THE OXFORD
REFERENCE
DICTIONARY

THE OXFORD REFERENCE DICTIONARY

EDITED BY
JOYCE M. HAWKINS

ILLUSTRATIONS EDITED BY
SUSAN LE ROUX

CLARENDON PRESS · OXFORD
1986

Oxford University Press, Walton Street, Oxford OX2 6DP

Oxford New York Toronto
Delhi Bombay Calcutta Madras Karachi
Petaling Jaya Singapore Hong Kong Tokyo
Nairobi Dar es Salaam Cape Town
Melbourne Auckland

and associated companies in
Beirut Berlin Ibadan Nicosia

Oxford is a trade mark of Oxford University Press

Published in the United States by
Oxford University Press, New York

British Library Cataloguing in Publication Data

The Oxford reference dictionary.
1. Encyclopedias and dictionaries
I. Hawkins, Joyce   II. Le Roux, Susan
032   AE5
ISBN 0-19-861148-X

Library of Congress Cataloging in Publication Data

The Oxford reference dictionary.
1. Encyclopedias and dictionaries.
I. Hawkins, Joyce.   II. Le Roux, Susan.
AG5.088   1986   031   86-8744
ISBN 0-19-861148-X

Printed in Great Britain
at the University Printing House, Oxford
by David Stanford
Printer to the University

CONTENTS

THE OXFORD REFERENCE DICTIONARY

ILLUSTRATIONS

APPENDICES

MAPS

PREFACE

The . . . Dictionary will be found to contain . . . a large amount
of useful and interesting information connected with literature,
art, and science, so that the charge usually preferred against
English dictionaries, namely, that they furnish but *dry sort of
reading*, will not apply to this dictionary.

Preface to *Ogilvie's Imperial Dictionary*, 1850

THIS book is designed to function both as a dictionary and as a concise
encyclopaedia. It includes biographical, historical, and geographical entries,
with over 6,000 articles on a wide variety of topics—arts, sciences, philosophy,
religion, mythology, technology, sport—in addition to conventional lexical
material.

The inclusion of encyclopaedic matter in an English dictionary is by no
means a new feature. Such matter is found in dictionaries from the 16th
century onwards, as it was in the earlier bilingual English and Latin
dictionaries upon which they drew. Proper names were included, with a
strong bias towards classical antiquity and the Bible, helping the reader to
understand the allusions that were characteristic of the literature of the
period; practical information, chiefly herbal and medical knowledge, was also
presented. Everyday words were the last to be admitted; technical or difficult
words and encyclopaedic information were of greater interest. Johnson's
Dictionary (1755) has disquisitions on selected subjects (including electricity
and opium), and an encyclopaedic element was still strong in the nineteenth
century. The American desire for a one-volume comprehensive reference
work, attractively produced, ensured the survival of this tradition in most
dictionaries of transatlantic origin, but in Britain the general tendency has
been to regard such matter as redundant and needlessly cluttering up the
pages; it is to be found (if at all) in sparse appendices. The burgeoning
vocabulary of the language, and the inevitable pressure on space, have made
it attractive for small dictionaries to restrict themselves to lexical information.
Even those that aspire to an integrated encyclopaedic element have, for the
most part, regarded selected proper names as acceptable material but have
made no attempt to offer encyclopaedic information on general topics. And
yet the distinction between information about 'words' and about 'things',
traditionally regarded as differentiating a dictionary from an encyclopaedia,
is not rigid; words refer to things, and understanding of words cannot be
separated from awareness of those things to which they refer.

In this book encyclopaedic treatment, including historical information, has
been given where this seemed necessary, interesting, or useful, the aim being
to present the non-specialist reader with the main aspects of a subject. The
fitting of so much material into a single volume has involved careful selection
of items; completeness could never be achieved and is not attempted, but we
hope that no major subject has been neglected. The choice of proper names

for inclusion has been guided by a number of considerations. Biographical entries are given for persons who are world-famous, pioneers, statesmen who were in power at a time of significant change in their country's history, and persons who have become legendary in their own spheres, together with a representative selection of lesser figures. Some persons' achievements and some subjects can be explained briefly, others cannot; readers who seek to compile or apply a 'league table' of importance based on the lengths of individual entries will find themselves frustrated. Geographical names include all independent countries of the world and their capital cities, continents, oceans, and major rivers and mountains, but the book is not intended to function as a gazetteer. The Appendices offer useful information which is more easily presented in tabulated form than in an encyclopaedic entry or dispersed through a number of such entries.

The illustrations supplement the text. Many have been chosen because their subjects can be explained more clearly by drawings than by words. By grouping items the relationships of separate elements to each other and to the whole can be indicated. Another function of the illustrations is to expand the encyclopaedic element of the book. In choosing subjects for illustration our aims have been to achieve a balance between the broad subject areas of science, natural history, and the arts, to indicate underlying principles or (where appropriate) historical development, and to open doors on some huge and complex subjects. The outline maps, included at the end of the book, present basic information.

The work has been edited in the English Dictionary Department of Oxford University Press, with encyclopaedic articles contributed by outside scholars who are specialists in their subjects. We are grateful to our colleagues in the Department for their help, interest, and encouragement, and in particular to Dr R. W. Burchfield, editor of the Oxford English Dictionary, who gave valuable advice when the dictionary was being planned and suggested the inclusion of the longer and more informative encyclopaedic articles, rather than the perfunctory entries that would usually be expected in a book of this size, that have given the book its distinctive character and made the work of its preparation so much more interesting for us all.

To write succinctly about complex subjects is not within everyone's power, and we are grateful to those scholars who accepted the challenge of presenting their knowledge in a limited space; some found it more difficult than they had expected but afterwards declared, with apparent sincerity, that they had enjoyed it. Particular mention must be made of Dr Malcolm Cooper, who showed himself well able and willing to write with detached, concise, and sometimes sardonic lucidity on the people and events of all periods of history.

For sustained help we must thank our two colleagues in the OED Department, R. C. Palmer, who worked with patient care, chiefly on the lexical material (including the etymologies), and prepared most of the Appendices, and R. C. Beatty, who wrote some of the science entries and edited others with competence and enthusiasm. A. M. Hughes, chief science editor of *A Supplement to the Oxford English Dictionary*, cheerfully tolerated our endless queries on articles and illustrations. M. Jones and Mrs M. P. A. Trumble gave conscientious help with presentation of the lexical entries. W. H. J. Baker, J. A. Hine, Miss E. M. Knowles, M. A. Mabe, and Dr W. R.

Trumble shared the proof-reading, and M. W. Grose and Mrs E. J. Pusey read through the text and made a number of useful suggestions. Mrs P. Lawton gave expert secretarial help with all stages of the work on the text, and Miss G. Metcalfe and Mrs J. Bartlam with the illustrations.

In preparing the illustrations we have received generous help and advice from a number of specialist museums and institutions and individual experts, and we are very grateful to them. In particular we must thank Mr Peter Clifford who worked closely with us throughout, suggesting appropriate subjects, undertaking substantial research and providing initial ideas for the contents, and checking the accuracy of the drawings at all stages; his precise and scholarly approach and his concern for detail have been invaluable.

In compiling the book we have sought to be informative (within the limits that space imposes), to interest, and occasionally to amuse. If readers can find that we have fulfilled any or all of these aims we shall feel well rewarded.

April 1986

J. M. H.
S. le R.

MAJOR CONTRIBUTORS

M. Booth (*Islam*)

M. Cooper (*History*)

J. V. Dumont (*Physical Anthropology*)

R. M. Flanders (*Art*)

P. Found (*Theatre, Cinema, Ballet*)

W. D. Hackmann (*Biographies of scientists*)

P. R. Hardie (*Classical History and Literature*)

I. J. Leslie (*Hinduism, Buddhism*)

A. Louth (*Theology*)

B. McMahon (*Astronomy*)

A. Mansbridge (*Music*)

A. W. L. Nayler (*Aeronautics*)

P. M. Neumann (*Mathematics*)

J. J. Roche (*Physics, Chemistry*)

S. A. Smiles (*Art*)

J. Stringer (*Literature*)

S. S. Wilson (*Technology*)

OTHER CONTRIBUTORS

J. Austoker, R. Bird, J. Campbell, J. Campling, B. Capp, P. G. Davey, A. R. Dexter, D. A. S. Fergusson, R. K. French, R. J. Gay, S. I. Gordon, D. M. Hamilton, H. Jones, J. R. Knight, M. R. Morris, P. J. Murray, C. Payne, M. H. Pelling, B. E. Reese, P. Russell, S. Seidenberg, J. R. Skelton, D. L. Stein, B. Teissier, M. P. A. Trumble, D. Walsh, A. Watson, A. Wear, P. J. Weindling.

Dr G. Abraham, A. J. Augarde, Professor J. Carey, H. Carpenter, Dr H. M. R. E. Mayr-Harting, Dr R. O'Hanlon, Sir David Piper, and the late Professor R. R. Porter contributed specimen entries when the book was being planned.

ILLUSTRATORS

John Brennan, Margaret Jones, and the staff of Illustra Design.

ACKNOWLEDGEMENTS

The following illustrations are based on copyright drawings, by kind permission of the copyright holders: The Car (Austin Rover Group Ltd.), Dress (D. Yarwood, *English Costume*, Batsford, 1952). In the Appendices, the table of the Beaufort Scale is reproduced by kind permission of the Meteorological Office (Crown Copyright).

NOTES

1. *Pronunciation*

Guidance on pronunciation follows the system of the International Phonetic Alphabet (see p. xi); it indicates the pronunciation that is standard in southern England.

2. *Inflexion*

Plurals of nouns, comparatives in *-er* and superlatives in *-est*, and forms of verbs are given only if they are irregular or if there might be doubt about the spelling. A doubled consonant in verbal inflexions (e.g. *rubbed, rubbing*; *sinned, sinning*) is shown in the form (**-bb-**), (**-nn-**), etc.

3. *Etymology*

This is given in square brackets at the end of an entry. It is usually omitted where the headword is a compound of two or more words (for which etymologies are given in their separate entries) or of an easily identifiable prefix (e.g. *anti-, pre-, un-*) and a whole word, or where the derivation is clear from the definition (e.g. *Chippendale, Spode*).

4. *Population*

Figures are given for countries and capital cities, but not for provinces, counties, etc. They are based on the latest information that was available when the entries were written.

5. *Proprietary status*

This dictionary includes some words which are, or are asserted to be, proprietary names or trade marks. Their inclusion does not imply that they have acquired for legal purposes a non-proprietary or general significance, nor is any other judgement implied concerning their legal status. In cases where the editor has some evidence that a word is used as a proprietary name or trade mark this is indicated by the letter [P] but no judgement concerning the legal status of such words is made or implied thereby.

PRONUNCIATION

1. CONSONANTS

b, *d*, *f*, *h*, *k*, *l*, *m*, *n*, *p*, *r*, *s*, *t*, *v*, *w*, and *z* have their usual English values. Other symbols are used as folllows:

g (*game*)	ŋ (lo*ng*)	ʃ (*sh*ip)
tʃ (*chair*)	θ (*thin*)	ʒ (mea*s*ure)
dʒ (*jet*)	ð (*there*)	j (*yes*)
x (Scots etc.: lo*ch*)		

Other consonants as in ar*c*, *c*ob *c*ry (but soft *c* before *e*, *i*, *y* as in i*c*e and *c*ity); *ch*ur*ch*; bla*ck*, lo*dge*; *game*, *g*ba*g* (but soft *g* before, *e*, *i*, *y* as in a*g*e and *g*in); *j*et; si*ng*; bla*nk*; *ph*oto; *qu*een; *sh*ot; bit*ch*; *th*in; bo*x*; *y*et.

2. VOWELS

short vowels		long vowels		diphthongs	
æ	(b*a*t)	ɑː	(d*ar*k)	eɪ	(s*ay*)
e	(b*e*t)	iː	(s*ee*m)	aɪ	(b*uy*)
ə	(*a*go)	ɔː	(b*or*n)	ɔɪ	(t*oy*)
ɪ	(s*i*t)	ɜː	(t*er*m)	əʊ	(s*o*)
ɒ	(t*o*p)	uː	(m*oo*n)	aʊ	(n*ow*)
ʌ	(b*u*t)			ɪə(r)	(p*eer*)
ʊ	(p*u*t)			eə(r)	(f*air*)
				ʊə(r)	(p*oor*)

(ə) signifies the indeterminate sound as in g*a*rden, carn*a*l, and rhyth*m*; (r) signifies a final r which is pronounced when the following word begins with a vowel sound.

Other vowels as in g*ai*n, f*ai*r, f*ar*, d*are*, s*aw*, s*ay*, b*ea*n, f*ear*, s*ee*n, s*eer*, h*er*d, h*ere*, f*ew*, th*ie*f, b*ie*r, b*ir*d, t*ire*, b*oa*t, b*oar*d, h*oe*, j*oi*n, m*oo*n, p*oor*, b*or*n, l*ou*d, s*our*, n*ow*, t*oy*, d*ue*, b*ur*n, p*ure*.

The following signify sounds not natural in English:

æ̃	(b*ai*n-marie, t*im*bre)	ø	(p*eu*)
ɑ̃	(contret*emps*)	œ	(b*œu*f)
ɔ̃	(b*on* voyage)	œ̃	(br*un*)

Main stress is indicated by ' preceding the relevant syllable; no attempt is made to indicate secondary stress.

Pronunciation of words of one syllable is not given when it conforms with the following basic pattern:

Single-letter vowels a = /æ/, e = /e/, i = /ɪ/, o = /ɒ/, u = /ʌ/; when lengthened by a succeeding single consonant followed by *e*, a = /eɪ/, e = /iː/, i = /aɪ/, o = /əʊ/, u = /juː/ (as in m*a*t and m*a*te; m*e*t and m*e*te, s*i*t and s*i*te, t*o*t and t*o*te, t*u*n and t*u*ne).

Pronunciation of two-syllable words is usually omitted when the first syllable is stressed and follows the basic pattern.

Pronunciation of compound words of easily recognized elements (e.g. *bathroom*, *headache*) is not given when the stress is on the first element.

Pronunciation of regularly formed derivates is not given when it can be easily deduced from the headword or from a preceding main word (e.g. *casually* from *casual* and *catty* from *cat*), unless there is a change of stress or some other notable feature (as with *certification*).

(iii) The following combinations, beginning a word, have the values shown: kn = /n/, rh = /r/, wh = /w/ or (by some speakers) /hw/ (not shown in individual entries), wr = /r/.

(iv) Pronunciation of the following suffixes and terminations should be noted:

-able /-əb(ə)l/
-age /-ɪdʒ/
-al (preceded by consonant) /-(ə)l/
-dom /-dəm/
-d (after *d* or *t*) /-ɪd/; (after other voiceless consonant) /-t/; (elsewhere) /-d/
-ess /-ɪs/
-est -ɪst/
-ful /-fʊl/
-fy /-faɪ/
-ible /-ɪb(ə)l
-ism /-ɪz(ə)m/
-ive /-ɪv/
-less /-lɪs/
-ment /-mənt/
-ness /-nɪs/
-ous /-əs/
-sion /-ʃ(ə)n or -ʒ(ə)n/
-some /-səm/
-tion /-ʃ(ə)n/
-y (preceded by consonant, but cf. **-fy**) /-ɪ/

ABBREVIATIONS

abbr./eviation etc.
abs./olute(ly)
acc./ording
adj./ective etc.
adjs. adjectives
adv./erb etc.
advs. adverbs
AF Anglo-French
Afr./ican
Afrik./aans
alt./eration etc.
app./arently
approx./imately
Arab./ic
Archit./ecture
assim./ilated etc.
assoc./iated etc.
Astron./omy Astrol./ogy
attrib./utive(ly)
Austral./ian
aux./iliary

Biol./ogy
Bot./any

c. century
c. circa
Chem./istry
Chin./ese
cogn./ate
collect./ive(ly)
colloq./uial(ly)
compar./ative
conj./unction
contr./action etc.
corrupt./ion

D = disputed usage
  (applied to a use that,
  although widely found,
  is still the subject of
  much adverse
  comment by informed
  users)
d./ied
dat./ive
derog./atory
dial./ect etc.
dim./inutive etc.
dist./inguished

Du./tch

Electr./icity
emphat./ic
Engl./ish
erron./eous(ly)
esp./ecially
est./imated etc.
euphem./ism etc.
exc./ept
excl./amation etc.

F French
f. from
fem./inine
fig./urative(ly)
fl./oruit
Flem./ish
foll./owing entry
freq./ently
frequent./ative
fut./ure

G German
Gael./ic
gen./itive
Geol./ogy
Gk Greek
Gmc Germanic
Gram./mar

Heb./rew
hist./orical(ly)
Hung./arian

i. intransitive
Icel./andic
ill./ustration etc.
imit./ative etc.
imper./ative(ly)
infl./uenced
int./erjection
interrog./ative(ly)
Ir./ish
iron./ically
irreg./ular(ly)
It./alian

Jap./anese
joc./ular(ly)

L Latin
LDu. Low Dutch
LG Low German
lit./eral(ly)

masc./uline
Math./ematics
MDu. Middle Dutch
Mex./ican
MHG Middle High
  German
Min./eralogy
MLG Middle Low
  German
Mus./ic etc.
myth./ology

n. noun
Naut./ical
neg./ative(ly)
N. Engl. north of
  England
neut./er
Norw./egian
ns. nouns

obj./ective
obs./olete
occas./ional(ly)
OE Old English
OF Old French
OHG Old High German
ON Old Norse
ONorw. Old Norwegian
opp. (as) opposed (to)
orig./in(ally)

P proprietary name
partic./iple
pass./ive(ly)
perh./aps
Pers./ian
phr./ase
Phys./ics
pl./ural
poet./ical(ly)
pop./ular(ly), population
Port./uguese
poss./essive
p.p. past participle

pr./onounced
prec./eding entry
predic./ative(ly)
Print./ing
prob./able etc.
pron./oun
pronunc./iation
prop./er(ly)
Prov./ençal

redupl./icated etc.
ref./erence etc.
refl./exive(ly)
rel./ated; relative
repr./esenting
rhet./orical(ly)
Rom./an, Romanic
Russ./ian

S.Afr. South Africa(n)
S.Amer. South
  America(n)
Sc./ottish
Scand./inavian
sing./ular
Skr. Sanskrit
Slav./onic
Sp./anish
superl./ative
Sw./edish

Theol./ogy
transl./ation etc.
Turk./ish

ult./imately
unkn./own
usu./al(ly)

v. verb
var./iant
v.aux. auxiliary verb
v.i. intransitive verb
v.refl. reflexive verb
v.t. transitive verb
v.t./i. transitive and
  intransitive verb
vulg./ar

w./ith
wd word

A

A, a *n.* **1.** the first letter of the alphabet. **2.** (*Mus.*) the sixth note in the scale of C major. —**A1**, (*colloq.*) first-rate, in perfect condition (see LLOYD'S).

A *abbr.* ampere(s).

Å *abbr.* ångström(s).

a /ə, *emphatic* eɪ/ *adj.* (called the *indefinite article*) **1.** one person or thing but not any specific one; one like. **2.** per. [OE]

a- *prefix* **1.** on (*afoot*), to (*ashore*), towards (*aside*). **2.** in (*nowadays*). **3.** in the process of (*a-begging, a-flutter*). [OE]

Aalto /'ɑːltəʊ/, Hugo Henrik Alvar (1898–1976), Finnish architect, one of the most inventive of his generation, who worked extensively in Europe and America as well as in Finland, where he was responsible for the design of a number of public buildings. He is notable for his expressive and inventive use of timber (Finland's basic building material) for structure and decoration, and for the use of mixed materials in designs that were beautiful as a result of purely functional concerns.

aardvark /'ɑːdvɑːk/ *n.* a nocturnal African animal (*Orycteropus afer*), with a bulky pig-like body, long ears, and a thick tail, that feeds on termites. [Afrik., = earth-pig]

Aaron /'eər(ə)n/ brother of Moses and traditional founder of the Jewish priesthood. —**Aaron's beard**, (see Ps. 133: 2) a popular name for several plants, especially a St John's wort *Hypericum calycinum*. **Aaron's rod**, a popular name for several tall plants with flowering stems, especially a mullein, *Verbascum thapsus*. (Aaron's rod sprouted and blossomed as a sign that he was designated by God as high priest of the Hebrews; see Numbers 17: 8.)

ab- *prefix* (**abs-** before *c, t*; **a-** before *m, p, v*) off, away, from. [F or L]

aback /ə'bæk/ *adv.* **taken aback**, disconcerted. [OE]

abacus /'æbəkəs/ *n.* (*pl.* **abacuses**) **1.** a frame containing grooves or parallel rods or wires with beads that slide to and fro, used for counting. Its provenance and date of origin are uncertain. The ancient Egyptians, Greeks, and Romans used a counting-board with vertical columns as an aid to reckoning; the frame may be a development of this, or may have been devised independently. It was in general use during the Middle Ages until the adoption of the nine figures and zero, and is still used in the Far East. **2.** (*Archit.*) the flat upper section of a capital, supporting the architrave (ill. TEMPLES). [L f. Gk *abax* slab, drawing-board f. Heb., = dust (from use of board sprinkled with sand or dust for drawing geometrical diagrams)]

abaft *adv.* in the stern half of a ship. —*prep.* nearer to the stern than. [f. A- + *baft* f. OE (*be* by, *æftan* behind)]

abalone /æbə'ləʊnɪ/ *n.* (*US*) an edible mollusc of the genus *Haliotis*, with an ear-shaped shell lined with mother-of-pearl. [Amer. Sp.]

abandon /ə'bændən/ *v.t.* **1.** to go away from without intending to return; to give up, to cease work on. **2.** to yield completely to an emotion or impulse. —*n.* reckless freedom of manner. —**abandonment** *n.* [f. OF (*à bandon* under another's control)]

abandoned /ə'bændənd/ *adj.* (of a person or behaviour) showing abandon, depraved. [f. prec.]

abase /ə'beɪs/ *v.t.* to humiliate, to degrade. —**abasement** *n.* [f. OF f. L (*bassus* short)]

abashed /ə'bæʃt/ *adj.* embarrassed, disconcerted, ashamed. [f. OF (*baïr* astound)]

abate /ə'beɪt/ *v.t./i.* to make or become less, to weaken. —**abatement** *n.* [f. OF f. L (AD-, *battuere* beat)]

abattoir /'æbətwɑː(r)/ *n.* a slaughterhouse. [F, as prec.]

abbacy /'æbəsɪ/ *n.* the office or jurisdiction of an abbot or abbess. [f. L (as ABBOT)]

Abbasid /'æbəsɪd/ *adj.* of a dynasty of caliphs ruling in Baghdad 750–1258, claiming descent from Abbas (566–652), uncle of Muhammad. —*n.* a member of this dynasty.

abbé /'æbeɪ/ *n.* a Frenchman entitled to wear ecclesiastical dress, with or without official duties. [F f. L (as ABBOT)]

abbess /'æbes/ *n.* a woman who is head of an abbey of nuns. [f. OF (as ABBOT)]

Abbevillian /æb'vɪlɪən/ *adj.* of the earliest lower palaeolithic hand-axe industries in Europe, named after the type-site at Abbeville on the River Somme in northern France and dated to *c.*500,000 BC. The hand-axes were made by hammering flakes off a flint with a hard stone, giving them a rough appearance. (See also ACHEULIAN.) —*n.* this industry. [f. *Abbeville*]

abbey /'æbɪ/ *n.* **1.** a building occupied by a community of monks or nuns. **2.** this community. **3.** a church or house that was formerly an abbey. —**the Abbey**, Westminster Abbey. [f. OF f. L *abbatia* abbacy]

Abbey Theatre a theatre in Abbey Street, Dublin, first opened in 1904, staging chiefly Irish plays. W. B. Yeats was associated with its foundation. In 1925 it became the first State-subsidized theatre in the English-speaking world.

abbot /'æbət/ *n.* a man who is head of an abbey of monks (now chiefly in Benedictine and Augustinian orders), usually elected by the monks for life or for a period of years and frequently holding certain episcopal rights. [OE, ult. f. Aram. *abba* father]

abbreviate /ə'briːvɪeɪt/ *v.t.* to shorten (esp. a word or title). —**abbreviation** /-'eɪʃ(ə)n/ *n.* [f. L *abbreviare* (*brevis* short)]

ABC *n.* **1.** the alphabet. **2.** the elementary facts of a subject. **3.** an alphabetically arranged guide. —*abbr.* Australian Broadcasting Corporation (formerly Commission).

abdicate /'æbdɪkeɪt/ *v.t./i.* to renounce, to resign from a throne, right, or high office. —**abdication** /-'keɪʃ(ə)n/ *n.* [f. L *abdicare* (AB-, *dicare* dedicate)]

abdomen /'æbdəmən/ *n.* **1.** the part of the body containing the stomach, bowels, intestines, and other digestive organs (ill. BODY 2); the front surface of the body from waist to groin. **2.** the hinder part of an insect (ill. INSECTS), crustacean, spider, etc. —**abdominal** /-'dɒmɪn(ə)l/ *adj.* [L]

abduct /æb'dʌkt/ *v.t.* to carry off (a person) illegally by force or deception. —**abduction** *n.*, **abductor** *n.* [f. L *abducere* (AB-, *ducere* lead)]

abed /ə'bed/ *adv.* (*archaic*) in bed. [OE as A-, BED]

Abel /'ɑːbel/, Niels Henrik (1802–29), Norwegian mathematician who, in his six productive years, published the first acceptable proof that equations of the fifth degree or above cannot be solved by methods analogous to those that had been known since the 16th c. for solving equations of degree 1, 2, 3 or 4, introduced rigorous argument into the theory of power series, and discovered startling new results on elliptic functions, as a result of which the theory of these and of their generalizations became one of the liveliest areas for 19th-c. mathematical research. After two years of travel, meeting mathematicians in Germany and France, he returned to Norway where he lived in poverty and died of consumption aged 26, at the height of his powers. —**Abelian** /ə'biːlɪən/ *adj.*

Abelard /'æbɪlɑːd/, Peter (1079–1142), French scholar, theologian, and philosopher, whose lively, restless, independent mind impressed his contemporaries but brought him into frequent conflict with his masters and led to his being twice condemned for heresy. He lectured in Paris until his academic career was cut short in 1118 by the tragic issue of his love affair with his pupil Héloïse, niece of Fulbert, a canon of Notre Dame. Abelard was castrated at Fulbert's instigation; he entered a monastery, and made Héloïse become a nun. Abelard continued his highly controversial teaching, applying reason to the deepest mysteries of the faith, notably the doctrine of the Trinity. His doctrine of the Atonement, emphasizing the love of Christ, manifest in his life and passion, which calls forth a human response of love, has had a continuing influence. The lovers are now buried in one grave in Paris.

Aberdeen /æbə'diːn/ a city and former county in Scotland, humorously credited with an extremely parsimonious population. —**Aberdeen Angus**, an animal of a Scottish breed of black hornless cattle. —**Aberdonian** /-'dəʊnɪən/ *adj. & n.*

aberrant /æˈberənt/ *adj.* departing from the normal type or accepted standard. [f. L *aberrare* (AB-, *errare* stray)]

aberration /æbəˈreɪʃ(ə)n/ *n.* **1.** departure from what is normal or accepted or regarded as right; a moral or mental lapse. **2.** (*Optics*) distortion of an image, the non-convergence of rays of light from a point to a single focus; *chromatic aberration*, a form of aberration due to the fact that light of different colours is refracted by different amounts as it passes through a lens, so that the resulting image is fringed with colours. **3.** (*Astron.*) the apparent change in the position of a celestial body caused by the observer's motion and the finite speed of light. As the earth has two motions, there is a *diurnal* as well as an *annual* aberration; *planetary* aberration is effected by the additional element of the motion of the planet itself, during the time occupied by the passage of its light to the earth. [as prec.]

abet /əˈbet/ *v.t.* (**-tt-**) to encourage or assist (an offender or offence). —**abetter** (in legal use **abettor**) *n.*, **abetment** *n.* [f. OF (*à* to, *beter* bait)]

abeyance /əˈbeɪəns/ *n.* **in abeyance,** (of a right or rule or problem etc.) suspended for a time. [f. OF (*à* to, *beer* gape)]

abhor /əbˈhɔː(r)/ *v.t.* (**-rr-**) to detest, to regard with disgust. —**abhorrence** /-ˈhɒrəns/ *n.* [f. L *abhorrere* shrink in dread]

abhorrent /əbˈhɒrənt/ *adj.* disgusting or hateful (*to* a person or one's beliefs); not according *to* (a principle). [as prec.]

abide /əˈbaɪd/ *v.t./i.* **1.** to tolerate, to endure. **2.** (*archaic, past* **abode** *or* **abided**) to remain, to dwell. —**abide by,** to act in accordance with (a promise etc.). [OE]

abiding *adj.* enduring, permanent. [f. prec.]

Abidjan /æbɪˈdʒɑːn/ the capital and chief port of the Ivory Coast; pop. (est. 1981) 1,686,100.

abigail /ˈæbɪɡeɪl/ *n.* a lady's maid. [character in Beaumont and Fletcher's *Scornful Lady*; cf. 1 Sam. 25]

ability /əˈbɪlɪtɪ/ *n.* the quality that makes an action or process possible; cleverness, talent. [f. OF f. L (*habilis* deft)]

ab initio /æb ɪˈnɪʃɪəʊ/ from the beginning. [L]

abject /ˈæbdʒekt/ *adj.* lacking all pride, made humble; wretched, without resources. —**abjectly** *adv.*, **abjection** /-ˈdʒekʃ(ə)n/ *n.* [f. L *abjectus* (AB-, *jacere* throw)]

abjure /əbˈdʒʊə(r)/ *v.t.* to renounce or repudiate. —**abjuration** /-ˈreɪʃ(ə)n/ *n.* [f. L *abjurare* deny on oath]

ablative /ˈæblətɪv/ *n.* (*Gram.*) the case (especially in Latin) that indicates the agent, instrument, or location of an action. —*adj.* (*Gram.*) of or in the ablative. [f. OF or L (*ablatus* carried away)]

ablaut /ˈæblaʊt/ *n.* a change of vowel in related words (e.g. *sing, sang, sung*), characteristic of Indo-European languages. [G]

ablaze /əˈbleɪz/ *predic. adj.* blazing; glittering; greatly excited. [f. A- + BLAZE]

able /ˈeɪb(ə)l/ *adj.* having the ability or capacity (*to* do something); clever, talented, competent. —**able-bodied** *adj.* fit and strong. —**ably** *adv.* [f. OF f. L *habilis* deft]

-able *suffix* forming adjectives in sense 'that may' (*comfortable, suitable*), now always in passive sense 'that can, may, or must be -d' (*eatable, payable*), 'that can be made the subject of' (*objectionable*), 'that is relevant to or in accordance with' (*fashionable*). [F, f. L -*abilis*]

ablution /əˈbluːʃ(ə)n/ *n.* (usu. in *pl.*) ceremonial washing of hands, vessels, etc.; (*colloq.*) ordinary washing of the body, a place for doing this. [f. OF or L *ablutio* (AB-, *luere* wash)]

abnegate /ˈæbnɪɡeɪt/ *v.t.* to give up or renounce (a pleasure or right etc.). —**abnegation** /-ˈɡeɪʃ(ə)n/ *n.* [f. L *abnegare* refuse]

abnormal /æbˈnɔːm(ə)l/ *adj.* different from what is normal. —**abnormally** *adv.*, **abnormality** /-ˈmælɪtɪ/ *n.* [f. F f. Gk (as ANOMALOUS)]

aboard /əˈbɔːd/ *adv. & prep.* on or into a ship, aircraft, train, etc. [f. A- + BOARD]

abode[1] /əˈbəʊd/ *n.* (*archaic* or *literary*) a dwelling-place. [f. ABIDE]

abode[2] /əˈbəʊd/ *past* of ABIDE.

abolish /əˈbɒlɪʃ/ *v.t.* to put an end to (a custom, institution, etc.). [f. F f. L *abolēre* destroy]

abolition /æbəˈlɪʃ(ə)n/ *n.* abolishing, being abolished, especially with reference to capital punishment or (*hist.*) Black slavery and the 19th-c. movement against this. [F or f. L (as prec.)]

abolitionist *n.* one who favours abolition, especially of capital punishment. [f. prec.]

abominable /əˈbɒmɪnəb(ə)l/ *adj.* detestable, loathsome; (*colloq.*) unpleasant. —**Abominable Snowman,** a large unidentified manlike or bearlike animal said to exist in the Himalayas, a yeti. —**abominably** *adv.* [f. OF f. L (as foll.)]

abominate /əˈbɒmɪneɪt/ *v.t.* to detest, to loathe. [f. L *abominari* deprecate]

abomination /əbɒmɪˈneɪʃ(ə)n/ *n.* **1.** detesting, loathing. **2.** an object of disgust. [f. OF (as prec.)]

aboriginal /æbəˈrɪdʒɪn(ə)l/ *adj.* indigenous, inhabiting a land from an early period, especially before the arrival of colonists; directly descended from early inhabitants. —*n.* an aboriginal inhabitant, especially (**Aboriginal**) of Australia (see foll.). [f. L (as foll.)]

aborigines /æbəˈrɪdʒɪniːz/ *n.pl.* (*sing.* **aborigine** is used informally, but *aboriginal* is preferable) aboriginal inhabitants, especially (**Aborigines**) of Australia. The Australian Aborigines, dark-skinned hunter-gatherers comprising several physically distinct groups, arrived in Australia in prehistoric times and brought with them the dingo. Before the arrival of Europeans they were scattered through the whole continent, including Tasmania. Their languages (except of Tasmania) are related to each other but not, apparently, to any other language family and have no literature of their own; estimated at several hundred in number they are almost or completely extinct, and of those that survive some have only a few hundred speakers in Australia. There are now roughly 160,000 Aborigines in Australia. Having become mostly urbanized many have recently moved to their traditional homeland areas in an attempt to preserve their culture. [L, prob. f. *ab origine* from the beginning]

abort /əˈbɔːt/ *v.t./i.* **1.** to cause an abortion of or to; to undergo abortion. **2.** to remain undeveloped, to stop (a growth or disease) in its early stages. **3.** to end prematurely and unsuccessfully. [f. L *aboriri* miscarry]

abortion /əˈbɔːʃ(ə)n/ *n.* **1.** the expulsion (either spontaneous or induced) of a foetus from the womb before it is able to survive, especially in the first 28 weeks of pregnancy. **2.** a stunted or misshapen creature or thing. [as prec.]

abortionist *n.* a person who practices abortion, esp. illegally. [f. prec.]

abortive /əˈbɔːtɪv/ *adj.* **1.** producing abortion. **2.** unsuccessful. [f. OF f. L (as ABORT)]

abound /əˈbaʊnd/ *v.i.* to be plentiful; to be rich *in*, to teem *with*. [f. OF f. L *abundare* overflow]

about /əˈbaʊt/ *prep.* **1.** in connection with, on the subject of. **2.** at a time near to. **3.** all round. **4.** near to hand. **5.** here and there in, at points throughout. —*adv.* **1.** approximately. **2.** at points near by, here and there. **3.** on the move, in action. **4.** all round, in every direction. **5.** in rotation or succession. (Tending to be replaced in many uses by *around* and *round*.) —**about turn,** a turn made so as to face the opposite direction; a reversal of opinion or policy etc. **be about to,** to intend to (do something) immediately; to be on the point or verge of. [OE (A-, *būtan* but)]

above /əˈbʌv/ *prep.* **1.** over, on the top of, higher than; over the level of. **2.** more than. **3.** higher in rank or importance etc. than. **4.** beyond the reach of; too good etc. for. —*adv.* **1.** at or to a higher point, overhead. **2.** in addition. **3.** further back on a page or in a book. **4.** (*rhet.*) in heaven. —*adj.* said, mentioned, or written above. —*n.* that which is above. —**above-board** *adv. & adj.* without concealment, open(ly). **above himself** etc., carried away by high spirits or conceit. [f. A- + OE *bufan* (*be* by, *ufan* above)]

abracadabra /æbrəkəˈdæbrə/ *n.* **1.** a supposedly magic formula or spell. **2.** gibberish. [L f. Gk; a cabbalistic word of a Gnostic sect, supposed when written triangularly, and worn, to cure fevers etc.; it is first found in a poem by Q. Serenus Sammonicus (early 3rd c. AD)]

abrade /əˈbreɪd/ *v.t.* to scrape or wear away by rubbing. [f. L *abradere* (AB-, *radere* scrape)]

abrasion /əˈbreɪʒ(ə)n/ *n.* scraping or wearing away; an area of damage caused thus. [as prec.]

abrasive /əˈbreɪsɪv/ *adj.* **1.** causing abrasion; capable of polishing by rubbing or rubbing or grinding. **2.** harsh and offensive in manner. —*n.* an abrasive substance. [as ABRADE]

Abraham /ˈeɪbrəhæm/ the Hebrew patriarch from whom all Jews trace their descent (Gen. 11: 27-25: 10). In Gen. 14 is made a contemporary of 'Amraphel king of Shinar', who may be Hammurabi (Shinar = Babylon). —**Plains of Abraham,** see separate entry.

abreaction /æbrɪˈækʃ(ə)n/ *n.* free expression and release of a previously repressed emotion. [f. AB- + REACTION]

abreast /əˈbrest/ *adv.* **1.** side by side and facing the same way. **2.** keeping up, not behind (*of* or *with* developments). [f. A- + BREAST]

abridge /ə'brɪdʒ/ *v.t.* to shorten into fewer words. —**abridgement** *n.* [f. OF f. L (as ABBREVIATE)]

abroad /ə'brɔːd/ *adv.* **1.** in or to a foreign country. **2.** over a wide area, in different directions. **3.** in circulation. [f. A- + BROAD]

abrogate /'æbrəgeɪt/ *v.t.* to repeal, to cancel. —**abrogation** /-'geɪʃ(ə)n/ *n.* [f. L *abrogare* (AB-, *rogare* propose law)]

abrupt /ə'brʌpt/ *adj.* **1.** sudden; disjointed, not smooth; curt. **2.** steep, precipitous. —**abruptly** *adv.*, **abruptness** *n.* [f. L *abruptus* (AB-, *rumpere* break)]

abscess /'æbsɪs/ *n.* a swollen area of body tissue in which pus gathers. [f. L *abscessus* a going away (AB-, *cedere* go)]

abscissa /æb'sɪsə/ *n.* (*pl.* -ae /-iː/) (*Math.*) a coordinate measured parallel to a horizontal axis. [f. L (AB-, *scindere* cut)]

abscond /əb'skɒnd/ *v.i.* to go away furtively, especially after wrongdoing. —**absconder** *n.* [f. L *abscondere* (AB-, *condere* stow)]

abseil /'æbseɪl/ *v.i.* to descend a steep rock-face using a doubled rope fixed at a higher point. —*n.* this process. [f. G (*ab* down, *seil* rope)]

absence /'æbs(ə)ns/ *n.* being away, the period of this; non-existence or lack *of*; inattentiveness (*of mind*). [as foll.]

absent /'æbs(ə)nt/ *adj.* not present; not existing. —/əb'sent/ *v.refl.* to keep *oneself* away. —**absent-minded** *adj.* forgetful; with one's mind on other things. —**absently** *adv.* [f. OF or L *absens* (*abesse* be away)]

absentee /æbs(ə)n'tiː/ *n.* one who absents himself. —**absentee landlord**, one not residing at the property he leases out. —**absenteeism** *n.* [f. prec.]

absinthe /'æbsɪnθ/ *n.* a liqueur originally flavoured with wormwood, now usually with other herbs. [f. F f. L f. Gk *apsinthion*]

absolute /'æbsəluːt, -juːt/ *adj.* complete, perfect; unrestricted, independent; not relative. —**absolute magnitude**, see MAGNITUDE. **absolute majority**, a majority over all rivals combined. **absolute pitch**, the ability to recognize or reproduce exactly the pitch of a note in music. **absolute temperature**, one measured from absolute zero. **absolute zero**, the temperature (−273.15 °C) at which the motion of particles that constitutes heat is at a minimum. [f. L (as ABSOLVE)]

absolutely /'æbsəluːtlɪ/ *adv.* **1.** completely, utterly, unreservedly. **2.** actually. **3.** in an absolute sense. **4.** /-'luːtlɪ/ quite so, yes. [f. prec.]

absolution /æbsə'luːʃ(ə)n/ *n.* formal forgiveness of a penitent's sins, declared by a priest. [f. OF f. L (as foll.)]

absolve /əb'zɒlv/ *v.t.* **1.** to clear *from* or *of* blame or guilt; to give absolution to. **2.** to free *from* an obligation. [f. L *absolvere* (AB-, *solvere* loosen)]

absorb /əb'sɔːb/ *v.t.* to take in, to incorporate as part of itself or oneself; to reduce the effect of, to deal easily with (shock etc.); to engross the attention of. —**absorbency** *n.*, **absorbent** *adj.* & *n.*, **absorption** *n.* [f. F or L *absorbēre* (AB-, *sorbēre* suck in)]

absorptive /əb'sɔːptɪv/ *adj.* able to absorb things; engrossing. [f. L (as prec.)]

abstain /əb'steɪn/ *v.i.* to restrain oneself, especially from drinking alcohol; to decline to use one's vote. —**abstainer** *n.*, **abstention** *n.* [f. AF f. L *abstinere* withhold]

abstemious /æb'stiːmɪəs/ *adj.* sparing or not self-indulgent, especially in eating and drinking. —**abstemiously** *adv.*, **abstemiousness** *n.* [f. L *abstemius* (AB-, *temetum* strong drink)]

abstinence /'æbstɪnəns/ *n.* abstaining, especially from food or alcohol. —**abstinent** *adj.* [f. OF f. L (as ABSTAIN)]

abstract[1] /'æbstrækt/ *adj.* **1.** having no material existence. **2.** theoretical rather than practical. —*n.* **1.** a summary. **2.** an abstract quality or idea. **3.** an example of abstract art. —**abstract noun**, a noun denoting quality or state. —**abstractly** *adv.*, **abstractness** *n.* [f. OF or L *abstractus* (AB-, *trahere* draw)]

abstract[2] /æb'strækt/ *v.t.* **1.** to take out, to remove. **2.** to make a written summary of. —**abstracted** *adj.* inattentive, with one's mind on other things. —**abstractor** *n.* [f. prec.]

abstract art painting or sculpture that dispenses with the physical appearance of the real world and concentrates instead on the relations between form and colour. Although such relations are the structural basis of all artistic design, their elevation into a self-sufficient aesthetic is essentially a

20th-c. phenomenon. The first abstract works of art are generally considered to date from *c.*1910-14, and since then abstract art has polarized into two main divisions: hard-edged and geometric (akin to the linear and classical) or flowing and organic (akin to the painterly and romantic).

abstract expressionism a term used to describe the art produced in New York in the 1940s and early 1950s in which large canvases were covered by means of spontaneous painterly gestures whose disposition primarily expressed an intangible emotive feeling as opposed to having any descriptive function. Of its participants de Kooning (1904-) retained some figurative elements, but many others avoided all such reference. Although initially inspired by European surrealism in its use of unconscious inspiration for pictorial creation, it is widely considered to be the first major American contribution to art and had enormous impact in Europe in the 1950s.

abstraction /æb'strækʃ(ə)n/ *n.* **1.** abstracting, removing. **2.** an abstract idea. **3.** inattentiveness. [F or f. L (as ABSTRACT[1])]

abstruse /æb'struːs/ *adj.* hard to understand, profound. —**abstrusely** *adv.*, **abstruseness** *n.* [F or f. L *abstrudere* conceal]

absurd /əb'sɜːd/ *adj.* wildly inappropriate; ridiculous. —**Theatre of the Absurd**, see THEATRE. —**absurdity** *n.*, **absurdly** *adv.* [f. F or L (AB-, *surdus* deaf, dull)]

abundant /ə'bʌndənt/ *adj.* more than enough, plenty; rich *in*. —**abundantly** *adv.*, **abundance** *n.* [f. L (as ABOUND)]

abuse /ə'bjuːz/ *v.t.* **1.** to make a bad or wrong use of; to maltreat. **2.** to attack verbally. —/ə'bjuːs/ *n.* **1.** misuse; an unjust or corrupt practice. **2.** abusive words, insults. [f. OF f. L (AB-, *uti* use)]

abusive /ə'bjuːsɪv/ *adj.* using insulting language, criticizing harshly. —**abusively** *adv.* [as prec.]

Abu Simbel /'æbuː 'sɪmb(ə)l/ a former village in southern Egypt, site of two rock-cut temples built by Rameses II (13th c. BC), a monument to the greatest of the pharaohs and a constant reminder to possibly restive Nubian tribes of Egypt's might. The great temple, with its façade (31 m, 102 ft., high) bearing four colossal seated statues of Rameses, faces due east, and is dedicated to Amun-Ra and other principal State gods of the period; the small temple is dedicated to Hathor and Nefertari, first wife of Rameses. In 1963 an archaeological salvage operation was begun, comparable in scale to the original construction of the temples, in which engineers sawed up the monument and carried it up the hillside to be rebuilt, with its original orientation, well above the rising waters of Lake Nasser, whose level was affected by the building of the High Dam at Aswan.

abut /ə'bʌt/ *v.t./i.* (**-tt-**) to adjoin, to border *on*; to touch at one side. [f. OF (*but* end) & L]

abutment /ə'bʌtmənt/ *n.* a lateral supporting structure of a bridge, arch, etc. (ill. BRIDGES). [f. prec.]

abysmal /ə'bɪzm(ə)l/ *adj.* extremely bad; extreme and deplorable. —**abysmally** *adv.* [f. OF f. L (as ABYSS)]

abyss /ə'bɪs/ *n.* a bottomless or deep chasm; an immeasurable depth. [f. L f. Gk *abussos* bottomless (*a*- not, *bussos* depth)]

abyssal /ə'bɪs(ə)l/ *adj.* at or of the ocean depths or floor, especially those below 1,000 metres containing relatively little marine life. [f. prec.]

Abyssinia /æbɪ'sɪnɪə/ a former name of Ethiopia. —**Abyssinian** *adj.* & *n.*

AC, a.c. *abbr.* alternating current.

Ac *symbol* actinium.

acacia /ə'keɪʃə/ *n.* a tree or shrub of the genus *Acacia*, some members of which yield gum arabic; a related tree, the false acacia or locust-tree (*Robinia pseudoacacia*) grown for ornament. [L f. Gk]

Academe /'ækədiːm/ *n.* (*literary*) **Groves of Academe**, a university environment. [f. Gk (as ACADEMY)]

academic /ækə'demɪk/ *adj.* **1.** of a college or university; scholarly as opposed to technical or practical. **2.** not of practical relevance. —*n.* a member of an academic institution. —**academically** *adv.* [f. F or L (as ACADEMY)]

academician /əkædə'mɪʃ(ə)n/ *n.* a member of an Academy. [f. ACADEMY]

Académie française /ækædemi frɑ'sez/ a French literary academy with a constant membership of 40, founded by Richelieu in 1635. Its functions include the compilation and periodic revision of a definitive dictionary of the French language, the first edition of which appeared in 1694. Its tendency is to defend traditional literary and linguistic rules and to discourage innovation. Nevertheless, membership is accounted a high literary honour and is coveted even by unorthodox writers who continue to experiment with the language (see FRENCH). [F, = French Academy]

Academy /əˈkædəmɪ/ **1.** a park and gymnasium in the outskirts of ancient Athens, sacred to the hero Academus, where Plato founded a school which survived until its dissolution by Justinian in AD 529. The name is applied by extension to the philosophical system of Plato, and also to the philosophical scepticism of the school in the 3rd and 2nd c. BC. **2.** a society of scholars or artists etc.; **the Academy,** the Royal Academy of Painting, Sculpture, and Architecture. —**Academy award,** any of the awards of the Academy of Motion Picture Arts and Sciences (Hollywood, USA) given annually for success in the film industry. [f. Gk *Acadēmos*]

academy /əˈkædəmɪ/ *n.* a school, especially for specialized training; (*Sc.*) a secondary school. [f. prec.]

Acadia /əˈkeɪdɪə/ a former French colony (*Acadie*; now Nova Scotia) on the eastern seaboard of North America. Founded in 1603, the colony was subject to considerable encroachment from British colonists and much of it was ceded to Britain by the Treaty of Utrecht in 1713. Some of its French inhabitants withdrew to French territory in the following year, and during the French and Indian War (1754–63) the remainder, who were considered to be a threat to the British position, were forcibly resettled in other British colonies to the south.

Acadian /əˈkeɪdɪən/ *adj.* of Acadia or Acadians. —*n.* a native or inhabitant of Acadia; a descendant of Acadian immigrants in Louisiana. [f. prec.]

acanthus /əˈkænθəs/ *n.* a Mediterranean herbaceous plant of the genus *Acanthus*, with prickly leaves; (*Gk Archit.*) a representation of its leaf (ill. TEMPLES). [L f. Gk (*akantha* thorn)]

ACAS /ˈeɪkæs/ *abbr.* Advisory, Conciliation, and Arbitration Service. The service was set up in 1975 to provide such facilities as a means of avoiding or resolving industrial disputes, and to promote the improvement of collective bargaining.

accede /ækˈsiːd/ *v.i.* **1.** to take office, to come *to* the throne. **2.** to agree *to* (a proposal etc.). [f. L *accedere* (AD-, *cedere* go)]

accelerate /əkˈseləreɪt/ *v.t./i.* to move faster or happen earlier; to cause to do this; to increase the speed of a motor vehicle. —**acceleration** /-ˈreɪʃ(ə)n/ *n.* [f. L *accelerare* (AD-, *celer* swift)]

accelerator /əkˈseləreɪtə(r)/ *n.* a device for increasing speed, a pedal that controls the throttle in a motor vehicle; an apparatus for imparting high speeds to charged particles. [f. prec.]

accelerometer /əkseləˈrɒmɪtə(r)/ *n.* an instrument for measuring acceleration or vibrations. [f. ACCELERATE + -METER]

accent /ˈæksent/ *n.* **1.** prominence given to a syllable by stress or pitch. **2.** a mark used with a letter or word to indicate pitch, stress, quality of vowel, etc. **3.** a particular (esp. local or national) mode of pronunciation. **4.** a distinctive feature or emphasis. —/ækˈsent/ *v.t.* **1.** to pronounce with an accent. **2.** to write accents on. **3.** to accentuate. —**accentual** /ækˈsentjuːəl/ *adj.* [L *accentus* (AD-, *cantus* song)]

accentor /əkˈsentə(r)/ *n.* a bird of the genus *Prunella*, e.g. the hedge-sparrow. [L, f. *ad* to +*cantor* singer]

accentuate /əkˈsentjueɪt/ *v.t.* to emphasize, to make prominent. —**accentuation** /-ˈeɪʃ(ə)n/ *n.* [f. L (as ACCENT)]

accept /əkˈsept/ *v.t.* **1.** to consent to receive, to take willingly; to answer (an invitation or suitor) affirmatively. **2.** to regard favourably; to tolerate or submit to. **3.** to take as valid. **4.** to undertake (a responsibility etc.). —**acceptance** *n.*, **acceptor** *n.* [f. OF or L *acceptare* (AD-, *capere* take)]

acceptable *adj.* worth accepting, welcome; tolerable. —**acceptably** *adv.*, **acceptability** /-ˈbɪlɪtɪ/ *n.* [as prec.]

access /ˈækses/ *n.* **1.** a way in, a means of approaching, reaching, or using. **2.** an outburst of emotion. —*v.t.* **1.** to obtain (data) from a computer. **2.** to accession. [f. OF or L (as ACCEDE)]

accessible /əkˈsesɪb(ə)l/ *adj.* that may be reached or obtained. —**accessibility** /-ˈbɪlɪtɪ/ *n.*, **accessibly** *adv.*, [F or f. L (as ACCEDE)]

accession /əkˈseʃ(ə)n/ *n.* **1.** acceding or attaining (*to* a throne, office, etc.). **2.** a thing added. —*v.t.* to record the addition of (a new item) to a library or museum. [as prec.]

accessory /əkˈsesərɪ/ *n.* **1.** an additional or extra thing; (usu.

in *pl.*) a small attachment or fitting. **2.** a person who helps in or is privy *to* an act, especially a crime. —*adj.* additional, contributing in a minor way. [f. L (as ACCEDE)]

accidence /ˈæksɪd(ə)ns/ *n.* the part of grammar that deals with the way words are inflected. [f. L. (as foll.)]

accident /ˈæksɪd(ə)nt/ *n.* an event that is unexpected or without apparent cause; an unintentional act, chance; an unfortunate (esp. a harmful) event. [f. OF f. L *accidens* (AD-, *cadere* fall)]

accidental /æksɪˈdent(ə)l/ *adj.* happening or done by accident. —*n.* (*Mus.*) a sign indicating temporary departure from a key signature. —**accidentally** *adv.* [f. L (as prec.)]

acclaim /əˈkleɪm/ *v.t.* to welcome with shouts of approval, to applaud enthusiastically; to hail as. —*n.* a shout of applause or welcome. —**acclamation** /ækləˈmeɪʃ(ə)n/ *n.* [f. L *acclamare* (AD-, *clamare* shout)]

acclimatize /əˈklaɪmətaɪz/ *v.t./i.* to make or become used to a new climate or conditions. —**acclimatization** /-ˈzeɪʃ(ə)n/ *n.* [f. F (à to, *climat* climate)]

acclivity /əˈklɪvɪtɪ/ *n.* an upward slope. [f. L *acclivitas* (AD-, *clivus* slope)]

accolade /ækəˈleɪd/ *n.* **1.** bestowal of praise. **2.** a sign at the bestowal of a knighthood, now usually a tap on the shoulder with the flat of a sword. [F (as AD, L *collum* neck)]

accommodate /əˈkɒmədeɪt/ *v.t.* **1.** to provide lodging or room for. **2.** to do a favour to, to oblige or supply (a person *with*). **3.** to adapt, to harmonize. [f. L *accommodare* (AD-, *commodus* fitting)]

accommodating *adj.* obliging, compliant. [f. prec.]

accommodation /əkɒməˈdeɪʃ(ə)n/ *n.* **1.** lodging, living-premises. **2.** adaptation, adjustment; a convenient arrangement. —**accommodation address,** one used on letters to a person unable to give a permanent address. [F or f. L (as ACCOMMODATE)]

accompaniment /əˈkʌmpənɪmənt/ *n.* **1.** an instrumental or orchestral part supporting or partnering a solo instrument, voice, or group. **2.** an accompanying thing. [f. F (as ACCOMPANY)]

accompanist /əˈkʌmpənɪst/ *n.* one who plays a musical accompaniment. [f. foll.]

accompany /əˈkʌmpənɪ/ *v.t.* **1.** to go with, to travel with as a companion or helper; to be done or found with. **2.** to provide in addition. **3.** (*Mus.*) to support or partner with an accompaniment. [f. F (as COMPANION)]

accomplice /əˈkʌmplɪs/ *n.* a partner in crime or wrong-doing. [f. F *complice* f. L (*complex* confederate)]

accomplish /əˈkʌmplɪʃ/ *v.t.* to succeed in doing, to complete. [f. OF f. L (AD-, *complere* complete)]

accomplished /əˈkʌmplɪʃt/ *adj.* skilled, having many accomplishments. [f. prec.]

accomplishment /əˈkʌmplɪʃmənt/ *n.* **1.** an acquired skill, especially a social one. **2.** accomplishing, completion. **3.** a thing achieved. [f. ACCOMPLISH]

accord /əˈkɔːd/ *v.t./i.* **1.** to be consistent *with.* **2.** to grant, to give. —*n.* conformity, agreement. —**of one's own accord,** without being asked or compelled. [f. F f. L *cor* heart]

accordance /əˈkɔːd(ə)ns/ *n.* conformity, agreement. —**accordant** *adj.* [as prec.]

according *adv.* **according as,** in a manner or to a degree that varies. **according to,** in a manner corresponding to; as stated by. [f. ACCORD]

accordingly *adv.* as the (stated) circumstances suggest. [f. prec.]

accordion /əˈkɔːdɪən/ *n.* a portable musical instrument with bellows, metal reeds, and keys and/or buttons. —**accordionist** *n.* [f. G. f. It. *accordare* tune]

accost /əˈkɒst/ *v.t.* to approach and speak to; (of a prostitute) to solicit. [f. F f. It. f. L *costa* rib)]

account /əˈkaʊnt/ *n.* **1.** a statement of money, goods, or services received or expended; a credit or similar business arrangement with a bank or firm; a record of this. **2.** a description, a report. **3.** importance, advantage. **4.** a reckoning. —*v.t./i.* to regard as. —**account for,** to give a reckoning of; to provide or serve as an explanation for; to kill or overcome. **on account of,** because of. [f. OF *aconter* (AD-, *conter* count)]

accountable *adj.* having to account (*for* one's actions); explicable. —**accountability** /-ˈbɪlɪtɪ/ *n.* [f. prec.]

accountant *n.* one who keeps or examines business accounts. —**accountancy** *n.* [as ACCOUNT]

accounting *n.* keeping or examining accounts; accountancy. [f. ACCOUNT]

accoutrements /əˈkuːtrəmənts/ n.pl. equipment, trappings. [F]

Accra /əˈkrɑː/ the capital of Ghana, a port on the Gulf of Guinea; pop. (est. 1980) 998,800.

accredit /əˈkredɪt/ v.t. to attribute, to credit (with a saying etc.); to send (an ambassador etc.) with credentials; to gain belief or influence for. —**accreditation** /-ˈteɪʃ(ə)n/ n., **accredited** adj. [f. F (as AD-, CREDIT)]

accretion /əˈkriːʃ(ə)n/ n. a growth or increase by gradual addition; matter added, adhesion of this. [f. L accretio (AD-, crescere grow)]

accrue /əˈkruː/ v.t./i. to come as a natural increase or advantage; to accumulate. [f. AF f. L (as prec.)]

accumulate /əˈkjuːmjʊleɪt/ v.t./i. to get more and more of; to increase in quantity or mass. —**accumulation** /-ˈleɪʃ(ə)n/ n. [f. L accumulare (AD-, cumulus heap)]

accumulator /əˈkjuːmjʊleɪtə(r)/ n. **1.** a rechargeable electric cell, a storage battery. **2.** a bet placed on a series of events with winnings from each staked on the next. **3.** a storage register in a computer. [f. prec.]

accurate /ˈækjʊərət/ adj. precise, conforming exactly to a standard or to truth. —**accuracy** n., **accurately** adv. [f. L accuratus done carefully (AD-, curare care)]

accursed /əˈkɜːsɪd/ adj. lying under a curse; (colloq.) detestable, annoying. [OE (A-, CURSE)]

accusation /ækjuːˈzeɪʃ(ə)n/ n. **1.** a statement accusing a person. **2.** accusing, being accused. [f. OF (as ACCUSE)]

accusative /əˈkjuːzətɪv/ n. (Gram.) the case expressing the object of a verb or preposition. —adj. (Gram.) of or in the accusative. [f. OF or L]

accusatorial /əkjuːzəˈtɔːrɪəl/ adj. (of procedure) in which the prosecutor is distinct from the judge (opp. inquisitorial). [f. L (as ACCUSE)]

accusatory /əˈkjuːzətərɪ/ adj. of or conveying an accusation. [f. L (as foll.)]

accuse /əˈkjuːz/ v.t. to state that one lays the blame for a fault or crime etc. upon. —**accuser** n. (f. OF f. L accusare (AD-, causa cause))

accustom /əˈkʌstəm/ v.t. to make or become used to. [f. OF f. L (as CUSTOM)]

accustomed /əˈkʌstəmd/ adj. customary; used to. [f. prec.]

ace /eɪs/ n. **1.** a playing-card etc. with one spot. **2.** one who excels in some activity. **3.** a stroke in tennis (especially a service) that is too good for an opponent to return. **4.** a point scored in rackets, badminton, etc. —**within an ace of,** on the verge of. [f. OF f. L as one]

Aceldama /əˈkeldəmə/ a field near ancient Jerusalem purchased for a cemetery with the blood-money received by Judas Iscariot (Matt. 27: 8, Acts 1: 19). [Aram., = field of blood]

acerbity /əˈsɜːbɪtɪ/ n. **1.** sharpness in speech or manner. **2.** sourness. [f. L acerbus sour-tasting]

acetate /ˈæsɪteɪt/ n. **1.** a salt or ester of acetic acid, especially its cellulose ester used to make textiles and gramophone records. **2.** fabric made from cellulose acetate. [f. foll.]

acetic /əˈkɛːtɪk/ adj. of or like vinegar. —**acetic acid,** the acid that gives vinegar its characteristic taste and smell. [f. F f. L acetum vinegar]

acetone /ˈæsɪtəʊn/ n. a colourless volatile liquid that dissolves organic compounds. [f. prec.]

acetylene /əˈsetɪliːn/ n. a hydrocarbon gas that burns with a bright flame used for cutting and welding metal. [as prec.]

Achaea /əˈkiːə/ **1.** a district of ancient Greece comprising SE Thessaly and the north coast of the Peloponnese. **2.** a Roman province comprising all the southern part of Greece.

Achaean /əˈkiːən/ adj. of Achaea or the Achaeans. —n. **1.** (in the Homeric poems) a Greek. **2.** (in classical times) an inhabitant of Achaea. [f. prec.]

Achaemenid /əˈkiːmənɪd/ adj. of the ruling dynasty in Persia 553–330 BC, descendants of the eponymous founder Achaemenes, that ended with the defeat of Darius III by Alexander the Great. —n. a member of this dynasty.

Achates /əˈkɑːtiːz/ (Gk & Rom. legend) a companion of Aeneas. His fidelity to his friend was so exemplary as to become proverbial (fidus (= faithful) Achates).

ache /eɪk/ n. a continuous or prolonged dull pain or mental distress. —v.i. to suffer or be the source of this. —**achy** adj. [f. OE. Dr Johnson is mainly responsible for the modern spelling, as he erroneously derived ache and the earlier form ake from Gk akhos (= pain, distress) and declared that the latter was 'more grammatically written ache']

achene /əˈkiːn/ n. a small dry one-seeded fruit that does not open, e.g. a strawberry pip. [f. Gk a not, khainō gape]

Acheulian /əˈʃuːlɪən/ adj. of the later stages of the lower palaeolithic hand-axe industries in Europe, named after the type-site at St Acheul near Amiens in northern France. The hand-axes of this period are differentiated from those of the preceding Abbevillian by the use of an implement made of wood, antler, or bone to hammer flakes off a flint, giving these a less rough appearance than that produced by a hard stone. In Africa, where the industry seems to have originated, and where it survived much longer than elsewhere, the entire lower palaeolithic hand-axe sequence is referred to as Acheulian, with the African lower Acheulian representing the Abbevillian of Europe; remains occur at Olduvai Gorge in northern Tanzania and at Kalambo Falls near the SE end of Lake Tanganyika. The industries as a whole are dated to c.500,000–200,000 BC. —n. this industry. [f. St Acheul]

achieve /əˈtʃiːv/ v.t. to reach or attain by effort; to earn (a reputation etc.); to accomplish. [f. OF (a chief to a head)]

achievement /əˈtʃiːvmənt/ n. **1.** something achieved; an act of achieving. **2.** (in heraldry) an escutcheon with adjuncts, or a bearing, especially in memory of a distinguished feat (ill. HERALDRY). [f. prec.]

Achilles /əˈkɪliːz/ (Gk legend) a hero of the Trojan War, son of Peleus and Thetis. During his infancy his mother plunged him in the Styx, thus making his body invulnerable except for the heel by which she held him. He was wounded in the heel during the Trojan war by an arrow shot by Paris, and died of this wound. —**Achilles' heel,** a weak or vulnerable point. **Achilles' tendon,** a tendon attaching the calf muscles to the heel.

achromatic /ækrəˈmætɪk/ adj. (in optics) free from colour; transmitting light without decomposing it into constituent colours. [f. F f. Gk (a not, CHROMATIC)]

acid /ˈæsɪd/ n. any of a class of substances that contain hydrogen and neutralize alkalis, turn blue litmus red, and of which the principal types are sour and able to corrode or dissolve metals (see below); any sour substance. —adj. sharp-tasting, sour; looking or sounding bitter. —**acid rain,** rain made acid by contamination, especially by waste gases from power stations, factories, etc. **acid test,** a crucial and conclusive test. (Acid is applied to a metal to test whether it is gold or not.) —**acidic** /əˈsɪdɪk/ adj., **acidity** /əˈsɪdɪtɪ/ n. [f. F or L (acēre be sour)]

The term was originally applied to the stony 'mineral acids', such as sulphuric acid, whose properties were attributed in the 17th c. to their consisting of particles with sharp points. Many organic compounds, however, also show acidic properties. The commonest modern definition of an acid is a substance which releases hydrogen ions when dissolved in water (or, by extension, in other alkaline substances), producing salts. Acids are now recognized as substances which are donors of hydrogen ions or protons or acceptors of electron pairs, but an unequivocal definition of the term has yet to be found. Acids play a highly important role in industry. Among the most useful mineral acids are sulphuric acid, which is the electrolyte commonly used in car batteries; hydrochloric acid, which is used in ore reduction, metal cleaning, and food processing; and nitric acid, which is used in the manufacture of explosives and fertilizers.

acidify /əˈsɪdɪfaɪ/ v.t. to make or become sour. [f. ACID]

acidosis /æsɪˈdəʊsɪs/ n. an over-acid condition of blood or body tissue. [as prec.]

acidulate /əˈsɪdjʊleɪt/ v.t. to make somewhat acid. [f. L acidulus somewhat sour]

acidulous /əˈsɪdʊləs/ adj. somewhat acid. [as prec.]

acknowledge /əkˈnɒlɪdʒ/ v.t. **1.** to agree to the truth or validity of, to admit. **2.** to report the receipt of. **3.** to show appreciation of. —**acknowledgement** n. [f. obs. v. knowledge]

acme /ˈækmɪ/ n. the highest point, the point of perfection. [Gk, = highest point]

acne /ˈæknɪ/ n. inflammation of the oil-glands of the skin, producing red pimples. [f. erron. Gk aknas for akmas (akmē facial eruption; cf. prec.)]

acolyte /ˈækəlaɪt/ n. a person assisting a priest in certain church services; an assistant. [f. F or L f. Gk akolouthos follower]

Aconcagua /ækɒnˈkɑːgwə/ the highest mountain in South America (6,960 m, 22,834 ft.) in the Andes of Argentina. It is an extinct volcano.

aconite /ˈækənaɪt/ n. a perennial plant of the buttercup family (genus *Aconitum*) with a poisonous root; a drug obtained from this. —**winter aconite,** a yellow-flowered plant of the genus *Eranthis*, blooming in winter. [f. F or L f. Gk]

acorn /ˈeɪkɔːn/ n. the fruit of the oak-tree, with a cup-like base. [OE]

acoustic /əˈkuːstɪk/ adj. of sound or the sense of hearing; of acoustics. —n. acoustics. —**acoustic guitar,** see GUITAR. **acoustics** n.pl. the properties or qualities (of a room etc.) affecting the transmission of sound; (as *sing.*) the science of sound. (See ill. SOUND.) —**acoustical** adj., **acoustically** adv. [f. Gk (akouō hear)]

acquaint /əˈkweɪnt/ v.t. to make aware or familiar. —**be acquainted with,** to know slightly. [f. OF f. L accognitare (AD-, cognoscere know)]

acquaintance n. 1. being acquainted. 2. a person one knows slightly. [as prec.]

acquiesce /ækwɪˈes/ v.i. to agree (tacitly), to raise no objection. —**acquiesce in,** to accept (an arrangement etc.). —**acquiescence** n., **acquiescent** adj. [f. L acquiescere (AD-, quiescere rest)]

acquire /əˈkwaɪə(r)/ v.t. to gain by and for oneself. —**acquired taste,** a liking gained by experience, not instantly. —**acquirement** n., **acquisition** /ækwɪˈzɪʃ(ə)n/ n. [f. OF f. L acquirere (AD-, quaerere seek)]

acquisitive /əˈkwɪzɪtɪv/ adj. keen to acquire things. —**acquisitively** adv., **acquisitiveness** n. [f. L (as prec.)]

acquit /əˈkwɪt/ v.t. (-tt-) to declare (a person) to be not guilty (of an offence etc.). —**acquit oneself,** to perform, to conduct oneself. [f. OF f. L acquitare pay debt]

acquittal /əˈkwɪt(ə)l/ n. 1. a verdict acquitting a person. 2. performance (of a duty). [f. prec.]

Acre /ˈeɪkə(r)/ a sea port of Israel. It was captured by the Christians in the Third Crusade in 1191, and recaptured, the last Christian stronghold in the Holy Land, in 1291.

acre /ˈeɪkə(r)/ n. a measure of land, originally as much as a yoke of oxen could plough in a day, afterwards limited by statute to 4840 sq. yds. (0.405 ha); a stretch of land. [OE]

acreage /ˈeɪkərɪdʒ/ n. the total number of acres; an extent of land. [f. prec.]

acrid /ˈækrɪd/ adj. bitterly pungent; bitter in manner or temper. —**acridity** /əˈkrɪdɪtɪ/ n. [f. L acer keen]

acrimonious /ækrɪˈməʊnɪəs/ adj. bitter in manner or temper. —**acrimoniously** adv., **acrimony** /ˈækrɪmənɪ/ n. [f. F or L (as ACRID)]

acrobat /ˈækrəbæt/ n. a performer of spectacular gymnastic feats. —**acrobatic** /-ˈbætɪk/ adj., **acrobatically** adv. [f. F f. Gk (akron summit, bainō walk)]

acrobatics /ækrəˈbætɪks/ n.pl. acrobatic feats. [f. prec.]

acronym /ˈækrənɪm/ n. a word formed from the initial letters of other words, e.g. *Nato, laser*. [f. Gk akron extremity, onoma name]

acropolis /əˈkrɒpəlɪs/ n. the citadel or upper fortified part of an ancient Greek city. —**the Acropolis,** that at Athens, containing the Parthenon, Erechtheum, and other noted buildings, mostly dating from the 5th c. BC. [f. Gk akron summit, polis city]

across /əˈkrɒs/ prep. & adv. 1. from side to side (of). 2. to or on the other side (of). 3. forming a cross with. 4. so as to be understood or accepted. —**across the board,** applying to all. **come** or **run across,** to meet or find by chance. [f. OF (croix cross)]

acrostic /əˈkrɒstɪk/ n. a word-puzzle or poem in which certain letters (usually the first or first and last in each line) form word(s). [f. F or Gk (akron end, stikhos row)]

acrylic /əˈkrɪlɪk/ adj. of material made from a synthetic polymer derived from acrylic acid. —n. an acrylic fibre, plastic, or resin. —**acrylic acid,** an unsaturated organic acid. [f. L acer pungent, olēre smell]

ACT abbr. Australian Capital Territory.

act n. 1. a thing done; the process of doing something. 2. a piece of entertainment. 3. a pretence. 4. a main division of a play or opera. 5. a decree or law made by a parliament. — v.t./i. 1. to perform actions, to behave; to perform functions; to have an effect. 2. to be an actor or actress. 3. to perform (a part) in a play etc.; to portray by actions. —**act of God,** the operation of uncontrollable natural forces. **Acts (of the Apostles),** a book of the New Testament immediately following the Gospels, relating the early history of the Church and dealing largely with the lives and work of St

Peter and St Paul. It is traditionally ascribed to St Luke. [f. OF & L actus (agere do)]

Actaeon /ækˈtiːən, ˈæk-/ (Gk myth.) a hunter who, because he accidentally saw Artemis bathing, was changed into a stag and killed by his own hounds.

actinic /ækˈtɪnɪk/ adj. having photochemical properties, as of short-wavelength radiation. [f. Gk aktis ray]

actinide /ˈæktɪnaɪd/ n. any of a series of fifteen radioactive metallic elements ranging from actinium (atomic number 89) to lawrencium (103). [f. foll.]

actinium /ækˈtɪnɪəm/ n. a radioactive metallic element, symbol Ac, atomic number 89, which occurs in pitchblende. It was first discovered in 1899. [f. Gk aktis ray]

action /ˈækʃ(ə)n/ n. 1. the process of doing or performing, exertion of energy or influence. 2. a thing done; a series of events in a drama etc. 3. a battle, fighting. 4. a way of moving or functioning, the mechanism of an instrument. 5. a lawsuit. —**action replay,** a play-back (at normal speed or in slow motion) of a televised incident in a sports match. **out of action,** not working. [f. OF f. L (as ACT)]

actionable adj. providing ground for an action at law. [f. prec.]

action painting abstract painting in which the artist applies paint by random actions. The term was first used in 1952 to describe the approach to art of certain New York painters. Although it is often used as a synonym for abstract expressionism, not all the artists associated with the latter can be considered as action painters.

activate /ˈæktɪveɪt/ v.t. 1. to make active. 2. to make radioactive. —**activation** /-ˈveɪʃ(ə)n/ n., **activator** n. [f. foll.]

active /ˈæktɪv/ adj. 1. consisting in or characterized by action, energetic; working, operative; having an effect. 2. radioactive. 3. (Gram.) attributing the action of the verb to the person or thing whence it proceeds (e.g. in *we saw him*). —n. (Gram.) the active voice or form of a verb. —**active voice,** (Gram.) that comprising the active forms of verbs. —**actively** adv., **activeness** n. [f. OF or L (as ACT)]

activist /ˈæktɪvɪst/ n. one who follows a policy of vigorous action in a cause, especially in politics. —**activism** n. [f. prec.]

activity /ækˈtɪvətɪ/ n. 1. being active, the exertion of energy. 2. a sphere or kind of action. 3. (esp. in *pl.*) actions, occupations. 4. radioactivity. [as ACTIVE]

actor n. a performer in a drama, film, etc. —**actress** n.fem. [L, = doer (as ACT)]

actual /ˈæktʃʊəl/ adj. existing in fact, real; current. [f. OF f. L (as ACT)]

actuality /æktʃʊˈælɪtɪ/ n. reality; (in *pl.*) existing conditions. [f. prec.]

actually /ˈæktʃʊəlɪ/ adv. 1. really. 2. at present. 3. strange as it may seem. [f. ACTUAL]

actuary /ˈæktʃʊərɪ/ n. an expert in statistics, especially one who calculates insurance risks and premiums. —**actuarial** /-ˈeərɪəl/ adj. [f. L actuarius bookkeeper]

actuate /ˈæktʃʊeɪt/ v.t. to activate (a movement or process), to cause to function; to cause (a person) to act. —**actuation** /-ˈeɪʃ(ə)n/ n., **actuator** n. [f. L (as ACTUAL)]

acuity /əˈkjuːətɪ/ n. sharpness, acuteness. [f. F or L (as ACUTE)]

acumen /ˈækjuːmən/ n. shrewdness. [L, = sharp thing]

acupuncture /ˈækjuːpʌŋktʃə(r)/ n. a method (originating in China) of pricking the tissues of the body with fine needles as medical treatment or to relieve pain. —**acupuncturist** n. [f. L acu with a needle + PUNCTURE]

acute /əˈkjuːt/ adj. 1. sharp or severe in its effect. 2. shrewd, perceptive. 3. (of a disease) not chronic, coming to a crisis. 4. (of sound) high, shrill. —**acute accent,** a mark (´) over a vowel to show its quality or length. **acute angle,** one of less than 90°. —**acutely** adv., **acuteness** n. [f. L acutus (acuere sharpen)]

AD abbr. of the Christian era. [abbr. of ANNO DOMINI]

ad n. (colloq.) an advertisement. [abbr.]

ad- prefix (usu. assimilated to **ac-** before c, k, q, to **af-** etc. before f, g, l, n, p, r, s, t; reduced to **a-** before sc, sp, st) implying motion or direction to; change into; addition, adherence, increase; simple intensification. [f. OF or L ad to]

adage /ˈædɪdʒ/ n. a traditional maxim, a proverb. [F f. L adagium (ad to, aiere say)]

adagio /əˈdɑːdʒɪəʊ/ adv. (Mus.) in slow time. —n. (pl. **-os**) (Mus.) a movement to be played in this way. [It.]

Adam[1] /ˈædəm/ (in Hebrew tradition) the first man.

—Adam's apple, the projection of cartilage at the front of the neck, especially in men. [f. Heb., = man]

Adam², Robert (1728-92), the principal architect of the 'Adam Revolution', son of William Adam, a leading Scottish architect. Robert's brothers also assisted him in the family practice. He began a Grand Tour in 1754, mainly in France and Italy, which gave him knowledge of ancient buildings and modern neoclassical theory. The brothers set up in London in 1758 and introduced a lighter, more decorative, style than the Palladianism of the previous half-century. Their *Works in Architecture* (1773, 1779, and posthumously 1822), published as advertisement, claim to have revolutionized architecture in Britain. Robert's actual buildings are almost exclusively domestic, and he was particularly successful as an interior designer.

adamant /ˈædəmənt/ *adj.* stubbornly resolute. —**adamantine** /-ˈmæntaɪn/ *adj.* [f. OF f. L f. Gk *adamas* very hard metal or stone]

adapt /əˈdæpt/ *v.t./i.* to make or become suitable for a new use or situation etc. —**adaptation** /-ˈteɪʃ(ə)n/ *n.* [f. F f. L *adaptare* (AD-, *aptus* fit)]

adaptable *adj.* able to be adapted or to adapt. —**adaptability** /-ˈbɪlɪti/ *n.* [f. prec.]

adaptor *n.* **1.** a device for making equipment compatible. **2.** a device for connecting several electric plugs to one socket. [f. ADAPT]

ADC *abbr.* aide-de-camp.

add *v.t./i.* **1.** to join (a thing *to* another) as an increase or supplement. **2.** to put (numbers or amounts) together to get their total. **3.** to make as a further remark. —**add up,** to find the total of; to amount *to*; (*colloq.*) to make sense, to seem reasonable. —**adder** *n.* [f. L *addere* put together]

addendum /əˈdendəm/ *n.* (*pl.* **-a**) something added; (in *pl.*) additional matter at the end of a book. [L, f. *addere* add]

adder *n.* **1.** a small venomous snake, especially the common viper. **2.** any of various harmless snakes of North America. **3.** (also **death adder**) a venomous snake of the cobra family, *Acanthophis antarcticus*, found in Australia and nearby islands. [OE, orig. *nadder*]

addict /ˈædɪkt/ *n.* a person who is addicted, especially to drugs. [as foll.]

addicted /əˈdɪktɪd/ *adj.* having an addiction *to*. [f. L *addicere* assign]

addiction /əˈdɪkʃ(ə)n/ *n.* the condition of doing or using something as a habit or compulsively (esp. of drug-taking, with adverse effects on ceasing); devotion *to* an interest. [as prec.]

addictive /əˈdɪktɪv/ *adj.* causing addiction. [as ADDICT]

Addis Ababa /ˈædɪs ˈæbəbə/ the capital of Ethiopia, situated at 2,440 m (*c.*8,000 ft.); pop. (est. 1980) 1,277,200.

Addison¹ /ˈædɪs(ə)n/, Joseph (1672-1719), English poet, dramatist, and essayist, whose name is inseparably linked with that of Sir Richard Steele for their co-operation in the daily journal *The Spectator*, and who was a close friend of Swift and other writers. A staunch Whig, he was an MP from 1708 until his death, holding various (chiefly minor) political offices. His tragedy *Cato* was produced with great success in 1713. In the history of English literature he is remarkable for his simple unornamented prose style which marked the end of the mannerisms and eccentricities of the 17th c. (See STEELE.)

Addison² /ˈædɪs(ə)n/, Thomas (1793-1860), English physician, the first to describe what is now called Addison's disease, a condition characterized by great weakness and frequently a bronze pigmentation of the skin, and to ascribe it correctly to defective functioning of the adrenal glands which were not previously known to be the seat of any definite malady. Distinguished for his remarkable zeal in the investigation of disease, Addison had a great reputation as a clinical teacher, and Guy's Hospital in London attained fame as a school of medicine during his connection with it as physician and lecturer.

addition /əˈdɪʃ(ə)n/ *n.* adding; a thing added. —**in addition,** as something added (*to*). [f. OF or L (as ADD)]

additional *adj.* added, extra. —**additionally** *adv.* [f. prec.]

additive /ˈædɪtɪv/ *n.* a thing added, especially a substance with special properties. —*adj.* involving addition. [f. L (as ADD)]

addle *v.t./i.* **1.** (of an egg) to become rotten and produce no chick. **2.** to muddle, to confuse. —**Addled Parliament,** the parliament of James I, summoned in 1614, so known because it refused to accede to the king's financial requests,

did not succeed in its attempts to curb his existing powers of taxation, and was dissolved without having passed any legislation. [OE, = filth]

address /əˈdres/ *n.* **1.** the place where a person lives or a firm is situated; particulars of this, especially for postal purposes. **2.** a speech to an audience. **3.** the part of a computer instruction that specifies the location of an item of stored information. —*v.t.* **1.** to write postal directions on. **2.** to speak or write to; to direct a remark or written statement to. **3.** to apply *oneself* or direct one's attention to. **4.** to take aim at (the ball, in golf). [f. OF f. L (as DIRECT)]

addressee /ædreˈsiː/ *n.* a person to whom a letter etc. is addressed. [f. prec.]

adduce /əˈdjuːs/ *v.t.* to cite as an instance or proof. [f. L *adducere* (AD-, *ducere* bring)]

adducible *adj.* that may be adduced. [f. prec.]

Adelaide /ˈædəleɪd/ the capital and chief port of South Australia, on the River Torrens; pop. (1983) 969,160.

Adélie Land /əˈdeɪli/ French territory in the coastal region of Antarctica, south of Australia.

Aden /ˈeɪd(ə)n/ a port commanding the entrance to the Red Sea, the capital (since 1967) of the People's Democratic Republic of Yemen (South Yemen); pop. (est. 1980) 343,000. A trading centre since Roman times, it was formerly under British rule, first as part of British India (from 1839), then from 1935 as a Crown Colony.

adenoids /ˈædənɔɪdz/ *n.pl.* enlarged lymphatic tissue between the back of the nose and throat, often hindering breathing. —**adenoidal** *adj.* [f. Gk *adēn* gland]

adenoma /ædɪˈnəʊmə/ *n.* a gland-like benign tumour. [as prec.]

adept /ˈædept/ *adj.* thoroughly proficient (*in* or *at*). —*n.* an adept person. [f. L (*adipisci* attain)]

adequate /ˈædɪkwət/ *adj.* sufficient, satisfactory; passable but not outstandingly good. —**adequacy** *n.*, **adequately** *adv.* [f. L *adaequare* make equal]

adhere /ədˈhɪə(r)/ *v.i.* **1.** to stick. **2.** to give one's support or allegiance *to*. **3.** to behave according *to* a rule etc. [f. F or L *adhaerēre* (AD-, *haerēre* stick)]

adherent *n.* a supporter (*of* a party or doctrine). —*adj.* adhering or sticking *to*. —**adherence** *n.* [as prec.]

adhesion /ədˈhiːʒ(ə)n/ *n.* **1.** adhering (*lit.* or *fig.*). **2.** the growing together of normally separate tissues as a result of inflammation or injury; such a formation. [f. F or L (as ADHERE)]

adhesive /ədˈhiːsɪv/ *adj.* having the property of adhering, sticky. —*n.* an adhesive substance. —**adhesive tape,** a strip of paper or transparent material coated with adhesive, used for fastening packages etc. —**adhesiveness** *n.* [f. F (as ADHERE)]

ad hoc /æd ˈhɒk/ for this purpose, special(ly). [L]

adieu /əˈdjuː/ *int.* & *n.* goodbye. [f. F (*à* to, *Dieu* God)]

Adi Granth /ˌɑːdɪ ɡrʌnt/ the single sacred scripture of Sikhism, compiled by religious teachers, containing religious poetry in several languages. After the death of the tenth and last guru (early 18th c.) the Adi Granth took the place of subsequent teachers. It is the main object of worship in the Sikh gurdwara. [Hindi (= first book), f. Skr.]

ad infinitum /æd ɪnfɪˈnaɪtəm/ without limit, for ever. [L]

adipose /ˈædɪpəʊs/ *adj.* of animal fat, fatty. —**adiposity** /-ˈpɒsɪti/ *n.* [f. L *adeps* fat]

Adirondack Mountains /ædɪˈrɒndæk/ (also **Adirondacks**) a range of mountains in New York State, source of the Hudson and Mohawk Rivers. Ancient glaciers have left rugged gorges, lakes, and waterfalls, and the region, with its forests, is now one of great scenic beauty.

adjacent /əˈdʒeɪs(ə)nt/ *adj.* lying near, contiguous (*to*). [f. L *adjacēre* (AD-, *jacēre* lie)]

adjective /ˈædʒɪktɪv/ *n.* a word indicating an attribute, used to describe or modify a noun. —**adjectival** /-ˈtaɪv(ə)l/ *adj.*, **adjectivally** *adv.* [f. OF f. L *adjicere* (AD- *jacere* throw)]

adjoin /əˈdʒɔɪn/ *v.t.* to be next to and joined with. [f. OF f. L *adjungere* (AD-, *jungere* join)]

adjourn /əˈdʒɜːn/ *v.t./i.* to postpone, to break off temporarily for later resumption. —**adjournment** *n.* [f. OF f. L (AD-, *diurnum* day)]

adjudge /əˈdʒʌdʒ/ *v.t.* to pronounce judgement on; to pronounce or award judicially. —**adjudg(e)ment** *n.* [f. OF f. L *adjudicare* (AD-, *judex* judge)]

adjudicate /əˈdʒuːdɪkeɪt/ *v.t./i.* to act as judge; to adjudge. —**adjudication** /-ˈkeɪʃ(ə)n/ *n.*, **adjudicator** *n.* [as prec.]

adjunct /ˈædʒʌŋkt/ n. a thing added or attached but subordinate (*to* or *of*). [f. L, as ADJOIN]

adjure /əˈdʒʊə(r)/ v.t. to command or urge solemnly. —**adjuration** /-ˈeɪʃ(ə)n/ n. [f. L *adjurare* put to an oath]

adjust /əˈdʒʌst/ v.t./i. 1. to arrange, to put into the correct order or position etc.; to regulate. 2. to make suitable (*to a need or purpose*); to harmonize (discrepancies); to adapt oneself to new conditions. 3. to assess (loss or damage). —**adjuster** n., **adjustment** n. [f. F f. L *juxta* near]

adjustable adj. that may be adjusted. [f. prec.]

adjutant /ˈædʒʊt(ə)nt/ n. an army officer assisting a superior officer in administrative duties; an assistant. —**adjutant bird**, a large stork of the genus *Leptoptilus*, of which the largest (*L. dubius*), found in India, is 1.8–2.1 m (6–7 ft.) tall. [f. L, frequent. of *adjuvare* help]

Adler /ˈædlə(r)/, Alfred (1870–1937), Austrian psychologist and psychiatrist. At first a disciple of Freud, he eventually rejected Freud's basic tenets, particularly the emphasis on biological instincts as determinants of personality. Holding that those of society and culture were at least as significant, he saw human action as motivated by future expectations rather than by past events, striving to express dominance and seeking perfection both in the self and in the individual's contribution to his group. He introduced the concept of the 'inferiority complex', asserting that the most important key to the understanding of both personal and mass problems was the sense of inferiority and the individual's striving to compensate for this.

ad lib v.t./i. (**-bb-**) (*colloq.*) to speak impromptu, to improvise. —adj. (*colloq.*) improvised. —adv. as one pleases, to any desired extent. [abbr. L *ad libitum* according to pleasure]

admin /ˈædmɪn/ n. (*colloq.*) administration. [abbr.]

administer /ədˈmɪnɪstə(r)/ v.t./i. 1. to manage (business affairs). 2. to give out (justice, a sacrament) formally; to present (an oath) to; to provide. 3. to act as administrator. [f. F f. L *administrare* (AD-, *ministrare* minister)]

administrate /ədˈmɪnɪstreɪt/ v.t./i. to act as administrator (of). [f. L (as prec.)]

administration /ədmɪnɪˈstreɪʃ(ə)n/ n. 1. administering, especially of public affairs. 2. the government. [f. OF or L (as ADMINISTER)]

administrative /ədˈmɪnɪstrətɪv/ adj. of or involving administration. [f. F or L (as prec.)]

administrator /ədˈmɪnɪstreɪtə(r)/ n. a manager of business affairs; one who is capable of organizing things; one authorized to manage an estate. [as ADMINISTER]

admirable /ˈædmərəb(ə)l/ adj. worthy of admiration; excellent. —**admirably** adv. [F f. L (as ADMIRE)]

admiral /ˈædmər(ə)l/ n. the commander-in-chief of a navy; a naval officer of high rank, the commander of a fleet or squadron. There are four grades: *Admiral of the Fleet*, *Admiral*, *Vice Admiral*, *Rear Admiral*. —**red admiral**, **white admiral**, European species of butterfly (*Vanessa atalanta* and *Ladoga camilla*), perhaps originally called *the admirable*. [f. OF f. L f. Arab., = commander (cf. AMIR). The modern maritime use is due to the office of 'Amir of the Sea' created by the Arabs in Spain and Sicily and adopted successively by the Genoese, French, and English under Edward III.]

Admiralty /ˈædmərəltɪ/ n. the former name of the department of State administering the Royal Navy. [as prec.]

admire /ədˈmaɪə(r)/ v.t. to regard with approval, respect, or satisfaction; to express admiration of. —**admiration** /ædmɪˈreɪʃ(ə)n/ n., **admirer** n. [f. F or L *admirari* (AD-, *mirari* wonder at)]

admissible /ədˈmɪsəb(ə)l/ adj. (of an idea etc.) worthy of being accepted or considered; (of evidence) allowable in law. —**admissibility** /-ˈbɪlɪtɪ/ n. [f. F or L (as ADMIT)]

admission /ədˈmɪʃ(ə)n/ n. 1. an acknowledgement (*of*). 2. admitting, being admitted; the fee for this. [f. foll.]

admit /ədˈmɪt/ v.t./i. (**-tt-**) 1. to recognize as true or valid; to confess *to*. 2. to allow to enter; to have room for. 3. to accept (a plea or statement). —**admit of**, to allow (a doubt, improvement, etc.) as possible. —**admittance** n. [f. L *admittere* (AD-, *mittere* send)]

admittedly /ədˈmɪtɪdlɪ/ adv. as an acknowledged fact. [f. prec.]

admixture /ædˈmɪkstʃə(r)/ n. a thing added as an ingredient; the adding of this. [f. AD- + MIXTURE]

admonish /ədˈmɒnɪʃ/ v.t. to reprove mildly but firmly; to urge or advise seriously; to warn. —**admonishment** n.,

admonition /-ˈnɪʃ(ə)n/ n. [f. OF f. L *admonere* (AD-, *monēre* warn)]

admonitory /ədˈmɒnɪtərɪ/ adj. admonishing. [as prec.]

ad nauseam /æd ˈnɔːzɪæm/ to an excessive or sickening degree. [L]

ado /əˈduː/ n. fuss, busy activity, trouble. [orig. in *much ado* = much to do]

adobe /əˈdəʊbɪ/ n. brick made of clay and dried in the sun; clay for this. It has been used extensively in South America, the south-western USA, and Africa. [Sp. f. Arab., = the brick]

adolescent /ædəˈles(ə)nt/ adj. growing up, between childhood and maturity. —n. an adolescent person. —**adolescence** n. [f. OF f. L *adolescere* grow up]

Adonis /əˈdəʊnɪs/ (*Gk myth.*) a beautiful youth loved by Aphrodite. He was killed by a boar (the flower anemone was said to have sprung from his blood), but was restored to life by Persephone when Zeus decreed that he should spend part of each year in the underworld with her and part on earth with Aphrodite. Adonis was a divinity of vegetation and fertility, his death and revival symbolizing the cycle of the life of plants, akin to the Babylonian Tammuz (the name Adonis may be simply the Semitic title *Adon* (= lord), by which he was known in Phoenicia). —n. a handsome young man. [L f. Gk f. Phoenician *adon* lord]

adopt /əˈdɒpt/ v.t. 1. to take into one's family *as* a relation, especially as one's child with legal guardianship; to choose (a course etc.); to take over (a name, idea, etc.); to choose as a candidate for office. 2. to accept responsibility for maintenance of (a road etc.). 3. to approve or accept (a report, accounts). —**adoption** /-ʃ(ə)n/ n. [f. F or L *adoptare* (AD-, *optare* choose)]

adoptive adj. related by adoption. [f. OF f. L (as prec.)]

adorable /əˈdɔːrəb(ə)l/ adj. worthy of adoration, very lovable; (*colloq.*) delightful. —**adorably** adv. [f. foll.]

adore /əˈdɔː(r)/ v.t. 1. to love deeply. 2. to worship as divine. 3. (*colloq.*) to like very much. —**adoration** /-ˈreɪʃ(ə)n/ n., **adorer** n. [f. OF f. L *adorare* worship (AD-, *orare* pray)]

adorn /əˈdɔːn/ v.t. to be an ornament to, to decorate with ornaments. —**adornment** n. [f. OF f. L *adornare* decorate]

adrenal /əˈdriːn(ə)l/ n. an adrenal gland. —**adrenal gland**, either of two ductless glands above the kidneys, secreting adrenalin. [f. AD- + RENAL]

adrenalin /əˈdrenəlɪn/ n. a hormone that stimulates the nervous system, secreted by the adrenal glands or prepared synthetically. [f. prec.]

Adriatic /eɪdrɪˈætɪk/ adj. of the Adriatic Sea. —n. the Adriatic Sea. —**Adriatic Sea**, an arm of the Mediterranean Sea lying between Italy and the Balkan Peninsula. **Marriage of the Adriatic**, a former Ascension-Day ceremony symbolizing the sea-power of Venice, during which the Doge dropped a ring into the water from his official barge.

adrift /əˈdrɪft/ adv. & predic. adj. 1. drifting. 2. (*colloq.*) amiss, out of touch, unfastened. [f. A- + DRIFT]

adroit /əˈdrɔɪt/ adj. skilful, ingenious. —**adroitly** adv., **adroitness** n. [F (*à droit* according to right)]

adsorb /ædˈsɔːb/ v.t. (of a solid) to hold (particles of a gas or liquid) to its surface. —**adsorbent** adj., **adsorption** n., **adsorptive** adj. [f. AD-, after absorb]

adulation /ædjʊˈleɪʃ(ə)n/ n. obsequious flattery. —**adulatory** adj. [f. L *adulari* fawn on]

Adullamite /əˈdʌləmaɪt/ n. a member of a dissident political group. The term was originally applied to a group of Liberal MPs who seceded from their party (which was then in power) from dissatisfaction with its attempt at Parliamentary reform and brought about defeat of the Reform Bill of 1866. [f. cave of *Adullam* (1 Sam. 22: 1–2) where all who were distressed, in debt, or discontented came to join David when he fled from Saul]

adult /ˈædʌlt/ adj. mature, grown-up. —n. an adult person. —**adulthood** n. [f. L (as ADOLESCENT)]

adulterant /əˈdʌltərənt/ n. a substance added in adulterating. [as foll.]

adulterate /əˈdʌltəreɪt/ v.t. to make impure or poorer in quality by an admixture of other substance(s). —**adulteration** /-ˈreɪʃ(ə)n/ n. [f. L *adulterare* corrupt]

adulterer /əˈdʌltərə(r)/ n. a person (esp. a man) who commits adultery. n.fem. [f. F f. L (as ADULTERY)]

adultery /əˈdʌltərɪ/ n. voluntary sexual intercourse of a married person with someone other than his or her spouse. —**adulterous** adj. [f. OF f. L]

adumbrate /ˈædʌmbreɪt/ v.t. **1.** to indicate faintly; to fore-shadow. **2.** to overshadow. —**adumbration** /-ˈbreɪʃ(ə)n/ n. [f. L adumbrare (AD-, umbra shade)]

advance /ədˈvɑːns/ v.t./i. **1.** to move or put forward; to progress; to rise in rank; **2.** to lend, to pay before a due date. **3.** to present (a suggestion or claim etc.). **4.** to bring (an event) to an earlier date. **5.** to raise (a price). —n. **1.** a forward movement, progress. **2.** a rise in price. **3.** a loan, payment beforehand. **4.** (in pl.) attempts to establish a friendly or business relationship. —attrib. adj. **1.** going before others. **2.** done or provided in advance. —**in advance,** ahead in time or place. [f. OF f. L (ab away, ante before)]

advanced adj. **1.** far on in progress or life; not elementary. **2.** (of ideas etc.) new and not yet generally accepted. [f. prec.]

advancement n. promotion of a person or plan. [f. ADVANCE]

advantage /ədˈvɑːntɪdʒ/ n. **1.** a favourable circumstance; benefit; superiority. **2.** the next point after deuce in ten-nis. —v.t. to be or give an advantage to. —**take advantage of,** to make use of, to exploit. —**advantageous** /ædvænˈteɪdʒəs/ adj., **advantageously** adv. [f. OF (as ADVANCE)]

Advent /ˈædvənt/ n. **1.** the season (with four Sundays) before Christmas Day; the coming of Christ. **2. advent,** the arrival of an important person, event, or development. [OE f. OF f. L adventus arrival (AD-, venire come)]

Adventist /ˈædvəntɪst/ n. a member of any of various sects believing that the second coming of Christ is imminent. As a denomination they originated in the USA, followers of William Miller (1782-1849), a millenarian preacher, who originally prophesied that Christ would return in 1843/4. The chief bodies now are the Second Advent Christians and the Seventh-day Adventists. [f. prec.]

adventitious /ædvenˈtɪʃəs/ adj. **1.** accidental, casual. **2.** ad-ded from outside. **3.** (Biol., of roots etc.) occurring in an unusual place (ill. PLANTS). —**adventitiously** adv. [f. L (as ADVENT)]

adventure /ədˈventʃə(r)/ n. **1.** an unusual and exciting or dangerous experience. **2.** willingness to take risks. —**adven-ture playground,** a playground where children are pro-vided with discarded materials etc. to use imaginatively in play. —**adventurous** adj., **adventurously** adv. [f. OF (as ADVENT)]

adventurer n. **1.** one who seeks adventures. **2.** one who is ready to take risks or be unscrupulous for personal gain. —**adventuress** n.fem. [f. prec.]

adverb /ˈædvɜːb/ n. a word indicating manner, degree, cir-cumstance, etc., used to modify an adjective, verb, or another adverb. —**adverbial** /ədˈvɜːbɪəl/ adj., **adverbially** adv. [f. F or L (ad to, verbum word)]

adversarial /ædvəˈseərɪəl/ adj. **1.** involving adversaries, contested. **2.** opposed, hostile. —**adversarially** adv. [f. foll.]

adversary /ˈædvəsərɪ/ n. an opponent, an enemy. [as foll.]

adverse /ˈædvɜːs/ adj. unfavourable; harmful. [f. OF f. L adversus (AD-, vertere turn)]

adversity /ədˈvɜːsɪtɪ/ n. misfortune, trouble. [as prec.]

advert /ˈædvɜːt/ n. (colloq.) an advertisement. [abbr.]

advertise /ˈædvətaɪz/ v.t./i. to praise publicly in order to promote sales; to make generally known; to offer or ask for by a notice in a newspaper etc. —**advertiser** n. [f. OF f. L (as ADVERSE)]

advertisement /ədˈvɜːtɪsmənt/ n. a public announcement advertising (for) something; advertising. [f. F (as prec.)]

advice /ədˈvaɪs/ n. **1.** an opinion given as to future action. **2.** information, news; formal notice of a transaction. —**take advice,** to seek it, to act according to it. [f. OF f. L (ad to, videre see)]

advisable /ədˈvaɪzəb(ə)l/ adj. worth recommending, ex-pedient. —**advisability** /-ˈbɪlɪtɪ/ n. [f. foll.]

advise /ədˈvaɪz/ v.t./i. **1.** to give advice (to), to recommend. **2.** to inform. —**adviser** n. [as ADVICE]

advisory /ədˈvaɪzərɪ/ adj. giving advice. [f. prec.]

advocacy /ˈædvəkəsɪ/ n. **1.** the advocating of a policy etc. **2.** the function of an advocate. [f. foll.]

advocate /ˈædvəkət/ n. one who advocates or speaks in favour of; one who pleads on behalf of another, especially in a lawcourt. —/-keɪt/ v.t. to recommend, to be in favour of. [f. OF f. L advocatus (AD-, vocare call)]

adze /ædz/ n. an axe-like tool with an arched blade, for trimming large pieces of wood. [OE]

Aegean /iːˈdʒiːən/ adj. of the Aegean Sea. —n. the Aegean Sea. —**Aegean Sea,** a part of the Mediterranean lying between Greece and Turkey.

aegis /ˈiːdʒɪs/ n. protection, sponsorship. [L f. Gk, = mythical shield of Zeus or Athene]

Ælfric /ˈælfrɪk/ (c.955-c.1020) Anglo-Saxon monk, a prose-writer and grammarian, whose chief works are the Catholic Homilies (990-2; collections of sermons) and the Lives of the Saints (993-6). Other surviving works include his popular Grammar which earned him the name of 'Gram-maticus'. He is celebrated for his stylistic excellence and his educational principles.

Aeneas /iːˈniːəs/ (Gk & Rom. legend) a Trojan leader, son of Anchises and Aphrodite. When Troy fell to the Greeks he escaped and after long wandering reached the Tiber. He was regarded by the Romans as the founder of their State, and is known as 'pious Aeneas' for his filial dutifulness and fidelity to his mission.

Aeneid /ˈiːnɪɪd/ a Latin hexameter epic poem in twelve books by Virgil, which relates the wanderings of the Trojan hero Aeneas (legendary founder of the Roman State) after the fall of Troy, his love-affair with the Carthaginian queen Dido, his visit to his dead father Anchises in the Under-world, his arrival in Italy, and his eventual victory over the hostile Italian peoples led by Turnus. Closely modelled on the epics of Homer, it also contains a not totally optimistic celebration of the ideals and achievements of Augustus. Virgil's wish that the poem (unfinished at his death) be burned was not respected by his literary executors.

aeolian /iːˈəʊlɪən/ adj. wind-borne. —**aeolian harp,** a stringed instrument giving musical sounds on exposure to wind. **Aeolian Islands,** the ancient name of the Lipari Islands. [f. foll.]

Aeolus /ˈiːələs/ (Gk myth.) the god of the winds. [Gk, = swift, changeable]

aeon /ˈiːən/ n. a long or indefinite period. [f. L f. Gk, = age]

aepyornis /iːpɪˈɔːnɪs/ n. a gigantic flightless extinct bird of the genus Aepyornis, resembling a moa, known from re-mains found in Madagascar. [L f. Gk aipus high, ornis bird]

aerate /ˈeəreɪt/ v.t. **1.** to expose to the action of air. **2.** to charge with carbon dioxide. —**aeration** /-ˈreɪʃ(ə)n/ n., **aerator** n. [f. L aer air]

aerial /ˈeərɪəl/ n. a wire or rod for transmitting or receiving aerial waves. —adj. **1.** from the air or aircraft. **2.** existing in the air. **3.** like air. [f. L (as AIR)]

aero- /eərəʊ-/ in comb. air, aircraft. [f. Gk (aēr air)]

aerobatics /eərəˈbætɪks/ n.pl. feats of expert flying of air-craft, especially for display. [f. AERO-, after acrobatics]

aerobic /eəˈrəʊbɪk/ adj. **1.** using oxygen from the air. **2.** (of exercises) designed to increase the intake of oxygen and improve the cardiovascular system. —**aerobics** n.pl. exercises of this kind. [f. F (as AERO- + Gk bios life)]

aerodrome /ˈeərədrəʊm/ n. an airfield or airport. [f. AERO-+ Gk dromos course]

aerodynamics /eərəʊdaɪˈnæmɪks/ n. (also as pl.) the dynamics of solid bodies moving through air. —**aero-dynamic** adj.

aerofoil /ˈeərəfɔɪl/ n. a body (e.g. an aircraft wing, fin, or tailplane) shaped to produce a desired aerodynamic reaction (e.g. lift) when it passes through air (ill. FLIGHT). [f. AERO-+ FOIL¹]

aeronaut /ˈeərənɔːt/ n. a balloonist or other aviator. [f. AERO- + Gk nautēs sailor]

aeronautics /eərəˈnɔːtɪks/ n. the science, art, or practice of the flight of aircraft. —**aeronautic** adj., **aeronautical** adj. [f. AERO- + NAUTICAL]

aeroplane /ˈeərəpleɪn/ n. a power-driven heavier-than-air aircraft with wings (ill. FLIGHT). The first true aeroplane to achieve controlled sustained flight was that designed, built, and flown by the Wright brothers in 1903. [f. F (as AERO-, PLANE¹)]

aerosol /ˈeərəsɒl/ n. a container holding a liquid or other substance and a propellant gas packed under pressure, dis-pensing its contents as a fine spray when the pressure is released; this substance. The propellant gas must be non-toxic and non-inflammable; for this reason one of the chlori-nated fluorocarbon refrigerants is often used, but fears have been expressed about the effects of accumulation of these gases in the upper atmosphere, where a photochemical re-action may reduce the amount of ozone. This in turn could lead to an increased amount of ultra-violet radiation reaching the earth, with consequent risks to health. Aerosols were first developed commercially in the USA in the early 1940s. [f. AERO- + SOL]

aerospace /ˈeərəʊspeɪs/ n. 1. earth's atmosphere and outer space. 2. the technology of aviation in this.

Aeschines /ˈiːskɪniːz/ (c.397–c.322 BC) Athenian orator and statesman, whose exchanges with his implacable opponent Demosthenes provide much of the evidence of the relations between Athens and Macedon 343–330 BC.

Aeschylus /ˈiːskɪləs/ (525/4–456 BC) Greek dramatist, who saw the collapse of tyranny and the rapid rise of democratic government at Athens, fought in the Persian Wars, and is regarded as the founder of Greek tragic drama. His seven extant plays are distinguished by magnificence of staging and spectacle (as in the oriental ceremony of the *Persians*), and by grandeur of language; his characters (e.g. Prometheus in *Prometheus Bound*) are strongly drawn, and behind them can be felt the presence and power of fate and of the gods; the chorus acts as a vehicle for profound reflections on events. His examination of the workings of providence is best seen in the *Oresteia*, a trilogy which traces the working-out, on the human and divine levels, of the blood-feud in the house of Agamemnon.

Aesir /ˈiːsə(r)/ (*Scand. myth.*) the collective name of the gods.

Aesop /ˈiːsɒp/ (early 6th c. BC) Greek teller of moral animal fables who lived as a slave on the island of Samos.

aesthete /ˈiːsθiːt/ n. a person who claims to have great understanding and appreciation of what is beautiful, especially in the arts. [f. Gk (as foll.)]

aesthetic /iːsˈθetɪk/ adj. concerned with or sensitive to what is beautiful; artistic, tasteful. —**aesthetics** n.pl. a branch of philosophy dealing with the principles of beauty and tastefulness. —**aesthetically** adv., **aestheticism** /-sɪz(ə)m/ n. [f. Gk (*aisthanomai* perceive)]

Aesthetic movement a literary and artistic movement devoted to 'art for art's sake' which blossomed in the 1880s, heavily influenced by the Pre-Raphaelites, Ruskin, and Walter Pater, in which the adoption of sentimental archaism as the ideal of beauty was carried to extravagant lengths and often accompanied by affectation of speech and manner and eccentricity of dress. Its chief followers, who included Oscar Wilde, Aubrey Beardsley, and others associated with the *Yellow Book*, were greatly ridiculed in *Punch* and in Gilbert and Sullivan's opera *Patience* (1881).

aetiology /iːtɪˈɒlədʒɪ/ n. 1. the study of causation. 2. the study of the causes of disease. 3. the cause of a disease. —**aetiological** /-əˈlɒdʒɪk(ə)l/ adj., **aetiologically** adv. [f. L f. Gk (*aitia* cause)]

afar /əˈfɑː(r)/ adv. far off, far away. [f. A- + FAR]

affable /ˈæfəb(ə)l/ adj. polite and friendly. —**affability** /-ˈbɪlɪtɪ/ n., **affably** adv. [F f. L *affabilis* (AD-, *fari* speak)]

affair /əˈfeə(r)/ n. 1. a matter, a concern; a thing done or to be done. 2. a temporary sexual relationship between two persons who are not married to each other. 3. (*colloq.*) a thing or event. 4. (in *pl.*) public or private business. [f. AF (*à faire* to do)]

affect /əˈfekt/ v.t. 1. to produce an effect on; (of disease) to attack; to touch the feelings of. 2. to pretend, to pose as. 3. to make a show of liking or using. [f. F or L *afficere* influence (AD-, *facere* do)]

affectation /æfekˈteɪʃ(ə)n/ n. a studied display (*of* modesty etc.); an artificial manner, pretence. [f. prec.]

affected /əˈfektɪd/ adj. 1. pretended, artificial. 2. full of affectation. [f. AFFECT]

affection /əˈfekʃ(ə)n/ n. 1. love, a liking. 2. a disease or diseased condition. [as prec.]

affectionate /əˈfekʃ(ə)nət/ adj. showing affection, loving. —**affectionately** adv. [f. prec.]

affiance /əˈfaɪəns/ v.t. to promise in marriage. [f. OF f. L *affidare* entrust]

affidavit /æfɪˈdeɪvɪt/ n. a written statement confirmed by an oath. [L, = has stated on oath]

affiliate /əˈfɪlɪeɪt/ v.t. to connect as a member or branch. —n. an affiliated person or organization. [f. L *affiliare* adopt (AD-, *filius* son)]

affiliation /əfɪlɪˈeɪʃ(ə)n/ n. affiliating, being affiliated. —**affiliation order**, a court order compelling the putative father of an illegitimate child to help support it. [f. prec.]

affinity /əˈfɪnɪtɪ/ n. 1. a liking or attraction. 2. a relationship, especially by marriage. 3. a resemblance or connection suggesting that there is a relationship. 4. (*Chem.*) the

tendency of substances to combine with others. [f. F f. L *affinis* bordering on]

affirm /əˈfɜːm/ v.t./i. to assert, to state as a fact; to declare solemnly in place of taking an oath. —**affirmation** /-ˈmeɪʃ(ə)n/ n., **affirmatory** /əˈfɜːm-/ adj. [f. OF f. L *affirmare* (AD-, *firmus* strong)]

affirmative /əˈfɜːmətɪv/ adj. affirming, answering that a thing is so. —n. an affirmative word or statement. —**affirmatively** adv. [as prec.]

affix /əˈfɪks/ v.t. 1. to stick on, to fasten. 2. to add (a signature etc.) in writing. —/ˈæfɪks/ n. a thing affixed; (*Gram.*) a prefix or suffix. [f. F or L *affigere* (AD-, *figere* fix)]

afflict /əˈflɪkt/ v.t. to distress physically or mentally. [f. L (AD-, *fligere* strike)]

affliction /əˈflɪkʃ(ə)n/ n. distress, suffering; a cause of this. [as prec.]

affluent /ˈæfluənt/ adj. wealthy; abundant. —n. a tributary stream. —**affluence** n., **affluently** adv. [f. OF f. L *affluere* (AD-, *fluere* flow)]

afford /əˈfɔːd/ v.t. 1. to have enough money, means, or time etc. for; to be able to spare; to be in a position *to* do. 2. to provide. [f. OE, = promote]

afforest /əˈfɒrɪst/ v.t. to convert into forest, to plant with trees. —**afforestation** /-ˈteɪʃ(ə)n/ n. [f. L *afforestare* (AD-, *foresta* forest)]

affray /əˈfreɪ/ n. a breach of the peace by fighting or rioting in public. [f. AF f. L, = remove from peace]

affront /əˈfrʌnt/ n. an open insult. —v.t. 1. to insult openly. 2. to face, to confront. [f. OF f. L (AD-, *frons* face)]

Afghan /ˈæfɡæn/ n. 1. a native of Afghanistan. 2. the language spoken there, Pashto. 3. (also **Afghan hound**) a dog of a breed with long silky hair. [f. Pashto]

Afghanistan /æfˈɡænɪstæn/ a mountainous country in central Asia dominated by the Hindu Kush, bordered by Iran to the west, Pakistan to the south and east, and Russia to the north; pop. (est. 1979) 15,500,000, though about 2–3 million are thought to have left as refugees since the Russian invasion at the end of that year; official languages, Pashto and a form of Persian (Dari); capital, Kabul. The principal industries are agriculture and sheep-raising. Conquered in the 4th c. BC by Alexander the Great, Afghanistan fell under Arab domination in the 7th c. AD, before being conquered by the Mongols under Genghis Khan. Part of the Indian Mogul empire, it became independent in the mid-18th c., and in the 19th and early 20th c. was the focal point for conflicting Russian and British interests on the Northwest Frontier, the British fighting three wars against the Afghans between 1839 and 1919. A constitutional monarchy since 1930, Afghanistan became progressively politically unstable in the 1970s and was invaded by the Russians in December 1979. Although the Russians have set up a puppet regime in Kabul, large parts of the country remain disaffected and the occupying forces have been subjected to continuing attack by Afghan guerrillas.

aficionado /əfɪsjəˈneɪdəʊ/ n. (*pl.* -os) a devotee of a sport or pastime. [Sp.]

afield /əˈfiːld/ adv. away from home, to or at a distance. [f. A- + FIELD]

afire /əˈfaɪə(r)/ adv. & predic. adj. on fire. [f. A- + FIRE]

aflame /əˈfleɪm/ adv. & predic. adj. 1. in flames, burning. 2. very excited [f. A- + FLAME]

afloat /əˈfləʊt/ adv. & predic. adj. 1. floating; at sea, on board ship. 2. flooded. 3. out of debt or difficulty. 4. in circulation, current. [f. A- + FLOAT]

afoot /əˈfʊt/ adv. & predic. adj. progressing, in operation. [f. A- + FOOT]

afore /əˈfɔː(r)/ adv. & prep. (*archaic* or *dial.* exc. in *Naut.* use) before. [f. A- + FORE]

aforesaid /əˈfɔːsed/ adj. mentioned previously.

aforethought /əˈfɔːθɔːt/ adj. premeditated.

a fortiori /eɪ fɔːtɪˈɔːraɪ/ with yet stronger reason (than a conclusion already accepted). [L]

afraid /əˈfreɪd/ predic. adj. 1. alarmed, frightened, anxious about consequences etc. 2. (*colloq.*) politely regretful. [orig. f. AFFRAY]

afresh /əˈfreʃ/ adv. anew, beginning again. [f. A- + FRESH]

Africa /ˈæfrɪkə/ the second-largest of the world's continents, a southward projection of the land-mass which constitutes the Old World, surrounded by sea except where the isthmus of Suez joins it to Asia and divided almost exactly in two by the Equator, the northern half being dominated by the Sahara Desert. Its indigenous inhabitants are dark-skinned peoples varying in colour from light copper in the north to black in equatorial and southern parts. Egypt in the north-east was one of the world's earliest centres of civilization, and the Mediterranean coast has been subject to European influence since classical times, but much of the continent remained unknown to the outside world until voyages of discovery along the coast between the 15th and 17th centuries. The interior was explored and partitioned by European nations in the second half of the 19th c., Liberia and Ethiopia alone remaining under African rule. Since the Second World War most of the former colonies have secured their independence, but decolonization has left a legacy of instability which in many areas has yet to be satisfactorily resolved.

African /ˈæfrɪkən/ n. **1.** of Africa or its people. **2.** (*S.Afr.*) Bantu. —n. **1.** an African Black. **2.** (*S.Afr.*) a Bantu of South Africa. —**African marigold**, an annual garden plant (*Tagetes erecta*) with yellow flowers, originally from Mexico. —**African violet**, an East African plant of the genus *Saintpaulia*, with purple, pink, or white flowers, grown as a house-plant in Britain. [f. prec.]

Africana /æfrɪˈkɑːnə/ n.pl. books, objects, etc., connected with Southern Africa. [f. AFRICA]

Africanize /ˈæfrɪkənaɪz/ v.t. to make African, to place under the control of African Blacks. —**Africanization** /-ˈzeɪʃ(ə)n/ n. [f. AFRICAN]

Afrikaans /æfrɪˈkɑːns/ n. a language that since 1925 has been one of the two official languages of the Republic of South Africa (the other being English). It is a development of 17th-c. Dutch brought to South Africa by settlers from Holland, and its subsequent isolation gave rise to various differences so that it is now considered to be a separate language. It is spoken by 4 million people—2 million white Afrikaners and about 2 million people of mixed race. [Du., = African]

Afrikaner /æfrɪˈkɑːnə(r)/ n. a white person in South Africa, especially a descendant of Dutch settlers, whose native language is Afrikaans. [Afrik.]

Afro /ˈæfrəʊ/ adj. (of a hair-style) full and bushy, as that naturally grown by some Blacks. [f. foll., or abbr. AFRICAN]

Afro- /æfrəʊ-/ in comb. African. [f. L Afer African]

Afro-American adj. of American Blacks or their culture. —n. an American Black.

Afro-Asiatic adj. (of languages) Hamito-Semitic.

afrormosia /æfrɔːˈməʊzɪə/ n. an African tree of the genus *Afrormosia*; its teak-like wood, used for furniture. [f. AFRO- + Ormosia genus of trees]

aft adv. in, near, or to the stern of a ship or the rear of an aircraft. [prob. f. earlier *baft* (see ABAFT)]

after prep. **1.** behind in place or order; later than. **2.** in spite of. **3.** as a result of. **4.** in pursuit or search of. **5.** about, concerning. **6.** in imitation or honour of. —adv. behind; later. —conj. at or in a time later than. —adj. later, following; nearer the stern in a boat. —**after-care** n. attention after leaving hospital etc. **after-effect** n. an effect that arises or persists after the primary action of something. [OE]

afterbirth n. the placenta and foetal membrane discharged from the womb after childbirth.

afterlife n. life in a later part of a person's lifetime, or after death.

aftermath /ˈɑːftəmæθ/ n. **1.** consequences, after-effects. **2.** new grass growing after mowing or harvest. [f. AFTER + math mowing]

aftermost adj. last, furthest aft. [f. AFTER + -MOST]

afternoon /ɑːftəˈnuːn/ n. the time from noon to evening.

afters /ˈɑːftəz/ n.pl. (colloq.) a course following the main course at a meal.

aftershave n. a lotion for use after shaving.

afterthought n. something thought of ˏr added later.

afterwards /ˈɑːftəwədz/, US **afterward** adv. later, subsequently. [OE f. AFT + -wards in the direction of]

Ag symbol silver. [f. L argentum]

again /əˈɡeɪn, əˈɡen/ adv. **1.** another time, once more; as before; in addition. **2.** furthermore, besides, likewise; on the other hand. [OE]

against /əˈɡeɪnst, əˈɡenst/ prep. **1.** in opposition to; to the disadvantage of; in contrast to. **2.** into collision or contact with. **3.** in anticipation of, in preparation for; so as to cancel or lessen the effect of; in return for. [f. prec.]

Aga Khan /ˌɑːɡə ˈkɑːn/ the leader of most of the Ismaili Muslims. Following the reign of the eighth Fatimid caliph a split in the Ismaili sect took place in 1094 over disagreement about the succession to the caliphate. The 'eastern' group, known as Nizaris after the candidate whom they supported, were based in Persia and known to those whom they opposed with violent methods as *Hashshīshīn* (hashish-takers) or, in its better-known form, 'Assassins'. The original *modus operandi* of the group did not survive; the Nizari community was reorganized in the 19th c. under the leadership of its imam (leader), known as the Aga Khan, who is traditionally based in the Indian subcontinent, although a much smaller remnant of the original Nizaris remains independent in Syria. The Aga Khan heads an enormous complex of services and welfare provisions for members of the community. [f. Turk. aga master, khan ruler]

Agamemnon /æɡəˈmemnən/ (*Gk legend*) king of Mycenae, or Argos, brother of Menelaus, and probably a historical person of the Mycenaean era. In the Homeric poems he is the commander-in-chief of the Greek expedition against Troy. On his return from Troy he was murdered by his wife Clytemnestra and her lover Aegisthus.

agapanthus /æɡəˈpænθəs/ n. an ornamental lily of the genus *Agapanthus*, native to South Africa, with blue or white flowers. [L f. Gk agapē love, anthos flower]

agape /əˈɡeɪp/ predic. adj. gaping, open-mouthed. [f. A- + GAPE]

agar /ˈeɪɡɑː(r)/ n. (also **agar-agar**) any of certain seaweeds of SE Asian seas, especially *Gracilaria lichenoides*, from which a gelatinous substance is extracted, used as a solidifying agent in bacterial culture media and in the East as food. [Malay]

agaric /ˈæɡərɪk/ n. a fungus of the family Agaricaceae, with a cap and stalk, including the common mushroom. [f. L f. Gk]

Agassiz /ˈæɡəsiːz/, Jean Louis Rodolphe (1807–73), Swiss-born zoologist, geologist, and palaeontologist, who in 1837 was the first to propose that much of Europe had once been in the grip of an ice age. Agassiz lived in America from 1846 onwards and became an influential teacher and writer on many aspects of natural history. He was an opponent of Darwin's theory of evolution, holding that organisms were immutable and independent of each other.

agate /ˈæɡət/ n. a kind of hard semiprecious stone, a variety of chalcedony, with streaked colouring. [F f. L f. Gk]

agave /əˈɡɑːvɪ/ n. a plant of the genus *Agave*, especially a tropical American plant with spiny leaves and a tall stem up to 12m (40ft.) high, flowering only once, when the plant is mature, in 10–70 years. Some species are an important source of fibre (especially sisal) or of alcoholic beverages (the Mexican pulque) and spirit (mescal); a few are ornamental. [f. Gk Agauē woman in myth (agauos illustrious)]

age n. **1.** the length of past life or existence. **2.** (colloq., esp. in pl.) a long time. **3.** a historical or other distinct period. **4.** the later part of life, old age. —v.t./i. (partic. **ageing**) to become or cause to become old or show signs of age; to mature. —**age-long, age-old** adjs. having existed for a very long time. **of age,** having reached the age (18, formerly 21) at which one has an adult's legal rights and obligations. **under age,** below this age. [f. OF f. L aetas age]

aged adj. **1.** /eɪdʒd/ of the age of (aged 3). **2.** /ˈeɪdʒɪd/ very old. [f. AGE]

ageless adj. never growing or appearing old or outmoded; eternal. [f. AGE + -LESS]

agency /ˈeɪdʒənsɪ/ n. **1.** the business or establishment of an agent. **2.** active or intervening action. [f. L (agere do)]

agenda /əˈdʒendə/ n. (pl. **-as**) a programme of items of business to be dealt with at a meeting etc. [L, f. agere do]

agent /ˈeɪdʒənt/ n. **1.** a person who acts for another in business etc. **2.** one who or that which exerts power or produces an effect. **3.** (also **secret agent**) a spy. [as prec.]

agent provocateur /æʒɑ̃ prəvɒkəˈtɜː(r)/ (pl. **-ts -rs**, pr. same) a person employed to detect suspected offenders by tempting them to overt action. [F, = provocative agent]

agglomerate /əˈɡlɒməreɪt/ v.t./i. to collect into a mass. —/-ət/ n. a mass, especially of fused volcanic fragments. —/-ət/ adj. collected into a mass. —**agglomeration** /-ˈreɪʃ(ə)n/ n. [f. L agglomerare (AD-, glomus ball)]

agglutinate /əˈɡluːtɪneɪt/ v.t./i. **1.** to stick or fuse together, to coalesce. **2.** (of language) to combine simple words without change of form to express compound ideas. —**agglutination** /-ˈeɪʃ(ə)n/ n., **agglutinative** /-ətɪv/ adj. [f. L agglutinare (AD-, gluten glue)]

aggrandize /əˈɡrændaɪz/ v.t. to increase the power, rank, or wealth of; to make seem greater. —**aggrandizement** /-ɪzmənt/ n. [f. F f. It. aggrandire f. L (AD-, grandis large)]

aggravate /ˈægrəveɪt/ v.t. **1.** to increase the gravity of. **2.** (colloq., D) to annoy. —**aggravation** /-ˈveɪʃ(ə)n/ n. [f. L aggravare make heavy (AD-, gravis heavy)]

aggregate /ˈægrɪgət/ n. **1.** a total, an amount assembled. **2.** broken stone, gravel, etc., used in making concrete. **3.** a mass of particles or minerals. —adj. combined, total. — /-geɪt/ v.t./i. to collect or form into an aggregate; to unite; (colloq.) to amount to. —**in the aggregate**, as a whole. — **aggregation** /-ˈgeɪʃ(ə)n/ n. [f. L aggregare herd together (AD-, grex flock)]

aggression /əˈgreʃ(ə)n/ n. unprovoked attacking or attack; a hostile act or behaviour. [f. F or L aggressio attack (AD-, gradi step)]

aggressive /əˈgresɪv/ adj. apt to make attacks, showing aggression; forceful, self-assertive. —**aggressively** adv., **aggressiveness** n. [as prec.]

aggressor /əˈgresə(r)/ n. one who makes an unprovoked attack or begins hostilities. [as AGGRESSION]

aggrieved /əˈgriːvd/ adj. having a grievance. [f. OF agrever make heavier (as GRIEF)]

aghast /əˈgɑːst/ adj. filled with consternation or dismay. [f. obs. v. agast frighten]

agile /ˈædʒaɪl/ adj. nimble, quick-moving; lively. —**agilely** adv., **agility** /əˈdʒɪlɪtɪ/ n. [F f. L agere do)]

Agincourt /ˈædʒɪnkɔː(r), -kɔːt/ a village of NW France, scene of a great English victory (1415) in the Hundred Years War, when a small invading army under Henry V defeated a much larger French force. Indiscipline, muddy ground, and Henry's sound defensive tactics led to heavy losses among the heavily armoured French knights. Following his victory, Henry was able to occupy Normandy and consolidate his claim to the French throne by marrying Catherine, daughter of the mad king Charles VI.

agitate /ˈædʒɪteɪt/ v.t./i. **1.** to disturb, to excite. **2.** to stir up (public) interest or concern. **3.** to shake briskly. —**agitation** /-ˈteɪʃ(ə)n/ n., **agitator** n. [f. L agitare frequent. of agere drive]

agley /əˈgleɪ/ adv. (Sc.) askew, awry. [f. A- + Sc. gley squint]

aglow /əˈgləʊ/ pred. adj. glowing. —adv. glowingly. [f. A- + GLOW]

AGM abbr. annual general meeting.

agnail /ˈægneɪl/ n. = HANGNAIL. [OE, = tight (metal) nail, hard excrescence in flesh]

Agnes /ˈægnɪs/, St (venerated as a virgin in Rome since the 4th c.). The legends of her martyrdom vary. Her emblem is a lamb (L agnus), and on her feast day (21 Jan.) two lambs providing wool for the pallium are blessed in her basilica in Rome.

Agni /ˈægnɪ/ (Hinduism) the Vedic god of fire, the priest of the gods and the god of the priests. As mediator between gods and men, he takes offerings to the gods in the smoke of sacrifice and returns to the earth as lightning. [Skr., = fire, cogn. with L ignis]

agnostic /ægˈnɒstɪk/ n. one who believes that nothing can be known of the existence of God or of anything but material phenomena. (See T. H. HUXLEY.) —adj. of this view. —**agnosticism** /-sɪz(ə)m/ n. [f. Gk a- not + GNOSTIC]

ago /əˈgəʊ/ adv. in the past. [f. obs. agone gone by]

agog /əˈgɒg/ adv. & predic. adj. eager, expectant. [f. F en gogues in fun]

agonize /ˈægənaɪz/ v.t./i. **1.** to suffer mental anguish; to suffer agony. **2.** to pain greatly. [f. foll.]

agony /ˈægənɪ/ n. extreme mental or physical suffering; a severe struggle. —**agony aunt**, (colloq.) the (female) editor of an agony column. **agony column**, the personal column of a newspaper; a regular newspaper or magazine feature containing readers' questions about personal difficulties, with replies from the columnist. [f. OF or L f. Gk (agōn struggle)]

agoraphobia /ægərəˈfəʊbɪə/ n. abnormal fear of crossing open spaces. —**agoraphobic** adj. & n. [f. Gk agora market-place + PHOBIA]

AGR abbr. advanced gas-cooled reactor.

Agra /ˈɑːgrə/ a city on the River Jumna in Uttar Pradesh, capital of the Mogul emperors from the early 16th c. to the mid-17th c. It is the site of the Taj Mahal.

agrarian /əˈgreərɪən/ adj. relating to agricultural land or its cultivation, or to landed property. [f. L (ager land)]

Agrarian Revolution the transformation of British agriculture during the 18th c., characterized by the acceleration of enclosures (see entry) and the consequent decline of the open-field system, as well as by the introduction of technological innovations such as the seed drill and the scientific rotation of crops.

agree /əˈgriː/ v.t./i. **1.** to hold a similar opinion; to consent (to). **2.** to become or be in harmony, to suit or be compatible with. **3.** to approve as correct; to reach agreement about. — **be agreed**, to have reached a similar opinion. [f. OF f. L (AD-, gratus pleasing)]

agreeable /əˈgriːəb(ə)l/ adj. **1.** pleasing. **2.** willing to agree. —**agreeably** adv. [as prec.]

agreement /əˈgriːmənt/ n. **1.** agreeing, harmony in opinion or feeling. **2.** a contract or promise. [as AGREE]

agribusiness /ˈægrɪbɪznɪs/ n. the group of industries concerned with the processing and distribution of agricultural produce or with farm machinery. [f. AGRICULTURE + BUSINESS]

Agricola /əˈgrɪkələ/, Gnaeus Julius (40–93), Roman senator and general, whose career is known chiefly from his Life by his son-in-law Tacitus. Governor of Britain from 78, he completed the subjugation of Wales, advanced into Scotland (where he built a number of forts), and defeated the Caledonian Highland tribes at the battle of Mons Graupius. His fleet circumnavigated Britain.

agriculture /ˈægrɪkʌltʃə(r)/ n. the process of cultivating land and rearing livestock (see below). —**agricultural** /-ˈkʌltʃər(ə)l/ adj., **agriculturist** /-ˈkʌl-/ n. [F, or f. L (ager field, cultura culture)]
The beginnings of agriculture date from the neolithic period, perhaps 9,000 years ago, and the gradual change from a life-style in which people obtained their food by hunting wild animals and gathering such berries, roots, etc., as nature provided to one in which they tended the animals they had caught, and planted crops in order to reap a harvest, is associated with the establishment of settled communities, as in the Tigris–Euphrates valley and beside the Nile. The type and development of farming have varied in different parts of the world, and methods used in one place have been (and still are) sometimes centuries ahead of those of another. In Britain, the system of land-holding whereby each man held scattered strips in large unfenced areas was replaced in the 18th c. (see AGRARIAN REVOLUTION) by enclosed fields, enabling individual farmers to make use of new implements and improve the quality of cattle and sheep by careful stock-breeding. Labour-saving machinery and improved methods of transport made increased production possible, important inventions being the reaping-machine, reaper-and-binder, combine harvester, and tractor; use of pesticides and fertilizers increased the yield from crops, while advances in the understanding of animal health did the same for livestock. In the 20th c. experiments in farm organization have aimed at greater efficiency in the use of both labour and land (e.g. in systems of collective farming, as in the USSR). Over-use of intensive methods of farming, however, has brought its own problems of soil erosion and environmental pollution.

agrimony /ˈægrɪmənɪ/ n. a perennial plant of the genus Agrimonia, especially one with small yellow flowers. —**hemp agrimony**, a wild perennial plant with mauve flowers and hairy leaves. [f. OF f. L f. Gk argemōnē poppy]

Agrippa¹ /əˈgrɪpə/, Marcus Vipsanius (64/3–12 BC), the right-hand man of Augustus (whose daughter Julia was his third wife) during the latter's rise to power and principate, and thrice consul. Indispensable in military and civilian affairs, he played an important part in the naval victories over Sextus Pompeius and Mark Antony, and held commands in western and eastern provinces. His many buildings in Rome (paid for out of his own pocket) included baths, aqueducts, and sewers.

Agrippa² /əˈgrɪpə/ = HEROD AGRIPPA.

agronomy /əˈgrɒnəmɪ/ n. the science of soil management and crop production. [f. F f. Gk (agros land, nemō arrange)]

aground /əˈgraʊnd/ adv. on or to the bottom of shallow water. [f. A- + GROUND]

ague /ˈeɪgjuː/ n. malarial fever; a fit of shivering. [f. OF f. L acuta (febris) acute fever]

AH abbr. of the Muslim era (see HEGIRA). [f. L anno Hegirae]

ah int. expressing surprise, delight, pity, etc. [f. F]

aha int. expressing surprise or triumph. [f. AH + HA]

ahead /əˈhed/ adv. further forward in space, time, or progress etc.; in advance. [orig. Naut., f. A- + HEAD]

ahimsa /əˈhɪmsɑː/ n. (in Hinduism, Buddhism, Jainism) the doctrine of non-violence or non-killing. [Skr. (a without, himsa injury)]

ahoy /əˈhɔɪ/ int. (Naut.) a call used in hailing. [f. AH + HOY]

Ahriman /ˈɑːrɪmən/ the evil spirit in the dualistic doctrine of Zoroastrianism. [Pers., f. Avestan *angramainyu* dark or destructive spirit]

Ahura Mazda /əhʊərə ˈmæzdə/ (later called *Ormazd*) the creator god of ancient Iran (and, in particular, of Zoroastrianism), the force for good and the opponent of Ahriman. [Avestan, = the living wise one]

aid *n.* **1.** help. **2.** one who or that which helps. —*v.t.* to help. [f. OF f. L (AD-, *juvare* help)]

aide /eɪd/ *n.* an aide-de-camp; (*US*) an assistant. [F]

aide-de-camp /eɪd də ˈkɑ̃ː/ *n.* (*pl.* **aides-de-camp** *pr.* same) an officer assisting a senior officer. [F]

AIDS /eɪdz/ *abbr.* acquired immune deficiency syndrome, a condition that breaks down a person's natural defences against illness.

ail *v.t./i.* (*archaic*) to make ill or uneasy; to be in poor health. [OE (*egle* troublesome)]

aileron /ˈeɪlərɒn/ *n.* a hinged flap on an aeroplane wing, controlling lift and lateral balance (ill. FLIGHT). [F, dim. of *aile* wing f. L *ala*]

ailing *adj.* ill, in poor health or condition. [f. AIL]

ailment *n.* a minor illness. [f. AIL]

aim *v.t./i.* **1.** to point, direct, or send towards a target; to take aim. **2.** to make an attempt, to intend. —*n.* **1.** the act of aiming. **2.** purpose, intention; goal. [f. OF f. L *aestimare* reckon]

aimless *adj.* without a purpose. —**aimlessly** *adv.*, **aimlessness** *n.* [f. AIM + -LESS]

ain't (*colloq.*) am not; is not, are not; has not, have not. [contr.]

Ainu /ˈaɪnuː/ *n.* (*pl.* same or **-s**) a member of the non-Mongoloid aboriginal inhabitants of the Japanese archipelago whose physical characteristics (light skin colour, round eyes, and exceptionally thick wavy hair) set them apart dramatically from the majority population of the islands and have stimulated much speculation as to their possible Caucasoid origin. Archaeological evidence suggests that the Ainu were resident in the area as early as 5000 BC, thereby pre-dating the great Mongoloid expansion. Forced by Japanese expansion to retreat to the northernmost islands (i.e. Hokkaido and Sakhalin) the Ainu are on the verge of cultural extinction and now number only a few hundred pure-blooded individuals. Assimilation has resulted in a shift from hunting and gathering to sedentary agriculture, and the Japanese language has all but replaced the unique Ainu language which is unrelated to any known form of speech. Traditional practices such as female tattooing and the *iomande* (bear sacrifice) have also declined as a result of Japanese cultural influence. [Ainu, = man]

air *n.* **1.** the mixture of gases (mainly oxygen and nitrogen) surrounding the earth and breathed by all land animals and plants. **2.** the atmosphere, open space in this; this as the place where aircraft operate. **3.** a light wind. **4.** an impression given; an affected manner. **5.** a melody, a tune. —*v.t./i.* **1.** to expose or be exposed to fresh or warm air so as to remove staleness or damp. **2.** to express publicly. —**air bed,** an inflatable mattress. **air brick,** a brick with holes to allow ventilation. **air-conditioned** *adj.* supplied with **air conditioning,** a system for regulating the humidity and temperature of a building. **air-cushion** *n.* an inflatable cushion; a layer of air providing support, especially for a vehicle of the hovercraft type. **air force,** a branch of the armed forces equipped for attacking and defending by means of aircraft (in Britain, the Royal Air Force, constituted in 1918 by amalgamating the Royal Flying Corps, formed in 1912, with the Royal Naval Air Service). **air freight,** freight carried by air. **air-freight** *v.t.* to send as air freight. **air letter,** a folding sheet of light paper that may be sent cheaply by airmail. **air pocket,** a partial vacuum in the air causing aircraft in flight to drop suddenly. **by air,** in or by aircraft. **in the air,** current, prevalent; uncertain, not yet decided. **on the air,** broadcast or broadcasting by radio or television. —**airer** *n.* [f. OF f. L f. Gk; sense 4 F, prob. f. OF *aire* disposition f. L *area*; sense 5 f. It *aria*]

airborne *adj.* **1.** transported by air or by aircraft. **2.** in flight after taking off.

aircraft *n.* (*pl.* same) a machine or structure designed for flight in the air. —**aircraft-carrier** *n.* a ship carrying and used as a base for aircraft. The first true aircraft carrier was HMS *Argus* (1918), though seaplane carriers had been used (chiefly for reconnaissance) in the First World War.

aircraftman *n.* the lowest rank in the RAF.

aircraftwoman *n.* the lowest rank in the WRAF.

aircrew *n.* the crew manning an aircraft.

Airedale /ˈeədeɪl/ *n.* a terrier of a large rough-coated breed. [place in W.Yorkshire]

airfield *n.* an area of land equipped with runways etc. for aircraft.

airflow *n.* a flow of air.

airgun *n.* a gun using compressed air to propel a missile.

airless *adj.* stuffy; without wind, calm and still. [f. AIR + -LESS]

airlift *n.* large-scale transport of troops, supplies, etc. by air, especially in an emergency. —*v.t.* to transport thus.

airline *n.* a service of air transport for public use; a company providing this.

airliner *n.* a large passenger-carrying aircraft.

airlock *n.* **1.** stoppage of a flow by trapped air in a pump or pipe. **2.** a compartment with an airtight door at each end, providing access to a pressurized chamber.

airmail *n.* mail carried by air. —*v.t.* to send by airmail.

airman *n.* (*pl.* **-men**) a male member of an air force; a male aviator.

airport *n.* an airfield with facilities for passengers and goods.

air raid an attack by aircraft with bombs etc. The first air raid in history took place when the Austrian army sent up hot-air balloons, with bombs but no pilots, to drift over Venice in the campaign of 1849. The first successful manned bombing flights were by Zeppelin raiders over England in the First World War.

airscrew *n.* an aircraft propeller.

airship *n.* a power-driven aircraft that is lighter than air. An airship may be *rigid*, having a rigid framework for maintaining the shape of its hull, *non-rigid* (also called a *blimp*), in which internal pressure maintains the shape of the envelope, *semi-rigid*, with a rigid longitudinal member to distribute the load and assist in maintaining the shape of its hull, or *hybrid*, with its design incorporating parts of an aeroplane or helicopter to supplement its lift. The airship developed from the balloon, elongated in shape and steered instead of having to drift with the wind; the problem was to build light enough engines. In 1852 a Frenchman, Henri Giffard, built an airship with a steam-engine slung (for reasons of safety) well below the gas-bag, but its speed was so slow that it could be steered only on a windless day. In 1884 the French government financed the building of one that was really controllable and able to return to its base; it was powered by a 6.75 kW electric motor. By the turn of the century Germany had taken the lead with the designs of Count von Zeppelin, whose machines were used in successful passenger services, in the First World War for bombing raids on England, and subsequently for trans-atlantic flights. In the 1930s, however, a series of disasters with hydrogen-filled airships, including the British *R101* at Beauvais, France (1930), and the German *Hindenburg* in 1937, cost many lives and gave such aircraft the tragic reputation which terminated interest in their use for about 40 years, while developments in heavier-than-air aircraft made them commercially obsolete. In the 1970s and 1980s, however, interest has revived, with non-flammable helium used instead of the potentially dangerous hydrogen as a lifting gas (see HELIUM and ill. FLIGHT).

airsick *adj.* affected with nausea from the motion of an aircraft. —**airsickness** *n.*

airspace *n.* the air above a country and subject to its jurisdiction.

airstrip *n.* a strip of ground prepared for take-off and landing of aircraft.

airtight *adj.* impermeable to air or gas.

airway *n.* **1.** a regular route of aircraft. **2.** a ventilating passage in a mine. **3.** a passage for air into the lungs; a device to secure this.

airwoman *n.* (*pl.* **-women**) a female member of an air force; a female aviator.

airworthy *adj.* (of aircraft) fit to fly. —**airworthiness** *n.*

airy *adj.* **1.** well-ventilated; breezy. **2.** light as air; unsubstantial. **3.** casual and light-hearted. —**airy-fairy** *adj.* fanciful, impractical. —**airily** *adv.*, **airiness** *n.* [f. AIR]

aisle /aɪl/ *n.* **1.** a side part of a church, divided by pillars from the main nave (ill. CHURCH). **2.** a passage between rows of pews or seats. [f. OF f. L *ala* wing]

aitch /eɪtʃ/ *n.* the letter H, h. [f. F]

aitchbone /ˈeɪtʃbəʊn/ *n.* the rump-bone of an animal; a cut of beef lying over this. [orig. *nache-bone* f. OF f. L *natis* buttock]

Ajanta /əˈdʒʌntə/ a village in south central India with caves containing Buddhist frescoes and sculptures of the 1st c. BC–7th c. AD, with the finest examples belonging to the Gupta period (5th–6th c. AD).

ajar /əˈdʒɑː(r)/ *adv. & predic. adj.* slightly open. [f. A- + obs. *char* turn]

Ajax /ˈeɪdʒæks/ (*Gk legend*) **1.** a Greek hero of the Trojan war, son of Telamon king of Salamis. **2.** another Greek, son of Oileus king of Locris, who was killed after a shipwreck on his homeward journey after the fall of Troy.

Akbar /ˈækbə(r)/, Jalaludin Muhammad (1542–1605), Mogul emperor of India. Coming to the throne in 1556, Akbar spread the Mogul empire over most of India and established administrative efficiency, a coherent commercial system, and religious toleration. He was the first ruler of India who sought to unite the many different peoples and religions rather than to be the leading representative of one dominant race or creed.

Akhenaten /æk(ə)ˈnɑːt(ə)n/ (= 'he who serves the Aten') the name taken by the pharaoh Amenophis IV (1353–1335 BC) when he founded his new capital, Akhetaten (see AMARNA) in celebration of his religious ideology. Unique in the history of ancient Egyptian religion, it advocated the recognition of the Aten (sun disc) as the sole deity, with the king as his only intermediary. The instigation of this belief became Akhenaten's main objective: temples to other gods were closed throughout the land, the name 'Amun' and the plural form 'gods' were systematically removed from inscriptions. His chief wife Nefertiti bore him six daughters but no sons, and he was succeeded by Tutankhamun, early in whose reign the new religion was abandoned.

akimbo /əˈkɪmbəʊ/ *adv.* (of arms) with hands on hips and elbows turned outwards. [orig. *in kenebow*, prob. f. ON, = bent in a curve]

akin /əˈkɪn/ *adj.* similar; related. [f. A- + KIN]

Akkad /ˈækæd/ the capital city (as yet undiscovered) which gave its name to an ancient kingdom, traditionally founded by Sargon (2334–2279 BC) in north central Mesopotamia (modern Iraq). Its power extended over Babylonia, Assyria, and Syria, and even penetrated into Asia Minor, until it was overwhelmed by invading tribes from the east *c.*2150 BC.

Akkadian /əˈkeɪdɪən/ *adj.* of Akkad or its people or language. —*n.* **1.** the Akkadian language, known from cuneiform inscriptions, the oldest Hamito-Semitic language for which we have any evidence, used in Mesopotamia from about 3000 BC. Two dialects of Akkadian, Assyrian and Babylonian, were widely spoken in the Middle East for the next 2,000 years before they gave way to Aramaic. **2.** a native or inhabitant of Akkad. [f. prec.]

Al *symbol* aluminium.

à la /ɑː lɑː/ after the manner of. [F]

Alabama /æləˈbæmə/ a State in the south-eastern USA bordering on the Gulf of Mexico. Visited by Spanish explorers in the mid-16th c., and later settled by the French, it passed to Britain in 1763 and to the US in 1783, becoming the 22nd State of the USA in 1819; capital, Montgomery.

alabaster /ˈæləbɑːstə(r)/ *n.* a translucent usually white form of gypsum, often carved into ornaments. —*adj.* of alabaster; white or smooth as alabaster. [f. OF f. L f. Gk]

à la carte /ɑː lɑː ˈkɑːt/ ordered as separate items from a menu. [F]

alacrity /əˈlækrɪtɪ/ *n.* prompt and eager readiness. [f. L (*alacer* brisk)]

Aladdin /əˈlædɪn/ hero of a story in the *Arabian Nights*, who acquired a lamp the rubbing of which brought a genie to do the will of the owner. —**Aladdin's cave**, a treasure-house of jewels or other valuables.

Alamein see EL ALAMEIN.

Alamo /ˈæləməʊ/ a mission in San Antonio, Texas, site of a siege in 1836 by Mexican forces during the Texan struggle for independence from Mexico. It was defended by a handful of volunteers (including the legendary Davy Crockett), all of whom were killed.

à la mode /ɑː lɑː ˈməʊd/ in fashion, fashionable. [F]

Alaric /ˈælərɪk/ (*c.*370–410), king of the Visigoths. Becoming king in 395, Alaric invaded first Greece (395–6) and then Italy (400–3), but was checked on each occasion by the Roman general Stilicho. He invaded Italy again in 408 and in 410 captured and sacked Rome.

alarm /əˈlɑːm/ *n.* **1.** a warning sound or signal; a device

giving this. **2.** an alarm clock. **3.** fear caused by expectation of danger or difficulty. —*v.t./i.* to frighten; to arouse to a sense of danger. —**alarm clock,** a clock with a device that rings at a set time. [f. OF f. It. (*all'arme!* to arms!)]

alarmist *n.* one who raises unnecessary or excessive alarm. [f. prec.]

alas /əˈlæs/ *int.* expressing sorrow or distress. [f. OF f. L *lassus* weary]

Alaska /əˈlæskə/ the largest State of the USA, in the extreme north-west of North America, with coasts in the Arctic Ocean, Bering Sea, and North Pacific. About one third of it lies within the Arctic Circle. It was discovered by Russian explorers (under Vitus Bering) in 1741, and further explored by Cook, Vancouver, and others during the last quarter of the 18th c. The territory was purchased from Russia in 1867 and became the 49th State of the USA in 1959; capital, Juneau. —**Alaskan** *adj. & n.*

alb *n.* a white vestment reaching to the feet, worn by some priests at church services (ill. VESTMENTS). [OE f. L *albus* white]

albacore /ˈælbəkɔː/ *n.* a tunny of a large West Indian or related species. [f. Port. f. Arab., = the young camel]

Alban /ˈɔːlbən/, St, the first British martyr, traditionally associated with the persecutions in Diocletian's reign (*c.* 305). He was a pagan of Verulamium (now St Albans, Herts.) who was converted and baptized by a fugitive priest whom he sheltered. When soldiers searched his house he put on the priest's cloak and was arrested and condemned to death. Feast day, 20 June.

Albania /ælˈbeɪnɪə/ a small country in SE Europe, bordering on the Adriatic Sea; pop. (1981) 2,752,300; official language, Albanian; capital, Tirana. Much of the land is mountainous and there are extensive forests, but the coastal areas are fertile. The economy is mainly agricultural but chemical and engineering industries are being developed and the rich mineral resources (which include copper and iron) exploited; all industry is nationalized. Although Albania was part of the Byzantine empire from the 6th c. and part of the Turkish from the 15th c., its mountain tribes always remained fiercely independent and central rule was never completely effective. It became an independent State as a result of the Balkan Wars in 1912, and after a brief period as a republic became a rather unstable monarchy under King Zog in 1928. Invaded by Italy in 1939, it became a Communist State under Enver Hoxha after the Second World War, and although first under the influence of the USSR and later under that of China, has generally remained isolationist in policy and outlook.

Albanian /ælˈbeɪnɪən/ *adj.* of Albania or its people or language. —*n.* **1.** a native or inhabitant of Albania. **2.** the official language of Albania, constituting a separate branch of the Indo-European language group, spoken by some 3 million speakers of whom 2 million live in Albania and 1 million in Yugoslavia. There are two distinct dialects, Tosk in the north and Gheg in the south. [f. prec.]

albatross /ˈælbətrɒs/ *n.* **1.** a long-winged bird related to the petrel, inhabiting the Pacific and Southern Oceans. **2.** (in golf) a score of 3 under par at a hole. [f. Sp. & Port. f. Arab., = the jug]

albedo /ælˈbiːdəʊ/ *n.* (*pl.* **-os**) the fraction of incident radiation reflected by a surface. [L, = whiteness (*albus* white)]

albeit /ɔːlˈbiːɪt/ *conj.* (*literary*) although. [f. *all be it,* = let it be completely true that]

Albert /ˈælbət/, Prince (1819–61), prince of Saxe-Coburg-Gotha, husband to Queen Victoria. An intelligent and energetic consort, Albert breathed considerable life into the British court in the first twenty years of his wife's reign. He was one of the driving forces behind the Great Exhibition of 1851, and a decade later, just before his premature death from typhoid fever, his moderating influence was crucial in keeping Britain out of the American Civil War.

Alberta /ælˈbɜːtə/ a prairie province in western Canada (from 1905), bounded on the south by the USA and on the west by the Rocky Mountains; capital, Edmonton.

Alberti /ælˈbeətɪ/, Leon Battista (1404–72), Italian architect, humanist, painter, writer on art, poet, and musician, justly described as 'the universal man of the early Renaissance'. Born in Genoa, he worked in Florence, and later in Rome (as a member of the papal court) and Mantua. In his works he emphasized the rational basis of all creative endeavour. He was the most representative figure in the change which took place at the Renaissance from the medieval attitude to art as a symbolic expression of theological truths to the humanistic outlook, and the new ideas of scientific naturalism found their fullest expression in his writings.

Albertus Magnus /ælˈbɜːtəs/, St (c.1206-80), Dominican theologian, philosopher, and scientist, who taught Aquinas. Nicknamed the 'universal doctor', he was a pioneer in the study of Aristotle and other pagan Greek and Arabic authors. He was particularly interested in the physical sciences (which led to a reputation for magical powers) and in the problem of reconciling Christianity with pagan philosophy.

Albigenses /ælbɪˈdʒensiːz/ n.pl. members of a heretical sect in southern France, 12th-13th c., named from the city of Albi. Their teaching was a form of Manichaean dualism, with a moral and social doctrine of extreme rigorism and an implacable hatred against the Church. The heresy spread rapidly, its advocates being admired for their austerity, until ruthlessly crushed in a crusade (1209-31) led by Simon de Montfort, and finally extirpated by the Dominican Inquisition.

albino /ælˈbiːnəʊ/ n. (pl. -os) a person or animal with a congenital lack of colouring pigment in the skin and hair (which are white) and the eyes (usually pink); a plant lacking normal colouring. —**albinism** /ˈælbɪnɪz(ə)m/ n. [Sp. & Port. f. L albus white]

Albion /ˈælbɪən/ (poet.) Britain. [OE f. L]

album /ˈælbəm/ n. **1.** a blank book in which a collection of postage stamps, photographs, autographs, etc. can be kept. **2.** a long-playing gramophone record with several items; a set of records. [L, = blank tablet (albus white)]

albumen /ˈælbjʊmɪn/ n. white of eggs [L (albus white)]

albumin /ˈælbjʊmɪn/ n. any of a class of water-soluble proteins found in egg-white, milk, blood, and some plants. [f. F (as prec.)]

Albuquerque /ˈælbəkɜːkɪ/, Alfonso de (1453-1515), Portuguese colonial statesman. He first travelled east in 1503, and, after being appointed Viceroy of the Portuguese Indies three years later, conquered Goa and made it the capital of the Portuguese empire in the east. An active and enlightened administrator, Albuquerque made further conquests on Ceylon, Malacca, Ormuz, the Sunda Isles, and along the Malabar Coast, but was relieved of office as a result of a court intrigue at home and died on the passage back to Portugal.

Alcaeus /ælˈsiːəs/ (born c.620 BC) Greek lyric poet from the island of Lesbos, active in its troubled politics. The surviving fragments of his poetry include political poems, drinking-songs, and love-songs. His works were an important model for the Roman poet Horace.

Alcatraz /ælkəˈtræz/ a rocky island in San Francisco Bay, California, named after its pelicans (Sp. álcatraces). It was the site in 1934-62 of a top-security Federal prison.

Alcestis /ælˈsestɪs/ (Gk legend) wife of Admetus king of Pherae in Thessaly, whose life she saved by consenting to die on his behalf. She was brought back from Hades by Hercules.

alchemy /ˈælkəmɪ/ n. a medieval form of chemistry (see below). —**alchemist** n. [f. OF f. L f. Arab., = the art of transmuting metals]
　Alchemy was based on the possible transmutation of all matter, and was far wider in scope than the familiar attempts to turn base metals into gold. It attracted such medieval scholars as Roger Bacon and Albertus Magnus, and was patronized by princes including the 16th-c. Emperors Maximilian II and Rudolf II. The influential German writer Paracelsus (16th c.) was primarily concerned with its medical application to his search for a chemical therapy for disease; his followers developed specialized chemical medicines and sought a universal elixir which they dreamed would prolong life and restore youth from old age. Alchemy made a considerable, if largely accidental, contribution to chemistry which separated slowly only from it; many leading scientists, including Newton, retained a belief or interest in transmutation. The rise of the mechanical philosophy in the 17th c. gradually undermined alchemy and other forms of the occult, and later alchemists chose to emphasize its mystical aspects in esoteric movements such as that of the Rosicrucians.

Alcibiades /ælsɪˈbaɪədiːz/ (c.450-404 BC) Athenian general and statesman. Educated in the household of Pericles, he became the pupil and friend of Socrates. In the Peloponnesian War he sponsored the unsuccessful expedition against Sicily, but fled to Sparta after being recalled for trial on a charge of sacrilege. He later held commands for Athens against Sparta and Persia, before his enemies finally forced him from Athens and had him murdered in Phrygia.

Alcock /ˈɔːlkɒk/, Sir John William (1892-1919), English aviator. He served as a pilot in the Royal Flying Corps during the First World War and was knighted after making the first direct non-stop transatlantic flight (16 hours 27 minutes) on 14-15 June 1919, from Newfoundland to Clifden, Ireland, with Sir Arthur Witten Brown in a converted Vickers Vimey bomber.

alcohol /ˈælkəhɒl/ n. a colourless volatile liquid, the intoxicant present in wine, beer, and spirits, also used as a solvent and fuel; liquor containing this; (Chem.) a compound of the same type as alcohol. [F or L f. Arab., = the kohl]

alcoholic /ælkəˈhɒlɪk/ adj. of or containing alcohol; caused by alcohol. —n. a person who suffers from alcoholism. [f. prec.]

alcoholism /ˈælkəhɒlɪz(ə)m/ n. habitual heavy drinking of alcohol; a diseased condition caused by this. [f. ALCOHOL]

Alcott /ˈɔːlkɒt/, Louisa May (1832-88), American novelist. From an early age she published sketches and stories to support her impractical father and her family, including Hospital Sketches (1863), which recounted her experiences as a nurse in the Civil War. Her novel for girls Little Women (1868-9), a largely autobiographical work concerning a New England family in the 19th c., achieved wide and lasting popularity. She wrote many others in the same vein as well as adult novels, and was involved in various reform movements, including women's suffrage.

alcove /ˈælkəʊv/ n. a recess in a wall, room, etc. [F f. Sp. f. Arab., = the vault]

Alcuin /ˈælkwɪn/ (c.735-804), English scholar and theologian, inspirer of the 'Carolingian Renaissance'. Born and educated at York, he was invited to Charlemagne's court and became his adviser in religious and educational matters. He improved the palace library, and, becoming Abbot of Tours in 796, established an important library and school there. He developed the type of minuscule handwriting which influenced the Roman type now used in printed books.

Aldebaran /ælˈdebərən/ a conspicuous red giant that is the brightest star in the constellation Taurus. [Arab., = the following (because it follows the Pleiades)]

aldehyde /ˈældɪhaɪd/ n. a volatile fluid with a suffocating smell, got by oxidation of alcohol; (Chem.) a compound of the same structure as this. [f. L, = alcohol deprived of hydrogen]

al dente /æl ˈdentɪ/ cooked so as to be still firm when bitten. [It., = to the tooth]

alder /ˈɔːldə(r)/ n. a tree of the genus Alnus, related to the birch; any of various similar trees (black, red, white alder) not related. [OE]

alderman /ˈɔːldəmən/ n. (pl. -men) **1.** (chiefly hist.) a co-opted member of an English county or borough council, next below mayor. **2.** (US & Austral.) an elected governor of a city. [f. OE aldor patriarch (ald old)]

Alderney /ˈɔːldənɪ/ n. a breed of small dairy cattle originally from Alderney in the Channel Islands; an animal of this breed.

ale /eɪl/ n. beer, especially (**real ale**) that regarded as brewed and stored in the traditional way, with secondary fermentation in the container from which it is dispensed. Ale and beer seem originally to have been synonyms, but after the introduction into England of 'the wicked weed called hops' (c.1624) beer was commonly flavoured with hops. [OE]

aleatory /ˈælɪətərɪ/ adj. depending on the throw of a die etc. or on chance; (in music and art) involving random choice, e.g. in the ordering of fragments of composed music or depending on chance procedures, such as the tossing of a coin, for its composition. [f. L (alea die)]

Alembert /ælãˈbeər/, Jean le Rond d' (1717-83), French philosopher and mathematician who collaborated with Diderot in the production of an encyclopaedia (see DIDEROT).

alembic /əˈlembɪk/ n. an apparatus formerly used in distilling. [f. OF f. L f. Arab. (= the still), f. Gr ambix cup]

Aleppo /əˈlepəʊ/ an ancient city in Syria, twice besieged (though not taken) in the Crusades.

alert /əˈlɜːt/ adj. watchful, vigilant; nimble. —n. a warning signal, notice to stand ready; a state or period of special vigilance. —v.t. to make alert, to warn of danger. [f. F f. It. all' erta to the watch-tower]

Aleut /əˈljuːt/ n. **1.** a native of the Aleutian Islands. **2.** the language of the Aleuts, distantly related to Eskimo. [orig. unkn.]

Aleutian Islands /ɔˈljuːʃ(ə)n/ (also **Aleutians**) a group of islands in US possession, extending SW from Alaska.

Alexander[1] /ælɪgˈzɑːndə(r)/ 'the Great' (356–323 BC), king of Macedon 336–323 BC, son of Philip II, tutored by the philosopher Aristotle. On his succession he immediately set about the invasion of the Persian empire; after liberating the Greek cities in Asia Minor, he defeated the Persians in Egypt, Syria, and Mesopotamia, and extended his conquests eastwards to Bactria and the Punjab. He died of a fever at Babylon, and his empire quickly fell apart after his death. Undoubtedly the greatest general of his country, and probably of antiquity, his remarkable achievements during his short life were due to his untiring energy, enquiring mind, and profound grasp of strategy both in war and in the foundation of new cities. His plans for the empire were grand and original but perhaps impossible of execution. Regarded as a god in his lifetime, he became a model for all later ancient imperialist conquerors and the subject of many fantastic legends.

Alexander[2] /ælɪgˈzɑːndə(r)/ the name of three kings of Scotland:
 Alexander I (c.1077–1124), son of Malcolm III, reigned 1107–24. During his reign the penetration of Anglo-Norman influences and the strengthening of feudal links between Scotland and England accelerated the drift of the hitherto remote northern kingdom into the mainstream of British social and political developments.
 Alexander II (1198–1249), son of William I, reigned 1214–49. He generally restored friendly relations with England, while extending royal authority within his own realm.
 Alexander III (1241–86), son of Alexander II, reigned 1249–86. He enjoyed a long and relatively peaceful reign, but his death in a riding accident left Scotland without a male heir to the throne, plunging the country into three decades of dynastic upheaval and struggle against English domination.

Alexander[3] /ælɪgˈzɑːndə(r)/ the name of three emperors of Russia:
 Alexander I (1777–1825), reigned 1801–25. Alexander came to the throne after the murder of his tyrannical father Paul, but, even though the new Tsar was a romantic liberal by temperament, he was unable to pursue reforming policies beyond limited administrative improvements. The first half of his reign was dominated by the military struggle with Napoleon, in which Russian arms, after many setbacks, finally emerged triumphant. In his later years Alexander became increasingly withdrawn and prone to religious conservatism and took less and less interest in improving the lot of his subjects.
 Alexander II (1818–81), son of Nicholas I, reigned 1855–81. A conservative by nature, Alexander realized the need for at least a measure of reform to rescue Russia from the economic and political crisis into which it had sunk in the last years of his father's reign. Although a series of reforms were introduced, including the emancipation of the serfs in 1861, Alexander was unwilling to go too far. As his reign progressed, radical opposition hardened, throwing up a series of terrorist groups, one of which succeeded in assassinating the Tsar with a bomb in March 1881.
 Alexander III (1845–94), son of Alexander II, reigned 1881–94. Coming to the throne after his father's murder, Alexander III stopped the policy of gradual liberal reform and fell back on repressive conservatism. Although his reign witnessed considerable economic development, his failure even to countenance social and political reform produced a dangerous situation to which his son and successor Nicholas II was to prove unequal.

Alexander[4] /ælɪgˈzɑːndə(r)/, Harold Rupert Leofric George, 1st Earl (1891–1969), British field marshal. In the Second World War he supervised the evacuation from Dunkirk, the withdrawal from Burma, and the victorious campaigns in North Africa (1943) and in Sicily and Italy (1943–5). After the war he became Governor-General of Canada (1946–52).

Alexander Nevski /ælɪgˈzɑːndə(r) ˈnefskɪ/ (1220–63), Russian saint and national hero, called 'Nevski' from the River Neva, on the banks of which he defeated the Swedes.

Alexandria /ælɪgˈzɑːndrɪə/ the chief port of Egypt; pop. (est. 1980) 2,521,000. Founded in 332 BC by Alexander the Great, after whom it is named, it became a major centre of Hellenistic and Jewish culture, with renowned libraries, and was the capital city until the Arab invasions c. AD 641.

alexandrine /ælɪgˈzændraɪn/ n. a verse of six iambic feet. —adj. in this metre. [f. F f. *Alexandre* = Alexander (the Great), subject of a poem in this metre]

alfalfa /ælˈfælfə/ n. lucerne. [Sp. f. Arab., = a green fodder]

Alfonso /ælˈfɒnsəʊ/ the name of 13 kings of Spain:
 Alfonso XIII (1886–1941), reigned 1886–1931. Alfonso ruled under the regency of his mother until 1902, during which time Spain lost her colonial possessions in the Philippines and Cuba to the USA. He appointed Primo de Rivera dictator in 1923, but after the opening of the National Assembly in 1927 Spain was stricken with a worsening political crisis. Martial law was declared in 1930, but this failed to stop the striking and rioting and a year later Alfonso was forced to abdicate.

Alfred /ˈælfrɪd/ 'the Great' (849–99), king of Wessex 871–99. Alfred's military resistance to Danish invaders saved the southwest part of the country from Norse occupation and made him one of the great heroic figures of his age. Apart from his military victories, Alfred was also responsible for a considerable revival of learning and literature in the west of England, himself translating Latin works into English.

alfresco /ælˈfreskəʊ/ adj. & adv. in the open air. [f. It.]

alga /ˈælgə/ n. (usu. in pl. **algae** /-dʒiː, -giː/) any of a large group of primitive mainly aquatic non-flowering photosynthetic plants, including seaweeds and many plankton. They may be single-celled or multicellular but, unlike higher plants, have no vascular (conducting) tissue and no absorbent root system. Algae constitute a form of life rather than a single related group and are now separated into a number of divisions or phyla, partly on the basis of their pigmentation. The primitive but widespread blue-green algae are related more to bacteria than to other algae; traces of them are reported in rocks several thousand million years old. The brown algae include the largest and most complex seaweeds, but another division, the green algae, are thought to be the ancestors of most land plants. Planktonic algae of various kinds provide the food which supports nearly all marine life. [L]

algebra /ˈældʒɪbrə/ n. the branch of mathematics that deals with formulae and equations in which symbols (usually letters) stand for unknown numbers or other entities. One of the earliest works on the subject was the *Arithmetica* by Diophantus of Alexandria (see entry). Abstract (or 'modern') algebra deals with systems (such as fields, rings, vector spaces, groups) that consist of elements (typically numbers, vectors, or geometrical transformations) and operations that may be performed with them (such as addition, multiplication, or composition of transformations). In abstract algebra attention is shifted from calculation that can be performed within particular systems to comparison between different systems. —**algebraic** /-ˈbreɪk/ adj., **algebraically** adv. [It., Sp., & L f. Arab., = reunion of broken parts, title of book written c.820 by Al-Khuwārizmī (see ALGORITHM)]

Algeria /ælˈdʒɪərɪə/ a North African country on the Mediterranean coast, consisting chiefly of desert, with fertile areas near the coast; pop. (est. 1983) 20,200,000; official language, Arabic; capital, Algiers. The people are mainly Arabs and Berbers and the economy is chiefly agricultural, though industrial development is proceeding; all major industries are under State control. The main exports are crude oil and (liquefied) natural gas, which are pumped from the Sahara to terminals on the coast. Algeria came under nominal Turkish rule in the 16th c., but the native peoples always retained a high degree of independence, dominating the Barbary coast until colonized by France in the mid-19th c. Heavily settled by French immigrants, Algeria was closely integrated with metropolitan France, but the refusal of the European settlers to grant equal rights to the native population led to increasing political instability and civil war in the 1950s, and in 1962 the country was granted independence as a result of a referendum. The departure of the French caused grave damage to the previously prosperous Algerian economy, with the result that the next two decades were characterized by slow attempts at economic recovery and limited external contacts. — **Algerian** adj. & n.

Algiers /ælˈdʒɪəz/ the capital of Algeria and a leading Mediterranean port; pop. approx. 3,250,000.

ALGOL n. a high-level computer language using algebra. [f. ALGO(RITHMIC) + L(ANGUAGE)]

Algol /ˈælgɒl/ an eclipsing binary star that is the second brightest in the constellation Perseus. [Arab., = the destruction]

Algonquian /ælˈgɒŋkwɪən/ n. (also **Algonkian**) **1.** a member of a large group of North American Indian tribes speaking related languages, pushed northward and westward by colonial expansion in the 18th and 19th c. **2.** any of their languages or dialects, forming one of the largest groups of American Indian languages and including Ojibwa, Cree, Blackfoot, Cheyenne, Fox, and Delaware, which are spoken mainly in the north Middle West of the USA, Montana, and south central Canada. Many English and American words have been adopted from this group, e.g. *moccasin, moose, pow-wow, squaw, toboggan.* —*adj.* of this people or their languages. [f. foll.]

Algonquin /ælˈgɒŋkwɪn/ n. **1.** an American Indian of a people encountered in the districts of Ottawa and Quebec; this people. **2.** their language. —*adj.* of the Algonquin or their language. [F, perh. f. native word = 'at the place of spearing fish and eels']

algorithm /ˈælgərɪð(ə)m/ n. a process or rules for calculation, especially by computer. [f. OF f. L f. Pers. *Al-Khuwārizmī* (name of 9th-c. mathematician)]

Alhambra /ælˈhæmbrə/ a fortified Moorish palace, the last stronghold of the Muslim kings of Granada, built between 1248 and 1354 near Granada in Spain. It is an outstanding piece of Moorish architecture with its marble courts and fountains, delicate columns and archways, and wall decorations of carved and painted stucco. [Arab., = red castle]

Ali /ˈɑːliː/, Muhammad (1942–) American boxer who won the world heavyweight title first in 1964 and regained it twice subsequently (1974, 1978). On joining the Black Muslim movement he gave up his real name (Cassius Clay) and became known as Muhammad Ali. He is a vital figure in the history of the sport, both for his physical skill, with great speed allied to a formidable physique, and for his colourful flamboyant character.

alias /ˈeɪlɪəs/ adv. called (by a certain name) at other times. —n. an assumed name. [L, = at another time]

Ali Baba /æli ˈbɑːbə/ the hero of a story supposed to be from the *Arabian Nights*, who discovered the magic formula ('Open Sesame!') which opened the cave in which forty robbers kept the treasure they had accumulated.

alibi /ˈælɪbaɪ/ n. (pl. **-bis**) **1.** a plea that an accused person was elsewhere when a specified act took place. **2.** (D) an excuse. [L, = at another place]

Alice /ˈælɪs/ heroine of stories by Lewis Carroll.

alidade /ˈælɪdeɪd/ n. a sighting device for angular measurement, formerly used with a quadrant, astrolabe, etc., now with a plane table. [f. L f. Arab., = the revolving radius]

alien /ˈeɪlɪən/ n. **1.** a foreign-born resident who is not naturalized in the country where he or she lives. **2.** a being from another world. —*adj.* **1.** foreign, not one's own, unfamiliar. **2.** differing in nature, inconsistent. **3.** repugnant. [f. OF f. L (*alius* other)]

alienate /ˈeɪlɪəneɪt/ v.t. **1.** to estrange, to make unfriendly or hostile. **2.** to transfer the ownership of; to divert. —**alienation** /-ˈneɪʃ(ə)n/ n. [f. L (as prec.)]

alight[1] /əˈlaɪt/ predic. adj. on fire, lit up. [prob. f. *on a light* (= lighted) *fire*]

alight[2] /əˈlaɪt/ v.i. to get down or off; to descend and settle. [OE]

align /əˈlaɪn/ v.t. **1.** to place in or bring into line, to co-ordinate. **2.** to ally with a party or cause. —**alignment** n. [f. F (à *ligne* into line)]

alike /əˈlaɪk/ predic. adj. like one another. —adv. in a like manner. [f. OE]

alimentary /ælɪˈmentəri/ adj. of food or nutrition; nourishing. —**alimentary canal,** the tubular passage through which food passes from mouth to anus in being digested and absorbed by the body (ill. BODY 2). [f. L *alimentarius* (*alere* nourish)]

alimony /ˈælɪməni/ n. (hist.) an allowance (now called *maintenance*) payable to a woman from her (ex-)husband pending or after a divorce or legal separation; (US) an allowance paid to a spouse or child. [as prec.]

aliphatic /ælɪˈfætɪk/ adj. (Chem.) (of compounds) related to fats; in which carbon atoms form open chains. [f. Gk *aleiphar* fat]

aliquot /ˈælɪkwɒt/ adj. that produces a quotient without a fraction when a given larger number is divided by it. —n. **1.** an aliquot part. **2.** a representative portion of a substance. [f. F f. L, = several]

alive /əˈlaɪv/ pred. adj. **1.** living. **2.** lively, active; alert or responsive *to*. **3.** teeming (*with*). [OE]

alkali /ˈælkəlaɪ/ n. (pl. **-is**) any of a class of substances that neutralize acids and form caustic or corrosive solutions in water (see below); a substance with similar but weaker properties, e.g. sodium carbonate. —**alkali metal,** any of the 6 chemically related metallic elements lithium, sodium, potassium, rubidium, caesium, and francium, whose hydroxides are alkalis. Being very reactive, they are not found in the free state in nature. They all display a valency of 1. [f. L f. Arab., = the calcined ashes]

Since the 17th c. alkalis or bases such as potash (potassium carbonate) and caustic soda (a mixture of sodium oxide and sodium hydroxide) have been thought of as substances which in some sense are opposed to acids. They neutralize acids, forming salts, have a caustic or acid taste, turn red litmus blue, and have a smooth soapy texture. It is now recognized that bases, at a molecular level, may be defined as any of the substances which accept a proton in solution or are capable of donating a pair of electrons to an acid. Whether a given substance functions as an acid or as a base depends upon its chemical environment. Well-known bases are sodium and potassium hydroxide, which are used to manufacture soaps and detergents; quicklime or calcium oxide, used in the manufacture of cement; and ammonia, which is used as a fertilizer and as a chemical intermediate.

alkaline /ˈælkəlaɪn/ adj. having the properties of an alkali. —**alkaline earth,** an oxide of an alkaline-earth metal. **alkaline-earth metal,** any of the 6 chemically related metallic elements beryllium, magnesium, calcium, strontium, barium, and radium, which resemble the alkali metals in being very reactive and in forming basic hydroxides, although these are comparatively insoluble. All these elements display a valency of 2. —**alkalinity** /-ˈlɪnɪti/ n. [f. prec.]

alkaloid /ˈælkəlɔɪd/ n. any of a large group of nitrogenous bases of plant origin, many of which are used as drugs (e.g. quinine). [f. G (as prec.)]

alkyl /ˈælkɪl/ n. (usu. *attrib.*) derived from or related to a hydrocarbon of the paraffin series. [f. G (as ALCOHOL)]

all /ɔːl/ adj. **1.** the whole amount, quantity, or extent of. **2.** the greatest possible. **3.** any whatever. —n. **1.** all persons concerned, everything. **2.** (in games) on both sides. —adv. entirely, quite; (colloq.) very. —**after all,** in spite of what has been said, done, or expected. **All Blacks,** the New Zealand international Rugby football team, so called from the colour of their uniforms. **all-clear,** n. a signal that a danger or difficulty is over. **All-Hallows** n. All Saints' Day. **all in,** exhausted. **all-in** attrib. inclusive of all. **all in all,** when everything is considered; of supreme importance. **all out,** using all possible strength, effort, etc. **all over,** completely finished; in or on all parts (of); typically; (colloq.) excessively or effusively attentive to. **all-purpose** adj. having many uses. **all right,** (predic.) satisfactory, safe and sound, in good condition; satisfactorily, as desired; (as int.) I consent or agree, (iron.) you deserve this. **all round,** in all respects; for each person. **all-round** adj. (of a person) versatile. **all-rounder** n. a versatile person. **All Saints' Day,** 1 Nov. **all set,** (colloq.) ready to start. **All Souls' Day,** 2 Nov. **all there,** (colloq.) mentally alert or normal. **all the same,** in spite of this. **all-time** adj. hitherto unsurpassed. **at all,** in any way, to any extent. **in all,** in total, altogether. [OE]

Allah /ˈælə/ n. the Muslim name of God. [f. Arab., = the god]

Allahabad /æləhəˈbɑːd/ an Indian city at the confluence of the Jumna with the Ganges. The capital of Uttar Pradesh, it is a place of Hindu pilgrimage.

allay /əˈleɪ/ v.t. to diminish (fear, suspicion, etc.); to relieve or alleviate pain. [OE (A-, LAY[1])]

Allecto /əˈlektəʊ/ (Gk myth.) one of the Furies. [Gk, = the implacable one]

allegation /ælɪˈɡeɪʃ(ə)n/ n. an assertion, especially one made without proof; alleging. [f. AF or L (*allegare* adduce)]

allege /əˈledʒ/ v.t. to declare, especially without proof; to advance as an argument or excuse. [f. AF f. L (*litigare* dispute at law, confused in sense w. *allegare* allege)]

allegedly /əˈledʒɪdli/ adv. as is said to be the case. [f. prec.]

Alleghany Mountains /æləˈgeɪni/ (also **Alleghanies**) a mountain range of the Appalachian system in the eastern USA.

allegiance /əˈliːdʒ(ə)ns/ n. support of a sovereign, government, or cause etc.; loyalty. [f. AF (as LIEGE)]

allegorize /ˈælɪgəraɪz/ v.t. to treat as or by means of an allegory. [f. foll.]

allegory /ˈælɪgɒrɪ/ n. a narrative or description in which things have a figurative or symbolical meaning. —**allegorical** /-ˈgɒrɪk(ə)l/ adj., **allegorically** adv. [f. OF f. L f. Gk (allos other, -agoria speaking)]

allegretto /ælɪˈgretəʊ/ adv. & adj. (Mus.) in fairly brisk time. —n. (pl. **-os**) (Mus.) an allegretto passage. [It., dim. of ALLEGRO]

allegro /əˈleɡrəʊ/ adv. (Mus.) in quick or lively tempo. —n. (pl. **-os**) (Mus.) an allegro passage. [It., = lively]

alleluia /ælɪˈluːjə/ int. & n. praise to God. [f. L f. Gk f. Heb., = praise the Lord]

allemande /ˈælmɑːnd/ n. **1.** any of several German dances; music for one of these, especially as a suite movement. **2.** a country-dance figure. [F, = German (dance)]

Allenby /ˈælənbɪ/, Edmund Henry Hynman, 1st Viscount (1861-1936), British general of the First World War, a veteran of the Boer War, who commanded the cavalry division and later the Third Army on the Western Front. In 1917 he was sent to the Middle East to lead the Egyptian Expeditionary Force. Having captured Jerusalem in December 1917, he went on to inflict total defeat on the Turkish forces in Palestine in 1918.

allergen /ˈælədʒ(ə)n/ n. a substance that causes an allergic reaction. —**allergenic** /-ˈdʒenɪk/ adj. [f. ALLERGY]

allergic /əˈlɜːdʒɪk/ adj. having an allergy or (colloq.) antipathy to; caused by allergy. [f. foll.]

allergy /ˈælədʒɪ/ n. a condition of reacting adversely to certain substances; (colloq.) an antipathy. [f. G f. Gk allos other + ENERGY]

alleviate /əˈliːvɪeɪt/ v.t. to lessen, to make less severe. —**alleviation** /-ˈeɪʃ(ə)n/ n., **alleviator** /-ˈliː-/ n. [f. L alleviare lighten (AD-, levare raise)]

alley n. **1.** a narrow passage, especially between or behind buildings. **2.** a channel for balls in bowling etc. **3.** a path bordered by hedges or shrubbery. [f. OF (aller go) f. L ambulare walk]

alliance /əˈlaɪəns/ n. a union or agreement to co-operate, especially of a State by treaty or families by marriage; **Alliance,** the Liberal Party and the Social Democratic Party in a political alliance. [f. OF (as ALLY)]

allied /ˈælaɪd/ adj. **1.** having a similar origin or character. **2.** in alliance with foreign States; **Allied,** of the Allies (see ALLY). [f. ALLY]

alligator /ˈælɪgeɪtə(r)/ n. crocodilian of the genus Alligator, found especially in the rivers of tropical America (A. mississippiensis); a smaller species (A. sinensis) found in the Yangtze region of China. It differs from the crocodile in various ways (see CROCODILE). [f. Sp. el lagarto (L lacerta lizard)]

alliteration /əlɪtəˈreɪʃ(ə)n/ n. occurrence of the same letter or sound at the beginning of several words in succession (as in sing a song of sixpence). —**alliterative** /əˈlɪtərətɪv/ adj. [f. L littera letter]

allocate /ˈæləkeɪt/ v.t. to assign or allot. —**allocable** /ˈæləkəb(ə)l/ adj., **allocation** /-ˈkeɪʃ(ə)n/ n. [f. L allocare (AD-, locus place)]

allot /əˈlɒt/ v.t. (**-tt-**) to distribute officially; to apportion as a share or task. [f. OF (a to, LOT)]

allotment /əˈlɒtmənt/ n. **1.** a small piece of (public) land let out for cultivation. **2.** apportioning. **3.** a share. [f. prec.]

allotrope /ˈælətrəʊp/ n. an allotropic form (for example, diamond and graphite are allotropes of carbon). [f. foll.]

allotropy /əˈlɒtrəpɪ/ n. the existence of several forms of a chemical element in the same state (gas, liquid, solid) but with different physical or chemical properties. —**allotropic** /æləˈtrɒpɪk/ adj. [f. Gk (allos different, tropos manner)]

allow /əˈlaʊ/ v.t./i. **1.** to permit, to let happen. **2.** to assign (a fixed sum) to. **3.** to add or deduct in estimating. **4.** to acknowledge as true or acceptable. —**allow for,** to take into consideration; to provide for. [orig. = praise, f. OF f. L (AD-, laudare praise, locare place)]

allowable /əˈlaʊəb(ə)l/ adj. that may be allowed. —**allowably** adv. [f. prec.]

allowance /əˈlaʊəns/ n. an amount or sum allowed; a deduction or discount. —v.t. to make an allowance to. —**make allowances for,** to regard as a mitigating circumstance. [as ALLOW]

alloy /ˈælɔɪ/ n. **1.** a substance that is a mixture wholly or mainly of metals. **2.** an inferior metal mixed especially with gold or silver. —v.t. **1.** to mix (metals). **2.** to debase by an

admixture; to weaken or spoil (pleasure etc. with). [f. OF (as ALLY)]

allspice /ˈɔːlspaɪs/ n. spice obtained from the berry of the pimento; this berry.

Allston /ˈɔːlst(ə)n/, Washington (1779-1843), American landscape painter, the most important artistic personality of the first generation of romanticism in the USA. His early works exhibit a taste for the monumental, apocalyptic, and melodramatic, in the same vein as J. M. W. Turner or John Martin (e.g. The Deluge, 1804, and his vast unfinished canvas, Belshazzar's Feast, 1817-43). More influential in America, however, were his later, visionary, and dreamlike paintings such as The Moonlight Landscape (1819).

allude /əˈljuːd/ v.i. to refer in passing or indirectly to (a thing presumed known). [f. L alludere (AD-, ludere play)]

allure /əˈljʊə(r)/ v.t. to entice; to attract or charm. —**allurement** n. [f. OF (a to, LURE)]

allusion /əˈluːʒ(ə)n/ n. a passing or indirect reference (to). [F or f. L (as ALLUDE)]

allusive /əˈluːsɪv/ adj. containing allusions. —**allusively** adv. [as prec.]

alluvium /əˈluːvɪəm/ n. (pl. **-ia**) a deposit of earth, sand, etc., left by a flood or flow, especially in a river valley. —**alluvial** adj. [L f. AD-, luere wash]

ally /ˈælaɪ/ n. a State or person co-operating with another for a special purpose, especially by treaty. —v.t. to combine in an alliance. —**the Allies,** the nations allied in opposition to the Central Powers in the First World War or to the Axis Powers in the Second World War. [f. OF f. L alligare (AD-, ligare bind)]

Almagest /ˈælmədʒest/ **1.** the title of an Arabic version of Ptolemy's astronomical treatise. **2.** (in the Middle Ages; also **almagest**) any of various other celebrated textbooks on astrology and alchemy. [f. Arab. al the, Gk megistē (suntaxis) the great (system)]

Alma Mater /ælmə ˈmeɪtə(r)/ the title used of a university or school by its past or present members. [L, = bounteous mother]

almanac /ˈɔːlmənæk/ n. **1.** (also **almanack**) an annual publication containing a calendar with astronomical data and sometimes other information. **2.** a yearbook of sport, theatre, etc. [f. L f. Gk]

Almanach de Gotha /ˈɔːlmənæk də ˈgəʊtə/ a formerly annual publication giving information about European royalty, nobility, and diplomats, published in French by Justus Perthes of Gotha since 1763.

Alma-Tadema /ælmə ˈtædɪmə/, Sir Lawrence (1836-1912), Dutch-born painter who settled in England in 1870 and was naturalized in 1873. With Leighton and Poynter he was typical of that meticulous painting style so popular in the late 19th c. that combined archaeological accuracy with contemporary concerns to produce idealized and often sentimental reconstructions of life in the classical world. His remarkable social and financial success has yet to be endorsed by posterity as an artistic one.

almighty /ɔːlˈmaɪtɪ/ adj. all-powerful; (colloq.) very great. —**the Almighty,** God. [OE (ALL, MIGHTY)]

almond /ˈɑːmənd/ n. the nut-like kernel of the fruit of two trees (sweet and bitter almond), varieties of Amydalus communis, allied to the plum and peach; either of these trees. [f. OF f. L f. Gk]

almoner /ˈɑːmənə(r)/ n. an official distributor of alms. [f. AF f. L (as ALMS)]

almonry /ˈɑːmənrɪ/ n. a place for the distribution of alms. [as prec.]

almost /ˈɔːlməʊst/ adv. all but; as the nearest thing to. [OE (as ALL, MOST)]

alms /ɑːmz/ n. (pl. same) (hist.) a donation of food or money given to the poor. [OE f. L f. Gk (eleos pity)]

almshouse n. a house founded by charity for the accommodation of poor (usually elderly) people.

almucantar /ælmjuːˈkæntə(r)/ n. a line of constant altitude above the horizon. [f. L or F f. Arab., = sundial (kantara arch)]

aloe /ˈæləʊ/ n. a plant of the genus Aloe, native to Africa, with erect spikes of flowers and with leaves that yield a bitter juice; (in pl.) a purgative drug made from this juice. —**American aloe,** a kind of agave. [OE f. L f. Gk]

aloft /əˈlɒft/ adv. high up, overhead; upward. [f. ON, = in air]

alone /əˈləʊn/ predic. adj. without anyone or anything else, without company, assistance, or addition. —*adv.* only, exclusively. [earlier *al one* (ALL, ONE)]

along /ə'lɒŋ/ *adv.* **1.** onward, into a more advanced state. **2.** in company with oneself or others. **3.** beside or through a part or the whole of a thing's length. —*prep.* beside or through (part of) the length of. —**all along,** from the beginning. **along with,** in addition to. [OE, orig. adj. = facing against]

alongshore *adv.* along or beside the shore.

alongside *adv.* at or to the side; close to the side of a ship, pier, or wharf. —*prep.* close to the side of.

aloof /ə'lu:f/ *adj.* unconcerned, lacking in sympathy. —*adv.* away, apart. —**aloofness** *n.* [orig. Naut., f. A- + LUFF]

aloud /ə'laʊd/ *adv.* in a normal voice so as to be audible; (*archaic*) loudly. [f. A- + LOUD]

alp *n.* pasture-land on mountains in Switzerland. [f. ALPS]

alpaca /æl'pækə/ *n.* **1.** a kind of llama of South America with long wool. **2.** its wool; fabric made from this. **3.** any of various similar fabrics. [Sp. f. Quechua (*pako* reddish-brown)]

alpenhorn /'ælpənhɔ:n/ *n.* a long wooden horn formerly used by herdsmen in the Alps. [G, = Alpine horn]

alpenstock /'ælpənstɒk/ *n.* a long iron-tipped staff used in mountain-climbing. [G, = Alpine stick]

alpha /'ælfə/ *n.* **1.** the first letter of the Greek alphabet, = a. **2.** a first-class mark in an examination. **3.** a designation of the brightest star in a constellation, or sometimes a star's position in a group. —**Alpha and Omega,** the beginning and the end. **alpha particles** *or* **rays,** helium nuclei emitted by radioactive substances (originally regarded as rays). [L f. Gk]

alphabet /'ælfəbet/ *n.* a set of letters used in a language; these in a fixed order; symbols or signs for these. (See ill. pp. 20-1.) —**phonetic alphabet,** symbols used to represent the sounds of speech. —**alphabetical** /-'betɪk(ə)l/ *adj.,* **alphabetically** *adv.* [f. L f. Gk *alpha, beta,* first two letters of Gk alphabet]

Alphabetic script developed as a consonantal system in the Levant during the second millennium BC and had assumed a linear form composed of twenty-two signs, known as 'Phoenician', by the 11th c. BC, before it was transmitted to Greece. With the introduction of the first full vocalic system, the earliest Greek alphabet of *c.*750 BC achieved the final structural development of writing which passed back to the Semites and thence to the rest of the world, remaining principally unaltered to the present day. The alphabet is the most flexible method of writing ever invented, passing from one language to another with minimal difficulty; it is hard to over-estimate its importance.

alphabetical /ælfə'betɪk(ə)l/ *adj.* in the order of the letters of the alphabet; using an alphabet. —**alphabetically** *adv.* [f. prec.]

alphabetize /'ælfəbətaɪz/ *v.t.* to put into alphabetical order. —**alphabetization** /-'zeɪʃ(ə)n/ *n.* [f. ALPHABET]

alphanumeric /ælfənju:'merɪk/ *adj.* containing both alphabetical and numerical symbols. [f. ALPHABET + NUMERICAL]

Alpine /'ælpaɪn/ *adj.* **1.** of the Alps or other high mountains. **2.** of or belonging to an extremely artificial sub-racial grouping of people who, as a population, are short (*c.*163cm (5ft. 4in.) tall on average) with intermediate colouring, and brachycephalic. —*n.* a plant suited to mountain regions or grown in rock gardens. [as foll.]

Alps /ælps/ a major European mountain range extending from the Mediterranean coast of France and NW Italy through Switzerland to the western Hungarian plain, with many peaks over 3,700m (12,000ft.). [f. F f. L f. Gk]

already /ɔ:l'redɪ/ *adv.* before the time in question; as early or soon as this. [f. ALL + READY]

Alsace /æl'sæs/ a French province west of the Rhine. It was annexed with part of Lorraine (the annexed territory was known as Alsace-Lorraine) after the Franco-Prussian war of 1870, and restored to France after the First World War.

Alsatian /æl'seɪʃ(ə)n/ *n.* a dog of a large strong smooth-haired breed of wolfhound. [f. L *Alsatia* Alsace]

also /'ɔ:lsəʊ/ *adv.* in addition, besides. —**also-ran** *n.* a horse or dog not among the first three to finish in a race; a person who has failed to win distinction in his activities. [OE (ALL, SO)]

Altaic /æl'taɪk/ *adj.* of the Altai Mountains in Central Asia, or a family of languages comprising the Turkic, Mongolian, and Tungusic groups. —*n.* this family of languages, whose

common features include vowel harmony, with all the vowels of a word belonging to the same class (i.e. either front or back).

Altamira /æltə'mi:rə/ the site of a cave with palaeolithic rock paintings, south of Santander in NE Spain, discovered in 1879. The paintings are boldly executed polychrome figures of animals, including deer, wild boar, aurochs, and especially bison, depicted with a sure realism; they are dated to the upper Magdalenian period.

altar /'ɒltə(r)/ *n.* the table on which bread and wine are consecrated in the Eucharist (ill. VESTMENTS); any structure on which offerings are made to a god. [OE f. L (*altus* high)]

Altdorfer /ælt'dɔ:fə(r)/, Albrecht (*c.*1485-1538), German painter. In his early works he was preoccupied with the problem of setting figures in a landscape which reflected the mood of the human activity; in his late years he painted pure landscapes, miniatures on vellum, and is an important figure in the history of the appreciation of scenery for its own sake. Altdorfer was employed by the Emperor Maximilian, and together with Dürer and others illustrated the margins of the Emperor's prayer-book. From 1526 he was town architect of Regensburg in Bavaria.

alter /'ɒltə(r)/ *v.t./i.* to make or become different, to change in character, size, place, etc. —**alteration** /-'reɪʃ(ə)n/ *n.* [f. OF f. L (*alter* other)]

altercate /'ɒltəkeɪt/ *v.i.* to dispute angrily, to wrangle. —**altercation** /-'keɪʃ(ə)n/ *n.* [f. L *altercari*]

alter ego /æltər 'i:gəʊ/ (*pl.* -**os**) an intimate friend; another aspect of oneself. [L, = other self]

alternate[1] /ɒl'tɜ:nət/ *adj.* (of things of two kinds) coming each after one of the other kind; (with *pl. n.*) every second one. —**alternate angles,** two angles on opposite sides and at opposite ends of a line that crosses two others. —**alternately** *adv.* [f. L, = do things by turns (*alter* other)]

alternate[2] /'ɒltəneɪt/ *v.t./i.* to arrange, perform, or occur alternately; to consist of alternate things. —**alternating current,** electric current that reverses direction at regular intervals. [as prec.]

alternation /ɒltə'neɪʃ(ə)n/ *n.* alternating. —**alternation of generations,** a pattern of reproduction occurring in the life cycles of many lower plants (e.g. ferns) and some invertebrate animals (especially coelenterates), involving a regular alternation between two distinct forms, differently produced and often very different from each other. Generation is alternately sexual and asexual (as in ferns) or dioecious and parthenogenetic (as in some jellyfish). [f. ALTERNATE[2]]

alternative /ɒl'tɜ:nətɪv/ *adj.* available in place of something else; (of life-style, medical treatment, etc.) using practices other than the conventional ones. —*n.* a choice available in place of another; each of two or more possibilities. —**Alternative Service Book,** a book containing the public liturgy of the Church of England published in 1980 for use as the alternative to the Book of Common Prayer. —**alternatively** *adv.* [as prec.]

alternator /'ɒltɜ:neɪtə(r)/ *n.* a dynamo producing alternating current. [f. ALTERNATE[2]]

alto /'æltəʊ/ *n.* (*pl.* -**os**) **1.** the highest adult male singing-voice; a female voice of similar range, a contralto; a singer with such a voice; a part written for it. **2.** an instrument of the second or third highest pitch in its family. [It., = high (singing)]

although /ɔ:l'ðəʊ/ *conj.* though. [f. ALL + THOUGH]

altimeter /'æltɪmi:tə(r)/ *n.* an instrument measuring altitude. [f. L *altus* + METER]

altitude /'æltɪtju:d/ *n.* height, especially as measured above sea-level or (of a star) above the horizon. [f. L (*altus* high)]

altocumulus /æltəʊ'kju:mjʊləs/ *n.* (*pl.* -**li** /-laɪ/) cloud like cumulus but at a higher level (ill. WEATHER). [f. L *altus* high + CUMULUS]

altogether /ɔ:ltə'geðə(r)/ *adv.* entirely, totally; on the whole. —**in the altogether,** (*colloq.*) nude. [f. ALL + TOGETHER]

altostratus /æltəʊ'streɪtəs/ *n.* (*pl.* -**ti** /-taɪ/) clouds forming a continuous layer at medium altitude (ill. WEATHER). [f. L. *altus* high + STRATUS]

altruism /'æltruɪz(ə)m/ *n.* regard for others as a principle of action, unselfishness. —**altruist** *n.,* **altruistic** /-'ɪstɪk/ *adj.,* **altruistically** *adv.* [f. F f. It. *altrui* somebody else]

alula /'æljʊlə/ *n.* the bastard wing of a bird (see BASTARD; ill. BIRDS). [dim. of L *ala* wing]

alum /'æləm/ *n.* a double sulphate of aluminium and another

Alphabets and Hieroglyphs

The development of a letter

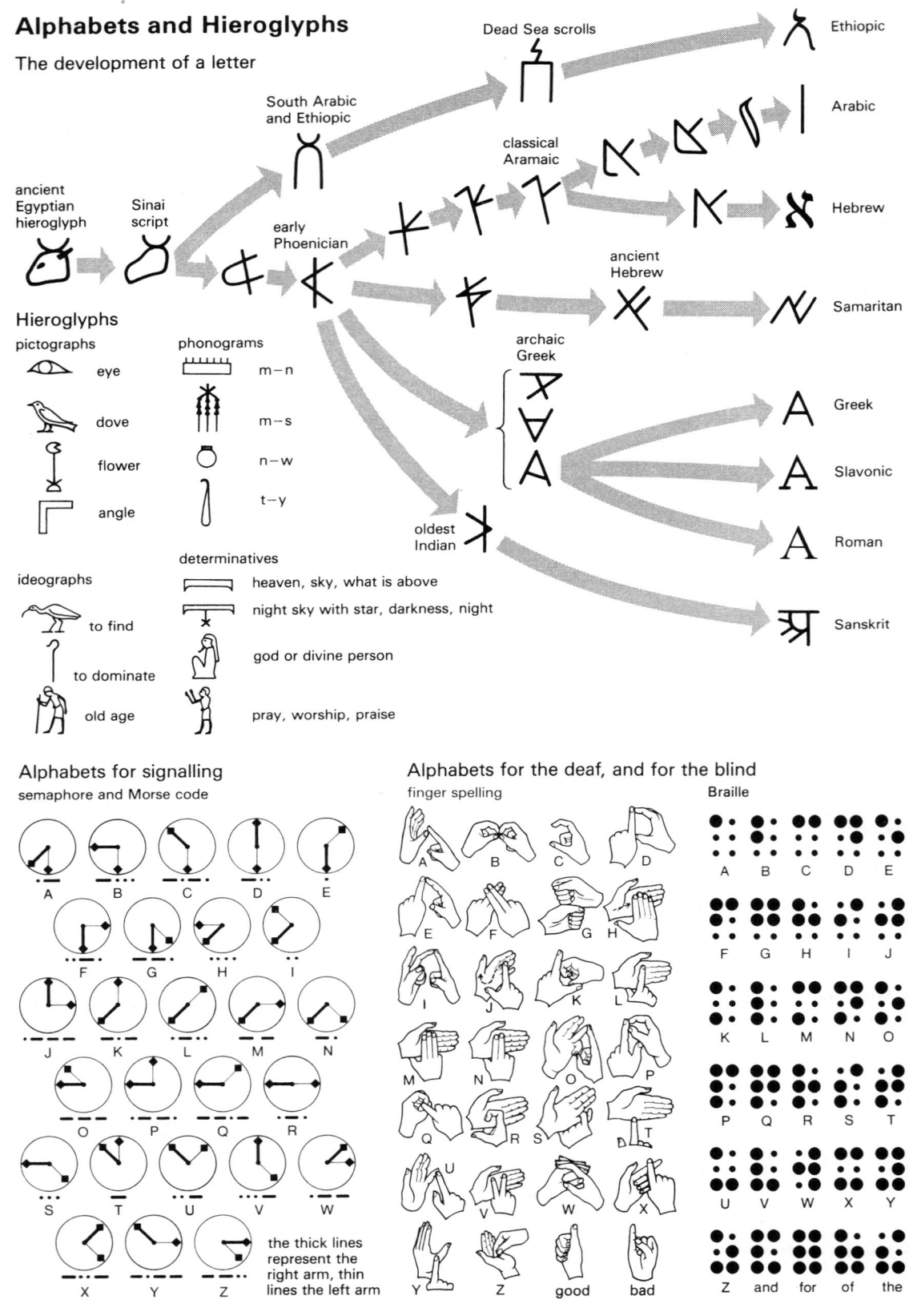

ancient Egyptian hieroglyph

Sinai script

early Phoenician

South Arabic and Ethiopic

Dead Sea scrolls

classical Aramaic

ancient Hebrew

archaic Greek

oldest Indian

Ethiopic

Arabic

Hebrew

Samaritan

Greek

Slavonic

Roman

Sanskrit

Hieroglyphs

pictographs

eye

dove

flower

angle

phonograms

m – n

m – s

n – w

t – y

ideographs

to find

to dominate

old age

determinatives

heaven, sky, what is above

night sky with star, darkness, night

god or divine person

pray, worship, praise

Alphabets for signalling

semaphore and Morse code

A B C D E
F G H I
J K L M N
O P Q R
S T U V W
X Y Z

the thick lines represent the right arm, thin lines the left arm

Alphabets for the deaf, and for the blind

finger spelling

A B C D
E F G H
I J K L
M N O P
Q R S T
U V W X
Y Z good bad

Braille

A B C D E
F G H I J
K L M N O
P Q R S T
U V W X Y
Z and for of the

Arabic

				Name	Translit.
ا	ا			'alif	'
ب	ب	ـبـ	ـب	bā'	b
ت	ت	ـتـ	ـت	tā'	t
ث	ث	ـثـ	ـث	thā'	th
ج	ج	ـجـ	ـج	jīm	j
ح	ح	ـحـ	ـح	ḥā'	ḥ
خ	خ	ـخـ	ـخ	khā'	kh
د	ـد			dāl	d
ذ	ـذ			dhāl	dh
ر	ـر			rā'	r
ز	ـز			zay	z
س	ـس	ـسـ	ـس	sīn	s
ش	ـش	ـشـ	ـش	shīn	sh
ص	ـص	ـصـ	ـص	ṣād	ṣ
ض	ـض	ـضـ	ـض	ḍād	ḍ
ط	ـط	ـطـ	ـط	ṭā'	ṭ
ظ	ـظ	ـظـ	ـظ	ẓā'	ẓ
ع	ـع	ـعـ	ـع	'ayn	'
غ	ـغ	ـغـ	ـغ	ghayn	gh
ف	ـف	ـفـ	ـف	fā'	f
ق	ـق	ـقـ	ـق	qāf	q
ك	ـك	ـكـ	ـك	kāf	k
ل	ـل	ـلـ	ـل	lām	l
م	ـم	ـمـ	ـم	mīm	m
ن	ـن	ـنـ	ـن	nūn	n
ه	ـه	ـهـ	ـه	hā'	h
و	ـو			wāw	w
ى	ـى	ـيـ	ـي	yā'	y

Hebrew

	Name	Translit.
א	aleph	'
ב	beth	b, bh
ג	gimel	g, gh
ד	daleth	d, dh
ה	he	h
ו	waw	w
ז	zayin	z
ח	ḥeth	ḥ
ט	ṭeth	ṭ
י	yodh	y
כ ך	kaph	k, kh
ל	lamedh	l
מ ם	mem	m
נ ן	nun	n
ס	samekh	s
ע	'ayin	'
פ ף	pe	p, ph
צ ץ	ṣadhe	ṣ
ק	qoph	q
ר	resh	r
שׂ	śin	ś
שׁ	shin	sh
ת	taw	t, th

Greek

	Name	Translit.
A α	alpha	a
B β	beta	b
Γ γ	gamma	g
Δ δ	delta	d
E ε	epsilon	e
Z ζ	zeta	z
H η	eta	ē
Θ θ	theta	th
I ι	iota	i
K κ	kappa	k
Λ λ	lambda	l
M μ	mu	m
N ν	nu	n
Ξ ξ	xi	x
O o	omicron	o
Π π	pi	p
P ρ	rho	r, rh
Σ σ ς	sigma	s
T τ	tau	t
Y υ	upsilon	u
Φ φ	phi	ph
X χ	chi	kh
Ψ ψ	psi	ps
Ω ω	omega	ō

Russian

	Translit.
А а	a
Б б	b
В в	v
Г г	g
Д д	d
Е е	e
Ё ё	ë
Ж ж	zh
З з	z
И и	i
Й й	ĭ
К к	k
Л л	l
М м	m
Н н	n
О о	o
П п	p
Р р	r
С с	s
Т т	t
У у	u
Ф ф	f
Х х	kh
Ц ц	ts
Ч ч	ch
Ш ш	sh
Щ щ	shch
Ъ ъ	" ('hard sign')
Ы ы	y
Ь ь	' ('soft sign')
Э э	é
Ю ю	yu
Я я	ya

element, especially potassium, used in medicine and in dyeing. [f. OF f. L *alumen*]

alumina /ə'lu:mınə/ *n.* an oxide of aluminium, e.g. corundum. [f. L *alumen* alum]

aluminium /ælju'mınıəm/ *n.* a light silvery-white metallic element, symbol Al, atomic number 13, having a valency of three. It is the most abundant metal in the earth's crust but it does not occur in uncombined form in nature and was obtained in the pure state only in 1825. Although very reactive, it forms a tough surface layer of oxide when exposed to air, protecting it against further corrosion. Its lightness, good thermal and electrical conductivity, and strength (when alloyed) have led to its widespread use in domestic utensils, engineering parts, and aircraft construction. The main commercial ore is bauxite, but aluminium is also a major constituent of clays and feldspars. [alt. (after *sodium* etc.) f. *aluminum*, earlier *aluminium* f. ALUM]

aluminize /ə'lu:mınaız/ *v.t.* to coat with aluminium. [f. prec.]

aluminum /ə'lu:mınəm/ *n.* (*US*) aluminium. [see ALUMINIUM]

alumnus /ə'lʌmnəs/ *n.* (*pl.* **-ni** /-naɪ/) a former pupil or student. [L, = nursling, pupil (*alere* nourish)]

alveolus /æl'vi:ələs/ *n.* (*pl.* **-li** /-laɪ/) **1.** a small cavity such as a tooth-socket or a cell in a honeycomb. **2.** any of the tiny air-filled sacs in the lungs from which oxygen passes into the blood and through which carbon dioxide is removed from it (ill. BODY 3). [L, dim. of *alveus* cavity]

always /'ɔ:lweız/ *adv.* at all times, on all occasions; whatever the circumstances; repeatedly. [f. ALL + WAY]

alyssum /'ælɪsəm/ *n.* any of various cruciferous plants of the genus *Alyssum* etc. with small usually yellow or white flowers. [L f. Gk, = curing (canine) madness]

Am *symbol* americium.

am 1st person sing. pres. of BE.

a.m. *abbr.* before noon. [abbr. of L *ante meridiem*]

amalgam /ə'mælgəm/ *n.* a mixture or blend; an alloy of mercury with another metal. [f. F or L, prob. f. Gk *malagma* emollient]

amalgamate /ə'mælgəmeıt/ *v.t./i.* to mix, to combine; (of metals) to alloy with mercury. —**amalgamation** /-meıʃ(ə)n/ *n.* [f. L (as prec.)]

amanuensis /əmænjʊ'ensıs/ *n.* (*pl.* **-enses**) a literary assistant, especially one who writes from dictation. [L, f. *a manu* at hand]

Amarna /ə'mɑ:nə/, **Tell el-** the modern name of Akhetaten (= 'the horizon of the Aten'), the short-lived capital of ancient Egypt, founded by Akhenaten in the fifth year of his reign 450km (280 miles) north of Thebes and dismantled by his successors. It is particularly famous for its lively and expressionistic art, which shows a conscious divergence from the old artistic conventions, and for the cuneiform tablets known as the Amarna Letters, discovered in 1887. These texts contain letters written by Assyrian and Mitannian kings, and by native chiefs and Egyptian governors in Syria and Palestine, providing valuable insight into Near Eastern diplomacy of the 14th c. BC.

amaryllis /æmə'rılıs/ *n.* a South African plant of the genus *Amaryllis*, with lily-like flowers, growing from a bulb; any of various related plants. [L f. Gk (girl's name)]

amass /ə'mæs/ *v.t.* to heap together, to accumulate. [f. F or L (AD-, *massa* mass)]

amateur /'æmətə(r)/ *n.* one who does something as a pastime not as a profession; one who lacks professional skill. —**amateurish** *adj.* [F f. It. f. L *amator* lover (*amare* love)]

Amati /ə'mɑ:tı/ a family of Italian violin-makers, of whom three generations worked in Cremona: Andrea (*c.*1520–1611), his sons Antonio (1550–1638) and Girolamo (1551–1635), and, most famous of them all, Nicolò (1596–1684). From Nicolò's workshop came Antonio Stradivari and Andreas Guarneri, great-uncle of the celebrated Giuseppe Guarneri 'del Gesù'. The Amatis were responsible for the classic shape of the violin, flattening the body by deepening the middle curvature, sharpening the corners, and rounding the sound-holes in a more elegant shape.

amatory /'æmətərı/ *adj.* of or showing sexual love. [f. L (*amare* love)]

amaze /ə'meız/ *v.t.* to surprise greatly, to overwhelm with wonder. —**amazement** *n.* [f. OE]

Amazon[1] /'æməz(ə)n/ (*Gk myth.*) any of a race of female warriors alleged to exist somewhere on the borders of the known world. Their name was explained by the Greeks as meaning 'without a breast', in connection with the fable that they destroyed the right breast so as not to interfere with the use of the bow, but this is probably the popular etymology of an unknown word. They caught the Greek imagination and appear in many legends. Amazons appear as allies of the Trojans in the Trojan war, and their queen, Penthesilea, was killed by Achilles. One of the labours of Hercules was to obtain the girdle of Hippolyta, queen of the Amazons. According to Athenian legend, Attica once suffered an invasion of Amazons, which Theseus repelled.

Amazon[2] /'æməz(ə)n/ a great river in South America, 6,570 km (4,080 miles) long, flowing into the Atlantic Ocean on the north coast of Brazil. It drains two-fifths of the continent and in terms of water-flow it is the largest river in the world. It bore various names after its discovery in 1500 and was finally named because of a legend that a tribe of female warriors lived somewhere on its banks. —**Amazonian** /-'zəʊnıən/ *adj.*

amazon /'æməz(ə)n/ *n.* a tall and strong or athletic woman; a female warrior. —**amazonian** /-'zəʊnıən/ *adj.* [f. AMAZON[1]]

ambassador /æm'bæsədə(r)/ *n.* a diplomat sent by a sovereign or State as a permanent representative or on a mission to another; an official messenger. —**ambassadorial** /-'dɔ:rıəl/ *adj.* [f. F, ult. f. L *ambactus* servant]

amber *n.* **1.** a yellowish-brown translucent fossil resin used in jewellery etc.; its colour. **2.** a yellow traffic-light used as a cautionary signal between red (= stop) and green (= go). —*adj.* made of or coloured like amber. [f. OF f. Arab.]
   Amber is found chiefly along the southern shores of the Baltic Sea. It burns with an agreeable odour, often entombs the bodies of insects etc. which were trapped in the resin before it hardened, and when rubbed becomes charged with static electricity and has the property of attracting small particles (the word *electric* is derived from the Greek word for *amber*). It has been used for ornaments since the mesolithic period and seems to have been the basic commodity of regular prehistoric trade routes from the Baltic along the Elbe and Vistula rivers down to the Adriatic Sea.

ambergris /'æmbəgrıs/ *n.* a grey waxlike substance found floating in tropical seas and present in the intestines of the sperm whale, used as a fixative in perfumes. [f. OF, = grey amber]

ambidextrous /æmbı'dekstrəs/ *adj.* able to use either hand equally well. [f. L (*ambi-* on both sides, *dexter* right-handed)]

ambience /'æmbıəns/ *n.* surroundings. [as foll.]

ambient /'æmbıənt/ *adj.* surrounding. [f. F or L (*ambi-* on both sides, *ire* go)]

ambiguous /æm'bıgjʊəs/ *adj.* having more than one possible meaning; doubtful, uncertain. —**ambiguously** *adv.*, **ambiguity** /-'gju:ıtı/ *n.* [f. L, = doubtful (*ambi-* both ways, *agere* drive)]

ambit *n.* scope or extent; bounds. [f. L *ambitus* circuit (as AMBIENT)]

ambition /æm'bıʃ(ə)n/ *n.* desire for distinction or for a specific attainment; its object. [f. OF f. L, = canvassing]

ambitious /æm'bıʃəs/ *adj.* full of ambition; needing great effort etc., on a large scale. —**ambitiously** *adv.* [as prec.]

ambivalence /æm'bıvələns/ *n.* co-existence in one person of opposite feelings towards a person or thing. —**ambivalent** *adj.* [f. G f. L (*ambo* both)]

amble *v.i.* to walk in a leisurely or casual manner. —*n.* a leisurely pace. [f. OF f. L *ambulare* walk]

Ambrose /'æmbrəʊz/, St (*c.*339–97), Doctor of the Church. He was a Roman governor at Milan when, a converted Christian though not yet baptized, he was elected bishop of Milan (374) by popular demand, and became a famous preacher and champion of orthodoxy. To him was partly due the conversion of St Augustine. His knowledge of Greek enabled him to introduce much Eastern theology into the West; he wrote on ascetical subjects, and encouraged monasticism. The so-called Athanasian Creed has been attributed to him. Feast day, 7 Dec.

ambrosia /æm'brəʊzıə/ *n.* the food of the gods in classical mythology; something delicious. —**ambrosial** *adj.* [L f. Gk, = elixir of life (*ambrotos* immortal)]

ambulance /'æmbjʊləns/ *n.* a specially equipped vehicle for conveying the sick or injured to hospital. (The word was used originally of a mobile field hospital.) [F (as foll.)]

ambulant /ˈæmbjʊlənt/ adj. able to walk about, not confined to bed. [f. L ambulare walk]

ambulatory /ˈæmbjʊlətərɪ/ adj. of or for walking; ambulant. —n. a place for walking, as in a cloister. [f. L (as prec.)]

ambuscade /æmbəsˈkeɪd/ n. an ambush. —v.t. to ambush. [f. F (as foll.)]

ambush /ˈæmbʊʃ/ n. the placing of troops etc. in concealment to make a surprise attack; such an attack. —v.t. to attack from an ambush, to lie in wait for. [f. OF (as BUSH)]

ameliorate /əˈmiːlɪəreɪt/ v.t./i. to make or become better. —**amelioration** /-ˈreɪʃ(ə)n/ n. [f. OF f. L (melior better)]

amen /ɑːˈmen, eɪ-/ int. (in prayers) so be it. [f. L f. Gk f. Heb., = certainly]

amenable /əˈmiːnəbəl/ adj. 1. tractable, responsive. 2. answerable (to the law etc.). —**amenability** /-ˈbɪlɪtɪ/ n., **amenably** adv. [AF f. F amener bring (as AD- + L minare drive animals f. minari threaten)]

amend /əˈmend/ v.t. to correct an error in; to make minor alterations in. —**amendment** n. [f. OF f. L, = emend]

amende honorable /æmɑ̃d ɒnɔːˈrɑblʲ/ a public or open apology and reparation. (Originally a punishment known in France from the 12th c. to the Revolution, involving a public and humiliating acknowledgement of crime, imposed in cases of public scandal and frequently required before execution.) [F, = honourable reparation]

amends /əˈmendz/ n.pl. **make amends,** to give compensation. [f. OF, = penalties (as AMEND)]

amenity /əˈmiːnɪtɪ/ n. a pleasant or useful feature or facility of a place etc.; a pleasant quality. [f. OF or L (amoenus pleasant)]

Amenophis /ɑːmenˈəʊfɪs/ the name of four Egyptian pharaohs of the 18th Dynasty (1550-1307 BC). —**Amenophis IV,** see AKHENATEN.

America /əˈmerɪkə/ 1. a continent of the New World or western hemisphere, consisting of two great land-masses, North and South America, joined by the narrow isthmus of Central America. North America was probably visited by Norse seamen in the 8th or 9th c., but for the modern world the continent was discovered by Christopher Columbus, who reached the West Indies in 1492 and the South American mainland in 1498. 2. the United States of America.
The name of America dates from the early 16th c. The traditional explanation is that it derives from the Latin form (Americus) of the name of the explorer Amerigo Vespucci, who sailed along the west coast of South America in 1501 while seeking a sea route to the Orient; he concluded that the land-mass was not a part of Asia. The name was later applied to the North and South continents. Another suggestion is that it was named after a Bristol merchant Richard Ameryk (or Amerik), who is said to have invested in Cabot's second voyage. As a customs collector he paid Cabot his pension of £20, but whether his name was used for the new land is a matter of speculation.

American /əˈmerɪkən/ adj. of the continent of America, especially the USA. —n. 1. a citizen of the USA; a native of America. 2. American English. [f. prec.]

American English the English language as spoken and written in the USA. Serious and cultured speech and writing does not differ greatly from that used in Britain, but during the 300 years in which American English has been developing many new words or meanings have been added to make the languages distinct from each other. These include adoptions from languages with which the early settlers came in contact (e.g. moccasin, pecan, racoon from Indian languages; prairie, shanty from French; corral, lasso, ranch from Spanish; boss, sleigh from Dutch), changes in meaning (e.g. corn, English = cereal plants, American = maize), survivals of 17th-18th-c. English (e.g. guess = suppose, fall = autumn, gotten = got), different words for the same thing (elevator = lift, sidewalk = pavement), and there are some notable differences in grammar and construction (e.g. the American to teach school, I just ate, a quarter of ten). There are also differences in spelling (e.g. color = colour) and pronunciation, but these are of slight importance in comparison with the use of words and phrases which give American English its distinctive character. Many American words have come into such general use outside the USA (e.g. blizzard, bogus, crank, deadline) that few people realize their transatlantic origin.

American football a form of football played in the USA between two teams of 11 players with an oval ball and an H-shaped goal, on a field marked out as a gridiron. Scoring is by points. Football in the USA dates as far back as 1609, when colonists from England were kicking an air-filled bladder as they had done in Britain, but the modern game developed from 1876 onwards, when the sport had been taken up in the colleges, and the Rugby Union code was adopted as the basis of the rules. Emphasis is placed on strategy and tactics in both attack and defence, and the game itself is violent enough to require the wearing of helmets and other protective clothing.

American Indian a member of a group of indigenous peoples of North and South America and the Caribbean Islands. They are characterized by medium skin pigmentation, coarse straight black hair, and certain blood features which are markedly different from those of the Mongoloid peoples whom they otherwise resemble and with whom they were formerly classified.

Americanism n. a word, sense, or phrase peculiar to or originating in the USA. [f. AMERICAN]

Americanize /əˈmerɪkənaɪz/ v.t. to make American in form or character. —**Americanization** /-ˈzeɪʃ(ə)n/ n. [as prec.]

American legion see LEGION.

American organ a type of reed organ resembling the harmonium but in which air is sucked (not blown) through reeds.

American Revolution (also known as the War of American Independence) the revolt of American colonists against British rule, 1775-83, triggered by colonial resentment at the commercial policies of Britain and by lack of American participation in political decisions which affected their interests. Disturbances such as the Boston Tea Party of 1773 developed into armed resistance in 1775 and full-scale war, with the Declaration of Independence a year later. The British were unable to provide sufficient manpower or co-ordinated leadership to crush the rebels, and following the American victory at Saratoga France and Spain lent their support, French sea-power eventually playing a crucial role in the decisive surrender of a British army at Yorktown in 1781. The war was ended by the Peace of Paris in 1783 and George Washington became the first President of the USA in 1789.

America's Cup a yachting trophy named after the yacht America which won it in 1851, originally presented by the Royal Yacht Squadron for a race round the Isle of Wight. The America's owners gave the trophy to the New York Yacht club as a perpetual international challenge trophy, and it remained in the club's possession for 132 years until the successful challenge by an Australian crew in September 1983.

americium /æməˈrɪsɪəm,-ʃɪəm/ n. an artificially made transuranic radioactive metallic element, symbol Am, atomic number 95, first obtained in 1945 by bombarding plutonium with neutrons. It emits gamma radiation and this property has led to its use in industrial measuring equipment. [f. AMERICA (where first made)]

Amerindian /æməˈrɪndɪən/ adj. & n. American Indian or Eskimo. [portmanteau wd]

amethyst /ˈæməθɪst/ n. a precious stone, purple or violet quartz. [f. OF f. L f. Gk, = not drunken (the stone being supposed to prevent drunkenness)]

Amharic /æmˈhærɪk/ n. the official language of Ethiopia, spoken by some 9 million people (approximately one third of the population) in the area of the capital, Addis Ababa, and the region to the north of it. It belongs to the Semitic language group but within the Ethiopic branch of this group is directly descended from Ge'ez. —adj. of or in this language. [f. Amhara, region of Ethiopia]

amiable /ˈeɪmɪəb(ə)l/ adj. friendly and pleasant; likeable. —**amiability** /-ˈbɪlɪtɪ/ n., **amiably** adv. [f. OF f. L, = amicable (confused with F aimable lovable)]

amicable /ˈæmɪkəb(ə)l/ adj. friendly, showing friendly feeling. —**amicably** adv. [f. L (amicus friend)]

amice[1] /ˈæmɪs/ n. a square of white linen worn by celebrant priests, formerly on the head, now on the neck and shoulders (ill. VESTMENTS). [ult. f. L amictus garment]

amice[2] /ˈæmɪs/ n. a cap, hood, or cape of religious orders. [f. OF f. L amucia; orig. unkn.]

amid /əˈmɪd/ prep. in the middle of, among. [f A- + MID]

amidships /əˈmɪdʃɪps/ adv. in or to the middle of a ship. [f. midship(s), after AMID]

amidst /əˈmɪdst/ var. of AMID.

amine /ˈeɪmiːn/ n. a compound in which an alkyl or other non-acidic radical replaces a hydrogen atom of ammonia. [f. AMMONIA]

amino acid /ə'miːnəʊ/ an organic acid derived from ammonia, especially as a constituent of proteins. [f. AMMONIA]

amir /ə'mɪə(r)/ n. a title of various Muslim rulers. [f. Arab., = commander]

Amis /'eɪmɪs/, Kingsley (1922–), English novelist and poet. He achieved popular success with his first novel *Lucky Jim* (1954) and its lower middle-class anti-establishment hero; the provincial university setting marked a new development in fiction that Amis confirmed in *That Uncertain Feeling* (1955) and *Take a Girl Like You* (1960). In *I Like it Here* (1958) Amis displays a deliberate cultivation of a prejudiced and philistine pose which later hardened into an increasingly conservative and hostile view of contemporary life and manners. His subsequent work, of great versatility, includes satiric comedies and several volumes of poetry.

amiss /ə'mɪs/ predic. adj. wrong, astray, faulty. —adv. wrongly; inappropriately. [prob. f. ON á mis so as to miss]

amity /'æmɪti/ n. friendship, a friendly relationship. [f. OF f. L amicus friend]

Amman /ə'mɑːn/ the capital of Jordan; pop. (1980) 750,000.

ammeter /'æmɪtə(r)/ n. an instrument for measuring electric current, usually in amperes. [f. AMPERE + METER]

Ammon /'æmən/ var. of AMUN.

ammonia /ə'məʊnɪə/ n. a pungent gas with a strong alkaline reaction; a solution of this in water. [f. SAL AMMONIAC]

ammonite /'æmənaɪt/ n. a fossil cephalopod of the order Ammonoidea, usually with a coil-shaped shell. [f. L, = horn of (Jupiter) Ammon]

ammunition /æmjʊ'nɪʃ(ə)n/ n. **1.** a supply of projectiles (especially bullets, shells, grenades) fired by guns etc. or hurled. **2.** points that can be used to advantage in an argument etc. [f. F la munition taken as l'amunition]

amnesia /æm'niːzjə/ n. loss of memory. —**amnesiac** adj. & n. [L f. Gk, = forgetfulness (a- not, mnaomai remember)]

amnesty /'æmnɪsti/ n. a general pardon, especially for political offences. [f. F or L f. Gk amnēstia forgetting (see prec.)]

amniocentesis /æmnɪəʊsen'tiːsɪs/ n. (pl. -teses) a prenatal diagnostic technique in which a sample of amniotic fluid is withdrawn from the uterus through a hollow needle and analysed for information about the foetus. [f. foll. + Gk kentēsis pricking]

amnion /'æmnɪɒn/ n. (pl. -ia) the innermost membrane enclosing the foetus and the fluid that surrounds it before birth. —**amniotic** /-'ɒtɪk/ adj. [Gk, = caul (amnos lamb)]

amoeba /ə'miːbə/ n. (pl. -as) a microscopic aquatic protozoan that constantly changes shape. —**amoebic** adj. [L f. Gk, = change]

amok /ə'mɒk/ adv. **run amok**, to run about wildly in violent rage. [Malay, = rushing in frenzy]

among /ə'mʌŋ/ prep. in an assembly of, surrounded by; in the number of; between. [OE, = in a crowd]

amongst /ə'mʌŋst/ var. of AMONG.

amoral /eɪ'mɒrəl/ adj. not based on or not having moral principles, neither moral nor immoral. —**amoralism** n. [f. Gk a- not + MORAL]

Amorite /'æməraɪt/ n. a member of a group of semi-nomadic tribes, bearing Semitic personal names, from the east Syrian steppe and desert region. In the late 3rd and early 2nd millennium BC they founded a number of States and dynasties, including Mari on the Euphrates and the First Dynasty of Babylon, associated with Hammurabi I (d. 1750 BC). —adj. of the Amorites. [f. Heb. f. Akkadian (Sumerian martu west)]

amorous /'æmərəs/ adj. of, showing, or feeling sexual love. —**amorously** adv., **amorousness** n. [OF f. L (amor love)]

amorphous /ə'mɔːfəs/ adj. having no definite shape or form; vague, not organized; (Min., Chem.) uncrystallized. [f. L f. Gk (a- not, morphē form)]

amortize /ə'mɔːtaɪz/ v.t. to pay off a debt gradually by means of a sinking fund; to write off the initial costs of (assets) gradually. —**amortization** /-'zeɪʃ(ə)n/ n. [f. OF f. L (ad mortem to death)]

Amos /'eɪmɒs/ **1.** a Hebrew minor prophet (c.760 BC). **2.** a book of the Old Testament containing his prophecies.

amount /ə'maʊnt/ v.i. to be equivalent in total value, quantity, significance, etc., to. —n. the total to which a thing amounts; a quantity. [f. F f. L (ad montem upward)]

amour propre /æmuə 'prɒpr/ self-esteem, vanity. [F]

amp n. **1.** an ampere. **2.** (colloq.) an amplifier. [abbr.]

amperage /'æmpərɪdʒ/ n. the strength of electric current, measured in amperes. [f. AMPERE]

Ampère /'æmpeə(r)/, André-Marie (1775-1836), French physicist, mathematician, and philosopher, a mathematical child prodigy who became one of the founders of electromagnetism and electrodynamics, and is best known for his analysis of the relationship between magnetic force and the electric current, begun shortly after he heard of Oersted's discovery in 1820. Ampère also developed a precursor of the galvanometer. The unit of electric current (see foll.) is named after him.

ampere /'æmpeə(r)/ n. the base unit of electric current (symbol A; established in 1948 for international use), that constant current which, if maintained in two straight parallel conductors of infinite length, of negligible circular cross-section, and placed 1 metre apart in a vacuum, would produce between these conductors a force equal to 2×10^{-7} newton per metre of length. [f. prec.]

ampersand /'æmpəsænd/ n. the sign & (= and). [corrupt. of '& per se and', = 'the sign & by itself is and']

amphetamine /æm'fetəmiːn/ n. a synthetic drug used as a stimulant and decongestant. [abbr. of chemical name]

amphibian /æm'fɪbɪən/ n. **1.** an animal living both on land and in water; a vertebrate animal of the class Amphibia, typically having an aquatic larval stage with gills (e.g. a tadpole) and an air-breathing four-legged adult stage. There are about 2,400 living species, divided into two main groups: tailless forms (frogs and toads) and those with tails (e.g. newts and salamanders). Amphibians, which evolved from fish ancestors in the Devonian period, were the first vertebrates to live on land, preceding the reptiles. Unlike reptiles, however, their eggs lack shells and require water or damp conditions to survive, and so they cannot be completely independent of a moist environment. (See ill. p. 25.) **2.** an amphibious vehicle etc. [f. Gk (amphi both, bios life)]

amphibious /æm'fɪbɪəs/ adj. **1.** living or operating both on land and in water. **2.** involving military forces landed from the sea. [as prec.]

amphitheatre /'æmfɪθɪətə(r)/ n. an oval or circular unroofed building with tiers of seats surrounding a central space (ill. THEATRE). [f. L f. Gk (amphi all round, theatron theatre]

Amphitrite /æmfɪ'traɪti/ (Gk myth.) a sea-goddess, wife of Poseidon.

amphora /'æmfərə/ n. (pl. -ae /-iː/) a Greek or Roman vessel with a narrow neck and two handles, tapering at the base, used for transporting and storing wine or oil. [L f. Gk (amphi- two, pherō carry)]

ample adj. plentiful, extensive; quite enough; large, of generous proportions. —**ampleness** n., **amply** adv. [f. F f. L amplus]

amplifier /'æmplɪfaɪə(r)/ n. an apparatus for increasing the strength of sounds or electrical signals. [f. foll.]

amplify /'æmplɪfaɪ/ v.t./i. **1.** to increase the strength of (sound or electrical signals). **2.** to add detail to (a story etc.); to expatiate. —**amplification** /-'keɪʃ(ə)n/ n. [f. OF f. L (as AMPLE)]

amplitude /'æmplɪtjuːd/ n. **1.** spaciousness, abundance. **2.** the maximum departure from average of oscillation, alternating current etc. [F or L f. L (as AMPLE)]

ampoule /'æmpuːl/ n. a small sealed glass vessel holding a liquid, especially for injection. [F f. L ampulla]

amputate /'æmpjʊteɪt/ v.t. to cut off by surgical operation. —**amputation** /-'teɪʃ(ə)n/ n. [f. L amputare (amb- about, putare prune)]

amputee /æmpjuː'tiː/ n. a person who has had a limb etc. amputated. [f. prec.]

Amritsar /æm'rɪtsə(r)/ a city in Punjab in NW India. Founded in 1577 by Ram Das, fourth guru of the Sikhs, it became the centre of the Sikh faith and is the site of its holiest temple.

Amsterdam /æmstə'dæm/ the capital and largest city of the Netherlands, one of the major ports and commercial centres of Europe, built on about 100 islands separated by the canals for which it is noted; pop. (est. 1981) 712,300.

amuck var. of AMOK.

Amu Darya /ɑːmuː 'dɑːrɪə/ a great river of central Asia, 2,400 km (1,500 miles) long, rising in the Pamirs and flowing into the Sea of Aral. In classical times it was known as the Oxus. For part of its length it forms the boundary between Afghanistan and the USSR.

Amphibians

Development of the common frog
(toads develop in a similar way)

frog-spawn

egg

jelly

tadpole at time
of hatching

mucous gland by which
the tadpole attaches
itself to weed

gill

toad-spawn

mouth closed

emerging
hind leg

gland and
gills gone

spiracle

mouth open

hind legs developed

forelegs emerging

eyes enlarged

(stages in development
not to scale)

tail is then absorbed
to complete metamorphosis

adult

Life cycle chart

Nov Dec Jan Feb Mar Apr May Jun Jul Aug Sept Oct

hibernation

active life

mating and spawning

metamorphosis

Tongue action of a toad

insect

tongue attached
to front of mouth

sticky saliva on
surface of tongue

time = $\frac{1}{10}$ second

(The frog feeds in a similar way,
but its tongue is forked.)

Warty newt

single egg

gills

emerging hind leg

tadpole at six weeks

adult male

amulet /ˈæmjʊlɪt/ n. a thing worn as a charm against evil. [f. L]

Amun /ˈæmən/ (also **Ammon**) a god of the ancient Egyptians (originally the local god of Thebes) whose worship spread to Greece, where he was identified with Zeus, and to Rome, where he was known as Jupiter Ammon. As a national god of Egypt he was associated in a triad with Mut and Khonsu. He is represented in human form (rarely as ram-headed). His priesthood was important in State affairs except for a brief period when Akhenaten introduced the worship of Aten.

Amundsen /ˈɑːmʊns(ə)n/, Roald (1872–1928), Norwegian polar explorer. The most successful of the turn-of-the-century polar explorers, Amundsen made his name with a successful three-year navigation of the Northwest Passage in the small sailing vessel *Gjöa* (1903–6). In December 1911 he beat the British explorer Scott in the famous race to reach the South Pole which cost the latter his life. In the 1920s Amundsen devoted himself to aerial exploration of the polar regions, eventually disappearing on a search for the missing Italian airship expedition led by Umberto Nobile.

amuse /əˈmjuːz/ v.t. **1.** to cause to laugh or smile. **2.** to occupy pleasantly. —**amusement** n. [f. OF (a to, muser stare)]

an /ən, emphatic æn/ adj. the form of a (the indefinite article) used before vowel sounds other than u /juː, jʊ/.

ana- /ænə-/ prefix (usu. **an-** before a vowel) **1.** up (in place or time). **2.** again. [f. Gk ana up]

Anabaptist /ænəˈbæptɪst/ n. a member of any of various 16th-c. religious groups practising adult baptism. [f. L f. Gk (ANA-, baptismos baptism]

anabolism /əˈnæbəlɪz(ə)m/ n. constructive metabolism, the synthesis of complex substances for body tissue etc. (opp. CATABOLISM). —**anabolic** /ænəˈbɒlɪk/ adj. [f. Gk anabolē ascent (ANA-, ballō throw)]

anachronism /əˈnækrənɪz(ə)m/ n. attribution of a custom or event etc. to a period to which it does not belong; a thing thus attributed; a person or thing out of harmony with the period. —**anachronistic** /-ˈnɪstɪk/ adj. [f. F or Gk (ANA-, khronos time)]

anacoluthon /ænəkəˈljuːθən/ n. (pl. **-tha**) a sentence or construction that lacks a proper grammatical sequence. [L f. Gk (an- not, akolouthos following)]

anaconda /ænəˈkɒndə/ n. a large aquatic and arboreal boa of tropical South America. [f. Sinhalese, = whip-snake; orig. of a snake in Sri Lanka]

Anacreon /əˈnækrɪən/ (born c.570 BC) Greek lyric poet who wrote for a number of courts in the Greek world. The surviving fragments of his work include love-songs and drinking-songs, iambic invectives, and elegiac epitaphs.

anaemia /əˈniːmɪə/ n. deficiency of red cells or of their haemoglobin in blood. [f. Gk, = lack of blood]

anaemic /əˈniːmɪk/ adj. suffering from anaemia; pale; lacking vitality. [f. prec.]

anaesthesia /ænɪsˈθiːzɪə/ n. loss of sensation, especially that induced by anaesthetics. [f. Gk (an- without, aesthēsia sensation)]

anaesthetic /ænɪsˈθetɪk/ n. a substance (e.g. a drug or gas) that produces loss of sensation and of ability to feel pain (see below). —adj. having this effect. [as prec.]

Attempts at anaesthesia were made from ancient times by stupefying patients with wine or the juices of narcotic plants, but it was not until the 1840s that unconsciousness was produced by inhalation of anaesthetic gases (ether and nitrous oxide) in dentistry and surgery. The first such use of ether dates from 1842 when an American surgeon, C. W. Long, removed a tumour from the neck of a patient who had inhaled its vapour. Chloroform was introduced as an alternative to ether (which for a time it superseded) by the Scottish physician Sir James Young Simpson, but both substances had disadvantages and other anaesthetic agents were sought. Today new materials and methods are constantly being introduced. Anaesthetics may be given as gases, by inhalation; as drugs in solution, by injection or enema; or (for localized effect) sprayed on the skin. There are four main types of anaesthesia: *general*, in which the patient loses consciousness; *spinal*, in which anaesthetic is injected into the fluid surrounding the spinal cord, and the portion of the body below the site of the injection is anaesthetized; *regional*, injecting around nerve-roots and nerve tracts as they emerge from the spinal column, anaesthetizing only that area of the body supplied by those nerves; and *local*, in which the drug is injected or sprayed directly at the site of the operative incision. Anaesthesia may also be produced by other means, including acupuncture and hypnosis. The introduction of anaesthesia removed the necessity for the surgeon to concentrate on speed, in order to end the patient's ordeal as soon as possible, and widened the scope of surgery enormously.

anaesthetize /əˈniːsθətaɪz/ v.t. to administer an anaesthetic to. —**anaesthetist** n., **anaesthetization** /-ˈzeɪʃ(ə)n/ n. [f. ANAESTHESIA]

anagram /ˈænəgræm/ n. a word or phrase formed by transposing the letters of another. [f. F f. ANA- + Gk gramma letter]

anal /ˈeɪn(ə)l/ adj. of or near the anus. [f. ANUS]

analgesia /ænælˈdʒiːzɪə/ n. relief of pain, loss of ability to feel pain while still conscious. [f. Gk (an- without, algēsia pain)]

analgesic /ænælˈdʒiːzɪk/ adj. producing analgesia. —n. an analgesic drug. [as prec.]

analogize /əˈnælədʒaɪz/ v.t./i. to represent or explain by analogy; to use analogy. [f. ANALOGY]

analogous /əˈnæləgəs/ adj. partially similar or parallel (to). —**analogously** adv. [f. L f. Gk (as ANALOGY)]

analogue /ˈænəlɒg/ n. an analogous thing. —**analogue computer**, one using physical variables (e.g. length, weight, voltage) to represent numbers. [F f. Gk (ana-according to, logos proportion)]

analogy /əˈnælədʒɪ/ n. correspondence or partial similarity of things; reasoning from parallel cases. —**analogical** /ænəˈlɒdʒɪk(ə)l/ adj. [f. F or L f. Gk (as prec.)]

analyse /ˈænəlaɪz/ v.t. **1.** to examine in detail. **2.** to ascertain the elements or structure of. **3.** to psychoanalyse. —**analysable** adj. [f. foll.]

analysis /əˈnæləsɪs/ n. (pl. **analyses**) **1.** the process of analysing; a statement of the result of this. **2.** psychoanalysis. **3.** the huge mathematical subject which, in the 19th c., emerged from the work of Cauchy and others as the modern version of calculus. Analysis is the theory of functions and limiting operations on them, continuity, differentiation, and integration, treated by the strictest standards of logical reasoning. —**analytic** /ænəˈlɪtɪk/ adj., **analytical** adj., **analytically** adv. [f. L f. Gk (ANA-, luō loosen)]

analyst /ˈænəlɪst/ n. **1.** one skilled in analysis, especially of chemical substances. **2.** a psychoanalyst. [f. F (as prec.)]

Ananias /ənəˈnaɪəs/ **1.** the husband of Sapphira, struck dead because he lied (Acts 5). **2.** the Jewish high priest before whom St Paul was brought (Acts 23).

anapaest /ˈænəpiːst/ n. a metrical foot with two short or unstressed syllables followed by one long or stressed syllable. [f. L f. Gk anapaistos (ana reversed (dactyl), -paistos f. paiō strike)]

anarchist /ˈænəkɪst/ n. one who believes that government and law should be abolished. —**anarchism** n., **anarchistic** /-ˈkɪstɪk/ adj. [as foll.]

anarchy /ˈænəkɪ/ n. disorder (esp. political), lack of government or control. —**anarchic** /æˈnɑːkɪk/ adj. [f. L f. Gk (an- without, arkhē rule)]

Anasazi /ænəˈsɑːzɪ/ adj. of an ancient culture of the southwestern USA from which the Pueblo culture (which continues to the present) developed. Its earliest phases are known as the Basket Maker period. [Navaho, = ancient one (also = 'enemy ancestor')]

anastigmatic /ænəstɪgˈmætɪk/ adj. free from astigmatism. [f. Gk an- not + ASTIGMATISM]

anathema /əˈnæθəmə/ n. **1.** a detested thing. **2.** a formal curse of the Church, excommunicating a person or denouncing a doctrine etc. [L f. Gk, = thing assigned (to evil)]

anathematize /əˈnæθəmətaɪz/ v.t. to curse. [f. prec.]

Anatolia /ænəˈtəʊlɪə/ (in history called Asia Minor; see entry) the western peninsula of Asia that now forms the greater part of Turkey, bounded by the Black Sea and the Aegean and Mediterranean Seas. Most of it consists of a high plateau; the mountain ranges in the east include Mount Ararat. —**Anatolian** adj. & n. [f. Gk anatolē east]

anatomize /əˈnætəmaɪz/ v.t. **1.** to dissect. **2.** to analyse. [as foll.]

anatomy /əˈnætəmɪ/ n. **1.** the science of bodily structure; the bodily structure of an animal or plant. **2.** analysis. —**anatomical** /ænəˈtɒmɪk(ə)l/ adj., **anatomically** adv. [f. F or L f. Gk (ANA-, temnō cut)]

Anaxagoras /ænækˈsægərəs/ (c.500–c.428 BC) Greek philosopher, the last of the Ionian school, who lived in Athens and was a teacher and friend of Pericles. Few fragments of his writings have survived. He held that all matter was infinitely divisible and initially held together in a motionless uniform mixture until put into a system of circulation directed by Spirit or Intelligence, which created the sky and earth, from which the sun, moon, and stars were formed. His astronomy was not particularly fruitful, but his concept of an independent moving cause prepared the way for a fully teleological view of nature. There is now some dispute as to whether he was the first to give the true explanation of eclipses.

Anaximander /ænæksɪˈmændə(r)/, (c.610-c.545 BC), Greek philosopher and astronomer of the Ionian school, who lived in Miletus. Apart from one verbatim quotation, all that is known about him comes from indirect sources. He is reputed to have drawn the earliest map of the inhabited world, to have introduced the gnomon sundial into Greece, and to have taught a primitive form of evolutionary theory, in that he argued that life began in water and that man originated from fish. More significantly, he taught that all phenomena resulted from a single law which set the primordial substance into a vortex motion. This separated out contrasting qualities, such as hot/cold, wet/dry, and eventually formed the universe, with a flat cylindrically shaped cold damp earth at the centre, surrounded by fiery sun, moon, and stars.

ANC abbr. African National Congress.

ancestor /ˈænsestə(r)/ n. **1.** a person from whom one is descended, especially one more remote than grandparents. **2.** an early type of animal, plant, or thing from which later ones have evolved. —**ancestral** /-ˈsestr(ə)l/ adj., **ancestress** /ˈæn-/ n. fem., **ancestry** n. [f. OF f. L (ante before, cedere go)]

anchor /ˈæŋkə(r)/ n. **1.** a heavy metal weight used to moor a ship to the sea-bottom or a balloon etc. to the ground. **2.** a thing that gives stability. —v.t./i. to secure or be moored with an anchor, to cast an anchor; to fix firmly. —**anchor escapement,** a form of escapement in clocks and watches in which the teeth of the crown- or balance-wheel act on the pallets by recoil. **anchor man,** one who co-ordinates activities, especially the compère in a broadcast; a strong member of a sports team who plays a vital part, e.g. the last runner in a relay race. [f. OE f. L f. Gk agkura]

anchorage /ˈæŋkərɪdʒ/ n. **1.** a place for anchoring. **2.** lying at anchor. [f. prec.]

anchorite /ˈæŋkəraɪt/ n. a hermit, a religious recluse. [f. L f. Gk (anakhōreō retire)]

anchovy /ˈæntʃəvɪ/ n. a small rich-flavoured fish of the herring family. [f. Sp. & Port. anchova]

ancient /ˈeɪnʃ(ə)nt/ adj. of times long past; having lived or existed for a long time. [f. AF f. L ante before]

ancillary /ænˈsɪlərɪ/ adj. subordinate, auxiliary (to). [f. L (ancilla handmaid)]

and /ənd, emphatic ænd/ conj. **1.** connecting words, clauses, and sentences in a simple relation or implying progression, causation, consequence, duration, number, addition, or variety. **2.** (colloq.) to (as in go and, try and). —**and/or,** together with or as an alternative. [OE]

Andalusia /ændəˈluːsɪə/ the southernmost region of Spain, bordering on the Atlantic Ocean and the Mediterranean Sea. —**Andalusian** adj. & n. [f. VANDAL; named by Muslim conquerors after the Vandals who had settled there in the 5th c.]

Andaman and Nicobar Islands /ˈændəmən, ˈnɪkəbɑː(r)/ a Union Territory of India, consisting of two groups of islands in the Bay of Bengal; capital, Port Blair, in the Andaman Islands.

andante /ænˈdæntɪ/ adv. (Mus.) in moderately slow tempo. —n. (Mus.) a movement to be played in this way. [It., = going]

Andersen /ˈændəs(ə)n/, Hans Christian (1805-75), Danish author, son of a shoemaker and a washerwoman. He attempted to become an actor in Copenhagen but failed in this and nearly starved; then friends took pity on him and he eventually won the generous patronage of King Frederick VI, and received a university education. He was acknowledged in Scandinavia as a novelist and travel-writer before publishing the first of the fairy-tales for which he is now celebrated. These appeared from 1835 and include such classics as 'The Snow Queen', 'The Ugly Duckling', and 'The Little Match Girl'. Andersen loved to see his native town of Odense illuminated in his honour, but he knew only too well how it felt to be humble and penniless, and some of his best-loved stories are those that tell of the plight of innocent helpless creatures in a harsh and dangerous world.

Anderson /ˈændəs(ə)n/, Elizabeth Garrett (1836-1917), pioneer of medical training for women. Debarred from entry to medical courses in Britain because of her sex, she studied privately and in 1865 obtained a licence to practise from the Society of Apothecaries. In the following year she opened a dispensary for women and children in Marylebone, which later became a hospital, the first to be staffed by medical women; its name was changed to the Elizabeth Garrett Anderson Hospital in 1918. Her influence was considerable in securing the admission of women to various qualifying bodies and to important medical societies.

Andes /ˈændiːz/ a major mountain range running the length of the Pacific coast of South America. It includes many volcanoes, and several peaks top 6,150m (20,000 ft.). —**Andean** /ænˈdiːən, ˈæn-/ adj.

Andhra Pradesh /ˈɑːndrə prəˈdeʃ/ a State in SE India; capital, Hyderabad.

andiron /ˈændaɪən/ n. a metal stand (usually one of a pair) supporting logs in a fireplace (ill. HOUSES). [f. OF andier, assim. to IRON]

Andorra /ænˈdɒrə/ a small autonomous principality in the southern Pyrenees, between France and Spain; pop. approx. 41,600; official language, Catalan; capital, Andorra la Vella. Its independence is said to arise from the granting of the lands by a son of Charlemagne to the counts of Urgel in Spain. Under a treaty of 1278 the sovereignty of Andorra is shared between France and the Spanish bishop of Urgel. —**Andorran** adj. & n.

Andrea del Sarto /ˈændrɪə del ˈsɑːtəʊ/ (1486-1531), Italian Renaissance painter who absorbed the style of poise and beauty developed by Bartolommeo and Raphael and influenced the mannerist experiments of his pupils Pontormo and Rosso (1494-1540). His reputation was largely made and marred by Vasari, who described his works as 'faultless' but represented him as a weakling under the thumb of a wicked wife—traits of character which Robert Browning (1855) and others have (unjustly) sought to link with the lack of vigour in his mellifluous style. He worked chiefly in Florence, where among his most important works are fresco cycles (Nativity of the Virgin, 1514; Madonna del Sacco, 1524) and grisailles which give the effect of relief sculpture. The appeal of his dreamy portraits and dark-eyed Madonnas has never failed with the unsophisticated world.

Andrew /ˈændruː/, St (1st c.), one of the twelve Apostles, brother of St Peter. Since c.750 he has been regarded as the patron saint of Scotland. An apocryphal work dating probably from the 3rd c. describes his death by crucifixion but makes no mention of the X-shaped cross associated with his name (ill. VESTMENTS). Feast day, 30 Nov.

Androcles /ˈændrəkliːz/ a runaway slave in a story by Aulus Gellius (2nd c. AD) who extracted a thorn from the paw of a lion which later recognized and refrained from attacking him when he faced it in the arena.

androgen /ˈændrəgən/ n. a male sex hormone or other substance that can cause certain male characteristics to develop or be maintained. [f. Gk andro- male]

androgynous /ænˈdrɒdʒɪnəs/ adj. hermaphrodite; (of a plant) with stamens and pistils in the same flowers. [f. Gk as prec. + gunē woman]

android /ˈændrɔɪd/ n. a robot with an apparently human form. [as ANDROGEN]

Andromache /ænˈdrɒməkɪ/ (Gk legend) wife of Hector. After the fall of Troy she became the slave of Neoptolemus (son of Achilles), and after his death married Helenus, a brother of Hector.

Andromeda /ænˈdrɒmɪdə/ **1.** (Gk legend) daughter of Cepheus, king of the Ethiopians. Her mother (Cassiopea) boasted that she herself (or her daughter) was more beautiful than the Nereids, whereupon Poseidon in vengeance sent a sea-monster to ravage the country. To abate his wrath Andromeda was fastened to a rock and exposed to the monster, from which she was rescued by Perseus. The story is of a type that is widely distributed and may have had a share in forming the legend of St George and the Dragon. The traditional site in later time was Joppa (= Jaffa). **2.** (Astron.) a constellation, conspicuous for its great spiral nebula (the **Andromeda Galaxy**) which is now known to be a spiral galaxy probably twice as massive as our own and located two million light-years away.

anecdote /ˈænɪkdəʊt/ n. a short account of an entertaining or interesting incident. —**anecdotal** /-ˈdəʊt(ə)l/ adj. [F or f. Gk anekdota unpublished things]

anechoic /ænɪˈkəʊɪk/ adj. free from echo. —**anechoic chamber,** a room designed to absorb nearly all the reverberation produced in it, used in acoustic experiments (ill. SOUND). [f. Gk *an-* without + ECHO]

anemometer /ænɪˈmɒmɪtə(r)/ n. an instrument for measuring the force of wind. [f. Gk *anemos* wind + METER]

anemone /əˈnemənɪ/ n. a plant of the genus *Anemone*, related to the buttercup, with white, red, or purple flowers. [f. L f. Gk, = wind-flower (*anemos* wind)]

anent /əˈnent/ prep. (Sc.) concerning. [OE *an efen* on a level with]

aneroid /ˈænərɔɪd/ n. an **aneroid barometer,** a barometer measuring air-pressure by the action of air on the lid of a box containing a vacuum, which causes a pointer to move, not by the height of a fluid column. [f. F f. Gk *a-* not, *nēros* water]

aneurysm /ˈænjʊrɪz(ə)m/ n. permanent abnormal dilatation of an artery. [f. Gk (*aneurinō* widen)]

anew /əˈnjuː/ adv. again; in a different way. [earlier *of newe*]

angel /ˈeɪndʒ(ə)l/ n. **1.** an attendant or messenger of God (see below); a representation of this, conventionally in human form with wings. **2.** a very virtuous, kind, or obliging person. —**angel cake,** very light sponge-cake. **angel-fish** n. a fish with wing-like fins. [f. OF f. L f. Gk *aggelos* messenger]

In the Bible angels are represented as an innumerable multitude of beings intermediate between God and man; they form the heavenly court. In the early Church interest in angels was peripheral; Dionysius the Pseudo-Areopagite speculatively arranged them in three hierarchies. In the Middle Ages there was speculation and controversy over their substance, form, and nature. Catholic Christianity in general teaches their existence, perfect spirituality, and creation before man, and enjoins a cult similar to that given to the saints; Protestants have shrunk from definition and speculation.

angelic /ænˈdʒelɪk/ adj. of or like an angel. —**Angelic Doctor,** the nickname of St Thomas Aquinas. —**angelically** adv. [as prec.]

angelica /ænˈdʒelɪkə/ n. an aromatic umbelliferous plant; its candied stalks, used in cookery. [f. L, = angelic (herb)]

Angelico /ænˈdʒelɪkəʊ/, Guido di Pietro, 'Fra Angelico' (1387-1455), Italian painter who became a Dominican friar at Fiesole in 1408, regarded in the 19th c. as a saint but now recognized as a highly professional artist, well aware of progressive developments in contemporary Florentine painting. His art makes use of Masaccio's achievements in the representation of volume, and of the architectural forms of Michelozzo and Brunelleschi, yet is more conservative in its preference for intense local colour and graceful linear rhythms. His most celebrated works are the frescos in the convent of San Marco, Florence (c.1438-47) and the *Scenes from the Lives of SS Stephen and Lawrence* (1447-9) in the private chapel of Pope Nicholas V in the Vatican.

angelus /ˈændʒɪləs/ n. a prayer of the Roman Catholic Church said at morning, noon, and sunset in commemoration of the Incarnation; a bell rung to announce this. [L *Angelus Domini* (= angel of the Lord), opening words of prayer]

anger /ˈæŋgə(r)/ n. extreme or passionate displeasure. — v.t. to make angry. [f. ON *angr* grief]

Angevin /ˈændʒɪvɪn/ n. **1.** a native or inhabitant of Anjou in France. **2.** a Plantagenet. —adj. of the Angevins. [F]

angina /ænˈdʒaɪnə/ n. (also **angina pectoris**) pain in the chest brought on by exertion, owing to an inadequate blood supply to the heart. [L f. Gk (*agkhonē* strangling)]

angiosperm /ˈændʒɪəʊspɜːm/ n. a member of the group of flowering plants that have seeds enclosed in an ovary (opp. GYMNOSPERM). [f. Gk *aggeion* vessel + *sperma* seed]

Angkor /ˈæŋkɔː(r)/ the capital of the ancient kingdom of Khmer, famous for its temples, especially the Angkor Wat (early 12th c.), decorated with relief sculptures. The site was overgrown with jungle when it was rediscovered in 1860.

Angle /ˈæŋg(ə)l/ n. a member of a North German tribe, originally inhabitants of what is now Schleswig-Holstein, who came to England in the 5th c., founding kingdoms in Mercia, Northumbria, and East Anglia, and finally gave their name to England and the English. [f. L f. *Angul* name of district in Germany]

angle[1] n. **1.** the space between two lines or surfaces that meet; the inclination of two lines etc. to each other; a corner. **2.** a point of view. —v.t./i. **1.** to move or place obliquely. **2.** to present (information etc.) from a particular point of view. [f. F or L *angulus*]

angle[2] v.i. **1.** to fish with hook and line. The first treatise on angling is that by Dame Juliana Barnes (1496); the most famous is Sir Izaac Walton's *Compleat Angler* (1653). **2.** to seek an objective deviously. —**angler** n. [OE]

Anglesey /ˈæŋgəlsɪ/ an island of NW Wales, separated from the mainland by the Menai Strait.

Anglican /ˈæŋglɪkən/ adj. of the reformed Church of England or any church in communion with it. —n. a member of the Anglican Church. —**Anglicanism** n. [f. L *Anglicanus,* = prec.]

Anglicism /ˈæŋglɪsɪz(ə)m/ n. a peculiarly English word or custom. [f. L *Anglicus* of Angles]

Anglicize /ˈæŋglɪsaɪz/ v.t. to make English in form or character. [as prec.]

Anglo- in comb. English; of English origin; English or British and. [as ANGLE]

Anglo-Catholic adj. of the section of the Church of England that emphasizes its unbroken connection with the early Church and seeks maximum accordance with the doctrine of the Catholic Church. —n. an adherent of Anglo-Catholic belief.

Anglo-French adj. & n. Anglo-Norman.

Anglo-Norman adj. of the Normans in England after the Norman Conquest, or their descendants or language. —n. the French language retained and separately developed in England after the Norman Conquest. It arose from the dialect of French carried to England by the Norman invaders in 1066, and remained the language of the English nobility for several centuries. It is still preserved in some archaic legal phraseology.

Anglophile /ˈæŋgləʊfaɪl/ n. one who greatly admires England or the English. [f. ANGLO- + -*phile* (Gk *philos* dear)]

Anglo-Saxon adj. of English Saxons before the Norman Conquest. —n. **1.** an Anglo-Saxon person. **2.** the English language of this period, also called Old English (see ENGLISH). **3.** a person of English descent.

Angola /æŋˈgəʊlə/ a country on the coast of Africa north of Namibia; pop. (est. 1983) 7,100,000; official language, Portuguese; capital, Luanda. The country is rich in mineral resources, including diamonds and oil. Discovered by the Portuguese at the end of the 15th c., the area was colonized by them a century later, and remained in Portuguese possession until it achieved independence in 1975 after a bitter anti-colonial war. —**Angolan** adj. & n.

angora /æŋˈgɔːrə/ n. **1.** a long-haired variety of cat, goat, or rabbit. **2.** soft fluffy fabric or yarn made from the hair of an angora rabbit or goat. [f. *Angora,* the former name of Ankara]

angostura /æŋgəˈstjʊərə/ n. the aromatic bitter bark of a South American tree, used as a flavouring. [f. *Angostura* (now Ciudad Bolívar), town in Venezuela]

angry /ˈæŋgrɪ/ adj. **1.** feeling or showing anger. **2.** inflamed. —**angrily** adv. [f. ANGER]

angst /æŋst/ n. anxiety; a feeling of guilt or remorse. [G]

Ångström /ˈæŋstrəm, ˈɔːŋstrœm/, Anders Jonas (1814-1874), Swedish physicist. He wrote on terrestrial magnetism and on the conduction of heat, but his most important work was in the new field of spectroscopy. He proposed a relationship between the emission and absorption spectra of chemical elements, discovered in 1862 the presence of hydrogen in the sun's atmosphere, and six years later published his atlas of the solar spectrum. He measured his optical wavelengths in units of one ten-millionth of a millimetre (10^{-10} metre), later named the ångström unit in his honour.

ångström /ˈæŋstrəm/ n. a unit of length used in measuring wavelengths of light. [f. prec.]

Anguilla /æŋˈgwɪlə/ the most northerly of the Leeward Islands in the West Indies; pop. approx. 7,000; official language, English; capital, Valley. The island is a British dependency with full self-government (see ST KITTS-NEVIS).

anguish /ˈæŋgwɪʃ/ n. severe (especially mental) suffering. —**anguished** adj. [f. OF f. L *angustia* tightness]

angular /ˈæŋgjʊlə(r)/ adj. **1.** having sharp corners or features, not plump or smooth. **2.** forming an angle. **3.** measured by angle. —**angularity** /-ˈlærɪtɪ/ n. [f. L *angulus* angle]

aniline /ˈænɪliːn/ n. an oily liquid got from coal tar, used in dye-making. [f. G (*anil* indigo, whence orig. obtained) f. Arab. *al nil* the indigo)]

animadvert /ænɪmədˈvɜ:t/ *v.i.* to pass hostile criticism or censure (*on*). —**animadversion** /-ˈvɜ:ʃ(ə)n/ *n.* [f. L (*animus* mind, *vertere* turn)]

animal /ˈænɪm(ə)l/ *n.* **1.** a living thing having sensation and usually the ability to move; such a being other than man; a quadruped. **2.** a brutish or uncivilized person. —*adj.* **1.** of or like an animal. **2.** bestial; carnal. [f. L *animalis* having breath (*anima* breath)]

animalcule /ænɪˈmælkjuːl/ *n.* a microscopic animal. [f. prec. + dim. -*cule*]

animate /ˈænɪmət/ *adj.* having life; lively. —/-eɪt/ *v.t.* **1.** to enliven. **2.** to give life to. **3.** to produce as an animated cartoon. **4.** to motivate. —**animated cartoon**, a film made by photographing a series of drawings or positions of puppets to create an illusion of movement. —**animation** /-ˈmeɪʃ(ə)n/ *n.*, **animator** *n.* [f. L *animare* give life to (*anima* life)]

animism /ˈænɪmɪz(ə)m/ *n.* attribution of a living soul to inanimate objects and natural phenomena. —**animistic** /-ˈmɪstɪk/ *adj.* [f. L *anima* life, soul)]

animosity /ænɪˈmɒsɪtɪ/ *n.* a spirit or feeling of hostility. [f. OF or L (as foll.)]

animus /ˈænɪməs/ *n.* a display of animosity; ill-feeling. [L, = spirit, mind]

anion /ˈænaɪən/ *n.* a negatively charged ion. —**anionic** /-ˈɒnɪk/ *adj.* [f. Gk *ana* up + ION]

aniseed /ˈænɪsiːd/ *n.* the aromatic seed of an umbelliferous plant *Pimpinella anisum*, used for flavouring. [f. OF f. L f. Gk *anison* dill]

Anjou /ɑ̃ˈʒuː/ a former province of western France, on the Loire. Henry II of England, as a Plantagenet, was Count of Anjou, but it was lost to the English Crown by King John in 1204.

Ankara /ˈæŋkərə/ (formerly **Angora**) an inland city of Asia Minor, the capital of Turkey since 1923; pop. (1980) 3,196,460. Prominent in Roman times as the capital (Ancyra) of Galatia, it later dwindled to insignificance until chosen by Kemal Atatürk in 1923 as his seat of government.

ankh /æŋk/ *n.* a cross with a loop as its upper arm, used in ancient Egypt as a symbol of life. [Egyptian, = life]

ankle *n.* the joint connecting the foot with the leg (ill. BODY 1); the part of the leg between this and the calf. [f. ON]

anklet /ˈæŋklɪt/ *n.* an ornament or fetter worn round the ankle. [f. prec. + -*let* (as in *bracelet*)]

ankylosis /æŋkaɪˈləʊsɪs/ *n.* stiffening of a joint by fusion of bones. [f. Gk (*agkulos* crooked)]

annals /ˈænəlz/ *n.pl.* a narrative of events year by year; written records. —**annalistic** /-ˈlɪstɪk/ *adj.* [f. F or L (*annus* year)]

Annapurna /ænəˈpɜ:nə/ a ridge of the Himalayas, in north central Nepal. Its highest peak rises to 8,078 m (26,503 ft.).

Anne[1] (1665–1714) queen of England and Scotland (known as Great Britain from 1707) and Ireland, 1702–14. The last of the Stuart monarchs, daughter of the Catholic James II (but herself a staunch Protestant), she eventually succeeded her brother-in-law William III on the throne, there presiding over the Act of Union which completed the unification of Scotland and England. Although Anne was pregnant eighteen times none of the five children born alive survived childhood, and by the Act of Settlement the throne passed to the House of Hanover on her death. —**Queen Anne's Bounty**, duties called 'first fruits and tenths', payable originally to the pope but made payable to the Crown by Henry VIII, and directed by Queeen Anne in 1704 to be used to provide for the augmentation of livings of the poorer clergy. The Bounty was later increased by parliamentary and private grants, and in 1948 its administration became the responsibility of the Church Commissioners.

Anne[2], St (1st c. BC), mother of the Virgin Mary, first mentioned by name in the apocryphal gospel of James (2nd c.). The extreme veneration of St Anne in the late Middle Ages was attacked by Luther and other reformers. Her feast day (26 July) is observed with special devotion in Brittany (of which she is the patron saint) and Canada.

Anne Boleyn see BOLEYN.

Anne of Cleves /kliːvz/ (1515–57), fourth wife of Henry VIII, whose marriage to her (1540) was the product of his minister Thomas Cromwell's attempt to forge a dynastic alliance with one of the Protestant German States. Henry, initially deceived by a flattering portrait of Anne painted by Holbein, took an instant dislike to his new wife and dissolved the marriage after six months. Cromwell paid for his blunder with his head.

anneal /əˈniːl/ *v.t.* to heat (metal or glass) and allow it to cool slowly, especially to toughen it. [OE, = bake]

annelid /ˈænəlɪd/ *n.* a segmented worm of the phylum Annelida, e.g. earthworm. [f. F f. L (*an(n)ulus* ring)]

annex /æˈneks/ *v.t.* **1.** to add or append as a subordinate part. **2.** to incorporate (territory) into one's own. **3.** (*colloq.*) to take without right. —**annexation** /-ˈseɪʃ(ə)n/ *n.* [f. F f. L *annectere* (AD-, *nectere* bind)]

annexe /ˈæneks/ *n.* a building attached to a larger or more important one or forming a subordinate part of a main building. [as prec.]

annihilate /əˈnaɪəleɪt/ *v.t.* to destroy completely. —**annihilation** /-ˈleɪʃ(ə)n/ *n.* [f. L *annihilare* (AD-, *nihil* nothing)]

anniversary /ænɪˈvɜːsərɪ/ *n.* the date on which an event took place in a previous year; a celebration of this. [f. L (*annus* year, *versus* turned)]

Anno Domini /ænəʊ ˈdɒmɪnaɪ/ *adv.* in the year of the Christian era. —*n.* (*colloq.*) advancing age. [L, = in the year of the Lord]

annotate /ˈænəʊteɪt/ *v.t.* to add explanatory notes to. —**annotation** /-ˈteɪʃ(ə)n/ *n.* [f. L *annotare* (AD-, *nota* mark)]

announce /əˈnaʊns/ *v.t.* to make publicly known; to make known the arrival or imminence of; to be a sign of. —**announcement** *n.* [f. OF f. L *annuntiare* (AD-, *nuntius* messenger)]

announcer *n.* one who announces items in broadcasting. [f. prec.]

annoy /əˈnɔɪ/ *v.t.* to anger slightly; to be troublesome to, to molest. —**annoyance** *n.* [f. OF f. L *in odio* hateful)]

annoyed /əˈnɔːd/ *adj.* somewhat angry. [f. prec.]

annual /ˈænjʊəl/ *adj.* **1.** reckoned by the year; recurring once every year. **2.** (of plants) living or lasting only one year or season. —*n.* **1.** a book etc. published in yearly issues. **2.** an annual plant. —**annual ring**, a ring in the cross-section of a tree, fish, etc., from one year's growth (ill. TREES). —**annually** *adv.* [f. OF f. L (*annus* year)]

annuity /əˈnjuːɪtɪ/ *n.* an investment yielding a fixed annual sum; a yearly grant or allowance. [as prec.]

annul /əˈnʌl/ *v.t.* (-ll-) to declare to be invalid; to cancel, to abolish. —**annulment** *n.* [f. OF f. L *annullare* (AD-, *nullus* none)]

annular /ˈænjʊlə(r)/ *adj.* ring-shaped, forming a ring. —**annular eclipse**, see ECLIPSE. [f. F or L (*an(n)ulus* ring)]

annulet /ˈænjuːlɪt/ *n.* a small ring (ill. HERALDRY); an encircling band. [f. L *an(n)ulus*]

Annunciation /ənʌnsɪˈeɪʃ(ə)n/ *n.* the announcement by the angel Gabriel to the Virgin Mary that she was to be the mother of Christ; the festival commemorating this (25 Mar.), also called Lady Day. [f. OF f. L (as ANNOUNCE)]

anode /ˈænəʊd/ *n.* the electrode by which current enters a device. [f. Gk *anodos* way up (*ana* up, *hodos* way)]

anodize /ˈænədaɪz/ *v.t.* to coat (metal) with a protective layer by electrolysis. [f. prec.]

anodyne /ˈænədaɪn/ *adj.* relieving pain, soothing. —*n.* an anodyne drug or circumstance. [f. L f. Gk (*an-* without, *odunē* pain)]

anoint /əˈnɔɪnt/ *v.t.* to apply oil or ointment to, especially as a religious ceremony; to smear (*with* grease etc.). [f. AF f. L *inungere*]

anomalous /əˈnɒmələs/ *adj.* deviant, irregular, abnormal. —**anomalously** *adv.* [f. L f. Gk (*an-* not, *homalos* even)]

anomaly /əˈnɒməlɪ/ *n.* an anomalous thing. [as prec.]

anon /əˈnɒn/ *adv.* soon, shortly. [OE *on an* into one]

anon. *abbr.* anonymous.

anonymous /əˈnɒnɪməs/ *adj.* with a name that is not known or not made public; written or given by such a person. —**anonymously** *adv.*, **anonymity** /ænəˈnɪmɪtɪ/ *n.* [f. L f. Gk (*an-* without, *onoma* name)]

anorak /ˈænəræk/ *n.* a waterproof jacket, usually with a hood attached. [Eskimo]

anorexia /ænəˈreksɪə/ *n.* lack of appetite for food. —**anorexia nervosa** /nɜːˈvəʊsə/, chronic anorexia caused by a psychological condition. —**anorexic** *n.* [L f. Gk (*an-* not, *orexis* appetite)]

another /əˈnʌðə(r)/ *adj.* additional, one more; a different (*thing* etc.); some other. —*n.* another person or thing. [earlier *an other*]

Anouilh /'ænu:i:/, Jean (1910-), French dramatist, who first achieved success with *Le Voyageur sans bagage* (*Traveller without Luggage*, 1937), and has since been one of the most popular playwrights in France. Among his works are the romantic comedy *L'Invitation au château* (*Ring Round the Moon*, 1947), *La Valse des toréadors* (*The Waltz of the Toreadors*, 1952), *L'Alouette* (*The Lark*, 1953, on Joan of Arc), *Becket* (1959), and *Antigone* (1944), a concealed drama of the Resistance which played in Nazi-occupied Paris.

Anselm /'ænselm/, St (*c.*1033-1109), Italian-born philosopher and theologian, who became Archbishop of Canterbury in 1293. His uncompromising insistence on the spiritual independence of his office twice led to his being exiled, after conflicts with William II and Henry I. Of his theological writings the most famous is the study on the Atonement (*Cur Deus Homo?*). Like later Schoolmen (and unlike most of his predecessors) he preferred to defend the faith by intellectual reasoning rather than by basing arguments on scriptural and other written authorities. Feast day, 21 April.

anserine /'ænsəraɪn/ *adj.* of or like a goose. [f. L (*anser* goose)]

answer /'ɑ:nsə(r)/ *n.* something said, written, or done in reaction to a question, statement, or circumstance; the solution to a problem. —*v.t./i.* **1.** to make an answer (to). **2.** to respond to the summons or signal of. **3.** to suit (a need or purpose). **4.** to be responsible *for* or *to*. **5.** to correspond *to* a description. —**answer back**, to answer a rebuke impudently. [OE, = swear against (a charge)]

answerable *adj.* **1.** responsible *to* or *for*. **2.** that can be answered. [f. prec.]

ant *n.* a small wingless or hymenopterous insect, all species of which live in highly organized groups. —**ant-eater** *n.* any of various mammals that feed on ants and termites. [OE]

antacid /æn'tæsɪd/ *adj.* preventing or correcting acidity. —*n.* an antacid substance. [f. ANTI- + ACID]

Antaeus /æn'ti:əs/ (*Gk myth.*) a giant, son of Poseidon and Earth, living in Libya. He compelled all comers to wrestle with him and overcame and killed them until he was defeated by Hercules. That he was made stronger when thrown, by contact with his mother the Earth, seems a later addition to the story.

antagonism /æn'tægənɪz(ə)m/ *n.* active opposition, hostility. [as foll.]

antagonist *n.* an opponent. [f. F or L f. Gk (as ANTAGONIZE)]

antagonistic /æntægə'nɪstɪk/ *adj.* showing antagonism, hostile. [as foll.]

antagonize /æn'tægənaɪz/ *v.t.* to arouse antagonism in. [f. Gk, = struggle against (*agōn* contest)]

Antananarivo /æntənænə'ri:vəʊ/ the capital of Madagascar; pop. approx. 700,000.

Antarctic /æn'tɑ:ktɪk/ *adj.* of the south polar regions. —*n.* the regions (both land and sea) round the South Pole. —**Antarctic Circle**, the parallel of latitude 66 ° 33' S, south of which the sun does not rise at midwinter or set at midsummer. [f. OF or L f. Gk *anti* opposite + ARCTIC]

Antarctica /æn'tɑ:ktɪkə/ a continent round the South Pole, situated mainly within the Antarctic Circle and almost entirely covered by ice-sheet. Only a few patches of moss and lichen grow—too few to support land animals, but there is abundant life in the sea, including whales, seals, and penguins. Exploration at first concentrated on reaching the South Pole. Scott pioneered the way in 1902, followed by Shackleton in 1908; in 1911 Amundsen was the first to reach the Pole, and Scott reached it a month later. The American aviator Richard Byrd flew over the South Pole in 1929. Although there is no permanent human habitation Norway, Australia, France, New Zealand, and the UK claim sectors of the continent (Argentina and Chile claim parts of the British sector); its exploitation is governed by international treaty of 1959.

ante /'æntɪ/ *n.* a stake put up by a poker player before drawing new cards; an amount to be paid in advance. —*v.t.* to put up (an ante). [f. ANTE-]

ante- *prefix* before, preceding. [L, = before]

antecedent /æntɪ'si:d(ə)nt/ *n.* **1.** a preceding thing or circumstance. **2.** (*Gram.*) a word or phrase to which another word (especially a relative pronoun) refers. **3.** (in *pl.*) a

person's or thing's past history. —*adj.* previous. [f. F or L (ANTE-, *cedere* go)]

antechamber *n.* an ante-room. [f. ANTE- + CHAMBER]

antedate /æntɪ'deɪt/ *v.t.* to be of earlier date than; to give a date earlier than the true one to. [f. ANTE- + DATE[1]]

antediluvian /æntɪdɪ'lu:vɪən/ *adj.* of the time before the Flood; (*colloq.*) very old. [f. ANTE- + L *diluvium* deluge]

antelope /'æntɪləʊp/ *n.* (*pl.* same or **-s**) a swift-running deerlike animal (e.g. chamois, gazelle) found especially in Africa. [f. OF or L f. Gk *antholops*]

antenatal /æntɪ'neɪt(ə)l/ *adj.* before birth; relating to pregnancy. [f. ANTE- + NATAL]

antenna /æn'tenə/ *n.* **1.** (*pl.* **-ae**) either of a pair of flexible sensory organs found on the heads of insects (ill. INSECTS), crustaceans, etc., a feeler. **2.** (*pl.* **-as**) a radio aerial. [L, = sail-yard]

antepenultimate /æntɪpɪ'nʌltɪmət/ *adj.* last but two.

ante-post /æntɪ'pəʊst/ *adj.* (of racing bets) made before the runners' numbers are displayed.

anterior /æn'tɪərɪə(r)/ *adj.* nearer the front; prior (*to*). [f. F or L, compar. of *ante* before]

ante-room /'æntɪru:m/ *n.* a small room leading to a main one.

anthem /'ænθəm/ *n.* **1.** a short choral composition, usually based on a passage of Scripture, for church use; a song of praise or gladness. **2.** a national anthem (see NATIONAL). [OE f. L (as ANTIPHON)]

Anthemius /æn'θi:mɪəs/ of Tralles (6th c.), Greek mathematician, engineer, and artist chosen by Justinian in 532 to design Santa Sophia in Constantinople. His experiments included study of the effects of compressed steam, and he had an extensive reputation in the classical world for both these and artistic pursuits.

anther /'ænθə(r)/ *n.* the part of a stamen containing pollen (ill. FLOWERS). [f. F or L f. Gk (*anthos* flower)]

anthill /'ænthɪl/ *n.* a mound of soil formed by ants over their nest.

anthology /æn'θɒlədʒɪ/ *n.* a collection of passages from literature, especially poetry and song. —**anthologist** *n.* [f. F or L f. Gk (*anthos* flower, *-logia* collection)]

Anthony[1] /'æntənɪ/, St (of Egypt; *c.*251-356), the founder of monasticism, a hermit who gave away his possessions and retired into the desert. The holiness and ordered discipline of his life attracted disciples, whom he organized into a community of hermits who lived under rule (this was an innovation). He used his influence in association with Athanasius against the Arians. In medieval times he was venerated as a healer. His emblems (pigs and bells) derive from the Hospitallers of St Antony (founded *c.*1100), who rang bells for alms and whose pigs were allowed to roam in the streets.

Anthony[2] /'æntənɪ/, St (of Padua; 1195-1231), Franciscan friar who converted many by his charismatic preaching. He is invoked as the finder of lost objects, possibly because of the story that a frightful apparition forced a novice to return a psalter borrowed without Anthony's permission. His devotion to the poor is commemorated by the alms known as St Anthony's bread.

anthozoan /ænθə'zəʊən/ *n.* a marine animal of the class Anthozoa which includes corals and sea anemones. [f. L f. Gk *anthos* flower, *zōa* animals]

anthracite /'ænθrəsaɪt/ *n.* a hard form of coal that burns with little flame and smoke. [f. Gk *anthrax* coal, carbuncle]

anthrax /'ænθræks/ *n.* a disease of sheep and cattle that can be transmitted to people. [L f. Gk (as prec.)]

anthropocentric /ænθrəpə'sentrɪk/ *adj.* regarding mankind as the centre of existence. [f. Gk *anthrōpos* human being]

anthropoid /'ænθrəpɔɪd/ *adj.* man-like in form. —*n.* an anthropoid ape. [as prec.]

anthropology /ænθrə'pɒlədʒɪ/ *n.* the study of mankind, now usually divided into two main sub-disciplines: study of the social organization and cultural systems of human groups (**social anthropology**), and study of the structure and evolution of man (**physical** or **biological anthropology**). —**anthropological** /-ə'lɒdʒɪk(ə)l/ *adj.*, **anthropologist** *n.* [f. Gk *anthrōpos* human being + -LOGY]
Interest in the activities of other cultures is as old as written records, and anthropology traces its antecedents to the Greek travellers Xenophanes (6th c. BC) and Herodotus. Travellers' reports (e.g. those of Marco Polo) continued to be a popular form of proto-anthropology in the Middle

Ages and Renaissance. The philosophical debates on the nature of man during the Enlightenment stimulated further interest in other cultures, but it was not until the advances of Saint-Simon and Comte that the foundation for a 'science of man' was laid. Modern academic anthropology traces its origin to the evolutionary theories of Darwin, which stimulated European interest in the 'primitive' peoples of the world who were seen to provide a living laboratory to test theories of cultural evolution and diffusion. The second half of the 19th c. saw an expansion of scholarly attention in and the quest for reliable information about the isolated and technologically less-developed peoples of the world. Initially ambitious comparative studies were undertaken on diverse topics including kinship systems, law, magic and religion, and culture, by a generation of library-bound scholars. At the turn of the present century advances by Durkheim saw a retreat from these evolutionary beginnings and a shift to the study of the ways in which societies maintain themselves. The functionalist revolution occasioned by Malinowski and Radcliffe-Brown in Britain and Boas in the USA saw an increasing emphasis on ethnographic fieldwork studies utilizing the technique of participant-observation that has since become the single most important feature distinguishing anthropology from its sister discipline sociology, and recently structuralism has become an important theoretical mode.

anthropomorphism /ænθrəpə'mɔ:fiz(ə)m/ *n.* the attribution of human form or personality to a god, animal, or thing. —**anthropomorphic** *adj.* [as foll.]

anthropomorphous /ænθrəpə'mɔ:fəs/ *adj.* of human form. [f. Gk (*anthrōpos* human being, *morphē* form)]

anti /'ænti/ *prep.* opposed to. —*n.* one who is opposed to a policy etc. [f. foll.]

anti- *prefix* opposed to; preventing. [f. Gk *anti* against]

anti-aircraft *adj.* used in attacking enemy aircraft.

antibiotic /æntɪbaɪ'ɒtɪk/ *n.* a substance capable of destroying or preventing the growth of bacteria or similar organisms. The first antibiotic to be produced for therapeutic use was penicillin (see entry). —*adj.* functioning in this way. [f. F f. Gk (ANTI-, *bios* life)]

antibody /'æntɪbɒdɪ/ *n.* a protein produced in the body in response to and then counteracting antigens. The capacity to develop immunity to infectious disease is essential for the survival of any animal. In vertebrates this is achieved by the formation of proteins which appear in the blood a few days after infection and which can combine specifically with the foreign substance. These proteins are known as antibodies and they are remarkably specific: immunity to diphtheria, for example, gives no protection against tetanus. All antibodies have the same basic structure of four polypeptide chains, small sections of which vary to determine their specific combining power. Combination with antibodies leads to the destruction of bacteria, viruses, or foreign substances and their elimination from the body. [transl. G *antikörper* (ANTI-, *körper* body)]

antic *n.* (usu. in *pl.*) absurd movements intended to cause amusement; odd or foolish behaviour. [f. It. *antico* antique, used as = grotesque]

Antichrist /'æntɪkraɪst/ *n.* an enemy of Christ, the great personal opponent of Christ expected by the early Christians to appear before the end of the world.

anticipate /æn'tɪsɪpeɪt/ *v.t.* **1.** to deal with or use before the proper time. **2.** to forestall. **3.** to be ahead of (a person) in taking some action etc.; to foresee and provide for. **4.** (D) to expect. [f. L *anticipare* (*anti* = ante, *capere* take)]

anticipation /æntɪsɪ'peɪʃ(ə)n/ *n.* anticipating; eager expectation. —**anticipatory** /-'peɪtərɪ/ *adj.* [f. prec.]

anticlimax /'æntɪklaɪmæks/ *n.* a trivial conclusion to something significant or impressive, especially where a climax was expected.

anticline /'æntɪklaɪn/ *n.* a land formation in which strata are folded so that they slope down on opposite sides of a ridge (ill. GEOLOGY). —**anticlinal** *adj.* [f. ANTI- + Gk *klinō* lean]

anticlockwise /æntɪ'klɒkwaɪz/ *adj. & adv.* moving in a curve in the opposite direction to the hands of a clock (see CLOCKWISE).

anticyclone /æntɪ'saɪkləʊn/ *n.* a system of winds rotating outwards from an area of high barometric pressure, producing fine weather.

antidote /'æntɪdəʊt/ *n.* a substance that counteracts the effect of a poison; anything that counteracts unpleasant

effects. —**antidotal** *adj.* [F or L f. Gk *antidotos* given against]

antifreeze *n.* a substance added to water (especially in the radiator of a motor vehicle) to lower its freezing-point and therefore make it less likely to freeze.

antigen /'æntɪdʒən/ *n.* a substance (e.g. a toxin) that causes the body to produce antibodies. [G (ANTI-, Gk *-genēs* of a kind)]

Antigone /æn'tɪgənɪ/ (*Gk legend*) daughter of Oedipus and Jocasta. When the strife between her brothers Eteocles and Polynices resulted in the latter's death she buried his body by night, against the order of King Creon, and was ordered by him to be buried alive. She took her own life before the sentence was carried out, and Creon's son Haemon, who was betrothed to her, killed himself over her body.

Antigua and Barbuda /æn'ti:gə, bɑ:'bu:də/ a country comprising part of the Leeward Islands in the West Indies; pop. approx. 100,000; official language, English; capital, St John's (on Antigua). Discovered in 1493 by Columbus and settled by the English in 1632, Antigua became a British colony with Barbuda as its dependency; the islands gained full independence as a member State of the Commonwealth in 1981. The economy, once dependent on sugar, is now much more diversified and contains a large element of tourism. —**Antiguan** *adj. & n.*, **Barbudan** *adj. & n.*

anti-hero *n.* a central character in a story or drama who noticeably lacks conventional heroic attributes.

antihistamine /æntɪ'hɪstəmi:n/ *n.* a substance that counteracts the effects of histamine, used in treating allergies.

antiknock *n.* a substance added to motor fuel to prevent or reduce knock.

Antilles /æn'tɪli:z/ a group of islands forming the greater part of the West Indies. The **Greater Antilles,** extending roughly east to west, comprise Cuba, Jamaica, Hispaniola (Haiti and the Dominican Republic), and Puerto Rico; the **Lesser Antilles,** to the south-east, include the Virgin Islands, Leeward Islands, Windward Islands, and various small islands to the north of Venezuela.

antilog /'æntɪlɒg/ *n.* (*colloq.*) an antilogarithm. [abbr.]

antilogarithm /æntɪ'lɒgərɪð(ə)m/ *n.* the number to which a given logarithm belongs.

antimacassar /æntɪmə'kæsə(r)/ *n.* a former name for a short cover put over the backs or arms of chairs etc. to keep them from getting dirty, or as an ornament. [f. ANTI- + *Macassar*, because originally used as a protection against the Macassar oil that was used on hair]

antimatter /'æntɪmætə(r)/ *n.* (hypothetical) matter composed solely of antiparticles (see ANTIPARTICLE).

antimony /'æntɪmənɪ/ *n.* a semi-metallic element, symbol Sb, atomic number 51, existing as a brittle silvery-white metal and in several non-metallic forms. The naturally-occurring sulphide was used as a cosmetic in ancient times, and was employed in alchemy. Antimony is widely used in alloys, especially with lead, where it increases hardness, and it is a component of the metal used for making printing-type where molten metal is used. [f. L *antimonium* (orig. unkn.)]

anting *n.* the rubbing or placing of ants etc. in their feathers by birds, perhaps in order to kill parasites. [f. ANT]

antinomian /æntɪ'nəʊmɪən/ *adj.* of the view that Christians are by grace released from the obligation of observing the moral law. —*n.* one who holds this view. It was attributed to St Paul by his opponents (Rom. 3: 8), and was held by many of the Gnostic sects, who held that as matter was so sharply opposed to spirit, bodily actions were indifferent. The teaching was revived at the Reformation as following from the Lutheran doctrine of justification by faith. [f. L (ANTI-, Gk *nomos* law)]

antinomy /æn'tɪnəmɪ/ *n.* contradiction between two laws or authorities that are both reasonable. [as prec.]

antinovel *n.* a novel in which the conventions of the form are studiously avoided.

Antioch /'æntɪɒk/ **1.** the capital of Syria under the Seleucid kings, now Antakya in Turkey near the Syrian border. **2.** a city in Phrygia near the Pisidian border, that became a Roman colony with the name Caesarea Antiochia.

Antiochus /æn'taɪəkəs/ the name of eight Seleucid kings:
Antiochus III 'the Great' (*c.*242–187 BC), reigned 223–187 BC, who restored and expanded the Seleucid empire. He defeated the vassal kingdoms of Parthia and Bactria, and conquered Armenia, Syria, and Palestine; when he invaded Europe he came into conflict with the Romans,

who defeated him by land and sea and severely limited his power.

Antiochus IV Epiphanes (*c*.215-163 BC), reigned 175-163 BC. His firm control of Judaea and his attempt to hellenize the Jews resulted in the revival of Jewish nationalism and the Maccabean revolt.

antiparticle *n.* an elementary particle having the same mass as a given particle but an opposite electric charge or magnetic moment. Aristotle's physics was much concerned with pairs of Pythagorean contraries, such as hot and cold, wet and dry, gravity and lightness, and so forth. Physics from the 17th c. onwards tended to dispense with such dualities, replacing them by graduated properties. Hot and cold, for example, became different degrees of a single quality rather than contrary qualities. Modern elementary particle physics has vigorously reasserted the importance of opposed dualities in nature. For every elementary particle there is a corresponding 'antiparticle': the positron or anti-electron, discovered in 1932, has the same mass as the electron but possesses an equal and opposite charge; the anti-proton has the same mass as the proton, but again with an equal and opposite charge. When particle and antiparticle collide they annihilate each other, producing other particles and an enormous release of energy.

Antimatter is a hypothetical substance composed of antiprotons, anti-electrons, and anti-neutrons; it is theoretically as stable as ordinary matter. It is speculated that galaxies or even clusters of galaxies may exist which are composed entirely of antimatter.

antipathy /æn'tɪpəθɪ/ *n.* a strong or deep-seated aversion; its object. —**antipathetic** /-'θetɪk/ *adj.* [f. F or L f. Gk (*antipathēs* opposed in feeling)]

antiperspirant /ænti'pɜ:spɪrənt/ *n.* a substance that prevents or reduces perspiration.

antiphon /'æntɪfən/ *n.* a hymn or psalm etc. in which versicles or phrases are sung alternately by two sections of a choir; a versicle or phrase from this. [f. L f. Gk (ANTI-, *phonē* sound)]

antiphonal /æn'tɪfən(ə)l/ *adj.* sung alternately by two sections of a choir. [f. prec.]

antipodes /æn'tɪpədi:z/ *n.pl.* places diametrically opposite each other on the earth; **the Antipodes**, Australasia in relation to Europe. —**antipodal** *adj.*, **antipodean** /-'di:ən/ *adj.* [F or L f. Gk, = having the feet opposite]

antipope *n.* a person set up as pope in opposition to one held by some supporters to be canonically chosen.

antiquarian /ænti'kweərɪən/ *adj.* of or dealing in antiques or rare books. —*n.* an antiquary. [as foll.]

antiquary /æn'tɪkwərɪ/ *n.* one who studies or collects antiques or antiquities. [f. L (*antiquus* ancient)]

antiquated /'æntɪkweɪtɪd/ *adj.* old, out of date, old-fashioned. [f. L (as foll.)]

antique /æn'ti:k/ *n.* an object of considerable age, especially an item of furniture or a decorative object sought by collectors. —*adj.* of or existing from an early date; old; old-fashioned. [F, or f. L = former, ancient (*ante* before)]

antiquity /æn'tɪkwɪtɪ/ *n.* **1.** ancient times, especially before the Middle Ages. **2.** great age. **3.** (in *pl.*) remains from ancient times. [f. OF f. L (as prec.)]

antirrhinum /ænti'raɪnəm/ *n.* a plant of the genus *Antirrhinum* with a flower that has an aperture between closed 'lips'. [L, f. Gk (*anti* counterfeiting, *rhis* snout)]

antiscorbutic /æntɪskɔ:'bju:tɪk/ *adj.* that prevents or cures scurvy. —*n.* an antiscorbutic medicine. [f. ANTI- + L *scorbutus* scurvy]

anti-Semitic /æntɪsɪ'mɪtɪk/ *adj.* hostile to Jews. —**anti-Semite** /-'si:maɪt/ *n.*, **anti-Semitism** /-'semɪtɪz(ə)m/ *n.*

antisepsis /ænti'sepsɪs/ *n.* the process or principles of using antiseptics.

antiseptic /ænti'septɪk/ *adj.* that counteracts sepsis, especially by destroying bacteria. —*n.* an antiseptic substance. In 1847 the Austrian physician Semmelweis ordered the use of a disinfectant solution by students attending women in childbirth, but without understanding why it prevented sepsis and without influencing his senior colleagues. Nearly twenty years later the antiseptic system was introduced into surgery by Lord Lister, who worked on the discoveries of Louis Pasteur. Until that time the mortality rate from surgical operations was very high because of infection of the tissues exposed at or after the operation, and septicaemia was a major hazard. Lister's introduction of antiseptics brought about a major revolution in the history of surgery. There were, however, a number of drawbacks: antiseptics

strong enough to counter infection often also damaged body tissue. Hence arose the aseptic method, the keeping of wounds free from all contact with micro-organisms that may cause sepsis.

antisocial /ænti'səʊʃ(ə)l/ *adj.* **1.** opposed or harmful to social institutions and laws; interfering with amenities enjoyed by others. **2.** not sociable.

antistatic /ænti'stætɪk/ *adj.* that counteracts the effects of static electricity.

antithesis /æn'tɪθəsɪs/ *n.* (*pl.* -**eses** /-əsi:z/) a direct opposite; contrast; contrast of ideas emphasized by the parallelism of contrasted words. —**antithetic** /-'θetɪk/ *adj.*, **antithetical** *adj.* [L f. Gk (*antitithēmi* set against)]

antitoxin /ænti'tɒksɪn/ *n.* an antibody that counteracts a toxin. —**antitoxic** *adj.*

antitrades /'æntɪtreɪdz/ *n.pl.* winds blowing above and in the opposite direction to trade winds. [f. ANTI- + TRADE (winds)]

antitrust *adj.* (*US*) opposed to trusts or other monopolies.

antitype *n.* **1.** one of the opposite type. **2.** that which a type or symbol represents. [f. Gk *antitupos* corresponding as an impression to the die (ANTI-, *tupos* stamp)]

antivivisection /æntɪvɪvɪ'sekʃ(ə)n/ *n.* opposed to experiments on live animals. —**antivivisectionist** *n.*

antler *n.* a branched horn of a stag or other (usually male) deer. —**antlered** *adj.* [f. AF; orig. unkn.]

Antonine /'æntənaɪn/ *adj.* of the Roman emperors Antoninus Pius and Marcus Aurelius Antoninus or their rule. —**Antonines** *n.pl.* these emperors. [f. L *Antoninus*]

Antonine Wall a defensive fortification about 59 km (37 miles) long, built across the narrowest part of southern Scotland between the Firth of Forth and the Firth of Clyde *c*. AD 140, in the time of Antoninus Pius. It was intended to mark the frontier of the Roman province of Britain, and consisted of a turf wall with a broad ditch in front and a counterscarp bank on the outer edge, with 29 small forts linked by a military road. The Romans, however, were unable to consolidate their position and *c*.181 the wall was breached and the northern tribes forced a retreat from the Forth–Clyde frontier, eventually to that established earlier at Hadrian's Wall.

Antoninus Pius /æntənaɪnəs 'paɪəs/ (86-161), Roman emperor 137-161, the first of the Antonines (whose reigns Gibbon regarded as the summit of virtuous good government). Adopted as successor by Hadrian, he ruled in harmony with the Senate and pursued a policy of moderation and liberality. He was no great conqueror, but under his rule the frontier of Britain was temporarily advanced to the Antonine Wall.

Antony[1] /'æntənɪ/ var. of ANTHONY.

Antony[2] /'ænt(ə)nɪ/, Mark (Marcus Antonius, *c.* 83-30 BC), Roman general and triumvir. A supporter of Julius Caesar, after whose murder he was appointed one of the triumvirate of 43 BC, with Octavian and Lepidus. After the battle of Philippi he took charge of the eastern empire, where he established his association with Cleopatra. Quarrels with Octavian led finally to his defeat at the sea-battle of Actium in NW Greece in 31 BC and to his suicide the next year in Alexandria.

antonym /'æntənɪm/ *n.* a word that is opposite in meaning to another. [f. F (ANTI-, Gk *onoma* name)]

Antrim /'æntrɪm/ a town and county of Northern Ireland.

antrum *n.* (*pl.* -**tra**) a cavity of the body, especially one of a pair in the upper jaw-bone. [L f. Gk, = cave]

Antwerp /'æntwɜ:p/ a city and sea-port of Belgium; pop. 923,547.

Anubis /ə'nju:bɪs/ (*Egyptian myth.*) the god of mummification, protector of tombs, represented as a seated jackal or with a jackal's head, or sometimes (in the Roman period) as a soldier in armour.

Anuradhapura /ɒnʊərədə'pʊərə/ a town in Sri Lanka, the ancient capital of the island (4th c. BC-AD 760), site of the sacred bo tree (descended from Buddha's original tree at Buddh Gaya in India) and of numerous Buddhist foundations.

anus /'eɪnəs/ *n.* the excretory opening at the end of the alimentary canal (ill. BODY 2). [L]

anvil *n.* an iron block on which a smith hammers metal into shape. [OE (*an* on, *filt-* beat)]

anxiety /æŋ'zaɪətɪ/ *n.* the state of being anxious; something causing this. [f. F or L (as foll.)]

anxious /'æŋʃəs/ *adj.* **1.** troubled, uneasy in mind. **2.** causing or marked by worry. **3.** eagerly wanting (to). —**anxiously** adv. [f. L anxius (angere choke)]

any /'enɪ/ adj. **1.** one or some (but no matter which) from three or more or from a quantity. **2.** an appreciable or significant (amount etc.). **3.** whichever is chosen. —pron. any one, any number or amount. —adv. at all, in some degree. [OE]

anybody /'enɪbɒdɪ/ n. & pron. **1.** any person. **2.** a person of importance. [f. ANY + BODY (= person)]

anyhow /'enɪhaʊ/ adv. **1.** anyway. **2.** in a disorderly manner.

anyone /'enɪwʌn/ n. & pron. anybody.

anything /'enɪθɪŋ/ n. & pron. any thing, a thing of any sort. —**anything but**, not at all. **like anything**, with great intensity.

anyway /'enɪweɪ/ adv. in any way or manner; in any case.

anywhere /'enɪ(h)weə(r)/ adv. in or to any place. —pron. any place.

Anzac /'ænzæk/ n. **1.** a member of the Australian and New Zealand Army Corps (1914-18). **2.** an Australian or a New Zealand person, especially a serviceman. —adj. of Anzacs. —**Anzac Day**, 25 April, commemorating the landing of the corps in Gallipoli. [acronym]

Anzus /'ænzəs/ the combination of Australia, New Zealand, and the USA for the security of the Pacific. [acronym]

aorist /'eɪərɪst/ n. the unqualified past tense of a verb (especially in Greek), without reference to duration or completion. [f. Gk, = indefinite]

aorta /eɪˈɔːtə/ n. the main artery carrying blood from the left ventricle of the heart. (ill. BODY 3). —**aortic** adj. [f. Gk (aeirō raise)]

apace /əˈpeɪs/ adv. swiftly. [f. OF à pas at (a considerable pace)]

Apache /əˈpætʃɪ/ n. (pl. same or **-s**) a member of an Athapaskan-speaking American Indian tribe which migrated from Canada to what are now the southwestern USA (primarily to Arizona and New Mexico with smaller numbers in Utah, Colorado, and Texas) over 1,000 years ago. The arid ecological conditions inhibited colonial expansion in the region with the result that the indigenous groups of the southwest (e.g. Apache, Navajo, and the various pueblo cultures) suffered less cultural disruption than most Amerindian groups. When contact finally came the Apache put up fierce resistance to colonial expansion and were, in the late 19th c., the last American Indian group to be conquered by the US cavalry—which has had a considerable effect on the popular imagination. Forcibly concentrated on reservations after 1887 and deprived of the freedom necessary to continue their traditional hunting and gathering by the policies of the US Bureau of Indian Affairs, Apache society has undergone profound restructuring in the 20th c. [Mexican Sp.]

apache /əˈpæʃ/ n. a violent street ruffian, originally in Paris c.1900. [f. prec.]

apart /əˈpɑːt/ adv. **1.** separately, not together. **2.** into pieces. **3.** aside, to or at a distance. —**apart from**, excepting, not considering. **tell apart**, to distinguish between. [f. OF (à to, part side)]

apartheid /əˈpɑːtheɪt/ n. the South African policy of racial separation and discrimination, separating Europeans and non-Europeans. Adopted by the successful Afrikaner National Party as a slogan in the 1948 election, apartheid intensified and institutionalized existing racial segregation, guaranteeing the dominance of the White minority. In the early 1960s domestic and international opposition to apartheid began to intensify, but despite rioting and terrorism at home and isolation abroad, the conservative White regime has maintained the apartheid system with only minor liberal alterations. (as APART, -HOOD)]

apartment /əˈpɑːtmənt/ n. **1.** (in pl.) a suite of rooms, usually rented furnished. **2.** (US) a flat. [f. F f. It. (a parte apart)]

apathy /'æpəθɪ/ n. lack of interest or concern, indifference. —**apathetic** /-'θetɪk/ adj., **apathetically** adv. [f. F f. L f. Gk (a- without, pathos suffering)]

apatite /'æpətaɪt/ n. a crystalline mineral of calcium phosphate and fluoride. [f. G f. Gk apatē deceit (from its deceptive forms)]

ape n. a monkey, especially of the tailless kind (gorilla, chimpanzee, orang-utan, gibbon). —v.t. to imitate. —**ape-man** n. an extinct primate postulated by Haeckel as intermediate between ape and man; a primitive man. [OE]

Apelles /əˈpeliːz/ (4th c. BC) court portrait painter to Alexander the Great. From written sources he must be considered the greatest painter of antiquity, though none of his works has survived. Amongst his recorded works was a picture of Aphrodite rising from the sea, and a picture entitled Calumny, both of which were emulated by Botticelli in the 15th c.

Apennines /'æpɪnaɪnz/ a mountain range running the length of Italy from the north-west to the southern tip of the peninsula.

aperient /əˈpɪərɪənt/ adj. laxative. —n. a laxative medicine. [f. L aperire to open]

aperitif /əˈperɪtiːf/ n. an alcoholic drink taken before a meal. [f. F f. L (as prec.)]

aperture /'æpətjʊə(r)/ n. an opening or gap; a space for admitting light in a camera or optical instrument. [f. L (as prec.)]

apex /'eɪpeks/ n. (pl. **apexes**) the highest point; the pointed end, the tip. [L]

aphelion /əˈfiːlɪən/ n. (pl. **-ia**) the point in a planet's or comet's orbit when it is furthest from the sun. [f. Gk aph' hēliou from the sun]

aphid /'eɪfɪd/ n. a plant louse such as greenfly or blackfly. [f. foll.]

aphis /'eɪfɪs/ n. (pl. **-ides** /-ɪdiːz/) an aphid. [the word was invented by Linnaeus, perh. a misreading of Gk koris bug]

aphorism /'æfərɪz(ə)m/ n. a short pithy saying. [f. F or L f. Gk aphorismos definition (horos boundary)]

aphrodisiac /æfrəˈdɪzɪæk/ adj. arousing sexual desire. —n. an aphrodisiac substance. [f. Gk f. foll.]

Aphrodite /æfrəˈdaɪtɪ/ (Gk myth.) the goddess of beauty, fertility, and sexual love, born of the sea-foam, identified by the Romans with Venus. Her cult was of eastern origin, and she was identified with Astarte, Ishtar, etc. The statue of Aphrodite (now lost) made by Praxiteles was the first important female nude. It was rejected by the people of the island of Cos, who found it too erotic, and acquired by Cnidos on the coast of Asia Minor, where it proved to be a great attraction to travellers, bringing fame to the town. [perh. f. Gk aphros foam]

apiary /'eɪpɪərɪ/ n. a place with a number of hives where bees are kept. —**apiarist** n. [f. L (apis bee)]

apical /'eɪpɪk(ə)l/ adj of, at, or forming an apex. [f. APEX]

apiculture /'eɪpɪkʌltʃə(r)/ n. bee-keeping. —**apiculturist** n. [f. L apis bee + CULTURE]

apiece /əˈpiːs/ adv. for each one. [orig. a piece]

Apis /'ɑːpɪs, 'æ-/ (Egyptian myth.) a god always depicted as a bull (symbolizing strength in war and in fertility), worshipped especially at Memphis, where he was recognized as a manifestation of Ptah, the city's patron, then of Ra (and the solar disc was placed between his horns), and later of Osiris. A live bull, carefully chosen, was considered to be his incarnation and kept in an enclosure. When it died it was mummified and ceremonially interred, and a young black bull with suitable markings was installed in its place.

aplomb /əˈplɒm/ n. assurance, self-confidence. [F, = straight as a plummet]

Apocalypse /əˈpɒkəlɪps/ n. **1.** the Revelation of St John the Divine, containing a prophetic description of the end of the world. **2.** **apocalypse**, great and dramatic events like those described in the Apocalypse. —**apocalyptic** /əpɒkəˈlɪptɪk/ adj., **apocalyptically** adv. [f. OF f. L f. Gk, = uncovering]

Apocrypha /əˈpɒkrɪfə/ the Biblical books received by the early Church as part of the Greek version of the Old Testament, but not included in the Hebrew Bible. They are included in the Vulgate (it was Jerome who introduced the term 'Apocrypha') and are regarded by the Roman Catholic Church as authoritative, but were refused the status of inspired Scripture at the Reformation. The books date from c.300 BC-c. AD 100, and are valuable as showing beliefs of the period when Christianity was not fully separated from Judaism.

apocryphal /əˈpɒkrɪf(ə)l/ adj. untrue, invented; of doubtful authenticity. [f. prec.]

apogee /'æpədʒiː/ n. the highest point, a climax; the point in the orbit of the moon or any planet or satellite when it is at its furthest point from the earth. [f. F or Gk apogeion away from the earth (gē earth)]

apolitical /eɪpəˈlɪtɪk(ə)l/ adj. not interested in or concerned with politics. [f. Gk a- not + POLITICAL]

Apollinarius /əpɒlɪˈneərɪəs/ (c.310-c.390) bishop of Laodicea in Asia Minor, instigator of the first great Christological heresy, which asserted that Christ had a human body and soul but no human spirit, this being replaced by the divine Logos. The fundamental objection to this was that unless Christ's manhood was complete he could not redeem the whole of human nature. —**Apollinarian** adj. & n.

Apollo /ə'pɒləʊ/ **1.** (*Gk myth.*) a Greek god, in art the ideal type of manly beauty, son of Zeus and Leto and brother of Artemis. He is associated especially with music, archery, prophecy, medicine, and the care of flocks and herds. **2.** the name given to the American space programme for landing men on the moon. Such a landing, to be achieved before 1970, was proposed by President J. F. Kennedy in 1961 following the first manned flights in space by the USSR, and achieved its declared object on 20 July 1969.

Apollonius /æpə'ləʊnɪəs/ of Rhodes (3rd c. BC), Greek poet of Alexandria, where he was chief librarian, who spent part of his life in Rhodes and was a rival of the poet Callimachus. His *Argonautica*, a poem in Homeric style on the expedition of the Argonauts, was the first to place love—Medea's love for Jason, vividly portrayed—in the foreground of the action of an epic poem.

Apollyon /ə'pɒljən/ the Devil, the 'angel of the bottomless pit' in Rev. 9: 11. [f. Gk, = destroyer]

apologetic /əpɒlə'dʒetɪk/ adj. making an apology; diffident. —**apologetics** n.pl. a reasoned defence, especially of Christianity. —**apologetically** adv. [f. F f. L f. Gk (*apologeomai* speak in defence)]

apologia /æpə'ləʊdʒɪə/ n. a formal defence of belief or conduct. [L f. Gk (see APOLOGY)]

apologist /ə'pɒlədʒɪst/ n. one who makes a formal defence of a belief etc. by argument. [f. F f. Gk *apologizomai* render an account]

apologize /ə'pɒlədʒaɪz/ v.i. to make an apology. [f. Gk (see prec.)]

apology /ə'pɒlədʒɪ/ n. **1.** regretful acknowledgement of an offence or failure. **2.** an explanation or defence of a belief etc. —**apology for,** a poor or scanty specimen of. [f. F or L f. Gk *apologia* (as APOLOGETIC)]

apophthegm /'æpəfθem/ n. a terse or pithy saying. [f. F or Gk (*apophtheggomai* speak out)]

apoplectic /æpə'plektɪk/ adj. of, suffering from, or liable to apoplexy; (*colloq.*) liable to fits of rage in which the face becomes very red. —**apoplectically** adv. [as foll.]

apoplexy /'æpəpleksɪ/ n. a sudden inability to feel and move, caused by blockage or rupture of a brain artery. [f. OF f. L f. Gk (*apoplēssō* disable by a stroke)]

apostasy /ə'pɒstəsɪ/ n. renunciation of one's religious faith or one's principles or party etc. [f. L f. Gk, = defection]

apostate /ə'pɒsteɪt/ n. one who renounces his former belief, principles, or party, etc. [f. OF or L f. Gk *apostatēs* deserter]

apostatize /ə'pɒstətaɪz/ v.i. to become an apostate. [f. prec.]

a posteriori /eɪ pɒsterɪ'ɔːraɪ/ reasoning from effects back to their causes. [L, = from what comes after]

Apostle /ə'pɒs(ə)l/ n. **1.** the name given in the Gospels and later to the twelve chief disciples of Christ, Saints Peter, Andrew, James, John, Philip, Bartholomew, Thomas, Matthew, James (the Less), Thaddaeus, Simon, and Judas Iscariot. After the suicide of Judas his place was taken by Matthias; the term was applied also to Paul and Barnabas. **2. apostle,** the first successful Christian missionary in a country; the leader of a new faith or reform. —**Apostles' Creed,** a statement of Christian belief used in the Western Church, dating (with minor variations in form) from the 4th c., by which time the legend that it was a joint composition by the twelve Apostles was current. **Apostle spoon,** a spoon with a figure of an Apostle on the handle. [OE f. L f. Gk (*apostellō* send forth)]

apostolic /æpə'stɒlɪk/ adj. of the Apostles or their teaching; of the pope. —**Apostolic Fathers,** the Christian writers from the age immediately following the Apostles. **apostolic succession,** the uninterrupted transmission of spiritual authority through successive popes and other bishops from the Apostles. The continuity has been disputed; the necessity of it is taught by the Roman Catholic Church but denied by most Protestants. [as prec.]

apostrophe /ə'pɒstrəfɪ/ n. **1.** the sign (') showing the possessive case, omission of letters or numbers, or the plurals of letters. **2.** an exclamatory passage addressed to a person or persons or an abstract idea. [L f. Gk (*apostrephō* turn away)]

apostrophize /ə'pɒstrəfaɪz/ v.t. to address in an apostrophe. [f. prec.]

apothecary /ə'pɒθɪkərɪ/ n. (*archaic*) a pharmaceutical chemist. [f. OF f. L f. Gk *apothēkē* storehouse]

apotheosis /æpəθɪ'əʊsɪs/ n. (pl. **-oses**) **1.** deification. **2.** a

deified ideal; the highest development of a thing. [L f. Gk (*theos* god)]

appal /ə'pɔːl/ v.t. (**-ll-**) to fill with horror or dismay, to shock deeply. —**appalling** adj. [f. OF *apalir* grow pale]

Appalachian Mountains /æpə'leɪʃ(ə)n/ (also **Appalachians**) a mountain system of eastern North America, which confined early European settlers to the eastern coastal belt.

apparatus /æpə'reɪtəs/ n. **1.** equipment for performing something, e.g. gymnastics or scientific experiments; bodily organs effecting a natural process. **2.** a complicted organization. [L (AD-, *parare* make ready)]

apparel /ə'pær(ə)l/ n. (*archaic*) clothing. —v.t. (**-ll-**) (*archaic*) to clothe. [f. OF f. Rom., = make ready (AD-, dim. of L *par* equal)]

apparent /ə'pærənt/ adj. **1.** readily visible or perceivable. **2.** seeming but not real. —**apparently** adv. [f. OF f. L (as APPEAR)]

apparition /æpə'rɪʃ(ə)n/ n. something remarkable or expected that appears; a ghost. [f. F or L (as APPEAR)]

appeal /ə'piːl/ v.t./i. **1.** to make an earnest or formal request; to call attention or resort *to* (evidence etc.) as support; to make a request (*to* a higher court) for alteration of the decision of a lower court; (in cricket) to ask the umpire to declare a batsman out. **2.** to be attractive or of interest *to.* —n. **1.** an act of appealing. **2.** an appealing quality, attraction. **3.** a request for donations to a cause. [f. F f. L *appellare* address (AD-, *pellere* drive)]

appear /ə'pɪə(r)/ v.i. **1.** to become or be visible; to give an impression, to seem. **2.** to present oneself formally or publicly. **3.** to be published. [f. OF f. L *apparēre* come in sight]

appearance n. appearing; an outward form as perceived, a semblance. —**keep up appearances,** to maintain a display or pretence of prosperity, good behaviour, etc. [as prec.]

appease /ə'piːz/ v.t. to make calm or quiet by making concessions etc. or by satisfying demands. —**appeasement** n. (in a derog. sense, used especially of the British Prime Minister's efforts, 1937–9, to placate, and so stave off the threatened aggression of, the Axis powers). [f. AF (*à* to, *pais* peace)]

appellant /ə'pelənt/ n. (*Law*) a person making an appeal to a higher court. [f. F (as APPEAL)]

appellation /æpə'leɪʃ(ə)n/ n. a name or title; nomenclature. [as prec.]

append /ə'pend/ v.t. to attach; to add, especially to a written document. [f. L *appendere* (AD-, *pendere* hang)]

appendage /ə'pendɪdʒ/ n. a thing attached to or forming a natural part of something larger or more important. [f. prec.]

appendicitis /əpendɪ'saɪtɪs/ n. inflammation of the appendix. [f. foll. + -ITIS]

appendix /ə'pendɪks/ n. (pl. **-ices** /-ɪsiːz/) **1.** supplementary matter at the end of a book etc. **2.** a small blind tube of tissue forming an outgrowth of the caecum (ill. BODY 2). [L (as APPEND)]

appertain /æpə'teɪn/ v.i. to belong or relate *to.* [f. OF f. L *appertinere* (AD-, *pertinēre* pertain)]

appetite /'æpɪtaɪt/ n. a natural craving or relish, especially for food or something pleasurable. [f. OF f. L *appetere* seek after]

appetizer /'æpɪtaɪzə(r)/ n. a small savoury or drink taken before a meal to stimulate the appetite. [f. foll.]

appetizing /'æpɪtaɪzɪŋ/ adj. (of food) stimulating the appetite, attractive to eat. —**appetizingly** adv. [f. F (as APPETITE)]

Appian Way /'æpɪən/ (L *Via Appia*) the principal southward road from Rome in classical times, named after the censor Appius Claudius Caecus who in 312 BC built the section to Capua (c.210 km, 132 miles); it was later extended to Brindisi on the SE coast of Italy.

applaud /ə'plɔːd/ v.t./i. to express strong approval (of), especially by clapping; to commend, to praise. —**applause** n. [f. L *applaudere* (AD-, *plaudere* clap hands)]

apple n. a round firm fruit with juicy flesh; the tree bearing this. —**apple of one's eye,** a cherished person or thing. **apple-pie order,** extreme neatness. [OE]

Appleton /'æp(ə)lt(ə)n/, Sir Edward Victor (1892–1965), English physicist. His investigation of the Kennelly-Heaviside (or E) layer of the atmosphere led him to the discovery of a higher region of ionized gases (the Appleton layer, now resolved into two layers F1 and F2) from which short-wave radio waves were reflected back to earth. This work, for which he was awarded the Nobel Prize for physics in 1947, was important for long-range radio transmission and radar.

appliance /ə'plaɪəns/ n. a device, a utensil; a fire-engine. [f. APPLY]

applicable /'æplɪkəb(ə)l/ adj. that may be applied (to), appropriate. —**applicability** /-'bɪlɪtɪ/ n. [OF or f. L (as APPLY)]

applicant /'æplɪkənt/ n. one who applies for something, especially employment. [f. foll.]

application /æplɪ'keɪʃ(ə)n/ n. 1. the act of applying something. 2. a thing applied. 3. a formal request. 4. sustained effort, diligence. 5. relevance. [f. F f. L (as APPLY)]

applicator /'æplɪkeɪtə(r)/ n. a device for applying a substance. [f. prec.]

applied /ə'plaɪd/ adj. (of knowledge etc.) put to practical use. [f. APPLY]

appliqué /ə'pli:keɪ/ n. ornamental work in which fabric is cut out and attached to the surface of another fabric. —v.t. (-quéd, -quéing) to decorate with appliqué. [F (as foll.)]

apply /ə'plaɪ/ v.t./i. 1. to make a formal request. 2. to put into contact, to spread on a surface. 3. to bring into use or action. 4. to be relevant. —**apply oneself**, to give one's attention and energy (to a task). [f. OF f. L applicare fasten to]

appoint /ə'pɔɪnt/ v.t. 1. to assign (a person) to a job or office; to set up by choosing members. 2. to fix or decide (a date or place etc.). —**well-appointed** adj. well-equipped or furnished. [f. OF (à point to a point)]

appointee /æpɔɪn'ti:/ n. a person appointed. [f. prec.]

appointment /ə'pɔɪntmənt/ n. 1. an arrangement to meet or visit at a particular time. 2. appointing a person to a job; the person appointed. 3. (in pl.) fittings, furnishings. [f. APPOINT]

apportion /ə'pɔ:ʃ(ə)n/ v.t. to share out; to assign as a share (to). —**apportionment** n. [f. F or L (as PORTION)]

apposite /'æpəzɪt/ adj. (of a remark) appropriate. —**appositely** adv., **appositeness** n. [f. L (apponere apply)]

apposition /æpə'zɪʃ(ə)n/ n. juxtaposition, especially (Gram.) of elements sharing a syntactic function. [as prec.]

appraise /ə'preɪz/ v.t. to estimate the value or amount of; to fix a price for (a thing) officially. —**appraisal** n. [earlier apprise, assim. to PRAISE]

appreciable /ə'pri:ʃəb(ə)l/ adj. enough to be seen or felt, considerable. —**appreciably** adv. [F (as foll.)]

appreciate /ə'pri:ʃɪeɪt/ v.t./i. 1. to value greatly; to be grateful for. 2. to recognize, to be sympathetically aware of; to assess realistically. 3. to raise or rise in value. —**appreciation** /-'eɪʃ(ə)n/ n. [f. L appretiare appraise (AD-, pretium price)]

appreciative /ə'pri:ʃɪv/ adj. expressing appreciation. [f. prec.]

appreciatory /ə'pri:ʃətərɪ/ adj. (of remarks etc.) expressing appreciation. [f. APPRECIATE]

apprehend /æprɪ'hend/ v.t. 1. to arrest, to seize. 2. to understand. [f. F or L apprehendere (AD-, prehendere grasp)]

apprehensible /æprɪ'hensɪb(ə)l/ adj. able to be grasped by the mind or perceived by the senses. [as prec.]

apprehension /æprɪ'henʃ(ə)n/ n. 1. dread, fearful, expectation. 2. arrest, capture. 3. understanding. [F or f. L (as APPREHEND)]

apprehensive /æprɪ'hensɪv/ adj. feeling apprehension, anxious. —**apprehensively** adv., **apprehensiveness** n. [f. F or L (as APPREHEND)]

apprentice /ə'prentɪs/ n. one who is learning a craft and is bound to an employer for a specified term by legal agreement in return for instruction; a novice (jockey). —v.t. to bind as an apprentice. —**apprenticeship** n. [f. OF (apprendre learn)]

apprise /ə'praɪz/ v.t. to inform, to notify. [f. F (apprendre learn; as APPREHEND)]

appro /'æprəʊ/ n. (colloq.) approval. [abbr.]

approach /ə'prəʊtʃ/ v.t./i. 1. to come near or nearer (to) in space or time. 2. to be similar or approximate to. 3. to make a tentative proposal. 4. to set about (a task). —n. 1. an act or means of approaching. 2. a way of dealing with a person or thing. 3. an approximation. 4. the final part of an aircraft's flight before landing. [f. OF f. L appropiare draw near (AD-, prope near)]

approachable /ə'prəʊtʃəb(ə)l/ adj. able to be approached; friendly, easy to talk to. —**approachability** /-'bɪlɪtɪ/ n. [f. prec.]

approbation /æprə'beɪʃ(ə)n/ n. approval, consent. [f. OF f. L approbatio (AD-, probare test)]

appropriate[1] /ə'prəʊprɪət/ adj. suitable, proper. —**appropriately** adv., **appropriateness** n. [f. L appropriare (AD-, proprius one's own)]

appropriate[2] /ə'prəʊprɪeɪt/ v.t. to take and use as one's own; to devote (money etc.) to a special purpose. —**appropriation** /-'eɪʃ(ə)n/ n., **appropriator** n. [f. prec.]

approval /ə'pru:v(ə)l/ n. 1. approving; favourable opinion. 2. consent. —**on approval**, returnable to the supplier (without obligation to purchase) if not suitable. [f. foll.]

approve /ə'pru:v/ v.t./i. 1. to give or have a favourable opinion (of). 2. to give assent to. [f. OF f. L approbare test (AD-, probus good)]

approximate[1] /ə'prɒksɪmət/ adj. almost (but not completely) exact or correct, near to the actual. —**approximately** adv. [f. L approximare (AD-, proximus very near)]

approximate[2] /ə'prɒksɪmeɪt/ v.t./i. to be or make approximate or near (to). —**approximation** /-'meɪʃ(ə)n/ n. [f. prec.]

appurtenances /ə'pɜ:tɪnənsɪz/ n.pl. belongings, accessories. [f. AF (as APPERTAIN)]

après-ski /æpreɪ'ski:/ adj. done or worn after skiing. [F]

apricot /'eɪprɪkɒt/ n. an orange-yellow stone-fruit allied to the plum and peach; its colour; the tree bearing it. [f. Port. or Sp. f. Arab. al the + barkuk, f. Gk f. L praecox early-ripe]

April /'eɪprɪ(ə)l/ n. the fourth month of the year. —**April fool**, the victim of a hoax on **April Fool's Day** (1 April). The custom of playing tricks on this day has been observed in many countries for hundreds of years, but its origin is unknown. [f. L Aprilis]

a priori /eɪ praɪ'ɔ:raɪ/ 1. reasoning from causes to effects. 2. assumed without investigation. 3. (of knowledge) existing in the mind independently of sensory experience. [L, = from what is before]

apron /'eɪprən/ n. 1. a garment worn over the front part of the body to protect the wearer's clothes. 2. a hard-surfaced area on an airfield where aircraft are manœuvred or loaded and unloaded. 3. an extension of a stage in front of a curtain. [orig. naperon, f. OF nape table-cloth f. L mappa]

apropos /'æprəpəʊ, -'pəʊ/ adj. & adv. relevant(ly). 2. by the way. —**apropos of**, concerning, with reference to. [f. F à propos to the purpose]

apse n. a recess with an arched or domed roof, especially at the end of a church. [as APSIS]

apsidal /'æpsɪd(ə)l/ adj. 1. of the form of an apse. 2. of apsides. [f. prec.]

apsis /'æpsɪs/ n. (pl. **apsides** /'æpsɪdi:z/) each of the points, on the orbit of a planet or satellite etc., nearest to or furthest from the body round which it moves. [L f. Gk (h)apsis arch, vault]

apt adj. 1. suitable, appropriate. 2. having a tendency. 3. quick at learning. —**aptly** adv., **aptness** n. [f. L aptus fitted]

apteryx /'æptərɪks/ n. a kiwi. [f. Gk a- without, pterux wing]

aptitude /'æptɪtju:d/ n. a natural ability or skill. [F f. L (as APT)]

Apuleius /æpjʊ'li:əs/ (born c.123) Latin writer from Africa. Renowned as a declaimer, he wrote a variety of rhetorical and philosophical works. His most famous work is the *Metamorphoses* (better known as *The Golden Ass*), a picaresque novel which recounts the adventures of one Lucius who is transformed into an ass, and which includes the Cupid and Psyche tale. His writings are characterized by an exuberant and bizarre use of language.

aqualung /'ækwəlʌŋ/ n. a portable underwater breathing apparatus consisting of cylinders of compressed air connected to a face-mask, first developed in 1943 by Jacques Cousteau and a French engineer Émile Gagnan. [f. L aqua water + LUNG]

aquamarine /ækwəmə'ri:n/ n. a bluish-green beryl; its colour. [f. L aqua marina sea water]

aquaplane /'ækwəpleɪn/ n. a board on which a person stands for riding on water, pulled by a speedboat. —v.i. 1. to ride on an aquaplane. 2. (of a vehicle) to glide uncontrollably on a wet surface. [f. L aqua water + PLANE]

aquarium /ə'kweərɪəm/ n. (pl. **-ums**) a tank or artificial pond for keeping and showing living fish and other aquatic life; a building containing such tanks etc. [f. L aquarius of water]

Aquarius /əˈkweərɪəs/ a constellation and the eleventh sign of the zodiac, the Water-carrier, which the sun enters about 21 Jan. It contains no bright stars but possesses several good examples of planetary nebulae. —**Aquarian** *adj.* & *n.* [L (as prec.)]

aquatic /əˈkwætɪk/ *adj.* growing or living in or near water; taking place in or on water. [f. F or L (*aqua* water)]

aquatint /ˈækwətɪnt/ *n.* a method of etching that gives an effect similar in some respects to that of a wash drawing; a print produced by this. The effect is produced by coating a copper plate (or plates) with a porous resin ground, painting the design on it with varnish, immersing it in nitric acid, and inking it, when the protected parts, being less corroded by the acid, will take up less ink. Invented in the 18th c., its use as a landscape medium was pioneered by the topographical artist Paul Sandby in the 1770s, while its combination with line etching reached supreme heights in Goya's graphic work. Although it was somewhat eclipsed by new graphic techniques in the 19th c. there has been a revival of interest in this medium in recent years. [f. F f. It. *acqua tinta* coloured water]

aqueduct /ˈækwɪdʌkt/ *n.* an artificial channel carrying water across country, especially in the form of a bridge across a valley or low ground. [f. L *aquae ductus* conduit (*aqua* water, *ducere* lead)]

aqueous /ˈeɪkwɪəs/ *adj.* of or like water; produced by water. —**aqueous humour,** see HUMOUR. [f. L (*aqua* water)]

Aquila /ˈækwɪlə/ a constellation, the Eagle, well seen during midsummer in the northern hemisphere. It contains the first-magnitude star Altair, twelfth brightest in the sky, and some rich star fields of the Milky Way.

aquilegia /ækwɪˈliːdʒɪə/ *n.* a plant of the genus *Aquilegia*, a columbine, especially with blue flowers. [L, of unknown meaning]

aquiline /ˈækwɪlaɪn/ *adj.* of or like an eagle; hooked like an eagle's beak. [f. L (*aquila* eagle)]

Aquinas /əˈkwaɪnəs/, St Thomas (1225–74), a Doctor of the Church, 'the Angelic Doctor', philosopher and theologian, an Italian Dominican friar. His enormous works include many commentaries on Aristotle as well as the *Summa Contra Gentiles* (intended as a manual for those disputing with Spanish Muslims and Jews), and the *Summa Theologiae* (intended as an undergraduate textbook, left unfinished at his death). He probably also wrote hymns for the feast of Corpus Christi. His achievement was to make the work of Aristotle acceptable in Christian Western Europe; his own metaphysics, his account of the human mind, and his moral philosophy, were a development of Aristotle's, and his famous arguments for the existence of God (the 'Five Ways') were indebted to Aristotle and to Arabic philosophers. In theology he maintained a distinction between what could be discovered without special revelation and what could be known only by communication from God. Faith was the acceptance of propositions revealed by God out of trust in God who had revealed them. Feast day, 7 March.

Aquitaine /ækwɪˈteɪn/ an ancient province of SW France, comprising at some periods the whole country from the Loire to the Pyrenees. By the marriage of Eleanor of Aquitaine to Henry II it became one of the English possessions in France.

Ar *symbol* argon.

Arab *n.* **1.** a member of a Semitic people originally inhabiting the Arabian peninsula and neighbouring countries, now also other parts of the Middle East and North Africa. **2.** a horse of a breed native to Arabia. —*adj.* of Arabs. [f. F, ult. f. Arab. '*arab*]

arabesque /ærəˈbesk/ *n.* **1.** an elaborate design using intertwined leaves, branches, and scrolls. **2.** a ballet dancer's position in which one leg is extended horizontally backwards and the arms are outstretched. **3.** a short usually florid piece of music. [F f. It. (*Arabo* Arab)]

Arabia /əˈreɪbɪə/ a peninsula of SW Asia, largely desert, lying between the Red Sea and the Persian Gulf and bounded on the north by Jordan and Iraq.

Arabian /əˈreɪbɪən/ *adj.* of Arabia or the Arabs (esp. with geographical reference). —**Arabian Nights,** (in full *Arabian Nights' Entertainments*, also called the 'Thousand and One Nights') a collection of fairy stories and romances written in Arabic, linked together by a framework of Persian origin though the tales themselves are for the most part not Arabian but Persian in character, probably collected in Egypt at some time during the 14th–16th cc. [f. prec.]

Arabian Sea the north-western part of the Indian Ocean, between Arabia and India.

Arabic /ˈærəbɪk/ *n.* the language of the Arabs (see below). —*adj.* of or in the Arabic language. —**arabic numerals,** the numerals (1, 2, 3, 4, etc.) which reached western Europe through Arabia by about AD 1200 but which probably originated in India. Different symbols are used in modern Arabic. [f. OF f. L f. Gk *Arabikos*]

Arabic is a Semitic language related to Hebrew and was originally confined to the Arabian peninsula, but during the Islamic conquests of the 7th c. it was carried eastwards to Iran and Syria and westwards to North Africa and Spain; it is now the official language of a number of countries in the Middle East and North Africa, being the native language of some 120 million people, and in addition is known to many millions of Muslims. There are many dialects of spoken Arabic but one common written language, which is based on 'classical' Arabic, the written form used in the Middle Ages when Arabic was the universal language of the Near and Middle East. It is the language of the Koran and of medieval Arabic literature, and was the chief medium of scientific and philosophical thought for some centuries, bequeathing to us words such as *alcohol, elixir, azimuth, zenith*. Arabic is written from right to left in a traditional script of uncertain origin which is used also for a number of other languages.

arable /ˈærəb(ə)l/ *adj.* (of land) suitable for growing crops. —*n.* land of this kind. [F or f. L (*arare* plough)]

Araby /ˈærəbɪ/ (*poetic*) Arabia.

Arachne /əˈræknɪ/ (*Gk legend*) a woman of Colophon in Lydia, a skilful weaver who challenged Athene to a contest. Athene destroyed her work and Arachne hanged herself, but Athene changed her into a spider.

arachnid /əˈræknɪd/ *n.* a member of the class Arachnida, comprising spiders, scorpions, ticks, and mites. [f. F or L f. Gk *arachnē* spider]

Aragon /ˈærəgən/ a region of Spain, bounded on the north by the Pyrenees and on the east by Catalonia and Valencia.

Aral Sea /ˈærəl/ an inland sea of the USSR, east of the Caspian Sea.

Aramaic /ærəˈmeɪɪk/ *n.* a Semitic language of ancient Syria which was used as the lingua franca in the Near East from the 6th c. BC and gradually replaced Hebrew as the language of the Jews in those parts. It was supplanted by Arabic in the 7th c. AD. A modern form of Aramaic is still spoken in small communities in Syria and Turkey. One of its most important descendants is Syriac; Aramaic was written in the Hebrew alphabet from which the various Syriac scripts developed. —*adj.* of or in Aramaic. [f. *Aram*, biblical name of Syria]

Aran /ˈærən/ *adj.* of a type of patterned knitwear characteristic of the **Aran Islands,** a group of three islands off the west coast of Ireland.

Aranda /əˈrændə/ *n.* (*pl.* same or -s) **1.** a member of an Aboriginal people of central Australia, noted for their complex system of kinship reckoning. **2.** their language. —*adj.* of the Aranda or their language. [native name]

Ararat /ˈærəræt/ either of two volcanic peaks of the Armenian plateau in eastern Turkey, near the frontiers of Russia and Iran, of which the higher (Great Ararat, 5,165 m, 16,946 ft.) last erupted in 1840. The mountains are the traditional site of the resting place of Noah's ark after the Flood (Gen. 8: 4).

Araucanian /ærɔːˈkeɪnɪən/ *n.* **1.** a member of an American Indian people of central Chile and adjacent regions of Argentina. **2.** the group of languages spoken by them. —*adj.* of the Araucanians or their language. [f. *Araucania* region of Chile]

Arawak /ˈærəwæk/ *n.* (*pl.* same or -s) **1.** a member of the American Indian peoples of the Greater Antilles and northern and western South America, speaking languages of the same linguistic family. They were forced out of the Antilles by the more warlike Carib Indians shortly before Spanish expansion in the Caribbean. **2.** this family of languages. —*adj.* of the Arawaks or their language. —**Arawakan** *adj.* & *n.*

arbiter /ˈɑːbɪtə(r)/ *n.* **1.** a person with great control or influence over something. **2.** a judge, an arbitrator. [L]

arbitrary /ˈɑːbɪtrərɪ/ *adj.* **1.** based on random choice or whim; capricious. **2.** despotic. —**arbitrarily** *adv.*, **arbitrariness** *n.* [f. F or L, = of an ARBITER]

arbitrate /ˈɑːbɪtreɪt/ *v.t./i.* to act as an arbitrator, to settle (a dispute) thus. —**arbitration** /-'treɪʃ(ə)n/ *n*. [f. L *arbitrari* judge]

arbitrator /ɑ:bɪtreɪtə(r)/ *n*. an impartial person chosen to settle a dispute between parties. [L]

arbor /'ɑ:bə(r)/ *n*. an axle or spindle on which a wheel etc. revolves in mechanism. [L, = tree]

Arbor Day /'ɑ:bə/ a day set apart by law for the public planting of trees, originally in Nebraska in 1872. It is now observed throughout USA, usually in late April or early May, and has been adopted in Canada, Australia, and New Zealand. [prec.]

arboreal /ɑ:'bɔ:rɪəl/ *adj*. of trees; living in trees. [f. L *arboreus* (*arbor* tree)]

arboretum /ɑ:bəri:təm/ *n*. (*pl*. -ta) a place where trees are grown for study and display. [L (*arbor* tree)]

arbour /'ɑ:bə(r)/ *n*. a shady retreat enclosed by trees or climbing plants. [f. AF f. L *herba* herb, assim. to L *arbor* tree]

arbutus /ɑ:'bju:təs/ *n*. **1**. an evergreen of the genus *Arbutus*, one with strawberry-like fruits. **2**. (*US*) a trailing plant that bears fragrant pink flowers in spring. [L]

arc *n*. **1**. part of the circumference of a circle or other curve (ill. SHAPES); anything shaped like this. **2**. a large luminous flow of electric current through gas. —*v.i*. (**arced, arcing** /-k-/) to form an arc, to move in a curve. —**arc lamp**, a lamp in which an arc is used to produce light. [f. OF f. L *arcus* bow, curve]

arcade /ɑ:'keɪd/ *n*. **1**. a covered walk, especially one lined with shops. **2**. a series of arches supporting or along a wall. [F (as ARCH)]

Arcadia /ɑ:'keɪdɪə/ a mountainous and, in antiquity, backward area in the central Peloponnese in Greece, in poetic fantasy the idyllic home of song-loving shepherds. —**Arcadian** *adj. & n*.

Arcady /'ɑ:kədɪ/ (*poet*.) Arcadia. [f. prec.]

arcane /ɑ:'keɪn/ *adj*. mysterious, secret, understood by few. [F, or f. L (*arcēre* shut up, *arca* chest)]

arch¹ *n*. a structure (usually curved) supporting the weight of what is above it or used ornamentally (ill. BRIDGES, BUILDING); something curved like this. —*v.t./i*. to form (into) an arch; to span with or like an arch. [f. OF f. L *arcus* arc]

arch² *adj*. consciously or affectedly playful. —**archly** *adv*., **archness** *n*. [f. foll. (2)]

arch- *prefix* **1**. chief, superior. **2**. pre-eminent, extremely bad. [f. OE or OF, f. L f. Gk (*arkhos* chief)]

archaeology /ɑ:kɪ'ɒlədʒɪ/ *n*. the study of civilizations through their material remains (see below and ill. pp. 38–9). —**archaeological** /-ə'lɒdʒɪk(ə)l/ *adj*., **archaeologist** *n*. [f. Gk, = ancient history (*arkhaios* old, -LOGY)]

Archaeology, as a careful study rather than a romantic interest, is not much more than a hundred years old. The major methodological advances began in the second half of the 19th c., and the subject has developed at an increasing pace ever since. Excavation to recover new evidence is one approach, and whereas before the 19th c. the quest was for objects it is now for information of all kinds. Stratigraphy yields evidence of sequence: in a simple undisturbed series of layers the oldest must be at the bottom and the youngest at the top—but the sequence is rarely so simple, and is likely to show phases of rebuilding, periods of abandonment, etc. Typology (study in changes in forms of pottery, tools, etc.) can link finds from one site with those of another. Specialists in many fields have essential contributions to make: palaeontology, botany, and geology are but three of the disciplines that can contribute to the dating and interpretation of evidence, and the archaeologist can now call on scientific aids (e.g. aerial photography, radio-carbon dating) at most stages of his work. Specialized branches of archaeology include marine archaeology (exploration and recovery of ancient shipwrecks, and study of inundated sites), and industrial archaeology (concerned with the recording, while they still survive, of buildings, machines, and communications of the early industrial period—in Britain, notably those of the Industrial Revolution), but the purpose of the work remains the same—to unravel the long and complicated story of man's past.

archaeomagnetism /ɑ:kɪə'mægnɪtɪz(ə)m/ *n*. the remanent magnetism of magnetic materials in clay and rocks which have been heated above a certain temperature. On cooling, the orientation and intensity of their magnetism becomes fixed, determined by the direction and intensity of the earth's magnetic field at that time and (under certain conditions) enabling the date of the object or sample to be calculated. [f. Gk *arkhaios* ancient + MAGNETISM]

archaeopteryx /ɑ:kɪ'ɒptərɪks/ *n*. the oldest known fossil bird (see BIRD). [f. Gk *arkhaios* ancient + *pterux* wing]

archaic /ɑ:'keɪɪk/ *adj*. ancient, of an early period in a culture; antiquated; (of a word) no longer in ordinary use. —**archaically** *adv*. [f. F f. Gk (*arkhē* beginning)]

archaism /'ɑ:keɪɪz(ə)m/ *n*. an archaic word or expression; use of what is archaic. —**archaistic** /-'ɪstɪk/ *adj*. [f. Gk (as prec.)]

archaize /'ɑ:keɪaɪz/ *v.t./i*. **1**. to imitate the archaic. **2**. to render archaistic. [f. Gk, = be old-fashioned (as prec.)]

Archangel /'ɑ:keɪndʒ(ə)l/ a port of the northern USSR, on the White Sea.

archangel /'ɑ:keɪndʒ(ə)l/ *n*. an angel of the highest rank. [OE, ult. f. Gk (as ARCH-, ANGEL)]

archbishop /ɑ:tʃ'bɪʃəp/ *n*. the chief bishop of a Church province. —**archbishopric** *n*. his office or diocese. [OE (as ARCH-, BISHOP)]

archdeacon /ɑ:tʃ'di:kən/ *n*. a church dignitary ranking next below bishop. —**archideaconal** /ɑ:kɪdɪ'ækən(ə)l/ *adj*. [OE, ult. f. Gk (as ARCH-, DEACON)]

archdeaconry *n*. an archdeacon's office or residence.

archdiocese /ɑ:tʃ'daɪəsɪs/ *n*. the diocese of an archbishop.

archduchy /'ɑ:tʃdʌtʃɪ/ *n*. the territory of an archduke. [as foll.]

archduke /'ɑ:tʃdju:k/ *n*. the chief duke; (*hist*.) the title of the son of the Emperor of Austria. —**archduchess** *n.fem*. [f. OF f. L (as ARCH-, DUKE)]

archer *n*. **1**. one who shoots with bow and arrows. **2**. **the Archer**, the constellation or sign of the zodiac Sagittarius. [f. OF f. L *arcus* bow]

archery *n*. the use of bow and arrows, especially as a sport. Bow and arrows were used in prehistoric times by hunters, and for recreation as well as in war by the ancient peoples of Egypt, India, and China. The sport of shooting developed as a pastime after the decline (16th c.) of the bow as a weapon. Modern archery is practised chiefly in the form of shooting at a target. [f. prec.]

archetype /'ɑ:kɪtaɪp/ *n*. **1**. the original model from which others are copied. **2**. a typical example. —**archetypal** *adj*. [f. L f. Gk (ARCH-, *tupos* stamp)]

archiepiscopal /ɑ:kɪɪ'pɪskəp(ə)l/ *adj*. of an archbishop or archbishopric. [f. L f. Gk (as ARCH-, *episkopos* bishop)]

Archilochus /ɑ:'kɪləkəs/ (8th or 7th c. BC) Greek iambic and elegiac poet, author of satirical verse and fables.

archimandrite /ɑ:kɪ'mændraɪt/ *n*. the superior of a large monastery in the Orthodox Church. [F or f. L f. Gk (as ARCH-, *mandra* monastery)]

Archimedean screw /ɑ:kɪ'mi:dɪən/ a device consisting of a large spiral screw in a tube, rotated by a handle, used for raising water. Its principle is also used in many other devices (e.g. a mincing machine). [f. foll.]

Archimedes /ɑ:kɪ'mi:di:z/ (*c*.287–212 BC) Greek mathematician and inventor, born at Syracuse and killed during the Roman invasion of that city. Popular history knew him as the inventor of marvellous machines used against the Romans in the siege of Syracuse, and of other devices such as the helical screw (still known by his name) for raising water, for his boast 'give me a place to stand on and I will move the earth', and for his discovery of the hydrostatic law (*Archimedes' principle*) that a body immersed in a fluid is subject to an upward force equal in magnitude to the weight of fluid it displaces. (Legend has it that he made this discovery while taking a bath, and ran through the streets shouting 'Eureka!'.) Among his mathematical discoveries are the ratio of the radius of a circle to its circumference, and formulas for the surface-area and volume of a sphere and of a cylinder.

archipelago /ɑ:kɪ'peləgəʊ/ *n*. (*pl*. -os) a sea with many islands; a group of islands. [f. It. f. Gk (as ARCH-, *pelagos* sea, orig. = the Aegean Sea)]

architect /'ɑ:kɪtekt/ *n*. a designer of buildings and large structures who prepares plans and supervises construction; a designer or creator *of*. [f. F, ult. f. Gk (as ARCH-, *tektōn* builder)]

architectonic /ɑ:kɪtek'tɒnɪk/ *adj*. **1**. of architecture or architects. **2**. constructive. [f. L f. Gk (as prec.)]

architecture /'ɑ:kɪtektʃə(r)/ *n*. the art or science of designing and constructing buildings; a style of building. —**architectural** /-'tektʃər(ə)l/ *adj*., **architecturally** *adv*. [F or f. L (as ARCHITECT)]

Archaeology

A stratigraphic section
revealed by digging a trench on an archaeological site

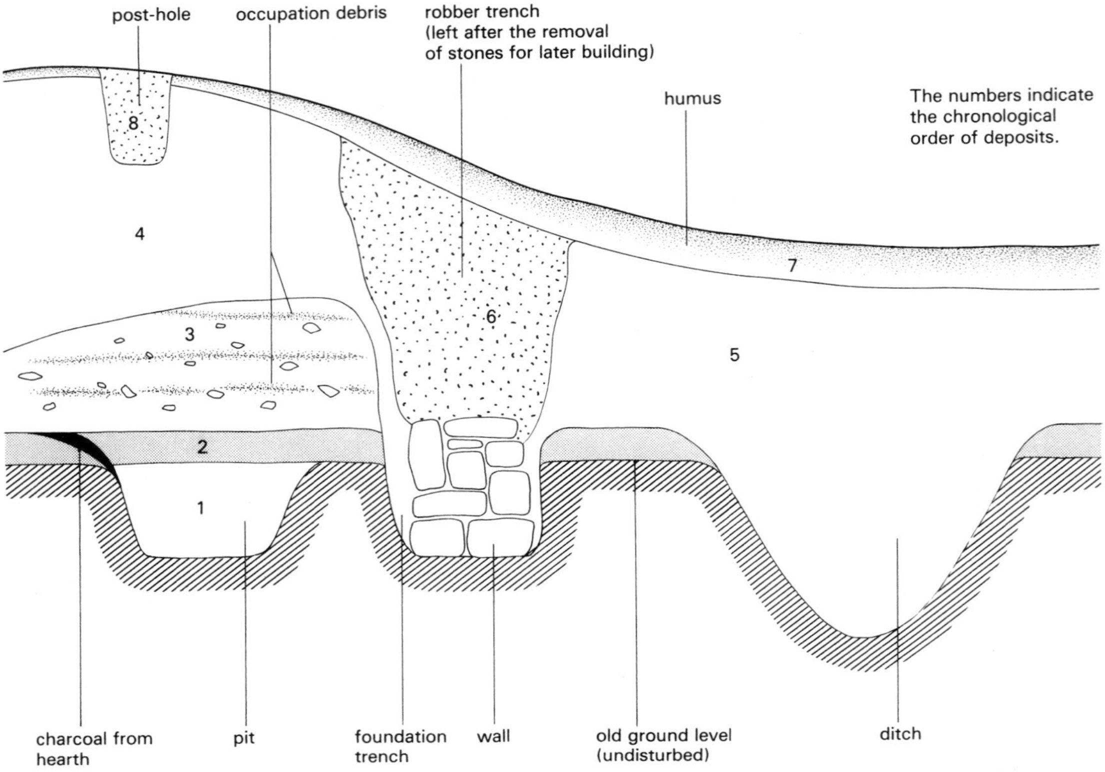

post-hole   occupation debris   robber trench
(left after the removal
of stones for later building)

humus

The numbers indicate
the chronological
order of deposits.

8

4

7

3

6

5

2

1

charcoal from
hearth

pit

foundation
trench

wall

old ground level
(undisturbed)

ditch

Some archaeological finds (not to scale)

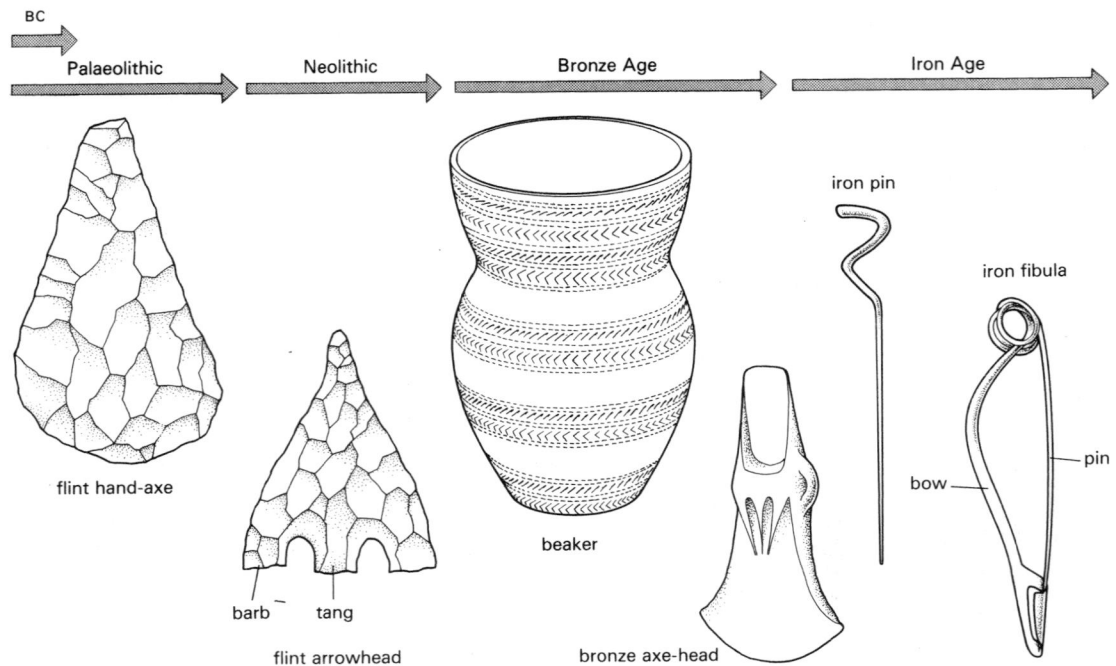

BC

Palaeolithic   Neolithic   Bronze Age   Iron Age

iron pin

iron fibula

flint hand-axe

bow

pin

barb   tang

beaker

flint arrowhead

bronze axe-head

Reconstruction

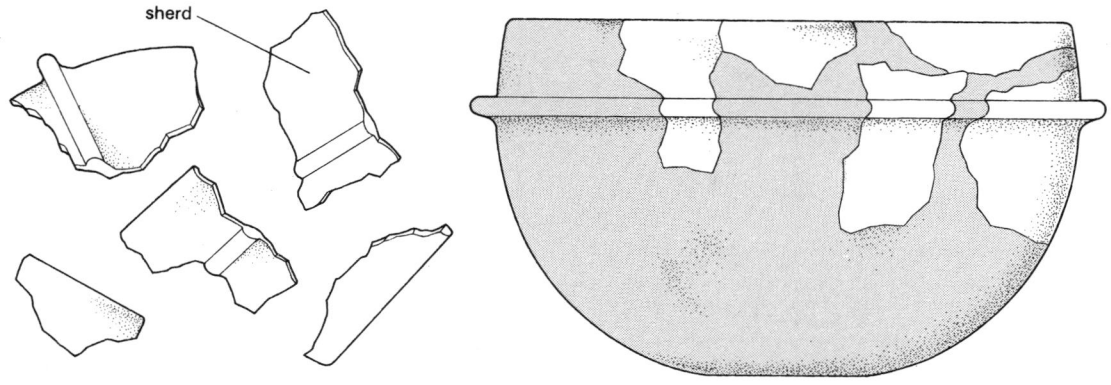

sherd

sherds as found on site

reconstructed neolithic bowl

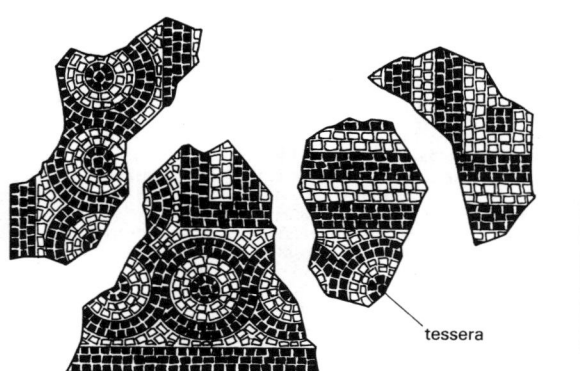

tessera

remaining pattern of tesserae
(as found during excavation)

reconstructed portion of Roman mosaic

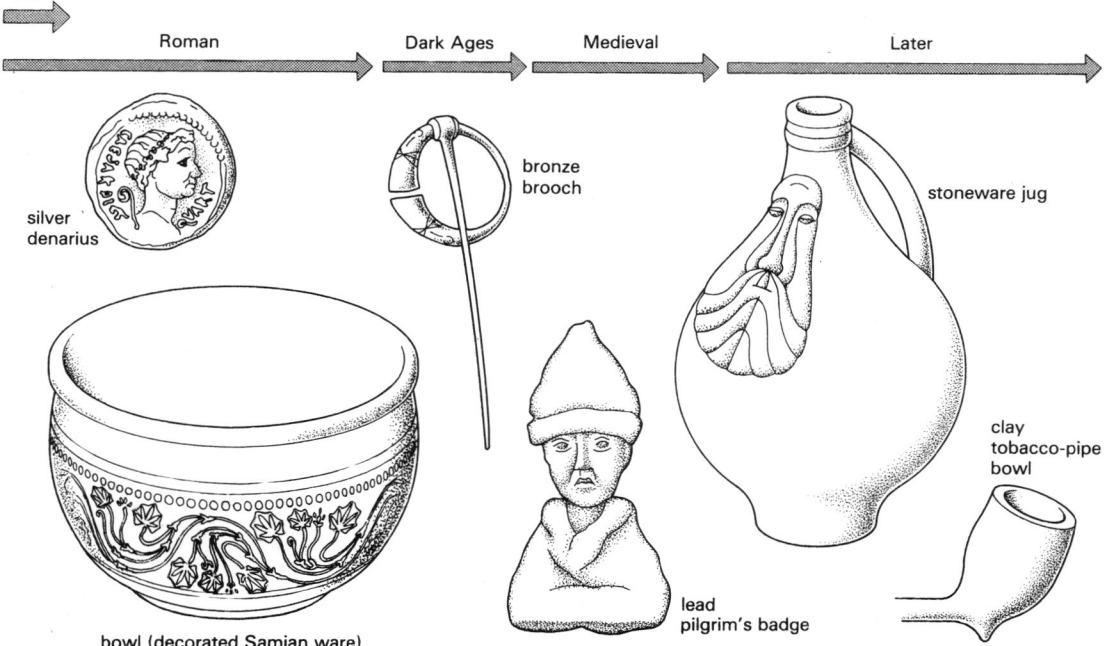

AD

Roman   Dark Ages   Medieval   Later

silver
denarius

bronze
brooch

stoneware jug

clay
tobacco-pipe
bowl

bowl (decorated Samian ware)

lead
pilgrim's badge

architrave /ˈɑːkɪtreɪv/ n. a horizontal beam resting on the tops of columns (ill. TEMPLES); a moulded frame round a doorway or window (ill. HOUSES). [F f. It. (as ARCH-, *trave* f. L *trabs* beam)]

archive /ˈɑːkaɪv/ n. (freq. in *pl.*) a collection of the historical documents or records of an institution or community. [f. F f. L f. Gk *arkheia* public records]

archivist /ˈɑːkɪvɪst/ n. one in charge of archives. [f. prec.]

archway /ˈɑːtʃweɪ/ n. an arched entrance or passage.

Arctic /ˈɑːktɪk/ adj. **1.** of the region round the North Pole (see below). **2. arctic,** very cold. —n. the Arctic regions. —**Arctic Circle,** an imaginary line round the Arctic region at the parallel of 66° 33′ N. [f. OF f. L f. Gk (*arktos* bear, Ursa Major)]

With the important exception of Greenland, most of the land in the Arctic is free from snow in the summer. Plants are able to grow (and a number of animals can live on them) even though about a metre below the surface the soil is permanently frozen. Real exploration of Arctic regions began in the 16th c. when northern European nations tried to find a way to the rich trade of China and the East Indies by way of a North-east or North-west passage (see entries) across the Arctic Ocean at a time when the longer but easier routes round Africa and South America were secured by Portugal and Spain. In the 19th c. attention turned to reaching the North Pole over the floating sea-ice (see NANSEN); in 1909 the American explorer R. E. Peary was the first man to reach the Pole; the American aviator Richard Byrd claimed to have flown over the North Pole in 1926. As air travel became more regular, flights were made over the polar ice. The last great advance in Arctic travel was the crossing of the polar ocean in 1958 by the atomic-powered submarine *Nautilus*, passing under the ice for 1,600 km from the Pacific to the Atlantic.

Arcturus /ɑːkˈtjʊərəs/ the brightest star in the northern sky, in the constellation Boötes. [f. Gk *arktos* bear, *ouros* guardian, because of its position in a line with the tail of Ursa Major]

Ardennes /ɑːˈden/ a forested upland region including parts of Belgium, Luxemburg, and northern France, the scene of fierce fighting in both World Wars.

ardent /ˈɑːd(ə)nt/ adj. eager, fervent, passionate. —**ardency** n. [f. OF f. L *ardens* burning]

ardour /ˈɑːdə(r)/ n. zeal, enthusiasm, passion. [f. OF f. L (*ardēre* burn)]

arduous /ˈɑːdjʊəs/ adj. hard to accomplish; needing much effort, laborious. —**arduously** adv. [f. L *arduus* steep, difficult]

are[1] 2nd person sing. & pl. and 3rd person pl. of BE.

are[2] /ɑː(r)/ n. a metric unit of measure, 100 square metres. [F f. L *area* (see foll.)]

area /ˈeərɪə/ n. **1.** the extent or measure of a surface. **2.** a region; a space set aside for a purpose. **3.** the field of an activity or subject. **4.** a space in front of the basement of a building. [L, = vacant piece of level ground]

areca /əˈriːkə/ n. a tropical Asiatic palm-tree of the genus *Areca*. [Port., f. Malayalam]

arena /əˈriːnə/ n. **1.** the level area in the centre of an amphitheatre or sports stadium etc. (ill. THEATRE). **2.** a scene of conflict, a sphere of action. [L, = sand]

aren't /ɑːnt/ (colloq.) are not. [contr.]

Areopagus /ærɪˈɒpəgəs/ **1.** a hill at Athens, where (Acts 17) St Paul preached on the Unknown God. **2.** the highest governmental council of ancient Athens, (later) a judicial court, meeting on this hill. [f. Gk, = hill of Ares]

Ares /ˈeəriːz/ (Gk myth.) the Greek war-god, son of Zeus and Hera. In Rome he was identified with Mars.

arête /æˈreɪt/ n. a sharp ridge on a mountain (ill. MOUNTAINS). [F f. L *arista* spiny process]

argali /ɑːˈgɑːlɪ/ n. a mountain-dwelling sheep of central Asia (*Ovis ammon ammon*), the largest Eurasian wild sheep, with massive curved horns. [Mongol]

argent /ˈɑːdʒənt/ n. & adj. (Her.) silver or white (colour). [F f. L *argentum* silver]

Argentina /ɑːdʒənˈtiːnə/ a country occupying much of the southern part of South America, characterized by heavily Europeanized cities and a large and often backward interior; pop. (1980) 27,862,771; official language, Spanish; capital, Buenos Aires. The economy is chiefly agricultural, and meat-packing is one of the principal industries, but there has been recent growth in textile, plastic, and engineering industries and development of natural mineral resources, particularly copper. Substantial deposits of oil and natural gas occur in various parts of the country and are of major importance to Argentina's industries. Colonized by the Spanish in the 16th c., Argentina declared its independence in 1816 and played a crucial role in the overthrow of European rule in the rest of South America. After a period of semi-dictatorial rule, the country emerged as a democratic republic in the mid-19th c., but has since had recurrent problems with political stability, periodically falling under military rule, most notably at the time of Juan Peron. In 1982 the Argentinian claim to the Falkland Islands led to an unsuccessful war with Britain. —**Argentinian** /-ˈtɪnɪən/ adj. & n. [f. L *argentum* silver, because the Rio de la Plata (= silver river) district exported it.]

Argive /ˈɑːgaɪv/ adj. **1.** of Argos or Argolis. **2.** (literary) Greek. —n. (literary) a Greek. [f. L f. Gk]

argon /ˈɑːgɒn/ n. an element of the noble gas group, symbol Ar, atomic number 18. First isolated in 1894, argon is the earth's commonest noble gas, making up nearly one per cent of its atmosphere by volume. The gas is used in electric-light bulbs to prolong the life of the filament, and also in industry, e.g. in arc welding and the growing of semiconductor crystals, where an inert atmosphere is important. [f. Gk *argos* idle (*a-* not, *ergon* work)]

Argonauts /ˈɑːgənɔːts/ n.pl. (Gk legend) the heroes who accompanied Jason on board the ship *Argo* on the quest for the Golden Fleece. Their story is one of the oldest Greek sagas, known to Homer, and may reflect early explorations in the Black Sea, but it is diversified with typical fairy-tale elements. [Gk, = sailor in the *Argo*]

Argos /ˈɑːgɒs/ an ancient Greek town of the eastern Peloponnese, from which the peninsula of Argolis derived its name.

argosy /ˈɑːgəsɪ/ n. (poet.) a merchant-ship; a fleet of these. [prob. f. It. *Ragusa nave* ship of Ragusa (in Dalmatia)]

argot /ˈɑːgəʊ/ n. the special jargon of a group. [F]

arguable /ˈɑːgjʊəb(ə)l/ adj. **1.** that may be asserted. **2.** open to doubt. —**arguably** adv. [f. foll.]

argue /ˈɑːgjuː/ v.t./i. **1.** to exchange views or angry words with expression of disagreement. **2.** to reason (for, against, or that); to treat by reasoning; to prove or indicate; to persuade into or out of. [f. OF f. L *argutari* prattle (*arguere* prove)]

argument /ˈɑːgjʊmənt/ n. **1.** a discussion involving disagreement; a quarrel. **2.** a reason advanced; a chain of reasoning. [as prec.]

argumentation /ɑːgjʊmenˈteɪʃ(ə)n/ n. arguing. [F f. L (as ARGUE)]

argumentative /ɑːgjʊˈmentətɪv/ adj. fond of arguing. —**argumentatively** adv. [f. F or L (as prec.)]

Argus /ˈɑːgəs/ **1.** (Gk myth.) a monster with many eyes, slain by Hermes. After his death he turned into a peacock, or Hera took his eyes to deck its tail. **2.** (Gk legend) the dog of Ulysses, who recognized his master on his return from Troy after an absence of 20 years.

argy-bargy /ˈɑːdʒɪbɑːdʒɪ/ n. (colloq.) a heated argument. [orig. Sc.]

aria /ˈɑːrɪə/ n. an extended piece for solo voice and accompaniment, especially in an opera or oratorio. [It.]

Ariadne /ærɪˈædnɪ/ (Gk myth.) daughter of Minos and Pasiphae. She helped Theseus to escape from the labyrinth of the Minotaur by providing him with a clue of thread. He then fled, taking her with him, but deserted her on the island of Naxos, where she was found and married by Dionysus. It is probable that she was originally a goddess, Minoan in origin.

Arian /ˈeərɪən/ adj. of Arianism. —n. a supporter of Arianism. [f. ARIUS]

Arianism /ˈeərɪənɪz(ə)m/ n. the principal heresy denying the divinity of Christ, named after its author Arius (see entry). Arianism maintained that the Son of God was not eternal but was created by the Father from nothing as an instrument for the creation of the world; the Son was therefore not coeternal with the Father, nor of the same substance. The heresy was condemned by the Council of Nicaea in 325 and again at Constantinople in 381, but though driven from the Empire it retained a foothold among Teutonic tribes until the conversion of the Franks to Catholicism (496). [f. prec.]

arid /ˈærɪd/ adj. **1.** dry, parched. **2.** uninteresting. —**aridly** adv., **aridity** /-ˈrɪdɪtɪ/ n., **aridness** n. [f. F or L (*arēre* be dry)]

Aries /ˈeəriːz/ a constellation and the eleventh sign of the zodiac, the Ram, which the sun enters at the vernal equinox (see PRECESSION OF THE EQUINOXES). —**Arian** adj. & n. [L, = ram]

aright /ə'raɪt/ adv. rightly. [OE (A-, RIGHT)]

Arion /ə'raɪən/ (7th c. BC) Greek poet and musician of Lesbos, said to have perfected the dithyramb. According to legend, sailors on a ship resolved to murder him but he leapt overboard and was carried safely ashore by one of the dolphins that had been attracted by his music.

Ariosto /ærɪ'ɒstəʊ/, Ludovico (1474-1533), Italian poet. His *Orlando Furioso* (final version 1532), about the exploits of Roland (Orlando) and other knights of Charlemagne, was the greatest of the Italian romantic epics. It was a continuation of Boiardo's *Orlando Innamorato* (1487), and influenced Spenser's *Faerie Queene*.

arise /ə'raɪz/ v.i. (past **arose**, p.p. **arisen** /ə'rɪz(ə)n/) **1.** to come into existence or to people's notice; to originate or result. **2.** (archaic) to get up; to rise from the dead. [OE (A-, RISE)]

Aristarchus[1] /ærɪ'stɑːkəs/ of Samos (3rd c. BC), Greek astronomer. Founder of an important school of Hellenic astronomy, he was aware of the rotation of the Earth and, by placing the sun at the centre of the universe, was able to account for the seasons. He knew that the sun must be larger than Earth and that the stars must be very distant. Many of his theories were more accurate than those of Ptolemy which replaced them.

Aristarchus[2] /ærɪ'stɑːkəs/ of Samothrace (c.217-145 BC), librarian at Alexandria who produced critical editions of the writings of Homer, Hesiod, Pindar, and other Greek authors, also commentaries and treatises upon their works, and is regarded as the originator of scientific scholarship.

Aristides /ærɪ'staɪdiːz/ 'the Just' (5th c. BC), Athenian statesman and general. In the Persian Wars he commanded the Athenian army at the battle of Plataea in 479 BC, and was subsequently prominent in founding the Athenian empire. His renowned honesty was contrasted with the deceitfulness of his colleague and rival Themistocles.

Aristippus /æ'rɪstɪpəs/ the name of two Greek philosophers: the elder (late 5th c. BC), a native of Cyrene and friend of Socrates, is often called the founder of the Cyrenaic school, probably by confusion with the younger, his grandson, who taught that immediate pleasure is the only purpose of action.

aristocracy /ærɪs'tɒkrəsɪ/ n. **1.** the hereditary upper classes, the nobility or élite. **2.** a State governed by these. **3.** the best representatives (of a category). —**aristocratic** /-tə'krætɪk/ adj. [f. F f. Gk (aristos best, -kratia power)]

aristocrat /'ærɪstəkræt/ n. a member of the aristocracy. [f. F (as prec.)]

Aristophanes /ærɪ'stɒfəniːz/ (c.450-c.385 BC) the greatest poet of Old Attic Comedy. His eleven surviving plays, characterized by fantasy of invention and exuberance of language, are largely occupied with topical themes; he satirizes politicians and intellectuals (e.g. Socrates), and parodies contemporary poets such as Aeschylus and Euripides. Political and social fantasy is a common theme, seen in the city of the birds ('Cloud-cuckoo-land') in the *Birds*, in the women's sex-strike for peace in the *Lysistrata*, and in the restoration of sight (and hence of proper discrimination) to the god of wealth in his last extant play, the *Plutus*.

Aristotelian /ærɪstə'tiːlɪən/ adj. of Aristotle or his philosophy. [f. L f. Gk]

Aristotle /'ærɪstɒt(ə)l/ (384-322 BC) Greek philosopher. A pupil of Plato, and tutor to Alexander the Great, in 335 BC he founded a school and library (the Lyceum) just outside Athens. His surviving written works, in the form of dry lecture notes, constitute a vast system of analysis, covering logic, physical science, zoology, psychology, metaphysics, ethics, politics, and rhetoric. In reasoning, he established the inductive method. In metaphysics, he reacted against the mystical speculation of Plato, whose Theory of Forms he rejected; for him form and matter were the inseparable constituents of all existing things. As an empirical scientific observer he had no rival in antiquity. The science in which he was most at home was biology, describing correctly the stomach of ruminants and the development of the chick embryo, and classifying animals by means of a scale ascending to man (without implying evolution). His work in this field was not fully appreciated until the 19th c.: Darwin acknowledges a debt to him. His influence in all fields has been immense: from the 9th c. it pervaded Islamic philosophy, theology, and science, and, after being lost to the West for some centuries, became the basis of scholasti-

cism; in astronomy, his rejection of the idea of the plurality of planets was a serious handicap to later thinking. An ancient tradition describes him as bald, with thin legs, small eyes, and a lisp, and as being noticeably well-dressed. A number of extant statues (e.g. one in the Vienna Museum) probably represent him.

arithmetic[1] /ə'rɪθmətɪk/ n. **1.** the part of mathematics that deals with numbers and the operations of addition, subtraction, multiplication, and division. Higher arithmetic, also called theory of numbers, is that part of arithmetic concerned mainly with deep properties of the integers. **2.** calculation by means of numbers. —**arithmetic unit**, the part of a computer where data are processed, as distinct from storage or control units. [f. OF f. L f. Gk arithmētikē (tekhnē) (art) of counting (arithmos number)]

arithmetic[2] /ærɪθ'metɪk/ adj. (also **arithmetical**) of arithmetic. —**arithmetical progression**, a sequence of numbers showing increase or decrease by a constant quantity, e.g. 1, 3, 5, 7. —**arithmetically** adv. [as prec.]

Arius /'eərɪəs/ (c.250-c.336) a priest of Alexandria, who initiated the heresy named after him (see ARIANISM).

Arizona /ærɪ'zəʊnə/ a State in the south-western USA, bordering on the Gulf of Mexico. It was acquired from Mexico in 1848 and 1854, and became the 48th State of the USA in 1912; capital, Phoenix.

ark n. **1.** Noah's boat or a model of this. **2. Ark of the Covenant**, a wooden chest in which the writings of Jewish Law were kept. [OE, f. L arca chest]

Arkansas /'ɑːkənsɔː/ a State in the south central USA, bordering on the Mississippi. It was acquired by the USA in 1803 as part of the Louisiana Purchase and became the 25th State in 1836; capital, Little Rock.

Arkwright /'ɑːkraɪt/, Sir Richard (1732-92), English pioneer of mechanical cotton-spinning, using first animal- then water-power, so that his spinning machines became known as water frames. He also improved the preparatory processes, including carding, and established spinning mills in Lancashire, Derbyshire, and Scotland. He became rich and powerful, succeeding by fairly ruthless determination and by incorporating the work of others (which led to a number of patent actions); nevertheless he must be regarded as one who made a great contribution to the establishment of the cotton industry.

arm[1] n. **1.** either of the two upper limbs of the human body, from shoulder to hand; something covering this, a sleeve. **2.** a raised side part of a chair, supporting a sitter's arm. **3.** a thing resembling an arm in shape or function. **4.** control, a means of reaching. —**arm-band** n. a band worn round the arm or sleeve. [OE]

arm[2] n. **1.** (usu. in pl.) a weapon. **2.** a branch of military forces. **3.** (in pl.) heraldic devices. —v.t./i. **1.** to equip with weapons etc.; to equip oneself in preparation for war. **2.** to make (a bomb etc.) ready to explode. —**up in arms**, protesting vigorously. [f. OF f. L arma weapons]

armada /ɑː'mɑːdə/ n. a fleet of warships, especially (**Armada**) a Spanish naval invasion force sent against England in 1588 by Philip II of Spain. The Armada, 129 ships strong and carrying almost 20,000 soldiers, was defeated in the Channel by a smaller English fleet before it could rendezvous with a Spanish army waiting in the Low Countries to be ferried across to England. The scattered survivors of the Armada tried to reach home by sailing north round Scotland, but many were lost to storms. [Sp. f. Rom., = army]

armadillo /ɑːmə'dɪləʊ/ n. (pl. **-os**) a burrowing mammal of South America with a body encased in bony plates, often rolling itself into a ball when captured. [Sp., dim. of armado armed man (ARM²)]

Armageddon /ɑːmə'ged(ə)n/ n. an ultimate or large-scale conflict, especially that between the forces of good and evil at the end of the world (Rev. 16: 16); the scene of this.

Armagh /ɑː'mɑː/ a town and county of Northern Ireland.

armament /'ɑːməmənt/ n. **1.** (usu. in pl.) military weapons and equipment. **2.** the process of equipping for war. [f. L (as ARM²)]

armature /'ɑːmətʃə(r)/ n. **1.** the wire-wound core of a dynamo or electric motor. **2.** a bar placed in contact with the poles of a magnet. **3.** a framework round which a clay or plaster sculpture is modelled. [F f. L armatura armour]

armchair n. **1.** a chair with side supports for a sitter's arms. **2.** (attrib.) theorizing, not practical or participating; amateur.

Armenia /ɑː'miːnɪə/ **1.** the country of the Armenians, a former kingdom in western Asia (Mount Ararat lies within it), most of which was under Turkish rule from the 16th c. and which is now divided between Turkey, Iran, and the USSR (see below). **2.** the Armenian SSR, a constituent republic lying south of the Caucasus; capital, Erivan.

In the early 19th c. the Russians advanced into the crumbling Ottoman empire, and in 1828 the Sultan was obliged to surrender part of the Armenian homeland. In 1915 the Turks, at war with Russia, suspected their Armenian subjects of sympathizing with kinsmen across the border and with the Western forces who had embarked on the Dardanelles campaign, and decided on mass deportation of 1,750,000 Armenians to the deserts of Syria and Mesopotamia. The long march involved massive loss of life and resulted in deep and lasting Armenian hatred towards the Turks.

Armenian /ɑːˈmiːnɪən/ *adj.* of Armenia or its people or language. *n.* **1.** a native or inhabitant of Armenia. **2.** a member of the reputedly Monophysite church established in Armenia *c.*300. **3.** the language of Armenia, which constitutes a separate branch of the Indo-European language group although its vocabulary has been substantially influenced by Iranian languages. There are some 4 million speakers of the modern language of whom about 3 million live in the Soviet Union. Its characteristic alphabet contains 38 letters and was invented in AD 400 by missionaries. [f. prec.]

armful *n.* a quantity that is as much as the arm can hold. [f. ARM¹ + -FUL]

armhole *n.* an opening in a garment through which the arm is inserted.

Arminian /ɑːˈmɪnɪən/ *adj.* of or following the doctrines of Jacobus Arminius (1560-1609), a Dutch Protestant theologian who rejected the Calvinist doctrines of predestination and election.

armistice /ˈɑːmɪstɪs/ *n.* a stopping of hostilities; a short truce. —**Armistice Day**, 11 Nov., the anniversary of the armistice that ended the First World War, now replaced by Remembrance Sunday and (in the USA) Veterans Day. [F or f. L (*arma* arms, *sistere* make stand)]

armlet /ˈɑːmlɪt/ *n.* a band worn round the arm or sleeve. [f. ARM¹ + -LET]

armorial /ɑːˈmɔːrɪəl/ *adj.* of coats of arms, heraldic. [f. foll.]

armour /ˈɑːmə(r)/ *n.* **1.** a protective covering for the body, formerly worn in fighting (see ill p. 43); a protective metal covering for an armed vehicle, ship, etc. **2.** armoured fighting vehicles collectively. [f. OF f. L (as ARM²)]

armoured /ˈɑːməd/ *adj.* **1.** furnished with armour. **2.** equipped with armoured vehicles. [f. prec.]

armourer /ˈɑːmərə(r)/ *n.* **1.** an official in charge of small arms. **2.** a maker of arms or armour. [f. ARMOUR]

armoury /ˈɑːmərɪ/ *n.* a place where arms are kept. [as prec.]

armpit *n.* the hollow under the arm below the shoulder. [f. ARM + PIT]

Armstrong /ˈɑːmstrɒŋ/, Louis (1900-71), known as 'Satchmo' (an abbreviation of 'Satchelmouth'), was born in New Orleans and grew up with the strains of ragtime about him, and became one of the great masters of Dixieland jazz. He learnt the trumpet in a waifs' home and played in jazz bands on the Mississippi river-boats, forming his own band in 1928. He was a distinctive singer as well as a trumpet player and had a brilliant talent for improvisation.

army *n.* **1.** an organized force armed for fighting on land (see below). **2.** a vast group. **3.** a body of people organized for a cause. [f OF (as ARM²)]

In Britain, until the mid-17th c. the army consisted chiefly of soldiers engaged only for the duration of particular campaigns. In 1644 Oliver Cromwell raised his New Model Army, and from then onwards a regular standing army was maintained at all times. At the Restoration in 1660 the army became dependent on the Crown, but after the Revolution of 1688 Parliament took over from the king the control and payment of the army.

Arne /ɑːn/, Thomas (1710-78), English composer who made a distinctive contribution to 18th-c. theatrical music, especially with his operas *Artaxerxes* (1762), in the Italian style, and *Thomas and Sally* (1760) and *Love in a Village* (1762), which are purely English in flavour. His famous song 'Rule, Britannia' was composed for the masque *Alfred* (1740).

arnica /ˈɑːnɪkə/ *n.* a composite plant of the genus *Arnica*,

with yellow flowers; a substance prepared from this, formerly used to treat bruises. [orig. unkn.]

Arno /ˈɑːnəʊ/ a river of northern Italy, flowing through Florence and Pisa.

Arnold /ˈɑːnəld/, Matthew (1822-88), English poet and critic, eldest son of Thomas Arnold, headmaster of Rugby. He published his first volume of poetry (which contained 'The Forsaken Merman') in 1849. In 1851 he became an inspector of schools, and, while he continued to publish poetry (including 'The Scholar Gipsy' (1853), a pastoral lament, and 'Dover Beach' (1867), a characteristic expression of the religious doubts and personal affirmations of the 19th c.) he turned increasingly to prose, becoming, with such works as *Culture and Anarchy*, one of the most influential social critics of his time, whose views on religion, education, and the need for a more European culture, provided a challenge to the materialism and complacency of Victorian prosperity.

aroma /əˈrəʊmə/ *n.* a smell, especially a pleasant one. [L f. Gk, = spice]

aromatic /ærəˈmætɪk/ *adj.* **1.** fragrant, having a pleasantly strong smell. **2.** (*Chem.*, of compounds) containing one or more rings of six carbon atoms, as in benzene. —*n.* an aromatic substance. —**aromatically** *adv.* [f. OF f. L f. Gk (as AROMA)]

arose /əˈrəʊz/ *past* of ARISE.

around /əˈraʊnd/ *adv.* **1.** on every side, all round; here and there. **2.** (*colloq.*) near at hand. —*prep.* **1.** on or along the circuit of; on every side of. **2.** about, (*US*) approximately at. [f. A- + ROUND]

arouse /əˈraʊz/ *v.t.* to rouse; to induce. [f. A- + ROUSE]

arpeggio /ɑːˈpedʒɪəʊ/ *n.* (*pl.* -os) the sounding of the notes of a chord in succession; a chord so played. [It. (*arpa* harp)]

arrack /ˈærək/ *n.* a kind of alcoholic spirit, especially that made from coco sap or rice. [f. Arab. *'arak*]

arraign /əˈreɪn/ *v.t.* to indict, to accuse; to find fault with (an action or statement), to challenge. —**arraignment** *n.* [f. AF f. L (AD-, *ratio* reason)]

arrange /əˈreɪndʒ/ *v.t./i.* **1.** to put into the required order, to adjust or place. **2.** to plan or prepare; to take measures or give instructions. **3.** to adapt, especially (music) for performance with different instruments or voices. —**arrangement** *n.* [f. OF (*à* to, *rangier* range)]

arrant /ˈærənt/ *adj.* downright, utter. [var. of ERRANT, orig. in *arrant* (= outlawed roving) *thief*]

arras /ˈærəs/ *n.* a richly decorated tapestry or wall-hanging. [f. *Arras*, town in France famous in the 13th-16th c. for tapestry weaving]

array /əˈreɪ/ *n.* an imposing series, a display; an ordered arrangement. —*v.t.* to arrange in order, to marshal (forces). [f. AF f. L (AD-, READY)]

arrears /əˈrɪəz/ *n.* the amount that is still outstanding or uncompleted, especially of a debt or of work to be done. —**in arrears**, not paid or done when it was due. [f. OF f. L (AD-, *retro* backwards)]

arrest /əˈrest/ *v.t.* **1.** to seize (a person) by the authority of the law. **2.** to stop or check (a movement or process). **3.** to catch and hold (attention). —*n.* **1.** an act of arresting, legal seizure of a person. **2.** a stoppage. —**arrester** *n.*, **arrestor** *n.* [f. OF f. L (*restare* remain)]

arrestable /əˈrestəb(ə)l/ *adj.* (of an offence) such that the offender may be arrested without a warrant. [f. prec.]

Arrhenius /əˈreɪnɪəs, əˈriː-/, Svante August (1859-1927), one of the founders of modern physical chemistry and the first Swede to win the Nobel Prize for chemistry, awarded in 1903 for his work on the physical chemistry of electrolytes.

arrière-pensée /ærɪeəˈpɑ̃seɪ/ *n.* an ulterior motive; a mental reservation. [F, = behind thought]

arris /ˈærɪs/ *n.* the sharp edge formed where two surfaces meet to form an angle, especially in architecture. [f. F *areste* = ARÊTE]

arrival /əˈraɪv(ə)l/ *n.* **1.** arriving, appearance on the scene. **2.** a person or thing that has arrived. [f. foll.]

arrive /əˈraɪv/ *v.i.* **1.** to reach a destination or a certain point on a journey. **2.** (of a time) to come. **3.** to be recognized as having achieved success in the world. **4.** (*colloq.*, of a baby) to be born. —**arrive at**, to reach (a decision or conclusion). [f. OF f. L (AD-, *ripa* shore)]

arriviste /ærɪˈviːst/ *n.* a person ruthlessly and obsessively aspiring to advancement. [F (*arriver* arrive)]

arrogant /ˈærəɡənt/ *adj.* proud and overbearing through

Armour

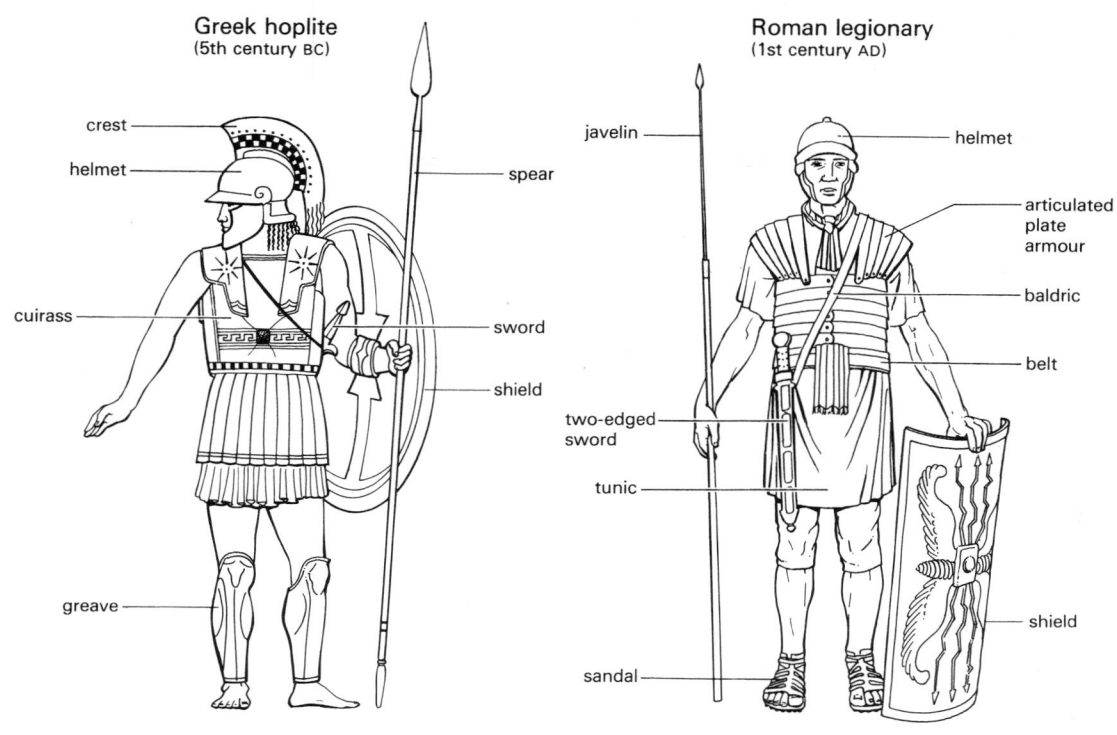

Greek hoplite
(5th century BC)

- crest
- helmet
- cuirass
- greave
- spear
- sword
- shield

Roman legionary
(1st century AD)

- javelin
- helmet
- articulated plate armour
- baldric
- belt
- two-edged sword
- tunic
- shield
- sandal

European armour

mail (c. 1226)

- mail hood
- surcoat
- sword

coat of plates (c. 1370)

- plastron
- chains to attach helmet and weapons
- lance rest

field armour (c. 1510)

- visor
- pauldron
- breastplate
- tasset
- vambrace
- gauntlet
- cuisse
- poleyn
- greave

mail		
1000	1100	1200

transition mail to plate

1300

plate		
1400	1500	1600

some comparative weights of complete armour

mail: 9.5 – 14kg
field armour: 18 – 32kg
jousting armour: up to 40kg

an exaggerated feeling of one's superiority. —**arrogance** *n.*, **arrogantly** *adv.* [f. OF (as foll.)]

arrogate /ˈærəgeɪt/ *v.t.* **1.** to claim or seize without right. **2.** to attribute unjustly. —**arrogation** /-ˈgeɪʃ(ə)n/ *n.* [f. L *arrogare* (AD-, *rogare* ask)]

arrow /ˈærəʊ/ *n.* a straight thin pointed shaft to be shot from a bow; a representation of this, especially to show direction. [OE]

arrowhead /ˈærəʊhed/ *n.* the pointed tip of an arrow.

arrowroot /ˈærəʊruːt/ *n.* a nutritious starch prepared from the root of an American plant; this plant.

arse *n.* (*vulg.*) the buttocks. [OE]

arsenal /ˈɑːs(ə)n(ə)l/ *n.* a place where weapons and ammunition are stored or manufactured. [F or f. It. f. Arab., = workshop]

arsenic /ˈɑːs(ə)nɪk/ *n.* a semi-metallic element, symbol As, atomic number 33, existing as a brittle steel-grey solid and in several other allotropic forms; (*pop.*) arsenic trioxide, its main commercial compound. Arsenic occurs naturally as an element and in various minerals, including the sulphides orpiment and realgar, which were formerly used as dyes and pigments. In its elemental form it has a few specialized uses, but several of its compounds, which like the element are highly poisonous, are widely used as herbicides, pesticides, etc. —**arsenical** /ɑːˈsenɪk(ə)l/ *adj.* [f. OF, ult. f. Pers. (*zar* gold)]

arson /ˈɑːs(ə)n/ *n.* the deliberate and criminal act of setting fire to a house or other building. —**arsonist** *n.* [AF f. L (*ardēre* burn)]

art[1] *n.* **1.** human creative skill or its application; the branch of creative activity concerned with the production of imitative and imaginative designs and expression of ideas, especially in painting; products of this. **2.** any skill; a craft or activity requiring imaginative skill. **3.** (in *pl.*) branches of learning (e.g. languages, literature, and history) requiring sympathetic understanding and creative skill as distinct from the technical skills of science. **4.** a specific ability, a knack. **5.** cunning, artfulness: a trick or stratagem. [f. OF f. L *ars*]

art[2] (*archaic*) 2nd person sing. pres. of BE.

Artaud /ɑːˈtəʊ/, Antonin (1896–1948), French actor, director, and poet, one of the seminal influences on experimental theatre after the Second World War. An advocate of surrealism in the 1920s, he later developed the concept of a non-verbal Theatre of Cruelty, freeing the spectator's unconscious, which was embodied in his play *Les Cenci* (1935) and in a series of essays published as *Le Théâtre et son double* (1938).

Artaxerxes /ɑːtəˈzɜːksiːz/ the name of two kings of ancient Persia:

    Artaxerxes I son of Xerxes, reigned 464–424 BC.
    Artaxerxes II son of Darius II, reigned 404–358 BC.

art deco /ɑːt ˈdekəʊ/ a new style in the decorative arts which was defined by the Exposition Internationale des Arts Décoratifs et Industriels held in Paris in 1925. Although applied principally to the decorative arts and interior design of the 1920s and 1930s the term can be extended to analogous styles in architecture and painting. Concentrating on stylishness tuned to domestic use and popular consumption, it is characterized by geometric patterning, sharp edges, and flat bright colours, and often involved the use of enamel, chrome, bronze, and highly polished stone. The simplicity of the style can be seen as classicizing in spirit, attested by the Egyptian and Greek motifs which were often adopted (e.g. the schematized Egyptian scarab). Although it led to a re-confirmation, in both Europe and America, of the role of the craftsman-designer, popularization of the style often resulted in the mass production of less refined objects.

artefact /ˈɑːtɪfækt/ *n.* a man-made object, especially a tool, weapon, or vessel as an archaeological item. [f. L *arte* by art, *facere* make]

Artemis /ˈɑːtɪmɪs/ (*Gk myth.*) a goddess who is probably pre-Hellenic. Daughter of Zeus, sister of Apollo, and a huntress, she is identified with Selene and Diana, and presided over birth, fertility, and fruitfulness. Her temple at Ephesus was one of the Seven Wonders of the World, but here her characteristics were those of an eastern nature-goddess, and her statue had rows of egg-shaped objects, either breasts or eggs (a symbol of fertility) across the chest. 'Great is Diana of the Ephesians' was the cry of the silversmiths at Ephesus when they found their trade in silver shrines of Diana threatened by St Paul's preaching (Acts 19: 24 ff.).

arteriosclerosis /ɑːtɪərɪəʊsklɪəˈrəʊsɪs/ *n.* hardening of the walls of arteries, so that blood circulation is hindered. [f. ARTERY + SCLEROSIS]

artery /ˈɑːtərɪ/ *n.* **1.** any of the tubes conveying blood away from the heart to all parts of the body. **2.** a main road or railway line. —**arterial** /ɑːˈtɪərɪəl/ *adj.* [f. L f. Gk (prob. f. *airō* raise)]

artesian /ɑːˈtiːʒ(ə)n/ a well in which water rises to the surface by natural pressure through a vertically drilled hole. [f. F《*Artois* an old province of France)]

artful *adj.* crafty, cunningly clever at getting what one wants. —**artfully** *adv.*, **artfulness** *n.* [f. ART[1]]

arthritis /ɑːˈθraɪtɪs/ *n.* a condition in which there is pain and stiffness in a joint or joints. —**arthritic** /ɑːˈθrɪtɪk/ *adj.* & *n.* [L f. Gk (*arthron* joint)]

arthropod /ˈɑːθrəpɒd/ *n.* an animal of the phylum Arthropoda, with a segmented body and jointed limbs, and typically encased in a hard outer skeleton. Insects, crustaceans, arachnids, centipedes, and millepedes are all arthropods, and, with well over a million species, the phylum is by far the largest in the animal kingdom. [f. Gk *arthron* joint + *pous podos* foot]

Arthur /ˈɑːθə(r)/ a reputed king of Britain, historically perhaps a 5th- or 6th-c. chieftain or general, on whose life and court a mass of legends, in various tongues, have become centred, including the exploits of adventurous knights and the quest for the Holy Grail. The stories are recounted by Malory and others. Geoffrey of Monmouth (12th c.) places his court at Caerleon-on-Usk; the Norman writer Wace (12th c.) mentions the 'Round Table', a device to enable the knights to be seated in such a way that none had precedence.

Arthurian /ɑːˈθjʊərɪən/ *adj.* of King Arthur. [f. prec.]

artichoke /ˈɑːtɪtʃəʊk/ *n.* a plant allied to the thistle; its flower, with thick leaf-like scales used as a vegetable: —**Jerusalem artichoke,** a kind of sunflower with tubers that are used as a vegetable. [f. It. f. Arab.; *Jerusalem* is a corrupt. of It. *girasole* sunflower]

article /ˈɑːtɪk(ə)l/ *n.* **1.** a particular item or commodity. **2.** a short self-contained piece of writing, in a newspaper, journal, etc., or in an encyclopaedia. **3.** a clause or item of an agreement. **4.** the definite or indefinite article (see below). —*v.t.* to bind by articles of apprenticeship. —**definite article,** 'the', **indefinite article,** 'a' or 'an' (or their equivalents in another language). [f. OF f. L *articulus* dim. of *artus* joint]

articular /ɑːˈtɪkjʊlə(r)/ *adj.* of a joint or joints of the body. [f. L (as prec.)]

articulate[1] /ɑːˈtɪkjʊlət/ *adj.* **1.** to express oneself clearly and fluently. **2.** (of speech) spoken clearly, in words. **3.** having joints. —**articulacy** *n.*, **articulately** *adv.*, **articulateness** *n.* [f. L (as ARTICLE)]

articulate[2] /ɑːˈtɪkjʊleɪt/ *v.t./i.* **1.** to speak or express clearly, to pronounce distinctly. **2.** to form a joint *with*. —**articulation** /-ˈleɪʃ(ə)n/ *n.* [as prec.]

articulated /ɑːˈtɪkjʊleɪtɪd/ *adj.* with parts connected or divided by a (flexible) joint or joints. [f. prec.]

artifice /ˈɑːtɪfɪs/ *n.* trickery, a piece of cunning; skill, ingenuity. [F f. L (*ars art*, *facere* make)]

artificer /ɑːˈtɪfɪsə(r)/ *n.* a skilled workman or mechanic. [f. F (as prec.)]

artificial /ɑːtɪˈfɪʃ(ə)l/ *adj.* produced by human art or effort, not originating naturally; affected, insincere. —**artificial insemination,** injection of semen into the uterus other than by copulation. **artificial respiration,** manual or mechanical stimulation of breathing. —**artificiality** /-ʃɪˈælɪtɪ/ *n.*, **artificially** *adv.* [f. OF or L (as ARTIFICE)]

artillery /ɑːˈtɪlərɪ/ *n.* heavy guns used for fighting on land; a branch of an army equipped with these. —**artilleryman** *n.* [f. OF (*artiller* equip)]

artisan /ɑːtɪˈzæn, ˈɑː-/ *n.* a skilled workman, a mechanic. [F f. It. f. L (*artire* instruct in arts)]

artist /ˈɑːtɪst/ *n.* **1.** one who practises any of the fine arts, especially painting. **2.** one who does something with skill or taste. **3.** an artiste. —**artistry** *n.* [f. F f. It. (*arte* art)]

artiste /ɑːˈtiːst/ *n.* a professional performer, especially a singer or dancer. [F (as prec.)]

artistic /ɑːˈtɪstɪk/ *adj.* of art or artists; skilfully or tastefully done; showing aptitude for the fine arts. —**artistically** *adv.* [f. prec.]

artless /ˈɑːtlɪs/ *adj.* **1.** free from artfulness, ingenuous. **2.**

not resulting from art, natural. **3.** crude, clumsy. —**artlessly** *adv.*, **artlessness** *n.* [f. ART¹]

art nouveau /ɑ: nu:ˈvəʊ/ a style of art, architecture, and design from the 1890s to the early 1900s in western Europe. As a decorative style it relied primarily on an organic and generative line that can be found equally in Beardsley's drawings, Mucha's posters, the architectural detail of van de Velde, and Guimard's designs for the Paris Métro. In its insistence on the introduction of good modern design into all aspects of life it became an international European style, but the movement nowhere survived the outbreak of the First World War to any significant extent. [F, = new art]

Arts and Crafts movement an English movement of the second half of the 19th c. which sought to revive, in an industrial age, the ideal of the handcrafted object. The notion of the craftsman employing traditional methods and style had both aesthetic and social implications. William Morris, influenced by J. J. Rousseau, and then by Pugin and Ruskin, translated the nostalgia for hand crafted goods into an organized business venture. (see MORRIS¹). In England the Arts and Crafts movement was closely associated with Pre-Raphaelitism and later with the Aesthetic movement. It influenced many artists and designers, including Walter Crane and C. R. Ashbee, who established the Guild and School of Arts and Crafts, London.

arty /ˈɑ:tɪ/ *adj.* (*colloq.*) pretentiously or quaintly artistic. —**artiness** *n.* [f. ART¹]

arum /ˈeərəm/ *n.* a plant of the genus *Arum* with small flowers enclosed in bracts. —**arum lily,** a cultivated white arum. [L f. Gk *aron*]

Arunachal Pradesh /ɑ:rəˈnɑ:tʃ(ə)l prəˈdeʃ/ a Union Territory of NE India, the North-east Frontier Agency of British India; capital, Itanagar.

Arunta /əˈrʌntə/ var. of ARANDA.

Aryan /ˈeərɪən/ *adj.* **1.** of the Indo-European family of languages. **2.** of the ancient inhabitants of the Iranian plateau speaking a language of this family. —*n.* **1.** a member of the Aryan peoples (not to be regarded as a race; see below). **2.** (in Nazi Germany) a non-Jewish European, a person of Nordic racial type. [f. Skr. *āryas* noble, earlier used as a national name]
   The idea current in the 19th c. of an Aryan race corresponding to a definite Aryan language was taken up by nationalistic, historical, and romantic writers. It was given especial currency by M. A. de Gobineau, who linked it with the theory of the essential inferiority of certain races. The term 'Aryan race' was later revived and used for purposes of political propaganda in Nazi Germany.

As *symbol* arsenic.

as /əz, emphat. æz/ *adv. & conj.* **1.** to the same extent; in the manner in which; in the capacity or form of; for instance. **2.** during or at the time of. **3.** for the reason that, seeing that. —*rel. pron.* that, who, which. —**as from**, on or after (a specified date). **as if,** as would be the case if. **as it were,** as if it was actually so, in a way. **as of,** as from, as at (a specified time). **as though,** as if. **as to,** with regard to. **as well,** advisable, desirable, reasonably. **as well (as),** in addition (to). **as yet,** until now. [f. OE *alswā* also]

asafoetida /æsəˈfiːtɪdə/ *n.* a resinous strong-smelling plant gum formerly used in medicine. [L f. Pers. *azā* mastic; *fetida* fetid]

asbestos /æsˈbestɒs/ *n.* a fibrous silicate mineral; a fire-resistant substance made from this. [f. OF f. L f. Gk, = unquenchable]

asbestosis /æsbesˈtəʊsɪs/ *n.* a lung disease caused by inhaling asbestos particles. [f. prec.]

ascend /əˈsend/ *v.t./i.* to move upwards, to rise; to climb. —**ascend the throne,** to become king or queen. [f. L *ascendere* (AD-, *scandere* climb)]

ascendancy /əˈsendənsɪ/ *n.* dominant power or control (*over*). [f. foll.]

ascendant /əˈsend(ə)nt/ *adj.* ascending, rising; gaining ascendancy; (*Astron.*) rising towards the zenith; (*Astrol.*, of a sign) just above the eastern horizon. —*n.* (*Astrol.*) the point of the ecliptic that is ascendant at a given time, e.g. at the birth of a child. A planet close to this point is held to have special influence upon the life of a child then born. —**in the ascendant,** at or near the peak of one's fortunes; (*pop.*) rising. [f. OF f. L (as ASCEND)]

ascension /əˈsenʃ(ə)n/ *n.* ascent, especially (**Ascension**) that of Christ into Heaven, witnessed by the Apostles.

—**Ascension Day,** the Thursday on which this is commemorated, the 40th day after Easter. [as prec.]

Ascension Island a small island in the South Atlantic, incorporated with St Helena; pop. (1984) 1,438. It was discovered by the Portuguese, traditionally on Ascension Day in 1501, but remained uninhabited until a small British garrison was stationed there on the arrival of Napoleon for imprisonment on St Helena in 1815. It is now a British telecommunications centre and a US air base. The island has been strategically important during (and since) the military operations in the Falkland Islands in 1982, serving as a base for British forces and a landing-point for aircraft travelling between Britain and the South Atlantic.

ascent /əˈsent/ *n.* **1.** ascending; rise. **2.** a way up, an upward path or slope. [f. ASCEND]

ascertain /æsəˈteɪn/ *v.t.* to find out for certain, especially by making enquiries. **ascertainable** *adj.*, **ascertainment** *n.* [f. OF (as CERTAIN)]

ascetic /əˈsetɪk/ *adj.* severely abstinent, austere; having the appearance of an ascetic. —*n.* a person leading an ascetic life, especially one doing this in a religious cause. —**ascetically** *adv.*, **asceticism** /-ɪsɪz(ə)m/ *n.* [f. L or f. Gk (*askētēs* monk, *askeō* exercise)]

ascidian /əˈsɪdɪən/ *n.* a tunicate of the order Ascidiacea, especially a sea-squirt. [f. Gk, dim. of *askos* wine-skin]

Asclepius /əˈskliːpɪəs/ (*Gk myth.*) a hero and god of healing, often represented bearing a staff with a serpent coiled round it. The scroll or tablet which he sometimes bears probably represents medical learning.

ascorbic acid /əˈskɔ:bɪk/ vitamin C, which prevents scurvy, found especially in citrus fruits and in vegetables. [f. Gk *a-* not + SCORBUTIC]

Ascot /ˈæskət/ a race-course near Windsor, Berks., and scene of an annual race-meeting in June, founded by Queen Anne in 1711. —**Ascot week,** this race-meeting.

ascribable /əˈskraɪbəb(ə)l/ *adj.* that may be ascribed. [f. foll.]

ascribe /əˈskraɪb/ *v.t.* to attribute. **ascription** /-ˈskrɪpʃ(ə)n/ *n.* [f. L *ascribere* (AD-, *scribere* write)]

asdic /ˈæzdɪk/ *n.* an early form of sonar. [f. initials of *Anti-Submarine Detection Investigation Committee*]

asepsis /eɪˈsepsɪs/ *n.* aseptic methods or conditions (see ANTISEPTIC). [f. Gk *a-* not + SEPSIS]

aseptic /eɪˈseptɪk/ *adj.* free from sepsis, especially that caused by micro-organisms, surgically sterile; aiming at the absence rather than the counteraction (cf. ANTISEPTIC) of septic matter. —**aseptically** *adv.* [f. Gk *a-* not + SEPTIC]

asexual /eɪˈseksjʊəl/ *adj.* without sex or sexuality; (of reproduction) not involving the fusion of gametes, —**asexually** *adv.* [f. Gk *a-* not + SEXUAL]

Asgard /ˈæzgɑ:d/ (*Scand. myth.*) a region in the centre of the universe, inhabited by the gods.

ash¹ *n.* (freq. in *pl.*) the whitish grey powdery residue left after combustion of any substance; (in *pl.*) the remains of a human body after cremation. —**the Ashes,** see separate entry. **Ash Wednesday,** the first day of Lent, so called from the former custom of sprinkling ashes on penitents' heads. [OE]

ash² *n.* a tree of the genus *Fraxinus* with silver-grey bark and pinnate foliage (ill. TREES); its hard close-grained wood. [OE]

ashamed /əˈʃeɪmd/ *adj.* (usu. *predic.*) feeling or affected by shame; reluctant or hesitant through shame. [OE (as A-, SHAME)]

ashbin *n.* a dustbin. [f. ASH¹]

ashen *adj.* of or like ashes, pale as ashes. [f. ASH¹]

Asher /ˈæʃə(r)/ **1.** Hebrew patriarch, son of Jacob and Zilpah (Gen. 30: 12, 13). **2.** the tribe of Israel traditionally descended from him.

Ashes, the a trophy for the winner of a series of test matches in cricket between England and Australia. The term originated in a mock obituary notice published in the *Sporting Times* 2 Sept. 1882, after the sensational victory of Australia: 'In Affectionate Remembrance of English Cricket Which died at the Oval on 29th August, 1882. Deeply lamented by a large circle of sorrowing friends and acquaintances. R.I.P. N.B.—The body will be cremated and the ashes taken to Australia.' Real ashes exist, kept in an urn at Lord's, and are said to be those of a bail (or a ball) burnt at Melbourne when England won the series of 1882–3.

Ashkenazi /æʃkɪˈnɑ:zɪ/ *n.* (*pl.* **-im**) a Jew of northern and eastern Europe, as distinct from a Sephardi. —**Ashkenazic** *adj.* [Heb., f. *Ashkenaz* (Gen. 10: 3)]

ashlar /'æʃlə(r)/ *n.* square-hewn stones, masonry made of these (ill. BUILDING); thin slabs of this used for facing walls. [f. OF f. L, dim. of *axis* board]

Ashmolean Museum /æʃ'məʊliən/ a museum of art and antiquities in Oxford, founded by the English antiquary Elias Ashmole (1617-92). In 1677 he deposited with Oxford University a number of items, some collected by himself, others forming the 'closett of Rarities' bequeathed to him by his friend John Tradescant (d. 1662), which formed the nucleus of the museum (opened in 1683), the first public institution of this kind in England, open to anyone who paid the entrance fee. From the first it was popular with the general public. The collection now includes archaeological material, European works of art, and Oriental works.

ashore /ə'ʃɔː(r)/ *adv.* to or on shore; on land. [f. A- + SHORE]

ashram /'æʃræm/ *n.* (in India etc.) a place of religious learning or retreat. [f. Skr., = hermitage]

Ashton /'æʃt(ə)n/, Sir Frederick (1904-), British dancer, choreographer, and ballet director. He became chief choreographer of the Vic-Wells Ballet in 1935, remaining with the company when it became the Sadler's Wells and finally the Royal Ballet, and being appointed associate director in 1952 and director 1963-70. As brilliant in creating new works as in adapting historical ballets, he shows a soft, fluid, lyrical classicism. His important ballets include *Façade*, *Symphonic Variations* (1946), *Romeo and Juliet* (1955), *La Fille mal gardée* (1960), *The Dream* (1964), and *A Month in the Country* (1976).

ashtray *n.* a receptacle for tobacco ash.

Ashurbanipal /æʃʊə'baːnɪp(ə)l/ (668-627 BC) the last great king of Assyria. His principal campaigns were to Egypt (where he was ultimately unsuccessful), to Babylon (where he suppressed a revolt), and to Elam (where he sacked Susa). He is celebrated for his library of over 20,000 clay tablets at Nineveh, which included literary, religious, scientific, and administrative documents, many of them copies of ancient texts.

ashy *adj.* like ash, ashen; covered with ashes. [f. ASH¹]

Asia /'eɪʃə/ the largest of the world's continents, constituting nearly one-third of the land mass, lying entirely north of the equator except for some SE Asian islands. It is connected to Africa by the isthmus of Suez, and generally divided from Europe (which forms part of the same land mass) by a line running through the Ural Mountains and the Caspian Sea. The continent is currently dominated by the USSR, China, and India, the last two descended from long imperial traditions and civilizations stretching back into the ancient world, the first a product of progressive eastern expansion by European Russia. Many of the peripheral areas, particularly in the south, were colonized by European nations between the 17th and 19th centuries, emerging as indepedent States only after the Second World War.

Asia Minor the westernmost part of Asia (see ANATOLIA), now comprising Asiatic Turkey. The first major civilization established there was that of the Hittites in the 2nd millennium BC. The Greeks colonized the western coast (see IONIA), while the kingdoms of Lydia and Phrygia developed independently. The land was subjugated by various invaders, including Cyrus of Persia (546 BC) and Alexander the Great (333 BC). It was subsequently the Roman province of Asia and then part of the Byzantine empire. Conquered by the Turks, it became part of the Ottoman empire from the end of the 13th c. until the establishment of modern Turkey after the First World War. (See TURKEY.)

Asian /'eɪʃ(ə)n, 'eɪʒ-/ *adj.* of Asia. —*n.* an Asian person. [f. L f. Gk]

Asiatic /eɪzɪ'ætɪk/ *adj.* of Asia. [as prec.]

aside /ə'saɪd/ *adv.* to or on one side, away from the main part or group. —*n.* words spoken aside. [f. A- + SIDE]

Asimov /'æsɪmɒf/, Isaac (1920-), Russian-born American author of science fiction and of books on science for the layman. He coined the term 'robotic' (see entry).

asinine /'æsɪnaɪn/ *adj.* like an ass, silly, stupid. —**asininity** /-'nɪnɪtɪ/ *n.* [f. L (*asinus* ass)]

ask /ɑːsk/ *v.t./i.* **1.** to call for an answer to or about, to address a question to. **2.** to seek to obtain from someone. **3.** to invite. [OE]

askance /ə'skæns/ *adv.* with a sideways look. —**look askance at**, to regard with distrust or disapproval. [orig. unkn.]

askew /ə'skjuː/ *adv.* & *pred. adj.* not straight or level, oblique(ly). [f. A- + SKEW]

aslant /ə'slɑːnt/ *adv.* on a slant, obliquely. —*prep.* obliquely across. [f. A- + SLANT]

asleep /ə'sliːp/ *predic. adj.* sleeping; (of a limb etc.) numb. —*adv.* into a state of sleep. [f. A- + SLEEP]

asocial /'eɪsəʊʃ(ə)l/ *adj.* not social; not sociable; (*colloq.*) inconsiderate. [f. Gk *a-* not + SOCIAL]

Asoka /ə'səʊkə/ (died *c.*232 BC) Buddhist emperor of India from *c.*269 BC, ruling over the greater part of the peninsula. He embarked on a campaign of conquest, but after his conversion to Buddhism renounced war and sent out missionaries as far afield as Syria and Ceylon to spread his new faith.

asp *n.* a small poisonous viper of Africa and southern Europe. [f. OF or L f. Gk]

asparagus /ə'spærəgəs/ *n.* a plant of the genus *Asparagus*, especially a species (*A. officinalis*) whose young shoots are cooked and eaten as a vegetable; this food. [L f. Gk]

aspect /'æspekt/ *n.* **1.** a person's or thing's appearance, especially to the mind, a feature by which a matter is considered. **2.** the direction a thing faces, the side of a building etc. facing a particular direction. **3.** (*Astrol.*) the relative position of planets etc., regarded as influencing events. [f. L (*adspicere* look at)]

aspen *n.* a kind of poplar with especially tremulous leaves. [OE (earlier *asp*)]

asperity /ə'sperɪtɪ/ *n.* harshness of temper or tone. [f. OF or L (*asper* rough)]

aspersion /ə'spɜːʃ(ə)n/ *n.* a damaging or derogatory remark. —**cast aspersions on**, to attack the reputation of. [f. L *aspergere* sprinkle]

asphalt /'æsfælt/ *n.* a tarlike bitumen made from petroleum; a mixture of this with sand and gravel for use in paving etc. Most asphalt is obtained from oil refineries, from the distillation of certain crude oils, but it can occur naturally in surface deposits. —*v.t.* to coat or pave with asphalt. [f. L f. Gk]

asphodel /'æsfədel/ *n.* a plant of the genus *Asphodeline* or *Asphodelus*, of the lily family; (*poet*) an immortal flower growing in Elysium. [f. L f. Gk]

asphyxia /æs'fɪksɪə/ *n.* lack of oxygen in the blood through impaired respiration, causing unconsciousness or death; suffocation. [f. Gk (*a-* not, *sphuxis* pulse)]

asphyxiate /æs'fɪksɪeɪt/ *v.t./i.* to cause asphyxia in; to suffocate. —**asphyxiation** /-'eɪʃ(ə)n/ *n.* [f. prec.]

aspic /'æspɪk/ *n.* a savoury jelly for holding meat, fish, egg, etc. [F, = asp (the colours of the jelly being compared to those of the asp)]

aspidistra /æspɪ'dɪstrə/ *n.* a plant of the genus *Aspidistra*, with broad tapering leaves, often grown as a house-plant. [f. Gk *aspis* shield]

aspirant /'æspɪrənt, ə'spaɪər-/ *n.* one who aspires, especially to an honour or position. —*adj.* aspiring. [F or f. L (as ASPIRE)]

aspirate¹ /'æspəreɪt/ *v.t.* **1.** to pronounce with an initial *h* or with release of breath. **2.** to draw (fluid) by suction from a cavity etc. [f. L as ASPIRE)]

aspirate² /'æspərət/ *n.* the sound of *h*; a consonant pronounced with this. —*adj.* pronounced with an aspirate. [as prec.]

aspiration /æspə'reɪʃ(ə)n/ *n.* **1.** ambition, strong desire. **2.** aspirating. **3.** the drawing of breath. [as ASPIRE]

aspirator /'æspəreɪtə(r)/ *n.* a device for drawing fluid from a cavity etc. [as foll.]

aspire /ə'spaɪə(r)/ *v.i.* to have an ambition or strong desire. [f. F or L *adspirare* breathe upon]

aspirin /'æsp(ə)rɪn/ *n.* a white powder, acetylsalicylic acid, used to relieve pain and reduce fever; a tablet of this. Aspirin was developed in Germany in the late 1890s, originally to reduce inflammation, and was discovered to have pain-relieving properties too. [G]

Asquith /'æskwɪθ/, Herbert Henry, 1st Earl of Oxford and Asquith (1852-1928), British statesman, who succeeded Campbell-Bannerman as Liberal leader and Prime Minister in 1908. In the years before the First World War his administration had to face a host of problems, most notably the conflict with the House of Lords caused by the introduction of Lloyd George's People's Budget in 1909, Irish demands for Home Rule, industrial unrest, and the women's suffrage movement. After the beginning of the war Asquith proved increasingly unequal to the task of leadership and was eventually displaced by Lloyd George at the end of 1916. He remained leader of the Liberal Party until 1926, but the party's fortunes declined sharply after the wartime split with Lloyd George.

ass[1] *n.* **1.** a quadruped of the horse genus with long ears, a donkey, regarded in ancient times as the embodiment of lust quite as much as stupidity. **2.** a stupid person. [OE f. L *asinus*]

ass[2] *n.* (*US, vulg.*) = ARSE.

assail /ə'seɪl/ *v.t.* **1.** to attack physically or verbally. **2.** to begin (a task) resolutely. —**assailant** *n.* [f. OF f. L *assilire* (AD-, *salire* leap)]

Assam /æ'sæm/ a State in NE India, formed in 1947; capital, Dispur. Parts have since been separated off as the States of Meghalaya and Nagaland and the Union Territories of Arunachal Pradesh and Mizoram. —**Assamese** /-'miːz/ *adj. & n.*

assassin /ə'sæsɪn/ *n.* **1.** one who assassinates another. **2. Assassin,** any of a number of Muslim fanatics in the time of the Crusades, sent on murder errands by Hasan-ben-Sabah (the 'Old Man of the Mountains') or later leaders and notorious for a series of killings of political and religious opponents (see AGA KHAN). [ult. f. Arab. (pl.) = hashish-takers, so called because they acted as if crazed by hashish]

assassinate /ə'sæsɪneɪt/ *v.t.* to kill (an important person) by violent means, usually for political or religious motives. —**assassination** /-'neɪʃ(ə)n/ *n.*, **assassinator** *n.* [as prec.]

assault /ə'sɔːlt/ *n.* a violent physical or verbal attack; (*euphem.*) rape; (*Law*) a threat or display of violence against a person. —*v.t.* to make an assault on, to attack. [f. OF f. L (as ASSAIL)]

assay /ə'seɪ/ *n.* a test of metal or ore to determine its ingredients and quality. —*v.t./i.* **1.** to make an assay of (metal). **2.** (*archaic*) to attempt. [f. OF, var. of *essai* essay]

assegai /'æsɪɡaɪ/ *n.* a light iron-tipped spear of South African peoples. [f. F or Port. f. Arab., = the spear]

assemblage /ə'semblɪdʒ/ *n.* **1.** coming together. **2.** an assembly; things assembled. [f. foll.]

assemble /ə'semb(ə)l/ *v.t./i.* to bring or come together; to fit or put (components, or a completed whole) together. —**assembler** *n.* [f. OF f. L (ad to, *simul* together)]

assembly /ə'semblɪ/ *n.* **1.** assembling. **2.** an assembled group; a deliberative body. —**assembly line,** machinery arranged in a sequence by which a product is progressively assembled. [as prec.]

assent /ə'sent/ *n.* (official) consent or approval. —*v.i.* to express agreement, to consent. —**assenter** *n.* [f. OF f. L *assentari* (AD-, *sentire* think)]

assert /ə'sɜːt/ *v.t.* **1.** to declare as true, to state. **2.** to enforce a claim to (rights). —**assert oneself,** to insist on one's rights or recognition; to take effective action. —**assertion** *n.*, **assertive** *n.* [f. L *asserere* (AD-, *serere* join)]

assess /ə'ses/ *v.t.* to estimate the value of (property) for taxation; to decide or fix the amount of (a tax, penalty, etc.). —**assessment** *n.* [f. F f. L *assidēre* sit by]

assessor /ə'sesə(r)/ *n.* **1.** one who assesses, especially for tax or insurance. **2.** one who advises a judge in court on technical matters. [f. OF f. L, = assistant-judge]

asset /'æset/ *n.* a possession having value, especially that which can be used or sold to meet debts etc.; a useful quality, skill, or person. [f. AF f. L (ad to, *satis* enough)]

asseverate /ə'sevəreɪt/ *v.t.* to state solemnly. —**asseveration** /-'reɪʃ(ə)n/ *n.* [f. L *asseverare* (AD-, *severus* serious)]

assiduous /ə'sɪdjʊəs/ *adj.* persevering, working with diligence and close attention. —**assiduity** /æsɪ'djuːɪtɪ/ *n.* **assiduously** *adv.*, **assiduousness** *n.* [f. L (as ASSESS)]

assign /ə'saɪn/ *v.t.* to allot; to put aside or specify for a particular purpose; to designate; to ascribe or attribute; (*Law*) to transfer formally. —**assignable** *adj.* [f. OF f. L *assignare* mark out to (*signum* sign)]

assignation /æsɪɡ'neɪʃ(ə)n/ *n.* **1.** an appointment to meet, especially by lovers in secret. **2.** assigning. [as prec.]

assignment /ə'saɪnmənt/ *n.* **1.** a thing assigned, especially a task or duty; a share. **2.** assigning. [f. ASSIGN]

assimilate /ə'sɪmɪleɪt/ *v.t./i.* **1.** to absorb or become absorbed. **2.** to make alike or similar (*to*). —**assimilable** *adj.*, **assimilation** /-'leɪʃ(ə)n/ *n.* [f. L *assimilare* (AD-, *similis* like)]

Assisi /ə'siːsɪ/ a town in central Italy, famous as the birth-place of St Francis.

assist /ə'sɪst/ *v.t./i.* to help. —**assistance** *n.* [f. F f. L *assistere* take one's stand by]

assistant /ə'sɪst(ə)nt/ *n.* one who assists, a helper; one who

serves customers in a shop. —*adj.* assisting, helping a senior and ranking next below him or her. [as prec.]

assizes /ə'saɪzɪz/ *n.pl.* a periodical county session, held until 1972, for the administration of civil and criminal justice. [f. F f. L (as ASSESS)]

associate[1] /ə'səʊsɪeɪt, -ʃɪeɪt/ *v.t./i.* **1.** to connect in one's mind. **2.** to join as a companion or colleague etc.; to act together for a common purpose; to have frequent dealings (*with*). **3.** to declare (oneself) as being in agreement *with*. —**associative** *adj.* [f. L *associare* (AD-, *socius* sharing, allied)]

associate[2] /ə'səʊsɪət, -ʃɪət/ *n.* **1.** a subordinate member of a society etc. **2.** a partner or colleague. —*adj.* **1.** associated **2.** having subordinate membership. [as prec.]

association /əsəʊsɪ'eɪʃ(ə)n, -ʃɪ-/ *n.* **1.** a body of persons organized for a common purpose. **2.** a mental connection of ideas. **3.** associating, companionship. —**Association football,** the kind of football played between two teams of 11 players with a round ball which may not be handled in play except by the goalkeeper. Scoring is by goals. (See ill. SPORTS.)

assonance /'æs(ə)nəns/ *n.* resemblance of sound between two syllables; a rhyme depending on identity in vowel-sounds only (as *sonnet/porridge*) or in consonants only (as *killed/cold*). —**assonant** *adj.*, **assonantal** /-'nænt(ə)l/ *adj.* [F f. L *assonare* (AD-, *sonus* sound)]

assort /ə'sɔːt/ *v.t./i.* **1.** to arrange in sorts, to classify. **2.** to suit or harmonize (*with*). [f. OF (à to, *sorte* sort)]

assorted /ə'sɔːtɪd/ *adj.* **1.** of various sorts, mixed. **2.** matched. [f. prec.]

assortment /ə'sɔːtmənt/ *n.* **1.** an assorted group or mixture. **2.** classification. [f. ASSORT]

assuage /ə'sweɪdʒ/ *v.t.* to soothe, to make less severe; to appease (an appetite). —**assuagement** *n.* [f. OF f. L *suavis* sweet]

assume /ə'sjuːm/ *v.t.* **1.** to take as true or sure to happen. **2.** to put on oneself (a role or attitude etc.); to undertake (an office). [f. L *assumere* (AD-, *sumere* take)]

assuming /ə'sjuːmɪŋ/ *adj.* presumptuous, arrogant. [f. prec.]

assumption /ə'sʌmpʃ(ə)n/ *n.* assuming, a thing assumed. —**the Assumption,** the taking of the Virgin Mary in bodily form into heaven; the festival commemorating this (15 Aug.). The doctrine dates from the 4th c. and is held by the Roman Catholic and Orthodox Churches. In the Church of England the feast was removed from the Book of Common Prayer in 1549 and has not been officially restored.

assurance /ə'ʃʊərəns/ *n.* **1.** a formal declaration or promise, a guarantee. **2.** self-confidence. **3.** certainty. **4.** insurance, especially of life. Insurance companies tend to use the term *assurance* of policies where a sum is payable after a fixed number of years or on the death of the insured person, and *insurance* of policies relating to events such as fire, accident, or death within a limited period. In popular usage the word *insurance* is used in both cases. [f. foll.]

assure /ə'ʃʊə(r)/ *v.t.* **1.** to make (a person) sure (*of* a fact), to convince; to tell confidently. **2.** to ensure the happening etc. of, to guarantee. **3.** to insure (especially life). [f. OF f. L AD-, *securus* safe]

assured /ə'ʃʊəd/ *adj.* made sure; confident. —**assuredly** /-rɪdlɪ/ *adv.* certainly. [f. prec.]

Assyria /ə'sɪrɪə/ an ancient country in what is now northern Iraq. It was originally centred on Ashur, a city-state on the west bank of the Tigris, which first became prominent and expanded its borders in the 14th c. BC. From the 8th to the late 7th c. BC Assyria was the dominant Near Eastern power and created an empire which stretched from the Persian Gulf to Egypt. The State fell in 612 BC, defeated by a coalition of Medes and Chaldeans. —**Assyrian** *adj. & n.*

Assyriology /əsɪrɪ'ɒlədʒɪ/ *n.* the study of the history, language, etc., of Assyria. [f. prec. + -LOGY]

Astarte /ə'stɑːtɪ/ (*Semitic myth.*) a Phoenician goddess of fertility and sexual love, whose cult was widespread. She became identified with the Egyptian Isis, the Greek Aphrodite, and others. In the Bible she is referred to as Ashtaroth or Ashtoreth, and her worship is linked with that of Baal.

astatine /'æstətiːn/ *n.* a radioactive element, symbol At, atomic number 85. The heaviest of the halogens, it occurs naturally in minute quantities but was first prepared artificially in 1940 by bombarding bismuth with alpha particles. [f. Gk *astatos* unstable]

aster *n.* a composite plant of the genus *Aster* with bright daisy-like flowers. [L f. Gk, = star]

asterisk /ˈæstərɪsk/ n. a star-shaped symbol (*) used to mark words etc. for reference or distinction. —v.t. to mark with an asterisk. [f. L f. Gk, = little star]

astern /əˈstɜːn/ adv. **1.** in or to the rear of a ship or aircraft, behind. **2.** backwards. [f. A- + STERN]

asteroid /ˈæstərɔɪd/ n. **1.** any of the minor planets. **2.** a starfish. [f. Gk (astēr star)]

asthma /ˈæsmə/ n. a respiratory disease (frequently connected with an allergy), often with paroxysms of difficult breathing. —**asthmatic** /æsˈmætɪk/ adj. & n. [f. L f. Gk (azō breathe hard)]

astigmatism /əˈstɪgmətɪz(ə)m/ n. a defect in an eye or lens, preventing rays of light from a point from being brought to a common focus. —**astigmatic** /æstɪgˈmætɪk/ adj., **astigmatically** adv. [f. Gk a- not + stigma point]

astir /əˈstɜː(r)/ adv. & predic. adj. in motion; out of bed. [f. A- + STIR]

Aston /ˈæst(ə)n/, Francis William (1877–1945), English physicist who worked in Cambridge with J. J. Thomson, and invented the mass spectrograph. With this apparatus he could separate electrically charged particles according to their atomic weights, and eventually discovered many of the 287 naturally occurring isotopes of non-radioactive elements, and in 1919 announced his whole-number rule governing their masses. He was awarded the Nobel Prize for chemistry in 1922.

astonish /əˈstɒnɪʃ/ v.t. to surprise very greatly. —**astonishment** n. [f. OF f. L (tonare thunder)]

astound /əˈstaʊnd/ v.t. to shock with surprise. [as prec.]

astragal /ˈæstrəg(ə)l/ n. a small moulding, of semicircular section, placed round the top or bottom of a column (ill. TEMPLES). [f. L f. Gk]

astrakhan /æstrəˈkæn/ n. the dark tightly curled fleece of lambs from Astrakhan in Russia; an imitation of this.

astral /ˈæstr(ə)l/ adj. of or connected with stars. —**astral body**, a supposed ethereal counterpart of the body. [f. L (astrum star)]

astray /əˈstreɪ/ adv. out of the right way. —**go astray**, to be missing; to fall into error or wrongdoing. [f. OF f. L extra away, vagari wander]

astride /əˈstraɪd/ adv. with one leg on either side (of); with feet wide apart. —prep. astride of; extending across. [f. A- + STRIDE]

astringent /əˈstrɪndʒ(ə)nt/ adj. **1.** that causes contraction of body tissue and checks bleeding. **2.** severe, austere. —n. an astringent substance. —**astringency** n. [F f. L (AD-, stringere bind)]

astrolabe /ˈæstrəleɪb/ n. an instrument formerly used for measuring the altitudes of stars etc. Its form and structure varied with the progress of astronomy and the purpose for which it was intended. In its earliest form (which dates from classical times) it consisted of a disc with the degrees of the circle marked round its edge, and a pivoted pointer along which a heavenly body could be sighted. From late medieval times it was used by mariners for calculating latitude, until replaced by the sextant. [f. OF f. L f. Gk, = star-taking]

astrology /əˈstrɒlədʒɪ/ n. study of the positions and movements of stars regarded as having an influence on human affairs (see below). —**astrologer** n., **astrological** /æstrəˈlɒdʒɪk(ə)l/ adj., **astrologically** adv. [f. OF f. L f. Gk (astron star, -LOGY)]

Astrology, long seen as applied astronomy, was developed by the Greeks and reached Christian Europe via the Arabs. It was a utilitarian science linked to medicine and agriculture, and also an ambitious philosophical system resting on the belief that the stars influenced the entire sublunar world. By studying eclipses, comets, and the movements of the planets in the zodiac, astrologers felt able to predict such effects as wars, plagues, and the weather. They found a key to a person's whole life in his horoscope, the disposition of the planets at his birth. In the Renaissance popes such as Paul III (1534–49) were enthusiastic patrons, and many rulers employed court astrologers for both political and medical assistance, Nostradamus (16th c.) being the best known. A papal bull of 1586 condemned judicial astrology, and the Protestant reformer Calvin was hostile, but its decline was slow and many leading scientists in the 17th c. thought it had at least a residual basis of truth. Though it had lost its intellectual standing by 1700, popular writers such as Old Moore (see Francis MOORE) gave it a widespread appeal which has survived to the present day.

It still retains a more reputable standing in many parts of the East.

astronaut /ˈæstrənɔːt/ n. a traveller in space. [f. Gk astron star, nautēs sailor]

astronautics /æstrəˈnɔːtɪks/ n. the science of space travel and its technology. —**astronautical** adj. [as prec.]

astronomical /æstrəˈnɒmɪk(ə)l/ adj. **1.** of astronomy. **2.** vast in amount. —**astronomically** adv. [as foll.]

astronomy /əˈstrɒnəmɪ/ n. the science of the heavenly bodies and their movements (see below and ill. pp. 49–50). —**astronomer** n. [f. OF f. L f. Gk (astron star, nemō arrange)]

From time immemorial man has charted the positions and motions of the sun and moon, stars and planets, his original naked-eye results later refined by the use of the telescope and interpreted by the mathematics of celestial mechanics and positional astronomy. The classification and interpretation of celestial objects depend now on the use of the most sophisticated instruments to measure positions and brightness: radio telescopes, infra-red detectors, ultraviolet and X-ray satellites are all used, while robot probes can visit the planets, nearest of our neighbours in space. Once the science of regular celestial phenomena, upon which timekeeping and navigation depended, astronomy has expanded to ask about the nature and content of the entire universe.

astrophysics /æstrəʊˈfɪzɪks/ n. the branch of astronomy concerned with the physics and chemistry of the heavenly bodies. The science draws heavily on the applications of known physical laws to understand the observations of astronomers, and reveals in turn new laws operating in the extreme conditions of temperature and density not attainable on earth. —**astrophysical** adj., **astrophysicist** n. [f. Gk astron star + PHYSICS]

Asturias /æˈstjʊərɪəs/ a region of NW Spain. —**Prince of the Asturias**, the former title of the eldest son of the king of Spain.

astute /əˈstjuːt/ adj. shrewd, seeing how to gain an advantage. —**astutely** adv., **astuteness** n. [f. F or L (astus craft)]

Asunción /əsʊnsɪˈɒn/ the capital and chief port of Paraguay; pop. (est. 1982) 720,000.

asunder /əˈsʌndə(r)/ adv. (formal) apart, in pieces. [OE on sundran into pieces]

Asura /əˈsjʊərə/ (Hinduism) an evil demon, enemy of the gods (in Veda frequently a god).

Aswan /æsˈwɑːn/ a city in southern Egypt near which are two dams across the Nile. The first was built in 1898–1902 to regulate the flooding of the Nile and control the supply of water for irrigation and other purposes. It is now superseded by the high dam, built in 1960–70 with Soviet aid, about 3.6 km (2¼ miles) long and 111 m (364 ft.) high, a feat of building comparable to that of the pyramids. Behind it is the enormous reservoir of Lake Nasser, and its controlled release not only ensures a steady supply of water for irrigation and domestic and industrial use but produces hydroelectric power sufficient to supply the greater part of Egypt's electricity.

asylum /əˈsaɪləm/ n. **1.** a place of refuge (formerly for criminals). **2.** (in full **political asylum**) protection given by a State to a political refugee from another country. **3.** (hist.) an institution for the care and shelter of insane or destitute persons. [f. L f. Gk, = refuge (a- not, sulon right of seizure)]

asymmetry /æˈsɪmətrɪ, eɪ-/ n. lack of symmetry. —**asymmetric** /-ˈmetrɪk/ adj., **asymmetrical** adj. [f. Gk a- not + SYMMETRY]

At symbol astatine.

at /ət, emphatic æt/ prep. **1.** having as position, time of day, state, or price. **2.** with motion or aim towards. —**at it**, working, in activity. [OE]

Atalanta /ætəˈlæntə/ (Gk legend) a huntress, averse to marriage, loved by Meleager. She would marry no one who could not beat her in a foot-race, but Melanion (or Hippomenes) won the race by throwing down three golden apples given to him by Aphrodite, which were so beautiful that Atalanta stopped to pick them up.

Atatürk /ˈætətɜːk/, Kemal (1881–1938), Turkish general and statesman. A successful general in the Gallipoli campaign in 1915. Atatürk organized the Turkish Nationalist Party after the war, and, elected President of a provisional government in 1920, launched a victorious campaign to drive Greek invaders from Turkish soil. With the official establishment of the Turkish republic in 1923, he was elected its first president and remained in power until his death, wielding almost dictatorial powers in his struggle to make Turkey a modern secular State. Known first as Mustapha Kemal, and then as Kemal Pasha, he took the name of Atatürk (= father-Turk) in 1934.

atavism /ˈætəvɪz(ə)m/ n. resemblance to remote ancestors rather than to parents, reversion to an earlier type. —**atavistic** /-ˈvɪstɪk/ adj. [f. F f. L atavus ancestor]

ate /et, eɪt/ past of EAT.

Aten /ˈɑːt(ə)n/ (Egyptian myth.) the name by which the sun or solar disc was worshipped particularly during the reign of Akhenaten.

Athanasian Creed /æθəˈneɪʃ(ə)n/ a profession of faith formerly much used in the Western Church, now less so. Its attribution to St Athanasius is now generally abandoned (see AMBROSE). [f. foll.]

Athanasius /æθəˈneɪʃəs/, St (c.296-373), bishop of Alexandria, a great and consistent upholder of orthodoxy, especially against Arianism. He aided the ascetic movement in Egypt and introduced knowledge of monasticism to the West. Feast day, 2 May.

Atharva-Veda /əˈtɑːvəveɪdə, -viː-/ n. a collection of hymns and spells in old Sanskrit, traditionally called the fourth Veda but originating outside Vedic society, perhaps in the indigenous fourth varna. [f. Skr. atharvan priest, vēda knowledge]

atheism /ˈeɪθɪɪz(ə)m/ n. belief that no God or gods exist(s). —**atheist** n., **atheistic** /-ˈɪstɪk/ adj. [f. F f. Gk (a-not, theos god)]

Athelstan /ˈæθ(ə)lstən/ (895-939), king of England 926-39. One of the most successful of England's Anglo-Saxon monarchs, Athelstan came to the thrones of Wessex and Mercia in 925 before becoming king of all England a year later. He successfully invaded both Scotland and Wales and inflicted a heavy defeat on an invading Danish army.

Athenaeum /æθɪˈniːəm/ a London club founded in 1824 for men of distinction in literature, art, and learning. [L, f. Gk Athēnaion temple of Athene]

Athene /əˈθiːniː/ (Gk myth.) the patron goddess of Athens, also extensively worshipped elsewhere in ancient Greece and its colonies, and almost certainly pre-Hellenic. Her cult-statues show her as female but fully armed, and in classical times the owl is regularly associated with her; she is identified with Minerva. A patroness of many arts and crafts, she became allegorized into a personification of wisdom. The principal myth concerning her is that she sprang, fully-armed and uttering her war-cry, from the head of Zeus.

Athens /ˈæθɪnz/ the capital of Greece, lying 6 km (nearly 4 miles) from its port Piraeus; pop. (1981) 3,027,331. It was a flourishing city-state from early times in ancient Greece, and by the mid-5th c. BC was established as leader of a league of Greek States from whom it exacted tribute. Under Pericles it became a cultural centre, and many of its best-known buildings (e.g. the Parthenon and Erechtheum) date from the extensive rebuilding that he commissioned. Athens recovered only slowly from defeat in the Peloponnesian War (404 BC). In 146 BC it became subject to Rome, but in the early Roman Empire enjoyed imperial favour and was still the cultural centre of the Greek world. Gothic invaders captured and sacked Athens in AD 267, and its importance declined as power and wealth were transferred to Constantinople. After its capture by the Turks in 1456 it declined to the status of a village until chosen as the capital of a newly independent Greece in 1834 after the successful revolt against Turkish rule.

atherosclerosis /æθərəʊsklɪəˈrəʊsɪs/ n. formation of fatty deposits in arteries, often with hardening. [f. G f. Gk athērē gruel]

athlete /ˈæθliːt/ n. one who competes or excels in physical games and exercises. —**athlete's foot**, a fungous disease of the feet. [f. L f. Gk (athlon prize)]

athletic /æθˈletɪk/ adj. of athletes; physically strong and active, muscular. —**athleticism** n. [f. F or L (as prec.)]

athletics n.pl. (occas. treated as sing.) the practice of or competition in physical exercises (running, jumping, throwing, etc.; see below); (US) physical sports and games of any kind. [f. prec.]
The sport of competing in athletics can be traced back at least to the Olympic Games in ancient Greece, but when they were abolished in AD 393 the sport became neglected. Evidence exists of athletic contests in England c.1154, but organized competitions were not held until the mid-19th c.

Athos /ˈæθɒs, ˈeɪ-/, **Mount** a mountainous peninsula projecting into the Aegean Sea from the coast of Macedonia, an autonomous district of Greece since 1927. It is inhabited by monks of the Eastern Orthodox Church in twenty monasteries; the earliest monastic settlement dates from 962. A curious rule of the monks forbids women, or even female animals, to set foot on the peninsula. —**Athonite** /ˈæθənaɪt/ adj. & n.

athwart /əˈθwɔːt/ adv. & prep. across from side to side. [f. A- + THWART]

Atlantic /ətˈlæntɪk/ adj. of the Atlantic Ocean. —n. the Atlantic Ocean. —**Atlantic Ocean**, the ocean lying between Europe and Africa on the east and North and South America on the west. The name was originally applied to the sea near the NW coast of Africa. [f. ATLAS]

Atlantis /ətˈlæntɪs/ (Gk legend) a fabled island in the ocean west of the Pillars of Hercules. It was beautiful and prosperous, and once ruled part of Europe and Africa, but its kings were defeated by the prehistoric Athenians when it attempted to conquer the rest (the story is told by Plato in the Timaeus), and it was overwhelmed by the sea. Memories of Atlantic islands, or of a great volcanic eruption, may lie behind the story.

Atlas /ˈætləs/ (Gk myth.) one of the Titans, who was punished for his part in their revolt against Zeus by being made to support the heavens (a popular explanation of why the sky does not fall). He became identified with the Atlas range in north-west Africa, or a peak of it (thought to be a sky-supporting mountain). According to a later story Perseus, with the aid of Medusa's head, turned him into a mountain.

atlas /ˈætləs/ n. a book of maps. [f. prec.]

Atlas Mountains a range of mountains in North Africa extending from Morocco to Tunisia and rising to over 4,000 m (13,000 ft.). (See ATLAS.)

atman /ˈætmən/ n. (Hinduism) the self or soul; the supreme principle of life in the universe. [Skr., = essence, highest personal principle of life]

atmosphere /ˈætməsfɪə(r)/ n. 1. the mixture of gases surrounding the earth (ill. WEATHER) or a heavenly body. 2. the air in a room etc. 3. a psychological environment; the tone or mood pervading a book or work of art etc. 4. pressure of about 1 kg per sq. cm, being that exerted by the atmosphere on the earth's surface. —**atmospheric** /-ˈferɪk/ adj. [f. Gk atmos vapour + SPHERE]

atmospherics /ætməsˈferɪks/ n. or n.pl. electrical disturbance in the atmosphere; interference in telecommunications caused by this.

atoll /ˈætɒl/ n. a ring-shaped coral reef enclosing a lagoon. [f. Maldive atolu]

atom /ˈætəm/ n. 1. the smallest particle of a chemical element (see below); this as a source of atomic energy. 2. a minute portion or thing. —**atom bomb**, an atomic bomb. [f. OF f. L f. Gk atomos indivisible]
Atomic theories have been known from antiquity, but did not receive their definitive verification until the present century. The atomic theory in ancient Greece was an attempt to explain the complexity of natural bodies and phenomena in terms of the arrangement and rearrangement of tiny indivisible particles, which differed from each other only in size, shape, and motion. The modern view of atoms is far more complex, in that atoms have an elaborate internal structure, they may under certain circumstances be transmuted into other atoms, they congregate together under electrical and gravitational forces, and there are about ninety naturally occurring species of atom and many others that can be created artificially. Atoms, which are roughly 10^{-8} cm in diameter, are each composed of a nucleus of about 10^{-12} cm diameter, containing neutrons and protons, which is surrounded by orbiting electrons. Each chemical element is composed of atoms of one kind only (see ELEMENT); the atoms of most elements can combine to form molecules.

atomic /əˈtɒmɪk/ adj. 1. of an atom or atoms. 2. using energy from atoms. —**atomic clock**, a clock using atomic vibrations as a standard of time. **atomic energy**, nuclear energy. **atomic mass**, = atomic weight. **atomic number**, the number of unit positive charges carried by the nucleus of an atom. **atomic theory**, the theory that all matter consists of atoms. **atomic weight**, the ratio between the mass of one atom of an element or isotope and one-twelfth the weight of an atom of the isotope carbon 12. [as prec.]

atomic bomb a bomb whose destructive power comes from the rapid release of nuclear energy by fission of heavy

Astronomy

Signs of the zodiac

Aries ♈

Taurus ♉

Gemini ♊

Northern hemisphere

the stars shown are visible at different times
of the year to observers in different latitudes

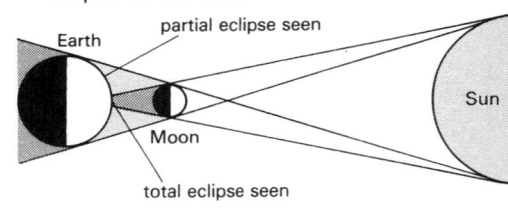

Cancer ♋

Leo ♌

Virgo ♍

Phases of the Moon

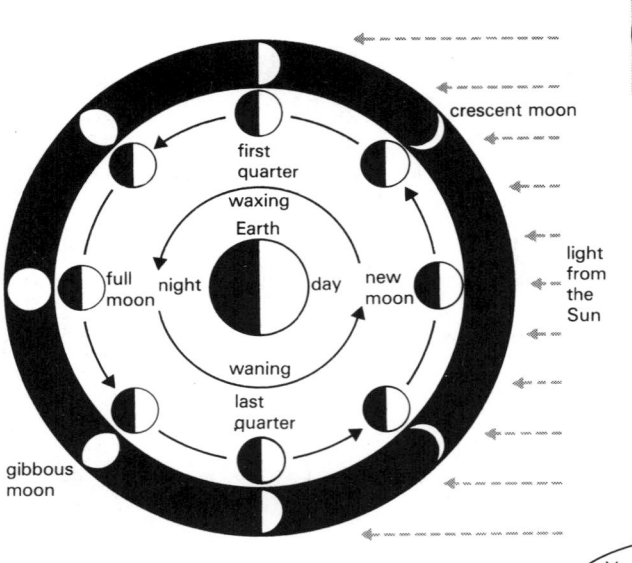

crescent moon

first quarter

waxing

Earth

night · day

full moon

new moon

light from the Sun

waning

last quarter

gibbous moon

the diagram shows how the light from
the Sun falls on the Moon, giving the
appearance as in the black ring

Eclipse of the Sun

partial eclipse seen

Earth

Sun

Moon

total eclipse seen

Comets

periodic comets travel on elliptical
orbits, reappearing at intervals

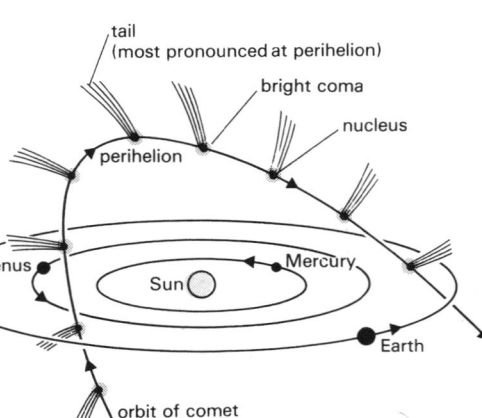

tail
(most pronounced at perihelion)

bright coma

nucleus

perihelion

Venus

Sun

Mercury

Earth

orbit of comet

Southern hemisphere

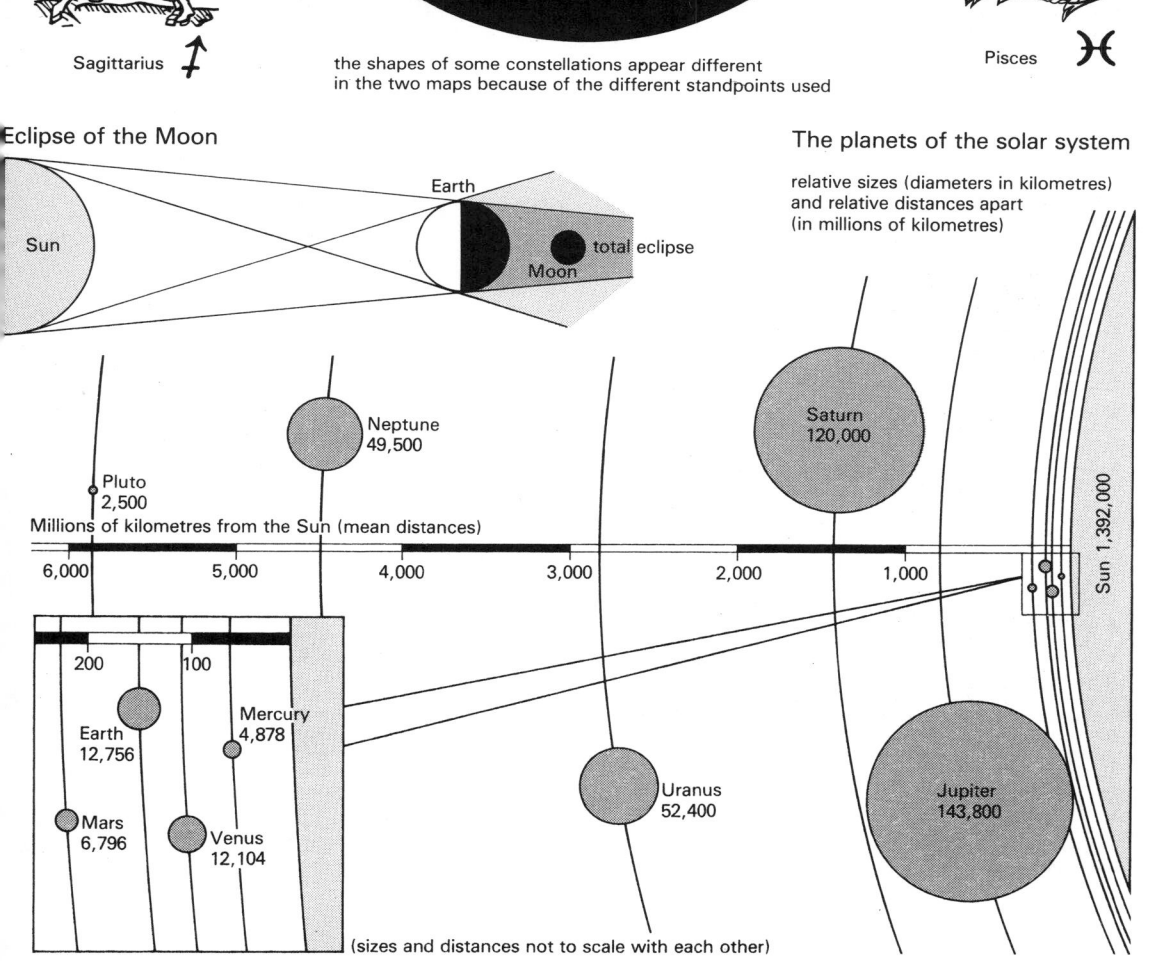

Libra ♎

Scorpio ♏

Sagittarius ↑

the shapes of some constellations appear different
in the two maps because of the different standpoints used

Capricorn ♑

Aquarius ♒

Pisces ♓

Eclipse of the Moon

Sun

Earth

Moon

total eclipse

The planets of the solar system

relative sizes (diameters in kilometres)
and relative distances apart
(in millions of kilometres)

Neptune
49,500

Saturn
120,000

Pluto
2,500

Millions of kilometres from the Sun (mean distances)

6,000   5,000   4,000   3,000   2,000   1,000

Sun 1,392,000

200   100

Earth
12,756

Mercury
4,878

Mars
6,796

Venus
12,104

Uranus
52,400

Jupiter
143,800

(sizes and distances not to scale with each other)

atomic nuclei, with damaging effects caused by heat, blast, and radioactivity. In it, a conventional explosive either pushes together two masses of fissile material or compresses a single mass. Small masses of such material are stable, but above a certain mass (critical mass) a chain reaction occurs with instantaneous release of energy. The first atomic bomb to be used in war was exploded by the USA 300 m above Hiroshima in Japan on 6 Aug. 1945, the second over Nagasaki three days later, resulting in the surrender of Japan and the end of the Second World War.

atomism /ˈætəmɪz(ə)m/ n. the philosophical theory that all matter consists of minute individual particles. —**atomistic** /-ˈmɪstɪk/ adj. [f. ATOM]

atomize /ˈætəmaɪz/ v.t. to reduce to atoms or fine particles. —**atomization** /-ˈzeɪʃ(ə)n/ n. [f. ATOM]

atomizer n. a device for reducing liquids to a fine spray. [f. prec.]

atonal /eɪˈtəʊn(ə)l/ adj. (Mus.) not written in any one key. —**atonality** /-ˈnælɪtɪ/ n. [f. Gk a- not + TONAL]

atone /əˈtəʊn/ v.i. to make amends (for). —**atonement** n. —**the Atonement**, the expiation of man's sin by Christ. **Day of Atonement**, the most solemn religious fast of the Jewish year, eight days after the Jewish New Year. [f. at one]

Atreus /ˈeɪtrɪəs/ (Gk legend) son of Pelops and brother of Thyestes, with whom he was at variance. He invited Thyestes to a banquet and served up to him the flesh of the latter's own children, at which the sun turned back on its course in horror.

atrium /ˈeɪtrɪəm/ n. (pl. -ia or -iums) 1. the central court of an ancient Roman house. 2. either of the two upper cavities in the heart (ill. BODY 3). [L]

atrocious /əˈtrəʊʃəs/ adj. very bad; wicked. —**atrociously** adv. [f. L atrox cruel]

atrocity /əˈtrɒsɪtɪ/ n. a wicked or cruel act, wickedness; a repellent thing. [f. F or L (as prec.)]

atrophy /ˈætrəfɪ/ n. wasting away through undernourishment or lack of use; emaciation. —v.t./i. to cause atrophy in; to suffer atrophy. [f. F or L f. Gk (a- without, trophē food)]

atropine /ˈætrəpɪn, -piːn/ n. a poisonous alkaloid found in deadly nightshade, used in medicine. [f. foll.]

Atropos /ˈætrɒpɒs/ (Gk myth.) one of the three Fates (see FATES). [Gk, = inflexible]

attach /əˈtætʃ/ v.t./i. 1. to fix to something else. 2. to join (oneself) as a companion etc.; to assign (a person) to a particular group. 3. to accompany or form part of. 4. to attribute; to be attributable. 5. to seize by legal authority. —**be attached to**, to be very fond of. [f. OF, = fasten]

attachable /əˈtætʃəb(ə)l/ adj. that may be attached. [f. prec.]

attaché /əˈtæʃeɪ/ n. a person attached to an ambassador's staff and having responsibility in a specific capacity. —**attaché case**, a small rectangular case for carrying documents etc. [F (as ATTACH)]

attachment /əˈtætʃmənt/ n. 1. attaching, being attached. 2. a thing (esp. a device) attached. 3. affection, devotion. 4. legal seizure. [f. ATTACH]

attack /əˈtæk/ v.t./i. 1. to act violently against; to make an attack. 2. to criticize strongly. 3. to act harmfully on. 4. to undertake (a task) with vigour. —n. 1. an act of attacking. 2. strong criticism. 3. a sudden onset of illness etc. —**attacker** n. [f. F f. It., = join battle]

attain v.t./i. to succeed in accomplishing, obtaining, or reaching. [f. AF f. L (AD-, tangere touch)]

attainable /əˈteɪnəb(ə)l/ adj. that may be attained. [f. prec.]

attainment /əˈteɪnmənt/ n. 1. attaining. 2. (usu. in pl.) what is attained, an achievement. [f. ATTAIN]

Attalid /ˈætəlɪdz/ adj. of the Hellenistic dynasty which ruled from Pergamum in Asia Minor, founded by Philetaerus, the son of Attalus, in 282 BC. The Attalid kings established Pergamum as a leading cultural centre of the Greek world, and celebrated their military victories in splendid sculptural monuments. The kingdom was bequeathed to Rome by Attalus III on his death in 133 BC. —n. a member of this dynasty. [f. Attalus]

attar /ˈætə(r)/ n. a fragrant oil, especially from rose-petals. [Pers. f. Arab. ('itr perfume)]

attempt /əˈtempt/ v.t. to make an effort to accomplish. —n. an effort to accomplish, overcome, or surpass something; an attack. [f. OF f. L attemptare (AD-, temptare try)]

attend /əˈtend/ v.t./i. 1. to be present (at); to go regularly

to. 2. to apply one's mind; to accompany. —**attendance** n. [f. OF f. L attendere (AD-, tendere stretch)]

attendant /əˈtend(ə)nt/ n. a person attending, especially to provide service. —adj. accompanying; waiting on. [f. prec.]

attention /əˈtenʃ(ə)n/ n. 1. applying one's mind, mental concentration; awareness. 2. consideration, care. 3. putting into good condition. 4. an attitude of concentration or readiness (also as a command). 5. (in pl.) small acts of kindness or courtesy. —int. an order to take notice or to assume an attitude of attention. [f. L (as ATTEND)]

attentive /əˈtentɪv/ adj. paying attention; devotedly courteous or considerate. —**attentively** adv., **attentiveness** n. [f. F (as ATTEND)]

attenuate /əˈtenjʊeɪt/ v.t. 1. to make slender or thin. 2. to reduce in force or value. —**attenuation** /-ˈeɪʃ(ə)n/ n. [f. L attenuare (AD-, tenuis thin)]

attest /əˈtest/ v.t./i. 1. to be evidence or proof of. 2. to declare to be true or genuine. —**attestation** /ætesˈteɪʃ(ə)n/ n. [f. F f. L attestari (AD-, testis witness)]

Attic /ˈætɪk/ adj. 1. of Athens or Attica. 2. of the ancient Greek dialect used there. —n. this dialect. [f. L f. Gk]

attic /ˈætɪk/ n. a room in the top storey of a house, immediately below the roof. [f. F, as foll.; orig. used of a small architectural feature above a larger one]

Attica /ˈætɪkə/ a triangular promontory, constituting the easternmost part of central Greece. Its chief city is Athens, whose territory it was in ancient times.

Attila /ˈætɪlə/ (406–53), king of the Huns 434–53. Having inflicted great devastation on the Eastern Roman Empire in 445–50, Attila invaded the Western Empire but was defeated at Châlons in 451. He and his army were the terror of Europe during his lifetime, earning Attila the nickname 'Scourge of God'.

attire /əˈtaɪə(r)/ n. (formal) clothes. [f. OF (à tire in order)]

attired /əˈtaɪəd/ adj. (formal) clothed. [f. prec.]

Attis /ˈætɪs/ (Anatolian myth.) the youthful consort of Cybele. A subsidiary figure in the early cult, at Rome he attained official status under Claudius. His death and resurrection were celebrated in a spring festival, with a sacrifice for the crops; his symbol was the pine-tree.

attitude /ˈætɪtjuːd/ n. 1. a way of regarding, a disposition or reaction (to). 2. a position of the body or its parts. 3. the position of an aircraft etc. in relation to given points. [F f. It. f. L (aptus fitted)]

Attlee /ˈætlɪ/, Clement Richard, 1st Earl Attlee (1883–1967), British statesman, leader of the Labour Party from 1935. As a result of the 1945 election Attlee became the first Labour Prime Minister to command an absolute majority in the House. His administration was notable at home for a series of measures setting up the modern Welfare State and abroad for progressive decolonization.

atto- /ætəʊ-/ prefix denoting a factor of 10^{-18} (attometre). [f. Da. or Norw. atten eighteen]

attorney /əˈtɜːnɪ/ n. one appointed to act for another in business or legal affairs; (US) a lawyer. —**Attorney-General** n. the chief legal officer, appointed by the government holding office. [f. OF (atorner assign)]

attract /əˈtrækt/ v.t. 1. to draw towards itself by unseen force. 2. to arouse interest, pleasure, or admiration in. —**attraction** n. [f. L attrahere (AD-, trahere pull)]

attractive /əˈtræktɪv/ adj. 1. that attracts or can attract. 2. good-looking. —**attractively** adv., **attractiveness** n. [f. F f. L (as prec.)]

attributable /əˈtrɪbjuːtəb(ə)l/ adj. that may be attributed. [f. foll.]

attribute[1] /əˈtrɪbjuːt/ v.t. (with to) to regard as belonging to, caused by, or originated by. —**attribution** /-ˈbjuːʃ(ə)n/ n. [f. L attribuere (AD-, tribuere allot)]

attribute[2] /ˈætrɪbjuːt/ n. 1. a quality ascribed to or characteristic of a person or thing. 2. an object associated with or symbolizing a person. [as prec.]

attributive /əˈtrɪbjʊtɪv/ adj. expressing an attribute; (Gram., of an adjective) placed before the noun it qualifies (cf. PREDICATIVE). —**attributively** adv. [f. F (as ATTRIBUTE[1])]

attrition /əˈtrɪʃ(ə)n/ n. 1. wearing away by friction. 2. gradual wearing down of strength and morale by harassment. [f. L attritio (AD- terere rub)]

attune /əˈtjuːn/ v.t. 1. to harmonize or adapt (one's mind etc.) to a matter or idea. 2. to bring into musical accord. [f. AD- + TUNE]

atypical /eɪˈtɪpɪk(ə)l/ adj. not belonging to any type. [f. Gk a- not + TYPICAL]

Au *symbol* gold. [f. L *aurum*]

aubergine /ˈəʊbəʒiːn/ *n.* **1.** the fruit of the egg-plant, used as a vegetable. **2.** its dark-purple colour. [F, ult. f. Skr.]

Aubrey /ˈɔːbri/, John (1626–97), English antiquarian and polymath, author of a collection of 'Lives' of eminent persons. He was a pioneer of field archaeology, most of his researches being centred on the earthworks and monuments in Wiltshire (particularly Avebury and Stonehenge), and became one of the first Fellows of the Royal Society in 1663.

aubrietia /ɔːˈbriːʃə/ *n.* a low-growing perennial rock-plant with mauve, purple, or pink flowers. [f. Claude *Aubriet*, Fr. botanist (d. 1743)]

auburn /ˈɔːbən/ *adj.* (of hair) reddish-brown. [orig. = yellowish-white, f. OF f. L (*albus* white)]

Aubusson /ˈəʊbuːsɔ̃/ *n.* a kind of tapestry made at the town of Aubusson in central France, famous since the 16th c., and especially in the 18th c., for the manufacture of tapestries and carpets; a carpet resembling this in design.

AUC *abbr.* ab urbe condita (Latin, = from the founding of the city, i.e. Rome).

Auckland /ˈɔːklənd/ **1.** the largest city and chief seaport of New Zealand; pop. (1982) 839,500. **2.** the province of New Zealand comprising the northern part of North Island.

auction /ˈɔːkʃ(ə)n/ *n.* a sale in which each article is sold to the highest bidder. —*v.t.* to sell by auction. [f. L (*augēre* increase)]

auctioneer /ɔːkʃəˈnɪə(r)/ *n.* one whose business is to conduct auctions. —*v.t.* to sell by auction. [f. prec.]

audacious /ɔːˈdeɪʃəs/ *adj.* daring, bold. —**audaciously** *adv.*, **audacity** /ɔːˈdæsɪtɪ/ *n.* [f. L (*audēre* dare)]

Auden /ˈɔːd(ə)n/, Wystan Hugh (1907–73), English poet. At Oxford he was the leading voice of a near-Marxist group (which included Day Lewis, MacNeice, and Spender) that responded to the public chaos of the 1930s. Auden collaborated with Isherwood in several Brechtian verse dramas (notably *The Ascent of F6*, 1936) and in *Journey to a War* (1939) recording a journey to China, and with MacNeice in *Letters from Iceland* (1937). Britten set many of his poems to music and later used Auden's text for his opera *Paul Bunyan*. In 1939, with Isherwood, he settled in America (becoming a US citizen in 1946) where he met Chester Kallmann, who became his lifelong friend and with whom he collaborated in several opera libretti including Stravinsky's *The Rake's Progress*. His poetry now became increasingly Christian in tone, reflecting man's isolation. His absence from Europe during the war led to a poor reception of his work in England, but the high quality of his later works, such as *Nones* (1951) and *The Shield of Achilles* (1955) reinstated him as a major poet; he was elected Professor of Poetry at Oxford in 1956. Auden's progress from the didactic poems of his youth to the complexity of his later works offered a wide variety of models. He was a master of verse form, accommodating traditional patterns to a fresh contemporary language.

audible /ˈɔːdɪb(ə)l/ *adj.* that can be heard (distinctly). —**audibility** /-ˈbɪlɪtɪ/ *n.*, **audibly** *adv.* [f. L (*audire* hear)]

audience /ˈɔːdɪəns/ *n.* **1.** a group of listeners or spectators. **2.** a formal interview. [f. OF f. L (as prec.)]

audio /ˈɔːdɪəʊ/ *n.* (*pl.* **-os**) and *in comb.* audible sound reproduced mechanically; its reproduction. —**audio frequency**, a frequency comparable to that of ordinary sound. **audio typist,** one who types from a recording. **audio-visual** *adj.* using both sight and sound. [f. L *audire* hear]

audit /ˈɔːdɪt/ *n.* an official scrutiny of accounts to see that they are in order. —*v.t.* to conduct an audit of. [f. L *auditus* hearing (as prec.)]

auditor /ˈɔːdɪtə(r)/ *n.* **1.** one authorized to audit accounts. **2.** a listener. [f. AF f. L (as AUDIO)]

auditorium /ɔːdɪˈtɔːrɪəm/ *n.* (*pl.* **-ums**) the part of a theatre etc. occupied by an audience (ill. THEATRE). [L (as foll.)]

auditory /ˈɔːdɪtərɪ/ *adj.* of or concerned with hearing. [f. L (as AUDITOR)]

Audubon /ˈɔːdəbən/, John James (1785–1851), American naturalist and artist, remembered for his great illustrated work *The Birds of America* (1827–38). His elementary education in France made him barely literate and he contributed little else to ornithology, except an early attempt to trace the movements of birds by banding them. His book was compiled during his wanderings round America trying and failing to make a living in various small towns. He portrayed even the largest birds life-size, and painted them not in conventionally formal postures but in dramatic

and sometimes violent action. Eventually he found a publisher in Britain and, published in parts, the book had lasting success, not only for the arresting quality of the engravings but also as a major contribution to the then rapidly growing knowledge of natural history.

au fait /əʊ ˈfeɪ/ well acquainted *with* a subject. [F]

Augean /ɔːˈdʒiːən/ *adj.* **1.** of the legendary king Augeus or his filthy stables, which Hercules cleaned in a day by diverting a river through them. **2.** filthy. [f. *Augeas*]

auger /ˈɔːgə(r)/ *n.* a tool for boring holes in wood, having a long shank with a helical groove, and a transverse handle. [OE (*nafu* nave of wheel, *gār* piercer)]

aught /ɔːt/ *n.* (*archaic* or *poet.*) anything. [OE]

augment¹ /ɔːgˈment/ *v.t.* to increase, to make greater. —**augmentation** /-ˈteɪʃ(ə)n/ *n.* [f. F or L (*augēre* increase)]

augment² /ˈɔːgmənt/ *n.* a vowel prefixed to past tenses in Greek and Sanskrit. [as prec.]

au gratin /əʊ ˈgrætæ̃/ cooked with a crust of breadcrumbs and grated cheese. [F (*gratter* grate)]

Augsburg /ˈaʊgzbɜːg/ a city of Bavaria. —**Augsburg Confession,** a statement of the Lutheran position, mainly drawn up by Melanchthon and approved by Luther before being presented to the Emperor Charles V at Augsburg on 25 June 1530.

augur /ˈɔːgə(r)/ *n.* an ancient Roman religious official who observed and interpreted omens in natural phenomena; a soothsayer. —*v.t./i.* to portend; to serve as an omen. —**augural** *adj.* [L]

August /ˈɔːgəst/ *n.* the eighth month of the year. [OE, f. AUGUSTUS]

august /ɔːˈgʌst/ *adj.* majestic, imposing. [f. F or L, = consecrated, venerable]

Augustan /ɔːˈgʌst(ə)n/ *adj.* **1.** of or belonging to the reign of Augustus Caesar, the outstanding period of Latin literature. **2.** (of any national literature) classical (in English literature, of the 17th–18th c.). —*n.* a writer of the Augustan age of any literature. [f. L f. AUGUSTUS]

Augustine¹ /ɔːˈgʌstɪn/, St (of Canterbury; died *c.*604), the first archbishop of Canterbury. Sent from Rome by Gregory the Great (then pope) to refound the Church in England, he and his party landed in Kent in 597 and were favourably received by King Ethelbert (whose wife was a Christian), who was afterwards converted. Augustine founded the first church and a monastery at Canterbury, and was consecrated as archbishop, but failed to reach agreement with representatives of the ancient Celtic Church which still survived in Britain and was at variance with Rome on questions of discipline and practice. Feast day, 26 May.

Augustine² /ɔːˈgʌstɪn/, St (of Hippo, 354–430), a Doctor of the Church. Born in North Africa of a pagan father and a Christian mother, he was early attracted to Manichaeism. He taught rhetoric in Rome and then in Milan, where he was influenced by the bishop Ambrose and embraced his Neoplatonic understanding of Christianity. Augustine henceforth lived a monastic life, first in retirement, then as priest and (after 395) as bishop of Hippo in North Africa. His episcopate was marked by continual controversy, with Manichees, Donatists, Pelagians and pagan philosophy. Most of his vast literary output was pastoral or polemical. The *City of God*, a vindication of the Church against paganism, is perhaps his most famous work, apart from his *Confessions* which contains a striking account of his early life and conversion. Augustine died during the siege of Hippo by the Vandals. His theology has dominated all later Western theology, with its profound psychological insight and its sense of man's utter dependence on grace, expressed in his doctrine of predestination, and of the Church and the sacraments.

Augustinian /ɔːgəˈstɪnɪən/ *adj.* of St Augustine of Hippo. —*n.* a member of any of the Roman Catholic religious orders that observe the 'rule of St Augustine' (based largely on his writings but not founded by him), especially the Augustinian Canons (founded in the 11th c.) and the Augustinian (or Austin) Friars, a mendicant order founded *c.*1250.

Augustus /ɔːˈgʌstəs/ (63 BC–AD 14) the first Roman emperor. Born Gaius Octavius (subsequently known as Octavian), grand-nephew of Julius Caesar, after whose murder he established his position in Italy as one of the triumvirate of 43 BC, he gained supreme power by his defeat of Antony at the battle of Actium in 31 BC. A constitutional settlement in 27 BC in theory restored the Republic but in practice regularized his sovereignty; in the same year he was given the title Augustus (L, = venerable). His rule was marked abroad by a series of expansionist military campaigns and at home by moral and religious reforms intended to restore old Roman values disrupted during the civil wars of previous decades. He energetically patronized the arts; the literature of his reign represents the high-point of Roman classicism.

auk /ɔːk/ n. a sea-bird of the family Alcidae, e.g. the great auk (flightless and extinct), little auk, guillemot, puffin, razorbill. [f. ON *álka*]

auld lang syne /ɔːld læŋ ˈsaɪn/ (Sc.) days of long ago. [Sc., = old long since]

aunt /ɑːnt/ n. a sister or sister-in-law of one's father or mother; (colloq.) an unrelated friend of a parent. —**Aunt Sally**, a figure used as a target in a throwing-game; a target of general abuse. [f. AF f. L *amita*]

auntie, aunty /ˈɔːntɪ/ n. (colloq.) an aunt.

au pair /əʊ ˈpeər/ (in full **au pair girl**) a young woman, usually from abroad, helping with housework etc. in return for board and lodging. [F]

aura /ˈɔːrə/ n. (pl. -as) the distinctive atmosphere attending a person or thing; a subtle emanation. [L f. Gk, = breeze]

aural /ˈɔːr(ə)l/ adj. of or concerning the ear or hearing. —**aurally** adv. [f. L *auris* ear]

Aurangzeb /ˈɔːrəŋzeb, ˈaʊ-/ (1618-1707), Mogul emperor of Hindustan 1658-1707, a period of great wealth and splendour for the empire. Having usurped the throne from his father, Aurangzeb assumed the title Alamgir—Conqueror of the World—and embarked on an expansionist policy. He increased the Mogul empire to its widest extent, but constant rebellions and wars greatly weakened it and it declined sharply after his death.

Aurelian /ɔːˈriːlɪən/ (Lucius Domitius Aurelianus, c.215-75) Roman emperor, acclaimed by the army in 270, and murdered in a military plot in 275. By a series of campaigns he reunited the empire and repulsed barbarian invaders. He built new walls round Rome and established the State worship of the sun.

Aurelius /ɔːˈriːlɪəs/, Marcus (121-180), Roman emperor 161-180, the adopted successor of Antoninus Pius. Much of his reign was occupied with wars against Germanic tribes invading the empire from the north. He himself was by nature a philosophical contemplative; his *Meditations* (in Greek) are a collection of aphorisms and reflections based on a Stoic outlook and written down for his own guidance. His equestrian statue now stands on the Capitol in Rome.

aureola /ɔːˈriːələ/, **aureole** /ˈɔːrɪəʊl/ n. 1. a celestial crown or halo, especially round the head or body of a portrayed divine figure. 2. a corona round the sun or moon. [L, = golden crown]

au revoir /əʊ rəˈvwɑːr/ goodbye for the moment. [F]

auricle /ˈɔːrɪk(ə)l/ n. 1. the external part of the ear. 2. an atrium of the heart; a small appendage to this (ill. BODY 4). —**auricular** /ɔːˈrɪkjʊlə(r)/ adj. [f. L, dim. of *auris* ear]

auriferous /ɔːˈrɪfərəs/ adj. yielding gold. [f. L (*aurum* gold, *ferre* bear)]

Auriga /ɔːˈraɪɡə/ the Charioteer or Wagoner, a constellation in the northern hemisphere, near Orion, including the brilliant yellow star Capella, sixth brightest in the sky, several interesting variable stars, and three well-known galactic clusters. It is crossed by the luminous band of the Milky Way.

Aurignacian /ɔːrɪɡˈneɪʃ(ə)n/ adj. of an early upper palaeolithic industry occurring throughout Europe and the Near East, named after the type-site, a cave at Aurignac in southern France, and dated in most places to c.32,000-27,000 BC. This period witnessed the first appearance of cave-paintings (e.g. those at Lascaux in the Dordogne region of France). —n. this industry. [f. *Aurignac*]

aurochs /ˈɔːrɒks/ n. 1. an extinct European wild ox. 2. a European bison. [G]

Aurora /ɔːˈrɔːrə/ (Rom. myth.) goddess of the dawn, corresponding to the Greek Eos. Most of the stories about her consist of kidnappings of handsome men to live with her (see TITHONUS). [L, = dawn]

aurora /ɔːˈrɔːrə/ n. (pl. -as, -ae /-iː/) a luminescent display of colours in the atmosphere at high northern (**aurora borealis**) or southern (**aurora australis**) latitudes, arising from electrical interactions between the Earth's magnetic field and streams of energetic charged particles from the sun. [as prec.]

Auschwitz /ˈaʊʃvɪts/ a town in Poland (Polish *Oświecim*), site of a Nazi concentration camp in the Second World War.

auscultation /ɔːskʌlˈteɪʃ(ə)n/ n. listening to the sounds of the heart, lungs, etc., for diagnosis. [f. L (*auscultare* listen to)]

auspice /ˈɔːspɪs/ n. 1. an omen. 2. (in pl.) patronage. [orig. = observation of bird-flight (in divination); F or f. L (*avis* bird)]

auspicious /ɔːˈspɪʃəs/ adj. showing signs that promise well, favourable. —**auspiciously** adv., **auspiciousness** n. [f. prec.]

Aussie /ˈɒzɪ/ n. & adj. (colloq.) Australian. [abbr.]

Austen /ˈɒstɪn/, Jane (1775-1817), English novelist, born at Steventon, Hampshire, where her father was rector. She never married but led an uneventful life in the midst of a large and lively family, writing the witty, epigrammatic, and satiric novels which were to make her world-famous. Her major works, which portray the social life of the upper classes and praise the virtues of reason and intelligence rather than those of passion and impulse, all end with a happy marriage, achieved after the surmounting of obstacles: *Sense and Sensibility* (1811), *Pride and Prejudice* (1813), *Northanger Abbey* (1818), *Mansfield Park* (1814), *Emma* (1815), and *Persuasion* (1818).

austere /ɔːˈstɪə(r)/ adj. stern, grim; severely simple; severe in self-discipline or abstinence. —**austerely** adv., **austerity** /ɔːˈsterɪtɪ/ n. [f. OF f. L f. Gk *austēros* severe]

Austerlitz /ˈaʊstəlɪts, ˈɒ-/ a town in central Czechoslovakia, scene in 1805 of Napoleon's defeat of the Austrians and Russians.

Austin Friars /ˈɒstɪn/ see AUGUSTINIAN FRIARS.

austral /ˈɔːstr(ə)l/ adj. 1. southern. 2. **Austral**, Australian; Australasian. [f. L *australis* (*Auster* south wind)]

Australasia /ɒstrəˈleɪʒə, ɔː-/ Australia, New Zealand, and neighbouring islands in the South Pacific. —**Australasian** adj. & n. [f. F (as AUSTRALIA, ASIA)]

Australia /ɒˈstreɪlɪə, ɔː-/ an island country and continent of the southern hemisphere in the SW Pacific, a member State of the British Commonwealth; pop. (1983) 15,451,800; official language, English; capital, Canberra. Much of the continent has a hot dry climate and a large part of the central area is desert or semi-desert; the most fertile areas are the eastern coastal plains and the SW corner of Western Australia. Agriculture has always been of vital importance to the economy, with cereal crops grown over wide areas and livestock producing wool, meat, and dairy products for export. There are significant mineral resources (including bauxite, coal, copper, iron, lead, uranium, and zinc), and fourteen oilfields produce nearly 70 per cent of the country's requirements. The people are mainly of European descent but there are about 160,000 Aborigines. [f. L *australis* southern (*Auster* south wind)]

Human habitation in Australia dates from prehistoric times (see ABORIGINES). The existence of an unknown southern land (*terra australis*) was postulated in ancient Greek geographical writings and the idea was passed on in medieval writings and maps. Pre-17th c. European sightings of Australia are claimed but not firmly attested. From 1606 onwards its western coast was explored by the Dutch, and in 1642 Tasman proved that it was an island; it was visited by an Englishman, William Dampier, in 1688 and 1699. In 1770 Captain James Cook landed at Botany Bay on the eastern side of the continent and formally took possession of New South Wales. British colonization began in 1788 (also the settling of convicts at Port Jackson, discontinued in 1840). The interior was gradually explored and opened up in the 19th c. and political consolidation resulted in the declaration of a Commonwealth in 1901, when the six colonies (New South Wales, Victoria, Queensland, South Australia, Western Australia, and Tasmania) federated as sovereign States. Australia supported Great Britain heavily in each of the two World Wars, being threatened herself by Japanese invasion during the second, but although still maintaining ties with the former mother country has more and more pursued her own interests both domestically and internationally, the latter with particular reference to SE Asia and the South Pacific.

Australian /ɒˈstreɪlɪən, ɔː-/ adj. of Australia or its people. —n. a native or inhabitant of Australia. [f. prec.]

Australian Capital Territory federal territory in New South Wales consisting of two enclaves ceded by New South Wales, one in 1911 to contain Canberra, the other in 1915 containing Jervis Bay.

Australian (National) Rules Football a form of football played by teams of 18 players with a ball shaped like that used in Rugby football. It is a fast-moving game with few rules apart from those aimed at protecting the player, forming the national code in the Australian Commonwealth and officially dating back to 1858.

Australoid /ˈɒstrəlɔɪd, ˈɔː-/ *adj.* of a race of people that diffused to Australia from Asia at a time of lower sea-level. The Vedda of Sri Lanka and the Aborigines of Australia are the modern representatives. Their physical attributes are: dark skin, black wavy to curly hair, abundant facial and body hair, dolichocephalic head, splayed nose, wide mouth, and thick lips. Male height varies from 150–180 cm (4 ft. 10 in.–6 ft.) with the women being *c*.10 cm (4 in.) shorter. —*n.* a person of Australoid ethnological type. [as AUSTRALIAN]

Australopithecus /ɒstreɪləˈpɪθɪkəs, ɔː-/ *n.* a genus of Southern and East African hominids of the Upper Pliocene and Lower Pleistocene, dating from *c*.5.5 million to 1 million years ago. —**Australopithecine** /-saɪn/ *adj.* & *n.* [f. L *australis* southern + Gk *pithēkos* ape]

Austria /ˈɒstrɪə, ˈɔː-/ a country in central Europe, much of it mountainous, with the River Danube flowing through the north-east; pop. (est. 1983) 7,551,300; official language, German; capital, Vienna. Agriculture and forestry are important (timber is a valuable source of wealth) and there are considerable heavy industries; hydroelectric power has been developed and is exported. The Celtic tribes settled in the area were conquered by the Romans in 15–9 BC and it remained part of the Roman Empire, with the Danube as its frontier, until overrun by Germanic peoples in the 5th c. AD. Dominated from the early Middle Ages by the Hapsburg family, Austria became the centre of a massive Central European empire which held sway over the area until the First World War. The collapse of the Hapsburg empire in 1918 left Austria a weak and unstable country which was easily incorporated within the Nazi Reich in 1938. After the Second World War the country remained under Allied military occupation until 1955. Since regaining her sovereignty Austria has emerged as a prosperous and stable democratic republic with decidedly westward leanings. —**Austrian** *adj.* & *n.*

autarchy /ˈɔːtɑːkɪ/ *n.* despotism, absolute rule. [f. Gk *autos* self, *arkhē* rule]

autarky /ˈɔːtɑːkɪ/ *n.* self-sufficiency, especially in economic affairs. [f. Gk (*autos* self, *arkeō* suffice)]

authentic /ɔːˈθentɪk/ *adj.* genuine, of legitimate or undisputed origin; trustworthy. —**authentically** *adv.*, **authenticity** /-ˈtɪsɪtɪ/ *n.* [f. OF f. L f. Gk, = principal, genuine]

authenticate /ɔːˈθentɪkeɪt/ *v.t.* to establish as valid or authentic. —**authentication** /-ˈkeɪʃ(ə)n/ *n.*, **authenticator** *n.* [f. L (as prec.)]

author /ˈɔːθə(r)/ *n.* **1.** the writer of a book or books, article(s), etc. **2.** the originator of a plan or policy etc. —**authorship** *n.* [f. AF f. L *auctor* (*augēre* increase)]

authoritarian /ɔːθɒrɪˈteərɪən/ *adj.* favouring or characterized by unqualified obedience to authority. —*n.* an authoritarian person. [f. AUTHORITY]

authoritative /ɔːˈθɒrɪtətɪv/ *adj.* reliable, as having authority; official. —**authoritatively** *adv.* [f. foll.]

authority /ɔːˈθɒrɪtɪ/ *n.* **1.** the power or right to enforce obedience. **2.** (esp. in *pl.*) a body having authority. **3.** personal influence arising from knowledge or position etc., a testimony based on this. **4.** a person to whom knowledge or influence is attributed; an expert. [f. OF f. L (as AUTHOR)]

authorize /ˈɔːθəraɪz/ *v.t.* to give authority to (a person) or for (an action etc.); to recognize officially. —**authorization** /-ˈzeɪʃ(ə)n/ *n.* [as prec.]

Authorized Version a popular appellation of the 1611 English translation of the Bible, ordered by James I (it is known in the USA as the 'King James Version') and produced by about 50 scholars. On the title-page are the words 'appointed to be read in churches', but it has never otherwise been officially 'authorized'. It immediately won the hearts of the people, loved for its intrinsic merits rather than promoted by official recommendation, and remained for centuries the Bible of every English-speaking country.

autism /ˈɔːtɪz(ə)m/ *n.* a mental condition, especially in children, preventing proper response to the environment. —**autistic** /ɔːˈtɪstɪk/ *adj.* [as AUTO-]

auto /ˈɔːtəʊ/ *n.* (*pl.* **-os**) (*US colloq.*) a motor car. [abbr. of AUTOMOBILE]

auto- /ˈɔːtə(ʊ)/ *in comb.* self; own; of or by oneself or itself, automatic. [f. Gk *autos* self]

autobahn /ˈɔːtəbɑːn/ *n.* a German, Austrian, or Swiss motorway. [G (*auto* motor car, *bahn* road)]

autobiography /ɔːtəbaɪˈɒɡrəfɪ/ *n.* the story of a person's life written by himself or herself; the writing of this. —**autobiographical** /-ˈɡræfɪk(ə)l/ *adj.*

autochthonous /ɔːˈtɒkθənəs/ *adj.* indigenous, aboriginal. [f. Gk, = sprung from that land itself (as AUTO-, *khthōn* land)]

autoclave /ˈɔːtəʊkleɪv/ *n.* **1.** a strong vessel used for chemical reactions at high pressures and temperatures. **2.** a sterilizer using high-pressure steam. [f. AUTO- + L *clavus* nail or *clavis* key]

autocracy /ɔːˈtɒkrəsɪ/ *n.* absolute government by one person; dictatorship. [f. Gk (as foll.)]

autocrat /ˈɔːtəkræt/ *n.* a sole ruler with absolute power; an authoritarian person. —**autocratic** /-ˈkrætɪk/ *adj.*, **autocratically** *adv.* [f. F f. Gk (as AUTO-, *kratos* power)]

autocross /ˈɔːtəʊkrɒs/ *n.* motor-racing across country or on unmade roads. The sport originated in England soon after the Second World War, but timed hill-climbs and speed trials had flourished earlier, *c*.1918-25. [f. AUTO(MOBILE) + CROSS]

Autocue /ˈɔːtəʊkjuː/ *n.* [P] a device showing a television speaker the script as an aid to memory.

auto-da-fé /ɔːtəʊdɑːˈfeɪ/ *n.* (*pl.* **-os-**) the ceremonial judgement of heretics by the Spanish Inquisition; the execution of heretics by public burning. [Port., = act of the faith]

autogiro /ɔːtəˈdʒaɪrəʊ/ *n.* (*pl.* **-os**) an aircraft in which the lift comes from its rotating wings. It differs from the helicopter in that its wings are not powered, but rotate in the slipstream. The aircraft itself is propelled forward by a conventional mounted engine and propeller. Originally the term 'autogiro' was the proprietary name used by its Spanish inventor, Juan de la Cierva, whose first autogiro flew in 1923. [Sp. (as AUTO-, *giro* gyration)]

autograph /ˈɔːtəɡrɑːf/ *n.* **1.** a person's signature, his or her handwriting. **2.** a manuscript in the author's handwriting. **3.** a document signed by its author. —*v.t.* to sign or write on in one's own hand. [F, or f. L f. Gk (*graphō* write)]

auto-immunity *n.* the state produced by the presence either of antibodies produced by an organism and reacting against a constituent of it, or of lymphoid cells sensitized against a constituent of the body's own tissues. —**auto-immune** *adj.*

automate /ˈɔːtəmeɪt/ *v.t.* to apply automation to, to operate by automation. [back-formation f. AUTOMATION]

automatic /ɔːtəˈmætɪk/ *adj.* **1.** working of itself without direct human intervention in the process. **2.** done from habit without conscious thought. **3.** following necessarily. **4.** (of a firearm) having a mechanism for continuous loading and firing. —*n.* **1.** an automatic gun etc. **2.** a motor vehicle with automatic transmission. —**automatic pilot**, a device in an aircraft or ship to keep it on a set course. **automatic transmission**, a system in a motor vehicle for automatic gear-change. —**automatically** *adv.* [as AUTOMATON]

automation /ɔːtəˈmeɪʃ(ə)n/ *n.* the production of goods etc. by automatic processes; use of automatic equipment in place of human effort. [f. prec.]

automatism /ɔːˈtɒmətɪz(ə)m/ *n.* **1.** involuntary action. **2.** unthinking routine. [f. F (as foll.)]

automaton /ɔːˈtɒmət(ə)n/ *n.* (*pl.* **-tons**, collect. **-ta**) **1.** a machine responding to automatic (esp. electronic) control. **2.** a person acting mechanically. [L f. Gk, = acting of itself]

automobile /ˈɔːtəməbiːl/ *n.* (*US*) a motor car. [F (as AUTO-, MOBILE)]

automotive /ɔːtəˈməʊtɪv/ *adj.* concerned with motor vehicles.

autonomic /ɔːtəˈnɒmɪk/ *adj.* functioning involuntarily. [as foll.]

autonomous /ɔːˈtɒnəməs/ *adj.* self-governing, acting independently. [f. Gk (AUTO- *nomos* law)]

autonomy /ɔːˈtɒnəmɪ/ *n.* the right of self-government, independence. [as prec.]

autopilot /ˈɔːtəʊpaɪlət/ *n.* an automatic pilot.

autopsy /ˈɔːtɒpsɪ/ *n.* a post-mortem. [f. F f. Gk (*autoptēs* eye-witness)]

autostrada /ˈɔːtəstrɑːdə/ *n.* (*pl.* **-de** /-deɪ/) an Italian motorway. [It. (as AUTOMOBILE, *strada* road)]

auto-suggestion *n.* suggestion arising unconsciously from within a person to influence his own actions etc.

autumn /ˈɔːtəm/ *n.* the season between summer and winter; a time of incipient decline. —**autumnal** /ɔːˈtʌmn(ə)l/ *adj.* [f. OF f. L *autumnus*]

Auvergne /əʊˈvɛːn/ an ancient province of south central France.

auxiliary /ɔːgˈzɪljərɪ/ adj. giving help; additional, subsidiary. —n. **1.** an auxiliary person or thing. **2.** an auxiliary verb. **3.** (in pl.) foreign or allied troops in the service of a nation at war. —**auxiliary verb,** a verb used to form tenses, moods, etc. of other verbs (e.g. have in they have gone). [f. L (auxilium help)]

auxin /ˈɔːksɪn/ n. a substance that stimulates the growth of plants, a growth hormone. [G, f. Gk auxō increase]

AV abbr. Authorized Version.

avail /əˈveɪl/ v.t./i. to be of use or advantage (to). —n. effectiveness, advantage. —**avail oneself of,** to make use of. [f. OF f. L valēre be strong]

available /əˈveɪləb(ə)l/ adj. capable of being used; at one's disposal. —**availability** /-ˈbɪlɪtɪ/ n. [f. prec.]

avalanche /ˈævəlɑːnʃ/ n. **1.** a mass of dislodged snow, rock, etc., sliding rapidly down a mountain. **2.** a great onrush. [F (avaler descend)]

Avalon /ˈævəlɒn/ **1.** (in Arthurian legend) the place to which Arthur was conveyed after death. **2.** (Welsh myth.) the kingdom of the dead.

avant-garde /ævɑ̃ˈgɑːd/ n. a leading group of innovators, especially in art and literature. —adj. (of ideas) new, progressive. [F, = vanguard]

Avar /ˈɑːvə(r)/ n. a member of a Turkic people prominent in SE Europe in the 6th–9th c. In the 7th c. their kingdom extended from the Black Sea to the Adriatic. They were finally subdued by Charlemagne (791–9). —adj. of this people.

avarice /ˈævərɪs/ n. greed for wealth or gain. —**avaricious** adj., **avariciously** adv. [f. OF f. L (avarus greedy)]

avatar /ˈævətɑː(r)/ n. (Hinduism) **1.** the descent to earth of a deity in a manifest form. **2.** of the ten incarnations of Vishnu. [f. Skr., = descent]

Ave /ˈɑːvɪ, ˈɑːveɪ/ n. (in full **Ave Maria,** = Hail, Mary) a devotional recitation and prayer to the Virgin Mary (cf. Luke 1: 28 & 42). [L, imper. of avēre fare well]

Avebury /ˈeɪvbərɪ/ a village in Wiltshire on the site of one of Britain's most impressive henge monuments of the late neolithic period (3rd millennium BC).

avenge /əˈvɛndʒ/ v.t. to take vengeance for (an injury) or on behalf of (a person). —**avenger** n. [f OF f. L (vindicare vindicate)]

avenue /ˈævənjuː/ n. **1.** a broad main street; a tree-lined approach or path. **2.** a way of approach. [F f. avenir come to f. L (AD-, venire come)]

aver /əˈvɜː(r)/ v.t. (-rr-) to assert, to affirm. —**averment** n. [f. OF (a- to + L verus true)]

average /ˈævərɪdʒ/ n. **1.** the generally prevailing rate, degree, or amount. **2.** a number obtained by adding several quantities together and dividing the total by the number of quantities. **3.** (Law) damage to or loss of a ship or cargo. —adj. of the usual or ordinary standard; calculated by making an average. —v.t. to amount to or produce as an average; to calculate the average of. [f. F f. It. f. Arab., = damaged goods]

Avernus /əˈvɜːnəs/ a lake near Naples in Italy, filling the crater of an extinct volcano, regarded by the ancients as the entrance to the Underworld.

Averroës /əˈvɛrəʊiːz/ (ibn-Rushd, c. 1126–98) Islamic philosopher, born at Cordoba in Spain, whose work crowned a 500-year tradition in Islamic thought. Of his scientific, philosophical, and religious writings the most influential were the commentaries on Aristotle which, through a reliance upon Neoplatonism, interpreted Aristotle's writings in such a way as to make them consistent with Plato's. Reality, he held, consists of hierarchical levels of being which flow from the Ultimate One, who can be identified with Allah. Averroës' commentaries exercised a strong and controversial influence upon the succeeding centuries of Western philosophy and science.

averse /əˈvɜːs/ predic. adj. unwilling, opposed, disinclined (to or from). [f. L (as AVERT)]

aversion /əˈvɜːʃ(ə)n/ n. **1.** a strong dislike (to or from), unwillingness. **2.** an object of dislike. [F or f. L (as foll.)]

avert /əˈvɜːt/ v.t. **1.** to turn away (eyes, thoughts, etc.). **2.** to prevent (a disaster etc.) from happening. [f. L (AB-, vertere turn)]

Avesta /əˈvɛstə/ n. the sacred scripture of Zoroastrianism, compiled by Zoroaster as a means of reforming an older tradition. (See ZEND-AVESTA.) [f. Pers. avastāk text]

Avestan /əˈvɛst(ə)n/ adj. **1.** of the Avesta. **2.** of Avestan. —n. the ancient east-Iranian language in which the Avesta is written (often incorrectly called Zend), closely related to Vedic Sanskrit. [f. prec.]

aviary /ˈeɪvɪərɪ/ n. a large cage or building for keeping birds. [f. L (avis bird)]

aviation /eɪvɪˈeɪʃ(ə)n/ n. the practice or science of flying aircraft. [F f. L (avis bird)]

aviator /ˈeɪvɪeɪtə(r)/ n. a pilot or member of an aircraft crew in the early days of aviation. [as prec.]

Avicenna /ævɪˈsɛnə/ (ibn-Sina, 980–1037) Islamic philosopher who exercised a dominant influence upon medieval Islam. Born in Persia, he worked as physician at the courts of local princes, and his surviving works include treatises on philosophy, medicine, and religion. His philosophical system, while drawing heavily from Aristotle, is closer to Neoplatonism, and was the major influence on the development of 13th-c. scholasticism. He produced a philosophical encyclopaedia Ash-Shifa (The Recovery), and his Canon of Medicine, which combined his own medical knowledge with Roman and Arabic medicine, was a popular text in the medieval world.

avid /ˈævɪd/ adj. eager, greedy. —**avidity** /əˈvɪdɪtɪ/ n., **avidly** adv. [f. F or L (avēre crave)]

Avignon /ˈæviːjɲɔ̃/ a city on the Rhône in southern France. From 1309 until 1377 it was the residence of the popes during their exile from Rome, and became papal property by purchase in 1348. After the papal court had returned to Rome two antipopes re-established a papal court in Avignon. The second of these was expelled in 1408, but the city remained in papal hands until the French Revolution.

avionics /eɪvɪˈɒnɪks/ n. or n.pl. the science of electronics applied to aeronautics. [f. AVI(ATION) + ELECTRONICS]

avocado /ævəˈkɑːdəʊ/ n. (pl. -os) **1.** a pear-shaped tropical fruit with rough skin and creamy flesh. **2.** its dark green colour. [Sp. = advocate) f. Aztec]

avocation /ævəˈkeɪʃ(ə)n/ n. a secondary activity done in addition to one's main work; (colloq.) one's occupation. [f. L (avocare call away)]

avocet /ˈævəsɛt/ n. a wading bird with long legs and an upturned bill. [f. F f. It.]

Avogadro /ævəˈgɑːdrəʊ/, Amadeo (1776–1856), Italian physicist, best known for his hypothesis (or law), formulated in 1811 but ignored for the next fifty years, according to which equal volumes of gases at the same temperature and pressure contain equal numbers of molecules (the term which he coined for an aggregation of atoms), and from which it became relatively simple to derive both molecular weights and a system of atomic weights. A constant named in his honour is Avogadro's number, which is the number of molecules in 1 gram-molecular weight (mole) of a substance, and has a value of 6.02×10^{23}.

avoid /əˈvɔːd/ v.t. to keep away or refrain from; to escape or evade. —**avoidable** adj., **avoidance** n. [f. AF, = clear out]

avoirdupois /ævədəˈpɔɪz/ n. a system of weights based on a pound of 16 ounces or 7,000 grains. [F, = goods of weight]

Avon /ˈeɪvən/ a county of SW England.

avow /əˈvaʊ/ v.t. to declare, to admit. —**avowal** n., **avowedly** /əˈvaʊɪdlɪ/ adv. [f. OF f. L (vocare call)]

avuncular /əˈvʌŋkjʊlə(r)/ adj. of or like a kindly uncle. [f. L avunculus maternal uncle (dim. of avus grandfather)]

await /əˈweɪt/ v.t. to wait for; to be in store for. [f. AF (as WAIT)]

awake /əˈweɪk/ v.t./i. (past **awoke** /əˈwəʊk/, p.p. **awoken** /əˈwəʊkən/) **1.** to wake, to cease from sleep; to become active. **2.** to rouse from sleep. —predic. adj. no longer or not yet asleep; alert. [OE]

awaken /əˈweɪkən/ v.t. to awake; to draw the attention of (a person to a fact etc.). [OE]

award /əˈwɔːd/ v.t. to give by official decision as a payment, prize, or penalty. —n. **1.** a decision of this kind. **2.** an amount or prize etc. awarded. [AF awarder (as WARD)]

aware /əˈweə(r)/ predic. adj. having knowledge or realization (of or that). [OE]

awash /əˈwɒʃ/ predic. adj. washed over by water or waves. [f. A- + WASH]

away /əˈweɪ/ adv. **1.** to or at a distance; into non-existence. **2.** constantly, persistently. **3.** without delay. —adj. played or playing on an opponent's ground. —n.

an away match or (in football pools) victory in this. [OE (A-, WAY)]

awe /ɔː/ n. respect or admiration charged reverence or fear. —v.t. to fill or inspire with awe. [ON]

aweigh /ə'weɪ/ adv. (of an anchor) just lifted from the bottom in weighing anchor. [f. A- + WEIGH]

awesome /'ɔːsəm/ adj. inspiring awe. [f. AWE + -SOME]

awestricken, awestruck adjs. filled with awe.

awful /'ɔːf(ə)l/ adj. 1. (colloq.) very bad or poor; notable of its kind. 2. awe-inspiring, terrifying. [f. AWE + -FUL]

awfully /'ɔːfʊlɪ, colloq. 'ɔːflɪ/ adv. 1. in a way that inspires awe. 2. (colloq.) very; badly.

awhile /ə'waɪl/ adv. for a short time. [OE, = a while]

awkward /'ɔːkwəd/ adj. 1. clumsy, having little skill. 2. difficult to handle, use, or deal with. 3. embarrassing, inconvenient; embarrassed. —**awkwardly** adv., **awkwardness** n. [f. obs. awk perverse, f. ON, = turned the wrong way]

awl n. a small pointed tool for pricking holes, especially in leather or wood. [OE]

awn n. the bristly head of the sheath of barley, oats, etc. [f. ON]

awning n. a canvas or plastic sheet stretched by supports from a wall as a shelter against sun and rain. [orig. unkn.]

awoke past of AWAKE.

awoken p.p. of AWAKE.

axe n. a chopping-tool with a long handle and a heavy blade. —v.t. to eliminate or reduce drastically. —**have an axe to grind**, to have a personal interest involved and to be anxious to take care of it. [OE]

axial /'æksɪəl/ adj. 1. of or forming an axis. 2. round an axis. —**axially** adv. [f. AXIS]

axil n. the upper angle where a leaf joins a stem, or between a branch and the trunk of a tree. [f. L axilla armpit (dim. of ala wing)]

axiology /æksɪ'ɒlədʒɪ/ n. (Philos.) the theory of value. —**axiological** /-'lɒdʒɪk(ə)l/ adj. [f. F f. Gk axia value]

axiom /'æksɪəm/ n. an established or accepted principle; a self-evident truth. —**axiomatic** /-'mætɪk/ adj. [f. F or L f. Gk (axios worthy)]

axis /'æksɪs/ n. (pl. **axes** /-siːz/) 1. an imaginary line about which an object rotates; a line about which a regular figure is symmetrically arranged. 2. any of a set of reference lines for measurement of coordinates etc. 3. the relation between countries, regarded as a common pivot on which they revolve, especially (**the Axis**) the political association of 1936 (becoming in 1939 a military alliance) between Italy and Germany, and later Japan. [L, = axle, pivot]

axle n. the bar or rod on which a wheel or wheels revolve(s); the rod connecting a pair of wheels of a vehicle. [f. ON]

Axminster /'æksmɪnstə(r)/ n. a machine-woven tufted carpet with cut pile. [name of town in Devon]

axolotl /'æksəlɒt(ə)l/ n. a newtlike amphibian found in Mexican lakes. [Nahuatl (atl water, xolotl servant)]

axon /'æksɒn/ n. a long appendage of a nerve cell, usually carrying signals from it. [f. Gk, = axis]

Ayers Rock /eəz/ a red rock-mass in Northern Territory, Australia, SW of Alice Springs. The largest monolith in the world, it is 348 m (1,143 ft.) high and about 9 km (6 miles) in circumference, rising in impressive isolation from the surrounding plain.

ayatollah /aɪə'tɒlə/ n. a Shiite religious leader in Iran. [Pers. f. Arab., = token of God]

aye[1] /aɪ/ adv. (archaic, dial., nautical, or formal) yes, —n. an affirmative answer or vote. [prob. f. pron. I expressing assent]

aye[2] /aɪ/ adv. (archaic) always. [f. ON]

Aymara /'aɪmərə/ n. 1. an American Indian people mainly inhabiting the plateau lands of Bolivia and Peru near Lake Titicaca; a member of this people. 2. their language. [Bolivian Sp.]

azalea /ə'zeɪlɪə/ n. a flowering shrubby plant of the genus or subgenus Azalea. [f. Gk, = dry (from the dry soil in which Linnaeus believed that it flourished)]

Azerbaijan /æzəbaɪ'dʒɑːn/ the Azerbaijan SSR, a constituent republic of the USSR, lying between the Black and Caspian Seas and containing the Baku oilfields. Until the early 19th c. it formed part of Persia; capital, Baku.

Azilian /ə'zɪlɪən/ adj. of an early mesolithic industry in Europe, named after the type-site, a cave at Mas d'Azil in the French Pyrenees, succeeding the Magdalenian and dated to 10,000–8,000 BC. It is characterized by flat bore harpoons, painted pebbles, and microliths. —n. this industry. [f. Mas d'Azil]

azimuth /'æzɪməθ/ n. 1. an arc of the sky from the zenith to the horizon. 2. the distance (measured as an angle) along the horizon clockwise from the north point to the point where the azimuth through a particular object (e.g. a star) meets the horizon. 3. a directional bearing. —**azimuthal** /-'muː θ(ə)l/ adj. [f. OF f. Arab. (al the, sumūt directions)]

Azores /ə'zɔːz/ a group of volcanic islands in the North Atlantic, 1,287 km (800 miles) west of Portugal, in Portuguese possession but partially autonomous; pop. (1981) 254,200; capital Ponta Delgada.

Azov /'æzɒf/, **Sea of** an inland sea of the southern USSR, separated from the Black Sea by the Crimea and communicating with it by a narrow strait.

Azrael /'æzreɪəl/ (Jewish & Muslim myth.) the angel who at death severs the soul from the body. [f. Heb., = help of God]

Aztec /'æztek/ n. 1. a member of the native people dominant in central Mexico at the time of the Spanish conquest; see below. 2. their language, also called Nahuatl. —adj. of the Aztecs or their language. [f. F or Sp. f. Nahuatl, = men of the north]

The people we call the Aztecs (who were also called Mexica or Tenochca) arrived in the central valley of Mexico after the collapse of the Toltec civilization in the 12th c., and at first were obliged to live in the less desirable, infertile regions, often on the brink of famine. By the early 15th c. they had risen to dominance of the area, and a century later commanded a territory that covered most of the central and southern part of present-day Mexico, exacting tribute from their subjects. They were a warring people who slew captives as human sacrifices to their chief god, but their life-style was comfortable as (for the rulers) luxurious, and the Spaniards under Cortés arrived to find a rich and elaborate civilization centred on the city of Tenochtitlán, which boasted vast pyramids, temples, and palaces with fountains, all so spectacular that they wondered if the sight was a dream.

azure /'æʒə(r), 'æʒjʊə(r)/ adj. & n. sky-blue; (in heraldry) blue. [f. OF f. L f. Arab. al the, lāzaward (f. Pers.) lapis lazuli]

B

B, b *n.* **1.** the second letter of the alphabet. **2.** (*Mus.*) the seventh note in the scale of C major.

B *symbol* boron.

b. *abbr.* born.

BA *abbr.* Bachelor of Arts.

Ba *symbol* barium.

baa /bɑː/ *n.* the bleat of a sheep or lamb. —*v.i.* (**baaed, baa'd**) to bleat. [imit.]

Baal /ˈbeɪ(ə)l/ (*pl.* **-im**) (*Semitic myth.*) any of the male deities of fertility whose cult was widespread in ancient Phoenician and Canaanite lands, strongly resisted by the Hebrew prophets. The name is found as a prefix to place-names (e.g. Baalbek) and as the last element in Phoenician names such as Hannibal and Jezebel. [f. Heb., = lord]

Baalbek /ˈbɑːlbek/ a town in eastern Lebanon, site of the ancient city of Heliopolis. Its principal monuments date from the Roman period, and include the Corinthian temples of Jupiter and Bacchus, and private houses with important mosaics.

baba /ˈbɑːbɑː/ *n.* (also **rum baba**) a sponge-cake soaked in rum syrup. [F]

Babbage /ˈbæbɪdʒ/, Charles (1791–1871), English mathematician and inventor, an outstanding example of a man ahead of his time, generally recognized as the pioneer of machine computing. His interest in the compilation of accurate tables of mathematical and astronomical functions through elimination of human error led to the construction (from 1823 onwards) of a mechanical computer or 'difference engine' which would not only perform calculations but also print the results. Because of the difficulties in constructing such a machine to a sufficient degree of accuracy, and of obtaining continuing financial support, neither this machine nor a subsequent analytical engine was ever finished, and Babbage became a frustrated and embittered man. Nevertheless he continued to innovate: in the field of operational research his analysis of the economies of the Post Office led to the introduction of the penny post, and he invented the heliograph and the ophthalmoscope. Tennyson's 'Every minute dies a man, Every minute one is born' drew from Babbage the remark that since the world's population was constantly increasing the second line should read 'And one and a sixteenth is born'. (Tennyson did in fact blur the assertion by changing 'minute' to 'moment'.)

babble *v.t./i.* **1.** to make incoherent sounds; to talk inarticulately or excessively; to say incoherently. **2.** to repeat or divulge foolishly. **3.** (of a stream etc.) to murmur as it trickles. —*n.* **1.** incoherent or foolish talk. **2.** a confused murmur. [imit.]

babe *n.* **1.** (*poet.*) a baby. **2.** an inexperienced or guileless person. **3.** (*US slang*) a young woman. [imit. of child's *ba ba*]

babel /ˈbeɪb(ə)l/ *n.* **1.** a confused noise, especially of voices. **2.** a scene of confusion. —**tower of Babel,** (in Gen. 11: 1–9) the tower built in an attempt to reach heaven, which God frustrated by confusing the languages of its builders so that they could not understand one another. The story was probably inspired by the Babylonian ziggurat, and may be an attempt to explain the existence of different languages. [f. Heb. *babel* Babylon f. Akkad. *bab ili* gate of God; cf. *balal* confuse]

Babi /ˈbɑːbiː/ *n.* a Persian eclectic sect, or a member of this, founded in 1844 by Mirza Ali Muhammad of Shiraz, emphasizing the coming of a new prophet or messenger of God (in Persian *Bab-ed-Din* gate (= intermediary) of the Faith, whence the founder's usual title of (*the*) *Bab*). The Baha'i faith is an offshoot of Babism. —**Babism** *n.* [f. Pers. & Arab. *bab* gate]

baboon /bəˈbuːn/ *n.* a large African and Arabian monkey with a doglike snout. [f. OF or L]

Babur /ˈbɑːbʊə(r)/ (1483–1530), the first Mogul emperor, descended from Tamerlane. He invaded India *c.*1525 and conquered the territory from the Oxus to Patna.

baby /ˈbeɪbiː/ *n.* **1.** a very young child or animal. **2.** the youngest member of a family etc.; a thing small of its kind; a childish person. **3.** (*slang*) a sweetheart. **4.** (*slang*) one's own concern or activity. —*v.t.* to treat like a baby. —**baby grand,** a small grand piano. **baby-sit** *v.i.* to look after a young child while its parents are out. **baby-sitter** *n.* one who baby-sits. —**babyhood** *n.*, **babyish** *adj.* [as BABE]

Babylon /ˈbæbɪlən/ **1.** the capital of Babylonia, first prominent under Hammurabi. The city (now in ruins) lay on the Euphrates and was noted for its luxury, its fortifications, and particularly for the 'Hanging Gardens' which were one of the Seven Wonders of the World. **2.** (among Blacks, especially Rastafarians) White society; the representatives of this, especially the police.

Babylonia /bæbɪˈləʊnɪə/ the ancient name for southern Mesopotamia (earlier called Sumer), which first became a political entity when an Amorite dynasty united Sumer and Akkad in the first half of the 2nd millennium BC. At this period its power ascended over Assyria and part of Syria. After *c.*1530 BC first the Hittites then other invaders, the Kassites, dominated the land, and it became part of the Assyrian empire. With the latter's decline Babylonia again became prominent under the Chaldeans 625–538 BC, only to fall to Cyrus the Great, whose entry into Babylon ended its power for ever.

baccalaureate /bækəˈlɔːrɪət/ *n.* the degree of a Bachelor of Arts or Science etc. [f. L *baccalaureus* (see BACHELOR), with pun on *bacca lauri* laurel berry]

baccarat /ˈbækərɑː/ *n.* a gambling card-game, played against the banker by punters each in turn staking that their hand will total nine. [F]

bacchanal /ˈbækən(ə)l/ *n.* **1.** a priest or worshipper of Bacchus. **2.** a drunken reveller or revelry. —*adj.* **1.** of Bacchus. **2.** riotous. [f. L (f. BACCHUS)]

Bacchanalia /bækəˈneɪlɪə/ *n.* **1.** a Roman festival in honour of Bacchus. **2.** drunken revelry. [L, as prec.]

bacchant /ˈbækənt/ *n.* **1.** a priest or worshipper of Bacchus. **2.** a drunken reveller. —**bacchante** /bəˈkænt/ *n.fem.* [f. F f. L *bacchari* celebrate Bacchanal rites]

Bacchic /ˈbækɪk/ *adj.* bacchanal. [f. L f. Gk, = of Bacchus]

Bacchus /ˈbækəs/ (*Gk myth.*) the other name of DIONYSUS.

Bach /bɑːx/, Johann Sebastian (1685–1750), German composer, the greatest of a large family of musicians, who was described by Wagner as 'the most stupendous miracle in all music', though in his lifetime his reputation as a composer was restricted to a fairly narrow circle. His enormous output included violin concertos, suites, the six Brandenburg Concertos, many clavier works, and (while serving St Thomas's Church in Leipzig) over 250 sacred cantatas as well as the St Matthew and St John Passions, the Christmas Oratorio, and the collection of large-scale Mass movements known to us as the B minor Mass and regarded as one of the great Christian works of art, though Bach did not conceive of it as a unity. He composed nothing without purpose: he was a devout Protestant in the Lutheran tradition and his chorales faithfully and movingly represent the message of their words; he was renowned for his organ-playing and his organ pieces are a summation of the North German tradition which he knew and revered; his last (unfinished) work, *The Art of Fugue*, is an awe-inspiring attempt to exhaust the possibilities of canon and fugue upon a single melody. Bach symbolizes the musical Baroque in Germany except in one respect: he left the composing of opera to his erstwhile compatriot Handel.

Of his 20 children, his eldest son Wilhelm Friedmann Bach (1710–84) became an organist and composer, Carl Philipp Emanuel Bach (1714–88) wrote much church music, over 200 keyboard sonatas, and a celebrated treatise on clavier-playing, and Johann Christian Bach (1735–82) became music-master to the British royal family and composed 13 operas and many instrumental works.

bachelor /ˈbætʃ(ə)lə(r)/ *n.* **1.** an unmarried man. **2.** one who holds the degree of Bachelor of Arts or Science etc. —**bachelor flat,** one suitable for a person living alone. **Bachelor of Arts** *or* **Science** etc., a person who has obtained a first degree in arts or sciences, or other faculty. [f. OF *bacheler* aspirant to knighthood]

bacillus /bə'sɪləs/ *n.* (*pl.* **bacilli** /-laɪ/) a rod-shaped bacterium, especially one causing disease by entering and multiplying in animal and other tissues. —**bacillary** *adj.* [L, dim. of *baculus* stick]

back¹ *n.* **1.** the hinder surface of the human body from shoulder to hip; the corresponding part of an animal's body. **2.** a similar ridge-shaped part, the keel of a ship. **3.** an outer or rear surface; the less active, less important, or less visible part; the side or part normally away from the spectator or direction of motion. **4.** the part of a garment covering the back. **5.** a defensive player near the goal in football etc. — *adj.* **1.** situated behind or in the rear. **2.** of or for past time. **3.** (of vowels) formed at the back of the mouth (as in *hard*, *hot*). —*adv.* **1.** to the rear, away from the front. **2.** in or into an earlier or normal position or condition; in or into the past. **3.** at a distance; in check. **4.** in return. —**at the back of one's mind,** borne in mind but not consciously thought of. **back-bencher** *n.* an MP not entitled to sit on the front benches in Parliament, i.e. one without senior office either in government or in opposition. **back boiler,** a boiler behind a domestic fire. **back formation,** an apparent root-word formed from a word that looks like (but is not) its derivative, as *laze* from *lazy*; formation of words in this way. **back of beyond,** (*colloq.*) a remote and benighted region. **back seat,** a seat at the back; a less prominent position. **back-seat driver,** a person who has no responsibility but is eager to advise someone who has. **back slang,** a form of slang using words spelt backwards, as *yob* for *boy*. **back-to-back** *adj.* (of houses) built with juxtaposed backs. **back to front,** with the back placed where the front should be. **get** *or* **put a person's back up,** to annoy or irritate him. **get off a person's back,** to stop annoying him. **have one's back to the wall,** to be fighting for survival. **put one's back into,** to put all one's strength into (efforts). **see the back of,** to be rid of. **turn one's back on,** to repudiate (former associates etc.). [OE]

back² *v.t./i.* **1.** to help with money, to give encouragement or support to; to lay a bet on the success of. **2.** to go or cause to go backwards. **3.** to provide with a lining or support at the back; to provide a musical accompaniment to. **4.** to be so situated that its rear abuts *on*. **5.** (of wind) to change gradually in an anticlockwise direction. —**back down,** to abandon a claim, viewpoint, etc. **back out,** to withdraw from an agreement. **back up,** to give encouragement or support to; to confirm (a statement). **back water,** to reverse a boat's forward motion by using the oars. —**backer** *n.* [f. BACK¹]

backache *n.* pain in the back.

backbiting *n.* spiteful talk about a person, especially in his or her absence.

backblocks *n.pl.* (*Austral. & NZ*) land in the remote interior.

backbone *n.* **1.** the spine. **2.** the main support of a structure. **3.** firmness of character.

backchat *n.* (*colloq.*) impudent repartee.

backdate *v.t.* to assign an earlier date than the actual one to (a document etc.); to make (agreements etc.) retrospectively valid.

backdrop *n.* a flat painted curtain at the back of a stage set.

backfire /bæk'faɪə(r)/ *v.i.* **1.** (of an engine or vehicle) to undergo premature explosion in the cylinder or exhaust-pipe. **2.** (of a plan etc.) to go wrong, especially so as to recoil on its originator. —*n.* an instance of backfiring.

backgammon /'bækgæmən/ *n.* a game for two, played on a special double board with pieces like draughtsmen moved according to the throw of a dice. It is among the most ancient of all games, combining elements of chance and skill, and passed from one civilization to another. [f. BACK¹ (because pieces go back and re-enter) + obs. *gamen* game]

background *n.* **1.** the back part of a scene etc., especially as the setting for the chief part; an unimportant or unobtrusive position. **2.** a person's education, knowledge, or social circumstances; explanatory or contributory information or circumstances.

backhand *n.* a stroke, especially in tennis, made with the back of one's hand towards one's opponent; the side of the court or player on which such strokes are made.

backhanded *adj.* **1.** delivered with the back of the hand. **2.** (of a compliment) oblique, ambiguous.

backhander *n.* **1.** a back-handed stroke. **2.** (*slang*) a reward for services rendered, a bribe.

backing *n.* **1.** support, encouragement; a body of supporters. **2.** material used to support or line the back of something. **3.** a musical accompaniment to a singer. [f. BACK²]

backlash *n.* a violent usually hostile reaction.

backless *adj.* without a back; (of a dress) cut low at the back. [f. BACK¹ + -LESS]

backlog *n.* arrears of uncompleted work etc. (orig. = a large log placed at the back of a fire to sustain it).

backpack *n.* a rucksack; a package of equipment carried similarly.

back-pedal *v.i.* (-ll-) **1.** to work the pedals of a bicycle backwards. **2.** to reverse one's previous action or opinion.

backside *n.* (*colloq.*) the buttocks.

backslide *v.i.* to relapse into error or bad ways.

backspace *v.i.* to cause a typewriter carriage or 'golf ball' to move backwards one space.

backstage *adj. & adv.* behind the curtain of a theatre, especially in the wings or dressing-rooms.

backstitch *v.t./i.* to sew by inserting the needle each time behind the place where it has just been brought out. —*n.* a stitch made in this way.

backstroke *n.* a swimming stroke performed on the back.

backtrack *v.i.* to retrace one's steps; to reverse one's action.

backward /'bækwəd/ *adj.* **1.** directed towards the back or to the starting-point. **2.** slow to make (mental etc.) progress. **3.** lacking confidence to come forward, shy. —*adv.* backwards. —**backwardness** *n.* [earlier *abackward*]

backwards /'bækwədz/ *adv.* **1.** towards the direction away from one's front; back foremost. **2.** (of the motion of a thing) towards its starting-point. **3.** in the reverse of the usual order; into a worse state; into the past. —**bend** *or* **lean over backwards,** to go to great lengths (*to*). **know something backwards,** to know it exhaustively. [as prec.]

backwash *n.* receding waves created by a moving ship.

backwater *n.* **1.** a stretch of stagnant water beside a stream. **2.** a place indifferent to progress or new ideas.

backwoods *n.* **1.** remote uncleared forest, as in North America. **2.** a remote or backward area. —**backwoodsman** *n.* (*pl.* **-men**)

backyard *n.* a yard at the back of a house.

Bacon¹ /'beɪkən/, Francis, Baron Verulam and Viscount St Albans (1561–1626), English lawyer and philosopher, the pre-eminent legal figure of the late Elizabethan and early Stuart periods, eventually rising to become Lord Chancellor under James I before falling from favour after impeachment on charges of corruption. His radical philosophical beliefs, expounded in several books which have become literary classics, proved very influential, dominating the field for a century after his death. In science he advocated the inductive method and rejected the formulation of a priori hypotheses; application of this inspired the founding of the Royal Society in 1660. There are those who credit him with having written the plays of Shakespeare.

Bacon² /'beɪkən/, Roger (*c.*1214-94), English medieval scholar. A Franciscan monk, Bacon taught at Oxford and Paris and was best known for his scientific work, particularly in the field of optics. Although widely acclaimed in scholarly circles he fell foul of his own order, which eventually imprisoned him as a heretic. He is alleged to have prophesied flying machines, mechanical propulsion, and optical instruments such as the telescope and microscope, and to have described spectacles and the manufacture of gunpowder.

bacon /'beɪkən/ *n.* dried and salted meat from the back or side of a pig. —**bring home the bacon,** (*slang*) to succeed in an undertaking. **save one's bacon,** (*slang*) to escape injury or punishment. [f. OF]

bactericide /bæk'tɪərɪsaɪd/ *n.* a substance that kills bacteria. —**bactericidal** *adj.* [f. BACTERIUM + -CIDE]

bacteriology /bæktɪərɪ'ɒlədʒɪ/ *n.* the scientific study of bacteria. —**bacteriological** /-'lɒdʒɪk(ə)l/ *adj.*, **bacteriologist** *n.* [f. foll. + -LOGY]

bacterium /bæk'tɪərɪəm/ *n.* (*pl.* **-ia**) any of several types of microscopic or ultramicroscopic single-celled organisms very widely distributed in nature, not only in soil, water, and air, but also on or in many parts of the tissues of plants and animals. Traditionally included in the plant kingdom they are now usually grouped as members of the Protista.

Bacteria form one of the main biologically interdependent groups of organisms in virtue of the chemical changes which many of them bring about (e.g. all forms of decay and the building up of nitrogen compounds in the soil; see CARBON CYCLE, NITROGEN CYCLE); the ability of some bacteria to incorporate atmospheric nitrogen into organic compounds is essential to life on earth. Bacterial classification is problematic because they are so uniform in shape, usually spherical (cocci) or rodlike (bacilli). Multiplication is usually by simple fission; some form spores, aerially dispersed; true sexual reproduction is rare. Because of the rapid growth rate and ease of culture of bacteria much modern biochemical knowledge has been derived from their study. The division between the apparently simple cells of bacteria and the larger nucleated cells of animals and plants is one of the most fundamental in biology, and bacterial cells are believed to be ancestral to nucleated cells. Bacteria were first observed by Leeuwenhoek in the 17th c. and first definitely implicated in a disease (anthrax) by Koch in 1876. —**bacterial** adj. [f. Gk *baktērion* dim. of *baktron* stick]

Bactria /ˈbæktrɪə/ the ancient name for a country that included the northern part of modern Afghanistan and parts of Soviet central Asia. Traditionally the home of Zoroaster and the Zend-Avesta, it was the seat of a powerful Indo-Greek kingdom in the 3rd and 2nd c. BC.

Bactrian /ˈbæktrɪən/ adj. of Bactria. —**Bactrian camel,** the two-humped camel of central Asia. [f. prec.]

bad adj. (compar. WORSE, superl. WORST) **1.** of poor quality, defective. **2.** putrid, decaying. **3.** in poor health, injured. **4.** morally defective, wicked; (of a child) naughty. **5.** unwelcome, disagreeable; harmful, detrimental; (of something unwelcome) serious, severe. —adv. (US) badly. —**bad blood,** unfriendly feelings. **bad debt,** one not recoverable. **bad language,** swear-words. **feel bad about,** to feel guilt or remorse about. **go to the bad,** to become criminal, dissolute, or immoral. **not bad,** (colloq.) good, fairly good. —**badness** n. [perh. f. OE *bæddel* hermaphrodite, womanish man]

bade /bæd, beɪd/ past of BID.

Baden-Powell /ˌbeɪd(ə)nˈpəʊəl/, Robert Stephenson Smyth, 1st Baron Baden-Powell of Gilwell (1857-1941), English soldier, founder of the Boy Scouts (1908), Girl Guides (1910), and related organizations, which proved to be the most important British youth movements of the 20th c. He had become a national hero after his successful defence of Mafeking in the early part of the Second Boer War, but retired in 1910 to devote himself to the Boy Scout movement.

badge n. something worn to show one's rank, membership, etc. [orig. unkn.]

badger /ˈbædʒə(r)/ n. a grey nocturnal burrowing animal of the weasel family. [perh. f. BADGE, from the distinctive markings on its head]

badinage /ˈbædɪnɑːʒ/ n. good-humoured mockery. [F]

badlands n.pl. strikingly eroded areas of the USA, characterized by sharp-crested ridges and pinnacles. Such topography is found where, owing to an arid climate or over-grazing, there is little vegetation to protect the land surface from erosion, so that streams and rivers have incised it with numerous gullies and ravines. The name was originally applied to parts of South Dakota and Nebraska, which the French trappers (applying the Indian name) found 'bad lands to cross'. Exposure of the rock layers has resulted in substantial finds of fossil vertebrates.

badly adv. (worse, worst) **1.** defectively, improperly. **2.** so as to inflict much injury, severely. **3.** (colloq.) very much. [f. BAD]

badminton /ˈbædmɪnt(ə)n/ n. a volleying game played by one or two players opposing an equivalent number across a net, using rackets and a shuttlecock. It derives its name from Badminton, Glos., the seat of the Duke of Beaufort, where the game is supposed to have evolved about 1870 from the ancient game of battledore and shuttlecock. From the outset it gained popularity with army officers who took it to India and played it out of doors. The first laws were drawn up in Poona in the mid-1870s.

Badon Hill /ˈbeɪd(ə)n/ according to some sources, the site of a successful defensive fight by King Arthur's forces against the Saxons in AD 516. Another source implies that the battle was fought c.500 but does not connect it with Arthur. The location of the site is uncertain.

Baedeker /ˈbeɪdekə(r)/ n. any of the guidebooks issued by the German publisher Karl Baedeker (1801-59) or his successors.

Baer /beə(r)/, Karl Ernest von (1792-1876), Russian biologist. His discovery that mammalian and human ova were not follicles of the ovary, but particles within these, was the chief of his many contributions to embryology. He also formulated a principle that in the developing embryo general characters appear before special ones, and his studies were used by Darwin in the theory of evolution.

Baffin /ˈbæfɪn/, William (c.1584-1622), English navigator and explorer who in 1616 discovered the largest island of the Canadian Arctic, which island (**Baffin Island**) and the strait (**Baffin Bay**) between it and Greenland are named after him. The record he established for attaining the most northerly latitude was not bested until the mid-19th c.

baffle v.t. **1.** to perplex, to bewilder. **2.** to frustrate. —n. a screen preventing the passage of sound etc. —**bafflement** n. [orig. unkn.]

bag n. **1.** a receptacle for carrying things, made of flexible material with an opening at the top; this with its contents. **2.** anything resembling this, as loose folds of skin under the eyes. **3.** the total number of game shot by a sportsman. **4.** (in pl., slang) a great quantity of. —v.t. (**-gg-**) **1.** to put in a bag. **2.** (slang) to secure possession of. —**bag and baggage,** with all one's belongings. **in the bag,** as good as secured. —**bagful** n. (pl. -fuls) [perh. f. ON]

bagatelle /bægəˈtel/ n. **1.** a board game in which small balls are struck into holes. **2.** a thing of no importance. **3.** a short piece of music, especially for the piano. [F f. It.]

Bagehot /ˈbædʒət/, Walter (1826-77), English economist and journalist, a banker and shipowner, editor of *The Economist* from 1860 until his death. His remarkable insight into economic and political questions is shown in his *The English Constitution* (1867), *Lombard Street* (1873), and *Economic Studies* (1880).

baggage /ˈbægɪdʒ/ n. **1.** luggage, especially that carried by sea or air. **2.** the portable equipment of an army. [f. OF (bagues bundles)]

baggy adj. hanging in loose folds. [f. BAG]

Baghdad /bægˈdæd/ the capital of Iraq, on the River Tigris. Under Caliph Harun-al-Rashid (d. 809) it became one of the greatest cities of Islam; pop. (1977) 3,205,645.

bagpipe n. (also in pl.) an instrument with reeds that are sounded by the pressure of wind emitted from a bag squeezed by the player's arm and fed with air either by breath or by means of small bellows strapped to the waist. It generally has at least two pipes, one (the chanter) giving the melody and any others sounding a drone or drones. The bagpipe has been a popular instrument in the West from the Middle Ages and also appears, in widely varying forms, in Central and Eastern Europe and Asia; it is now associated especially with Scotland, Northumberland, and Ireland.

bah /bɑː/ int. expressing contempt or disgust. [prob. f. F]

Baha'i /bɑːˈhɑːi/ n. a monotheistic religion, or a follower of this, founded in Persia in the 19th c. by Baha-ullah (1817-92) and his son Abdul Baha (1844-1921), that is a development of Babism (see below). —**Baha'ism** n. [f. Pers. *bahā* splendour]
    The central tenet of the Baha'i faith is that the essence of all religions is one; thus all religious teachers are the messengers of one God. Its quest is for the general peace of mankind, whose unification it regards as necessary and inevitable; membership is open to all who accept its teachings, and members are now found in most countries of the world. Almost from its inception followers of this faith have been persecuted in Persia. The seat of its governing body, the Universal House of Justice, is in Haifa in Israel, adjacent to the golden-domed shrine of the Bab (see BABI) where his bones were buried in 1909 after freedom was given to religious minorities in the Ottoman empire.

Bahamas /bəˈhɑːməz/ a country consisting of an archipelago off the SE coast of Florida, part of the West Indies; pop. (1980) 241,000; official language, English; capital, Nassau. It was here that Columbus made his first landfall in the New World (12 Oct. 1492). The islands were depopulated in the 16th c. as the Spaniards carried off most of the inhabitants to slavery and death. In 1648 a group of English Puritans settled there, and the islands were administered as a British colony from the 18th c. until they gained independence, as a member of the Commonwealth, in 1973. The subtropical climate and extensive beaches make tourism the main industry. —**Bahamian** adj. & n.

Bahrain /bɑːˈreɪn/ a sheikdom consisting of a group of

islands in the Persian Gulf; pop. (1981) 350,798; official language, Arabic; capital, Manama. The islands, famous in ancient times for their pearls, were ruled by the Portuguese in the 16th c. and the Persians in the 17th c. They became a British protectorate in 1861 under a treaty by which the sheikh pledged himself to refrain from 'the prosecution of war, piracy, or slavery', and independent in 1971. Bahrain's economy is almost wholly dependent on the refining and export of oil, chiefly that coming by pipeline from Saudi Arabia. —**Bahraini** adj. & n.

Baikal /baɪˈkɑːl/, **Lake** a large lake in southern Siberia.

bail[1] n. **1.** money or property pledged as security that an arrested person will appear in court to stand trial if released temporarily. **2.** permission for a person's release on such security. —v.t. to procure the release of (an arrested person) by becoming security for him or her. —**bail out**, to rescue from financial difficulties. —**on bail**, released after bail is pledged. [f. OF (bailler take charge of) f. L baiulare carry a load]

bail[2] n. **1.** (in cricket) either of the two cross-pieces resting on the three stumps of the wicket (ill. SPORTS). **2.** a bar separating horses in an open stable. **3.** a bar holding paper against the platen of a typewriter. [f. OF bailler enclose]

bail[3] v.t. to scoop out (water) that has entered a boat; to clear (a boat) of water. [f. F baille bucket]

bailey /ˈbeɪlɪ/ n. the outer wall of a castle; a court enclosed by this (ill. CASTLES). —**Old Bailey**, see separate entry. [rel. to BAIL[2]]

Bailey bridge /ˈbeɪlɪ/ a bridge made in prefabricated sections designed for rapid assembly. [f. D. C. Bailey (d. 1985), the designer]

bailie /ˈbeɪlɪ/ n. a municipal officer and magistrate in Scotland. [as foll.]

bailiff /ˈbeɪlɪf/ n. **1.** a sheriff's officer who serves writs and performs arrests. **2.** a landlord's agent or steward. **3.** the leading civil officer in each of the Channel Islands. [f. OF f. L (baiulus manager)]

bailiwick /ˈbeɪlɪwɪk/ n. the jurisdiction of a bailie or (in the Channel Islands) a bailiff. [f. BAILIE + wick district]

bain-marie /bæmæˈrɪ/ n. a vessel of hot water in which a dish of food is placed for slow cooking. [F f. L balneum mariae bath of Mary (supposed Jewish alchemist)]

Bairam /baɪˈrɑːm/ n. either of two annual Muslim festivals, **Greater Bairam**, celebrated concurrently with the annual pilgrimage (hadj) in the twelfth month of the Muslim lunar calendar and continuing for 3-4 days, and **Lesser Bairam**, which follows the month of ritual fasting (Ramadan), the ninth month of the year, and lasts 2-3 days. [Turk. & Pers.]

Baird /beəd/, John Logie (1888-1946), Scottish pioneer of television. He started his work in the early 1920s, gave a demonstration in London in 1926, and made the first transatlantic transmission and demonstration of colour television in 1928.

bairn /beən/ n. (Sc.) a child. [OE, rel. to BEAR[1]]

bait n. food (real or sham) used to entice fish etc.; an enticement. —v.t. **1.** to put bait on or in (a fish-hook, trap, etc.). **2.** to attack (a chained bear etc.) with dogs for sport; to torment or provoke. [f. ON, rel. to BITE]

baize n. a coarse usually green woollen material used to cover tables, doors, etc. [f. F bai chestnut-coloured]

bake v.t./i. **1.** to cook or be cooked by dry heat, especially in an oven. **2.** to harden or be hardened by exposure to heat. —**baked beans**, cooked haricot beans (usually tinned and prepared with tomato sauce). [OE]

bakehouse n. a house or room for baking bread.

bakelite /ˈbeɪk(ə)laɪt/ n. a plastic made from phenol etc. and formaldehyde, used in electrical appliances etc. as an insulator. [G, f. L. H. Baekeland Belgian-American inventor (d. 1944)]

baker n. one who bakes and sells bread. —**baker's dozen**, thirteen (from the old custom of giving the retailer a free loaf for every twelve he bought). [f. BAKE]

bakery n. a place where bread is made or sold. [as prec.]

Bakewell /ˈbeɪkwel/, Robert (1725-95), English pioneer in scientific methods of livestock breeding and husbandry, who from his Leicestershire farm produced pedigree herds of sheep and cattle. Proper irrigation of his grassland gave him four cuts a year, while feeding and rigorously selective breeding greatly improved the meat-production from his animals. The first expenses of his experiments appear to have exceeded the profits, for he became bankrupt in 1776.

Bakewell tart /ˈbeɪkwel/ a tart containing an almond-flavoured pudding mixture over a layer of jam. [town in Derbyshire]

baking adj. (colloq., of weather etc.) intolerably hot. [f. BAKE]

baking-powder n. a mixture of sodium bicarbonate, cream of tartar, etc., used as a raising agent.

baksheesh /bækˈʃiːʃ/ n. (in the Middle East) a gratuity, alms. [Pers.]

Bakst /bækst/, Léon (1866-1924), real name Lev Semuilovich Rosenberg, Russian painter and designer. Associated with Diaghilev's magazine The World of Art from 1899, he became one of the most influential members of the Diaghilev circle and the Ballets Russes. He designed the décor for such Diaghilev productions as Carnaval, Sheherazade (both 1910), Spectre de la rose (1911), L'après-midi d'un faune, Daphnis and Chloë (both 1912), and The Sleeping Princess (1921).

Baku /bæˈkuː/ the capital of Azerbaijan, a centre of the oil industry, on the shore of the Caspian Sea.

Balaclava /bæləˈklɑːvə/ a Crimean village, scene of a battle (1854) in the Crimean War. A Russian attempt to break the siege of Sebastopol was repulsed by the Franco-British army in a confused engagement most famous for the Charge of the Light Brigade. —n. (in full **Balaclava helmet**) a knitted cap covering the head and neck, with an opening for the face.

balalaika /bæləˈlaɪkə/ n. a guitar-like instrument (made in various sizes) with a triangular body, popular in Slavonic countries (ill. MUSICAL NOTATION). [Russ.]

balance /ˈbæləns/ n. **1.** a weighing-apparatus with two scales or pans hanging from a cross-bar. **2.** (also **balance-wheel**) a mechanism regulating the speed of a clock or watch. **3.** the stable condition arising from even distribution of weight or amount. **4.** a preponderating weight or amount. **5.** the agreement or difference between credits and debits; a statement of this. **6.** the difference between a sum paid and a sum due; the amount left over. —v.t./i. **1.** to offset, to weigh (considerations etc.) against each other. **2.** to distribute (weights) evenly; to be, put, or keep in a state of balance. **3.** to compare the credit and debit sides of (an account) and make any necessary entry to equalize them; (of an account) to have its two sides equal. —**balance of payments**, the difference in value between the amount paid by a country for its imports and that paid to it for its exports (including invisible earnings). **balance of power**, a situation in which the chief States have roughly equal power; the power to decide events, held by a small group when the larger groups are of equal strength to each other. **balance of trade**, the difference in value between imports and exports. **balance sheet**, a written statement of assets and liabilities. **in the balance**, with the outcome still undecided. **on balance**, taking all things into consideration. [f. OF f. L bilanx two-scaled (balance) (BI-, lanx scale)]

Balanchine /bælɑ̃ˈʃiːn, ˈbæləntʃiːn/, George (1904-83), real name Georgi Melitonovich Balanchivadze, Russian-American dancer, choreographer, and ballet director. Diaghilev made him chief choreographer of his Ballets Russes in 1925; from this time dates his life-long friendship with Stravinsky. In 1934 he went to the USA, and started the company which later became the New York City Ballet. One of the greatest choreographers in ballet history, he became a dominant force of neoclassicism and a master of the plotless ballet. His numerous works include Firebird (1949), Nutcracker (1954), A Midsummer Night's Dream (1962), and Slaughter on Tenth Avenue (1968). He also choreographed opera, musicals, and films.

Balboa /bælˈbəʊə/, Vasco Núñez de (1475-1517), Spanish explorer, especially of Central America. Settling in San Domingo in the new Spanish colony of Hispaniola in 1501, Balboa later joined an expedition to Darien as a stowaway, but rose to command it after a mutiny (1510-11). In 1513 he reached the western coast of the isthmus after an epic 25-day march, thereby becoming the first European to see the Pacific Ocean. The arrival of a colonial governor in Panama marked a drastic downturn in Balboa's fortunes, however, and in 1517, after a series of disagreements with his superior, he was executed on a trumped-up charge of sedition.

Balcon /ˈbælkən/, Michael (1896-1977), British film producer. He was responsible for several early Hitchcock films but is mainly remembered for his long association with Ealing Studios, during which he produced such famous comedies as Kind Hearts and Coronets, Passport to Pimlico, and *Whisky Galore* (all 1949), *The Man in the White Suit*, and *The Lavender Hill Mob* (both 1952).

balcony /ˈbælkənɪ/ *n.* **1.** a platform with a rail or balustrade, on the outside of a building, with access from an upper-storey door or window. **2.** an upper tier of seats in a cinema or above the dress circle in a theatre (ill. THEATRE). [f. It., as BALK]

bald /bɔːld/ *adj.* **1.** with a hairless scalp; (of animals etc.) lacking the usual hairs, feathers, etc. of the species. **2.** (of a tyre) having its tread worn away. **3.** (of style) plain and unelaborated. —**bald eagle,** a kind of eagle (*Haliaetus leucocephalus*) with white feathers on its head and neck, the emblematic bird of the USA. [orig. unkn.]

baldachin /ˈbældəkɪn/ *n.* (also **baldaquin**) a canopy over a throne etc. [f. It. *Baldaco* (= Baghdad), where the original brocade of the canopy was made]

Balder /ˈbɔːldə(r)/ (*Scand. myth.*) a son of Odin and god of the summer sun. He was invulnerable to all things except mistletoe, with which the evil spirit Loki by a trick induced the blind god Hödur to kill him.

balderdash /ˈbɔːldədæʃ/ *n.* nonsense. [earlier sense (16th c.) 'frothy liquid'; orig. unkn.]

balding /ˈbɔːldɪŋ/ *adj.* becoming bald. [f. BALD]

baldric /ˈbɔːldrɪk/ *n.* a strap, worn across the body, on which a shield or sword is hung (ill. ARMOUR). [f. OF *baudrei*]

bale[1] *n.* a large bundle of merchandise (e.g. cloth) or hay. — *v.t.* to make into a bale. —**baler** *n.* [f. MDu., rel. to BALL[1]]

bale[2] *v.i.* **bale out,** to escape from an aircraft by parachute. [= BAIL[1]]

Balearic Islands /bælɪˈærɪk/ (also **Balearics**) a group of Mediterranean islands off the east coast of Spain, forming a province of that country, with four large islands (Majorca, Minorca, Ibiza, Formentera) and seven smaller ones; pop. (1970) 558,287; capital, Palma (on Majorca). Occupied by the Romans after the destruction of Carthage, the islands were subsequently conquered by Vandals and Moors, and then by Aragon in the 14th c.

baleen /bəˈliːn/ *n.* whalebone. [f. OF f. L *balaena* whale]

baleful /ˈbeɪlfəl/ *adj.* having a deadly or malign influence. —**balefully** *adv.* [f. bale (OE *b(e)alu*) destruction, evil]

Balfour /ˈbælfʊə(r)/, Arthur James, 1st Earl of Balfour (1848–1930), British Conservative statesman and philosopher. An MP from 1874, Balfour entered the Cabinet of his uncle, the Earl of Salisbury, in 1886, and succeeded him as Prime Minister in 1902. His premiership saw the formation of the Committee of Imperial Defence and the creation of the Entente Cordiale with France, but the party split over the issue of tariff reform in 1905, forcing Balfour's resignation. During the First World War Balfour served as First Lord of the Admiralty (1915–16) and Foreign Secretary (1916–19), in which capacity he issued in 1917 the declaration, known by his name, in favour of a Jewish national home in Palestine.

Bali /ˈbɑːlɪ/ a mountainous island of Indonesia; pop. 2,174,105; capital, Singaradja. —**Balinese** /-ˈniːz/ *adj. & n.* (*pl.* same).

Baliol /ˈbeɪlɪəl/, John de (*c.*1250–1313), king of Scotland 1292–6. One of several baronial claimants to the vacant Scottish throne, Baliol became king as a result of the support of the English king Edward I, but his subsequent attempt to break free from feudal domination was crushed, and following his deposition the leadership of the struggle for independence passed first to Sir William Wallace and then to Robert the Bruce.

balk /bɔːk/ *v.t./i.* **1.** to shy or jib *at.* **2.** to thwart. [= BAULK]

Balkan /ˈbɔːlkən, ˈbɒl-/ *adj.* of the Balkan Peninsula or States. —**the Balkans,** the Balkan States. **Balkan Peninsula,** a peninsula of SE Europe, south of the Danube and Sava rivers, home of various peoples (Albanians, Vlachs, Greeks, Serbs, Bulgars, and Turks) with differing cultures. **Balkan States,** the countries of this peninsula. [Turk.]

From the 3rd to 7th c. the peninsula, nominally ruled by the Byzantine emperors, was invaded by successive migrations of Slavs; later, parts of it were conquered by Venice and other States. In 1356 the Ottoman invasion began: Constantinople fell to the Turks in 1453, and by 1478 most of the peninsula was in their power; the subject nations, though largely retaining their languages and religions, did not recover independence until the 19th c. In 1912–13 Turkey was attacked and defeated by other Balkan peoples in alliance, and after the First World War the peninsula was divided between Greece, Bulgaria, Albania,

and Yugoslavia, with Turkey retaining only Constantinople and the surrounding land.

Balkis /ˈbɔːlkɪs, ˈbɒl-/ the name of the Queen of Sheba in Arabic literature.

ball[1] /bɔːl/ *n.* **1.** a rounded object, solid or hollow, especially for use in a game. **2.** a single delivery of a ball by a bowler in cricket or a pitcher in baseball. **3.** a rounded mass or part; (in *pl.*, *vulg.*) the testicles. —*v.t./i.* to form into a ball. —**ball (and socket) joint,** a form of joint with a rounded end in a concave cup or socket, having great freedom of movement (ill. BODY 2). **ball-bearing** *n.* a bearing using small steel balls. **ball-point (pen),** a pen with a tiny ball as its writing-point. **on the ball,** (*colloq.*) alert. **set the ball rolling,** to open a discussion. [f. ON]

ball[2] /bɔːl/ *n.* a formal social gathering for dancing. [f. F f. L f. Gk]

ballad /ˈbæləd/ *n.* a simple song, especially one with a repeated melody; a poem or song in short stanzas telling a story. [f. OF f. Prov. *balada* dancing-song (as BALL[2])]

ballade /bæˈlɑːd/ *n.* a poem with one or more sets of three verses with 7, 8, or 10 lines each ending with the same refrain line, and a short final verse. [F, = prec.]

balladeer /bæləˈdɪə(r)/ *n.* a composer or performer of ballads. [f. BALLAD]

ballast /ˈbæləst/ *n.* **1.** heavy material placed in the hold of a ship or the car of a balloon to give it stability. **2.** coarse stones etc. forming the bed of a railway or road. —*v.t.* to weight with ballast. [f. LG or Scand.]

ballcock *n.* a device with a floating ball controlling the water-level in a cistern.

ballerina /bæləˈriːnə/ *n.* a woman ballet-dancer, especially one taking leading roles in classical ballet. [It. (*ballare* dance)]

ballet /ˈbæleɪ/ *n.* a form of dancing and mime to music (see below); a performance of this. [F f. It. (as BALL[2])]

The art of ballet grew up in Renaissance Italy and reached its first great flowering in France at the court of Louis XIV who employed a young Italian, Lully, as his dancing master. The great schools of 'romantic' and 'classical' ballet developed in the 19th c., the former represented by such dancers as Marie Taglioni (1804–84) and Carlotta Grisi (1819–99) and the latter by the choreographer Marius Petipa (1818–1910), whose works include *The Sleeping Beauty* (1890) to music by Tchaikovsky. The early 20th c. was dominated by the productions of Diaghilev's Ballets Russes, involving the collaboration of outstanding dancers, choreographers, stage designers, and composers, but an equally important influence was that of the American dancer Isadora Duncan, who abandoned the traditional role of ballet as a narrative art for one of subjective response directly to the music. This forms the basis of the 'modern dance' movement, with which the names of Martha Graham (1894–) and Merce Cunningham (1919–) are associated.

balletomane /ˈbælɪtəmeɪn/ *n.* a ballet enthusiast. [f. prec. + -*mane* (as MANIA)]

ballista /bəˈlɪstə/ *n.* (*pl.* -ae) a machine of ancient warfare for hurling large stones etc. [L, f. Gk *ballō* throw]

ballistic /bəˈlɪstɪk/ *adj.* of projectiles. —**ballistic missile,** one powered only during the initial stages of its flight and falling by gravity on its target. [f. prec.]

ballistics *n.* the science of projectiles and firearms. [f. prec.]

balloon /bəˈluːn/ *n.* **1.** a small inflatable rubber bag with a neck, used as a child's toy or decoration. **2.** a large rounded envelope inflated with hot air or gas to make it rise in the air, often one with a basket etc. for passengers (ill. FLIGHT); see below. **3.** a balloon-shaped line containing the words or thoughts of a character in a comic strip or cartoon. —*v.t./i.* **1.** to swell out like a balloon. **2.** to travel by balloon. **3.** to hit or kick (a ball) high in the air. [f. F or It. (*balla* ball)]

A small hot-air balloon was demonstrated in Lisbon in 1709, but attracted little attention. Napoleon, as a young general, used balloons for military observation in 1794, information about the enemy's movements being communicated by signalling. Barrage balloons, arranged in protective cordons round cities, were used in the First and Second World Wars to deter bombing attacks. Free balloons, both manned and unmanned, have had important functions in atmospheric research and weather prediction.

Man's efforts to fly succeeded on 21 Nov. 1783 when two Frenchmen, de Rozier and the Marquis d'Arlandes, were airborne under a hot-air balloon (built by the Montgolfier brothers) for 25 minutes and covered more than 8 km

(5 miles). In 1804 two other intrepid Frenchmen, Biot and Gay-Lussac, undertook an ascent (the first ever made solely in the cause of science) to examine magnetic force and the constitution of the higher atmosphere and its electrical properties. Ballooning in the 19th c. was a story of steady and astonishing achievement, with flights across the English Channel and the Alps. By the end of the century the sport was so fashionable in London as to be rated a social grace, but lapsed at the end of the Edwardian era with the arrival of heavier-than-air flight. Interest in it has recently revived.

balloonist *n.* one who travels by balloon. [f. prec.]

ballot /ˈbælət/ *n.* the process of voting to select a representative or course of action etc. usually in secret and on ballot-papers; the total of votes cast by this method. — *v.t./i.* to vote or cause to vote by ballot. —**ballot-box** *n.* a container for ballot-papers. **ballot-paper** *n.* a paper used in voting by ballot, usually having the names of candidates etc. printed on it. [f. It., = small ball; such voting was orig. by small balls]

ballroom *n.* a large room for formal dancing.

bally /ˈbæli/ *adj. & adv.* (*colloq.*) a milder form of intensive 'bloody'. [voicing of *bl—y*, squeamish printing of BLOODY]

ballyhoo /bælɪˈhuː/ *n.* loud noise, fuss; extravagant publicity. [orig. unkn.]

balm /bɑːm/ *n.* **1.** a fragrant medicinal gum exuded by certain trees, balsam. **2.** an aromatic ointment. **3.** a healing or soothing influence. **4.** a herb (*Melissa officinalis*) with lemon-scented leaves. [f. OF f. L BALSAM]

Balmoral Castle /bælˈmɒr(ə)l/ a holiday residence of the British royal family near Braemar in Scotland. The estate was bought in 1847 by Prince Albert, who rebuilt the castle.

balmy /ˈbɑːmi/ *adj.* **1.** resembling balm, fragrant or soothing; (of air) soft and warm. **2.** (*slang*) = BARMY. [f. BALM]

baloney /bəˈləʊni/ *n.* var. of BOLONEY.

balsa /ˈbɒlsə/ *n.* (also **balsa-wood**) a very light strong wood from a tropical American tree (*Ochroma pyramidale*), used for models etc. [Sp., = raft]

balsam /ˈbɔːlsəm/ *n.* **1.** a resinous exudation from certain trees, balm; an ointment, especially of a substance dissolved in oil or turpentine; a tree producing balsam. **2.** any of various flowering plants of the genus *Impatiens*, especially one cultivated for its showy flowers. [OE f. L *balsamum*]

Baltic /ˈbɔːltɪk, ˈbɒl-/ *adj.* of the Baltic Sea, States, or languages. —*n.* the Baltic Sea. —**Baltic languages**, a group of languages today represented only by Lithuanian and Latvian, others having died out over the centuries. It belongs to the Indo-European language group but shares a number of features with Slavonic languages. **Baltic Sea,** an almost land-locked sea in northern Europe, connected with the North Sea by a channel, and bordered by Sweden, Finland, the USSR, Poland, Germany, and Denmark. **Baltic States,** the former independent republics of Estonia, Latvia, and Lithuania. [f. L (*Balthae* dwellers near the Baltic Sea)]

Baltimore /ˈbɔːltɪmɔː(r), ˈbɒl-/ a seaport in north Maryland; pop. 774,113. [f. Lord *Baltimore* (d. 1632), English proprietor of territory which later became Maryland]

baluster /ˈbæləstə(r)/ *n.* a short pillar with a curving outline, especially in a balustrade; a post helping to support a rail. [f. F, ult. f. Gk *balaustion* flower of wild pomegranate, from resemblance in shape]

balustrade /bæləˈstreɪd/ *n.* a row of balusters with a rail or coping as an ornamental parapet to a balcony, terrace, etc. [f. F, as prec.]

Balzac /ˈbælzæk/, Honoré de (1799–1850), French novelist, who studied law in Paris before turning to literature in 1819. His first successful novel was *Les Chouans* (1829). Thereafter his output became prodigious and his great series of co-ordinated interconnected novels and stories known collectively as *La Comédie humaine* appeared in 1842–8. The whole is a panorama of French society during the late 18th to early 19th c. and the underlying theme is the role of money in shaping personal and social relations. The breadth of Balzac's vision, and the vitality of his creations, have earned him a reputation as a writer of universal genius, and his work is an essential reference-point in the history of the European novel. Having struggled with insolvency most of his life he finally married the wealthy Polish lady, Mme Eveline Hanska, with whom he had corresponded since 1832 (*Lettres à l'Étrangère*, 1899–1906) shortly before his death.

Bamako /ˈbæməkəʊ/ the capital of Mali, pop. 600,000.

bamboo /bæmˈbuː/ *n.* any of a large group of tree-like grasses of the genus *Bambusa*, especially characteristic of eastern Asia; its hollow stem used to make canes, furniture, etc., or as food. The pulp and fibre of some species are used in paper-making, or distilled to extract substances for use in medicines and chemical reactions. [f. Du. f. Port. *Mambu*, f. Malay]

bamboozle /bæmˈbuːz(ə)l/ *v.t.* (*colloq.*) to hoax, to cheat; to mystify, to perplex. —**bamboozlement** *n.* [orig. unkn.]

ban *v.t.* (-**nn**-) to prohibit officially (*from*); to forbid. —*n.* an official prohibition. [OE, = summon]

banal /bəˈnɑːl/ *adj.* commonplace, trite. —**banality** /bəˈnælɪtɪ/ *n.* [F (as BAN); orig. = 'compulsory', hence = 'common to all']

banana /bəˈnɑːnə/ *n.* a long finger-shaped yellow fruit; the tropical tree (*Musa sapientum*) bearing it. —**banana republic,** (*derog.*) a small tropical country dependent on its fruit exports and regarded as economically unstable. [Port. or Sp., f. Afr. name]

band[1] *n.* **1.** a narrow strip, hoop, or loop. **2.** a range of values, wavelengths, etc. between two given limits. —*v.t.* to put a band on or round. —**band-saw** *n.* a power saw consisting of a toothed steel belt running over wheels. [f. ON, rel. to BIND]

band[2] *n.* **1.** an organized group of people with a common purpose. **2.** a group of musicians (especially players of wind and percussion instruments) organized for playing together. —*v.t./i.* to unite in an organized group. [f. OF, perh. f. Goth. *bandwa* signal]

Banda /ˈbændə/, Hastings Kamuzu (1906–), Malawi statesman, who studied medicine in the USA and practised in Britain before returning to lead his country to independence. As its first President he created a highly autocratic regime, but his prestige overcame the tribal divisions which plagued many newly independent African countries so that Malawi, a poor country with few resources, became an oasis of calm in a troubled region.

bandage /ˈbændɪdʒ/ *n.* a strip of material used to bind a wound. —*v.t.* to bind with a bandage. [F, as BAND[1]]

bandanna /bænˈdænə/ *n.* a large handkerchief with spots or other pattern. [f. Hindi, = tie-dyeing (rel. to BAND[1], BIND)]

bandbox *n.* a box for hats etc.

bandeau /ˈbændəʊ/ *n.* (*pl.* **-eaux** /-əʊz/) a strip of material worn round the hair or inside a hat. [F, as BAND[1]]

bandicoot /ˈbændɪkuːt/ *n.* **1.** a kind of very large rat (*Bandicota indica*) in India. **2.** a ratlike Australasian marsupial of the family Peramelidae. [Telugu, = pig-rat]

bandit *n.* a robber or outlaw, especially one of a gang attacking travellers. —**banditry** *n.* [f. It., = outlawed (as BANISH)]

bandmaster *n.* the conductor of a musical band.

bandoleer, bandolier /bændəˈlɪə(r)/ *n.* a shoulder-belt with loops for ammunition. [f. Du. or F, prob. rel. to BANNER]

bandstand *n.* a platform for musicians, especially outdoors.

bandwagon /ˈbændwægən/ *n.* a wagon for a band of musicians to ride in, as in a parade. —**climb** or **jump on the bandwagon,** to attach oneself to a successful party or cause.

bandwidth *n.* (in telecommunications etc.) a range of frequencies.

bandy[1] *v.t.* to exchange (words etc. *with*); to pass on (a rumour etc.) thoughtlessly. —*n.* a game resembling ice hockey but played with a ball not a puck. [perh. f. F *bander* take sides, oppose]

bandy[2] *adj.* (of legs) curving apart at the knees. [perh. f. obs. *bandy* hockey-stick]

bane *n.* **1.** a cause of ruin or trouble. **2.** (*archaic*) a poison (now only in plant-names, as *henbane*). —**baneful** *adj.* [OE]

bang *v.t./i.* **1.** to make a sudden loud noise like an explosion; to strike or shut noisily. **2.** to collide. —*n.* **1.** a banging noise. **2.** a sharp blow. —*adv.* **1.** with a banging sound. **2.** (*colloq.*) abruptly, exactly. [imit.]

banger *n.* anything that makes a loud bang, as a firework; (*colloq.*) a noisy old car; (*slang*) a sausage. [f. BANG]

Bangkok /bænˈkɒk/ the capital and chief port of Thailand; pop. (est. 1983) 49,459,000.

Bangladesh /bæŋɡləˈdeʃ/ a Muslim country of the Indian subcontinent, in the Ganges delta; pop. (1981) 89,940,000; official language, Bengali; capital, Dhaka. From 1857 the area formed part of India, under British rule, until 1947 when it became (as East Pakistan) one of the two geographical units of Pakistan. In response to serious internal political problems an independent republic was proclaimed in East Pakistan in 1971, taking the name of Bangladesh (Bengali, = land of Bengal), which became a member State of the Commonwealth in 1972. It is the world's chief producer of jute, which forms its main export, but the country remains one of the poorest in the world. The region is subject to frequent cyclones which cause immense damage and loss of life and crops. —**Bangladeshi** adj. & n.

bangle n. a large decorative ring worn round the arm or ankle. [f. Hindi bangri]

Bangui /ˈbæŋgiː/ the capital of the Central African Republic; pop. 350,000.

banian /ˈbænjən/ n. an Indian fig-tree (Ficus benghalensis) with spreading branches from which roots grow downwards to the ground and form new trunks. [Port. f. Skr., = trader (from such a tree under which traders built a pagoda)]

banish v.t. 1. to condemn to exile. 2. to dismiss from one's mind or presence. —**banishment** n. [f. OF, rel. to BAN]

banister /ˈbænɪstə(r)/ n. any of the posts supporting a stair handrail (ill. HOUSES); (in pl.) these posts together with the rail. [corrupt. of BALUSTER]

banjo /ˈbændʒəʊ/ n. (pl. **-os**) a stringed instrument like a guitar, with a circular body. Its origin is supposed to be Africa, and it was in use among slaves of the southern USA. It became the characteristic instrument of Negro minstrels, and in the 20th c. found a place in jazz bands. —**banjoist** n. [corrupt. of earlier bandore, ult. f. Gk pandoura three-stringed lute]

Banjul /bænˈdʒuːl/ (formerly Bathurst) the capital of the Gambia; pop. (1983) 44,536.

bank[1] n. 1. a stretch of sloping ground, especially that on either side of a river. 2. a raised mass of sand etc. in the bed of the sea or of a river. 3. a flat-topped mass of snow or cloud. —v.t./i. 1. to provide with or form a bank. 2. to heap; to pile coal-dust etc. on (a fire) so that it burns slowly. 3. to tilt laterally in rounding a curve. [f. ON, rel. to BENCH]

bank[2] n. 1. an establishment where money is deposited in accounts, withdrawn, and borrowed. 2. a place for storing a reserve supply (e.g. of blood). 3. the pool of money in a gambling-game. —v.t./i. to deposit (money) at a bank; to have an account at or with a bank. —**bank holiday**, a weekday kept as a public holiday, when banks are officially closed. In the 19th c. certain Saints' days (about 33 per annum) were kept as holidays at the Bank of England. In 1834 these were reduced to Good Friday, 1 May, 1 Nov., and Christmas Day. An Act of 1871 formally recognized certain days as bank holidays, and the number and date of these has been altered subsequently. [f. F or It. (as foll.), referring to the fact that early bankers transacted their business at a bench (banco) in the market-place]

bank[3] n. a series of similar objects grouped in a row; a tier of oars in a galley. [f. OF banc bench (as BANK[1])]

banker n. 1. one who runs a bank. 2. the keeper of the bank in a gambling-game. [f. BANK[2]]

banking n. the business of running a bank. [f. BANK[2]]

banknote n. a strip of paper serving as currency, originally a promissory note from a bank.

Bank of England the central bank of England (see CENTRAL), originally incorporated in 1694 to raise and lend money to William III towards carrying on the war with France. It has the right of issuing legal-tender notes, manages the National Debt, and administers exchange-control regulations. The government is its chief customer; it was nationalized in 1946.

bankrupt /ˈbæŋkrʌpt/ adj. 1. declared by a court of law to be unable to meet debts in full, the estate therefore being administered on behalf of creditors; financially ruined, insolvent. 2. destitute of. —n. a person officially declared bankrupt. —v.t. to make bankrupt. —**bankruptcy** n. [f. It., = broken bench (cf. BANK[2])]

Banks /bæŋks/, Sir Joseph (1743-1820), English naturalist who accompanied Captain Cook on his first voyage round the world and collected and recorded many new species of plants. Banks became an influential figure in science: he was President of the Royal Society for over 40 years, and helped to establish the botanic gardens at Kew near London not only as a repository of thousands of living specimens from all over the world but as a centre for the introduction of plants to new regions, including breadfruit for the West Indies and tea from China to India. He also imported merino sheep from Spain and sent them on to Australia.

His herbarium and library in London became a centre of taxonomic research, and after his death became part of the British Museum.

banksia /ˈbæŋksɪə/ n. a flowering shrub of the Australian genus Banksia. [f. prec.]

banner n. 1. a large cloth carrying an emblem or slogan, carried on a crossbar or between two poles at public demonstrations. 2. the flag of a king, knight, etc., serving as a rallying-point. —**banner headline,** one extending across a newspaper page. [f. AF f. L bandum standard]

Bannister /ˈbænɪstə(r)/, Sir Roger Gilbert (1929-), British middle-distance runner, the first man to run the mile in under 4 minutes (6 May 1954) which, in its day, was the most coveted achievement in athletics.

bannock /ˈbænək/ n. (Sc. & N. Engl.) a round flat loaf, usually unleavened. [OE]

Bannockburn /ˈbænəkbɜːn/ a village in central Scotland, scene of a decisive Scottish victory when the much larger English army of Edward II, advancing to break the siege of Stirling Castle in 1314, was outmanœuvred and defeated by Robert the Bruce on difficult ground a few miles from the castle. Bruce's victory virtually ended for several decades the Plantagenet attempt to reduce Scotland to the status of a vassal kingdom.

banns n.pl. an announcement in church, usually read out on three successive Sundays, of an intended marriage, to give opportunity of objection. The custom of announcing a forthcoming marriage during a church service was adopted early, but seems to have developed especially after Charlemagne's order for inquiry before marriage into possible consanguinity between the parties. It was ordered in England in 1200, and made compulsory throughout Christendom in 1215. The matter is regulated by statute, and the obtaining of a marriage licence is a civil and canonical equivalent. [pl. of BAN]

banquet /ˈbæŋkwɪt/ n. a sumptuous meal; an elaborate and formal dinner. —v.i. to take part in a banquet. —**banqueter** n. [f. F, dim. of banc bench]

banshee /ˈbænʃiː/ n. (Ir. & Sc.) a female spirit whose wail outside a house is superstitiously believed to portend death within. [Ir., = woman of the fairies]

bantam /ˈbæntəm/ n. a kind of small domestic fowl, of which the cock is very pugnacious. [f. Bantam seaport in Java]

bantamweight n. a boxing-weight between flyweight and featherweight (see BOXING-WEIGHT).

banter n. playful good-humoured teasing. —v.t./i. to exchange banter, to joke in a good-humoured way; to chaff. [orig. unkn.]

Banting[1] /ˈbæntɪŋ/, Sir Frederick Grant (1891-1941), Canadian surgeon who, in 1921, working with a science student, Charles Best, isolated the internal secretion of the pancreas, insulin. Banting had no significant experience in physiological research and the production of insulin originated from a wrongly conceived, badly conducted, and incorrectly interpreted series of experiments. None the less the discovery was a complex and dramatic event which revolutionized the treatment of diabetes, and he was awarded a Nobel Prize for medicine in 1923.

Banting[2] /ˈbæntɪŋ/, William (1797-1878), English undertaker who advocated a method of reducing weight by dieting.

Bantu /bænˈtuː/ n. (pl. same or **-us**) 1. a large group of Black peoples in central and southern Africa (see below); a member of this group. 2. the group of languages spoken by them. —adj. of the Bantu or their languages. [Bantu, = people]
The Bantu people migrated to southern Africa, through the lake region of East Africa, by the 3rd c. AD. They are basically of Negro stock but vary considerably in physical appearance through admixture with other African peoples during and after their initial entry into southern Africa. It is believed that the Bantu introduced iron metallurgy to southern Africa at the time of their entry. Bantu languages belong to the Niger-Congo language group, and there are more than 300 of them (with 100 million speakers), of which Swahili is the most important. Their chief characteristics are that nearly all the words are tonal, and that all nouns belong to one of a set of classes, usually about eighteen. Most Bantu languages were not written down until the 19th c. Originally Arabs trading along the coast had brought their Arabic script, which was used for Swahili, but elsewhere the Roman alphabet has been used, sometimes with additional characters. Linguistic evidence suggests that the original

home of these languages may have been in the Cameroon region.

Bantustan /bæntu:'stɑ:n/ *n.* any of the territories, officially called Bantu homelands, reserved for Black Africans in the Republic of South Africa. [f. prec. + *-stan* (as in HINDUSTANI)]

banyan /'bænɪən/ *n.* var. of BANIAN.

baobab /'beɪəʊbæb/ *n.* an African tree (*Adansonia digitata*) with a massive trunk and large edible pulpy fruit. [prob. native name]

bap *n.* a soft flat bread roll. [Sc.; orig. unkn.]

baptism /'bæptɪz(ə)m/ *n.* admission to the Church by the rite of sprinkling with or immersing in water, chiefly administered to infants, with name-giving. **-baptism of fire,** initiation in a painful experience, such as exposure to gunfire. **—baptismal** /-'tɪzm(ə)l/ *adj.* [as BAPTIZE]

Baptist /'bæptɪst/ *n.* **1.** a member of a Christian sect practising baptism of adults by immersion (see below). **2. the Baptist,** the title of St John who baptized Christ. [as BAPTIZE]

Baptists form one of the largest Protestant bodies, to be found in every continent and especially in the USA. The exiled John Smyth founded the first group in Amsterdam in 1609, and in 1612 some of his followers returned to London and established a Baptist Church in England. Churches arising from this practice were known as General Baptists, and those founded by a group of Calvinists, who held that salvation was only for a particular few, as Strict or Particular Baptists. Rigid Calvinism was gradually modified and the merging of the two groups, begun in 1813, was largely completed by the end of the 19th c.

baptistery /'bæptɪstərɪ/ *n.* a part of a church, or (formerly) a separate building, used for baptism; an immersion receptacle in a Baptist chapel. [f. Gk *baptistērion* bathing-place (as foll.)]

baptize /bæp'taɪz/ *v.t.* **1.** to administer baptism to, to christen. **2.** to name or nickname. [f. OF f. L f. Gk *baptizō* immerse, baptize]

bar[1] *n.* **1.** a long piece of rigid material; an oblong piece (of chocolate, soap, etc.); the heating element of an electric fire. **2.** a strip of silver below the clasp of a medal, serving as an extra distinction. **3.** a band of colour etc., a stripe. **4.** a rod or pole that fastens, confines, or obstructs something; a barrier; a sandbank or shoal at the mouth of a harbour or estuary; a restriction. **5.** (*Mus.*) any of the vertical lines dividing a piece of music into equal units; a section between two of these. **6.** a partition (real or imaginary) across a lawcourt, separating the judge, jury, and certain lawyers from the public; **the Bar,** barristers. **7.** a counter across which alcoholic drinks are served; the room containing this; a counter for special service (e.g. *heel bar* for shoe repairs). — *v.t.* (*-rr-*) **1.** to fasten with a bar, bolt, etc.; to shut *in* or *out.* **2.** to obstruct, prevent, or prohibit; to exclude. —*prep.* excluding. [f. OF *barre*]

bar[2] *n.* a unit of pressure, 10⁵ newton per sq. metre, approximately one atmosphere, used especially in meteorology. [f. Gk. *baros* weight]

Barabbas /bə'ræbəs/ the robber whom Pontius Pilate released from prison to the Jews instead of Jesus Christ (Mk. 15: 6–15).

barathea /bærə'θiːə/ *n.* a kind of fine cloth, especially of wool woven with silk. [orig. unkn.]

barb *n.* **1.** a small spine curving back from the point of an arrow or fish-hook, making it difficult to withdraw from what it has pierced. **2.** a wounding remark. **3.** a fleshy appendage from the mouth of some fishes. **4.** a lateral filament branching from the shaft of a feather (ill. BIRDS). [f. OF f. L. *barba* beard]

Barbados /bɑ:'beɪdəʊz, -dəs/ the most easterly of the Caribbean islands; pop. (1980) 248,983; official language, English; capital, Bridgetown. The geographical position of Barbados has influenced its history. Difficult of access in the days of sailing-ships, it became a British colony in 1652 and remained British without interruption until 1966 when it gained independence as a member State of the Commonwealth. The economy is based on tourism, sugar, and light manufacturing industries. **—Barbadian** *adj. & n.*

barbarian /bɑ:'beərɪən/ *n.* an uncivilized person. —*adj.* uncivilized. [as BARBAROUS]

barbaric /bɑ:'bærɪk/ *adj.* typical of a barbarian, rough and unrefined. [as BARBAROUS]

barbarism /'bɑ:bərɪz(ə)m/ *n.* **1.** an uncivilized condition or practice. **2.** an unacceptable linguistic usage. [as BARBAROUS]

barbarity /bɑ:'bærɪtɪ/ *n.* savage cruelty; a savagely cruel act. [as BARBAROUS.]

Barbarossa /bɑ:bə'rɒsə/ see FREDERICK I.

barbarous /'bɑ:bərəs/ *adj.* uncivilized; savagely cruel. — **barbarously** *adv.* [f. L. f. Gk, orig. = non-Greek, then = outside the Romano-Greek world]

Barbary /'bɑ:bərɪ/ *n.* an old name for the western part of North Africa. **Barbary ape,** a macaque of North Africa and Gibraltar. [ult. f. Arab., = BERBER]

barbecue /'bɑ:bɪkjuː/ *n.* a metal frame or portable grill for cooking meat, especially over an open fire; meat so cooked; an open-air party using this. —*v.t.* to cook on a barbecue. [f. Sp. f. Haitian]

barbed *adj.* **1.** furnished with a barb or barbs. **2.** (of remarks) having cruel undertones. **—barbed wire,** wire set with small spikes, used as fencing. [f. BARB]

barbel /'bɑ:b(ə)l/ *n.* **1.** a beardlike filament at the mouth of some fishes. **2.** a large European freshwater fish of the genus *Barbus* with such filaments. [f. OF (as BARB)]

barbell *n.* a metal rod used in weight-lifting, with adjustable weighted discs at either end.

barber *n.* a men's hairdresser (see below). **—barber-shop** *adj.* of a style of highly chromatic part-singing by male quartets. [AF f. L *barba* beard]

Formerly the barber was also a regular practitioner in surgery and dentistry. The Company of Barber-surgeons was incorporated by Edward IV in 1461; under Henry VIII (1540) the title was altered to 'Company of Barbers and Surgeons' (to which women were admitted), and surgery passed out of the hands of the barbers. (See DENTISTRY, SURGERY.)

barbican /'bɑ:bɪkən/ *n.* an outer defence of a castle or city, especially a double tower over a gate or bridge (ill. CASTLES). [f. OF; orig. unkn.]

barbiturate /bɑ:'bɪtjʊərət/ *n.* a soporific and sedative drug derived from barbituric acid. [f. foll.]

barbituric acid /bɑ:bɪ'tjʊərɪk/ an acid, malonyl urea, from which barbiturates are derived. [f. F f. G, f. *Barbara* woman's name]

Barbizon school /'bɑ:bɪz(ə)n/ a group of French landscape painters, who came together in the 1840s, opposed to academic painting conventions and concerned with landscape painting for its own sake. They took their name from the small village, near Paris, where they worked. Théodore Rousseau was the leader of the group which included Daubigny, Diaz, Miller, and Dupré. Influenced by Constable and Dutch 17th-c. traditions they painted direct from nature, in the form of studies which were completed later in the studio. They were unlike the impressionists in this respect, but shared the same desire to return to nature for aesthetic inspiration. Their fresh naturalistic approach was closely linked to the spirit of the realist movement, though with a much more limited subject-range.

Barbour /'bɑ:bə(r)/, John (*c.* 1320–95), Scottish poet, Archdeacon of Aberdeen (1357), who probably taught at Oxford and Paris. The only poem ascribed to him with certainty is *The Bruce*, a verse chronicle relating the deeds of Robert Bruce, king of Scotland, and his follower James Douglas, which contains a celebrated account of Bannockburn.

Barbuda see ANTIGUA AND BARBUDA.

barbule /'bɑ:bju:l/ *n.* a filament branching from the barb of a feather (ill. BIRDS). [f. L (dim. of *barba* beard)]

barcarole /bɑ:kə'rɒl, -'rəʊl/ *n.* **1.** a gondolier's song. **2.** a piece of music with steady lilting rhythm, especially for piano. [f. F f. It. (*barca* boat)]

Barcelona /bɑ:sɪ'ləʊnə/ a city and province of Catalonia in NE Spain; pop. (city) 1,752,627.

Bar-Cochba /'kɒkbə/ the name found in Christian sources (Jewish sources call him Simeon) for the leader of a Jewish rebellion in AD 132 against Hadrian's project to rebuild Jerusalem as a non-Jewish city, replacing the Jewish Temple with a temple of Jupiter. He claimed to be, and was accepted as, the Messiah. A number of letters in his handwriting have been found in archaeological excavations in Israel. [f. Aram., = son of a star]

bard[1] *n.* **1.** a Celtic minstrel; a Welsh poet honoured at an Eisteddfod. **2.** (*archaic*) a poet. **—the Bard of Avon,** Shakespeare. [Celtic]

bard[2] *v.t.* to place slices of bacon over (meat etc.) before roasting. [f. F *barde* (orig. = horse's breastplate), ult. f. Arab.]

bare *adj.* **1.** not clothed, not covered; scantily furnished. **2.** empty. **3.** plain, not elaborated. **4.** scanty, only just sufficient. —*v.t.* to uncover, to reveal. —**barely** *adv.*, **bareness** *n.* [OE]

bareback *adj.* & *adv.* on a horse without a saddle.

Barebones Parliament /ˈbeəbəʊnz/ the nickname of Cromwell's Parliament of 1653, from one of its members, Praise-God Barbon, an Anabaptist leather-seller in Fleet Street.

barefaced *adj.* shameless, impudent.

barefoot *adj.* & *adv.* without shoes, stockings, etc., on the feet.

bareheaded *adj.* without a hat.

barely *adv.* scarcely, only just. [f. BARE]

Barents /ˈbærənts/, Willem (d. 1597), Dutch explorer. The leader of several expeditions in search of the Northeast Passage to Asia, Barents discovered Spitsbergen and reached Novaya Zemlya, off the coast of which he died. Traces of his winter quarters were discovered undisturbed in the 1870s. The Barents Sea, north of Russia, is named after him.

bargain /ˈbɑːgɪn/ *n.* an agreement made with obligations on both sides, or on the terms of a sale; something obtained as a result of this, a thing got cheaply. —*v.i.* **1.** to discuss the terms of a sale or agreement. **2.** to expect or be prepared *for.* [f. OF *bargaignier*]

barge *n.* a long flat-bottomed boat carrying freight on rivers or canals; a large ornamental boat for State occasions etc. —*v.i.* to lurch or move clumsily *into, around,* etc. —**barge in,** to intrude without ceremony. [f. OF, perh. f. L & rel. to BARQUE]

barge-board *n.* a board or ornamental screen under the edge of a gable. [orig. unkn.]

bargee /bɑːˈdʒiː/ *n.* a person in charge of a barge (for freight); a member of its crew. [f. BARGE]

baritone /ˈbærɪtəʊn/ *n.* a male voice between tenor and bass; a singer having such a voice; a part written for it. [f. It. f. Gk *barus* heavy]

barium /ˈbeərɪəm/ *n.* a silver-white metallic element of the alkaline-earth metal group, symbol Ba, atomic number 56, first isolated by Sir Humphrey Davy in 1808. Barium and its compounds have a number of specialized uses, e.g. in water purification, the glass industry, pigments, and insecticides. It is used as an ingredient of signal flares and fireworks, where it imparts a bright yellowish-green colour to the flame. Its soluble compounds are poisonous, and the carbonate is used in rat poisons. —**barium meal,** a mixture including barium sulphate, which is opaque to X-rays, used in radiography of the alimentary canal. [f. BARYTA]

bark[1] *n.* the tough outer skin of the trunks and branches of trees (ill. TREES). —*v.t.* **1.** to strip bark from (trees). **2.** to scrape the skin off (part of the body) accidentally. [f. Scand., perh. rel. to BIRCH]

bark[2] *v.t./i.* **1.** (of a dog or fox) to utter a sharp explosive cry. **2.** to speak or utter in a sharp commanding tone. —*n.* a sound of or like barking. —**bark up the wrong tree,** to direct one's efforts to the wrong quarter. [OE, perh. var. of BREAK]

barley /ˈbɑːlɪ/ *n.* a cereal plant of the genus *Hordeum,* or its grain, used as food and in making malt liquors and spirits. —**barley sugar,** a sweet made of boiled sugar. **barley-water** *n.* a drink made from pearl barley (see PEARL). [OE]

barmaid *n.* a woman who serves behind the bar of a public house etc.

barman *n.* (*pl.* **-men**) a man who serves behind the bar of a public house etc.

Barmecide /ˈbɑːmɪsaɪd/ the patronymic of a noble Persian family in the time of the Abbasid caliphs. According to the *Arabian Nights* one of them set before a beggar rich dish-covers with nothing below, pretending that they contained a sumptuous banquet, whence the phrase **Barmecide feast,** illusory or disappointing benefits.

bar mitzvah /ˈmɪtzvə/ **1.** a Jewish boy aged 13 when he takes on the responsibilities of an adult under the Jewish law. **2.** the solemnization of this event by calling upon the boy to read from the Scriptures in a synagogue service. [Heb., = son of commandment]

barmy *adj.* (*slang*) crazy. [f. OE *barm* froth on top of fermenting liquor]

barn *n.* a simple roofed building for storing grain etc. on a farm. —**barn dance,** a kind of country dance; a social gathering for dancing, originally held in a barn. **barn owl,** a kind of owl, brownish above with white under-parts. [OE, = barley-house]

Barnabas /ˈbɑːnəbəs/, St (1st c.), a Levite, born in Cyprus, who became one of the earliest disciples of Christ at Jerusalem. He introduced St Paul to the Apostles and accompanied him in the first missionary journey to Cyprus and Asia Minor, returning to Cyprus after they disagreed and separated. He is the traditional founder of the Cypriot Church, and legend asserts that he was martyred at Salamis in Cyprus in AD 61. Feast day, 11 June.

barnacle /ˈbɑːnək(ə)l/ *n.* a shellfish that clings to coastal rocks, ships' bottoms, etc. —**barnacle goose,** an Arctic goose (*Branta Leucopsis*) visiting Britain in winter. [orig. unkn.]

Barnard /ˈbɑːnɑːd/, Christiaan (Neethling) (1922–), South African surgeon, pioneer of human heart transplantation. He performed the first operation of this kind in Dec. 1967.

Barnardo /bəˈnɑːdəʊ/, Thomas John (1845–1905), British philanthropist, founder of a chain of homes ('Dr Barnado's Homes') for destitute children, the first of which was opened in London in 1870.

barney /ˈbɑːnɪ/ *n.* (*slang*) a noisy dispute. [orig. unkn.; perh. dial.]

barnstorm *v.i.* to travel through rural areas as an actor or political campaigner. —**barnstormer** *n.*

barograph /ˈbærəgrɑːf/ *n.* a self-recording barometer. [as foll. + Gk *graphō* write]

barometer /bəˈrɒmɪtə(r)/ *n.* an instrument measuring atmospheric pressure, used to forecast weather. The principle of the mercury barometer was established by the Italian physicist Torricelli (see entry) in 1644. A successful aneroid barometer (less sensitive than the mercury type but portable and more convenient) was devised in France in the 1840s. —**barometric** /bærəˈmetrɪk/ *adj.* [f. Gk *baros* weight, *metron* measure]

baron /ˈbærən/ *n.* **1.** a member of the lowest order of the British peerage, styled *Lord —;* a foreign nobleman of equivalent rank (styled *Baron —*). **2.** one who controls the trade in a specified commodity, a magnate. **3.** (*hist.*) one who held land from the king in the Middle Ages. —**baroness** *n.fem.* [f. AF f. L *baro* man (prob. = free man or king's man; orig. not a title of dignity)]

baronet /ˈbærənɪt/ *n.* a member of the lowest hereditary titled British order, ranking next below a baron. —**baronetcy** *n.* [f. BARON]

baronial /bəˈrəʊnɪəl/ *adj.* of or suitable for a baron. [as prec.]

barony /ˈbærənɪ/ *n.* the rank or domain of a baron. [f. BARON]

baroque /bəˈrɒk/ *adj.* of the ornate style of architecture and art of the 17th and 18th c.; of comparable musical developments *c.*1600–1750. —*n.* baroque style or ornamentation; baroque art collectively. [F f. Port., orig. = misshapen pearl]

barouche /bəˈruːʃ/ *n.* a four-wheeled horse-drawn carriage with seats for two couples facing each other. [f. G f. It. f. L *birotus* (BI-, *rota* wheel)]

barque /bɑːk/ *n.* a sailing-ship square-rigged on the foremast and mainmast and fore-and-aft rigged on the mizen (ill. SAILING-SHIPS). Until the mid-19th c. barques were relatively small sailing-ships, but later were built up to about 3,000 tons or more, sometimes with four or five masts. They are now virtually obsolete as trading vessels but some are used as sail training ships. [f. F, prob. f. L *barca* ship's boat]

barquentine /ˈbɑːkəntiːn/ *n.* a three-masted vessel with the foremast square-rigged, the main and mizen fore-and-aft rigged (ill. SAILING-SHIPS). [f. prec., after *brigantine*]

barrack /ˈbærək/ *v.t./i.* (of spectators etc.) to shout derisively (at). [prob. = Austral. sl. *borak* banter, of Aboriginal orig.]

barracks /ˈbærəks/ *n.* a large building or group of buildings in which soldiers are housed; a large plain and ugly building. —**barrack-room lawyer,** a pompously argumentative person. [f. F f. It. or Sp., = soldier's tent]

barracuda /bærəˈkuːdə/ *n.* **1.** a large voracious West Indian sea-fish of the family Sphyraenidae. **2.** (also **barracouta** /-ˈkuːtə/) a long slender sea-fish (*Thyrsites atun*) of the Pacific etc. (In South Africa the same fish is called *snoek.* [Amer. Sp.]

barrage /ˈbærɑːʒ/ *n.* **1.** a heavy continuous artillery bombardment; a rapid succession of criticisms, questions, etc. **2.** an artificial barrier in a river, acting as a dam. —**barrage**

balloon, a large balloon anchored to the ground, as part of a barrier against aircraft. [F, as BAR¹]

barratry /ˈbærətrɪ/ n. fraud or culpable negligence by a ship's master or crew at the expense of the owner or insurer. [f. OF (barat deceit)]

barre /bɑː(r)/ n. a horizontal bar at waist-level, used by dancers to steady themselves when exercising. [F, = BAR¹]

barrel /ˈbærəl/ n. **1.** a large rounded usually wooden container for liquids etc., with slightly bulging sides and flat circular ends. **2.** the amount it contains, often used as a measure of capacity (in brewing = 36 imperial gallons; in the oil industry = 35 imperial or 42 US gallons). **3.** a cylindrical tube-like part, especially the part of a gun through which the shot is fired. —v.t. (-ll-) to store in a barrel. —**barrel vault,** a vault with a uniform concave roof. [f. OF, perh. as BAR¹]

barrel-organ n. **1.** an automatic pipe-organ much used in churches in the 19th c. Projections on a cylinder (barrel) that was turned by a handle (which also worked the bellows) opened pipes to produce the required notes for a pre-determined tune. **2.** a 19th-c. street-instrument (not of the organ type) producing notes by means of metal tongues struck by pins fixed in the barrel. The tone resembles that of a piano.

barren /ˈbærən/ adj. **1.** (of land) unable to produce crops or vegetation, infertile. **2.** unable to bear young; not producing fruit. **3.** not productive of results. [f. AF, ult. orig. unkn.]

Barrett /ˈbærət/, Elizabeth, see BROWNING.¹

barricade /bærɪˈkeɪd/ n. a barrier, especially one hastily erected across a street. —v.t. to block or defend with a barricade. [F, f. Sp. barrica cask (as BARREL)]

Barrie /ˈbærɪ/, Sir James Matthew (1860-1937), Scottish dramatist and novelist, son of a weaver, who wrote several sentimental stories before turning to drama. He achieved success with Quality Street (1901), the ever-popular comedy The Admirable Crichton (1902), and Dear Brutus (1917), and is above all remembered for his internationally celebrated children's play Peter Pan (1904) about the boy who would not grow up, the copyright of which he bequeathed to the Great Ormond Street Children's Hospital.

barrier /ˈbærɪə(r)/ n. **1.** a fence, rail, etc., barring advance or preventing access. **2.** a gate at a railway-station where tickets have to be shown. **3.** a circumstance that prevents progress or communication etc. —**barrier reef,** a coral reef cut off from the nearest land by a channel. [f. AF (as BAR¹)]

barrister /ˈbærɪstə(r)/ n. a lawyer entitled to represent clients in the higher lawcourts. [f. BAR¹]

barrow¹ /ˈbærəʊ/ n. **1.** a two-wheeled hand-cart, especially for selling things in the street. **2.** a wheelbarrow. [OE, rel. to BEAR¹]

barrow² /ˈbærəʊ/ n. a mound of earth constructed in ancient times to cover one or more burials (often marked on maps as tumulus). The earliest barrows occurred in NW Europe in the late 5th and 4th millenniums BC and were elongated in shape (long barrows). In the late 4th millennium BC round barrows came into use, and continued to be constructed intermittently up to the 10th c. AD. The somewhat uniform appearance that these monuments tend to display today belies a wide range of burial practices and construction techniques. [OE, = hill, hillock]

Barry /ˈbærɪ/, Sir Charles (1795-1860), English architect who made his reputation with his Italianate design of the Travellers' Club in Pall Mall, London (1830-2), and in 1836 won a competition to design the new Houses of Parliament after the old buildings had been destroyed by fire. These he formed in Gothic style, with details contributed by A. W. N. Pugin.

Barrymore /ˈbærɪmɔː(r)/ the name of an American family of actors. Lionel (1878-1954) withdrew from the theatre in 1925 and spent the rest of his life in films, where he had a long and distinguished career. Ethel (1879-1959), a beautiful woman with a warm and distinguished presence, gave some of her finest performances in later life. In 1928 a NewYork theatre was named after her. John (1882-1942), who was noted for his romantic good looks and perfect diction, was an excellent light comedian as well as a serious actor. His most spectacular success was as Hamlet, both in New York (1922) and in London (1925).

bartender /ˈbɑːtendə(r)/ n. a barman or barmaid.

barter /ˈbɑːtə(r)/ v.t./i. to deal with (goods) in exchange for others of equivalent value; to trade in this way. —n. such trade or exchange. [prob. f. OF barater, as BARRATRY]

Barth /bɑːt, bɑːθ/, Karl (1886-1968), Swiss Protestant theo-

logian. Under the shadow of the First World War he was led to a radical questioning of contemporary religious philosophy, with its positive attitude to science and the arts, its sympathy with mysticism, and its stress on feeling. Regarding this outlook as fundamentally erroneous, he sought a return to the principles of the Reformation and the teachings of the Bible. He emphasized the supremacy and transcendence of God and the worthlessness of human reason, asserting that our understanding of God is centred exclusively upon his revelation in Christ, and that man is utterly dependent upon his revelation in Christ, and that man is utterly dependent upon divine grace. Though in English-speaking countries the greatest impact of his theology was in the 1930s, his potent astringent influence continued, and his personal prestige, based largely on his distinctive and forthright standpoint, has given him the position of the outstanding Protestant theologian of the 20th c.

Bartholomew /bɑːˈθɒləmjuː/, St (1st c.), one of the twelve Apostles. He is said to have been flayed alive in Armenia, and is hence regarded as the patron saint of tanners. Feast day, 12 Aug. —**Massacre of St Bartholomew,** the massacre of Huguenots throughout France ordered by Charles IX at the instigation of his mother, Catherine de Médicis, and begun without warning on the feast of St Bartholomew, 1572.

Bartók /ˈbɑːtɒk/, Béla (1881-1945), Hungarian composer, better known in his native country as a collector, with Kodály, of Magyar folk-songs, and as a pianist. He emigrated to the USA in 1940, and there produced one of the works for which he is most famous, the Concerto for Orchestra (1943), dying in poverty two years later. His music is not obviously influenced by Hungarian idioms, and in his only opera, Duke Bluebeard's Castle (1911), he reveals an interest in Debussy and Schoenberg and also in recent developments in the study of psychology which led him to depict Bluebeard not as the standard bloodthirsty monster but as a personification of the loneliness and disillusionment of man. Bartók's string quartets, composed before he left for America, are regarded as his crowning achievement, combining perfectly balanced form and the-matic integrity with the presentation of deeply personal emotions.

Bartolommeo /bɑːtɒlɒˈmeɪəʊ/, Fra Baccio della Porta (c. 1472-1517), Florentine painter, who belonged to the period of transition from the early to the High Rennaissance. Deeply influenced by Savonarola, he entered the Domini-can Order in 1499. His large-scale works are restrained and austere, and his ideals were balance and simplicity. He was one of the first to replace modern costume with generalized drapery in his religious figures.

Baruch /ˈbɑːrʊk/ a book of the Apocrypha, attributed in the text to Baruch, the scribe of Jeremiah (Jer. 36).

baryon /ˈbærɪɒn/ n. a nucleon or hyperon. [f. Gk barus heavy; so called because their mass is greater than, or equal to, that of the proton]

baryta /bəˈraɪtə/ n. barium oxide or hydroxide. [f. Gk barus heavy]

barytes /bəˈraɪtiːz/ n. barium sulphate, used in some white paints. [as prec.]

basal /ˈbeɪs(ə)l/ a. of or forming the base of something. [f. BASE¹]

basalt /ˈbæsɔːlt/ n. a dark igneous rock, often forming columnar strata. —**basaltic** /bəˈsɔːltɪk/ adj. [f. L f. Gk (basanos touchstone)]

bascule /ˈbæskjuːl/ n. a lever apparatus used in a **bascule bridge,** a kind of drawbridge worked by counterweights (ill. BRIDGES). [F, = see-saw]

base¹ n. **1.** the lowest part of anything, the part on which it rests. **2.** a basis; a main principle or starting-point. **3.** the headquarters of an expedition or military force etc., from where its operations are directed. **4.** the main or underlying ingredient of a mixture. **5.** a substance, (not necessarily soluble in water) that can combine with an acid to form a salt. The term includes alkalis but has wider application (see ALKALI). **6.** the number on which a system of calculation is based, e.g. 10 in decimal counting, 2 in the binary system. **7.** (in baseball) any of the four stations that a batsman must reach in turn in scoring a run. —v.t. to use as a base or foundation, or as evidence for a conclusion etc. [F, or f. L f. Gk basis stepping]

base² adj. **1.** lacking moral worth, cowardly, contemptible. **2.** (of metals) not precious; (of coins) adulterated with inferior metal. —**basely** adv., **baseness** n. [f. F bas of low height, f. L bassus short]

baseball n. a game evolved from rounders, with teams of

9 players who in turn seek to strike the ball thrown by an opponent (the *pitcher*) and traverse a circuit of four points (*bases*). Long regarded as the American national game, it was played in simple form in both England and America (under the name 'base ball') from the mid-18th c., and is mentioned in Jane Austen's novel *Northanger Abbey*. The basic modern rules date from *c.*1845.

baseless *adj.* with no foundation in fact. [f. BASE¹ + -LESS]

baseline *n.* a line used as a base or starting-point; the line at each end of a tennis-court (ill. SPORTS).

basement /ˈbeɪsmənt/ *n.* a storey below ground level. [prob. Du. f. as BASE¹]

basenji /bəˈsendʒɪ/ *n.* a breed of small rarely-barking African hunting-dog. [Bantu]

bash *v.t.* 1. to strike violently. 2. to attack violently with blows, words, or hostile actions. —*n.* a heavy blow. —**have a bash,** (*colloq.*) to have a try. [imit., perh. B(ANG + SM)ASH]

bashful *adj.* self-consciously shy. —**bashfully** *adv.*, **bashfulness** *n.* [f. obs. *bash* (*v.*) = ABASH + -FUL]

BASIC /ˈbeɪsɪk/ *n.* a computer language using familiar English words. [acronym, *Beginner's All-purpose Symbolic Instruction Code*]

basic /ˈbeɪsɪk/ *adj.* 1. forming a base or starting-point; forming a standard minimum before additions. 2. of fundamental importance. 3. (of rock or soil) having a low silica content in proportion to the lime or other bases present. — **Basic English,** a simplified form of English with a select vocabulary of 850 words for international use. **basic slag,** a fertilizer containing phosphates, formed as a by-product in steel manufacture. —**basically** *adv.* [f. BASE¹]

Basie /ˈbeɪsɪ/, 'Count' (1904–84), American jazz bandleader. He took up the piano at an early age, looking to figures such as 'Fats' Waller and Willie 'the Lion' Smith for his models, and became famous as leader of his own 'big band' from 1935.

Basil /ˈbæz(ə)l/, St, 'the Great' (*c.*330–379), a Doctor of the Church, brother of St Gregory of Nyssa and St Macrina. He was called from the hermit life to defend orthodoxy against the Arian emperor Valens, and in 370 was appointed bishop of Caesarea in Cappadocia. Eloquent, learned, and statesmanlike, he was endowed with a talent for organization, and the monastic rule which he put forward is still the basis of that followed in the Eastern Church. Feast day, 14 June.

basil /ˈbæz(ə)l/ *n.* an aromatic herb of the genus *Ocimum*. [f. OF f. L f. Gk *basilikos* royal]

basilica /bəˈzɪlɪkə/ *n.* an oblong hall or church with a double colonnade and an apse. [L f. Gk, = royal (house)]

basilisk /ˈbæzɪlɪsk/ *n.* 1. a mythical reptile (also called a *cockatrice*), hatched by a serpent from a cock's egg. Its breath, and even its glance, was fatal. 2. a tropical crested lizard of the genus *Basiliscus*. [f. L f. Gk, dim. of *basileus* king (so called, acc. to Pliny, from a spot resembling a crown on its head)]

basin /ˈbeɪs(ə)n/ *n.* 1. a rounded open vessel for liquids etc.; a wash-basin. 2. a depression where water collects; the tract of country drained by a river. 3. an almost land-locked harbour. —**basinful** *n.* [f. OF f. L *ba(s)cinus*, perh. f. Gaulish]

basis /ˈbeɪsɪs/ *n.* (*pl.* **bases** /ˈbeɪsiːz/) 1. a foundation or support. 2. a main principle, a starting-point. [L f. Gk, = BASE¹]

bask /bɑːsk/ *v.i.* (usu. with *in*) to lie or rest comfortably in a pleasant warmth; to enjoy (one's popularity, glory, etc.). —**basking shark,** a very large shark (*Cetorhinus maximus*) accustomed to lie near the surface of water. [f. ON, rel. to BATHE]

Baskerville /ˈbæskəvɪl/, John (1706–75), English printer, who designed the typeface that bears his name.

basket /ˈbɑːskɪt/ *n.* a container made of interwoven cane, wire, etc.; the amount contained in it. —**basket weave,** one with a pattern resembling basketwork. —**basketful** *n.* [AF & OF; orig. unkn.]

basketball *n.* a game played between teams of 5 or 6 players in which a goal is scored when the ball is thrown into a net fixed on a ring about 3 m (10 ft.) above the ground. It originated in the USA in 1891, the invention of Dr J. A. Naismith (1861–1939), at Springfield, Mass.

Basket Maker a member of a culture of the south-western USA, forming the early stages of the Anasazi culture from the 1st c. BC until *c.*700 AD, so called from the basketry and other woven fragments found in early cave sites.

basketry /ˈbɑːskɪtrɪ/ *n.* 1. baskets and other objects woven from flexible canes etc. 2. the art of weaving these. [f. BASKET]

basketwork *n.* basketry.

Basque /bɑːsk/ *n.* 1. a member of a people living in the western Pyrenees on both sides of the French–Spanish border. 2. their language. (See below.) —*adj.* of the Basques or their language. [F f. L *Vasco* (see below)]
Culturally the Basques are one of the most distinct groups in Europe. While they do not differ physically from other European groups, their language, Basque, is not of the Indo-European language family and is unrelated to any other known tongue, though some similarities with Caucasian languages have been noted. This complex language, inherited from the ancient Vascones and pre-dating the Roman conquest of the Iberian peninsula, is the only remnant of the languages spoken in SW Europe before the region was Romanized. It is spoken by some 700,000 people in the Pyrenees, but evidence of place-names suggests that it was originally current in a much wider area.

bas-relief /ˈbæsrɪliːf/ *n.* low relief; a sculpture or carving in low relief. [f. It. *basso rilievo*]

bass¹ /beɪs/ *adj.* deep-sounding; of the lowest musical pitch. —*n.* 1. a male voice of the lowest range; a singer with such a voice; a part written for it. 2. bass pitch. 3. (*colloq.*) a double bass; a bass guitar. —**bass-viol** *n.* a viola da gamba. [as BASE², alt. after It. *basso*]

bass² /bæs/ *n.* (*pl.* **basses,** *collect.* **bass**) any of several marine fish of the perch family. [OE]

basset /ˈbæsɪt/ *n.* (in full **basset-hound**) a short-legged hound of a kind originally used for hunting hares. [F, dim. of *bas* low]

bassinet /bæsɪˈnet/ *n.* a child's wicker cradle with a hood. [F, dim. of *bassin* basin]

bassoon /bəˈsuːn/ *n.* a bass instrument of the oboe family. —**bassoonist** *n.* [f. F f. It. *bassone* (*basso* BASE²)]
The bassoon dates from about the 1660s. It has a range of about three-and-a-half octaves, and is a standard orchestral instrument. It is often used for comic effect but also has a capacity for melancholy which has not been overlooked by composers. The contrabassoon, or double bassoon, has a range an octave deeper than the bassoon's.

bast /bæst/ *n.* fibrous material obtained from the inner bark of the lime-tree or other sources and used for matting etc.; phloem (ill. TREES). [OE]

bastard /ˈbɑːstəd/ *adj.* 1. born of parents not married to each other. 2. hybrid. 3. (*Bot. & Zool.*) resembling (the species whose name is appropriated). —*n.* 1. a bastard person. 2. (*colloq.*) a disliked or difficult person or thing. — **bastard wing,** the group of feathers borne on a small joint in the middle of a bird's wing, taken as the analogue of the thumb in mammals. [f. OF f. L, perh. f. *bast* pack-saddle (used by muleteers as a bed)]

bastardize *v.t.* to declare (a person) illegitimate. [f. prec.]

bastardy *n.* the condition of being a bastard, illegitimacy. [f. BASTARD]

baste¹ /beɪst/ *v.t.* to moisten (roasting meat) with melted fat to prevent it from drying. [orig. unkn.]

baste² /beɪst/ *v.t.* to stitch loosely together (preparatory to regular sewing). [f. OF, = sew lightly]

Bastet /ˈbæstet/ (*Egyptian myth.*) a goddess usually shown as a woman with the head of a cat, wearing one gold ear-ring.

Bastille /bæsˈtiːl/ a fortress in Paris built in the 14th c. and used in the 17th–18th c. as a State prison. It became a symbol of despotism and its storming by the mob on 14 July 1789 marked the start of the French Revolution; the anniversary of this event is kept as a national holiday. [f. OF f. Prov. (*bastir* build)]

bastinado /bæstiˈnɑːəʊ/ *n.* (*pl.* **-os**) a torture consisting of repeated blows with a light cane on the soles of the feet. —*v.t.* to torture in this way. [f. Sp. (*baston* stick)]

bastion /ˈbæstɪən/ *n.* 1. a projecting part of a fortification (ill. CASTLES). 2. a fortified place near hostile territory. 3. an institution etc. serving as a stronghold. [F f. It. (*bastire* build)]

bat¹ 1. *n.* an implement (usually of wood) with handle and a flat or curved surface for striking the ball in games (see ill. SPORTS); a turn at using this. 2. a batsman. —*v.t./i.* (**-tt-**) to use a bat; to hit with a bat. —**off one's own bat,** without prompting or assistance. [f. OE *batt* club f. OF (*battre* hit)]

bat² *n.* a furry mouselike mammal of the order Chiroptera, active at night, flying by means of a winglike membrane on its forelimbs (ill. MAMMALS). —**blind as a bat,** completely blind. [f. Scand., orig. *bakke*]

bat[3] *v.t.* (-tt-) to flutter. —**not bat an eyelid,** (*colloq.*) to show no surprise or alarm. [var. of obs. *bate* flutter]

batch /bætʃ/ *n.* **1.** a quantity of loaves or cakes produced at a single baking. **2.** a quantity or number of persons or things coming or dealt with together; an instalment. [f. OE, rel. to BAKE]

bated /'beɪtɪd/ *adj.* **with bated breath,** holding one's breath in anxiety or suspense. [f. ABATE]

Bates /beɪts/, Henry Walter (1825–92), English naturalist, a friend and colleague of A. R. Wallace with whom he travelled in Brazil, and author of *The Naturalist on the River Amazons* (1863). The phenomenon known as 'Batesian mimicry' is named after him: noting the resemblance of certain animals, especially insects, to their natural backgrounds, and the fact that certain edible species of butterfly resemble those avoided by predators, Bates suggested that, by natural selection, those who 'mimic' in this way are more likely to survive.

bath /bɑ:θ/ *n.* (*pl.* **baths** /bɑ:ðz/) **1.** a long open vessel in which one sits to wash the body; water for this; the process of washing in it; (in *pl.*) a building where baths may be taken by the public. **2.** (in *pl.*) a public swimming-pool. **3.** a liquid in which something is immersed; its container. —*v.t./i.* to immerse in a bath; to take a bath. —**Order of the Bath,** an order of knighthood, so called from the ceremonial bath which originally preceded installation. [OE]

Bath bun /bɑ:θ/ a round spiced bun with currants and icing. [*Bath*, spa town in Avon]

bath chair a kind of wheelchair for invalids. [as prec.]

bathe /beɪð/ *v.t./i.* **1.** to immerse in or treat with liquid; to lie immersed in water etc. **2.** to go swimming. **3.** (of light or warmth) to envelop. —*n.* an instance of bathing. —**bathing-suit** *n.* a garment worn for swimming. —**bather** *n.* [rel. to BATH[1]]

bathos /'beɪθɒs/ *n.* unintentional descent from the sublime to the commonplace or absurd. [Gk, = depth]

bathroom *n.* a room with a bath, wash-basin, etc.; (*euphem.*) a lavatory.

Bathsheba /bæθ'ʃi:bə/ the wife of Uriah the Hittite (2 Sam. 11). She became one of the wives of David, who had caused her husband to be killed in battle, and was the mother of Solomon.

bathyscaphe /'bæθɪskæf/ *n.* a manned vessel for deep-sea diving, with special buoyancy gear. [F, f. Gk *bathus* deep + *skaphos* ship]

bathysphere /'bæθɪsfɪə(r)/ *n.* a spherical diving-vessel for deep-sea observation. [f. Gk *bathus* deep + SPHERE]

batik /'bætɪk/ *n.* a method, originally Javanese, of printing coloured designs on textiles by waxing the parts not to be dyed, so as to repel the pigment; fabric treated thus. [Javanese, = painted]

batiste /bæ'ti:st/ *n.* a fine light cotton or linen fabric. [F, f. *Baptiste* of Cambrai, first maker]

batman /'bætmən/ *n.* (*pl.* **-men**) a soldier acting as personal servant to an officer. [f. OF f. L *bastum* pack-saddle]

baton /bæt(ə)n/ *n.* **1.** a long thin stick used by a conductor to direct performers; a short stick carried and passed on in a relay race; a drum major's stick; a staff of office; a policeman's truncheon. **2.** (in heraldry) a narrow bend truncated at each end. **3.** a stroke replacing a figure on the face of a clock or watch. —**baton sinister,** (in heraldry) a baton from sinister to dexter, used as a mark of bastardy. [f. F f. L *bastum* stick]

batrachian /bə'treɪkɪən/ *n.* any of a class of amphibians (Batrachia or Salientia) that discard gills and tails, e.g. frog and toad. —*adj.* of these animals. [f. Gk *batrachos* frog]

batsman /'bætsmən/ *n.* (*pl.* **-men**) a player who is batting in cricket or baseball; one who is good at this. [f. BAT[1]]

battalion /bə'tælɪən/ *n.* a large body of men ready for battle, especially an infantry unit forming part of a brigade; a large group of persons with a common purpose. [f. F f. It. (*battaglia* battle)]

batten[1] /'bæt(ə)n/ *n.* **1.** a long narrow piece of squared timber. **2.** a strip of wood or metal fastening or holding something in place. —*v.t.* to strengthen or fasten with battens. [f. OF (*battre* beat)]

batten[2] /'bæt(ə)n/ *v.i.* to grow fat or prosperous *on*. [ON, rel. to BETTER]

Battenberg /'bæt(ə)nbɜ:g/ *n.* (in full **Battenberg cake**) a kind of cake made in a rectangular shape with alternating pink and yellow squares, covered with marzipan. [perh. f. name of village in W. Germany]

batter[1] *v.t./i.* to hit with repeated hard blows; to knock heavily and insistently *at.* —*n.* a beaten mixture of flour, eggs, and milk for cooking. —**battered baby, wife,** etc., one subjected to repeated violence. [f. AF (as BATTERY)]

batter[2] *n.* a batsman in baseball. [f. BAT[1]]

battering-ram *n.* a swinging beam, formerly with an iron ram's-head end, used to breach walls etc. [f. BATTER[1]]

battery /'bætərɪ/ *n.* **1.** a portable container of a cell or cells for converting chemical into electrical energy (see below). **2.** a series of cages for the intensive keeping of poultry or cattle etc. **3.** a set of connected similar units of equipment. **4.** (*Law*) unlawful physical violence inflicted on a person. [f. F L *battuere* beat]

The first electric battery was made in 1800 by Alessandro Volta, who caused a current to pass through a wire by attaching it to two different metals (zinc and copper) in a salt solution. Dry batteries derive from a Leclanché cell, with the electrolyte in the form of a paste or jelly instead of a liquid.

battle *n.* **1.** a fight between large organized forces. **2.** a contest; a hard struggle. —*v.i.* to struggle hard. —**battle-cry** *n.* a war-cry; a slogan. [f. OF f. L, = gladiatorial exercises (as prec.)]

battleaxe *n.* **1.** a heavy axe used in ancient warfare. **2.** (*colloq.*) a formidable or domineering woman.

battledore /'bæt(ə)ldɔ:(r)/ *n.* a small racket used with a shuttlecock in the volleying game of **battledore and shuttlecock,** which dates at least from the 18th c. The game of badminton may have developed from it. [perh. f. Prov. *batedor* beater, orig. a paddle-like instrument used in washing etc.]

battledress *n.* the everyday uniform of a soldier etc.

battlefield *n.* the site of a battle.

battleground *n.* a battlefield.

battlement /'bæt(ə)lmənt/ *n.* (usu. in *pl.*) a parapet with lower sections at intervals, originally for firing from (ill. CASTLES). [f. OF *batailler* fortify (as BATTLE)]

battleship *n.* a warship with the heaviest armour and largest guns.

batty /'bætɪ/ *adj.* (*slang*) crazy; eccentric. [f. BAT[2]]

bauble /'bɔ:b(ə)l/ *n.* a showy but valueless ornament. [f. OF *ba(u)bel* toy]

Baucis /'bɔ:kɪs/ (*Gk myth.*) the wife of Philemon (see PHILEMON[1]).

baud /bɔ:d/ *n.* (intelecommunications and computers) a unit of signal transmission speed equal to one information unit per second; (*loosely*) a unit of data transmission speed of one bit per second. [f. J. M. E. *Baudot*, French engineer (d. 1903)]

Baudelaire /'bəʊdəleə(r)/, Charles (1821–67), French poet and critic. In 1842 he inherited a large fortune and lived extravagantly until his family intervened and put his inheritance in trust, allowing him only a limited income, which he supplemented by following a literary career. He began writing reviews, and made translations of Edgar Allen Poe. His *Les Fleurs du mal* (1857), one of the great collections of French verse, is a series of 101 exquisitely composed lyrics in a variety of metres, exploring his own sense of isolation, exile and sin, boredom and melancholy, the attraction of evil and vice, and the fascination and degradation of Paris life. On publication he was fined and six of the poems were banned as offensive to public morals. By 1864 his resources were exhausted and he lived a dissipated life in Brussels while trying to earn a living by lecturing; he returned to Paris (1866) with general paralysis and died in obscurity, though by the end of the 19th c. leaders of the symbolist movement were acknowledging a debt to him. Like his poetic genius, his critical writing was little appreciated in his time but his stature is now universally recognized. His essays on Paris salons, on Delacroix, Gautier, Flaubert, and Wagner, were collected posthumously in *Curiosités esthétiques* and *L'Art romantique* (1868).

Bauhaus /'baʊhaʊs/ the school of design established by Gropius in Weimar in Germany in 1919, whence it moved to Dessau in 1925. Its style is characterized by emphasis on architectonic form and smooth linearity, employing the resources of modern technology while continuing to take account of the tradition of the Arts and Crafts movement. Gropius fostered the idea of the artist as craftsman and saw the school as exemplifying the need for co-operation amongst artists working in different disciplines, from architecture to painting, sculpture, weaving, and the design of objects for utilitarian use; Breuer's tubular steel chair is perhaps the best-known consumer design to have emerged. The socialist principles on which Bauhaus ideas rested incurred the inevitable hostility of the Nazis and the school was closed in 1933. The resultant movement abroad of teachers and pupils has ensured the international dissemination of its style and ideas.

baulk /bɔːk/ *n.* **1.** a strip of ground left unploughed; a strip of earth left between excavation trenches. **2.** the area of a billiard-table within which the cue balls are placed at the start of a game. **3.** a roughly squared length of timber. [OE f. ON]

bauxite /ˈbɔːksaɪt/ *n.* an earthy mineral, the chief source of aluminium. [F, f. *Les Baux* in S. France]

Bavaria /bəˈveərɪə/ a former State of South Germany, now in the Federal Republic. —**Bavarian** *adj.* & *n.*

bawdy /ˈbɔːdɪ/ *adj.* humorously indecent. —*n.* bawdy talk or writing. —**bawdily** *adv.*, **bawdiness** *n.* [f. obs. *bawd* woman brothel-keeper]

bawl /bɔːl/ *v.t./i.* to call out loudly; to weep noisily. —**bawl out**, (*colloq.*) to reprimand severely. [imit.]

Bax /bæks/, Sir Arnold (1883-1953), English composer, who was greatly influenced by the poetry of Yeats and by Irish folk music. He was born in London and had no Irish blood, but travelled in Ireland and wrote short stories under the pseudonym Dermot O'Byrne. His tone-poems are the best known of his works today, but he also composed seven symphonies, chamber works, choral music, and some attractive piano pieces.

bay[1] *n.* a broad inlet of the sea where the land curves inwards. [f. OF f. Sp. *bahia*]

bay[2] *n.* **1.** a section of wall between buttresses or columns. **2.** a recess in a room or building, especially one formed by a projecting window. **3.** any of a series of compartments in a building or structure; a partitioned or marked area forming a unit. **4.** the cul-de-sac where a side-line terminates at a railway station. —**bay window**, a window projecting from the line of a building. [f. OF (*ba(y)er* gape)]

bay[3] *n.* the Mediterranean laurel *Laurus nobilis*, with fragrant deep-green leaves that are used for seasoning. —**bay rum**, perfume (especially for the hair) originally distilled from rum and bayberry leaves. [f. OF f. L *baca* berry]

bay[4] *n.* the deep drawn-out cry of a large dog or of hounds in pursuit of a hunted animal. —*v.i.* to utter this cry. —**at bay**, facing one's attackers, as a cornered animal. **hold** or **keep at bay**, to fight off (pursuers). [f. OF (as BAY[2])]

bay[5] *adj.* (esp. of a horse) reddish-brown. —*n.* a reddish-brown horse. [f. OF f. L *badius*]

Bayard /ˈbeɪɑːd/, Pierre du Terrail, Seigneur de (1473-1524), French soldier of great valour and chivalry, known as the knight 'sans pent et sans reproche' (fearless and above reproach).

bayberry *n.* a fragrant West Indian tree, *Pimenta acris*. [as prec.]

Bayer /ˈbaɪə(r)/, Johann Friedrich Wilhelm Adolf von (1835-1917), German organic chemist, best known for the discovery of synthetic indigo. He was taught by both Bunsen and Kekulé. A very fine chemical experimenter, he had a profound influence on organic chemistry and subsequently on the emerging field of biochemistry. He was awarded the 1905 Nobel Prize for chemistry for his work on dyes and hydro-aromatic compounds.

Bayeux Tapestry /baɪˈjɜː/ a superb example of Anglo-Saxon embroidery (it is not really a tapestry) executed between 1066 and 1077, probably at Canterbury, for Odo, bishop of Bayeux and half-brother of William the Conqueror, and now exhibited at the museum of Bayeux in Normandy. It is 48 cm (19 inches) wide and, although incomplete, 70 m (230 ft.) long. In 79 racy and colourful scenes, accompanied by a Latin text and arranged like a strip cartoon, it tells the story of the Norman Conquest and the events that led up to it. It is an important historical record, relating incidents not recorded elsewhere, and is a source of information on such things as armour, clothes, and boats. The colours, of which there are eight, are used for decorative rather than descriptive purposes.

Baylis /ˈbeɪlɪs/, Lilian Mary (1874-1937), English theatre manageress. An intensely religious and single-minded woman, she devoted herself to the founding and running of popular homes for drama and opera in London. Under her management the Old Vic acquired a reputation as the world's leading house of Shakespearean productions, and

her initiative in reopening the old Sadler's Wells Theatre in 1931 led to the development of the Royal Ballet and the English National Opera.

Bay of Pigs Cochinos Bay, a bay on the SW coast of Cuba, where on 17 Apr. 1961 about 1,500 Cuban exiles, with the support of the American CIA, made an unsuccessful attempt to invade the country and overthrow the regime of Fidel Castro. The newly inaugurated President Kennedy refused the expected US air support, and the operation was a fiasco. Castro's prestige and popularity rose as a result of this, and Kennedy emphasized the need for strict presidential control of the CIA and its overseas activities.

bayonet /ˈbeɪənɪt/ *n.* a stabbing blade that can be attached to the muzzle of a rifle for use in hand-to-hand fighting. —*v.t.* to wound with a bayonet. —**bayonet fitting**, a type of attachment in which a cylindrical part is pushed into a socket and twisted slightly so that it is secured by engagement of parts. [f. F, perh. f. *Bayonne* in SW France, where the weapon is said to have been first made or first used]

Bayreuth /ˈbaɪrɔɪt, -ˈrɔɪt/ a town in Bavaria, Germany, where Wagner made his home from 1874 and where he is buried. Festivals of his operas are held regularly in a theatre specially built (1872-6) to house performances of *Der Ring des Nibelungen*.

bazaar /bəˈzɑː(r)/ *n.* **1.** a market in oriental countries. **2.** a sale of goods to raise funds for charity. [f. Pers.]

bazooka /bəˈzuːkə/ *n.* a tubular anti-tank rocket-launcher. [orig. = trombone-like instrument; perh. rel. to Du. *bazuin* trumpet]

BBC *abbr.* British Broadcasting Corporation, a public corporation originally having the monopoly of broadcasting in Britain, financed by a grant-in-aid from Parliament. It was established in 1927 by royal charter to carry on work previously performed by the British Broadcasting Company.

BC *abbr.* before Christ (in dating).

BCE *abbr.* before the Common Era (in dating).

bdellium /ˈdelɪəm/ *n.* a resin used especially as a perfume; the tree (esp. of the genus *Commiphora*) yielding this. [L f. Gk f. Heb.]

Be *symbol* beryllium.

be /bɪ, *emphatic* biː/ *v.i.* (*pres.* **am, are, is**; *past* **was, were**; *p.p.* **been**; *partic.* **being**) **1.** to exist; to occur; to occupy a given position in space or time. **2.** to have a certain quality, identity, meaning, cost, etc. —*v.aux.* used with parts of other verbs to form passive, continuous tenses, or (with infin.) to express destiny, duty, etc. —**be-all (and end-all)** *n.* one's consuming purpose. **be that as it may**, whatever the facts of the matter may be. **for the time being**, for the moment. **have been**, (*colloq.*) to have come or gone as a visitor. **let be**, to leave undisturbed. **the — to be**, the future (person of a named function). [OE]

be- *prefix* **1.** forming verbs implying transitive action (*bemoan*), completeness (*becalm*), thoroughness (*belabour*), attitude or treatment (*befriend*). **2.** forming adjectives with the suffix *-ed* in sense 'having' (*bespectacled*). [OE, = BY]

beach *n.* a pebbly or sandy shore, especially of the sea between high and low water-mark. —*v.t.* to haul up (a boat) on the beach. —**beach-head** *n.* a fortified position set up on a beach by landing forces. [orig. unkn.]

beachcomber /ˈbiːtʃkəʊmə(r)/ *n.* one who lives by salvaging objects washed up on the beach; a loafer who lives on what he can earn casually on a waterfront. —**beachcombing** *n.*

beacon /ˈbiːkən/ *n.* **1.** a signal-fire set up in a high or prominent position; a high hill suitable for such a fire. **2.** a warning or guiding light; a Belisha beacon. **3.** a signal station such as a lighthouse. [OE]

bead *n.* **1.** a small perforated piece of hard material for making necklaces etc.; (in *pl.*) a necklace or string of beads, a rosary. **2.** a drop of moisture; a small bubble. **3.** a small knob forming the sight of a gun. **4.** a strip on the inner edge of a pneumatic tyre for gripping the wheel. **5.** a small globular moulding, often applied in rows like a series of beads. —*v.t.* **1.** to adorn with beads. **2.** to coat (a surface) with beads of moisture. —**draw a bead on**, to take aim at. [OE, = prayer (from its use in rosaries)]

beading *n.* **1.** a decoration of beads. **2.** a moulding or carving like a series of beads. **3.** a strip of material with one side rounded, used to trim the edge of wood. **4.** the bead of a tyre.

beadle /ˈbiːd(ə)l/ *n.* **1.** a ceremonial officer of a church, college, etc. **2.** (*Sc.*) a church officer attending on a minister.

3. (*hist.*) a minor officer of a parish, dealing with petty offenders etc. [f. OF f. Gmc]

beady *adj.* (of eyes) small and glittering. [f. BEAD]

beagle /'bi:g(ə)l/ *n.* a small hound of a kind originally used in hunting hares etc. on foot. [f. OF *beegueule* noisy person, prob. f. *beer* open wide + *gueule* throat]

beagling *n.* hunting with beagles. [f. prec.]

beak *n.* **1.** a bird's horny projecting jaws. **2.** a similar mouth-like part or other projection. —**beaked** *adj.* [f. OF, of Celtic origin]

beaker /'bi:kə(r)/ *n.* **1.** a tall narrow drinking-cup, often without a handle. **2.** an open glass vessel with straight sides and a lip for pouring liquids, used in laboratories. **3.** a wide-mouthed pottery vessel found in graves of the late neolithic period (3rd millennium BC) in western Europe (ill. ARCHAEOLOGY). —**Beaker Folk**, users of such prehistoric vessels. For a long time they were thought of as a mobile population directly responsible for the rapid spread of beaker pottery, but more recent theory holds that the distribution of these vessels can be accounted for by trade and exchange. [ON, perh. f. Gk *bikos* drinking-vessel]

beam *n.* **1.** a long sturdy piece of timber or other solid material used in building houses etc. **2.** the cross-bar of a balance. **3.** (in *pl.*) the horizontal cross-timbers of a ship; a ship's greatest breadth. **4.** a ray or stream of light or other radiation. **5.** radio waves transmitted undispersed, especially as used to guide aircraft or missiles. **6.** a radiant look, a smile. —*v.t./i.* **1.** to radiate (light, affection, etc.). **2.** to direct (radio signals); to shine. **3.** to smile radiantly. — **on one's beam-ends**, (*colloq.*) near the end of one's resources. [OE, = tree]

bean *n.* **1.** any of the oval edible seeds of various leguminous plants; a plant producing beans. **2.** a similar-shaped seed of other plants (e.g. cocoa, coffee). —**full of beans**, (*colloq.*) lively, in high spirits. **spill the beans**, (*slang*) to divulge secrets. [OE]

beanfeast *n.* a festive entertainment, originally one given annually by an employer to his employees. [f. prec., beans and bacon being regarded as an indispensable dish]

beano /'bi:nəʊ/ *n.* (*pl.* **-os**) (*slang*) a party, a merry time. [abbr. BEANFEAST]

bear[1] /beə(r)/ *v.t./i.* (*past* **bore**; *p.p.* **borne**) **1.** to carry; to support. **2.** to bring or take. **3.** to have as a visible feature or as a name, meaning, etc. **4.** to hold or cherish in the mind. **5.** to give birth to; to produce (fruit or flowers). **6.** to hold up (a load) without collapsing; to sustain (a cost); to endure, to tolerate; to be fit for. **7.** to make one's way in a given direction. **8.** to exert pressure, to thrust. —**bear on**, to be relevant to. **bear out**, to confirm. **bear up**, to remain cheerful, not despair. **bear with**, to tolerate patiently. **bear witness to**, to provide evidence of the truth of. **bring to bear**, to focus (pressure etc.). **be borne in upon**, to become convincing to. [OE]

bear[2] /beə(r)/ *n.* **1.** a large heavy powerful mammal of the family Ursidae, with thick fur. **2.** a rough uncouth or surly person. **3.** one who sells shares on the Stock Exchange for future delivery, hoping to buy them at a lower price in the mean time. The term (which dates from the 18th c.) is probably derived from the proverb 'to sell the bear's skin before one has caught the bear'. The associated term *bull* appears later, and was perhaps suggested by *bear*. — **bear-hug** *n.* a powerful hug. **Great Bear**, Ursa Major. **Little Bear**, Ursa Minor. [OE]

bearable *adj.* endurable. [f. BEAR[1]]

beard /bɪəd/ *n.* hair on the chin etc. of an adult man; similar hair in certain animals, e.g. goats. —*v.t.* to confront boldly. —**bearded** *adj.* [OE]

Beardsley /'bɪədzlɪ/, Aubrey Vincent (1872–98), English artist and illustrator. Encouraged by Burne-Jones, his early work was influenced by the Pre-Raphaelites and his discovery of Japanese prints. His illustrations for Malory's *Morte d'Arthur* (1893) brought him to public notice, and in 1894 he became editor of the quarterly periodical *The Yellow Book*. In that year he illustrated Oscar Wilde's *Salome* and thereby gained much notoriety. The chief English representative of aestheticism in art, his genius for linear arabesque and acute sense of visual design give his prints and drawings a unique place in the corpus of English art: the quality of his designs for *The Rape of the Lock* bears witness to the tragedy of his early death.

bearer *n.* **1.** one who carries or helps to carry a load, especially equipment on an expedition. **2.** one who brings

a letter or message; the actual presenter of a cheque. [f. BEAR[1]]

beargarden *n.* (*colloq.*) a scene of rowdy behaviour.

bearing *n.* **1.** bodily attitude as expressing character. **2.** relationship, relevance. **3.** (usu. in *pl.*) the part of a machine bearing the friction. **4.** the compass direction of one point in relation to another; (in *pl.*) relative position. (See ill. NAVIGATION). **5.** a heraldic charge or device. [f. BEAR[1]]

bearskin *n.* a guardsman's tall furry cap.

beast *n.* **1.** an animal, especially a wild four-footed kind. **2.** an offensively brutal or sensuous man; (*colloq.*) any objectionable person. [f. L *bestia*]

beastly *adj.* **1.** of or like a beast, especially in obedience to animal instincts. **2.** (*colloq.*) objectionable, highly unpleasant. [f. prec.]

beat *v.t./i.* (*past* **beat**; *p.p.* **beaten**) **1.** to hit repeatedly, especially with a stick; to strike persistently; to shape or flatten by blows. **2.** to mix vigorously to a frothy or smooth consistency. **3.** (of the heart) to pulsate rhythmically. **4.** to overcome, to do better than; to be too difficult for. **5.** to sail to windward by a series of alternate tacks across the wind. — *n.* **1.** a regular repeated stroke, a sound of this; the rhythmic pulsation of the heart. **2.** the principal recurring accent in music or verse; a form of pop music with strongly-marked rhythm. **3.** a route regularly patrolled by a policeman or sentinel. —*predic. adj.* (*slang*) exhausted, tired out. —**beat about the bush**, to approach a subject in a roundabout way. **beat a retreat**, to withdraw to a safer position. **beat down**, to force (a seller) to lower his price; (of the sun, rain, etc.) to come down with great force. **beaten track**, a well-worn or frequented route. **beat it**, (*slang*) to go away. **beat off**, to repel (an attacker). **beat the bounds**, to perform the ancient ceremony of going round a parish boundary striking certain points with willow rods. **beat time**, to wave a stick or tap in time with music. **beat up**, to assault systematically with punches, kicks, etc. [OE]

beater *n.* **1.** an implement for beating things; a device for tapping a triangle (percussion instrument; ill. ORCHESTRA). **2.** a person employed to rouse game at a shoot. [f. BEAT]

beatific /bi:ə'tɪfɪk/ *adj.* **1.** (of smiles etc.) showing great happiness. **2.** making blessed. [f. F or L (*beatus* blessed, *facere* make)]

beatify /bi:'ætɪfaɪ/ *v.t.* to make blessed; (of the pope) to declare (a person) to be in heaven (the first step to canonization). —**beatification** /-fɪ'keɪʃ(ə)n/ *n.* [as prec.]

beatitude /bi:'ætɪtju:d/ *n.* **1.** blessedness. **2.** (in *pl.*) the pronouncements by Christ in the Sermon on the Mount beginning 'Blessed are . . .' (Matt.5:3–11). [f. L (*beatus* blessed)]

Beatles /'bi:t(ə)lz/ English rock group consisting of George Harrison (1943–), John Lennon (1940–80), Paul McCartney (1942–), and Ringo Starr (real name Richard Starkey, 1940–). In the 1960s both their music and their ideas caught the imagination of their generation throughout the world and focused attention on the fact that young people could make their own music.

Beaufort scale /'bəʊfət/ a scale of wind velocity ranging from 0 (calm) to 12 (hurricane). [f. Sir F. *Beaufort*, English admiral (d. 1857), the inventor]

Beaujolais /'bəʊʒəleɪ/ *n.* a red or white burgundy from Beaujolais, France.

Beaumarchais /bəʊmɑːr'ʃeɪ/, Pierre Augustin Caron de (1732–90), French dramatist, best known for his comedies *Le Barbier de Séville* (1775) and *Le Mariage de Figaro* (1784) which inspired operas by Rossini and Mozart.

Beaumont /'bəʊmɒnt/, Francis (1584–1616), English dramatist, who entered the Inner Temple in 1600 and collaborated with John Fletcher in *Philaster* (1609), *The Maid's Tragedy* (1610–11), and many other plays. *The Knight of the Burning Pestle* (?1607) is attributed to Beaumont alone. He retired *c.*1613 when he married profitably; he is buried in Westminster Abbey.

beautician /bju:'tɪʃ(ə)n/ *n.* one who gives beautifying treatments to the face or body. [f. BEAUTY]

beautiful /'bju:tɪf(ə)l/ *adj.* **1.** having beauty, pleasing to the eye, ear, or mind. **2.** admirable or excellent of its kind. — **beautifully** *adv.* [f. BEAUTY + -FUL]

beautify /'bju:tɪfaɪ/ *v.t.* to make beautiful. —**beautification** /-fɪ'keɪʃ(ə)n/ *n.* [f. foll.]

beauty /'bju:tɪ/ *n.* **1.** qualities of form, face, etc., that together please one or more of the senses or the mind; a person or thing having these. **2.** a fine specimen; a pleasing or advantageous feature. —**beauty parlour**, an establishment giving beautifying treatments. **beauty queen,** a woman judged the most beautiful in a contest. **beauty sleep,** sleep that is said to make or keep a person beautiful. **beauty-spot** *n.* a place famous for its beautiful scenery; a birthmark or artificial patch on the face, said to heighten beauty. [f. AF f. L (*bellus* pretty)]

Beauvoir /'bəʊvwɑː r/, Simone de (1908-), French existentialist novelist and feminist whose best-known work is the treatise *Le Deuxième Sexe* (*The Second Sex*, 1949). She formed a lifelong association with Sartre, whom she met in 1929.

beaver[1] *n.* **1.** an amphibious rodent of the genus *Castor* with soft brown fur and a broad tail, able to cut down trees by gnawing and to build dams in which to make lodges and raise young. **2.** its fur; a hat made of this (ill. DRESS). **3. Beaver,** a member of a junior branch of the Scout Association, consisting of boys aged six and seven. —*v.i.* **beaver away,** to work hard. [OE]

beaver[2] *n.* (*hist.*) the lower portion of the face-guard of a helmet, when worn with a visor. In the 14th c. the term was applied to the movable face-guard; in the early part of the 15th c. the beaver was formed of overlapping plates, which could be raised or depressed to any degree desired by the wearer. In the 16th c. it again became confounded with the visor, and could be pushed up entirely over the top of the helmet, or drawn down. [f. OF *baviere* bib]

Beaverbrook /'biːvəbrʊk/, William Maxwell Aitken, 1st Baron (1879-1964), British Conservative politician and newspaper proprietor, who made his fortune in Canadian business before coming to Britain and winning election to Parliament in 1910. A wartime Cabinet Minister, he built up a substantial newspaper empire, centred on the Daily Express, in the 1920s, and during the early years of the Second World War served again in the Cabinet, being Minister of Aircraft Production during the crucial years of 1940-2.

bebop /'biːbɒp/ *n.* a kind of jazz with highly syncopated rhythms. [imit.]

becalm /bɪ'kɑːm/ *v.t.* (usu. in *pass.*) to keep (a ship) motionless through absence of wind. [f. BE- + CALM]

became *past* of BECOME.

because /bɪ'kɒz/ *conj.* for the reason that, since. —*adv.* by reason *of.* [f. BE- + CAUSE]

béchamel sauce /'beɪʃəm(ə)l/ a kind of fine white sauce. [invented by Marquis de *Béchamel* (d. 1703), courtier of Louis XIV]

Bechstein /'bekstaɪn/, Friedrich Wilhelm Carl (1826-1900), German piano-builder. His name is used to designate a piano manufactured by him or by the firm which he founded in 1856.

beck[1] *n.* (*archaic*) a gesture. —**at the beck and call of,** subject to constant orders from. [f. *beck* (*v.*) inferred from BECKON]

beck[2] *n.* (*N.Engl.*) a brook, a stream. [ON]

Becket /'bekɪt/, St Thomas (*c.*1118-70), close and influential friend of Henry II who made him his chancellor and later (1162) Archbishop of Canterbury, a position Becket accepted with reluctance, foreseeing the inevitable clash between the interests of the King and those of the Church to which his service and loyalty were now transferred. He soon found himself in open opposition to Henry first on a matter of taxation and later over the coronation of Henry's son, and the King in anger uttered words which sent four knights to Canterbury in revenge. Becket was assassinated in his cathedral in the late afternoon of 29 Dec. He proved to be more potent in death than he had ever been in life: the murder aroused indignation throughout Europe, miracles were soon reported at his tomb, and Henry was obliged to do public penance there. The shrine became a major centre of pilgrimage until its destruction under Henry VIII (1538). Feast day, 29 Dec.

Beckett /'bekɪt/, Samuel Barclay (1906-), Irish dramatist, novelist, and poet, who spent five solitary years in Germany, France and London, reviewing, translating, writing poems and a study of Proust (1931), before settling permanently in France. His trilogy comprising *Molloy* (1951), *Malone Dies* (1951), and *The Unnameable* (1953) was originally published in French; all three are desolate terminal interior monologues irradiated with flashes of black humour. His highly distinctive despairing yet exhilarating voice made its greatest impact with *Waiting for Godot* (1952), one of the most influential plays of the post-war period, and from this time Beckett established his association with the Theatre of the Absurd. His use of the stage and of dramatic

narrative and symbolism revolutionized drama in England. Subsequent plays include *Endgame* (1957), a one-act drama of frustration, irascibility, and senility, *Krapp's Last Tape* (1959), *Breath* (1966), a thirty-second play consisting of a pile of rubbish, a breath, and a cry, and *Not I* (1973), a disembodied monologue delivered by an actor of indeterminate sex of whom only the 'Mouth' is illuminated. Beckett was awarded the Nobel Prize for literature in 1969.

Beckford /'bekfəd/, William (1759-1844), English writer, the son of a Lord Mayor of London from whom he inherited an enormous fortune which he spent lavishly. He travelled in Europe, collected works of art and curios, and commissioned the building of Fonthill, a Gothic extravaganza where he lived in almost complete and somewhat mysterious seclusion from 1796. He is remembered as the author of the fantastic oriental romance, *Vathek* (1786, originally written in French), and also wrote two notable travel-books.

beckon /'bekən/ *v.t./i.* to signal or summon by a gesture. [OE, rel. to BEACON]

become /bɪ'kʌm/ *v.t./i.* (*past* **became**; *p.p.* **become**) **1.** to come or grow to be, to begin to be. **2.** to suit, to be becoming to. —**become of,** to happen to. [f. BE- + COME]

becoming *adj.* giving a pleasing appearance or effect, suitable. —**becomingly** *adv.* [f. prec.]

Becquerel /'bekərel/, Antoine-Henri (1852-1908), French physicist, who shared the 1903 Nobel Prize for physics with the Curies for his discovery of natural radioactivity in uranium salts (1896), and made a systematic study of the properties of this form of radiation. Initially, the rays emitted by radioactive substances were named after him.

becquerel /'bekərel/ *n.* a unit of radioactivity, corresponding to one disintegration per second. [f. prec.]

bed *n.* **1.** a base or support to sleep or rest on, a piece of furniture with a mattress and covering. **2.** a garden plot in which plants are grown. **3.** the bottom of the sea or a river etc.; the foundation of a road or railway. **4.** a stratum or layer. —*v.t./i.* (**-dd-**) **1.** to put or go to bed. **2.** to plant in a garden bed. **3.** to place or fix in a foundation. [OE]

bedaub /bɪ'dɔːb/ *v.t.* to smear all over, especially with paint. [f. BE- + DAUB]

bedbug *n.* a small flat evil-smelling blood-sucking insect (*Cimex lectularius*) infesting dirty beds.

bedclothes *n.pl.* sheets, blankets, etc., used on a bed.

bedding *n.* **1.** things used to make a bed (e.g. mattress, bedclothes; straw and hay for horses etc.). **2.** geological strata. —**bedding plant,** a plant suitable for a garden bed. [f. BED]

Beddoes /'bedəʊz/, Thomas Lovell (1803-49), English dramatic poet, much influenced by Jacobean tragedy. His finest play *Death's Jest-book*, posthumously published in 1850, shows his characteristic preoccupation with death and penchant for the macabre.

Bede /biːd/, the Venerable (*c.*673-735), monk of Jarrow, the 'Father of English History'. He is best known for his historical works including the *Ecclesiastical History of the English People* (completed 731), a primary source for early English history, with vivid descriptions and based on careful research, separating fact from hearsay and tradition. This and specific works on the calculation of Easter did much to establish the practice of dating events from the Incarnation. He was honoured after his death with the title Venerable in recognition of the holiness of his life. Feast day, 27 May.

bedevil /bɪ'dev(ə)l/ *v.t.* (**-ll-**) to trouble or vex; to confuse or perplex; to torment or abuse. —**bedevilment** *n.* [f. BE- + DEVIL]

bedfellow *n.* one occupying the same bed; an associate.

Bedfordshire /'bedfədʃɪə(r) an east midland county of England.

bedizen /bɪ'daɪz(ə)n/ *v.t.* to deck out gaudily. [f. BE- + obs. *dizen* deck out]

bedlam /'bedləm/ *n.* a scene of wild uproar or uproar. 'Bedlam' was originally the popular name of the hospital of St Mary of Bethlehem, founded as a priory in 1247 at Bishopsgate, London, and by the 14th c. a mental hospital. In 1675 a new hospital was built in Moorfields, and this in turn was replaced by a building in the Lambeth Road in 1815 (now the Imperial War Museum), and transferred to Beckenham in Kent in 1931.

bedouin /'beduːɪn/ *n.* (*pl.* same) a nomadic Arab of the desert. [f. OF ult. f. Arab. (*bedw* desert)]

bedpan *n.* a pan for use as a lavatory by a person confined to bed.

bedpost *n.* any of the upright supports of a bedstead.

bedraggled /bɪˈdræg(ə)ld/ *adj.* wet and dishevelled. [f. BE- + DRAGGLE]

bedridden /ˈbedrɪd(ə)n/ *adj.* permanently confined to bed by infirmity. [f. BED + *ridden* (see RIDE)]

bedrock *n.* **1.** solid rock beneath loose soil. **2.** basic facts or principles.

bedroom *n.* a room with a bed and other furniture for sleeping in.

Beds. *abbr.* Bedfordshire.

bedside *n.* a position by a bed.

bedsit, bedsitter *ns.* (*colloq.*) a bed-sitting-room. [f. foll.]

bed-sitting-room *n.* a room serving as bedroom and sitting-room.

bedsore *n.* a sore caused by prolonged lying in bed.

bedspread *n.* a cloth or cover put over a bed when this is not in use.

bedstead /ˈbedsted/ *n.* the framework of a bed.

bedstraw *n.* a herbaceous plant of the genus *Galium*, formerly used as straw for beds.

bee *n.* a four-winged stinging insect, living in colonies and collecting nectar and pollen to produce wax and honey (ill. INSECTS). —**a bee in one's bonnet,** (*colloq.*) an obsession. [OE]

beech *n.* **1.** a forest tree of the genus *Fagus*, with smooth bark and glossy leaves (ill. TREES). **2.** any of various similar chiefly evergreen trees of the genus *Notofagus*, growing in cooler regions of the countries of the southern hemisphere. **3.** the wood of any of these. [OE]

Beecham /ˈbiːtʃəm/, Sir Thomas (1879-1961), English conductor and impresario, possessor of a keen wit, who was associated in one way or another with most of the leading British orchestras, founding the London Philharmonic in 1932 and the Royal Philharmonic in 1947. In the decade preceding the Second World War he was artistic director of the Royal Opera House. An ardent champion of Delius (whose friend and biographer he became) Beecham was a notable interpreter of Mozart, Haydn, Sibelius, Richard Strauss, and French composers.

beechmast /ˈbiːtʃmɑːst/ *n.* beech nuts collectively. [f. BEECH + MAST²]

beef *n.* **1.** the meat of an ox, bull, or cow; (*pl.* **beeves**) an ox etc. bred for meat. **2.** (*colloq.*) muscular strength, brawn. **3.** (*slang*) a complaint. —*v.i.* (*slang*) to grumble. —**beef tea,** stewed extract of beef, given to invalids etc. **beef up,** (*slang*) to strengthen, to reinforce. [f. AF f. L *bos bovis* ox]

beefeater /ˈbiːfiːtə(r)/ *n.* a guard at the Tower of London, or a member of the Yeomen of the Guard, wearing Tudor dress as uniform. [f. obs. sense 'dependant, well-fed menial']

beefy *adj.* like beef; brawny, muscular. —**beefiness** *n.* [f. BEEF]

beehive *n.* a hive.

beeline *n.* a straight line of travel between two points. —**make a beeline for,** to head directly for.

Beelzebub /ˈbiːlzɪbʌb/ (in the Gospels) the Devil, (in 2 Kings 1) the god of the Philistine city Ekron. The name is not found elsewhere in contemporary sources. [f. L, rendering (i) Gk *Beelzeboub* (Matt. 12:24), (ii) Heb. *ba'alzebub* lord of flies]

been *p.p.* of BE.

beep *n.* a short high-pitched sound, especially that of a car-horn. —*v.i.* to make this sound. [imit.]

beer *n.* an alcoholic drink made from fermented malt and flavoured especially with hops (see ALE). —**small beer,** something insignificant. —**beery** *adj.* [OE]

Beerbohm /ˈbɪəbəʊm/, Sir Henry Maximilian ('Max') (1872-1956), English caricaturist, essayist, and critic. A central figure of the Aesthetic movement, he was well placed to comment on the avant-garde tendencies of the period, which he did with elegance and wit in collections of essays and of caricatures. His one completed novel *Zuleika Dobson* (1911) is a fantasized distillation of the atmosphere of *fin-de-siècle* Oxford.

beeswax /ˈbiːzwæks/ *n.* wax secreted by bees for honeycombs and used for polishing wood.

beeswing /ˈbiːzwɪŋ/ *n.* a filmy crust on old port wine.

beet *n.* (*pl.* same or **-s**) a plant of the genus *Beta* grown for its succulent root and used for sugar. [OE f. L]

Beethoven /ˈbeɪthəʊv(ə)n/, Ludwig van (1770-1827), German composer, born at Bonn in the Rhineland, who settled in Vienna in 1792 and remained there for the rest of his

life. Always a man of brusque manner, his eccentricities grew after his discovery in 1798 that he was growing deaf, an affliction which worsened steadily in the next twenty years. Like Haydn, his teacher in Vienna, he was preeminently an instrumental composer, and he poured powerful new life into the forms of sonata, symphony, and concerto that had matured during the latter part of the 18th c., reshaping them as masterfully as his hero Napoleon (with whom he became disillusioned after the latter proclaimed himself emperor) was reshaping the map of Europe. Such works as the 'Eroica' and Fifth Symphonies, the so-called 'Emperor' Concerto, and the 'Appassionata' Sonata ripened in the climate of the Napoleonic Wars, but when the wars were over Beethoven turned in upon himself. In the piano sonatas of 1816-22 and the string quartets of 1824-6 the old structural forms are only latent; in his Ninth (and last) Symphony he broke with them altogether in the finale by introducing voices to sing Schiller's *Ode to Joy*. With his titanic expansion of 18th c. forms and techniques and the penetration of his later works with personal emotion he crowns the classic age of music and heralds the Romantic.

beetle¹ *n.* an insect of the order Coleoptera, with front wings converted to hard wing-cases closing over its back wings; (*pop.*) a similar (often black) insect. [OE, rel. to BITE]

beetle² *n.* a heavy-headed tool for crushing or ramming things. [OE, rel. to BEAT¹]

beetle-browed *adj.* with brows projecting in a threatening way. [f. *beetle* (orig. unkn.) + BROW]

beetling *adj.* projecting threateningly, overhanging. [as prec.]

Beeton /ˈbiːt(ə)n/, Mrs Isabella Mary (1836-65), English author of a book of cookery and household management first published serially (1859-61).

beetroot *n.* the red root of the garden beet, used in salads etc.

befall /bɪˈfɔːl/ *v.i./t.* (*past* **befell;** *p.p.* **befallen**) to happen (to). [f. BE- + FALL]

befit /bɪˈfɪt/ *v.t.* (**-tt-**) to be suited to or proper for. [f. BE- + FIT]

befog /bɪˈfɒg/ *v.t.* (**-gg-**) to envelop as with fog, to confuse. [f. BE- + FOG]

before /bɪˈfɔː(r)/ *adv. & prep.* **1.** ahead (of), in front (of); in the presence of. **2.** at a time previous (to). **3.** in preference to. —*conj.* earlier than the time when. —**before Christ,** (of a date) reckoned backwards from the birth of Christ. [f. BE- + FORE]

beforehand *adv.* in advance, in readiness or anticipation.

befriend /bɪˈfrend/ *v.t.* to act as a friend to, to help. [f. BE- + FRIEND]

befuddle /bɪˈfʌd(ə)l/ *v.t.* to stupefy, to confuse with or as with alcoholic drink. [f. BE- + FUDDLE]

beg *v.t./i.* (**-gg-**) **1.** to ask for as a gift or favour, to request earnestly or humbly; to live by seeking charity. **2.** to ask for formally; to take or ask leave to do something. —**beg the question,** to assume the truth, in reasoning, of a thing that is still to be proved. **go begging,** to be available but unwanted. [rel. to BID]

began *past* of BEGIN.

beget /bɪˈget/ *v.t.* (**-tt-;** *past* **begot** (*archaic* **begat**); *p.p.* **begotten**) to be the father of; to give rise to (an effect). [f. BE- + GET]

beggar /ˈbegə(r)/ **1.** one who lives by begging; a very poor person. **2.** (*colloq.*) a person, a fellow. —*v.t.* **1.** to reduce to extreme poverty. **2.** to render (description etc.) inadequate —**beggarly** *adj.*, **beggary** *n.* [f. BEG]

begin /bɪˈgɪn/ *v.t./i.* (**-nn-;** *past* **began;** *p.p.* **begun**) **1.** to perform the earliest or first part of (an activity or process etc.). **2.** to be the first to do something; to take the first step, to start speaking; (*colloq.*) to show any likelihood. **3.** to come into existence. **4.** to have its first element or starting-point (at some point in space or time). [OE]

beginner *n.* one who is just beginning, especially to learn a skill. —**beginner's luck,** good luck supposed to attend a beginner. [f. prec.]

beginning *n.* the first part of something; the time or place at which something begins; source, origin. —**beginning of the end,** the first clear signs of an (often unfavourable) outcome. [f. BEGIN]

begone /bɪˈgɒn/ *int.* go away at once! [f. BE + GONE]

begonia /bɪˈgəʊnɪə/ *n.* a garden plant of the genus *Begonia* with showy flowers and brightly coloured leaves. [f. M. *Bégon*, French patron of science (d. 1710)]

begot, begotten *past* & *p.p.* of BEGET.

begrudge /bɪˈgrʌdʒ/ *v.t.* to grudge. [f. BE- + GRUDGE]

beguile /bɪˈgaɪl/ *v.t.* **1.** to charm or divert; to make (time) pass pleasantly. **2.** to deceive, to trick. —**beguilement** *n.* [f. BE- + obs. *guile* deceive]

beguine /bɪˈgiːn/ *n.* a West Indian dance; its music or rhythm. f. F (*béguin* infatuation)]

begum /ˈbeɪgəm/ *n.* (in Pakistan and India) the title of a Muslim married woman, = Mrs; a Muslim woman of high rank. [f. Urdu f. Turk., = princess]

begun *p.p.* of BEGIN.

behalf /bɪˈhɑːf/ *n.* **on behalf of,** in the interests of, as the representative of. [earlier *bihalve* on the part of (BE-, *half* side)]

behave /bɪˈheɪv/ *v.i.* **1.** to act or react (in a specified way). **2.** to show good manners;to conduct (oneself) well. [f. BE- + HAVE]

behaviour /bɪˈheɪvjə(r)/ *n.* a way of behaving, manners. [f. prec.]

behavioural *adj.* of or concerned with behaviour. —**behavioural science,** any discipline that studies behaviour, e.g. sociology. [f. prec.]

behaviourism *n.* the study of actions by analysis into stimulus and response; advocacy of this as the only valid method in psychology. (See J. B. WATSON.) —**behaviourist** *n.*, **behaviouristic** /-ˈrɪstɪk/ *adj.* [f. BEHAVIOUR]

behead /bɪˈhed/ *v.t.* to cut off the head of, especially in execution. [f. BE- + HEAD]

beheld *past* of BEHOLD.

behest /bɪˈhest/ *n.* (*literary*) a command, a request. [OE]

behind /bɪˈhaɪnd/ *adv.* & *prep.* **1.** to the rear (of); further back in space or time (than). **2.** in an inferior position (to). **3.** in support (of). **4.** remaining after others have left. **5.** in arrears (with). —*n.* (*colloq.*) the buttocks. —**behind the times,** antiquated in ideas or practices. **behind time,** late, unpunctual. [OE]

behindhand /bɪˈhaɪndhænd/ *adv.* & *predic. adj.* in arrears; behind time; out of date.

behold /bɪˈhəʊld/ *v.t.* (*past* & *p.p.* **beheld**) (*archaic* or *literary*) to observe, to see. [f. BE- + HOLD]

beholden /bɪˈhəʊld(ə)n/ *predic. adj.* under an obligation (to). [obs. p.p. of BEHOLD]

behoove /bɪˈhuːv/ *v.t. impers.* (*US*) = BEHOVE.

behove /bɪˈhəʊv/ *v.t. impers.* to be incumbent on ; to be fitting for. [f. BE- + OE *hof* rel. to HEAVE]

Behring /ˈbeɪrɪŋ/, Emil Adolf von (1854–1917), German bacteriologist and immunologist, one of the founders of immunology, who discovered in 1890 that animals can produce substances in the blood which counteract the effects of toxins released by invading bacteria. Behring and his colleagues quickly applied this knowledge of 'antitoxins' (now known to be types of antibody) to curing diphtheria and tetanus by injecting patients with blood serum taken from animals previously exposed to the disease. He was awarded a Nobel Prize in 1901.

beige /beɪʒ/ *adj.* & *n.* sandy fawn. [F]

Beijing /beɪˈdʒɪ/ Pinyin form of PEKING.

being /ˈbiːɪŋ/ *n.* **1.** existence. **2.** essence or nature, constitution. **3.** something (esp. a person) that exists and has life. [f. BE]

Beirut /beɪˈruːt/ the capital and a port of Lebanon; pop. 702,000.

bejewelled /bɪˈdʒuːəld/ *adj.* adorned with jewels. [f. BE- + JEWEL]

Bel (*Babylonian* & *Assyrian myth.*) = BAAL. —**Bel and the Dragon,** a book of the Apocrypha containing stories of Daniel, including his miraculous liberation from the lions' den.

bel *n.* a unit (= ten decibels) used in comparing power levels in electrical communication. [f. A. G. BELL[1]]

belabour /bɪˈleɪbə(r)/ *v.t.* **1.** to attack physically or verbally. **2.** to labour (a subject). [f. BE- + LABOUR]

belated /bɪˈleɪtɪd/ *adj.* coming late or too late. —**belatedly** *adv.* [f. BE- + LATE]

belay /bɪˈleɪ/ *v.t.* to secure (a rope) by winding it round a peg or spike etc. —*n.* the securing of a rope in this way. [f. Du. *beleggen*]

bel canto /bel ˈkæntəʊ/ a style of operatic singing concentrating on beauty of sound and vocal technique. [It., = fine song]

belch *v.t./i.* **1.** to emit wind from the stomach through the mouth. **2.** (of a chimney, gun, etc.) to discharge (smoke etc.). —*n.* an act of belching. [OE]

beleaguer /bɪˈliːgə(r)/ *v.t.* (*literary*) **1.** to besiege. **2.** to harass or oppress. [f. Du. *belegeren* camp round (*leger* camp)]

belemnite /ˈbeləmnaɪt/ *n.* a common fossil of sharp-pointed tapering shape. [f. Gk *belemnon* dart]

Belfast /belˈfɑːst/ the capital of Northern Ireland, a port at the mouth of the River Lagan; pop.(1983) 322,600.

belfry /ˈbelfrɪ/ *n.* a bell tower (chiefly attached to a church); the bell-chamber in this. [orig. = siege-tower; f. OF f.Gmc]

Belgium /ˈbeldʒəm/ a country in western Europe on the south shore of the North Sea and English Channel, now highly industrialized; pop. (1981) 8,863,374; official languages, Flemish and French; capital, Brussels. The country takes its name from the Belgae, a Celtic people conquered by the Romans in the 1st c. BC. A low-lying area, prosperous in medieval times as a result of textile production and commerce, Belgium was on the border of French, Dutch, and Hapsburg spheres of influence in the 16th–18th c. and, as a result, frequently the site of military operations. After falling at various times under the rule of Burgundy, Spain, Austria, France, and the Netherlands it gained formal independence in 1839 as a consequence of a nationalist revolt that began in 1830, and Prince Leopold of Saxe-Coburg was elected as king. Occupied and devastated during both world wars, Belgium made a quick recovery after 1945, taking the first step towards European economic integration with the formation of the Benelux customs union with the Netherlands and Luxemburg in 1947. —**Belgian** *adj.* & *n.*

Belgrade /belˈgreɪd/ the capital of Yugoslavia, at the junction of the river Sava with the Danube; pop. (1981) 1,455,000.

Belial /ˈbiːljəl/ the Devil, Satan. [f. Heb., = worthless]

belie /bɪˈlaɪ/ *v.t.* (*past* & *p.p.* **belied**; *pres. p.* **belying**) **1.** to fail to confirm, to show to be untrue; to fail to live up to (one's reputation, promise, etc.). **2.** to give a false idea of. [f. BE- + LIE[1]]

belief /bɪˈliːf/ *n.* **1.** the act of believing. **2.** something firmly believed. **3.** trust, confidence in. **4.** acceptance of a doctrine etc., one's religion. [f. BELIEVE]

believable /bɪˈliːvəb(ə)l/ *adj.* that may be believed. [f. foll.]

believe /bɪˈliːv/ *v.t./i.* **1.** to accept as true or conveying truth. **2.** to think, to suppose. **3.** to have (religious) faith; to have faith *in*; to have confidence *in*. —**believer** *n.* [OE]

Belisarius /belɪˈseərɪəs/ (?505–65) general under Justinian.

Belisha beacon /bɪˈliːʃə/ a flashing orange globe on a striped post, marking a pedestrian crossing. [f. L. Hore-*Belisha*, Minister of Transport 1934]

belittle /bɪˈlɪt(ə)l/ *v.t.* to imply to be of little consequence. —**belittlement** *n.* [f. BE- + LITTLE]

Belize /beˈliːz/ a country on the Caribbean coast of Central America; pop. (est. 1981) 148,300; official language, English; capital, Belmopan. Remains of the Maya civilization have been found in this area. The British settled there in the 17th c., proclaiming the area (as British Honduras) a Crown colony in 1862. It adopted the name Belize (from a Mayan word, = muddy water) in 1973, and in 1981 became an independent State within the Commonwealth. Guatemala, which bounds it on the west and south, has always claimed the territory on the basis of old Spanish treaties. —**Belizian** *adj.* & *n.*

Bell[1], Alexander Graham (1847–1922), Scottish scientist and inventor, who became interested in sound waves, speech, and helping the deaf. Emigrating to the USA, he worked on transmission of messages by telegraphy and then by telephony, using electromagnetic principles. The three patents he took out between 1875 and 1877 were disputed by Edison, but upheld. Bell also invented the gramophone as a successful rival to Edison's phonograph, founded the huge Bell Telephone Company, and investigated the stability of flying machines.

Bell[2], Currer, Ellis, and Acton, see BRONTË.

bell[1] *n.* **1.** a cup-shaped metal instrument that makes a ringing sound when struck (see below). **2.** the sound of a bell, used as a signal (*one to eight bells* indicating the half-hours of a nautical watch). **3.** a bell-shaped object or flower. **4.** a device making a ringing or buzzing sound for attracting attention in a house etc. —**bell-bottomed** *adj.* (of trousers) widening from the knee down. **bell-ringing** *n.* the ringing of church bells or handbells with changes etc. [OE]

Bells vary enormously in weight and size, from the huge

broken bell at the Kremlin, dating from 1733 and weighing over 170 tons, to small handbells ranged in pitch order on a table. The oldest bell in England is thought to be that at Claughton, Lancs., cast in 1296. Bells occur all over the world, have various powers assigned to them, and possess their own special mystique, whether sinister and awesome or joyous.

bell[2] *n.* the bay of a stag. —*v.i.* to make this sound. [OE]

belladonna /belə'dɒnə/ *n.* deadly nightshade, a plant (*Atropa belladonna*) with purple flowers and poisonous black berries; a drug prepared from this. [f. It., = beautiful lady]

belle /bel/ *n.* a beautiful or the most beautiful woman. [F f. L (*bellus* beautiful)]

belle époque /bel ɪ'pɒk/ the period of settled and comfortable life preceding the First World War. [F, = fine period]

Bellerophon /bɪ'lerəfən/ (*Gk legend*) a hero who slew the monster Chimaera with the help of the winged horse Pegasus.

belles-lettres /bel'letr/ *n.pl.* writings or studies of a literary nature. [F, = fine letters]

bellicose /'belikəʊz/ *adj.* eager to fight, warlike. —**bellicosity** /-'kɒsɪtɪ/ *n.* [f. L (*bellum* war)]

belligerent /bɪ'lɪdʒərənt/ *adj.* engaged in a war or conflict; bellicose. —*n.* a person or nation participating in a war. —**belligerence** *n.*, **belligerency** *n.* [f. L (*bellum* war, *gerere* wage)]

Bellini[1] /be'liːnɪ/ the name of a family of Venetian painters. Jacopo (*c.*1400-70) was trained by Gentile da Fabriano: few of his paintings survive, but over 230 drawings are preserved in two sketchbooks (Louvre and British Museum). His elder son, Gentile (*c.*1429-1507) was prominent as a portraitist and narrative painter. Giovanni, the younger son (*c.*1430-1516) transformed Venice into a major centre of Renaissance painting. He was deeply influenced by his brother-in-law Mantegna, but Giovanni's painting is always more fluent and poetic, and its serene contemplative qualities have hardly been equalled. In the 15th c. his work is dominated by Madonnas and other sacred subjects, but he showed astonishing adaptability as an old man, painting the newly fashionable pagan themes and mysterious allegories. Stylistically, he brought a sense of volume to a predominantly linear art, and, around 1500, moved to a more atmospheric method of painting which paralleled that of his young pupils, Giorgione and Titian.

Bellini[2] /be'liːnɪ/, Vincenzo (1801-35), Italian composer of 11 operas before his untimely death in France. He is most famous for *La sonnambula*, *Norma* (both 1831), and *I Puritani* (1835); the soprano aria 'Casta diva' ('Chaste goddess'), in which Norma prays for peace between the Romans and the Druids, is the supreme example of his gift for long-breathed melody, while in the last act of that opera, where Norma chooses to sacrifice her life, Bellini achieves his finest expression of tragic doomed grandeur.

Belloc /'belɒk/, Hilaire (1870-1953), versatile British writer (poet, essayist, historian, novelist), and Liberal MP (1906-10). A devout Roman Catholic, he collaborated with G. K. Chesterton in works often directly opposing the socialism of G. B. Shaw and H. G. Wells, notably in *The Servile State* (1912). He wrote biographies of Danton, Robespierre, Napoleon, and Cromwell, and numerous travel works including *The Path to Rome* (1902), but is today best known for his popular light verse, such as *The Bad Child's Book of Beasts* (1896) and *Cautionary Tales* (1907).

Bellow /'beləʊ/, Saul (1915-), American novelist, born in Canada of Russian-Jewish parentage. His works range from the richly comic *The Adventures of Augie March* (1953), a picaresque account of a young Chicago Jew, to the semi-autobiographic *Herzog* (1964). He was awarded the Nobel Prize for literature in 1976.

bellow /'beləʊ/ *v.i./t.* to emit a deep loud roar; to utter loudly. —*n.* a loud roar, originally that of a bull. [orig. unkn.]

bellows /'beləʊz/ *n.pl.* **1.** a device which, when squeezed, drives a blast of air into a fire, through organ pipes, etc. **2.** the expandable part of a camera etc. [rel. to foll.]

belly /'belɪ/ *n.* **1.** the abdomen; the stomach. **2.** the underside of a four-legged animal. **3.** the cavity or bulging part of anything. —*v.i./t.* to swell out. —**belly-ache** *n.* stomach pain; (*v.i.*) (*slang*) to complain querulously. **belly-dance** *n.* an oriental dance by a woman, with voluptuous movements of the belly. **belly-dancer** *n.* [OE, = bag]

Belmopan /belməʊ'pæn/ the capital of Belize; pop. (est. 1980) 4,500.

belong /bɪ'lɒŋ/ *v.i.* **1.** (with *to*) to be the property of; to be rightly assigned to as a duty, right, part, etc.; to be a member of (a club, family, etc.). **2.** to fit an environment etc.; to be rightly placed. [f. BE- + obs. *long* belong]

belongings *n.pl.* personal possessions. [f. prec.]

Belorussia /beləʊ'rʌʃə/ (also known as White Russia) the Belorussian SSR, a constituent republic of the USSR in the west of the country; capital, Minsk. [f. Russ. (*belyi* white, *Russiya* Russia)]

Belorussian /beləʊ'rʌʃ(ə)n/ *adj.* of Belorussia or its people or language. —*n.* **1.** a native of Belorussia. **2.** its East Slavonic language. [f. prec.]

beloved /bɪ'lʌvɪd/ *adj.* much loved (*predic.* /-'lʌvd/). —*n.* a beloved person. [f. BE- + LOVE]

below /bɪ'ləʊ/ *adv.* **1.** at or to a lower point or level. **2.** further down a page, further on in a book etc. —*prep.* lower in position, amount, rank, etc., than; downstream from. [f. BE- + LOW[1]]

Belsen /'bels(ə)n/ a village in the north of West Germany, site of a Nazi concentration camp in the Second World War.

Belshazzar /bel'ʃæzə(r)/ (in Dan. 5) son of Nebuchadnezzar and last king of Babylon, who was killed in the sack of the city by Cyrus (538 BC) and whose doom was foretold by writing which appeared on the walls of his palace at a great banquet. In inscriptions and documents from Ur, however, he was the son of Nabonidos, last king of Babylon, and did not himself reign.

belt *n.* **1.** a strip of leather etc. worn round the waist or diagonally across the chest to secure clothes or hold weapons etc. **2.** a strip of colour, a special surface, trees, etc., round or on something; a zone or region. **3.** a flexible strip carrying machine-gun cartridges; an endless strap connecting pulleys etc. **4.** (*slang*) a heavy blow. —*v.t.* **1.** to put a belt round. **2.** to thrash with a belt; (*slang*) to hit with force. **3.** to move rapidly. —**below the belt**, unfair, unfairly. **belt up**, to fasten one's safety belt; (*slang*) to stop talking. **tighten one's belt**, to live more frugally. [OE f. L *balteus*]

beluga /bɪ'luːgə/ *n.* **1.** a large white sturgeon (*Huso huso*); caviare from this. **2.** a white whale (*Delphinapterus leucas*). [Russ. (*belyi* white)]

belvedere /'belvɪdɪə(r)/ *n.* a raised turret or summer-house from which to view scenery. [It., = beautiful view]

bemoan /bɪ'məʊn/ *v.t.* to lament, complain of. [f. BE- + MOAN]

bemuse /bɪ'mjuːz/ *v.t.* to stupefy or bewilder. [f. BE- + MUSE]

Benares /bɪ'nɑːrɪz/ see VARANASI.

bench *n.* **1.** a long seat of wood or stone. **2.** a work-table for a carpenter, scientist, etc. **3.** a judge's seat in court; a lawcourt; (*collect.*) judges and magistrates. —**bench-mark** *n.* a surveyor's mark indicating a point in a line of levels; a standard or point of reference. **King's** *or* **Queen's Bench**, a division of the High Court of Justice. **on the bench**, serving as a judge or magistrate. [OE, rel. to BANK[1]]

bencher *n.* a senior member of any of the Inns of Court. [f. BENCH]

bend[1] *v.t./i.* (*past & p.p.* bent exc. in *bended knee*) **1.** to force (what was straight) into a curve or angle; to become curved or angular; to modify (rules) to suit oneself. **2.** to direct (one's energies) *to*. **3.** to incline from the vertical; to submit or bow (*to, before*); to force to submit. **4.** to turn (one's steps etc.) in a new direction. —*n.* **1.** a curve, departure from a straight course; the bent part of a thing. **2.** (in *pl.*) sickness due to too rapid decompression e.g. after diving. [OE, rel. to BIND]

bend[2] *n.* **1.** any of various knots used to tie one rope to another. **2.** (in heraldry) a stripe from the dexter chief to the sinister base (ill. HERALDRY). —**bend sinister**, (in heraldry) a stripe from the sinister chief to the dexter base, sometimes used as a sign of bastardy. [OE, = band, bond]

beneath /bɪ'niːθ/ *adv. & prep.* **1.** below, under. **2.** not worthy of. —**beneath contempt**, not even worth despising. [OE (rel. to NETHER)]

Benedict /'benɪdɪkt/, St (*c.*480-*c.*550), a hermit, the 'Patriarch of Western monasticism', compiler of a monastic rule (chiefly at Monte Cassino in Italy) though he does not seem to have been ordained or to have contemplated founding an order. He was buried at Monte Cassino in the same grave as his sister, St Scholastica. Feast day, 21 March.

The rule of St Benedict was gradually adopted by most western monastic houses, sometimes with their own modifications. Relaxations of discipline were followed by attempts at reform, and resulted in the formation of separate orders, which remained largely independent of any wider organization. The Benedictines have rendered invaluable services to civilization, preparing the social organization of the Middle Ages during the chaos after the fall of the Roman Empire, preserving ideals of scholarship, and maintaining or restoring the use of good art in liturgical worship.

Benedictine /benɪˈdɪktɪn/ n. **1.** a monk of an order following the rule of St Benedict, also called Black Monks from the colour of their habits; a nun of a corresponding order. **2.** [P] a liqueur of a kind originally made by these monks. — adj. of St Benedict or the Benedictines. [f. prec.]

benediction /benɪˈdɪkʃ(ə)n/ n. a spoken blessing, especially at the end of a religious service or as a special Roman Catholic service. —**benedictory** adj. [f. OF f. L (benedicere bless)]

benefaction /benɪˈfækʃ(ə)n/ n. a charitable gift or endowment, especially to an institution. [as foll.]

benefactor /ˈbenɪfæktə(r)/ n. one who has given financial or other help, especially to an institution. —**benefactress** n. fem. [f. L (as BENEFIT)]

benefice /ˈbenɪfɪs/ n. a living held by a vicar, rector, etc. [f. OF f. L beneficium kind deed]

beneficent /bɪˈnefɪs(ə)nt/ adj. conferring blessings or favours. —**beneficence** n. [f. L (as BENEFIT)]

beneficial /benɪˈfɪʃ(ə)l/ adj. advantageous, having benefits. —**beneficially** adj. [f. L (as BENEFICE)]

beneficiary /benɪˈfɪʃərɪ/ n. a recipient of benefits, especially as designated in a will. [f. L (as BENEFICE)]

benefit /ˈbenɪfɪt/ n. **1.** a favourable, helpful, or profitable factor or circumstance. **2.** a payment to which one is entitled from an insurance policy or government funds. **3.** a public performance or game of which the proceeds go to a charitable cause etc. —v.t./i. **1.** to do good to. **2.** to receive benefit (from or by). —**benefit of clergy,** the privilege, to which clergymen were formerly entitled, of being tried before an ecclesiastical court not a secular one, or (in certain cases) of being exempt from the sentence imposed. **benefit of the doubt,** concession that a person is innocent, correct, etc., although doubt exists. **benefit society,** a society for mutual insurance against illness or the effects of old age. [f. AF f. L benefactum (bene facere do well)]

Benelux /ˈbenɪlʌks/ a collective name for Belgium, the Netherlands, and Luxemburg, especially with reference to their economic co-operation established in 1948. [f. their initial letters]

benevolent /bɪˈnev(ə)lənt/ adj. wishing to do good to others, friendly and helpful; (of a fund) charitable. —**benevolence** n., **benevolently** adv. [f. OF f. L bene volens well wishing]

Bengal /beŋˈgɔːl/ a former province of NE India, divided in 1947 into West Bengal (now a State of India) and East Bengal (now Bangladesh).

Bengali /beŋˈgɔːlɪ/ adj. of the region of Bengal or its people or language. —n. **1.** a member of a people living in this region. **2.** their language, spoken by some 125 million people. It is a descendant of Sanskrit, written in a version of the Sanskrit Devanagari script, and is the official language of Bangladesh. [f. prec.]

benighted /bɪˈnaɪtɪd/ adj. **1.** overtaken by night. **2.** intellectually or morally ignorant. [f. BE- + NIGHT]

benign /bɪˈnaɪn/ adj. kindly; propitious; (of climate) mild; (of disease) mild, not malignant. —**benignly** adv. [f. OF f. L benignus]

benignant /bɪˈnɪgnənt/ adj. kindly, especially to inferiors; beneficial. —**benignancy** n., **benignantly** adv. [f. prec.]

benignity /bɪˈnɪgnɪtɪ/ n. kindliness. [f. BENIGN]

Benin /beˈnɪn/ a country of western Africa, immediately west of Nigeria; pop. (est. 1981) 3,641,000; official language, French; capital, Porto Novo. Known as Dahomey, and a centre of the slave trade, the country was conquered by the French in 1893 and became part of French West Africa. In 1960 it became fully independent and in 1975 adopted the name of Benin, a former African kingdom (in what is now southern Nigeria) that was powerful in the 14th-17th c. and was famous for its bronze and ivory sculptures. —**Beninese** /-ˈniːz/ adj. & n.

benison /ˈbenɪz(ə)n/ n. (archaic) a blessing. [f. OF f. L benedictio benediction]

Benjamin /ˈbendʒəmɪn/ **1.** Hebrew patriarch, youngest

and favourite son of Jacob (Gen. 35:8, 42, etc.). **2.** the smallest tribe of Israel, traditionally descended from him.

Bennett /ˈbenɪt/, (Enoch) Arnold (1867-1931), English novelist who began a versatile literary career in London writing for periodicals and editing the journal Woman. He lived in Paris (1902-12) where he was greatly influenced by the French realists, and wrote several successful plays, but his fame rests on his novels and stories set in the Potteries (the 'Five Towns') of his youth, notably Anna of the Five Towns (1902), The Old Wives' Tale (1908), and the Clayhanger series (1902-8), in which he portrays provincial life and culture in documentary detail.

Ben Nevis /ben ˈnevɪs/ the highest mountain in the British Isles (1,343 m, 4,406 ft.), in western Scotland.

bent¹ p.p. of BEND¹. —adj. curved or having an angle; (slang) dishonest, illicit. —n. a natural tendency or bias; a talent (for). —**bent on,** determined on, seeking to do.

bent² n. **1.** any of various coarse stiff grasses etc. **2.** the flower-stalk of grasses, especially when old and dry. [= OE beonet]

Bentham /ˈbentəm, -θəm/, Jeremy (1748-1832), English philosopher, the first major proponent of utilitarianism, advocating the organization of society to secure 'the greatest happiness for the greatest number' and concerned to reform the law by giving it a clear theoretical justification. He went beyond general theoretical foundations and produced intricate classifications of kinds of pleasures and pains, motives, dispositions, and offences, and attacked the concept of natural rights, which he called 'nonsense on stilts'. He also made plans for a model prison, which were taken seriously but never put into practice. Bentham exercised a decisive influence over 19th-c. British thought, particularly with reference to political reform.

benthos /ˈbenθɒs/ n. the flora and fauna found at the bottom of a sea or lake. [Gk, = depth of sea]

bentwood n. wood artificially curved for making furniture.

benumb /bɪˈnʌm/ v.t. to make numb; to paralyse or deaden. [f. BE- + NUMB]

Benz /bents/, Karl Friedrich (1844-1929), German engineer, one of the great pioneers of the motor car, building the first car (a three-wheeled vehicle) to be driven by an internal-combustion engine, at Mannheim in Germany in 1885.

benzene /ˈbenziːn/ n. a substance obtained from coal-tar and used as a solvent, fuel, and in the manufacture of plastics. [f. BENZOIN]

benzine /ˈbenziːn/ n. a spirit obtained from petroleum and used as a cleansing agent. [f. foll.]

benzoin /ˈbenzəʊɪn/ n. the aromatic resin of an East Indian tree, Styrax benzoin; a white crystalline constituent of this. —**benzoic** /-ˈzəʊɪk/ adj. [f. F f. Arab. lubān jāwī incense of Java]

benzol /ˈbenzɒl/ n. benzene, especially in its unrefined state. [f. prec.]

Beowulf /ˈbeɪəwʊlf/ a legendary Swedish hero celebrated in the Old English epic poem 'Beowulf'. The historical events referred to in the poem belong to the first part of the 6th c., but the date of the poem itself is less certain since it includes both heathen and Christian religious elements.

bequeath /bɪˈkwiːð/ v.t. to leave (personal estate) to a person by will; to transmit to posterity. [OE (BE- + root of QUOTH)]

bequest /bɪˈkwest/ n. bequeathing; a thing bequeathed. [rel. to prec.]

berate /bɪˈreɪt/ v.t. to scold or rebuke severely. [f. BE- + RATE]

Berber /ˈbɜːbə(r)/ n. **1.** a member of a Caucasoid people of North African stock including the aboriginal races, speaking allied languages (now mainly in Morocco and Algeria). **2.** their Hamito-Semitic language or group of languages. —adj. of the Berbers or their language. [f. Arab. barbar]

berberis /ˈbɜːbərɪs/ n. a cultivated prickly yellow-flowered shrub of the genus Berberis. [f. L & OF (orig. unkn.)]

berceuse /beəˈsɜːz/ n. an instrumental piece of music in the style of a lullaby. [F (bercer rock to sleep)]

bereave /bɪˈriːv/ v.t. (chiefly in pass.; p.p. **bereaved**) to deprive of a near relative, spouse, etc., by death. [OE (reave take away forcibly)]

bereft /bɪˈreft/ adj. deprived (of). [f. prec.]

Berenice /berɪˈnaɪsɪ/ (3rd c. BC) Egyptian queen, wife of Ptolemy III. During his absence on an expedition in Syria she dedicated her hair as a votive offering for his safe return. The hair was stolen, and legend said that it was carried to the heavens where it became the constellation *Coma Berenices*.

beret /ˈbereɪ/ *n.* a round flat cap of felt or cloth. [F, rel. to BIRETTA]

Berg /beəg/, Alban (1885–1935), Austrian composer who studied with Schoenberg in Vienna, and together with Anton Webern became his greatest pupil. The emotional content of his music has done much to ease public acceptance of his use of 12-note music and serial techniques, and one of his best-loved works is the Violin Concerto (1935), composed as a memorial after the death of the 18-year-old daughter of Alma and Walter Gropius. His two operas, *Wozzeck* (1914–21) and *Lulu* (1928–35), the former based on a play by Georg Büchner and the latter on two plays by Wedekind, combine an expressionist violence with a deep compassion for his unfortunate hero and heroine. His music, together with that of Schoenberg and Webern, was condemned by Hitler as 'degenerate art', but he remained in Austria during the Second World War, dying in Vienna after suffering blood poisoning from an insect bite.

berg *n.* an iceberg. [abbr.]

bergamot /ˈbɜːgəmɒt/ *n.* **1.** a perfume from the rind of a citrus fruit; the tree (*Citrus bergamia*) bearing this fruit. **2.** an aromatic herb, especially *Monardia didyma*. [f. *Bergamo* in Italy]

Bergerac see CYRANO DE BERGERAC.

Bergman /ˈbɜːgmən/, Ingmar (1918–), Swedish film and theatre director. After several films about the problems of the young he turned to studies of feminine psychology, one of which, *Smiles of a Summer Night* (1955), made him internationally famous. He achieved further worldwide success with *The Seventh Seal* and *Wild Strawberries* (both 1957), each of them, together with several subsequent films, concerned with man's isolation from God. In *Persona* (1966), *Cries and Whispers* (1972), and *Autumn Sonata* (1978) Bergman turned from metaphysics to study the relationships between women. *Fanny and Alexander* (1982) was announced as being his last film. Bergman is also important as a theatre director, notably at Stockholm's Royal Dramatic Theatre, and many of his players worked frequently with him in both media.

bergschrund /ˈbeəkʃrʊnt/ *n.* a crevasse or gap at the junction of a steep upper slope with a glacier or névé (ill. MOUNTAINS). [G]

Bergson /ˈbɜːgs(ə)n/, Henri (1859–1941), French philosopher, whose ideas influenced the novelist Proust (whose cousin he married in 1891), impressed William James (who became a close friend), and reached a wide public throughout Europe. His philosophy is dualistic, dividing the world into life (or consciousness) and matter. In his most famous work *Creative Evolution* (1907) he interprets evolution as the continuous operation of a vital impulse (*élan vital*), which is a manifestation of a single original impulse seeking to impose itself upon matter, which resists it; latterly Bergson identified this force with a God whose being and purpose are love. We perceive matter through intellect, but it is through intuition (which is superior to intellect) that we perceive this life force and the reality of time, which is an indivisible flow of experience and not as measured in units. After the First World War Bergson spent much time attempting to promote international peace and co-operation. He was awarded the Nobel Prize for literature for 1927.

beriberi /berɪˈberɪ/ *n.* a tropical disease of the nervous system, caused by deficiency of vitamin B. [Sinhalese, f. *beri* weakness]

Bering /ˈbeərɪŋ/, Vitus Jonassen (1681–1741), Danish navigator and explorer of Arctic Asia, who led several Russian expeditions aimed at discovering whether Asia and North America were connected by land. He sailed along the coast of Siberia, and in 1741 reached Alaska from the east. On the return journey his ship was wrecked and he died on an island which now bears his name. Also named after him are the Bering Sea (the northern most part of the Pacific) and Bering Strait (between Asia and America, connecting the Bering Sea with the Arctic Ocean).

Berkeley /ˈbɑːklɪ/, George (1685–1753), Irish-born philosopher and bishop. His philosophical system originated in criticisms of Locke's. Berkeley denied the existence of matter, holding that only minds and mental events exist, and supported his view by a number of ingenious arguments. He maintained that material objects exist only by being

perceived. To the objection that a tree, for example, would cease to exist if no one was looking at it he replied that God perceives everything, and that this gives trees, rocks, and stones an existence as continuous as common sense supposes: they are ideas in the mind of God. If there were no God material objects would leap in and out of existence; this was, in his view, a weighty argument for the existence of God.

berkelium /bɑːˈkiːlɪəm, ˈbɜːklɪəm/ *n.* an artificially made transuranic radioactive metallic element, symbol Bk, atomic number 97, first obtained in 1949 by bombarding americium with helium ions. [f. *Berkeley* in California (where first made)]

Berks *abbr.* Berkshire.

Berkshire /ˈbɑːkʃɪə(r)/ *abbr.* a southern inland county of England.

Berlin[1] /bɜːˈlɪn/ the former capital of Prussia and Germany, divided since the Second World War into two parts: West Berlin, a State of the Federal Republic of Germany, forming an enclave within the German Democratic Republic, pop. (1981) 1,879,100; and East Berlin, the zone of the city that was Soviet-occupied at the end of the Second World War, now the capital of the German Democratic Republic, pop. (1980) 1,166,641. A fortified wall separating the two sectors was erected in 1961 by the Communist authorities to curb the flow of refugees to the West.

Berlin[2] /bəˈlɪn/, Irving (1888–), Russian-born American song-writer, born Israel Baline, who emigrated with his family to the USA when he was four. He began writing songs when he was 16 and in 1911 had a best-selling hit with *Alexander's Ragtime Band*. He formed his own publishing business in 1919 and in 1921 built, with Sam H. Harris, the Music Box Theater. Some of his best songs were written for films; his greatest commercial success was the song 'White Christmas' from *Holiday Inn* (1942).

Berlioz /ˈbeəlɪəʊz/, Hector (1803–69), French composer, one of the most original of his time. He took as his inspiration such giants as Shakespeare and Beethoven, and his private life was as dramatic as his music. His *Symphonie fantastique* (1830) reflects his unhappy passion for Harriet Smithson, an Irish actress he had seen playing Ophelia, with a programme describing happy times with his beloved (represented by an *idée fixe*, or recurring melody) followed by fearful scenes where she is transformed into a very active participant in a Witches' Sabbath. A subsequent affair with a young pianist drove him to plan, in full detail, her murder and that of her lover, and in turn inspired the monodrama *Lélio* (1831–2) as a sequel to the *Symphonie*. Berlioz was an innovative orchestrator, and his *Grand traité d'instrumentation et d'orchestration moderne* (1843) affords a fascinating glimpse of his approach to the instruments of his day.

berm *n.* a narrow strip or ledge, especially that between a ditch and the base of a parapet in a fortification. [f. F f. Du., prob. rel. to ON *barmr* brim]

Bermuda /bɜːˈmjuːdə/ (also **Bermuda Islands, Bermudas**) a country comprising a group of about 150 small islands off the coast of North Carolina; pop. (1980) 57,237; official language, English; capital, Hamilton. The climate is subtropical and tourism is the principal industry. The islands (now a British dependency with full internal self-government) were sighted early in the 16th c. by the Spaniard, Juan Bermúdez, from whom they take their name, but remained uninhabited until 1609 when an English expedition, on its way to Virginia, was shipwrecked there; its leader, Sir George Somers, later returned from Virginia to claim the islands for Britain. —**Bermuda ketch, sloop,** etc., one that has a high tapering sail (**Bermuda rig**); ill. SAILING-SHIPS. **Bermuda Triangle,** the name given to an area of sea between Bermuda and Florida, credited since the mid-19th c. with a number of unexplained disappearances of ships and aircraft. —**Bermudian** *adj. & n.*

Bernadette /bɜːnəˈdet/, St (1844–79), Marie Bernarde Soubirous (see LOURDES).

Bernadotte[1] /beənəˈdɒt/, Folke, Count (1895–1948), Swedish statesman. A member of the Swedish royal family, Bernadotte gained a deserved reputation as a neutral arbiter in international disputes. Charged with the position of UN mediator in Palestine after the Second World War, he was assassinated by Jewish extremists.

Bernadotte[2] /beənəˈdɒt/, Jean Baptiste (1763–1844), French soldier, one of Napoleon's marshals. He was adopted by Charles XIII of Sweden in 1810 and became king (as Charles XIV) in 1818, thus founding the present royal house.

Bernard[1] /ber'nɑːrd/, Claude (1813-78), French physiologist, pioneer of modern knowledge of the functioning of the body. Bernard used animal experiments to show the role of the pancreas in digestion, the method of regulation of body temperature, and the function of the nerves to the body's internal organs. He realized that the constant composition of the body fluids, the '*milieu interieur*', was essential for the optimal functioning of the body. He also discovered the biological importance of glycogen and investigated the action of curare, the paralysing drug still used in anaesthesia.

Bernard[2] /'bɜːnəd/, St (1090-1153), a saintly monk of strong personality, abbot of Clairvaux in France, where he founded a monastery which became one of the chief centres of the Cistercian order. Enjoying papal favour, he was an important religious force in Europe, and the Cistercian order grew rapidly under his influence. His writings reveal above all a faith inspired by sublime mysticism. Feast day, 20 Aug.

Bernard[3] /'bɜːnəd/, St (*c*.996-*c*.1081), a priest who founded two hospices to aid travellers in the Alps. The St Bernard passes, where the hospices were situated, and St Bernard dogs, once kept by the monks and trained to aid travellers, are named after him. Feast day, 28 May.

Berne /bɜːn/ a city on the river Aar, founded in 1191 and the capital of Switzerland since 1848; pop. (1982) 145,700 — **Berne Convention,** an international copyright agreement of 1885, later revised. The USA has never been party to it.

Bernhardt /'bɜːnhɑːt/, Sarah (1844-1923), real name Rosine Bernard, French romantic and tragic actress. The 'divine Sarah' made her début in 1862, and her earliest successes (due largely to her beautiful voice and magnetic personality) were in Victor Hugo's *Ruy Blas* and *Hernani*, and as Phaedra in Racine's tragedy. The loss of a leg late in life, as the result of an accident, did not diminish her activity; numerous legends about her eccentricities were in circulation, some provoked by her undoubted unconventionality, others apocryphal.

Bernini /beə'niːni/, Gianlorenzo (1598-1680), Italian sculptor, painter, and architect, the outstanding figure of the Italian baroque, son of a sculptor (Pietro Bernini, 1562-1629). His works are original in their vigour, movement, and dramatic and emotional power, and he used a variety of materials (bronze, stucco, stone, and marble) to fuse sculpture, architecture, and painting into a magnificent decorative whole. Working chiefly in Rome, he became architect to St Peter's in 1629, for which he made the great baldacchino over the high altar, decorated the apse with the group of the Church Fathers supporting the chair of St Peter, and designed the colonnade round the piazza in front of the church. Although to the neo-classical taste of the 18th c. Bernini's approach to sculpture was anathema, changes of fashion and taste in the 20th c. have brought a more sympathetic recognition of his achievement.

Bernoulli /bɜː'nuːiː/ the name of a Swiss family that produced many eminent mathematicians and scientists within three generations. Jakob (Jacques or James) Bernoulli (1654-1705) made substantial discoveries in the calculus, which he used to solve minimization problems, and he contributed to geometry and the theory of probabilities. His brother Johann (Jean or John, 1667-1748) also contributed to differential and integral calculus. Both were professors of mathematics at Basle. Daniel Bernoulli (1700-82), son of Johann, was professor of mathematics at St Petersburg and then held successively the chairs of botany, physiology, and physics at Basle. Although his original studies were in medicine, his greatest contributions were to hydrodynamics and various branches of mathematical physics. Other members of the family were also well-known mathematicians, astronomers, and scientists in their day.

berry *n.* any small roundish juicy fruit without a stone; (*Bot.*) a fruit with seeds enclosed in pulp (e.g. banana, tomato). [OE]

berserk /bə'sɜːk/ *adj.* uncontrollably violent. —**go berserk,** to fly into a violent rage, to lose control. [orig. = Norse warrior, f. Icel. = bear-coat]

berth *n.* **1.** a fixed bunk on a ship, train, etc., for sleeping in. **2.** a ship's place at a wharf; room for a ship to swing at anchor. —*v.t./i.* **1.** to moor (a ship) in a berth; to come to a mooring. **2.** to provide with a sleeping-berth. —**give a wide berth to,** to keep at a safe distance from. [f. BEAR[2]]

Bertillon /beərtiːjɔ̃/, Alphonse (1853-1914), French criminologist who devised a system of body-measurements for the identification of criminals. It was widely used in France and other countries until superseded by the technique of finger-printing at the beginning of the 20th c.

beryl /'berɪl/ *n.* a transparent often pale-green precious stone; a mineral species including this and the emerald. [f. OF f. L f. Gk *bērullos*]

beryllium /bə'rɪlɪəm/ *n.* a very light hard greyish-white metallic element of the alkaline-earth metal series, symbol Be, atomic number 4. First isolated in 1828, its chief use is in alloys, especially where lightness and a high melting-point are important, as in aircraft or space vehicles. The main commercial ore is beryl. [f. prec.]

Berzelius /bɜː'ziːlɪəs/, Jöns Jakob (1779-1848), Swedish chemist, who was created a baron on his wedding-day in 1835. Regarded by his contemporaries as a remarkably gifted analytical chemist he studied about 2,000 compounds, and by 1818 had determined the atomic weights of most of the then known elements, using oxygen as the standard. He discovered three new elements: cerium (1803), selenium (1817), and thorium (1829), suggested the basic principles of the modern notation of chemical formulae, and introduced the terms isomerism, polymer, protein, and catalysis.

Bes /bes/ (*Egyptian myth.*) a grotesque god depicted as having short legs, an obese body, and an almost bestial face, whose comic but frightening aspect had the effect of dispelling evil spirits.

beseech /bɪ'siːtʃ/ *v.t.* (*past & p.p.* **besought** /-'sɔːt/) to implore, to ask earnestly for. [f. BE- + SEEK]

beset /bɪ'set/ *v.t.* (**-tt-;** *past & p.p.* **beset**) to surround, to hem in; (of troubles etc.) to assail persistently. [f. BE- + SET]

beside /bɪ'saɪd/ *prep.* **1.** by the side of; near. **2.** compared with. —**beside oneself,** frantic with worry, anger, etc. **beside the point,** irrelevant. [f. BE- + SIDE]

besides /bɪ'saɪdz/ *adv. & prep.* in addition (to). [f. prec.]

besiege /bɪ'siːdʒ/ *v.t.* **1.** to lay seige to. **2.** to crowd round oppressively, to harass with requests etc. [f. BE- + SIEGE]

besom /'biːz(ə)m/ *n.* a broom made of twigs tied round a stick. [OE]

besot /bɪ'sɒt/ *v.t.* (**-tt-;** esp. in *pass.*) to infatuate. [f. BE- + SOT]

bespeak /bɪ'spiːk/ *v.t.* (*past* **bespoke**; *p.p.* **bespoken,** as *adj.* **bespoke**) **1.** to engage beforehand; to commission (a product). **2.** to be an indication of. [f. BE- + SPEAK]

bespectacled /bɪ'spektək(ə)ld/ *adj.* wearing spectacles. [f. BE- + SPECTACLE]

bespoke /bɪ'spəʊk/ *adj.* (of clothes etc.) made to order; (of a tailor etc.) dealing in such goods. [f. BESPEAK]

Bessemer /'besɪmə(r)/, Sir Henry (1813-98), English engineer and inventor, of French Huguenot extraction, remembered for the steel-making process which bears his name (see foll.). The most important part of his career dates from the Crimean War, when the obvious imperfections in the artillery of the British army brought forward a large number of more or less able inventors. His proposals for the redesign of guns received little encouragement from the British War Office but a great deal from the Emperor Napoleon; experiments proved, however, that the material available for gun construction was inadequate for its purpose. Bessemer's efforts were then directed to the production of a stronger material, and led to a series of experiments and patents.

Bessemer process a process formerly much used for removing carbon, silicon, etc., from molten pig-iron by the passage of air, thus converting it into a material suitable for steel-making. The process was invented by Henry Bessemer, but followed earlier work by William Kelly in the USA. By 1860 Bessemer had evolved his convertor, a large steel vessel lined with a refractory material and pivoted in such a way that it could be tilted to three positions. When the axis was horizontal it could be loaded with steel scrap on to which molten iron was poured. With the axis vertical a blast of air was blown through the mixture; the oxygen in the air combined with the carbon and some other elements to provide the heat needed to melt the steel scrap and reduce the amount of carbon and other impurities to a low level. After removal of molten slag from the surface and the addition of a small quantity of manganese the convertor was tilted far enough to allow the finished steel to be poured out. It was the first successful method of making steel in quantity at low cost, so enabling it to be used on a large scale, but has been replaced by more modern techniques (see STEEL).

best *adj.* (*superl.* of GOOD) of the most excellent or desirable kind. —*adv.* (*superl.* of WELL) in the best manner; to the greatest degree; most usefully. —*n.* that which is best; the chief merit; (*colloq.*) one's best clothes. —*v.t.* (*colloq.*) to defeat or outwit. —**at best**, on the most hopeful or favourable view. **best end**, the rib end of neck of lamb, meatier than the scrag end. **best man**, a bridegroom's chief attendant. **best part**, most *of*. **best-seller** *n.* a book that sells in very large numbers. **do one's best**, do all one can. **get or have the best of**, to win (a fight etc.). **make the best of**, to be as contented as possible with; to do what one can with (something of limited potential). [OE, for *betest* (cf. BETTER)]

bestial /'bestɪəl/ *adj.* of a beast; beast-like in cruelty, blind lust, etc. —**bestiality** /-'ælɪtɪ/ *n.* [f. OF f. L (*bestia* beast)]

bestiary /'bestɪərɪ/ *n.* a medieval treatise on beasts. [f. L (as prec.)]

bestir /bɪ'stɜ:(r)/ *v.t.* (**-rr-**) to rouse or exert (*oneself*). [f. BE- + STIR]

bestow /bɪ'stəʊ/ *v.t.* to confer. —**bestowal** *n.* [f. BE- + STOW]

bestrew /bɪ'stru:/ *v.t.* (*p.p.* **bestrewed, bestrewn**) to strew; to lie scattered over. [f. BE- + STREW]

bestride /bɪ'straɪd/ *v.t.* (*past* **bestrode**; *p.p.* **bestridden**) 1. to sit astride on. 2. to stand astride over. [f. BE- + STRIDE]

bet *v.i./t.* (**-tt-**; *past & p.p.* **bet, betted**) 1. to risk one's money against another's on the outcome of an event; to risk (an amount) thus. 2. (*colloq.*) to think most likely. —*n.* 1. an act of betting. 2. a sum staked. —**you bet**, (*slang*) you may be sure. [perh. = ABET]

beta /'bi:tə/ *n.* 1. the second letter of the Greek alphabet, = b. 2. a second-class mark in an examination. 3. a designation of the second brightest star in a constellation, or sometimes a star's position in a group. —**beta-blocker** *n.* a drug that prevents the stimulation of receptors (**beta receptors**) in the central nervous system that cause increased cardiac activity. **beta particles** *or* **rays**, fast-moving electrons emitted by radioactive substances, formerly regarded as rays. [f. Gk]

betake /bɪ'teɪk/ *v.refl.* (*past* **betook**; *p.p.* **betaken**) to go *to*. [f. BE- + TAKE]

betatron /'bi:tətrɒn/ *n.* an apparatus for accelerating electrons in a circular path. [f. BETA + (ELEC)TRON]

betel /'bi:t(ə)l/ *n.* the leaf of the plant *Piper betle*, chewed in the east with betel-nut. —**betel-nut** *n.* the areca nut. [f. Port. f. Malayalam]

Betelgeuse /'bi:t(ə)lʒɜ:z/ a first-magnitude variable star in the constellation of Orion. Its Arabic name apparently means 'armpit of the Great One'. Variations in brightness by a factor of two can occur over periods of a few years, and are associated with pulsations in the outer envelope of this red giant.

bête noire /beɪt 'nwɑ:(r)/ (*pl.* **bêtes noires** *pr.* same) a person's chief dislike. [F, lit. = black beast]

bethink /bɪ'θɪŋk/ *v.refl.* (*past & p.p.* **bethought**) to stop to think, to recollect. [f. BE- + THINK]

Bethlehem /'beθlɪhem/ a small town 8 km (5 miles) south of Jerusalem, first mentioned in Egyptian records of the 14th c. BC. The native city of King David and reputed birthplace of Jesus Christ, it contains a church built by Constantine in 330 over the supposed site of Christ's birth. St Jerome lived and worked in Bethlehem from 384, and it became a monastic centre.

betide /bɪ'taɪd/ *v.t./i.* to happen (to), now chiefly in **woe betide** (a person), orig. a curse, now a warning. [f. BE- + obs. *tide* befall]

betimes /bɪ'taɪmz/ *adv.* (*literary*) in good time, early. [f. BE- + TIME]

Betjeman /'betʃəmən/, Sir John (1906-84), English poet, whose first collection (*Mount Zion*) was published in 1931. Others followed, including *New Bats in Old Belfries* (1945), *Collected Poems* (1958), and his blank-verse autobiography *Summoned by Bells* (1960), a nostalgic description of his boyhood and his life at Oxford University. His poems are witty and gently satiric, a comedy of manners, place-names, and contemporary allusions, capturing the spirit of his age and making him the most popular poet since Kipling. His 'topographical predilection' is displayed in many of his works, including those on architecture, such as *Ghastly Good Taste* (1933), and he fostered interest in Victorian and Edwardian buildings, campaigning enthusiastically for their preservation. He was appointed Poet Laureate in 1972.

betoken /bɪ'təʊkən/ *v.t.* to be a sign of, to indicate. [f. BE- + TOKEN]

betony /'betənɪ/ *n.* a purple-flowered plant *Betonica officinalis*, formerly used in medicine. [f. OF f. L, perh. f. name of Iberian tribe]

betray /bɪ'treɪ/ *v.t.* 1. to be disloyal to; to give up or reveal disloyally (to an enemy). 2. to reveal involuntarily; to be evidence of. 3. to lead astray. —**betrayal** *n.*, **betrayer** *n.* [f. BE- + obs. *tray* f. F f. L *tradere* hand over]

betroth /bɪ'trəʊð/ *v.t.* to engage to marry a specified person. —**betrothal** *n.*, **betrothed** *adj. & n.* [f. BE- + TRUTH]

better *adj.* (*compar.* of GOOD) 1. of a more excellent or desirable kind. 2. partly or fully recovered from illness. 3. greater (*part* etc.). —*adv.* (*compar.* of WELL[1]) in a better manner; to a greater degree; more usefully. —*n.* that which is better; (in *pl.*) one's superiors. —*v.t.* to improve; to surpass (a feat). —*v.refl.* to improve one's position in life. —**better half**, (*colloq.*) one's spouse. **get the better of**, to defeat or outwit. **had better**, would find it more advantageous to. [OE]

betterment *n.* improvement. [f. prec.]

betting-shop *n.* a bookmaker's shop or office.

between /bɪ'twi:n/ *adv. & prep.* 1. in the space, time, condition, etc., bounded by (two limits). 2. to and from; reciprocally felt or done by. 3. by the sharing or joint action of. 4. taking one and rejecting the other of. —**between ourselves, between you and me**, speaking in confidence. **in between**, in an intermediate position. [OE (ult. rel. to TWO)]

betwixt /bɪ'twɪkst/ *prep. & adv.* between, now only in **betwixt and between**, (*colloq.*) neither one thing nor the other. [f. OE (as prec.)]

Bevan /'bev(ə)n/, Aneurin (1897-1960), British Labour politician. In a Parliamentary career stretching from 1929 to 1960, Bevan's most notable contribution was the creation of the National Health Service during his time as Minister of Health 1945-51. The leader of the left wing of the Labour Party, he was defeated by Hugh Gaitskell in the contest for the party leadership in 1955.

bevel /'bev(ə)l/ *n.* 1. a joiner's or mason's tool for adjusting angles. 2. a slope from the horizontal or vertical; a sloping edge or surface. —*v.t./i.* (**-ll-**) to reduce (a square edge) to a sloping one; to slope at an angle. [f. OF (*baer* gape)]

beverage /'bevərɪdʒ/ *n.* any drink. [f. OF f. L *bibere* drink]

Beveridge /'bevərɪdʒ/, William Henry, 1st Baron (1879-1963), British economist. Long-time Director of the London School of Economics, Beveridge was the chairman of the wartime committee appointed to investigate social insurance problems. His report, completed in 1942, was the blueprint for post-war legislation leading to the drawing up of a national insurance scheme.

bevy /'bevɪ/ *n.* a large group (*of*). [orig. unkn.]

bewail /bɪ'weɪl/ *v.t.* to wail over, to mourn for. [f. BE- + WAIL]

beware /bɪ'weə(r)/ *v.i.* (only *imper. & infin.*) to be on one's guard. —**beware of**, to be cautious of, to guard against. [f. BE + obs. *ware* cautious]

Bewick /'bju:ɪk/, Thomas (1755-1828), English animal artist and wood engraver whose best works are the shrewdly observed and expressive animal studies which illustrate such books as *The History of British Birds* (1797, 1804).

bewilder /bɪ'wɪldə(r)/ *v.t.* to perplex or confuse. —**bewilderment** *n.* [f. BE- + obs. *wilder* to lose one's way]

bewitch /bɪ'wɪtʃ/ *v.t.* 1. to captivate, to delight greatly. 2. to cast a spell on. [f. BE- + WITCH]

beyond /bɪ'jɒnd/ *adv. & prep.* 1. at or to the far side (of). 2. outside the scope or understanding of. 3. in addition (to). —*n.* the unknown after death. [OE (*be* by, rel. to YON]

bezel /'bez(ə)l/ *n.* 1. the sloping edge of a chisel; an oblique face of a cut gem. 2. a rim holding a glass cover etc. or a gem in position. [f. OF; orig. unkn.]

bezique /bɪ'zi:k/ *n.* a card-game for two players, using a double pack of 64 cards (ace to seven only); a combination of the queen of spades and jack of diamonds in this game. [F, perh. f. Pers. = juggler]

Bhagavadgita /bɑ:gəvɑ:d'gi:tə/ *n.* the 'Song of the Lord' (i.e. Krishna), the most famous religious text of Hinduism, an independent work incorporated into the Mahabharata. Composed between the 2nd c. BC and 2nd c. AD, it is the earliest exposition of devotional religion (*bhakti*). Presented as a dialogue between the Kshatriya prince Arjuna and his divine charioteer Krishna, the poem stresses the importance of doing one's duty and of faith in God. [Skr.]

bhakti /ˈbɑːktɪ/ n. (*Hinduism*) devotional worship directed to one supreme deity, usually Vishnu (especially in his incarnations as Rama and Krishna) or Siva, by whose grace salvation may be attained by all regardless of sex, caste, or class. This is the religion of the majority of Hindus today. [Skr.]

bhang /baeŋ/ n. Indian hemp; its dried leaves smoked or chewed as a narcotic and intoxicant. [f. Port. f. Skr.]

Bhutan /buːˈtɑːn/ a small independent kingdom, a protectorate of the Republic of India, lying on the south-east of the Himalayas; pop. (est. 1981) 1,174,000; official language, Dzongkha; capital, Thimphu. —**Bhutanese** /-təˈniːz/ adj. & n.

Bi symbol bismuth.

bi- /baɪ-/ prefix two, twice (*bilateral, bi-weekly*). [L]

biannual /baɪˈænjʊəl/ adj. twice-yearly.

bias /ˈbaɪəs/ n. **1.** a predisposition or prejudice. **2.** distortion of a statistical result by a neglected factor. **3.** (in bowls) the oblique course of a bowl or the lopsided form causing it. **4.** an oblique direction in cutting cloth. —v.t. (p.t. & p.p. **biased**) to give a bias to, to influence unfairly. —**bias binding**, a strip of material cut diagonally, used to bind edges. [f. OF, perh. ult. f. Gk *epikarsios* oblique]

bib n. **1.** a cloth etc. tied over a child's chest at meals to protect its clothes. **2.** the part of an apron or overall covering the chest. [perh. f. archaic *bib* drink (f. L *bibere*)]

Bible /ˈbaɪb(ə)l/ n. **1.** the Christian scriptures (Old and New Testament). See below. **2.** **bible**, a copy of these; the scriptures of another religion; an authoritative book. [f. OF f. L f. Gk *biblia* books, orig. dim of *bublos* papyrus]

The respect shown by Christ and the early Church to the scriptures of Judaism formed the basis of the Christian attitude to the Old Testament, the message therein being complemented by that of the New Testament, with the two together forming a single record of God's revelation. Although there was some allegorical interpretation, in the earlier phases of the modern scientific movement (16th and 17th c.) both Protestants and Catholics held to belief in the truth of the Bible's assertions on matters not only of history, doctrine, and ethics but also of cosmology and natural science, and it was not until the 19th c. that critical study began to interpret the Bible in its historical perspective and the circumstances and purpose of its compilation. Protestant reformers sought to make the Bible available to the laity in the vernacular (Luther's German translation of the New Testament appeared in 1522), and there are now translations of all or part of it in 1763 languages.

bibliography /bɪblɪˈɒɡrəfɪ/ n. **1.** a list of books by a given author or on a given topic. **2.** the study of the history of books and their production. —**bibliographer** n., **bibliographical** /-ˈɡraefɪk(ə)l/ adj. [f. Gk (as prec., *graphia* writing)]

bibliophile /ˈbɪblɪəfaɪl/ n. a lover of books. [f. F (as prec. + Gk *philos* friend)]

Bibliothèque nationale /bɪblɪətek næsjɒˈnɑːl/ the national library of France, in Paris. It had its origins in the libraries of medieval French kings who amassed their collections in the way that was then usual —by plunder and gifts. In the long reign of Louis XIV, when France was very prosperous, it grew to more than 70,000 volumes and part of the present building was erected. Its present name first came to be used during the French Revolution.

bibulous /ˈbɪbjʊləs/ adj. addicted to alcoholic drink. [f. L *bibere* drink)]

bicameral /baɪˈkæmər(ə)l/ adj. having two legislative chambers. [f. BI- + L *camera* chamber]

bicarbonate /baɪˈkɑːbəneɪt/ n. a carbonate containing a double proportion of carbon dioxide, especially sodium bicarbonate.

bicentenary /baɪsenˈtiːnərɪ/ n. a two-hundredth anniversary.

bicentennial /baɪsenˈtenɪəl/ adj. occurring every two hundred years. —n. a bicentenary.

biceps /ˈbaɪseps/ n. a muscle with two heads or attachments, especially that which bends the elbow. [L, = two-headed]

bicker v.i. to quarrel pettily. [orig. unkn.]

biconcave /baɪˈkɒnkeɪv/ adj. (of a lens) concave on both sides.

biconvex /baɪˈkɒnveks/ adj. (of a lens) convex on both sides.

bicuspid /baɪˈkʌspɪd/ adj. having two cusps. —n. any of the eight bicuspid teeth (between the molars and canines). [f. BI- + L *cuspis* sharp point]

bicycle /ˈbaɪsɪk(ə)l/ n. a road vehicle with two wheels one behind the other, driven by pedals worked by the rider (see below). —v.i. to ride on a bicycle. —**bicycle clip,** each of a pair of clips for securing a cyclist's trouser-leg at the ankle. —**bicyclist** n. [f. F (BI-, Gk *kuklos* wheel)]

A two-wheeled conveyance (called a velocipede) was patented by Karl von Drais in Germany in 1817: a rider sat on a bar between the wheels and propelled himself by pushing the ground with each foot alternately. It was introduced into France and into England, where it was called a 'pedestrian curricle' (or 'hobby-horse' or 'dandy-horse'), and achieved a certain popularity. A lever-drive arrangement worked by treadles was fitted to the back wheel c.1840, and in 1861 in France Pierre Michaux and his son added cranks and pedals to the front wheel; this machine became copied elsewhere. The early bicycle was a cumbersome and uncomfortable machine, with a heavy frame and iron tyres, putting considerable strain on the rider's limbs and hence known as the 'bone-shaker'. Springs and wire-spoke wheels were introduced in the 1860s, also solid rubber tyres (c.1867), and the front wheel was made much larger so that the distance covered for each push of the pedals was longer. This machine became known as the 'ordinary' bicycle (and later by the derisory name 'penny-farthing') after the introduction in the late 1870s of 'safety' bicycles with two medium-sized wheels and with the rider's seat set further back, reducing the chances of pitching head-first over the handlebars from a high position. The successful Rover safety bicycle of 1884/5, with smaller wheels and with a toothed gear-wheel connected by an endless chain with the hub of the rear wheel, was essentially the modern machine. The diamond-shaped frame was common by the 1890s, and the next really new development did not take place until 1962 when the cross-frame was introduced, with one large tube as the main horizontal member from which two parallel tubes project (one for the seat and one for the handlebars), and with small wheels. Many key modern technologies were developed for the bicycle, including wire-spoked wheels, ball-bearings, and pneumatic tyres. The machine had a great social effect and remains of major importance in both rich and poor countries.

bid v.t./i. (**-dd-**; past & p.p. **bid**) **1.** to offer (a certain sum) as the price one is willing to pay, especially at an auction; to make a bid or bids; (in card-games) to state (the number of tricks) one undertakes to win in a given suit. **2.** (past **bade**, p.p.**bidden** or **bid**) to instruct or invite to; to utter (a greeting, farewell). —n. **1.** an act of bidding; a sum etc. bid. **2.** an attempt. —**bid fair to,** to seem likely to. **make a bid for,** to attempt to secure. [OE]

biddable /ˈbɪdəb(ə)l/ adj. docile, obedient. [f. BID]

bidding n. **1.** a person's command or invitation. **2.** the bids made at an auction or in a card-game. [f. BID]

biddy n. **old biddy,** (*slang*) an elderly woman. [pet-form of woman's Christian name *Bridget*]

bide v.t./i. (*archaic* or *dial.*) to remain. —**bide one's time,** to await one's best opportunity. [OE]

bidet /ˈbiːdeɪ/ n. a low basin for sitting astride to wash the genital and anal regions. [F, = pony]

biennial /baɪˈenɪəl/ adj. **1.** lasting or living for two years. **2.** happening every second year. —n. a plant that springs one year and flowers, fruits, and dies the next. [f. L (BI-, *annus* year)]

bier /bɪə(r)/ n. a movable stand on which a coffin or corpse rests. [OE (rel. to BEAR²)]

biff n. (*slang*) a smart blow. —v.t. to strike (a person). [imit.]

bifid /ˈbaɪfɪd/ adj. divided by a deep cleft into two parts. [f. L (BI-, *findere* split)]

bifocal /baɪˈfəʊk(ə)l/ adj. having two foci (of spectacle lenses having part for near and part for distant vision). —**bifocals** n.pl. spectacles with such lenses (see SPECTACLE).

bifurcate /ˈbaɪfəkeɪt/ v.t./i. to divide into two branches. —**bifurcation** /-ˈkeɪʃ(ə)n/ n. [f. L *bifurcare* (BI-, *furca* fork)]

big adj. (**-gg-**) **1.** large in size, amount, or intensity; outstandingly large of its kind; grown up, elder. **2.** important, outstanding. **3.** boastful; (*colloq.*) ambitious, generous. **4.** advanced in pregnancy (especially of animals). —adv. (*colloq.*) on a grand scale, ambitiously. —**Big Brother,** a seemingly benevolent but in fact ruthless dictator. [character in George Orwell's novel *1984*] **big end,** the end of a connecting-rod in an engine, encircling the crankshaft.

big-head *n.* (*colloq.*) a conceited person. **big-hearted** *adj.* generous. **big time,** (*slang*) the highest rank among entertainers etc. **big top,** the main tent at a circus. [orig. unkn.]

bigamy /ˈbɪgəmɪ/ *n.* the crime of making a second marriage while a first is still valid. —**bigamist** *n.*, **bigamous** *adj.* [f. OF f. L (BI-, Gk *gamos* marriage)]

big bang according to current cosmological theories, the event which marks the origin of our universe. In the beginning, a fireball of radiation at unbelievably high temperatures but occupying a tiny volume is believed to have formed. The density at this time was also extremely high, and the fireball expanded and cooled, infinitely fast at first, but more slowly as elementary particles condensed out from the radiation to form the matter which later accumulated into galaxies and stars. Currently, the galaxies are still retreating from one another in the wake of this initial explosion, and it is not known whether they contain sufficient mass to halt the expansion through their mutual gravitational attraction. What was left of the original radiation continued to cool, and may now be observed with microwave detectors at a temperature of three degrees above absolute zero.

Big Ben a bell that strikes the hours in the clock-tower of the Houses of Parliament in London. It weighs about 13½ tons, and was named either after Sir Benjamin Hall, First Commissioner of Works (1855-8) when the bell was ordered, or after a famous prize-fighter of the time.

big crunch the compression of the entire universe to a point of infinite density and temperature that will ensue if the now receding galaxies possess enough mass for their gravitational influence to halt and reverse the expansion of the universe. Conditions at this instant will resemble those of the big bang, suggesting that a re-expansion of the universe in further cycles of creation may occur.

bighorn *n.* either of two North American sheep (*Ovis canadensis* and *O. dalli*) with transversely ribbed horns that in the male may curve in a huge spiral.

bight /baɪt/ *n.* **1.** a loop of rope. **2.** a wide shallow bay on a coast. [OE]

bigot /ˈbɪgət/ *n.* an obstinate and intolerant adherent of a creed or view. —**bigoted** *adj.*, **bigotry** *n.* [F]

bigwig *n.* (*colloq.*) an important person.

Bihar /bɪˈhɑː(r)/ a State in NE India; capital, Patna.

Bihari /bɪˈhɑːrɪ/ *n.* **1.** a native or inhabitant of Bihar. **2.** a group of three closely related languages, descended from Sanskrit, spoken principally in Bihar. The three languages are Bhojpuri with 20 million speakers in western Bihar and eastern Uttar Pradesh, Maithili with 15 million speakers in northern Bihar and Nepal, and Magahi with 5 million speakers in central Bihar. [f. prec.]

bijou /ˈbiːʒuː/ *adj.* small and elegant. [F, = jewel]

bike *n.* (*colloq.*) a bicycle or motor cycle. —*v.i.* (*colloq.*) to ride on this. [abbr.]

bikini /bɪˈkiːnɪ/ *n.* a woman's scanty two-piece beach garment. [f. *Bikini*, an atoll in the West Pacific where an atomic bomb was tested in 1946]

bilateral /baɪˈlætər(ə)l/ *adj.* of, on, or having two sides; involving two parties. —**bilateralism** *n.*, **bilaterally** *adv.* [f. L (BI-, *latus* side)]

bilberry /ˈbɪlbərɪ/ *n.* a small shrub (*Vaccinium myrtillus*) growing on heaths, moors, etc.; its purple-black berry. [Scand.]

bile *n.* **1.** a bitter yellowish fluid produced by the liver and stored in the gall-bladder, aiding digestion of fats. **2.** (*archaic*) one of the four humours (see HUMOUR). —**bile duct,** a duct conveying bile to the duodenum (ill. BODY 2). [f. F f. L *bilis*]

bilge /bɪldʒ/ *n.* **1.** the nearly flat part of a ship's bottom (ill. SAILING-SHIPS). **2.** (also **bilge-water**) the foul water that collects there. **3.** (*slang*) worthless ideas or talk. [prob. var. of BULGE]

bilharzia /bɪlˈhɑːtsɪə/ *n.* a tropical disease caused by a flatworm parasitic in the pelvis. [f. T. *Bilharz*, German physician (d. 1862)]

bilingual /baɪˈlɪŋgw(ə)l/ *adj.* speaking or written in two languages. [f. L (BI-, *lingua* language)]

bilious /ˈbɪljəs/ *adj.* **1.** affected by sickness assumed to be caused by a disorder of the bile. **2.** of a sickly yellowish hue. —**biliousness** *n.* [f. BILE]

bilk *v.t.* to cheat (*of* what is due); to avoid paying (a creditor etc.). [orig. unkn.]

bill¹ *n.* **1.** a statement of charges for goods or services

supplied. **2.** the draft of a proposed law. **3.** a poster or placard; a programme of entertainment. **4.** (*US*) a banknote. —*v.t.* **1.** to announce on a poster or in a programme. **2.** to advertise *as.* **3.** to send a note of charges to. —**bill of exchange,** a written order to pay a sum on a given date to the drawer or a named person. **bill of fare,** a menu. **bill of lading,** an inventory of goods to be shipped, signed by the carrier. [f. AF f. L *bulla* seal]

bill² *n.* **1.** a bird's beak, especially when slender or flattened. **2.** a narrow promontory. —*v.i.* (of doves) to stroke each other's bills. —**bill and coo,** to exchange caresses. [OE]

bill³ *n.* (*hist.*) a weapon with a hooked blade. [OE]

billabong /ˈbɪləbɒŋ/ *n.* (*Austral.*) a river branch forming a backwater or stagnant pool. [f. Aboriginal *Bilibang* Bell River (*billa* water)]

billboard *n.* a hoarding for advertisements. [f. BILL¹ + BOARD]

billet¹ /ˈbɪlɪt/ *n.* **1.** an order to a householder to lodge and board soldiers etc.; a place so provided. **2.** (*colloq.*) a job. —*v.t.* to place (soldiers etc.) in a billet. [f. AF (dim. of *bille* BILL¹)]

billet² /ˈbɪlɪt/ *n.* **1.** a thick piece of firewood. **2.** a small bar of metal. **3.** (in heraldry) a bearing shaped like a rectangle placed on end (ill. HERALDRY). [f. F (dim. of *bille* tree-trunk)]

billet-doux /bɪlɪˈduː/ *n.* (*pl.* **billets-doux** -ˈduːz/) (*joc.*) a love-letter. [F, = sweet note]

billhook *n.* a tool with a hooked blade, used for pruning etc. [f. BILL³ + HOOK]

billiards /ˈbɪljədz/ *n.* a game played on an oblong cloth-covered table with three balls struck with cues. There are many forms of the game, and its origin and age are uncertain until the 16th-17th c., when it is well attested. The reference to billiards in Shakespeare's 'Antony and Cleopatra' is an anachronism. —**bar billiards,** a game in which balls are to be struck into holes on a table. [f. F *billard* cue, dim. of *bille* tree-trunk]

billingsgate /ˈbɪlɪŋzgeɪt/ *n.* coarse abuse. [f. *Billingsgate*, a London fish-market dating from the 16th c., known for the invective traditionally ascribed to the fish-porters]

billion /ˈbɪljən/ *adj.* & *n.* (*pl.* **billion** except as below) **1.** a million million. **2.** (*US* and increasingly *British*) a thousand million. **3.** **billions** (*pl.*, *colloq.*) great numbers *of.* —**billionth** *adj.* [f. F (BI-, MILLION)]

Bill of Rights 1. a bill passed in October 1689 confirming the deposition of James II and the accession of William and Mary, guaranteeing the Protestant succession, and laying down principles of parliamentary supremacy. **2.** the first 10 amendments to the Constitution of the USA, proposed by Congress in 1789 and ratified in 1791, spelling out individual rights that are regarded as inalienable. The First Amendment gives citizens freedom of religion, assembly, speech, and the press, and the right of petition. The next seven secure the rights of property and guarantee the rights of persons accused of crime. The Ninth protects rights held concurrently by the people and the federal government, and the Tenth assures the reserved rights of the States.

billow /ˈbɪləʊ/ *n.* a large wave. —*v.i.* to rise or roll like waves. —**billowy** *adj.* [f. ON]

billy *n.* a billycan. [abbr.]

billycan /ˈbɪlɪkæn/ *n.* a tin or enamelled container with a lid and handle, used as a cooking-vessel, especially in Australia. [perh. f. Aboriginal *billa* water]

billy-goat /ˈbɪlɪgəʊt/ *n.* a male goat. [f. *Billy* pet-form of *William* + GOAT]

bimetallic /baɪmɪˈtælɪk/ *adj.* using or made of two metals.

bin *n.* a large rigid container, usually with a lid, for storing coal, grain, flour, etc.; a dustbin. [OE]

binary /ˈbaɪnərɪ/ *adj.* involving a pair or pairs. —*n.* a binary star. —**binary compound,** one containing two chemical elements or radicals. **binary digit,** either of the two digits used in the binary scale. **binary scale,** a numerical system using only the two digits 0 and 1. **binary star,** a gravitationally-bound pair of stars revolving round a common centre. By no means uncommon, such pairs may be widely separated, or they may interact tidally if close together, one stripping material from the other. Close binary pairs may eclipse one another if their orbital plane lies in the line of sight. [f. L *bini* two together]

binaural /baɪnˈɔːr(ə)l, bɪ-/ *adj.* of or used with both ears; (of sound) recorded by two microphones and usually transmitted separately to the two ears. [f. BI- + AURAL]

bind /baɪnd/ *v.t./i.* (*past* & *p.p.* **bound**) **1.** to tie or fasten

Birds

Main parts of a bird

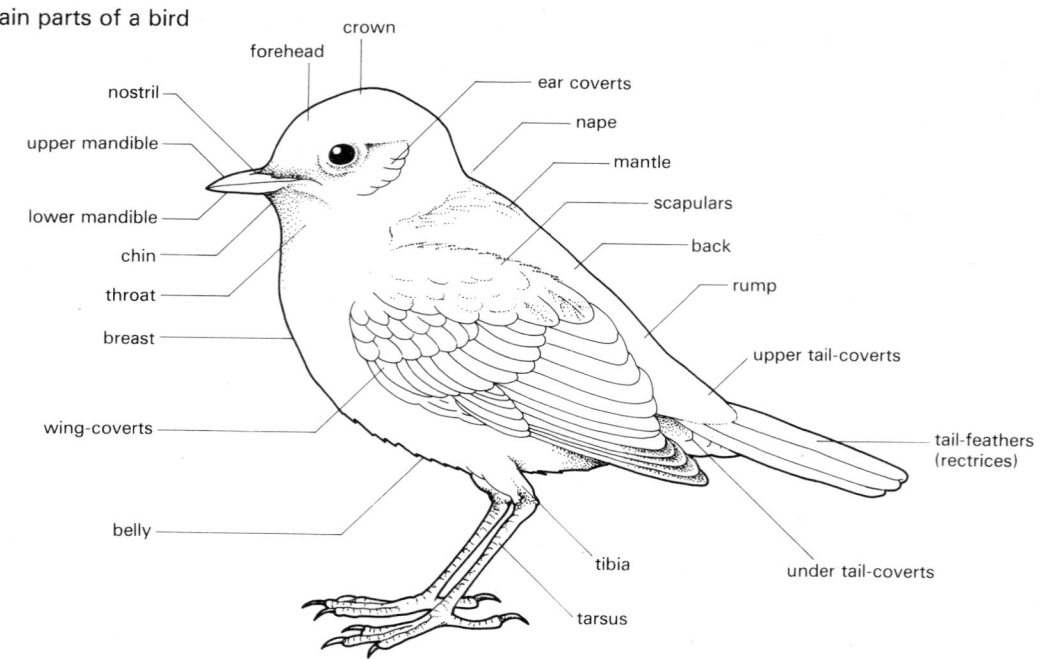

forehead

crown

nostril

ear coverts

upper mandible

nape

lower mandible

mantle

chin

scapulars

throat

back

breast

rump

wing-coverts

upper tail-coverts

belly

tail-feathers
(rectrices)

tibia

under tail-coverts

tarsus

Wing

wrist

alula

primary coverts

secondary coverts

primaries

secondaries

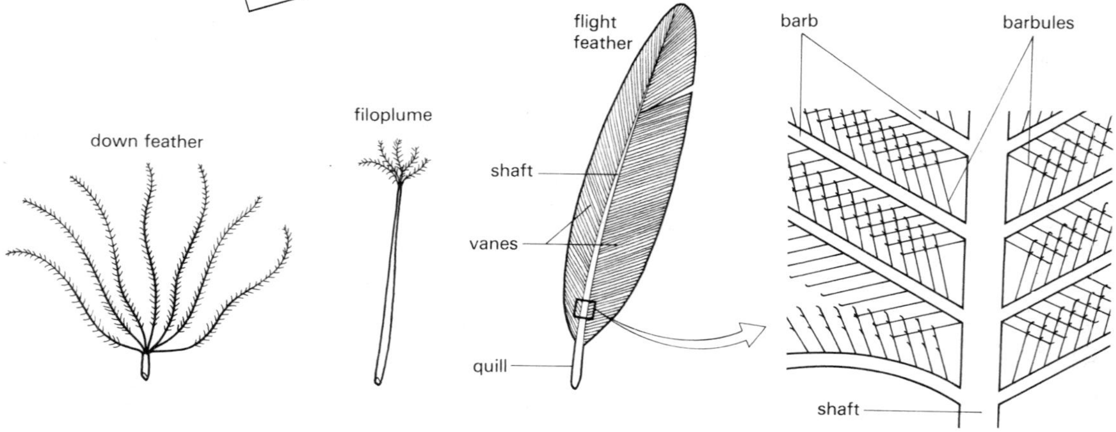

down feather

filoplume

flight
feather

barb

barbules

shaft

vanes

quill

shaft

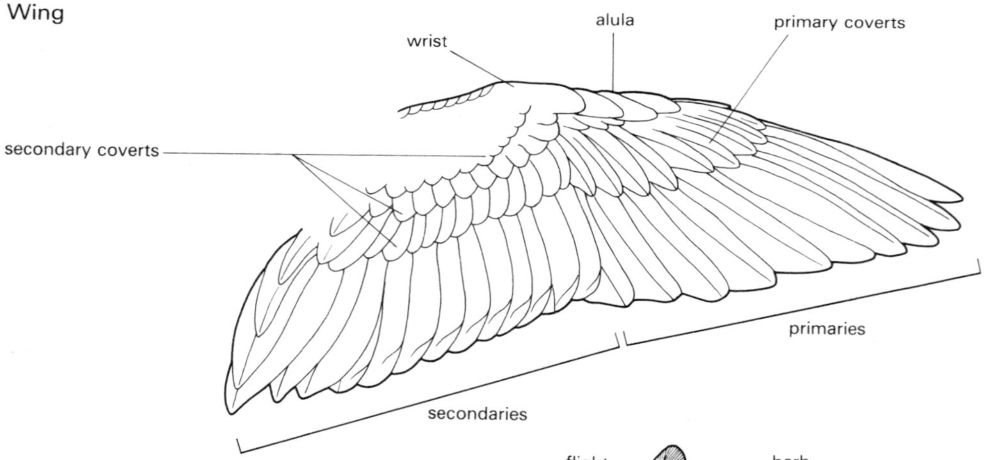

Beaks, feet, and flight

strong talons for
gripping prey

flesh-eater

seed-eater

insect-eater

gliding

soaring

hovering

(birds not to scale)

surface
feeder

webbed feet
for swimming

fish-eater

feet adapted to
gripping a slender
support

together; to encircle *with*; to bandage (*up*). **2.** to secure or restrain by fastening; to fasten sheets of (a book) into a cover; to cover the edge of (a thing) with strengthening or decorative material. **3.** to be obligatory; to compel, to impose a duty on. **4.** to stick together. **5.** to constipate. **6.** (*slang*) to grumble. —*n.* (*slang*) a nuisance, a bore. —**bind over,** (*Law*) to put under an obligation (*to* keep the peace etc.). [OE]

binder /'baɪndə(r)/ *n.* **1.** a loose cover for papers. **2.** a bookbinder. **3.** a substance that binds things together. **4.** a machine that binds harvested corn into sheaves. [f. prec.]

bindery *n.* a bookbinder's workshop. [f. prec.]

binding /'baɪndɪŋ/ *n.* something that binds, especially the gluing etc. and covers of a book. —*adj.* obligatory (*on*). [f. BIND]

bindweed /'baɪndwiːd/ *n.* convolvulus.

bine *n.* the twisting stem of a climbing plant, especially the hop. [dial. form of BIND]

Binet /biːneɪ/, Alfred (1857–1911), French psychologist, father of intelligence testing as it is known today. He was requested by the French government to devise a test which would detect intellectually slow schoolchildren who might not benefit from the normal school curriculum at a time when school attendance became mandatory in France, and from 1905, together with another French psychologist, Theodore Simon, he produced tests thought to task general reasoning capacities rather than the perceptual-motor skills which had previously been used as an indicator of intellectual ability. Believing that bright and dull schoolchildren were simply advanced or retarded in their mental growth, Binet devised a 'mental-age' scale which described a student's performance in relation to the average performance of students of the same physical age.

binge /bɪndʒ/ *n.* (*slang*) a drinking-bout or spree. [prob. dial., = soak]

bingo¹ /'bɪŋɡəʊ/ *int.* an exclamation at a sudden action or event. [imit. of sudden sound; cf. dial. *bing*]

bingo² /'bɪŋɡəʊ/ *n.* a popular gambling game that is a variety of lotto, played with cards on which numbered squares have to be covered as the numbers are called at random. The player first covering all or a set of these wins a prize. [perh. f. winner's exclam. of *bingo* (see prec.)]

binnacle /'bɪnək(ə)l/ *n.* a case or stand for a ship's compass. [earlier *bittacle*, f. Sp. or Port. f. L *habitaculum* lodging]

binocular /bɪ'nɒkjʊlə(r), baɪ-/ *n.* (usu. in *pl.* and /bɪ-/) field- or opera-glasses etc. for use with both eyes. —/usu. baɪ-/ *adj.* for or using both eyes. [f. L *bini* two together, *oculus* eye]

binomial /baɪ'nəʊmɪəl/ *n.* an algebraic expression consisting of two terms linked by a plus or minus sign. —*adj.* consisting of two terms so linked. —**binomial theorem,** formula for finding any power of a binomial without multiplying at length. [f. F (BI-, Gk *nomos* part)]

binturong /'bɪntjʊərɒŋ/ *n.* a prehensile-tailed civet (*Arctitis binturong*) of South Asia. [Malay]

bio- /baɪəʊ-/ *prefix* of life or living things. [f. Gk *bios* life]

biochemistry /baɪəʊ'kemɪstrɪ/ *n.* the study of the chemistry of living organisms. —**biochemical** *adj.*, **biochemist** *n.*

biodegradable /baɪəʊdɪ'greɪdəb(ə)l/ *adj.* capable of being decomposed by bacteria.

bioengineering /baɪəʊendʒɪ'nɪərɪŋ/ *n.* the application of engineering techniques to biological processes.

biography /baɪ'ɒɡrəfɪ/ *n.* a written account of a person's life; the writing of biographies. —**biographer** *n.*, **biographical** /baɪə'ɡræfɪk(ə)l/ *adj.* [f. BIO- + -GRAPHY]

biological /baɪə'lɒdʒɪk(ə)l/ *adj.* of or relating to biology. — **biological warfare,** the use of organisms to spread disease among the enemy. —**biologically** *adv.* [f. foll.]

biology /baɪ'ɒlədʒɪ/ *n.* the science of living organisms, dealing with their morphology, physiology, anatomy, behaviour, origin, and distribution. The word was coined in the 19th c. as it began to be realized that all living things share fundamental similarities. —**biologist** *n.* [f. BIO- + -LOGY]

biometry /baɪ'ɒmɪtrɪ/ *n.* the analysis of biological phenomena by statistical methods. —**biometric** /baɪə'metrɪk/ *adj.* [f. BIO- + Gk *metron* measure]

bionic /baɪ'ɒnɪk/ *adj.* forming or possessing an electronically operated body part or parts. [f. BIO-, after *electronic*]

biophysics /baɪəʊ'fɪzɪks/ *n.* the science of the physical properties of living organisms and their constituents, and the investigation of biological phenomena in general by means of the techniques of modern physics. —**biophysical** *adj.*, **biophysicist** *n.*

biopsy /'baɪɒpsɪ/ *n.* an examination of tissue cut from the living body, as a means of diagnosis; surgical removal of such tissue. [f. BIO-, after *autopsy*]

biorhythm /'baɪəʊrɪð(ə)m/ *n.* any of the internal cycles said to govern a person's physiological, emotional, and intellectual activity.

biosphere /'baɪəsfɪə(r)/ *n.* the regions of the earth's crust and atmosphere occupied by living organisms.

biotic /baɪ'ɒtɪk/ *adj.* of life or living things. [f. F or L f. Gk (*bios* life)]

biotin /'baɪətɪn/ *n.* a vitamin in yeast and egg-yolks, controlling growth. [G, as prec.]

bipartisan /baɪpɑː'tɪzæn/ *adj.* involving or agreed to by two parties.

bipartite /baɪ'pɑːtaɪt/ *adj.* consisting of two parts; shared by two parties. [f. L (BI-, *partiri* divide)]

biped /'baɪped/ *n.* a two-footed animal. —*adj.* two-footed. [f. L (BI-, *pes* foot)]

bipinnate /baɪ'pɪnət/ *adj.* having leaflets and the petioles bearing them arranged pinnately (ill. PLANTS).

biplane /'baɪpleɪn/ *n.* an aeroplane with two sets of wings, one above the other (ill. FLIGHT).

bipolar /baɪ'pəʊlə(r)/ *adj.* having two poles or extremities.

birch /bɜːtʃ/ *n.* **1.** a tree of the genus *Betula* with smooth bark and slender branches. **2.** a rod of birch twigs, used for flogging delinquents. —*v.t.* to flog with a birch. [OE]

bird /bɜːd/ *n.* **1.** an egg-laying vertebrate animal of the class Aves, with feathers, two wings, and two feet (see below). **2.** (*slang*) a young woman; a person (especially a strange one). **3.** (*rhyming-slang*, f. *birdlime* = time) a prison sentence. —**bird of paradise,** a New Guinea bird with brilliant plumage. **bird of passage,** a migrant, a transient visitor. **bird-watcher** *n.* one who studies birds in their natural surroundings. [orig. unkn.]

The earliest known fossil bird, *Archaeopteryx*, comes from the Jurassic period, about 140 million years ago, and clearly shows the close relationship of birds to the dinosaur-like reptiles from which they are descended: it had feathers, and forelimbs modified as wings, but retained teeth, a long tail containing vertebrae, and other reptilian features. Modern birds, of which there are about 8,600 living species, are anatomically a comparatively uniform group, probably because of the structural demands that flight imposes. Their bones are often hollow for the sake of lightness. They are warm-blooded, and their feathers, besides making flight possible, function as an insulating layer to help conserve their body heat. Birds are primarily diurnal animals, with good colour vision, good hearing, and a poor sense of smell. They exhibit complex social and migratory behaviour, but are considered to behave more instinctively and with less ability to adapt than mammals. (See ill. pp. 82–3.)

birdie /'bɜːdɪ/ *n.* **1.** (*children's colloq.*) a bird. **2.** (in golf) a hole played in one stroke under par. [f. BIRD]

biretta /bɪ'retə/ *n.* a square cap worn by (esp. Roman Catholic) priests. [f. It. or Sp. dim. f. L *birrus* cape]

Biro /'baɪərəʊ/ *n.* [P] a kind of ball-point pen. [f. L. *Biró*, Hungarian inventor (d. 1985)]

birth *n.* **1.** the emergence of young from the mother's body. **2.** origin, parentage. —**birth certificate,** an official document giving the date and place etc. of a person's birth. **birth-control** *n.* prevention of undesired pregnancy. **birth-rate** *n.* the number of births in one year for every 1,000 people. **give birth to,** to produce (young); to cause. [f. ON (rel. to BEAR²)]

birthday *n.* the anniversary of the day of one's birth.

birthmark *n.* an unusual coloured mark on a person's skin at or from the time of birth.

birthplace *n.* the place of a person's birth.

birthright *n.* rights belonging to a person by birth, especially as the eldest son.

birthstone *n.* (in astrology) a gemstone associated with a particular month or sign of the zodiac and thought to bring good luck if worn by a person born then.

Biscay /'bɪskeɪ/, **Bay of** part of the North Atlantic between the north coast of Spain and the west coast of France, notorious for storms.

biscuit /'bɪskɪt/ *n.* **1.** a flat thin unleavened cake, usually dry and crisp. **2.** porcelain after firing but before glazing. **3.** a light-brown colour. [f. OF f. L *biscoctus* twice baked]

bisect /baɪˈsekt/ v.t. to divide into two (strictly, equal) parts. —**bisection** n., **bisector** n. [f. BI- + L secare cut]

bisexual /baɪˈseksjʊəl/ adj. 1. sexually attracted both to men and women. 2. having male and female sexual organs in one individual. —**bisexuality** /-ˈælɪtɪ/ n.

bishop /ˈbɪʃəp/ n. 1. a senior clergyman in charge of a diocese. 2. a mitre-shaped chess piece. —**Bishops' Bible**, the version of 1568, which remained the official English version until publication of the Authorized Version in 1611. [OE, ult. f. Gk. episkopos overseer]

bishopric /ˈbɪʃəprɪk/ n. the office or diocese of a bishop. [f. prec.]

Bismarck /ˈbɪzmɑːk/, Otto Eduard Leopold, Prince von (1815–98), German statesman. As minister-president and foreign minister of Prussia from 1862, Bismarck was the driving force behind the unification of Germany, orchestrating wars with Denmark (1864), Austria (1866), and France (1870–1) in order to achieve his end. As Chancellor of the new German empire from 1871 to 1890, he continued to dominate the political scene, attempting to crush opposition to the central government at home (see KULTURKAMPF) while consolidating Germany's position as a European power by creating a system of alliances. Although Bismarck was able to work very well with the ageing Wilhelm I, he quarrelled with Wilhelm II and was forced to resign in 1890.

bismuth /ˈbɪzməθ/ n. a brittle reddish-white metallic element, symbol Bi, atomic number 83; a compound of it used as a medicine. Bismuth occurs in the free state in nature but was not identified as a separate element until the 18th c. It is a relatively poor conductor of heat and electricity. Its main use is as a component of alloys required to have a low melting-point. [f. G wismut, orig. unkn.]

bison /ˈbaɪs(ə)n/ n. (pl. same) 1. the European wild ox Bison bonasus (no longer surviving in the wild state). 2. the North American buffalo Bison bison. [f. L f. Gmc]

bisque[1] /bɪsk/ n. an extra turn, stroke, etc., allowed to an inferior player in some games. [F]

bisque[2] /biːsk/ n. unglazed white porcelain. [f. BISCUIT]

bisque[3] /bɪsk/ n. rich soup made from shellfish. [F; orig. unkn.]

Bissau /bɪˈsaʊ/ the capital of Guinea-Bissau; pop. (1979) 109,500.

bistre /ˈbɪstə(r)/ n. a brown pigment prepared from soot; the colour of this. [F; orig. unkn.]

bistro /ˈbiːstrəʊ/ n. (pl. -os) a continental wine-bar or small restaurant. [F]

bit[1] n. a small piece or quantity; a short distance or time; a small coin. —**a bit**, (colloq.) somewhat. **bit by bit**, gradually. **bit part**, a small part in a play or film. [OE (rel. to BITE)]

bit[2] n. 1. the mouthpiece of a bridle (ill. HORSE). 2. the part of a tool that cuts, grips, etc.; the boring-piece of a drill (ill. CARPENTRY). [OE (rel. to BITE)]

bit[3] n. (in computers) a unit of information expressed as a choice between two possibilities. [f. b(inary dig)it)]

bitch n. 1. a female dog; a female fox, otter, etc. 2. (derog.) a spiteful or unpleasant woman. —v.i. to speak spitefully; (colloq.) to grumble. [OE]

bitchy /ˈbɪtʃɪ/ adj. spiteful, catty. —**bitchiness** n. [f. prec.]

bite v.t./i. (past bit; p.p. bitten) 1. to cut into or wound with the teeth; to take (a piece) off with the teeth. 2. (of an insect) to sting; (of a snake) to pierce with its fangs. 3. to snap at; (of a fish) to accept bait. 4. to cause smarting pain. 5. (of a wheel, screw, etc.) to grip the surface. —n. 1. an act of biting; a wound made by biting etc. 2. a mouthful of food; a snack. 3. the taking of bait by a fish. 4. incisiveness, pungency. [OE]

Bithynia /bɪˈθɪnɪə/ the ancient name for the region of NW Asia Minor west of Paphlagonia and bordering the Black Sea and the Sea of Marmara.

bitter adj. 1. having a sharp astringent taste, not sweet; (of beer) strongly flavoured with hops. 2. piercingly cold. 3. painful to the mind. 4. showing grief or resentment; virulent, resentful. —n. bitter beer; (in pl.) liquors impregnated with bitter herbs. —**bitter-sweet** adj. sweet but with a bitter element. **to the bitter end**, to the last extremity however painful. —**bitterly** adv., **bitterness** n. [OE (prob. rel. to BITE)]

bittern /ˈbɪtɜːn/ n. a marsh bird of the genus Botaurus, allied to herons, especially one known for the male's booming note in the breeding-season. [f. OF f. L butio bittern, taurus bull]

bitty adj. made up of bits, scrappy. [f. BIT[1]]

bitumen /ˈbɪtjʊmɪn/ n. a mixture of tarlike hydrocarbons derived from petroleum. —**bituminous** /-ˈtjuːmɪnəs/ adj. [L]

bivalve /ˈbaɪvælv/ adj. (of shellfish) having two shells united by a hinge. —n. a bivalve shellfish, e.g. the oyster.

bivouac /ˈbɪvʊæk/ n. an encampment without tents, as of troops in the field. —v.i. (-ck-) to camp thus. [f. F, prob. f. G beiwacht additional guard; orig. of the citizens' patrol at Aargau and Zurich, assisting the night-watch at times of special need]

bizarre /bɪˈzɑː(r)/ adj. strikingly odd in appearance or effect. [F, orig. = brave, soldierly]

Bizet /ˈbiːzeɪ/, Alexandre Césare Léopold, known as Georges (1838–75), French composer. His first major work was the symphony in C major (1855). Among his best-known works are the suites from his incidental music to Daudet's play L'Arlésienne (1872), and above all the opera Carmen which after a lukewarm reception in 1875 has become one of the best-loved works in the repertory.

Bk symbol berkelium.

blab v.t./i. (-bb-) to talk indiscreetly, to let out (secrets) by indiscreet talk. [prob. imit.]

Black, Joseph (1728–99), Scottish chemist, renowned for his study of the chemistry of gases and for formulating the concepts of latent heat and thermal capacity. He developed accurate techniques for following chemical reactions by weighing reactants and products. In studying the chemistry of alkalis he isolated a gas which he termed 'fixed air' (now known to be carbon dioxide), and investigated its chemistry, including its characteristic reaction with lime water.

black adj. 1. colourless from the absence or absorption of light, of the colour of coal or soot. 2. dark-skinned; **Black**, of or for Negroes; of their culture etc. 3. (of the sky) dusky, overcast. 4. sinister, wicked; dismal, sullen, frowning; portending trouble or difficulty; (of humour) morbid, cynical. 5. (of goods etc.) banned by workers on strike from being handled by other trade-unionists. —n. 1. black colour or pigment; black (especially mourning) clothes or material. 2. a black ball or piece in a game. 3. the credit side of an account; in the black, solvent. 4. **Black**, a Negro. —v.t. 1. to make black. 2. to polish with blacking. 3. to declare (goods) to be 'black'. —**black and blue**, discoloured by bruises. **Black and Tans**, an armed force recruited to fight Sinn Fein in 1921, who wore a mixture of constabulary and military uniform. **black and white**, photographed etc. in shades of grey and not in colour; comprising only opposite extremes; in black and white, recorded in writing or print. **black box**, the flight-recorder in an aircraft. **black bread**, coarse rye bread. **black coffee**, coffee without milk. **Black Country**, the industrial district of the Midlands west of Birmingham, so called from the smoke and dust of the coal and iron trades in the 19th c. **black eye**, one with the surrounding skin darkened by bruises. **Black Friars**, Dominicans, so called from their black cloaks. **black ice**, thin transparent ice on a road etc. **black letter**, a heavy style of type used by early printers. **black magic**, magic involving the invocation of devils. **Black Maria**, a police vehicle for conveying prisoners. **black mark**, a mark of discredit. **black market**, illicit traffic in rationed or officially restricted goods. **black mass**, a sacrificial rite in honour of Satan, parodying the Eucharist. **Black Monk**, a Benedictine, so called from the colour of the habit. **black-out** n. a covering of all windows etc. to prevent light being seen by enemy aircraft; a temporary ban on the release of news; (colloq.) a momentary loss of consciousness. **black out**, to impose a black-out on; to suffer a 'black-out'. **black pepper**, pepper from the unripe berries complete with husks. **Black Power**, a movement seeking civil rights, political power, etc., for Blacks. **black sheep**, a discreditable character in an otherwise well-behaved group. **black tie**, a man's black bow-tie worn with a dinner-jacket. **Black Watch**, the Royal Highland Regiment, whose uniform includes a dark tartan. **black widow**, a venomous spider of the genus Latrodectus, found in tropical and subtropical regions. The female of the North American species L. mactans devours its mate. —**blackly** adv., **blackness** n. [OE]

blackball v.t. to reject (a proposed member of a club etc.) in a ballot, originally by voting with a black ball.

blackberry n. the dark edible fruit of the bramble; this shrub.

blackbird n. 1. a songbird of the thrush family (Turdus

merula), the male of which is black. **2.** (*US*) the grackle or a similar bird.

blackboard *n.* a board with a smooth dark surface, used in classrooms etc. for writing on in chalk.

blackcock *n.* a male black grouse.

blackcurrant *n.* the small dark edible berry of the shrub *Ribes nigrum*; this shrub.

Black Death an epidemic of plague (chiefly bubonic) that decimated the population of Europe in the mid-14th c. It originated in central Asia and spread rapidly through Europe, carried by the fleas of black rats, reaching England in 1349 and killing between one third and one half of the population in a matter of months. Less severe outbreaks of plague occurred at irregular intervals throughout the next few centuries. The name dates from 1833 and is a translation from the German; the significance of 'black' is uncertain.

blacken /ˈblækən/ *v.t./i.* **1.** to make or become black. **2.** to speak ill of, to defame. [f. BLACK]

Blackett /ˈblækɪt/, Patrick Maynard Stuart, Baron (1897–1974), English physicist. During the Second World War he was involved in operational research, of great importance in the U-boat war, and was a member of the Maud Committee which dealt with the development of the atomic bomb. He modified Wilson's cloud chamber (a device for detecting ionized particles) for the study of cosmic rays, and in 1948 was awarded the Nobel Prize for physics for his discoveries in nuclear physics and cosmic radiation.

blackfly *n.* a black aphid infesting plants.

Black Forest a hilly wooded region of southern West Germany lying to the east of the Rhine valley.

blackguard /ˈblægɑːd/ *n.* an unprincipled villain, a scoundrel. —**blackguardly** *adj.* [f. BLACK + GUARD; orig. collect. *n.*, = royal scullions, vagrants, etc.]

blackhead *n.* a black-topped pimple on the face etc.

black hole a region in outer space with a gravitational field so intense that no matter or radiation can escape from it, formed most likely when a massive star exhausts its nuclear fuel and begins to collapse under the force of its own gravity. If the star is massive enough, no known force can counteract the increasing gravity, and it will collapse to a point of infinite density. Before this stage is reached, light itself will be trapped and the later stages of collapse lost from sight. A traveller unfortunate enough to pass near to a black hole would be torn apart by strong tidal forces as he crossed the boundary of the region within which light is trapped; in any case, he could never hope to return once that point had been passed. It is speculated that black holes of millions of solar masses may lurk at the centre of some galaxies, swallowing passing stars and increasing in mass. Such cannibalistic objects may provide the enormous energies seen in quasars.

blacking *n.* black polish for shoes. [f. BLACK]

blacklead *n.* graphite.

blackleg *n.* (*derog.*) a person who refuses to join an appropriate trade union, or who participates in strike-breaking by working for an employer whose regular workmen are on strike. —*v.i.* (-**gg**-) to act as a blackleg. [f. BLACK + LEG, for unknown reason]

blacklist /ˈblæklɪst/ *n.* a list of persons etc. in disfavour. —*v.t.* to put on a blacklist.

blackmail *n.* exaction of payment in return for not carrying out a threat, especially to reveal discreditable secrets; payment exacted thus; use of threats or moral pressure. —*v.t.* to exact payment by blackmail; to threaten, to coerce. —**blackmailer** *n.* [f. obs. *mail* rent]

Blackmore /ˈblækmɔː(r)/, Richard Doddridge (1825–1900), English writer who became a fruit-farmer and published novels, poems, and translations. His fame rests almost entirely on his enduringly popular romantic novel *Lorna Doone* (1869), set in 17th-c. Exmoor.

Black Prince the 16th-c. name given, for unknown reasons, to Edward Plantagenet (1330–76), eldest son of Edward III of England. A soldier of considerable ability, the Black Prince was responsible for some of the greatest English triumphs of the early years of the Hundred Years War, most notably that at Poitiers in 1356. His health failed at a relatively early age and he predeceased his father, although his own son eventually came to the throne as Richard II.

Black Rod (in full *Gentleman Usher of the Black Rod*) the chief gentleman usher of the Lord Chamberlain's department of the royal household, who is also usher to the House of Lords, so called from the ebony staff, surmounted

by a golden lion, which he carries as his symbol of office. When the monarch is to deliver a speech in the House of Lords he summons the Commons to attend by knocking on their door (which has been shut against him) with his staff.

Black Sea a tideless virtually land-locked sea between the USSR, Turkey, Bulgaria, and Romania, connected to the Mediterranean Sea through the Bosporus and Sea of Marmara.

blacksmith *n.* a smith who works in iron.

blackthorn *n.* a thorny shrub *Prunus spinosa* bearing white flowers and sloes.

bladder *n.* a sac in the bodies of humans and animals for holding liquids, especially the urinary bladder (ill. BODY 2); an animal's bladder, or a bag resembling this, inflated or otherwise prepared for various uses. —**bladder-wrack** *n.* a seaweed with air-filled swellings among its fronds. [OE]

blade *n.* **1.** the cutting part of a knife etc.; the flat wide part of a spade, oar, etc. **2.** the flat narrow leaf of grasses; the broad part of a leaf, as distinct from its stalk. **3.** a broad flattish bone. [OE]

Blake /bleɪk/, William (1757–1827), English artist and poet. He trained as an engraver but, despite the encouragement of patrons, never achieved prosperity or the recognition that his highly original works were posthumously accorded. His volumes of poetry, which, through a personal mythology, express a mystic sense of the energy of the universe and a protest against hypocrisy and constraint in conventional religion and art, mark a rejection of the Age of Enlightenment and the dawn of Romanticism; they include *Songs of Innocence* (1789), *Songs of Experience* (1794), and various long symbolic and prophetic works. His major prose work, *The Marriage of Heaven and Hell* (engraved *c.*1790–3) is a collection of paradoxical and revolutionary aphorisms. His watercolours and engravings (illustrating, notably, the Book of Job and the works of Dante) are equally striking and unconventional, and are now very highly regarded.

blame *v.t.* to hold responsible and criticize (*for*); to fix the responsibility (for misfortunes etc.) *on* a person. —*n.* responsibility for a bad result or attribution of it to a person. —**blameless** *adj.*, **blameworthy** *adj.* [f. OF, ult. = BLASPHEME]

blanch /blɑːntʃ/ *v.t./i.* **1.** to make white by extracting the colour from or by depriving (plants) of light. **2.** to peel (almonds) by scalding; to dip (vegetables) in boiling water. **3.** to become pale with fear etc. [f. OF (as BLANK)]

Blanchard /ˈblɑːnʃɑːd/, Jean Pierre François (1753–1809), French balloonist. Before the invention of the balloon he designed a flapping-wing machine with four wings and a rudder, which he later tried (unsuccessfully) on a hydrogen balloon. Together with American Dr John Jeffries he made the first crossing of the English Channel by air, flying by balloon from Dover to Calais on 7 Jan. 1785, and was the first to fly a balloon in the USA. Essentially a showman, by his many flights he stimulated others to awareness of the possibility of flight, but was killed in Paris making practice jumps by parachute from a balloon.

blancmange /bləˈmɒnʒ/ *n.* a flavoured jelly-like pudding made with cornflour and milk. [f. OF, = white food]

bland *adj.* mild in flavour or properties; insipid, dull; soothing in manner, suave. —**blandly** *adj.*, **blandness** *n.* [f. L *blandus* soft, caressing]

blandish /ˈblændɪʃ/ *v.t.* to flatter, to cajole. —**blandishment** *n.* (usu. in *pl.*) [f. OF *blandir* flatter f. L (as prec.)]

blank *adj.* **1.** not written, printed, or recorded on; with spaces left for details or signature. **2.** showing no interest or emotion. **3.** sheer, unadorned. —*n.* **1.** a blank space in a document etc.; an empty surface. **2.** a dash put in place of an omitted word. **3.** a blank cartridge. —*v.t.* to screen *off* or *out*. —**blank cartridge,** one containing no bullet. **blank cheque,** one with the amount left for the payee to fill in. **blank verse,** unrhymed verse, usually in iambic pentameters. **draw a blank,** to be unsuccessful, to get no response. [f. OF *blanc* white f. Gmc]

blanket /ˈblæŋkɪt/ *n.* **1.** a thick covering made of woollen or other fabric, used for warmth, chiefly as bedding. **2.** a thick covering mass or layer. —*adj.* general, covering all cases or classes. —*v.t.* to cover with a blanket. **2.** to suppress (a scandal etc.). [f. OF (dim. of *blanc* BLANK)]

blare /bleə(r)/ *v.i./t.* to make a loud sound like a trumpet; to utter loudly. —*n.* a blaring sound. [f. Du., imit.]

blarney/ ˈblɑːnɪ/ *n.* deceptive flattery. —*v.t./i.* to use or subject to such flattery. [f. *Blarney* Castle near Cork, a stone of which is said to confer a cajoling tongue on anyone kissing it]

blasé /ˈblɑːzeɪ/ *adj.* bored or unimpressed, especially through familiarity. [F]

blaspheme /blæsˈfiːm/ *v.t./i* to utter blasphemy against, to talk impiously. —**blasphemer** *n.* [f. OF f. L f. Gk *blasphēmeō* speak ill of]

blasphemy /ˈblæsfəmɪ/ *n.* grossly irreverent talk about God or sacred things. —**blasphemous** *adj.* [as prec.]

blast /blɑːst/ *n.* 1. an explosion, a destructive wave of air from this; a strong gust of wind etc. 2. the loud sound made by a trumpet, car horn, etc. —*v.t.* 1. to blow up (rocks etc.) with explosives. 2. to blow destructively on, to wither or blight (*lit.*, and in curses or as *int.* of annoyance). —**(at) full blast**, at full capacity or speed. **blast off**, (of a rocket or spacecraft) to launch into space. **blast-off** *n.* this launching. [OE (rel. to BLOW)]

blasted /ˈblɑːstɪd/ *adj.* cursed, damnable. —*adv.* damnably. [f. BLAST]

blast-furnace *n.* a smelting-furnace into which compressed hot air is driven. This is the major means of smelting iron ore to produce molten iron. It consists of a tall steel tower, roughly cylindrical in shape and lined with a refractory material, charged from the top with a mixture of iron ore, coke, and limestone. Hot air is blown into the base of the tower through nozzles. The oxygen in the air reacts with the carbon in the coke to produce carbon monoxide which in turn combines with oxygen from the iron ore to produce carbon dioxide and pure iron. As the carbon dioxide passes up the tower it again reacts with carbon to produce carbon monoxide, and the cycle is repeated. The limestone combines with ash from the coke to form a liquid slag which absorbs sulphur in the iron and is collected at the bottom of the tower, floating above a pool of molten iron. The iron and the slag are tapped off separately from time to time and the gas exhausted from the top of the tower, after cleaning, is used to preheat the incoming blast of air and then is used as fuel for raising steam to drive the blowing-engines (air compressors) or to heat the coke-ovens. The whole process is therefore a well-integrated method of producing iron continuously on a large scale.

blatant /ˈbleɪt(ə)nt/ *adj.* flagrant, unashamed; loudly obtrusive. —**blatantly** *adv.* [orig. = clamorous; coined by Spenser]

blather /ˈblæðə(r)/ *v.i.* (*colloq.*) to chatter foolishly. —*n.* (*colloq.*) foolish chatter. [f. ON]

Blavatsky /blæˈvætski/, Helena Petrovna (1831–91), Russian spiritualist, founder of the Theosophical Society.

blaze[1] *n.* 1. a bright flame or fire. 2. a brilliant display (*of* lights, colours, publicity). 3. a dramatic outburst of emotion. —*v.i.* 1. to burn or shine fiercely. 2. to display sudden emotion, usually anger. —**blaze away**, to fire a gun continuously. [OE, = torch]

blaze[2] *n.* 1. a white mark on the face of an animal, especially a horse. 2. a mark made in the bark of a tree to indicate a route. —*v.t.* to mark (a tree or path) with blazes. —**blaze a trail**, to show the way for others to follow. [orig. unkn.]

blaze[3] *v.t.* to proclaim. [f. MLG & MDu., rel. to BLOW[1]]

blazer /ˈbleɪzə(r)/ *n.* a light jacket often in the colours, or with the badge, of a team or school. [f. BLAZE[1]]

blazon /ˈbleɪz(ə)n/ *n.* a heraldic shield, a coat of arms. —*v.t.* to proclaim; to describe or paint (a coat of arms); to inscribe with arms, names, etc., in colours. —**blazonry** *n.* [f. OF *blason* shield]

bleach *v.t./i.* to whiten by chemicals or exposure to sunlight. —*n.* a bleaching substance or process. —**bleaching powder**, chloride of lime. [OE]

bleak *adj.* 1. cold and wind-swept. 2. unpromising, dreary, grim. —**bleakly** *adv.*, **bleakness** *n.* [orig. = pale; rel. to BLEACH]

bleary *adj.* dim-sighted from watering of the eyes. —**blearily** *adv.* [f. LG]

bleat *n.* the tremulous cry of a sheep, goat, or calf. —*v.i.* to utter this cry; to say or speak feebly or plaintively. [OE, imit.]

bleed *v.t./i* (*past & p.p.* **bled**) 1. to leak blood or other fluid; (of a dye) to run. 2. to draw off blood or surplus fluid from; (*colloq.*) to extort money from. —*n.* an act of bleeding. [OE (rel. to BLOOD)]

bleep *v.i.* to emit an intermittent high-pitched signal. —*n.* such a signal. [imit.]

blemish /ˈblemɪʃ/ *v.t.* to spoil the beauty or perfection of. —*n.* a defect, a flaw. [f. OF *blesmir* make pale]

blench *v.i.* to flinch. [OE, = deceive; rel. to BLINK]

blend *v.t./i.* 1. to mix (different varieties) to get a required flavour, texture, etc. 2. to mingle or merge (*with*). 3. (of colours etc.) to pass imperceptibly into each other. 4. to harmonize. —*n.* a mixture of different varieties. [f. ON]

blende /blend/ *n.* native zinc sulphide. [G (*blenden* deceive, because while often resembling lead ore it yielded no lead)]

blender *n.* a device for blending soft or liquid foods. [f. BLEND]

Blenheim /ˈblenɪm/ a village in Bavaria, scene of a battle in 1704 (see MARLBOROUGH).

blenny *n.* a small sea-fish (especially of the genus *Blennius*) with spiny fins and slimy scales. [f. L f. Gk *blennos* mucus, from the mucous coating of its scales]

Blériot /ˈbleərɪəʊ/, Louis (1872–1936), French pioneer in aviation. Trained as an engineer, he built a successful flapping-wing model aircraft in 1901 and one of the first successful monoplanes in 1907. On 25 July 1909 he made aviation history by being the first to fly the English Channel, from Calais to Dover, in a monoplane (a balloon crossing had been made by Blanchard in 1785). Later he became an aircraft manufacturer, and between 1909 and 1914 his factory built over 800 aeroplanes of 40 different types; by the end of the First World War it was producing 18 aircraft a day.

bless *v.t.* 1. to invoke God's favour on; to sanctify by the sign of the cross; to consecrate (food etc.). 2. to glorify (God); to attribute one's good luck to (one's stars etc.). —**be blessed with**, to be fortunate enough to possess. [OE, rel. to BLOOD]

blessed /ˈblesɪd/ *predic. adj.* holy; beatified; (*iron. slang*) cursed.

blessing *n.* 1. an invocation of God's favour; a grace before or after a meal. 2. something one is thankful for, a benefit. [f. BLESS]

blether var. of BLATHER.

blew *past* of BLOW.

blewits /ˈbluːɪts/ *n.* an edible mushroom with a lilac stem. [prob. f. BLUE]

Bligh /blaɪ/, William (1754–1817), British naval officer who, as captain, commanded HMS *Bounty*. He eventually rose to become a Vice-Admiral, although his harsh temperament got him into trouble on at least one occasion other than the mutiny, when he was deposed by disaffected officers while acting as governor of New South Wales (1805–8).

blight /blaɪt/ *n.* 1. a disease causing plants to shrivel up etc.; a fungus or aphid causing it. 2. an obscure malignant influence. —*v.t.* 1. to affect (plants) with blight. 2. to frustrate or spoil. [orig. unkn.]

blighter /ˈblaɪtə(r)/ *n.* (*colloq.*) a person or thing, especially an annoying one. [f. prec.]

Blighty /ˈblaɪtɪ/ *n.* (*military slang*) home (especially Britain) after service abroad; a wound ensuring one's return home. [f. Hind., = foreign, European]

blimey /ˈblaɪmɪ/ *int.* of astonishment, contempt, etc. [corrupt. of (*God*) *blind me*]

blimp *n.* 1. a small non-rigid airship. 2. a soundproof cover for a cine-camera. 3. **(Colonel) Blimp**, a diehard reactionary (named after a cartoon character representing a pompous obese elderly man). [orig. unkn.]

blind /blaɪnd/ *adj.* 1. lacking the power of sight; (of a corner etc.) not allowing a clear view of the road ahead; (of flying) relying solely on instruments. 2. without foresight or discernment; reckless; not governed by purpose. —*v.t.* to deprive of sight; to dazzle with bright light; to beguile so as to rob of judgement; to overawe. —*n.* 1. a screen for a window; a shop's awning. 2. a pretext, a ruse. —**blind alley**, a street closed at one end. **blind date**, a social engagement between a man and woman who have not previously met. **blind spot**, a spot on the retina insensitive to light (ill. BODY2); an area in which discernment is lacking. **blind stitch** etc., sewing visible on one side only. **turn a blind eye to**, to pretend not to notice. —**blindly** *adv.*, **blindness** *n.* [OE]

blindfold *adj. & adv.* with the eyes bandaged. —*n.* a cloth placed over a person's eyes. —*v.t.* to block the sight of with a blindfold. [orig. *blindfelled* = struck blind]

blind man's buff a game in which a blindfold player tries to catch others, who push him about. A sport with universal appeal, it is played under different names in many countries, and goes back to remote antiquity. In the Middle Ages it was played by adults in the street, with greater emphasis on the 'buffs' than is usual in its later version as a children's (indoor) party game. [f. obs. *buff* = buffet]

blindworm *n.* a slow-worm [from its small eyes].

blink *v.t./i.* **1.** to move the eyelids quickly down and up; to look with eyes opening and shutting. **2.** to shine with an unsteady or intermittent light. **3.** to shirk consideration of (facts etc.). —*n.* **1.** an act of blinking. **2.** a momentary gleam. [rel. to BLENCH]

blinkers *n.pl.* screens on a horse's bridle to prevent it seeing sideways. [f. BLINK]

blinking *adj. & adv.* (*slang, euphem.*) bloody (= damned). [f. BLINK]

blip *n.* a spot of light on a radar screen; a quick popping sound. —*v.i.* (**-pp-**) to make a blip. [imit.]

Bliss Sir Arthur (1891-1975), English composer, director of music at the BBC from 1942 to 1944 and Master of the Queen's Music from 1953 to 1975. He showed an interest in avant-garde music, particularly that of Schoenberg and Stravinsky, when he was in his twenties, composing in 1922, at Elgar's behest, *A Colour Symphony* for the Three Choirs Festival. In later years, however, he tended more to traditional forms, as in his symphony for orator, chorus, and orchestra *Morning Heroes* (1930), composed as a memorial to the victims of the First World War (who included his brother).

bliss *n.* perfect happiness; the perfect joy of heaven. — **blissful** *adj.*, **blissfully** *adv.* [OE f. Gmc (= blithe)]

blister *n.* a bubble on the skin filled with watery fluid, caused by friction etc.; a similar swelling on painted wood etc. —*v.t./i* **1.** to develop blisters; to raise blisters on. **2.** to criticize sharply. [orig. unkn.]

blithe /blaɪð/ *adj.* joyous, carefree; casual, careless. [OE]

blitz /blɪts/ *n.* a sudden intensive (usually aerial) attack; **the Blitz,** the German air-raids on London in 1940. —*v.t.* to attack or destroy by a blitz. [abbr. of foll.]

blitzkrieg /'blɪtskriːg/ *n.* an intensive campaign intended to bring about a speedy victory, especially as used by Germany against various countries of Europe in the Second World War. [G, = lightning war]

blizzard /'blɪzəd/ *n.* a severe snowstorm. [orig. unkn.]

bloat *v.t.* to cause to swell out, to make turgid. [f. obs. *bloat* swollen (orig. unkn.)]

bloated *adj.* puffed up with pride of wealth, self-indulgence, etc. [f. BLOAT]

bloater *n.* a herring half-dried in smoke. [perh. rel. to ON *blautr* soaked]

blob *n.* a thick drop; a small round mass. [imit.]

bloc /blɒk/ *n.* a combination of countries, parties, etc., to foster a common interest. [F, = BLOCK]

Bloch /blɒx/, Ernest (1880-1959), Swiss-born composer of Jewish descent, who lived in the USA from 1916. His opera *Macbeth* was produced in 1909. Many of his works (which include the *Israel Symphony* (1912-16), *Schelomo*, a rhapsody for cello and orchestra (1916), and numerous orchestral compositions are inspired by Jewish folk-music and liturgy.

block *n.* **1.** a solid piece of wood, stone, or other hard substance; this as used for chopping or hammering on, or from which horses are mounted; **the block,** that on which condemned people were beheaded. **2.** a large building divided into flats or offices. **3.** a group of buildings bounded by streets. **4.** an obstruction; an inability or mental resistance caused by psychological factors. **5.** a large section of seats, shares, etc. as a unit; (*attrib.*) made or treated as a large unit. **6.** a piece of wood or metal engraved for printing. **7.** a pulley mounted in a case. —*v.t.* **1.** to obstruct or impede; to restrict the use or conversion of (currency). **2.** to sketch *in* or *out* roughly. —**block and tackle,** a system of pulleys and ropes, especially for lifting things. **block-buster** *n.* a bomb powerful enough to destroy a whole block of buildings. **block diagram,** one showing the general arrangement of parts in an apparatus. **block letters,** letters written separately as in print, usually in capitals. **block mountain,** one formed by faults (ill. GEOLOGY). **block vote,** a vote by a delegate to a conference etc. proportional in value to the number of persons represented. [f. OF f. LDu.]

blockade /blɒˈkeɪd/ *n.* the cutting off of a place by enemy forces to prevent goods etc. reaching or leaving it. —*v.t.* to subject to a blockade. [f. BLOCK]

blockhead *n.* a slow-witted person.

blockhouse *n.* a reinforced concrete military shelter; a timber building used as a fort, with loopholes for guns.

bloke *n.* (*colloq.*) a man, a fellow. [Shelta]

blond (of a woman or her hair usu. **blonde**) *adj.* fair-haired; (of hair) fair. —*n.* a fair-haired person. [f. F f. L, = yellow]

Blondin /blɒ̃dæ̃/, Charles (Jean-François Gravelet, 1824-97), French acrobat, who walked across a tightrope suspended over Niagara Falls in 1859 and on subsequent occasions with acrobatics.

blood /blʌd/ *n.* **1.** the fluid, usually red, circulating in the arteries and veins of animals (see below). **2.** the taking of life. **3.** passion, temperament. **4.** race, descent, parentage (see below); blood-relations. **5.** a dandy. —*v.t.* to give (hounds) their first taste of blood; to initiate (a person). — **blood-bath** *n.* a massacre. **blood count,** the number of corpuscles in a given volume of blood. **blood-curdling** *adj.* extremely horrific. **blood group,** any of the types into which human blood is divided according to its compatibility in transfusion (see LANDSTEINER). **blood-money** *n.* a fine paid by a killer to his victim's next-of-kin. **blood orange,** a variety of orange with red-streaked pulp. **blood-poisoning** *n.* infection of the bloodstream by bacteria. **blood pressure,** varying pressure of blood in the vessels, measured for diagnosis. **blood-relation** *n.* one related by birth, not marriage. **blood sports,** sports involving the killing of animals. **blood-stained** *adj.* stained with blood; guilty of bloodshed. **blood test,** an examination of a person's blood for diagnosis etc. **blood-vessel** *n.* a vein, artery, or capillary conveying blood. **in cold blood,** with premeditated violence. [OE]
Most animal bodies depend upon a circulating fluid for transporting substances from one part to another. In vertebrates this fluid is blood, circulating in veins and arteries and pumped by the heart, carrying food, salts, oxygen, hormones, and cells and molecules of the immune system to tissues, and removing waste products; by virtue of its large volume and rapid circulation it evens out the temperature of the bodily parts. Blood consists of a mildly alkaline fluid (plasma) in which are suspended a number of different types of cell: red cells (erythrocytes), white cells (leucocytes), and platelets. Plasma consists chiefly of water and is driven easily along even the smallest blood-vessels. Red blood-cells (which give blood its colour) carry the protein haemoglobin, which can combine with oxygen and also with carbon dioxide, thus enabling the blood to carry oxygen from the lungs to the tissues and carbon dioxide in the reverse direction. The main function of white blood-cells (of which there are several types) is to protect the body against the invasion of foreign agents (e.g. bacteria) into its tissues. Platelets and other factors present in plasma are concerned in the clotting of blood, preventing haemorrhage.
Blood was formerly thought to be the medium of heredity, whence such phrases as *the blood royal, we are of the same blood, gambling is in his blood,* and *blood will tell.*

bloodhound *n.* a large keen-scented dog used in tracking.

bloodless *adj.* **1.** without blood, pale from loss of blood. **2.** involving no bloodshed. **3.** without vitality; unemotional. [f. BLOOD + -LESS]

bloodshed *n.* the spilling of blood, slaughter.

bloodshot *adj.* (of eyeballs) tinged with blood.

bloodstock *n.* pedigree horses.

bloodstream *n.* the blood circulating in the body.

bloodsucker *n.* **1.** a creature that sucks blood, a leech. **2.** an extortionate person.

bloodthirsty *adj.* eager for bloodshed.

bloody /'blʌdɪ/ *adj.* **1.** of, like, or smeared with blood. **2.** involving bloodshed; cruel, bloodthirsty. **3.** (*slang*) cursed, damnable. —*adv.* (*slang*) damnably. —*v.t.* to stain with blood. —**Bloody Assizes,** the trials held in SW England in 1685 of the supporters of the Duke of Monmouth after their defeat at Sedgemoor. The government's representative, Judge Jeffreys, sentenced several hundred rebels to death and about 1,000 others to transportation to America as plantation slaves. **bloody-minded** *adj.* deliberately uncooperative. —**bloodily** *adv.*, **bloodiness** *n.* [f. BLOOD]

bloom *n.* **1.** the flower of a plant (especially one grown chiefly for this). **2.** greatest beauty or perfection; freshness; flush, glow. **3.** the powdery deposit on grapes, plums, etc. — *v.i.* **1.** to bear blooms, to be in bloom. **2.** to be in full beauty or vigour. —**in bloom,** flowering. [f. ON]

bloomer *n.* (*slang*) a blunder. [f. BLOOM]

bloomers *n.pl.* **1.** loose knee-length trousers formerly worn by women. **2.** (*colloq.*) knickers with legs. [f. Mrs A.

Bloomer, Amer. social reformer (d. 1894) who advocated costume called 'rational dress' for women, invented by Mrs E. S. Miller and consisting of a short jacket, full skirt reaching to just below the knee, and trousers down to the ankle]

Bloomfield /'blu:mfiəld/, Leonard (1887-1949), American linguistics scholar who counts as one of the founders of American linguistic structuralism. He wrote about Indo-European philology, Malayo-Polynesian languages, American-Indian languages, and theoretical linguistics but the work which reached the widest public was *Language* (1933), a textbook which contained important sections on historical and comparative linguistics but was largely dedicated to an account of the techniques and aims of the new descriptive linguistics (see DESCRIPTIVE).

blooming *adj.* & *adv.* **1.** in bloom; flourishing. **2.** (*slang*) expressing mild annoyance or dislike) confounded. [f. BLOOM]

Bloomsbury set, group, etc. /'blu:mzbəri/ a school of writers and aesthetes living in Bloomsbury in the early 20th c. [f. *Bloomsbury* district of London]

blossom /'blɒsəm/ *n.* a flower or mass of flowers, especially of a fruit tree. —*v.i.* **1.** to open into blossom. **2.** to evolve or mature *into*. **3.** to thrive. [OE]

blot *n.* **1.** a small stain of ink etc. **2.** a disfiguring feature. **3.** something bringing disgrace. —*v.t.* (**-tt-**) **1.** to stain with ink or other liquid. **2.** to dry with blotting-paper. —**blot out**, to obliterate; to obscure from view. **blotting-paper** *n.* absorbent paper for drying wet ink. [prob. f. Scand.]

blotch /blɒtʃ/ *n.* a discoloured patch on the skin; any large irregular patch of colour. —**blotchy** *adj.* [f. obs. *plotch* and BLOT]

blotter *n.* a pad of blotting-paper. [f. BLOT]

blotto /'blɒtəʊ/ *adj.* (*slang*) very drunk. [orig. unkn.]

blouse /blaʊz/ *n.* **1.** a shirt-like garment worn by women. **2.** a waist-length jacket forming part of a soldier's or airman's battledress. [F; orig. unkn.]

blow[1] /bləʊ/ *v.t./i* (*past* **blew** /blu:/; *p.p.* **blown** /bləʊn/) **1.** to direct a current of air from the mouth; to move rapidly as a current of air; to breathe hard; (of a whale) to eject air and water when surfacing. **2.** to sound (a wind instrument), (of such an instrument) to sound; to send out (bubbles etc.) or clear (the nose) by breathing. **3.** to break open with explosives, to send flying (*off* etc.) by explosion; to melt (a fuse) or be melted under an overload. **4.** to propel by a current of air; to shape (molten glass) by blowing. **5.** (*slang*) to reveal (a secret etc.). **6.** (*slang*, esp. as *int.*) to curse. **7.** (*slang*) to squander; to bungle. —*n.* an act of blowing; exposure to fresh air. —**blow-dry** *v.t.* to use a hand-held drier to style washed hair while drying it. **blow-hole** *n.* a hole for blowing or breathing through; an outlet for the escape of air or gas etc. **blow one's own trumpet**, to boast. **blow-out** *n.* an uncontrolled eruption of oil or gas from a well; a burst in a tyre; (*colloq.*) a large meal. **blow up**, to shatter or be shattered in an explosion; to inflate with air; (*colloq.*) to enlarge (a photograph). [OE]

blow[2] /bləʊ/ *n.* a hard stroke with the hand or a weapon; a sudden shock or misfortune. [orig. unkn.]

blowfly *n.* a fly that lays its eggs on meat.

blowlamp *n.* a portable burner producing a very hot flame that can be directed on to a small area.

blowpipe *n.* **1.** a tube for blowing air through, to increase the heat of a flame or in glass-blowing. **2.** a tube through which poisonous darts are blown.

blowzy /'blaʊzi/ *adj.* red-faced, coarse-looking; slatternly. [f. obs. *blowze* beggar's wench]

blubber *n.* whale fat. —*v.i.* to sob noisily. —*adj.* (of lips) thick, swollen. [prob. imit.]

bludgeon /'blʌdʒ(ə)n/ *n.* a short stick with a heavy end. —*v.t.* **1.** to beat with a bludgeon. **2.** to coerce. [orig. unkn.]

blue /blu:/ *adj.* **1.** having the colour of the clear sky. **2.** sad, despondent. **3.** indecent. —*n.* **1.** blue colour or pigment; blue clothes or material. **2.** the distinction of representing Oxford or Cambridge in a sport; one holding this. **3.** (in *pl.*) a despondent state, slow melancholy music of Black American origin. —*v.t.* (*partic.* **blueing**) **1.** to make blue. **2.** (*colloq.*) to squander. —**blue baby**, one with congenital blueness of the skin from a heart defect. **blue blood**, aristocratic birth. **blue book**, a Parliamentary or Privy-Council report. **blue cheese**, cheese with veins of blue mould. **blue-collar worker**, a manual or industrial worker. **blue-eyed boy**, (*colloq.*) a favourite. **blue-pencil** *v.t.* to delete with a blue pencil, to censor. **Blue Peter**, a blue flag with a white square raised when a ship leaves port. **Blue Riband** (*or* **Ribbon**) **of the Atlantic**, a trophy for the ship making the fastest sea-crossing of the Atlantic. **blue ribbon**, the ribbon of the Garter; the highest honour in any sphere; a small strip of blue ribbon formerly worn by certain abstainers from alcoholic beverages. **blue tit**, a tit with bright blue tail, wings, and top of head. **blue whale**, a rorqual, the largest known living mammal. **once in a blue moon**, very rarely. **out of the blue**, unexpectedly. —**blueness** *n.* [f. OF *bleu* f. Gmc]

Bluebeard /'blu:bɪəd/ the hero of a tale by Perrault. Bluebeard killed several wives in turn because they showed undue curiosity about a locked room (which contained the bodies of his previous wives). Local tradition in Brittany identifies him with Gilles de Retz (c.1400-40), a perpetrator of atrocities, though he had only one wife (who left him).

bluebell *n.* a plant with blue bell-shaped flowers, the wild hyacinth (*Endymion non-scriptus*) or (*Sc.*) harebell (*Campanula rotundifolia*).

bluebottle *n.* a large buzzing fly with a blue body.

blueprint *n.* a blue-and-white photographic print of plans, technical drawings, etc.; a detailed plan.

bluestocking *n.* a pretentiously intellectual woman. [f. the '*Blue Stocking*' Club', 18th-c. literary coterie, led by three ladies, formed to substitute for the card-playing, which then formed the chief recreation at evening parties, more intellectual modes of spending the time, including conversation on literary subjects, in which eminent men of letters often took part. Many of these eschewed formal dress and one habitually wore grey or 'blue' worsted stockings instead of black silk.]

bluff[1] *v.t./i.* to make pretence of strength etc. to gain an advantage; to deceive by this. —*n.* an act of bluffing. [orig. a term in the game of poker, f. Du. *bluffen* brag]

bluff[2] *adj.* **1.** (of cliffs etc.) having a vertical or steep broad front. **2.** frank or abrupt and hearty in manner. —*n.* a bluff cliff or headland. [orig. unkn.]

bluish /'blu:ɪʃ/ *adj.* fairly blue. [f. BLUE]

Blumenbach /'blu:mənbɑ:x/, Johann Friedrich (1752-1840), German physiologist and comparative anatomist who, out of respect for his formulation of one of the earliest racial classifications, is called the founder of Physical Anthropology. His research led to the division of modern man into five broad categories: Caucasian (white), Mongolian (yellow), Malayan (brown), Ethiopian (black), and American (red).

Blunden /'blʌnd(ə)n/, Edmund Charles (1869-1974), English poet and critic, whose *Undertones of War* (1928) is a sensitive account of his experiences in the First World War. His writings show his deep love of the English countryside.

blunder *v.i.* to make a serious or foolish mistake; to move clumsily and uncertainly. —*n.* a serious or foolish mistake. [prob. f. Scand.]

blunderbuss /'blʌndəbʌs/ *n.* a type of muzzle-loading usually flintlock gun for close-range use, common in the 18th c., with a flared muzzle, firing many balls at one shot. [f. Du., = thunder-gun]

blunt *adj.* **1.** without a sharp edge or point, not sharp. **2.** abrupt and outspoken. —*v.t.* to make blunt or less sharp. —**bluntly** *adv.*, **bluntness** *n.* [perh. f. Scand. (ON *blunda* shut the eyes)]

blur *v.t.* (**-rr-**) to make or become less distinct; to smear (writing etc.). —*n.* **1.** a thing seen or heard indistinctly. **2.** a smear. [perh. rel. to BLEARY]

blurb *n.* descriptive or commendatory matter, especially a description of a book printed on its jacket. [said to have been originated in 1907 by G. Burgess, Amer. humorist, in a comic book jacket embellished with a drawing of a pulchritudinous young lady whom he facetiously dubbed Miss Blinda Blurb]

blurt *v.t.* (usu. with *out*) to utter abruptly or tactlessly. [imit.]

blush *v.i.* **1.** to develop a pink tinge in the face from shame or embarrassment; to be ashamed or embarrassed *to*. **2.** to be red or pink. —*n.* an act of blushing; a rosy glow. [OE]

bluster *v.i.* to behave noisily or boisterously; (of winds etc.) to blow fiercely. —*n.* noisy self-assertive talk, threats. —**blustery** *adj.* [imit.]

Blyton /'blaɪt(ə)n/, Enid (1897-1968), English writer of over 600 books for children. Her writings attracted considerable criticism from educationists and others because of their mediocrity and limited vocabulary, and for some years libraries refused to stock them, but they were commercially successful. Her most celebrated character was Noddy (created in 1949).

BMX *n.* **1.** organized bicycle racing on a dirt track. **2.** a kind of bicycle for use in this. [abbr. *bicycle moto-cross*]

boa /ˈbəʊə/ *n.* **1.** a large South American non-poisonous snake of the genus *Boa* that kills its prey by constriction so that it suffocates; (*loosely*) a snake of similar habits elsewhere, a python. **2.** a woman's long furry or feathered wrap for the throat. —**boa constrictor**, a Brazilian species of boa. [L]

Boadicea /bəʊədɪˈsiːə/ = BOUDICCA.

boar *n.* **1.** a wild pig (*Sus scrofa*) formerly common in forested areas of Europe. **2.** an uncastrated male domestic pig. [OE]

board *n.* **1.** a flat thin piece of sawn timber, usually long and narrow; a flat piece of wood or other firm substance used in games, for posting notices, etc. **2.** material resembling boards, made of compressed fibres; thick stiff card used for book-covers. **3.** provision of meals, usually for payment. **4.** the directors of a company or other official group meeting together. **5.** (in *pl.*) a theatre stage, the acting profession. — *v.t./i.* **1.** to go aboard (a ship, aircraft, etc.). **2.** to cover or close *up* with boards. **3.** to provide with or receive meals, usually for payment. —**board game**, a game played on a specially marked board. **on board**, on or on to a ship, aircraft, oil rig, etc. [OE]

boarder *n.* one who boards with a person, especially a pupil who boards at a boarding-school. [f. prec.]

boarding-house *n.* a house at which board and lodging may be obtained for payment. [f. BOARD]

boarding-school *n.* a school that provides pupils with board and lodging. [f. BOARD]

boardroom *n.* a room in which a board of directors etc. regularly meet.

Boas /ˈbəʊs/, Franz (1858-1942), American anthropologist. Against the general trend of contemporary theory he founded the approach to anthropology that became dominant in the 20th c., insisting that cultrual development must be explored by means of field studies reconstructing histories of particular cultures rather than by assuming there to be total, hierarchical, and racially correlated culture. He did much to destroy the theory of 'Nordic' superiority over 'inferior peoples'; his writings were burnt by the Nazis.

boast *v.t./i.* to speak with great pride and try to impress people, to extol one's own excellence etc.; to be the proud possessor of. —*n.* an act of boasting; something one boasts of. [f. AF; orig. unkn.]

boastful *adj.* boasting frequently, full of boasting. — **boastfully** *adv.*, **boastfulness** *n.* [f. BOAST + -FUL]

boat *n.* **1.** a small vessel propelled on water by paddle, oars, sail, or engine; (*loosely*) a ship; (*US*) a sea-going vessel. **2.** a boat-shaped vessel for gravy etc. —*v.i.* to go in a boat, especially for pleasure. —**boat-hook** *n.* a long pole with a hook and spike at the end for moving boats. **boat-house** *n.* a shed at the water's edge in which boats are kept. **boat-train** *n.* one timed to catch a boat. **in the same boat**, suffering the same troubles. [OE]

Boat is the generic name for small open craft used (for practical purposes or for pleasure) on inland waterways and near coasts, as distinct from ships, which are sea-going. Some exceptions to this general definition are fishing boats, gunboats, patrol boats, mail boats, etc., some yachts, and submarines, possibly because they were originally called 'submarine boats'. Usage (especially by people ashore) is not always precise or consistent: railway companies run 'boat trains' to take passengers to what everyone would call a 'ship'.

boater *n.* a flat-topped straw hat with a brim. [f. BOAT]

boatman *n.* (*pl.* -men) one who conveys by boat or hires out boats.

Boat Race an annual rowing competition on the Thames in London between eights of Oxford and Cambridge Universities. First rowed at Henley in 1829 (when Oxford won), then from Westminster to Putney in 1836 (when Cambridge were successful) it became an annual event in 1839. In 1845 the course was moved to its present location from Putney to Mortlake (6.8 km, 4¼ miles). The idea of such a race was originated largely by Charles Wordsworth (nephew of the poet), who had inaugurated the University cricket match a few years earlier.

boatswain /ˈbəʊs(ə)n/ *n.* a ship's officer in charge of the crew, rigging, etc.

bob¹ *v.i.* (**-bb-**) to make a jerky movement, to move quickly up and down; to curtsy quickly. —*n.* a bobbing movement. —**bob up**, (*colloq.*) to appear or re-emerge suddenly. [imit.]

bob² *n.* **1.** a hair-style in which the hair is cut short to hang evenly. **2.** a weight on a pendulum. —*v.t.* to cut (the hair) in a bob. [orig. unkn.]

bob³ *n.* (*pl.* same) (*slang*) a shilling, five pence. [orig. unkn.]

bobbin /ˈbɒbɪn/ *n.* a cylinder holding a spool of thread in machine sewing, lace-making, etc. [f. F]

bobble *n.* a small ornamental woolly ball. [dim. of BOB²]

bobby /ˈbɒbɪ/ *n.* (*colloq.*) a policeman. [f. Sir *Robert* Peel, Home Secretary at the passing of the Metropolitan Police Act, 1828]

bob-sleigh /ˈbɒbsleɪ/, **bob-sled** *ns.* a sleigh with two axles, each of which has two runners, steered either by ropes or by a wheel; the winter sport in which such sleighs, normally manned by crews of four or two, are guided down a specially prepared descending track of solid ice with banked bends. — **bob-sleighing**, **bob-sledding** *ns.* [perh. f. BOB²]

bobstay *n.* a rope holding the bowsprit down (ill. SAILING-SHIPS). [perh. f. BOB¹]

bobtail *n.* a docked tail, a horse or dog having such a tail. [f. BOB²]

Boccaccio /bɒˈkɑːtʃɪəʊ/, Giovanni (1313-75), Italian novelist, poet, and humanist, son of a Florentine merchant. He was a friend and admirer of Dante and endeavoured, apparently with little success, to interest Petrarch in his fellow poet. In 1348 he witnessed the Black Death in Florence. His most famous work, the *Decameron* (1348-58) is a collection of tales supposedly told by a group of ten young people fleeing from the pestilence. Boccaccio is an important figure in the history of narrative fiction and has provided inspiration to major writers in most periods of literature, including Chaucer, Shakespeare, Dryden, Keats, Longfellow, and Tennyson.

Boccherini /bɒkəˈriːni/, Luigi (1743-1805), Italian composer, famous in his teens as a virtuoso cellist, important chiefly for his works for the cello.

bode *v.t./i.* to be a sign of, to portend. —**bode ill** *or* **well**, to be a bad or good sign. [OE]

bodega /bəˈdiːgə/ *n.* a cellar or shop selling wine. [Sp.]

Bodhisattva /bɒdɪˈsatvə/ *n.* one who is destined to become enlightened (the term is applied to the Buddha before his enlightenment). While the goal of the ancient schools of Buddhism (Hinayana, Theravada) is to attain nirvana oneself, that of Mahayana Buddhism is to become a bodhisattva, postponing one's own salvation in order to help others on the spiritual path. [Skr., = one whose essence is perfect knowledge]

bodice /ˈbɒdɪs/ *n.* **1.** the upper part of a woman's dress, down to the waist. **2.** a woman's vest-like undergarment. [orig. *pair of bodies* = whalebone corset]

bodily /ˈbɒdɪlɪ/ *adj.* of the human body or physical nature. —*adv.* **1.** as a whole. **2.** in the body, in person. [f. BODY]

bodkin /ˈbɒdkɪn/ *n.* a blunt thick needle for drawing tape etc. through a hem. [orig. unkn.]

Bodleian Library /ˈbɒdlɪən/ (*colloq.* **Bodley**) the library of Oxford University. The first library was founded in the 14th c. and benefited from the manuscript collections donated by Humphrey, duke of Gloucester (1391-1447). It was refounded by Sir Thomas Bodley (1545-1613), diplomat and scholar, for the use both of the University of Oxford and the 'republic of the learned', and opened in 1602. In 1610 the Stationers' Company agreed to give to the library a copy of every book printed in England, and by various Copyright Acts it is now one of the five libraries entitled to receive on demand a copy of every book published in the UK. It also houses one of the world's most extensive collections of Western and Oriental manuscripts.

body /ˈbɒdɪ/ *n.* **1.** the physical structure, including bones, flesh, and organs, of a human being or animal (alive or dead). (See ill. pp. 92-5.) **2.** a corpse. **3.** the trunk apart from the head and limbs; the main or central part of something; the majority *of*. **4.** a group of persons or things regarded as a unit. **5.** (*colloq.*) a person. **6.** a distinct piece of matter. **7.** solidity, substantial character etc. — **body-blow** *n.* a very severe setback. **body-building** *n.* strengthening of the body by exercises. **body language**, involuntary movements or attitudes by which a person communicates his feelings or moods etc. (usually unwittingly) to others. **bodyline bowling**, (*Cricket*) persistent fast bowling on the leg side, threatening the batsman's body. **body politic,** the nation in its corporate character. **in a body,** collectively. [OE]

bodyguard n. a person or group of persons escorting and guarding a dignitary etc.

body-snatcher n. (hist.) one who illicitly disinterred corpses for dissection. Prior to the Anatomy Act, 1832, there was no provision for supplying bodies to medical students for anatomical study, and disinterment was profitable though illegal. —**body-snatching** n.

bodywork n. the structure of a vehicle body.

Boer /'bəʊə(r), bʊə(r)/ n. an Afrikaner; (hist.) an early Dutch inhabitant of the Cape. —adj. of Boers. [Du., = farmer]

Boer Wars two wars fought by Great Britain in South Africa. The first (1880–1) began with the revolt of the Boer settlers in the Transvaal against British rule and ended after the British defeat at Majuba Hill with the establishment of an independent Boer Republic under British suzerainty. The second (1899–1902) was caused by the Boer refusal to grant equal rights to recent British immigrants and by the imperialist ambitions of Cecil Rhodes and some Conservative policitians. In the early stages of the war the Boers gained a series of remarkable victories, but after the arrival of Roberts and Kitchener the British succeeded in capturing the Boer capital Pretoria and driving the Boer leader Kruger into exile. The second half of the war was dominated by guerrilla warfare, victory eventually being obtained through the use of almost half a million British and imperial troops and the employment of blockhouses, barbed wire, and concentration camps to control the countryside.

Boethius /bəʊ'i:θɪəs/ (Anicius Manlius Severinus, c.480–524) Roman statesman and philosopher. After rising to high office under Theodoric, king of Italy, he was arrested, imprisoned, and finally executed on a charge of treason. A man of wide-ranging abilities, he wrote Latin commentaries and translations of Aristotle in addition to works on education, science, philosophy, and logic. His greatest work, *The Consolation of Philosophy*, written in a mixture of prose and verse while in prison, argued that the soul can attain happiness in affliction by realizing the value of goodness and meditating on the reality of God. While drawing upon Stoicism and Neoplatonism its thought echoed Christian sentiments and exercised considerable influence throughout the Middle Ages, especially among the scholastic theologians. It was frequently translated into European languages; renderings into English include those by King Alfred, Chaucer, and Queen Elizabeth I.

boffin /'bɒfɪn/ n. (colloq.) a person engaged in (esp. secret) scientific research. [orig. unkn.]

bog n. a piece of wet spongy ground, especially on peat. — v.t. (-gg-; usu.in pass. with down) to stick fast in wet ground; to impede the progress of. —**bog myrtle,** a fragrant-leaved shrub found in bogs. **bog oak,** wood of oak etc. preserved in peat. —**boggy** adj. [f. Ir. or Gael. bogach]

bogey /'bəʊgɪ/ n. (in golf) a score of one stroke above par at a hole. [perh. f. BOGY as imaginary player]

boggle v.i. to take alarm or hesitate (at). [f. dial. bogle = BOGY]

bogie /'bəʊgɪ/ n. a wheeled undercarriage pivoted below a locomotive etc. [orig. unkn.]

Bogotá /bɒgə'tɑː/ the capital of Colombia, situated in the eastern Andes at 2,610 m (c.8,560 ft.); pop. (est. 1981) 4,486,200.

bogus /'bəʊgəs/ adj. sham, spurious. [orig. unkn.]

bogy /'bəʊgɪ/ n. an evil spirit; an object of dread. [orig. (Old) Bogey the Devil]

bogyman /'bəʊgɪmæn/ n. (pl. **-men**) a person (often imaginary) causing fear or difficulty. [f. prec.]

Bohemia /bəʊ'hi:mɪə/ an area of Czechoslovakia. A former Slavonic kingdom, it fell under Austrian rule in 1526, and by the Treaty of Versailles (1919) became a province of Czechoslovakia.

Bohemian /bəʊ'hi:mɪən/ adj. **1.** of Bohemia. **2.** of irregular and socially unconventional habits. —n. a person of Bohemian habits. [f. prec.]

Bohr /bɔ:(r)/, Niels Hendrik David (1885–1962), Danish physicist, one of the major early figures in the development of quantum physics. He worked with J. J. Thomson at Cambridge and with Rutherford at Manchester. Bohr's theory of the structure of the atom was a radical departure since it incorporated quantum theory for the first time, and is the basis for the present-day quantum mechanical models. He postulated that electrons orbited the nucleus at fixed distances, each orbit having a quantum (fixed amount) of energy, released (or absorbed) when electrons jumped from one quantum orbit to another. Taking the simplest case, the hydrogen atom, he could now account for the lines in its spectrum. In 1927 he proposed the principle of 'complementarity', that natural phenomena could be looked at in mutually exclusive ways, which accounted for the paradox of regarding subatomic particles both as waves and as particles. Bohr had returned to Copenhagen in 1916, and in the 1930s he was joined by Jewish and other physicists fleeing from Nazi persecution. In 1943, at risk of imprisonment as a patriot, he escaped from German-occupied Denmark and helped to develop the atomic bomb, working first in Britain and then in the USA. He became increasingly concerned about the human implications of atomic weapons and stressed the need for international co-operation in the study of the peaceful applications of atomic energy. Niels Bohr was awarded the 1922 Nobel Prize for physics for his contribution to atomic energy, and his son, Aage Niels Bohr (1922–) shared the 1975 Prize for his studies in the physics of the atomic nucleus.

boil[1] v.t./i. **1.** to bubble up (of liquid reaching the temperature at which it gives off vapour, or of the containing vessel); to bring to boiling-point; to cook or be cooked in boiling liquid, to subject to the heat of boiling liquid. **2.** (of the sea etc.) to seethe like boiling liquid. **3.** to be greatly disturbed by anger or other strong emotion. —n. the act or point of boiling. —**boil over** to spill over in boiling. [f. AF f. L bullire (bulla bubble)]

boil[2] n. an inflamed pus-filled swelling under the skin. [OE]

Boileau(-Despréaux) /'bwɑ:ləʊ despreɪ'əʊ/, Nicholas (1636–1711), French critic and poet, friend of Racine, Molière, and La Fontaine. His *Satires* appeared in 1666–1711, and his didactic poem, *Art Poétique* (1674, based on Horace's *Ars Poetica*) defining principles of composition and criticism, earned him international recognition as the legislator and model for French neo-classicism at its apogee. Boileau was less important as a poet than as a founder of French literary criticism, where his influence has been profound.

boiler n. **1.** a tank in which a house's hot water is stored; a closed vessel in which water is heated to supply steam for an engine etc. **2.** a large tub for boiling laundry. [f. BOIL[1]]

boiling-point n. **1.** the temperature at which a liquid begins to boil. **2.** a state of great anger or excitement. [f. BOIL[1]]

boisterous /'bɔɪstərəs/ adj. noisily exuberant; (of the wind or sea) stormy, turbulent. [orig. unkn.]

bold /bəʊld/ adj. **1.** confident and courageous, adventurous; shameless, impudent. **2.** standing out distinctly, conspicuous. —**bold face,** type with thick heavy lines. —**boldly** adv., **boldness** n. [OE]

bole n. the trunk of a tree. [f. ON]

bolero n. (pl. **-os**) **1.** /bə'leərəʊ/ a Spanish dance; the music for this. **2.** /'bɒlərəʊ/ a woman's short jacket with no front fastening (ill. DRESS). [Sp.]

Boleyn /bʊ'lɪn, 'bʊ-/, Anne (1507–36), second wife of Henry VIII and mother of Elizabeth I. Although the King had fallen deeply in love with Anne, and had divorced Catherine of Aragon in order to marry her, she fell from favour when she failed to provide him with the male heir he so desperately wanted. She was eventually executed because of suspected infidelities which were probably more the product of Henry's own suspicion, and of his desire for a new queen, than of any act of Anne's.

Bolivar /bɒlɪ'vɑ:(r)/, Simon (1783–1830), Venezuelan patriot and statesman, called 'the Liberator'. More than any other man Bolivar was responsible for the liberation of South America from Spanish rule. Although his military career was not without its failures, and although his dream of a South American federation was never realized, he liberated one area of the country after another and eventually had one country, Bolivia, named after him.

Bolivia /bə'lɪvɪə/ a land-locked country in South America; pop. approx. 6,000,000; official language, Spanish; capital, La Paz; legal capital and seat of the judiciary, Sucre. Bolivia's chief topographical feature is the Altiplano, the great central plateau between the two chains of the Andes, at an average height of 3,850 m (12,500 ft.) above sea-level. The main exports include tin and other minerals and natural gas; the coca plant, from the leaves of which cocaine is produced, grows freely. Oil is produced in quantities that are sufficient for home consumption. Part of the Inca empire, Bolivia became one of the most important parts of Spain's American empire following the discovery of major

The Body: 1

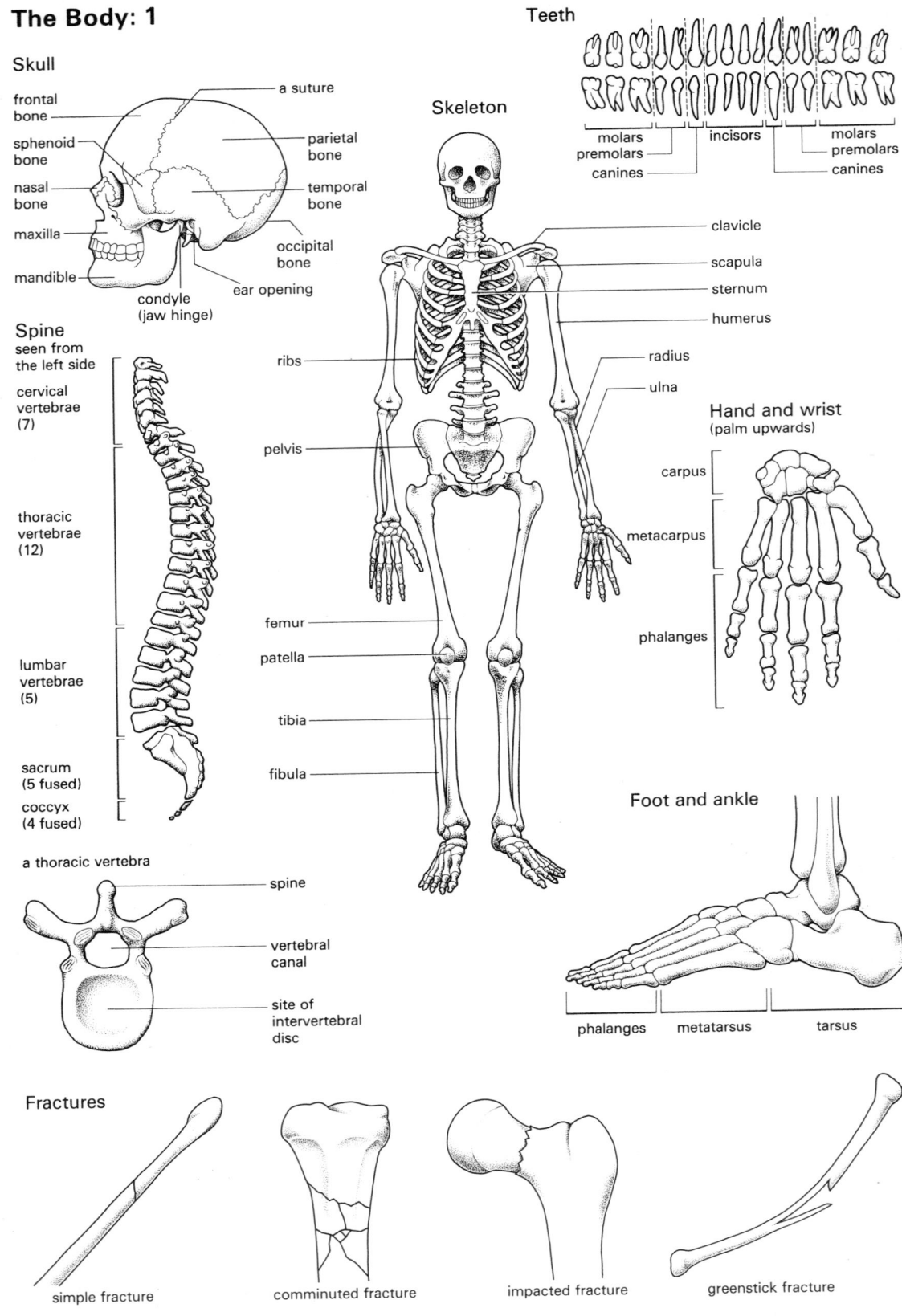

Skull

- frontal bone
- sphenoid bone
- nasal bone
- maxilla
- mandible
- a suture
- parietal bone
- temporal bone
- occipital bone
- ear opening
- condyle (jaw hinge)

Spine

seen from the left side

- cervical vertebrae (7)
- thoracic vertebrae (12)
- lumbar vertebrae (5)
- sacrum (5 fused)
- coccyx (4 fused)

a thoracic vertebra

- spine
- vertebral canal
- site of intervertebral disc

Teeth

- molars
- premolars
- canines
- incisors
- molars
- premolars
- canines

Skeleton

- clavicle
- scapula
- sternum
- humerus
- ribs
- radius
- ulna
- pelvis
- femur
- patella
- tibia
- fibula

Hand and wrist
(palm upwards)

- carpus
- metacarpus
- phalanges

Foot and ankle

- phalanges
- metatarsus
- tarsus

Fractures

- simple fracture
- comminuted fracture
- impacted fracture
- greenstick fracture

The Body: 2

Ball and socket joint

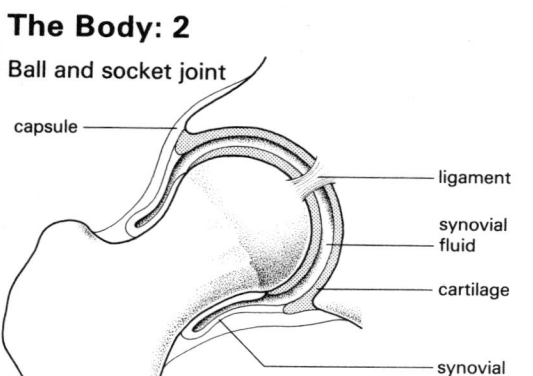

capsule

ligament

synovial fluid

cartilage

synovial membrane

Parts of a muscle

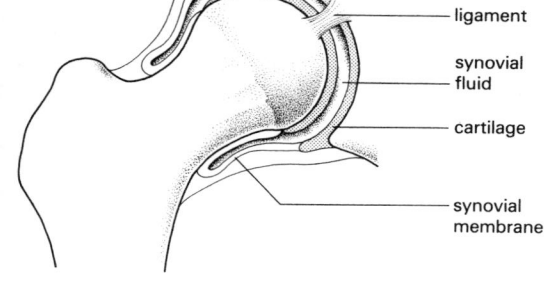

origin

body of muscle

tendon

insertion

Lower abdomen

male

spine   ureter

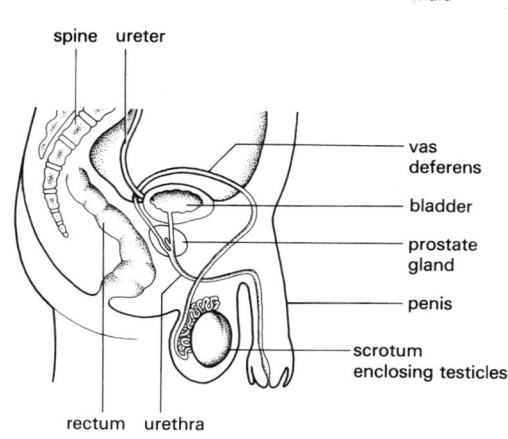

vas deferens

bladder

prostate gland

penis

scrotum enclosing testicles

rectum   urethra

female

spine   ovary

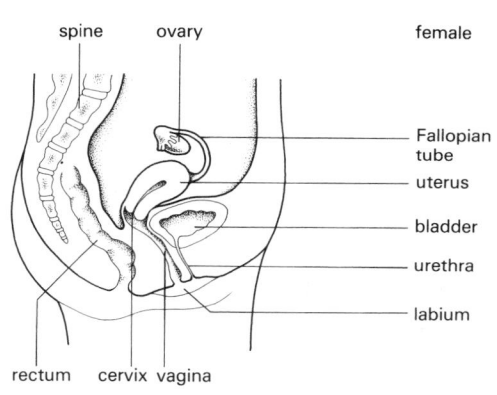

Fallopian tube

uterus

bladder

urethra

labium

rectum   cervix vagina

The alimentary canal

Nose, mouth, and throat

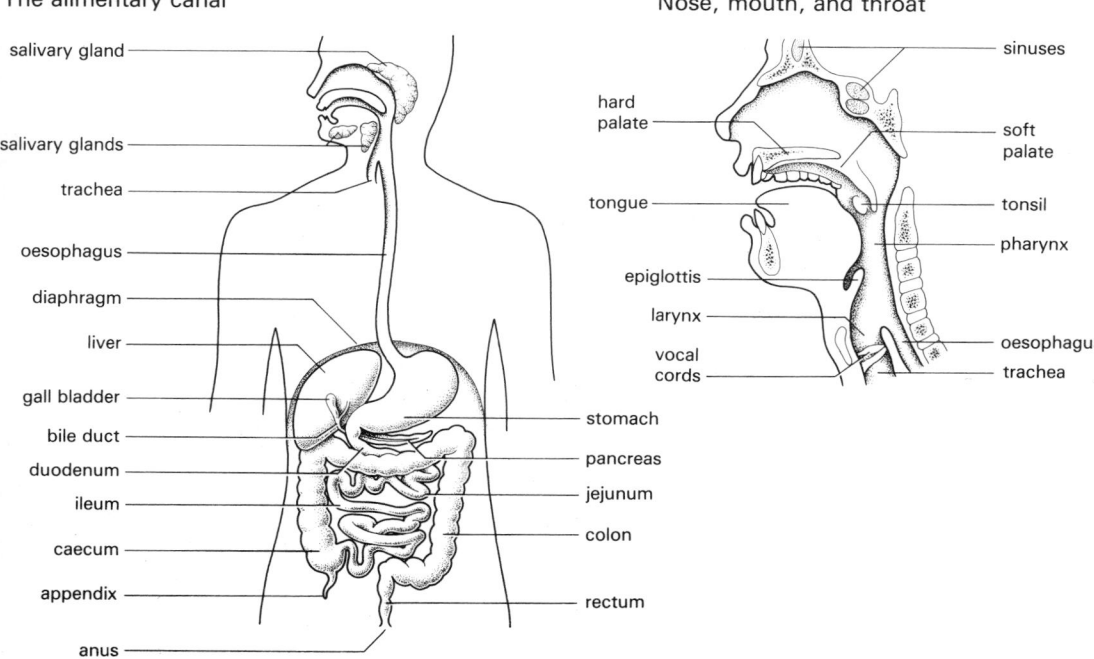

salivary gland

salivary glands

trachea

oesophagus

diaphragm

liver

gall bladder

bile duct

duodenum

ileum

caecum

appendix

anus

stomach

pancreas

jejunum

colon

rectum

sinuses

hard palate

soft palate

tongue

tonsil

pharynx

epiglottis

larynx

vocal cords

oesophagus

trachea

The Body: 3

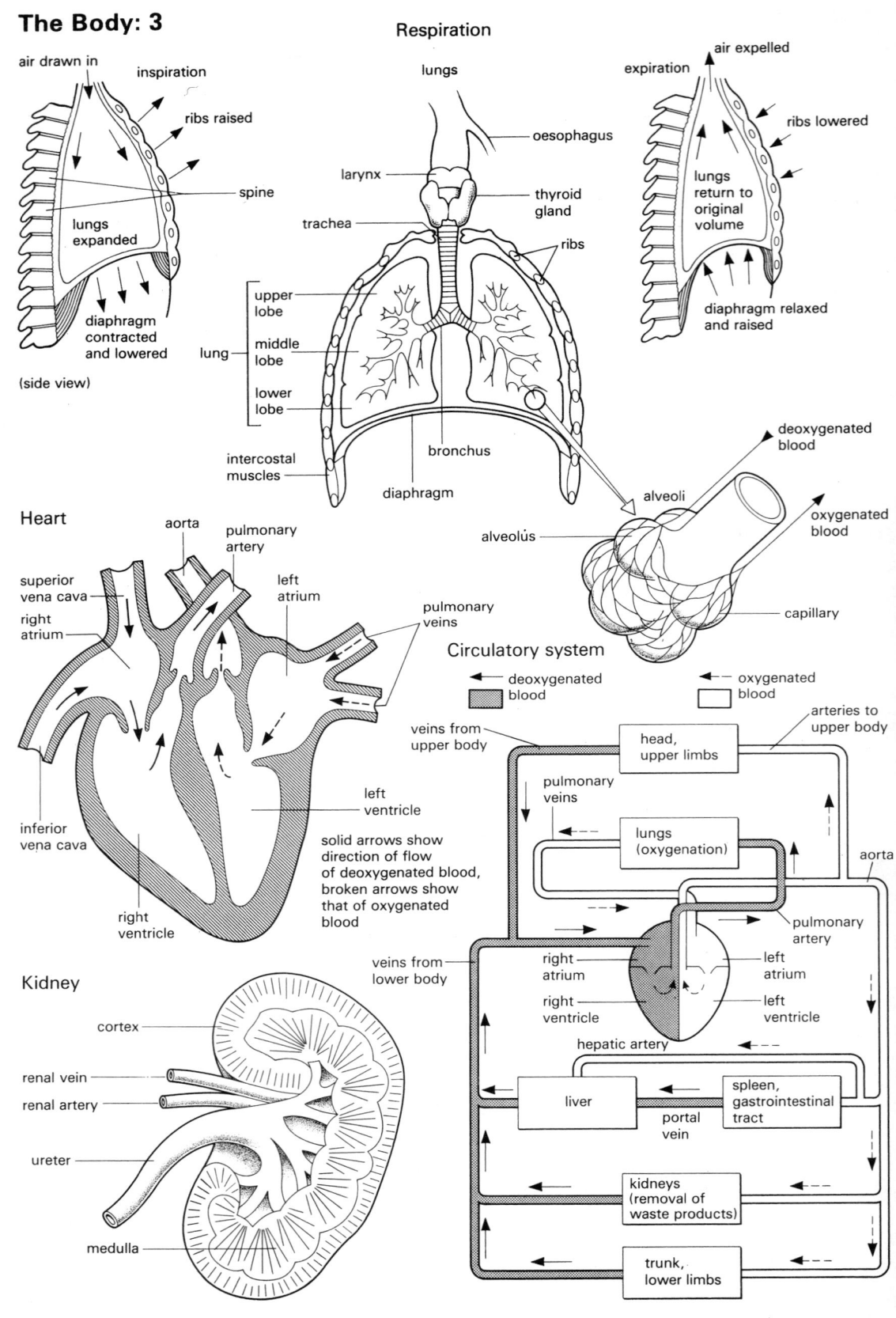

Respiration

air drawn in
inspiration
ribs raised
spine
lungs expanded
diaphragm contracted and lowered
(side view)

lungs
oesophagus
larynx
thyroid gland
trachea
ribs
upper lobe
middle lobe
lower lobe
lung
intercostal muscles
bronchus
diaphragm

expiration
air expelled
ribs lowered
lungs return to original volume
diaphragm relaxed and raised

deoxygenated blood
oxygenated blood
alveoli
alveolus
capillary

Heart

aorta
pulmonary artery
superior vena cava
right atrium
left atrium
pulmonary veins
inferior vena cava
left ventricle
right ventricle

solid arrows show direction of flow of deoxygenated blood, broken arrows show that of oxygenated blood

Circulatory system

deoxygenated blood
oxygenated blood

veins from upper body
pulmonary veins
head, upper limbs
arteries to upper body
lungs (oxygenation)
aorta
veins from lower body
right atrium
right ventricle
left atrium
left ventricle
pulmonary artery
hepatic artery
liver
portal vein
spleen, gastrointestinal tract
kidneys (removal of waste products)
trunk, lower limbs

Kidney

cortex
renal vein
renal artery
ureter
medulla

The Body: 4

Brain

frontal lobe

cerebrum

parietal lobe

occipital lobe

thalamus

optic nerve

pituitary gland

hypothalamus

cerebellum

pineal body

spinal cord

Tongue

pharyngeal part

oral part

bitter

sour

salt

sweet

papillae

areas for taste

Skin
(section)

sebaceous gland

hair

sweat pore

erector muscle

epidermis

dermis

pressure sensory receptor

subcutaneous fat

sweat gland

nerves

Fingerprints
(unique to each individual)

the six basic formations

double loop

tented loop

radial loop

arch

whorl

ulnar loop

Ear

ossicles

semicircular canals

auditory nerve

cochlea

eardrum

Eustachian tube

auricle (not to scale)

middle ear

inner ear

Eye

conjunctiva

eyelash

aqueous humour

cornea

iris

vitreous humour

pupil

lens

retina

blind spot

optic nerve

silver deposits soon after Pizarro's destruction of the Incas.
It was freed from the Spanish in 1825 and named after the
great liberator Bolivar, but since then it has been crippled
by endemic poverty and political instability, losing land
(including its Pacific coast) to surrounding countries in
19th- and early 20th-c. wars and suffering from almost
continual coups and changes of government. —**Bolivian**
adj. & n. [f. prec.]

boll/ bəʊl/ n. a round seed-vessel (of cotton, flax, etc.) —
boll-weevil n. a destructive insect infesting the cotton-
plant. [f. MDu. bolle, rel. to BOWL¹]

Bollandists /ˈbɒləndɪsts/ n.pl. the Jesuit editors of the Acta
Sanctorum, a critical edition of the lives of the saints, based
on authentic sources and first edited by John Bolland
(1596-1665).

bollard /ˈbɒləd/ n. 1. each of a line of short posts for keeping
traffic off a path etc. 2. a post on a ship or quay to which a
mooring rope may be tied. [perh. f. BOLE]

boloney /bəˈləʊnɪ/ n. (slang) nonsense. [orig. unkn.]

Bolshevik /ˈbɒlʃɪvɪk/ n. 1. a member of the wing of the
Social-Democratic party in Russia which, from 1903, favoured revolutionary tactics (see below). 2. (loosely) any socialist
extremist. —**Bolshevism** n., **Bolshevist** n. [Russ., =mem-
ber of the majority; cf. Menshevik]
  The Bolsheviks formed the majority faction of the Russian
Socialist Party, led by Lenin, advocating no co-operation
with moderate reformers and fomentation of revolution by
a small political élite prepared to shape the ideas of the
working class. After the successful overthrow of the Russian
government in 1917 they eventually succeeded in seizing
complete control of the country from the various other
revolutionary groups. In March 1918 they were renamed
the (Russian) Communist Party.

Bolshie /ˈbɒlʃɪ/ adj. (slang) 1. Bolshevik, left-wing. 2. rebellious, uncooperative. —n. (slang) a Bolshevik. [abbr.]

Bolshoi Ballet /ˈbɒlʃɔɪ/ a Moscow ballet company, the
most prestigious in the world, dating from 1776. The New
Bolshoi Petrovsky Theatre (the present Bolshoi Theatre)
opened in 1825 and by 1850 the company numbered 155
dancers. The first production of Swan Lake, with music
by Tchaikovsky, was given in 1877. After the October
Revolution the company was reorganized and new Soviet
ballets such as the The Red Poppy (1927) were introduced.
The company first appeared in London in 1956 and in New
York in 1959, and performs regularly at the Kremlin Palace
Theatre. [Russ., = great]

bolster /ˈbəʊlstə(r)/ n. 1. a long under-pillow across a bed.
2. a pad or support in a machine or instrument. —v.t. to
support or prop (up), to strengthen. [OE]

bolt¹ /bəʊlt/ n. 1. a bar sliding into a socket, for fastening a
door. 2. a heavy pin for holding metal plates etc. together,
usually secured with a nut. 3. an act of bolting. 4. a discharge
of lightning. 5. an arrow shot from a crossbow. —v.t./i 1.
to secure (a door) with bolts, to keep in or out by bolting a
door; to fasten together with metal bolts. 2. to eat (food)
very rapidly. 3. to dash off suddenly, (of a horse) to run off
out of control. 4. to run to seed prematurely. —**bolt-hole**
n. a means or place of escape. **bolt upright**, rigidly upright.
[OE]

bolt² /bəʊlt/ v.t. to sift (flour etc). [f. OF bul(e)ter (orig.
unkn.)]

Boltzmann /ˈbɒltsmən/, Ludwig (1844-1906), Austrian
physicist who made fundamental contributions to the
kinetic theory of gases, classical statistical mechanics, and
thermodynamics. He was one of the first European scientists
to recognize the importance of the electro-magnetic theory
of James Clerk Maxwell, but had difficulty in getting his
own work on statistical mechanics accepted until the new
discoveries in atomic physics at the turn of the century.
Boltzmann introduced the so-called Maxwell-Boltzmann
equation for the change in distribution of atoms due to
collisions, and he correlated entropy with probability when
he brought thermodynamics and molecular physics
together.

bomb /bɒm/ n. a destructive device containing explosive or
incendiary material, gas, etc., which is thrown, dropped
from an aircraft, or placed in position; **the bomb,** a nuclear
bomb as the ultimate weapon. —v.t. to attack with bombs,
especially from the air. [f. F, ult. f. Gk bombos loud
humming]

bombard /bɒmˈbɑːd/ v.t. 1. to attack persistently with
heavy guns. 2. to assail with questions, abuse, etc. 3.

(Physics) to direct a stream of high-speed particles at. —
bombardment n. [f. F (as prec.)]

bombardier /bɒmbəˈdɪə(r)/ n. 1. a non-commissioned
officer in the artillery. 2. (US) a person in an aircraft who
releases bombs. [f. F (as prec.)]

bombast /ˈbɒmbæst/ n. pompous or grandiloquent language. —**bombastic** /-ˈbæstɪk/ adj., **bombastically** adv. [f.
obs. bombace cotton wadding]

Bombay /bɒmˈbeɪ/ a city and port on the west coast of
India, that country's largest city and a commercial centre,
long noted for its textile industry; pop. 8,300,000.

Bombay duck a small fish eaten as a relish when dried,
especially with curry. [corrupt. of bombil, Marathi name of
the fish]

bombazine /ˈbɒmbəziːn/ n. a twilled worsted dress-
material, especially the black kind formerly much used for
mourning. [f. F ult. f. Gk (bombux silk)]

bomber /ˈbɒmə(r)/ n. 1. an aircraft used to drop bombs. 2.
a person using bombs illegally. [f. BOMB]

bombshell n. an overwhelming surprise or disappointment.

bona-fide /ˈbəʊnə ˈfaɪdɪ/ adj. genuine, sincere. —**bona fides**
/-iːz/, honest intention, sincerity. [L, = (in) good faith]

bonanza /bəˈnænzə/ n. a source of wealth or prosperity, an
unexpected success (orig. a mining term). [Sp., = fair
weather, prosperity]

Bonaparte /ˈbəʊnəpɑːt/ the name of a Corsican family
including the three French rulers named Napoleon.

Bonaventura /bɒnəvenˈtjʊərə/, St (1221-74) Giovanni di
Fidanza, a Franciscan theologian, the 'seraphic doctor',
from 1257 Minister General of his order, who wrote the
official biography of St Francis and had a lasting influence
as a spiritual writer. Feast day, 15 (formerly 14) July.

bon-bon n. a sweet. [F (bon good)]

Bond, James, a secret agent in the spy novels of Ian
Fleming.

bond n. 1. something that binds together or (usu. in pl.)
restrains. 2. a binding agreement; a deed by which a person
binds himself to pay another; a certificate issued by a
government or company, undertaking to repay borrowed
money together with any due interest. 3. the linkage of
atoms in a molecule. 4. any of various methods (English
bond, Flemish bond, etc.; ill. BUILDING) of holding a wall
together by making bricks overlap. —v.t. 1. to unite or
reinforce with a bond. 2. to place goods in bond. —**bond
(paper),** a high-quality writing paper. **in bond,** stored by
the Customs in special warehouses until the importer has
paid the duty. [var. of BAND¹]

bondage n. slavery, captivity; subjection to any constraining force. [f. OE bonda husbandman, later assoc. with BOND]

bonded adj. (of goods) placed in bond; (of warehouses)
containing such goods. [f. BOND]

bone n. 1. any of the hard pieces (other than teeth, nails,
and cartilage) making up the skeleton in vertebrates (see
below); (in pl.) a skeleton, especially as remains. 2. the
material of which bones consist or a similar substance. 3.
(in pl.) the basic essentials of a thing. —v.t. to remove the
bones from. —**bone china,** china made of clay mixed with
bone ash. **bone-dry** adj. completely dry. **bone-meal** n.
ground bones used as fertilizer. **bone of contention,** the
subject of a dispute. **bone-shaker** n. an old jolting vehicle;
(hist.) an early type of bicycle (see BICYCLE). **have a bone
to pick,** to have something to complain about or dispute
with. **make no bones about,** to admit or allow without
fuss. **to the bone,** to the bare minimum. [OE].
  The human skeleton is conventionally regarded as consisting of two main parts: the skull, spine, and ribs, which
support and protect body tissues and organs, and the limb
bones and their attachments which function in conjunction
with muscles as levers to provide movement. Bone itself is
a living tissue, composed of special cells which secrete
around them a material consisting of calcium salts (which
provide hardness and strength in compression) and collagen
fibres (which provide tensile strength); its formation is a
complex process, beginning in the embryo. The material
of bone varies considerably in density and compactness,
that near the surface of a bone generally being more
compact. Many bones have a central cavity containing
marrow, a tissue which is the source of most of the cells of
the blood and is also a site for the storage of fats. The
calcium salts in bone are crucial in the regulation of the
level of calcium throughout the body.

bonfire n. a large open-air fire. —**Bonfire Night,** that of

5 November, when bonfires are lit in memory of the Gunpowder Plot. [earlier *bonefire* = fire in which bones are burnt]

bongo /ˈbɒŋgəʊ/ *n.* (*pl.* **-os, -oes**) each of a pair of small drums usually held between the knees and beaten with the fingers. [Amer. Sp.]

bonhomie /ˈbɒnəmiː/ *n.* friendly geniality. [F (f. *bonhomme* good-natured man)]

Boniface /ˈbɒnɪfeɪs/, St (680–754), apostle of Germany, who laid the foundations of a settled ecclesiastical organization there. Originally named Wynfrith, he was born in Devon and went as a missionary to Frisia and Germany. His courage in felling the sacred oak of Thor won him instant success and many converts. In 741 he was given authority to reform the whole Frankish Church. The first papal legate north of the Alps, Boniface greatly assisted the spread of papal influence. He was martyred in Frisia. Feast day, 5 June.

Bonn /bɒn/ the capital of the Federal Republic of Germany, situated on the Rhine; pop. (1980) 288,100.

bonnet /ˈbɒnɪt/ *n.* **1.** an outdoor head-dress tied with strings below the chin, now chiefly worn by babies. **2.** a Scotch cap. **3.** a hinged cover over the engine of a motor vehicle. [f. OF *bonet* (orig. = the material of which caps were made)]

bonny /ˈbɒnɪ/ *adj.* (chiefly *Sc.*) **1.** handsome, healthy-looking. **2.** pleasant. —**Bonny Prince Charlie,** a romantic Jacobite name given to Charles Edward Stuart, elder son of the Stuart claimant to the British throne and leader of the 1745-6 Jacobite uprising. [perh. f. F *bon* good]

bonsai /ˈbɒnsaɪ/ *n.* an artificially dwarf potted tree or shrub; the method of growing these. [Jap.]

bonus /ˈbəʊnəs/ *n.* something paid or given in addition to the normal amount; an extra benefit. [L, = good]

bon voyage /bɔ̃ vwaːˈjaːʒ/ an expression of good wishes to someone beginning a journey. [F]

bony /ˈbəʊnɪ/ *adj.* of or like bone; thin with prominent bones; (of fish) having a skeleton of bone rather than cartilage (see FISH¹). —**boniness** *n.* [f. BONE]

bonze *n.* a Buddhist priest in Japan or adjacent countries. [f. F or Port. f. Jap.]

boo *int.* expressing disapproval or contempt. —*n.* the sound *boo.* —*v.t./i.* to utter boos, to jeer at. [imit.]

boob¹ *n.* (*slang*) **1.** a silly mistake. **2.** a foolish person. —*v.i.* (*slang*) to make a silly mistake. [f. BOOBY]

boob² *n.* (usu. in *pl.*; *slang*) a woman's breast. [f. earlier *bub,* *bubby*; cf. G dial. *bübbi* teat]

booby *n.* a stupid or childish person. —**booby prize,** a prize awarded to the person coming last in a contest. **booby trap,** a hidden trap rigged up for a practical joke; a disguised explosive device. **booby-trap** *v.t.* to place a booby trap in or on. [f. Sp. *bobo* f. L *balbus* stammering]

boogie-woogie /ˈbuːgɪˈwuːgɪ/ *n.* a style of playing blues on the piano, marked by persistent bass rhythm. [orig. unkn.]

book /bʊk/ *n.* **1.** a set of printed sheets bound together in a cover for reading; a written work intended for printing as a book. **2.** a bound set of blank sheets for writing notes, accounts, exercises, etc. in; (in *pl.*) a set of accounts. **3.** a series of cheques, stamps, tickets, etc., bound together like a book. **4.** a main division of a literary work, or of the Bible. **5.** a record of bets made. **6.** a libretto, the script of a play. —*v.t./i.* **1.** to enter the name of in a book or list; to record a charge against. **2.** to reserve in advance; to make a reservation. —**book club,** a society supplying its members with selected books on special terms. **book-ends** *n.* a pair of props designed to keep a row of unshelved books upright. **book in,** to register one's arrival at a hotel etc. **book-plate** *n.* a label with the owner's name etc. pasted at the front of a book. **book token,** a voucher exchangeable for books of a given value. **bring to book,** to call to account. **by the book,** strictly in accordance with regulations. [OE]

bookbinder *n.* one who binds books professionally. —**bookbinding** *n.*

bookcase *n.* a piece of furniture with shelves for books.

bookie /ˈbʊkɪ/ *n.* (*colloq.*) a bookmaker. [abbr.]

bookish /ˈbʊkɪʃ/ *adj.* addicted to reading; deriving one's knowledge from books, not from experience. [f. BOOK]

bookkeeper *n.* one who keeps accounts, especially as a profession. —**bookkeeping** *n.*

booklet /ˈbʊklɪt/ *n.* a small thin usually paper-covered book. [f. BOOK + -LET]

bookmaker *n.* a professional taker of bets. —**bookmaking** *n.*

bookmark *n.* a strip of card, leather, etc. inserted in a book to mark the reader's place.

Book of Common Prayer the official service book of the Church of England. It was compiled through the desire of Cranmer and others to simplify and condense the Latin service books of the medieval Church and produce in English a simple, convenient, and comprehensive guide for priest and people. It was first issued in 1549 under Edward VI, and its use ordered by Act of Parliament; after revision in the light of Protestant criticism it was reissued in 1552; abolished by the Catholic Queen Mary, reinstated under Elizabeth I (1559), it was again abolished (through Puritan objections), but revised and reissued in 1662, a version which remained almost unchanged until the 20th c.; a revised version was proposed in 1928. Measures of 1965 and 1974 authorized the use also of alternative services that follow forms sanctioned by the Church authorities, in an attempt to meet people's diverse spiritual needs, and the Alternative Service Book (issued in 1980) presents these services (in modern English) in their final form.

bookseller *n.* a dealer in books.

bookworm *n.* **1.** a person addicted to reading. **2.** a larva that feeds on paper etc. in books.

Boole /buːl/, George (1815-64), English mathematician, entirely self-taught, professor at Cork in Ireland from 1849 until his death. He wrote important works on differential equations and various other branches of mathematics, but is remembered chiefly for his development of an algebraic description of reasoning, now known as Boolean algebra. The branch of mathematics known as mathematical (or symbolic) logic developed mainly from his ideas.

boom¹ *n.* a deep resonant sound. —*v.i.* to make or speak with a boom. [imit.]

boom² *n.* a period of sudden prosperity or commercial activity. —*v.i.* to enjoy a boom. [perh. = BOOM¹]

boom³ *n.* **1.** a long pole fixed at one end to support the bottom of a sail, microphone, etc. (ill. SAILING-SHIPS). **2.** a barrier across a harbour. [f. Du., = BEAM]

boomerang /ˈbuːməræŋ/ *n.* **1.** a flat curved strip of wood, used by Australian Aborigines, usually of a kind that when thrown returns to the thrower. **2.** a scheme etc. that recoils unfavourably on its originator. —*v.i.* (of a scheme) to recoil thus. [Aboriginal]

boon¹ *n.* something to be thankful for, a blessing. [f. ON, = prayer]

boon² *adj.* **boon companion,** a pleasant sociable companion. [f. OF f. L *bonus* good]

Boone /buːn/, Daniel (c.1735-1820), American pioneer. Moving west from his native Pennsylvania, Boone made trips into the unexplored area of Kentucky from 1767 onwards, organizing settlements and successfully defending them against hostile Indians. He later moved further west to Missouri, being granted land there in 1799. As a hunter, trail-blazer, and fighter against the Indians he became a legend even during his own long life.

boor /bʊə(r)/ *n.* an ill-mannered person. —**boorish** *adj.,* **boorishness** *n.* [f. LDu.]

boost *v.t.* to increase the strength or reputation of; (*colloq.*) to push from below. —*n.* an act of boosting. [orig. unkn.]

booster *n.* a device for increasing voltage or signal strength; an auxiliary engine or rocket for initial acceleration; an injection etc. renewing the effect of an earlier one. [f. BOOST]

boot¹ *n.* **1.** an outer foot-covering, often of leather, coming above the ankle. **2.** a luggage compartment at the back of a car. —*v.t.* to kick. [f. ON]

boot² *n.* **to boot,** as well, into the bargain. [OE, = advantage]

bootee /buːˈtiː/ *n.* a baby's knitted or crocheted boot. [f. BOOT¹]

Boötes /bəʊˈəʊtiːz/ the Herdsman, a northern constellation containing Arcturus. [f. Gk, = ox-driver]

Booth /buːð/, William (1829-1912), founder of the Salvation Army. Of partly Jewish origin, he was for some time a Methodist revivalist preacher. He had a great love for the poor, whose souls he sought to save by his preaching while at the same time ministering to their bodily needs. Though he was ignorant of theology, the strength of his emotions and sympathies, combined with shrewd commercial sense, made the movement one of the most successful religious revivals of modern times.

booth /buːð/ *n.* a small temporary shelter for a stall etc.

at a market or fair; an enclosure or compartment for telephoning, voting, etc. [f. ON]

bootleg *adj.* smuggled, illicit (orig. of liquor so called because concealed in the boots). —**bootlegger** *n.*

bootless *adj.* unavailing. [f. BOOT² + -LESS]

booty /ˈbuːtɪ/ *n.* plunder gained in war etc., loot. [f. G, = exchange]

booze *n.* (*colloq.*) alcoholic drink. —*v.i.* (*colloq.*) to drink heavily. —**boozer** *n.*, **boozy** *adj.* [f. Du., = drink to excess]

bop *n.* bebop. [abbr.]

boracic /bəˈræsɪk/ *adj.* of borax. —**boracic acid,** boric acid. [f. BORAX]

borage /ˈbɒrɪdʒ/ *n.* a herb (*Borago officinalis*) with blue flowers and hairy leaves. [f. OF, ult. f. Arab., = father of sweat (from its use as a diaphoretic)]

borax /ˈbɔːræks/ *n.* a white powder, a compound of boron, used in making glass, enamels, and detergents. [f. OF, ult. f. Pers.]

Bordeaux /bɔːˈdəʊ/ *n.* red or white wine from the Bordeaux district of SW France; a similar wine from elsewhere.

border /ˈbɔːdə(r)/ *n.* **1.** an edge or boundary; the part near this. **2.** the dividing-line between two countries; the district on either side of this. **3.** a strip of ground round the edge of a garden. **4.** an edging to a garment etc. —*v.t./i.* **1.** to provide with a border; to serve as a border to. **2.** (with *on*) to adjoin; to come close to (a condition). —**the Border,** that between England and Scotland. [f. OF *bordure*, rel. to BOARD]

borderland *n.* **1.** the district near a border. **2.** a condition between two extremes. **3.** an area for debate.

borderline *n.* a boundary; the limit of a category etc. — *adj.* on or near the borderline.

Borders /ˈbɔːdəz/ a local government region in southern Scotland.

Bordone /bɔːˈdəʊnɪ/, Paris (1500-71), Venetian painter whose reputation in his own day rivalled that of Titian, under whom he may have studied. His chiaroscuro and rich colouring were highly praised and his popularity brought him commissions from all over Europe, but his works were too conventional and unoriginal for lasting fame.

bore¹ *v.t./i.* **1.** to make (a hole or well etc.), especially with a revolving tool; to make a hole (in) thus; to drill (the shaft of a well). **2.** to hollow out (a tube) evenly. **3.** (of a racehorse) to push another horse out of the way. —*n.* **1.** the hollow of a gun barrel or of the cylinder in an internal-combustion engine; its diameter. **2.** a borehole made to find water etc. [OE; cf. ON *bora* borehole]

bore² *v.t.* to weary by tedious talk or dullness. —*n.* a dull or wearisome person or thing. —**boredom** *n.*, **boring** *adj.* [orig. unkn.]

bore³ *n.* a high tidal wave with a steep front that occurs when two tides meet or when the spring flood tide rushes up a narrowing estuary. [f. Scand.]

bore⁴ *past* of BEAR¹.

borehole *n.* a deep hole bored in the ground especially to find water.

Borg /bɔːg/, Bjorn (1956-), Swedish tennis-player, who in 1980 won the men's singles championship at Wimbledon for the fifth year in succession, beating the record of three consecutive wins held by Fred Perry.

Borgia /ˈbɔːdʒə/ the name of an Italian noble family of Spanish origin, two of whose members rose to the papacy in the second half of the 15th c. as Calixtus III (d. 1458) and Alexander VI (d. 1503). The Borgias were much resented as foreigners in Italy and Alexander's son Cesare (*c.*1475-1507) gained a particularly bad reputation as a result of his attempts to establish himself as the ruler of central Italy. Though notorious for his violence and crimes he was an able soldier and an early believer in the unity of Italy. His sister Lucrezia (1480-1519) was associated by rumour with Cesare's crimes, and her second husband, Alfonso of Aragon, was murdered by his direction; she afterwards married Alfonso d'Este, heir of the Duke of Ferrara, and her court became a centre for artists, poets, and scholars.

boric acid /ˈbɔːrɪk/ an acid derived from borax, used as an antiseptic. [f. BORON]

Boris Godunov see GODUNOV.

Born /bɔːn/, Max (1882-1970), German theoretical physicist, one of the founders of quantum mechanics. In 1921 he was appointed professor of theoretical physics at Göttingen, where he established a powerful group of theoreticians, but

in 1933, being a Jew, he had to flee the Nazi régime and settled in Britain. After retirement from the chair of natural philosophy at Edinburgh University he returned to Göttingen to write mainly on the philosophy of physics and the social responsibility of scientists. He provided a link between wave mechanics and quantum theory by postulating a probabilistic interpretation of Schrödinger's wave equation, for which he was awarded the Nobel Prize for physics in 1954. He wrote extremely popular textbooks on optics and atomic physics.

born¹ *p.p.* of BEAR¹. —*adj.* **1.** existing as a result of birth. **2.** qualified by natural disposition or ability. **3.** destined or of a certain status or origin by birth. —**born of,** owing its origin to.

-borne *adj.* with prefixed noun in sense 'carried or transported by'. [*p.p.* of BEAR¹]

Borneo /ˈbɔːnɪəʊ/ a large island of the Malay archipelago, comprising Kalimantan (a region of Indonesia), Sabah and Sarawak (now parts of Malaysia), and Brunei. —**Bornean** *adj.*

Borodin /ˈbɒrədɪn/, Alexander (1833-87), Russian composer (illegitimate son of a Russian prince), one of the group known as 'The Five' or 'The Mighty Handful' (the others were Balakirev, Musorgsky, Rimsky-Korsakov, and Cui). He earned his living as a scientist, but showed early musical talent. He composed symphonies, string quartets, songs, and piano music, but is best known for the epic opera *Prince Igor* (completed after his death by Rimsky-Korsakov and Glazunov).

boron /ˈbɔːrɒn/ *n.* a non-metallic element, symbol B, atomic number 5, which can exist in crystalline form or as a brown powder. The element, which is not found in the free state in nature, was first isolated by Sir Humphrey Davy in 1807. Boron and its compounds have a wide variety of specialized industrial uses, and trace amounts of it are essential to the growth of plants. [f. BORAX w. ending of *carbon*, which it resembles in some respects]

borough /ˈbʌrə/ *n.* **1.** an administrative division of London or of New York City; a territorial division in Alaska, corresponding to a county. **2.** a town with a corporation and with privileges conferred by royal charter or defined by statute; (*hist.*) a town sending representatives to Parliament. —**pocket borough,** (*hist.*) a borough where elections were controlled by a wealthy private person or family. **rotten borough,** (in the 19th c.) a borough that was still represented by an MP although the population had become severely reduced in numbers. The choice of MP was often in the hands of one person or family. Such boroughs were abolished by the Reform Act of 1832. [OE; orig. = fortress, fortified town]

Borromini /bɒrəˈmiːnɪ/, Francesco (1599-1667), Italian architect, one of the leading figures of Roman baroque. His style, at once passionate and mathematical, using subtle architectural forms but austere methods of decoration, was of tremendous importance in the development of the baroque in Italy, and even more in Austria and South Germany; it was repeatedly denounced in the 18th-19th c. Arriving at Rome in 1614, he worked as a mason at St Peter's, and on the Palazzo Barberini with Maderna and Bernini. Always neurotic, he committed suicide in a fit of melancholia.

Borrow /ˈbɒrəʊ/, George (1803-81), English writer whose travels in England, Europe, Russia, and the East provided material, inextricably combined with fiction, for his picaresque narrative *Lavengro* (1851) in which he meets gypsies, tinkers, and murderers and describes much of his comparative study of the languages of the countries he visits. He continues his adventures in *The Romany Rye* (1857), and *The Bible in Spain* (1843) gives a vivid account of a country racked by Civil War during the author's travels as a distributor of Bibles.

borrow /ˈbɒrəʊ/ *v.t./i.* to get the temporary use of (a thing) on condition that it is returned; to obtain money thus; to adopt or use (ideas etc. of another). [OE]

Borstal /ˈbɔːst(ə)l/ *n.* the former name for an institution for reforming and training young offenders. [f. *Borstal* in Kent]

bortsch /bɔːtʃ/ *n.* a highly seasoned Russian or Polish soup of various ingredients including beetroot and cabbage. [f. Russ. *borshch*]

borzoi /ˈbɔːzɔɪ/ *n.* a large Russian wolfhound with a narrow head and silky coat. [Russ., = swift]

Bosch /bɒʃ/, Hieronymus (*c.*1450-1516), Dutch painter who took his name from his birthplace ('s Hertogenbosch), a strangely individual figure whose style has little in common with the mainstream of painting in the Low Countries. His works are characterized by creatures of fantasy, half-human half-animal, and demons, interspersed with human figures in a setting of imaginary architecture and landscape; his basic themes show an innocent central figure (Christ or a saint) besieged by horrific representations of evil and temptation, or stress in morbid vein the fearful consequences of human sin and folly. His turbulent and grotesque fantasy has appealed to modern taste and caused the surrealists to claim him as the forerunner of their school.

bosh *n. & int. (slang)* nonsense. [f. Turk., = empty]

Boskop /ˈbɒskɒp/ a town in the Transvaal, South Africa, where a skull dome was found in 1913. The fossil itself is undated and morphologically shows no primitive features. At the time of discovery, this find became the type-fossil of a distinct 'Boskop race' but is now thought to be related to the Bushman-Hottentot types.

bos'n /ˈbəʊs(ə)n/ contr. of BOATSWAIN.

Bosnia and Hercegovina /ˈbɒznɪə, hɜːtsɪɡəˈviːnə/ a constituent republic of Yugoslavia. —**Bosnian** *adj. & n.*

bosom /ˈbʊz(ə)m/ *n.* the breast, especially of a woman, or the part of a dress covering it; the enclosing space formed by the breast and arms. —**bosom friend,** an intimate friend. [OE]

boson /ˈbəʊzɒn/ *n.* a particle obeying the relations stated by Bose and Einstein, with integral spin. [f. S. N. *Bose,* Indian physicist (d. 1974)]

Bosporus /ˈbɒspərəs/ a strait connecting the Black Sea and the Sea of Marmara, with Istanbul at its south end. It separates Europe from Asia Minor, and is spanned by one of the world's longest suspension bridges.

boss[1] *n. (colloq.)* an employer or manager. —*v.t. (colloq.)* to be the boss of; to order *about.* [f. Du. *baas* master]

boss[2] *n.* a round projecting knob or stud, as in the centre of a shield; a carved projection where ribs of vaulting cross. [f. OF; orig. unkn.]

boss-eyed *adj.* cross-eyed, having only one good eye. [f. *boss* miss a shot; orig. unkn.]

bossy *adj. (colloq)* fond of ordering people about. —**bossiness** *n.* [f. BOSS[1]]

Boston /ˈbɒst(ə)n/ the capital city and a seaport of Massachusetts; pop. (1982) 560,847. It was founded *c.*1630 and named after Boston in Lincolnshire ('St Botulph's town'), which has associations with the Pilgrim Fathers. —**Boston tea-party,** a violent demonstration by American colonists who in 1773 boarded vessels moored in the harbour of Boston, Massachusetts, dressed as Red Indians, and threw the cargoes of tea into the water in protest at the imposition of a tax on tea by the British Parliament, in which the colonists had no representation. It occasioned the general revolt of the American colonies and the War of Independence.

bosun, bo'sun /ˈbəʊs(ə)n/ contr. of BOATSWAIN.

Boswell /ˈbɒzwəl/, James (1740–95), Scottish author and biographer. After travelling through Europe, where he met Rousseau and Voltaire, he practised law in England and Scotland, though his ambitions were directed towards literature and politics. A visit to Corsica in 1765 inspired him with zeal for the cause of Corsican liberty and resulted in his first substantial work, *An Account of Corsica* (1768). He first met Johnson in London (1762–3) and Boswell's *Journal of a Tour to the Hebrides* (1785) describes their travels together in 1773. The rest of his life was devoted to an unsuccessful pursuit of a political career and to assembling material for the most celebrated biography in the English language, *The Life of Samuel Johnson* (1791), which gives a vivid and intimate portrait of Johnson and an invaluable panorama of the age and its personalities, presented with the curious mix of naïve enthusiasm and sad worldliness that is the essential Boswell.

Bosworth Field /ˈbɒzwəθ/ the scene, near Market Bosworth in Leicestershire, of a battle (1485) in the Wars of the Roses, at which Henry Tudor defeated the Yorkist king Richard III, who died there. The battle is generally considered to mark the end of the Wars of the Roses, but Henry, crowned soon afterwards as Henry VII, was not really secure until a last Yorkist challenge was crushed at the battle of Stoke two years later.

botanize /ˈbɒtənaɪz/ *v.i.* to collect or study plants. [f. foll.]

botany /ˈbɒtənɪ/ *n.* the science of the structure, physiology, classification, and distribution of plants. —**botanical** /bəˈtænɪk(ə)l/ *adj.* [f. F or L f. Gk (*botanē* plant)]
The study of plants has a long history: Theophrastus (*c.*300 BC) wrote about their form and function, and they remained of interest thereafter, especially because of their medicinal properties. John Ray (1627–1705) produced the first systematic account of English flora, and by the mid-18th c. Linnaeus had devised a systematic method of naming and classifying plants which is still used (though modified) today. Study of plant anatomy developed in the 17th c., and of plant physiology a century later, with important advances such as the discovery of photosynthesis. In the 20th c. botanical studies have contributed much to the development of agriculture and horticulture with discoveries such as plant hormones (widely used to accelerate or delay growth and the fruiting of crop plants), systematic breeding techniques, and advances in the understanding of plant biology and pathology.

Botany Bay a bay near Sydney, New South Wales, Australia, which was the site of Captain Cook's landing in 1770 and of an early penal settlement. Its name refers to the variety of its plant life.

botch *v.t.* to bungle, to do badly; to patch or put together clumsily. —*n.* bungled or spoilt work. [orig. unkn.]

both /bəʊθ/ *adj. & pron.* the two, not only one. —*adv.* with equal truth in two cases. [f. ON]

Botha /ˈbəʊtə/, Louis (1862–1919), South African soldier and statesman. One of the most successful Boer leaders in the Boer War, Botha became commander-in-chief in 1900 and waged guerrilla warfare against the more numerous British forces until the war ended. In 1910 he became the first President of the Union of South Africa, holding the post until his death.

bother /ˈbɒðə(r)/ *v.t./i.* **1.** to give trouble, worry, or annoyance to. **2.** to take trouble. **3.** to concern oneself *with.* —*n.* a person or thing causing bother. [orig. unkn.]

bothersome /ˈbɒðəsəm/ *adj.* troublesome. [f. prec. + -SOME]

Bothwell /ˈbɒθwel/, James Hepburn, 4th Earl of (*c.*1536–78), third husband of Mary Queen of Scots. He was implicated in the murder of Darnley.

bo-tree /ˈbəʊtriː/ *n.* the Buddhist name for a large Indian fig-tree (*Ficus religiosa*) related to the banyan, sometimes worshipped as a symbol of the Buddha since he attained nirvana beneath such a tree. [Sinhalese *bo* (Skr. *boahi* perfect knowledge)]

Botswana /bɒtˈswɑːnə/ an inland country of southern Africa, a member State of the Commonwealth; pop. (1981) approx. 937,000; official language, English; capital, Gaborone. The area was made the British Protectorate of Bechuanaland in 1885. In 1966 it became a republic within the Commonwealth under the presidency of Sir Seretse Khama. Cattle-raising is the chief industry, though minerals (including diamonds, copper, nickel, and coal) were discovered in the 1960s and are becoming increasingly important as exports.

Botticelli /bɒtɪˈtʃelɪ/, Alessandro di Mariano Filipepi (1445–1510), called Sandro, Florentine painter. A pupil of Filippo Lippi, he had his own studio by 1470 and enjoyed the patronage of the Medici from 1475. His mythological paintings such as *Primavera* (*c.*1478) and *The Birth of Venus* (*c.*1480) show the influence of Neoplatonic philosophy derived from Lorenzo de' Medici's circle. The preaching of Savonarola in the 1490s is said by Vasari to have altered the course of his art, which became increasingly ecstatic, intense, and mannered (e.g. in *Mystic Nativity,* 1500). During his lifetime his reputation was apparently restricted to a small circle and he died in obscurity. His fame was resurrected in the second half of the 19th c., when the Pre-Raphaelites imitated his now elongated figures, Ruskin sang his praises, and Walter Pater wrote eloquently of him.

bottle *n.* **1.** a narrow-necked glass or plastic container for storing liquid; the amount that will fill it. **2.** a hot-water bottle. **3.** a baby's feeding-bottle. **4.** *(slang)* courage. —*v.t.* **1.** to seal or store in bottles or jars. **2.** (with *up*) to confine; to restrain (feelings etc.). —**bottle-brush** *n.* a cylindrical brush for cleaning inside bottles; any of various plants with flowers of this shape. **bottle-green** *adj.* dark green. **bottle-neck** *n.* a narrow stretch of road where traffic cannot flow freely. **bottle-party** *n.* one to which each guest brings a bottle of drink. [f. OF, rel. to BUTT[4]]

bottom /ˈbɒtəm/ *n.* **1.** the lowest part of anything, that on which it rests; the buttocks. **2.** the lowest or most distant point; the less honourable end of a table, class, etc. **3.** the ground under a stretch of water. **4.** a ship's keel or hull; a ship. —*adj.* lowest in position, rank, or degree. —*v.t./i.* **1.** to provide with a bottom. **2.** (of prices, usu. with *out*) to reach the lowest level. —**at bottom,** basically. **bottom line,** the amount of total assets after profit and loss etc. are calculated; (*fig.*) the essential thing. **get to the bottom of,** to find the real cause of. [OE]

botulism /ˈbɒtjʊlɪz(ə)m/ *n.* poisoning by a bacillus found in inadequately preserved food etc. [f. L *botulus* sausage]

Boucher /ˈbuːʃeɪ/, François (1703-70), French painter and decorative artist whose elegant, often frivolous, works sum up the spirit of the rococo style in France. As protégé of Mme de Pompadour and her brother the Marquis de Marigny, Boucher enjoyed both royal and aristocratic patronage; in 1755 he was appointed director of the Gobelins tapestry factory and, in 1765, King's Painter. In the spirit of Watteau, Boucher displayed little interest in the grand manner, preferring to paint light-hearted mythological subjects and *scènes galantes*. His art reflected the elegant social life of the period, his output ranging from large decorative paintings, popular engravings, tapestry design, and décors for the opera, to minor commissions such as the painting of fans and slippers. Boucher's artificial, rather frivolous subject-matter was by no means universally admired, incurring for example the disapproval of Diderot, who found his work lacking in *la vérité*.

Boucher de Perthes /buːʃeɪ də pert/, Jacques (1788-1868), French antiquarian who produced some of the first evidence of man-made stone tools in association with the bones of extinct (Pleistocene) animals from the valley of the River Somme in northern France. In the decade following 1837 he argued that these tools (and their makers) belonged to a remote pre-Celtic 'antediluvian' age, but it was not until the 1850s, when geologists supported his claims, that his findings were accepted.

bouclé /ˈbuːkleɪ/ *n.* yarn with looped or curled ply; a fabric made from this. [F, = curled]

Boudicca /ˈbuːdɪkə/ (pop. *Boadicea*, d. AD 62) a queen of the ancient Britons, ruler of the Iceni tribe in eastern England. She led her forces in revolt against the Romans and sacked Colchester, St Albans, and London before being completely defeated by the Roman governor Paulinus. Boudicca committed suicide soon after her defeat, but her name became a symbol of native resistance to the Roman occupation.

boudoir /ˈbuːdwɑː(r)/ *n.* a woman's private room. [F (*bouder* sulk)]

bougainvillaea /buːɡənˈvɪlɪə/ *n.* a tropical shrub of the genus *Bougainvillaea*, with large coloured bracts. [f. foll.]

Bougainville /ˈbuːɡənvɪl/, Louis Antoine de (1729-1811), French explorer. After a distinguished early military career, most notably as aide-de-camp to Montcalm during the unsuccessful defence of French Canada in 1759, Bougainville joined the French Navy and between 1766 and 1769 led the first successful French circumnavigation of the globe, visiting many of the islands of the South Pacific and compiling an invaluable scientific record of his findings. Afterwards he served in the American Revolution before retiring to devote himself to science. The largest of the Solomon Islands is named after him.

bouget /ˈbuːʒeɪ/ *n.* (in heraldry) a representation of an ancient water-vessel (ill. HERALDRY). [earlier spelling of BUDGET]

bough /baʊ/ *n.* any of the main branches of a tree. [OE]

bought *past* & *p.p.* of BUY.

bouillon /ˈbuːjɔ̃/ *n.* thin clear soup. [F (*bouillir* boil)]

boulder /ˈbəʊldə(r)/ *n.* a large stone worn smooth by weather or water. [f. Scand.]

boulevard /ˈbuːləvɑːd/ *n.* a broad often tree-lined street (in France etc.); (*US*) a broad main road. [F. f. G, = bulwark (orig. of promenade on demolished fortification)]

Boulez /ˈbuːlez/, Pierre (1925-), French composer and conductor who introduced to French audiences not only modern composers but also music of the Renaissance and baroque periods. In 1976 he became director of the French government's research institute into techniques of modern composition, and in his own works explored thoroughly and imaginatively the possibilities of serial music and of aleatory procedures. His use of instruments, both traditional and electronic, is brilliantly effective.

boult var. of BOLT².

Boulting /ˈbəʊltɪŋ/, John (1913-85) and Roy (1913-), twin brothers who worked together, interchanging responsibilities as film producer and director. They made a number of memorable films, including *Brighton Rock* (1947) and *Seven Days to Noon* (1950). From the late 1950s their main output was comedy and farce, including *Private's Progress* (1956) and *I'm All Right Jack* (1959).

Boulton /ˈbəʊlt(ə)n/, Matthew (1728-1809), pioneer, with his partner James Watt, in the manufacture of steam-engines, providing the commercial expertise, optimism, and capacity for achievement necessary for such engines to succeed on a large scale.

bounce *v.t./i.* 1. to rebound or cause to rebound; (*slang*, of a cheque) to be returned by the bank as worthless. 2. to rush noisily or boisterously. —*n.* 1. an act or the power of bouncing. 2. a self-confident manner, swagger. —**bouncy** *adj.* [orig. unkn.]

bouncer *n.* 1. a bumper in cricket. 2. a person employed to eject troublesome people from a night-club etc. [f. prec.]

bouncing *adj.* (usu. of a baby) big and healthy. [f. BOUNCE]

bound¹ *v.i.* to spring or leap, to move by leaps; (of a ball etc.) to recoil from a wall or the ground. —*n.* a springy upward or forward movement; the recoil of a ball etc. [f. AF, orig. = resound]

bound² *n.* (usu. in *pl.*) the limit of a territory; a limitation, a restriction. —*v.t.* to set bounds to; to be the boundary of. —**beat the bounds,** see BEAT¹. **out of bounds,** beyond one's permitted area. [f. AF. f. L; orig. unkn.]

bound³ *adj.* heading *for* a place or in a given direction. [f. ON, = ready]

bound⁴ *p.p.* of BIND. —*adj.* 1. obliged by law or duty *to*; certain *to*. 2. tied or fastened. —**bound up with,** closely associated with.

boundary /ˈbaʊndərɪ/ *n.* 1. a line marking the limit of land etc. 2. (in cricket) the limit of the field; a hit to this, scoring 4 or 6 runs. —**boundary layer,** the layer of fluid adjacent to the surface of a moving body, or of air to an aircraft in motion. [F. BOUND²]

bounden /ˈbaʊnd(ə)n/ *adj.* (of duty etc.) obligatory. [archaic p.p. of BIND]

boundless *adj.* unlimited. [f. BOUND² + -LESS]

bountiful /ˈbaʊntɪfʊl/ *adj.* 1. generous in giving. 2. ample. [f. BOUNTY]

Bounty /ˈbaʊntɪ/ HMS *Bounty* was bound from Tahiti to the Cape of Good Hope and the West Indies when on 28 April 1789 part of the crew mutinied against their commander, Lieutenant Bligh, either because he was an unduly stern disciplinarian or (more probably) because of the attractions of the women and way of life of the South Sea Islands. Bligh and 18 companions, set adrift in an open boat, succeeded in reaching Timor in the East Indies, nearly 6,400 km (4,000 miles) away. The mutineers returned to Tahiti whence some of them went on to Pitcairn Island, founding a settlement there which was not discovered until 1808; this was eventually adopted by the British government as a colony.

bounty /ˈbaʊntɪ/ *n.* 1. liberality in giving; a generous gift. 2. a sum paid as an official reward, especially by the State. [f. OF f. L (*bonus* good)]

bouquet /buːˈkeɪ/ *n.* 1. a bunch of flowers for carrying in the hand. 2. a compliment. 3. the perfume of a wine. — **bouquet garni** /ˈɡɑːniː/, a bunch or bag of mixed herbs for flavouring a stew etc. [F, f. OF *bois* wood]

Bourbaki /buəˈbɑːkɪ/, Nicolas. The pseudonym under which a group of mathematicians, mainly French, have been attempting to publish a complete account of the foundations of all known pure mathematics. Their approach is highly abstract and strictly axiomatic in style and spirit, intending to lay bare the structure of the entire field. Volumes in different areas of mathematics have been appearing since 1939 and, in spite of their idiosyncrasies, have been highly influential among mathematicians.

Bourbon /ˈbuəbən/ the surname of a branch of the royal family of France, who became the ruling monarchs when Henry IV succeeded to the throne in 1589 and reached the peak of their power under Louis XIV in the late 17th c. The last Bourbon king was Louis Philippe, and the French monarchy came to an end when he was overthrown in 1848. Members of this family became kings of Spain (1700-1931) and of Naples.

bourbon /ˈbɜːbən/ *n.* (*US*) whisky distilled from maize and rye. [f. *Bourbon* County, Kentucky, where first made]

bourgeois /ˈbuəʒwɑː/ *adj.* of or associated with the middle classes; conventional, materialistic. —*n.* a bourgeois person. [F, = BURGESS]

bourgeoisie /buəʒwɑːˈziː/ *n.* (usu. *derog.*) the bourgeois class. [F. (f. prec.)]

bourn /buən/ *n.* a small stream. [S. Engl. var. of BURN²]

bourne /bɔːn/ *n.* (*archaic*) a limit. [f. F *borne* f. OF *bodne*, = BOUND²]

bourse /buəs/ *n.* a money-market; **Bourse,** the Paris equivalent of the Stock Exchange. [F, = purse, f. L *bursa*]

bout *n.* **1.** a turn or spell of an activity; an attack *of* an illness. **2.** a boxing or wrestling match. [f. obs. *bought* bending]

boutique /buːˈtiːk/ *n.* a small shop or department selling clothes and other items of fashion. [F]

bouzouki /buːˈzuːkɪ/ *n.* a Greek stringed instrument of the lute family, plucked with a plectrum, played in popular music. [mod. Gk]

bovine /ˈbəʊvaɪn/ *adj.* of or like an ox; dull, stupid. [f. L (*bos* ox)]

bow¹ /bəʊ/ *n.* **1.** a shallow curve or bend; a thing of this form. **2.** a weapon for shooting arrows, with string stretched across the ends of a curved piece of wood etc. **3.** a flexible stick with stretched horsehair for playing a violin etc. (ill. ORCHESTRA). **4.** a knot made with a loop or loops, a ribbon etc. so tied. —*v.t.* to use the bow on (a violin etc., or *abs.*). — **bow-legged** *adj.* having bandy legs. **bow-tie** *n.* a necktie tied in a bow. **bow-window** *n.* a curved bay window. [OE]

bow² /baʊ/ *v.t./i.* **1.** to incline the head or body, especially in formal salutation; to incline (the head) thus. **2.** to cause to bend under a weight. —*n.* an act of bowing. —**bow and scrape,** to be obsequiously polite. **take a bow,** to acknowledge applause. [OE]

bow³ /baʊ/ *n.* (often in *pl.*) the fore-end of a boat or ship; the rower nearest the bow. [f. LG or Du., rel. to BOUGH]

bowdlerize /ˈbaʊdləraɪz/ *v.t.* to expurgate (a book or author). —**bowdlerization** /-ˈzeɪʃ(ə)n/ *n.* [f. T. *Bowdler,* who in 1818 published an expurgated edition of Shakespeare]

bowel /ˈbaʊəl/ *n.* a division of the alimentary canal below the stomach, the intestine; (in *pl.*) innermost parts. [f. OF f. L (dim. of *botulus* sausage)]

Bowen /ˈbəʊɪn/, Elizabeth Dorothea Cole (1899–1973), Anglo-Irish novelist and writer of short stories. Her skill in describing landscape (urban and rural) and her sensibility to changes of light and atmosphere are distinguishing features of her prose; she wrote most confidently within a middle- and upper-middle-class social range. Among her best-known novels are *The Death of the Heart* (1938), and *The Heat of the Day* (1949) which centres on a tragic wartime love affair.

bower /ˈbaʊə(r)/ *n.* a leafy shelter, an arbour. —**bower-bird** *n.* any of various passerine birds natie to Australia and New Guinea, the males of which build decorated 'bowers' during courtship. [OE, = dwelling]

bowie /ˈbəʊɪ/ *n.* (in full **bowie knife**) a long hunting-knife with a double-edged point. [f. J. *Bowie* Amer. soldier (d. 1836)]

bowl¹ /bəʊl/ *n.* **1.** a round open vessel for food or liquid. **2.** the rounded part of a tobacco-pipe, spoon, etc. **3.** the contents of a bowl. **4.** (*US*) an outdoor stadium (orig. bowl-shaped) for football. [OE]

bowl² /bəʊl/ *n.* a hard ball weighted or shaped so as to run in a curve; (in *pl.*) see BOWLS. —*v.t.* **1.** to play bowls; to roll (a ball etc.) along the ground. **2.** (in cricket) to deliver (a ball); to dismiss (a batsman) by delivering a ball that hits the wicket. **2.** to move (*along*) rapidly in a vehicle etc. — **bowling-alley** *n.* one of a series of enclosed channels for playing skittles; a building containing these. **bowling-green** *n.* a lawn for playing bowls. **bowl over,** to knock down; to amaze or disconcert. [f. F f. L *bulla* bubble]

bowler¹ /ˈbəʊlə(r)/ *n.* **1.** one who plays bowls. **2.** (in cricket) the player who delivers the ball. [f. BOWL²]

bowler² /ˈbəʊlə(r)/ *n.* a stiff felt hat with a rounded crown (ill. DRESS). [f. J. *Bowler,* London hatter who designed it, 1850]

bowline /ˈbəʊlɪn/ *n.* **1.** a rope from a ship's bow keeping the sail taut against the wind. **2.** a knot forming a non-slipping loop at the end of a rope. [f. BOW³ + LINE]

bowling /ˈbəʊlɪŋ/ *n.* (also **tenpin bowling**) an indoor game for individual players or for teams, in which a player tries to knock down with a ball ten 'pins' placed in a triangle, the apex of which is 18.3 m (60 ft.) away at the end of a 'lane' of smooth polished wood. Related games were played in ancient Egypt; in Germany, congregations played at bowling in church cloisters (*c.*1400), with the target representing the Devil and the player who hit it adjudged free of sin (Luther approved of the game). In England, Edward III banned the game in 1361 (like football and golf it interfered with the practice of archery, which was of military use). Henry VIII built alleys at Whitehall but condemned the game in 1511 for its association with gambling. In 1895 the American Bowling Congress gave the game rules and standardized its equipment.

bowls /bəʊlz/ *n.* a game played with bowls (see BOWL¹) on grass, or with round balls in a room. One of the oldest games known in Britain, it is now played chiefly out of doors. An intentional imbalance (*bias*) of balls was introduced in the 16th c., greatly increasing the tactical scope of the game by allowing balls to run in curved paths round obstructions. It is fashionable to discount the legend, first published in a political pamphlet in 1624, that on 19 July 1588 Sir Francis Drake (who was known to like the game) was playing bowls on Plymouth Hoe when news came that the Spanish Armada had been sighted, and refused to leave until he had finished the game, but it could be true.

bowsprit /ˈbəʊsprɪt/ *n.* a long spar running forward from a ship's bow (ill. SAILING-SHIPS). [f. MLG or MDu. (as BOW³, SPRIT)]

Bow Street Runners /bəʊ/ the common name for London's police force during the first half of the 19th c., coined because the main police court was situated in Bow Street.

box¹ *n.* **1.** a container for solids, usually with flat sides and a lid; the quantity contained in this. **2.** a separate compartment, as for several people in a theatre, for horses in a stable etc., or witnesses in a lawcourt. **3.** a box-like shelter, as for a sentry, person telephoning, etc.; a small country-house for shooting, fishing, etc. **4.** a confined space. **5.** a receptacle at a newspaper office for replies to an advertisement. **6.** a coachman's seat. —*v.t.* to put in or provide with a box. —**box girder,** a girder made of plates fastened in a box shape. **box in** or **up,** to shut into a small space restricting movement. **box junction,** a road intersection with a yellow-striped area which a vehicle may not enter (except when turning right) until its exit is clear. **box number,** the number of a box in a newspaper office. **box-office** *n.* an office for booking seats at a theatre etc. **box-pleat** *n.* a combination of two parallel pleats forming a raised strip. **box-room** *n.* a room for storing boxes etc. **box-spring** *n.* each of a set of vertical springs in a mattress. [OE, f. L *pyxis, buxis* (as BOX³)]

box² *v.t./i.* **1.** to fight with the fists, especially in boxing-gloves as a sport. **2.** to slap (a person's ears). —*n.* a hard slap on the ears etc. [orig. unkn.]

box³ *n.* an evergreen shrub (*Buxus sempervirens*) much used in hedging and topiary; its wood. [OE f. L *buxus,* var. of L *pyxis* box of boxwood]

Box and Cox two people who take turns at using or doing the same thing. [f. characters in a farce (1847) by J. M. Morton, a printer and a hatter to whom a landlady let the same room without their knowing it, the one being out at work all night and the other all day.]

Boxer *n.* a member of a fanatical Chinese secret organization in the late 19th c. Abetted by the Dowager Empress, in 1899 it led a Chinese uprising against Western domination and besieged the foreign legations in Peking. The uprising was eventually crushed by a combined European force, aided by Japan and the USA, and the foreign powers took their opportunity to strengthen their hold over the Chinese. [f. Chinese name, = righteous harmony boxers (fists)]

boxer *n.* **1.** one who boxes for sport. **2.** a dog of a breed of medium size with a smooth brown coat. [f. BOX²]

boxing *n.* the sport of fist-fighting by two men (usually wearing padded gloves) in a roped square. It was organized in its modern form under the Queensberry Rules, compiled in the 1860s. It is both an amateur and a professional sport, with contestants divided into categories according to their weight, and fights are divided into 3-minute rounds. — **boxing-glove** *n.* a padded glove worn in the sport of boxing. **boxing-weight** *n.* the weight at which boxers are matched. British professional scale, upper weight limits: flyweight 8 stone, bantamweight 8 stone 6 lbs, featherweight 9 stones, lightweight 9 stones 9 lbs, light welterweight 10 stone, welterweight 10 stone 7 lbs, light middleweight 11 stone, middleweight 11 stone 6 lbs, light heavyweight 12 stone 7 lbs, heavyweight (no limit; any weight above 12 stone 7 lbs). The weights and divisions are modified in the amateur scale. [f. BOX²]

Boxing Day the first weekday after Christmas, when Christmas-boxes used to be presented. [f. (money-)BOX³]

boy *n.* **1.** a male child. **2.** a young man. **3.** a (young) male employee or servant. —**the boys,** a group of men, especially in a social context. **boy-friend** *n.* a girl's or woman's regular male companion. —**boyhood** *n.*, **boyish** *adj.* [orig. unkn.]

boycott /ˈbɔɪkɒt/ *v.t.* to combine in refusing to have dealings with (a person, group, etc.) or handle (goods etc.). —*n.* an act of boycotting. [f. Capt. *Boycott*, land-agent in Ireland, so treated in 1880. The Irish Land League ordered him to reduce rents after a bad harvest, and when he refused the tenants avoided any communication with him]

Boyle /bɔɪl/, Robert (1627-91), English natural philosopher, of aristocratic birth, a founder member of the Royal Society. He rejected the chemical views of the alchemists and Aristotelians and advanced a corpuscular view of matter, a precursor of the modern theory of chemical elements and a cornerstone of his mechanical philosophy which became very influential. He is best known for his experiments with the air pump, assisted intially by Robert Hooke, which led to the famous law named after him that the volume of a fixed quantity of gas at constant temperature is inversely proportional to its pressure; this was published by Boyle in 1662 with information supplied by R. Towneley, and subsequently but independently by Edmé Mariotte in France in 1676.

Boyne /bɔɪn/ a river in the Republic of Ireland, scene of the victory of a Protestant (largely English) army under William III over the Catholic (Irish and French) forces of the recently deposed James II in 1690. Although the campaign dragged on for some months afterwards, the Battle of the Boyne effectively destroyed for some time James's chances of regaining his throne.

Boz /bɒz/ the pseudonym used by Charles Dickens in his *Pickwick Papers* and contributions to the *Morning Chronicle*.

BP *abbr.* before the present (esp. in geological dating).

Br *symbol* bromine.

bra /brɑː/ *n.* a brassière. [abbr.]

Brabant /brəˈbænt/ a former duchy in western Europe, now divided between Belgium and the Netherlands.

brace *n.* **1.** a device that clamps things together or holds and supports them in position. **2.** (in *pl.*) straps to hold up the trousers, fastened to the waistband and passing over the shoulders. **3.** (esp. of game; *pl.* same) a pair. **4.** a rope attached to the yard of a ship for trimming a sail. **5.** a connecting mark { or } in printing. —*v.t.* **1.** to clamp or hold up by a brace, to fasten tightly, to steady against pressure or shock. **2.** to invigorate. —**brace and bit,** a revolving tool with a D-shaped handle, for boring holes (ill. CARPENTRY). [f. OF f. L *bracchia* arms]

bracelet /ˈbreɪslɪt/ *n.* an ornamental band or chain worn on the wrist or arm. [f. OF, dim. of *bracel* f. L *bracchiale* (as prec.)]

brachiopod /ˈbrækɪəpɒd/ *n.* an invertebrate of the phylum Brachiopoda like a bivalve mollusc, found especially as a fossil. [f. Gk *brakhiōn* arm + *pous podos* foot]

brachiosaurus /ˌbrækɪəˈsɔːrəs/ *n.* a huge dinosaur of the genus *Brachiosaurus*, with the forelegs longer than the hind legs. [f. Gk *brakhiōn* arm + *sauros* lizard]

brachycephalic /ˌbrækɪsɪˈfælɪk/ *adj.* having a short rounded skull whose width is at least 80% of its length, i.e. with a cephalic index of equal to or greater than 80. Examples of brachycephalic populations occur in Central Europe from central France to central Russia, and from north Italy to Prussia. —**brachycephalous** /-ˈsefələs/ *adj.*, **brachycephaly** *n.* [f. Gk *brakhus* short, *kephalē* head]

bracken /ˈbrækən/ *n.* a large fern of heaths and hillsides; a mass of such ferns. [f. ON]

bracket /ˈbrækɪt/ *n.* **1.** a flat-topped projection from a wall supporting a statue, arch, etc.; a shelf fixed with an angled prop to a wall. **2.** a mark used in pairs ( ) [ ] { } to enclose words or figures. **3.** a group of people classified together as similar or falling between given limits. —*v.t.* **1.** to enclose (words etc.) in brackets. **2.** to group in the same category. —**bracket clock,** a clock designed to stand on a shelf or wall-bracket. [f. Sp. f. L *bracae* breeches]

brackish *adj.* (of water) slightly saline. [f. LG or Du.]

bract *n.* a small modified often scale-like leaf below the calyx of a flower (ill. PLANTS). [f. L *bractea* thin metal sheet]

bracteole /ˈbræktɪəʊl/ *n.* a small bract (ill. PLANTS). [f. L (as prec.)]

brad *n.* a thin flat nail with the head in the form of a slight enlargement at the top (ill. CARPENTRY). [f. ON, = spike]

bradawl /ˈbrædɔːl/ *n.* a small non-spiral hand-tool for boring holes for brads and screws (ill. CARPENTRY). [f. BRAD + AWL]

Bradbury¹ /ˈbrædbərɪ/, Malcolm Stanley (1932-) English

novelist and critic. His first three novels (*Eating People is Wrong*, 1959; *Stepping Westward*, 1965; and *The History Man*, 1975) are satirical campus novels with widely differing backgrounds, and *Rates of Exchange* (1983) is a witty satiric commentary on cultural exchange. His critical works, which include studies of Waugh (1962) and Bellow (1982), show a respect for pluralism with an admiration for the experimental and fictive devices of the American novel.

Bradbury² /ˈbrædbərɪ/, Ray Douglas (1920-), American writer of science fiction, whose works include *Martian Chronicles* (1950) and *Fahrenheit 451* (1951). He is a richly imaginative writer with a distinctive blend of sentiment and cynicism.

Bradley /ˈbrædlɪ/, James (1693-1762), English astronomer, appointed Savilian professor of astronomy at Oxford in 1721 and Astronomer Royal in 1742. His attempt to measure the distance of the stars by means of stellar parallax resulted in his discovery of the aberration of light announced in 1729, which he ascribed correctly to the combined effect of the velocity of light and the earth's annual orbital motion. He also observed the oscillation of the earth's axis, which he termed 'nutation'. His catalogue of star positions was published posthumously in two volumes in 1798 and 1805.

Bradman /ˈbrædmən/, Sir Donald George (1908-), Australian cricketer whose career extended from 1927 to 1949. He scored 117 centuries in 338 innings in first-class cricket.

Bradshaw /ˈbrædʃɔː/ *n.* a timetable of (esp. British) passenger trains. [f. G. *Bradshaw* (d. 1853), British printer and engraver, first publisher of *Bradshaw's Railway Guide*, a timetable of all passenger trains in Britain, issued until 1961]

brae /breɪ/ *n.* (*Sc.*) a steep slope, a hillside. [f. ON, = eyelash]

brag *v.t./i.* (-**gg**-) to talk boastfully; to boast. —*n.* boastful talk. [orig. unkn.]

Bragg /bræg/, Sir William Henry (1862-1942), English physicist and a founder of solid state physics. His early work was on the ionization of X-rays and radioactivity, but in 1912 he began to collaborate with his son, William (later Sir Lawrence) Bragg (1890-1971) in developing the technique of X-ray diffraction for determining the atomic structure of crystals; for this they shared the 1915 Nobel Prize for physics. During the First World War he worked on submarine detection for the Admiralty; afterwards he returned to University College, London, where he established a research school for crystallography, and moved to the Royal Institution of which he became the director in 1923. His son was appointed head of the same establishment in 1953. Their diffraction analysis of organic crystals was of fundamental importance in the emerging field of molecular biology.

braggart /ˈbrægət/ *n.* boastful person. —*adj.* boastful. [f. BRAG]

Brahe /ˈbrɑːə/, Tycho (1546-1601), the greatest naked-eye astronomer, a Danish nobleman of great wealth but uncertain temper. He boasted a fine metal nose, substituted for his own which he lost in a duel. He built the great observatory of Uraniborg at Hveen in Åresund, which he equipped with many new and accurate instruments, using these to observe the planetary motions and star positions with great precision. His detailed tables of the position of Mars, in particular, were to be used later by his protégé Kepler to work out the laws of planetary dynamics. He was aware of the effects of atmospheric refraction on his observations, and made appropriate corrections. His observations of cometary orbits, published in the book *De Nova Stella* (1577), demonstrated that they followed regular sun-centred paths, but despite this he adhered to a geocentric picture of the orbits of the planets. The 'new star' which he observed in 1572, since named after him, is now known to have been a supernova.

Brahma /ˈbrɑːmə/ the creator-god of late Vedic religion (see foll.), who later formed a triad with Vishnu and Siva. Little worshipped after the 5th c. AD, he has one known temple dedicated to him in India today. [masc. form of neut. BRAHMAN]

Brahman /ˈbrɑːmən/ *n.* the supreme being of the Upanishads, often identified with the inner core of the individual (*atman*). It is the eternal and conscious ground of the universe, the source of dharma, and the special sphere of the priestly brahmin class. A neuter term, Brahman was personified in Hindu mythology as the male creator god (Brahma). [Skr., = sacred knowledge]

brahman /ˈbrɑːmən/ var. of BRAHMIN.

Brahmana /ˈbrɑːmənə/ *n.* any of the lengthy commentaries on the Vedas, composed in Sanskrit *c.*900-700 BC, containing exegetical material relating to Vedic sacrificial ritual. [as BRAHMAN]

Brahmaputra /brɑːməˈpuːtrə/ a river of southern Asia, rising in Tibet and flowing 2,900 km (1,800 miles) through the Himalayas and NE India to join the Ganges at its delta (in Bangladesh) on the Bay of Bengal.

brahmin /ˈbrɑːmɪn/ *n.* a member of the Hindu priestly class, versed in sacred knowledge (i.e. the Veda). His function is to study and teach the Veda and to perform sacrifices. —**brahminical** /-ˈmɪnɪk(ə)l/ *adj.* [f. Skr. (*brahman* priest)]

brahminism /ˈbrɑːmɪnɪz(ə)m/ *n.* (also **Brahmanism**) the complex sacrificial religion that emerged in post-Vedic India (*c.*900 BC) under the influence of the dominant priesthood (brahmins). It was as a reaction to brahmin orthodoxy that heterodox sects such as Buddhism and Jainism were formed. [f. prec.]

Brahms /brɑːmz/, Johannes (1833-97), German composer and pianist. Welcomed as a genius in Leipzig by Schumann in 1853, he lived for most of the last 35 years of his life in Vienna. Firmly opposed to the 'New German' school of Liszt and the young Wagner, he eschewed programme music and opera and concentrated his energies on 'pure' and traditional forms. He wrote four symphonies, two piano concertos, the Violin Concerto and the Double Concerto, chamber and piano music, choral works including the highly successful *German Requiem* (1857-68), and nearly 200 songs, all of which, if classical in conception, are undeniably romantic and frequently lyrical in expression.

braid *n.* 1. a woven band of silk or thread used for trimming. 2. a plaited tress of hair. —*v.t.* 1. to trim with braid. 2. to plait. 3. (esp. in *p.p.*; of a stream) to divide (esp. at low water) into several channels. [OE]

Braille /breɪl/ *n.* a system of representing letters etc. by raised dots, which blind people can read by touch. (ill. ALPHABETS). —*v.t.* to represent in Braille. [f. L. *Braille*, its inventor (d. 1852), a blind French teacher who perfected his system in 1834]

brain *n.* 1. that part of the nervous system in the vertebrate that is contained in the skull (see below; ill. BODY 4); a structure of analogous function found in many invertebrates. 2. an intelligent person; (also in *pl.*) one who organizes a complex plan or idea. 3. (often in *pl.*) intellectual power. 4. an electronic device with functions comparable to the brain's. —*v.t.* to kill by a heavy blow on the head. —**brain-child** *n.* a person's inspired idea. **brain-drain** *n.* the loss of talented or professional people by emigration. **brain-stem** *n.* the stemlike portion of the brain connecting the cerebral hemispheres with the spinal cord. **brains trust,** a group of experts giving impromptu answers to questions (as a form of entertainment). **on the brain,** obsessively in one's thoughts. [OE]

The human brain comprises that part of the nervous system contained in the skull. Like that of other vertebrates it arises, during development of the embryo, from the anterior end of a tube of nervous tissue which becomes the spinal cord. The brain directs an animal's activity and exerts control over internal physiological processes; in humans and perhaps some other animals it is the seat of consciousness. It consists of three main parts. (i) The forebrain, greatly developed into the cerebrum in man, consists of two 'hemispheres', joined by a bridge of nerve fibres and is responsible for the exercise of thought and control of the faculty of speech. Its wrinkled surface or cortex is coated with nerve-cells, which appear grey in contrast to the white of the deeper nerve-fibres. Deep in its substance are the thalamus and the hypothalamus, which has a number of functions, being concerned with the regulation of temperature and water balance, with hunger, thirst, and the sex drive, and with the experience of emotions such as anger. The left half of the cerebrum is associated with the right side of the body, regulating its posture and movements and appreciation of bodily sensations, and the right half with the left side. The functions of most of the cerebral cortex, the nature of the physical embodiment of memory and of consciousness itself, remain unknown. (ii) The midbrain, the upper part of the tapering brain-stem, contains cells concerned in eye-movements. (iii) The hindbrain, the lower part of the brain-stem, contains the cells responsible for breathing and others which regulate the action of the heart, the flow of digestive juices, etc. The cerebellum, which lies behind the brain-stem, plays an important role in the execution of highly skilled movements. In invertebrate animals the brain is similar but less developed; in the lower animals a collection of ganglia has an analogous function.

brainless *adj.* lacking intelligence. [f. BRAIN + -LESS]

brainpower *n.* mental ability or intelligence.

brainstorm *n.* 1. a sudden extreme mental disturbance. 2. (*US*) a sudden bright idea.

brainstorming *n.* (*US*) a spontaneous discussion in a search for new ideas.

brainwash *v.t.* to implant new ideas in the mind of (a person) and eliminate established ones by subjecting him systematically to great mental pressure.

brainwave *n.* 1. an electrical impulse in the brain. 2. (*colloq.*) a sudden bright idea.

brainy *adj.* intellectually active or clever. —**braininess** *n.* [f. BRAIN]

braise /breɪz/ *v.t.* to cook (meat) slowly in fat or with very little liquid in a closed vessel. [f. F (*braise* live coals)]

brake[1] *n.* a device for checking the motion of a wheel, vehicle, etc. (ill. CAR). —*v.t./i.* to apply a brake; to retard by a brake. —**brake-drum** *n.* a cylinder attached to a wheel, on which the brake-shoe presses. **brake-horsepower** *n.* the power of an engine measured by the force needed to brake it. **brake-shoe** *n.* a long curved block acting on a wheel to brake it. [orig. unkn.]

brake[2] *n.* a clump of bushes, a thicket. [f. OE, = branch, stump]

brake[3] *n.* an estate car. [var. of *break* carriage-frame, wagonette (orig. unkn.)]

Bramah /ˈbræmə/, Joseph (1749-1814), English inventor, one of the most versatile and influential engineers of the Industrial Revolution. Best known for his hydraulic press, used for heavy forging, he was responsible also for other important machine tools. In 1784 he patented a very successful lock, unpicked until 1851. To develop the precision machines needed for its manufacture he engaged Henry Maudslay who became a major innovator of machine tools and in turn encouraged other innovators. Bramah's own inventions included milling and planing machines, a beer-engine, a machine for numbering banknotes, and a water-closet.

Bramante /brəˈmænti/, Donato di Angelo (1444-1514), the outstanding Italian architect of the High Renaissance. Strongly influenced by the remains of antiquity he adapted the circular temple to Christian usage, his work expressing the Renaissance striving for the ideal of classical perfection. Employed by Pope Julius II, his most important tasks were the works at the Vatican and the designing of the new St Peter's (begun in 1506), where his Greek-cross plan, crowned with a central dome, was the starting-point for all subsequent work on the basilica. Bramante's character seems to have been forceful and unscrupulous, and he was probably responsible for setting up his kinsman Raphael in Rome in opposition to Michelangelo.

bramble *n.* a rough prickly shrub of the genus *Rubus* with long trailing shoots, especially the blackberry; its fruit. — **brambly** *adj.* [OE, rel.to BROOM]

brambling *n.* a small brightly coloured finch (*Fringilla montifringilla*). [f. G, rel. to prec.]

bran *n.* ground husks of grain, sifted out from the flour. — **bran-tub** *n.* a lucky dip with prizes hidden in bran. [f. OF; orig. unkn.]

branch /brɑːntʃ/ *n.* 1. a limb from the trunk or bough of a tree. 2. a lateral extension of a river, road, railway, etc. 3. a subdivision of a family, study, etc. 4. a local establishment of a bank or other central organization. —*v.t.* to diverge from the main part; (often with *off*) to divide into branches; to put out branches. —**branch out,** to extend one's field of interest. [f. OF f. L *branca* paw]

brand *n.* 1. a trade mark, identifying label, etc., on goods; a particular make of goods. 2. a mark of ownership burnt on livestock with a hot iron, the iron used for this. 3. a stigma, mark of disgrace. 4. a piece of burning or charred wood. —*v.t.* 1. to assign a trade mark or proprietary label to (goods). 2. to mark with a hot iron as a mark of ownership or disgrace; to stigmatize. 3. to impress on the memory. — **brand-new** *adj.* completely new. [OE]

brandish /ˈbrændɪʃ/ *v.t.* to wave (weapons etc.) threateningly or in display. [f. OF f. Gmc]

brandy /ˈbrændɪ/ *n.* a strong spirit distilled from wine. — **brandy-snap** *n.* a crisp rolled gingerbread wafer. [f. Du. *brandewijn* burnt (distilled) wine]

Braque /brɑːk/, Georges (1882-1963), French painter who, with Picasso, inaugurated cubism. Painting at first in the manner of the Fauves, with pure pigments and bright colours, he was impressed with the structural composition of the Cézanne exhibition of 1907 so that when he met Picasso in the following year he was ripe to join him in the researches which led to cubism, and the two worked in close association until Braque's mobilization in 1914 for the First World War. Braque was the first to make the collages which developed into synthetic cubism, introducing real elements and commercial lettering into pictures to contrast the real with the 'illusory' painted image. In 1915 he suffered a severe head wound, but contrived to paint in cubist style from 1917, and by the 1930s was recognized as an international master of still life.

brash *adj.* vulgarly or obnoxiously self-assertive, impudent. [dial.]

Brasilia /brəˈzɪlɪə/ the capital (since 1960) of Brazil, built on a site that was chosen (in 1956) in an attempt to draw people away from the crowded coastal areas; pop. (1980) 1,176,748.

brass /brɑːs/ *n.* **1.** a widely-used alloy of copper and zinc, sometimes including minor constituents such as tin. **2.** brass objects or wind-instruments collectively; a brass memorial tablet in a church; a brass ornament worn by a horse. **3.** (*hist.*) bronze. **4.** (*colloq.*) money. **5.** (*slang*) impudence. — *adj.* made of brass. —**brass band**, a band playing brass instruments. **brass-rubbing** *n.* the taking of impressions on paper of memorial brasses. **brass tacks**, (*colloq.*) essential details. [OE]

brasserie /ˈbræsərɪ/ *n.* a bar where food can be obtained as well as drinks; an informal licensed restaurant. [F, = brewery (*brasser* brew)]

Brassey /ˈbræsɪ/, Thomas (1805-70), English engineer, the greatest railway contractor of the 19th c., who built over 10,000 km (6,500 miles) of railways in Europe, North and South America, Australia, and India. Brassey had a genius for recruiting and organizing men, both labourers and managers, who gave of their best. After building the railway from London to Southampton he was responsible for building that from Paris to Rouen and later to Le Havre, for which purposes he sent thousands of British navvies over to France to show his large labour force how to work. Despite this, one large viaduct (550 m long) collapsed but was rebuilt in record time so that the line was opened on time, as were all his subsequent lines. He never went to law over disputes and the reputation he gained for British civil engineering was of lasting value. His one failure was the Grand Trunk Railway of Canada, where lack of experience of local conditions caused costs to exceed estimates considerably, though Brassey bore much of the loss himself. It was said of him that he altered the world more effectively than the conquests of Alexander the Great.

brassica /ˈbræsɪkə/ *n.* a plant of the genus *Brassica* (cabbage, turnip, etc.). [L]

brassière /ˈbræsɪeə(r)/ *n.* a woman's undergarment supporting the breasts. [F]

brassy /ˈbrɑːsɪ/ *adj.* **1.** bold and vulgar; pretentious, showy. **2.** loud and strident. —**brassiness** *n.* [f. BRASS]

brat *n.* (*derog.*) a child. [orig. unkn.]

Braun[1] /braʊn/, Karl Ferdinand (1850-1918), German physicist who made notable contributions to wireless telegraphy and to the development of the cathode ray tube, the essential precursor of television. He discovered the rectification properties of certain crystals and invented the coupled system of radio transmission. His demonstration that a beam of electrons could be deflected by a voltage difference between deflector plates in an evacuated tube, or by a magnetic field, led to the Braun tube, the forerunner of the cathode ray tube. He was awarded the Nobel Prize for physics, jointly with Guglielmo Marconi, in 1909.

Braun[2] /braʊn/, Werner von (1912-77), German designer of rocket engines in the 1930s and during the Second World War. After the war he joined the US team in New Mexico, leading the efforts which resulted in successful launches of satellites, interplanetary missions, and the landing of men on the moon in 1969.

bravado /brəˈvɑːdəʊ/ *n.* an outward display of fearlessness. [Sp.]

brave *adj.* able or ready to face danger, pain, etc. **2.** splendid, spectacular. —*v.t.* to face bravely or defiantly. —*n.* a North American Indian warrior. —**bravely** *adj.*, **bravery** /ˈbreɪvərɪ/ *n.* [f. F. f. Sp.]

bravo[1] /ˈbrɑːvəʊ/ *n.* (*pl.* **-os**) & *int.* a cry of approval; well done! [F f. It. (as foll.)]

bravo[2] /ˈbrɑːvəʊ/ *n.* (*pl.* **-oes**) a hired ruffian or killer. [F f. It. (as BRAVE)]

bravura /brəˈvʊərə/ *n.* a brilliant or ambitious performance; a piece of vocal etc. music calling for technical virtuosity. [It.]

brawl *n.* a noisy quarrel or fight. —*v.i.* **1.** to take part in a brawl. **2.** (of a stream) to flow noisily. —**brawler** *n.* [f. Prov., rel. to BRAY]

brawn *n.* **1.** muscle, muscular strength. **2.** pressed jellied meat made from a pig's head etc. —**brawny** *adj.* [f. AF f. Gmc]

Bray, Vicar of the hero of an 18th-c. song who kept his benefice from Charles II's reign to George I's by changing his beliefs to suit the times. The song is apparently based on an anecdote of an unidentified vicar of Bray, Berks., in T. Fuller *Worthies of England* (1662).

bray *n.* a donkey's loud strident cry; any loud harsh sound. —*v.i.* to emit a bray. [f. OF, perh. f. Celtic]

braze *v.t.* to solder with an alloy of brass and zinc. [f. F *braser* (*braise* live coals)]

brazen /ˈbreɪz(ə)n/ *adj.* **1.** shameless and defiant. **2.** of or like brass; harsh in tone or colour. —*v.t.* to face (a situation) *out* boldly and defiantly after doing wrong. [OE, as BRASS]

brazier[1] /ˈbreɪzɪə(r)/ *n.* a metal stand with burning coal as a portable heater. [f. F *brasier* (*braise* hot coals)]

brazier[2] /ˈbreɪzɪə(r)/ *n.* a worker in brass. [prob. f. BRASS, after *glass*, *glazier*]

Brazil[1] /brəˈzɪl/ a country in NE South America, the largest of that continent, comprising almost half its total area, and the fourth-largest in the world; pop. (1980) 119,098,922; official language, Portuguese; capital, Brasilia. In the north lies the Amazon basin with its tropical rain forests. Economically, Brazil is still mainly an agricultural country, but is rich in mineral resources (not yet fully exploited), including iron, gold, phosphates, and uranium. The land is split into an industrialized coastal belt, which makes it the most industrially advanced country in South America, and a vast underdeveloped interior. Colonized by the Portuguese in the 16th c., Brazil became an independent kingdom in 1826, remaining a liberal monarchy until the institution of a republic in 1889. It fell under dictatorial rule between the World Wars, and although not as troubled by instability as some of its neighbours, is still prone to socio-political unrest. —**Brazilian** *adj.* & *n.*

Brazil[2] *n.* (also **Brazil nut**) a large three-sided nut from a Brazilian tree. [f. prec.]

Brazzaville /ˈbræzəvɪl/ the capital and a major port of the People's Republic of the Congo, on the Congo River; pop. approx. 2,100,000.

breach *n.* **1.** a breaking of or failure to observe a law, contract, etc. **2.** a breaking of relations, estrangement. **3.** a gap or opening (in fortifications etc). —*v.t.* to make a breach in. —**breach of the peace**, a disturbance, an affray. **breach of promise**, the breaking of a promise to marry. [f. OF f. Gmc, rel. to BREAK]

bread /bred/ *n.* flour moistened, kneaded, and baked in loaves, usually with leaven. —*v.t.* to coat with breadcrumbs for frying. —**bread-fruit** *n.* the fruit of a Pacific tree (*Artocarpus communis*) with white pulp like new bread. [OE]

breadboard *n.* **1.** a board for cutting bread on. **2.** a board on which an experimental electric circuit is set out.

breadcrumbs *n.pl.* bread crumbled for use in cooking.

breadth /bredθ/ *n.* **1.** the distance or measurement from side to side of a thing. **2.** great extent. **3.** freedom from limitations set by prejudice, intolerance, etc. [f. OE, rel. to BROAD]

breadwinner *n.* the member of a family who earns the money to support the other(s).

break /breɪk/ *v.t./i.* (*past* **broke**; *p.p.* **broken**) **1.** to separate or cause to separate into pieces under a blow or strain; to damage, to make or become inoperative; to break the bone in (a part of the body). **2.** to stop for a time, to make or become discontinuous; (of weather) to change suddenly after a fine spell. **3.** to fail to keep (a law or promise etc.). **4.** to make a way suddenly or violently. **5.** to emerge or appear suddenly (from); to reveal (news etc.); to become known. **6.** to surpass (a record). **7.** to solve (a cipher). **8.** to make or become weak; to overwhelm with grief etc.; to destroy the spirit etc. of (a person). **9.** to change course etc. suddenly; (of a voice) to change its even tone, either with emotion or (of a boy's voice) by becoming suddenly deeper at puberty; (of waves) to fall in foam. **10.** (of boxers) to come out of a clinch. *—n.* **1.** the act or process of breaking. **2.** a point where a thing is broken, a gap. **3.** an interval, an interruption, a pause in activity. **4.** a sudden dash. **5.** (*slang*) a piece of luck. **6.** (in cricket) a change of direction of a ball on bouncing. **7.** points scored continuously in billiards etc. —**break away**, to free oneself from constraint; to secede. **break the bank**, to exhaust its funds (in gambling etc.). **break dancing**, a kind of street dancing to a loud beat, with wriggling and bending of the arms and legs, in which the dancers may spin to the floor and revolve on their backs. **break down**, to experience mechanical failure; to make or become ineffective; to suffer an emotional collapse; to reduce to its constituent parts by chemical action or analysis. **break even**, to emerge from a transaction with neither profit nor loss. **break in**, to enter forcibly; to interpose a remark; to accustom to a habit or duties etc.; to wear until comfortable. **break-in** *n.* a forcible entry by a thief etc. **breaking-point**, *n.* the point at which a person or thing gives way under stress. **break into**, to enter forcibly; to begin suddenly to utter, perform, etc. **break off**, to detach by breaking; to bring abruptly to an end; to cease talking etc. **break open**, to use force to open. **break out**, to escape by force from prison etc.; to begin or develop suddenly; to become suddenly covered *in* a rash. **break-out** *n.* a forcible escape. **break up**, to break into small pieces; to separate, (of schoolchilden) to disperse for the holidays. **break wind**, to emit wind from the anus. **break with**, to end one's friendship with. [OE]

breakable *adj.* easily broken. [f. prec.]

breakage *n.* damage by breaking; an instance of this. [f. BREAK]

breakaway *n.* a breaking of one's ties, secession. *—adj.* that has broken away or seceded.

breakdown *n.* **1.** a failure of mechanical action health, mental stability, etc. **2.** an analysis of statistics.

breaker *n.* a heavy wave breaking on a coast or over a reef (ill. COASTS). [f. BREAK]

breakfast /'brekfəst/ *n.* the first meal of the day. *—v.i.* to have breakfast. [f. BREAK + FAST²]

breakneck *adj.* (of speed) dangerously fast.

breakthrough *n.* **1.** a major advance or discovery. **2.** the act of breaking through an obstacle etc.

breakup *n.* disintegration, collapse; dispersal.

breakwater *n.* a barrier protecting a harbour etc. against heavy waves.

bream *n.* (*pl.* same) a yellowish freshwater fish of the genus *Abramis*; (also **sea-bream**) a similarly shaped fish of the family Sparidae. [f. OF]

breast /brest/ *n.* **1.** either of the two protuberant milk-secreting organs on the upper front of a woman's body; the corresponding (usually rudimentary) part of a man's body. **2.** the upper front of the human body or of a garment covering it; the corresponding part in animals. **3.** the breast as a source of emotion. *—v.t.* to advance to meet with one's breast; to reach the top of (a hill). —**breast-feed** *v.t.* to feed (a baby) with milk from the breast. **breast-stoke** *n.* a swimming stroke performed face downwards, with sweeping movements of the arms. [OE]

breastbone *n.* the flat vertical bone in the chest joined to the ribs.

breastplate *n.* a piece of armour covering the chest (ill. ARMOUR).

breastwork *n.* a low temporary defensive wall or parapet.

breath /breθ/ *n.* **1.** air drawn into and expelled from the lungs; exhaled air as perceived by the senses. **2.** a breathing in; breathing, ability to breathe. **3.** a slight movement of air; a whiff (of perfume). **4.** a hint or slight rumour (of suspicion etc.). —**breath-test**, a test of breath to discover the amount of alcohol in the body. **hold one's breath**, to cease breathing temporarily from excitement etc. **out of breath**, panting after strenuous exercise. **under one's breath**, in a whisper. [OE]

breathalyse /'breθəlaɪz/ *v.t.* to test with a breathalyser. [f. foll.]

breathalyser *n.* an instrument measuring the amount of alcohol in a person's blood from a sample of his exhaled breath. [f. BREATH + ANALYSE]

breathe /briːð/ *v.t./i.* **1.** to draw air into and expel it from the lungs; to be alive; to draw into or expel from the lungs on the breath. **2.** to utter or mention; to speak softly. **3.** to pause for breath. **4.** to exude or instil (a quality or feeling). —

breathe again *or* **freely**, to feel relieved of fear etc.

breathing-space *n.* time to breathe, a chance to recover from effort. [f. BREATH]

breather /'briːðə(r)/ *n.* a pause for rest; a spell of fresh air. [f. prec.]

breathless *adj.* panting after exertion; holding one's breath with excitement. [f. BREATH + -LESS]

breathtaking *adj.* spectacular, very exciting.

Brecht /brext/, Bertolt (1898-1956), German dramatist, producer, and poet. His early plays showed kinship with expressionism and in 1928 he achieved outstanding success with *The Threepenny Opera* (an adaptation of John Gay's *The Beggar's Opera*) with music by Kurt Weill. From 1933 he lived in the USA and Scandinavia, returning in 1949 to East Berlin where he founded the Berlin Ensemble. His enormous impact on 20th-c. drama derives from his attempts to develop a Marxist 'epic theatre', exploiting his famous 'alienation effect' which rejected Aristotelian principles, disposed of dramatic climaxes, and used songs to comment on the action as in *The Life of Galileo* (1937-9), *Mother Courage* (1941), and *The Caucasian Chalk Circle* (1948).

bred *past* & *p.p.* of BREED.

breech *n.* **1.** the back part of a rifle or gun barrel. **2.** (*archaic*) the buttocks. —**breech birth**, a birth in which the baby's buttocks or feet emerge first. [OE]

breeches /'brɪtʃɪz/ *n.pl.* knee-length trousers, now worn for riding or in ceremonial dress (ill. DRESS). —**Breeches Bible**, the Geneva Bible of 1560 with *breeches* for *aprons* in Gen. 3: 7. **breeches buoy**, a lifebuoy with canvas breeches, slung on a rope for hauling people off a wreck etc. [pl. of prec.]

breed *v.t./i.* (*past* & *p.p.* **bred**) **1.** to bear young. **2.** to keep (animals) in order to produce young. **3.** to train or bring up. **4.** to give rise to. **5.** to produce (fissile material) in a breeder reactor. *—n.* **1.** a strain of an animal or plant species evolved by selective breeding. **2.** family, lineage. **3.** a sort or kind. [OE, rel. to BROOD]

breeder *n.* one who breeds animals. —**breeder reactor**, a nuclear reactor which can create more fissile material than it consumes. [f. prec.]

breeding *n.* **1.** the production of young from animals, propagation. **2.** good manners resulting from training or background. [f. BREED]

breeze¹ *n.* a cool or gentle wind. *—v.i.* (*colloq.*) to come *in*, to move *along* etc., in a casual jaunty manner. [f. Sp. *briza* north-east wind]

breeze² *n.* small cinders. —**breeze block**, a lightweight building block made from breeze with sand and cement. [f. F *braise* live coals]

breezy *adj.* **1.** pleasantly windy or wind-swept. **2.** casual and jaunty in manner. [f. BREEZE¹]

Bren *n.* (also **Bren gun**) a lightweight quick-firing machine-gun. [f. *Br*no in Czechoslovakia (where orig. made), *En*field in Greater London (where later made)]

Brendan /'brend(ə)n/, St (*c.*486-*c.*575), abbot of Clonfert. The legend of the 'Navigation of St Brendan' (*c.*1050), describing his voyage with a band of monks to a promised land (possibly the Orkneys and Hebrides) was widely popular in the Middle Ages.

brent-goose *n.* (also **brent**) the smallest kind of wild goose, *Branta bernicla*. [orig. unkn.]

Bresson /'bresɔ̃/, Robert (1907-), French film director whose spare individual style depicts with meticulous detail the subject he wishes to explore, but omits everything extraneous to it. He preferred not to use professional actors. His films, which appear infrequently and are given thematic coherence by his Catholic beliefs, include *Diary of a Country Priest* (1951), *The Trial of Joan of Arc* (1962), *The Devil, Probably* (1977), and *L'Argent* (1983).

Brest-Litovsk /brestlɪ'tɒfsk/ a Polish town on the Russian frontier (now in the USSR), in which was signed the treaty of peace between Germany and Russia in March 1918.

brethren /'breðrɪn/ *n.pl.* brothers (*archaic* except with ref. to monastic orders, certain sects, etc.). [f. BROTHER]

Breton /'bretən/ *adj.* of the Bretons or their language. *—n.* **1.** a native or inhabitant of Brittany. **2.** the language of the Bretons, belonging to the Brythonic branch of the Celtic language group. It is the only Celtic language now spoken on the European mainland, representing the modern development of the language brought from Cornwall and South Wales in the 5th and 6th c. by Britons fleeing from the Saxon invaders. Until the 20th c. it was widely spoken in Brittany, but it is now effectively excluded from the education system and its use is rare in the younger generation. [OF, = Briton]

Breughel var. of BRUEGEL and BRUEGHEL.

Breuil /'brøɪ/, Henri (1877-1961), French archaeologist, noted for his work on palaeolithic cave-paintings.

breve /bri:'v/ n. 1. a mark (˘) placed over a short or unstressed vowel. 2. (*Mus.*) a note equal to two semibreves. [var. of BRIEF]

breviary /'bri:vɪərɪ/ n. a book containing the daily office of the Roman Catholic Church. [f. L *breviarium* summary (*brevis* brief)]

brevity /'brevɪtɪ/ n. conciseness of written or spoken expression; shortness, especially of duration. [f. L (as prec.)]

brew /bru:/ v.t./i. 1. to make (beer etc.) by infusion, boiling, and fermentation; to make (tea etc.) by infusion; to undergo such processes. 2. (of evil results) to develop, to gather force. —n. a liquid or amount of liquid made by brewing; the process of brewing; the quality of what is brewed. — **brewer** n. [OE]

brewery /'bru:ərɪ/ n. a place where beer is brewed commercially. [f. prec.]

Brian Boru /braɪən bə'ru:/ (926-1014) king of Munster in SW Ireland. Having defeated the Danes he became high king of Ireland, but was killed after a victory over the Danes at Clontarf.

briar[1,2] var. of BRIER[1,2].

bribe n. money etc. offered to procure a corrupt action or decision in favour of the giver. —v.t. to give a bribe to. — **bribery** /'braɪbərɪ/ n. [f. OF *briber* beg]

bric-à-brac /'brɪkəbræk/ n. miscellaneous old ornaments, furniture, trinkets, etc. [f. obs. F, = at random]

brick n. 1. a small usually rectangular block of baked or dried clay, used in building; the material of this; building work consisting of such blocks. 2. a brick-shaped loaf, block of ice-cream, etc. —adj. made of brick. —v.t. to block *up* or fill *in* with bricks. —**brick-red** adj. having the red colour of bricks. [f. LG or Du.]

brickbat n. 1. a piece of brick, especially as a missile. 2. an uncomplimentary remark.

bricklayer n. a workman who builds with bricks.

brickwork n. a structure of or building in bricks (ill. BUILDING).

bridal /'braɪd(ə)l/ adj. of a bride or wedding. [OE, orig. as n. = wedding feast]

Bride /braɪd/, St, see BRIDGET[1].

bride n. a woman on or just before her wedding-day; a newly-married woman. [OE]

bridegroom n. a man on or just before his wedding-day; a newly-married man.

bridesmaid n. an unmarried woman or girl attending the bride at a wedding.

bridewell /'braɪdwel/ n. (*hist.*) a prison or reformatory. [f. St *Bride's* (or Bridget's) *Well* in London, between Fleet Street and the Thames, where such a building (formerly a royal palace) stood]

bridge[1] n. 1. a structure carrying a road, railway, etc. over a river, ravine, etc. (see ill. p. 107); a thing joining or connecting parts. 2. the upper bony part of the nose. 3. a piece of wood etc. over which the strings of a violin are stretched. 4. the raised platform on a ship from which the captain directs its course. 5. a false tooth or teeth supported by the natural teeth on each side. —v.t. to connect by or as by a bridge. —**Bridge of Sighs**, a 16th c. covered bridge in Venice between the doges' palace and the State prison, crossed by prisoners on their way to torture or execution.

bridging-loan n. a loan to cover the short interval between buying one thing and selling another (especially houses). [OE]

bridge[2] /brɪdʒ/ n. a card-game derived from whist, in which one player's cards are exposed and played by his partner. Its two main forms are **auction bridge** (with competitive bidding for the right to name the trump suit), which was popular with the British in India in the 19th c., and **contract bridge**, where only the tricks bid and won count towards the game and which has now largely superseded other forms, under the influence of the American player Ely Culbertson (1891-1955). [orig. unkn., but prob. of Levantine origin since some form of the game seems to have been long known in the Near East]

bridgehead n. a fortified position established in hostile territory, especially on the far side of a river as a base for further advance.

Bridges /'brɪdʒɪz/, Robert (1844-1930), English poet, who studied and for a time practised medicine. Author of many beautiful lyrics, Bridges was perhaps too subtle and severe a poet to appeal to a very wide public, though his long philosophical poem in the Victorian tradition, *The Testament of Beauty* (1929) was instantly popular. He wrote two influential essays, *Milton's Prosody* (1893) and *John Keats* (1895). His greatest contribution to literature was the publication of his friend Gerard Manley Hopkins's poems in 1918. From 1913 to 1930 he was Poet Laureate. Bridges was intimately associated with Oxford University Press, taking an active interest in questions of type, spelling, and phonetics, and did much to encourage taste and accuracy in printing.

Bridget[1] /'brɪdʒɪt/, St (of Ireland), traditionally abbess of Kildare in the early 6th c. She was venerated in Ireland as a virgin saint, noted in miracle stories for her compassion, and her cult soon spread over most of western Europe. Details such as her sacred fire described by Gerald of Wales suggest that she may represent the Irish goddess Brig.

Bridget[2] /'brɪdʒɪt/, St (of Sweden; c.1303-73). After her husband's death she devoted herself to religion and founded the Order of Brigettines (c.1346) at Vadstena in Sweden. The revelations which she was held to have received in visions were highly regarded in the Middle Ages.

bridle /'braɪd(ə)l/ n. the harness round a horse's head by which the rider controls it (ill. HORSE); a restraining thing or influence. —v.t./i. 1. to put a bridle on; to curb or restrain. 2. to draw up the head in pride or resentment. — **bridle-path** n. one suitable for horse-riding. [OE]

Brie /bri:/ n. a kind of soft ripe cheese. [f. *Brie* in N. France.]

brief adj. 1. of short duration. 2. concise. —n. 1. a summary of the facts of a case drawn up for a barrister; a case taken on by a barrister. 2. (in *pl.*) very short pants. —v.t. to give a brief to (a barrister); to provide with the essential facts beforehand. —**briefly** adv. [f. AF f. L *breve* dispatch (*brevis* short)]

briefcase n. a flat case for carrying documents.

brier[1] /'braɪə(r)/ n. a wild rose or other prickly bush. [OE]

brier[2] /'braɪə(r)/ n. a shrubby heath (*Erica arborea*) of southern Europe; a tobacco-pipe made from its woody root. [f. F *bruyère* heath]

brig n. a square-rigged sailing-ship with two masts (ill. SAILING-SHIPS). [abbr. BRIGANTINE]

brigade /brɪ'geɪd/ n. 1. a military unit forming part of a division. 2. a body of people organized for a special purpose. [f. F. f. It. *brigata* company (*brigare* be busy with, f. *briga* strife)]

brigadier /brɪgə'dɪə(r)/ n. an officer commanding a brigade; a staff officer with similar status, next in rank above a colonel. [F (as prec.)]

brigand /'brɪgənd/ n. a member of a robber gang, a bandit. —**brigandage** n. [f. OF f. It. (as BRIGADE)]

brigantine /'brɪgəntiːn/ n. a sailing-ship with two masts, the foremast square-rigged, used in the 18th and 19th c. for short coastal and trading voyages. The name comes from the fact that they were favourite vessels of sea brigands. [f. OF or It. (as BRIGAND)]

Bright /braɪt/, John (1811-89), English Liberal politician and reformer. A noted orator, Bright was the leader, along with Richard Cobden, of the campaign to repeal the Corn Laws.

bright /braɪt/ adj. 1. emitting or reflecting much light, shining. 2. (of colour) intense, conspicuous. 3. intelligent, talented. 4. cheerful, vivacious. —adv. brightly. —**brightly** adv., **brightness** n. [OE]

brighten /'braɪt(ə)n/ v.t./i. to make or become brighter. [f. prec.]

brill n. a European flat-fish (*Scophthalmus rhombus*). [orig. unkn.]

brilliant /'brɪlɪənt/ adj. 1. bright, sparkling. 2. strikingly talented or intelligent. 3. showy. —n. a diamond of the finest cut and brilliance, with many facets. —**brilliance** n., **brilliancy** n. [f. F *brillant* shining, f. It. *brillare*; orig. unkn.]

brilliantine /'brɪlɪəntiːn/ n. a substance to make the hair glossy. [f. F (as prec.)]

brim n. the edge or lip of a cup or other vessel; the projecting edge of a hat. —v.t./i. (-mm-) to fill or be full to the brim. —**brim over**, to overflow. [orig. unkn.]

Bridges

Girder bridges

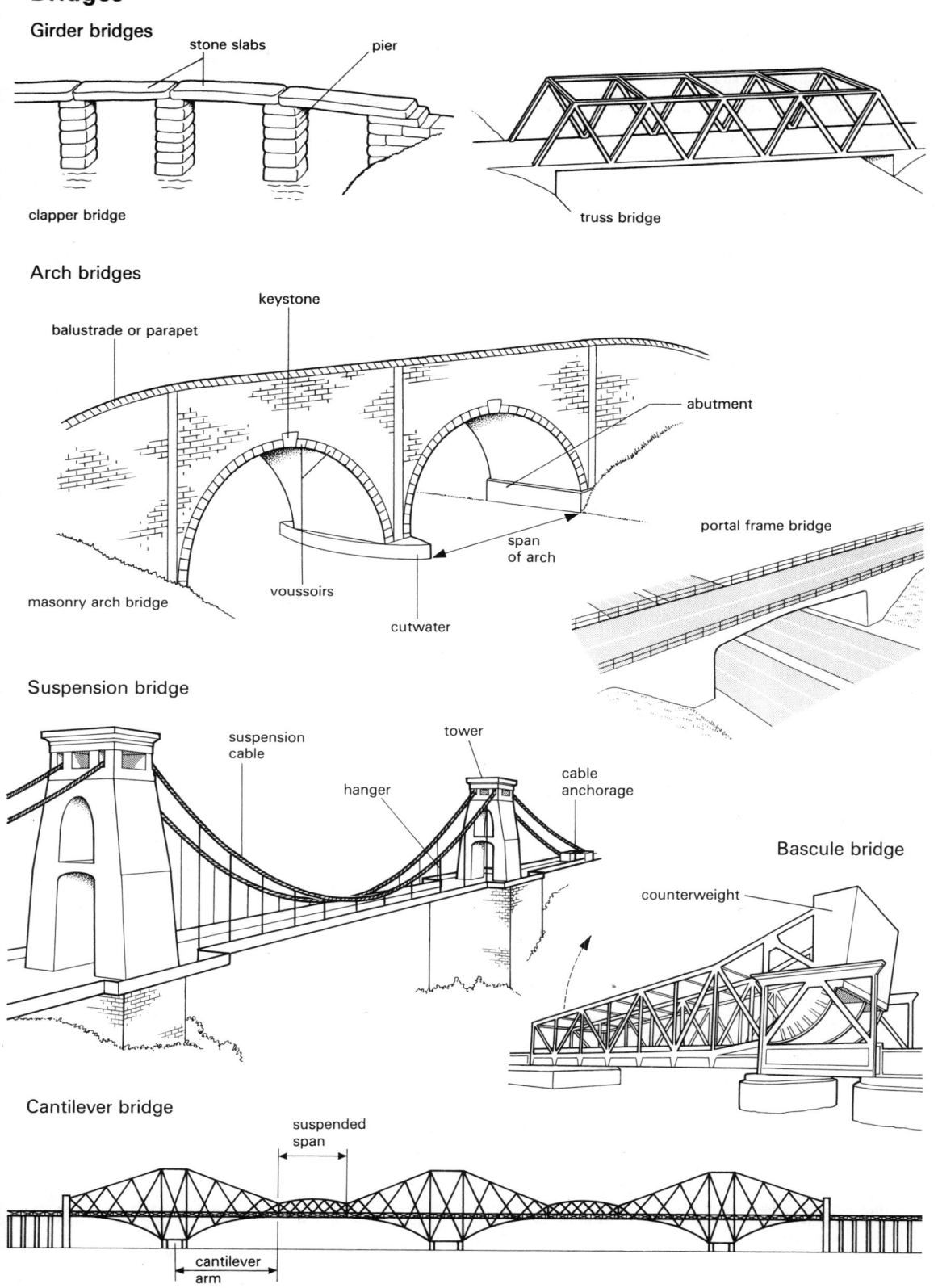

stone slabs

pier

clapper bridge

truss bridge

Arch bridges

balustrade or parapet

keystone

abutment

masonry arch bridge

voussoirs

span of arch

cutwater

portal frame bridge

Suspension bridge

suspension cable

tower

hanger

cable anchorage

Bascule bridge

counterweight

Cantilever bridge

suspended span

cantilever arm

brimstone *n.* (*archaic*) sulphur. [f. BURN¹ + STONE]

brindled /ˈbrɪnd(ə)ld/ *adj.* (esp. of dogs or cattle) brownish or tawny with streaks of other colour. [f. Scand.]

Brindley /ˈbrɪndlɪ/, James (1716–72), pioneer British canal builder, starting in 1760 with the Bridgewater canal to bring coal from the Duke of Bridgewater's mines at Worsley to Manchester. This included an aqueduct over the River Irwell at Barton, a wonder of the age. Altogether he designed some 600 km (375 miles) of waterway, completing the main canal system connecting all the major rivers of England. Brindley believed in building contour canals with the minimum of locks, embankments, cuttings, or tunnels, at the expense of greater lengths. His philosophy has proved correct in that canals built with many locks were the first to be abandoned.

brine *n.* water saturated with salt. —*v.t.* to soak in brine. —**briny** *adj.* [OE]

bring *v.t./i.* (*past & p.p.* **brought** /brɔːt/) **1.** to come carrying, leading, etc. **2.** to cause to be present, to result in. **3.** to put forward (charges etc.?) in court. **4.** to cause to reach a given state. **5.** to induce *to.* —**bring about,** to cause to happen. **bring-and-buy-sale,** a sale at which people bring items for sale and buy those brought by others. **bring down,** to cause to fall; to lower (prices). **bring forth,** to give birth to. **bring forward,** to move to an earlier time; to transfer from a previous page or account. **bring in,** to introduce; to yield as income or profit. **bring off,** to attempt successfully. **bring on,** to cause to develop rapidly. **bring out,** to bring into prominence; to publish. **bring up,** to supervise the education etc. of (a growing child); to call attention to (a subject); to vomit; to come to a sudden halt. [OE]

brink *n.* **1.** the edge of a steep place or stretch of water. **2.** the point immediately before some dangerous action, experience, etc. [f. ON]

brinkmanship *n.* the art of pursuing a dangerous policy to the brink of war etc. before desisting. [f. prec., after *sportsmanship*]

brio /ˈbriːəʊ/ *n.* vivacity. [It.]

briquette /brɪˈket/ *n.* a block of compressed coal-dust. [F, dim. of *brique* BRICK]

Brisbane /ˈbrɪzbən/ an Australian seaport, the capital of Queensland; pop. (est. 1983) 1,138,370.

brisk *adj.* moving quickly, active, lively. —**briskly** *adv.*, **briskness** *n.* [prob. f. F BRUSQUE]

brisket /ˈbrɪskɪt/ *n.* a joint of meat cut from an animal's breast. [f. AF, perh. f. ON]

brisling /ˈbrɪzlɪŋ/ *n.* a small herring or sprat. [Norw. & Da.]

bristle /ˈbrɪs(ə)l/ *n.* **1.** a short stiff hair. **2.** one of the stiff pieces of hair or wire etc. in a brush. —*v.t./i* **1.** to show anger or temper. **2.** (of hair or feathers) to stand upright; (of an animal etc.) to make the hair bristle. —**bristle with,** to have in abundance. [OE]

bristletail *n.* a wingless insect of the order Thysanura (ill. INSECTS).

bristly /ˈbrɪslɪ/ *adj.* full of bristles; rough and prickly. [f. BRISTLE] .

Britain /ˈbrɪt(ə)n/ (in full **Great Britain**) the island containing England, Wales, and Scotland, and including the small adjacent islands. After the OE period *Britain* was used only as a historical term until about the time of Henry VIII and Edward VI, when it came into practical politics in connection with the efforts made to unite England and Scotland. In 1604 James I was proclaimed 'King of Great Britain', and this name was adopted for the United Kingdom at the Union of 1707, after which *South Britain* and *North Britain* were frequent in Acts of Parliament for England and Scotland respectively. (See GREAT BRITAIN.) —**Battle of Britain,** the series of air raids directed against Britain by the German air force (June 1940–April 1941), successfully resisted by the RAF, thereby frustrating this preliminary to a planned invasion of Britain. [f. F f. L *Brittania*, OE *Breoton* and variants]

Britannia /brɪˈtænjə/ *n.* a personification of Britain, shown as a woman with shield, helmet, and trident. It is said that one of Charles II's ladies, the Duchess of Richmond, sat as a model for Britannia to replace the figure which appears on Roman coins from the time of Hadrian or earlier and that King Charles was so pleased with the result that he ordered one of his new naval ships to be given this name. The first warship to be called *Britannia* was in service in 1682, and the name has been associated with the Royal Navy ever since. —**Britania metal,** a silvery alloy of tin,

antimony, and copper. **Britannia silver,** silver that is about 96% pure. [f. L (see prec.)]

Britannic /brɪˈtænɪk/ *adj.* of Britain (chiefly in *His* or *Her Britannic Majesty*). [as prec.]

Briticism /ˈbrɪtɪsɪzm/ *n.* an idiom used in Britain but not in the USA etc. [f. foll., after *Gallicism*]

British /ˈbrɪtɪʃ/ *adj.* of Great Britain or the United Kingdom. —**the British,** the people of Great Britain or the United Kingdom. **Royal British Legion,** see LEGION. [OE]

British Academy an institution founded in 1901 for the promotion of historical, philosophical, and philological studies.

British Columbia /kəˈlʌmbɪə/ a province of Canada (from 1871), on the west coast, formed in 1866 by the union of Vancouver Island (a British colony from 1849) and the mainland area which was called New Caledonia; capital, Victoria.

British Council an organization established in 1934. Its royal charter (1930) defines its aims as the promotion of a wider knowledge of Britain and English abroad, and the development of closer cultural relations with other countries. Most of its funds are provided by Parliament.

British Empire British overseas possessions, acquired for commercial, strategic, or territorial reasons. The colonization of North America started in the early 17th c., although the colonies south of Canada were lost in the American Revolution in the late 18th c. British domination of India began under the auspices of the East India Company, also in the 17th c., while a series of small colonies, mostly in the West Indies, were gained during the colonial wars with France between the late 17th–early 19th c. Australia, New Zealand, and various possessions in the Far East were added in the 19th c. (notably Hong Kong), while extensive possessions in Africa came Britain's way in the last few decades of the 19th c. at the height of the imperialist age. The movement of the British colonies towards independence began in the mid-19th c. with the granting of self-government to Canada, Australia, New Zealand, and South Africa. This trend was accelerated by the two World Wars, with most of the remaining colonies gaining independence in the decade and a half following the end of the Second World War.

British Library the national library of Britain containing the former library departments of the British Museum (in which it is housed), to which George II presented the royal library in 1757. As one of the six copyright libraries it receives a copy of every book published in the UK. It was established separately from the British Museum in 1972, and new premises are being prepared.

British Museum a national museum of antiquities etc. in Bloomsbury, London, occupying the site of Montagu House, which was acquired in 1753 to house the library and collections of Sir Hans Sloane and the Harleian manuscripts purchased with funds granted by Parliament. The present buildings were erected from 1823 onwards. The original holdings have been greatly increased by gifts and purchases and by acquisitions from excavations, and now comprise one of the world's finest collections, particularly of Egyptian, Assyrian, Greek, Roman, and Oriental antiquities, including the Elgin Marbles and the Rosetta Stone. During the 19th c. the natural history collections grew so extensively that it became necessary to find new quarters for them, and in 1881 they were moved to South Kensington; in 1963 the Natural History Museum was made completely independent. The library departments of the British Museum were transferred in 1972 to the British Library.

Briton /ˈbrɪt(ə)n/ *n.* **1.** a member of the people living in South Britain before the Roman conquest. **2.** a native of Great Britain. [f. L f. Celt.]

Brittany /ˈbrɪtənɪ/ a NW district of France, an ancient province and duchy.

Britten /ˈbrɪt(ə)n/, Edward Benjamin, Lord Britten of Aldeburgh, (1913–76), English musician, whose talents as a composer were matched by his outstanding abilities as conductor and pianist. His compositions dazzle in their unrelenting sharpness of vision, and his operas and other vocal works, the best known of his music, are doubly moving for their commemoration of his long friendship with the tenor Peter Pears. *Peter Grimes* (1945), after Crabbe's poem *The Borough* (1810), heralded a new beginning for English music following the privations of the Second World War, and in *Curlew River* (1964), *The Burning Fiery Furnace* (1966), and *The Prodigal Son* (1968) he invented a new musical genre, the church parable. He made settings of a wide and varied range of writers, including Rimbaud (*Les Illuminations*, 1939), Michelangelo (*Seven Sonnets*, 1940), John Donne (nine *Holy Sonnets*, 1945), Henry James (*The Turn of the Screw*, 1954), Shakespeare (*A Midsummer Night's Dream*, 1960), and at the end of his life Thomas Mann (*Death in Venice*, 1973); his pacifism found public expression in the *War Requiem* (1961), which combines the Latin Mass with war poems by Wilfred Owen. Few composers have caught the public's imagination in their lifetime as vividly as did Britten; each new work was eagerly awaited and absorbed.

brittle *adj.* hard but fragile; easily destroyed. **—brittleness** *n.* [OE]

broach[1] *v.t.* **1.** raise (a subject) for discussion. **2.** to pierce (a cask) to draw liquor. **—n. 1.** a tool for enlarging holes. **2.** a roasting-spit. **—broach spire,** a church spire rising from a square tower without a parapet. [f. OF f. L *broccus* projecting]

broach[2] *v.t./i.* (usu. with *to*) to veer or cause (a ship) to veer and present its side to the wind and waves. [orig. unkn.]

broad /brɔːd/ *adj.* **1.** large in extent from one side to the other, wide; (after measurements) in breadth; extensive. **2.** full and complete; (of hints) explicit; (of accent) strongly regional. **3.** tolerant, liberal. **4.** in general terms, not detailed. **5.** (of humour) somewhat coarse. **—n.** the broad part. **— broad bean,** an edible bean, *Vicia faba*, or one of its large flat seeds. **Broad Church,** the section of the Anglican Church favouring toleration, not strict adherence to dogma. **broad-minded** *adj.* having tolerant views. **the Broads,** large areas of open fresh water in East Anglia, formed by the widening of rivers. The removal of peat in medieval times (with subsequent flooding) was probably an important factor in their formation. [OE]

broadcast *v.t./i* (past & *p.p.* **broadcast**) **1.** to transmit (programmes or information) by radio or television; to speak or perform thus. **2.** to disseminate (information) widely. **3.** to scatter (seed) at random rather than in rows. **—n.** a radio or television programme or transmission. **—adv.** by random sowing. **—broadcaster** *n.*

broadcloth *n.* a fine woollen or worsted cloth used in tailoring (orig. woven on a wide loom).

broaden /ˈbrɔːd(ə)n/ *v.t./i.* to make or become broad. [f. BROAD]

broadloom *adj.* (of carpets) woven in broad widths.

broadsheet *n.* a large sheet of paper printed on one side only, especially with information.

broadside *n.* **1.** the firing of all the guns that are on one side of a ship. **2.** a fierce verbal attack. **3.** the side of a ship above the water between bow and quarter. **—broadside on,** sideways on.

broadsword *n.* a sword with a broad blade for cutting rather than thrusting.

Broadway a street traversing the length of Manhattan Island, New York. The longest street in the world, it extends for 241 km (150 miles), and is famous for its theatres which formerly made its name synonymous with show-business.

brocade /brəˈkeɪd/ *n.* a fabric woven with raised pattern. **— v.t.** to weave thus. [f. Sp. and Port. f. It. (*brocco* twisted thread)]

broccoli /ˈbrɒkəlɪ/ *n.* a hardy variety of cauliflower with greenish flower-heads. [It.]

broch /brɒk, brɒx/ *n.* a circular dry-stone tower of a type found in northern Scotland and the adjacent islands, somewhat resembling present-day cooling towers in shape and serving as fortified dwellings, dating from *c.*100 BC-100 AD. [f. ON *borg* castle]

brochure /ˈbrəʊʃʊə(r)/ *n.* a booklet or pamphlet giving descriptive information. [F, = stitching (*brocher* stitch)]

Brocken /ˈbrɒkən/ the name of the highest of the Harz Mountains in nothern Germany, reputed to be the scene of witches' Walpurgis-night revels. **—Brocken spectre,** a magnified shadow of the spectator thrown on a bank of cloud in high mountains when the sun is low, and often encircled by rainbow-like bands. This phenomenon was first observed on the Brocken.

broderie anglaise /brəʊdrɪ ɑ̃ɡˈleɪz/ open embroidery on white linen or cambric. [F, = English embroidery]

brogue[1] /brəʊɡ/ *n.* a strong outdoor shoe with ornamental perforated bands; a rough shoe of untanned leather. [f. Ir. & Gael. f. ON]

brogue[2] /brəʊɡ/ *n.* a strong regional, especially Irish, accent. [perh. allusive use of prec.]

broil *v.t./i.* to cook (meat) on a fire or gridiron; to make or become very hot, as from sunshine. [f. OF *bruler* burn]

broiler *n.* a young chicken reared for broiling or roasting. [f. prec.]

broke *past* of BREAK. **—adj.** (*colloq.*) having no money, bankrupt.

broken *p.p.* of BREAK. **—adj.** that has been broken; (of a person) crushed in spirit, beaten; (of a language) spoken imperfectly (by a foreigner); (of sleep or time) disturbed, interrupted. **—broken chord,** (*Mus.*) a chord in which the notes are played successively, not simultaneously. **brokendown** *adj.* worn or sick, inoperative through mechanical failure. **broken-hearted** *adj.* overwhelmed by grief. **broken home,** a family lacking one parent, as by divorce or separation. **broken reed,** a person who proves unreliable in an emergency.

Broken Hill the former name of Kabwe, a town in Zambia, site of a cave that has yielded human fossils in association with tools belonging to the early middle Stone Age of the Upper Pleistocene in Southern Africa, *c.*125,000 years old. The fossils are of the type *Homo sapiens rhodesiensis* (African Neanderthaloid) that apparently belong to the most recent threshold of human evolution from which fully modern man developed.

broker *n.* **1.** an agent buying and selling for others, a middleman or stockbroker. **2.** an official licensed to sell or appraise distrained goods. [f. AF; orig. unkn.]

brokerage /ˈbrəʊkərɪdʒ/ *n.* a broker's fee or commission. [f. prec.]

brolly *n.* (*colloq.*) an umbrella. [abbr.]

bromide /ˈbrəʊmaɪd/ *n.* **1.** a compound of bromine, used in sedatives. **2.** a soothing statement. [f. foll.]

bromine /ˈbrəʊmiːn/ *n.* a non-metallic dark-red liquid element of the halogen group with a poisonous rank-smelling vapour, symbol Br, atomic number 35, first discovered in 1826. The uncombined element has few uses but bromine compounds are used as petrol additives, insecticides, sedatives, laboratory reagents, etc. The main commercial source for bromine is sea-water. [f. F f. Gk *brōmos* stench]

bronchial /ˈbrɒŋkɪəl/ *adj.* of the bronchi (see BRONCHUS) or the smaller tubes into which they divide. [f. BRONCHUS]

bronchitis /brɒŋˈkaɪtɪs/ *n.* inflammation of the mucous membrane in the bronchial tubes. [f. foll.]

bronchus /ˈbrɒŋkəs/ *n.* (*pl.* **-chi** /-kaɪ/) either of the two main divisions of the windpipe, leading to the lungs (ill. BODY 3). [L f. Gk.]

bronco /ˈbrɒŋkəʊ/ *n.* (*pl.* **-os**) a wild or half-tamed horse of the western USA. [Sp., = rough]

Brontë /ˈbrɒnteɪ/, Charlotte (1816-55), Emily (1818-48), and Anne (1820-49), English novelists, the three surviving daughters of Patrick Prunty or Brontë, perpetual curate of Haworth in Yorkshire. Having lost their mother in 1821 they were educated (with their black-sheep brother, Branwell) largely at home. A lonely childhood in a remote neighbourhood intensified the imaginative powers that were to produce their remarkable novels; apart from work as governesses and, for Emily and Charlotte, a visit to Brussels, their experience of the outside world was unusually limited. All died young, Emily of consumption after publication but before the success of her masterpiece, *Wuthering Heights* (1847), Anne, also of consumption, after publishing two novels, and Charlotte shortly after her marriage to the Revd A. B. Nicholls, when she was already famous for her romantic *tour-de-force*, *Jane Eyre* (1847), and for her restrained *Shirley* (1849) and *Villette* (1853). Their works were published under the pseudonyms Currer, Ellis, and Acton Bell, including their unsuccessful first efforts, a joint book of poems, of which Emily's are now highly regarded.

brontosaurus /brɒntəˈsɔːrəs/ *n.* a large herbivorous dinosaur of the genus *Brontosaurus* of the Jurassic and Cretaceous periods. [f. Gk *brontē* thunder + *sauros* lizard]

bronze *n.* **1.** an alloy of copper and tin. **2.** its brownish colour. **3.** an object (especially a work of art) made of bronze. **—adj.** made of or coloured like bronze. **—v.t.** to give a bronze surface or colour to; (of the sun etc.) to tan. **— bronze medal,** one awarded as the third prize. [f. F f. It., prob. f. Pers. *birinj* copper]

Bronze was first smelted in the Near East, the Aegean, and the Balkans in the late 4th and early 3rd millennium BC. It is harder than pure copper and therefore superior for making weapons and tools. Until the introduction of iron, bronze remained the sole metal for utilitarian purposes, and afterwards it continued in general use to the end of antiquity for sculpture, many domestic objects, and (after the 5th c. BC) for small-denomination coins. The bronze coin was introduced into Britain in 1860, but continued to be called a 'copper'.

Bronze Age the second stage in the classification of prehistoric periods (see PREHISTORY) when certain weapons and tools were usually made of bronze rather than stone. It began in the Near East and SE Europe in the late 4th and early 3rd millennium BC and is associated with the first European civilizations, the spread of the wheel, and the establishment of far-reaching trade networks. It is equated with the beginnings of urban life in China (beginning c. 2000 BC), but develops only in the final stages of some of the Meso-American civilizations (c.AD 1000). In NW Europe the Bronze Age is unaccompanied by developments in civilized life but merely follows on from the Stone Age; in Africa and Australasia it does not appear at all. It ends in most areas with the general use of iron technology, in the 8th c. BC in northern Europe and in the 5th c. AD in China; in Greece and other Aegean countries it ends c.1200 BC with the start of a Dark Age.

brooch /brəʊtʃ/ n. an ornamental clasp fastening by a pin at the back. [f. as BROACH[1]]

brood n. 1. the young of a bird or other creature produced at one hatching or birth. 2. the children in a family. —v.i. 1. to ponder anxiously or resentfully. 2. to sit as a hen on eggs to hatch them. [OE]

broody adj. 1. (of a hen) wanting to brood. 2. engrossed and thoughtful. [f. prec.]

brook[1] /brʊk/ n. a small stream. [OE]

brook[2] /brʊk/ v.t. (usu. with negative) to tolerate, to allow. [OE]

broom n. 1. a yellow-flowered shrub of acid soils, *Cytisus* (or *Sarothamnus*) *scoparius*; any shrub of the genus *Cytisus* or the allied genus *Genista*, with yellow, white, etc. flowers. 2. a long-handled implement for sweeping floors, originally made with twigs from this. —**new broom,** a newly appointed person eager to make changes. [OE]

broomstick n. a broom-handle.

broth /brɒθ/ n. the water in which meat or fish has been boiled; a soup made from this. [OE]

brothel /ˈbrɒθ(ə)l/ n. a house where prostitutes may be visited. [orig. = worthless man, prostitute, f. OE]

brother /ˈbrʌðə(r)/ n. 1. a man or boy in relation to the other sons and daughters of his parents. 2. a man who is a close friend or associate; a male fellow member of the same church, trade union, or other association, or of the human race. 3. a monk who is not a priest. —**brother-in-law** n. (pl. **brothers-in-law**) the brother of one's husband or wife; the husband of one's sister. —**brotherly** adj. [OE]

brotherhood /ˈbrʌðəhʊd/ n. 1. friendly feeling as between brothers. 2. an association of men with common (often religious) beliefs or interests. [f. BROTHER + -HOOD]

brougham /ˈbruːəm/ n. (hist.) a one-horse closed carriage with the driver's seat outside; a motor-car with the driver's seat open. [f. Lord *Brougham* (d. 1868)]

brought /brɔːt/ past & p.p. of BRING.

brow /braʊ/ n. 1. (usu. in pl.) an eyebrow. 2. the forehead. 3. the projecting upper part or edge of a hill or cliff. —**brow-band** n. the strap of a bridle passing over a horse's brow (ill. HORSE). [OE]

browbeat v.t. to intimidate.

Brown[1] /braʊn/, Sir Arthur Whitten (1886–1948), aviator, born in Glasgow of American parents, knighted in 1919 for his pioneer transatlantic flight with Alcock.

Brown[2] /braʊn/, John (1800–59), American abolitionist, commemorated in the popular marching-song 'John Brown's Body'. The leader of an unsuccessful uprising in Virginia in 1859, he was captured and executed after he had seized the arsenal at Harper's Ferry, intending to arm the Black slaves and start a revolt. Although the revolt never materialized, Brown became a hero of the American abolitionists who played a crucial part in the outbreak of the American Civil War soon afterwards.

Brown[3] /braʊn/, Lancelot (1716–83), English landscape gardener, known as 'Capability' because he would tell his patrons that their estates had 'great capabilities'. He created natural-looking landscape parks, broken by serpentine waters and clumps of trees. Famous examples of his work are

at Blenheim Palace in Oxfordshire and Chatsworth in Derbyshire.

brown /braʊn/ adj. of a colour between orange and black; dark-skinned, sun-tanned; (of bread) brown from the colour of the wholemeal, or other coarse flour used. —n. brown colour or pigment; brown clothes or material. —v.t./i. to make or become brown. —**brown bear,** a large bear (*Ursus arctos*) of the northern hemisphere with shaggy usually brownish fur. **brown paper,** unbleached paper used for packing. **brown sugar,** sugar only partially refined. [OE]

Browne /braʊn/, Sir Thomas (1605–82), English physician, author of *Religio Medici* (1642), a confession of Christian faith (qualified by an eclectic and generally sceptical attitude), and a collection of opinions on a vast number of subjects more or less connected with religion, expressed with a wealth of fancy and wide erudition.

Brownian motion or **movement** /ˈbraʊnɪən/ the irregular movements of microscopic particles in a fluid, caused by molecules of the fluid colliding with them. [f. R. *Brown* Scottish botanist (d. 1858) who discovered the phenomenon]

brownie /ˈbraʊnɪ/ n. 1. a benevolent elf. 2. **Brownie,** a junior Guide. [f. BROWN]

Browning[1] /ˈbraʊnɪŋ/, Elizabeth Barrett (1806–61), English poet, a semi-invalid from the age of 15. She is chiefly remembered today for her sensational romance with Robert Browning who rescued her from her domineering father and eloped with her to Italy in 1846. During her life her poetic reputation stood higher than Browning's; she was seriously considered a possible successor to Wordsworth as Poet Laureate. Her best-known works are her love poems *Sonnets from the Portuguese* (1850) and her verse novel *Aurora Leigh* (1857).

Browning[2] /ˈbraʊnɪŋ/, Robert (1812–89), English poet, son of a clerk in the Bank of England, who received most of his education from his father's library. The success of his long poem *Paracelsus* (1835) resulted in friendships with the writer John Forster and theatrical manager W. C. Macready who encouraged him to write for the stage; *Strafford* (1837) was successfully produced at Covent Garden but the poor reception of *Sordello* (1840) eclipsed his reputation for many years. In 1846 he married and eloped to Italy with Elizabeth Barrett; Elizabeth and Renaissance Italy inspired his greatest work and his reputation revived with *Men and Women* (1855) and *Dramatis Personae* (1864). His greatest triumph was *The Ring and the Book* (1868–9), a series of dramatic monologues, a form which Browning developed to perfection. Browning's experiments in form and content and his technical virtuosity have considerably influenced modern poets, notably Eliot and Pound.

browning n. browned flour or other additive to colour gravy. [f. BROWN]

browse /braʊz/ v.i. 1. to read or inspect items on display etc. casually. 2. (of animals) to crop or feed on leaves and young shoots. —n. an act or spell of browsing. [f. OF *broust* young shoot, prob. f. Gmc]

Bruce[1] /bruːs/ see ROBERT I 'the Bruce'.

Bruce[2] /bruːs/, James (1730–94), Scottish explorer. Consul-General at Algiers from 1763 to 1765, Bruce set off from Cairo in 1768 on an expedition to Abyssinia, discovering the source of the Blue Nile, after many hardships, in late 1770. Many of his accounts were dismissed by contemporaries as fabrications, but have since been vindicated by other observers.

brucellosis /bruːsəˈləʊsɪs/ n. a bacterial disease causing abortion in domestic animals and recurrent fever in humans consuming their products. [f. Sir D. *Bruce*, Scottish physician (d. 1931)]

Bruckner /ˈbrʊknə(r)/, Anton (1824–96), Austrian composer and virtuoso organist. He went to Vienna as professor of harmony, counterpoint, and organ at the Conservatory when he was 44. His friendship with Wagner began in 1865 but, although he dedicated his Third Symphony (1873–8) to him, he derived little from Wagner's music beyond a sense of the large-scale and a massive slow-moving harmonic thought. His music moved to 'maturity equally slowly, and Bruckner allowed himself to be persuaded by critical friends to alter the orchestration of his symphonies; for the most part editors have traced his original intentions, and the symphonies, together with the Masses, form the cornerstone upon which his fame rests.

Bruegel /ˈbrɔɪg(ə)l/, Pieter (c.1525–69), Flemish artist, also known as 'Peasant Bruegel' and 'Pieter Bruegel the elder'. He joined the Antwerp guild in 1551 and after travelling to Italy settled there for eight years, producing graphic work in the main. In 1563 he moved to Brussels and worked in a variety of different genres, establishing his reputation as an artist of wide range and ability, with such pictures as *Hunters in the Snow* (1565), *The Procession to Calvary* (1564), and *The Blind Leading the Blind*. Both of his two sons (who spell their name *Brueghel*) worked chiefly in Antwerp. Pieter Brueghel the younger (1564-1638) is known primarily as a very able copyist of his father's work, while Jon ('Velvet') Brueghel (1568-1623) was a celebrated still-life and mythological painter.

bruise /bru:z/ *n.* an injury caused by a blow etc. that discolours the skin without breaking it. —*v.t./i.* to injure in this way; to be susceptible to bruises; to hurt mentally. [orig. = crush, f. OE]

bruit /bru:t/ *v.t.* (*archaic*) to spread (a report) *abroad* or *about*. [F, = noise]

Brummell /ˈbrʌm(ə)l/, George Bryan, 'Beau' (1778-1840), Regency dandy, arbiter of British fashion for the first decade and a half of the 19th c., owing his social position to his close friendship with the Prince of Wales (later George IV). Brummell quarrelled with his patron and fled to France to avoid his creditors in 1816, eventually dying penniless in a mental asylum in Caen.

brunch *n.* (*colloq.*) a meal combining breakfast and lunch. [portmanteau word]

Brunei /ˈbru:naɪ/ a small oil-rich sultanate on the NW coast of Borneo, a British protectorate until it became fully independent in 1984; pop. (1982) about 200,000; official language, Malay; capital, Bandar Seri Begawan. By the early 16th c. Brunei's power extended over the whole of the island of Borneo and parts of the Philippines, but declined as Portuguese and Dutch influence grew, and in 1888 it was placed under British protection. Its main industries are crude oil production and gas liquefying and distilling. —**Bruneian** *adj.*

Brunel /bruˈnel/, Sir Marc Isambard (1769-1849), engineer who was born in France but fled to the USA during the French Revolution, where he invented a mechanical method of producing ships' blocks. He came to England in 1799 and persuaded the government to finance first models then full-sized machines at Portsmouth dockyard; these must be regarded as the first examples of automation. He also designed other machines for woodworking, boot-making, knitting, and printing; he was a versatile civil engineer and built bridges, landing stages, and the first tunnelling shield, with which he built the first tunnel under the Thames, between 1825 and 1843.
His son Isambard Kingdom Brunel (1806-59) was equally versatile, designing the famous Clifton suspension bridge at Bristol, then in 1833 becoming chief engineer of the Great Western railway before turning to steamship construction with the *Great Western* (1837), the first successful trans-atlantic steamship. A little-known but remarkable achievement was Brunel's design in 1855 of a prefabricated hospital for the Crimean War. Both father and son have a brilliant record of achievement.

Brunelleschi /bruːneˈleskɪ/, properly Filippo di Ser Brunellesco (1377-1446), the most famous Florentine architect of the 15th c. He trained as a goldsmith, but began to study architecture soon after 1401 and went to Rome. He is often credited with the 'discovery' of perspective—i.e. he studied the mathematical laws underlying appearances, by use of which artists could give an appearance of reality and depth. He revived Roman architectural forms, and above all studied Roman construction; he was an engineer rather than a designer. His greatest feat was the construction of the dome of Florence cathedral, evolving a method, based on his Roman studies, of raising the dome without the use of temporary supports.

brunette /bruːˈnet/ *n.* a woman with dark brown hair. [F, dim. of *brun* brown]

Brunhild /ˈbruːnhɪlt/ (in the Nibelungenlied) wife of Gunther, who instituted the murder of Siegfried. In the Norse versions she is a Valkyrie whom Sigurd (the Norse counterpart of Siegfried) wins by penetrating the wall of fire behind which she lies in an enchanted sleep.

Bruno /ˈbruːnəʊ/, St (*c.*1032-1101), German founder of the Carthusian order (1086). He was never formally canonized but in 1514 his order obtained papal leave to keep his feast day (6 Oct.).

Brunswick /ˈbrʌnzwɪk/ a city and ancient duchy of north-ern Germany.

brunt *n.* the chief stress or strain (*of* an attack or res-ponsibility etc.). [orig. unkn.]

brush *n.* **1.** an implement with bristles, hairs, etc., set in a solid base for cleaning, painting, dressing the hair, etc.; an application of this. **2.** a fox's bushy tail. **3.** a brushlike piece of carbon or metal for making an electrical connection, especially with a moving part. **4.** a short, usually unpleasant, encounter *with*. —*v.t.* **1.** to sweep clean, arrange, etc., with a brush. **2.** to touch lightly in passing. **3.** to apply or remove with a brush. —**brush aside**, to dismiss as irrelevant. **brush off**, to dismiss abruptly. **brush-off** *n.* an abrupt dismissal, a rebuff. **brush up**, to clean or smarten up; to revive one's former knowledge of. [f. AF *brousse*, OF *brosse*]

brushed *adj.* (of fabrics) finished with a nap. [f. prec.]

brushwood *n.* cut or broken twigs etc. undergrowth.

brushwork *n.* manipulation of the brush in painting; a painter's style in this.

brusque /brʊsk/ *adj.* abrupt or offhand in manner. — **brusquely** *adv.*, **brusqueness** *n.* [F, f. It. *brusco* sour]

Brussels /ˈbrʌs(ə)lz/ a city on the River Senne, the capital of Brabant since the 14th c. and of Belgium since it achieved independence in 1830; pop. (1981) 997,293. The Commission of the European Communities has its head-quarters here.

Brussels sprouts /ˈbrʌs(ə)lz/ the edible leaf-buds, resem-bling tiny cabbages, growing thickly on the stem of a variety of cabbage (*Brassica oleracea gemmifera*). [f. prec.]

brutal /ˈbruːt(ə)l/ *adj.* very cruel, merciless. —**brutality** /-ˈtælɪtɪ/ *n.*, **brutally** *adv.* [f. BRUTE]

brutalize *v.t./i.* to make or become brutal; to treat brutally. [f. prec.]

brute *n.* a brutal or (*colloq.*) disagreeable person. —*adj.* unable to reason; animal-like in stupidity, sensuality, etc.; unthinking, exerted etc. without mental effort. —**brutish** *adj.* [f. F. f. L *brutus* stupid]

Brutus[1] /ˈbruːtəs/ great-grandson of Aeneas and legendary founder of the British people, said to have brought a group of Trojans to England and founded Troynovant or New Troy (later called London), becoming the progenitor of a line of kings. His story is told (or more probably invented) by the historian Geoffrey of Monmouth (12th c.).

Brutus[2] /ˈbruːtəs/, Lucius Junius, traditional founder of the Roman Republic. According to the legend (probably with a historical core), in 510 BC after the rape of his wife Lucretia by the son of King Tarquin the Proud, and her subsequent suicide, he led a popular uprising against the king (his uncle) and drove him from Rome; he and the father of Lucretia were elected as the first consuls of the Republic (509 BC).

Brutus[3] /ˈbruːtəs/, Marcus Junius (85-42 BC), Roman sena-tor who claimed descent from Lucius Junius Brutus. With Cassius he was a leader of the conspirators who assassinated Julius Caesar in the name of the Republic in 44 BC. He and Cassius were defeated by Caesar's supporters, Antony and Octavian, at the battle of Philippi in 42 BC, after which he committed suicide.

bryony /ˈbraɪənɪ/ *n.* either of two climbing hedge-plants, *Bryonia dioica* and *Tamus communis*. [f. L f. Gk]

bryophyte /ˈbraɪəfaɪt/ *n.* a member of the Bryophyta, a group of plants comprising the mosses and liverworts (ill. PLANTS). [ult. f. Gk (*bruon* moss, *phuton* plant)]

Brythonic /braɪˈθɒnɪk/ *adj.* of the Celts of southern Britain or their languages. —*n.* the southern group of the Celtic languages, including Welsh, Cornish, and Breton. It grew from the language spoken by the Britons at the time of the Roman invasion, and borrowed a number of Latin words during the Roman occupation. When in the 5th c. Britain was invaded by Germanic-speaking peoples the language of the Britons died out in most parts but survived in the mountainous and more remote west —Wales, Cumberland, parts of the Scottish lowlands, and Cornwall —and was carried by British emigrants across the Channel, where it survives as the Breton language in Brittany. [f. Welsh *Brython* Britons]

B.Sc. *abbr.* Bachelor of Science.

bubble *n.* **1.** a globular film of liquid enclosing air or gas; an air-filled cavity in glass etc. **2.** a transparent domed canopy. —*v.t.* to send up or rise in bubbles; to make the sound of bubbles. —**bubble and squeak**, cooked potato and cabbage fried together in a cake. **bubble cap**, (in oil refining) each of a series of small domed structures that allow vapour to rise against descending liquids (ill. OIL).

bubble gum, chewing-gum that can be blown into bubbles. —**bubbly** adj. [imit.]

bubonic /bjuːˈbɒnɪk/ adj. **bubonic plague,** a contagious bacterial disease characterized by inflamed swelling is (*buboes*) in the groin or armpit. [f. Gk *boubōn* groin]

buccaneer /bʌkəˈnɪə(r)/ n. a pirate, originally on the Spanish-American coast; an unscrupulous adventurer. —**buccaneering** adj. & n. [f. F (*boucan* barbecue, of Brazilian origin)]

Bucephalus /bjuːˈsefələs/ the favourite horse of Alexander the Great, which was tamed by him as a boy and accompanied him on his campaigns until its death, after a battle, in 326 BC.

Buchan¹ /ˈbʌk(ə)n/, Alexander (1829–1907), Scottish meteorologist who wrote a standard textbook on the subject. After scrutinizing temperature records over a nine-year period, he proposed that at certain times the temperature deviated from the normal for that season; it is now thought that these 'Buchan's cold spells' are probably distributed at random. He also produced maps and tables of atmospheric circulation, and of ocean currents and temperatures, based largely on information gathered by the HMS *Challenger* expedition during 1872–6.

Buchan² /ˈbʌkən/, John, 1st Baron Tweedsmuir (1875–1940), novelist, who combined a literary career with public life (he was Governor-General of Canada 1935–40). He wrote non-fictional works but is remembered for his action-packed adventure stories, often featuring recurring heroes (such as Richard Hannay). Popular among these are *The Thirty-Nine Steps* (1915), *Greenmantle* (1916), and *The Three Hostages* (1924).

Bucharest /buːkəˈrest/ the capital of Romania; pop. 1,960,097.

Buchenwald /ˈbʊkənvaːlt, ˈbʊx-/ a village in East Germany, near Weimar, site of a Nazi concentration camp in the Second World War.

buck¹ n. **1.** a male deer, rabbit, or hare. **2.** (*archaic*) a fashionable young man. —v.t./i. (of a horse) to jump vertically with back arched; to throw (the rider) thus. —**buck up,** (*slang*) to hurry up; to cheer up. [OE]

buck² n. (in poker) an object placed as a reminder before the player whose turn it is to deal. —**pass the buck,** (*colloq.*) to shift responsibility (and possible blame) to another. [orig. unkn.]

buck³ n. (*US slang*) a dollar [orig. unkn.]

bucket /ˈbʌkɪt/ n. **1.** a round flat-bottomed container with a handle, for carrying liquids etc.; the amount contained in this. **2.** a scoop in a dredger etc.; a compartment in a water-wheel. —v.t./i. **1.** to travel or drive fast and bumpily. **2.** to rain or pour down heavily. [perh. f. OE, = pitcher]

Buckingham Palace /ˈbʌkɪŋəm/ the London residence of the British sovereign since 1837, adjoining St James's Park, Westminster. It was built for the Duke of Buckingham in the early 18th c., bought by George III in 1761, and redesigned by John Nash for George IV in 1825; the façade facing the Mall was redesigned in 1913.

Buckinghamshire /ˈbʌkɪŋəmʃɪə(r)/ a southern county of England.

buckle n. a metal clasp with a hinged pin for securing a strap, belt, etc. —v.t./i. **1.** to fasten with a buckle. **2.** to crumple or cause to crumple under pressure. [f. OF f. L *buccula* cheek-strap of helmet]

buckler n. a small round shield with a handle. [as prec.]

buckram /ˈbʌkrəm/ n. coarse linen or cloth stiffened with paste, used for binding books etc. [f. AF, perh. f. *Bokhara* in central Asia]

Bucks. abbr. Buckinghamshire.

buckshee /bʌkˈʃiː/ adj. & adv. (*slang*) free of charge. [corrupt of BAKSHEESH]

buckshot n. coarse lead shot. [f. BUCK¹ + SHOT]

buckskin n. leather from a buck's skin; a thick smooth cotton or woollen fabric.

buckthorn n. a thorny shrub (*Rhamnus cathartica*) with berries that were formerly used as a purgative. [f. BUCK¹ + THORN]

buckwheat n. a plant of the genus *Fagopyrum*, with dark seeds used for horse and poultry food etc. [Du., = beech-wheat.]

bucolic /bjuːˈkɒlɪk/ adj. of herdsmen or shepherds, pastoral. —n. a pastoral poem. [f. L f. Gk (*boukolos* herdsman)]

bud n. the rudiment of a shoot, foliage, or flower; a leaf or flower not fully open; an asexual growth separating from an organism to form a new animal. —v.t./i. (**-dd-**) **1.** to put forth buds. **2.** to graft the bud of (a plant) on another plant. **3.** (esp. in *partic.*) to begin to grow or develop. [orig. unkn.]

Budapest /buːdəˈpest/ the capital of Hungary, formed in 1873 by the union of the hilly Buda on the right bank of the Danube with the low-lying Pest on the left bank; pop. (1980) 2,060,000.

Buddha /ˈbʊdə/ n. the title of successive teachers (past and future) of Buddhism, an honorific applied to an enlightened man. It usually denotes the founder of Buddhism, Siddhartha Gautama of the Sakyas (see SAKYAMUNI). Born a Kshatriya prince in the Nepalese Terai c.563 BC, he renounced kingdom, wife, and child to become an ascetic. After taking religious instruction from various teachers, he attained enlightenment (nirvana) c.525 BC through meditation beneath a bo-tree in the village of Buddh Gaya in NE India. He then taught all who wanted to learn, regardless of sex, class, or caste, until his death in c.480 BC. [Skr., = enlightened (*budh* wake up, know)]

Buddhism /ˈbʊdɪz(ə)m/ n. the religion founded by Siddhartha Gautama, entitled the Buddha, in NE India in the 5th c. BC as a reaction against the sacrificial religion of orthodox brahminism. It is a religion without a god, in which human mistakes and human doom are linked in a relentless chain of cause and effect. There are two major traditions or 'vehicles': Theravada (often called Hinayana), and Mahayana; and, emerging from the latter, Vajrayana. The basic teachings of Buddhism are contained in the 'four noble truths': all existence is suffering; the cause of suffering is desire; freedom from suffering is nirvana; and the means of attaining nirvana is prescribed in the 'eightfold path' that combines ethical conduct, mental discipline, and wisdom. Central to this religious path are the doctrine of 'no-self' (*anatta*; Skr. *an-atman*) and the practice of meditation. The three 'jewels' of Buddhism are the Buddha, the doctrine (*dharma*), and the sangha. —**Buddhist** n. & adj. [f. prec.]

buddleia /ˈbʌdlɪə/ n. a garden shrub or tree of the genus *Buddleia*, with small fragrant lilac, white, red, pink, or yellow flowers in clusters, especially *B. davidii* which bears lilac flowers that attract many butterflies. [f. A. *Buddle* English botanist (d. 1715)]

buddy n. a friend, a mate. [perh. f. BROTHER]

budge /bʌdʒ/ v.t./i. (chiefly in negative contexts) **1.** to move in the least degree. **2.** to abandon or cause to abandon an opinion. [f. F *bouger*]

budgerigar /ˈbʌdʒərɪgɑː(r)/ n. an Australian grass parakeet, often kept as a cage-bird. [Aboriginal, = good cockatoo]

budget /ˈbʌdʒɪt/ n. an estimate or plan of income and expenditure, especially those of a country; the amount of money needed or available. —v.t./i. to allot or allow *for* in a budget. —**budgetary** adj. [f. OF f. L *bulga* bag]

budgie /ˈbʌdʒɪ/ n. (*colloq.*) a budgerigar. [abbr.]

Buenos Aires /ˈbweɪnɒs ˈaɪriːz/ the capital city and a port of Argentina; pop. (1980) 2,908,000.

buff n. **1.** a velvety dull-yellow leather; the colour of this. **2.** (*colloq.*) an enthusiast [orig. for going to fires, from the buff uniforms once worn by New York volunteer firemen]. —v.t. to polish (metal etc.) by rubbing; to make velvety like buff. —**in the buff,** naked. [orig. = buffalo, f. F *buffle*]

buffalo /ˈbʌfələʊ/ n. (*pl* -oes, collect. -o) an ox, especially *Bubalis bubalis* of Asia, or *Syncerus caffer* of Africa, or (especially) *Bison bison* of North America. [prob. f. Port. f. L f. Gk *boubalos*]

Buffalo Bill William Frederick Cody (1846–1917), American plainsman. Cody gained his nickname for killing a record number of buffalo in a single day, and, after working as an army scout and in a host of other itinerant jobs, devoted his life to show business, particularly a 'Wild West' show, which travelled all over the country giving performances purporting to portray life in the American West. As a result more of these dramatics than of any real frontier exploits, Cody became a national figure, and his death in 1917 was widely seen as symbolizing the end of an era.

buffer¹ n. **1.** thing that deadens impact, especially a shock-absorber fitted (in pairs) on a railway vehicle or at the end of a track. **2.** a substance that maintains the degree of acidity in a solution. —**buffer state,** a small country between two powerful ones, thought to reduce the chance of war between these. [f. *buff* sound as of a soft body when struck]

buffer² n. (*slang*) a man, a fellow. [perh. f. prec.]

buffet[1] /ˈbʊfeɪ/ n. **1.** a place where light meals may be bought (usually at a counter) and eaten. **2.** /also ˈbʌfɪt/ a sideboard or recessed cupboard for dishes etc. **3.** provision of food where guests serve themselves. —**buffet car,** a railway coach in which refreshments are served. [F, = stool]

buffet[2] /ˈbʌfɪt/ n. a blow, especially with the hand. —v.t. to deal such blows to; to contend with (waves etc.) [f. OF, dim. of bufe blow]

Buffon /buːˈfɔ̃/, Georges-Louis Leclerc, Comte de (1707-88), French naturalist, appointed Keeper of the Jardin du Roi (Royal Botanical Garden) in 1739, which began his lifelong interest in natural history. He suggested that on scientific evidence the earth was much older than was generally accepted and he saw all life as the physical property of matter, thereby stressing the unity of all living species and minimizing the apparent differences between animals and plants. His work gives the impression that he is groping towards a concept of evolution, formulated in the next century by Darwin. These thoughts were expressed in a remarkable compilation of the animal kingdom, the Histoire naturelle, begun in 1749. At his death 36 volumes had been published, to which another 8 volumes were added posthumously.

buffoon /bəˈfuːn/ n. a jester, a clown. —**buffoonery** n. [f. F f. It. f. L buffo clown]

bug n. **1.** a hemipterous insect, especially a bedbug; any small insect. **2.** (colloq.) a virus, an infection; an obsessive enthusiasm or enthusiast. **3.** (slang) a concealed microphone. **4.** (slang) a defect in a machine etc. —v.t. (-gg-) (slang) **1.** to conceal a microphone in. **2.** to annoy. [orig. unkn.]

bugbear n. a cause of annoyance; an object of baseless fear, a bogy. [f. obs. bug bogy]

bugger n. (vulgar) a hateful or contemptible person or thing; a sodomite. —int. (vulgar) expressing annoyance. [f. Du., ult. f. L Bulgarus Bulgarian heretic]

buggery n. sodomy. [as prec.]

buggy n. a light horse-drawn vehicle for one or two persons; a small sturdy motor vehicle. [orig. unkn.]

bugle[2] /ˈbjuːg(ə)l/ n. an instrument like a small trumpet, for sounding signals. —v.i. to sound a bugle. —**bugler** n. [orig. = buffalo; f. OF f. L buculus young bull]

bugle[2] /ˈbjuːg(ə)l/ n. a creeping woodland plant (Ajuga reptans) with blue flowers. [f. L bugula]

bugloss /ˈbjuːglɒs/ n. **1.** a plant related to borage, of various genera. **2.** a plant of the genus Echium, especially E. vulgare (also called biper's bugloss) with white bristly hairs and blue flowers. [f. F or L f. Gk bouglossos ox-tongued, with ref. to the shape and roughness of its leaves]

buhl /buːl/ n. inlaid work of brass, tortoiseshell, etc. [f. A. C. Boule, French wood-carver (d. 1732)]

build /bɪld/ v.t. (past & p.p. built /bɪlt/) to construct by putting parts or material together; to develop or establish (a reputation etc.). —n. style of construction; proportions of the body. —**build up,** to establish or be established gradually. [OE]

builder n. one who builds, especially a contractor who builds houses. [f. prec.]

building n. **1.** the construction of houses etc. **2.** a permanent built structure that can be entered. —**building society,** a society of investors that lends money to people buying houses etc. The earliest building societies date from the first part of the 19th c. They consisted of a group of people contributing to a fund which was used to purchase a house for each of its members, and were dissolved when this had been achieved. Later in the 19th c. societies were established on a permanent basis, and some still retain the word 'Permanent' in their titles.

buildup **1.** n. a favourable description in advance. **2.** a gradual approach to a climax.

built /bɪlt/ past & p.p. of BUILD. —adj. having a specified bodily build. —**built-up** adj. increased in height etc. by the addition of parts; (of an area) fully occupied by houses etc.

Bujumbura /buːdʒəmˈbʊərə/ the capital of Burundi, on Lake Tanganyika; pop. (1979) 151,000.

bulb n. **1.** the globular base of the stem in plants such as the onion and daffodil, from which roots grow down and leaves grow up (ill. PLANTS). **2.** an object or part shaped like this; an electric lamp, its glass container. —**bulbous** /ˈbʌlbəs/ adj. [f. L f. Gk bolbos onion]

Bulgar /ˈbʌlgɑː(r)/ n. **1.** a member of an ancient Finnish tribe that conquered the Slavs of the lower Danube area in the 7th c. AD and settled in what is now Bulgaria, becoming Slavonic in language. **2.** a native or inhabitant of Bulgaria. —adj. Bulgarian. [f. L Bulgarus]

Bulgaria /bʌlˈgeərɪə/ a country in SE Europe on the western shores of the Black Sea; pop. (1982) 8,929,000; official language, Bulgarian; capital, Sofia. Until the Second World War Bulgaria was predominantly an agricultural country, but since then the industrial sector has been effectively built up and there is a substantial engineering industry. Conquered during the Dark Ages by Bulgar tribes from the east, the country became part of the Ottoman empire in the 14th c., remaining under Turkish rule until the Russo-Turkish wars of the late 19th c. Bulgaria fought on the German side in both World Wars, generally not enjoying good relations with her Balkan neighbours. Occupied by the Russians after the Second World War, the State has since become one of the most consistently pro-Russian members of the Warsaw Pact.

Bulgarian /bʌlˈgeərɪən/ adj. of Bulgaria or its people or language. —n. **1.** a native or inhabitant of Bulgaria. **2.** the official language of Bulgaria, belonging to the Slavonic group of languages within which it is most closely related to Serbo-Croat. [f. prec.]

bulge n. **1.** an irregularly rounded swelling. **2.** (colloq.) a temporary increase in numbers. —v.i. to form a bulge. [f. L bulga bag]

bulk n. **1.** size or magnitude, especially when great. **2.** the greater part of. **3.** a large shape, body, or person. **4.** a large quantity. —v.t./i. **1.** to increase the size or thickness of. **2.** to seem (large etc.) in size or importance. —**bulk buying,** buying in large amounts, especially by one buyer of much of a producer's output. [ON]

bulkhead n. an upright partition between compartments in a ship, aircraft, etc. [f. bulk stall + HEAD]

bulky adj. taking up much space, inconveniently large. —**bulkiness** n. [f. BULK]

bull[1] /bʊl/ n. **1.** an uncastrated male of the ox family; the male of the whale, elephant, and other large animals. **2. the Bull,** the constellation or sign of the zodiac Taurus. **3.** the bull's-eye of a target. **4.** one who buys shares on the Stock Exchange in the hope of selling them at a higher price later (cf. BEAR[2]). —**bull-nosed** adj. with a rounded end. —**bull-terrier** n. a dog of a breed originally produced by crossing a bulldog and a terrier. [f. ON]

bull[2] /bʊl/ n. a papal edict. [f. L bulla seal]

bulldog n. a dog of strong courageous breed with a broad head and short thick neck.

bulldoze /ˈbʊldəʊz/ v.t. **1.** to move or clear with a bulldozer. **2.** (colloq.) to intimidate; to force one's way. [orig. = coerce by threats of violence; perh. f.BULL[1], DOSE]

bulldozer n. a powerful tractor with a broad vertical blade in front for moving earth etc. [f. prec.]

bullet /ˈbʊlɪt/ n. a small cylindrical projectile fired from a gun etc. [f. F (dim. of boule ball)]

bulletin /ˈbʊlɪtɪn/ n. a short official statement of news, the condition of a patient, etc. [F f. It. dim. of bulletta passport (L bulla seal)]

bullfighting n. the sport of baiting and usually killing a bull. Bullfighting is the national spectator sport of Spain, found also in some parts of Latin America and southern France, taking place in an outdoor arena. An early type of bullfighting was practised by Minoans, Greeks, and Romans, and the sport seems to have been introduced into Spain in about the 11th c. —**bullfighter** n.

bullfinch n. a songbird with a short beak and pinkish breast.

bullfrog n. a large American frog with a bellowing cry.

bullion /ˈbʊljən/ n. gold or silver in bulk before coining, or valued by weight. [AF, = mint (as BOIL[1])]

bullock /ˈbʊlək/ n. a castrated bull. [OE, dim. of BULL[1]]

Bull Run /bʊl/ a small river in East Virginia, USA, scene of two important battles (1861 and 1862) in which the Federal side was defeated in the American Civil War.

bull's-eye n. **1.** the centre of a target. **2.** a large hard minty sweet. **3.** a hemisphere or thick disc of glass as a window in a ship, a small circular window; a hemispherical lens, a lantern with this; a boss at the centre of a sheet of blown glass. [f. BULL[1]]

bully[1] /ˈbʊlɪ/ n. a person using strength or power to hurt or coerce others by intimidation. —v.t. to behave as a bully towards, to intimidate. [prob. f. Du., orig. as a term of endearment]

bully[2] /ˈbʊlɪ/ n. the start of play in hockey, at which two

Building Techniques

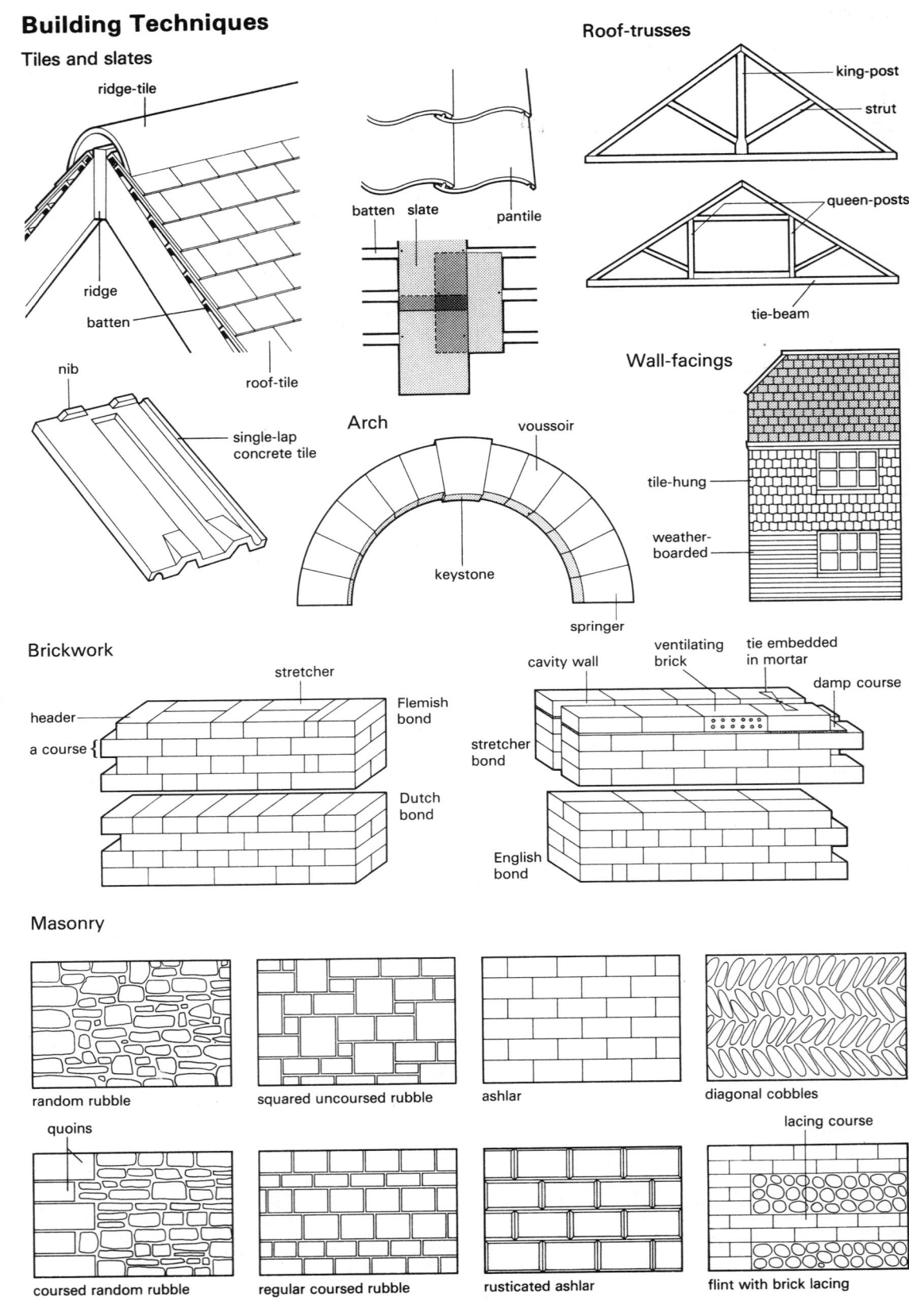

Tiles and slates

ridge-tile

ridge

batten

nib

roof-tile

single-lap
concrete tile

batten slate pantile

Arch

voussoir

keystone

springer

Roof-trusses

king-post

strut

queen-posts

tie-beam

Wall-facings

tile-hung

weather-
boarded

Brickwork

stretcher

header

a course {

Flemish
bond

Dutch
bond

cavity wall

ventilating
brick

tie embedded
in mortar

damp course

stretcher
bond

English
bond

Masonry

random rubble

squared uncoursed rubble

ashlar

diagonal cobbles

quoins

coursed random rubble

regular coursed rubble

rusticated ashlar

lacing course

flint with brick lacing

opposing players tap the ground and each other's sticks three times before hitting the ball. —*v.i.* to start play thus. [orig. unkn.]

bulrush /ˈbʊlrʌʃ/ *n.* any of several tall reed-like plants, *Scirpus lacustris* or (now more usually) *Typha latifolia*. [f. BULL¹, in sense 'coarse']

bulwark /ˈbʊlwək/ *n.* **1.** a defensive wall, especially of earth; a protecting person or thing. **2.** (usu. in *pl.*) a ship's side above deck (ill. SAILING-SHIPS). [f. MDu.]

Bulwer-Lytton see LYTTON.

bum¹ *n.* (*slang*) the buttocks. [orig. unkn.]

bum² *n.* (*US slang*) a loafer, a dissolute person. [f. G *bummler* loafer]

bumble *v.i.* **1.** to blunder, to act ineptly. **2.** to ramble *on* in speaking. **3.** to buzz loudly. [f. BOOM¹]

bumble-bee *n.* a large bee with a loud hum.

bummalo /ˈbʌmələʊ/ *n.* (*pl.* same) a small fish (*Harpodon nehereus*) of South Asian coasts. [perh. f. Marathi]

bump *n.* **1.** a dull-sounding blow or impact. **2.** a swelling produced by this. **3.** any lump or unevenness on a surface; a prominence on the skull, associated by phrenologists with mental faculties. —*v.t./i* to hit or come (*against* or *into*) with a bump; to hurt thus; to travel with jolts. —**bump into**, (*colloq.*) to meet by chance. **bump off**, (*slang*) to murder. **bump up**, to increase (prices etc.). —**bumpily** *adv.*, **bumpiness** *n.*, **bumpy** *adj.* [imit.]

bumper *n.* **1.** a horizontal bar attached at either end of a motor vehicle to reduce damage in a collision. **2.** (in cricket) a ball that rises high after pitching. **3.** a wine-glass filled to the brim. —*adj.* (of crops etc.) exceptionally abundant. [f. BUMP]

bumpkin *n.* an awkward or simple country person. [f. Du.]

bumptious /ˈbʌmpʃəs/ *adj.* offensively self-confident. [f. BUMP, after *fractious*]

bun *n.* **1.** a small round cake often with currants. **2.** hair fastened in a rounded mass at the back of the head. [orig. unkn.]

bunch *n.* **1.** a set of things growing or fastened together. **2.** (*slang*) a gang or group. —*v.t./i.* **1.** to make into a bunch. **2.** to gather into close folds. **3.** to form a group or crowd. —**bunchy** *adj.* [orig. unkn.]

bundle *n.* a collection of things fastened or wrapped together. —*v.t.* **1.** to make into a bundle. **2.** to throw hastily *into* a receptacle; to send (a person) unceremoniously *out* etc. [perh. f. OE, = binding; also f. Du. *bundel*]

bung *n.* a large stopper, especially for the mouth of a cask. —*v.t.* **1.** to stop with a bung. **2.** (*slang*) to throw, to put. —**bunged up**, blocked. [f. Du.]

bungalow /ˈbʌŋgələʊ/ *n.* a one-storeyed house. [orig. in India, f. Gujarati f. Hindi, = of Bengal]

bungle *v.t.* to mismanage, to blunder through lack of skill. —*n.* a bungled attempt. —**bungler** *n.* [imit., cf. *bumble*]

Bunin /ˈbuːniːn/, Ivan Alekseyevich (1870-1953), Russian poet and novelist, who attained great popularity in the early 20th c. His first book of poems was published in 1891, and he translated works by Tennyson, Byron, and Longfellow. An opponent of modernism, he made love and rural life the most prominent themes in his prose works, which include *The Village* (a novel, 1910), *The Gentleman from San Francisco* (short stories, 1916), and *The Well of Days* (autobiography, 1910). He opposed the October Revolution and left Russia in 1918, eventually reaching France and permanent exile. In 1933 he became the first Russian to be awarded the Nobel Prize for literature.

bunion /ˈbʌnjən/ *n.* a swelling on the foot, especially on the big toe. [f. OF (*buigne* bump on head)]

bunk¹ *n.* a shelf-like bed, usually one in a tiered series, as in a ship etc. [orig. unkn.]

bunk² *n.* **do a bunk**, (*slang*) to go away hurriedly. [orig. unkn.]

bunk³ *n.* (*slang*) bunkum. [abbr.]

bunker *n.* **1.** a compartment for coal; a reinforced underground shelter. **2.** a sandy hollow constructed as an obstacle on a golf-course. —*v.t.* to fill the bunkers of (a ship) with fuel. [orig. unkn.]

Bunker Hill the first pitched battle (1775) of the American War of Independence (actually fought on Breed's Hill near Boston, Massachusetts). Although the British were able to drive the American rebels from their positions, the good performance of the untrained American irregulars gave considerable impetus to the revolution.

bunkum *n.* nonsense, claptrap. [f. a verbose congressman from *Buncombe* County in North Carolina *c.*1820]

bunny *n.* (*children's colloq.*) a rabbit. [f. dial. *bun* rabbit]

Bunsen /ˈbʌns(ə)n/, Robert Wilhelm Eberhard (1811-99), German chemist, a pioneer of chemical spectroscopy and photochemistry. His first important research was on organo-arsenic compounds, and he lost the use of his right eye in an explosion. In the 1860s he collaborated with Gustav Kirchhoff to develop the field of spectroscopy, when it was discovered that each element produced light of a characteristic wavelength. They realized that spectral analysis could be used for detecting new elements and for determining the composition of terrestrial and celestial matter (the sun and stars), and discovered the element caesium in 1860 and rubidium in the following year. Bunsen enjoyed designing chemical apparatus, including the Bunsen battery (1841), grease-spot photometer (1844), absorptiometer (1855), actinometer (with Sir Henry Roscoe, 1856), effusion apparatus (1857), filter pump (1868), ice calorimeter (1870), and the vapour calorimeter (1887). His best-known device, the Bunsen (gas) burner (see foll.) was developed in 1855, after a design by Peter Desdega or Michael Faraday.

Bunsen burner a laboratory instrument with a vertical tube burning a mixture of air and gas to produce great heat. [f. prec.]

Bunter /ˈbʌntə(r)/, Billy. A schoolboy, noted for fatness and gluttony, in stories by Frank Richards (pseudonym of Charles Hamilton, 1875-1961).

bunting¹ *n.* flags and similar festive decorations; a loosely-woven fabric used for these. [orig. unkn.]

bunting² *n.* a small bird allied to the finches. [orig. unkn.]

Buñuel /buːˈnwel/, Luis (1900-83), Spanish film director, of whom it is said that he distinguished the cinema as much as the cinema did its best to extinguish him. In jokes, fierce independence, and original ideas he strayed far from the chic and fashionable. His early work was banned, and he had to leave Spain and go into exile in Mexico. His fiercest scorn was directed at the great institutions of civilization — the State and the Church —particularly at the idea that they conferred distinction or protection or allowed licence for dictatorship. He was profoundly influenced by surrealism (all his films propose a 'reality' composed as much of dreams and illusions as of verifiable events), and his first film *Un Chien andalou* (1928) was written and directed jointly with Salvador Dali, with whom he parted company when Dali supported Franco. Outstanding among his later works were the powerful and disturbing *Nazarin* (1958) and *Viridiana* (1961), and *The Discreet Charm of the Bourgeoisie* (1972).

Bunyan /ˈbʌnjən/, John (1628-88), English writer, son of a brazier. He served with the Parliamentary army during the Civil War, an experience perhaps reflected in his allegory *The Holy War* (1682). After a period of religious torment, he joined, in 1653, the Nonconformist Church at Bedford where he preached and came into conflict with the Quakers. He was arrested in 1660 for preaching without a licence and spent most of the next 12 years in prison, where he wrote his spiritual autobiography *Grace Abounding* (1666) and began his major work *The Pilgrim's Progress* (1678-84), an allegory in the form of a dream by the author. The work is remarkable for the beauty and simplicity of its language, the reality of its impersonations, and its humour; it has been translated into more than 100 languages.

Buonaparte /ˈbwɒnəpɑːt/ var. of BONAPARTE.

buoy /bɔɪ/ *n.* **1.** an anchored float marking a navigable course or reefs etc. **2.** a lifebuoy. —*v.t.* **1.** to mark with a buoy. **2.** (also with *up*) to keep afloat; to sustain and encourage (a person, courage, etc.). [prob. f. MDu., perh. f. OF *boie* chain ult. f. Gk *boeiai* (*dorai*) ox-hides, straps]

buoyant /ˈbɔɪənt/ *adj.* **1.** able to stay afloat. **2.** constantly cheerful or light-hearted. —**buoyancy** *n.* [f. F or Sp. (as prec.)]

bur *n.* a seed or seed-head with hooked bristles, clinging to the hair or clothes. [f. Scand.]

Burbage /ˈbɜːbɪdʒ/, Richard (*c.*1567-1619), the first outstanding English actor, creator of most of Shakespeare's great tragic roles —Hamlet, Othello, Lear, and Richard III. He was also associated in the building of the Globe Theatre, scene of his greatest triumphs. His father James (*c.*1530-97) built the first permanent playhouse in London, The Theatre, in 1576.

burble *v.i.* to make a murmuring noise; to speak ramblingly. [imit.]

burbot /ˈbɜːbət/ n an eel-like freshwater fish (*Lota lota*). [rel. to OF *barbote*]

burden n. **1.** a thing carried, especially something heavy; an oppressive responsibility, expense, etc. **2.** a ship's carrying capacity. **3.** the refrain of a song; the main theme of a speech etc. —v.t. to place a heavy load on, to encumber; to oppress. —**burden of proof,** the obligation to prove one's case. [OE, f. BEAR¹]

burdensome adj. troublesome, oppressive. [f. prec. + -SOME]

burdock /ˈbɜːdɒk/ n. a plant of the genus *Arctium*, with dock-like leaves and bur-like flower-heads. [f. BUR + DOCK⁴]

bureau /ˈbjʊərəʊ/ n. (pl. **-eaux**) **1.** a writing-desk with drawers. **2.** an office or department for transacting specific business; a government department. [F, = desk, orig. its baize covering, ult. f. Gk *purros* red]

bureaucracy /bjʊəˈrɒkrəsɪ/ n. government by the officials of a central administration rather than by elected representatives; such officials, often regarded as inflexible or unimaginative; excessive official routine. [f. prec., after *aristocracy* etc.]

bureaucrat /ˈbjʊərəkræt/ n. an official in a bureaucracy. — **bureaucratic** /-ˈkrætɪk/ adj. [as prec.]

burette /bjʊəˈret/ n. a graduated glass tube with a tap, for measuring small amounts of liquid in chemical analysis. [F]

burgee /bɜːˈdʒiː/ n. a small triangular or swallow-tailed flag on a yacht (ill. SAILING-SHIPS). [perh. for *burgee's* (owner's) *flag* f. F *bourgeois* owner etc.]

burgeon /ˈbɜːdʒ(ə)n/ v.i. (literary) to begin to grow rapidly, to flourish. [f. OF f. L *burra* wool]

Burgess /ˈbɜːdʒɪs/, Anthony John Burgess Wilson (1917-), English novelist and critic whose varied career has included a period as an education officer in Malaya and Borneo (1954-60) which inspired his first three novels, set in the Far East (*Time for a Tiger*, 1956; *The Enemy in the Blanket*, 1958; and *Beds in the East*, 1959). *A Clockwork Orange* (1962), an alarming vision of violence, high technology, and authoritarianism, appeared in a film version by Stanley Kubrick in 1971. His many other works include his comic trilogy which traces the literary, amorous, and digestive triumphs and misfortunes of the fitfully-inspired poet Enderby, the ambitious novel *Earthly Powers* (1980) in which real and fictitious characters mingle to produce an international panorama of the 20th c., critical works (notably on Joyce), screenplays, and a biography of Shakespeare.

burgess /ˈbɜːdʒɪs/ n. a citizen of a town or borough; (hist.) an MP for a borough, corporate town, or university. [f. OF f. L *burgus* borough]

burgh /ˈbʌrə/ n. a Scottish borough. [Sc. form of BOROUGH]

burgher /ˈbɜːɡə(r)/ n. a citizen of a (chiefly foreign) town. [f. G or Du. (*burg* BOROUGH)]

Burghley /ˈbɜːlɪ/, William Cecil, 1st Baron (1521-98), English statesman, Lord Treasurer, and Queen Elizabeth I's most trusted councillor and minister.

burglar /ˈbɜːɡlə(r)/ n. one who commits burglary. —**burglarious** /-ˈɡleərɪəs/ adj. [f. AF *burgler* plunderer]

burglary /ˈbɜːɡlərɪ/ n. illegal entry into a building to commit theft etc. [as prec.]

burgle v.t. to enter and rob (a house), to rob the house of (a person). [f. BURGLAR]

burgomaster /ˈbɜːɡəmɑːstə(r)/ n. the mayor of a Dutch or Flemish town. [Du. (*burg* borough)]

Burgoyne /ˈbɜːɡɔɪn/, John (1722-92), English general and playwright, known as 'Gentleman Johnny', who capitulated to the Americans at Saratoga (1777) in the American War of Independence.

burgundy /ˈbɜːɡəndɪ/ n. a red or white wine from Burgundy in eastern France; a similar wine from elsewhere. [place-name]

burial /ˈberɪəl/ n. **1.** the burying of a dead body; a funeral. **2.** (*Archaeol.*) a grave or its remains. [f. BURY]

burin /ˈbjʊərɪn/ n. a tool for engraving on copper or wood; a prehistoric flint tool with a narrow chisel edge. [F]

Burke¹ /bɜːk/, Edmund (1729-97), British man of letters and politician. The son of Dublin lawyer, Burke produced a large corpus of political writings, much of it dealing with the issue of political emancipation in Britain and her colonies. His speeches were magnificently eloquent but lengthy and not well delivered; his contemporaries called him the 'the dinner-gong'. In the last years of his life he devoted himself to attacking the radical excesses of the

French Revolution, opposing the idea of peace with a regime that he saw as pernicious.

Burke² /bɜːk/, John (1787-1848), Irish-born genealogical and heraldic writer, first compiler of a 'Peerage and Baronetage' (1826), issued periodically since 1847.

Burke³ /bɜːk/, Robert O'Hara (1820-61), Irish explorer and adventurer. After service in the Austrian army and the Irish constabulary, Burke emigrated to Australia in 1853 and became Inspector of Police in Victoria. In 1860-1 he successfully crossed Australia from south to north in the company of W. J. Wills (the first white men to do so). On the return journey, however, both he and his companion died of starvation.

Burke⁴ /bɜːk/, William (1792-1829), Irish navvy, living in Edinburgh, who was hanged for having dug up corpses from cemeteries and smothered at least 15 persons in order to sell the bodies for dissection (see BODY-SNATCHER). William Hare, his landlord and fellow Irishman, was his accomplice.

Burkina /bɜːˈkiːnə/ an inland country of western Africa, bounded on its south by the Ivory Coast, Ghana, and Togo; pop. (est. 1981) 6,251,000; official language, French; capital, Ouagadougou. The country was a French protectorate from 1898, originally attached to Soudan (now Mali) and later partitioned between the Ivory Coast, Soudan, and Niger. In 1958 it became an autonomous republic within the French Community and a fully independent republic in 1960. —**Burkinan** adj. & n.

burlesque /bɜːˈlesk/ n. a composition in which a serious subject is treated comically or a trivial one with mock solemnity; this as a branch of literature etc. — adj. of the nature of burlesque. —v.t. to make or give a burlesque of. [F. f. It. (*burla* mockery)]

burly adj. of strong sturdy build. [orig. = stately; prob. f. BOWER]

Burma /ˈbɜːmə/ a country in SE Asia on the Bay of Bengal, centred on the Irrawaddy River; pop. (1983) 35,313,905; official language, Burmese; capital, Rangoon. Rice has traditionally been the mainstay of the country's economy, and teak is a valuable export. Burma is rich in minerals, including lead and zinc; petroleum products are the most important. An independent empire under the Pagan dynasty in the 11th-13th c., Burma fell to the Mongols and was generally split into small rival States until unified once again in 1757. As a result of the Burmese Wars of 1823-86 Burma was gradually annexed by the British, remaining under British administration until the Second World War. Occupied by the Japanese in 1942, the country became an independent republic in 1948, taking the formal name of the Union of Burma. Since that time it has suffered periodic political disturbances, partially as a result of the general instability of SE Asia and partially as a result of religious and political differences within Burma itself. A new constitution was adopted in 1974.

Burmese /bɜːˈmiːz/ adj. of Burma or its people or language. —n. (pl. same) **1.** a native of Burma. **2.** the official language of Burma, spoken by three-quarters of its population (some 26 million people), a tonal language belonging to a branch of the Sino-Tibetan language group. It has a distinctive alphabet consisting almost entirely of circles or parts of circles in various combinations, which arose as a consequence of writing on palm leaves where straight lines were impossible. [f. prec.]

burn¹ v.t./i. (past & p.p. **burned, burnt**) **1.** to consume or be consumed by fire; to blaze or glow with fire. **2.** to use or be used as fuel; to give out or cause to give out light or heat. **3.** to injure by fire or great heat, to suffer such injury; to scorch or char in cooking. **4.** to produce (a mark etc.) by fire; to harden (bricks) by fire. **5.** to feel a hot sensation. **7.** to be filled *with* a violent emotion. —n. a mark or injury caused by burning. —**burn down,** to destroy or be destroyed by burning. **burning-glass** n. a lens to concentrate the sun's rays on an object and burn it. [OE]

burn² n. (*Sc.*) a brook. [OE]

Burne-Jones /bɜːnˈdʒəʊnz/, Sir Edward Coley (1833-98), English painter of medieval and literary themes, friend of William Morris and Dante Gabriel Rossetti. He created an escapist dreamlike world in his paintings, which are much influenced by 15th-c. Italian artists, especially Botticelli; he also made many designs for tapestry and stained glass.

burner n. the part of a lamp, gas cooker, etc., that emits and shapes the flame. [f. BURN¹]

Burnett /bəˈnet/, Francis (Eliza) Hodgson (1849-1924), English author of novels and other works, remembered chiefly for her novels for children, including *Little Lord Fauntleroy* (1886) and *The Secret Garden* (1911).

Burney /'bɜːnɪ/, Fanny (1752–1840), English novelist who won fame and the praise of Samuel Johnson with her first novel *Evelina* (1778). She served Queen Charlotte at court (1786–91) and in 1793 married General d'Arblay with whom she was interned in France by Napoleon. Her diaries and letters provide a vivid record of her time and the distinguished circles in which she moved.

burning *adj*. **1.** that burns; ardent, intense. **2.** (of a question) hotly discussed. [f. BURN¹]

burnish /'bɜːnɪʃ/ *v.t.* to polish by rubbing. [f. OF *brunir* (*brun* brown)]

burnous /bɜː'nuːs/ *n*. an Arab or Moorish hooded cloak. [F f. Arab. f. Gk *birros* cloak]

Burns /bɜːnz/, Robert (1759–96), Scottish poet, son of a poor farmer in Ayrshire. He early developed an inclination for literature and also a tendency to dissipation. His *Poems, chiefly in the Scottish Dialect* (1786) was an immediate success and he was lionized by Edinburgh society. His best poems include his satires, 'Holy Willie's Prayer' (1785), 'The Twa Dogs' (1786), and 'The Jolly Beggars' (1786), and the broad humour of his narrative poem 'Tam o' Shanter' (1791); his songs, many of which were published in *The Scots Musical Museum* (1787–1803), have always been popular—'Auld Lang Syne', 'Ye Banks and Braes', and 'Scots wha hae'—as are his sentimental lyrics and rhetorical poems. His attractive appearance and gregarious temperament led him into many amorous entanglements. After returning unsuccessfully to farming he became an excise officer (1791) in Dumfries. Burns wrote, with equal facility in English and Scots, vividly and passionately on themes of country life, love, and animals, and with a deep sympathy for the oppressed. He was above all a patriot and his popularity with his fellow-countrymen is celebrated annually on his birthday on 25 Jan., with feasting and drinking.

burnt *past* & *p.p.* of BURN¹. —*adj*. **burnt ochre, sienna,** etc., pigment darkened by burning. **burnt offering,** a sacrifice offered by nature.

burp *v.t./i.* (*colloq.*) to belch; to cause (a baby) to belch. —*n*. (*colloq.*) a belch. [imit.]

burr¹ *n*. **1.** a whirring sound; a rough pronunciation of the letter r; a regional accent characterized by this. **2.** a rough edge on metal or paper. **3.** a small drill. —*v.i.* to make a burr. [imit.]

burr² var. of BUR.

burrow /'bʌrəʊ/ *n*. a hole or tunnel dug by a fox, rabbit, etc. as a dwelling. —*v.t./i.* **1.** to dig a burrow; to form by burrowing. **2.** to investigate or search (*into*). [var. of BOROUGH]

bursar /'bɜːsə(r)/ *n*. **1.** a person who manages the finances of a college etc. **2.** a student holding a bursary. [f. F or L *bursa* bag)]

bursary *n*. **1.** a grant or scholarship awarded to a student. **2.** the bursar's office in a college. [f. prec.]

burst *v.t./i.* (*past* & *p.p.* burst) **1.** to force open by internal pressure; to be full to overflowing. **2.** to make one's way with sudden violence; to appear or come suddenly. —*n*. **1.** a bursting, a split. **2.** a sudden outbreak or explosion. **3.** a sudden effort, a spurt. —**burst into,** to break into (blossom, flame, tears, etc.). **burst out,** to exclaim suddenly; to begin suddenly. [OE]

Burton /'bɜːt(ə)n/, Sir Richard Francis (1821–90), explorer, anthropologist, and translator, one of the most flamboyant characters of his day. He joined the Indian Army in 1842 and subsequent travels took him to the forbidden City of Mecca, to expeditions in Africa (where, with Speke, he discovered Lake Tanganyika), to the Crimea, to Salt Lake City, and as consul to Brazil, Damascus, and Trieste. He published over 40 volumes of travel, several of folklore, and two of poetry and translations. He is best remembered for his unexpurgated version of the *Arabian Nights* (1885–8), *The Kama Sutra* (1883), *The Perfumed Garden* (1886), and other works of Arabian erotica. His interest in sexual behaviour and deviance and his detailed ethnographical notes led him to risk prosecution many times under the Obscene Publications Act of 1857.

Burundi /bʊ'rʌndɪ/ a country on the east side of Lake Tanganyika; pop. (est. 1984) 4,480,000; official languages, French and Kirundi; capital, Bujumbura. The area formed part of German East Africa until the First World War, after which it was administered by Belgium. It became an independent monarchy in 1962, and a republic in 1966. —**Burundian** *adj*. & *n*.

bury /'berɪ/ *v.t.* **1.** to deposit (a corpse) in the earth, a tomb, or the sea; to put underground; to put out of sight. **2.** to involve *oneself* deeply *in* (a study etc.). —**bury the hatchet,** to cease quarrelling. [OE]

bus *n*. (*pl*. **buses**) a long-bodied passenger vehicle, especially one serving the public on a fixed route (see below). —*v.t./i.* (**bused, busing**) to go by bus; to transport by bus, especially to counteract racial segregation. [abbr. of OMNIBUS]
   The bus originated in Paris in 1827. It was originally a horse-drawn vehicle, known as an omnibus (= 'a vehicle for all'), with the entrance at the rear. Later versions were motor-driven, first by petrol engines and then from *c.*1930 onwards by diesel engines. From early days passengers were carried on the roof as well as inside the vehicle, and from this practice there developed the form of the double-decker bus with upper and lower sections.

busby /'bʌzbɪ/ *n*. a tall fur cap worn by hussars as part of military ceremonial uniform. [orig. unkn.]

bush¹ /bʊʃ/ *n*. **1.** a shrub or clump of shrubs; a thick growth (of hair etc.). **2.** wild uncultivated country, forest (in Australia, Africa, etc.). —**bush-baby** *n*. a small African tree-climbing lemur. [f. OE & ON]

bush² /bʊʃ/ *n*. **1.** a metal lining for a round hole in which something fits or revolves. **2.** an electrically insulating sleeve. —*v.t.* to fit with a bush. [f. MDu. *busse* box]

bushel /'bʊʃ(ə)l/ *n*. a measure of capacity (8 gallons, about 36.4 litres) for corn, fruit, etc. The bushel formerly had a great variety of other values, varying not only from place to place but in the same place according to the commodity in question. Frequently it was a weight (not a measure) of so many pounds. [f. OF *buissel*, perh. of Gaulish orig.]

bushido /buː'ʃiːdəʊ/ *n*. the strict ethical code of the Japanese samurai involving military skill, fearlessness, and obedience to authority. Under the influence of Zen Buddhism and Confucianism it came to denote the virtues of the ideal man (kindness, honesty, etc.). [Jap., = military knight's way]

bushman *n*. (*pl*. **-men**) **1.** a dweller or traveller in the Australian bush. **2. Bushman,** a member or the language of an aboriginal people in South Africa.

bushranger *n*. (*hist*.) an Australian brigand living in the bush.

bushy /'bʊʃɪ/ *adj*. **1.** growing thickly like a bush. **2.** covered with bushes. [f. BUSH¹]

business /'bɪznɪs/ *n*. **1.** a person's regular occupation or profession. **2.** a thing that is one's concern, a task or duty. **3.** a thing or things needing to be dealt with. **4.** (*derog*.) an affair, subject, or device. **5.** buying and selling, trade; a commercial house or firm. —**business man** *or* **woman,** one engaged in commerce. **mean business,** to be in earnest. **mind one's own business,** to refrain from meddling. [OE (as BUSY)]

businesslike *adj*. practical, methodical. [f. prec. + -LIKE]

busker *n*. a singer or other entertainer who performs in the street. —**busking** *n*. [f. obs. *busk* peddle]

buskin *n*. a thick-soled boot worn by tragic actors in ancient Greece. [prob. f. OF]

Busoni /buː'zəʊnɪ/, Ferruccio Benvenuto (1866–1924), Italian composer and conductor, a brilliant pianist (his best-known works are for that instrument), who from 1894 made his home in Berlin. His music found mixed favour in his lifetime but has become increasingly admired for its visionary nature. Deriving from the impressionistic late works of Liszt, it ventured into harmonic and rhythmic territory that became the preserve of Webern, Bartók, and Messiaen.

bust¹ *v.t./i.* (*past* & *p.p.* **bust, busted**) (*colloq*.) to break or burst. —*adj*. (*colloq*.) broken, burst; bankrupt. —*n*. (*colloq*.) a sudden (esp. financial) failure. —**bust-up** *n*. a quarrel. [f. BURST]

bust² *n*. **1.** a sculptured representation of the head, shoulders, and chest. **2.** the upper front of a woman's etc. body; the measurement round this. [f. F f. It.]

bustard /'bʌstəd/ *n*. a large tall ostrich-like swift-running bird of the family Otididae. These birds, the heaviest flying-birds in the world, are chiefly centred in Africa but some species are found in southern Europe and in Asia, and one (*Choriotis australis*) in Australia. [prob. f. AF f. L *avis tarda* slow bird ('slow' unexplained)]

bustle¹ /'bʌs(ə)l/ *v.i.* to make a show of activity, to hurry (*about*). —*n*. excited activity. [perh. f. obs. *busk* prepare, rel. to BOUND³]

bustle² /'bʌs(ə)l/ n. (hist.) a pad used to puff out a woman's skirt at the back (ill. DRESS). [orig. unkn.]

busy /'bɪzɪ/ adj. 1. actively engaged in doing something; ceaselessly active, always employed; meddlesome. 2. full of business or activity. —v.t. to occupy or keep busy. —**busily** adv. [OE]

busybody n. a meddlesome person.

but /bət, emphatic bʌt/ conj. nevertheless, however; on the other hand; otherwise than; without the result that. —prep. except, apart from, other than. —adv. only, no more than. —n. an objection. [OE (f. BY, OUT); orig. = outside]

butane /'bjuːteɪn/ n. a hydrocarbon of the paraffin series, used in liquid form as fuel. [f. BUTYL]

butch /bʊtʃ/ adj. (slang) masculine, tough-looking. [orig. unkn.]

butcher /'bʊtʃə(r)/ n. 1. a dealer in meat; one who slaughters animals for food. 2. one who kills or has people killed needlessly or brutally. —v.t. 1. to slaughter or cut up (an animal) for meat. 2. to kill needlessly or cruelly. 3. to perform or deal with very ineptly. [f. OF bo(u)chier (boc buck)]

Butler¹ /'bʌtlə(r)/, Samuel (1612–80), English poet. His reputation rests on his satirical poem *Hudibras* (1663–80, 3 parts), a mock romance derived from *Don Quixote*, with a loose narrative framework which give the author ample opportunity for digressions which included attacks on academic pedantry, the theological differences within the Puritan sects, the politics of the Civil War, and other contemporary concerns, in a distinctive style (8-syllable couplets with comic rhymes). It was highly approved by Charles II, who granted the author a pension, but Butler is said to have died in penury.

Butler² /'bʌtlə(r)/, Samuel (1835–1902), English novelist. The son of a clergyman, he emigrated in 1859 and became a successful sheep farmer in New Zealand. Returning to England in 1864 he studied painting for 10 years and turned to literature, publishing his satirical anti-utopian novel *Erewhon* (1872) and its sequel *Erewhon Revisited* (1901), several works of scientific controversy challenging aspects of Darwinism, and his semi-autobiographical *The Way of All Flesh* (1903), a witty ironic study of the relations of parents to children and the stultifying effects of inherited family traits.

butler /'bʌtlə(r)/ n. the chief manservant of a household, in charge of the wine-cellar. [f. AF buteler (bouteille bottle)]

butt¹ v.t./i. 1. to push with the head like a ram or goat. 2. to meet or cause to meet edge to edge. —n. 1. an act of butting. 2. a butted join. —**butt in**, to interfere. [f. AF buter strike, thrust]

butt² n. 1. an object of ridicule etc.; a person habitually mocked or teased. 2. a mound behind a target; (in pl.) a shooting-range. [f. OF but goal]

butt³ n. the thicker end of a tool or weapon; the stub of a cigarette or cigar. [f. Du. bot stumpy]

butt⁴ n. a large cask. [f. AF f. L buttis]

butter n. a fatty food substance made from cream by churning. —v.t. to spread, cook, or serve with butter. —**butter-bean** n. a large dried white Lima bean. **butterfingers** n. a clumsy person always dropping things. **butter muslin**, thin loosely woven cloth originally used for wrapping butter. **butter up**, (colloq.) to flatter. [OE, ult. f. Gk bouturon]

buttercup n. a meadow plant of the genus *Ranunculus* with yellow cup-shaped flowers.

butterfly n. any of a large group of insects of the order Lepidoptera, distinguished from moths in most instances by diurnal behaviour, clubbed or dilated antennae, thin bodies, and the usually erect position of the wings when at rest (ill. INSECTS). —**butterfly nut**, a kind of wing-nut. **butterfly stroke**, (in swimming) a stroke in which both arms are lifted forwards simultaneously. [orig. unkn.]

buttermilk n. the somewhat acid liquid left after churning butter.

butterscotch n. a hard kind of toffee. [perh. orig. of *Scotch* manufacture]

buttery¹ adj. like or containing butter.

buttery² /'bʌtərɪ/ n. a place in a college etc. where provisions are kept and supplied. [f. BUTT⁴]

buttock /'bʌtək/ n. (usu. in pl.) either of the two fleshy rounded parts on the lower rear of a human or animal body. [dim. of butt ridge]

button /'bʌt(ə)n/ n. 1. a small disc or knob attached to a garment etc. to fasten it by passing through a hole, or to serve as an ornament or badge. 2. a small rounded object of similar form, especially a knob to operate an electrical device. —v.t./i. to fasten (up) with buttons. —**button mushroom**, a small unopened mushroom. [f. OF bouton]

buttonhole n. 1. a slit through which a button is passed to fasten clothing etc. 2. a flower worn in the buttonhole of a coat-lapel. —v.t. to accost and detain (a reluctant listener).

buttress /'bʌtrɪs/ n. 1. a projecting support built against a wall (ill. CHURCH). 2. a support or reinforcement. —v.t. 1. to support with a buttress or buttresses. 2. to give support and help to. [f. OF (ars) bouterez thrusting (arch), f. bouter BUTT⁴]

butyl /'bjuːtɪl/ n. the radical C₄H₉ derived from butane. [f. L butyrum butter]

buxom /'bʌksəm/ adj. (esp. of women) plump and healthy-looking. [earlier = pliant, rel. to BOW²]

Buxtehude /'bʊkstəhuːdə/, Dietrich (c.1637–1707), Danish organist and composer. He worked as an organist in Lübeck from 1668 until his death, expanding the series of Sunday evening concerts traditionally given there to include a wide range of sacred vocal, organ, and chamber music. His skill as an organist inspired Bach to walk over 200 miles from Anstadt to hear him play, and his own organ works (preludes, fugues, chorale variations, etc.) give some idea of his mastery of the instrument as well as of his great contrapuntal gifts as a composer.

buy /baɪ/ v.t. (past & p.p. **bought** /bɔːt/) 1. to obtain in exchange for money etc.; to win over by bribery. 2. (slang) to believe, to accept the truth of. —n. a purchase. —**buy off**, to pay to be rid of. **buy out**, to pay (a person) to give up an ownership etc. **buy up**, to buy all available stock of; to absorb (a firm) by purchase. [OE]

buyer n. one who buys; an agent who selects and purchases stock for a large shop. —**buyer's market**, trading conditions favourable to the buyer. [f. BUY]

buzz v.t./i. 1. to make a sibilant hum like a bee; to be filled with a confused murmur. 2. to be filled with activity or excitement; to move excitedly about etc. 3. to threaten (an aircraft) by flying close to it. —n. a buzzing sound; (slang) a telephone call. —**buzz off**, (slang) to go away. **buzz word**, a word (esp. technical or jargon) used more to impress than to inform. [imit.]

buzzard /'bʌzəd/ n. a large kind of predatory hawk of the genus *Buteo*. [f. OF f. L buteo falcon]

buzzer n. an electrical device producing a buzzing sound as a signal. [f. BUZZ]

bwana /'bwɑːnə/ n. sir, master (a form of address in Africa). [Swahili]

by /baɪ/ prep. 1. near, beside. 2. along, via, passing through or beside; avoiding. 3. in circumstances of, during. 4. through the agency or means of; (of an animal) having as its sire. 5. as soon as, not later than. 6. according to, using a standard or unit. 7. succeeding, with a succession of. 8. to the extent of. 9. concerning, in respect of. 10. as surely as one believes in (God etc.). —adv. 1. close at hand. 2. aside, in reserve. 3. past. —adj. subordinate, incidental; secondary, side. —n. = BYE¹. —**by and by**, before long. **by the by** (or bye), incidentally. **by and large**, on the whole. **by oneself**, without companions; by one's own unaided efforts. [OE]

bye¹ /baɪ/ n. 1. (in cricket) a run scored from a ball that passes the batsman without being hit. 2. the status of an unpaired competitor in a game, who proceeds to the next round as if having won. [= BY]

bye² /baɪ/ int. (also **bye-bye**) (colloq.) goodbye. [abbr.]

by-election n. the election of an MP in place of one who has died or resigned.

bygone adj. past, antiquated. —n. (in pl.) a past offence or injury (in phr. let bygones be bygones).

by-law n. a regulation made by a local authority or corporation. [perh. f. Scand. by town, assoc. with BY]

byline n. a line in a newspaper etc. naming the writer of an article.

bypass n. 1. a main road taking through traffic round a town or congested area. 2. a secondary channel, pipe, etc. for use when the main one is closed. —v.t. 1. to avoid by means of a bypass; to provide with a bypass. 2. to avoid consulting (a person) or omit (procedures etc.) in order to act quickly.

by-play n. subsidiary action in a play, usually without speech.

by-product *n.* a product arising incidentally in the manufacture of something else; a secondary result.

Byrd[1] /bɜːd/, Richard Evelyn (1888-1957), American polar explorer, a career naval officer and aviator, leader of four scientific expeditions to the Antarctic. He claimed to have made the first aeroplane flight over the North Pole in 1926, made that over the South Pole in 1929, and led further expeditions to the Antarctic in 1933-4 and 1939-41.

Byrd[2] /bɜːd/, William (1543-1623), Roman Catholic composer under the Anglican Elizabeth I. He wrote for both Churches, and two of his finest works are the Anglican Great Service and the Latin Four-part Mass. As well as his expressive and beautifully crafted sacred music he left a huge quantity of music for virginals, of which the variations on popular tunes of the day remain widely known and loved, over 40 consort songs, a genre brought by him to a rich perfection, and consort music.

byre /ˈbaɪə(r)/ *n.* a cow-shed. [OE, rel. to BOWER]

by-road *n.* a minor road.

Byron /ˈbaɪrən/, George Gordon, 6th Baron (1788-1824), English poet, born with a club foot which profoundly affected his temperament. Angered by contemptuous criticism of his first volume of verse (*Hours of Idleness*, 1807) Byron retaliated with his satire *English Bards and Scotch Reviewers* (1809). Soon afterwards he left England for extensive travels in Europe described in *Childe Harold's Pilgrimage* (1812-18), a work presenting, in the pilgrim, a truly 'Byronic' hero, aloof, cynical, melancholy, and rebellious. He became famous overnight and was lionized by literary and aristocratic circles. His marriage to Anne Isabella Milbanke in 1815 ended after the birth their daughter Ada, while rumours of his incestuous relationship with his half-sister (Augusta Leigh) mounted and debts associated with his ancestral home, Newstead Abbey, increased. Ostracized and embittered Byron left England permanently, stayed with Shelley in Geneva, finally to settle in Italy. In *Beppo* (1818) he found a new ironic colloquial voice which he fully developed in his epic satire *Don Juan* (1819-24), a work which attacked hypocrisy and social conventions with subtle irony and wit. Though criticized on moral grounds, Byron's poetry exerted enormous influence on the Romantic movement, as his name became a symbol of deep romantic melancholy. At the end of his life he was training troops for the Greeks against the Turks, a cause for which he had great enthusiasm.

byssinosis /bɪsɪˈnəʊsɪs/ *n.* a lung disease caused by prolonged inhalation of textile fibre dust. [f. Gk *bussinos* made of linen]

bystander *n.* one who stands by but does not take part in something, a mere spectator.

byte /baɪt/ *n.* a fixed number of binary digits in a computer, often representing a single character. [orig. unkn.]

byway *n.* a minor road or path.

byword *n.* a person or thing cited as a notable example; a familar saying.

Byzantine /bɪˈzæntaɪn, baɪ-/ *adj.* of Byzantium or the Eastern Roman Empire; resembling its complicated and devious politics. —*n.* a native or inhabitant of Byzantium. [f. foll.]

Byzantium /bɪˈzæntɪəm, baɪ-/ an ancient Greek city on the European side of the south end of the Bosporus, founded in the 7th c. BC and refounded as Constantinople by Constantine.

C

C, c *n.* **1.** the third letter of the alphabet. **2.** (*Mus.*) the first note of the natural major scale. **3.** (as a Roman numeral) 100.

C *abbr.* **1.** Celsius, centigrade, **2.** coulomb.

C *symbol* **1.** carbon. **2.** (also ©) copyright.

c. *abbr.* **1.** century. **2.** chapter. **3.** cent.

c. *abbr. circa*, about.

Ca *symbol* calcium.

Caaba var. of KAABA.

cab *n.* **1.** a taxi; (*hist.*) a cabriolet or its improved successor the hansom; any of various types of horse-drawn public carriage with two or four wheels. **2.** the driver's compartment in a train, lorry, or crane. [abbr. of CABRIOLET]

cabal /kə'bæl/ *n.* **1.** a secret intrigue. **2.** a political clique. [f. F f. L, = CABBALA]

cabaret /'kæbəreɪ/ *n.* an entertainmeent provided in a restaurant or night-club while guests eat or drink at tables; such a night-club etc. [F, = tavern]

cabbage /'kæbɪdʒ/ *n.* **1.** a vegetable with thick green or purple leaves, usually forming a round head. **2.** (*colloq.*) a person who lives inactively or without interest. [f. OF *caboche* head]

cabbala /kə'bɑːlə/ *n.* a pretended tradition of mystical interpretation of the Old Testament, using esoteric methods (including ciphers), that reached the height of its influence in the later Middle Ages. [L f. Heb., = tradition]

cabbalistic /kæbə'lɪstɪk/ *adj.* of or like the cabbala; having a mystical sense, occult. [f. prec.]

cabby, cabbie /'kæbɪ/ *n.* (*colloq.*) a taxi-driver. [f. CAB]

caber /'keɪbə(r)/ *n.* a roughly-trimmed tree-trunk used in the Scottish Highland sport of **tossing the caber.** There is no universal standard size for the caber, but once tossed it must never be shortened; the Braemar caber is 19 ft. (5.79 m) long and weighs 120 lb (54.5 kg). [f. Gael. *cabar* pole]

cabin /'kæbɪn/ *n.* **1.** a small shelter or house, especially of wood. **2.** a room or compartment in a ship, aircraft, etc., for passengers or crew. **3.** a driver's cab. —**cabin-boy** *n.* a man or boy waiting on officers or passengers on a ship. **cabin cruiser,** a large motor boat with a cabin. [f. OF f. L *capanna*]

cabinet /'kæbɪnɪt/ *n.* **1.** a cupboard or container with drawers, shelves, etc., for storing or displaying articles; a piece of furniture housing a radio or television set etc. **2.** **Cabinet,** the group of ministers reponsible for implementing government policy (see below). —**cabinet-maker** *n.* a skilled joiner. [f. prec.]
The kings of England always had advisers. After the Restoration in 1660 a Cabinet (or Cabinet Council) developed, consisting of the major office-bearers and the king's most trusted members of the Privy Council, meeting as a committee in a private room (the *cabinet*, whence its name) and taking decisions without consulting the full Privy Council. In the time of Queen Anne it became the main machinery of executive government and the Privy Council became formal. From about 1717 the monarch (George I) ceased to attend, and from that time the Cabinet met independently. George III became obliged, through insanity and age, to leave more and more to his ministers, but it was not until after the Reform Act of 1832 that the royal power was dissolved and Cabinets came to depend, for their existence and policies, upon the support of a majority in the House of Commons.

cable /'keɪb(ə)l/ *n.* **1.** a thick rope of wire or hemp; an encased group of insulated wires for transmitting electricity or for telecommunications; the anchor chain of a ship. **2.** a cablegram. **3.** (in full **cable stitch**) a knitted pattern looking like twisted rope. —*v.t./i.* to communicate with or transmit by cablegram. —**cable-car** *n.* any of the cars in a **cable railway,** mounted on an endless cable and drawn up and down a mountain side etc. by an engine at one end. **cable television,** transmission of television programmes by cable to subscribers. [f. AF f. L *caplum* halter, f. Arab.]

cablegram *n.* a telegraph message sent by undersea cable. [f. CABLE + -GRAM]

caboose /kə'buːs/ *n.* (*US*) a guard's van, especially on a goods train. [f. Du.; orig. unkn.]

Cabot /'kæbət/, John (d. *c.*1498), Venetian explorer and navigator. He and his son Sebastian (d. 1557) sailed from Bristol in 1497 with a patent from Henry VII and discovered the mainland of North America a year before Columbus. The site of their landfall is uncertain (it may have been Cape Breton Island, or Labrador, or Newfoundland), but they believed themselves to be on the NE coast of Asia; Cabot returned to Bristol and reported his success. He undertook a second expedition in 1498 and appears to have returned to Bristol afterwards. Sebastian made further voyages of exploration after his father's death.

cabriole /'kæbrɪəʊl/ *n.* a kind of curved leg characteristic of 17th–18th-c. furniture, especially that of Chippendale type. [F, f. It. *capriolare* leap in the air; from resemblance to a leaping animal's foreleg]

cabriolet /'kæbrɪəleɪ/ *n.* a light two-wheeled carriage with a hood, drawn by one horse, introduced into London from Paris in the early 19th c. [F, f. *cabriole* goat's leap]

cacao /kə'keɪəʊ/ *n.* (*pl.* **-os**) the seed from which cocoa and chocolate are made; the tree (*Theobroma cacao*) producing it. [Sp. f. Nahuatl]

cachalot /'kæʃəlɒt/ *n.* a sperm whale. [F f. Sp. & Port.]

cache /kæʃ/ *n.* a place for hiding treasures or stores; things so hidden. —*v.t.* to put in a cache. [F (*cacher* hide)]

cachet /'kæʃeɪ/ *n.* **1.** a distinguishing mark or seal. **2.** prestige. **3.** internal evidence of authenticity. **4.** a wafer enclosing an unpleasant medicine. [F (*cacher* press, f. L *coactare* constrain)]

cackle *n.* **1.** the clucking of a hen. **2.** noisy inconsequential talk. **3.** a loud silly laugh. —*v.i.* to emit a cackle; to utter or express with a cackle. —**cut the cackle,** (*colloq.*) to come to the point. [imit.]

cacophony /kə'kɒfənɪ/ *n.* harsh discordant sound. —**cacophonous** *adj.* [f. F f. Gk (*kakos* bad, *phōnē* sound)]

cactus /'kæktəs/ *n.* (*pl.* **-i** /-aɪ/, **-uses**) a succulent plant of the family Cactaceae, with a thick fleshy stem, usually spines but no leaves, and brilliantly coloured flowers. [L f. Gk]

cad *n.* a person (especially a man) who behaves dishonourably. —**caddish** *adj.* [abbr. of CADDIE in the sense 'odd-job man']

cadaver /kə'deɪvə(r)/ *n.* a corpse. [f. L (*cadere* fall)]

cadaverous /kə'dævərəs/ *adj.* corpselike, gaunt and pale. [as prec.]

caddie /'kædɪ/ *n.* **1.** a person who assists a golfer during a match, carrying his clubs etc. **2.** a small container holding articles ready for use. —*v.i.* to act as caddie. [orig. Sc., f. F CADET]

caddis-fly /'kædɪsflaɪ/ *n.* a feebly flying frequently nocturnal insect of the order Trichoptera, living near water (ill. INSECTS). —**caddis-worm** *n.* its larva. [orig. unkn.]

caddy[1] /'kædɪ/ *n.* a small box for holding tea. [earlier *catty* weight of 1⅓ lb., f. Malay *kātī*]

caddy[2] /'kædɪ/ var. of CADDIE.

cadence /'keɪd(ə)ns/ *n.* **1.** the fall of the voice, especially at the end of a phrase or sentence; tonal inflection. **2.** rhythm in sound. **3.** a melodic or harmonic progression or device conventionally associated with the end of a musical composition, section, or phrase. [f. It. *cadenza* f. L *cadere* fall]

cadency /'keɪd(ə)nsɪ/ *n.* the status of a younger branch of a family. [as prec.]

cadenza /kə'denzə/ *n.* a flourish inserted into the final cadence of any section of a vocal aria or a movement in a concerto, sonata, or other solo instrumental work. From the late 17th-18th c. such insertions were improvised by the performer, but in the 19th c. composers frequently wrote out their cadenzas. [see CADENCE]

cadet /kə'det/ *n.* **1.** a member of a corps receiving elementary military or police training. **2.** a younger son. [F, f. dim. of L *caput* head]

cadge/ kædʒ/ *v.t./i.* to ask for as a gift; to beg. —**cadger** *n.* [orig. unkn.]

cadmium /ˈkædmɪəm/ *n.* a bluish-white metallic element, symbol Cd, atomic number 48, physically resembling tin but chemically related to zinc. Discovered in 1817, cadmium is obtained as a by-product of the extraction of zinc from its ores; the metal does not occur in the free state in nature. It is used as a component in low-melting-point alloys, as a coating on other metals to protect them against corrosion, and in the manufacture of pigments. Both the metal and its components are highly toxic. [f. obs. *cadmia* calamine, ult. f. Gk *kadm(e)ia* (*gē*) Cadmean (earth), f. foll.]

Cadmus /ˈkædməs/ (*Gk legend*) brother of Europa whom he was sent to seek when she disappeared, and traditional founder of Thebes in Boeotia. To get water he killed a dragon which guarded a spring, and when (by Athene's advice) he sowed the dragon's teeth there came up a harvest of armed men, whom Cadmus disposed of by setting them to fight one another. He is also reputed to have introduced the alphabet into Greece.

cadre /ˈkɑːdə(r)/ *n.* a group forming a nucleus of trained persons round which a military or political unit can be formed. [F f. It. f. L *quadrus* square]

caecilian /sɪˈsɪlɪən/ *n.* a member of the order Apoda of amphibians, mainly tropical and wormlike. [f. L *caecilia* a kind of lizard]

caecum /ˈsiːkəm/ *n.* (*pl.* -ca) a tubular pouch forming the first part of the large intestine (ill. BODY 1). [L (*caecus* blind)]

Cædmon /ˈkædmən/ (7th c.) English poet, said by Bede to have been an illiterate herdsman who received in a vision the power of song and put into English verse passages from the Scriptures. The only authentic fragment of his work is the hymn quoted by Bede.

Caerphilly /keəˈfɪlɪ/ *n.* a mild crumbly white cheese. [name of town in Wales where orig. sold]

Caesar /ˈsiːzə(r)/ *n.* **1.** Julius Caesar. **2.** the title of Roman emperors, especially from Augustus to Hadrian. **3.** a dictator, an autocrat. —**Caesar's wife**, a person required to be above suspicion. [L, family name of Julius Caesar]

Caesarean /sɪˈzeərɪən/ *adj.* **Caesarean birth** *or* **section,** delivery of a child by cutting into the mother's womb through the wall of the abdomen, so called from the story that Julius Caesar was born in this way. [f. L (as prec.)]

caesium/ ˈsiːzɪəm/ *n.* a soft silver-white metallic element of the alkali metal group, symbol Cs, atomic number 55. Discovered by spectroscopic means in 1860 by Bunsen and Kirchhoff, caesium is the most reactive of all metals apart from francium. It melts at 28.5 °C and so is liquid in a warm room. It is not used commercially in large quantities, although it has a few specialized applications. A specified transition of the caesium-133 atom is used in defining the second as a unit of time (see SECOND²]. [f. L *caesius* bluish- or greyish-green, f. its spectrum lines]

caesura /sɪˈzjʊərə/ *n.* a short pause in the rhythm of a line of verse. [L (*caedere* cut)]

café /ˈkæfeɪ/ *n.* a tea-shop or small restaurant. [F, = coffee (-house)]

cafeteria /kæfɪˈtɪərɪə/ *n.* a restaurant in which customers serve themselves from a counter or display. [f. Amer. Sp., = coffee-shop]

caffeine /ˈkæfiːn/ *n.* an alkaloid stimulant found in tea leaves and coffee beans. [f. F (*café* coffee)]

caftan /ˈkæft(ə)n/ *n.* **1.** a long coat-like garment, often with a sash or belt, worn by men in countries of the Near East. **2.** a woman's long loose dress. [f. Turk.]

Cage /keɪdʒ/, John (1912–), American composer, pianist, and writer, born in Los Angeles where he studied music with Schoenberg after a period in New York. He returned to New York in 1942 and there developed his ideas on the role of chance in music: his *Music of Changes* (for piano, 1951) was composed according to decisions made by tossing a coin. In 1938 he invented the 'prepared piano' (with pieces of metal, rubber, etc., inserted between the strings to alter the tone), and he occasionally uses electronic instruments. Perhaps his most notorious work is *4′ 33″* (1952), in which the 'performance' consists of four minutes thirty-three seconds of silence.

cage 1. *n.* a structure with bars or wires, especially for containing animals or birds. **2.** any similar framework, an enclosed platform in which people travel in a lift or the shaft of a mine. —*v.t.* to confine in a cage. [f. OF f. L *cavea*]

cagey /ˈkeɪdʒɪ/ *adj.* (*colloq.*) cautious about giving information, secretive. —**cagily** *adv.*, **caginess** *n.* [orig. unkn.]

cagoule /kəˈguːl/ *n.* a thin hooded waterproof jacket reaching to the knees. [F]

cahoots /kəˈhuːts/ *n.pl.* (*US slang*) **in cahoots with,** in collusion with. [orig. unkn.]

Cain /keɪn/ (in Gen. 4) the eldest son of Adam and murderer of his brother Abel. —**raise Cain,** (*colloq.*) to make a disturbance.

Cainozoic /kaɪnəˈzəʊɪk/ *adj.* of the most recent era of geological time, following the Mesozoic era and lasting from about 65 million years ago to the present day. It includes the Tertiary and Quaternary periods, and is characterized by the rapid evolution of mammals (whence the name). —*n.* this era. [f. Gk *kainos* new + *zōion* animal]

caique /kɑːˈiːk/ *n.* a light rowing-boat used on the Bosporus; a Levantine sailing-ship. [F f. It. f. Turk. *kayik*]

cairn *n.* a mound of rough stones set up as a monument or landmark. —**cairn terrier,** a small shaggy terrier with short legs. [f. Gael. *carn*]

cairngorm *n.* a yellow or wine-coloured semi-precious stone from the Cairngorm mountains in Scotland. [f. Gael. *carn gorm* blue cairn]

Cairo /ˈkaɪrəʊ/ the capital of Egypt, a port on the Nile near the head of the delta, and the largest city in Africa; pop. (est. 1983) 11,000,000. Founded by the Fatimid Dynasty in 969 it was later fortified against the Crusaders by Saladin, whose citadel (built *c.*1179) still survives. Cairo's many mosques include that of Al Azhar (972), housing an Islamic university.

caisson /ˈkeɪs(ə)n/ *n.* a watertight chamber inside which work can be carried out on underwater structures. [F f. It. *cassone*]

cajole /kəˈdʒəʊl/ *v.t.* to coax. —**cajolery** *n.* [f. F *cajoler*]

cake *n.* **1.** a baked sweet breadlike food made from a mixture of flour, fats, sugar, eggs, etc. **2.** other food cooked in a flat round shape. **3.** a flattish compact mass. **4.** cattle-cake. —*v.t./i.* to form into a compact mass; to encrust *with* a hardened or sticky mass. [ON]

calabash /ˈkæləbæʃ/ *n.* **1.** a tropical American tree of the genus *Crescentia*, with fruit in the form of large gourds. **2.** this or a similar gourd whose shell serves for holding liquid etc. **3.** a bowl or pipe made from a gourd. [f. F f. Sp., perh. f. Pers. *karbuz* melon]

calabrese /kæləˈbreɪseɪ/ *n.* a variety of sprouting broccoli. [It., = Calabrian]

Calabria /kəˈlæbrɪə/ the SW (formerly the SE) promontory of Italy. In antiquity the name was applied to the flat and arid but fertile SE promontory or 'heel' of Italy. The Lombards seized Calabria *c.* AD 700, whereupon the Byzantines transferred its name to the SW promontory or 'toe' of Italy, the Calabria of today. —**Calabrian** *adj. & n.*

calamine /ˈkæləmaɪn/ *n.* a pink powder, chiefly zinc carbonate or oxide, used especially in skin lotions. [f. F f. L *cadmia* (see CADMIUM)]

calamity /kəˈlæmɪtɪ/ *n.* a grievous disaster or adversity. —**calamitous** /-mɪtəs/ *adj.* —**Calamity Jane,** the nickname of Martha Jane Burke (née Canary; d. 1903), a famous American horse-rider and markswoman. A colourful character (but not the beautiful heroine into which popular fiction transformed her) she was a prostitute, wore male clothing, carried a gun, and engaged in drinking bouts. [f. F f. L]

calcareous /kælˈkeərɪəs/ *adj.* of or containing calcium carbonate. [f. L *calx* lime]

calceolaria /kælsɪəˈleərɪə/ *n.* a South American plant of the genus *Calceolaria*, with a slipper-shaped flower. [f. L, dim. of *calceus* shoe]

calcify /ˈkælsɪfaɪ/ *v.t./i.* to harden by a deposit of calcium salts; to convert or be converted into calcium carbonate. —**calcification** /-ˈkeɪʃ(ə)n/ *n.* [f. L *calx* lime]

calcine /ˈkælsaɪn/ *v.t./i.* to reduce (a substance) or be reduced to quicklime or powder by heating to a high temperature without melting it. —**calcination** /-sɪˈneɪʃ(ə)n/ *n.* [f. OF or L (as prec.)]

calcite /ˈkælsaɪt/ *n.* crystalline calcium carbonate. [as foll.]

calcium /ˈkælsɪəm/ *n.* a greyish-white metallic element of the alkaline-earth metal group, symbol Ca, atomic number 20, first isolated by Sir Humphry Davy in 1808. A common element in the earth's crust, it occurs naturally in limestone, fluorite, and gypsum, but never uncombined. The metal now has a number of specialized uses. Calcium is also essential to life: many physiological processes depend on the movement of calcium ions, and calcium salts are an essential constituent of bone, teeth, and shells. [f. L *calx* lime]

calculable /ˈkælkjʊləb(ə)l/ *adj.* that may be calculated. [f. foll.]

calculate /ˈkælkjʊleɪt/ *v.t./i.* **1.** to ascertain, especially by using mathematics or by reckoning. **2.** to plan deliberately; to rely *on*. **3.** (*US colloq.*) to suppose, to believe. — **calculation** /-ˈleɪʃ(ə)n/ *n.* [f. L (as CALCULUS)]

calculated *adj.* **1.** done with awaresness of the likely consequences. **2.** designed or suitable *to* do. [f. prec.]

calculating *adj.* (of a person) shrewd, scheming. [f. CALCULATE]

calculator *n.* a device, especially a small electronic one, used in making calculations. [as prec.]

calculus /ˈkælkjʊləs/ *n.* **1.** a particular system of calculation or reasoning, especially the branch of mathematics that deals with differentiation and integration. Calculus emerged in the 17th c. from the work of Leibnitz, Newton, and their predecessors as the method of finding rates of change of varying quantities. It was developed for its main applications in mechanics and in geometry, where it provides techniques for finding tangents of curves and areas of curvilinear figures. **2.** (*pl.* -**li**) a stone or concretion found in some part of the body. [L, = small stone (used on an abacus)]

Calcutta /kælˈkʌtə/ the capital of the State of West Bengal, an important port and industrial centre and the second largest city of India; pop. (est.) 9,200,000. Founded *c.*1690 by the East India Company, it was the capital of India from 1833 to 1912. —**Black Hole of Calcutta**, a dungeon in Fort William, Calcutta, where, following the capture of Calcutta by the Nawab of Bengal in 1756, 156 English prisoners were confined in a narrow cell 20 ft. square for the night of 20 June, only 23 of them still being alive the next morning.

Calderón de la Barca /ˈkɔːldərɒn, ˈkɒl-/, Pedro (1600–81), Spanish dramatist and poet, author of some 120 plays.

Caledonian /kælɪˈdəʊnɪən/ *adj.* of Scotland or (in Roman times) Caledonia (= northern Britain). —*n.* (usu. *joc.*) a Scotsman. —**Caledonian Canal**, a system of lochs and canals in Scotland from Inverness on the east coast to Fort William in the west, linking the North Sea with the Atlantic Ocean. The work of Thomas Telford, it was opened in 1832. [f. L *Caledonia*]

calendar /ˈkælɪndə(r)/ *n.* **1.** a system fixing a year's beginning, length, and subdivision (see GREGORIAN, JULIAN calendar). **2.** a chart showing the days, weeks, and months of a particular year; an adjustable device showing the day's date etc. **3.** a register or list of special dates or events, documents chronologically arranged, etc. —*v.t.* **1.** to enter in a calendar. **2.** to analyse and index (documents). [f. AF f. L *calendarium* account-book (as CALENDS)]

calender /ˈkælɪndə(r)/ *n.* a machine for rolling cloth, paper, etc. to glaze or smooth it. —*v.t.* to press in a calender. [f. F]

calends /ˈkælɪndz/ *n.pl.* the first day of the month in the ancient Roman calendar. [f. OF f. L *calendae* (from the proclaiming of the order of days)]

calf[1] /kɑːf/ *n.* (*pl.* **calves** /kɑːvz/) young of cattle, also of the deer, elephant, whale, and certain other animals; calfskin. —**calf-love** *n.* immature romantic love. [OE]

calf[2] /kɑːf/ *n.* (*pl.* **calves** /kɑːvz/) the fleshy hind part of the human leg below the knee. [ON]

calfskin *n.* leather made from the skin of calves. [f. CALF[1]]

calibrate /ˈkælɪbreɪt/ *v.t.* **1.** to mark (a gauge) with a scale of readings; to correlate the readings of (an instrument etc.) with a standard. **2.** to find the calibre of. —**calibration** /-ˈbreɪʃ(ə)n/ *n.*, **calibrator** *n.* [f. foll.]

calibre /ˈkælɪbə(r)/ *n.* **1.** the internal diameter of a gun-barrel or tube; the diameter of a bullet or shell. **2.** strength or quality of character; ability, importance. [f. F, ult. f. Arab., = mould]

calico /ˈkælɪkəʊ/ *n.* (*pl.* -**oes**) cotton cloth, especially plain white or unbleached; (*US*) printed cotton fabric. —*adj.* **1.** of calico. **2.** (*US*) multicoloured. [f. *Calicut* town in India]

California /kælɪˈfɔːnɪə/ a State on the Pacific coast of the USA, ceded by Mexico in 1848. The discovery of gold there in the same year led to a rapid influx of settlers. California became the 31st State of the USA in 1850; capital, Sacramento. —**Californian** *adj.* & *n.*

californium /kælɪˈfɔːnɪəm/ *n.* an artificially made transuranic radioactive metallic element, symbol Cf, atomic number 98, first obtained in 1950 by bombarding curium with helium ions. It is now used in industry and medicine as a source of neutrons. [f. CALIFORNIA (where first made)]

Caligula /kəˈlɪɡjʊlə/ the nickname (lit. 'baby boot') of the Roman emperor Gaius, given to him as an infant by the soldiers on account of the military boots which he wore while in camp on the Rhine with his parents Germanicus and Agrippina. (See GAIUS.)

caliph /ˈkælɪf, ˈkeɪ-/ *n.* (*hist.*) a leader of the Muslim community in matters both temporal and spiritual (see below). —**caliphate** *n.* [f. OF f. Arab., = successor (i.e. one succeeding Muhammad)]

The first caliph (Abu Bakr), who had been one of the Prophet Muhammad's earliest converts and most devoted disciples, was instituted by acclamation of the small Muslim community following the death of Muhammad in AD 632. He and the following three caliphs had had personal links with the Prophet and were dedicated to developing the community along the path he had marked out, being responsible for implementation of the precepts of Islamic rule and legislation; this also entailed military leadership as the community expanded across and beyond the Arabian Sea. Subsequently the caliphate became a hereditary position with the establishment of the Ummayyad and Abbasid dynasties (respectively 661–750 and 750–945), with the latter ruling in Baghdad until 1258 and then in Egypt until the Ottoman conquest (1517), though by the 11th c. most of the caliph's authority had been passed to a hierarchy of officials. The title was then held by the Ottoman sultans until the nationalist revolution of 1922, and the caliphate was abolished by Atatürk in 1924.

calix /ˈkeɪlɪks/ *n.* (*pl.* -**ices** /-ɪsiːz/) a cuplike cavity or organ. [L, = cup]

call /kɔːl/ *v.t./i.* **1.** to shout or speak *out* loudly to attract attention; (of a bird etc.) to utter its call. **2.** to summon; to order to take place; to invite (attention etc.). **3.** to rouse deliberately from sleep, to summon to get up. **4.** to name, describe, or regard as. **5.** to communicate or converse with by telephone or radio. **6.** to name (a suit) in bidding at cards; to attempt to predict the result of tossing a coin etc. **7.** to make a brief visit (*at* a place, *on* a person). —*n.* **1.** a shout or cry; the characteristic cry of a bird etc.; a signal on a bugle etc. **2.** a summons, an invitation; a demand or claim; a need, an occasion. **3.** a player's right or turn to bid or call trumps at cards; a bid etc. thus made. **4.** an act of telephoning, a conversation over the telephone. **5.** the option of buying stock at a given date. —**call-box** *n.* a telephone kiosk. **call-girl** *n.* a prostitute accepting appointments by telephone. **call up**, to summon to do military service. **call-up** *n.* a summons to do military service. **on call**, ready or available when needed. —**caller** *n.* [OE f. ON]

Callas /ˈkæləs/, Maria (real name Calageropoulos, 1923–77), operatic coloratura soprano, born in America of Greek parents. Her highly individual voice and great dramatic talent were responsible for the revival of works by Rossini, Bellini, and Donizetti, and her range included Wagnerian roles as well as the Italian repertory.

calligraphy /kəˈlɪɡrəfɪ/ *n.* beautiful handwriting; hand-writing. —**calligrapher** *n.*, **calligraphist** *n.*, **calligraphic** /kælɪˈɡræfɪk/ *adj.* [f. Gk (*kallos* beauty, *graphē* writing)]

Callimachus /kəˈlɪməkəs/ (*c.*305–*c.*240 BC) Hellenistic poet and scholar, originally from Cyrene, who worked in the great library at Alexandria. His scholarly works included a vast critical catalogue of previous Greek literature. As a poet he exemplified a new ideal of short or episodic poetry, self-conscious, highly-polished, and learnedly allusive.

calling *n.* a profession or trade; a vocation. [f. CALL]

Calliope /kəˈlaɪəpɪ/ (*Gk & Rom. myth.*) the Muse of epic poetry. [Gk, = beautiful-voiced]

calliope /kəˈlaɪəpɪ/ *n.* (*US*) a musical instrument, used in carnivals etc., with a set of steam whistles that produce musical notes, played by a keyboard. [f. prec.]

calliper /ˈkælɪpə(r)/ *n.* (usu. in *pl.*) **1.** a pair of hinged arms for measuring diameters. **2.** a metal support for a weak or injured leg. [var. of CALIBRE]

callisthenics /kælɪsˈθenɪks/ *n.pl.* exercises to develop elegance and grace of movement. [f. Gk *kallos* beauty + *sthenos* strength]

callosity /kəˈlɒsɪtɪ/ *n.* abnormal hardness of the skin; a callus. [f. F or L (as foll.)]

callous /ˈkæləs/ *adj.* **1.** unfeeling, unsympathetic. **2.** (of skin) hardened. [f. L *callosus* (as CALLUS)]

callow /ˈkæləʊ/ *adj.* immature and inexperienced. —**callowly** *adv.*, **callowness** *n.* [OE, prob. f. L *calvus* bald]

callus /ˈkæləs/ *n.* an area of hard thickened skin or tissue; bony material formed when a bone-fracture heals. [L]

calm /kɑːm/ *adj.* **1.** quiet and still, not windy. **2.** not excited or agitated. **3.** confident. —*n.* a calm condition or period. — *v.t./i.* to make or become calm. —**calms of Cancer**, a belt of high pressure surrounding the earth around latitudes 30°–35°N. **calms of Capricorn**, a similar belt 30°–35°S. —**calmly** *adv.*, **calmness** *n.* [f. L f. Gk *kauma* heat]

calomel /ˈkæləmel/ *n.* a compound of mercury, used as a purgative. [perh. f. Gk *kalos* beautiful, *melas* black]

Calor gas /ˈkælə/ [P] liquefied butane etc. stored under pressure in containers for use where mains gas is not available. [L *calor* heat]

caloric /ˈkælərɪk/ *adj.* of heat; of calories. [f. F (as foll.)]

calorie /ˈkælərɪ/ *n.* a unit of quantity for measuring heat, the amount needed to raise one gram (*small calorie*) or one kilogram (*large calorie*) of water 1 °C; a large calorie as a unit for measuring the energy value of foods. [F f. L *calor* heat]

calorific /kæləˈrɪfɪk/ *adj.* producing heat. [f. L (*calor* heat)]

calorimeter /kæləˈrɪmɪtə(r)/ *n.* an instrument for measuring the quantity of heat in a body. [as prec. + -METER]

caltrop /ˈkæltrɒp/ *n.* (also **caltrap**) **1.** (*hist.*) a four-spiked iron ball thrown on the ground to impede cavalry horses; (in heraldry) a representation of this (ill. HERALDRY). **2.** a plant with spiked flower-heads resembling caltrops. [f. OF *kauketrape* (*cauchier* tread, *trappe* trap); sense 2 f. OE]

calumniate /kəˈlʌmnɪeɪt/ *v.t.* to slander, to defame. —**calumniation** /-ˈeɪʃ(ə)n/ *n.* [f. L *calumniari*]

calumny /ˈkæləmnɪ/ *n.* slander; malicious representation. —**calumnious** /kəˈlʌmnɪəs/ *adj.* [f. L]

Calvary /ˈkælvərɪ/ *n.* **1.** the place (just outside ancient Jerusalem) where Christ was crucified. **2.** a representation of the Crucifixion. [f. L *calvaria* skull, transl. of Gk *golgotha* f. Aram. (Matt. 27: 33)]

calve /kɑːv/ *v.i.* to give birth to a calf. [OE (as CALF[1])]

Calvin /ˈkælvɪn/, John (1509–64), French Protestant theologian, the most important of the second generation of Reformers. Embracing Protestantism, he fled France, going first to Basle, where in 1536 he published the first edition of the *Institutes of the Christian Religion*, his systematic presentation of reformed Christianity, which was revised and extended throughout his life. This he tried to put into practice, first in Geneva, then in Strasbourg, then again in Geneva from 1541 until his death. Unlike Luther, Calvin envisaged a complete restructuring of society in accordance with Christian principles, an ideal which in practice proved inhumanly austere. The private morality of citizens was monitored, the power of excommunication readily used, and Calvin did not shrink from torture and persecution, most notoriously in the case of Servetus, Spanish theologian and physician, executed for Trinitarian and Christological heresy. His influence on Protestantism, through the *Institutes* and his vast work of scholarly and theological commentary on the Scriptures, has been enormous. (See foll.)

Calvinism /ˈkælvɪnɪz(ə)m/ *n.* the theological system of John Calvin and his successors, which finds concise expression in the *Institutes of the Christian Religion* (final edition, 1559). It is presented as derived from the Scriptures, Old and New Testaments being of equal authority, the true interpretation of which is assured by the inner witnesss of the Holy Spirit. Luther's characteristic doctrine of justification by faith alone becomes an overriding emphasis on the grace of God which culminates in the central place given to the doctrine of predestination. Later Calvinism (beginning with Calvin's successor in Geneva, Theodore Beza) is much occupied by this doctrine and the question of signs by which the elect can be known, and in the 17th c. there was division between strict Calvinists and so-called Arminians who played down the doctrine. For Calvin himself it is not all-important, being rather the final assurance of the Christian life, and he finds room for a powerful doctrine of the Eucharist which stresses the role of the Spirit in a way that recalls the Greek Fathers. —**Calvinist** *n.*, **Calvinistic** *adj.* [f. prec.]

calx *n.* (*pl.* **calces** /ˈkælsiːz/) the powdery or friable substance left after the burning of a metal or mineral. [L, = lime]

Calypso /kəˈlɪpsəʊ/ (*Gk legend*) a nymph who kept Odysseus

on her island, Ogygia, for seven years. [Gk, = she who conceals]

calypso /kəˈlɪpsəʊ/ *n.* (*pl.* **-os**) a West Indian song with a variable rhythm and topical, usually improvised, lyrics. [orig. unkn.]

calyx /ˈkeɪlɪks/ *n.* (*pl.* **calyces** /-ɪsiːz/) a whorl of leaves forming the outer case of a bud or the envelope of a flower. [L f. Gk (*kaluptō* hide)]

cam *n.* a projecting part on a wheel or shaft in machinery, shaped so that its circular motion, as it turns, transmits an up-and-down or back-and-forth motion to another part. [f. Du. *kam* comb (*kamrad* cog-wheel)]

camaraderie /kæməˈrɑːdərɪ/ *n.* comradeship, mutual trust and friendship. [F]

Camargue /kæˈmɑːg/, **the** a region of the Rhône delta in SE France, characterized by numerous shallow salt lagoons. The region is known for its white horses and as a nature reserve.

camber /ˈkæmbə(r)/ *n.* a convex or arched shape given to the surface of a road, deck, etc.; the banked outer curve of a bend in a road etc. —*v.t.* to construct with a camber. [f. F (= arched) f. L *camurus* curved inwards]

cambium /ˈkæmbɪəm/ *n.* cellular tissue from which xylem and phloem grow (ill. TREES). [L, = exchange]

Cambodia /kæmˈbəʊdɪə/ = KAMPUCHEA. —**Cambodian** *adj. & n.*

Cambrian /ˈkæmbrɪən/ *adj.* **1.** Welsh. **2.** of the first period of the Palaeozoic era, following the Precambrian era and preceding the Ordovician period, lasting from about 590 to 505 million years ago. It was a time of widespread seas, and is the first period in which fossils (notably trilobites) can be used in geological dating. Rocks of this period were first recognised in Wales (whence its name). —*n.* this period. [f. L *Cambria* var. of *Cumbria* f. Welsh (as CYMRIC)]

cambric /ˈkæmbrɪk/ *n.* thin linen or cotton cloth. [f. *Cambrai*, town in N. France where orig. made]

Cambridge /ˈkeɪmbrɪdʒ/ a city in Cambridgeshire on the River Cam, the seat of a major English university organized as a federation of colleges. The first historical trace of Cambridge as a University (*studium generale*) is in 1209; a number of scholars migrated from Oxford to Cambridge in 1209–14 after a conflict with townsmen during which two or three students were hanged. Its first recognition came in a royal writ to the Chancellor of Cambridge in 1230. The first college, Peterhouse, was founded in 1284 and another nine followed in the 14th and 15th centuries, but the University did not achieve real eminence until the 16th-c. Reformation when it produced Tyndale, Coverdale, Cranmer, and Latimer. After a prolonged period of stagnation, Cambridge was revived by its growth as a centre of scientific research in the late 19th and early 20th c. Women's colleges were founded in the mid-19th c., but women did not receive full academic status until 1948. In 1982–3 there were 9,827 undergraduates in residence (6,513 men, 3,314 women) and 2,458 postgraduates (1,846 men, 612 women).

Cambridgeshire /ˈkeɪmbrɪdʒʃə(r)/ an east midland county of England. —*n.* a handicap horse-race run annually at Newmarket in Suffolk, England, in early October, inaugurated in 1839.

Cambs. *abbr.* Cambridgeshire.

Cambyses /kæmˈbaɪsiːz/ (d. 522 BC) son of Cyrus, king of Persia 530–522 BC. His main achievement was the conquest of Egypt in 525 BC.

came *past of* COME.

camel /ˈkæm(ə)l/ *n.* **1.** a large ruminant quadruped with a long neck and one hump (*Arabian camel*) or two humps (*Bactrian camel*), adapted to living in sandy deserts. **2.** fawn colour. —**camel('s) hair**, fabric made of this or similar hair; fine soft hair used in artists' brushes. [OE f. L f. Gk f. Semitic]

camellia /kəˈmɛlɪə/ *n.* a shrub of the genus *Camellia*, especially a flowering evergreen from China and Japan. [f. J. *Camellus*, 17th-c. Jesuit and botanist]

Camelot /ˈkæmɪlɒt/ (in Arthurian legend) the place where King Arthur held his court, stated by Malory to be Winchester.

Camembert /ˈkæməmbeə(r)/ *n.* a kind of small soft rich cheese. [name of town in Normandy, France, where orig. made]

cameo /ˈkæmɪəʊ/ *n.* (*pl.* **-os**) **1.** a small piece of hard stone carved in relief, especially with two coloured layers cut so that one serves as a background to the design. **2.** something small but well executed, especially a short descriptive literary sketch or an acted scene. [f. OF & L]

camera /ˈkæmərə/ *n.* an apparatus for taking photographs, motion pictures, or television pictures (see below and PHOTOGRAPHY). —*in camera,* (*Law*) in a judge's private room; privately, not in public. [L, = vault, f. Gk *kamara* thing with arched cover]
   The photographic camera consists essentially of a light-tight chamber fitted in front with a lens to focus an image of the object being photographed on to the light-sensitive film or plate at the rear; an aperture, closed by a shutter, admits light for the brief period needed for the image to register. Cameras were developed during the 19th c. and originally used metal and then glass plates with a sensitized coating. Later, flexible roll-film of coated celluloid was used, enabling cameras to be made much smaller and more portable, and the tendency towards miniaturization has continued. Reflex cameras originally used two lenses, one to give an image for viewing on a ground-glass screen, the other to focus the image on the film; single-lens reflex cameras achieve a similar result by a complex arrangement of reflecting mirrors. The television camera contains an 'electron gun' that converts an image into an electrical signal which is amplified for transmission (see TELEVISION and ill. LIGHT).

cameraman *n.* (*pl.* **-men**) a person whose job is to operate a camera, especially in film-making or television.

camera obscura /əbˈskjʊərə/ an apparatus that uses a darkened box or room with an aperture for projecting an image of a distant object on a screen within. Aristotle was aware of the principle on which this depends, and early astronomers used a form of it to watch the solar eclipse. In the early 17th c. Johann Kepler used it to record astronomical phenomena, and artists to trace an accurate outline of a subject. By the 18th c. it had become a craze and both amateurs and professionals (such as Canaletto) were using it for topographical painting. The *camera lucida* (L, = light chamber) was a similar device using a prism, and was employed mainly in copying drawings. [L, = dark chamber]

Cameroon /kæməˈruːn/ a country on the west coast of Africa between Nigeria and Gabon; pop. (est. 1980) 8,320,000; official languages, French and English; capital, Yaoundé. From 1884 to 1916 the territory was a German protectorate; it was then administered under League of Nations, later UN, trusteeship, part by France and part by Britain. In 1960 French Cameroons became an independent republic, to be joined in 1961 by part of the British Cameroons; the remainder became part of Nigeria. The French and British halves of the territory at first had separate governments but in 1972 merged as a United Republic. —**Cameroonian** *adj.* & *n.*

camisole /ˈkæmɪsəʊl/ *n.* a woman's bodice-like garment or undergarment. [F f. It. or Sp., = shirt]

camomile /ˈkæməmaɪl/ *n.* an aromatic composite plant of the genus *Anthemis* or *Matricaria* with flowers that are used as a tonic. [f. OF f. L f. Gk, = earth-apple (from the apple-like smell of the flowers)]

camouflage /ˈkæməflɑːdʒ/ *n.* the disguising of guns, ships, etc. by colouring or covering them to make them blend with their surroundings; this disguise; a means of disguise or concealment. —*v.t.* to hide by camouflage. [F (*camoufler* disguise) f. It.]

camp[1] *n.* **1.** a place where troops are lodged or trained. **2.** an ancient fortified site. **3.** temporary accommodation of tents, huts, etc. for holiday-makers, detainees, etc. **4.** the adherents of a doctrine or party. —*v.i.* to live in a camp; to make a camp. —**camp-bed** *n.* a folding portable bed. **camp-follower** *n.* a civilian worker in a military camp; an adherent of a group or theory. —**camper** *n.* [F f. It. f. L *campus* level ground]

camp[2] *adj.* affectedly exaggerated for theatrical effect; effeminate, homosexual. —*n.* a camp manner or style. —*v.t./i.* to act in a camp way. [orig. unkn.]

campaign /kæmˈpeɪn/ *n.* **1.** a series of military operations in a definite area or for a particular objective. **2.** an organized course of action for a particular purpose, especially to arouse public interest. —*v.i.* to take part in a campaign. —**campaigner** *n.* [f. F, = open country (as CAMP[1])]

campanology /kæmpəˈnɒlədʒɪ/ *n.* the study of bells and their founding, ringing, etc. —**campanologist** *n.* [f. L *campana* bell]

campanula /kəmˈpænjʊlə/ *n.* a plant of the genus *Campanula* with bell-shaped usually blue, pink, or white flowers. [dim. of L *campana* bell]

Campbell[1] /ˈkæmb(ə)l/, Mrs Patrick (1865-1940), née Beatrice Stella Tanner, English actress, renowned for her wit and eccentricity. She created the parts of Paula in *The Second Mrs Tanqueray* (1893), Agnes in *The Notorious Mrs Ebbsmith* (1895), both by Pinero, and the title role in *Magda* (1896), the English version of Sudermann's *Heimat*. George Bernard Shaw wrote for her the part of Eliza Doolittle in *Pygmalion* (1914) and exchanged letters with her over a long period.

Campbell[2] /ˈkæmb(ə)l/, Thomas (1777-1844), Scottish poet, the son of a Glasgow merchant. He published *The Pleasures of Hope* (1799) and *Gertrude of Wyoming* (1809) among other volumes of verse, and is now chiefly remembered for his patriotic lyrics such as 'The Battle of Hohenlinden' and 'Ye Mariners of England', and for his ballads.

Camp David the retreat in the Appalachian Mountains, Maryland, of the President of the USA.

camphor /ˈkæmfə(r)/ *n.* a white translucent strong-smelling crystalline substance used in insect-repellents and medicines and in making plastics. [f. OF or L f. Arab. f. Skr.]

camphorated /ˈkæmfəreɪtɪd/ *adj.* containing camphor. [f. prec.]

Campion /ˈkæmpɪən/, St Edmund (1540-81), Jesuit priest and martyr. Ordained deacon of the Church of England but with Roman Catholic sympathies, he went abroad, becoming a Catholic and a Jesuit priest (1578). He was a member of the first Jesuit mission to England (1580). In 1581 he was arrested, charged with conspiracy against the Crown, tortured, and executed at Tyburn.

campion /ˈkæmpɪən/ *n.* a plant of the genus *Silene, Melandrium,* or *Lychnis,* with usually pink or white notched flowers. [orig. unkn.; transl. of Gk name of a plant used for garlands]

campsite *n.* a camping-site, especially one equipped for holiday-makers.

campus /ˈkæmpəs/ *n.* the grounds of a university or college; a university, especially as a teaching institution. [L, = field]

camshaft *n.* a shaft carrying cams.

Camus /kæˈmuː/, Albert (1913-60), French novelist, dramatist, and essayist, born in Algeria, the son of a farm labourer. He made his name as a journalist during the Second World War and became editor of the left-wing daily *Combat* (1944-7). Through his novels he illustrated the philosophy of the absurd, notably in *L'Étranger* (*The Outsider*, 1942) and *La Peste* (*The Plague*, 1947) and in his essays, *Le Mythe de Sisyphe* (*The Myth of Sisyphus*, 1942) and *L'Homme révolté* (*The Rebel*, 1951). He wrote several plays including *Caligula* (1945) and adaptations for the stage. In 1957 he was awarded the Nobel Prize for literature, and by the time of his death at the age of 46 he had achieved international recognition.

can[1] /kən, emphatic kæn/ *v.aux.* (3 *sing. pres.* **can;** *past* **could**) **1.** to be able to, to know how to. **2.** to have the right to, to be permitted to. [OE, = know]

can[2] *n.* a metal or plastic container for liquids; a tin container in which food or drink is hermetically sealed for preservation. —*v.t.* (**-nn-**) to put or preserve in a can. — **canned music,** music recorded for reproduction. [OE]
   Canning was introduced in the 19th c. The principle on which it is based was devised by a French confectioner, Nicolas Appert (1810), as a means of supplying preserved food for French troops. Food was heated to a high temperature in glass jars which were then sealed until used. The reason for its success was not known until the work of Louis Pasteur: heat destroyed the micro-organisms present in food, and sealing prevented others from entering. In the same year the technique was applied in England, using glass or metal containers, and tin-coated steel containers became widely used. Lids were soldered until the early 20th c., when a method was devised of sealing the cover to the can. The invention of tinned food considerably preceded the equally important invention of the tin-opener: opening was by means of a hammer and chisel until a domestic implement was devised in the mid-19th c.

Canaan /ˈkeɪnən/ the land, later known as Palestine, which the Israelites gradually conquered and occupied during the latter part of the 2nd millennium BC. The earliest known mention of the country by this name occurs in the Mari documents of the 18th c. BC. —**Canaanite** /-naɪt/ *adj.* & *n.*

Canada /ˈkænədə/ the second-largest country in the world, a member State of the Commonwealth, covering the entire northern half of North America with the exception of Alaska; pop. (1981) 24,343,181; official languages, English and French; capital, Ottawa. Both agriculture and industry are highly developed, and there are vast mineral resources. The Vikings established a settlement on the NE tip of Newfoundland *c.* AD 1000. John Cabot reached the east coast in 1497, Jacques Cartier explored the St Lawrence in 1535, and Samuel de Champlain founded Quebec in 1608 and penetrated the interior (1609-16). Eastern Canada was colonized by the French mainly in the 17th c., with the British emerging as the ruling colonial power after the Seven Years War (Treaty of Paris, 1763). Canada became a federation of provinces in 1867, and the last step in the attainment of its legal independence from the UK was taken with the signing of the Constitution Act of 1982. Through the late 19th and early 20th centuries the vast Canadian West was gradually opened up, but the country remains sparsely populated for its size. Although periodically affected by the dissatisfactions of part of the French-speaking minority, Canada has generally remained both stable and prosperous.

Canadian /kəˈneɪdɪən/ *adj.* of Canada or its people. —*n.* a native or inhabitant of Canada. —**Canadian shield,** see SHIELD. [f. prec.]

canal /kəˈnæl/ *n.* **1.** an artificial channel carrying water for irrigation, drainage, or power, or for inland navigation (see below). **2.** a tubular passage in a plant or animal body. [f. OF or It. f. L *canalis*].

Examples of irrigation canals date from the 5th millennium BC in Iraq. Early canals are also to be found in Egypt and China, where the Grand Canal, 1,700 km (1,060 miles) in length, begun in 109 BC, was completed in 1327. Many notable canals are designed to shorten sea passages: in France the Canal du Midi joined the Atlantic and Mediterranean in 1681, the Suez Canal joined the latter to the Red Sea in 1869, and in 1914 the Panama Canal joined the Atlantic and Pacific Oceans. The great advantage of inland water transport is its economy, due to the low resistance to movement of vessels and the level nature of the route. (Where changes in level are needed some form of lock is generally used.) In England canals were the arteries of the Industrial Revolution, greatly reducing the cost of transport to below that of land transport over inadequate roads. Brindley and Telford were the great canal builders between 1760 and 1840, by which time a network of some 6,800 km (4,250 miles) of canal was in being. Thereafter canal use declined in Britain, through the rise in railways and the restricted size of the early canals, but in Europe and North America canal use has grown in route length and in size of vessels. The Rhine, Rhône, and Danube will shortly be linked, while the Great Lakes are accessible to ocean-going vessels by means of the St Lawrence Seaway.

Canaletto /kænəˈletəʊ/, Giovanni Antonio Canal (1697-1768), Venetian view painter, especially popular with the English aristocracy, who commissioned his paintings of the Grand Canal and the festivals of Venice as mementos of their Grand Tour. His early work is dramatic and freely handled, reflecting his training as a theatrical scene painter, but *c.*1730 he changed to a smoother more precise style, almost photographic in its topographical accuracy. From 1746 to 1755 Canaletto was in England, in a search for patronage which was of limited success, partly owing to the mannered mechanical style of his later work. His most important patron, Joseph Smith (British consul in Venice), sold a large collection of Canaletto's paintings and drawings to George III, and they remain in the British Royal Collection.

canalize /ˈkænəlaɪz/ *v.t.* **1.** to make a canal through; to provide with canals. **2.** to channel. —**canalization** /-ˈzeɪʃ(ə)n/ *n.* [f. CANAL)]

canapé /ˈkænəpeɪ/ *n.* a small piece of bread, pastry, or biscuit with a savoury topping. [F]

canary /kəˈneərɪ/ *n.* a small songbird with yellow feathers, the finch *Serinus canarius.* [f. *Canary* Islands, f. L *canis* dog, one of the islands being noted in Roman times for large dogs]

Canary Islands /kəˈneərɪ/ (also **Canaries**) a group of islands, in Spanish possession since the 15th c., situated off the NW coast of Africa; pop. (est. 1975) 1,275,643.

canasta /kəˈnæstə/ *n.* a card-game of Uruguayan origin, resembling rummy. [Sp., = basket]

Canberra /ˈkænbərə/ the capital and seat of the federal government of Australia; pop. (1982) 230,800.

cancan /ˈkænkæn/ *n.* a lively stage-dance with high kicking, performed by women in long skirts and petticoats. Originally a decent and measured social dance invented by M. Masarié in 1830 as a variant of the quadrille, it appeared

after 1844 in the French music-halls, developing there an increasingly uninhibited emphasis on the throwing up of the legs of the dancers and the display of their underwear, so that it was forbidden by the authorities. The best-known examples, however, are in Offenbach's operettas, notably *Orpheus in the Underworld.*

cancel /ˈkæns(ə)l/ *v.t./i.* (**-ll-**) **1.** to state that (a previous arrangement or decision) will not take place or be executed; to discontinue; to annul, to make void. **2.** to neutralize, to counterbalance. **3.** to obliterate or delete (writing etc.); to mark so as to prevent further use. **4.** (*Math.*) to strike out (an equal factor) on each side of an equation etc. —**cancellation** /-ˈleɪʃ(ə)n/ *n.* [f. F f. L (*cancelli* cross-bars)]

Cancer /ˈkænsə(r)/ a constellation and the fourth sign of the zodiac, the Crab, which the sun enters at the summer solstice. It is most noted for its beautiful cluster of stars known as Praesepe or the Beehive, which appears as a misty patch of light to the naked eye, but was first resolved into individual stars by the telescope observations of Galileo. —**calms of Cancer,** see CALM. **tropic of Cancer,** see TROPIC [L, = crab]

cancer /ˈkænsə(r)/ *n.* **1.** a tumour, especially a malignant one; a disease featuring this (see below). **2.** an evil influence or corruption. —**cancerous** *adj.*, **cancroid** /ˈkæŋkrɔɪd/ *adj.* [= prec.]

Cancer is a disorder of the processes of growth, development, and repair during which cells undergo morphological and metabolic deviations from those inherent properties of the cells of the tissue of origin. Cancers result from the disruption in the control mechanisms normally exerted over cell reproduction and differentiation. A new growth of tissue arises spontaneously, is atypical in structure, loses or alters its normal biochemical characteristics, and follows an inexorable and purposeless growth pattern in which there is a failure of the normal control mechanisms to operate. As a consequence of these intrinsic cellular defects cancer cells do not conform to the restraints imposed on the proliferation of normal body cells. They do not form discrete isolated tumours but tend both to infiltrate neighbouring tissues and to spread to distant parts of the body, forming secondary growths or metastases. It is this disturbance of the fundamental cellular control processes, leading to the consequent disorder of cell behaviour, which characterizes cancer. As its etiology is so imperfectly understood cancer defies definition and the above description does no more than detail in basic and general terms the abnormal changes underlying the cancerous process.

candela /kænˈdiːlə/ *n.* the base unit of luminous intensity (symbol cd; established in 1948 for international use; amended in 1967), the luminous intensity, in the perpendicular direction, of a surface of 1/600,000 square metre of a black body at the temperature of freezing platinum under a pressure of 101,325 newtons per square metre. [L, = candle (*candēre* shine)]

candelabrum /kændɪˈlɑːbrəm/ *n.* (*pl.* **-bra**) a large branched candlestick or light-holder. [L (as prec.)]

candid *adj.* **1.** frank, not hiding one's thoughts. **2.** (in photography) informal, of a picture taken usually without the subject's knowledge. —**candidly** *adv.*, **candidness** *n.* [f. F or L *candidus* white]

candidate /ˈkændɪdət/ *n.* **1.** a person who seeks or is nominated for an office, award, etc. **2.** a person or thing likely to gain a specified distinction or position. **3.** one taking an examination. —**candidacy** *n.*, **candidature** *n.* [f. F or L, = white-robed (see prec.), from the white robes worn by Roman candidates for office]

candle *n.* a usually cylindrical stick of wax or tallow enclosing a wick for giving light when burning. —**candle-light** *n.* the light of candles. **cannot hold a candle to,** is very inferior to. [OE f. L (*candēre* shine)]

Candlemas /ˈkændlməs/ *n.* the feast of the Purification of the Virgin Mary (2 Feb.), when candles are blessed. [OE (as CANDLE, MASS²)]

candlepower *n.* a unit of luminous intensity.

candlestick *n.* a holder for one or more candles.

candlewick *n.* a fabric with a raised tufted pattern worked in thick soft cotton yarn; this yarn.

candour /ˈkændə(r)/ *n.* candid speech or quality, frankness. [f. F or L *candor* whiteness (*candēre* shine)]

candy *n.* **1.** sugar crystallized by repeated boiling and slow evaporation. **2.** (*US*) sweets, a sweet. —*v.t.* to preserve (fruit etc.) by coating or impregnating with candy. —**candy-floss** *n.* a fluffy mass of spun sugar round a stick. **candy-stripes** *n.pl.* alternate stripes of white and colour.

candy-striped adj. [earlier sugar candy, f. F f. Arab. (kand sugar, ult. f. Skr.)]

candytuft n. a garden plant of the genus Iberis with white, pink, or purple flowers in flat tufts. [f. Candia in Crete]

cane n. **1.** the hollow jointed stem of tall reeds and grasses (e.g. bamboo, sugar-cane); the solid stem of slender palms (e.g. Malacca); a plant with such a stem; the stems of these used as material for wickerwork etc. **2.** a stem or a length of it, or a slender rod, used as a walking-stick or to support a plant etc. or as a stick for use in corporal punishment. —v.t. **1.** to beat with a cane. **2.** to weave cane into (a chair etc.). —**cane-sugar**, sugar obtained from the juice of sugar-cane. [f. OF f. L f. Gk kanna reed, f. Semitic]

canine /ˈkeɪnaɪn/ adj. of a dog or dogs. —n. **1.** a dog. **2.** a canine tooth (ill. BODY 1). —**canine tooth**, a strong pointed tooth between the incisors and molars. [f. L caninus (canis dog)]

canister /ˈkænɪstə(r)/ n. a metal box or other container; a cylinder, filled with shot or tear-gas, that bursts and releases its contents on impact. [f. L f. Gk kanastron wicker basket (kanna reed)]

canker /ˈkæŋkə(r)/ n. **1.** a disease that destroys the wood of trees and plants; a disease causing ulcerous sores in animals. **2.** a corrupting influence. —**cankerous** adj. [OE f. L (as CANCER)]

canna /ˈkænə/ n. a tropical plant of the genus Canna, with ornamental leaves and bright yellow, red, or orange flowers. [L (as CANE)]

cannabis /ˈkænəbɪs/ n. a hemp plant of the genus Cannabis; a preparation of this for smoking or chewing as an intoxicant or hallucinogenic drug. [L f. Gk]

cannery /ˈkænərɪ/ n. a canning-factory. [f. CAN²]

cannibal /ˈkænɪb(ə)l/ n. a person who eats human flesh (see below); an animal that eats its own species. —**cannibalism** n., **cannibalistic** /-ˈlɪstɪk/ adj. [f. Sp., var. of Caribes name of West Indian tribe (Caribs) formerly noted for their practice of cannibalism]

Archaeological evidence suggests that cannibalism has occurred since palaeolithic times in many places throughout the world, although now, if it exists at all, it is limited to isolated parts of Melanesia and South America. Cannibalism is rarely associated with starvation, which is probably the least common motive for its occurrence; more often it is associated with ritual, religious, or magical beliefs. Anthropologists distinguish two categories of cannibalism: endocannibalism, in which the remains of relatives or other members of one's own group are consumed, and exocannibalism, in which the remains of one's enemies are consumed. The motivation underlying these two forms differs: in endocannibalism respect and reverence are shown toward one's deceased kinsmen; in exocannibalism the act is often associated with ritualized vengeance or with the means of absorbing the vitality or other qualities of vanquished foes. The parts of the body eaten and the methods of their preparation for consumption varied widely between societies and the particular organs or portions consumed frequently had ritual signficance.

cannibalize /ˈkænɪb(ə)laɪz/ v.t. to use (a machine etc.) as a source of spare parts for others. —**cannibalization** /-ˈzeɪʃ(ə)n/ n. [f. prec.]

Canning /ˈkænɪŋ/, George (1770–1827), Foreign Secretary of Great Britain 1807–9 and 1822–7. Canning resigned his post in 1809 after a disagreement with his rival Castlereagh over a disastrous expedition in the Napoleonic Wars, but returned to office following the latter's suicide in 1822, whereupon he presided over a reversal of Britain's hitherto conservative foreign policy, being particularly responsible for the support of nationalist movements in various parts of Europe. He succeeded Lord Liverpool as Prime Minister on the latter's death in 1827, but died himself six months later.

Cannizzaro /kænɪˈzɑːrəʊ/, Stanislao (1826–1910), Italian chemist, remembered for his revival of Avogadro's hypothesis, which had been neglected for fifty years. He also discovered a reaction (named after him) in which an aldehyde is converted into an acid and an alcohol in the presence of a strong alkali.

cannon /ˈkænən/ n. **1.** (pl. same) an old type of large heavy gun of a size which required it to be mounted for firing, discharging solid metal balls. It dates (in Europe) from the early 14th c. **2.** an automatic shell-firing gun used in aircraft. **3.** the hitting of two balls successively by a player's ball in billiards. —v.i. to collide heavily against or into. —**cannon-bone** n. a tube-shaped bone between a horse's

hock and fetlock (ill. HORSE). **cannon-fodder** n. men regarded merely as material to be expended in war. [f. F f. It., = great tube (as CANE); sense 2 formerly carom]

cannonade /kænəˈneɪd/ n. continuous heavy gunfire. —v.t. to bombard with a cannonade. [as prec.]

cannot /ˈkænɒt/ = can not. [CAN¹]

canny /ˈkænɪ/ adj. shrewd and cautious; worldly-wise. —**cannily** adv., **canniness** n. [f. CAN¹]

canoe /kəˈnuː/ n. a keelless boat, pointed at both ends and propelled by a paddle or paddles, in which the paddler faces forward, often in a kneeling position (see below). —v.i. (partic. **canoeing**) to go in or paddle a canoe. —**canoeist** n. [f. Sp. & Haitian canoa]

The term was applied to a small open boat used by primitive peoples, originally to those of West Indian aborigines (canoa is the native name found in use by Columbus) which were hollowed out of a single tree-trunk. It was extended to embrace similar craft, in which paddles were the motive force, all over the world, some of which (particularly among the Pacific islands) were remarkably large vessels in which two banks of paddlers, up to 20 or 30 a side, were used.

canon /ˈkænən/ n. **1.** a general rule, law, principle, or criterion; a church decree or law. **2.** a member of a cathedral chapter. **3.** a body of sacred or other writings accepted as genuine. **4.** the central unchanging part of the RC Mass. **5.** (Mus.) a passage or piece of music in which a theme is taken up by several parts successively. —**canon law**, ecclesiastical law, based on the New Testament, tradition, pronouncements by popes and councils of the Church, and decisions in particular cases. [OE f. L f. Gk kanōn rule]

canonical /kəˈnɒnɪk(ə)l/ adj. **1.** according to or ordered by canon law. **2.** included in the canon of Scripture; authoritative, accepted. **3.** of a cathedral canon or chapter. **4.** (in pl.) the canonical dress of clergy. [f. L (as prec.)]

canonize /ˈkænənaɪz/ v.t. **1.** to declare officially to be a saint, usually with a ceremony. **2.** to admit to the canon of Scriptures. **3.** to sanction by church authority. —**canonization** /-ˈzeɪʃ(ə)n/ n. [f. L (as CANON)]

Canopic jar or **vase** /kəˈnəʊpɪk/ each of a set of (usually four) urns for containing the different organs (liver, lungs, etc.) of an embalmed body in an ancient Egyptian burial. The lids, originally plain, were later modelled as the human, falcon, dog, and jackal heads of the four sons of Horus, protectors of the jars. [f. L f. Canopus town in ancient Egypt]

canopy /ˈkænəpɪ/ n. **1.** a hanging cover forming a shelter above a throne, bed, or person etc.; any similar covering. **2.** the expanding part of a parachute. —v.t. to supply or be a canopy to. [f. L f. Gk, = mosquito-net (kōnōps gnat)]

Canova /kəˈnəʊvə/, Antonio (1757–1822), Italian sculptor who by the early 19th c. had developed an international reputation as the pre-eminent exponent of neo-classicism. Canova's sculpture readily reflected that 'noble simplicity' and 'calm grandeur' defined by Winckelmann as the essence of true classicism. His works range from heroic groups of classical subjects to funeral monuments and life-size busts: while on the one hand his fine carving reflects the ideality of his antique sources, his sense of invention and sophisticated treatment of problems such as multiple view-points were, in every sense, modern. His commissions included papal and royal monuments and figures executed for Napoleon and his family; Canova even attracted the commission for the statue of George Washington for North Carolina.

cant¹ n. **1.** insincere pious or moral talk. **2.** jargon. —v.i. to use cant. [prob. f. L cantare (see CHANT)]

cant² n. a tilted or sloping position; a sloping surface, a bevel. —v.t./i. to tilt, to slope. [LG or Du., =edge, f. L cant(h)us iron tire]

can't /kɑːnt/ (colloq.) cannot. [CAN¹]

Cantab. abbr. Cantabrigian, of Cambridge University.

cantabile /kænˈtɑːbɪlɪ/ adv. (Mus.) in a smooth flowing style. —n. (Mus.) a piece to be performed in this way. [It., = suitable for singing]

Cantabrigian /kæntəˈbrɪdʒɪən/ adj. of Cambridge or Cambridge University. —n. a citizen of Cambridge; a member of Cambridge University. [f. Cantabrigia, Latinized name of CAMBRIDGE]

cantaloup /ˈkæntəluːp/ n. a small round ribbed melon with orange flesh. [F, f. Cantaluppi near Rome, where first grown in Europe]

cantankerous /kænˈtæŋkərəs/ adj. bad-tempered, quarrelsome. —**cantankerously** *adv.*, **cantankerousness** *n.* [perh. f. Ir. *cant* outbidding + *rancorous*]

cantata /kæn'tɑːtə/ *n.* (*Mus.*) a short narrative or descriptive composition with vocal solos and usually a chorus and orchestral accompaniment. Cantatas in the early 17th c. were of the nature of extended songs, but towards the end of the century the form began to expand until it comprised several sections, combining recitative, aria, and instrumental music. The great sacred cantatas of Bach and his contemporaries frequently incorporated melodies from the Lutheran chorales, sometimes harmonized simply so that the congregation could join in the singing at that point. The cantata declined after 1750, but isolated examples appear in the 20th c., e.g. by Britten (*Cantata academica*, 1959) and Stravinsky (*Cantata*, 1951-2). [It., = sung (air) f. *cantare* sing]

canteen /kæn'tiːn/ *n.* 1. a restaurant for the employees of a factory, office, etc.; a shop for provisions or liquor in a barracks or camp. 2. a case or box containing a set of cutlery. 3. a soldier's or camper's water-flask. [f. F or Ir., = cellar]

canter *n.* a gentle gallop (ill. HORSE). —*v.t./i.* to go or cause to go at a canter. [short for *Canterbury gallop* etc., from the supposed easy pace of medieval pilgrims to Canterbury in Kent]

Canterbury /'kæntəbərɪ/ a city in Kent, St Augustine's centre for the conversion of England to Christianity, now the seat of the archbishop, Primate of All England. St Augustine had been ordered to organize England into two ecclesiastical provinces, with archbishops at London and York. From the first, however, the place of London was taken by Canterbury.

cantharides /kæn'θærɪdiːz/ *n.pl.* the dried remains of a kind of beetle (*Lytta vesicatoria*). It has been used in medicine for its irritant action on the skin, and as an aphrodisiac. [L f. Gk]

canticle /'kæntɪk(ə)l/ *n.* 1. a song or chant with words taken from the Bible. 2. **Canticles**, the Song of Solomon. [f. OF or L, dim. of *canticum* (*cantus* song)]

cantilever /'kæntɪliːvə(r)/ *n.* a projecting beam, bracket, or girder supporting a balcony, bridge (ill. BRIDGES), or similar structure; a beam or girder fixed at one end only. [orig. unkn.]

cantle *n.* the upward-curving hind part of a saddle (ill. HORSE). [f. AF f. L *cantellus*, dim. of *cantus* (see CANT²)]

canto /'kæntəʊ/ *n.* (*pl.***-os**) any of the sections into which a long poem is divided. [It., = song, f. L *cantus* (as CHANT²)]

canton /'kæntɒn/ *n.* a subdivision of a country; a State of the Swiss confederation. [OF, = corner (rel. to CANT²)]

Cantonese /kæntə'niːz/ *n.* (*pl.* same) 1. a native or inhabitant of the city of Canton in China. 2. a Chinese language spoken in southern China and in Hong Kong. —*adj.* of Canton or its people or language. [name of city]

Cantor /'kæntɔː(r)/, Georg (1845-1918), Russian-born mathematician who spent most of his life in Germany, professor at Halle from 1869 until his death. He introduced the theory of sets which was later to be adopted as a satisfactory medium in which to express most concepts of mathematics. His analysis of the notion of real number and his study of infinite sets have led to a proper understanding of transfinite cardinal and ordinal numbers and of the logical foundations of most of mathematics.

cantor /'kæntɔː(r)/ *n.* the leader of the liturgical singing of a church choir; a precentor in a synagogue. —**cantorial** /-'tɔːrɪəl/ *adj.* [L, = singer (*canere* sing)]

Canute var. of CNUT.

canvas /'kænvəs/ *n.* 1. strong coarse cloth used for making tents and sails and as a surface for oil-painting; a painting on canvas. 2. a racing-boat's covered end. [f. OF f. L CANNABIS]

canvass /'kænvəs/ *v.t./i.* 1. to solicit votes (from); to ascertain the opinions of; to ask for custom from. 2. to propose (an idea or plan etc.). —*n.* canvassing, especially of electors. —**canvasses** *n.* [f. prec., orig. = toss in a sheet, hence = shake up, agitate]

canyon /'kænjən/ *n.* a deep gorge. [f. Sp., = tube, f. L (as CANE)]

caoutchouc /'kaʊtʃʊk/ *n.* unvulcanized rubber. [F f. Carib *cahuchu*]

CAP *abbr.* Common Agricultural Policy (of the EEC), a system for establishing common prices for most agricultural products, a single fund for price supports, and levies on imports.

cap *n.* 1. a soft brimless head-covering, usually with a peak.

2. a head-covering worn in a particular profession; an academic mortar-board; a cap awarded as a sign of membership of a sports team. 3. a caplike cover or top. —*v.t.* (**-pp-**) 1. to put a cap on; to cover the top or end of 2. to award a sports cap to. 3. to form the top of. 4. to surpass, to excel. [f. OE f. L *cappa*, perh. f. *caput* head]

capable /'keɪpəb(ə)l/ *adj.* having a certain ability or capacity *of;* competent. —**capability** /-'bɪlɪtɪ/ *n.*, **capably** *adv.* [F f. L (*capere* hold)]

capacious /kə'peɪʃəs/ *adj.* roomy, able to hold much. —**capaciously** *adv.*, **capaciousness** *n.* [f. L *capax* (*capere* hold)]

capacitance /kə'pæsɪt(ə)ns/ *n.* ability to store an electric charge; the measure of this, the ratio of the change in the electric charge of a body to a corresponding change in its potential. [f. CAPACITY]

capacitor /kə'pæsɪtə(r)/ *n.* a device having capacitance, usually consisting of conductors separated by an insulator. [f. foll.]

capacity /kə'pæsɪtɪ/ *n.* 1. the ability to contain or accommodate. 2. ability, capability. 3. the maximum amount that can be contained or produced etc. 4. function, position, legal competency. —**to capacity**, fully, to the full. [f. F f. L (as CAPACIOUS)]

caparison /kə'pærɪs(ə)n/ *n.* a horse's trappings; equipment, finery. —*v.t.* to adorn. [f. F f. Sp., = saddle-cloth (as CAPE¹)]

cape¹ *n.* a cloak; a similarly shaped part or garment covering the shoulders. [F f. L *cappa* CAP]

cape² *n.* a coastal promontory. —**the Cape**, the Cape of Good Hope; the province containing it, Cape Province. [f. OF f. L *caput* head]

Cape Horn the southernmost point of South America, on an island south of Tierra del Fuego, belonging to Chile. It was discovered by the Dutch navigator Schouten in 1616 and named after Hoorn, his birthplace. The ocean region is notorious for storms, and until the opening of the Panama Canal in 1914 lay on the only sea route between the Atlantic and Pacific Oceans.

Čapek /'tʃɑːpek/, Karel (1890-1938), Czech novelist and dramatist, born in Bohemia. He wrote several plays with his brother, Josef Čapek (1887-1945) (a painter and stage-designer) including *The Insect Play* (1921), a satire on human society and totalitarianism. Čapek's best-known independent work was *R.U.R.* (1920), set 'on a remote island in 1950-60' the title 'Rossum's Universal Robots' and the concept of the mechanical robot introduced a new word to the English language and opened up a whole new vein of science fiction. His other works include the play *The Makropoulos Affair* (1923), utopian romances, novels, travel works, and essays.

Cape of Good Hope a mountainous promontory near the southern extremity of Africa, south of Cape Town. It was sighted towards the end of the 15th c. by the Portuguese explorer Dias and named Cape of Storms, and was rounded for the first time by Vasco da Gama in 1497.

Cape Province the southern province of the Republic of South Africa; capital, Cape Town.

caper¹ /'keɪpə(r)/ *v.i.* to jump or run about playfully. —*n.* 1. a playful jump or leap. 2. a prank. 3. (*slang*) an activity. [abbr. of CAPRIOLE]

caper² /'keɪpə(r)/ *n.* a bramble-like shrub; (in *pl.*) its buds pickled for use in sauces etc. [f. L f. Gk *kapparis*]

capercaillie /kæpə'keɪlɪ/ *n.* the largest kind of European grouse, *Tetrao urogallus*, formerly native to the Scottish Highlands, where it was reintroduced from Scandinavia after becoming extinct in Scotland. [f. Gaelic, = horse of the forest]

Capetian /kə'piːʃ(ə)n/ *n.* a member of a dynasty of kings of France, founded by Hugo Capet in 987 in succession to the Carolingian dynasty. It survived until 1328, giving way to the House of Valois. The extinction of the direct line of Capetians gave rise to Edward III's claim to the French throne and the start of the Hundred Years War.

Cape Town the legislative capital of the Republic of South Africa, at the foot of Table Mountain; pop. (est. 1978) 892,200.

Cape Verde Islands /vɜːd/ a country consisting of a group of islands in the Atlantic off the coast of Senegal, named after the most westerly cape of Africa; pop. (1980) 296,093; official language, Portuguese; capital, Praia. Settled by the Portuguese in the 15th c., the islands formed a Portuguese colony until they became independent in 1975. They have links with Guinea-Bissau, with which they were formerly administered, but the plan for federation with Guinea-Bissau was dropped in 1980. —**Cape Verdean** /ˈvɜːdɪən/ adj. & n.

capillary /kəˈpɪlərɪ/ adj. like a hair, hairlike in diameter. —n. **1.** a capillary tube. **2.** any of the very fine ramified blood-vessels connecting arteries and veins. —**capillary attraction, repulsion,** the tendency of liquid to be drawn up or down in a capillary tube. —**capillarity** /-ˈlærɪtɪ/ n. [f. L (capillus hair)]

capital /ˈkæpɪt(ə)l/ n. **1.** the most important town or city of a country or region, usually its seat of government and administrative centre. **2.** the money or other assets with which a company starts business; accumulated wealth; capitalists collectively. **3.** a capital letter. **4.** the head of a column or pillar (ill. CHURCH). —adj. **1.** principal, most important; (colloq.) excellent. **2.** involving punishment by death; very serious. **3.** (letters of the alphabet) of the form and size used to begin a name or sentence. —**capital gain,** profit from the sale of investment or property. **capital punishment,** see separate entry. **capital sum,** a lump sum of money, especially that payable to an insured person. **capital transfer tax,** a tax on capital that is transferred from one person or another, as by gift or bequest. **make capital out of,** to use (a situation etc.) to one's own advantage. [f. OF f. L (caput head)]

capitalism /ˈkæpɪt(ə)lɪz(ə)m/ n. an economic system in which trade and industry are controlled by private owners and for profit. [f. prec.]

capitalist /ˈkæpɪt(ə)lɪst/ n. **1.** a person using or possessing capital, a rich person. **2.** a believer in capitalism. —adj. of or favouring capitalism. —**capitalistic** /-ˈɪstɪk/ adj. [as prec.]

capitalize /ˈkæpɪt(ə)laɪz/ v.t./i. **1.** to convert into capital; to provide with capital. **2.** to write or print with a capital letter; to begin (a word) with a capital letter. —**capitalize on,** to use to one's advantage. —**capitalization** /-ˈzeɪʃ(ə)n/ n. [f. F (as CAPITAL)]

capital punishment infliction of death by an authorized public authority as punishment for a crime. It was recognized by ancient legal systems, and methods of execution varied: the Babylonians used drowning, the Hebrews stoning, the Greeks allowed a free man to take poison (but slaves were beaten to death); Roman methods included hurling from the Tarpeian rock, strangulation, exposure to wild beasts, and crucifixion. In medieval Europe hanging and beheading were the usual methods; religious heretics were burnt at the stake. In more recent times, only hanging was used in Britain, the guillotine was introduced into France in the 18th c., the garrotte was used by Spain, and in the USA the chief methods of execution were the electric chair and the gas chamber. In the 19th c. in Britain the death penalty, previously available for a wide range of offences (some quite trivial) was restricted to cases of treason and murder, and in 1965 abolished for murder. Many western countries have abolished it.

capitation /kæpɪˈteɪʃ(ə)n/ n. a tax or fee levied per person. [F or f. L, = poll-tax (caput head)]

Capitol /ˈkæpɪt(ə)l/ **1.** the temple of Jupiter in ancient Rome. **2.** the seat of the US Congress in Washington DC. Its site was chosen by George Washington, who laid the first stone in 1793. [f. OF f. L (caput head)]

capitulate /kəˈpɪtjʊleɪt/ v.i. to surrender. —**capitulation** /-ˈleɪʃ(ə)n/ n. [f. L capitulare put under headings, f. capitulum dim. of caput head]

capon /ˈkeɪpɒn/ n. a domestic cock castrated and fattened for eating. [OE f. AF f. L capo]

Capone /kəˈpəʊn/, Al (1899–1947), American gangster, born in Italy, notorious for his domination of organized crime in Chicago in the 1920s.

Cappadocia /kæpəˈdəʊʃə/ the ancient name for the region in the centre of Asia Minor (modern Turkey) between Lake Tuz and the Euphrates, north of Cilicia. —**Cappadocian** adj. & n.

Capri /ˈkæpriː, kəˈpriː/ an island off the west coast of Italy, in the Bay of Naples.

caprice /kəˈpriːs/ n. **1.** a whim; a tendency to capricious behaviour. **2.** a work of lively fancy in art or music. [F f. It. capriccio sudden start (orig. = horror)]

capricious /kəˈprɪʃəs/ adj. guided by caprice, impulsive; unpredictable. —**capriciously** adv., **capriciousness** n. [as prec.]

Capricorn /ˈkæprɪkɔːn/ a constellation and the tenth sign of the zodiac, the Goat, which the sun enters at the winter

solstice. In the northern hemisphere it is visible in late summer. —**calms of Capricorn,** see CALM. **tropic of Capricorn,** see TROPIC. [f. OF f. L (caper goat, cornu horn)]

Capsian /ˈkæpsɪən/ adj. of a palaeolithic industry of North Africa and southern Europe (c. 8000–4500 BC) noted for its microliths. —n. this industry. [f. L Capsa = Gafsa in Tunisia]

capsicum /ˈkæpsɪkəm/ n. the sweet pepper, a tropical plant of the genus Capsicum with hot-tasting seeds; its fruit. [perh. f. L capsa case]

capsize /kæpˈsaɪz/ v.t./i. to overturn (a boat); to be overturned. [perh. f. Sp. capuzar sink by the head (cabo head, chapuzar dive)]

capstan /ˈkæpst(ə)n/ n. **1.** a thick revolving post round which a cable or rope is wound as it turns, e.g. to raise a ship's anchor. **2.** a revolving spindle carrying the spool on a tape-recorder. —**capstan lathe,** a lathe with a revolving tool-holder. [f. Prov. f. L (capere seize)]

capsule /ˈkæpsjuːl/ n. **1.** a small soluble case in which a dose of medicine is enclosed for swallowing. **2.** a plant's seed-case that splits open when ripe. **3.** a detachable compartment of an aircraft or nose-cone of a rocket. —adj. concise, highly condensed. [F f. L (capsa case)]

capsulize /ˈkæpsjʊlaɪz/ v.t. to put (information etc.) into a compact form. [f. prec.]

captain /ˈkæptɪn/ n. **1.** a person given authority over a group or team. **2.** the person commanding a ship; a naval officer ranking next below commodore. **3.** an army officer ranking next below major. **4.** the pilot of a civil aircraft. —v.t. to be captain of. —**captaincy** n. [f. OF f. L, = chief (caput head)]

caption /ˈkæpʃ(ə)n/ n. a short title or heading; a description or explanation printed with an illustration etc.; words shown on a cinema or television screen. —v.t. to provide with a caption. [f. L (capere take)]

captious /ˈkæpʃəs/ adj. fond of finding fault, raising petty objections. —**captiously** adv., **captiousness** n. [f. OF or L (as prec.)]

captivate /ˈkæptɪveɪt/ v.t. to capture the affection or fancy of, to charm. —**captivation** /-ˈveɪʃ(ə)n/ n. [f. L captivare take captive (as foll.)]

captive /ˈkæptɪv/ adj. taken prisoner; restrained, confined; (of an audience or market) having no choice but to listen or comply. —n. a captive person or animal. [f. L captivus (capere take)]

captivity /kæpˈtɪvɪtɪ/ n. the state of being held captive. —**the Captivity,** that of the Jews in Babylon, to which they were deported by Nebuchadnezzar in 586 BC and from which they were released by Cyrus in 538 BC. [as prec.]

captor /ˈkæptə(r)/ n. one who captures. [L (as CAPTURE)]

capture /ˈkæptʃə(r)/ v.t. **1.** to take prisoner, to seize; to obtain by force, trickery, attraction, or skill. **2.** to portray (a likeness etc.) in permanent form. **3.** to absorb (an atomic particle). **4.** (of a stream) to divert the upper course of (another) into its own waters by encroaching on the other's basin. **5.** (of a star or planet) to bring (an object) within its gravitational field. **6.** to put (data) into a form accessible by computer. —n. **1.** the act of capturing. **2.** a thing or person captured. [F f. L (as prec.)]

Capuchin /ˈkæpjʊtʃɪn/ n. **1.** a Franciscan friar of the new rule of 1528. **2.** (**capuchin**) a monkey or pigeon with a hood-like crown. [F f. It. (cappuccio cowl)]

capybara /kæpɪˈbɑːrə/ n. a large South American rodent (Hydrochoerus capybara) allied to the guinea-pig. [Tupi]

car n. **1.** a motor car (see separate entry and ill. p. 130–1). **2.** a railway carriage of a specified type; (US) any railway carriage or van. **3.** the passenger compartment of an airship, balloon, cable railway, or lift. —**car-park** n. an area for parking cars. [f. AF f. L carrum]

Caracalla /kærəˈkælə/ the nickname (lit. 'a hooded Gallic cloak') of Marcus Aurelius Antoninus (188–217), Roman emperor 211–217, son of the emperor Septimius Severus. Sole ruler after the murder of his brother Geta in 212, he campaigned first in Germany and then in the east, where he hoped to repeat the conquests of Alexander the Great, but was assassinated in Mesopotamia. By an edict of 212 he granted Roman citizenship to all free inhabitants of the Roman Empire.

Caracas /kəˈrækəs/ the capital of Venezuela, famous as the birthplace of the revolutionary leader Simón Bolívar; pop. (est. 1981) 3,041,000.

caracul var. of KARAKUL.

carafe /kə'ræf/ *n.* a glass container in which water or wine is served at table. [F, ult. f. Arab., = drinking-vessel]

caramel /'kærəm(ə)l/ *n.* **1.** burnt sugar or syrup used for colouring or flavouring food. **2.** a kind of toffee tasting like this. **3.** light-brown colour. [F f. Sp.]

caramelize /'kærəməlaɪz/ *v.t./i.* to turn into caramel. —**caramelization** /-'zeɪʃ(ə)n/ *n.* [f. prec.]

carapace /'kærəpeɪs/ *n.* the upper shell of a tortoise or crustacean. [F f. Sp.]

carat /'kærət/ *n.* a unit of weight for precious stones, 200 mg; a unit of measurement for the purity of gold, pure gold being 24 carat. [F, ult. f. Gk *keration* fruit of carob (dim. of *keras* horn)]

Caravaggio /kærə'vædʒɪəʊ/, properly Michelangelo Merisi da Caravaggio (1573-1610), Italian painter who was an important figure in the transition from late mannerism to the baroque, and had a far-reaching European influence, affecting Ribera, Rubens, Georges de la Tour, and, indirectly, Rembrandt. Born near Bergamo, he trained under a pupil of Titian, and was in Rome by 1592. Here he developed his characteristic style: using dramatic lighting, foreshortening, and unexpected poses, often making the figures seem unnervingly close to the spectator, he adopted a literal, realistic approach to traditional subjects, which revitalized religious art and rescued it from the nebulous unreality of late 16th-c. painting. In *The Death of the Virgin* the model was, reputedly, a drowned prostitute. Several of his altarpieces were rejected by the clergy on the grounds of indecorum, but he had powerful defenders, including cardinals and noblemen. Caravaggio's life was short and violent: forced to flee from Rome in 1606 after killing a man in a brawl, he spent his remaining years in Naples, Malta, and Sicily, dying of fever in 1610.

caravan /'kærəvæn/ *n.* **1.** an enclosed carriage equipped for living in, able to be towed by a vehicle; a covered cart used similarly, towed by a horse. **2.** a company (especially of merchants) travelling together, especially across desert country. —*v.i.* (**-nn-**) to travel or live in a caravan. [f. F f. Pers.]

caravanserai /kærə'vænsəraɪ/ *n.* (in eastern countries) an inn with a large central courtyard for accommodation of travelling caravans. [f. Pers., = caravan-place]

caraway /'kærəweɪ/ *n.* an aromatic umbelliferous plant (*Carum carvi*) with spicy seeds that are used for flavouring cake etc. [f. Sp. f. Arab., perh. f. Gk *caron* cumin]

carbide /'kɑːbaɪd/ *n.* a binary compound of carbon, especially calcium carbide which is used in making acetylene gas. [f. CARBON]

carbine /'kɑːbaɪn/ *n.* a short rifle, originally for cavalry use. [earlier & F *carabine*, weapon of the *carabin* mounted musketeer]

carbohydrate /kɑːbə'haɪdreɪt/ *n.* **1.** an energy-producing compound of carbon with oxygen and hydrogen, e.g. starch, sugar, glucose. **2.** starchy food, considered to be fattening. [f. CARBON + HYDRATE]

carbolic /kɑː'bɒlɪk/ *adj.* **carbolic acid**, phenol. **carbolic soap**, soap containing this. [f. foll.]

carbon /'kɑːbən/ *n.* **1.** a non-metallic element, symbol C, atomic number 6 (see below). **2.** a carbon copy; carbon paper. **3.** a rod of carbon used in an arc lamp. —**carbon copy**, a copy made with carbon paper; an exact copy. **carbon cycle**, see separate entry. **carbon dioxide**, a colourless odourless gas formed by burning carbon or breathed out by animals in respiration. **carbon 14**, a radioisotope with mass 14 used in dating prehistoric objects. **carbon monoxide**, a poisonous colourless almost odourless gas formed by burning carbon incompletely, occurring e.g. in the exhaust of motor engines. **carbon paper**, thin pigmented paper placed between sheets of paper for reproducing what is written or typed on the top sheet. **carbon tetrachloride**, a colourless liquid used as a solvent in dry cleaning etc. [f. F f. L *carbo* charcoal]
    The element occurs naturally as diamond and graphite; charcoal and coke are also composed of carbon. It has many economic uses, but its unique significance is that carbon compounds form the physical basis of all living organisms. Carbon has the property of combining with itself and other elements to form molecules consisting of rings or long chains of atoms, and an immense variety of compounds can therefore exist. The chemistry of such compounds found in living things or their remains was once thought to obey laws different from those governing other substances, whence the original separation of 'organic chemistry' as a distinct branch of the subject.

carbonaceous /kɑːbə'neɪʃəs/ *adj.* consisting of or containing carbon; of or like coal or charcoal. [f. prec.]

carbonade /kɑːbə'neɪd/ *n.* a rich beef stew containing beer. [F]

carbonate /'kɑːbənɪt/ *n.* a salt of carbonic acid. —*v.t.* to impregnate with carbon dioxide; to make (drinks) effervescent with this. [f. F. (as CARBON)]

carbon cycle **1.** the cycle in which carbon is absorbed from and replaced in the atmosphere. Carbon dioxide from the air is converted into more complex substances by plants, which are eaten by animals, and is finally released again into the air by the respiration of plants and animals or when organic substances decay. **2.** a cycle of thermonuclear reactions in stellar regions, in which carbon acts as a catalyst in the conversion of hydrogen into helium. The consequent energy released is held to be the source of the energy radiated by the sun and stars.

carbonic /kɑː'bɒnɪk/ *adj.* of carbon. —**carbonic acid**, a weak acid formed from carbon dioxide and water. [f. CARBON]

carboniferous /kɑːbə'nɪfərəs/ *adj.* **1.** producing coal. **2.** **Carboniferous**, of the fifth period of the Palaeozoic era, following the Devonian and preceding the Permian, lasting from about 360 to 286 million years ago. During this period seed-bearing plants first appeared, corals were widespread, and extensive limestone deposits were formed, rivers formed deltas, and luxuriant vegetation developed on coastal swamps. This vegetation was later drowned and buried under mud and sand, and subsequently became coal. In the USA the Pennsylvanian and Mississippian periods correspond to the Carboniferous of other areas. —**Carboniferous** *n.* this period. [f. CARBON + *-ferous* bearing (L *ferre* bear)]

carbonize /'kɑːbənaɪz/ *v.t.* **1.** to convert into carbon; to reduce to charcoal or coke. **2.** to coat with carbon. —**carbonization** /-'zeɪʃ(ə)n/ *n.* [f. CARBON]

carborundum /kɑːbə'rʌndəm/ *n.* a compound of carbon and silicon, used especially as an abrasive. [f. CARBON + CORUNDUM]

carboy /'kɑːbɔɪ/ *n.* a large globular bottle enclosed in a frame, used for transporting liquids safely. [f. Pers., = large glass flagon]

carbuncle /'kɑːbʌŋk(ə)l/ *n.* **1.** a severe abscess in the skin. **2.** a bright-red gem cut in a knob-like shape. [f. OF f. L, = small coal (*carbo* coal)]

carburation /kɑːbjʊ'reɪʃ(ə)n/ *n.* the process of charging air with a spray of liquid hydrocarbon fuel. [f. CARBON]

carburettor /kɑːbjʊ'retə(r)/ *n.* an apparatus for the carburation of air in an internal-combustion engine. [as prec.]

carcass /'kɑːkəs/ *n.* **1.** the dead body of an animal, especially one prepared for cutting up as meat; the bony part of the body of a bird before or after cooking. **2.** a framework; the foundation structure of a tyre. [f. AF; orig. unkn.]

Carchemish /'kɑːkɪmɪʃ/ an ancient city situated in a strategic position on the upper Euphrates, a Hittite stronghold, annexed by Sargon II of Assyria in 717 BC.

carcinogen /kɑː'sɪnədʒən/ *n.* a substance that induces cancer. —**carcinogenic** /-'dʒenɪk/ *adj.* [f. foll.]

carcinoma /kɑːsɪ'nəʊmə/ *n.* (*pl.* **-mata**) a cancerous tumour. [L f. Gk (*karkinos* crab)]

card¹ *n.* **1.** thick stiff paper or thin cardboard; a piece of this for writing or printing on, especially to send messages or greetings or to record information; a flat usually rectangular piece of thin pasteboard, plastic, etc., recording membership or identifying the bearer; (in *pl.*, *colloq.*) an employee's documents held by his employer. **2.** a playing-card; (in *pl.*) card-playing. **3.** a programme of events at a race-meeting etc. **4.** (*colloq.*) an odd or amusing person. —**card-carrying** *adj.* being a registered member of a political party, trade union, etc. **card-sharp** *n.* a swindler at card-games. **card vote**, a block vote (see BLOCK). **on the cards**, likely, possible. [f. OE f. L f. Gk *khartēs* papyrus-leaf]

card² *n.* a toothed instrument or wire brush for raising nap on cloth or for disentangling fibres before spinning. —*v.t.* to brush or comb with a card. [f. OF f. L *carere* card]

cardamom /'kɑːdəməm/ *n.* spice from the seed-capsules of various East Indian plants, especially *Elettaria cardamomum*, a plant of the ginger family. [f. L or F f. Gk (*kardamon* cress, *amōmon* a spice-plant)]

cardboard *n.* stiff paper or pasteboard, especially for making cards or boxes.

cardiac /'kɑːdɪæk/ *adj.* of the heart. [f. F or L f. Gk (*kardia* heart)]

The Car

The internal-combustion engine — four-stroke cycle

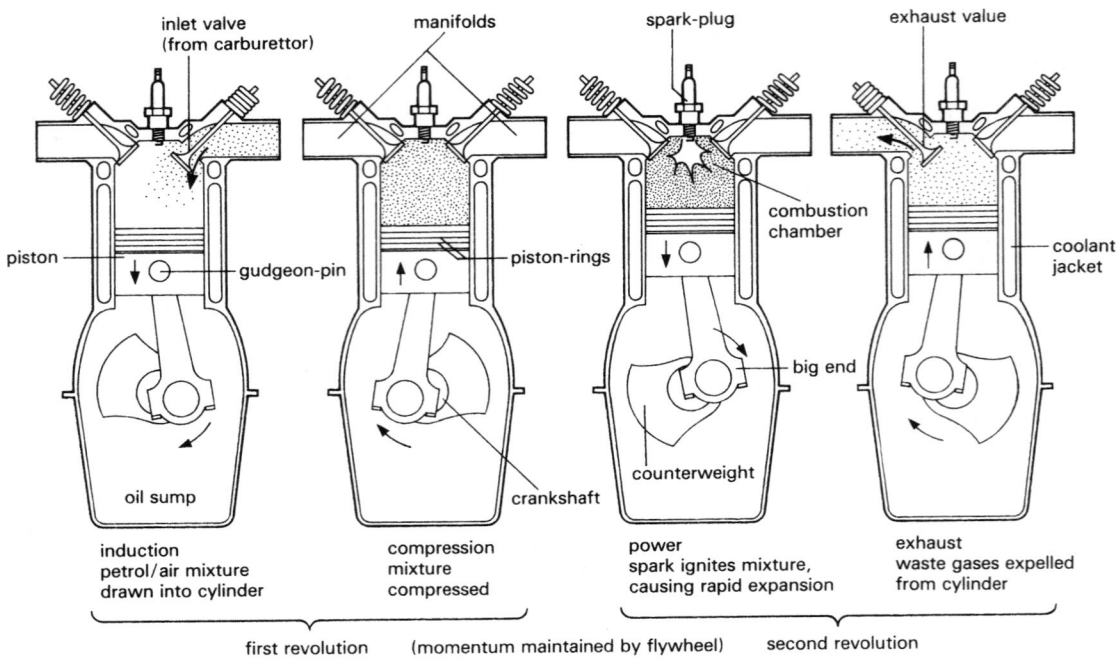

inlet valve (from carburettor)

manifolds

spark-plug

exhaust value

piston

gudgeon-pin

piston-rings

combustion chamber

coolant jacket

big end

counterweight

oil sump

crankshaft

induction
petrol/air mixture
drawn into cylinder

compression
mixture
compressed

power
spark ignites mixture,
causing rapid expansion

exhaust
waste gases expelled
from cylinder

first revolution   (momentum maintained by flywheel)   second revolution

Engine

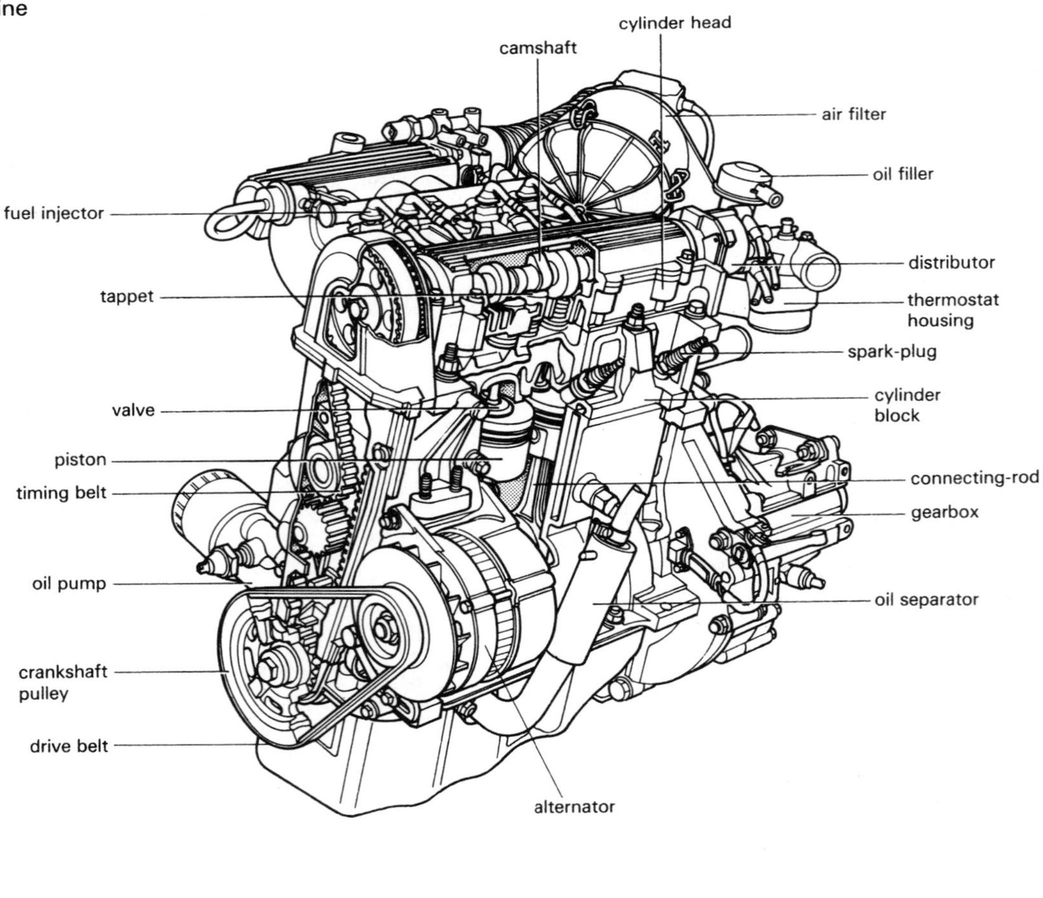

camshaft

cylinder head

air filter

oil filler

fuel injector

distributor

tappet

thermostat housing

spark-plug

valve

cylinder block

piston

connecting-rod

timing belt

gearbox

oil pump

oil separator

crankshaft pulley

drive belt

alternator

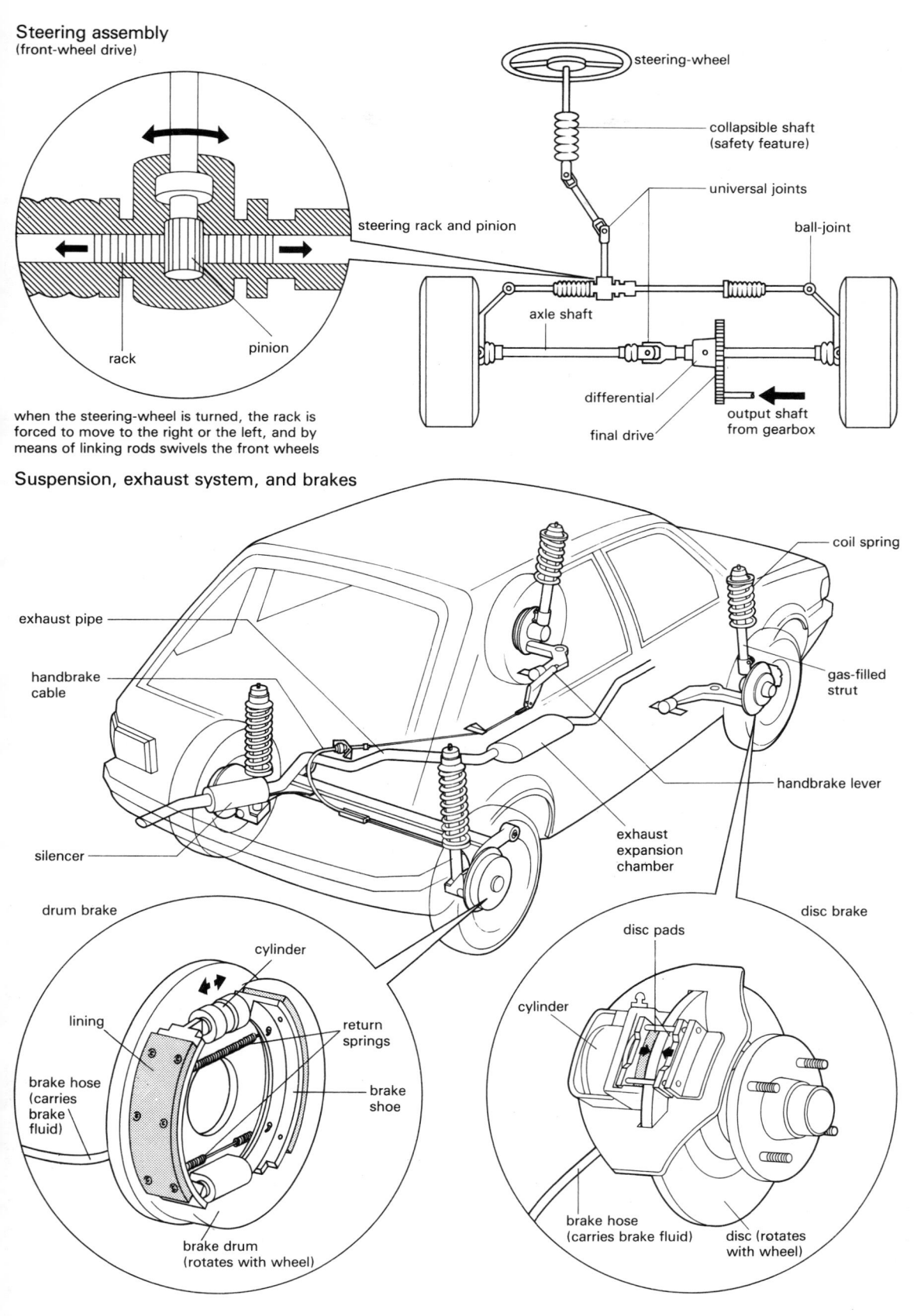

Steering assembly
(front-wheel drive)

steering-wheel

collapsible shaft
(safety feature)

universal joints

ball-joint

steering rack and pinion

rack

pinion

axle shaft

differential

final drive

output shaft
from gearbox

when the steering-wheel is turned, the rack is
forced to move to the right or the left, and by
means of linking rods swivels the front wheels

Suspension, exhaust system, and brakes

coil spring

exhaust pipe

handbrake
cable

gas-filled
strut

handbrake lever

silencer

exhaust
expansion
chamber

drum brake

cylinder

lining

return
springs

brake hose
(carries
brake
fluid)

brake
shoe

brake drum
(rotates with wheel)

disc brake

disc pads

cylinder

brake hose
(carries brake fluid)

disc (rotates
with wheel)

Cardiff /ˈkɑːdɪf/ the capital of Wales, at the mouth of the River Taff; pop. (1981) 278,900.

cardigan /ˈkɑːdɪɡən/ n. a knitted jacket. [named after 7th Earl of Cardigan (d. 1868), who led the disastrous Charge of the Light Brigade in the Crimean War]

cardinal /ˈkɑːdɪn(ə)l/ adj. 1. chief, fundamental. 2. deep scarlet as worn by cardinals. —n. 1. a member of the Sacred College of the Roman Catholic Church. Cardinals hold the highest rank next to the pope, who is chosen from their number. 2. a small scarlet American songbird of the genus *Richmondena*. —**cardinal numbers,** the whole numbers (1, 2, 3, etc.) representing a quantity, as opposed to ordinal numbers. **cardinal points,** the four main points of the compass, North, South, East, and West. **cardinal virtues,** justice, prudence, temperance, fortitude, faith, hope, charity. [f. OF f. L (*cardo* hinge)]

cardiology /kɑːdɪˈɒlədʒɪ/ n. the branch of medicine concerned with diseases and abnormalities of the heart. —**cardiological** /-ˈlɒdʒɪk(ə)l/ adj., **cardiologist** n. [f. Gk *kardia* heart + -LOGY]

care /keə(r)/ n. 1. serious attention and thought; caution to avoid damage or loss. 2. protection, charge, supervision. 3. a thing to be done or seen to. —v.t./i. 1. to feel concern or interest. 2. to feel affection or a liking *for* or willingness *to* do. 3. to provide *for*. —**care of,** at the address of (one who will deliver or forward things). **in care,** taken into the care of a local authority. [OE, = sorrow]

careen /kəˈriːn/ v.t. 1. to tilt, to lean over. 2. (*US*) to swerve. [f. F f. L *carina* keel]

career /kəˈrɪə(r)/ n. 1. one's advancement through life, especially in a profession; a profession or occupation, especially one offering advancement. 2. swift forward movement. —v.i. to move swiftly or wildly. [f. F, ult. f. L *carrus* car]

careerist n. a person who is predominantly concerned with advancement in a career. [f. prec.]

carefree n. light-hearted through being free from anxiety or responsibility.

careful adj. giving serious attention and thought, painstaking; done with care and attention; cautious. —**carefully** adv., **carefulness** n. [f. CARE + -FUL]

careless adj. not giving or given serious attention and thought; unthinking, insensitive; casual and light-hearted. —**carelessly** adv., **carelessness** n. [f. CARE + -LESS]

carer n. one who looks after a sick or disabled person at home.

caress /kəˈres/ v.t. to touch or stroke lovingly, to caress. —n. a loving touch, a kiss. [f. F f. L *carus* dear]

caret /ˈkærət/ n. a mark showing an omission (and intended insertion) in something printed or written. [L, = is lacking]

caretaker n. 1. a person employed to look after a house or building etc. 2. (*attrib.*) exercising temporary power.

careworn adj. showing the effects of prolonged worry.

cargo n. (*pl.* **-oes**) goods carried on a ship or aircraft. [Sp., as CHARGE]

Caria /ˈkɛərɪə/ the ancient name for the region of SW Asia Minor south of the river Maeander and NW of Lycia. —**Carian** adj. & n.

Carib /ˈkærɪb/ n. a member or the language of the pre-Columbian American Indian inhabitants of the Lesser Antilles and parts of the neighbouring South American coast, or of their descendants. —adj. of the Caribs or their language. [f. Sp. *Caribe* f. Haitian]
  A fearsome maritime people, the Caribs forced the peaceful Arawak-speaking peoples of the Antilles to migrate to South America to escape their depredations. Still expanding at the time of Spanish conquest the Caribs were supplanted, in turn, by European colonialism and have all but disappeared in the West Indies (where only a few hundred still remain on the island of Dominica). On mainland South America Carib-speaking groups occupy territory in the NE and Amazon regions, living in small autonomous communities. Peculiarly, the Carib language was spoken only by men; their women, who were captured in raids on other tribes, spoke only Arawak. Male captives were tortured and eaten—hence giving the Carib name not only to the Caribbean Sea but also to the root of the English word 'cannibal'.

Caribbean /kærɪˈbiːən/ adj. of the Caribbean Sea. —n. the Caribbean Sea. —**Caribbean Sea,** a sea lying between the Antilles and the mainland of Central and South American. [f. CARIB]

caribou /ˈkærɪbuː/ n. (*pl.* same) a North American reindeer. [F, prob. f. Amer. Ind.]

caricature /ˈkærɪkətjʊə(r)/ n. a grotesque representation, especially of a person by exaggeration of characteristics; a ridiculously poor imitation or version. —v.t. to make or give a caricature of. —**caricaturist** n. [F f. It. (*caricare* exaggerate)]

caries /ˈkɛəriːz/ n. (*pl.* same) decay in bones or teeth. [L]

carillon /kəˈrɪljən, ˈkæ-/ n. a set of bells sounded either from a keyboard or mechanically. [F]

carioca /kærɪˈəʊkə/ n. a Brazilian dance resembling the samba; music for this. [Port.]

Carlovingian /kɑːləˈvɪndʒɪən/ adj. & n. = CAROLINGIAN.

Carlyle /kɑːˈlaɪl/, Thomas (1795–1881), Scottish historian and political philosopher. He had already embarked on a literary career when he married Jane Welsh in 1826, later celebrated for her brilliant letters. The Carlyles moved to London in 1834, shortly after the publication of the idiosyncratic *Sartor Resartus* (1833–4), where he established himself as 'the sage of Chelsea', revered almost as a prophet, and renowned for his history of the French Revolution (1837), his popular public lectures (*On Heroes and Hero-Worship*, 1840), and his attacks on the dehumanizing effects of utilitarian economics. He exalted the medieval past as a time of harmony and violently attacked the consequences of the Industrial Revolution, abhorred materialism, and showed genuine compassion for the poor; his views became increasingly anti-democratic. His important works include an edition of Cromwell's letters and speeches (1845) and a lengthy life of Frederick the Great (1858–65); a more human perspective is seen in his letters and in J. A. Froude's notoriously frank biography (1882–4).

Carmelite /ˈkɑːməlaɪt/ n. a member of the Carmelite order (see below). —adj. of the Carmelite order. [f. L, f. Mt. *Carmel* in Palestine, place of foundation]
  The 'Order of Our Lady of Mount Carmel' (also called 'White Friars' from the colour of their cloaks) was founded in Palestine by St Berthold *c.*1154; a corresponding order of nuns was established in 1452. In the 16th c., after discipline in the order had become relaxed, the 'discalced' reform movement, begun by St Teresa of Avila and St John of the Cross towards the end of the century, gradually spread, restoring the stricter rule. The order is contemplative and has produced great mystics.

carminative /ˈkɑːmɪnətɪv/ adj. curing flatulence. —n. a carminative drug. [f. F or L *carminare* heal (by incantation)]

carmine /ˈkɑːmaɪn/ adj. of vivid crimson colour. —n. 1. this colour. 2. a red pigment made from cochineal. [f. F or L (perh. as CRIMSON)]

carnage /ˈkɑːnɪdʒ/ n. great slaughter. [F f. It. f. L *caro* flesh]

carnal /ˈkɑːn(ə)l/ adj. of the body or flesh, not spiritual; sensual, sexual. —**carnality** /-ˈnælɪtɪ/ n., **carnally** adv. [f. L (as prec.)]

Carnap /ˈkɑːnæp/, Rudolf (1891–1970), German-American philosopher, one of the originators of logical positivism, a founder and most influential member of the Vienna Circle, noted for his contributions to logic, the analysis of language, the theory of probability, and the philosophy of science. He thought the philosopher's task was to construct logically rigorous languages capable of expressing the truths of science, and attempted to fix meaning by stipulation and to define necessity in terms of it. At the heart of his view was the belief (modified over the years) that a statement is meaningful only if it can be verified by sensory observation; this led to a robust dismissal of the problems of traditional metaphysics.

carnassial /kɑːˈnæsɪəl/ n. a carnassial tooth. —adj. **carnassial tooth,** a carnivore's premolar tooth, adapted for cutting (ill. MAMMALS). [f. F *carnassier* carnivorous]

carnation /kɑːˈneɪʃ(ə)n/ n. a cultivated clove-scented pink. [earlier *coronation*]

Carné /ˈkɑːneɪ/, Marcel (1903–), French film director, whose partnership with the scriptwriter Pierre Prévert produced some memorable films, including *Le Jour se lève* (1939), *Les Enfants du Paradis* (1945), and *Les Portes de la Nuit* (1946). His films are characterized by a fatalistic outlook and masterly evocation of atmosphere. Carné held a dominant position among film-makers of the 1930s and 1940s, but more recent evaluation, with modern taste for flexibility and freedom, has disliked the cold visual perfection of the studio-bound and rehearsed artistry of his films.

Carnegie /kɑːˈneɪgɪ/, Andrew (1835-1919), son of a Scottish immigrant weaver, who built up a huge fortune in the steel industry in the USA through his own shrewdness and energy. He retired from business in 1901 and devoted his wealth to charitable purposes on both sides of the Atlantic. One of his most notable achievements was the creation of the Carnegie Peace Fund to promote international peace.

carnelian /kɑːˈniːlɪən/ var. of CORNELIAN².

carnet /ˈkɑːneɪ/ *n.* the documents of identification etc. that are needed to permit a vehicle to be driven across a frontier or to use a camping-site. [F, = notebook]

carnival /ˈkɑːnɪvəl/ *n.* 1. festivities and public merry-making, usually with a procession. 2. (*US*) a fun-fair or circus. [f. It. f. L *carnelevarium* Shrove-tide, f. *caro* meat, *levare* put away, with ref. to the austerities of Lent]

carnivore /ˈkɑːnɪvɔː(r)/ *n.* a carnivorous animal or plant. [f. foll.]

carnivorous /kɑːˈnɪvərəs/ *adj.* feeding on flesh or other animal matter; belonging to the Carnivora, a large order of mainly carnivorous mammals (bears, cats, dogs, foxes, seals, etc.). [f. L (*caro* flesh)]

Carnot /ˈkɑːnəʊ/, Nicolas Léonard Sadi (1796-1832), French scientist, noted for his contributions to thermodynamics. An army officer for most of his short life, Carnotbecame interested in the principles of operation of steam-engines and, in a book published in 1824, analysed the efficiency of such engines, using the notion of a cycle of reversible temperature and pressure changes of the gases within. Although Carnot's work had no influence on contemporary engine design, it was recognized after his death as being of crucial importance to the theory of thermodynamics.

carob /ˈkærəb/ *n.* the horn-shaped edible pod of a Mediterranean evergreen tree, *Ceratonia siliqua*. [f. F, ult. f. Arab.]

carol /ˈkærəl/ *n.* a joyful song, especially a Christmas hymn. —*v.t./i.* (-ll-) to sing carols; to sing joyfully. —**caroller** *n.* [f. OF; orig. unkn.]

Carolean /kærəˈliːən/ *adj.* of the time of Charles I or II of England. [f. L *Carolus* Charles]

Caroline /ˈkærəlaɪn/ *adj.* = CAROLEAN.

Carolingian /kærəˈlɪndʒɪən/ *adj.* of the Frankish dynasty founded by Charlemagne. —*n.* a member of this dynasty. [f. F f. *Karl* Charles]

Carothers /kəˈrʌðəz/, Wallace Hume (1896-1937), American industrial chemist who in 1928 was appointed director of research in organic chemistry by the firm of E. I. du Pont de Nemours. He took up the study of long-chain molecules, now called polymers, developed (with J. A. Nieuwland) the synthetic rubber 'neoprene', and in the early 1930s the first melt-spun synthetic fibre, 'Nylon 66'. He committed suicide at the age of 41 before nylon had been commercially exploited, and it was left to others to follow his lead and discover the polyester fibres.

carotid /kəˈrɒtɪd/ *adj.* of the two main arteries, one on each side of the neck, carrying blood to the head. —*n.* a carotid artery. [f. F f. Gk (*karoō* stupefy, compression of these arteries being thought to cause stupor)]

carouse /kəˈraʊz/ *v.i.* to have a noisy or lively drinking-party. —*n.* such a party. —**carousal** *n.* [f. G *gar aus* (drunk) right out]

carousel /kærʊˈsel/ *n.* 1. (*US*) a merry-go-round. 2. a rotating conveyor or delivery system. [F f. It.]

carp¹ *n.* (*pl.* same) a freshwater fish of the genus *Cyprinus*, especially a species often bred in ponds. [f. OF f. Prov. or L]

carp² *v.i.* to find fault, to complain pettily. [f. ON, = brag]

carpal /ˈkɑːp(ə)l/ *adj.* of the wrist-bone. [f. CARPUS]

Carpathian Mountains /kɑːˈpeɪθɪən/ (also **Carpathians**) a mountain system extending SE from southern Poland and Czechoslovakia into Romania.

carpel /ˈkɑːp(ə)l/ *n.* any of the segments of a compound pistil of a flower (ill. FLOWERS); a simple pistil, in which the seeds develop. [f. F f. Gk *karpos* fruit]

carpenter /ˈkɑːpɪntə(r)/ *n.* a craftsman in woodwork, one who makes or repairs wooden structures. —*v.i.* to do or make by carpenter's work. —**carpentry** *n.* (See ill. pp. 134-5.) [f. OF f. L (*carpentum* wagon)]

carpet /ˈkɑːpɪt/ *n.* 1. a thick textile covering for floors or stairs. 2. a carpet-like expanse, a thick layer underfoot. —*v.t.* 1. to cover with or as with a carpet. 2. (*colloq.*) to

reprimand. —**carpet-bag** *n.* a travelling-bag of the kind formerly made of carpet-like material. **carpet-bagger** *n.* a political candidate without local connections; (*hist.*) any of the adventurers from the northern States who went into the southern States after the American Civil War, in order to profit from the post-war reorganization (so called from the carpet-bag which held all their possessions). **carpet-sweeper** *n.* a household device with revolving brushes for sweeping carpets. **on the carpet**, (*colloq.*) being reprimanded. [f. OF or L (*carpere* pull to pieces)]

carport *n.* an open-sided shelter for a car, projecting from the side of a house.

carpus /ˈkɑːpəs/ *n.* (*pl.* **-pi** /-paɪ/) the set of small bones connecting the hand and forearm, especially the wrist in man (ill. BODY 1). [f. Gk *karpos* wrist]

Carracci /kɑːˈrɑːtʃɪ/ the name of a family of Italian painters from Bologna. Agostino (1557-1602) is remembered more for his teaching than his painting and probably dictated the training of the students in the so-called Carracci Academy at Bologna. His brother Annibale (1560-1609) was the most famous member of the family. His early work of the 1580s and 1590s revealed his ability in religious and landscape painting, but it was his move to Rome in 1595 that established his genius in the creation of paintings and decoration in the Grand Manner, in particular the Farnese Gallery in Rome. His combination of strong composition, tonal control, and use of gesture were to prove of immense and lasting influence in the 17th c., while his landscapes initiated the classical landscape with ruins developed by Claude and Poussin. His cousin Lodovico (1555-1619) established the Carracci studio in Bologna and helped pass on that style.

carrack /ˈkærək/ *n.* a large merchant ship of northern and southern Europe in the 14th-17th c., the forerunner and first example of the larger three-masted ship which dominated naval architecture until the general introduction of steam propulsion in the mid-19th c. (See GALLEON.) [f. F f. Sp. f. Arab.]

carriage /ˈkærɪdʒ/ *n.* 1. a wheeled passenger vehicle, usually horse-drawn. 2. a railway passenger vehicle. 3. the conveying of goods etc.; the cost of this. 4. a moving part carrying or holding something in a machine. 5. a gun-carriage. 6. the posture of the body when walking. —**carriage clock**, a small portable clock with a rectangular case and a handle on top. [as CARRY]

carriageway *n.* the part of the road on which vehicles travel.

carrier /ˈkærɪə(r)/ *n.* 1. a person or thing that carries something; a person or company conveying goods or passengers for payment. 2. a support or receptacle for carrying something; a carrier bag. 3. a person or animal that transmits a disease without being affected by it. 4. an aircraft-carrier. —**carrier bag**, a paper or plastic bag, with handles, for holding shopping etc. **carrier pigeon**, a homing pigeon used to carry messages tied to its leg or neck. **carrier wave**, a high-frequency electromagnetic wave modulated in amplitude or frequency to convey a telecommunications signal. [f. CARRY]

carrion /ˈkærɪən/ *n.* dead putrefying flesh. —**carrion crow**, a black crow (*Corvus corone*) that feeds on carrion and small animals. [f. AF f. L *caro* flesh]

Carroll /ˈkær(ə)l/, Lewis (pseudonym of Charles Lutwidge Dodgson, 1832-98), English writer and lecturer in mathematics at Oxford (1855-81), celebrated as author of the sophisticated children's classics (written for the daughter of the dean of his college, H. G. Liddell) *Alice's Adventures in Wonderland* (1865) and *Through the Looking Glass* (1871), both illustrated by Tenniel, describing a child's dream adventure. He also wrote nonsense verse, notably *The Hunting of the Snark* (1876), and experimented in portrait photography.

carrot /ˈkærət/ *n.* 1. an umbelliferous plant (*Daucus carota*) with a tapering orange-coloured edible root; this root, used as a vegetable. 2. a means of enticement; —**carroty** *adj.* [f. F f. L f. Gk *karōton*]

carry /ˈkærɪ/ *v.t./i.* 1. to hold up or support while moving; to take with one from one place to another. 2. to support the weight or responsibility of. 3. to be pregnant with. 4. to conduct or transmit. 5. to take (a process etc.) to a specified point. 6. to involve, to entail or imply. 7. to transfer (a figure) to a column of higher value. 8. to hold (the body or oneself) in a specified way. 9. (of a newspaper or broadcast etc.) to include in its contents; (of a shop) to keep a regular stock of. 10. (of sound) to be audible at a distance; (of a gun etc.) to propel to a specified distance. 11. to win or

Carpentry

Some basic hand- and power tools

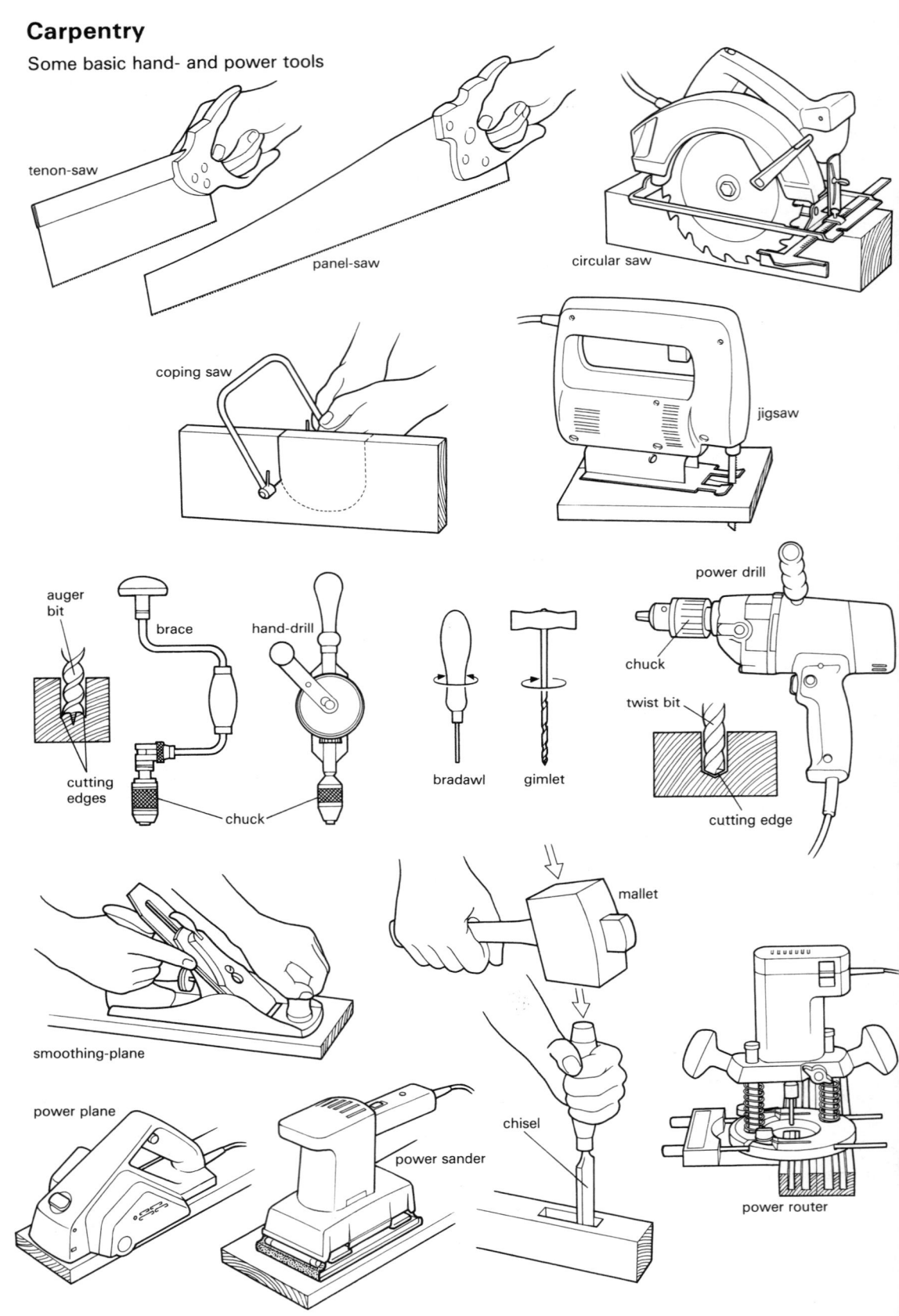

tenon-saw

panel-saw

circular saw

coping saw

jigsaw

auger
bit

brace

hand-drill

power drill

chuck

bradawl

gimlet

twist bit

cutting
edges

chuck

cutting edge

smoothing-plane

mallet

power plane

power sander

chisel

power router

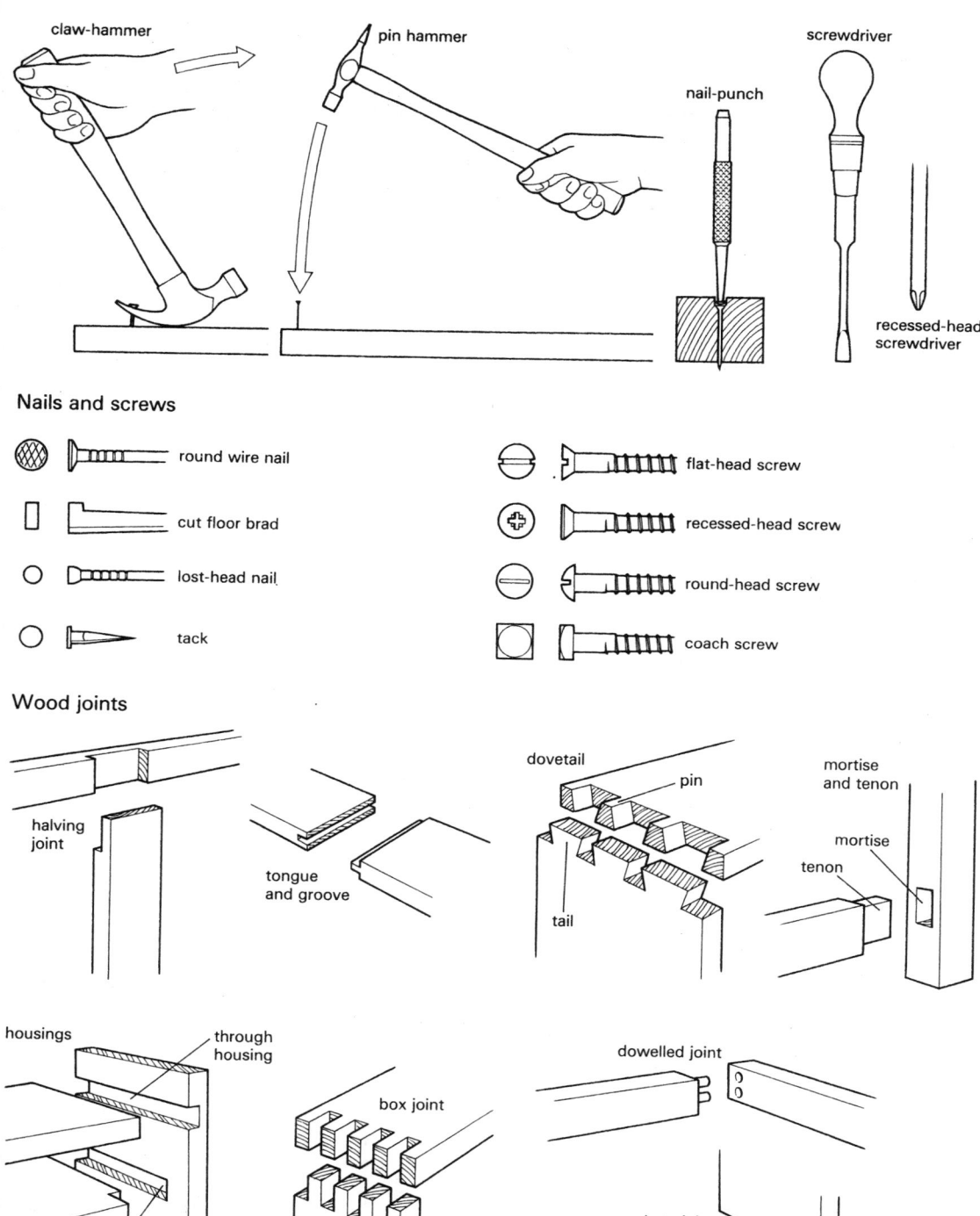

claw-hammer

pin hammer

nail-punch

screwdriver

recessed-head
screwdriver

Nails and screws

round wire nail

cut floor brad

lost-head nail

tack

flat-head screw

recessed-head screw

round-head screw

coach screw

Wood joints

halving
joint

tongue
and groove

dovetail

pin

tail

mortise
and tenon

mortise

tenon

housings

through
housing

stopped housing

box joint

dowelled joint

rebate joint

capture; to win over (an audience); to win victory or acceptance for (a proposal etc.). —*n.* an act of carrying; (in golf) the flight of a ball before pitching. —**be carried away,** to be uncontrollably excited. **carry-cot** *n.* a portable cot for a baby. **carry forward,** to transfer to a new page or account. **carry off,** to take away (especially by force); (of a disease) to cause the death of; to win (a prize); to deal with (a situation) successfully. **carry on,** to continue; to engage in; (*colloq.*) to behave excitedly, to complain lengthily; to flirt or have an affair (*with*). **carry out,** to put (an idea etc.) into practice. **carry over,** to carry forward; to postpone. **carry weight,** to be influential or important. [f. AF (as CAR)]

cart *n.* a small strong vehicle with two or four wheels for carrying loads, usually drawn by a horse; a light vehicle for pulling by hand. —*v.t.* **1.** to convey in a cart. **2.** (*slang*) to carry or take laboriously. —**cart-horse** *n.* a horse of heavy build, fit for drawing carts. **cart-wheel** *n.* a handspring in which the body turns with limbs spread like the spokes of a wheel, balancing on each hand in turn. **cart-wright** *n.* a maker of carts. [ON & OE]

carte blanche /kɑːt blɑ̃ʃ/ full discretionary power given to a person. [F, = blank paper]

cartel /kɑːˈtel/ *n.* a union of business firms to control prices etc. [f. G. f. F f. It., dim. of *carta* card]

Cartesian /kɑːˈtiːzjən/ *adj.* of Descartes or his philosophy. —*n.* a follower of Descartes. —**Cartesian coordinates,** those measured from intersecting straight axes. **Cartesian diver,** a toy device that rises and falls in liquid when the cover of a vessel is subjected to varying pressure. [f. L (*Cartesius* Descartes)]

Carthage /ˈkɑːθɪdʒ/ a city on the north coast of Africa near Tunis, traditionally founded by Phoenicians from Tyre (in modern Lebanon) in 814 BC. It became a major force in the Mediterranean, with interests in North Africa, Spain, and Sicily, which brought it into conflict with Greece until the 3rd c. BC and then with Rome in the Punic Wars, until the Romans finally destroyed it in AD 146. —**Carthaginian** /kɑːθəˈdʒɪnɪən/ *adj.* & *n.* [f. Semitic, = new town]

Carthusian /kɑːˈθjuːzɪən/ *n.* a member of the Carthusian order (see below). —*adj.* of the Carthusian order. [f. L *Cart(h)usia* Chartreuse]
    The Carthusian order is a strictly contemplative order of monks founded at the Grande Chartreuse (whence the name) in SE France by St Bruno in 1084. Their eremitical way of life, largely inspired by early eastern monasticism, is remarkable for its austerity and self-denial. The order includes a few houses of nuns.

Cartier /ˈkɑːtɪeɪ/, Jacques (1491-1557), French explorer of Canada, who made three exploring voyages to Canada between 1534 and 1541, sailing up the St Lawrence River and attempting to establish a settlement on the site of what is now Montreal.

cartilage /ˈkɑːtɪlɪdʒ/ *n.* tough flexible tissue attached to the bones of vertebrates; a structure of this (ill. BODY 2). [F f. L *cartilago*]

cartilaginous /kɑːtɪˈlædʒɪnəs/ *adj.* of or like cartilage; (of fish) having a cartilaginous skeleton (opp. *bony*; see FISH[1]). [f. prec.]

cartography /kɑːˈtɒɡrəfɪ/ *n.* map-drawing. —**cartographer** *n.*, **cartographic** /-ˈɡræfɪk/ *adj.* [f. F (*carte* map)]

carton /ˈkɑːt(ə)n/ *n.* a light box or container made of cardboard or plastic. [F, f. as foll.]

cartoon /kɑːˈtuːn/ *n.* **1.** a humorous drawing in a newspaper etc., especially as a topical comment; a sequence of such drawings telling a comic or serial story; an animated cartoon on film. **2.** an artist's full-size drawing as a sketch for a work of art. —*v.t.* to draw a cartoon of. —**cartoonist** *n.* [f. It. (*carta* card)]

cartouche /kɑːˈtuːʃ/ *n.* **1.** a scroll-like ornamentation in architecture etc. **2.** an oval emblem containing hieroglyphics that give the birth-name and coronation name of an ancient Egyptian king. [F, = cartridge (as prec.)]

cartridge /ˈkɑːtrɪdʒ/ *n.* **1.** a case containing a charge of propellant explosive for firearms or blasting, with bullet or shot if for small arms. **2.** a sealed container holding film, magnetic tape, etc., ready for insertion as a unit. **3.** a component on the pick-up head of a record-player, carrying the stylus. —**cartridge paper,** thick strong paper for drawing etc. [f. prec.]

Cartwright /ˈkɑːtraɪt/, Edmund (1743-1823), English engineer, remembered chiefly as the inventor in 1785 of the power loom, but his record of achievements is a remarkable

one. Starting as a clergyman he became interested in textile machinery and despite financial failures continued to innovate, with a wool-combing machine (1789), a rope-making machine (1792), and in 1797 an engine which used alcohol rather than steam, a thermodynamic development far ahead of its time. His achievements were recognized eventually by the government in 1809, who voted him £10,000, a just reward for innovations which had a profound effect on textile manufacture.

Caruso /kəˈruːsəʊ/, Enrico (1873-1921), Italian operatic tenor of the highest popularity. He appeared in both French and Italian opera, winning immense financial awards for appearances in person and for the recordings which made him a household name even among those who never attended operatic performances.

carve *v.t./i.* **1.** to produce or shape by cutting; to cut designs etc. in (hard material). **2.** to cut (meat) into slices for serving. **3.** to make (a career etc.) by effort. —**carve up,** to divide into parts or shares. [OE]

carvel-built /ˈkɑːv(ə)lˈbɪlt/ *adj.* (of a boat) made with planks joined smoothly and not overlapping. [f. F, ult. f. Gk *karabos* light ship]

carver *n.* **1.** one who carves. **2.** a knife or (in *pl.*) knife and fork for carving meat. **3.** a chair with arms that forms one of a set of dining-room chairs. [f. CARVE]

carving *n.* a carved object or design. [f. CARVE]

Cary /ˈkeərɪ/, (Arthur) Joyce (Lunel) (1888-1957), English novelist. His colourful exuberant novels include some set in Africa, where he had served briefly in the colonial service. In *The Horse's Mouth* (1944), one of a trilogy, he achieved a memorable portrait of an outrageous artist.

caryatid /kærɪˈætɪd/ *n.* a sculptured female figure used as a supporting pillar in a building (ill. TEMPLES). [f. F, ult. f. Gk, = priestess of Caryae in Greece)]

Casanova /kæzəˈnəʊvə, kæs-/ *n.* a man notorious for many love-affairs. [f. G. J. Casanova de Seingalt, Italian adventurer (d. 1798), famous for his memoirs, in French, describing his adventurous life, and particularly his pursuit of women, in a large number of European countries]

cascade /kæsˈkeɪd/ *n.* a small waterfall, especially one in a series; something arranged like this. —*v.i.* to fall in or like a cascade. [F, ult. f. L *casus* case]

cascara /kæsˈkɑːrə/ *n.* the bark of a North American buckthorn, used as a laxative. [Sp., = sacred bark]

case[1] *n.* **1.** an instance of a thing's occurring; an actual or hypothetical situation. **2.** a condition of disease or injury, a person suffering from this. **3.** an instance or condition of one receiving professional guidance, especially by a doctor. **4.** a matter under investigation e.g. by police. **5.** a lawsuit; the sum of arguments on one side in this; a set of facts or arguments supporting something. **6.** (*Gram.*) the relation of a word to others in a sentence; the form of a noun, adjective, or pronoun expressing this. —**case-law** *n.* law as established by cases decided. **in any case,** whatever the facts are. **in case,** lest something should happen; in the event of. [f. OF f. L *casus* (*cadere* fall)]

case[2] *n.* **1.** a container or protective covering; this with its contents. **2.** a suitcase or other item of luggage. **3.** (*Printing*) a partitioned receptacle for type. —*v.t.* to enclose in a case. —**case-harden** *v.t.* to harden the surface of (metal, especially iron by carbonizing); to make unfeeling or unsympathetic. **lower case,** non-capital letters in printing-type. **upper case,** capital letters in printing-type. [f. OF f. L *capsa* (*capere* hold)]

casemate /ˈkeɪsmeɪt/ *n.* **1.** a room built inside the thick wall of a fortification. **2.** an armoured enclosure for guns on a warship. [F & It., perh. f. Gk *khasma* gap]

Casement /ˈkeɪsmənt/, Sir Roger David (1864-1916), Irish nationalist. He was a member of the British consular service in Africa and after retiring from this in 1912 went to Germany soon after the outbreak of the First World War to try to organize support for an Irish uprising. He was captured on his return to Ireland before the Easter rebellion of 1916, and subsequently hanged by the British for treason. Diaries reputedly written by him, containing descriptions of homosexual practices (suspicion of which had biased opinion against him) were not made available to the public until 1959.

casement /ˈkeɪsmənt/ *n.* a window hinged to open at the side (ill. HOUSES); (*poet.*) a window. [f. L *cassimentum* (*cassa* CASE[2])]

cash *n.* money in coin or notes; immediate payment at the time of purchase; (*colloq.*) wealth. —*v.t.* to give or obtain cash for. —**cash and carry,** a system of (esp. wholesale) trading in which the buyer pays for goods in cash and takes them away himself. **cash crop,** a crop grown for selling. **cash flow,** movement of money out of and into a business, affecting its ability to make payments. **cash in (on),** to profit (from); to use to one's advantage. **cash on delivery,** a system of paying for goods when they are delivered. **cash register,** a machine in a shop etc. with mechanism for recording the amount of each sale. Such a device was first patented in the USA in 1879. [f. F (as CASE²)]

cashew /ˈkæʃuː/ n. an edible kidney-shaped nut; the tropical tree (*Anacardium occidentale*) producing this. [f. Port. f. Tupi]

cashier¹ /kæˈʃɪə(r)/ n. a person in charge of cash transactions in a bank or shop etc. [f. Du. or F (as CASH)]

cashier² /kæˈʃɪə(r)/ v.t. to dismiss from service, especially with disgrace. [f. Flemish f. F f. L *cassare* quash]

cashmere /ˈkæʃmɪə(r)/ n. a very fine soft wool, especially that of the Kashmir goat; fabric made from this. [f. *Kashmir* in Asia]

casing /ˈkeɪsɪŋ/ n. a protective covering. [f. CASE²]

casino /kəˈsiːnəʊ/ n. (pl. -os) a public room or building for gambling and other amusements. [It., dim. of *casa* house f. L *casa* cottage]

cask /kɑːsk/ n. a barrel, especially one for alcoholic liquor; its contents. [f. F or Sp. (*casco* helmet)]

casket /ˈkɑːskɪt/ n. 1. a small usually ornamental box for holding valuables etc. 2. (US) a coffin. [perh. f. AF, ult. f. L *capsa* CASE²]

Caslon /ˈkæzlən/, William (1692–1766), English typographer, who established a type foundry (continued by his son William, 1720–78), supplying printers on the Continent as well as in England. His name is applied to the type cut there, or an imitation of this.

Caspian Sea /ˈkæspɪən/ a land-locked sea enclosed by the USSR and Iran. It is the world's largest body of inland water and its surface lies 28 m (92 ft.) below sea-level.

Cassandra /kəˈsændrə/ (*Gk legend*) daughter of Priam king of Troy. She was loved by Apollo, who gave her the gift of prophecy, but when she cheated him he turned this into a curse by causing her prophecies, though true, to be disbelieved. —n. a person who prophesies disaster.

cassata /kəˈsɑːtə/ n. an ice-cream cake containing fruit and nuts. [It.]

cassava /kəˈsɑːvə/ n. a tropical plant of the genus *Manihot*, with tuberous roots; starch or flour from this, used to make bread and tapioca. [f. Amer. Ind. *casavi*]

casserole /ˈkæsərəʊl/ n. a covered dish in which meat etc. is cooked and served; food cooked in this. —v.t. to cook in a casserole. [F, ult. f. Gk *kuathion* little cup]

cassette /kəˈset/ n. a small sealed case containing a reel of film or magnetic tape. [F, dim. of *casse* CASE²]

cassia /ˈkæsɪə/ n. 1. a kind of cinnamon. 2. a plant of the genus *Cassia*, yielding senna-leaves. [f. L f. Gk f. Heb.]

Cassiopeia /kæsɪəˈpiːə/ 1. (*Gk myth.*) wife of Cepheus king of Ethiopia, and mother of Andromeda. She boasted herself more beautiful than the Nereids, thus incurring the wrath of Poseidon. 2. (*Astron.*) a northern constellation, recognizable by the 'W' shape of its five brightest stars.

Cassius /ˈkæsjəs/ (Gaius Cassius Longinus, d. 42 BC) Roman general, with Marcus Junius Brutus one of the leaders of the conspiracy in 44 BC to assassinate Julius Caesar. He and Brutus were defeated by Caesar's supporters, Antony and Octavian, at the battle of Philippi in 42 BC; in the course of the battle he committed suicide.

cassock /ˈkæsək/ n. a long usually black or red garment worn by certain clergy and members of a church choir (ill. VESTMENTS). [f. F f. It. *cassaca* horseman's coat]

cassowary /ˈkæsəweərɪ/ n. a large flightless bird of the genus *Casuarius*, related to the emu. [f. Malay]

cast /kɑːst/ v.t./i. (past & p.p. **cast**) 1. to throw, to emit; to shed. 2. to send, direct, or cause to fall (*on, over,* etc.). 3. to record or register (a vote). 4. to shape (molten metal or plastic material) in a mould; to make (a product) thus. 5. to assign (an actor) *as* a character; to allocate roles in (a play or film etc.). 6. to utter (aspersions *on*). 7. to reckon or add up (figures); to calculate (a horoscope). —n. 1. the throwing of a missile, dice, fishing-line or net, etc. 2. an object of metal, clay, etc., made in a mould; a moulded mass of solidified material, especially plaster protecting a broken limb. 3. a set of actors taking parts in a play or film etc. 4. the form, type, or quality (*of* features, the mind, etc.). 5. a tinge of colour. 6. a slight squint. —**cast about for,** to try

to find or think of. **cast down,** to depress, to deject. **casting vote,** the deciding vote when votes on two sides are equal. **cast iron,** see IRON. **cast-iron** adj. made of cast iron; very strong, unchallengeable. **cast off,** to discard; to release a ship from its moorings; (in knitting) to loop stitches off a needle to form an edge. **cast-off** n. an abandoned thing; a garment that the owner will not wear again. **cast on,** (in knitting) to make the first row of loops on a needle. [f. ON]

Castalia /kæˈsteɪlɪə/ a spring on Mount Parnassus, sacred to Apollo and the Muses. —**Castalian** adj.

castanet /kæstəˈnet/ n. (usu. in pl.) a small concave piece of hardwood, ivory, etc., struck against another by the fingers as a rhythmic accompaniment, especially to a Spanish dance (ill. MUSICAL NOTATION). [f. Sp. f. L *castanea* chestnut]

castaway /ˈkɑːstəweɪ/ n. a shipwrecked person. —adj. 1. discarded. 2. shipwrecked.

caste /kɑːst/ n. 1. a Hindu hereditary class (see below); this class system; the position it confers. 2. a more or less exclusive social class or system of classes. —**casteism** /-tɪz(ə)m/ n. [f. Sp. & Port. *casta* lineage, fem. of *casto* pure (as CHASTE)]

The term occurs first in Spanish, but was applied by the Portuguese in the 16th c. to denote the rigid social divisions found in India. The caste system, which ranks groups of individuals according to birth and occupation and is governed by rules of marriage and social intercourse within the group, extends even to the non-Hindu segments of South Asian society such as Indian Christians and Muslims. The term is frequently confused with the ancient and traditional division of society into four classes (varna) from which the caste system is erroneously said to have evolved. The true origin of caste may be the early trade and professional guilds listed in later Vedic literature.

castellated /ˈkæstəleɪtɪd/ adj. built with battlements; castle-like. —**castellation** /-ˈleɪʃ(ə)n/ n. [f. L (as CASTLE)]

caster var. of CASTOR.

castigate /ˈkæstɪgeɪt/ v.t. to rebuke or punish severely. —**castigation** /-ˈgeɪʃ(ə)n/ n., **castigator** n. [f. L *castigare* reprove (*castus* pure)]

Castile /kæˈstiːl/ the central plateau of the Iberian peninsula, a former Spanish kingdom. Castile became an independent kingdom in the 10th c. and, with Aragon to the east, dominated the Spanish scene during the Middle Ages. The marriage of Isabella of Castile to Ferdinand of Aragon in 1469 effectively unified Spain into a single country.

Castilian /kæˈstɪlɪən/ adj. of Castile in Spain. —n. 1. a native or inhabitant of Castile. 2. the language of Castile, pure literary Spanish. [f. prec.]

castle /ˈkɑːs(ə)l/ n. 1. a large fortified building or group of buildings (ill. pp. 138–9). The term is also applied in proper names to ancient British or Roman earthworks. 2. (in chess) a rook (ROOK²). —v.t./i. (in chess) to move (the king) two squares towards a rook and the rook to the square which the king has crossed; (of the king or player) to make such a move. —**castles in the air,** a visionary unattainable scheme, a day-dream. [f. AF f. L, dim. of *castrum* fort]

Castlereagh /ˈkɑːs(ə)lreɪ/ Robert Stewart, Viscount Castlereagh (1769–1822), British statesman. Having already held office as Secretary of Ireland and War Secretary, Castlereagh became Foreign Secretary in 1812, and as such represented his country at the Congress of Vienna, playing a central part in the establishment of a conservative system of relations between the great European powers, based on the maintenance of the balance of power. He committed suicide in 1822, his mind having apparently given way under the strain of work.

Castor /ˈkɑːstə(r)/ 1. (*Gk myth.*) one of the Dioscuri. 2. (*Astron.*) the more northerly of the two bright stars in the constellation Gemini. It is of special interest as a multiple star system, the three components visible in a moderate telescope being close binaries.

castor /ˈkɑːstə(r)/ n. 1. a small swivelled wheel (often one of a set) fixed to the leg or underside of a piece of furniture so that this can be moved easily. 2. a small container for sugar or salt, with a perforated top for sprinkling the contents. —**castor sugar,** finely granulated white sugar. [f. CAST]

castor oil /ˈkɑːstə(r)/ oil from seeds of the plant *Ricinus communis*, used as a purgative and lubricant. [orig. unkn.]

castrate /kæˈstreɪt/ v.t. 1. to remove the testicles of, to geld. 2. to deprive of vigour. —**castration** n. [f. L *castrare*]

castrato /kæˈstrɑːtəʊ/ n. (pl. -ti /-tiː/) (*hist.*) a male singer

Castles

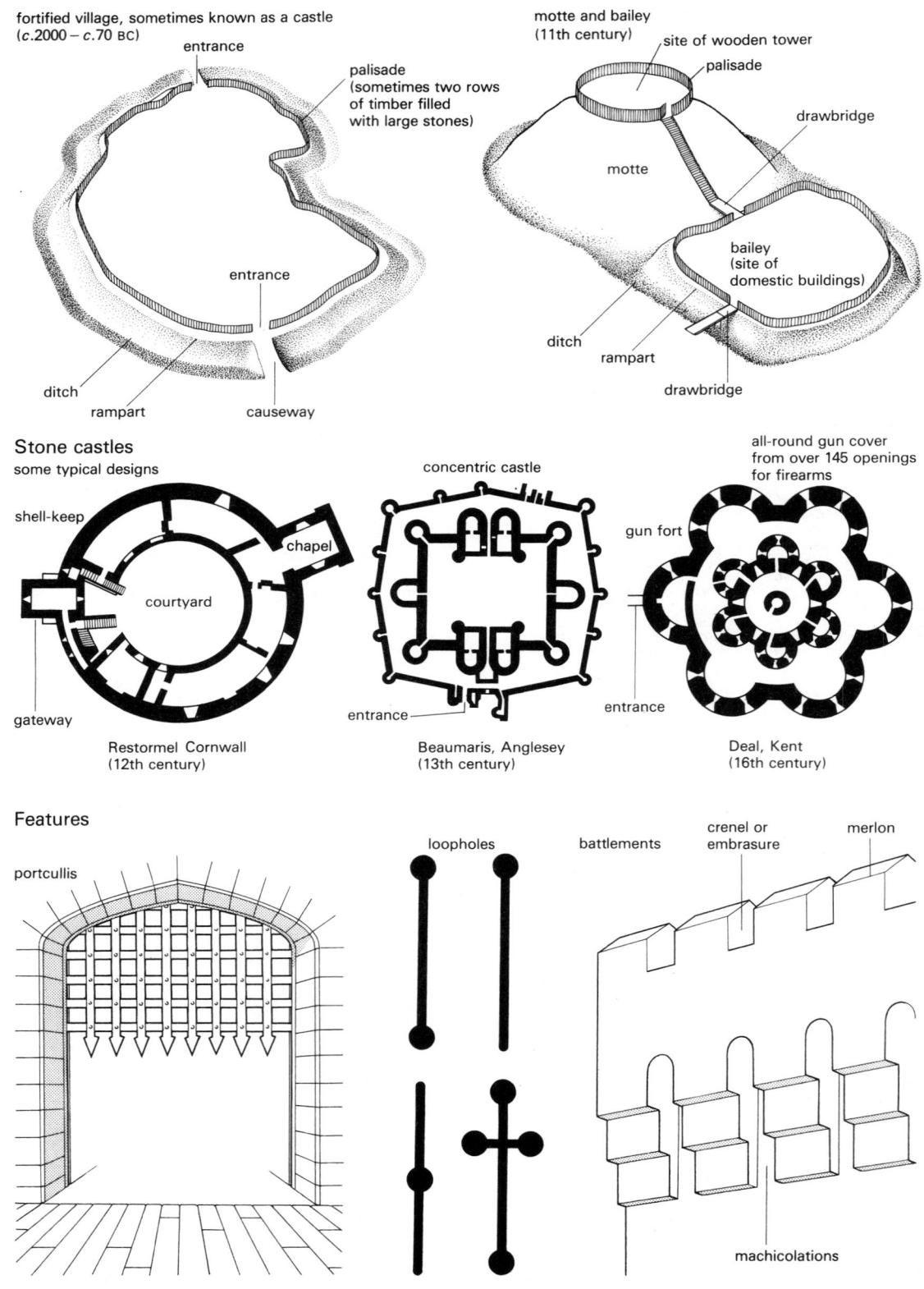

fortified village, sometimes known as a castle
(*c*.2000 – *c*.70 BC)

entrance

palisade
(sometimes two rows
of timber filled
with large stones)

entrance

ditch

rampart

causeway

motte and bailey
(11th century)

site of wooden tower

palisade

drawbridge

motte

bailey
(site of
domestic buildings)

ditch

rampart

drawbridge

Stone castles
some typical designs

shell-keep

chapel

courtyard

gateway

Restormel Cornwall
(12th century)

concentric castle

entrance

Beaumaris, Anglesey
(13th century)

all-round gun cover
from over 145 openings
for firearms

gun fort

entrance

Deal, Kent
(16th century)

Features

portcullis

loopholes

battlements

crenel or
embrasure

merlon

machicolations

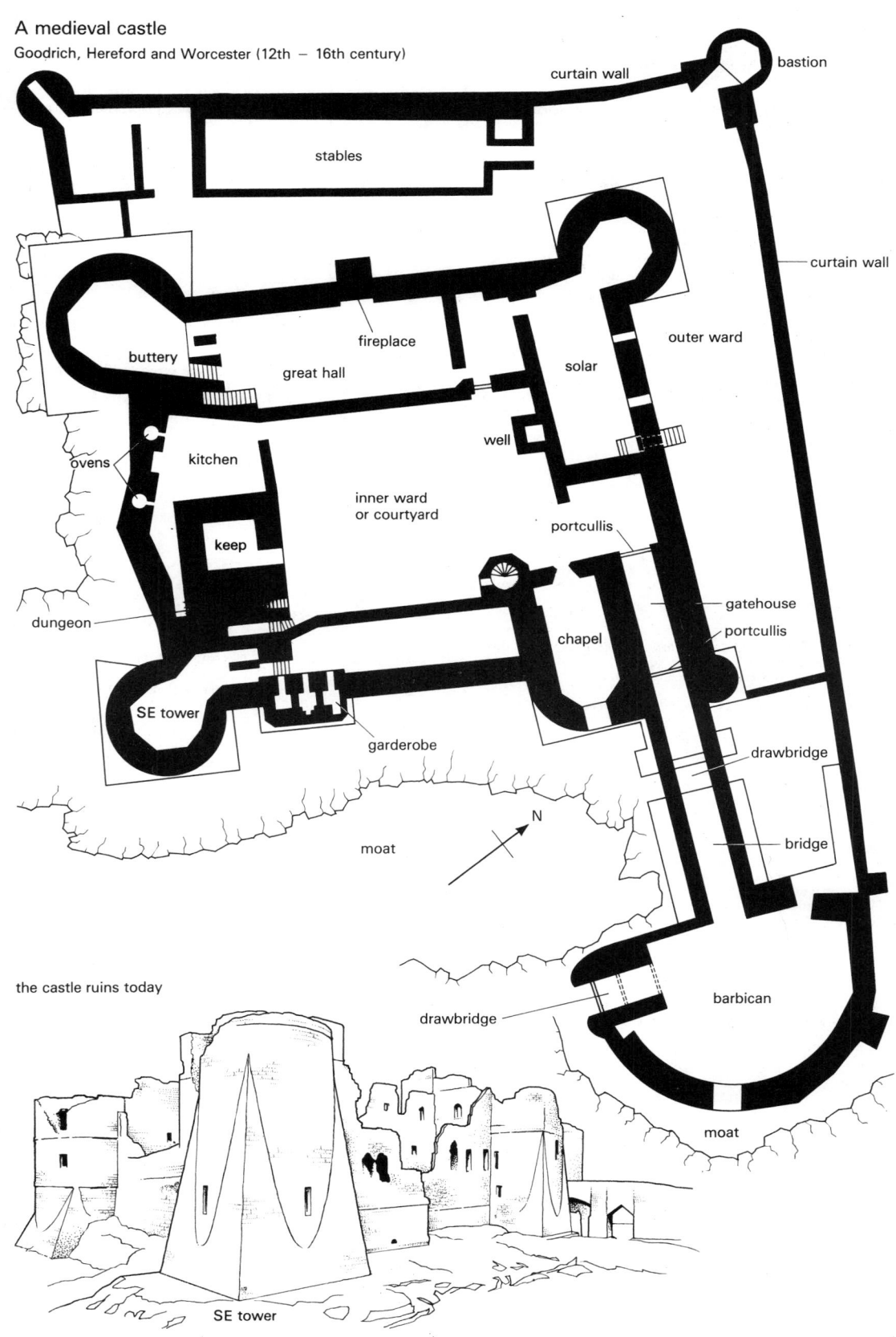

A medieval castle
Goodrich, Hereford and Worcester (12th – 16th century)

curtain wall

bastion

stables

curtain wall

fireplace

outer ward

buttery

solar

great hall

well

ovens

kitchen

inner ward
or courtyard

portcullis

keep

gatehouse

portcullis

dungeon

chapel

SE tower

garderobe

drawbridge

N

bridge

moat

drawbridge

the castle ruins today

barbican

moat

SE tower

castrated in boyhood to preserve a soprano or alto voice. [It. (as prec.)]

Castro /ˈkæstrəʊ/, Fidel (1927-), Cuban statesman. Castro led a successful uprising against the regime of President Batista in 1959, setting up a Communist regime in Cuba which he has led ever since.

casual /ˈkæʒjʊəl/ adj. **1.** happening by chance. **2.** unconcerned, made or done without great care or thought. **3.** not regular or permanent. **4.** (of clothes) informal. —n. **1.** a casual worker. **2.** (usu. in pl.) casual clothes or shoes. —**casually** adv., **casualness** n. [f. OF & L (casus CASE¹)]

casualty /ˈkæʒjʊəltɪ/ n. **1.** a person killed or injured in war or in an accident; a thing lost or destroyed in some occurrence. **2.** an accident or mishap. [f. L (as prec.)]

casuarina /kæzjʊəˈriːnə/ n. a tree of the genus Casuarina, native to Australia and tropical SE Asia, with jointed branches resembling gigantic horse-tails. [f. CASSOWARY, f. fancied resemblance to its feathers]

casuistry /ˈkæʒjʊɪstrɪ/ n. clever but often false reasoning, especially about moral issues. —**casuist** n., **casuistic** /-ˈɪstɪk/ adj. [f. F f. Sp. f. L casus CASE¹]

cat n. **1.** a small furry domesticated carnivorous quadruped, Felis catus; a member of the genus Felis (e.g. lion, tiger, leopard (the great Cats)); a catlike animal of other species. **2.** (colloq.) a malicious or spiteful woman. **3.** the cat-o'-nine tails. —**cat-and-dog life**, one full of quarrels. **cat-and-mouse game**, the practice of taking slight action repeatedly against a weaker party. **cat burglar**, one who enters by climbing a wall or drainpipe etc. to an upper storey. **cat-o'-nine tails**, a whip with nine knotted lashes. **cat's cradle**, a child's game with string forming looped patterns between the fingers. **Cats-eye** n. [P] any of a line of reflector studs marking the centre or edge of a road (patented in 1934). **cat's-paw** n. a person used as a tool by another (from the fable of the monkey who used the paw of his friend the cat to rake roasted chestnuts out of the fire). [OE f. L cattus]

cata- /kætə-/ prefix (usu. **cat-** before a vowel or h) **1.** down (cataract). **2.** wrongly (catachresis). [f. Gk kata down]

catabolism /kəˈtæbəlɪz(ə)m/ n. destructive metabolism, the breakdown of complex substances in the body (opp. ANABOLISM). —**catabolic** /kætəˈbɒlɪk/ adj. [f. Gk (CATA-, bolē throwing)]

catachresis /kætəˈkriːsɪs/ n. incorrect use of words. —**catachrestic** adj. [L f. Gk (CATA-, khrēsis f. khraomai use)]

cataclysm /ˈkætəklɪz(ə)m/ n. a violent upheaval or disaster; a sudden great change caused by this. [f. F f. L f. Gk (CATA-, klusmos flood)]

cataclysmic /kætəˈklɪzmɪk/ adj. of or involving a cataclysm. —**cataclysmic variable**, a class of variable star which includes dwarf novae, classical novae, and others exhibiting single or repeated outbursts. [f. prec.]

catacomb /ˈkætəkuːm/ n. a subterranean place for burial of the dead, consisting of galleries of passages with recesses excavated in their sides for tombs. The term catacumbas was used as early as the 5th c. in connection with the subterranean cemetery under the Basilica of St Sebastian, on the Appian Way, near Rome, in which the bodies of the Apostles Peter and Paul were said to have been deposited. In later times it was applied (in the plural) to all the subterranean cemeteries lying around Rome (which, after having been long covered up and forgotten, were fortuitously discovered in 1578), and extended to similar works elsewhere. Since Roman legislation regarded every burial-place as sacrosanct, Christians could use the catacombs in the era of the persecutions, and their violation was extremely rare. The stucco paintings which often covered the walls are the first examples of Christian art. [f. F f. L catacumbas; orig. unkn.]

catafalque /ˈkætəfælk/ n. a decorated platform for supporting the coffin of a distinguished person during a funeral or lying-in-state. [F f. It.; orig. unkn.]

Catalan /ˈkætəlæn, -lən/ adj. of Catalonia or its people or language. —n. **1.** a native or inhabitant of Catalonia. **2.** a Romance language most closely related to Provençal. Traditionally it is the language of Catalonia, but it is also spoken in Andorra (where it has official status), the Balearic Islands, and some parts of southern France. [F f. Sp.]

catalepsy /ˈkætəlɛpsɪ/ n. a trance or seizure with unconsciousness and rigidity of the body. —**cataleptic** /-ˈlɛptɪk/ adj. & n. [f. F or L f. Gk (CATA-, lēpsis seizure)]

catalogue /ˈkætəlɒg/ n. a list of items, usually in systematic order and often with a description of each. —v.t. to make

a catalogue of; to enter in a catalogue. —**cataloguer** n. [F f. L f. Gk (CATA-, legō choose)]

Catalonia /kætəˈləʊnɪə/ a region of NE Spain.

catalyse /ˈkætəlaɪz/ v.t. to accelerate or produce by catalysis. [f. foll.]

catalysis /kəˈtælɪsɪs/ n. (pl. **-lyses** /-siːz/) the action of a catalyst. [f. Gk, = dissolution (CATA-, luō set free)]

catalyst /ˈkætəlɪst/ n. a substance that aids or accelerates a chemical reaction without itself undergoing change; a person or thing that precipitates a change. [f. prec.]

catalytic /kætəˈlɪtɪk/ adj. of or using a catalyst; of catalysis. —**catalytic cracker**, a device in which catalytic cracking is carried out. **catalytic cracking**, the cracking of petroleum oils by a process using a catalyst. [f. CATALYSIS]

catamaran /kætəməˈræn/ n. **1.** a boat with twin hulls side by side. **2.** a raft of yoked logs or boats. [f. Tamil, = tied wood]

catamite /ˈkætəmaɪt/ n. the passive partner (especially a boy) in homosexual practices. [f. L f. Gk, = GANYMEDE]

catapult /ˈkætəpʌlt/ n. **1.** a forked stick etc. with elastic for shooting small stones. **2.** an ancient type of military machine for hurling large stones etc. **3.** a mechanical device for launching a glider, an aircraft from a ship's deck, etc. —v.t./i. **1.** to launch with or hurl from a catapult. **2.** to fling forcibly. **3.** to leap or be hurled forcibly. [f. F or L f. Gk (CATA- pellō hurl)]

cataract /ˈkætərækt/ n. **1.** a large waterfall; a rush of water. **2.** a condition in which the lens of the eye becomes progressively opaque. [f. L f. Gk, = down-rushing; sense 2 prob. f. obs. sense = portcullis]

catarrh /kəˈtɑː(r)/ n. inflammation of mucous membrane; a watery discharge in the nose or throat due to this. —**catarrhal** adj. [f. F f. L f. Gk (CATA-, rheō flow)]

catastrophe /kəˈtæstrəfɪ/ n. a great and usually sudden disaster; a disastrous end. **catastrophic** /kætəˈstrɒfɪk/ adj., **catastrophically** adv. [f. L f. Gk (CATA-, strephō turn)]

catatonia /kætəˈtəʊnɪə/ n. schizophrenia with intervals of catalepsy and occasionally violence; catalepsy. —**catatonic** /-ˈtɒnɪk/ adj. & n. [f. Gk (CATA-, tonos tension)]

catcall n. a shrill whistle of disapproval. —v.i. to make a catcall.

catch v.t./i. (past & p.p. **caught** /kɔːt/) **1.** to capture in a trap, in the hand(s) etc., or after a chase; to lay hold of; to catch out (a batsman). **2.** to be in time for and board (a train etc.). **3.** to detect or surprise; to trap into a mistake or contradiction etc. **4.** to get or contract by infection, contagion, or example. **5.** to grasp with the senses or mind; to perceive and reproduce (a likeness etc.). **6.** to become or cause to become fixed or entangled; to check suddenly. **7.** to draw the attention of, to captivate. **8.** to begin to burn. —n. **1.** the act of catching. **2.** something caught or worth catching. **3.** a concealed difficulty or disadvantage; a question etc. involving this for a victim. **4.** a device for fastening something. **5.** (Mus.) a round, especially with words arranged to produce a humorous effect. —**catch-all** n. a thing for including many items. **catch-as-catch-can** n. wrestling in which few or no holds are barred. **catch crop**, a crop that grows quickly and is harvested while the main crop is growing. **catch hold of**, to grasp, to seize in the hand(s). **catch it**, (colloq.) to be scolded or punished. **catch on**, (colloq.) to become popular; to understand what is meant. **catch out**, to detect in a mistake; to get (a batsman) out by catching the ball direct from his bat. **catch-phrase** n. a phrase in frequent current use; a slogan. **catch up**, to come abreast with (a person etc. ahead); to make up arrears. [f. AF f. L captare try to catch (capere take)]

catcher n. one who catches; a baseball fielder who stands behind the batter. [f. prec.]

catching adj. infectious; catchy. [f. CATCH]

catchment n. collection of rainfall. —**catchment area**, an area from which rainfall drains into a river or reservoir; an area served by a school, hospital, etc. [as prec.]

catchpenny adj. intended to sell quickly.

catch-22 n. (colloq.) a dilemma where the victim is bound to suffer, no matter which course of action etc. he takes. [title of a comic novel by J. Heller (1961), set in the Second World War, in which the hero wishes not to fly any more missions and decides to go crazy, only to be told that anyone who wants to get out of combat duty is not really crazy]

catchweight adj. & n. (Sport) accepting a contestant at the weight he happens to be, not a fixed weight.

catchword n. **1.** a memorable word or phrase in frequent current use, a slogan. **2.** a word so placed as to draw attention.

catchy /adj./ **1.** (of a tune etc.) easy to remember. **2.** tricky, involving a catch. [f. CATCH.]

catechism /ˈkætɪkɪz(ə)m/ *n.* a summary of the principles of a religion in the form of questions and answers; a series of questions. [f. L (as foll.)]

catechize /ˈkætɪkaɪz/ *v.t.* to put a series of questions to; to instruct by use of the Church catechism. [f. L f. Gk (*katēkheō* make clear)]

catechumen /kætɪˈkjuːmən/ *n.* a convert to Christianity who is being instructed before baptism. [as prec.]

categorical /kætɪˈgɒrɪk(ə)l/ *adj.* unconditional, explicit. —**categorical imperative,** (in Kant's ethical theory) a moral obligation, unconditional and derived from pure reason, to act only as if the principle on which the action is based could become a universal law. —**categorically** *adv.* [f. CATEGORY]

categorize /ˈkætɪgəraɪz/ *v.t.* to place in a category. —**categorization** /-ˈzeɪʃ(ə)n/ *n.* [f. foll.]

category /ˈkætɪgərɪ/ *n.* a class or division (of things etc.). [f. F or L f. Gk, = statement (*katēgoros* accuser)]

catenary /kəˈtiːnərɪ/ *n.* a curve formed by a uniform chain hanging freely from two points that are not in the same vertical line (ill. SHAPES). —*adj.* forming or like such a curve, [f. L *catena* chain]

cater /ˈkeɪtə(r)/ *v.i.* **1.** to supply food; to provide meals, amusements, etc. *for.* **2.** to pander *to* (bad inclinations). [f. obs. *cater* (now *caterer*), f. OF *acater* buy]

caterer /ˈkeɪtərə(r)/ *n.* one whose trade is to supply food for social events. [f. prec.]

caterpillar /ˈkætəpɪlə(r)/ *n.* the larva of a butterfly or moth; a similar larva of various insects. [f. F, lit. = hairy cat]

Caterpillar track [P] a band of linked steel plates passing round wheels on each side of a tractor etc. for travel on rough ground.

caterwaul /ˈkætəwɔːl/ *v.i.* to make a cat's shrill howling cry. [f. CAT + -*waul* (imit.)]

catfish *n.* a large fish of the sub-order Siluroidea, with whisker like barbels round its mouth.

catgut *n.* fine strong thread made from the dried intestines of sheep etc., used for the strings of musical instruments and for surgical suture. [some have conjectured a humorous reference to the resemblance of the sound to caterwauling]

catharsis /kəˈθɑːsɪs/ *n.* **1.** purgation. **2.** relief of strong feelings or tension, e.g. by giving vent to these in drama or art (the emotional effect of tragedy described in Aristotle's *Poetics*). [f. Gk (*kathairō* cleanse)]

cathartic /kəˈθɑːtɪk/ *adj.* effecting catharsis; purgative. —*n.* a cathartic substance. [f. prec.]

Cathay /kæˈθeɪ/ (also *Khitai*) (*hist. & poet.*) the name by which China was known to medieval Europe, the Khitans being a people of Manchu race, to the NE of China, who established an empire over northern China during the two centuries ending in 1123.

cathedral /kəˈθiːdr(ə)l/ *n.* the principal church of a bishop's see. —*adj.* of or having a cathedral. [f. OF or L f. Gk *kathedra* seat]

Catherine II /ˈkæθərɪn/, 'the Great' (1729–96), Russian empress, reigned 1762–96. A German princess, Catherine deposed her husband Peter III in 1762 and ruled in his place. She attempted a wide-reaching series of social and political reforms, but entrenched aristocratic interests prevented these from developing very far, and in later years her reign became increasingly conservative. Abroad, Russia played an important part in European affairs, participating in the three partitions of Poland and forming close links with Prussia and Austria, while to the south and east further territorial advances were made at the expense of the Turks and Tartars.

Catherine de Medici /kæθərɪn də ˈmedɪtʃɪ, -ˈdiːtʃɪ/ (1519–89), queen of France. The wife of Henry II of France, Catherine ruled as regent during the minorities of their three sons, Francis II, Charles IX, and Henry III. She proved unable or unwilling to control the confused situation during the French religious wars, contributing substantially to the disorder and bloodshed through her own plotting and her instigation of the massacre of the Huguenots on St Bartholomew's Eve 1572.

Catherine of Aragon /ˈkæθərɪn, ˈærəgən/ (1485–1536), first wife of Henry VIII, youngest daughter of Ferdinand and Isabella of Spain, mother of Mary I. Originally married to Henry's elder brother Arthur, Catherine was eventually married to Henry several years after Arthur had died at the age of fifteen. The marriage was a reasonably happy one until about 1525 when the king, concerned by Catherine's failure to produce a male heir, fell in love with Anne Boleyn. His attempts to divorce his wife on the debatable grounds that Catherine's involvement with his brother made the marriage illegal did not gain the approval of the Vatican and led to a break with Rome.

Catherine wheel /ˈkæθərɪn/ a firework that rotates when lit. [f. St *Catherine*, said to have been tortured on a spiked wheel (and then beheaded) at Alexandria in the 4th c.]

catheter /ˈkæθɪtə(r)/ *n.* a tube inserted into a body-cavity (especially the bladder) to drain fluid. [f. Gk (*kathiēmi* send down)]

cathode /ˈkæθəʊd/ *n.* the electrode by which current leaves a device. —**cathode ray tube,** a vacuum tube in which a beam of electrons from the cathode produces a luminous image on a fluorescent screen (as in a television set and an oscilloscope). [f. Gk *kathodos* way down (*kata* down, *hodos* way)]

The study of the discharge of high-voltage electricity through glass tubes containing gases at low pressure late last century revealed that a highly energetic radiation was being emitted from the region of the cathode or negative terminal of the tube. J. J. Thomson in 1897 established that cathode rays consisted of streams of high-velocity electrons. Cathode rays now have many applications in science and industry. The modern television tube, for example, is an advanced form of cathode-ray tube. It is highly evacuated and produces cathode rays through the evaporation of electrons from a heated cathode. The electrons are accelerated and focused by a specially designed and positively charged anode, and fall on a luminous screen where they produce a pin-point of light. A metal grid or mesh inserted between cathode and anode may be charged positively or negatively, thereby increasing or reducing the brightness of the spot. When an external signal is not being received by the tube, special electrical circuits cause the electron beam to set up a scanning pattern which covers the whole screen with uniform illumination. When a signal is received at the grid from a television transmitter it controls the intensity of the electron beam, and, therefore, the brightness of the spot on the screen, in such a manner that the electrical signals received are translated into the pictures seen on the screen.

catholic /ˈkæθəlɪk/ *adj.* universal, including many or most things. —**catholicity** /-ˈlɪsɪtɪ/ *n.* [f. OF or L f. Gk (*kata* in respect of, *holos* whole)]

Catholic *adj.* **1.** including all Christians, or all of the Western Church. **2.** Roman Catholic. —*n.* a Roman Catholic. —**Catholicism** /-ˈθɒlɪsɪz(ə)m/ *n.* [= prec.]

Catiline /ˈkætɪlaɪn/ (Lucius Sergius Catilina, d. 62 BC), Roman nobleman and conspirator. Repeatedly thwarted in his ambition to be elected consul, in 63 BC he planned an uprising in Italy; his fellow-conspirators in Rome were successfully suppressed and executed on the initiative of the consul Cicero, and Catiline died fighting in Etruria in early 62 BC.

cation /ˈkætaɪən/ *n.* a positively charged ion (opp. *anion*). —**cationic** /-ˈɒnɪk/ *adj.* [f. Gk. *kata* down + ION]

catkin *n.* a spike of small soft flowers (usually hanging) on trees such as willow and hazel. [f. Du., = kitten]

catmint *n.* a blue-flowered plant (*Nepeta cataria*) with a strong smell that is attractive to cats.

catnap *n.* a short sleep. —*v.i.* (-**pp**-) to have a catnap.

catnip *n.* catmint.

Cato /ˈkeɪtəʊ/, Marcus Porcius 'the Censor' (234–149 BC), Roman statesman, orator, and writer, for later ages the embodiment of traditional Roman values. Of peasant stock, as a young man he fought in the Second Punic War, and thereafter remained an implacable enemy of Carthage. As censor in 184 BC he engaged in a vigorous programme of moral and social reform, and attempted to stem the growing influence of Greek culture on Roman life. His many writings included a lost history of Rome and an extant work on agriculture. His grandson, Cato the Younger (95–46 BC), was an opponent of the dictatorial ambitions of Julius Caesar.

catsuit *n.* a close-fitting garment covering the body from neck to feet, with sleeves and trouser legs.

cattle *n.pl.* cows, bulls, oxen. —**cattle-grid** *n.* a grid covering a ditch, allowing vehicles to pass over but not cattle, sheep, etc. [f. OF *chatel* (cf. CHATTEL), as CAPITAL]

catty *adj.* catlike; malicious, speaking spitefully. —**cattily** *adv.*, **cattiness** *n.* [f. CAT]

Catullus /kə'tʌləs/, Gaius Valerius (*c.*84–*c.*54 BC), Roman poet, originally from Verona. His one book of verse contains poems in a variety of metres on a variety of subjects; he is best known for his intensely expressed poems to Lesbia, the nickname of one Clodia, probably the fast-living wife of the prominent Q. Metellus Celer. He also wrote personal poems to other friends and enemies, and a number of longer mythological pieces. His importance for later Latin poetry lies both in the impetus he gave to the development of love-elegy, and in his cultivation of an Alexandrian refinement and learning.

catwalk /'kætwɔ:k/ *n.* a raised narrow pathway.

Caucasian /kɔ:'keɪzɪən, -ʒ(ə)n/ *adj.* **1.** of the Caucasus. **2.** of the 'white' or light-skinned race of mankind (see below). —*n.* a Caucasian person. —**Caucasian languages**, a group of languages spoken in the region of the Caucasus. Of the 40 known only a few are committed to writing. The main language of the group is Georgian, which belongs to the southern group. [f. CAUCASUS, supposed place of origin]
This is one of the major racial divisions of man defined by Blumenbach. The physical attributes of Caucasians are highly variable: a wide range in body build, variable in nose-form and in the quantity and type of body and facial hair; a wide range in head-shape and in the form of the lips and mouth; and skin-colour ranging from extremely light to dark. The original distribution of this race extended from the Arctic to Africa north of the Sahara, and from the Azores in the North Atlantic to Samarkand in Soviet Central Asia.

Caucasoid /'kɔ:kəsɔɪd/ *adj.* of the Caucasian division of mankind. [as prec.]

Caucasus /'kɔ:kəsəs/ a mountain range in Georgia, USSR, between the Black and Caspian Seas, rising to over 5,500 m (18,000 ft.).

Cauchy /'kəʊʃɪ/, Augustin Louis, Baron (1789–1857), prolific and enormously influential French mathematician. It is said that more concepts and theorems have been named after Cauchy than after any other mathematician. His textbooks and many of his original writings introduced new standards of criticism and rigorous argument in the calculus from which grew the field of mathematics known as analysis. He transformed the theory of complex functions by discovering his integral theorems and introducing the calculus of residues. He founded the modern theory of elasticity, produced fundamental new ideas about the solution of differential equations, and contributed substantially in 1845 to the founding of the theory of groups.

caucus /'kɔ:kəs/ *n.* **1.** (often *derog.*) the committee of a local branch of a political party, making plans, decisions, etc. **2.** (*US*) a meeting of party leaders to decide policy etc. **3.** (*Austral.*) the parliamentary members of a political party who decide policy etc.; a meeting of these. [US wd, perh. f. Algonquin, = adviser]

caudal /'kɔ:d(ə)l/ *adj.* of, like, or at the tail. [f. L *cauda* tail]

caudate /'kɔ:'deɪt/ *adj.* having a tail. [as prec.]

caught *past* & *p.p.* of CATCH.

caul /kɔ:l/ *n.* a membrane enclosing a foetus in the womb; part of this sometimes found on a child's head at birth. The superstition existed among many sailors at least until the early 20th c. that possession of the caul of a new-born child was a sure protection against death by drowning. [perh. f. OF, = small cap]

cauldron /'kɔ:ldrən/ *n.* a large deep cooking-pot for boiling things in. [f. AF f. L *caldarium* hot bath]

cauliflower /'kɒlɪflaʊə(r)/ *n.* a cabbage with a large white flower-head. —**cauliflower ear**, an ear thickened by repeated blows. [f. F *chou fleuri* flowered cabbage]

caulk /kɔ:k/ *v.t.* to make watertight by filling seams or joints with waterproof material, or by driving edges of plating together. [f. OF f. L *calcare* tread]

causal /'kɔ:z(ə)l/ *adj.* of or forming a cause; relating to cause and effect. —**causally** *adv.* [f. L (as CAUSE)]

causality /kɔ:'zælɪtɪ/ *n.* the relationship between cause and effect; the principle that everything has a cause. [f. prec.]

causation /kɔ:'zeɪʃ(ə)n/ *n.* the act of causing; causality. [F or f. L (as CAUSE)]

causative /'kɔ:zətɪv/ *adj.* acting as or expressing a cause. [f. OF or L (as CAUSE)]

cause /kɔ:z/ *n.* **1.** a thing that produces an effect; a person or thing that makes something happen. **2.** a reason or motive; justification. **3.** a principle, belief, or purpose for which efforts are made, a movement or charity. **4.** a matter to be settled at law; a case offered at law. —*v.t.* to be the cause of, to produce, to make happen. [f. OF f. L *causa*]

cause célèbre /kɔ:z se'lebrə/ (*pl.* **-s -s**, pr. same) a lawsuit or other issue that rouses great interest. [F]

causeway /'kɔ:zweɪ/ *n.* a raised road across low or wet ground. [earlier *cauce(way)*, f. OF f. L *calx* limestone]

caustic /'kɔ:stɪk/ *adj.* **1.** that burns or corrodes things by chemical action. **2.** sarcastic. —**caustic curve**, a curve formed by the intersection of rays reflected or refracted from a curved surface (ill. SHAPES). **caustic soda**, sodium hydroxide. —**causticity** /-'tɪsɪtɪ/ *n.*, **caustically** *adv.* [f. L f. Gk (*kaustos* burnt)]

cauterize /'kɔ:təraɪz/ *v.t.* to burn (tissue) with a caustic substance or hot iron to destroy infection or stop bleeding. —**cauterization** /-'zeɪʃ(ə)n/ *n.* [f. F f. L f. Gk (*kautērion* branding-iron)]

caution /'kɔ:ʃ(ə)n/ *n.* **1.** avoidance of rashness, attention to safety. **2.** a warning against danger etc.; a warning and reprimand. **3.** (*colloq.*) an amusing person or thing. —*v.t.* to warn; to warn and reprimand. [f. OF f. L (*cavere* take heed)]

cautionary /'kɔ:ʃ(ə)nərɪ/ *adj.* that gives or serves as a warning. [f. prec.]

cautious /'kɔ:ʃəs/ *adj.* having or showing caution. —**cautiously** *adv.*, **cautiousness** *n.* [f. CAUTION]

cavalcade /'kævəlkeɪd/ *n.* a procession or company of people on horseback or in cars etc. [F f. It. (*cavalcare* ride, f. L *caballus* horse)]

Cavalier /kævə'lɪə(r)/ *n.* a supporter of Charles I in the English Civil War. The term originally had pejorative connotations, referring to the supposedly overenthusiastic attitude of the king's supporters towards the prospect of war. [F f. It. (as CHEVALIER)]

cavalier /kævə'lɪə(r)/ *n.* a courtly gentleman. —*adj.* arrogant, offhand. [as prec.]

cavalry /'kæv(ə)lrɪ/ *n.* (usu. as *pl.*) troops who fight on horseback or in armoured vehicles. [f. F f. It. f. L *caballus* horse]

cave *n.* a hollow in the side of a hill or cliff, or underground. —*v.i.* to explore caves. —**cave-painting** *n.* picture(s) of animals etc. on the interior of a cave, especially by prehistoric peoples. **cave in**, to fall or cause to fall inwards, to collapse; to withdraw one's opposition. [f. OF f. L *cavus* hollow]

caveat /'kævɪæt/ *n.* a warning; a proviso. [L, = let him beware]

Cavell /'kæv(ə)l/, Edith (1865–1915), English nurse, executed by the Germans in 1915. Arrested by the German military authorities for helping British soldiers to escape from occupied Belgium, she was shot as a spy, a serious blunder on the part of the Germans who thereby gave British propaganda considerable fuel for allegations of German atrocities.

caveman *n.* (*pl.* **-men**) a prehistoric man living in caves; a man with a rough primitive manner towards women.

Cavendish /'kævəndɪʃ/, Henry (1731–1810), English natural philosopher, nephew of the 3rd Duke of Devonshire. He was of independent means so that he did not have to study for a profession. Indeed, he was described as the 'richest of the learned, and the most learned of the rich'. A shy and eccentric man, he pursued his research for its own sake in his private laboratory, and troubled little about publishing his results. He identified hydrogen ('inflammable air') as a separate gas, studied carbon dioxide ('fixed air'), and determined their densities relative to common air in 1766, established that water was a compound in 1784, and determined the density of the earth by means of John Mitchel's torsion balance in 1798. The full extent of his discoveries in electrostatics was not known until his manuscripts were published by James Clerk Maxwell in 1879: he had anticipated Coulomb, Ohm, and Faraday, deduced the inverse square law of electrical attraction and repulsion, and discovered specific inductive capacity (not his term). The Cavendish Laboratory at Cambridge was named in his honour in 1874.

cavern /'kævən/ *n.* a large cave. —**cavernous** *adj.* [f. or L (*cavus* hollow)]

caviare /'kævɪɑ:(r)/ *n.* the pickled roe of sturgeon or other large fish. [f. It. f. Turk.]

cavil /'kævɪl/ *v.i.* (**-ll-**) to raise petty objections (*at*). —*n.* a petty objection. [f. F f. L (*cavilla* mockery)]

cavity /'kævɪtɪ/ *n.* a hollow within a solid body. —**cavity wall,** a double wall with an internal space (ill. BUILDING). [f. F or L (as CAVE)]

cavort /kə'vɔːt/ *v.i.* to prance or caper excitedly. [perh. f. CURVET]

Cavour /kə'vʊə(r)/, Camillo Benso, Count di (1810–61), Italian statesman. Premier of Sardinia from 1852, Cavour was the driving force behind the unification of Italy, organizing the movement behind his monarch Victor Emmanuel II and actively participating in international affairs, notably the Crimean War and the Franco-Austrian War, in order to win wide support for the project, which finally came to fruition with unification in 1860–1.

caw *n.* the harsh cry of a rook, raven, or crow etc. —*v.i.* to make a caw. [imit.]

Caxton /'kækstən/, William (c.1422–91), the first English printer. Having learned the art of printing on the Continent, Caxton printed his first English text in 1474 and went on to produce about 80 other texts (many of them his own translations of French romances) before his death, doing more than any other person to popularize printed books in Britain.

cayenne /keɪ'en/ *n.* (in full **cayenne pepper**) pungent red powdered pepper made from capsicum. [f. Tupi, assim. to *Cayenne* capital of French Guiana]

Cayley¹ /'keɪlɪ/, Arthur (1821–95), English mathematician and barrister, who wrote almost 1,000 mathematical papers on topics in algebra and geometry. These include articles on determinants, the newly developing group theory, and the algebra of matrices. He also studied dynamics and physical astronomy. The Cayley numbers, a generalization of complex numbers, are named after him.

Cayley² /'keɪlɪ/, Sir George (1773–1857), the father of British aeronautics, a mechanical genius best known for his understanding of the principles of flight, his model gliders, and his 'man-carrier', a glider which carried his coachman across Brompton Dale, Yorkshire, in 1853. At one time MP for Scarborough, his research, inventions, and devices covered schemes and devices for land reclamation, artificial limbs, theatre architecture, railways, lifeboats, finned projectiles, optics, electricity, hot-air engines, and what was later called the caterpillar tractor (1825). He was a founder of the original Regent Street Polytechnic Institution (1838).

cayman /'keɪmən/ *n.* (*pl.* **-s**) a South American alligator, especially of the genus *Caiman*. [f. Sp. & Port. f. Carib]

Cayman Islands /'keɪmən/ (also **Caymans**) three islands in the Caribbean Sea, a British dependency, south of Cuba; pop. (1983) 18,750; official language, English; capital, George Town. Columbus, discovering the islands in 1503, named them *Las Tortugas* (Sp., = the turtles) because of their abundance of turtles. A British colony was established towards the end of the 17th c., and in the 19th c. the Caymans became noted for the building of schooners.

CB *abbr.* citizens' band.

CBI *abbr.* Confederation of British Industry, the employers' federation in the UK, founded in 1965.

Cd *symbol* cadmium.

cd *abbr.* candela.

CE *abbr.* Common Era.

Ce *symbol* cerium.

cease /siːs/ *v.t./i.* to bring or come to an end; to stop. —**cease-fire** *n.* a signal (in war) to stop firing; a halt in hostilities. [f. OF f. L *cessare*]

ceaseless *adj.* without cease, not ceasing. [f. prec. + -LESS]

Cecilia /sɪ'siːljə/, St (2nd or 3rd c.), one of the most venerated martyrs in the early Roman Church. Her body is said to have been found entire and uncorrupted in 1599 in the church in Rome which bears her name. She is frequently represented as playing on the organ, and is the patron saint of church music. Feast day, 22 Nov.

cedar /'siːdə(r)/ *n.* an evergreen coniferous tree of the genus *Cedrus*; its hard fragrant wood. [f. OF f. L f. Gk *kedros*]

cede /siːd/ *v.t.* to give up one's rights to or possession of. [f. L *cedere* yield]

cedilla /sɪ'dɪlə/ *n.* a mark written under *c* especially in French, to show that it is sibilant (as in *façade*). [f. Sp., dimin. of *zeda* z]

ceilidh /'keɪlɪ/ *n.* (orig. *Sc.* & *Ir.*) an informal gathering for traditional music, dancing, etc. [Gael.]

ceiling /'siːlɪŋ/ *n.* **1.** the under-surface of the top of a room etc. **2.** the maximum altitude a given aircraft can normally reach. **3.** an upper limit (of prices, performance, etc.). [orig. unkn.]

celandine /'seləndaɪn/ *n.* either of two yellow-flowered plants, **greater celandine** (*Chelidonium majus*) and **lesser celandine** (*Ranunculus ficaria*). [f. OF f. L f. Gk (*chelidon* the swallow)]

Celebes /se'liːbɪz/ see SULAWESI.

celebrant /'selɪbrənt/ *n.* an officiating priest, especially at the Eucharist. [as foll.]

celebrate /'selɪbreɪt/ *v.t./i.* **1.** to mark (an occasion) with festivities; to engage in such festivities. **2.** to perform (religious rites); to officiate at the Eucharist etc. **3.** to praise widely, to extol. —**celebration** /-'breɪʃ(ə)n/ *n.* [f. L *celebrare* (*celeber* renowned)]

celebrated *adj.* widely known. [f. prec.]

celebrity /sɪ'lebrɪtɪ/ *n.* a well-known person; fame. [as CELEBRATE]

celeriac /sɪ'lerɪæk/ *n.* a variety of celery with large edible root. [f. CELERY]

celerity /sɪ'lerɪtɪ/ *n.* (*archaic* & *literary*) swiftness. [f. L (*celer* swift)]

celery /'selərɪ/ *n.* a vegetable (*Apium graveolens*) with blanched stems eaten raw in salads or cooked. [f. F, ult. f. Gk *selinon* parsley]

celesta /sɪ'lestə/ *n.* a small keyboard instrument with hammers striking metal plates to give a bell-like sound. [f. F *céleste* (as foll.)]

celestial /sɪ'lestɪəl/ *adj.* **1.** of the sky or heavenly bodies. **2.** of heaven, divine. —**celestial equator,** a great circle of the sky in a plane parallel to the earth's axis (ill. NAVIGATION). **celestial mechanics,** the mathematical description of the positions and motions of astronomical objects on the celestial sphere. **celestial pole,** the point on the celestial sphere directly above the earth's geographic pole (north or south). This is the point in the sky around which the stars and planets rotate during the course of the night, currently (in the northern hemisphere) within one degree of the bright star Polaris, but because of the precession of the equinoxes it appears to trace out a circle on the celestial sphere over a period of some 26,000 years. **celestial sphere,** the abstract sphere of unit radius on which the positions of celestial objects are projected to form a map of the heavens whose poles and equator are projections of the corresponding terrestrial features. —**celestially** *adv.* [f. L (*caelum* sky)]

celibate /'selɪbət/ *adj.* remaining unmarried or abstaining from sexual relations, especially for religious reasons. —*n.* a celibate person. —**celibacy** *n.* [f. L *caelebs* bachelor]

cell *n.* **1.** a very small room, e.g. for a monk in a monastery or for confining a prisoner. **2.** a compartment in a honeycomb. **3.** a microscopic structure which is effectively the unit of life (see below). **4.** a container with materials for producing electricity by chemical action; a device for converting chemical or radiant energy into electrical energy. **5.** a small group of people forming a centre or nucleus of political (often subversive) activities. [f. L *cella* store-room]

Nearly all organisms are composed of cells (the simplest consist of a single cell), which are microscopic structures bounded by a membrane and capable of metabolism, self-repair, and reproduction. The word was first applied to dead cork cells by Robert Hooke in 1665, but the universal importance of living cells was not appreciated until the 19th c. Cells arise most commonly by the division of other cells, but sometimes by fusion (as of gametes in sexual reproduction). There are two basic types of cell: those of bacteria, lacking nuclei and other complex structures, and animal and plant cells, which are larger and more complex and possess a nucleus. This nucleus contains the genetic information (see DNA), the surrounding cytoplasm contains various structures and carries out most of the cell's metabolism, and the cell membrane regulates the exchange of materials with its environment. The activities of the cell are to a large extent controlled by the information in its DNA. In large organisms such as humans there are many specialized types of cell lacking some of the features described above; for example, red blood cells have no nuclei, and nerve cells in adults, although nucleated, are unable to reproduce. Most plant cells differ from those of animals in having a thick wall of cellulose outside the cell membrane, a large fluid-filled cavity within the cytoplasm, and (in green plants) structures that contain chlorophyll.

cellar /'selə(r)/ *n.* **1.** a room below ground-level, used for storage (especially of wine). **2.** a person's or institution's stock of wine. [f. AF f. L *cellarium* (as prec.)]

Cellini /tʃeˈliːnɪ/, Benvenuto (1500-71), Florentine gold-smith and metal-worker, one of the most important manner-ist sculptors. While in the service of Francis I of France, 1540-5, he created the salt-cellar of gold and enamel (now in Vienna), which is the greatest example of goldsmith's work that has survived from the Italian Renaissance. The rest of his life was spent in Florence; here he cast the bronze *Perseus* (1545-54) which is regarded as his masterpiece. His autobiography, translated by Goethe in the 18th c., is famous for its racy style and its vivid picture of a proud, quarrelsome, Renaissance craftsman.

cello /ˈtʃeləʊ/ n. (pl. **-os**) a violoncello, an instrument like a large violin with four strings and a range of over three octaves, played supported on the floor in an upright or slanting position between the seated player's knees (ill. ORCHESTRA). —**cellist** n. [abbr. of VIOLONCELLO]

Cellophane /ˈseləfeɪn/ n. [P] a thin transparent wrapping material made from viscose (first produced in Switzerland in 1908). [f. CELLULOSE, cf. DIAPHANOUS]

cellular /ˈseljʊlə(r)/ adj. consisting of cells; (of blankets etc.) woven with an open mesh. —**cellularity** /-ˈlærɪtɪ/ n. [f. foll.]

cellule /ˈseljuːl/ n. a small cell or cavity. [F, or f. L *cellula* (*cella* CELL)]

celluloid /ˈseljʊlɔɪd/ n. a plastic made from camphor and cellulose nitrate. Invented in the USA, it was patented in Britain in 1871 as a material for dental plates. [f. foll.]

cellulose /ˈseljʊləʊz, -əʊs/ n. 1. the main constituent of plant-cell walls and derived textile fibres (see below). 2. (*pop.*) paint or lacquer made from solutions of cellulose acetate or nitrate. [f. F or L (as CELLULE)]

Cellulose, the main structural material of plants, is a carbohydrate consisting of long unbranched chains of glu-cose molecules and is the most abundant organic compound on earth. It is a major constituent of wood, from which it is produced industrially. Paper and plant-based textile fibres such as cotton consist largely of cellulose, and in chemically modified forms it is used in the manufacture of rayon, certain plastics, and many other products. It is important in the human diet since it is a constituent of dietary fibre.

Celsius[1] /ˈselsɪəs/, Anders (1701-44), Swedish astronomer, best known for his thermometer scale. He was appointed professor of astronomy at Uppsala in 1730, and six years later joined an expedition to measure a meridian in the north, which successfully verified Newton's theory that the earth is flattened at the poles. In 1742 he advocated a metric thermometer scale with 100° as the freezing-point of water and 0° as the boiling-point, but the thermometer which was introduced at the Uppsala Observatory in 1747 had its scale reversed. It was long known as the 'Swedish thermometer' and only in the early 19th c. did Celsius' name become associated with it.

Celsius[2] /ˈselsɪəs/ adj. of or using the Celsius (centigrade) scale of temperature (see prec.).

Celt /kelt/ n. a member of one of a group of western European peoples (including the ancient Gauls and Britons; see below); modern Bretons, Cornish, Gaels, Irish, Manx, Welsh). [f. L f. Gk *Keltoi*]

The Celts occupied a large part of Europe in the Iron Age. Their unity is recognizable by common speech (see CELTIC) and common artistic tradition, but they did not constitute one race or group of tribes ethnologically. The origins of their culture can be traced back to the Bronze Age of the upper Danube in the 13th c. BC, with successive stages represented by the urnfield and Hallstatt cultures. Spread-ing over western and central Europe from perhaps as early as 900 BC, they reached the height of their power in the La Tène period of the 5th-1st c. BC. The ancients knew them as fierce fighters and superb horsemen, with savage religious rites conducted by the Druid priesthood. They were farm-ers, who cultivated fields on a regular basis with ox-drawn ploughs in place of manual implements, revolutionary changes which permanently affected people's way of life. But Celtic political sense was weak, and the numerous tribes, continually warring against each other, were crushed between the migratory Germans and the power of Rome, to be ejected or assimilated by the former or conquered outright by the latter.

Celtic /ˈkeltɪk/ adj. of the Celts and kindred peoples, or their languages. —n. a sub-group of the Indo-European language group, today spoken in the British Isles and in Brittany, divided into two groups, Goidelic (consisting of Irish, Scots Gaelic, and Manx) and Brythonic (consisting of Welsh, Cornish, and Breton). There is widespread evidence that a Celtic language was spoken in mainland Europe before and during the Roman period. [f. L (as CELT) or F]

cement /sɪˈment/ n. a grey powder made by burning lime and clay, which sets to a stonelike mass when mixed with water and is used as a building material, mortar, etc.; any soft substance that sets firm. —v.t. to join with or like cement; to apply cement to, to line with cement. —**cemen-tation** /-ˈteɪʃ(ə)n/ n. [f. OF f. L *caementum* quarry stone]

cemetery /ˈsemɪtərɪ/ n. a burial ground other than a churchyard. [f. L f Gk *koimētērion* dormitory]

cenotaph /ˈsenətɑːf/ n. a sepulchral monument to persons buried elsewhere. —**the Cenotaph**, a monument, designed by Sir Edward Lutyens, erected in 1919-20 in Whitehall, London, as a memorial to the British servicemen who died in the First World War. An inscription now commemorates also those who died in the Second World War. [f. Gk, = empty tomb]

censer /ˈsensə(r)/ n. a small container in which incense is burnt, swung on chains in a religious ceremony to disperse its fragrance. [f. AF (as INCENSE[1])]

censor /ˈsensə(r)/ n. an official with the power to suppress parts of books, films, letters, news, etc., on grounds of obscenity, risk to security, etc. —v.t. to treat (books, films, etc.) in this way. —**censorship** n. [L, = magistrate who registered citizens and could exclude from public functions on moral grounds]

censorious /senˈsɔːrɪəs/ adj. severely critical, fault-finding. [f. prec.]

censure /ˈsenʃə(r)/ n. strong criticism or condemnation, a rebuke. —v.t. to blame and rebuke. [f. OF f L (*censēre* assess; cf. CENSOR)]

census /ˈsensəs/ n. an official count of a population or of a class of things. [L, as CENSOR]

cent n. one hundredth of a US dollar or certain other metric units of currency; a coin of this value. [f. F, It. or L (*centum* hundred)]

Centaur /ˈsentɔː(r)/ n. 1. (*Gk myth.*) a member of a tribe of wild creatures with the upper part of a man and the hindquarters of a horse. The legend of their existence may have arisen from the ancient inhabitants of Thessaly having tamed horses and appearing to their neighbours mounted on horseback. 2. (*Astron.*) the southern constellation Centaurus.

Centaurus /senˈtɔːrəs/ a southern constellation, the Cen-taur, famous for its brightest member, alpha Centauri, third-brightest in the sky and actually a triple star system of which the least bright component is the nearest star beyond our solar system, at a distance of 4.34 light-years.

centaury /ˈsentɔːrɪ/ n. a plant of the genus *Centaurium* with small pink flowers usually in clusters, especially the common centaury of the herbalists (*C. erythraea*). [f. L f. Gk, = centaur, because said to have been discovered and used medicinally by Chiron the Centaur, tutor of Achilles]

centenarian /sentɪˈneərɪən/ n. a person a hundred or more years old. [as foll.]

centenary /senˈtiːnərɪ/ n. a hundredth anniversary. —adj. of such an anniversary. [f. L (*centeni* 100 each)]

centennial /senˈtenɪəl/ adj. & n. centenary. [as prec.]

centesimal /senˈtesɪm(ə)l/ adj. reckoning or reckoned by hundredths. [f. L (*centum* hundred)]

centi- in comb. 1. one hundredth. 2. a hundred. [f. L *centum* hundred]

centigrade /ˈsentɪgreɪd/ adj. of or having a temperature scale of a hundred degrees, 0° being the freezing-point and 100° the boiling-point of water. [f. CENTI- + L *gradus* step]

centigram /ˈsentɪgræm/ n. one hundredth of a gram.

centilitre /ˈsentɪliːtə(r)/ n. one hundredth of a litre.

centimetre /ˈsentɪmiːtə(r)/ n. one hundredth of a metre, about 0.4 inch.

centipede /ˈsentɪpiːd/ n. a many-legged arthropod of the class Chilopoda, having one pair of legs to each segment (cf. MILLEPEDE). [f. F or L (*centum* hundred, *pes pedis* foot)]

Central /ˈsentr(ə)l/ a local government region in central Scotland.

central /ˈsentr(ə)l/ adj. 1. of, at, from, or forming the centre. 2. chief, most important. —**central bank**, a national (not commercial) bank, issuing currency. **Central Criminal Court**, the Old Bailey. **central heating**, a method of warming a building from one source by circulat-ing hot water, hot air, or steam in pipes, or by linked radiators. **Central Intelligence Agency,** a federal agency in the USA, established in 1947, responsible for co-ordinating government intelligence activities. **central nervous system,** the brain and spinal cord. **Central Powers,** Germany and Austria–Hungary before 1914. —**centrality** /-'trælɪtɪ/ n., **centrally** adv. [F or f. L (*centrum* centre)]

Central African Republic a country of central Africa, bounded by Chad, Sudan, Zaïre, and the Cameroon Republic; pop. (est. 1981) 2,379,000; official language, French; capital, Bangui. Formerly the French colony of Ubanghi Shari, it became a republic within the French Community in 1958 and a fully independent State in 1960. In 1976 its President, Jean Bédel Bokassa, declared himself Emperor and changed the country's name to Central African Empire, but it reverted to the name of Republic after he had been ousted in 1979 following widespread unrest and allegations of atrocities.

Central America the narrow southern part of North America, south of Mexico.

centralism /'sentrəlɪz(ə)m/ n. a centralizing policy, especially in administration. —**centralist** n. [f. prec.]

centralize /'sentrəlaɪz/ v.t. to concentrate (administration etc.) at a single centre; to subject to such a system. —**centralization** /-'zeɪʃ(ə)n/ n. [f. CENTRAL]

centre /'sentə(r)/ n. **1.** the middle point or part; a pivot or axis of rotation. **2.** a point towards which interest is directed or from which administration etc. is organized; a main source of dispersal. **3.** a place where certain activities or facilities are concentrated. **4.** those members of a political party or group holding moderate opinions, between two extremes. **5.** a centre-forward. —*adj.* of or at the centre. —*v.t./i.* **1.** to place in or at the centre. **2.** to concentrate or be concentrated *in* or *on.* **3.** to kick or hit from the wing towards the middle of the pitch in football or hockey. —**centre-forward, centre-half** ns. the middle player in the forward (or half-back) line in football etc. **centre of gravity,** the point round which the mass of a body is evenly distributed. **centre-piece** n. an ornament for the middle of a table etc., a principal item. [f. OF or L f. Gk *kentron* sharp point]

centreboard n. a movable board lowered through a ship's keel to prevent leeway (ill. SAILING-SHIPS).

centrifugal /sen'trɪfjʊg(ə)l, -'fjuː-/ adj. moving away from the centre or axis. —**centrifugal force,** the apparent tendency of a rotating body to move outwards from the centre of rotation (see CENTRIFUGE). **centrifugal machine,** one in which the rotation causes this. —**centrifugally** adv. [f. L *centrum* centre + *fugere* flee]

centrifuge /'sentrɪfjuːdʒ/ n. a machine using centrifugal force to separate substances of different densities (e.g. milk and cream; see below). —*v.t.* to subject to centrifugal motion; to separate by using a centrifuge. [F (as prec.)]

Centrifugal force is generated in a mechanically-driven bowl or cylinder, usually of metal, which turns inside a stationary casing. Higher forces are generated using smaller machines, since these contain less material and can be rotated faster without damaging the apparatus. There are two main types of centrifuge. In one type (used, for example, for separating cream from milk, or particles from a liquid in which they are suspended) constituents of greater density are impelled to the periphery and those of lesser density collect near the middle, so that a heterogeneous liquid eventually separates into distinct layers. In the other type, a filtering centrifuge, liquid in which particles are suspended is placed inside a révolving cylinder that has a perforated wall lined with a filter (e.g. a cloth or fine screen): liquid passes through the wall, impelled by centrifugal force, leaving behind a cake of solids on the filter medium.

centripetal /sen'trɪpɪt(ə)l, -'piː-/ adj. moving towards the centre or axis. [f. L (*centrum* centre, *petere* seek)]

centrist /'sentrɪst/ n. one who adopts a middle position in politics etc. —**centrism** n. [f. CENTRE]

centurion /cen'tjʊərɪən/ n. an officer in the Roman army, originally one commanding a hundred infantrymen. [f. L (as foll.)]

century /'sentjʊrɪ, -tʃərɪ/ n. **1.** a period of a hundred years, especially one reckoned from the birth of Christ. **2.** (in cricket) a batsman's score of at least one hundred runs in an innings. [f. L *centuria* (*centum* hundred)]

cephalic /sɪ'fælɪk/ adj. of or in the head. —**cephalic index,** the ratio of the maximum skull width to maximum skull length, multiplied by 100. [f. F f. L f. Gk (*kephalē* head)]

cephalopod /'sefələpɒd/ n. a mollusc of the class Cephalopoda, having a distinct head with a ring of tentacles round the mouth. The group, which is entirely marine, contains about 700 living species, including octopuses, squid, cuttlefish, and nautiluses, but fossil species are much more numerous, and include the ammonites and belemnites. Cephalopods have large brains and are the most intelligent of all invertebrates, octopuses in particular having been shown to exhibit considerable learning ability. They are also notable for their well-developed eyes, which are quite similar to the vertebrate eye, and their ability to swim by a form of jet propulsion. Giant squid, which are rarely found but can grow to at least 18 m (60 ft.) long including tentacles, are the world's largest invertebrates. [f. Gk *kephalē* head + *pous podos* foot]

cepheid /'siːfɪɪd/ n. a star of regularly varying brightness, caused by pulsations of the surface layers. A precise relationship exists between the total luminosity of the star and the period of pulsation, allowing its distance to be inferred. [f. delta *Cephei*, the original example, in the constellation *Cepheus* named after a mythical king]

ceramic /sɪ'ræmɪk/ adj. of pottery or similar substances. —n. **1.** a ceramic article or substance. **2.** (in pl.) the art of making pottery etc. [f. Gk (*keramos* pottery)]

Cerberus /'sɜːbərəs/ (*Gk myth.*) the monstrous watch-dog with three heads (or fifty heads, according to Hesiod) guarding the entrance to Hades. The heroes who visited Hades during their lifetime (e.g. Aeneas) appeased him with a cake (whence the phrase 'a sop to Cerberus'); Orpheus lulled him to sleep with his lyre; one of the twelve labours of Hercules was to bring him up from the Underworld.

cercus /'sɜːkəs/ n. (pl. **-ci** /-siː/) each of a pair of small appendages found at the hind end of the abdomen of certain insects and other arthropods (ill. INSECTS). [f. Gk *kerkos* tail]

cereal /'sɪərɪəl/ adj. of edible grain. —n. **1.** an edible grain or the grass producing it. **2.** a breakfast food made from this. [f. L *cerealis* f. CERES]

cerebellum /serɪ'beləm/ n. a small part of the brain, located in the back of the skull. [L, dim. of CEREBRUM]

cerebral /'serɪbr(ə)l/ adj. of the brain; intellectual. —**cerebral palsy,** spastic paralysis resulting from brain damage before or at birth, with jerky or uncontrolled movements. [f. L *cerebrum* brain]

cerebration /serɪ'breɪʃ(ə)n/ n. activity of the brain. [as prec.]

cerebro-spinal /serɪbrəʊ'spaɪn(ə)l/ adj. of the brain and spinal chord. [f. foll. + SPINAL]

cerebrum /'serɪbrəm/ n. the principal part of the brain, located in the front of the skull (ill. BODY 4). [L]

ceremonial /serɪ'məʊnɪəl/ adj. of a ceremony, used in ceremonies; formal. —n. ceremony; a system of rules for ceremonies. —**ceremonially** adv. [f. L (as CEREMONY)]

ceremonious /serɪ'məʊnɪəs/ adj. full of ceremony; elaborately performed. —**ceremoniously** adv. [as foll.]

ceremony /'serɪmənɪ/ n. **1.** a set of formal acts, especially those used in a religous or public occasion. **2.** formal or elaborate politeness. [f. OF or L *caerimonia* religous worship]

Ceres /'sɪəriːz/ **1.** (*Rom. myth.*) an ancient Italian corn-goddess, commonly identified in antiquity with Demeter. **2.** (*Astron.*) the largest of the asteroids, and the first to be discovered (1 Jan. 1801).

cerise /sə'riːz/ adj. & n. light clear red. [F, = cherry]

cerium /'sɪərɪəm/ n. a soft iron-grey metallic element of the lanthanide series, symbol Ce, atomic number 58. The most abundant of the rare-earth elements, cerium was first isolated in pure form in 1875, although as a mixture with other rare earths it had been identified by Berzelius and others at the beginning of the 19th c. The pure metal is alloyed to make cigarette-lighter flints, and cerium dioxide is widely used for polishing glass. [f. CERES, asteroid discovered (1801) just before the element]

certain /'sɜːt(ə)n/ adj. **1.** feeling sure, convinced. **2.** known without doubt; that can be relied on to happen, be effective, etc. **3.** that will not be further specified or defined. **4.** small in amount but definitely there. [f. OF f. L *certus* settled]

certainly adv. without doubt; yes. [f. prec.]

certainty n. **1.** an undoubted fact; an indubitable prospect. **2.** absolute conviction. [f. AF (as CERTAIN)]

certifiable /'sɜːtɪfaɪəb(ə)l/ adj. that can be certified. [f. CERTIFY]

certificate /sə'tɪfɪkət/ n. an official written or printed statement attesting certain facts. —**certificated** adj., **certification** /-ˈkeɪʃ(ə)n/ n. [f. F or L (as foll.)]

certify /ˈsɜːtɪfaɪ/ v.t. to state formally on a certificate; to declare (a person) officially to be insane. [f. OF f. L (as CERTAIN)]

certitude /ˈsɜːtɪtjuːd/ n. a feeling of certainty. [as prec.]

cerulean /səˈruːlɪən/ adj. sky-blue. [f. L caeruleus (caelum sky)]

Cervantes /sɜːˈvæntiːz/, Miguel de (1547-1616) (full surname Cervantes Saavedra), Spanish novelist and dramatist, born of an ancient and impoverished family. He lost the use of his left hand at the battle of Lepanto (1571), was captured by pirates (1575), and spent the next five years as a prisoner in Algiers. The rest of his life was spent trying to earn a living from literature and humble government employment. His first novel La Galatea (1585) was followed by his masterpiece Don Quixote (1605, 1615), a satirical romance about an amiable knight who imagines himself called upon to roam the world in search of adventure on his horse Rosinante, accompanied by the shrewd squire Sancho Panza. Don Quixote and Quixotism have been described as the genius of the Spanish nation but he has been adopted by many other countries, is the source of plots of several 17th-c. English plays, and continues to inspire innumerable imitations. Among Cervantes' other surviving works are sixteen plays and Novelas Ejemplares (1613; short stories).

cervix /ˈsɜːvɪks/ n. (pl. **-vices** /-vɪsiːz/) the neck; a necklike structure, especially the opening of the womb (ill. BODY 2). —**cervical** /səˈvaɪk(ə)l, ˈsɜːvɪk(ə)l/ adj. [L]

Cesarewitch /sɪˈzærəwɪtʃ, -ˈzaːr-/ a handicap horse-race run annually at Newmarket in Suffolk, England, in late October, inaugurated in 1839 and named in honour of the state visit of the Russian prince who became Alexander II. [f. Russ. tsesarévich title of heir to Russian throne]

cessation /seˈseɪʃ(ə)n/ n. ceasing; a pause. [f. L (cessare cease)]

cession /ˈseʃ(ə)n/ n. the act of ceding. [f. OF or L (as CEDE)]

cesspit /ˈsespɪt/ n. a covered pit for temporary storage of liquid waste or sewage. [f. foll.]

cesspool /ˈsespuːl/ n. = prec. [perh. alt. f. earlier cesperalle f. suspiral water-pipe]

cetacean /sɪˈteɪʃ(ə)n/ n. a member of the mammalian order Cetacea, containing whales, dolphins, and porpoises. —adj. of cetaceans. [f. L f. Gk kētos whale]

cetane /ˈsiːteɪn/ n. a hydrocarbon of the paraffin series, found in petroleum. [f. SPERMACETI]

Ceylon /sɪˈlɒn/ the former name (until 1972) of Sri Lanka.

Cézanne /seɪˈzæn/, Paul (1839-1906), French painter, associated with the impressionists but concerned less with fleeting impressions than with the structural analysis of nature, which made him a forerunner of cubism. Born in Aix-en-Provence, he was a schoolfellow of Zola, who introduced him to Manet and Courbet. He exhibited with the impressionists in 1874 and 1877, and was closest to Pissarro, near whose home he settled in 1872. His work, consisting mainly of still life and landscape, is dominated by his search for the cube, the cone, and the cylinder in nature. An exhibition in 1895 strengthened his influence on the younger French artists, and his painting became known in England through the Post-Impressionist exhibitions of 1910 and 1912, where it was made the foundation of the new aesthetic attitude of Clive Bell and Roger Fry, emphasizing pure form, which dominated English criticism in the 1930s.

Cf symbol californium.

cf. abbr. compare. [f. L confer]

Chablis /ˈʃæbliː/ n. a white burgundy. [f. Chablis in E. France]

Chad an inland country in north central Africa, bordering in the north on Libya; pop. (est.) 4,000,000; official language, French; capital, Ndjaména. Much of the northern area is desert, merging into the Sahara, but there are mineral deposits of uranium, tungsten, and perhaps oil. The population comprises a remarkable mixture of peoples, languages, and religions, living mainly by agriculture with cotton as the chief crop. French expeditions entered the region in 1890, and by 1913 the country was organized as a French colony. It became autonomous within the French Community in 1958, and fully independent as a republic in 1960. —**Chadian** adj. & n.

chadar, chador ns. variants of CHUDDAR.

Chadic /ˈtʃædɪk/ adj. of a group of languages spoken in the region of Lake Chad in north central Africa, of which the most important is Hausa.

Chadwick /ˈtʃædwɪk/, Sir James (1891-1974), English physicist, appointed in 1923 as assistant director to Rutherford at the Cavendish Laboratory, Cambridge, where he researched the artificial disintegration (transmutation) of elements such as beryllium when bombarded by alpha particles, which led, in 1932, to the discovery of the neutron, for which he received the 1935 Nobel Prize for physics. In the Second World War he was involved with the atomic bomb project, and afterwards stressed the importance of university research into nuclear physics.

chafe /tʃeɪf/ v.t./i. 1. to rub (the skin etc.) to restore warmth. 2. to make or become sore by rubbing. 3. to become irritated or impatient. [f. OF chauffer f. L calefacere make warm]

chafer /ˈtʃeɪfə(r)/ n. a large slow-moving beetle, especially a cockchafer. [OE]

chaff /tʃɑːf/ n. 1. corn-husks separated from the seed by threshing etc.; chopped hay or straw as cattle-food; worthless stuff. 2. good-humoured teasing or joking. —v.t. to tease or joke in a good-humoured way. [OE]

chaffer /ˈtʃæfə(r)/ v.i. to bargain or haggle. [OE]

chaffinch /ˈtʃæfɪntʃ/ n. a common European finch (Fringilla coelebs). [OE (as CHAFF, FINCH)]

chafing-dish /ˈtʃeɪfɪŋ/ n. a pan with a heater under it for cooking food or keeping it warm at the table. [f. CHAFE]

Chagall /ʃəˈgɑːl/, Marc (1887-1985), Russian-born painter, of Jewish family, who from 1910 spent most of his working life in Paris, where he joined the avant-garde circle of Soutine, Delaunay, and Modigliani. He returned to Russia and set up an art school in 1917, but his style of painting—imaginative, inspired by folk art and by the more sophisticated naïveté of the fauves—was not acceptable to the authorities, and he returned to Paris in 1923; from 1941 to 1947 he lived in the USA. His achievements include graphic work (illustrations to Gogol's Dead Souls and La Fontaine's Fables, 1923-30), theatre design (the costumes and décor for Stravinsky's Firebird, 1945, murals for the Metropolitan Opera House, New York, 1966) and a series of paintings inspired by the Bible, culminating in 17 large pictures (now in a museum at Nice). His autobiography, Ma vie, was published in 1931.

chagrin /ˈʃægrɪn/ n. a feeling of annoyance and embarrassment or disappointment. —v.t. to affect with chagrin. [F]

Chain /tʃeɪn/, Sir Ernst Boris (1906-79), British biochemist, born in Germany. (See FLOREY.)

chain n. 1. a series of connected metal links or rings, used for hauling, supporting, or restraining things or worn as an ornament; a connected series or sequence. 2. a number of shops, hotels, etc., owned by a single company. 3. a unit of length for measuring land, 66 ft. (see GUNTER). —v.t. to fasten or restrain with a chain. —**chain-gang** n. a group of prisoners chained together for manual work. **chain-letter** n. a letter of which the recipient is asked to make copies and send these to others, who will do the same. **chain-mail** n. armour made from interlaced rings (ill. ARMOUR). **chain reaction**, a chemical or nuclear reaction the products of which themselves cause further reactions; a series of events in which each causes or influences the next. **chain-saw** n. a saw consisting of an endless loop of chain with teeth set in it. **chain-smoke** v.i to smoke many cigarettes in a continuous succession. **chain-stitch** n. an ornamental sewing or crochet stitch like a chain; a stitch made by a sewing machine using a single thread that is hooked through its own loop on the under-side of the fabric sewn. **chain store**, one of a series of shops owned by the same firm and selling similar goods. [f. OF f. L catena]

chair n. 1. a movable seat with a back, for one person. 2. a position of authority at a meeting, the chairmanship. 3. a professorship. 4. (US) the electric chair. —v.t. 1. to seat in a chair of honour. 2. to carry in triumph on the shoulders of a group. 3. to act as chairman of. —**chair-lift** n. a series of chairs suspended from an endless cable for carrying passengers up a mountain etc. [f. AF f. L f. Gk cathedra]

chairman n. (pl. **-men**) the person presiding over a meeting; the regular president of a committee, board of directors, etc. —**chairwoman** n. (pl. **-women**), **chairperson** n., **chairmanship** n.

chaise longue /ʃeɪz ˈlɒŋg/ a low chair with the seat long enough to support the sitter's legs. [F, = long chair]

Chalcedon /kælˈsiːd(ə)n/ a city in Asia Minor, where the fourth ecumenical council of the Church was held in 451, at which was drawn up the important statement of faith affirming the two natures, human and divine, united in the single person of Christ unconfusedly, unchangeably, indivisibly, and inseparably. —**Chalcedonian** /-sɪˈdəʊnɪən/ adj.

chalcedony /kælˈsed(ə)nɪ/ n. a type of quartz including many varieties of precious stone, e.g. onyx and jasper. [f. L f. Gk; both the origin of the name (which is unlikely to be from CHALCEDON) and its early application are obscure]

chalcolithic /kælkəˈlɪθɪk/ adj. of a period in which both stone and bronze implements were used. [f. Gk khalkos copper + lithos stone]

Chaldea /kælˈdiːə/ the country of the Chaldeans, the southern part of Babylonia (the names are virtually synonymous). [f. Assyrian Kaldu]

Chaldean /kælˈdiːən/ adj. of the Chaldeans or their language. —n. **1.** a member of a Semitic people originating from Arabia, who settled in the neighbourhood of Ur c.800 BC and ruled Babylonia 625-538 BC. They were famous as astronomers. The biblical reference to 'Ur of the Chaldees' in the time of Abraham is an anachronism. **2.** their Semitic language. [f. prec.]

Chaldee /kælˈdiː/ n. a Chaldean. [f. L (as prec.)]

chalet /ˈʃæleɪ/ n. **1.** a Swiss mountain hut or cottage; a house in similar style. **2.** a small hut in a holiday camp etc. [Swiss F]

chalice /ˈtʃælɪs/ n. a vessel like a large goblet for holding wine, one from which wine is drunk at the Eucharist (ill. VESTMENTS). [f. OF f. L calix cup]

chalk /tʃɔːk/ n. a white soft limestone used for burning into lime; a stick of this or similar substance, white or coloured, used for writing or drawing. —v.t. to mark, draw, rub, etc., with chalk. —**by a long chalk**, by far. **chalk-stripe** n. a textile pattern of thin white stripes on a dark background. **chalk up**, to register (a success etc.). —**chalky** adj. [OE f. L CALX]

challenge /ˈtʃælɪndʒ/ n. **1.** a call to demonstrate one's ability or strength, especially in a contest. **2.** a call or demand to respond, a sentry's call for a person to identify himself. **3.** a formal objection, e.g. to a juryman. **4.** a challenging task. —v.t. **1.** to issue a challenge to. **2.** to raise a formal objection to. **3.** to question the truth or rightness of. **4.** (abs., usu. in partic.) to offer problems that test one's abilities, to be stimulating. —**challenger** n. [f. OF f. L calumnia calumny]

Challenger Deep /ˈtʃælɪndʒə(r)/ the deepest part of the Mariana Trench in the Pacific Ocean, discovered by HMS Challenger II in 1948 (ill. SEA).

chalybeate /kəˈlɪbɪət/ adj. (of water or springs) impregnated with iron salts. [f. L f. Gk khalups steel]

chamber /ˈtʃeɪmbə(r)/ n. **1.** an assembly hall; the council or other body that meets in it. **2.** (in pl.) a set of rooms in a larger building, a judge's room for hearing cases that do not need to be taken in court. **3.** a cavity or compartment in the body of an animal or plant, or in machinery. **4.** (archaic) a room, especially a bedroom. —**chamber music**, music written for a small number of players, suitable for performing in a room or small hall. **Chamber of Commerce**, an association of business men etc. to promote local commercial interests. **chamber-pot** n. a receptacle for urine etc., used in the bedroom. [f. OF f. L camera vaulted chamber]

Chamberlain[1] /ˈtʃeɪmbəlɪn/, Arthur Neville (1869-1940), son of Joseph Chamberlain. A Conservative MP from 1918, he succeeded Baldwin as Prime Minister in 1937 and proved a strong leader, but his policy of personal diplomacy and appeasement of Hitler caused increasing discontent in his own party. Although Chamberlain is unfairly blamed for failing to prevent a war which was almost certainly inevitable, his war leadership was certainly inadequate and in May 1940 he was replaced by Winston Churchill.

Chamberlain[2] /ˈtʃeɪmbəlɪn/, Joseph (1836-1914), a successful industrialist who became a Liberal MP (1876), leaving the party in 1886 because of Gladstone's support of Irish Home Rule and leading the Liberal Unionists into an alliance with the Conservatives. As Colonial Secretary he was the spokesman for imperialist interests, playing a leading role in the Second Boer War.

chamberlain /ˈtʃeɪmbəlɪn/ n. an official managing a royal or noble household. [f. OF f. Gmc (as CHAMBER)]

chambermaid n. a woman employed to clean and tidy bedrooms in a hotel etc.

Chambers /ˈtʃeɪmbəz/, Sir William (1723-96), architect, born in Sweden of Scottish parents, founder-member of

the British Royal Academy and designer of Somerset House in London (1776). Travels in the Far East and studies in France and Italy helped to mould his eclectic but conservative style.

chameleon /kəˈmiːlɪən/ n. **1.** a small lizard able to change colour according to its surroundings. **2.** a changeable or inconstant person. [f. L. f. Gk, = ground-lion]

chamfer /ˈtʃæmfə(r)/ v.t. to bevel symmetrically. —n. a chamfered edge or corner. [f. F (chant edge, fraint broken)]

chamois /ˈʃæmwɑː/ n. **1.** (pl. same /-wɑːz/) a small wild antelope of goat size, found in the mountains of Europe and Asia. **2.** /ˈʃæmɪ/ (also **chamois-leather**) soft yellowish leather from sheep, goats, deer, etc., or a piece of this, used for washing or polishing things. [F]

chamomile var. of CAMOMILE.

champ v.t./i. **1.** to munch noisily; to make a chewing action or noise. **2.** to show impatience. [imit.]

champagne /ʃæmˈpeɪn/ n. **1.** a naturally sparkling white wine from Champagne in France; a similar wine from elsewhere. **2.** a pale straw colour. [f. Champagne, former province in E. France]

champion /ˈtʃæmpɪən/ n. **1.** (freq. attrib.) a person or thing that has defeated or surpassed all rivals in a competition. **2.** a person who fights or argues in support of another or of a cause. —v.t. to support as a champion. [f. OF f. L campio fighter (campus field)]

championship n. **1.** the status of a champion in a sport etc.; a contest held to decide the champion. **2.** advocacy, defence (of a cause etc.). [f. prec. + -SHIP]

Champlain /ʃæmˈpleɪn/, Samuel de (1567-1635), French explorer and colonial statesman. Champlain began his seaborne career in the service of Spain, but later entered French service, making his first voyage to Canada in 1603. Between 1604 and 1607 he explored the eastern seaboard of North America and in 1608 established the colony of Quebec, of which he became Lieutenant Governor. Much of his subsequent career was spent exploring the Canadian interior and defending his settlements against hostile Indians. After his capture and imprisonment by the English (1629-32), he returned to Canada for a final spell as Governor (1633-5).

champlevé /ˈʃɑ̃ləveɪ/ adj. of or using a style of enamel-work decoration in which hollows are made in a metal surface and filled with enamel. —n. this style. [F, = raised field]

chance /tʃɑːns/ **1.** the way things happen without known cause or agency; the supposed force governing such happenings, luck, fate. **2.** a possibility, likelihood. **3.** an opportunity. —adj. happening by chance. —v.t./i. **1.** to happen by chance. **2.** to take one's chance of, to risk. —**by chance**, as it turns or turned out; without being planned. **chance on**, to come upon or find by chance. **chance one's arm**, (colloq.) to take a chance although failure is possible. **take a chance**, to take a risk, to act in the hope that a particular thing will (or will not) happen. **take chances**, to behave riskily. **take one's chance**, to trust to luck. [f. AF f. L cadere fall]

chancel /ˈtʃɑːns(ə)l/ n. the part of a church, often screened off, containing the altar (ill. CHURCH). [f. OF f. L cancelli grating]

chancellor /ˈtʃɑːns(ə)lə(r)/ n. **1.** a State or law official of various kinds; the chief minister of State in West Germany and Austria. **2.** the non-resident head of a university. —**Chancellor of the Exchequer**, the finance minister of the UK, who prepares the budget. His office dates from the reign of Henry III, and was originally that of assistant to the treasurer of the Exchequer; it has become of prime importance since that of Treasurer came to be held not by an individual but by the Lords Commissioners of the Treasury (see TREASURY). [f. AF f. L cancellarius secretary]

chancellery /ˈtʃɑːns(ə)lərɪ/ n. **1.** a chancellor's department, residence, or staff. **2.** = CHANCERY 2. [f. foll.]

Chancery /ˈtʃɑːnsərɪ/ n. the Lord Chancellor's division of the High Court of Justice. [contr. of CHANCELLERY]

chancery /ˈtʃɑːnsərɪ/ n. **1.** a public records office. **2.** an office attached to an embassy or consulate. [= prec.]

chancy /ˈtʃɑːnsɪ/ adj. risky, uncertain. [f. CHANCE]

chandelier /ʃændəˈlɪə(r)/ n. an ornamental branched support for a number of lights, hung from a ceiling. [f. F (as CANDLE)]

Chandigarh /tʃʌndɪˈɡɑː(r)/ a Union Territory in India created in 1966; a city in this Territory, capital of Punjab.

chandler /ˈtʃɑːndlə(r)/ n. a dealer in ropes, canvas, and other supplies for ships. [f. F (CANDLE)]

change /tʃeɪndʒ/ v.t./i. 1. to make or become different; to pass from one form or phase into another. 2. to take or use another instead of; to put fresh clothes or coverings etc. on; to go from one (vehicle, route, etc.) to another; to exchange. 3. to give small money in change for; to give different currency for. —n. 1. changing, alteration; money in small units; money returned as the balance when the price is less than the amount tendered. 3. the menopause. 4. (in bell-ringing, usu. in pl.) the different orders in which the bells of a peal may be rung. —**change hands**, to pass to a new owner. **change of heart**, a great alteration in one's attitude or feelings. **change of life**, the menopause. **change one's mind**, to adopt a new purpose or way of thinking. **change over**, to change from one system or situation to another. **change-over** n. such a change. **change-ringing** n. ringing a peal of bells in a series of different orders. [f. AF f. L cambire barter]

changeable /ˈtʃeɪndʒəb(ə)l/ adj. liable to change, inconstant. [f. prec.]

changeling /ˈtʃeɪndʒlɪŋ/ n. a child or thing believed to have been substituted secretly for another, especially by elves etc. [f. CHANGE + -LING]

channel n. 1. the sunken bed of a watercourse; the navigable part of a waterway. 2. a piece of water (wider than a strait) connecting two seas. 3. a passage along which a liquid may flow; a sunken course or line along which something may move. 4. any course by which news or information etc. may travel. 5. a band of broadcasting frequencies reserved for a particular programme. 6. a path for transmitting electrical signals or (in computers) data. —v.t. (-ll-) 1. to form channels or grooves in. 2. to direct along a channel or desired route. —**the Channel**, the English Channel (see ENGLISH). [f. OF f. L canalis canal]

Channel Islands a group of islands in the English Channel off the NW coast of France, of which the largest are Jersey, Guernsey, and Alderney. They are the only portions of the former dukedom of Normandy that still owe allegiance to England, to which they have been attached since the Norman Conquest in 1066.

Channel Tunnel a proposed tunnel under the English Channel, linking the coasts of England and France. Such a scheme was first put forward in 1802 by a French engineer, who perceived the possibility of tunnelling through the layer of soft chalk rock that is continuous from one side of the Channel to the other. Napoleon showed interest, but Britain was again at war with France in 1803 and no move was made. The proposal was revived again at intervals and digging actually started in 1882, but fear of invasion from the Continent brought hostile reaction in Britain until the 1950s, when the development of air power and guided missiles had made the Channel no longer the natural defence that it had been hitherto.

Chanson de Geste /ʃɑ̃sɔ̃ də ˈʒest/ any of a group of French historical verse romances, mostly connected with Charlemagne, composed in the 11th–13th c. [F, = song of heroic deeds]

chant /tʃɑːnt/ n. 1. a melody for psalms and other unmetrical texts, in which an indefinite number of syllables are sung to one opening note. 2. a measured monotonous song. —v.t. to sing, especially a chant; to shout or call rhythmically. [f. OF f. L cantare sing]

chanter n. 1. one who chants. 2. the melody-pipe of bagpipes. [f. prec.]

chanterelle /ʃɑːntəˈrel/ n. a yellow edible funnel-shaped fungus (Cantharellus cibarius). [F, f. L f. Gk kantharos drinking-vessel]

chantry /ˈtʃɑːntrɪ/ n. a chapel endowed for the saying of masses for the founder's soul. [f. AF (chanter chant)]

Chanute /ˈʃænuːt/, Octave (1832–1910), Franco-American aviation pioneer, who went to America at the age of 6. Educated as a railway engineer, he built the first glider in 1896 and later produced others of which the most successful was the biplane type which made over 700 flights without accident and inspired the Wright brothers. His encouragement to them and to the serious study of aeronautics greatly assisted them in making the world's first controlled powered flight on 17 Dec. 1903.

chaos /ˈkeɪɒs/ n. 1. utter confusion or disorder. 2. formless primordial matter. —**chaotic** /-ˈɒtɪk/ adj., **chaotically** adv. [F or L f. Gk]

chap[1] n. (colloq.) a man, a fellow. [abbr. of archaic chapman pedlar]

chap[2] v.t./i. (-pp-) (of skin) to split or crack, (of wind etc.) to cause to develop chaps. —n. (usu. in pl.) a crack in the skin. [perh. rel. to Du. kappen chop off]

chap[3] n. the lower jaw or half of the cheek, especially of a pig, as food. [var. of CHOP[3]; orig. unkn.]

chaparral /tʃæpəˈræl, ʃæ-/ n. (US) dense tangled brushwood, especially in the south-western USA and Mexico. [Sp. (chaparra evergreen oak)]

chapati, chapatti variants of CHUPATTY.

chap-book n. (hist.) a small pamphlet of tales, ballads, tracts, etc., hawked by chapmen. [as CHAPMAN]

chapel /ˈtʃæp(ə)l/ n. 1. a place used for Christian worship, other than a cathedral or parish church; a service in this. 2. a separate part of a cathedral or church, with its own altar. 3. a section of a trade union in a printing works. The name reflects the early connection of printing with the production of religious texts. [f. OF f. L, dim. of cappa cloak; the first chapel was a sanctuary in which St Martin's sacred cloak was kept by capellani (chaplains)]

chaperon /ˈʃæpərəʊn/ n. an older or married woman in charge of a young unmarried woman on social occasions. —v.t. to act as a chaperon to —**chaperonage** n. [F, = hood]

chaplain /ˈtʃæplɪn/ n. a clergyman attached to a private chapel, institution, regiment, ship, etc. —**chaplaincy** n. [f. AF f. L (see CHAPEL)]

chaplet /ˈtʃæplɪt/ n. 1. a wreath for the head. 2. a short rosary. [f. OF f. L cappa cap]

Chaplin /ˈtʃæplɪn/, Sir Charles Spencer ('Charlie') (1889–1977), English film actor and director, considered by many the greatest screen mimic and clown. In 1914 he made 35 short slapstick comedies, mostly playing the Tramp, which remained his usual characterization for more than 25 years. He soon achieved world-wide fame, making his first full-length film The Kid in 1921. The peak of his career was marked by The Gold Rush (1925), The Circus (1928), and City Lights (1931), all of which—like Modern Times (1936) and The Great Dictator (1940), his first sound film and his last appearance as a tramp—he also directed. His four later films were of less interest.

Chapman /ˈtʃæpmən/, George (c. 1560–1634), English poet and dramatist. He is chiefly known for his translation of Homer, animated by 'a daring fiery spirit' (Pope) and commemorated in a sonnet by Keats, but Swinburne and others have drawn attention to the remarkable quality of his dramatic works. Chapman was renowned as a scholar and is perhaps the 'rival poet' of Shakespeare's 'Sonnets'.

chapman n. (pl. -men) (hist.) a pedlar. [OE (cēap barter, MAN)]

chapter /ˈtʃæptə(r)/ n. 1. a division of a book; (fig.) a period of time. 2. the canons of a cathedral or the monks of a particular order etc.; a meeting of these. —**chapter house**, a building used for such meetings. [f. OF f. L capitulum, dim. of caput head]

char[1] v.t./i. (-rr-) to make or become black by burning; to burn to charcoal. [back-formation f. CHARCOAL]

char[2] n. a charwoman. —v.t. (-rr-) to work as a charwoman. [earlier chare f. OE cerr a turn]

char[3] n. (pl. same) a small trout of the genus Salvelinus. [orig. unkn.]

charabanc /ˈʃærəbæŋ/ n. a long vehicle, originally horse-drawn and open, later an early form of motor coach, with seating on transverse benches facing forward. [f. F char-à-bancs benched carriage]

character /ˈkærɪktə(r)/ n. 1. the distinguishing qualities of a person, group, or thing; a person's moral qualities; moral strength. 2. reputation; good reputation. 3. a person having specified qualities; an eccentric. 4. a person in a play, novel, etc. 5. a description of a person's qualities, a testimonial. 6. (often in pl.) an inscribed letter or graphic symbol, as in an alphabet. 7. a physical characteristic of a biological species. [f. OF f. L f. Gk, = stamp, impression]

characteristic /kærɪktəˈrɪstɪk/ adj. distinctive of a particular individual, class, etc. —n. a characteristic feature or quality. —**characteristically** adv. [f. F (as prec.)]

characterize /ˈkærɪktəraɪz/ v.t. 1. to sum up the qualities of. 2. to be characteristic of. —**characterization** /-ˈzeɪʃ(ə)n/ n. [f. F or L f. Gk (as CHARACTER)]

charade /ʃəˈrɑːd/ n. 1. (in pl.) a game in which a word has to be guessed from clues to each syllable given in acted scenes. 2. an absurd pretence. [F f. Prov. (charra chatter)]

charcoal /'tʃɑːkəʊl/ *n.* the black carbonized residue of partially burnt wood etc., ued as a filtering material, as fuel, or for drawing. —**charcoal grey**, very dark grey. [rel. to COAL]

charge *n.* **1.** the price asked for goods or services. **2.** a formal accusation. **3.** an admonition given about one's duty or responsibility; a task or duty. **4.** custody. **5.** an impetuous attack in battle etc. **6.** the quantity of material used in an apparatus in a single operation, especially of explosive in a gun. **7.** the amount of electricity contained in a substance; energy stored chemically for conversion into electricity. **8.** a heraldic device or bearing. —*v.t./i.* **1.** to ask as a price; to ask (a person) for a price; to debit (a cost) *to* an account. **2.** to accuse formally of a crime. **3.** to entrust *with* a task; to admonish *to*. **4.** to advance impetuously; to attack thus. **5.** to give an electric charge to; to store energy in; to load with the requisite amount of explosive etc. **6.** to saturate with liquid, vapour, or chemical. —**in charge**, in command. **take charge,** to take control. [f. OF f. L *carricare* load (*carrus* car)]

chargé d'affaires /ʃɑːʒeɪ dæˈfeə(r)/ (*pl.* **-és** /-eɪ/) an ambassador's deputy; an envoy to a minor country. [F, = entrusted with affairs]

Charge of the Light Brigade a British cavalry charge during the battle of Balaclava in the Crimean War. A misunderstanding between the commander of the Light Brigade, Lord Cardigan, and his superiors, Lords Raglan and Lucan, led to the British cavalry being committed to an attack up a valley heavily held on three sides by the Russians. Immortalized in verse by Tennyson, the charge in fact decimated some of the finest light cavalry in the world to very little military purpose.

charger *n.* **1.** a cavalry horse. **2.** an apparatus for charging a battery. [f. CHARGE]

chariot /'tʃærɪət/ *n.* a two-wheeled horse-drawn vehicle used in ancient warfare and racing. Chariots were known in Mesopotamia from the end of the 3rd millennium BC, and spread from there to Europe and Asia. —**charioteer** /-ɪəˈtɪə(r)/ *n.* [f. OF (*char* car)]

charisma /kəˈrɪzmə/ *n.* the capacity to inspire devotion and enthusiasm; divinely conferred power or talent. —**charismatic** /kærɪzˈmætɪk/ *adj.* [L f. Gk (*kharis* favour, grace)]

charitable /'tʃærɪtəb(ə)l/ *adj.* **1.** generous in giving to those in need; lenient in judging others. **2.** connected with organized charities. —**charitably** *adv.* [f. foll.]

charity /'tʃærɪti/ *n.* **1.** kindness or voluntary giving to those in need; an organization for helping those in need; help so given. **2.** leniency in judging others; love towards others. [f. OF f. L *caritas* (*carus* dear)]

charlady *n.* a charwoman. [f. CHAR²]

charlatan /'ʃɑːlətən/ *n.* one falsely claiming to have a special knowledge or skill. —**charlatanism** *n.* [F f. It., = babbler]

Charlemagne /'ʃɑːləmeɪn/ (742–814), military and political colossus of the Dark Ages, who ruled the Franks in northern Europe 768–814. Famed in legend for being defeated at Roncesvalles, his successful conquests were prodigious. Had he not conquered the Saxons, whom he severely Christianized, and the Bavarians, Germany could hardly have come into existence. He gave to government new moral drive and religious responsibility. The political cohesion of his empire could not last, but the influence of his court scholars persisted in the Carolingian Renaissance. His coronation by Pope Leo III in Rome on Christmas Day, 800, is taken to have inaugurated the Holy Roman Empire, though he himself despised 'Babylonic pride' in rulers and remained at heart a Frank.

Charles¹ /tʃɑːlz/ the name of two kings of Britain:
Charles I (1600–49), son of James I, reigned 1625–49. His reign was dominated by the deepening religious and constitutional crisis that eventually resulted in the English Civil War. The King's attempt to rule without Parliament (1629–40) eventually failed when he became involved in war with Scotland, and the Long Parliament proved so uncooperative that an open breach and war between the two sides followed in 1642. The King was finally defeated and surrendered to the Scots in 1646. Handed over to Parliament in 1647, he escaped and negotiated with the Scots to fight on his behalf in return for religious concessions, but the Royalist forces were defeated at Preston (1648) and the English army demanded Charles's death. He was tried by a special parliamentary court and beheaded in London in January 1649.

Charles II (1630–85), son of Charles I, reigned 1660–85. After his father's death Charles II was crowned in Scotland, but was forced into exile after the defeat of his invading army at Worcester in 1651. He remained in exile on the Continent for nine years before he was restored after the collapse of Cromwell's regime in 1660. Charles displayed considerable adroitness in handling the difficult constitutional situation left by the preceding two decades of strife, but his failure to produce a Protestant heir left the future of the Stuart dynasty in doubt after his death.

Charles² /tʃɑːlz/ the name of ten kings of France:
Charles VII (1403–61), reigned 1422–61. His reign witnessed the final defeat of the English forces in France and the end of the Hundred Years War. At the time of his father's death, the English were in firm occupation of much of northern France, including Reims (thus denying Charles his coronation). After the intervention of Joan of Arc, however, the French experienced a dramatic military revival. Charles was crowned in 1429 and the English gradually driven out until in 1453 only Calais remained in their hands. Charles achieved a considerable modernization of the administration of the army and did a great deal to lay the foundations of French power in the following decades, being so well aided in these and other tasks as to earn the sobriquet 'the Well-Served'.

Charles³ /tʃɑːlz/ the name of four kings of Spain:
Charles I (1500–58), reigned 1516–56, Holy Roman Emperor (as Charles V) 1519–56. The son of Philip I of Spain and grandson of the Emperor Maximilian I, Charles came to the throne of Spain in 1516 and united it with that of the Empire when he inherited the latter in 1519. Tied down by such wide responsibilities, Charles was never able to give proper consideration or attention to national and international problems. In Germany his reign was characterized by the struggle against the newly formed Protestant religion, in Spain he had to confront a serious revolt in Castile, and for most of his reign he was engaged in a war with France (1521–44). Exhausted by these struggles, Charles handed Naples (1554), the Netherlands (1555), and Spain (1556) over to his son Philip II and the imperial crown (1556) to his brother Ferdinand, and retired to a monastery in Spain.
Charles II (1661–1700), reigned 1665–1700. The last Hapsburg to be king of Spain, Charles inherited a kingdom already in the throes of decline and proved unequal to the task of regenerating it. His choice of Philip of Anjou, grandson of Louis XIV of France, as his successor brought on the War of the Spanish Succession, which began after his death.
Charles IV (1748–1819), reigned 1788–1808. A weak ruler, Charles was dominated by his mother Maria Louisa and his favourite Manuel de Godoy (Prime Minister from 1792). He was unable to stand up to Napoleon, with the result that his fleet was destroyed along with that of France at Trafalgar in 1805. Following the French invasion of Spain in 1807, Charles was forced to abdicate. He died in exile in Rome.

Charles⁴ /tʃɑːlz/ (1682–1718), king of Sweden (as Charles XII) 1697–1718. One of the most accomplished soldier-kings of his time, Charles embarked on the Great Northern War, three years after his accession, against the encircling powers of Denmark, Poland-Saxony, and Russia. In the early years he won a series of brilliant victories, most notably against the Russians at Narva in 1700, but in 1709 he embarked on an ill-fated expedition deep into Russia which ended in disaster at Poltava. Following the destruction of his army, Charles was interned in Turkey until 1715, leaving his country to fight on leaderless against almost all the surrounding nations. He resumed his military career after his return but was killed while besieging the Norwegian fortress of Fredrikshald in 1718.

Charleston /'tʃɑːlstən/ *n.* a lively American dance of the 1920s, with side-kicks from the knee. [f. *Charleston* in S. Carolina]

charlock /'tʃɑːlɒk/ *n.* a mustardlike weed (*Sinapis arvensis*) with yellow flowers. [OE]

charlotte /'ʃɑːlɒt/ *n.* **1.** a pudding made of stewed apple or other fruit with a covering or layer of crumbs, biscuits, etc. **2.** a moulded dessert consisting of a creamy filling enclosed in sponge fingers. [F]

Charlotte Dundas /ʃɑːlət dʌnˈdæs/ the first vessel to use steam propulsion commercially, built on the River Clyde. The engine drove a single paddle-wheel and the ship made her first voyage in 1802.

charm *n.* **1.** attractiveness, the power of arousing love or admiration; an attractive feature. **2.** an act, object, or words believed to have occult power; a trinket on a bracelet etc. —*v.t.* **1.** to delight; to influence by personal charm. **2.** to influence by or as if by magic. —**charmer** *n.* [f. OF f. L *carmen* song, spell]

charming *adj.* delightfully attractive. —**charmingly** *adv.* [f. prec.]

charnel-house /ˈtʃɑːn(ə)l/ a place where the bodies or bones of the dead are kept. [F f. L (as CARNAL)]

Charollais /ˈʃærəleɪ/ *n.* a French breed of large white beef-cattle; an animal of this breed. [f. Monts du *Charollais* in E. France]

Charon /ˈkeərən/ (*Gk myth.*) the aged ferryman who, for a fee of one obol, ferried the souls of the dead across the rivers Styx and Acheron to Hades. It was usual for the Greeks to place a coin in the mouth of the dead for this fee.

chart *n.* **1.** a map for those navigating on water or in the air; an outline map for showing special information. **2.** a diagram, graph, or table giving information in tabular form; (in *pl.*) those listing the recordings currently most popular. —*v.t.* to make a chart of, to map. [f. F f. L *charta* card]

charter *n.* **1.** a document from a ruler or government, conferring rights or laying down a constitution. **2.** the chartering of an aircraft, ship, etc. —*v.t.* **1.** to grant a charter to; to found by charter. **2.** to let or hire (an aircraft, ship, etc.) for private use. —**chartered accountant, surveyor,** etc., one belonging to a professional body that has a royal charter. **charter flight,** a flight by chartered aircraft. [f. OF f. L, dim. of *charta* card]

Chartism *n.* a popular movement in Britain for electoral and social reform, 1837–48, whose principles were set out in a manifesto called *The People's Charter*. —**Chartist** *n.* [f. prec.]

chartreuse /ʃɑːˈtrɜːz/ *n.* **1.** a pale green or yellow aromatic brandy liqueur. **2.** its green colour. **3.** fruit enclosed in jelly. [f. *Chartreuse*, monastery near Grenoble]

charwoman *n.* (*pl.* -**women**) a woman hired by the hour to clean a house or other building. [f. CHAR²]

chary /ˈtʃeərɪ/ *adj.* cautious, wary; sparing *of*. [OE, rel. to CARE]

Charybdis /kəˈrɪbdɪs/ (*Gk legend*) a dangerous whirlpool in a narrow channel of the sea (later identified with the Strait of Messina, where there is no whirlpool), opposite the cave of Scylla.

chase¹ /tʃeɪs/ *v.t./i.* **1.** to go quickly after in order to capture, overtake, or drive away. **2.** to hurry. **3.** (*colloq.*) to try to attain. —*n.* **1.** chasing, pursuit; hunting, especially as a sport. **2.** unenclosed park-land, originally for hunting. [f. OF f. L *captare* (*capere* catch)]

chase² /tʃeɪs/ *v.t.* to engrave or emboss (metal). [f. F (as CASE²)]

chaser *n.* **1.** a horse for steeplechasing. **2.** a drink taken after another of a different kind. [f. CHASE¹]

chasm /ˈkæz(ə)m/ *n.* **1.** a very deep cleft in the ground etc. **2.** a wide difference of feeling, interests, etc. [f. L f. Gk, = gaping hollow]

chassis /ˈʃæsɪ, -iː/ *n.* (*pl.* **chassis** /-iːz/) the base-frame of a motor vehicle, carriage, etc.; a metal frame to carry radio etc. equipment. [f. F f. L (as CASE²)]

chaste /tʃeɪst/ *adj.* **1.** virgin, celibate; not having sexual intercourse except with one's spouse. **2.** simple in style, not ornate. —**chastely** *adv.* [f. OF f. L *castus*]

chasten /ˈtʃeɪs(ə)n/ *v.t.* to subdue the pride of. [f. OF f. L *castigare* castigate]

chastise /tʃæˈstaɪz/ *v.t.* to punish, especially by beating. —**chastisement** *n.* [app. rel. to prec.]

chastity /ˈtʃæstɪtɪ/ *n.* **1.** virginity, celibacy. **2.** simplicity of style. [f. OF f. L (*castus* chaste)]

chasuble /ˈtʃæzjʊb(ə)l/ *n.* a loose sleeveless outer vestment worn by a priest celebrating the Eucharist (ill. VESTMENTS). [f. OF, ult. f. L *casula* hooded cloak, dim. of *casa* cottage]

chat *n.* a friendly informal conversation. —*v.i.* (-**tt**-) to hold a chat. —**chat up,** (*colloq.*) to chat to a person flirtatiously or with a particular motive. **chat show,** a television programme in which people are interviewed. [f. CHATTER]

chateau /ˈʃætəʊ/ *n.* (*pl.* -**eaux** /-əʊz/) a large French country house or castle. [F, = castle]

Chateaubriand /ʃætəʊbriːˈɑ̃/, François-René, Vicomte de (1768–1848), French writer and diplomat, a major figure of early French romanticism. The Revolution interrupted his career and in 1791 he travelled to America, returning in 1792 to fight with the Royalists. Between 1793 and 1800 he lived in exile in England where he published his *Essai sur les révolutions* (1797). His literary reputation was established with *Atala* (1801) but he won great celebrity with *Le Génie du Christianisme* (1802), a work of Christian apologetics which contributed to the post-revolution religious revival in France. His political career began with the restoration of Louis XVIII—as a minister at Ghent, then as ambassador in London (1822). *Mémoires d'outre-tombe* (1849–50), considered a masterpiece, gives an eloquent account of the author's life against the background of political upheaval.

chatelaine /ˈʃæt(ə)leɪn/ *n.* **1.** the mistress of a large house. **2.** (*hist.*) a set of short chains attached to a woman's belt, for carrying keys etc. [F (as prec.)]

chattel /ˈtʃæt(ə)l/ *n.* (usu. in *pl.*) a movable possession (as opposed to a house or land). [f. OF (as CATTLE)]

chatter /ˈtʃætə(r)/ *v.i.* **1.** to talk quickly, incessantly, trivially, or indiscreetly. **2.** (of a bird) to emit short quick notes. **3.** (of the teeth) to click repeatedly together. —*n.* chattering talk or sound. [imit.]

chatterbox *n.* a talkative person.

Chatterton /ˈtʃætət(ə)n/, Thomas (1753–70), English poet with a precocious literary talent, chiefly remembered for his fabricated poems purported to be the work of Thomas Rowley, an imaginary 15th-c. monk. Poverty and lack of recognition drove him to suicide at the age of 17. The Rowley poems were first published in 1777 by Thomas Tyrwhitt and controversy about their authenticity continued until Skeat proved them to be spurious in his 1871 edition. Chatterton's tragic life had a powerful effect on the Romantic poets who followed.

chatty *adj.* **1.** fond of chatting. **2.** resembling chat. —**chattily** *adv.*, **chattiness** *n.* [f. CHAT]

Chaucer /ˈtʃɔːsə(r)/, Geoffrey (c.1342–1400), English poet, son of a London vintner. He held various positions at court and in the Customs service, and travelled to Europe on numerous diplomatic missions during which he may have met Boccaccio and Petrarch. He enjoyed the patronage of John of Gaunt (to whom he was related by marriage) and received pensions from Richard II and Henry IV. Chaucer translated part of the French poem, *Le Roman de la Rose*; his *The Book of the Duchess* (c.1370) was perhaps influenced by Dante's *Divine Comedy*. These poems, and *The Parliament of Fowls* (c.1380) are in the European dream allegory tradition; *Troilus and Criseyde* (1385) was based on Boccaccio's *Il Filostrato*. His best-known work, *The Canterbury Tales* (begun 1387), is a cycle of linked tales told by a group of pilgrims (ranging from Knight to Plowman, all vividly introduced in *The Prologue*) who meet in Southwark in London before their pilgrimage to Canterbury. Chaucer helped to establish the East Midland dialect of Middle English as the fully developed English literary language; many regard his work as the starting-point of English literature. He is buried in Poets' Corner in Westminster Abbey.

chauffeur /ˈʃəʊfə(r), ʃəʊˈfɜː(r)/ *n.* a person employed to drive a car. —*v.t.* to drive as chauffeur. —**chauffeuse** /-z/ *n.fem.* [F, = stoker]

chauvinism /ˈʃəʊvɪnɪz(ə)m/ *n.* **1.** exaggerated or aggressive patriotism. **2.** excessive or prejudiced support or loyalty for one's cause or group. —**chauvinist** *n.*, **chauvinistic** /-ˈnɪstɪk/ *adj.* [f. *Chauvin*, Napoleonic veteran, character in French play (1831)]

cheap *adj.* **1.** low in price, worth more than it cost; charging low prices, offering good value; **2.** poor in quality, of low value; showy but worthless, silly. —*adv.* cheaply. —**cheaply** *adv.*, **cheapness** *n.* [f. obs. phr. *good cheap* (*cheap* bargain, f. OE ult. f. L *caupo* innkeeper)]

cheapen *v.t./i.* to make or become cheap; to depreciate, to degrade. [f. prec.]

cheapjack *n.* a seller of shoddy goods at low prices. —*adj.* of poor quality, shoddy.

cheat *v.t./i.* to trick or deceive, to deprive *of* by trickery; to act fraudulently or dishonestly. —*n.* **1.** one who cheats. **2.** a deception, a fraud. [as ESCHEAT]

check¹ *n.* **1.** a stopping or slowing of motion, a pause; a loss of the scent in hunting. **2.** a restraint. **3.** a control to secure accuracy; a test or examination to see that something is correct or in good working order. **4.** a receipt; a bill in a restaurant. **5.** (*US*) a cheque. **6.** (in chess) exposure of a king to possible capture. —*v.t./i.* **1.** to stop or slow the motion of suddenly, to restrain; to make a sudden stop. **2.** to test or examine for correctness or good working order. **3.** (*US*) to correspond when compared. **4.** (in chess) to threaten (an opponent's king). —**check in,** to register one's arrival at a hotel, airport, etc. **check on** or **up** or **up on,** to examine or investigate the correctness, honesty, etc., of. **check out,** to leave a hotel, airport, etc., with proper formalities; to test (a possibility). **check-out** n. checking out; a place where goods are paid for by customers in a supermarket. **check-up** n. a thorough examination, especially a medical one. [f. OF, ult. f. Pers., = king]

check[2] n. a cross-lined pattern of small squares. [prob. f. CHEQUER]

checked adj. having a check pattern. [f. CHECK[2]]

checkers n.pl. (usu. treated as sing.) (US) the game of draughts. [var. of CHEQUER]

checkmate n. **1.** (in chess) a check from which the king cannot escape. **2.** a final defeat. —v.t. **1.** to put in checkmate. **2.** to defeat finally, to foil. [f. OF, ult. f. Pers. shāh māt the king is dead]

Cheddar /ˈtʃedə(r)/ n. a hard cheese of a kind originally made at Cheddar in Somerset.

cheek n. **1.** either side of the face below the eye. **2.** impudent speech; quiet arrogance. —v.t. to speak impudently to. —**cheek-bone** n. the bone below the eye. **cheek by jowl,** in juxtaposition. —**cheek-piece** n. a strap of a bridle passing over a horse's cheek (ill. HORSE). [OE]

cheeky adj. impertinent, saucy. —**cheekily** adv., **cheekiness** n. [f. CHEEK]

cheep n. the weak shrill cry of a young bird. —v.i. to make this cry. [imit.]

cheer n. **1.** a shout of encouragement or applause. **2.** cheerfulness. —v.t./i. **1.** to raise a cheer; to applaud or urge on with cheers. **2.** to comfort or gladden. —**cheer up,** to make or become more cheerful. [f. AF, = face, ult. f. Gk kara head]

cheerful adj. in good spirits, visibly happy; pleasantly bright. —**cheerfully** adv., **cheerfulness** n. [f. CHEER + -FUL]

cheerio /tʃɪərɪˈəʊ/ int. (colloq.) expressing good wishes on parting; goodbye. [f. CHEER]

cheerless adj. gloomy, comfortless. [f. CHEER + -LESS]

cheery adj. ebulliently cheerful. —**cheerily** adv. [f. CHEER]

cheese /tʃiːz/ n. **1.** a food made from milk curds or occasionally from whey; a shaped mass of this. **2.** a thick stiff jam. —**cheese-paring** adj. & n. stingy, stinginess. —**cheesy** adj. [OE, f. L caseus]

cheesecake n. a tart filled with sweetened curds.

cheesecloth n. a thin loosely woven cotton fabric.

cheetah /ˈtʃiːtə/ n. a very swift feline resembling a leopard, sometimes used in hunting. [Hindi, perh. f. Skr. chitraka speckled]

chef /ʃef/ n. a male cook (esp. the head cook) in a restaurant etc. [F, = head]

chef-d'œuvre /ʃeɪˈdɜːvr/ n. (pl. **chefs-d'œuvre,** pr. same) a masterpiece. [F]

Chekhov /ˈtʃekɒf/, Anton Pavlovich (1860–1904), Russian dramatist and short-story writer, who studied medicine in Moscow where he began writing short humorous stories for journals. His first successful play was Ivanov (1887) but his status rests on his four later plays, The Seagull (1895), Uncle Vanya (1900), The Three Sisters (1901), and The Cherry Orchard (1904). These productions established the reputation and style of the Moscow Arts Theatre, of which Stanislavsky was a co-founder; in 1901 Chekhov married Olga Knipper, an actress at the theatre. In his revolutionary form of drama, using innovative idiomatic dialogue where communication between characters can convey non-communication, and where the smallest surface details can adopt a symbolic significance, Chekhov had an immense influence on 20th-c. drama. Shaw paid tribute to him in Heartbreak House.

Chelsea /ˈtʃelsɪ/ n. **Chelsea bun,** a kind of rolled currant bun. **Chelsea pensioner,** an inmate of Chelsea Royal Hospital for old or disabled soldiers. **Chelsea ware,** a kind of porcelain made at Chelsea in the 18th c. [name of London borough]

chemical /ˈkemɪk(ə)l/ adj. of, using, or produced by chemistry or chemicals —n. a substance obtained by or used in a chemical process. —**chemical engineering,** the industrial applications of chemistry. **chemical warfare,** warfare using poison gas and other chemicals. —**chemically** adv. [f. F f. L (as ALCHEMY)]

chemise /ʃəˈmiːz/ n. a loose-fitting undergarment formerly worn by women, hanging straight from the shoulders; a dress of similar shape. [f. OF f. L camisia shirt]

chemist /ˈkemɪst/ n. **1.** a dealer in medicinal drugs etc. **2.** a scientist specializing in chemistry. [f. F (as ALCHEMIST)]

chemistry /ˈkemɪstrɪ/ n. **1.** the scientific study of substances and their elements and of how they react when combined, etc. **2.** the chemical properties, reactions, etc., of a substance. [f. prec.]

chemotherapy /keməʊˈθerəpɪ/ n. treatment of disease by drugs and other chemical substances. [f. CHEMICAL + THERAPY]

chenille /ʃəˈniːl/ n. a tufty velvety cord or yarn, used for trimming furniture; a fabric made from this. [F, = hairy caterpillar, f. L canicula little dog]

cheongsam /tʃɪɒŋˈsæm/ n. a Chinese woman's garment with a high neck and slit skirt. [Chinese]

Cheops /ˈkiːɒps/ n. KHUFU.

cheque /tʃek/ n. a written order for a bank to pay a stated sum from the drawer's account; a printed form for writing this. —**cheque-book** n. a book of printed forms for writing cheques. **cheque card,** a card issued by a bank, guaranteeing payment of cheques up to a stated amount. [var. of CHECK[1]]

chequer /ˈtʃekə(r)/ n. (chiefly in pl.) a pattern of squares of alternating colours, as on a chessboard. —v.t. **1.** to mark with such a pattern or variegate. **2.** to vary with different elements; (in p.p.) marked by vicissitudes of fortune. [f. EXCHEQUER]

Chequers /ˈtʃekəz/ a Tudor mansion in the Chilterns near Princes Risborough, Bucks., presented to the British nation in 1917 by Lord and Lady Lee of Fareham to serve as a country seat of the Prime Minister in office.

cherish /ˈtʃerɪʃ/ v.t. to tend lovingly; to be fond of; to cling to (a hope or feeling). [f. OF (cher f. L carus dear)]

cheroot /ʃəˈruːt/ n. a cigar with both ends open. [f. F f. Tamil]

Cherokee /ˈtʃerəkiː/ n. (pl. same) a member of an American Indian tribe formerly inhabiting much of the southern USA. [native name]

cherry /ˈtʃerɪ/ n. **1.** a small soft round stone-fruit. **2.** a tree of the genus Prunus bearing this or grown for its ornamental flowers; the wood of this tree. **3.** the bright red colour of ripe cherries. —adj. bright red. —**cherry brandy,** a liqueur of brandy in which cherries have been steeped. [f. OF f. L perh. f. Gk kerasos]

Chersonese /tʃɜːsəˈniːz/ the ancient name for (i) the Thracian or Gallipoli peninsula on the north side of the Hellespont, (ii) the Crimea (the Tauric Chersonese). [f. Gk khersonēsos peninsula]

chert /tʃɜːt/ n. a flintlike form of quartz. [orig. unkn.]

cherub /ˈtʃerəb/ n. **1.** (pl. **cherubim**) an angelic being of an order usually grouped with the seraphim. **2.** a representation, in art, of a winged chubby child; a pretty or well-behaved child. —**cherubic** /-ˈruːbɪk/ adj. [OE, f. Heb.]

Cherubini /keruˈbiːnɪ/, Luigi (1760–1842), Italian composer. Born in Florence, he spent most of his composing career in Paris, where he discarded the Italian operatic style in his attempts to create a truer drama involving less artificial characters; in this he was following the lead of Gluck, and when he visited Vienna in 1805 he in his turn influenced Beethoven (especially in Fidelio). Cherubini's sacred music (including seven Masses and two Requiem Masses) is scrupulous in its attention to the demands of the words.

chervil /ˈtʃɜːvɪl/ n. a herb (Anthriscus cerefolium) used to flavour salads etc. [OE f. L f. Gk khairephullon]

Ches. abbr. Cheshire.

Cheshire /ˈtʃeʃə(r)/ a north midlands county of England. —**Cheshire cheese,** a crumbly cheese originally made in Cheshire. **like a Cheshire cat,** with a broad fixed grin. The phrase was popularized through Lewis Carroll's Alice's Adventures in Wonderland (1865). Its origin is uncertain: suggested explanations include a reference to Cheshire cheeses made in the shape of a cat, or to the lion rampant on Cheshire inn-signs.

chess n. a game of skill played between two persons on a chequered board divided into 64 squares. Each player has 16 'men' (king, queen, 2 bishops, 2 knights, 2 castles or rooks, 8 pawns), which are moved according to strict rules in simulation of a battle where the object is to manœuvre the opponent's king into a position (checkmate) from which escape is impossible. Many moves are named after the great players who originated them. The game seems to be a descendant (5th c.) of an earlier Indian game and to have reached Persia and Arab countries and spread thence until by the 13th c. it was known all over western Europe. [f. OF *esches*, pl. of *eschec* (CHECK¹); in medieval Latin the game was called *scacci*, but Spanish and Portuguese preserved the Arabic name *chat-ranj* f. Skr. *chaturanga*, = the four *angas* or members of an army (elephants, horses, chariots, foot-soldiers)]

chessboard *n.* the board used in chess (see prec.).

chest *n.* **1.** a large strong box for storing or transporting things. **2.** the part of the body enclosed by the ribs and breast-bone; the upper front surface of the body. —**chest of drawers**, a piece of furniture consisting of a set of drawers in a frame, for storing clothes etc. [OE f. L f. Gk *kistē*]

chesterfield /'tʃestəfiːld/ *n.* a sofa with padded back, seat, and ends. [f. 19th-c. Earl of *Chesterfield*]

Chesterton /'tʃestət(ə)n/, Gilbert Keith (1874-1936), English essayist, novelist, and poet, who made his name in journalism. With Belloc he opposed the agnostic socialism of Wells and Shaw, praising the virtues of the Merry England of 'Beef and Beer'. His best-known novel is *The Napoleon of Notting Hill* (1904), but he is also widely remembered for his creation of detective priest Father Brown, who first appears in *The Innocence of Father Brown* (1911). Chesterton became a Roman Catholic in 1922.

chestnut /'tʃesnʌt/ *n.* **1.** a tree with hard brown nuts, those of the Spanish or sweet chestnut (*Castanea sativa*) being edible; its nut; the wood of this tree. **2.** deep reddish-brown. **3.** a horse of reddish-brown or yellowish-brown colour. **4.** a small hard patch on a horse's leg (ill. HORSE). **5.** an old joke or anecdote. —*adj.* deep reddish-brown or (of horses) yellowish-brown. [f. obs. *chesten* (f. OF f. L f. Gk *kastanea*) + NUT]

cheval-glass /ʃə'væl/ *n.* a tall mirror swung on an upright frame. [f. F *cheval* horse, frame]

chevalier /ʃevə'lɪə(r)/ *n.* a member of certain orders of knighthood, or of the French Legion of Honour etc. [f. AF f. L (*caballus* horse)]

Cheviot Hills /'tʃevɪət, 'tʃiː-/ (also **Cheviots**) a range of hills on the border between England and Scotland.

chevron /'ʃevrən/ *n.* a V-shaped line, stripe, or bar, especially one worn on the sleeve of a uniform to denote rank. [f. OF f. L *caper* goat; cf. L *capreoli* pair of rafters]

chew *v.t.* to work or grind between the teeth; to make this movement. —*n.* the act of chewing; something for chewing. —**chewing-gum** *n.* flavoured gum for prolonged chewing. **chew over**, (*colloq.*) to think over. [OE]

chez /ʃeɪ/ *prep.* at the home of. [F, f. OF f. L *casa* cottage]

chi /kaɪ/ *n.* the twenty-second letter of the Greek alphabet, = kh, ch.

Chiang Kai-shek /tʃjæŋ kaɪ'ʃek/ (1887-1975), Chinese leader who achieved military prominence as a general in the army of Sun Yat-sen, and after the latter's death in 1925 launched a campaign to unite China. In the 1930s he concentrated more on defeating the Chinese Communists than on resisting the invading Japanese, but despite his efforts he proved unable to establish order and was defeated by the Communists after the end of the Second World War. Forced to abandon mainland China in 1949, he set up a separate Nationalist Chinese State on Taiwan.

Chianti /kɪ'ænti/ *n.* a dry, usually red, Italian wine. [name of town in Tuscany]

chiaroscuro /kɪɑːrə'skʊərəʊ/ *n.* treatment of light and shade in painting; light and shade effects in nature. [It. (*chiaro* bright, *oscuro* dark)]

Chibcha /'tʃɪbtʃə/ *n.* (*pl.* same) a member or the language of an Indian people of Colombia with an ancient civilization that was flourishing at the time the Spaniards first encountered them in 1537; a member of this people. —*adj.* of the Chibcha or their language. —**Chibchan** *adj.* & *n.* [Sp.]

chic /ʃiːk/ *n.* fashionable elegance or stylishness in dress etc. —*adj.* fashionably elegant, stylish. [F]

Chicago /ʃɪ'kɑːgəʊ/ a city in Illinois, on Lake Michigan, the third largest city of the USA and the original home of the skyscraper; pop. (1982) 2,997,155.

chicane /ʃɪ'keɪn/ *v.t./i.* to practise or subject to chicanery; to trick. —*n.* **1.** chicanery. **2.** an artificial barrier on a motor-racing course etc. [F, = quibble]

chicanery /ʃɪ'keɪnəri/ *n.* quibbles or subterfuges used to gain an advantage. [f. F (as prec.)]

Chichén Itzá /tʃiː'tʃen ɪt'sɑː/ a site in northern Yucatan, Mexico, which was the centre of the Maya empire after AD

918, with elaborate ceremonial buildings centred on a sacred well.

Chichimec /tʃiː'tʃiːmek/ *n.* (*pl.* same) a member of a horde of invaders who entered the central valley of Mexico from the north west *c.*950-1300, and came to be known as the Toltec after the founding of their capital, Tula, in 968. In 1300 Chichimec farmers left their drought-stricken land and converged on Tula, contributing to its destruction. [Sp. f. Nahuatl]

chick *n.* **1.** a young bird before or after hatching. **2.** (*slang*) a young woman. [f. CHICKEN]

chicken /'tʃɪkɪn/ *n.* **1.** a young bird, especially of the domestic fowl. **2.** the flesh of the domestic fowl as food. —*adj.* (*slang*) afraid to do something, cowardly. —*v.i.* (*slang*) to opt *out* through cowardice. —**chicken-feed** *n.* (*colloq.*) an unimportant or small amount of money etc. **chicken-hearted** *adj.* cowardly. **chicken-pox** *n.* a disease, especially of children, with an eruption of small blisters. **chicken-wire** *n.* light wire netting with hexagonal mesh. [OE]

chick-pea *n.* the legume *Cicer arietinum*; its edible seed. [*chick* for earlier *chich* f. F f. L *cicer*]

chickweed *n.* a small weed, *Stellaria media*, with tiny white flowers.

chicle /'tʃɪk(ə)l/ *n.* a gum-like substance obtained from the sapodilla tree, used chiefly in chewing-gum. [Sp., Nahuatl]

chicory /'tʃɪkəri/ *n.* **1.** a blue-flowered plant (*Cichorium intybus*) grown for salads etc.; its root ground for use with or instead of coffee. Its crown is known in the USA as *endive*. **2.** (*US*) = ENDIVE 1. [f. F f. L f. Gk]

chide *v.t.* (*past* **chided**, **chid**; *p.p.* **chided**, **chidden**) (*archaic* & *literary*) to scold. [OE]

chief *n.* **1.** a leader or ruler; the head of a tribe, clan, etc.; a person with the highest authority. **2.** (in heraldry) the upper third of a shield (ill. HERALDRY). —*adj.* highest in rank or authority; most important. [f. OF f. L *caput* head]

chiefly *adv.* pre-eminently, above all; mainly but not exclusively. [f. prec.]

chieftain /'tʃiːftən/ *n.* the chief of a clan or tribe. [f. OF f. L *capitaneus* captain]

chiff-chaff *n.* a small song-bird (*Phylloscopus collybita*) of the warbler family. [imit.]

chiffon /'ʃɪfɒn/ *n.* **1.** a light diaphanous fabric of silk, nylon, etc. **2.** a very light-textured pudding made with beaten egg-white. [F (*chiffe* rag)]

chiffonier /ʃɪfə'nɪə(r)/ *n.* **1.** a movable low cupboard with a top used as a sideboard. **2.** (*US*) a tall chest of drawers. [f. F, = rag-picker, chest of drawers for odds and ends]

chigger *n.* a chigoe; a harvest-bug. [var. of CHIGOE]

chignon /'ʃiːnjɔ̃/ *n.* a coil or mass of hair worn by women at the back of the head. [F, orig. = nape]

chigoe /'tʃɪgəʊ/ *n.* a tropical flea that burrows into the skin. [Carib]

chihuahua /tʃɪ'wɑːwə/ *n.* a dog of a very small smooth-haired breed originating in Mexico. [f. *Chihuahua* State and city in Mexico]

chilblain /'tʃɪlbleɪn/ *n.* an inflamed swelling on a finger, toe, etc., caused by exposure to cold and by poor blood-circulation. [f. CHILL + OE *blain* swelling, sore]

child /tʃaɪld/ *n.* (*pl.* **children** /'tʃɪldrən/) **1.** a young person of either sex before puberty; an unborn or newborn human being; a childish person. **2.** a son or daughter; a descendant; a product *of*. —**child's play**, something very easy to do. [OE]

childbirth *n.* the process of giving birth to a child.

childhood *n.* the period or condition of being a child. [f. CHILD + -HOOD]

childish *adj.* immature like a child; unsuited to an adult. —**childishly** *adv.*, **childishness** *n.* [f. CHILD]

childless *adj.* having no children. [f. CHILD + -LESS]

childlike *adj.* having the good qualities of a child, simple and innocent.

Chile /'tʃɪli/ a country occupying a long coastal strip down the southern half of the west of South America, between the Andes and the Pacific Ocean; pop. (est. 1979) 11,000,000; official language, Spanish; capital, Santiago. The country's mineral wealth is considerable and includes copper, iron, nitrates, coal, and oil; Chile is one of the world's chief exporters of copper. Most of Chile was incorporated in the Inca empire and became part of the Spanish Viceroyalty of Peru after Pizarro's conquest, although the tribes of the south generally held out successfully against both imperial powers. Chilean independence was proclaimed in 1810 by O'Higgins and finally achieved in 1818 with help from Argentina. Chilean territory was pushed northwards in 1879-83 at the expense of Bolivia, and although difficulties with Argentina were solved without war in 1902, relations with her eastern neighbour have since periodically deteriorated. Chile has been ruled by a right-wing military dictatorship since the overthrow of the Marxist democrat Allende in 1973. —**Chilean** adj. & n.

chill n. **1.** unpleasant coldness. **2.** an illness with feverish shivering. **3.** coldness of manner.—adj. chilly. —v.t./i. **1.** to make or become cold; to harden (molten metal) by contact with cold material; to preserve (meat etc.) at a low temperature without freezing. **2.** to depress or dispirit. [OE]

chilli /'tʃɪlɪ/ n. (pl. **chillies**) the small red hot-tasting dried pod of a type of capsicum, used as a relish or made into seasoning. [f. Sp. f. Aztec]

chilly adj. rather cold, unpleasantly cold; cold and unfriendly in manner. [f. CHILL]

Chiltern Hills /'tʃɪltən/ (also **Chilterns**) a range of hills in southern England, north of the Thames. —**apply for the Chiltern Hundreds,** (of an MP) to apply for the stewardship of a district (formerly called a *hundred*) which includes part of the Chiltern Hills and is Crown property, and hence to be allowed to resign his seat. Resignation is not normally permitted once an MP has been elected, but the holding of an office of profit under the Crown disqualifies a person from being an MP, and by a legal fiction this stewardship is held to be such an office.

chime n. a tuned set of bells; a series of notes sounded by these. —v.t./i. (of bells) to sound; (of a clock) to indicate (the hour) by chiming.—**chime in,** to interject a remark; to agree or correspond with. [OE f. L f. Gk kumbalon cymbal]

Chimera /kɪ'mɪərə/ (Gk myth.) a fire-breathing monster with a lion's head, goat's body, and serpent's tail, killed by Bellerophon. [f. L f. Gk, = she-goat]

chimera /kɪ'mɪərə/ n. a thing of hybrid character. —**chimerical** /-'merɪk(ə)l/ adj. [= prec.]

chimney /'tʃɪmnɪ/ n. **1.** a structure carrying off the smoke or steam of a fire, furnace, engine, etc.; the part of this projecting above a roof (ill. HOUSES). **2.** a glass tube protecting the flame of a lamp. **3.** a narrow vertical cleft in a rock-face (ill. MOUNTAINS). —**chimney-breast** n. the projecting part of a wall round a chimney-flue. **chimney-pot** n. an earthenware or metal tube at the top of a chimney. **chimney-stack** n. a number of chimneys standing together. **chimney-sweep** n. one who removes soot from inside chimneys. [f. OF f. L f. Gk kaminos oven]

chimpanzee /tʃɪmpən'zi:/ n. a Central and West African ape of the genus *Pan*, of which there are two species: *P. troglodytes*, which resembles man more closely than does any other ape, and the pygmy chimpanzee *P. paniscus*. [f. F f. African native name]

Chimu /tʃi:'mu:/ n. (pl. same) a member or the language of a South American Indian civilization of Peru, the largest and most important civilization before the Inca. The large-scale irrigation systems and increased urbanization which marked their great efflorescence in the 14th c. anticipated subsequent developments by their Inca conquerers, to whom they passed their culture and engineering skills. Chimu social organization, with its distinctive hierarchical structure, was imperfectly copied by the Inca who had not yet established a permanent ruling class at the time of the Spanish conquest. The Chimu language died out in the 19th c. [Sp., f. American Indian]

chin n. the front of the lower jaw. [OE]

China /'tʃaɪnə/ a country in eastern Asia, the third-largest and most populous in the world; pop. (1982) 1,008,175,288; official language, Chinese; capital, Peking. It is essentially an agricultural country, cereals being produced in the northern provinces and rice and sugar in the south; cotton, tea, hemp, jute, and flax are the most important crops, while the culture of silkworms is one of the oldest industries. Mineral resources are considerable and include coal, iron ore, and oil, in which the country has been self-sufficient since 1973. Chinese civilization stretches back until at least the 3rd millennium BC, the country being ruled by a series of dynasties, including a Mongol one in the 13th-14th c., until the Ch'ing (or Manchu) dynasty was overthrown by Sun Yat-sen in 1912. The country was stricken first by civil war and then by Japanese invasion, and soon after the end of the Second World War the corrupt and ineffective Kuomintang government was overthrown by the Commu-

nists, the People's Republic of China being declared in 1949 (see MAO TSE-TUNG). Until quite recently, China remained generally closed to Western economic or political penetration, both under its old imperial rulers and its new Communist ones. In the ancient and medieval past, however, China was undoubtedly more civilized in many ways than Europe, and after the stagnation and chaos of the late 19th and early 20th centuries the country is now emerging as a world power.

china /'tʃaɪnə/ n. fine earthenware, porcelain. —**china clay,** kaolin. [f. Pers. f. CHINA]

chinagraph /'tʃaɪnəɡrɑːf/ n. a kind of pencil that can write on china and glass. [f. CHINA + -GRAPH]

China Sea a part of the Pacific Ocean off the coast of China, divided by the island of Taiwan into the East China Sea in the north and the South China Sea in the south.

chinchilla /tʃɪn'tʃɪlə/ n. **1.** a small South American rodent of the genus *Chinchilla*; its soft grey fur. **2.** a variety of silver-coloured domestic cat. **3.** a variety of rabbit bred for its fur; this fur. [Sp., dim. of chinche bug]

Chindit /'tʃɪndɪt/ n. a member of the allied forces fighting behind Japanese lines in Burma 1943-5. [f. Burmese chinthé a mythical creature]

chine¹ n. **1.** an animal's backbone; a joint of meat containing part of this. **2.** a mountain ridge. —v.t. to cut through the backbone of (a carcass). [f. OF f. Gmc (rel. to SHIN and L spina spine)]

chine² n. a deep narrow ravine on the Isle of Wight or Dorset coast. [OE cinu chink]

Chinese /tʃaɪ'ni:z/ n. (pl. same) **1.** a native of China; a person of Chinese descent. **2.** the language spoken in China (see below). —adj. of China or its people or language. —**Chinese lantern.** a collapsible paper lantern; a plant (*Physalis alkekengi*) grown for its inflated papery orange calyx. [f. CHINA]

Chinese is a member of the Sino-Tibetan language group, a tonal language with no inflexions, declension, or conjugations. It is estimated that there are some 800 million speakers in China and neighbouring countries. There are many dialects, including Mandarin (based on the pronunciation of Peking), and Cantonese (spoken in the south-east and in Hong Kong). Chinese script is ideographic; the characters were in origin pictographic, with each sign standing for an object, and they gradually gave way to non-pictorial ideographs representing not only tangible objects but also abstract concepts. Despite its complexity the script makes written communication possible between people speaking mutually incomprehensible dialects. Examples of Chinese writing date back well beyond 1000 BC. Traditionally Chinese books were arranged in vertical columns and read from right to left, but they are now usually composed horizontally. Until the beginning of the 20th c. the greater part of written Chinese was in a style which imitated that of the Chinese classics, most of which were written before 200 BC, and this written style became far removed from current speech. A reform movement was started to make the literature available to the masses, and many simplified characters were introduced. A system of spelling (*Pinyin*) using the Roman alphabet has been officially adopted, in stages, since 1958.

Ch'ing the name of a Chinese dynasty established by the Manchus, 1644-1912. Its overthrow in 1912 ended imperial rule in China and plunged the country into prolonged civil war.

chink¹ n. a narrow opening or slit. [rel. to CHINE²]

chink² n. a sound like glasses or coins being struck together. —v.t./i. to make or cause to make this sound. [imit.]

chinoiserie /ʃɪn'wɑːzərɪ/ n. imitation of Chinese motifs in furniture or decoration; examples of this. [F]

Chinook /tʃɪ'nʊk/ n. (pl. same) a member of a North American Indian tribe originally inhabiting the region round Columbus River in Oregon.

chinook /tʃɪ'nʊk/ n. a warm dry wind which blows down the eastern slopes of the Rocky Mountains; (erron.) a warm wet oceanic wind west of them. [f. prec.]

chintz n. a cotton fabric with a printed pattern, usually glazed, used for furnishings. [f. Hindi f. Skr. citra variegated]

chip v.t./i. (-pp-) **1.** to knock or break (a piece) off, away; to break the edge or surface of; to shape or carve thus. **2.** to make (potatoes) into chips. —n. **1.** a piece chipped off; the mark left by this. **2.** a long fried strip of potato. **3.** a counter used in a game. **4.** a microchip. —**chip off the old**

block, a child who is very like his father. **chip on one's shoulder,** a feeling of resentment or bitterness about something. **chip in,** (*colloq.*) to interrupt; to contribute money. [f. OE *cipp, cyp* beam]

chipboard *n.* material made of compressed wood chips and resin.

chipmunk /ˈtʃɪpmʌŋk/ *n.* a small striped North American animal of the genus *Tamias*, resembling a squirrel. [Algonquian]

chipolata /tʃɪpəˈlɑːtə/ *n.* a small spicy sausage. [F f. It. (*cipolla* onion)]

Chippendale /ˈtʃɪpəndeɪl/ *n.* an elegant 18th-c. style of furniture, named after its designer, Thomas Chippendale, English cabinet-maker (d. 1779).

chiromancy /ˈkaɪrəmænsɪ/ *n.* palmistry. —**chiromancer** *n.* [f. Gk *kheir* hand]

chiropody /kɪˈrɒpədɪ/ *n.* treatment of ailments of the foot. —**chiropodist** *n.* [f. Gk *kheir* hand + *pous* foot]

chiropractic /kaɪrəˈpræktɪk/ *n.* treatment of disease by manipulation of the spine and joints. —**chiropractor** *n.* [f. Gk *kheir* hand + *praktikos* (cf. PRACTICAL)]

chirp *n.* the short sharp note of a small bird or a grasshopper. —*v.i.* to make this sound. [imit.]

chirrup /ˈtʃɪrəp/ *n.* a series of chirps. —*v.i.* to make this sound. [trilled form of CHIRP]

chisel /ˈtʃɪz(ə)l/ *n.* a tool with a bevelled cutting-edge for shaping wood, stone, or metal (ill. CARPENTRY). —*v.t.* (**-ll-**) to cut or shape with a chisel. [f. OF f. L *caedere* cut]

chit¹ *n.* a shoot, a sprout. —*v.i.* (of seed) to sprout, to germinate. [orig. unkn.]

chit² *n.* a young child; a small young woman. [orig. = whelp, cub, kitten, perh. f. CHIT¹]

chit³ *n.* a short written note, especially of an order made, a sum owed, etc. [earlier *chitty,* f. Hindi f. Skr. *citra* mark]

chit-chat *n.* chat, gossip. [redupl. of CHAT]

chitin /ˈkaɪtɪn/ *n.* a substance forming the horny constituent in the exoskeleton of arthropods. —**chitinous** *adj.* [f. F f. Gk *khitōn* garment]

chitterlings *n.pl.* the smaller intestines of a pig, cooked as food. [orig. unkn.]

chivalry /ˈʃɪv(ə)lrɪ/ *n.* courtesy and consideration, especially to weaker people; the medieval knightly system with its ethical and social code. —**chivalrous** *adj.* [f. OF f. L, = horseman (as CAVALIER)]

chive *n.* (chiefly in *pl.*) a small herb (*Allium schoenoprasum*) related to the onion, used for flavouring. [f. OF f. L *cepa* onion]

chivvy /ˈtʃɪvɪ/ *v.t.* to keep urging (a person) to hurry, to harass. [f. *chevy,* prob. f. ballad of *Chevy Chase,* place on Scottish Border]

chloral /ˈklɔːr(ə)l/ *n.* (in full **chloral hydrate**) a white crystalline compound used as a sedative or anaesthetic. [F (*chlore* chlorine, *alcool* alcohol)]

chloride /ˈklɔːraɪd/ *n.* a binary compound of chlorine; a bleaching agent containing this. [f. CHLORINE]

chlorinate /ˈklɔːrɪneɪt/ *v.t.* to treat or disinfect with chlorine. —**chlorination** /-ˈneɪʃ(ə)n/ *n.* [f. foll.]

chlorine /ˈklɔːriːn/ *n.* a non-metallic gaseous element of the halogen group, symbol Cl, atomic number 17, first isolated in 1774 and named in 1810 by Sir Humphry Davy for its colour. It is obtained mainly from sea water and from salt deposits. The yellowish-green gas is toxic and has a powerful irritating smell; it was used as a poison gas in the First World War. Chlorine is added to water supplies as a disinfectant, and is a constituent of many commercial chemical compounds, including bleaches, antiseptics, insecticides, dyes, and synthetic rubbers. [f. Gk *khlōros* green]

chloroform /ˈklɒrəfɔːm/ *n.* a thin colourless liquid whose inhaled vapour produces unconsciousness. —*v.t.* to make unconscious with this. [f. F (as prec.)]

chlorophyll /ˈklɒrəfɪl/ *n.* the green colouring-matter in plants. [f. F f. Gk *khlōros* green, *phullon* leaf]

choc *n.* (*colloq.*) chocolate; a chocolate. —**choc-ice** *n.* a small bar of ice-cream coated with chocolate. [abbr.]

chock *n.* a block or wedge used to prevent something from moving. —*v.t.* to wedge with a chock or chocks. —**chock-a-block** *adj.* & *adv.* crammed or crowded together. **chock-full** *adj.* crammed full. [prob f. OF *ço(u)che*; orig. unkn.]

chocolate /ˈtʃɒk(ə)lət,/ *n.* **1.** an edible powder, paste, or solid block made from cacao seeds; a sweet made of or coated with this; a drink made with it. **2.** dark-brown colour. —*adj.* **1.** made of chocolate; flavoured or coated with chocolate. **2.** chocolate-coloured. [f. F or Sp. f. Aztec *chocolatl*]

Choctaw /ˈtʃɒktɔː/ *n.* (*pl.* same) a member or the language of a North American Indian tribe originally inhabiting Mississippi and Alabama. [f. Choctaw *Chahta*]

choice *n.* the act or power of choosing; a person or thing chosen; a variety from which to choose. —*adj.* of special quality. [f. OF f. Gmc, rel. to CHOOSE]

choir /kwaɪə(r)/ *n.* **1.** an organized body of singers especially in a church. **2.** the part of a church etc. where they sit. [f. OF f. L *chorus*]

choke /tʃəʊk/ *v.t./i.* **1.** to stop the breathing of by compressing or blocking the windpipe or (of smoke etc.) by being unfit to breathe; to be unable to breathe from such a cause; to make or become speechless from emotion. **2.** to clog, to smother. —*n.* **1.** choking, a choking sound. **2.** a valve controlling the flow of air into a petrol engine. **3.** an inductance coil to smooth variations of alternating current. —**choke off,** (*colloq.*) to silence or discourage, usually by snubbing. [f. OE *ācēocian* (A-, *cēoce* cheek)]

choker *n.* a high collar; a close-fitting necklace. [f. prec.]

choler /ˈkɒlə(r)/ *n.* **1.** (*hist.*) one of the four humours. **2.** (*poet.* or *archaic*) anger, irascibility. [f. OF f. L f. Gk (*kholē* bile)]

cholera /ˈkɒlərə/ *n.* an infectious often fatal disease with acute diarrhoea. Cholera came to Europe from the East, spreading along the ancient trade routes, through Asia and eastern Europe from its traditional home in the Ganges valley. With the great increase of international trade and commerce in the 19th c. the disease found its way to western Europe, the first large epidemic being in 1831-2, and the low standard of public and personal hygiene at that time gave it every chance of spreading. It is the classic example of a mainly water-borne disease, and where the domestic watersupply has been purified cholera epidemics have nearly always ceased. A vaccine is now available. [f. L (as prec.)]

choleric /ˈkɒlərɪk/ *adj.* irascible; angry. [f. OF (as CHOLER)]

cholesterol /kəˈlestərɒl/ *n.* a fatty steroid alcohol found in animal tissues and thought to promote arteriosclerosis. [f. Gk *kholē* bile + *stereos* stiff]

Chomsky /ˈtʃɒmskɪ/, Avram Noam (1928-), American linguistics scholar associated since 1957 with the theory of generative-transformational grammar which reacted against the static and taxonomic forms of American linguistic structuralism. He views language as the result of innate capacity, common to all persons, arguing that linguistics is a part of psychology. Chomsky was also a leading critic of the American involvement in the Vietnam war of 1961-76.

chondrite /ˈkɒndraɪt/ *n.* a meteorite containing granules (*chondrules*), the most abundant type of meteorite in the solar system. [f. G f.Gk *khondros* granule]

chook /tʃʊk/ *n.* (*Austral.* & *NZ*) a domestic fowl, a chicken. [prob. f. dial. *chuck* chick]

choose /tʃuːz/ *v.t./i.* (*past* chose /tʃəʊz/; *p.p.* chosen /ˈtʃəʊz(ə)n/) to select from a greater number; to decide or desire as a matter of preference. [OE]

choosey /ˈtʃuːzɪ/ *adj.* (*colloq.*) careful and cautious in choosing, hard to please. [f. prec.]

chop¹ *v.t./i.* (**-pp-**) **1.** to cut with a heavy blow, usually with an axe or knife; to cut up small in cookery; to make a chopping blow *at.* **2.** to strike (a ball) with a heavy edgewise blow. —*n.* **1.** a chopping stroke or blow. **2.** a thick slice of meat, usually including a rib. [var. of CHAP²]

chop² *v.t./i.* (**-pp-**) **chop and change,** to keep changing. [perh. var. of obs. *chap* barter]

chop³ *n.* (usu. in *pl.*) the jaws of a person or animal. [var. of CHAP³]

Chopin /ˈʃəʊpæ̃/, Fryderyk (Frédéric) (1810-49), Polish composer and pianist. He left Poland in 1830 and in 1831, while in Stuttgart, heard that Warsaw had been captured by the Russians. He never returned to his native land, moving to Paris in 1831 and remaining there, apart from a tour of Britain as a concert pianist and a year in Majorca and Spain, for the rest of his short life. For some years he was the lover of the French writer George Sand, but their affair ended before his death from tuberculosis. He was famous as a pianist, and his piano music represents for many the perfect expression of poetry in music. His works range from the dreamy lyricism of the Nocturnes to the fire and spirit of the Polonaises, while some of the larger-scale works such as the four Ballades combine and contrast these qualities. The Victorian conception of him as a consumptive drawing-room balladeer of the keyboard has long been exposed as a false trail leading hearers away from the true, poetic, heroic Chopin.

chopper *n.* **1.** a short axe with large blade; a butcher's cleaver. **2.** (*slang*) a helicopter. [f. CHOP[1]]

choppy *adj.* **1.** (of the sea) full of short broken waves. **2.** jerky, abrupt. —**choppiness** *n.* [f. CHOP[1]]

chopsticks *n.pl.* a pair of sticks held in one hand and used in China etc. to lift food to the mouth. [f. pidgin English *chop* quick]

chop-suey /tʃɒp'su:ɪ/ *n.* a Chinese dish of small pieces of meat fried with rice and vegetables. [Chinese, = mixed bits]

choral /'kɔ:r(ə)l/ *adj.* written for a choir or chorus; sung or spoken by these. —**choral society,** a society formed to sing choral music. [f. L (as CHORUS)]

chorale /kɒ'rɑ:l/ *n.* a metrical hymn sung in unison, originally in the Lutheran Church; a harmonized form of this. [f. G (as prec.)]

chord[1] /kɔ:d/ *n.* a group of notes sounded together in harmony. [orig. *cord* f. ACCORD]

chord[2] /kɔ:d/ *n.* **1.** a straight line joining the ends of an arc (ill. SHAPES). **2.** (*poet.*) a string of a harp etc. [var. of CORD]

chordate /'kɔ:deɪt/ *adj.* of the phylum Chordata, having a notochord. —*n.* a member of this phylum, which includes all the vertebrates as well as a few invertebrate groups, characterized by having a notochord at some stage of the life cycle. [f. L *chorda* CHORD[1], after *Vertebrata* etc.]

chore /tʃɔ:(r)/ *n.* a recurrent or tedious task. [rel. to CHAR[2]]

choreograph /'kɒrɪəgrɑ:f/ *v.t.* to provide choreography for. [f. foll.]

choreography /kɒrɪ'ɒgrəfɪ/ *n.* the composition of ballet or stage-dances. —**choreographer** *n.*, **choreographic** /-'græfɪk/ *adj.* [f. Gk *khoreia* choral dancing to music (as CHORUS)]

chorister /'kɒrɪstə(r)/ *n.* a member of a church choir. [f. OF (*quer* choir)]

chortle *n.* a loud gleeful chuckle. —*v.i.* to utter a chortle. [blend of CHUCKLE and SNORT]

chorus /'kɔ:rəs/ *n.* **1.** an organized group of singers; a group of singing dancers in an opera, musical comedy, etc. or in an ancient Greek play. **2.** a thing sung or said by many at once; the refrain of a song, which the audience join the performer in singing. **3.** a character speaking the prologue etc. in a play. —*v.t./i.* to say or sing in chorus. [L f. Gk]

chose, chosen *past & p.p. of* CHOOSE.

Chou En-lai /tʃəʊ en'laɪ/ (also *Zhou Enlai*, 1898–1976), Chinese statesman. One of the founders of the Chinese Communist party, he joined Sun Yat-sen in 1924 and organized the revolt in Shanghai in 1927 before forming a partnership with Mao Tse-tung, whose lieutenant he became. On the formation of the Communist regime in 1949 Chou became Premier.

chough /tʃʌf/ *n.* a red-legged crow of the genus *Pyrrhocorax*. [imit.]

choux pastry /ʃu:/ a very light pastry enriched with eggs. [F, orig. = cabbages]

chow /tʃaʊ/ *n.* a long-haired dog of a Chinese breed. [short for *chow-chow*, perh. f. pidgin English]

chowder /'tʃaʊdə(r)/ *n.* (*US*) a thick soup of clams (or fish) and vegetables. [perh. f. F (*chaudière* pot)]

chow mein /tʃaʊ 'meɪn/ *n.* a Chinese dish of fried noodles usually with shredded meat and vegetables. [f. Chinese, = fried flour]

Chrétien de Troyes /kretɪæ̃ də 'trwɑ:/ (12th c.) French poet who lived and worked at the court of Marie de Champagne and is regarded as the greatest of the writers of courtly romances. He probably wrote a romance of Tristan; his four extant volumes of romances are: *Erec* (*c.*1170), *Cligés* (1176), *Yvain* (*c.*1177–81), and *Lancelot* (*c.*1177–81). His unfinished *Perceval*, part of which survives, introduced the Holy Grail to literature. His writings greatly influenced subsequent Arthurian literature.

chrism /'krɪz(ə)m/ *n.* consecrated oil. [OE f. L f. Gk *khrisma* anointing]

Christ /kraɪst/ *n.* the Messiah of Jewish prophecy; the title (now treated as a name) of Jesus, regarded as fulfilling this prophecy. [OE f. L f. Gk *khristos* anointed one (transl. of Heb., = Messiah)]

Christadelphian /krɪstə'delfɪən/ *n.* a member of a religious sect founded in America in 1848 by John Thomas, rejecting the beliefs and development associated with the term 'Christian', calling themselves 'Christadelphians' (= brothers of Christ) and claiming to return to the beliefs and practices of the earliest disciples. The core of their faith is that Christ will return in power to set up a world-wide theocracy beginning at Jerusalem, and that belief in this is necessary for salvation. [f. CHRIST + Gk *adelphos* brother]

christen /'krɪs(ə)n/ *v.t.* to admit to the Christian Church by baptism; to give a name or nickname to. [OE, = make Christian]

Christian /'krɪstjən/ *adj.* **1.** of the doctrines of Christianity, believing in or based on these. **2.** showing the qualities of a Christian, kindly, humane. —*n.* **1.** an adherent of Christianity. **2.** a kindly or humane person. —**Christian era,** the era reckoned from the birth of Christ. **Christian name,** a personal name given at baptism. [f. L (*Christus* Christ)]

Christiania /krɪstɪ'ɑ:nɪə/ *n.* (in skiing) a turn in which the skis are kept parallel, used for stopping short. [former name of Oslo]

Christianity /krɪstɪ'ænɪtɪ/ *n.* **1.** the Christian religion, based on the belief that Christ was the incarnate Son of God and on his teaching (see below). **2.** Christian character or quality. [f. OF (as prec.)]

At first Christianity was simply a Jewish sect which believed that Jesus of Nazareth was the Messiah (or 'Christ', = anointed one). Largely owing to the former Pharisee, Paul of Tarsus, it quickly became an independent, mainly Gentile, organization. In the early centuries Christians experienced intermittent persecution from the State, though there was no clear legal basis for this until the reign of the Emperor Decius (AD 250). By the 3rd c. Christianity was widespread throughout the Roman Empire; in 313 Constantine ended persecution and in 380 Theodosius recognized it as the State religion. There were frequent disputes between Christians mainly over the status of Christ and the nature of the Trinity, and later over grace and Church organization. Division between East and West, in origin largely cultural and linguistic, intensified, culminating in the Schism of 1054, sealed by the Crusades. In the West the organization of the Church, focused on the Roman papacy, was fragmented by the Reformation of the 16th c. In the 20th c. the ecumenical movement has sought to heal these ancient wounds.

Christian Science the doctrine of spiritual healing upheld by the 'Church of Christ Scientist', founded in Boston (1879) by Mrs Mary Baker Eddy to promote her beliefs. She taught that mind is the only reality, matter an illusion, and suffering and death the effects of a mistaken belief in the reality of matter. The movement flourished and spread to other English-speaking countries and to Germany. After the death of the foundress in 1910 the organization passed into the hands of a board of directors. Worship consists of readings from the Bible and from the works of Mary Baker Eddy. —**Christian Scientist,** an adherent of this doctrine.

Christie /'krɪstɪ/, Dame Agatha (1890–1976), English author of detective fiction. The first of her novels, *The Mysterious Affair at Styles* (1920; introducing the Belgian detective Hercule Poirot who reappeared in many further novels), was followed by 66 further works in the genre, including *The Murder of Roger Ackroyd* (1926), *Murder on the Orient Express* (1934), *Death on the Nile* (1937), and *Ten Little Niggers* (1939); the settings for some of these were provided by her experiences while accompanying her second husband, Sir Max Mallowan (1904–78), on his archaeological expeditions in the Middle East. Her other works include two self-portraits and several plays: *The Mousetrap* (1952) has had a record run of over 30 years on the London stage, and a number of her stories have been filmed. Her prodigious international success has been achieved by her brisk humorous dialogue and her ingenious plots which sustain suspense while misdirecting the reader.

christie /'krɪstɪ/ *n.* = Christiania (ill. SPORTS). [abbr.]

Christingle /krɪ'stɪŋg(ə)l/ *n.* a lighted candle set in an orange received at a Christingle service. —**Christingle service,** a children's Advent service, originally in the Moravian Church and recently popularized outside it, at which each participant is given an orange (symbolizing the world) set with a candle (symbolizing Christ as the Light of the World) and other symbolical decorations. [f. CHRIST; origin of second element unknown]

Christmas /'krɪsməs/ *n.* the Christian festival commemorating the birth of Christ (see below); the festive period about this time. —**Christmas-box** *n.* a present or gratuity given at Christmas, especially to employees. **Christmas**

card, a card sent with greetings at Christmas. The Christmas card, as we know it, dates from the mid-19th c.
Christmas Day, 25 Dec. **Christmas Eve,** 24 Dec.
Christmas pudding, rich plum pudding eaten at Christmas. **Christmas rose,** a white-flowered winter-blooming hellebore, *Helleborus niger.* **Christmas tree,** a young conifer (or imitation of one) decorated with lights etc. at Christmas. The Christmas tree originated in Germany, where it was known from the 16th c., and spread elsewhere from there. It became fashionable in England after Prince Albert introduced it into his family. [OE, = CHRIST, MASS²]
The festival of Christ's birth has been celebrated in the Western Church from the end of the 4th c., and in the East formerly on 6 Jan. in conjunction with the Epiphany. There is no biblical or other direct evidence of the season of Christ's nativity, and the date may have been chosen to oppose the pagan celebration of the rebirth of the sun after the winter solstice. It has always been marked by the merrymaking characteristic of the Roman Saturnalia and similar festivals, and many of the things now associated with Christmas (e.g. evergreens, lights, red colour) belong to the rituals of 'bringing back the year' which it replaced.

Christopher /ˈkrɪstəfə(r)/, St, legendary martyr, adopted as the patron saint of travellers. According to tradition he was martyred in Asia Minor. He is represented as a giant who carried travellers across a river; once he carried a child whose weight bowed him down, as the child was Christ and his weight that of the world. His feast day (25 July) was dropped from the Roman calendar in 1969. [f. Gk, = one who bore Christ]

Christ's Hospital a boys' school founded in London in 1552 for poor children, which has since moved to Horsham, Sussex. Pupils wear a distinctive uniform of long dark-blue belted gowns and yellow stockings.

chromatic /krəˈmætɪk/ adj. **1.** of colour, in colours.
2. (*Mus.*) with notes not belonging to the diatonic scale.
—**chromatic scale,** one that proceeds by semitones. [f. F or L f. Gk (*khrōma* colour)]

chromatin /ˈkrəʊmətɪn/ n. a readily stained constituent of the nucleus of a cell. [G, f. Gk *khrōma* colour]

chromatography /krəʊməˈtɒɡrəfɪ/ n. separation of a mixture into its component substances by passing it over material which absorbs these at different rates so that they appear as layers, often of different colours. [f. G (as prec. + -GRAPHY)]

chrome /krəʊm/ n. chromium, especially as a plating; a yellow pigment obtained from a compound of chromium. [F, f. Gk *khrōma* colour, from the brilliant colours of its compounds]

chromium /ˈkrəʊmɪəm/ n. a hard metallic element, symbol Cr, atomic number 24, first isolated in 1798. It is often plated on to other metals for decorative purposes and to prevent corrosion, and it is an important component of many alloys, notably stainless steel. Chromium compounds, many of which are brightly coloured, are used as pigments, in dyeing, and in the tanning of leather. [f. CHROME]

chromosome /ˈkrəʊməsəʊm/ n. any of a number of rod-like or threadlike structures found in the nuclei of the cells of living organisms and containing the genes. They can normally be seen as separate structures only when the cell is dividing. A normal undivided chromosome contains a single DNA double helix (associated with protein) in which the genes are arranged in linear order. The number of chromosomes per cell varies between species. Man has 23 pairs (see DIPLOID) of which one pair determines the sex of the individual: a female carries two similar X-chromosomes in each cell while a male has one X- and one smaller Y-chromosome. The genetic material of a bacterium is now also referred to as a chromosome. [G, f. Gk *khrōma* colour *sōma* body)]

chromosphere /ˈkrəʊməsfɪə(r)/ n. the region immediately above the photosphere of the sun which, together with the corona, constitutes its outer atmosphere. Material in this region is at temperatures of 10,000–20,000 °C, and is subject to magnetic forces originating within the sun that may occasionally lift and propel it outwards for thousands of kilometres as solar flares. [f. Gk *khrōma* colour + SPHERE]

chronic /ˈkrɒnɪk/ adj. (of diseases etc.) long-lasting, persistent; suffering from a chronic disease. —**chronically** adv. [f. F f. L f. Gk (*khronos* time)]

chronicle /ˈkrɒnɪk(ə)l/ n. a record of events in the order of their occurrence. —v.t. to record in a chronicle.
—**Chronicles,** either of two books of the Old Testament

recording the history of Israel and Judah from the Creation until the return from Exile (536 BC), with interest concentrated on the religious aspects, especially the Temple and worship. —**chronicler** n. [f. AF f. L f. Gk *khronika* (as prec.)]

chronogram /ˈkrɒnəɡræm/ n. a phrase etc. of which the Roman-numeral letters, when added, give a date, e.g. LorD haVe MerCIe Vpon Vs = 50 + 500 + 5 + 1000 + 100 + 1 + 5 + 5 = 1666. [f. Gk *khronos* time + -GRAM]

chronology /krəˈnɒlədʒɪ/ n. arrangement of events according to date or in order of occurrence. —**chronological** /krɒnəˈlɒdʒɪk(ə)l/ adj., **chronologically** adv. [f. Gk *khronos* time + -LOGY]

chronometer /krəˈnɒmɪtə(r)/ n. a time-measuring instrument, especially one keeping accurate time in spite of movement or of variations in temperature, humidity, and air pressure. The longitude of a ship at sea may be found by comparing local time with Greenwich Mean Time; the former can be computed by astronomical observation, but without an accurate marine time-keeper it was not easy to ascertain Greenwich time. By 1785 French and English clockmakers had evolved a chronometer with an accuracy of better than one second a day, employing special balance-wheels and springs. Modern chronometers use a quartz crystal kept in oscillation at a constant frequency by electronic means. Since the advent of radio time-signals the need for expensive marine chronometers scarcely exists. [f. Gk *khronos* time + -METER]

chrysalis /ˈkrɪsəlɪs/ n. (pl. **chrysalides** /-ˈsælɪdiːz/) a butterfly or moth at the quiescent stage between the larval and adult phases; the case enclosing it. [f. L f. Gk (*khrusos* gold)]

chrysanthemum /krɪˈsænθəməm/ n. an autumn-flowering plant of the genus *Chrysanthemum,* grown in many colours. [L f. Gk (*khrusos* gold, *anthemon* flower)]

chryselephantine /krɪselɪˈfæntaɪn/ adj. (of sculpture) overlaid with gold and ivory. [f. Gk (*khrusos* gold, *elephas* ivory)]

chrysoberyl /krɪsəʊˈberɪl/ n. a yellowish-green gem. [f. L f. Gk (*khrūsos* gold, BERYL)]

chrysolite /ˈkrɪsəlaɪt/ n. a precious stone, a variety of olivine. [f. OF f. L f. Gk (*khrūsos* gold, *lithos* stone)]

Chrysostom /ˈkrɪsəstəm/, St John (c.347–407), bishop of Constantinople, Doctor of the Church. His name (Gk, = golden-mouthed) is a tribute to the eloquence of his preaching, and his sermons on books of the Bible established his title as the greatest of Christian expositors. As Patriarch of Constantinople his combination of honesty, asceticism, and tactlessness in his attempts at reforming the corrupt state of the court, clergy, and people offended many, including the Empress Eudoxia, who with some reason took all attempts at moral reform as a censure on herself; he was banished and died in exile. Feast day, 27 Jan.

chub n. (pl. same) a thick-bodied river-fish (*Leuciscus cephalus*) of the carp family. [orig. unkn.]

chubby adj. plump, plump-faced. [f. CHUB]

chuck¹ v.t. **1.** (*colloq.*) to throw carelessly or casually. **2.** to touch playfully (*under the chin*). —n. an act of chucking. —**chuck out,** (*slang*) to expel; to throw away. [perh. f. F *chuquer* knock]

chuck² n. **1.** the part of a lathe holding the workpiece; the part of a drill holding the bit (ill. CARPENTRY). **2.** a cut of beef from the neck to the ribs. [var. of CHOCK]

chuckle n. a quiet or suppressed laugh. —v.i. to give a chuckle. [f. *chuck* cluck]

chuddar /ˈtʃʌdə(r)/ n. a large piece of cloth worn as a kind of cloak, leaving only the face exposed, by Muslim women in certain countries. [f. Pers.]

chug n. the dull short repeated sound of an engine running slowly. —v.i. (-**gg**-) to move with or make this sound. [imit.]

chukker /ˈtʃʌkə(r)/ n. (also **chukka**) a period of play in polo. [f. Hindi f. Skr. *cakra* wheel]

chum n. (*colloq.*) a close friend. —v.i. (-**mm**-) —**chum up,** (*colloq.*) to form a close friendship. [prob. abbr. of *chamber-fellow*]

chummy adj. (*colloq.*) friendly. —**chumminess** n. [f. CHUM]

chump n. **1.** the thick blunt end of loin of lamb etc. **2.** (*colloq.*) a stupid person. [blend of CHUNK and LUMP]

chunk n. a thick lump cut off; a substantial amount. [prob. var. of CHUCK²]

chunky adj. **1.** in chunks, containing chunks. **2.** short and thickset. [f. prec.]

chupatty /tʃʌˈpætɪ/ *n.* a small flat thin cake of coarse unleavened bread. [f. Hindi]

church *n.* a building for public Christian worship (ill. pp. 158-9); a service in this. —*v.t.* to perform the church service of thanksgiving for (a woman after childbirth). —**the Church,** the whole body of Christian believers; a particular group of these; the clergy, the clerical profession. **Church Slavonic,** see SLAVONIC. [OE f. Gk *kuriakon* Lord's (house)]

Churchill /ˈtʃɜːtʃɪl/, Sir Winston Leonard Spencer (1874-1965), British statesman. After an early career as a soldier and war correspondent, Churchill was elected as a Conservative MP in 1901, but joined the Liberals after the Conservative Party split over free trade. Having served as President of the Board of Trade, Home Secretary, and First Lord of the Admiralty, he lost his position of prominence after the Dardanelles fiasco and left politics to return to the army. Out of Parliament between 1922 and 1924, he returned as Conservative Chancellor of the Exchequer under Baldwin, failing to cope adequately with the economic crisis, and after the government's fall in 1929 did not hold office again for a decade. Something of a political outcast, Churchill persistently warned of the threat of German military expansion in the 1930s, and on the outbreak of war returned to public life as First Lord of the Admiralty. He replaced Chamberlain as Prime Minister in May 1940 and served as war leader until 1945, becoming a symbol of British resistance in the darkest days of the conflict. After the victory, defeated in the general election of 1945, he campaigned for Western unity against the Communist threat and was returned to office in 1951, finally resigning at the age of 80 in 1955. A powerful orator, he was the originator or popularizer of a number of slogans and phrases. His writings include *The Second World War* (1948-53) and *A History of the English-speaking Peoples* (1956-8); he was awarded the Nobel Prize for literature in 1953.

churchman *n.* (*pl.* -men) 1. a clergyman. 2. a member of a Church.

Church of England the English branch of the Western or Latin Church, rejecting the pope's authority since the Reformation and having the monarch as its titular head and nominator of its bishops and archbishops. A synod held at Whitby in 664 resolved the earlier conflict between the indigenous Celtic Church, dominated by missionaries from Ireland and Scotland, and the Roman customs, introduced by St Augustine's mission (597), in favour of the latter. The English Church remained part of the Western Catholic Church until the 16th c. when, against a background of religious dissatisfaction and growing national self-awareness, Henry VIII failed to obtain a divorce from Catherine of Aragon and subsequently repudiated papal supremacy, bringing the Church under the control of the Crown. Some of Henry's advisers, notably Thomas Cromwell and Archbishop Cranmer, were deeply influenced by the Protestant Reformation, and the influence of Continental Protestantism reached a peak in the reign of Edward VI. The Church achieved its definitive form under Elizabeth I, when the Book of Common Prayer became its service-book and the Thirty-nine Articles its statement of doctrine. The aim of the Church of England has been, while rejecting the claims of Rome, to maintain its continuity with earlier tradition.

Church of Scotland the national (Presbyterian) Church of Scotland. At the Reformation the Calvinist party in Scotland, under John Knox, reformed the established Church and organized it on Presbyterian lines (1560). During the next century there were repeated attempts by the Stuart monarchs to impose episcopalianism, and the Church of Scotland was not finally established as Presbyterian until 1690. Its statement of doctrine is the *Westminster Confession* (1643). Like many Protestant Churches it has had a complicated history of schism and reunification.

churchwarden *n.* 1. a lay representative of a parish who helps with the business of a church. 2. a long-stemmed clay pipe.

churchyard *n.* the enclosed ground round a church, especially as used for burials.

churlish *adj.* rude and unfriendly, ungracious; mean, grudging. —**churlishly** *adv.*, **churlishness** *n.* [OE]

churn *n.* 1. a vessel in which milk or cream is shaken to produce butter. 2. a large milk-can in which milk is carried from a farm. —*v.t./i.* 1. to shake (milk or cream) in a churn;

to produce (butter) thus. 2. to stir or swirl violently, to break *up* the surface of. —**churn out,** to produce in quantity. [OE]

Churrigueresque /tʃʌrɪɡəˈresk/ *adj.* of the lavishly ornamented late Spanish baroque style. [f. J. de *Churriguera*, Spanish architect (d. 1725)]

chute /ʃuːt/ *n.* a sloping or vertical channel or slide for conveying things to a lower level. [F, = fall, with some senses of SHOOT]

chutney /ˈtʃʌtnɪ/ *n.* a pungent relish of fruits, vinegar, spices, etc. [f. Hindi]

CIA *abbr.* Central Intelligence Agency.

ciborium /sɪˈbɔːrɪəm/ *n.* (*pl.* -ia) 1. (*Archit.*) a canopy; a canopied shrine. 2. a covered receptacle for the reservation of the Eucharist (ill. VESTMENTS). [L f. Gk, = seed-vessel of water-lily, cup made from it]

cicada /sɪˈkɑːdə/ *n.* a grasshopper-like insect of the genus *Cicada,* that makes a loud rhythmic chirping. [L]

cicatrice /ˈsɪkətrɪs/ *n.* the scar left by a healed wound. [f. OF or L]

cicely /ˈsɪs(ə)lɪ/ *n.* **sweet cicely,** an aromatic umbelliferous herb, *Myrrhis odorata.* [f. L f. Gk *seselis,* assim. to the woman's name *Cicely*]

Cicero /ˈsɪsərəʊ/, Marcus Tullius (106-43 BC), Roman statesman, orator, and writer. The greatest forensic and political orator of his time, in politics he was a somewhat conservative upholder of Republican values and a supporter of Pompey against the ambitions of Julius Caesar; his proudest success was the suppression, during his consulship of 63 BC, of the conspiracy of Catiline. He died in the proscriptions of 43 BC, a victim of Antony, whom he had savagely attacked in the *Philippics* after the death of Julius Caesar. As an orator and writer he established a model for Latin prose; his surviving works include many speeches, treatises on rhetoric, philosophical works (chiefly adaptations into Latin of the teachings of the several Greek schools), and books of letters, which form a close record of his personal and political interests and activities.

cicerone /tʃɪtʃəˈrəʊnɪ, sɪs-/ *n.* (*pl.* -ni /-niː/) a guide who shows antiquities to visitors. [It. f. L CICERO]

CID *abbr.* Criminal Investigation Department.

Cid /sɪd/, **The** the title in Spanish literature of Ruy Diaz, count of Bivar, 11th-c. champion of Christianity against the Moors.

-cide *suffix* person or substance that kills (*regicide, insecticide*); killing (*homicide*). [f. L *caedere* kill]

cider /ˈsaɪdə(r)/ *n.* a fermented drink made from apples. [f. OF, ult. f. Heb., = strong drink]

cigar /sɪˈɡɑː(r)/ *n.* a roll of tobacco leaves for smoking. [f. F or Sp.]

cigarette /sɪɡəˈret/ *n.* a small cylinder of shredded tobacco etc. rolled in thin paper for smoking. [F, dim. of *cigare*]

ciliate /ˈsɪlɪət/ *adj.* having cilia. —*n.* a member of the class Ciliata consisting of protozoa which have a relatively complex body structure and are characterized by possessing cilia. [f. CILIUM]

Cilicia /sɪˈlɪʃə/ the ancient name for the eastern half of the south coast of Asia Minor. —**Cilician** *adj.*

cilium /ˈsɪlɪəm/ *n.* (*pl.* cilia) a minute hair fringing a leaf, an insect's wing, etc; a hairlike vibrating organ on animal or vegetable tissue. [L, = eyelid]

Cimabue /tʃɪməˈbuːɪ/, real name Cenni di Peppi (c.1240-1302), Florentine painter, a contemporary of Dante, who refers to him in the *Divine Comedy.* Later writers claimed he was the teacher of Giotto, and initiator of the movement away from Byzantine stylization and towards greater realism which culminated in the Renaissance. However, only one work can be securely attributed to him, a *St John* forming part of a larger mosaic in Pisa (1301), though tradition has credited him with many works of outstanding quality from the end of the 13th c., such as the cycle of frescoes, including a *Crucifixion,* in the Upper Church of St Francis in Assisi.

Cimmerian /sɪˈmɪərɪən/ *n.* a member of an ancient nomadic people, the earliest known inhabitants of the Crimea, who overran Asia Minor in the 7th c. BC. They overthrew Phrygia c.676 BC, and terrorized Ionia, but were gradually destroyed by epidemics and in wars with Lydia and Assyria. —*adj.* of the Cimmerians. [f. L f. Gk]

cinchona /sɪŋˈkəʊnə/ *n.* a South American evergreen tree or shrub of the genus *Cinchona;* its bark, the source of

Church Architecture

Structure

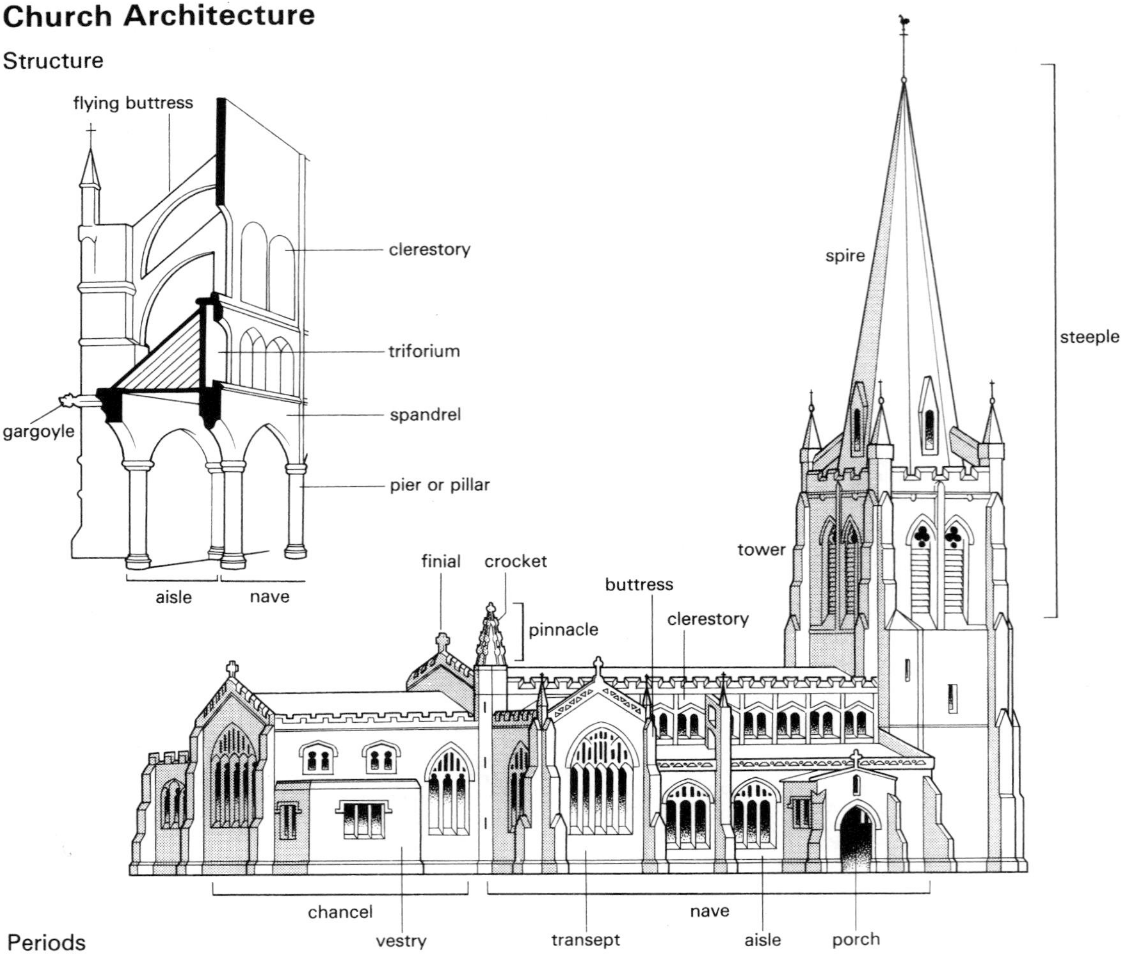

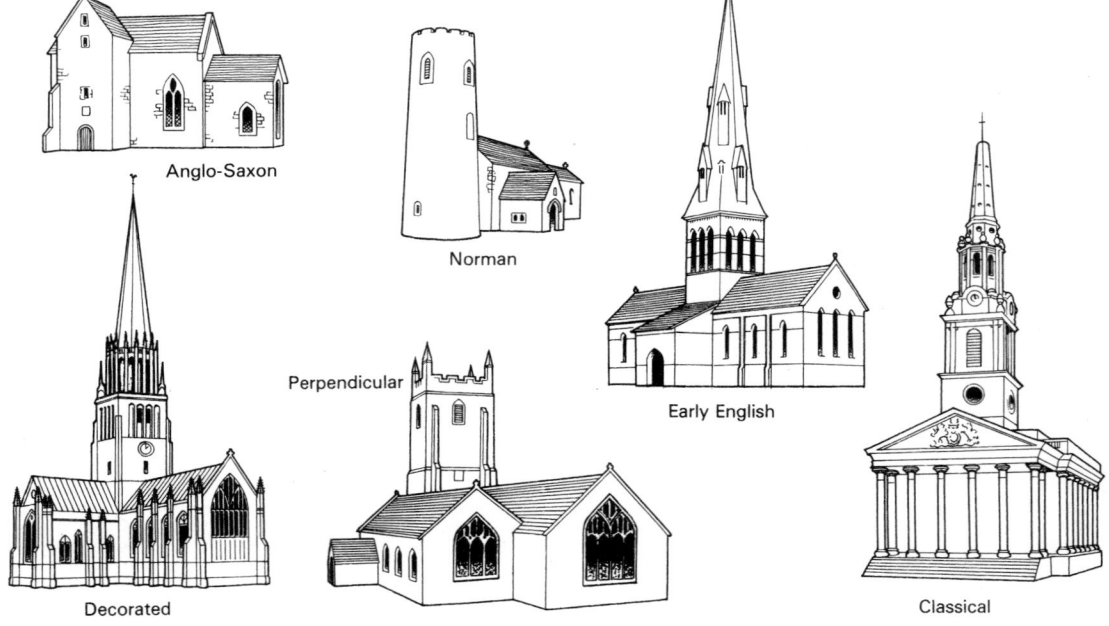

flying buttress

clerestory

triforium

spandrel

gargoyle

pier or pillar

aisle

nave

finial

crocket

pinnacle

buttress

clerestory

tower

spire

steeple

chancel

vestry

transept

nave

aisle

porch

Periods

(note: some churches include architectural details which are earlier or later than the main periods which they illustrate)

Anglo-Saxon

Norman

Perpendicular

Early English

Decorated

Classical

Windows

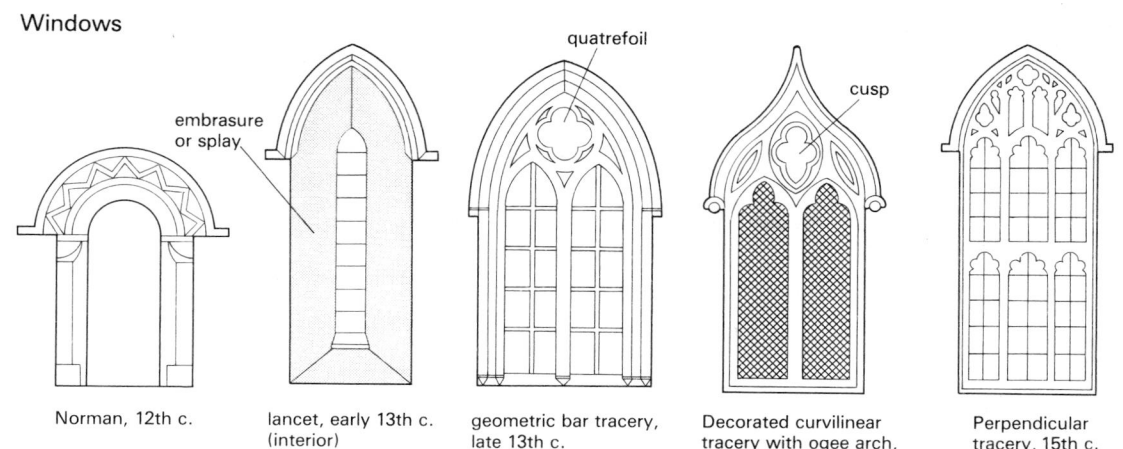

embrasure or splay

quatrefoil

cusp

Norman, 12th c.

lancet, early 13th c. (interior)

geometric bar tracery, late 13th c.

Decorated curvilinear tracery with ogee arch, 14th c.

Perpendicular tracery, 15th c.

Vaults

Hammer-beam roof

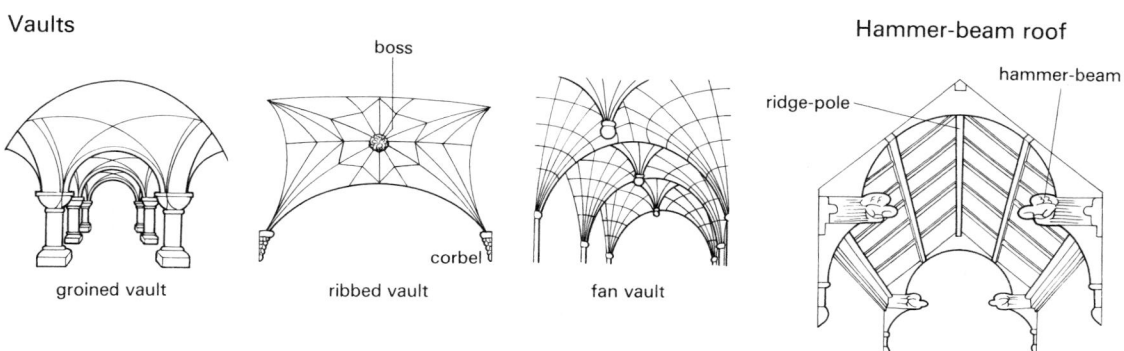

boss

corbel

groined vault

ribbed vault

fan vault

hammer-beam

ridge-pole

Monastic buildings

church

gatehouse

cloister

chapter house

infirmary

abbot's lodging

store-rooms

kitchen

garth

refectory

dormitory

bakehouse

mill

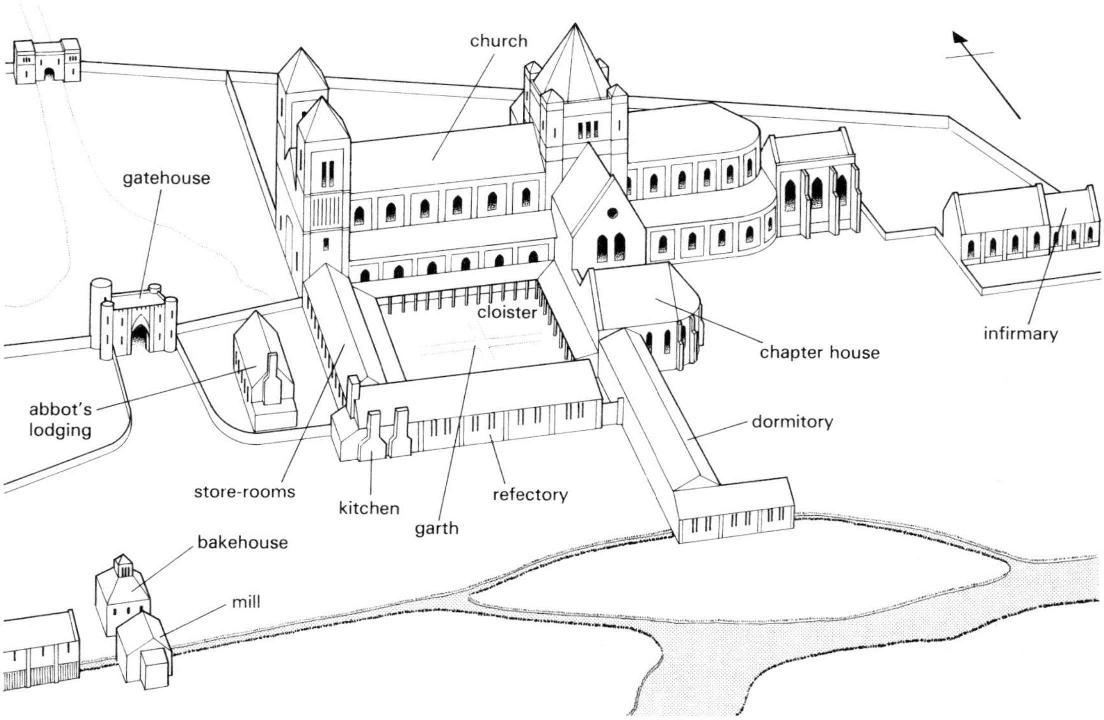

quinine. [f. Countess of *Chinchón* who introduced the drug to Spain, 1640]

cincture /ˈsɪŋktʃə(r), -tʃʊə(r)/ *n.* (*literary*) a girdle, belt, or border. —*v.t.* to surround with a cincture. [f. L *cinctura* (*cingere* gird)]

cinder /ˈsɪndə(r)/ *n.* the residue of coal, wood, etc., after it has ceased to flame; (in *pl.*) ashes. [OE]

Cinderella /sɪndəˈrelə/ *n.* a person or thing that is persistently neglected in favour of others. [character in fairy-tale by Perrault; analogous stories exist in folk-lore of various countries]

cine- /sɪnɪ-/ *prefix* cinematographic (as in *cine-camera*, *cine-projector*). [abbr.]

cinema /ˈsɪnəmə/ *n.* 1. a theatre where motion-picture films are shown. It is thought that the Central Hall, Colne, Lancashire, built in 1907, was the first cinema in Britain, films having been regarded earlier as a passing novelty. Cinema design in the USA developed rapidly after 1912, evolving into the fantastic 'movie palaces' of the 1920s, whose British equivalent appeared in the 1930s. 2. films as an art or industry (see below). —**cinematic** /-ˈmætɪk/ *adj.* [f. F *cinéma* abbr. *cinématographe* (see CINEMATOGRAPH)]

Photographic motion pictures projected on to a screen became available to the general public from about 1895. The earliest pictures, shown either as side-shows at fairgrounds or as items in music-hall programmes, were all short and silent; they included slapstick comedy, trick pictures, short romances, and five-minute dramas. More important were the films recording actual happenings, such as the Derby of 1896, the Boer War, the funeral of Queen Victoria, and travel all over the world. From 1900 to 1914 the film industry was international, led by France, Italy, Britain, and America; films made in any country could be sold in any other, and their length increased from a few minutes to two hours. During the First World War the demand for films grew at a time when European producers were least able to meet it, and America became the foremost film-making country, Hollywood in California, with its strong clear light, being the chief centre of production. America consolidated this position in the 1920s, developing the star-system and film publicity simultaneously. The cinema became the people's entertainment, lavish, luxurious, often lurid, available at the price of a few pence. Sound films evolved in the late 1920s, and (because of the language barrier) forced national film industries to develop independently. In 1932 a three-colour process known as Technicolor was adopted, adding gaiety and brilliance to the spectacle but (unlike the introduction of sound) often no greater sense of realism. Since the Second World War the increasing popularity of television has seriously threatened the prosperity of the cinema industry, taking over the 'domestic' film and, with its immediacy of transmission, the newsreel. New techniques, such as wide screens, were hurried forward, and costly and elaborate productions, including a number of science fiction and horror films, had some success in attracting audiences back to the cinema.

CinemaScope /ˈsɪnəməskəʊp/ *n.* [P] a wide-screen process in which special lenses are used to compress a wide image into a standard frame and then expand it again during projection. The resulting image is almost two and a half times as wide as it is high. The process was copyrighted by Twentieth Century-Fox in 1952, and similar processes were later adopted by other studios.

cinematheque /sɪnəməˈtek/ *n.* a film library or repository; a small cinema. [f. F (CINEMA, *bibliothèque* library)]

cinematograph /sɪnəˈmætəɡrɑːf/ *n.* a machine for projecting motion-picture films on to a screen. [f. F *cinématographe* (machine patented by the Lumière brothers in 1895), f. Gk *kinēma* motion + -GRAPH]

cinematography /sɪnɪməˈtɒɡrəfɪ/ *n.* the art of making motion-picture films. —**cinematographer** *n.*, **cinematographic** /-ˈɡræfɪk/ *adj.* [as prec.]

cinéma-vérité /sɪnəmə ˈverɪteɪ/ *n.* a style of documentary film-making developed in the late 1950s and early 1960s, and made possible by the development for television of hand-held 16 mm cameras and portable sound equipment. In order to achieve immediacy and truth there was no script and no director, and the film crew consisted only of a cameraman and a sound-man. The style developed concurrently in France and in the USA, where it was known as direct cinema. [F, = film truth]

cineraria /sɪnəˈreərɪə/ *n.* a composite plant, a variety of

Senecio cruentus, with bright daisy-like flowers. [L, = of ashes, f. the hoary leaves of allied species]

cinerary urn /ˈsɪnərərɪ/ an urn for holding a dead person's ashes after cremation. [f. L (as prec.)]

cinnabar /ˈsɪnəbɑː(r)/ *n.* 1. red mercuric sulphide; the pigment obtained from this, vermilion. 2. a moth with reddish-marked wings. [f. L f. Gk]

cinnamon /ˈsɪnəmən/ *n.* a spice from the aromatic inner bark of a SE Asian tree; its colour, a yellowish-brown. [f. OF f. L, ult. f. Semitic]

cinquefoil /ˈsɪŋkfɔɪl/ *n.* 1. a plant of the genus *Potentilla*, with a compound leaf of five leaflets. 2. a five-cusped ornament etc. (ill. HERALDRY). [f. L (*quinque* five, *folium* leaf)]

Cinque Ports /sɪŋk/ a group of medieval ports in SE England (originally five: Dover, Hastings, Hythe, Romney, and Sandwich; Rye and Winchelsea were added later) formerly allowed various trading privileges in exchange for providing the bulk of England's navy. The origins of the association are unknown, but it existed long before its first real charter was granted by Edward I. Most of the old privileges were abolished in the 19th c. and the Wardenship of the Cinque Ports is now a purely honorary post. [f. OF f. L, = five ports]

cipher /ˈsaɪfə(r)/ *n.* 1. a set of letters or symbols representing others, used to conceal the meaning of a message etc. 2. the symbol O, representing nought or zero. 3. any Arabic numeral. —*v.t.* to write in cipher. [f. OF f. L f. Arab., = zero]

circa /ˈsɜːkə/ *prep.* about (a specified date or number). [L]

circadian /sɜːˈkeɪdɪən/ *adj.* (of physiological activities etc.) occurring about once every twenty-four hours. [f. L *circa* about, *dies* day]

Circassian /sɜːˈkæsɪən/ *adj.* of a group of tribes of the Caucasus, whose women were remarkable for their beauty. —*n.* a member of these tribes. [f. *Circassia* district in N. Caucasus (Russ. *Cherkés* tribe calling themselves Adighe)]

Circe /ˈsɜːsɪ/ (*Gk legend*) an enchantress who lived with her wild animals on the fabled island of Aeaea. When Odysseus visited the island his companions were changed into pigs by her potions, but he protected himself by the herb called *moly* and forced her to restore his men into human form. The island was later identified with the promontory of Circeii on the coast of Italy near Naples, where the great bulk of Monte Circeo rises like an island floating in the marshes.

circle /ˈsɜːk(ə)l/ *n.* 1. a round plane figure with its circumference equidistant from the centre at all points (ill. SHAPES). 2. a circular or roundish structure, enclosure, etc.; a curved upper tier of seats at a theatre etc.; a road or railway without ends, on which traffic circulates continuously. 3. persons grouped round a centre of interest; a restricted group or set. —*v.t./i.* 1. to move in a circle; to revolve round. 2. to form a circle round, to surround. [f. OF f. L *circulus* dim. of *circus* ring]

circlet /ˈsɜːklɪt/ *n.* an ornamental band worn round the head. [f. prec. + -LET]

circuit /ˈsɜːkɪt/ *n.* 1. a line enclosing an area, the route or distance round; a motor-racing track. 2. a closed path for an electric current; the apparatus through which a current passes. 3. a judge's itinerary through a district to hold courts, such a district; a group of Methodist churches served by a set of itinerant preachers. 4. a chain of theatres, cinemas, etc., under a single management. 5. a sequence of sporting events. —**circuit-breaker** *n.* an automatic device for interrupting an electric current. [f. OF f. L *circuitus* (*circum* round, *ire* go)]

circuitous /sɜːˈkjuːɪtəs/ *adj.* going a long way round, indirect. [f. L (as prec.)]

circuitry /ˈsɜːkɪtrɪ/ *n.* a system of electric circuits; the equipment forming this. [f. CIRCUIT]

circular /ˈsɜːkjʊlə(r)/ *adj.* 1. in the form of a circle. 2. travelling in a circle; (of reasoning) following a vicious circle. 3. (of letters etc.) addressed to a number of people, not individual. —*n.* a circular letter, leaflet, etc. —**circular saw**, a rotating toothed disc for sawing wood etc. (ill. CARPENTRY). —**circularity** /-ˈlærɪtɪ/ *n.* [f. AF f. L *circularis* (*circulus* circle)]

circularize /ˈsɜːkjʊləraɪz/ *v.t.* to send circulars to. [f. prec.]

circulate /ˈsɜːkjʊleɪt/ *v.t./i.* 1. to go round continuously; to hand or be passed from person to person. 2. to send circulars to. [f. L (as CIRCLE)]

circulation /sɜːkjʊˈleɪʃ(ə)n/ n. **1.** movement from and back to a starting-point, especially that of the blood from and to the heart (ill. BODY 3). **2.** transmission or distribution (of information, books, etc.). **3.** the number of copies of a newspaper etc. sold or distributed. [f. prec.]

circulatory /sɜːkjʊˈleɪtərɪ/ adj. of the circulation of the blood. [f. CIRCULATE]

circumcise /ˈsɜːkəmsaɪz/ v.t. to cut off the foreskin of (a male person) as a religious rite or surgically; to cut off the clitoris of (a female person), to perform the operation of infibulation on. —**circumcision** /-ˈsɪʒ(ə)n/ n. [f. OF f. L (circum round, caedere cut)]

circumference /sɜːˈkʌmfərəns/ n. the line enclosing a circle or circular object; the distance round this. [f. OF f. L (circum round, ferre carry)]

circumflex /ˈsɜːkəmfleks/ n. (in full **circumflex accent**) a mark (ˆ) over a vowel to show contraction, length, or special quality. [f. L (circum round, flexus bent)]

circumlocution /sɜːkəmləˈkjuːʃ(ə)n/ n. speaking in a roundabout or indirect way; a roundabout expression. —**circumlocutory** /-ˈlɒkjʊtərɪ/ adj. [f. L (circum round, locutio speaking)]

circumnavigate /sɜːkəmˈnævɪgeɪt/ v.t. to sail round (the world etc.). —**circumnavigation** /-ˈgeɪʃ(ə)n/ n. [f. L (circum round, navigare navigate)]

circumscribe /ˈsɜːkəmskraɪb/ v.t. **1.** to draw a line round; (in geometry) to draw (a figure) round another so as to touch it at points without cutting it. **2.** to mark the limits of, to restrict. —**circumscription** /-ˈskrɪpʃ(ə)n/ n. [f. L (circum round, scribere write)]

circumspect /ˈsɜːkəmspekt/ adj. cautious, taking everything into account. —**circumspection** /-ˈspekʃ(ə)n/ n. [f. L (circum round, specere look)]

circumstance /ˈsɜːkəmstəns/ n. **1.** a fact or occurrence. **2.** (in pl.) the conditions connected with or affecting an event or person or action, financial position. **3.** ceremony, fuss. [f. OF f. L (circum round, stare stand)]

circumstantial /sɜːkəmˈstænʃ(ə)l/ adj. **1.** giving full details. **2.** (of evidence) consisting of facts that strongly suggest something without providing direct proof. —**circumstantiality** /-ʃɪˈælɪtɪ/ n., **circumstantially** adv. [f. L (as prec.)]

circumvent /sɜːkəmˈvent/ v.t. to evade or find a way round (a difficulty); to outwit. —**circumvention** n. [f. L (circum round, venire come)]

circus /ˈsɜːkəs/ n. **1.** a travelling show of performing animals, acrobats, clowns, etc. (see below). **2.** (colloq.) a scene of lively action. **3.** (colloq.) a group of people in a common activity, especially sport. **4.** an open space in a town, on which streets converge. **5.** (hist.) an arena for sports and games. [L, = ring]

Roman circuses in no way resembled those of the present day: they were arenas used for chariot-racing and gladiatorial combats. The modern circus dates from the late 18th c., when ex-sergeant-major Philip Astley gave horse-riding displays in London, at first in a field and then in 'Astley's Royal Amphitheatre of Arts', an arena to which he had added a stage for singing, dancing, and pantomime. This form of entertainment proved so popular that similar shows were started elsewhere in England and in other countries of Europe, some permanent, others as 'tenting' circuses, with performers and equipment travelling in caravans and wagons (later by train). From the early 19th c. they were often combined with the travelling menageries and wild animals' performances that had become very popular, of which the most celebrated was the combined circus and menagerie owned by the Sangers. America was the home of the really big circus. Barnum and his partners opened their first show at Brooklyn in 1871, and combined in 1880 with his great rivals Cooper and Bailey. After losing itspopularity in England in the early 20th c., the circus enjoyed a revival through the large and elaborate productions of C. B. Cochran (1912) and after the First World War by new circuses such as that of Bertram Mills, but circuses are now rare in Britain. In the USSR, however, the State-subsidized circus continues to flourish.

cire perdue /sɪər ˈpɜːdjuː/ a method of casting bronze by using an inner and an outer mould, with molten metal poured in after the wax layer between these has been melted away. [F, = lost wax]

cirque /sɜːk/ n. a deep bowl-shaped hollow at the head of a valley or on a mountain-side (ill. MOUNTAINS). [F f. L circus ring]

cirrhosis /sɪˈrəʊsɪs/ n. a chronic disease of the liver, especially suffered by alcoholics, in which the liver hardens into many small projections. [f. Gk kirrhos tawny]

cirriped /ˈsɪrɪped/ n. a marine crustacean in a valved shell, e.g. a barnacle. [f. L cirrus curl (from form of legs) + pes foot]

cirrocumulus /sɪrəʊˈkjuːmjuːləs/ n. (pl. -li /-laɪ/) a form of usually high cloud consisting of small roundish fleecy clouds in contact with one another, known as 'mackerel sky' (ill. WEATHER). [f. CIRRUS + CUMULUS]

cirrostratus /sɪrəʊˈstreɪtəs/ n. (pl. -ti /-taɪ/) thin usually high white cloud composed mainly of fine ice-crystals and producing halo phenomena. [f. foll. + STRATUS]

cirrus /ˈsɪrəs/ n. (pl. cirri /-raɪ/) **1.** a form of cloud, usually high, with diverging filaments or wisps (ill. WEATHER). **2.** a tendril or appendage of a plant or animal. [L, = curl]

Cisneros /θiːsˈneɪrəʊs/, Francisco Jiménez de (1437–1517), Spanish statesman. One of the major contributors to the growth of Spanish power in the late 15th and early 16th c., Cisneros became primate of Spain in 1495 and later a Cardinal and Inquisitor General for Castile and Léon.

cissy var. of SISSY.

cist /kɪst/ n. a prehistoric burial chest or chamber excavated in rock or formed of stones or hollowed tree-trunks, especially a stone coffin formed of slabs placed on edge and covered on the top by one or more horizontal slabs. [Welsh, = chest]

Cistercian /sɪsˈtɜːʃ(ə)n/ n. a member of the Cistercian order (see below). —adj. of the Cistercian order. [f. F f. L Cistercium Cîteaux near Dijon in France, where founded]

The Cistercian order was founded in 1098 for strict observance of the Rule of St Benedict, and Cistercian houses spread throughout Europe in the 12th–13th c. The monks are now divided into two observances, the strict observance (following the original rule), known popularly as Trappists, and the common observance, which has certain relaxations.

cistern /ˈsɪstɜːn/ n. a tank for storing water (especially in a roof-space) supplying taps, or as part of a flushing lavatory; an underground reservoir. [f. OF f. L (cista box, f. Gk kistē)]

cistus n. a shrub of the genus Cistus with large white, pink, or purple flowers. [f. Gk]

citadel /ˈsɪtəd(ə)l/ n. **1.** a fortress, usually on high ground, protecting or dominating a city. **2.** a meeting-hall of the Salvation Army. [f. F or It., f. L civitas city]

cite /saɪt/ v.t. **1.** to quote or mention as an example or to support an argument. **2.** to mention in an official dispatch. **3.** to summon to appear in a lawcourt. —**citation** /-ˈteɪʃ(ə)n/ n. [f. F f. L (ciēre set moving)]

citizen /ˈsɪtɪz(ə)n/ n. a native or naturalized member of a State; an inhabitant of a city. —**citizens' band,** a system of local radio intercommunication by individuals on special frequencies. —**citizenry** n., **citizenship** n. [f. AF f. L civitas city]

citrate /ˈsɪtreɪt/ n. a salt of citric acid. [f. foll.]

citric /ˈsɪtrɪk/ adj. derived from citrus fruit. —**citric acid,** the sharp-tasting acid in lemon-juice etc. [f. F f. L citrus citron]

citron /ˈsɪtrən/ n. a large yellow-skinned fruit like a lemon; the tree (Citrus medica) bearing it. [F f. L citrus]

citronella /sɪtrəˈnelə/ n. a fragrant oil obtained from a grass (Cymbopogon nardus) of S. Asia; this grass. [as prec.]

citrus /ˈsɪtrəs/ n. a tree of the genus Citrus, including citron, lemon, and orange; the fruit of such a tree. [L]

city /ˈsɪtɪ/ n. a large town, especially one created by royal charter and containing a cathedral. —**the City,** the part of London governed by the Lord Mayor and Corporation; the business quarter of this; commercial circles. **city fathers,** the officials administering a city. **city-state** n. (hist.) a city that is also an independent State, characteristic of ancient Greece. [f. OF f. L civitas (civis citizen)]

cityscape n. a view of a city, city scenery. [f. CITY, after landscape]

civet /ˈsɪvɪt/ n. **1.** (in full **civet-cat**) any of various small catlike animals of the family Viverridae, especially Civettictis civetta of central Africa. **2.** the strong musky perfume obtained from its anal glands. [f. F, ult. f. Arab., = the perfume]

civic /ˈsɪvɪk/ adj. of a city; of citizens or citizenship. —**civic centre,** the area where municipal offices are situated. [f. OF or L (civis citizen)]

civics /ˈsɪvɪks/ *n.pl.* the study of the rights and duties of citizenship. [f. prec.]

civil /ˈsɪv(ə)l, -ɪl/ *adj.* **1.** of or belonging to citizens. **2.** of ordinary citizens, non-military. **3.** polite, obliging, not rude. **4.** (*Law*) concerning private rights and not criminal offences. **5.** (of the length of the day, year, etc.) fixed by custom or law, not natural or astronomical. —**civil defence,** an organization for protecting civilians in an air raid or other enemy action. **civil disobedience,** refusal to comply with a law or laws as a peaceful protest. **civil engineer,** one who designs or maintains works of public utility, e.g. roads and bridges. **civil liberty,** freedom of action subject to the law. **civil list,** the annual allowance by Parliament for the sovereign's household expenses etc. It is made in lieu of the revenues from royal patrimonies, which are assigned to the Treasury for public use. **civil marriage,** one solemnized with a civil (not religious) ceremony. **civil rights,** the rights of citizens, especially (*US*) of Blacks, to liberty, equality, etc. **Civil Service, civil war,** see separate entries. —**civilly** *adv.* [f. OF f. L *civilis* (as CIVIC)]

civilian /sɪˈvɪljən/ *n.* a person not in the armed forces or police force. —*adj.* of or for civilians. [f. prec.]

civility /sɪˈvɪlɪtɪ/ *n.* politeness; an act of politeness. [f. OF f. L (as CIVIL)]

civilization /sɪvɪlaɪˈzeɪʃ(ə)n/ *n.* **1.** an advanced stage or system of social development; those peoples of the world regarded as having this. **2.** a people or nation (especially of the past) regarded as an element of social evolution. [f. foll.]

civilize /ˈsɪvɪlaɪz/ *v.t.* to bring out of a barbarous or primitive stage of society to a more developed one; to refine and educate. [f. F *civiliser* (as CIVIL)]

Civil Service the body of full-time officers employed by a State in the administration of civil (non-military) affairs. The Roman Empire had such a service, and there was one in China from the 7th c.; in the 19th c. many European countries copied Napoleon's system of an organized hierarchy. The term 'Civil Service' was originally applied to the part of the service of the East India Company carried on by covenanted servants who did not belong to the army or navy. —**Civil Servant,** a member of the Civil Service.

civil war war between citizens of the same country:
   English Civil War the war between Charles I and his Parliamentary opponents, 1642–9. After several years of warfare, the better-organized Parliamentary forces gained the upper hand in 1644–5. Royalist resistance collapsed in 1646 and an attempt by Charles to regain power in alliance with the Scots was defeated at Preston in 1648, Charles himself being executed at the behest of the Parliamentary army in 1649. Fought against a background of confused political and religious issues, the English Civil War dramatically changed the nature of English society and government, even though the attempt to find an alternative to the monarchy eventually ended with the restoration of Charles II after the death of Oliver Cromwell, the dominant figure of the entire period.
   American Civil War the war between the northern US States (usually known as the Union) and the Confederate States of the South, 1861–5. The southern States, having seceded from the Federal Union over the issues of slavery and States' rights, maintained a military resistance to the superior industrial strength of the north for four years. Although its armies won some impressive victories in the first two years of the war, the Confederacy failed to gain foreign recognition and was gradually overwhelmed by superior military might and naval blockade. By the time the main Confederate army surrendered in April 1865, most of the South, including its capital Richmond, had already fallen to Union soldiers.
   Spanish Civil War the conflict between Nationalist and Republican forces in Spain, 1936–9. It began with a widespread military uprising against the leftist republican government in July 1936; the Nationalists were extensively aided by Germany and Italy, the Republicans by Russia and by an International Brigade of volunteers from Europe and America. In bitter fighting the Nationalists, led by Franco, gradually gained control of the countryside but failed to capture the capital, Madrid. Various attempts to bring the war to an end failed until after long periods of prolonged stalemate Franco finally succeeded in capturing Barcelona and Madrid in early 1939.

civvies /ˈsɪvɪz/ *n.pl.* (*slang*) civilian clothes. [abbr.]

Civvy Street (*slang*) civilian life. [abbr.]

Cl *symbol* chlorine.

cl *abbr.* centilitre(s).

clack *v.i.* to make a sharp sound as of boards struck together; to chatter. —*n.* a clacking noise or talk. [imit.]

Clactonian /klækˈtəʊnɪən/ *adj.* of the lower palaeolithic industries represented by the flint implements found at Clacton, Essex, dated to *c.*250,000–200,000 BC. —*n.* these industries.

clad[1] *past & p.p.* of CLOTHE.

clad[2] *v.t.* (**-dd-**) to provide with cladding. [f. prec.]

cladding *n.* a protective coating or covering on a structure, material, etc. [f. prec.]

clade /kleɪd/ *n.* a group of organisms that have evolved from a common ancestor. [f. Gk *klados* branch]

cladistics /kləˈdɪstɪks/ *n.* the systematic classification of groups of organisms on the basis of the order of their assumed divergence from ancestral species. [f. prec.]

claim *v.t.* **1.** to demand as one's due or property. **2.** to represent oneself as having; to profess *to*; to assert *that*. **3.** to have as an achievement or victim etc.; to deserve (attention etc.). —*n.* **1.** a demand for a thing considered one's due. **2.** the right or title (*to*). **3.** an assertion. **4.** a thing (especially land) claimed. [f. OF f. L *clamare* call out]

claimant *n.* a person making a claim, especially in a lawsuit. [f. prec.]

Clair, René (1898–1981), real name Chomette, French film director, the fantastic nature of whose work contained elements of surrealism, though humour and satire were always at their core. He made a number of silent films, notably *An Italian Straw Hat* (1927), and his early sound films included the classics *Sous les Toits de Paris* (1930), *Le Million,* and *A Nous la Liberté* (both 1931). His British and American work was less successful, but he regained his touch on returning to France in films such as *Les Belles de Nuit* (1952). He was invariably involved in writing the scripts.

clairvoyance /kleəˈvɔɪəns/ *n.* the supposed faculty of seeing mentally things in the future or out of sight; exceptional insight. —**clairvoyant** *n. & adj.* [F (*clair* clear, *voyant* seeing)]

clam *n.* an edible bivalve mollusc, especially *Mercenaria mercenaria* and *Mya arenaria.* —*v.i.* (**-mm-**) **clam up,** (*slang*) to become silent. [app. f. *clam* clamp]

clamber *v.i.* to climb laboriously with hands and feet. —*n.* a difficult climb. [prob. f. *clamb* (obs. past tense of CLIMB)]

clammy *adj.* unpleasantly damp and sticky. —**clammily** *adv.,* **clamminess** *n.* [f. *clam* daub]

clamour /ˈklæmə(r)/ *n.* a loud or vehement shouting or noise; a loud protest or demand. —*v.t./i.* to make a clamour; to utter with a clamour. —**clamorous** *adj.* [f. OF f. L (*clamare* call out)]

clamp[1] *n.* a device, especially a brace or band of iron etc., for strengthening, pressing, or holding things together. —*v.t.* to strengthen or fasten with a clamp; to fix firmly. —**clamp down on,** to become strict about, to suppress. **clamp-down** *n.* [f. LG or Du.]

clamp[2] *n.* a pile of bricks for burning; potatoes etc. stored in the open under straw and earth, peat, etc. [prob. f. Du., rel. to CLUMP]

clan *n.* a group of families with a common ancestor, especially in Scotland; a large family or social group; a group with a strong common interest. —**clannish** *adj.,* **clansman** *n.* [f. Gael. f. L *planta* sprout]

clandestine /klænˈdestɪn/ *adj.* surreptitious, secret. —**clandestinely** *adv.* [f. F or L (*clam* secretly)]

clang *n.* a loud resonant metallic sound. —*v.t./i.* to make or cause to make a clang. [imit.; cf. L *clangere* resound]

clangour /ˈklæŋɡə(r)/ *n.* prolonged clanging. —**clangorous** *adj.* [f. L (as prec.)]

clank *n.* a metallic sound as of metal striking metal. —*v.t./i.* to make or cause to make a clank. [imit.]

clap *v.t./i.* (**-pp-**) **1.** to strike the palms (or *hands*) repeatedly together, especially in applause; to applaud thus. **2.** to put or place with vigour or determination. —*n.* **1.** an act of clapping, especially as applause; an explosive sound, especially of thunder. **2.** a friendly slap. —**clap eyes on,** (*colloq.*) to catch sight of. **clapped out,** (*slang*) worn out, exhausted. [OE, = throb, beat]

clapper *n.* the tongue or striker of a bell. —**clapper-board** *n.* a device in film-making that makes a sharp clap for synchronizing picture and sound. [f. CLAP]

clapper bridge a rough bridge consisting of a series of

slabs or planks resting on piles of stones (ill. BRIDGES). [perh. f. L. *claperius* heap of stones (orig. unkn.)]

claptrap *n.* insincere or pretentious talk, nonsense.

claque /klæk/ *n.* a hired group of applauders in a theatre etc. [F (*claquer* clap)]

Clare /kleə(r)/, St (1194–1253), foundress of the 'Poor Clares', an order of Franciscan nuns named after her. Born at Assisi, she joined St Francis *c.*1212, and when a few years later he set up a separate community for women to live on Franciscan lines she became its abbess. The order spread through Italy and into Europe.

Clarendon /ˈklærəndən/, Edward Hyde, Earl of (1609–74), English statesman and historian, Lord Chancellor under Charles II and Chancellor of Oxford University from 1660 until his fall in 1667, and author of a successful and prestigious history of the English civil war. The new printing house into which Oxford University Press moved in 1713, and the laboratory which houses the university physics department (founded in 1872), are named after him.

claret /ˈklærət/ *n.* 1. red wine, especially from Bordeaux. 2. reddish-violet colour. [F, orig. = clarified wine (*clarus* clear)]

clarify /ˈklærɪfaɪ/ *v.t./i.* 1. to make or become clear to see or easier to understand. 2. to free (a liquid etc.) from impurity or opaqueness. —**clarification** /-fɪˈkeɪʃ(ə)n/ *n.* [f. OF f. L (*clarus* clear)]

clarinet /klærɪˈnet/ *n.* a single-reed wood-wind instrument dating from the early 18th c. (ill. ORCHESTRA) It has a range of just over three octaves, but the highest notes are not generally scored for except by some modern composers seeking a squeaky harsh sound. It has been a standard orchestral instrument since the late 18th c. —**clarinettist** *n.* [f. F, dim. of *clarine* a kind of bell]

clarion /ˈklærɪən/ *n.* 1. a clear rousing sound. 2. (*hist.*) a shrill war-trumpet. [f. L (*clarus* clear)]

clarity /ˈklærɪtɪ/ *n.* clearness. [as prec.]

Clark, William (1770–1838), US army officer who jointly commanded the Lewis and Clark expedition (1804–6) across the American continent.

Clarke /klɑːk/, Arthur Charles (1917–), English writer of science fiction stories and novels, including *The Nine Billion Names of God* (1967) and *A Space Odyssey* (1968), and of many non-fiction works on space travel.

clash *v.t./i.* 1. to strike making a loud harsh sound as of light metal objects struck together. 2. to conflict, to disagree; to coincide inconveniently (*with*). 3. (of colours) to produce an unpleasant visual effect by not being harmonious. —*n.* 1. a sound of clashing. 2. conflict, a disagreement. 3. a clashing of colours. [imit.]

clasp /klɑːsp/ *n.* 1. a device with interlocking parts for fastening. 2. a grasp, a handshake, an embrace. 3. a bar on a medal-ribbon. —*v.t.* 1. to fasten with a clasp. 2. to grasp, to hold closely or embrace. —**clasp-knife** *n.* a folding knife with a catch to hold the blade open. [orig. unkn.]

class /klɑːs/ *n.* 1. a set of persons or things grouped together, or graded or differentiated (especially by quality) from others; a division or order of society; a division of candidates by merit in an examination; a grouping of animals or plants next below a phylum. 2. distinction, high quality. 3. a set of students taught together; the occasion when they meet. —*v.t.* to place in a class, to classify. [f. L *classis* division of Roman people]

classic /ˈklæsɪk/ *adj.* 1. of acknowledged excellence; outstandingly important, remarkably typical. 2. of ancient Greek and Roman art, literature, and culture; resembling this, especially in harmony and restraint. 3. having historic associations. —*n.* 1. a classic work, example, writer, etc. 2. (in *pl.*) the study of ancient Greek and Roman literature, culture, etc. [f. L *classicus* of the highest class (as CLASS)]

classical /ˈklæsɪk(ə)l/ *adj.* 1. of ancient Greek and Roman art, literature, culture, etc. (see below). 2. simple and harmonious in style. 3. (of music) serious, following established forms; of the period *c.*1750–1800. —**classical scholar,** an expert in ancient Greek and Roman languages and culture. —**classically** *adv.* [as prec.]

Classical art refers, in the first instance, to the art of the Greeks and Romans: the term was originally applied to literature and its present usage in the visual arts dates back to the 17th c., when it was assumed that antique art had set the standard for all future achievement. In the late 18th c. it took on a second meaning as the antithesis to Romantic. In the 20th c. classicism tends to denote clarity, logicality,

and adherence to recognized canons of form and conscious craftsmanship, in contrast to an irrational display of personal emotion.

classicism /ˈklæsɪsɪz(ə)m/ *n.* following of the classic style. [f. CLASSIC]

classicist /ˈklæsɪsɪst/ *n.* a classical scholar. [as prec. + IST]

classifiable /ˈklæsɪfaɪəb(ə)l/ *adj.* that can be classified. [f. CLASSIFY]

classificatory /klæsɪfɪˈkeɪtərɪ/ *adj.* of or involving classification. [as prec.]

classify /ˈklæsɪfaɪ/ *v.t.* 1. to arrange in classes or categories; to assign a class to. 2. to designate as officially secret or not for general disclosure. —**classification** /-ˈkeɪʃ(ə)n/ *n.* [back-formation f. *classification* f. F (as CLASS)]

classless *adj.* without distinctions of social class. [f. CLASS + -LESS]

classroom *n.* a room where a class of students is taught.

classy /ˈklɑːsɪ/ *adj.* (*colloq.*) superior, stylish. —**classily** *adv.*, **classiness** *n.* [f. CLASS]

clatter *n.* a sound as of hard objects struck together or falling; noisy talk. —*v.i.* to make a clatter; to fall, move, etc., with a clatter. [OE (imit.)]

Claude /kləʊd/ French landscape painter, Claude Gellée, called Le Lorrain and in England known as Claude Lorraine (1600–82), living in Rome from 1627, whose paintings are harmonious evocations of the pastoral serenity of the Golden Age. Apprenticed as a pastry-cook to the Roman painter Agostino Tassi, he became his assistant and worked with him on villa decoration. The influence of the late mannerists is evident in the nuns and picturesque paraphernalia of his early paintings, but in his mature works he concentrates on the poetic power of light and atmosphere, letting the sun shine directly out of the picture, and raising the viewpoint so that the eye can roam over a spacious panorama to the distant horizon. His paintings were so much in demand that he recorded them in the form of sketches in his *Liber Veritatis* to guard against forgeries. Claude was particularly admired in England, where he inspired a revolution in landscape gardening in the mid-18th c. and was a profound influence on the painters Wilson and Turner.

Claudius /ˈklɔːdɪəs/ Tiberius Claudius Nero Germanicus (10 BC–AD 54), Roman emperor 41–54. Neglected in early life because of his physical infirmities, and largely devoted to historical and antiquarian studies, he was proclaimed emperor by the Praetorian Guard after the murder of Caligula. He took part personally in the invasion of Britain in 43. The power of his wives and freedmen was notorious; his fourth wife, Agrippina, the mother of Nero, is said to have killed him with a dish of poisoned mushrooms.

clause /klɔːz/ *n.* 1. a distinct part of a sentence, containing a finite verb. 2. a single part in a treaty, law, contract, etc. [f. OF f. L *clausula* conclusion (as CLOSE)]

Clausewitz /ˈklaʊzəvɪts/, Karl von (1780–1831), Prussian soldier and military theorist, whose monumental study *On War* was perhaps the most influential strategical work of the century. Unfortunately his efforts to place military operations in the context of national and international politics were misinterpreted by his disciples (including many of the 19th and early 20th centuries' most important soldiers and statesmen) as establishing war as the ultimate and most desirable means of political action.

claustrophobia /klɔːstrəˈfəʊbɪə/ *n.* abnormal fear of being in a confined space. —**claustrophobic** *adj.* [f. L *claustrum* enclosed space + PHOBIA]

clavichord /ˈklævɪkɔːd/ *n.* a stringed keyboard instrument with a very soft tone, developed in the 14th c. and in use from the early 15th. The strings are struck by brass blades, or 'tangents', to produce a clear and quiet tone for domestic music-making. It was a favourite instrument of both Johann Sebastian Bach and his son C. P. E. Bach [f. L (*clavis* key, *chorda* string)]

clavicle /ˈklævɪk(ə)l/ *n.* the collar-bone (ill. BODY 1). [f. L, dim. of *clavis* key]

clavier /ˈkleɪvɪə(r)/ *n.* a keyboard; an instrument with this; an organ manual. [F, or f. G f. L, orig. = key-bearer (*clavis* key)]

claw *n.* 1. the pointed nail of an animal's or bird's foot; a foot armed with claws. 2. the pincers of a shellfish. 3. a device for grappling and holding things. —*v.t.* to scratch or maul or pull with the claws; to scratch with the fingernails. —**claw back,** to recoup (money etc.) that has just been given away, e.g. in taxation. **claw-hammer** *n.* a hammer with one side of the head forked for extracting nails (ill. CARPENTRY). [OE]

Clay, Cassius, see Muhammad ALI.

clay *n.* a stiff sticky earth, especially used for making bricks, pottery, etc. —**clay pigeon**, a breakable disc thrown up from a trap as a target for shooting. [OE]

claymore *n.* **1.** a Scottish two-edged broadsword. **2.** a broadsword (often single-edged) with a basket-like structure protecting the hilt. [Gael., = great sword]

clean *adj.* **1.** free from dirt or impurities, not soiled; not yet used, preserving what is regarded as the original state; free from obscenity or indecency; attentive to personal hygiene and cleanness; (of a nuclear weapon) producing relatively little fall-out; containing nothing dishonourable, (of a licence) without endorsements. **2.** complete, clear-cut; evenly shaped, without projections or roughness. —*adv.* **1.** completely, entirely. **2.** in a clean manner. —*v.t./i.* to make or become clean. —*n.* a process of cleaning. —**clean-cut** *adj.* sharply outlined. **clean out**, to clean the inside of; (*slang*) to use up all the supplies or money of. **clean-shaven** *adj.* with beard or moustache shaved off. **clean sheet**, a record not showing any offences. **clean up**, to make clean or tidy; to restore order or morality to; (*colloq.*) to make a gain or profit. **make a clean breast of**, to confess fully about. —**cleanness** *n.* [OE]

cleaner *n.* **1.** a person employed to clean rooms. **2.** (usu. in *pl.*) an establishment for cleaning clothes. **3.** a device or substance for cleaning things. [f. prec.]

cleanly[1] /ˈkliːnlɪ/ *adv.* in a clean manner. [f. CLEAN]

cleanly[2] /ˈklenlɪ/ *adj.* habitually clean, with clean habits. —**cleanliness** *n.* [as prec.]

cleanse /klenz/ *v.t.* to make clean or pure. —**cleanser** *n.* [f. CLEAN]

clear *adj.* **1.** not clouded or murky or spotted; transparent; (of the conscience) free from guilt. **2.** readily perceived by the senses or mind. **3.** able to discern readily and accurately; confident or convinced (*about, that*). **4.** (of a road etc.) unobstructed, open. **5.** net, without deduction, complete; unhampered, free (*of* debt, commitments, etc.). —*adv.* clearly; completely; apart, out of contact. —*v.t./i.* **1.** to make or become clear. **2.** to free from or of obstruction, suspicion, etc.; to show or declare to be innocent (*of*); to approve (a person) for special duty, access to information, etc.; to pass (a cheque) through a clearing-house. **3.** to pass over or by without touching; to pass through (a customs office etc.). **4.** to make (an amount of money) as a net gain or to balance expenses. —**clear away**, to remove completely; to remove used crockery etc. after a meal; (of mists etc.) to disappear. **clear-cut** *adj.* sharply defined. **clearing bank**, a large bank belonging to a clearing-house. **clearing-house** *n.* a bankers' establishment where cheques etc. are exchanged, only the balances being paid in cash; an agency for collecting or distributing information etc. **clear off**, to get rid of, to complete payment of (a debt etc.); (*colloq.*) to go away. **clear out**, to empty; to remove; (*colloq.*) to go away. **clear up**, to tidy up; to solve (a mystery etc.); (of weather) to become fine. **clear a thing with**, to get approval or authorization of it from (a person). —**clearly** *adv.*, **clearness** *n.* [f. OF f. L *clarus* bright, clear]

clearance *n.* **1.** the act or process of clearing or being cleared; permission, authorization. **2.** a space allowed for one object to move within or past another. [f. prec.]

clearing *n.* an open space in woodland from which trees have been cleared. [f. CLEAR]

clearway *n.* a main road (other than a motorway) on which vehicles may not ordinarily stop.

cleat *n.* **1.** a projecting piece of metal, wood, etc., bolted on for securing ropes to, or to strengthen woodwork. **2.** a projecting piece fastened to a spar, gangway, boot, etc., to prevent slipping. **3.** a wedge serving as a support. [OE]

cleavage *n.* **1.** the process of splitting, the way in which a thing tends to split. **2.** the hollow between full breasts. [f. foll.]

cleave[1] *v.t./i.* (*past* **clove**, **cleft**, **cleaved**; *p.p.* **cloven** /ˈkləʊv(ə)n/, **cleft**, **cleaved**) to chop, to split or become split, especially along the grain or line of cleavage; to make a way through (the air etc.). [OE]

cleave[2] *v.i.* (*literary*) to stick fast or adhere *to*. [OE]

cleaver *n.* a heavy chopping tool used by butchers. [f. CLEAVE[1]]

cleavers *n.* (as *sing.* or *pl.*) a plant (*Galium aparine*) with hooked bristles on its stem that catch in clothes etc. [f. CLEAVE[2]]

clef *n.* a symbol on a staff in a musical score, locating a particular note on it and showing the pitch of the notes following that symbol, e.g. **alto** (*or* **C**) **clef**, **bass** (*or* **F**) **clef**, **treble** (*or* **G**) **clef** (ill. MUSICAL NOTATION). The clef signs evolved from the letters for which they stand. [F, = key]

cleft *p.p.* of CLEAVE[1]. —*adj.* split, partly divided. —*n.* a space made by cleaving, a fissure. —**cleft palate**, a congenital split in the roof of the mouth. **in a cleft stick**, in a dilemma.

clematis /ˈklemətɪs/ *n.* a climbing plant of the genus *Clematis*, chiefly with white, pink, or purple flowers. [L f. Gk (*klēma* vine branch)]

Clemenceau /klemɑ̃ˈsəʊ/, Georges (1841-1929), French statesman. A radical politician and journalist, Clemenceau made his name as a critic of government corruption and an exponent of the recapture of Alsace and Lorraine, lost to Germany in the Franco-Prussian War. A persistent opponent of the government during the early years of the First World War, he became Premier himself in November 1917 and saw France through to victory in 1918. At the Versailles peace talks he pushed hard for a punitive settlement with Germany and retired from politics soon afterwards, having failed to be elected President in 1920.

Clemens /ˈklemənz/, Samuel Langhorne (1835-1910) see Mark TWAIN.

Clement /ˈklemənt/ of Alexandria, St (*c.*150-*c.*215), Greek theologian, head of the theological school at Alexandria from 190 to 202, when he was forced to flee from persecution. He was succeeded by his pupil Origen. In his writings Clement explained and supplemented the Christian faith with the ideas of Greek philosophy.

clement /ˈklemənt/ *adj.* **1.** (of weather) mild. **2.** merciful. —**clemency** *n.* [f. L]

clementine /ˈklemɒntiːn/ *n.* a kind of small orange. [F]

clench *v.t.* **1.** to close (the teeth or fingers) tightly; to grasp firmly. **2.** to clinch (a nail or rivet). —*n.* a clenching action, a clenched state. [OE]

Cleopatra /klɪəˈpætrə/ (69-30 BC) the last Ptolemaic ruler of Egypt (as Cleopatra VII from 51 BC), famous for her brief liaison with Julius Caesar and for her longer political and romantic alliance with Mark Antony (the famous meeting described by Shakespeare took place at Tarsus in 41 BC), by whom she had three children. She and Antony were defeated by Octavian at the battle of Actium in 31 BC, after which she committed suicide by the bite of an asp.

Cleopatra's Needles a pair of granite obelisks erected at Heliopolis by Tuthmosis III *c.*1475 BC. They were moved to Alexandria in 12 BC and moved again in 1878, one being set up on the Thames Embankment in London and the other in Central Park, New York. They have no connection with Cleopatra.

clerestory /ˈklɪəstərɪ/ *n.* the part of the wall of a cathedral or large church, with a series of windows, above the aisle roof (ill. CHURCH). [f. CLEAR + STOREY]

clergy *n.* (usu. as *pl.*) the body of those ordained for religious service; clergymen. [f. OF (as CLERK)]

clergyman *n.* (*pl.* **-men**) a member of the clergy, especially of the Church of England.

cleric /ˈklerɪk/ *n.* a clergyman. [f. L f. Gk (*klēros* heritage, priestly order)]

clerical /ˈklerɪk(ə)l/ *adj.* **1.** of the clergy or a clergyman. **2.** of or done by clerks. —**clerical collar**, an upright white collar fastening at the back, worn by clergy. [as prec.]

clerihew /ˈklerɪhjuː/ *n.* a short witty, comic, or nonsensical verse, usually in two rhyming couplets with free metre in lines of unequal length. [f. E. *Clerihew* Bentley, English writer (d. 1956), its inventor]

clerk /klɑːk/ *n.* **1.** a person employed in an office, bank, etc., to keep records, accounts, etc. **2.** a secretary or agent of a local council (*town clerk*), court, etc. **3.** a lay officer of a church (*parish clerk*). —**clerk of (the) works**, an overseer of building works etc. [f. OE & OF (as CLERIC)]

Cleveland /ˈkliːvlənd/ a county of NE England.

clever /ˈklevə(r)/ *adj.* quick at learning or understanding things, skilful; ingenious. —**cleverly** *adv.*, **cleverness** *n.* [perh. rel. to CLEAVE[2], w. sense 'quick to seize']

clevis /ˈklevɪs/ *n.* a U-shaped piece of metal at the end of a beam for attaching tackle etc. [f. OE, rel. to CLEAVE[1]]

clew /kluː/ *n.* the lower or after corner of a sail (ill. SAILING-SHIPS); the small cords suspending a hammock. —*v.t.* to draw the lower ends of (a sail) *up* to the upper yard or mast for furling. [OE, orig. = ball of thread]

cliché /ˈkliːʃeɪ/ n. a hackneyed phrase or opinion. [F, orig. = metal casting of stereotype]

click n. a slight sharp sound as of a dropping latch. —v.t./i. **1.** to make or cause to make a click; to fasten with a click. **2.** (slang) to become clear or understandable; to be successful; to become friendly with. [imit.]

client /ˈklaɪənt/ n. a person using the services of a lawyer, architect, or professional person other than a doctor, or of a business; a customer. [f. L cliens (cluere hear, obey)]

clientele /kliːɒnˈtel/ n. clients or customers collectively. [f. L & F (as prec.)]

cliff n. a steep rock-face, especially on the coast. —**cliffhanger** n. a serial film etc. in which the viewer etc. is left in suspense at the end of each episode. [OE]

climacteric /klaɪˈmæktərɪk/ n. the period of life when physical powers begin to decline. [f. F or L f. Gk (as CLIMAX)]

climactic /klaɪˈmæktɪk/ adj. of a climax. [f. CLIMAX]

climate /ˈklaɪmət/ n. **1.** the prevailing weather conditions of an area; a region with certain weather conditions. **2.** the prevailing trend of opinion or feeling. —**climatic** /-ˈmætɪk/ adj. [f. OF or L f. Gk klima slope]

climax /ˈklaɪmæks/ n. **1.** the event or point of the greatest intensity or interest, culmination. **2.** sexual orgasm. —v.t./i. to reach or bring to a climax. [L f. Gk, = ladder]

climb /klaɪm/ v.t./i. **1.** to go up or over by effort. **2.** to move upwards, to go higher; (of a plant) to grow up a support. **3.** to rise in social rank etc. by one's own efforts. —n. **1.** the action of climbing. **2.** a hill etc. climbed or to be climbed. —**climb down,** to go downwards by effort; to retreat from a position taken up in argument. **climb-down** n. such a retreat. **climbing-frame** n. a structure of jointed bars etc. for children to climb on. [OE]

climber n. **1.** a mountaineer. **2.** a climbing plant. **3.** one who strives to rise socially. [f. prec.]

clime n. (literary) a region; a climate. [f. L clima (as CLIMATE)]

clinch v.t./i. **1.** to confirm or settle (an argument or bargain) conclusively. **2.** (of boxers) to come too close together for a full-arm blow; (colloq.) to embrace. **3.** to secure (a nail or rivet) by driving the point sideways when it is through. —n. a clinching action, a clinched state. [var. of CLENCH]

clincher n. a decisive point that settles an argument, proposition, etc. [f. prec.]

cling v.i. (past & p.p. clung) **1.** to maintain one's grasp, to hold on tightly. **2.** to become attached, to stick fast. **3.** to be stubbornly faithful. [OE]

clingstone n. a kind of peach or nectarine in which the stone is difficult to separate from the flesh.

clinic /ˈklɪnɪk/ n. **1.** a private or specialized hospital. **2.** a place or session at which specialized medical treatment or advice is given. [f. F f. Gk (as foll.)]

clinical /ˈklɪnɪk(ə)l/ adj. **1.** of or for the treatment of patients; taught or learnt at the hospital bedside. **2.** dispassionate, coldly detached. —**clinical death,** death judged by observation of a person's condition. —**clinically** adv. [f. L f. Gk (klinē bed)]

clinician /klɪˈnɪʃ(ə)n/ n. one who is skilled in the practice of clinical medicine, psychiatry, etc. [f. CLINIC]

clink[1] n. a sharp ringing sound. —v.t./i. to make or cause to make this sound. [f. Du.; imit.]

clink[2] n. (slang) prison. [orig. unkn.]

clinker n. a mass of slag or lava; the stony residue from burnt coal. [f. Du. (as CLINK[1])]

clinker-built adj. (of a boat) having its external planks overlapping and secured with clinched nails. [f. clink, dial. var. of CLINCH]

Clio /ˈklaɪoʊ/ (Gk & Rom. myth.) the Muse of epic poetry and history. [Gk kleiō celebrate]

clip[1] n. **1.** a device for holding things together or affixing something. **2.** a piece of jewellery fastened by a clip. **3.** a set of attached cartridges for a firearm. —v.t. (-pp-) to grip tightly; to fix with a clip. —**clip-on** adj. attached by a clip. [OE]

clip[2] v.t. (-pp-) **1.** to cut or trim with shears or scissors. **2.** to punch a small piece from (a ticket etc.) to show that it has been used; to cut from a newspaper etc. **3.** to omit (letters etc.) from (a word pronounced). **4.** (colloq.) to hit sharply. —n. **1.** the act of clipping. **2.** something clipped; a yield of wool clipped from sheep; an extract from a film. **3.** (colloq.) a sharp blow. **4.** (colloq.) a rapid pace. [f. ON, prob. imit.]

clipboard n. a small portable board with a spring clip for holding papers.

clipper n. **1.** a fast sailing-ship (see below). **2.** (usu. in pl.) an instrument for clipping hair. [f. CLIP[2]]

The term 'clipper' is loosely used as a generic name for types of very fast sailing-ship; it is said to refer to the fact that such ships could 'clip' the passage-time of the regular packet ships, themselves very fast in their day, and was first applied to the speedy schooners built in Virginia and Maryland in the early 19th c. The hull design was long and low with a very sharply-raked stem, and was later combined with the three-masted square rig, making the beautiful clipper-ships of the mid-19th c. the finest productions of the age of sail. The first British clippers were built for the tea trade, a profitable cargo, with the first arrivals in London from China each year commanding the highest prices. The opening of the Suez Canal in 1869 struck at the raison d'être of the tea-clippers, making the long trip round the Cape of Good Hope unprofitable.

clipping n. a piece clipped off; a newspaper cutting. [f. CLIP[2]]

clique /kliːk/ n. a small exclusive group of people. —**cliquish** adj., **cliquy** adj. [F, orig. = clicking noise]

clitoris /ˈklɪtərɪs/ n. a small erectile part of the female genitals, at the upper end of the vulva. —**clitoral** adj. [L f. Gk]

Clive /klaɪv/, Robert (1725-74), British general and colonial administrator who rose to fame as a commander in the East India Company's army during the struggle with France for India in the 1750s, his most notable victory being at Plassey in 1757 against a Franco-Indian force many times the size of his own. After a five-year spell in politics in England, he went back to India as Governor of Bengal, but on his return to England had to face a parliamentary inquiry, and, although cleared of accusations of peculation, became so afflicted by illness and depression that he committed suicide.

cloaca /kloʊˈeɪkə/ n. (pl. -ae /-iː/) the excretory opening at the end of the intestinal canal in birds, reptiles, etc. [L, = sewer]

cloak n. a sleeveless outdoor garment hanging loosely from the shoulders. —v.t. **1.** to cover with a cloak. **2.** to conceal, to disguise. —**cloak-and-dagger** adj. involving intrigue and espionage. [f. OF cloke, var. of cloche bell (from its shape)]

cloakroom n. a room where outdoor clothes and luggage may be left by visitors; (euphem.) a lavatory.

clobber[1] n. (slang) clothing, personal belongings. [orig. unkn.]

clobber[2] v.t. (slang) **1.** to hit repeatedly, to beat up. **2.** to defeat. **3.** to criticize severely. [orig. unkn.]

cloche /klɒʃ/ n. **1.** a portable translucent cover for protecting outdoor plants. **2.** a woman's close-fitting bell-shaped hat (ill. DRESS). [F, = bell, f. L (as foll.)]

clock[1] n. **1.** an instrument measuring and recording the passage of time, with a regulating device (so that it operates at a uniform speed) and constant motive power, usually indicating hours, minutes, etc., by hands on a dial or by displayed figures (see below). **2.** a clocklike measuring device; (colloq.) a speedometer, taximeter, or stop-watch. **3.** the seed-head of a dandelion. —v.t. to time (a race) with a stop-watch; (with up) to attain or register (a stated time, distance, or speed). —**clock golf,** a game in which a golf-ball is putted into a hole from successive points round a circle. **clock in** or **on,** to register one's arrival at work, especially by means of an automatic clock. **clock off** or **out,** to register one's departure similarly. [f. LG or Du. f. L clocca bell]

The first true mechanical clock dates from c.1280. Such clocks were large weight-driven structures fitted into towers, and known as turret clocks; they had no dial or clock-hands, but sounded a signal which alerted a keeper to toll a bell. In the 14th c. public striking-clocks made their appearance, using a foliot or weighted arm as an oscillating flywheel controlled by a toothed wheel and an escapement mechanism. The first spring-driven clocks appeared c.1500, and led to the development of watches (i.e. spring clocks small enough to be carried on the person). The 17th c. (c.1670 in England) saw the anchor escapement, and the use of the swinging pendulum by Huygens from 1657. This was a great advance because its period of swing is independent of the friction of gears to which the foliot was subject; grandfather clocks and bracket clocks using this reached a high pitch of excellence in the hands of great

English clockmakers such as Tompion. By 1620 another important invention was in use, the balance-wheel, followed (in the last quarter of the 17th c.) by the balance-spring, whose frequency of oscillation was controlled by a spiral spring of the now familiar type. Electrically driven clocks were introduced by 1840, and the quartz clock in 1927-30, using a quartz crystal maintained in oscillation at a fixed high frequency. A more accurate type of pendulum clock was manufactured by the Shortt-Synchronome Corporation 1921-4, with the master pendulum enclosed in an airtight nearly evacuated chamber. Most accurate of all is the caesium clock, depending on the vibration of atoms of caesium. (For the development towards accuracy, see ill. TIME.)

clock[2] n. an ornamental pattern on the side of a stocking or sock. [orig. unkn.]

clockwise adj. & adv. moving in a curve from left to right, corresponding in direction to the hands of a clock.

clockwork n. a mechanism with spring and gears, like that used (from the 15th c., instead of weights) to drive clocks; (attrib.) driven by clockwork.

clod n. a lump of earth, clay, etc. [var. of CLOT]

clodhoppers n.pl. (colloq.) large heavy shoes.

clog n. a shoe with a thick wooden sole. —v.t./i. (-gg-) to cause an obstruction in; to become blocked. [orig. unkn.]

cloisonné /klwa:'zɒneɪ/ n. a technique of enamel decoration in which the colours are kept apart by thin metal strips. —adj. of or using this technique. [F, f. cloison partition, ult. f. L claudere close]

cloister n. 1. a covered walk, often round a quadrangle with a wall on the outer and a colonnade on the inner side, especially in a monastery, convent, college, or cathedral (ill. CHURCH). 2. monastic life or seclusion. —v.t. to seclude in a convent etc. —**cloistral** adj. [f. OF f. L claustrum enclosed place (claudere shut)]

cloistered adj. secluded, sheltered; monastic. [f. prec.]

clone n. a group of plants or organisms produced asexually from one stock or ancestor; one such organism; (colloq.) a person regarded as identical with another. —v.t. to propagate as a clone. —**clonal** /'kləʊn(ə)l/ adj. [f. Gk klōn twig]

clonk n. a sharp heavy sound of an impact. —v.t./i. 1. to make this sound. 2. (colloq.) to hit. [imit.]

close[1] /kləʊs/ adj. 1. near in space or time; near in relationship or association; nearly alike; (of a race or contest) in which the competitors are almost equal. 2. dense, compact, with only slight intervals; detailed, leaving no gaps or weaknesses. 3. oppressively warm or humid. 4. closed, shut; limited to certain persons. 5. hidden, secret; secretive. 6. niggardly. —adv. at a short distance or interval. —n. 1. a street closed at one end. 2. a precinct of a cathedral. —at close quarters, very close together. close harmony, harmony in which the notes of a chord are close together. **close-hauled** adj. with sails hauled aft to sail close to the wind (ill. SAILING-SHIPS). **close-knit** adj. closely united. **close season,** the season when the killing of game etc. is illegal. **close shave,** a narrow escape. **close-up** n. a photograph etc. taken at close range. —**closely** adv., **closeness** n. [f. OF f. L clausus (claudere shut)]

close[2] /kləʊz/ v.t./i. 1. to shut, to block up. 2. to bring or come to an end; to be or declare to be not open to the public. 3. to bring or come closer or into contact; to make (an electric circuit etc.) continuous. —n. a conclusion, an end. —**closed-circuit** adj. (of television) transmitted by wires to a restricted circuit of receivers. **close down,** to cease working, trading, or transmitting. **closed shop,** a business etc. where employees must belong to an agreed trade union. **closed universe,** the condition that there is sufficient matter in the universe to halt the expansion driven by the big bang and cause eventual re-collapse. Current observations suggest that the amount of visible matter is only a tenth of that required for closure, but apparent uncertainties in the masses of galaxies leave open the possibility of there being large quantities of 'dark matter'. **close in,** to approach from all sides so as to shut in or entrap; (of days) to get successively shorter. **close with,** to accept the offer made by (a person); to join battle or start fighting with. **closing-time** n. the time when a public house etc. ends business. [f. OF clos f. L claudere shut]

closet /'klɒzɪt/ n. a cupboard or small room; a water-closet. —v.t. to shut away, especially in private conference or study. [f. OF, dim. of clos enclosed space (as prec.)]

closure /'kləʊʒə(r)/ n. a closing or closed state; a decision in Parliament to take a vote without further debate. —v.t.

to apply closure to (a motion, speaker, etc.). [f. OF f. L clausura (claudere close)]

clot n. a thick mass of coagulated liquid, especially of blood exposed to air. —v.i. (-tt-) to form into clots. —**clotted cream,** thick cream obtained by slow scalding. [OE]

cloth n. 1. woven or felted material; a piece of this for a special purpose; a dishcloth, tablecloth, etc. 2. clerical clothes, the clergy. [OE]

clothe /kləʊð/ v.t. (past & p.p. **clothed** or **clad**) to put clothes on, to provide with clothes; to cover as with clothes. [OE as CLOTH]

clothes /kləʊðz, -əʊz/ n.pl. things worn to cover the body and limbs; bedclothes. —**clothes-horse** n. a frame for airing washed clothes. **clothes-line** n. a rope or wire on which washed clothes are hung out to dry. **clothes-peg** n. a clip or forked device for securing clothes to a clothes-line. [OE (orig. pl. of CLOTH)]

clothier /'kləʊðɪə(r)/ n. a seller of men's clothes. [f. CLOTH]

clothing /'kləʊðɪŋ/ n. clothes collectively. [f. CLOTH]

Clotho /'kləʊθəʊ/ (Gk myth.) one of the three Fates (see FATES). [Gk, = she who spins]

cloud n. 1. a visible mass of condensed watery vapour floating high above the ground (ill. WEATHER). 2. a mass of smoke or dust; a large moving mass of insects etc. in the sky. 3. a state of gloom, trouble, or suspicion. —v.t./i. to cover or darken with clouds or gloom or trouble; to become overcast or gloomy. —**cloud chamber,** a device containing vapour for tracking the paths of charged particles, X-rays, and gamma rays. **cloud-cuckoo-land** n. a realm of fantasy or unrealistic ideas (transl. of Gk name of realm in Aristophanes' Birds built by the birds to separate the gods from mankind). [OE]

cloudburst n. a sudden violent rainstorm.

cloudless adj. without clouds. [f. CLOUD + -LESS]

cloudy adj. 1. covered with clouds, overcast. 2. not clear, not transparent. —**cloudiness** n. [f. CLOUD]

Clouet /'klu:eɪ/ the name of a family of painters descended from Jean Clouet the elder (b. 1420), a Fleming, who was painter to the Duke of Burgundy in 1475. The more famous Jean Clouet (c.1485-1541), thought to be his son, was a portrait painter belonging to the school of Flemish naturalism; his drawings have been compared to those of Holbein. His son François (d. 1572) worked in the international mannerist style and painted portraits and genre scenes.

Clough /klʌf/, Arthur Hugh (1819-61), English poet. A fellow of Oriel College, Oxford, he resigned in 1848 because of religious doubts, and some of his best-known poems express his spiritual anguish. Matthew Arnold's poem Thyrsis was written to commemorate his death.

clout n. 1. a heavy blow. 2. (archaic) a piece of cloth or clothing. —v.t. to hit hard. [OE]

clove[1] n. the dried flower-bud of a tropical myrtle (Eugenia caryophyllata) used as a spice. [f. OF f. L clavus nail (from the shape)]

clove[2] n. a small segment of a compound bulb, especially of garlic. [OE, rel. to CLEAVE[1]]

clove[3] past of CLEAVE[1].

clove hitch a knot used for securing a rope to a spar or to another rope. [old p.p. of CLEAVE[1]]

cloven p.p. of CLEAVE[1]. —adj. split, partly divided. —**cloven hoof,** a hoof that is divided, as of oxen, sheep, or goats.

clover n. a fodder plant of the genus Trifolium, with leaves of three leaflets. —**in clover,** in ease and luxury. [OE]

Clovis /'kləʊvɪs/ the name of a city in eastern New Mexico in the USA, applied to the remains of a prehistoric industry first found at the Blackwater Draw site near by, and especially to a type of projectile point often found in association with bones of the mammoth. The points are heavy, leaf-shaped, with parallel or slightly convex sides, and some are fluted for part of their length. They precede the Folsom type, dating from the 10th millennium BC and earlier.

clown n. a performer, especially in a circus, who does comical tricks and actions (see GRIMALDI); a person acting like a clown. —v.i. to behave like a clown. —**clownish** adj. [orig. unkn.]

cloy v.t. to satiate or sicken, especially with richness, sweetness, or excess. [f. AF (cf. ENCLAVE)]

club n. 1. a heavy stick thick at one end, used as a weapon etc.; a stick with a shaped head, used in golf. 2.

a playing-card of the suit (**clubs**) marked with black clover-leaves. **3.** an association of persons meeting periodically for a shared activity; an organization or premises offering its members social amenities, meals, temporary accommodation, etc.; an organization offering subscribers certain benefits. —*v.t./i.* (**-bb-**) **1.** to strike with a club etc. **2.** to combine, especially in making up a sum of money for a purpose. —**club-foot** *n.* a congenitally deformed foot. **club-moss** *n.* a pteridophyte with upright spikes of spore-cases. **club-root** *n.* a disease of cabbages etc. with a swelling at the base of the stem. [ON]

clubbable *adj.* sociable, fit for membership of a club. [f. CLUB]

clubhouse *n.* the premises used by a club.

cluck *n.* a guttural cry like that of a hen. —*v.i.* to emit a cluck. [imit.]

clue *n.* a fact or idea that gives a guide to the solution of a problem; a word or words indicating what is to be inserted in a crossword puzzle. —*v.t.* to provide with a clue. —**not to have a clue**, (*colloq.*) to be ignorant or incompetent. [var. of CLEW]

clump *n.* a cluster or mass (of trees, tall plants, etc.). —*v.t.* **1.** to form a clump, to arrange in a clump. **2.** to walk with a heavy tread. **3.** (*colloq.*) to hit. [f. LG or Du.]

clumsy /'klʌmzɪ/ *adj.* heavy and lacking in dexterity or grace; large and difficult to handle or use; done without tact or skill. —**clumsily** *adv.*, **clumsiness** *n.* [f. obs. *clumse* be numb with cold, prob. f. Scand.]

clung past & p.p. of CLING.

Cluny /'kluːnɪ/ a town in eastern France where a monastery was founded in 910 with the object of returning to the strict Benedictine rule, cultivation of the spiritual life, and stress on the choir office. Other houses followed suit, and the order became centralized and influential in the 11th–12th c. —**Cluniac** /-iæk/ *adj. & n.*

cluster *n.* a small close group; a group of stars bound together by gravity, either as a loose assemblage (*open or galactic cluster*) or as a compact sphere (*globular cluster*), found within or orbiting a galaxy. —*v.t./i.* to gather in a cluster. [OE]

clutch[1] *v.t./i.* to seize eagerly, to grasp tightly; try to grasp *at.* —*n.* **1.** a tight grasp; (in *pl.*) grasping hands, cruel or relentless grasp or control. **2.** (in motor vehicles) a device for connecting the engine to the transmission; the pedal operating this. [OE]

clutch[2] *n.* a set of eggs for hatching; the chickens hatched from these. [var. of N. Engl. *cletch*, f. ON]

clutter *n.* a crowded untidy collection of things; untidy state. —*v.t.* to crowd untidily, to fill with clutter. [rel. to CLOT]

Clwyd /'kluːɪd/ a county in NE Wales.

Clyde /klaɪd/ a river in SW Scotland, famous for the shipbuilding industries along its banks.

Clydesdale /'klaɪdzdeɪl/ *n.* a breed of heavy draught-horses originally bred near the River Clyde; an animal of this breed.

Clytemnestra /klaɪtɪm'nestrə/ (*Gk legend*) sister of Helen and the Dioscuri, wife of Agamemnon (see AGAMEMNON).

Cm *symbol* curium.

cm *abbr.* centimetre(s).

CND *abbr.* Campaign for Nuclear Disarmament. Its first president was Bertrand Russell (1958).

Cnut /kə'njuːt/ (*c*.994–1035), Danish king of England, reigned 1017–35. Having succeeded his father as king of Denmark in 1014, Cnut became king of England after the murder in 1016 of Edmund Ironside, king of Wessex, ending a prolonged struggle for the throne. As king, he presided over a period of relative peace, depending more and more on English rather than Danish advisers. He is most commonly remembered for the occasion on which he demonstrated his inability to stop the rising tide to fawning courtiers who had told him he was all-powerful.

Co *symbol* cobalt.

Co. *abbr.* company.

c/o *abbr.* care of.

co- *prefix* together with, jointly. [L]

coach *n.* **1.** a single-decker bus, usually comfortably equipped for longer journeys; a railway carriage; a closed horse-drawn carriage. **2.** an instructor or trainer in sport; a private tutor. —*v.t.* to train or teach as a coach. —**coach screw**, a large screw with a square head, turned by a spanner (ill. CARPENTRY). [f. F f. Magyar]

coachwork *n.* the bodywork of a road or railway vehicle.

coagulant /kəʊ'ægjʊlənt/ *n.* a substance that causes coagulation. [f. foll.]

coagulate /kəʊ'ægjʊleɪt/ *v.t./i.* to change from a liquid to a semisolid; to clot, to curdle. —**coagulation** *n.* [f. L *coagulare* (*coagulum* rennet)]

coal *n.* a hard black mineral, found below ground and used as fuel and in making gas, tar, etc. (see below); a piece of this, one that is burning. —*v.t./i.* to put coal into (a ship etc.); to take in a supply of coal. —**coal-face** *n.* the exposed surface of coal in a mine. **coal gas**, mixed gases extracted from coal and used for lighting and heating. **coal measures,** a series of rocks formed by seams of coal and intervening strata. **coals to Newcastle**, a thing brought to a place where it is already plentiful, an unnecessary action. **coal-scuttle** *n.* a container for coal to supply a domestic fire. **coal tar**, tar extracted from bituminous coal. **coal-tit** *n.* a small greyish bird with a dark head. [OE]

Coal is the most abundant form of solid fuel, formed from the remains of trees and other plant material, mostly during the Carboniferous period. It consists chiefly of carbon, formed by the plants from carbon dioxide in the air by the process of photosynthesis, and this stored energy is released when the coal is burnt with oxygen from the air to produce carbon dioxide again. There is a wide variety of coal types, from black anthracite (almost pure carbon) through bituminous coal which contains tarry substances (mostly hydrocarbon compounds which form gases when heated), to lignite, a soft brown coal of later formation and with lower calorific value. Coal is widely used as a fuel in industry for the production of heat and electric power, formerly also for producing gas. Although oil and natural gas are competitive fuels at present, both are finite in quantity, whereas coal deposits are sufficient for several hundred years. Layers of coal near the surface are mined by opencast methods, removing and later replacing the covering soil. Deeper layers are mined by sinking shafts and digging the coal layers by machine, leaving pillars to support the ground above. Both methods have severe social problems; surface mining can leave derelict areas, while underground mining is dirty and dangerous work which cannot at present be done entirely by machines.

coalesce /kəʊə'les/ *v.i.* to come together and form one whole. —**coalescence** *n.*, **coalescent** *adj.* [f. L *coalescere* (CO-, *alescere* grow up)]

coalfield *n.* an area yielding coal.

coalition /kəʊə'lɪʃ(ə)n/ *n.* fusion into one whole; a temporary alliance of political parties. [f. L (as COALESCE)]

coaming *n.* a raised border round a ship's hatches etc. to keep out water. [orig. unkn.]

coarse *adj.* **1.** rough or loose in texture, made of large particles. **2.** lacking refinement of manner or perception, crude, vulgar; (of language) obscene. **3.** inferior, common. —**coarse fish,** freshwater fish other than salmon and trout. —**coarsely** *adv.*, **coarseness** *n.* [orig. unkn.]

coarsen *v.t./i.* to make or become coarse. [f. prec.]

coast *n.* the border of the land nearest the sea, the sea-shore. (see ill. p. 168) —*v.i.* **1.** to ride or move, usually downhill, without the use of power. **2.** to sail along the coast. —**coastal** *adj.* [f. OF f. L *costa* rib, flank]

coaster *n.* **1.** a ship that travels along the coast. **2.** a small tray or mat for a bottle or glass. [f. COAST]

coastguard *n.* a body of persons employed to keep watch on coasts, prevent smuggling, etc.; a member of this.

coastline *n.* the line of the sea-shore, especially with regard to its configuration.

coat *n.* **1.** an outer garment with sleeves and often extending below the hips, an overcoat, jacket, etc. **2.** a natural covering, especially an animal's fur or hair. **3.** a covering of paint etc. laid on a surface at any one time. —*v.t.* to cover *with* a coat or layer; (of paint etc.) to form a covering to. —**coat of arms,** the heraldic bearings or shield of a person or corporation. **coat of mail**, see MAIL[2]. [f. OF f. Gmc]

coating *n.* **1.** a covering layer. **2.** material for coats. [f. COAT]

co-author *n.* a joint author. —*v.t.* to be joint author of.

coax *v.t.* **1.** to persuade gradually or by flattery; to obtain by such means. **2.** to manipulate carefully or slowly. [f. 'make a *cokes* of' (obs. *cokes* fool)]

coaxial /kəʊ'æksɪəl/ *adj.* having a common axis; (of an electric cable or line) transmitting by means of two concentric conductors separated by an insulator. [f. CO- + AXIAL]

cob *n.* **1.** a roundish lump. **2.** a corn-cob (see CORN[1]). **3.** a

Coasts

Erosion features

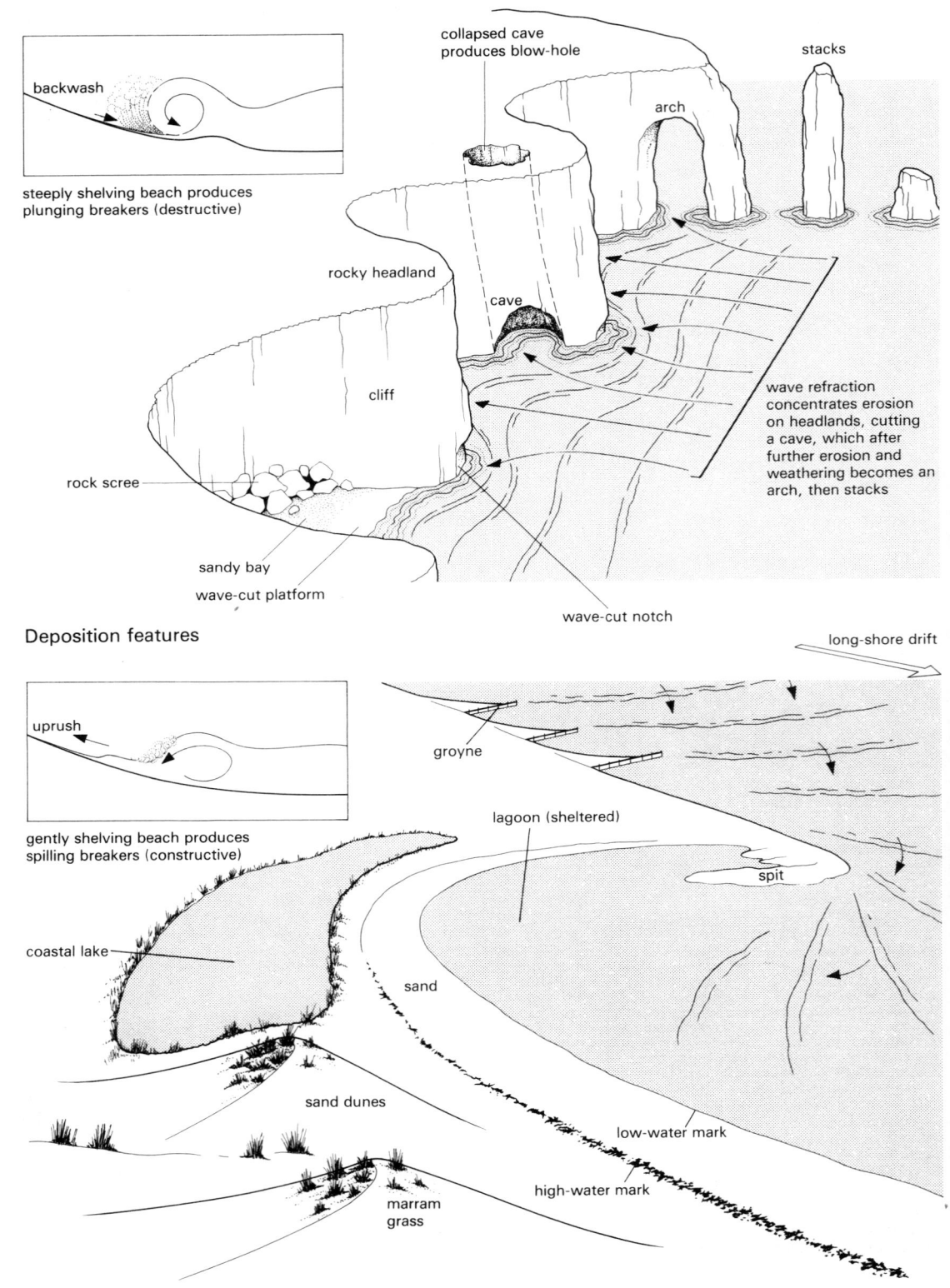

backwash

steeply shelving beach produces
plunging breakers (destructive)

collapsed cave
produces blow-hole

stacks

arch

rocky headland

cave

cliff

wave refraction
concentrates erosion
on headlands, cutting
a cave, which after
further erosion and
weathering becomes an
arch, then stacks

rock scree

sandy bay

wave-cut platform

wave-cut notch

Deposition features

uprush

gently shelving beach produces
spilling breakers (constructive)

long-shore drift

groyne

lagoon (sheltered)

spit

coastal lake

sand

sand dunes

low-water mark

high-water mark

marram
grass

sturdy riding-horse with short legs. **4.** a male swan. **5.** a large hazel-nut. **6.** a loaf rounded on the top. [orig. unkn.]

cobalt /ˈkəʊbɔːlt, -plt/ *n.* **1.** a hard silvery-white metallic element similar in many respects to nickel, symbol Co, atomic number 27. The metal was known to Paracelsus, though its discovery is usually credited to G. Brandt (d. 1768) in 1733. There are important deposits from which it is mined in Zaïre and in Canada. Its main use is as a component of magnetic alloys and those designed for use at high temperatures. Cobalt compounds have been used since ancient times to colour ceramics, and they are also widely used as catalysts. The element is essential in small quantities to living organisms. **2.** a pigment made from cobalt. —*adj.* the deep-blue colour characteristic of this pigment. [f. G *kobalt*, prob. = *kobold* goblin or demon of the mines, the ore having been so called by the miners on account of its worthlessness (as then supposed) and from its bad effects upon their health and upon the silver ores with which it occurred, effects due mainly to the arsenic and sulphur with which it was combined]

cobber *n.* (*Austral. & N.Z. colloq.*) a friend, a mate. [perh. f. dial. *cob* take a liking to]

Cobbett /ˈkɒbɪt/, William (1762–1835), English political reformer. A brilliant radical journalist, Cobbett was one of the leaders of the post-1815 campaign for political and social reform in England. Despite brief periods in prison and exile, Cobbett did much to expose the shortcomings of early 19th-c. industrial society, although his own reforming ideas looked back rather than forward.

cobble[1] *n.* (in full **cobble-stone**) a small rounded stone used for paving. —*v.t.* to pave with cobbles. [f. COB]

cobble[2] *v.t.* to mend or patch up (especially shoes); to repair or put together roughly. [back-formation f. foll.]

cobbler *n.* **1.** a shoe-repairer. **2.** an iced drink of wine, sugar, and lemon. **3.** a fruit pie topped with scones. [orig. unkn.]

Cobden /ˈkɒbd(ə)n/, Richard (1804–65), British political reformer. A Manchester industrialist, Cobden was one of the leading spokesmen of the free-trade movement in Britain, leading, with John Bright, the Anti-Corn Law League in its successful campaign for the repeal of the Corn Laws in the early 1840s.

COBOL /ˈkəʊbɒl/ *n.* a computer language for use in commerce. [*Common Business Oriented Language*]

cobra /ˈkəʊbrə, ˈkɒ-/ *n.* a venomous hooded Indian or African snake of the genus *Naja*. [Port., f. L *colubra* snake]

cobweb *n.* the fine network spun by a spider; a thread of this. —**cobwebby** *adj.* [f. obs. *coppe* spider]

coca /ˈkəʊkə/ *n.* a South American shrub, *Erythroxylon coca*; its leaves, chewed as a stimulant. [Sp. f. Quechua]

cocaine /kɒˈkeɪn, kəʊ-/ *n.* a drug from coca, used as a local anaesthetic and as a stimulating drug. [f. COCA]

coccyx /ˈkɒksɪks/ *n.* (*pl.* **coccyges** /-dʒiːz/) a small triangular bone at the base of the spinal column (ill. BODY 1). [L f. Gk *kokkux* cuckoo (from being shaped like its bill)]

cochineal /ˈkɒtʃɪniːl/ *n.* a bright-red colouring matter made from the dried bodies of a Mexican insect *Dactylopius coccus*. [f. F or Sp. f. L *coccineus* scarlet f. Gk]

cochlea /ˈkɒklɪə/ *n.* (*pl.* **cochleae** /-lɪiː/) the spiral cavity of the inner ear (ill. BODY 4). [L, = snail-shell, f. Gk]

cock[1] *n.* **1.** a male bird, especially of the domestic fowl. **2.** the firing-lever in a gun, raised to be released by the trigger; a cocked position. **3.** a tap or valve controlling the flow of a liquid. —*v.t.* **1.** to make upright or erect; to move (the eye or ear) attentively or knowingly; to set aslant or turn up the brim of (a hat). **2.** to raise the cock of (a gun). —**cock-a-doodle-doo** *int.* the sound of a cock crowing. **cock-a-hoop** *adj.* exultant. **cock-a-leekie** *n.* a Scottish soup of cock boiled with leeks. **cock-and-bull story**, one that is absurd or incredible. **cock a snook**, see SNOOK. **cock-crow** *n.* dawn. **cocked hat**, a brimless triangular hat pointed at front, back, and top. **cock-eyed** *adj.* (*colloq.*) crooked, askew; absurd, not practical. **cock-fight** *n.* a fight between cocks as a sport. **cock-shy** *n.* a target for throwing at, a throw at this; an object of ridicule or criticism. [f. OE & F]

cock[2] *n.* a small conical pile of hay or straw. [perh. f. Scand.]

cockade /kɒˈkeɪd/ *n.* a rosette etc. worn in the hat as a badge. [f. F (as COCK[1])]

cockatoo /kɒkəˈtuː/ *n.* a crested parrot. [f. Du. f. Malay]

cockchafer /ˈkɒktʃeɪfə(r)/ *n.* a large pale-brown beetle.

Cockcroft /ˈkɒkkrɒft/, Sir John Douglas (1897–1967), English physicist, who joined Rutherford's group at the Cavendish Laboratory, Cambridge, in 1922, and ten years later, working with E. T. S. Walton, succeeded in 'splitting the atom' by means of artificially accelerated protons. With their novel high-energy particle accelerator the researchers bombarded lithium atoms with protons (the nuclei of hydrogen atoms) and produced alpha particles (helium nuclei); this pioneering experiment demonstrated the transmutation of elements and Einstein's theory of the equivalence of mass and energy. It ushered in the whole field of nuclear and particle physics relying on particle accelerators, and for their work the two shared the 1951 Nobel Prize for physics. After the Second World War Cockcroft emerged as one of the leading scientific figures, and was the first director of the Atomic Energy Research Establishment at Harwell.

cocker *n.* (in full **cocker spaniel**) a small spaniel with a golden-brown coat. [f. COCK[1], as starting woodcock]

cockerel /ˈkɒkər(ə)l/ *n.* a young cock. [dim. of COCK[1]]

cockle *n.* **1.** an edible bivalve shellfish; its shell. **2.** a pucker or wrinkle in paper, glass, etc. **3.** (in full **cockle-shell**) a small shallow boat. —*v.t./i.* to make or become puckered. [f. OF *coquille* shell f. L f. Gk (as CONCH)]

cockney /ˈkɒknɪ/ *n.* **1.** a native of London, especially of the East End (according to Minsheu (early 17th c.) 'one born within the sound of Bow Bells'). **2.** the dialect or accent historically associated with this area. A distinctive feature is its use of rhyming slang (see RHYME). —*adj.* of cockneys or their dialect. [f. obs. *cokeney* cock's egg, orig. sense prob. small or ill-shaped egg, hence 'milksop', 'townsman']

cockpit *n.* **1.** the compartment for the pilot (and crew) of an aircraft or spacecraft; the driver's seat in a racing-car; a space for the helmsman in some small yachts. **2.** an arena of war or other conflict. **3.** a place made for cock-fights.

cockroach *n.* a dark-brown beetle-like insect infesting kitchens and bathrooms. [f. Sp. *cucaracha*]

cockscomb *n.* the crest of a cock.

cocksure *adj.* presumptuously or arrogantly confident; absolutely sure. [f. *cock* = God + SURE]

cocktail *n.* **1.** a mixed alcoholic drink, especially of spirit with bitters etc. **2.** an appetizer containing shellfish or fruit. [orig. unkn.]

cocky *adj.* pertly self-confident. —**cockily** *adv.*, **cockiness** *n.* [f. COCK[1]]

coco /ˈkəʊkəʊ/ *n.* a tropical palm-tree (*Cocos nucifera*) from which coconuts come. [Sp. & Port., = grimace]

cocoa /ˈkəʊkəʊ/ *n.* a powder made with crushed cacao seeds, often with other ingredients; a drink made from this. The Aztec Indians were the first to make such a drink, and in the 16th c. the Spaniards brought it to Europe, where it was enjoyed as an expensive luxury. —**cocoa bean**, a cacao seed. **cocoa butter,** a fatty substance obtained from this. [alt. of CACAO]

coconut /ˈkəʊkənʌt/ *n.* the large brown seed of the coco, with a hard shell and edible white lining enclosing a milky juice. —**coconut matting**, matting made of fibre from coconut husks. **coconut shy**, a fairground amusement where balls are thrown to dislodge coconuts from a stand. [f. COCO + NUT]

cocoon /kəˈkuːn/ *n.* the silky case spun by an insect larva to protect itself as a chrysalis, especially that of a silkworm; a protective covering. —*v.t.* to wrap or coat in a cocoon. [f. F f. Prov. (*coca* shell)]

cocotte /kəˈkɒt/ *n.* a small fireproof dish for serving food. [F]

Cocteau /kɒkˈtəʊ/, Jean Maurice (1889–1963), French dramatist and film director. His plays include *La Machine infernale* (1934), based on the Oedipus legend, *Les Parents terribles* (1938), and *L'Aigle à deux têtes* (1946). He is better known outside France, however, for his films, some of which were adaptations of his plays. His reputation as a film-maker rests mainly on *Le Sang d'un poète* (1930), *La Belle et la bête* (1946), *Orphée* (1950), and *Le Testament d'Orphée* (1960), all of which show how poetry derives from the ordinary rather than from the obscure; they mingle myth and reality, often by the use of trick photography. His dramatic writing, with its singular blend of poetry, irony, and fantasy, proved a constant source of inspiration and controversy.

COD *abbr.* cash (*US* collect) on delivery.

cod *n.* (*pl.* same) a large sea fish (also **codfish**). —**cod-liver oil**, oil from cod livers, rich in vitamins A and D. [orig. unkn.]

coda *n.* the final passage of a movement or piece of music, often elaborate and distinct; the concluding section of a ballet. [It. f. L *coda* tail]

coddle *v.t.* **1.** to treat as an invalid; to protect attentively, to pamper. **2.** to cook (an egg) in water just below boiling-point. [prob. var. of CAUDLE]

code *n.* **1.** a system of words, letters, or symbols used to represent others for secrecy or brevity. **2.** a system of prearranged signals for transmitting messages. **3.** a set of instructions used in programming a computer. **4.** a systematic set of laws or rules. **5.** a prevailing standard of moral behaviour. —*v.t.* to put into code. [f. OF f. L *codex*]

codeine /'kəʊdiːn/ *n.* an alkaloid obtained from opium, used to relieve pain or induce sleep. [f. Gk *kōdeia* poppy-head]

codex /'kəʊdeks/ *n.* (*pl.* **codices** /-dɪsiːz/) **1.** an ancient manuscript text in the book-form which between 1st–4th c. AD gradually replaced the continuous roll previously used for written documents. **2.** a collection of pharmaceutical descriptions of drugs etc. [L, = wood block, tablet, book (as these tablets were often coated with wax and inscribed)]

codger /'kɒdʒə(r)/ *n.* (*colloq.*) a person, especially a strange one. [perh. var. of CADGER]

codicil /'kɒdɪsɪl/ *n.* an addition to a will explaining, modifying, or revoking it or part of it. [f. L, dim. of CODEX]

codify /'kəʊdɪfaɪ/ *v.t.* to arrange (laws etc.) systematically into a code. —**codification** /-ɪ'keɪʃ(ə)n/ *n.*, **codifier** *n.* [f. CODE]

codling[1] *n.* (also **codlin**) **1.** a kind of cooking apple, usually oblong and yellowish. **2.** a moth whose larva feeds on apples. [f. F *quer de lion* lion-heart]

codling[2] *n.* a small codfish. [f. COD]

codpiece *n.* an appendage like small bag or a flap at the front of a man's breeches in 15th–16th-c. dress. [f. obs. *cod* scrotum]

Cody /'kəʊdɪ/, William Frederick, see BUFFALO BILL.

coeducation /kəʊedjuːˈkeɪʃ(ə)n/ *n.* education of pupils of both sexes together. —**coeducational** *adj.*

coefficient /kəʊɪˈfɪʃ(ə)nt/ *n.* (*Math.*) a quantity placed before and multiplying another quantity; (*Physics*) a multiplier or factor by which a property is measured.

coelacanth /'siːləkænθ/ *n.* a fish of the family Coelacanthidae, originally thought to have a hollow spine, extinct but for one species (*Latimeria chalumnae*). [f. Gk *koilos* hollow + *acantha* spine]

coelenterate /siːˈlentəreɪt/ *n.* a member of the phylum Coelenterata, aquatic animals (including sea-anemones, hydras, jellyfish, and corals) with a simple tube-shaped or cup-shaped body and a digestive system with a single opening surrounded by a ring of tentacles. —*adj.* of coelenterates. [f. Gk *koilos* hollow + *enteron* intestine]

coeliac /'siːlɪæk/ *adj.* of the belly. —**coeliac disease,** an intestinal disease causing defective digestion of fats. [f. L f. Gk (*koilia* belly)]

coenobite /'siːnəbaɪt/ *n.* a member of a monastic community. —**coenobitic** /-ˈbɪtɪk/ *adj.*, **coenobitical** *adj.* [f. OF or L f. Gk *koinobion* convent (*koinos* common, *bios* life)]

coequal /kəʊˈiːkwəl/ *adj.* & *n.* (*archaic* or *literary*) equal.

coerce /kəʊˈɜːs/ *v.t.* to impel or force (*into* obedience etc.). —**coercion** *n.* [f. L *coercēre* (CO-, *arcēre* restrain)]

coercive /kəʊˈɜːsɪv/ *adj.* using coercion. [as prec.]

coeval /kəʊˈiːvəl/ *adj.* having the same age, existing at the same epoch. —*n.* a coeval person, a contemporary. [f. L *coaevus* (CO-, *aevum* age)]

coexist /kəʊɪɡˈzɪst/ *v.i.* to exist together (*with*). [f. L *coexistere* (CO-, *existere* exist)]

coexistence *n.* coexisting. —**peaceful coexistence,** mutual tolerance of nations with different ideologies or political and social systems. —**coexistent** *adj.* [f. prec.]

coextensive /kəʊɪkˈstensɪv/ *adj.* extending over the same space or time.

C. of E. *abbr.* Church of England.

coffee /'kɒfiː/ *n.* **1.** a drink made from the roasted and ground beanlike seeds of a tropical shrub of the genus *Coffea*; a cup of this; these seeds; the shrub. **2.** the pale brown colour of coffee mixed with milk. —**coffee bar,** a place serving coffee and light refreshments from a counter. **coffee morning,** a morning social gathering at which coffee is served, usually in aid of a good cause. **coffee shop,** an informal restaurant, especially at a hotel. **coffee-table** *n.* a small low table. **coffee-table book,** a large expensive illustrated book, too large for a bookshelf. [f. Turk. f. Arab.]

coffer *n.* **1.** a large strong box for valuables; (in *pl.*) a treasury, funds. **2.** a sunken panel in a ceiling etc. —**coffer-dam** *n.* a watertight enclosure pumped dry for work in building bridges etc., or for repairing a ship. [f. OF f. L f. Gk *kophinos* basket]

coffin *n.* a box in which a corpse is buried or cremated. —*v.t.* to put in a coffin. [f. OF, = little basket (as prec.)]

cog *n.* any of a series of projections on the edge of a wheel or bar transferring motion by engaging with another series; an unimportant member of an organization etc. —**cog-wheel** *n.* a wheel with cogs. [prob. f. Scand.]

cogent /'kəʊdʒ(ə)nt/ *adj.* convincing, compelling. —**cogency** *n.*, **cogently** *adv.* [f. L *cogere* compel]

cogging *n.* the process of passing heated metal ingots between a pair of rollers as the first stage in rolling them into the shape required. [f. COG]

cogitate /'kɒdʒɪteɪt/ *v.t./i.* to ponder, to meditate. —**cogitation** /-ˈteɪʃ(ə)n/ *n.*, **cogitative** *adj.* [f. L *cogitare* think]

cognac /'kɒnjæk/ *n.* brandy, especially that distilled in the town of Cognac in western France. [f. *Cognac*]

cognate /'kɒɡneɪt/ *adj.* related or descended from a common ancestor; (of a word) having the same linguistic family or derivation. —*n.* a relative; a cognate word. [f. L *cognatus* (CO-, *gnatus* born)]

cognition /kɒɡˈnɪʃ(ə)n/ *n.* knowing, perceiving, or conceiving as an act or faculty distinct from emotion and volition; the result of this. —**cognitional** *adj.*, **cognitive** /'kɒɡnɪtɪv/ *adj.* [f. L *cognoscere* (CO-, *gnoscere* know)]

cognizance /'kɒɡnɪz(ə)ns/ *n.* **1.** knowledge or awareness, perception. **2.** sphere of observation or concern. **3.** a distinctive device or mark. [f. OF f. L (as prec.)]

cognizant /'kɒɡnɪz(ə)nt/ *adj.* having knowledge or taking note of. [f. prec.]

cognomen /kɒɡˈnəʊmen/ *n.* a nickname; an ancient Roman's personal name or epithet. [L]

cognoscente /kɒnjəˈʃentɪ/ *n.* (*pl.* **-ti**) a connoisseur. [It.]

cohabit /kəʊˈhæbɪt/ *v.i.* to live together as husband and wife (usually of a couple who are not married to each other). —**cohabitation** /-ˈteɪʃ(ə)n/ *n.* [f. L *cohabitare* (CO-, *habitare* dwell)]

cohere /kəʊˈhɪə(r)/ *v.i.* **1.** (of parts or a whole) to stick together, to remain united. **2.** (of reasoning etc.) to be logical or consistent. [f. L *cohaerēre* (CO-, *haerēre* stick)]

coherent /kəʊˈhɪərənt/ *adj.* cohering; (of reasoning) connected logically; not rambling in speech or in reasoning. —**coherence** *n.*, **coherently** *adv.* [as prec.]

cohesion /kəʊˈhiːʒ(ə)n/ *n.* sticking together; the force with which molecules cohere, a tendency to cohere. —**cohesive** *adj.* [as COHERE]

cohort /'kəʊhɔːt/ *n.* **1.** a Roman military unit, one tenth of a legion; a band of warriors. **2.** persons banded or grouped together; a group having a common statistical characteristic. [f. F or L *cohors*]

coif *n.* (*hist.*) a close-fitting cap. [f. OF f. L *cofia* helmet]

coiffeur /kwaˈfɜː(r)/ *n.* a hairdresser. —**coiffeuse** *n.fem.* [F]

coiffure /kwaˈfjʊə(r)/ *n.* a hairstyle. [F]

coign /kɔɪn/ *n.* a projecting corner, chiefly in **coign of vantage,** a place from which a good view can be obtained. [old form of COIN (Shak. *Macbeth* I. vi. 7)]

coil *v.t./i.* to arrange or be arranged in spirals or concentric rings; to move sinuously. —*n.* a coiled length of rope etc.; a coiled arrangement; a single turn of a coiled thing; a flexible loop as a contraceptive device in the womb; a coiled wire for the passage of an electric current. [f. OF f. L *colligere* collect]

coin *n.* a small stamped disc of metal as official money; coins collectively. —*v.t.* **1.** to make (money) by stamping metal; to make (metal) into coins. **2.** to invent (a new word or phrase). [f. OF, = stamping-die, f. L *cuneus* wedge]

coinage /'kɔɪnɪdʒ/ *n.* **1.** coining; coins; a system of coins in use. Coinage is reputed to be the invention of the Lydians of Asia Minor, probably in the mid-7th c. BC. **2.** a coined word or phrase. [as prec.]

coincide /kəʊɪnˈsaɪd/ *v.i.* **1.** to occur at the same time; to occupy the same portion of space. **2.** to agree or be identical (*with*). [f. L *coincidere* (CO-, *incidere* fall on)]

coincidence /kəʊˈɪnsɪd(ə)ns/ *n.* coinciding; a remarkable concurrence of events or circumstances without apparent causal connection. —**coincident** *adj.* [as prec.]

coincidental /kəʊɪnsɪˈdent(ə)l/ *adj.* occurring by coincidence; in the nature of a coincidence. —**coincidentally** *adv.* [f. prec.]

Cointreau /ˈkwæntrəʊ/ n. [P] a colourless orange-flavoured liqueur.

coir /kɔɪə(r)/ n. coconut fibre used for ropes, matting, etc. [f. Malayalam, = cord]

coition /kəʊˈɪʃ(ə)n/ n. coitus. [f. L coire (CO-, ire go)]

coitus /ˈkəʊɪtəs/ n. sexual intercourse. —**coital** adj. [L, as prec.]

coke n. the solid substance left after gases have been extracted from coal. —v.t. to convert (coal) into coke. [prob. f. dial. colk core (orig. unkn.)]

col /kɒl/ n. 1. a depression in a chain of mountains (ill. MOUNTAINS). 2. a region of low pressure between anticyclones. [F f. L, = neck]

col- prefix see COM-.

cola /ˈkəʊlə/ n. a West African tree with seed producing an extract used as a tonic etc.; a carbonated drink flavoured with this. [West African]

colander /ˈkʌləndə(r)/ n. a perforated bowl-shaped vessel used to strain off liquid in cooking. [f. L colare strain]

Colbert /ˈkɒlbeə(r)/, Jean Baptiste (1619-83), French statesman, one of Louis XIV's most competent ministers, who achieved an impressive series of reforms, particularly of the country's finances. He also improved industry and commerce and established the French navy as one of the most formidable in Europe. His reforms, however, could not keep pace with the demands of Louis' war policies and of the extensive royal building programme, and by the end of Louis' reign French finances were in a desperate situation.

Colchis /ˈkɒlkɪs/ the Greek name for the region south of the Caucasus mountains at the east end of the Black Sea, the goal of Jason's expedition for the Golden Fleece.

cold adj. 1. of or at a low temperature, especially when compared with the human body; not heated, cooled after heat; feeling cold. 2. dead; (slang) unconscious. 3. lacking geniality, affection, or enthusiasm. 4. depressing, dispiriting. 5. (of colour) suggestive of cold. 6. remote from the thing sought; (of the scent in hunting) grown faint. 7. unrehearsed. —adv. in a cold state. —n. 1. prevalence of low temperature; cold condition. 2. an infectious illness of the nose or throat or both, with catarrh and sneezing. —**cold-blooded** adj. having a body temperature that varies with that of the environment; callous, cruel. **cold chisel,** a chisel for cutting cold metal. **cold comfort,** poor consolation. **cold cream,** an ointment for cleansing and softening the skin. **cold frame,** an unheated frame for growing small plants. **cold shoulder,** deliberate unfriendliness. **cold-shoulder** v.t. to be unfriendly to. **cold storage,** storage in a refrigerator; in cold storage, put aside but still available. **cold war,** hostilities short of armed conflict, consisting in threats, violent propaganda, subversive political activities or the like, specifically those between the USSR and the Western powers after the Second World War. **get** or **have cold feet,** to feel afraid or reluctant. **throw** or **pour cold water on,** to be discouraging about, to belittle. —**coldly** adv., **coldness** n. [OE, cogn. w. L gelu frost]

cole n. any of various plants of the cabbage family, especially (**cole-seed**) rape. [f. ON f. L caulis]

coleopterous /kɒlɪˈɒptərəs/ adj. of the order Coleoptera (comprising beetles and weevils) of insects with front wings serving as sheaths for the hinder wings. [f. Gk (koleon sheath, pteron wing)]

Coleridge /ˈkəʊlərɪdʒ/, Samuel Taylor (1772-1834), English poet, critic, and philosopher, whose intense friendship with William Wordsworth began in 1797. Their jointly produced Lyrical Ballads (1798) revolutionized literary taste and sensibility and effectively started the English Romantic movement; Coleridge's own great contribution to the movement is found in his supernatural poems, 'The Ancient Mariner', 'Christabel', and 'Kubla Khan'. The simplicity and lucidness of his poetical expression contrasts with the involved fashion of his prose. He was instrumental in introducing 18th-c. German thought into England, and his debt to Kant and German philosophy may be seen in his major critical work, Biographia Literaria (1817). His unhappy marriage, his continuing opium addiction, and his hopeless love for Sarah Hutchinson contributed to his decline, recorded in his pessimistic poem 'Dejection: an Ode' (1802), and his ardent support for the French Revolution also turned to disillusion. His final position was that of Romantic conservative and Christian radical.

coleslaw /ˈkəʊlslɔː/ n. a salad of sliced raw cabbage coated in dressing. [f. COLE]

Colette /kɒˈlet/ the pen-name of Sidonie Gabrielle (1873-1954), French novelist, noted for her sensuous feeling for nature and for her vivid insight into the crises of womanhood, often in the older woman, as in Chéri (1920) and La Fin de Chéri (1921).

coleus /ˈkəʊlɪəs/ n. a plant of the genus Coleus with variegated coloured leaves. [f. Gk koleos sheath]

colic /ˈkɒlɪk/ n. a severe spasmodic abdominal pain. —**colicky** adj. [f. F f. L (as COLON²)]

colitis /kɒˈlaɪtɪs/ n. inflammation of the lining of the colon. [f. COLON²]

collaborate /kəˈlæbəreɪt/ v.i. to work jointly (with), especially at a literary or artistic production; to co-operate with the enemy. —**collaboration** /-ˈreɪʃ(ə)n/ n., **collaborator** n. [f. L collaborare (COL-, laborare work)]

collage /kɒˈlɑːʒ/ n. a form or work of art in which various materials are arranged and glued to a backing. [F, = gluing]

collagen /ˈkɒlədʒ(ə)n/ n. a protein found in animal tissue and bone, yielding gelatin on boiling. [f. F f. Gk kolla glue]

collapse /kəˈlæps/ v.t./i. 1. to fall down or in suddenly. 2. to lose strength, force, or value suddenly; to cause to collapse. —n. the act or process of collapsing; a breakdown. [f. L collapsus (COL-, labi slip)]

collapsible /kəˈlæpsɪb(ə)l/ adj. made so as to fold compactly. [f. prec.]

collar /ˈkɒlə(r)/ n. 1. a neckband, upright or turned over, of a coat, dress, shirt, etc. 2. a strap of leather etc. put round an animal's neck. 3. a restraining or connecting band, ring, or pipe in a machine etc. —v.t. (slang) to seize, to appropriate. —**collar-beam** n. a horizontal beam connecting two rafters (ill. HOUSES). **collar-bone** n. the bone joining the breast-bone and shoulder-blade, the clavicle. [f. AF f. L (collum neck)]

collate /kəˈleɪt/ v.t. to compare (texts etc.) in detail (with); to collect and arrange systematically. —**collator** n. [f. L collat- p.p. stem of conferre bring together]

collateral /kɒˈlætərəl/ adj. 1. side by side, parallel; additional but subordinate, contributory; connected but aside from the main subject, course, etc. 2. descended from the same stock but by a different line. —n. a collateral person or security. —**collateral security,** an additional security pledged; a security lodged by a third party, or consisting of stocks, shares, property, etc., as opposed to a personal guarantee. —**collaterally** adv. [f. L (COL-, lateralis lateral)]

collation /kɒˈleɪʃ(ə)n/ n. 1. collating, being collated. 2. a light meal. [f. L (as COLLATE); sense 2 f. Collationes Patrum (= Lives of the Fathers) read in Benedictine monasteries and followed by a light repast]

colleague /ˈkɒliːg/ n. a fellow official or worker, especially in a profession or business. [f. F f. L collega partner in office (COL-, legare depute)]

collect¹ /kəˈlekt/ v.t./i. 1. to bring or come together, to assemble, to accumulate; to seek and obtain (books, stamps, etc.) systematically for addition to others; to get (contributions, tax, etc.) from a number of people. 2. to call for, to fetch. 3. to regain control of, to concentrate, to recover (oneself, one's thoughts, courage, etc.); (in p.p.) not perturbed or distracted. —adj. & adv. (US) to be paid for by the recipient (of a telephone call, parcel, etc.). —**collection** n., **collector** n. [f. OF f. L colligere (COL-, legere pick)]

collect² /ˈkɒlekt/ n. a short prayer of the Anglican or Roman Catholic Church, usually to be read on an appointed day. [as prec.]

collectable /kəˈlektəb(ə)l/ adj. suitable for being collected. —n. (usu. in pl.) a collectable item. [f. COLLECT¹]

collective /kəˈlektɪv/ adj. formed by, constituting, or denoting a collection; taken as a whole, aggregate, common. —n. 1. a collective farm. 2. a collective noun. —**collective bargaining,** negotiation of wages etc. by an organized body of employees. **collective farm,** a jointly operated amalgamation of several smallholdings. **collective noun,** a singular noun denoting a collection or number of individuals (e.g. cattle, flock, troop). **collective ownership,** ownership of land etc. by all for the benefit of all. **collective unconscious,** (in the theory of C. G. Jung) that part of the unconscious (mind) which derives from the ancestral experiences of a group, or is shared by all human beings, and is additional to the personal unconscious. —**collectivity** /-ˈtɪvɪtɪ/ n., **collectively** adv. [f. F or L (as COLLECT¹)]

collectivism n. the theory or practice of collective ownership of land and means of production. —**collectivist** n. [f. prec.]

colleen /kəˈliːn/ n. (Ir.) a girl. [Ir., dim. of caile country-woman]

college /ˈkɒlɪdʒ/ n. **1.** an establishment for higher or professional education; a body of teachers and students within a university, their premises; a small university; a school. **2.** an organized body of persons with shared functions and privileges. —**College of Arms**, a royal corporation, founded in 1483, consisting of the Earl Marshal, kings-of-arms, heralds, and pursuivants, exercising jurisdiction in matters armorial, recording proved pedigrees, and granting armorial bearings. [f. OF or L (as COLLEAGUE)]

collegiate /kəˈliːdʒɪət/ adj. of a college or college student. —**collegiate church**, a church (other than a cathedral) with a chapter of canons but without bishops, or (Sc. & US) associated jointly with others under a group of pastors. [f. L (as COLLEGE)]

collide /kəˈlaɪd/ v.i. to come into collision or conflict (with). [f. L collidere (COL, laedere strike and hurt)]

collie /ˈkɒlɪ/ n. a sheep-dog with a long pointed muzzle and usually long hair. [perh. f. coll coal (as being orig. black)]

collier /ˈkɒlɪə(r)/ n. **1.** a coal-miner. **2.** a ship that carries coal as its cargo. [f. COAL]

colliery n. a coal-mine and its buildings. [as prec.]

Collins /ˈkɒlɪnz/, (William) Wilkie (1824–89), English novelist, a friend and collaborator of Charles Dickens. He is remembered as the writer of the first full-length detective stories in English; his finest works in this genre were *The Woman in White* (1860) and *The Moonstone* (1868). His ingenious and meticulously constructed plots influenced Dickens's later works.

collision /kəˈlɪʒ(ə)n/ n. colliding, the striking of one body against another. —**collision course**, a course or action that is bound to end in a collision. [f. L (as COLLIDE)]

collocate /ˈkɒləkeɪt/ v.t. to place (esp. words) together or side by side. —**collocation** /-ˈkeɪʃ(ə)n/ n. [f. L collocare (COL-, locare place)]

colloid /ˈkɒlɔɪd/ n. **1.** a gluey substance. **2.** a non-crystalline substance with very large molecules, forming a viscous solution with special properties; a finely divided substance dispersed in a gas, liquid, or solid. —**colloidal** adj. [f. Gk kolla glue]

collop /ˈkɒləp/ n. a slice of meat, an escalope. [f. Scand., = fried bacon and eggs]

colloquial /kəˈləʊkwɪəl/ adj. belonging or proper to ordinary or familiar conversation, not formal or literary. —**colloquially** adv. [as COLLOQUY]

colloquialism n. a colloquial word or phrase; use of these. [f. prec.]

colloquy /ˈkɒləkwɪ/ n. talk, a conversation. [f. L colloquium (COL-, loqui speak)]

collusion /kəˈluːʒ(ə)n/ n. a secret agreement or co-operation, especially for fraud or deceit. —**collusive** adj. [f. OF or L collusio (COL-, ludere play)]

collywobbles /ˈkɒlɪwɒb(ə)lz/ n.pl. (colloq.) rumblings or pain in the stomach; an apprehensive feeling. [f. COLIC + WOBBLE]

Cologne /kəˈləʊn/ German city on the west bank of the Rhine; pop. (1981) 967,700. Founded by the Romans, Cologne rose to prominence through the see established there, the Archbishop of Cologne becoming one of the most powerful German secular princes in the Middle Ages. At that time it was famous for the shrine of the Wise Men of the East, the 'Three Kings of Cologne'.

cologne /kəˈləʊn/ n. eau-de-Cologne or other lightly scented liquid, used to cool or scent the skin. [abbr.]

Colombia /kəˈlɒmbɪə/ a country in the extreme NW of South America, having a coastline on both the Atlantic and the Pacific Ocean; pop. (est. 1981) 28,100,000; official language, Spanish; capital, Bogotá. The Pacific coastal plain is humid and swampy, and most of the population is concentrated in the temperate valleys of the Andes. The economy is mainly agricultural, coffee being the chief export. Mineral resources are rich and include gold, silver, platinum (one of the world's richest deposits), emeralds, and salt, as well as oil, coal, and natural gas. Inhabited by the Chibcha and other Indian peoples, Colombia was conquered by the Spanish in the early 16th c., and under Spanish rule the capital Bogotá developed such a reputation for intellectual and social life as to be called 'the Athens of South America'. Like the rest of Spain's South American empire, Colombia achieved independence in the early

19th c., although the resulting Republic of Great Colombia lasted only until 1830, when first Venezuela and then Ecuador broke away to become independent States in their own right. The remaining State was known as New Granada, changing its name to Colombia in 1863. The country was stricken by civil war between 1949 and 1953, and since then has struggled with endemic poverty and social problems. —**Colombian** adj. & n.

Colombo /kəˈlʌmbəʊ/ the capital and chief port of Sri Lanka; pop. (1981) 585,776.

colon[1] /ˈkəʊlən/ n. a punctuation mark (:), used (i) to show that what follows is an example, list, or summary of what precedes it, or a contrasting idea; (ii) between numbers that are in proportion. [f. L f. Gk kōlon limb, clause]

colon[2] /ˈkəʊlɒn/ n. the lower and greater part of the large intestine (ill. BODY 2). —**colonic** /-ˈlɒnɪk/ adj. [f. OF or L f. Gk]

colonel /ˈkɜːn(ə)l/ n. an officer commanding a regiment, of rank next below brigadier. —**colonelcy** n. [f. F f. It. (colonna column)]

colonial /kəˈləʊnɪəl/ adj. of a colony or colonies. —n. an inhabitant of a colony. [F, or f. COLONY]

colonialism n. the policy of acquiring or maintaining colonies; (derog.) an alleged policy of exploitation of colonies. —**colonialist** n. [f. prec.]

colonist /ˈkɒlənɪst/ n. a settler in or inhabitant of a colony. [f. COLONY]

colonize /ˈkɒlənaɪz/ v.t./i. to establish a colony (in); to join a colony. —**colonization** /-ˈzeɪʃ(ə)n/ n. [as prec.]

colonnade /kɒləˈneɪd/ n. a row of columns, especially supporting entablature or roof. [F (colonne column)]

colony /ˈkɒlənɪ/ n. **1.** a settlement or settlers in a new country fully or partly subject to the mother country; their territory. **2.** a group of one nationality, occupation, etc., forming a community in a city. **3.** a group of animals that live close together. [f. L (colonus farmer, f. colere cultivate)]

colophon /ˈkɒləfən/ n. a tailpiece in a manuscript or book, giving the writer's or printer's name, date, etc.; a publisher's or printer's imprint, especially on a title-page. [L f. Gk, = summit, finishing touch]

Colorado /kɒləˈrɑːdəʊ/ a State in the central USA, named from the great Colorado River which rises there and flows into the Gulf of California. Part of it was acquired by the Louisiana Purchase in 1803 and the rest ceded by Mexico in 1848. It became the 31st State in 1876; capital, Denver. —**Colorado beetle**, a yellow and black beetle, the larva of which is very destructive to the potato plant.

coloration /kʌləˈreɪʃ(ə)n/ n. colouring; an arrangement of colours. [F or f. L (colorare colour)]

coloratura /kɒlərəˈtʊərə/ n. an elaborate ornamentation of a vocal melody; a soprano skilled in coloratura singing. [It. f. L (as prec.)]

colossal /kəˈlɒs(ə)l/ adj. immense; (colloq.) remarkable, splendid. —**colossally** adv. [F (colosse colossus)]

Colosseum /kɒləˈsiːəm/ the medieval name given to the Amphitheatrum Flavium, a vast amphitheatre in Rome begun by Vespasian c.AD 75 and continued and completed by Titus and Domitian. It was capable of holding 50,000 people, with seating in three tiers and standing-room above; an elaborate system of staircases served all parts. The arena, floored with timber and surrounded by a fence, was the scene of gladiatorial combats, fights between men and beasts, and large-scale mock battles.

Colossians /kəˈlɒʃ(ə)nz/ **Epistle to the Colossians,** a book of the New Testament, an epistle of St Paul to the Church at Colossae in Phrygia.

colossus /kəˈlɒsəs/ n. (pl. -i) **1.** a statue of more than life size. **2.** a gigantic person or personified empire etc. —**Colossus of Rhodes,** a huge bronze statue of the sun-god Helios, one of the Seven Wonders of the World, said by Pliny to have been over 30.5 m (100 ft.) high. It stood beside (not astride) the harbour entrance at Rhodes for about 50 years but was destroyed in an earthquake in 224 BC. [L f. Gk]

colostomy /kəˈlɒstəmɪ/ n. an artificial opening through which the bowel can empty, made surgically by bringing part of the colon to the surface of the abdomen. [f. as COLON[2] + Gk stoma mouth]

colour /ˈkʌlə(r)/ n. **1.** the sensation produced on the eye by rays of light resolved (as by a prism) into different wavelengths or by selective reflection (black being the effect produced by no light or by a surface reflecting no rays, and white the effect produced by rays of unresolved light). (See below.) **2.** a particular variety of this. **3.** the use of all colours (not only black and white), e.g. in photography. **4.** a colouring substance. **5.** pigmentation of the skin, especially when dark. **6.** ruddiness of complexion. **7.** (in *pl.*) a coloured ribbon etc. given to regular or leading members of a sports team; the flag of a ship or regiment. **8.** a show of reason; a pretext. **9.** quality, mood, or variety in music, literature, etc. —*v.t./i.* **1.** to put colour on, to paint, stain, or dye; to take on colour, to blush. **2.** to give a special character or bias to. —**colour bar,** discrimination between white and non-white persons. **colour-blind** *adj.* unable to distinguish between certain colours. **colour scheme,** a systematic combination of colours. **primary colours,** (of light) red, green, and violet, (of paints etc.) red, blue, and yellow, giving all others by mixture. **secondary colour,** a mixture of two primary colours. [f. OF f. L]

White light is composed of a mixture of colours, and (as Newton established) is separated by a prism into its constituent colours, ranging from violet light, which has the highest frequency (shortest wavelength), to red light, which has the lowest frequency (longest wavelength). Colour perceived depends chiefly on the relative intensities of the mixture of optical frequencies present in the light received. The human retina possesses three types of specialized receptors which are able to distinguish between these various frequencies, and the gradual increase in frequency from the red end to the violet end of the visible spectrum is perceived as six or seven distinct bands or hues, with progressive colour shading within each hue.

colourant /ˈkʌlərənt/ *n.* colouring-matter. [f. prec.]

coloured *adj.* having colour; wholly or partly of non-white descent, or (**Coloured,** in South Africa) of mixed white and non-white descent. —*n.* a coloured person; **Coloured,** (in South Africa) a person of mixed white and non-white descent. [f. COLOUR]

colourful *adj.* full of colour or interest; with vivid details. —**colourfully** *adv.* [f. COLOUR + -FUL]

colouring *n.* **1.** the disposition of colours. **2.** a substance giving colour. **3.** an artist's use of colour. **4.** facial complexion. [f. COLOUR]

colourless *adj.* without colour; lacking character or vividness. [f. COLOUR + -LESS]

colt /kəʊlt/ *n.* **1.** a young male horse. **2.** an inexperienced player in a team. [OE, = young donkey or camel]

Coltrane /ˈkɒltreɪn/, John (1926–67), American jazz musician. His instrument was the saxophone, and he formed his own band in 1960; he was a leading figure in avant-garde jazz.

coltsfoot /ˈkəʊltsfʊt/ *n.* a weed (*Tussilago farfara*) with large leaves and yellow flowers. Its Latin name refers to the fact that a cough medicine (L *tussis* cough) was formerly made from it.

Columba /kəˈlʌmbə/, St (*c.*521–97), Irish-born abbot and missionary. After founding several churches and monasteries in his own country he established himself *c.*563 with twelve companions on the island of Iona off the west coast of Scotland, and lived there for 34 years evangelizing the mainland and establishing monasteries in the neighbouring islands. Feast day, 9 June.

Columbine /ˈkɒlʌmbaɪn/ a character in Italian comedy, the mistress of Harlequin; she appears in the harlequinade of English pantomime as a short-skirted dancer.

columbine /ˈkɒləmbaɪn/ *n.* a garden plant (aquilegia) with slender pointed projections on its petals. [f. OF f. L *columba* pigeon, from the resemblance of the flower to clustered pigeons]

Columbus /kəˈlʌmbəs/, Christopher (1451–1506), Italian explorer. A Genoese by birth, Columbus persuaded Ferdinand and Isabella of Spain to sponsor an expedition to sail westwards across the Atlantic in search of Asia and prove that the world was round. Sailing with three small ships in 1492, he discovered the New World (actually various Caribbean islands; he himself remained convinced that he had in fact found the coast of Asia) and returned home to a hero's welcome. Columbus made three further voyages to the New World between 1493 and 1504, but failed to find the expected riches of semi-mythical Cathay. A romantic visionary, unsuited either to organization or to intrigue, Columbus was out of his depth in the faction-ridden politics both at the Spanish court and within the new colonies he established. Out of favour, he died in poverty and obscurity at Valladolid in NW Spain.

column /ˈkɒləm/ *n.* **1.** a pillar, usually of circular section and with a base and capital (ill. TEMPLES). **2.** something

shaped like this. **3.** a vertical division of a page in printed matter; a part of a newspaper devoted to a particular subject or by a regular writer. **4.** a vertical row of figures in accounts etc. **5.** a long narrow formation of troops or vehicles etc. —**columnar** /kəˈlʌmnə(r)/ *adj.* [f. OF & L, = pillar]

columnist /ˈkɒləmɪst/ *n.* a person regularly writing a newspaper column. [f. prec.]

com- *prefix* (becoming **col-** before l, **cor-** before r, and **con-** before other consonants) with, jointly; altogether. [f. L *cum* with]

coma /ˈkəʊmə/ *n.* (*pl.* **-ae**) a state of prolonged deep unconsciousness. [f. L f. Gk, = deep sleep]

Comanche /kəˈmæntʃi/ *n.* **1.** a North American Indian people of Texas and Oklahoma. **2.** their language. —*adj.* of this people or their language. [Sp.]

comatose /ˈkəʊmətəʊs/ *adj.* in a coma, drowsy. [f. COMA]

comb /kəʊm/ *n.* **1.** a toothed strip of rigid material for tidying and arranging the hair or for keeping it in place; part of a machine having a similar design or purpose. **2.** the red fleshy crest of a fowl, especially the cock. **3.** a honeycomb. —*v.t./i.* to draw a comb through (hair); to dress (wool etc.) with a comb; (*colloq.*) to search (a place etc.) thoroughly. —**comb out,** to remove with a comb; (*colloq.*) to search out and get rid of (anything unwanted). [OE]

combat /ˈkɒmbæt/ *n.* a fight, struggle, or contest. —*v.t./i.* to engage in a fight; to oppose, to strive against. [f. F f. L (COM-, *batuere* fight)]

combatant /ˈkɒmbət(ə)nt/ *adj.* fighting, for fighting. —*n.* a person engaged in fighting. [as prec.]

combative /ˈkɒmbətɪv/ *adj.* pugnacious. [f. COMBAT]

combe /kuːm/ *var.* of COOMB.

combination /kɒmbɪˈneɪʃ(ə)n/ *n.* **1.** combining, being combined; a combined state. **2.** a combined set of persons or things; a sequence of numbers or letters used to open a combination lock. **3.** (in *pl.*) a one-piece undergarment for body and legs. —**combination lock,** a lock which can be opened only by a specific sequence of movements. —**combinative** /ˈkɒmbɪnətɪv/ *adj.* [as foll.]

Combination Acts British laws of 1799–1800 making illegal the confederacy of persons to further their own interests, affect the rate of wages, etc. Formulated in the wake of naval mutinies and the Irish rebellion, and to prevent seditious revolutionary ideas from spreading to England after the French Revolution, the laws were supposed to apply to masters and men alike, but in fact the masters were allowed to combine freely and restrictions were enforced against working-class unions; most of the legislation was repealed in 1824.

combine[1] /kəmˈbaɪn/ *v.t./i.* to join or be joined into a group, set, or mixture; to co-operate. [f. OF or L *combinare* (COM-, *bini* two together)]

combine[2] /ˈkɒmbaɪn/ *n.* a combination of persons or firms acting together in business. —**combine harvester,** a combined reaping and threshing machine. [f. prec.]

combings /ˈkəʊmɪŋz/ *n.pl.* loose hair removed by a brush or comb. [f. COMB]

combust /kəmˈbʌst/ *v.t.* to subject to combustion. [as COMBUSTION]

combustible /kəmˈbʌstɪb(ə)l/ *adj.* capable of or used for burning. —*n.* a combustible thing. —**combustibility** /-ˈbɪlɪtɪ/ *n.* [as foll.]

combustion /kəmˈbʌstʃ(ə)n/ *n.* the process of burning, a chemical process (accompanied by heat and light) in which substances combine with oxygen. [f. F or L (*combustere* burn up)]

come /kʌm/ *v.i.* **1.** to move, be brought towards, or reach a place thought of as near or familiar to the speaker or hearer. **2.** to reach a specified point, condition, or result. **3.** to occur, to happen, to become present instead of future. **4.** to take or occupy a specified position in space or time. **5.** to become perceptible or known. **6.** to be available. **7.** to be descended, to be the result (*of*). **8.** (*colloq.*) to behave like. **9.** (in *imper.*) an exclamation of mild protest or encouragement. —**come about,** to happen. **come across,** to meet or find unexpectedly. **come along,** to make progress; (as *imper.*) hurry up. **come-back** *n.* a return to one's former successful position; (*colloq.*) a retort or retaliation. **come by,** to obtain. **come-down** *n.* a downfall; an anticlimax. **come-hither** *adj.* flirtatious, inviting. **come out,** to emerge, to become known; to go on strike; to be published; to declare oneself (*for* or *against*); to be satisfactorily visible in a photograph etc.; to erupt, to become covered *in* (a rash etc.); to emerge from an examination etc. with a specified result; to be solved. **come out with,** to say, to disclose. **come over,** (of a feeling etc.) to affect (a person); (*colloq.*) to be affected with (a feeling). **come round,** to pay an informal visit; to recover consciousness; to be converted to another person's opinion; (of a date) to recur. **come to,** to amount to, to be equivalent to; to recover consciousness. **come to pass,** to happen. **come up,** to arise for discussion etc., to occur. **come-uppance** *n.* (*colloq.*) a deserved punishment or rebuke. **come up with,** to present or produce (an idea etc.); to draw level with. —**comer** *n.* [OE]

Comecon /ˈkɒmɪkɒn/ the English name for an economic organization of Soviet-bloc countries, founded in 1949 and analogous to the European Economic Community. [short for *Council for Mutual Economic Aid* (or *Assistance*), transl. Russ. title]

comedian /kəˈmiːdɪən/ *n.* a humorous performer on the stage, television, etc.; an actor who plays comic parts. —**comedienne** /-ˈen/ *n.fem.* [as COMEDY.]

Comédie française /kɒmedi frɑ̃ˈseɪz/ the French national theatre founded in 1680 and reconstituted by Napoleon in 1803. [F]

comedy /ˈkɒmɪdɪ/ *n.* **1.** a light amusing play or film, usually with a happy ending; the branch of drama that consists of such plays. **2.** humour, humorous incidents in life. [f. OF f. L f. Gk (*kōmos* revel)]

comely /ˈkʌmlɪ/ *adj.* handsome, good-looking. **comeliness** *n.* [prob. as BECOME]

comestibles /kəˈmestɪb(ə)lz/ *n.pl.* (*formal* or *joc.*) things to eat. [f. F f. L (*comedere* eat)]

comet /ˈkɒmɪt/ *n.* a luminous object seen in the night sky, originally considered a supernatural omen, but now recognized as an object orbiting the sun, consisting of an icy nucleus and a tail of evaporated gas and dust particles. Originating in a belt of material perhaps more than a light-year from the sun, comets are seen in the inner solar system only if perturbed from their orbits by the outer planets. Most escape back to interstellar space, but a few are trapped near the sun, and reappear regularly as periodic comets, of which the best known is Halley's. —**cometary** *adj.* [f. F f. L f. Gk, = long-haired]

comfit /ˈkʌmfɪt/ *n.* (*archaic*) a sweet consisting of a nut etc. in sugar. [f. OF f. L *confectum* (CON-, *facere* make)]

comfort /ˈkʌmfət/ *n.* **1.** a state of physical or mental well-being or contentment. **2.** relief of suffering or grief, consolation; a person or thing that gives this. **3.** (in *pl.*) things that allow ease or well-being in life. —*v.t.* to give comfort to, to soothe in grief, to console. —**comforter** *n.* [f. OF f. L *confortare* strengthen (CON-, *fortis* strong)]

comfortable /ˈkʌmfətəb(ə)l/ *adj.* **1.** giving or feeling ease and contentment; not close or restricted. —**comfortably** *adv.* [as prec.]

comfrey /ˈkʌmfrɪ/ *n.* a tall bell-flowered plant of the genus *Symphytum*, growing in damp shady places. [f. AF f. L *conferva* (CON-, *fervēre* boil)]

comfy /ˈkʌmfɪ/ *adj.* (*colloq.*) comfortable. [abbr.]

comic /ˈkɒmɪk/ *adj.* of or like comedy; causing amusement or laughter. —*n.* **1.** a comedian. **2.** a paper (usually for children) with series of strip cartoons. —**comical** *adj.*, **comically** *adv.* [f. L (as COMEDY)]

coming /ˈkʌmɪŋ/ *adj.* approaching next; likely to be important in the near future. —*n.* arrival. [f. COME]

Comintern /ˈkɒmɪntɜːn/ *n.* the Third International (1919–43; see INTERNATIONAL). [f. Russ., = communist international]

comity /ˈkɒmɪtɪ/ *n.* courtesy, friendship; an association of nations etc. for their mutual benefit. —**comity of nations,** nations' friendly recognition of each other's laws and customs. [f. L (*comis* courteous)]

comma *n.* the punctuation-mark (,), indicating a slight pause or break between parts of a sentence, or separating words or figures in a list. [f. L f. Gk, = clause]

command /kəˈmɑːnd/ *n.* **1.** a statement, given with authority, that some action must be performed. **2.** the right to control others, authority. **3.** ability to use something, mastery. **4.** forces or a district under a commander. —*v.t./i.* **1.** to give a command or order to; to have authority over. **2.** to deserve and get. **3.** to dominate (a strategic position) from a superior height, to look down over. —**Command paper,** a paper laid before Parliament by royal command. **command performance,** a performance of a film, show, etc., by royal request. [f. AF f. L, = COMMEND]

commandant /ˈkɒmənd(ə)nt/ *n.* a commanding officer, especially of a military academy or prisoner-of-war camp. [F (as COMMAND)]

commandeer /kɒmənˈdɪə(r)/ *v.t.* to seize for military use; to seize for one's own purposes. [f. S.Afr. Du. f. F, = command]

commander /kəˈmɑːndə(r)/ *n.* **1.** one who commands, especially a naval officer of rank next below captain. **2.** (in full **Knight Commander**) a member of the higher class in some orders of knighthood. —**commander-in-chief** *n.* the supreme commander. [f. OF (as COMMAND)]

commandment /kəˈmɑːndmənt/ *n.* a divine command, especially (**Commandment**) one of the ten given to Moses (Exod. 20: 1–17). [as prec.]

commando /kəˈmɑːndəʊ/ *n.* (*pl.* -os) **1.** a party called out for military purposes. **2.** (in the Boer War) a unit of the Boer army composed of the militia of an electoral district. **3.** (in the Second World War) a member of a military unit specially trained for making raids and assaults; such a unit. [Port. (as COMMAND)]

commedia dell'arte /kɒmiːdɪə delˈɑːteɪ/ improvised drama performed by professional actors developed in 16th-c. Italy, and extended throughout Europe until the end of the 18th c., in which stock character types (e.g. Harlequin, Columbine, Pantaloon) adapted their comic dialogue and action according to a few basic plots (commonly love intrigues) and to popular needs. It had an enormous influence on European drama as seen in the work of Jonson, Molière, and Goldoni. [It., = comedy of art]

comme il faut /kɒm iːl ˈfəʊ/ proper, properly, as it should be. [F, = as is necessary]

commemorate /kəˈmeməreɪt/ *v.t.* to keep in memory by a celebration or ceremony; to be a memorial to. —**commemoration** /-ˈreɪʃ(ə)n/ *n.*, **commemorative** *adj.* [f. L *commemorare* (COM-, *memor* mindful)]

commence /kəˈmens/ *v.t.* to begin. —**commencement** *n.* [f. OF f. L (COM-, *initiare* initiate)]

commend /kəˈmend/ *v.t.* **1.** to praise; to recommend. **2.** to entrust, to commit. —**commendation** /-ˈdeɪʃ(ə)n/ *n.*, **commendatory** /-ˈmen-/ *adj.* [f. L *commendare* (COM-, *mandare* entrust)]

commendable /kəˈmendəb(ə)l/ *adj.* praiseworthy. —**commendably** *adv.* [f. OF (as prec.)]

commensal /kəˈmens(ə)l/ *adj.* living in a form of symbiosis that is beneficial to one species and neither harmful nor beneficial to the other. —*n.* a plant or animal living thus. —**commensalism** *n.* [f. F or L (COM-, *mensa* table)]

commensurable /kəˈmenʃərəb(ə)l/ *adj.* measurable by the same standard (*with* or *to*); proportionate *to*. [f. L (as MEASURE)]

commensurate /kəˈmenʃərət/ *adj.* coextensive (*with*); proportionate (*to* or *with*). [as prec.]

comment /ˈkɒment/ *n.* a brief critical or explanatory remark or note, an opinion. —*v.i.* to utter or write comments. [f. L, = contrivance, interpretation (*comminisci* devise)]

commentary /ˈkɒmentərɪ/ *n.* a series of descriptive comments on an event or performance; a set of explanatory notes on a text etc. [as prec.]

commentate /ˈkɒmənteɪt/ *v.i.* to act as a commentator. [f. foll.]

commentator *n.* the speaker or writer of a commentary; one who comments on current events. [L (as COMMENT)]

commerce /ˈkɒmɜːs/ *n.* buying and selling, all forms of trading, including banking, insurance, etc. [F or f. L *commercium* (COM-, *merx* merchandise)]

commercial /kəˈmɜːʃ(ə)l/ *adj.* of or engaged in commerce; concerned chiefly with financial profit; (of broadcasting) in which advertisements are included to provide finance. —*n.* a broadcast advertisement. —**commercial traveller,** a firm's representative visiting shops etc. to obtain orders. —**commercially** *adv.* [f. prec.]

commercialism *n.* commercial practices and attitudes. [f. prec.]

commercialize *v.t.* to make commercial; to seek to make profitable. —**commercialization** /-ˈzeɪʃ(ə)n/ *n.* [f. COMMERCIAL]

Commie /ˈkɒmɪ/ *n.* (*slang, derog.*) a Communist. [abbr.]

commination /kɒmɪˈneɪʃ(ə)n/ *n.* threatening of divine vengeance. —**comminatory** /ˈkɒmɪneɪtərɪ/ *adj.* [f. L (COM-, *minare* threaten)]

commingle /kəˈmɪŋg(ə)l/ *v.t./i.* (*literary*) to mix together. [f. COM- + MINGLE]

comminute /ˈkɒmɪnjuːt/ v.t. **1.** to reduce to small fragments. **2.** to divide (property) into small portions. — **comminuted fracture,** one producing multiple fragments of bone (ill. BODY 2). —**comminution** /-ˈnjuːʃ(ə)n/ n. [f. L comminuere (COM-, minuere lessen)]

commiserate /kəˈmɪzəreɪt/ v.i. to express pity, to sympathize. —**commiseration** /-ˈreɪʃ(ə)n/ n., **commiserative** adj. [f. L commiserari (COM-, miserari pity)]

commissar /ˈkɒmɪsɑː(r)/ n. (hist.) a head of a government department of the USSR. [f. Russ. f. F (as COMMISSARY)]

commissariat /kɒmɪˈseərɪət/ n. **1.** the department responsible for the supply of food etc. for an army; the food supplied. **2.** (hist.) a government department of the USSR. [F (as foll.)]

commissary /ˈkɒmɪsərɪ/ n. **1.** a deputy, a delegate. **2.** (US) a store where food and other supplies are sold at a military base. **3.** (US) a restaurant in a film studio or factory etc. [f. L, = person in charge (as COMMIT)]

commission /kəˈmɪʃ(ə)n/ n. **1.** the giving of authority to a person to perform a task; the task so given; such a person's authority or instructions. **2.** a body or board of persons constituted to perform certain duties. **3.** a warrant conferring authority, especially that of an officer in the armed forces above a certain rank. **4.** the payment or percentage received by an agent. **5.** committing, performance (e.g. of a crime). —v.t. **1.** to give a commission to; to employ (a person) to do a piece of work. **2.** to prepare (a ship) for active service. **3.** to bring (a machine etc.) into operation. —**commission agent,** a bookmaker. **in** or **out of commission,** ready or not ready for use. [f. OF f. L (as COMMIT)]

commissionaire /kəmɪʃ(ə)ˈneə(r)/ n. an attendant at the door of a theatre, office, etc. [F, as foll.]

commissioner /kəˈmɪʃ(ə)nə(r)/ n. **1.** one who is appointed by commission (e.g. the head of Scotland Yard). **2.** a member of a commission. **3.** an official representing the government in a district, department, etc. —**Commissioner for Oaths,** a solicitor authorized to administer oaths in affidavits etc. [f. L (as COMMISSION)]

commissure /ˈkɒmɪsjʊə(r)/ n. the joint between two bones; a junction or seam. [f. L, = junction]

commit /kəˈmɪt/ v.t. (-tt-) **1.** to be the doer of (a crime etc.). **2.** to entrust for safe keeping or treatment. **3.** to pledge, to bind with an obligation. —**commit to memory,** to memorize. [f. L committere entrust (COM-, mittere send)]

commitment /kəˈmɪtmənt/ n. **1.** committing, being committed. **2.** an engagement or involvement that restricts freedom of action or choice. **3.** an obligation or pledge. [f. prec.]

committal /kəˈmɪt(ə)l/ n. the action of committing, especially to prison or for burial or cremation. [as prec.]

committee /kəˈmɪtɪ/ n. a group of persons appointed by (and usually out of) a larger body, to attend to special business or manage the business of a club etc. [f. COMMIT]

commode /kəˈməʊd/ n. **1.** a chamber-pot mounted in a chair or box with a cover. **2.** a chest of drawers. [F f. L commodus convenient]

commodious /kəˈməʊdɪəs/ adj. roomy. [f. F f. L, as prec.]

commodity /kəˈmɒdɪtɪ/ n. an article of trade, especially a product as opposed to a service. [f. OF or L (as COMMODE)]

commodore /ˈkɒmədɔː(r)/ n. a naval officer next below rear-admiral; the commander of a squadron or other division of a fleet; the president of a yacht club. [f. Du. f. F, = commander]

common /ˈkɒmən/ adj. **1.** shared by, coming from, or affecting all concerned; of or belonging to the whole community, public. **2.** occurring often; ordinary, of the most familiar or numerous kind. **3.** without special rank or position; (in pl.) the common people. **4.** of inferior quality; ill-bred, unrefined. **5.** (Gram., of a noun) referring to any one of a class; (of gender) referring to individuals of either sex. —n. an area of unfenced grassland for all to use. —**Common Era,** the Christian era. **common law,** unwritten law based on custom and precedent. **common-law husband** or **wife,** one recognized by common law without an official ceremony, usually after a period of cohabitation. **Common Market,** the European Economic Community. **common or garden,** (colloq.) ordinary. **common-room** n. a room for social use by students or teachers at a college etc. **common sense,** good practical sense in everyday matters. **common time,** (Mus.) four crotchets in a bar. **in common,** shared by several (especially as an interest or characteristic); in joint use. **the Commons,** the House of Commons. **commonly** adv., **commonness** n. [f. OF f. L]

commonality /kɒməˈnælɪtɪ/ n. **1.** the sharing of an attribute. **2.** a common occurrence. [var. of foll.]

commonalty /ˈkɒmən(ə)ltɪ/ n. the common people; the general body (of mankind) etc. [as COMMON]

commoner /ˈkɒmənə(r)/ n. **1.** a member of the common people (below the rank of peer). **2.** a student without financial support from a college. [as COMMON]

commonplace adj. ordinary, usual; lacking in originality or individuality. —n. a commonplace event, topic, etc., or remark. [transl. of L & Gk (lit. common place), = general theme]

commonsensical /kɒmənˈsensɪk(ə)l/ adj. having or marked by common sense. [f. common sense]

commonwealth /ˈkɒmənwelθ/ n. **1.** an independent State or community. **2.** a republic or democratic State. **3.** a federation of States. —**the Commonwealth,** (i) the republican government of Britain between the execution of Charles I in 1649 and the Restoration in 1660; (ii) an association of the UK and various independent States (previously subject to Britain) and dependencies. **Commonwealth Day,** the name since 1959 of what was formerly called Empire Day, celebrated until 1965 on 24 May (Queen Victoria's birthday) and after that on the Queen's official birthday, originally commemorating assistance given to Britain by the colonies in the Boer War of 1899–1902. **New Commonwealth,** those countries which have achieved self-government within the Commonwealth since 1945. [f. COMMON + WEALTH]

commotion /kəˈməʊʃ(ə)n/ n. uproar, fuss and disturbance. [f. OF or L (as COM-, MOTION)]

communal /ˈkɒmjʊn(ə)l/ adj. shared between the members of a group or community. —**communally** adv., **communalistic** /-ˈlɪstɪk/ adj. [F f. L (as foll.)]

commune[1] /ˈkɒmjuːn/ n. **1.** a group of people, not all of one family, sharing living arrangements and goods. **2.** a small district of local government in France and certain other European countries. —**the Commune (of Paris),** (i) a body which usurped the municipal government of Paris and in this capacity played a leading part in the Reign of Terror until suppressed in 1794; (ii) the government on communalistic principles established in Paris for a short time in 1871 after the Franco-Prussian war and the collapse of the Second Empire. [f. L communia (communis common)]

commune[2] /kəˈmjuːn/ v.i. to communicate mentally or spiritually, to feel in close touch (with). [F, = share]

communicable /kəˈmjuːnɪkəb(ə)l/ adj. that can be communicated. [f. OF or L (as COMMUNICATE)]

communicant /kəˈmjuːnɪkənt/ n. **1.** a person who receives Holy Communion; one who does this regularly. **2.** one who communicates information [as foll.]

communicate /kəˈmjuːnɪkeɪt/ v.t./i. **1.** to impart, to transmit; to make known; to succeed in conveying information. **2.** to have social dealings (with). **3.** to be connected. **4.** to receive Holy Communion. [f. L communicare (as COMMON)]

communication /kəmjuːnɪˈkeɪʃ(ə)n/ n. **1.** communicating. **2.** something that communicates information, sent or transmitted from one person to another; a letter or message. **3.** a means of communicating, e.g. a road, railway, telegraph line, radio, etc. **4.** (in pl.) the science and practice of transmitting information. —**communication cord,** a cord or chain to be pulled by a passenger wishing to stop the train in an emergency. **communications satellite,** one used for intercontinental television and telephone etc. communications (ill. SPACE). [as prec.]

communicative /kəˈmjuːnɪkətɪv/ adj. ready and willing to talk and impart information. [as COMMUNICATE]

communion /kəˈmjuːnɪən/ n. **1.** fellowship, having ideas and beliefs in common. **2.** a body of Christians of the same denomination. **3.** social dealings. —**(Holy) Communion,** the Eucharist. **communion of saints,** fellowship of Christians past and present. [f. OF or L (communis common)].

communiqué /kəˈmjuːnɪkeɪ/ n. an official communication or report. [F, = communicated]

communism /ˈkɒmjʊnɪz(ə)m/ n. **1.** a system of society with vesting of property in the community, each member working for the common benefit according to his capacity and receiving according to his needs. **2. Communism,** a movement or political party advocating communism, especially as derived from Marxism; a communistic form of society established in the 20th c. in the USSR and elsewhere (see below). [f. F (commun common)]

Communism took practical form with the triumph of the Bolsheviks in the Russian Revolution in 1917, and although it has adopted many different forms in different countries, it has generally been defined in terms of the Soviet system. Perhaps the most important political force in the 20th c., Communism embraces a revolutionary ideology based on the overthrow of the capitalist system, and, in theory at least, on the notion of constant progress towards the perfect stateless society.

communist /ˈkɒmjʊnɪst/ n. **1.** a supporter of communism. **2. Communist,** a member or supporter of a Communist Party. —**communistic** /-ˈnɪstɪk/ adj. [as prec.]

community /kəˈmjuːnɪtɪ/ n. **1.** a body of people living in one place, district, or country; a group having a religion, race, profession, etc., in common; a commune. **2.** fellowship (of interest etc.); the state of being shared or held in common; joint ownership or liability. —**community centre,** a place providing social, recreational, and educational facilities for a neighbourhood. **community home,** a centre for housing young offenders. **community service,** performance of specified unpaid services to the community as an alternative to a prison sentence. **community singing,** organized singing in chorus by a large gathering of people. [f. OF f. L (as COMMON)]

commutative /kəˈmjuːtətɪv/ adj. (of a mathematical operation) producing the same result regardless of the order in which the quantities are taken (e.g. $3 + 4 = 7, 4 + 3 = 7$). [f. F or L (as foll.)]

commute /kəˈmjuːt/ v.t./i. **1.** to travel regularly by train, bus, or car to and from one's daily work in a city etc. **2.** to exchange for; to change (one form of payment or obligation) for or into another; to change (a punishment) to another less severe. —**commutation** /-ˈteɪʃ(ə)n/ n. [f. L commutare (COM-, mutare change)]

commuter n. one who commutes to and from work. [f. prec.]

Comoros /kɒˈmɔːrəʊz/ a country consisting of a group of islands in the Indian Ocean north of Madagascar; pop. (est. 1979) 385,000; official languages, French and Arabic; capital, Moroni. The islands were first visited by the English at the end of the 16th c. At that time and for long afterwards Arab interest was dominant. In the mid-19th c. they came under French protection, until in 1974 all but one of the four major islands voted for independence. —**Comoran** adj. & n.

compact[1] /kəmˈpækt/ adj. closely or neatly packed together; concise. —v.t. to make compact. —/ˈkɒm-/ n. a small flat case for face-powder. —**compact disc,** a disc without grooves, on which sound is recorded digitally for reproduction by means of a laser beam directed on to it. —**compactly** adv., **compactness** n. [f. L compingere (COM-, pingere fasten)]

compact[2] /ˈkɒmpækt/ n. an agreement, a contract. [f. L compactum (COM-, as PACT)]

companion /kəmˈpænjən/ n. **1.** one who associates with or accompanies another; a woman paid to live with and accompany another. **2.** a member of the lowest grade of some orders of knighthood. **3.** a handbook or reference book dealing with a specified subject. **4.** a thing that matches or accompanies another. —**companion-way** n. a staircase from a ship's deck to the saloon or cabins. —**companionship** n. [f. OF f. L (COM-, panis bread)]

companionable adj. sociable, friendly. —**companionably** adv. [f. prec.]

company /ˈkʌmpənɪ/ n. **1.** being with another or others. **2.** a number of people assembled, guests; a person's associates; a body of persons assembled for a common (esp. commercial) object; a group of actors etc.; a subdivision of an infantry battalion. —**part company,** to go different ways after being together; to cease associating (with). [f. AF (as COMPANION)]

comparable /ˈkɒmpərəb(ə)l, (D) -ˈpær-/ adj. that can be compared (with or to). —**comparability** /-ˈbɪlɪtɪ/ n., **comparably** adv. [f. OF f. L (as COMPARE)]

comparative /kəmˈpærətɪv/ adj. perceptible or estimated by comparison; of or involving comparison; considered in relation to each other. —n. (Gram.) the comparative degree. —**comparative adjective, adverb,** one in the comparative degree. **comparative degree,** the form expressing a higher degree of a quality (e.g. braver, more quickly). [f. L (as foll.)]

compare /kəmˈpeə(r)/ v.t./i. **1.** to estimate the similarity of (one thing with or to another; two things); to liken or regard as similar (to); to bear comparison with. **2.** to form the comparative and superlative degrees of (an adjective or adverb). —n. (literary) comparison. [f. OF f. L comparare (COM-, par equal)]

comparison /kəmˈpærɪs(ə)n/ n. comparing. —**bear comparison,** to be able to be compared favourably with. **degrees of comparison,** (Gram.) the positive, comparative, and superlative (of adjectives and adverbs). [as prec.]

compartment /kəmˈpɑːtmənt/ n. a division separated by partitions, e.g. in a railway carriage; a watertight division of a ship. [f. F f. It. f L compartiri (COM-, partiri share)]

compartmental /kɒmpɑːtˈment(ə)l/ adj. of or divided into compartments or categories. [f. prec.]

compartmentalize /kɒmpɑːtˈment(ə)laɪz/ v.t. to divide into compartments or categories. [f. prec.]

compass /ˈkʌmpəs/ n. **1.** an instrument showing the magnetic north and bearings from it (see below and ill. NAVIGATION). **2.** (often in pl.) an instrument for taking measurements and describing circles, with two legs connected at one end by a movable joint. **3.** circumference, boundary; area, extent, scope; the range of a voice or musical instrument. —**compass rose,** a circle showing the 32 principal points of the compass. [f. OF f. L (COM-, passus step)]

In early times navigation was by observation of landmarks or of the stars. The mariner's compass is reported in China c.1100, western Europe 1187, Arabia c.1220, and Scandinavia c.1300; its actual use may well be considerably earlier in each of these areas. In very small and simple compasses the compass-card is fixed and the magnetic needle swings round above it; in all aircraft and ships' magnetic compasses, however, the card is laid on top of the needle and attached to it, so that the needle swings it round. In a ship the compass-card not only rotates on a pivot but is arranged so that it nearly floats on a quantity of alcohol; this liquid lessens the weight on the pivot, making the compass more sensitive, and the casing of the whole is swung on gimbals so that it remains face upwards in spite of the rocking of the ship. This kind of compass, which points to the magnetic north (whose position varies over the years) is subject to a number of errors (deviations can be caused by adjacent metal fitments etc.) but is carried as an emergency instrument even when a gyro-compass is fitted.

compassion /kəmˈpæʃ(ə)n/ n. a feeling of pity inclining one to be helpful or show mercy. [f. OF f. L (COM-, pati suffer)]

compassionate /kəmˈpæʃənət/ adj. sympathetic, showing compassion. —**compassionate leave,** leave granted on grounds of bereavement etc. —**compassionately** adv. [f. prec.]

compatible /kəmˈpætɪb(ə)l/ adj. **1.** able to co-exist (with); mutually tolerant. **2.** (of equipment etc.) able to be used in combination. —**compatibility** /-ˈbɪlɪtɪ/ n. [F f. L (as COMPASSION)]

compatriot /kəmˈpætrɪət/ n. a fellow-countryman. [f. F f. L (COM-, patria mother country)]

compeer /kəmˈpɪə(r)/ n. a person of equal standing; a comrade. [f. OF (as COM-, PEER[2])]

compel /kəmˈpel/ v.t. (-ll-) **1.** to use irresistible force or influence so as to cause (a person etc.) to do something; to allow no choice of action. **2.** to arouse (a feeling) irresistibly. [f. L compellere (COM-, pellere drive)]

compelling adj. arousing strong interest or admiration. [f. prec.]

compendious /kəmˈpendɪəs/ adj. comprehensive but brief. [f. OF f. L (as foll.)]

compendium /kəmˈpendɪəm/ n. (pl. -ia) **1.** a concise summary or abridgement. **2.** a collection of table-games etc. [L, = saving, short cut (COM-, pendere weigh)]

compensate /ˈkɒmpənseɪt/ v.t./i. **1.** to make suitable payment in return for (loss, damage, etc.); to recompense. **2.** to counterbalance. —**compensatory** adj. [f. L compensare (COM-, frequent. of pendere weigh)]

compensation /kɒmpənˈseɪʃ(ə)n/ n. compensating, being compensated; a thing (esp. money) that compensates. [f. OF f. L (as prec.)]

compère /ˈkɒmpeə(r)/ n. a person who introduces artistes at a variety show etc. —v.t. to act as compère to. [F, = godfather]

compete /kəmˈpiːt/ v.i. to take part in a contest, race, etc.; to strive (with or against). [f. L competere strive after (COM-, petere seek)]

competence /ˈkɒmpɪtəns/ n. (also **competency**) **1.** being competent, ability; legal capacity. **2.** a comfortably adequate income. [f. foll.]

competent /ˈkɒmpɪt(ə)nt/ adj. having the required knowledge, ability, or authority; effective, adequate. —**competently** adv. [f. OF or L (as COMPETE)]

competition /kɒmpɪˈtɪʃ(ə)n/ n. **1.** an event in which persons compete. **2.** competing (for) by examination, in trade, etc. **3.** those competing with one. [as COMPETE]

competitive /kəmˈpetɪtɪv/ adj. of or involving competition; (of prices etc.) comparing favourably with those of rivals. —**competitively** adv. [as COMPETE]

competitor /kəmˈpetɪtə(r)/ n. one who competes; a rival, especially in trade. [as prec.]

compile /kəmˈpaɪl/ v.t. to collect and arrange (information) into a list, volume, etc.; to produce (books etc.) thus. —**compilation** /-ˈleɪʃ(ə)n/ n., **compiler** n. [f. OF or L compilare plunder]

complacent /kəmˈpleɪsənt/ adj. self-satisfied, calmly content. —**complacency** n., **complacently** adv. [f. L complacēre (COM-, placēre please)]

complain /kəmˈpleɪn/ v.i. to express dissatisfaction. —**complain of,** to say that one is suffering from (a pain etc.); to state a grievance concerning. [f. OF f. L (COM-, plangere lament)]

complainant /kəmˈpleɪnənt/ n. the plaintiff (in certain lawsuits). [as prec.]

complaint /kəmˈpleɪnt/ n. **1.** a statement of dissatisfaction, utterance of a grievance, a formal accusation. **2.** a cause of dissatisfaction; an illness. [as COMPLAIN]

complaisant /kəmˈpleɪz(ə)nt/ adj. inclined to please or defer to others; acquiescent. —**complaisance** n. [F (as COMPLACENT)]

complement /ˈkɒmpləmənt/ n. that which makes a thing complete; the full number required to man a ship, fill a conveyance, etc.; the word or words added to a verb to complete the predicate; the deficiency of an angle from 90°. —v.t. to complete; to form a complement to. [f. L (as COMPLETE)]

complementary /kɒmpləˈmentərɪ/ adj. completing, forming a complement; (of two or more things) complementing each other. —**complementary colour,** a colour of light that when combined with a given colour makes white light (e.g. blue with yellow). [f. prec.]

complete /kəmˈpliːt/ adj. having all its parts, entire; finished; thorough, in every way. —v.t. to make complete; to finish; to fill in (a form etc.). —**complete with,** having as an important feature or addition. —**completely** adv., **completeness** n. [f. OF or L (as COMPLEMENT)]

completion /kəmˈpliːʃ(ə)n/ n. completing, being completed. [as prec.]

complex /ˈkɒmpleks/ adj. consisting of several parts, composite; complicated. —n. **1.** a complex whole. **2.** a group of usually repressed ideas etc. causing abnormal behaviour or mental state. **3.** a set of buildings. —**complexity** n. [f. F or L complecti embrace, assoc. with complexus plaited]

complexion /kəmˈplekʃ(ə)n/ n. **1.** the natural colour, texture, and appearance of the skin, especially of the face. **2.** character, aspect. [f. OF f. L (as prec.)]

compliant /kəmˈplaɪənt/ adj. complying, obedient. —**compliance** n. [f. COMPLY]

complicate /ˈkɒmplɪkeɪt/ v.t. to make involved, intricate, or difficult. [f. L complicare (COM-, plicare fold)]

complication /kɒmplɪˈkeɪʃ(ə)n/ n. **1.** an involved condition, an entangled state of affairs. **2.** a complicating circumstance; a secondary disease or condition aggravating an already existing one. [as prec.]

complicity /kəmˈplɪsɪtɪ/ n. partnership in evil action. [f. obs. complice accomplice]

compliment /ˈkɒmplɪmənt/ n. a polite expression of praise; an act implying praise; (in pl.) formal greetings accompanying a note, present, etc. —/-ment/ v.t. to pay a compliment to. [F f. L (as COMPLEMENT)]

complimentary /kɒmplɪˈmentərɪ/ adj. expressing a compliment; given free of charge by way of compliment. [f. prec.]

compline /ˈkɒmplɪn/ n. the last of the canonical hours of prayer; the service said at this. [f. OF f. L (as foll.)]

comply /kəmˈplaɪ/ v.i. to act in accordance (with). [f. It. f. L complēre fill up]

component /kəmˈpəʊnənt/ adj. forming one of the parts of a whole. —n. a component part. [f. L (as COMPOUND[1])]

comport /kəmˈpɔːt/ v.t./i. (literary) to conduct or behave oneself. —**comport with,** to suit, to befit. —**comportment** n. [f. L comportare (COM-, portare carry)]

compose /kəmˈpəʊz/ v.t. **1.** to create in music or writing. **2.** to form, to make up. **3.** (in printing) to set up (type), to arrange (an article etc.) in type. **4.** to arrange artistically, neatly, or for a specified purpose. **5.** to make (oneself, one's feelings, etc.) calm. —**composed of,** made up of, consisting of. [f. F f. L componere (COM-, ponere put)]

composed adj. calm, self-possessed. —**composedly** /-ɪdlɪ/ adv. [f. prec.]

composer n. one who composes (esp. music). [f. COMPOSE]

composite /ˈkɒmpəzɪt, -zaɪt/ adj. **1.** made up of various parts. **2.** (of a plant, e.g. daisy, dandelion) of the family Compositae, in which the flower-head is made up of many individual flowers which together look like one bloom. **3.** (Archit.) of mixed Ionic and Corinthian style (ill. TEMPLES). —n. a composite thing or plant. [F f. L (as COMPOUND[1])]

composition /kɒmpəˈzɪʃ(ə)n/ n. **1.** an act or method of putting together into a whole, composing. **2.** a thing composed, a piece of writing or (esp.) music. **3.** the constitution of a substance etc.; the arrangement of parts in a picture etc. **4.** a compound artificial substance, especially one serving the purpose of a natural one. **5.** a financial compromise. —**compositional** adj. [f. OF f. L (as prec.)]

compositor /kəmˈpɒzɪtə(r)/ n. one who sets up type for printing. [f. AF f. L (as COMPOSE)]

compost /ˈkɒmpɒst/ n. a mixture of decayed organic mixture used as a fertilizer; a mixture usually of soil and other ingredients for growing seedlings, cuttings, etc. —v.t. to make into compost; to treat with compost. [f. OF f. L (as COMPOSITE)]

composure /kəmˈpəʊʒə(r)/ n. tranquil demeanour, calmness. [f. COMPOSE]

compote /ˈkɒmpəʊt, -pɒt/ n. fruit preserved or cooked in syrup. [F (as COMPOSITE)]

compound[1] /ˈkɒmpaʊnd/ n. a thing made up of two or more ingredients; a substance consisting of two or more elements chemically united in fixed proportions; a word formed by a combination of words. —/kəmˈpaʊnd/ v.t./i. **1.** to mix or combine (ingredients or elements); to make up (a composite whole); to increase or complicate (difficulties etc.). **2.** to settle (a matter) by mutual agreement; to condone or conceal (an offence or liability) for personal gain; to come to terms (with a person). —/ˈkɒmpaʊnd/ adj. made up of two or more ingredients; combined, collective. —**compound fracture,** one complicated by a wound. **compound interest,** see INTEREST. **compound time,** (Mus.) that with a ternary subdivision of the unit (e.g. into three, six, nine). [f. OF f. L componere put together]

compound[2] /ˈkɒmpaʊnd/ n. an enclosure or fenced-in space; (in India, China, etc.) the enclosure in which a house or factory stands. [f. Port. or Du. f. Malay kampong]

comprehend /kɒmprɪˈhend/ v.t. **1.** to grasp mentally, to understand. **2.** to include. —**comprehensible** adj., **comprehension** n. [f. OF or L comprehendere (COM-, prehendere grasp, seize)]

comprehensive adj. including much or all, inclusive. —n. a comprehensive school. —**comprehensive school,** a large secondary school providing courses for children of all abilities. —**comprehensively** adv. [as prec.]

compress /kəmˈpres/ v.t. to squeeze together; to bring into a smaller space. —/ˈkɒmpres/ n. a pad of lint etc. pressed on to some part of the body to stop bleeding, relieve inflammation, etc. [f. OF or L compressare frequent. of comprimere (COM-, premere press)]

compression /kəmˈpreʃ(ə)n/ n. compressing; reduction in the volume of fuel mixture in an internal-combustion engine before ignition. [f. prec.]

compressor /kəmˈpresə(r)/ n. a machine for compressing air or other gases. [f. COMPRESS]

comprise /kəmˈpraɪz/ v.t. to include, to consist of. [f. F (as COMPREHEND)]

compromise /ˈkɒmprəmaɪz/ n. **1.** a settlement made by each side giving up part of its demands; the process of making this. **2.** an intermediate way between conflicting courses, opinions, etc. —v.t./i. **1.** to settle (a dispute) or modify (principles) by compromise; to make a compromise. **2.** to bring under suspicion or into danger by indiscreet action. [f. OF f. L compromittere (COM-, promittere put forth)]

Compton /ˈkɒmpt(ə)n/, Arthur Holly (1892-1962), American physicist who, in 1923, observed that the wavelength of X-rays increased when scattered by electrons. This became known as the Compton effect and demonstrates the dual particle and wave properties of electromagnetic radiation and matter predicted by quantum theory. He shared the 1927 Nobel Prize for physics with C. T. R. Wilson, the inventor of the cloud chamber, a device that Compton had used in this research. During the Second World War he developed plutonium production at Chicago for the Manhattan Project (see entry).

Compton-Burnett /ˈkɒmptənbɜːˈnet/, Dame Ivy (1884-1969), English novelist. She embarked on her serious literary career with *Pastors and Masters* (1925) which, with other early works, notably *Brothers and Sisters* (1929), reflected her brittle deflationary wit and satirical exuberance. Her highly individual novels, composed almost entirely in dialogue, including *A House and Its Head* (1935), *A Family and a Fortune* (1939), and *Manservant and Maidservant* (1947), set in large gloomy houses, portray inward-looking self-contained high Victorian households ruled by a tyrannical parent or grandparent. They deal with domestic crime ranging from adultery, incest, child abuse, to murder and fraud, providing the author with an ideal environment in which to examine the misuse of power.

comptroller *n.* var. of CONTROLLER (in titles of some financial officers).

compulsion /kəmˈpʌlʃ(ə)n/ *n.* compelling, being compelled; an irresistible urge. [f. F f. L (as COMPEL)]

compulsive /kəmˈpʌlsɪv/ *adj.* tending to compel; resulting or acting from or as if from compulsion, especially contrary to one's conscious wishes; irresistible. [as prec.]

compulsory /kəmˈpʌlsərɪ/ *adj.* that must be done, required by the rules etc. —**compulsorily** *adv.* [as COMPULSION]

compunction /kəmˈpʌŋkʃ(ə)n/ *n.* pricking of the conscience; a slight regret or scruple. [f. OF f. L (COM-, *pungere* prick)]

computable /kəmˈpjuːtəb(ə)l/ *adj.* that can be computed. —**computability** /-ˈbɪlɪtɪ/ *n.* [f. foll.]

compute /kəmˈpjuːt/ *v.t./i.* to reckon or calculate; to use a computer. —**computation** /kɒmpjuːˈteɪʃ(ə)n/ *n.* [f. F or L *computare* reckon]

computer /kəmˈpjuːtə(r)/ *n.* 1. an automatic electronic apparatus for analysing and storing data, making calculations, or controlling operations that are expressible in numerical or logical terms. 2. one who or that which computes. —**analogue computer,** one using physical quantities (e.g. voltage, weight, length) to represent numbers. Such computers are used for certain specialized tasks (such as simulation) where digital processing is unsuitable, but are generally far less flexible than digital computers. **digital computer,** one making calculations etc. with data represented by digits or in similar discrete form (see below). [f. prec.]
The characteristic feature of all digital computers is the ability to store, and hence change rapidly, the operating program; they can operate at their own speed (up to several million instructions per second) and can therefore perform tasks too large to be completed in a human time-scale. The two major components of a computing system are the hardware (its physical elements) and the software (programs controlling the system). The three main elements of the hardware are the central processing unit (which processes the data), the memory (which stores the data before and after processing), and the peripheral (input/output) devices, which link the computer with the outside world by enabling information to be fed into the machine and produced by it (as a printout, magnetic tape, or display on a VDU) after processing. Information is converted into binary form (see BINARY SCALE) for storage and manipulation, the digits 0 and 1 representing the 'off' and 'on' positions of electronic switches. Computers are unusual tools in that their function can be altered by the software, without physical change, and hence a single machine can be used for a variety of disparate purposes.
Computing history is usually considered to start with Charles Babbage (see entry) who, between 1822 and 1871, designed a series of uncompleted machines able to perform calculations on different formulae. In 1936 the English mathematician Alan Turing showed that a single machine (the future computer) could process any problem if given rules for the solution. The Second World War provided the stimulus for the construction of practical machines in Germany, the UK, and the USA. Since 1945 there has been an accelerating reduction in size and cost coupled with increased speed and reliability as valves (first generation) were replaced by transistors (second generation)

and these by integrated circuits of diminishing size and increasing complexity (third generation). Subsequent work is being directed as much to programming techniques as to further advances in hardware.

computerize /kəmˈpjuːtəraɪz/ *v.t.* to equip with, perform, or produce by computer. —**computerization** /-ˈzeɪʃ(ə)n/ *n.* [f. prec.]

comrade /ˈkɒmrəd/ *n.* an associate or companion in some activity; a fellow socialist or communist. —**comradely** *adj.*, **comradeship** *n.* [f. F f. Sp., orig. = room-mate (as CHAMBER)]

Comte /kɔ̃t/, Auguste (1798-1857), French positivist philosopher. A republican who rebelled against his Catholic upbringing, he sought to come to terms with the changing political and industrial world. In his historical study of the progress of the human mind he discerned three phases—the theological, the metaphysical, and the positive; with the discrediting of the former types of explanation only the last phase survives in mature sciences, where there is simply a study of relations of succession and resemblance which are subsumed under laws. Comte attempted to show that sciences each evolve from one another developing their own laws in due course, and held that the latest and last science was sociology which had not yet reached its positive stage.

con[1] *v.t.* (-nn-) (*slang*) to persuade or swindle (a person) after winning his confidence. —*n.* (*slang*) a confidence trick. [abbr. of CONFIDENCE]

con[2] *v.t.* (-nn-) to peruse, study, or learn by heart. [form of CAN[1]]

con[3] *v.t.* (-nn-) to direct the steering of (a ship). [orig. *cond* f. F *conduire* (as CONDUCT)]

con[4] *adv.* & *prep.* (of an argument or reason) against. —*n.* a reason against (see PRO[2]). [f. L *contra* against]

con- *prefix* see COM-.

Conakry /ˈkɒnəkri/ the capital and chief port of Guinea; pop. (est. 1980) 763,000.

concatenate /kɒnˈkætɪneɪt/ *v.t.* to link together, to form a sequence of. —**concatenation** /-ˈneɪʃ(ə)n/ *n.* [f. L *concatenare* (CON-, *catena* chain)]

concave /kɒnˈkeɪv/ *adj.* curved like the interior of a circle or sphere. —**concavity** /-ˈkævɪtɪ/ *n.* [f. L (CON-, *cavus* hollow)]

conceal /kənˈsiːl/ *v.t.* to keep secret or hidden. —**concealment** *n.* [f. OF f. L *concelare* hide]

concede /kənˈsiːd/ *v.t.* 1. to admit to be true. 2. to grant (a privilege, right, etc.) 3. to admit defeat in (a contest, election, etc.). [f. F or L *concedere* (CON-, *cedere* cede)]

conceit /kənˈsiːt/ *n.* 1. excessive pride in oneself. 2. a fanciful notion. [f. CONCEIVE]

conceited *adj.* having too high an opinion of one's qualities or attributes. [f. prec.]

conceivable /kənˈsiːvəb(ə)l/ *adj.* that can be (mentally) conceived. —**conceivably** *adv.* [f. foll.]

conceive /kənˈsiːv/ *v.t./i.* 1. to become pregnant (with). 2. to form (ideas etc.) in the mind; to imagine, to think *of*. [f. OF f. L *concipere* (CON-, *capere* take)]

concentrate /ˈkɒnsəntreɪt/ *v.t./i.* 1. to employ all one's thought, attention, efforts, etc. (*on*); to bring or come together to one place. 2. to increase the strength of (a liquid etc.) by removing water etc. —*n.* a concentrated substance. [f. after F *concentrer* (as CON-, CENTRE)]

concentrated *adj.* 1. (of a liquid) having more than natural or original strength, not diluted. 2. intense. [f. prec.]

concentration /kɒnsənˈtreɪʃ(ə)n/ *n.* 1. concentrating, being concentrated. 2. the amount or strength of a substance in a mixture; a mental state of exclusive attention. —**concentration camp,** a place for the detention of political prisoners etc., especially in Nazi Germany; any of the camps (instituted by Lord Kitchener) where non-combatants of a district were accommodated during the Second Boer War of 1899-1902.

concentric /kənˈsentrɪk/ *adj.* having a common centre. —**concentrically** *adv.* [f. OF f. L (as CENTRE)]

concept /ˈkɒnsept/ *n.* a generalized idea or notion. [f. L (as CONCEIVE)]

conception /kənˈsep(ʃ)(ə)n/ *n.* 1. conceiving, being conceived. 2. the result of this, an idea. —**conceptional** *adj.* [f. OF f. L (as prec.)]

conceptual /kənˈseptjʊ(ə)l/ *adj.* of mental concepts. [as CONCEPT]

conceptualism /kənˈseptjʊəlɪz(ə)m/ *n.* the theory that

universals exist, but only as mental concepts. —**conceptualist** n. [f. prec.]

conceptualize /kən'septjʊ(ə)laɪz/ v.t. to form a mental concept of. [f. CONCEPTUAL]

concern /kən'sɜ:n/ v.t. to be relevant or important to; to affect or worry; to relate to, to be about. —n. 1. a thing of interest or importance to one. 2. anxiety, worry. 3. (in pl.) one's affairs. 4. a business or firm; (colloq.) a thing. —**be concerned in,** to take part in. **concern oneself,** to feel an interest or anxiety (in, about, etc.); to have a desire to deal with. —**concernment** n. [f. F or L concernere (CON-, cernere sift, discern)]

concerned adj. 1. anxious, troubled. 2. involved, interested. —**concernedly** /-ɪdlɪ/ adv., **concernedness** /-ɪdnɪs/ n. [f. prec.]

concerning prep. about, with regard to. [f. CONCERN]

concert /'kɒnsət/ n. 1. a musical entertainment by several performers. 2. a combination of voices or sounds. 3. agreement, working together. —**concert pitch,** a pitch, slightly higher than the ordinary, internationally agreed for concert performances. The present International Standard Pitch for 'concert A' is 440 cycles per second, the previous standard being slightly lower at between 435 (European) and 439 (British). This note is generally carried about through the medium of a tuning-fork and in an orchestra is given out by the oboe, one of the instruments least affected by temperature change. [F f. It. (as CONCERTO)]

concerted /kən'sɜ:tɪd/ adj. 1. effected by mutual agreement, done in co-operation. 2. (Mus.) arranged in parts for voices or instruments. [as prec.]

concertina /kɒnsə'ti:nə/ n. a portable musical instrument like an accordion but smaller. —v.t./i. to compress or collapse in folds like those of a concertina. [f. CONCERT]

concerto /kən'tʃɜ:təʊ/ n. (pl. -os or -i /-i:/) a composition (usually in three movements) for one or more solo instruments accompanied by an orchestra (see below). —**concerto grosso** /'grɒsəʊ/, a composition with a small group of solo instruments accompanied by an orchestra. [It. (as CONCERT); grosso big]
In the 16th and early 17th c. the term was used fairly broadly, as in its application to the motets for voices and organ by the Italian composer Viadana (1602). Later in the 17th c. came the concerto grosso of Corelli and his contemporaries, in which a small body of instruments was offset against a larger ensemble. The concerto for an individual player was developed by J. S. Bach in his harpsichord concertos, and Handel's organ concertos were also an important development, being among the first to provide a cadenza in which the soloist could display his skill by extemporization. By this time the concerto was usually a three-movement form, and the classical composers continued this principle. Mozart composed nearly fifty concertos for various instrumental combinations, and established the modern style, but since the 19th c. it has been usual for the composer to write out the cadenza.

concession /kən'seʃ(ə)n/ n. 1. conceding. 2. a thing conceded, especially a grant of land for extraction of minerals, trading rights, etc.; a reduction in price for certain categories of person. —**concessionary** adj. [f. F or L (as CONCEDE)]

concessionaire /kənseʃə'neə(r)/ n. the holder of a concession. [F (as prec.)]

concessive /kən'sesɪv/ adj. (Gram.) expressing a concession, of words such as although or even if. [f. L (as CONCEDE)]

conch /kɒntʃ/ n. the spiral shell of certain shellfish; such a shellfish, especially a large gastropod. [f. L concha f. Gk]

conchology /kɒŋ'kɒlədʒɪ/ n. the study of shells and shellfish. —**conchologist** n. [f. CONCH + -LOGY]

concierge /'kɒnsɪeəʒ/ n. (in France and French-speaking areas) a doorkeeper or porter (esp. of a block of flats). [F, f. L conservius fellow-slave]

conciliate /kən'sɪlɪeɪt/ v.t. to win over from anger or hostility, to win the goodwill of; to reconcile (disagreeing parties). —**conciliation** /-'eɪʃ(ə)n/ n. **conciliator** n., **conciliatory** adj. [f. L conciliare combine, gain (concilium council)]

concise /kən'saɪs/ adj. brief but comprehensive in expression. —**concisely** adv., **conciseness** n., **concision** /-'sɪʒ(ə)n/ n. [f. F or L (CON-, caedere cut)]

conclave /'kɒŋkleɪv/ n. a private meeting; a meeting-place or assembly of cardinals for the election of a pope. [f. OF f. L, = lockable room (clavis key)]

conclude /kən'klu:d/ v.t./i. 1. to bring or come to an end;

to arrange or settle (a treaty etc.) finally. 2. to draw a conclusion (that). [f. L concludere (CON-, claudere shut)]

conclusion /kən'klu:ʒ(ə)n/ n. 1. ending, an end. 2. a settling or concluding (of peace etc.). 3. a judgement or opinion based on reasoning, a proposition in logic reached from previous ones. [as prec.]

conclusive /kən'klu:sɪv/ adj. decisive, completely convincing. —**conclusively** adv. [as CONCLUDE]

concoct /kən'kɒkt/ v.t. to prepare, especially by mixing a variety of ingredients; to invent (a story or plot). —**concoction** /-'kɒkʃ(ə)n/ n. [f. L concoquere (CON-, coquere cook)]

concomitant /kən'kɒmɪtənt/ adj. accompanying. —n. an accompanying thing. —**concomitance** n. [f. L concomitari (CON-, comes companion)]

concord /'kɒŋkɔ:d/ n. 1. agreement, harmony. 2. (Mus.) a chord or interval satisfactory in itself. 3. (Gram.) agreement between words in gender, number, etc. —**concordant** /kən'kɔ:dənt/ adj. [f. OF f. L (CON-, cor heart)]

concordance /kən'kɔ:dəns/ n. 1. agreement. 2. an alphabetical index of the words used by an author or in a book. [as prec.]

concordat /kən'kɔ:dæt/ n. an official agreement, especially between Church and State. [f. F or L p.p. of concordare (as CONCORD)]

concourse /'kɒŋkɔ:s/ n. 1. a crowd, a gathering. 2. a large open area in a railway station etc. [f. OF f. L (as CONCUR)]

concrete /'kɒŋkri:t/ n. a mixture of cement with sand or gravel, used in building (see below). —adj. 1. existing in material form, real. 2. definite, positive. 3. (Gram., of a noun) denoting a thing, not a quality or state etc. —v.t./i. 1. to cover with or embed in concrete. 2. /kən'kri:t/ to form into a mass, to solidify. —**concrete music,** music prepared from recorded (natural or man-made) sounds. **concrete poetry,** poetry using typographical devices to enhance its effect. [f. F f. L concrescere grow together]
Concrete was used by the Romans as a building material. Its modern use dates from the 19th c. (see PORTLAND CEMENT). Reinforced concrete was developed in France and England in the mid-19th c.; metal rods, bars, or mesh embedded in the concrete provided the tensile strength which concrete itself lacks. Prestressed concrete was invented by a German builder c.1886 and further developed by the French engineer Eugène Freyssinet in the early 20th c.; in it the reinforcing metal bars are stretched while the concrete is wet and released when it has set round them, thereby compressing the concrete longitudinally and reducing its tendency to bend under a load. It has been used with notable success in the building of bridges.

concretion /kən'kri:ʃ(ə)n/ n. a hard solid mass; the forming of this by coalescence. [as prec.]

concubine /'kɒŋkjʊbaɪn/ n. a woman cohabiting with a man to whom she is not married; a secondary wife in polygamous societies. —**concubinage** /kən'kju:bɪnɪdʒ/ n. [f. OF f. L (CON-, cubare lie)]

concupiscence /kən'kju:pɪsəns, kɒnkjʊ'pɪ-/ n. intense sexual desire. —**concupiscent** adj. [f. L concupiscere begin to desire]

concur /kən'kɜ:(r)/ v.i. (-rr-) 1. to agree in opinion. 2. to happen together, to coincide. [f. L concurrere (CON-, currere run)]

concurrence /kən'kʌrəns/ n. 1. agreement. 2. simultaneous occurrence of events. [f. prec.]

concurrent /kən'kʌrənt/ adj. 1. existing or acting together or at the same time. 2. running in the same direction; (of three or more lines) meeting at or tending to one point. —**concurrently** adv. [as CONCUR]

concuss /kən'kʌs/ v.t. to subject to concussion. [f. L concutere (CON-, quatere shake)]

concussion /kən'kʌʃ(ə)n/ n. 1. injury to the brain caused by a heavy blow, fall, etc. 2. violent shaking. [as prec.]

condemn /kən'dem/ v.t. 1. to express utter disapproval of. 2. to pronounce guilty, to convict; to sentence to a punishment; to assign an unpleasant future or fate to. 3. to pronounce unfit for use or habitation. —**condemnation** /kɒndem'neɪʃ(ə)n/ n., **condemnatory** /kən'demnətərɪ/ adj. [f. OF f. L condemnare (CON-, damnare damn)]

condensation /kɒnden'seɪʃ(ə)n/ n. 1. condensing. 2. condensed material (esp. water on cold windows etc.). 3. abridgement. [f. L (as foll.)]

condense /kən'dens/ v.t./i. 1. to make denser or more concentrated. 2. to change or be changed from gas or vapour into liquid. 3. to express in few words. —**condensed milk,**

milk thickened by evaporation and sweetened. [f. F or L *condensare* (CON-, *densus* thick)]

condenser *n.* **1.** an apparatus or vessel for condensing vapour. **2.** a capacitor. **3.** a lens system for concentrating light. [f. prec.]

condescend /kɒndɪˈsend/ *v.i.* to be gracious enough (*to* do), especially while showing one's feeling of dignity or superiority; to disregard one's superiority (*to* a person). —**condescension** *n.* [f. OF f. L *condescendere* (CON-, *descendere* descend)]

condign /kənˈdaɪn/ *adj.* (of punishment etc.) severe and well-deserved. [f. OF f. L (CON-, *dignus* worthy)]

condiment /ˈkɒndɪmənt/ *n.* a seasoning or relish for food. [f. L (*condire* pickle)]

condition /kənˈdɪʃ(ə)n/ *n.* **1.** a stipulation, a thing upon the fulfilment of which depends something else. **2.** the state of being of a person or thing. **3.** a state of physical fitness or (of things) fitness for use. **4.** an ailment or abnormality. **5.** (in *pl.*) circumstances, especially those affecting the functioning or existence of something. —*v.t.* **1.** to bring into the desired state or condition; to make fit; to train or accustom. **2.** to modify, to have a strong effect on. —**conditioned reflex,** a reflex response to a non-natural stimulus, established by training (see PAVLOV). **on condition that,** with the condition that. [f. OF f. L, = thing agreed on (CON-, *dicere* say)]

conditional *adj.* **1.** dependent (*on*); not absolute, containing a condition or stipulation. **2.** (*Gram.*, of a clause, mood, etc.) expressing a condition. —**conditionally** *adv.* [f. prec.]

condole /kənˈdəʊl/ *v.i.* to express sympathy (*with* a person *on* a loss etc.). —**condolence** *n.* [f. L *condolēre* (CON-, *dolēre* grieve)]

condom /ˈkɒndəm/ *n.* a contraceptive sheath. [orig. unkn.]

condominium /kɒndəˈmɪnɪəm/ *n.* joint control of a State's affairs by two or more other States. [L (CON-, *dominium* sovereignty)]

condone /kənˈdəʊn/ *v.t.* to forgive or overlook (an offence or wrongdoing). —**condonation** /kɒndəˈneɪʃ(ə)n/ *n.* [f. L *condonare* (CON-, *donare* give)]

condor /ˈkɒndə(r)/ *n.* a very large vulture (*Vultur gryphus*) of South America; a smaller (and rare) vulture, the California condor (*Gymnogyps californianus*) of North America. [Sp. f. Quechua *cuntur*]

conduce /kənˈdjuːs/ *v.i.* to tend to lead or contribute *to* (a result). —**conducive** *adj.* [f. L (as foll.)]

conduct /ˈkɒndʌkt/ *n.* **1.** behaviour (esp. in its moral aspect). **2.** the manner of directing and managing (a business or war). —/kənˈdʌkt/ *v.t.* **1.** to lead or guide. **2.** to direct or manage (a business etc.). **3.** to be conductor of (an orchestra etc.). **4.** to transmit (heat, electricity, etc.) by conduction. —**conduct oneself,** to behave (*well, badly,* etc.). [f. OF f. L *conducere* (CON-, *ducere* lead)]

conductance /kənˈdʌkt(ə)ns/ *n.* the power of a specified body to conduct electricity. [f. prec.]

conduction /kənˈdʌkʃ(ə)n/ *n.* the transmission or conducting of heat, electricity, etc. [as CONDUCT]

conductive /kənˈdʌktɪv/ *adj.* having the property of conducting heat or electricity. —**conductivity** /kɒndʌkˈtɪvɪtɪ/ *n.* [f. CONDUCT]

conductor /kənˈdʌktə(r)/ *n.* **1.** a person who directs the performance of an orchestra, choir, etc. **2.** one who collects fares in a bus etc. **3.** a substance that conducts heat or electricity. [f. F f. L (as CONDUCT)]

conductress /kənˈdʌktrɪs/ *n.fem.* a woman bus conductor. [f. prec.]

conduit /ˈkɒndɪt, -djʊɪt/ *n.* a channel or pipe for conveying liquids; a tube or trough for protecting insulated electric wires. [f. OF f. L (as CONDUCT)]

condyle /ˈkɒndaɪl/ *n.* a rounded process at the end of a bone, forming an articulation with another bone (ill. BODY 1). [F f. L f. Gk *kondulos* knuckle]

cone *n.* **1.** a solid figure with a circular plane base, narrowing to a point (ill. SHAPES); a thing of similar shape, solid or hollow. **2.** the dry fruit of a pine or fir (ill. TREES). **3.** an ice-cream cornet. [f. F f. L f. Gk]

coney *n.* var. of CONY.

confabulate /kənˈfæbjʊleɪt/ *v.i.* to converse, to chat. —**confabulation** /-ˈleɪʃ(ə)n/ *n.* [f. L *confabulari* (CON-, *fabula* tale)]

confection /kənˈfekʃ(ə)n/ *n.* a dish or delicacy made with sweet ingredients; a cake or sweet. [f. OF f. L (*conficere* prepare)]

confectioner *n.* a maker or retailer of confectionery. [f. prec.]

confectionery *n.* confections, especially sweets. [f. prec.]

confederacy /kənˈfedərəsɪ/ *n.* a league or alliance, especially (**the Confederacy**) that of the Confederate States. [f. AF (as foll.)]

confederate /kənˈfedərət/ *adj.* allied. —*n.* **1.** an ally, especially (in bad sense) an accomplice. **2. Confederate,** a supporter of the Confederate States. —/-reɪt/ *v.t./i.* to bring or come into alliance (*with*). —**Confederate States,** the 11 southern States (Alabama, Arkansas, Florida, Georgia, Louisiana, Mississippi, North Carolina, South Carolina, Tennessee, Texas, Virginia) which seceded from the United States in 1860-1 and formed a confederacy of their own (thus precipitating the American Civil War) which was finally overthrown in 1865, after which they were reunited to the USA. [f. L (CON-, FEDERATE)]

confederation /kənfedəˈreɪʃ(ə)n/ *n.* **1.** forming or being formed in alliance etc. **2.** a union or alliance of States. [f. prec.]

confer /kənˈfɜː(r)/ *v.t./i.* (**-rr-**) **1.** to grant, to bestow. **2.** to hold a conference or discussion. —**conferrable** *adj.* [f. L *conferre* (CON-, *ferre* bring)]

conference /ˈkɒnfərəns/ *n.* consultation; a meeting (esp. a regular one) for discussion. [as prec.]

conferment /kənˈfɜːmənt/ *n.* the conferring (of a degree, honour, etc.). [f. CONFER]

confess /kənˈfes/ *v.t./i.* **1.** to acknowledge, own, or admit (a fault, wrongdoing, etc.); to admit reluctantly. **2.** to declare one's sins formally, especially to a priest. **3.** (of a priest) to hear the confession of. [f. OF f. L *confitēri* (CON-, *fatēri* declare, avow)]

confessedly /kənˈfesɪdlɪ/ *adv.* by personal or general admission. [f. prec.]

confession /kənˈfeʃ(ə)n/ *n.* **1.** the confessing (of an offence etc., or of sins to a priest). **2.** a thing confessed; a declaration of one's religious beliefs, a statement of one's principles. [as prec.]

confessional *n.* an enclosed stall in a church, in which a priest sits to hear confessions. —*adj.* of a confession. [f. prec.]

confessor *n.* **1.** a priest who hears confessions and gives spiritual counsel. **2.** one who avows his religion in the face of danger. [f. AF f. L (as CONFESS)]

confetti /kənˈfetɪ/ *n.* small bits of coloured paper thrown by wedding guests at the bride and bridegroom. [It. (as CONFECTION)]

confidant /kɒnfɪˈdænt/ *n.* (*fem.* **confidante** *pr.* same) a person trusted with knowledge of one's private affairs. [as foll.]

confide /kənˈfaɪd/ *v.t./i.* **1,** to tell (secrets *to*). **2.** to entrust (an object of care or a task *to*). —**confide in,** to talk confidentially to. [f. L *confidere* (CON-, *fidere* trust)]

confidence /ˈkɒnfɪd(ə)ns/ *n.* **1.** firm trust; a feeling of certainty, sense of self-reliance, boldness. **2.** something told confidentially. —**confidence man,** one who robs by means of a confidence trick. **confidence trick,** a swindle in which the victim is persuaded to trust someone who gives a false impression of honesty. **in a person's confidence,** trusted with his secrets. [f. L (as prec.)]

confident *n.* feeling or showing confidence, bold. [F f. L (as CONFIDE)]

confidential /kɒnfɪˈdenʃ(ə)l/ *adj.* **1.** spoken or written in confidence. **2.** entrusted with secrets. **3.** confiding. —**confidentiality** /-ʃɪˈælɪtɪ/ *n.*, **confidentially** *adv.* [f. prec.]

configuration /kənfɪgjʊəˈreɪʃ(ə)n/ *n.* manner of arrangement, shape, outline. [f. L *configuratio* (CON-, *figurare* fashion)]

confine /kənˈfaɪn/ *v.t.* to keep or restrict within certain limits; to imprison. —/ˈkɒnfaɪn/ *n.* (usu. in *pl.*) a limit or boundary of an area. —**be confined,** to be undergoing childbirth. [f. F f. L (CON-, *finis* limit)]

confinement *n.* **1.** confining, being confined. **2.** the period of childbirth. [f. prec.]

confirm /kənˈfɜːm/ *v.t.* **1.** to provide support for the truth or correctness of. **2.** to establish more firmly; to encourage (*in* an opinion etc.). **3.** to make formally definite or valid. **4.** to administer the rite of confirmation to. —**confirmative** *adj.*, **confirmatory** /-ˈfɜː-/ *adj.* [f. OF f. L *confirmare* (CON-, *firmus* firm)]

confirmation /kɒnfəˈmeɪʃ(ə)n/ *n.* **1.** confirming; corroboration. **2.** a religious rite confirming a baptized person as a member of the Christian Church. [as prec.]

confirmed *adj.* firmly settled in some habit or condition. [f. CONFIRM]

confiscate /ˈkɒnfɪskeɪt/ *v.t.* to take or seize by authority. —**confiscation** /-ˈkeɪʃ(ə)n/ *n.* [f. L *confiscare* (CON-, *fiscus* treasure)]

conflagration /kɒnfləˈgreɪʃ(ə)n/ *n.* a great and destructive fire. [f. L *conflagratio* (CON-, *flagrare* blaze)]

conflate /kənˈfleɪt/ *v.t.* to blend or fuse together (especially two variant texts into one). —**conflation** *n.* [f. L *conflare* (CON-, *flare* blow)]

conflict /ˈkɒnflɪkt/ *n.* **1.** a fight, a struggle. **2.** the clashing (*of* opposed principles etc.). —/kənˈflɪkt/ *v.i.* **1.** to struggle (*with*). **2.** to clash or be incompatible. [f. L *confligere* (CON-, *fligere* strike)]

confluence /ˈkɒnfluəns/ *n.* flowing together; the place where the two rivers unite. [as foll.]

confluent /ˈkɒnfluənt/ *adj.* flowing together, uniting. —*n.* a stream joining another. [f. L *confluere* (CON-, *fluere* flow)]

conform /kənˈfɔːm/ *v.t./i.* **1.** to comply *with* rules or general custom. **2.** to make or be conformable. —**conform to** or **with**, to comply or be in accordance with. [f. OF f. L *conformare* (CON-, *forma* shape)]

conformable *adj.* **1.** similar (*to*). **2.** consistent (*with*), adaptable (*to*). —**conformably** *adv.* [as prec.]

conformation /kɒnfəˈmeɪʃ(ə)n/ *n.* the way in which a thing is formed, its structure. [as CONFORM]

conformist /kənˈfɔːmɪst/ *n.* one who conforms to an established practice. —**conformism** *n.* [as prec.]

conformity *n.* conforming with established practice; agreement, suitability. [f. OF f. L (as CONFORM)]

confound /kənˈfaʊnd/ *v.t.* **1.** to perplex, to baffle; to confuse. **2.** (*archaic*) to defeat or overthrow. —*int.* of annoyance (*confound it!*). [f. AF f. L *confundere* mix up]

confounded *adj.* (*colloq.*) damned. [f. prec.]

confrère /ˈkɒnfreə(r)/ *n.* a fellow-member of a profession etc. [F, = fellow-brother]

confront /kənˈfrʌnt/ *v.t.* **1.** to meet or stand facing; to face in hostility or defiance. **2.** (of a difficulty etc.) to present itself to. **3.** to bring (a person) face to face *with* (accusers etc.). —**confrontation** /kɒnfrʌnˈteɪʃ(ə)n/ *n.* [f. F f. L *confrontare* (CON-, *frons* face)]

Confucianism /kənˈfjuːʃ(ə)nɪz(ə)m/ *n.* a system of philosophical and ethical teachings founded by Confucius in the 6th c. BC and developed by Mencius (Meng-tzu) in the 4th c. BC, one of the two major Chinese ideologies (see TAOISM). The basic concepts are ethical ones: love for one's fellows, filial piety, decorum, virtue; and the ideal of the superior man. The publication in AD 1190 of the four great Confucian texts revitalized Confucianism throughout China. A second series of texts, the 'five classics', includes the I Ching. [f. foll.]

Confucius /kənˈfjuːʃəs/ (Latinization of Chinese *Kongfuze* Kong the master) the most influential Chinese philosopher (551–479 BC), founder of Confucianism. The most reliable source of his teachings is the Lun yu (Chinese, = conversations), published in 1890. —**Confucian** *adj.*

confuse /kənˈfjuːz/ *v.t.* **1.** to bring into disorder, to mix up. **2.** to throw the mind or feelings of (a person) into disorder; to destroy the composure of. **3.** to mix up in the mind, to fail to distinguish between. **4.** to make unclear. —**confusedly** /-ˈfjuːzɪdlɪ/ *adv.* [back-formation f. *confused* (as CONFOUND)]

confusion *n.* the act or result of confusing; a confused state. [as prec.]

confute /kənˈfjuːt/ *v.t.* to prove (a person or thing) to be in error. —**confutation** /kɒnfjuːˈteɪʃ(ə)n/ *n.* [f. L *confutare* restrain]

conga /ˈkɒŋgə/ *n.* a Latin-American dance of African origin, usually with a number of persons in a single line. —**conga drum**, a tall narrow low-toned drum beaten with the hands (ill. MUSICAL NOTATION). [Amer. Sp., f. Sp. *conga* of the Congo]

congé /ˈkɔ̃ʒeɪ/ *n.* unceremonious dismissal; leave-taking. [f. OF f. L *commeatus* leave of absence (*commeare* go and come)]

congeal /kənˈdʒiːl/ *v.t./i.* to become or cause to become semi-solid by cooling; (of blood etc.) to coagulate. —**congelation** /ˈkɒndʒəˈleɪʃ(ə)n/ *n.* [f. OF f. L *congelare* freeze (CON-, *gelu* ice)]

congener /ˈkɒndʒenə(r)/ *n.* a thing or person of the same kind or class. [f. L (CON-, GENUS)]

congenial /kənˈdʒiːnɪəl/ *adj.* pleasant because like oneself in temperament or interests; suited or agreeable (*to*). —**congeniality** /-ˈælɪtɪ/ *n.*, **congenially** *adv.* [f. CON- + GENIAL]

congenital /kənˈdʒenɪt(ə)l/ *adj.* existing or as such from birth. —**congenitally** *adv.* [f. L (CON-, *genitus* begotten)]

conger /ˈkɒŋgə(r)/ *n.* a large sea eel of the family Congridae. [f. OF f. L f. Gk]

congeries /kənˈdʒɪərɪːz/ *n.* (*pl.* same) a disorderly collection, a mass or heap. [L (as foll.)]

congest /kənˈdʒest/ *n.* (usu. in *p.p.*) to affect with congestion. [f. L *congere* (CON-, *gerere* bring)]

congestion /kənˈdʒestʃ(ə)n/ *n.* abnormal accumulation or obstruction, especially of traffic etc. or of blood in a part of the body. [as prec.]

conglomerate /kənˈglɒmərət/ *adj.* gathered into a rounded mass. —*n.* **1.** a conglomerate mass. **2.** a group or corporation formed by the merging of separate firms. —/-reɪt/ *v.t.* to collect into a coherent mass. —**conglomeration** /-ˈreɪʃ(ə)n/ *n.* [f. L *conglomerare* (CON-, *glomus* ball)]

Congo /ˈkɒŋgəʊ/ **1.** the former name of the Zaïre River. **2.** a country in Africa, with a short Atlantic coastline, lying on the Equator with Zaïre to the east, and the Zaïre River and its tributary the Ubanghi forming most of its eastern boundary; pop. approx. 2,100,000; official language, French; capital, Brazzaville. There are some oil deposits but production is low. Colonized in the 19th c. by France and Belgium, the area has suffered severely as a result of the decolonizing process, being the scene of continued fighting in the 1960s and 1970s. —**Congolese** *adj.* & *n.*

congratulate /kənˈgrætjʊleɪt/ *v.t.* to express pleasure at the happiness, excellence, or good fortune of (a person *on* an event etc.). —**congratulate oneself,** to think oneself fortunate. —**congratulatory** *adj.* [f. L *congratulari* (CON-, *gratulari* show joy)]

congratulation /kəngrætjʊˈleɪʃ(ə)n/ *n.* congratulating; an expression of this. [as prec.]

congregate /ˈkɒŋgrɪgeɪt/ *v.t./i.* to collect or gather into a crowd. [f. L *congregare* (CON-, *grex* flock)]

congregation /kɒŋgrɪˈgeɪʃ(ə)n/ *n.* a gathering of persons, especially for religious purposes; a body of persons regularly attending a particular church etc. [f. OF or L (as prec.)]

congregational *adj.* **1.** of a congregation. **2. Congregational,** of or adhering to Congregationalism. [f. prec.]

Congregationalism *n.* a form of church organization in which each local church is independent and autonomous. The system derives from the belief that Christ is the sole head of his Church and all members of the Church, as Christians, are 'priests unto God'. Originally known as Independents, Congregationalists formed the backbone of Cromwell's army, but were persecuted under the 1662 Act of Uniformity. The independence of Congregational churches did not prevent them from forming County Associations for mutual support; in 1832 these Associations combined, and in 1972 the Congregational Church in England and Wales combined with the Presbyterian Church of England to form the United Reformed Church. —**Congregationalist** *n.* [f. prec.]

congress /ˈkɒŋgres/ *n.* **1.** a formal meeting of delegates for discussion. **2. Congress,** a national legislative assembly; that of the USA, which was established by the Constitution of 1787 and composed of two houses, the upper or Senate, made up of two members for each State, each sitting for six years (one-third of whom come up for re-election every two years), and the lower, or House of Representatives, composed of 435 members (re-elected every two years) divided between the States on the basis of population by the method of major fractions in which each State elects one member for each ratio quotient and major fraction thereof. —**Library of Congress,** the US national library, in Washington, DC. It was established in 1800, originally for the benefit of members of Congress, and was at first housed in the Capitol, moving to its present site in 1897. [f. L (CON-, *gradi* walk)]

congressional /kənˈgreʃ(ə)n(ə)l/ *adj.* of a congress. [f. prec.]

Congreve /ˈkɒŋgriːv/, William (1670–1729), English dramatist, who gave up law for literature and achieved fame with *The Old Bachelor* (1693). Of his other plays, the best known are *The Double Dealer* (1693) and *The Way of the World* (1700), both brilliant examples of the sparkling and at times coarse wit of Restoration comedy. He wrote little for the stage after 1700. He lived comfortably, holding several sinecures and enjoying the company of Swift, Pope, Steele, and the Duchess of Marlborough who bore him a daughter.

congruent /ˈkɒŋgruənt/ *adj.* **1.** suitable, consistent (*with*). **2.** (of geometric figures) coinciding exactly when superimposed. —**congruence** *n.*, **congruency** *n.* [f. F or L (*congruere* agree)]

congruous /ˈkɒŋgruəs/ *adj.* suitable, agreeing; fitting. —**congruity** /-ˈgruɪtɪ/ *n.* [f. L *congruus* (as prec.)]

conic /ˈkɒnɪk/ *adj.* of a cone. —**conic section,** a figure formed by the intersection of a cone and a plane. [f. L f. Gk (as CONE)]

conical /ˈkɒnɪk(ə)l/ *adj.* cone-shaped. [as prec.]

conifer /ˈkɒnɪfə(r), ˈkəʊn-/ *n.* a tree that bears cones. —**coniferous** /-ˈnɪfərəs/ *adj.* [f. L (as CONE, *ferre* bear)]

conjectural /kənˈdʒektʃər(ə)l/ *adj.* based on or involving conjecture. [as foll.]

conjecture /kənˈdʒektʃə(r)/ *n.* **1.** formation of an opinion on incomplete grounds; guessing. **2.** a guess. —*v.t./i.* to guess. [f. OF or L *conjicere* (CON-, *jacere* throw)]

conjoin /kənˈdʒɔɪn/ *v.t./i.* to join or combine. [f. OF f. L *conjungere* (CON-, *jungere* join)]

conjoint /ˈkɒndʒɔɪnt/ *adj.* associated, conjoined. [as prec.]

conjugal /ˈkɒndʒʊg(ə)l/ *adj.* of marriage or the relationship of husband and wife. —**conjugally** *adv.* [f. L (*conjunx* spouse)]

conjugate /ˈkɒndʒʊgeɪt/ *v.t./i.* **1.** to give the different forms of (a verb). **2.** to unite; to become fused. —*adj.* joined together, coupled, fused. —*n.* a conjugate word or thing. [f. L *conjugare* yoke together (CON-, *jugum* yoke)]

conjugation /kɒndʒʊˈgeɪʃ(ə)n/ *n.* (*Gram.*) a system of verbal inflection. [as prec.]

conjunct /kənˈdʒʌŋkt/ *adj.* jointed together; combined; associated. [f. L (as CONJOIN)]

conjunction /kənˈdʒʌŋkʃ(ə)n/ *n.* **1.** joining, connection. **2.** (*Gram.*) a word used to connect clauses or sentences, or words in the same clause (e.g. *and, but, if*). **3.** a combination of events or circumstances. **4.** the apparent proximity of two heavenly bodies. [as prec.]

conjunctiva /kɒndʒʌŋkˈtaɪvə/ *n.* the mucous membrane connecting the eyeball and inner eyelids (ill. BODY 4). [L (as foll.)]

conjunctive /kənˈdʒʌŋktɪv/ *adj.* serving to join; (*Gram.*) of the nature of a conjunction. [as CONJOIN]

conjunctivitis /kəndʒʌŋktɪˈvaɪtɪs/ *n.* inflammation of the conjunctiva. [f. CONJUNCTIVA]

conjuncture /kənˈdʒʌŋktʃə(r)/ *n.* a combination of events; a state of affairs. [F f. It. (as CONJOIN)]

conjure /ˈkʌndʒə(r)/ *v.t./i.* **1.** to perform tricks which appear to be magical, especially by movements of the hands. **2.** to summon (a spirit) to appear. —**conjure up,** to produce as if from nothing; to evoke. [f. OF *conjurer* plot, exorcize, f. L *conjurare* bind together by oath]

conjuror *n.* a skilled performer of conjuring tricks. [f. prec.]

conker *n.* a horse-chestnut fruit; (in *pl.*) a children's game played with these on strings. [f. dial. *conker* snail-shell]

connate /ˈkɒneɪt/ *adj.* **1.** born with a person, innate. **2.** formed at the same time. **3.** (of leaves etc.) united from the start of life (ill. PLANTS). [f. L *connatus* (CON-, *nasci* be born]

connect /kəˈnekt/ *v.t./i.* **1.** to join, to be joined; to construct a line etc. from (one point to another). **2.** to associate mentally or practically; (usu. in *pass.*) to unite or associate in a relationship etc. **3.** (of a train etc.) to be synchronized at its destination *with* another, allowing passengers to transfer. **4.** to be meaningful or relevant; to form a logical sequence. —**connecting-rod,** the rod between the piston and the crankpin etc. [f. L *connectere* (CON-, *nectere* bind)]

Connecticut /kəˈnetɪkət/ a State of the USA bordering on the Atlantic. A Puritan settlement in the 17th c., it was one of the original 13 States of the USA (1788); capital, Hartford.

connection /kəˈnekʃ(ə)n/ *n.* **1.** connecting; being connected or related. **2.** a relationship or association of ideas. **3.** a connecting part. **4.** a relative or close associate. **5.** a group of associates or clients. **6.** a connecting train etc. [as prec.]

connective *adj.* serving to connect, especially of body tissues connecting and supporting organs etc. [f. CONNECT]

connector *n.* a thing that connects others. [as prec.]

conning-tower *n.* a raised structure on a submarine, containing the periscope; an armoured pilot-house on a warship. [f. CON³]

connive /kəˈnaɪv/ *v.i.* **connive at,** to disregard or tacitly consent to (wrongdoing). —**connivance** *n.* [f. F or L *connivēre* shut the eyes to]

connoisseur /kɒnəˈsɜː(r)/ *n.* an expert judge (*of* or in matters of taste, especially in the fine arts). [F (*connaître* know)]

connote /kəˈnəʊt/ *v.t.* (of words) to imply in addition to the literal meaning; to mean, to signify. —**connotation** /kɒnəˈteɪʃ(ə)n/ *n.*, **connotative** /ˈkɒnəteɪtɪv/ *adj.* [f. L *connotare* (CON-, *notare* note)]

connubial /kəˈnjuːbɪəl/ *adj.* of marriage or the relation of husband and wife. [f. L (CON-, *nubere* marry)]

conquer /ˈkɒŋkə(r)/ *v.t./i.* to overcome and control militarily; to be victorious; to overcome by effort. —**conqueror** *n.* [f. AF f. L *conquirere* win]

conquest /ˈkɒŋkwest/ *n.* **1.** conquering. **2.** conquered territory; something won; a person whose affections have been won. —**the Conquest** *or* **Norman Conquest,** the conquest of England by William of Normandy in 1066. [as prec.]

conquistador /kɒnˈkwɪstədɔː(r)/ *n.* (*pl.* **-ores** /-ɔːˈriːz/) a conqueror, especially one of the Spanish soldiers and adventurers who conquered South and Central America in the 16th c. While the initial object of most of their expeditions was the search for the fabled riches of the area, they ended by overthrowing the Aztec, Mayan, and Inca civilizations and establishing Spanish colonies. [Sp.]

Conrad /ˈkɒnræd/, Joseph (Teodor Josef Konrad Korzeniowski, 1857-1924), British novelist (he became a British subject in 1886), born of Polish parents in the Russian-dominated Ukraine. He was orphaned at an early age, went to sea in 1874, became a Master Mariner in 1894, when he settled in England and produced his first novel *Almayer's Folly* (1895). He established his reputation with *The Nigger of the Narcissus* (1897) and *Lord Jim* (1900), and continued his success with *Nostromo* (1904) in which he explores man's vulnerability and corruptibility, a theme he carries to terrifying conclusions in his story 'Heart of Darkness' (1902) and *The Secret Agent* (1907). The sea supplies the setting for most of his works and his narrative technique is characterized by breaks in time sequence, sometimes using a narrator, Marlow, to provide a commentary similar to a Greek chorus. He was a leading modernist and is considered by some critics to be among the great novelists in the English language.

consanguineous /kɒnsæŋˈgwɪnɪəs/ *adj.* descended from the same ancestor, akin. —**consanguinity** *n.* [f. L (CON-, *sanguis* blood)]

conscience /ˈkɒnʃ(ə)ns/ *n.* the moral sense of right and wrong, especially as felt by a person and affecting his behaviour. —**conscience clause,** a clause in a law, ensuring respect for the consciences of those affected. **conscience money,** a sum paid to relieve one's conscience. **conscience-stricken** *adj.* made uneasy by a bad conscience. [f. OF f. L (as CONSCIOUS)]

conscientious /kɒnʃɪˈenʃəs/ *adj.* obedient to conscience; showing or done with careful attention. —**conscientious objector,** a person who for reasons of conscience objects to military service etc. —**conscientiously** *adv.*, **conscientiousness** *n.* [as prec.]

conscious /ˈkɒnʃəs/ *adj.* **1.** awake and aware of one's surroundings and identity. **2.** knowing, aware (*of* or *that*). **3.** (of actions, emotions, etc.) realized or recognized by the doer etc., intentional. —*n.* the conscious mind. —**consciously** *adv.* [f. L *conscire* be privy to (CON-, *scire* know)]

consciousness *n.* awareness; a person's conscious thoughts and feelings as a whole. [f. prec.]

conscript /kənˈskrɪpt/ *v.t.* to summon for compulsory State (esp. military) service. —/ˈkɒnskrɪpt/ *n.* a conscripted person. [back-formation f. *conscription* f. L *conscribere* enrol]

consecrate /ˈkɒnsɪkreɪt/ *v.t.* **1.** to make or declare sacred, to dedicate formally to a religious or divine purpose. **2.** to devote *to* a purpose. —**consecration** /-ˈkreɪʃ(ə)n/ *n.* [f. L *consecrare* (CON-, *sacrare* dedicate)]

consecutive /kənˈsekjʊtɪv/ *adj.* **1.** following continuously, in unbroken or logical order. **2.** (*Gram.*) expressing consequence. —**consecutively** *adv.* [f. F f. L (CON-, *sequi* follow)]

consensus /kənˈsensəs/ *n.* agreement in opinion; a majority view. [L (as foll.)]

consent /kənˈsent/ *v.i.* to express willingness or agree (*to*), to give permission (*that*). —*n.* voluntary agreement, permission. —**age of consent,** the age at which a girl's consent to sexual intercourse is valid in law. [f. OF f. L *consentire* agree (CON-, *sentire* feel)]

consequence /'kɒnsɪkwəns/ *n.* **1.** what follows logically or effectively from some causal action or condition. **2.** importance. [as foll.]

consequent /'kɒnsɪkwənt/ *adj.* following as a consequence (*on* or *upon*); logically consistent. —*n.* a thing that follows another. —**consequently** *adv.* [f. OF f. L *consequi* (as CONSECUTIVE)]

consequential /kɒnsɪ'kwenʃ(ə)l/ *adj.* **1.** consequent; resulting indirectly. **2.** self-important. —**consequentially** *adv.* [f. L *consequentia* consequence]

conservancy /kən'sɜːvənsɪ/ *n.* a body controlling a port, river, etc., or concerned with the preservation of natural resources. [f. AF f. L (as foll.)]

conservation /kɒnsə'veɪʃ(ə)n/ *n.* preservation, especially of the natural environment. —**conservation of energy,** the principle that the quantity of energy of any system of bodies not subject to external action remains constant. [as CONSERVE]

conservationist *n.* a supporter or advocate of environmental conservation. [f. prec.]

conservative /kən'sɜːvətɪv/ *adj.* **1.** tending to conserve, averse to rapid changes; (of views, taste, etc.) avoiding extremes. **2.** (of an estimate etc.) purposely low. —*n.* **1.** a conservative person. **2. Conservative,** a member or supporter of the Conservative Party. —**conservatism** *n.*, **conservatively** *adv.* [f. L (as CONSERVE)]

Conservative Party a political party disposed to maintain existing institutions and promote private enterprise. The modern Conservative Party in Britain emerged from the old Tory Party under Peel in the 1830s and 1840s. Under Disraeli it was the party committed to traditional institutions, social reform, and the defence of the Empire. After the First World War the Conservatives benefited from the decline of their traditional opponents, the Liberals, and dominated the political scene until defeated in the general election of 1945 by the Labour Party.

conservatoire /kən'sɜːvətwɑː(r)/ *n.* a (usually European) school of music or other arts. [F (as foll.)]

conservatory /kən'sɜːvətərɪ/ *n.* a greenhouse for tender plants, especially one with a communicating entrance from a house. [as CONSERVE]

conserve /kən'sɜːv/ *v.t.* to keep from harm, decay, or loss, especially for future use. —*n.* jam, especially that made from fresh fruit. [f. OF f. L *conservare* (CON-, *servare* keep safe)]

consider /kən'sɪdə(r)/ *v.t.* **1.** to think about, especially in order to reach a conclusion; to examine the merits of; (in *p.p.*, of an opinion etc.) formed after careful thought. **2.** to make allowances or be thoughtful for. **3.** to think to be; to have the opinion *that*. **4.** to look attentively at. [f. OF f. L *considerare* (orig. an augural term, f. *sidus* star)]

considerable /kən'sɪdərəb(ə)l/ *adj.* not negligible, fairly great in amount or extent etc.; of some importance. —**considerably** *adv.* [as prec.]

considerate /kən'sɪdərət/ *adj.* thoughtful for others, careful not to cause inconvenience or hurt. —**considerately** *adv.* [f. L (as CONSIDER)]

consideration /kənsɪdə'reɪʃ(ə)n/ *n.* **1.** careful thought. **2.** being considerate, kindness. **3.** a factor influencing a decision or course of action. **4.** a compensation, reward. —**in consideration of,** in return for, on account of. **take into consideration,** to make allowance for. [f. OF f. L (as prec.)]

considering *prep.* in view of, taking into consideration; (*ellipt.*, *colloq.*) in view of the circumstances. [f. CONSIDER]

consign /kən'saɪn/ *v.t.* to hand over or deliver; to assign or commit *to*; to send (goods) *to*. [f. F or L *consignare* mark with a seal]

consignee /kɒnsaɪ'niː/ *n.* a person to whom something is consigned. [f. prec.]

consignment *n.* **1.** consigning. **2.** a batch of goods etc. consigned. [f. CONSIGN]

consist /kən'sɪst/ *v.i.* **1.** to be composed *of.* **2.** to be consistent *with.* —**consist in,** to have as its basis or essential feature. [f. L *consistere* (CON-, *sistere* stop)]

consistency /kən'sɪstənsɪ/ *n.* **1.** degree of density, firmness, or solidity, especially of thick liquids. **2.** being consistent. [f. F or L (as prec.)]

consistent /kən'sɪst(ə)nt/ *adj.* **1.** compatible or in harmony (*with*). **2.** (of a person) constant to the same principles of thought or action. —**consistently** *adv.* [as CONSIST]

consistory /kən'sɪstərɪ/ *n.* **1.** a council of cardinals, or of the pope and cardinals. **2. Consistory (Court),** an Anglican bishop's court to deal with ecclesiastical problems and offences. [f. AF f. L (as CONSIST)]

consolation /kɒnsə'leɪʃ(ə)n/ *n.* consoling; a consoling circumstance. —**consolation prize,** a prize given to a competitor who just fails to win one of the main prizes. —**consolatory** *adj.* [as foll.]

console[1] /kən'səʊl/ *v.t.* to comfort, especially in grief or disappointment. [f. F f. L *consolari*]

console[2] /'kɒnsəʊl/ *n.* **1.** a bracket supporting a shelf etc. **2.** a frame containing the keys and stops of an organ; a panel for switches, controls, etc. **3.** a cabinet for radio etc. equipment. [F]

consolidate /kən'sɒlɪdeɪt/ *v.t./i.* **1.** to make or become strong or solid. **2.** to combine into one whole. —**consolidation** /-'deɪʃ(ə)n/ *n.* [f. L *consolidare* (CON-, *solidus* solid)]

Consolidated Fund the Exchequer account at the Bank of England into which public monies (such as tax receipts) are paid and from which the main payments are made that are not dependent on annual votes in Parliament. These include interest on the National Debt, grants to the Royal Family, and payments on the Civil List. It was established by William Pitt the Younger in 1786 and so called because it 'consolidated various revenues into a single fund'.

consols /'kɒnsɒlz/ *n.pl.* British government securities. [abbr. of *consolidated annuities*]

consommé /kən'sɒmeɪ/ *n.* clear meat soup. [F]

consonance /'kɒnsənəns/ *n.* agreement or harmony. [as foll.]

consonant /'kɒnsənənt/ *n.* a speech sound in which the breath is at least partially obstructed, combining with a vowel to form a syllable; a letter representing this. —*adj.* in agreement or harmony *with*; agreeable *to.* —**consonantal** /-'nænt(ə)l/ *adj.* [f. F f. L *consonare* (CON-, *sonare* sound)]

consort[1] /'kɒnsɔːt/ *n.* **1.** a wife or husband, especially of a reigning monarch. **2.** a ship sailing with another. —/kən'sɔːt/ *v.i.* **1.** to associate or keep company (*with, together*). **2.** to be in harmony (*with*). [f. F f. L *consors* sharer (CON-, *sors* lot)]

consort[2] /'kɒnsɔːt/ *n.* an ensemble of voices and/or instruments in English music from about 1570 to 1720. The term 'broken consort' refers to an ensemble of mixed instruments (e.g. viols, recorders, and lutes) and 'whole consort' to a complete set of a single type. —**consort song,** a song for solo voice and a consort usually of viols. [earlier form of CONCERT]

consortium /kən'sɔːtɪəm/ *n.* (*pl.* **-ia**) an association, especially of several business companies. [L (as CONSORT[1])]

conspectus /kən'spektəs/ *n.* a general view or survey; a synopsis. [L (*conspicere* look at attentively)]

conspicuous /kən'spɪkjʊəs/ *adj.* clearly visible, attracting attention; noteworthy, striking. —**conspicuously** *adv.*, **conspicuousness** *n.* [f. L (as prec.)]

conspiracy /kən'spɪrəsɪ/ *n.* an act of conspiring; an unlawful combination or plot. —**conspiracy of silence,** an agreement not to talk about something. [as CONSPIRE]

conspirator /kən'spɪrətə(r)/ *n.* a person who conspires. —**conspiratorial** /-'tɔːrɪəl/ *adj.*, **conspiratorially** *adv.* [as foll.]

conspire /kən'spaɪə(r)/ *v.i.* **1.** to plan secretly with others, especially for some unlawful purpose. **2.** (of events) to seem to be working together. [f. OF f. L *conspirare* agree, plot (CON-, *spirare* breathe)]

Constable /'kʌnstəb(ə)l/, John (1776–1837), English painter. Never a prodigy, his style developed slowly towards a radical naturalism that took prosaic landscape and subjected it to rigorous visual analysis (e.g. *The Hay Wain,* 1820). Increasingly, however, his interests in paint handling as such, and a more generalized view of nature, saw the development of a florid, almost mannered, late style that replaced observation with expressive, almost rhetorical, statements about growth, change, and decay (e.g. *The Valley Farm,* 1835). Although he had no immediate followers in England, the exhibition of his work at Paris in 1824 was a revelation to French artists such as Delacroix and contemporary landscape painters. His personal achievement ranks, with that of Turner, as the greatest splendour of English landscape painting.

constable /'kʌnstəb(ə)l, 'kʌn-/ *n.* **1.** a policeman; a policeman or policewoman of the lowest rank. **2.** the governor of a royal castle. **3.** (*hist.*) the principal officer of the royal household. —**Chief Constable,** the head of the police force of an area. [f. OF f. L *comes stabuli* count of the stable]

constabulary /kənˈstæbjʊlərɪ/ *n.* a police force. [as prec.]

constancy /ˈkɒnst(ə)nsɪ/ *n.* the quality of being unchanging and dependable; faithfulness. [as foll.]

constant /ˈkɒnst(ə)nt/ *adj.* **1.** continuous; frequently occurring. **2.** unchanging, faithful, dependable. —*n.* anything that does not vary; (*Math. & Physics*) a quantity or number of constant value. —**constantly** *adv.* [f. OF f. L *constare* (CON-, *stare* stand)]

Constantine /ˈkɒnstəntaɪn/ 'the Great' (d. 337), Roman emperor from 306, who in his youth spent time at the court of Diocletian where he learned the new Byzantine ideas of absolute sovereignty. In 312 he defeated his rival Maxentius at a battle near Rome, adopting the labarum as a standard (reportedly after a vision of the Cross; probably because a Christian symbol secured the loyalty of the army, which was largely Christian). Shortly afterwards toleration and imperial favour were given to the Christian faith. His policy was to unite the Church to the secular State by the closest possible ties, and he involved himself in its internal affairs. After 324 he fixed his capital at Byzantium (rebuilt and inaugurated as Constantinople in 330), a move which led to an increasing imperial control of the Eastern Church and incidentally left the bishop of Rome as the most prominent figure in the West; the secular importance of the papacy in the Middle Ages dates from this time. His reign, though not free from blemishes, was marked by humanizing reforms and by liberal endowment of church building, especially at the holy sites in Palestine; in the Eastern Church he is venerated as a saint (feast day, 21 May).

Constantinople /kɒnstæntɪˈnəʊp(ə)l/ a city (modern Istanbul) on the European side of the south end of the Bosporus, founded in 324 and inaugurated (330) as the second capital of the Roman Empire by Constantine the Great on the site of Byzantium. Subsequently the seat of the Byzantine emperors, it was captured by the Ottoman Turks in 1453.

constellation /kɒnstəˈleɪʃ(ə)n/ *n.* a group of stars forming a recognizable pattern in the sky and identified by some imaginative name describing their form or identifying them with a mythological figure. Eighty-eight are officially recognized by modern astronomers, many identical with those of the ancient Egyptians. [f. F f. L *constellatio* (CON-, *stella* star)]

consternation /kɒnstəˈneɪʃ(ə)n/ *n.* amazement or dismay causing mental confusion. [f. F or L (CON-, *sternere* throw down)]

constipate /ˈkɒnstɪpeɪt/ *v.t.* to affect with constipation. [f. L *constipare* (CON-, *stipare* stuff full)]

constipation /kɒnstɪˈpeɪʃ(ə)n/ *n.* a condition with hardened faeces and difficulty in emptying the bowels. [as prec.]

constituency /kənˈstɪtjʊənsɪ/ *n.* a body of voters who elect a representative; an area so represented. [as foll.]

constituent /kənˈstɪtjʊənt/ *adj.* **1.** composing or helping to make a whole. **2.** able to make or change a constitution; electing a representative. —*n.* **1.** a constituent part. **2.** a member of a constituency. [as foll.]

constitute /ˈkɒnstɪtjuːt/ *v.t.* **1.** to compose, to be the essence or components of. **2.** to appoint or set up (an assembly etc.) in legal form. **3.** to form or establish. [f. L *constituere* (CON-, *statuere* set up)]

constitution /kɒnstɪˈtjuːʃ(ə)n/ *n.* **1.** an act or method of constituting, composition. **2.** the condition of a person's body as regards health, strength, etc. **3.** the form in which a State is organized; the body of fundamental principles by which a State or organization is governed. [as prec.]

constitutional *adj.* of, in harmony with, or limited by the constitution. —*n.* a walk taken regularly as healthy exercise. —**constitutionality** /-ˈnælɪtɪ/ *n.,* **constitutionally** *adv.* [f. prec.]

constitutive /ˈkɒnstɪtjuːtɪv/ *adj.* **1.** able to form or appoint, constituent. **2.** essential. [as CONSTITUTE]

constrain /kənˈstreɪn/ *v.t.* **1.** to urge irresistibly or by necessity. **2.** to confine forcibly, to imprison. **3.** (in *p.p.*) forced, embarrassed. [f. OF f. L *constringere* (CON-, *stringere* bind)]

constraint /kənˈstreɪnt/ *n.* constraining, being constrained; a restriction; restraint of natural feelings, a constrained manner. [as prec.]

constrict /kənˈstrɪkt/ *v.t.* to compress, to make narrow

or tight. —**constriction** *n.,* **constrictive** *adj.* [f. L (as CONSTRAIN)]

constrictor *n.* **1.** a muscle that draws together or narrows a part. **2.** a snake that kills by compressing its prey. [f. prec.]

construct /kənˈstrʌkt/ *v.t.* **1.** to make by fitting parts together, to build or form. **2.** (*Geom.*) to delineate (a figure). —/ˈkɒn-/ *n.* a thing constructed, especially by the mind. —**constructor** /-ˈstrʌktə(r)/ *n.* [f. L *construere* (CON-, *struere* pile, build)]

construction /kənˈstrʌkʃ(ə)n/ *n.* **1.** constructing; a thing constructed. **2.** the syntactical connection of words in a sentence. **3.** an interpretation or explanation of a statement or action. —**constructional** *adj.* [as prec.]

constructive /kənˈstrʌktɪv/ *adj.* tending to form a basis for ideas, positive, helpful. —**constructively** *adv.* [as CONSTRUCT]

constructivism /kɒnˈstrʌktɪvɪz(ə)m/ *n.* an artistic movement which gained momentum in the 1920s as two distinct trends — that of Russian constructivism and a separate international movement. The Russian movement stemmed from the work of artists such as Tatlin (1885–1953), Antony Pevsner, and Naum Pevsner (Gabo), who sought to 'construct' sculptural forms using materials as various as sheet metal, tubing, wire, perspex, and glass, and were as concerned with negative space as positive form. Opinion varies as to the founder and to the specific moment of the movement's birth. Tatlin, influenced by Picasso's cubist collages, was experimenting with 'hanging reliefs' of wood and iron as early as 1913, and his theories were most spectacularly expressed in his projected monument of 1920 to the Third Communist International, a leaning spiral with vertical glass chambers continually revolving at varying speeds. The constructivist school outside Russia was more diverse and is consequently less capable of categorization. Related ideas can be detected in aspects of the de Stijl movement in Holland and the Bauhaus in Germany, and the later presence in England of Gabo, Pevsner, and others exerted some influence there. —**constructivist** *n.* [f. Russ. *konstruktivizm* as prec.)]

construe /kənˈstruː/ *v.t.* **1.** to interpret (words or actions). **2.** to combine (words *with* others) grammatically. **3.** to analyse the syntax of (a sentence). **4.** to translate word for word. [as CONSTRUCT]

consubstantial /kɒnsəbˈstænʃ(ə)l/ *adj.* of one substance. [f. L (as CON-, SUBSTANTIAL)]

consubstantiation /kɒnsəbstænʃɪˈeɪʃ(ə)n/ *n.* the doctrine, associated especially with Luther, that in the Eucharist, after consecration of the elements, the real substances of the body and blood of Christ coexist with those of the bread and wine. The theory was formulated in opposition to the medieval doctrine of transubstantiation. [as prec.]

consul /ˈkɒns(ə)l/ *n.* **1.** an official appointed by the State to live in a foreign city and protect the State's citizens and other interests there. **2.** (*hist.*) either of the two annually elected chief magistrates in ancient Rome. —**consular** /ˈkɒnsjʊlə(r)/ *adj.* [L, rel. to CONSULT]

consulate /ˈkɒnsjʊlət/ *n.* the position, office, or residence of a consul. [as prec.]

consult /kənˈsʌlt/ *v.t./i.* **1.** to seek information or advice from (a person, book, etc.); to take counsel (*with*). **2.** to take (feelings etc.) into consideration. [f. F f. L *consultare* frequent. of *consulere* take counsel]

consultant /kənˈsʌltənt/ *n.* a person qualified to give expert professional advice, especially in a branch of medicine. —**consultancy** *n.* [as prec.]

consultation /kɒnsəlˈteɪʃ(ə)n/ *n.* consulting; a meeting for this purpose. [f. OF or L (as CONSULT)]

consultative /kənˈsʌltətɪv/ *adj.* of or for consultation. [f. CONSULT]

consume /kənˈsjuːm/ *v.t.* **1.** to eat or drink; to use up; to destroy. **2.** (in *p.p.*) possessed *by* or entirely preoccupied *with* (envy etc.). —**consumable** *adj.* [f. L *consumere* (CON-, *sumere* take up)]

consumer *n.* one who consumes, especially one who uses a product; a person who buys or uses goods or services. [f. prec.]

consumerism *n.* **1.** protection or promotion of consumers' interests. **2.** high consumption of goods, the belief in this. [f. prec.]

consummate /kənˈsʌmɪt/ *adj.* complete; perfect; supremely skilled. —/ˈkɒnsəmeɪt/ *v.t.* to make perfect or complete; to complete (a marriage) by sexual intercourse.

—**consummation** /kɒnsə'meɪʃ(ə)n/ *n.* [f. L *consummare* complete (CON,- *summus* utmost)]

consumption /kən'sʌmpʃ(ə)n/ *n.* **1.** consuming; the amount consumed. **2.** the purchase and use of goods etc. **3.** pulmonary tuberculosis. [as CONSUME]

consumptive /kən'sʌmptɪv/ *adj.* tending to or affected with pulmonary tuberculosis. —*n.* a consumptive person. [as prec.]

contact /'kɒntækt/ *n.* **1.** the condition or state of touching, meeting, or communicating. **2.** a person who is or may be contacted for information, assistance, etc. **3.** a person likely to carry a contagious disease through being near an infected person. **4.** a connection for the passage of an electric current. —/also kən'tækt/ *v.t.* to get in touch with (a person); to begin communication or personal dealings with. —**contact lens,** a small usually plastic lens placed against the eyeball to correct faulty vision. [f. L *contingere* (CON-, *tangere* touch)]

contagion /kən'teɪdʒən/ *n.* the spreading of disease by bodily contact; a disease so transmitted; a corrupting moral influence. [f. L *contagio* (as prec.)]

contagious /kən'teɪdʒəs/ *adj.* (of a person) likely to transmit disease by bodily contact; (of a disease) transmitted in this way. [f. L *contagiosus* (as CONTAGION)]

contain /kən'teɪn/ *v.t.* **1.** to have, hold, or be able to hold within itself; to include or comprise; to consist of, to be equal to; (of a number) to be divisible by (a factor) without remainder. **2.** to enclose, to prevent from moving or extending; to control or restrain (feelings etc.). [f. OF f. L *continēre* (CON-, *tenēre* hold)]

container *n.* **1.** a box, jar, etc., for containing particular things. **2.** a large boxlike receptacle of standard design for the transport of goods. [f. prec.]

containerize *v.t.* to transport by container; to convert to this method of transporting goods. —**containerization** /-'zeɪʃ(ə)n/ *n.* [f. prec.]

containment *n.* the action or policy of preventing the expansion of a hostile country or influence. [f. CONTAIN]

contaminate /kən'tæmɪneɪt/ *v.t.* to pollute, especially with radioactivity; to infect. —**contaminant** *n.,* **contamination** /-'neɪʃ(ə)n/ *n.,* **contaminator** *n.* [f. L *contaminare* (CON-, *tamin-* rel. to *tangere* touch)]

contemn /kən'tem/ *v.t.* (*literary*) to despise; to disregard. [f. OF or L *contemnere* despise]

contemplate /'kɒntəmpleɪt/ *v.t./i.* **1.** to survey with the eyes or mind. **2.** to regard (an event) as possible; to intend. **3.** to meditate. —**contemplation** /-'pleɪʃ(ə)n/ *n.* [f. L *contemplari* (CON-, *templum* area within which an augur took the auspices)]

contemplative /kən'templətɪv/ *adj.* of or given to (esp. religious) contemplation, meditative. —*n.* a person devoted to religious contemplation. [f. OF f. L (as prec.)]

contemporaneous /kəntempə'reɪnɪəs/ *adj.* existing or occurring at the same time (*with*). —**contemporaneity** /-'niːɪtɪ/ *n.* [f. L *contemporaneus* (CON-, *tempus* time)]

contemporary /kən'tempərərɪ/ *adj.* **1.** belonging to the same time or period; of the same age. **2.** modern in style or design. —*n.* a contemporary person or thing. [f. L (as prec.)]

contempt /kən'tempt/ *n.* **1.** the feeling that a person or thing is worthless or beneath consideration, or deserving extreme reproach or scorn; the condition of being held in contempt. **2.** (in full **contempt of court**) disrespect for or disobedience to a court of law. [as CONTEMN]

contemptible /kən'temptɪb(ə)l/ *adj.* deserving contempt. —**contemptibility** /-'bɪlɪtɪ/ *n.,* **contemptibly** *adv.* [as CONTEMN]

contemptuous *adj.* feeling or showing contempt. —**contemptuously** *adv.,* **contemptuousness** *n.* [as CONTEMPT]

contend /kən'tend/ *v.i.* **1.** to struggle or compete; to argue (*with*). **2.** to assert or maintain (*that*). —**contender** *n.* [f. OF or L *contendere* (CON-, *tendere* stretch, strive)]

content[1] /'kɒntent/ *n.* **1.** (usu. in *pl.*) what is contained in a thing, especially in a vessel, book, or house. **2.** capacity, volume. **3.** the amount (of a constituent) contained. **4.** the substance (of a speech etc.) as distinct from the form. [f. L (as CONTAIN)]

content[2] /kən'tent/ *predic. adj.* satisfied, adequately happy; willing (*to* do). —*v.t.* to make content, to satisfy. —*n.* a contented state, satisfaction. [f. OF f. L (as CONTAIN)]

contented /kən'tentɪd/ *adj.* satisfied; willing to be content *with.* —**contentedly** *adv.* [f. prec.]

contention /kən'tenʃ(ə)n/ *n.* **1.** contending, argument or

dispute. **2.** the point contended for in an argument. [f. prec.]

contentious /kən'tenʃəs/ *adj.* **1.** quarrelsome. **2.** likely to cause argument. [as prec.]

contentment *n.* a contented state, tranquil happiness. [f. CONTENT[2]]

conterminous /kɒn'tɜːmɪnəs/ *adj.* having a common boundary (*with*). [f. L *conterminus* (CON-, *terminus* boundary)]

contest /'kɒntest/ *n.* contending, strife; a competition. —/kən'test/ *v.t.* **1.** to dispute (a claim or statement). **2.** to contend or compete for (a prize, a seat in parliament, etc.) or in (an election). [f. L *contestari* (CON-, *testis* witness)]

contestant /kən'testənt/ *n.* one who takes part in a contest. [f. prec.]

context /'kɒntekst/ *n.* **1.** the parts that precede and follow a word or passage and fix its precise meaning. **2.** attendant circumstances. —**contextual** /kən'tekstjʊəl/ *adj.* [f. L (CON-, *texere* weave)]

contiguous /kən'tɪgjʊəs/ *adj.* next (*to*); touching, in contact. —**contiguity** /kɒntɪ'gjuːɪtɪ/ *n.,* **contiguously** *adv.* [as CONTINGENT]

continent[1] /'kɒntɪnənt/ *n.* any of the main continuous bodies of land (Europe, Asia, Africa, North America, South America, Australia, Antarctica). —**the Continent,** the mainland of Europe as distinct from the British Isles. [f. L *terra continens* continuous land (as foll.)]

continent[2] /'kɒntɪnənt/ *adj.* able to control the movements of the bowels and bladder. —**continence** *n.* [f. L (as CONTAIN)]

continental /kɒntɪ'nent(ə)l/ *adj.* **1.** of or characteristic of a continent. **2. Continental,** characteristic of the Continent. —**Continental breakfast,** a light breakfast of coffee and rolls etc. **continental quilt,** a duvet. **continental rise,** the moderately inclined slope between the continental slope and the deep ocean floor (ill. SEA). **continental shelf,** the shallow sea-bed bordering a continent. **continental slope,** the relatively steep slope between the outer edge of the continental shelf and the ocean bed. [f. prec.]

continental drift the postulated movement of the existing continents to their present positions after having at one time formed a single land-mass. The idea of continental drift is generally ascribed to the German meteorologist Alfred Wegener, although similar but less detailed suggestions had been put forward by earlier writers. Wegener's theory was based on similarities in the types of rock and in the flora and fauna (both fossil and living) of the continents, and in the correspondence of the outline of the coasts of South America and Africa, but the concept that the masses of rock forming the continents could drift across the rocks that form the weaker suboceanic portion of the earth's crust gained little credence before the 1960s. Since then information from the floors of the oceans, from seismic studies, from palaeomagnetic surveys, and from radiometric dating of rocks have shown that the theory is valid. It is now evident that the present continental land masses of South America, Africa, Australia, Antarctica, and the Indian subcontinent once formed a single supercontinent, termed Gondwanaland, which began splitting up about 200-150 million years ago. The precise geophysical mechanisms involved in the drift of the continents and, indeed, plate tectonics—a theory which expands upon that of continental drift—are still hotly debated. (See ill. GEOLOGY.)

contingency /kən'tɪndʒ(ə)nsɪ/ *n.* an event that may or may not occur; an unknown or unforeseen circumstance. [as foll.]

contingent /kən'tɪndʒ(ə)nt/ *adj.* conditional or dependent (*on* or *upon* especially an uncertain event or circumstance); that may or may not occur; fortuitous. —*n.* a body of troops, ships, etc., forming part of a larger group. —**contingently** *adv.* [f. L (as CONTACT)]

continual /kən'tɪnjʊəl/ *adj.* constantly or frequently recurring; always happening. —**continually** *adv.* [as CONTINUE]

continuance /kən'tɪnjʊəns/ *n.* continuing in existence or operation; duration. [as CONTINUE]

continuation /kəntɪnjʊ'eɪʃ(ə)n/ *n.* continuing; a thing that continues something else. [as CONTINUE]

continue /kən'tɪnjuː/ *v.t./i.* **1.** to maintain or keep up, not to stop (an action etc.). **2.** to resume or prolong (a narrative, journey, etc., or *abs.*); to prolong, to be a sequel to. **3.** to remain, to stay; not to become other than. [f. OF f. L *continuare* (as CONTINUOUS)]

continuity /kɒntɪˈnjuːɪtɪ/ *n.* **1.** being continuous; unbroken succession; logical sequence. **2.** maintenance of consistency in successive shots or scenes of a film etc. **3.** linkage between broadcast items. [as CONTINUOUS]

continuo /kənˈtɪnjʊəʊ/ *n.* (*pl.* **-os**) (*Mus.*) a continuous bass accompaniment played usually on a keyboard instrument. [It. (as foll.)]

continuous /kənˈtɪnjʊəs/ *adj.* without an interval or break, uninterrupted; connected throughout in space or time. —**continuously** *adv.* [f. L (as CONTAIN)]

continuum /kənˈtɪnjʊəm/ *n.* (*pl.* **-nua**) a thing of continuous structure. [L (as prec.)]

contort /kənˈtɔːt/ *v.t.* to twist or force out of normal shape. —**contortion** *n.* [f. L *contorquēre* (CON-, *torquēre* twist)]

contortionist /kənˈtɔːʃənɪst/ *n.* a performer who can twist his body into unusual positions. [f. prec.]

contour /ˈkɒntʊə(r)/ *n.* **1.** an outline. **2.** a line on a map joining points at the same altitude. **3.** a line separating differently coloured parts of a design. —*v.t.* to mark with contour lines. [f. F f. It. (*contornare* draw in outline)]

contra- *prefix* against, opposed to. [f. L *contra* against]

contraband /ˈkɒntrəbænd/ *n.* smuggled goods, smuggling; prohibited trade. —*adj.* forbidden to be imported or exported. [f. Sp. f. It. (as CONTRA-, *bando* proclamation)]

contrabassoon /kɒntrəbəˈsuːn/ *n.* see BASSOON.

contraception /kɒntrəˈsepʃ(ə)n/ *n.* prevention of pregnancy, the use of contraceptives. [f. CONTRA- + (CON)CEPTION]

contraceptive /kɒntrəˈseptɪv/ *adj.* preventing pregnancy. —*n.* a contraceptive device or drug. [as prec.]

contract /ˈkɒntrækt/ *n.* a written or spoken agreement, especially one enforceable by law; the document recording it. —/kənˈtrækt/ *v.t./i.* **1.** to make or become smaller; to draw (muscles, the brow, etc.) together. **2.** to shorten (a word) by combination or elision. **3.** to make a contract (*with*); to form or enter into (a marriage, debt, etc.); to arrange for (work) to be done by contract. —**contract bridge,** a form of bridge in which only tricks bid and won count towards the game. **contract in** *or* **out,** to elect to enter or not to enter a scheme or commitment. [f. OF f. L *contractus* (CON-, *trahere* draw)]

contractable *adj.* (of disease) that may be contracted. [f. prec.]

contractible *adj.* able to be made smaller or drawn together. [f. CONTRACT]

contractile /kənˈtræktaɪl/ *adj.* capable of or producing contraction. —**contractility** /kɒntrækˈtɪlɪtɪ/ *n.* [as prec.]

contraction /kənˈtrækʃ(ə)n/ *n.* **1.** contracting. **2.** shortening a word or words by combination or elision; a contracted form. [f. CONTRACT]

contractor /kənˈtræktə(r)/ *n.* one who makes a contract, especially to build houses. [as prec.]

contractual /kənˈtræktjʊəl/ *adj.* of or in the nature of a contract. —**contractually** *adv.* [f. CONTRACT]

contradict /kɒntrəˈdɪkt/ *v.t.* to deny; to deny the statement made by; (of facts, statements, etc.) to be at variance or conflict with. —**contradiction** *n.*, **contradictory** *adj.* [f. L *contradicere* (CONTRA-, *dicere* say)]

contradistinction /kɒntrədɪsˈtɪŋkʃ(ə)n/ *n.* distinction by contrast; contrast.

contraflow *n.* a flow (esp. of road traffic) in a direction opposite to, and alongside, that of the usual or established flow.

contralto /kənˈtræltəʊ/ *n.* (*pl.* **-os**) the lowest female singing-voice; a singer with such a voice; a part written for it. [It. (CONTRA-, ALTO)]

contraption /kənˈtræpʃ(ə)n/ *n.* a machine or device, especially a strange or cumbersome one. [orig. unkn.]

contrapuntal /kɒntrəˈpʌnt(ə)l/ *adj.* of or in counterpoint. —**contrapuntally** *adv.* [f. It. *contrappunto* counterpoint]

contrariwise /kənˈtreərɪwaɪz/ *adv.* on the other hand, in the opposite way; perversely. [f. foll.]

contrary[1] /ˈkɒntrərɪ/ *adj.* opposed in nature, tendency, or direction; in opposition *to*; (of a wind) impeding, unfavourable. —*n.* the opposite of a person or thing. —*adv.* in opposition or contrast *to*. —**on the contrary,** in contrast to what has just been implied or stated. [f. AF f. L *contrarius* (*contra* against)]

contrary[2] /kənˈtreərɪ/ *adj.* doing the opposite of what is expected or advised, wilful. —**contrariness** *n.* [var. pronunc. of prec.]

contrast /ˈkɒntrɑːst/ *n.* **1.** juxtaposition or comparison showing striking differences; a difference so revealed. **2.** a person or thing having noticeably different qualities (*to*). **3.** the degree of difference between tones in a photograph or television picture. —/kənˈtrɑːst/ *v.t./i.* to set in opposition to reveal a contrast; to have or show a contrast (*with*). [f. F f. It. f. L *contrastare* (CONTRA-, *stare* stand)]

contravene /kɒntrəˈviːn/ *v.t.* to violate or infringe (a law); to contradict, to conflict with. —**contravention** /-ˈvenʃ(ə)n/ *n.* [f. L *contravenire* (CONTRA-, *venire* come)]

contretemps /ˈkɔ̃trətɑ̃/ *n.* an unfortunate occurrence; an unexpected mishap. [F]

contribute /kənˈtrɪbjuːt, (D) ˈkɒn-/ *v.t./i.* to give jointly with others (*to* a common fund); to supply (an article) for publication with others. —**contribute to,** to help to bring about. —**contributor** *n.* [f. L *contribuere* (CON-, *tribuere* bestow)]

contribution /kɒntrɪˈbjuːʃ(ə)n/ *n.* contributing; a thing contributed. [f. OF or L (as prec.)]

contributory /kənˈtrɪbjʊtərɪ/ *adj.* that contributes; using contributions. [as CONTRIBUTE]

contrite /ˈkɒntraɪt/ *adj.* penitent, feeling great guilt. —**contritely** *adv.*, **contrition** /kənˈtrɪʃ(ə)n/ *n.* [f. OF f. L *contritus* bruised (CON-, *terere* rub)]

contrivance /kənˈtraɪv(ə)ns/ *n.* contriving; something contrived, especially a device or plan. [f. foll.]

contrive /kənˈtraɪv/ *v.t./i.* to devise, plan, or make resourcefully or with skill; to manage (*to* do). —**contriver** *n.* [f. OF *controver* find, imagine, f. It.]

control /kənˈtrəʊl/ *n.* **1.** the power of directing or restraining; self-restraint; a means of restraining or regulating; (usu. in *pl.*) switches and other devices by which a machine is controlled. **2.** a place where something is controlled or verified. **3.** a standard of comparison for checking the results of an experiment. **4.** a personality said to direct the actions and words of a spiritualist medium. —*v.t.* **1.** to have control of, to regulate; to serve as a control to. **2.** to check or verify. —**control tower,** a tall building at an airport from which air traffic is controlled. **in control,** in charge (*of*). **out of control,** unrestrained, without control. —**controllable** *adj.* [f. AF *contreroller* keep copy of accounts, f. L (CONTRA-, *rotulus* roll)]

controller *n.* a person or thing that controls; a person in charge of expenditure. [as prec.]

controversial /kɒntrəˈvɜːʃ(ə)l/ *adj.* causing or subject to controversy. [as foll.]

controversy /ˈkɒntrəvɜːsɪ, (D) kənˈtrɒvəsɪ/ *n.* a prolonged argument or dispute. [as foll.]

controvert /ˈkɒntrəvɜːt/ *v.t.* to dispute or deny. [f. F f. L (CONTRA-, *vertere* turn)]

contumacy /ˈkɒntjʊməsɪ/ *n.* stubborn refusal to obey or comply. —**contumacious** /kɒntjʊˈmeɪʃəs/ *adj.* [f. L *contumax* (CON-, perh. rel. to *tumēre* swell)]

contumely /ˈkɒntjuːmlɪ/ *n.* insulting language or treatment; disgrace. —**contumelious** /kɒntjuːˈmiːlɪəs/ *adj.* [f. L (perh. as prec.)]

contuse /kənˈtjuːz/ *v.t.* to bruise. —**contusion** *n.* [f. L *contundere* (CON-, *tundere* thump)]

conundrum /kəˈnʌndrəm/ *n.* a riddle or hard question, especially one with a pun in its answer. [orig. unkn.]

conurbation /kɒnɜːˈbeɪʃ(ə)n/ *n.* an extended urban area, especially consisting of several towns and merging suburbs. [f. CON- + L *urbs* city]

convalesce /kɒnvəˈles/ *v.i.* to recover health after an illness. [f. L *convalescere* (CON-, *valescere* grow strong)]

convalescent /kɒnvəˈles(ə)nt/ *adj.* recovering from an illness. —*n.* a convalescent person. —**convalescence** *n.* [f. prec.]

convection /kənˈvekʃ(ə)n/ *n.* **1.** the transmission of heat by movement of the heated substance. **2.** (*Meteorol.*) a vertical movement of air. —**convective** *adj.* [f. L *convectio* (CON-, *vehere* carry)]

convector /kənˈvektə(r)/ *n.* a heating appliance that circulates warm air. [as prec.]

convene /kənˈviːn/ *v.t./i.* to summon or arrange (a meeting etc.); to assemble. —**convener** *n.* [f. L *convenire* (CON-, *venire* come)]

convenience /kənˈviːnɪəns/ *n.* **1.** the quality of being convenient, suitability; freedom from difficulty or trouble;

advantage. **2.** a useful thing; a lavatory, especially a public one. —**convenience food,** food requiring very little preparation. [as prec.]

convenient /kən'viːnɪənt/ adj. serving one's comfort or interests, suitable, free of trouble or difficulty; available or occurring at a suitable time or place. —**conveniently** adv. [f. L convenire suit, agree with (as CONVENE)]

convent /'kɒnvənt/ n. a religious community, especially of nuns, under vows; a building occupied by this. [f. AF f. L (as CONVENE)]

conventicle /kən'ventɪk(ə)l/ n. (chiefly hist.) a secret meeting, especially of religious dissenters. [f. L (as prec.)]

convention /kən'venʃ(ə)n/ n. **1.** a formal assembly or conference. **2.** a formal agreement or treaty. **3.** general agreement on social behaviour etc. by the implicit consent of the majority. **4.** a custom or customary practice. [f. OF f. L (as CONVENE)]

conventional adj. depending on or according with a convention; (of a person) attentive to social conventions; usual, of agreed significance; not spontaneous or sincere or original; (of weapons or a power) non-nuclear. —**conventionalism** n., **conventionality** /-'nælɪtɪ/ n., **conventionally** adv. [f. F or L (as prec.)]

converge /kən'vɜːdʒ/ v.i. to come together or towards the same point. —**converge on,** to approach from different directions. —**convergence** n., **convergent** adj. [f. L convergere (CON-, vergere incline)]

conversant /kən'vɜːsənt/ adj. well acquainted (with a subject etc.). [f. OF (as CONVERSE[1])]

conversation /kɒnvə'seɪʃ(ə)n/ n. the informal exchange of ideas by spoken words; an instance of this. [f. OF f. L (as CONVERSE[1])]

conversational adj. of or in a conversation; colloquial. —**conversationally** adv. [f. prec.]

conversationalist n. a person fond of or good at conversation. [f. prec.]

converse[1] /kən'vɜːs/ v.i. to hold a conversation, to talk (with). —/'kɒnvɜːs/ n. (archaic) conversation. [f. OF f. L conversari keep company (as CONVERT)]

converse[2] /'kɒnvɜːs/ adj. opposite, contrary, reversed. —n. a converse statement, idea or proposition. —**conversely** /kən'vɜːslɪ/ adv. [f. L (as CONVERT)]

convert /kən'vɜːt/ v.t./i. **1.** to change or be able to be changed in form or function (into). **2.** to cause (a person) to change his beliefs, opinion, party, etc. **3.** to change (money etc.) into a different form or currency. **4.** to make structural alterations in (a building) for a new purpose. **5.** to complete (a try in Rugby football) by kicking a goal. —/'kɒnvɜːt/ n. a person converted, especially to a new religion. —**conversion** n., **converter** n. [f. OF f. L convertere (CON-, vertere turn)]

convertible /kən'vɜːtɪb(ə)l/ adj. able to be converted. —n. a motor car with folding or detachable roof. —**convertibility** /-'bɪlɪtɪ/ n. [OF f. L (as prec.)]

convex /'kɒnveks/ adj. with the outline or surface curved like the exterior of a sphere or circle. —**convexity** /kən'veksɪtɪ/ n. [f. L convexus vaulted]

convey /kən'veɪ/ v.t. **1.** to transport or carry (goods, passengers, etc.). **2.** to communicate (an idea, meaning, etc.). **3.** to transfer the legal title to (property). **4.** to transmit (sound etc.). —**conveyable** adj. [f. OF f. L conviare (CON-, via way)]

conveyance n. **1.** conveying. **2.** a means of transport, a vehicle. **3.** the transfer of property; a deed effecting this. —(in legal sense) **conveyancer** n., **conveyancing** n. [f. prec.]

conveyor n. (also **conveyer**) a person or thing that conveys. —**conveyor belt,** an endless moving belt for conveying articles in a factory etc. [f. CONVEY]

convict /kən'vɪkt/ v.t. to prove or find guilty (of). —/'kɒnvɪkt/ n. a convicted prisoner. [f. L convincere (CON-, vincere conquer)]

conviction /kən'vɪkʃ(ə)n/ n. **1.** convicting, being convicted. **2.** being convinced, a convinced state; a firm belief. [as prec.]

convince /kən'vɪns/ v.t. to persuade firmly (of, that). —**convincible** adj. [f. L (as CONVICT)]

convivial /kən'vɪvɪəl/ adj. fond of good company, sociable and lively. —**conviviality** /-'ælɪtɪ/ n. **convivially** adv. [f. L convivium feast (CON-, vivere live)]

convocation /kɒnvə'keɪʃ(ə)n/ n. convoking; an assembly convoked, especially the provincial synod of Anglican clergy

or the legislative assembly of a university. —**convocational** adj. [as foll.]

convoke /kən'vəʊk/ v.t. to call together; to summon to assemble. [f. L convocare (CON-, vocare call)]

convoluted /'kɒnvəluːtɪd/ adj. coiled, twisted; complex. [f. L convolutus (CON-, volvere roll)]

convolution /kɒnvə'luːʃ(ə)n/ n. coiling; a coil or twist; complexity; a sinuous fold in the surface of the brain. [as prec.]

convolvulus /kən'vɒlvjʊləs/ n. a twining plant of the genus Convolvulus or Calystegia, bindweed. [L (as CONVOLUTED)]

convoy /'kɒnvɔɪ/ v.t. to escort as a protection. —n. **1.** convoying. **2.** a group of ships, vehicles, etc., travelling together or escorted. [f. OF (as CONVEY)]

convulse /kən'vʌls/ v.t. (usu. in pass.) to affect with convulsions; to cause to laugh uncontrollably. —**convulsive** adj. [f. L convellere (CON-, vellere pull)]

convulsion /kən'vʌlʃ(ə)n/ n. **1.** (often in pl.) a violent irregular motion of the limbs or body caused by involuntary contraction of the muscles. **2.** a violent disturbance. **3.** (in pl.) uncontrollable laughter. [f. prec.]

cony /'kəʊnɪ/ n. a rabbit; its fur. [f. AF f. L cuniculus]

coo n. a soft murmuring sound like that of the dove. —v.t./i. to emit a coo; to talk or say in a soft or amorous voice. [imit.]

cooee /'kuːiː/ n. a cry used to attract attention. —v.i. to emit a cooee. —int. (colloq.) used to attract attention. [imit., orig. Aboriginal]

Cook[1] /kʊk/, James (1728–79), English explorer. Cook first went to sea as a common sailor, but rose to the rank of Master in the Royal Navy as a result of his navigational skills, charting the St Lawrence Channel and the coasts of Newfoundland and Labrador during his service in North America (1759–67). Between 1768 and 1771 he conducted an expedition to the Pacific to observe the transit of Venus, charting the coasts of Australia, New Zealand, and New Guinea before returning via the Cape of Good Hope. Promoted to Commander, he returned to the Pacific in 1772–5 to search for the fabled Antarctic continent, visiting Tahiti, the New Hebrides, and New Caledonia on a voyage notable for the success of Cook's health measures (only one member of his crew dying during the entire voyage). His final voyage (1776–9), to discover a passage round North America from the Pacific side, was marked by further pioneer charting work, but eventually ended in disaster when Cook was killed in a skirmish with native peoples in Hawaii. Cook's surveying work added immeasurably to contemporary knowledge of the Pacific; he died a European hero.

Cook[2] /kʊk/, Thomas (1808–92), English tourist agent. Zealous in the cause of temperance, in 1841 he organized the first publicly advertised excursion train in England, carrying 570 passengers from Leicester and Loughborough and back, to attend a temperance meeting, for the price of one shilling. The success of this induced him to make the organizing of excursions at home and abroad a regular occupation.

cook /kʊk/ v.t./i. **1.** to prepare (food) by heating; to undergo cooking. **2.** (colloq.) to alter or falsify (accounts etc.). —n. one who cooks, esp. professionally or in a specified way. —**cook up,** (colloq.) to invent or concoct (a story, an excuse, etc.). [OE f. L coquus]

cooker n. **1.** an appliance or vessel for cooking food. **2.** a fruit (esp. an apple) suitable for cooking. [f. prec.]

cookery n. the art or practice of cooking. [f. COOK]

cookie /'kʊkɪ/ n. **1.** (US) a sweet biscuit. **2.** (Sc.) a plain bun. [f. Du. koekje dim. of koek cake]

cool adj. **1.** of or at a fairly low temperature, fairly cold, not hot; suggesting or achieving coolness. **2.** calm, unexcited; lacking enthusiasm, restrained; calmly audacious. —n. coolness; cool air, a cool place. —v.t./i. (often with down or off) to make or become cool. —**cooling tower,** a tall structure for cooling hot water before reuse, especially in industry (ill. ELECTRICAL POWER). **cooling-off period,** an interval to allow for a change of mind before action. **cool off,** to calm down. —**coolly** /'kuːllɪ/ adv., **coolness** n. [OE, rel. to COLD]

coolant /'kuːlənt/ n. a cooling agent, especially a fluid to remove heat from an engine. [f. prec.]

cooler n. **1.** a vessel in which a thing is cooled. **2.** (slang) a prison cell. [f. COOL]

coolie /'kuːlɪ/ n. an unskilled native labourer in Eastern countries. [perh. f. Kuli, tribe in India]

coomb /ku:m/ n. a valley on the side of a hill; a short valley running up from the coast. [OE]

coop n. a cage for keeping poultry. —v.t. to keep in a coop; (often with *in* or *up*) to confine (a person). [f. LG or Du., ult. f. L *cupa* cask]

Cooper /ˈku:pə(r)/, James Fenimore (1789-1851), American novelist. After being dismissed from Yale he spent a short time in the US Navy and then settled down as a country proprietor and novelist. *The Pioneers* (1823) was the first of *The Leather Stocking Tales*, called after the deerskin leggings of their hero Natty Bumppo; the sequels were *The Last of the Mohicans* (1826), *The Prairie* (1827), *The Pathfinder* (1840), and *The Deerslayer* (1841), giving a vivid picture of American Indian and frontier life. During the years 1826-33 he travelled in Europe and published highly critical accounts of European society, including *England, with Sketches of Society in the Metropolis* (1837), and later vigorously expressed the defects and dangers of democracy in America in *The American Democrat* (1838).

cooper n. a maker or repairer of casks and barrels. [as prec.]

co-operate /kəʊˈɒpəreɪt/ v.i. to work or act together (*with*). —**co-operation** /-ˈreɪʃ(ə)n/ n., **co-operator** n. [f. L *cooperari* (CO-, *opus* work)]

co-operative /kəʊˈɒpərətɪv/ adj. 1. of or providing co-operation; willing to co-operate. 2. (of a business) owned and run jointly by its members with profits shared among them. —n. a co-operative farm or society. —**co-operatively** adv. [as prec.]

co-opt /kəʊˈɒpt/ v.t. to appoint to membership of a body by the invitation or votes of the existing members. —**co-option** n., **co-optive** adj. [f. L *cooptare* (CO-, *optare* choose)]

co-ordinate /kəʊˈɔːdɪnət/ adj. equal in rank or importance (esp. of the parts of a compound sentence); consisting of co-ordinate things. —n. 1. a co-ordinate thing. 2. (*Math.*, usu. **coordinate**) each of a system of magnitudes used to fix the position of a point, a line, or a plane. 3. (in *pl.*) matching items of clothing. —/-neɪt/ v.t. to make co-ordinate; to bring (parts, movements, etc.) into a proper relationship; to cause (the limbs, parts, etc.) to function together or in proper order. —**co-ordinately** adv., **co-ordination** /-ˈneɪʃ(ə)n/ n., **co-ordinative** adj., **co-ordinator** n. [f. CO- + L *ordinare* arrange, order]

coot n. a water-bird of the genus *Fulica* with a horny white patch on its forehead. [prob. f. LG]

cop n. (*slang*) a policeman. —v.t. (**-pp-**) (*slang*) 1. to catch or arrest (an offender). 2. to receive, to obtain or suffer. —**cop out**, (*slang*) to withdraw, to give up. **cop-out** n. (*slang*) a cowardly evasion or escape. [perh. f. obs. F *cap* arrest f. *caper* seize]

copal /ˈkəʊp(ə)l/ n. the resin of various tropical trees, used for varnish. [Sp. f. Aztec]

copartner /kəʊˈpɑːtnə(r)/ n. a partner or associate. —**copartnership** n. [f. CO- + PARTNER]

cope[1] v.i. to deal effectively or contend *with*; (*colloq.*) to manage successfully. [f. OF f. L f. Gk *kolaphos* blow with fist]

cope[2] n. a long cloaklike vestment worn by priests in ceremonies and processions (ill. VESTMENTS). —v.t. to cover with a cope or coping. [OE, f. L *cappa* cap, cape]

copeck /ˈkəʊpek/ n. a Russian coin, one hundredth of a rouble. [f. Russ. *kopeika*]

Copenhagen /kəʊpənˈheɪgən/ the capital and chief port of Denmark; pop. (1982) 575,217.

Copernicus /kəˈpɜːnɪkəs/, Nicolaus (original name Koppernigk, 1473-1543), Polish astronomer, canon of the cathedral at Frauenberg, the figure most closely associated with the overthrow of the ancient Greek Earth-centred cosmology. He developed his theories of a moving Earth, which he first published in outline in 1530, to a generally favourable reception. Not until 1543, however, was the full substance of his studies published in *De Revolutionibus Orbium Coelestium*, a copy of which, according to tradition, first reached Copernicus on his deathbed. Eschewing the complex system of epicyclic motions required to explain planetary motions in the Ptolemaic theory, he proposed the simpler model of a system of planets, including the Earth, all orbiting the sun. Still influenced by classical ideas of perfection, he supposed the orbits of the planets to be determined by combinations of perfect circles; but the most important break with tradition was in removing the Earth from the centre of the universe, a move which was to find

much opposition in the Roman Catholic Church during the next century.

copier /ˈkɒpɪə(r)/ n. a person or machine that copies (documents etc.). [f. COPY]

co-pilot /ˈkəʊpaɪlət/ n. the second pilot in an aircraft.

coping /ˈkəʊpɪŋ/ n. the top (usually sloping) row of masonry in a wall. —**coping-stone** n. a stone used in a coping. [f. COPE[2]]

coping saw /ˈkəʊpɪŋ/ a D-shaped saw for cutting curved outlines in wood (ill. CARPENTRY). [f. OF *coper* cut (as COPE[2])]

copious /ˈkəʊpɪəs/ adj. abundant, plentiful; producing much. —**copiously** adv. [f. OF or L (*copia* plenty)]

Copland /ˈkəʊplənd/, Aaron (1900-), American composer, pianist, and conductor. The son of immigrant Jewish parents from Lithuania, he was concerned to establish a distinctive 'American' style in music, borrowing from jazz in his Piano Concerto (1926) and *Music for the Theater* (1925), from Shaker music in the evocative and popular *Appalachian Spring* (1944), and from other folk and traditional songs in the ballet scores *Billy the Kid* (1938) and *Rodeo* (1942). He furthered the cause of his country's music in his work as a conductor and in his establishment of the American Composers' Alliance (1937).

Copley /ˈkɒplɪ/, John Singleton (1738-1815), American painter. His shrewd and forceful realism marked him out as one of the most talented of colonial portraitists: his power of characterization enabled him to create the most convincing expressions of the aristocratic ideal in 18th-c. American painting, and he had a special gift for the portrayal of older people of the professional classes. Urged by Reynolds and Benjamin West, he sailed for Europe in 1774, and settled in England, remaining there until his death. He enjoyed a short period of success, especially with history pictures such as *The Death of Chatham* (1779-80), but his popularity waned and his last years were menaced by debt.

copper[1] /ˈkɒpə(r)/ n. 1. a reddish-brown ductile metallic element, symbol Cu, atomic number 29 (see below). 2. a bronze coin (see PENNY). 3. a large metal vessel for boiling things, especially laundry. —adj. made of or coloured like copper. —v.t. to cover with copper. —**Copper Age**, the prehistoric period when some weapons and tools were made of copper, either before or in place of bronze. **copper beech**, a variety of beech with copper-coloured leaves. **copper-bottomed** adj. having the bottom sheathed with copper (esp. of a ship or pan); reliable; genuine. [OE f. L *cuprum* = *cyprium aes* Cyprus metal (Cyprus was the principal source of copper in Roman times)]

Copper is found in the native state as well as in the form of ores. It was the earliest metal to be used by man, first by itself and then later alloyed with tin to form bronze. A ductile easily worked metal, it is a very good conductor of heat and electricity. Copper is a component of many alloys, but it is still used mainly in its pure state, especially for electrical wiring. Copper compounds are used in the production of green pigments, insecticides, and fungicides. In trace amounts the element is essential to living organisms.

copper[2] n. (*slang*) a policeman. [f. COP]

copperhead n. a venomous American or Australian snake with a reddish-brown head.

copperplate n. 1. a polished copper plate for engraving or etching; a print made from this. 2. a fine style of handwriting.

coppice /ˈkɒpɪs/ n. an area of small trees and undergrowth. [f. OF f. L (as COPE[2])]

copra /ˈkɒprə/ n. dried coconut-kernels. [Port. f. Malay-alam]

copse n. a coppice. [shortened form]

Copt n. 1. a native Egyptian in and after the Hellenistic period. 2. a member of the Coptic Church. [f. F f. Arab., ult. f. Gk *Aiguptios* Egyptian]

Coptic /ˈkɒptɪk/ adj. of the Copts or Coptic. —n. a language that represents the final stage of ancient Egyptian, with an alphabet largely based on the Greek but with some letters borrowed from Egyptian demotic, and now surviving only as the liturgical language of the Coptic Church. In the 3rd c. AD Coptic was the prevailing language of Christian Egypt. After the Arab conquest in 642 it began to give way to Arabic but did not die out as a spoken language until the 17th c. —**Coptic Church**, the native Christian Church in Egypt, traditionally founded by St Mark. It became isolated from the rest of Christendom in 451 when it adhered to the Monophysite doctrine condemned by the Council of Chalcedon, and its numbers declined when the conquest of Egypt by Muslim Arabs in the 7th c. was followed by centuries of persecution. There is a small Uniat Coptic Church dating from 1741. [f. prec.]

copula /ˈkɒpjʊlə/ n. a connecting word, especially a part of the verb *to be* connecting the predicate with the subject. [L, = fastening]

copulate /ˈkɒpjʊleɪt/ v.i. to come together sexually (*with*), as in the act of mating. —**copulation** /-ˈleɪʃ(ə)n/ n. [f. L *copulare* fasten together]

copy /ˈkɒpɪ/ n. 1. a thing made to look like another; a specimen of a book, magazine, etc. 2. matter to be printed; material for a newspaper article. 3. the text of an advertisement. —v.t./i. to make a copy (of); to imitate, to do the same as. —**copy-typist** n. one who makes typewritten copies of documents etc. **copy-writer** n. a writer of copy for publication, especially publicity material. [f. OF f. L *copia* abundance, in medieval sense = transcript, f. phr. *facere copiam describendi* give permission to transcribe]

copy-book n. a book containing models of handwriting for learners to imitate. —adj. tritely conventional; exemplary.

copyhold n. (*hist.*) tenure of land in accordance with the transcript of manorial records; land so held.

copyist n. a person who makes copies; an imitator. [f. COPY]

copyright n. the exclusive legal right to print, publish, perform, film, or record literary, artistic, or musical material, normally vested in the creator of such material (see below). —adj. protected by copyright. —v.t. to secure a copyright of (material). —**copyright libraries**, the British Library, Bodleian, Cambridge University. National Library of Wales, Scottish National Library, and Trinity College, Dublin, which are entitled by law to receive from the publisher a free copy of every book published in the UK.
    Protection of rights was made necessary by the invention of printing (15th c.). Rulers issued monopoly rights to individuals or guilds, and at first the only protection available to the author was against publication of his work without his permission; once published it was out of his control. The first English statute recognizing the author's rights was passed in 1710, and gave him protection for 28 years only; in 1790 a similar copyright law was passed in the USA. In Britain, in general copyright subsists for the author's lifetime plus 50 years; in the USA protection lasts for 28 years, renewable for a second 28-year term. Legislation has recently been introduced to protect rights in computer programs and computer-stored material.

coquette /kɒˈket/ n. a flirtatious woman or girl. —v.i. to flirt. —**coquettish** adj., **coquetry** /ˈkɒkɪtrɪ/ n. [F, = wanton, dim. of *coq* cock]

cor- prefix see COM-.

coracle /ˈkɒrək(ə)l/ n. a small boat, occasionally circular but more often rectangular with rounded corners, constructed of wickerwork and made watertight originally with animal hides but more recently with pitch or some other watertight material, used for river and coastal transport by the ancient Britons and still used by fishermen on the rivers and lakes of Wales and Ireland. [f. Welsh *corwgl* (*corwg* = Ir. *currach* boat)]

coral /ˈkɒr(ə)l/ n. 1. a hard usually red, pink, or white calcareous substance secreted by many species of coelenterates for support or habitation, and sometimes building up to form reefs and islands; that forming the skeleton of the precious coral (*corallium*) of the Mediterranean and Red Sea; (*loosely*) a similar substance produced by marine algae etc. 2. a structure formed of such substances. 3. any of numerous species of usually colonial marine coelenterates producing a horny, calcareous, or soft skeleton; an individual polyp or colony of these, especially of the order Madreporaria (the stony or true corals) which have a calcareous skeleton and are the main reef-forming types. 3. the yellowish- or reddish-pink colour of some corals. —adj. 1. made of coral. 2. yellowish- or reddish-pink. [f. OF f. L f. Gk *korallion*, prob. of Semitic origin]

coralline /ˈkɒrəlaɪn/ adj. of or like coral. —n. a seaweed with a hard jointed stem. [f. It. *corallino* dim. of *corallo* (as prec.)]

Coral Sea a part of the Pacific lying between Australia, New Guinea, and Vanuatu.

cor anglais /kɔːr ˈɑ̃ɡleɪ/ an alto woodwind instrument of the oboe family. [F, = English horn]

corbel /ˈkɔːb(ə)l/ n. a stone or timber projection from a wall, acting as a supporting bracket (ill. CHURCH). —**corbelled** adj. [f. OF, dim. of *corp* crow (as foll.)]

corbie /ˈkɔːbɪ/ n. (*Sc.*) a raven, a black crow. [f. OF *corb*, *corp* f. L *corvus*]

Corcyra /kɔːˈsaɪərə/ the former name of Corfu.

cord n. 1. thick string or a piece of this; a similar structure in the body; electric flex. 2. a ribbed fabric, especially corduroy; (in *pl.*) corduroy trousers. 3. a measure of cut wood (usually 128 cu. ft, 3.6 cu. m). —v.t. 1. to secure with cord. 2. (in *p.p.*, of cloth) ribbed. [f. OF f. L f. Gk *khordē* string of musical instrument]

cordate /ˈkɔːdeɪt/ adj. heart-shaped (of leaves, ill. PLANTS). [f. L *cor* heart]

Corday /kɔːˈdeɪ/, Charlotte (1768-93), French noblewoman, a supporter of the revolutionary Girondist party, who assassinated Marat in his bath and was guillotined for her crime.

cordial /ˈkɔːdɪəl/ adj. heartfelt, sincere; warm, friendly. —n. a fruit-flavoured drink. —**cordiality** /-ˈælɪtɪ/ n., **cordially** adv. [f. L *cordialis* (*cor* heart)]

cordite /ˈkɔːdaɪt/ n. a cordlike smokeless explosive. [f. CORD]

Cordoba /ˈkɔːdəbə/ a city in southern Spain, founded by the Carthaginians, held by the Moors from 711 to 1236. As capital of the most powerful of the Arab Spanish States it flourished as a centre of learning, earning the title of 'the Athens of the West'. It began to decline after the overthrow of the caliphate in 1031.

cordon /ˈkɔːd(ə)n/ n. 1. a line or circle of police, soldiers, guards, etc., esp. one preventing access to or from an area. 2. an ornamental cord or braid. 3. a fruit-tree trained to grow as a single stem. —v.t. (often with *off*) to enclose or separate with a cordon of police. [f. It. & F (as CORD)]

cordon bleu /kɔːdɔ̃ ˈblɜː/ 1. of the highest class in cookery. 2. a cook of this class. [F, = blue ribbon, orig. that worn by Knights-grand-cross of the French order of the Holy Ghost, the highest order of chivalry under the Bourbon kings; hence extended to other first-class distinctions]

corduroy /ˈkɔːdərɔɪ/ n. a thick cotton fabric with velvety ribs; (in *pl.*) corduroy trousers. [f. CORD ribbed fabric + obs. *duroy* coarse woollen fabric]

core n. 1. the horny central part of certain fruits, containing the seeds. 2. the central or most important part of anything; the central region of the earth (ill. GEOLOGY). 3. the region of fissile material in a nuclear reactor. 4. a unit of structure in a computer, storing one bit (see BIT²) of data. 5. the inner strand of an electric cable. 6. the piece of soft iron forming the centre of a magnet or induction coil. —v.t. to remove the core from. [orig. unkn.]

Corelli /kəˈrelɪ/, Arcangelo (1653-1713), Italian violinist and composer. His best-known works are for the violin: four sets of trio sonatas, one of sonatas for solo violin, and one of *concerti grossi* (for a solo group of instruments and small orchestra). With their idiomatic writing and beautiful melodies they had an important influence abroad, on Purcell, Bach, Handel, and Couperin, among others.

coreopsis /kɒrɪˈɒpsɪs/ n. a plant of the genus *Coreopsis*, with daisy-like usually yellow flowers. [L, f. Gk *koris* bug + *opsis* appearance (from the shape of the seed)]

co-respondent /kəʊrɪˈspɒnd(ə)nt/ n. the person (esp. the man) said to have committed adultery with the respondent in a divorce case.

Corfu /kɔːˈfuː/ one of the largest of the Ionian islands, off the west coast of Greece; pop. (1971) 89,664.

corgi /ˈkɔːɡɪ/ n. a dog of short-legged Welsh breed with a foxlike head. [Welsh]

coriander /kɒrɪˈændə(r)/ n. an aromatic herb, *Coriandrum sativum*; its seeds used as flavouring. [f. OF f. L f. Gk]

Corinthian /kəˈrɪnθɪən/ adj. 1. of ancient Corinth in southern Greece. 2. (*Archit.*) of the order characterized by acanthus-leaf capitals and ornate decoration, used especially by the Romans (ill. TEMPLES). —(**Epistle to the**) **Corinthians**, either of two books of the New Testament, epistles of St Paul to the Church at Corinth in Greece. [f. L f. Gk *Korinthios*]

Coriolanus /kɒrɪəˈleɪnəs/, Gnaeus Marcius (5th c. BC), Roman general, said to have left Rome after opposing the distribution of corn to the starving people and being charged with tyrannical conduct. He led a Volscian army against Rome in 491 BC, and was turned back only by the pleas of his mother Veturia and his wife Volumnia; he was subsequently put to death by the Volscians.

Coriolis /kɒrɪˈəʊlɪs/, Gaspard Gustave de (1792-1843),

French engineer and mathematician whose name is applied to the effect (which he described) whereby a body moving relative to a rotating frame of reference is accelerated in that frame in a direction perpendicular both to its direction of motion and to the axis of rotation of the frame. It helps to explain, for example, the movement of an air mass or the rotation of a rocket over the surface of the earth.

cork *n.* **1.** the outer bark of a South European oak (*Quercus suber*), a buoyant light-brown substance. **2.** a bottle-stopper of cork or other material. **3.** a float made of cork. —*v.t.* (often with *up*) to stop or confine; to restrain (the feelings etc.). [f. LG or Du. f. Sp. *alcorque*]

corkage /'kɔ:kɪdʒ/ *n.* a charge made by a restaurant etc. for serving wine (esp. when brought from elsewhere). [f. prec.]

corked *adj.* stopped with cork; (of wine) spoilt by a decayed cork. [f. CORK]

corkscrew *n.* **1.** a spiral steel device for extracting corks from bottles. **2.** (often *attrib.*) a thing with a spiral shape. —*v.i.* to move spirally, to twist.

corm *n.* the bulblike underground stem of certain plants. [f. L f. Gk *kormos* trunk with boughs lopped off]

cormorant /'kɔ:mərənt/ *n.* a large black voracious sea-bird, *Phalocrorax carbo*. [f. OF f. L *corvus marinus* sea-raven]

corn[1] *n.* a cereal before or after harvesting, especially wheat, oats, barley, or (*US*) maize; a grain or seed of a cereal plant. —**corn-cob** *n.* the cylindrical centre of an ear of maize, to which the grains are attached. **corn on the cob,** maize cooked and eaten in this form. **corn dolly,** a symbolic or decorative figure made of plaited straw. **Corn Laws,** see separate entry. [OE]

corn[2] *n.* a small tender horny place on the skin, especially on the toe. [f. AF f. L *cornu* horn]

Corn. *abbr.* Cornwall.

corncrake *n.* a bird (*Crex crex*) with a harsh grating cry. [f. CORN[1]]

cornea /'kɔ:nɪə/ *n.* the transparent membrane covering the iris and pupil of the eyeball (ill. BODY 4). —**corneal** *adj.* [f. L *cornea (tela)* horny tissue (*cornu* horn)]

corned *adj.* (of beef) preserved in salt or brine. [f. CORN[1]]

Corneille /kɔ:'neɪ/, Pierre (1606-84), French dramatic poet, leader of classical French tragedy until he was eclipsed by Racine. *Médée* (1635), *Le Cid* (1637), and *Cinna* (1640) are among his masterpieces. His characters, more sublime than those of Racine, are often torn between duty and passion but may rise to superhuman heights of self-sacrifice.

cornel /'kɔ:n(ə)l/ *n.* a tree of the genus *Cornus*, e.g. cornelian cherry, dogwood. [f. G, ult. f. L *cornus*]

cornelian /kɔ:'ni:lɪən/ *n.* a dull red variety of chalcedony. [f. OF, after L *caro* flesh]

cornelian cherry /kɔ:'ni:lɪən/ a European berry-bearing tree, *Cornus mas*. [f. CORNEL]

corner *n.* **1.** a place where converging sides or edges meet; a projecting angle, especially where two streets meet. **2.** an internal space or recess formed by the meeting of two walls etc.; an angle of a ring in boxing etc., especially one where a contestant rests between rounds; a difficult position, especially one with no escape. **3.** a secluded or remote place; a region or quarter, especially a remote one. **4.** the action or result of buying the whole available stock of a commodity. **5.** a free kick or hit from the corner of the field in football and hockey. —*v.t./i.* **1.** to force (a person) into a difficult or inescapable position. **2.** to establish a corner in (a commodity). **3.** (esp. of or in a vehicle) to go round a corner. —**corner-stone** *n.* a stone in the projecting angle of a wall, a foundation-stone; an indispensable part or basis. [f. AF f. L *cornarium* (*cornu* horn)]

cornet /'kɔ:nɪt/ *n.* **1.** a brass instrument resembling a trumpet but shorter and wider. **2.** a conical wafer for holding ice-cream. —**cornettist, cornetist** /-'netɪst/ *n.* [f. OF dim. f. L *cornu* horn, trumpet]

cornflakes *n.pl.* a breakfast cereal of toasted maize flakes.

cornflour *n.* fine-ground flour made from maize, rice, etc.

cornflower *n.* a plant (especially a blue-flowered kind, *Centaurea cyanus*) that grows wild in cornfields.

cornice /'kɔ:nɪs/ *n.* a horizontal moulding in relief, especially along the top of an internal wall or as the topmost part of an entablature (ill. TEMPLES). [f. F f. It.]

Cornish /'kɔ:nɪʃ/ *adj.* of Cornwall or its people or language. —*n.* the ancient language of Cornwall, belonging to the Brythonic branch of the Celtic language group. It was formerly spoken in Cornwall but gradually died out in the 17th-18th c., though attempts are being made to revive

it. —**Cornish pasty,** seasoned meat and vegetables baked in a pastry envelope. [f. CORNWALL]

Corn Laws legislation first introduced in 1815 in an attempt to maintain the prosperity enjoyed by British agriculture during the Napoleonic Wars. The original Corn Law allowed foreign grain to be imported only after the price of home-grown wheat had risen above 80 shillings a quarter, but this had the unintended effect of forcing bread prices so high that both consumer and producer suffered. A sliding scale of import duties was introduced in 1828, but opposition to the Corn Laws continued to mount and they were eventually repealed by Peel in 1846, an act which split the Conservative Party.

cornucopia /kɔ:nju'kəʊpɪə/ *n.* a symbol of plenty consisting of a goat's horn overflowing with flowers, fruit, and corn; abundance. [L (*cornu copiae* horn of plenty)]

Cornwall /'kɔ:nw(ə)l/ a county occupying the extreme SW peninsula of England. The Celtic language of the ancient Cornish kingdom was still spoken there until the 18th c.

corny *adj.* (*colloq.*) trite; feebly humorous; sentimental, old-fashioned. —**cornily** *adv.*, **corniness** *n.* [f. CORN[1]]

corolla /kə'rɒlə/ *n.* the whorl of petals forming the inner envelope of a flower. [L, dim. of CORONA]

corollary /kə'rɒlərɪ/ *n.* a proposition that follows from one already proved; the natural consequence (*of*). [f. L *corollarium* money paid for garlands, gratuity]

corona /kə'rəʊnə/ *n.* (*pl.* **-ae** /-i:/) **1.** the outermost region of the sun, normally visible only during a total solar eclipse, when it is seen as a pearly glow round the disc of the obscuring moon, extending for several times the radius of the sun. It consists of an extremely rarefied gas of electrically charged particles, heated to a temperature of millions of degrees by sound waves originating in the surface layers of the sun. There is evidence of such regions in other stars. **2.** a glow round an electric conductor. **3.** any of various crownlike parts of the body. **4.** (in a flower) an appendage on top of a seed or on the inner side of a corolla. —**coronal** *adj.* [L, = garland, crown]

coronary /'kɒrənərɪ/ *adj.* of the arteries supplying blood to the heart. —*n.* a coronary artery or thrombosis. —**coronary thrombosis,** blockage of a coronary artery by a clot of blood. [as prec.]

coronation /kɒrə'neɪʃ(ə)n/ *n.* the ceremony of crowning a sovereign or consort. —**Coronation stone,** the stone of Scone on which Scottish kings were crowned, brought to England by Edward I and now preserved in the coronation chair at Westminster Abbey. [f. OF f. L *coronatio* (*coronare* crown)]

coroner /'kɒrənə(r)/ *n.* an officer holding inquests into deaths thought to be violent or accidental, and inquiries into cases of treasure trove. [f. AF (as CROWN)]

coronet /'kɒrənɪt, -net/ *n.* **1.** a small crown (ill. HERALDRY); a band of jewels worn as a head-dress. **2.** the lowest part of a horse's pastern (ill. HORSE). [f. OF, dim. of *corone* crown]

Corot /'kɒrəʊ/, Jean-Baptiste Camille (1796-1875), French landscape artist, trained in the neo-classical tradition, who was an important influence on the impressionist landscape painters, especially Pissarro. At 26 he abandoned a commercial career for art. He was in Italy, the subject of many of his landscapes, in 1825-8 and again in 1834 and 1843. Corot was friendly with the Barbizon group, but his works remained poetic and essentially classical in spirit, becoming more misty and ethereal in the 1850s and 1860s. Throughout his career he painted charmingly direct portraits and figure studies, and he retained his powers into old age, *The Studio* (1870) and *Sens Cathedral* (1874) being among his masterpieces.

corpora *pl.* of CORPUS.

corporal[1] /'kɔ:pər(ə)l/ *n.* a non-commissioned army or RAF officer next below a sergeant. [f. F f. It.]

corporal[2] /'kɔ:pərəl/ *adj.* of the human body. —**corporal punishment,** that inflicted on the body, especially by beating. —**corporality** /-'ælɪtɪ/ *n.* [f. OF f. L (*corpus* body)]

corporate /'kɔ:pərət/ *adj.* forming a corporation or group; of or belonging to a group. [f. L *corporare* form into a body (as prec.)]

corporation /kɔ:pə'reɪʃ(ə)n/ *n.* **1.** a group of people authorized to act as an individual, especially in business. **2.** the civic authorities of a borough, town, or city. **3.** (*colloq.*) a protruding abdomen. [as prec.]

corporative /'kɔ:pərətɪv/ *adj.* of a corporation; governed by or organized in corporations, especially of employers and employed. [f. CORPORATE]

corporeal /kɔːˈpɔːrɪəl/ *adj.* bodily, physical; material. —**corporeality** /-ˈælɪtɪ/ *n.*, **corporeally** *adv.* [f. L (*corpus* body)]

corposant /ˈkɔːpəz(ə)nt/ *n.* a luminous electrical discharge (also known as *St Elmo's fire*) sometimes seen on a ship or aircraft during a storm. [f. Sp. *corpo santo* holy body]

corps /kɔː/ *n.* (*pl.* same /kɔːz/) **1.** a military force or division. **2.** a group of persons engaged in some activity. [F (as CORPSE)]

corps de ballet /kɔː də ˈbæleɪ/ a company of ballet-dancers. [F]

corps diplomatique /kɔː dɪpləmæˈtiːk/ the diplomatic corps (see DIPLOMATIC). [F]

corpse /kɔːps/ *n.* a dead (usu. human) body. [f. OF f. L *corpus* body]

corpulent /ˈkɔːpjʊlənt/ *adj.* bulky in body, fat. —**corpulence** *n.* [f. L *corpulentus* (as foll.)]

corpus /ˈkɔːpəs/ *n.* (*pl.* **corpora** /ˈkɔːpərə/) a body or collection of writings, texts, etc. —**Corpus Christi,** (= body of Christ) the feast commemorating the institution and gift of the Eucharist, celebrated on the Thursday after Trinity Sunday. In medieval times it was the occasion when the guilds of many towns performed religious plays. [L, = body]

corpuscle /ˈkɔːpʌs(ə)l/ *n.* a minute body or cell in an organism, especially (in *pl.*) the red or white cells in the blood of vertebrates. —**corpuscular** /-ˈpʌskjʊlə(r)/ *adj.* [f. L *corpusculum* dim. of prec.]

corral /kɒˈrɑːl/ *n.* an enclosure for wild animals or (*US*) cattle or horses. —*v.t.* (**-ll-**) to put or keep in a corral. [Sp. & Port., f. as KRAAL]

correct /kəˈrekt/ *adj.* **1.** true, accurate. **2.** (of conduct) proper, in accordance with taste or a standard. —*v.t.* **1.** to set right (an error, omission, etc.); to mark the errors in; to substitute the right thing for (a wrong one). **2.** to admonish; to punish (a person or fault). **3.** to counteract (a harmful or divergent tendency etc.); to eliminate an aberration from (a lens etc.); to bring into accordance with a standard. —**correctly** *adv.*, **correctness** *n.*, **corrector** *n.* [f. L *corrigere* (COR-, *regere* guide)]

correction /kəˈrekʃ(ə)n/ *n.* **1.** correcting. **2.** a thing substituted for what is wrong. **3.** (*archaic*) punishment. [f. OF f. L (as CORRECT)]

correctitude /kəˈrektɪtjuːd/ *n.* consciously correct behaviour. [blend of CORRECT, RECTITUDE]

corrective /kəˈrektɪv/ *adj.* serving to correct or counteract something harmful. —*n.* a corrective measure or thing. [F or f. L (as CORRECT)]

Correggio /kɒˈredʒɪəʊ/, Antonio Allegri (*c.*1489–1534), Italian painter, influenced by Mantegna and Leonardo, from whom he derived the soft indistinct outlines of his style of sentimental elegance and conscious allure. He was probably in Parma, the scene of his greatest activity, by 1518. There he decorated two domes, those of S. Giovanni Evangelista (1520) and Parma cathedral (*The Assumption of the Virgin*, 1526), developing the illusionism of Mantegna, henceforth almost always used in ceiling decoration, whereby the figures are seen in sharp foreshortening as if the event really were taking place in the sky above. His mythologies, such as *The Loves of Jupiter*, have a lyrical sensuous air which anticipates the rococo of the 18th c.

correlate /ˈkɒrɪleɪt/ *v.t./i.* to have or bring into a mutual relation or dependence (*with* or *to*). —*n.* each of two related or complementary things. —**correlation** /-ˈleɪʃ(ə)n/ *n.* [f. L *correlatio* (COR-, *relatio* relation)]

correlative /kɒˈrelətɪv/ *adj.* having a mutual relationship; (*Gram.*, of words) corresponding to each other and used regularly together (as *neither* and *nor*). —**correlativity** /-ˈtɪvɪtɪ/ *n.* [f. L (COR-, *relativus* relative)]

correspond /kɒrɪˈspɒnd/ *v.i.* **1.** to be analogous (*to*) or in agreement (*with*). **2.** to communicate by interchange of letters (*with*). [f. F f. L *correspondere* (COR-, *respondere* answer)]

correspondence *n.* **1.** agreement or similarity. **2.** communication by letters; the letters sent or received. —**correspondence course,** a course of study conducted by post. [f. OF f. L (as prec.)]

correspondent *n.* **1.** a person writing letters to another, esp. regularly. **2.** a person employed by a newspaper to write regularly on a particular subject. [as prec.]

corridor /ˈkɒrɪdɔː(r)/ *n.* **1.** a passage from which doors lead into rooms; a passage in a train giving access to compartments along its length. **2.** a strip of territory of one

State passing through that of another. **3.** a route which aircraft must follow, especially over foreign territory. [F f. It. (*correre* run)]

corrie *n.* (*Sc.*) a round hollow on a mountainside. [Gaelic]

corrigendum /kɒrɪˈgendəm/ *n.* (*pl.* **-da**) a thing to be corrected, especially an error in a book. [L (*corrigere* correct)]

corrigible /ˈkɒrɪdʒɪb(ə)l/ *adj.* able to be corrected; submissive. —**corrigibly** *adv.* [f. F f. L (as prec.)]

corroborate /kəˈrɒbəreɪt/ *v.t.* to confirm or give support to (a person, a statement or belief). —**corroboration** /-ˈreɪʃ(ə)n/ *n.*, **corroborative** /kəˈrɒbərətɪv/ *adj.* **corroborator** *n.*, **corroboratory** /kəˈrɒbərətərɪ/ *adj.* [f. L *corroborare* (COR-, *robur* strength)]

corroboree /kəˈrɒbərɪ/ *n.* a festive or warlike dance of Australian aboriginals; a noisy party. [Aboriginal]

corrode /kəˈrəʊd/ *v.t./i.* to wear away, especially by chemical action; to destroy gradually; to decay. —**corrosion** *n.* [f. L *corrodere* (COR-, *rodere* gnaw)]

corrosive /kəˈrəʊsɪv/ *adj.* tending to corrode. —*n.* a corrosive substance. [f. OF (as prec.)]

corrugated /ˈkɒrʊgeɪtɪd/ *adj.* formed into regular alternate folds and grooves, especially so as to strengthen (iron etc., or for use as roofing) or make (cardboard or paper) more resilient. —**corrugation** /-ˈgeɪʃ(ə)n/ *n.* [f. L *corrugare* (COR-, *ruga* wrinkle)]

corrupt /kəˈrʌpt/ *adj.* **1.** morally depraved, wicked; influenced by or using bribery. **2.** (of a text etc.) made suspect or unreliable by errors or alterations. —*v.t./i.* to make or become corrupt. —**corruption** *n.*, **corruptive** *adj.* [f. OF or L *corruptus* (COR-, *rumpere* break)]

corruptible /kəˈrʌptɪb(ə)l/ *adj.* able to be (esp. morally) corrupted. —**corruptibility** /-ˈbɪlɪtɪ/ *n.* [f. prec.]

corsage /kɔːˈsɑːʒ/ *n.* (*US*) a small bouquet worn by a woman. [f. OF (as CORPSE)]

corsair *n.* a pirate ship; a pirate. [f. F f. L *cursarius* (as COURSE)]

corselette /ˈkɔːslɪt/ *n.* a woman's foundation garment combining corset and brassière. [f. CORSLET]

corset /ˈkɔːsɪt/ *n.* a close-fitting undergarment worn to compress and shape the figure or as a surgical support. —*v.t.* **1.** to provide with a corset. **2.** to control closely. —**corsetry** *n.* [f. OF dim. of *cors* body (as CORPSE)]

Corsica /ˈkɔːsɪkə/ an island off the west coast of Italy, belonging to France, birthplace of Napoleon I (who was known as 'the Corsican'); pop. (1982) 240,178; capital, Ajaccio. —**Corsican** *adj. & n.*

corslet /ˈkɔːslɪt/ *n.* **1.** a garment (usually tight-fitting) covering the body. **2.** (*hist.*) armour covering the trunk of the body. [f. OF, as prec.]

cortège /kɔːˈteɪʒ/ *n.* a procession, especially for a funeral. [F]

Cortés /ˈkɔːtez/, Hernando (1485–1547), Spanish conqueror of Mexico. The first of the conquistadors, Cortés successfully overthrew the Aztec empire with a tiny army of adventurers, taking its capital city in 1519 and deposing the emperor Montezuma.

cortex /ˈkɔːteks/ *n.* (*pl.* **cortices** /-ɪsiːz/) the outer covering of the kidney or other organ (ill. BODY 3); the outer grey matter of the brain. —**cortical** *adj.*, **corticated** *adj.* [L, = bark]

cortisone /ˈkɔːtɪzəʊn/ *n.* a hormone used medically against inflammation and allergy. [abbr. of chemical name]

corundum /kəˈrʌndəm/ *n.* extremely hard crystallized alumina, used especially as an abrasive. [f. Tamil f. Skr., = ruby]

coruscate /ˈkɒrəskeɪt/ *v.i.* to sparkle, to shine. —**coruscation** /-ˈskeɪʃ(ə)n/ *n.* [f. L *coruscare* glitter]

corvette /kɔːˈvet/ *n.* a small naval escort vessel; (*hist.*) a flush-decked warship with one tier of guns. [F, f. MDu. *corf* kind of ship]

corymb /ˈkɒrɪmb/ *n.* a flat-topped cluster of flowers on a long stem with the stems lengthening away from the centre (ill. PLANTS). [f. F or L f. Gk, = cluster]

cos¹ /kɒs/ *n.* a crisp lettuce with narrow leaves. [f. *Cos*, island in the Aegean, where it originated]

cos² /kɒs, -z/ *abbr.* cosine.

cos³ /kɒz/ *conj.* (*colloq.*) because. [abbr.]

cosec. /ˈkəʊsek/ *abbr.* cosecant.

cosecant /kəʊˈsiːkənt/ *n.* the secant of the complement of a given angle. [f. CO- + SECANT]

cosh *n.* (*colloq.*) a heavy blunt weapon. —*v.t.* (*colloq.*) to hit with a cosh. [orig. unkn.]

cosine /ˈkəʊsaɪn/ *n.* the ratio of the side adjacent to the acute angle (in a right-angled triangle) to the hypotenuse. [f. CO- + SINE]

cosmetic /kɒzˈmetɪk/ *adj.* **1.** designed to beautify the skin, hair, etc.; (of a body treatment or surgery) improving or restoring the normal appearance. **2.** superficially improving or beneficial. —*n.* a cosmetic preparation, especially for the face. —**cosmetically** *adv.* [f. F f. Gk (*kosmeō* adorn)]

cosmic /ˈkɒzmɪk/ *adj.* of the cosmos, especially as distinct from the earth; of or for space travel. —**cosmic rays** *or* **radiation,** high energy radiation from outer space. [f. COSMOS[1]]

cosmogony /kɒzˈmɒɡənɪ/ *n.* the origin of the universe; a theory about this. [f. Gk (as COSMOS[1], -*gonia* begetting)]

cosmology /kɒzˈmɒlədʒɪ/ *n.* the science of the creation and development of the universe. While ancient cosmologies supposed the world to be supported on the backs of elephants standing upon tortoises, or placed Earth at the centre of a universe of concentric crystal spheres, modern science debates whether an infinite and unchanging universe is maintained by the continuous creation of matter from the void, or whether a big bang both created and dispersed matter in an expansion which continues today, and which may be reversed if the universe is dense enough. The last of these interpretations is favoured by the detection of a radiation field permeating the universe, believed to be the cool remnant of the initial fireball. —**cosmological** /-ˈlɒdʒɪk(ə)l/ *adj.*, **cosmologist** *n.* [f. COSMOS + -LOGY]

cosmonaut /ˈkɒzmənɔːt/ *n.* a Russian astronaut. [f. COSMOS[1], after *astronaut*]

cosmopolitan /kɒzməˈpɒlɪt(ə)n/ *adj.* of or from many parts of the world; free from national limitations or prejudices. —*n.* a cosmopolitan person. —**cosmopolitanism** *n.* [f. Gk *kosmopolitēs* citizen of the world]

cosmos[1] /ˈkɒzmɒs/ *n.* the universe as a well-ordered whole. [Gk, = order, ornament, world, or universe]

cosmos[2] /ˈkɒzmɒs/ *n.* a garden plant of the genus *Cosmos*, with pink, white, or purple flowers. [as prec.]

Cossack /ˈkɒsæk/ *n.* a member of those Russians who sought a free life in the steppes or on the frontiers of imperial Russia and were allowed privileges by the Tsars, including autonomy for their settlements in southern Russia (especially the Ukraine) and Siberia in return for service in protecting the frontiers; a descendant of these, noted for warlike qualities and for horsemanship. [ult. f. Turki, = nomad, adventurer (first used of an unrelated nomadic people, the Kazakhs, of S. Siberia)]

cosset /ˈkɒsɪt/ *v.t.* to pamper. [f. earlier = pet lamb, f. AF f. OE *cotsǣta* cottager]

cost *v.t.* **1.** (*past & p.p.* **cost**) to be obtainable for (a certain sum), to have as a price; to require as an effort; to involve as a loss or sacrifice. **2.** (*past & p.p.* **costed**) to fix or estimate the cost of. —*n.* what a thing costs, a price; an expenditure of time or effort; a loss or sacrifice; (in *pl.*) legal expenses. —**at all costs**, no matter what the cost or risk may be. **cost-effective** effective in relation to its cost. **cost of living,** the level of prices especially of basic necessities. **cost price,** the price paid for a thing by one who later sells it. [f. OF f. L *constare* stand at a price]

costal /ˈkɒst(ə)l/ *adj.* of the ribs. [f. F f. L (*costa* rib)]

co-star *n.* a cinema or stage star appearing with another or others of equal importance. —*v.t.* (-**rr**-) to include as a co-star.

Costa Rica /kɒstə ˈriːkə/ a country in Central America on the Isthmus of Panama, with Nicaragua to the north and Panama to the south-east. The population is chiefly of European stock; pop. (est. 1981) 2,276,676; official language, Spanish; capital, San José. Colonized by Spain in the early 16th c., Costa Rica achieved independence in 1823 and finally emerged as a separate country in 1838 after 14 years within the Federation of Central America. Since then it has been one of the most stable and prosperous States in the region, enjoying high literacy and standards of living. The economy is chiefly agricultural, and the forests which cover most of the land produce valuable timber. In 1948 the army was abolished, the President declaring it unnecessary as the country loved peace. —**Costa Rican** *adj. & n.*

coster *n.* a costermonger. [abbr.]

costermonger /ˈkɒstəmʌŋɡə(r)/ *n.* a person who sells fruit, vegetables, etc., from a barrow in the street. [f. *costard* large apple f. OF *coste* rib (as COSTAL)]

costive /ˈkɒstɪv/ *adj.* constipated. [f. OF f. L (as CONSTIPATE)]

costly *adj.* costing much, expensive. —**costliness** *n.* [f. COST]

costume /ˈkɒstjuːm/ *n.* a style of dress, especially as associated with a particular place or time; a set of clothes; clothes or a garment for a particular activity; an actor's clothes for a part. —**costume jewellery,** jewellery made of inexpensive materials. [F f. It., f. L *consuetudo* custom]

costumier /kɒˈstjuːmɪə(r)/ *n.* one who makes or deals in costumes. [F (as prec.)]

cosy /ˈkəʊzɪ/ *adj.* comfortable and warm, snug. —*n.* a cover to keep hot a teapot or boiled egg. —*v.t.* (often with *along*) (*colloq.*) to reassure, to delude. —**cosily** *adv.*, **cosiness** *n.* [orig. Sc.; etym. unkn.]

cot[1] *n.* a bed with high sides for a baby or very young child; a small light bed. —**cot-death** *n.* an unexplained death of a sleeping baby. [f. Hindi, = bedstead, hammock]

cot[2] *n.* a small shelter; a cote; (*poetic*) a cottage. [OE, rel. to COTE]

cot[3] *abbr.* cotangent.

cotangent /ˈkəʊtændʒ(ə)nt/ *n.* the tangent of the complement of a given angle. [f. CO- + TANGENT]

cote *n.* a shed, stall, or shelter, especially for birds or animals. [OE]

coterie /ˈkəʊtərɪ/ *n.* an exclusive group of people sharing an interest. [F, orig. = association of tenants]

Cotman /ˈkɒtmən/, John Sell (1782–1842), English artist, whose importance as a landscape painter transcends his position as drawing-master to the East Anglian gentry. His early watercolours (e.g. *Greta Bridge*, 1805) have been compared in their compositional daring to Chinese painting. In 1817–20 he visited Normandy and developed a more richly coloured style. From 1834 he lived and taught in London and there developed his considerable skills as an engraver to become one of the most distinctive British etchers of the 19th c.

cotoneaster /kətəʊnɪˈæstə(r)/ *n.* a shrub or small tree bearing red or orange berries. [f. L *cotoneum* quince]

Cotswold Hills /ˈkɒtswəʊld/ (also **Cotswolds**) a range of limestone hills, largely in Gloucestershire, noted for sheep pastures and formerly a centre of the woollen industry.

cottage /ˈkɒtɪdʒ/ *n.* a small simple house, especially in the country. —**cottage cheese,** a soft white cheese made from curds of skim milk without pressing. **cottage industry,** one carried on at home. **cottage pie,** a dish of minced meat topped with mashed potato. [f. AF (as COT[2])]

cottager *n.* one who lives in a cottage. [f. prec.]

cottar /ˈkɒtə(r)/ *n.* (also **cotter**[1]) (*hist. & Sc.*) a farm-labourer having free use of a cottage. [f. COT[2]]

cotter[2] *n.* a bolt or wedge for securing parts of machinery etc. —**cotter pin,** a cotter, a split pin put through a cotter to keep it in place. [orig. unkn.]

cotton /ˈkɒt(ə)n/ *n.* a soft white fibrous substance covering the seeds of tropical plants of the genus *Gossypium*; such a plant; thread or cloth made from this. —*v.i.* **cotton on (to),** (*slang*) to understand; to form a liking or attachment for. —**cotton wool,** fluffy wadding of a kind originally made from raw cotton. —**cottony** *adj.* [f. OF f. Arab.]

cotyledon /kɒtɪˈliːd(ə)n/ *n.* the first leaf produced by a plant embryo (ill. PLANTS). [L f. Gk (*kotulē* cup)]

couch[1] /kaʊtʃ/ *n.* **1.** a piece of furniture like a sofa but with the back extending along half its length and only one raised end; a sofa or settee. **2.** a bed-like structure on which a doctor's patient can lie for examination. —*v.t./i.* **1.** to express in words of a certain kind. **2.** to lay as on a couch. **3.** to lie in a lair etc. or in ambush. **4.** to lower (a spear) to the position for attack. [f. OF f. L *collocare* lay in place]

couch[2] /kuːtʃ, kaʊtʃ/ *n.* (in full **couch-grass**) a grassy weed (*Elymus repens*) with long creeping roots. [var. of QUITCH]

couchant /ˈkaʊtʃ(ə)nt/ *adj.* (in heraldry, of an animal) lying with the body resting on the legs and the head raised. (ill. HERALDRY). [F, as COUCH[1]]

couchette /kuːˈʃet/ *n.* a railway carriage with seats that are convertible into sleeping-berths; a berth in this. [F, = little bed]

Coué /ˈkuːeɪ/, Émile (1857–26), French psychologist, advocate of a system of optimistic auto-suggestion. —**Couéism** *n.*

cougar /ˈkuːɡə(r)/ *n.* (*US*) a puma. [F, f. Guarani]

cough /kɒf/ *v.t./i.* **1.** to expel air or other matter from the lungs with a sudden sharp sound; (of an engine etc.) to make a similar sound. **2.** (*slang*) to confess. —*n.* the act or sound of coughing; a condition of the respiratory organs causing coughing. —**cough mixture,** a medicine to relieve a cough. **cough up,** to eject or say with coughs; (*slang*) to bring out or give (money or information) reluctantly. [imit., rel. to Du. *kuchen*]

could /kʊd/ *v.aux.* **1.** *past* of CAN[1]. **2.** to feel inclined to. —**could be,** (*colloq.*) might be; that may be true.

couldn't /ˈkʊd(ə)nt/ (*colloq.*) = could not.

Coulomb /ˈkuːlɒm/, Charles-Augustin de (1736–1806), French military engineer. He had a good grasp of mathematics and was a skilful experimenter, conducting fundamental research on structural mechanics, elasticity, friction, electricity, and magnetism. He is best known for Coulomb's Law, established with a sensitive torsion balance in 1785, according to which the forces between two electrical charges are proportional to the product of the sizes of the charges and inversely proportional to the square of the distance between them. At last the inverse-square law of electrostatic force had been verified and the quantity of electric charge could be defined. A unit of charge, the coulomb, has been named in his honour.

coulomb /ˈkuːlɒm/ *n.* a unit of electric charge, the quantity of electricity conveyed in one second by a current of one ampere. [f. prec.]

coulter /ˈkoʊltə(r)/ *n.* a vertical blade in front of a plough-share. [OE f. L *culter* knife]

council /ˈkaʊns(ə)l/ *n.* an advisory, deliberative, or administrative body; a meeting of the local administrative body of a county, city, town, etc. —**council house,** a house owned and let by a local council. [f. AF f. L *concilium* assembly; cf. COUNSEL]

councillor /ˈkaʊns(ə)lə(r)/ *n.* a member of a council, especially of a local administrative council. [alt. of COUNSELLOR]

counsel /ˈkaʊns(ə)l/ *n.* **1.** advice formally given; consultation, especially to seek or give advice; professional guidance. **2.** a legal adviser (esp. a barrister); a group of these. —*v.t.* (**-ll-**) **1.** to advise, to recommend. **2.** to give professional guidance to (a person in need of psychological help). —**counsel of despair,** an action to be taken when all else fails. **counsel of perfection,** ideal but impracticable advice. **keep one's own counsel,** not to confide in others. **King's** or **Queen's Counsel,** counsel to the Crown, taking precedence over other barristers. **take counsel,** to consult *with*. [f. OF f. L *consilium* (*consulere* consult)]

counsellor /ˈkaʊns(ə)lə(r)/ *n.* an adviser; one who gives counsel. [as prec.]

count[1] /kaʊnt/ *v.t./i.* **1.** to find the number of (things etc.), especially by assigning successive numerals; to repeat numerals in order. **2.** to include or be included in a reckoning or consideration. **3.** to have a certain value or significance. **4.** to regard or consider. —*n.* **1.** counting, a calculation. **2.** a total. **3.** any of the points being considered. **4.** each of the charges in a legal indictment. —**count on,** to rely on, to expect. **count out,** to exclude, to disregard; to complete a count of 10 seconds over (a fallen boxer etc.); to procure an adjournment of (the House of Commons) for lack of a quorum. **count up,** to find the total of. **keep** or **lose count,** to know or not know how many there have been. **out for the count,** defeated, unconscious. [f. OF f. L *computare* compute]

count[2] /kaʊnt/ *n.* a foreign nobleman equivalent in rank to an earl. [f. OF f. L *comes* companion]

countdown *n.* counting numerals backwards to zero, especially before launching a spacecraft etc.

countenance /ˈkaʊntɪnəns/ *n.* **1.** a facial expression, the face; composure of the face. **2.** moral support or approval. —*v.t.* to give approval to (an act); to encourage or connive at (a person or practice). —**keep one's countenance,** to maintain composure, to refrain from laughing. [f. OF (*contenir* contain)]

counter[1] /ˈkaʊntə(r)/ *n.* **1.** a flat-topped fitment in a shop etc. over which goods are sold or served or business is conducted with customers. **2.** a small disc used in table-games for scoring etc. **3.** a token representing a coin. **4.** a device for counting. —**under the counter,** surreptitiously, illegally. [f. OF f. L *computatorium* (as COMPUTE)]

counter[2] /ˈkaʊntə(r)/ *v.t./i.* **1.** to oppose, to contradict. **2.** to make or meet by a countermove; to baffle or frustrate thus. **3.** to give a return blow in boxing. —*adv.* in the opposite direction or manner. —*adj.* opposite. —*n.* **1.** a return action or blow; a countermove. **2.** the stiff part of a

shoe or boot round the heel. **3.** the curved part of a ship's stern. [f. foll.]

counter- *prefix* forming verbs, nouns, adjectives, and adverbs, implying retaliation or reversal (*counterstroke, counter-clockwise*), rivalry or opposition (*counter-attraction, counter-current*), reciprocity or correspondence (*countersign, counterpart*). [f. OF *contre* f. L *contra* against]

counteract /kaʊntəˈrækt/ *v.t.* to neutralize, hinder, or defeat by contrary action. —**counteraction** *n.*, **counteractive** *adj.*

counter-attack *n.* an attack made to meet an enemy's or opponent's attack. —*v.t./i.* to make a counter-attack (on).

counterbalance *n.* a weight or influence that balances another. —*v.t.* to be a counterbalance to, to neutralize thus.

countercheck *n.* **1.** an obstruction checking movement or operating against another check. **2.** a second test for verifying another. —*v.t.* to verify by a second test.

counter-clockwise *adj.* & *adv.* anticlockwise.

counter-espionage *n.* action taken to uncover and frustrate enemy espionage.

counterfeit /ˈkaʊntəfiːt, -fɪt/ *adj.* made in imitation of and of inferior material, usually to defraud; not genuine, forged. —*n.* a counterfeit thing. —*v.t.* to make a counterfeit of in order to defraud, to forge. [f. p.p. of OF *contrefaire* f. L, = make in opposition]

counterfoil /ˈkaʊntəfɔɪl/ *n.* the part of a cheque, receipt, etc., retained as a record by the person issuing it.

counter-intelligence *n.* counter-espionage.

countermand /kaʊntəˈmɑːnd/ *v.t.* to revoke or cancel (a command). —*n.* a command cancelling a previous one. [f. OF f. L *contramandare* (CONTRA-, *mandare* order)]

countermarch *n.* a march in the opposite direction. —*v.t./i.* to march or cause to march back.

countermeasure *n.* an action taken to counteract a danger or threat.

countermove *n.* a move or action taken in opposition to another.

counterpane /ˈkaʊntəpeɪn/ *n.* a bedspread. [f. OF f. L *culcita puncta* quilted mattress]

counterpart /ˈkaʊntəpɑːt/ *n.* a person or thing like or naturally complementary to another; a duplicate.

counterpoint *n.* a melody added as an accompaniment to a given melody; the art or mode of adding melodies as an accompaniment according to fixed rules (see below). —*v.t.* to add counterpoint to; to set in contrast. [f. OF f. L *contrapunctum* pricked or marked opposite, i.e. to the original melody]

The practice of adding a part or parts to an existing melody according to more or less strict rules arose in sacred music of the 9th c., and from simple progressions in parallel octaves and fifths the intricate art of counterpoint developed until in the 16th and early 17th c. it embraced rhythmically and melodically distinct movement in as many parts as the composer felt he could control. Fugue and canon are familiar contrapuntal forms.

counterpoise /ˈkaʊntəpɔɪz/ *n.* the balancing of each other by two weights or forces; a counterbalancing weight or force. —*v.t.* to counterbalance; to compensate for. [f. OF f. L (CONTRA-, *pensum* weight)]

counter-productive *adj.* having the opposite of the desired effect.

Counter-Reformation *n.* the revival of the Roman Catholic Church in Europe from the mid-16th–mid-17th c. Though stimulated by Protestant opposition, reform movements within the Roman Catholic Church had begun almost simultaneously with the Lutheran schism, aimed at countering the abuses of the Renaissance age. The Jesuit order became the spearhead of the movement both within Europe and as a missionary force in America and the East, while the power of the papacy triumphed over those Catholics who wished for conciliation with the Protestants and over those French and Spanish bishops who opposed papal claims. Spain, the strongest military power of the day, constituted itself the secular arm of the Counter-Reformation in Europe, and the Inquisition was extended to other countries. Although most of northern Europe remained Protestant, South Germany and Poland were brought back to the Roman obedience.

counter-revolution *n.* a revolution opposing a former one or reversing its results.

countersign /ˈkaʊntəsaɪn/ *v.t.* to add a confirming signature to (a document already signed by another). —*n.* a word required in answer to a sentry's challenge; an identificatory mark. —**counter-signature** /-sɪg-/ n. [f. F f. It. (as COUNTER-, SIGN)]

countersink /ˈkaʊntəsɪŋk/ v.t. (past & p.p. **-sunk**) to shape the top of (a screw-hole) with a tapered enlargement so that a screw-head lies level with or below the surface; to sink (a screw etc.) in such a hole.

counterstroke /ˈkaʊntəstrəʊk/ n. a stroke given in return.

counter-tenor n. a male singing-voice higher than tenor but with its quality; a singer with such a voice; a part written for it.

countervail /ˈkaʊntəveɪl/ v.t. to counterbalance; to avail against. [f. AF f. L contra valēre be of worth against]

counterweight /ˈkaʊntəweɪt/ n. a counterbalancing weight.

countess /ˈkaʊntɪs/ n. the wife or widow of an earl or count; a woman holding the rank of an earl or count. [f. OF f. L comitissa (as COUNT²)]

countless /ˈkaʊntlɪs/ adj. too many to be counted.

countrified /ˈkʌntrɪfaɪd/ adj. rustic in appearance or manners. [f. foll.]

country /ˈkʌntrɪ/ n. **1.** the territory of a nation; the State of which one is a member. **2.** the national population (esp. as electors). **3.** a land or region with regard to its aspect or associations. **4.** open regions of fields and woods etc. as distinct from towns or the capital (often attrib.). **5.** country-and-western. —**country-and-western** n. rural or cowboy songs to the guitar. **country club,** a sporting social club in a rural area. **country dance,** a traditional English dance, often with couples face to face in lines. **go to the country,** to appeal to the body of electors after an adverse or doubtful vote in the House of Commons, or at the end of a government's term of office, by effecting the dissolution of Parliament and holding a general election. [f. OF f. L contrata (terra) land lying opposite (as CONTRA-)]

countryman n. (pl. **-men**) **1.** a person living in rural parts. **2.** a fellow-member of a State or district. —**countrywoman** n.fem. (pl. **-women**)

countryside n. country districts.

country-wide adj. extending throughout a nation.

county /ˈkaʊntɪ/ n. **1.** a territorial division of a country, forming the chief unit of local administration and justice; (US) a political and administrative division next below a State. **2.** the people of a county; long-established families of a high social level. —**county council,** the elected governing body of an administrative county. **county court,** a local court for civil cases. **county town,** a town that is the administrative centre of a county. [f. AF f. L comitatus (as COUNT²)]

couvade /kuːˈvɑːd/ n. a primitive people's custom whereby a husband feigns illness and is put to bed when his wife is giving birth to a child. [F (couver hatch, f. L cubare lie down)]

coup /kuː/ n. a successful stroke or move, a coup d'état. [F f. L colpus blow]

coup de grâce /kuː də ˈgrɑːs/ a finishing stroke. [F]

coup d'état /kuː deɪˈtɑː/ the sudden overthrow of a government, especially by force.[F]

coupé /ˈkuːpeɪ/ n. a closed two-door car with a sloping back. [F (couper cut)]

Couperin /ˈkuːpəræ̃/, François (1668–1733), French composer, organist, and harpsichordist. As a composer at the court of Louis XIV he participated in concerts at Versailles, Fontainebleau, and Sceaux, and many of his over 230 harpsichord pieces, nearly all with descriptive titles, were composed for such royal surroundings. He combined elements of the prevailing Italian style with the French tradition, and the resulting delicacy of idiom and strength of invention have been aptly compared with the painting of Watteau. His treatise on playing the harpsichord (1716) influenced Bach.

couple /ˈkʌp(ə)l/ n. **1.** a man and woman who are engaged or married to each other. **2.** a pair of partners in a dance etc. **3.** two things, or (loosely) several things. —v.t./i. **1.** to link or associate together. **2.** to copulate. [f. OF f. L copula fastening]

couplet /ˈkʌplɪt/ n. two successive lines of verse, especially when rhyming and of the same length. [F (as prec.)]

coupling /ˈkʌplɪŋ/ n. **1.** a link connecting two railway vehicles or two parts of machinery. **2.** the arrangement of items on a gramophone record.

coupon /ˈkuːpɒn/ n. **1.** a small often detachable piece of

printed paper entitling the holder to specified goods or a service or some concession. **2.** a small printed form of application or entry for a competition etc. [F (couper cut)]

courage /ˈkʌrɪdʒ/ n. readiness to face and endure danger or difficulty; the ability to control or suppress fear or its disturbing effects; a courageous mood or inclination. —**have the courage of one's convictions,** to have the courage to do what one believes to be right. [f. OF f. L (cor heart)]

courageous /kəˈreɪdʒəs/ adj. having or showing courage. —**courageously** adv. [as prec.]

Courbet /kʊəˈbeɪ/, Gustave (1819–77), French painter, who set himself up as the leader of the realist school of painting, choosing his themes from contemporary life and not excluding what was ugly or vulgar. He was an innovator in his choice of subject-matter, which he used for its pictorial value rather than for emotional impact.

courgette /kʊəˈʒet/ n. a small green or yellow vegetable marrow. [F (courge gourd)]

courier /ˈkʊrɪə(r)/ n. **1.** a special messenger. **2.** a person employed to guide and assist a group of tourists. [f. F f. It. corriere f. L (currere run)]

course /kɔːs/ n. **1.** an onward movement in space or time; a direction taken or intended; the direction or channel followed by a river etc. **2.** the successive development of events, the ordinary sequence or order; a line of conduct or action. **3.** a series of lectures, lessons, etc., in a particular subject; a sequence of medical treatment. **4.** each successive part of a meal. **5.** a golf-course; a racecourse. **6.** a continuous row of masonry at one level in a building. —v.t./i. **1.** to use hounds to hunt (esp. hares). **2.** to move or flow freely. —**in the course of,** in the process of. **in due course,** at about the expected time. **of course,** as is or was to be expected, without doubt, admittedly. [f. OF f. L cursus (currere run)]

courser /ˈkɔːsə(r)/ n. **1.** a fast-running African or Asian bird. **2.** (poetic) a swift horse. [f. L (as prec.)]

court /kɔːt/ n. **1.** a courtyard; a yard surrounded by houses, with entry from the street. **2.** an enclosed or marked area for some games, e.g. squash and tennis. **3.** (also **Court**) a sovereign's establishment with courtiers and attendants; this as representing a country; a reception at court. **4.** (in full **court of law**) a judicial body hearing legal cases; the place where this meets; the judges of a court. —v.t. to treat flatteringly or with special attention; to seek to attract the favour or love of; to seek to win; to make oneself vulnerable to. —**court-card** n. a playing-card that is a king, queen, or jack. **court-house** n. the building in which a court of law is held; (US) the building containing the administrative offices of a county. **court martial,** (pl. **courts martial**) a judicial court of naval, military, or air force officers for trying charges involving offences against military law; trial by such a court. **court-martial** v.t. (-ll-) to try by court martial. **Court of Arches,** the ecclesiastical court of appeal for the province of Canterbury, so known because it was formerly held at the church of St Mary-le-Bow, famous for its arched crypt. **Court of St James's,** the court of the British sovereign. **court shoe,** a woman's light shoe with a low-cut upper. **go to court,** to take legal action. **hold court,** to preside over one's admirers. **out of court,** (of a settlement) without reaching trial; not worth discussing. **pay court to,** to court (a person) to win favour. **put out of court,** to refuse or make it inappropriate to consider. [f. AF f. L cohors yard, retinue]

courteous /ˈkɜːtɪəs/ adj. polite, considerate. —**courteously** adv. [f. OF (as prec.)]

courtesan /kɔːtɪˈzæn/ n. a prostitute with clients among the wealthy or nobility. [f. F f. It. (cortigiano courtier)]

courtesy /ˈkɜːtəsɪ/ n. courteous behaviour, a courteous act. —**by courtesy of,** by permission of. **courtesy light,** a light in a car that is switched on automatically by opening the door. [f. OF (as COURTEOUS)]

courtier /ˈkɔːtɪə(r)/ n. a companion of the sovereign at court. [f. AF (as COURT)]

courtly /ˈkɔːtlɪ/ adj. polished or refined in manners. —**courtly love,** the conventional medieval tradition of knightly love and etiquette. —**courtliness** n. [f. COURT]

courtship n. courting, especially of an intended wife; a period of courting.

courtyard n. a space enclosed by walls or buildings.

couscous /ˈkuːskuːs/ n. a North African dish of crushed wheat or coarse flour steamed over broth, often with meat or fruit added. [F f. Arab. (kaskasa to pound)]

cousin /ˈkʌz(ə)n/ n. **1.** (also **first cousin, cousin german**) a son or daughter of one's uncle or aunt; (also **first cousin once** (*or* **twice** etc.) **removed**) a son or daughter (or grandson etc.) of one's first cousin, one's parent's (or grandparent's etc.) cousin; (also **second cousin**) a son or daughter of one's parent's first cousin. **2.** (*hist.*) the title used by one sovereign addressing another. —**cousinly** *adj.* [f. OF f. L *consobrinus*]

Cousteau /ˈkuːstəʊ/, Jacques-Yves (1910–), French oceanographer and film director. A naval officer keenly interested in underwater exploration, he began using a camera under water in 1939 as an aid to research. He made a number of short films recording underwater expeditions and three feature films, *The Silent World* (1956), *World Without Sun* (1964), and *Voyage to the Edge of the World* (jointly with Philippe Cousteau, 1976). He has also made several series for television.

couture /kuːˈtjʊə(r)/ *n.* the design and making of high-quality fashionable clothes. [F, = sewing, dressmaking]

couturier /kuːˈtjʊərieɪ/ *n.* a fashion designer. —**couturière** /-ieə(r)/ *n. fem.* [F]

couvade /kuːˈvaːd/ *n.* a custom of some primitive peoples by which the husband feigns illness and is put to bed when his wife is giving birth to a child. [F (*couver* hatch f. L *cubare* lie down)]

cove[1] *n.* **1.** a small bay or inlet of the coast; a sheltered recess. **2.** a curved moulding at the junction of a ceiling and a wall. —*v.t.* **1.** to provide (a room etc.) with a cove. **2.** to slope (the sides of a fireplace) inwards. [OE, = chamber]

cove[2] *n.* (*slang*) a fellow, a man. [orig. unkn.]

coven /ˈkʌv(ə)n/ *n.* an assembly of witches. [f. OF *covent* (as CONVENT)]

covenant /ˈkʌvənənt/ *n.* a formal agreement, (*Law*) a sealed contract; the biblical compact between God and the Israelites. —*v.t./i.* to agree, especially by legal covenant (*with* a person). [f. OF *co*(*n*)*venir* (as CONVENE)]

covenanter *n.* **1.** one who covenants. **2. Covenanter,** a supporter of the Scottish National Covenant of 1638 and the Solemn League and Covenant (1643; see separate entry), proclamations defending Presbyterianism and resisting the religious policies of Charles I. The name was later applied to those who opposed the reintroduction of episcopacy to Scotland in 1662. The Covenanters were ruthlessly persecuted in 1678–85. [f. prec.]

Covent Garden /ˈkʌvənt/ a district in central London, originally the convent garden of the Abbey of Westminster. It was the site for 300 years of London's chief fruit and vegetable market, which in 1974 was moved to Nine Elms, Battersea. The first Covent Garden Theatre was opened in 1732 and such famous plays as Goldsmith's *She Stoops to Conquer* (1773) and Sheridan's *The Rivals* (1775) were first performed there. It was several times destroyed and reconstructed, and since 1946 has been the home of London's chief opera and ballet companies.

Coventry /ˈkɒvəntrɪ/ **send to Coventry,** to refuse to speak to or associate with. The origin of the phrase is unknown. One suggestion is based on Clarendon's statement that during the English Civil War Royalists taken prisoner at Birmingham were sent to Coventry, which was a Parliamentary stronghold; soldiers of the rival faction who were sent there would be cut off from social intercourse—whence, perhaps, the phrase. [name of town in W. Midlands]

cover /ˈkʌvə(r)/ *v.t.* **1.** to lie or extend over, to form or occupy the whole surface of. **2.** to conceal or protect (a thing) by placing something on or in front of it; to provide (a person) with something that covers; to protect, to clothe; to strew thoroughly *with.* **3.** to enclose or include; to deal with (a subject). **4.** to travel (a specified distance etc.). **5.** to be enough money to pay for. **6.** to investigate or describe as a reporter. **7.** (of a fortification or gun etc.) to have within its range; to protect from a commanding position; to keep a gun aimed at; to have within one's range of fire; to protect by firing against the enemy. **8.** to protect or oppose (another player) in field-games. **9.** (of a stallion etc.) to mate with. **10.** to deputize temporarily *for.* **11.** (in *p.p.*) wearing a hat, having a roof. —*n.* **1.** a thing that covers, a lid, a top. **2.** the binding of a book; one board of this. **3.** an envelope or other postal wrapping. **4.** shelter, protection. **5.** a screen, a pretence; a pretended identity. **6.** funds from an insurance to meet a liability or contingent loss, protection by insurance. **7.** a supporting force protecting another from attack. **8.** an individual place-setting at a meal. **9.** cover-point (ill. SPORTS). —**cover charge,** an extra charge per person in a restaurant etc. **cover girl,** a girl whose picture appears on magazine covers. **covering letter** *or* **note,** one

sent with and explaining goods or documents. **cover note,** a temporary certificate of current insurance. **cover-point** *n.* a cricket fieldsman covering point. **cover-up** *n.* a concealment, especially of facts. **take cover,** to seek shelter. **under cover,** in secret, sheltered from the weather. **under cover of,** hidden or protected by (e.g. darkness); with an outward show of (e.g. friendship). [f. OF f. L *cooperire* (CO-, *operire* cover)]

coverage /ˈkʌvərɪdʒ/ *n.* the area or amount covered or reached; the reporting of events in a newspaper etc. [f. prec.]

coverall /ˈkʌvərɔːl/ *n.* a thing that covers entirely; (usu. in *pl.*) a full-length protective garment.

Coverdale /ˈkʌvədeɪl/, Miles (1488–1568), translator of the first complete printed English Bible (1535), produced while he was in exile on the Continent for preaching against confession and images. In 1539, with R. Grafton, he issued the Great Bible; under Elizabeth I he became a Puritan leader.

coverlet /ˈkʌvəlɪt/ *n.* a covering, especially a bedspread. [f. AF (as COVER, *lit* bed)]

covert /ˈkʌvət/ *adj.* disguised, not open or explicit. —*n.* **1.** a wood or thicket affording cover for game. **2.** a feather covering the base of a bird's wing-feather or tail-feather (ill. BIRDS). —**covertly** *adv.* [as COVER]

covet /ˈkʌvɪt/ *v.t.* to envy another the possession of, to long to possess. [f. OF f. L (as CUPIDITY)]

covetous /ˈkʌvɪtəs/ *adj.* coveting, avaricious, grasping. —**covetously** *adv.,* **covetousness** *n.* [as prec.]

covey /ˈkʌvɪ/ *n.* **1.** a brood of partridges (esp. flying together). **2.** a small group of people. [f. OF f. L (*cubare* lie)]

cow[1] *n.* (*pl.* **cows,** *archaic* **kine**) **1.** the fully-grown female of any bovine animal, especially of the domestic species used as a source of milk and beef. **2.** the female of other large animals, especially the elephant, whale, or seal. —**cow-lick** *n.* a projecting lock of hair. **cow-pat** *n.* a flat round piece of cow-dung. [OE]

cow[2] *v.t.* to intimidate, to dispirit. [f. ON *kúga* oppress]

Coward /ˈkaʊəd/, Sir Noël Pierce (1899–1973), English playwright, actor, and composer. His plays of the 1920s, which matched the contemporary mood of smart sophistication, established his popularity, and his continuing production of plays, revues, musical plays, operettas, and films, spiced with wit and sweetened with sentimentality, added to it. Among his best-known works are the plays *Private Lives* (1930), *Cavalcade* (1931), *Blithe Spirit* (1941), and the operetta *Bitter Sweet* (1929).

coward /ˈkaʊəd/ *n.* a person easily giving way to fear and lacking courage. [f. OF f. L *cauda* tail]

cowardice /ˈkaʊədɪs/ *n.* cowardly feelings or conduct. [as prec.]

cowardly *adj.* of or like a coward, lacking courage; (of an action) done against one who cannot retaliate. —**cowardliness** *n.* [f. COWARD]

cowbell *n.* a bell hung round a cow's neck.

cowboy *n.* **1.** (in the western US) a man in charge of cattle. **2.** (*colloq.*) an unscrupulous or reckless business man.

cowcatcher *n.* a fender fitted on the front of a locomotive to push aside cattle or other obstacles on the line.

cower *v.i.* to crouch or shrink back, especially in fear; to huddle up. [f. LG *kuren* lie in wait]

Cowes /kaʊz/ a town on the Isle of Wight, famous internationally as a yachting centre.

cowherd *n.* a person who looks after cows at pasture.

cowhide *n.* a cow's hide; leather or a whip made from this.

cowl *n.* **1.** a monk's hood or hooded garment. **2.** a hood-shaped covering, especially of a chimney or shaft. (ill. HOUSES). [OE f. L *cucullus* hood of cloak]

cowling *n.* a removable cover over the engine of a vehicle or aircraft. [f. prec.]

co-worker *n.* one who works in collaboration with another.

Cowper /ˈkuːpə(r)/, William (1731–1800), English poet. He suffered from acute melancholia and turned to evangelical Christianity for consolation. With the curate John Newton he wrote *Olney Hymns* (1779) to which Cowper contributed 'Oh! for a closer walk with God' amongst other congregational favourites. His famous comic ballad, *John Gilpin* appeared in 1782; his long poem *The Task* (1785) is notable for its intimate sketches of rural scenes. After the death of his close friend Mary Unwin he wrote 'The Castaway'

(1803) expressing man's isolation, a theme which recurs in many of his poems.

cowpox *n.* a disease of cows, caused by a virus which is used in vaccination against smallpox.

cowrie /ˈkaʊrɪ/ *n.* a gastropod of the family Cypraeidae, with a glossy shell and an opening that consists of a slit running the length of one side. Such shells were used from the mesolithic period onwards as ornaments, and shells of *Cypraea moneta* are used in parts of Africa and southern Asia as money. [f. Urdu & Hindi]

cowslip *n.* a wild plant (*Primula veris*) with small yellow flowers. [OE (as COW¹, *slyppe* slimy substance, i.e. dung)]

cox *n.* a coxswain, especially of a racing boat. —*v.t./i.* to act as cox (of). [abbr.]

coxcomb /ˈkɒkskəʊm/ *n.* **1.** a conceited showy person. **2.** (*hist.*) a medieval jester's cap. —**coxcombry** *n.* [=*cock's comb*]

coxswain /ˈkɒkswein, ˈkɒks(ə)n/ *n.* **1.** the steersman of a rowing-boat or other small boat. **2.** the senior petty officer in a small ship. —*v.t./i.* to act as coxswain (of). [f. obs. *cock* small boat + SWAIN]

coy *adj.* affectedly modest or bashful; archly reticent. —**coyly** *adv.*, **coyness** *n.* [f. OF f. L *quietus* quiet]

coyote /kɔɪˈəʊtɪ, ˈkɔɪəʊt/ *n.* the North American prairie-wolf (*Canis latrans*). [Mex. Sp. f. Aztec]

coypu /ˈkɔɪpuː/ *n.* a beaver-like water-rodent, originally from South America. [native name in Chile]

cozen /ˈkʌz(ə)n/ *v.t./i.* (*literary*) to cheat, to defraud; to act deceitfully. —**cozenage** *n.* [perh. rel. to COUSIN]

c.p. *abbr.* candlepower.

Cpl. *abbr.* Corporal.

c.p.s. *abbr.* cycles per second.

Cr *symbol* chromium.

crab *n.* **1.** a shellfish, especially of the group Brachyura, with ten legs, of which the front pair are modified into pincers; the flesh of this as food. **2. the Crab**, the constellation or sign of the zodiac Cancer. —*v.t./i.* (*colloq.*) (**-bb-**) to criticize adversely or captiously; to act so as to spoil. — **catch a crab**, to get an oar jammed underwater by a faulty stroke in rowing. **crab-apple** *n.* the fruit of an apple tree, *Malus sylvestris*, that bears small fruit with a harsh sour flavour. **crab-louse** *n.* a parasite infesting the hairy parts of the body. [OE, rel. to LG *krabben*, ON *krafla* scratch]

Crabbe /kræb/, George (1754–1832), English poet. His early life was spent at Aldeburgh, Suffolk, where he experienced much hardship. Crabbe's grimly realistic narrative poems, written in heroic couplets, were once immensely popular; they include the story of Peter Grimes, made the subject of an opera by Benjamin Britten.

crabbed /ˈkræbɪd/ *adj.* **1.** bad-tempered, crabby. **2.** (of writing) difficult to read or decipher. [f. CRAB]

crabby *adj.* irritable, morose. —**crabbily** *adv.*, **crabbiness** *n.* [as prec.]

Crab Nebula an irregular patch of luminous gas in the constellation Taurus, believed to be the remnant of a supernova explosion seen by Chinese astronomers in 1054. At its centre is the first pulsar to be observed visually. The nebula is also a strong source of high-energy radiation.

crabwise *adv.* sideways or backwards like the movement of a crab.

crack *n.* **1.** a sudden sharp explosive sound. **2.** a sharp blow. **3.** a narrow opening; a line of division where something is broken but has not come completely apart. **4.** (*colloq.*) a wisecrack, a joke. —*adj.* (*colloq.*) first-rate. —*v.t./i.* **1.** to break without coming completely apart; to become broken thus; to gape with cracks. **2.** to make or cause to make the sound of a crack; to hit sharply. **3.** to break the case of (a nut); to break into (a safe etc.); to find the solution to (a code or problem). **4.** (of the voice) to become suddenly harsh, as with emotion. **5.** to yield suddenly or cease to resist under strain. **6.** to tell (a joke). **7.** to break down (heavy oils) in order to produce lighter ones. **8.** (in *p.p.*, *colloq.*) crazy, infatuated. —**crack a bottle**, to open it and drink the contents. **crack-brained** *adj.* crazy. **crack down on**, (*colloq.*) to take severe measures against. **crack of dawn**, daybreak. **crack up**, (*colloq.*) to have a physical or mental breakdown; to praise highly (usu. in *pass.*, esp. in *not all it etc is cracked up to be*). **get cracking**, (*colloq.*) to make a start. **have a crack at**, (*colloq.*) to attempt. [OE, = resound]

cracker *n.* **1.** an explosive firework. **2.** a small paper toy in the form of a roll that makes a cracking sound when

pulled apart. **3.** a thin crisp savoury biscuit; (*US*) a biscuit. [f. prec.]

crackers *predic. adj.* (*slang*) crazy. [f. prec.]

crackle /ˈkræk(ə)l/ *n.* the sound of repeated slight cracks as of burning wood. —*v.i.* to emit a crackle. [f. CRACK]

crackling *n.* the crisp skin of roast pork. [f. prec.]

cracknel /ˈkrækn(ə)l/ *n.* a light crisp kind of biscuit. [f. F f. MDu. (as CRACK)]

crackpot *adj.* (*colloq.*) eccentric, unpractical. —*n.* (*colloq.*) an eccentric or unpractical person.

-cracy /krəsɪ/ *suffix* with sense 'rule or ruling body of'. [f. F f. Gk (*kratos* strength)]

cradle /ˈkreɪd(ə)l/ *n.* **1.** a small bed or cot for a baby, usually on rockers. **2.** a place regarded as the origin of something. **3.** a supporting framework or structure. —*v.t.* to place in a cradle; to contain or shelter as in a cradle. [OE]

craft /krɑːft/ *n.* **1.** a special skill or technique; an occupation needing this. **2.** cunning, craftiness. **3.** (*pl.* same) a ship or boat, an aircraft or spacecraft. —*v.t.* to make in a skilful manner. [OE, = OHG *kraft* strength]

craftsman *n.* (*pl.* **-men**) one who practises a craft; a skilled person. —**craftsmanship** *n.*

crafty *adj.* cunning, using underhand methods; ingenious. —**craftily** *adv.*, **craftiness** *n.* [as CRAFT]

crag *n.* a steep rugged rock. —**craggy** *adj.*, **cragginess** *n.* [Celtic]

crake *n.* a bird of the rail family, especially the corncrake. [f. ON, imit. of cry]

cram *v.t./i.* (**-mm-**) **1.** to fill to excess; to force (*in* or *into*). **2.** to feed to excess. **3.** to study intensively for an examination. [OE]

cramp *n.* **1.** a sudden painful involuntary contraction of muscle(s). **2.** (in full **cramp-iron**) a kind of clamp, especially for holding masonry or timbers. —*v.t.* **1.** to affect with cramp. **2.** to restrict or confine narrowly. **3.** to fasten with a cramp. —**cramp a person's style**, to prevent him from acting freely or to his best ability. [f. OF f. MDu., f. adj. meaning 'bent']

cramped *adj.* (of a space) too narrow; (of handwriting) small and with the letters close together. [f. prec.]

crampon /ˈkræmpən/ *n.* an iron plate with spikes fixed to a boot for climbing on ice. [f. F (as prec.)]

cranberry /ˈkrænbərɪ/ *n.* a small acid red berry; the shrub bearing it (*Vaccinium oxycoccus* or *V. macrocarpon*). [after G *kranbeere* crane-berry]

crane *n.* **1.** a machine for moving heavy objects, usually by suspending them from a projecting arm or beam. **2.** a large wading bird of the family Gruidae, with long legs, neck, and bill. —*v.t./i.* to stretch (one's neck) in order to see something. —**crane-fly** *n.* a two-winged insect of the family Tipulidae, with very long legs. **crane's-bill** *n.* a plant of the genus *Geranium*. [OE]

cranium /ˈkreɪnɪəm/ *n.* (*pl.* **-ia**) the bones enclosing the brain; the skull. —**cranial** *adj.* [L f. Gk]

crank¹ *n.* the part of an axle or shaft bent at right angles for converting reciprocal into circular motion, or vice versa. —*v.t.* to move by means of a crank; to start (*up*) (a car engine) by turning a crank. [OE]

crank² *n.* an eccentric person. [back-formation f. CRANKY]

crankcase *n.* the case enclosing a crankshaft.

crankpin *n.* the pin by which the connecting-rod is attached to the crank.

crankshaft *n.* a shaft driven by a crank.

cranky *adj.* **1.** shaky. **2.** crotchety, eccentric; ill-tempered. —**crankily** *adv.*, **crankiness** *n.* [perh. f. obs. *crank* rogue feigning sickness]

Cranmer /ˈkrænmə(r)/, Thomas (1489–1556), Anglican cleric and martyr. He was appointed Archbishop of Canterbury in 1532 after his support for Henry VIII in the annulment of the king's marriage with Catherine of Aragon. Protestant in outlook, he was largely responsible for English liturgical reform, particularly under Edward VI, and for the compilation of the Book of Common Prayer. After the accession of Mary Tudor, Cranmer was tried for high treason, then for heresy, and finally burnt at the stake in Oxford.

crannog /ˈkrænəg/ *n.* a lake-dwelling in Scotland or Ireland, examples of which are found from the neolithic period until medieval times. [Irish (*crann* tree, beam)]

cranny *n.* a crevice. —**crannied** *adj.* [f. OF f. L *crena* notch]

crap *n.* (*vulgar*) faeces; nonsense, rubbish. —*v.i.* (**-pp-**) (*vulgar*) to defecate. —**crappy** *adj.* [f. Du.; orig. = chaff, refuse from fat-boiling]

crape *n.* crêpe, usually of black silk etc., especially for mourning dress. [as CRÊPE]

craps *n.pl.* a game of chance played with dice, popular in the USA since the mid-19th c. —**shoot craps**, to play this. [perh. f. *crab* lowest throw at dice]

crapulent /ˈkræpʊlənt/ *adj.* suffering or resulting from intemperance. —**crapulence** *n.*, **crapulous** *adj.* [f. L f. Gk *kraipalē* drunken headache]

crash[1] *n.* **1.** a sudden violent percussive noise as of something breaking by impact; a fall or impact accompanied by this; a burst of loud sound. **2.** a sudden downfall or collapse (especially of a government or a business). **3.** (*attrib.*) done rapidly or urgently. —*v.t./i.* **1.** to fall, collide, or proceed with a crash, to cause to do this; to make the noise of a crash. **2.** (of an aircraft or pilot) to fall violently to land or sea. **3.** to collapse financially. **4.** to pass (an instruction etc. to stop, especially a red light). **5.** (*colloq.*) to enter or take part in (a party etc.) uninvited. —*adv.* with a crash. —**crash-dive** *v.i.* (of a submarine) to submerge hurriedly in an emergency; (of an aircraft) to dive and crash; (*n.*) the action of this. **crash-helmet** *n.* a helmet worn to protect the head in case of a crash. **crash-land** *v.t./i.* (of an aircraft or pilot) to land hurriedly with a crash. [imit.]

crash[2] *n.* a coarse plain linen or cotton fabric. [f. Russ. *krashenina*]

crashing *adj.* (*colloq.*) overwhelming. [f. CRASH[1]]

crass /kræs/ *adj.* gross; grossly stupid. —**crassly** *adv.*, **crassness** *n.* [f. L *crassus* thick]

-crat *suffix* forming nouns meaning 'a supporter or member of a -cracy'. [f. F f. Gk (as -CRACY)]

crate[1] *n.* **1.** a packing-case made of wooden slats, for conveying fragile goods. **2.** (*slang*) an old aircraft or car. —*v.t.* to pack in a crate. [perh. f. Du. *krat* basket]

crater /ˈkreɪtə(r)/ *n.* the mouth of a volcano; a bowl-shaped cavity, especially that made by the explosion of a shell or bomb. [L f. Gk, = mixing-bowl]

cravat /krəˈvæt/ *n.* **1.** a short scarf. **2.** a broad neck-tie. [f. F f. G f. Serbo-Croatian, = Croat]

-cratic, -cratical *suffixes* forming adjectives from nouns in *-crat*. [f. -CRAT]

crave *v.t./i.* to desire greatly, to long *for;* to ask earnestly for. [OE]

craven /ˈkreɪv(ə)n/ *adj.* cowardly, abject. —*n.* a craven person. [perh. f. OF *cravanté* f. L *crepare* burst]

craving *n.* a strong desire, an intense longing. [f. CRAVE]

craw *n.* the crop of a bird or insect. —**stick in one's craw**, to be unacceptable. [f. MLG or Du.]

crawfish *n.* a large spiny sea-lobster. [var. of CRAYFISH]

Crawford /ˈkrɔːfəd/, Osbert Guy Stanhope (1886–1957), British archaeologist, a pioneer in the use of aerial photography for the detection of previously unlocated or buried archaeological sites and monuments.

crawl *v.i.* **1.** to progress with the body on or close to the ground or other surface, or on hands and knees. **2.** to walk or move or (of time) pass slowly. **3.** (*colloq.*) to seek favour by behaving in a servile way. **4.** to be covered or filled *with*. **5.** (of the skin etc.) to creep. —*n.* **1.** crawling. **2.** a slow rate of motion. **3.** a high-speed overarm swimming stroke. [orig. unkn.]

crayfish *n.* a small lobster-like freshwater crustacean; a crawfish. [f. OF *crevice* crab f. G]

crayon /ˈkreɪən/ *n.* a stick or pencil of coloured wax etc. for drawing. —*v.t.* to draw or colour with crayons. [F (*craie* chalk)]

craze *n.* a great but usually temporary enthusiasm; the object of this. —*v.t.* to make crazy. [orig. = break, shatter; perh. f. ON]

crazy /ˈkreɪzɪ/ *adj.* **1.** insane; foolish, lacking sense. **2.** (*colloq.*) extremely enthusiastic (*about*). **3.** (of a building etc.) unsound. —**crazy paving**, paving made up of irregular pieces. —**like crazy**, (*colloq.*) like mad, very much. —**crazily** *adv.*, **craziness** *n.* [f. prec.]

creak *n.* a harsh strident noise, as of an unoiled hinge. —*v.i.* to make or move with a creak; to be in poor condition. —**creaky** *adj.*, **creakily** *adv.* [imit.]

cream *n.* **1.** the part of milk with a high fat content; its yellowish-white colour. **2.** a creamlike preparation or ointment; a food or drink with the consistency of or compared to cream. **3.** the best part *of.* —*v.t.* **1.** to remove the cream from (milk). **2.** to make creamy; to beat to a creamy consistency. **3.** to apply cosmetic cream to. **4.** to form cream, froth, or scum. —**cream cheese**, a soft rich cheese made of cream or unskimmed milk without pressing. **cream off**, to remove the best or a required part of. **cream of tartar**, purified tartar used in medicine and cooking. [f. OF f. L (as CHRISM)]

creamery /ˈkriːmərɪ/ *n.* a place where dairy products are processed or sold. [f. prec.]

creamy *adj.* like cream; rich in cream. —**creamily** *adv.*, **creaminess** *n.* [f. CREAM]

crease *n.* **1.** a line caused by folding or crushing. **2.** a line defining the position of the bowler or batsman in cricket (ill. SPORTS). —*v.t./i.* **1.** to make creases in; to develop creases. **2.** (*slang*) to stun, to tire out. [earlier *creast* = CREST]

create /kriːˈeɪt/ *v.t./i.* **1.** to bring into existence, to give rise to; to originate. **2.** to invest (a person) with a rank. **3.** (*slang*) to make a fuss. [f. L *creare*]

creation /krɪˈeɪʃ(ə)n/ *n.* **1.** creating. **2.** all created things. **3.** a thing created, especially by human intelligence. —**the Creation**, the creation of the world. [f. OF f. L (as prec.)]

creationism *n.* the theory attributing the origin of matter and biological species to special creation, not to evolution. [f. prec.]

creative /krɪˈeɪtɪv/ *adj.* able to create; inventive, imaginative. —**creativity** /-ˈtɪvɪtɪ/ *n.*, **creatively** *adv.* [f. CREATE]

creator /krɪˈeɪtə(r)/ *n.* one who creates something; **the Creator**, God. [f. OF f. L (as CREATE)]

creature /ˈkriːtʃə(r)/ *n.* **1.** a created being, especially an animal; a person. **2.** one in a subservient position. —**creature comforts**, good food, clothes, surroundings, etc. [f. OF f. L (as CREATE)]

crèche /kreɪʃ/ *n.* a day nursery for babies. [F]

Crécy /ˈkresɪ/ a village in Picardy in northern France, scene of the first great English victory (1346) of the Hundred Years War. The invading English army of Edward III was attacked in a strong defensive position by a much larger French force. English longbowmen, however, wrought havoc in the ranks of the attacking French knights, whose disorganized charges made little impact on the English position. After repeated assaults lasting almost until nightfall, the French army retreated in confusion, leaving thousands of dead on the field, including a large portion of the nobility.

credence /ˈkriːd(ə)ns/ *n.* **1.** belief. **2.** a small table, shelf, or niche for the Eucharistic elements before consecration (ill. VESTMENTS). [f. OF f. L (as CREDIT)]

credentials /krɪˈdenʃ(ə)lz/ *n.pl.* a letter or letters of introduction; evidence of achievement or trustworthiness. [f. L (as CREDIT)]

credibility /kredɪˈbɪlɪtɪ/ *n.* being credible. —**credibility gap**, the seeming difference between what is said and what is true. [f. foll.]

credible /ˈkredɪb(ə)l/ *adj.* believable, worthy of belief. —**credibly** *adv.* [f. L (as CREDIT)]

credit /ˈkredɪt/ *n.* **1.** belief or confidence in a person, his words, or actions. **2.** a source of honour or good reputation; the power or influence it gives. **3.** the acknowledgement of merit or achievement; (usu. in *pl.*) the acknowledgement of a contributor's services to a book, film, etc. **4.** trust that a person will pay later for goods supplied; power to buy in this way; a person's financial standing. **5.** the sum at a person's disposal in a bank; an entry in an account of a sum paid into it; this sum. **6.** the side of an account recording such entries. **7.** (*US*) a certificate of the completion of a course by a student. —*v.t.* **1.** to believe, to take to be true or reliable. **2.** to enter on the credit side of an account (an amount *to* a person, a person *with* an amount). **3.** to attribute. —**credit card**, a card authorizing the purchase of goods on credit. **credit with**, to ascribe (a quality or feeling) to. **give credit for**, to recognize that (a person) has a quality etc. **on credit**, by arrangement to pay later. **to one's credit**, in one's favour. [f. F f. L (*credere* believe, trust)]

creditable *adj.* praiseworthy, bringing honour or respect. —**creditably** *adv.* [f. prec.]

creditor /ˈkredɪtə(r)/ *n.* a person to whom money is owed. [f. AF f. L (as prec.)]

credo /ˈkriːdəʊ, ˈkreɪ-/ *n.* (*pl.* **-os**) a creed. [L, = I believe]

credulity /krɪˈdjuːlɪtɪ/ *n.* an inclination to believe too readily. [f. foll.]

credulous /ˈkredjʊləs/ *adj.* too ready to believe; (of

behaviour) showing credulity. —**credulously** adv. [f. L (as CREDIT)]

Cree n. **1.** an Indian people of central North America; a member of this people. **2.** their Algonquian language. —adj. of this people or their language. [f. Canadian-French Cris f. Algonquian]

creed n. a system of religious belief; a formal summary of Christian doctrine; a set of beliefs or principles. —**creedal** adj. [OE f. L credo]

Creek n. **1.** an American Indian tribe now settled in Oklahoma; a member of this tribe. **2.** their Muskogean language. **3.** a confederacy of several tribes and languages of which the Creek proper were the most numerous. —adj. of this people or their language. [f. foll.]

creek n. an inlet on the sea-coast; a short arm of a river; (Austral. & NZ) a stream, a brook; (US) a tributary of a river. —**up the creek**, (slang) in difficulties; crazy. [f. ON or MDu.; ult. orig. unkn.]

creel n. a fisherman's large wicker basket. [orig. Sc; ult. orig. unkn.]

creep v.i. (past & p.p. **crept**) **1.** to move slowly with the body prone and close to the ground; to move stealthily or cautiously, to advance very gradually; (of a plant) to grow along the ground or up a vertical surface. **2.** to experience a shivering sensation due to repugnance or fear. **3.** to develop gradually. —n. **1.** creeping. **2.** (slang) an unpleasant person. **3.** a gradual change in the shape of a metal under stress. —**the creeps**, (colloq.) a nervous feeling of revulsion or fear. [OE]

creeper n. a person or thing that creeps; a creeping or climbing plant. [f. prec.]

creepy adj. causing nervous revulsion or fear; having this feeling. —**creepy-crawly** n. (colloq.) a small creeping insect. —**creepily** adv., creepiness n. [f. CREEP]

creese n. var. of KRIS.

cremate /krɪˈmeɪt/ v.t. to dispose of a corpse by burning it to ashes (see below). —**cremation** n. [f. L cremare burn]
The practice of cremation was not common in primitive times, but in the ancient civilized world it was the normal custom except in Egypt, Judaea, and China. Belief in the resurrection of the body made the practice repugnant to the early Christians, and by the 5th c. Christian influence had caused it to be abandoned throughout the Roman Empire. It was revived in the West in the 19th c.; in the East it has remained the most general method of disposal of the dead.

crematorium /kremɑˈtɔːrɪəm/ n. (pl. **-ia**) a place where corpses are cremated. [L (as prec.)]

crematory /ˈkremətərɪ/ adj. of or pertaining to cremation. —n. (US) a crematorium. [f. CREMATE]

crème de menthe /krem də ˈmɑ̃t/ n. a green peppermint liqueur. [F, = cream of mint]

crenate /ˈkriːneɪt/ adj. with a notched edge or rounded teeth. —**crenated** adj. (ill. PLANTS). [f. L crena notch]

crenel /ˈkren(ə)l/ n. an open space or indentation in an embattled parapet, originally for shooting through etc. (ill. CASTLES). [f. OF f. dim. of L crena notch]

crenellate /ˈkrenəleɪt/ v.t. to furnish with battlements or loopholes. —**crenellation** /-ˈleɪʃ(ə)n/ n. [f. F (as prec.)]

Creole /ˈkriːəʊl/ n. **1.** a descendant of European settlers in the West Indies or Central or South America; a white descendant of French settlers in the southern USA. **2.** a person of mixed European and Black descent. **3.** a creolized language. —adj. **1.** that is a Creole; of Creole or Creoles. **2.** **creole**, of local origin or descent. [f. F f. Sp., prob. f. Port. crioulo home-born slave]

creolize /ˈkriːəlaɪz/ v.t. to make (the language of a dominant group, in modified form) into the sole language of the group dominated. [f. prec.]

creosote /ˈkriːəsəʊt/ n. a dark-brown oil distilled from coal tar, used as a wood preservative; a colourless oily fluid distilled from wood tar, used as an antiseptic. —v.t. to treat with creosote. [f. G f. Gk, = flesh-preserver]

crêpe /kreɪp/ n. **1.** a gauzelike fabric with a wrinkled surface. **2.** a durable wrinkled sheet rubber used for shoe-soles etc. —**crêpe paper**, a thin crinkled paper. **crêpe Suzette**, a small sweet pancake served flambé. [F f. L (as CRISP)]

crepitate /ˈkrepɪteɪt/ v.i. to make a crackling sound. —**crepitation** /ˈteɪʃ(ə)n/ n. [f. L crepitare (frequent. of crepare creak)]

crept past & p.p. of CREEP.

crepuscular /krɪˈpʌskjʊlə(r)/ adj. **1.** of twilight; (of animals)

appearing or active in twilight. **2.** dim, not yet fully enlightened. [f. L crepusculum twilight]

crescendo /krɪˈʃendəʊ/ adv. (Mus.) with a gradual increase of loudness. —n. (pl. **-os**) **1.** a passage to be played this way. **2.** progress towards a climax. [It. (as foll.)]

crescent /ˈkres(ə)nt/ n. **1.** the waxing moon; the moon as seen in the first or last quarter; this as an emblem of Turkey or Islam (see below). **2.** anything of crescent shape, especially a street of houses. —adj. **1.** increasing. **2.** crescent-shaped. [f. AF f. L (crescere grow)]
As an emblem of Turkey or Islam the crescent has an ambiguous history. In the non-Islamic Western world it was regarded as the quintessential emblem of 'the Muslim Orient' from the mid-15th c. Early uses of the symbol do not suggest a specific religious significance (although the new moon itself is of great importance in Islam, for its appearance defines the first and last days of Ramadan and the start of the annual pilgrimage). It was first adopted officially by Sultan Selim III for use on the flag of his newly organized army and navy, but was given up when he was deposed in 1807. It was re-instituted in 1827, and subsequently became the central motif of many national flags (e.g. Turkey, Tunisia, Egypt until 1958, Pakistan, Malaysia, Mauritania, Algeria).

cress n. any of various cruciferous plants with pungent edible leaves. [OE]

Cressida /ˈkresɪdə/ (in medieval legends of the Trojan War) the daughter of Calchas, a priest. She was faithless to her lover Troilus, a son of Priam.

crest n. **1.** a comb or tuft on a bird's or animal's head. **2.** a plume, as on a helmet etc. (ill. ARMOUR). **3.** the top of a mountain, roof, or ridge; the surface line of the neck in animals (ill. HORSE); a curl of foam on a wave. **4.** a device above the shield and helmet on a coat of arms, or on notepaper etc. (ill. HERALDRY). —v.t./i. **1.** to reach the crest of. **2.** (of a wave) to form a crest. **3.** to serve as a crest to, to crown. [f. OF f. L crista]

crestfallen adj. dejected, abashed.

cretaceous /krɪˈteɪʃ(ə)s/ adj. **1.** of the nature of chalk. **2.** **Cretaceous**, of the final period of the Mesozoic era, following the Jurassic and preceding the Tertiary, lasting from about 144 to 65 million years ago, during which time the climate was warm and the sea-level rose. It is characterized especially in NW Europe by the deposition of chalk (whence its name). This period saw the emergence of the first flowering plants and the continued dominance of dinosaurs, although they died out before the end of it. —**Cretaceous** n. this period. [f. L cretaceus (creta chalk)]

Crete /kriːt/ an island in the eastern Mediterranean, noted for remains of the Minoan civilization. It fell to Rome in 67 BC and was subsequently ruled by Byzantines, Venetians, and Turks; it has been under Greek rule since 1913; pop. (1971) 456,208. —**Cretan** adj. & n.

cretin /ˈkretɪn/ n. a person with deformity and mental retardation caused by thyroid deficiency; (colloq.) a stupid person. —**cretinism** n., **cretinous** adj. [f. Swiss F (as CHRISTIAN)]

cretonne /ˈkretɒn/ n. a colour-printed cotton cloth used for chair-covers etc. [F, f. Creton in Normandy]

crevasse /krɪˈvæs/ n. a deep open crack, especially in the ice of a glacier (ill. MOUNTAINS). [F (as foll.)]

crevice /ˈkrevɪs/ n. a narrow opening or fissure especially in a rock or wall. [f. OF crevace (crever burst)]

crew[1] /kruː/ n. **1.** the body of persons manning a ship, aircraft, etc.; these other than the officers. **2.** a group of people, especially working together. —v.t./i. to act as a crew (for); to supply a crew for. —**crew cut**, a closely cropped man's haircut. **crew neck**, a close-fitting round neckline, especially of a pullover. [orig. = reinforcement; f. OF creue increase f. L (crescere grow)]

crew[2] past of CROW.

crewel /ˈkruːəl/ n. a thin worsted yarn for tapestry and embroidery. —**crewel-work** n. a design in this on linen. [orig. unkn.]

crib n. **1.** a wooden framework for holding animals' fodder. **2.** a child's bed or cot. **3.** a model of the manger scene at Bethlehem. **4.** the cards given by other players to the dealer at cribbage; (colloq.) cribbage. **5.** a literal translation for the use of students; (colloq.) an instance of plagiarism. —v.t./i. (**-bb-**) **1.** to confine in a small space. **2.** to pilfer; to copy unfairly or without acknowledgement. [OE]

cribbage n. a card-game for two or more persons, with a 'crib' (see CRIB 4). The game was invented by the English poet Sir John Suckling (1609-42) and seems to be developed from an older game called Noddy. [orig. unkn.]

Crichton /ˈkraɪt(ə)n/, James (1560-85), Scottish adventurer, frequently known as 'the Admirable Crichton'. An accomplished swordsman, staunch Catholic, and intellectual prodigy, Crichton led a mercurial career abroad, supposedly disputing scientific questions in twelve languages in Paris at the age of 17, serving in the French army, and making a considerable impact on Italian universities before being killed in a brawl in Mantua.

Crick, Francis Harry Compton (1916-), British biophysicist who together with J. D. Watson proposed a model for the structure of the DNA molecule, for which he shared a Nobel Prize in 1962.

crick *n.* a sudden painful stiffness in the neck or back. —*v.t.* to cause a crick in. [orig. unkn.]

cricket[1] /ˈkrɪkɪt/ *n.* an open-air summer game played with ball, bats, and two wickets between teams of 11 players each (ill. SPORTS). Scoring is by runs. Members of the batting side take it in turns to defend each wicket from attack by a ball bowled by a member of the fielding side and to strike the ball out of reach of the fieldsmen, so that the batsman can score one or more runs by running to (and from) the wicket at the opposite end before the ball is returned. The game was first played in England in Tudor times and has spread as a major sport throughout the Commonwealth. The laws (which are complicated) were first drawn up in 1744. —**not cricket**, (*colloq.*) not fair play (from the game's tradition of fair play and generous applause for the achievements of players of both sides). —**cricketer** *n.* [orig. unkn.]

cricket[2] /ˈkrɪkɪt/ *n.* a jumping chirping insect. [f. OF (*criquer* creak); imit.]

cri de coeur /kriː də kɜː/ a passionate appeal, a complaint or protest. [F, = cry from the heart]

cried *past & p.p.* of CRY.

crier /ˈkraɪə(r)/ *n.* one who cries, especially an official making public announcements in lawcourts or in the street. [f. AF (as CRY)]

crikey /ˈkraɪkɪ/ *int.* (*slang*) expressing astonishment. [euphem. for *Christ*]

crime *n.* an act (usually a serious offence) punishable by law; an evil act; such acts collectively; (*colloq.*) a shame, a senseless act. [F *L crimen* accusation, offence]

Crimea /kraɪˈmɪə/ a peninsula of the USSR lying between the Sea of Azov and the Black Sea. It was the scene of inconclusive but bloody fighting between Russia and Turkey, France, and Britain in 1854-6. —**Crimean** *adj.*

Crimean War /kraɪˈmiːən/ a mid-19th-c. war between Russia and an alliance of Great Britain, France, Sardinia, and Turkey. Russian aggression against Turkey led to war in 1853, with Turkey's European allies intervening to destroy Russian naval power in the Black Sea in 1854. The main theatre of the war was the Crimean peninsula where an Anglo-French army eventually captured the fortress city of Sebastopol in 1855 after a lengthy siege. A peace treaty was signed early in 1856, but although the allied armies had been successful the war was chiefly remembered for the deficiencies it exposed in the British army, particularly with regard to medical services; both sides sustained heavy losses.

criminal /ˈkrɪmɪn(ə)l/ *n.* a person guilty of crime. —*adj.* of, involving, or concerning crime; guilty of crime. — **criminality** /-ˈnælɪtɪ/ *n.* **criminally** *adv.* [f. L (as CRIME)]

criminology /krɪmɪˈnɒlədʒɪ/ *n.* the scientific study of crime. —**criminologist** *n.* [as CRIME + -LOGY]

crimp *v.t.* to press into small folds or ridges; to corrugate; to make waves in (hair). —*n.* a crimped thing or form. [prob. f. MDu. or MLG]

crimson /ˈkrɪmz(ə)n/ *adj.* of a rich deep red inclining to purple. —*n.* crimson colour. [ult. f. Arab. (as KERMES)]

cringe /krɪndʒ/ *vi.* to shrink back in fear, to cower; to behave obsequiously (*to*). [rel. to CRANK[1]]

crinkle *n.* a wrinkle, a crease. —*v.t./i.* to form crinkles (in). —**crinkly** *adj.* [frequent. of OE *crincan* yield (rel. to prec.)]

crinoid /ˈkrɪnɔɪd/ *adj.* lily-shaped —*n.* a crinoid echinoderm. [f. Gk *krinoeidēs* (*krinon* lily)]

crinoline /ˈkrɪnəlɪn, -liːn/ *n.* **1.** a stiffened or hooped petticoat formerly worn to make a long skirt stand out. **2.** a stiff fabric of horsehair etc. used for linings, hats, etc. [F f. L (*crinis* hair, *linum* thread)]

cripes /kraɪps/ *int.* (*vulgar*) expressing astonishment. [perversion of CHRIST]

cripple *n.* a person who is permanently lame. —*v.t.* to make a cripple of, to lame; to disable, to weaken or damage seriously. [OE, cogn. w. CREEP]

crisis /ˈkraɪsɪs/ *n.* (*pl.* **crises** /-siːz/) a decisive moment; a time of danger or great difficulty. [L f. Gk, = decision]

crisp *adj.* **1.** hard but brittle, breaking with a snap; slightly stiff. **2.** (of air) cold and bracing. **3.** (of style or manner) brisk and decisive. —*n.* a thin fried slice of potato (sold in packets etc.). —*v.t./i.* to make or become crisp. —**crisply** *adv.*, **crispness** *n.*, **crispy** *adj.* [f. L *crispus* curled]

crispbread *n.* a thin crisp biscuit of crushed rye etc.

criss-cross *n.* a pattern of crossing lines. —*adj.* crossing, in cross lines. —*adv.* crosswise, at cross purposes. —*v.t./i.* to mark or form or move in a criss-cross pattern. [orig. f. *Christ's cross*]

criterion /kraɪˈtɪərɪən/ *n.* (*pl.* **-ia**) a principle or standard by which a thing is judged. [Gk, = means of judging (as foll.)]

critic /ˈkrɪtɪk/ *n.* **1.** one who censures. **2.** one who reviews or judges the merit of literary, artistic, etc., works. [f. L f. Gk (*kritēs* judge)]

critical /ˈkrɪtɪk(ə)l/ *adj.* **1.** fault-finding, censorious; expressing criticism. **2.** of or at a crisis, decisive, crucial. **3.** marking the transition from one state etc. to another; (of a nuclear reactor) maintaining a self-sustaining chain-reaction. —**critical path**, the sequence of stages determining the minimum time needed for a complex operation. —**critically** *adv.* [f. L (as prec.)]

criticism /ˈkrɪtɪsɪz(ə)m/ *n.* **1.** finding fault, censure. **2.** the work of a critic; a critical article, essay, or remark. [f. CRITIC]

criticize /ˈkrɪtɪsaɪz/ *v.t./i.* **1.** to find fault (with), to censure. **2.** to discuss critically. [as prec.]

critique /krɪˈtiːk/ *n.* **1.** a critical essay or analysis. **2.** a criticism. [F (as CRITIC)]

croak *n.* a deep hoarse cry or sound as of a raven or frog. —*v.t./i.* **1.** to utter or speak with a croak. **2.** (*slang*) to die; to kill. [imit.]

Croat /ˈkrəʊæt/ *n.* **1.** a native or inhabitant of Croatia in Yugoslavia. **2.** the language of the Croats. —**Croatian** /-ˈeɪʃ(ə)n/ *adj. & n.* [f. L f. Serbo-Croatian *Hrvat*]

Croatia /krəʊˈeɪʃə/ a constituent republic of Yugoslavia. —**Croatian** *adj. & n.*

Croce /ˈkrɒtʃeɪ/, Benedetto (1866-1952), Italian philosopher. Born into a family of wealthy landowners, Croce spent most of his life engaged in academic pursuits. His philosophy, which coincided with a revival of historical idealism in Italy, arose out of his aesthetic theory. Aesthetic experience is interpreted as an intuition of the universal spirit which manifests itself in the practical activities of human personality. While reflection upon these intuitions requires rational concepts the former are more primitive than the latter; consequently history and art are seen as more primitive than science. Practical action is grounded in economic activity yet this must be made subject to the regulation of an ethic which expresses universal spiritual values. Croce broke with the Fascist regime in 1925 and thereafter became a leading antagonist. Following the demise of Fascism he became leader of the Liberal party and served briefly as a Cabinet minister in 1944.

crochet /ˈkrəʊʃeɪ/ *n.* needlework in which the yarn is looped into a pattern of stitches by means of a hooked needle. —*v.t./i.* to make in or do crochet. [F (*croc* hook)]

crock[1] *n.* (*colloq.*) a person who suffers from ill health or lameness etc.; a worn-out vehicle, ship, etc. [orig. Sc., perh. f. Flem.]

crock[2] *n.* an earthenware pot or jar; a broken piece of this. [OE]

crockery *n.* earthenware vessels, plates, etc. [f. CROCK[2]]

crocket /ˈkrɒkɪt/ *n.* a small ornamental carving on the inclined side of a pinnacle etc. (ill. CHURCH). [f. OF (as CROCHET)]

Crockford /ˈkrɒkfəd/ short for *Crockford's Clerical Directory*, a reference book of Anglican clergy first issued in 1860. [f. J. *Crockford* (d. 1865), nominal first publisher]

crocodile /ˈkrɒkədaɪl/ *n.* **1.** a reptile of the order Crocodilia (see foll.), usually of the genus *Crocodylus*, found in tropical regions. Its long snout is narrower than that of the alligator, and when the jaws are closed the fourth tooth on each side of the lower jaw projects outside the snout, whereas in the alligator it fits into a socket in the upper jaw. **2.** its skin, used to make bags, shoes, etc. **3.** (*colloq.*) a line of schoolchildren etc. walking in pairs. —**crocodile tears,** insincere grief (from the belief that the crocodile wept while devouring, or to allure, its victim). [f. OF f. L f. Gk *krokodilos*]

crocodilian /krɒkə'dɪlɪən/ *n.* a large heavy amphibious reptile of the order Crocodilia, which includes crocodiles, alligators, and caymans. Crocodilians have a long snout, strong jaws, short legs with webbed toes and with claws, and a powerful tail. In evolutionary sequence they are the last living link with prehistoric reptiles resembling the dinosaurs, and are the closest living relatives of the birds. —*adj.* of the crocodilians. [f. prec.]

crocus /'krəʊkəs/ *n.* a dwarf spring-flowering plant of the genus *Crocus*, growing from a corm, with yellow, purple, or white flowers. —**autumn crocus,** a similar plant blooming in autumn after its leaves have died down. [L f. Gk, of Semitic orig.]

Croesus /'kriːsəs/ the last king of Lydia *c.*560–546 BC, friendly to Greeks despite his subjugation of the Greek cities on the coast of Asia Minor, and proverbial for his wealth. His empire, with its capital at Sardis, was overthrown by the Persian king Cyrus. At this point his fate becomes the theme of legend; Cyrus is said to have cast him on a pyre from which he was saved by the miraculous intervention of Apollo.

croft *n.* an enclosed piece of (usually arable) land; a small rented farm, especially in the Scottish Highlands. —*v.i.* to farm a croft; to live as a crofter. [OE]

crofter *n.* one who rents a croft. [f. prec.]

croissant /'krwɑːsɑ̃/ *n.* a crescent-shaped bread roll. [F, = crescent]

Cro-Magnon /krəʊ'mænjɒn/ the name of a hill of Cretaceous limestone in the Dordogne department of France, in a cave at the base of which skeletons of five individuals were found in 1868 among deposits of upper palaeolithic age. It had previously been supposed that modern man did not exist in palaeolithic times. The name is now applied in a more general sense to describe a particular race of modern man (*Homo sapiens sapiens*) that is associated with the upper palaeolithic Aurignacian industry found throughout western Europe and particularly SW France from between *c.*34,000 and 29,000 years BP. The geographical origin of the fully modern Cro-Magnon 'race' is uncertain but its appearance in western Europe heralded the apparent decline and disappearance of the existing Neanderthal populations and their middle palaeolithic industries. The group persisted in mesolithic and neolithic times, and some authorities consider that it survived in the Guanches, the earliest inhabitants (now extinct) of the Canary Islands.

Crome /krəʊm/, John (1768–1821), English artist, born in Norwich. His fame as a landscape painter rests on his traditional position between the beginnings of naturalism in Richard Wilson (d. 1782) and its maturity in John Constable. He helped found the Norwich Society of Artists in 1803, and was its acknowledged principal. Although his landscapes are obviously indebted to Dutch artists such as Hobbema and Rembrandt, the unity of pictorial and emotional tone in such pictures as *Slate Quarries* shows a tendency towards the more personal interpretation of nature that would be developed between 1800 and 1850.

cromlech /'krɒmlek/ *n.* **1.** a megalithic chamber tomb, a dolmen. **2.** (in Brittany) a circle of upright prehistoric stones. [Welsh (*crwm* curved, *llech* flat stone)]

Crompton /'krɒmptən/, Samuel (1753–1827), English inventor of the spinning mule (see MULE[1] 2).

Cromwell[1] /'krɒmwel/, Oliver (1599–1658), English general and statesman. A Puritan squire from Huntingdon, Cromwell was among the Parliamentary opponents of Charles I, but only became a national figure as a soldier during the English Civil War, playing a decisive part in the victories of Marston Moor and Naseby and in the formation of the New Model Army. His rise to pre-eminence continued with his victories at Preston, Dunbar, and Worcester and his subjugation of Ireland, and with the collapse of parliamentary government after the King's execution he became Lord Protector, an office he held from 1653 until his death.

Cromwell[2] /'krɒmwel/, Thomas (*c.*1485–1540), chief minister to Henry VIII. Rising from humble origins in the service of Cardinal Wolsey, Cromwell succeeded the latter as the King's chief adviser. During the 1530s he presided over the King's divorce from Catherine of Aragon and

break with the Roman Catholic Church, as well as the dissolution of the monasteries and a series of administrative reforms strengthening the central government. He fell from favour over Henry's marriage to Anne of Cleves and was executed on a trumped-up charge of treason.

crone *n.* a withered old woman. [f. Du. *croonje* carcass]

Cronin /'krəʊnɪn/, Archibald Joseph (1896–1981), Scottish novelist who practised as a physician until the success of his first novel made him devote himself to writing. His novels include *Hatter's Castle* (1931), *The Citadel* (1937), telling of the struggles of an idealistic young doctor, and *The Stars Look Down* (1935), about a mining community, all written with rare sympathy and understanding and a rich panorama of characters.

Cronus /'krəʊnəs/ (*Gk myth.*) the youngest son of Heaven and Earth, and leader of his brothers the Titans. By the advice of his mother he castrated his father, who therefore no longer approached Earth but left room for the Titans between them. Cronus then married his sister Rhea and swallowed all his male children because he was fated to be overcome by one of them. Rhea wrapped a stone in swaddling-clothes when Zeus was born and hid the baby away in Crete. Cronus swallowed the stone, and Zeus eventually dethroned him as ruler of the universe. The story is largely derived from Asia Minor and is almost certainly pre-Hellenic.

crony *n.* a close friend. [f. Gk *khronios* of long standing (*khronos* time)]

crook /krʊk/ *n.* **1.** the hooked staff of a shepherd or bishop. **2.** a bent or curved thing; a hook; a bend, a curve. **3.** (*colloq.*) a rogue, a swindler; a professional criminal. —*adj.* (*Austral.* & *NZ*) unsatisfactory, unpleasant; ailing, injured. —*v.t./i.* to bend, to curve. [f. ON]

crooked /'krʊkɪd/ *adj.* **1.** not straight or level; bent, curved, twisted. **2.** not straightforward, dishonest. —**crookedly** *adv.,* **crookedness** *n.* [f. prec.]

Crookes /krʊks/, Sir William (1832–1919), English physicist and chemist who combined scientific research in his private laboratory with business, and edited several photographic and scientific journals. He lacked mathematical skills but was a brilliant experimenter in the mould of Faraday, his model, and employed several adept assistants. His interest in spiritualism and psychic research caused several controversies. In 1861, shortly after the spectroscopic discoveries of Bunsen and Kirchhoff, he discovered the element thallium. This led him indirectly to the invention of the radiometer in 1875, a device with mica vanes rotated by daylight radiation which confirmed the kinetic theory of gases. In 1876 he began investigating electrical discharges (cathode rays) in vacuum tubes, for which he developed the Crookes' tube (the precursor of the X-ray tube). He finally took up the study of radioactivity, and in 1903 invented the spinthariscope for detecting alpha particles.

croon *v.t./i.* to hum or sing in a low subdued voice and sentimental manner. —*n.* such singing. —**crooner** *n.* [orig. Sc. & N. Engl., f. MDu., MLG *kronen* groan, lament]

crop *n.* **1.** the produce of cultivated plants, especially cereals; a season's total yield; a group or amount produced at one time. **2.** the handle of a looped whip. **3.** hair cut very short. **4.** the pouch in a bird's gullet where food is prepared for digestion. —*v.t./i.* (**-pp-**) **1.** to cut or bite off; to cut (hair) very short. **2.** to sow (land) *with* a crop; to bear crops. —**crop-eared** *adj.* with the ears or hair cut short. **crop up,** to occur unexpectedly or by chance. [OE]

cropper *n.* a crop-producing plant of a specified quality. —**come a cropper,** (*slang*) to fall heavily, to fail badly. [f. prec.]

croquet /'krəʊkeɪ/ *n.* **1.** a game, played on a lawn, in which wooden balls are driven with mallets through square-topped hoops. It owes its origin to *paille maille* (or *Pell-Mell*; whence the name of the London street *Pall Mall*, where it was played), a game known in France from the 16th c. **2.** an act of croqueting. —*v.t./i.* to drive away (an opponent's ball) by placing one's own against it and striking one's own. [perh. dial. var. of F *crochet* hook]

croquette /krəʊ'ket/ *n.* a roll of potato, meat, etc. coated in breadcrumbs and fried. [F (*croquer* crunch)]

crore /krɔː(r)/ *n.* (in India) 10 million, one hundred lakhs. [f. Hindi f. Skr. *koti* apex]

crosier /'krəʊzɪə(r), -ʒə(r)/ *n.* the hooked staff carried by a bishop as a symbol of office (ill. VESTMENTS). [f. OF *crossier* crook-bearer, *croisier* cross-bearer]

cross[1] *n.* **1.** an upright post with a transverse bar, as used in antiquity for crucifixion, especially **(the Cross)** that on which Christ was crucified; a representation of this as the emblem of Christianity, a staff surmounted by a cross; a monument in the form of a cross. **2.** a thing or mark of similar shape, especially the figure made by two short intersecting lines (+ or ×). **3.** a decoration indicating rank in some orders of knighthood or awarded for personal valour. **4.** an intermixture of breeds, a hybrid; a mixture or compromise *between* two or more things. **5.** a crosswise movement of an actor, football, boxer's fist, etc. **6.** a trouble or annoyance. —*adj.* **1.** transverse, reaching from side to side; intersecting. **2.** contrary, opposed, reciprocal. **3.** annoyed or angry (*with*) —**be at cross purposes**, to misunderstand or conflict with one another. **on the cross**, diagonally. —**crossly** *adv.*, **crossness** *n.* [OE, ult. f. L *crux*]

cross[2] *v.t./i.* **1.** to go across (a road, river, sea, any area), to cross a road etc. **2.** to intersect or be across one another; to cause to be in this position. **3.** to draw a line or lines across. **4.** to make the sign of the cross over (esp. *oneself*). **5.** to pass in opposite or different directions. **6.** to thwart, to frustrate; to anger by refusing to acquiesce. **7.** to interbreed; to cross-fertilize. —**cross one's heart**, to make the sign of the cross over it as a sign of sincerity. **cross one's mind**, (of an idea etc.) to occur to one. **cross off**, to remove from a list etc. **cross out**, to cancel, to obliterate. [f. prec.]

crossbar *n.* a horizontal bar, especially between uprights.

cross-bench *n.* a bench in Parliament for members not belonging to the government or main opposition.

crossbill *n.* a bird of the genus *Loxia* with a bill whose jaws cross when closed.

crossbow *n.* a bow fixed across a wooden stock, with a groove for the arrow and a mechanism for drawing and releasing the string.

cross-breed *v.t.* to produce a hybrid of. —*n.* a hybrid animal or plant. —**cross-bred** *adj.* hybrid.

cross-check *v.t./i.* to check by an alternative method of verification. —*n.* a check of this kind.

cross-country *adj. & adv.* across fields, not keeping to main or direct roads.

cross-cut *n.* a diagonal cut, path, etc. —**cross-cut saw**, a saw for cutting across the grain of wood.

crosse *n.* the netted crook used in lacrosse. [F as CROCHET]

cross-examine *v.t.* to examine (especially an opposing witness in a lawcourt) so as to check or extend previous testimony. —**cross-examination** *n.*

cross-eyed *adj.* having one or both eyes turned towards the nose.

cross-fertilize *v.t.* to fertilize (an animal or plant) from one of a different species. —**cross-fertilization** *n.*

crossfire *n.* a firing of guns in two crossing directions; opposition, interrogation, etc., from several sides at once.

cross-grained *adj.* **1.** (of wood) with the grain in crossing directions. **2.** (of a person) perverse, intractable.

crossing *n.* **1.** place where things cross. **2.** a place at which one may cross. **3.** a journey across water. [f. CROSS[2]]

cross-legged *adj.* with the legs crossed, or with the ankles crossed and knees apart.

cross-patch *n.* a bad-tempered person.

cross-ply *adj.* (of a tyre) having the fabric layers with the cords lying crosswise.

cross-question *v.t.* to cross-examine.

cross-reference *n.* a reference from one part of a book etc. to another.

crossroads *n.pl.* the intersection of two roads. —**at the crossroads**, at the point where a decision must be made or a course of action chosen.

cross-section *n.* **1.** a transverse section; a representation or diagram of a thing as if cut through. **2.** a representative sample. —**cross-sectional** *adj.*

cross-stitch *n.* a stitch formed by two crossing stiches.

cross-talk *n.* **1.** unwanted transfer of signals between communication channels. **2.** repartee.

crossways *adv.* = CROSSWISE.

cross-wind *n.* a wind blowing across the direction of travel.

crosswise *adv.* (also **crossways**) in the manner of a cross, across, with one crossing the other.

crossword *n.* a puzzle in which vertically and horizontally crossing words indicated by clues have to be fitted into a grid of squares. Invention of the crossword is attributed to a journalist, Arthur Wynne, whose puzzle (called a 'word-cross') appeared in a Sunday newspaper, the *New York World*, on 21 Dec. 1913.

crotch *n.* the place where things (especially the legs of a body or a garment) fork. [perh. f. OF *croc(he)* hook]

crotchet /ˈkrɒtʃɪt/ *n.* (*Mus*) a note equal to two quavers or half a minim (ill. MUSICAL NOTATION) [f. OF (as prec.)]

crotchety *adj.* peevish. [f. prec.]

crouch *v.i.* to lower the body with the knees bent close against the chest; to be in this position. —*n.* crouching. [f. OF *crochir* be bent (as CROTCH)]

croup[1] /kruːp/ *n.* an inflammation of the larynx and trachea of children, with a hard cough and difficult breathing. [f. *croup* to croak (imit.)]

croup[2] /kruːp/ *n.* the rump (especially of a horse) (ill. HORSE). [f. OF (rel. to CROP)]

croupier /ˈkruːpɪə(r)/ *n.* a person in charge of a gambling-table raking in and paying out money. [F, orig. = rider on the croup]

crouton /ˈkruːtɒn/ *n.* a small piece of fried or toasted bread served with soup etc. [F (as CRUST)]

crow /krəʊ/ *n.* **1.** a large black bird of the genus *Corvus* or family Corvidae, including the jackdaw, raven, and rook. **2.** the cry of a crow, the crowing of a cock. —*v.i.* (*past* in 1st sense also **crew** /kruː/ **1.** (of a cock) to utter a loud shrill cry. **2.** (of a baby) to utter happy sounds. **3.** to express gleeful satisfaction (*over*). —**as the crow flies**, in a straight line. **crow's foot**, a wrinkle at the outer corner of the eye. **crow's nest** *n.* a barrel fixed at the mast-head of a sailing ship as a shelter for the look-out. [OE]

crowbar *n.* an iron bar with a flattened end, used as a lever.

crowd *n.* a large number of people gathered together without orderly arrangement; a mass of spectators, an audience; (*colloq.*) a company, a set, a lot. —*v.t./i.* to come or cause to come together in a crowd; to fill, to occupy, to cram (*into* or *with*); to inconvenience by crowding or coming aggressively close to. —**crowd out**, to keep out by crowding. —**crowded** *adj.* [OE *crūdan* press, drive]

crown *n.* **1.** a monarch's ornamental and usually jewelled headdress. **2.** (often **Crown**) *the* monarch (especially as head of State); *the* power or authority of the monarch. **3.** a wreath for the head, as an emblem of victory; a reward for or consummation of effort. **4.** the top part of a thing, especially of the head or a hat; the highest or central point of an arched or curved thing; the part of a tooth projecting from the gum, an artificial replacement for this or a part of this. **5.** a figure of a crown as a mark or emblem. **6.** a British coin worth 25p (formerly 5 shillings). **7.** a former size of paper, 504 × 384 mm. —*v.t.* **1.** to put a crown on; to invest with a regal crown or office; to be a crown to, to encircle or rest on the top of; to be the consummation, reward, or finishing-touch to. **2.** (*slang*) to hit on the head. **3.** to promote (a piece in draughts) to king. —**Crown Colony**, a colony subject to direct control by the British government. **Crown Court**, a court of criminal jurisdiction in England and Wales. **Crown Derby**, a kind of china made at Derby and often marked with a crown. **crown glass**, see GLASS. **crown jewels**, the sovereign's regalia, including a crown, sceptre, and orb, used on ceremonial occasions. **Crown Prince**, the male heir to a throne. **Crown Princess**, the wife of a Crown Prince; the female heir to a throne. **crown wheel**, a wheel with teeth or cogs at right angles to its plane. [f. AF f. L *corona*]

crozier var. of CROSIER.

CRT *abbr.* cathode-ray tube.

cruces *pl.* of CRUX.

crucial /ˈkruːʃ(ə)l/ *adj.* decisive, critical; (*colloq.*) (**D**) very important. —**crucially** *adv.* [F, f. L *crux* cross]

crucible /ˈkruːsɪb(ə)l/ *n.* a melting-pot for metals etc.; a severe test. [f. L *crucibulum* (as prec.)]

cruciferous /kruːˈsɪfərəs/ *adj.* of the family Cruciferae, having flowers with four equal petals arranged crosswise. [f. L, = cross-bearing (as CRUCIAL)]

crucifix /ˈkruːsɪfɪks/ *n.* a model of the cross, especially with a figure of Christ on it. [f. OF f. L, = fixed to a cross]

crucifixion /kruːsɪˈfɪkʃ(ə)n/ *n.* crucifying, being crucified (see below); **the Crucifixion**, that of Christ. [f. L (as prec.)]
Crucifixion was a form of capital punishment used by various ancient peoples including the Persians, Carthaginians, and Romans; it was normally confined to slaves and other persons with no civil rights. The condemned man

was first flogged and then made to carry a cross-beam to the place of execution, where a stake had been fixed in the ground. He was fastened to the beam by nails or cords, and it was drawn up and fixed to the stake so that his feet were clear of the ground; sometimes the feet were fastened to the upright. Some support for the body was provided by a projecting ledge, but a foot-rest is rarely attested. Death apparently resulted from exhaustion, perhaps caused by the difficulty of breathing when the body's weight is suspended by the arms in this way; it could be hastened by breaking the legs. The penalty was abolished by the emperor Constantine.

cruciform /ˈkruːsɪfɔːm/ adj. cross-shaped. [f. L crux cross + -FORM]

crucify /ˈkruːsɪfaɪ/ v.t. **1.** to put to death by fastening to a cross (see CRUCIFIXION). **2.** to persecute, to torment; to destroy in argument etc. [f. OF f. L (as CRUCIFIX)]

cruck /krʌk/ n. one of the paired curved timbers extending to the ground in the framework of a house-roof (ill. HOUSES). [var. of CROOK]

crude /kruːd/ adj. in the natural state, not refined; lacking finish, unpolished; rude, blunt. —**crudely** adv., **crudity** n. [f. L crudus raw, rough]

cruel /ˈkruːəl/ adj. indifferent to or gratified by another's suffering; causing pain or suffering. —**cruelly** adv., **cruelty** n. [f. L crudelis (as prec.)]

cruet /ˈkruːɪt/ n. a small glass bottle for holding oil or vinegar for use at table; a stand holding this and salt, pepper, and mustard pots. [f. OF, dim. of crue pot (rel. to CROCK²)]

Crufts an annual dog-show held in London, first organized in 1886 by Charles Cruft, British dog-breeder.

cruise /kruːz/ v.i. **1.** to sail about without precise destination, or calling at a series of places. **2.** (of a motor vehicle or aircraft) to travel at a moderate economical speed. **3.** (of a vehicle or driver) to travel at random, esp. slowly. —n. a cruising voyage. —**cruise missile**, one able to fly at low altitude and guide itself by reference to the features of the region traversed. [prob. f. Du. (kruis cross)]

cruiser /ˈkruːzə(r)/ n. a warship of high speed and medium armament; a cabin cruiser (see CABIN). [f. Du. (as prec.)]

cruiserweight n. light heavyweight (see HEAVYWEIGHT).

crumb /krʌm/ n. **1.** a small fragment, especially of bread; a small particle or amount of. **2.** the soft inner part of bread. —v.t. **1.** to cover with bread crumbs. **2.** to crumble (bread). —**crumby** adj. [OE]

crumble v.t./i. to break or fall into small fragments; (of power, reputation, etc.) to collapse gradually. —n. a dish of cooked fruit with a crumbly topping. —**crumbly** adj. [f. prec.]

crumbs /krʌmz/ int. expressing dismay or surprise. [euphem. for Christ]

crummy adj. (slang) dirty, squalid; inferior, worthless. —**crumminess** n. [var. of CRUMBY]

crumpet /ˈkrʌmpɪt/ n. **1.** a flat soft cake of yeast mixture, toasted and eaten with butter. **2.** (slang) the head. **3.** (slang) a sexually attractive woman or women. [orig. unkn.]

crumple v.t./i. to crush or become crushed into creases; to collapse, to give way. [f. obs. crump curl up]

crunch v.t./i. to crush noisily with the teeth; to grind under foot (gravel, dry snow, etc.); to make a crunching sound. —n. **1.** crunching; a crunching sound. **2.** (colloq.) a decisive event. —**when it comes to the crunch**, (colloq.) when there is a show-down. [imit.]

crupper n. a strap holding a harness back by passing under a horse's tail. [f. AF (as CROUP²)]

crusade /kruːˈseɪd/ n. **1. Crusade**, any of a series of military expeditions undertaken by Christian western Europe in the 11th–13th c. to rescue the Holy Land from the Saracens (see below). **2.** a vigorous campaign in favour of a cause. —v.t./i. to engage in a crusade. [earlier croisade (F, f. croix cross)]

The first Crusade (1096–9) resulted in the capture of Jerusalem and the establishment of Crusader States in the Holy Land, but the second (1147–9) failed to stop a Muslim resurgence, and Jerusalem fell to Saladin in 1187. The third (1189–92) recaptured some lost ground but not Jerusalem, while the fourth (1202–04) was diverted against the Byzantine Empire, which was fatally weakened by the resultant sack of Constantinople. The fifth (1217–21) was side-tracked to Egypt, where it accomplished nothing, and although the sixth (1228–9) resulted in the return of Jerusalem to Christian hands the city was lost to the Turks

in 1244. The seventh (1248–54) ended in disaster in Egypt, while the eighth and last (1270–1) petered out when its leader Louis IX of France died on his way east, and the Holy Land was left in Muslim hands until the 20th c. Although undertaken in a religious cause, the Crusades were carried on like most other medieval wars and were generally badly organized and indecisive.

crusader n. **1.** one who engages in a crusade. **2. Crusader**, one who took part in the Crusades. [f. prec.]

cruse /kruːz/ n. (archaic) an earthenware pot or jar. [OE]

crush v.t./i. **1.** to press heavily or with violence so as to break, injure or wrinkle; to squeeze tightly; to press or pound into small fragments. **2.** to become crushed. **3.** to defeat or subdue completely. —n. **1.** a crowded mass of people pressed together. **2.** a drink made from the juice of crushed fruit. **3.** (slang) an infatuation. [f. OF croissir gnash (the teeth)]

crushable /ˈkrʌʃəb(ə)l/ adj. that can be crushed; easily crushed. [f. prec.]

crust n. **1.** the hard outer part of bread; the similar casing of anything. **2.** the rocky outer skin of the earth (ill. GEOLOGY). **3.** a deposit, especially from wine on a bottle. **4.** (slang) impudence. —v.t./i. to cover with or form into a crust; to become covered with a crust. —**crustal** adj. [f. OF f. L crusta rind, shell]

crustacean /krʌˈsteɪʃ(ə)n/ n. a member of the Crustacea, a large class of hard-shelled mainly aquatic animals including crabs, lobsters, shrimps, wood-lice, etc. —adj. of crustaceans. [f. L (as prec.)]

crusty adj. **1.** having a crisp crust. **2.** irritable, curt. —**crustily** adv., **crustiness** n. [f. CRUST]

crutch n. **1.** a support for a lame person, usually with a cross-piece fitting under the armpit or shaped so that the weight is supported on the forearm; any support. **2.** the crotch. [OE]

crux /krʌks/ n. (pl. **cruces** /ˈkruːsiːz/) the decisive point, the crucial element of a problem. —**Crux Australis**, the Southern Cross. [L, = cross]

cry /kraɪ/ v.t./i. (past & p.p. **cried**) **1.** to make a loud shrill sound; to call out loudly in words; (of an animal) to utter its cry. **2.** to shed tears. **3.** (often with out) to appeal, demand, or show need for. **4.** (of a hawker etc.) to proclaim (wares) for sale. —n. **1.** a loud inarticulate utterance of pain, grief, joy, etc.; a loud excited utterance of words; the loud natural utterance of an animal, that of hounds on a scent. **2.** an urgent appeal or entreaty; a public demand. **3.** a watchword, a rallying call. **4.** a spell of weeping. —**cry-baby** n. a person who weeps easily or without good reason. **cry down**, to disparage. **cry off**, to withdraw from a promise or undertaking. **cry up**, to praise, to extol. **cry wolf**, see WOLF. **in full cry**, in close pursuit. [f. OF f. L quiritare wail]

crying adj. (esp. of injustice) flagrant, demanding redress. [f. prec.]

cryogenics /kraɪəˈdʒenɪks/ n. the branch of physics dealing with very low temperatures and their effects. Modern techniques have reduced temperatures to a tiny fraction of 1 kelvin; the laws of physics suggest, however, that the absolute zero of temperature is in principle unattainable. Low temperature environments are becoming increasingly important in science and in industry. At very low temperatures many elements and alloys entirely lose their electrical resistance and become superconductors; this has many applications, in the production of powerful electromagnets, for example. At very low temperatures also the thermal 'noise' produced by vibrating atoms is greatly reduced and various types of electrical devices, including detectors of electromagnetic signals, become much more sensitive and discriminating. [f. Gk kruos frost + -GENIC]

cryosurgery /kraɪəʊˈsɜːdʒərɪ/ n. surgery in which local application of intense cold is used for anaesthesia or therapy. [f. Gk kruos frost + SURGERY]

crypt /krɪpt/ n. a vault, especially one beneath a church, used as a burial-place. [f. L f. Gk kruptē (kruptos hidden)]

cryptic /ˈkrɪptɪk/ adj. secret, mysterious; obscure in meaning. —**cryptically** adv. [as prec.]

cryptogam /ˈkrɪptəgæm/ n. a plant with no true flowers or seeds; a fern, moss, or fungus. —**cryptogamous** /-ˈtɒgəməs/ adj. [f. F (as CRYPT, Gk gamos marriage)]

cryptogram /ˈkrɪptəgræm/ n. a thing written in cipher. [as CRYPT + -GRAM]

cryptography /krɪpˈtɒgrəfɪ/ n. the art of writing in or

deciphering codes or ciphers. —**cryptographer** n., **crypto-graphic** /-tə'græfɪk/ adj. [as CRYPT + -GRAPHY]

crystal /'krɪst(ə)l/ n. **1.** a kind of clear transparent colourless mineral; a piece of this. **2.** highly transparent glass, flint glass; articles made of this. **3.** an aggregation of molecules with a definite internal structure and the external form of a solid enclosed by symmetrically arranged plane faces. —adj. made of crystal; like or clear as crystal. —**crystal ball**, a glass globe used in crystal-gazing. **crystal-gazing** n. concentrating one's gaze on a crystal to obtain a picture by hallucination etc. [OE f. OF, ult. f. Gk krustallos ice, crystal]

crystalline /'krɪst(ə)laɪn/ adj. **1.** of, like, or clear as crystal. **2.** having the structure and form of a crystal. —**crystallinity** /-'lɪnɪtɪ/ n. [f. OF (as prec.)]

crystallize /'krɪstəlaɪz/ v.t./i. **1.** to form into crystals. **2.** (of ideas or plans) to become definite. —**crystallized fruit**, fruit preserved in sugar. —**crystallization** /-'zeɪʃ(ə)n/ n. [f. CRYSTAL]

crystallography /krɪstə'lɒgrəfɪ/ n. the science of crystal structure. —**crystallographer** n. [f. CRYSTAL + -GRAPHY]

crystalloid /'krɪst(ə)lɔɪd/ n. a substance having a crystalline structure. [f. CRYSTAL]

Crystal Palace a large building of iron and glass, like a giant greenhouse, designed by (Sir) Joseph Paxton for the Great Exhibition of 1851 in Hyde Park, London, and re-erected at Sydenham near Croydon; it was accidentally burnt down in 1936.

Cs symbol caesium.

c/s abbr. cycles per second.

CSE abbr. Certificate of Secondary Education.

Ctesiphon /'tesɪf(ə)n/ an ancient city on the Tigris near Baghdad, capital of the Parthian kingdom from c.224 and then of Persia under the Sassanian dynasty. It was taken by the Arabs in 636.

Cu symbol copper.

cu. abbr. cubic.

cub n. **1.** the young of a fox, bear, lion, etc. **2.** an ill-mannered young man. **3.** (colloq.)an inexperienced reporter. **4.** Cub, a Cub Scout. —v.t./i. (**-bb-**) **1.** to bring forth (cubs). **2.** to hunt fox-cubs. —**Cub Scout**, a member of the junior branch of the Scout Association, consisting of boys aged eight to ten-and-a-half. [orig. unkn.]

Cuba /'kjuːbə/ a Caribbean country, the largest and furthest west of the islands of the West Indies, situated at the mouth of the Gulf of Mexico; pop. (est. 1983) 9,939,800; official language, Spanish; capital, Havana. Sugar is the mainstay of the economy and is the principal export; other main exports include nickel and tobacco. One of the first parts of the New World to be discovered and colonized by Spain, Cuba remained under Spanish rule until the Spanish-American War of 1898. Thereafter it was nominally independent but heavily under American influence, until granted full autonomy in 1934. The country was stricken by instability, however, and after several periods of dictatorship was taken over by a Communist rebellion in 1959, since which time it has leant heavily on Russian aid under the presidency of Fidel Castro. In 1962 Cuba became the focus of cold war manœuvres when on 22 Oct. President Kennedy announced a US blockade of the island in order to compel the USSR to dismantle the missile bases which it had installed there. On 28 Oct. Khrushchev agreed to do so, and the crisis was over; the prospect of nuclear war had never seemed closer. —**Cuban** adj. & n.

cubby-hole /'kʌbɪhəʊl/ n. a very small room; a small snug place. [f. dial. cub stall f. LG]

cube /kjuːb/ n. **1.** a solid contained by six equal squares (ill. SHAPES); a cube-shaped block. **2.** the product of a number multiplied by its square. —v.t. **1.** to find the cube of (a number). **2.** to cut (food) into small cubes. —**cube root**, the number which produces a given number when cubed. [F or L f. Gk]

cubic /'kjuːbɪk/ adj. **1.** of three dimensions. **2.** involving the cube (and no higher power) of a number. —**cubic metre** etc., the volume of a cube whose edge is one metre etc. [f. F or L (as prec.)]

cubical /'kjuːbɪk(ə)l/ adj. cube-shaped. [f. prec.]

cubicle /'kjuːbɪk(ə)l/ n. a small separate sleeping-compartment; an enclosed space screened for privacy. [f. L (cubare lie)]

cubism /'kjuːbɪz(ə)m/ n. a style of art (esp. painting) in which objects are so presented as to give the effect of an assemblage of geometrical figures. This style, created by Picasso and Braque, was inaugurated by Picasso's Dem-

oiselles d'Avignon (1906-7) and Braque's Nude (1907-8). It was a reaction against the optical realism of impressionism, and developed from Cézanne's structural analysis; its aim was to depict the permanent structure of things as perceived in their solid tangible reality. In the first phase, known as analytical cubism, the artists confined their colour range and subject-matter, made the picture-space artificially shallow, and depicted objects as a series of planes, as they would be seen from a variety of different viewpoints. In the later phase, synthetic cubism (1912 onwards), they experimented with collages, sticking pieces of newspaper, matchboxes, etc., on to the canvas and combining them with drawing or painting. The movement ended c.1920, but its influence was strong until the 1940s. —**cubist** n. [f. F (as CUBE)]

cubit /'kjuːbɪt/ n. an ancient measure of length, approximately equal to the length of the forearm. [f. L cubitum elbow]

cuboid /'kjuːbɔɪd/ adj. cube-shaped, like a cube. —n. a rectangular parallelepiped. [f. Gk (as CUBE)]

cuckold /'kʌkəʊld/ n. a husband whose wife is unfaithful to him. —v.t. to make a cuckold of. —**cuckoldry** n. [f. OF (cucu cuckoo)]

cuckoo /'kʊkuː/ n. **1.** a migratory bird (Cuculus canorus) with a characteristic cry, which deposits its eggs in the nests of small birds. **2.** a bird of the family Cuculidae, with or without this habit. —adj. (slang) crazy, foolish. —**cuckoo-pint** n. wild arum (Arum maculatum). **cuckoo-spit** n. a froth exuded by the larvae of certain insects on leaves, stems, etc. [f. OF (imit.)]

cucumber /'kjuːkʌmbə(r)/ n. a long green fleshy vegetable used in salads; the plant producing this. [f. OF f. L cucumer]

cud n. the half-digested food that a ruminant chews at leisure. —**chew the cud**, to reflect, to ponder. [OE, rel. to OHG kuti, quiti glue]

cuddle v.t./i. to hug, to embrace fondly; to lie close and snug; to nestle together. —n. a prolonged and fond hug. —**cuddlesome** adj., **cuddly** adj. [perh. f. dial. couth snug]

cudgel /'kʌdʒ(ə)l/ n. a short thick stick used as a weapon. —v.t. (**-ll-**) to beat with a cudgel. —**cudgel one's brains**, to think hard about a problem. **take up the cudgels for**, to defend vigorously. [OE]

cue[1] n. something said or done (especially by an actor in a play) which serves as a signal for another to say or do something; a stimulus to perception etc.; a signal, a hint. —v.t. to give a cue to. —**cue in**, to insert a cue for; to give information to. [orig. unkn.]

cue[2] n. a billiard-player's rod for striking the ball. —v.t./i. to use a cue; to strike with a cue. [var. of QUEUE]

cuff[1] n. **1.** the thicker end-part of a sleeve; a separate band worn round the wrist. **2.** (in pl., colloq.) handcuffs. —**cuff-link** n. one of a pair of fasteners for shirt cuffs. **off the cuff**, extempore, without preparation. [orig. unkn.]

cuff[2] v.t. to strike with the open hand. —n. a cuffing blow. [perh. imit.]

Cufic var. of KUFIC.

cuirass /kwɪ'ræs/ n. a piece of armour consisting of a breastplate and back-plate fastened together (ill. ARMOUR). [f. OF f. L coriaceus (corium leather)]

cuisine /kwɪ'ziːn/ n. a style or method of cooking. [F, = kitchen]

cuisse /kwɪs/ n. (hist., usu. in pl.) thigh armour (ill. ARMOUR). [f. OF f. L (coxa hip)]

Culbertson /'kʌlbəts(ə)n/, Ely (1891-1955), American authority on contract bridge, whose activities in the early 1930s helped to establish this form of the game in preference to auction bridge.

Culdees /kʌl'diːz/ n.pl. the name given to certain Irish and Scottish monks in the 8th and following centuries. They appear to have been anchorites in origin, who banded together, usually in groups of 13 (on the analogy of Christ and his Apostles). They were gradually brought under canonical rule along with the secular clergy. [prob. f. Ir. célé dé companion]

cul-de-sac /'kʌldəsæk, 'kʊl-/ n. (pl. **culs-de-sac** pr. same) a street or passage closed at one end. [F, = sack-bottom]

culinary /'kʌlɪnərɪ/ adj. of or for cooking. [f. L (culina kitchen)]

cull v.t. **1.** to pick (a flower etc.), to select. **2.** to select from a herd etc. and kill (surplus animals). —n. culling; an animal or animals culled. [f. OF f. L colligere collect]

Culloden /kə'lɒd(ə)n/ a moor near Inverness in NE Scotland, site of the final engagement of the Jacobite uprising of 1745-6, the last pitched battle fought on British soil.

Having withdrawn into the Highlands before the Hanoverian army commanded by the Duke of Cumberland, the small and poorly supplied Jacobite army turned on its pursuers. Superior fire-power smashed the attacking Highland clan regiments, and a ruthless pursuit after the battle effectively prevented any chance of saving the Jacobite cause.

culminate /ˈkʌlmɪneɪt/ v.i. to reach its highest point (in). —**culmination** /-ˈneɪʃ(ə)n/ n. [f. L culminare (culmen summit)]

culottes /kjuːˈlɒts/ n.pl. women's trousers styled to resemble a skirt. [F, = knee-breeches]

culpable /ˈkʌlpəb(ə)l/ adj. deserving blame. —**culpability** /-ˈbɪlɪtɪ/ n., **culpably** adv. [f. OF f. L (culpare to blame)]

culprit /ˈkʌlprɪt/ n. a person accused of or guilty of an offence. [perh. abbr. of AF formula said by Clerk of Crown to prisoner pleading Not Guilty, Culpable: prest d'averrer etc. (You are) guilty: (I am) ready to prove it]

cult n. a system of religious worship especially as expressed in ritual; devotion or homage to a person or thing. [f. F or f. L (colere cultivate, worship)]

cultivate /ˈkʌltɪveɪt/ v.t. 1. to prepare and use (soil) for crops. 2. to produce (crops) by tending them. 3. to apply oneself to improving or developing (the mind, an acquaintance, etc.). 4. to spend time and care in developing; to develop the friendship of. —**cultivation** /-ˈveɪʃ(ə)n/ n. [f. L cultivare (cultiva (terra) arable land, as prec.)]

cultivator /ˈkʌltɪveɪtə(r)/ n. 1. a device for breaking up ground. 2. one who cultivates. [f. prec.]

Cultural Revolution a political upheaval in China, 1966-8, initiated by Marshal Lin Piao's calls for a return to revolutionary Maoist beliefs and attacks on the liberal ideals which had become prevalent in the early 20th c. Largely carried forward by the Red Guard, the Cultural Revolution resulted in a large-scale bloodless purge in party posts and the appearance of a virtual cult around the Chinese leader Mao Tse-tung, who had been in semi-retirement since 1959. It led, however, to considerable economic dislocation and was gradually brought to a halt by Chou En-lai.

culture /ˈkʌltʃə(r)/ n. 1. refined understanding of the arts and other human intellectual achievement. 2. the customs and civilization of a particular time or people. 3. improvement by care and training. 4. the cultivation of plants, rearing of bees, silkworms, etc. 4. a quantity of bacteria grown for study. —v.t. to grow (bacteria) for study. —**cultural** adj. [f. F or L (as CULT)]

cultured adj. having or showing culture. —**cultured pearl**, a pearl formed by an oyster after the insertion of a foreign body into its shell. [f. prec.]

culvert /ˈkʌlvət/ n. a drain that crosses under a road, canal, etc. [orig. unkn.]

cum /kʊm/ prep. with, together with; also used as. [L]

cumber v.t. (literary) to hamper, to hinder, to inconvenience. [f. ENCUMBER]

Cumberland /ˈkʌmbələnd/, William Augustus, Duke of Cumberland (1721-65), third son of George II. Hanoverian commander at the battle of Culloden, Cumberland gained great notoriety (and the nickname 'the Butcher') for the severity of his suppression of the Jacobite clans in the aftermath of his victory.

cumbersome /ˈkʌmbəsəm/ adj. hampering; inconvenient in size, weight, or shape. [f. prec.]

Cumbria /ˈkʌmbrɪə/ 1. an ancient kingdom of northern Britain. 2. a county of NW England.

cumin /ˈkʌmɪn/ n. a herb (Cuminum cyminum) with aromatic seeds. [f. OF f. L f. Gk (prob. of Semitic origin)]

cummerbund /ˈkʌməbʌnd/ n. a sash worn round the waist. [f. Hindi & Pers., = loin-band]

cumquat var. of KUMQUAT.

cumulate /ˈkjuːmjʊleɪt/ v.t./i. to accumulate; to combine (catalogue entries etc.). [f. L cumulare (cumulus heap)]

cumulative /ˈkjuːmjʊlətɪv/ adj. increasing or increased in amount, force, etc., by successive additions. —**cumulatively** adv. [as prec.]

cumulonimbus /kjuːmjʊləʊˈnɪmbəs/ n. a form of cloud consisting of a tall dense mass, present during thunderstorms (ill. WEATHER). [f. foll. + NIMBUS]

cumulus /ˈkjuːmjʊləs/ n. (pl. -li) a form of cloud consisting of rounded masses heaped on a horizontal base (ill. WEATHER). [L, = heap]

Cunard /kjuːˈnɑːd/, Sir Samuel (1787-1865), British-Canadian ship-owner. A native of Nova Scotia, Cunard

was one of the pioneers of the regular transatlantic passenger service, founding the steamship company which still bears his name with the aid of a contract to carry the mails between Britain and Canada.

cuneiform /ˈkjuːnɪfɔːm/ adj. of or using an ancient system of writing with wedge-shaped marks impressed on soft clay with a straight length of reed, bone, wood, or metal, or incised into stone etc. —n. this writing. It was used (though perhaps not invented) by the Sumerians, whose originally pictographic script had by the 3rd millennium BC become simplified into stylized patterns of short straight strokes (some with phonetic values) that were more suitable for impressing on the clay which had become increasingly the material on which writing was done. The dissemination of their civilization led to its use in modified forms for a number of languages in the Near East until towards the end of the 1st millennium BC. Cuneiform scripts remained undeciphered until the 19th c. when H. C. Rawlinson, British consul in Baghdad, discovered at Behistun in Persia a rock bearing a trilingual inscription; one text was in Persian characters, already partially deciphered, which served as a key to the others. [f. F f. L cuneus wedge + forma shape]

cunning adj. 1. skilled in ingenuity or deceit, selfishly clever or crafty; ingenious. 2. (US) attractive, quaint. —n. craftiness, skill in deceit. [f. ON, = knowing (as CAN¹)]

cunt n. (vulgar) the female genitals. [f. ON kunta, MLG, MDu. kunte]

cup n. 1. a small bowl with a handle, used for drinking from; its contents, the amount that it holds. 2. a cup-shaped thing. 3. flavoured wine, cider, etc. 4. an ornamental vessel as the prize for a race or contest. 5. one's fate or fortune. —v.t. (-pp-) to form (esp. one's hands) into the shape of a cup; to hold as in a cup. —**Cup Final**, the final football etc. match in a competition for a cup. —**cupful** n. (pl. -fuls) [OE]

cupboard /ˈkʌbəd/ n. a recess or piece of furniture with a door and (usually) shelves, in which things may be stored. —**cupboard love**, a display of affection meant to secure some gain.

Cupid /ˈkjuːpɪd/ (Rom. myth.) the god of love, identified by the Romans with Eros. He is often pictured as a beautiful naked boy with wings, carrying bow and arrows with which he wounds his victims. [f. L Cupido (cupere desire)]

cupidity /kjʊˈpɪdɪtɪ/ n. greed for gain. [f. OF or L (as CUPID)]

cupola /ˈkjuːpələ/ n. 1. a small dome on a roof. 2. a furnace for melting metals. 3. a ship's or fort's revolving gun-turret. [It. f. L (cupa cask)]

cuppa /ˈkʌpə/ n. (colloq.) a cup of (tea). [corrupt.]

cupreous /ˈkjuːprɪəs/ adj. of or like copper. [f. L (cuprum copper)]

cupric /ˈkjuːprɪk/ adj. of copper. [as prec.]

cupro-nickel /kjuːprəʊˈnɪk(ə)l/ n. an alloy of copper and nickel. [as CUPREOUS]

cur n. 1. a worthless or bad-tempered dog. 2. a contemptible person. [perh. f. ON kurr grumbling]

curable /ˈkjʊərəb(ə)l/ adj. that can be cured. [f. CURE]

curaçao /ˈkjʊərəsəʊ/ n. a liqueur flavoured with the peel of bitter oranges. [name of Caribbean island producing these oranges]

curacy /ˈkjʊərəsɪ/ n. a curate's office; the tenure of it. [f. CURATE]

curare /kjʊəˈrɑːrɪ/ n. the bitter extract of various plants, used by South American Indians as a poison on arrows. [f. Carib]

curate /ˈkjʊərət/ n. the assistant to a parish priest. [f. L (as CURE)]

curator /kjʊəˈreɪtə(r)/ n. a person in charge of a museum or other collection. [as prec.]

curative /ˈkjʊərətɪv/ adj. tending or able to cure. —n. a curative thing. [F f. L (as CURE)]

curb n. 1. a check, a restraint. 2. a strap or chain fastened to a bit and passing under a horse's lower jaw, used as a check. 3. a border or edging, the frame round the top of a well; a kerb. —v.t. 1. to restrain. 2. to put a curb on (a horse). [f. OF f. L curvare (as CURVE)]

curd n. (often in pl.) a coagulated substance formed by the action of acids on milk, made into cheese or eaten as food. [orig. unkn.]

curdle v.t./i. to congeal, to form into curds. —**make one's blood curdle**, to fill one with horror. [f. prec.]

cure *v.t.* **1.** to restore to health; to relieve *of* a disease; to eliminate (a disease, evil, etc.). **2.** to preserve (meat, fruit, tobacco, or skins) by salting, drying, etc. **3.** to vulcanize (rubber). —*n.* a thing that cures; a restoration to health; a course of medicinal or healing treatment. [f. OF f. L *curare* take care of (*cura* care)]

curé /ˈkjʊərei/ *n.* a parish priest in France etc. [F (as CURATE)]

curette /kjʊˈret/ *n.* a surgeon's small scraping-instrument. —*v.t.* to scrape with this. —**curettage** *n.* [F, f. *curer* cleanse (as CURE)]

curfew /ˈkɜːfjuː/ *n.* a signal or time after which people must remain indoors; (*hist.*) a signal for the extinction of fires at a fixed evening hour. [f. AF *coeverfu* (as COVER, FUEL)]

Curia /ˈkjʊərɪə/ *n.* the papal court, especially those functionaries through whom the government of the Roman Catholic Church is administered. [L, = senate-house at Rome]

Curie /ˈkjʊəri/, Marie (1867-1934) and Pierre (1859-1906), pioneers of radioactivity. Born Marja Sklodowska in Poland, Marie studied physics at the Sorbonne in Paris and married Pierre in 1895. They worked together on the mineral pitchblende, seeking to discover why it was so radioactive even after uranium had been extracted from it. Pierre earned their living by teaching, while Marie lugged the sacks and stirred the cauldron with a long iron bar, and working in a rough shed they discovered the elements polonium and radium in the mineral; for this they shared the 1903 Nobel Prize for physics with Becquerel. Marie succeeded to her husband's chair of physics at the Sorbonne after his accidental death, and continued her work on radioactivity, receiving a second Nobel Prize in 1911, this one for chemistry, for her isolation of radium; she was the first scientist to be awarded two Prizes. She also studied radioactive decay and the applications of radioactivity to medicine, pioneered mobile X-ray units, headed the French Radiological Service during the First World War, and afterwards worked in the newly-established Radium Institute. She died of leukaemia, undoubtedly caused by prolonged exposure to radioactive materials; neither the Curies nor anyone else had realized the dangers. Pierre's early researches were on piezoelectricity (which he discovered with his brother Jacques in 1880) and on the effects of temperature on magnetism. He discovered that at a certain temperature (the Curie point) ferromagnetic substances lose their magnetism and exhibit paramagnetism. Their elder daughter, Irène, married the physicist J.-F. Joliot. The curie, a unit of radioactivity, was named after Pierre and the element curium after Marie and Pierre Curie.

curie /ˈkjʊəri/ *n.* **1.** a unit of radioactivity, corresponding to 3.7×10^{10} disintegrations per second. **2.** a quantity of radioactive substance having this activity. [f. P. CURIE]

curio /ˈkjʊərɪəʊ/ *n.* (*pl.* **-os**) a rare or unusual object. [abbr. of foll.]

curiosity /kjʊərɪˈɒsɪtɪ/ *n.* **1.** an eager desire to know; inquisitiveness. **2.** a strange or rare thing. [as foll.]

curious /ˈkjʊərɪəs/ *adj.* **1.** eager to know or learn; inquisitive. **2.** strange, surprising, odd. —**curiously** *adv.* [f. OF f. L *curiosus* careful (as CURE)]

curium /ˈkjʊərɪəm/ *n.* an artificially made transuranic radioactive metallic element, symbol Cm, atomic number 96, first obtained in 1944 by bombarding plutonium with helium ions. [f. M. and P. CURIE]

curl *v.t./i.* **1.** to bend or coil into a spiral; to move in a spiral form. **2.** to play curling. —*n.* **1.** a coiled lock of hair; anything spiral or curved inwards. **2.** a curling movement. —**curl up,** to lie or sit with the knees drawn up; to writhe with horror, shame, etc. [f. obs. *crulle* curly f. Du.]

curler *n.* a device for curling the hair. [f. prec.]

curlew /ˈkɜːljuː/ *n.* a wading bird of the genus *Numenius*, with a long slender curved bill. [f. OF]

curlicue /ˈkɜːlɪkjuː/ *n.* a decorative curl or twist. [f. CURLY + CUE² (= pigtail) or Q]

curling *n.* a game played on ice, in which large flat rounded stones are hurled along a defined space (the *rink*) towards a mark (the *tee*). In its earlier form it seems to have been akin to quoits, but is now more like bowls. Scotland's 'ain game' may have originated in the Low Countries: two of Breughel's landscapes (16th c.) show a similar game being played on frozen ponds. There are references to the game from 1620 onwards, and it developed in Scotland whence it spread to other countries where the climatic conditions are suitable. [f. CURL]

curly *adj.* having or arranged in curls; moving in curves. [f. CURL]

curmudgeon /kəˈmʌdʒ(ə)n/ *n.* a bad-tempered person. [orig. unkn.]

currant /ˈkʌrənt/ *n.* **1.** the dried fruit of a small seedless grape, used in cookery. **2.** any of various shrubs of the genus *Ribes* producing black, red, or white berries; such a berry. [f. AF, = (grapes of) Corinth, the orig. source)]

currawong /ˈkʌrəwɒŋ/ *n.* a small crowlike Australian bird of the genus *Strepera*, with a resonant call. [Aboriginal]

currency /ˈkʌrənsɪ/ *n.* **1.** the money in use in a country. **2.** being current, prevalence. [f. foll.]

current /ˈkʌrənt/ *adj.* **1.** belonging to the present time, happening now. **2.** (of money, an opinion, rumour, word) in general circulation or use. —*n.* **1.** a body of water, air, etc., moving in a definite direction, especially through a stiller surrounding body. **2.** the general tendency or course *of* events or opinions. **3.** the movement of electrically charged particles; a quantity representing the intensity of this. —**current account,** a bank account from which money may be drawn without notice. [f. OF f. L *currere* run]

currently *adv.* at the present time. [f. prec.]

curricle /ˈkʌrɪk(ə)l/ *n.* a light open horse-drawn carriage, usually with two horses abreast. [f. L *curriculum* (see foll.)]

curriculum /kəˈrɪkjʊləm/ *n.* (*pl* **-la**) a course of study. —**curriculum vitae** /ˈviːtaɪ/, an account of one's previous career. [L, = racecourse (*currere* run)]

currier /ˈkʌrɪə(r)/ *n.* a leather-dresser. [f. OF f. L (*corium* leather)]

curry¹ *n.* a dish of meat, fish, eggs, etc., cooked with hot-tasting spices, usually served with rice. —*v.t.* to make (meat etc.) into a curry. —**curry powder,** a preparation of turmeric and other spices for making curry. [f. Tamil *kari* sauce]

curry² *v.t.* **1.** to groom (a horse) with a curry-comb. **2.** to treat (tanned leather) to improve its properties. —**curry-comb** *n.* a pad with rubber or plastic projections for grooming a horse. —**curry favour,** to ingratiate oneself. [f. OF f. L *conredare* f. Gmc (as READY)]

curse *n.* **1.** a solemn utterance wishing a person to suffer destruction or punishment; an evil resulting from this. **2.** a violent exclamation of anger, a profane oath. **3.** a thing that causes evil or harm. —*v.t./i.* to utter a curse against; to utter expletive curses. —**the curse,** (*colloq.*) menstruation. **be cursed with,** to have as a burden or source of harm. [OE]

cursed /ˈkɜːsɪd/ *adj.* damnable, abominable. [f. prec.]

cursive /ˈkɜːsɪv/ *adj.* (of writing) done with joined characters. —*n.* cursive writing. [f. L (*scriptura*) *cursiva* f. *currere* run]

cursor /ˈkɜːsə(r)/ *n.* **1.** a transparent slide with a hair-line, forming part of a slide-rule. **2.** the indicator on a VDU screen, showing a particular position in displayed matter. [L, = runner (as prec.)]

cursory /ˈkɜːsərɪ/ *adj.* hasty, hurried. —**cursorily** *adv.* [f. L, = of a runner (as prec.)]

curt *adj.* noticeably or rudely brief. —**curtly** *adv.*, **curtness** *n.* [f. L *curtus* cut short]

curtail /kɜːˈteɪl/ *v.t.* to cut short, to reduce. —**curtailment** *n.* [f. obs. *curtal* horse with docked tail f. OF (as prec.)]

curtain /ˈkɜːt(ə)n/ *n.* a piece of cloth etc. hung up as a screen, usually movable sideways or upwards, especially at a window or between the stage and auditorium of a theatre; the rise or fall of the stage curtain at the beginning or end of an act or scene; (in *pl.*, *slang*) the end. —*v.t.* to furnish or cover with curtains; to shut *off* with a curtain or curtains. —**curtain-call** *n.* an audience's summons to an actor or actors to take a bow after the fall of the curtain. **curtain-raiser** *n.* a short opening theatre-piece; a preliminary event. **curtain-wall** *n.* the plain wall of a fortified place, connecting two towers etc. [f. OF f. L *cortina* transl. Gk *aulaia* (*aulē* court)]

Curtiss /ˈkɜːtɪs/, Glenn Hammond (1878-1930), pioneer American pilot and designer of aircraft and engines. Like some motor manufacturers he began by building and selling bicycles; then he built motor cycles (1901), on one of which he achieved 136.3 mph in 1907, and his first aeroplane in 1909. He obtained America's first pilot's licence, and won the first international Gordon Bennett Cup in 1911. In 1912 he built the world's first successful flying boat.

curtsy /ˈkɜːtsɪ/ *n.* a woman's or girl's salutation made by bending the knees and lowering the body. —*v.i.* to make a curtsy. [var. of COURTESY]

curvaceous /kɜːˈveɪʃəs/ *adj.* (*colloq.*) (of a woman) having a shapely curved figure. [f. CURVE]

curvature /ˈkɜːvətʃə(r)/ *n.* curving; curved form. [f. OF f. L (as foll.)]

curve *n.* a line of which no part is straight; a surface of which no part is flat; a curved form or thing; a curved line on a graph. —*v.t./i.* to bend or shape so as to form a curve. —**curvy** *adj.* [f. L *curvus* curved]

curvet /kɜːˈvet/ *n.* a horse's short frisky leap. —*v.i.* to perform a curvet. [f. It. dim. of *corva* (as prec.)]

curvilinear /kɜːvɪˈlɪnɪə(r)/ contained by or consisting of curved lines. [f. CURVE, after *rectilinear*]

Cushing /ˈkʊʃɪŋ/, Harvey Williams (1869-1939), American surgeon who introduced techniques that greatly increased the likelihood of success in neurosurgical operations, and was the first to describe (in 1932) a hormonal disorder named after him.

cushion /ˈkʊʃ(ə)n/ *n.* **1.** a fabric case filled with a mass of soft or springy material, used to make a seat etc. more comfortable. **2.** a soft pad or other means of support or of protection against jarring; a means of protection against shock; the elastic lining of the rim of a billiard table, from which the balls rebound. **3.** the body of air supporting a hovercraft etc. —*v.t.* **1.** to provide or protect with a cushion or cushions. **2.** to mitigate the adverse effects of. [f. OF f. L *culcita* mattress]

Cushitic /kʌˈʃɪtɪk/ *adj.* of a group of East African languages of Hamitic type, spoken mainly in Ethiopia and Somalia. —*n.* this group of languages. [f. *Cush*, ancient country in Nile valley]

cushy /ˈkʊʃɪ/ *adj.* (*colloq.*, of a job etc.) pleasant and easy. [f. Hindi, = pleasant]

cusp *n.* a point at which two curves meet; a projecting point between small arcs in Gothic tracery (ill. CHURCH); the horn of the crescent moon etc. [f. L *cuspis* point, apex]

cuss *n.* (*colloq.*) **1.** a curse. **2.** an awkward or difficult person. —*v.t./i.* (*colloq.*) to curse. [vulgar pronunc. of CURSE]

cussed /ˈkʌsɪd/ *adj.* (*colloq.*) awkward and stubborn. —**cussedness** *n.* [f. prec.]

custard /ˈkʌstəd/ *n.* a dish or sauce made with milk and beaten eggs, usually sweetened; a sweet sauce made with milk and flavoured cornflour. [f. AF f. OF *crouste* crust]

Custer /ˈkʌstə(r)/, George Armstrong (1839-76), US cavalry general, who earned distinction in numerous battles in the American Civil War but led his men to their deaths in a clash with the Indians at Little Bighorn in Montana. Assessment of him varies, and controversy over his conduct in the final battle still continues.

custodian /kʌsˈtəʊdɪən/ *n.* a guardian or keeper, especially of a public building. [f. foll.]

custody /ˈkʌstədɪ/ *n.* **1.** guardianship, protective care. **2.** imprisonment. —**take into custody,** to arrest. —**custodial** /-ˈstəʊdɪəl/ *adj.* [f. L *custodia* (*custos* guardian)]

custom /ˈkʌstəm/ *n.* **1.** the usual way of behaving or acting; established usage as a power or as having the force of law. **2.** a business patronage, regular dealings or customers. **3.** (in *pl.*) the duty levied on imports; (often treated as *sing.*) the government department or officials administering this. —**custom-built** *adj.* built to a customer's order. **custom-house** *n.* an office at a port or frontier etc. at which customs duties are levied. [f. OF f. L *consuetudo*]

customary *adj.* in accordance with custom, usual. —**customarily** *adv.* [f. L (as prec.)]

customer *n.* a person who buys goods or services from a shop or business; (*colloq.*) a person one has to deal with. [f. AF (as CUSTOM)]

cut *v.t./i.* (*past* and *p.p.* **cut**) **1.** to penetrate or wound with a sharp-edged instrument (also *fig.*). **2.** to divide or detach with a knife etc.; to shape, make, or shorten thus; to be able to cut or be cut; to have (a tooth) appear through the gum. **3.** to execute (*a caper* etc.) or make (*a sorry figure* etc.). **4.** to reduce by removing part of; to cease to provide; to switch off (electricity, an engine, etc.). **5.** to divide a pack of cards; to select (a card) thus. **6.** to absent oneself from; to renounce (a connection), to ignore or refuse to recognize (a person). **7.** to edit (a film); to go quickly *to* another shot. **8.** to hit (a ball) with a chopping motion in cricket etc. **9.** to pass *through* etc. as a shorter way. **10.** (*US*) to dilute (spirits for drinking). —*n.* **1.** the act of cutting; a division, wound, or hurt made by this; a stroke with a sword, whip, or cane. **2.** a piece of meat cut from a carcass. **3.** the way a

thing is cut, the style in which clothes are made. **4.** a reduction or cessation. **5.** an excision of part of a play, film, book, etc. **6.** (*slang*) a commission, a share of the profits etc. **7.** a stroke made by cutting a ball in cricket etc. **8.** a cutting remark. **9.** the ignoring of or refusal to recognize a person etc. —**a cut above,** noticeably superior to. **cut and dried,** prepared in advance, ready; inflexible. **cut and run,** (*slang*) to run away. **cut back,** to reduce, to prune. **cut-back** *n.* a reduction. **cut both ways,** to serve both sides of an argument. **cut corners,** to do a task etc. perfunctorily or incompletely. **cut down,** to reduce (expenses etc.). **cut in,** to interrupt; to move in front of another vehicle (especially in overtaking) leaving too little space. **cut it out,** (*slang*, *imper.*) stop doing that. **cut line,** a line above which service must be made in squash (ill. SPORTS). **cut one's losses,** to abandon an unprofitable scheme before the losses become too great. **cut no ice,** (*slang*) to be of no importance or effect. **cut off,** to end abruptly; to intercept, to interrupt; to prevent from continuing; to disinherit. **cut-off** *n.* the point at which a thing is cut off; a device for stopping a flow. **cut out,** to remove, to omit; to outdo or supplant; to cease or cause to cease functioning; (in *pass.*) to be suited (*for, to* be or do). **cut-out** *n.* a thing cut out; a device for automatic disconnection; the release of exhaust gases, etc. **cut-price** *adj.* for sale at a reduced price. **cut-rate** *adj.* available at a reduced rate. **cut a tooth,** to have a tooth beginning to emerge from the gum. **cut one's teeth on,** to acquire experience from. **cut up,** to cut into small pieces; (in *pass.*) to be greatly distressed. **cut up rough,** to show anger or resentment. [perh. OE]

cutaneous /kjuːˈteɪnɪəs/ *adj.* of the skin. [f. L (as CUTIS)]

cutaway *adj.* **1.** (of a diagram etc.) having some parts absent to reveal the interior. **2.** (of a coat) with the front below the waist cut away.

cute /kjuːt/ *adj.* (*colloq.*) clever, ingenious; (*US*) attractive, quaint. —**cutely** *adv.*, **cuteness** *n.* [f. ACUTE]

Cuthbert /ˈkʌθbət/, St (d. 687), English monk and missionary, who became bishop of Lindisfarne. Feast day, 20 Mar.

cuticle /ˈkjuːtɪk(ə)l/ *n.* the skin at the base of the finger-nail or toe-nail. [f. L *cuticula* (as foll.)]

cutis /ˈkjuːtɪs/ *n.* the true skin beneath the epidermis. [L, = skin]

cutlass /ˈkʌtləs/ *n.* (*hist.*) a short sword with a slightly curved blade. [f. F f. L (as foll.)]

cutlery /ˈkʌtlərɪ/ *n.* knives, forks, and spoons for use at table. [f. OF f. L *cultellus* dim. of *culter* knife]

cutlet /ˈkʌtlɪt/ *n.* a neck-chop of mutton or lamb; a small piece of veal etc. for frying; a flat cake of minced meat etc. [f. OF f. L (*costa* rib)]

cutter *n.* **1.** a tailor etc. who takes measurements and cuts cloth. **2.** a small fast sailing-ship (ill. SAILING-SHIPS). **3.** a small boat carried by a larger ship. [f. CUT]

cutting *n.* **1.** a piece cut from a newspaper etc. **2.** a piece cut from a plant for propagation. **3.** an excavated channel through high ground, for a railway or road. [f. CUT]

cutthroat *n.* **1.** a murderer. **2.** a razor with a long blade set in a handle. —*adj.* **1.** intense and ruthless. **2.** (of a card-game) three-handed.

cuttlefish /ˈkʌt(ə)lfɪʃ/ *n.* a ten-armed mollusc of the genus *Sepia* that ejects a black fluid when threatened. [OE, rel. to *cod* bag (ref. to the ink-bag)]

Cutty Sark the only survivor of the British tea-clippers (see CLIPPER), launched in 1869 and now preserved as a museum ship at Greenwich, London. The name comes from a poem by Robert Burns which tells of a Scottish farmer who was chased by the young witch Nannie who wore only her 'cutty sark' (= short shift); the ship's figurehead is a representation of the witch with her arm outstretched to catch the tail of the farmer's grey mare on which he was escaping.

cutwater *n.* **1.** the forward edge of a ship's prow. **2.** a wedge-shaped projection from a pier or bridge (ill. BRIDGES).

Cuvier /ˈkuːvɪeɪ/, Georges Jean Léopold Nicolas Frédéric, Baron (1769-1832), French naturalist who founded the science of palaeontology with a study of fossil elephants. Pioneering also in comparative anatomy, he was the first to classify the lower invertebrate animals. Later he realized that each such species could be derived from another by small changes in their structure, an observation which proved crucial in the emergence of the theory of evolution. He himself believed resolutely in the conventional view that the world had been created by God and quarrelled publicly with the early proponents of evolutionary ideas, notably Lamarck. He sought favour with the new political regimes of early 19th-c. France, and was given responsibility for the reorganization of the French universities.

Cuzco /ˈkʌskəʊ/ a city in the Andes in southern Peru that was the capital of the Inca empire until the Spanish conquest (1533).

c.v. *abbr.* curriculum vitae.

cwm /kuːm/ *n.* (in Wales) = COOMB; a cirque. [Welsh]

cwt. *abbr.* hundredweight.

cyan /ˈsaɪən/ *adj. & n.* (in photography) greenish-blue. [f. Gk *kuan(e)os* dark blue]

cyanic /saɪˈænɪk/ *adj.* of or containing cyanogen. [f. CYANOGEN]

cyanide /ˈsaɪənaɪd/ *n.* a highly poisonous substance used in the extraction of gold and silver. [f. foll.]

cyanogen /saɪˈænədʒɪn/ *n.* an inflammable poisonous gas. [f. F f. Gk *kuanos* dark-blue mineral + -GEN]

cyanosis /saɪəˈnəʊsɪs/ *n.* blue discoloration of the skin due to lack of oxygen in the blood. [as prec.]

Cybele /sɪˈbiːlɪ/ (*Anatolian myth.*) a mother-goddess worshipped especially in Phrygia and later in Greece (where she was associated with Demeter), Rome, and the Roman provinces, with her consort Attis.

cybernetics /saɪbəˈnetɪks/ *n.* the science of the systems of control and communications in animals and machines. —**cybernetic** *adj.* [f. Gk *kubernētēs* steersman]

Cyclades /ˈsɪklədiːz/ *n.pl.* a group of islands in the Aegean Sea, regarded in antiquity as circling around the sacred island of Delos. They are the site of a Bronze Age civilization noted for developments in metallurgy and for angular figurines in white marble. —**Cycladic** /saɪˈklædɪk/ *adj.* [L f. Gk *kuklos* circle)]

cyclamate /ˈsaɪkləmeɪt, ˈsɪk-/ *n.* an artificial sweetening agent. [f. chemical name]

cyclamen /ˈsɪkləmən/ *n.* a plant of the genus *Cyclamen*, with pink, red, or white flowers with reflexed petals. [L f. Gk (perh. f. *kuklos* circle)]

cycle /ˈsaɪk(ə)l/ *n.* **1.** a recurrent round or period (of events, phenomena, etc.); the time needed for one such round or period; cycles per second, hertz. **2.** a recurrent series of operations or states; a series of songs, poems, etc., usually on a single theme. **3.** a bicycle, a tricycle, or motor cycle. —*v.i.* **1.** to ride a bicycle or tricycle. **2.** to move in cycles. [f. OF, or f. L f. Gk *kuklos* circle]

cyclic /ˈsaɪklɪk/ *adj.* **1.** recurring in cycles; belonging to a chronological cycle. **2.** (*Chem.*) with the constituent atoms forming a ring. [f. F or L (as prec.)]

cyclist /ˈsaɪklɪst/ *n.* a rider of a bicycle. [f. CYCLE]

cyclo- *comb. form* of CYCLE.

cyclo-cross /ˈsaɪkləʊkrɒs/ *n.* cross-country racing on bicycles, a sport mainly confined to Europe (especially Luxemburg, the Low Countries, and Russia) but found also in the USA, especially near Chicago.

cyclone /ˈsaɪkləʊn/ *n.* a system of winds rotating inwards to an area of low barometric pressure; a violent hurricane of a limited diameter (ill. WEATHER). —**cyclonic** /-ˈklɒnɪk/ *adj.* [f. Gk *kuklōma* wheel, coil of snake (as CYCLE)]

Cyclopean /saɪkləˈpiːən/ *adj.* (of ancient masonry) made of massive irregular blocks. [f. L f. Gk (*Kuklōps* Cyclops, see foll.)]

Cyclopes /ˈsaɪkləpiːz/ *n.pl.* (*sing.* **Cyclops**) (*Gk myth.*) (in Homer) a race of one-eyed giants who are savage and pastoral; (in Hesiod) three one-eyed giants who make thunderbolts and are craftsmen.

cyclostyle /ˈsaɪkləstaɪl/ *n.* an apparatus printing copies of writing from a stencil. —*v.t.* to print or reproduce with this. [f. CYCLO- + STYLE]

cyclotron /ˈsaɪklətrɒn/ *n.* an apparatus for accelerating charged atomic particles by subjecting them repeatedly to an electric field as they revolve in orbits of increasing diameter in a constant magnetic field. It was invented in 1929 by the American physicist E. O. Lawrence, who was awarded a Nobel Prize in 1939. [f. CYCLO- + -TRON]

cygnet /ˈsɪgnɪt/ *n.* a young swan. [f. AF f. L (as foll.)]

Cygnus /ˈsɪgnəs/ a summer constellation, the Swan (named after a disguise adopted by Zeus on one of his many earthly escapades) or Northern Cross. It contains a host of objects of great astronomical interest, including the yellow supergiant star Deneb, the brightest dwarf nova SS Cygni, and the X-ray source Cygnus X-1 which is believed to be a binary star system which includes a black hole. [L, = swan]

cylinder /ˈsɪlɪndə(r)/ *n.* a uniform solid or hollow body

with straight sides and a circular section; a thing of this shape, e.g. a container for liquid gas etc., or a part of a machine, especially the piston-chamber in an engine.

cylinder seal, a small cylindrical object of precious or semi-precious stone, shell, clay, faience, glass, occasionally metal, and possibly wood, which is usually pierced through its long axis for suspension and is always engraved with a design. It is particularly characteristic of Mesopotamia from the late 4th-1st millennium BC, where it served first as a mark of property and later as a signature to authenticate clay documents. —**cylindrical** /-ˈlɪndrɪk(ə)l/ *adj.* [f. L f. Gk (*kulindō* to roll)]

cymbal /ˈsɪmb(ə)l/ *n.* each of a pair of concave brass plates forming a musical instrument, clashed together or struck to make a ringing sound (ill. ORCHESTRA). —**cymbalist** *n.* [f. L f. Gk (*kumbē* cup)]

cyme /saɪm/ *n.* a flower group with a single terminal flower on each stem (ill. PLANTS). [F, var. of *cime* summit [f. L f. Gk]

Cymric /ˈkɪmrɪk/ *adj.* Welsh. [f. Welsh *Cymru* Wales]

Cynewulf /ˈkɪnɪwʊlf/ (late 8th-9th c.), Anglo-Saxon poet, probably from Northumbria or Mercia. Of the many poems that have been attributed to him modern scholarship restricts attribution to four poems in the Exeter Book and the Vercelli Book which end with his name in runes: *Juliana*; *Elene*, the story of the Finding of the Cross by St Helena; *The Fates of the Apostles*; and *Christ II*, a poem on the Ascension.

Cynic /ˈsɪnɪk/ *n.* a member of an ancient Greek sect of philosophers founded by Antisthenes, a pupil of Socrates, who were characterized by an ostentatious contempt for ease, wealth, and the enjoyments of life. The most famous was Diogenes, a pupil of Antisthenes, who carried these principles to an extreme of asceticism. The movement flourished in the 3rd c. BC and revived in the 1st c. AD, when the Cynic beggar philosophers became a common sight in the Roman Empire. —*adj.* of the Cynics. [f. L f. Gk *kunikos* (*kuōn* dog, nickname of Diogenes]

cynic /ˈsɪnɪk/ *n.* one who has little faith in human sincerity or goodness. —**cynical** *adj.*, **cynically** *adv.*, **cynicism** *n.* [= prec.]

cynosure /ˈsaɪnəzjʊə(r), ˈsɪn-/ *n.* a centre of attraction or admiration. [F, or f. L f. Gk, = dog's tail (name for Ursa Minor)]

cypher var. of CIPHER.

cypress /ˈsaɪprəs/ a coniferous tree of the genus *Cupressus*, with dark foliage, taken as a symbol of mourning. [f. OF f. L f. Gk]

Cyprian /ˈsɪprɪən/, St (d. 258), bishop of Carthage, author of an esteemed work on the nature of true unity in the Church in its relation to the episcopate, martyred in the reign of the emperor Valerian. Feast day, (in the RC Missal) 16 Sept.; in the Book of Common Prayer (by confusion with Cyprian, a converted magician of Antioch, who lived *c.*300) 26 Sept.

Cypriot /ˈsɪprɪət/ *n.* **1.** a native or inhabitant of Cyprus. **2.** the dialect of Greek used there. —*adj.* of Cyprus or its people or language. [f. foll.]

Cyprus /ˈsaɪprəs/ a large island in the eastern Mediterranean about 80 km (50 miles) south of the Turkish coast; pop. (est. 1980) 662,000; official languages, Greek and Turkish; capital, Nicosia. The island was colonized from Greece in the first half of the 14th c. BC. In classical times it was noted for its copper (which is named after it) and its cult of Aphrodite. Placed at the crossroads of a number of ancient civilizations, its Greek population was successively subject to Assyrian, Egyptian, Persian, Ptolemaic, and Roman overlordship. In medieval times it was ruled by Byzantines, Arabs, Franks, and Venetians, until conquered in 1571 by the Turks, who held it until 1878 when it was placed under British administration. It was annexed by Britain in 1914 and made a Crown Colony in 1925. The island's recent history has been dominated by tension between the two major communities, the Greek Cypriots (some of whom favour *enosis* or union with Greece) and the Turkish Cypriots. After a period of virtual civil war from 1955 Cyprus became an independent republic within the Commonwealth in 1959, but its constitution proved unworkable. In 1974 Turkey invaded the island and established a 'Turkish Federated State' in northern Cyprus; this has not been recognized by the UN.

Cyrano de Bergerac /sɪrɑːnəʊ də ˈbeəʒəræk/, Savinien (1619-55), soldier, libertine, and duellist, famous for his grotesque appearance and long nose. He became a dramatist and novelist and is the subject of a highly successful play by Edmond Rostand. Two of his novels are about flights to the moon, with propulsion by bottles of dew (which vanished sunward in the morning), lodestones, and finally an array of rockets.

Cyrenaic /saɪrɪˈneɪɪk/ *adj.* of the hedonistic school of philosophy founded *c*.400 BC by Aristippus of Cyrene (a town in North Africa), a pupil of Socrates. Its ethical doctrines anticipated those of the Epicureans. —*n.* a philosopher of this school. [f. L f. Gk (*Kurēnē* Cyrene)]

Cyril[1] /ˈsɪrɪl/, St (d. 444), Patriarch of Alexandria, Doctor of the Church, best known for his vehement opposition to the views of Nestorius whose condemnation he secured at the Council of Ephesus in 431. His extensive writings show his precision, accuracy, and skill as a theologian but often reveal intransigence and misunderstanding of his opponents' thought. Feast day, 9 Feb.

Cyril[2] /ˈsɪrɪl/, St (826–69), Greek missionary, to whom is ascribed the invention of the Cyrillic alphabet (see foll.). He and his brother Methodius (*c*.815–85) became known as the 'Apostles of the Slavs'. Dispatched to Moravia, they taught in the vernacular, which they adopted also for the liturgy, and circulated a Slavonic version of the Scriptures. They met with hostility from the German bishops there, but received papal support. Feast day in the Eastern Church 11 May, in the Western Church 14 Feb.

Cyrillic /sɪˈrɪlɪk/ *adj.* of one of the two principal Slavonic alphabets (the other is the Roman) in use today. It was based on Greek uncials, and was reputedly introduced by St Cyril and his brother St Methodius in their missionary work amongst southern Slavs. It has remained, with some changes, the method of writing the languages (which include Russian) of those Slavonic peoples whose Christianity and culture came, directly or indirectly, from the Greek civilization of medieval Constantinople. [f. CYRIL[2]]

Cyrus /ˈsaɪrəs/ 'the Great', son of Cambyses, king of Persia 559–529 BC and founder of the Achaemenid dynasty. He subjected the Medes after the capture of their king Astyages in 549 BC, and went on to conquer Asia Minor, Babylonia, Syria, Palestine, and most of the Iranian plateau. He ruled his empire with wisdom and moderation.

cyst /sɪst/ *n.* a sac formed in the body, containing morbid matter. [f. Gk *kustis* bladder]

cystic *adj.* 1. of the bladder. 2. like a cyst. [f. F (as prec.)]

cystitis /sɪsˈtaɪtɪs/ *n.* inflammation of the bladder. [f. Gk *kustis* bladder]

-cyte /-saɪt/ *suffix* denoting a mature biological cell. [as foll.]

cytology /saɪˈtɒlədʒɪ/ *n.* the study of biological cells. —**cytological** /-ˈlɒdʒɪk(ə)l/ *adj.* [f. Gk *kutos* vessel + -LOGY]

cytoplasm /ˈsaɪtəplæz(ə)m/ *n.* the protoplasmic content of a cell other than the nucleus. —**cytoplasmic** *adj.* [f. CYTO- + PLASMA]

czar var. of TSAR.

Czech /tʃek/ *n.* 1. a native of the western and central parts of Czechoslovakia, namely Bohemia and Moravia. 2. the Slavonic language spoken by some 10 million people in these parts. 3. a Czechoslovakian. —*adj.* of the Czechs or their language. [Polish spelling of Bohemian *Cech*]

Czechoslovak /tʃekəˈsləʊvæk/ (also **Czechoslovakian** /-ˈvækɪən/) *n.* a native of Czechoslovakia. —*adj.* of Czechoslovakia or its people. [f. prec. + SLOVAK]

Czechoslovakia /tʃekəsləˈvækɪə/ a country in central Europe, between Germany in the west and the USSR in the east; pop. (1980) 15,280,148; official languages, Czech and Slovak; capital, Prague. The country has long been industrialized. Economic planning is in the hands of the government, industry is nationalized, and agriculture is mainly run by State or co-operative farms. Czechoslovakia was created out of the northern part of the old Austro-Hungarian empire after the latter's collapse at the end of the First World War. It incorporated the Czechs (who had enjoyed freedom within their own State of Bohemia until the rise of Hapsburg power in the 16th and 17th c.) of Bohemia and Moravia in the west with the Slovaks of Slovakia in the east. Czech history between the two World Wars represents a brave and enlightened attempt at integration, undermined by economic trouble and eventually crushed by the Nazi takeover of first the Sudetenland (1938) and then the rest of Bohemia-Moravia (1939). After the Second World War, power was seized by the Communists and since then Czechoslovakia has remained under Russian domination, an attempt at liberalization being crushed by Soviet military intervention in 1968. —**Czechoslovakian** *adj.* & *n.*

Czerny /ˈtʃeənɪ/, Karl (1791–1857), Austrian pianist, teacher, and composer. He was a pupil of Beethoven, the teacher of Liszt, and a pianist/composer at a time when the piano was undergoing important structural developments. The bulk of his output is made up of over 1,000 exercises and studies for this instrument, but he also composed operas, symphonies, and sacred works.

D

D, d *n.* **1.** the fourth letter of the alphabet. **2.** (*Mus.*) the second note in the scale of C major. **3.** (as a Roman numeral) 500. **4.** = DEE.

d. *abbr.* **1.** daughter. **2.** died. **3.** (until 1971) penny, pence (short for L *denarius*).

dab[1] *v.t./i.* (**-bb-**) **1.** to press briefly and lightly. **2.** to aim a feeble blow (*at*), to strike lightly. —*n.* **1.** an act of dabbing, a light blow. **2.** a small amount of a soft substance applied to a surface. **3.** (in *pl.*, *slang*) fingerprints. [imit.]

dab[2] *n. & adj.* (*colloq.*, also **dab hand**) an adept [orig. unkn.]

dab[3] *n.* a flat-fish of the genus *Limanda*. [orig. unkn.]

dabble *v.t./i.* **1.** to wet partly or intermittently; to move the feet, hands, or bill lightly in water or mud. **2.** to study or work casually (*in* a subject). [f. DAB[1]]

dabchick *n.* a small water-bird of the grebe family. [prob. f. *dap* dip + CHICK]

Dacca /ˈdækə/ var. of DHAKA.

dace /deɪs/ *n.* (*pl.* same) a small freshwater fish, especially of the genus *Leuciscus*, related to the carp. [f. OF *dars* dart]

dachshund /ˈdækshʊnd/ *n.* a small dog of a short-legged long-bodied breed. [G, = badger-dog]

Dacia /ˈdeɪʃə/ an ancient country of SE Europe in what is now the northern and western part of Romania.

dactyl /ˈdæktɪl/ *n.* a metrical foot with one long or stressed syllable followed by two short or unstressed syllables. —**dactylic** /-ˈtɪlɪk/ *adj.* [f. Gk *dactulos* finger]

dad *n.* (*colloq.*) father. [imit. of child's *da da*]

Dada /ˈdɑːdɑː/ *n.* an international movement in art and literature about 1915–20, repudiating conventions and intended to shock (see below). —**Dadaism** /-dəɪz(ə)m/ *n.*, **Dadaist** *n.*
Dada is a French word for a child's hobby-horse, said to have been chosen at random from a dictionary and used as a label by a group of artists and writers who were refugees from the First World War in Switzerland. The movement was born in Zurich in 1916 and spread to Paris, Cologne, and New York. It was essentially nihilistic and self-destructive and was absorbed by the Surrealists during the 1920s, although, unlike Surrealism, it was always against politics (and against everything else, including, logically, Dada). The leading figures were the poet Tzara, the sculptor Arp, and the painters Ernst and Duchamp.

daddy *n.* (*colloq.*) father; the oldest or most important person or thing. [f. DAD]

daddy-long-legs *n.* a crane-fly.

dado /ˈdeɪdəʊ/ *n.* (*pl.* **-os**) **1.** the lower part of the wall of a room etc. when it is coloured or faced differently from the upper part. **2.** the plinth of a column. **3.** the cube of a pedestal. [It., = DIE[1]]

Dadra and Nagar Haveli /ˈdɑːdrə, ˈnɑːgə həˈveɪli/ a Union Territory in western India; capital, Silvassa.

Daedalus /ˈdaɪdələs/ (*Gk legend*) a craftsman who is said to have built the labyrinth for Minos, king of Crete. Minos imprisoned him and his son Icarus, but they escaped on wings which Daedalus made. Icarus was killed when he flew so near the sun that the wax attaching his wings was melted and he fell into the Aegean Sea, but Daedalus reached Sicily safely. Daedalus was considered the inventor of carpentry and of such things as the saw, axe, plumb-line, auger, and glue, as well as the mast and yards of boats, and is credited with making figures which had open eyes, walked, and moved their arms. It is uncertain whether a historical artist gave rise to the legends, or whether Daedalus is a mythological figure representing accomplished craftsmanship.

daemon *n.* see DEMON.

daffodil /ˈdæfədɪl/ *n.* a yellow narcissus with a trumpet-shaped crown. [earlier *affodil*, f. as ASPHODEL]

daft /dɑːft/ *adj.* (*colloq.*) silly, foolish, crazy. [OE, = mild]

da Gama see GAMA.

dagger *n.* **1.** a short pointed two-edged weapon used for stabbing. **2.** an obelus. —**at daggers drawn,** hostile and on the point of quarrelling. **look daggers,** to glare angrily. [perh. f. *dag* pierce]

dagoba /ˈdɑːgəbə/ *n.* see STUPA. [Sinhalese f. Skr., = containing relics]

Dagon /ˈdeɪgɒn/ a national deity of the ancient Philistines, represented as a fish-tailed man. [f. Heb., = dear little fish]

daguerreotype /dəˈgerəʊtaɪp/ *n.* an early kind of photograph taken on a silver-coated copper plate and developed by exposure to mercury vapour, giving a positive image of white on silver. [f. name of inventor, Louis *Daguerre* (d. 1851)]

dahlia /ˈdeɪlɪə/ *n.* a composite plant of the genus *Dahlia*, of Mexican origin, cultivated for its many-coloured single or double flowers. [f. name of A. *Dahl* (d. 1789), Swedish botanist]

Dáil /dɔɪl/ *n.* (also **Dáil Éireann** /ˈeɪrən/) the lower house of parliament in the Republic of Ireland, composed of 166 members elected on a basis of proportional representation. It was first established in 1919 when the Irish republicans elected to Westminster in the 1918 election proclaimed an Irish State. [Irish, = assembly (of Ireland)]

daily /ˈdeɪlɪ/ *adj.* done, produced, or occurring every day or weekday. —*adv.* every day. —*n.* **1.** a daily newspaper. **2.** (*colloq.*) a charwoman employed on a daily basis. —**daily bread,** one's livelihood. [f. DAY]

Daimler /ˈdaɪmlə(r)/, Gottlieb (1834–90), German engineer who contributed to the development of the internal-combustion engine. An employee of Nikolaus Otto, he produced a small engine using the Otto cycle in 1884 and made it propel a bicycle in 1886, using petrol vapour. He was a pioneer in the manufacture of motor cars, and was the original designer of the type /pr. deɪmlə(r)/ named after him.

dainty *adj.* **1.** small and pretty, delicate. **2.** fastidious, especially about food. —*n.* a delicacy. —**daintily** *adv.*, **daintiness** *n.* [f. OF L *dignitas* worth]

daiquiri /ˈdaɪkɪrɪ/ *n.* a cocktail of rum, lime-juice, etc. [f. *Daiquiri*, a rum-producing district in Cuba]

dairy *n.* a room or building where milk and milk products are processed; a shop where these are sold. —**dairy farm,** a farm producing chiefly milk and its derivatives. [OE, = kneader of dough]

dairymaid *n.* a woman employed in a dairy.

dairyman *n.* (*pl.* **-men**) a dealer in milk etc.

dais /ˈdeɪɪs/ *n.* a low platform, especially at one end of a room or hall. [f. L *discus* disc, in med. L = table]

daisy /ˈdeɪzɪ/ *n.* a small European composite flower (*Bellis perennis*) with a yellow disc and white rays; any of various similar flowers. —**daisy wheel,** a disc with characters on its circumference used as a printer in word processing. [OE, = day's eye]

Dakar /ˈdækɑː(r)/ the capital of Senegal, a port on the Atlantic coast of West Africa; pop. approx. 1,000,000.

Dakota /dəˈkəʊtə/ a former territory of the USA, organized in 1889 into the States of North Dakota and South Dakota.

Dalai Lama /ˈdælaɪ ˈlɑːmə/ an honorific applied to a series of reincarnate lamas. Believed to be the reincarnation of the bodhisattva Ávalokitesvara, the Dalai Lama is the head of the dominant Tibetan Buddhist order and was, until the establishment of Chinese Communist rule in 1959, the spiritual and temporal ruler of Tibet. He lived in the strictest seclusion and was worshipped with almost divine honours. When he died, the lamas professed to search for a child who gave evidence that the soul of the deceased had entered into him; when found, the child succeeded to the office. [Mongolian *dalai* ocean + LAMA]

dale *n.* a valley, especially in north England. [OE]

Dalek /ˈdɑːlek/ *n.* a type of robot appearing in 'Dr Who', a BBC Television science-fiction serial. [invented word, named after an encyclopaedia volume covering DAL–LEK]

Dalhousie /dælˈhaʊzɪ/, James Ramsay, 1st Marquis (1812–60), British colonial administrator who, as Governor-General of India between 1847 and 1856, was responsible for a series of reforms and innovations, notably the introduction of railways and of telegraphic communications. His policies, however, took insufficient account of the conservatism of the native peoples of India and contributed to the mounting discontent with British rule which eventually led to the Indian Mutiny.

Dali /'dɑːliː/, Salvador (1904-), Spanish Cubist painter, who went to Paris in 1928 and in 1929 was welcomed by André Breton into the Surrealist movement. He was expelled from it—by Breton—in 1938, since he rejected its Marxist connections, while retaining the Freudian elements. His pictures are extremely detailed representations of improbable juxtapositions, partly abstract, claimed to be paranoiac in content and deriving from the subconscious. He was in the USA 1940-55, after which he returned to Spain as an avowed supporter of Franco. He made two films with Buñuel (1928, 1930), contributed a dream sequence of Hitchcock's *Spellbound* (1945) and, so far, has written two autobiographies.

Dallapiccola /dæl æ'pikələ/, Luigi (1904-75), Italian composer and pianist. His concern for liberty and opposition to Fascism is expressed in two of his best-known works, *Canti di Prigionia* (1938-41) and the opera *Il Prigioniero* (1944-8). His musical style combines the serial technique of Schoenberg and Webern, a typically Italian love of grateful vocal writing, and a concern for colour and sonority.

dally *v.i.* **1.** to dawdle, to waste time. **2.** to amuse oneself; to flirt. —**dalliance** *n.* [f. OF *dalier* chat]

Dalmatian /dæl'meɪʃ(ə)n/ *adj.* of Dalmatia, the central region of the coast of Yugoslavia. —*n.* a dog of a large white breed with dark spots.

dalmatic /dæl'mætɪk/ *adj.* a long loose vestment with slit sides and wide sleeves, worn by deacons and bishops on ceremonial occasions. [f. L *dalmatica* (*vestis*) robe of Dalmatian wool]

Dalriada /dæl'riːədə/ an ancient Gaelic kingdom in northern Ireland whose people (known as *Scoti*) established a colony in SW Scotland from about the late 5th c. By the 9th c. Irish Dalriada had declined but the people of Scottish Dalriada gradually acquired dominion over the whole of Scotland, giving that country its present name.

Dalton /'dɔːlt(ə)n/, John (1766-1844), English chemist, Quaker schoolmaster, son of a weaver, possessor of insatiable curiosity, the founding father of modern atomic theory. His interest in meteorology led to the study of gases, and in 1801 he formulated the celebrated law of partial pressures named after him, according to which the total pressure of a mixture of gases is equal to the sum of the pressures that each gas would exert separately. Because of criticism he decided to furnish experimental proof; he took up his friend William Henry's study on the solubility of gases, and this resulted in his most fundamental work: his atomic theory and concept of atomic weight. He defined an atom as the smallest part of a substance that could participate in a chemical reaction, argued that elements are composed of atoms, and that elements combine in definite proportions. This allowed him, in 1803, to produce the first table of comparative atomic weights. In 1794 he published the first detailed description of 'Daltonism' or colour-blindness, based on his own inability to distinguish green from red.

dam[1] *n.* a barrier built across a river etc. to hold back water and control its flow (see below and ill. ELECTRICAL POWER). —*v.t.* (**-mm-**) **1.** to hold back with a dam. **2.** to obstruct, to block (*up*). [f. G *tam*]

One of the earliest dams, dating from *c.*2500 BC, is to be found in Egypt, and there are others in Iran, Iraq, and China, made of earth or masonry. Earth dams are still used, with a waterproof core of clay to prevent seepage and with the earth compacted and protected from erosion. Where site conditions are suitable concrete is used. Gravity dams rely on the weight of the dam for stability; arch dams, with a curved structure having its convex face upstream, rely on lateral thrust from solid rock abutments to resist the horizontal pressure of water, just as an arch bridge supports a vertical load. The main uses for dams are to generate electricity by means of water turbines, to store water for irrigation, industrial, or domestic water supplies, and to supply canals with water. It is estimated that at present one-tenth of the stream-flow of the world's rivers is regulated by dams; by the year 2000 two-thirds could be regulated.

dam[2] *n.* the mother especially of a quadruped. [var. of DAME]

damage /'dæmɪdʒ/ *n.* **1.** something done or suffered that reduces the value or usefulness of the thing affected or spoils its appearance. **2.** (*slang*) the cost. **3.** (in *pl.*) money claimed or awarded as compensation for loss or injury. —*v.t.* to cause damage to. [OF f. L *damnum* loss]

damascene /'dæməsiːn/ *v.t.* to decorate (metal) with inlaid or wavy patterns. [f. foll.]

Damascus /də'mɑːskəs/ the capital of Syria since the country's independence in 1946; pop. (est.) 2,250,000. It has existed as a city for over 4,000 years and has always been a centre of trade and travel.

damask /'dæməsk/ *n.* figured woven silk or linen, especially white table-linen with designs shown up by reflection of light. —*adj.* **1.** made of damask. **2.** coloured like a damask rose, velvety pink. —**damask rose**, a fragrant rose grown especially to make attar. [f. prec.]

dame *n.* **1. Dame**, the title of a woman Knight Commander or holder of the Grand Cross in orders of chivalry; a woman with this title. **2.** a comic middle-aged female character in modern pantomime, usually played by a man. **3.** (*archaic, joc.,* or *US slang*) a woman. —**dame school**, (*hist.*) a small primary school of the 18th c., usually kept by one female teacher, for the children of poor families. [f. OF f. L *domina* lady]

damn /dæm/ *int.* an exclamation of anger or annoyance. —*v.t.* **1.** to curse. **2.** to condemn as a failure, to censure. **3.** to doom to hell. **4.** to be the ruin of; to show to be guilty. —*n.* an uttered curse. —*adj.* & *adv.* (*colloq.*) damned. —**damn all**, (*slang*) nothing at all. [f. OF f. L (*damnum* loss)]

damnable /'dæmnəb(ə)l/ *adj.* hateful, annoying. —**damnably** *adv.* [f. DAMN]

damnation /dæm'neɪʃ(ə)n/ *n.* eternal punishment in hell. —*int.* damn. [f. DAMN]

damned /dæmd/ *adj.* hateful, annoying. —*adv.* extremely. —**do one's damnedest**, to do one's utmost. [f. DAMN]

Damocles /'dæməkliːz/ a courtier who excessively praised the happiness of Dionysius, ruler of Syracuse (4th c. BC). To show him how precarious this happiness was, Dionysius seated him at a banquet with a sword hung by a single hair over his head. —**sword of Damocles**, an imminent danger at a time of apparent well-being.

Damon /'deɪmən/ a Syracusan whose friend Phintias was sentenced to death. Damon went bail for Phintias, who returned at the last moment and saved him, and was reprieved. —**Damon and Pythias** (erron. for *Phintias*), faithful friends.

damp *adj.* slightly or moderately wet. —*n.* **1.** diffused moisture, especially as an inconvenience or danger. **2.** foul or explosive gas in a mine. —*v.t.* **1.** to make damp. **2.** to make sad or dull, to discourage; to reduce the vigour of. **3.** to reduce the vibration of. —**damp course**, a layer of damp-proof material built into a wall near the ground to prevent damp from rising (ill. BUILDING). —**damply** *adv.*, **dampness** *n.* [f. G, = vapour]

dampen *v.t.* to damp. [f. DAMP]

damper *n.* **1.** a device that reduces shock, noise, vibration, or oscillation; a pad that silences a piano-string except when removed by a note's being struck or by use of a pedal (ill. MUSICAL NOTATION). **2.** a movable metal plate that regulates the flow of air into the fire in a stove or furnace. [f. DAMP]

Dampier /'dæmpɪə(r)/, William (1652-1715), English explorer and adventurer. Having already established a reputation as a hydrographer, Dampier was involved in buccaneering activities in Panama before setting out on a privateering expedition along the west coast of America in 1683. He crossed the Pacific to the Philippines, China, and Australia, was marooned on the Nicobar Islands in 1688, and eventually got back to England in 1691. In 1699 he revisited Australia, commissioned by the British government to explore the coast, and circumnavigated the globe again, despite being wrecked on Ascension Island on the way home. His later privateering activities were marred by drunkenness and brutality which caused trouble both with his own crews and with the British authorities.

damsel /'dæmz(ə)l/ *n.* (*archaic* or *literary*) a young woman. [f. OF, dim. of L *domina* (see DAME)]

damselfly /'dæmz(ə)lflaɪ/ *n.* an insect of the order Odonata, like a dragonfly but with wings that fold while it rests. [f. prec.]

damson /'dæmz(ə)n/ *n.* a small dark-purple plum; its colour; the tree that bears it. [f. L *damascenum* (*prunum*) Damascus plum]

Dan 1. Hebrew patriarch, son of Jacob and Bilhah (Gen. 30: 6). **2.** the tribe of Israel traditionally descended from him. **3.** a city in the extreme north of Canaan.

dan *n.* a degree of proficiency in judo etc.; one who reaches this. [Jap.]

Dana /'deɪnə/, James Dwight (1813-95), American naturalist, geologist, and mineralogist, an influential teacher whose works became standard textbooks in their subjects. At the age of 24 he produced *A System of Mineralogy*, founding a classification of minerals based on chemistry and physics; in spite of the reorganization of material made necessary by the development of scientific techniques the book still appears under his name. His view of the earth as a unit, with its physical features changing and developing progressively, was an evolutionary one, but he did not accept the theory of the evolution of species, constructed by Charles Darwin (with whom he corresponded), until the last edition of his *Manual of Geology*, published shortly before his death.

Danae /'dænɑː/ (*Gk myth.*) the daughter of Acrisius, king of Argos. An oracle foretold that she would bear a son who would kill her father. In an attempt to evade this he imprisoned her in a tower, but Zeus visited her in the form of a shower of gold and she conceived Perseus, who after many adventures killed Acrisius by accident.

Danaids /'dænɑːdz/ *n.pl.* (*Gk legend*) the daughters of Danaus, king of Argos, who were compelled to marry the sons of his brother Aegyptus but murdered their husbands on the wedding night, except for Hypermnestra, who helped her husband to escape. They were punished in Hades by being set to fill a leaky jar with water.

dance /dɑːns/ *v.t./i.* **1.** to move with rhythmical steps or movements, usually to music; to perform (a specified dance). **2.** to move in a lively way, to bob up and down. —*n.* **1.** a piece of dancing, a special form of this. **2.** a social gathering for dancing. **3.** a piece of music for dancing to. —**dance attendance on,** to follow about and help dutifully. **lead a person a dance,** to cause him much trouble. —**dancer** *n.* [f. OF *danser*, ult. orig. unkn.]

Dance of Death a medieval conceit in which skeletal figures seized popes, kings, merchants, beggars, emphasizing the equality of all men before Death. The earliest dated painting (*c.*1425) was a mural in a Parisian cemetery, but the most famous example is the series of 41 woodcuts after drawings by Holbein (*c.*1523-6), based on a mural in Basle, first printed in Lyons in 1538 and immediately popular.

dancetty /'dæn'setɪ/ *adj.* (in heraldry, of a line) drawn with broad indentations (ill. HERALDRY). [f. F *danché* f. L *dens* tooth]

dandelion /'dændɪlaɪən/ *n.* a common composite plant (*Taraxacum officinale*) with jagged leaves and a large bright-yellow flower on a hollow stalk, succeeded by a globular head of seeds with downy tufts. [f. F *dent-de-lion*, f. L (= lion's tooth)]

dander *n.* (*colloq.*) anger, fighting spirit. [orig. unkn.]

dandified /'dændɪfaɪd/ *adj.* like a dandy. [f. DANDY]

dandle *v.t.* to dance (a child) on one's knees or in one's arms. [orig. unkn.]

dandruff /'dændrʌf/ *n.* flakes of scurf on the scalp and amongst the hair. [orig. unkn.]

dandy *n.* **1.** a man who pays excessive attention to the smartness of his appearance and clothes. **2.** (*colloq.*) an excellent thing. —*adj.* (*colloq.*) splendid, first-rate. [perh. orig. = *Andrew* in *Jack-a-dandy*]

Dane *n.* **1.** a native of Denmark. **2.** (*hist.*) a Northman invader of England in the 9th-11th c. —**Great Dane,** a dog of a large short-haired breed. [f. ON *Danir* (L *Dani*)]

Danegeld /'deɪngeld/ *n.* a land-tax levied in Anglo-Saxon England (especially 991-1016), originally to bribe the invading Danes to go away, turned into a permanent levy for national defence by the Norman kings. [OE, = Dane payment]

Danelaw /'deɪnlɔː/ *n.* the NE part of England settled or held by the Danes from the late 9th c. and administered according to their laws until after the Norman Conquest. [OE, = Danes' law]

danger /'deɪndʒə(r)/ *n.* liability or exposure to harm or death; a thing that causes this. [f. OF f. L *dominus* lord]

dangerous /'deɪndʒərəs/ *adj.* involving or causing danger. —**dangerously** *adv.* [f. prec.]

dangle *v.t./i.* **1.** to hang loosely; to hold or carry (a thing) so that it sways loosely. **2.** to hold out (a bait or temptation) enticingly. [corresp. to Sw. *dangla*]

Daniel /'dænj(ə)l/ **1.** a Hebrew prophet (6th c. BC), captive at Babylon, who spent his life at the court there, interpreted the dreams of Nebuchadnezzar, and was delivered by God from the lions' den into which he had been thrown as the result of a trick. The stories are regarded as legendary. **2.** the book of the Old Testament bearing his name but probably of the 2nd c. BC. —*n.* an upright judge, a person of infallible wisdom (alluding to Sus. 45-64, where Daniel showed the evidence against Susannah to be false).

Danish /'deɪnɪʃ/ *adj.* of Denmark or its people or language. —*n.* the official language of Denmark (where it is spoken by 5 million inhabitants) and also of Greenland and the Faeroes. It belongs to the Scandinavian language group. —**Danish blue,** a soft white cheese with veins of blue mould. **Danish pastry,** a yeast cake topped with icing, nuts, etc. [f. L *Danensis*]

dank *adj.* unpleasantly cold and damp. [prob. f. Scand. (Sw. *dank* marshy spot)]

d'Annunzio /dɑː'nʊntsɪəʊ/, Gabriele (1863-1938), Italian poet, novelist, and dramatist. A fervent patriot, in the First World War he effectively urged the entry of Italy on the side of the Allies and himself took part in some spectacular exploits. All his work exudes a sensuous enjoyment of life; the Nietzchian hedonists (untroubled by conscience) who are the heroes of his novels may be said to anticipate Fascism. His flamboyance, his grand passion for the actress Eleanora Duse, and the erotic and decadent aspects of some of his works, made him a controversial figure both as a man and as a writer.

Dante Alighieri /'dæntɪ ælɪg'jeərɪ/ (1265-1321), Italian poet and philosopher, born in Florence of a Guelph family. He became active in political life, and in 1301 went into exile in various Italian cities after his party lost power. Early in life he fell in love with the girl whom he celebrates under the name of 'Beatrice'. His first major work, as an innovative poet of courtly love, was the collection of his poems for her, after her death, into a visionary narrative, the 'Vita Nuova' (*c.*1292-4). He promised more for her, and eventually achieved this in his masterpiece (finished just before his death), the 'Commedia' ('Divina' was added by Boccaccio), a classical and Christian autobiographical epic in the form of an imagined visit to Hell and Purgatory (the 'Inferno' and 'Purgatorio') with Virgil as guide, and finally to the spheres of Heaven (the 'Paradiso') with Beatrice, now a blessed spirit, as guide. His works are vividly pictorial with dramatic encounters, a gift to illustrators. His writings included a pioneering work (in Latin) on the value of vernacular Italian as a literary language, displacing Latin.

Danton /'dɑːtɔ̃/, Georges Jacques (1759-94), French revolutionary, a noted orator, who won great popularity among the Paris mob in the early days of the French Revolution. Initially an ally of Robespierre and the Jacobins, he later revolted against their radicalism and attempted to form an opposition, only to be arrested and executed on Robespierre's orders.

Danube /'dænjuːb/ a river about 2,850 km (1,770 miles) long that rises in the Black Forest in SW Germany and flows into the Black Sea. The cities of Vienna, Budapest, and Belgrade are situated on it.

Danubian /dæ'njuːbɪən/ *adj.* of the River Danube. —**Danubian principalities,** the former principalities of Moldavia and Wallachia, now forming part of Romania.

Daphne /'dæfnɪ/ (*Gk myth.*) a nymph who was turned into a laurel-bush to save her from the pursuit of Apollo. [see foll.]

daphne /'dæfnɪ/ *n.* a flowering shrub of the genus *Daphne* (e.g. spurge laurel), mezereon. [f. Gk, = laurel]

Daphnis /'dæfnɪs/ (*Gk legend*) a Sicilian shepherd, son or favourite of Hermes. According to one version of the legend he was struck with blindness for his infidelity to the nymph Echenaïs who loved him; he consoled himself by making pastoral music, of which he was the inventor, or it was first invented by the other shepherds, who sang of his misfortunes.

dapper /'dæpə(r)/ *adj.* neat and smart, especially in dress. [f. MLG, MDu., = strong, stout]

dapple *v.t.* to mark with spots or patches of colour or shade. [orig. unkn.]

dapple-grey *adj.* grey with darker markings. —*n.* a dapple-grey horse. [f. prec.]

Darby and Joan a devoted old married couple. The source of the names is usually considered to be a poem in the *Gentleman's Magazine* (1735) containing the lines 'Old Darby, with Joan by his side, You've often regarded with wonder: He's dropsical, she is sore-eyed, Yet they're never happy asunder'.

Dardanelles /dɑːdəˈnelz/ a narrow strait between Europe and Asiatic Turkey, anciently called the Hellespont. It was the scene of an unsuccessful attack on Turkey by British and French troops in 1915, with Australian and New Zealand contingents playing a major part.

dare /deə(r)/ v.t. (3 sing. pres. usu. **dare** before an expressed or implied infinitive without *to*) **1.** to have the courage or impudence (*to*); to face as a danger. **2.** to challenge to do something risky. —*n.* a challenge to do something risky. —**I dare say**, I am prepared to believe, I do not deny, it is very likely. [OE (cf. Gk *tharseō* be bold)]

daredevil *n.* a recklessly daring person.

Dar es Salaam /dɑːr es səˈlɑːm/ the former capital and chief port of Tanzania, founded in 1866 by the sultan of Zanzibar, who built his summer palace there; pop. (1978) approx. 757,346.

daring /ˈdeərɪŋ/ *n.* adventurous courage. —*adj.* bold, adventurous; boldly dramatic or unconventional. [f. DARE]

dariole /ˈdærɪəʊl/ *n.* a savoury or sweet dish cooked and served in a small mould; this mould. [f. OF]

Darius /dəˈraɪəs/ 'the Great' (*c.*550–486 BC), king of Persia 521–486 BC. He divided the empire into provinces governed by satraps, and (a true successor of Cyrus) centralized authority while allowing each province its own form of government and institutions. He developed commerce, building a network of roads, exploring the Indus valley, and connecting the Nile with the Red Sea by canal. His campaigns were designed to consolidate the empire. After suppressing a revolt of the Greek cities in Ionia (499–494 BC) he prepared to punish the mainland Greeks for their interference, but his expeditions ended in a Greek victory at Marathon (490 BC), and he died soon afterwards.

Darjeeling /dɑːˈdʒiːlɪŋ/ *n.* a type of tea grown in Darjeeling, a town and district of West Bengal.

dark *adj.* **1.** with little or no light. **2.** (of colour) of a deep shade closer to black than to white; having a brown or black skin, complexion, or hair. **3.** gloomy, dismal. **4.** secret; mysterious; remote and unexplored. —*n.* **1.** absence of light; a time of darkness, night or nightfall. **2.** a dark colour or area. —**Dark Continent**, Africa. **dark horse**, a competitor of whose abilities little is known before the contest. **dark-room** *n.* a room where light is excluded so that photographs can be processed. **in the dark**, with no light; lacking information. —**darkly** *adv.*, **darkness** *n.* [OE]

Dark Ages a term denoting the obscurity or barbarity of the period between the fall of the Roman Empire and the high Middle Ages in the West, *c.*500–1100. Obscurity can delight historians who piece together the evidence; barbarity may imply an underestimate of classical influences on the newly settled Germanic peoples. Broadly, however, there was political fragmentation, a hiatus in city life, a lack of major learned centres, and an emphasis on waterways rather than roads. The Devil was accorded great power, symptomatic of an age which made peculiarly little distinction between nature and the supernatural (good or evil), and inhibiting of human development. The Dark Ages may be said to have ended when St Anselm became the first medieval thinker to deny that the Devil had a rightful dominion over men.

The term *Dark Age* has been applied to a similar period in the history of Greece and other Aegean countries from the end of the Bronze Age until the beginning of the historical period, when the region seems to have been heavily depopulated, its material culture stagnant, there was no building of palaces and fortresses, and the art of writing (associated with the palace bureaucracies) was apparently lost. The period falls between two cultural phases that have been comparatively well explored, but some features such as ship-building and the extraction of silver, and strong oral tradition resulting in the emergence of the Homeric poems as we have them, are at variance with the generally humble picture of Dark Age Greece and suggest that it has been painted too black.

darken *v.t./i.* to make or become dark. —**never darken a person's door**, to stay away from him because one is unwelcome. [f. DARK]

darling *n.* a beloved or lovable person or thing, a favourite. —*adj.* beloved; (*colloq.*) charming. [OE, = little dear]

Darling River a river of SE Australia, flowing 2,757 km (1,712 miles) in a generally south westward course to join the Murray River.

darn[1] *v.t.* to mend by weaving yarn across a hole. —*n.* a place mended by darning. —**darning** *n.* a piece of such mending; things to be darned. **darning-needle** *n.* a long sewing-needle used in darning. [orig. unkn.]

darn[2], **darned** /dɑːnd/ = DAMN, DAMNED. [corruption]

darnel /ˈdɑːnəl/ *n.* a grass (*Lolium temulentum*) that grows in some countries as a weed among corn. It was known first as the English name for the weed called *Lolium* in the Vulgate. Now rare in Britain, it appears to have been more common formerly when seed-corn was imported from Mediterranean regions, where it abounds. It is a health hazard when infested by ergot, to which it is particularly susceptible, dangerous to grazing animals and formerly liable to contaminate rye flour. [f. F dial. *darnelle*]

Darnley /ˈdɑːnlɪ/, Lord (1545–67), Henry Stewart (or Stuart), Scottish nobleman, second husband of his cousin Mary Queen of Scots and father of James I of England. He was implicated in the murder of Riccio, her secretary, and was killed in mysterious circumstances at Edinburgh.

dart *n.* **1.** a small pointed missile used as a weapon or in the game of *darts* (see below). **2.** a darting movement. **3.** a tapering stitched tuck in a garment. —*v.t./i.* **1.** to spring or move suddenly (*out, past*, etc.). **2.** to direct (a glance etc.) rapidly. [f. OF *dars*]

Darts is a predominantly British indoor game in which light usually feathered darts are thrown at a target (**dartboard**) marked with concentric circles and a bull's-eye in the centre, and now divided by radiating lines into numbered sectors. The game is associated with village inns, taverns, and public houses, and dates from the time of George III or earlier.

Dartmoor /ˈdɑːtmʊə(r)/ **1.** a moorland district in Devon that was a royal forest in Saxon times, now a national park. **2.** a prison near Princetown in this district, originally built to hold French prisoners of war from the Napoleonic Wars.

Darwin[1] /ˈdɑːwɪn/, Charles Robert (1809–82), natural historian, geologist, voyager/collector, revolutionary thinker, botanist and zoologist of remarkable powers, who propounded the theory of evolution by natural selection, to the consternation of certain theologians at this threat to the beliefs that they found comfortable. Grandson of the eminent physician Erasmus Darwin and son of a Shrewsbury doctor and the daughter of the potter Josiah Wedgwood, he failed to complete his medical training at Edinburgh and just scraped a degree at Cambridge in vague preparation for a life in the Church. At twenty-two, seizing his one great opportunity, a post as gentleman-naturalist to HMS *Beagle* on her circumnavigation of the globe, he set out as an untried amateur and returned five years later to take his place amongst the élite of the learned societies. Marrying his cousin Emma Wedgwood and retiring into a massively productive isolation in Kent, visited only by a chosen handful of scientists, he published an astonishing series of books, monographs, and papers. *On the Origin of Species* (1859) and *The Descent of Man* (1871) changed our concept of nature and of man's place within it. The Newton of biology, he is buried in Westminster Abbey.

Darwin[2] /ˈdɑːwɪn/ the capital of the Northern Territory, Australia; pop. 46,655.

dash *v.t./i.* **1.** to run rapidly, to rush. **2.** to knock, drive, or throw forcefully, to shatter thus; to destroy (hopes etc.); to daunt. **3.** to write hastily. **4.** (*slang*) damn. **5.** (*slang*) to give as a bribe. —*n.* **1.** a short rapid run, a rush; (*US*) a sprinting-race. **2.** impetuous vigour; lively spirit or appearance. **3.** a slight admixture (of liquid or flavouring). **4.** a horizontal stroke (—) in writing or printing to mark a break in the sense, omitted words, etc. **5.** the longer of the two signals used in the Morse code. **6.** a dashboard. —**cut a dash**, to make a brilliant show in appearance or behaviour. [imit.]

dashboard *n.* a board below the windscreen of a motor vehicle, carrying various instruments and controls.

dashing *adj.* spirited, lively; showy. [f. DASH]

dastardly /ˈdæstədlɪ/ *adj.* contemptible and cowardly. [prob. f. *dazed*, or obs. *dasart* dullard]

data /ˈdeɪtə, ˈdɑː-/ *n.pl.*, also ((**D**) as *sing.*, although the sing. form is *datum*) facts or information used as a basis for inference or reckoning, or prepared for being processed by a computer; quantities or characters for such processing. — **data bank**, a large store or source of data. **data processing**, automatic performance of operations on data. [L, = things given (*dare* give)]

database /ˈdeɪtəbeɪs/ *n.* an organized store of data for computer processing.

datable /ˈdeɪtəb(ə)l/ *adj.* capable of being dated. [f. DATE[1]]

date[1] *n.* **1.** the numbered day of the month. **2.** a statement (usually day, month, and year) on a document, coin, etc., of when it was composed or issued; the period to which something belongs; the time at which a thing happens or is to happen. **3.** (*colloq.*) an appointment to meet; (*US*) a person of the opposite sex with whom one has a social engagement. —*v.t./i.* **1.** to mark with a date; to assign a date to. **2.** to have existed *from*. **3.** to be or become out of date; to show up the age of. **4.** (*colloq.*) to make a social engagement with. —**out of date**, no longer fashionable, current, or valid. **to date**, until now. **up to date**, in current fashion; in accordance with what is now known or required. [f. OF f. L *data* = (letter) given (at specified time and place)]

date[2] *n.* the oblong brown sweet edible fruit of a palm tree (*Phoenix dactylifera*) of western Asia and North Africa; (also **date-palm**) this tree. [f. OF f. L f. Gk *daktulos* finger, from the shape of its leaf]

date-line *n.* **1.** the imaginary north-south line through the Pacific Ocean, partly along the meridian farthest (i.e. 180°) from Greenwich, east and west of which the date differs (east being one day earlier). It was officially adopted worldwide in 1884 (see GREENWICH MEAN TIME). **2.** a line in a newspaper at the head of a dispatch etc. showing the date and place of writing.

date-stamp *n.* an adjustable rubber stamp for marking the date of receipt etc. on a document; its mark. —*v.t.* to mark with a date-stamp.

dative /ˈdeɪtɪv/ *n.* (*Gram.*) the case expressing the indirect object or a recipient. —*adj.* (*Gram.*) of or in the dative. [f. L (*casus*) *dativus* (case) of giving]

datum /ˈdeɪtəm, ˈdɑː-/ *n.* **1.** (*pl.* **data**) see DATA. **2.** (*pl.* **-ums**) the starting-point from which something is measured or calculated. [sing. of DATA]

daub /dɔːb/ *v.t.* **1.** to coat or smear roughly with a soft substance; to lay on (such a substance). **2.** to paint crudely or unskilfully. —*n.* **1.** plaster or other substance daubed on a surface, a smear. **2.** a crude painting. [f. OF f. L *dealbare* to whitewash (DE-, *albus* white)]

Daudet /ˈdəʊdeɪ/, Alphonse (1840-97), French novelist, best known for his sketches of life in his native Provence (*Lettres de mon moulin*, 1868), for his semi-autobiographical *Le petit chose* (1868), and as the creator of Tartarin, a caricature of the Frenchman of the Midi, whose comic exploits are first related in *Tartarin de Tarascon* (1872). His other novels portray the social, political, and professional life of Paris.

daughter /ˈdɔːtə(r)/ *n.* **1.** a female child in relation to her parents(s); a female descendant or product *of*. **2.** (*Phys.* & *Biol.*, *attrib.*) an element or cell etc. produced by disintegration or division of another. —**daughter-in-law** *n.* a son's wife. [OE]

daunt /dɔːnt/ *v.t.* to discourage, to intimidate. [f. OF f. L *domitare* (*domare* tame)]

dauntless *adj.* not to be daunted, intrepid. [f. DAUNT + -LESS]

dauphin /ˈdɔːfɪn/ *n.* the title borne by the eldest son of the king of France from 1349 to 1830. Originally a personal name, it became the title of the lords of an area of SE France which was thence called Dauphiné. In 1349 the French Crown acquired the lands and the title, and Charles V, ceding it to his eldest son in 1368, established the practice of passing both title and lands to the Crown prince. [f. L *delphinus* dolphin]

davenport /ˈdævənpɔːt/ *n.* **1.** a writing-desk with drawers and a hinged flap. **2.** (*US*) a large sofa. [19th-c. maker's name]

David[1] /ˈdeɪvɪd/ (died *c.*970 BC) youngest son of Jesse of Bethlehem, and slayer of a Philistine (see GOLIATH). On the death of Saul (whose son Jonathan was his close friend) he became king of Judah and later of the whole of Israel, making Jerusalem his capital and reigning there for 33 years. He is traditionally regarded as the author of the Psalms, but it is unlikely that more than a fraction of the Psalter is his work.

David[2] /ˈdeɪvɪd/ the name of two kings of Scotland:
   David I (1084-1153), son of Malcolm III, reigned 1124-53. He reasserted some measure of Scottish independence from English feudal domination at the time of the civil wars of Stephen and Matilda, but was decisively defeated at the Battle of the Standard in Yorkshire in 1138.
   David II (1324-71), son of Robert the Bruce, reigned 1329-71. His long reign witnessed a renewal of the Wars of Independence, with Edward III taking advantage of the Scots king's minority to introduce the son of John de Baliol

as an English puppet in his place. After coming of age David was defeated by the English at Neville's Cross (1346) and spent eleven years in captivity. His death without issue in 1371 left the throne to the Stuarts.

David[3] /daˈviːd/, Jacques-Louis (1748-1825), French neo-classical painter of scenes from Roman history, stoic and austere in their style and morality, and recorder of events in the Revolutionary and Napoleonic eras. He became actively involved in the Revolution, voted the death of Louis XVI, and supported Robespierre: in *The Tennis-Court Oath* (1789) and *The Death of Marat* (1793) he treated contemporary events with a grandeur hitherto reserved for history painting. Imprisoned after the fall of Robespierre, he returned to prominence under Napoleon, recording Napoleonic ceremonies in a less austere style. His last years were spent in exile in Brussels. David responded best to direct contact with nature, as in his portraits, and was an excellent teacher; his pupils included Ingres.

David[4] /ˈdeɪvɪd/, St (6th c.), patron saint of Wales. Little is known of his life; the claim that he was elected bishop of the Welsh Church because of his eloquence, and that he made a pilgrimage to Jerusalem, where he was consecrated, seem not to be historically valid. Feast day, 1 Mar.

Davies /ˈdeɪvɪs/, Peter Maxwell (1934-), English composer, conductor, and teacher. From 1971 he has made his home in Orkney, where the landscape and solitude have had an undoubted effect upon his music. He has composed in a variety of styles for the theatre, ranging from the opera *Taverner* (1970), in which a strong dramatic impulse is given full outlet, to the violent and pitiful depiction of madness in *Eight Songs for a Mad King* (1969).

Davis /ˈdeɪvɪs/, William Morris (1850-1934), American geographer, geologist, and meteorologist, who established one of the most important concepts of geomorphology, the cycle of erosion, according to which newly uplifted land is gradually eroded (typically by rivers) and the land surface passes through several stages, ending with the formation of flat plains.

Davis Cup /ˈdeɪvɪs/ the award for the men's international team competition in lawn tennis (officially the International Lawn Tennis Challenge Trophy). It was the gift of Dwight F. Davis (1879-1945), a leading American player, in 1900.

davit /ˈdævɪt/ *n.* a kind of small crane on board ship. [f. AF, dim. of *Davi* David]

Davy /ˈdeɪvɪ/, Sir Humphry (1778-1829), English chemist, a pioneer of electrochemistry and the inventor of a miner's safety lamp. After indifferent schooling and an apprenticeship with an apothecary-surgeon he discovered nitrous oxide (laughing gas), and as a result was invited to join the Royal Institution in London. He applied Volta's electrochemical battery to chemistry and, by means of electrolytic decomposition, discovered the elements sodium, potassium, magnesium, calcium, strontium, and barium during 1807-8. Davy identified and named the element chlorine after he had demonstrated that, contrary to Lavoisier, oxygen was not a constituent of acids, determined the properties of iodine, and demonstrated that diamond was a form of carbon. He appointed Faraday his assistant in 1813, and it has been said that this was his greatest discovery.

Davy Jones /ˈdeɪvɪ ˈdʒəʊnz/ (*nautical slang*) the evil spirit of the sea, first mentioned in the 18th c. —**Davy Jones's locker**, the bottom of the sea, especially as the grave of those who are drowned or die at sea. [orig. unkn.]

Davy lamp /ˈdeɪvɪ/ an early type of safety lamp for miners, with wire gauze enclosing the flame, named after Sir Humphry Davy who invented it in 1816. The action of the gauze was to quench, by its sudden cooling effect, any flame which might tend to emerge from inside and ignite the methane found in underground collieries. A very similar lamp was devised almost simultaneously by George Stephenson.

daw *n.* a jackdaw. [OE]

dawdle *v.i.* to proceed slowly and idly. [orig. unkn.]

dawn *n.* **1.** the first light of day. **2.** the beginning *of*. —*v.i.* **1.** to begin to grow light. **2.** to begin to appear or become evident. —**dawn chorus**, early-morning bird-song. **dawn on**, to begin to be understood by. [f. OE, as DAY]

day *n.* **1.** the time between sunrise and sunset; daylight; the time for one rotation of the earth, 24 hours, especially from one midnight to the next; the hours given to work. **2.** a specified or appointed date; a period, era, or lifetime. **3.** a period of prosperity or success. **4.** a day's endeavour, especially as bringing success. —**day-bed** *n.* a bed for

daytime rest. **day-boy, day-girl** *ns.* a school pupil attending a boarding school but living at home. **day centre,** a place where social and other facilities are provided for elderly or handicapped people during the day. **day in, day out,** continuously. **day nursery,** a place where young children are looked after while their parents are at work. **day release,** a system of allowing employees days off work for education. **day-return** *n.* a ticket sold at a reduced rate for a journey both ways in one day. **day-room** *n.* a room for use during the day only. **day-star** *n.* the sun or other morning star. [OE]

Dayak /ˈdaɪæk/ var. of DYAK.

daybreak *n.* the first light of day, dawn.

day-dream *n.* a pleasant fantasy or reverie. —*v.i.* to indulge in day-dreams.

Day-Lewis /deɪˈluːɪs/, Cecil (1904–72), British poet and critic, born in Ireland. During the 1930s he was associated with a group of left-wing poets which included Auden and Spender, and his early volumes of verse (*Transitional Poems*, 1929; *The Magnetic Mountain*, 1933) have a distinct revolutionary flavour. At this time he also wrote detective fiction under the pseudonym of 'Nicholas Blake'. After 1940 he became an increasingly establishment figure, consolidating his literary reputation with translations of Valéry and Virgil, further collections of original verse and an autobiography, *The Buried Day* (1960). He was Professor of Poetry at Oxford 1951–6, and was appointed Poet Laureate in 1968.

daylight *n.* **1.** the light of day; dawn. **2.** understanding or knowledge that has dawned. —**daylight robbery,** (*colloq.*) an excessive charge. **daylight saving,** the achieving of longer evening daylight, especially in summer, by making clocks show a later time. **scare the (living) daylights out of,** (*slang*) to terrify.

daytime *n.* the time of daylight.

daze *v.t.* to stupefy, to bewilder. —*n.* a state of being dazed. [f. ON, = weary]

dazzle *v.t.* **1.** to make temporarily unable to see by excess of light. **2.** to impress or overpower by a display of knowledge, ability, etc. —*n.* bright dazzling light. [f. prec.]

dB *abbr.* decibel(s).

DC *abbr.* **1.** (also **d.c.**) direct current. **2.** District of Columbia.

D-Day *n.* **1.** the day (6 June 1944) on which British and American forces invaded northern France in the Second World War. **2.** the day on which an important operation is to begin. [*D* for *day*]

DDT *n.* a white chlorinated hydrocarbon used as an insecticide. [f. chemical name]

de- *prefix* **1.** down, away. **2.** completely. **3.** removing, reversing. [f. L *de* off, from]

deacon /ˈdiːkən/ *n.* (in Episcopal churches) a clergyman ranking below bishop and priest; (in Nonconformist churches) a layman attending to church business; (in the early Church) a minister of charity. —**deaconess** *n.fem.* [OE f. L f. Gk *diakonos* servant]

dead /ded/ *adj.* **1.** no longer alive. **2.** numb, having lost sensation. **3.** unappreciative, insensitive *to.* **4.** no longer effective or in use, extinct; inactive; lacking vigour, interest, or activity; (of a ball in games) out of play. **5.** abrupt, complete; exact, unqualified. —*adv.* completely, exactly. —*n.* an inactive or silent time. —**dead-alive** *adj.* very dreary. **dead beat,** (*colloq.*) exhausted. **dead-beat escapement,** one that stops 'dead' without recoil. **dead end,** the closed end of a passage etc.; a course etc. with no prospects. **dead heat,** the result of a race in which two or more competitors finish exactly level. **dead letter,** a law or practice that is no longer observed. **dead man's handle,** a controlling-handle on an electric train etc. that disconnects the power supply if released. **dead march,** a funeral march. **dead nettle,** a plant of the genus *Lamium* with nettle-like leaves but not stinging. **dead-pan** *adj.* & *adv.* with an expressionless face. **dead reckoning,** calculation of a ship's position by log and compass etc. when observations are impossible. **dead set,** a determined attack. **dead shot,** one who never misses the target. **dead water,** the water in a ship's wake close to the stern. **dead weight,** a heavy inert weight. **dead wood,** useless persons or things. [OE]

deaden /ˈdedən/ *v.t./i.* to deprive of or lose vitality, loudness, feeling, etc.; to make insensitive *to.* [f. DEAD]

deadline *n.* a time-limit. [orig. = the line round a military prison (at Andersonville, Georgia, USA; *c.*1864) beyond which a prisoner was liable to be shot down]

deadlock *n.* a situation in which no progress can be made. —*v.t./i.* to bring or come to a deadlock.

deadly /ˈdedlɪ/ *adj.* **1.** causing or able to cause fatal injury, death, or serious damage. **2.** intense; deathlike. **3.** accurate. —*adv.* as if dead; extremely. —**deadly nightshade,** see BELLADONNA. **seven deadly sins,** those held to result in damnation for a person's soul (traditionally pride, covetousness, lust, envy, gluttony, anger, sloth; listed (with minor variation) by the monk John Cassian (d. 435), St Gregory the Great, and St Thomas Aquinas). —**deadliness** *n.* [as DEAD]

Dead Sea a bitter salt lake or inland sea in the Jordan valley on the Israel-Jordan border. Its surface is 400 m (1,300 ft.) below sea-level. —**Dead Sea scrolls,** a once considerable collection of Hebrew and Aramaic manuscripts discovered in caves near Qumran, at the NE end of the Dead Sea, between 1947 and 1956, chiefly in fragments. They belonged to the library of a splinter Jewish sect, generally equated with the Essenes, who settled in a large building (or monastery) at Qumran from the mid-1st c. BC until the Jewish revolt against Roman rule AD 66–70, and are presumed to have been hidden, stored in the jars in which they were found, for safe-keeping when the destruction of the centre seemed imminent. They include texts of many books of the Old Testament, commentaries, psalms, an apocalyptic work, and documents containing the rules of the life of the religious community. They are important for the evidence they provide on the history of the Old Testament text, scripts of the period, and the life and doctrines of a Jewish sect at the time when Christianity was born.

deaf /def/ *n.* **1.** wholly or partly without hearing. **2.** refusing to listen. —**deaf aid,** a hearing-aid. **deaf mute,** a person who is both deaf and dumb. —**deafness** *n.* [OE]

deafen /ˈdefən/ *v.t.* to overwhelm with sound; to make deaf or temporarily unable to hear by a very loud noise. —**deafening** *adj.* [f. DEAF]

deal[1] *v.t./i.* (*past & p.p.* **dealt** /delt/) **1.** to distribute or hand *out* among several people etc.; to distribute cards to players. **2.** to assign as a share or deserts; to inflict. **3.** to do business; to trade *in.* —*n.* **1.** dealing or a player's turn to deal at cards; the round of play following this. **2.** (*colloq.*) a business transaction or agreement. **3.** (*colloq.*) treatment. **4.** (*colloq.*) a large amount. —**deal with,** to do business with; to take action about; to be what is needed by (a situation etc.); to discuss (a subject) in a book or speech etc. [OE]

deal[2] *n.* sawn fir or pine timber; a deal board of standard size. [f. MLG, MDu. *dele* plank]

dealer *n.* **1.** a person dealing at cards. **2.** a trader. **3.** a jobber on the Stock Exchange. [f. DEAL[1]]

dealings *n.pl.* a person's conduct or transactions *with* another. [f. DEAL[1]]

dean *n.* **1.** a clergyman who is head of the chapter of a cathedral or collegiate church. **2.** a college fellow responsible for student discipline; the head of a university faculty or department or of a medical college. —**area** *or* **rural dean,** the head of clergy in a division of an archdeaconry. [f. AF f. L *decanus* (*decem* ten); orig. = chief of group of ten]

deanery *n.* **1.** a dean's house or office. **2.** a rural dean's group of parishes. [f. DEAN]

dear *adj.* **1.** much loved; cherished; precious *to.* **2.** (as a polite form of address) esteemed. **3.** costing more than it is worth; having high prices. —*n.* a dear person. —*adv.* dearly, at a high price. —*int.* expressing surprise, distress, or pity. —**dearly** *adv.,* **dearness** *n.* [OE]

dearth /dɜːθ/ *n.* scarcity, lack. [as DEAR]

death /deθ/ *n.* **1.** the process of dying, the end of life; final cessation of vital functions; the state of being dead. **2.** an event etc. that ends life, a cause of death. **3.** the ending or destruction of something. —**at death's door,** close to death. **death cap,** a poisonous toadstool (*Amanita phalloides*). **death certificate,** an official statement of the date, place, and cause of a person's death. **death duty,** (*hist.*) a tax levied on property after the owner's death. **death knell,** the tolling of a bell to mark a person's death; an event that heralds a thing's extinction. **death-mask** *n.* a cast taken of a dead person's face. **death penalty,** punishment by being put to death. **death rate,** the number of deaths per thousand of population per year. **death-roll** *n.* a list or number of those killed in an accident, battle, etc. **death's head,** a picture of a skull as a symbol of death. **death-trap** *n.* a dangerous place, vehicle, etc. **death-warrant** *n.* an order for the execution of a condemned person; something that

causes the end of an established practice etc. **death-watch beetle,** a small beetle whose larva bores in wood and makes a ticking sound, formerly supposed to portend a death.
death-wish *n.* a desire (usually unconscious) for the death of oneself or another. **put to death,** to kill, to execute. **to death,** extremely, to the utmost limit. **to the death,** until one or other is killed. [OE]

deathbed *n.* a bed on which a person is dying or dies.

deathly *adj.* suggestive of death. —*adv.* in a deathly way. [f. DEATH]

deb *n.* (*colloq.*) débutante. [abbr.]

débâcle /deɪˈbɑːkl/ *n.* a sudden disastrous collapse, rout, etc. [F (*débâcler* unbar)]

debar /dɪˈbɑː(r)/ *v.t.* (**-rr-**) to exclude, to prohibit.

debase /dɪˈbeɪs/ *v.t.* to lower in quality or value; to depreciate (coins) by use of an alloy etc. —**debasement** *n.* [f. DE- + obs. *base* abase]

debatable /dɪˈbeɪtəb(ə)l/ *adj.* open to dispute. [f. foll.]

debate /dɪˈbeɪt/ *n.* a formal discussion, an open argument. —*v.t./i.* to hold a debate about; to discuss, to consider. [f. F (as DE-, BATTLE)]

debauch /dɪˈbɔːtʃ/ *v.t.* to make dissolute; to lead into debauchery. —*n.* a bout of debauchery. [f. F; ult. orig. unkn.]

debauchery /dɪˈbɔːtʃərɪ/ *n.* excessive sensual indulgence. [f. prec.]

Debbrett /dɪˈbret/, John (*c.*1750-1822), compiler of a 'Peerage of England, Scotland and Ireland' first issued in 1803 and until fairly recently issued annually.

debenture /dɪˈbentʃə(r)/ *n.* a certificate or bond acknowledging a debt and providing for payment of interest at fixed intervals. [f. L *debentur* are owing (*debēre* owe)]

debilitate /dɪˈbɪlɪteɪt/ *v.t.* to cause debility in. [f. L (as foll.)]

debility /dɪˈbɪlɪtɪ/ *n.* feebleness, weakness, especially of health. [f. OF f. L (*debilis* weak)]

debit /ˈdebɪt/ *n.* an entry in an account-book of a sum owed; the sum itself, the total of such sums. —*v.t.* to enter as a debit (in). [f. F f. L *debitum* debt]

debonair /debəˈneə(r)/ *adj.* having a carefree self-assured manner. [f. OF (*de bon aire* of good disposition)]

debouch /dɪˈbaʊtʃ/ *v.i.* to come out from a ravine or wood etc. into open ground; (of a river or road) to merge into a larger or wider one. [f. F (DE-, *bouche* mouth)]

debrief /diːˈbriːf/ *v.t.* to interrogate (a person) about a completed undertaking in order to obtain information about it.

debris /ˈdebriː, ˈdeɪ-/ *n.* scattered broken pieces, rubbish, wreckage. [f. F (DE- *briser* break)]

de Broglie /də ˈbrəʊlji:/, Louis (1892-   ) French physicist, whose name is applied to the wave which in wave mechanics is taken as accounting for or representing the wave-like properties of particles of matter, especially elementary particles. He was awarded a Nobel Prize in 1929.

debt /det/ *n.* money etc. that is owed; an obligation; a state of owing. [f. OF f. L *debitum* (*debēre* owe)]

debtor /ˈdetə(r)/ *n.* a person owing money etc. [as prec.]

debug /diːˈbʌg/ *v.t.* (**-gg-**) **1.** to remove bugs from. **2.** (*slang*) to remove concealed listening devices from (a room etc.) or defects from (a machine etc.).

debunk /diːˈbʌŋk/ *v.t.* (*colloq.*) to show the good reputation of (a person etc.) to be false; to expose the falseness of (a claim etc.).

Debussy /dəˈbjuːsiː/, Achille-Claude (1862-1918), French composer and critic, whose music was stimulated and influenced by events in Paris that ranged from the impressionist and symbolist movements, and the current preoccupation with the old church modes and with plainchant, to the sonorities of a Javanese gamelan at the World Exhibition in Paris in 1889. Cultivating a distinctively French musical outlook (eventually styling himself 'music-ien français'), he was an innovator of the first degree, using block chords, harmony based on the whole-tone scale, and a declamatory yet lyrical style of vocal composition. His opera *Pelléas et Mélisande* (1893-5) turns away from Wagner in its reticence and its focusing not on the motives and thoughts of the protagonists but on their position 'at the mercy of life or destiny'. Such works as the *Prélude à l'après-midi d'un faune* (1894, produced by Diaghilev as a ballet in 1912 with Nijinsky in the title role) and *La mer* (inspired by Hokusai's painting of a wave) led to criticisms

that he allowed effect to take the place of structure, but it was his feeling for colour and texture (not only in his orchestral works but also in the impressionistic piano Préludes, Images, Estampies, etc.) that made him such an important influence on later composers, including Webern, Berg, Bartók, Varèse, and Boulez.

début /ˈdeɪbuː, -bjuː/ *n.* a first appearance (as a performer, in society, etc.). [F (*débuter* lead off)]

débutante /ˈdebjuːtɑːnt/ *n.* a young woman making her social début. [F (as prec.)]

Dec. *abbr.* December.

deca- *in comb.* **1.** tenfold, having ten. **2.** ten (esp. of a unit in the metric system, as *decagram*). [f. Gk *deka* ten]

decade /ˈdekeɪd/ *n.* a ten-year period; a series or group of ten. [f. F f. L f. Gk (*deka* ten)]

decadence /ˈdekəd(ə)ns/ *n.* **1.** deterioration, decline (esp. of a nation, art or literature after reaching a peak). **2.** decadent attitude or behaviour. [f. F f. L (as foll.)]

decadent /ˈdekəd(ə)nt/ *adj.* **1.** declining, of a period of decadence. **2.** self-indulgent. [f. F f. L (as DECAY)]

decaffeinated /diːˈkæfɪneɪtɪd/ *adj.* having had the caffeine removed or reduced. [f. DE- + CAFFEINE]

decagon /ˈdekəgən/ *n.* a plane figure with ten sides and ten angles. —**decagonal** / -ˈkægən(ə)l/ *adj.* [f. L f. Gk (DECA-, *-gōnos* angled)]

decagram /ˈdekəgræm/ *n.* a metric unit of mass, equal to 10 grams.

decalitre /ˈdekəliːtə(r)/ *n.* a metric unit of capacity, equal to 10 litres.

Decalogue /ˈdekəlɒg/ *n.* the Ten Commandments. [f. OF or L f. Gk (*hoi deka logoi* the ten commandments)]

Decameron /dɪˈkæmərən/ a work by Boccaccio, written between 1348 and 1358, containing 100 tales supposedly told in 10 days by a party of 7 young ladies and 3 young men who had fled from the plague in Florence. [It. f. Gk (*deka* ten, *hēmera* day)]

decametre /ˈdekəmiːtə(r)/ *n.* a metric unit of length, equal to 10 metres.

decamp /dɪˈkæmp/ *v.i.* **1.** to break up or leave camp. **2.** to take oneself off, to abscond. [f. F (as DE-, CAMP[1])]

decanal /dɪˈkeɪn(ə)l, ˈdekə-/ *adj.* of a dean; of the dean's or south side of a choir. [f. L (*decanus* dean)]

decant /dɪˈkænt/ *v.t.* to pour off (wine, liquid, a solution) leaving a sediment behind; to transfer as if by pouring. [f. L *decanthare* f. Gk *kanthos* lip of beaker]

decanter /dɪˈkæntə(r)/ *n.* a stoppered glass bottle into which wine or spirit is decanted. [f. prec.]

decapitate /dɪˈkæpɪteɪt/ *v.t.* to behead. —**decapitation** /-teɪʃ(ə)n/ *n.* [f. L (DE-, *caput* head)]

decapod /ˈdekəpɒd/ *n.* a ten-footed crustacean, e.g. a crab. [f. F f. L f. Gk (as DECA-, *pous pod-* foot)]

decarbonize /diːˈkɑːbənaɪz/ *v.t.* to remove the carbon from (an internal-combustion engine etc.). —**decarbonization** /-ˈzeɪʃ(ə)n/ *n.* [f. DE- + CARBON]

decathlon /dɪˈkæθlən/ *n.* an athletic contest in which each competitor takes part in the ten different events which it comprises, which has featured in the Olympic Games since 1912. [f. Gk *deka* ten, *athlon* contest]

decay /dɪˈkeɪ/ *v.t./i.* **1.** to rot or decompose, to cause to do this. **2.** to decline or cause to decline in quality, power, wealth, energy, beauty, etc. **3.** (of a substance) to undergo change by radioactivity. —*n.* **1.** a rotten or ruinous state. **2.** decline in health, loss of quality. **3.** radioactive change. [f. OF f. L (DE-, *cadere* fall)]

Deccan /ˈdekən/ a triangular plateau of southern India, bounded by the Malabar and Coromandel coasts, and by the Vindhaya mountains in the north.

decease /dɪˈsiːs/ *n.* (chiefly *Law*) death. —*v.i.* to die. [f. OF f. L *decessus* (*cedere* go)]

deceased *adj.* dead. —*n.* a person who has died (esp. recently). [f. prec.]

deceit /dɪˈsiːt/ *n.* the concealing of truth in order to mislead, a dishonest trick; the tendency to use deceit. —**deceitful** *adj.*, **deceitfully** *adv.*, **deceitfulness** *n.* [as foll.]

deceive /dɪˈsiːv/ *v.t./i.* **1.** to make (a person) believe what is false, to mislead purposely; to use deceit. **2.** to be unfaithful to, esp. sexually. —**deceive oneself,** to persist in a mistaken belief. —**deceiver** *n.* [f. OF f. L *decipere* (DE-, *capere* take)]

decelerate /diːˈseləreɪt/ *v.t./i.* to reduce the speed (of). —**deceleration** /-ˈreɪʃ(ə)n/ *n.* [f. DE-, after ACCELERATE]

December /dɪˈsembə(r)/ n. the twelfth month of the year. [f. OF f. L (*decem* ten, because orig. the tenth month in the Roman calendar)]

decency /ˈdiːs(ə)nsɪ/ n. correct and tasteful behaviour; compliance with recognized propriety; avoidance of obscenity; (in pl.) the requirements of correct behaviour. [f. L (as DECENT)]

decennial /dɪˈsenɪ(ə)l/ adj. lasting for ten years; recurring every ten years. [f. L (*decem* ten, *annus* year)]

decent /ˈdiːs(ə)nt/ adj. **1.** seemly, not immodest or obscene or indelicate; respectable. **2.** acceptable, quite good. **3.** (colloq.) kind, obliging. —**decently** adv. [f. F or L (*decēre* be seemly)]

decentralize /diːˈsentrəlaɪz/ v.t. to transfer from a central to a local authority; to distribute among local centres. —**decentralization** /-ˈzeɪʃ(ə)n/ n.

deception /dɪˈsepʃ(ə)n/ n. deceiving, being deceived; a thing that deceives. [f. OF or L (as DECEIVE)]

deceptive /dɪˈseptɪv/ adj. apt to mislead, easily mistaken for something else. —**deceptively** adv. [as prec.]

deci- in comb. one-tenth. [f. L *decimus* tenth]

decibel /ˈdesɪb(e)l/ n. a unit used in the comparison of power levels in electrical communication or the intensities of sounds, freq. used to express a single power level or sound intensity relative to some reference level (stated or understood).

decide /dɪˈsaɪd/ v.t./i. to bring or come to a resolution; to settle (an issue etc.) in favour of one side or another; to give a judgement. [f. F or L (DE-, *caedere* cut)]

decided adj. **1.** (usu. attrib.) definite, unquestionable. **2.** having clear opinions, determined. —**decidedly** adv. [f. prec.]

decider n. a game, race, etc., to decide between competitors finishing equal in a previous contest. [f. DECIDE]

deciduous /dɪˈsɪdjʊəs/ adj. (of a tree) shedding its leaves annually; (of leaves, horns, teeth, etc.) shed periodically or normally. [f. L (DE-, *cadere* fall)]

decigram /ˈdesɪɡræm/ n. a metric unit of mass, equal to one-tenth of a gram.

decilitre /ˈdesɪliːtə(r)/ n. a metric unit of capacity, equal to one-tenth of a litre.

decimal /ˈdesɪm(ə)l/ adj. of tenths or ten, proceeding or reckoning by tens; of decimal coinage. —n. a decimal fraction. —**decimal coinage** or **currency**, that in which the units are decimal multiples or fractions of each other. **decimal fraction**, one with a power of 10 as the denominator, especially when written as figures after the decimal point. **decimal point**, the dot placed after the unit figure in the decimal notation. **decimal system**, that in which each denomination, weight, or measure is 10 times the value of the one immediately below it. [f. L *decimus* tenth (*decem* ten)]

decimalize /ˈdesɪməlaɪz/ v.t. to express as a decimal, to convert to a decimal system. —**decimalization** /-ˈzeɪʃ(ə)n/ n. [f. prec.]

decimate /ˈdesɪmeɪt/ v.t. to destroy one-tenth of; (D) to destroy a large proportion of. —**decimation** /-ˈmeɪʃ(ə)n/ n. [f. L *decimare* take the tenth man (*decimus* tenth), referring to the ancient Roman custom of putting to death one in every ten soldiers taking part in a mutiny or similar crime]

decimetre /ˈdesɪmiːtə(r)/ n. a metric unit of length, equal to one-tenth of a metre.

decipher /dɪˈsaɪfə(r)/ v.t. to convert (a text written in cipher or unfamiliar script) into an understandable script or language; to establish the meaning of (poor writing, anything puzzling). —**decipherment** n.

decipherable adj. able to be deciphered. [f. prec.]

decision /dɪˈsɪʒ(ə)n/ n. **1.** an act of deciding. **2.** settlement (of an issue etc.). **3.** a conclusion reached, a resolve made. **4.** the tendency to decide firmly. [f. OF or L (as DECIDE)]

decisive /dɪˈsaɪsɪv/ adj. **1.** that decides an issue or contributes to a decision. **2.** showing decision and firmness, positive. —**decisively** adv. [f. F f. L (as prec.)]

Decius /ˈdiːsɪəs/, Gaius Messius Quintus (d. 251), Roman emperor 249–251, noted for his persecution of the Christians which resulted from his belief that the restoration of State cults was essential to the preservation of the empire. —**Decian** adj.

deck n. **1.** a platform in a ship covering the hull's area (or part of this) at any level and serving as a floor; a ship's accommodation on a particular deck. **2.** a floor or compartment of a bus etc. **3.** the component that carries the magnetic

tape, disc, etc., in sound-reproduction equipment or a computer. **4.** (US) a pack of cards. **5.** (slang) the ground. —v.t. **1.** to furnish with or cover as a deck. **2.** (often with out) to array, to adorn. —**below deck(s)**, in(to) the space under the main deck. **deck-chair** n. a portable folding chair (orig. used on deck in passenger ships). **deck-hand** n. a man employed on a ship's deck in cleaning and odd jobs. [f. MDu., = roof, cloak]

-decker in comb. having a specified number of decks. [f. DECK]

declaim /dɪˈkleɪm/ v.t./i. to speak or utter rhetorically or affectedly; to practise oratory; to inveigh against. —**declamation** /dekləˈmeɪʃ(ə)n/ n., **declamatory** /dɪˈklæmətərɪ/ adj. [f. L (as CLAIM)]

declaration /dekləˈreɪʃ(ə)n/ n. declaring; an emphatic or deliberate statement; a formal announcement. [f. L (as DECLARE)]

Declaration of Independence a document drawn up by Thomas Jefferson, Benjamin Franklin, John Adams, Roger Sherman, and Robert Livingston declaring the USA to be independent of the British Crown, signed on 4 July 1776 by the Congressional representatives of eleven States.

Declaration of Indulgence any of the declarations made by the two Stuart kings Charles II and James II dispensing with repressive legislation against religious nonconformists. The first two declarations, issued by Charles II in 1662 and 1672, were rejected by Parliament. Two, issued by James II in 1687–8, represented attempts to stimulate a Roman Catholic revival, and led to the trial of seven Anglican bishops who refused to comply with the King's wishes.

declare /dɪˈkleə(r)/ v.t./i. **1.** to announce openly or formally; to pronounce; to assert emphatically; (in p.p.) that is such by his own admission. **2.** to acknowledge the possession of (dutiable goods, income, etc.). **3.** (in cricket) to choose to close one's side's innings before all the wickets have fallen. **4.** to name the trump suit in a card-game. —**declare oneself**, to reveal one's intentions or identity. —**declarative** /-ˈklærətɪv/ adj., **declaratory** /-ˈklærətərɪ/ adj. [f. L *declarare* (DE-, *clarus* clear)]

declension /dɪˈklenʃ(ə)n/ n. **1.** variation of the form of a noun etc. to give its grammatical case; the class by which a noun etc. is declined. **2.** falling-off, deterioration. [f. OF (as DECLINE)]

declination /deklɪˈneɪʃ(ə)n/ n. **1.** a downward bend. **2.** the angular distance of a star etc. north or south of the celestial equator. **3.** the deviation of a compass needle east or west from the true north. —**declinational** adj. [f. L (as foll.)]

decline /dɪˈklaɪn/ v.t./i. **1.** to deteriorate, to lose strength or vigour, to decrease. **2.** to refuse (an invitation or challenge) formally and courteously; to give or send a refusal. **3.** to slope downwards; to bend down, to droop. **4.** (Gram.) to give the forms of (a noun or adjective) corresponding to the cases. —n. **1.** a gradual loss of vigour etc. **2.** deterioration, decay. [f. OF f. L *declinare* (DE-, *clinare* bend)]

declivity /dɪˈklɪvɪtɪ/ n. a downward slope. [f. L *declivitas* (DE-, *clivus* slope)]

declutch /diːˈklʌtʃ/ v.i. to disengage the clutch of a motor vehicle.

decoct /dɪˈkɒkt/ v.t. to make a decoction of. [f. L *decoquere* boil down]

decoction /dɪˈkɒkʃ(ə)n/ n. boiling down to extract an essence; the essence produced. [f. OF or L (as prec.)]

decode /diːˈkəʊd/ v.t. to convert (a coded message) into an understandable language.

decoke /diːˈkəʊk/ v.t. (colloq.) to decarbonize. —n. (colloq.) the process of decarbonizing.

décolletage /deɪkɒlˈtɑːʒ/ n. a low neckline of a woman's dress etc. [F (DE-, *collet* collar of dress)]

décolleté /deɪˈkɒlteɪ/ adj. having a low neckline. [F (as prec.)]

decompose /diːkəmˈpəʊz/ v.t./i. **1.** to decay, to rot. **2.** to separate (a substance) into its elements. —**decomposition** /-kɒmpəˈzɪʃ(ə)n/ n.

decompress /diːkəmˈpres/ v.t. to subject to decompression.

decompression /diːkəmˈpreʃ(ə)n/ n. release from compression; the gradual reduction of air pressure on a person who has been subjected to it (especially underwater). —**decompression chamber,** an enclosed space for this. **decompression sickness,** the condition caused by a sudden lowering of the air pressure and the formation of bubbles in the blood.

decongestant /diːkənˈdʒest(ə)nt/ *n.* a medicinal substance that relieves congestion.

decontaminate /diːkənˈtæmɪneɪt/ *v.t.* to remove (esp. radioactive) contamination from. —**decontamination** /-ˈneɪʃ(ə)n/ *n.*

décor /ˈdeɪkɔː(r), deɪ-/ *n.* the furnishing and decoration of a room or stage. [F (as foll.)]

decorate /ˈdekəreɪt/ *v.t.* **1.** to furnish with adornments; to serve as an adornment to. **2.** to paint or paper etc. (a room or house). **3.** to invest with an order, medal, or other award. —**Decorated style,** a style of English Gothic architecture (*c.*1250-1350) with increasing use of decoration. —**decorative** /ˈdekərətɪv/ *adj.* [f. L *decorare* (*decus* beauty)]

decoration /dekəˈreɪʃ(ə)n/ *n.* **1.** decorating; a thing that decorates; (in *pl.*) flags etc. put up on a festive occasion. **2.** a medal etc. conferred and worn as an honour. [f. F or L (as prec.)]

decorator /ˈdekəreɪt(ə)r/ *n.* a person who decorates, especially one who paints or papers houses professionally. [f. DECORATE]

decorous /ˈdekərəs/ *adj.* having or showing decorum. —**decorously** *adv.* [f. L *decorus* seemly]

decorum /dɪˈkɔːrəm/ *n.* behaviour or usage conforming with decency or politeness, seemliness. [L (as prec.)]

decoy /ˈdiːkɔɪ/ *n.* a thing or person used to lure an animal or other person into a trap or danger; a bait, an enticement. —/dɪˈkɔɪ/ *v.t.* to lure by means of a decoy. [perh. f. Du. (*de* the, *kooi* f. L *cavea* cave)]

decrease /dɪˈkriːs/ *v.t./i.* to make or become smaller or fewer. —/ˈdiː-/ *n.* decreasing; the amount by which a thing decreases. [f. OF f. L *decrescere* (DE-, *crescere* grow)]

decree /dɪˈkriː/ *n.* an official or authoritative order having legal force; a judgement or decision of certain law-courts. —*v.t.* to ordain by decree. —**decree nisi** /ˈnaɪsaɪ/, a provisional order for divorce, made absolute unless cause to the contrary is shown within a fixed period (L *nisi* unless). [f. OF f. L *decretum* thing decided]

decrepit /dɪˈkrepɪt/ *adj.* weakened by age or hard use, dilapidated. —**decrepitude** *n.* [f. L (DE-, *crepare* creak)]

decretal /dɪˈkriːt(ə)l/ *n.* a papal decree. [f. L (as DECREE)]

decry /dɪˈkraɪ/ *v.t.* to disparage, to depreciate.

decussate /dɪˈkʌsət/ *adj.* X-shaped; with pairs of opposite leaves etc. each at right angles to the pair below (ill. PLANTS). [f. L *decussare* divide in cross shape, f. *decussis* numeral ten or shape X (*decem* ten)]

Dedekind /ˈdeɪdɪkɪnd/, Richard (1831-1916), German mathematician, professor at Brunswick from 1862 until his death. His analysis of the properties that characterize real numbers and his description of real numbers as Dedekind sections of rational numbers solved the 2,000-year-old question of what numbers are and supplied a satisfactory foundation on which mathematical analysis could be rigorously based. He is remembered also for his theory of rings of algebraic integers which, simplifying and extending the work of Eduard Kummer, cast the theory of algebraic numbers into its very general modern form. Like Georg Cantor, he introduced collections of numbers, treating these collections as entities that are of interest in their own right, whose relationships to each other may be studied by means of set theory. Thus he was one of the principal founders of abstract algebra and 'modern maths'.

dedicate /ˈdedɪkeɪt/ *v.t.* to devote to a sacred person or purpose; to devote (esp. *oneself*) to a special task or purpose; (of an author or composer) to address (a book, piece of music, etc.) *to* a person as an honour or recognition; (in *p.p.*) devoted to a vocation etc., having single-minded loyalty. —**dedicator** *n.* [f. L *dedicare* (DE-, *dicare* declare)]

dedication /dedɪˈkeɪʃ(ə)n/ *n.* dedicating; the words with which a book etc. is dedicated. [f. OF or L (as prec.)]

dedicatory /ˈdedɪkeɪtərɪ/ *adj.* of or forming a dedication. [f. DEDICATE]

deduce /dɪˈdjuːs/ *v.t.* to infer, to draw as a logical conclusion. —**deducible** *adj.* [f. L *deducere* (DE-, *ducere* lead)]

deduct /dɪˈdʌkt/ *v.t.* to subtract, to take away; to withhold (a portion or amount). [f. L (as prec.)]

deductible *adj.* that may be deducted, especially from one's tax or taxable income. [f. prec.]

deduction /dɪˈdʌkʃ(ə)n/ *n.* **1.** deducting; an amount deducted. **2.** deducing, the inferring of particular instances

from a general law. **3.** a conclusion reached. [f. OF or L (as DEDUCE)]

deductive *adj.* of or reasoning by deduction. [f. L (as DEDUCE)]

dee *n.* the letter D; a thing shaped like this. [name of the letter]

deed *n.* **1.** a thing consciously done; a brave, skilful, or conspicuous act. **2.** actual fact, performance. **3.** a document effecting the legal transfer of ownership and bearing the disposer's signature. —**deed-box** *n.* a strong box for keeping deeds and other documents. **deed of covenant,** an agreement to pay a regular amount annually to a charity etc., enabling the charity to recover the tax paid by the donor on this amount of his outcome. **deed poll,** a deed made by one party only, especially to change a name. [OE, rel. to DO[1]]

deem *v.t.* to regard, to consider, to judge. [OE]

deemster /ˈdiːmstə(r)/ *n.* either of the two judges in the Isle of Man. [f. prec.]

deep *adj.* **1.** extending far down or in from the top, surface, or edge; extending to or lying at a specified depth. **2.** situated far down, back, or in. **3.** coming or brought from far down or in; low-pitched, full-toned, not shrill. **4.** intense, vivid, extreme. **5.** heartfelt, absorbing; fully absorbed or overwhelmed. **6.** profound, penetrating, difficult to understand. —*n.* **1.** a deep place (esp. *the* sea) or state. **2.** the position of a fieldsman distant from the batsman in cricket. —*adv.* deeply; far down or in. —**deep-fry** *v.t.* to fry (food) in fat or oil that covers it. **deep-laid** (of a scheme) secret and elaborate. **deep-rooted, -seated** *adjs.* (of feelings or convictions) firmly established, profound. **Deep South,** the States of South Carolina, Georgia, Alabama, Mississippi, and Louisiana in the south-eastern USA, which formed the heartland of the Confederacy defeated in the American Civil War and retain a traditional cultural identity. **go off the deep end,** to give way to anger or emotion. **in deep water,** in trouble or difficulty. —**deeply** *adv.*, **deepness** *n.* [OE]

deepen *v.t./i.* to make or become deep or deeper. [f. DEEP]

deep-freeze /diːpˈfriːz/ *n.* a freezer; storage in a freezer. —*v.t.* (*past* **deep-froze**; *p.p.* **deep-frozen**) to store in a deep-freeze.

deer *n.* (*pl.* same) a four-footed ruminant animal of the family Cervidae, of which the male usually has antlers (ill. MAMMALS). [OE]

deerskin *n.* leather from a deer's skin.

deerstalker /ˈdɪəstɔːkə(r)/ *n.* a soft cloth cap with peaks in front and behind.

deface /dɪˈfeɪs/ *v.t.* to spoil the appearance of; to make illegible. —**defacement** *n.*

de facto /diː ˈfæktəʊ, deɪ/ in fact, existing in fact (whether by right or not). [L]

defalcate /ˈdiːfælkeɪt/ *v.i.* to misappropriate money. —**defalcator** *n.* [f. L *defalcare* lop with a sickle (DE-, *falx* sickle)]

defalcation /diːfælˈkeɪʃ(ə)n/ *n.* **1.** misappropriation of money; the amount misappropriated. **2.** a shortcoming. [f. prec.]

defame /dɪˈfeɪm/ *v.t.* to attack the good reputation of, to speak ill of. —**defamation** /defəˈmeɪʃ(ə)n/ *n.*, **defamatory** /dɪˈfæmətərɪ/ *adj.* [f. OF f. L *diffamare* (DIS-, *fama* report)]

default /dɪˈfɔːlt, -ˈfɒlt/ *n.* failure to fulfil an obligation, especially to appear, pay, or act in some way. —*v.i.* to fail to meet an (esp. pecuniary) obligation. —**go by default,** to be absent, to be ignored because of absence. **in default of,** because of or in case of the lack or absence of. [f. OF f. L (as FAIL)]

defaulter *n.* one who defaults, especially a soldier guilty of a military offence. [f. prec.]

defeat /dɪˈfiːt/ *v.t.* to overcome in a battle or other contest; to frustrate, to baffle. —*n.* defeating, being defeated. [f. AF f. L *disfacere* (DIS-, *facere* do)]

defeatist *n.* one who expects or accepts defeat too readily. —**defeatism** *n.* [f. prec.]

defecate /ˈdiːfɪkeɪt/ *v.i.* to expel faeces from the bowels. —**defecation** /-ˈkeɪʃ(ə)n/ *n.* [f. L *defaecare* purify (DE-, *faex* dregs)]

defect /dɪˈfekt/ *n.* /also ˈdiː-/ a lack of something essential to adequacy or completeness, an imperfection; a shortcoming, a failing. —*v.i.* to abandon one's country or cause in favour of another. —**defector** *n.* [f. L *deficere* fail]

defection /dɪˈfekʃ(ə)n/ n. the abandonment of one's country or cause. [f. L (as prec.)]

defective /dɪˈfektɪv/ adj. 1. having defects, imperfect, incomplete. 2. mentally subnormal. —**defectively** adv., **defectiveness** n. [f. OF or L (as DEFECT)]

defence /dɪˈfens/ n. 1. defending from or resistance against attack; a means of achieving this; (in pl.) fortifications etc. 2. a justification put forward in response to an accusation. 3. the defendant's case in a lawsuit; counsel for the defendant. 4. the players in the defending position in a game. —**defence mechanism**, the body's reaction against disease organisms; a mental process avoiding conscious conflict. [f. OF f. L (as DEFEND)]

defenceless adj. having no defence, unable to defend oneself. [f. prec. + -LESS]

defend /dɪˈfend/ v.t./i. 1. to resist an attack made on, to protect. 2. to uphold by argument, to speak or write in favour of; to conduct the defence in a lawsuit. —**defender** n. [f. OF f. L defendere (DE-, fendere strike)]

defendant n. the person accused or sued in a lawsuit. [f. prec.]

Defender of the Faith a title (transl. L Fidei defensor) conferred on Henry VIII by Pope Leo X in 1521 in recognition of his treatise defending the seven sacraments against Luther. It was recognized by Parliament as an official style of the English monarch in 1544, and has been borne by all subsequent sovereigns.

defensible /dɪˈfensɪb(ə)l/ adj. able to be defended or justified. —**defensibility** /-ˈbɪlɪtɪ/ n., **defensibly** adv. [f. L (as DEFEND)]

defensive adj. done or intended for defence, protective. —**on the defensive**, in an attitude or position of defence; expecting criticism. —**defensively** adv. [f. F f. L (as DEFEND)]

defer[1] /dɪˈfɜː(r)/ v.t. (-rr-) to put off to a later time, to postpone. —**deferred payment**, payment by instalments for goods supplied. **deferred shares** (or **stock**), shares or stock with the least entitlement to a dividend. —**deferment** n., **deferral** n. [orig. same as DIFFER]

defer[2] /dɪˈfɜː(r)/ v.i. (-rr-) to yield or make concessions in opinion or action (to a person). [f. F f. L deferre confer, give]

deference /ˈdefərəns/ n. courteous regard, compliance with another's wishes or advice. —**in deference to**, out of respect for. [f. F (as prec.)]

deferential /defəˈrenʃ(ə)l/ adj. showing deference. —**deferentially** adv. [f. prec.]

defiance /dɪˈfaɪəns/ n. defying, open disobedience, bold resistance. [f. OF (as DEFY)]

defiant /dɪˈfaɪənt/ adj. showing defiance. —**defiantly** adv. [f. prec.]

deficiency /dɪˈfɪʃ(ə)nsɪ/ n. being deficient; a lack or shortage (of); a thing lacking, a deficit. —**deficiency disease**, a disease caused by lack of some essential element in the diet. [f. foll.]

deficient /dɪˈfɪʃ(ə)nt/ adj. incomplete or insufficient in some essential respect. [f. L deficere be lacking]

deficit /ˈdefɪsɪt/ n. the amount by which a total falls short of what is required; the excess of liabilities over assets. [f. F f. L (as prec.)]

defile[1] /dɪˈfaɪl/ v.t. to make dirty, to pollute; to corrupt. —**defilement** n. [for earlier defoul f. OF, = trample down]

defile[2] /dɪˈfaɪl/ n. /also ˈdiː-/ a gorge or pass through which troops etc. can pass only in file. —v.i. to march in file. [f. F (as DE-, FILE[1])]

definable /dɪˈfaɪnəb(ə)l/ adj. able to be defined. [f. foll.]

define /dɪˈfaɪn/ v.t. 1. to give the exact meaning of (a word etc.). 2. to describe or explain the scope of. 3. to outline clearly, to mark out the boundary of. [f. OF f. L definire finish (finis boundary)

definite /ˈdefɪnɪt/ adj. having exact and discernible limits; clear and distinct, not vague. —**definite article**, see ARTICLE. —**definitely** adv. [f. L (as prec.)]

definition /defɪˈnɪʃ(ə)n/ n. 1. defining; a statement of the precise meaning of a word etc. 2. the degree of distinctness in the outline of an object or image. [f. OF f. L (as prec.)]

definitive /dɪˈfɪnɪtɪv/ adj. (of an answer, treaty, verdict, etc.) final, decisive, unconditional; (of an edition of a book etc.) most authoritative. [as prec.]

deflate /dɪˈfleɪt/ v.t./i. 1. to let out the air or gas from (a balloon, tyre, etc.). 2. to lose or cause to lose confidence or

conceit. 3. to apply deflation to (the economy), to pursue a policy of deflation. [f. DE- + INFLATE]

deflation /dɪˈfleɪʃ(ə)n/ n. deflating; reduction of the amount of money in circulation to increase its value as a measure against inflation. —**deflationary** adj. [f. prec.]

deflect /dɪˈflekt/ v.t./i. to turn aside from a straight course or intended purpose; to deviate or cause to deviate (from). —**deflexion**, **deflection** ns., **deflector** n. [f. L deflectere (DE-, flectere bend)]

deflower /diːˈflaʊə(r)/ v.t. 1. to deprive (a woman) of virginity; to ravage. 2. to remove the flowers from (a plant). [f. OF f. L (as DE-, FLOWER)]

Defoe /dɪˈfəʊ/, Daniel (1660–1731), English novelist and journalist, born in London, the son of a butcher. His very varied career included several unsuccessful business ventures and secret service work for both Whigs and Tories, but he was best known to his contemporaries as a political journalist. His verse satire The True-Born Englishman (1701), in defence of William of Orange, won him fame and the King's friendship. However, he was pilloried and imprisoned for his pamphlet The Shortest Way with the Dissenters (1702) in which he (though himself a Dissenter) ironically demanded the suppression of dissent. Having produced more than 500 pamphlets, books, and a thrice-weekly political journal The Review (1704–13), he was nearly 60 when he turned to fiction, producing in 1719 his greatest and most enduring novel, Robinson Crusoe; other fictional and semi-fictional works followed, notably Captain Singleton (1720), Moll Flanders and Colonel Jack (1722), A Journal of the Plague Year (1722), and Roxana (1724). He was a master of vivid narrative with a journalist's eye for realistic detail, and is regarded by many as the first true English novelist, and the spokesman of the rising middle classes.

defoliate /diːˈfəʊlɪeɪt/ v.t. to remove the leaves from, especially as a military tactic. —**defoliant** n., **defoliation** /-ˈeɪʃ(ə)n/ n. [f. L defoliare (DE-, folium leaf)]

deform /dɪˈfɔːm/ v.t. to spoil the appearance or form of, to put out of shape. —**deformation** /diːfɔːˈmeɪʃ(ə)n/ n. [f. L deformare (DE- forma shape)]

deformed adj. misshapen. [f. prec.]

deformity /dɪˈfɔːmɪtɪ/ n. deformed state; a malformation, especially of a body or limb. [as DEFORM]

defraud /dɪˈfrɔːd/ v.t. to cheat by fraud. [f. OF or L (DE-, fraus fraud)]

defray /dɪˈfreɪ/ v.t. to provide the money to pay (a cost or expense). —**defrayal** n. [f. F f. L fredum fine]

defrost /diːˈfrɒst/ v.t. to remove the frost or ice from; to unfreeze (frozen food).

deft adj. neatly skilful or dextrous, adroit. —**deftly** adv., **deftness** n. [var. of DAFT in obs. sense 'meek']

defunct /dɪˈfʌŋkt/ adj. no longer existing or in use; extinct, dead. [f. L (DE-, p.p. of fungi perform)]

defuse /diːˈfjuːz/ v.t. to remove the fuse from (an explosive, a bomb); to reduce the tension or potential danger in (a crisis, difficulty, etc.).

defy /dɪˈfaɪ/ v.t. 1. to resist openly, to refuse to obey. 2. (of a thing) to present insuperable obstacles to. 3. to challenge (a person) to do or prove something. [f. OF f. L fides faith]

Degas /dəˈɡɑː/, Edgar (1834–1917), French artist, born in Paris of a wealthy family. His early work evinced his training at the École des Beaux-Arts, where he greatly admired Ingres. This academic influence was to survive in his life-long concentration on the human form, characterized by a sure sense of draughtsmanship, even after his introduction to the impressionist circle. He exhibited with Manet, Monet, Renoir, Cézanne, Sisley, Pissarro, and Fantin-Latour, evidence of his firm position in the inner circle of impressionist painters in Paris. Degas has in common with the impressionists an imagery which concentrates on everyday events. He explored subjects as diverse as horse-racing, bathers, and ballet-dancers, often finely executed in pastel, and he also produced a series of bronze statuettes, unique in his group. There is evidence that his daring compositional experiments were influenced by photography.

de Gaulle see GAULLE.

degauss /diːˈɡaʊs/ v.t. to demagnetize; to neutralize the magnetism of (a ship) by means of an encircling current-carrying conductor, as a precaution against magnetic mines.

degenerate[1] /dɪˈdʒenərət/ adj. having lost the qualities that are normal and desirable or proper to its kind. —n. a degenerate person or animal. —**degeneracy** n. [as foll.]

degenerate[2] /dɪˈdʒenəreɪt/ v.i. to become worse or lower in standard; to become degenerate. —**degeneration** /-'reɪʃ(ə)n/ n. [f. L (*degener* ignoble, f. DE-, *genus* race)]

degrade /dɪ'greɪd/ v.t. **1.** to reduce to a lower rank. **2.** to bring into dishonour or contempt. **3.** to reduce to a lower organic type or a simpler structure. —**degradation** /degrə'deɪʃ(ə)n/ n. [f. OF f. L *degradare* (DE-, *gradus* step)]

degrading /dɪ'greɪdɪŋ/ adj. humiliating, lowering one's self-respect. [f. prec.]

degree /dɪ'griː/ n. **1.** a stage in an ascending or descending series; a stage in intensity or amount etc.; a category of crime or criminality; a step in direct genealogical descent. **2.** a unit of measurement in an angle or arc; a unit in a scale of temperature, hardness, etc. **3.** an academic diploma awarded for proficiency in a specified subject, or as an honour. —**by degrees**, a little at a time, gradually. [f. OF f. L (DE-, *gradus* step)]

de Havilland /də 'hævɪlənd/, Sir Geoffrey (1882-1965), English aircraft designer and manufacturer. Having built the BE series of fighters in the First World War he started the company named after him (1920), and designed and built many famous light aircraft including the Moth series and also the Gipsy series of aircraft engines, the Mosquito of the Second World War, and some of the first jet-propelled aircraft.

dehisce /dɪ'hɪs/ v.i. to gape, to burst open (especially of a seed-vessel). —**dehiscence** n., **dehiscent** adj. [f. L *dehiscere* (DE-, *hiscere* begin to gape)]

dehumanize /diː'hjuːmənaɪz/ v.t. to remove human characteristics from; to make impersonal. —**dehumanization** /-'zeɪʃ(ə)n/ n. [f. DE- + HUMAN]

dehydrate /diː'haɪdreɪt/ v.t./i. to remove the water or moisture from; to make or become dry. —**dehydration** /-'dreɪʃ(ə)n/ n. [f. DE- + Gk *hudōr* water]

Deianira /daɪə'naɪrə/ (*Gk myth.*) the wife of Hercules, who was tricked into smearing poison on a garment which caused his death.

de-ice /diː'aɪs/ v.t. to remove the ice from; to prevent the formation of ice on. —**de-icer** n.

deify /diː'ɪfaɪ/ v.t. to make a god of; to regard or worship as a god. —**deification** /-fɪ'keɪʃ(ə)n/ n. [f. OF f. L *deificare* (*deus* god)]

deign /deɪn/ v.i. to think fit or condescend *to* do. [f. OF f. L *dignari* (*dignus* worthy)]

deism /'diːɪz(ə)m/ n. belief in the existence of a god (creator of the world) without accepting revelation (cf. THEISM), especially the system of natural religion developed in England in the 17th-18th c. by anti-Christian rationalists influenced by Locke's empiricism. Never widely accepted in England, it had a great influence in France (where Voltaire and J.-J. Rousseau were among its exponents) and in Germany. —**deist** n., **deistic** /-'ɪstɪk/ adj. [f. L *deus* god]

deity /'diːɪtɪ, (D) 'deɪ-/ n. divine status or nature; a god; **the Deity**, God. [f. OF f. L (as prec.)]

déjà vu /deɪʒa: 'vuː/ the illusory feeling of having already experienced a present situation; something tediously familiar. [F, = already seen]

deject /dɪ'dʒekt/ v.t. (often in *p.p.*) to put in low spirits, to depress. —**dejectedly** adv., **dejection** n. [f. L *dejicere* cast down (DE-, *jacere* throw)]

de jure /diː 'dʒʊərɪ, deɪ 'jʊəreɪ/ rightful; by right. [L]

Dekker /'dekə(r)/, Thomas (1570?-1632), English playwright, author of *The Shoemaker's Holiday* (1600), a cheerful comedy of London life. Middleton collaborated with him in the first part of *The Honest Whore* (1604), and John Ford and William Rowley in *The Witch of Edmonton* (1623). His writings are marked by a racy wit, sunny simplicity, and sympathy for the poor and oppressed.

dekko /'dekəʊ/ n. (*slang*) a look. [f. Hindi]

Delacroix /'deləkrwa:/, Ferdinand-Victor-Eugène (1798-1863), French painter, the greatest of the French romantics, though he himself claimed to be 'un pur classique'. His main artistic education came from study of Old Masters, especially Rubens and Veronese. In 1832 he visited Morocco, which both provided exotic subject-matter and stimulated his life-long interest in colour. From the 1830s he experimented with complementary colours, purifying his palette to exclude black and earth colours, in an anticipation of impressionist methods which led Cézanne to say 'we are all in Delacroix'. Delacroix never painted modern life, preferring literary, historical, and typically romantic subject-matter, but to his great admirer, Baudelaire, he was modern because he expressed the spirit of his age. His *Journal* (1822-4 and 1847-63) is a revealing record of his

views on literature, music, and art, as well as of his personal struggles and philosophy.

de la Mare /də læ 'meə(r)/, Walter (1873-1956), English poet and novelist whose highly individual works, addressed to adults and children, have a dream-like quality suggesting eeriness and mystery. These include the poem 'The Listeners' (1912) and for children the story of *The Three Mulla Mulgars* (1910) and the verse collection *Peacock Pie* (1913).

Delaware /'deləweə(r)/ a State of the USA on the Atlantic coast, one of the original 13 States of the USA (1787); capital, Dover.

delay /dɪ'leɪ/ v.t./i. to make or be late, to hinder; to postpone, to defer; to wait, to loiter. —n. an act or process of delaying; a hindrance; the time lost by inaction or inability to proceed. —**delayed-action** adj. operating after an interval of time. [f. OF (prob. as DIS-, *laier* leave)]

delectable /dɪ'lektəb(ə)l/ adj. delightful, enjoyable. —**delectably** adv. [f. OF f. L (*delectare* delight)]

delectation /diːlek'teɪʃ(ə)n/ n. enjoyment, delight. [f. OF (as prec.)]

delegacy /'delɪgəsɪ/ n. a body of delegates. [f. foll.]

delegate /'delɪgət/ n. a person appointed as a representative; a member of a deputation or committee. —/-geɪt/ v.t. to appoint or send as a representative; to entrust (a task) *to* an agent. [f. L *delegare* (DE-, *legare* depute)]

delegation /delɪ'geɪʃ(ə)n/ n. **1.** delegating. **2.** a body of delegates. [as prec.]

delete /dɪ'liːt/ v.t. to cross out or remove (a letter, word, etc.). —**deletion** n. [f. L *delēre* efface]

deleterious /delɪ'tɪərɪəs/ adj. harmful to the body or mind. [f. L f. Gk]

delft n. (also **delftware**) a kind of glazed earthenware, usually decorated in blue, made at Delft in Holland. [name of town]

Delhi /'delɪ/ a Union Territory of India, containing Old and New Delhi. —**Old Delhi**, a city of India on the River Jumna. It was made the capital of the Mogul empire in 1638 by Shah Jahan, who there built the Red Fort containing the imperial Mogul palace. **New Delhi**, the present capital of India, adjoining Old Delhi, originally built 1912-29 to replace Calcutta as the capital of British India; pop. (1981) 6,196,414.

Delian /'diːlɪən/ adj. of Delos. —n. a native or inhabitant of Delos. —**Delian League**, the modern name given to the alliance of Greek city-states formed in 478-447 BC against the Persians, with its headquarters on Delos. Command of the joint forces and control of the treasury were in Athenian hands, and Athens used the alliance increasingly in her own interest; after the end of the war with Persia the treasury was moved from Delos to Athens and disaffection among the allies was firmly suppressed. Pericles encouraged the conversion of the alliance into an empire, the contributions became a form of tribute, and the reserve brought from Delos was used for the rebuilding of Athenian temples. The league was disbanded on the defeat of Athens in the Peloponnesian War (404 BC), but again united under Athens' leadership against Spartan aggression in 377-338 BC.

deliberate /dɪ'lɪbərət/ adj. **1.** intentional, fully considered. **2.** unhurried, slow and careful. —/-reɪt/ v.i. to think carefully (about); to take counsel. —**deliberately** adv. [f. L *deliberare* (DE-, *librare* weigh f. *libra* balance)]

deliberation /dɪlɪbə'reɪʃ(ə)n/ n. careful consideration; careful slowness. [f. OF f. L (as prec.)]

deliberative /dɪ'lɪbərətɪv/ adj. of or for deliberation. [f. F or L (as DELIBERATE)]

Delibes /də'liːb/, (Clément Philibert) Léo (1836-91), French composer and organist. He wrote a number of operas and operettas, but his best-known works are the ballets *Coppélia* (1870) and *Sylvia* (1876).

delicacy /'delɪkəsɪ/ n. **1.** delicateness. **2.** avoidance of immodesty or giving offence. **3.** a choice food. [f. foll.]

delicate /'delɪkət/ adj. **1.** fine or pleasing in texture or construction etc.; (of colour or taste etc.) pleasantly subtle, not strong. **2.** deft, sensitive; (esp. of actions) considerate. **3.** tender, easily harmed; liable to illness; requiring deftness or tact. **4.** avoiding coarseness or impropriety. —**delicately** adv., **delicateness** n. [f. OF or L; orig. unkn.]

delicatessen /delɪkə'tes(ə)n/ n. a shop selling prepared foods and delicacies; such food. [Du. or G f. F *délicatesse* (as prec.)]

delicious /dɪ'lɪʃəs/ adj. highly pleasing, especially to the taste or smell. —**deliciously** adv. [f. OF f. L (deliciae delight)]

delight /dɪˈlaɪt/ v.t./i. **1.** to please greatly. **2.** to take great pleasure in; to be highly pleased to do. —n. great pleasure; a thing that gives it. [f. OF f. L delectare]

delightful adj. giving delight. —**delightfully** adv. [f. prec.]

Delilah /dɪˈlaɪlə/ a woman who betrayed Samson to the Philistines (Judges 16); hence, a seductive treacherous woman.

delimit /dɪˈlɪmɪt/ v.t. to fix the limits or boundaries of. —**delimitation** /-ˈteɪʃ(ə)n/ n. [f. F f. L delimitare (DE-, limes boundary)]

delineate /dɪˈlɪnɪeɪt/ v.t. to show by a drawing or description. **delineation** /-ˈeɪʃ(ə)n/ n. [f. L delineare (DE-, linea line)]

delinquent /dɪˈlɪŋkwənt/ adj. committing an offence; failing in a duty. —n. an offender (esp. **juvenile delinquent**). —**delinquency** n. [f. L delinquere offend]

deliquesce /delɪˈkwes/ v.i. to become liquid, to melt; to dissolve in moisture absorbed from the air. —**deliquescence** n., **deliquescent** adj. [f. L deliquescere begin to be liquid)]

delirious /dɪˈlɪrɪəs/ adj. affected with delirium; raving, wildly excited; ecstatic. —**deliriously** adv. [f. foll.]

delirium /dɪˈlɪrɪəm/ n. a disordered state of mind with incoherent speech and hallucinations; a mood of frenzied excitement. —**delirium tremens** /ˈtriːmenz/, a form of delirium with tremors and terrifying delusions due to prolonged consumption of alcohol. [L, f. delirare be deranged, orig. = deviate from a ridge in ploughing]

Delius /ˈdiːlɪəs/, Frederick (1862–1934), English composer, born in Yorkshire of German parents, who spent his life abroad, settling in France in the 1890s. From 1928, left paralysed, blind, and helpless after what was thought to be an attack of syphilis, he transmitted his work through the medium of a Yorkshireman, Eric Fenby. Best known for such pastoral works as Brigg Fair (1907) and On Hearing the First Cuckoo in Spring (1912), Delius also wrote two operas which are still performed, A Village Romeo and Juliet (1900–1) and Fennimore and Gerda (1909–10), which, together with his songs, reveals his love of Scandinavian life and literature: he had visited Norway in 1887 and there became a close friend of Grieg.

deliver /dɪˈlɪvə(r)/ v.t. **1.** to convey or distribute (letters or goods etc.) to a destination or destinations; to transfer possession of, to give up or hand over to another. **2.** to utter (a speech or sermon); to aim or launch (a blow, attack, ball). **3.** to set free, to rescue (from). **4.** to assist at the birth of or in giving birth; (also **be delivered of**) to give birth to. —**deliver the goods**, (colloq.) to carry out one's part of a bargain. —**deliverer** n. [f. OF (as DE-, LIBERATE)]

deliverance n. rescue, setting free. [as prec.]

delivery n. delivering, being delivered; the periodical distribution of letters or goods etc.; the manner of delivering a ball, speech, etc. [f. AF (as DELIVER)]

dell n. a small wooded hollow. [OE, rel. to DALE]

Della Robbia /delə ˈrɒbɪə/, Luca (1400–82), Florentine sculptor, trained in the workshop of Florence cathedral, for which he executed a marble Singing Gallery of child musicians (1431–8) in his characteristically sweet and charming style. He invented vitreous glazes to colour sculpture modelled in terracotta, thus making it possible for polychromatic sculpture to be used in outdoor settings without suffering from damp. The workshop, and the secret of the technique, were passed on to his nephew, Andrea (1434–1525), but the later productions of the family declined in quality as a result of mass-production.

Delos /ˈdiːlɒs/ a small island regarded as the centre of the Cyclades. According to legend the birthplace of Apollo and Artemis, it was from earliest historical times sacred to Apollo.

delouse /diːˈlaʊs/ v.t. to rid of lice.

Delphi /ˈdelfɪ, -faɪ/ one of the most important religious sanctuaries of the ancient Greek world, dedicated to Apollo and situated on the lower southern slopes of Mt. Parnassus above the Gulf of Corinth. Reputedly the navel of the earth, it was the seat of the Delphic Oracle, whose often riddling responses to a wide range of religious, political, and moral questions were delivered in a state of ecstasy by the Pythia, the priestess of Apollo; a male prophet put the question to her and interpreted her answer. Influential in the earlier periods of Greek history, its influence declined in Hellenistic times although it was still a centre of information for the Greek world. Under the Roman Empire there were other oracles and other methods of divination (e.g. astrology) which provided alternative sources of prophecy, and its decline was almost complete when Christianity became the official religion under Constantine.

Delphic /ˈdelfɪk/ adj. of or like the ancient Greek oracle at Delphi; obscure, enigmatic. [f. prec.]

delphinium /delˈfɪnɪəm/ n. a garden plant of the genus Delphinium, with tall spikes of usually blue flowers. [L f. Gk, = larkspur (delphin dolphin)]

delta n. **1.** the fourth letter of the Greek alphabet, = d. **2.** a triangular alluvial tract at a river's mouth enclosed or watered by diverging outlets. **3.** a designation of the fourth-brightest star in a constellation, or sometimes the star's position in a group. —**delta wing**, a triangular swept-back wing of an aircraft. —**deltaic** /delˈteɪɪk/ adj. [Gk, f. Phoenician daleth door]

delude /dɪˈluːd/ v.t. to fool, to deceive. [f. L deludere (DE-, ludere play)]

deluge /ˈdeljuːdʒ/ n. **1.** a great flood; **the Deluge,** Noah's flood. **2.** a heavy fall of rain. **3.** an overwhelming rush. —v.t. to flood; to overwhelm. [f. OF f. L diluvium]

delusion /dɪˈluːʒ(ə)n/ n. a false belief or impression; a vain hope; a hallucination. —**delusive** adj. [f. L (as DELUDE)]

de luxe /də ˈlʌks, ˈlʊks/ of a superior kind or quality; sumptuous. [F, = of luxury]

delve v.t./i. **1.** to search (into books etc.) for information. **2.** (archaic) to dig. [OE]

demagnetize /diːˈmægnɪtaɪz/ v.t. to remove the magnetization of. —**demagnetization** /-ˈzeɪʃ(ə)n/ n.

demagogue /ˈdeməgɒg/ n. a political agitator appealing to popular wishes or prejudices. —**demagogic** /-ˈgɒgɪk/ adj., **demagogy** /ˈdem-/ n. [f. Gk [dēmos people, agōgos leading)]

demand /dɪˈmɑːnd/ n. **1.** a request made as of right or peremptorily; an urgent claim. **2.** popular desire for goods or services. —v.t. **1.** to make a demand for. **2.** to insist on being told. **3.** to require, to call for. —**in demand,** much sought after. **on demand,** as soon as asked for. [f. OF f. L demandare (DE-, mandare to commission)]

demanding adj. requiring much skill or effort; making many demands. [f. prec.]

demarcation /diːmɑːˈkeɪʃ(ə)n/ n. the marking of a boundary or limits, especially between work considered by trade unions to belong to different trades. [f. Sp. (demarcar mark bounds of)]

démarche /ˈdeɪmɑːʃ/ n. a step or proceeding in diplomacy, especially one initiating a fresh policy.ˈ[F (démarcher take steps)]

dematerialize /diːməˈtɪərɪəlaɪz/ v.t./i. to make or become non-material or spiritual.

demean /dɪˈmiːn/ v.t. to lower the dignity of. [f. DE- + MEAN²]

demeanour /dɪˈmiːnə(r)/ n. bearing, outward behaviour. [f. OF (as DE-, LIBERATE) drive animals f. minari threaten)]

demented /dɪˈmentɪd/ adj. driven mad, crazy. [f. OF or L (demens out of one's mind)]

dementia /dɪˈmenʃə/ n. insanity with loss of intellectual power due to brain disease or injury. —**dementia praecox** /ˈpriːkɒks/, schizophrenia. [L (as prec.)]

demerara /deməˈreərə/ n. a kind of raw cane-sugar, originally and chiefly from Demerara, a region of Guyana, the crystals of which have a yellowish-brown colour.

demerit /diːˈmerɪt/ n. a fault, an undesirable quality. [f. OF or L (demerēri deserve)]

demesne /dɪˈmiːn, -meɪn/ n. **1.** the land attached to a mansion etc.; territory, a domain; landed property, an estate. **2.** possession (of land) as one's own. **3.** a region or sphere (of). [f. AF, = belonging to a lord, f. L (dominus lord)]

Demeter /dɪˈmiːtə(r)/ (Gk myth.) the corn-goddess, identified in Italy with Ceres, daughter of Cronos and mother of Persephone. [f. Gk mētēr mother]

demi- /ˈdemɪ/ prefix half-. [f. F f. L dimidius]

demigod /ˈdemɪgɒd/ n. a partly divine being; the offspring of a mortal and a god or goddess; a godlike person.

demijohn /ˈdemɪdʒɒn/ n. a large bottle in a wicker case. [corruption of F dame-jeanne Lady Jane]

demilitarize /diːˈmɪlɪtəraɪz/ v.t. to remove military organization or forces from (a zone etc.). —**demilitarization** /-ˈzeɪʃ(ə)n/ n.

De Mille /də ˈmɪl/, Cecil Blount (1881–1959), American film producer-director. In 1915 he created in *Carmen*, the first of the lavish spectacles that were to become synonymous with his name. *The Ten Commandments* (1923) was his best-known film; he remade it more than 30 years later. The Bible also provided the source material for *The King of Kings* (1927), *The Sign of the Cross* (1932), and *Samson and Delilah* (1949), history inspired *Cleopatra* (1934) and *The Crusades* (1935), while *The Plainsman* (1937) and *Union Pacific* (1939) were westerns. The quintessential Hollywood showman, he displayed unrivalled skill in creating spectacular effects and handling crowds.

demi-mondaine /demɪmɔ̃ˈdeɪn/ n. a woman of the *demi-monde*. [f. foll.]

demi-monde /ˈdemɪmɒnd/ n. **1.** women of doubtful repute in society. **2.** a group behaving with doubtful legality etc. [F, = half-world]

demise /dɪˈmaɪz/ n. **1.** death. **2.** transfer of an estate by lease or a will. —v.t. to transfer (an estate or title) to another. [f. AF, = abdicate (as DISMISS)]

demisemiquaver /demɪˈsemɪkweɪvə(r)/ n. a note in music equal to half a semiquaver (ill. MUSICAL NOTATION).

demist /diːˈmɪst/ v.t. to clear mist from (a windscreen etc.). —**demister** n.

demo /ˈdemaʊ/ n. (pl. **-os**) (colloq.) a demonstration, especially to express opinion. [abbr.]

demob /diːˈmɒb/ v.t. (**-bb-**) (colloq.) to demobilize. [abbr.]

demobilize /diːˈməʊbɪlaɪz/ v.t. to release from military service. —**demobilization** /-ˈzeɪʃ(ə)n/ n.

democracy /dɪˈmɒkrəsɪ/ n. **1.** government by all the people, direct or representative; a State having this. **2.** a form of society ignoring hereditary class distinctions and tolerating minority views. [f. F f. L f. Gk (*dēmos* the people, -CRACY)]

democrat /ˈdeməkræt/ n. **1.** an advocate of democracy. **2.** **Democrat**, (*US*) a member of the Democratic Party. [f. F (as prec. + -CRAT)]

democratic /deməˈkrætɪk/ adj. of or according to democracy; supporting or constituting democracy. —**democratically** adv. [f. F f. L f. Gk (as DEMOCRACY)]

Democratic Party one of the two chief political parties in the USA (the other being the Republican Party). The name dates from c.1828, but the party existed earlier under other names; it claims Thomas Jefferson as its founder. In modern times the party is broadly liberal, supporting social reform and international commitment.

democratize /dɪˈmɒkrətaɪz/ v.t. to make democratic. —**democratization** /-ˈzeɪʃ(ə)n/ n. [f. DEMOCRATIC]

Democritus /dɪˈmɒkrɪtəs/ (5th c. BC) Greek philosopher, one of the founders of the atomic theory, according to which all things in an infinite universe are composed of the random groupings of atoms moving in a void. The later sobriquet 'the laughing philosopher' alludes to his ethical ideal of cheerfulness.

demodulation /diːmɒdjʊˈleɪʃ(ə)n/ n. the process of extracting a modulating radio signal from a modulated wave etc.

demography /dɪˈmɒgrəfɪ/ n. the study of statistics of births, deaths, diseases, etc., as illustrating the conditions of life in communities. —**demographic** /deməˈgræfɪk/ adj., **demographically** adv. [f. Gk *dēmos* the people + -GRAPHY]

demolish /dɪˈmɒlɪʃ/ v.t. **1.** to pull or knock down (a building); to destroy. **2.** to refute (a theory); to overthrow (an institution). **3.** (joc.) to eat up. —**demolition** /deməˈlɪʃ(ə)n/ n. [f. F f. L *demoliri* (DE-, *moliri* construct)]

demon /ˈdiːmən/ n. **1.** a devil, an evil spirit; a cruel or forceful person; a personified evil passion. **2.** (also **daemon**) a supernatural being in Greek mythology. —**demonic** /dɪˈmɒnɪk/ adj. [f. L f. Gk *daimōn* inferior deity, spirit]

demonetize /diːˈmɒnɪtaɪz/ v.t. to withdraw (a coin etc.) from use as money. —**demonetization** /-ˈzeɪʃ(ə)n/ n. [f. F (as DE-, L *moneta* money)]

demoniac /dɪˈməʊnɪæk/ adj. **1.** possessed by an evil spirit. **2.** of or like a demon. **3.** fiercely energetic, frenzied. —n. a demoniac person. —**demoniacal** /diːməˈnaɪək(ə)l/ adj. [f. OF f. L f. Gk (*daimonion* dim. of *daimōn*; see prec.)]

demonology /diːməˈnɒlədʒɪ/ n. the study of beliefs about demons. [f. DEMON + -LOGY]

demonstrable /ˈdemənstrəb(ə)l/ adj. able to be shown or proved. —**demonstrably** adv. [f. L (as foll.)]

demonstrate /ˈdemənstreɪt/ v.t./i. **1.** to show evidence of; to describe and explain by help of specimens or experiments; to prove the truth of logically. **2.** to take part in a public demonstration. [f. L *demonstrare* (DE-, *monstrare* show)]

demonstration /demənˈstreɪʃ(ə)n/ n. **1.** demonstrating; an instance of this. **2.** a show of feeling. **3.** an organized gathering or procession to express the opinion of a group publicly. **4.** a display of military force. [f. OF or L (as prec.)]

demonstrative /dɪˈmɒnstrətɪv/ adj. **1.** showing or proving. **2.** given to or marked by the open expression of feelings. **3.** (*Gram.*, of an adjective or pronoun) indicating the person or thing referred to (e.g. *this, those*). —**demonstratively** adv. [f. OF f. L (as DEMONSTRATE)]

demonstrator /ˈdemənstreɪtə(r)/ n. one who demonstrates; one who teaches by demonstration, especially in a laboratory. [f. L (as DEMONSTRATE)]

demoralize /dɪˈmɒrəlaɪz/ v.t. to weaken the morale of, to dishearten. —**demoralization** /-ˈzeɪʃ(ə)n/ n. [f. F (as DE-, MORAL)]

Demosthenes /dɪˈmɒsθəniːz/ (384–322 BC) the greatest Athenian orator. His political speeches are largely taken up with the cause of Greek liberty against the pretensions of Philip II of Macedon, whom he attacked in the *Philippics*. Unsurpassed in the force, directness, and flexibility of his oratory, his devotion to liberty was unquestionable, but his methods and policies were not the best suited to attain this, and those of his opponents were no less directed to maintaining the power and independence of Athens. The real problem of his day was how the Greek city-states could be united to counter the military power of the new national State of Macedon, and failure to achieve this (except with Thebes) led to their defeat in 338 BC. Demosthenes was finally driven to suicide in exile.

demote /diːˈməʊt/ v.t. to reduce to a lower rank or class. —**demotion** n. [f. DE- + PROMOTE]

demotic /dɪˈmɒtɪk/ adj. (of language or writing) of the popular form. —n. **1.** demotic script, the popular simplified form of ancient Egyptian writing, a cursive script based partially on hieratic, which dates from c.650 BC and was gradually replaced by Greek in the Ptolemaic period. **2.** the popular form of modern Greek (see GREEK). [f. Gk (*dēmos* people)]

demur /dɪˈmɜː(r)/ v.t. (**-rr-**) to raise objections, to be unwilling. —n. objecting (usu. *without demur*). [f. OF f. L DE-, *morari* delay]

demure /dɪˈmjʊə(r)/ adj. quiet and serious or affectedly so. —**demurely** adv., **demureness** n. [perh. f. p.p. of OF *demorer* remain (as prec.)]

demurrer /dɪˈmʌrə(r)/ n. a legal objection to the relevance of an opponent's point. [f. AF (as DEMUR)]

den n. **1.** a wild beast's lair. **2.** a place of crime or vice. **3.** a small private room for study etc. [OE]

denarius /dɪˈneərɪəs/ n. (pl. **-rii** /-rɪaɪ/) an ancient Roman silver coin. [L (*deni* ten each)]

denary /ˈdiːnərɪ/ adj. of ten, decimal. [f. L (as prec.)]

denationalize /diːˈnæʃ(ə)nəlaɪz/ v.t. to transfer (an industry, institution, etc.) from national to private ownership. —**denationalization** /-ˈzeɪʃ(ə)n/ n.

denature /diːˈneɪtʃə(r)/ v.t. **1.** to change the nature or properties of. **2.** to make (alcohol) unfit for drinking. [f. F (as DE-, NATURE)]

dendrochronology /dendrəʊkrəˈnɒlədʒɪ/ n. a method of dating timber by study of its annual growth-rings. Trees add a ring of growth each year, and variations in climate affect the width of these rings, with a dry year producing limited growth and a wet year luxuriant growth and a broader ring. By matching sequences of these rings from a tree of known date (e.g. one still alive) with those from an earlier (dead) tree overlapping in age, a master plot of tree-ring patterns can be built up, and timber of unknown date from within the area of this plot can be dated exactly by matching its rings. [f. Gk *dendron* tree + CHRONOLOGY]

dendrology /denˈdrɒlədʒɪ/ n. the study of trees. [f. Gk *dendron* tree + -LOGY]

dene /diːn/ n. a narrow wooded valley. [OE, rel. to DEN]

dengue /ˈdeŋgɪ/ n. an infectious tropical fever causing acute pain in the joints. [West Indian Sp. f. Swahili]

deniable /dɪˈnaɪəb(ə)l/ adj. able to be denied. [f. DENY]

denial /dɪˈnaɪ(ə)l/ n. **1.** denying. **2.** refusal of a request or wish. **3.** a statement that a thing is not true or existent. **4.** a disavowal. [f. DENY]

denier /ˈdenjə(r)/ *n.* a unit of weight for measuring the fineness of silk, rayon, or nylon yarn. [orig. name of small coin; f. OF f. L *denarius*]

denigrate /ˈdenɪgreɪt/ *v.t.* to blacken the reputation of; to defame. —**denigration** /-ˈgreɪʃ(ə)n/ *n.*, **denigrator** *n.* [f. L *denigrare* (DE- *niger* black)]

denim /ˈdenɪm/ *n.* a twilled cotton fabric used for overalls, jeans, etc.; (in *pl.*) a garment made of this. [for *serge de Nim* (*Nîmes* in S. France)]

Denis /ˈdenɪs/, St (*c.*250), patron saint of France. According to a 6th-c. biography he was one of a group of seven sent to convert Gaul, became bishop of Paris, and was martyred. He was later identified with Dionysius the Areopagite. Feast day, 9 Oct.

denizen /ˈdenɪz(ə)n/ *n.* **1.** an inhabitant or occupant (of a place). **2.** a foreigner admitted to residence and certain rights. **3.** a naturalized foreign word, animal, or plant. [f. AF (*deinz* within f. L *de intus*)]

Denmark /ˈdenmaːk/ a Scandinavian country consisting of the greater part of the Jutland peninsula and the neighbouring islands, between the North Sea and the Baltic; pop. (est. 1982) 5,116,464; official language, Danish; capital, Copenhagen. Denmark emerged as a separate country during the Viking period of the 10th and 11th c. In the 14th c. Denmark and Norway were united under a Danish king, the union being joined between 1389–97 and 1523 by Sweden. Territory was lost to Sweden as a result of wars in the mid-17th c. and Norway was ceded to Sweden after the Napoleonic Wars. More territory was lost to the south when Schleswig-Holstein was taken by Prussia in 1864 (although the northern part of Schleswig was returned to Denmark in 1920). Denmark remained neutral in the First World War, but was occupied by the Germans for much of the Second. Since the war, however, Denmark has been stable and prosperous, her economy built largely around agriculture, particularly dairy products.

denominate /dɪˈnɒmɪneɪt/ *v.t.* to give a name to; to call or describe (a person or thing) as. [f. L *denominare* (as DE-, NOMINATE)]

denomination /dɪnɒmɪˈneɪʃ(ə)n/ *n.* **1.** a name or designation, especially a characteristic or class name. **2.** a Church or religious sect. **3.** a class of units of measurement or money. [f. OF or L (as prec.)]

denominational /dɪnɒmɪˈneɪʃ(ə)n(ə)l/ *adj.* of a particular religious denomination. [f. prec.]

denominator /dɪˈnɒmɪneɪtə(r)/ *n.* the number below the line in a vulgar fraction, showing how many parts the whole is divided into, the divisor. —**least** *or* **lowest common denominator**, the lowest common multiple of the denominators of several fractions; the common feature of the members of a group. [f. F or L (as DENOMINATE)]

denote /dɪˈnəʊt/ *v.t.* **1.** to be the name for, to be the sign or symbol of. **2.** to indicate, to give to understand; to signify. —**denotation** /diːnəʊˈteɪʃ(ə)n/ *n.* [f. F or L *denotare* (DE-, *notare* mark)]

dénouement /deɪˈnuːmɑ̃/ *n.* the unravelling of a plot, especially the final resolution in a play, novel, etc. [F, = unknotting]

denounce /dɪˈnaʊns/ *v.t.* **1.** to inform against, to accuse publicly. **2.** to announce withdrawal from (a treaty etc.). [f. OF f. L *denuntiare* make known (DE-, *nuntius* messenger)]

de novo /dɪ ˈnəʊvəʊ/ afresh, starting again. [L]

dense *adj.* **1.** closely compacted in substance; crowded together. **2.** crass, stupid. —**densely** *adv.*, **denseness** *n.* [f. F or L *densus*]

density /ˈdensɪtɪ/ *n.* **1.** closeness of substance. **2.** the degree of consistency measured by the quantity of mass in a unit volume. **3.** the opacity of a photographic image. [f. F or L (as prec.)]

dent *n.* a depression in a surface left by a blow or pressure. —*v.t./i.* to make a dent in; to become dented. [prob. f. INDENT]

dental /ˈdent(ə)l/ *adj.* **1.** of or for the teeth; of dentistry. **2.** (of a consonant) pronounced with the tongue-tip against the upper front teeth or the ridge of the teeth. —**dental floss**, fine strong thread used to clean between the teeth. **dental surgeon**, a dentist. [f. L *dentalis* (*dens* tooth)]

dentate /ˈdenteɪt/ *adj.* toothed, having toothlike notches. [f. L *dentatus* (as prec.)]

dentifrice /ˈdentɪfrɪs/ *n.* a powder, paste, etc., for cleaning the teeth. [F f. L (*dens* tooth, *fricare* rub)]

dentine /ˈdentiːn/ *n.* the hard dense tissue forming the main part of teeth. [f. L *dens* tooth]

dentist /ˈdentɪst/ *n.* a person who is qualified to treat the teeth, extract them, fit artificial ones, etc. —**dentistry** *n.* [f. F f. L (*dens* tooth)]

Dental disease was recognized in ancient times in Babylonia and in Egypt, from where a papyrus of *c.*1500 BC contains prescriptions for diseases of the teeth and gums, though preventive and restorative work seem to have been unknown. The Etruscans had reached a high level of dental surgery by the 9th c. BC, and dentistry was highly developed in ancient India: Hindu writings describe extraction, scaling, and filling, and the fitting of artificial teeth. In early medieval times barbers and barber-surgeons were the dentists (see BARBER). Dentistry was taught in some hospitals from the early 19th c., and the first separate school of dental surgery was started at Baltimore in the USA in 1839. Some instruments, notably the forceps, are of great antiquity, but many date from the early 19th c.; the principle of the dental drill was invented in 1829 by James Nasmyth, the Scottish engineer who invented the steam-hammer. The development of anaesthetics and X-rays greatly benefited dentistry. The modern tendency is for the preservation of the natural teeth for as long as possible.

dentition /denˈtɪʃ(ə)n/ *n.* **1.** the type and arrangement of teeth in a species etc. **2.** teething. [f. L (*dentire* teethe)]

denture /ˈdentʃə(r)/ *n.* a set of artificial teeth. [F f. L (as DENTAL)]

denude /dɪˈnjuːd/ *v.t.* to make naked or bare; to strip of a covering, property, etc. —**denudation** /diːnjuːˈdeɪʃ(ə)n/ *n.* [f. L *denudare* strip (DE-, *nudus* naked)]

denunciation /dɪnʌnsɪˈeɪʃ(ə)n/ *n.* denouncing. —**denunciatory** /dɪˈnʌnsɪətərɪ/ *adj.* [f. F or L (as DENOUNCE)]

deny /dɪˈnaɪ/ *v.t.* **1.** to declare untrue or non-existent. **2.** to disavow or repudiate. **3.** to refuse (a request, applicant, thing *to* a person). —**deny oneself,** to restrict (one's food, drink, or pleasure). [f. OF f. L *denegare* (DE-, *negare* say no)]

deodar /ˈdiːədɑː(r)/ *n.* the Himalayan cedar (*Cedrus deodara*), the tallest of the cedars (sometimes 60 m in height), with pendulous tips to its slightly drooping branches and bearing large barrel-shaped cones. [f. Hindi f. Skr., = divine tree]

deodorant /dɪˈəʊdərənt/ *adj.* that removes or conceals unwanted odours. —*n.* a deodorant substance. [f. foll.]

deodorize /dɪˈəʊdəraɪz/ *v.t.* to destroy the odour of. —**deodorization** /-ˈzeɪʃ(ə)n/ *n.* [f. DE- + L *odor* smell]

deoxyribonucleic acid /dɪɒksɪraɪbəʊnjuːˈkliːɪk/ see DNA. [f. DE- + OXYGEN + RIBONUCLEIC]

dep. *abbr.* **1.** departs. **2.** deputy.

depart /dɪˈpɑːt/ *v.i.* to go away, to leave; (of a train, bus, etc.) to set out, to leave; to diverge or deviate. —**depart this life**, to die. [f. OF f. L *dispertire* divide]

departed *adj.* & *n.* bygone; (*the*) deceased. [f. prec.]

department *n.* **1.** a separate part of a complex whole, a branch, especially of a municipal or State administration, university, or shop. **2.** an administrative district in France etc. **3.** an area of activity. —**department store,** a large shop supplying many kinds of goods from various departments. —**departmental** /diːpɑːtˈment(ə)l/ *adj.* [f. F (as DEPART)]

departure /dɪˈpɑːtʃə(r)/ *n.* **1.** going away; a deviation *from* (the truth, a standard); the starting of a train, aircraft, etc. **2.** setting out on a course of action or thought. [f. OF (as DEPART)]

depend /dɪˈpend/ *v.i.* **1.** (with *on* or *upon*, or *absol.*) to be controlled or determined by. **2.** (with *on* or *upon*) to be unable to do without, to need for success etc. **3.** to trust confidently, to feel certain about. **4.** (*archaic*) to hang down. [f. OF f. L *dependēre* (DE-, *pendēre* hang)]

dependable *adj.* that may be depended on. —**dependability** /-ˈbɪlɪtɪ/ *n.*, **dependably** *adv.* [f. prec.]

dependant *n.* one who depends on another for support. [f. F (as DEPEND)]

dependence *n.* depending, being dependent; reliance. [as prec.]

dependency *n.* a country or province controlled by another. [as DEPENDANT]

dependent *adj.* **1.** depending (*on*). **2.** unable to do without something (especially a drug). **3.** maintained at another's cost. **4.** (of a clause, phrase, or word) in a subordinate relation to a sentence or word. —*n.* (*US*) = DEPENDANT. [var. of DEPENDANT]

depict /dɪˈpɪkt/ v.t. to represent in drawing or colours; to portray in words, to describe. —**depiction** n. [f. L depingere (DE-, pingere paint)]

depilate /ˈdepɪleɪt/ v.t. to remove hair from. —**depilation** /-ˈleɪʃ(ə)n/ n. [f. L depilare (DE-, pilus hair)]

depilatory /dɪˈpɪlətərɪ/ adj. that removes unwanted hair. —n. a depilatory substance. [f. prec.]

deplete /dɪˈpliːt/ v.t. to empty, to exhaust; to reduce the numbers or quantity of. —**depletion** n. [f. L deplere (DE-, plēre fill)]

deplorable /dɪˈplɔːrəb(ə)l/ adj. lamentable, regrettable; exceedingly bad, shocking. —**deplorably** adv. [f. foll.]

deplore /dɪˈplɔː(r)/ v.t. to regret deeply; to find deplorable. [f. F or It. f. L deplorare (DE-, plorare bewail)]

deploy /dɪˈplɔɪ/ v.t. **1.** to spread (troops) out from a column into a line. **2.** to bring (forces, arguments, etc.) into effective action. —**deployment** n. [f. F f. L displicare scatter and deplicare explain (plicare fold)]

deponent /dɪˈpəʊnənt/ adj. (of a verb, esp. in Greek and Latin) passive in form but active in meaning. —n. **1.** a deponent verb. **2.** a person making a deposition under oath. [f. L deponere put down, lay aside]

depopulate /diːˈpɒpjʊleɪt/ v.t. to reduce the population of. —**depopulation** /-ˈleɪʃ(ə)n/ n. [f. L depopulari lay waste (DE-, populus people)]

deport /dɪˈpɔːt/ v.t. **1.** to remove (an unwanted person) from a country. **2.** to behave or conduct oneself (in a specified manner). [f. OF f. L deportare (DE-, portare carry)]

deportation /diːpɔːˈteɪʃ(ə)n/ n. the removal of an unwanted person from a country. [f. prec.]

deportee /diːpɔːˈtiː/ n. a person who has been or is to be deported. [f. DEPORT]

deportment /dɪˈpɔːtmənt/ n. bearing, behaviour. [f. F (as DEPORT)]

depose /dɪˈpəʊz/ v.t./i. **1.** to remove from power; to dethrone. **2.** to bear witness that, to testify to, especially on oath in court. [f. OF f. L (as foll.)]

deposit /dɪˈpɒzɪt/ n. **1.** a thing stored or entrusted for safe-keeping; a sum placed in a bank. **2.** a sum required and paid as a pledge or first instalment. **3.** a layer of precipitated matter, a natural accumulation. —v.t. **1.** to store or entrust for keeping (esp. a sum in a bank). **2.** to pay as a pledge. **3.** to lay down; (of water etc.) to leave (matter) lying. —**deposit account**, a savings account at a bank requiring notice for withdrawal. [f. p.p. of L deponere (as DEPONENT)]

depositary /dɪˈpɒzɪtərɪ/ n. a person to whom a thing is entrusted. [f. L (as prec.)]

deposition /depəˈzɪʃ(ə)n, diː-/ n. **1.** deposing; a dethronement. **2.** sworn evidence, the giving of this. **3.** the taking down of Christ from the Cross. [f. OF f. L (as DEPOSE)]

depositor n. a person who deposits money or property. [f. DEPOSIT]

depository /dɪˈpɒzɪtərɪ/ n. a storehouse; = DEPOSITARY. [f. L (as DEPOSIT)]

depot /ˈdepəʊ/ n. **1.** a storehouse, especially one for military supplies. **2.** the headquarters of a regiment. **3.** a place where goods are deposited or from which goods, vehicles, etc., are dispatched; a bus station; (US) a railway station. [f. F (as DEPOSIT)]

deprave /dɪˈpreɪv/ v.t. to make morally bad, to corrupt. —**depravation** /deprəˈveɪʃ(ə)n/ n. [f. OF or L depravare (DE-, pravus crooked)]

depravity /dɪˈprævɪtɪ/ n. moral corruption, wickedness. [f. DE- + obs. pravity f. L (as prec.)]

deprecate /ˈdeprɪkeɪt/ v.t. **1.** to express a wish against or disapproval of. **2.** to try to avert (a person's anger etc.). —**deprecation** /-ˈkeɪʃ(ə)n/ n., **deprecatory** /ˈdeprɪkətərɪ/ adj. [f. L deprecari pray (a thing) away (DE-, precari pray)]

depreciate /dɪˈpriːʃɪeɪt/ v.t./i. **1.** to diminish in value, price, or purchasing power. **2.** to disparage, to belittle. [f. L depretiare (DE-, pretiare value f. pretium price)]

depreciation /dɪpriːsɪˈeɪʃ(ə)n/ n. a decline in value, especially that due to wear and tear; the allowance made for this. [f. prec.]

depreciatory /dɪˈpriːʃətərɪ/ adj. disparaging. [f. DEPRECIATE]

depredation /deprɪˈdeɪʃ(ə)n/ n. (usu. in pl.) plundering, destruction. [f. F f. L (DE-, praedari plunder)]

depress /dɪˈpres/ v.t. **1.** to lower the spirits of, to sadden. **2.** to reduce the activity of (esp. trade). **3.** to press down

(a lever etc.). —**depressed area,** an area of economic depression. [f. OF f. L depressare (DE-, premere press)]

depressant adj. causing depression. —n. a depressant agent or influence. [f. prec.]

depression /dɪˈpreʃ(ə)n/ n. **1.** a state of extreme dejection, often with physical symptoms. **2.** a long period of financial and industrial slump (see below). **3.** a lowering of atmospheric pressure; the winds caused by this. **4.** a sunken place or hollow on a surface. **5.** pressing down.

The Great Depression of 1929–34 began with an agricultural crisis caused by over-production and led to a financial collapse, with massive speculation, a sudden loss of confidence, and consequent withdrawal of funds, resulting in widespread business failures and massive unemployment (13.7 million in the USA, 5.6 million in Germany, and 2.8 million in Britain). The most dramatic results of the Depression were the introduction of extensive State-controlled economic planning, such as the American New Deal, and the rise of right-wing movements such as the German Nazi Party.

depressive adj. tending to depress; involving mental depression. —n. a person suffering from depression. [f. F or L (as DEPRESS)]

deprivation /deprɪˈveɪʃ(ə)n/ n. depriving; loss of a desired thing. [f. foll.]

deprive /dɪˈpraɪv/ v.t. to prevent from the use or enjoyment of; to dispossess or strip of. —**deprived child,** one lacking a normal home life. —**deprival** n. [f. OF f. L deprivare (DE-, privare deprive)]

De profundis /deɪ prəˈfʊndiːs/ Psalm 130, beginning thus in Latin (= 'Out of the depths (have I cried)').

Dept. abbr. Department.

depth n. **1.** deepness; the measurement from the top down, from the surface inwards, or from the front to the back. **2.** profundity, abstruseness; sagacity. **3.** intensity of a colour, darkness, etc. **4.** (often in pl.) the deepest or most central part. —**depth charge,** a bomb exploding under water, for dropping on a submerged submarine etc., devised in Britain and used during the First World War. **in depth,** thoroughly. **in-depth** adj. thorough. **out of one's depth,** in water too deep to stand in; engaged on a task beyond one's powers. [as DEEP]

deputation /depjʊˈteɪʃ(ə)n/ n. a body of persons appointed to represent others. [f. L (as foll.)]

depute /dɪˈpjuːt/ v.t. to delegate (a task) to a person; to appoint as one's deputy. [f. OF f. L deputare regard as, allot]

deputize /ˈdepjʊtaɪz/ v.i. to act as deputy (for). [f. foll.]

deputy /ˈdepjʊtɪ/ n. **1.** a person appointed to act as a substitute for another. **2.** a parliamentary representative in some countries. [f. p.p. of OF deputer (as DEPUTE)]

De Quincey /də ˈkwɪnsɪ/, Thomas (1785–1859), English essayist and critic, who ran away from school to homeless wanderings in Wales and London where he was befriended by a young prostitute, Ann. He then went to Oxford where he first took opium for toothache and became a lifelong addict. His acquaintance with Wordsworth and Coleridge drew him to the Lake District in 1809; he moved to Edinburgh in 1829. He won instant fame with his Confessions of an English Opium Eater (1822), a study of his addiction and its psychological effects from the euphoric early reveries to the appalling nightmares of the later stages. His work, mainly journalism written under pressure to support his family, included 'On the knocking on the Gate in "Macbeth"' (1827); 'Suspiria de Profundis' (1845), and 'The English Mail Coach' (1849), in which he traced how childhood experiences are crystallized in dreams into symbols which can form the dreamer's personality. His writing is distinguished by eclectic learning, pungent black humour, and a stately singular style.

derail /dɪˈreɪl/ v.t. to cause (a train) to leave the rails. —**derailment** n. [f. F (as DE-, RAIL¹)]

derange /dɪˈreɪndʒ/ v.t. to throw into confusion, to disrupt; to make insane. —**derangement** n. [f. F (as DE-, rang rank, order)]

Derby /ˈdɑːbɪ/ n. **1.** an annual horse-race for three-year-olds, founded in 1780 by the 12th Earl of Derby (d. 1834), run on Epsom Downs in England on the last Wednesday in May or the first Wednesday in June. **2.** a similar race elsewhere. **3.** an important sporting contest.

Derby. abbr. Derbyshire.

Derbyshire /ˈdɑːbɪʃɪə(r)/ a north midland county of England.

derelict /ˈderɪlɪkt/ adj. abandoned, left to fall into ruin (esp. of a ship at sea or decrepit property). —n. an abandoned property, especially a ship; a person forsaken by society, a social misfit. [f. L *derelictus* (DE-, *relinquere* leave behind)]

dereliction /derɪˈlɪkʃ(ə)n/ n. **1.** abandoning, being abandoned. **2.** neglect *of duty*. **3.** a shortcoming. [f. L (as prec.)]

derestrict /diːrɪˈstrɪkt/ v.t. to remove a restriction (esp. a speed-limit) from. —**derestriction** n.

deride /dɪˈraɪd/ v.t. to laugh scornfully at; to treat with scorn. [f. L *deridēre* (DE-, *ridēre* laugh)]

de rigueur /də rɪˈɡɜː(r)/ required by custom or etiquette. [F, = of strictness]

derision /dɪˈrɪʒ(ə)n/ n. scorn, ridicule. [f. OF f. L (as DERIDE)]

derisive /dɪˈraɪsɪv/ adj. scornful, showing derision. —**derisively** adv. [f. prec.]

derisory /dɪˈraɪsərɪ/ adj. **1.** showing derision. **2.** deserving derision; too insignificant for serious consideration. [f. L (as DERIDE)]

derivation /derɪˈveɪʃ(ə)n/ n. **1.** deriving. **2.** the formation of a word from a word or root; the tracing or a statement of this. [f. F or L (as DERIVE)]

derivative /dɪˈrɪvətɪv/ adj. derived from a source, not original. —n. **1.** a derivative word or thing. **2.** (Math.) a quantity measuring the rate of change of another. [f. F f. L (as foll.)]

derive /dɪˈraɪv/ v.t./i. **1.** to trace or obtain *from* a source. **2.** to originate, to be descended, *from*. **3.** to show or assert the descent or formation of (a word etc.) *from*. [f. OF or L *derivare* (as DE-, *rivus* stream)]

dermatitis /dɜːməˈtaɪtɪs/ n. inflammation of the skin. [f. Gk *derma* skin]

dermatology /dɜːməˈtɒlədʒɪ/ n. the study of the skin and its diseases. —**dermatologist** n. [as prec. + -LOGY]

dermis /ˈdɜːmɪs/ n. the layer of skin below the epidermis. (ill. BODY 4). [after EPIDERMIS]

derogate /ˈderəɡeɪt/ v.i. to detract *from* (a merit, right, etc.). —**derogation** /-ˈɡeɪʃ(ə)n/ n. [f. L *derogare* (DE-, *rogare* ask)]

derogatory /dɪˈrɒɡətərɪ/ adj. involving disparagement or discredit; depreciatory. [as prec.]

derrick /ˈderɪk/ n. **1.** a kind of crane with an arm pivoted at the base of a central post or to a floor. **2.** the framework over an oil-well etc., holding the drilling machinery. [orig. = gallows, f. name of London hangman *c.*1600]

derring-do /derɪŋˈduː/ n. (*literary*) heroic courage or action. [orig. = *daring to do*]

derris /ˈderɪs/ n **1.** a tropical climbing plant of the genus *Derris*. **2.** an insecticide made from its powdered root. [L f. Gk, = leather covering (in allusion to its pods)]

derv n. a fuel oil used in heavy road-vehicles. [f. *diesel-engined road vehicle*]

dervish /ˈdɜːvɪʃ/ n. a member of any of several Sufi religious groups, vowed to poverty and austerity and holding esoteric beliefs. Some of the orders perform ecstatic rituals (such as dancing or ritual chanting), and are known as *dancing*, *whirling*, or *howling dervishes* according to the practice of their order. The order of whirling dervishes, founded in Anatolia in the 13th c. by the poet and mystic Mevlana, was dissolved in 1925 by order of Atatürk. [f. Turk. f. Pers., = poor, a mendicant]

desalinate /dɪˈsælɪneɪt/ v.t. to remove the salt from (esp. sea-water). —**desalination** /-ˈneɪʃ(ə)n/ n. [f. DE- + SALINE]

descant /ˈdeskænt/ n. a free soprano part added to a tune; (*poetic*) a song, a melody. — /dɪsˈkænt/ v.i. to talk lengthily *upon*. [f. OF f. L (DIS-, *cantus* song)]

Descartes /deɪˈkɑːt/, René (1596–1650), French philosopher, mathematician, and man of science, often called the father of modern philosophy. Aiming to reach totally secure foundations for knowledge he began by attacking all his beliefs with sceptical doubts. What was left was the certainty of his own conscious experience, and with it of his existence: '*Cogito, ergo sum*' (I think, therefore I exist). From this certainty he proceeded by arguing for the existence of God (as the first cause) and the reality of the physical world, and developed a dualistic theory: the world was composed of mind (conscious experience) and matter; their interaction remained unsolved. His approach set the agenda for the part of modern philosophy called theory of knowledge. In mathematics his name is attached to the Cartesian method whereby points in the plane are located

by their coordinates with respect to rectangular axes fixed in the plane, and lines or curves may then be described by giving the value of the y-coordinates of their points as functions of the x-coordinates. By this method algebraic techniques, and, later, the techniques of calculus, could be used to solve geometrical problems. A cautious man and a practising Catholic, Descartes suppressed his heretical doctrines of the Earth's rotation and the infinity of the universe; fragments of his work in this field were published after his death. From 1628 to 1649 he lived in Holland, then departed for Sweden at the invitation of Queen Christina, a passionate and learned lady who required daily lessons from him at five o'clock in the morning; the unaccustomed early rising and the bitter Scandinavian winter brought on the pneumonia from which he died.

descend /dɪˈsend/ v.t./i. **1.** to go or come down; to slope downwards. **2.** to make a sudden attack or unexpected visit (*on*). **3.** to sink or stoop *to* (an unworthy act), to pass by inheritance *to*. —**be descended from**, to come by descent from (a specified person etc.). [f. OF f. L *descendere* (DE-, *scandere* climb)]

descendant n. a person descended from another. [f. F (as prec.)]

descent /dɪˈsent/ n. **1.** the act of descending. **2.** a way by which one may descend; a downward slope. **3.** lineage, family origin. **4.** a sudden attack. **5.** decline, fall. [as DESCEND]

describe /dɪˈskraɪb/ v.t. **1.** to set forth in words; to recite the characteristics of. **2.** to mark out, to draw, to move in (a specified line or curve). [f. L *describere* (DE-, *scribere* write)]

description /dɪˈskrɪpʃ(ə)n/ n. **1.** describing; an account or verbal picture. **2.** a sort or class. [as prec.]

descriptive /dɪˈskrɪptɪv/ adj. serving or seeking to describe; (of linguistics or grammar etc.) studying the structure of a language at a given time, avoiding comparisons with other languages or other historical phases and without social evaluations. [as DESCRIBE]

descry /dɪˈskraɪ/ v.t. to catch sight of, to succeed in discerning. [f. OF *descrier* (as CRY); orig. = announce, proclaim]

desecrate /ˈdesɪkreɪt/ v.t. to treat (a sacred thing) with irreverence or disrespect. —**desecration** /-ˈkreɪʃ(ə)n/ n., **desecrator** n. [f. DE- + CONSECRATE]

desegregate /diːˈseɡrɪɡeɪt/ v.t. to abolish racial segregation in. —**desegregation** /-ˈɡeɪʃ(ə)n/ n.

desert[1] /dɪˈzɜːt/ v.t./i. to abandon, to leave without intention of returning; to leave military service unlawfully. —**deserter** n., **desertion** n. [f. F f. L (*deserere* forsake)]

desert[2] /ˈdezət/ n. a dry barren often sand-covered area of land. —adj. uninhabited, barren. [f. OF f. L *desertus* (as prec.)]

desert[3] /dɪˈzɜːt/ n. **1.** deserving, being worthy of reward or punishment. **2.** (in *pl.*) a deserved recompense. [f. OF (as DESERVE)]

deserve /dɪˈzɜːv/ v.t. to be entitled to, especially by one's conduct or qualities. [f. OF f. L *deservire* (DE-, *servire* serve)]

deservedly /dɪˈzɜːvɪdlɪ/ adv. as deserved, justly. [f. prec.]

deserving adj. worthy (*of*), worth rewarding or supporting. [f. DESERVE]

déshabillé /deɪzæˈbiːeɪ/ n. the state of being only partly dressed. [F, = undressed]

De Sica /də ˈsiːkə/, Vittorio (1901–74), Italian film director and actor. He acted in over 150 films, including some in English, but in 1940 began also to direct. His first notable production, *The Children Are Watching Us* (1942), inaugurated the collaboration with the scriptwriter Cesare Zavattini which was to create four neo-realist masterpieces: *Shoeshine* (1946), *Bicycle Thieves* (1948)—De Sica's best-known work—*Miracle in Milan* (1951), and *Umberto D* (1952). The last marked the end of his most creative directing, and of his numerous later films only a few—including *Two Women* (1960) and especially *The Garden of the Finzi-Continis* (1971)—revealed signs of his former brilliance.

desiccate /ˈdesɪkeɪt/ v.t. to remove the moisture from; to dry (a foodstuff) to preserve it. —**desiccation** /-ˈkeɪʃ(ə)n/ n., **desiccator** n. [f. L *desiccare* (DE-, *siccus* dry)]

desideratum /dɪsɪdəˈreɪtəm, -ˈrɑː-/ n. (*pl.* -**ta**) a thing that is lacking but needed or desired. [L (as DESIRE)]

design /dɪˈzaɪn/ n. **1.** a preliminary outline or drawing for something that is to be made; the art of producing these. **2.** a scheme of lines or shapes forming a decoration. **3.** a general arrangement or layout; an established form of a product. **4.** an intention or purpose; a mental plan, a scheme of attack or approach. —v.t./i. **1.** to prepare a design for; to be a designer. **2.** to intend or set aside for some purpose. **—by design,** on purpose. **have designs on,** to plan to harm or appropriate. [f. F f. L (as foll.)]

designate /ˈdezɪgneɪt/ v.t. **1.** to specify, to indicate as having some function. **2.** to describe as, to give or serve as a name or distinctive mark to. **3.** to appoint to a position. —/-nət/ adj. appointed to but not yet installed in office. [f. L designare (DE-, signum mark)]

designation /dezɪgˈneɪʃ(ə)n/ n. designating; a name or title. [f. OF (as prec.)]

designedly /dɪˈzaɪnɪdlɪ/ adv. intentionally. [f. DESIGN]

designer n. one who makes designs, especially for clothes or manufactured products. [f. DESIGN]

designing adj. crafty, scheming. [as prec.]

desirable adj. worth having or wishing for; causing desire; (of a course of action) advisable. [f. foll.]

desire /dɪˈzaɪə(r)/ n. **1.** an unsatisfied longing, a feeling of potential pleasure or satisfaction in obtaining or possessing something. **2.** an expression of this, a request. **3.** an object of desire. **4.** strong sexual urge. —v.t./i. to have a desire for; to ask for; (archaic) to wish. **—leaves much to be desired,** is very imperfect. [f. OF f. L desiderare long for]

desirous predic. adj. having a desire, desiring. [f. AF (as prec.)]

desist /dɪˈzɪst, -ˈsɪst/ v.i. to cease (from). [f. OF f. L desistere (DE-, sistere stop)]

desk n. **1.** a piece of furniture with a flat or sloped surface serving as a rest for writing or reading at. **2.** a counter behind which a receptionist or cashier sits. **3.** the section of a newspaper office dealing with specified topics. **4.** the position of the music-stand at which a player (especially of a stringed instrument) sits in an orchestra. [f. L (as DISCUS)]

desolate /ˈdesələt/ adj. **1.** left alone, solitary. **2.** deserted, uninhabited, barren, dismal. **3.** forlorn and wretched. —/-leɪt/ v.t. **1.** to depopulate, to devastate. **2.** to make (a person) wretched. [f. L desolatus (DE-, solus alone)]

desolation /desəˈleɪʃ(ə)n/ n. **1.** a desolate or barren state. **2.** being forsaken, loneliness. **3.** grief, wretchedness. [as prec.]

despair /dɪsˈpeə(r)/ n. complete loss or absence of hope; a thing that causes this. —v.i. to lose all hope (of). [f. OF f. L desperare (DE-, sperare hope)]

despatch var. of DISPATCH.

desperado /despəˈrɑːdəʊ/ n. (pl. -oes) a desperate or reckless person, especially a criminal. [as foll. w. Sp. suffix]

desperate /ˈdespərət/ adj. **1.** leaving no or little room for hope; extremely dangerous or serious. **2.** reckless from despair; violent, lawless. **3.** staking all on a small chance. **—desperately** adv. [as prec.]

desperation /despəˈreɪʃ(ə)n/ n. despair; a reckless state of mind, readiness to take any way out of a desperate situation. [f. L (as DESPAIR)]

despicable /ˈdespɪkəb(ə)l, dɪˈspɪk-/ adj. deserving to be despised, contemptible. **—despicably** adv. [f. L (despicari despise, as foll.)]

despise /dɪsˈpaɪz/ v.t. to regard as inferior or worthless; to feel contempt for. [f. OF f. L despicere look down on (DE-, specere look at)]

despite /dɪˈspaɪt/ prep. in spite of. —n. (literary) **1.** disdain. **2.** malice, hatred. [f. OF f. L despectus (as prec.)]

despoil /dɪˈspɔɪl/ v.t. (literary) to plunder, to rob. **—despoliation** /dɪspəʊlɪˈeɪʃ(ə)n/ n. [f. OF or L (as SPOIL)]

despond /dɪˈspɒnd/ v.i. to lose heart, to be dejected. [f. L despondēre abandon (DE-, spondēre promise)]

despondent /dɪˈspɒndənt/ adj. having lost heart, dejected. **—despondency** n., **despondently** adv. [as prec.]

despot /ˈdespɒt/ n. an absolute ruler; a tyrant. [f. F f. L f. Gk despotēs master]

despotic /deˈspɒtɪk/ adj. having unrestricted power, tyrannous. **—despotically** adv. [f. prec.]

despotism /ˈdespətɪz(ə)m/ n. rule by a despot; a country ruled by a despot. [f. DESPOT]

Des Prés /de ˈpreɪ/, Josquin (c.1440-1521), the leading composer of the early Renaissance. Best known for his Italian song 'El grillo', with its imitations of the chirrup of the cricket, he composed both secular and sacred music prolifically.

dessert /dɪˈzɜːt/ n. the sweet course of a meal; a course of fruit, nuts, etc., at the end of dinner. [f. F desservir clear the table]

dessertspoon n. a spoon between a tablespoon and a teaspoon in size. **—dessertspoonful** n. (pl. **-fuls**) [f. prec.]

De Stijl see STIJL.

destination /destɪˈneɪʃ(ə)n/ n. a place to which a person or thing is going. [f. OF or L (as foll.)]

destine /ˈdestɪn/ v.t. to settle or determine the future of; to appoint, to set apart for a purpose. [f. F f. L destinare]

destiny /ˈdestɪnɪ/ n. fate considered as a power; what is destined to happen to a person etc.; the predetermined course of events. [f. OF (as prec.)]

destitute /ˈdestɪtjuːt/ adj. without resources, in great need of food, shelter, etc.; devoid of. **—destitution** /-ˈtjuːʃ(ə)n/ n. [f. L destituere forsake (DE-, statuere place)]

destroy /dɪˈstrɔɪ/ v.t. **1.** to pull or break down; to make useless. **2.** to kill (esp. a sick or unwanted animal) deliberately. **3.** to nullify, to neutralize the effect of; to put out of existence. [f. OF f. L destruere (DE-, struere build)]

destroyer n. **1.** a person or thing that destroys. **2.** a fast warship designed to protect other ships. [f. prec.]

destruct /dɪˈstrʌkt/ v.t./i. (US) to destroy (one's own equipment) deliberately; to be destroyed thus. —n. (US) the action of destructing. [f. L (as DESTROY), or back-formation f. DESTRUCTION]

destructible adj. able to be destroyed. [F or f. L (as DESTROY)]

destruction /dɪˈstrʌkʃ(ə)n/ n. destroying, being destroyed; a cause of this. [f. OF f. L (as DESTROY)]

destructive /dɪˈstrʌktɪv/ adj. **1.** destroying, causing destruction. **2.** (of criticism etc.) merely negative, refuting etc. without offering amendments or alternatives. [as prec.]

desuetude /dɪˈsjuːɪtjuːd/ n. a state of disuse. [f. F or L desuetudo (DE-, suescere be accustomed)]

desultory /ˈdesəltərɪ/ adj. going constantly from one subject to another; disconnected, unmethodical. **—desultorily** adv., **desultoriness** n. [f. L (desultor one who vaults, f. salire leap)]

detach /dɪˈtætʃ/ v.t. **1.** to unfasten or separate and remove (from). **2.** to send (part of a force) on a separate mission. [f. F (as DE-, ATTACH)]

detached adj. **1.** separate, standing apart. **2.** unemotional, impartial. [f. prec.]

detachment n. **1.** detaching, being detached. **2.** a lack of emotion or concern, impartiality. **3.** a portion of an army etc. separately employed. [f. F (as DETACH)]

detail /ˈdiːteɪl/ n. **1.** an item, a small or subordinate particular; these collectively, the treatment of them. **2.** minor decoration in a building, picture, etc. **3.** a small military detachment. —v.t. **1.** to give particulars of, to describe fully. **2.** to assign for special duty. **—in detail,** describing the individual parts or events fully. [f. F (DE-, tailler cut)]

detailed adj. having or involving many details; thorough. [f. prec.]

detain /dɪˈteɪn/ v.t. **1.** to keep in confinement or under restraint. **2.** to keep waiting, to delay. [f. OF f. L detinēre (DE-, tenēre hold)]

detainee /diːteɪˈniː/ n. a person detained in custody, usually on political grounds. [f. prec.]

detect /dɪˈtekt/ v.t. to discover the existence or presence of; to discover (a person) in the performance of some wrong or secret act. **—detector** n. [f. L detegere (DE-, tegere cover)]

detectable adj. that may be detected. [f. prec.]

detection /dɪˈtekʃ(ə)n/ n. detecting, being detected; the work of a detective. [f. DETECT]

detective /dɪˈtektɪv/ n. a person, especially a member of a police force, employed to investigate crimes. —adj. serving to detect. **—detective story** etc., one describing a crime and the detection of criminals (see below). [f. DETECT]

The first detective stories in English literature are generally reckoned to be Poe's 'The Murders in the Rue Morgue' (1841) and Wilkie Collins's *The Moonstone* (1868). Conan Doyle's 'Sherlock Holmes' stories achieved world-wide popularity; other outstanding examples are G. K. Chesterton's 'Father Brown' stories, and E. C. Bentley's *Trent's Last Case* (1913), which set the pattern for the next quarter century of detective novels, generally regarded as the Golden Age of that genre. Among the classics are the works of Agatha Christie and D. L. Sayers, with their tradition of giving the reader full information presented so as to mislead, and ultimate vindication of law and order. From c.1950 the American school of tough detective fiction began to erode but never destroyed the classic British formula.

détente /deɪˈtɑːt/ n. the easing of strained relations, especially between States. [F, = relaxation]

detention /dɪˈtenʃ(ə)n/ n. detaining, being detained; being kept in school after hours as a punishment. —**detention centre,** an institution for the brief detention of young offenders. [f. F or L (as DETAIN)]

deter /dɪˈtɜː(r)/ v.t. (**-rr-**) to discourage or prevent (*from*) through fear or dislike of the consequences. —**determent** n. [f. L deterrere (DE-, terrēre frighten)]

detergent /dɪˈtɜːdʒ(ə)nt/ n. a cleansing agent, especially a synthetic substance used with water for removing dirt etc. —adj. cleansing. [f. L detergēre (DE-, tergēre wipe)]

deteriorate /dɪˈtɪərɪəreɪt/ v.t./i. to make or become worse. —**deterioration** /-ˈreɪʃ(ə)n/ n. [f. L (deterior worse)]

determinant /dɪˈtɜːmɪnənt/ adj. determining, decisive. —n. **1.** a determining factor. **2.** the quantity obtained by adding the products of the elements of a square matrix according to a certain rule. [f. L (as DETERMINE)]

determinate /dɪˈtɜːmɪnət/ adj. limited, of definite scope or nature. [as prec.]

determination /dɪtɜːmɪˈneɪʃ(ə)n/ n. **1.** firmness of purpose, resoluteness. **2.** the process of deciding, determining, or calculating. [f. OF f. L (as DETERMINE)]

determinative /dɪˈtɜːmɪnətɪv/ adj. serving to define, qualify, or direct. —n. a determinative thing. [f. F (as foll.)]

determine /dɪˈtɜːmɪn/ v.t./i. **1.** to find out or calculate precisely; to settle; to decide; to be the decisive factor in regard to. **2.** to decide firmly, to resolve. —**be determined,** to have decided firmly. [f. OF f. L determinare (DE-, terminus end, limit)]

determined adj. showing determination, resolute, unflinching. —**determinedly** adv. [f. prec.]

determinism /dɪˈtɜːmɪnɪz(ə)m/ n. the theory that human action is not free but is determined by motives regarded as external forces acting on the will. —**determinist** n., **deterministic** /-ˈnɪstɪk/ adj. [f. DETERMINE]

deterrent /dɪˈterənt/ adj. deterring. —n. a deterrent thing or factor. [f. L (as DETER)]

detest /dɪˈtest/ v.t. to hate, to loathe. —**detestation** /-ˈsteɪʃ(ə)n/ n. [f. L detestari call to witness]

detestable adj. intensely disliked, hateful. [f. prec.]

dethrone /diːˈθrəʊn/ v.t. to remove from a throne, to depose. —**dethronement** n.

detonate /ˈdetəneɪt/ v.t./i. to explode or cause to explode with a loud report. —**detonation** /-ˈneɪʃ(ə)n/ n. [f. L detonare (DE-, tonare thunder)]

detonator n. a device for detonating an explosive. [f. prec.]

detour /ˈdiːtʊə(r)/ n. a divergence from one's direct or intended route, a roundabout course. [f. F détourner turn away (as DE-, TURN)]

detract /dɪˈtrækt/ v.t./i. to take away (some amount) *from* a whole. —**detract from,** to reduce the credit due to, to depreciate. —**detraction** n., **detractor** n. [f. L detrahere (DE-, trahere draw)]

detriment /ˈdetrɪmənt/ n. harm, damage; a thing causing this. —**detrimental** /-ˈment(ə)l/ adj., **detrimentally** adv. [f. OF or L detrimentum (deterere wear away)]

detritus /dɪˈtraɪtəs/ n. matter produced by erosion, as gravel or rock-debris. [f. F f. L (as prec.)]

de trop /də ˈtrəʊ/ not wanted, in the way. [F, = excessive]

Deucalion /djuːˈkeɪlɪən/ (*Gk myth.*) the Greek Noah, son of Prometheus. When Zeus flooded the earth in wrath at the impiety of mankind, Deucalion and his wife Pyrrha took refuge on the top of Parnassus (or built an ark in which they were carried there). When the flood had subsided, to repopulate the world they were advised by Zeus (or by an oracle) to throw stones over their shoulders; those thrown by Deucalion became men, and those thrown by Pyrrha women.

deuce[1] /djuːs/ n. **1.** (in tennis) the score of 40 all, at which two consecutive points are needed to win. **2.** the two on dice. [f. OF f. L duos (duo two)]

deuce[2] /djuːs/ n. misfortune, the Devil (*colloq.* used esp. as an exclamation of surprise or annoyance). [f. LG duus (as prec.), the two at dice being the worst throw]

deuced /ˈdjuːsɪd, djuːst/ adj. & adv. damned. [f. prec.]

deus ex machina /ˌdeɪəs eks ˈmækɪnə/ an unexpected power or event saving a seemingly impossible situation, especially in a play or novel. [L transl. Gk, = god from the machinery (w. ref. to the machinery by which, in ancient Greek theatre, gods were shown in the air)]

deuterium /djuːˈtɪərɪəm/ n. a heavy isotope of hydrogen,

symbol D or ^{2}H, atomic number 1, differing from the commonest isotope in having a neutron as well as a proton in the nucleus. It is present to about 1 part in 6,000 in naturally occurring hydrogen. Discovered in 1931, it is used as a moderator in nuclear reactors and a fuel in thermonuclear bombs. [f. Gk deuteros second]

deuteron /ˈdjuːtərɒn/ n. the nucleus of a deuterium atom, consisting of a proton and a neutron. [as prec.]

Deuteronomy /djuːtəˈrɒnəmɪ/ the fifth book of the Old Testament, containing a repetition, with hortatory comments, of the Ten Commandments and most of the laws in Exod. 21-4. [f. L f. Gk (deuteros nomos second law), from a mistranslation of Hebrew words (Deut. 17: 18) meaning 'a copy or duplicate of this law']

Deutschmark /ˈdɔɪtʃmɑːk/ n. the currency unit in the Federal Republic of Germany. [G, = German mark (MARK[2])]

deva /ˈdeɪvə/ n. a divine being of either of two classes of gods in the Vedic period. In Indian mythology, whether Hindu, Buddhist or Jain, the term denotes a deity or benevolent spirit; in ancient Iran (see ZOROASTRIANISM), it denotes an evil spirit or demon. [Skr., = god]

de Valera /də vəˈleərə/, Eamon (1882-1975), Irish statesman, one of the leaders of the Easter 1916 uprising against the British, condemned to death but eventually released a year later. He led Sinn Fein 1917-26 and was President of the provisional government in 1919-22. He founded the Fianna Fáil party in 1926 and served as President of the Irish Free State 1932-7. After the formation of the Irish Republic, de Valera served as Prime Minister on three separate occasions before ending his political career as President (1959-73).

devalue /diːˈvælju:/ v.t. to reduce the value of, to reduce the value of (a currency) in relation to other currencies or to gold. —**devaluation** /-ˈeɪʃ(ə)n/ n.

Devanagari /deɪvəˈnɑːgərɪ/ n. the alphabet in which Sanskrit, Hindi, and other Indian languages are usually written. [Skr., = divine town script]

devastate /ˈdevəsteɪt/ v.t. to lay waste, to cause great destruction to. —**devastation** /-ˈsteɪʃ(ə)n/ n. [f. L devastare (DE-, vastare lay waste)]

devastating adj. crushingly effective, overwhelming. [f. prec.]

develop /dɪˈveləp/ v.t./i. **1.** to make or become bigger, fuller, or more elaborate or systematic; to bring or come to an active or visible state or to maturity, to reveal or be revealed. **2.** to begin to exhibit or suffer from. **3.** to construct new buildings on (land); to convert (land) to a new use so as to use its resources. **4.** to treat (a photographic film etc.) to make the picture visible. —**developing country,** a poor or primitive country that is developing better economic and social conditions. —**developer** n. [f. F développer]

development n. **1.** developing, being developed. **2.** a thing that has developed, especially an event or circumstance. **3.** developed land. **4.** (*Mus.*) elaboration of a theme, especially in the second part of a sonata movement. —**development area,** one where new industries are encouraged in order to counteract unemployment there. —**developmental** /-ˈment(ə)l/ adj. [f. prec.]

Devi /ˈdeɪvɪ/ (*Hinduism*) the supreme goddess, often identified with Parvati. [Skr., = goddess]

deviant /ˈdiːvɪənt/ adj. that deviates from the normal. —n. a deviant person or thing. [as foll.]

deviate /ˈdiːvɪeɪt/ v.i. to turn aside or diverge (*from* a course of action, rule, etc.). —**deviator** n. [f L. deviare (DE-, via way)]

deviation /diːvɪˈeɪʃ(ə)n/ n. deviating; departing from an accepted political (esp. Communist) doctrine. —**deviationist** n. [f. F f. L (as prec.)]

device /dɪˈvaɪs/ n. **1.** a thing made or adapted for a particular purpose. **2.** a plan, a scheme; a trick. **3.** an emblematic or heraldic design. —**leave a person to his own devices,** to leave him to do as he wishes without help or advice. [f. OF f. L (as DEVISE)]

devil /ˈdev(ə)l/ n. **1.** the supreme spirit of evil (usu. **the Devil;** see below); an evil spirit, a demon, a superhuman malignant being; a personified evil spirit, force, or quality. **2.** a wicked or cruel person; a mischievously energetic, clever, or self-willed person. **3.** (*colloq.*) a person, a fellow. **4.** fighting spirit, mischievousness. **5.** (*colloq.*) something difficult or awkward. **6.** a literary hack used by an employer; a junior legal counsel. —v.t./i. (**-ll-**) **1.** to cook (food) with hot seasoning. **2.** to act as a devil (for an author or barrister).

3. (*US*) to harass, to worry. —**between the devil and the deep blue sea,** in a dilemma. **a devil of,** (*colloq.*) a considerable or remarkable. **devil-may-care** *adj.* cheerful and reckless. **devil's advocate,** one who tests a proposition by arguing against it. **devil's coach-horse,** a large rove-beetle. **the devil's own,** very difficult or unusual. **the devil to pay,** trouble to be expected. **give the Devil his due,** to acknowledge the merits or achievement of a person otherwise disfavoured. **play the devil with,** to cause severe damage to. [OE f. L f. Gk *diabolos* slanderer]
The Devil is the supreme spirit of evil in Jewish and Christian theology, enemy of God and tempter of mankind. In theological tradition he was regarded as the chief of the fallen angels, cast out of heaven for rebellion against God, but there was no fixed teaching on the exact nature of his sin; known also as Satan, he was held to preside over those condemned to eternal fire (see HELL). In the narrative of the Fall, the serpent which tempted Eve has traditionally been regarded as his embodiment, and in Rev. 12: 7-9 he is identified with the dragon cast out by Michael and his angels.

devilish *adj.* of or like a devil; mischievous. —*adv.* (*colloq.*) very, extremely. [f. prec.]

devilment *n.* mischief, wild spirits. [f. DEVIL]

devilry *n.* wickedness, reckless mischief; black magic. [f. DEVIL]

devious /ˈdiːvɪəs/ *adj.* winding, circuitous; not straightforward, underhand. —**deviously** *adv.*, **deviousness** *n.* [f. L *devius* (DE-, *via* way)]

devise /dɪˈvaɪz/ *v.t.* **1.** to plan or invent by careful thought. **2.** (*Law*) to leave (real estate) by will. [f. OF f. L *dividere* divide]

devoid /dɪˈvɔɪd/ *predic. adj.* (with *of*) quite lacking or free from. [f. OF (as DE-, VOID)]

devolution /diːvəˈluːʃ(ə)n/ *n.* delegation of power, especially by a central government to a local or regional administration. [f. L (as foll.)]

devolve /dɪˈvɒlv/ *v.i.* (of work or duties) to pass or be passed on to another; (of property etc.) to descend or pass (*to* or *upon*). [f. L *devolvere* (DE-, *volvere* roll)]

Devon /ˈdevən/ a county of SW England.

Devonian /dɪˈvəʊnɪən/ *adj.* of the fourth period of the Palaeozoic era, following the Silurian and preceding the Carboniferous, lasting from about 408 to 360 million years ago. During this period fish became abundant, the first amphibians evolved, and the first forests appeared. —*n.* this period. [f. L *Devonia* Devonshire]

Devonshire /ˈdevənʃɪə(r)/ = DEVON.

devote /dɪˈvəʊt/ *v.t.* to apply or give over *to* a particular activity or purpose. [f. L *devovēre* (DE-, *vovēre* vow)]

devoted *adj.* showing devotion, very loyal or loving. —**devotedly** *adv.* [f. prec.]

devotee /devəˈtiː/ *n.* a person who is devoted to something, an enthusiast. [f. DEVOTE]

devotion /dɪˈvəʊʃ(ə)n/ *n.* **1.** great love or loyalty, enthusiastic zeal. **2.** religious worship; (in *pl.*) prayers. —**devotional** *adj.* [f. OF or L (as DEVOTE)]

devour /dɪˈvaʊə(r)/ *v.t.* **1.** to eat hungrily or greedily. **2.** (of fire etc.) to engulf, to destroy. **3.** to take in greedily with the eyes or ears. **4.** to absorb the attention of. [f. OF f. L *devorare* (DE-, *vorare* swallow)]

devout /dɪˈvaʊt/ *adj.* earnestly religious; earnest, sincere. —**devoutly** *adv.* [f. OF f. L *devotus* (as DEVOTE)]

dew *n.* atmospheric vapour condensing in small drops on cool surfaces between evening and morning; beaded or glistening moisture resembling this. —**dew-claw** *n.* the rudimentary inner toe of some dogs. **dew-point** *n.* the temperature at which the air can hold no more water vapour, and dew forms. **dew-pond** *n.* a shallow, usually artificial, pond once supposed to be fed by atmospheric condensation. —**dewy** *adj.* [OE]

dewar /ˈdjuːə(r)/ *n.* a double-walled flask with the space between its walls evacuated to reduce transfer of heat. [f. Sir J. *Dewar*, British physicist (d. 1923)]

dewberry *n.* a bluish fruit like a blackberry; the shrub (*Rubus caesius*) bearing it. [f. prec.]

dewdrop *n.* a drop of dew.

Dewey[1] /ˈdjuːɪ/, John (1859-1952), American philosopher and educationist. His pragmatic philosophy (called *instrumentalism*) holds that thought is an instrument, producing theories designed to solve practical problems over a wide range (in logic, metaphysics, morals, art, etc.); truth is not final and static but changes as these problems change. In education, he observed that most schools were proceeding along traditional lines and failing to take account of the findings of child psychologists or of the needs of a changing and democratic social environment, and argued strongly for learning by experience and necessity rather than through authoritarian instruction: education should meet and develop the child's own interests and abilities. In the 1930s he was a prominent campaigner in favour of civil liberties and against militarism.

Dewey[2] /ˈdjuːɪ/, Melville (1851-1931), American librarian who devised the decimal system, named after him, of classifying books by their subject-matter.

dewlap *n.* a fold of loose skin hanging from the throat of cattle and other animals. [f. DEW + LAP[1]]

dexter *adj.* of or on the right-hand side (the observer's left) of a shield etc. (ill. HERALDRY). [L, = on the right]

dexterity /dekˈsterɪtɪ/ *n.* skill in handling things; manual or mental adroitness. [f. F f. L (as DEXTER)]

dexterous var. of DEXTROUS.

dextrous /ˈdekstrəs/ *adj.* having or showing dexterity. —**dextrously** *adv.* [f. L (as prec.)]

DFC *abbr.* Distinguished Flying Cross.

DFM *abbr.* Distinguished Flying Medal.

Dhaka /ˈdækə/ the capital of Bangladesh, on the Ganges delta; pop. (est. 1979) 2,500,000.

dharma /ˈdɑːmə/ *n.* the eternal law of the Hindu cosmos, inherent in the very nature of things, upheld (but neither created nor controlled) by the gods. The concept is both descriptive and prescriptive: what is and what should be. In the context of individual action, it denotes the social rules codified in the lawbooks (e.g. The Laws of Manu); in Buddhism, it is the true doctrine as preached by the Buddha; in Jainism, it is both virtue and a fundamental substance, the medium of motion. [Skr., = decree, custom]

dhoti /ˈdəʊtɪ/ *n.* the loincloth worn by male Hindus. [Hindi]

dhow /daʊ/ *n.* a lateen-rigged ship of the Arabian Sea. [orig. unkn.]

di- *prefix* two, double-. [Gk (*dis* twice)]

dia- *prefix* (**di-** before a vowel) **1.** through. **2.** apart. **3.** across. [Gk *dia* through]

diabetes /daɪəˈbiːtiːz/ *n.* a disease (also called **diabetes mellitus**) in which sugar and starch are not properly metabolized by the body. In 1922, as a result of the work of F. G. Banting and others, it was discovered that the disease is due to a deficiency in the production or effectiveness of the hormone insulin, which is produced in certain cells of the pancreas. Diabetes is characterized by thirst, emaciation, excessive production of urine containing glucose, and abnormally high levels of sugar in the blood. It is one of the earliest known diseases, being recorded in an Egyptian papyrus of *c.*1500 BC. The word *mellitus* (L, = sweet) was added to distinguish this disease from the much rarer diabetes insipidus, a disorder of the pituitary gland characterized by the passing of large quantities of urine but not involving sugar metabolism. [orig. = siphon; L f. Gk (*diabainō* go through)]

diabetic /daɪəˈbetɪk/ *adj.* of or having diabetes, for diabetics. —*n.* a person suffering from diabetes. [f. prec.]

diabolic, diabolical /daɪəˈbɒlɪk, -k(ə)l/ *adjs.* of the Devil; devilish, inhumanly cruel or wicked; fiendishly clever or cunning or annoying. —**diabolically** *adv.* [f. OF or L (as DEVIL)]

diabolism /daɪˈæbəlɪz(ə)m/ *n.* worship of the Devil; sorcery. [f. Gk (as DEVIL)]

diachronic /daɪəˈkrɒnɪk/ *adj.* concerned with the historical development of a subject. —**diachronic linguistics,** historical linguistics (see HISTORICAL). [f. F (DIA-, Gk *khronos* time)]

diaconal /daɪˈækən(ə)l/ *adj.* of a deacon. [f. L (as DEACON)]

diaconate /daɪˈækənət/ *n.* **1.** the office of a deacon. **2.** a body of deacons. [as prec.]

diacritical /daɪəˈkrɪtɪk(ə)l/ *adj.* distinguishing, distinctive. —**diacritical mark** (*or* **sign**), a sign used to indicate different sounds or values of a letter (an accent, diaeresis, cedilla, etc.). [f. Gk (as DIA-, CRITICAL)]

diadem /ˈdaɪədem/ *n.* **1.** a crown or headband worn as a sign of sovereignty. **2.** sovereignty. **3.** a crowning distinction or glory. [f. OF f. L f. Gk (*deō* bind)]

diaeresis /daɪˈɪərəsɪs/ *n.* (*pl.* **-reses** /-siːz/) a mark (as in *naïve*) over a vowel indicating that it is sounded separately. [L f. Gk, = separation]

Diaghilev /dɪˈægɪlef/, Serge Pavlovich (1872-1929), Russian ballet impresario. After the closure of his magazine *The World of Art* (1899-1904) he began taking opera and ballet productions to Paris, bringing about the gradual formation of his Ballets Russes, which he directed until his death. Initially with Nijinsky as his star performer, and later with Massine, he effected a complete reformation of the European ballet scene, becoming a catalyst of the most important artistic trends during the 1910s and 1920s, though not himself a choreographer. The company never performed in Russia.

diagnose /ˈdaɪəgnəʊz/ v.t. to make a diagnosis of (a disease, a mechanical fault, etc.); to infer the presence of (a specified disease etc.) from symptoms. [f. foll.]

diagnosis /daɪəgˈnəʊsɪs/ n. (pl. **-oses** /-siːz/) the identification of a disease by means of the patient's symptoms, a formal statement of this; the ascertainment of the cause of a mechanical fault etc. [L f. Gk (DIA-, *gignōskō* recognize)]

diagnostic /daɪəgˈnɒstɪk/ adj. of or assisting diagnosis. —n. a symptom. —**diagnostician** /-ˈstɪʃ(ə)n/ n. [f. Gk (as prec.)]

diagonal /daɪˈægən(ə)l/ adj. crossing a straight-sided figure from corner to corner, slanting, oblique. —n. a straight line joining two opposite corners. —**diagonally** adv. [f. L f. Gk (DIA-, *gōnia* angle)]

diagram /ˈdaɪəgræm/ n. a drawing showing the general scheme or outline of an object and its parts; a graphic representation of a course or the results of an action or process. —**diagrammatic** /-ˈmætɪk/ adj., **diagrammatically** adv. [f. L f. Gk (as DIA-, -GRAM)]

dial /ˈdaɪəl/ n. **1.** the plate on the front of a clock or watch, marking the hours etc.; a similar flat plate marked with a scale for the measurement of something, and having a movable pointer indicating the amount registered. **2.** a movable disc with finger-holes over a circle of numbers, manipulated in order to make a connection with another instrument; a plate or disc etc. on a radio or television set for selecting a wavelength or channel. **3.** (slang) a person's face. —v.t./i. (**-ll-**) to select or regulate by means of a dial; to make a telephone connection by using a dial or numbered buttons; to ring up (a number etc.) thus. [f. L (*dies* day)]

dialect /ˈdaɪəlekt/ n. a form of speech peculiar to a district or class; a subordinate variety of a language showing sufficient differences from the standard language in vocabulary, pronunciation, or idiom for it to be considered as distinct. —**dialectal** /-ˈlekt(ə)l/ adj., **dialectology** n. [f. F or L f. Gk, = discourse (*dialegomai* converse)]

dialectic /daɪəˈlektɪk/ n. **1.** (also in pl., occas. treated as sing.) the art of investigating the truth of opinions; the testing of truth by discussion, logical disputation. **2.** criticism dealing with metaphysical contradictions and their solutions; the existence or action of opposing social forces etc. —adj. of disputation or dialectics. [f. OF or L f. Gk *dialektikē* (*tekhnē* art) of debate]

dialectical /daɪəˈlektɪk(ə)l/ adj. of dialectic. —**dialectical materialism**, the theory propagated by Marx and Engels according to which political events or social phenomena are to be interpreted as a conflict of social forces (the 'class struggle') produced by the operation of economic causes, and history is to be interpreted as a series of contradictions and their solutions (the thesis, antithesis, and synthesis of Hegel's philosophy). [f. prec.]

dialogue /ˈdaɪəlɒg/ n. a conversation; the written form of this; a passage of conversation in a novel etc.; a discussion between the representatives of two groups etc. [f. OF f. L f. Gk (*dialegomai* converse)]

dialysis /daɪˈælɪsɪs/ n. (pl. **-lyses** /-siːz/) the separation of particles by differences in their ability to pass through a suitable membrane; the process of allowing blood to flow past such a membrane on the other side of which is another liquid, so that certain dissolved substances in the blood may pass through the membrane and the blood itself be purified or cleansed in cases of renal failure, poisoning, etc.; an occasion of undergoing this process. The dialysis may take place outside the body in an artificial kidney or inside it using a natural membrane such as the peritoneum. [f. L f. Gk, = dissolution (as DIA-, *luō* set free)]

diamanté /dɪəˈmɑːteɪ/ adj. decorated with powdered crystal or other sparkling substance. [F, = set with diamonds]

diameter /daɪˈæmɪtə(r)/ n. a straight line passing from side to side through the centre of a circle or sphere (ill. SHAPES); a transverse measurement, width, or thickness; the unit of linear magnifying power. [f. OF f. L f. Gk, = measuring across (as DIA-, -METER)]

diametrical /daɪəˈmetrɪk(ə)l/ adj. **1.** of or along a diameter. **2.** (of opposites etc.) complete, direct. —**diametrically** adv. (f. Gk (as prec.)]

diamond /ˈdaɪəmənd/ n. **1.** a very hard transparent precious stone of pure crystallized carbon. **2.** a rhombus. **3.** a playing-card of the suit (**diamonds**) marked with red rhombuses. —**diamond wedding**, the 60th (or 75th) anniversary of a wedding. [f. OF f. L f. Gk *adamas* adamant]

Diana /daɪˈænə/ (Rom. myth.) an early Italian goddess anciently identified with Artemis. There is no real evidence that she was a moon-goddess, though she often occurs in English literature in this character. [prob. = bright one]

dianthus /daɪˈænθəs/ n. a flowering plant of the genus *Dianthus*, including the carnation. [f. Gk *Dios* of Zeus + *anthos* flower]

diapason /daɪəˈpeɪs(ə)n, -z-/ n. the entire compass of a musical instrument or voice; a fixed standard of musical pitch; either of the two main organ-stops extending through the whole compass. [f. L f. Gk, = through all (notes)]

diaper /ˈdaɪəpə(r)/ n. (US) a baby's nappy. [f. OF f. L f. Gk (as DIA-, *aspros* white)]

diaphanous /daɪˈæfənəs/ adj. (of a fabric etc.) light and delicate and almost transparent. [f. L f. Gk (DIA-, -*phanēs* showing)]

diaphragm /ˈdaɪəfræm/ n. **1.** the muscular partition between the thorax and the abdomen in mammals (ill. BODY 2, 3). **2.** a thin sheet used as a partition etc.; a vibrating disc in a microphone, telephone, loudspeaker, etc., and acoustic systems etc. **3.** a device for varying the lens aperture in a camera etc. **4.** a thin contraceptive cap fitting over the cervix of the uterus. [f. L f. Gk (DIA-, *phragma* fence)]

diarist /ˈdaɪərɪst/ n. one who keeps a diary. [f. DIARY]

diarrhoea /daɪəˈriːə/ n. the condition of excessively frequent and loose bowel movements. [f. L f. Gk (DIA-, *rheō* flow)]

diary /ˈdaɪərɪ/ n. a daily record of events or thoughts; a book for this or for noting future engagements. [f. L *diarium* (*dies* day)]

Diaspora /daɪˈæspərə/ n. the Dispersion of the Jews (see DISPERSION); the Jews thus dispersed. [Gk, f. *dia* through, *speirō* scatter]

diastase /ˈdaɪəsteɪs/ the enzyme converting starch to sugar, important in digestion. [F f. Gk, = separation]

diastole /daɪˈæst(ə)lɪ/ n. the dilatation of the heart rhythmically alternating with systole to form the pulse. —**diastolic** /daɪəˈstɒlɪk/ adj. [L f. Gk (DIA-, *stellō* send)]

diathermy /ˈdaɪəθəmɪ/ n. the application of high-frequency electric currents to produce heat within the body. In medical use the tissues are warmed but not sufficiently to change their nature; in surgical use there is sufficient heating to produce a local change such as destruction of tissue or coagulation of bleeding vessels. —**diathermic** adj. [f. G f. Gk *dia* through, *thermon* heat]

diatom /ˈdaɪətəm/ n. a microscopic one-cell alga of the division Bacillariophyta, found as plankton and forming fossil deposits. [f. L f. Gk, = cut in half]

diatomic /daɪəˈtɒmɪk/ adj. consisting of two atoms; having two replaceable atoms or radicals. [f. DI- + ATOM]

diatonic /daɪəˈtɒnɪk/ adj. (Mus., of a scale, interval, etc.) involving only notes proper to the prevailing key without chromatic alteration. [f. F or L f. Gk (DIA-, *tonikos* tonic)]

diatribe /ˈdaɪətraɪb/ n. a forceful verbal attack, abusive criticism. [F f. L f. Gk *diatribē* spending of time, discourse]

dibber /ˈdɪbə(r)/ n. a hand-tool for making holes in the ground for seeds or young plants. [f. foll.]

dibble /ˈdɪb(ə)l/ n. a dibber. —v.t./i. to prepare (soil) with a dibble, to sow or plant with a dibble. [perh. rel. to DAB¹]

dice n. (properly pl. of DIE² but often as sing.) a small cube with the faces bearing usually 1-6 spots used in games of chance; a game played with one or more of these. —v.t./i. **1.** to gamble with dice. **2.** to cut into small cubes. —**no dice**, (slang) no success or prospect of it. [f. DIE²]

dicey /ˈdaɪsɪ/ adj. (slang) risky, unreliable. [f. prec.]

dichotomy /daɪˈkɒtəmɪ/ n. a division into two parts or kinds. [f. L f. Gk (*dikho-* apart, *-tomia* cutting)]

dichroic /daɪˈkrəʊɪk/ adj. (of doubly refracting crystals) showing two colours; (of a mirror) reflecting the light of one colour and transmitting that of others. —**dichroism** n. [f. Gk (DI-, *khroos* colour)]

dichromatic /daɪkrəˈmætɪk/ adj. **1.** two-coloured. **2.** having vision sensitive to only two of the three primary colours. [f. DI- + Gk *khrōma* colour]

Dickens /ˈdɪkɪnz/, Charles Huffham (1812-70), English novelist, son of an improvident Royal Navy pay clerk (the model for Micawber in *David Copperfield*). In 1824 his father was imprisoned for debt, and Charles worked briefly in a London blacking factory. This boyhood degradation deeply affected him, prompting him to write on themes such as the Poor Law (*Oliver Twist*, 1837-8), the ill-treatment of schoolchildren (*Nicholas Nickleby*, 1838-9), the dehumanizing effect of business ethics (*Dombey and Son*, 1847-8), the outdated legal system (*Bleak House*, 1852-3), industrialism (*Hard Times*, 1854), imprisonment for debt (*Little Dorrit*, 1855), and class distinction (*Great Expectations*, 1860-1). A master of laughter and tears, with a gift for satirical humour that is never absent from his works, Dickens created the greatest gallery of characters in English fiction, many of them grotesques (e.g. Fagin, Scrooge, Mrs Gamp, Uriah Heep). He enjoyed immense popularity, his reading tours in England and America receiving tumultuous acclaim, though *Martin Chuzzlewit* (1843-4) upset the Americans in its portrayal of American stereotypes. Serial publication helped him to monitor audience reaction, which strongly influenced his art. Through his works, public readings, and speeches Dickens aroused the Victorian conscience and captured the popular imagination as no other novelist has done.

dickens /ˈdɪkɪnz/ n. (*colloq.*) deuce, the Devil (esp. in exclamations). [prob. f. surname *Dickens*]

Dickensian /dɪˈkenzɪən/ adj. of Charles Dickens or his works; resembling situations described in them. [f. DICKENS]

dicker v.i. to bargain, to haggle. [perh. f. *dicker* set of ten (hides), as unit of trade]

Dickinson /ˈdɪkɪns(ə)n/, Emily Elizabeth (1830-86), American poet who lived in seclusion in Amherst, Massachussets. Her withdrawal and inner struggle is reflected in her mystical poems, expressed in her own elliptical language. Of her nearly 2,000 poems only seven were published in her lifetime; the first selection appeared in 1890. At first regarded as an eccentric minor poet, she is now considered a writer of unusual originality.

dicky adj. (*slang*) unsound, likely to collapse or fail. —n. (*colloq.*) a false shirt-front. [f. *Dicky* dim. of Richard]

dicotyledon /daɪkɒtɪˈliːd(ə)n/ n. a flowering plant having two cotyledons. —**dicotyledonous** adj.

Dictaphone /ˈdɪktəfəʊn/ n. [P] a machine for recording and playing back dictated words. [f. DICTATE + Gk *phōnē* voice]

dictate /dɪkˈteɪt/ v.t./i. 1. to say or read aloud (words to be written down or recorded). 2. to state or order with the force of authority; to give peremptory orders. —/ˈdɪkteɪt/ n. (usu. in *pl.*) an authoritative instruction. —**dictation** /-ˈteɪʃ(ə)n/ n. [f. L *dictare* (*dicere* say)]

dictator /dɪkˈteɪtə(r)/ n. a ruler (often a usurper) with unrestricted authority; a person with supreme authority in any sphere; a domineering person. —**dictatorship** n. [f. L (as prec.)]

dictatorial /dɪktəˈtɔːrɪəl/ adj. of or like a dictator; imperious, overbearing. —**dictatorially** adv. [as prec.]

diction /ˈdɪkʃ(ə)n/ n. 1. a person's manner of enunciation in speaking or singing. 2. the choice of words and phrases in speech or writing. [f. F or L *dictio* (*dicere* say)]

dictionary /ˈdɪkʃ(ə)nərɪ/ n. a book that lists (usually in alphabetical order) and explains the words of a language (often with information on pronunciation, inflected forms, and etymology) or gives the equivalent words in another language (see below); a similar book explaining the terms of a particular subject. [f. L (as prec.)]

Dictionaries are of two kinds: those in which the meanings of the words of one language or dialect are given in another, and those in which the words of a language are treated in this language itself; the former are the earlier. The tradition of making (and subsequently collecting) glossaries arose when the language or dialect used in literary works was no longer intelligible. It began among the Greeks, especially of the 1st-5th c. AD, and continued in medieval times. In the 16th c. the market was for 'bilingual' dictionaries, especially Latin-English. In 1604 schoolmaster Robert Cawdrey produced *A Table Alphabetical of English Words* (based on an earlier word-list); it was written to help 'Ladies . . . or other unskilful persons'. Dictionaries contained only words regarded as 'difficult' until Kersey broke with this tradition in 1702 by including the common words

of the language and discarding some of the more fantastic formations. Bailey's dictionary (1721) of about 40,000 words, giving great attention to etymology, was extremely popular in the 18th c. and his great folio dictionary (1730) was used by Samuel Johnson as the basis of his own work, the most famous of all time, which remained the authoritative English dictionary for over a century (see JOHNSON). The 19th c. saw the publication of Noah Webster's *An American Dictionary of the English Language* (1878), containing about 70,000 words, and the initiation of the great *Oxford English Dictionary* (see MURRAY), which remains the supreme achievement in lexicography. (See also GRIMM, LITTRÉ.) In the 20th c. small dictionaries have multiplied and find a ready market.

dictum /ˈdɪktəm/ n. (*pl.* **-ta**) a formal expression of opinion; a saying. [L (p.p. of *dicere* say)]

did *past* of DO[1].

didactic /dɪˈdæktɪk, daɪ-/ adj. meant to instruct; (of a person) tediously pedantic. —**didactically** adv., **didacticism** /-tɪsɪz(ə)m/ n. [f. Gk (*didaskō* teach)]

diddle v.t. (*slang*) to cheat, to swindle. [back-formation f. Jeremy *Diddler*, character in play (1803)]

Diderot /ˈdiːdərəʊ/, Denis (1713-84), French philosopher and man of letters, a leading member of the Enlightenment and principal director of the *Encyclopédie* through which he disseminated and popularized scientific knowledge and philosophic doctrines. His major philosophic writings include *Lettre sur les aveugles* (1749), a philosophic treatise tending to atheism which caused his temporary imprisonment, and *Pensées sur l'interpretation de la nature* (1754), anticipating evolutionary ideas on the nature and origin of life. His *Salons* (1759-81) inaugurated the genre of art criticism in France.

didn't (*colloq.*) = did not.

Dido /ˈdaɪdəʊ/ (in the *Aeneid*) queen of Carthage who fell in love with the shipwrecked Aeneas and killed herself when he deserted her. According to ancient tradition, which may be founded on fact, she was the daughter of a king of Tyre (where she was known as Elissa) and granddaughter of Ithobaal (= Ethbaal, father of Jezebel), and left Tyre with a group of Phoenicians, afterwards founding the city of Carthage.

die[1] /daɪ/ v.i. (*partic.* **dying** /ˈdaɪɪŋ/) 1. to cease to live, to expire, to lose vital force. 2. to cease to exist or function, to disappear, to fade away; (of flame) to go out. 3. to wish longingly or intently. 4. to be exhausted or tormented. —**die away**, to become weaker or fainter to the point of extinction. **die back**, (of a plant) to decay from the tip towards the root. **die down**, to become less loud or strong. **die-hard** n. a conservative or stubborn person. **die out**, to become extinct, to cease to exist. **never say die**, keep up courage, not give in. [prob. f. ON]

die[2] /daɪ/ n. 1. see DICE. 2. an engraved device for stamping a design on coins, medals, etc.; a device for stamping, cutting, or moulding material into a particular shape. —**die-casting** n. a process or product of casting from metal moulds. **die-sinker** n. an engraver of dies. **die-stamping** n. embossing paper etc. with a die. **straight as a die**, quite straight, very honest. [f. OF f. L *datum* p.p. of *dare* give]

dielectric /daɪəˈlektrɪk/ adj. that does not conduct electricity. —n. a dielectric substance usable for insulating. [f. Gk *dia* through + ELECTRIC]

diesel /ˈdiːz(ə)l/ n. 1. (also **diesel engine**) a type of internal-combustion engine in which ignition of fuel is produced by the heat of air that has been highly compressed (see below). 2. a vehicle driven by such an engine. 3. the fuel for this. —**diesel-electric** adj. driven by electric current from a generator driven by a diesel engine. **diesel oil**, the heavy petroleum fraction used in diesel engines. [f. R. *Diesel*]

The diesel engine was patented by the German engineer Dr Rudolf Diesel (d. 1913) in 1892, though a similar engine was already being made in England to the design of Herbert Ackroyd-Stuart. Air is compressed alone, inside the engine, causing its temperature to rise; fuel oil is sprayed into the combustion chamber when the compressed air is at a high enough temperature to ignite the fuel, which then burns and raises the temperature and pressure of the mixture to very high values at the start of the expansion process. The advantage of compression-ignition over conventional spark-ignition is that a high compression ratio can be employed, since there is no danger of the explosive combustion of a fuel/air mixture as with a petrol engine. The consequent high expansion ratio gives the diesel engine a higher thermal efficiency, over 40% in large engines. Hence the diesel engine is widely used in ships, in railway locomotives, for stationary uses such as electricity generation, and for road vehicles, particularly commercial vehicles, and recently for taxis and private cars.

diet[1] /ˈdaɪət/ *n.* the sort of foods one habitually eats; a precribed course of food to which a person is restricted. —*v.t./i.* to restrict oneself to a special diet, especially in order to control one's weight; to restrict (a person) to a special diet. —**dietary** *adj.* [f. OF f. L f. Gk *diaita* way of life]

diet[2] /ˈdaɪət/ *n.* a conference or congress (especially as the English name for some foreign parliamentary assemblies). [f. L *dieta* (*dies* day)]

dietetic /daɪəˈtetɪk/ *adj.* of diet and nutrition. [f. L f. Gk (as DIET[1])]

dietetics *n.pl.* the scientific study of diet and nutrition. [f. prec.]

dietitian /daɪəˈtɪʃ(ə)n/ *n.* an expert in dietetics. [f. DIET[1]]

differ *v.i.* **1.** to be unlike; to be distinguishable *from*. **2.** to disagree in opinion (*from*). [f. OF f. L *differre* orig. = bear apart]

difference *n.* **1.** being different or unlike. **2.** a point in which things differ; the amount or degree of unlikeness. **3.** the quantity by which amounts differ, the remainder left after subtraction. **4.** a disagreement in opinion, a dispute, a quarrel. —**make all the difference,** to be very important or significant. **split the difference,** to take the average of two proposed amounts. [f. OF f. L (as foll.)]

different *adj.* unlike, of other nature, form, or quality (*from* or (**D**) *to*); separate, distinct; unusual. —**differently** *adv.* [f. OF f. L (as DIFFER)]

differential /dɪfəˈrenʃ(ə)l/ *adj.* **1.** of or showing or depending on a difference; constituting or relating to specific differences. **2.** (*Math.*) relating to infinitesimal differences. —*n.* **1.** an agreed difference in wage between industries or between different classes of workers in the same industry. **2.** a difference between rates of interest etc. **3.** a differential gear. —**differential calculus,** a method of calculating rates of change, maximum and minimum values, etc. **differential gear,** a gear enabling a motor vehicle's rear wheels to revolve at different speeds in rounding corners. [f. L (as DIFFERENCE)]

differentiate /dɪfəˈrenʃɪeɪt/ *v.t.* **1.** to constitute the difference between or in. **2.** to recognize as different, to distinguish, to discriminate. **3.** to develop differences, to become different. **4.** (*Math.*) to calculate the derivative of. —**differentiation** /-ˈeɪʃ(ə)n/ *n.* [as prec.]

difficult /ˈdɪfɪk(ə)lt/ *adj.* needing much effort or skill; troublesome, perplexing; not easy to please or satisfy. [back form. f. foll.]

difficulty /ˈdɪfɪk(ə)ltɪ/ *n.* being difficult; a difficult problem or thing, a hindrance to progress; (often in *pl.*) trouble or distress, especially shortage of money. [f. L *difficultas* (as FACULTY)]

diffident /ˈdɪfɪd(ə)nt/ *adj.* lacking self-confidence, hesitating to put oneself or one's ideas forward. —**diffidence** *n.*, **diffidently** *adv.* [f. L *diffidere* mistrust (DIS-, *fidere* trust)]

diffract /dɪˈfrækt/ *v.t.* to break up (a beam of light) into a series of dark and light bands or coloured spectra, or (a beam of radiation or particles) into a series of high and low intensities. —**diffractive** *adj.* [f. L, = break apart (DE-, *frangere* break)]

diffraction /dɪˈfrækʃ(ə)n/ *n.* diffracting. —**diffraction grating,** a plate of glass or polished metal ruled with very close equidistant parallel lines, producing a spectrum by means of the transmitted or reflected light. [f. prec.]

diffuse /dɪˈfjuːs/ *adj.* spread out, not concentrated; wordy, not concise. —/-ˈfjuːz/ *v.t.* to spread widely or thinly; (esp. of fluids) to intermingle by diffusion. —**diffusible** /-z-/ *adj.*, **diffusive** /-s-/ *adj.* [f. F or L *diffusus* extensive (*fundere* pour)]

diffusion /dɪˈfjuːʒ(ə)n/ *n.* diffusing, being diffused; the interpenetration of substances by the natural movement of their particles. [f. L (as prec.)]

dig *v.t./i.* (-**gg**-; *past* & *p.p.* **dug**) **1.** to break up and remove or turn over (ground etc.) with a tool, the hands, claws, etc.; to make (a way, hole, etc.) or obtain by digging; to excavate archaeologically. **2.** to thrust (a sharp object) *into* or *in*; to prod or nudge. **3.** to make a search (*for* or *into*). —*n.* **1.** a piece of digging; an archaeological excavation. **2.** a prod or nudge. **3.** a cutting or sarcastic remark. **4.** (in *pl.*, *colloq.*) lodgings. —**dig one's heels** *or* **toes in,** to be

obstinate, to refuse to give way. **dig in,** to mix into the soil by digging; (*colloq.*) to begin eating. **dig oneself in,** to dig a defensive trench or pit; to establish one's position. [perh. f. OE]

digest /dɪˈdʒest/ *v.t.* **1.** to assimilate food in the stomach and bowels. **2.** to understand and assimilate mentally. **3.** to summarize. —/ˈdaɪdʒest/ *n.* a methodical summary, especially of laws; a periodical synopsis of current literature or news. [f. L *digerere* distribute, dispose]

digestible /dɪˈdʒestɪb(ə)l/ *adj.* able to be digested. [f. prec.]

digestion /dɪˈdʒestʃ(ə)n/ *n.* the process of digesting; the power of digesting food. [f. DIGEST]

digestive /dɪˈdʒestɪv/ *adj.* of or aiding digestion. —*n.* a digestive substance. —**digestive biscuit,** a sweet kind of wholemeal biscuit. [f. OF or L (as DIGEST)]

digger *n.* **1.** one who digs; a mechanical excavator. **2.** (*colloq.*) an Australian or New Zealander.

diggings *n.pl.* **1.** a mine or goldfield. **2.** (*colloq.*) lodgings. [f. DIG]

digit /ˈdɪdʒɪt/ *n.* **1.** any of the numerals from 0 to 9. **2.** a finger or toe. [f. L *digitus* finger, toe]

digital /ˈdɪdʒɪt(ə)l/ *adj.* of digits. —**digital clock, watch,** one showing the time by displayed digits, not by hands. **digital computer,** a computer operating on data represented as a series of digits. **digital recording,** a recording with sound-information represented in digits for more accurate transmission. —**digitally** *adv.* [f. L *digitalis* (as prec.)]

digitalis /dɪdʒɪˈteɪlɪs/ *n.* a drug prepared from dried foxglove leaves, used as a heart-stimulant. [as prec., generic name of foxglove, f. its thimble-shaped flower]

dignified *adj.* having or showing dignity. [f. foll.]

dignify /ˈdɪgnɪfaɪ/ *v.t.* to confer dignity on, to ennoble; to give a high-sounding name to. [f. OF f. L (*dignus* worthy)]

dignitary /ˈdɪgnɪtərɪ/ *n.* a person holding a high rank or position, especially ecclesiastical. [f. foll.]

dignity /ˈdɪgnɪtɪ/ *n.* **1.** a composed and serious manner or style, showing suitable formality. **2.** worthiness of honour or respect. **3.** a high rank or position. —**beneath one's dignity,** not worthy enough for one to do. **stand on one's dignity,** to insist on being treated with respect. [f. L *dignitas* (*dignus* worthy)]

digraph /ˈdaɪgrɑːf/ *n.* a union of two letters representing one sound (as *ph*, *ea*). [f. DI- + Gk -*graphos* written]

digress /daɪˈgres/ *v.i.* to depart from the main subject temporarily in speech or writing. —**digression** *n.* [f. L *digredi* depart (*gradus* step)]

dike /daɪk/ *n.* a long wall or embankment against flooding; a ditch; a low wall of turf or stone. —*v.t.* to provide or protect with dikes. [f. ON or Du.]

diktat /ˈdɪktɑːt/ *n.* a categorical statement or decree. [G, = DICTATE]

dilapidated /dɪˈlæpɪdeɪtɪd/ *adj.* in a state of disrepair or ruin. —**dilapidation** /-ˈdeɪʃ(ə)n/ *n.* [f. L *dilapidare* squander (*lapis* stone)]

dilatation /dɪləˈteɪʃ(ə)n/ *n.* dilation; widening of the cervix, e.g. for surgical curettage. [as foll.]

dilate /daɪˈleɪt/ *v.t./i.* **1.** to make or become wider or larger. **2.** to speak or write at length. —**dilation** *n.* [f. OF f. L *dilatare* spread out (*latus* wide)]

dilatory /ˈdɪlətərɪ/ *adj.* **1.** slow to act, not prompt. **2.** designed to cause delay. [f. L *dilatorius* (*dilator* delayer)]

dilemma /dɪˈlemə, daɪ-/ *n.* a situation in which a choice has to be made between alternatives that are both undesirable; (**D**) a difficult situation. [L f. Gk, = double proposition]

dilettante /dɪlɪˈtæntɪ/ *n.* (*pl.* -**ti** /-tiː/, -**tes**) who dabbles in a subject without serious study of it. —**dilettantism** *n.* [It., f. *dilettare* (f. L *delectare*) delight]

diligent /ˈdɪlɪdʒ(ə)nt/ *adj.* careful and hard-working; showing care and effort. —**diligence** *n.*, **diligently** *adv.* [f. OF f. L *diligens* assiduous f. *diligere* love]

dill *n.* a yellow-flowered herb (*Anethum graveolens*) with scented leaves and seeds used for flavouring pickles. [OE]

dilly-dally *v.i.* to waste time by indecision etc. [redupl. of DALLY]

dilute /daɪˈljuːt/ *v.t.* **1.** to reduce the strength of (a fluid) by adding water or other solvent. **2.** to weaken or reduce the forcefulness of. —*adj.* diluted. —**dilution** *n.* [f. L *diluere* wash away, dilute]

dim *adj.* **1.** faintly luminous or visible, not bright. **2.** indistinct, not clearly perceived or remembered. **3.** not seeing clearly; (*colloq.*) stupid. —*v.t./i.* (**-mm-**) to become or make dim. —**dimly** *adv.*, **dimness** *n.* [OE]

dime /daɪm/ *n.* (*US*) a ten-cent coin. [orig. = tithe, f. OF f. L *decima* (*pars*) tenth part]

dimension /daɪ'menʃ(ə)n/ *n.* a measurable extent of any kind, as length, breadth, thickness, area, or volume; (in *pl.*) size; extent or scope in a particular aspect. —**dimensional** *adj.* [f. OF f. L (DI-, *mensio* measure)]

dimidiate /dɪ'mɪdɪət/ *adj.* halved, split in two. —**dimidiation** /-'eɪʃ(ə)n/ *n.* (ill. HERALDRY) [f. L *dimidiare* (DI-, *midium* half)]

diminish /dɪ'mɪnɪʃ/ *v.t./i.* to make or become smaller or less (in fact or appearance); to lessen the reputation of (a person). —**law of diminishing returns,** the fact that expenditure, taxation, etc., beyond a certain point does not produce a proportionate yield. [f. earlier *minish* (f. OF, as MINCE) and *diminue* f. OF f. L *diminuere* break up small]

diminuendo /dɪmɪnjʊ'endəʊ/ *adv.* (*Mus.*) with a gradual decrease of loudness. —*n.* (*pl.* **-os**) (*Mus.*) a passage to be played in this way. [It. (as prec.)]

diminution /dɪmɪ'njuːʃ(ə)n/ *n.* diminishing, being diminished; decrease. [f. OF f. L (as DIMINISH)]

diminutive /dɪ'mɪnjʊtɪv/ *adj.* **1.** remarkably small, tiny. **2.** (of a derivative or suffix) used to imply something small (actually or in token of affection etc.) of the kind denoted by the simple word. —*n.* a diminutive word. [as prec.]

dimity /'dɪmɪtɪ/ *n.* a cotton fabric woven with checks or stripes of heavier thread. [f. It. or L f. Gk *dimitos* of double thread]

dimple *n.* a small hollow or dent, especially in the cheek or chin. —*v.t./i.* to produce dimples in; to show dimples. [prob. f. OE, cf. OHG *tumphilo* deep place in water]

din *n.* a prolonged loud and distracting noise. —*v.t./i.* (**-nn-**) **1.** to force (information) *into* a person by continually repeating it. **2.** to make a din. [OE]

dinar /'diːnɑː(r)/ *n.* a currency unit in Yugoslavia and in several countries of the Middle East and North Africa. [f. Arab. & Pers. f. Gk f. L *denarius* silver coin]

dine *v.t./i.* **1.** to eat dinner. **2.** to give dinner to (esp. socially). —**dining-car** *n.* a railway coach in which meals are served. **dining-room** *n.* a room in which meals are eaten. [f. OF *di(s)ner* f. L *disjejunare* break one's fast (DIS-, *jejunare* fast)]

diner *n.* **1.** a person who dines. **2.** a small dining-room. **3.** a dining-car on a train. [f. prec.]

ding-dong *n.* the sound of alternating strokes as of two bells. —*adj.* (of a contest) in which each contestant alternately has the advantage. —*adv.* with vigour and energy. [imit.]

dinghy /'dɪŋgɪ, -ŋɪ/ *n.* a ship's small boat; a small pleasure boat (ill. SAILING-SHIPS); a small inflatable rubber boat. [f. Hindi, = Indian river-boat]

dingle *n.* a deep wooded valley or dell. [orig. unkn.]

dingo /'dɪŋgəʊ/ *n.* (*pl.* **-oes**) a wild or half-domesticated Australian dog, *Canis dingo.* [Aboriginal]

dingy /'dɪndʒɪ/ *adj.* dull-coloured, drab; dirty-looking. —**dingily** *adv.*, **dinginess** *n.* [orig. unkn.]

dinkum /'dɪŋkəm/ *adj.* (*Austral. & NZ colloq.*) genuine, real. [orig. unkn.]

dinky *adj.* (*colloq.*) neat and attractive; small, dainty. [dim. of Sc. *dink* neat, trim]

dinner *n.* the chief meal of the day, whether at midday or evening; a formal evening meal in honour of a person or event. —**dinner-jacket,** a man's short usually black jacket for evening wear. [f. OF (as DINE)]

dinosaur /'daɪnəsɔː(r)/ *n.* an extinct reptile of the Mesozoic era, often of enormous size. Some dinosaurs were herbivores, others carnivores; all died out (for reasons which are still in dispute) at the end of the Cretaceous period. [f. L f. Gk (*deinos* terrible, *sauros* lizard)]

dint *n.* a dent. —*v.t.* to mark with dints. —**by dint of,** by force or means of. [f. OE & ON; ult. orig. unkn.]

diocese /'daɪəsɪs/ *n.* the district under the pastoral care of a bishop. —**diocesan** /daɪ'ɒsɪs(ə)n/ *adj.* [f. OF f. L f. Gk *dioikēsis* administration]

Diocletian /daɪə'kliːʃ(ə)n/ (Gaius Aurelius Valerius Diocletianus, d. 316) Roman emperor 284–305, a low-born Dalmatian, elevated to the throne by the army. Faced with military problems on many frontiers and insurrection in the provinces, in 293 he divided the empire between himself (in the east) and Maximian (in the west). His genius was as an organizer, and many of his administrative measures lasted for centuries. An enthusiast for what he believed was the old Roman religion, tradition, and discipline, which he held could reinforce imperial unity, he insisted on maintenance of Roman law in the provinces, and it was against this background that the persecution of the Christians began in 303, probably on the insistence of his assistant, Galerius. In 304 he suffered a collapse in health and abdicated in the following year, retiring to Dalmatia; the remains of his palace survive at Split, on the coast of Yugoslavia.

diode /'daɪəʊd/ *n.* a thermionic valve having two electrodes; a semiconductor rectifier having two terminals. [f. DI- + ELECTRODE]

dioecious /daɪ'iːʃəs/ *adj.* **1.** (*Bot.*) with male and female organs on separate plants. **2.** (*Zool.*) having the two sexes produce separate individuals. [f. DI- + Gk *-oikos* -housed]

Diogenes /daɪ'ɒdʒɪniːz/ (*c.*400–*c.*325 BC) founder of the Cynics. He lived at Athens in extreme poverty (legend says in a tub) and with an ostentatious disregard for social conventions that led to his being nicknamed *Kuōn* (the dog), from which appellation the name of the Cynics is derived. His main principles were that happiness is attained by satisfying only one's basic natural needs (and in the cheapest and easiest way), practising self-sufficiency, and that what is natural cannot be dishonourable or indecent and should be done in public. His originality apparently consisted more in the way he applied his philosophy in everyday life than in his theories as such. He became a legendary figure, and among the many stories told of him is that he took a lantern in daylight, saying that he was seeking an honest man.

Dionysian /daɪə'nɪzɪən/ *adj.* **1.** of Dionysus or his worship. **2.** sensual, unrestrained. [f. DIONYSUS]

Dionysius Exiguus /daɪə'nɪsɪəs ɪg'zɪgjʊəs/ a Scythian monk who lived at Rome *c.*500–550, famous for his contributions to ecclesiastical chronology and his corpus of canon law. He introduced the system of the 'Christian era' that is still in use, (wrongly) accepting 753 AUC as the year of the Incarnation. He is said to have dubbed himself 'Exiguus' (little) owing to his extreme humility.

Dionysius the Areopagite /daɪə'nɪsɪəs, ærɪ'ɒpəgaɪt/, St (1st c.), traditionally the first bishop of Athens, whose conversion by St Paul is recorded in Acts 17: 34. He was later confused with St Denis and with a 5th-c. mystical theologian, 'Dionysius the pseudo-Areopagite', whose writings on the soul's journey towards unity with God, combining Christianity with Neoplatonism, exercised a profound influence on medieval theology. Feast day, 9 Oct.

Dionysus /daɪə'naɪsəs/ (*Gk myth.*) a Greek god, also known as Bacchus, son of Zeus and Semele, a god of the fertility of nature, associated with emotional religious rites, and (though not originally) a god of wine who loosens care and inspires to music and poetry.

Diophantus /daɪə'fæntəs/ (date uncertain; prob. between 150 BC and AD 280) Greek mathematician of Alexandria, the first to attempt an algebraical notation. In his *Arithmetica* he shows how to solve simple and quadratic equations. It was Diophantus' work which led Fermat to take up the theory of numbers, in which he made his world-famous discoveries.

Dioscuri /daɪ'ɒskjʊərɪ/ (*Gk myth.*) the title of Castor and Polydeuces (Latinized as *Pollux*), brothers of Helen, born to Leda after her seduction by Zeus. Castor was mortal, the son of Tyndareus and Leda; his twin, Pollux, was immortal, the son of Zeus and Leda; at Pollux's request they shared his immortality between them, spending half their time below the earth and the other half in Olympus. It is an unsettled controversy whether they are in origin heroes or 'faded' gods. They are often identified with the constellation Gemini, and were the patrons of mariners. [Gk, = sons of Zeus]

dioptre /daɪ'ɒptə(r)/ *n.* a unit of refractive power of a lens. [f. F f. L f. Gk *dioptra* optical instrument]

diorama /daɪə'rɑːmə/ *n.* **1.** a scenic painting in which changes in colour and direction of illumination simulate sunrise etc. **2.** a small representation of a scene with three-dimensional figures, viewed through a window etc. **3.** a small-scale model or film-set. [f. Gk *dia* through + *horama* thing seen]

dioxide /daɪ'ɒksaɪd/ *n.* an oxide containing two atoms of oxygen.

dip *v.t./i.* (**-pp-**) **1.** to put or let down into a liquid, to immerse; to dye (a fabric) thus; to wash (sheep) in vermin-killing liquid; to go under water and emerge quickly; to go down, to go below any surface or level. **2.** to lower for a moment and then raise again; to lower the beam of (a vehicle's headlights) to reduce dazzle. **3.** to slope or extend downwards. **4.** to put a hand or ladle etc. *into* to take something out; to look cursorily *into* (a book etc.). — *n.* **1.** dipping, being dipped. **2.** (*colloq.*) a bathe in the sea etc. **3.** a liquid in which a thing is dipped; a sauce or dressing in which food is dipped before eating. **4.** the downward slope of a road etc.; a depression in the skyline etc. —**dip-stick** *n.* a rod for measuring the depth of a liquid, especially oil in a vehicle's engine. **dip-switch** *n.* a switch for dipping a vehicle's headlights. [OE]

diphtheria /dɪfˈθɪərɪə/ *n.* an acute infectious bacterial disease with inflammation of a mucous membrane especially of the throat. [f. F f. Gk *diphthera* piece of leather, f. the toughness of the false membrane developed]

diphthong /ˈdɪfθɒŋ/ *n.* a union of two vowels (letters or sounds) pronounced in one syllable (as in *coin, loud, toy*). —**diphthongal** /-ˈθɒŋɡ(ə)l/ *adj* [f. F f. L f. Gk (DI-, *phthongos* sound)]

diplodocus /dɪˈplɒdəkəs/ *n.* a giant herbivorous dinosaur of the order Sauropoda, remains of which have been found in the Upper Jurassic of western North America. [f. Gk *diploos* double + *dokos* beam]

diploid /ˈdɪplɔɪd/ *adj.* having chromosomes in homologous pairs. —*n.* a diploid cell or organism. [G, f. Gk *diplous* double + *eidos* form]

diploma /dɪˈpləʊmə/ *n.* **1.** a certificate awarded by a college etc. to a person who has successfully completed a course of study; a document conferring honour or privilege. **2.** an official document, a charter. [L f. Gk, = folded paper (*diplous* double)]

diplomacy /dɪˈpləʊməsɪ/ *n.* the management of international relations or skill in this; tact. [f. F (as DIPLOMATIC)]

diplomat /ˈdɪpləmæt/ *n.* **1.** a member of the diplomatic service. **2.** a tactful person. [f. F (as foll.)]

diplomatic /dɪpləˈmætɪk/ *adj.* of or involved in diplomacy; tactful. —*n.* (in *sing.* or *pl.*) the palaeographic and critical study of diplomas (sense 2). —**diplomatic immunity**, exemption of diplomatic staff etc. abroad from arrest, taxation, etc. **diplomatic service**, the branch of public service concerned with the representation of a country abroad. —**diplomatically** *adv.* [f. F (as DIPLOMA)]

diplomatist /dɪˈpləʊmətɪst/ *n.* a diplomat.

dipper *n.* **1.** a thing that dips. **2.** a diving bird, especially the water ouzel. [f. prec.]

dipsomania /dɪpsəˈmeɪnɪə/ *n.* an uncontrollable craving for alcohol. —**dipsomaniac** *n.* [f. Gk *dipsa* thirst + MANIA]

dipterous /ˈdɪptərəs/ *adj.* two-winged, belonging to the order Diptera (insects with one pair of membranous wings, e.g. fly, mosquito). [f. Gk (DI-, *pteron* wing)]

diptych /ˈdɪptɪk/ *n.* a painting, especially an altar-piece, on two leaves closing like a book. [f. L f. Gk, = pair of writing tablets (DI-, *ptukhē* fold)]

Dirac /dɪˈræk/, Paul Adrian Maurice (1902–84), English theoretical physicist. He applied Einstein's theory of relativity to quantum mechanics in order to describe the behaviour of the electron, including its spin, and later predicted the existence of a short-lived fundamental particle, the positive electron or positron, discovered by Carl David Anderson in 1932. He also developed a quantum theory of radiation, and was the co-inventor of the Fermi–Dirac statistics, which describe the behaviour of a class of sub-atomic particles, later called fermions. Dirac shared with Schrödinger the 1933 Nobel Prize for physics, for their contribution to wave mechanics.

dire *adj.* dreadful, calamitous, ominous; extreme and requiring urgent remedy. [f. L *dirus*]

direct /dɪˈrɛkt, daɪ-/ *adj.* **1.** extending or moving in a straight line or by the shortest route, not crooked or oblique. **2.** straightforward, going straight to the point; frank, not ambiguous. **3.** without intermediaries; personal. **4.** (of descent) linear, not collateral. **5.** complete, greatest possible. —*adv.* in a direct way or manner; by a direct route. —*v.t.* **1.** to control, to manage, to govern the actions of; to command; to supervise the acting etc. of (a play or film etc.). **2.** to tell (a person) the way (*to*); to address (a letter etc. *to*). **3.** to cause (a blow, remark, effort, attention, etc.) to have a specified direction or target. —**direct action**, exertion of pressure on the community by action (e.g. a strike or sabotage) seeking an immediate effect, rather than by parliamentary means. **direct current**, an electric current flowing in one direction only. **direct debit**, the

regular debiting of a person's bank account at the request of a creditor. **direct-grant school**, one receiving money from the government and not from a local authority, and in return observes certain conditions as to the admission of pupils. **direct object**, the primary object of action of a transitive verb. **direct speech**, words quoted as actually spoken, not modified by being reported. **direct tax**, one levied on income as distinct from one on goods or services. —**directness** *n.* [f. L *dirigere* (*regere* keep straight, rule)]

direction *n.* **1.** directing, supervision. **2.** (usu. in *pl.*) an order or instruction. **3.** a line along which or a point to or from which a person or thing moves or looks; the tendency or scope of a subject, aspect. [f. F or L (as prec.)]

directional *adj.* **1.** of or indicating direction. **2.** sending or receiving radio signals in one direction only. [f. prec.]

directive *n.* a general instruction for a procedure or action. —*adj.* serving to direct. [as DIRECT]

directly *adv.* in a direct line or manner; at once, without delay. —*conj.* as soon as. [f. DIRECT]

Directoire /dɪˈrɛktwɑː(r)/ *n.* the French Directory; (*attrib.*) in imitation of the styles in dressmaking, art, etc., prevalent during the period of the Directory. [F, as DIRECTORY]

director *n.* one who directs, especially a member of the board managing the affairs of a company etc.; a person who directs a play, film, etc.; a spiritual advisor. —**directorial** /-ˈtɔːrɪəl/ *adj.*, **directorship** *n.*, **directress** *n. fem.* [f. AF f. L, = governor (as DIRECT)]

directorate *n.* **1.** the office of director. **2.** a board of directors. [f. prec.]

directory *n.* a book with a list of telephone subscribers, inhabitants of a district, members of a profession etc., with various details. [as DIRECT]

Directory /dɪˈrɛktərɪ/ *n.* the executive of the French Revolutionary National Convention, constituted in 1795. The Directory was composed of five members, elected at the rate of one a year, and represented an attempt to avoid the one-man dictatorship previously achieved by Robespierre. It maintained an aggressive foreign policy, but proved too weak to control events at home and was overthrown by Napoleon in 1799.

dirge *n.* a slow mournful song; a lament for the dead. [f. L *dirige* imper. of *dirigere* direct, first wd in Latin antiphon (from Psalm 5: 8) in Office of the Dead]

dirigible /ˈdɪrɪdʒɪb(ə)l/ *adj.* capable of being guided. —*n.* a dirigible balloon airship. or [as DIRECT]

dirk *n.* a kind of dagger, especially of a Scottish Highlander. [orig. unkn.]

dirndl /ˈdɜːnd(ə)l/ *n.* a woman's dress imitating Alpine peasant costume, with a fitted bodice and full skirt; (also **dirndl skirt**) a full gathered skirt with a tight waistband. [G, dim. of *dirne* girl]

dirt *n.* **1.** unclean matter that soils something. **2.** earth, soil. **3.** foul or malicious words or talk. **4.** excrement. —**dirt cheap**, (*colloq.*) very cheap. **dirt road**, a road without a made surface. **dirt-track** *n.* a racing track made of earth or rolled cinders etc. **treat like dirt**, to treat (a person) with contempt. [ON, = excrement]

dirty *adj.* **1.** soiled by dirt, unclean; (of a nuclear weapon) causing considerable fall-out. **2.** obscene, lewd. **3.** dishonourable, unfair. **4.** (of weather) rough, squally. **5.** (of a colour) not pure or clear. —*v.t./i.* to make or become dirty. —**dirty look**, (*colloq.*) a look of disapproval or disgust. **dirty word**, an obscene word; a word for something disapproved of. —**dirtily** *adv.*, **dirtiness** *n.*

dis- *prefix* (**di-** before certain consonants) implying reversal of an action or state, the direct opposite of the simple word, the removal of a thing or quality, completeness or intensification of the action, expulsion from. [L]

disability /dɪsəˈbɪlɪtɪ/ *n.* something that disables or disqualifies a person; a physical incapacity caused by injury, disease, etc.

disable /dɪsˈeɪb(ə)l/ *v.t.* to deprive of an ability; (esp. in *p.p.*) to cripple, to deprive of or reduce the power of acting, walking, etc. —**disablement** *n.*

disabuse /dɪsəˈbjuːz/ *v.t.* to free *of* a false idea etc., to disillusion.

disadvantage /dɪsədˈvɑːntɪdʒ/ *n.* an unfavourable circumstance or condition; damage to one's interest or reputation. —*v.t.* to put at a disadvantage. —**disadvantageous** /-ˈteɪdʒəs/ *adj.*

disadvantaged *adj.* in unfavourable conditions; lacking normal social etc. opportunities. [f. prec.]

disaffected /dɪsəˈfektɪd/ adj. discontented; disloyal. —**disaffection** n.

disagree /dɪsəˈgriː/ v.i. 1. to hold a different opinion; to quarrel. 2. (of factors or circumstances) to fail to correspond. —**disagree with**, to differ in opinion from; to have an adverse effect on. —**disagreement** n.

disagreeable adj. unpleasant, not to one's liking; (of a person) not amiable. —**disagreeably** adv.

disallow /dɪsəˈlaʊ/ v.t. to refuse to allow or accept as valid.

disappear /dɪsəˈpɪə(r)/ v.i. to cease to be visible, to pass from sight or existence. —**disappearance** n.

disappoint /dɪsəˈpɔɪnt/ v.t. to fail to fulfil the desire or expectation of; to frustrate (a hope, purpose, etc.). [f. OF (as DIS-, APPOINT)]

disappointment n. a person, thing, or event that proves disappointing; the resulting distress. [f. prec.]

disapprobation /dɪsæprəˈbeɪʃ(ə)n/ n. disapproval.

disapprove /dɪsəˈpruːv/ v.i. to have or express an unfavourable opinion (of). —**disapproval** n.

disarm /dɪˈsɑːm/ v.t./i. 1. to deprive of weapons or the means of defence; to reduce or give up one's own armaments. 2. to defuse (a bomb). 3. to pacify the hostility or suspicions of. [f. OF (as DIS-, ARM²)]

disarmament /dɪsˈɑːməmənt/ n. the reduction of military forces and armaments. [f. prec.]

disarrange /dɪsəˈreɪndʒ/ v.t. to undo the arrangement of, to disorganize. —**disarrangement** n.

disarray /dɪsəˈreɪ/ n. disorder. —v.t. to throw into disorder.

disassociate /dɪsəˈsəʊsɪeɪt/ v.t. = DISSOCIATE.

disaster /dɪˈzɑːstə(r)/ n. a sudden or great misfortune; a complete failure. —**disastrous** adj., **disastrously** adv. [f. F f. It. (as DIS-, L astrum star, planet)]

disavow /dɪsəˈvaʊ/ v.t. to disclaim knowledge of or responsibility for. —**disavowal** n.

disband /dɪsˈbænd/ v.t./i. to break up (a group etc.); (of a group) to disperse. —**disbandment** n.

disbar /dɪsˈbɑː(r)/ v.t. (-rr-) to deprive (a barrister) of the right to practise law. —**disbarment** n.

disbelieve /dɪsbɪˈliːv/ v.t./i. to refuse or be unable to believe; to be sceptical. —**disbelief** n., **disbeliever** n.

disburden /dɪsˈbɜːd(ə)n/ v.t. to relieve of a burden; to remove (a load, anxieties, etc.).

disburse /dɪsˈbɜːs/ v.t. to pay out (money). —**disbursal** n., **disbursement** n. [f. OF (as DIS-, bourse purse)]

disc n. 1. a thin circular plate of any material; something shaped or looking like this, as the sun's face. 2. a layer of cartilage between the vertebrae (ill. BODY 1). 3. a gramophone record. 4. (in computers) a disc with a surface on which data can be recorded (usu. magnetically) and stored. —**disc brake**, a brake consisting of a disc operated by the action of friction pads on it (ill. CAR). **disc drive**, (in computers) a device for controlling and using a disc pack, having a rotation mechanism. **disc jockey**, a presenter of a broadcast programme featuring recordings of popular music. **disc pack**, a data storage medium consisting of an assembly of rigid magnetic discs mounted on a spindle, with a removable protective cover. [f. F or f. L discus]

discard /dɪsˈkɑːd/ v.t. to put aside as useless or unwanted; to reject (a playing card) from a hand. —/ˈdɪs-/ n. a discarded thing.

discern /dɪˈsɜːn/ v.t. to perceive clearly with the mind or senses; to make out by thought or by gazing, listening, etc. [f. OF f. L discernere (DIS-, cernere separate)]

discernible adj. able to be discerned. [f. prec.]

discerning adj. having good judgement or insight. [f. DISCERN]

discernment n. good judgement or insight. [as prec.]

discharge /dɪsˈtʃɑːdʒ/ v.t. 1. to send out or emit (missiles, liquids, etc.), (of a wound etc.) to emit a liquid; to unload from a ship. 2. to release (a prisoner); to allow (a patient, jury, etc.) to leave; to relieve (a bankrupt) of residual liability; to dismiss from employment or office. 3. to acquit oneself of, to pay or perform (a duty or obligation). 4. to fire (a gun); to release the electric charge of; to remove the cargo from (a ship etc.). —also ˈdɪs-/ n. 1. discharging, being discharged. 2. that which is discharged, especially matter from a wound or sore. 3. the release of an electric charge, especially with a spark. 4. a written certificate of release, dismissal, etc. [f. OF (as DIS-, CHARGE)]

disciple /dɪˈsaɪp(ə)l/ n. a follower or adherent of a leader, teacher, etc.; one of Christ's original followers. [f. L discipulus (discere learn)]

disciplinarian /dɪsɪplɪˈneərɪən/ n. one who enforces or believes in strict discipline. [f. foll.]

disciplinary /ˈdɪsɪplɪnərɪ, -ˈplɪn-/ adj. of or for discipline. [as foll.]

discipline /ˈdɪsɪplɪn/ n. 1. training or a way of life aimed at self-control and obedience; order maintained or observed among pupils, soldiers, and others under control; control exercised over the members of an organization. 2. punishment given to correct a person or enforce obedience. 3. a branch of instruction or learning. —v.t. to train to obedience and order; to punish. [f. L (discere learn)]

disclaim /dɪsˈkleɪm/ v.t. to renounce a claim to, to disown, to deny (responsibility etc.).

disclaimer n. a statement disclaiming something; a renunciation. [f. prec.]

disclose /dɪsˈkləʊz/ v.t. 1. to make known. 2. to expose to view. —**disclosure** n. [f. OF (as DIS-, CLOSE²)]

disco n. (pl. -os) (colloq.) a discothèque; a dancing-party with records; equipment for this. [abbr.]

Discobolus /dɪsˈkɒbələs/ 'the Discus-thrower', the title of a statue by the Greek sculptor Myron (5th c. BC). Several copies survive.

discolour /dɪsˈkʌlə(r)/ v.t./i. to spoil the colour of, to stain; to become changed in colour or stained. —**discoloration** /-ˈreɪʃ(ə)n/ n. [f. OF or L (as DIS-, colorare colour)]

discomfit /dɪsˈkʌmfɪt/ v.t. to humiliate or disconcert completely. —**discomfiture** /-fɪtʃə(r)/ n. [f. OF desconfire (as DIS-, L conficere put together)]

discomfort /dɪsˈkʌmfət/ n. lack of comfort; a thing causing this. —v.t. to make uncomfortable.

discompose /dɪskəmˈpəʊz/ v.t. to disturb the composure of. —**discomposure** n.

disconcert /dɪskənˈsɜːt/ v.t. to disturb the self-possession of, to fluster. [f. F (as DIS-, CONCERT)]

disconnect /dɪskəˈnekt/ v.t. to break the connection of; to put out of action by disconnecting parts. —**disconnection** n.

disconnected adj. (esp. of speech or writing) lacking orderly connection, having abrupt transitions. [f. prec.]

disconsolate /dɪsˈkɒnsələt/ adj. forlorn, downcast, disappointed. [f. L disconsolatus (DIS-, consolare console)]

discontent /dɪskənˈtent/ n. dissatisfaction, lack of contentment; a grievance. —v.t. to make dissatisfied. —**discontentment** n.

discontented adj. dissatisfied, feeling discontent. [f. prec.]

discontinue /dɪskənˈtɪnjuː/ v.t./i. to cease, to cause to cease; to cease from, to give up. —**discontinuance** n. [f. OF f. L discontinuare (DIS- continuare continue)]

discontinuous /dɪskənˈtɪnjʊəs/ adj. lacking continuity in space or time, intermittent. —**discontinuity** /-ˈjuːɪtɪ/ n.

discord /ˈdɪskɔːd/ n. 1. opposition of views, strife; a harsh noise, clashing sounds. 2. (Mus.) a lack of harmony between notes sounded together. [f. OF f. L (as DIS-, cor heart)]

discordant /dɪsˈkɔːd(ə)nt/ adj. disagreeing; not in harmony, clashing. —**discordance** n. [f. prec.]

discothèque /ˈdɪskəʊtek/ n. a club etc. where amplified recorded popular music is played for dancing; the equipment for playing such records. [F, = record-library]

discount /ˈdɪskaʊnt/ n. an amount deducted from the full or normal price; an amount deducted for the immediate payment of a sum not yet due (e.g. on a bill of exchange). —v.t. 1. -ˈkaʊnt/ to disregard partly or wholly. 2. /ˈdɪs-/ to buy or sell at a discount; to deduct an amount from (a price etc.). —**at a discount**, below full or normal price; (fig.) not at the true value. [f. F or It. (as DIS-, COUNT¹)]

discountenance /dɪsˈkaʊnt(ə)nəns/ v.t. 1. to refuse to approve of. 2. to disconcert.

discourage /dɪsˈkʌrɪdʒ/ v.t. to deprive of courage or confidence; to dissuade, to deter; to show disapproval of. —**discouragement** n. [f. OF (as DIS-, COURAGE)]

discourse /ˈdɪskɔːs/ n. 1. conversation; a speech or lecture. 2. a written treatise on a subject. —/-ˈkɔːs/ v.i. 1. to converse; to speak or write at length on a subject. 2. to utter a discourse. [f. L discursus (as DISCURSIVE)]

discourteous /dɪsˈkɜːtɪəs/ adj. lacking courtesy. —**discourteously** adv., **discourtesy** n.

discover /dɪsˈkʌvə(r)/ v.t. to acquire knowledge or sight of by effort or chance; to be the first to do this in a particular case. [f. OF f. L discooperire (DIS-, cooperire cover)]

discovery n. discovering; a thing discovered. [f. prec.]

discredit /dɪsˈkredɪt/ v.t. **1.** to harm the good reputation of. **2.** to refuse to believe; to cause to be disbelieved. —n. **1.** harm to a reputation, a person or thing causing this. **2.** lack of credibility.

discreditable adj. bringing discredit, shameful. —**discreditably** adv. [f. prec.]

discreet /dɪsˈkriːt/ adj. **1.** showing caution and good judgement in what one does; not giving away secrets. **2.** unobtrusive. —**discreetly** adv. [f. OF f. L discretus separate, discretio discernment]

discrepancy /dɪsˈkrepənsɪ/ n. a difference, failure to correspond, inconsistency. —**discrepant** adj. [f. L, = discordance of sound]

discrete /dɪsˈkriːt/ adj. separate, individually distinct; discontinuous. [f. L (discernere distinguish, separate)]

discretion /dɪsˈkreʃ(ə)n/ n. **1.** good judgement, prudence; ability to keep secrets. **2.** freedom or authority to act according to one's judgement. —**years** or **age of discretion**, the age at which a person is considered capable of managing his own affairs. [f. OF f. L (as DISCERN)]

discretionary adj. done or used at a person's discretion. [f. prec.]

discriminate /dɪsˈkrɪmɪneɪt/ v.t./i. **1.** to make or see a distinction (between); to distinguish unfairly against or in favour of a person on grounds of sex, race, colour, etc. **2.** to have good taste or judgement. —**discrimination** /-ˈneɪʃ(ə)n/ n., **discriminatory** /-ˈkrɪm-/ adj. [f. L (discrimen distinction)]

discriminating adj. showing good judgement, discerning. [f. prec.]

discursive /dɪsˈkɜːsɪv/ adj. wandering from topic to topic. [f. L (discurrere run to and fro)]

discus /ˈdɪskəs/ n. a heavy thick-centred disc thrown in ancient and modern sports (ill. SPORTS). Throwing the discus is mentioned in the writings of Homer, and was contested in the Olympic Games in about 708 BC. [L f. Gk diskos]

discuss /dɪsˈkʌs/ v.t. to consider (a subject) by talking or writing about it; to hold a conversation about. —**discussion** n. [f. L discutere shake to pieces]

disdain /dɪsˈdeɪn/ n. scorn, contempt. —v.t. to regard with disdain; to refrain or refuse from disdain. —**disdainful** adj., **disdainfully** adv. [f. OF f. L dedignare think unworthy]

disease /dɪˈziːz/ n. an unhealthy condition of the body, a plant, or some part thereof, caused by infection, diet, or faulty functioning of a physiological process; a particular kind of this; an abnormal mental condition. [f. OF (as DIS-, EASE)]

diseased adj. affected with disease; abnormal, disordered. [f. prec.]

disembark /dɪsɪmˈbɑːk/ v.t./i. to go or put ashore. —**disembarkation** /-ˈkeɪʃ(ə)n/ n.

disembarrass /dɪsɪmˈbærəs/ v.t. **1.** to free from embarrassment. **2.** to rid or relieve (of). —**disembarrassment** n.

disembody /dɪsɪmˈbɒdɪ/ v.t. to free (a soul, spirit, etc.) from the body or concrete form. —**disembodiment** n.

disembowel /dɪsɪmˈbaʊəl/ v.t. (**-ll-**) to remove the bowels or entrails of. —**disembowelment** n. [f. DIS- = utterly + obs. embowl disembowel]

disenchant /dɪsɪnˈtʃɑːnt/ v.t. to free from enchantment or illusion. —**disenchantment** n.

disencumber /dɪsɪnˈkʌmbə(r)/ v.t. to free from encumbrance.

disengage /dɪsɪnˈɡeɪdʒ/ v.t./i. to detach, to loosen, to release from engagement; to become detached. —**disengagement** n.

disengaged adj. at leisure, uncommitted; detached. [f. prec.]

disentangle /dɪsɪnˈtæŋɡ(ə)l/ v.t./i. to free or become free of tangles or complications. —**disentanglement** n.

disestablish /dɪsɪˈstæblɪʃ/ v.t. to end the established state of, to deprive (the Church) of its State connection. —**disestablishment** n.

disfavour /dɪsˈfeɪvə(r)/ n. dislike, disapproval; being disliked. —v.t. to regard or treat with disfavour.

disfigure /dɪsˈfɪɡə(r)/ v.t. to spoil the appearance of. —**disfigurement** n.

disfranchise /dɪsˈfræntʃaɪz/ v.t. to deprive of rights as a citizen or of a franchise held. —**disfranchisement** n.

disgorge /dɪsˈɡɔːdʒ/ v.t. to eject from the throat; to pour forth.

disgrace /dɪsˈɡreɪs/ n. loss of favour or respect, downfall from a position of honour; a thing that causes this. —v.t. to bring disgrace to, to degrade; to dismiss from favour or honour. [f. F f. It. (as DIS-, GRACE)]

disgraceful adj. causing disgrace, shameful. —**disgracefully** adv. [f. prec.]

disgruntled /dɪsˈɡrʌnt(ə)ld/ adj. sulkily discontented. [f. DIS- = utterly + gruntle obs. frequent. of GRUNT]

disguise /dɪsˈɡaɪz/ v.t. to conceal the identity of, to make unrecognizable; to conceal or obscure. —n. something worn to disguise one's identity; a disguised state. [f. OF (as DIS-, GUISE)]

disgust /dɪsˈɡʌst/ n. strong dislike, repugnance. —v.t. to cause disgust in. [f. OF f. It. (as DIS-, GUSTO)]

dish n. **1.** a shallow flat-bottomed container for holding food; its contents; (in pl.) all the utensils after use at a meal. **2.** a particular kind of food. **3.** a dish-shaped object or cavity. **4.** (colloq.) an attractive young woman. —v.t. **1.** to make dish-shaped. **2.** (colloq.) to frustrate, to ruin. —**dish out**, (slang) to distribute (carelessly). **dish up**, to put (food) in dishes ready for serving, to prepare to serve a meal; (slang) to present as fact or argument. **dish-water** n. water in which dishes have been washed. [OE f. L discus disc]

dishabille /dɪsəˈbiːl/ var. of DÉSHABILLÉ.

disharmony /dɪsˈhɑːmənɪ/ n. lack of harmony, discord. —**disharmonious** /-ˈməʊnɪəs/ adj.

dishcloth n. a cloth for washing dishes.

dishearten /dɪsˈhɑːt(ə)n/ v.t. to make despondent, to cause to lose courage or confidence. —**disheartenment** n.

dishevelled /dɪˈʃev(ə)ld/ adj. ruffled and untidy. —**dishevelment** n. [f. OF (as DIS-, chevel hair)]

dishonest /dɪsˈɒnɪst/ adj. not honest. —**dishonestly** adv., **dishonesty** n.

dishonour /dɪsˈɒnə(r)/ n. loss of honour or respect, shame or disgrace; a thing that causes this. —v.t. **1.** to bring dishonour upon, to disgrace. **2.** to refuse to accept or pay (a cheque etc.). [f. OF f. L dishonorare (DIS-, HONOUR)]

dishonourable /dɪsˈɒnərəb(ə)l/ adj. bringing dishonour, shameful, ignominious. —**dishonourably** adv. [f. prec.]

dishwasher n. **1.** a machine for washing dishes. **2.** a water wagtail.

disillusion /dɪsɪˈluːʒ(ə)n/ v.t. to free from illusion or mistaken belief. —n. being disillusioned. —**disillusionment** n.

disincentive /dɪsɪnˈsentɪv/ n. a thing or factor discouraging a particular action.

disincline /dɪsɪnˈklaɪn/ v.t. to make unwilling. —**disinclination** /-klɪˈneɪʃ(ə)n/ n.

disinfect /dɪsɪnˈfekt/ v.t. to cleanse of infection, to remove bacteria from. —**disinfection** n.

disinfectant adj. having disinfecting properties. —n. a disinfecting substance. [f. prec.]

disinflation /dɪsɪnˈfleɪʃ(ə)n/ n. a policy designed to counteract inflation without producing the disadvantages of deflation. —**disinflationary** n.

disingenuous /dɪsɪnˈdʒenjʊəs/ adj. insincere, giving a false appearance of candour. —**disingenuously** adv., **disingenuousness** n.

disinherit /dɪsɪnˈherɪt/ v.t. to reject as one's heir, to deprive of the right of inheritance (esp. by making a new will). —**disinheritance** n. [f. DIS- + INHERIT in obs. sense 'make heir']

disintegrate /dɪˈsɪntɪɡreɪt/ v.t./i. to separate or cause to separate into component parts, to break up; to deprive of or lose cohesion; (of a nucleus) to emit one or more particles or divide into smaller nuclei. —**disintegration** /-ˈɡreɪʃ(ə)n/ n., **disintegrator** n.

disinter /dɪsɪnˈtɜː/ v.t. (**-rr-**) to dig up (esp. a corpse) from the ground. —**disinterment** n.

disinterest /dɪsˈɪntərest/ n. **1.** impartiality. **2.** (**D**) lack of concern.

disinterested adj. **1.** impartial, not influenced by involvement or advantage. **2.** (**D**) uninterested. —**disinterestedly** adv., **disinterestedness** n. [f. prec.]

disjoin /dɪsˈdʒɔɪn/ v.t. to separate, to disunite, to part. [f. OF f. L disjungere (DIS-, jungere join)]

disjoint /dɪsˈdʒɔɪnt/ v.t. to take to pieces at the joints; to dislocate; to disturb the working or connection of. [as prec.]

disjointed adj. (of talk) disconnected. [f. prec.]

disjunction /dɪsˈdʒʌŋkʃ(ə)n/ n. disjoining, separation. [f. OF or L (as DISJOIN)]

disjunctive /dɪsˈdʒʌŋktɪv/ *adj.* involving separation; (of conjunctions such as *or* and *but*) introducing an alternative or contrast. [f. L (as prec.)]

disk var. of DISC.

diskette /dɪsˈket/ *n.* a floppy disc, not necessarily of small size. [f. prec. + -ETTE]

dislike /dɪsˈlaɪk/ *n.* a feeling that a person or thing is unpleasant, unattractive, etc.; the object of this. —*v.t.* to have a dislike for, not to like.

dislocate /ˈdɪsləkeɪt/ *v.t.* to disturb the normal connection of, to displace a bone in (a joint); to disrupt, to put out of order. —**dislocation** /-ˈkeɪʃ(ə)n/ *n.* [f. OF or L *dislocare* (DIS-, *locare* place)]

dislodge /dɪsˈlɒdʒ/ *v.t.* to disturb or move from an established position. —**dislodgement** *n.*

disloyal /dɪsˈlɔɪl/ *adj.* unfaithful, lacking loyalty. —**disloyally** *adv.*, **disloyalty** *n.*

dismal /ˈdɪzm(ə)l/ *adj.* causing or showing gloom, miserable, dreary; (*colloq.*) feeble, inept. —**dismally** *adv.* [f. OF f. L *dies mali* unlucky days (of which there were held to be two in each month)]

dismantle /dɪsˈmænt(ə)l/ *v.t.* to pull down, to take to pieces; to deprive of defences, equipment, etc.

dismay /dɪsˈmeɪ/ *n.* a feeling of helplessness and alarm in the face of some danger or difficulty. —*v.t.* to fill with dismay. [f. OF (as DIS-, MAY[1])]

dismember /dɪsˈmembə(r)/ *v.t.* **1.** to remove the limbs from. **2.** to partition (a country etc.), to divide up. —**dismemberment** *n.* [f. OF (as DIS-, L *membrum* limb)]

dismiss /dɪsˈmɪs/ *v.t.* **1.** to send away, to cause to leave one's presence; to disperse. **2.** to order to terminate employment or service (esp. with dishonour). **3.** to put out of one's thoughts, to cease to feel or discuss; to treat (a subject) summarily; to reject (a lawsuit etc.) without further hearing. **4.** to put out (a batsman or side) in cricket (*for* a stated score). —**dismissal** *n.*, **dismissive** *adj.* [f. OF f. L *dimissus* (as DIS-, *mittere* send)]

dismount /dɪsˈmaʊnt/ *v.t./i.* **1.** to get off or down from an animal one is riding; to cause to fall off, to unseat. **2.** to remove (a thing, esp. a gun) from its mounting.

Disney, /ˈdɪznɪ/, Walter Elias ('Walt') (1901–66), American animator and film producer. He became famous with the creation of Mickey Mouse in 1928, followed by the Silly Symphony series (1929) involving the Three Little Pigs. In 1934 he began to produce the first feature-length cartoon with sound and colour, *Snow White and the Seven Dwarfs* (1937). Later came *Pinocchio* (1940), *Dumbo* (1941), *Bambi* (1943), and many others, as well as *Fantasia* (1940), which combined pieces of classical music with appropriate animation. *Treasure Island* (1950) was the first of many live-action features, of which the musical *Mary Poppins* (1964) was the most successful. He also produced nature documentaries, beginning with *Seal Island* (1949) and including *The Living Desert* (1953). Disneyland in California and Walt Disney World in Florida are amusement parks incorporating all the elements of Disney fantasy.

disobedient /dɪsəˈbiːdɪənt/ *adj.* disobeying, rebellious. —**disobedience** *n.*, **disobediently** *adv.*

disobey /dɪsəˈbeɪ/ *v.t./i.* fail or refuse to obey; to disregard (a rule, order, etc.).

disorder /dɪsˈɔːdə(r)/ *n.* **1.** lack of order, confusion; a commotion, a riot. **2.** disturbance of a normal state or function; an ailment, a disease. —*v.t.* to put into disorder, to upset. [f. OF (as DIS-, ORDAIN)]

disorderly *adj.* untidy, confused; riotous, contrary to public order or morality. —**disorderly house,** a brothel. [f. prec.]

disorganize /dɪsˈɔːɡənaɪz/ *v.t.* to upset the order or system of, to throw into confusion. —**disorganization** /-ˈzeɪʃ(ə)n/ *n.*

disorient /dɪsˈɔːrɪənt/ *v.t.* to disorientate.

disorientate /dɪsˈɔːrɪənteɪt/ *v.t.* to confuse (a person) as to his bearings. —**disorientation** /-ˈteɪʃɪ(ə)n/ *n.*

disown /dɪsˈəʊn/ *v.t.* to refuse to recognize or acknowledge, to repudiate; to reject connection with.

disparage /dɪsˈpærɪdʒ/ *v.t.* to speak slightingly of, to belittle. —**disparagement** *n.*, **disparagingly** *adv.* [f. OF *desparagier* marry unequally (as DIS-, *parage* equality of rank f. L *par* equal)]

disparate /ˈdɪspərət/ *adj.* essentially different, unrelated, not comparable. [f. L *disparare* separate, infl. in sense by *dispar* unequal]

disparity /dɪsˈpærɪtɪ/ *n.* inequality, difference, incongruity. [f. F f. L (*dispar* unequal)]

dispassionate /dɪsˈpæʃ(ə)nət/ *adj.* free from emotion, impartial. —**dispassionately** *adv.*

dispatch /dɪˈspætʃ/ *v.t.* **1.** to send off to a destination or for a purpose. **2.** to give the death-blow to, to kill; to finish or dispose of promptly or quickly. —*n.* **1.** dispatching, being dispatched. **2.** promptness, efficiency. **3.** a written (official) message; a news report sent to a newspaper or news agency. —**dispatch-box** *n.* a case for carrying official documents. **dispatch-rider** *n.* an official messenger on a motor cycle. [f. It. *dispacciare* or Sp. *despachar*]

dispel /dɪˈspel/ *v.t.* (-ll-) to drive away, to scatter (darkness, fog, fears, etc.). [f. L *dispellere* (DIS-, *pellere* drive)]

dispensable /dɪˈspensəb(ə)l/ *adj.* that can be dispensed with. [f. L (as DISPENSE)]

dispensary /dɪˈspensərɪ/ *n.* a place (especially a room) where medicines are dispensed. [f. L (as DISPENSE)]

dispensation /dɪspenˈseɪʃ(ə)n/ *n.* **1.** dispensing, distributing. **2.** ordering or management, especially of the world by Providence. **3.** an exemption from a penalty, rule, or obligation. [f. OF or L (as foll.)]

dispense /dɪˈspens/ *v.t./i.* to distribute, to deal out, to administer; to make up and give out (medicines etc.) according to prescriptions. —**dispense with,** to do without; to make unnecessary. [f. OF f. L *dispensare*, frequent. of *dispendere* weigh or pay out]

dispenser *n.* **1.** a person who dispenses (especially medicine). **2.** a device for dispensing commodities in fixed quantities. [f. prec.]

disperse /dɪˈspɜːs/ *v.t./i.* **1.** to scatter; to drive, go, or send in different directions. **2.** to send to or station at different points. **3.** to put in circulation, to disseminate. **4.** to separate (white light) into coloured constituents. —**dispersal** *n.*, **dispersive** *adj.* [f. L *dispergere* (DIS-, *spargere* scatter)]

dispersion /dɪˈspɜːʃ(ə)n/ *n.* **1.** dispersing, being dispersed. **2. the Dispersion,** the scattering of Jews among Gentiles from the time of the Captivity onwards; the Jews thus scattered. [f. prec.]

dispirit /dɪˈspɪrɪt/ *v.t.* (often in *p.p.*) to make despondent. [f. DIS- + SPIRIT]

displace /dɪsˈpleɪs/ *v.t.* to move from its place; to oust, to take the place of; to remove from office. —**displaced person,** one removed from his home country by military or political pressure; originally, a civilian deported from a German-occupied country to work in Germany during the Second World War and thereafter homeless.

displacement *n.* **1.** displacing, being displaced. **2.** the amount of fluid displaced by a thing floating or immersed in it; the amount by which a thing is shifted from its place. [f. prec.]

display /dɪˈspleɪ/ *v.t.* to exhibit, to show; to reveal, to betray, to allow to appear. —*n.* **1.** displaying. **2.** a thing or things displayed, a show; ostentation. **3.** a bird's special pattern of behaviour as a means of visual communication. [f. OF f. L *displicare* (DIS-, *plicare* fold)]

displease /dɪsˈpliːz/ *v.t.* to arouse the disapproval or indignation of, to offend; to be unpleasing to. [f. OF (as DIS-, L *placere* please)]

displeasure /dɪsˈpleʒə(r)/ *n.* a displeased feeling, indignation, dissatisfaction. [as prec.]

disport /dɪˈspɔːt/ *v.t./i.* to play, to frolic; to enjoy *oneself*. [f. OF (as DIS-, L *portare* carry)]

disposable *adj.* able to be disposed of; at one's disposal; designed to be thrown away after use. —*n.* a disposable article. [f. DISPOSE]

disposal *n.* disposing, disposing of. —**at one's disposal,** available for one's use. [f. foll.]

dispose /dɪˈspəʊz/ *v.t./i.* **1.** to place suitably or in order, to arrange. **2.** to incline, to make willing or desirous; to bring (a person, the mind) into a certain state; (in *pass.*) to have a specified tendency of mind. **3.** to determine the course of events. —**dispose of,** to get rid of; to deal with, to finish; to prove (an argument etc.) incorrect. [f. OF (as POSE), assoc. with foll.]

disposition /dɪspəˈzɪʃ(ə)n/ *n.* **1.** setting in order, arrangement. **2.** the relative position of parts. **3.** a temperament; a natural tendency, an inclination. **4.** (usu. in *pl.*) a plan, preparations. [f. OF f. L (*disponere* arrange)]

dispossess /dɪspəˈzes/ *v.t.* to deprive (a person) of the possession *of*; to oust, to dislodge. —**dispossession** *n.*

disproof /dɪsˈpruːf/ *n.* disproving, a refutation.

disproportion /dɪsprə'pɔːʃ(ə)n/ *n.* lack of proportion; being out of proportion.

disproportionate /dɪsprə'pɔːʃ(ə)nət/ *adj.* out of proportion, relatively too large or too small. —**disproportionately** *adv.* [f. prec.]

disqualify /dɪs'kwɒlɪfaɪ/ *v.t.* to make or declare ineligible or unsuitable; to debar from a competition. —**disqualification** /-'keɪʃ(ə)n/ *n.*

disquiet /dɪs'kwaɪət/ *n.* uneasiness, anxiety. —*v.t.* to cause disquiet to.

disquietude /dɪs'kwaɪətjuːd/ *n.* a state of disquiet.

disquisition /dɪskwɪ'zɪʃ(ə)n/ *n.* a long elaborate treatise or discourse upon a subject. [F f. L (DIS-, *quaerere* seek)]

Disraeli /dɪz'reɪlɪ/, Benjamin, 1st Earl of Beaconsfield (1804–81), British statesman of Italian-Jewish descent, Prime Minister 1868 and 1874–80. A novelist of some distinction in early life, Disraeli first sat in Parliament in 1837, taking a central part in the reconstruction of the Conservative Party after Peel, slowly reuniting it and educating it out of protectionism and into parliamentary reform, arousing its interest in the working man and enthusiasm for the Empire. He was largely responsible for the Second Reform Act of 1867 which doubled the electorate. As Prime Minister between 1874 and 1880 he enacted a useful series of social reforms, involved Britain in the purchase of the Suez Canal, and made Queen Victoria Empress of India. On the Continent the prestige of Britain was revived and her influence in international affairs increased. Against the handicaps of belonging to the wrong race, religion, social class, and educational background, Disraeli made his way by force of genius, energy, and quick imagination. His career is one of the most remarkable in the 19th c.

disregard /dɪsrɪ'gɑːd/ *v.t.* to pay no attention to, to treat as of no importance. —*n.* lack of attention, indifference, neglect.

disrepair /dɪsrɪ'peə(r)/ *n.* bad condition due to lack of repairs.

disreputable /dɪs'repjʊtəb(ə)l/ *adj.* of bad repute, not respectable in character or appearance; discreditable. —**disreputably** *adv.*

disrepute /dɪsrɪ'pjuːt/ *n.* lack of good repute, discredit.

disrespect /dɪsrɪ'spekt/ *n.* lack of respect, discourtesy. —**disrespectful** *adj.*, **disrespectfully** *adv.*

disrobe /dɪs'rəʊb/ *v.t./i.* to remove clothes (from).

disrupt /dɪs'rʌpt/ *v.t.* to interrupt the flow or continuity of, to bring disorder to; to break apart. —**disruption** *n.*, **disruptive** *adj.* [f. L *disrumpere* (DIS-, *rumpere* break)]

dissatisfaction /dɪsætɪs'fækʃ(ə)n/ *n.* lack of satisfaction or contentment; a cause of this.

dissatisfy /dɪ'sætɪsfaɪ/ *v.t.* to fail to satisfy, to make discontented.

dissect /dɪ'sekt/ *v.t.* 1. to cut into pieces, especially so as to examine parts or structure. 2. to analyse, to examine or criticize in detail. —**dissection** *n.*, **dissector** *n.* [f. L *dissecare* (DIS-, *secare* cut)]

dissemble /dɪ'semb(ə)l/ *v.t./i.* to conceal or disguise (intention, character, feeling, etc.); to talk or act hypocritically or insincerely. [f. OF f. L *dissimulare* (DIS-, *simulare* simulate)]

disseminate /dɪ'semɪneɪt/ *v.t.* to scatter about, to spread (ideas etc.) widely. —**dissemination** /-'neɪʃ(ə)n/ *n.*, **disseminator** *n.* [f. L *disseminare* (DIS-, *semen* seed)]

dissension /dɪ'senʃ(ə)n/ *n.* discord arising from dissent. [f. OF f. L (as foll.)]

dissent /dɪ'sent/ *v.i.* to disagree openly, to hold a different view or belief (*from*). —*n.* such a difference of view or belief; an expression of this. [f. L *dissentire* (DIS-, *sentire* feel)]

dissenter *n.* one who dissents; **Dissenter**, a member of a sect that has separated from the Church of England, a Nonconformist. [f. prec.]

dissentient /dɪ'senʃɪənt, -ʃ(ə)nt/ *adj.* dissenting from an established view. —*n.* a dissentient person. [as DISSENT]

dissertation /dɪsə'teɪʃ(ə)n/ *n.* a detailed discourse, especially as submitted for a higher degree in a university. [f. L *dissertare*, frequent. of *disserere* examine]

disservice /dɪs'sɜːvɪs/ *n.* a harmful action, especially one done in a misguided attempt to help.

dissident /'dɪsɪd(ə)nt/ *adj.* disagreeing, at variance. —*n.* a person who is at variance, especially with established authority. —**dissidence** *n.* [F, or f. L *dissidēre* (DIS-, *sedēre* sit)]

dissimilar /dɪ'sɪmɪlə(r)/ *adj.* unlike, not similar. —**dissimilarity** /-'lærɪtɪ/ *n.*

dissimulate /dɪ'sɪmjʊleɪt/ *v.t./i.* to dissemble. —**dissimulation** /-'leɪʃ(ə)n/ *n.* [f. L *dissimulare* (DIS-, *simulare* simulate)]

dissipate /'dɪsɪpeɪt/ *v.t./i.* to dispel, to disperse; to squander, to fritter away. [f. L *dissipare* scatter around]

dissipated *adj.* given to dissipation, dissolute. [f. prec.]

dissipation /dɪsɪ'peɪʃ(ə)n/ *n.* dissipating; a frivolous or dissolute way of life. [as DISSIPATE]

dissociate /dɪ'səʊsɪeɪt, -ʃɪ-/ *v.t./i.* to separate or disconnect in thought or fact; to become dissociated. —**dissociate oneself from**, to declare oneself unconnected with. **dissociation** /-'eɪʃ(ə)n/ *n.*, **dissociative** *adj.* [f. L *dissociare* (DIS-, *socius* companion)]

dissoluble /dɪ'sɒljʊb(ə)l/ *adj.* that can be disintegrated, loosened, or disconnected. [F, or f. L (DIS-, SOLUBLE)]

dissolute /'dɪsəluːt, -ljuːt/ *adj.* morally lax, licentious. [f. L (as DISSOLVE)]

dissolution /dɪsə'luːʃ(ə)n, -'ljuː-/ *n.* 1. dissolving, being dissolved, especially of a partnership or of a parliament for a new election; the breaking up or abolition (of an institution). 2. death. —**Dissolution of the Monasteries**, the abolition of monasteries in England by Henry VIII under two Acts (1536, 1539) by which they were suppressed and their assets vested in the Crown. Though monasteries were much criticized in the later Middle Ages for their wealth, moral laxity, and stress on the contemplative life, Henry's motives were personal: to replenish his treasury, and to establish royal supremacy in ecclesiastical affairs. [f. OF or L (as foll.)]

dissolve /dɪ'zɒlv/ *v.t./i.* 1. to make or become liquid, especially by immersion or dispersion in a liquid. 2. to disappear gradually; to cause to do this. 3. to dismiss or disperse (an assembly, especially a parliament). 4. to annul or put an end to (a marriage or partnership). —**dissolve into**, to give way to (tears, laughter). [f. L *dissolvere* (DIS-, *solvere* loosen)]

dissonant /'dɪsənənt/ *adj.* not in harmony, harsh-toned; incongruous. —**dissonance** *n.* [f. OF or L *dissonare* (DIS-, *sonare* sound)]

dissuade /dɪ'sweɪd/ *v.t.* to give advice or exercise influence to discourage or divert (a person *from*). —**dissuasion** *n.*, **dissuasive** *adj.* [f. L *dissuadēre* (DIS-, *suadēre* persuade)]

distaff /'dɪstɑːf/ *n.* a cleft stick holding wool or flax for spinning. —**distaff side**, the branch of a family descended from a female parent or ancestor. [OE (as MLG *dise(ne)* bunch of flax, STAFF)]

distance /'dɪstəns/ *n.* 1. the length of space between one point and another; a space of time. 2. a distant point, a remoter field of vision. 3. being far off; remoteness, reserve. —*v.t.* 1. to place or cause to seem far off. 2. to leave far behind in a race etc. —**keep one's distance**, to remain apart or aloof. [f. OF f. L (*distare* stand apart)]

distant /'dɪst(ə)nt/ *adj.* 1. far away, at a specified distance; remote in position, time, relationship, or concept. 2. avoiding familiarity, aloof. —**distantly** *adv.* [as prec.]

distaste /dɪs'teɪst/ *n.* a dislike, an aversion (*for*).

distasteful *adj.* causing distaste, disagreeable *to*. —**distastefully** *adv.* [f. prec.]

distemper[1] /dɪ'stempə(r)/ *n.* a disease of dogs and some other animals, with catarrh and weakness. —*v.t.* (*archaic*, usu. in *p.p.*) to upset, to derange. [f. L *distemperare* (DIS-, *temperare* mix in correct proportion)]

distemper[2] /dɪ'stempə(r)/ *n.* a kind of paint using glue or size instead of an oil-base, for use on walls. —*v.t.* to paint with this. [f. OF or L *distemperare* soak (as prec.)]

distend /dɪ'stend/ *v.t./i.* to swell or stretch out by pressure from within. —**distensible** *adj.*, **distension** *n.* [f. L *distendere* (DIS-, *tendere* stretch)]

distich /'dɪstɪk/ *n.* a verse couplet. [f. L f. Gk (DI-, *stikhos* line)]

distil /dɪ'stɪl/ *v.t.* 1. to purify, to extract the essence from (a substance) by vaporizing it with heat then condensing it with cold and re-collecting the resulting liquid; to make (whisky, an essence, etc.) by distilling raw materials. 2. to fall or cause to fall in drops. —**distillation** /-'leɪʃ(ə)n/ *n.* [f. L *distillare* (DE-, *stilla* drop)]

distillate /dɪ'stɪleɪt/ *n.* a product of distillation. [f. prec.]

distiller *n.* one who distils, especially a maker of alcoholic liquor. [f. DISTIL]

distillery *n.* a place where alcoholic liquor is distilled. [as prec.]

distinct /dɪˈstɪŋkt/ *adj.* **1.** not identical, separate, different in quality or kind. **2.** clearly perceptible, definite, and unmistakable. —**distinctly** *adv.*, **distinctness** *n.* [f. p.p. of L *distinguere* (as DISTINGUISH)]

distinction /dɪˈstɪŋkʃ(ə)n/ *n.* **1.** seeing or making a difference, discrimination. **2.** a difference seen or made; a thing that differentiates. **3.** distinguished character, excellence. **4.** the showing of special consideration. **5.** a title or mark of honour. [f. OF f. L (as DISTINGUISH)]

distinctive *adj.* distinguishing, characteristic. —**distinctively** *adv.* [as prec.]

distingué /dɪˈstæŋɡeɪ/ *adj.* having a distinguished air or manners. [F (as foll.)]

distinguish /dɪˈstɪŋɡwɪʃ/ *v.t./i.* **1.** to observe or identify a difference in; to differentiate, to draw distinctions (*between*); to characterize, to be a mark or property of. **2.** to make out by listening, looking, etc. **3.** to make *oneself* prominent or noteworthy (*by* some achievement). [f. F or L *distinguere* (DIS-, *stinguere* extinguish)]

distinguishable *adj.* able to be distinguished. [f. prec.]

distinguished *adj* eminent, having distinction. [f. DISTINGUISH]

distort /dɪˈstɔːt/ *v.t.* to pull or twist out of shape; to transmit (a sound etc.) inaccurately; to misrepresent (facts etc.). —**distortion** *n.* [f. L *distorquēre* (DIS-, *torquēre* twist)]

distract /dɪˈstrækt/ *v.t.* to draw away the attention of (a person, the mind, etc.); to confuse, to bewilder. [f. L (DIS-, *trahere* draw)]

distraction /dɪˈstrækʃ(ə)n/ *n.* **1.** distracting, being distracted. **2.** a thing that distracts the attention or impairs concentration. **3.** an amusement, a relaxation. **4.** mental confusion or distress. [f. OF or L (as prec.)]

distrain /dɪˈstreɪn/ *v.i.* to levy distraint (*upon* a person or goods). [f. OF f. L *distringere* (DIS-, *stringere* draw tight)]

distraint /dɪˈstreɪnt/ *n.* the seizure of goods as a method of enforcing payment. [f. prec.]

distrait /dɪˈstreɪ/ *adj.* (*fem.* **distraite** /-eɪt/) inattentive; distraught. [F (as DISTRACT)]

distraught /dɪˈstrɔːt/ *adj.* much troubled in mind; demented with worry etc. [alt. of obs. *distract* adj. (as DISTRACT)]

distress /dɪˈstres/ *n.* **1.** anguish or suffering caused by pain, sorrow, worry, or exhaustion; a state of difficulty or helplessness; lack of money or necessaries. **2.** (*Law*) distraint. —*v.t.* to cause distress to, to make unhappy. [f. OF (rel. to DISTRAIN)]

distressed *adj.* affected by distress, impoverished. —**distressed area**, a region of much poverty and unemployment. [f. prec.]

distributary /dɪˈstrɪbjʊtərɪ/ *n.* a river or glacier branch that does not return to the main stream after leaving it (as in a delta). [f. foll.]

distribute /dɪˈstrɪbjuːt, (D) ˈdɪs-/ *v.t.* to divide and give a share of to each of a number; to spread about, to scatter, to put at different points; to arrange, to classify. —**distribution** /-ˈbjuːʃ(ə)n/ *n.* [f. L *distribuere* (DIS-, *tribuere* assign)]

distributive /dɪˈstrɪbjʊtɪv/ *adj.* of, concerned with, or produced by distribution; (*Gram.* & *Logic*) referring to each individual of a class, not to the class collectively. —*n.* a distributive word (e.g. *each, neither, every*). [f. F or L (as prec.)]

distributor /dɪˈstrɪbjʊtə(r)/ *n.* **1.** one who distributes things, especially an agent who markets goods. **2.** a device in an internal-combustion engine for passing the current to each sparking-plug in turn. [f. DISTRIBUTE]

district /ˈdɪstrɪkt/ *n.* a region or territory regarded as a geographical or administrative unit; a division of a county. —**district attorney**, (*US*) the prosecuting officer of a district. **district nurse**, a local nurse visiting patients at their homes. [F f. L, = territory of jurisdiction (as DISTRAIN)]

distrust /dɪsˈtrʌst/ *n.* lack of trust, suspicion. —*v.t.* to feel distrust in. —**distrustful** *adj.*

disturb /dɪˈstɜːb/ *v.t.* **1.** to break the rest or quiet or calm of; to agitate, to worry. **2.** to move from a settled position. **3.** (in *p.p.*) emotionally or mentally unstable or abnormal. [f. OF f. L *disturbare* (DIS-, *turbare* to disorder)]

disturbance *n.* an interruption of tranquillity; agitation; a tumult, an uproar. [as prec.]

disunion /dɪsˈjuːnɪən/ *n.* separation, lack of union; discord.

disunite /dɪsjuːˈnaɪt/ *v.t./i.* to remove unity from; to cause to separate, to experience separation. —**disunity** /-ˈjuːnɪtɪ/ *n.*

disuse /dɪsˈjuːz/ *v.t.* to cease to use. —/-ˈjuːs/ *n.* a disused state.

disyllable /dɪˈsɪləb(ə)l, daɪ-/ *n.* a word or metrical foot of two syllables. —**disyllabic** /-ˈlæbɪk/ *adj.* [f. DI- + SYLLABLE]

ditch *n.* a long narrow excavated channel, especially for drainage or to mark a boundary. —*v.t./i.* **1.** to make or repair ditches. **2.** to drive (a vehicle) into a ditch; (*slang*) to make a forced landing on the sea, to bring (an aircraft) down thus. **3.** (*slang*) to abandon, to discard, to leave in the lurch; to frustrate. —**dull as ditch-water**, very dull. [OE]

dither /ˈdɪðə(r)/ *v.i.* to be nervously hesitant or unsure; to tremble, to quiver. —*n.* a state of dithering, nervous excitement or apprehension. [var. of *didder* = DODDER[1]]

dithyramb /ˈdɪθɪræm/ *n.* a Greek choric hymn, wild in character; a passionate or inflated poem, speech, or writing. —**dithyrambic** /-ˈræmbɪk/ *adj.* [f. L f. Gk]

dittany /ˈdɪtənɪ/ *n.* a herb of the genus *Dictamnus*, formerly supposed to be of medicinal value. [f. OF f. L *dictamnus* f. Gk (perh. f. *Diktē* mountain in Crete where (among other places) the herb grew)]

ditto /ˈdɪtəʊ/ *n.* (*pl.* **-os**) the aforesaid, the same (in accounts, inventories, etc.), symbolized by two small marks (*ditto marks* ,,) placed under the word or item repeated; (*colloq.*) an expression of agreement. [It. f. L (as DICTUM)]

ditty *n.* a short simple song. [f. OF *dité* composition f. L (as DICTATE)]

diuretic /daɪʊəˈretɪk/ *adj.* causing an increased secretion of urine. —*n.* a diuretic drug. [f. OF or L f. Gk (DIA-, *oureō* urinate)]

diurnal /daɪˈɜːn(ə)l/ *adj.* **1.** of the day, not nocturnal. **2.** daily; occupying one day. [f. L (*dies* day)]

diva /ˈdiːvə/ *n.* a great woman singer, a prima donna. [It. f. L, = goddess]

divalent /daɪˈveɪlənt/ *adj.* (*Chem.*) having a valence of two. [f. DI- + -*valent* (as VALENCE)]

divan /dɪˈvæn/ *n.* a low couch or bed without a back or ends. [F or It. ult. f. Pers., = bench]

dive *v.t./i.* **1.** to plunge, especially head first, into water; (of an aircraft) to plunge steeply downwards; (of a submarine or diver) to submerge; to go down or out of sight suddenly. **2.** to rush or move suddenly. **3.** to put (one's hand) *into* one's pocket, handbag, etc. —*n.* **1.** an act of diving (ill. SPORTS); a sharp downward movement or dart. **2.** (*colloq.*) a disreputable place, a drinking-den. —**dive-bomb** *v.t.* to drop bombs on from a diving aircraft. **diving-bell** *n.* an open-bottomed structure supplied with air, in which a diver can be lowered into deep water. **diving-board** *n.* a springboard for diving from. **diving-suit** *n.* a watertight suit, usually with a helmet and an air-supply for work underwater. [OE; rel. to DEEP, DIP]

diver *n.* **1.** one who dives, especially a person who works underwater in a diving-suit. **2.** a diving bird, especially of the genus *Gavia*. [f. prec.]

diverge /daɪˈvɜːdʒ/ *v.i.* to go in different directions from a common point, to become further apart; to go aside *from* a track or path. —**divergent** *adj.*, **divergence** *n.* [f. L (DIS-, *vergere* incline)]

divers /ˈdaɪvəz/ *adj.* (*archaic*) various, several. [f. OF (as foll.)]

diverse /daɪˈvɜːs/ *adj.* of different kinds, varied. [f. L *diversus* (DIS-, *vertere* turn)]

diversify /daɪˈvɜːsɪfaɪ/ *v.t.* to make diverse, to vary; to spread (an investment) over several enterprises or products. —**diversification** /-fɪˈkeɪʃ(ə)n/ *n.* [f. OF f. L (as prec.)]

diversion /daɪˈvɜːʃ(ə)n/ *n.* **1.** diverting something from its course. **2.** the diverting of attention, a manœuvre to achieve this; a pastime, a recreation. **3.** an alternative route when a road is temporarily closed to traffic. —**diversionary** *adj.* [f. L (as foll.)]

diversity /daɪˈvɜːsɪtɪ/ *n.* being diverse; a variety. [f. OF (as DIVERS)]

divert /daɪˈvɜːt/ *v.t.* **1.** to turn aside from its course; to cause to go by a different route. **2.** to distract (the attention); to entertain or amuse. [f. F f. L (DIS-, *vertere* turn)]

divertissement /diːvɜːˈtiːsmɑ̃/ *n.* a short ballet etc. between acts or longer pieces; a diversion or entertainment. [F (as prec.)]

Dives /ˈdaɪviːz/ the Latin word for 'rich man', occurring in the Vulgate, Luke 16, whence commonly taken for the name of the rich man in that parable.

divest /daɪˈvest/ *v.t.* to strip (a person) *of* clothes; to deprive or rid *of*. [f. OF (as DIS-, L *vestire* clothe)]

divide /dɪˈvaɪd/ *v.t./i.* 1. to separate *into* parts, to split or break up; to separate (one thing) from another; to become or be able to be divided. 2. to mark out into parts or groups, to classify. 3. to cause to disagree, to set at variance. 4. to distribute, to share out. 5. to find how many times a number contains another. 6. to separate (an assembly etc.) into two sets in voting, to be thus separated. —*n.* 1. a watershed. 2. (*fig.*) a dividing line. —**divided skirt**, culottes. **Great Divide**, the main range of the Rocky Mountains which forms the watershed between the eastern and western drainage systems of North America. [f. L *dividere* force apart]

dividend /ˈdɪvɪdend/ *n.* 1. a number to be divided. 2. a share of profits paid to shareholders or to winners in a football pool. 3. the benefit from an action. [f. AF f. L (as prec.)]

divider *n.* 1. a screen etc. dividing a room. 2. (in *pl.*) measuring compasses. [f. prec.]

divination /dɪvɪˈneɪʃ(ə)n/ *n.* insight into the unknown or the future by allegedly supernatural means. [f. OF or f. L (as DIVINE[2])]

divine[1] /dɪˈvaɪn/ *adj.* 1. of, from, or like God or a god; sacred. 2. (*colloq.*) excellent, delightful. —*n.* a theologian or clergyman. —**divine right of kings**, the doctrine that a monarch in the hereditary line of succession has authority derived directly from God, independently of the subjects' will, and that rebellion is the worst of political crimes. Enunciated in the 16th c., under the Stuarts it was upheld by almost all the leading Anglican divines, but many of its strenuous upholders found no difficulty in accommodating themselves to the Revolution of 1688, by which the Stuart dynasty was expelled from the throne. —**divinely** *adv.* [f. OF f. L (*divus* god)]

divine[2] /dɪˈvaɪn/ *v.t./i.* to discover by intuition, inspiration, or guessing; to foresee; to practise divination. —**divining-rod** *n.* a dowsing-rod (see DOWSE). —**diviner** *n.* [f. F f. L *divinare* (as prec.)]

divinity /dɪˈvɪnɪtɪ/ *n.* 1. being divine; a god; godhead. 2. theology. [f. OF f. L (as DIVINE[1])]

divisible /dɪˈvɪzɪb(ə)l/ *adj.* able to be divided. —**divisibility** /-ˈbɪlɪtɪ/ *n.* [F or f. L (as DIVIDE)]

division /dɪˈvɪʒ(ə)n/ *n.* 1. dividing, being divided; a process of dividing a number by another; a disagreement or discord; (in Parliament) the separation of members into two sections for counting votes. 2. one of the parts into which a thing is divided; a major unit of administration or organization. —**division sign**, the sign ÷ indicating that one quantity is to be divided by another. —**divisional** *adj.* [f. OF f. L (as DIVIDE)]

divisionism *n.* see POINTILLISM. —**divisionist** *n.* [as prec.]

divisive /dɪˈvaɪsɪv/ *adj.* tending to cause disagreement. [f. L (as DIVIDE)]

divisor /dɪˈvaɪzə(r)/ *n.* the number by which another is to be divided. [f. F or L (as DIVIDE)]

divorce /dɪˈvɔːs/ *n.* 1. legal dissolution of a marriage. 2. severance, separation. —*v.t.* 1. to separate by divorce; to end a marriage with (one's husband or wife) by divorce. 2. to detach, to separate. [f. OF f. L (DIS-, *vortere* = *vertere* turn)]

divorcee /dɪvɔːˈsiː/ *n.* a divorced person. [f. prec.]

divot /ˈdɪvət/ *n.* a piece of turf cut out by a blow, especially by the head of a golf-club. [orig. Sc.; etym. unkn.]

divulge /daɪˈvʌldʒ/ *v.t.* to disclose or reveal (a secret etc.). —**divulgence** *n.* [f. L (DIS-, *vulgare* publish)]

divvy *n.* (*colloq.*) a dividend. —*v.t.* (*colloq.*, with *up*) to share out. [abbr. of DIVIDEND]

Diwali /dɪˈwɑːlɪ/ *n.* the Hindu festival of lights celebrated in October or November in honour of the goddess of wealth (Lakshmi). [f. Hindi f. Skr., = row of lamps (*dīpa* lamp)]

Dixie /ˈdɪksɪ/ *n.* the Southern States of the USA. The name is used in the song *Dixie* (1859) by Daniel D. Emmett, a popular marching-song sung by Confederate soldiers in the American Civil War. [orig. unkn.]

dixie *n.* a large iron cooking-pot used by campers etc. [f. Hindi *degchī* f. Pers., dim. of *deg* pot]

Dixieland *n.* 1. Dixie. 2. a kind of jazz with a strong two-beat rhythm. [f. DIXIE]

DIY *abbr.* do-it-yourself.

dizzy *adj.* giddy, feeling confused; making giddy. —*v.t.* to make dizzy, to bewilder. —**dizzily** *adv.*, **dizziness** *n.* [OE]

DJ *abbr.* 1. a disc jockey. 2. a dinner-jacket.

Djakarta var. of JAKARTA.

Djibouti var. of JIBOUTI.

dl *abbr.* decilitre(s).

D-layer *n.* the lowest stratum of the ionosphere. [f. *D* (arbitrary)]

D.Litt. *abbr.* Doctor of Letters. [f. L *Doctor Litterarum*]

dm *abbr.* decimetre(s).

DNA *abbr.* deoxyribonucleic acid, a substance that is a major constituent of chromosomes. DNA molecules carry the genetic information necessary for the organization and functioning of most living cells and control the inheritance of characteristics (see MENDELISM). The structure of a DNA molecule was first proposed by J. D. Watson and F. H. Crick in 1953: each consists of two strands coiled round each other to form a double helix, a structure like a spiral ladder; it is the 'rungs' of the ladder that carry the information. Each rung consists of a pair of chemical groups called bases (of which there are four types). The different rungs function rather like different letters of the alphabet, which are without meaning in themselves but in sequences produce meaningful words, and long sequences of bases similarly 'spell out' genetic information. These control the manufacture of proteins needed by the cell; genes are 'copied' in the nucleus into the similar RNA, which then passes out into the cytoplasm and forms a template for the synthesis of particular proteins, especially enzymes. The DNA molecule also has the special property of self-replication: the strands separate and each provides a template for the synthesis of a new complementary strand with which it recombines, thus producing two identical copies of the original double helix.

Dnieper /ˈdniːpə(r)/ a river of the USSR flowing some 2,200 km (1,370 miles) through Belorussia and Ukraine to the Black Sea. The cities of Kiev and Dnepropetrovsk are situated on it. Dams have been built at a number of points to provide hydroelectric power and water for Ukraine's industries.

Dniester /ˈdniːstə(r)/ a river of the USSR flowing 1,410 km (876 miles) from the Carpathian Mountains through Moldavia to the Black Sea.

D-notice *n.* an official request to news editors not to publish items on specified subjects, for reasons of security. [f. *defence* + NOTICE]

do[1] /do, *emphat.* duː/ *v.t./i.* (3 *sing. pres.* **does** /dʌz/; *past* **did**; *p.p.* **done** /dʌn/; *partic.* **doing**) 1. to perform, to carry out, to fulfil or complete. 2. to produce, to make; to bring about, to provide. 3. to deal with, to set in order; to work out, to solve; to work at, to be occupied with; to cook; to translate or transform; (*slang*) to cheat, to rob or burgle; to prosecute or convict. 4. to cover in travelling; (*colloq.*) to visit, to see the sights of. 5. to undergo. 6. to provide food etc. for; (*colloq.*) to satisfy, to be suitable or convenient to. 7. to produce (a play etc.); to play the part of, to act like. 8. to fare, to get on, to achieve something. 9. to be suitable or acceptable, to serve a purpose. 10. to be in progress. —*v. aux.*, with infinitive or elliptically, for emphasis, in inversion, in questions and negations, or in place of the verb. —**do away with**, to get rid of, to abolish, to kill. **do down**, (*colloq.*) to overcome, to cheat, to swindle. **do for**, to be satisfactory or sufficient for; (*colloq.*) to destroy, to ruin, to kill; (*colloq.*) to act as a housekeeper for. **do-gooder** *n.* person meaning to do social good but unrealistic or intrusive in the process. **do in**, (*slang*) to ruin, to kill; (*colloq.*) to exhaust, to tire out. **do-it-yourself** *adj.* & *n.* (work) done or to be done by an amateur handyman at home. **do or die**, to persist regardless of danger. **do out**, to clean or redecorate (a room). **do over**, (*slang*) to attack, to beat up. **do something for**, (*colloq.*) to enhance the appearance or quality of. **do up**, to fasten, to wrap up; to refurbish, to renovate. **do with**, to use, to treat. **do without**, to forgo, to manage without. **to do with**, in connection with, related to. [OE]

do[2] /duː/ *n.* (*pl.* **dos**, **do's**) 1. an elaborate event, party, or operation. 2. (*colloq.*) a swindle, a hoax. —**dos and don'ts**, the rules of behaviour. **fair dos**, fair shares. [f. prec.]

do[3] var. of DOH.

Dobermann pinscher /ˈdəʊbəmən ˈpɪnʃə(r)/ a large dog of a German breed with a smooth coat and docked tail. [f.

L *Dobermann* (19th-c. German dog-breeder), G *pinscher* terrier]

doc *n.* (*colloq.*) doctor. [abbr.]

Docetist /dəˈsiːtɪst/ *n.* a member of the Docetae, a sect of early Christian heretics who held that Christ's body was not human but a phantom or of celestial substance. —**Docetism** *n.* [f. Gk *dokeō* seem, appear]

docile /ˈdəʊsaɪl/ *adj.* submissive, easily managed. —**docilely** *adv.*, **docility** /-ˈsɪlɪtɪ/ *n.* [f. L (*docēre* teach)]

dock[1] *n.* an artificially enclosed body of water for the loading, unloading, and repair of ships; (in *pl.*) a range of docks with wharves and offices. —*v.t./i.* **1.** to bring or come into dock. **2.** to join (two or more spacecraft) together in space, to become joined thus. —**in dock**, (*colloq.*) in hospital or (of a vehicle) laid up for repairs. [f. MDu. *docke*]

dock[2] *n.* an enclosure in a criminal court for the accused. [prob. f. Flem. *dok* cage]

dock[3] *n.* a weed of the genus *Rumex*, with broad leaves that are rubbed on the skin to alleviate the pain of nettle-stings. [OE]

dock[4] *v.t.* **1.** to cut short (an animal's tail). **2.** to reduce or take away a part of (wages, supplies, etc.). [f. *dock* fleshy part of tail, perh. rel. to MLG *dokke* bundle of straw]

dock[5] *n.* **1.** the solid fleshy part of an animal's tail (ill. HORSE); the crupper of a saddle or harness. [perh. f. MLG *dokke* bundle of straw]

docker *n.* a person employed to load and unload ships. [f. DOCK[1]]

docket /ˈdɒkɪt/ *n.* a document or label listing goods delivered or the contents of a package, or recording the payment of customs dues etc. —*v.t.* to enter on a docket, to label with a docket. [orig. unkn.]

dockland *n.* the district near docks. [f. DOCK[1]]

dockyard *n.* an area with docks and equipment for building and repairing ships. [f. DOCK[1]]

doctor /ˈdɒktə(r)/ *n.* **1.** a qualified practitioner of medicine, a physician. **2.** a person who holds a doctorate. —*v.t.* **1.** to treat medically. **2.** to castrate or spay (an animal). **3.** to patch up (machinery etc.); to tamper with or falsify. —**Doctor of the Church**, the title of certain Christian theologians, originally Gregory the Great, Ambrose, Augustine, and Jerome. [f. OF f. L (*docēre* teach)]

doctoral /ˈdɒktər(ə)l/ *adj.* of or for the degree of doctor. [f. prec.]

doctorate /ˈdɒktərət/ *n.* the highest university degree in any faculty. [f. DOCTOR]

doctrinaire /dɒktrɪˈneə(r)/ *n.* a person who applies principles pedantically without allowance for circumstances. —*adj.* theoretical and unpractical. [F (as foll.)]

doctrine /ˈdɒktrɪn/ *n.* what is taught, a body of instruction; a principle of religion, a political etc. belief, a set of such principles. —**doctrinal** /-ˈtraɪn(ə)l/ *adj.* [f. OF f. L (as DOCTOR)]

document /ˈdɒkjʊmənt/ *n.* a thing, especially a title-deed, writing, or inscription, that provides a record or evidence. —*v.t.* to prove by or provide with documents. —**documentation** /-ˈteɪʃ(ə)n/ *n.* [f. OF f. L, = proof (as DOCTOR)]

documentary /dɒkjʊˈmentərɪ/ *adj.* consisting of documents; providing a factual record or report. —*n.* a documentary film (see below). [f. prec.]
Documentaries are factual films depicting real people, events, or landscapes either lyrically or as a means of social comment. The lyrical vein was first seen in Robert Flaherty's study of Eskimo life *Nanook of the North* (1922), but the social purpose emerged most strongly in the 1930s, notably in Britain under the influence of John Grierson. Such films were used as propaganda by both sides in the Second World War, but after the war their production sharply declined until the growth of television provided a new outlet; they are now made mainly for this medium.

dodder[1] *v.i.* to tremble or totter, especially from age. —**dodderer** *n.*, **doddery** *adj.* [var. of obs. dial. *dadder*]

dodder[2] *n.* a threadlike climbing parasitic plant of the genus *Cascuta*. [= MLG *dod(d)er*, MHG *toter*]

dodecagon /dəʊˈdekəgən/ *n.* a plane figure with twelve sides and angles. [f. Gk (*dōdeka* twelve, *-gonos* angled)]

dodecahedron /dəʊdekəˈhiːdrən/ *n.* a solid figure with twelve faces (ill. SHAPES). [f. Gk (*dōdeka* twelve, *hedra* base)]

Dodecanese /dəʊdɪkəˈniːz/ a group of twelve islands in the SE Aegean, of which the largest is Rhodes, which were occupied by Italy in 1912 during the war with Turkey and ceded to Greece in 1947; capital, Rhodes. [f. Gk (*dōdeka* twelve, *nēsos* island)]

dodecaphonic /dəʊdekəˈfɒnɪk/ *adj.* of a compositional method, developed in the 20th c., in which the twelve notes of the octave are treated equally, without the focusing on a 'home-note' (the tonic) of traditional harmony. [f. Gk *dōdeka* twelve + PHONIC]

dodge /dɒdʒ/ *v.t./i.* to move quickly to one side, or round, about, or behind an obstacle, to elude a pursuer, blow, etc.; to evade by cunning or trickery. —*n.* a quick movement to avoid something; a clever trick or expedient. [orig. unkn.]

dodgem /ˈdɒdʒəm/ *n.* a small electrically driven car in an enclosure at a fun-fair, in which the driver tries to bump other cars and dodge those trying to bump his or her car. [f. prec. + 'EM]

Dodgson, Charles Lutwidge, see Lewis CARROLL.

dodgy *adj.* (*colloq.*) awkward, unreliable, tricky. [f. DODGE]

dodo /ˈdəʊdəʊ/ *n.* (*pl.* **-os**) a large extinct bird (*Raphus cucullatus*) of Mauritius etc. —**as dead as the dodo**, entirely obsolete. [f. Port., = simpleton]

Dodoma /dəˈdəʊmə/ the capital of Tanzania.

DOE *abbr.* Department of the Environment.

doe /dəʊ/ *n.* the female of the fallow deer, reindeer, hare, or rabbit. [OE]

doer /ˈduːə(r)/ *n.* one who does something; one who acts rather than merely talking or thinking. [f. DO[1]]

does /dʌz/ see DO[1].

doeskin *n.* the skin of a fallow deer; leather made from this.

doesn't /ˈdʌz(ə)nt/ (*colloq.*) = does not.

doff *v.t.* to take off (a hat or clothing). [= *do off*]

dog *n.* **1.** a four-legged carnivorous animal of the genus *Canis*, of many breeds (wild and domesticated); the male of this or of a fox or wolf. **2.** a person, a despicable person. **3.** a mechanical device for gripping something. —*v.t.* to follow closely and persistently, to pursue, to track. —**dog-collar** *n.* a collar for a dog; (*colloq.*) a clerical collar. **dog days**, the hottest period of the year. **dog-eared** *adj.* (of a book) with the corners worn or battered with use. **dog-eat-dog** *n.* ruthless competition. **dog-end** *n.* (*slang*) a cigarette-end. **dog in the manger**, one who clings to a thing he cannot use, preventing others from enjoying it. **dog's breakfast**, (*colloq.*) a mess. **dog's life**, a life of misery or harassment. **dog-star** *n.* the chief star of the constellation Canis Major or Minor, especially Sirius. **dog-tired** *adj.* tired out. **dog-watch** *n.* one of the two-hour watches on a ship (4–6 or 6–8 p.m.). **go to the dogs**, (*slang*) to deteriorate, to be ruined. [OE]

dogcart *n.* a two-wheeled driving-cart with cross seats back to back.

doge /dəʊdʒ/ *n.* (*hist.*) the chief magistrate in the former republics of Venice and Genoa. [F f. It. f. L *dux* leader]

dogfight *n.* **1.** a close combat between fighter aircraft. **2.** an uproar, a fight like that between dogs.

dogfish *n.* (*pl.* usu. same) any of several small sharks, especially *Scyliorhinus Caniculus*.

dogged /ˈdɒgɪd/ *adj.* tenacious, grimly persistent. —**doggedly** *adv.* [f. DOG]

doggerel /ˈdɒgər(ə)l/ *n.* poor or trivial verse. [app. f. DOG (with disparaging force as in *dogrose*)]

Doggett's Coat and Badge /ˈdɒgɪt/ a rowing contest held each year among Thames watermen for an orange livery with a silver badge. It was instituted in 1715 by an Irish comedian, Thomas Doggett, and is now the oldest sculling race in the world.

doggie /ˈdɒgɪ/ *n.* (*children's colloq.*) a dog. [f. DOG]

doggo *adv.* **lie doggo**, (*slang*) to lie motionless or hidden. [prob. f. DOG]

doggy *adj.* of or like a dog; devoted to dogs. —*n.* = DOGGIE. [f. DOG]

doghouse *n.* (*US*) a dog's kennel. —**in the doghouse**, (*slang*) in disgrace.

dogma /ˈdɒgmə/ *n.* **1.** a principle or tenet; a system of these, especially as laid down by the authority of a Church. **2.** an arrogant declaration of opinion. [L f. Gk (*dokeō* seem)]

dogmatic /dɒgˈmætɪk/ *adj.* **1.** of or in the nature of a dogma. **2.** asserting or given to asserting dogmas or opinions; intolerantly authoritative. —**dogmatically** *adv.* [f. prec.]

dogmatism /ˈdɒgmətɪz(ə)m/ *n.* the tendency to be dogmatic. [as foll.]

dogmatize /ˈdɒgmətaɪz/ *v.t./i.* to speak dogmatically; to express (a principle etc.) as a dogma. [f. F f. L f. Gk (as DOGMA)]

dogrose *n.* a wild hedge-rose, *Rosa canina.*

dogsbody /ˈdɒgzbɒdɪ/ *n.* (*colloq.*) a drudge.

dogwood *n.* a shrub (*Cornus sanguinea*) with dark red branches, greenish-white flowers, and purple berries, found in woods and hedgerows.

doh /dəʊ/ *n.* (*Mus.*) the first note of a major scale in tonic sol-fa (see entry). [f. It. *do*]

Doha /ˈdəʊhə/ the capital of Qatar; pop. (est.) 200,000.

doily /ˈdɔɪlɪ/ *n.* a small ornamental lace or paper mat used on a plate for cakes etc. [orig. name of a fabric, f. surname]

doing /ˈduːɪŋ/ *partic.* of DO¹. —*n.* **1.** activity, effort. **2.** (in *pl.*, *slang*) adjuncts, things needed. [f. DO¹]

Dolby /ˈdɒlbɪ/ *n.* [P] a system used in tape-recording to reduce unwanted sounds at high frequency. [f. R. *Dolby* (1933–) the inventor]

doldrums /ˈdɒldrəmz/ *n.pl.* **1.** low spirits; a period of inactivity. **2.** an equatorial ocean region often marked by calms. [perh. after *dull* and *tantrum*]

dole *n.* **1.** a charitable distribution, a thing given sparingly or reluctantly. **2. the dole,** (*colloq.*) a State benefit payable to insured persons who are unable to obtain employment. —*v.t.* to deal *out* sparingly. —**on the dole,** (*colloq.*) receiving State benefit for the unemployed. [OE, rel. to DEAL¹]

doleful /ˈdəʊlf(ə)l/ *adj.* mournful, sad; dreary, dismal. —**dolefully** *adv.* [f. *dole* grief f. OF f. L (*dolēre* grieve)]

dolerite /ˈdɒləraɪt/ *n.* a coarse basaltic rock. [f. F f. Gk *doleros* deceptive (because its contents are difficult to distinguish)]

dolichocephalic /dɒlɪkəʊsɪˈfælɪk/ *adj.* having a skull that is longer than it is wide, with a cephalic index of less than or equal to 75.9. Examples of dolichocephalic populations occur in the peoples of the Iberian Peninsula, Sardinia, Corsica, Sicily, south Italy, parts of France, the British Isles, Norway, and Sweden. —**dolichocephalous** /-ˈsefələs/ *adj.*, **dolichocephalism** /-ˈsef-/ *n.*, **dolichocephaly** /-ˈsef-/ *n.* [f. Gk *dolikhos* long + CEPHALIC]

Dolin /ˈdəʊlɪn, ˈdɒl-/, Anton (1904–83), real name Sydney Francis Patrick Chippendall Healey-Kay, British dancer, choreographer, teacher, actor, and writer. In 1935 he founded with Markova the Markova–Dolin Ballet, which toured until 1938, and in 1940 he joined the Ballet Theatre in New York. From another troupe newly formed with Markova the London Festival Ballet emerged in 1950, of which he became artistic director and first soloist until 1961. Later he pursued a worldwide freelance career as a teacher.

doll *n.* **1.** a small model of a human figure, especially a baby or child, as a child's toy; a ventriloquist's dummy. **2.** (*slang*) a young woman. —*v.t.* (*colloq.*) to dress *up* smartly. [pet-form of name *Dorothy*]

dollar /ˈdɒlə(r)/ *n.* the currency unit in the USA and certain other countries. Its ancestors were the Spanish peso (widely used as currency in North and South America in the 17th–18th c.) and the Bohemian *Joachimsthaler* of the early 16th c. The Spanish 'dollar' was formally retained as the standard unit of currency (with decimal subdivisions) in 1785. The first true American dollar was minted in 1794, but Spanish dollars continued in use and remained legal tender until 1857. The origin of the dollar sign $ is uncertain. It may be a modification of the figure 8 (representing 8 reals, the value of the peso), with upright strokes symbolizing the two architectural columns (representing the Pillars of Hercules) which for several centuries were conspicuous on the obverse of the Spanish peso; there are other less plausible suggestions. [f. LG f. G *thaler* (*Joachimsthaler*, coin from *Joachimstal* in Germany)]

Dollfuss /ˈdɒlfʊs/, Engelbert (1892–1934), Chancellor of Austria. After coming to power in 1932, Dollfuss attempted to govern without parliament in order better to oppose Nazi attempts to force Anschluss (union) with Germany. During an attempted Nazi coup in July 1934, he was assassinated by German SS troops dressed as Austrian soldiers, but his successor was able to prevent Anschluss until 1938.

dollop /ˈdɒləp/ *n.* (*colloq.*) a shapeless lump of food etc. [perh. f. Scand.]

dolly *n.* **1.** (*children's colloq.*) a doll. **2.** a movable platform for a cine-camera. —**dolly-bird** *n.* (*colloq.*) an attractive and stylish young woman. [f. DOLL]

dolman sleeve /ˈdɒlmən/ a loose sleeve cut in one piece with the body of a garment. [f. Turk.]

dolmen /ˈdɒlmən/ *n.* a megalithic chamber tomb with a

large flat stone laid on upright ones. [F, perh. f. Cornish *tolmēn* hole of stone]

dolomite /ˈdɒləmaɪt/ *n.* a mineral or rock of calcium magnesium carbonate. —**dolomitic** /-ˈmɪtɪk/ *adj.* [F, f. D. de *Dolomieu* French geologist (d. 1802)]

Dolomite Mountains /ˈdɒləmaɪt/ (also **Dolomites**) a range of the Alps in northern Italy, so named because the characteristic rock of the region is dolomitic limestone.

dolour /ˈdɒlə(r)/ *n.* (*literary*) sorrow, distress. —**dolorous** *adj.* [f. OF f. L (as DOLEFUL)]

dolphin *n.* a sea mammal (*Delphinus delphis*) like a porpoise but larger and with a slender pointed snout (ill. MAMMALS). There are many ancient (and some modern) stories of the dolphin's intelligence and friendliness towards man. [f. L *delphinus* f. Gk]

dolt /dəʊlt/ *n.* a stupid person. [prob. rel. to *dol* obs. var. of DULL]

Dom /dɒm/ *n.* a title prefixed to the names of some Roman Catholic dignitaries, and Benedictine and Carthusian monks. [f. L *dominus* master]

-dom *suffix* forming nouns, (1) from nouns or adjectives, denoting rank, condition, or domain (*earldom*, *freedom*, *kingdom*), (2) from nouns, denoting collective plural or in sense 'the ways of' —*s* (*officialdom*). [OE]

domain /dəˈmeɪn/ *n.* an area under one rule, a realm; an estate or lands under one control; a sphere of control or influence. [f. F, var. of DEMESNE]

dome /dəʊm/ *n.* a rounded vault forming a roof; a dome-shaped thing. [f. F f. It. *duomo* cathedral f. L *domus* house]

domed *adj.* having a dome or domes; shaped like a dome. [f. prec.]

Dome of the Rock an Islamic shrine in Jerusalem, surrounding the sacred rock on which, according to tradition, Abraham prepared to sacrifice his son (Gen. 22: 9) and from which the Prophet Muhammad made his miraculous midnight ascent into heaven. Built in the area of Solomon's Temple and dating from the end of the 7th c., to Muslims it is the third most holy place, after Mecca and Medina. The expanse of rough irregular rock that forms its centre contrasts starkly with the strict Byzantine geometry and ornate decoration of the surrounding structure, while the exterior is of rich mosaic work capped by a golden dome.

Domesday Book /ˈduːmzdeɪ/ a survey of property in England, excluding only London, Winchester, and the four northern counties, compiled on the orders of William the Conqueror in 1086 in order to provide a proper basis for taxation. The most comprehensive survey of property carried out in medieval times, it caused considerable popular discontent at the time of its compilation, and was given its name because, like the Day of Judgement, there could be no appeal against it.

domestic /dəˈmestɪk/ *adj.* of the home or household or family affairs; of one's own country, not foreign or international; fond of home life; (of an animal) kept by or living with man. —*n.* a household servant. —**domestic science**, home economics (see HOME). —**domestically** *adv.* [f. F f. L (*domus* house)]

domesticate /dəˈmestɪkeɪt/ *v.t.* to tame (an animal) to live with humans; to accustom to home life and management. [f. L (as prec.)]

domesticity /dɒməsˈtɪsɪtɪ/ *n.* being domestic; domestic or home life. [f. DOMESTIC]

domicile /ˈdɒmɪsaɪl/ *n.* a dwelling-place; (*Law*) a place of permanent residence, the fact of residing. [f. OF f. L (*domus* house)]

domiciled *adj.* having a domicile at or in. [f. prec.]

domiciliary /dɒmɪˈsɪlɪərɪ/ *adj.* of a dwelling-place (especially of the visit of a doctor, officials, etc., to a person's home). [f. F f. L (as DOMICILE)]

dominant /ˈdɒmɪnənt/ *adj.* dominating, prevailing; (of an inherited characteristic) appearing in offspring even when a corresponding opposite characteristic is also inherited. —*n.* (*Mus.*) the fifth note of the diatonic scale of any key. —**dominance** *n.* [F, f. L *dominari* (as foll.)]

dominate /ˈdɒmɪneɪt/ *v.t./i.* to have a commanding influence over; to be the most influential or conspicuous; (of a high place) to have a commanding position over. —**domination** /-ˈneɪʃ(ə)n/ *n.* [f. L *dominari* (*dominus* lord)]

domineer /dɒmɪˈnɪə(r)/ *v.i.* to behave in an arrogant and overbearing way. [f. Du. f. F *dominer* (as prec.)]

Dominic /ˈdɒmɪnɪk/, St (c.1170–1221), Spanish priest,

founder of the order named after him (see DOMINICAN). In 1203 he began his mission to convert the heretics known as the Albigenses, who were flourishing in SW Europe. In this he met with little success, but from it arose his foundation of a religious order dedicated to preaching and teaching. An austere figure and less popular than St Francis of Assisi, his contemporary, Dominic was a man of great integrity, humility, and courage. He is traditionally, but erroneously, held to have instituted the rosary. Feast day (now) 8 Aug.

Dominica /dɒmɪˈniːkə/ a mountainous island in the West Indies, the loftiest of the Lesser Antilles; pop. (1981) 74,069; official language, English; capital, Roseau. It was named by Columbus who discovered it on a Sunday (L *dies domenica* the Lord's day) in 1493, and after much Anglo-French rivalry came into British possession at the end of the 18th c., becoming an independent republic within the Commonwealth in 1978. —**Dominican** adj. & n.

Dominican /dəˈmɪnɪkən/ adj. of St Dominic or his order of friars and nuns (see below). —n. a Dominican friar or nun. [f. L (*Dominicus*, Latinized name of *Domingo* de Guzmán, St Dominic)]

The Dominican order was founded by St Dominic in 1216, and followed the established rule of St Augustine. It is known also as Black Friars (from the black cloak worn over a white habit) or in France as Jacobins. Its members are specially devoted to preaching and study, and their chief interest was, and is, educational. During the Middle Ages they supplied many leaders of European thought, including Albertus Magnus and St Thomas Aquinas; the popes used them for preaching crusades and for staffing the Inquisition. They followed the Portuguese and Spanish explorers, and though with the rise of new orders at the Reformation (especially the Jesuits, often their rivals) they fell into the background, they remain one of the most influential orders and retain their original characteristics as champions of learning and orthodoxy.

Dominican Republic /dəˈmɪnɪkən/ a country in the Caribbean, the Spanish-speaking eastern portion of the island named Hispaniola by Columbus, who discovered it in 1492; pop. (1981) 5,647,977; official language, Spanish; capital, Santo Domingo. The Republic is the former Spanish colony of Santo Domingo, the part of Hispaniola which Spain retained when she ceded the western portion (now Haiti) to France in 1697. After the colony of Santo Domingo had itself been made over to France in 1795 and twice been overrun by Haiti, a Republic was proclaimed in 1844. The history of the Republic has been turbulent, culminating in the ruthless dictatorship (1930-61) of Rafael Trujillo Molina. An unsettled period followed, with civil war and US military intervention; a new constitution was introduced in 1966. The country occupies a strategic position on major sea routes leading from both Europe and the USA to the Panama Canal. —**Dominican** adj. & n.

dominion /dəˈmɪnjən/ n. 1. sovereignty, control. 2. the territory of a sovereign or government, a domain. 3. (*hist.*) the title of the self-governing territories of the British Commonwealth. [f. OF f. L (*dominus* lord)]

domino[1] /ˈdɒmɪnəʊ/ n. a loose cloak with a mask for the upper part of the face, formerly worn at masquerades. [F, prob. as prec. but unexplained]

domino[2] /ˈdɒmɪnəʊ/ n. each of 28 small oblong pieces marked with (usually) 0-6 pips in each half; (in *pl.*) the game played with these. It was played anciently in China but was unknown in Europe (where it may have arisen independently) before the 18th c., and was introduced to England possibly by French prisoners by about 1800. —**domino theory**, the theory that one (especially a political) event precipitates others in a causal sequence, like a row of dominoes falling over. [perhaps named from the semblance of the black back of the domino to the masquerade garment of the same name: see prec.]

Domitian /dəˈmɪʃ(ə)n/ (Titus Flavius Domitianus 51-96), Roman emperor 81-96, son of Vespasian. An energetic but autocratic ruler, his assassination ended the Reign of Terror of his last few years. His absolutism found expression in large building programmes, including monumental palace-buildings on the Palatine Hill in Rome.

Don a river of the southern USSR, flowing into the Sea of Azov.

don[1] n. 1. a head, fellow, or tutor of a college, especially at Oxford or Cambridge. 2. **Don**, a Spanish title prefixed to a man's Christian name. [Sp., f. L *dominus* lord]

don[2] v.t. (**-nn-**) to put on (clothing etc.). [= do on]

Donald Duck a Disney cartoon character, a duck with a rubbery rear, twistable neck, and a big mouth, who first appeared in 1934. His lines were quacked by Clarence Nash (d. 1985).

donate /dəʊˈneɪt/ v.t. to give or contribute (money etc.), especially voluntarily to a fund or institution. [back-formation f. foll.]

Donatello /dɒnəˈtɛləʊ/, Donato di Niccolo (1386-1466), Florentine sculptor, one of the pioneers of scientific perspective. He is famous especially for his lifelike sculptures, including the bronze *David*, his most classical work. He was in Padua from 1443 to 1453, where he made the *Gattamelata*, the first equestrian statue to be created since antiquity. On his return to Florence he reacted somewhat against classical principles, evolving a very moving late style in which distortion is used to convey dramatic and emotional intensity, e.g. his *John the Baptist* and the carved wooden statue *St Mary Magdalene*.

donation /dəʊˈneɪʃ(ə)n/ n. an act of donating; an amount donated. [f. OF f. L (*donum* gift)]

Donatist /ˈdəʊnətɪst/ n. a member of a Christian sect which arose in North Africa in 311 out of a dispute about the election of the bishop of Carthage, and which maintained that it was the only true and pure Church and that the ordinations of others were invalid. —**Donatism** n. [f. L, = follower of Donatus, bishop of Carthage, or a schismatic leader of the same name]

Donatus /dəˈneɪtəs/, Aelius (4th c.) Roman grammarian. His two grammatical treatises, the *Ars Minor* (*Lesser Art*) and the *Ars Maior* (*Major Art*) were favourite school-books in the Middle Ages.

done /dʌn/ p.p. of DO[1]. —adj. 1. completed; cooked. 2. (of an action or behaviour etc.) socially acceptable. 3. (as *int.* in reply to an offer etc.) accepted. 4. (*colloq.*) tired out (often with *in* or *up*). —**be done with**, to have finished with. **done for**, in serious trouble. **have done with**, to finish dealing with.

Donizetti /dɒnɪˈtseti/, Gaetano (1797-1848), the leading Italian composer between the death of Bellini (1835) and Verdi's first great success in 1842. His tragedies—*Anna Bolena* (1830), *Maria Stuarda* (1835), and *Lucia di Lammermoor* (1835)—all reveal the prevailing taste for librettos set in the wild and romantic north, and his comedies *L'elisir d'amore* (1832) and *La fille du régiment* (1840) reveal him as a master rivalling Rossini.

donjon /ˈdɒndʒ(ə)n/ n. the great tower or keep of a castle. [archaic spelling of DUNGEON]

Don Juan /ˈdʒuːən/ legendary Spanish nobleman of dissolute life. According to a Spanish story first dramatized by Gabriel Tellez (d. 1641) and subsequently by Molière and in Mozart's opera *Don Giovanni*, he was Don Juan Tenorio of Seville. The name is used allusively of a heartless seducer of women, a libertine. [f. DON[1]]

donkey /ˈdɒŋkɪ/ n. 1. a domestic ass (see ASS[1]). 2. (*colloq.*) a stupid person. —**donkey engine**, a small auxiliary engine. **donkey jacket**, a workman's thick weatherproof jacket. **donkey's years**, (*colloq.*) a very long time. **donkey-work** n. the laborious part of a job. [perh. f. proper name *Duncan* (cf. NEDDY)]

Donkin /ˈdɒŋkɪn/, Bryan (1768-1855), English engineer who made pioneering contributions in several fields, including paper-making and printing, patenting (with Richard Bacon) the first rotary press. Following the work of Nicholas Appert in France he successfully developed the method of food preservation by heat sterilization and sealing the food inside a container made of sheet steel—the ubiquitous tin can (see TIN).

Donna /ˈdɒnə/ n. the title of an Italian, Spanish, or Portuguese lady. [It., f. L *domina* mistress; cf. DON[1]]

Donne /dʌn/, John (1572-1631), English poet and divine, who was born into a devout Catholic family but renounced his faith c.1593. After troubled early years, when his prospects of worldly advancement were ruined by his secret marriage to his patron's niece, he turned to a successful career in the Church, becoming dean of St Paul's in 1621 and one of the most celebrated of the metaphysical poets; his love poetry (*Song and Sonnets*), satires, and divine poems all display his brilliant wit, passionate temperament, verbal ingenuity, and creative vigour. Out of fashion in the 18th-19th c., his works are now widely admired, interest having been aroused partly by T. S. Eliot's reappraisal.

donnish adj. like a college don; pedantic. [f. DON[1]]

donor /ˈdəʊnə(r)/ n. one who gives or donates something;

one who provides blood for transfusion, semen for insemination, or an organ or tissue for transplantation. [f. AF f. L *donator* (as DONATION)]

Don Quixote see QUIXOTE.

don't /dəʊnt/ (*colloq.*) = do not. —*n.* a prohibition. [f. DO[1]]

doodle *v.t./i.* to scribble or draw, esp. absent-mindedly. —*n.* a scribble or drawing made by doodling. [orig. = foolish person; cf. LG *dudelkopf*]

doom *n.* a grim fate or destiny, death or ruin; a condemnation. —*v.t.* to condemn or destine *to.* [OE, = statute]

doomsday /ˈduːmzdeɪ/ *n.* the day of the Last Judgement. —**till doomsday**, for ever. [f. prec.]

door /dɔː(r)/ *n.* **1.** a hinged, sliding, or revolving barrier for closing the entrance to a building, room, cupboard, etc. (ill. HOUSES); this as representing a house etc.; a doorway. **2.** an entrance or exit, the means of access or approach. —**door-keeper** *n.* a doorman. **door-to-door** *adj.* (of selling etc.) done at each house in turn. [OE]

doorbell *n.* a bell in a house rung at the front door by visitors to signal arrival.

doorknob *n.* a knob for turning to release the latch of a door.

doorman *n.* (*pl.* **-men**) a person on duty at the entrance to a large building.

doormat *n.* **1.** a mat at an entrance, for wiping the shoes. **2.** a feebly submissive person.

doorstep *n.* **1.** a step leading to the outer door of a house etc.; a point in front of this. **2.** (*slang*) a thick slice of bread. —**on one's doorstep**, very close.

doorstop *n.* a device for keeping a door open or to prevent it from striking a wall etc. when opened.

doorway *n.* an opening filled by a door.

dope *n.* **1.** a thick liquid used as a lubricant etc.; varnish. **2.** (*slang*) a drug, especially a narcotic; a drug or stimulant given to an athlete etc. to affect performance. **3.** (*slang*) information. **4.** (*slang*) a stupid person. —*v.t./i.* **1.** to treat with dope. **2.** to give a drug or stimulant to; to take addictive drugs. [f. Du. *doop* sauce]

dopey /ˈdəʊpɪ/ *adj.* (*slang*) half asleep; stupefied by or as by a drug; stupid. —**dopiness** *n.* [f. prec.]

doppelgänger /ˈdɒp(ə)lɡeŋə(r)/ *n.* the wraith of a living person. [G, = double-goer]

Doppler effect /ˈdɒplə(r)/ the apparent increase (or decrease) in the frequency of sound, light, and other waves when the source and the observer become closer (or more distant). [f. C. J. *Doppler* Austrian physicist (d. 1853)]

dorado /dəˈrɑːdəʊ/ *n.* (*pl.* **-os**) a blue and silver sea-fish of the genus *Coryphaena*, showing brilliant colours when it dies out of water. [Sp., = gilt]

Dordogne /dɔːˈdɔɪn/ an inland department of SW France containing numerous caves and rock-shelters that have yielded abundant remains of early man and his artefacts and art. Fossils of both Neanderthal and Cro-Magnon man have been recovered from its caves and rock-shelters. The walls and ceilings of many of the caves and shelters have served as surfaces upon which the people of the upper palaeolithic expressed their artistic representations of animals, 'hunting magic', and abstract designs. The cave and shelter fillings have also yielded engraved and sculpted bones, antlers, ivory, and clay that have been produced by the populations responsible for the murals. The cave at Lascaux is but a single example of the vast richness of the department's art and archaeology.

Dorian /ˈdɔːrɪən/ *n.* a member of the tribes speaking the Doric dialect of Greek who probably originated from NW Greece and by the 8th c. BC had settled most of the Peloponnese, the southernmost Aegean islands, and the SW corner of Asia Minor. While culturally distinct in architecture and dialect, the Dorians retained their political system only in Sparta and Crete where the ruling military class subjected the local peoples as serfs and dependants. (See DARK AGES.) —*adj.* of the Dorians. [f. L f. Gk]

Doric /ˈdɒrɪk/ *adj.* **1.** (of a dialect) broad, rustic. **2.** (*Archit.*) of the oldest and simplest of the Greek orders (ill. TEMPLES). —*n.* rustic English or (esp.) Scots. [f. L f. Gk (*Doris* in Greece)]

dormant /ˈdɔːmənt/ *adj.* sleeping, lying inactive as in a sleep; temporarily inactive; (of plants) alive but not actively growing. —**dormancy** *n.* [f. partic. of OF *dormir* sleep f. L *dormire*]

dormer *n.* a projecting upright window in a sloping roof (ill. HOUSES). [f. OF (as prec.)]

dormitory /ˈdɔːmɪtərɪ/ *n.* **1.** a sleeping-room with several beds, especially in a school or institution. **2.** (in full **dormitory town**) a small town or suburb from which people travel to work in a city etc. [f. L (*dormire* sleep)]

dormouse /ˈdɔːmaʊs/ *n.* (*pl.* **-mice** /-maɪs/) a mouselike hibernating rodent of the family Gliridae. [orig. unkn.]

dormy /ˈdɔːmɪ/ *adj.* as many holes ahead in the score of golf as there are holes left to play. [orig. unkn.]

dorsal /ˈdɔːs(ə)l/ *adj.* of or on the back. —**dorsally** *adv.* [F, or f. L (*dorsum* back)]

Dorset /ˈdɔːsɪt/ a county of SW England.

dory /ˈdɔːrɪ/ *n.* (also **John Dory**) an edible sea-fish, *Zeus faber.* [f. F *dorée* gilded]

dosage /ˈdəʊsɪdʒ/ *n.* the giving of a dose; the size of a dose. [f. foll.]

dose *n.* **1.** the amount of medicine to be taken at one time; an amount of flattery, punishment, etc.; an amount of radiation received by a person or thing. **2.** (*slang*) a venereal infection. —*v.t.* to give a dose or doses of medicine to; to treat (a person or animal) *with.* [F f. L f. Gk *dosis* gift]

dosimeter /dəʊˈsɪmɪtə(r)/ *n.* a device for measuring the amount of a dose; a recording device to measure ionizing radiation, especially one worn by a person exposed to potentially harmful radiation. [f. DOSE + -METER]

doss *v.i.* (*slang*) to sleep, especially in a doss-house. —**doss down**, (*slang*) to sleep on a makeshift bed. **doss-house** *n.* (*slang*) a cheap lodging-house. [prob. = *doss* ornamental cover for seat-back, f. OF *dos* back (as DORSAL)]

dossier /ˈdɒsɪə(r), -ɪeɪ/ *n.* a set of documents containing information about a person or event. [F, f. label on back (*dos,* as prec.)]

Dostoevsky /dɒstɔɪˈefskɪ/, Fedor Mikhailovich (1821–81), Russian novelist who was arrested in 1849 as a member of the socialist Petrashevsky Circle and after a macabre mock execution sent to Siberia for four years, followed by four years as a private soldier. During his imprisonment he suffered a spiritual crisis and rejected his early socialist ideals, replacing them with orthodox religion and a faith in the Russian people; this period is reflected in *Notes from the House of the Dead* (1860–1). He made visits abroad during the 1860s, including one to London, which he saw as the centre of the capitalist world, and used this image to express the corruption of the modern scientific world in *Notes from Underground* (1864). The series of novels that are most admired include *Crime and Punishment* (1866), *The Idiot* (1868), *The Devils* (1872), and *The Brothers Karamazov* (1880). In these he revels his genius for character analysis and conveys his religious and political ideas and basic philosophy—that human beings are morally improved by having to undergo physical pain and public humiliation. He influenced the development of the Russian novel through the use of urban settings and by powerful narrative tension.

dot *n.* **1.** a small round mark or spot; this as part of *i* or *j* or as a decimal point. **2.** the shorter of the two signals used in the Morse code. —*v.t.* (**-tt-**) **1.** to mark with a dot or dots; to cover parts of as with dots. **2.** (*slang*) to hit. —**dotted line,** a line of dots on a document to show the place for a signature. **dot the i's and cross the t's,** to be minutely accurate; to emphasize details. **on the dot,** exactly on time. **the year dot,** (*colloq.*) far in the past. [perh. = OE *dott* head of boil]

dotage /ˈdəʊtɪdʒ/ *n.* feeble-minded senility. [f. DOTE]

dotard /ˈdəʊtəd/ *n.* a person who is in his dotage. [f. foll.]

dote *v.i.* to be silly or infatuated. —**dote on,** to be excessively fond of. [cf. MDu. *doten* be silly]

dotterel /ˈdɒtər(ə)l/ *n.* a small migrant plover, *Eudromias morinellus.* [f. prec.; named from the ease with which it is caught, a supposed sign of stupidity]

dottle *n.* the remnant of unburnt tobacco in a pipe. [f. DOT]

dotty *adj.* (*colloq.*) feeble-minded, eccentric, silly. —**dottiness** *n.* [f. DOT]

Douai /ˈduːeɪ/ a town in Flanders where colleges were established for English Roman Catholic scholars exiled under Elizabeth I. It gave its name to an English translation of the Bible, completed there in the early 17th c., that was used in the Roman Catholic Church until recently.

double[1] /ˈdʌb(ə)l/ *adj.* **1.** consisting of two parts or things. **2.** twofold, multiplied by two; twice as much or many. **3.** having twice the usual quantity, size, strength, etc.; having some part double; (of a flower) having more than one circle of petals. **4.** folded, stooping. **5.** ambiguous, deceitful, hypocritical. **6.** (of a musical instrument) lower in pitch by an octave. —*adv.* at or to twice the amount etc.; two together. —*n.* **1.** a double quantity or thing; a double measure of spirits etc.; twice as much or many. **2.** the counterpart of a person or thing, a person who looks exactly like another. **3.** (in *pl.*) a game between two pairs of players. **4.** a pair of victories over the same team or of championships at the same game etc.; a system of betting in which the winnings and stake from the first bet are transferred to a second; a doubling of an opponent's bid in bridge; a hit on the narrow ring between the outer circles in darts. —**at the double,** running, hurrying. **double agent,** one who spies simultaneously for two rival countries. **double axe,** a double-bladed axe with a perforation between the blades for the handle, especially as a characteristic Minoan and Mycenaean tool and one of the most common Minoan religious symbols. **double-barrelled** *adj.* (of a gun) having two barrels; (of a name) having two parts with a hyphen. **double-bass** /beɪs/ *n.* the largest and lowest-pitched instrument of the violin family, now possessing four strings (formerly three) and sounding an octave below the cello, with a range of nearly three octaves (ill. ORCHESTRA). **double-breasted** *adj.* (of a coat etc.) having fronts that overlap to fasten across the breast. **double-check** *v.t.* to verify twice or in two ways. **double chin,** a chin with a fold of loose flesh below it. **double cream,** thick cream with a high fat-content. **double-cross** *v.t.* to deceive or betray (a person one is supposedly helping); (as *n.*) an act of doing this. **double-dealing** *n.* deceit, especially in business; (as *adj.*) practising deceit. **double-decker** *n.* a bus with two decks. **double Dutch,** gibberish. **double eagle,** a figure of a two-headed eagle. **double-edged** *adj.* having two cutting-edges; (*fig.*) damaging to the user as well as his opponent. **double entry,** a system of book-keeping in which each transaction is entered as a debit in one account and a credit in another. **double figures,** the numbers from 10 to 99. **double glazing,** two layers of glass in a window to reduce loss of heat and exclude noise. **double helix,** a pair of parallel helices with a common axis, especially in the structure of the DNA molecule. **double-jointed** *adj.* having joints that allow unusual bending of the fingers etc. **double or quits,** a gamble to decide whether a player's loss or debt be doubled or cancelled. **double-park** *v.i.* to park a vehicle alongside one that is already parked at the roadside. **double pneumonia,** that affecting both lungs. **double-quick** *adj.* & *adv.* very quick(ly). **double standard,** a rule or principle applied more strictly to some than to others (or to oneself). **double star,** two stars that are actually or apparently very close together. **double-stopping** *n.* the sounding of two strings at once on a violin etc. **double take,** a delayed reaction to a situation etc. immediately after one's first reaction. **double-talk** *n.* verbal expression that is (usually deliberately) ambiguous or misleading. **double-think** *n.* a mental capacity to accept contrary opinions at the same time. **double time,** payment of an employee at twice the normal rate. —**doubly** *adv.* [f. OF f. L *duplus*]

double² /ˈdʌb(ə)l/ *v.t./i.* **1.** to make or become double, to increase twofold, to multiply by two; to amount to twice as much. **2.** to fold or bend over on itself, to become folded. **3.** to act (two parts) in the same play etc.; to be an understudy etc. (*for*); to play a twofold role (as). **4.** to turn sharply in flight or pursuit; (of a ship) to sail round (a headland). **5.** to make a call in bridge increasing the value of points to be won or lost on (an opponent's bid). —**double back,** to take a new direction opposite to the previous one. **double-talk** *n.* verbal expression that is (deliberately) ambiguous etc. **double-think** *n.* the mental capacity to accept contrary opinions etc. at the same time. **double up,** to bend or curl up with pain or laughter, to cause to do this; to share or cause to share a room, quarters, etc., with another or others. [as prec.]

double entendre /duːbl ɑ̃ˈtɑ̃dr/ a phrase affording two meanings, one usually indecent. [obs. F, = double understanding]

doublet /ˈdʌblɪt/ *n.* **1.** a man's close-fitting jacket, with or without sleeves, worn in the 15th–17th c. (ill. DRESS). **2.** either of a pair of similar things. [as DOUBLE¹]

doubloon /dʌbˈluːn/ *n.* a former Spanish gold coin. [f. F or Sp. (as DOUBLE¹)]

doubt /daʊt/ *n.* a feeling of uncertainty about something, an undecided state of mind; an inclination to disbelieve; an uncertain state of things; a lack of full proof or clear indication. —*v.t./i.* to feel uncertain or undecided (about); to hesitate to believe; to call in question. —**no doubt,**

certainly, probably, admittedly. **without (a) doubt,** certainly. —**doubter** *n.* [f. OF f. L *dubitare*]

doubtful *adj.* feeling doubt; causing doubt, unreliable, undecided. —**doubtfully** *adv.*, **doubtfulness** *n.* [f. DOUBT + -FUL]

doubtless *adv.* certainly, probably. [f. DOUBT + -LESS]

douche /duːʃ/ *n.* a jet of liquid applied to a part of the body for cleansing or for a medicinal purpose; a device for producing such a jet. —*v.t./i.* to treat with a douche; to use a douche. [F f. It. *doccia* pipe f. L (as DUCT)]

dough /dəʊ/ *n.* **1.** a thick mixture of flour etc. and liquid, for baking. **2.** (*slang*) money. —**doughy** *adj.* [OE]

doughnut /ˈdəʊnʌt/ *n.* a small sweetened fried cake of dough. [f. prec.]

doughty /ˈdaʊtɪ/ *adj.* (*archaic* or *joc.*) valiant, stouthearted. —**doughtily** *adv.*, **doughtiness** *n.* [OE]

Douglas /ˈdʌɡləs/ *n.* **Douglas fir, pine,** *or* **spruce,** a large conifer of the genus *Pseudotsuga*, originally of western North America. [f. D. *Douglas*, Sc. botanist (d. 1834)]

dour /dʊə(r)/ *adj.* stern, severe, obstinate. —**dourly** *adv.*, **dourness** *n.* [prob. f. Gaelic *dúr* dull, obstinate]

douse /daʊs/ *v.t.* **1.** to plunge into water, to throw water over. **2.** to extinguish (a light). [perh. rel. to MDu., LG *dossen* strike]

dove /dʌv/ *n.* **1.** a bird of the family Columbidae, with short legs, small head, and large breast. **2.** an advocate of peace or peaceful policy. **3.** a gentle or innocent person. [f. ON (perh. imit.)]

dovecote /ˈdʌvkɒt/ *n.* a shelter with nesting-holes for domesticated pigeons.

dovetail *n.* a joint formed by a mortise with a tenon shaped like a dove's spread tail (ill. CARPENTRY). —*v.t./i.* **1.** to fit together with dovetails. **2.** to fit together or combine neatly.

dowager /ˈdaʊədʒə(r)/ *n.* a woman with a title or property derived from her late husband; (*colloq.*) a dignified elderly woman. [f. OF (*douage*, as DOWER)]

dowdy /ˈdaʊdɪ/ *adj.* (of clothes) unattractively dull; (of a person) dressed in dowdy clothes. —**dowdily** *adv.*, **dowdiness** *n.* [orig. unkn.]

dowel /ˈdaʊəl/ *n.* a headless wooden or metal pin for holding two pieces of wood or stone together. —*v.t.* (**-ll-**) to fasten with a dowel (ill. CARPENTRY). [f. MLG *dovel*]

dowelling *n.* round rods for cutting into dowels. [f. prec.]

dower /ˈdaʊə(r)/ *n.* **1.** a widow's share for life of her husband's estate. **2.** (*archaic*) a dowry. —*v.t.* **1.** (*archaic*) to give a dowry to. **2.** to endow *with* talent etc. —**dower house,** a smaller house near a big one, forming part of a widow's dower. [f. OF f. L *dotarium* (dos dowry)]

Dow-Jones index *or* **average** /daʊˈdʒəʊnz/ a figure indicating the relative price of American securities based on the current average rates of an agreed select list of industrial and other stocks. The first index was devised in 1897 on the basis of twelve stocks; its scope was later widened. [f. C. H. *Dow* (d. 1902) and E. D. *Jones* (d. 1920), Amer. economists]

Down /daʊn/ a county of Northern Ireland.

down¹ /daʊn/ *adv.* **1.** at, in, or towards a lower place, level, value, or condition, or a place etc. regarded as lower; to a finer consistency or smaller amount or size; southwards, further south; away from a central place or capital city or university; in or into a less strong or less active or losing position or condition; into quiescence; incapacitated *with* (an illness etc.). **2.** from an erect or vertical position to a horizontal one. **3.** so as to be deflated. **4.** from an earlier to a later time. **5.** in writing; in or into a recorded form. **6.** to its source or place. **7.** as a payment at the time of purchase. —*prep.* **1.** downwards along, through, or into; from the top to the bottom of; along. **2.** at or in a lower part of. —*adj.* directed downwards; (of travel) away from a capital or centre. —*v.t.* (*colloq.*) to knock or bring down; to swallow. —*n.* **1.** an act of putting down. **2.** a reverse of fortune (often in *ups and downs*). —**down and out,** penniless, destitute. **down-and-out** *n.* a destitute person. **down-hearted** *adj.* dejected. **down in the mouth,** looking unhappy. **down on,** holding in disfavour. **down payment,** a partial payment made at the time of purchase. **down stage,** at or to the front of a theatre stage. **down-to-earth** *adj.* practical, realistic. **down tools,** to cease work; to go on strike. **down to the ground,** (*colloq.*) completely. **down under,** in the antipodes, especially Australia. **down with** *int.* of disgust with or rejection of a stated person or thing. **have a down on,** to hold in disfavour. [f. earlier *adown* (f. DOWN³)]

down² *n.* the first covering of young birds, a bird's under-plumage (ill. BIRDS); fine soft feathers or short hairs; a fluffy substance. [f. ON]

down[3] *n.* **1.** (also **downland**) an area of high open land. **2.** (in *pl.*) chalk uplands especially of southern England. [OE, rel. to DUNE]

downbeat *n.* an accented beat in music, when the conductor's baton moves downwards. —*adj.* **1.** pessimistic, gloomy. **2.** relaxed.

downcast *adj.* **1.** (of the eyes) looking downwards. **2.** (of a person) dejected.

downfall *n.* a fall from prosperity or power; a cause of this.

downgrade *v.t.* to lower in grade or rank.

downhill *adv.* down a slope; in a descending direction. —*adj.* sloping downwards, declining. —**go downhill,** to deteriorate.

Downing Street /ˈdaʊnɪŋ/ a street in Westminster, London, between Whitehall and St James's Park. It was built by the diplomat Sir George Downing (d. 1684), described by Pepys as 'a most ungrateful villain'. His friend and benefactor Colonel Okey was one of the people who had signed the death warrant of Charles I; Downing betrayed him to the Royalists (who then executed Okey), and the street now named after him was his reward. In 1732 No. 10 was acquired on a Crown lease by Sir Robert Walpole, Britain's first Prime Minister, who accepted it on behalf of all future Lords of the Treasury (still the formal title of the Prime Minister). This house is the official town residence of the Prime Minister, No. 11 that of the Chancellor of the Exchequer, and the Foreign and Commonwealth Office is also situated in this street, whence the allusive use of its name to refer to the British government, Prime Minister, etc.

downpipe *n.* a pipe for carrying rain-water from a roof to a drain.

downpour *n.* a heavy fall of rain.

downright *adj.* plain, straightforward; utter, complete. —*adv.* thoroughly, completely.

Down's syndrome /daʊnz/ an abnormal congenital condition in which a person has a broad flattened skull, slanting eyes, and mental deficiency (also called *mongolism* from some physical resemblance to Mongoloid peoples). [f. J. L. H. *Down* physician (d. 1896)]

downstairs *adv.* down the stairs; to or on a lower floor. —*adj.* situated downstairs. —*n.* a downstairs floor.

downstream *adj.* & *adv.* in the direction in which a stream flows; moving downstream.

downtown *adj.* (*US*) of a lower or more central part of a town or city. —*adv.* (*US*) in or into this part. —*n.* (*US*) a downtown area.

downtrodden *adj.* oppressed, badly treated.

downturn *n.* a decline, especially in an economic or business activity.

downward /ˈdaʊnwəd/ *adv.* (also **downwards** /-z/) towards what is lower, inferior, less important, or later. — *adj.* moving or extending downwards. [f. DOWN[1] + -WARD]

downwind *adj.* & *adv.* in the direction in which the wind is blowing.

downy *adj.* **1.** of or like down, soft and fluffy. **2.** (*slang*) aware, knowing. [f. DOWN[2]]

dowry /ˈdaʊərɪ/ *n.* property or money brought by a bride to her husband. [f. AF & OF, = dower]

dowse[1] /daʊz/ *v.i.* to search for underground water or minerals by holding a Y-shaped stick or rod (*dowsing-rod*) which dips abruptly when over the right spot. —**dowser** *n.* [orig. unkn.]

dowse[2] /daʊs/ var. of DOUSE.

doxology /dɒkˈsɒlədʒɪ/ *n.* a liturgical formula of praise to God. [f. L f. Gk (*doxa* glory, -LOGY)]

doyen /ˈdɔɪən/ *n.* a senior member of a body of colleagues. —**doyenne** /-ˈen/ *n. fem.* [F. (as DEAN)]

Doyle /dɔɪl/, Sir Arthur Conan (1859-1930), Scottish-born novelist, who qualified in medicine at Edinburgh, creator of the archetypal private detective Sherlock Holmes and his friend and foil the ingenuous Dr Watson, who are embodied in a cycle of stories. The first of these, *A Study in Scarlet* (1887) was followed by a series of historical and other romances for half a century. Notable among them are *Micah Clarke* (1889), *The White Company* (1891), *The Exploits of Brigadier Gerard* (1896), and *Rodney Stone* (1896). *The Lost World* (1912), an early work of science fiction, introduced the scientist-explorer Professor Chal-

lenger, for whose photograph the author himself posed wearing a false beard and whiskers. Doyle's patriotism was shown in his defence of British policy in the second Boer War (in which he served), for which he was knighted. During his later years, following the death of his son in the First World War, he became much interested in spiritualism.

doz. *abbr.* dozen.

doze *v.i.* to be half asleep, to sleep lightly. —*n.* a short light sleep. —**doze off,** to fall lightly asleep. [orig. unkn.]

dozen /ˈdʌz(ə)n/ *n.* **1.** (for plural usage see HUNDRED) twelve, a set of twelve. **2.** (in *pl.*) very many. —**talk nineteen to the dozen,** to talk incessantly. [f. OF ult. f. L *duodecim* twelve]

dozy /ˈdəʊzɪ/ *adj.* drowsy; (*colloq.*) stupid, lazy. [f. DOZE]

D.Phil. *abbr.* Doctor of Philosophy.

DPP *abbr.* Director of Public Prosecutions.

Dr *abbr.* Doctor.

drab *adj.* **1.** dull, uninteresting. **2.** of a dull brownish colour. —*n.* drab colour. —**drably** *adv.*, **drabness** *n.* [f. obs. *drap* cloth f. OF f. L]

Drabble /ˈdræb(ə)l/, Margaret (1939-), English novelist, whose early works, such as *The Garrick Year* (1964) and *The Millstone* (1966) are much concerned with the conflicts of career and motherhood. Her later novels (e.g. *The Needle's Eye*, 1972, and *The Ice Age*, 1977) have a larger canvas and a more documentary approach to English social life.

drachm /dræm/ *n.* a weight formerly used by apothecaries, one eighth of an ounce. [f. OF or L (as foll.)]

drachma /ˈdrækmə/ *n.* (*pl.* **-as**) **1.** the unit of currency of Greece. **2.** silver coin of ancient Greece. [L f. Gk *drakhmē*]

Draconian /drəˈkəʊnɪən/ *adj.* (of laws) very harsh, cruel. [f. *Drakōn* (*c.*620 BC), said to have established severe laws in ancient Athens]

Dracula /ˈdrækjʊlə/ the king of the vampires in Bram Stoker's novel *Dracula* (1897), located in a lonely castle in Transylvania. Vlad Tepeş (Vlad the Impaler), also known as Dracula, was a 15th-c. prince of Wallachia, renowned for his cruelty, and the novelist has woven this name into a sinister tale of a region with which vampires and werewolves were traditionally associated.

draft /drɑːft/ *n.* **1.** a rough preliminary outline of a scheme or written version of a speech, document, etc. **2.** a written order for the payment of money by a bank; drawing of money by this. **3.** a detachment from a larger group for a special duty or purpose; selection of this; (*US*) conscription. —*v.t.* **1.** to prepare a draft of (writing or a scheme). **2.** to select for a special duty or purpose; (*US*) to conscript. [phonetic spelling of DRAUGHT]

draftsman *n.* (*pl.* **-men**) one who drafts documents.

drag *v.t./i.* (**-gg-**) **1.** to pull or pass along with effort, difficulty, or friction; to trail or allow to trail along the ground; (*colloq.*) to take (a person *to*, especially against his will). **2.** to use a grapnel, to search (the bottom of a lake or river etc.) with grapnels, nets, etc. **3.** (*colloq.*) to draw *on* or *at* (a cigarette etc.). —*n.* **1.** a hindrance to progress; a longitudinal retarding force exerted by air on aircraft etc. in flight (ill. FLIGHT). **2.** a retarded motion. **3.** (*colloq.*) a boring or tiresome person, duty, etc. **4.** a lure drawn before hounds as a substitute for a fox; a hunt using this; an apparatus for dredging etc.; a drag-net. **5.** (*slang*) a draw on a cigarette etc. **6.** (*slang*) women's clothes worn by men. —**drag one's feet,** to be deliberately slow or reluctant to act. **drag in,** to introduce a subject) irrelevantly. **drag-net** *n.* a net drawn through a river or across ground to trap fish or game; a systematic hunt for criminals etc. **drag on,** to continue tediously. **drag out,** to prolong at length. **drag race,** an acceleration race between cars over a short distance. **drag up,** (*colloq.*) to introduce or revive (an unwelcome subject). [OE or ON (as DRAW)]

draggle *v.t./i.* to make dirty, wet, or limp by trailing; to hang trailing. [f. prec.]

dragon /ˈdrægən/ *n.* **1.** a mythical monster like a reptile, usually with wings and able to breathe out fire (see below). **2.** a fierce person. [f. OF f. L f. Gk *drakōn* serpent]

The dragon is probably the commonest emblem in Far Eastern art, and the most ancient. A form with five claws on each foot (Oriental dragons normally have four) was adopted as the chief imperial emblem in China. Fundamentally the dragon represented fertilizing power, cosmic energy revealing itself in nature. It resided especially in water, in rivers, lakes, and the sea; in springtime it moved in heaven among the clouds. In the art of the West the dragon appears in such contexts as St George slaying the dragon as a symbol of threat and destruction, and is used as a heraldic emblem (ill. HERALDRY).

dragon-fly n. an insect of the order Neuroptera, with a long body and two pairs of transparent wings (ill. INSECTS).

dragoon /drə'guːn/ n. **1.** a cavalryman (orig. a mounted infantryman). **2.** a fierce fellow. —v.t. to force *into* doing something. [orig. = carbine, f. F *dragon* (as prec.)]

drain v.t./i. **1.** to draw off liquid from; to draw off (a liquid). **2.** to flow or trickle away. **3.** to dry or become dry as liquid flows away; to exhaust of strength or resources. **4.** to drink (a liquid), to empty (a glass etc.) by drinking the contents. —n. **1.** a channel, conduit, or pipe carrying off a liquid, sewage, etc. **2.** a constant outlet or expenditure. —**down the drain**, (*colloq.*) lost, wasted. **drain-pipe** n. a pipe for carrying off surplus water or liquid sewage from a building. **draining-board** n. a sloping grooved surface beside a sink on which washed dishes etc. are left to drain.

drainage n. **1.** draining; a system of drains. **2.** what is drained off. [f. prec.]

drake n. a male duck. [app. f. second element in OHG *antrehho*]

Drake, Sir Francis (c.1540–96), Elizabethan sailor and explorer, the most daring and successful of English privateers in the Spanish West Indies. In 1577 he was backed by Elizabeth I in an enterprise of circumnavigation with the prospect of loot in Spanish seas. Having passed through the Magellan Straits he plundered the South American settlements before sailing his ship, the *Golden Hind*, up the Californian coast. From there he traversed the Pacific, sailed round the Cape of Good Hope, and arrived back in Plymouth in 1580 a rich man, being knighted in the following year. His successful raid on Cadiz in 1587 (the operation known as 'singeing the king of Spain's beard') delayed the sailing of the Armada by a year by destroying its supply-ships, and the next year he played an important part in its defeat in the Channel. Like his cousin, Sir John Hawkins, Drake died at sea during their unsuccessful expedition to the West Indies.

dram n. **1.** a small drink of spirits. **2.** = DRACHM. [f. OF *drame* or L *drama* (as DRACHM)]

drama /'drɑːmə/ n. **1.** a play for acting on stage or for broadcasting. **2.** the art of writing and presenting plays. **3.** a dramatic series of events; dramatic quality. [L f. Gk (*draō* do)]

dramatic /drə'mætɪk/ adj. of drama, sudden and exciting or unexpected; vividly striking; (of a gesture etc.) overdone or absurd. —**dramatically** adv. [f. L f. Gk (as prec.)]

dramatics n.pl. (often treated as *sing.*) **1.** the performance of plays. **2.** exaggerated behaviour. [f. prec.]

dramatis personae /'dræmətɪs pɜː'səʊnaɪ/ the characters in a play; a list of these. [L, = persons of the drama]

dramatist /'dræmətɪst/ n. a writer of dramas. [f. DRAMA]

dramatize /'dræmətaɪz/ v.t./i. **1.** to make (a novel etc.) into a play. **2.** to make a dramatic scene of; to behave dramatically. —**dramatization** /-'zeɪʃ(ə)n/ n. [as prec.]

drank past of DRINK.

drape v.t. to cover loosely, hang, or adorn, with cloth etc.; to arrange (clothes, hangings) in graceful folds. —n. (in *pl.*, US) curtains. [f. OF f. L *drappus* cloth]

draper n. a retailer of textile fabrics. [as prec.]

drapery n. **1.** a draper's trade or fabrics. **2.** fabric arranged in loose folds. [f. prec.]

drastic /'dræstɪk/ adj. having a strong or far-reaching effect, severe. —**drastically** adv. [f. Gk *drastikos* (*draō* do)]

drat int. of anger or annoyance, (*colloq.*) curse. —**dratted** adj. [for '*Od* (= God) *rot*]

draught /drɑːft/ n. **1.** a current of air in a room etc., or in a chimney. **2.** pulling, traction. **3.** the depth of water needed to float a ship. **4.** the drawing of liquor from a cask etc. **5.** a single act of drinking; the amount so drunk. **6.** the drawing in of a fishing-net; the fish caught in this. —**draught beer**, beer drawn from a cask, not bottled. **draught-horse** n. a horse used for pulling heavy loads, a cart, plough, etc. **feel the draught**, (*slang*) to feel the effect of financial or other difficulties. [perh. f. ON]

draughts /drɑːfts/ n. a game for two players, with initially 12 pieces (of equal value) each, on a **draughtboard** (the same as a chessboard). The game as played nowadays dates essentially from the 16th c., though it was called 'draughts'

c.1400 and similar games were played from ancient Egyptian times onwards. [pl. of prec.]

draughtsman n. (*pl.* **-men**) **1.** one who makes drawings, plans, or sketches. **2.** a piece in the game of draughts. —**draughtsmanship** n. [f. DRAUGHT]

draughty adj. (of a room etc.) letting in sharp currents of air. [as prec.]

Dravidian /drə'vɪdɪən/ n. **1.** a member of a dark-skinned people of southern India and Sri Lanka. **2.** the group of languages spoken by them, including Tamil, Telugu, and Kanarese. It is thought that before the arrival of speakers of Indo-Aryan languages c.1000 BC the Dravidian languages were spoken over much of India. —adj. of the Dravidians or their languages. [f. Skr. *Dravida*, a province of S. India]

draw v.t./i. (*past* **drew** /druː/; *p.p.* **drawn**) **1.** to pull or cause to move towards or after one; to pull up, over, or across; to pull (curtains etc.) open or shut. **2.** to attract; to take in; to elicit or evoke; to induce. **3.** to take out, to remove; to obtain by lot, to draw lots. **4.** to take or get from a source; to obtain (water) from a well or tap; to bring out (liquid from a vessel, blood from the body); to disembowel. **5.** to infer (a conclusion). **6.** to trace (a line or mark); to produce (a picture) by lines and marks; to represent (a thing) thus. **7.** to formulate or perceive (a comparison, distinctions). **8.** to compose or write out (a document, cheque, etc.). **9.** to finish (a contest or game) with neither side winning. **10.** to make one's way, to move. **11.** to make a call *on* a person, his skill, etc. **12.** (of a ship) to require (a specified depth of water) to float in. **13.** to search (a cover) for game. —n. **1.** an act of drawing, a pull. **2.** a person or thing that draws custom, attention, etc. **3.** a drawing of lots, a raffle. **4.** a drawn game. **5.** a suck on a cigarette etc. —**draw back**, to withdraw from an undertaking. **draw in,** (of days) to become shorter; to persuade to join. **draw in one's horns**, to become less assertive or ambitious. **draw the line at**, to set a limit (of tolerance etc.) at. **draw on,** to approach, to come near. **draw out**, to prolong; to elicit, to induce to talk; (of days) to become longer. **draw-string** n. one that can be pulled to tighten an opening. **draw up,** to compose or draft (a document etc.); to bring into order; to come to a halt; to make *oneself* stiffly erect. **quick on the draw,** quick to react. [OE (as DRAG)]

drawback n. a thing that impairs satisfaction, a disadvantage.

drawbridge n. a bridge, especially over a moat, hinged at one end for drawing up (ill. CASTLES).

drawer /'drɔːə(r)/ n. **1.** one who or that which draws, especially a person who draws a cheque etc. **2.** (also /drɔː/) a boxlike storage compartment without a lid, for sliding in and out of a table etc. **3.** (in *pl.*) an undergarment worn next to the body below the waist. [f. DRAW]

drawing n. **1.** the art of representing by line with a pencil etc. **2.** a picture etc. drawn thus. —**drawing-board** n. a board on which paper is stretched while a drawing is made. **drawing-pin** n. a flat-headed pin for fastening paper etc. to a surface.

drawing-room n. a room for comfortable sitting or entertaining in a private house. [f. earlier *withdrawing-room*]

drawl v.t./i. to speak with drawn-out vowel-sounds. —n. a drawling utterance or way of speaking. [prob. f. LG, Du. *dralen* linger]

drawn p.p. of DRAW. —adj. looking strained from fear or anxiety.

dray n. a low cart without sides for heavy loads, especially beer-barrels. —**drayman** n. (*pl.* **-men**) [OE, = drag-net (as DRAW)]

dread /dred/ v.t. to fear greatly; to look forward to with great apprehension. —n. great fear or apprehension. —adj. dreaded; (*archaic*) dreadful, awe-inspiring. [OE]

dreadful adj. terrible; (*colloq.*) troublesome, very bad. —**dreadfully** adv. [f. DREAD + -FUL]

dream n. **1.** a series of pictures or events in the mind of a sleeping person. **2.** a day-dream, a fantasy; an ideal or aspiration. **3.** a beautiful or ideal person or thing. —v.t./i. (*past* & *p.p.* **dreamt** /dremt/ or **dreamed**) **1.** to experience a dream; to imagine as in a dream. **2.** (with *neg.*) to think of as a possibility. —**dream-land** n. an ideal or imaginary land. **dream up,** to imagine, to invent. **like a dream,** (*colloq.*) easily, effortlessly. —**dreamer** n. [f. OE]

dreamless adj. without dreaming. [f. DREAM]

dreamy adj. **1.** dreamlike. **2.** given to dreaming or fantasy, vague. —**dreamily** adv., **dreaminess** n. [as prec.]

dreary *adj.* dismal, dull, gloomy. —**drearily** *adv.*, **dreariness** *n.* [OE (*drēor* gore)]

dredge[1] /dredʒ/ *n.* an apparatus for bringing up oysters etc. or clearing out mud etc. from a river or the sea bottom. —*v.t./i.* to bring *up* or clean out with a dredge; to use a dredge. [f. Sc. *dreg* perh. rel. to MDu. *dregghe*]

dredge[2] *v.t.* to sprinkle with flour, sugar, etc. [f. obs. *dredge* sweetmeat f. OF perh. ult. f. Gk *tragēmata* spices]

dredger[1] *n.* a dredge, a boat with a dredge. [f. DREDGE[1]]

dredger[2] *n.* a container with a perforated lid, used for sprinkling flour etc. [f. DREDGE[2]]

dregs *n.pl.* sediment, grounds, lees; the worst or most useless part. [prob. f. ON]

drench *v.t.* **1.** to make thoroughly wet. **2.** to force (an animal) to take a dose of medicine. —*n.* a dose of medicine for an animal. [OE (as DRINK)]

Dresden /ˈdrezd(ə)n/ *n.* **1.** (also **Dresden china** etc.) china of a kind made at Meissen near Dresden (a town in East Germany), with elaborate decoration and delicate colourings. **2.** (*attrib.*) characterized by delicate or frail prettiness.

dress *v.t./i.* **1.** to put clothes upon; to provide oneself with and wear clothes; to put on one's clothes; to put on evening dress. **2.** to arrange or adorn (the hair, a shop window, etc.). **3.** to clean or treat (a wound etc.). **4.** to prepare (a bird, crab, or salad) for cooking or eating. **5.** to finish the surface of (a fabric, leather, stone). **6.** to apply manure to. **7.** to correct the alignment of (troops). —*n.* **1.** clothing, especially the visible part of it; formal or ceremonial costume. **2.** a woman's or girl's garment of bodice and skirt. **3.** an external covering, an outward form. —**dress-circle** *n.* the first gallery in a theatre, where evening dress was formerly required (ill. THEATRE). **dress down**, to scold; to reprimand. **dress rehearsal**, the final rehearsal in full costume. **dress up**, to put on special clothes; to make (a thing) more attractive or interesting. [f. OF f. L *directus* direct]

dressage /ˈdresɑːʒ/ *n.* the training of a horse in obedience and deportment; a display of this. [F (*dresser* train, as prec.)]

dresser[1] *n.* a kitchen sideboard with shelves for dishes etc. [f. OF (*dresser* prepare, as DRESS)]

dresser[2] *n.* **1.** one who helps to dress actors or actresses. **2.** a surgeon's assistant in operations. [f. DRESS]

dressing *n.* **1.** putting clothes on. **2.** a sauce or stuffing etc. for food. **3.** a bandage, ointment, etc., for a wound. **4.** manure etc. spread over the land. **5.** a substance used to stiffen textile fabrics during manufacture. —**dressing down**, a scolding. **dressing-gown** *n.* a loose gown worn when one is not fully dressed. **dressing-room** *n.* a room for dressing or changing clothes, especially in a theatre etc., or attached to a bedroom. **dressing-table** *n.* a piece of bedroom furniture with a mirror and usually drawers, for use while dressing, arranging the hair, applying make-up, etc.

dressmaker *n.* a person who makes women's clothes. —**dressmaking** *n.*

dressy *adj.* smart, elegant, wearing stylish clothes. —**dressily** *adv.*

drew *past* of DRAW.

drey /dreɪ/ *n.* a squirrel's nest. [orig. unkn.]

Dreyfus /ˈdreɪfəs/, Alfred (1859–1935), French army officer whose trial on charges of spying for Germany caused a major political crisis in the Third Republic. Falsely accused of providing military secrets to the Germans in 1894, the trial, imprisonment, and eventual rehabilitation of the Jewish Dreyfus polarized deep-set anti-militarist and anti-Semitic trends in a society still coming to terms with defeat and revolution in 1870–1. Notable among the Dreyfusards, as supporters of the supposed spy were known, was the novelist Émile Zola, whose *J'accuse*, published in 1898, ruthlessly exposed attempts to cover up official mistakes.

dribble *v.t./i.* **1.** to allow saliva to flow from the mouth; to flow or cause to flow in drops. **2.** to move the ball forward in football or hockey with slight touches of the feet or stick. —*n.* **1.** an act of dribbling. **2.** a dribbling flow. [frequent. of *drib* obs. var. of DRIP]

driblet /ˈdrɪblɪt/ *n.* a small amount. [as prec. + -LET]

dribs and drabs small scattered amounts. [*drib* as DRIBBLE; *drab* redupl.]

drier /ˈdraɪə(r)/ *n.* a device for drying hair, laundry, etc. [f. DRY]

drift *n.* **1.** being driven along, especially by a current; a slow movement or variation; a slow deviation of a ship, projectile, etc. from a course. **2.** a mass of snow or sand driven along or heaped up by the wind; fragments of rock heaped up by wind, water, etc. **3.** the policy of merely waiting on events, inaction. **4.** (in mining) a horizontal passage following a mineral vein. **5.** (*S. Afr.*) a ford. —*v.t./i.* **1.** to be carried by or as if by a current of air or water, (of a current) to cause to drift; to heap or be heaped in drifts. **2.** to move casually or aimlessly. —**drift mine**, a mine using a horizontal passage (see sense 4). **drift-net** *n.* a net used in sea-fishing and allowed to drift with the tide. [f. ON & MHG *trift* movement of cattle (cogn. w. DRIVE)]

drifter *n.* **1.** an aimless person. **2.** a boat used for fishing with a drift-net. [f. prec.]

driftwood *n.* wood floating on moving water or washed ashore by it.

drill[1] *n.* **1.** a tool or machine for boring holes (ill. CARPENTRY) or sinking wells. **2.** instruction in military exercises; thorough training, especially by a repeated routine; (*colloq.*) a recognized procedure. —*v.t./i.* **1.** to make (a hole) with a drill; to make a drill on. **2.** to train or be trained by means of drill. [f. MDu. *drillen* bore]

drill[2] *n.* **1.** a small furrow for sowing seed in. **2.** a machine for making a furrow, sowing, and covering the seed. **3.** a row of seeds so sown. —*v.t.* to plant in drills. [perh. = obs. *drill* rivulet]

drill[3] *n.* a strong twilled cotton or linen fabric. [f. G *drilich* f. L *trilix* having three threads]

drill[4] *n.* a West African baboon (*Mandrillus leucophaeus*) related to the mandrill. [prob. African name; cf. MANDRILL]

drily /ˈdraɪlɪ/ *adv.* in a dry manner. [f. DRY]

drink *v.t./i.* (*past* **drank**; *p.p.* **drunk**) **1.** to swallow (a liquid); to swallow the contents of (a vessel); to take alcoholic liquor, especially to excess; to bring (*oneself*) to a specified state by drinking. **2.** (of a plant, sponge, etc.) to absorb (moisture). —*n.* liquid for drinking; a glass etc. or portion of this, especially alcoholic; intoxicating liquor, the excessive use of it. —**the drink**, (*slang*) the sea. **drink a person's health**, to pledge good wishes to him by drinking. **drink in**, to listen to or understand eagerly. **drink to**, to drink a toast to, to wish success to. **drink up**, to drink all or the remainder (of). —**drinker** *n.* [OE]

drinkable *adj.* suitable for drinking. [f. prec.]

drip *v.t./i.* (**-pp-**) to fall or let fall in drops; to be so wet (*with* a liquid) as to shed drops. —*n.* **1.** a small falling drop of liquid; a liquid falling in drops, the sound of this; a drip-feed. **2.** (*slang*) a feeble or dull person. [f. MDa. *drippe* (cf. DROP)]

drip-dry *v.t./i.* to dry easily when hung up; to leave to dry in this way. —*adj.* made of a fabric that will dry easily without creasing.

drip-feed *n.* feeding by liquid a drop at a time, especially intravenously; apparatus for this. —*v.t.* to apply a drip-feed to.

dripping *n.* fat melted from roasting meat. [f. DRIP]

dripstone *n.* a projection above a wall or window etc., to divert water from the parts below.

drive *v.t./i.* (*past* **drove**; *p.p.* **driven** /ˈdrɪv(ə)n/) **1.** to urge in some direction by blows, threats, violence, etc. **2.** to cause to go in some direction; to direct and control (a vehicle or locomotive); to convey in a vehicle; to operate a motor vehicle, to be competent to do so; to travel in a private vehicle. **3.** to impel or carry along; to hit (a ball) forcibly; to force or hit (a nail or stake) *into*; to bore (a tunnel etc.); (of a power-source) to set or keep (machinery) going. **4.** to compel; to force into a state of being (*mad* etc.); to overwork. **5.** to be moved by wind, esp. rapidly. **6.** to carry on, to conclude. **7.** to dash, to rush; to work hard *at*. —*n.* **1.** an excursion or journey in a vehicle. **2.** a street or road, especially a scenic one. **3.** a driveway. **4.** a forcible stroke of a ball. **5.** capacity or desire to achieve things; organized effort to some end. **6.** the transmission of power to machinery, the wheels of a motor vehicle etc. **7.** a social event of numerous simultaneous card-games etc. —**drive at**, to seek, to intend, to mean. **drive-in** *adj.* (of a cinema, bank, etc.) for the use of passengers seated in cars; (*n.*) a cinema, bank, etc., of this type. **driving-licence** *n.* a licence permitting one to drive a motor vehicle. **driving-test** *n.* an official test of competence to drive a motor vehicle. **driving-wheel** *n.* a wheel communicating motive power in machinery. [OE]

drivel /ˈdrɪv(ə)l/ *n.* silly talk, nonsense. —*v.i.* (**-ll-**) **1.** to talk drivel. **2.** to run at the nose or mouth. [OE]

driven *p.p.* of DRIVE.

driver *n.* **1.** a person who drives (especially a motor vehicle). **2.** a golf-club for driving from a tee. [f. DRIVE]

driveway *n.* a road serving as an approach for vehicles, especially a private one to a house etc.

drizzle *n.* very fine rain. —*v.i.* (of rain) to fall in very fine drops. —**drizzly** *adj.* [perh. rel. to OE *drēosan* fall]

droll /drəʊl/ *adj.* oddly or strangely amusing. —**drolly** /ˈdrəʊl-lɪ/ *adv.* [f. F *drôle*]

drollery /ˈdrəʊlərɪ/ *n.* quaint humour. [f. prec.]

dromedary /ˈdrɒmɪdərɪ, ˈdrʌm-/ *n.* a light one-humped (esp. Arabian) camel bred for riding. [f. F or L f. Gk *dromas* runner]

drone *n.* **1.** a non-working male of the honey-bee; an idler. **2.** a deep humming sound; the bass-pipe of a bagpipe, its continuous note. —*v.t./i.* to make a deep humming sound; to speak or utter monotonously. [OE]

drool /druːl/ *v.i.* to dribble, to slobber; to show unrestrained admiration (*over*). [contr. of DRIVEL]

droop /druːp/ *v.t./i.* to bend or hang downwards, especially through tiredness or weakness; to languish, to flag; to let (the eyes or head) drop. —*n.* a drooping attitude, a loss of spirit. —**droopy** *adj.* [f. ON (as foll.)]

drop *n.* **1.** a small round portion of liquid such as hangs or falls separately or adheres to a surface; a thing in the shape of a drop, especially a sweet or a pendant; (in *pl.*) a liquid medicine to be measured by drops; a minute quantity; a glass etc. of intoxicating liquor. **2.** an act of dropping, a fall of prices, temperature, etc. **3.** a thing that drops or is dropped; a drop-curtain. **4.** a steep or vertical descent; the distance of this. **5.** (*slang*) a hiding-place for stolen or illicit goods etc. **6.** (*slang*) a bribe. —*v.t./i.* **1.** to fall by the force of gravity from not being held; to allow to fall, to cease to hold. **2.** to fall or cause to fall in drops; to shed (tears, blood). **3.** to set down (a passenger, parcel, etc.). **4.** to fell with a blow, bullet, etc.; to sink to the ground, esp. from exhaustion or injury. **5.** to fall naturally *asleep*, (*back*) *into* a habit, etc. **6.** to fall in a direction, condition, amount, degree, or pitch. **7.** to lower, to direct downwards; to become lower; to perform (a curtsy). **8.** to move to or be left in a position further back. **9.** to cease to associate with, deal with, or discuss; to cease, to lapse. **10.** to utter or be uttered casually; to send casually; to come or go casually *by* or *in* as a visitor, or *into* a place. **11.** to lose (money, esp. in gambling); to omit in speech. **12.** to send (the ball) or score (a goal) in football by a drop-kick. **13.** to give birth to (esp. a lamb). —**at the drop of a hat,** promptly, instantly. **drop-curtain** *n.* a painted curtain that can be lowered on to a theatre stage. **drop-kick** *n.* a kick at football made by dropping the ball and kicking it as it touches the ground. **drop off,** to fall asleep; to drop (a passenger). **drop on a person,** to be severe with him. **drop out,** to cease to take an active part. **drop-out** *n.* one who withdraws from conventional society. **drop scone,** a scone made by dropping a spoonful of mixture on to a cooking surface. [OE]

droplet *n.* a small drop. [f. DROP]

dropper *n.* a device for releasing a liquid in drops. [f. DROP]

droppings *n.pl.* what falls or has fallen in drops, especially the dung of some animals and birds. [f. DROP]

dropsy *n.* a disease in which watery fluid collects in the cavities or tissues of the body. —**dropsical** *adj.* [for earlier *hydropsy* f. OF f. L f. Gk (*hudōr* water)]

drosophila /drəˈsɒfɪlə/ *n.* a fruit-fly of the genus *Drosophila*, used extensively in genetic research. [f. Gk *drosos* dew, moisture + *philos* loving]

dross /drɒs/ *n.* scum separated from metals in melting; impurities, rubbish. [OE]

drought /draʊt/ *n.* an abnormally prolonged spell without rain. [OE (as DRY)]

drove[1] *n.* a herd or flock being driven or moving together; a moving crowd. [OE (as DRIVE)]

drove[2] *past* of DRIVE.

drover *n.* a driver of cattle. [f. DROVE[1]]

drown *v.t./i.* **1.** to suffocate by submersion in water or other liquid; to flood, to drench. **2.** to alleviate (a sorrow etc.) with drink. **3.** to overpower (a sound) with a louder noise. —**drowned valley,** a valley that has become submerged at its lower end by the sea or a lake. [rel. to ON *drukna* be drowned; cogn. w. DRINK]

drowse /draʊz/ *v.i.* to be lightly asleep. [back-formation f. foll.]

drowsy /ˈdraʊzɪ/ *adj.* very sleepy, almost asleep. —**drowsily** *adv.*, **drowsiness** *n.* [rel. to OE *drūsian* be languid]

drub *v.t.* (**-bb-**) to beat, to thrash; to defeat thoroughly. —**drubbing** *n.* [ult. f. Arab.]

drudge *n.* one who does dull, laborious, or menial work. —*v.i.* to work hard or laboriously, to toil. —**drudgery** *n.* [perh. rel. to DRAG]

drug *n.* a medicinal substance; a narcotic, hallucinogen, or stimulant, especially one causing addiction. —*v.t./i.* (**-gg-**) to add a drug to (food or drink); to give drugs to, to stupefy; to take drugs as an addict. —**drug on the market,** a commodity that is plentiful but no longer in demand. [f. OF *drogue*]

drugget /ˈdrʌgɪt/ *n.* a coarse woven fabric used for floor coverings etc. [f. F *droguet*]

druggist *n.* a pharmaceutical chemist. [f. F (as DRUG)]

drugstore *n.* (*US*) a chemist's shop also selling light refreshments and other articles.

Druid /ˈdruːɪd/ *n.* **1.** a priest of the ancient Celts in Gaul, Britain, and Ireland (see below). **2.** a member of any of various movements attempting to revive Druid practices. **3.** an officer of the Gorsedd. —**Druidism** *n.*, **Druidic** /-ˈɪdɪk/ *adj.*, **Druidical** *adj.* [f. F or L f. Celtic]

Our picture of the Druids is based chiefly on the hostile account of them in the writings of Julius Caesar and Tacitus. Caesar reports that they had judicial and priestly functions, were proficient in natural philosophy, and held responsibility for the education of young Gaulish nobles, a duty which they carried on in oral poetry; they worshipped in 'groves' (clearings in the forest) and cut mistletoe from the sacred oak with a golden sickle. The religion was stamped out by the Romans with unrelenting ferocity, either because of the human sacrifices that it involved or lest it should become a focus for resistance to Roman rule. Druidism of the Roman period may well contain elements of older faiths. Its association with Stonehenge, however, is now rejected (there is no mention of any constructed temple in the classical accounts), but the modern Druidical order seeks to make ceremonial use of the site.

drum *n.* **1.** a musical instrument or toy sounded by striking, made of a hollow cylinder or hemisphere with skin or parchment stretched over the opening(s) (ill. MUSICAL NOTATION and ORCHESTRA); its player; the sound produced by striking it; (in *pl.*) the percussion section of an orchestra or band. **2.** a cylindrical object, structure, or container. **3.** the ear-drum. —*v.t./i.* (**-mm-**) **1.** to play a drum; to make the sound of a drum, to tap or beat continuously or rhythmically with the fingers etc. **2.** to drive facts or a lesson *into* a person by persistence. **3.** (of a bird or insect) to make a loud noise with the wings. —**drum brake,** a brake consisting of shoes acting on a revolving drum (ill. CAR). **drum major,** the leader of a marching band. **drum majorette,** a female drum major. **drum out,** to dismiss with ignominy. **drum up,** to produce or obtain by vigorous effort. [f. LG *trommel*]

drumhead *n.* the part of a drum that is struck.

drumlin /ˈdrʌmlɪn/ *n.* a long oval mound of glacial drift or diluvial formation, with its longer axis parallel to the direction of the flow. [f. Gael. & Ir. *druim* ridge]

drummer *n.* a player of a drum. [f. DRUM]

drumstick *n.* **1.** a stick for beating a drum. **2.** the lower joint of the leg of a cooked fowl.

drunk *adj.* lacking proper control of oneself from the effects of alcoholic drink; overcome *with* joy, success, etc. —*n.* **1.** a drunken person. **2.** (*slang*) a bout of drinking. [p.p. of DRINK]

drunkard /ˈdrʌŋkəd/ *n.* a person who is habitually drunk. [f. prec.]

drunken *adj.* drunk, often drunk; involving or caused by excessive alcoholic drinking. —**drunkenly** *adv.*, **drunkenness** /-kən-nɪs/ *n.* [as DRUNK]

drupe /druːp/ *n.* a fleshy or pulpy fruit enclosing a stone with a kernel, e.g. a plum. [f. L f. Gk *druppa* olive]

Drury Lane /ˈdrʊərɪ/, Theatre Royal, London's most famous theatre. The first theatre on the site opened in 1663 (see PATENT THEATRE), the second—notable for David Garrick's association with it—in 1674, and the third in 1794. The present theatre, dating from 1812, was not particularly successful until the 1880s, when it became famous for its melodramas and spectacles. Since the 1920s it has staged musicals, including *The Desert Song* (1927), *Glamorous Night* (1935), *Oklahoma!* (1947), *My Fair Lady* (1958), and *Hello, Dolly!* (1965).

Druse /druːz/ *n.* a member of a political and religious sect

Dress

English costume through the ages

Early British (pre-Roman)

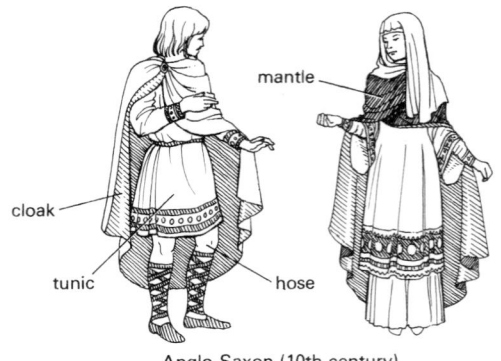

mantle

cloak

tunic   hose

Anglo-Saxon (10th century)

Norman (early 12th century)

hose

Plantagenet (late 14th century)

doublet

jerkin

underskirt

Tudor (early 16th century)

ruff

farthingale

Elizabethan (late 16th century)

muff

breeches

Stuart (mid-17th century)

periwig

tricorn

petticoat

Queen Anne (early 18th century)

waistcoat

fan

pannier

stockings

Georgian (late 18th century)

beaver hat

reticule

tailcoat

Empire
gown

Regency (early 19th century)

cape

bonnet

overskirt

Early Victorian (mid-19th century)

bowler

turban

bustle

cane

Late Victorian (late 19th century)

top hat

bolero
jacket

frock-coat

parasol

spats

Edwardian (early 20th century)

cap

cloche hat

fur

plus-fours

1920s and 1930s

felt hat

worsted
suit

overcoat

1950s

miniskirt

1960s

of Muslim origin, concentrated in Lebanon, with smaller groups in Syria and Israel. The sect broke away from Ismaili Shiite Islam in the 11th c. over a disagreement about the succession to the imamate (leadership), a position in which spiritual and political leadership were and are indissolubly linked. The Druses followed the seventh caliph of the Fatimid dynasty, al-Hakim b'illah (996–1021), who is claimed to have disappeared and whose return is expected. They regard al-Hakim as a deity, and thus are considered heretics by the Muslim community at large. [F f. Arab., prob. f. their founder *al-Darazî* (11th c.)]

dry /draɪ/ *adj*. (**drier, driest**) **1.** without moisture, not wet; not rainy, deficient in rainfall; not yielding water, milk, etc.; parched, dried up; (*colloq*.) thirsty. **2.** prohibiting or opposed to the sale of alcoholic liquor at some or all times. **3.** unconnected with or not using liquid. **4.** solid, not liquid. **5.** without butter etc. **6.** (of a liquid) having disappeared by evaporation, draining, wiping, etc. **7.** (of a wine) free from sweetness. **8.** plain, unelaborated, uninteresting; cold, impassive; (of wit) expressed with pretended seriousness. —*v.t./i.* to make or become dry; to preserve (food) by the removal of moisture. —**dry battery** *or* **cell**, a battery or cell in which the electrolyte is absorbed in a solid. **dry-clean** *v.t.* to clean (clothes etc.) with organic solvents that evaporate quickly, without using water. **dry dock**, a dry enclosure for building or repairing ships. **dry-fly** *adj*. (of fishing) using an artificial fly that floats. **dry-ice** *n*. solid carbon dioxide used as a refrigerant. **dry land**, land as distinct from sea etc. **dry measure**, a measure for dry goods. **dry out**, to make or become fully dry; (of a drug addict etc.) to undergo treatment to cure an addiction. **dry painting**, see SAND-PAINTING. **dry-point** *n*. a needle for engraving without acid on a bare copper plate; an engraving produced by this. **dry-rot** *n*. a decayed state of wood when not well ventilated; the fungi causing this; any moral or social decay. **dry run**, (*colloq*.) a rehearsal. **dry-shod** *adj*. & *adv*. without wetting one's shoes. **dry up**, to dry washed dishes; to make completely dry; to cease to yield liquid; to become unproductive; (of an actor) to forget one's lines; (in *imper.*) to cease to talk. —**dryness** *n*. [OE]

dryad /ˈdraɪæd/ *n*. a wood-nymph. [f. OF f. L f. Gk (*drus* oak)]

Dryden /ˈdraɪd(ə)n/, John (1631–1700), English poet, critic, and dramatist. He wrote his first major poem *Heroique Stanzas* (1658) on the death of Cromwell, and later celebrated Charles II's return with two panegyrics. During 1663–81 Dryden wrote almost a play a year (the theatres had been reopened), of which the greatest was the blank verse *All for Love* (1678), based on Shakespeare's *Antony and Cleopatra*. His verse satires, including *Absalom and Achitophel* (1681) and *MacFlecknoe* (1682), demonstrate his developing mastery of the heroic couplet. Following James II's accession Dryden became a Catholic, and lost the position of Poet Laureate, which he had held since 1668, on the accession of the Protestant William III. Dr Johnson, with justification, described Dryden as the 'father of English criticism'. His major critical work is *Of Dramatic Poesie* (1668) but much of his criticism is found in his Prefaces and Prologues. His splendid achievements as a translator include a version of Virgil's *Georgics*, and *Fables Ancient and Modern* (1699).

dryer var. of DRIER.

dryly var. of DRILY.

Dryopithecus /draɪəˈpɪθɪkəs/ *n*. a genus of fossil anthropoid apes that existed in Europe, Asia, and Africa from the early Miocene to early Pliocene periods (*c*.23–10 million years ago). It is believed that the family to which mankind belongs diverged from these between about 20 and 10 million years ago, through an as yet unspecified species of Dryopithecus. —**dryopithecine** /-saɪn/ *adj*. [f. Gk *drus* tree + *pithēkos* ape]

drystone *adj*. (of a wall etc.) made of stones without mortar.

DSC *abbr*. Distinguished Service Cross.

D.Sc. *abbr*. Doctor of Science.

DSM *abbr*. Distinguished Service Medal.

DSO *abbr*. Distinguished Service Order.

d.t., d.t.'s *abbr*. delirium tremens.

dual /ˈdjʊəl/ *adj*. composed of two parts, twofold, double. —*n*. (*Gram*.) a dual number or form. —**dual carriageway**, a road with a dividing strip between traffic flowing in opposite directions. **dual-control** *n*. two linked sets of controls, enabling either of two persons to operate a car or aircraft. —**duality** /djʊˈælɪtɪ/ *n*. [f. L *dualis* (*duo* two)]

dub[1] *v.t.* (**-bb-**) **1.** to make (a person) a knight by touching his shoulders with a sword. **2.** to give a specified name to. **3.** to smear (leather) with grease. [f. OF *adober* equip with armour, repair]

dub[2] *v.t.* (**-bb-**) to make an alternative sound-track of (a film) especially in a different language; to add (sound effects, music) to a film or broadcast. [abbr. of DOUBLE]

dubbin *n*. (also **dubbing**) a thick grease for softening and waterproofing leather. [f. DUB[1]]

dubiety /djuːˈbaɪətɪ/ *n*. a feeling of doubt. [f. L (as foll.)]

dubious /ˈdjuːbɪəs/ *adj*. **1.** hesitating, doubtful. **2.** unreliable; of questionable or suspected character. —**dubiously** *adv*. [f. L *dubiosus* (*dubium* doubt)]

Dublin /ˈdʌblɪn/ the capital of the Republic of Ireland, situated at the mouth of the River Liffey; pop. (1981) 525,882.

ducal /ˈdjuːk(ə)l/ *adj*. of or like a duke. [f. F (as DUKE)]

ducat /ˈdʌkət/ *n*. a gold coin formerly current in most European countries. [f. It. or L, = duchy]

Duccio di Buoninsegna /ˈduːtʃɪʊ dɪ bwɔʊnɪnˈseɪnjə/ (active 1278–1319), the leading painter of Siena in the late 13th and early 14th c., who makes the transition from Byzantine to Gothic. The only fully documented surviving work by him is the great *Virgin in Majesty* (the *Maestà*) for the high altar of Siena cathedral (completed 1311). Duccio was a master of pictorial narrative, conveying emotion through facial expression, sequence of colour, and arrangement of scenery, yet keeping the composition within Byzantine conventions. After him, even far into the 15th c., Sienese painting was influenced by his sensitive line, his resplendent colours, and his tenderness.

duchess /ˈdʌtʃɪs/ *n*. the wife or widow of a duke; a woman holding the rank of duke in her own right. [f. OF f. L *ducissa* (as DUKE)]

duchy /ˈdʌtʃɪ/ *n*. the territory of a duke or duchess; the royal dukedom of Cornwall or Lancaster. [f. OF f. L *ducatus* (as DUKE)]

duck[1] *n*. **1.** a swimming bird of the genus *Anas* and kindred genera, especially the domesticated form of the mallard or wild duck; the female of this; its flesh as food. **2.** the score of 0 in cricket. **3.** (*colloq*., esp. as a form of address) dear. —*v.t./i.* **1.** to bob down, especially to avoid being seen or hit; to dip the head under water and emerge; to plunge (a person) briefly in water. **2.** (*colloq*.) to dodge or avoid (a task etc.). —**duck-boards** *n.pl.* wooden slats forming a narrow path in a trench or over mud. **ducks and drakes**, the game of making a flat stone skim along the surface of water (*play ducks and drakes with*, to squander). **like water off a duck's back**, producing no effect. [OE (*dūcan* dive)]

duck[2] *n*. a strong linen or cotton cloth; (in *pl*.) trousers made of this. [f. MDu.]

duckbill *n*. a platypus.

duckling *n*. a young duck. [f. DUCK[1] + -LING]

duckweed *n*. a plant of the genus *Lemna* that forms a covering on the surface of still water.

ducky *n*. (*colloq*., esp. as a form of address) dear. [f. DUCK[1]]

duct *n*. a channel or tube for conveying a fluid, cable, etc.; a tube in the body conveying secretions etc. —*v.t.* to convey through a duct. [f. L *ductus* aqueduct (*ducere* lead)]

ductile /ˈdʌktaɪl/ *adj*. **1.** (of a metal) capable of being drawn into wire. **2.** pliable, docile. —**ductility** /-ˈtɪlɪtɪ/ *n*. [f. F or L (as prec.)]

ductless *adj*. without a duct. —**ductless gland**, a gland that passes its secretions directly into the bloodstream, not through a duct. [f. DUCT + -LESS]

dud *n*. (*slang*) **1.** a thing that fails to work, a useless thing. **2.** (in *pl*.) clothes, rags. —*adj*. (*slang*) defective, useless. [orig. unkn.]

dude /djuːd/ *n*. (*US*) a dandy; a city man. [prob. f. G dial. *dude* fool]

dudgeon /ˈdʌdʒ(ə)n/ *n*. resentment, indignation, usu. in *in high dudgeon*, very angry. [orig. unkn.]

due /djuː/ *adj*. **1.** owed as a debt or obligation; payable immediately. **2.** merited, appropriate; that ought to be given *to* a person. **3.** ascribable *to* a cause, agent, etc. **4.** under engagement *to* do something or arrive at a certain time; to be looked for or foreseen. —*adv*. (of a point of the compass) exactly, directly. —*n*. **1.** what one owes; (usu. in *pl*.) a fee or amount payable. **2.** a person's right, what is owed him. —**become** *or* **fall due**, to become payable. **due to**, (D) because of. [f. OF f. L *debitus* (*debēre* owe)]

duel /ˈdjuːəl/ *n*. a formal fight with deadly weapons between two persons; a two-sided contest. —*v.i.* (**-ll-**) to fight a duel. —**duellist** *n.* [f. It. *duello* or L *duellum* (= *bellum*) war]

duenna /dju'enə/ *n.* an older woman acting as a chaperon to girls, especially in a Spanish family. [Sp. f. L *domina* (as DON¹)]

duet /dju:'et/ *n.* a musical composition for two performers; the performers. —**duettist** *n.* [f. G or It. f. L (*duo* two)]

Dufay /du:'faɪ/, Guillaume (*c.*1400–74), Franco-Flemish composer and singer, who spent much of his life in Italy and Savoy. A noted teacher, he was one of the first great Renaissance composers. His works include much church music (his own Requiem Mass, now lost, was sung at his funeral), motets, and 84 songs.

duff¹ *adj.* (*slang*) worthless, useless, counterfeit. —*n.* a boiled pudding. [northern pronunc. of DOUGH]

duff² *v.t.* (*slang*) to bungle. [perh. back-formation f. DUFFER]

duffel var. of DUFFLE.

duffer *n.* an inefficient or stupid person. [perh. f. Sc. *doufart* stupid person]

duffle *n.* a heavy woollen cloth. —**duffle bag,** a cylindrical canvas bag closed by a draw-string. **duffle coat,** a hooded overcoat of duffle, fastened with toggles. [f. *Duffel* town in Belgium]

Dufy /'du:fɪ/, Raoul (1877–1953), French painter and textile designer. His mature style shows deft outline drawings of forms on brilliant background washes evocative of Mediterranean sunlight. His favourite subjects were racing scenes, boating scenes, and the glitter and sparkle of the Riviera, London, or Nice—drawing-room art of splendid attractiveness.

dug¹ *past* & *p.p.* of DIG.

dug² *n.* an udder, a teat. [orig. unkn.]

dugong /'du:gɒŋ/ *n.* an Asian sea-mammal, *Dugong dugon*. [f. Malay]

dug-out *n.* **1.** a canoe made by hollowing a tree-trunk. **2.** a roofed shelter, especially for troops in the trenches.

duke /dju:k/ *n.* a person holding the highest hereditary title of nobility; a sovereign prince ruling a duchy or small State. —**dukedom** *n.* [f. OF f. L (*dux* leader)]

dulcet /'dʌlsɪt/ *adj.* sweet-sounding. [f. OF f. L (*dulcis* sweet)]

dulcimer /'dʌlsɪmə(r)/ *n.* **1.** a musical instrument consisting of a shallow closed box over which metal strings are stretched to be struck by wood, cane, or wire hammers, the prototype of the piano. **2.** a musical instrument of the zither type, fretted and with steel strings which are stopped with one hand and plucked with a plectrum by the other, played in Kentucky and Alabama as an accompaniment to songs and dances. [f. OF perh. f. L *dulce melos* sweet melody]

dull *adj.* **1.** not bright, vivid, or clear; (of weather) overcast. **2.** tedious, not interesting or exciting. **3.** not sharp; (of pain) indistinctly felt; (of sound) not resonant. **4.** slow in understanding, stupid; without keen perception. **5.** listless, depressed; (of trade etc.) slow, sluggish. —*v.t./i.* to make or become dull. —**dully** /'dʌl-lɪ/ *adv.*, **dullness** *n.* [f. MLG, MDu. *dul* = OE *dol* stupid]

dullard /'dʌləd/ *n.* a mentally dull person. [f. prec.]

duly /'dju:lɪ/ *adv.* in due time or manner; rightly, properly, sufficiently. [f. DUE]

Duma /'du:mə/ *n.* an elective legislative assembly introduced in Russia by Tsar Nicholas II in 1905 in response to popular unrest. In practice the Duma had little effective power. [Russ.] = elective municipal council]

Dumas /'dju:mɑ:/, Alexandre (1802–70), French novelist and dramatist, known as 'Dumas *père*', a pioneer of the Romantic theatre in France. He achieved great popularity with his swiftly moving dramas, mostly on historical subjects, such as *Henry III et sa cour* (1829), *Antony* (1831), and *La Tour de Nesle* (1832). Even more successful were his historical novels on which his reputation now rests, including *The Three Musketeers* (1844–5) and its sequels following the adventures of d'Artagnan, and *The Count of Monte Cristo* (1844–5), a masterpiece of mystery and adventure. His son Alexandre Dumas (1824–95), 'Dumas *fils*', also a novelist and dramatist, won fame with his novel *La Dame aux camélias* (1848) which formed the basis of Verdi's opera *La Traviata* (1853).

dumb /dʌm/ *adj.* **1.** unable to speak; silenced by surprise, shyness, etc.; inarticulate; taciturn, reticent. **2.** stupid, ignorant. **3.** (of action) performed without speech. **4.** giving no sound. —**dumb show,** gestures instead of speech. **dumb**

waiter, a small movable set of shelves for serving food; a lift for food etc. —**dumbly** *adv.*, **dumbness** *n.* [OE]

dumb-bell *n.* a short bar with a weight at each end used in pairs for exercising the muscles.

dumbfound /dʌm'faʊnd/ *v.t.* to nonplus, to make speechless with surprise. [f. DUMB + CONFOUND]

Dumfries and Galloway /dʌmfri:s, 'gæləweɪ/ a local government region in SW Scotland.

dumdum bullet /'dʌmdʌm/ a soft-nosed bullet that expands on impact. [f. *Dum-Dum* in India, where first produced]

dummy *n.* **1.** a model of the human form, especially as used to display clothes or by a ventriloquist; an imitation object, an object serving to replace a real or normal one. **2.** a baby's rubber teat. **3.** a stupid person; a person taking no real part, a figure-head. **4.** a player or an imaginary player in some card-games, whose cards are exposed and played by a partner. —*adj.* sham, imitation. —*v.i.* to use a feigned pass or swerve in football etc. —**dummy run,** a trial attempt, a rehearsal. [f. DUMB]

dump *v.t.* **1.** to deposit as rubbish; to put down firmly or clumsily; (*colloq.*) to abandon or get rid of. **2.** to sell (excess goods) in a new market (especially abroad) at a lower price than in an original market. —*n.* **1.** a place or heap for depositing rubbish; an accumulated pile of ore, earth, etc.; a temporary store of ammunition etc. **2.** (*colloq.*) an unpleasant or dreary place. [perh. rel. to Norw. *dumpa* fall suddenly]

dumpling /'dʌmplɪŋ/ *n.* **1.** a baked or boiled ball of dough, as part of a stew or containing apple etc. **2.** a small fat person. [perh. f. *dump* small round object + -LING]

dumps *n.pl.* (*colloq.*) low spirits, depression, usu. in *down in the dumps*. [prob. f. MDu. *domp* exhalation, mist (as DAMP)]

dumpy *adj.* short and stout. —**dumpiness** *n.* [f. *dump* (cf. DUMPLING)]

dun¹ *adj.* greyish-brown; (of a horse) having a golden sand-coloured body. —*n.* **1.** dun colour. **2.** a dun horse. [OE]

dun² *v.t.* (**-nn-**) to ask persistently for payment of a debt. —*n.* a demand for payment. [abbr. of obs. *dunkirk* privateer, f. *Dunkirk* in France]

Dunbar /dʌn'bɑ:(r)/, William (?1456–?1513), Scottish poet and priest, awarded a royal pension by James IV. His first great poem 'The Thrissill and the Rois' (1503), a political satire, celebrated the marriage of James IV to Mary Tudor, while his best-known poem, the 'Lament for the Makaris', is a powerful elegy on the deaths of Chaucer and other fellow poets. A versatile craftsman, Dunbar wrote in a variety of stanza forms with much humour and satirical power; his vitality and originality were in sharp contrast to much poetry of the preceeding century.

Duncan /'dʌŋkən/, Isadora (1878–1927), American dancer and teacher. Clad appropriately in a loosely falling tunic, she developed a form of 'free' barefoot dancing akin to that of classical Greece and based on natural impulses. Though not popular in America she was much admired in Europe, where she settled, founding a school in Berlin and making many visits to Russia, where she may have influenced Fokine. She had several well-publicized love affairs, lost her two children by drowning, and herself died through strangulation when her trailing scarf became entangled in the wheels of a car.

dunce *n.* one who is slow at learning, a dullard. [f. DUNS Scotus]

Dundee cake /dʌn'di:/ a rich fruit-cake usually decorated with split almonds. [f. *Dundee* city in Scotland]

dunderhead /'dʌndəhed/ *n.* a stupid person. [perh. rel. to dial. *dunner* resounding noise]

dune /dju:n/ *n.* a mound or ridge of sand etc. formed by wind (ill. COASTS). [F, f. MDu. (as DOWN³)]

dung *n.* the excrement of animals; manure. —*v.t.* to apply dung to, to manure (land). —**dung-beetle** *n.* a beetle whose larvae develop in dung. [OE]

dungaree /dʌŋgə'ri:/ *n.* a strong coarse cotton cloth; (in *pl.*) overalls or trousers made of this. [f. Hindi]

dungeon /'dʌndʒ(ə)n/ *n.* an underground cell for prisoners. [f. OF f. L *domnio* (*dominus* lord)]

dunghill *n.* a heap of dung or refuse in a farmyard.

dunk *v.t.* to dip (bread etc.) into a soup or beverage before eating it; to immerse. [f. G *tunken* dip]

Dunkirk /dʌn'kɜ:k/ French Channel port, scene of the

evacuation of the British Expeditionary Force in 1940. Forced to retreat to the Channel by the German breakthrough at Sedan, 225,000 British troops, as well as 110,000 of their French allies, were evacuated from Dunkirk between 27 May and 2 June by warships, requisitioned civilian ships, and a host of small boats, under constant attack from the air. No British soldiers were left on the beach (although large quantities of arms and equipment had to be left behind), and it is remembered as a success rather than a retreat—'snatching glory out of defeat'.

dunlin /'dʌnlɪn/ n. the red-backed sandpiper, *Calidris alpina*. [prob. f. DUN¹]

Dunlop /'dʌnlɒp/, John Boyd (1840-1921), Scottish veterinary surgeon, working in Belfast, the first person to devise a successful pneumatic tyre (1888), which was manufactured by the company named after him (see PNEUMATIC).

Dunmow Flitch /'dʌnməʊ/ a flitch of bacon awarded in a contest on Whit Monday, according to an ancient custom of Great Dunmow in Essex, to a married couple who will go to the priory and, kneeling on two sharp-pointed stones, swear that they have not quarrelled or repented of their marriage within a year and a day after its celebration. The prize is said to have been offered in 1244 (though its origin may have been earlier). [f. DUN¹]

Dunne /dʌn/, John William (1875-1949), English philosopher. His theory that all time exists simultaneously (*serialism*) was an attempt to explain the phenomenon of precognition in dreams etc.

dunnock /'dʌnək/ n. the hedge-sparrow, *Prunella modularis*. [f. DUN¹]

Duns Scotus /'skəʊtəs/, John (c.1260-1308), Scottish-born Franciscan philosopher whose reasoning earned him the title of the 'Subtle Doctor'. In opposition to the teaching of Aquinas he argued that faith was a matter of will, not dependent on logical proofs; his conception of form (i.e. the nature of things, by which they are what they are) and matter differed from that of Aquinas; and he was the first great theologian to defend the theory of the Immaculate Conception. His system was accepted by the Franciscans as their doctrinal basis and exercised a profound influence in the Middle Ages. In the Renaissance his followers were ridiculed by humanists and reformers for the subtleties of their reasoning; they, in turn, hurled abuse at the 'new learning', and the term *Duns* or *Dunce*, soon passed into the sense of 'dull obstinate person impervious to the new learning' and of 'blockhead incapable of learning'.

Dunstable /'dʌnstəb(ə)l/, John (c.1390-1453), the leading English composer of the early 15th c., also an astrologer and mathematician. His works include masses and motets, and he was probably the first to write an instrumental accompaniment for church music.

Dunstan /'dʌnst(ə)n/, St (c.909-988), a monk and later abbot at Glastonbury who insisted on full observance of the Benedictine rule, and under whom the monastery became famous for its learning. He was appointed archbishop of Canterbury by King Edgar in 960, and together they carried through a reform of Church and State. The restoration of monastic life, which seems to have been virtually extinct in England by the mid-10th c., was almost wholly Dunstan's work. He zealously supported the cause of learning and himself achieved fame as a musician, illuminator, and metal-worker. Feast day, 19 May.

duo /'dju:əʊ/ n. (pl. **-os**) a pair of performers; a duet. [L, = two]

duodecimal /dju:əʊˈdesɪm(ə)l/ adj. of twelfths or twelve; proceeding or reckoning by twelves. [f. L (*duodecim* twelve)]

duodenum /dju:əʊˈdiːnəm/ n. the first part of the small intestine immediately below the stomach (ill. BODY 2). —**duodenal** adj. [L (as prec.), from its length of 12 fingers' breadth]

duologue /'dju:əlɒg/ n. a dialogue between two persons. [f. L or Gk *duo* two, after MONOLOGUE]

dupe /dju:p/ n. a victim of deception. —v.t. to deceive, to trick. [F, lit. = hoopoe]

duple /'dju:p(ə)l/ adj. of two parts. —**duple time**, (*Mus.*) that with two beats to the bar. [f. L (*duo* two)]

duplex /'dju:pleks/ adj. having two parts; (of a set of rooms) on two floors. [L, = double]

duplicate /'dju:plɪkət/ adj. exactly like another example; existing in two examples, having two corresponding parts; doubled, twice as large or as many; (of card-games) with the same hand played by different players. —n. one of two things exactly alike, especially that made after the other; an exact copy of a letter or document. —/-keɪt/ v.t. to make or be an exact copy of; to double; to multiply by two; to repeat (an action etc.) especially unnecessarily. —**duplication** /-ˈkeɪʃ(ə)n/ n. [f. L (as prec.)]

duplicator n. a machine for producing documents in multiple copies. [f. prec.]

duplicity /dju:ˈplɪsɪtɪ/ n. double-dealing, deceitfulness. —**duplicitous** adj. [f. OF or L (as DUPLEX)]

Dur. abbr. Durham (county).

durable /'djʊərəb(ə)l/ adj. likely to last; (of goods) remaining useful for a long period; resisting wear, decay, etc. —**durability** /-ˈbɪlɪtɪ/ n. [f. OF f. L (*durare* endure)]

dura mater /djʊərə ˈmeɪtə(r)/ the tough outer membrane enveloping the brain and spinal cord. [L, = hard mother, transl. of Arabic phrase ('mother' in Arabic indicating the relationship of things)]

duration /djʊəˈreɪʃ(ə)n/ n. the time during which a thing continues. [as prec.]

Dürer /'djʊərə(r)/, Albrecht (1471-1528) German painter from Nuremberg, deeply influenced by the forms and ideas of Italian Renaissance art. Dürer was fascinated by scientific problems such as perspective and proportion, and wrote a treatise on the latter (1528), partly inspired by the studies of Leonardo. His interest in ideal form, however, was combined with meticulous attention to detail and with a feeling for individual nature which reflects the realism of the northern tradition. He travelled in Germany in 1490-4, and then set up a workshop at Nuremberg where he produced his great series of woodcuts and engravings, including the *Apocalypse* (1498), *The Great Passion* (1510), and *The Life of the Virgin* (1510). From c.1512 he was court painter to the Emperor Maximilian; his graphic works were influential throughout Europe, including Italy. His landscape watercolours, apparently done for his own pleasure, are remarkably advanced for their time in their treatment of light and atmosphere.

duress /djʊəˈres/ n. the use of force or threats, esp. illegally; imprisonment. [f. OF f. L *duritia* (*durus* hard)]

Durga /'dʊəgə/ (*Hinduism*) a fierce goddess, wife of Siva (see PARVATI), often identified with Kali. She is usually depicted riding a tiger or lion and slaying the buffalo demon, and with eight or ten arms. [Skr., = inaccessible]

Durham /'dʌrəm/ a town and county of NE England.

during /'djʊərɪŋ/ prep. throughout or at a point in the duration of. [f. obs. *dure* continue f. OF (as DURATION)]

Durkheim /'dʊəkhaɪm/, Émile (1858-1917), French philosopher, a founder of modern sociology. He stressed the collective consciousness and the common values of society as the source of religion, morality, and social order.

Durrell /djʊəˈrel/, Lawrence George (1912-), English novelist and poet. Born in India, he travelled widely, living in Paris in the 1930s and thereafter mainly in the Eastern Mediterranean. First recognized as a poet, Durrell produced several verse collections before achieving fame with his *Alexandria Quartet* (*Justine*, 1957; *Balthazar*, 1958; *Mountolive*, 1958; *Clea*, 1960), the central topic of which is 'an investigation of modern love'. Set in Alexandria before the Second World War, the novels are bound together in a web of political and sexual intrigue, and written in an ornate lyrical and sensual style. His travel books include *Prospero's Cell* (1945) on Corfu and *Bitter Lemons* (1957) on Cyprus.

dusk n. the darker stage of twilight. [f. OE *dox* dark, swarthy]

dusky adj. shadowy, dim; dark-coloured. —**duskily** adv.; **duskiness** n. [f. prec.]

dust n. 1. finely powdered earth or other matter. 2. pollen; a fine powder of any material. 3. a dead person's remains. 4. confusion, turmoil. —v.t. 1. to clear of dust by wiping; to clear furniture etc. of dust. 2. to sprinkle (powder or dust) over, to sprinkle (an object) thus. —**bite the dust,** to be killed. **dust-cart** n. a vehicle for collecting household refuse. **dust-cover** n. a sheet or cloth to keep the dust off furniture etc.; a dust-jacket. **dust-jacket** n. a paper wrapper on a book. **dust-sheet** n. a dust-cover for furniture. **dust-up** n. (*colloq.*) a fight, a disturbance. **throw dust in (a person's) eyes,** to mislead him. [OE]

dustbin n. a container for household refuse.

dust-bowl n. an arid or unproductive dry region. The term is applied specifically to an area in the prairie States of the USA that was subject to dust storms and drought in the 1930s when the land was returned to grazing after having been cultivated since the First World War, and the hooves of livestock pulverized the unprotected soil.

A graphic and moving description is given in John Steinbeck's novel *The Grapes of Wrath* (1939). Increased rainfall, re-grassing, and erosion-preventing measures such as contour ploughing have since reduced the area.

duster *n.* a cloth for dusting furniture etc. [f. DUST]

dustman *n.* (*pl.* **-men**) a man employed to empty dustbins.

dustpan *n.* a pan into which dust is brushed from a floor.

dusty *adj.* **1.** covered with or full of dust. **2.** like dust. **3.** (of a colour) dull or vague. **—dusty answer,** a curt rejection of a request. **not so dusty,** (*colloq.*) fairly good. **—dustily** *adv.*, **dustiness** *n.* [OE (as DUST)]

Dutch *adj.* of the Netherlands or its people or language (see etymology below). **—***n.* the Dutch language, which belongs to the Germanic language group and is most closely related to German and English. It is spoken by the 13 million inhabitants of the Netherlands and is also the official language of Surinam in South America and the Netherlands Antilles in the Caribbean. The same language is also spoken in parts of Belgium where it is called Flemish. An offshoot of Dutch is Afrikaans which was taken to Africa by Dutch settlers in the 17th c. **—the Dutch,** the people of the Netherlands. **Dutch auction,** one in which the price is reduced until a buyer is found. **Dutch barn,** a farm shelter for hay etc., consisting of a roof on poles. **Dutch cap,** a contraceptive diaphragm. **Dutch courage,** courage induced by alcoholic drink. **Dutch elm disease,** a fungous disease of elms, first found in the Netherlands. **Dutch oven,** a metal box for cooking, of which the open side is turned towards an ordinary fire; a covered cooking-pot. **Dutch treat,** a party, outing, etc., at which each participant pays for his own share. **go Dutch,** to share the expenses on an outing etc. **in Dutch,** (*slang*) in disgrace. **talk like a Dutch uncle,** to speak severely but kindly. [f. MDu. *dutsch*, OHG *diutisc* national. In Germany the adj. was used (in the 9th c.) as a rendering of L *vulgaris* to distinguish the 'vulgar tongue' from the Latin of the Church and the learned; hence it came to be applied to any dialect, and generically to German as a whole. From the language, it was naturally extended to those who spoke it, whence arose the name of the country, *Deutschland* = Germany. In the 15th and 16th c. in England 'Dutch' included the language and people of the Netherlands as part of the 'Low Dutch' or Low German domain. After the United Provinces became an independent State, using the Low German of Holland as the national language, the term 'Dutch' was gradually restricted in England to the Netherlands.]

dutch *n.* (*slang*) a costermonger's wife. [abbr. of DUCHESS]

Dutchman *n.* (*pl.* **-men**) a man of Dutch birth or nationality. **—I'm a Dutchman,** a phrase implying refusal or disbelief.

duteous /ˈdjuːtɪəs/ *adj.* (*literary*) dutiful. [f. DUTY]

dutiable /ˈdjuːtɪəb(ə)l/ *adj.* requiring payment of duty. [f. DUTY]

dutiful /ˈdjuːtɪf(ə)l/ *adj.* doing or observant of one's duty, obedient. **—dutifully** *adv.* [f. DUTY + -FUL]

duty /ˈdjuːtɪ/ *n.* **1.** a moral or legal obligation, what one is bound or ought to do; the binding force of what is right; a business, office, or function arising from these, an engagement in these. **2.** deference, an expression of respect to a superior. **3.** a tax levied on certain goods, imports, events, or services. **—do duty for,** to serve as or pass for (something else). **duty-bound** *adj.* obliged by duty. **duty-free shop,** a shop at an airport etc. at which goods can be bought free of duty. **on, off, duty,** actually engaged, not engaged, in one's regular work or some obligation. [f. AF (as DUE)]

duvet /ˈduːveɪ/ *n.* a thick soft quilt used instead of bedclothes. [F]

Dvořák /ˈdvɔːʒæk/, Antonin (1841–1904), Czech composer, brought up in Bohemia at a time of strong national consciousness, who combined the idioms of folk dances and songs (not only Czech but also American) with the central German and Austrian tradition from Haydn and Mozart to Brahms and Wagner. His widely popular 'New World' (Ninth) Symphony dates from a period (1892–5) spent in the USA as director of the National Conservatory of Music, New York, and contains reminiscences of Negro spirituals, including 'Swing low, sweet chariot', as well as Bohemian melodies. Dvořák's chamber music, the Cello Concerto (1895), and the operas *The Jacobin* (1887–8), and *Rusalka* (1900) are now beginning to receive the recognition they deserve.

dwarf /dwɔːf/ *n.* (*pl.* **-fs**) **1.** a person, animal, or plant much below normal size. **2.** a small mythological being with magical powers. **—***adj.* of a kind very small in size. **—***v.t.* **1.** to stunt in growth. **2.** to make seem small by contrast or distance. **—dwarf nova,** a type of cataclysmic variable star varying up to a hundredfold in light output during the space of a few days. These eruptions occur semi-regularly, and are believed to be due to a fluctuating transfer of material from one member of a binary pair of stars to the other. [OE]

dwell *v.i.* (*past & p.p.* **dwelt**) to live as an occupant or inhabitant. **—dwell on** or **upon,** to think or speak or write at length on. **—dweller** *n.* (OE, = lead astray)

dwelling *n.* a house, a residence. [f. prec.]

dwindle *v.i.* to become gradually less or smaller; to lose importance. [f. *dwine* fade away f. OE]

Dy *symbol* dysprosium.

Dyak /ˈdaɪæk/ *n.* **1.** a member of the indigenous non-Muslim inhabitants of Borneo (see below). **2.** their language, = Iban. [f. Malay *dayak* up-country]

The Dyak peoples are sub-divided into several named groups including the Land Dyak of SW Borneo and the Sea Dyak of Sarawak. Reckoned to be early inhabitants of the island, forced inland by subsequent migrations of Malays to the coasts, the people live in long-house communities, and intertribal warfare and head-hunting were formerly characteristic of Dyak society. The term 'Sea Dyak' is a misnomer, since the population to which it is applied is primarily a riverine hill-dwelling people whose economy is based on rice cultivation; it was introduced originally to distinguish the more aggressive peoples of the interior, who carried out raids on their coastal neighbours by going down to the sea and then mounting expeditions, from the more passive Land Dyaks of the coast.

dybbuk /ˈdɪbʌk/ *n.* (*pl.* **-im, -s**) (in Jewish folklore) the malevolent spirit of a dead person that enters and controls the body of a living person until exorcized. [f. Heb. (*dābak* cling)]

dye /daɪ/ *n.* a substance used to change the colour of hair, fabric, wood, etc.; a colour produced by this. **—***v.t.* (*partic.* **dyeing**) to impregnate with dye; to make (a thing) a specified colour thus. **—dyed in the wool,** out-and-out, unchangeable. **—dyer** *n.* [OE]

Dyfed /ˈdʌvɪd/ a county of SW Wales.

dying see DIE[1].

dyke var. of DIKE.

dynamic /daɪˈnæmɪk/ *adj.* **1.** of motive force (opp. *static*). **2.** of force in actual operation (opp. *potential*). **3.** of dynamics. **4.** (of a person) active, energetic. **—dynamically** *adv.* [f. F f. Gk (*dunamis* force, power)]

dynamics *n.* (usu. treated as *sing.*) **1.** the mathematical study of motion and the forces causing it; the branch of any science in which forces or changes are considered. **2.** motive forces, physical or moral, in any sphere. **3.** (*Mus.*) gradations or amount of volume of sound. [f. prec.]

dynamism /ˈdaɪnəmɪz(ə)m/ *n.* energizing or dynamic action or power. [f. Gk *dunamis* power]

dynamite /ˈdaɪnəmaɪt/ *n.* **1.** a high explosive (see below). **2.** a potentially dangerous person or thing. **—***v.t.* to charge or blow up with dynamite. [as prec.]

Dynamite is a plastic high explosive introduced by Alfred B. Nobel in 1866, consisting of nitroglycerine absorbed by a solid substance to improve handling quality. The solid may be inert (e.g. kieselguhr, a form of silicon dioxide), or active (e.g. a mixture of sodium nitrate and wood pulp). In particular ammonium nitrate may be added to improve safety during handling, and to reduce cost. Minor ingredients include calcium carbonate to neutralize acidity, and a freezing-point depressant to prevent freezing during cold weather. Dynamite is chiefly used for commercial blasting.

dynamo /ˈdaɪnəməʊ/ *n.* (*pl.* **-os**) a machine converting mechanical into electrical energy, especially by rotating coils of copper wire in a magnetic field. [abbr. of *dynamo-electric machine* (as DYNAMIC)]

dynamometer /daɪnəˈmɒmɪtə(r)/ *n.* an instrument measuring the energy expended. [f. F f. Gk *dunamis* force + -METER]

dynast /ˈdɪnæst/ *n.* a ruler; a member of a dynasty. [f. L f. Gk (*dunamai* be able)]

dynasty /ˈdɪnəstɪ/ *n.* a line of hereditary rulers; a succession of leaders in any field. **—dynastic** /-ˈnæstɪk/ *adj.* [f. F or L f. Gk (as prec.)]

dyne /daɪn/ *n.* a unit of force, the force that, acting for 1 second on a mass of 1 g, gives it a velocity of 1 cm per second. [F, f. Gk *dunamis* force]

dys- *prefix* bad, difficult. [f. Gk *dus-*]

dysentery /ˈdɪs(ə)ntrɪ/ *n.* a disease with inflammation of the intestines, causing severe diarrhoea. [f. OF or L f. Gk (DYS-, *entera* bowels)]

dyslexia /dɪsˈleksɪa/ *n.* abnormal difficulty in reading and spelling, caused by a condition of the brain. —**dyslexic** *adj.* & *n.* [f. G f. Gk (DYS-, *lexis* speech)]

dyspepsia /dɪsˈpepsɪə/ *n.* indigestion. —**dyspeptic** *adj.* & *n.* [L f. Gk (DYS-, *peptos* cooked, digested)]

dysprosium /dɪsˈprəʊzɪəm/ *n.* a soft metallic element of the lanthanide series, symbol Dy, atomic number 66, discovered in 1886. Purified dysprosium has various specialized uses, including as a component in certain magnetic alloys. [f. Gk *dusprositos* hard to get at]

dystrophy /ˈdɪstrəfɪ/ *n.* defective nutrition. —**muscular dystrophy,** hereditary progressive weakening and wasting of the muscles. [L f. Gk (DYS-, *-trophia* nourishment)]

Dzongkha /ˈzɒŋkə/ *n.* a Tibetan dialect that is the official language of Bhutan. [Tibetan, = language of the fortress]

E

E, e n. **1.** the fifth letter of the alphabet. **2.** (*Mus.*) the third note in the scale of C major.

E *symbol* (preceding a number) indicating conformity with an EEC standard of quantities and capacities permitted for certain prepackaged products.

E. *abbr.* east, eastern.

e *symbol* indicating conformity with EEC standards for the indicated weights or volume of certain prepackaged products.

each *adj.* every one of (two or more persons or things) regarded separately. —*pron.* each person or thing. —**each other,** one another. **each way,** (of a bet) backing a horse etc. to win and to be placed. [OE, = ever alike]

eager /ˈiːgə(r)/ *adj.* full of keen desire, enthusiastic. —**eager beaver,** (*colloq.*) a very or excessively diligent person. —**eagerly** *adv.*, **eagerness** n. [f. AF f. L *acer*]

eagle n. **1.** a large bird of prey of the family Accipitridae, with keen vision and powerful flight; the figure of an eagle, especially as the symbol of the USA or (*hist.*) as a Roman or French ensign. **2.** (in golf) a hole played in two under par or bogey. —**eagle eye,** keen sight or watchfulness. —**eagle-eyed** *adj.* [f. AF f. L *aquila*]

eaglet /ˈiːglɪt/ n. a young eagle. [f. prec. + -LET]

E. & O.E. *abbr.* errors and omissions excepted.

ear[1] n. **1.** the organ of hearing in man and animals, especially the external part of this (ill. BODY 4). **2.** the faculty of discriminating sound. **3.** an ear-shaped thing. —**all ears,** listening attentively. **ear-drum** n. the internal membrane of the ear. **ear-piercing** *adj.* shrill. **ear-plug** n. a piece of wax etc. placed in the ear to protect against water, noise, etc. **ear-ring** n. an ornament worn on the lobe of the ear. **ear-splitting** *adj.* extremely loud. **ear-trumpet** n. a trumpet-shaped tube formerly used as an aid to hearing by the partially deaf. **give one's ears,** to make any sacrifice *for* a thing, *to* do, *if.* **have** or **keep an ear to the ground,** to be alert to rumours or the trend of opinion. **have a person's ear,** to have a person's favourable attention. **up to the ears,** (*colloq.*) deeply involved or occupied (*in*). [OE]

ear[2] n. the seed-bearing head of a cereal plant. [OE]

earache n. pain in the inner ear.

earful n. (*colloq.*) **1.** copious talk. **2.** a reprimand. [f. EAR[1] + -FUL]

earl /ɜːl/ n. a British nobleman ranking between marquis and viscount. —**Earl Marshal,** the officer presiding over the Heralds' College, with ceremonial duties on royal occasions. [OE]

earldom /ˈɜːldəm/ n. the position or domain of an earl. [f. EARL + -DOM]

early /ˈɜːlɪ/ *adj.* & *adv.* before the due, usual, or expected time; not far on in day, night, or time; not far on in a period, development, or process of evolution; forward in flowering, ripening, etc. —**early bird,** (*colloq.*) one who arrives or gets up early. **early days,** early in time for something (to happen etc.). **Early English (style),** the first stage of English Gothic architecture (13th c.), with narrow pointed windows and pointed arches. **early on,** at an early stage. [OE (as ERE)]

earmark n. an identifying mark; an owner's mark on the ear of an animal. —*v.t.* **1.** to set aside for a special purpose. **2.** to mark (an animal) with an earmark.

earn /ɜːn/ *v.t.* **1.** to bring in as income or interest. **2.** (of a person, conduct, etc.) to obtain or be entitled to as a reward of work or merit. [OE]

earnest[1] /ˈɜːnɪst/ *adj.* ardently serious, showing intense feeling. —**in earnest,** serious, seriously, with determination. —**earnestly** *adv.*, **earnestness** n. [OE (cf. ON *ern* vigorous)]

earnest[2] /ˈɜːnɪst/ n. money paid as an instalment, especially to confirm a contract; a token, a foretaste. [prob. var. of *erles* f. L *arrhula* dim. of *arr(h)a* pledge]

earnings *n.pl.* money earned. [f. EARN]

earphone n. a device worn over or put to the ear to receive radio or telephone etc. communication.

earshot n. hearing-distance.

earth /ɜːθ/ n. **1.** (also **Earth**) the planet on which we live (see below). **2.** the present abode of man, as distinct from heaven and hell. **3.** land and sea, as distinct from sky; dry land, the ground. **4.** soil. **5.** connection to earth as the completion of an electrical circuit, either accidental (with resulting leakage of current or dangerous differences of potential) or intentional (as for the purpose of providing a return path for a current). **6.** the hole of a badger, fox, etc. **7.** (*colloq.*) a huge sum, a vast amount. —*v.t.* **1.** to connect (an electrical circuit) to earth. **2.** to cover (the roots of a plant) with earth. —**come back to earth,** to return to realities. **earth-nut** n. any of various plants or their tubers, especially the peanut. **earth sciences,** those concerned with the earth or part of it. **earth-shaking** *adj.* having a violent effect. **gone to earth,** in hiding. **on earth,** existing anywhere. **run to earth,** to find after a long search. [OE]

Earth is the third closest planet to the sun in the solar system and has one natural satellite, the moon. It has an equatorial radius of 6,378 km (3,963 miles), an average density 5.5 times that of water, and is believed to have formed about 4,600 million years ago. Internally it consists of three concentric layers: core, mantle, and crust (see ill. GEOLOGY). The crust, which forms the surface of the solid earth, is only a few kilometres thick, although thicker beneath the continents than beneath the oceans. The mantle consists mainly of silicate rocks, and constitutes the bulk of the earth's volume. Beneath it is the core, which extends to the centre of the earth, consisting largely of iron and nickel; its outer part is liquid and is thought to be the seat of the earth's magnetic field. According to the theory of plate tectonics (see entry) the crust and upper part of the mantle are divided into a series of rigid plates, which lie on top of a more plastic region. Earth, which is three-quarters covered by oceans and has a dense atmosphere of nitrogen and oxygen, is the only planet known to support life.

earthbound *adj.* **1.** attached (*lit.* or *fig.*) to the earth or earthly things. **2.** moving towards the earth.

earthen *adj.* made of earth or baked clay. [f. EARTH]

earthenware n. pottery made of coarse baked clay.

earthly *adj.* of the earth or man's life on it, terrestrial. —**no earthly,** (*colloq.*) absolutely no use. **not an earthly,** (*slang*) no chance whatever. —**earthliness** n. [f. EARTH]

earthquake n. a convulsion of the earth's surface. While gentle earth tremors can occur in any region of the globe, the more severe ones usually occur near the edges of the major 'plates' that make up the earth's crust. The point at which an earthquake shock originates is called the focus and the point immediately above this on the earth's surface is the epicentre. The intensity of the earthquake is reported as measured by the Richter scale. Major earthquakes generally measure between about 7 and 9, though in theory there is no upper limit on the scale.

earthwork n. an artificial bank of earth in a fortification or in road-building.

earthworm n. an annelid worm (of various genera) living in the ground.

earthy *adj.* **1.** of or like earth or soil. **2.** gross, coarse. **3.** worldly. —**earthiness** n. [f. EARTH]

earwig n. a small insect of the order Dermaptera, with pincers at its tail end (ill. INSECTS). [OE (EAR[1], *wig* prob. rel. to *wiggle*); once thought to enter the head through the ear]

ease /iːz/ n. **1.** freedom from pain or trouble; freedom from constraint. **2.** facility. —*v.t./i.* **1.** to relieve from pain or anxiety. **2.** to relax, to slacken, to make or become less burdensome. **3.** to cause to move by gentle force. —**at ease,** free from anxiety or constraint; (of soldiers etc.) in a relaxed attitude, with the feet apart. **ease off** or **up,** to become less burdensome or severe. [f. OF *aise* f. L *adjacens* lying near]

easel /ˈiːz(ə)l/ n. a standing wooden support for an artist's canvas, a blackboard, etc. [f. Du. *ezel* ass]

easement /ˈiːzmənt/ n. a legal right of way or similar right over another's ground or property. [f. OF (as EASE)]

easily /ˈiːzɪlɪ/ *adv.* **1.** in an easy manner, without difficulty. **2.** by far. **3.** very probably. [f. EASE]

east *n.* **1.** the point of the horizon where the sun rises at the equinoxes; the compass point corresponding to this; the direction in which this lies. **2.** (usu. **East**) the part of a country or town lying to the east; the regions or countries lying to the east of Europe; the Communist States of eastern Europe. —*adj.* **1.** towards, at, or facing the east. **2.** (of wind) blowing from the east. —*adv.* towards, at, or near the east. —**East End,** the eastern part of London, including the docks. **east-north-east, east-south-east** *adjs.* & *advs.* midway between east and north-east, or south-east; (*ns.*) the compass point in this position. **East Side,** the eastern part of Manhattan. [OE]

East Anglia /ˈæŋglɪə/ an ancient division of England, now a region of eastern England consisting of the counties of Norfolk, Suffolk, and parts of Essex and Cambridgeshire.

East China Sea see CHINA SEA.

Easter /ˈiːstə(r)/ *n.* the feast of the Resurrection of Christ, the greatest and oldest feast of the Christian Church, celebrated on the first Sunday after the first full moon after the vernal equinox (21 March). The derivation of the name is uncertain. According to Bede, it was connected with an Anglo-Saxon goddess Eostre whose festival was in spring; at any rate it seems clear that the Christian feast superseded an old pagan festival. —**Easter egg,** an edible artificial (usually chocolate) egg given as a gift at Easter. The egg is an ancient symbol of renewed life. Easter eggs, originally called 'pace eggs' (*Pasch* = Easter; see PASCHAL), were known as early as the 13th c. They were ordinary hard-boiled eggs, with the shells dyed different colours. **Easter rising,** the insurrection in Dublin and other cities in Ireland against British rule, Easter 1916. It ended with the surrender of the insurgents, some of whose leaders were subsequently executed.

Easter Island an island in the SE Pacific west of Chile, named by the Dutch navigator Roggeveen who visited it on Easter Day, 1722. It is administered by Chile and is famous for its many monolithic statues of human heads (up to 10 metres high); pop. (est., 1971) 1,400.

easterly /ˈiːstəlɪ/ *adj.* & *adv.* in an eastern position or direction; (of wind) blowing from the east (approximately). [f. EAST]

eastern /ˈiːstən/ *adj.* of or in the east. —**Eastern Church,** the Orthodox Church. **Eastern Empire,** see ROMAN EMPIRE. —**easternmost** *adj.* [f. EAST]

easterner *n.* a native or inhabitant of the east. [f. prec.]

East India Company a trading company formed in 1600 to develop commerce in the newly discovered East Indies (formerly called East India). In the second half of the 18th c., after a series of victories over local princes, the Company took over the administration of British India, maintaining its own army and political service. Government remained in the hands of the company until 1858 when the British Crown took over in the wake of the Indian Mutiny.

East Indies the many islands off the SE coast of Asia, now often called the Malay Archipelago.

easting *n.* (*Naut.* etc.) **1.** a distance travelled or measured eastward. **2.** an easterly direction. [f. EAST]

Eastman /ˈiːstmən/, George (1854–1932), American inventor of the hand-held Kodak camera (1888) designed to use a flexible roll-film coated with light-sensitive emulsion, and of the film itself—inventions which did much to popularize amateur photography.

East Sussex /ˈsʌsɪks/ a county of SE England.

eastward /ˈiːstwəd/ *adj.* & (also **eastwards** /-z/) *adv.* towards the east. —*n.* an eastward direction or region. [f. EAST + -WARD]

easy /ˈiːzɪ/ *adj.* **1.** not difficult, achieved without great effort. **2.** free from pain, trouble, or anxiety. **3.** free from awkwardness, strictness, etc., relaxed and pleasant. **4.** compliant, obliging. —*adv.* with ease, in an effortless or relaxed manner; (as *int.*) go carefully. —**easy chair,** a large comfortable chair. **easy on the eye,** pleasant to look at. **Easy Street,** (*colloq.*) a state of affluence. **go easy,** to be sparing or cautious (*with* or *on*). **I'm easy,** (*colloq.*) I have no preference. **take it easy,** to proceed gently, to relax. —**easiness** *n.* [f. AF (as EASE)]

easygoing *adj.* placid and tolerant, relaxed in manner.

eat *v.t./i.* (*past* **ate** /et, eɪt/, *p.p.* **eaten**) **1.** to take into the mouth, to chew and swallow (food); to consume food, to take a meal. **2.** (often with *away*) to destroy, to consume; (also with *at*) to trouble, to vex. —**eat one's heart out,** to suffer greatly from anxiety or longing. **eating apple** etc., one suitable for eating raw. **eats** *n.pl.* (*colloq.*) food, a meal.

eat up, to eat or consume completely; to traverse (distance) rapidly. **eat one's words,** to retract them abjectly. [OE]

eatable *adj.* that may be eaten. —*n.* (usu. in *pl.*) food. [f. EAT]

eater *n.* **1.** one who eats. **2.** an eating apple etc. [f. EAT]

eau-de-Cologne /ˌəʊdəkəˈləʊn/ *n.* a perfume originally made at Cologne. [F, = water of Cologne]

eaves *n.pl.* the projecting lower edge of a roof (ill. HOUSES). [OE, rel. to OVER]

eavesdrop /ˈiːvzdrɒp/ *v.i.* (**-pp-**) to listen secretly to a private conversation. —**eavesdropper** *n.* [f. prec.]

ebb *n.* **1.** the outward movement of the tide, away from the land. **2.** decline, poor condition. —*v.i.* to flow back; to recede, to decline. [OE]

ebonite /ˈebənaɪt/ *n.* vulcanite. [f. foll.]

ebony /ˈebənɪ/ *n.* the hard heavy black wood of a tropical tree especially of the genus *Diospyros.* —*adj.* made of ebony; black like ebony. [f. L f. Gk *ebenos* ebony-tree]

ebullient /ɪˈbʌlɪənt/ *adj.* exuberant, high-spirited. —**ebullience** *n.*, **ebulliency** *n.* [f. L *ebullire* (EX-, *bullire* boil)]

ebullition /ebəˈlɪʃ(ə)n/ *n.* boiling; a sudden outburst of passion or emotion. [as prec.]

EC *abbr.* East Central.

eccentric /ɪkˈsentrɪk/ *adj.* **1.** odd or capricious in behaviour or appearance. **2.** not placed centrally; not having its axis placed centrally; (of a circle) not concentric (*to* another circle); (of an orbit) not circular. —*n.* **1.** an eccentric person. **2.** a disc fixed eccentrically on a revolving shaft, for changing rotatory to to-and-fro motion. —**eccentrically** *adv.*, **eccentricity** /-ˈtrɪsɪtɪ/ *n.* [f. L f. Gk (*ek* out of, *kentron* centre)]

Eccles cake /ˈek(ə)lz/ a round cake of pastry filled with currants. [f. *Eccles* in Greater Manchester]

Ecclesiastes /ɪkliːzɪˈæstiːz/ a book of the Old Testament traditionally ascribed to Solomon but no longer seriously held to be his work. Its date is uncertain; it was one of the latest books to be accepted into the Hebrew canon. The author exhorts to wisdom, industry, and the fear of God, but the general tone is pessimistic, with observations on the futility of human life. [f. Gk, = public speaker, preacher]

ecclesiastic /ɪkliːzɪˈæstɪk/ *n.* a clergyman. [f. F or L f. Gk (*ekklēsia* church)]

ecclesiastical *adj.* of the Church or clergy. [f. prec.]

Ecclesiasticus /ɪkliːzɪˈæstɪkəs/ a book of the Apocrypha, also called 'The Wisdom of Jesus the son of Sirach', containing moral and practical maxims and probably composed or compiled in the early 2nd c. BC. The origin of its name is uncertain; the theory that it represents the Latin *Liber ecclesiasticus* (= book of the Church), so called owing to its use as a book of instruction in the early Church, is untenable.

ecclesiology /ɪkliːzɪˈɒlədʒɪ/ *n.* the study of church building and decoration. [f. Gk *ekklēsia* church + -LOGY]

ECG *abbr.* electrocardiogram.

echelon /ˈeʃəlɒn/ *n.* **1.** a formation of troops or ships, aircraft, etc., in parallel rows with the end of each row projecting further laterally than the one in front. **2.** a grade or rank in an organization. [F, = rung of ladder]

echidna /ɪˈkɪdnə/ *n.* an Australian egg-laying animal (*Tachyglossus aculeatus*) resembling a hedgehog. [L f. Gk, = viper]

echinoderm /ɪˈkaɪnədɜːm, ˈekɪn-/ *n.* an animal of the phylum Echinodermata, a group of marine invertebrates including starfish and sea-urchins, many of which have spiny skins. As well as the characteristic symmetry of their bodies, echinoderms are notable for possessing a unique system of hydraulic tubes used to extend numerous small saclike organs ('tube feet') for locomotion, feeding, etc. Echinoderms are well represented as fossils, and are first found in the Cambrian period. Their embryological development indicates that they are distantly related to the vertebrates. [f. Gk *ekhinos* hedgehog, sea-urchin + *derma* skin]

echo /ˈekəʊ/ *n.* (*pl.* **-oes**) **1.** repetition of sound by the reflection of sound-waves; a secondary sound so produced (see below). **2.** a reflected radio or radar beam. **3.** a close imitation or imitator. —*v.t./i.* **1.** (of a place) to resound with an echo; to repeat (a sound) thus; (of a sound) to be repeated, to resound. **2.** to repeat (a person's words); to imitate the opinions of. —**echo-sounder** *n.* a sounding apparatus for determining the depth of sea beneath a ship by measuring the time taken for an echo to be received (see ASDIC, SONAR). **echo-sounding** *n.* [f. OF or L f. Gk]

There are two mythological explanations of echoes. (i) Echo was a nymph vainly loved by the god Pan, who finally sent the shepherds mad and they tore her in pieces; but Earth hid the fragments which can still sing and imitate other sounds. (ii) According to Ovid, Hera had deprived Echo of speech in order to stop her chatter, and Echo could only repeat what others had said. On being repulsed by Narcissus she wasted away with grief until there was nothing left of her but her voice.

echoic /eˈkəʊɪk/ adj. (of a word) imitating the sound it represents, onomatopoeic. —**echoically** adv. [f. ECHO]

echolocation /ekəʊləˈkeɪʃ(ə)n/ n. the location of objects by means of the echo reflected from them by a sound-signal, as of ultrasonic sounds emitted by bats or by man-made devices.

éclair /eɪˈkleə(r), ɪ-/ n. a finger-shaped cake of choux pastry filled with cream and iced. [F, = lightning]

éclat /ˈeɪklɑː/ n. brilliant success or display; renown, esteem. [F, lit. = burst of light]

eclectic /ɪˈklektɪk/ adj. selecting ideas or beliefs from various sources. —n. an eclectic person. —**eclectically** adv., **eclecticism** /-sɪz(ə)m/ n. [f. Gk (eklegō pick out)]

eclipse /ɪˈklɪps/ n. 1. the obscuring of light from one heavenly body by another (ill. ASTRONOMY). 2. loss of light, brilliance, or importance. —v.t. 1. to cause an eclipse of; to intercept (light). 2. to outshine, to surpass. —**annular eclipse,** one leaving a complete ring of the solar surface open to view, occurring when the moon passes before the sun at a greater distance than average. **partial eclipse,** one that is not total. **total eclipse,** one where the entire surface of the luminous body is obscured. [f. OF, ult. f. Gk ekleipō fail to appear]

ecliptic /ɪˈklɪptɪk/ n. the apparent path across the heavens of the sun during the year (ill. NAVIGATION), so called because lunar and solar eclipses will occur only when the moon crosses this path. —adj. of an eclipse or the ecliptic. [f. L f. Gk (as prec.)]

eclogue /ˈeklɒg/ n. a short poem, especially a pastoral dialogue such as those of Theocritus and Virgil. [f. L f. Gk, = selection (as ECLECTIC)]

eco- prefix ecology, ecological. [f. ECOLOGY]

ecoclimate /ˈiːkəʊklaɪmət/ n. climate as an ecological factor. [f. ECO- + CLIMATE]

ecology /iːˈkɒlədʒɪ/ n. the study of organisms in relation to one another and to their surroundings (see ill. pp. 258-9). —**ecological** /-ˈlɒdʒɪk(ə)l/ adj., **ecologist** n. [f. Gk oikos home + -LOGY]

economic /iːkəˈnɒmɪk, ek-/ adj. 1. of economics. 2. maintained for profit, on business lines; adequate to pay or recoup expenditure with some profit; practical, considered with regard to human needs. —**economically** adv. [f. F or L f. Gk (as ECONOMY)]

economical adj. careful in the use of resources, avoiding waste; thrifty. —**economically** adv. [as prec.]

economics n. 1. the science of the production and distribution of wealth; the application of this to a particular subject. 2. (as pl.) the financial aspects of something. [f. ECONOMIC]

economist /ɪˈkɒnəmɪst/ n. an expert on or student of economics. [f. Gk (as ECONOMY)]

economize /ɪˈkɒnəmaɪz/ v.t./i. to be economical, to make economies, to reduce expenditure; (usu. with on) to use sparingly. [as prec.]

economy /ɪˈkɒnəmɪ/ n. 1. the wealth and resources of a community; the administration or condition of these. 2. careful management of (esp. financial) resources, frugality; an instance of this. [f. F or L f. Gk oikonomia stewardship (oikos house, nemō manage)]

ecosystem /ˈiːkəʊsɪstəm/ n. a system of interacting organisms in a particular habitat. [f. ECO- + SYSTEM]

ecru /ˈeɪkruː/ n. a light fawn colour. [F, = unbleached]

ecstasy /ˈekstəsɪ/ n. 1. an overwhelming feeling of joy, rapture. —**ecstatic** /ekˈstætɪk/ adj., **ecstatically** adv. [f. OF f. L f. Gk ekstasis standing outside oneself]

ECT abbr. electroconvulsive therapy.

ecto- prefix outside. [f. Gk ektos]

ectomorph /ˈektəmɔːf/ n. a person with a lean build of body, thought likely to be an introvert. (One of W. H. Sheldon's three constitutional types: cf. ENDOMORPH, MESOMORPH.) [f. ECTO- + Gk morphē form]

-ectomy /-ektəmɪ/ suffix forming nouns, denoting a surgical operation in which some part is removed (tonsillectomy). [f. Gk ektomē excision]

ectopic /ekˈtɒpɪk/ adj. (Path.) in an abnormal place or position. [f. Gk ektopos out of place]

ectoplasm /ˈektəplæz(ə)m/ n. a viscous substance supposed to emanate from the body of a spiritualist medium during a trance. [f. ECTO- + PLASMA]

Ecuador /ˈekwədɔː(r)/ an equatorial country in South America, on the Pacific coast, pop. (1981) approx. 8,000,000; official language, Spanish; capital, Quito. Ranges and plateaux of the Andes separate the coastal plain from the tropical jungles of the Amazon basin. The economy remains backward and largely agricultural despite some improvement due to oil exports after major oilfields were discovered in 1972. Incorporated in the late 16th c. into the Inca empire, Ecuador was conquered by the Spanish in 1534 and remained part of Spain's American empire until independence was won in 1822. Ecuador has remained independent since leaving the Federation of Grand Colombia in 1830, but has since lost territory in border disputes with its more powerful neighbours. —**Ecuadorean** adj. & n.

ecumenical /iːkjuːˈmenɪk(ə)l/ adj. of or representing the whole Christian world; seeking world-wide Christian unity. —**ecumenicalism** n., **ecumenism** /iːˈkjuːmənɪz(ə)m/ n. [f. L f. Gk (oikoumenē the inhabited earth)]

eczema /ˈeksɪmə/ n. a skin disorder with inflammation and itching. —**eczematous** /ekˈziːmətəs/ adj. [L f. Gk (ek out, zeō boil)]

ed. abbr. 1. edited (by); edition; editor. 2. educated.

Edam /ˈiːdæm/ n. a spherical Dutch cheese, usually pale yellow with a red rind. [f. Edam in Holland]

Edda /ˈedə/ a body of ancient Icelandic literature contained in two 13th-c. books, the Elder or Poetic Edda, a collection of Old Norse poems on mythical or traditional subjects, and the Younger or Prose Edda (attributed to the Icelandic historian Snorri Sturluson), a handbook to Icelandic poetry with prosodic and grammatical treatises and quotations and prose paraphrases from old poems. The Eddas are the chief source of our knowledge of Scandinavian mythology. [ON]

Eddington /ˈedɪŋt(ə)n/, Sir Arthur Stanley (1882-1944), founder of the modern science of astrophysics. His book The Internal Constitution of the Stars (1930) established the fundamental principles of stellar structure and gave some hint of the nature of the energy sources within stars (not fully understood until the discovery of nuclear fusion). He is renowned also for his observations of star positions during the solar eclipse of 1919, which demonstrated the bending of light by gravity and triumphantly vindicated Einstein's recently formulated theory of General Relativity.

eddy /ˈedɪ/ n. an area of water swirling in a circular motion; smoke, fog, etc., moving like this. —v.t./i. to move in eddies. [f. OE ed- again, back]

Eddy /ˈedɪ/, Mrs Mary Baker (1821-1910), foundress of the Church of Christ Scientist (see CHRISTIAN SCIENCE). Long a victim to various ailments, she believed herself cured by a mesmerist, P. P. Quimby. After his death (1866) she evolved her own system of spiritual healing, set out in her book Science and Health (1875).

edelweiss /ˈeɪd(ə)lvaɪs/ n. an alpine plant (Leontopodium alpinum) with woolly white bracts round the flower-heads. [G (edel noble, weiss white)]

Eden /ˈiːd(ə)n/ (also **Garden of Eden**) in the Old Testament, the abode of Adam and Eve at their creation, from which they were expelled for disobedience. [f. L f. Gk f. Heb. (= delight, perh. f. Babylonian edinu a plain]

edentate /ɪˈdenteɪt/ adj. having few or no teeth. —n. an edentate animal, especially a mammal. [f. L edentatus (EX-, dens tooth)]

Edgar /ˈedgə(r)/ (c.944-75), king of England 959-75. He became king of Northumbria and Mercia in 957 when these regions renounced their allegiance to his elder brother Edwy, and succeeded to the throne of England on Edwy's death two years later. One of the strongest of the Anglo-Saxon kings of England, Edgar was renowned for his support of organized religion, playing a decisive part in the growth of monasticism.

edge /edʒ/ n. 1. the cutting side of a blade; the sharpness of this; (fig.) effectiveness. 2. an edge-shaped thing, especially the crest of a ridge. 3. the meeting-line of surfaces; the boundary-line of a region or surface; the brink of a precipice. —v.t./i. 1. to give or form a border to. 2. to insinuate (a thing or oneself, in etc.). 3. to advance (esp. gradually and obliquely). 4. to give a sharp edge to. —**have the edge on,** (colloq.) to have an advantage over. **on edge,** tense and irritable. **set one's teeth on edge,** (of a taste or

Ecology

Energy flow and the cycling of chemicals

The maintenance of life depends upon: a) continual input of sunlight and one-way flow of energy ($\Rightarrow$)

b) continual cycle of chemicals through the system (e.g. oxygen ➡ and carbon ➡)

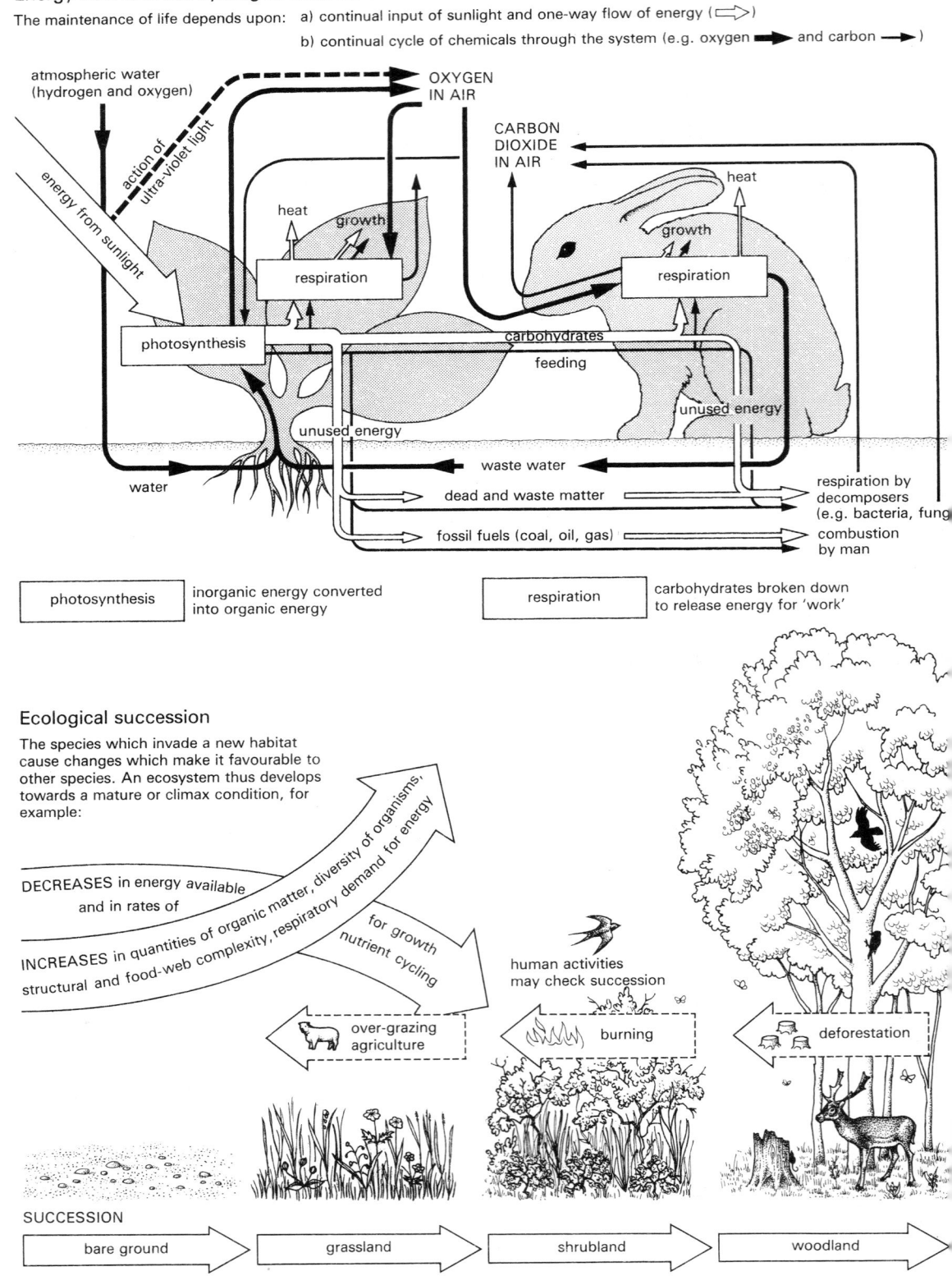

photosynthesis	inorganic energy converted into organic energy

respiration	carbohydrates broken down to release energy for 'work'

Ecological succession

The species which invade a new habitat cause changes which make it favourable to other species. An ecosystem thus develops towards a mature or climax condition, for example:

DECREASES in energy available and in rates of

INCREASES in quantities of organic matter, diversity of organisms, structural and food-web complexity, respiratory demand for energy

for growth

nutrient cycling

human activities may check succession

over-grazing agriculture

burning

deforestation

SUCCESSION

bare ground → grassland → shrubland → woodland

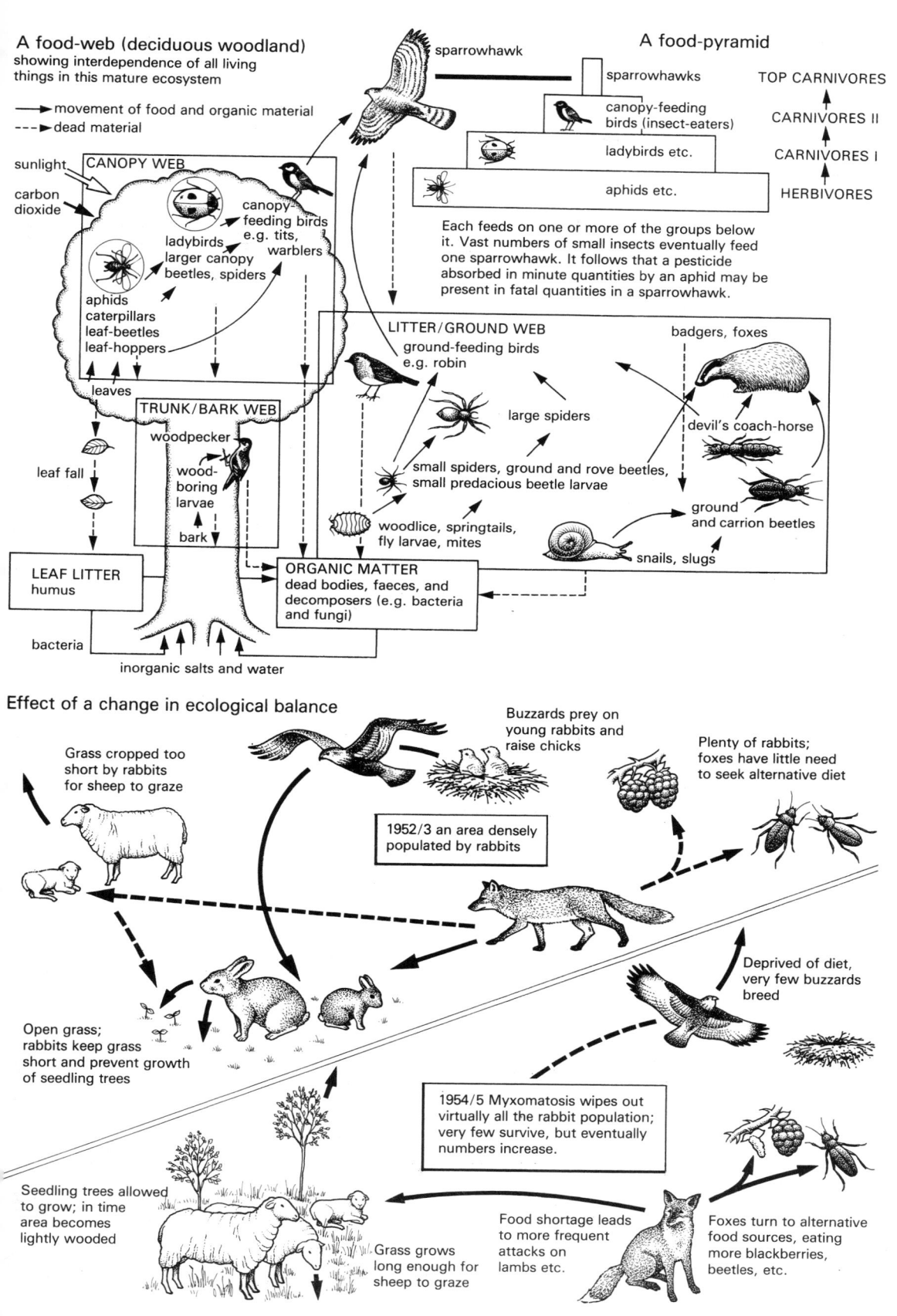

A food-web (deciduous woodland)
showing interdependence of all living
things in this mature ecosystem

→ movement of food and organic material
---→ dead material

sparrowhawk

A food-pyramid

sparrowhawks — TOP CARNIVORES

canopy-feeding birds (insect-eaters) — CARNIVORES II

ladybirds etc. — CARNIVORES I

aphids etc. — HERBIVORES

Each feeds on one or more of the groups below
it. Vast numbers of small insects eventually feed
one sparrowhawk. It follows that a pesticide
absorbed in minute quantities by an aphid may be
present in fatal quantities in a sparrowhawk.

sunlight
carbon
dioxide

CANOPY WEB

ladybirds
larger canopy
beetles, spiders

canopy-
feeding birds
e.g. tits,
warblers

aphids
caterpillars
leaf-beetles
leaf-hoppers

leaves

LITTER/GROUND WEB
ground-feeding birds
e.g. robin

badgers, foxes

large spiders

devil's coach-horse

TRUNK/BARK WEB

woodpecker

wood-
boring
larvae

bark

leaf fall

small spiders, ground and rove beetles,
small predacious beetle larvae

woodlice, springtails,
fly larvae, mites

ground
and carrion beetles

snails, slugs

LEAF LITTER
humus

ORGANIC MATTER
dead bodies, faeces, and
decomposers (e.g. bacteria
and fungi)

bacteria

inorganic salts and water

Effect of a change in ecological balance

Buzzards prey on
young rabbits and
raise chicks

Plenty of rabbits;
foxes have little need
to seek alternative diet

Grass cropped too
short by rabbits
for sheep to graze

1952/3 an area densely
populated by rabbits

Deprived of diet,
very few buzzards
breed

Open grass;
rabbits keep grass
short and prevent growth
of seedling trees

1954/5 Myxomatosis wipes out
virtually all the rabbit population;
very few survive, but eventually
numbers increase.

Seedling trees allowed
to grow; in time
area becomes
lightly wooded

Grass grows
long enough for
sheep to graze

Food shortage leads
to more frequent
attacks on
lambs etc.

Foxes turn to alternative
food sources, eating
more blackberries,
beetles, etc.

sound) to cause an unpleasant nervous sensation. **take the edge off,** to dull, to weaken, to make less intense. [OE]

Edgehill /edʒ'hɪl/ the first pitched battle of the English Civil War (1642), fought at the village of Edgehill in the West Midlands. The royal army failed to exploit a chance of decisive victory through the failure of its cavalry commanders to control their victorious troopers, and the Parliamentary army under the Earl of Essex was able to stay between the King and London. The missed opportunity denied Charles I his chance to win a quick victory in that year.

edgeways *adv.* (also **edgewise**) with the edge foremost or uppermost. —**get a word in edgeways,** to contribute to a conversation dominated by another or others.

Edgeworth /'edʒwɜ:θ/, Maria (1767–1849), Anglo-Irish novelist. Her humorous but sympathetic portrayal of Irish life in novels such as *Castle Rackrent* (1800) won her the friendship of Sir Walter Scott.

edging *n.* a thing forming an edge, a border. [f. EDGE]

edgy *adj.* irritable, anxious, on edge. —**edgily** *adv.*, **edginess** *n.* [f. EDGE]

edible /'edɪb(ə)l/ *adj.* fit to be eaten. —*n.* an edible thing. —**edibility** /-'bɪlɪtɪ/ *n.* [f. L (*edere* eat)]

edict /'i:dɪkt/ *n.* an order proclaimed by authority. [f. L (*edicere* proclaim)]

edifice /'edɪfɪs/ *n.* a building, especially a large imposing one. [f. OF f. L *aedificium*]

edify /'edɪfaɪ/ *v.t.* to benefit spiritually; to improve morally. —**edification** /-fɪ'keɪʃ(ə)n/ *n.* [f. OF f. L *aedificare* build]

Edinburgh /'edɪnbərə/ the capital of Scotland from 1437, lying close to the southern shore of the Firth of Forth; pop. (1984) 440,902. The city grew up round the 11th-c. castle built by Malcolm III on a rocky ridge which dominates the landscape.

Edison /'edɪs(ə)n/, Thomas Alva (1847–1931), the archetypal American inventor. Starting from the humblest beginnings, with three months of school education, he was employed at the age of 12 as a newsboy and at 15 as a telegraph operator, from which he developed an interest in electricity and its applications. He took out the first of over 1,000 patents at the age of 21; his most important inventions were automatic telegraph systems, the mimeograph, the carbon microphone for telephones, the phonograph (precursor of the gramophone), the carbon filament lamp, the nickel-iron or NIFE accumulator (one of the few alternatives to the ubiquitous lead-acid battery), and discovered the 'Edison effect', the passage of electricity from the filament to a metal plate inside an incandescent lamp globe, thus the precursor of the thermionic valve. His development of electric lighting led him to devise complete systems for generating and distributing electricity, originally with direct current. Perhaps his most significant invention was that of the industrial laboratory employing teams of scientists and engineers, though ironically this led to the demise of the individual inventor so splendidly typified by Edison himself.

edit /'edɪt/ *v.t.* **1.** to assemble or prepare (written material) for publication; to arrange or modify (another's work) for publication. **2.** to act as editor of (a newspaper etc.). **3.** to prepare (data) for processing by computer. **4.** to take extracts from and collate (a film etc.) so as to form a unified sequence. **5.** to reword for a purpose. [f. F (as foll.)]

edition /ɪ'dɪʃ(ə)n/ *n.* **1.** the edited or published form of a book etc. **2.** the copies of a book, newspaper, etc., issued at one time; the whole number of products of the same kind issued at one time. **3.** a person etc. considered as resembling another. [f. F f. L (*edere* publish)]

editor /'edɪtə(r)/ *n.* **1.** one who edits. **2.** one who directs the content and writing of a newspaper or a particular section of one. **3.** the head of a department of a publishing house. —**editorship** *n.* [L (as EDIT)]

editorial /edɪ'tɔ:rɪəl/ *adj.* of an editor or editing. —*n.* a newspaper article commenting on a current topic, written or sanctioned by the editor. —**editorially** *adv.* [f. prec.]

Edomite /'i:dəmaɪt/ *adj.* of Edom, an ancient region south of the Dead Sea, or its people. —*n.* a member of an ancient people traditionally descended from Esau, living in Edom.

EDP *abbr.* electronic data processing.

educable /'edjʊkəb(ə)l/ *adj.* able to be educated. [f. foll.]

educate /'edjʊkeɪt/ *v.t.* to train or instruct intellectually, morally, and socially; to provide schooling for. —**educated**

guess, one based on experience. —**educative** *adj.*, **educator** *n.* [f. L (rel. to EDUCE)]

education /edjʊ'keɪʃ(ə)n/ *n.* systematic instruction; a course of this; development of character or mental powers. —**educational** *adj.*, **educationally** *adv.* [f. F or L (as prec.)]

educationist *n.* (also **educationalist**) an expert in educational methods. [f. prec.]

educe /ɪ'dju:s/ *v.t.* to bring out, to develop from latent or potential existence. —**eduction** /ɪ'dʌkʃ(ə)n/ *n.* [f. L *educere* draw out]

Edward /'edwəd/ the name of six kings of England since the Conquest and two of the United Kingdom:

Edward I (1239–1307), son of Henry III, reigned 1272–1307, nicknamed 'the Hammer of the Scots'. After coming to the throne Edward did much to solidify the central administration weakened by Henry's fecklessness, but soon became involved in the wars which were eventually to impose a dangerous financial burden on the realm. His campaign against the Welsh prince Llewelyn ended with the annexation of Wales in 1284, but from 1291 onwards Edward became increasingly preoccupied with his attempt to impose feudal superiority on Scotland. There he dealt successfully with a revolt in 1296 but a second uprising dragged on from 1297 until 1305. On his way north to deal with a third revolt, led this time by Robert the Bruce, he died, leaving his weak son Edward II to deal with a situation which was to prove beyond him.

Edward II (1284–1327), son of Edward I, reigned 1307–27. He was the first English Prince of Wales, but the story that as an infant he was presented to the Welsh crowd by his father as their future sovereign, a native prince who could speak no English, is apocryphal. A weak and foolish monarch, Edward soon proved unequal to the problems left him by his more military father. Early trouble with his barons led to civil war, and two years later his defeat by the Scots at Bannockburn further weakened his position and he temporarily lost power to Thomas, Earl of Lancaster. With the help of new favourites, the Despensers, Edward eventually managed to overthrow and kill Lancaster, but his wife, Isobel of France, allied herself with the exiled Roger de Mortimer, who invaded England and deposed Edward in favour of his son. Edward died in Berkeley Castle in Gloucestershire soon after his deposition, almost certainly at the hands of murderers.

Edward III (1312–77), son of Edward II, reigned 1327–77. Edward assumed personal control of his kingdom in 1330, executing Roger de Mortimer who had deposed his father Edward II. He restored order and reconciled the baronial opposition, but was soon involved in the wars which were to dominate much of his reign. Edward resumed his grandfather's policy of undermining Scottish independence by supporting the pretender to the Scottish throne Edward de Baliol, and started the Hundred Years War with France by advancing his claim to the French throne. Although he won dramatic victories in both theatres, final victory eluded him, and following his premature decline into senility, effective government fell into the hands of his unpopular fourth son, John of Gaunt.

Edward IV (1442–83), son of Richard Duke of York, reigned 1461–83. Following his father's death in the early stages of the Wars of the Roses, Edward inherited the Yorkist claim to the throne, and after defeating his opponents in two battles deposed the Lancastrian king Henry VI and reigned in his place as Edward IV. The early years of his reign were troubled by Lancastrian plots, but the most serious threat arose in 1470-1 as a result of an alliance between his old Lancastrian enemies and his disaffected former lieutenant, the Earl of Warwick. Edward was briefly forced into exile, but returned to crush his opponents, thereafter ruling in relative peace until his death. His rule was characterized by vigorous and successful attempts to reform royal government, although in his last few years he seems to have given way to some extent to personal pleasure.

Edward V (1470–c.1483), son of Edward IV, reigned 1483 but was not crowned. Illegitimized following his father's death, on debatable evidence of the illegality of Edward IV's marriage, the youthful prince's throne was taken by his uncle Richard III. (See PRINCES IN THE TOWER.)

Edward VI (1537–53), son of Henry VIII, reigned 1547–53. During his brief reign as a minor England was effectively ruled by two Protectors, the Duke of Somerset and the Duke of Northumberland. Although the young and sickly king had little direct influence over the policies pursued by his guardians, his Protestant beliefs contributed significantly to the establishment of Protestantism as the State religion, a development which was to survive the Catholic reaction which followed under his elder sister and successor, Mary I.

Edward VII (1841–1910), son of Victoria, reigned 1901–10, known as 'the Peacemaker' for no very good reason. His reign, however, was a period of peace. An extrovert and something of a playboy, Edward was kept away from the serious conduct of royal affairs during the long reign of his mother, but although he played little part in government upon finally coming to the throne, his popularity and interest in public appearances generally increased the prestige of the monarchy. He died suddenly in 1910 before his attitude to the then current crisis over the government's plans to create a large number of new peers could have any impact on events.

Edward VIII (1894–1972), son of George V, reigned 1936 but was not crowned. A popular Prince of Wales, Edward abdicated eleven months after coming to the throne in order to marry the American divorcee Mrs Wallis Simpson. Created Duke of Windsor, he served as Governor-General of the Bahamas during the Second World War before spending the rest of his life in France.

Edwardian /edˈwɔːdɪən/ adj. belonging to or characteristic of the reign of Edward VII (1901–10). —n. a person of this period. [f. EDWARD]

Edward the Confessor (c.1003–66), king of England 1042–66, son of Ethelred the Unready. Famed for his piety, Edward was dominated through much of his reign by his wife's father Earl Godwin, and in later years took less and less interest in affairs of State, effective control falling to Godwin's son, who eventually succeeded Edward as Harold II. Edward was buried in Westminster Abbey and canonized in 1161.

Edward the Martyr (c.963–78), king of England 975–8. Although he successfully succeeded his father Edgar in 975, the youthful Edward was soon faced by a challenge for the throne from his half-brother Ethelred, who eventually had him murdered at Corfe in 978. Edward was subsequently made a saint and became the subject of a considerable medieval cult.

Edwy /ˈedwɪ/ (died 959), king of England 955–9. An ineffective monarch, Edwy alienated a large part of his kingdom during his short reign, and, after Mercia and Northumbria had renounced him in favour of his brother Edgar in 957, he ruled only over the lands south of the Thames.

EEC abbr. European Economic Community.

EEG abbr. electroencephalogram.

eel n. 1. a snakelike fish. 2. an evasive person. [OE]

eerie /ˈɪərɪ/ adj. gloomy and strange, weird. —**eerily** adv., **eeriness** n. [OE; orig. = timid]

efface /ɪˈfeɪs/ v.t. 1. to rub or wipe out (a mark, recollection, or impression). 2. to surpass, to eclipse. —**efface oneself**, to treat or regard oneself as unimportant. —**effacement** n. [f. F (as EX-¹, FACE)]

effect /ɪˈfekt/ n. 1. a result or consequence of an action etc. 2. the state of being operative; efficacy. 3. an impression produced on a spectator or hearer etc. 4. (in pl.) property. 5. (in pl.) sounds and visual features giving realism to a play, film, etc. —v.t. to bring about, to accomplish, to cause to occur. —**bring** or **carry into effect,** to accomplish. **give effect to,** to make operative. **in effect,** for practical purposes, in reality. **take effect,** to become operative. **to that effect,** having that result or implication. **with effect from,** coming into operation at (a stated time). [f. OF or L (as EFFICIENT)]

effective /ɪˈfektɪv/ adj. 1. having an effect, powerful in effect; striking, remarkable. 2. actual, existing. 3. operative. —**effectively** adv., **effectiveness** n. [f. L (as prec.)]

effectual /ɪˈfektʃʊəl, -tjʊəl/ adj. answering its purpose, sufficient to produce an effect; valid. —**effectually** adv. [f. L (as EFFECT)]

effectuate /ɪˈfektʃʊeɪt, -tjʊeɪt/ v.t. to cause to happen. [as prec.]

effeminate /ɪˈfemɪnət/ adj. (of a man) womanish in appearance or manner. —**effeminacy** n. [f. L effeminatus (EX-¹, femina woman)]

effervesce /efəˈves/ v.i. 1. to give off bubbles of gas. 2. to show great liveliness. —**effervescence** n., **effervescent** adj. [f. L effervescere (EX-¹, fervescere begin to be hot)]

effete /ɪˈfiːt/ adj. worn out, lacking vitality; feeble. —**effeteness** n. [f. L effetus worn out by bearing young (as FOETUS)]

efficacious /efɪˈkeɪʃəs/ adj. producing or able to produce

the desired effect. —**efficacy** /ˈefɪkəsɪ/ n. [f. L efficax (as foll.)]

efficient /ɪˈfɪʃ(ə)nt/ adj. 1. productive with the minimum waste of effort. 2. (of a person) capable, acting effectively. 3. producing an effect. —**efficiency** n. **efficiently** adv. [f. L efficere accomplish (EX-¹, facere make, do)]

effigy /ˈefɪdʒɪ/ n. a portrait or image of a person. [f. L effigies (EX-¹, fingere fashion)]

effloresce /eflɔːˈres/ v.i. 1. to burst into flower. 2. (of a substance) to turn to fine powder on exposure to air; (of salts) to come to the surface and crystallize; (of a surface) to become covered with such salt particles. —**efflorescence** n., **efflorescent** adj. [f. L efflorescere (EX-¹, florescere begin to bloom)]

effluence /ˈeflʊəns/ n. a flowing out of light or electricity etc.; that which flows out. [as foll.]

effluent /ˈeflʊənt/ adj. flowing out. —n. a thing that flows out, especially a stream from a larger stream, or sewage. [f. L effluere flow out]

effluvium /eˈfluːvɪəm/ n. (pl. -ia) an outflow of a substance, especially an unpleasant or harmful one. [L (as prec.)]

efflux /ˈeflʌks/ n. an outflow. [f. L effluxus (as EFFLUENT)]

effort /ˈefət/ n. 1. strenuous physical or mental exertion; the application of this, an attempt; the force exerted. 2. (colloq.) something accomplished. [F, f. OF esforcier f. L fortis strong]

effortless adj. done without effort, requiring no effort. —**effortlessly** adv. [f. prec. + -LESS]

effrontery /ɪˈfrʌntərɪ/ n. shameless insolence, impudence. [f. F f. L effrons shameless (EX-¹, frons forehead)]

effulgent /ɪˈfʌldʒ(ə)nt/ adj. radiant, bright. —**effulgence** n. [f. L effulgēre (EX-¹, fulgēre shine)]

effuse /ɪˈfjuːz/ v.t. to pour forth, to send out (a liquid or light, or fig.). [f. L effundere (EX-¹, fundere pour)]

effusion /ɪˈfjuːʒ(ə)n/ n. an outpouring, especially (derog.) of unrestrained literary work. [f. OF or L (as prec.)]

effusive /ɪˈfjuːsɪv/ adj. demonstrative, gushing. —**effusively** adv., **effusiveness** n. [f. L (as EFFUSE)]

eft n. a newt. [OE]

EFTA /ˈeftə/ abbr. European Free Trade Association.

e.g. abbr. for example. [abbr. of L exempli gratia]

egalitarian /ɪgælɪˈteərɪən/ adj. of or advocating equal rights for all. —n. an egalitarian person. —**egalitarianism** n. [f. F (égal equal)]

egg¹ n. 1. a spheroidal body produced by the female of birds etc. containing the germ of a new individual, especially that of the domestic fowl for eating; a female ovum. 2. (colloq.) a person (qualified in some way). —**egg-cup** n. a small cup for holding a boiled egg. **egg-flip, egg-nog** ns. a drink of alcoholic spirit with beaten egg, milk, etc. **eggplant** n. a plant (Solanum melongena) with deep purple fruit used as a vegetable; its fruit, aubergine. **with egg on one's face,** (colloq.) made to look foolish. —**eggy** adj. [f. ON]

egg² v.t. to urge on. [f. ON (as EDGE)]

egghead n. (colloq.) an intellectual person.

eggshell n. the shell of an egg. —adj. 1. (of china) thin and fragile. 2. (of paint) with a slight gloss.

eglantine /ˈegləntaɪn/ n. sweet-brier. [f. F f. L acus needle]

ego /ˈiːgəʊ, ˈe-/ n. (pl. -os) 1. the self, the part of the mind that reacts to reality and has a sense of individuality. 2. self-esteem. —**ego-trip** n. (colloq.) an activity undertaken to boost one's own self-esteem or feelings. [L, = I]

egocentric /egəʊˈsentrɪk/ adj. self-centred. —**egocentricity** /-ˈtrɪsɪtɪ/ n. [f. EGO + -CENTRIC]

egoism /ˈegəʊɪz(ə)m/ n. 1. self-interest as the moral basis of behaviour; systematic selfishness. 2. egotism. —**egoist** n., **egoistic** /-ˈɪstɪk/ adj., **egoistically** adv. [f. EGO]

egotism /ˈegəʊtɪz(ə)m/ n. the practice of talking too much about oneself; self-conceit; selfishness. —**egotist** n., **egotistic** /-ˈtɪstɪk/ adj., **egotistically** adv. [f. EGO, with intrusive -t-]

egregious /ɪˈgriːdʒəs/ adj. outstandingly bad; (archaic) remarkable. [f. L, = illustrious, lit. 'standing out from the flock']

egress /ˈiːgres/ n. an exit; the right of going out. [f. L (egredi walk out)]

egret /ˈiːgrɪt/ n. a kind of heron (Egretta alba) with long white feathers. [f. F aigrette]

Egypt /ˈiːdʒɪpt/ a country in NE Africa bordering on the

Mediterranean Sea, consisting largely of desert, with its population concentrated chiefly along the fertile valley of the River Nile; pop. (est. 1983) 47,000,000; official language, Arabic; capital, Cairo. The chief cash crop is cotton, and Egypt is self-sufficient in energy, having considerable reserves of petroleum and natural gas as well as hydro-electric power produced by the Aswan High Dam. Its antiquities make tourism a major industry.

Egypt's history spans 5,000 years, dating back to the neo-lithic period when nomadic hunters settled in the Nile valley. The ancient kingdoms of Upper and Lower Egypt became united, according to tradition, under Menes (*c.*3000 BC), founder of the first of the 31 dynasties which succes-sively ruled ancient Egypt. The period of the Old Kingdom (*c.*2575-2134 BC, 4th-8th Dynasty), the 'Pyramid Age', was characterized by strong central government, with the political and religious centre at Memphis. The Middle Kingdom (*c.*2040-1640 BC, 11th-14th Dynasty) is con-sidered to be the classical age of ancient Egyptian culture; its collapse was brought about by infiltration of Asiatics, culminating in the Hyksos usurpation. The New Kingdom (*c.*1550-1070 BC, 18th-20th Dynasty), the 'empire' period, with its capital at Thebes, begins with the expulsion of the Hyksos. Egyptian claims in Syria and Palestine became definitive and involved direct confrontation with her principal rivals, Mitanni and the Hittites; Nubia was administered directly from Egypt. These foreign interests brought Egypt considerable wealth as well as technological and cultural innovations, but by the end of the period a decline in the power of the pharaohs and an increase in that of the priests resulted in a weakening of the central government. Egypt fell successively to Libyans, Ethiopians, Assyrians, and Persians, and indigenous rule was finally ended by Alexander the Great, who took Egypt in 332 BC. From then until AD 1922 someone other than the Egyptians ruled Egypt.

On Alexander's death the Macedonian Ptolemy I acquired Egypt, and for three centuries the country was the centre of Hellenistic culture because of the considerable role played by Alexandria, home of a cosmopolitan Greek-speaking population who cultivated the arts and sciences, until on the death of Cleopatra it became a Roman province. After the Arab conquest in 642 Egypt was an Islamic country. From 1517 it formed part of the Ottoman empire except for a brief period (1798-1801) under French rule following Napoleon's invasion. The opening of the Suez Canal in 1869 made Egypt strategically important, and when the Turks became allies of Germany in the First World War the British (who had installed themselves following an Egyptian nationalist revolt in 1882) declared the country a British protectorate. Independence was granted in 1922 and a kingdom was established, becoming a republic after the overthrow of the monarchy in 1953.

Egyptian /ɪˈdʒɪpʃ(ə)n/ *adj.* of Egypt or its people or lan-guage. —*n.* 1. a native or inhabitant of Egypt. 2. the Hamitic language of the ancient Egyptians, represented in its oldest stages by hieroglyphic inscriptions and in its latest form by Coptic. [f. EGYPT]

Egyptology /iːdʒɪpˈtɒlədʒɪ/ *n.* the study of Egyptian antiquities. —**Egyptologist** *n.* [f. EGYPT + -LOGY]

eh /eɪ/ *int.* (*colloq.*) expressing inquiry or surprise, or inviting assent, or asking for repetition or explanation. [instinctive excl.]

Ehrlich /ˈɛːlɪk/, Paul (1854-1915), German scientist who was one of the founders of immunology, developed tech-niques for staining tissues, and was a pioneer of chemo-therapy, convinced that each disease could be killed off by an appropriate 'magic bullet'. Success in this last field came in 1911 when a synthetic compound of arsenic, Salvarsan, proved effective against syphilis.

eider /ˈaɪdə(r)/ *n.* a large northern duck, especially of the genus *Somateria*. [f. Icel.]

eiderdown *n.* a quilt stuffed with feathers, down, or other soft material. [f. prec.]

Eiffel /ˈaɪf(ə)l/, Alexandre Gustave (1832-1923), French engineer best known as the designer and builder of the **Eiffel Tower,** a wrought-iron structure erected in Paris for the exhibition of 1889 and still a famous landmark, though at first greatly disliked. Before that he had built several notable wrought-iron arch bridges, including one over the Douro River in Portugal. In 1885 he designed the inner structure of the Statue of Liberty in New York harbour. The Eiffel Tower, with a height of 300 metres (984 ft.) was the tallest man-made structure for many years.

Eiffel later used it for experiments in aerodynamics, and built one of the first wind tunnels in 1912.

eight /eɪt/ *adj.* & *n.* 1. one more than seven; the symbol for this (8, viii, VIII). 2. a size etc. denoted by eight. 3. an eight-oared rowing-boat or its crew. —**have one over the eight,** (*slang*) to get slightly drunk. [OE]

eighteen /eɪˈtiːn/ *adj.* & *n.* 1. one more than seventeen; the symbol for this (18, xviii, XVIII). 2. a size etc. denoted by eighteen. —**eighteenth** *adj.* & *n.* [f. EIGHT + -TEEN]

eightfold *adj.* & *adv.* 1. eight times as much or as many. 2. consisting of eight parts. [f. EIGHT + -FOLD]

eighth /eɪtθ/ *adj.* next after the seventh. —*n.* one of eight equal parts of a thing. —**eighthly** *adv.* [OE (cf. EIGHT)]

eightsome *adj.* for eight people. —**eightsome reel,** a lively Scottish dance for eight people. [f. EIGHT + -SOME]

eighty /ˈeɪtɪ/ *adj.* & *n.* 1. eight times ten; the symbol for this (80, lxxx, LXXX). 2. (in *pl.*) the numbers, years, or degrees of temperature from 80 to 89. —**eightieth** *adj.* & *n.* [OE (cf. EIGHT)]

Eisenhower /ˈaɪzənhaʊə(r)/, Dwight David (1890-1969), American general and statesman, 34th President of the USA 1953-61. In the Second World War he was Commander-in-Chief of Allied forces in North Africa and Italy 1942-3 and Supreme Commander of Allied Expeditionary Forces in western Europe 1943-5.

Einstein /ˈaɪnstaɪn/, Albert (1879-1955), German-born theoretical physicist, founder of the theory of relativity, and perhaps the greatest scientist of the 20th c. In 1905 he published several remarkable papers: one dealt with the photoelectric emission in terms of Planck's quantum theory of light, for which he was awarded the 1921 Nobel Prize for physics, another dealt with the Brownian motion in liquids and demonstrated that this effect was caused by the action of molecules, and a third described his Special Theory of Relativity, postulating a constant velocity of light which led to his famous equation relating mass and energy ($E = mc^2$), the basis of atomic energy. After several academic posts he moved, in 1914, to Berlin as a member of the Prussian Academy of Sciences and to direct the Kaiser Wilhelm Institute for Physics. For ten years he tried to incorporate gravitation into his theory, and achieved success at last with his General Theory of Relativity published in 1915. Einstein became a household name when one of the predictions of his theory, the bending of light when passing close to the sun, was observed during the solar eclipse of 1919. A Jew, a Zionist, and a pacifist, he was attacked by the Nazis, and when Hitler came to power in 1933 he settled in the USA and joined the Institute for Advanced Study at Princeton. He spent the remainder of his life searching without success for a unified field theory which would combine electromagnetism, gravitation, relativity, and quantum mechanics. In 1939 he wrote a letter to President Roosevelt, at the request of several prominent physicists, outlining the military potential of nuclear energy and the dangers of a Nazi lead in this field. His letter greatly influenced the decision to build an atomic bomb, though he took no part in the Manhattan Project. After the war he spoke out passionately against nuclear weapons and repression. The artificial element einsteinium has been named in his honour.

einsteinium /aɪnˈstaɪnɪəm/ *n.* an artificially made trans-uranic radioactive metallic element, symbol Es, atomic number 99, identified in 1952 in debris from the first hydrogen bomb explosion. [f. prec.]

Eire /ˈeərə/ the former name of the Republic of Ireland (see IRELAND), still often used in newspapers etc. to distinguish the country from Northern Ireland and from the island as a whole. [Ir.]

Eisenstein /ˈaɪz(ə)nstaɪn/, Sergei Mikhailovich (1898-1948), Russian film director, one of the great innovators of the cinema, particularly in his use of montage in which he presented images, perhaps independent of the main action, to create maximum psychological impact. Chosen by the Russian authorities to direct a film commemorating the revolution of 1905, Eisenstein's response was *The Battleship Potemkin* (1925), about the mutiny on a battleship of the Black Sea fleet, considered one of the greatest films ever made. *Alexander Nevsky* (1938) was an immediate success in the Soviet Union, though in spite of its dramatic power, striking imagery, and imaginative use of Prokofiev's music it could not compare with the stimulating experimentalism of his earlier work and was less well received abroad. His last completed work was *Ivan the Terrible*, Part I (1944),

Part II (1946, not released until 1958 because of Stalin's disapproval of the presentation of Ivan's character).

eisteddfod /aɪsˈteðvɒd/ n. an annual meeting of Welsh poets and musicians for competitions. [Welsh, = session]

either /ˈaɪðə(r), ˈiːðə(r)/ adj. & pron. one or the other of two; each of two. —adv. or conj. **1.** as one possibility; as one choice or alternative, which way you will. **2.** (with neg. or interrog.) any more than the other, moreover. [OE]

ejaculate /ɪˈdʒækjʊleɪt/ v.t./i. **1.** to utter suddenly, to exclaim. **2.** to emit (esp. semen) from the body. —**ejaculation** /-ˈleɪʃ(ə)n/ n., **ejaculatory** adj. [f. L ejaculari shoot out (jaculum javelin)]

eject /ɪˈdʒekt/ v.t. **1.** to expel. to compel to leave; to dispossess (a tenant). **2.** to send out, to emit. —**ejection** n., **ejectment** n. [f. L (EX-¹, jacere throw)]

ejector n. a device for ejecting something. —**ejector seat,** a device for the ejection of the pilot of an aircraft etc. in an emergency. [f. prec.]

eke /iːk/ v.t. (with out) to make (a living) or support (an existence) with difficulty; to supplement (an income etc.). [OE; cogn. w. L augēre increase]

elaborate¹ /ɪˈlæbərət/ adj. minutely worked out; highly developed or complicated. —**elaborately** adv. [f. L elaborare (EX-¹, laborare work)]

elaborate² /ɪˈlæbəreɪt/ v.t./i. to work out or explain in detail. —**elaboration** /-ˈreɪʃ(ə)n/ n. [as prec.]

Elagabalus /iːləˈgæbələs/ (born Varius Avitus Bassianus, 204–22) Roman emperor 218–22. He took his name from Elah-Gabal, the sun-god of Emesa in Syria, whose hereditary priest he was. In his fifteenth year he was raised to power under the title of Marcus Aurelius Antoninus, his mother alleging he was the son of Caracalla. He promoted the worship of the sun-god in Rome, in the form of a black stone, and celebrated the midsummer festival with a ceremonial no less ludicrous than obscene, leading a dissipated life and ignoring State affairs. Both he and his mother were murdered in 222 after complicated intrigues.

El Alamein /ˈæləmeɪn/ the site of the decisive British victory in the North African campaign of 1940–3, 90 km (60 miles) west of Alexandria, where the German Afrika Korps under Rommel was checked in its advance towards the Nile by the British Eighth Army under Montgomery.

Elam /ˈiːlæm/ an ancient kingdom east of the Tigris, established in the 4th millennium BC, with its capital at Susa. —**Elamite** /ˈiːləmaɪt/ adj. & n.

élan /eɪˈlɑ̃/ n. vivacity, dash. [F (élancer launch)]

eland /ˈiːlənd/ an African antelope of the genus Taurotragus, the largest of living antelopes, with spirally twisted horns. [Du., = elk]

elapse /ɪˈlæps/ v.i. (of time) to pass away. [f. L elabi (EX-¹, labi glide)]

elasmobranch /ɪˈlæzməbræŋk/ n. a fish of the class Chondrichthyes (shark, skate, etc.). [f. Gk elasmos beaten metal + bragkhia gills]

elastic /ɪˈlæstɪk/ adj. **1.** able to resume its normal length, bulk, or shape after being stretched or crushed; springy. **2.** (of the feelings or a person) buoyant; flexible, adaptable. —n. elastic cord or fabric, usually woven with strips of rubber. —**elastically** adv., **elasticity** /-ˈstɪsɪtɪ/ n. [f. Gk, = propulsive (elaunō drive)]

elasticated /ɪˈlæstɪkeɪtɪd/ adj. (of fabric) made elastic by weaving with rubber thread. [f. prec.]

elastomer /ɪˈlæstəmə(r)/ n. a natural or synthetic rubber or rubber-like plastic. —**elastomeric** /-ˈmerɪk/ adj. [f. ELASTIC, after isomer]

elate /ɪˈleɪt/ v.t. to inspirit, to stimulate; (esp. in p.p.) to make elated or proud. —**elation** n. [f. L efferre elat- raise]

E-layer n. the Heaviside layer.

Elba /ˈelbə/ a small island off the west coast of Italy, famous as the place of Napoleon's first exile (1814–15); pop. (1971) 26,830.

Elbe /elb/ a river of Germany flowing 1,159 km (720 miles) from Czechoslovakia to the North Sea. Major cities upon it are Dresden, Magdeburg, and Hamburg.

elbow /ˈelbəʊ/ n. **1.** the joint between the forearm and upper arm; the corresponding part in an animal (ill. HORSE). **2.** the part of the sleeve of a garment covering this. **3.** an elbow-shaped bend etc. —v.t. to thrust or jostle (oneself or one's way in, out, etc.). —**elbow-grease** n. (colloq.) vigorous polishing; hard work. **elbow-room** n. plenty of room to move or work in. **out at (the) elbows,** worn, ragged, poor. [OE (as ELL, BOW¹)]

elder¹ adj. (of persons, especially related ones) senior, of greater age. —n. **1.** (in pl.) persons of greater age or venerable because of age. **2.** an official in the early Christian Church and some modern Churches. —**elder statesman,** an influential experienced person (especially a politician) of advanced age. [OE (compar. of OLD)]

elder² n. a tree (Sambucus nigra) with white flowers and dark berries. [OE]

elderberry n. the berry of the elder tree.

elderly adj. somewhat old, past middle age. [f. ELDER¹]

eldest adj. first-born, oldest surviving. [OE (superl. of OLD)]

El Dorado /dəˈrɑːdəʊ/ the name of a fictitious country (according to some, a city) abounding in gold, believed by the Spanish and by Sir Walter Raleigh to exist upon the Amazon. The origin of the belief, which led Spanish conquistadors to converge on the area in search of treasure, appears to have been rumours of an Indian ruler, in what is now Colombia, who ritually coated his body with gold dust and then plunged into a sacred lake while his subjects threw in gold and jewels. [Sp., = the gilded]

eldorado /eldəˈrɑːdəʊ/ n. (pl. -os) a place of great abundance. [f. prec.]

eldritch /ˈeldrɪtʃ/ adj. (Sc.) weird; hideous. [perh. rel. to ELF]

Eleanor Cross /ˈelɪnə(r)/ any of the stone crosses erected by Edward I to mark the stopping-places of the cortège that brought the body of his queen, Eleanor of Castile, from Nottinghamshire to London in 1290. Three of the twelve crosses survive.

Eleatic /elɪˈætɪk/ adj. of Elea, an ancient Greek city in SW Italy, or the school of philosophers there about the 6th c. BC, especially Xenophanes, Parmenides, and Zeno. —n. an Eleatic philosopher.

elecampane /elɪkæmˈpeɪn/ n. a plant (Inula helenium) with bitter aromatic leaves and root. [corruption of medieval name Enula campana]

elect /ɪˈlekt/ v.t. to choose by voting; to choose (a thing, to do); (Theol. of God) to choose (a person) for salvation (see ELECTION). —adj. chosen; select; choice; (after a noun) chosen but not yet in office. [f. L eligere pick out]

election /ɪˈlekʃ(ə)n/ n. **1.** electing, being elected; the process of electing, especially Members of Parliament. **2.** (Theol.) God's choice of some persons in preference to others. In medieval times the nature and conditions of election were much disputed, and formed a fundamental issue in the teaching of Calvin, who held that God's choice was wholly without relation to faith or good works.

electioneer /ɪlekʃəˈnɪə(r)/ v.i. to take part in an election campaign. [f. prec.]

elective /ɪˈlektɪv/ adj. **1.** chosen or appointed by election. **2.** (of a body) having power to elect. **3.** optional, not urgently necessary. [f. F f. L (as ELECT)]

elector /ɪˈlektə(r)/ n. **1.** one who has the right to elect or take part in an election. **2. Elector,** (hist.) any of the German princes entitled to elect the Emperor.

electoral /ɪˈlektər(ə)l/ adj. of or ranking as electors. —**electoral college,** a body of persons who cast votes for the election of a leader; (in the USA) the body of electors, chosen by popular vote in each State, who elect the US President and vice-president. [f. prec.]

electorate /ɪˈlektərət/ n. **1.** the body of electors. **2.** the office or dominions of a German Elector. [f. ELECTOR]

Electra /ɪˈlektrə/ (Gk legend) daughter of Agamemnon and Clytemnestra. She urged her brother Orestes to kill Clytemnestra and Aegisthus in revenge for the murder of Agamemnon. The development of her story is due to the Greek dramatists and poets, not to tradition. —**Electra complex,** (Psychol.) a daughter's feeling of attraction towards her father and hostility towards her mother, the counterpart in females of the Oedipus complex (with reference to Electra's having caused her mother to be killed for having murdered Electra's father).

electric /ɪˈlektrɪk/ adj. **1.** of, worked by, or charged with electricity; producing or capable of generating electricity. **2.** causing sudden and dramatic excitement. —n. an electric light, vehicle, etc.; (in pl.) electrical equipment. —**electric blanket,** a blanket heated by an internal electric element. **electric chair,** a chair used to electrocute as a form of execution. **electric eel,** an eel-like fish (Electrophorus electricus) capable of giving an electric shock. **electric eye,** a photoelectric cell operating a relay when a beam of light is broken. **electric field,** see FIELD. **electric fire,** an

Electrical Power

Simple a.c. electric generator

A coil of wire ABCD is fixed to the spindle EF.
When the coil is rotated in the magnetic field a
voltage is induced in the wire as it cuts the lines
of force. The two slip-rings each have a fixed
carbon block (brush) pressed against them as
they rotate, and the current passes out through
one and returns through the other, lighting the
lamp on the way. The principle of generating
electricity is the same in power-stations, where a
rotating turbine drives the generator.

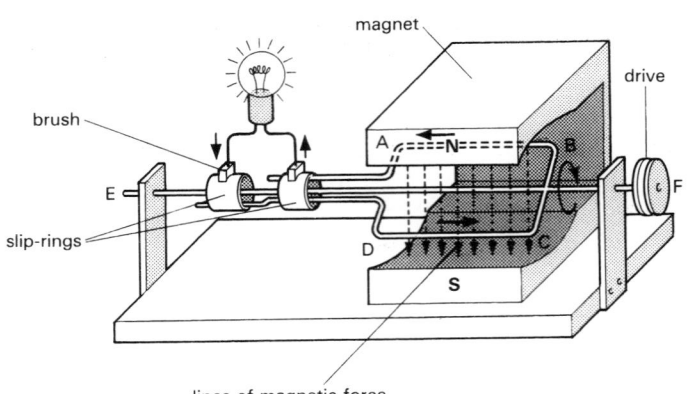

Hydroelectric power

The turbine is driven by the moving water
from a reservoir, a river, or a tidal estuary

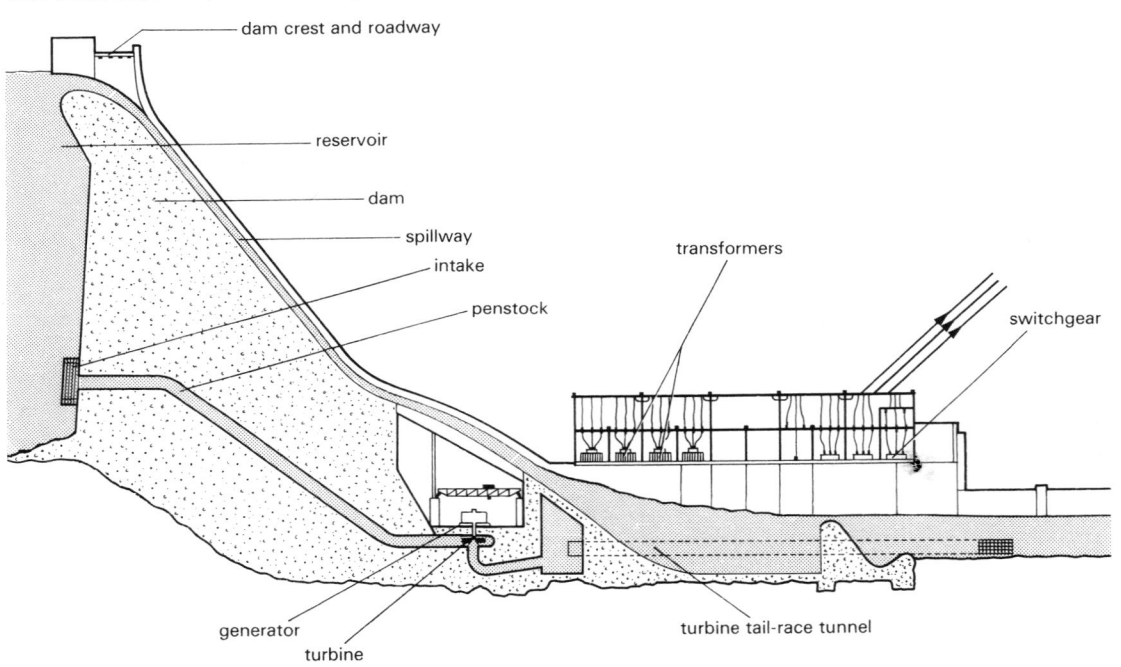

Electricity supply

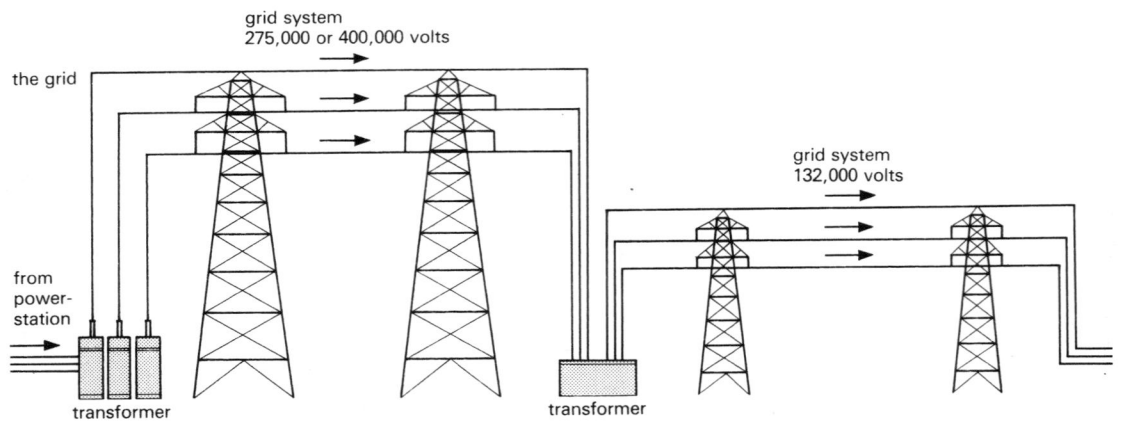

Stages in producing electricity in a thermal power-station

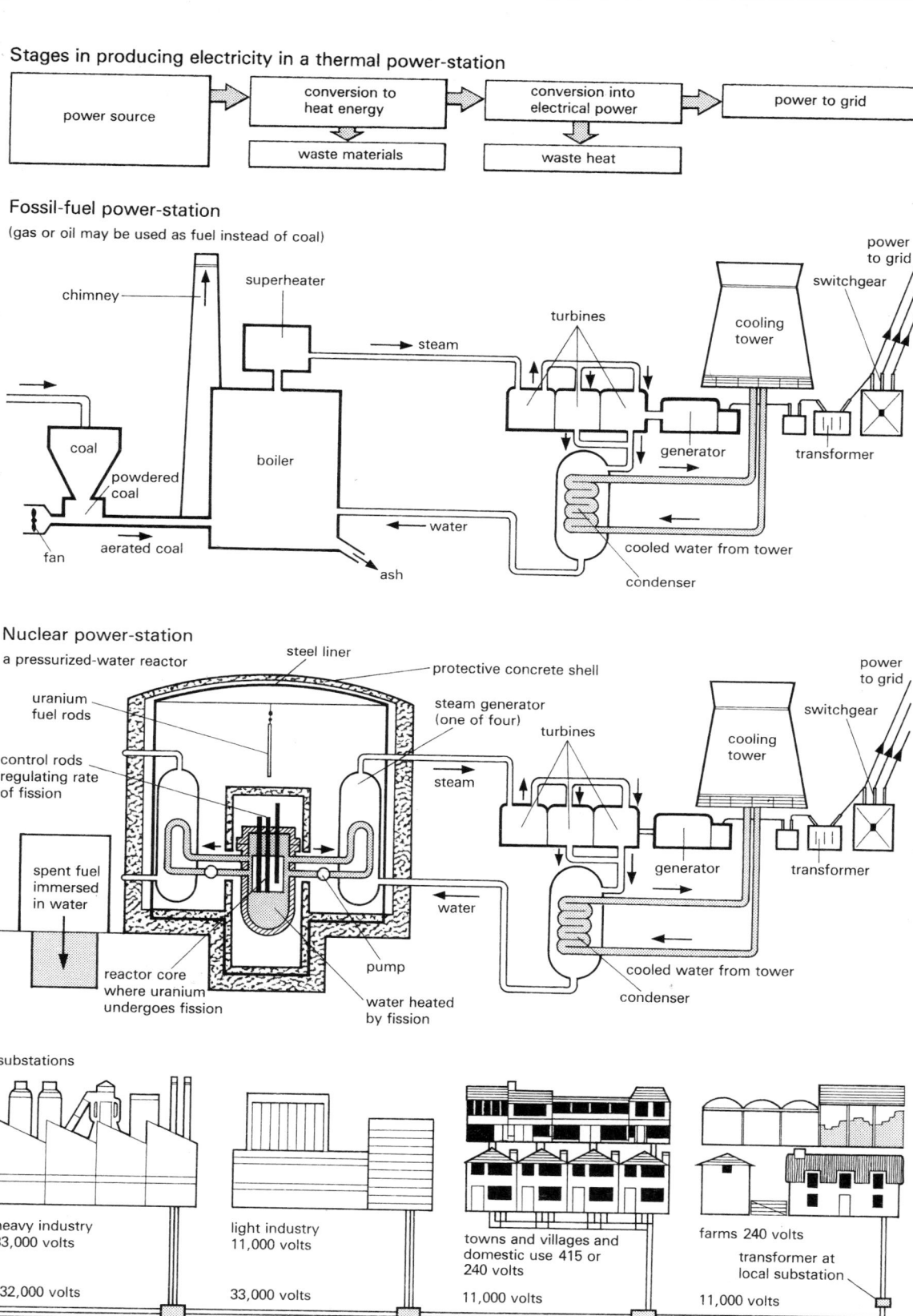

power source → conversion to heat energy → conversion into electrical power → power to grid

waste materials

waste heat

Fossil-fuel power-station

(gas or oil may be used as fuel instead of coal)

chimney

superheater

steam

turbines

cooling tower

power to grid

switchgear

coal

powdered coal

boiler

generator

transformer

fan

aerated coal

water

cooled water from tower

ash

condenser

Nuclear power-station

a pressurized-water reactor

steel liner

protective concrete shell

uranium fuel rods

steam generator (one of four)

control rods regulating rate of fission

turbines

steam

cooling tower

power to grid

switchgear

spent fuel immersed in water

generator

transformer

reactor core where uranium undergoes fission

pump

water heated by fission

water

cooled water from tower

condenser

substations

heavy industry 33,000 volts

light industry 11,000 volts

towns and villages and domestic use 415 or 240 volts

farms 240 volts

transformer at local substation

132,000 volts

33,000 volts

11,000 volts

11,000 volts

transformers at substations

appliance giving heat from an electrically charged wire coil or bar. **electric light,** a light produced by electricity in any of various devices (e.g. an incandescent lamp, fluorescent lamp, arc lamp). The first successful electric lamps were developed almost simultaneously by Joseph Swan in England and Thomas Edison in America in 1879. **electric shock,** the effect of a sudden discharge of electricity through the body of a person etc. [f. L f. Gk *ēlektron* amber, from the static electricity found in it]

electrical /ɪˈlektrɪk(ə)l/ *adj.* **1.** of or concerned with electricity. **2.** suddenly exciting. —**electrically** *adv.* [f. prec.]

electrician /ɪlekˈtrɪʃ(ə)n/ *n.* a person whose profession is installing and maintaining electrical equipment. [f. ELECTRIC]

electricity /ɪlekˈtrɪsɪtɪ/ *n.* **1.** a form of energy occurring in elementary particles (electrons, protons) and hence in larger bodies containing them (see below); the branch of science concerned with this. **2.** a supply of electricity. [as prec.]

When a piece of dry amber is rubbed with cloth it develops the power of attracting small pieces of paper. This manifestation of electricity has been known from antiquity, but the scientific elucidation of the nature of electricity proved to be an extraordinarily difficult problem. In the 18th c. it was discovered that there are two opposite kinds of electricity: like electricities repel each other and unlike electricities attract. Benjamin Franklin named these positive and negative electric. Some of the mystery surrounding electricity was resolved late last century when J. J. Thomson located the seat of negative electricity in subatomic particles called electrons; that of positive electricity was found to lie in larger particles, protons, in the atomic nucleus. All electrical and magnetic phenomena are due ultimately to protons and electrons. Electric current in the wires of domestic appliances, for example, consists in the slow drift of electrons (back and forth if it is an alternating current). Electric forces are responsible for binding protons and electrons together in atoms, binding atoms together to form matter, and for many other natural phenomena.

The town of Godalming in Surrey, England, was the first in the world to have electricity supplied for public and private usage, in a three-year experiment from 1881 (a few private schemes were inaugurated a little earlier), after which the town reverted to gas lighting; the electricity supply was generated at first by water-power, then by a steam-engine. Use of electrical power in homes and factories did not become common until the years between the two World Wars.

electrify /ɪˈlektrɪfaɪ/ *v.t.* **1.** to charge with electricity. **2.** to convert (a railway, factory, etc.) to the use of electric power. **3.** to excite or startle suddenly. —**electrification** /-fɪˈkeɪʃ(ə)n/ *n.* [f. ELECTRIC]

electro- /ɪlektrəʊ-/ *in comb.* of, by, or caused by electricity. [as ELECTRIC]

electrocardiogram /ɪlektrəʊˈkɑːdɪəɡræm/ *n.* the record obtained by an electrocardiograph. [f. ELECTRO- + CARDIO- + -GRAM]

electrocardiograph /ɪlektrəʊˈkɑːdɪəɡrɑːf/ *n.* an instrument that receives electrical impulses as they vary during the cardiac cycle and transforms them into a graphic record. When the heart muscle contracts and relaxes, changes in potential are produced, which can be picked up from the skin surface by electrodes applied to various parts of the body. The electrocardiograph contains a delicate galvanometer consisting essentially of a silvered wire connected to the electrodes, which vibrates in a magnetic field in response to the change in potential. While it vibrates, an electrographic record is obtained upon a moving photographic plate or a tape. The electrical activity of the heartbeat was first recorded by the Dutch physiologist William Einthoven in 1903. [as prec. + -GRAPH]

electroconvulsive therapy /ɪlektrəʊkənˈvʌlsɪv/ therapy using the convulsive response to electric shocks.

electrocute /ɪˈlektrəkjuːt/ *v.t.* to kill or execute by electric shock. —**electrocution** /-ˈkjuːʃ(ə)n/ *n.* [f. ELECTRO-, after *execute*]

electrode /ɪˈlektrəʊd/ *n.* a conductor through which electricity enters or leaves an electrolyte, gas, vacuum, etc. [f. ELECTRIC + Gk *hodos* way]

electrodynamics /ɪlektrəʊdaɪˈnæmɪks/ *n.* the study of electricity in motion.

electroencephalogram /ɪlektrəʊenˈsefələɡræm/ *n.* a record traced by an electroencephalograph. [f. ELECTRO- + ENCEPHALO- + -GRAM]

electroencephalograph /ɪlektrəʊenˈsefələɡrɑːf/ *n.* an

instrument recording the electrical activity of the brain, introduced in 1929 by Dr J. Berger of Jena (now in East Germany). [as prec. + -GRAPH]

electrolyse /ɪˈlektrəlaɪz/ *v.t.* to subject to or treat by electrolysis. [f. foll.]

electrolysis /ɪlekˈtrɒlɪsɪs/ *n.* chemical decomposition by electric action; the breaking up of tumours, hair-roots, etc., by electric action. —**electrolytic** /-əˈlɪtɪk/ *adj.* [f. ELECTRO- + -LYSIS]

electrolyte /ɪˈlektrəlaɪt/ *n.* a solution able to conduct an electric current, especially in an electric cell or battery; a substance that can dissolve to produce this. [f. ELECTRO- + -LYTE]

electromagnet /ɪlektrəʊˈmæɡnɪt/ *n.* a soft metal core made into a magnet by an electric current passing through a coil surrounding it (ill. MAGNETISM). The first simple electromagnet capable of supporting its own weight was made by William Sturgeon of Manchester, a self-taught electrical engineer, in 1825.

electromagnetic /ɪlektrəʊmæɡˈnetɪk/ *adj.* having both electrical and magnetic properties. —**electromagnetic radiation,** the kind of radiation that includes visible light, radio waves, gamma rays, etc., in which electric and magnetic fields vary simultaneously (see RADIATION). —**electromagnetically** *adv.*

electromagnetism /ɪlektrəʊˈmæɡnətɪz(ə)m/ *n.* magnetic forces produced by electricity; the study of these. Hans Christian Oersted in 1820 was the first to establish that a flow of electricity in a conductor affects a nearby magnetic compass exactly as an ordinary magnet does. Electromagnetism now has an enormous variety of applications. Electric motors are usually driven by electromagnets. Electric bells and automatic switches of various sorts, certain kinds of loudspeakers and television tubes, magnetic tapes, certain kinds of current-measuring instruments and certain navigational systems, all make use of electromagnetism as their most important principle of operation. (See also FIELD.)

electromotive /ɪlektrəʊˈməʊtɪv/ *adj.* producing or tending to produce an electric current. —**electromotive force,** a force set up by difference of potential in an electric circuit.

electron /ɪˈlektrɒn/ *n.* a stable elementary particle with an indivisible charge of negative electricity, found in all atoms and acting as a carrier of electricity in solids, with mass of approximately 9×10^{-31} kg (see below). —**electron lens,** a device for focusing a stream of electrons by electric and magnetic fields. **electron-volt** *n.* a unit of energy, the amount gained by an electron when accelerated through a potential difference of one volt. [f. ELECTRIC]

Electrons, which orbit the nucleus in atoms, are responsible for an enormous variety of natural phenomena: electric currents in metals and in semiconductors consist of a flow of electrons; light, radio waves, X-rays, and a large proportion of heat radiation are all produced by accelerating and decelerating electrons; electrons are chiefly responsible for the binding together of atoms in molecules, for magnetism, and for the conduction of heat through metals. Electronics and electrical engineering are largely concerned with harnessing the forces and energies of electrons.

electronic /ɪlekˈtrɒnɪk/ *adj.* **1.** produced by or involving a flow of electrons. **2.** of electrons or electronics. —**electronic music,** music produced by electronic means and recorded on tape. —**electronically** *adv.* [f. prec.]

electronics *n.* **1.** the branch of physics and technology dealing with the behaviour of electrons in a vacuum, gas, semiconductor, etc. **2.** (as *pl.*) electronic circuits. [f. prec.]

electron microscope a type of microscope (first developed in the early 1930s) giving high magnification and resolution by employing a beam of electrons instead of light and focusing it by means of magnetic or electrostatic fields. Because the de Broglie wavelength of a high-speed electron is very much shorter than that of light, a correspondingly greater resolving power is possible, so that magnifications of up to one million can be achieved. In one type of instrument the electron beam is focused on to a very thin specimen and the transmitted beam is made to impinge on a fluorescent screen to give a visible image representing the electron-stopping power of different parts of the specimen. Other types use reflection from the specimen or a scanning beam that is measured electrically and the signal fed to a television monitor.

electroplate /ɪˈlektrəʊpleɪt/ *v.t.* to coat with a thin layer of silver, chromium, etc., by electrolysis. The commercial use of this process dates from the mid-19th c. —*n.* objects so plated.

Electronics
Some symbols and components

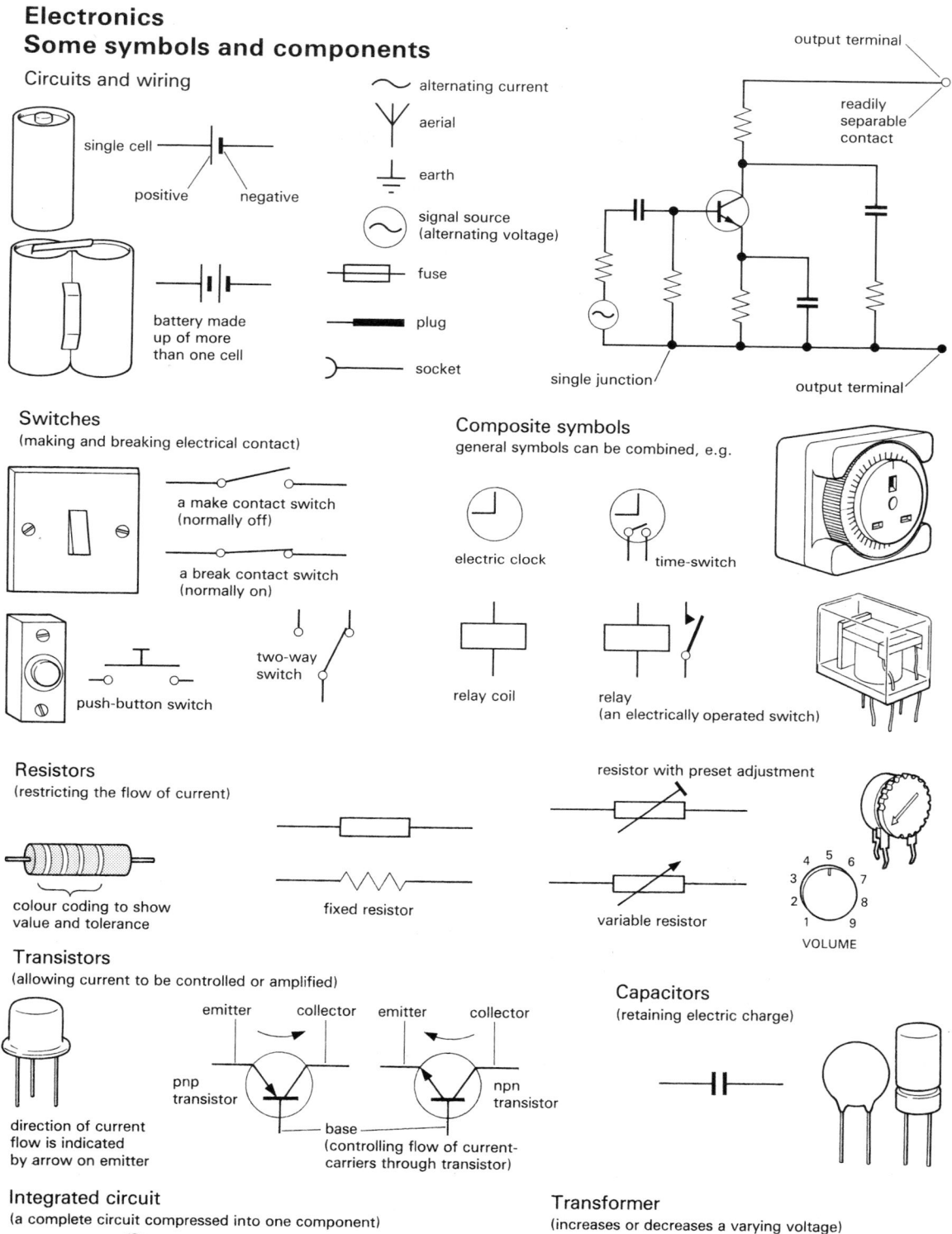

Circuits and wiring

single cell — positive — negative

battery made up of more than one cell

~ alternating current

aerial

earth

signal source (alternating voltage)

fuse

plug

socket

output terminal

readily separable contact

single junction

output terminal

Switches
(making and breaking electrical contact)

a make contact switch (normally off)

a break contact switch (normally on)

push-button switch

two-way switch

Composite symbols
general symbols can be combined, e.g.

electric clock

time-switch

relay coil

relay (an electrically operated switch)

Resistors
(restricting the flow of current)

colour coding to show value and tolerance

fixed resistor

variable resistor

resistor with preset adjustment

4 5 6
3 7
2 8
1 9
VOLUME

Transistors
(allowing current to be controlled or amplified)

emitter   collector   emitter   collector

pnp transistor

npn transistor

base
(controlling flow of current-carriers through transistor)

direction of current flow is indicated by arrow on emitter

Capacitors
(retaining electric charge)

Integrated circuit
(a complete circuit compressed into one component)

inputs

outputs

Transformer
(increases or decreases a varying voltage)

core

tappings

winding

electroscope /ɪˈlektrəskəup/ n. an instrument for detecting and measuring electricity, especially to indicate the ionization of air by radioactivity. [f. ELECTRO- + -SCOPE]

electro-shock /ɪlektrəuˈʃɒk/ n. electric shock. —**electro-shock therapy**, electroconvulsive therapy.

electrostatics /ɪlektrəuˈstætɪks/ n. the study of electricity at rest.

electrotechnology /ɪlektrəutekˈnɒlədʒɪ/ n. the science of the technological application of electricity.

electrotherapy /ɪlektrəuˈθerəpɪ/ n. the treatment of diseases by the use of electricity. [f. ELECTRO- + THERAPY]

elegant /ˈelɪgənt/ adj. graceful in appearance or manner; tasteful, refined. —**elegance** n., **elegantly** adv. [f. F or L, rel. to eligere (as ELECT)]

elegiac /elɪˈdʒaɪək/ adj. used for elegies; mournful. —n. (in pl.) elegiac verses. —**elegiac couplet** or **metre**, a dactylic hexameter and pentameter. [f. F or L (as foll.)]

elegy /ˈelɪdʒɪ/ n. a sorrowful or serious poem or song; a lament for the dead; a poem in elegiac metre. [f. F or L f. Gk (elegos mournful poem)]

element /ˈelɪmənt/ n. **1.** a component part, a contributing factor. **2.** a substance composed of atoms of the same atomic number (see below). **3.** any of the four substances (earth, water, air, and fire) in ancient and medieval philosophy. **4.** a being's natural abode or environment. **5.** a wire that gives out heat in an electric cooker, heater, etc. **6.** (in pl.) atmospheric agencies, especially wind and storm. **7.** (in pl.) the bread and wine of the Eucharist. —**in one's element**, in one's accustomed or preferred surroundings, doing what one is skilled at and enjoys. [f. OF f. L]

All stable matter consists of elements (of which 105 are currently known; see p. 970) either individually or in combination. Each element is a substance composed of atoms all of which have the same atomic number and therefore the same number of electrons orbiting the nucleus; this number differs for each element, a fact which accounts for their different chemical properties. Electrons can be regarded as occupying definite orbits or 'shells' surrounding the nucleus, and it is the number in the outermost shell that determines how an atom of a particular element interacts and forms bonds with other atoms to form molecules and compounds. Certain elements of widely differing atomic number (e.g. halogens, noble gases) are similar chemically because the outermost 'shells' contain the same number of electrons, and this configuration of outer electrons makes possible the general classification in the periodic table. Elements are often classified into metals (comprising the majority) and non-metals. Uranium and almost all of the elements with a smaller atomic number than this occur naturally, but most of the thirteen heavier ones are known only from having been synthesized in nuclear reactions. (For the origin of the elements in the universe see NUCLEOSYNTHESIS.)

elemental /elɪˈment(ə)l/ adj. **1.** of or like the elements or the forces of nature, powerful, tremendous. **2.** basic, essential. [f. prec.]

elementary /elɪˈmentərɪ/ adj. **1.** dealing with the simplest facts of a subject, rudimentary. **2.** (Chem.) not analysable. —**elementarily** adv., **elementariness** n. [f. L (as ELEMENT)]

elementary particle any of several subatomic particles which are not known to be composed of simpler particles and which are characterized by having a definite mass, a lifetime that is long compared with the interaction time, and well-defined electromagnetic properties, and are capable of an independent existence.

The discovery of the electron in 1897 and the subsequent discoveries of the photon, the atomic nucleus, the proton, and the neutron led to the recognition that the atom itself is composed of more elementary particles, and also that there are other elementary particles, such as the photon, which do not exist in atoms, and which can exist quite independently of atoms. Theoretical and experimental research from the 1930s to the present has led to the discovery of numerous other 'elementary' particles, most of which are unstable with very short half-lives. The best known of these are the neutrino, which is a stable neutral particle of very small or even zero rest mass; the positron, which is a positively charged electron; and the mesons, which are responsible for the strong interactions between the particles of the nucleus.

Elementary particles are classified into four major groups: quanta, leptons (which include electrons and neutrinos), mesons, and baryons (which include protons and neutrons).

There has been an enormous investment of theoretical and experimental effort to establish the properties of these particles, to classify them, and to fit them into a coherent theoretical framework. This effort has led to the postulation of many new hypothetical particles such as 'quarks' and 'gluons', and to the identification of a range of new but poorly understood particle properties including those termed 'parity', 'strangeness', 'isospin number', 'helicity', 'charm', and 'colour' (no connection with visual colour).

elephant /ˈelɪfənt/ n. the largest living land animal, with a trunk and ivory tusks. Of several species once distributed over the world, including Britain, only two survive, the Indian elephant (Elephas maximus) and the African (Loxodonta africana). The African elephant is larger than the Indian, though there is a smaller variety of it (which may be a different species) in parts of Africa. The Indian elephant is used for heavy work and as a beast of burden in India and some countries of SE Asia. [f. OF f. L f. Gk elephas, orig. = ivory (which was known to the Greeks long before the elephant)]

elephantiasis /elɪfənˈtaɪəsɪs/ n. a skin disease causing gross enlargement of a limb etc. [L f. Gk (as prec.)]

elephantine /elɪˈfæntaɪn/ adj. **1.** of elephants. **2.** huge, clumsy, unwieldy. [f. L f. Gk (as ELEPHANT)]

elevate /ˈelɪveɪt/ v.t. to raise or lift up; to enhance morally or intellectually; (in p.p.) exalted in rank or status. [f. L elevare lift (EX-[1], levis light)]

elevation /elɪˈveɪʃ(ə)n/ n. **1.** elevating, being elevated. **2.** the height above a given (especially sea) level; a high position; the angle (especially of a gun or the direction of a heavenly body) with the horizontal. **3.** a flat drawing showing one side of a building. [f. OF or L (as prec.)]

elevator n. **1.** a person or thing that elevates; a hoisting-machine. **2.** the movable part of a tailplane, used for changing an aircraft's attitude to its flight-path (ill. FLIGHT). **3.** (US) a lift (see LIFT n. 3). [f. ELEVATE]

eleven /ɪˈlev(ə)n/ adj. & n. **1.** one more than ten; the symbol for this (11, xi, XI). **2.** a size etc. denoted by eleven. **3.** a team of eleven players at cricket, football, etc. —**eleven-plus** n. an examination taken in some districts of England and Wales at the age 11-12 before entering secondary school. [OE, perh. = one left over (ten)]

elevenfold adj. & adv. eleven times as much or as many; consisting of eleven parts. [f. prec. + -FOLD]

elevenses /ɪˈlevənzɪz/ n. light refreshment taken at about 11 a.m. [f. ELEVEN]

eleventh adj. next after the tenth. —n. one of eleven equal parts. —**eleventh hour**, the last possible moment. [OE (as ELEVEN)]

elf n. (pl. **elves** /elvz/) a supernatural being in Germanic mythology; a dwarf, a little creature. —**elfish** adj. [OE]

elfin /ˈelfɪn/ adj. of elves, elflike. [f. ELF]

Elgar /ˈelgɑː(r)/, Sir Edward William (1857-1934), the strongest creative personality to appear in British music for nearly two hundred years. A self-taught provincial from Worcester—he always remained a countryman at heart—he learnt more from the scores of Liszt and Wagner than he could have done at any Victorian school of music. He applied their techniques first in the then fashionable form of the cantata; he was in his forties before he made his mark with a novel orchestral work, a set of variations on an 'Enigma' theme dedicated to 'my friends pictured within'. But Elgar's pictures are portraits in a mirror; each variation may suggest a friend but it also reflects the man himself—sensitive, emotional, playful, but also (in the finale) the face of a late Victorian imperialist. He went on to breathe life into the dying form of oratorio, but the essential Elgar was later more perfectly embodied in his symphonies and concertos.

Elgin Marbles /ˈelgɪn/ a collection of marble sculptures and architectural fragments, chiefly from the frieze and pediment of the Parthenon, executed under the supervision of Phidias from 447 BC, which Lord Elgin acquired from the occupying Turkish authorities in 1801-3 and which he sold to the British nation in 1816 for £35,000. Their original exhibition in London had an enormous impact, it being the first time authentic classical Greek sculpture had been on public display. They are regarded as a classical masterpiece, housed in the British Museum, and at the centre of a widely publicized repatriation request from the Greek government, who do not accept the legality of the Turkish sale.

El Greco /ˈgrekəu/ (Sp., = the Greek) (1541-1614), Spanish painter of Greek origin whose real name was Domenikos

Theotokopoulos. Trained as an icon painter in Crete, he travelled to Venice, where it is believed he became a pupil of Titian. After being in Rome 1570-6 he settled finally in Toledo in 1577, where he remained for the rest of his life. His portraits and religious works, with their distorted perspective, elongated figures, and psychological tension, can have an unnerving effect. His colours can be both bright and discordant, and his works capture the religious fervour and mysticism of the Counter-Reformation in Spain with a sensitive expressionism outreaching his contemporaries.

Elia /ˈiːlɪə/ the pseudonym adopted by Charles Lamb in his *Essays of Elia* (1823).

elicit /ɪˈlɪsɪt/ *v.t.* to draw out (a latent thing, especially a response etc.). [f. L *elicere* (EX-¹, *lacere* entice)]

elide /ɪˈlaɪd/ *v.t.* to omit (a vowel or syllable) in pronunciation. [f. L *elidere* crush out]

eligible /ˈelɪdʒɪb(ə)l/ *adj.* fit or entitled to be chosen (*for* an office, award, etc.); desirable or suitable, especially for marriage. —**eligibility** /-ˈbɪlɪtɪ/ *n.* [f. F f. L (as ELECT)]

Elijah /ɪˈlaɪdʒə/ (9th c. BC) a Hebrew prophet in the time of Jezebel, who maintained the worship of Jehovah against that of Baal and other pagan gods. Legends say that he was miraculously fed by ravens, raised a widow's son from the dead, and was carried to heaven in a chariot of fire (1 Kings 17-2 Kings 2).

eliminate /ɪˈlɪmɪneɪt/ *v.t.* to remove, to get rid of; to exclude from consideration; to exclude from a further stage of competition through defeat etc. —**elimination** /-ˈneɪʃ(ə)n/ *n.*, **eliminator** *n.* [f. L *eliminare* (EX-¹, *limen* threshold)]

Eliot¹ /ˈelɪət/, George (pseudonym of Mary Ann Evans, 1819-80), English novelist. Early influenced by Evangelicalism she later adopted agnostic views, but her lofty moral concepts of love and duty retained a religious authority. She became assistant editor of the *Westminster Review* (1851) and joined George Henry Lewes in a union without marriage until his death in 1878. Her first work of fiction, *Scenes of Clerical Life* (1858), was praised for its domestic realism, pathos, and humour and *Adam Bede* (1859) established her as a leading novelist, a reputation she consolidated in *The Mill on the Floss* (1860), *Silas Marner* (1861), and other writings. Her masterpiece is *Middlemarch* (1871-2); its brilliant depiction of provincial Victorian intellect and society has made it one of the greatest English novels.

Eliot² /ˈelɪət/, Thomas Stearns (1888-1965), Anglo-American poet, critic, and dramatist, who was greatly encouraged by Ezra Pound. His early verse collections, *Prufrock and other Observations* (1917) and *Poems* (1919) struck a new note in modern poetry. In his newly founded quarterly *Horizon* he published *The Waste Land* (1922), which established him as the voice of a disillusioned generation. In 1927 he became a British subject and an Anglican, describing himself as 'classical in literature, royalist in politics, and Anglo-Catholic in religion'; the same preoccupation with tradition was expressed in his influential critical works. *Four Quartets* (1943) communicated in modern idiom the fundamentals of Christian faith. His attempts to revive poetic drama resulted in *Murder in the Cathedral* (1935), *The Family Reunion* (1939), and *The Cocktail Party* (1959). *Old Possum's Book of Practical Cats* (1939) was his classic children's verse collection; it achieved stage success in a musical adaptation *Cats* in 1981. He was awarded the Nobel Prize for literature in 1947.

Elisha /ɪˈlaɪʃə/ a Hebrew prophet, disciple and successor of Elijah.

elision /ɪˈlɪʒ(ə)n/ *n.* omission of a vowel or syllable in pronouncing (as in *I'm*, *let's*; *e'en*) or of a passage in a book etc. [f. L (as ELIDE)]

élite /eɪˈliːt/ *n.* **1.** a select group or class; *the* best (of a group). **2.** a size of letters in typewriting (12 per inch). [f. F (as ELECT)]

élitism /eɪˈliːtɪz(ə)m/ *n.* recourse to or advocacy of leadership or dominance by a select group. —**élitist** *n.* [f. prec.]

elixir /ɪˈlɪksə(r)/ *n.* **1.** an alchemist's preparation designed to change metal into gold or (*elixir of life*) to prolong life indefinitely; a remedy for all ills. **2.** an aromatic medicinal drug. [f. L f. Arab., prob. f. Gk *xērion* powder for wounds]

Elizabeth I /ɪˈlɪzəbəθ/ (1533-1603), daughter of Henry VIII, queen of England and Ireland 1558-1603. Succeeding her Catholic sister Mary, Elizabeth was successful in uniting a deeply divided nation and re-establishing a moderate form of Protestantism as the religion of the State. Although frequently courted, Elizabeth never married and indeed

owed much of her popularity and success to the cult of the Virgin Queen created around her. Her reign was dominated by the threat of a Catholic restoration (eventually leading to the execution of Mary Queen of Scots) and by war with Spain, during which the country was saved from invasion by the defeat of the Armada in 1588. Her reign also witnessed a great flowering of national culture, particularly in the field of literature, in which Shakespeare, Marlowe, and Spenser were all active.

Elizabeth II (1926-), daughter of George VI, queen of the United Kingdom from 1952. She has done much to maintain the popularity of the monarchy at home and abroad through an extensive series of royal tours and public appearances.

Elizabethan /ɪlɪzəˈbiːθ(ə)n/ *adj.* belonging to or characteristic of the reign of Queen Elizabeth I. —*n.* a person of this period. [f. ELIZABETH]

elk *n.* **1.** a large deer (*Alces alces*) of northern Europe and Asia, the moose. **2.** (*US*) the wapiti. [prob. OE]

ell *n.* (*hist.*) a measure of length, = 45 inches. [OE, = forearm (cogn. with L *ulna*)]

Ellington /ˈelɪŋt(ə)n/, Edward Kennedy ('Duke') (1899-1974), American composer, pianist, and band-leader, the most distinctive and influential figure in the history of jazz. His band established its fame in the early 1930s, and some of its members remained with him for over 30 years. Ellington wrote over 900 compositions; his first world-wide success was *Mood Indigo* (1930).

ellipse /ɪˈlɪps/ *n.* a regular oval, the figure produced when a cone is cut by a plane making a smaller angle with the base than the side of the cone makes (ill. SHAPES). [f. F f. L f. Gk *elleipsis* deficit]

ellipsis /ɪˈlɪpsɪs/ *n.* (*pl.* **ellipses** /-siːz/) the omission of words needed to complete a construction or sense; a set of three dots etc. indicating such an omission. [as prec.]

ellipsoid /ɪˈlɪpsɔɪd/ *n.* a solid of which all plane sections through one axis are ellipses and all other plane sections are ellipses or circles. [f. ELLIPSE]

elliptical /ɪˈlɪptɪk(ə)l/ *adj.* **1.** of or in the form of an ellipse. **2.** of or containing an ellipsis. —**elliptically** *adv.* [f. Gk (as ELLIPSE)]

elm *n.* a tree of the genus *Ulmus*, especially *U. procera* with rough serrated leaves; its wood. [OE]

Elmo /ˈelmoʊ/, St, (*pop.*) St Peter González (c.1190-1246), a Dominican preacher who worked among seafaring folk on the coasts of Spain, and after his death was canonized as the patron saint of seamen. —**St Elmo's fire**, see CORPOSANT.

elocution /eləˈkjuːʃ(ə)n/ *n.* the art or style of expressive speaking. —**elocutionary** *adj.*, **elocutionist** *n.* [f. L (as ELOQUENT)]

elongate /ˈiːlɒŋɡeɪt/ *v.t.* to lengthen, to extend, to draw out. —**elongation** /-ˈɡeɪʃ(ə)n/ *n.* [f. L *elongare* (EX-¹, *longus* long)]

elope /ɪˈloʊp/ *v.i.* to run away secretly with a lover, especially in order to get married. —**elopement** *n.* [f. AF, perh. rel. to LEAP]

eloquence /ˈeləkwəns/ *n.* fluent and effective use of language. [f. OF f. L (as foll.)]

eloquent *adj.* having eloquence; expressive (*of*). —**eloquently** *adv.* [f. OF f. L *eloqui* (EX-¹, *loqui* speak)]

El Salvador /ˈsælvədɔː(r)/ a country in Central America, on the Pacific coast; pop. (est. 1981) 4,939,400; official language, Spanish; capital, San Salvador. Its economy is mainly agricultural, coffee, cotton, and sugar-cane being the chief crops. Conquered by the Spanish in 1524, El Salvador gained its independence in 1821 and joined the Central American Federation in 1824, before finally emerging as an independent republic in 1839. In the late 1970s and early 1980s the country has fallen into increasingly severe internal unrest, characterized by guerrilla warfare, harsh repressive measures, and a large refugee problem.

else *adv.* (with indefinite or interrog. pronoun) besides; instead; otherwise, if not. —**or else**, (*colloq.*) expressing threat or warning. [OE, rel. to L *alius* other]

elsewhere *adv.* in or to some other place.

elucidate /ɪˈluːsɪdeɪt/ *v.t.* to throw light on, to explain. —**elucidation** /-ˈdeɪʃ(ə)n/ *n.*, **elucidatory** *adj.* [f. L *elucidare* (EX-¹, *lucidus* bright)]

elude /ɪˈljuːd/ *v.t.* to escape adroitly from (danger etc.); to avoid compliance with or fulfilment of (a law, obligation, etc.); to baffle (a person or the memory etc.). —**elusion** *n.*, **elusive** *adj.* [f. L *eludere* (EX-¹, *ludere* play)]

elver *n.* a young eel. [var. of *eelfare* (EEL, FARE)]

elves *pl.* of ELF.

elvish *adj.* = ELFISH.

Élysée /eɪliːzeɪ/ (in full **Élysée Palace**, Fr. *Palais de l'Élysée*) a building in Paris, on the Champs Élysées, the official residence of Presidents of France since 1873, whence the use of its name as a synonym for the President and his advisers, or the government of the day. It was once owned by Mme de Pompadour.

Elysium /ɪˈlɪzɪəm/ **1.** (*Gk myth.*) the fields at the ends of the earth to where (according to Homer and Hesiod) certain favoured heroes, exempted from death, were translated by the gods. This concept appears to be a survival from Minoan religion. When a later age concerned itself with the fate of the blessed *dead*, Elysium was transferred to the nether regions, in conformity with Greek ideas and the Homeric picture of the House of Hades. **2.** a place of ideal happiness. —**Elysian** *adj.* [f. L f. Gk *Elusion* (*pedion* plain)]

Elzevir /ˈelzəvɪə(r)/ a family of Dutch printers, 15 of whom were active 1583–1712. Louis (1542–1617), born at Louvain, founded the business at Leiden *c.*1580. Their fame depends largely on their elegant editions of the works of classical authors (1634–6).

em *n.* (*Printing*) a unit of measurement equal to the space occupied by m. [name of letter *M*]

'em /əm/ *pron.* (*colloq.*) them.

em- see EN-.

emaciate /ɪˈmeɪsɪeɪt, -ʃ-/ *v.t.* to make thin or feeble. —**emaciation** /-ˈeɪʃ(ə)n/ *n.* [f. L *emaciare* (EX-[1], *macies* leanness)]

emanate /ˈeməneɪt/ *v.t./i.* to originate or proceed (*from* a source, person, etc.); to cause to do this. —**emanation** /-ˈneɪʃ(ə)n/ *n.* [f. L *emanare* (EX-[1], *manare* flow)]

emancipate /ɪˈmænsɪpeɪt/ *v.t.* to free from slavery or from (esp. political or social) restraint. —**emancipation** /-ˈpeɪʃ(ə)n/ *n.*, **emancipator** *n.*, **emancipatory** *adj.* [f. L *emancipare* (EX-[1], *mancipare* transfer ownership of)]

emancipist /ɪˈmænsɪpɪst/ *n.* (*Austral. hist.*) an ex-convict who had served his term. [f. prec.]

emasculate /ɪˈmæskjʊleɪt/ *v.t.* **1.** to castrate. **2.** to deprive of strength or force. —/-ət/ *adj.* **1.** castrated; effeminate. **2.** deprived of strength or force. —**emasculation** /-ˈleɪʃ(ə)n/ *n.*, **emasculatory** *adj.* [f. L *emasculare* (EX-[1], *masculus* dim. of *mas* male)]

embalm /ɪmˈbɑːm/ *v.t.* **1.** to preserve (a corpse) from decay. **2.** to preserve from decay or oblivion. **3.** to make fragrant. —**embalmment** *n.* [f. OF (as EM-, BALM)]

embankment /ɪmˈbæŋkmənt/ *n.* an earth or stone bank keeping back water or carrying a road, railway, etc. [f. EM- + BANK]

embargo /emˈbɑːɡəʊ/ *n.* (*pl.* **-oes**) an order forbidding foreign ships to enter, or any ships to leave, the country's ports; a prohibition or restraint, especially of commerce. —*v.t.* to place under an embargo. [Sp., f. *embargar* arrest (as IN-[1], BAR[1])]

embark /ɪmˈbɑːk/ *v.t./i.* **1.** to put or go on board ship (*for* a destination). **2.** to engage *in* or *on* an enterprise. [f. F (as EM-, BARQUE)]

embarkation /embɑːˈkeɪʃ(ə)n/ *n.* embarking on a ship. [f. prec.]

embarrass /ɪmˈbærəs/ *v.t.* **1.** to make (a person) feel awkward or ashamed. **2.** to encumber; to perplex; to complicate (a question etc.). —**embarrassment** *n.* [f. F f. Sp. f. It. (*imbarrare* bar in)]

embassy /ˈembəsɪ/ *n.* the offices or residence of an ambassador; an ambassador and his staff; a deputation to a foreign government. [f. OF (as AMBASSADOR)]

embattled /ɪmˈbæt(ə)ld/ *adj.* **1.** prepared or arrayed for battle. **2.** fortified with battlements. **3.** (in heraldry) like battlements in form (ill. HERALDRY). [f. EM- + BATTLE]

embed /ɪmˈbed/ *v.t.* (**-dd-**) to fix firmly in a surrounding mass.

embellish /ɪmˈbelɪʃ/ *v.t.* to beautify, to adorn; to enhance (a narrative) with fictitious additions. —**embellishment** *n.* [f. OF *embellir* (*bel* handsome f. L)]

ember *n.* (usu. in *pl.*) a small piece of live coal etc. in a dying fire. [OE]

ember days a group of three days in each season, observed as days of fasting and prayer in some Churches. Their early history and original purpose is obscure; at first there were apparently only three groups, perhaps taken over from pagan religious observances connected with seed-time, harvest, and autumn vintage. They are now associated almost entirely with the ordination of ministers. [OE, perh. f. *ymbryne* period]

embezzle /ɪmˈbez(ə)l/ *v.t.* to divert (money etc.) fraudulently to one's own use. —**embezzlement** *n.*, **embezzler** *n.* [f. AF (*besiler* = OF *besillier* maltreat, ravage)]

embitter /ɪmˈbɪtə(r)/ *v.t.* to arouse bitter feelings in; to make bitter. —**embitterment** *n.*

emblazon /ɪmˈbleɪz(ə)n/ *v.t.* to blazon. —**emblazonment** *n.*

emblem /ˈembləm/ *n.* a symbol; a heraldic or representative device. —**emblematic** /-ˈmætɪk/ *adj.* [f. L *emblēma* inlaid work f. Gk (*emballō* insert)]

embody /ɪmˈbɒdɪ/ *v.t.* **1.** to make (an idea etc.) actual or discernible; (of a thing) to be an expression of. **2.** to include, to comprise. —**embodiment** *n.*

embolden /ɪmˈbəʊld(ə)n/ *v.t.* to make bold, to encourage. [f. EM- + BOLD]

embolism /ˈembəlɪz(ə)m/ *n.* an obstruction of an artery etc. by a clot of blood, an air-bubble, etc. [f. L f. Gk (*emballō* insert)]

embolus /ˈembələs/ *n.* (*pl.* **-li** /-laɪ/) a thing causing an embolism. [as prec.]

emboss /ɪmˈbɒs/ *v.t.* to carve or decorate with a design in relief. —**embossment** *n.* [f. OF (as EM-, BOSS[2])]

embrace /ɪmˈbreɪs/ *v.t.* **1.** to hold closely in the arms, especially as a sign of affection; (*absol.* of two people) to embrace each other; to clasp, to enclose. **2.** to accept, to adopt (an idea, belief, etc.). **3.** to take in with the eye or mind. —*n.* holding in the arms, a clasp. [f. OF f. L *bracchium* arm]

embrasure /ɪmˈbreɪʒə(r)/ *n.* **1.** the bevelling of a wall at the sides of a window etc. (ill. CHURCH). **2.** an opening between the merlons of an embattled parapet (ill. CASTLES). [f. F (*embraser* splay)]

embrocation /embrəˈkeɪʃ(ə)n/ *n.* a liquid for rubbing on the body to relieve muscular pain. [f. F or L f. Gk *embrokhē* lotion]

embroider /ɪmˈbrɔɪdə(r)/ *v.t.* **1.** to decorate (cloth etc.) with needlework. **2.** to embellish (a narrative). [f. AF *enbrouder* f. Gmc]

embroidery *n.* **1.** embroidering; embroidered work. **2.** elaboration, as of a narrative by inessential detail. [f. prec.]

embroil /ɪmˈbrɔɪl/ *v.t.* **1.** to bring (affairs etc.) into confusion. **2.** to involve (a person) in hostility (*with* another). —**embroilment** *n.* [f. F *embrouiller* entangle, mix]

embryo /ˈembrɪəʊ/ *n.* (*pl.* **-os**) an unborn or unhatched offspring; a human offspring in the first eight weeks from conception; a rudimentary plant in a seed; a thing in a rudimentary stage. —*adj.* undeveloped, immature. —**in embryo** undeveloped. —**embryonic** /-ˈɒnɪk/ *adj.* [L f. Gk *embruon* (EM-, *bruō* swell, grow)]

embryology /embrɪˈɒlədʒɪ/ *n.* the science of the embryo. [f. prec. + -LOGY]

emend /ɪˈmend/ *v.t.* to correct or remove errors from (a text etc.), to seek to do this. —**emendation** /iːmenˈdeɪʃ(ə)n/ *n.* [f. L *emendare* (EX-[1], *menda* fault)]

emerald /ˈemər(ə)ld/ *n.* a bright-green precious stone; the colour of this. —**Emerald Isle**, Ireland. [f. OF f. L *smaragdus* f. Gk]

emerge /ɪˈmɜːdʒ/ *v.i.* to come up or out into view; to become known or recognized, (of facts) to be revealed; (of a difficulty) to occur. —**emergence** *n.*, **emergent** *adj.* [f. L *emergere* (EX-[1], *mergere* plunge)]

emergency /ɪˈmɜːdʒ(ə)nsɪ/ *n.* a sudden state of danger, conflict, etc., requiring immediate action; a condition needing immediate treatment, a patient with this. —*adj.* for use in an emergency. [f. L (as prec.)]

emeritus /ɪˈmerɪtəs/ *adj.* retired and retaining a title as an honour. [L, = that has earned his discharge by service]

Emerson /ˈeməs(ə)n/, Ralph Waldo (1803–82), American philosopher and poet, who was ordained and became a pastor in Boston, but owing to his sceptical views on the nature of the sacraments resigned and left for Europe (1832). In England he met Coleridge, Wordsworth, and Carlyle through whom he became associated with German idealism. On his return he evolved the new quasi-religious concept of transcendentalism which found expression in his essay *Nature* (1836); his mystic idealism and reverence for nature was immensely influential in American life and thought. He was involved in the anti-slavery campaign and continued to write poems and prose until his last decade, when his mental faculties sharply declined.

emery /ˈeməri/ n. a coarse corundum for polishing metal etc. —**emery-board** n. emery-coated nail-file. [f. F f. It. f. Gk *smēris* polishing powder]

emetic /ɪˈmetɪk/ adj. that causes vomiting. —n. an emetic medicine. [f. Gk (*emeō* vomit)]

EMF abbr. electromotive force.

emigrant /ˈemɪgrənt/ n. one who emigrates. —adj. emigrating. [as foll.]

emigrate /ˈemɪgreɪt/ v.i. to leave one's own country to settle in another. —**emigration** /-ˈgreɪʃ(ə)n/ n. [f. L *emigrare* (EX-¹, MIGRATE)]

émigré /ˈemɪgreɪ/ n. an emigrant, especially a political exile. [F as prec.)]

eminence /ˈemɪnəns/ n. **1.** distinction, recognized superiority. **2.** a piece of rising ground. --**His, Your,** etc., **Eminence,** a title used in addressing or referring to a cardinal. [f. L (as EMINENT)]

éminence grise /eɪmɪnɑ̃s ˈgriːz/ one who exercises power or influence without holding office. [F, = grey cardinal (orig. applied to Cardinal Richelieu's secretary)]

eminent /ˈemɪnənt/ adj. distinguished, notable, outstanding. —**eminently** adv. [f. L, orig. = jutting out]

emir /eˈmɪə(r)/ n. the title of various Muslim rulers. [f. F (as AMIR)]

emirate /ˈemɪərət/ n. the rank, domain, or reign of an emir. [f. prec.]

emissary /ˈemɪsəri/ n. a person sent on a special diplomatic mission. [f. L, = scout, spy (as foll.)]

emit /ɪˈmɪt/ v.t. (**-tt-**) to send out (light, heat, etc.); to utter (a cry etc.). —**emission** n., **emissive** adj. [f. L *emittere* (EX-¹, *mittere* send)]

emollient /ɪˈmɒlɪənt/ adj. softening or soothing the skin. —n. an emollient substance. [f. L *emollire* (EX-¹, *mollis* soft)]

emolument /ɪˈmɒljʊmənt/ n. a profit from employment, a salary. [f. OF or L, prob. orig. = payment for corn-grinding (*molere* grind)]

emote /ɪˈməʊt/ v.i. to act with a show of emotion. [back-formation f. foll.]

emotion /ɪˈməʊʃ(ə)n/ n. a strong mental or instinctive feeling such as love or fear. [f. F (*émouvoir* excite, as MOVE)]

emotional adj. of or expressing emotion(s); liable to excessive emotion. —**emotionalism** n., **emotionally** adv. [f. prec.]

emotive /ɪˈməʊtɪv/ adj. of or tending to excite emotion; arousing feeling. [f. L *emovere* disturb (EX-¹, *movere* move)]

empanel /ɪmˈpæn(ə)l/ v.t. (**-ll-**) to enter (a jury) on a panel. [f. AF (as EM-, PANEL)]

empathize /ˈempəθaɪz/ v.t./i. to treat with empathy; to use empathy. [f. foll.]

empathy /ˈempəθi/ n. the power of identifying oneself mentally with (and so fully comprehending) a person or object of contemplation. —**empathic** /-ˈpæθɪk/ adj. [transl. G *einfühlung* (*ein* in, *fühlung* feeling), after Gk *empatheia* (EM-, *pathēs* f. *pathos* feeling)]

Empedocles /emˈpedəkliːz/ (*c*.493-*c*.433 BC) Greek philosopher from Sicily, whose theory of matter was a step on the road towards atomism. His hexameter poem *On Nature* teaches that the universe is composed of the four imperishable elements of fire, air, water, and earth, which mingle and separate under the influence of the opposing principles of Love and Strife. He was also a religious teacher, miracle-worker, statesman, and orator. According to legend he leapt into the crater of Mount Etna in Sicily in order that he might be thought a god.

emperor /ˈempərə(r)/ n. the sovereign of an empire. —**emperor penguin,** the largest known species of penguin, *Aptenodytes forsteri*. [f. OF f. L *imperator* (*imperare* command)]

emphasis /ˈemfəsɪs/ n. (*pl.* **emphases** /-siːz/) **1.** special importance or prominence attached to a thing. **2.** the stress on a syllable or word(s) or on note(s) in music. **3.** vigour or intensity of expression, feeling, etc. [L f. Gk *emphainō* exhibit]

emphasize /ˈemfəsaɪz/ v.t. to put emphasis on, to stress. [f. prec.]

emphatic /ɪmˈfætɪk/ adj. full of emphasis, forcibly expressive; (of words) bearing stress, used to give emphasis. —**emphatically** adv. [f. L f. Gk (as EMPHASIS)]

emphysema /emfɪˈsiːmə/ n. a swelling due to air in body tissues. [L f. Gk (*emphusaō* puff up)]

empire /ˈempaɪə(r)/ n. **1.** an extensive group of countries or States under the supreme rule of one State or person. **2.** a large commercial organization etc. owned or directed by one person or group. **3.** supreme dominion (*over*). —**the Empire,** the British Empire; the Holy Roman Empire; the period of the reign of Napoleon I as Emperor of the French (1804-15), also called 'First Empire' to distinguish it from the 'Second Empire' of Napoleon III (1852-70). **empire-building** n. deliberate accumulation of territory, authority, etc. [f. OF f. L *imperium* (as EMPIRE)]

Empire State Building a skyscraper in Fifth Avenue, New York, which was for long the tallest building in the world. When first erected, in 1930-1, it measured 381 m (1,250 ft.); the addition of a television mast in 1951 brought its height to 449 m (1,472 ft.). It is named after New York, the Empire State.

Empire style a style of furniture, interior decoration, and dress which started in Paris after the French Revolution and spread through Europe, corresponding to the Regency style in England. Basically the style is neo-classical but with an increment of archaeological interest, an attempt to copy what was known of ancient furniture and motifs, with particular affectation of Egyptian motifs probably reflecting interest in Napoleon's Egyptian campaigns. In women's dress there was a distinctive high-waisted fashion embellished with dazzling embroidery (ill. DRESS).

empirical /emˈpɪrɪk(ə)l/ adj. relying on observation and experiment, not on theory. —**empirically** adv. [f. Gk (*empeiria* experience)]

empiricism /ɪmˈpɪrɪsɪz(ə)m/ n. **1.** the use of empirical methods. **2.** the theory that regards sense-experience(s) as the only source of knowledge. —**empiricist** n. [f. L f. Gk *empeirikos* (as prec.)]

emplacement /ɪmˈpleɪsmənt/ n. **1.** putting in position. **2.** a platform for guns. [f. F (as EM-, PLACE)]

employ /ɪmˈplɔɪ/ v.t. to use the services of (a person) in return for payment; to use (a thing, time, energy, etc.) to some effect; to keep occupied. —n. **in the employ of,** employed by. —**employer** n. [f. OF f. L *implicari* be involved]

employable adj. able to be employed. [f. prec.]

employee /emplɔɪˈiː, -ˈplɔɪɪ/ n. a person employed for wages. [f. EMPLOY]

employment n. employing, being employed; one's regular trade or profession. —**employment exchange,** a State office concerned with finding employment for those seeking it. [as prec.]

emporium /emˈpɔːrɪəm/ n. (*pl.* **-ia, -iums**) a centre of commerce, a market; a large shop, a store. [L f. Gk *emporos* merchant)]

empower /ɪmˈpaʊə(r)/ v.t. to give power or authority to.

empress /ˈemprɪs/ n. the wife or widow of an emperor; a woman emperor. [f. OF (as EMPEROR)]

Empson /ˈempsən/, William (1906-84), English poet, whose intricate closely reasoned poems reflect his training as a mathematician. His *Seven Types of Ambiguity* (1930) was an influential piece of literary criticism.

empty adj. **1.** containing nothing; (of a house etc.) unoccupied or unfurnished. **2.** (*colloq.*) hungry. **3.** foolish, meaningless, vacuous. —v.t./i. to remove the contents of; to transfer (the contents of one thing *into* another); to become empty; (of a river) to discharge itself. —n. an empty bottle, box, etc. —**empty-handed** adj. having or bringing nothing. **empty-headed** adj. foolish, lacking sense. —**emptily** adv., **emptiness** n. [OE (*æmetta* leisure)]

empyrean /empaɪˈriːən/ n. the highest heaven, as the sphere of fire in ancient cosmology or the abode of God. —adj. of this. —**empyreal** adj. [f. L f. Gk (*pur* fire)]

EMS abbr. European Monetary System.

emu /ˈiːmjuː/ n. a large flightless Australian bird, *Dromaius novaehollandiae*, capable of running at speeds of up to 50 k.p.h. (30 m.p.h.). [f. Port. *ema* crane]

emulate /ˈemjʊleɪt/ v.t. to try to equal or excel; to imitate. —**emulation** /-ˈleɪʃ(ə)n/ n., **emulative** adj., **emulator** n. [f. L *aemulari* (as foll.)]

emulous /ˈemjʊləs/ adj. eagerly or jealously imitative (*of*); actuated by rivalry. [f. L *aemulus* rival]

emulsify /ɪˈmʌlsɪfaɪ/ v.t. to convert into an emulsion. [as foll.]

emulsion /ɪˈmʌlʃ(ə)n/ n. **1.** a fine dispersion of one liquid in another, especially as paint, medicine, etc. **2.** a mixture of a silver compound in gelatin etc. as a coating for a photographic plate or film. —**emulsive** *adj.* [f. F f. L *emulgēre* (EX-[1], *mulgēre* milk)]

en *n.* (*Printing*) a unit of measurement equal to half an em. [name of letter N]

en- *prefix* (**em-** before *b*, *m*, *p*) **1.** = IN-[1], forming verbs (1) from nouns, in the sense 'put into or on' (*embed*), (2) from nouns or adjectives, in the sense 'bring into the condition of' (*enslave*), often with suffix -EN (*enlighten*), (3) from verbs, in the sense 'in, into, on' (*enfold*) or intensively (*entangle*). [f. F f. L *in-*]. **2.** in, inside (*energy*, *enthusiasm*). [f. Gk *en-*]

enable /ɪˈneɪb(ə)l/ *v.t.* to give the means or authority (*to do*); to make possible.

enact /ɪˈnækt/ *v.t.* **1.** to ordain, to decree. **2.** to play (a part on the stage or in life). —**enactive** *adj.*

enactment *n.* a law enacted. [f. prec.]

enamel /ɪˈnæm(ə)l/ *n.* **1.** a glasslike (usually opaque) ornamental or preservative coating on metal. **2.** a hard smooth coating; a cosmetic simulating this; the hard coating of teeth. **3.** a painting done in enamel. —*v.t.* (**-ll-**) to coat, inlay, or portray with enamel. [f. AF f. Gmc]

enamour /ɪˈnæmə(r)/ *v.t.* (usu. in *p.p.*) to inspire with love or liking (*of*). [f. OF *enamourer* (*amour* love)]

en bloc /ɒn ˈblɒk/ in a block, all at the same time. [F]

encamp /ɪnˈkæmp/ *v.t./i.* to settle in a military or other camp. —**encampment** *n.*

encapsulate /ɪnˈkæpsjʊleɪt/ *v.t.* **1.** to enclose (as) in a capsule. **2.** to summarize; to isolate. —**encapsulation** /-ˈleɪʃ(ə)n/ *n.* [f. EN- + L *capsula* capsule]

encase /ɪnˈkeɪs/ *v.t.* to confine (as) in a case. —**encasement** *n.*

encash /enˈkæʃ/ *v.t.* to convert into cash. —**encashment** *n.*

en.caustic /enˈkɔːstɪk/ *adj.* (of painting) using pigments mixed with hot wax, which are burned in as an inlay. —*n.* the art or product of this. [f. L f. Gk (as EN-, CAUSTIC)]

enceinte /ɑːˈsæt/ *adj.* pregnant. [F, = ungirdled]

encephalitis /ensefəˈlaɪtɪs/ *n.* inflammation of the brain. [f. Gk *egkephalos* brain]

encephalogram /enˈsefələgræm/ *n.* an electroencephalogram. [as prec. + -GRAM]

encephalograph /enˈsefələgrɑːf/ *n.* an electroencephalograph. [as ENCEPHALITIS + -GRAPH]

enchain /ɪnˈtʃeɪn/ *v.t.* **1.** to chain up. **2.** to hold (the attention or emotions) fast. [f. F (as EN-, CHAIN)]

enchant /ɪnˈtʃɑːnt/ *v.t.* to charm, to delight; to bewitch. —**enchanter, enchantment** *ns.*, **enchantress** *n.fem.* [f. F f. L *incantare*, frequent. of *canere* sing]

encircle /ɪnˈsɜːk(ə)l/ *v.t.* to surround; to form a circle round. —**encirclement** *n.* [f. EN- + CIRCLE]

enclave /ˈenkleɪv/ *n.* the territory of one State surrounded by that of another. [F (*enclaver* shut in, f. L *clavis* key)]

enclitic /enˈklɪtɪk/ *adj.* (of a word) pronounced with so little emphasis that it forms part of the preceding word. —*n.* such a word. [f. L f. Gk (EN-, *klinō* lean)]

enclose /ɪnˈkləʊz/ *v.t.* **1.** to shut in on all sides, to surround with a wall or fence etc.; to shut up in a receptacle (esp. in an envelope besides a letter). **2.** (in *p.p.*, of a religious community) secluded from the outside world. [f. OF f. L (as INCLUDE)]

enclosure /ɪnˈkləʊʒə(r)/ *n.* **1.** the act of enclosing; the enclosing of common land to make it private property (see below). **2.** an enclosed space or area. **3.** a thing enclosed with a letter. [as prec.]
The conversion from the traditional medieval system of open-field farming to that of enclosed fields caused considerable unrest at various times, most notably in the mid-16th c. when the enclosure of much common land for sheep-farming resulted in widespread deprivation in large parts of the English countryside. The pressures of an expanding population, along with the advances made in the Agrarian Revolution, hastened the pace of enclosures during the 18th c., and by the early 19th c. the available agricultural land had been almost completely enclosed.

encode /ɪnˈkəʊd/ *v.t.* to put into code. —**encoder** *n.*

encomium /enˈkəʊmɪəm/ *n.* (*pl.* **-ums**) formal or bombastic praise. [f. L f. Gk]

encompass /ɪnˈkʌmpəs/ *v.t.* to surround; to contain.

encore /ˈɒŋkɔː(r)/ *n.* an audience's demand for further performance or repetition of an item; such an item. —*v.t.* to call for an encore of (an item), to call back (a performer) for this. —/also -ˈkɔː(r)/ *int.* again, once more. [F, = once more]

encounter /ɪnˈkaʊntə(r)/ *v.t.* **1.** to meet by chance or unexpectedly. **2.** to find oneself faced with (a problem etc.). **3.** to meet as an adversary. —*n.* a meeting by chance or in conflict. [f. OF f. L *contra* against]

encourage /ɪnˈkʌrɪdʒ/ *v.t.* **1.** to give courage or confidence to. **2.** to urge; to stimulate, to promote. —**encouragement** *n.* [f. F (as EN-, COURAGE)]

encroach /ɪnˈkrəʊtʃ/ *v.i.* to intrude (*on* or *upon*); to advance gradually beyond due limits. —**encroachment** *n.* [f. OF *encrochier* (*croc* hook)]

encrust /ɪnˈkrʌst/ *v.t./i.* to cover with or form a crust; to overlay with a crust of silver etc. [f. F (as EN-, CRUST)]

encumber /ɪnˈkʌmbə(r)/ *v.t.* to be a burden to; to hamper, to impede. [f. OF f. Rom.]

encumbrance *n.* a burden, an impediment. [f. prec.]

encyclical /ɪnˈsɪklɪk(ə)l/ *adj.* for wide circulation. —*n.* a papal encyclical letter. [f. L f. Gk (EN-, *kuklos* circle)]

encyclopaedia /ensaɪkləˈpiːdɪə/ *n.* a book or set of books giving information on many subjects, or on many aspects of one subject (see below). [L f. Gk *egkuklios* all-round, *paideia* education]
The word 'encyclopaedia' comes from a Greek phrase meaning 'all-round education', the circle of arts and sciences considered by the ancient Greeks as essential to a liberal education, but their emphasis was on the spoken word and it was left to the Romans to record their knowledge in readable form. Roman encyclopaedic works include those of Cato, Varro, Celsus (1st c. AD), and Pliny the Elder, with articles grouped under main topics, as were the Latin medieval compilations such as those of Isidore of Seville and Francis Bacon (1620). The first known use of the word 'encyclopaedia' as the title of a book occurs in 1559, in a Latin compilation by the German writer Paul Scaliger. After the Renaissance similar works were produced in vernacular languages and an alphabetical arrangement became adopted. The 18th c. saw the publication of the *Cyclopaedia* of Ephraim Chambers (1728) and the great French *Encyclopédie* (1751–76), under the direction of Diderot, whose contributors included Voltaire, Rousseau, and other brilliant but controversial writers; F. A. Brockhaus produced a successful German encyclopaedia (1796–1811); Larousse's *Grand Dictionnaire Universel* was published in 1866–76. The *Encyclopaedia Britannica* began in 1768–71 as a dictionary of the arts and sciences issued by a 'Society of Gentlemen in Scotland'; its second edition, in ten volumes, added history and biography; the current edition is the largest encyclopaedia in the English language.

encyclopaedic *adj.* (of knowledge or information) comprehensive. [f. prec.]

encyclopaedist *n.* a writer of an encyclopaedia. [f. ENCYCLOPAEDIA]

end *n.* **1.** the extreme limit, the furthest point; the extreme part or surface of a thing. **2.** a finish or conclusion; the latter part; destruction, death. **3.** a purpose, an object. **4.** a result, an outcome. **5.** a remnant, a piece left over. **6.** the half of a sports pitch etc. occupied by one side. **7.** the part or share with which a person is concerned. —*v.t./i.* to bring or come to an end, to finish; to result *in*. —**the end,** (*colloq.*) the limit of endurability. **end it all,** (*colloq.*) to commit suicide. **end on,** with the end facing one or adjoining the end of the next object. **end-product** *n.* the final product of manufacture, a transformation, etc. **ends of the earth,** the remotest regions. **end to end,** with the end of one adjoining the end of the next in a series. **end up,** to reach a certain state or action eventually. **in the end,** finally. **keep one's end up,** to do one's part despite difficulties. **make ends meet,** to live within one's income. **no end,** (*colloq.*) to a great extent. **no end of,** (*colloq.*) much or many of. **on end,** upright; continuously. **put an end to,** to stop, to abolish, to destroy. [OE]

endanger /ɪnˈdeɪndʒə(r)/ *v.t.* to bring into danger.

endear /ɪnˈdɪə(r)/ *v.t.* to make dear (*to*).

endearment *n.* **1.** an act or words expressing affection. **2.** liking, affection. [f. prec.]

endeavour /ɪnˈdevə(r)/ *v.t.* to try earnestly (*to do*). —*n.* an earnest attempt. [f. EN- + F *devoir* duty]

endemic /enˈdemɪk/ *adj.* regularly or only found among a (specified) people or in a (specified) country. —*n.* an endemic disease or plant. —**endemically** *adv.* [f. F or L f. Gk (EN-, *dēmos* people)]

ending *n.* the end or final part, especially of a story; the inflected final part of a word. [f. END]

endive /ˈendɪv/ n. 1. a curly leaved plant (*Cichorium endivia*) used in salads. 2. (*US*) a chicory crown. [f. OF, ult. f. L *intibum*]

endless /ˈendlɪs/ adj. without end, infinite; incessant; continual; (*colloq.*) innumerable. —**endless belt** *or* **chain** etc., one with the ends joined for continuous action over wheels etc. [f. END + -LESS]

endmost adj. nearest the end. [f. END + -MOST]

endo- prefix internal(ly). [f. Gk *endon* within]

endocrine /ˈendəʊkraɪn, -krɪn/ adj. (of a gland) secreting directly into the blood. [f. ENDO- + Gk *krinō* sift]

endogenous /enˈdɒdʒɪnəs/ adj. growing or originating from within. [f. ENDO- + -GENOUS]

endomorph /ˈendəʊmɔːf/ n. a person with a soft round build of the body, thought likely to be an extrovert (see ECTOMORPH). [f. ENDO- + Gk *morphē* form]

endorphin /enˈdɔːfɪn/ n. any of a group of peptides that occur naturally in the brain and have an effect similar to that of morphine, serving to inhibit pain. [f. F (as ENDO-, MORPHINE)]

endorse /ɪnˈdɔːs/ v.t. 1. to confirm, to approve. 2. to write a comment etc. on (a document); to sign the back of (a cheque). 3. to enter the details of a conviction for an offence on (a licence). —**endorsement** n. [f. L *indorsare* (IN-¹, *dorsum* back)]

endoscope /ˈendəskəʊp/ n. an instrument used for viewing the internal parts of the body. —**endoscopy** /ˈdɒskəpɪ/ n. [f. ENDO- + -SCOPE]

endow /ɪnˈdaʊ/ v.t. 1. to bequeath or give a permanent income to (a person, institution, etc.). 2. (esp. in *p.p.*) to provide with talent or ability. [f. AF (as EN-, DOWER)]

endowment n. endowing; an endowed income. —**endowment assurance** *or* **insurance policy** etc., a form of life insurance with payment of a fixed sum to the insured person on a specified date, or to his estate if he dies earlier. [f. prec.]

endpaper n. a stout blank leaf of paper fixed across the beginning or end of a book and the inside cover.

endue /ɪnˈdjuː/ v.t. to provide (a person *with* qualities etc.). [f. OF f. L *inducere* draw on, assoc. with *induere* put on (clothes)]

endurable adj. able to be endured. [f. ENDURE]

endurance n. 1. the power of enduring. 2. the ability to withstand prolonged strain. [OF (as ENDURE)]

endure /ɪnˈdjʊə(r)/ v.t./i. 1. to undergo (pain etc.); to tolerate, to bear. 2. to last. [f. OF f. L *indurare* harden (IN-¹, *durus* hard)]

endways adv. (also **endwise**) 1. with the end uppermost or foremost. 2. end to end.

Endymion /enˈdɪmɪən/ (*Gk myth.*) a remarkably beautiful young man, either a king of Elis in the NE Peloponnese or a Carian. Of the various tales told about him the most celebrated is that he was loved by the Moon (Selene) who caused him to sleep everlastingly so that she could enjoy his beauty for ever. According to another version he obtained from Zeus eternal youth and the gift of sleeping as long as he wished.

enema /ˈenɪmə/ n. the insertion of liquid through the anus into the rectum, especially to expel its contents; a liquid or syringe used for this. [L f. Gk (*enīemi* inject)]

enemy /ˈenəmɪ/ n. a person actively hostile to another and seeking to defeat or harm him; a hostile nation or army, a member of this; an adversary, an opponent. —adj. of or belonging to the enemy. [f. OF f. L *inimicus* (IN-², *amicus* friend)]

energetic /enəˈdʒetɪk/ adj. full of energy; powerfully active. —**energetically** adv. [f. Gk (as ENERGY)]

energize /ˈenədʒaɪz/ v.t. to give energy to; to provide (a device) with energy for operation. [f. foll.]

energy /ˈenədʒɪ/ n. 1. capacity for activity, force, vigour. 2. the ability of matter or radiation to do work (see below). [f. F or L f. Gk *energeia* (*ergon* work)]
The modern scientific concept of energy was formulated in the 19th c. mainly through the study of the generation of mechanical power by means of heat-engines and electrical machines, which were increasingly supplementing the more traditional agencies such as wind and flowing water as alternatives to human labour. Energy can be neither created nor destroyed, but only changed from one form into another. These forms include kinetic energy (energy of motion), potential energy (the energy an object has by virtue of its position), heat energy, electrical energy, and so on.

Einstein (among others) showed that matter can also be regarded as a form of energy, as the two are in principle interconvertible. The standard unit of energy is the joule.

enervate /ˈenəveɪt/ v.t. to deprive of vigour or vitality. —**enervation** /-ˈveɪ(ə)n/ n. [f. L *enervare* (EX-¹, *nervus* sinew)]

enfant terrible /ɑ̃fɑ̃ teˈriːbl/ a person who causes embarrassment by indiscreet behaviour; an unruly child. [F, = terrible child]

enfeeble /ɪnˈfiːb(ə)l/ v.t. to make feeble. —**enfeeblement** n. [f. OF (as EN-, FEEBLE)]

enfilade /enfɪˈleɪd/ n. gunfire directed along a line from end to end. —v.t. to direct an enfilade at. [F, f. *enfiler* (EN-, *fil* thread)]

enfold /ɪnˈfəʊld/ v.t. to wrap (a person *in* or *with*); to clasp, to embrace.

enforce /ɪnˈfɔːs/ v.t. to compel observance of (a law etc.); to impose (an action or one's will etc. *on* a person); to persist in (a demand etc.). —**enforceable** adj., **enforcement** n. [f. OF *enforci(e)r* f. L *fortis* strong]

enfranchise /ɪnˈfræntʃaɪz/ v.t. 1. to give (a person) the right to vote. 2. to give (a town) municipal rights, especially representation in parliament. 3. to free (a slave etc.). —**enfranchisement** /-ɪzmənt/ n. [f. OF *enfranchir* (*franc* free)]

engage /ɪnˈɡeɪdʒ/ v.t./i. 1. to take into one's employment, to hire. 2. to arrange beforehand to occupy (a room, seat, etc.). 3. to promise, to pledge. 4. to occupy the attention of; to occupy oneself. 5. to come or bring into battle (with). 6. to interlock (parts of a gear etc.) so as to transmit power; to become interlocked thus. [f. F (as IN-, GAGE¹)]

engaged adj. 1. having promised to marry. 2. occupied or reserved by a person etc.; occupied with business etc. 3. (of a telephone line) already in use. [f. prec.]

engagement n. 1. engaging, being engaged. 2. an appointment made with another person. 3. a promise to marry a specified person. 4. a battle. —**engagement ring**, a finger-ring given by a man to a woman when they promise to marry. [F (as ENGAGE)]

engaging adj. attractive, charming. [f. ENGAGE]

Engels /ˈeŋ(ə)lz/, Friedrich (1820–95), German socialist, founder with Karl Marx of modern Communism. Engels collaborated with Marx in the writing of the *Communist Manifesto* (1848), but was forced to flee abroad after involvement in the revolution in Baden in 1848–9. He lived the rest of his life in England, making a career as a manufacturer in Manchester before moving to London in 1869. An influential author in his own right, Engels was perhaps more important as the publicist and patron of his colleague Marx.

engender /ɪnˈdʒendə(r)/ v.t. to give rise to (a feeling etc.). [f. OF f. L (as IN-¹, GENERATE)]

engine /ˈendʒɪn/ n. 1. a mechanical contrivance of parts working together, especially as a source of power. 2. a railway locomotive; a fire-engine; a steam-engine. 3. (*archaic*) a machine of war; an instrument; a means. [f. OF f. L *ingenium* talent, device]

engineer /endʒɪˈnɪə(r)/ n. 1. a person skilled in some branch of engineering; a civil engineer (see CIVIL). 2. a person who makes or is in charge of engines or other equipment. 3. one who designs and constructs military works, especially a soldier so trained. —v.t./i. 1. to act as an engineer; to plan and construct or control as engineer. 2. (*colloq.*) to contrive, to bring about. [f. OF f. L *ingeniator* (as prec.)]

engineering n. the application of science for the control and use of power, especially in roads and other works of public utility, machines, and electrical apparatus. [f. prec.]

England /ˈɪŋɡlənd/ a part of Great Britain and the United Kingdom, largely made up of the area south of the River Tweed and containing the capital, London; pop. (1981) 46,362,836. There were settlements in England from at least palaeolithic times, and considerable remains exist of neolithic and Bronze Age cultures. These were followed by the arrival of the Celtic peoples whose civilization spread over the whole country. The Romans under Julius Caesar raided the south of Britain in 55 and 54 BC, but full-scale invasion did not take place until a century later; the country was then administered as a Roman province until the Teutonic conquest of Gaul in the early 5th c. and the subsequent withdrawal of the last Roman garrison. In the 3rd–7th c. Germanic-speaking tribes, traditionally known as Angles, Saxons, and Jutes, raided and then settled, establishing independent kingdoms, and when that of Wessex became dominant in the 9th c. England emerged as a distinct political entity before being conquered by William, Duke of Normandy, in 1066. The neighbouring principality of Wales was gradually conquered during the Middle Ages and politically incorporated in the 16th c. During the period of Tudor rule (1485-1603) England emerged as a Protestant State with a strong stable monarchy and as a naval power. Scotland and England have been ruled by one monarch from 1603, and the two crowns were formally united in 1707. (See GREAT BRITAIN.)

English /'ɪŋglɪʃ/ adj. of England or its people or language. —n. the language of England (see below); its literary or standard form. —**english** v.t. (archaic) to render into English. —**the English**, the people of England. **the King's** or **Queen's English**, the English language correctly spoken or written. [OE (as ANGLES)]

English is the principal language of Great Britain, the USA, Ireland, Australia, and many other countries. There are some 300 million native speakers, and it is the medium of communication for many millions more in all parts of the world. Its history can be divided into three stages: Old English (up to 1150), Middle English (1150-1500), and Modern English (1500 onwards). Old English is usually said to have begun with the settlement of Germanic-speaking tribes (Angles, Saxons, and Jutes) in Britain in the mid-5th c. It was an inflected language, and the gradual decay of these endings is one of the chief changes that took place over the centuries, until by the 15th c. most of them had been lost. Old English was essentially a spoken language, but by the time of Alfred the Great something like a standard literary language was emerging, and by the late 10th c. the dialect of Wessex was becoming dominant. In addition to native Celtic elements and words surviving from the period of Roman rule, extension of vocabulary was brought by the spread of Christian culture, with some words adopted or translated from Latin, and by Scandinavian invaders in the 9th-10th c. After the Norman Conquest, Anglo-Norman was the language of the ruling classes, but from the 14th c. English again became the standard. Despite the influence of French, the Germanic nature of English has been maintained in its syntax and morphology. All changes were gradual, including those in pronunciation; by the 16th c. many vowels were sounded much as they are today.

The spread of the language has its origins in colonization from the Middle Ages onwards and the consolidation of the British Empire particularly in the 19th c. It developed locally (as it has in the British Isles) into many different varieties. Even since the break-up of the Empire, English has gained in influence largely through its use as a medium of international communication and now probably ranks as the world's unofficial lingua franca.

English Channel the sea channel separating southern England from northern France. It is 35 km (22 miles) wide at its narrowest point.

Englishman n. (pl. **-men**) one who is English by birth, descent, or naturalization. —**Englishwoman** n.fem. (pl. **-women**)

engorged /ɪn'gɔːdʒd/ adj. crammed full; congested with blood. [f. F (as EN-, GORGE)]

engraft /ɪn'grɑːft/ v.t. to graft (a shoot of one plant on or into another); to implant; to incorporate (a thing into another).

engrail /ɪn'greɪl/ v.t. to indent the edge of, to give a serrated appearance to (ill. HERALDRY). [f. OF engresler (EN-, gresle hail)]

engrave /ɪn'greɪv/ v.t. **1.** to inscribe or cut (a design) on a hard surface; to inscribe (a surface) thus. **2.** to impress deeply on the memory.

engraving n. a print made from an engraved plate. [f. prec.]

engross /ɪn'grəʊs/ v.t. **1.** to absorb the attention of, to occupy fully. **2.** to write out in large letters or in legal form. —**engrossment** n. [f. AF engrosser (en gros whole-sale); f. en in, grosse large writing]

engulf /ɪn'gʌlf/ v.t. to flow over and swamp, to overwhelm.

enhance /ɪn'hɑːns/ v.t. to heighten or intensify (a quality or power etc.). —**enhancement** n. [f. AF prob. alt. f. OF enhaucier f. L altus high]

enigma /ɪ'nɪgmə/ n. a puzzling thing or person; a riddle or paradox. —**enigmatic** /-'mætɪk/ adj., **enigmatically** adv. [f. L f. Gk ainigma]

enjoin /ɪn'dʒɔɪn/ v.t. to command, to order; to impose (an action on a person); (Law) to prohibit by injunction (from doing). [f. OF f. L injungere attach]

enjoy /ɪn'dʒɔɪ/ v.t. to take pleasure in; to have the use or benefit of; to experience. —**enjoy oneself**, to experience pleasure. —**enjoyment** n. [f. OF (as EN-, JOY)]

enjoyable adj. pleasant, giving enjoyment. —**enjoyably** adv. [f. prec.]

enkephalin /en'kef(ə)lɪn/ n. either of two morphine-like peptides in the brain thought to be concerned with the perception of pain. [f. Gk egkephalos brain]

enkindle /ɪn'kɪnd(ə)l/ v.t. to cause to blaze up; to arouse.

enlarge /ɪn'lɑːdʒ/ v.t./i. **1.** to make or become larger or wider; to reproduce (a photograph) on a larger scale. **2.** to describe in greater detail. —**enlargement** n. [f. OF (as EN-, LARGE)]

enlighten /ɪn'laɪt(ə)n/ v.t. to instruct or inform (a person on a subject); to free from superstition etc.

enlightenment n. enlightening. —**the Enlightenment**, the 18th-c. philosophy allegedly placing too much emphasis on reason and individualism as against tradition. [f. prec.]

enlist /ɪn'lɪst/ v.t./i. **1.** to enrol in the armed services. **2.** to secure as a means of help or support. —**enlistment** n.

enliven /ɪn'laɪv(ə)n/ v.t. to make lively or cheerful. —**enlivenment** n.

en masse /ɑ̃ 'mæs/ all together. [F]

enmesh /ɪn'meʃ/ v.t. to entangle (as) in a net.

enmity /'enmɪtɪ/ n. the state or feeling of being an enemy, hostility. [f. OF (as ENEMY)]

Ennius /'enjəs/, Quintus (239-169 BC), Roman writer, origi-nally from Calabria in SW Italy. Brought to Rome by Cato the Censor he was largely responsible for the creation of a native Roman literature based on Greek models. Of his many works (surviving only in fragments) the most import-ant was the Annals, a hexameter epic on the history of Rome, which was a major influence on such poets as Lucretius and Virgil.

ennoble /ɪ'nəʊb(ə)l/ v.t. to make (a person) a noble; to make noble. —**ennoblement** n. [f. F (as EN-, NOBLE)]

ennui /'ɒnwiː, ɒ'nwiː/ n. mental weariness caused by idle-ness or lack of interest, a feeling of boredom. [F, f. L in odio hateful]

Enoch /'iːnɒk/ **1.** the eldest son of Cain. **2.** the first city, built by Cain and named after Enoch (Gen. 4:17). **3.** a Hebrew patriarch (said to have 'walked with God'), father of Methuselah. Two works ascribed to him, the Book of Enoch and the Book of the Secrets of Enoch, date from the 2nd-1st c. BC and 1st c. AD respectively. A third treatise likewise dates from the Christian era.

enormity /ɪ'nɔːmɪtɪ/ n. **1.** monstrous wickedness; a dreadful crime; a serious error. **2.** (D) great size. [f. F f. L (as foll.)]

enormous /ɪ'nɔːməs/ adj. extraordinarily large, vast, huge. —**enormously** adv. [f. L enormis (EX-¹, norma pat-tern, standard)]

enough /ɪ'nʌf/ adj. as much or as many as required. —n. the amount or quantity that is enough. —adv. to the required degree, adequately; fairly; very, quite. —**have had enough of**, to want no more of; to be satiated with or tired of. **sure enough**, undeniably, as expected. [OE]

enounce /ɪ'naʊns/ v.t. to enunciate, to pronounce. [f. F énoncer (as ENUNCIATE)]

en passant /ɑ̃ 'pæsɑ̃/ by the way. [F, = in passing]

enquire /ɪn'kwaɪə(r)/ v.t./i. to ask to be told (a person's name, business, etc.); to seek information (about etc.). —**enquiry** n. [= INQUIRE]

enrage /ɪn'reɪdʒ/ v.t. to make furious. [f. F (as EN-, RAGE)]

enrapture /ɪn'ræptʃə(r)/ v.t. to delight intensely.

enrich /ɪn'rɪtʃ/ v.t. to make rich or richer; to increase the strength or wealth or value of. —**enrichment** n. [f. OF (as EN-, RICH)]

enrol /ɪn'rəʊl/ v.t./i. (-ll-) to write the name of (a person) on a list; to enlist; to incorporate as a member; to enrol oneself. —**enrolment** n. [f. OF (as EN-, ROLL)]

en route /ɑ̃ 'ruːt/ on the way. [F]

ensconce /ɪn'skɒns/ v.t. to settle comfortably.

ensemble /ɑ̃'sɒ̃bl/ n. **1.** a thing viewed as a sum of its parts. **2.** a set of matching items of dress. **3.** a group of actors, dancers, musicians, etc., performing together; (Mus.) a concerted passage for an ensemble. [F, f. L insimul (IN-¹, simul at the same time)]

enshrine /ɪn'ʃraɪn/ v.t. to enclose (as) in a shrine; to serve as a shrine for.

enshroud /ɪn'ʃraʊd/ v.t. to cover completely (as) with a shroud; to hide from view.

ensign /'ensaɪn, -s(ə)n/ n. **1.** a banner or flag, especially a nation's military or naval flag. **2.** a standard-bearer. **3.** (hist.) the lowest commissioned infantry officer. **4.** (US) the lowest commissioned officer in the navy. [f. OF f. L insignia]

ensilage /'ensɪlɪdʒ/ n. silage. [F (as EN-, SILAGE)]

enslave /ɪn'sleɪv/ v.t. to make into a slave. —**enslavement** n.

ensnare /ɪn'sneə(r)/ v.t. to catch (as) in a snare.

ensue /ɪn'sju:/ v.i. to happen later or as a result. [f. OF f. L (IN-¹, sequi follow)]

en suite /ã 'swi:t/ forming a single unit. [F, = in sequence]

ensure /ɪn'ʃʊə(r)/ v.t. to make certain or secure; to make safe (against risks). [f. AF (as EN-, SURE)]

ENT abbr. ear, nose, and throat.

entablature /ɪn'tæblətʃə(r)/ n. (Archit.) an upper part supported by columns, including the architrave, frieze, and cornice (ill. TEMPLES). [f. It., f. intavolare board up (tavola table)]

entail /ɪn'teɪl/ v.t. **1.** to necessitate or involve unavoidably. **2.** (Law) to bequeath (an estate) inalienably to a named succession of beneficiaries. —n. an entailed estate or succession.

entangle /ɪn'tæŋg(ə)l/ v.t. to cause to get caught in a snare or tangle; to involve in difficulties; to complicate. —**entanglement** n.

entente /ã'tãt/ n. a friendly understanding or association, especially between States. —**entente cordiale** /kɔ:dɪ'a:l/, that between Britain and France resulting from diplomatic exchanges in 1904. Although not an alliance in its own right, the entente did draw Britain away from a position of isolation vis-à-vis the rest of Europe and towards a common policy with France and Russia. (See also TRIPLE ENTENTE.) [F, = understanding (as INTENT)]

enter v.t./i. **1.** to go or come in or into; to come on stage (esp. as a direction); to penetrate. **2.** to write (a name, details, etc.) in a list, book, etc.; to register as a competitor; to record (a plea etc.) formally. **3.** to admit or obtain admission for (a pupil, a person as a member, etc.). —**enter into**, to take part in (a conversation etc.); to subscribe to or become bound by (an agreement, contract, etc.); to form part of (a calculation, plan, etc.); to sympathize with (feelings). **enter on** or **upon**, to assume possession of (property) or the functions of (an office); to begin; to begin to deal with. [f. OF f. L intrare (intra within)]

enteric /en'terɪk/ adj. of the intestines. [f. Gk (enteron intestine)]

enteritis /entə'raɪtɪs/ n. inflammation of the intestines. [as prec. + -ITIS]

enterprise /'entəpraɪz/ n. an undertaking, especially a bold or difficult one; readiness to be involved in such undertakings. [f. OF entreprendre var. of emprendre f. L (as IN-¹, prehendere take)]

enterprising adj. showing enterprise; energetic and resourceful. [f. prec.]

entertain /entə'teɪn/ v.t. **1.** to amuse, to occupy agreeably. **2.** to receive as a guest; to receive guests. **3.** to harbour, to cherish, to consider favourably (an idea etc.). [f. F f. L (INTER-, tenēre hold)]

entertainer n. one who provides entertainment, especially as a professional. [f. prec.]

entertaining adj. amusing, diverting. [f. ENTERTAIN]

entertainment n. entertaining; a thing that entertains, especially before a public audience. [f. prec.]

enthral /ɪn'θrɔ:l/ v.t. (-ll-) to captivate, to please greatly. —**enthralment** n. [f. EN- + THRALL]

enthrone /ɪn'θrəʊn/ v.t. to place on a throne, especially ceremonially. —**enthronement** n.

enthuse /ɪn'θju:z, -'θu:z/ v.t./i. (colloq.) to be or make enthusiastic. [back-formation f. foll.]

enthusiasm /ɪn'θju:zɪæz(ə)m, -'θu:-/ n. intensity of feeling or interest, great eagerness. [f. F or L f. Gk (entheos possessed by a god)]

enthusiast n. a person full of enthusiasm for something. [as prec.]

enthusiastic /ɪnθju:zɪ'æstɪk, -θu:-/ adj. having or showing enthusiasm. —**enthusiastically** adv. [f. prec.]

entice /ɪn'taɪs/ v.t. to persuade by an offer of pleasure or reward. —**enticement** n. [f. OF prob. f. L titio firebrand]

entire /ɪn'taɪə(r)/ adj. **1.** whole, complete. **2.** in one piece; continuous. **3.** unqualified, absolute. [f. AF f. L integer (IN-², tangere touch)]

entirely adv. wholly, solely. [f. prec.]

entirety /ɪn'taɪərətɪ/ n. completeness; the sum total (of). —**in its entirety**, in its complete form. [f. ENTIRE]

entitle /ɪn'taɪt(ə)l/ v.t. **1.** to give a right or just claim to. **2.** to give a title to (a book etc.). —**entitlement** n. [f. AF f. L intitulare (IN-¹, titulus title)]

entity /'entɪtɪ/ n. a thing with distinct existence; a thing's existence in itself. [f. F or L (ens partic. of esse be)]

entomb /ɪn'tu:m/ v.t. to place in a tomb; to serve as a tomb for. —**entombment** n.

entomology /entə'mɒlədʒɪ/ n. the study of insects. —**entomological** /-'lɒdʒɪk(ə)l/ adj., **entomologist** n. [f. F or L f. Gk (entomon insect)]

entourage /ɒntʊə'ra:ʒ/ n. the people attending an important person. [F (entourer surround)]

entr'acte /'ɒntrækt/ n. an interval between the acts of a play; a dance or music etc. performed then. [F (entre between, acte act)]

entrails /'entreɪlz/ n.pl. **1.** the bowels, the intestines. **2.** the inner parts of a thing. [f. OF f. L intralia (inter among)]

entrance¹ /'entrəns/ n. **1.** going or coming in; the coming of an actor on to a stage. **2.** a door or passage etc. by which one enters. **3.** the right of admission; the fee charged for this. [f. OF (as ENTER)]

entrance² /ɪn'tra:ns/ v.t. **1.** to enchant, to delight. **2.** to put into a trance. —**entrancement** n.

entrant /'entrənt/ n. one who enters an examination, profession, etc. [F (as ENTER)]

entrap /ɪn'træp/ v.t. (-pp-) to catch (as) in a trap; to beguile. [f. OF (as EN-, TRAP)]

entreat /ɪn'tri:t/ v.t. to ask earnestly, to beg. [f. OF (as EN-, TREAT)]

entreaty n. an earnest request. [f. prec.]

entrecôte /'ɒntrəkəʊt/ n. a boned steak cut off a sirloin. [F, = between-rib]

entrée /'ɒntreɪ/ n. **1.** the right of admission. **2.** a dish served between fish and meat courses; (US) the main dish of a meal. [F, = entry]

entrench /ɪn'trentʃ/ v.t. **1.** to establish firmly (in a position, office, etc.). **2.** to surround with a trench as a fortification. —**entrenchment** n.

entrepôt /'ɒntrəpəʊ/ n. a warehouse for temporary storage of goods in transit. [F (entreposer store, as INTERPOSE)]

entrepreneur /ɒntrəprə'nɜ:(r)/ n. one who undertakes a commercial enterprise with a chance of profit or loss; a contractor acting as an intermediary. —**entrepreneurial** adj. [F (as ENTERPRISE)]

entropy /'entrəpɪ/ n. a measure of the disorder of the molecules in substances etc. that are mixed or in contact with each other, indicating the amount of energy that (although it still exists) is not available for use because it has become more evenly distributed instead of being concentrated. (See below.) [f. G (as EN-, Gk tropē transformation)]

The concept of entropy first arose in the 19th c. as a mathematical quantity in thermodynamics. It was later given a physical interpretation as representing the degree of disorder of the constituents of any physical system. Thermodynamic theory indicates that the entropy of an isolated system can increase but will never decrease, and that the universe therefore appears to be steadily running down and may eventually reach a 'heat death' where the temperature is even throughout the whole universe.

entrust /ɪn'trʌst/ v.t. to give (an object of care) with trust; to assign responsibility to (a person).

entry /'entrɪ/ n. **1.** entering; the liberty to do this. **2.** a place of entrance, a door, gate, etc. **3.** a passage between buildings. **4.** an item entered in a diary, list, etc.; the recording of this. **5.** a person or thing entered in a race, competition, etc.; a list of such competitors. [f. OF (as ENTER)]

entwine /ɪn'twaɪn/ v.t. to twine round; to interweave.

enumerate /ɪ'nju:məreɪt/ v.t. to count; to specify (items). —**enumeration** /-'reɪʃ(ə)n/ n., **enumerative** adj. [f. L enumerare (EX-¹, numerare number)]

enumerator n. a person employed in census-taking. [f. prec.]

enunciate /ɪ'nʌnsɪeɪt/ v.t. **1.** to pronounce (words) clearly. **2.** to state in definite terms. —**enunciation** /-'eɪʃ(ə)n/ n. [f. L enuntiare (EX-¹, nuntiare announce)]

enuresis /enjʊə'ri:sɪs/ n. involuntary urination. [f. Gk enoureō urinate in (ouron urine)]

envelop /ɪnˈveləp/ v.t. to wrap up; to surround, to cover on all sides. —**envelopment** n. [f. OF (as EN-; cf. DEVELOP)]

envelope /ˈenvələup, ˈɒn-/ n. 1. a folded paper container for a letter etc. 2. a wrapper, a covering. 3. the gas container of a balloon or airship (ill. FLIGHT). [f. F (as prec.)]

enviable /ˈenvɪəb(ə)l/ adj. such as to cause envy, desirable. —**enviably** adv. [f. ENVY]

envious /ˈenvɪəs/ adj. feeling or showing envy. —**enviously** adv. [f. AF (as ENVY)]

environment /ɪnˈvaɪərənmənt/ n. surroundings, especially as affecting people's lives; conditions or circumstances of living. —**environmental** /-ˈment(ə)l/ adj. [f. OF (as ENVIRONS)]

environmentalist /ɪnvaɪərenˈment(ə)lɪst/ n. one who is concerned with the protection of the environment from pollution etc. [f. prec.]

environs /ɪnˈvaɪərənz/ n.pl. the district round a town etc. [f. OF (viron circuit, neighbourhood, f. virer turn)]

envisage /ɪnˈvɪzɪdʒ/ v.t. to have a mental picture of (a thing or conditions not yet existing); to conceive as possible or desirable. [f. OF (as EN-, VISAGE)]

envoy /ˈenvɔɪ/ n. 1. a messenger or representative. 2. (in full **envoy extraordinary**) a diplomatic agent ranking below ambassador. [f. F (envoyer send)]

envy /ˈenvɪ/ n. a feeling of discontented longing aroused by another's better fortune etc.; the object of this feeling. —v.t. to feel envy of. [f. OF f. L invidia]

enwrap /ɪnˈræp/ v.t. (**-pp-**) to wrap up or enfold.

enzyme /ˈenzaɪm/ n. any of a class of large molecules, consisting entirely or chiefly of protein, found in all cells and essential to life, that act as catalysts of biochemical reactions in all living organisms. They may work within a cell or (as with digestive enzymes) outside it. The shape of each enzyme is such that it catalyses only a specific type of reaction. [f. Gk en in + zumē leaven]

Eocene /ˈiːəʊsiːn/ adj. of the second epoch of the Tertiary period, following the Palaeocene and preceding the Oligocene, lasting from about 54.9 to 38 million years ago. It was a time of rising world temperatures. —n. this epoch. [f. Gk ēōs dawn + kainos new]

eolithic /iːəˈlɪθɪk/ adj. of the earliest age of man that is represented by the use of worked flint implements. [f. F f. Gk ēōs dawn + lithos stone]

Eos /ˈiːɒs/ see AURORA. [Gk, = dawn]

EP abbr. extended-play (record).

epaulette /ˈepəlet/ n. an ornamental shoulder-piece worn on a uniform. [f. F (épaule shoulder)]

épée /ˈeɪpeɪ/ n. a sharp-pointed sword used (with the end blunted) in fencing. [f. F]

epergne /ɪˈpɜːn/ n. an ornament for a dinner-table, with small bowls or vases on branched supports. [orig. unkn.]

ephedrine /ˈefədrɪn/ n. an alkaloid drug used to relieve asthma etc. [f. Ephedra, genus of plants yielding it]

ephemera /ɪˈfemərə/ n.pl. things of only short-lived usefulness. [f. L f. Gk (as foll.)]

ephemeral /ɪˈfemər(ə)l/ adj. lasting or living only a day or a few days; transitory. [f. Gk ephēmeros lasting only a day (epi on, hēmera day)]

Ephesians /ɪˈfiːʒ(ə)nz/ **Epistle to the Ephesians**, a book of the New Testament ascribed to St Paul, an epistle to the Church at Ephesus on the coast of Asia Minor.

ephod /ˈefɒd/ n. a Jewish priestly vestment. [f. Heb.]

Ephraim /ˈiːfreɪm/ 1. Hebrew patriarch, son of Joseph (Gen. 41: 52). 2. the tribe of Israel traditionally descended from him.

epi- /epɪ-/ prefix upon, above, in addition. [f. Gk]

epic /ˈepɪk/ n. a long poem narrating the adventures or achievements of a heroic figure or a nation; a book or film based on this. —adj. of or like an epic; grand, heroic. [f. L f. Gk (epos word, narrative song)]

epicanthus /epɪˈkænθəs/ n. a downward fold of skin which sometimes covers the inner angle (canthus) of the eye, especially in Mongolian peoples. —**epicanthic** adj. [f. EPI- + L canthus corner of the eye]

epicene /ˈepɪsiːn/ adj. of, for, or denoting both sexes; having the characteristics of both sexes or of neither sex. —n. an epicene person. [f. L f. Gk (EPI-, koinos common)]

epicentre /ˈepɪsentə(r)/ n. the point at which an earthquake reaches the earth's surface; the central point of a difficulty. [f. Gk (as EPI-, CENTRE)]

Epictetus /epɪkˈtiːtəs/ (c.55–c.135) Stoic philosopher, originally a slave, who taught in Rome and later in Epirus in NW Greece. He addressed himself to the multitude, preaching the common brotherhood of man and advocating indifference to the blows of fortune and submission to the workings of Providence. Posthumous publications of his teaching, including the *Manual (Enchiridion)*, had a great influence on Marcus Aurelius.

epicure /ˈepɪkjʊə(r)/ n. a person of refined tastes in food and drink etc. —**epicurism** n. [f. L f. EPICURUS]

epicurean /epɪkjʊəˈriːən/ adj. fond of refined sensuous pleasure and luxury. —n. a person with epicurean tastes. [f. foll.]

Epicurus /epɪˈkjʊərəs/ (341–270 BC) Greek philosopher who taught in his garden at Athens (whence the sect named after him is known as the 'Garden'). His physics (later expounded by the Roman writer Lucretius) is based on the theory of a materialist universe, unregulated by divine Providence, composed of indestructible atoms moving in a void. From this follows his moral theory (later misrepresented as licence for indulgence of the appetites), a hedonism seeking the minimization of pain by avoidance of unnecessary fears and desires in private and public life, leading to the quietist ideal of freedom from disturbance. —**Epicurean** /-ˈriːən/ adj. & n., **Epicureanism** /-ˈriːən-/ n.

epidemic /epɪˈdemɪk/ adj. (esp. of a disease) prevalent among a community at a particular time. —n. an epidemic disease. [f. F f. L f. Gk epidēmia prevalence of disease (EPI-, dēmos the people)]

epidemiology /epɪdiːmɪˈɒlədʒɪ/ n. the branch of medicine concerned with the control of epidemics. [as prec. + -LOGY]

epidermis /epɪˈdɜːmɪs/ n. the outer layer of the skin, the cuticle (ill. BODY 4). —**epidermal** adj. [L f. Gk (EPI-, derma skin)]

epidiascope /epɪˈdaɪəskəʊp/ n. an optical projector giving images of both opaque and transparent objects. [f. EPI- + DIA- + -SCOPE]

epidural /epɪˈdjʊər(ə)l/ adj. (of an anaesthetic) injected into the dura mater round the spinal cord. —n. an epidural injection. [f. EPI- + DURA (MATER)]

epiglottis /epɪˈglɒtɪs/ n. the cartilage at the root of the tongue, depressed to cover the wind-pipe in swallowing (ill. BODY 2). —**epiglottal** adj. [Gk (EPI-, glōtta tongue)]

epigram /ˈepɪgræm/ n. a short poem with a witty ending; a pointed saying. —**epigrammatic** /-grəˈmætɪk/ adj. [f. F or L f. Gk (as EPI-, -GRAM)]

epigraph /ˈepɪgrɑːf/ n. an inscription. —**epigraphic** /-ˈgræfɪk/ adj. [f. Gk (as EPI-, -GRAPH)]

epigraphy /eˈpɪgrəfɪ/ n. the study of inscriptions. —**epigraphist** n. [as prec.]

epilepsy /ˈepɪlepsɪ/ n. a nervous disorder with seizures accompanied by changes in the rhythm of the electrical currents of the brain. There are several different forms: *grand mal* involves loss of consciousness, and convulsions; *petit mal* lasts for only a few seconds, with partial loss of consciousness. —**epileptic** /-ˈleptɪk/ adj. & n. [f. F or L f. Gk (epilambanō take hold of)]

epilogue /ˈepɪlɒg/ n. the concluding part of a book etc.; a speech or short poem addressed to an audience by an actor at the end of a play. [f. F f. L f. Gk (EPI-, logos speech)]

Epiphany /ɪˈpɪfənɪ/ n. a feast of the Church kept on 6 Jan., having originated in the East where it has been celebrated from the 3rd c. in honour of Christ's baptism. It was introduced into the Western Church in the 4th c. where it became associated with the manifestation of Christ to the Gentiles in the persons of the Magi. [f. OF f. L f. Gk (EPI-, phainō show)]

episcopacy /eˈpɪskəpəsɪ/ n. government by bishops. —**the episcopacy**, the bishops. [f. L (as foll.)]

episcopal /eˈpɪskəp(ə)l/ adj. of a bishop or bishops; (of a Church) governed by bishops. —**episcopally** adv. [f. F or L (episcopus bishop)]

episcopalian /epɪskəˈpeɪlɪən/ adj. of episcopacy. —n. an adherent of episcopacy; a member of an episcopal Church. —**episcopalianism** n. [f. prec.]

episcopate /eˈpɪskəpət/ n. the office or tenure of a bishop. —**the episcopate**, the bishops. [f. L (as EPISCOPAL)]

episiotomy /epɪsɪˈɒtəmɪ/ n. a surgical cut made at the opening of the vagina during childbirth, to aid delivery. [f. Gk epision pubic region + -TOMY]

episode /ˈepɪsəʊd/ n. an incident in a narrative, one part of several in a serial story; an incident or event as part of a sequence; an incidental narrative or series of events. [f. Gk (EPI-, eisodos entrance)]

episodic /epɪ'sɒdɪk/ *adj.* sporadic, occurring irregularly; incidental. —**episodically** *adv.* [f. prec.]

epistemology /epɪstɪ'mɒlədʒɪ/ *n.* the theory of the method or grounds of knowledge. —**epistemological** /-ə'lɒdʒɪk(ə)l/ *adj.* [f. Gk *epistēmē* knowledge + -LOGY]

epistle /ɪ'pɪs(ə)l/ *n.* **1.** any of the letters in the New Testament, written by the Apostles. **2.** (usu. *joc.*) any letter. **3.** a poem etc. in the form of a letter. [f. OF f. L f. Gk *epistolē* (EPI-, *stellō* send)]

epistolary /ɪ'pɪstələrɪ/ *adj.* of or suitable for letters. [f. F or L (as prec.)]

epitaph /'epɪtɑ:f/ *n.* the words inscribed on a tomb or appropriate to a dead person. [f. OF f. L f. Gk *epitaphion* funeral oration (EPI-, *taphos* tomb)]

epithalamium /epɪθə'leɪmɪəm/ *n.* (*pl.* -ia) a nuptial song or poem. [f. L f. Gk (EPI-, *thalamos* bridal chamber)]

epithelium /epɪ'θi:lɪəm/ *n.* (*pl.* -ia) the tissue forming the outer layer of the body or lining an open cavity; the epidermis of young cells. —**epithelial** *adj.* [L (EPI-, Gk *thēlē* teat)]

epithet /'epɪθet/ *n.* an adjective expressing a quality or attribute, a descriptive word. —**epithetic** /-'θetɪk/ *adj.*, **epithetically** *adv.* [f. F or L f. Gk (EPI-, *tithēmi* place)]

epitome /e'pɪtəmɪ/ *n.* a person who embodies a quality etc.; a thing that represents another in miniature. [L f. Gk, = abridgement]

epitomize *v.t.* to be an epitome of. [f. prec.]

EPNS *abbr.* electroplated nickel silver.

epoch /'i:pɒk/ *n.* a period of history etc. marked by notable events; the beginning of an era in history, life, etc.; the division of a geological period, corresponding to a series in rocks. —**epoch-making** *adj.* very important or remarkable. —**epochal** *adj.* [f. L f. Gk, = pause]

eponym /'epənɪm/ *n.* a person after whom a place etc. is named. —**eponymous** /ɪ'pɒnɪməs/ *adj.* [f. Gk (EPI-, *onoma* name)]

epoxy /ɪ'pɒksɪ/ *adj.* of or derived from a compound in which an oxygen atom and two carbon atoms form a ring. —**epoxy resin,** a synthetic thermosetting resin. [f. EPI- + OXY-]

epsilon /ep'saɪlən/ *n.* the fifth letter of the Greek alphabet, = e. [Gk, = bare E (*psilos* bare)]

Epsom salts /'epsəm/ magnesium sulphate used as a purgative etc. [f. *Epsom* in Surrey]

Epstein /'epstaɪn/, Sir Jacob (1880-1959), sculptor. New York born, but established in London from 1905, he introduced the language of 20th-c. art, evolved in part from cubism, into the academic traditions of British sculpture, causing initially (even into the 1930s) public scandal and uproar. His *Rima* in Hyde Park was tarred and feathered, but his most successful and original work was the early *Rock Drill* (1913-15), a key-piece of vorticism. Later, he developed a forceful highly personal and expressive style, modelled not carved, in portraiture of the famous: his *Einstein* is a superb example.

equable /'ekwəb(ə)l/ *adj.* even, not varying; (of climate) moderate; (of a person) not easily disturbed. —**equably** *adv.* [f. L *aequabilis* (as foll.)]

equal /'i:kw(ə)l/ *adj.* the same in number, size, degree, merit, etc.; evenly balanced; having the same rights or status; uniform in operation. —*n.* a person or thing equal to another, especially a person equal in rank or status. —*v.t.* (-ll-) to be equal to; to achieve something that is equal to. —**be equal to,** to have the strength or capacity for. —**equally** *adv.* [f. L *aequalis* (*aequus* even, equal)]

equalitarian /i:kwɒlɪ'teərɪən/ *adj.* var. of EGALITARIAN.

equality /i:'kwɒlɪtɪ/ *n.* the condition of being equal. [f. OF f. L (as EQUAL)]

equalize /'i:kwəlaɪz/ *v.t./i.* to make or become equal; (in games) to reach an opponent's score. —**equalization** /-'zeɪʃ(ə)n/ *n.* [f. EQUAL]

equalizer *n.* a goal etc. that equalizes a score. [f. prec.]

equanimity /ekwə'nɪmɪtɪ, i:k-/ *n.* mental composure; acceptance of fate. [f. L (*aequus* even, *animus* mind)]

equate /ɪ'kweɪt/ *v.t.* to regard as equal or equivalent (*to* or *with*). [f. L *aequare* (*aequus* equal)]

equation /ɪ'kweɪʒ(ə)n/ *n.* **1.** equating, making equal, balancing. **2.** a statement of equality between two mathematical expressions (conveyed by the sign =). **3.** a formula indicating a chemical reaction by the use of symbols. [f. OF or L (as prec.)]

equator /ɪ'kweɪtə(r)/ *n.* an imaginary line round the earth or other body, equidistant from the poles. —**celestial equator,** see CELESTIAL. [f. OF or L (as EQUATE)]

equatorial /ekwə'tɔ:rɪəl/ *adj.* of or near the equator. [f. prec.]

Equatorial Guinea /'gɪnɪ/ a small country of West Africa on the Gulf of Guinea, comprising several offshore islands and a coastal settlement between Cameroon and Gabon; pop. (est. 1981) 372,000; official language, Spanish; capital, Malabo (on the island of Bioco). Formerly a Spanish colony, the country became fully independent in 1968. It is the only independent Spanish-speaking State in the continent of Africa.

equerry /'ekwərɪ/ *n.* an officer of the British royal household attending members of the royal family. [earlier *esquiry* f. obs. F *escurie* stable]

equestrian /ɪ'kwestrɪən/ *adj.* of horse-riding; on horseback. —*n.* a rider or performer on a horse. [f. L *equestris* (*equus* horse)]

equi- *prefix* equal. [f. L *aequi-* (*aequus* equal)]

equiangular /i:kwɪ'æŋgjʊlə(r)/ *adj.* having equal angles.

equidistant /i:kwɪ'dɪst(ə)nt/ *adj.* at equal distances.

equilateral /i:kwɪ'lætər(ə)l/ *adj.* having all sides equal. [f. EQUI- + L *latus* side]

equilibrate /i:kwɪ'laɪbreɪt/ *v.t./i.* to cause (two things) to balance; to balance. —**equilibration** /-'breɪʃ(ə)n/ *n.* [f. L *aequilibrare* (EQUI-, *libra* balance)]

equilibrium /i:kwɪ'lɪbrɪəm/ *n.* (*pl.* -ia) a state of balance; composure. [L (as prec.)]

equine /'ekwaɪn/ *adj.* of or like a horse. [f. L (*equus* horse)]

equinoctial /i:kwɪ'nɒkʃ(ə)l, ek-/ *adj.* of, happening at or near, an equinox. —*n.* the celestial equator. —**equinoctial line,** the celestial equator. **equinoctial point,** see EQUINOX. [as foll.]

equinox /'ekwɪnɒks/ *n.* **1.** the time or date at which the sun crosses the equator, and day and night are everywhere of equal length. **2.** the position of the sun on the celestial sphere at either of these times (also called the *equinoctial point*). —**autumn** *or* **autumnal equinox,** about 22 Sept. **spring** *or* **vernal equinox,** about 20 March. [f. OF or L (as EQUI-, *nox* night)]

equip /ɪ'kwɪp/ *v.t.* (-pp-) to supply with what is needed. [f. F, prob. f. ON *skipa* man (ship)]

equipage /'ekwɪpɪdʒ/ *n.* requisites, an outfit; a carriage and horses with attendants. [as prec.]

equipment /ɪ'kwɪpmənt/ *n.* equipping; the necessary outfit, tools, apparatus, etc. [as EQUIP]

equipoise /'ekwɪpɔɪz/ *n.* **1.** equilibrium. **2.** a counterbalancing thing. [f. EQUI- + POISE]

equitable /'ekwɪtəb(ə)l/ *adj.* fair, just; valid in equity rather than law. —**equitably** *adv.* [f. F (as EQUITY)]

equitation /ekwɪ'teɪʃ(ə)n/ *n.* riding on a horse; horsemanship. [f. F or L (*equitare* ride horse)]

equity /'ekwɪtɪ/ *n.* **1.** fairness; the principles of justice as supplementing law. **2.** the value of shares issued by a company. **3.** (in *pl.*) stocks and shares not bearing fixed interest. [f. OF f. L *aequitas* (*aequus* equal, fair)]

equivalent /ɪ'kwɪv(ə)lənt/ *adj.* equal in value, amount, importance, etc.; corresponding; meaning the same; having the same result. —*n.* an equivalent thing, amount, etc. —**equivalence** *n.* [f. OF f. L (as EQUI-, *valere* be worth)]

equivocal /ɪ'kwɪvək(ə)l/ *adj.* of double or doubtful meaning; of uncertain nature; questionable, dubious. —**equivocally** *adv.* [f. L *aequivocus* (as EQUI-, *vocare* call)]

equivocate /ɪ'kwɪvəkeɪt/ *v.i.* to use equivocal terms to conceal the truth. —**equivocation** /-'keɪʃ(ə)n/ *n.*, **equivocator** *n.* [f. L (as prec.)]

er /ɜ:, ə, etc./ *int.* expressing hesitation. [imit.]

ER *abbr.* **1.** Queen Elizabeth (L *Elizabetha Regina*). **2.** King Edward (L *Edwardus Rex*).

Er *symbol* erbium.

era /'ɪərə/ *n.* a system of chronology starting from a noteworthy event; a historical or other period, the date beginning this; a major division of geological time. [L, = number expressed in figures (orig. pl. of *aes* money)]

eradicable /ɪ'rædɪkəb(ə)l/ *adj.* able to be eradicated. [f. foll.]

eradicate /ɪ'rædɪkeɪt/ *v.t.* to root out, to destroy completely. —**eradication** /-'keɪʃ(ə)n/ *n.*, **eradicator** *n.* [f. L *eradicare* (EX-[1], *radix* root)]

erase /ɪ'reɪz/ *v.t.* to rub out; to obliterate, to remove all traces of; to remove a recording from (magnetic tape). [f. L *eradere* (EX-¹, *radere* scrape)]

eraser *n.* a thing that erases, especially a piece of rubber etc. for removing pencil marks. [f. prec.]

Erasmus /ɪˈræzməs/, Desiderius (*c.*1469-1536), Dutch Christian humanist, during his lifetime the most famous scholar in Europe, and the first best-selling author in printing history. He was a man of vast if not always deep erudition, of uncommon intellectual powers, averse to metaphysical speculation. Though he had himself paved the way for the Reformation by his merciless satires on the Church, his scholarly character, which abhorred violence and sought tranquillity, prevented him from joining the Protestants and threw him back on the tradition of the Church as the safeguard of stability. In the later years of his life he became suspect to both parties.

erasure /ɪˈreɪʒə(r)/ *n.* 1. erasing. 2. an erased word etc. [f. ERASE]

Erato /ˈerətəʊ/ (*Gk & Rom. myth.*) the Muse of lyric poetry and hymns. [Gk, = lovely]

Eratosthenes /erəˈtɒsθəniːz/ (*c.*275-194 BC) Hellenistic scholar and geographer, pupil of Callimachus and head of the library at Alexandria. Active in the fields of literary criticism and chronology, he was also the first systematic geographer of antiquity; he calculated the circumference of the earth to a high degree of accuracy and (with much less accuracy) the magnitude and distance of the sun and moon.

erbium /ˈɜːbɪəm/ *n.* a soft metallic element of the lanthanide series, symbol Er, atomic number 68. [f. *Ytterby* in Sweden]

ere /eə(r)/ *prep. & conj.* (*archaic* or *poetic*) before. [OE, orig. a compar. (cf. ERSTWHILE)]

Erechtheum /ɪˈrekθɪəm/ a marble temple built on the Acropolis in Athens in *c.*421-*c.*406 BC, with shrines to Athene, Poseidon, and Erechtheus, a legendary king of Athens. A masterpiece of the Ionic order, it is most famous for its southern portico in which the entablature is supported by six caryatids.

erect /ɪˈrekt/ *adj.* upright, vertical; (of hair) bristling; (of the penis etc.) enlarged and rigid from sexual excitement. —*v.t.* 1. to raise, to set upright, to build. 2. to establish. —**erection** *n.* [f. L *erigere* set up]

erectile /ɪˈrektaɪl/ *adj.* that can become erect (esp. of body tissue by sexual excitement). [f. F (as prec.)]

erector *n.* a person or thing that erects something; a muscle causing erection (ill. BODY 4). [f. ERECT]

eremite /ˈerɪmaɪt/ *n.* a hermit, especially a Christian recluse. —**eremitic** /-ˈmɪtɪk/ *adj.*, **eremitical** *adj.* [f. OE (as HERMIT)]

erg *n.* a unit of work or energy. [f. Gk *ergon* work]

ergo /ˈɜːgəʊ/ *adv.* therefore. [L]

ergonomics /ɜːgəˈnɒmɪks/ *n.* the study of the efficiency of persons in their working environment. —**ergonomic** *adj.*, **ergonomically** *adv.* [f. Gk *ergon* work + -*nomics* (as ECONOMICS)]

ergot /ˈɜːgət/ *n.* 1. a disease of rye etc. caused by a fungus. 2. a drug prepared from the fungus. 3. a horny protuberance on the inner side of a horse's fetlock (ill. HORSE). [F, f. OF *argot* cock's spur (from the appearance of the diseased grain etc.)]

Ericsson¹ /ˈerɪks(ə)n/, John (1803-89), versatile Swedish engineer who worked also in Britain and America. His successful invention of the marine screw propeller (1836) led to his move to the USA, where he achieved fame by building the ironclad *Monitor*, the first ship to have a revolving armoured turret, which fought an inconclusive battle on the Union side in the American Civil War. Ericsson was also a pioneer of solar energy, constructing a steam pump supplied from a boiler heated by a concentrating mirror.

Ericsson² /ˈerɪks(ə)n/, Leif (*c.*1000), Norwegian explorer, son of Eric the Red. He sailed westward from Greenland in about 1000, discovering land (variously identified as Labrador, Newfoundland, or New England) which he named Vinland because of the vines he found growing there.

Eric the Red /ˈerɪk/ (10th c.) Norwegian explorer who left Iceland in 982 in search of land to the west, exploring Greenland and establishing a Norse settlement there in 986. His explorations were later continued by his son Leif Ericsson.

Erie /ˈɪərɪ/, **Lake** one of the five Great Lakes of North America.

Erin /ˈɪərɪn/ an ancient or poetic name for Ireland. [Irish]

Erinys /eˈrɪnɪs/ *n.* (*pl.* -**yes** /-iːz/) (*Gk myth.*) a Fury. [Gk]

Eritrea /erɪˈtreɪə/ a province of Ethiopia, on the Red Sea. An Italian colony from 1890, it federated with Ethiopia in 1952 and was integrated as a province in 1962. —**Eritrean** *adj. & n.*

Erlang /ˈɜːlæŋ/, Agner Krarup (1878-1929), Danish mathematician whose name is used to designate various formulae, functions, etc., derived by him or arising out of his work.

erl-king *n.* (*Germanic myth.*) a bearded golden-crowned giant who lures little children to the land of death. [f. G *erlkönig* alder-king, mistranslation of Da. *ellerkonge* king of the elves]

ermine /ˈɜːmɪn/ *n.* 1. an animal of the weasel family (*Mustela erminea*) with brown fur turning white (except for the dark tip of its tail) in winter (cf. STOAT). 2. its white fur, used in the robes of judges, peers, etc. 3. (in heraldry) white fur marked with black spots (ill. HERALDRY). [f. OF, prob. f. L (*mus*) *Armenius* Armenian (mouse)]

erminois /ɜːmɪˈnɔɪz/ *n.* a heraldic fur, or with sable 'spots' (ill. HERALDRY). [f. OF, = ermine]

erne /ɜːn/ *n.* the sea eagle, *Haliaetus albicilla*. [OE]

Ernie /ˈɜːnɪ/ a device used (from 1956) for drawing the prize-winning numbers of Premium Bonds. [f. initial letters of *electronic random number indicator equipment*]

erode /ɪˈrəʊd/ *v.t.* to wear away or destroy gradually. —**erosion** *n.*, **erosional** *adj.*, **erosive** *adj.* [f. F or L *erodere* (EX-¹, *rodere* gnaw)]

erogenous /ɪˈrɒdʒɪnəs/ *adj.* causing sexual desire, particularly sensitive to sexual stimulation. [f. Gk *erōs* sexual love + -GENOUS]

Eros /ˈɪərɒs/ 1. (*Gk myth.*) the god of love (see CUPID). 2. (*Astron.*) an asteroid, discovered in 1898, that comes at times nearer to Earth than any heavenly body except the moon. 3. the name given to the winged figure of an archer over the fountain in Piccadilly Circus made by Sir Alfred Gilbert, erected as a memorial to the Earl of Shaftesbury, the philanthropist, and unveiled in 1899. [Gk, = sexual love]

erotic /ɪˈrɒtɪk/ *adj.* of or causing sexual excitement or desire. —**erotically** *adv.* [f. F f. Gk (*erōs* sexual love)]

erotica /ɪˈrɒtɪkə/ *n.pl.* erotic literature or art. [f. prec.]

eroticism /ɪˈrɒtɪsɪz(ə)m/ *n.* erotic character, sexual excitement. [f. EROTIC]

err /ɜː(r)/ *v.i.* to be mistaken or incorrect; to do wrong, to sin. [f. OF f. L *errare* wander, stray]

errand /ˈerənd/ *n.* a short journey for taking a message, collecting goods, etc.; the object of a journey. —**errand of mercy**, a journey to relieve distress etc. [OE]

errant¹ /ˈerənt/ *adj.* erring. [as ERR]

errant² /ˈerənt/ *adj.* travelling in search of adventure. —**errantry** *n.* [f. OF f. L *itinerare* (*iter* journey)]

erratic /ɪˈrætɪk/ *adj.* uncertain in movement; irregular in conduct or opinion etc. —**erratic block**, a large rock brought from a distance by a glacier. —**erratically** *adv.* [f. OF f. L *erraticus* (as ERR)]

erratum /eˈrɑːtəm/ *n.* (*pl.* -**ta**) an error in printing or writing. [L (as ERR)]

erroneous /ɪˈrəʊnɪəs/ *adj.* incorrect. —**erroneously** *adv.* [f. OF or L (*erro* vagabond, as ERR)]

error /ˈerə(r)/ *n.* a mistake; the condition of being wrong in opinion or conduct; a wrong opinion; the amount of inaccuracy in a calculation or measurement. [f. OF f. L (as ERR)]

ersatz /ˈeəzæts/ *n.* a substitute or imitation. —*adj.* synthetic, imitation. [G, = replacement]

Erse /ɜːs/ *adj. & n.* Irish Gaelic (see GAELIC). [early Sc. form of IRISH]

erstwhile /ˈɜːstwaɪl/ *adj.* former, previous. —*adv.* (*archaic*) formerly. [OE superl. (as ERE) + WHILE]

eructation /iːrʌkˈteɪʃ(ə)n/ *n.* belching. [f. L (EX-¹, *ructare* belch)]

erudite /ˈeruːdaɪt/ *adj.* learned, showing great learning. —**erudition** /-ˈdɪʃ(ə)n/ *n.* [f. L *erudire* instruct (EX¹, *rudis* untrained)]

erupt /ɪˈrʌpt/ *v.i.* 1. to break out suddenly or dramatically. 2. (of a volcano) to shoot out lava etc. 3. (of a rash) to appear on the skin. —**eruption** *n.*, **eruptive** *adj.* [f. L *erumpere* (EX-¹, *rumpere* break)]

erysipelas /erɪˈsɪpɪləs/ *n.* acute inflammation of the skin, with deep red coloration. [L f. Gk]

erythrocyte /ɪˈrɪθrəʊsaɪt/ *n.* a red blood-corpuscle. [f. Gk *eruthros* red + -CYTE]

Es *symbol* einsteinium.

Esau /'iːsɔː/ the elder son of Isaac and Rebecca, who sold his birthright to his brother Jacob (Gen. 25). He is the traditional ancestor of the Edomites.

escalate /'eskəleɪt/ *v.t./i.* to increase or develop (usually rapidly) by stages; to become more intense, to cause to do so. —**escalation** /-'leɪʃ(ə)n/ *n.* [back-formation f. foll.]

escalator /'eskəleɪtə(r)/ *n.* a staircase with an endless chain of steps moving up or down. The name was first applied (originally as a proprietary term) to a moving stairway at the Paris Exposition of 1900. A similar device had been invented earlier by J. W. Reno of the USA, and by 1896–8 such staircases were being installed in department stores. —**escalator clause**, a clause in a contract providing for a change in the price etc. under certain conditions. [f. *escalade* climb wall by ladder + ELEVATOR]

escallop /ɪ'skæləp/ *n.* a scallop; (in heraldry) a scallop-shell as a device (ill. HERALDRY). [as foll.]

escalope /'eskələʊp/ *n.* a slice of boneless meat, especially from a leg of veal. [F, orig. = shell]

escapade /eskə'peɪd/ *n.* a piece of daring or reckless adventure. [F, f. Prov. (as foll.)]

escape /ɪ'skeɪp/ *v.t./i.* to get free of restriction or control, to get free *from*; (of gas etc.) to leak from a container etc.; to elude, to avoid (punishment, commitment, etc.); to elude the notice or memory of; (of words etc.) to issue unawares from (a person, the lips). —*n.* escaping; a means or act or the fact of escaping; a leakage of gas etc.; temporary relief from reality or worry. —**escape clause**, one specifying the conditions under which a party to a contract is free from obligations. **escape velocity**, the minimum velocity needed to escape from the gravitational field of a body. —**escaper** *n.* [f. AF f. EX-¹ + L *cappa* cloak]

escapee /eskeɪ'piː/ *n.* one who has escaped. [f. prec.]

escapement /ɪ'skeɪpmənt/ *n.* the part of a watch or clock mechanism connecting and regulating its motive power. [f. F (as ESCAPE)]

escapism /ɪ'skeɪpɪz(ə)m/ *n.* a tendency to seek distraction or relief from reality. —**escapist** *n.* [f. ESCAPE]

escapology /eskə'pɒlədʒɪ/ *n.* the methods and technique of escaping from captivity or confinement. —**escapologist** *n.* [f. ESCAPE + -LOGY]

escarpment /ɪ'skɑːpmənt/ *n.* a long steep slope at the edge of a plateau. [f. F (as SCARP)]

eschatology /eskə'tɒlədʒɪ/ *n.* a doctrine of death and the afterlife. —**eschatological** /-'lɒdʒɪk(ə)l/ *adj.* [f. Gk *eskhatos* last + -LOGY]

escheat /ɪs'tʃiːt/ *n.* (*hist.*) the lapse of property to the government etc. on the owner's dying intestate without heirs; the property so lapsing. —*v.t./i.* to hand over or revert as an escheat; to confiscate. [f. OF f. L *excidere* (EX-¹, *cadere* fall)]

eschew /ɪs'tʃuː/ *v.t.* to avoid, to abstain from. [f. OF f. Gmc (as SHY¹)]

escort /'eskɔːt/ *n.* a person or group of persons, vehicles, ships, etc., accompanying a person or thing for protection or as a courtesy; a person accompanying another of the opposite sex socially. —/ɪ'skɔːt/ *v.t.* to act as an escort to. [f. F f. It. *scorgere* conduct)]

escritoire /eskrɪ'twɑː(r)/ *n.* a writing-desk with drawers etc. [F, f. L *scriptorium*]

escudo /e'skjuːdəʊ/ *n.* (*pl.* **-os**) the monetary unit of Portugal. [Sp. & Port., f. L *scutum* shield]

esculent /'eskjʊlənt/ *adj.* fit for food. —*n.* an esculent substance. [f. L (*esca* food)]

escutcheon /ɪ'skʌtʃ(ə)n/ *n.* a shield or emblem bearing a coat of arms. —**blot on one's escutcheon**, a stain on one's reputation. [f. AF f. L *scutum* shield]

Esdras /'ezdrəs/ **1.** either of two books of the Apocrypha, of which the first is mainly a compilation from Chronicles, Nehemiah, and Ezra, and the second is a record of angelic revelations. **2.** (in the Vulgate) the books of Ezra and Nehemiah.

esker /'eskə(r)/ *n.* a long ridge of gravel in a river valley, originally deposited by a stream formed from the melting of ice under a glacier (ill. MOUNTAINS). [f. Ir. *eiscir*]

Eskimo /'eskɪməʊ/ *n.* (*pl.* **-os** or same) a member or the language of a people inhabiting the Arctic coast of North America and of eastern Siberia (see below). —*adj.* of the Eskimos or their language. [Da. f. F f. Algonquian, lit. = 'eaters of raw flesh']
This North American aboriginal people formerly occupied the habitable coasts and islands of the Arctic western hemisphere from east Greenland and north Newfoundland to Alaska and the westernmost Aleutian Islands, with a small number extending across the Bering Strait to the east coast of Siberia. A semi-nomadic hunting-and-gathering people, they are noted for their adaptation to a harsh environment and for the low level of social integration they effect (with co-operation being limited to very narrowly defined kinship units: the nuclear family).

The Eskimo languages belong to the Eskimo-Aleut family and are divided into two main branches: the Inupik or Inuk (spoken in Greenland, Labrador, the Arctic coast of Canada and northern Alaska) and the Yupik or Yuk (spoken in southern Alaska and Siberia). There are approximately 40,000 Eskimo-speakers in Greenland, 25,000 in Alaska, 15,000 in Canada, and several hundred in Siberia.

ESN *abbr.* educationally subnormal.

esoteric /iːsəʊ'terɪk/ *adj.* intelligible only to those with special knowledge. [f. Gk (compar. of *esō* within)]

ESP *abbr.* extra-sensory perception.

espadrille /espə'drɪl/ *n.* a light canvas shoe with a plaited fibre sole. [F f. Prov. (as ESPARTO)]

espalier /ɪ'spælɪə(r)/ *n.* a lattice-work along which the branches of a tree or shrub are trained; a tree or shrub so trained. [F f. It. (*spalla* shoulder)]

esparto /e'spɑːtəʊ/ *n.* a coarse grass (*Stipa tenacissima*) of Spain and North Africa, used in paper-making. [Sp. f. L f. Gk *sparton* rope]

especial /ɪ'speʃ(ə)l/ *adj.* special, exceptional. [f. OF f. L (as SPECIAL)]

especially *adv.* particularly, more than in other cases. [f. prec.]

Esperanto /espə'ræntəʊ/ *n.* an artificial language designed in 1887 by L. L. Zamenhof, Polish physician, as a medium of communication for persons of all languages. Its words are based mainly on roots commonly found in Romance and other European languages, and while it has the advantage of grammatical regularity and ease of pronunciation it retains the structure of these languages, which makes Esperanto no easier than any other European language for a speaker whose native tongue falls outside this group. [pen-name (f. L *sperare* hope) of its inventor]

espionage /'espɪɒnɑːʒ/ *n.* spying, the use of spies. [F (*espion* spy)]

esplanade /esplə'neɪd/ *n.* a level open area, especially for walking on or separating a fortress from a town. [F f. Sp. f. L *explanare* make level]

espousal /ɪ'spaʊz(ə)l/ *n.* **1.** the espousing of a cause. **2.** (often in *pl.*) betrothal, marriage. [f. OF f. L *sponsalia* (as foll.)]

espouse /ɪ'spaʊz/ *v.t.* **1.** to adopt or support (a cause). **2.** to marry; to give (a woman) in marriage. [f. OF f. L *sponsare* (*spondēre* betroth)]

espresso /e'spresəʊ/ *n.* (*pl.* **-os**) strong concentrated coffee made under steam pressure; a machine for making this. [It., = pressed out]

esprit /'espriː/ *n.* sprightliness; wit. —**esprit de corps** /də 'kɔː/ devotion and loyalty to a body by its members. [F, = SPIRIT]

espy /ɪ'spaɪ/ *v.t.* to catch sight of. [f. OF (as SPY)]

Esq. *abbr.* esquire.

-esque /-esk/ *suffix* forming adjectives in the sense 'after the style of' (*romanesque*). [F f. It. f. L -*iscus*]

esquire /ɪ'skwaɪə(r)/ *n.* **1.** a title added to a man's surname when no other title is used, especially as a form of address in letters. **2.** (*archaic*) a squire. [f. OF f. L *scutarius* shield-bearer (*scutum* shield)]

-ess /-ɪs/ *suffix* forming nouns denoting females (*actress, goddess*). [f. F, ult. f. Gk -*issa*]

essay /'eseɪ/ *n.* a short prose composition on a subject; an attempt. —/e'seɪ/ *v.t.* to attempt. [f. F f. L *exagium* weighing; = ASSAY]

essayist /'eseɪɪst/ *n.* a writer of essays. [f. prec.]

essence /'es(ə)ns/ *n.* **1.** all that makes a thing what it is; an indispensable quality or element. **2.** an extract got by distillation etc.; a perfume, a scent. —**in essence**, fundamentally. **of the essence**, indispensable. [f. OF f. L *essentia* (*esse* be)]

Essene /e'siːn, 'e-/ *n.* a member of a Jewish ascetic sect of the 2nd c. BC–2nd c. AD in Palestine, who lived in highly organized groups and held property in common. The suggestion that St John the Baptist and even Christ himself were Essenes is highly improbable. [f. L f. Gk]

essential /ɪ'senʃ(ə)l/ *adj.* necessary, indispensable; of or constituting a thing's essence. —*n.* an indispensable or fundamental element or thing. —**essential oil**, a volatile oil with an odour characteristic of the plant from which it is extracted. —**essentiality** /-ʃɪ'ælɪtɪ/ *n.*, **essentially** *adv.* [f. L (as ESSENCE)]

Essex /'esɪks/ a county of eastern England.

establish /ɪ'stæblɪʃ/ *v.t.* **1.** to set up (a system, business, etc.) on a permanent basis; to settle (a person etc. *in* an office etc.). **2.** to cause to be generally accepted, to prove, to place beyond dispute. —**Established Church**, the Church recognized by the State. [f. OF f. L *stabilire* make stable]

establishment *n.* **1.** establishing, being established. **2.** an organized body permanently maintained (e.g. the army, navy, Civil Service). **3.** a business firm or public institution. **4.** a household, a staff of servants etc. **5.** a church system established by law. —**the Establishment**, people established in positions of power and authority, exercising influence in public life or other activity and thought of as a group generally resisting changes. [f. prec.]

estate /ɪ'steɪt/ *n.* **1.** landed property. **2.** a residential or industrial area with an integrated design or purpose. **3.** a person's assets and liabilities, especially at death. **4.** a property where rubber, tea, grapes, etc., are cultivated. **5.** a class forming part of the body politic and sharing in government. **6.** (*archaic*) state, condition. —**estate agent**, one whose business is the sale or lease of houses and land, the steward of an estate. **estate car**, a motor car with the interior extended at the rear to accommodate passengers and goods. **the Three Estates (of the Realm)**, (in England) the Lords Spiritual, Lords Temporal, and the commons. [f. OF f. L *status*]

esteem /ɪ'stiːm/ *v.t.* to have a high regard for, to think favourably of; to consider to be. —*n.* high regard or favour. [f. OF f. L (as ESTIMATE)]

ester /'estə(r)/ *n.* a chemical compound formed by the interaction of an acid and an alcohol. [G, prob. f. *essig* vinegar + = *äther* ether]

Esther /'estə(r)/ **1.** a Jewish woman who was chosen on account of her beauty by King Ahasuerus (generally supposed to be Xerxes) to be his queen. **2.** the book of the Old Testament containing an account of this, with further material in a book of the Apocrypha.

estimable /'estɪməb(ə)l/ *adj.* worthy of esteem. [F, f. L (as foll.)]

estimate /'estɪmət/ *n.* an approximate judgement of number, amount, quality, character, etc.; a price quoted for work etc. to be undertaken. /-eɪt/ *v.t.* **1.** to form an estimate or opinion of; to form an estimate *that*. **2.** to fix by estimate (*at*). —**estimator** *n.* [f. L *aestimare* fix price of]

estimation /estɪ'meɪʃ(ə)n/ *n.* estimating; a judgement of worth. [f. OF or L (as prec.)]

estoile /e'stɔɪl/ *n.* (in heraldry) a charge in the form of a star with wavy points or rays (ill. HERALDRY). [OF, = star]

Estonia /e'stəʊnɪə/ a territory on the south coast of the Gulf of Finland, under Danish and then Swedish rule until ceded to Russia in 1721. It was proclaimed an independent republic in 1918 but was incorporated in the USSR in 1940 as a constituent republic, the Estonian SSR; capital, Tallinn.

Estonian /e'stəʊnɪən/ *adj.* of Estonia or its people or language. —*n.* **1.** a native or inhabitant of Estonia. **2.** the native language of Estonia, spoken by about a million people, one of the Finno-Ugric group of languages, most closely related to Finnish. [f. prec.]

estrange /ɪ'streɪndʒ/ *v.t.* to cause (a person) to turn away in feeling or affection (*from* another). —**estrangement** *n.* [f. AF f. L *extraneare* treat as a stranger (as STRANGE)]

estuary /'estjʊərɪ/ *n.* the wide tidal mouth of a river. [f. L *aestuarium* tidal channel (*aestus* tide)]

ETA *abbr.* **1.** estimated time of arrival. **2.** /'etə/ a Basque separatist movement [Basque abbr.].

eta /'iːtə/ *n.* the seventh letter of the Greek alphabet, = ē. [Gk]

et al. *abbr.* and others. [f. L *et alii*, etc.]

etc. *abbr.* et cetera.

et cetera /et 'setərə/ and the rest, and so on. —**etceteras** *n.pl.* extras, sundries. [L]

etch *v.t./i.* **1.** to reproduce (a picture etc.) by engraving a

metal plate with acid, especially to print copies; to engrave (a plate) with acid; to practise this craft (see foll.). **2.** (*fig.*) to impress deeply (*on*). [f. Du. f. G f. OHG *azzen* cause to eat]

etching *n.* a print made from an etched plate; the art of producing etched prints. The first etchings date from the early 16th c., though the basic principle, that of corroding a design into a metal plate, had been utilized earlier for the decoration of armour. [f. prec.]

ETD *abbr.* estimated time of departure.

eternal /ɪ'tɜːn(ə)l/ *adj.* existing always, without end or (usually) beginning; unchanging; constant, too frequent. —**the Eternal**, God. —**eternally** *adv.* [f. L *aeternus* (*aevum* age)]

eternity /ɪ'tɜːnɪtɪ/ *n.* infinite (esp. future) time; endless life after death; being eternal; (*colloq.*) a very long time. —**eternity ring**, a finger-ring with gems set all round it. [f. OF f. L (as prec.)]

ethane /'eθeɪn, 'iːθ-/ *n.* a hydrocarbon gas of the paraffin series. [as ETHER]

Ethelred /'eθəlred/ 'the Unready' (= lacking good advice, rash) (*c.*969-1016), king of England 978-1016. Succeeding his murdered half-brother Edward the Martyr, Ethelred proved quite unequal to the task of confronting the Danes, resorting to the payment of tribute (Danegeld) to keep them from attacking, and losing his throne briefly (1013-14) to the Danish king Sven Forkbeard.

ether /'iːθə(r)/ *n.* **1.** a volatile liquid produced by the action of acids on alcohol, used as a solvent or anaesthetic. **2.** clear sky, the upper air. **3.** the medium formerly assumed to permeate space and transmit electromagnetic radiation. [f. OF or L f. Gk *aithēr* (*aithō* burn, shine)]

ethereal /ɪ'θɪərɪəl/ *adj.* light, airy; delicate, especially in appearance; heavenly. —**ethereally** *adv.* [f. L f. Gk (as prec.)]

ethic /'eθɪk/ *n.* a set of moral principles. —*adj.* ethical. [f. OF or L f. Gk (as ETHOS)]

ethical *adj.* **1.** relating to morals, especially as concerning human conduct. **2.** morally correct. **3.** (of a medicine or drug) not advertised to the general public and usually available only on a doctor's prescription. —**ethically** *adv.* [f. prec.]

ethics *n.* **1.** the science of morals in human conduct. **2.** (as *pl.*) moral principles or code. [f. ETHIC]

Ethiopia /iːθɪ'əʊpɪə/ a country in NE Africa, bordering on the Red Sea; pop. (1981) 31,000,000; official language, Amharic; capital, Addis Ababa. Its earliest recorded civilization, known to the ancient Egyptians as Punt, dates from the 2nd millennium BC. In ancient times Ethiopians (= 'burnt-faced men') were often confused with Indians. Christianized in the 4th c., Ethiopia was isolated by Muslim conquests to the north three centuries later, remaining remote and little known until the late 19th c. It successfully resisted Italian attempts at colonization in the 1890s but was conquered by Italy in 1935. The Emperor Haile Selaise was restored by the British in 1941 and ruled until overthrown in a Marxist coup in 1975. In recent years the military government has been faced with serious opposition in the eastern province of Eritrea (originally integrated into the country in 1962). Ethiopia is one of the poorest countries in the world. Agriculture is chiefly at subsistence level, and serious crop failures have resulted in widespread famines. International help was organized on a massive scale following 1984 about the plight of refugees. —**Ethiopian** *adj.* & *n.* [as foll.]

Ethiopic /iːθɪ'ɒpɪk/ *n.* the liturgical language of the Coptic Church of Ethiopia (see GE'EZ). —*adj.* of this language. [f. L f. Gk (*Aithops* Ethiopian, f. *aithō* burn, *ops* face)]

ethnic /'eθnɪk/ *adj.* **1.** of a group of mankind distinguished from others by race or by having a common national or cultural tradition. **2.** (of clothes etc.) resembling the peasant clothes of an ethnic group or primitive people. —**ethnical** *adj.*, **ethnically** *adv.* [f. L f. Gk (*ethnos* nation)]

ethnology /eθ'nɒlədʒɪ/ *n.* the comparative scientific study of human peoples. —**ethnological** /-ə'lɒdʒɪk(ə)l/ *adj.*, **ethnologist** *n.* [as prec. + -LOGY]

ethology /iː'θɒlədʒɪ/ *n.* **1.** the science of character-formation. **2.** the science of animal behaviour. —**ethologist** *n.* [f. Gk *ēthos* character, disposition + -LOGY]

ethos /'iːθɒs/ *n.* the characteristic spirit or attitudes of a community etc. [Gk, = character, disposition]

ethyl /'eθɪl/ *n.* a radical derived from ethane, present in alcohol and ether. [G (as ETHER)]

ethylene /'eθɪliːn/ *n.* a hydrocarbon of the olefin series. [f. prec.]

etiolate /'iːtɪəleɪt/ *v.t.* to make (a plant) pale by excluding light; to give a sickly hue to (a person). —**etiolation** /-'leɪʃ(ə)n/ *n.* [f. F f. Norman *étieuler* make into haulm f. L *stipula* straw]

etiquette /'etɪket/ *n.* conventional rules of social behaviour or professional conduct. [F, = ticket]

Etna /'etnə/ a volcano in Sicily, the highest European volcano (3,323 m, 10,902 ft.). It has a long history of eruptions.

Eton College /'iːt(ə)n/ a public school near Windsor, Berks., founded in 1440 by Henry VI to prepare scholars for King's College, Cambridge. —**Eton wall game,** one of the oldest forms of football in existence, played only on a site at Eton College where a red brick wall (built in 1717) separates a playing field from the Slough road. The game consists chiefly of 'bullies' or scrimmages against the wall; the player with the ball attempts to force a way through the opposition, keeping the ball against the wall. Progress is slow, and although points are scored in various ways goals are a rarity. The famous wall game between scholars (or Collegers) and non-scholars (or Oppidans) on St Andrew's Day (30 Nov.) dates back to at least 1820.

Etruscan /ɪ'trʌskən/ *adj.* of ancient Etruria (see below) or its people or language. —*n.* 1. a native of ancient Etruria. 2. its language, which is not of the Indo-European family and has never been satisfactorily deciphered. [f. L *Etruscus*]
The Etruscans were the earliest historical inhabitants of the area (Etruria) between the Arno and the Tiber (roughly the modern Tuscany). Their empire in Italy was at its height *c.*500 BC, and their sophisticated civilization was an important influence on the Romans, who completely subdued them by the end of the 3rd c. BC.

et seq. *abbr.* (also **et seqq.**) and the following (page(s), matter, etc.). [f. L *et sequentia*]

-ette /-et/ *suffix* forming nouns denoting smallness (*kitchenette*), imitation or substitution (*flannelette*), or female status (*suffragette*). [f. F]

étude /eɪ'tjuːd/ *n.* a short musical composition (usually for one instrument). [F, = study]

etymology /etɪ'mɒlədʒɪ/ *n.* 1. the origin and development of a word's form and its meaning; an account of this. 2. the study of the origin of words. —**etymological** /-'lɒdʒɪk(ə)l/ *adj.*, **etymologist** *n.* [f. OF f. L f. Gk (*etumon* original form of word)]

Eu *symbol* europium.

eu- *prefix* well, easily. [Gk]

eucalyptus /juːkə'lɪptəs/ *n.* 1. (also **eucalypt**) a tall evergreen tree of the genus *Eucalyptus*. 2. an oil obtained from it used as an antiseptic etc. [f. EU- + Gk *kaluptos* covered (the unopened flower being protected by a cap)]

Eucharist /'juːkərɪst/ *n.* 1. a Christian sacrament in which bread and wine are consecrated and consumed (see below). 2. the consecrated elements, especially the bread. —**Eucharistic** /-'rɪstɪk/ *adj.* [f. OF f. L f. Gk, = thanksgiving]
The origins of the Eucharist are found in the synoptic Gospels and 1 Cor. 10, 11. From the first it was accepted that the Eucharist conveyed to the believer the body and blood of Christ, but there were different interpretations of the sense in which Christ was present (see CONSUBSTANTIATION, TRANSUBSTANTIATION).

euchre /'juːkə(r)/ *n.* an American card-game for 2, 3, or 4 persons, played with a pack of 32 cards (the 2, 3, 4, 5, 6 of each suit being rejected), from which each player is dealt 5 cards. A player may 'pass' or decline to play; if he plays he must take three tricks to win the point, losing two points to his opponent(s) if he fails to do so. [orig. unkn.]

Euclid /'juːklɪd/ (*c.*300 BC) Greek mathematician who taught at Alexandria in Egypt, famous for his great textbook, entitled *Elements*, on plane geometry, the theory of numbers, irrationals, and solid geometry, which was the standard work on geometry until recent times.

Euclidean /juː'klɪdɪən/ *adj.* of Euclid. —**Euclidean geometry,** that of ordinary experience, based on the postulates used by Euclid (that parallel lines never meet, that the sum of the angles of a triangle is 180°). **Euclidean space,** that for which Euclidean geometry is valid. [f. prec.]

eugenics /juː'dʒenɪks/ *n.* the science of the production of fine (esp. human) offspring by control of inherited qualities (see GALTON). —**eugenic** *adj.*, **eugenically** *adv.* [f. EU- + Gk *gen-* give birth to]

Euler /'ɔɪlə(r)/, Leonhard (1707–83), Swiss-born mathematician, who worked in St Petersburg and Berlin for most of his life. He wrote on all branches of mathematics and made significant discoveries in most. His work is characterized by a vigorous originality and an innocent but harmless lack of rigour. Nevertheless, it was his attempts to elucidate the nature of functions and his successful though logically dubious study of infinite series which led his successors, notably Abel, Bolzano, and Cauchy, to introduce ideas of convergence and rigorous argument into mathematics. Perhaps his best-known and best-loved theorem is his startling discovery of a connection between the most important constants in mathematics, the equation $e^{i\pi} = -1$. His enormous output of books and articles, and his extensive correspondence with scientists all over Europe, were scarcely affected by the blindness which afflicted him from 1771.

eulogize /'juːlədʒaɪz/ *v.t.* to extol, to praise. [f. foll.]

eulogy /'juːlədʒɪ/ *n.* a speech or writing in praise of a person; an expression of praise. —**eulogistic** /-'dʒɪstɪk/ *adj.* [f. L f. Gk *eulogia* praise (as EU-, -LOGY)]

Eumenides /juː'menɪdiːz/ (*Gk myth.*) kindly powers sending fertility, but who, being of the earth, were often confused with the Erinyes or Furies. [Gk, = kindly ones]

eunuch /'juːnək/ *n.* a castrated man, especially one formerly employed in a harem or as a court official especially in the Orient or under the Roman Empire. [f. L f. Gk, = bedchamber attendant]

euphemism /'juːfɪmɪz(ə)m/ *n.* the use of a mild or indirect expression instead of a blunt or direct one; such an expression. —**euphemistic** /-'mɪstɪk/ *adj.*, **euphemistically** *adv.* [f. Gk (EU-, *phēmē* speaking)]

euphonium /juː'fəʊnɪəm/ *n.* a tenor tuba. [as foll.]

euphony /'juːfənɪ/ *n.* pleasantness of sounds, especially of words; a pleasing sound. —**euphonious** /-'fəʊnɪəs/ *adj.* [f. F f. L f. Gk (EU-, *phōnē* sound)]

euphoria /juː'fɔːrɪə/ *n.* a feeling of well-being or elation. —**euphoric** /-'fɒrɪk/ *adj.* [f. Gk *euphoros* (EU-, *pherō* bear)]

Euphrates /juː'freɪtiːz/ a river of SW Asia, length about 2,430 km (1,510 miles), that rises in the mountains of eastern Turkey and flows through Syria and Iraq to join the Tigris, forming the Shatt al-Arab which flows into the Persian Gulf.

euphuism /'juːfjuːɪz(ə)m/ *n.* an affected or high-flown style of writing. —**euphuistic** /-'ɪstɪk/ *adj.*, **euphuistically** *adv.* [orig. of writing in imitation of Lyly's *Euphues* (16th c.)]

Eurasian /jʊə'reɪʒ(ə)n/ *adj.* 1. of mixed European and Asian parentage. 2. of Europe and Asia. —*n.* a Eurasian person. [f. EUROPEAN + ASIAN]

Euratom /jʊər'ætəm/ *n.* the European Atomic Energy Community. [abbr.]

eureka /jʊə'riːkə/ *int.* (announcing a discovery etc.) I have found it. [Gk *heurēka* (*heuriskō* find); attributed to Archimedes]

eurhythmics /juː'rɪðmɪks/ *n. pl.* harmony of bodily movement, especially as developed (originally by the Swiss composer Émile Jaques-Dalcroze, d. 1950) with music and dance into a system of education. [f. EU- f. Gk *rhuthmos* proportion, rhythm]

Euripides /jʊə'rɪpɪdiːz/ (*c.*485–*c.*406 BC) Greek dramatist, the latest (after Aeschylus and Sophocles) of the three great tragedians. His 19 surviving plays show important innovations in the handling of the traditional myths, reflecting the contemporary Athenian intellectual enlightenment. He was notorious for introducing a low realism into grand subject-matter, had a deep interest in feminine psychology (e.g. in the *Medea*), was a penetrating portrayer of abnormal and irrational states of mind (e.g. in the *Bacchae* and *Hippolytus*), and had a fondness for involved adventure-plots (e.g. the rescue of Iphigenia from Tauris). The influence of the developing art of rhetoric is pervasive, and his use of the traditional chorus displays an increasing lyricism and detachment from the main action.

Euro- /jʊərəʊ/ *in comb.* Europe, European.

Eurocommunism *n.* Communism in the countries of Western Europe, independent of Soviet influence.

Eurocrat /'jʊərəʊkræt/ *n.* a bureaucrat of the European Communities. [f. EURO- + -CRAT]

Eurodollar *n.* a dollar held in a bank in Europe etc.

Europa /jʊə'rəʊpə/ (*Gk myth.*) daughter of Agenor king of Tyre, or of Phoenix (= 'the Phoenician'). Wooed by Zeus in the form of a bull, she was carried off to Crete, where she bore him three sons: Minos, Rhadamanthus, and Sarpedon.

Europe /'jʊərəp/ 1. a continent of the northern hemisphere consisting of the western part of the land mass of which Asia forms the eastern (and greater) part, and including Scandinavia and the British Isles. It contains approximately 20 per cent of the world's population. The western part of Europe was consolidated within the Roman Empire, but the subsequent barbarian invasions brought political chaos which was only gradually resolved in the medieval and post-medieval periods, the last modern European nation States emerging in the 19th c. Politically and economically pre-eminent in the 18th and 19th centuries, Europe has been overshadowed as a result of the rise of the superpowers in the 20th c., but it still maintains a general standard of living and political stability well in advance of that of most of the Third World. **2.** the European Economic Community.

European /jʊərə'piːən/ adj. of, in, or extending over Europe. —n. **1.** a native or inhabitant of Europe; a descendant of such persons. **2.** one who is interested in Europe as a unity. [f. prec.]

European Economic Community an economic association of European countries set up by the Treaty of Rome (1957). The original members were Belgium, France, the Federal Republic of Germany, Italy, Luxemburg, and the Netherlands; Denmark, Ireland, and the UK joined in 1973, Greece in 1981, and Spain and Portugal in 1986; Greenland withdrew in 1985. Its aims include the free movement of labour and capital between member countries, especially by the abolition of customs barriers and cartels, and the fostering of common agricultural and trading policies.

europium /jʊə'rəʊpɪəm/ n. a soft metallic element of the lanthanide series, symbol Eu, atomic number 63. Europium was first purified (as europium oxide) in 1901. The oxide is used together with yttrium oxide as a red phosphor in colour television screens. [f. EUROPE]

Eurydice /jʊə'rɪdɪsɪ/ (Gk myth.) wife of Orpheus.

Eusebius /juːˈsiːbɪəs/ (c.260–c.340) bishop of Caesarea on the coast of Palestine, and church historian. His *Ecclesiastical History* is the principal source for the history of Christianity (especially in the Eastern Church) from the Apostolic age until his own day.

Eustachian tube /juːˈsteɪʃɪən/ the narrow passage from the pharynx to the cavity of the middle ear (ill. BODY 4). [f. B. *Eustachi* It. anatomist (d. 1574)]

Euterpe /jʊˈtɜːpɪ/ (Gk & Rom. myth.) the Muse of flutes. [Gk, = well-pleasing]

euthanasia /juːθə'neɪzɪə/ n. the bringing about of a gentle and easy death in the case of incurable and painful disease; such a death. [Gk (as EU-, *thanatos* death)]

eV abbr. electron-volt(s).

evacuate /ɪ'vækjʊeɪt/ v.t. **1.** to send (people) away from a place of danger; to empty (a place) thus; to withdraw from. **2.** to make empty; to empty the contents of. —**evacuation** /-'eɪʃ(ə)n/ n. [f. L *evacuare* (EX-[1], *vacuus* empty)]

evacuee /ɪvækjuː'iː/ n. a person sent away from a place of danger. [f. prec.]

evade /ɪ'veɪd/ v.t. to avoid or escape from, especially by guile or trickery; to avoid doing or answering directly. [f. F f. L (EX-[1], *vadere* go)]

evaluate /ɪ'væljʊeɪt/ v.t. to find or state the number or amount of; to appraise, to assess. —**evaluation** /-'eɪʃ(ə)n/ n. [f. F (as EX-[1], VALUE)]

evanesce /iːvə'nes, e-/ v.i. to fade from sight, to disappear. [f. L *evanescere* (EX-[1], *vanus* empty)]

evanescent adj. (of an impression etc.) quickly fading. —**evanescence** n. [f. prec.]

evangelical /iːvæn'dʒelɪk(ə)l/ adj. **1.** of the Protestant Churches, as basing their claim pre-eminently on the gospel. **2.** (formerly, in Germany and Switzerland) the Lutheran Churches as contrasted with the Calvinist (Reformed) Churches. **3.** (in the Church of England) of the school (originating in the 18th c.) that lays special stress on personal conversion and salvation by faith in the Atonement. —**evangelicalism** n. [f. L f. Gk (as EVANGELIZE)]

evangelism /ɪ'vændʒəlɪz(ə)m/ n. preaching or promulgation of the gospel. [as prec.]

evangelist /ɪ'vændʒ(ə)lɪst/ n. **1.** the writer of any one of the four Gospels. **2.** a preacher of the gospel. —**evangelistic** /-'lɪstɪk/ adj. [f. OF f. L (as foll.)]

evangelize /ɪ'vændʒ(ə)laɪz/ v.t. to preach the gospel to; to convert to Christianity. —**evangelization** /-'zeɪʃ(ə)n/ n. [f. L f. Gk (*euaggelion* good news)]

Evans /'ev(ə)nz/, Sir Arthur John (1851–1941), British archaeologist, best known for his excavations at Knossos in Crete, which lasted intermittently from 1900 to 1935, and the resulting discovery of the Bronze Age civilization of Crete, which he termed Minoan.

evaporable /ɪ'væpərəb(ə)l/ adj. able to be evaporated. [f. foll.]

evaporate /ɪ'væpəreɪt/ v.t./i. **1.** to turn into vapour; to lose or cause to lose moisture as vapour. **2.** to become lost or disappear; to cause to do this. —**evaporated milk**, unsweetened milk concentrated by partial evaporation and tinned. —**evaporation** /-'reɪʃ(ə)n/ n. [f. L *evaporare* (EX-[1], as VAPOUR)]

evasion /ɪ'veɪʒ(ə)n/ n. **1.** evading. **2.** an evasive answer etc. [f. OF f. L (as EVADE)]

evasive /ɪ'veɪsɪv/ adj. seeking to evade; not direct in answer etc. —**evasively** adv., **evasiveness** n. [as prec.]

Eve /iːv/ (in Hebrew tradition) the first woman, wife of Adam. According to Genesis 3: 20 she was so named because she was the mother of all living beings, but the Hebrew name may have meant 'serpent' and so she became associated with the primitive myth that all life originated in a primeval serpent. It was a common medieval conceit that the Latin form of her name (*Eva*) spelt backwards was the first word of the angel's address to Mary (*Ave*) at the Annunciation, symbolizing the reversal, through the Incarnation, of Eve's fall.

eve /iːv/ n. the evening or day before a festival etc.; the time just before an event; (archaic) evening. [= EVEN[2]]

Evelyn /'iːvlɪn/, John (1620–1706), English writer, traveller, connoisseur of the arts, pioneer of English forestry and gardening, humanist, and Christian, a man of means and of untiring curiosity and energy, and a friend of Samuel Pepys. In his diaries he recorded in great detail the extraordinary variety of his life. He was a main founder of the Royal Society, through which he met Robert Boyle and Isaac Newton. Surviving both the plague and the Great Fire of London he saw his country governed by six monarchies and one republic.

even[1] /'iːv(ə)n/ adj. **1.** level, free from irregularities, smooth. **2.** uniform in quality, constant. **3.** equal in amount, value, etc.; equally balanced. **4.** in the same plane or line (with). **5.** equable, calm. **6.** (of a number such as 4 or 6) integrally divisible by 2; bearing such a number; not involving fractions. —v.t./i. (often with *up*) to make or become even or equal. —adv. (a) inviting comparison of the negation, assertion, etc., with an implied one that is less strong or remarkable; (b) introducing an extreme case. —**be** or **get even with**, to have one's revenge on. **even chance**, an equal chance of success or failure. **even-handed** adj. impartial, fair. **even money**, **evens** n.pl. betting-odds offering a gambler the chance of winning the amount he staked. **even now**, now as well as previously, at this very moment. **even so**, despite some other consideration. —**evenly** adv., **evenness** n. [OE]

even[2] /'iːv(ə)n/ n. (poetic) evening. [OE]

evening /'iːvnɪŋ/ n. **1.** the end of the day, especially from about 6 p.m. (or earlier sunset) to bedtime. **2.** the decline or last period (of life etc.). —**evening dress**, formal dress for evening wear. **evening primrose**, a plant of the genus *Oenothera*, with yellow flowers that open in the evening. **evening star**, a planet, especially Venus, when seen in the west after sunset. [OE]

evensong n. the service of evening prayer in the Church of England. [f. EVEN[2] + SONG]

event /ɪ'vent/ n. a thing that happens or takes place, especially one of importance; the fact of a thing occurring; an item in an (especially sports) programme. —**at all events**, **in any** or **either event**, whatever happens. **in the event**, as it turned out. **in the event of**, if (the specified event) occurs. **in the event that**, if. [f. L (*evenire* happen)]

eventful adj. marked by noteworthy events. —**eventfully** adv. [f. prec.]

eventide /'iːvəntaɪd/ n. (archaic) evening. [f. EVEN[2] + TIDE]

eventual /ɪ'ventʃʊ(ə)l/ adj. occurring in due course or at last. —**eventually** adv. [as EVENT]

eventuality /ɪventʃʊ'ælɪtɪ/ n. a possible event or result. [f. prec.]

eventuate /ɪ'ventʃʊeɪt/ v.i. to result, to be the outcome. [as EVENT]

ever /'evə(r)/ adv. **1.** at all times, always; at any time. **2.** (as an emphatic word) in any way, at all. —**did you ever?**, (colloq.) did you ever hear or see the like? **ever since**, throughout the period since (then). **ever so**, (colloq.) very; very much. **ever such a**, (colloq.) a very. [OE]

Everest /'evərɪst/, **Mount** the highest mountain in the world (8,848 m, 29,028 ft.), in the Himalayas on the border of Nepal and Tibet. It is named after Sir George Everest (1790-1866), surveyor-general of India, and was first climbed in 1953 by the New Zealand mountaineer and explorer (Sir) Edmund Hillary and the Sherpa mountaineer Tenzing Norgay.

evergreen adj. retaining its green leaves throughout the year. —n. an evergreen tree or shrub.

everlasting /evə'lɑːstɪŋ/ adj. **1.** lasting for ever; lasting a long time. **2.** (of flowers) keeping their shape and colour when dried. —n. **1.** eternity. **2.** an everlasting flower, especially one of the genus *Helichrysum*. —**everlastingly** adv.

evermore /evə'mɔː(r)/ adv. for ever, always.

every /'evrɪ/ adj. **1.** each single. **2.** each at a specified interval in a series. **3.** all possible; the utmost degree of. —**every bit as,** (colloq.) quite as. **every now and then,** from time to time. **every one,** each one. **every other,** each second in a series. **every so often,** at intervals, occasionally. [OE, = ever each]

everybody pron. every person.

everyday adj. occurring or used every day; ordinary, commonplace.

Everyman /'evrɪmæn/ an ordinary or typical person. [name of leading character in 15th-c. morality play]

everyone pron. everybody.

everything pron. **1.** all things. **2.** the thing of chief importance.

everywhere adv. in every place; (colloq.) in many places.

evict /ɪ'vɪkt/ v.t. to expel (a tenant) by legal process. —**eviction** n. [f. L (EX-¹, *vincere* conquer)]

evidence /'evɪd(ə)ns/ n. **1.** an indication, a sign, the facts available as proving or supporting a notion etc. **2.** (Law) information given personally or drawn from a document etc. and tending to prove a fact; testimony admissible in court. —v.t. to indicate, to be evidence of. —**in evidence,** conspicuous. **turn King's or Queen's evidence,** said of an accused person who testifies for the prosecution against the person(s) associated with him in an alleged crime. [f. OF f. L (as foll.)]

evident adj. obvious, plain, manifest. —**evidently** adv. [f. OF or L (EX-¹, *vidēre* see)]

evidential /evɪ'denʃ(ə)l/ adj. of or providing evidence. [f. EVIDENCE]

evil /'iːv(ə)l, -ɪl/ adj. morally bad, wicked; harmful, tending to harm; disagreeable. —n. an evil thing; wickedness. —**evil eye,** a malicious look superstitiously believed to do material harm. —**evilly** adv. [OE]

evildoer n. a sinner. —**evildoing** n.

evince /ɪ'vɪns/ v.t. to indicate or exhibit (a quality). [f. L (as EVICT)]

eviscerate /ɪ'vɪsəreɪt/ v.t. to disembowel. —**evisceration** /-'reɪʃ(ə)n/ n. [f. L *eviscerare* (EX-¹, *viscera* bowels)]

evocative /ɪ'vɒkətɪv/ adj. tending to evoke (esp. feelings or memories). [f. foll.]

evoke /ɪ'vəʊk/ v.t. to inspire or draw forth (memories, a response, etc.). —**evocation** /evə'keɪʃ(ə)n/ n. [f. L *evocare* (EX-¹, *vocare* call)]

evolute /'iːvəljuːt, -luːt/ n. the locus of the centres of curvature of another curve that is its involute (ill. SHAPES). [f. L (as EVOLVE)]

evolution /iːvə'luːʃ(ə)n/ n. **1.** evolving. **2.** the origination of species by development from earlier forms, not by special creation (see below); the gradual development of a phenomenon, organism, etc. **3.** a change in the disposition of troops or ships. —**evolutionary** adj. [f. L, = unrolling (as EVOLVE)]
The philosophical speculation that primitive organisms may become more complex, change into one another, ascend some imaginary hierarchy, a ladder of life, a great chain of being (often with bouts of spontaneous generation along the way) is an idea that may be traced back to the ancient Greeks. The forebears of the modern scientific concept, however, are Erasmus Darwin in England and Lamarck in France. Species transformation by the inheritance of acquired characteristics (the single-minded neck-stretching giraffe in pursuit of the tender topmost leaves of bushes bequeaths his hard-won muscles to his offspring) was at least a serious secular attempt to understand apparent relationships in the plant and animal kingdom, but it

was Charles Lyell's *Principles of Geology* (1830-3), which demonstrated that the structure of the surface of the earth could be explained as the product of slow small changes accumulating in vertiginous stretches of a time almost without end, that gave Charles Darwin the idea of nature which he needed to discover the principle of evolution by natural selection. *On the Origin of Species* (1859) proposed that, once isolated from each other in some way, pre-existent varieties within a population might give rise to new species by differential adaptation to their new surroundings; combined with recent genetical theory, and the new understanding of the role of DNA, this is the great unifying concept in modern biology.

evolutionist n. one who upholds the theory that species developed by evolution rather than by special creation. [f. prec.]

evolve /ɪ'vɒlv/ v.t./i. **1.** to develop gradually by a natural process; **2.** to work out or devise (a theory, plan, etc.). **3.** to unfold, to open out. **4.** to give off (gas, heat, etc.). [f. L (EX-¹, *volvere* roll)]

ewe /juː/ n. a female sheep. [OE]

ewer /'juːə(r)/ n. a water-jug with a wide mouth. [f. OF f. L *aqua* water]

ex¹ prep. **1.** (of goods) sold from. **2.** outside, without, exclusive of. —**ex dividend,** (of stocks and shares) not including the next dividend. [L, = out of]

ex² n. (colloq.) a former husband or wife. [f. EX-¹]

ex-¹ prefix (**ef-** before f; **e-** before some consonants) forming (1) verbs in the sense 'out', 'forth' (*exclude, exit*), 'upward' (*extol*), 'thoroughly' (*excruciate*), 'bring into a state' (*exasperate*), (2) nouns from the titles of office, status, etc., in the sense 'formerly' (*ex-convict*). [f. L *ex* out of]

ex-² prefix = 'out' (*exodus*). [f. Gk]

exa- in comb. denoting a factor of 10^{18}. [perh. f. HEXA-]

exacerbate /ek'sæsəbeɪt/ v.t. to make (pain, anger, etc.) worse; to irritate. —**exacerbation** /-'beɪʃ(ə)n/ n. [f. L *exacerbare* (EX-¹, *acerbus* bitter)]

exact /ɪg'zækt/ adj. accurate, correct in all details; precise, (of a person) tending to precision. —v.t. to demand and enforce payment etc. of; to demand, to require urgently, to insist on. —**exact science,** one in which absolute precision is possible. —**exactness** n., **exactor** n. [f. L *exigere* (EX-¹, *agere* drive)]

exacting adj. making great demands, calling for much effort. [f. prec.]

exaction /ɪg'zækʃ(ə)n/ n. **1.** exacting (of money etc.). **2.** the thing exacted. **3.** an illegal or exorbitant demand, extortion. [f. EXACT]

exactitude /ɪg'zæktɪtjuːd/ n. exactness, precision. [as prec.]

exactly adv. **1.** accurately, precisely. **2.** (said in reply) I quite agree. [f. EXACT]

exaggerate /ɪg'zædʒəreɪt/ v.t. to make (a thing, or absol.) seem larger or greater than it really is, in speech or writing; to enlarge or alter beyond normal or due proportions. —**exaggeration** /-'reɪʃ(ə)n/ n. [f. L *exaggerare* heap up (EX-¹, *agger* heap)]

exalt /ɪg'zɔːlt/ v.t. **1.** to raise in rank or power etc. **2.** to praise highly. **3.** to dignify, to ennoble. —**exaltation** /-'teɪʃ(ə)n/ n. [f. L *exaltare* (EX-¹, *altus* high)]

exam /ɪg'zæm/ n. (colloq.) an examination. [abbr.]

examination /ɪgzæmɪ'neɪʃ(ə)n/ n. examining, being examined; the testing of proficiency or knowledge by oral or written questions; the formal questioning of a witness etc. in a lawcourt. [f. OF f. L (as foll.)]

examine /ɪg'zæmɪn/ v.t. **1.** to inquire into the nature or condition etc. of. **2.** to look closely at. **3.** to test the proficiency of by a series of questions or exercises. **4.** to question formally. —**examiner** n. [f. OF f. L *examinare* (*examen* tongue of balance)]

examinee /ɪgzæmɪ'niː/ n. one who is being examined, especially in a test of proficiency. [f. prec.]

example /ɪg'zɑːmp(ə)l/ n. **1.** a thing characteristic of its kind or illustrating a general rule; a problem or exercise designed to do this. **2.** a person or thing or conduct worthy of imitation. **3.** a fact or thing seen as a warning to others. —**for example,** by way of illustration. [f. OF f. L *exemplum*]

exasperate /ɪg'zæspəreɪt, -zɑːs-/ v.t. to irritate intensely. —**exasperation** /-'reɪʃ(ə)n/ n. [f. L *exasperare* (EX-¹, *asper* rough)]

Excalibur /eksˈkælɪbə(r)/ (in Arthurian legend) the name of King Arthur's magic sword.

ex cathedra /eks kəˈθiːdrə/ with full authority (esp. of a papal pronouncement). [L, = from the chair]

excavate /ˈekskəveɪt/ v.t. to make (a hole or channel) by digging, to dig out (soil); to reveal or extract by digging. —**excavation** /-ˈveɪʃ(ə)n/ n., **excavator** n. [f. L excavare (EX-[1], cavus hollow)]

exceed /ɪkˈsiːd/ v.t. **1.** to be more or greater than, to surpass. **2.** to go beyond (a limit etc.); to do more than is warranted by (instructions etc.). [f. OF f. L excedere go beyond]

exceedingly adv. very, extremely. [f. prec.]

excel /ɪkˈsel/ v.t./i. (-ll-) to be superior to; to be pre-eminent. [f. L excellere; cf. celsus lofty]

excellence /ˈeksələns/ n. great worth or quality. [f. OF or L (as prec.)]

Excellency n. **His, Her, Your,** etc., **Excellency,** a title used in addressing or referring to certain high officials. [f. L (as EXCEL)]

excellent adj. extremely good. —**excellently** adv. [f. OF (as EXCEL)]

excentric var. (in technical senses) of ECCENTRIC.

except /ɪkˈsept/ v.t. to exclude from a general statement or condition etc. —prep. not including, other than. —conj. (archaic) unless. [f. L excipere take out]

excepting prep. except. [f. prec.]

exception /ɪkˈsepʃ(ə)n/ n. **1.** excepting. **2.** a thing or case excepted or apart, especially a thing not following a general rule. —**take exception,** to object (to). **with the exception of,** except. [f. OF f. L (as EXCEPT)]

exceptionable adj. open to objection. [f. prec.]

exceptional adj. forming an exception, unusual; outstanding. —**exceptionally** adv. [f. EXCEPT]

excerpt /ˈeksɜːpt/ n. a short extract from a book, film, etc. —/ɪkˈsɜːpt/ v.t. to take excerpts from. —**excerption** /-ˈsɜːpʃ(ə)n/ n. [f. L excerpere (EX-[1], carpere pluck)]

excess /ɪkˈses/ n. **1.** the exceeding of due limits; (usu. in pl.) immoderate or outrageous behaviour. **2.** the amount by which one number or quantity exceeds another. **3.** an agreed amount subtracted from the total payment to be made to an insured person who makes a claim. —/ˈekses/ adj. that exceeds a limit or given amount; required as an excess. —**excess baggage,** that exceeding the weight-allowance and liable to an extra charge. **in excess of,** more than. [f. OF f. L (as EXCEED)]

excessive /ɪkˈsesɪv/ adj. too much, too great, more than what is normal or necessary. —**excessively** adv. [f. prec.]

exchange /ɪksˈtʃeɪndʒ/ n. **1.** the act or process of giving one thing and receiving another in its place; the giving of money for its equivalent in money of the same or another country. **2.** the central telephone office of a district, where connections are effected. **3.** the place where merchants, brokers, etc., gather to transact business. **4.** an office where certain information is given. **5.** a system of settling debts between persons (especially in different countries) without the use of money, by bills of exchange (see BILL[1]). —v.t./i. to give or receive (a thing) in place of (or for) another; to give one and receive another of (things or persons); to make an exchange with someone else. —**exchange rate,** the value of one currency in terms of another. **in exchange,** as a thing exchanged (for). [f. OF (as EX-[1], CHANGE)]

exchangeable adj. able to be exchanged. [f. prec.]

exchequer /ɪksˈtʃekə(r)/ n. **1. Exchequer,** the former government department dealing with national revenue (see below); a royal or national treasury. **2.** one's private funds. [f. OF f. L scaccarium chess-board, w. ref. to former keeping of accounts on chequered table-cloth]
The Normans created two departments dealing with finance. One was the Treasury, which received and paid out money on behalf of the monarch, the other was the Exchequer which was itself divided into two parts, lower and upper. The lower Exchequer was an office for receiving money and was connected to the Treasury (see entry); the upper Exchequer was a court of law dealing with cases related to revenue, and was merged with the High Court of Justice in 1880. The Exchequer now denotes the account at the Bank of England into which tax receipts and other public monies are paid, the balance of which forms the Consolidated Fund. Its name survives also in the title 'Chancellor of the Exchequer'.

excise[1] /ˈeksaɪz/ n. duty or tax levied on goods produced or sold within a country, and on various licences etc. —v.t.

to charge excise on; to make (a person) pay excise. [f. MDu. (as CENSUS)]

excise[2] /ɪkˈsaɪz/ v.t. to remove by cutting out or away (a passage from a book, tissue from the body, etc.). —**excision** /-ˈsɪʒ(ə)n/ n. [f. L excidere (EX-[1], caedere cut)]

excitable /ɪkˈsaɪtəb(ə)l/ adj. (esp. of a person) easily excited. —**excitability** /-ˈbɪlɪtɪ/ n. [f. foll.]

excite /ɪkˈsaɪt/ v.t. to rouse the feelings or emotion of (a person); to bring into play, to rouse up (feelings etc.); to provoke or bring about (an action etc.); to stimulate (a bodily organ etc.) to activity. [f. OF or L excitare, frequent. of exciēre set in motion]

excitement n. **1.** a thing that excites. **2.** an excited state of mind. [f. prec.]

exciting adj. arousing great interest or enthusiasm. —**excitingly** adv. [f. EXCITE]

exclaim /ɪkˈskleɪm/ v.t./i. to cry out, especially in anger, surprise, pain, etc.; to utter or say in this manner. [f. F or L exclamare (EX-[1], clamare shout)]

exclamation /ekskləˈmeɪʃ(ə)n/ n. **1.** exclaiming. **2.** a word or words etc. exclaimed. —**exclamation mark,** the punctuation mark (!) placed after and indicating an exclamation. [f. OF or L (as prec.)]

exclamatory /ɪkˈsklæmətərɪ/ adj. of or serving as an exclamation. [as prec.]

exclude /ɪkˈskluːd/ v.t. **1.** to shut or keep out from a place, group, or privilege etc. **2.** to remove from consideration. **3.** to make impossible, to preclude. —**exclusion** n. [f. L excludere (EX-[1], claudere shut)]

exclusive /ɪksˈkluːsɪv/ adj. excluding, not inclusive; excluding all others; tending to exclude others, esp. socially; (of shops or goods) high-class, catering for the wealthy; (of goods for sale, a newspaper article, etc.) not available or appearing elsewhere. —**exclusive of,** not counting. —**exclusively** adv., **exclusiveness** n., **exclusivity** /-ˈsɪvɪtɪ/ n. [as prec.]

excommunicate /ekskəˈmjuːnɪkeɪt/ v.t. to deprive (a person) of membership and especially the sacraments of the Church. —/-ət/ adj. excommunicated. —/-ət/ n. an excommunicated person. —**excommunication** /-ˈkeɪʃ(ə)n/ n. [f. L excommunicare put out of the community (EX-[1], communis common)]

excoriate /eksˈkɔːrɪeɪt/ v.t. **1.** to remove part of the skin of (a person etc.), as by abrasion; to strip off (skin). **2.** to censure severely. —**excoriation** /-ˈeɪʃ(ə)n/ n. [f. L excoriare (EX-[1], corium hide)]

excrement /ˈekskrɪmənt/ n. faeces. —**excremental** /-ˈment(ə)l/ adj. [f. F or L (as EXCRETE)]

excrescence /ɪkˈskresəns/ n. an abnormal or morbid outgrowth on a body or plant; an ugly addition. —**excrescent** adj. [f. L (EX-[1], crescere grow)]

excreta /ekˈskriːtə/ n.pl. faeces and urine. [L (as foll.)]

excrete /ɪkˈskriːt/ v.t. to expel from the body as waste. —**excretion** n., **excretory** adj. [f. L (EX-[1], cernere sift)]

excruciating /ɪkˈskruːʃɪeɪtɪŋ/ adj. acutely painful; (colloq.) (of humour etc.) shocking, poor. [f. L excruciare torment (EX-[1], crux cross)]

exculpate /ˈekskʌlpeɪt/ v.t. to free from blame; to clear (a person from a charge). —**exculpation** /-ˈpeɪʃ(ə)n/ n., **exculpatory** /-ˈkʌlpətərɪ/ adj. [f. L exculpare (EX-[1], culpa blame)]

excursion /ɪkˈskɜːʃ(ə)n/ n. a short journey or ramble for pleasure and returning to the starting-point. [f. L (EX-[1], currere run)]

excursive adj. digressive. [as prec.]

excuse /ɪkˈskjuːz/ v.t. **1.** to try to lessen the blame attaching to (an act or fault or the person committing it); (of a fact or circumstance) to mitigate or justify thus; to overlook or forgive (a person or offence). **2.** to release from an obligation or duty; to gain exemption for. **3.** to allow to leave. —/ɪkˈskjuːs/ n. a reason put forward to mitigate or justify an offence; an apology. —**excuse me,** a polite apology for interrupting or disagreeing etc. **excuse oneself,** to ask permission or apologize for leaving. [f. OF f. L excusare (EX-[1], causa accusation)]

ex-directory adj. (of a telephone number) omitted from the directory at the subscriber's request.

exeat /ˈeksɪæt/ n. leave of absence from college etc. [L, = let him go out]

execrable /ˈeksɪkrəb(ə)l/ adj. abominable. —**execrably** adv. [f. OF f. L (as foll.)]

execrate /ˈeksɪkreɪt/ v.t./i. to express loathing for, to detest;

to utter curses. —**execration** /-'kreɪʃ(ə)n/ *n*. [f. L *ex-(s)ecrari* (EX-[1], *sacrare* sacred f. *sacer* sacred, accursed)]

executant /ɪg'zekjʊt(ə)nt/ *n*. a performer, especially of music. [f. F (as foll.)]

execute /'eksɪkju:t/ *v.t*. **1**. to carry into effect, to perform (a plan, duty, etc.). **2**. to produce (a work of art). **3**. to inflict capital punishment on. **4**. to make (a legal document) valid by signing, sealing, etc. [f. OF f. L *executare* (EX-[1], *sequi* follow)]

execution /eksɪ'kju:ʃ(ə)n/ *n*. **1**. carrying out, performance. **2**. an infliction of capital punishment. **3**. skill in or manner of a performance. [f. OF f. L (as prec.)]

executioner *n*. one who carries out a death sentence. [f. prec.]

executive /ɪg'zekjʊtɪv/ *adj*. concerned with executing laws, agreements, etc., or with other administration or management. —*n*. a person or body having executive authority or in an executive position in a business organization etc.; the executive branch of government etc. [f. L (as EXECUTE)]

executor /ɪg'zekjʊtə(r)/ *n*. a person appointed by a testator to carry out the terms of a will. —**executorial** /-'tɔ:rɪəl/ *adj*., **executrix** *n. fem*. [f. AF f. L (as EXECUTE)]

exegesis /eksɪ'dʒi:sɪs/ *n*. (*pl*. **exegeses** /-si:z/) an explanation, especially of a passage of Scripture. —**exegetic** /-'dʒetɪk/ *adj*. [f. Gk, f. *exēgeomai* interpret]

exemplar /ɪg'zemplə(r)/ *n*. a model, a type; an instance. [f. OF f. L (as EXAMPLE)]

exemplary /ɪg'zemplərɪ/ *adj*. **1**. fit to be imitated, very good. **2**. serving as an example or as a warning. [f. L (as EXAMPLE)]

exemplify /ɪg'zemplɪfaɪ/ *v.t*. to give or serve as an example of. —**exemplification** /-'keɪʃ(ə)n/ *n*. [f. L (as EXAMPLE)]

exempt /ɪg'zempt/ *adj*. freed (from an obligation or liability etc. imposed on others). —*v.t*. to make exempt (*from*). —**exemption** *n*. [f. L (*eximere* take out)]

exequies /'eksɪkwɪz/ *n. pl*. funeral rites. [f. OF f. L *exsequiae* (as EXECUTE)]

exercise /'eksəsaɪz/ *n*. **1**. activity requiring physical effort, done to improve the health; (often in *pl*.) a particular bodily task devised for this. **2**. the use or application (of a mental faculty, right, etc.); the practice (of a virtue or function etc.). **3**. (often in *pl*.) military drill or manœuvres. —*v.t*. **1**. to use or apply (a mental faculty, right, etc.); to practise (a virtue or function etc.). **2**. to take or cause to take exercise; to give exercise to. **3**. to perplex, to worry. [f. OF f. L (*exercēre* keep at work)]

exert /ɪg'zɜ:t/ *v.t*. to bring into use, to bring (influence, pressure, etc.) to bear. —**exert oneself**, to use efforts or endeavours. —**exertion** *n*. [f. L *exserere* put forth]

exeunt /'eksɪʊnt/ *v.i*. (as a stage direction) they leave the stage. —**exeunt omnes** /'ɒmnɪ:z/, all go off. [L (as EXIT[2])]

exfoliate /eks'fəʊlɪeɪt/ *v.i*. to come off in scales or layers; (of a tree) to throw off bark thus. —**exfoliation** /-'eɪʃ(ə)n/ *n*. [f. L *exfoliare* (EX-[1], *folium* leaf)]

ex gratia /eks 'greɪʃə/ done or given as a concession, not from an (especially legal) obligation. [L, = from kindness]

exhale /eks'heɪl/ *v.t./i*. to breathe out; to give off or be given off in a vapour. —**exhalation** /-hə'leɪʃ(ə)n/ *n*. [f. OF f. L *exhalare* (EX-[1], *halare* breathe)]

exhaust /ɪg'zɔ:st/ *v.t*. **1**. to consume or use up the whole of; to use up the strength or resources of, to tire out. **2**. to empty (a vessel etc. *of* its contents); to draw off (air). **3**. to study or expound on (a subject) completely. —*n*. **1**. the expulsion or exit of steam or waste gases from an engine etc.; such gases etc. **2**. the pipe or system through which they are expelled. [f. L *exhaurire* drain]

exhaustible *adj*. liable to be exhausted. [f. prec.]

exhaustion /ɪg'zɔ:stʃ(ə)n/ *n*. exhausting, being exhausted; complete loss of strength. [as EXHAUST]

exhaustive *adj*. that exhausts a subject; thorough, comprehensive. —**exhaustively** *adv*. [f. EXHAUST]

exhibit /ɪg'zɪbɪt/ *v.t*. to show or display, especially publicly; to manifest (a quality etc.). —*n*. a thing exhibited, especially in an exhibition or as evidence in a lawcourt. —**exhibitor** *n*. [f. L *exhibēre* (EX-[1], *habēre* hold)]

exhibition /eksɪ'bɪʃ(ə)n/ *n*. **1**. exhibiting, being exhibited. **2**. a public display of works of art etc. **3**. a minor scholarship, especially from the funds of a school or college etc. [f. OF f. L (as prec.)]

exhibitioner *n*. a student receiving an exhibition. [f. prec.]

exhibitionism *n*. a tendency towards display or extravagant behaviour; a perverted mental condition characterized by indecent exposure of the genitals. —**exhibitionist** *n*. [f. EXHIBITION]

exhilarate /ɪg'zɪləreɪt/ *v.t*. to enliven or gladden. —**exhilaration** /-'reɪʃ(ə)n/ *n*. [f. L *exhilarare* (EX-[1], *hilaris* cheerful)]

exhort /ɪg'zɔ:t/ *v.t*. to urge or admonish earnestly. —**exhortation** /egzɔ:'teɪʃ(ə)n/ *n*., **exhortative** *adj*., **exhortatory** *adj*. [f. L (EX-[1], *hortari* exhort)]

exhume /eks'hju:m/ *v.t*. to dig up or unearth (especially a buried corpse). —**exhumation** /-'meɪʃ(ə)n/ *n*. [f. F f. L (EX-[1], *humare* bury)]

ex hypothesi /eks haɪ'pɒθəsɪ/ according to the hypothesis proposed. [L]

exigency /'eksɪdʒənsɪ/ *n*. (also **exigence**) an urgent need or demand; an emergency. —**exigent** *adj*. [f. F & L *exigere* (as EXACT)]

exiguous /eg'zɪgjʊəs/ *adj*. scanty, small. —**exiguity** /-'gju:ɪtɪ/ *n*., **exiguousness** *n*. [f. L *exiguus* scanty (*exigere* weigh exactly)]

exile /'eksaɪl, eg-/ *n*. **1**. being expelled from one's native country; a long absence abroad. **2**. a person in exile. —*v.t*. to send into exile. —**the Exile**, the Captivity of the Jews in Babylon. [f. OF f. L *exilium* banishment]

exist /ɪg'zɪst/ *v.i*. **1**. to have a place in reality. **2**. (of circumstances etc.) to occur, to be found. **3**. to live, to sustain life; to continue in being. [prob. back-formation f. foll. (cf. L *existere*)]

existence /ɪg'zɪst(ə)ns/ *n*. **1**. the fact or a manner of existing or living; continuance in life or being. **2**. all that exists. —**existent** *adj*. [f. OF or L *existentia* (EX-[1], *sistere* redupl. of *stare* stand)]

existential /egzɪ'stenʃ(ə)l/ *adj*. of or relating to existence; concerned with human experience as viewed by existentialism. —**existentially** *adv*. [f. L (as prec.)]

existentialism /egzɪ'stenʃ(ə)lɪz(ə)m/ *n*. a philosophical theory that emphasizes the existence of the individual, who, being free and responsible, is held to be what he makes himself by the self-development of his essence through acts of the will (which, in the Christian form of the theory, leads to God). The term denotes recurring themes in modern philosophy and literature rather than a single school of thought. Kierkegaard is generally taken to be the first existentialist philosopher, and the theory was developed chiefly in continental Europe. —**existentialist** *n*. [f. G (as prec.)]

exit[1] /'eksɪt, 'egz-/ *n*. **1**. the act or right of going out. **2**. a passage or door as the way out. **3**. an actor's departure from the stage. —*v.i*. to make one's exit. [f. L *exitus* going out (as foll.)]

exit[2] /'eksɪt, 'egz-/ *v.i*. (as a stage direction) he or she leaves the stage. [L (*exire* go out)]

exo- *prefix* external(ly). [f. Gk *exō* outside]

exocrine /'eksəkraɪn, -krɪn/ *adj*. (of a gland) secreting through a duct. [f. EXO- + Gk *krinō* sift]

Exodus /'eksədəs/ a book of the Old Testament relating the departure of the Israelites under Moses from their bondage in Egypt. —*n*. this departure, ascribed by scholars to any of various dates within the limits *c*.1580–*c*.1200 BC. Although there is a strong and fervent tradition about the events, the variety of sources and purpose of the narrative make it impossible to treat this as a straightforward historical account, though such considerations have never inhibited speculation about the date and the route involved. [L f. Gk, = way out]

exodus /'eksədəs/ *n*. a mass departure. [= prec.]

ex officio /eks ə'fɪʃɪəʊ/ by virtue of one's office. —**ex-officio** *adj*. of a position held thus. [L]

exonerate /ɪg'zɒnəreɪt/ *v.t*. to free or declare free from blame. —**exoneration** /-'reɪʃ(ə)n/ *n*., **exonerative** /ɪg'zɒnərətɪv/ *adj*. [f. L *exonerare* (EX-[1], *onus* burden)]

exorbitant /ɪg'zɔ:bɪtənt/ *adj*. (of a price or demand etc.) grossly excessive. [f. L (as EX-[1], ORBIT)]

exorcise /'eksɔ:saɪz/ *v.t*. to drive out (an evil spirit) by invocation etc.; to free (a person or place) thus. —**exorcism** *n*., **exorcist** *n*. [f. F or L f. Gk *exorkizō* (*horkos* oath)]

exordium /ek'sɔ:dɪəm/ *n*. (*pl*. **-iums**) the introductory part of a discourse or treatise. [L (EX-[1], *ordiri* begin)]

exotic /ɪg'zɒtɪk/ *adj*. introduced from abroad, not native; remarkably strange or unusual. —*n*. an exotic plant etc. —**exotically** *adv*. [f. L f. Gk (as EXO-)]

exotica /ɪg'zɒtɪkə/ *n.pl*. remarkably strange or rare objects. [L (as prec.)]

expand /ɪkˈspænd/ v.t./i. **1.** to increase in size, bulk, or importance. **2.** to unfold or spread out. **3.** to express at length (condensed notes, an algebraic expression, etc.). **4.** to be genial or effusive. —**expanding universe,** the universe regarded as continually expanding so that the galaxies are carried farther apart (see HUBBLE). —**expander** n. [f. L *expandere* spread]

expanse /ɪkˈspæns/ n. a wide area or extent of land, space, etc. [as prec.]

expansible /ɪkˈspænsɪb(ə)l/ adj. that can be expanded. —**expansibility** /-ˈbɪlɪtɪ/ n. [f. EXPAND]

expansion /ɪkˈspæn(ə)n/ n. expanding; an enlargement, an increase. [as prec.]

expansionism n. advocacy of expansion, especially in territory. —**expansionist** n. [f. prec.]

expansive /ɪkˈspænsɪv/ adj. **1.** able or tending to expand. **2.** extensive. **3.** effusive, genial. —**expansively** adv., **expansiveness** n. [as EXPAND]

expatiate /ɪkˈspeɪʃɪeɪt/ v.i. to speak or write at length (*on*). —**expatiation** /-ˈeɪʃ(ə)n/ n., **expatiatory** adj. [f. L *exspatiari* walk about (EX-¹, *spatium* space)]

expatriate /eksˈpætrɪeɪt/ v.t. to expel, or to remove *oneself*, from one's native country. —/-ət/ adj. expatriated. —/-ət/ n. an expatriated person. —**expatriation** /-ˈeɪʃ(ə)n/ n. [f. L *expatriare* (EX-¹, *patria* native land)]

expect /ɪkˈspekt/ v.t. **1.** to regard as likely, to assume as a future event or occurrence. **2.** to look for as due. **3.** (*colloq.*) to think, to suppose. —**be expecting,** (*colloq.*) to be pregnant. [f. L *ex(s)pectare* (*spectare* look)]

expectancy n. a state of expectation; a prospect or prospective chance. [f. prec.]

expectant adj. expecting, having expectation. —**expectant mother,** a pregnant woman. —**expectantly** adv. [as EXPECT]

expectation /ekspekˈteɪʃ(ə)n/ n. **1.** expecting, looking forward with hope or fear etc. **2.** what one expects; the probability (*of* an event); the probable duration (*of* life); (in *pl.*) prospects of inheritance. [as prec.]

expectorant /ekˈspektərənt/ adj. that causes one to expectorate. —n. an expectorant medicine. [as foll.]

expectorate /ekˈspektəreɪt/ v.t./i. to cough or spit out (phlegm etc.) from the chest or lungs; to spit. —**expectoration** /-ˈreɪʃ(ə)n/ n. [f. L *expectorare* (EX-¹, *pectus* breast)]

expedient /ɪkˈspiːdɪənt/ adj. advantageous, advisable on practical rather than moral grounds; suitable, appropriate. —n. a means of achieving an end, a resource. —**expedience** n., **expediency** n., **expediently** adv. [f. L *expedire* (as foll.)]

expedite /ˈekspɪdaɪt/ v.t. to assist the progress of, to hasten (an action, measure, etc.); to accomplish (business) quickly. [f. L *expedire* free from difficulties, put in order]

expedition /ekspəˈdɪʃ(ə)n/ n. **1.** a journey or voyage for a particular purpose especially exploration; the people or ships etc. undertaking this. **2.** promptness, speed. [f. OF f. L (as prec.)]

expeditionary adj. of or used in an expedition [f. prec.]

expeditious /ekspəˈdɪʃəs/ adj. acting or done with speed and efficiency. —**expeditiously** adv. [as prec.]

expel /ɪkˈspel/ v.t. (-**ll**-) to send or drive out by force; to compel (a person) by process of law to leave a school or country etc. [f. L *expellere* (EX-¹, *pellere* drive)]

expend /ɪkˈspend/ v.t. to spend or use up (money, time, etc.). [f. L *expendere* (EX-¹, *pendere* weigh)]

expendable adj. that may be sacrificed or dispensed with; not worth preserving. [f. prec.]

expenditure /ekˈspendɪtʃə(r)/ n. expending (especially of money); the amount expended. [f. EXPEND]

expense /ɪkˈspens/ n. a cost incurred; (in *pl.*) the costs incurred in doing a job etc., reimbursement for these; the spending of money, a thing on which money is spent. —**at the expense of,** so as to cause loss or damage or discredit to. **expense account,** the record of an employee's expenses payable by an employer. [f. OF f. L *expensa* (as EXPEND)]

expensive adj. costing much, of a high price. —**expensively** adv., **expensiveness** n. [as EXPEND]

experience /ɪkˈspɪərɪəns/ n. personal observation of or involvement with a fact, event, etc.; knowledge or skill based on this; an event that affects one. —v.t. to have experience of, to undergo; to feel. [f. OF f. L (*experiri* make trial of)]

experienced adj. having had much experience; skilled from this. [f. prec.]

experiential /ɪkspɪərɪˈenʃ(ə)l/ adj. involving or based on experience. [f. EXPERIENCE]

experiment /ɪkˈsperɪmənt/ n. a procedure tried on the chance of success, or to test an hypothesis etc. or demonstrate a known fact. —/also -ent/ v.i. to make an experiment (*on* or *with*). —**experimentation** /-ˈteɪʃ(ə)n/ n. [f. OF or L (as EXPERIENCE)]

experimental /ɪksperɪˈment(ə)l/ adj. of, based on, or using an experiment; in the nature of an experiment. —**experimentalism** n., **experimentally** adv. [f. prec.]

expert /ˈekspɜːt/ adj. highly practised and skilful, or well informed, in a subject. —n. a person who is expert in a subject; (*attrib.*) of or being an expert. —**expertly** adv. [f. OF f. L (as EXPERIENCE)]

expertise /ekspɜːˈtiːz/ n. expert skill or knowledge or judgement. [F]

expiate /ˈekspɪeɪt/ v.t. to make amends for (a wrong); to pay the penalty of. —**expiable** adj., **expiation** /-ˈeɪʃ(ə)n/ n., **expiatory** adj. [f. L *expiare* seek to appease (EX-¹, *pius* devout)]

expiratory /ɪkˈspaɪrətərɪ/ adj. of breathing out. [f. foll.]

expire /ɪkˈspaɪə(r)/ v.t./i. **1.** (of a period, the validity of a thing, etc.) to come to an end. **2.** to breathe out (air, or *absol.*); to die. —**expiration** /ekspɪˈreɪʃ(ə)n/ n. [f. OF f. L *exspirare* (EX-¹, *spirare* breathe)]

expiry /ɪkˈspaɪrɪ/ n. the termination of a period of validity. [f. prec.]

explain /ɪkˈspleɪn/ v.t. to make clear or intelligible, to give the meaning of; to make known in detail; to account for (conduct etc.). —**explain away,** to minimize the significance of. **explain oneself,** to justify one's conduct or attitude etc. [f. L *explanare* (EX-¹, *planus* flat, plain)]

explanation /ekspləˈneɪʃ(ə)n/ n. explaining; a statement or circumstance that explains something. [as prec.]

explanatory /ɪkˈsplænətərɪ/ adj. serving or intended to explain. [as EXPLAIN]

expletive /ɪkˈspliːtɪv/ n. an oath or meaningless exclamation; a word used to fill out a sentence etc. —adj. serving as an expletive. [f. L (*explēre* fill out)]

explicable /ˈeksplɪkəb(ə)l, ɪkˈsplɪk-/ adj. that can be explained. [as foll.]

explicate /ˈeksplɪkeɪt/ v.t. to explain or develop (an idea etc.). —**explication** /-ˈkeɪʃ(ə)n/ n. [f. L *explicare* unfold (EX-¹, *plicare* fold)]

explicit /ɪkˈsplɪsɪt/ adj. **1.** expressly stated, not merely implied; stated in detail; definite. **2.** outspoken. —**explicitly** adv., **explicitness** n. [f. F or L (as prec.)]

explode /ɪkˈspləʊd/ v.t./i. **1.** to expand suddenly with a loud noise owing to the release of internal energy; to cause to do this. **2.** to give vent suddenly to emotion or violence. **3.** to increase suddenly or rapidly. **4.** to expose or discredit (a theory etc.). **5.** (usu. in *p.p.*) to show parts of (a diagram etc.) in relative positions but somewhat separated. [f. L *explodere* drive off the stage by clapping (EX-¹, *plaudere* clap)]

exploit /ˈeksplɔɪt/ n. a bold or daring feat. —/ɪkˈsplɔɪt/ v.t. to use or develop for one's own ends, to take advantage of. —**exploitation** /-ˈteɪʃ(ə)n/ n. [f. OF (as EXPLICATE)]

explore /ɪkˈsplɔː(r)/ v.t. **1.** to travel extensively through (a country etc.) in order to learn or discover about it. **2.** to inquire into. **3.** to examine by touch. —**exploration** /ekspləˈreɪʃ(ə)n/ n., **exploratory** /ɪkˈsplɔrətərɪ/ adj., **explorer** n. [f. F f. L *explorare*]

explosion /ɪkˈspləʊʒ(ə)n/ n. **1.** exploding; a loud noise due to this. **2.** a sudden outbreak of feeling etc. **3.** a sudden or rapid increase. [f. L (as EXPLODE)]

explosive /ɪkˈspləʊsɪv/ adj. **1.** able or tending or likely to explode. **2.** likely to cause a violent outburst etc., dangerously tense. —n. an explosive substance. —**explosively** adv. [f. prec.]

exponent /ɪkˈspəʊnənt/ n. **1.** a person who explains or interprets something. **2.** a person who favours or promotes an idea etc. **3.** a type or representative. **4.** a raised symbol beside a numeral (e.g. 3 in 2 3³) indicating how many times it is to be multiplied by itself. [f. L *exponere* (EX-¹, *ponere* put)]

exponential /ekspəˈnenʃ(ə)l/ adj. **1.** of or indicated by a mathematical exponent. **2.** (of an increase etc.) more and more rapid. —**exponential curve,** one based on an exponential equation, increasing sharply in steepness (ill. SHAPES). [f. prec.]

export /ˈekspɔːt/ v.t. /also -ˈspɔːt/ to send out (goods) for sale in another country. —n. **1.** exporting. **2.** an exported article; (usu. in pl.) the amount exported. —**exportation** /-ˈteɪʃ(ə)n/ n., **exporter** /-ˈpɔːt-/ n. [f. L exportare (EX-[1], portare carry)]

exportable /ɪkˈspɔːtəb(ə)l/ adj. that can be exported. [f. prec.]

expose /ɪkˈspəʊz/ v.t. **1.** to leave uncovered or unprotected, especially from the weather; to allow light to reach (a photographic film or plate); to leave (a baby) in the open to die. **2.** to subject to (a risk etc.). **3.** to reveal, to make known or visible; to show up in a true (usually unfavourable) light. —**expose oneself**, to expose one's body indecently. [f. OF f. L (as EXPONENT)]

exposé /ekˈspəʊzeɪ/ n. an orderly statement of facts; a revealing of a discreditable thing. [F (as prec.)]

exposition /ekspəˈzɪʃ(ə)n/ n. **1.** expounding, an explanatory account. **2.** a large public exhibition. **3.** (Mus.) the part of a movement in which themes are presented. [f. OF or L (as EXPOSE)]

ex post facto /eks pəʊst ˈfæktəʊ/ retrospective, retrospectively. [L, = from what is done afterwards]

expostulate /ɪkˈspɒstjʊleɪt/ v.i. to make a reasoned protest, to remonstrate. —**expostulation** /-ˈleɪʃ(ə)n/ n., **expostulatory** adj. [f. L (as EX-[1], POSTULATE)]

exposure /ɪkˈspəʊʒə(r)/ n. **1.** exposing, being exposed. **2.** the exposing of a photographic film or plate; the duration of this; the part of a film exposed for one picture. [f. EXPOSE]

expound /ɪkˈspaʊnd/ v.t. to set forth in detail; to explain, to interpret. [f. OF (as EXPONENT)]

express /ɪkˈspres/ v.t. **1.** to represent or make known in words or by gestures, conduct, etc. **2.** to squeeze out (juice etc.). **3.** to send by express service. —adj. **1.** definitely stated, explicit. **2.** sent or delivered by a specially fast service. **3.** (of a train) travelling at high speed and with few stops. —n. **1.** an express train etc. **2.** (US) a service for the rapid transport of parcels etc. —adv. at high speed, by express. —**express oneself**, to say what one means or thinks. —**expressly** adv. [f. OF f. L exprimere, orig. = press out]

expressible /ɪkˈspresɪb(ə)l/ adj. that can be expressed. [f. prec.]

expression /ɪkˈspreʃ(ə)n/ n. **1.** expressing; a word or phrase; a collection of symbols in mathematics expressing a quantity. **2.** a look or facial aspect; the showing of feeling in the manner of speaking or of performing music; the representation of feeling in art. [as EXPRESS]

expressionism /ɪkˈspreʃ(ə)nɪz(ə)m/ n. a style of painting in which the artist or writer seeks to express emotional experience rather than impressions of the physical world, especially through the use of violent colour and linear distortions; a similar style or movement in literature, drama, music, etc. (See below.) —**expressionist** n. & adj. [f. prec.]

The beginnings of expressionism can be traced to Van Gogh, Gauguin, and Munch in the 1880s and 1890s, but the term was not used until the early 20th c., when it was applied to the fauves and early cubists. Major expressionist painters include Soutine, Chagall, and Roualt in France, Nolde in Germany, Kokoschka in Austria. The word has been used as a synonym for modernism, identified with whatever is thought best in modern art; it can also be applied to earlier art, such as that of El Greco, in which non-naturalistic distortions have an expressive effect. In the theatre, the term has been associated with the works of Ernst Toller, Strindberg, Wedekind, and early Brecht, and embraces a wide variety of moods—satirical, grotesque, visionary, exclamatory, violent, but always anti-naturalistic. The epitome of expressionism in German cinema was Robert Heine's The Cabinet of Dr. Caligari (1919). Expressionism took little root in Britain, though traces of its influence can be found in the verse dramas of Auden and Isherwood, and later in the cinema (e.g. Carol Reed's version of Graham Greene's The Third Man, 1949).

expressionless adj. without positive expression, not revealing one's thoughts or feelings. [f. prec. + -LESS]

expressive adj. serving to express; full of expression. —**expressively** adv., **expressiveness** n. [f. F f. L (as EXPRESS)]

expressway n. (US) an urban motorway.

expropriate /eksˈprəʊprieɪt/ v.t. to take away (property)

from its owner; to dispossess (a person). —**expropriation** /-ˈeɪʃ(ə)n/ n. [f. L expropriare (EX-[1], proprium property)]

expulsion /ɪkˈspʌlʃ(ə)n/ n. expelling, being expelled. [f. L (as EXPEL)]

expulsive /ɪkˈspʌlsɪv/ adj. expelling. [f. prec.]

expunge /ɪkˈspʌndʒ/ v.t. to erase or remove (a passage from a book etc.). [f. L expungere prick out (for deletion)]

expurgate /ˈekspɜːgeɪt/ v.t. to remove matter thought to be objectionable from (a book etc.); to remove (such matter). —**expurgation** /-ˈgeɪʃ(ə)n/ n., **expurgator** n. [f. L expurgare (EX-[1], purgare cleanse)]

exquisite /ˈekskwɪzɪt, (D) ekˈskwɪzɪt/ adj. **1.** extremely beautiful or delicate. **2.** highly sensitive; acute, keen. —n. a person of refined (especially affected) tastes. —**exquisitely** adv. [f. L exquirere search out (EX-[1], quaerere seek)]

ex-serviceman /eksˈsɜːvɪsmən/ n. (pl. -men) a former member of the armed forces.

extant /ekˈstænt, ˈek-/ adj. still existing. [f. L ex(s)tare (EX-[1], stare stand)]

extemporaneous /ekstempəˈreɪnɪəs/ adj. spoken or done without preparation. —**extemporaneously** adv. [as EXTEMPORE]

extemporary /ɪkˈstempərərɪ/ adj. extemporaneous. [as foll.]

extempore /ekˈstempərɪ/ adj. & adv. without preparation, offhand. [L, lit. = out of the time (ex out of, tempus time)]

extemporize /ɪkˈstempəraɪz/ v.t./i. to speak, utter, or perform extempore. —**extemporization** /-ˈzeɪʃ(ə)n/ n. [f. prec.]

extend /ɪkˈstend/ v.t./i. **1.** to lengthen in space or time; to increase in scope. **2.** to stretch or lay out at full length; to reach or be continuous over a certain area; to have a certain scope. **3.** to offer or accord a feeling, invitation, etc., to. —**extended family**, one including relatives living near. **extended-play** adj. (of a gramophone record) playing for longer than most singles. **extend oneself** or **be extended**, to have one's abilities taxed to the utmost. —**extender** n. [f. L extendere (EX-[1], tendere stretch)]

extensible /ɪkˈstensɪb(ə)l/ adj. (also **extendible**) that can be extended. [f. prec.]

extension /ɪkˈstenʃ(ə)n/ n. **1.** extending, being extended. **2.** a part enlarging or added on to a main structure etc.; an additional period of time; a subsidiary telephone on the same line as the main one, its number. **3.** extramural instruction by a university or college etc.

extensive adj. large; far-reaching. —**extensively** adv., **extensiveness** n. [f. F or L (as EXTEND)]

extent /ɪkˈstent/ n. the space over which a thing extends; a large area; range, scope, or degree. [f. AF f. L (as EXTEND)]

extenuate /ɪkˈstenjʊeɪt/ v.t. to lessen the seeming seriousness of (an offence or guilt) by partial excuse. —**extenuation** /-ˈeɪʃ(ə)n/ n. [f. L extenuare (EX-[1], tenuis thin)]

exterior /ɪkˈstɪərɪə(r)/ adj. outer, outward; coming from outside. —n. the exterior part or aspect; an outdoor scene in filming. [f. L, compar. of exterus outside]

exterminate /ɪkˈstɜːmɪneɪt/ v.t. to destroy (a disease, people, etc.) utterly. —**extermination** /-ˈneɪʃ(ə)n/ n., **exterminator** n. [f. L exterminare (EX-[1], terminare put an end to, f. terminus boundary)]

external /ekˈstɜːn(ə)l/ adj. of or situated on the outside or visible part; coming from the outside or an outside source; of a country's foreign affairs; outside the conscious subject; (of medicine etc.) for use on the outside of the body; of students taking the examinations of, but not attending, a university. —n. (in pl.) external features or circumstances; non-essentials. —**externality** /-ˈnælɪtɪ/ n., **externally** adv. [f. L externus (as EXTERIOR)]

externalize /ekˈstɜːnəlaɪz/ v.t. to give or attribute external existence to. —**externalization** /-ˈzeɪʃ(ə)n/ n. [f. prec.]

extinct /ɪkˈstɪŋkt/ adj. no longer existing, obsolete; no longer burning, (of a volcano) no longer active. [f. L exstinguere (EX-[1], stinguere quench)]

extinction /ɪkˈstɪŋkʃ(ə)n/ n. making or becoming extinct, dying out. [as prec.]

extinguish /ɪkˈstɪŋgwɪʃ/ v.t. **1.** to cause (a fire or light etc.) to cease to burn or function. **2.** to terminate, to make extinct, to destroy; to wipe out (a debt). [f. L (as EXTINCT)]

extinguisher n. a fire extinguisher (see FIRE).

extirpate /ˈekstɜːpeɪt/ v.t. to destroy, to root out. —**extirpation** /-peɪʃ(ə)n/ n. [f. L exstirpare (EX-[1], stirps stem)]

extol /ɪkˈstəʊl/ v.t. (-ll-) to praise enthusiastically. [f. L *extollere* (EX-¹, *tollere* raise)]

extort /ɪkˈstɔːt/ v.t. to obtain (money, a secret, etc.) by force, threats, or intimidation etc. [f. L *extorquere* (EX-¹, *torquere* twist)]

extortion /ɪkˈstɔːʃ(ə)n/ n. extorting, especially of money; illegal exaction. [as prec.]

extortionate /ɪkˈstɔːʃ(ə)nət/ adj. (of prices) excessively high; (of demands) excessive. —**extortionately** adv. [f. prec.]

extortioner n. one who practises extortion. [f. EXTORTION]

extra /ˈekstrə/ adj. additional; more than is usual or necessary or expected. —adv. more than usually; additionally. —n. an extra thing; a thing charged extra; a person engaged temporarily for a minor part in a film etc.; a special issue of a newspaper etc.; a run in cricket not scored from a hit with the bat. —**extra cover**, a fieldsman in cricket on the line between cover-point and mid-off but beyond these. [prob. for EXTRAORDINARY]

extra- prefix forming adjectives in the sense 'outside', 'beyond the scope of'. [f. L *extra* outside]

extract /ɪkˈstrækt/ v.t. 1. to take out by effort or force (anything firmly rooted or fixed). 2. to obtain (money, an admission etc.) against a person's will. 3. to obtain (juice etc.) by pressure, distillation, etc. 4. to derive (pleasure etc. *from*). 5. to quote or copy out (a passage from a book etc.). 6. to find (the root of a number). —/ˈekstrækt/ n. 1. a short passage from a book etc. 2. a substance got by distillation etc.; a concentrated preparation. [f. L *extrahere* (EX-¹, *trahere* draw)]

extraction /ɪkˈstrækʃ(ə)n/ n. 1. extracting, especially of a tooth. 2. lineage. [f. F f. L (as prec.)]

extractive /ɪkˈstræktɪv/ adj. of or involving extraction. —**extractive industry**, one obtaining minerals etc. from the ground. [f. EXTRACT]

extractor /ɪkˈstræktə(r)/ n. a person or thing that extracts. —**extractor fan**, a ventilating fan in a window etc. to remove stale air. [as prec.]

extra-curricular /ekstrəkəˈrɪkjʊlə(r)/ adj. not part of the normal curriculum.

extraditable /ˈekstrədaɪtəb(ə)l/ adj. liable to or (of a crime) warranting extradition. [f. foll.]

extradite /ˈekstrədaɪt/ v.t. to hand over (a person accused of a crime) to the State wishing to try him. —**extradition** /-ˈdɪʃ(ə)n/ n. [f. F (as EX-¹, TRADITION)]

extramarital /ekstrəˈmærɪt(ə)l/ adj. (of sexual relationships) outside marriage.

extramural /ekstrəˈmjʊər(ə)l/ adj. (of university teaching) additional to normal degree courses. [f. L *extra muros* outside the walls]

extraneous /ɪkˈstreɪnɪəs/ adj. of external origin; not belonging (*to* the matter in hand). —**extraneously** adv. [f. L *extraneus* (*extra* outside)]

extraordinary /ɪkˈstrɔːdɪnərɪ, ekstrəˈɔː-d-/ adj. unusual or remarkable; out of the usual course, additional; specially employed; unusually great. —**extraordinarily** adv. [f. L (*extra ordinem* outside the usual order)]

extrapolate /ekˈstræpəleɪt/ v.t./i. to estimate from known values, data, etc. (others which lie outside the range of those known). —**extrapolation** /-ˈleɪʃ(ə)n/ n. [f. EXTRA- + INTERPOLATE]

extra-sensory /ekstrəˈsensərɪ/ adj. (of perception) derived by means other than the known senses.

extra-terrestrial /ekstrətɪˈrestrɪ(ə)l/ adj. outside the earth or its atmosphere.

extravagant /ɪkˈstrævəgənt/ adj. 1. spending (especially money) excessively. 2. costing much. 3. passing the bounds of reason, absurd. —**extravagance** n., **extravagantly** adv. [f. L (EXTRA-, *vagari* wander)]

extravaganza /ekstrævəˈgænzə/ n. a fanciful literary, musical, or dramatic composition; a spectacular theatrical production. [f. It. *estravaganza* (as prec.)]

extravasate /ekˈstrævəseɪt/ v.t./i. to force out (blood etc.) from its vessel; (of blood, lava, etc.) to flow out. —**extravasation** /-ˈseɪʃ(ə)n/ n. [f. L *extra* outside + *vas* vessel]

extreme /ɪkˈstriːm/ adj. reaching a high or the highest degree; severe, going to great lengths; politically far to the left or right; outermost, furthest from the centre; utmost; last. —n. one or other of two things as remote or as different as possible, the thing at either end; an extreme degree; the first or last of a series. —**go to extremes**, to take an extreme course of action. **in the extreme**, to an extreme degree. [f. OF f. L (superl. of *exterus* outer)]

extremely adv. in an extreme degree, very. [f. prec.]

extremist n. one who holds extreme (esp. political) views. —**extremism** n. [f. EXTREME]

extremity /ɪkˈstremɪtɪ/ n. an extreme point, an end; extreme distress or difficulty; (in *pl.*) the hands and feet. [f. OF or L (as EXTREME)]

extricable /ˈekstrɪkəb(ə)l/ adj. that can be extricated. [f. foll.]

extricate /ˈekstrɪkeɪt/ v.t. to free or disentangle (*from* a difficulty etc.). —**extrication** /-ˈkeɪʃ(ə)n/ n. [f. L *extricare* (EX-¹, *tricae* entanglements)]

extrinsic /ekˈstrɪnsɪk/ adj. not inherent or intrinsic; extraneous, not belonging (*to*). —**extrinsically** adv. [f. L *extrinsecus* outwardly (as EXTRA-)]

extrovert /ˈekstrəvɜːt/ adj. (also **extroverted**) directing one's thoughts and interests to things outside oneself; socially unreserved. —n. an extrovert person. —**extroversion** /-ˈvɜːʃ(ə)n/ n. [as EXTRA- + *vertere* turn]

extrude /ekˈstruːd/ v.t. to thrust or force out; to shape (metal, plastics, etc.) by forcing through a die. —**extrusion** n., **extrusive** adj. [f. L (EX-¹, *trudere* thrust)]

exuberant /ɪgˈzjuːbərənt/ adj. lively, effusive, high-spirited; (of a plant etc.) prolific, luxuriant; (of health, emotion, etc.) overflowing, abundant. —**exuberance** n., **exuberantly** adv. [f. F f. L *exuberare* (EX-¹, *uber* fruitful)]

exude /ɪgˈzjuːd/ v.t./i. to ooze out; to give out (moisture); to emit (a smell); to show (pleasure etc.) freely. —**exudation** /eksjuˈdeɪʃ(ə)n/ n. [f. L (EX-¹, *sudare* sweat)]

exult /ɪgˈzʌlt/ v.i. to rejoice greatly. —**exultation** /eksʌlˈteɪʃ(ə)n/ n. [f. L (EX-¹, *saltare* dance)]

exultant adj. exulting, rejoicing. [f. prec.]

eye /aɪ/ n. 1. the organ of sight in man and animals (ill. BODY 4); the iris of an eye; the region round an eye. 2. a particular visual faculty. 3. a thing like an eye, e.g. a spot on a peacock's tail or butterfly's wing, the leaf-bud of a potato; the hole of a needle; a calm region in the centre of a hurricane etc. —v.t. (*partic.* **eyeing**) to look at, to observe (esp. with curiosity or suspicion). —**all eyes**, watching intently. **all my eye**, (*slang*) nonsense. **cast** *or* **run an eye over**, to examine quickly. **catch a person's eye**, to succeed in attracting a person's attention. **close** *or* **shut one's eyes to**, to ignore, to disregard. **do in the eye**, to defraud or thwart. **an eye for an eye**, retaliation in kind. **eye-liner** n. a cosmetic applied as a line round the eye. **eye-opener** n. a surprising or revealing fact or circumstance. **eye-rhyme** n. correspondence of words in spelling but not in pronunciation (e.g. *dear* and *pear*). **eye-shade** n. a device to protect the eyes from strong light. **eye-shadow** n. a cosmetic applied to the skin round the eyes. **eye-strain** n. weariness of the eyes. **eye-tooth** n. a canine tooth in the upper jaw, below the eye. **get one's eye in**, to become accustomed to prevailing conditions especially in sport. **half an eye**, the slightest degree of perceptiveness. **have eyes for**, to be interested in, to wish to acquire. **in** *or* **through the eyes of**, from the point of view of, in the judgement of. **in the public eye**, receiving much publicity. **keep an eye on**, to watch carefully, to take care of. **keep an eye open** *or* **out for**, to watch for. **keep one's eyes open** *or* (*slang*) **peeled** *or* **skinned**, to be watchful. **make eyes at**, to look at amorously or flirtatiously. **one in the eye**, a setback or discomfiture (*for*). **see eye to eye**, to agree. **set eyes on**, to catch sight of. **up to the eyes**, deeply engaged or involved *in*. **with an eye to**, with a view to. [OE]

eyeball n. the ball of the eye, within the lids and sockets. —**eyeball to eyeball**, (*colloq.*) confronting closely.

eyebath n. a small cup shaped to fit round the eye, for applying lotion to the eye.

eyebright n. a plant of the genus *Euphrasia*, formerly used as a remedy for weak eyes.

eyebrow n. the fringe of hair growing on the ridge above the eye-socket. —**raise an eyebrow** *or* **one's eyebrows**, to show surprise or disbelief.

eyeful n. a thing thrown or blown into the eye; (*colloq.*) a thorough look; (*colloq.*) a visually striking person or thing. [f. EYE -FUL]

eyeglass n. a lens for a defective eye.

eyehole n. 1. the socket containing the eye. 2. a hole to look through.

eyelash *n.* any of the fringe of hairs on the edge of the eyelid (ill. BODY 4).

eyelet /ˈaɪlɪt/ *n.* a small hole for passing cord or rope through; a metal ring for strengthening this. [f. OF *oillet* dim. of *oil* eye]

eyelid *n.* either of the two folds of skin that can be moved together to cover the eye.

eyepiece *n.* the lens or lenses to which the eye is applied at the end of a microscope, telescope, etc.

eyesight *n.* the faculty or power of seeing.

eyesore *n.* a thing that offends the sight; an ugly object etc.

eyewash *n.* **1.** a lotion for the eye. **2.** (*slang*) nonsense, insincere talk.

eyewitness *n.* a person who can give evidence of an incident from personal observation of it.

Eyre /eə(r)/, Edward John (1815–1901), English explorer and colonial statesman. Having emigrated to Australia at the age of 17, Eyre established himself as a sheep-farmer and in 1840–1 undertook explorations in the interior deserts of the continent. He later served as Lieutenant-Governor of New Zealand (1846–53) and Governor of St Vincent (1854–60) and Jamaica (1864–6). He was recalled from the last post for putting down a native revolt with undue severity but was eventually cleared of all charges.

eyrie /ˈaɪərɪ, ˈɪərɪ/ *n.* the nest of an eagle or other bird of prey built high up; a house etc. perched high up. [f. OF *aire* lair f. L *ager* piece of ground]

Ezekiel /ɪˈziːkɪəl/ **1.** a Hebrew major prophet of the 6th c. BC who prophesied the forthcoming destruction of Jerusalem and the Jewish nation, and inspired hope for the future well-being of a restored State. **2.** a book of the Old Testament containing his prophecies.

Ezra /ˈezrə/ **1.** a Jewish priest and scribe who played a central part in the reform of Judaism in the 5th or 4th c. BC, following Nehemiah in taking measures to secure the racial purity of the Jews. **2.** a book of the Old Testament dealing with the return of the Jews from Babylon and the rebuilding of the Temple.

F

F, f *n.* (*pl.* **Fs**, **F's**) **1.** the sixth letter of the alphabet. **2.** (*Mus.*) the fourth note in the scale of C major.

F *abbr.* **1.** Fahrenheit. **2.** farad(s). **3.** Fellow of. **4.** fine (pencil-lead).

F *symbol* fluorine.

f. *abbr.* **1.** female; feminine. **2.** focal length. **3.** folio. **4.** following page etc.

f *abbr.* (*Mus.*) forte.

FA *abbr.* Football Association.

fa var. of FAH.

fab *adj.* (*colloq.*) marvellous. [abbr. of FABULOUS]

Fabergé /ˈfɑːbɛərʒeɪ/, Peter Carl (1846-1920), Russian jeweller, famed for his small intricate ornaments.

Fabian /ˈfeɪbɪən/ *n.* a member of the Fabian Society, an English socialist society founded in 1884, numbering among its members Sidney and Beatrice Webb and George Bernard Shaw, advocating social change through gradual reform rather than by violent revolutionary action. — **Fabianism** *n.* [f. foll.]

Fabius /ˈfeɪbɪəs/ (Quintus Fabius Maximus Verrucosus Cunctator, d. 203 BC) Roman general and statesman. After Hannibal's defeat of the Roman army at Cannae in 216 BC, he successfully pursued a strategy of caution and delay in order to wear down the Carthaginian invaders, whence his nickname Cunctator ('the Delayer').

fable /ˈfeɪb(ə)l/ *n.* **1.** a story, especially a supernatural one, not based on fact; a short moral tale especially about animals; legendary tales. **2.** a lie, lies. **3.** a thing only supposed to exist. [f. OF f. L *fabula* discourse]

fabled *adj.* celebrated in fable, legendary. [f. prec.]

fabric /ˈfæbrɪk/ *n.* **1.** woven, knitted, or felted material; a plastic resembling this. **2.** the walls, floors, and roof of a building. **3.** a structure (*lit.* or *fig.*). [f. F f. L (*faber* metal-worker)]

fabricate /ˈfæbrɪkeɪt/ *v.t.* **1.** to construct, to manufacture. **2.** to invent (a story); to forge (a document). — **fabrication** /-ˈkeɪʃ(ə)n/ *n.*, **fabricator** *n.* [f. L (as prec.)]

fabulous /ˈfæbjʊləs/ *adj.* **1.** famed in fable, legendary. **2.** incredible, absurd. **3.** (*colloq.*) marvellous. — **fabulously** *adv.* [f. F or L (as FABLE)]

façade /fəˈsɑːd/ *n.* **1.** the face or front of a building. **2.** an outward (esp. deceptive) appearance. [F (as foll.)]

face *n.* **1.** the front of the head from the forehead to the chin; the expression of the facial features; a grimace. **2.** the surface of a thing, especially the functional surface of a tool etc.; the upper or forward-facing side, the front; the dial-plate of a clock. **3.** an outward appearance, an aspect. **4.** composure; effrontery, nerve. **5.** esteem. **6.** a typeface. —*v.t./i.* **1.** to have or turn the face towards; to be opposite to. **2.** to meet resolutely, not to shrink from; to meet (an opponent) in a contest; to present itself to. **3.** to cover the surface of (a wall etc.) with a facing; to put a facing on (a garment etc.). —**face card**, a court card. **face-cloth** *n.* a face-flannel; a smooth-surfaced woollen cloth. **face-flannel** *n.* a cloth for washing one's face. **face-lift** *n.* the operation of having one's face lifted; a procedure to improve a thing's appearance. **face to face**, facing, confronting each other. **face up to**, to face resolutely. **face value**, the value printed or stamped on money; what a thing seems to mean or imply. **have the face**, to be shameless enough. **in (the) face of**, despite. **lose face**, to be humiliated. **make** *or* **pull a face**, to grimace. **on the face of it**, to outward appearances. **put a bold** *or* **good face on**, to accept (a difficulty etc.) cheerfully. **save face**, to preserve esteem, to avoid humiliation. **set one's face against**, to resist determinedly. **show one's face**, to let oneself be seen. **to a person's face**, openly in his presence. [f. OF f. L *facies*]

faceless /ˈfeɪslɪs/ *adj.* **1.** without identity, purposely not identifiable. **2.** lacking character. [f. FACE + -LESS]

facer *n.* a sudden unexpected difficulty. [f. FACE]

facet /ˈfæsɪt/ *n.* **1.** one aspect of a problem etc. **2.** one side of a many-faceted cut gem etc. —**faceted** *adj.* [f. F (as FACE)]

facetious /fəˈsiːʃəs/ *adj.* intending or intended to be amus-

ing. —**facetiously** *adv.*, **facetiousness** *n.* [f. F f. L *facetiae* wit]

facia /ˈfeɪʃə/ *n.* **1.** the instrument panel of a motor vehicle. **2.** the plate over a shop-front with the name etc. [var. of FASCIA]

facial /ˈfeɪʃ(ə)l/ *adj.* of or for the face. —*n.* a beauty treatment for the face. —**facially** *adv.* [f. L (as FACE)]

facile /ˈfæsaɪl/ *adj.* **1.** easily achieved but of little value. **2.** easy, easily done; working easily, fluent. [f. F or L *facilis* (*facere* make, do)]

facilitate /fəˈsɪlɪteɪt/ *v.t.* to make easy or less difficult; to make (an action or result) more easily achieved. —**facilitation** /-ˈteɪʃ(ə)n/ *n.* [f. F f. It. (as prec.)]

facility /fəˈsɪlɪtɪ/ *n.* **1.** ease, absence of difficulty; fluency, dexterity. **2.** (esp. in *pl.*) the opportunity or equipment for doing something. [f. F or L (as FACILE)]

facing *n.* a layer of material over a part of a garment etc., for contrast or strength; an outer layer covering the surface of a wall etc. [f. FACE]

facsimile /fækˈsɪmɪlɪ/ *n.* an exact copy of writing, a picture, etc. [L, = make a likeness]

fact *n.* a thing that is known to be true or to exist; truth, reality; a thing assumed as a basis for argument. —**facts and figures**, the precise details. **facts of life**, (*colloq.*) the realities of a situation; knowledge of human sexual functions. **in fact**, in reality, in short. [f. L *factum* (as FACILE)]

faction /ˈfækʃ(ə)n/ *n.* a small group with special aims within a larger one. —**factional** *adj.* [f. F f. L]

factious /ˈfækʃəs/ *adj.* of a faction, characterized by factions. [f. F or L (as FACTION)]

factitious /fækˈtɪʃəs/ *adj.* made for a special purpose; artificial. —**factitiously** *adv.* [f. L (as FACILE)]

factor /ˈfæktə(r)/ *n.* **1.** a circumstance etc. contributing to a result. **2.** a whole number etc. that when multiplied with another produces a given number. **3.** a business agent; an agent or deputy; (*Sc.*) a land-steward. **4.** a gene or other agent determining a hereditary character. [f. F or L (*facere* make, do)]

factorial /fækˈtɔːrɪəl/ *n.* the product of a number and all the whole numbers below it. —*adj.* of a factor or factorial. [f. prec.]

factorize /ˈfæktəraɪz/ *v.t.* to resolve into factors. —**factorization** /-ˈzeɪʃ(ə)n/ *n.* [f. FACTOR]

factory /ˈfæktərɪ/ *n.* a building or buildings in which goods are manufactured. —**Factory Acts**, legislation regulating the operation of factories in order to improve the working conditions of employees. The first effective Act was that of 1833, which provided for the use of inspectors. **factory farm**, one employing industrial or intensive methods of rearing livestock. **factory ship**, one that processes and freezes its catch while still at sea. [f. Port. or L (as FACTOR)]

factotum /fækˈtəʊtəm/ *n.* an employee doing all kinds of work. [L, = do the whole lot]

factual /ˈfæktjʊ(ə)l/ *adj.* based on or concerning facts. —**factually** *adv.* [f. FACT]

faculty /ˈfæk(ə)ltɪ/ *n.* **1.** an aptitude or ability for a particular activity; an inherent mental or physical power. **2.** a department of a university teaching a particular subject; (*US*) the staff of a university or college. **3.** authorization, especially by Church authority. [f. OF f. L *facultas* (*facilis* easy)]

fad *n.* **1.** a craze; a peculiar notion. —**faddish** *adj.* [prob. f. FIDDLE-FADDLE]

faddy *adj.* having arbitrary likes and dislikes, especially about food. —**faddiness** *n.* [f. prec.]

fade *v.t./i.* to lose or cause to lose colour, freshness, or strength; to disappear gradually; to bring (a sound or picture) gradually *in* or *out* of perception. —*n.* an act of fading. —**fade away** *or* **out**, to become weaker or less distinct; to die away; to disappear. [f. OF (*fade* dull, insipid)]

faeces /ˈfiːsiːz/ *n.pl.* waste matter discharged from the bowels. —**faecal** /ˈfiːk(ə)l/ *adj.* [L]

Faeroe Islands /ˈfeərəʊ/ (also **Faeroes**) a group of islands in the North Atlantic between Iceland and the Shetlands, belonging to Denmark but partly autonomous; pop. (1976) 41, 211; capital, Thorshavn. —**Faeroese** /-ˈiːz/ *adj.* & *n.*

fag[1] *v.t./i.* (**-gg-**) **1.** to tire (*out*), to exhaust. **2.** to toil; (as a junior schoolboy) to run errands for a senior boy. —*n.* **1.** (*colloq.*) drudgery. **2.** (*slang*) a cigarette. **3.** a schoolboy who fags. —**fag-end** *n.* a cigarette end. [orig. unkn.]

fag[2] *n.* (*US slang*) a homosexual. [abbr. of foll.]

faggot /ˈfægət/ *n.* **1.** a ball or roll of seasoned chopped liver etc. baked or fried. **2.** a bundle of sticks, herbs, metal rods, etc. **3.** (*slang*) an unpleasant woman. **4.** (*US slang*) a homosexual. [f. OF f. It.]

faggoting *n.* embroidery in which threads are fastened together like faggots. [f. prec.]

fah /faː/ *n.* (*Mus.*) the fourth note of the major scale in tonic sol-fa (see entry). [f. *famuli* (see GAMUT)]

Fahrenheit /ˈfærənhaɪt/ *adj.* of the scale of temperature on which water freezes at 32° and boils at 212°. [f. G. *Fahrenheit* German physicist (d. 1736)]

faience /ˈfaɪɑ̃s/ *n.* decorated and glazed earthenware and porcelain. [f. F f. *Faenza* in Italy]

fail *v.t./i.* **1.** not to succeed; to be unsuccessful in (an examination etc.); to grade (a candidate) as not having passed an examination. **2.** to disappoint, to let down. **3.** to neglect or forget, to be unable. **4.** to be absent or deficient; (of crops) to produce a very poor harvest. **5.** to become weak or ineffective, to cease functioning; to become bankrupt. —*n.* a failure in an examination. —**fail-safe** *adj.* reverting to a safe condition in the event of a breakdown etc. **without fail**, for certain, whatever happens. [f. OF f. L *fallere* deceive]

failed *adj.* unsuccessful. [f. prec.]

failing *n.* a fault, a weakness. —*prep.* in default of, if not. [f. FAIL]

failure /ˈfeɪljə(r)/ *n.* **1.** failing, non-performance, lack of success. **2.** cessation of normal function through weakness etc. **3.** deficiency, as through a poor harvest. **4.** an unsuccessful person or thing. [f. FAIL]

fain *predic. adj.* willing or obliged (*to*). —*adv.* gladly. [OE]

faint *adj.* **1.** indistinct, pale, dim. **2.** weak from hunger etc. **3.** timid; feeble. —*v.i.* to lose consciousness, to become faint. —*n.* an act of fainting, a state of having fainted. —**faint-hearted** *adj.* cowardly, timid. —**faintly** *adv.*, **faintness** *n.* [f. OF, p.p. of *feindre* feign]

fair[1] *adj.* **1.** just, unbiased, in accordance with the rules. **2.** blond, not dark, pale. **3.** of only moderate quality or amount. **4.** favourable, satisfactory, promising; unobstructed. **5.** (of a copied document) neat, without corrections. **6.** beautiful. **7.** (*slang*) complete, unquestionable. —*adv.* **1.** in a fair manner. **2.** exactly, completely. —**fair and square**, exactly; above-board, straightforward(ly). **fair game**, a thing one may reasonably or legitimately pursue etc. **fair play**, equitable conduct or conditions. **the fair sex**, women. **fair-weather friend**, a friend or ally who is unreliable in difficulties. **in a fair way to**, likely to. [OE]

fair[2] *n.* **1.** a periodical gathering for the sale of goods, often with entertainments. **2.** a fun-fair. **3.** an exhibition, especially to promote particular products. [f. OF f. L *feriae* holiday]

fairground *n.* an outdoor area where a fair is held.

fairing[1] *n.* a streamlining structure added to a ship or aircraft. [f. FAIR[1]]

fairing[2] *n.* an object bought at a fair. [f. FAIR[2]]

Fair Isle an island about half-way between the Orkneys and Shetlands, noted for the characteristic coloured designs in knitting which are named after it. There is a legend that a Spanish galleon was wrecked there after the defeat of the Armada in 1588, and that the designs were learnt from its survivors.

fairly *adv.* **1.** in a fair manner. **2.** moderately. **3.** to a noticeable degree. [f. FAIR[1]]

fairway *n.* **1.** a navigable channel. **2.** a part of a golf-course between a tee and the green, kept free of rough grass.

fairy *n.* **1.** a small imaginary being with magical powers. **2.** (*slang*) a male homosexual. —**fairy godmother**, a benefactress. **fairy lights**, small coloured lights especially for outdoor decorations. **fairy ring**, a ring of darker grass caused by fungi. **fairy story** *or* **-tale** *n.* a tale about fairies; an incredible story, a falsehood. [f. OF (as FAY, -ERY)]

fairyland /ˈfeərɪlænd/ *n.* the home of the fairies; an enchanted place.

fait accompli /feɪt əˈkɒmpliː/ a thing that has been done and is past arguing against. [F]

faith *n.* **1.** complete trust, unquestioning confidence. **2.** strong belief, especially in a religious doctrine; a system of beliefs, a religion. **3.** loyalty, trustworthiness. —**bad faith**, dishonest intention. **faith-cure, -healing**, etc., a cure etc. depending on faith rather than on medical treatment. **good faith**, sincere intention. [f. AF f. L *fides*]

faithful *adj.* **1.** showing faith; loyal, trustworthy, constant. **2.** accurate. **3. the Faithful**, believers in a religion, followers. —**faithfulness** *n.* [f. FAITH + -FUL]

faithfully *adv.* in a faithful manner. —**yours faithfully**, a formula for ending a business or formal letter. [f. prec.]

faithless *adj.* **1.** false, unreliable, disloyal. **2.** without religious faith. [f. FAITH + -LESS]

fake *n.* a thing or person that is not genuine. —*adj.* counterfeit, not genuine. —*v.t.* to make (a thing) so that it falsely appears genuine; to feign. [f. obs. *feak*, *feague* thrash f. G]

fakir /ˈfeɪkɪə(r)/ *n.* a Muslim or Hindu religious mendicant or ascetic. [Arab., = poor man]

Falasha /fæˈlɑːʃə/ *n.* (*pl.* same) a member of a group of people in Ethiopia holding the Jewish faith. After much persecution they were airlifted to Israel in 1984-5. [Amharic, = exile, immigrant]

falchion /ˈfɔːltʃ(ə)n/ *n.* a broad curved sword. [f. OF f. L *falx* scythe]

falcon /ˈfɔːlkən/ *n.* a small hawk trained to hunt game-birds for sport. [f. OF f. L *falco*]

falconry *n.* the breeding and training of hawks. [f. F (as prec.)]

Falkland Islands /ˈfɔːlklənd, ˈfɒl-/ (also **Falklands**) a group of two main islands and nearly 100 smaller ones in the South Atlantic, about 500 km (300 miles) east of the Magellan Strait. The climate is bleak, with long winters and much snow; the moors are the home of many species of bird. Most of the islanders are occupied in sheep-farming. First visited by European explorers in the late 16th c., the Falklands were successively colonized by the French and Spanish before final occupation by Britain in 1832-3, following the expulsion of an Argentinian garrison. Argentina has since refused to recognize British sovereignty and has continued to refer to the islands by their old Spanish name—the Malvinas. In 1982 an Argentinian invasion led to a two-month war ending in a successful British re-occupation.

fall /fɔːl/ *v.i.* (*past* **fell**; *p.p.* **fallen**) **1.** to go or come down freely, to descend. **2.** to cease to stand, to come suddenly to the ground from a loss of balance etc. **3.** to become detached and descend, to slope or hang down; to become lower, to subside; to lose status or position; to yield to temptation; to succumb (*to*); to be overthrown or vanquished, to perish; (of the face) to show dismay or disappointment. **4.** to take or have a particular direction or place; to come by chance or duty. **5.** to occur. **6.** to pass *in* or *into* a specified condition; to become. —*n.* **1.** the act or manner of falling; succumbing to temptation. **2.** the amount by which something falls; the amount that falls. **3.** (esp. in *pl.*) a waterfall. **4.** a wrestling-bout; a throw in this in which both shoulders touch the mat for one second. **5.** (*US*) autumn. —**the Fall (of man)**, the first act of disobedience of Adam and Eve (Gen. 2 ff.) whereby man lost his primal innocence and happiness and entered upon his actual condition of sin and toil. This belief was, from the first, part of the background against which the Christian doctrine of redemption was expounded. **fall away**, to become few or thin; to desert; to vanish. **fall back**, to retreat. **fall back on**, to have recourse to in an extremity. **fall down (on)**, to fail (in). **fall flat**, to be a failure, to fail to win applause. **fall for**, (*colloq.*) to be captivated or deceived by. **fall foul of**, to collide or quarrel with. **fall-guy** *n.* (*slang*) an easy victim, a scapegoat. **fall in**, to take or cause to take one's place in a military formation; (of a building etc.) to collapse. **fall in with**, to meet (by chance); to agree or coincide with. **fall off**, to decrease; to deteriorate. **fall on** *or* **upon**, to assault; to meet. **fall on one's feet**, to get out of a difficulty successfully. **fall out**, to quarrel; to result, to occur; to leave or cause to leave one's place in a military formation. **fall-out** *n.* radioactive debris in the air, from a nuclear explosion. **fall over**, to stumble and come to the ground. **fall over oneself**, (*colloq.*) to be eager or hasty; to be very confused. **fall short**, to be deficient or inadequate. **fall short of**, to fail to reach or obtain. **fall through**, to fail, (of a plan etc.) to come to nothing. **fall to**, to begin. [OE]

Falla /ˈfæljə/, Manuel de (1876-1946), Spanish composer and pianist. He received his musical education in his home town, Cádiz, and in Madrid, and in 1907 went to Paris, remaining until the outbreak of the First World War in becoming friends with Ravel and Debussy. In 1939, after the Spanish Civil War, during which he proclaimed himself a pacifist, he settled in Argentina. He was one of the most important representatives of Spanish nationalism abroad and his works remain popular, especially the ballet *The Three-cornered Hat* (produced by Diaghilev in 1919 with designs by Picasso).

fallacy /ˈfæləsɪ/ *n.* a mistaken belief; faulty reasoning or misleading argument; a tendency to mislead or delude. —**fallacious** /fəˈleɪʃəs/ *adj.* [f. L (*fallere* deceive)]

fallible /ˈfælɪb(ə)l/ *adj.* capable of making mistakes. —**fallibility** /-ˈbɪlɪtɪ/ *n.*, **fallibly** *adv.* [as prec.]

Fallopian tube /fəˈləʊpɪən/ either of two tubes along which egg-cells travel from the ovaries to the womb (ill. BODY 2). [f. *Fallopius*, Italian anatomist (d. 1562)]

fallow[1] /ˈfæləʊ/ *adj.* (of land) ploughed but left unsown; uncultivated. —*n.* fallow land. [OE]

fallow[2] /ˈfæləʊ/ *adj.* of a pale brownish or reddish yellow. —**fallow deer,** a species (*Dama dama*) smaller than the red deer. [OE]

false /fɔːls, fɒls/ *adj.* 1. wrong, incorrect. 2. deceitful, treacherous, unfaithful *to*; deceptive. 3. spurious, sham, artificial. 4. improperly so called. —**false alarm,** an alarm needlessly given. **False Cross,** a group of four stars in the southern sky that may be confused with the Southern Cross (ill. NAVIGATION). **false pretences,** misrepresentation with intent to deceive. **false teeth,** artificial teeth. —**falsely** *adv.*, **falseness** *n.* [f. OE & OF f. L *falsus* (*fallere* deceive)]

falsehood *n.* an untrue thing; a lie, lying. [f. prec. + -HOOD]

falsetto /fɔːlˈsetəʊ, fɒl-/ (*pl.* **-os**) an artificial voice above the normal range, especially by a male tenor. [It., dim. of *falso* false]

falsies /ˈfɔːlsɪz, ˈfɒl-/ *n.pl.* (*colloq.*) pads etc. to make the breasts seem larger. [f. FALSE]

falsify /ˈfɔːlsɪfaɪ, ˈfɒl-/ *v.t.* to alter fraudulently; to misrepresent (facts etc.). —**falsification** /-fɪˈkeɪʃ(ə)n/ *n.* [f. F or L (*falsificus* making false)]

falsity *n.* being false. [f. FALSE]

falter /ˈfɔːltə(r)/ *v.t./i.* to stumble; to move or function unsteadily; to say or speak hesitatingly; to lose strength. [orig. unkn.]

fame *n.* renown; the state of being famous; (*archaic*) reputation. [f. OF f. L *fama*]

famed *adj.* famous, much spoken of (*for*). [f. FAME]

familial /fəˈmɪlɪ(ə)l/ *adj.* of or relating to a family or its members. [F, f. L *familia* family]

familiar /fəˈmɪlɪə(r)/ *adj.* 1. well acquainted *with*. 2. well known (*to*); often encountered or experienced. 3. informal, esp. excessively so. —*n.* 1. an intimate friend. 2. a familiar spirit. —**familiar spirit,** a demon serving a witch etc. —**familiarity** /-ˈærɪtɪ/ *n.*, **familiarly** *adv.* [f. OF f. L (as FAMILY)]

familiarize /fəˈmɪlɪəraɪz/ *v.t.* 1. to make well acquainted. 2. to make well known. —**familiarization** /-ˈzeɪʃ(ə)n/ *n.* [f. F (as FAMILIAR)]

family /ˈfæmɪlɪ/ *n.* 1. a set of parents and children or of relatives; a person's children; the members of a household. 2. all the descendants of a common ancestor; lineage; a race or group of peoples from a common stock; a group of languages derived from one early language. 3. a group of objects distinguished by common features. 4. a group of allied genera of animals or plants, usually a subdivision of an order. —**family man,** one with a family; one who is fond of home life. **family name,** a surname. **family planning,** birth-control. **family tree,** a genealogical chart. **in the family way,** (*colloq.*) pregnant. [f. L *familia* household (*famulus* servant)]

famine /ˈfæmɪn/ *n.* extreme scarcity, especially of food. [f. OF f. L *fames* hunger]

famish /ˈfæmɪʃ/ *v.t./i.* to reduce or be reduced to extreme hunger. —**be famished** *or* **famishing,** (*colloq.*) to be very hungry. [f. OF (as prec.)]

famous /ˈfeɪməs/ *adj.* 1. well known, celebrated. 2. (*colloq.*) excellent. —**famously** *adv.* [f. AF & OF f. L (as FAME)]

fan[1] *n.* 1. a mechanical apparatus with rotating blades for ventilation. 2. a device (usually folding and sector-shaped when spread out) waved in the hand to cool the face etc.; anything spread out in this shape. —*v.t./i.* (**-nn-**) 1. to cool or kindle by agitating the air around; to blow gently upon. 2. to spread (*out*) in a fan shape. —**fan belt,** the belt transmitting the torque from a motor-vehicle engine to the fan which cools the radiator. **fan-jet** *n.* a turbofan. **fan tracery** *or* **vault(ing),** ornamental vaulting with fanlike ribs (ill. CHURCH). [OE, f. L *vannus* winnowing-basket]

fan[2] *n.* a devotee of a specified amusement, performer, etc. —**fan club,** one organized for a celebrity's admirers. **fan mail,** letters to a celebrity from fans. [abbr. of foll.]

fanatic /fəˈnætɪk/ *n.* a person filled with excessive and often misguided enthusiasm for something. —*adj.* excessively enthusiastic. —**fanatical** *adj.*, **fanatically** *adv.*, **fanaticism** /-ɪsɪz(ə)m/ *n.* [f. F or L (*fanum* temple)]

fancier /ˈfænsɪə(r)/ *n.* a connoisseur, an enthusiast; an amateur breeder of some plant or animal. [f. FANCY]

fanciful /ˈfænsɪf(ə)l/ *adj.* 1. existing only in imagination or fancy. 2. indulging in fancy. —**fancifully** *adv.* [f. foll. + -FUL]

fancy /ˈfænsɪ/ *n.* 1. the faculty of imagination; a mental image. 2. a supposition. 3. a caprice; a liking or whim. 4. those who have a certain hobby, fanciers. —*adj.* 1. elaborate, ornamental. 2. capricious, extravagant. —*v.t.* 1. to imagine. 2. (*colloq.*) to feel a desire for; to find sexually attractive; to have an unduly high opinion of (*oneself*, one's ability, etc.). 3. to be inclined to think (*that*). 4. to breed or grow (animals or plants) with attention to certain points. —**fancy dress,** costume for masquerading as a different person etc. at a party etc. **fancy-free** *adj.* not in love. **fancy man,** (*slang*) a woman's lover, a pimp. **fancy that!** *or* **just fancy!,** how strange! **fancy woman,** (*slang*) a mistress. [contr. of FANTASY]

fandango /fænˈdæŋɡəʊ/ *n.* (*pl.* **-oes**) a lively Spanish dance; music for this. [Sp., perh. of Black orig.]

fanfare /ˈfænfeə(r)/ *n.* a short showy or ceremonious sounding of trumpets etc. [F, imit.]

fang *n.* 1. a canine tooth, especially of a dog or wolf. 2. a serpent's venom-tooth. 3. the root of a tooth or its prong. [OE f. ON]

fanlight *n.* a small (orig. semi-circular) window over a door or other window. [f. FAN[1] + LIGHT[1]]

fanny /ˈfænɪ/ *n.* (*slang*) the female genitals; the buttocks. [orig. unkn.]

fantail *n.* a pigeon with a fan-shaped tail.

fantasia /fænˈtɑːzɪə, -ˈteɪzɪə/ *n.* a musical or other composition in which form is subordinate to imagination, or which is based on familiar tunes. [It., = fantasy]

fantasize /ˈfæntəsaɪz/ *v.t./i.* to imagine, to create a fantasy (about); to day-dream. [f. FANTASY]

fantastic /fænˈtæstɪk/ *adj.* 1. extravagantly fanciful, fabulous; grotesque, quaint. 2. (*colloq.*) excellent, extraordinary. —**fantastically** *adv.* [f. OF f. L f. Gk (as foll.)]

fantasy /ˈfæntəsɪ/ *n.* 1. imagination, especially when extravagant; a mental image, a day-dream. 2. a fanciful invention or composition, a book or film etc. relating fanciful events. [f. OF f. L f. Gk *phantasia* appearance]

far *adv.* (*compar.* **farther, further;** *superl.* **farthest, furthest**) 1. at, to, or by a great distance; a long way or a long way off in space or time. 2. to a great extent or degree, by much. —*adj.* distant, remote; more distant. —**as far as,** right to (a place); to the extent that. **by far,** by a great amount. **far and away,** by far. **far and wide,** over a large area. **far-away** *adj.* remote; (of a look) dreamy; (of a voice) sounding as if from a distance. **a far cry,** a long way. **Far East,** China, Japan, and other countries of East and SE Asia. **far-fetched** *adj.* (of an explanation etc.) strained, unconvincing. **far-flung** *adj.* extending far. **far-reaching** *adj.* of wide application or influence. **far-seeing** *adj.* showing foresight, prudent. **Far West,** the regions of North America in the Rocky Mountains and along the Pacific coast; (*formerly*) the area west of the earliest European settlements (now called the *Middle West*). **in so far as,** to the extent that. **so far,** to such an extent, to this point; until now. **so far as,** as far as; in so far as. [OE]

farad /ˈfærəd/ *n.* a unit of capacitance such that one coulomb of charge causes a potential difference of one volt. [f. foll.]

Faraday /ˈfærədeɪ/, Michael (1791-1867), English physicist and chemist, discoverer of electromagnetic induction and the concept of the classical field theory. The son of a blacksmith, he came from a poor but closely-knit family and was largely self-educated. At the age of 14 he was apprenticed to a London bookbinder and bookseller, but in 1812 he was appointed by Sir Humphry Davy his laboratory assistant at the Royal Institution. Initially, he concentrated on analytical chemistry, liquefied chlorine in 1823, discovered benzene in 1825, and studied the composition of optical glass. However, his most important work was to be in electromagnetism, a study begun in 1821 when he demonstrated electromagnetic rotation (the rotation of a wire carrying an electric current round a permanent magnet). In 1831 he discovered electromagnetic induction, the condition under which a permanent magnet could generate electricity, and the key to the development of the electric dynamo and motor. Similar investigations were performed in America by Joseph Henry (1797-1878). Central to these discoveries was Faraday's concept of magnetic lines of force, the basis of the classical field theory of electromagnetic behaviour which Clerk Maxwell was to express in mathematical form. He also discovered the two laws of electrolysis named after him, which established the relationship between electric force and matter (chemical affinity) at the molecular level, and demonstrated the connection between magnetism and light by rotating the plane of polarization of polarized light by means of a powerful electromagnet (the Faraday effect). He retired in 1862 to a house at Hampton Court provided by Queen Victoria.

farandole /færən'dəʊl/ n. a lively Provençal dance; the music for this. [F f. Prov.]

farce n. **1.** a comedy based on ludicrously improbable events; this genre of theatre. **2.** absurdly futile proceedings or pretence. —**farcical** adj., **farcically** adv. [F (orig. = stuffing) f. OF f. L farcire to stuff (with ref. to interludes)]

fare /feə(r)/ n. **1.** the price charged to a passenger on public transport; a fare-paying passenger. **2.** food provided. —v.i. to progress, to get on. [OE]

farewell /feə'wel/ int. goodbye! —n. a leave-taking.

farina /fə'raɪnə, fə'riːnə/ n. flour or meal of corn, nuts, or starchy roots. [L]

farinaceous /færɪ'neɪʃəs/ adj. of or like farina, starchy. [f. prec.]

farm n. an area of land and its buildings used under one management for growing crops, rearing animals, etc.; any place for breeding animals; a farmhouse. —v.t./i. **1.** to use (land) for growing crops, rearing animals, etc.; to breed (fish etc.) commercially; to work as a farmer. **2.** to take the proceeds of (a tax) on payment of a fixed sum. —**farm-hand** n. a worker on a farm. **farm out,** to delegate (work) to others. [f. OF f. L firma fixed payment; orig. applied to leased land]

farmer n. an owner or manager of a farm. [f. FARM]

farmhouse n. a dwelling-place attached to a farm.

farmost adj. furthest. [f. FAR]

farmstead /'fɑːmsted/ n. a farm and its buildings.

farmyard n. the yard of a farmhouse.

faro /'feərəʊ/ n. a gambling card-game. [f. F pharaon pharaoh (said to have been name of king of hearts)]

Farquhar /'fɑːkə(r)/, George (1678-1707), English writer of comedies, of which the best are *The Recruiting Officer* (1706) and *The Beaux' Stratagem* (1707). The atmosphere of realism and genial merriment in his plays contrasts markedly with the artificial comedy of the period.

farrago /fə'rɑːgəʊ/ n. (pl. **-os**) a hotchpotch, a medley. [L, = mixed fodder (far corn)]

Farrell /'færəl/, James Gordon (1935-79), English novelist. His first substantial novel, *Troubles* (1970), is set in Ireland against a background of Sinn Fein violence; *The Siege of Krishnapur* (1973) deals with events of the Indian Mutiny; and *The Singapore Grip* (1978) describes the fall of Singapore to the Japanese. These works reflect a sense of the end of the Empire and the stubborn refusal of the characters to recognize the course of history. He was accidentally drowned and left unfinished *The Hill Station* (1981).

farrier /'færɪə(r)/ n. a smith who shoes horses. —**farriery** n. [f. OF f. L ferrarius (ferrum iron, horseshoe)]

farrow /'færəʊ/ v.t./i. (of a sow) to give birth, to give birth to (pigs). —n. farrowing; a litter of pigs. [OE]

Farsi /'fɑːsɪ/ n. a language (also known as Persian), spoken by over 23 million people in Iran and Afghanistan, belonging to the Indo-Iranian language group. It is attested from the 6th c. BC when Old Persian was the language of the Persian Empire, which at one time spread from the Mediterranean to India. Old Persian was written in cuneiform, but in the 2nd c. BC the Persians created their own alphabet (Pahlavi), which remained in use until the Islamic conquest in the

7th c.; since then Persian or Farsi has been written in the Arabic script. [Pers.; cf. PARSEE]

fart v.i. (vulgar) to emit wind from the anus. —n. (vulgar) an emission of wind from the anus. [OE]

farther /'fɑːðə(r)/ adv. & adj. at or to a greater distance, more remote. [var. of FURTHER]

farthest /'fɑːðɪst/ adv. & adj. at or to the greatest distance, most remote. [var. of FURTHEST]

farthing /'fɑːðɪŋ/ n. (hist.) a quarter of a penny, a coin of this value (legal tender until 1961). [OE, f. fēortha fourth]

farthingale /'fɑːðɪŋgeɪl/ n. (hist.) a hooped petticoat (ill. DRESS). [f. F verdugale f. Sp. (verdugo rod)]

fasces /'fæsiːz/ n. a bundle of rods with a projecting axe-blade carried before an ancient Roman magistrate as a symbol of authority. [L, pl. of fascis bundle]

fascia /'feɪʃə/ n. **1.** (Archit.) a long flat surface of wood or stone. **2.** a stripe, a band. **3.** = facia. [L, = band, door-frame]

fascicle /'fæsɪk(ə)l/ n. an instalment of a book. [f. L fasciculus dim. of fascis bundle]

fascinate /'fæsɪneɪt/ v.t. **1.** to capture the interest of; to charm irresistibly. **2.** (of a snake etc.) to paralyse (a victim) with fear. —**fascination** /-'neɪʃ(ə)n/ n., **fascinator** n. [f. L fascinare (fascinum spell)]

Fascism /'fæʃɪz(ə)m/ n. an extreme right-wing totalitarian political system or such views, originally as prevailing in Italy (1922-43) where it was founded by Mussolini. It spread to other European countries (Hitler developed a more racialist brand of authoritarianism in Germany) and to South America. —**Fascist** n. & adj. [f. It. (fascio bundle, organized group, f. L fascis bundle; see FASCES)]

fashion /'fæʃ(ə)n/ n. **1.** the current popular custom or style, especially in dress. **2.** a manner of doing something. —v.t. to form or make (into). —**after a fashion,** to some extent, barely adequately. **in fashion,** fashionable at the present time. **out of fashion,** no longer fashionable. [f. AF f. L factio (facere make)]

fashionable adj. following or in keeping with the current fashion; characteristic of or patronized by fashionable people. —**fashionably** adv. [f. prec.]

fast[1] /fɑːst/ adj. **1.** moving or done quickly; enabling or causing quick motion; (of a clock etc.) showing a time later than the correct time; (of photographic film) very sensitive to light and needing only a short exposure. **2.** (of a person) immoral, dissipated. **3.** firm, fixed, firmly attached; (of a colour) not fading when washed etc.; (of a friend) close. —adv. **1.** quickly, in quick succession. **2.** firmly, tightly. —**fast breeder (reactor),** a reactor using mainly fast neutrons. **fast neutron,** a neutron with high kinetic energy. **fast one,** (slang) an unfair or deceitful action. [OE]

fast[2] /fɑːst/ v.i. to abstain from food or certain food, especially as a religious observance. —n. fasting; a period of fasting. [OE]

fasten /'fɑːs(ə)n/ v.t./i. **1.** to fix firmly, to tie or join together; to join or close up. **2.** to fix (one's glance or attention) intently. **3.** to become fastened. **fasten off,** to tie or secure the end of a thread etc. **fasten on** or **upon,** to seize on (as a victim etc.). [OE (as FAST¹)]

fastener /'fɑːsnə(r)/ n. (also **fastening**) a device that fastens something. [f. prec.]

fastidious /fæ'stɪdɪəs/ adj. very careful in matters of choice or taste; easily disgusted, squeamish. —**fastidiously** adv., **fastidiousness** n. [f. L fastidium aversion)]

fastness /'fɑːstnɪs/ n. a stronghold. [OE (as FAST¹)]

fat n. **1.** very plump; well-fed; (of an animal) made plump for slaughter. **2.** containing much fat; covered with fat. **3.** thick, substantial. **4.** fertile. —n. **1.** an oily or greasy substance found in animal bodies etc. **2.** the fat part of an animal's flesh (opp. lean). —v.t. (**-tt-**) to fatten. —**a fat chance,** (slang) very little chance. **fat-head** (colloq.) a stupid person. **the fat is in the fire,** there will be trouble. **a fat lot,** (slang) very little. **kill the fatted calf,** to celebrate, especially at a prodigal's return. **live off the fat of the land,** to live luxuriously. —**fatness** n. [OE]

fatal /'feɪt(ə)l/ adj. causing or ending in death; ruinous, disastrous, fateful. —**fatally** adv. [f. OF or L (as FATE)]

fatalism /'feɪtəlɪz(ə)m/ n. the belief that all that happens is predetermined and therefore inevitable. —**fatalist** n., **fatalistic** /-'lɪstɪk/ adj. [f. prec.]

fatality /fə'tælɪtɪ/ n. **1.** a death by accident or in war etc. **2.** a fatal influence; a predestined liability to disaster. [f. F or L (as FATAL)]

Fata Morgana /'fɑːtə mɔː'gɑːnə/ a kind of mirage most

frequently seen in the Strait of Messina between Italy and Sicily, attributed in early times to fairy agency. [It., = fairy Morgan, sister of King Arthur, whose legend was carried to Sicily by Norman settlers, where her reputation as an enchantress survived so that by the 19th c. the mirages were attributed to her agency]

fate *n.* **1.** an irresistible power or force controlling all events. **2.** what is destined; a person's destiny or fortune; death, destruction. —*v.t.* (esp. in *pass.*) to preordain. [f. It. & L *fatum*]

fateful *adj.* controlled by fate; decisive, important. —**fatefully** *adv.* [f. FATE + -FUL]

Fates /feɪts/ *n.pl.* (*Gk myth.*) the goddesses who presided over the birth and life of men. The gods were thought of as spinning, with a thread, the great realities—death, trouble, riches, homecoming—around a man, as if he were a spindle. From this image come the 'harsh spinners', usually three: Clotho who presided over the moment of a man's birth and held a distaff, Lachesis who with her spindle spun out the events and actions of his life, and Atropos who cut the thread of human life with her shears. [pl. of FATE]

father /ˈfɑːðə(r)/ *n.* **1.** a male parent; a male guardian through adoption. **2.** (usually in *pl.*) a forefather; a founder or originator, an early leader; (in *pl.*) elders, leading members. **3. Father**, God, especially the first person of the Trinity. **4.** a priest, especially of a religious order, or as a title or form of address. **5.** venerable person, especially as a title in personifications. —*v.t.* **1.** to beget; to originate (a scheme etc.). **2.** to fix the paternity of (a child) or the responsibility for (a book, idea, etc.) *on* or *upon*. —**father-figure** *n.* an older man who is respected like a father, a trusted leader. **father-in-law** *n.* (*pl.* **fathers-in-law**) one's wife's or husband's father. **Father of the House**, the member of the House of Commons with the longest continuous service. **Father's Day**, a day (usually the third Sunday in June) for a special tribute to fathers. **Fathers (of the Church)**, those early ecclesiastical writers, especially of the first five centuries, whose writings on Christian doctrines were regarded as especially authoritative. —**fatherhood** *n.* [OE]

Father Christmas the personification of Christmas as a benevolent old man with a flowing white beard, wearing a red gown and hood trimmed with white fur, and carrying a sack of Christmas presents. Traditionally he arrives from the far north, but his origin is obscure and his attributes are comparatively recent. In late medieval Europe he became associated with St Nicholas (Santa Claus). In England Father Christmas was not St Nicholas but a personification of Christmas, a genial red-robed old man, who appeared in many 16th-c. masques and in mumming plays. He was not then a gift-bringer, but acquired that attribute from St Nicholas in the 19th c. when there was a great revival of Christmas festivities.

fatherland *n.* one's native country.

fatherly *adj.* of or like a father. [f. FATHER]

fathom /ˈfæð(ə)m/ *n.* a measure of 6 feet, especially in soundings. —*v.t.* **1.** to understand. **2.** to measure the depth of (water). [OE, = the outstretched arms]

fatigue /fəˈtiːg/ *n.* **1.** extreme tiredness. **2.** weakness in metals etc. from variations of stress. **3.** a soldier's non-combatant duty; (in *pl.*) clothing worn for this. —*v.t.* to cause fatigue in; to tire. [f. F f. L *fatigare* exhaust]

Fatima /ˈfætɪmə/ (d. 632) daughter of the Prophet Muhammad and wife of Ali ibn Abi Talib, fourth caliph of the Muslim community. The descendants of Muhammad all trace their lineage through her, and she is revered especially by Shiite Muslims as the mother of the imams Hasan and Husayn.

Fatimite /ˈfætɪmaɪt/ (also **Fatimid**) *adj.* of an Arabian dynasty claiming descent from Fatima (see prec.) which ruled in parts of northern Africa from 908 to 1171, and during some of that period in Egypt and Syria. —*n.* a member of this dynasty. [f. prec.]

fatstock *n.* livestock fattened for slaughter.

fatten *v.t./i.* to make or become fat. [f. FAT]

fatty *adj.* like or containing fat. —**fatty acid,** a member of a series of acids occurring in or derived from natural fats etc. [f. FAT]

fatuous /ˈfætjʊəs/ *adj.* silly, purposeless. —**fatuity** /fəˈtjuːɪtɪ/ *n.*, **fatuously** *adv.* [f. L *fatuus*]

faucet /ˈfɔːsɪt/ *n.* a tap for a barrel etc.; (*US*) any tap. [f. F *fausset* vent-peg f. Prov. (*falsar* bore)]

Faulkner /ˈfɔːknə(r)/, William (1897-1962), American novelist, born in Mississippi. The history and legends of the South and of his own family provided material for his greatest books. Among his novels set in Jefferson in the mythical county of Yoknapatawpha County (Mississippi) are *Sartoris* (1929) and his tour-de-force, *The Sound and the Fury* (1929), in which Faulkner views the decline of the South through the eyes of 33-year-old 'idiot' Benjay. This work displays a technical brilliance which he further demonstrated in *As I Lay Dying* (1930), and with *Absalom, Absalom!* (1936) he confirmed his reputation as one of the finest of modern novelists. His several volumes of short stories were collected in 1950. He was awarded the Nobel Prize for literature in 1949.

fault /fɔːlt, fɒlt/ *n.* **1.** a defect or blemish. **2.** an offence or misdeed; the responsibility or blame for this; (in tennis etc.) an incorrect serve; (in show-jumping) a penalty for an error. **3.** a break in the continuity of rock strata (ill. GEOLOGY). —*v.t./i.* **1.** to find fault with, to blame. **2.** to cause a fault in (rock strata); (of rock) to have a fault. —**at fault,** blameworthy. **find fault with,** to criticize unfavourably. **to a fault,** excessively. [f. OF f. L *fallere* deceive]

faultless *adj.* without faults. —**faultlessly** *adv.* [f. FAULT + -LESS]

faulty *adj.* having a fault or faults, imperfect. —**faultily** *adv.*, **faultiness** *n.* [f. FAULT]

faun /fɔːn/ *n.* a Latin rural deity with a goat's horns, legs, and tail. [f. OF or L *Faunus*, Latin god identified with Gk Pan]

fauna /ˈfɔːnə/ *n.* (*pl.* **-as**) the animals of a particular region or period. [f. name of rural goddess, sister of Faunus (see prec.)]

Fauntleroy /ˈfɔːntlərɔɪ/ the gentle hero of Francis Hodgson Burnett's novel *Little Lord Fauntleroy* (1885). The name is applied to the style of dress (velvet suits with lace collars and cuffs) which the book popularized.

Fauré /ˈfɔːreɪ/, Gabriel (1845-1924), French composer and organist, director of the Conservatoire in Paris until increasing deafness forced him to retire in 1920. He composed songs throughout his career, creating delicate miniatures in 'Lydia' and 'Clair de lune' and an elegiac masterpiece in the song-cycle *La bonne Chanson* (1892-4). He was also successful with large-scale works, such as the Requiem Mass (1887-9) and the opera *Pénélope* (1913), but his restrained style and general lack of interest in dramatic effect prevented his recognition as a great French composer until after the Second World War.

Faust /faʊst/ a wandering astronomer and necromancer who lived in Germany *c.*1488-1541 and was reputed to have sold his soul to the Devil. He was the hero of dramas by Marlowe and Goethe and of a novel by Thomas Mann. —**Faustian** *adj.*

faute de mieux /fəʊt də ˈmjɜː/ for want of any better alternative. [F]

fauve /fəʊv/ *n.* a member of a movement in painting, chiefly associated with Matisse, which flourished in Paris from 1905, characterized mainly by a vivid and arbitrary use of colour, with strident dissonances to express feelings and emotions. The name was coined by the French art critic Louis Vauxcelles at the Autumn Salon of 1905; coming across a quattrocento-like statue in the midst of works by Matisse and his associates, he remarked, 'Donatello au milieu des fauves!' Fauvism was one of the reactions against impressionism; its adherents included Dufy, Derain, and Vlaminck. The movement petered out *c.*1909, but had an important influence on the use of colour by subsequent artists. —**fauvism** *n.*, **fauvist** *n.* [F, = wild beast]

faux pas /fəʊ ˈpɑː/ *n.* (*pl.* same /ˈpɑːz/) a tactless mistake, a blunder. [F, = false step]

favour /ˈfeɪvə(r)/ *n.* **1.** liking, goodwill, approval. **2.** a kind or helpful act. **3.** partiality. **4.** a badge or ornament worn as a mark of favour. —*v.t.* **1.** to regard or treat with favour or partiality. **2.** to support, to promote, to prefer; to oblige *with*; to be to the advantage of, to facilitate. **3.** (*colloq.*) to resemble in features. **4.** (in *p.p.*) having special advantages; having specified looks. —**in** or **out of favour,** approved or disapproved of. **in favour of,** in support of; to the advantage of. [f. OF f. L *favor* (*favēre* show goodwill to)]

favourable *adj.* **1.** well disposed, approving. **2.** pleasing. **3.** satisfactory; helpful, suitable. —**favourably** *adv.* [as prec.]

favourite /ˈfeɪvərɪt/ *adj.* preferred to all others. —*n.* a favourite person or thing, especially a person favoured by a monarch or superior; (in sport) a competitor thought most likely to win. [f. obs. F f. It. (as FAVOUR)]

favouritism n. unfair favouring of one person or group at the expense of another. [f. prec.]

Fawkes /fɔːks/, Guy (1570–1606), a conspirator in the Gunpowder Plot of 1605, recruited for his ability to deal with gunpowder.

fawn[1] n. **1.** a deer in its first year. **2.** a light yellowish-brown colour. —adj. fawn-coloured. —v.t. to give birth to (a fawn). [f. OF f. L *fetus* offspring]

fawn[2] v.i. (esp. of a dog etc.) to try to win affection by grovelling etc.; to lavish caresses (on or upon); to behave servilely. [OE (as FAIN)]

fay n. (literary) a fairy. [f. OF f. L *fata* the Fates]

FBA abbr. Fellow of the British Academy.

FBI abbr. (US) Federal Bureau of Investigation.

Fe symbol iron.

fealty /ˈfiːəltɪ/ n. the duty of a feudal tenant or vassal to his lord; allegiance. [f. OF f. L (as FIDELITY)]

fear n. **1.** an unpleasant emotion caused by exposure to danger, the expectation of pain, etc.; alarm. **2.** awe and reverence. **3.** a danger, a likelihood. —v.t./i. **1.** to have fear, to expect with fear or anxiety; to be afraid of; to shrink from (doing). —**no fear!**, (colloq.) certainly not! [OE, = sudden calamity, danger]

fearful adj. **1.** afraid, reluctant through fear. **2.** causing fear. **3.** (colloq.) extreme, annoying. —**fearfully** adv. [f. prec. + -FUL]

fearless adj. without fear, brave. —**fearlessly** adv., **fearlessness** n. [f. FEAR + -LESS]

fearsome adj. frightening, formidable. [f. FEAR + -SOME]

feasible /ˈfiːzɪb(ə)l/ adj. practicable, possible. —**feasibility** /-ˈbɪlɪtɪ/ n., **feasibly** adv. [f. OF f. L *facere* do]

feast n. **1.** a large meal, a banquet. **2.** a joyful religious festival. **3.** something giving great pleasure. —v.t./i. **1.** to partake of a feast, to eat and drink heartily (on). **2.** to give a feast to. **3.** to give pleasure to, to regale. [f. OF f. L (*festus* festal)]

feat n. a remarkable act or achievement. [f. OF f. L (as FACT)]

feather /ˈfeðə(r)/ n. **1.** any of the appendages growing from a bird's skin, with a horny stem and fine strands on both sides; a piece of this as a decoration etc. **2.** (collect.) plumage; game-birds. —v.t./i. **1.** to cover or line with feathers. **2.** to turn (an oar) so that it passes through the air edgeways; to make this movement. —**feather bed**, a mattress stuffed with feathers. **feather-bed** v.t. to make things easy for, to pamper. **feather-brained, -headed** adjs. silly. **feather in one's cap**, an achievement to one's credit. **feather one's nest**, to enrich oneself. **in fine** or **high feather**, in good spirits. —**feathery** adj. [OE]

feathering n. **1.** plumage. **2.** the feathers of an arrow. **3.** a feather-like structure or marking. [f. prec.]

featherweight n. **1.** a boxing-weight between bantamweight and lightweight (see BOXING-WEIGHT). **2.** a person or thing of very light weight.

feature /ˈfiːtʃə(r)/ n. **1.** (usu. in pl.) a part of the face, especially with regard to the appearance. **2.** a characteristic or notable part of a thing. **3.** a prominent article in a newspaper etc. **4.** a feature film. —v.t./i. **1.** to give prominence to. **2.** to be a feature of. **3.** to be a participant (in). —**feature film**, the main film in a cinema programme. [f. OF f. L *factura* formation (*facere* make)]

featureless adj. lacking distinct features. [f. prec. + -LESS]

Feb. abbr. February.

febrile /ˈfiːbraɪl/ adj. of a fever, feverish. [f. F or L (*febris* fever)]

February /ˈfebruərɪ/ n. the second month of the year. [f. OF f. L (*februa* purification feast held in this month)]

Fechner /ˈfexnə(r)/, Gustav Theodor (1801–87), German poet, physicist, and psychologist, who sought to define the quantitative relationship between degrees of physical stimulation and the resulting sensation, the study of which he termed 'psycho-physics' (1859). By associating sensations with numerical values, he hoped to make psychology a truly objective science.

feckless adj. feeble, incompetent, helpless. —**fecklessness** n. [f. Sc. *feck* (*effeck* var. of EFFECT) + -LESS]

fecund /ˈfiːkənd/ adj. prolific, fertile; fertilizing. —**fecundity** /fɪˈkʌndɪtɪ/ n. [f. F or L *fecundus* fruitful]

fecundate /ˈfiːkəndeɪt/ v.t. to make fecund, to fertilize. —**fecundation** /-ˈdeɪʃ(ə)n/ n. [f. L *fecundare* (as prec.)]

fed past & p.p. of FEED.

federal /ˈfedər(ə)l/ adj. **1.** of a system of government in which several States unite but remain independent in internal affairs; of such States or their central government. **2.** relating to or favouring central as opposed to provincial government. **3.** **Federal**, (US) of the northern States in the American Civil War. —**federalism** n., **federalist** n., **federally** adv. [f. L (*foedus* covenant)]

federalize v.t. to make federal, to organize in a federal system. —**federalization** /-ˈzeɪʃ(ə)n/ n. [f. prec.]

federate /ˈfedəreɪt/ v.t./i. to unite on a federal basis or for a common object. —/ˈfedərət/ adj. so united. [f. L *foederare* (as FEDERAL)]

federation /fedəˈreɪʃ(ə)n/ n. **1.** an act of federating. **2.** a federal group. —**federative** /ˈfedərətɪv/ adj. [f. F f. L (as FEDERAL)]

fee n. **1.** the sum payable to an official or professional person for services; the charge for joining a society, taking an examination, etc.; the money paid for the transfer to another employer of a footballer etc.; (in pl.) regular payment for instruction at a school etc. **2.** an inherited estate of land, unlimited (**fee simple**) or limited (**fee-tail**) as to the class of heir. [f. AF f. L *feudum*, perh. f. Frankish *fehu-od* cattle-property]

feeble adj. weak; lacking strength, energy, or effectiveness. —**feeble-minded** adj. mentally deficient. —**feebleness** n., **feebly** adv. [f. OF f. L *flebilis* lamentable]

feed v.t. (past & p.p. **fed**) **1.** to supply with food, to put food into the mouth of; to give as food to animals. **2.** (esp. of animals or babies, or colloq.) to take food, to eat. **3.** to maintain a supply of (material required into a machine etc.), to keep (a machine, fire, etc.) supplied thus. **4.** to gratify; to encourage with. **5.** to send passes to (a player) in football etc. —n. **1.** food for animals; a measured allowance of this. **2.** feeding. **3.** a meal (esp. for babies, or colloq.). **4.** material supplied to machines etc. —**fed up**, (colloq.) discontented or bored (with). **feed on**, to consume; to be nourished or strengthened by. [OE]

feedback n. **1.** return to the input of a part of the output of a system or process; a signal so returned. **2.** information about the result of an experiment etc.; response.

feeder n. **1.** one that feeds in a specified way. **2.** the feeding apparatus in a machine. **3.** a child's bib. **4.** a tributary, branch road, branch railway line, etc., that links with the main system. [f. prec.]

feel v.t./i. (past & p.p. **felt**) **1.** to examine or search by touch; to perceive by touch, to have a sensation of. **2.** to be conscious of (an emotion etc.). **3.** to experience, to be affected by (an emotion or physical condition). **4.** to seem, to give an impression of being. **5.** to have a vague or emotional impression; to consider, to think; to be consciously, to consider oneself. **6.** to sympathize with, to have pity for. —n. **1.** an act of feeling; the sense of touch. **2.** the sensation characterizing a material, situation, etc. —**feel like**, (colloq.) to have a wish for, to be inclined towards. **feel one's way**, to proceed cautiously (lit. or fig.). [OE]

feeler n. **1.** an organ in certain animals for testing things by touch. **2.** a tentative proposal or suggestion. —**feeler gauge**, a gauge with blades that can be inserted to measure gaps. [f. prec.]

feeling n. **1.** the capacity to feel, the sense of touch. **2.** an emotion; (in pl.) emotional susceptibility. **3.** an opinion or notion. **4.** sympathy with others. **5.** earnestness. —adj. sensitive, sympathetic; heartfelt. [f. FEEL]

feet pl. of FOOT.

feign /feɪn/ v.t. to pretend; to simulate. [f. OF f. L *fingere* mould, fashion]

feint /feɪnt/ n. a sham attack, blow, etc. to divert an opponent's attention from the main attack; a pretence. —v.i. to make a feint. —adj. (of paper etc.) having faintly ruled lines. [f. F (as prec.)]

feldspar /ˈfeldspɑː(r)/ n. any of a group of usually white or flesh-red rock-forming minerals which are aluminium silicates combined with various other metallic ions. The feldspar group is the most widespread of any group of minerals, making up about 60 per cent of the earth's crustal material. [f. G *feldspat(h)* (*feld* field, *spat(h)* spar)]

felicitate /fɪˈlɪsɪteɪt/ v.t. to congratulate. [f. L *felicitare* make very happy (*felix* happy)]

felicitation /fɪlɪsɪˈteɪʃ(ə)n/ n. (usu. in pl.) a congratulation. [f. prec.]

felicitous /fɪˈlɪsɪtəs/ adj. well-chosen, apt. —**felicitously** adv. [f. foll.]

felicity /fɪˈlɪsɪtɪ/ *n.* **1.** great happiness. **2.** a pleasing manner or style. [f. OF f. L (*felix* happy)]

feline /ˈfiːlaɪn/ *adj.* of cats; catlike. —*n.* an animal of the cat family. —**felinity** /fɪˈlɪnɪtɪ/ *n.* [f. L (*feles* cat)]

fell[1] *v.t.* **1.** to cut down (a tree); to strike down by a blow or cut. **2.** to stitch down (the edge of a seam). [OE (causative of FALL)]

fell[2] *n.* a hill; a stretch of hills or moorland, especially in northern England. [ON]

fell[3] *adj.* ruthless, destructive. —**at one fell swoop,** in a single (deadly) action. [f. OF (as FELON)]

fell[4] *n.* an animal's skin or hide with the hair. [OE]

fell[5] *past* of FALL.

fellatio /feˈlɑːtɪəʊ/ *n.* stimulation of the penis by sucking. [f. L *fellare* suck]

fellow /ˈfeləʊ/ *n.* **1.** a comrade or associate. **2.** a counterpart, an equal. **3.** (*colloq.*) a man or boy. **4.** an incorporated senior member of a college; a research student receiving a fellowship. **5.** a member of a learned society. —*attrib.* or *adj.* of the same class, associated in a joint action. —**fellow-feeling** *n.* sympathy with a person whose experience etc. one shares. **fellow-traveller** *n.* a sympathizer with but not a member of a political (esp. the Communist) party. [OE f. ON]

fellowship *n.* **1.** friendly association with others, companionship. **2.** a body of associates. **3.** the position or income of a fellow of a college or learned society; the stipend granted to a graduate for a period of research. [f. prec.]

felon /ˈfelən/ *n.* one who has committed a felony. [f. OF f. L *fel(l)o* (orig. unkn.)]

felony /ˈfelənɪ/ *n.* (*hist.*) any of a class of crimes which may loosely be said to have been regarded by the law as of graver character than those called misdemeanours. The class (which included murder, wounding, arson, rape, and robbery) comprised those offences the penalty of which formerly included forfeiture of land and goods, together with others added to the list by statute. Forfeiture was abolished in 1870, but procedural differences applied until 1967 when (in English law) all distinctions between felonies and misdemeanours were removed; the distinction never existed in Scotland. In the USA most jurisdictions distinguish between felonies and misdemeanours, the distinction usually depending on the penalties or consequences attaching to the crime. —**felonious** /fɪˈləʊnɪəs/ *adj.*, **feloniously** *adv.* [f. OF (as prec.)]

felspar var. of FELDSPAR.

felt[1] *n.* a cloth of matted and pressed fibres of wool etc. —*v.t./i.* to make into felt; to cover with felt; to become matted. —**felt(-tip** *or* **-tipped) pen,** a pen with a felt point. [OE]

felt[2] *past & p.p.* of FEEL.

felucca /fɪˈlʌkə/ *n.* a small ship with lateen sails and/or oars, used on Mediterranean coasts. [f. It. f. Sp. f. Arab., perh. f. Gk *epholkion* small boat towed after a ship]

female /ˈfiːmeɪl/ *adj.* **1.** of the sex that can bear offspring or produce eggs; (of plants) fruit-bearing; of women or female animals or plants. **2.** (of a screw, socket, etc.) made hollow to receive the corresponding inserted part. —*n.* a female person, animal, or plant. [f. OF f. L *femella* (*femina* woman), assim. to MALE]

feminine /ˈfemɪnɪn/ *adj.* **1.** of a woman; having qualities associated with women. **2.** (*Gram.*) of or denoting the gender proper to women's names. **3.** (of a rhyme or line-ending) having a stressed syllable followed by an unstressed one. —*n.* the feminine gender; a feminine word. —**femininity** /-ˈnɪnɪtɪ/ *n.* [f. OF or L (*femina* woman)]

feminism /ˈfemɪnɪz(ə)m/ *n.* advocacy of women's rights on the basis of the equality of the sexes. —**feminist** *n.* [as prec.]

femme fatale /fæm fæˈtɑːl/ *n.* a dangerously attractive woman. [F]

femto- /ˈfemtəʊ-/ *in comb.* denoting a factor of 10^{-15} (*femtometre*). [f. Da. or Norw. *femten* fifteen]

femur /ˈfiːmə(r)/ *n.* the thigh-bone (ill. BODY 1). —**femoral** /ˈfemər(ə)l/ *adj.* [L, = thigh]

fen *n.* a low marshy area of land. —**the Fens,** low-lying districts of Lincolnshire, Cambridgeshire, and neighbouring counties in eastern England. Formerly marshland, they have been drained for agriculture since the 17th c., originally by Dutch engineers. [OE]

fence *n.* **1.** a barrier or railing enclosing a field, garden, etc.; a structure for a horse to jump over in a competition etc. **2.** a guard or guide or gauge in a machine. **3.** a dealer in stolen goods. —*v.t./i.* **1.** to surround (as) with a fence; to enclose or separate with a fence. **2.** to practise the sport of fencing; to be evasive, to parry. **3.** to deal in (stolen goods). [f. DEFENCE]

fencing /ˈfensɪŋ/ *n.* **1.** fences; material for fences. **2.** the sport of fighting with foils or other kinds of sword. Skilful use of a sword according to established rules and movements was practised by the ancient Egyptians, Persians, Greeks, and Romans not only in war but as a pastime. [f. prec.]

fend *v.t./i.* **1.** to ward *off*, to repel. **2.** to provide *for*. [f. DEFEND]

fender *n.* **1.** a low frame bordering a fireplace to keep in falling coals etc. **2.** a pad or bundle of rope etc. hung over a vessel's side to protect it against impact. **3.** (*US*) the bumper of a motor vehicle. [f. prec.]

fenestella /fenɪˈstelə/ *n.* a niche in a church wall south of the altar holding a piscina and often a credence (ill. VESTMENTS). [L, dim. of *fenestra* window]

Fenian /ˈfiːnɪən/ *n.* a member of the Irish Republican Brotherhood, a revolutionary nationalist organization founded in the USA in 1858 by James Stephens, a veteran of the failed 1848 Irish uprising. The Fenians staged an unsuccessful revolt in Ireland in 1867 and were responsible for isolated revolutionary acts against the British until the early 20th c., when they were gradually eclipsed by the IRA. —*adj.* of Fenians or Fenianism. —**Fenianism** *n.* [f. Ir. *féne* name of ancient Irish people, confused with *fíann* guard of legendary kings]

fennel /ˈfen(ə)l/ *n.* a yellow-flowered herb (*Foeniculum vulgare*) used for flavouring. [OE & f. OF f. L *faeniculum*]

fenny *adj.* characterized by fens. [f. FEN]

fenugreek /ˈfenjuːɡriːk/ *n.* a leguminous plant (*Trigonella foenum-graecum*) with aromatic seeds. [f. OF f. L, = Greek hay]

feoff /fef/ *n.* a fief. [AF var. of FIEF]

feral /ˈfɪər(ə)l/ *adj.* wild; uncultivated; in a wild state after escape from captivity; brutal. [f. L *ferus* wild]

Ferdinand /ˈfɜːdɪnənd/ (1452–1516), king of Spain. A prince of the House of Aragon, Ferdinand married Isabella of Castile in 1469 and succeeded to the throne of Castile (as Ferdinand V) with her in 1474. When he became king of Aragon (as Ferdinand II) in 1479 he effectively united Spain as one country. While on the throne he waged the final war against the Moors (1482–92), capturing Granada and ending Muslim rule in the Iberian peninsula. He and his wife earned the title 'the Catholic Kings'.

ferial /ˈfɪərɪəl/ *adj.* (of a day) not a festival or fast. [f. OF or L *ferialis* (*feriae* holiday)]

Ferm. *abbr.* Fermanagh.

Fermanagh /fəˈmænə/ a county of Northern Ireland.

Fermat /ˈfeəmɑː/, Pierre de (1601–65), French lawyer and counsellor, whose professional activities were overshadowed by his success and fame as a mathematician. His study of the problems of finding tangents to curves, finding areas under curves, and maxima and minima, led directly to the general methods of the calculus introduced by Newton and Leibnitz. He made many beautiful discoveries about integers, for which he is seen as the founder of the theory of numbers. His most famous assertion is that if n is greater than 2 then there is no integer whose nth power can be expressed as the sum of two smaller nth powers. This statement, known as Fermat's Last Theorem, attracts more attention from both professionals and amateurs than any other mathematical problem, but after more than 300 years it has still been neither proved nor disproved.

ferment /ˈfɜːment/ *n.* **1.** fermentation; a fermenting agent. **2.** excitement. —/fəˈment/ *v.t./i.* **1.** to undergo or subject to fermentation. **2.** to excite. [f. OF or L *fermentum* (*fervēre* boil)]

fermentation /fɜːmenˈteɪʃ(ə)n/ *n.* **1.** a chemical change involving effervescence and the production of heat, induced by an organic substance such as yeast. **2.** excitement. —**fermentative** /fəˈmentətɪv/ *adj.* [f. L (as prec.)]

Fermi /ˈfɜːmɪ/, Enrico (1901–54), Italian-born American atomic physicist, a key figure in the development of the atomic bomb and nuclear energy. Working at first in his native Italy, he established the statistical laws—found independently by Paul Dirac—which apply to the particles forming the atom, a mathematical tool of great value in atomic, nuclear, and solid-state physics. In 1934 he began work on artificial radioactivity, predicted the existence of the neutrino, and produced radioactive isotopes by bombarding the atomic nuclei of elements with neutrons; this work was to culminate in the discovery of nuclear fission by Hahn and Fritz Strassmann in 1938. In that year Fermi was awarded the Nobel Prize for physics, and left Italy to escape Fascist persecution, settling in the USA. He directed the first controlled nuclear chain reaction at the University of Chicago in December 1942, joined the Manhattan Project, and worked on the atomic bomb at Los Alamos. The artificial element fermium and a class of sub-atomic particles, the fermions, are named after him.

fermion /ˈfɜːmɪɒn/ n. a particle obeying the relations stated by Fermi and Dirac, with half-integral spin. [f. prec.]

fermium /ˈfɜːmɪəm/ n. an artificially made transuranic radioactive metallic element, symbol Fm, atomic number 100, identified in 1953 in debris from the first hydrogen bomb explosion. [f. E. FERMI]

fern n. a kind of flowerless plant, usually with feathery fronds. —**ferny** adj. [OE]

ferocious /fəˈrəʊʃəs/ adj. fierce, savage. —**ferociously** adv., **ferocity** /fəˈrɒsɪtɪ/ n. [f. L ferox]

Ferranti /fəˈræntɪ/, Sebastian Ziani de (1864–1930), English electrical engineer, one of the great pioneers of electricity generation and distribution in Britain, his particular contribution being the use of high voltages for economical transmission over a distance.

ferret /ˈfɛrɪt/ n. a variety of the common polecat, used in catching rabbits, rats, etc. —v.t./i. 1. to hunt with ferrets. 2. to rummage, to search. —**ferret out,** to discover or produce by searching. [f. OF f. L (fur thief)]

ferric /ˈfɛrɪk/ adj. of iron; containing iron in trivalent form. [f. L ferrum iron]

Ferris wheel /ˈfɛrɪs/ a giant revolving vertical wheel with passenger cars on its periphery, used for rides at fun-fairs etc. [f. name of inventor G. W. G. Ferris, Amer. engineer (d. 1896)]

ferro- in comb. containing iron; of iron. [as FERRIC]

ferroconcrete /fɛrəʊˈkɒnkriːt/ n. reinforced concrete.

ferromagnetism /fɛrəʊˈmægnɪtɪz(ə)m/ n. a form of magnetism found in substances (such as iron, cobalt, nickel, and their alloys) with high magnetic permeability and with some ability to retain their magnetization after the magnetizing field is removed. —**ferromagnetic** /-mægˈnɛtɪk/ adj.

ferrous /ˈfɛrəs/ adj. containing iron; containing iron in divalent form. [f. L ferrum iron]

ferrule /ˈfɛruːl, -uːl/ n. a metal ring or cap strengthening the end of a stick etc. [f. OF virelle f. L (viriae bracelet)]

ferry /ˈfɛrɪ/ v.t./i. 1. to go or convey in a boat across water; (of a boat) to pass to and fro across water. 2. to transport from one place to another, especially as a regular service. —n. a boat etc. used for ferrying; the place or service of ferrying. —**ferryman** n. [f. ON]

fertile /ˈfɜːtaɪl/ adj. 1. (of soil) rich in the materials needed to support vegetation; fruitful (lit. or fig.). 2. (of animals and plants) able to produce young or fruit. 3. (of seeds or eggs) capable of developing into a new plant or animal. 4. (of the mind) easily producing ideas, inventive. 5. (of nuclear material) able to become fissile by the capture of neutrons. —**Fertile Crescent,** a crescent-shaped area of cultivable land extending from the eastern Mediterranean via the fertile steppe between the Arabian Desert and the mountains of Asia Minor to the Tigris-Euphrates valley and the Persian Gulf. —**fertility** /fəˈtɪlɪtɪ/ n. [f. F f. L fertilis]

fertilize /ˈfɜːtɪlaɪz/ v.t. 1. to make (soil etc.) fertile. 2. to introduce pollen or sperm into (a plant, egg, or female animal) so that seed or young develops. —**fertilization** /-ˈzeɪʃ(ə)n/ n. [f. prec.]

fertilizer n. a chemical or natural substance added to soil to make it more fertile. [f. prec.]

fervent /ˈfɜːv(ə)nt/ adj. ardent, impassioned. —**fervency** n., **fervently** adv. [f. OF f. L (fervēre boil)]

fervid /ˈfɜːvɪd/ adj. fervent. —**fervidly** adv. [f. L (as prec.)]

fervour /ˈfɜːvə(r)/ n. passion, zeal. [as FERVENT]

fescue /ˈfɛskjuː/ n. a grass of the genus Festuca, valuable for pasture and fodder. [f. OF f. L festuca stalk, straw]

fess n. (in heraldry) a horizontal stripe across the middle of a shield, broader than a bar (ill. HERALDRY). [f. OF f. L fascia band]

festal /ˈfɛst(ə)l/ adj. of a feast or festival; joyous. —**festally** adv. [f. OF f. L (as FEAST)]

fester v.t./i. 1. to make or become septic. 2. to cause continuing annoyance. 3. to rot, to stagnate. [f. OF f. L fistula pipe, flute]

festival /ˈfɛstɪv(ə)l/ n. 1. a day or time of celebration. 2. a cultural event comprising a series of concerts, plays, films, etc., held regularly. [f. OF f. L (as foll.)]

festive /ˈfɛstɪv/ adj. of or characteristic of a festival; joyous. —**festively** adv. [f. L (festum, as FEAST)]

festivity /fɛˈstɪvɪtɪ/ n. gaiety, festive celebration; (in pl.) festive proceedings. [f. OF or L (as prec.)]

festoon /fɛˈstuːn/ n. a chain of flowers, ribbons, etc., hung in a curve as a decoration; something arranged similarly. —v.t. to adorn with or form into festoons. [f. F f. It. (as FEAST)]

Festschrift /ˈfɛstʃrɪft/ n. a published collection of writings in honour of a scholar. [G, = festival-writing]

fetch /fɛtʃ/ v.t./i. 1. to go for and bring back. 2. to cause to come, to draw forth; to be sold for (a price). 3. (colloq.) to deal (a blow etc.). 4. (Naut.) to arrive at; to sail close-hauled without tacking. —n. 1. an act of fetching. 2. a dodge, a trick. —**fetch up,** (colloq.) to arrive, to stop; to vomit. [OE]

fetching adj. attractive. [f. prec.]

fête /feɪt/ n. an outdoor function with a sale of goods, amusements, etc., especially to raise funds for some purpose. —v.t. to honour or entertain lavishly. [F (as FEAST)]

fetid /ˈfɛtɪd, ˈfiːt-/ adj. stinking. [f. L (fetēre stink)]

fetish /ˈfɛtɪʃ/ n. 1. an object worshipped as magical by primitive peoples. 2. a thing evoking irrational devotion or respect. 3. a thing abnormally stimulating or attracting sexual desire. —**fetishism** n., **fetishist** n. [f. F f. Port. feitiço charm, orig. adj. = made by art, f. L facticius]

fetlock n. the part of the back of a horse's leg above the hoof where a tuft of hair grows (ill. HORSE). [rel. to G fessel pastern]

fetter /ˈfɛtə(r)/ n. a shackle for holding a prisoner by the ankle; a bond, (in pl.) captivity; a restraint. —v.t. to put into fetters; to restrict. [OE, rel. to FOOT]

fettle n. condition, trim. [OE, = girdle]

fetus /ˈfiːtəs/ var. of FOETUS.

feu /fjuː/ n. (Sc.) a perpetual lease at a fixed rent; land so held. —v.t. (Sc.) to grant (land) on feu. [f. OF (as FEE)]

feud[1] /fjuːd/ n. a prolonged mutual hostility, especially between families or groups. —v.i. to conduct a feud. [f. OF f. MDu. (rel. to FOE)]

feud[2] /fjuːd/ n. a fief. [f. L feudum (as FEE)]

feudal /ˈfjuːd(ə)l/ adj. of, resembling, or according to the feudal system. —**feudal system,** a medieval European politico-economic system based on the relation of vassal and superior arising from the holding of lands on condition of homage and military service or labour. The nobility held lands from the Crown in exchange for a specified amount of military service; the peasantry lived on their lord's land and had to provide him with labour or a share of his own produce in exchange for protection. The feudal system began to break down in England in the 13th and 14th c., although feudal tenures were not actually abolished by statute until 1666. —**feudalism** n., **feudalist** n., **feudalistic** /-ˈlɪstɪk/ adj. [f. L feudalis (as prec.)]

fever /ˈfiːvə(r)/ n. 1. an abnormally high body temperature, often with delirium; a disease characterized by this. 2. nervous agitation or excitement. —v.t. to affect with fever or excitement. —**fever pitch,** a state of extreme excitement. [f. OE & AF f. L febris]

feverfew /ˈfiːvəfjuː/ n. an aromatic herb (Chrysanthemum parthenium) with feathery leaves, formerly used to reduce fever. [OE f. L febrifuga (as prec., fugare put to flight)]

feverish adj. having the symptoms of fever; excited, restless. —**feverishly** adv., **feverishness** n. [f. FEVER]

few adj. not many. —n. a small number. —**a few,** some, several. **few and far between,** scarce. **a good** or **quite a few,** a fair number (of). **no fewer than,** as many as. —**fewness** n. [OE]

fey /feɪ/ adj. strange, other-worldly; (Sc.) fated to die soon. —**feyness** n. [OE]

fez n. (pl. **fezzes**) a flat-topped conical red cap with a tassel worn by men in some Muslim countries. [Turk., perh. f. Fez in Morocco]

ff. abbr. following pages etc.

ff abbr. (Mus.) fortissimo.

fiancé /fɪˈɒseɪ/ n. a man or (**fiancée**) woman to whom a person is engaged to be married. [F (fiancer betroth)]

Fianna Fáil /ˈfiːənə fɔɪl/ an Irish political party, traditionally more republican than its rival Fine Gael. It was formed by De Valera in 1926 from moderate members of Sinn Fein. [Ir. *fianna* bands of hunters, *fál* of the defensive fortification. The term *fál* was applied to the rampart of mountains surrounding the central plain of Ireland. The phrase *Fianna Fáil* was used in 15th-c. poetry in the neutral sense 'people of Ireland', but the founders of the political party interpreted it to mean 'soldiers of destiny'.]

fiasco /fɪˈæskəʊ/ *n.* (*pl.* **-os**) a ludicrous or humiliating failure. [It., = bottle (with unexplained allusion)]

fiat /ˈfaɪæt/ *n.* an authorization; a decree. [L, = let it be done]

fib *n.* a trivial lie. —*v.i.* (**-bb-**) to tell a fib. —**fibber** *n.* [perh. f. obs. *fible-fable* nonsense (f. FABLE)]

Fibonacci /fiːbəˈnɑːtʃi/, Leonardo (*c.*1200), Italian mathematician (also called Leonardo Pisano) after whom is named the series of numbers 1, 1, 2, 3, 5, 8, 13, etc., in which each number after the first two is the sum of the two preceding numbers.

fibre /ˈfaɪbə(r)/ *n.* **1.** any of the threads or filaments forming animal and vegetable tissue and textile substance. **2.** a piece of glass in the form of a thread. **3.** a substance formed of fibres. **4.** character. [f. F f. L *fibra*]

fibreboard *n.* flexible board made of compressed fibres of wood etc.

fibreglass *n.* glass in fibrous form; material made from this (e.g. fabric for curtains, matter for use in thermal insulation); plastic containing such glass, used as a structural material e.g. for boat-hulls. Fibreglass was developed commercially in the USA in the 1930s; the word was originally a proprietary term.

fibre optics the use of thin flexible fibres of glass or other transparent solids to transmit light-signals, using the total internal reflection of light. The fibres, which may be used singly or in bundles, and which need not be straight, are less than 1 mm in thickness and have a high refractive index. Early applications included their use in the medical practice of endoscopy, for inspection of internal organs. In optical communications, a system consists of a transmitter, a length of fibre, and a receiver. The transmitter converts an electrical signal into optical energy by modulation of a light-source, which can be a semiconductor laser or a light-emitting diode. The modulated light is passed into the fibre, propagated through it by a series of total internal reflections at the fibre walls, and received by a light-detector which converts the optical signal back into electrical form; the receiver then converts this back into the original form. Because of the high frequencies employed nearly 2,000 channels can be used to carry that number of signals simultaneously.

fibril /ˈfaɪbrɪl/ *n.* a small fibre. [dim. of FIBRE]

fibroid /ˈfaɪbrɔɪd/ *adj.* of or like fibrous tissue. —*n.* a fibroid tumour in the uterus. [f. FIBRE]

fibrosis /faɪˈbrəʊsɪs/ *n.* development of excessive fibrous tissue. [f. FIBRE]

fibrositis /faɪbrəˈsaɪtɪs/ *n.* rheumatic inflammation of fibrous tissue. [as foll. + -ITIS]

fibrous /ˈfaɪbrəs/ *adj.* of or like fibre. [as FIBRE]

fibula /ˈfɪbjʊlə/ *n.* (*pl.* **-ae** /-iː/) **1.** the bone on the outer side of the lower leg (ill. BODY 1). **2.** an ancient brooch or clasp (ill. ARCHAEOLOGY). [L, = brooch]

fiche /fiːʃ/ *n.* (*pl.* same) a microfiche. [abbr.]

Fichte /ˈfɪxtə/, Johann Gottlieb (1762-1814), German philosopher, a pupil of Kant from whose dualism he later dissented. His philosophy is a pure idealism: the thinking self or ego is the only basic reality; the world around it, comprehensively classified as the 'non-ego', is posited by the ego in defining and limiting itself. In his later writings he sought reality not in the ego but in the 'divine idea which lies at the base of all experience', and of which the world of the senses is a manifestation. Fichte preached moral virtues and was an eloquent patriot; his political addresses had some influence on the development of German nationalism and the overthrow of Napoleon.

fickle *adj.* inconstant, changeable, especially in loyalty. —**fickleness** *n.*, **fickly** *adv.* [OE]

fiction /ˈfɪkʃ(ə)n/ *n.* **1.** an invented idea, statement, or narrative; literature describing imaginary events and people. **2.** a conventionally accepted falsehood. —**fictional** *adj.* [f. OF f. L (as FEIGN)]

fictionalize *v.t.* to make into a fictional narrative. [f. prec.]

fictitious /fɪkˈtɪʃəs/ *adj.* imagined or made up, not real or genuine. [f. L (as prec.)]

fictive /ˈfɪktɪv/ *adj.* created or creating by imagination. [f. F or L (as FICTION)]

fiddle *n.* **1.** (*colloq.* or *derog.*) a stringed instrument played with a bow, especially a violin. **2.** (*slang*) an instance of cheating or fraud. —*v.t./i.* **1.** to play restlessly (*with*), to move aimlessly. **2.** (*slang*) to cheat, to swindle, to falsify, to get by cheating. **3.** to play (on) the fiddle. —**as fit as a fiddle**, in very good health. **play second fiddle**, to take a subordinate role. [OE, ult. as VIOL]

fiddle-faddle /ˈfɪd(ə)lfæd(ə)l/ *n.* trivial matters. —*v.i.* to fuss, to trifle. —*int.* nonsense. [redupl. of prec.]

fiddler *n.* **1.** a player on the fiddle. **2.** (*slang*) a swindler. **3.** a small crab of the genus *Uca*, the male having one large claw held in a position like a violinist's arm. [f. FIDDLE]

Fiddler's Green the sailor's Elysium, in which wine, women, and song figure prominently.

fiddlesticks *int.* nonsense.

fiddling *adj.* petty, trivial. [f. FIDDLE]

fiddly *adj.* (*colloq.*) awkward to do or use. [as prec.]

fidelity /fɪˈdelɪti/ *n.* **1.** faithfulness, loyalty. **2.** accuracy; precision in the reproduction of sound. [f. F or L (*fidelis* faithful)]

fidget /ˈfɪdʒɪt/ *v.t./i.* to move or act restlessly or nervously; to be or make uneasy. —*n.* **1.** one who fidgets. **2.** (in *pl.*) fidgeting movements. —**fidgety** *adj.* [f. obs. or dial. *fidge* twitch]

fiduciary /fɪˈdjuːʃɪəri/ *adj.* of, held, or given in trust; (of a paper currency) depending for its value on public confidence or securities. —*n.* a trustee. [f. L (*fiducia* trust)]

fie /faɪ/ *int.* expressing disgust or shame. [f. OF f. L]

fief /fiːf/ *n.* **1.** land held under a feudal system or in fee. **2.** one's sphere of operation or control. [F, as FEE]

field /fiːld/ *n.* **1.** an area of open land, especially for pasture or crops; an area rich in some natural product, e.g. a coalfield, oilfield. **2.** a piece of land for a specified purpose, especially an area marked out for a game. **3.** the participants in a contest or sport; all the competitors or all but the one(s) specified; the fielding side in cricket. **4.** an expanse of ice, sea, snow, etc. **5.** a place of battle or campaign. **6.** an area or sphere of operation, observation, intellectual activities, etc. **7.** the area in which a force is effective, the force exerted by such a field (see below and ill. MAGNETISM). **8.** the background of a picture, coin, flag, etc.; (in heraldry) the surface of an escutcheon. **9.** (in computers) a part of a record, representing a unit of information. —*attrib.* **1.** (of an animal or plant) found in open country, wild. **2.** (of artillery etc.) light and mobile for use on campaign. **3.** carried out or working in the natural environment, not in the laboratory etc. —*v.t./i.* **1.** to act as a fieldsman in cricket etc.; to stop and return (a ball). **2.** to select (a team or individual) to play in a game. **3.** to deal with (a succession of questions etc.). —**field-day** *n.* a military exercise or review, an important or successful occasion. **field-events** *n.pl.* athletic sports other than races. **field-glasses** *n.pl.* binoculars for outdoor use. **Field-Marshal** *n.* an army officer of the highest rank. **field officer**, an army officer of a rank above a captain and below a general. **Field of the Cloth of Gold**, see separate entry. **field sports**, outdoor sports, especially hunting, shooting, and fishing. **hold the field**, not to be superseded. **take the field**, to begin a campaign. [OE]

The means by which a magnet attracts a piece of iron or another magnet some distance away, even when wood or stone is interposed, has perplexed natural philosophers from antiquity and is still poorly understood. The explanation most widely accepted today was originally proposed by Michael Faraday. According to present theory a magnet produces an intermediate 'condition' in space, called a magnetic field, which in turn acts directly on iron objects or on other magnets placed in the field; this condition can exist even in the absence of any material medium and is not directly affected by the presence of any such medium. Electric fields are similar hypothetical 'conditions' in space introduced to explain the action of one stationary electric charge upon another. It is now known that the magnetism of any body is due to tiny electric currents circulating in that body, and that electric charges in motion are responsible for all magnetic fields. When electric charges accelerate, a third type of field is produced, the electromagnetic radiation field. Light, radiowaves, microwaves, infra-red and ultraviolet radiation, and X-rays are all electromagnetic radiation produced by accelerating electric charges. To summarize: stationary electric charges produce electric fields, steadily moving charges produce in addition a magnetic field, and accelerating charges produce electromagnetic radiation.

fielder *n.* a fieldsman. [f. prec.]

fieldfare *n.* a kind of thrush (*Turdus pilaris*). [perh. f. FIELD + FARE]

Fielding /ˈfiːldɪŋ/, Henry (1707-54), English novelist. After he had written several comedies and farces including *Tom Thumb* (1730), his fierce political satire *The Historical Register for 1736* provoked the introduction of censorship in the Licensing Act of 1737 and ended his career as a playwright. He subsequently turned to political journalism and fiction. His first major novel, *Joseph Andrews* (1742), begins as a parody of his rival Richardson's *Pamela*. His greatest achievement, *Tom Jones* (1749), with its ingeniously constructed plot, traces the fortunes of the highly sexed hero while presenting a vivid panorama of 18th-c. London society. Fielding attempted, in these comic epics in prose, 'to laugh mankind out of their follies and vices'; they were significant contributions to the development of the English novel. In 1748 Fielding became JP for Westminster; he wrote several pamphlets on the suppression of crime and established the Bow Street Runners, predecessors of the London police. *A Journal of a Voyage to Lisbon* (1755) was written in Portugal where he died.

Field of the Cloth of Gold a meeting-place of Henry VIII of England and Francis I of France near Calais in 1520, so called because of the magnificent display made by the rival monarchs. Little of importance was achieved at the meeting which was most significant as a symbol of Henry's determination to play a full part in European dynastic politics.

fieldsman *n.* (*pl.* **-men**) a player (other than the bowler or pitcher) of the side deployed in the field while the opposing players are batting in cricket, baseball, etc.

fieldwork *n.* **1.** practical work done outside libraries and laboratories by surveyors, scientists, etc. **2.** a temporary fortification. —**fieldworker** *n.*

fiend /fiːnd/ *n.* **1.** an evil spirit, a devil; a very wicked or cruel person. **2.** (*slang*) a devotee or addict. —**fiendish** *adj.*, **fiendishly** *adv.* [OE]

fierce *adj.* vehemently aggressive or frightening in temper or action, violent; eager, intense; strong or uncontrolled. —**fiercely** *adv.*, **fierceness** *n.* [f. OF f. L *ferus* savage]

fiery /ˈfaɪərɪ/ *adj.* **1.** consisting of fire, flaming; like fire in appearance, bright red; intensely hot. **2.** spirited, passionate, intense. —**fierily** *adv.*, **fieriness** *n.* [f. FIRE]

fiesta /fɪˈestə/ *n.* a festival, a holiday. [Sp. (as FEAST)]

Fife /faɪf/ a local government area of east central Scotland.

fife /faɪf/ *n.* a small shrill flute used in military music. [f. G *pfeife* pipe]

fifteen /fɪfˈtiːn/ *adj.* & *n.* **1.** one more than fourteen; the symbol for this (15, xv, XV). **2.** the size etc. denoted by fifteen. **3.** a team of fifteen players, especially in rugby football. —**fifteenth** *adj.* & *n.* [OE (as FIVE, -TEEN)]

fifth *adj.* next after the fourth. —*n.* **1.** one of five equal parts of a thing. **2.** (*Mus.*) an interval or chord spanning five alphabetical notes (e.g. C to G). —**fifth column,** a group working for the enemy within a country at war. The term dates from the Spanish Civil War when General Mola, leading four columns of troops towards Madrid, declared that he had a fifth column inside the city. **fifth columnist,** a member of this, a traitor. —**fifthly** *adv.* [OE (cf. FIVE)]

fifty /ˈfɪftɪ/ *adj.* & *n.* **1.** five times ten; the symbol for this (50, l, L). **2.** (in *pl.*) the numbers, years, or degrees of temperature from 50 to 59. —**fifty-fifty** *adj.* & *adv.* equal, equally. —**fiftieth** *adj.* & *n.* [OE (as FIVE)]

fig¹ *n.* **1.** a soft pear-shaped fruit; the tree bearing it (*Ficus carica*). **2.** a thing of little value. —**fig-leaf** *n.* a device for concealing something, especially the genitals. [f. OF f. L *ficus*]

fig² *n.* dress, equipment; condition. [f. obs. *feague* (as FAKE)]

fig. *abbr.* figure.

fight /faɪt/ *v.t./i.* (*past & p.p.* **fought** /fɔːt/) **1.** to contend or struggle (against) in physical combat or in war; to carry on (a battle). **2.** to contend or struggle in any way (about), to strive *for*; to strive to overcome. **3.** to make *one's way* by fighting or effort. —*n.* **1.** fighting, a battle or combat; a conflict or struggle, a vigorous effort. **2.** the power or inclination to fight. **3.** a boxing-match. —**fighting chance,** an opportunity of succeeding by a great effort. **fighting fit,** fit and ready. **fight shy of,** to avoid. [OE]

fighter *n.* **1.** one who fights; one who does not yield without

a struggle. **2.** a fast military aircraft designed for attacking other aircraft. [f. prec.]

figment /ˈfɪgmənt/ *n.* a thing invented or existing only in the imagination. [f. L *figmentum* (as FEIGN)]

figuration /fɪgjʊˈreɪʃ(ə)n/ *n.* an act or mode of formation; ornamentation. [f. F or L (as FIGURE)]

figurative /ˈfɪgjʊrətɪv, -gə-/ *adj.* **1.** metaphorical, not literal; characterized by figures of speech. **2.** of pictorial or sculptural representation. —**figuratively** *adv.* [f. L (as foll.)]

figure /ˈfɪgə(r)/ *n.* **1.** external form, bodily shape; a geometrical space enclosed by lines or surfaces. **2.** a person as seen but not identified, or as contemplated mentally; an appearance as giving a certain impression. **3.** a representation of the human form etc.; an image or likeness. **4.** a diagram, an illustration; a decorative pattern; a series of movements forming a single unit in dancing etc.; a succession of notes forming a single idea in music. **5.** the symbol of a number, a numeral (especially 0-9); a value, an amount of money; (in *pl.*) arithmetical calculations. —*v.t./i.* **1.** to appear or be mentioned, esp. prominently. **2.** to represent in a diagram or picture. **3.** to imagine, to picture mentally. **4.** to embellish with a pattern. **5.** to mark with numbers or prices. **6.** to calculate, to do arithmetic. **7.** to be a symbol of. **8.** (*US*) to understand, to consider; (*colloq.*) to be likely or understandable. —**figure-head** *n.* a carved image at a ship's prow; a person nominally at the head but with no real power. **figure (of speech),** an expression using words differently from their literal meaning, especially a metaphor. **figure out,** to work out by arithmetic or logic. [f. OF f. L *figura* (*fingere* fashion)]

figurine /ˈfɪgjʊriːn/ *n.* a statuette. [F f. It. (as prec.)]

Fiji /ˈfiːdʒiː/ a group of some 840 islands, of which about 100 are inhabited, in the South Pacific (the International Date Line has been diverted to the east of the island group); pop. (1983) 671,712; official language, English; capital, Suva. The population, which is mostly engaged in agriculture and fishing, contains an almost equal mix of native Pacific islanders and Indians, the latter being descendants of those brought in to work the sugar plantations in the 19th c. Discovered by Tasman in 1643 and visited by Captain Cook in 1774, the Fiji Islands became a British Crown Colony in 1874 and an independent State, a member of the Commonwealth, in 1970. —**Fijian** *adj.* & *n.*

filament /ˈfɪləmənt/ *n.* a threadlike strand or fibre; the conducting wire or thread in an electric bulb (now usually of tungsten). —**filamentary** /-ˈmentərɪ/ *adj.* [f. F or L (*filum* thread)]

filbert /ˈfɪlbət/ *n.* a nut of the cultivated hazel; the tree bearing it (*Corylus maxima*). [f. AF *philbert*, the nut being ripe about St Philibert's day (20 Aug.)]

filch *v.t.* to pilfer, to steal. [orig. unkn.]

file¹ *n.* **1.** a folder or box etc. for holding loose papers; its contents. **2.** a collection of (usually related) data stored under one reference in a computer. **3.** a line of people or things one behind the other. —*v.t./i.* **1.** to place in a file or among records; to submit (an application for divorce, a petition, etc.); (of a reporter) to send (a story etc.) to a newspaper. **2.** to walk in a line. [f. F f. L *filum* thread]

file² *n.* a tool with a roughened steel surface for smoothing or shaping wood etc. —*v.t.* to smooth or shape with a file. [OE]

filial /ˈfɪlɪ(ə)l/ *adj.* of or due from a son or daughter. —**filially** *adv.* [f. OF or L (*filius* son, *filia* daughter)]

filibuster /ˈfɪlɪbʌstə(r)/ *n.* **1.** a person engaging in unauthorized warfare against a foreign State. **2.** one who obstructs progress in a legislative assembly; such obstruction. —*v.i.* to act as a filibuster. [ult. f. Du. *vrijbuiter* (as FREEBOOTER)]

filigree /ˈfɪlɪgriː/ *n.* fine ornamental work in gold etc. wire; similar delicate work. —**filigreed** *adj.* [f. F *filigrane* f. It. (L *filum* thread, *granum* seed)]

filing *n.* (usu. in *pl.*) a particle rubbed off by a file. [f. FILE²]

Filioque /fɪlɪˈəʊkwiː/ the word (L, = and from the Son) inserted in the Western version of the Nicene Creed to assert the doctrine of the procession of the Holy Ghost from the Son as well as from the Father, which is not admitted by the Eastern Church. It was one of the central issues in the Great Schism of 1054.

Filipino /fɪlɪˈpiːnəʊ/ *n.* (*pl.* **-os**) a native of the Philippine Islands. —*adj.* of Filipinos or the Philippine Islands. [Sp., = Philippine]

fill *v.t./i.* **1.** to make or become full (*with*); to occupy completely, to spread over or through; to block up (a cavity or hole); to drill and put a filling into (a decayed tooth); (of a sail) to be distended by the wind. **2.** to appoint a person to hold (a vacant post); to hold or discharge the duties of (an office etc.); to carry out or supply (an order, commission, etc.); to occupy (vacant time). —*n.* as much as one wants or can bear of food etc.; enough to fill a thing. —**fill the bill**, to be suitable or adequate. **fill in**, to add information to complete (a form or document etc.); to complete (a drawing etc.) within the outline; to fill (a hole etc.) completely; to act as a substitute (*for*); to spend (time) in a temporary activity; (*colloq.*) to give the required information to. **fill out**, to enlarge to the required size; to become enlarged or plump. **fill up**, to make or become completely full; to fill in (a document); to fill the petrol tank of (a car etc.). [OE (cf. FULL)]

filler *n.* material used to fill a cavity or increase the bulk; an item filling space in a newspaper etc. [f. FILL]

fillet /ˈfɪlɪt/ *n.* **1.** a boneless piece of meat or fish. **2.** a headband, a hair ribbon; a narrow strip or ridge. **3.** (*Archit.*) a narrow flat band between mouldings. —*v.t.* **1.** to remove the bones from; to divide (a fish etc.) into fillets. **2.** to bind or provide with a fillet or fillets. [f. OF f. L *filum* thread]

filling *n.* **1.** the material used to fill a cavity in a tooth. **2.** the material between the bread in a sandwich. —**filling-station** *n.* an establishment selling petrol etc. to motorists. [f. FILL]

fillip /ˈfɪlɪp/ *n.* **1.** a stimulus, an incentive; **2.** a flick with the finger or thumb. —*v.t.* to give a fillip to. [imit.]

filly /ˈfɪlɪ/ *n.* **1.** a young female horse. **2.** (*slang*) a lively young woman. [f. ON (as FOAL)]

film *n.* **1.** a thin coating or covering layer. **2.** a strip or sheet of plastic or some other flexible base coated with a light-sensitive emulsion for exposure in a camera. **3.** a motion picture; a story represented by this; (in *pl.*) the cinema industry. **4.** a slight veil or haze etc.; a dimness or morbid growth affecting the eyes. —*v.t.* **1.** to make a film or motion picture of (a scene, story, etc.). **2.** to cover or become covered with a film. —**film star**, a celebrated actor or actress in films. **film-strip** *n.* a series of transparencies in a strip for projection. [OE *filmen* membrane]

filmy *adj.* thin and transparent. —**filmily** *adv.*, **filminess** *n.* [f. prec.]

filoplume /ˈfaɪləpluːm/ *n.* a slender feather of a type found between and beneath the flight feathers of some birds (ill. BIRDS). [f. L *filum* thread, *pluma* feather]

filter *n.* **1.** a device for removing impurities from a liquid or gas passed through it; a screen for absorbing or modifying light, X-rays, etc.; a device for suppressing electrical or sound waves of frequencies not required. **2.** an arrangement for filtering traffic. —*v.t./i.* **1.** to pass or cause to pass through a filter; to make a way gradually (*through*, *into*, etc.), to leak *out*. **2.** (of traffic) to be allowed to pass in a certain direction while other traffic is held up (especially at traffic lights). —**filter-paper** *n.* a porous paper for filtering. **filter-tip** *n.* a cigarette with a filter for purifying smoke; the filter itself. [f. F f. L f. Gmc (as FELT¹, the earliest filters being of felt)]

filth *n.* repugnant or extreme dirt; obscenity. [OE (cf. FOUL)]

filthy *adj.* **1.** extremely or disgustingly dirty; obscene. **2.** (*colloq.*, of the weather) very unpleasant. —*adv.* in a filthy way; (*colloq.*) extremely. —**filthily** *adv.*, **filthiness** *n.* [f. prec.]

filtrate /ˈfɪltreɪt/ *v.t.* to filter. —*n.* a filtered liquid. —**filtration** /-ˈtreɪʃ(ə)n/ *n.* [f. FILTER]

fin *n.* **1.** a thin flat organ for propelling and steering, growing on fish and cetaceans at various parts of the body (ill. FISH); an underwater swimmer's flipper. **2.** a small projection on an aircraft or rocket for ensuring stability; any similar projection or attachment. [OE]

finagle /fɪˈneɪɡ(ə)l/ *v.t./i.* (*colloq.*) to act or obtain dishonestly. [f. dial. *fainaigue* cheat]

final /ˈfaɪn(ə)l/ *adj.* situated at the end, coming last; conclusive, decisive. —*n.* **1.** the last or deciding heat or game in sports etc. **2.** the last edition of a day's newspaper. **3.** (usu. in *pl.*) a final examination. —**final cause**, an ultimate purpose. **final clause**, (*Gram.*) a clause expressing purpose. —**finally** *adv.* [f. OF or L (*finis* end, goal)]

finale /fɪˈnɑːlɪ/ *n.* the last movement or section of a piece of music or drama etc. [It. (as prec.)]

finalist /ˈfaɪnəlɪst/ *n.* a competitor in the final of a competition etc. [f. FINAL]

finality /faɪˈnælɪtɪ/ *n.* the quality or fact of being final. [f. F or L (as FINAL)]

finalize /ˈfaɪnəlaɪz/ *v.t.* to put into a final form, to complete. —**finalization** /-ˈzeɪʃ(ə)n/ *n.* [f. FINAL]

finance /faɪˈnæns, fɪ-, ˈfaɪ-/ *n.* **1.** the management of money; support in money for an enterprise. **2.** (in *pl.*) money resources. —*v.t.* to provide the capital for (a person or enterprise). —**finance company** *or* **house**, a company concerned mainly with providing money for hire-purchase transactions. [f. OF (*finer* settle debt, as FINE²)]

financial /faɪˈnænʃ(ə)l, fɪ-/ *adj.* of finance. —**financial year**, a year reckoned from 1 or 6 April for taxing and accounting. —**financially** *adv.* [f. prec.]

financier /faɪˈnænsɪə(r), fɪ-/ *n.* a person engaged in large-scale finance. [F (as FINANCE)]

finch *n.* any of several small songbirds, especially of the genus *Fringilla*. [OE]

find /faɪnd/ *v.t.* (*past* & *p.p.* **found** /faʊnd/) **1.** to discover or get possession of by chance or effort; to become aware of. **2.** to obtain, to succeed in obtaining. **3.** to seek out and provide. **4.** to ascertain by inquiry, calculation, etc. **5.** to perceive or experience; to regard or discover from experience. **6.** (of a jury, judge, etc.) to decide and declare. **7.** to reach by a natural process. —*n.* a discovery; a thing or person discovered, especially when of value. —**find oneself**, to discover what one is, to discover one's vocation. **find one's feet**, to be able to walk; to develop one's independent ability. **find out**, to discover or detect (a wrongdoer etc.); to get information (about). [OE]

finder *n.* **1.** one who finds. **2.** a small telescope attached to a large one to locate an object. **3.** a viewfinder. [f. FIND]

finding *n.* (often in *pl.*) a conclusion reached by an inquiry etc. [f. FIND]

fine¹ *adj.* **1.** of high quality; excellent, of notable merit (also *iron.*); pure, refined; (of gold or silver) containing a specified proportion of pure metal. **2.** of handsome appearance or size, beautiful, imposing; not rough. **3.** (of the weather) bright; free from rain, fog, etc. **4.** small, thin, or sharp of its kind; in small particles. **5.** (of speech) tritely complimentary, euphemistic. **6.** smart, showy, ornate. **7.** fastidious, affectedly refined. **8.** (in cricket) behind and at a narrow angle to the wicket. —*n.* **1.** fine weather. **2.** (in *pl.*) small particles in mining, milling, etc. —*adv.* finely; (*colloq.*) very well. —*v.t./i.* (often with *away*, *down*, *off*) to make or become pure, clear, thinner, etc. —**cut** *or* **run it fine**, to allow very little margin of time etc. **fine arts**, those appealing to the mind or the sense of beauty, especially painting, sculpture, and architecture. **fine-spun** *adj.* delicate; (of a theory) too subtle, unpractical. **fine-tooth comb**, a comb with narrow close-set teeth (*go over with a fine-tooth comb*, to search thoroughly). **not to put too fine a point on it**, to speak bluntly. —**finely** *adv.*, **fineness** *n.* [f. OF f. L *finire* finish]

fine² *n.* a sum of money (to be) paid as a penalty. —*v.t.* to punish by a fine. —**in fine**, in sum. [f. OF f. L *finis* end (in medieval times = sum paid on settling lawsuit)]

finery /ˈfaɪnərɪ/ *n.* showy dress or decoration. [f. FINE¹]

fines herbes /fiːnz ˈeəb/ *n.pl.* mixed herbs used in cooking. [F, = fine herbs]

finesse /fɪˈnes/ *n.* **1.** refinement; subtle or delicate manipulation; artful tact in handling a difficulty. **2.** (in card-games) an attempt to win a trick by playing a card that is not the highest held. —*v.t./i.* **1.** to achieve by finesse. **2.** (in card-games) to make a finesse (with). [F (as FINE¹)]

finger /ˈfɪŋɡə(r)/ *n.* **1.** any of the five terminal members of the hand, any of these excluding the thumb. **2.** the part of a glove for a finger. **3.** a finger-like object or structure. **4.** a measure of liquor in a glass, based on the breadth of a finger. —*v.t.* to feel or turn about with the fingers; to play (music or an instrument) with the fingers. —**finger-board** *n.* a flat strip at the top end of a stringed instrument, against which the strings are pressed to determine notes. **finger-bowl** *n.* a small bowl for rinsing the fingers during a meal. **finger-mark** *n.* a mark left on a surface by a finger. **finger-nail** *n.* the nail at the tip of a finger. **finger-plate** *n.* a plate fixed to a door above the handle to prevent finger-marks. **finger spelling**, manual signs for communication with the deaf (ill. ALPHABETS). **finger-stall** *n.* a sheath to cover an injured finger. **get** *or* **pull one's finger out**, (*slang*) to cease prevaricating and start to act. **put one's finger on**, to locate or identify exactly. [OE]

fingering *n.* the manner or technique of using the fingers, especially to play an instrument; an indication of this in a musical score. [f. prec.]

fingerprint *n.* an impression made on a surface by the fleshy pad at the end of a finger, especially as a means of identification (ill. BODY 4). No two persons in the world have exactly the same pattern of ridges and marks on these parts, and the patterns can be classified and recorded systematically. Sir William Herschel (1833-1917) had introduced the use of fingerprints for identification purposes in India in the late 1870s. It was adopted in Britain, as a means of identifying criminals, in 1901.

fingertip *n.* the tip of a finger. —**have at one's fingertips,** to be thoroughly familiar with (a subject etc.).

finial /ˈfɪnɪ(ə)l/ *n.* an ornamental top to a gable, canopy, etc. (ill. CHURCH). [f. AF f. L *finis* end]

finicky /ˈfɪnɪkɪ/ *adj.* (also **finical, finicking**) 1. excessively detailed, fiddly. 2. over-particular, fastidious. [prob. slang extension of FINE[1]]

finis /ˈfɪnɪs, ˈfiːn-/ *n.* the end, especially of a book. [L]

finish /ˈfɪnɪʃ/ *v.t./i.* (often with *off* or *up*) to bring or come to an end, to come to the end of; to complete the manufacture of (cloth etc.) by surface treatment. —*n.* 1. the end, the last stage; the point at which a race etc. ends. 2. a method, material, or texture used for surface treatment of wood, cloth, etc. —**finishing-school** *n.* a private school where girls are prepared for entry into fashionable society. **finish off,** to kill. **finish with,** to have no more to do with. [f. OF f. L (*finis* end)]

finite /ˈfaɪnaɪt/ *adj.* limited, not infinite; (of a part of the verb) having a specific number and person. [f. L (*finire* end, set limit to)]

Finland /ˈfɪnlənd/ a Scandinavian country with a coastline on the Baltic Sea and an extensive network of inland waterways; pop. (1982) 4,844,000; official languages, Finnish and Swedish; capital, Helsinki. The country is highly industrialized, principal export earnings being from timber and the paper industry, shipbuilding, and engineering. Converted to Christianity by Eric IX of Sweden in the 12th c., Finland became an area of Swedish-Russian rivalry. A Grand Duchy from the 16th c., it was ceded to Russia in 1809, regaining full independence after the Russian Revolution. Wars with the USSR in 1939-40 and 1941-4 cost Finland Karelia and Petsamo, and although Finland has been neutral since the war, she has remained, at least partially, under Soviet influence.

Finn[1] /fɪn/ the principal hero of a cycle of Irish legends, father of Ossian. He is supposed to have lived in the 3rd c. AD.

Finn[2] *n.* a native of Finland. [OE]

finnan /ˈfɪnən/ *n.* (also **finnan haddock**) haddock cured with the smoke of green wood, turf, or peat. [f. *Findhorn* in Scotland]

Finnic /ˈfɪnɪk/ *adj.* 1. of the group of peoples allied to the Finns. 2. of the group of languages allied to Finnish. [f. FINN]

Finnish /ˈfɪnɪʃ/ *adj.* of the Finns or their language. —*n.* a language spoken by some five and a half million people in Finland (where it is one of the two official languages), the NW Soviet Union, and Sweden, belonging to the Finno-Ugric group and closely related to Estonian. It is noted for its complexity; a Finnish noun has 15 different case-forms. [f. FINN]

Finno-Ugric /fɪnəʊˈuːgrɪk/ *adj.* of a group of the Ural-Altaic languages, divided into Finnic languages (of which the most important are Finnish and Estonian), and Ugric languages (of which the most important is Hungarian). The languages are also spoken in scattered areas of central Russia, which is thought to be the original homeland of their speakers. —*n.* this group of languages. —**Finno-Ugrian** *adj.* & *n.* [f. FINN + UGRIC, UGRIAN]

fiord /fjɔːd/ *n.* (also **fjord**) a long narrow inlet of the sea between high cliffs. [Norw. f. ON; cf. FIRTH]

fipple /ˈfɪp(ə)l/ *n.* the plug at the mouth-end of a wind instrument. —**fipple flute,** a flute played by blowing endwise, e.g. a recorder. [cf. Icel. *flipi* lip of horse]

fir *n.* an evergreen coniferous tree of the genus *Abies* or various other genera, with needles placed singly on the shoots; its wood. —**fir-cone** *n.* its fruit. **noble fir,** a common fir (*Abies procera*) of fine and lofty appearance (ill. TREES). [prob. f. ON]

fire *n.* 1. the state or process of combustion causing heat and light, the active principle operative in this, flame or incandescence. The earliest evidence for the use of fire dates from about 500,000 years ago (see PEKING MAN). 2. destructive burning. 3. burning fuel in a grate or furnace; an electric or gas fire (see ELECTRIC, GAS). 4. the firing of guns. 5. angry or excited feeling, enthusiasm, vivacity. 6.

burning heat, fever. —*v.t./i.* 1. to send (a missile) from a gun etc.; to detonate. 2. to deliver or utter in rapid succession. 3. to dismiss (an employee) from a job. 4. to set fire to with the intention of destroying. 5. to catch fire; (of an internal-combustion engine) to undergo ignition. 6. to supply (a furnace etc.) with fuel. 7. to stimulate (the imagination); to fill with enthusiasm. 8. to bake or dry (pottery, bricks, etc.). 9. to become heated or excited. 10. to cause to glow, to redden. —**catch fire,** to ignite, to start to burn. **fire-alarm** *n.* a device giving warning of a fire. **fire-ball** *n.* a large meteor; a ball of flame from a nuclear explosion; an energetic person. **fire-bomb** *n.* an incendiary bomb. **fire-break** *n.* an obstacle to the spread of fire in a forest etc. **fire-brick** *n.* a fireproof brick used in a grate. **fire-brigade** *n.* an organized body of men trained and employed to extinguish fires. **fire-clay** *n.* a clay used to make fire-bricks. **fire-drill** *n.* a rehearsal of the procedure to be used in case of fire. **fire-eater** *n.* a conjuror who appears to swallow fire; a quarrelsome person. **fire-engine** *n.* a vehicle carrying the equipment for fighting large fires. **fire-escape** *n.* an emergency staircase or apparatus for escape from a building on fire. **fire extinguisher,** an apparatus with a jet for discharging liquid chemicals or foam to extinguish a fire. **fire-guard** *n.* a protective screen or grid placed in front of a fire. **fire-irons** *n.pl.* the tongs, poker, and shovel for tending a domestic fire. **fire-lighter** *n.* a piece of inflammable material used to help start a fire in a grate. **Fire of London,** see GREAT FIRE. **fire-power** *n.* the destructive capacity of guns etc. **fire-practice** *n.* fire-drill. **fire-raising** *n.* arson. **fire station,** the headquarters of a fire-brigade. **fire-storm** *n.* a high wind or storm following a fire caused by bombs. **fire-trap** *n.* a building without proper provision for escape in case of fire. **fire-watcher** *n.* a person keeping watch for fires, especially those caused by bombs. **fire-water** *n.* (*colloq.*) strong alcoholic liquor. **on fire,** burning; excited. **open fire,** to start firing guns etc. **set fire to, set on fire,** to cause to burn or ignite. **set the world on fire,** to do something remarkable or sensational. **under fire,** being fired on (by the enemy etc.); being rigorously criticized or questioned. —**firer** *n.* [OE]

firearm *n.* (usu. in *pl.*) a gun, pistol, or rifle.

firebox *n.* the fuel-chamber of a steam-engine or boiler.

firebrand *n.* 1. a piece of burning wood. 2. a person who causes trouble.

firecracker *n.* (*US*) an explosive firework.

firedamp *n.* a miners' name for methane, which is explosive when mixed in a certain proportion with air.

firedog *n.* an andiron (ill. HOUSES).

firefly *n.* a kind of beetle emitting phosphorescent light (there are about 2,000 species).

firelight *n.* light from the fire in a fireplace.

fireman *n.* (*pl.* **-men**) 1. a member of a fire-brigade. 2. one who tends the furnace of a steam-engine fire.

fireplace *n.* an open recess for a domestic fire, at the base of a chimney (ill. HOUSES); its surrounding structure.

fireproof *adj.* able to resist fire or great heat. —*v.t.* to make fireproof.

fireside *n.* the area round a fireplace; one's home or home-life.

firewood *n.* wood for use as fuel.

firework *n.* 1. a device containing combustible chemicals that cause explosions or spectacular effects. 2. (in *pl.*) an outburst of passion, especially anger.

firing *n.* 1. the discharge of guns. 2. fuel. —**firing-line** *n.* the front line in a battle, the leading part in an activity etc. **firing-squad** *n.* a group that fires the salute at a military funeral or shoots a condemned person.

firm[1] *adj.* solid, stable, steady, not fluctuating; resolute, determined; not easily shaken; (of an offer etc.) not liable to cancellation after acceptance. —*adv.* firmly. —*v.t./i.* to become or cause to become firm or secure. —**firmly** *adv.* [f. OF f. L *firmus*]

firm[2] *n.* a business concern or its members. [earlier = signature, f. Sp. & It. f. L *firmare* ratify (as prec.)]

firmament /ˈfɜːməmənt/ *n.* the sky regarded as a vault or arch. [f. OF f. L (as FIRM[1])]

first *adj.* 1. foremost in time, order, or importance. 2. most willing or likely. 3. basic, evident. —*n.* 1. the person or thing that is first; the first day of a month; a first occurrence of something notable. 2. first-class honours in a university degree. —*adv.* 1. before anyone or anything else; before someone or something else. 2. for the first time. 3. in preference. —**at first**, at the beginning. **at first hand,** directly, from the original source. **first aid,** help given to the injured until medical treatment is available. **first blood,** the first success in a contest. **first-born** adj. eldest; (n.) the eldest child. **first class,** the best group or category; the best accommodation in a train, ship, etc.; the class of mail to be most quickly delivered; the highest category of achievement in an examination. **first-class** adj. & adv. of or by the first class; excellent. **first-day cover,** an envelope with stamps postmarked on the first day of issue. **first finger,** that next to the thumb. **first-foot** n. (Sc.) the first person to cross the threshold in the New Year; (v.i.) to be the first to do this. **first-fruit** n. (usu. in pl.) the first agricultural produce of the season; the first results of work etc. **First Lady,** (US) the wife of the President. **first light,** dawn. **first night,** the first public performance of a play etc. **first offender,** one against whom no previous conviction is recorded. **first officer,** the mate on a merchant ship. **first past the post,** winning an election by having most votes though not necessarily an absolute majority. **first-rate** adj. & adv. excellent; (colloq.) very well. **in the first place,** as the first consideration. **First World War,** see WORLD WAR. [OE (superl. from stem of FORE)]

firsthand adj. & adv. from the original source, direct.

firstly adv. first, to begin with. [f. FIRST]

firth n. a narrow inlet of sea; an estuary. [f. ON (as FIORD)]

fiscal /ˈfɪsk(ə)l/ adj. of the public revenue. —n. a legal official in some countries; (Sc.) a procurator fiscal. [f. F or L (fiscus treasury)]

fish¹ n. (pl. usu. same) **1.** a vertebrate cold-blooded animal with gills and fins living wholly in water (see below and ill. p. 303); any animal living in water, e.g. a cuttlefish, a jellyfish. **2.** the flesh of fish as food. **3.** (colloq.) a person. **4.** (in pl.) **the Fish** or **Fishes,** the constellation or sign of the zodiac Pisces. —v.t./i. **1.** to try to catch fish (in). **2.** to search (for) in water or by reaching into something; (colloq.) to bring out thus. **3.** to seek for (compliments, information, etc.) by hinting or indirect questioning. —**fish cake,** a small fried cake of shredded fish and mashed potato. **fish-eye lens,** a wide-angled lens with a distorting effect. **fish finger,** a small oblong piece of fish in batter or bread-crumbs. **fish-hook** n. a barbed hook for catching fish. **fish-kettle** n. an oval pan for boiling fish. **fish-meal** n. ground dried fish as a fertilizer etc. **fish-net** adj. (of a fabric) made with an open mesh. **fish out of water,** a person not in his element. **fish-tail** n. a thing shaped like a fish's tail. **other fish to fry,** more important things to do. [OE]

Fish represent a form of life rather than a single related group. The most primitive class are the jawless fishes, which first appeared about 500 million years ago and are represented today by the lampreys. Jawed fishes appeared about 100 million years later, and present-day forms can be divided into two main classes: cartilaginous fish and bony fish. The former includes sharks, dogfish, skates, and rays. As their name suggests, they have a skeleton of cartilage rather than bone, and they also lack a swim-bladder to give them buoyancy, so that they must remain in motion constantly in order not to sink to the sea bottom. Bony fish, which constitute the great majority of the 30,000 or so living fish species, typically have a swim-bladder and also possess fins with much greater manœuvrability than those of cartilaginous forms.

fish² n. a piece of wood or iron etc. to strengthen a mast, beam, etc. —**fish-plate** n. a flat plate of iron etc. connecting railway rails. [f. F ficher fix f. L figere]

Fisher /ˈfɪʃə(r)/, Sir Ronald Aylmer (1890-1962), English statistician and geneticist, who made major contributions to the development of statistics in the 20th c. He published influential books on statistical theory, the design of experiments, statistical methods for research workers, and the relationship between Mendelian genetics and evolutionary theory. He himself also carried out experimental work in agriculture and on the genetics of blood groups.

fisher n. **1.** a fishing animal. **2.** (archaic) a fisherman. [f. FISH¹]

fishery n. **1.** a place where fish are caught. **2.** the business of fishing. [f. FISH¹]

fishing n. the sport of trying to catch fish. —**fishing-line, -rod** ns. a line and rod with a fish-hook, used in this. [f. FISH¹]

fishmonger n. a dealer in fish.

fishwife n. a woman who sells fish.

fishy adj. **1.** of or like a fish. **2.** (slang) dubious, suspect. —**fishily** adv., **fishiness** n. [f. FISH¹]

fissile /ˈfɪsaɪl/ adj. capable of undergoing nuclear fission; tending to split. [f. L (as FISSURE)]

fission /ˈfɪʃ(ə)n/ n. **1.** a method of biological reproduction by the division of a cell etc. **2.** nuclear fission. —v.t./i. to undergo or cause to undergo fission. —**fission bomb,** an atomic bomb. [f. L (as foll.)]

fissionable adj. capable of undergoing nuclear fission. [f. prec.]

fissure /ˈfɪʃə(r)/ n. a cleft made by splitting or separation of parts. —v.t./i. to split, to crack. [f. OF or L (findere fiss- cleave)]

fist n. the tightly closed hand. [OE]

fisticuffs /ˈfɪstɪkʌfs/ n.pl. fighting with the fists. [f. fisty (obs. adj. f. prec.) + CUFF]

fistula /ˈfɪstjʊlə/ n. **1.** a long pipelike ulcer. **2.** an abnormal or surgically made passage in the body. —**fistular** adj., **fistulous** adj. [L, = pipe]

fit¹ adj. **1.** well suited or qualified. **2.** competent, worthy; in a suitable condition, ready. **3.** in good health or condition. **4.** proper, befitting. —v.t./i. (-tt-) **1.** to make or be of the right shape and size (for). **2.** to put or go into position. **3.** to adapt, to make or be suitable or competent. **4.** to supply or equip with. —n. the way a thing fits. —**fit in,** to be or cause to be harmonious or in a suitable relationship; to find space or time for. **fit out** or **up,** to supply or equip with. **see** or **think fit,** to decide or choose (to do). —**fitly** adv., **fitness** n. [orig. unkn.]

fit² n. **1.** a sudden seizure of epilepsy, hysteria, etc., usually with unconsciousness; a brief attack of an illness or its symptoms. **2.** a sudden short bout or burst. —**by** or **in fits and starts,** spasmodically. **have a fit,** (colloq.) to be greatly surprised or outraged. **in fits,** laughing uncontrollably. [orig. = position of danger; etym. unkn.]

fitful adj. active or occurring spasmodically or intermittently. —**fitfully** adv. [f. FIT² + -FUL]

fitment n. a piece of fixed furniture. [f. FIT¹]

fitter n. **1.** a person concerned with the fitting of clothes etc. **2.** a mechanic who fits together and adjusts machinery. [f. FIT¹]

fitting n. **1.** the process of having a garment etc. fitted. **2.** (in pl.) the fixtures and fitments of a building. —adj. proper, befitting. [f. FIT¹]

Fitzgerald¹ /fɪtsˈdʒer(ə)ld/, Edward (1809-83), English scholar, famous for his English poetic version of the Rubái-yát of Omar Khayyám.

Fitzgerald² /fɪtsˈdʒer(ə)ld/, (Francis) Scott (Key) (1896-1940), American novelist. His first novel This side of Paradise (1920) made him instantly famous, and shortly afterwards he married the glamorous Zelda Sayre; together they embarked on a high-living, big-spending, party-going 'jazz-age' life. His short stories, which chronicled the mood and manners of the times, were collected in Flappers and Philosophers (1920) and Tales of the Jazz Age (1922; containing 'The Diamond as Big as the Ritz'). Probably his finest novel was The Great Gatsby (1925), a tale of romantic and destructive passion played against a backdrop of Long Island glamour and New York squalor. By now Zelda was suffering from a nervous breakdown, Scott from the effects of their violent lives, and Tender is the Night (1934) reflects his own sense of impending disaster. His unfinished The Last Tycoon (1941) analyses his own deterioration.

Fitzgerald³ /fɪtsˈdʒer(ə)ld/, George Francis (1851-1901), Irish physicist, who suggested that length, time, and mass depended on the relative motion of the observer, while the speed of light was constant. This hypothesis, postulated independently by Lorentz (see entry), prepared the way for Einstein's special theory of relativity.

five adj. & n. **1.** one more than four; the symbol for this (5, v, V). **2.** the size etc. denoted by five. —**five-year plan,** a plan for the economic development of the USSR in five years, inaugurated in 1928 (and later repeated); a similar plan adapted in other countries. [OE]

fivefold adj. & adv. **1.** five times as much or as many. **2.** consisting of five parts. [f. FIVE + -FOLD]

fiver n. (colloq.) a £5 note. [f. FIVE]

fives /faɪvz/ n. a ball-game played with padded gloves in a walled court, with three walls (Eton fives) or four (Rugby fives). [pl. of FIVE. The significance of the word fives is unknown; its slang use to mean 'a hand' is not found until the early 19th c., whereas forms of the game date from much earlier.]

Fish

A cartilaginous fish
(e.g. shark, dogfish)

inclined pectoral fins provide lift

tail provides forward thrust

gill slits

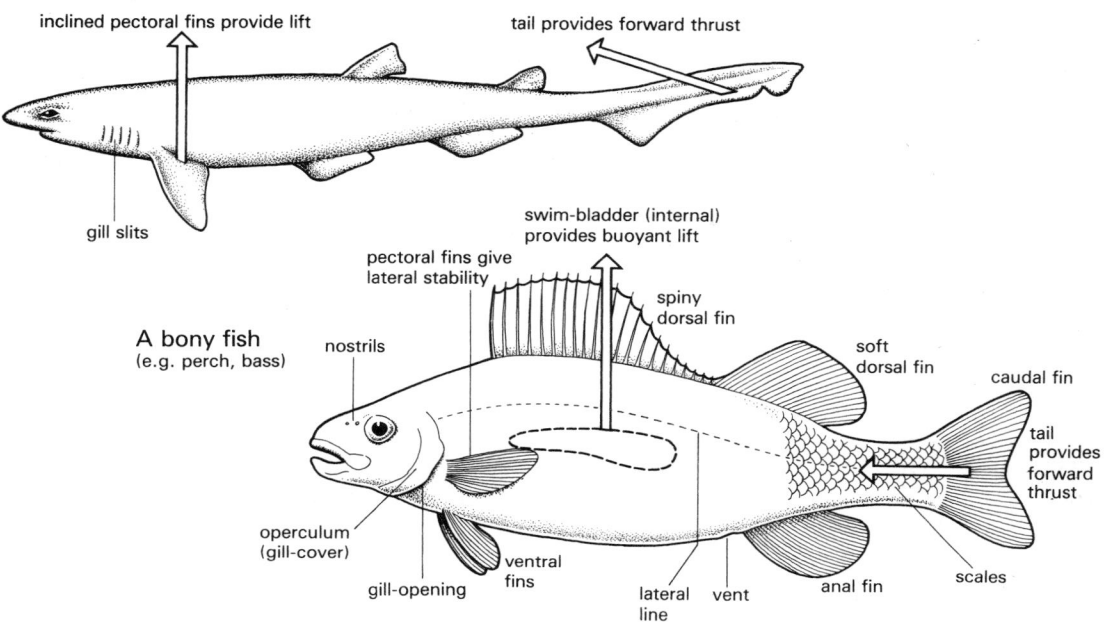

A bony fish
(e.g. perch, bass)

swim-bladder (internal) provides buoyant lift

pectoral fins give lateral stability

spiny dorsal fin

soft dorsal fin

caudal fin

nostrils

tail provides forward thrust

operculum (gill-cover)

gill-opening

ventral fins

lateral line

vent

anal fin

scales

Main internal organs

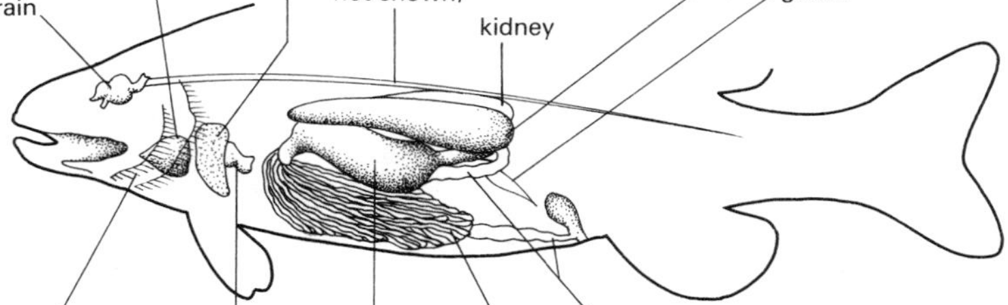

heart   liver   spinal cord (surrounding vertebrae not shown)   swim-bladder

brain   kidney   gonad

gills

gall-bladder   stomach   intestine

pyloric caeca

Gills
(horizontal section through mouth and gills)

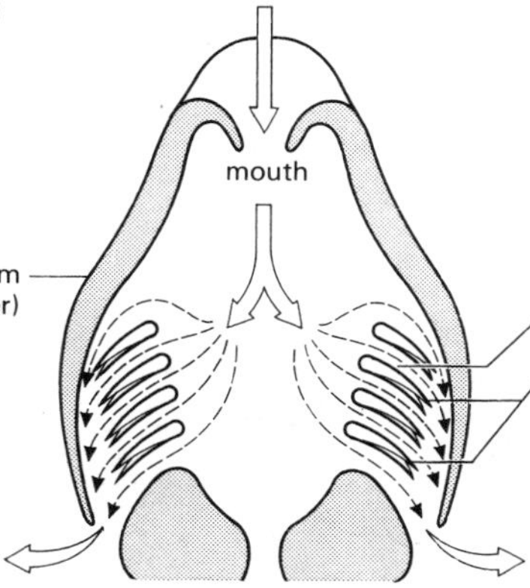

water drawn in

mouth

operculum (gill-cover)

gill slits

gill filaments (oxygen from water absorbed into bloodstream)

water driven out (carbon dioxide leaves bloodstream)

Lateral line
(sensory system)

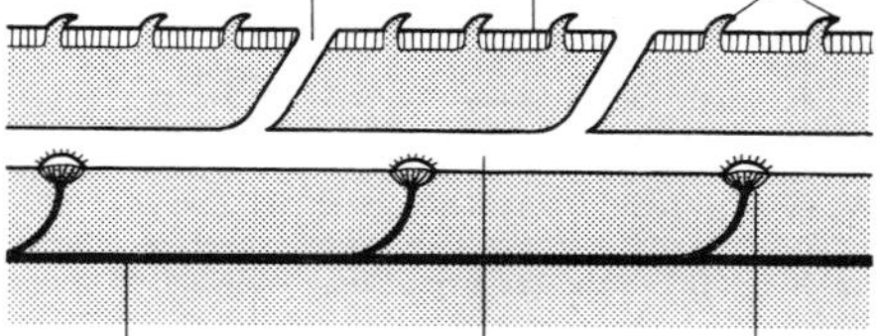

opening   body wall   scales

nerve   jelly-filled canal   sense-organ

Movements and currents in the surrounding water cause pressure changes which produce vibrations in the jelly-filled canal, activating sensory nerve endings. It is believed that in this way the fish receives information about current flow and the presence of nearby organisms.

fix *v.t./i.* **1.** to make firm or stable, to fasten, to secure; to implant (an idea or memory) in the mind. **2.** to place definitely or permanently. **3.** to decide, to settle, to specify (a price, date, etc.). **4.** to direct (the eyes or attention) steadily. **5.** to determine the exact nature, position, etc., of; to identify, to locate. **6.** to make (the eyes or features) rigid; to become rigid; to congeal, to stiffen. **7.** to repair. **8.** (*colloq.*) to punish or kill. **9.** (*colloq.*) to secure the support of (a person) or result of (a race etc.) fraudulently. **10.** (*slang*) to inject (*oneself*) with a narcotic. **11.** to make (a colour, photographic image, etc.) fast or permanent. **12.** (of a plant) to assimilate (nitrogen, carbon dioxide) by forming a non-gaseous compound. —*n.* **1.** a dilemma, a difficult position. **2.** the act of finding a position, or a position found, by bearings etc. **3.** (*slang*) a dose of a narcotic drug. —**be fixed (for)**, (*colloq.*) to be situated (as regards). **fixed star**, a star so far from Earth as to appear motionless except for the diurnal revolution of the heavens (opp. *planet, comet,* etc.). **fix up**, to choose, to decide on. **fix up,** to arrange, to organize; to accommodate. [ult. f. L *figere fix-fix*]

fixate /fɪkˈseɪt/ *v.t.* **1.** to direct one's gaze on. **2.** (chiefly in *pass.*) to cause to acquire an abnormal attachment to persons or things. [f. L (as FIX)]

fixation /fɪkˈseɪʃ(ə)n/ *n.* **1.** the act or process of being fixated. **2.** an obsession, a concentration on one idea. **3.** the process of fixing (see FIX 12). [f. L (*fixare* fix)]

fixative /ˈfɪksətɪv/ *adj.* tending to fix or secure. —*n.* a fixative substance. [f. FIX]

fixedly /ˈfɪksɪdlɪ/ *adv.* in a fixed way, intently. [f. FIX]

fixer *n.* a person or thing that fixes; (*colloq.*) one who makes (esp. illicit) arrangements; a substance for fixing a photographic image etc. [f. FIX]

fixings *n.pl.* (*US*) **1.** apparatus, equipment. **2.** the trimmings of a dress or dish. [f. FIX]

fixity *n.* fixed state, stability, permanence. [f. obs. *fix* fixed]

fixture /ˈfɪkstʃə(r)/ *n.* **1.** a thing fixed in position; (in *pl.*) articles belonging to a house etc. **2.** a sporting event or date fixed for it. [alt. of obs. *fixure* (as FIX)]

fizz *v.i.* **1.** to effervesce. **2.** to hiss, to splutter. —*n.* **1.** a hissing sound. **2.** effervescence; (*colloq.*) an effervescent drink. [imit.]

fizzle *v.i.* to make a feeble hiss. —*n.* a fizzling sound. —**fizzle out**, to end feebly. [as prec.]

fizzy *adj.* effervescent. —**fizziness** *n.* [f. FIZZ]

fjord var. of FIORD.

fl. *abbr.* **1.** floruit. **2.** fluid.

flab *n.* (*colloq.*) fat, flabbiness. [imit. or f. FLABBY]

flabbergast /ˈflæbəgɑːst/ *v.t.* (*colloq.*) to astound. [perh. f. foll. + AGHAST]

flabby *adj.* limp and hanging loose; feeble. —**flabbily** *adv.*, **flabbiness** *n.* [alt. of *flappy* (f. FLAP)]

flaccid /ˈflæksɪd/ *adj.* flabby; drooping. —**flaccidity** /-ˈsɪdɪtɪ/ *n.*, **flaccidly** *adv.* [f. F or L (*flaccus* flabby)]

flag[1] *n.* **1.** a piece of material, usually oblong or square and attached by one edge to a pole, rope, etc., used as a country's emblem or as a standard, signal, etc. **2.** a small metal plate showing that a taxi is for hire. **3.** a small paper etc. device resembling a flag. —*v.t.* (**-gg-**) **1.** to inform or signal (as) with a flag, especially (often with *down*) to signal (a vehicle or driver) to stop. **2.** to mark with a flag or tag. —**flag-day** *n.* a day on which money is raised from passers-by etc. for a cause and small paper flags are given as tokens. **flag of convenience**, a foreign flag under which a ship is registered to avoid taxes etc. **flag-officer** *n.* an admiral, vice-admiral, or rear-admiral; the commodore of a yacht-club. **flag of truce**, a white flag, indicating a desire to parley. **flag-pole** *n.* a flagstaff. [perh. f. obs. *flag* drooping]

flag[2] *v.i.* (**-gg-**) to lose momentum or vigour; to become limp or feeble. [as prec.; orig. unkn.]

flag[3] *n.* a flagstone; (in *pl.*) a pavement of these. —*v.t.* (**-gg-**) to pave with flags. [cf. ON *flaga* slab of stone]

flag[4] *n.* a plant with a bladed leaf (especially *Iris pseudacorus*), usually growing on moist ground. [orig. unkn.]

flagellant /ˈflædʒələnt/ *n.* one who flagellates himself or others. —*adj.* of flagellation. [f. L *flagellare* whip (as FLAGELLUM)]

flagellate[1] /ˈflædʒəleɪt/ *v.t.* to whip, to flog, especially as a religious discipline or sexual stimulus. —**flagellation** /-ˈleɪʃ(ə)n/ *n.* [as prec.]

flagellate[2] /ˈflædʒələt/ *adj.* having flagella (see foll.). —*n.* a protozoon having flagella. [f. foll.]

flagellum /fləˈdʒeləm/ *n.* (*pl.* **-a**) **1.** (*Bot.*) a runner, a creeping shoot. **2.** (*Biol.*) a lashlike appendage. [L, = whip, dim. of *flagrum* scourge]

flageolet /flædʒəˈlet/ *n.* a fipple flute with two thumb-holes. [F. Prov.]

flagon /ˈflægən/ *n.* a large rounded vessel for holding liquids, usually with a handle and lid. [f. AF f. L (as FLASK)]

flagrant /ˈfleɪɡrənt/ *adj.* glaringly bad; notorious or scandalous. —**flagrancy** *n.*, **flagrantly** *adv.* [f. F or L (*flagrare* blaze)]

flagship *n.* a ship that carries an admiral and flies his flag; the principal vessel of a shipping-line.

flagstaff *n.* a pole on which a flag is hoisted.

flagstone *n.* a flat slab of stone for paving.

flail *n.* a short heavy stick swinging at the end of a wooden staff, used as an implement for threshing. —*v.t./i.* to wave or swing wildly; to beat (as) with a flail. [OE, prob. f. L *flagellum* whip]

flair *n.* a natural ability or talent for selecting or doing what is best, useful, etc.; style, finesse. [F, = power of scent]

flak *n.* **1.** anti-aircraft fire. **2.** a barrage of criticism. —**flak jacket**, a heavy protective jacket reinforced with metal. [G, abbr. of *fliegerabwehrkanone* pilot-defence-gun]

flake *n.* **1.** a small light piece; a piece of snow; a thin broad piece shaved or split off. **2.** dog-fish as food. —*v.t./i.* to take or come *away* or *off* in flakes; to fall in or sprinkle with flakes. —**flake out**, (*colloq.*) to fall asleep or faint (as) with exhaustion. —**flaky** *adj.* [cf. ON *flakna* flake off]

flambé /ˈflɑːbeɪ/ *adj.* (of food) covered with spirit and served alight. [F, = singed]

flamboyant /flæmˈbɔɪənt/ *adj.* showy or florid in appearance or manner. —**flamboyance** *n.*, **flamboyantly** *adv.* [F (as prec.)]

flame *n.* **1.** ignited gas burning visibly; a tongue-shaped portion of this. **2.** a bright light or bright red colour. **3.** passion, especially of love. —*v.i.* **1.** to burn with flames, to blaze. **2.** (of a person or temper) to explode in anger. **3.** to shine or glow like a flame. —**flame-thrower** *n.* a weapon throwing a spray of flame. **flame-tree** *n.* any of several trees with brilliant red or yellow flowers. [f. OF f. L *flamma*]

flamenco /fləˈmeŋkəʊ/ *n.* (*pl.* **-os**) a Spanish gypsy style of song or dance. [Sp., = flamingo]

flaming *adj.* **1.** burning with flames. **2.** very hot or bright. **3.** (*colloq.*) passionate. **4.** (*colloq.*) damned. [f. FLAME]

flamingo /fləˈmɪŋɡəʊ/ *n.* (*pl.* **-os**) a tall long-necked wading-bird of the family Phoenicopteridae, with pink, scarlet, and black plumage. [f. Port. f. Prov. (as FLAME)]

flammable /ˈflæməb(ə)l/ *adj.* that may be set on fire. —**flammability** /-ˈbɪlɪtɪ/ *n.* [f. L (as FLAME)]

flan *n.* an open sponge or pastry case filled or spread with a fruit or savoury filling. [F, orig. = round cake]

Flanders /ˈflɑːndəz/ a medieval principality in the SW part of the Low Countries, now divided between Belgium, France, and Holland. The area was the scene of considerable military activity during the First World War when British troops held the sector of the Western Front round the town of Ypres. —**Flanders poppy**, a red poppy used as an emblem of the soldiers of the Allies who fell in the First World War; an artificial red poppy made for wearing on Remembrance Sunday, sold in aid of needy ex-service people.

flange /flændʒ/ *n.* a rim or projection, especially for strengthening or attachment to another object. [perh. f. *flange, flanch* widen outwards]

flank *n.* **1.** the fleshy part of the side of the body between the ribs and the hip. **2.** the side of a mountain etc. **3.** the left or right side of a body of troops. —*v.t.* to be or be posted at or move along the flank or side of. [f. OF f. Gmc]

flannel *n.* **1.** a kind of woven woollen usually napless cloth; (in *pl.*) flannel garments, especially trousers. **2.** a cloth used for washing oneself. **3.** (*slang*) nonsense, flattery. —*v.t.* (**-ll-**) **1.** to wash with a flannel. **2.** (*slang*) to flatter. —**flannelled** *adj.* [perh. f. Welsh *gwlanen* (*gwlan* wool)]

flannelette /flæn(ə)ˈlet/ *n.* a napped cotton fabric resembling flannel. [f. prec.]

flap *v.t./i.* (**-pp-**) **1.** to swing or sway about; to cause to do this, to move up and down. **2.** to hit at (a fly etc.) with a flat object. **3.** (*colloq.*, of ears) to listen intently. **4.** (*colloq.*) to be agitated or panicky. —*n.* **1.** a flat broad piece attached at one edge, acting as a cover, extension, etc.; an aileron on an aircraft, a hinged or sliding section used to control lift (ill. FLIGHT). **2.** the action or sound of flapping. **3.** a light blow, usually with something flat. **4.** (*colloq.*) a state of agitation or fuss. —**flappy** *adj.* [prob. imit.]

flapdoodle /ˈflæpduːd(ə)l/ *n.* nonsense. [orig. unkn.]

flapjack *n.* **1.** a sweet oatcake. **2.** a small pancake. [f. FLAP (in dial. sense 'toss') + JACK]

flapper *n.* **1.** a broad flat device, a flap. **2.** (*colloq.*) a young (esp. unconventional) woman in the 1920s. [f. FLAP]

flare /fleə(r)/ *v.t./i.* **1.** to blaze with a bright unsteady flame. **2.** to burst into sudden activity or anger. **3.** to widen gradually. —*n.* **1.** a flame or bright light used as a signal or for illumination. **2.** an outburst of flame. **3.** a dazzling unsteady light; unwanted light resulting from reflection within a lens. **4.** a flared shape, a gradual widening. —**flare path,** a line of lights to guide aircraft landing or taking off. **flare up,** to burst into flame; to become suddenly angry. [orig. unkn.]

flash *n.* **1.** a sudden short blaze of flame or light. **2.** a brief outburst of feeling, a transient display of wit etc.; an instant; a brief news item on the radio etc. **3.** a photographic flashlight. **4.** a coloured cloth patch as an emblem on military uniform. —*v.t./i.* **1.** to give out a flash, to gleam. **2.** to burst suddenly into view or perception. **3.** to send or reflect like a flash or in flashes; to cause to shine briefly. **4.** to rush past suddenly. **5.** to send (news etc.) by radio or telegraph. **6.** (*colloq.*) to show suddenly or ostentatiously; (*slang*) to display oneself indecently. —*adj.* (*colloq.*) gaudy, showy, smart. —**flash cube,** a set of four flashbulbs arranged as a cube and operated in turn. **flash in the pan,** a seemingly brilliant but fleeting success; a promising start followed by failure. [orig. imit., of the sea]

flashback *n.* a return to a past event, especially as a scene in a film.

flashbulb *n.* a bulb giving a bright light for flashlight photography.

flasher *n.* **1.** an automatic device for flashing lights intermittently. **2.** (*slang*) a person who exposes himself indecently. [f. FLASH]

flashing *n.* a strip of metal acting as waterproofing at a joint of roofing etc. (ill. HOUSES). [f. dial. *flash* seal with lead sheets, or obs. *flash* lightning]

flashlight *n.* **1.** a device producing a brief bright light for indoor etc. photography. **2.** an electric torch.

flashpoint *n.* the temperature at which vapour from oil etc. will ignite; the point at which anger breaks out.

flashy *adj.* gaudy, showy, cheaply attractive. —**flashily** *adv.*, **flashiness** *n.* [f. FLASH]

flask /flɑːsk/ *n.* **1.** a vacuum-flask. **2.** a narrow-necked bulbous bottle as used in chemistry. **3.** a small flat bottle for spirits, carried in the pocket etc. [f. F & It. f. L (cf. FLAGON)]

flat *adj.* **1.** horizontal, level; spread out, lying at full length. **2.** smooth, without bumps or indentations. **3.** absolute, downright; dull, uninteresting, monotonous; (of a drink) that has lost its effervescence; (of a battery etc.) no longer able to generate electric current. **4.** (of a tyre) deflated, especially from a puncture. **5.** (*Mus.*, of a note) below the normal or correct pitch; a semitone lower than the corresponding note or key of natural pitch. —*adv.* **1.** in a flat manner. **2.** (*Mus.*) below the correct pitch. **3.** (*colloq.*) absolutely, completely, exactly. —*n.* **1.** a group of rooms, usually on one floor, forming a residence. **2.** a flat thing or part, level ground; low land; (*colloq.*) a flat tyre; a section of stage scenery mounted on a frame. **3.** (*Mus.*) a note that is a semitone lower than the corresponding one of natural pitch; the sign indicating this (ill. MUSICAL NOTATION). —**the flat,** the season of flat races for horses. **flat-fish** *n.* a type of fish with a flattened body (e.g. sole, plaice). **flat feet,** feet with less than the normal arch beneath. **flat-footed** *adj.* having flat feet; (*colloq.*) resolute, uninspired, unprepared. **flat-iron** *n.* a heavy iron for pressing linen etc., heated by external means. **flat-out** *adv.* at top speed, using all one's strength or resources. **flat race,** a race over level ground, without jumps. **flat rate,** an unvarying rate or charge. **flat spin,** a nearly horizontal spin in an aircraft; (*colloq.*) agitation or panic. **that's flat,** (*colloq.*) that is definite. —**flatly** *adv.*, **flatness** *n.* [f. ON]

flatlet /ˈflætlɪt/ *n.* a small flat, usually of one or two rooms. [f. FLAT + -LET]

flatten *v.t./i.* **1.** to make or become flat. **2.** to defeat or refute decisively, to humiliate. [f. FLAT]

flatter *v.t.* to pay exaggerated or insincere compliments to, especially to win favour; to cause to feel honoured; (of a portrait etc.) to represent (a person) too favourably.

—**flatter oneself,** to delude oneself smugly. —**flatterer** *n.* [perh. rel. to OF *flater* smooth down]

flattery *n.* exaggerated or insincere praise. [f. prec.]

flatulent /ˈflætjʊlənt/ *adj.* **1.** causing, caused by, or troubled with the formation of gas in the alimentary canal. **2.** inflated, pretentious. —**flatulence, flatulency** *ns.* [F f. L (*flatus* wind in stomach)]

flatworm *n.* a type of worm with a flattened body, e.g. the tapeworm.

Flaubert /ˈfləʊbeə(r)/, Gustave (1821–80), French novelist. His first published (and greatest) novel *Madame Bovary* (1857) relates the adulteries and suicide of a doctor's wife in provincial Normandy and is noted for its rigorous psychological development, a quality which marks all his mature work. This sensational work was judged offensive to public morals, but Flaubert and his printer were acquitted after trial. Flaubert's *Correspondence* (1887–93), with searching reflections on the art of fiction, shows the novelist as an extravagant romantic, an enthusiastic traveller, and the lover of the poet Louise Colet (1808–76).

flaunt *v.t./i.* to display proudly; to show off, to parade. [orig. unkn.]

flautist /ˈflɔːtɪst/ *n.* a flute-player. [f. It. (*flauto* flute)]

Flavian /ˈfleɪvɪən/ *adj.* of the dynasty of Roman emperors including Vespasian and his sons Titus and Domitian. —*n.* a member of this dynasty. [f. L *Flavius* name of family]

flavour /ˈfleɪvə(r)/ *n.* a distinctive taste; a mingled sensation of smell and taste; an indefinable characteristic quality. —*v.t.* to give a flavour to, to season. —**flavoursome** *adj.* [f. OF *flaor,* perh. f. L *flatus* blowing & *foetor* stench, assim. to *savour*]

flavouring *n.* a thing used to flavour food or drink. [f. prec.]

flaw[1] *n.* an imperfection, a blemish; a crack, a breach; an invalidating defect in a document etc. —*v.t.* to make a flaw in, to spoil. [perh. f. ON *flaga* slab (as FLAG[3])]

flaw[2] *n.* a squall of wind. [f. MDu. *vlaghe*]

flax *n.* a blue-flowered plant (*Linum usitatissimum*) cultivated for its seed and for the textile fibre obtained from its stem; its fibre. —**flax-seed** *n.* linseed. [OE]

flaxen *adj.* of flax; pale yellow. [f. FLAX]

Flaxman /ˈflæksmən/, John (1755–1826), English neo-classical sculptor. He worked for the potter, Josiah Wedgwood, 1775–87, designing medallion portraits and plaques, and was in Rome 1787–94 studying the antique and Italian medieval art. In 1793 he published engraved illustrations to Homer, greatly influenced by Greek vase-painting, which won him international fame. On his return to England he became a busy sculptor, executing many church monuments. He is one of the very few English sculptors to have had a European reputation, though this was based largely on his drawings.

flay *v.t.* **1.** to strip off the skin or hide of; to peel off. **2.** to criticize severely. [OE]

F-layer *n.* the highest and most strongly ionized layer in the ionosphere.

flea *n.* a small wingless jumping insect feeding on human and other blood (ill. INSECTS). —**flea-bite** *n.* a slight injury or inconvenience. **flea-bitten** *adj.* bitten by or infested with fleas; shabby. **a flea in one's ear,** a sharp reproof. **flea market,** (*colloq.*) a street market selling second-hand goods etc. [OE]

fleck *n.* a small spot of colour; a small particle, a speck. —*v.t.* to mark with flecks. [f. ON, or MLG or Du.]

Flecker /ˈflekə(r)/, (Herman) James Elroy (1884–1915), English poet, whose best-known works are 'The Golden Journey to Samarkand' (1913) and the verse drama *Hassan,* published posthumously in 1922, for which Delius wrote incidental music.

fled *past* & *p.p.* of FLEE.

fledge *v.t.* **1.** to provide (a bird, arrow, etc.) with feathers or down. **2.** to rear (a young bird) until it can fly. **3.** (in *p.p.*) able to fly; mature, independent, trained. [f. obs. adj. *fledge* fit to fly]

fledgeling /ˈfledʒlɪŋ/ *n.* **1.** a young bird. **2.** an inexperienced person. [f. prec.]

flee *v.t./i.* (*past* & *p.p.* **fled**) to run away (from), to leave hurriedly; to seek safety in flight; to vanish. [OE]

fleece *n.* **1.** the woolly coat of a sheep etc.; the wool shorn from a sheep in one shearing. **2.** a soft fabric for lining etc. —*v.t.* **1.** to strip or rob of money, property, etc. **2.** to remove the fleece from (a sheep). —**fleecy** *adj.* [OE]

fleet *n.* **1.** a naval force, a navy; a group of ships under one commander. **2.** a number of vehicles under one proprietor. —*v.i.* to pass rapidly. —*adj.* swift, nimble. —**fleetly** *adv.*, **fleetness** *n.* [OE]

fleeting *adj.* brief, passing rapidly. [OE, = float, swim]

Fleet Street a London street between the Strand and the City, in or near which most of the leading national newspapers have offices, whence the allusive use of its name to refer to the British press. It is named after the River Fleet, which is now covered in.

Fleming[1] /ˈflemɪŋ/ *n.* a native of Flanders. [OE f. ON & Du. (*Vlaanderen* Flanders)]

Fleming[2] /ˈflemɪŋ/, Sir Alexander (1881-1955), Scottish doctor and scientist, who spent most of his career at St Mary's Hospital, London, where he investigated the body's defences against bacteriological infection. In 1928 he discovered the effect of penicillin on bacteria, and twelve years later a team of Oxford scientists, led by Florey and Chain, established its therapeutic use. In 1942 Fleming was propelled into the limelight, as a British scientific hero, by a government eager for 'good news', and so achieved fame retrospectively for his work in the 1920s. A string of honours followed: fellowship of the Royal Society (1943), a knighthood (1944), and the award of the Nobel Prize for medicine, jointly with Florey and Chain, in 1945.

Fleming[3] /ˈflemɪŋ/, Ian (Lancaster) (1908-64), English thriller-writer, creator of the fictional secret agent James Bond.

Flemish /ˈflemɪʃ/ *adj.* of Flanders or its people or their language. —*n.* one of the two official languages of Belgium, the other being French. It is essentially the same language as Dutch; the apparent differences are a matter of spelling convention. —**Flemish bond,** see BOND[1]. [f. Du. (as prec.)]

flesh *n.* **1.** the soft substance between the skin and bones. **2.** the tissue of animal bodies (excluding fish and sometimes fowl) as food. **3.** the body as opposed to the mind or soul. **4.** the visible surface of the human body; the pulpy part of a fruit or plant; plumpness, fat. —*v.t./i.* (with *out*) to make or become substantial. —**the flesh,** the physical or sensual appetites. **flesh and blood,** the human body, human nature, mankind (*one's flesh and blood,* near relations). **flesh-coloured** *adj.* yellowish pink. **flesh-wound** *n.* a wound not reaching a bone or vital organ. **in the flesh,** in bodily form, in person. [OE]

fleshly *adj.* **1.** mortal, worldly. **2.** sensual. [OE]

fleshpots *n.pl.* luxurious living.

fleshy *adj.* of or like flesh, plump, pulpy. —**fleshiness** *n.* [f. FLESH]

Fletcher /ˈfletʃə(r)/, John (1579-1625), English dramatist. Before dying of the plague he had produced some 15 plays with Beaumont, including *Philaster* (1609), *The Maid's Tragedy* (1610-11), 16 plays of which he was the sole author, such as *The Faithful Shepherdess* (1610) and *The Woman's Prize* (1604-17), and others in collaboration with Massinger, Jonson, Chapman, and with Shakespeare in *The Two Noble Kinsmen* (1612-13) and *Henry VIII* (c.1613). His reputation was at its highest during the Restoration when he ranked with Shakespeare and Jonson.

fleur-de-lis /flɜːdəˈliː/ *n.* (also -**lys**; *pl.* **fleurs-** *pr.* same) the heraldic lily of three petals (ill. HERALDRY); the former royal arms of France. [f. OF, = flower of lily]

fleury /ˈflɜːrɪ/ *adj.* (in heraldry) decorated with fleurs-de-lis (ill. HERALDRY). [f. OF *flo(u)ré* (*flour* flower)]

flew *past* of FLY[1].

flex[1] *v.t.* to bend (a joint or limb); to move (a muscle) to bend a joint. [f. L *flectere flex-* bend]

flex[2] *n.* flexible insulated wire. [abbr. of foll.]

flexible /ˈfleksɪb(ə)l/ *adj.* **1.** that bends easily without breaking, pliable. **2.** adaptable to circumstances. **3.** easily persuaded, manageable. —**flexibility** /-ˈbɪlɪtɪ/ *n.*, **flexibly** *adv.* [f. OF or L (as FLEX[1])]

flexion /ˈflekʃ(ə)n/ *n.* bending; a bent state or part. [f. L *flexio* (as FLEX[1])]

flexitime /ˈfleksɪtaɪm/ *n.* a system of flexible working hours. [f. FLEXIBLE + TIME]

flibbertigibbet /ˈflɪbətɪdʒɪbɪt/ *n.* a gossiping or frivolous person. [imit. of chatter]

flick *n.* **1.** the sudden release of a bent finger or thumb. **2.** a quick light blow or stroke. **3** (*colloq.*) a cinema film; **the flicks,** a cinema performance. —*v.t.* to strike or knock or move with a flick. —**flick-knife** *n.* a knife with a blade that springs out when a button etc. is pressed. **flick through,** to look cursorily through (a book etc.). [imit.]

flicker *v.i.* **1.** to burn or shine unsteadily or fitfully. **2.** to quiver, to flutter. **3.** (of hope etc.) to occur briefly. —*n.* **1.** a flickering light or movement. **2.** a brief spell (of hope, recognition, etc.). [OE]

flier var. of FLYER.

flight[1] /flaɪt/ *n.* **1.** an act or manner of flying; the movement or passage of a thing through the air; the distance flown. (See ill. pp. 308-9.) **2.** a journey made by an aircraft or airline. **3.** a group of birds etc. flying together; a volley (*of* arrows etc.). **4.** a series (*of* stairs in a straight line, of hurdles etc. for racing). **5.** an exceptional effort *of* fancy etc. **6.** the tail of a dart. —**flight-deck** *n.* the cockpit of a large aircraft; the deck of an aircraft-carrier. **flight-lieutenant** *n.* an RAF officer next below squadron leader. **flight-recorder** *n.* an electronic device in an aircraft, recording information about its flight. **flight sergeant,** the RAF rank next above sergeant. **in the first** *or* **top flight,** taking a leading place, excellent of its kind. [OE (cf. FLY[1])]

flight[2] /flaɪt/ *n.* fleeing, an escape from danger etc. —**put to flight,** to cause to flee. **take (to) flight,** to flee. [OE (as FLEE)]

flightless /ˈflaɪtlɪs/ *adj.* (of a bird) lacking the power of flight. [f. FLIGHT + -LESS]

flighty *adj.* (usu. of a woman) frivolous, changeable. —**flightily** *adv.*, **flightiness** *n.* [f. FLIGHT]

flimsy /ˈflɪmzɪ/ *adj.* **1.** lightly or carelessly assembled; easily damaged or knocked apart. **2.** (of an excuse etc.) unconvincing. —**flimsily** *adv.*, **flimsiness** *n.* [orig. unkn.]

flinch *v.i.* to draw back, to shrink (*from* an action); to wince. [f. OF *flenchir* f. Gmc]

Flinders /ˈflɪndəz/, Matthew (1774-1814), English explorer. In the company of George Bass, Flinders explored the coast of New South Wales in 1795-1800, before being commissioned by the Royal Navy to circumnavigate Australia. Between 1801 and 1803 he charted much of the west coast of the continent for the first time, but was wrecked on his voyage home and imprisoned by the French on Mauritius until 1810.

fling *v.t./i.* (*past* & *p.p.* **flung**) **1.** to throw, esp. forcefully or hurriedly. **2.** to put or send hurriedly or summarily. **3.** to put *on* or take *off* (clothes) hurriedly or casually. **4.** to rush, to go angrily or violently. —*n.* **1.** the action of flinging. **2.** a vigorous dance. **3.** a short bout of self-indulgence. [perh. f. ON]

flint *n.* **1.** a hard stone of nearly pure silica found in pebbly lumps steel-grey within and encrusted with white; a piece of this, especially as a prehistoric tool or weapon. **2.** a piece of hard alloy used to produce a spark. **3.** anything hard and unyielding. **flint glass,** see GLASS. —**flinty** *adj.* [OE]

flintlock *n.* an old type of gun fired by a spark from a flint.

flip[1] *v.t.* (-**pp**-) to turn over quickly, to flick; to toss (a thing) with a jerk so that it turns over in the air. —*n.* **1.** the action of flipping. **2.** (*colloq.*) a short trip. —**flip side,** the reverse side of a gramophone record. **flip through,** to look cursorily through (a book etc.). [prob. f. FILLIP]

flip[2] *n.* a drink of heated beer and spirit. [perh. = prec.]

flip[3] *adj.* (*colloq.*) glib, flippant. [f. FLIP[1]]

flippant /ˈflɪpənt/ *adj.* treating a serious matter lightly, disrespectful. —**flippancy** *n.*, **flippantly** *adv.* [f. FLIP[1]]

flipper *n.* **1.** a limb used by turtles, seals, etc., in swimming. **2.** a flat rubber etc. attachment worn on the foot in underwater swimming. **3.** (*slang*) the hand. [f. FLIP[1]]

flipping *adj.* & *adv.* (*slang*, expressing mild annoyance) damned. [f. FLIP[1]]

flirt *v.t./i.* **1.** to behave lightheartedly in an amorous manner, to pretend courtship. **2.** to toy *with* an idea etc., to interest oneself superficially. **3.** to trifle *with* a danger etc. **4.** to wave or move briskly in short jerks. —*n.* one who flirts amorously. —**flirtation** /-ˈteɪʃ(ə)n/ *n.*, **flirtatious** /-ˈteɪʃəs/ *adj.*, **flirtatiously** *adv.* [imit., orig. = move or throw with a jerk]

flit *v.i.* (-**tt**-) **1.** to move lightly and rapidly. **2.** to make short flights. **3.** to abscond, to disappear secretly (especially from one's abode to escape a creditor). —*n.* an act of flitting. [f. ON (rel. to FLEET)]

flitch *n.* a side of bacon. [OE]

flitter *v.i.* to flit about. —**flitter-mouse** *n.* a bat (BAT[2]). [f. FLIT]

float *v.t./i.* **1.** to rest or move on the surface of a liquid; to cause to do this; to move or be suspended *in* a liquid or gas. **2.** (*slang*) to move about in a leisurely way. **3.** to hover *before* the eyes or mind. **4.** (of a currency) to have a fluctuating exchange rate; to cause or allow (a currency) to have this. **5.** to start (a company, scheme, etc.). —*n.* **1.** a raft. **2.** a floating device to control the flow of water, petrol, etc. **3.** a structure enabling an aircraft to float on water. **4.** a cork or quill used on a fishing-line as an indicator; a cork supporting the edge of a fishing-net. **5.** a low-bodied lorry or cart, especially one used for display in a procession. **6.** a sum of money retained for minor expenditure or change-giving. **7.** a tool for smoothing plaster. **8.** (in *sing.* or *pl.*) the footlights in a theatre. —**float glass, float process,** see GLASS. **floating dock,** a floating structure usable as a dry dock. **floating kidney,** one unusually movable. **floating population,** a population not settled in a definite place. **floating rib,** any of the ribs not joined to the breastbone. **floating voter,** a voter not permanently supporting any one political party. [OE]

floatation var. of FLOTATION.

flocculent /ˈflɒjʊlənt/ *adj.* like tufts of wool; in or showing tufts. —**flocculence** *n.* [f. L (as FLOCK²)]

flock¹ *n.* **1.** a number of sheep, goats, or birds regarded as a group or unit. **2.** a large crowd of people; a number of people in the care of a priest or teacher etc. —*v.i.* to move or assemble in large numbers. [OE]

flock² *n.* a lock or tuft of wool etc.; wool or cotton waste used as a stuffing. [f. OF f. L *floccus*]

Flodden /ˈflɒd(ə)n/ the scene of the decisive battle of the Anglo-Scottish war of 1513. A Scottish army under James IV was defeated by a smaller but better-led English force under the Earl of Surrey (sent northwards by Henry VIII, who was on campaign in France) near the Northumbrian village of Branxton. The Scottish king and most of his nobles were among the heavy Scots losses.

floe /fləʊ/ *n.* a sheet of floating ice. [f. Norw.]

flog *v.t.* (**-gg-**) **1.** to beat with a whip, stick, etc. **2.** (*slang*) to sell. —**flog a dead horse,** to waste one's efforts. **flog to death,** (*colloq.*) to talk about or promote at tedious length. —**flogging** *n.* [orig. unkn.]

flood /flʌd/ *n.* **1.** an influx or the overflowing of water beyond its normal confines, especially over land; the water that overflows; an outpouring, an outburst of great quantity. **2.** the inflow of the tide. **3.** (*colloq.*) a floodlight. —*v.i.* **1.** to overflow; to cover or be covered with a flood. **2.** to come (*in*) in great quantities. **3.** to drive *out* (of a home etc.) by flood. **4.** to have a uterine haemorrhage. —**the Flood,** that brought by God upon the earth in the time of Noah (Gen. 6 ff.) to destroy mankind because of the wickedness of the human race. Parallel stories are found in Mesopotamian sources (e.g. the Gilgamesh epic); the flood that forms part of Chinese mythology was not a retribution for sin. Archaeological evidence at Ur and Kish shows that the Tigris-Euphrates valley was subject to periodic inundations but cannot be equated directly with the Biblical narrative. **flood plain,** the level area over which a river spreads in flood (ill. RIVERS). **flood-tide** *n.* a rising tide. [OE, rel. to FLOW]

floodgate *n.* a gate that can be opened or closed to control the flow of water, especially the lower gate of a lock.

floodlight *n.* a large powerful light (usually one of several) to illuminate a building, sportsground, etc. —*v.t.* to illuminate with this.

floor /flɔː(r)/ *n.* **1.** the lower surface of a room, on which one stands. **2.** the bottom of the sea, a cave, etc. **3.** the rooms etc. on the same level in a building. **4.** the part of a legislative assembly etc. where members sit and speak; the right to speak next in a debate etc. **5.** a level area. **6.** a minimum level for prices, wages, etc. —*v.t.* **1.** to provide with a floor. **2.** to knock (a person) down. **3.** to baffle or nonplus; to overcome. —**floor manager,** the stage manager of a television production. **floor show,** an entertainment presented on the floor of a night-club etc. [OE]

floorboard *n.* a long wooden board used for flooring.

floorcloth *n.* a cloth for washing floors.

flooring *n.* boards etc. used as a floor. [f. FLOOR]

floozie *n.* (also **floosie**) (*colloq.*) a girl or woman, especially a disreputable one. [cf. FLOSS and dial. *floosy* fluffy]

flop *v.i.* (**-pp-**) **1.** to fall or sit etc. (*down*) suddenly, awkwardly, or with a slight thud. **2.** to hang or sway limply or heavily. **3.** to make a dull flapping sound. **4.** (*slang*) to fail. —*n.* **1.** a flopping motion or sound. **2.** (*slang*) a failure. —*adv.* with a flop. [var. of FLAP]

floppy *adj.* tending to flop, not firm or rigid. —**floppy disc,** a flexible disc for the storage of machine-readable data. —**floppiness** *n.* [f. FLOP]

Flora /ˈflɔːrə/ (*Rom. myth.*) the goddess of flowering plants.

flora /ˈflɔːrə/ *n.* (*pl.* **-as**) the plants of a particular region or period. [L, f. prec.]

floral /ˈflɔːr(ə)l, ˈflɒ-/ *adj.* of or decorated with flowers. —**florally** *adv.* [f. L (as FLOWER)]

Florence /ˈflɒrəns/ a city of Tuscany in northern Italy; pop. (est. 1981) 453,293. From the 14th to the 16th c., especially under the Medici family, it was the centre of the Italian Renaissance.

Florentine /ˈflɒrəntaɪn/ *adj.* of Florence in Italy. —*n.* a native of Florence. [f. F or L]

florescence /flɔːˈres(ə)ns, flɒ-/ *n.* flowering time or state (*lit.* or *fig.*). [f. L *florescere* (*florēre* bloom)]

floret /ˈflɔːrɪt/ *n.* a small flower; each of the small flowers of a composite flower. [f. L *flos floris* flower]

Florey /ˈflɔːrɪ/, Howard Walter, Baron (1898-1968), Australian pathologist who, in collaboration with Sir Ernst Chain, isolated and purified penicillin, developed techniques for its large-scale production, and performed the first clinical trials. For their work Florey and Chain shared a 1945 Nobel Prize with the discoverer of penicillin, Sir Alexander Fleming.

floribunda /flɒrɪˈbʌndə/ *n.* a rose or other plant bearing dense clusters of flowers. [L, = freely flowering (as prec. +-*bund-* (cf. *moribund*) infl. by L *abundus* copious)]

florid /ˈflɒrɪd/ *adj.* **1.** ornate, elaborate, showy. **2.** ruddy, flushed. [f. F or L *floridus* (*flos floris* flower)]

Florida /ˈflɒrɪdə/ a State forming a peninsula of the southeastern USA, chiefly under Spanish dominion from the 16th c. and purchased from Spain in 1819. It became the 27th State of the Union in 1845; capital, Tallahassee.

florin /ˈflɒrɪn/ *n.* a gold or silver coin, especially the former English two-shilling coin (10p). [f. OF f. It. (*fiore* flower), the original coin having the figure of a lily]

florist /ˈflɒrɪst/ *n.* one who deals in or grows flowers. [f. L *flos floris* flower]

floruit /ˈflɒrʊɪt/ *n.* the period or date at which a person lived or worked. [L, = he or she flourished]

flory *adj.* = FLEURY.

floss *n.* **1.** the rough silk enveloping a silkworm's cocoon. **2.** untwisted silk thread for embroidery. **3.** dental floss (see DENTAL). —**flossy** *adj.* [f. F *floche*]

flotation /fləʊˈteɪʃ(ə)n/ *n.* the launching of a commercial enterprise etc. [alt. of *floatation*, f. FLOAT after *rotation* etc.]

flotilla /fləˈtɪlə/ *n.* a small fleet; a fleet of small ships. [Sp. (*flota* fleet)]

flotsam /ˈflɒtsəm/ *n.* wreckage found floating. —**flotsam and jetsam,** odds and ends; vagrants etc. [f. AF (*floter* float)]

flounce¹ *v.i.* to go or move abruptly or angrily, with jerking movements. —*n.* a flouncing movement. [perh. imit.]

flounce² *n.* an ornamental frill round a woman's skirt etc. —*v.t.* to trim with flounces. [alt. of *frounce* fold, pleat, f. OF]

flounder¹ *v.i.* to move or struggle helplessly or clumsily; to progress with great difficulty, to struggle. —*n.* an act of floundering. [imit.]

flounder² *n.* a flat-fish, especially a small edible species (*Pleuronectes flesus*). [f. AF, prob. f. Scand.]

flour /ˈflaʊə(r)/ *n.* a fine meal or powder made by milling and usually sifting cereals, especially wheat; a fine soft powder. —*v.t.* to sprinkle with flour. —**floury** *adj.* [different spelling of FLOWER in sense 'finest part']

flourish /ˈflʌrɪʃ/ *v.t./i.* **1.** to grow vigorously and healthily; to prosper, to thrive, to be in one's prime. **2.** to wave, to brandish. —*n.* **1.** an ornamental curve in writing. **2.** a dramatic gesture with the hand etc. **3.** (*Mus.*) a florid passage, a fanfare. [f. OF f. L *florēre* (as FLORET)]

flout /flaʊt/ *v.t.* to disobey openly and scornfully. [perh. f. Du. *fluiten* whistle, hiss (cf. FLUTE)]

flow /fləʊ/ *v.i.* **1.** to glide along as a stream, to move freely like a liquid or gas. **2.** (of blood, money, or electric current) to circulate. **3.** to proceed steadily and continuously. **4.** to hang easily, to undulate. **5.** to be plentiful; to be plentifully supplied *with*. **6.** to gush out (*from*); to result from. **7.** (of the tide) to rise. —*n.* **1.** a flowing movement or mass; a flowing liquid, the amount of this. **2.** an outpouring. **3.** a rise of the tide. —**flow chart** *or* **diagram** *or* **sheet,** a diagram showing the movement or development of things through a series of processes. [OE]

flower /ˈflaʊə(r)/ *n.* the part of a plant from which the fruit or seed is developed (see ill. pp. 322-3); a blossom (and its stem) used especially in groups for decoration; a plant

Flight

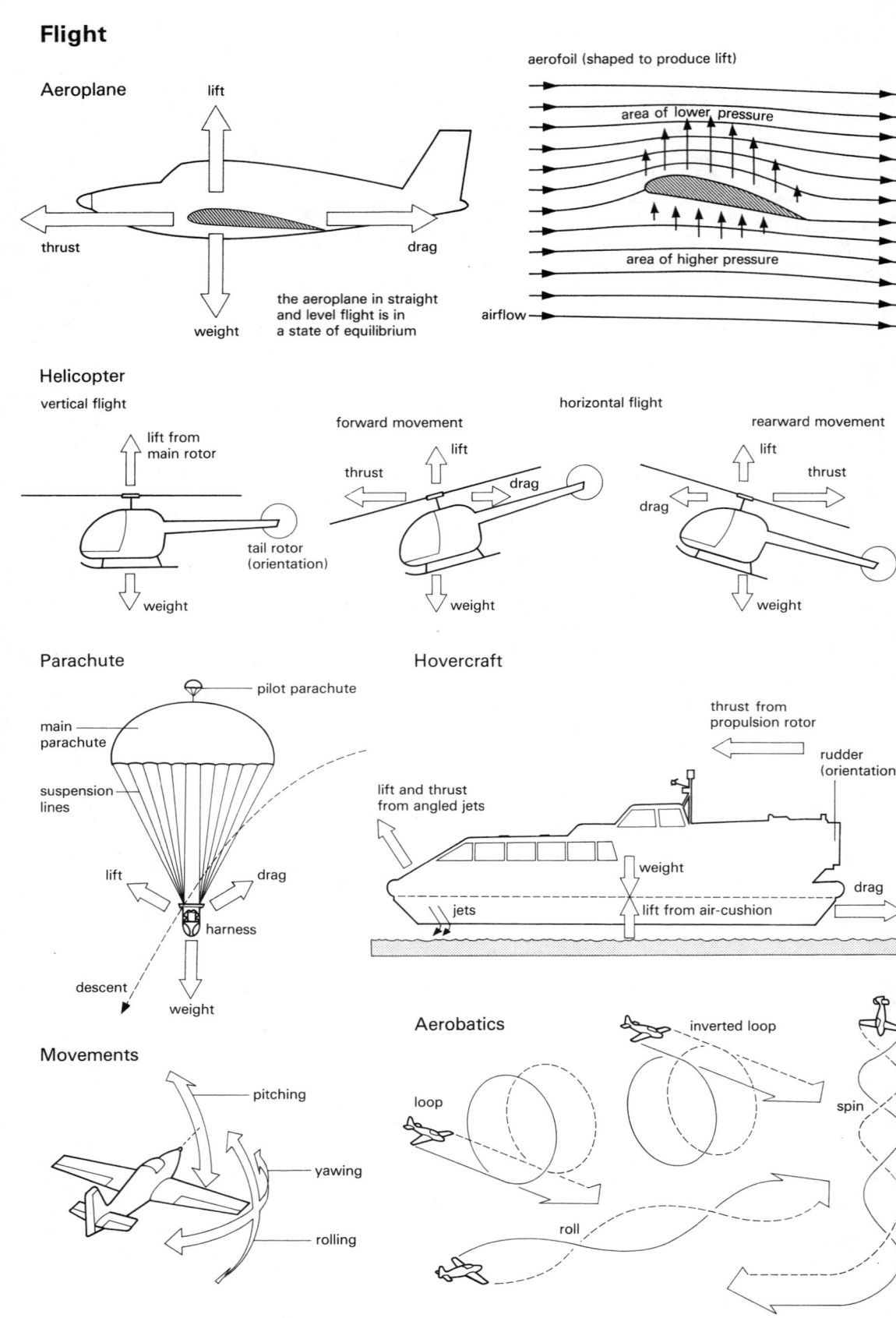

Aeroplane

lift

thrust

drag

weight

the aeroplane in straight
and level flight is in
a state of equilibrium

aerofoil (shaped to produce lift)

area of lower pressure

area of higher pressure

airflow

Helicopter

vertical flight

horizontal flight

lift from
main rotor

tail rotor
(orientation)

weight

forward movement

thrust

lift

drag

weight

rearward movement

lift

thrust

drag

weight

Parachute

pilot parachute

main
parachute

suspension
lines

lift

drag

harness

descent

weight

Hovercraft

thrust from
propulsion rotor

rudder
(orientation)

lift and thrust
from angled jets

weight

jets

lift from air-cushion

drag

Movements

pitching

yawing

rolling

Aerobatics

inverted loop

loop

spin

roll

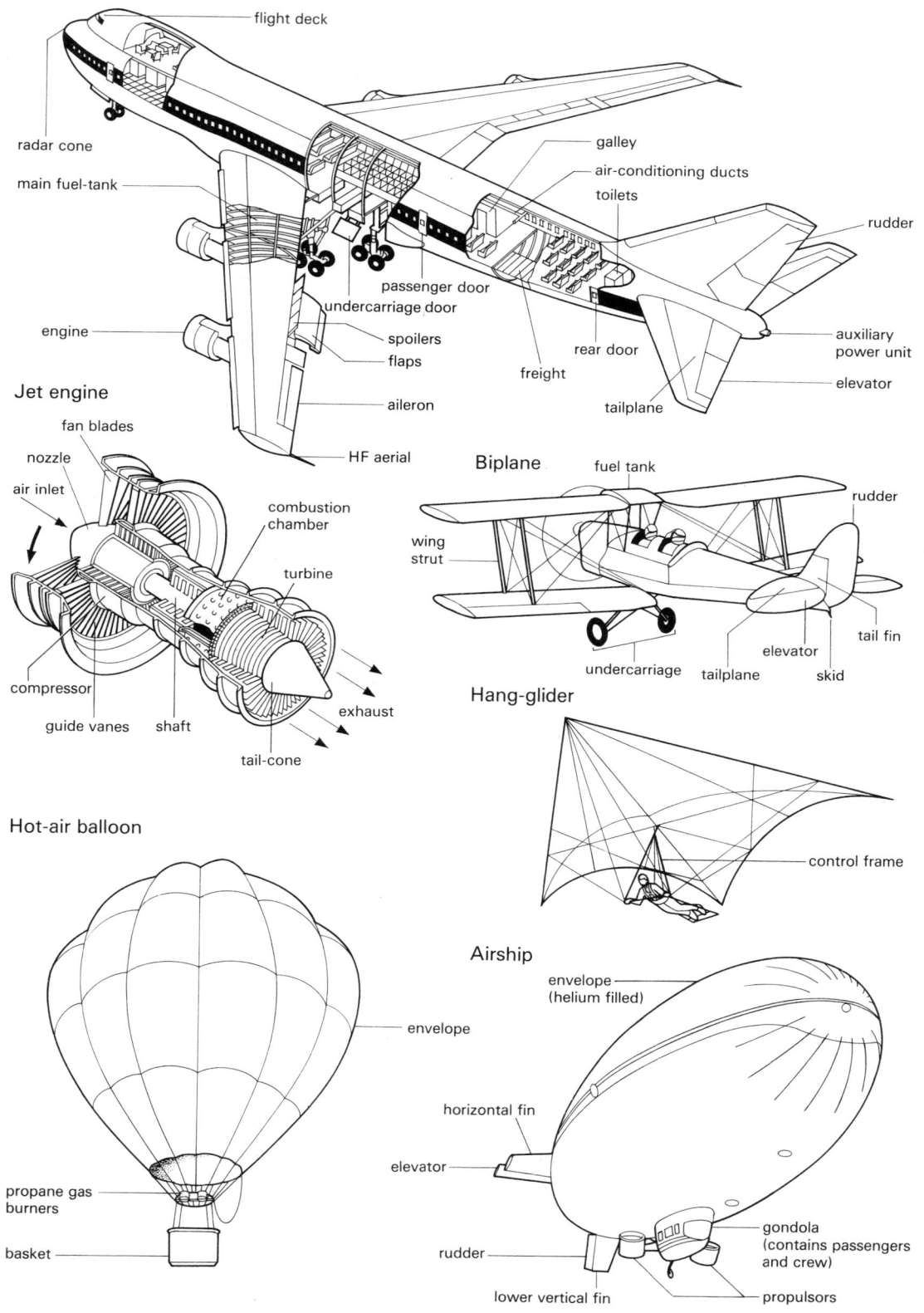

Jet aircraft (Boeing 747)

flight deck

radar cone

main fuel-tank

engine

galley

air-conditioning ducts

toilets

rudder

passenger door

undercarriage door

spoilers

flaps

aileron

HF aerial

rear door

freight

auxiliary power unit

elevator

tailplane

Jet engine

fan blades

nozzle

air inlet

combustion chamber

turbine

compressor

guide vanes

shaft

tail-cone

exhaust

Biplane

fuel tank

rudder

wing strut

tail fin

undercarriage

tailplane

elevator

skid

Hang-glider

control frame

Hot-air balloon

envelope

propane gas burners

basket

Airship

envelope (helium filled)

horizontal fin

elevator

rudder

lower vertical fin

gondola (contains passengers and crew)

propulsors

cultivated or noted for its flowers. —*v.t./i.* **1.** to bloom or blossom, to cause to do this. **2.** to reach a peak. —**the flower of,** the best part of. **flowers of sulphur,** the fine powder produced when sulphur evaporates and condenses. **in flower,** with the flowers out. [f. OF f. L *flos floris*]

flowerpot *n.* a pot in which a plant may be grown.

flowery *adj.* **1.** abounding in flowers. **2.** (of language) ornate, elaborate. —**floweriness** *n.* [f. FLOWER]

flown *p.p.* of FLY[1].

flu /fluː/ *n.* (*colloq.*) influenza. [abbr.]

fluctuate /ˈflʌktjʊeɪt/ *v.i.* to vary erratically, to rise and fall. —**fluctuation** /-ˈeɪʃ(ə)n/ *n.* [f. L *fluctuare* (*fluctus* wave)]

flue /fluː/ *n.* the smoke-duct in a chimney; a channel for conveying heat. [orig. unkn.]

fluent /ˈfluːənt/ *adj.* (of a person) able to speak quickly and easily; (of speech) flowing easily, coming readily. —**fluency** *n.*, **fluently** *adv.* [f. L (*fluere* flow)]

fluff *n.* **1.** a light downy substance, e.g. that shed from fabric. **2.** (*slang*) a bungle or mistake (in a performance etc.). —*v.t./i.* **1.** to shake or puff into a soft mass. **2.** (*slang*) to make a mistake in, to bungle. [prob. dial. alt. of *flue* fluff]

fluffy /ˈflʌfɪ/ *adj.* having or covered with a mass of fluff. —**fluffily** *adv.*, **fluffiness** *n.* [f. prec.]

fluid /ˈfluːɪd/ *n.* a substance, as a gas or liquid, that is capable of flowing freely; a fluid part or secretion. —*adj.* able to flow freely; not solid or rigid, fluctuating. —**fluid mechanics,** the study of the mechanical properties of fluids. **fluid ounce,** one twentieth of a pint; (*US*) one sixteenth of a pint. —**fluidity** /-ˈɪdɪtɪ/ *n.* [f. F or L (*fluere* flow)]

fluidics /fluːˈɪdɪks/ *n.* the technique of using small interacting flows and fluid jets for amplification, switching, etc. [f. prec.]

fluidize /ˈfluːɪdaɪz/ *v.t.* to cause (a mass of granular material, e.g. sand) to behave like a fluid by passing a current of gas, vapour, or liquid upwards through it. The technique has various applications, e.g. in the transporting of powdered material and in cleaning a catalyst in oil refining. —**fluidization** /-ˈzeɪʃ(ə)n/ *n.* [f. FLUID]

fluke[1] /fluːk/ *n.* a thing that happens or succeeds by chance, a piece of luck. —*v.t.* to achieve, hit, etc., by a fluke. —**fluky** *adj.* [perh. f. dial. *fluke* guess]

fluke[2] /fluːk/ *n.* **1.** a flat-fish, a flounder. **2.** a parasitic worm of the class Trematoda, found in sheep's liver. [OE]

fluke[3] /fluːk/ *n.* **1.** the triangular flat end of an anchor arm. **2.** the lobe of a whale's tail. [perh. f. prec.]

flummery /ˈflʌmərɪ/ *n.* **1.** a sweet milk dish. **2.** nonsense, empty talk. [f. Welsh *llymru*]

flummox /ˈflʌməks/ *v.t.* (*colloq.*) to bewilder, to disconcert. [prob. dial., imit.]

flung *past* & *p.p.* of FLING.

flunk *v.t./i.* (*US colloq.*) to fail, especially in an examination. [cf. FUNK and obs. *flink* be a coward]

flunkey /ˈflʌŋkɪ/ *n.* (usu. *derog.*) **1.** a footman. **2.** a toady, a snob. **3.** (*US*) a cook, waiter, etc. [perh. f. FLANK, with sense 'one who flanks']

fluoresce /fluəˈres/ *v.i.* to be or become fluorescent. [f. foll.]

fluorescent *adj.* (of a substance) absorbing radiation and emitting it in the form of light. —**fluorescent lamp,** one with such a substance. —**fluorescence** *n.* [f. FLUORSPAR, after *opalescent*]

fluoridate /ˈfluərɪdeɪt/ *v.t.* to add traces of fluoride to (drinking-water etc.), especially to prevent tooth-decay. —**fluoridation** /-ˈdeɪʃ(ə)n/ *n.* [f. foll.]

fluoride /ˈfluəraɪd/ *n.* a binary compound of fluorine. [f. FLUORINE]

fluorinate /ˈfluərɪneɪt/ *v.t.* to fluoridate; to introduce fluorine into. [f. foll.]

fluorine /ˈfluəriːn/ *n.* a pale yellow non-metallic gaseous element of the halogen group, symbol F, atomic number 9. The most reactive of all elements, fluorine is common in combined form in nature but the element itself was not isolated until 1886. Its compounds are used as catalysts and to protect against dental decay, and hydrocarbons combined with fluorine form an important group of very unreactive substances used to form non-stick surfaces and as lubricants. [F (as FLUORSPAR)]

fluorocarbon /fluərəʊˈkɑːbən/ *n.* a synthetic compound of carbon and fluorine. [f. prec. + CARBON]

fluorspar /ˈfluəspɑː(r)/ *n.* calcium fluoride as a mineral. [f. *fluor* mineral used as flux (L, f. *fluere* flow) + SPAR[3]]

flurry /ˈflʌrɪ/ *n.* a gust, a squall; a sudden burst of activity; nervous hurry, agitation. —*v.t.* to confuse or agitate. [imit.]

flush[1] *v.t./i.* **1.** to become or cause to become red in the face, to blush. **2.** to cleanse (a drain, lavatory, etc.) by the flow of water; to dispose of (a thing) thus. **3.** (of water) to rush or spurt out. **4.** to inflame with pride or passion. **5.** to make level. —*n.* **1.** a reddening of the face, a blush; a feeling of feverish heat. **2.** a rush of excitement or elation. **3.** a rush of water; cleansing by flushing. **4.** freshness, vigour. —*adj.* **1.** level, in the same plane. **2.** (*colloq.*) having plenty of money etc. [perh. = foll., influenced by *flash* and *blush*]

flush[2] *v.t./i.* **1.** to take wing and fly up or away, to cause to do this. **2.** to reveal, to drive *out*. [imit.; cf. *fly, rush*]

flush[3] *n.* a hand of cards all of one suit. —**straight flush,** a flush that is also a sequence. **royal flush,** a straight flush headed by an ace. [f. OF f. L (as FLUX)]

fluster *v.t./i.* to confuse or agitate; to make nervous; to bustle. —*n.* a confused or agitated state. [orig. unkn.]

flute /fluːt/ *n.* **1.** an instrument of the wood-wind family made in silver, stainless steel, or occasionally wood, having holes along it stopped by fingers or (since the 19th c.) keys, and a blow-hole in the side near the end (ill. ORCHESTRA). The flute has a range of three octaves. Since the 14th c. it has had an association with military music as a marching instrument (fife and drums), and it has been a standard orchestral instrument since the early 18th c. **2.** its player. **3.** a semicylindrical vertical groove in a pillar; a similar groove elsewhere. —*v.t./i.* **1.** to play (on) the flute. **2.** to speak or utter in flute-like tones. **3.** to make ornamental grooves in. [f. OF, prob. f. Prov. *flaüt*]

fluting /ˈfluːtɪŋ/ *n.* a series of ornamental grooves. [f. FLUTE]

flutter *v.t./i.* **1.** to flap (the wings) in flying or trying to fly. **2.** to wave or flap quickly and irregularly; to move about restlessly; (of the pulse) to beat feebly and irregularly. —*n.* **1.** fluttering. **2.** a state of nervous excitement. **3.** a rapid fluctuation in pitch or loudness. **4.** (*colloq.*) a small bet or speculation. [OE (as FLEET)]

fluvial /ˈfluːvɪ(ə)l/ *adj.* of or found in rivers. [f. L (*fluvius* river)]

flux *n.* **1.** a continuous succession of changes. **2.** flowing; the inflow of the tide. **3.** a substance mixed with a metal etc. to aid fusion. [f. OF or L *fluxus* (*fluere* flow)]

fly[1] /flaɪ/ *v.t./i.* (*past* **flew** /fluː/, *p.p.* **flown** /fləʊn/) **1.** to move through the air by means of wings. **2.** (of an aircraft etc. or its occupants) to travel through the air or space; to transport in an aircraft. **3.** (of a cloud etc.) to pass quickly through the air. **4.** to go or move quickly, to pass swiftly; to flee (from); (*colloq.*) to depart hastily. **5.** (of a flag, hair, etc.) to wave; to raise (a flag) so that it waves. **6.** to make (a kite) rise and stay aloft. **7.** to be driven or scattered; to come or be forced suddenly *off, open*, etc. —*n.* **1.** flying. **2.** a flap on a garment to contain or cover a fastening, (usu. in *pl.*) this fastening on trousers; a flap at the entrance of a tent. **3.** (in *pl.*) the space over the proscenium in a theatre. **4.** (in *pl.*) the space over the proscenium in a theatre. **5.** the part of a flag furthest from the staff. —**fly a kite,** (*colloq.*) to sound out public opinion. **fly-by-night** *adj.* unreliable, irresponsible; (*n.*) a person of this kind. **fly-half** *n.* the stand-off half in Rugby football. **fly in the face of,** to disregard or disobey openly. **fly off the handle,** (*colloq.*) to become uncontrollably angry. **fly-past** *n.* a ceremonial flight of aircraft past a person or place. [OE]

fly[2] /flaɪ/ *n.* **1.** a two-winged insect, especially of the order Diptera (ill. INSECTS). **2.** some other winged insect, e.g. a firefly, mayfly. **3.** a disease of plants or animals caused by flies. **4.** a natural or artificial fly as a bait in fishing. —**fly-blown** *adj.* (of meat etc.) tainted by flies' eggs. **fly-fish** *v.i.* to fish with a fly. **fly in the ointment,** a minor irritation that spoils enjoyment. **fly on the wall,** an unnoticed observer. **fly-paper** *n.* a sticky treated paper for catching flies. **fly-spray** *n.* a liquid sprayed from a canister to kill flies. **fly-trap** *n.* a plant (*Dionaea muscipula*) able to catch flies. **there are no flies on him,** (*slang*) he is very astute. [OE (as foll.)]

fly[3] *adj.* (*slang*) knowing, clever. [orig. unkn.]

flycatcher *n.* a bird (especially of the genus *Muscicapa*) that catches insects in the air.

flyer *n.* **1.** an airman or an woman. **2.** a fast-moving animal or vehicle. **3.** an ambitious or outstanding person. [f. FLY[1]]

flying *n.* flight. —*adj.* **1.** that flies. **2.** (of a flag etc.) fluttering, waving. **3.** hasty. **4.** (of an animal) able to make long leaps by the use of membranes etc. **5.** (of a vehicle etc.) designed for rapid movement. —**flying boat,** an aircraft that can land on and take off from water and whose main body is a hull which supports it in the water (see SEAPLANE). **flying buttress,** a buttress formed from a separate column, usually forming an arch with the wall it supports (ill. CHURCH). **flying fish,** a tropical fish of either of two genera (*Dactylopterus* and *Exocetus*) with winglike fins, able to rise into the air. **flying fox,** a fruit-eating bat of the genus *Pteropus*. **flying officer,** an RAF officer next below flight lieutenant. **flying picket,** a picket organized for moving from place to place. **flying saucer,** an unidentified saucer-shaped object reported as seen in the sky. **flying squad,** a police detachment or other body organized for rapid movement. **flying start,** a start in which the starting-point is passed at full speed; (*fig.*) a vigorous start giving an initial advantage. **with flying colours,** with great credit gained in a test etc. [f. FLY[1]]

Flying Dutchman a legendary spectral ship supposed to be seen in the region of the Cape of Good Hope and presaging disaster. The legend is the basis of a music-drama (1843) by Wagner.

flyleaf *n.* a blank leaf at the beginning or end of a book.

flyover *n.* a bridge that carries one road or railway over another.

flysheet *n.* a tract or circular of 2 or 4 pages.

flyweight *n.* the lightest professional boxing-weight (see BOXING-WEIGHT).

flywheel *n.* a heavy wheel on a revolving shaft to regulate machinery or accumulate power.

FM *abbr.* **1.** Field Marshal. **2.** frequency modulation.

Fm *symbol* fermium.

f-number /ef-/ *n.* the ratio of the focal length and effective diameter of a lens, used in photography to calculate the amount of light passing through the lens. [f. focal + NUMBER]

FO *abbr.* **1.** Flying Officer. **2.** (*hist.*) Foreign Office.

foal *n.* the young of the horse or a related animal. —*v.t.* (of a mare etc.) to give birth to (a foal, or *abs.*). —**in** or **with foal,** (of a mare etc.) pregnant. [OE]

foam *n.* **1.** a collection of small bubbles formed on or in a liquid by agitation, fermentation, etc.; the froth of saliva or perspiration. **2.** a substance resembling foam, e.g. rubber or plastic in a cellular mass. —*v.i.* to emit foam, to froth; to run in a foam. —**foam at the mouth,** to be very angry. —**foamy** *adj.* [OE]

fob[1] *n.* **1.** an ornamental attachment to a watch-chain, key-ring, etc. **2.** a small pocket for a watch etc. in the waistband of trousers. [prob. f. G]

fob[2] *v.t.* (**-bb-**) **fob off,** to deceive into accepting or being satisfied (*with* an inferior thing, excuse, etc.); to palm or pass off (a thing) *on* (*to*) a person. [f. obs. *fop* to dupe]

f.o.b. *abbr.* free on board.

focal /ˈfəʊk(ə)l/ *adj.* of or at a focus. —**focal distance** or **length,** the distance between the centre of a mirror or lens and its focus. —**focally** *adv.* [f. L (as FOCUS)]

Foch /fɒʃ/, Ferdinand (1851–1929), French military officer, one of the most influential proponents of the doctrine of offensive warfare which was to cost the French dear in the early years of the First World War. During that war Foch rose steadily to become Supreme Commander of all Allied Forces on the Western Front in early 1918, and served as the senior French representative at the Armistice negotiations which ended hostilities.

fo'c's(')le /ˈfəʊks(ə)l/ *var.* of FORECASTLE.

focus /ˈfəʊkəs/ *n.* (*pl.* **focuses, foci** /ˈfəʊsaɪ/) **1.** the point at which rays or waves meet after reflection or refraction; the point from which rays etc. appear to proceed; the point at which an object must be situated for a lens or mirror to give a well-defined image; an adjustment of the eye or a lens to give a clear image; a state of clear definition. **2.** a centre of interest or activity etc. —*v.t./i.* (*p.t.* **focused**) **1.** to bring into focus; to adjust the focus of (a lens or the eye); to converge or cause to converge to a focus. **2.** to concentrate or be concentrated *on*. [L, = hearth]

fodder *n.* dried hay or straw etc. for horses, cattle, etc. —*v.t.* to give fodder to. [OE, rel. to FOOD]

foe *n.* (chiefly *poetic*) an enemy. —**foeman** *n.* [OE]

foetid /ˈfiːtɪd/ *var.* of FETID.

foetus /ˈfiːtəs/ *n.* an unborn or unhatched offspring, especially a human embryo more than eight weeks after conception. —**foetal** *adj.* [f. L *fetus* young offspring]

fog *n.* **1.** a thick cloud of water droplets or smoke suspended at or near the earth's surface. **2.** cloudiness obscuring the image on a photographic negative etc. —*v.t./i.* (**-gg-**) **1.** to

cover or become covered (as) with fog. **2.** to perplex. —**fog-bank** *n.* a mass of fog at sea. **fog-bound** *adj.* unable to leave because of fog. **fog-horn** *n.* a horn sounding a warning to ships in fog. **fog-lamp** *n.* a powerful lamp for use in fog. [perh. = *fog* rank grass, perh. of Scand. orig.]

foggy *adj.* full of fog; of or like fog, indistinct. —**not have the foggiest,** (*colloq.*) to have no idea at all. —**fogginess** *n.* [f. FOG]

fogy /ˈfəʊgɪ/ *n.* (also **fogey**) an old-fashioned person (usu. *old fogy*). [orig. unkn.]

foible /ˈfɔɪb(ə)l/ *n.* a small weakness in a person's character. [F, obs. form of *faible* (as FEEBLE)]

foil[1] *v.t.* to baffle, to frustrate, to defeat. [perh. f. OF *fouler* to full cloth, to trample, f. L (as FULLER)]

foil[2] *n.* **1.** metal hammered or rolled into thin sheets. **2.** a person or thing that enhances the qualities of another by contrast. [f. OF f. L *folium* leaf]

foil[3] *n.* a light blunt-edged sword used in fencing. [orig. unkn.]

foist *v.t.* to force (an inferior, unwelcome, or undeserved thing) *on* (a person). [orig. of palming false dice, f. Du. *vuisten* take in the hand]

Fokine /ˈfəʊkiːn/, Mikhail Mikhailovich (in the West he called himself Michel (1880–1942), Russian dancer and choreographer. Though an excellent, expressive, and technically strong dancer, he was more important as one of the great ballet reformers, striving for a greater dramatic, stylistic, and directional unity. From 1909, as Diaghilev's chief choreographer, he produced such works as *Firebird* (music by Stravinsky, 1910), *Petrushka* (1911), *Daphnis and Chloë* (1912), and *The Golden Cockerel* (1914). He never returned to Russia after 1918, settling in New York in 1923. His *œuvre* comprises over 60 titles, but few of his later ballets compare with his earlier work.

Fokker /ˈfɒkə(r)/, Anthony Herman Gerard (1890–1939), Dutch pioneer aircraft designer and pilot. He built his first aircraft in 1908, the monoplane Eindecker, a type used by Germany as a fighter aircraft in the First World War, and designed the successful Trimotor F-7 airliners (1925), later versions of which provided the backbone of Continental airlines in the 1930s.

fold[1] /fəʊld/ *v.t./i.* **1.** to bend or close (a flexible thing) over upon itself; to bend part of (a thing) *back* or *down*; to become or be able to be folded. **2.** to embrace (*in* the arms or *to* the breast); to clasp (the arms etc.) *about* or *round*; to wrap, to envelop. **3.** (in cookery) to mix (an ingredient) *in* lightly without stirring or beating. —*n.* **1.** folding. **2.** a folded part; a line made by folding. **3.** a hollow among hills. **4.** a curvature of geological strata (ill. GEOLOGY). —**fold one's arms,** to place them across the chest, together or entwined. **fold one's hands,** to clasp them. **fold up,** to collapse (*lit.* or *fig.*); to cease to function. [OE]

fold[2] *n.* **1.** a sheep-fold. **2.** the body of believers, the members of a Church. —*v.t.* to enclose (sheep) in a fold. [OE]

-fold /fəʊld/ *suffix* forming adjectives and adverbs from cardinal numbers, in sense 'in an amount multiplied by', 'with so many parts'. [OE, orig. = folded in so many layers]

folder *n.* **1.** a folding cover or holder for loose papers. **2.** a folded leaflet. [f. FOLD[1]]

foliaceous /fəʊlɪˈeɪʃəs/ *adj.* of or like leaves; laminated. [f. L (*folium* leaf)]

foliage /ˈfəʊlɪɪdʒ/ *n.* leaves, leafage. [f. F *feuillage* (*feuille* leaf, as prec.)]

foliar /ˈfəʊlɪə(r)/ *adj.* of leaves. —**foliar feed,** a feed supplied to the leaves of plants. [f. L *folium* leaf]

foliate /ˈfəʊlɪət/ *adj.* leaflike, having leaves. —/-eɪt/ *v.t./i.* to split or beat into thin layers. —**foliation** /-ˈeɪʃ(ə)n/ *n.* [as prec.]

folic /ˈfəʊlɪk, ˈfɒ-/ *adj.* **folic acid,** a B-group vitamin, deficiency of which causes human anaemia. [f. L *folium* leaf (because found especially in green leaves)]

Folies-Bergère /fɒlɪ beəˈʒeə(r)/ a variety theatre in Paris, opened in 1869. In an age of decorum its reputation was for pleasurable impropriety.

folio /ˈfəʊlɪəʊ/ *n.* (*pl.* **-os**) **1.** a leaf of paper etc., especially one numbered only on the front. **2.** a sheet of paper folded once, making two leaves of a book; a book made of such sheets. —*adj.* (of a book etc.) made of folios, of the largest size. —**in folio,** made of folios. [L, ablative of *folium* leaf]

foliot /ˈfəʊlɪət, ˈfɒ-/ *n.* a type of clock escapement consisting of a bar with adjustable weights on the ends (ill. TIME). [f. OF, perh. f. *folier* play the fool, dance about]

folk /fəʊk/ n. **1.** a nation or people. **2.** the people of a specified class; (often in pl.) people in general; one's parents or relatives. **3.** folk-music. —attrib. of popular origin. —**folk-music, folk-song,** ns. music or song traditional in a country, or in the style of this.

folklore n. the traditional beliefs etc. of a community; the study of these. —**folklorist** n.

folksy /ˈfəʊksɪ/ adj. adopting the characteristics of ordinary people or of folk-art; simple, unpretentious, friendly. [f. FOLK]

folkweave n. a rough loosely woven fabric.

follicle /ˈfɒlɪk(ə)l/ n. a small sac or vesicle in the body, especially one containing a hair-root. —**follicular** /fɒˈlɪkjʊlə(r)/ adj. [f. L (dim. of follis bellows)]

follow /ˈfɒləʊ/ v.t./i. **1.** to go or come after (a person or thing proceeding ahead). **2.** to go along (a road etc.). **3.** to come next in order or time. **4.** to take as a guide or leader, to conform to; to practise (a trade or profession), to undertake (a course of study etc.). **5.** to understand the meaning or tendency of (an argument, speaker). **6.** to be aware of the present state or progress of (events etc.). **7.** to provide with a sequel or successor. **8.** to result from; to be necessarily true as a result of something else. —**follow on,** to continue; (of a cricket team) to have to bat again immediately after a first innings. **follow-on** n. an instance of this. **follow out,** to carry out, to adhere strictly to (instructions etc.). **follow suit,** to play a card of the suit led; to conform to another's actions. **follow through,** to continue (an action etc.) to its conclusion. **follow up,** to pursue; to develop; to supplement (one thing with another). **follow-up** n. a further or continued action, a measure, etc. [OE]

follower n. one who follows; a supporter or devotee. [f. prec.]

following n. a body of supporters or devotees. —adj. that follows or comes after. —prep. after in time, as a sequel to. —**the following,** what follows; now to be given or named. [f. FOLLOW]

folly n. **1.** foolishness; a foolish act, behaviour, idea, etc. **2.** a costly ornamental building that serves no practical purpose. [f. OF folie (fol mad, as FOOL)]

Folsom /ˈfəʊlsəm/ the name of a village in NE New Mexico in the USA, applied to the remains of a prehistoric industry first found there, and especially to a distinctive type of fluted lanceolate projectile point or spearhead, flaked from stone, found at the site in association with the bones of an extinct bison. These points have now been found throughout much of central North America but are commonest in eastern Colorado and New Mexico. The industry dates from c.11,000–10,000 to c.8000 BP. It is generally thought that the development of the Folsom industry reflects a change in prehistoric economy from the hunting of mammoth, prevalent during the preceding period, to the hunting of bison. The impact of the initial Folsom site discovery in 1926 cannot be underestimated, for before 1926 it was held that man entered the New World no earlier than 3,000–4,000 years ago. The direct association of the Folsom point with an extinct late Pleistocene bison clearly demonstrated man's presence at an early date and forced a radical rethinking of the date of man's discovery and population of the New World. It is now known that man was in the New World long, perhaps 20,000 years, before the blossoming of the Folsom 'culture'. (See CLOVIS.)

foment /fəˈment/ v.t. to instigate or stir up (trouble, discontent, etc.). [f. F f. L fomentum poultice (fovēre warm, cherish)]

fomentation /fəʊmenˈteɪʃ(ə)n/ n. **1.** fomenting. **2.** a hot lotion applied to part of the body to relieve pain or inflammation. [f. OF or L (as prec.)]

fond adj. **1.** affectionate, loving; doting. **2.** (of hopes, beliefs, etc.) foolishly credulous or optimistic. —**fond of,** having a liking for. —**fondly** adv., **fondness** n. [f. obs. fon fool, be foolish]

fondant /ˈfɒnd(ə)nt/ n. a soft sweet of flavoured sugar. [F, = melting f. L fundere pour]

fondle v.t. to caress. [back-formation f. fondling fondled person, f. FOND]

fondue /ˈfɒndjuː, -duː/ n. a dish of flavoured melted cheese. [F, p.p. of fondre melt (as FONDANT)]

font¹ n. a receptacle in a church for baptismal water (ill. VESTMENTS). —**fontal** adj. [OE f. OIr. f. L fons fountain]

font² US var. of FOUNT¹.

fontanelle /fɒntəˈnel/ n. the membranous space in an infant's skull at the angles of the parietal bones. [f. F (fontaine fountain)]

Fonteyn /fɒnˈteɪn/, Dame Margot (1919–), real name Peggy Hookham, British dancer. With her beautiful physique, exquisite line, innate musicality, and refined artistry, she is one of the greatest 20th-c. ballerinas. She created her first major role in Ashton's Le Baiser de la fée (1935), later dancing all the ballerina roles of the standard classics and creating many others. Her partnership with Nureyev revivified her career.

food n. **1.** any substance(s) that can be taken into the body to maintain life and growth. **2.** a solid substance of this kind. —**food-chain** n. (similarly **food-pyramid;** ill. ECOLOGY) a series of plants and animals each of which serves as a source of nourishment for the one(s) above it in the series (ill. SEA). **food for thought,** something that needs thinking about. **food-gatherer** n. a member of a people at a primitive stage of civilization obtaining food from natural sources not through agriculture. **food-gathering** n. this practice. **food-poisoning** n. an illness caused by bacteria or toxins in food. **food processor,** an electrically driven device with blades for mixing or slicing food. **food value,** the nourishing power of a food. **food-web** n. an interdependent group of food-chains. [OE, rel. to FEED]

foodstuff n. a substance used as a food.

fool¹ n. **1.** a person who acts or thinks unwisely or imprudently, a stupid person. **2.** (hist.) a jester, a clown. **3.** a dupe. —v.t./i. to act in a joking or teasing way; to play or trifle (about, around); to cheat or deceive (a person) out of something or into doing. —**act or play the fool,** to behave in a silly way. **be no or nobody's fool,** to be shrewd or prudent. **fool's errand,** a fruitless errand. **fool's gold,** iron pyrites. **fool's paradise,** illusory happiness. **make a fool of,** to make (a person) look foolish; to trick or deceive. [f. OF fol f. L follis bellows, empty-headed person]

fool² n. a dessert of fruit crushed and mixed with cream or custard. [perh. f. prec.]

foolery n. foolish acts or behaviour. [f. FOOL¹]

foolhardy adj. rashly or foolishly bold, reckless. —**foolhardiness** n. [f. OF (as FOOL¹, HARDY)]

foolish adj. (of a person or action) lacking good sense or judgement, unwise. —**foolishly** adv., **foolishness** n. [f. FOOL¹]

foolproof adj. (of a procedure, machine, etc.) so straightforward or simple as to be incapable of misuse or mistake.

foolscap /ˈfuːlskæp, -lz-/ n. a size of paper, about 330 × 200 (or 400) mm. [f. use of fool's cap (jester's cap with bells) as watermark]

foot /fʊt/ n. (pl. **feet**) **1.** the end part of the leg beyond the ankle (ill. BODY 1). **2.** the lowest part of a page, table, hill, etc.; the end of a bed where the feet are normally. **3.** the part of a sock etc. covering the foot. **4.** (pl. also **foot**) a linear measure of 12 inches (30.48 cm) originally based on the measurement of a man's foot. **5.** a division of verse including one stressed syllable. **6.** step, pace, tread. **7.** (hist.) infantry. —v.t. to pay (a bill). —**feet of clay,** a fundamental weakness in a person of supposed merit. **foot-and-mouth (disease),** a contagious virus disease of cattle etc. **foot-brake** n. a foot-operated brake on a vehicle. **foot-bridge** n. a bridge for pedestrians only. **foot-slog** v.i. (colloq.) to walk or march. **have one foot in the grave,** to be near death or very old. **my foot!** (colloq.) an exclamation of contemptuous contradiction. **on foot,** walking not riding. **put one's feet up,** to have a rest. **put one's foot down,** to be firm or insistent; to accelerate a motor vehicle. **put one's foot in it,** to blunder. **under one's feet,** in the way (lit. & fig.). **under foot,** on the ground. [OE]

footage n. a length in feet, especially of exposed cinema film. [f. FOOT]

football n. **1.** a large inflated ball, usually of leather. **2.** an outdoor game between two teams, played with this (see below). —**football pool(s),** a form of gambling on the results of football matches, the entry money being awarded in prizes. **footballer** n.

There is a strong and natural inclination to kick at a rounded object and propel it. Interpretations of the significance of the procedure involving two teams, a ball, and a goal, have varied: one traces its origin to fertility rites in ancient Egypt, another regards it as a symbolic hunt. A form of football was played at an early date in China (c.300 BC) and in ancient Greece and Rome; the ball was handled as well as kicked. In medieval England it was a rowdy game, played in the streets, and attempts were made to ban it; in Tudor times it caused 'fighting, brawling . . murder, and great effusion of blood'; in 1424 James I banned it by Act of Parliament because it interfered with the practice of archery, which was of practical use in warfare, but still it persisted, with no rules except those agreed locally and no limit on the number of participants. By the 19th c. forms of football were played regularly in the public schools, but it was not until the middle of the century that the establishment of common rules made it possible to hold matches between different schools, clubs, and (eventually) countries.

footfall *n.* the sound of a footstep.

foothill *n.* one of the low hills near the bottom of a mountain or range.

foothold *n.* a place where the foot can be supported securely; (*fig.*) a secure initial position.

footing *n.* **1.** a foothold, a secure position. **2.** the position or status of a person in relation to others. [f. FOOT]

footlights *n.pl.* a row of lights at the front of a stage at the level of the actors' feet (ill. THEATRE).

footling /'fu:tlɪŋ/ *adj.* (*slang*) trivial, silly. [f. *footle* play the fool (orig. unkn.)]

footloose *adj.* free to act as one pleases.

footman *n.* (*pl.* **-men**) a liveried servant for attending at the door or at table.

footnote *n.* a note printed at the foot of a page.

footpad *n.* (*hist.*) an unmounted highwayman. [f. FOOT + *pad* (archaic slang) = road, f. Du. & LG *pad* path]

footpath *n.* a path for pedestrians, a pavement.

footplate *n.* a platform for the driver and fireman in a locomotive.

footprint *n.* an impression left by a foot or shoe.

footsore *adj.* with sore feet, especially from walking.

footstep *n.* a step taken in walking; the sound of this. —**follow in a person's footsteps**, to do as he did.

footstool *n.* a stool for resting the feet on when sitting.

footway *n.* a path for pedestrians only.

footwear *n.* shoes, socks, etc.

footwork *n.* the use or manner of using the feet in sports, dancing, etc.

fop *n.* a dandy. —**foppery** *n.*, **foppish** *adj.* [perh. f. obs. *fop* fool]

for /fə(r), *emphat.* fɔ:(r)/ *prep.* **1.** in defence, support, or favour of; in the interest or to the benefit of. **2.** suitable or appropriate to. **3.** in respect or reference to, regarding, so far as concerns. **4.** at the price of; in exchange with, corresponding to; as a penalty or reward resulting from. **5.** with a view to, in hope or quest of, in order to get. **6.** in the direction of, towards, to reach. **7.** so as to have begun by (a specified time). **8.** through or over (a distance or period), during. **9.** in the character of, as being. **10.** because of, on account of. **11.** in spite of, notwithstanding. **12.** considering or making due allowance in respect of. —*conj.* seeing that, since, because. —**be for it,** (*colloq.*) to be about to get punishment or other trouble. **for ever,** for all time (see also FOREVER). **O** or **oh for,** I wish I had. [OE (prob. as FORE)]

for- *prefix* forming verbs etc. meaning (1) away or off (*forget, forgive*); (2) prohibition (*forbid*); (3) abstention or neglect (*forgo, forsake*). [OE]

f.o.r. *abbr.* free on rail.

forage /'fɒrɪdʒ/ *n.* **1.** food for horses and cattle. **2.** foraging. —*v.t./i.* to go searching, to rummage; to collect forage (from). —**forager** *n.* [f. OF f. Gmc (as FODDER)]

forasmuch /fɒrəz'mʌtʃ/ *adv.* **forasmuch as,** (*archaic*) since, because. [= *for as much*]

foray /'fɒreɪ/ *n.* a sudden attack, a raid. —*v.i.* to make a foray. [f. OF *forrier* forager (as FODDER)]

forbade, forbad *past* of FORBID.

forbear[1] /fɔ:'beə(r)/ *v.t./i.* (*past* **forbore**; *p.p.* **forborne**) to abstain (from) or refrain. [OE (FOR-, BEAR[1])]

forbear[2] var. of FOREBEAR.

forbearance *n.* patient self-control, tolerance. [f. FORBEAR[1]]

forbid /fə'bɪd/ *v.t.* (**-dd-**; *past* **forbade** /-'bæd/, **forbad**; *p.p.* **forbidden**) to order not *to do*; to refuse to allow (a thing, or a person to have a thing); to refuse a person entry to. —**Forbidden City,** a name applied to Lhasa (see entry) and Peking, to the central part of which foreigners are still not freely admitted. [f. FOR-, BID]

forbidding *adj.* uninviting, repellent, stern. [f. prec.]

forbore *past* of FORBEAR[1].

forborne *p.p.* of FORBEAR[1].

force[1] *n.* **1.** strength, power, impetus, intense effort; co-ercion, compulsion; military strength. **2.** an organized body of soldiers, police, workers, etc. **3.** binding power, validity, effect, precise significance. **4.** influence, efficacy. **5.** a measurable and determinable influence tending to cause the motion of a body (see below); the intensity of this; a person or thing likened to this.—*v.t./i.* **1.** to constrain (a person) by force or against his will. **2.** to make (a way) into or through by force, to break open by force. **3.** to drive or propel violently or against resistance. **4.** to impose or press (a thing) *on* or *upon* a person. **5.** to cause or produce by effort. **6.** to strain or increase to the utmost, to overstrain. **7.** to hasten the growth or maturity of (a plant, pupil, etc.) artificially. —**forced labour,** compulsory labour, usually under harsh conditions. **forced landing,** an unavoidable landing of an aircraft in an emergency. **forced march,** a lengthy and vigorous march especially by troops. **force-feed** *v.t.* to feed (esp. a prisoner) against his will. **force a person's hand,** to make him act prematurely or unwillingly. **force the issue,** to make an immediate decision necessary. **in force,** valid, in great strength or numbers. [f. OF f. L *fortis* strong]

Force in physics is that which causes a mass to undergo acceleration or deformation, or the quantity 'mass times acceleration' itself. In a static situation such as a building opposing forces may be equally balanced so that there is no net acceleration, but some deformation of the material will still occur. Force was first described mathematically by Newton in his laws of motion, and the present-day standard unit of force, the newton, is named after him. Newton's first law, the principle of inertia, states that a moving body will naturally tend to maintain its present motion for ever in a straight line. A force is not, therefore, as earlier thinkers had supposed, necessary for maintaining motion itself; its effect is rather to cause a body to tend to accelerate (or decelerate). This is the substance of Newton's second law of motion, that force equals mass times acceleration. In the everyday world, impacts of bodies, tensions in wires, and air and water pressures, all constitute forces. Physicists, however, consider that such phenomena are ultimately dependent on four fundamental forces that govern the inter-action between all particles of matter: the strong nuclear force which binds protons and neutrons to one another in the atomic nucleus; the weak nuclear force responsible for some radioactive phenomena; the electromagnetic force acting between charged particles; and the gravitational force.

force[2] *n.* (*N. Engl.*) a waterfall. [f. ON *fors*]

forceful *adj.* powerful and vigorous; (of speech) impressive, compelling. —**forcefully** *adv.*, **forcefulness** *n.* [f. FORCE[1] + -FUL]

force majeure /fɔ:s mæ'ʒɜ:(r)/ irresistible force; unforeseen circumstances excusing a person from the fulfilment of a contract. [F, = superior strength]

forcemeat /'fɔ:smi:t/ *n.* meat etc. chopped and seasoned for a stuffing or garnish. [f. OF *farsir* stuff (as FARCE)]

forceps /'fɔ:seps/ *n.* (*pl.* same) surgical pincers. [L]

forcible /'fɔ:sɪb(ə)l/ *adj.* done by or involving force; forceful. —**forcibly** *adv.* [f. OF (as FORCE[1])]

Ford[1], Ford Madox (formerly Ford Hermann Hueffer 1873-1939), English novelist, grandson of the Pre-Raphaelite painter Ford Madox Brown. He collaborated with Conrad on *The Inheritors* (1901) and *Romance* (1903). His own major works were the novel *The Good Soldier* (1915) and the tetralogy *Parade's End* (1924-8), a remarkable record in fiction of the change and disruption caused by the First World War. As founder of the *English Review* (1908) and the Paris-based *Translantic Review* (1924) he published works by the most prominent authors of his day (e.g. Hemingway, Joyce, Pound, and Wells), exerting an important influence on the course of 20th-c. literature.

Ford[2], Henry (1863-1947), American pioneer of mass-production for motor vehicles, who had a profound influence on their widespread use by making them available so cheaply. He was brought up on a farm but was more interested in mechanical matters. By 1903 he had evolved a reliable car and founded his own firm, making several different models. In 1909 Ford produced his famous Model T of which 15 million were made over the next 19 years at gradually reducing prices that were due to large-scale manufacture of a standard model, to a succession of simple tasks performed by unskilled or semi-skilled labour, and to the use of a conveyor-belt for assembly. Ford went on to produce in 1917 a cheap and effective farm tractor, the Fordson, which had a great effect on agricultural mechanization. It can fairly be said that Henry Ford was a philanthropist, for his aim was to provide cheap transport and cheap food for the millions, while with his profits he endowed the Ford Foundation, a major charitable trust.

ford *n.* a shallow place where a river or stream may be crossed by wading, in a motor vehicle, etc. —*v.t.* to cross (water) thus. —**fordable** *adj.* [OE (rel. to FARE)]

fore *adj.* situated in front. —*n.* the front part, the bow of a ship. —*int.* (in golf) as a warning to a person likely to be hit by a ball. —**fore and aft,** at the bow and stern; all over the ship. **fore-and-aft** *adj.* (of a sail or rigging) lengthwise, not on yards. **to the fore,** in front, conspicuous. [OE]

fore- *prefix* forming (1) verbs in senses 'in front' (*foreshorten*), 'beforehand' (*forewarn*); (2) nouns in senses 'situated in front' (*forecourt*), 'front part of' (*forehead*), 'of or near the bow of a ship' (*forecastle*), 'preceding' (*forerunner*). [f. prec.]

forearm[1] /ˈfɔːrɑːm/ *n.* the arm between the elbow and the wrist or fingertips; the corresponding part in an animal (ill. HORSE).

forearm[2] /fɔːrˈɑːm/ *v.t.* to arm beforehand, to prepare.

forebear /ˈfɔːbeə(r)/ *n.* (usu. in *pl.*) an ancestor. [f. FORE- + obs. *beer* (BE)]

forebode /fɔːˈbəʊd/ *v.t.* to be an advance sign of, to portend; to have a presentiment of (usu. evil) or *that*.

foreboding *n.* an expectation of trouble. [f. prec.]

forecast /ˈfɔːkɑːst/ *v.t.* (*past* & *p.p.* **-cast** or **-casted**) to predict or estimate beforehand. —*n.* forecasting; a prediction.

forecastle /ˈfəʊks(ə)l/ *n.* the forward part of a ship where formerly the crew were accommodated (ill. SAILING-SHIPS).

foreclose /fɔːˈkləʊz/ *v.t.* **1.** to take possession of the mortgaged property of (a person) when the loan is not duly repaid; to stop (a mortgage) from being redeemable. **2.** to exclude, to prevent. —**foreclosure** *n.* [f. OF *forclore* (for-out of, as CLOSE[1])]

forecourt *n.* an enclosed space in front of a building; the part of a filling-station where petrol is dispensed.

foredoom /fɔːˈduːm/ *v.t.* to doom or condemn beforehand.

forefather *n.* (usu. in *pl.*) an ancestor, a member of a past generation of a family or people.

forefinger *n.* the finger next to the thumb.

forefoot *n.* (*pl.* **-feet**) a front foot of an animal.

forefront *n.* the foremost part; the leading position.

foregoing /fɔːˈɡəʊɪŋ/ *adj.* preceding, previously mentioned. [as foll.]

foregone /ˈfɔːɡɒn/ *adj.* previous, preceding. —**foregone conclusion,** an easily foreseen or predictable result. [OE (as FORE-, GO)]

foreground *n.* **1.** the part of a view or picture nearest the observer. **2.** the most conspicuous position.

forehand *n.* (in tennis etc.) a stroke made with the palm of the hand facing the opponent. —*adj.* (also **forehanded**) of or made with this stroke.

forehead /ˈfɒrɪd, ˈfɔːhed/ *n.* the part of the head above the eyebrows.

foreign /ˈfɒrən/ *adj.* **1.** of, from, situated in, or characteristic of a country or language other than one's own; dealing with other countries; of another district, society, etc. **2.** unfamiliar, strange, uncharacteristic. **3.** coming from outside. —**foreign aid,** money etc. given or lent by one country to another. **Foreign and Commonwealth Office,** the UK government department dealing with foreign affairs. **Foreign Legion,** see separate entry. **Foreign Secretary,** the head of this. [f. OF f. L *foris* outside]

foreigner *n.* a person born in or coming from another country. [f. prec.]

Foreign Legion a military formation of foreign volunteers, especially that founded in the 1830s to fight France's colonial wars and composed, except for the higher ranks, of non-Frenchmen. Most of the Legion's most famous campaigns were in French North Africa in the late 19th and early 20th c., although it also fought in both World Wars, in various 19th-c. colonial wars, and most recently in the unsuccessful French resistance to the Vietnamese and Algerian independence movements. Although its original purpose has been lost, the Legion is still in existence, in greatly reduced form.

foreknow /fɔːˈnəʊ/ *v.t.* to know beforehand. —**foreknowledge** /fɔːˈnɒlɪdʒ/ *n.*

foreland *n.* a promontory, a cape.

foreleg *n.* a front leg of an animal.

forelimb *n.* a front limb of an animal.

forelock *n.* a lock of hair just above the forehead. —**take time by the forelock,** to seize an opportunity.

foreman *n.* (*pl.* **-men**) **1.** a workman supervising others. **2.** the president and spokesman of a jury.

foremast *n.* the mast nearest the bow of a ship (ill. SAILING-SHIPS).

foremost *adj.* most advanced in position; most notable, best. —*adv.* in the first place, most importantly. [f. superl. of OE *forma* first, assim. to FORE and -MOST]

forename *n.* a first or Christian name.

forenoon *n.* the day till noon, the morning.

forensic /fəˈrensɪk/ *adj.* of or used in courts of law. —**forensic medicine,** the application of medical knowledge to legal problems. —**forensically** *adv.* [f. L (as FORUM)]

foreordain /fɔːrɔːˈdeɪn/ *v.t.* to destine beforehand. —**foreordination** /-dɪˈneɪʃ(ə)n/ *n.*

forepaw *n.* a front paw of an animal.

foreplay *n.* stimulation preceding sexual intercourse.

forerunner *n.* a predecessor; an advance messenger.

foresail /ˈfɔːseɪl/, -s(ə)l/ *n.* the principal sail on the foremast.

foresee /fɔːˈsiː/ *v.t.* (*past* **-saw**; *p.p.* **-seen**) to see or be aware of beforehand.

foreseeable /fɔːˈsiːəb(ə)l/ *adj.* able to be foreseen. —**in the foreseeable future,** in the period ahead during which the general course of events can reasonably be predicted. [f. prec.]

foreshadow /fɔːˈʃædəʊ/ *v.t.* to be a warning or indication of (a future event).

foreshore *n.* the shore between high- and low-water marks.

foreshorten /fɔːˈʃɔːt(ə)n/ *v.t.* to show or portray (an object) with apparent shortening due to visual perspective.

foresight *n.* **1.** regard or provision for the future. **2.** foreseeing. **3.** the front sight of a gun.

foreskin *n.* the loose skin covering the end of the penis.

forest /ˈfɒrɪst/ *n.* a large area of land covered chiefly with trees and undergrowth; the trees in this; a dense concentration (of things). —*v.t.* to plant with trees, to make into a forest. [f. OF f. L *forestis* (*silva* wood) outside (walls of park)]

forestall /fɔːˈstɔːl/ *v.t.* to act in advance of in order to prevent; to deal with beforehand. [f. OE, = an ambush, plot (as FORE-, STALL)]

forestay *n.* a stay from the head of the foremast to a ship's deck to support the foremast (ill. SAILING-SHIPS).

forester *n.* **1.** an officer in charge of a forest. **2.** a dweller in a forest. [f. FOREST]

forestry *n.* the science or management of forests. [as prec.]

foretaste *n.* a taste or experience of something in advance.

foretell /fɔːˈtel/ *v.t.* (*past* & *p.p.* **-told**) to predict, to prophesy; to be a precursor of.

forethought *n.* care or provision for the future; deliberate intention.

forever /fəˈrevə(r)/ *adv.* continually, persistently.

forewarn /fɔːˈwɔːn/ *v.t.* to warn beforehand.

forewoman *n.* (*pl.* **-women**) **1.** a woman worker supervising others. **2.** the woman foreman of a jury.

foreword *n.* the introductory remarks at the beginning of a book, often by a person other than the author.

forfeit /ˈfɔːfɪt/ *n.* a penalty, a thing surrendered as a penalty. —*v.t.* to lose or surrender as a penalty. —*adj.* lost or surrendered as a forfeit. —**forfeiture** *n.* [f. OF *forfaire* transgress f. L *foris* outside, *facere* do]

forgather /fɔːˈɡæðə(r)/ *v.i.* to assemble, to associate. [f. Du. *vergaderen*]

forgave *past* of FORGIVE.

forge[1] *v.t.* **1.** to make or write in fraudulent imitation. **2.** to shape (metal) by heating and hammering. —*n.* a furnace etc. for melting and refining metal; a workshop with this; a blacksmith's workshop. —**forger** *n.* [f. OF f. L *fabrica* (as FABRIC)]

forge[2] *v.i.* to advance or move forward gradually or steadily. [perh. alt. f. FORCE[1]]

forgery /ˈfɔːdʒərɪ/ *n.* **1.** the act of forging. **2.** a forged document etc. [f. FORGE[1]]

forget /fəˈɡet/ *v.t./i.* (**-tt-**; *past* **forgot**; *p.p.* **forgotten**, *US* **forgot**) to lose remembrance of or *about*, not to remember; to neglect or overlook; to cease to think of. —**forget oneself,**

to put others' interests first; to behave without due dignity. [OE (as FOR-, GET)]

forgetful *adj.* apt to forget, neglectful. —**forgetfully** *adv.*, **forgetfulness** *n.* [f. prec. + -FUL]

forget-me-not *n.* a plant of the genus *Myosotis* with small blue flowers.

forgive /fə'gɪv/ *v.t.* (*past* **forgave**; *p.p.* **forgiven** /-'gɪv(ə)n/) **1.** to cease to feel angry or resentful towards (a person) or about (an offence). **2.** to pardon. **3.** to remit (a debt). [OE (as FOR-, GIVE)]

forgiveness *n.* the act of forgiving; the state of being forgiven. [f. prec.]

forgiving *adj.* inclined readily to forgive. [f. FORGIVE]

forgo /fɔː'ɡəʊ/ *v.t.* (*past* **forwent**; *p.p.* **forgone**) to go without, to relinquish; to omit or decline to take or use (a pleasure, advantage, etc.). [OE (as FOR-, GO)]

forgot *past* (& *US p.p.*) of FORGET.

forgotten *p.p.* of FORGET.

fork *n.* **1.** a pronged implement used in eating and cooking; a similar much larger implement used for digging, lifting, etc. **2.** a divergence of a stick, road, etc, into two parts; the place of this; one of the two parts. **3.** the forked support for a bicycle wheel. **4.** a pronged device pushed under a load to be lifted. —*v.t./i.* **1.** to form a fork or branch by separating into two parts; to take one road at a fork. **2.** to dig, lift, or throw with a fork. —**fork-lift truck**, a vehicle with a fork for lifting and carrying loads. **fork out**, (*slang*) to pay (usu. reluctantly). [OE f. L *furca*]

forlorn /fɔː'lɔːn/ *adj.* sad and abandoned; in a pitiful state. —**forlorn hope**, a faint remaining hope or chance. —**forlornly** *adv.* [p.p. of obs. *forlese* (as FOR-, LOSE); *forlorn hope* f. Du. *verloren hoop* lost troop (orig. of storming-party)]

form *n.* **1.** shape, arrangement of parts, visible aspect. **2.** a person or animal as visible or tangible. **3.** the mode in which a thing exists or manifests itself. **4.** a printed document with blank spaces for information to be inserted. **5.** a class in school. **6.** a customary method; a set order of words. **7.** a species, a kind. **8.** behaviour according to rule or custom; correct procedure. **9.** (of an athlete, horse, etc.) condition of health and training; (in racing etc.) details of previous performances; (*slang*) a criminal record. **10.** one of the ways in which a word may be spelt, pronounced, or inflected. **11.** the arrangement and style in a literary or musical composition. **12.** a bench. **13.** a hare's lair. —*v.t./i.* **1.** to fashion or shape. **2.** to mould by discipline, to train or instruct. **3.** to develop or establish as a concept, institution, or practice; to organize (*into* a company etc.) **4.** to be the material of, to make up, to be. **5.** to take shape, to come into existence. **6.** to construct (a word) by inflexion etc. **7.** (often with *up*) to bring or move into formation. —**on** *or* **off form**, performing or playing well or badly. [f. OF f. L *forma*]

-form *suffix* forming adjectives (usu. as **-iform**) in senses 'having the form of' (*cuneiform*), 'having such a number of forms' (*uniform*). [as prec.]

formal /'fɔːm(ə)l/ *adj.* **1.** used or done or held in accordance with rules, convention, or ceremony; excessively stiff or methodical. **2.** valid or correctly so called because of its form; explicit. **3.** of or concerned with (outward) form, especially as distinct from content or matter. **4.** perfunctory, following form only. **5.** precise, symmetrical. —**formally** *adv.* [f. L (as FORM)]

formaldehyde /fɔː'mældɪhaɪd/ *n.* the aldehyde of formic acid, used as a disinfectant and preservative. [f. FORMIC + ALDEHYDE]

formalin /'fɔːməlɪn/ *n.* an aqueous solution of formaldehyde. [f. prec.]

formalism /'fɔːməlɪz(ə)m/ *n.* **1.** strict or excessive adherence to or concern with form or forms. **2.** treatment of mathematics as the manipulation of meaningless symbols. **3.** a symbolic and stylized manner of theatrical production. —**formalist** *n.* [f. FORMAL]

formality /fɔː'mælɪtɪ/ *n.* a formal act, regulation, or custom (often lacking real significance); a thing done simply to comply with a rule or convention; rigid observance of rules or convention. [f. F or L (as FORMAL)]

formalize /'fɔːməlaɪz/ *v.t.* to make formal; to give a definite (esp. legal) form to. —**formalization** /-'zeɪʃ(ə)n/ *n.* [f. FORMAL]

format /'fɔːmæt/ *n.* **1.** the shape and size (of a book etc.). **2.** style or manner of arrangement or procedure. **3.** the arrangement of data etc. for a computer. —*v.t.* (**-tt-**) to

arrange in a format, especially for a computer. [F f. G, f. L *formatus* (*liber*) shaped (book), as foll.]

formation /fɔː'meɪʃ(ə)n/ *n.* **1.** forming. **2.** a thing formed; a particular arrangement (e.g. of troops; a set of rocks or strata with a common characteristic. [f. OF or L (*formare* to shape, as FORM)]

formative /'fɔːmətɪv/ *adj.* serving to form or fashion; of formation. [f. OF or L (as prec.)]

forme /fɔːm/ *n.* a body of type secured in a chase for printing at one impression. [var. of FORM]

former *adj.* of the past, earlier. —**the former**, (often *absol.*), the first or first-mentioned of two. [compar. of OE *forma* first (cf. FOREMOST)]

formerly *adv.* in former times. [f. prec.]

Formica /fɔː'maɪkə/ *n.* [P] a hard durable plastic laminate used on surfaces. [orig. unkn.]

formic acid /'fɔːmɪk/ a colourless irritant volatile acid contained in the fluid emitted by ants. [f. L *formica* ant]

formidable /'fɔːmɪdəb(ə)l, (D) -'mɪd-/ *adj.* **1.** inspiring fear or dread. **2.** likely to be difficult to overcome or deal with. —**formidably** *adv.* [F, or f. L (*formidare* dread)]

formless *adj.* without a definite or regular form. [f. FORM + -LESS]

formula /'fɔːmjʊlə/ *n.* (*pl.* **-as**, **-ae** /-iː/) **1.** a set of chemical symbols showing the constituents of a substance. **2.** a mathematical rule expressed in figures. **3.** a fixed form of words, especially one used on social or ceremonious occasions; a form of words embodying or enabling an agreement. **4.** a list of ingredients. **5.** the classification of a racing car, especially by engine capacity. **6.** (*US*) an infant's food made according to a prescribed recipe. —**formulaic** /-'leɪɪk/ *adj.* [L, dim. of *forma* form]

formulary /'fɔːmjʊlərɪ/ *n.* a collection of formulas or set forms. [f. F or L (as prec.)]

formulate /'fɔːmjʊleɪt/ *v.t.* to express in a formula; to express clearly and precisely. —**formulation** /-'leɪʃ(ə)n/ *n.* [f. FORMULA]

fornicate /'fɔːnɪkeɪt/ *v.i.* (of people not married to each other) to have sexual intercourse voluntarily. —**fornication** /-'keɪʃ(ə)n/ *n.*, **fornicator** *n.* [f. L *fornicare* (*fornix* brothel)]

forsake /fɔː'seɪk/ *v.t.* (*past* **forsook** /-'sʊk/; *p.p.* **forsaken**) **1.** to give up, to renounce. **2.** to withdraw one's help or companionship from. [OE (as FOR-, *sacan* quarrel)]

forsooth /fɔː'suːθ/ *adv.* (*archaic*, now usu. *iron.*) indeed, truly, no doubt. [OE (as FOR, SOOTH)]

Forster /'fɔːstə(r)/, Edward Morgan (1879-1970), English novelist, a master of social comedy, sometimes with pagan supernatural elements, contrasting British (and Christian) inhibition and philistinism with passionate Mediterranean culture and, in his last novel *A Passage to India* (1924), with Hindu religious sensibility. A homosexual, Forster felt conventional narrow-mindedness acutely. *Maurice* (finished in 1914) and some other homosexual stories appeared posthumously. Forster exerted, through essays and journalism, a humane civilizing influence.

forswear /fɔː'sweə(r)/ *v.t.* (*past* **forswore**; *p.p.* **forsworn**) **1.** to abjure, to renounce. **2.** (in *p.p.*) perjured. —**forswear oneself**, to perjure oneself. [OE (as FOR-, SWEAR)]

forsythia /fɔː'saɪθɪə/ *n.* an ornamental shrub of the genus *Forsythia*, with bright yellow flowers. [f. W. *Forsyth* English botanist (d. 1804)]

fort *n.* a fortified military building or position. —**hold the fort**, to act as a temporary substitute, to cope with an emergency. [f. F or It. f. L *fortis* strong]

forte[1] /'fɔːteɪ/ *n.* one's strong point, a thing in which one excels. [f. F *fort* strong (as prec.)]

forte[2] /'fɔːteɪ/ *adj.* & *adv.* (*Mus.*) loud, loudly. —*n.* (*Mus.*) loud playing; a passage played loudly. [It., = strong, loud]

fortepiano /'fɔːtɪpɪænəʊ/ *n.* (*pl.* **-os**) a pianoforte, especially with reference to an instrument of the 18th to early 19th c. [It. (*forte* loud, *piano* soft)]

forth *adv.* (*archaic* exc. in set phrases) forward, into view; onwards in time; forwards; out from a starting-point. [OE]

forthcoming *adj.* **1.** approaching, coming or available soon; **2.** produced when wanted. **3.** (of a person). **3.** willing to give information, responsive.

forthright *adj.* straightforward; outspoken; decisive.

forthwith /fɔːθ'wɪð/ *adv.* at once, without delay. [f. earlier *forthwithal* (FORTH, WITH, ALL)]

fortification /fɔːtɪfɪ'keɪʃ(ə)n/ *n.* **1.** the act of fortifying. **2.** (usu. in *pl.*) defensive works, walls, etc. [f. F f. L (as foll.)]

fortify /'fɔːtɪfaɪ/ *v.t./i.* **1.** to strengthen physically, mentally, morally, etc. **2.** to provide with or erect fortifications. **3.** to strengthen (wine) with alcohol; to add extra nutrients, especially vitamins, to (food). [f. OF f. L *fortificare* (*fortis* strong)]

fortissimo /fɔːˈtɪsɪməʊ/ *adj.* & *adv.* (*Mus.*) very loud, very loudly. —*n.* (*pl.* -os) (*Mus.*) very loud playing; a passage played very loudly. [It., superl. of FORTE²]

fortitude /ˈfɔːtɪtjuːd/ *n.* courage in pain or adversity. [f. F f. L (*fortis* strong, brave)]

Fort Knox /nɒks/ a US military reservation in Kentucky, famous as the site of the US Depository (built in 1936) which holds the bulk of the nation's gold bullion in its vaults.

fortnight *n.* two weeks. [OE, = fourteen nights]

fortnightly *adj.* done, produced, or occurring once a fortnight. —*adv.* every fortnight. —*n.* a fortnightly magazine etc. [f. prec.]

fortran /ˈfɔːtræn/ *n.* a computer language used especially for scientific calculations. [f. *Formula Translation*]

fortress /ˈfɔːtrɪs/ *n.* a fortified building or town. [f. OF f. L *fortis* strong]

fortuitous /fɔːˈtjuːɪtəs/ *adj.* happening by chance, accidental. —**fortuitously** *adv.*, **fortuitousness** *n.*, **fortuity** *n.* [f. L (*forte* by chance)]

fortunate /ˈfɔːtjʊnət, -tʃənət/ *adj.* lucky, auspicious. —**fortunately** *adv.* [f. L (as foll.)]

fortune /ˈfɔːtjuːn, -tʃuːn/ *n.* **1.** chance or luck as a force in human affairs. **2.** the luck (good or bad) that befalls a person or enterprise. **3.** a person's destiny. **4.** good luck; prosperity, great wealth, a huge sum of money. —**fortune-teller** *n.* a person who claims to foretell one's destiny. **make a fortune,** to become very rich. [f. L *fortuna* luck, chance]

forty *adj.* & *n.* **1.** four times ten; the symbol for this (40, xl, XL). **2.** (in *pl.*) the numbers, years, degrees of temperature, etc., from 40 to 49. —**forty winks,** a short sleep. —**fortieth** *adj.* & *n.* [OE (as FOUR)]

forum /ˈfɔːrəm/ *n.* **1.** the public square or market-place in an ancient Roman city, used for judicial and other business. **2.** a place of or meeting for public discussion; a court, a tribunal. [L]

forward /ˈfɔːwəd/ *adj.* **1.** lying in one's line of motion, onward or towards the front. **2.** relating to the future. **3.** precocious, bold in manner, presumptuous. **4.** approaching maturity or completion; (of a plant etc.) well-advanced, early. —*n.* an attacking player near the front in football, hockey, etc. —*adv.* **1.** to the front, into prominence; in advance, ahead. **2.** onward so as to make progress. **3.** towards the future. **4.** (also **forwards**) towards the front in the direction one is facing; in the normal direction of motion or of traversal; with a continuous forward motion. —*v.t.* **1.** to send (a letter etc.) on to a further destination; to dispatch (goods etc.). **2.** to help to advance; to promote. —**forwardness** *n.* [OE (as FORTH, -WARD)]

fosse /fɒs/ *n.* a long ditch or trench, especially in fortification. [f. OF f. L *fossa* ditch]

Fosse Way an ancient road in Britain, so called from the fosse or ditch on each side. It probably ran from Axminster to Lincoln, via Bath and Leicester (about 300 km, 200 miles), and marked the limit of the first stage of the Roman occupation (mid-1st c. AD).

fossick /ˈfɒsɪk/ *v.i.* (*Austral.* & *NZ slang*) to rummage, to search *about*; to search for gold etc. in abandoned workings. [per. f. dial. *fossick* bustle about]

fossil /ˈfɒs(ə)l/ *n.* **1.** the remains or impression of a (usu. prehistoric) plant or animal hardened in a rock (see below). **2.** an antiquated or unchanging person or thing. —*adj.* **1.** of or like a fossil. **2.** found buried, dug from the ground. —**fossil fuel,** coal, oil, etc. formed in the geological past (esp. opp. *nuclear fuel*). [f. F f. L *fossilis* (*fodere* dig)]

Fossils are usually the hard parts of organisms, the bones or shells, preserved as moulds or casts in rock. The original material may have been chemically replaced by a very different mineral. Rarely, the fossils of organisms such as jellyfish, which do not have a bony component, are preserved in fine-grained rocks such as shales. The study of fossils and the fossil record has provided much of the information upon which the present subdivisions of the geological time-scale are based. (See ill. GEOLOGY.)

fossilize /ˈfɒsɪlaɪz/ *v.t./i.* to become or cause to become a fossil. —**fossilization** /-ˈzeɪʃ(ə)n/ *n.* [f. prec.]

foster *v.t.* **1.** to promote the growth or development of; to encourage or harbour (a feeling); (of circumstances) to be favourable to. **2.** to bring up a child that is not one's own. —*adj.* (in *comb.*, as *foster-brother, -mother*) having a family connection by fostering not by birth. —**foster home,** a home in which a foster-child is brought up. [OE, = nourishment (as FOOD)]

fought *past* & *p.p.* of FIGHT.

Foucault /ˈfuːkəʊ/, Jean Bernard Léon (1819–68), French physicist, inventor of the gyroscope. He is chiefly remembered for the huge pendulum which he hung from the roof of the Panthéon in Paris in 1851: as the pendulum swung, the path of its swing slowly rotated, demonstrating the rotation of the Earth beneath it. He obtained the first reasonably accurate determination of the velocity of light by using the rotating mirror technique developed by Wheatstone in the 1830s, introduced the modern technique of silvering glass for the reflecting telescope, pioneered astronomical photography, discovered eddy currents (the Foucault currents induced in cores of electrical equipment such as generators and transformers), and improved a host of devices such as the arc lamp and the induction coil.

foul *adj.* **1.** offensive, loathsome, stinking; filthy, soiled; (*colloq.*) disgusting. **2.** (of language etc.) obscene, disgustingly abusive. **3.** (of weather) rough, stormy. **4.** containing noxious matter; clogged, choked; overgrown with barnacles etc. **5.** unfair, against the rules. **6.** in collision; (of a rope etc.) entangled. —*n.* **1.** a foul stroke or piece of play. **2.** a collision, an entanglement. —*adv.* unfairly, contrary to the rules. —*v.t./i.* **1.** to make or become foul. **2.** to commit a foul against (a player). **3.** to become or cause to become entangled; to collide with. —**foul-mouthed** *adj.* using abusive or offensive language. **foul play,** unfair play in sport; a treacherous or violent act, especially murder. **foul up,** to become or cause to become blocked or entangled; to spoil or bungle. —**foully** *adv.* [OE]

foulard /fuːˈlɑːd/ *n.* a thin soft material of silk or silk and cotton. [F]

found¹ *v.t.* **1.** to establish, especially with an endowment; to originate or initiate (an institution etc.), to be the original builder of (a town etc.). **2.** to lay the base of (a building); to construct or base (a story, theory, rule, etc.) *on* or *upon.* —**ill-founded** *adj.* unjustified. **well-founded** *adj.* justified, reasonable. —**founder**¹ *n.* [f. OF f. L *fundare* (*fundus* bottom)]

found² *v.t.* to melt and mould (metal); to fuse (the materials for glass); to make (a thing) thus. —**founder**² *n.* [f. OF f. L *fundere* pour]

found³ *past* & *p.p.* of FIND.

foundation /faʊnˈdeɪʃ(ə)n/ *n.* **1.** establishing, especially of an endowed institution; such an institution (e.g. a college, hospital, school) or its revenues. **2.** the solid ground or base on which a building rests; (in *sing.* or *pl.*) the lowest part of a building usually below ground-level. **3.** a basis, an underlying principle. **4.** the material or part on which other parts are overlaid; (in full **foundation garment**) a woman's supporting undergarment, e.g. a corset. —**foundation-stone** *n.* a stone laid ceremonially to celebrate the founding of a building; (*fig.*) a basis. [f. OF f. L (as FOUND¹)]

founder¹·² see FOUND¹·².

founder³ *v.i.* (of a horse or rider) to fall to the ground, to fall from lameness, to stick in mud etc.; (of a plan etc.) to fail; (of a ship) to fill with water and sink. [f. OF f. L *fundus* bottom]

foundling *n.* an abandoned infant of unknown parents. [f. p.p. of FIND]

foundry *n.* a workshop for or the business of casting metal. [f. FOUND²]

fount¹ /faʊnt, fɒnt/ *n.* a set of printing-type of the same face and size. [f. F (as FOUND²)]

fount² *n.* a source; (*poetic*) a spring, a fountain. [back-formation f. foll.]

fountain /ˈfaʊntɪn/ *n.* **1.** a jet or jets of water made to spout for ornamental purposes or for drinking; a structure provided for this. **2.** a spring; the source (*of* wisdom etc.). —**fountain-head** *n.* the source. **fountain-pen** *n.* a pen with a reservoir holding ink. [f. OF f. L *fontana* (*fons fontis* spring)]

four /fɔː(r)/ *adj.* & *n.* **1.** one more than three; the symbol for this (4, iv, IV). **2.** the size etc. denoted by four. **3.** a team of four; a four-oared boat or its crew. —**four-in-hand** *n.* a vehicle with four horses driven by one person. **the four last things,** death, judgement, heaven, and hell. **four-letter word,** a short word referring to the sexual or excretory functions and regarded as vulgar or obscene. **four-poster** *n.* a bed with four posts supporting a canopy.

four-square *adj.* solidly based, steady; (*adv.*) squarely, resolutely. **four-stroke** *adj.* (of an internal-combustion engine) having a cycle of four strokes of a piston, in which a cylinder fires once (ill. CAR). **four-wheel drive**, drive acting on all four wheels of a vehicle. **on all fours**, on hands and knees. [OE]

fourfold *adj.* & *adv.* four times as much or as many; consisting of four parts. [f. FOUR + -FOLD]

Fourier /ˈfuəriɛi/, Jean Baptiste Joseph (1768–1830), French public servant and mathematician whose theory of the diffusion of heat involved him in the solution of partial differential equations by the method of separation of variables and superposition. This led him to study the series and integrals that are now known by his name. Fourier's belief, controversial at the time, that a wide class of periodic phenomena could be described by means of series of trigonometrical functions was substantially vindicated by the results of later mathematicians, who had to invent extremely delicate techniques of mathematical analysis for that purpose. The theory of Fourier series now provides one of the most important methods for solving many partial differential equations that occur in physics and engineering.

foursome *n.* a group of four persons; a golf match between two pairs with partners playing the same ball. [f. FOUR + -SOME]

fourteen /fɔːˈtiːn/ *adj.* & *n.* **1.** one more than thirteen; the symbol for this (14, xiv, XIV). **2.** the size etc. denoted by fourteen. —**fourteenth** *adj.* & *n.* [OE (as FOUR, -TEEN)]

fourth *adj.* next after the third. —*n.* one of the four equal parts of a thing. —**fourth estate**, the press. —**fourthly** *adv.* [OE (cf. FOUR)]

fowl *n.* (*pl.* **fowls** or *collect.* **fowl**) **1.** a domestic cock or hen kept for eggs and flesh; the flesh of birds as food. **2.** a bird (*archaic exc. in comb.*) —*v.i.* to hunt or shoot or snare wildfowl. —**fowler** *n.* [OE]

Fowler /ˈfaʊlə(r)/, Henry Watson (1858–1933), English lexicographer and author of prescriptive works on style and idiom. With his brother Francis George Fowler (1870–1918) he compiled the *Concise Oxford Dictionary* (1911), adopting certain principles which continued to be followed in the smaller Oxford dictionaries for more than half a century. In 1926 his most famous work appeared, *Modern English Usage* (still known affectionately as 'Fowler'), in which major hazards of English were pointed out and recommendations made with 'a cheerful attitude of infallibility'. In isolation from the current linguistic controversies and from the growing support for a 'descriptive' approach, he displayed such acknowledged and respected sensitivity to all aspects of the English language that those departing from his recommendations knew that they risked censure.

Fox, George (1624–91), founder of the Society of Friends. The son of a Leicestershire weaver, he began his life of preaching in 1647, teaching that truth is the inner voice of God speaking to the soul. Despite frequent imprisonment he attracted followers ('Friends of the Truth') whom he formed into a stable organization.

fox *n.* **1.** a wild four-legged animal (*Vulpes vulpes*) of the dog family with red fur and a bushy tail; its fur. **2.** a cunning person. —*v.t.* **1.** to deceive, to baffle; **2.** (esp. in *p.p.*) to discolour (the pages of a book etc.) with brownish marks. —**fox-terrier** *n.* a kind of short-haired terrier. [OE]

Foxe /fɒks/, John (1516–87), English religious writer and martyrologist, who relinquished his fellowship at Magdalen College, Oxford, in 1545 because he was unwilling to conform to the religious statutes. He fled to the Continent on the accession of Catholic Mary I, and published in Strasburg an early draft of his *Actes and Monuments*, popularly known as *The Book of Martyrs*, which appeared in England in 1563. This passionate account of suffering and persecution under Bloody Mary inspired hatred for Catholicism for generations.

foxglove *n.* a tall plant (*Digitalis purpurea*) with purple or white flowers like glove-fingers.

foxhole *n.* a hole in the ground used as a shelter against missiles or as a firing-point.

foxhound *n.* a kind of hound bred and trained to hunt foxes.

foxtrot *n.* a ballroom dance with slow and quick steps; the music for this. —*v.i.* to dance the foxtrot.

foxy *adj.* **1.** foxlike. **2.** sly, cunning. **3.** reddish-brown. —**foxily** *adv.*, **foxiness** *n.* [f. FOX]

foyer /ˈfɔiei, ˈfwæjei/ *n.* the entrance hall or an open space in a theatre etc. for the audience's use during an interval; the entrance hall of a hotel etc. [F, = hearth, home]

Fr *symbol* francium.

Fr. *abbr.* **1.** Father. **2.** French.

fr. *abbr.* franc(s).

fracas /ˈfrækɑː/ *n.* (*pl.* same /-kɑːz/, (*US*) **fracases**) a noisy disturbance or quarrel. [F f. It.]

fraction /ˈfrækʃ(ə)n/ *n.* **1.** a numerical quantity that is not a whole number (e.g. ½, 0.5). **2.** a small part, piece, or amount. **3.** a portion of a mixture obtained by distillation etc. [f. OF f. L (*frangere* break)]

fractional *adj.* **1.** of fractions; being a fraction. **2.** very slight. —**fractional distillation,** separation of parts of a mixture by making use of their different physical properties. —**fractionally** *adv.* [f. prec.]

fractionate /ˈfrækʃəneit/ *v.t.* to break up into parts; to separate (a mixture) by fractional distillation. —**fractionation** *n.*, **fractionator** *n.* [f. FRACTION]

fractious /ˈfrækʃəs/ *adj.* irritable, peevish. —**fractiously** *adv.*, **fractiousness** *n.* [f. prec. in obs. sense 'brawling']

fracture /ˈfræktʃə(r)/ *n.* a breakage, especially of a bone or cartilage (ill. BODY 1). —*v.t./i.* to cause a fracture in; to suffer a fracture. [f. F or L (as FRACTION)]

fragile /ˈfrædʒail/ *adj.* easily broken, weak; of delicate constitution, not strong. —**fragilely** *adv.*, **fragility** /frəˈdʒiliti/ *n.* [f. F or L *fragilis* (as FRACTION)]

fragment /ˈfrægmənt/ *n.* a part broken off; the remainder of an otherwise lost or destroyed whole; the extant remains or an unfinished portion of a book etc. —/also -ˈment/ *v.t./i.* to break or separate into fragments. —**fragmentary** *adj.*, **fragmentation** /-ˈteiʃ(ə)n/ *n.* [f. F or L *fragmentum* (as prec.)]

fragrance /ˈfreigrəns/ *n.* sweetness of smell; a sweet scent. [f. F or L (as foll.)]

fragrant /ˈfreigrənt/ *adj.* sweet-smelling. —**fragrantly** *adv.* [f. F or L (*fragrare* smell sweet)]

frail *adj.* fragile, delicate; transient; morally weak. —**frailly** *adv.* [f. OF (as FRAGILE)]

frailty *n.* frail quality; a weakness, a foible. [as prec.]

frame *v.t.* **1.** to construct, to put together or devise (a complex thing, idea, theory, etc.); to adapt or fit *to* or *into*. **2.** to articulate (words). **3.** to set in a frame; to serve as a frame for; (*slang*) to concoct a false charge or evidence against, to devise a plot against. —*n.* **1.** the case or border enclosing a picture, window, door, etc. **2.** the human or animal body, especially with reference to its size. **3.** the basic rigid supporting structure of a building, motor vehicle, aircraft, bicycle, etc.; (in *pl.*) the structure of spectacles holding the lenses. **4.** construction, build, structure; the established order or system; a temporary state (*of mind*). **5.** a single complete image or picture on a cinema film or transmitted in a series of lines by television. **6.** a boxlike structure of glass etc. for protecting plants. **7.** the triangular structure for positioning the balls in snooker etc.; a round of play in snooker etc. **8.** (*US slang*) a frame-up. —**frame of reference,** a system of geometrical axes for defining position, a set of standards or principles governing behaviour, thought, etc. **frame-up** *n.* (*colloq.*) a conspiracy to make an innocent person appear guilty. [OE, = be helpful]

framework *n.* an essential supporting structure; a basic system.

franc *n.* the unit of currency in France, Belgium, Switzerland, etc. [f. *Francorum Rex* king of the Franks, legend on the earliest gold coins so called (14th c.)]

France[1] /frɑːns/ a country in western Europe, with coastlines on the Atlantic Ocean and Mediterranean Sea; pop. (1982) 54,335,000; official language, French; capital, Paris. Although it is an industrial country agriculture remains important, and many regions are famous for their wines. Prehistoric remains, cave paintings, and megalithic monuments attest the long history of human habitation. Julius Caesar subdued the area in the 1st c. BC and it became the Roman province of Gaul. It was politically splintered by barbarian invasions from the 3rd c. onwards and, although briefly united under the Merovingian and Carolingian kings, did not emerge as a permanently unified State until the ejection of the English and Burgundians at the end of the Middle Ages. Under the Valois and Bourbon dynasties France rose to contest European hegemony in the 16th–18th c., and after the overthrow of the monarchy in the French Revolution briefly dominated Europe under Napoleon. Defeated in the Franco-Prussian war (1870–1), severely handled in the First World War and occupied by the

Germans in the Second, France has revived in the post-war era as a major European power.

France² /frɑ̃s/, Anatole (pseudonym of Jacques-Anatole-François Thibault, 1844-1922), French novelist and man of letters. He wrote poems and criticism, developed wide interests in journalism and radical politics, and achieved success as a novelist with *Le Crime de Sylvestre Bonnard* (1881). *L'Histoire contemporaine* (1897-1901), a social and political satire, introduced the disenchanted provincial professor Bergeret. The Dreyfus case had aroused France's sympathies of which *L'Île des pingouins* (1908) contains an ironic account with clear Marxist overtones. *Les dieux ont soif* (1912) is a study of fanaticism during the French Revolution. Qualities of graceful erudition and clarity of thought are displayed in all his works and notably in his short stories. He was awarded the Nobel Prize for literature in 1921.

franchise /ˈfræntʃaɪz/ n. **1.** the right to vote in a State election. **2.** full membership of a corporation or State, citizenship. **3.** a right or privilege granted to a person or corporation. **4.** authorization to sell a company's goods etc. in a particular area. —v.t. to grant a franchise to. [f. OF (*franc* free, as FRANK)]

Francis /ˈfrɑːnsɪs/, St, of Assisi (1181/2-1226), founder of the Franciscan order. Born of a rich family, he became dissatisfied with his worldly life, and in 1208, hearing read in church Christ's words bidding his disciples to leave all (Matt. 10: 7-19), understood them as a personal call and set out to save souls. Before long he had gathered a band of like-minded followers, and he drew up for them a simple rule of life based on sayings from the Gospels. He was the first person known to have shown the stigmata (1224). His generosity, simple faith, deep humility, and love of nature have made him one of the most cherished saints. Feast day, 4 Oct.

Francis I /ˈfrɑːnsɪs/ (Fr. *François*), king of France 1515-47. Francis was widely hailed as the epitome of the Renaissance prince, and indeed culture and the arts did flourish in France under his patronage, but his reign was completely dominated by wars which left the country weakened and on the brink of serious religious upheaval. Francis's struggle with the Emperor Charles V, much of which took place in Italy, was to prove but the first round in the struggle for European mastery with Spain which was to go on until the reign of Louis XIV.

Franciscan /frænˈsɪskən/ n. a monk or nun of the Franciscan order (see below). —adj. of the Franciscan order. [f. F f. L (*Franciscus* Francis)]
The Franciscan order of friars minor or Grey Friars was founded by St Francis of Assisi (1209). His ideal of complete poverty proved incompatible with the organization of a large membership, and the original simple rule was modified, to his great regret (1221 and 1223), and successive laxities and reforms led to the formation of separate branches. The nuns are known as Poor Clares, after their founder, St Clare (1215). There is also an order of tertiaries or lay brothers (founded 1221). The friars have been important preachers and missionaries.

Francis Xavier, St, see XAVIER.

francium /ˈfrænsɪəm/ n. a radioactive metallic element, discovered in 1939, that is the heaviest member of the alkali-metal group and is chemically similar to caesium, symbol Fr, atomic number 87. All its isotopes have short half-lives (the most stable about 22 minutes) and only one occurs naturally, produced by the radioactive decay of actinium 227. [f. FRANCE, country of its discoverer (M. Perey)]

Franck /frɑ̃k/, César (1822-90), Belgian composer. In 1836 he moved to Paris, where he became one of the most influential figures in French musical life. He was a noted organist, and the sonorities of that instrument found their way into his orchestral works. He is at his best when formal considerations restrict a tendency to massiveness and over-chromaticism, and it is his instrumental works that have proved most durable, particularly the Piano Quintet (1879), the Symphonic Variations for piano and orchestra (1885), the hugely popular Violin Sonata (1886), the D minor Symphony (1886-8), and the String Quartet (1889).

Franco /ˈfræŋkəʊ/, Francisco (1892-1975), Spanish dictator. After service in Morocco, where he helped to form the Spanish Foreign Legion, Franco was among the leaders of the military uprising against the republican government which led to the Spanish Civil War. In October 1936 he became leader of the Nationalist forces, and when the last loyalist strongholds finally surrendered in early 1939 he assumed dictatorial powers and set up a Fascist regime. Despite pressure from Germany and Italy, Franco kept Spain neutral during the Second World War, and continued to rule until his death in 1975.

Franco- in comb. French and (*Franco-German*). [f. L (as FRANK)]

franglais /ˈfrɑ̃gleɪ/ n. a corrupt version of French using many words and phrases borrowed from English. [F (*français* French, *anglais* English)]

Frank n. a member of a Germanic people that conquered Gaul in the 6th c. —**Frankish** adj. [OE]

frank adj. candid, open, outspoken, undisguised, unmistakable. —v.t. to mark (a letter etc.) to record the payment of postage. —n. a franking signature or mark. —**frankly** adv., **frankness** n. [f. OF f. L *francus* free (as foll., since only Franks had full freedom in Frankish Gaul)]

Frankenstein /ˈfræŋkənstaɪn/ n. (more correctly **Frankenstein's monster**) a thing that becomes terrifying to its creator. [Character in Mary Shelley's novel *Frankenstein* (1818), who constructed a human monster and endowed it with life. It became filled with hatred for its creator and eventually killed him.]

frankfurter /ˈfræŋkfɜːtə(r)/ n. a seasoned smoked sausage. [f. G *Frankfurter wurst* Frankfurt sausage (*Frankfurt* in West Germany)]

frankincense /ˈfræŋkɪnsens/ n. an aromatic gum resin burnt as incense. [f. OF (as FRANK in obs. sense 'of high quality', INCENSE²)]

Franklin /ˈfræŋklɪn/, Benjamin (1706-90), American statesman, one of the signatories to the peace between the USA and Great Britain after the American War of Independence, inventor, and scientist. He became a wealthy printer and publisher and published, amongst other things, the *Pennsylvania Gazette* and *Poor Richard's Almanack*. His main scientific achievements were the formulation of a theory of electrical (electrostatic) action based on the concept of a single electric 'fluid' which was widely used in the second half of the 18th c., and a demonstration of the electrical nature of lightning (his suggestion was first taken up in France by Jean François d'Alibard), which led to the invention of the lightning conductor. His inventions include the Pennsylvanian fireplace or Franklin stove, and bifocal spectacles.

frantic /ˈfræntɪk/ adj. wildly excited, frenzied; characterized by great hurry or anxiety, desperate, violent; (*colloq.*) extreme. —**frantically** adv. [f. OF f. L (as PHRENETIC)]

frappé /ˈfræpeɪ/ adj. (esp. of wine) iced, chilled. [F, p.p. of *frapper* strike, ice (drinks)]

fraternal /frəˈtɜːn(ə)l/ adj. of brothers, brotherly. —**fraternal twins**, twins developed from separate ova and not necessarily similar. —**fraternally** adv. [f. L (*frater* brother)]

fraternity /frəˈtɜːnɪtɪ/ n. **1.** a religious brotherhood. **2.** a guild or group of people sharing interests or beliefs etc. **3.** brotherliness. **4.** (*US*) a male students' society in a college or university. [f. OF f. L (as prec.)]

fraternize /ˈfrætənaɪz/ v.i. to associate or make friends (*with*); (of troops) to enter into friendly relations *with* enemy troops or inhabitants of an occupied country. —**fraternization** /-ˈzeɪʃ(ə)n/ n. [f. F & L (as FRATERNAL)]

fratricide /ˈfrætrɪsaɪd/ n. **1.** the crime of killing one's own brother or sister. **2.** one who is guilty of this. —**fratricidal** adj. [F, or f. L (*frater* brother, -CIDE)]

Frau /fraʊ/ n. (pl. **Frauen**) a German woman; the title of a German wife or widow, = Mrs. [G]

fraud /frɔːd/ n. **1.** criminal deception. **2.** a dishonest artifice or trick; an impostor. **3.** a person or thing not fulfilling a claim or expectation. [f. OF f. L]

fraudulent /ˈfrɔːdjʊlənt/ adj. of, involving, or guilty of fraud. —**fraudulence** n., **fraudulently** adv. [f. OF or L (as prec.)]

fraught /frɔːt/ adj. **1.** filled or attended *with* (danger etc.). **2.** (*colloq.*) causing or suffering anxiety or distress. [p.p. of obs. *fraught* load with cargo, f. MDu. (as FREIGHT)]

Fräulein /ˈfrɔɪlaɪn/ n. an unmarried German woman; the title of a German spinster, = Miss. [G, dim. of FRAU]

Fraunhofer /ˈfraʊnhəʊfə(r)/, Joseph von (1787-1826), German skilled optician and pioneer in spectroscopy. He observed and mapped a large number of fine dark lines in the solar spectrum and plotted their wavelengths. These lines, named after him, had already been observed by Wollaston in 1802. They were explained by Bunsen and

Gustav Kirchhoff in 1859, and were used to determine the chemical elements present in the spectra of the sun and stars. He became noted for his finely ruled diffraction gratings, used by him to determine the wavelengths of specific colours of light and of the major spectral lines.

fray[1] *v.t./i.* to become or cause to become worn through by rubbing; to become ragged at the edge (*lit.*, or *fig.* of nerves, temper, etc.). [f. F f. L *fricare* rub]

fray[2] *n.* a fight, a conflict; a brawl. [as AFFRAY]

Frazer /ˈfreɪzə(r)/, Sir James George (1854-1941), Scottish classicist and a founder of British social anthropology and ethnology. The first chair in anthropology (at Liverpool University) was created for him in 1907. Born five years before the publication of Darwin's *Origin of Species*, Frazer's work throughout his lifetime reflected his pre-eminent position as an intellectualist evolutionist. Nowhere is this more clearly seen than in his twelve-volume series of essays *The Golden Bough: A Study in Magic and Religion* (1890-1915) in which he proposed a theory of evolutionary development in human modes of thought from the magical and religious to the scientific through which, he believed, all societies pass. Although his evolutionary sequence is now disregarded, his important distinction between magic (the attempt to manipulate events by technical means based upon misconception or pseudo-scientific natural laws) and religion (the appeal to the supernatural for help) continues to underlie much contemporary anthropology. While Frazer's lasting contribution to anthropology (and more widely: it caught the literary imagination and influenced D. H. Lawrence, T. S. Eliot, and others) was *The Golden Bough*, he was a prolific writer in other fields as well, and within his own lifetime he was highly regarded as a biblical scholar and classicist.

frazzle *n.* a worn or exhausted state. [perh. f. FRAY[1] + dial. *fazzle* tangle]

freak *n.* **1.** a capricious or unusual idea, act, etc. **2.** a monstrosity, an abnormal person or thing. **3.** an unconventional person; one who freaks out; a drug addict. —*v.t./i.* (with *out*) (*slang*) **1.** to undergo or cause to undergo hallucinations through drug-taking etc. or a strong emotional experience. **2.** to adopt an unconventional life-style. —**freak-out** *n.* (*slang*) the experience of freaking out. —**freakish** *adj.* [prob. f. dial.]

freckle *n.* a light brown spot on the skin. —*v.t./i.* to spot or be spotted with freckles. [f. ON]

Frederick[1] /ˈfredrɪk/ (Ger. *Friedrich*) the name of three Holy Roman Emperors:
Frederick I 'Barbarossa' (= 'Redbeard'), (*c.*1123-90), emperor 1152-90. One of the strongest rulers of his age, Barbarossa made a sustained attempt to bring Italy and the papacy under military subjugation but was eventually checked at the Battle of Legnano in 1176. He was drowned while crossing a river on his way to the Third Crusade, but legend says that he still sleeps in a cavern in the Kyffhäuser mountains until the needs of his country shall summon him forth.

Frederick[2] /ˈfredrɪk/ (Ger. *Friedrich*) the name of three kings of Prussia:
Frederick II 'the Great' (1712-86), reigned 1740-86. On his succession to the throne Frederick promptly claimed Silesia, launching Europe into the War of the Austrian Succession. He soon proved to be a brilliant soldier, building the Prussian army into the best fighting force in Europe. During the Seven Years War (1756-63) he fought against a coalition of France, Russia, Austria, Sweden, and Saxony, and despite some setbacks successfully brought his country out of the war in a better position than it had enjoyed at the outset. The most famous soldier of his age, Frederick also made his name as a patron of culture and enacted a series of legal and administrative reforms in his kingdom.

free *adj.* (*compar.* **freer** /ˈfriːə(r)/, *superl.* **freest** /ˈfriːɪst/) **1.** not a slave or under the control of another, having personal rights and social and political liberty; (of a State, citizens, or institutions) subject neither to foreign domination nor to despotic government. **2.** not fixed or held down, able to move without hindrance; permitted *to* do; unrestricted, not controlled by rules; (of a translation) not literal. **3.** (with *of* or *from*) without, not subject to or affected by. **4.** without payment, costing nothing to the recipient. **5.** not occupied or in use; without engagements; clear of obstructions. **6.** coming, given, or giving readily; impudent. **7.** (*Chem.*) not combined; (*Phys.*) not bound in an atom or molecule; (of power or energy) disengaged, available. —*adv.* freely; without cost or payment. —*v.t.* to make free, to set at

liberty; to relieve *from*; to rid or ease *of*; to clear, to disentangle. —**free and easy**, informal. **free association**, association of ideas, by a person undergoing a psychological test, without suggestion or control by the tester. **free-born** *adj.* born as a free citizen. **Free Church**, a nonconformist Church, **Free Church of Scotland**, that which seceded from the Presbyterian establishment 1843-1929. **free enterprise**, freedom of private business from State control. **free fall**, movement under the force of gravity only. **free fight**, a general fight in which all present may join, without rules. **free-for-all** *n.* a free fight, an unrestricted discussion etc. **free hand**, freedom to act at one's own discretion. **free-hand** *adj.* (of a drawing) done without instruments such as a ruler or compasses. **free-handed** *adj.* generous. **free house**, an inn or public house not controlled by a brewery and therefore able to sell any brand of beer etc. **free kick**, a kick in football taken without interference from opponents, as a minor penalty. **free lance**, a person whose services are available to any would-be employer, not one only. **free-lance** *adj.* of a free lance; (*v.i.*) to act as a free lance. **free-loader** *n.* (*slang*) a sponger. **free love**, sexual relations irrespective of marriage. **free market**, a market in which prices are determined by unrestricted competition. **free on board** *or* **rail**, without charge for delivery to a ship, railway wagon, etc. **free port**, one open to all traders, or free from duty on goods in transit. **free-range** *adj.* (of hens etc.) given freedom of movement in seeking food etc. **free speech**, the freedom to express opinions of any kind. **free-spoken** *adj.* not concealing one's opinions. **free-standing** *adj.* not supported by another structure. **free-style** *adj.* (of a swimming-race) in which any stroke may be used; (of wrestling) with few restrictions on the holds permitted. **free-thinker** *n.* one who rejects dogma or authority in religious belief. **free trade**, trade left to its natural course without import restrictions etc. **free vote**, a parliamentary vote in which members are not bound by party policy. **free wheel**, the driving-wheel of a bicycle able to revolve with the pedals at rest. **free-wheel** *v.i.* to ride a bicycle with the pedals at rest; to move or act without constraint. **free will**, the power of acting without the constraint of necessity or fate, the ability to act at one's own discretion. **free world**, the non-Communist countries' collective name for themselves. —**freely** *adv.* [OE]

-free *in comb.* free of or from (*duty-free, fancy-free*). [f. prec.]

freeboard *n.* the part of a ship's side between the water-line and the deck.

freebooter *n.* a pirate. [f. Du. *vrijbuiter* (as FREE, BOOTY)]

freedman *n.* (*pl.* **-men**) an emancipated slave. [f. p.p. of *free* v. (FREE) + MAN]

freedom /ˈfriːdəm/ *n.* **1.** the condition of being free or unrestricted; personal or civic liberty; liberty of action (*to*). **2.** frankness, undue familiarity. **3.** exemption (*from*); the unrestricted use (*of* a house etc.); honorary membership or citizenship. —**freedom of speech**, the right to express one's views freely. [OE (cf. FREE)]

freehold *n.* the holding of land or property in absolute possession. —*adj.* held thus. —**freeholder** *n.*

freeman *n.* (*pl.* **-men**) **1.** one who is not a slave or serf. **2.** one who has the freedom of a city etc.

Freemason /ˈfriːmeɪs(ə)n/ *n.* a member of an international fraternity for mutual help and fellowship, called *Free and Accepted Masons*, having an elaborate ritual and system of secret signs. The original *free masons* were probably emancipated skilled itinerant stonemasons who (in and after the 14th c.) found work wherever important buildings were being erected, the *accepted masons* being honorary members (originally supposed to be eminent for architectural or antiquarian learning) who began to be admitted early in the 17th c., all of whom recognized their fellow craftsmen by secret signs. The distinction of being an 'accepted mason' became a fashionable object of ambition, and before the end of the 17th c. the purpose of the fraternities seems to have been chiefly social and convivial. In 1717 four of these societies or 'lodges' in London united to form a 'grand lodge', with a new constitution and ritual, and a new objective of mutual help and fellowship among members. The London 'grand lodge' became the parent of other 'lodges' in Britain and around the world, and there are now bodies of Freemasons in many countries of the world.

Freemasonry *n.* **1.** the system and institutions of Freemasons (see prec.). **2. freemasonry**, a secret or tacit fellowship, instinctive sympathy. [f. prec.]

freesia /ˈfriːzjə, -ʒə/ *n.* a bulbous African plant of the genus

Freesia, with fragrant flowers. [f. F. T. H. *Freese* German physician (d. 1876)]

Freetown the capital and chief port of Sierra Leone; pop. 274,000.

freeway *n.* an express highway, especially with limited access.

freeze *v.t./i.* (*past* **froze**; *p.p.* **frozen**) **1.** to turn into ice or some other solid by cold; to cover or become covered with ice. **2.** to be or feel very cold; to make or become rigid from cold; to adhere by frost. **3.** to preserve (food) by refrigeration below freezing-point. **4.** to become or cause to become motionless through fear, surprise, etc. **5.** to fix (prices, wages, etc.) at a certain level; to make (assets) unavailable. —*n.* **1.** a state or period of frost; the coming of a period of frost. **2.** the fixing or stabilization of prices, wages, etc. —**freeze-dry** *v.t.* to freeze and dry by evaporation of ice in a high vacuum. **freeze on to**, (*slang*) to take or keep a tight hold of. **freeze up**, to freeze completely; to obstruct by the formation of ice etc. **freeze-up** *n.* a period or conditions of extreme cold. **freezing-point** *n.* the temperature at which a liquid, especially water, freezes. [OE]

freezer *n.* a refrigerated container or compartment in which food is preserved at a very low temperature. [f. prec.]

Frege /ˈfreɪgə/, Gottlob (1848–1925), German philosopher and mathematician, founder of modern logic. His aim was to introduce rigour into mathematical proofs and establish the certainty of mathematical truth, and he developed a logical system for the expression of mathematics which was a vast improvement on the syllogistic logic which it replaced; he also worked on general questions of philosophical logic and semantics. His theory of meaning, based on his use of a distinction between what a linguistic term refers to and what it expresses, is still influential. Frege tried to provide a rigorous foundation for mathematics on the basis of purely logical principles, but abandoned the attempt when Bertrand Russell pointed out that his system was inconsistent.

freight /freɪt/ *n.* **1.** the transport of goods in containers or by water or air (or (*US*) by land). **2.** the goods transported, a cargo, a load. **3.** a charge for the transport of goods. —*v.t.* to transport (goods) by freight; to load with freight. [f. MLG or MDu. *vrecht* var. of *vracht* (as FRAUGHT)]

freighter *n.* a ship or aircraft designed to carry freight; (*US*) a freight-wagon. [f. prec.]

freightliner *n.* a train carrying goods in containers.

Frémont /ˈfriːmɒnt/, John Charles (1813–90), American explorer and statesman. Known as the Pathfinder for his efforts at opening up the American West, Frémont was responsible for exploring several viable routes to the Pacific across the Rockies in the 1840s. His public career, however, was stormy, involving two resignations from the army (one from a high position during the American Civil War), an unsuccessful bid for the Presidency in 1856, and a scandal over railway speculation which lost him his fortune in the 1870s. He served as Governor of Arizona in 1878–83 before eventually dying in New York.

French *adj.* of France or its people or language; having French characteristics. —*n.* **1.** the French language (see below). **2.** (*euphem.*) bad language. **3.** dry vermouth. —**the French** (*pl.*), the people of France. **French bean**, the kidney or haricot bean used as unripe sliced pods or as ripe seeds. **French bread**, bread in a long crisp loaf. **French Canadian**, a native of the French-speaking area of Canada. **French chalk**, finely powdered talc used as a marker, dry lubricant, etc. **French Community**, an association, set up in 1958, consisting of France, her overseas territories and departments, and various independent African States formerly under French rule. Some African States have since left the Community but retain close links with France. **French dressing**, a salad dressing of seasoned oil and vinegar. **French fried potatoes** *or* **fries**, (*US*) potato chips. **French horn**, an instrument of the brass family, a coiled tube with a wide-flaring bell facing backwards, having a range of about three-and-a-half octaves (ill. OR-CHESTRA). The coiled horn first appeared around the 1660s, probably in France; the valved horn in use today came in *c.*1815. **French leave**, absence without permission. **French letter**, (*colloq.*) a condom. **French polish**, shellac polish for wood. **French window**, a glazed door in an outside wall. [OE (as FRANK)]

French is spoken as a native language by some 75 million people in France and neighbouring countries and also in Canada, and is the official language of a number of African States, having spread as a result of French colonization. It is a Romance language which has developed from the version of the Latin spoken in Gaul after its conquest in 58–51 BC. A number of dialects of French arose, but in recent centuries, since Paris became the French capital, the northern dialects have gained the ascendancy. A feature of French which began in the Middle Ages is the nasal pronunciation of certain vowels, found in no other living West European speeches except Portuguese. From the 11th to the 14th c. France was the leading country in Europe. Its influence and language spread, and in most European countries it became customary for the upper classes to learn French. From the 13th c. until well into the 20th c. it was the language of diplomacy, used for international negotiations. In 1635 the French Academy was founded (see ACADÉMIE FRANÇAISE), determining what should be considered correct French, and although modern writers continue to experiment with the language modern literary French remains much the same as the language of the 17th c.

French is the international postal language (whence the use of *aérogramme* on air-letter forms)—a status that it has held since a decision of the Universal Postal Union on its foundation in 1875.

frenchify /ˈfrentʃɪfaɪ/ *v.t.* (usu. in *p.p.*) to make French in form, manners, etc. [f. prec.]

Frenchman *n.* (*pl.* **-men**) a man of French birth or nationality. —**Frenchwoman** *n.fem.* (*pl.* **-women**)

French Revolution the overthrow of the Bourbon monarchy in France. It was the first of a series of European political upheavals, in which various groups in French society found common cause in opposing the feudal structure of the State, with its privileged Establishment and discredited monarchy. It began with the meeting of the legislative assembly in May 1789, when the French government was already in crisis. The Bastille was stormed in July of the same year and thereafter the Revolution became steadily more radical with the rise of orators such as Robespierre in Paris and attempts at intervention from abroad resulting in the execution of Louis XVI (Jan. 1793) and the Reign of Terror (Sept. 1793–July 1794). The Revolution failed to produce a stable form of republican government, and after several different forms of administration had been tried, the last, the Directory, was overthrown by Napoleon in 1799.

frenetic /frəˈnetɪk/ *adj.* frantic, frenzied; fanatic. —**frenetically** *adv.* [f. OF f. L f. Gk (*phrēn* mind)]

frenzy /ˈfrenzɪ/ *n.* wild excitement or agitation; a delirious fury. —*v.t.* (usu. in *p.p.*) to drive to frenzy. —**frenziedly** *adv.* [f. OF f. L (as prec.)]

frequency /ˈfriːkwənsɪ/ *n.* **1.** commonness of occurrence; frequent occurrence. **2.** the rate of recurrence (of vibration etc.); the number of cycles of a carrier wave per second; a band or group of such values. —**frequency modulation**, the varying of a carrier-wave frequency. [f. L (as foll.)]

frequent /ˈfriːkwənt/ *adj.* occurring often or in close succession; habitual, constant. —/frɪˈkwent/ *v.t.* to attend or go to habitually. —**frequently** *adv.*, **frequentation** /-teɪʃ(ə)n/ *n.* [f. F or L *frequens*, orig. = crowded]

frequentative /frɪˈkwentətɪv/ *adj.* (*Gram.*, of a verb etc.) expressing frequent repetition or intensity of action. —*n.* a frequentative verb etc. [as prec.]

fresco /ˈfreskəʊ/ *n.* (*pl.* **-os**) a method of wall-painting, or a picture done, in which pure powdered pigments, mixed only in water, are applied to a wet freshly laid lime-plaster ground. The colours penetrate into the surface and as it dries they become fixed and insoluble in water. The fresco painter has to work rapidly, before the plaster dries, and corrections are almost impossible; but, once completed, the fresco will last as long as the wall itself. Fresco was used in the wall-paintings at Pompeii, and by the great masters of the Italian Renaissance, Giotto, Masaccio, Piero della Francesca, Raphael, and Michelangelo. It works best in dry climates, and has been used chiefly in Italy (except Venice) and rarely in northern Europe, although attempts were made to revive it by the German Nazarenes and English Pre-Raphaelites in the 19th c. [It., = cool, fresh]

fresh *adj.* **1.** newly made or obtained; other, different, not previously known or used. **2.** lately arrived *from*. **3.** not stale or musty; not faded. **4.** (of food) not preserved by salting, tinning, freezing, etc. **5.** not salty. **6.** pure, untainted; refreshing. **7.** not weary, vigorous; (of a wind) brisk. **8.** cheeky, amorously impudent; inexperienced. —*adv.* newly, recently (esp. in comb.: *fresh-baked, fresh-cut*). —**freshly** *adv.*, **freshness** *n.* [f. OF *freis fresche* f. Gmc]

freshen *v.t./i.* to make or become fresh. [f. prec.]

fresher *n.* (*slang*) a freshman. [f. FRESH]

freshet /ˈfreʃɪt/ *n.* a stream of fresh water flowing into the sea; a flood of a river. [f. OF (as FRESH)]

freshman *n.* (*pl.* **-men**) a first-year student at university or (*US*) high school.

freshwater *adj.* (of fish etc.) of fresh (not salt) water, not of the sea.

Fresnel /frəˈnel/, Augustin Jean (1788–1827), French physicist and civil engineer. He took up the study of polarized light in 1814 and postulated that light moved in a wave-like motion, which had already been suggested by, among others, Huygens and Thomas Young (1773–1829). They, however, assumed the waves to be longitudinal, while by 1821 Fresnel was sure that they vibrated transversely to the direction of propagation, and he used this to explain successfully the phenomenon of double refraction. He invented a large lens, made up of a series of concentric rings, for lighthouses and searchlights.

fret[1] *v.t./i.* (**-tt-**) **1.** to worry, to vex; to be worried or distressed. **2.** to wear or consume by gnawing or rubbing. —*n.* worry, vexation. [OE *fretan* (as FOR-, EAT)]

fret[2] *n.* an ornamental pattern of continuous combinations of straight lines joined usually at right angles. —*v.t.* (**-tt-**) to adorn with a fret or with carved or embossed work. [f. OF *frete* trellis-work]

fret[3] *n.* a bar or ridge on the finger-board of a guitar etc. to guide fingering. [orig. unkn.]

fretful *adj.* constantly fretting, querulous. —**fretfully** *adv.* [f. FRET[1] + -FUL]

fretsaw *n.* a narrow saw stretched on a frame for cutting thin wood in patterns. [f. FRET[2] + SAW[1]]

fretwork *n.* ornamental work in wood with a fretsaw.

Freud /frɔɪd/, Sigmund (1856–1939), Austrian neurologist and psychotherapist, the first to draw attention to the significance of unconscious processes in normal and neurotic behaviour, and founder of psychoanalysis as both a theory of personality and a therapeutic practice (see PSYCHOANALYSIS). The study of neurotic ailments led him to various conclusions relating to mental processes in general, such as the existence of an unconscious element in the mind which influences consciousness, and of conflicts in it between various sets of forces (including repression), he emphasized the importance of a child's semi-consciousness of sex as a factor in mental development, while his theory of the sexual origin of neuroses drew wide publicity and aroused great controversy. Born of a Jewish family, he left Vienna after the German annexation of Austria in 1938 and joined his son in London, where he lived for the rest of his life. His publications include *The Interpretation of Dreams* (1899), *The Psychopathology of Everyday Life* (1904), and *Totem and Taboo* (1913).

Freudian /ˈfrɔɪdɪən/ *adj.* of Freud or his theories or methods of psychoanalysis. —**Freudian slip**, an unintentional error that seems to reveal unconscious feelings. [f. prec.]

Frey /freɪ/ (also **Freyr** /ˈfreɪə(r)/) (*Scand. myth.*) god of fertility and dispenser of rain and sunshine.

Freya /ˈfreɪə/ (*Scand. myth.*) goddess of love and of the night, the northern Venus, sister of Frey. She is sometimes indistinguishable from Frigga.

Fri. *abbr.* Friday.

friable /ˈfraɪəb(ə)l/ *adj.* easily crumbled. —**friability** /-ˈbɪlɪtɪ/ *n.* [f. F or L (*friare* crumble)]

friar /ˈfraɪə(r)/ *n.* a member of certain non-enclosed religious orders of men (especially Augustinians, Carmelites, Dominicans, and Franciscans), founded in the Middle Ages. —**friar's balsam**, a tincture of benzoin etc. used especially for inhaling. [f. OF f. L *frater* brother]

friary *n.* a monastery of friars. [f. prec.]

fricassee /ˈfrɪkəsiː, -ˈsiː/ *n.* a dish of stewed or fried pieces of meat served in a thick sauce. —*v.t.* to make a fricassee of. [F (*fricasser* cut up and stew in sauce)]

fricative /ˈfrɪkətɪv/ *adj.* (of a consonant, e.g. *f, th*) sounded by the friction of the breath in a narrow opening. —*n.* a fricative consonant. [f. as foll.)]

friction /ˈfrɪkʃ(ə)n/ *n.* **1.** the rubbing of one object against another. **2.** the resistance an object encounters in moving over another. **3.** clash of wills, temperaments, opinions, etc. —**frictional** *adj.* [f. F f. L (*fricare* rub)]

Friday /ˈfraɪdeɪ, -dɪ/ *n.* the day of the week following

Thursday. —*adv.* (*colloq.*) on Friday. —**girl** *or* **man Friday**, an assistant doing general duties in an office etc. [f. Man Friday, character in Defoe's *Robinson Crusoe*]. [OE, = day of FRIGGA]

fridge *n.* (*colloq.*) a refrigerator. [abbr.]

friend /frend/ *n.* **1.** a person with whom one enjoys mutual affection and regard (usu. exclusive of sexual or family bonds). **2.** a sympathizer, a helper; a helpful thing or quality; one who is not an enemy. **3.** some person already mentioned or under discussion. **4.** (usu. in *pl.*) a regular contributor of money or other assistance to an institution. **5. Friend**, a member of the Society of Friends (see entry), a Quaker. [OE]

friendless *adj.* without friends. [f. prec. + -LESS]

friendly *adj.* acting as or like a friend, well-disposed, kindly; on amicable terms (*with*); characteristic of friends, showing or prompted by kindness. —*n.* a friendly match. —*adv.* in a friendly manner. —**friendly match**, a match played for enjoyment and not in competition. **Friendly Society**, a society for insurance against sickness etc. —**friendliness** *n.* [f. FRIEND]

Friendly Islands see TONGA.

friendship *n.* a friendly relationship or feeling. [OE (as FRIEND, -SHIP)]

frier var. of FRYER.

Friesian /ˈfriːʒjən/ *n.* one of a breed of large black-and-white dairy cows, originally from Friesland, a northern province of the Netherlands. [var. of FRISIAN]

frieze /friːz/ *n.* **1.** the part of an entablature between the architrave and the cornice (ill. TEMPLES); a horizontal band of sculpture filling this. **2.** a band of decoration, especially along a wall near the ceiling. [f. F f. L *Phrygium* (*opus*) Phrygian work]

frigate /ˈfrɪgɪt/ *n.* a naval escort-vessel like a large corvette; (*hist.*) the warship next in size to ships of the line. [f. F f. It.]

Frigga /ˈfrɪgə/ (*Scand. myth.*) wife of Odin and goddess of married love and of the hearth. (See FREYA.) Friday is named after her.

fright /fraɪt/ *n.* **1.** sudden or extreme fear; an instance of this. **2.** a person or thing looking grotesque or ridiculous. [OE]

frighten *v.t.* to fill with fright; to force or drive (*away* or *off*) by fright. [f. prec.]

frightful *adj.* dreadful, shocking, ugly; (*colloq.*) extreme, extremely bad. —**frightfully** *adv.* [f. FRIGHT + -FUL]

frigid /ˈfrɪdʒɪd/ *adj.* **1.** lacking friendliness or enthusiasm, dull. **2.** (of a woman) sexually unresponsive. **3.** (esp. of climate or air) cold. —**frigidity** /-ˈdʒɪdɪtɪ/ *n.*, **frigidly** *adv.* [f. L *frigidus* (*frigēre* be cold)]

frill *n.* **1.** a strip of material gathered or pleated and fixed along one edge as a trimming. **2.** (in *pl.*) unnecessary embellishments or accomplishments. —*v.t.* to decorate with a frill. —**frilled** *adj.*, **frilly** *adj.* [orig. unkn.]

fringe *n.* **1.** a border or edging of tassels or loose threads. **2.** the front hair hanging over the forehead; **3.** the margin or outer limit of an area, population, etc. **4.** an area or part of minor importance. —*v.t.* to adorn with a fringe; to serve as a fringe to. —**fringe benefit**, an employee's benefit additional to the normal wage or salary. —**fringe medicine**, systems of treatment of diseases, injuries, etc., that are not regarded by the medical profession as part of orthodox treatment. [f. OF f. L *fimbria* fibres, fringe]

frippery /ˈfrɪpərɪ/ *n.* showy finery or ornament, especially in dress; empty display in speech, literary style, etc. [f. F *friperie* (OF *frepe* rag)]

Frisbee /ˈfrɪzbɪ/ *n.* [P] a concave plastic disc for skimming through the air as an outdoor game. [perh. f. *Frisbie* American baker whose pie-tins could be used similarly]

Frisian /ˈfrɪzɪən/ *adj.* of Friesland, a northern province of the Netherlands, or its people or language. —*n.* **1.** a native of Friesland. **2.** the Germanic language spoken there, most closely related to English and Dutch, with about 300,000 speakers. [f. L *Frisii* (*pl.*) f. OFris.]

frisk *v.t./i.* **1.** to leap or skip playfully. **2.** (*slang*) to feel over and search (a person) for a weapon etc. —*n.* **1.** a playful leap or skip. **2.** (*slang*) a search of a person. [f. OF *frisque* lively]

frisky *adj.* lively, playful. —**friskily** *adv.*, **friskiness** *n.* [f. prec.]

frisson /ˈfriːsɔ̃/ *n.* an emotional thrill. [F, = shiver]

Frith /frɪθ/, William Powell (1819–1909), English painter,

From Flowers to Fruits

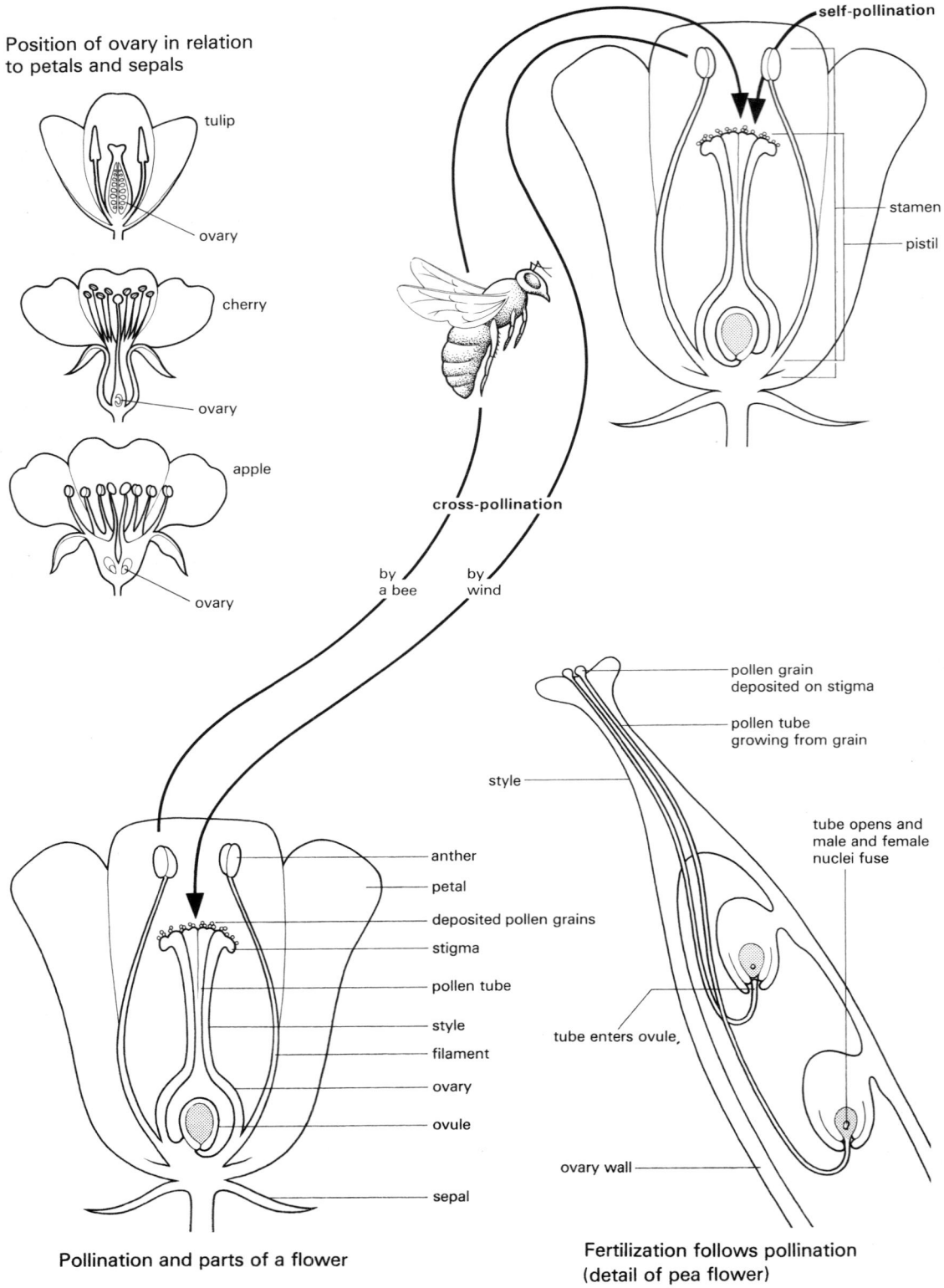

Position of ovary in relation to petals and sepals

tulip

ovary

cherry

ovary

apple

ovary

self-pollination

stamen

pistil

cross-pollination

by a bee

by wind

pollen grain deposited on stigma

pollen tube growing from grain

style

tube opens and male and female nuclei fuse

anther

petal

deposited pollen grains

stigma

pollen tube

style

filament

ovary

ovule

tube enters ovule

ovary wall

sepal

Pollination and parts of a flower

Fertilization follows pollination (detail of pea flower)

Some flowers and their fruits

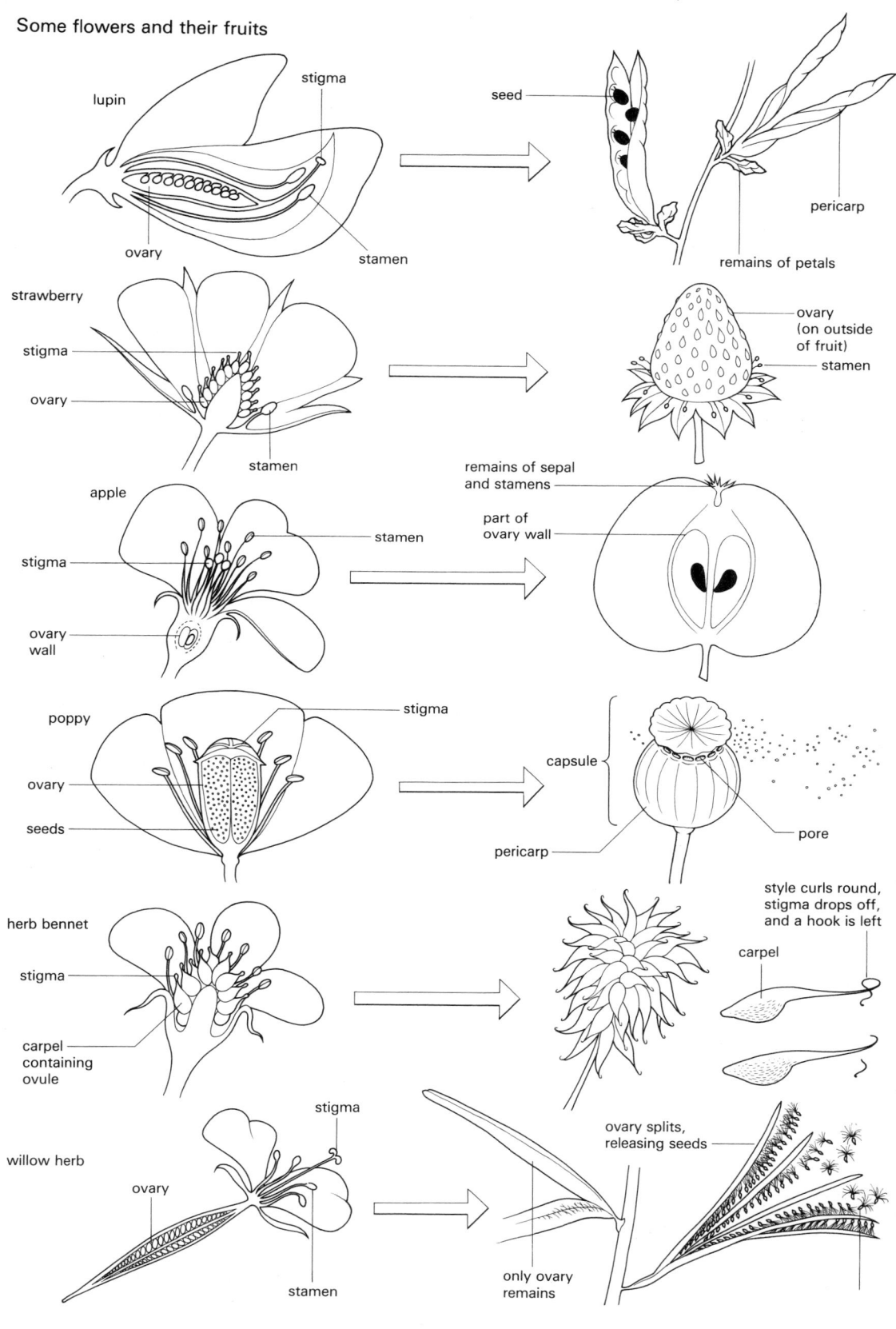

lupin
stigma
ovary
stamen
seed
pericarp
remains of petals

strawberry
stigma
ovary
stamen
ovary (on outside of fruit)
stamen

apple
stamen
stigma
ovary wall
remains of sepal and stamens
part of ovary wall

poppy
stigma
ovary
seeds
capsule
pericarp
pore

herb bennet
stigma
carpel containing ovule
style curls round, stigma drops off, and a hook is left
carpel

willow herb
stigma
ovary
stamen
ovary splits, releasing seeds
only ovary remains

best known for his panoramic scenes of Victorian middle-class life, executed in fine detail with great technical dexterity.

frith var. of FIRTH.

fritter[1] *v.t.* (usu. with *away*) to waste (money, time, energy, etc.) triflingly or indiscriminately. [f. obs. *fritters* fragments]

fritter[2] *n.* a small flat piece of fried batter containing meat or fruit etc. [f. OF *friture* f. L *frigere* fry]

frivolous /ˈfrɪvələs/ *adj.* paltry, trifling; lacking seriousness, silly. —**frivolity** /-ˈvɒlɪtɪ/ *n.*, **frivolously** *adv.* [f. L *frivolus* silly, trifling]

frizz *v.t.* to form (hair) into a mass of small curls. —*n.* frizzed hair or a frizzed state. —**frizzy** *adj.* [f. F *friser*]

frizzle[1] *v.t./i.* **1.** to fry or cook with a sizzling noise. **2.** to burn or shrivel (up). [f. obs. *frizz* fry, with imit. ending]

frizzle[2] /ˈfrɪz(ə)l/ *v.t./i.* to form into tight curls. —*n.* frizzled hair. —**frizzly** *adj.* [orig. unkn.; earlier than FRIZZ]

fro /frəʊ/ *adv.* **to and fro**, see TO. [f. ON, = from]

Frobisher /ˈfrəʊbɪʃə(r)/, Sir Martin (*c.*1535–94), English sailor and explorer. Having first gone to sea as a boy, he went on to lead an expedition in search of the Northwest Passage, discovering what became called Frobisher Bay and landing in Labrador before returning safely despite the loss of one of his three tiny ships and the desertion of another (1576). He returned to Canada in each of the following two years in a fruitless search for gold, before serving in Drake's West Indies expedition of 1585–6 and playing a prominent part in the defeat of the Spanish Armada (for which he was knighted). He died in Plymouth from wounds received in the siege of the Spanish fort at Crozon in Brittany.

frock *n.* **1.** a woman's or girl's dress. **2.** a monk's or priest's gown. **3.** a smock. —*v.t.* to invest with priestly office. —**frock-coat** *n.* a man's long-skirted coat not cut away in front (ill. DRESS); a military coat of this shape. [f. OF *froc*]

Froebel /ˈfrɜːb(ə)l/, Friedrich Wilhelm (1782–1852), German educationist, founder of the kindergarten system. Believing that play materials, practical occupations, and songs were needed to develop a child's real nature, when his two brothers died he undertook the education of their children, opening a school in his native Thuringia to put his theories into practice. In 1837 he opened a school for younger children, naming it the Kindergarten (= children's garden), and later developed a system of specialized training for teachers. In the reactionary period after the 1848 uprisings, however, his reforms fell into disfavour, with the result that his schools were closed by Prussian authorities in 1851.

frog[1] *n.* **1.** a small tailless smooth-skinned leaping amphibian of the order Anura, especially the common frog (genus *Rana*; ill. AMPHIBIANS). **2. Frog**, (*derog.*) a Frenchman (with ref. to use of edible frogs' legs in French cooking). **3.** the horny substance in the sole of a horse's foot. —**frog in one's throat**, (*colloq.*) hoarseness. [OE]

frog[2] *n.* an ornamental coat-fastening of a spindle-shaped button and loop. [orig. unkn.]

frogman *n.* (*pl.* **-men**) a person equipped with a rubber suit and flippers etc. for underwater swimming.

frogmarch *v.t.* to hustle forward holding and pinning the arms from behind; to carry (a person) face downwards by means of four persons each holding a limb. —*n.* the process of frogmarching a person.

frolic /ˈfrɒlɪk/ *v.i.* (**-ck-**) to play about cheerfully. —*n.* cheerful play; a prank; a merry party. [f. Du. *vrolijk* (*vro* glad)]

frolicsome *adj.* merry, playful. [f. prec. + -SOME]

from /frɒm, *emphat.* frɒm/ *prep.* expressing separation or origin, followed by: a person, place, time, etc., that is the starting-point of a motion or action; a place, object, etc., whose distance or remoteness is stated; a source, giver, sender; a thing or person avoided, deprived, etc.; a reason, cause, motive; a thing distinguished or unlike; a lower limit; a state changed for another; adverbs or prepositions of time or place. [OE]

frond *n.* a leaflike part of a fern or palm. [f. L *frons frondis* leaf]

front /frʌnt/ *n.* **1.** the side or part normally nearer to or towards the spectator or direction of motion. **2.** any face of a building, especially that of the main entrance. **3.** the foremost part of an army, a line of battle, the ground towards the enemy, the scene of actual fighting; a sector of activity compared to a military front; an organized political group. **4.** a forward or conspicuous position. **5.** an outward appearance; a bluff, a pretext; a person etc. serving to cover subversive or illegal

activities. **6.** the promenade of a seaside resort. **7.** the forward edge of an advancing mass of cold or warm air. **8.** the auditorium of a theatre. —*adj.* of the front; situated in front; (of vowels) formed at the front of the mouth (as in *see*). —*v.t./i.* **1.** to have the front facing or directed (*on, to, towards, upon*). **2.** (*slang*) to act as a front or cover *for*. **3.** to furnish with a front. —**front-bencher** *n.* a leading member of the government or opposition in Parliament. **front runner**, the contestant most likely to succeed. **in front**, in an advanced or facing position. **in front of**, before, in advance of; in the presence of, confronting. [f. OF f. L *frons frontis* forehead]

frontage *n.* **1.** the front of a building. **2.** the land abutting on a street or water, or between the front of a building and a road. **3.** the extent of a front. **4.** the way a thing faces; an outlook. [f. prec.]

frontal *adj.* **1.** of or on the front; of the front as seen by an onlooker. **2.** of the forehead. —*n.* **1.** a covering for the front of an altar (ill. VESTMENTS). **2.** a façade. [as FRONT]

frontier /ˈfrʌntɪə(r)/ *n.* **1.** a border between two countries, the district on each side of it. **2.** the limits of attainment or knowledge in a subject. [f. AF f. L (as FRONT)]

frontispiece /ˈfrʌntɪspiːs/ *n.* an illustration facing the title-page of a book. [f. F or L, = façade (as prec., *specere* look)]

frost *n.* **1.** freezing; the prevalence of a temperature below the freezing-point of water. **2.** frozen dew or vapour. **3.** a chilling influence, unfriendliness. —*v.t./i.* **1.** to cover (as) with frost; to injure (a plant etc.) with frost. **2.** to make (glass) non-transparent by giving it a rough frostlike surface. —**frost-bite** *n.* injury to the tissue of the body due to freezing. **frost-bitten** *adj.* affected with frost-bite. [OE (as FREEZE)]

frosting *n.* a sugar icing for cakes. [f. prec.]

frosty *adj.* **1.** cold with frost; covered (as) with frost. **2.** unfriendly in manner. —**frostily** *adv.*, **frostiness** *n.* [f. FROST]

froth /frɒθ/ *n.* **1.** foam. **2.** idle talk or ideas. —*v.t./i.* to emit or gather froth; to make (beer etc.) froth. —**frothy** *adj.* [f. ON]

froward /ˈfrəʊəd/ *adj.* (*archaic*) perverse, difficult to deal with. [f. FRO + -WARD]

frown *v.i.* to wrinkle the brows, especially in displeasure or deep thought. —*n.* the action of frowning; a look of displeasure or deep thought. —**frown at** or **on**, to disapprove of. [f. OF (*froigne* surly look, f. Celt.)]

frowsty *adj.* stuffy, fusty. [var. of foll.]

frowzy *adj.* **1.** fusty. **2.** slatternly, dingy. [orig. unkn.]

froze, frozen *past & p.p.* of FREEZE.

FRS *abbr.* Fellow of the Royal Society.

fructify /ˈfrʌktɪfaɪ/ *v.t./i.* to bear or cause to bear fruit. [f. OF f. L (as FRUIT)]

fructose /ˈfrʌktəʊz/ *n.* a sugar found in fruit juice, honey, etc. [f. L (as FRUIT)]

frugal /ˈfruːg(ə)l/ *adj.* **1.** sparing or economical, especially as regards food. **2.** meagre, costing little. —**frugality** /-ˈgælɪtɪ/ *n.*, **frugally** *adv.* [f. L (*frugi* thrifty)]

fruit /fruːt/ *n.* **1.** the product of a plant or tree that contains seed (see ill. pp. 322–3); this used as food; these products collectively. **2.** (usu. in *pl.*) vegetable products fit for food. **3.** the product of action, the result; (in *pl.*) profits. —*v.t./i.* to bear or cause to bear fruit. —**fruit-cake** *n.* one containing dried fruit. **fruit machine**, a coin-operated gambling machine, often using symbols resembling fruit. **fruit sugar**, fructose. [f. OF f. L *fructus* (*frui* enjoy)]

fruiterer /ˈfruːtərə(r)/ *n.* a dealer in fruit. [f. prec.]

fruitful /ˈfruːtfəl/ *adj.* **1.** producing much fruit. **2.** producing good results, successful. —**fruitfully** *adv.*, **fruitfulness** *n.* [f. FRUIT + -FUL]

fruition /fruːˈɪʃ(ə)n/ *n.* the bearing of fruit (*lit.* or *fig.*); the realization of aims or hopes. [f. OF f. L (*frui* enjoy), erron. assoc. with FRUIT]

fruitless /ˈfruːtlɪs/ *adj.* **1.** not bearing fruit. **2.** useless, unsuccessful. —**fruitlessly** *adv.*, **fruitlessness** *n.* [f. FRUIT + -LESS]

fruity /ˈfruːtɪ/ *adj.* **1.** of fruit, tasting or smelling like fruit; full of fruit. **2.** (of a voice etc.) full and rich quality. **3.** (*colloq.*) full of rough humour or (usu. scandalous) interest. —**fruitily** *adv.*, **fruitiness** *n.* [f. FRUIT]

frump *n.* an unattractive dowdy woman. —**frumpish** *adj.* [perh. f. dial. *frumple* wrinkle f. MDu. (as FOR-, RUMPLE)]

frustrate /frʌˈstreɪt/ *v.t.* to make (efforts) ineffective; to prevent (a person) from achieving a purpose; (in *p.p.*)

discontented because unable to achieve desires. —**frustration** n. [f. L (*frustra* in vain)]

frustum /'frʌstəm/ n. (pl. **-ta**) the lower part of a cone or pyramid whose top is cut off by a plane parallel to the base (ill. SHAPES). [L, = piece cut off]

Fry, Elizabeth (1780-1845), English Quaker prison reformer who was in the forefront of the early 19th-c. campaign for penal reform, concerning herself with conditions in English prisons, the lot of convicts transported to Australia, and the large vagrant population in London and the south-east.

fry[1] v.t./i. to cook or be cooked in hot fat. —n. 1. the internal parts of animals usually eaten fried. 2. fried food. —**frying-pan** n. a shallow pan used in frying (*out of the frying-pan into the fire*, from a bad situation to a worse). **fry-up** n. miscellaneous fried food. [f. OF f. L *frigere*]

fry[2] n. young or newly hatched fishes. —**small fry**, people of little importance; children. [f. ON, = seed]

fryer n. 1. one who fries. 2. a vessel for frying food, especially fish. [f. FRY[1]]

ft. abbr. foot, feet.

Fuchs /foks/, Sir Vivian Ernest (1908-   ), English explorer and geologist, director of the Falkland Islands (Dependencies) Survey 1947-50 and 1960-73, and leader of the Commonwealth Trans-Antarctic Expedition 1957-8.

fuchsia /'fjuː.ʃə/ n. a shrub of the genus *Fuchsia*, with drooping red or purple or white flowers. [f. L *Fuchs*, German botanist (d. 1566)]

fuck v.t./i. (*vulgar*) 1. to have sexual intercourse (*with*). 2. to make *off*; to idle *about* or *around*. 3. to mess *up*. —int. (*vulgar*) expressing anger or annoyance. —n. (*vulgar*) 1. the act of or a partner in sexual intercourse. 2. the slightest amount. —**fucking** adj. & adv. (*vulgar*, often as a mere intensive). [orig. unkn.]

fuddle v.t. to confuse or stupefy, especially with alcoholic liquor. —n. confusion; intoxication. [orig. unkn.]

fuddy-duddy /'fʌdɪdʌdɪ/ adj. (*slang*) old-fashioned or quaintly fussy. —n. (*slang*) such a person. [orig. unkn.]

fudge n. 1. a soft toffee-like sweet made of milk, sugar, and butter. 2. nonsense. —v.t. to put together in a makeshift or dishonest way, to fake. [perh. f. obs. *fadge* fit]

fuel /'fjuː(ə)l/ n. 1. material for burning as a fire or as a source of heat or power; material used as a source of nuclear energy. 2. food as a source of energy. 3. a thing that sustains or inflames passion etc. —v.t./i. (**-ll-**) 1. to supply with fuel; to inflame (a feeling etc.). 2. to take in or get fuel. —**fuel cell**, a cell producing electricity direct from a chemical reaction. **fuel injection**, the direct introduction of fuel under pressure into the combustion unit of an internal-combustion engine (ill. CAR). [f. AF f. L *focus* hearth]

fug n. (*colloq.*) stuffiness of the air in a room. —**fuggy** adj., **fugginess** n. [orig. unkn.]

fugitive /'fjuːdʒɪtɪv/ adj. 1. fleeing, that runs or has run away. 2. fleeting, transient; (of literature) of passing interest, ephemeral. —n. one who flees, e.g. from justice or an enemy. [f. OF f. L (*fugere* flee)]

fugue /fjuːg/ n. a piece of music in which three or more parts or 'voices' (described thus whether vocal or instrumental) enter successively in imitation of each other. The first voice enters with a short melody (the *subject*) and is 'answered' by the second voice transposing the subject up a perfect fifth or down a perfect fourth. Subject and voice continue to alternate in this way until all the voices have entered. This 'exposition' is followed by an 'episode' introducing new material or developing existing motives. Further entries of the subject may be made in different keys, but the piece will end with its appearance in the original key. [F or f. It., f. L *fuga* flight]

führer /'fjʊərə(r)/ n. a tyrannical leader. [G, = leader (part of title assumed by Adolf Hitler)]

Fujiyama /fuːdʒɪ'jɑːmə/ a dormant (or perhaps extinct) volcano which is Japan's highest peak (3,810 m, 12,385 ft.). It has a snow-capped cone of exceptional beauty. Its last eruption was in 1707.

-ful /-fʊl/ suffix forming (1) adjectives from nouns, in sense 'full of' (*beautiful*), 'having the qualities of' (*masterful*), or from adjectives (*direful*); or from verbs in sense 'apt to' (*forgetful*); (2) nouns (pl. **-fuls**) in sense 'amount that fills' (*glassful*, *handful*, *spoonful*). [f. FULL]

fulcrum /'fʊlkrəm/ n. (pl. **fulcra**) the point on which a lever is supported. [L, = post of couch (*fulcire* prop)]

fulfil /fʊl'fɪl/ v.t. (**-ll-**) to carry out (a task, prophecy, promise, command, or law); to satisfy (conditions, a desire,

a prayer); to answer (a purpose). —**fulfil oneself**, to develop fully one's gifts and character. —**fulfilment** n. [OE (as FULL[1], FILL)]

full[1] /fʊl/ adj. 1. holding all that its limits will allow; having eaten to one's limit or satisfaction. 2. abundant, copious, satisfying. 3. having an abundance *of*. 4. engrossed in thinking *of*. 5. complete, perfect, reaching the specified or usual or utmost limit. 6. (of a tone) clear and deep. 7. plump, rounded; (of clothes) made of much material hanging in folds. —adv. 1. very; quite, fully. 2. exactly. —**full back**, a defensive player near the goal in football, hockey, etc. **full-blooded** adj. vigorous, sensual; not hybrid. **full-blown** adj. fully developed. **full board**, the provision of bed and all meals at a hotel etc. **full-bodied** adj. rich in quality, tone, etc. **full brother, sister**, a brother or sister with both parents the same. **full face**, with all the face visible to the spectator. **full house**, a large or full attendance at a theatre etc.; a hand in poker with three of a kind and a pair. **full-length** adj. not shortened or abbreviated; (of a mirror or portrait) showing the whole of the human figure. **full moon**, the moon with the whole disc illuminated; the time when this occurs. **full pitch, full toss**, a ball pitched right up to the batsman in cricket. **full-scale** adj. not reduced in size, complete. **full stop**, the punctuation mark (.) used at the end of a sentence or abbreviation; a complete cessation. **full time**, the total normal duration of work etc. **full-time** adj. occupying or using the whole of the available working time. **full toss**, a ball pitched right up to the batsman in cricket. **in full**, without abridgement, to or for the full amount. **in full view**, entirely visible. **to the full**, to the utmost extent. [OE]

full[2] /fʊl/ v.t. to clean and thicken (cloth). [back-formation f. foll.]

Fuller /'fʊlə(r)/, Thomas (1608-61), English cleric, preacher, and historian, whose best-known and most characteristic work, *The Worthies of England* (a description of the counties, with short biographies of local personages) appeared in 1662, after his death. His writings are marked with humour and a quaint wit that is sometimes a little incongruous with the subject.

fuller n. one who fulls cloth. —**fuller's earth**, a type of clay used in fulling. [OE f. L *fullo*]

fullness n. being full. —**the fullness of time**, the appropriate or destined time. [f. FULL[1]]

fully adv. completely, entirely; no less than. —**fully-fashioned** adj. (of women's clothing) shaped to fit the body. [f. FULL[1]]

fulmar /'fʊlmə(r)/ n. an Arctic sea-bird (*Fulmarus glacialis*) related to the petrel. [f. ON (as FOUL, *mar* gull)]

fulminant /'fʊlmɪnənt/ adj. 1. fulminating. 2. (of a disease) developing suddenly. [f. F or L (as foll.)]

fulminate /'fʌlmɪneɪt, 'fʊ-/ v.i. 1. to express censure loudly and forcefully. 2. to explode violently, to flash like lightning. —**fulmination** /-'neɪʃ(ə)n/ n., **fulminator** n. [f. L (*fulmen* lightning)]

fulsome /'fʊlsəm/ adj. (of flattery etc.) cloying, disgustingly excessive. [f. FULL[1]]

Fulton /'fʊlt(ə)n/, Robert (1765-1815), American pioneer of the steamship. He came to England at an early age and in London studied painting under Benjamin West. Urged by James Watt and others, he turned to engineering and invented an apparatus for raising and lowering canal boats, a device for sawing marble, and a machine for twisting hemp into rope. During the Napoleonic Wars he spent some time in France and proposed both torpedoes and submarines, constructing a steam-propelled 'diving-boat' which in 1801 submerged to a depth of 7.6 m (25 ft.). Unable to obtain support for his ideas in Europe he returned to America in 1806 and built the *Clermont*, a paddle-steamer powered by a steam-engine. This made a successful trip in 1807, and 18 other steamships were subsequently built (including some for Russia), inaugurating the era of commercial steam navigation.

fumble v.t./i. to use the hands awkwardly, to grope about; to handle clumsily or nervously. —n. an act of fumbling. [f. LG or Du.]

fume /fjuːm/ n. (usu. in pl.) exuded gas, smoke, or vapour, especially when harmful or unpleasant. —v.t./i. 1. to emit fumes; to issue in fumes. 2. to be very angry. 3. to subject to fumes, especially of ammonia to darken oak etc. [f. OF f. L *fumus* smoke]

fumigate /'fjuːmɪgeɪt/ v.t. to disinfect or purify with the action of fumes. —**fumigation** /-'geɪʃ(ə)n/ n., **fumigator** n. [f. L (as prec.)]

fun *n.* lively or playful amusement; a source of this. —**for** *or* **in fun**, not seriously. **make fun of** *or* **poke fun at**, to tease, to ridicule. [f. obs. v. *fun* befool (as FOND)]

function /ˈfʌŋkʃ(ə)n/ *n.* **1.** the activity proper to a person or institution or by which a thing fulfils its purpose; an official or professional duty. **2.** a public ceremony or occasion. **3.** a social gathering, especially a large one. **4.** (*Math.*) a quantity whose value depends on varying values (of others). —*v.i.* to fulfil a function, to operate. [f. F f. L (*fungi funct-* perform)]

functional *adj.* **1.** of or serving a function; designed or intended to be practical rather than necessarily attractive or pleasing. **2.** affecting a function of a bodily organ but not its structure. —**functionally** *adv.* [f. prec.]

functionalism *n.* belief in or stress on the practical application of a thing. The idea that beauty results from or is identical to function is found in Xenophon (4th c. BC) and in 18th-c. aesthetic theory, but has had its greatest impact in architecture, whose language it entered at least as early as the 1840s. In 1901 Louis Sullivan originated the phrase 'form follows function' and Frank Lloyd Wright amplified this as 'form and function are one'. Functionalism was preached as a new aesthetic creed by Le Corbusier (*Towards a New Architecture*, 1927), who defined a house as a machine for living in, and it became popular also in the severely utilitarian furniture design of the 1930s. By the mid-20th c., however, functionalism was seen as one element in the aesthetic basis of the practical arts but no longer preached as the sole principle of beauty. —**functionalist** *n.* [f. prec.]

functionary *n.* a person or official performing certain duties. [as prec.]

fund *n.* **1.** a permanently available stock. **2.** a stock of money, especially one set apart for a purpose; (in *pl.*) money resources. —*v.t.* to provide with money; to make (a debt) permanent at a fixed interest. —**in funds**, having money to spend. [f. L *fundus* bottom]

fundamental /fʌndəˈment(ə)l/ *adj.* of, affecting, or serving as a base or foundation, essential, primary. —*n.* **1.** (usu. in *pl.*) a fundamental rule or principle. **2.** (in full **fundamental note**) the lowest note of a chord. —**fundamental particle**, an elementary particle. —**fundamentally** *adv.* [f. F or L (*fundamentum* foundation, as prec.)]

fundamentalism *n.* strict maintenance of traditional orthodox religious beliefs; a religious movement which developed among various Protestant bodies in the USA after the First World War, based on strict adherence to certain tenets (e.g. the literal inerrancy of Scripture) held to be fundamental to the Christian faith. —**fundamentalist** *n.* [f. prec.]

funeral /ˈfjuːnər(ə)l/ *n.* **1.** a burial or cremation of the dead with ceremonies. **2.** (*slang*) one's (usu. unpleasant) concern. —*attrib. adj.* of or used at funerals. [f. OF f. L (*funus funer-* burial)]

funerary /ˈfjuːnərərɪ/ *adj.* of or used at a funeral or funerals. [f. L (as prec.)]

funereal /fjuːˈnɪərɪəl/ *adj.* of or appropriate to a funeral, dismal, dark. —**funereally** *adv.* [as prec.]

fun-fair *n.* a fair consisting of amusements and side-shows.

fungicide /ˈfʌndʒɪsaɪd/ *n.* a substance that kills fungus. —**fungicidal** /-saɪd(ə)l/ *adj.* [f. FUNGUS + -CIDE]

fungoid /ˈfʌŋɡɔɪd/ *adj.* fungus-like. —*n.* a fungoid plant. [f. foll.]

fungus /ˈfʌŋɡəs/ *n.* (*pl.* **-gi** /-gaɪ/) any of a large group of non-flowering plants including mushrooms, toadstools, moulds, and yeasts (see below). **2.** a spongy morbid growth. —**fungal** *adj.*, **fungous** *adj.* [L]
Fungi lack chlorophyll and are therefore incapable of photosynthesis; most live either on dead matter or as parasites, but some form associations with other plants, notably growing with algae to form lichens. Many species play an ecologically vital role in breaking down dead organic matter, others are an important source of antibiotics, others cause disease in plants, animals, and humans. Although believed to be an ancient group, fungi are scarce as fossils, and their relationship with other plants is obscure; they are sometimes classified as a separate kingdom, distinct from the green plants.

funicular /fjuːˈnɪkjʊlə(r)/ *adj.* (of a railway especially on a mountain) operating by a cable with ascending and descending cars counterbalanced. —*n.* such a railway. [f. L *funiculus* dim. of *funis* rope]

funk *n.* (*slang*) **1.** fear, panic. **2.** a coward. —*v.t./i.* (*slang*) to be afraid (of); to try to evade. —**blue funk**, (*slang*) extreme panic. [orig. unkn.]

funky /ˈfʌŋkɪ/ *adj.* (*slang*) **1.** (esp. of music) down-to-earth, emotional. **2.** fashionable. **3.** having a strong smell. [orig. unkn.]

funnel /ˈfʌn(ə)l/ *n.* **1.** a narrow tube or pipe widening at the top, for pouring liquid etc. into a small opening. **2.** a metal chimney on a steam-engine or ship. —*v.t./i.* (**-ll-**) to move or cause to move (as) through a funnel. [f. Prov. *fonilh* f. L (*in*)*fundibulum* f. IN-¹, *fundere* pour]

funny /ˈfʌnɪ/ *adj.* **1.** amusing, comical. **2.** strange, hard to account for; (*colloq.*) slightly unwell, eccentric, etc. —**funny-bone** *n.* the part of the elbow over which a very sensitive nerve passes. —**funnily** *adv.*, **funniness** *n.* [f. FUN]

fur *n.* **1.** the short fine soft hair of certain animals. **2.** an animal skin with the fur on it, used especially for making or trimming clothes etc.; a garment made or lined with this. **3.** (in heraldry) a representation of tufts on a plain ground (ill. HERALDRY). **4.** (*collect.*) furred animals. **5.** the crust or coating formed on the tongue in sickness, in a kettle by hard water, etc. —*v.t./i.* (**-rr-**) **1.** (esp. in *p.p.*) to line or trim with fur. **2.** (often with *up*) to make or become coated with a fur deposit. —**make the fur fly**, to cause trouble or dissension. [f. OF *forrer* (*forre, fuerre* sheath)]

furbelow /ˈfɜːbɪləʊ/ *n.* **1.** a gathered strip or pleated border of a skirt or petticoat. **2.** (in *pl.*) showy ornaments. [f. F *falbala*]

furbish /ˈfɜːbɪʃ/ *v.t.* (often with *up*) to polish, to clean up or renovate. [f. OF *forbir*]

furcate /ˈfɜːkeɪt/ *adj.* forked, branched. —*v.i.* to fork, to divide. —**furcation** /-ˈkeɪʃ(ə)n/ *n.* [f. L (*furca* fork)]

Furies /ˈfjʊərɪz/ *n.pl.* (*Gk myth.*) spirits of punishment who executed the curses pronounced upon criminals, tortured the guilty with stings of conscience, or inflicted famines and pestilences. They were anciently confused with the Eumenides. [pl. of FURY]

furious /ˈfjʊərɪəs/ *adj.* very angry, full of fury, raging, frantic. —**furiously** *adv.* [f. OF f. L (as FURY)]

furl *v.t./i.* to roll up and bind (a sail etc.); to become furled. [f. F *ferler* f. OF (*ferm* firm, *lier* bind)]

furlong /ˈfɜːlɒŋ/ *n.* one-eighth of a mile. The term originally meant the length of the furrow in the common field, which was theoretically regarded as a square containing ten acres; as a lineal measure the furlong therefore varied according to the extent assigned at various times and places to the acre. As early as the 9th c. it was regarded as the equivalent of the Roman *stadium*, which was one-eighth of a Roman mile, and hence *furlong* has always been used as a name for the eighth part of an English mile, whether this coincided with the agricultural measure or not. [OE (as FURROW, LONG¹)]

furlough /ˈfɜːləʊ/ *n.* leave of absence, especially that granted to a serviceman. —*v.t./i.* (*US*) to grant a furlough to; to spend a furlough. [f. Du. (as FOR-, LEAVE)]

furnace /ˈfɜːnɪs/ *n.* an enclosed structure for intense heating by fire, especially of metals or water; a very hot place. [f. OF f. L *fornax* (*fornus* oven)]

furnish /ˈfɜːnɪʃ/ *v.t.* **1.** to provide (a house or room etc.) with furniture. **2.** to supply *with* a thing. [f. OF *furnir* (cf. FRAME, FROM)]

furnishings *n.pl.* the furniture and fitments in a house or room etc. [f. prec.]

furniture /ˈfɜːnɪtʃə(r)/ *n.* **1.** the movable equipment of a house or room etc., e.g. tables, chairs, and beds. **2.** a ship's equipment. **3.** accessories, e.g. the handles and lock on a door. [f. F (as FURNISH)]

furore /fjʊəˈrɔːrɪ/ *n.* an uproar of enthusiastic admiration or fury. [It., f. L *furor* madness]

furrier /ˈfʌrɪə(r)/ *n.* a dealer in or dresser of furs. [f. OF]

furrow /ˈfʌrəʊ/ *n.* **1.** a narrow cut in the ground made by a plough. **2.** a rut, a groove, a wrinkle. **3.** a ship's track. —*v.t.* **1.** to plough. **2.** to make furrows or grooves etc. in. [OE]

furry /ˈfɜːrɪ/ *adj.* like or covered with fur. [f. FUR]

further /ˈfɜːðə(r)/ *adv.* **1.** more far in space or time. **2.** more, to a greater extent. **3.** in addition. —*adj.* **1.** more distant or advanced. **2.** more, additional. —*v.t.* to promote or favour (a scheme etc.). —**further education,** that for persons above school age. [OE (compar. of FORTH)]

furtherance *n.* the furthering of a scheme etc. [f. prec.]

furthermore *adv.* in addition, besides.

furthermost *adj.* most distant.

furthest /ˈfɜːðɪst/ adj. most distant. —adv. to or at the greatest distance. [superl. f. FURTHER]

furtive /ˈfɜːtɪv/ adj. done by stealth; sly, stealthy. —**furtively** adv., **furtiveness** n. [f. F or L (furtum theft)]

fury /ˈfjʊərɪ/ n. **1.** wild and passionate anger, rage. **2.** the violence of a storm, disease, etc. **3. Fury,** each of the Furies (see entry). **4.** an angry or malignant woman. —**like fury,** (colloq.) with great force or effort. [f. OF f. L furia (as FURORE)]

furze n. a spiny evergreen shrub of the genus Ulex with yellow flowers, gorse. —**furzy** adj. [OE]

fuse[1] /fjuːz/ v.t./i. **1.** to melt with intense heat; to blend into a whole by melting. **2.** to mix or blend together. **3.** to provide (an electric circuit) with a fuse or fuses. **4.** (of an appliance) to fail owing to the melting of a fuse; to cause (an appliance) to do this. —n. a device with a strip or wire of easily melted metal placed in an electric circuit so as to interrupt an excessive current by melting. [f. L fundere fuspour, melt]

fuse[2] /fjuːz/ n. a device or component of combustible matter for detonating a bomb etc. or an explosive charge. —v.t. to fit a fuse to. [f. It. f. L fusus spindle]

fuselage /ˈfjuːzəlɑːʒ/ n. the body of an aeroplane. [F (fuseler cut in spindle form, as prec.)]

fusible /ˈfjuːzɪb(ə)l/ adj. that may be melted. —**fusibility** /-ˈbɪlɪtɪ/ n. [f. L (as FUSE[1])]

fusil /ˈfjuːzɪl/ n. (hist.) a light musket. [F f. L (focus hearth)]

fusilier /fjuːzɪˈlɪə(r)/ n. a member of any of several British regiments formerly armed with fusils. [F (as prec.)]

fusillade /fjuːzɪˈleɪd/ n. **1.** a continuous discharge of firearms. **2.** a sustained outburst of criticism etc. [F (fusiller shoot, as prec.)]

fusion /ˈfjuːʒ(ə)n/ n. **1.** fusing or melting together; blending, coalition. **2.** nuclear fusion (see NUCLEAR). [f. F or L (as FUSE[1])]

fuss n. **1.** excited commotion, bustle. **2.** excessive concern about a trivial thing. **3.** a sustained protest or dispute. —v.t./i. to behave with nervous concern; to agitate, to worry. —**make a fuss,** to complain vigorously. **make a fuss of,** to treat with excessive attention etc. [orig. unkn.]

fusspot n. (colloq.) a person given to fussing.

fussy adj. inclined to fuss; over-elaborate, fastidious. —**fussily** adv., **fussiness** n. [f. FUSS]

fustian /ˈfʌstɪən/ n. **1.** a thick twilled cotton cloth usually dyed dark. **2.** bombast. —adj. **1.** made of fustian. **2.** bombastic, worthless. [f. OF f. L, orig. ref. to cloth from Fostat suburb of Cairo]

fusty adj. musty, stuffy, stale-smelling; antiquated. —**fustiness** adj. [f. OF, = smelling of the cask (fust cask)]

futile /ˈfjuːtaɪl/ adj. useless, ineffectual, frivolous. —**futility** /-ˈtɪlɪtɪ/ n. [f. L futilis, lit. = leaky]

future /ˈfjuːtʃə(r)/ adj. **1.** belonging to the time coming after the present; about to happen or be or become. **2.** (Gram., of a tense) describing an event yet to happen. —n. **1.** future time, events, or condition. **2.** a prospect of success etc. **3.** (Gram.) a future tense. **4.** (in pl.) goods and stocks for future delivery. —**in future,** from this time onwards. [f. OF f. L futurus fut. partic. of esse be]

futurism n. a movement in art, literature, music, etc., departing from traditional forms so as to express movement and growth. Launched by the Italian poet Filippo Marinetti in 1909, futurism was designed to shake the public out of their cultural torpor. Its participants demanded the incorporation into art of 20th-c. experience, particularly the celebration of new technology, dynamism, and the altered sensibilities of modern man. The use of manifestos and public demonstrations to publicize the movement ensured the wide dissemination over Europe of its art and theory, with important repercussions particularly in Russia. Although effectively ended by the First World War, the group's attitude to art and its techniques of propaganda had a lasting influence on Dada and other new artistic groupings. —**futurist** n. [f. prec.]

futuristic /fjuːtʃəˈrɪstɪk/ adj. **1.** suitable for the future, ultra-modern. **2.** of futurism. [f. FUTURE]

futurity /fjuːˈtjʊərɪtɪ/ n. future time; (in sing. or pl.) future events. [as prec.]

futurology /fjuːtʃəˈrɒlədʒɪ/ n. the forecasting of the future, especially from present trends in society. [f. FUTURE + -LOGY]

fuzz[1] n. **1.** fluff; fluffy or frizzed hair. [prob. f. LG or Du.]

fuzz[2] n. (slang) the police; a policeman. [orig. unkn.]

fuzzy adj. **1.** like fuzz. **2.** blurred, indistinct. —**fuzzily** adv., **fuzziness** n. [f. FUZZ]

G

G, g /dʒiː/ *n.* (*pl.* **Gs, G's**) **1.** the seventh letter of the alphabet. **2.** (*Mus.*) the fifth note in the scale of C major.

G *abbr.* **1.** gauss. **2.** giga-.

g. *abbr.* **1.** gram(s). **2.** gravity; acceleration due to gravity.

Ga *symbol* gallium.

gab *n.* (*colloq.*) talk, chatter. —**gift of the gab,** eloquence, loquacity. [var. of GOB²]

gabardine /ˈɡæbədiːn/ *n.* a twill-woven cloth, especially of worsted. [var. of GABERDINE]

gabble *v.t./i.* to talk or utter inarticulately or too fast. —*n.* fast unintelligible talk. —**gabbler** *n.* [f. MDu., imit.]

gabby *adj.* (*colloq.*) talkative. [f. GAB]

gaberdine /ˈɡæbədiːn/ *n.* **1.** (*hist.*) a loose long upper garment worn especially by Jews. **2.** gabardine. [f. OF *gauvardine*]

gable /ˈɡeɪb(ə)l/ *n.* **1.** the triangular upper part of a wall at the end of a ridged roof (ill. HOUSES); an end wall with a gable. **2.** a gable-shaped canopy. —**gabled** *adj.* [f. ON & OF]

Gabon /ɡæˈbɒn/ a country on the west coast of Africa on the Gulf of Guinea, north of Congo; pop. (est. 1982) 2,000,000; official language, French; capital, Libreville. Formerly a French territory and from 1910 to 1957 part of French Equatorial Africa, the country became autonomous within the French Community in 1958 and fully independent in 1960. It is one of the major oil-producing African States, and also has rich deposits of manganese. —**Gabonese** /ɡæbəˈniːz/ *adj.* & *n.*

Gaborone /kæbʊˈruːni/ the capital of Botswana; pop. (est.) 60,000.

Gabriel /ˈɡeɪbrɪəl/ **1.** one of the seven archangels enumerated in the Book of Enoch, a messenger of God (Dan. 8, 9, Luke 1). **2.** (in Muslim religion) one of the four principal angels. [f. Heb., = man of God]

Gad **1.** Hebrew patriarch, son of Jacob and Zilpah (Gen. 30: 11). **2.** the tribe of Israel traditionally descended from him.

gad¹ *v.i.* (**-dd-**) to go *about* idly or in search of pleasure. [f. obs. *gadling* companion f. OE]

gad² *int.* (also **by gad**) expressing surprise or emphatic assertion. [= *God*]

gadabout /ˈɡædəbaʊt/ *n.* one who gads about.

Gadaffi /ɡəˈdɑːfɪ/, Muammar al- (1942–), head of the State of Libya since 1970 after leading the coup which overthrew King Idris in 1969. Formerly an officer in the Libyan army, he established himself as the leader of a socialist republic, acquiring a reputation for unpredictability in his dealings with the West and with his Arab neighbours.

gadfly *n.* **1.** a fly that bites cattle. **2.** an irritating person. [f. obs. *gad* spike f. ON]

gadget /ˈɡædʒɪt/ *n.* a small mechanical device or tool. —**gadgetry** *n.* [orig. unkn.]

gadoid /ˈɡeɪdɔɪd/ *adj.* of the cod family Gadidae. —*n.* a gadoid fish. [f. Gk *gados* cod]

gadolinium /ɡædəˈlɪnɪəm/ *n.* a metallic element of the lanthanide series, symbol Gd, atomic number 64. It resembles steel in appearance and is strongly magnetic below room temperature. First isolated in pure form (as the oxide) in 1886, it is now used as a phosphor in colour television sets. [f. J. *Gadolin*, Finnish mineralogist (d. 1852)]

Gaea /ˈɡeɪə/ = GE.

Gael /ɡeɪl/ *n.* a Scottish Celt; a Gaelic-speaking Celt. [f. Gaelic *Gaidheal*]

Gaelic /ˈɡeɪlɪk, ˈɡæ-/ *n.* a language spoken in Ireland and Scotland in two distinct varieties, referred to also as Irish (or Erse; see IRISH) and Scots Gaelic respectively, forming, together with Manx, the Goidelic group of the Celtic language group. From about the 5th c. AD the language was carried to Scotland by settlers from Ireland (see DALRIADA), and became the language of most of the Highlands and islands; in time the Scottish variety diverged to the point where it was clearly a different dialect. Scots Gaelic, however, has no official status and now is spoken by only about 75,000 people in the far west of Scotland; there is a small but flourishing literary movement. A number of English words are taken from it, e.g. *bog, cairn, slogan, whisky.* —*adj.* of Gaelic or the Gaels. [f. GAEL]

gaff¹ *n.* **1.** a stick with an iron hook for landing large fish; a barbed fishing-spear. **2.** a spar to which the head of a fore-and-aft sail is bent (ill. SAILING-SHIPS). —*v.t.* to seize (a fish) with a gaff. [f. Prov. *gaf* hook]

gaff² *n.* **blow the gaff,** (*slang*) to divulge a plot or secret. [orig. unkn.]

gaffe /ɡæf/ *n.* a social blunder. [F]

gaffer *n.* **1.** an old fellow (also as a title or form of address). **2.** a foreman, a boss. [prob. contraction of GODFATHER]

gag *n.* **1.** a thing thrust into or tied across the mouth to prevent speech or hold the mouth open for an operation. **2.** a joke or comic scene in a play, film, etc. **3.** a thing restricting free speech; a Parliamentary closure. —*v.t./i.* (**-gg-**) **1.** to apply a gag to. **2.** to silence, to deprive of free speech. **3.** to make gags in a play, film, etc. **4.** to choke, to retch. [perh. imit. of choking]

gaga /ˈɡɑːɡɑː/ *adj.* (*slang*) senile; fatuous, slightly crazy. [F]

gage¹ *n.* **1.** a pledge, a thing deposited as security. **2.** the symbol of a challenge to fight, especially a glove thrown down. [f. OF (cf. WED)]

gage² *n.* a greengage. [abbr.]

gage³ *US & Naut.* var. of GAUGE.

gaggle *n.* **1.** a flock of geese. **2.** a disorderly group. [imit.]

gaiety /ˈɡeɪətɪ/ *n.* being gay, mirth; merry-making, amusement; bright appearance. [f. F (as GAY)]

gaily *adv.* in a gay manner. [f. GAY]

gain *v.t./i.* **1.** to obtain or secure. **2.** to acquire as profit etc., to earn; to make a profit; to be benefited, improve, or advance *in* some respect. **3.** to obtain as an increment or addition. **4.** (of a clock etc.) to become fast, or fast by (a specified time). **5.** to come closer to something pursued, to catch up *on* or *upon*. **6.** to reach (a desired place). **7.** to win (land from the sea, a battle). —*n.* **1.** an increase of wealth or possessions. **2.** an improvement, an increase in amount or power. **3.** the acquisition of wealth. —**gain ground,** to make progress. **gain time,** to improve one's chances by causing or accepting a delay. —**gainer** *n.* [f. OF *gaigner* till, acquire]

gainful *adj.* (of employment) paid; lucrative. —**gainfully** *adv.* [f. GAIN + -FUL]

gainsay /ɡeɪnˈseɪ/ *v.t.* to deny, to contradict. [f. obs. *gain-* against + SAY]

Gainsborough /ˈɡeɪnzbərə/, Thomas (1727–88), English painter of portraits and landscapes. Born in Suffolk, he worked there 1746–60, thereafter in fashionable Bath (1760–74), and finally in London (1774–88). Landscape was always his greatest love, and his mature landscapes are poetic and broadly painted, reflecting the influence of Rubens: in the 1780s he found a lucrative way to combine them with peasant figures in his 'fancy pictures'. His light rapid brushwork was especially suited to the depiction of effects of light, whether in twilight landscapes or in shimmering silks and satins; in his later years he painted by candle-light, so that such effects became even more delicate and subtle.

gait *n.* manner of walking; the manner of forward motion of a horse etc. [var. of dial. *gate* road, going]

gaiter *n.* a covering of cloth, leather, etc., for the leg below the knee, for the ankle, or for part of a machine etc. [f. F *guêtre*]

Gaius /ˈɡaɪəs/ Gaius Julius Caesar Germanicus (12–41), also known as Caligula, Roman emperor 37–41. His short and autocratic reign, which ended with his assassination, has become a byword for tyrannical excess. The story that he appointed his horse consul appears to be without foundation.

gal *n.* (*colloq.*) a girl. [repr. var. pronunc.]

gal. *abbr.* gallon(s).

gala /ˈɡɑːlə, ˈɡeɪlə/ *n.* a festive occasion; a festive gathering for sports. [f. F or It. f. Sp. f. Arab., = presentation garment]

galactic /gə'læktɪk/ *adj.* of a galaxy or galaxies. [f. Gk *galaktias*, var. of *galaxias* (as GALAXY)]

Galahad /'gæləhæd/ (in Arthurian legend) a knight of immaculate purity, destined to retrieve the Holy Grail.

galantine /'gæləntiːn/ *n.* white meat boned, spiced, etc., and served cold. [f. OF, alt. f. *galatine* jellied meat]

galanty /'gæləntɪ/ *n.* **galanty show**, see SHADOW-SHOW. [perh. f. It. *galanti* gallants]

Galapagos Islands /gə'læpəgəs/ a Pacific archipelago on the Equator, about 1,045 km (650 miles) west of Ecuador, to which it belongs. The abundant wildlife of the islands includes giant tortoises, flightless cormorants, and many other endemic species. The observations made here by Charles Darwin in 1835, when official naturalist on HMS *Beagle*, helped him to form his theory of natural selection. [Sp., = tortoises]

Galatea /gælə'tiːə/ (*Gk myth.*) **1.** a sea-nymph courted by the Cyclops Polyphemus, who in jealousy killed his rival Acis. **2.** the name given to the statue fashioned by Pygmalion and brought to life (see PYGMALION).

Galatia /gə'leɪʃə/ **1.** the ancient name for the region in central Asia Minor, centred on Ankara, settled by invading Celts (the Galatians) in the 3rd c. BC. **2.** a Roman province formed in 25 BC including Galatia proper and additional territories. —**Galatian** *adj.* & *n.*

Galatians /gə'leɪʃ(ə)nz/ *Epistle to the Galatians*, a book of the New Testament, an epistle of St Paul to the Church at Galatia.

galaxy /'gæləksɪ/ *n.* **1.** an aggregate of gas, dust, and millions or billions of stars, bound together by gravity, in form either elliptical, irregular, or disc-shaped (usually with well-defined spiral arms); **Galaxy**, that which contains the Earth (see below). **2. Galaxy**, the Milky Way. **3.** a brilliant company. [f. OF f. L Gk *galaxias* (*gala* milk)]

The Galaxy in which the Earth is located is a collection of approximately 100,000 million stars. It has two main components: the halo, 100,000 light-years across, containing a relatively sparse population of cool dim stars and the globular clusters (see CLUSTER), and the disc, a few thousand light-years thick, rich in gas, dust, and young stars, where the spiral arms denote regions of most recent star formation. Our sun is located slightly above the mid-plane of the disc, and about two-thirds of the way out from the centre. The centre of the disc exhibits a thickening, called the nuclear bulge, in which high-velocity gas motions seem to be occurring. The central few light-years of the Galaxy contain energetic radio and infra-red sources, associated apparently with disturbed complexes of ionized hydrogen. These streaming gas-clouds behave as if ejected explosively from something not yet understood, perhaps a massive black hole, at the precise centre.

Galba /'gælbə/ Servius Sulpicius Galba (*c.*3 BC–AD 69), Roman emperor AD 68–9. He had had a distinguished career and was a governor in Spain when invited to succeed the murdered emperor Nero in AD 68, quickly obtaining the allegiance of all the Roman military forces. Once in power, however, he lacked the cool judgement that his task required, aroused hostility by his notorious parsimony, and alienated the legions in Germany by removing their commander. In mid-January AD 69 he was murdered in a conspiracy organized by Otho, who succeeded him.

gale[1] *n.* **1.** a very strong wind, especially (on the Beaufort scale) of 32–54 m.p.h.; a storm. **2.** an outburst, especially of laughter. **3.** (*poetic*) a breeze. [orig. unkn.]

gale[2] *n.* (usu. in **sweet-gale**) bog myrtle (*Myrica gale*). [OE]

Galen /'geɪlən/ (129–199) Greek physician from Pergamum in Asia Minor, where he tended the gladiators, who became court-physician in Rome. He was the author of numerous works which attempt to systematize the whole of medicine. His pathology was founded on Hippocrates' doctrine of the four humours, but he was especially productive as a practical anatomist and experimental physiologist. He demonstrated that the arteries carry blood not (as had been thought) air, but postulated the presence of minute pores in the wall between the ventricles of the heart, allowing blood to pass through, a theory which was accepted until medieval times. His works reached Europe in the 12th c. in Latin translations from Arabic texts, and were widely influential.

Galicia /gə'lɪʃə/ a province of NW Spain. —**Galician** *adj.* & *n.*

Galilean[1] /gælɪ'liːən/ *adj.* of Galileo. —**Galilean satellites**, the four largest moons of Jupiter, discovered by Galileo in 1610 and independently by Simon Marius. Visible through almost any small telescope, they are worlds in their own right, airless but with individual geological features: Io has many volcanoes which erupt frequently to cover the surface in bright sulphurous lava, the others have rocky cores topped by a mantle of ice, heavily marked by either grooves (Ganymede), criss-crossing lines (Europa), or craters (Callisto and Ganymede). **Galilean telescope**, the first type of astronomical telescope, used by Galileo, with a bi-convex objective and bi-concave eyepiece.

Galilee /'gælɪlɪ/ the northern part of ancient Palestine, west of the Jordan, now in Israel. —**Sea of Galilee**, (also called Lake Tiberias) a lake in northern Israel. The River Jordan flows through it from north to south. —**Galilean**[2] /-'liːən/ *adj.* & *n.*

Galileo Galilei /gælɪleɪəʊ gælɪ'leɪɪ/ (1564–1642), Italian astronomer and physicist, one of the founding fathers of modern science. His important discoveries include the constancy of the time of a pendulum's swing, later applied to the regulation of clocks. He formulated the law of uniform acceleration for falling bodies, and described the parabolic trajectory of projectiles, important to the development of classical mechanics. In 1609 he improved the primitive telescope, applied it to astronomy, and made a number of startling observations, including mountains on the moon, sunspots, the stars of the Milky Way, the four satellites of Jupiter, and the phases of Venus. His acceptance (and supporting evidence) of the Copernican system with the Earth and other planets moving round the sun was rejected by the Catholic Church and led to his appearing before the Inquisition in 1633. Under threat of torture he publicly recanted his heretical views and was released into permanent house arrest; he spent his last days blind but still working on problems of astronomy and physics.

gall[1] /gɔːl/ *n.* **1.** the bile of animals. **2.** bitterness; asperity; rancour. **3.** (*slang*) impudence. —**gall-bladder** *n.* a vessel containing bile after its secretion by the liver (ill. BODY 2). [ON]

gall[2] /gɔːl/ *n.* a sore made by chafing; mental soreness or its cause; a place rubbed bare. —*v.t.* **1.** to rub sore. **2.** to vex, to humiliate. [f. MLG or MDu.]

gall[3] /gɔːl/ *n.* a growth produced by insects etc. on plants and trees, especially the oak. [f. OF f. L *galla*]

gallant /'gælənt/ *adj.* **1.** brave. **2.** fine, stately. **3.** /also gə'lænt/ very attentive to women. —*n.* /also gə'lænt/ a ladies' man. [f. OF (*galer* make merry)]

gallantry /'gæləntrɪ/ *n.* **1.** bravery. **2.** devotion to women. **3.** a polite act or speech. [f. F (as prec.)]

galleon /'gæljən/ *n.* a type of ship that was a development of the carrack, following the successful experiments of Sir John Hawkins in 1570 in eliminating the high forecastle (which caught the wind), with which all large ships were then built, and so producing a ship that was more weatherly and manœuvrable. This new design reached Spain *c.*1587 and the resulting galleon, originally designed as a warship, over the next 30–40 years became the principal type of trading ship. Although the design was essentially English the name was never adopted in England or northern Europe. [f. MDu. f. F *galion*, or f. Sp. *galeón*]

gallery /'gælərɪ/ *n.* **1.** a room or building for showing works of art. **2.** a balcony, especially in a hall or church; the highest tier of seats in a theatre; its occupants. **3.** a covered walk partly open at the side, a colonnade; a narrow passage in the thickness of a wall or on corbels, open towards the interior of a building. **4.** a long narrow room or passage. **5.** a group of spectators at a golf match etc. **6.** a horizontal underground passage in a mine etc. —**play to the gallery**, to seek to win approval by appealing to unrefined taste. [f. F f. It. f. L *galeria*]

galley /'gælɪ/ *n.* **1.** (*hist.*) a long flat one-decked vessel usually rowed by slaves or criminals. **2.** an ancient oared warship (see below). **3.** a kitchen in a ship or aircraft. **4.** a long tray for set-up type in printing. **5.** (in full **galley proof**), a proof in a long narrow form. [f. OF f. L or Gk]

The galley was the oared fighting-ship of the Mediterranean, dating from about 3000 BC and lasting into the 18th c. AD. Such ships may have had up to three banks of oars (see TRIREME), or angled benches with several men to each oar, but firm evidence is lacking. The weapon was the ram, a pointed spur fixed to the bow of the galley on or just below the waterline; the ancient Greek technique of fighting was to ram and then depart at speed; the Romans preferred to grapple and fight on deck, or use catapult weapons. With its slim light-draught design the galley was an unstable vessel suitable only for calm waters. Galleys were fitted with one or two masts, which were lowered or beached before action.

Gallic /ˈgælɪk/ *adj.* **1.** of Gaul or the Gauls. **2.** typically French. [f. L (*Gallus* a Gaul)]

Gallican /ˈgælɪkən/ *adj.* of the ancient church of Gaul or France; of a doctrine (reaching its peak in the 17th c.) asserting the freedom of the Roman Catholic Church, especially in France, from the ecclesiastical authority of the papacy (cf. ULTRAMONTANE). —*n.* an adherent of this doctrine. —**Gallicanism** *n.* [as prec.]

Gallicism /ˈgælɪsɪz(ə)m/ *n.* a French idiom. [f. prec.]

gallinaceous /gælɪˈneɪʃəs/ *adj.* of the order including domestic poultry, pheasants, etc. [f. L (*gallina* hen)]

Gallipoli /gəˈlɪpəlɪ/ a peninsula on the European side of the Dardanelles, scene of heavy fighting during the First World War. In early 1915, after a naval attempt to force the Dardanelles had failed, the Allies decided to invade the Gallipoli peninsula, hoping thereby to remove Turkey from the war and open supply lines to Russia's Black Sea ports. Although the Turks were caught at a severe disadvantage, the Allies failed to take their opportunity and the campaign bogged down in trench warfare. After each side had suffered a quarter of a million casualties, the Allies successfully evacuated the peninsula without further loss in January 1916.

gallium /ˈgælɪəm/ *n.* a soft bluish-white metallic element, symbol Ga, atomic number 31, which liquefies at 30 °C. Discovered in 1875, gallium now has a number of uses, e.g. in thermometers designed for high temperatures, and as a semiconductor in electronic components. [f. L *Gallia* Gaul, in honour of France, country of its discoverer (Lecoq de Boisbaudran)]

gallivant /gælɪˈvænt/ *v.i.* (*colloq.*) to gad about. [perh. corrupt. of *gallant* to flirt (as GALLANT)]

Gallo- /gæləʊ-/ *in comb.* French. [f. L *Gallus* a Gaul]

gallon /ˈgælən/ *n.* a measure of capacity (4546 cc; for wine, or *US*, 3785 cc); (usu. in *pl.*, *colloq.*) a large amount. [f. OF *jalon* f. Rom.]

gallop /ˈgæləp/ *n.* the fastest pace of a horse etc., with all the feet off the ground together in each stride (ill. HORSE); a ride at this pace. —*v.t./i.* **1.** (of a horse etc. or its rider) to go at a gallop; to make (a horse) gallop. **2.** to read, talk, etc., fast; to progress rapidly. [f. OF (as WALLOP)]

galloway /ˈgæləweɪ/ *n.* **1.** a horse of a small strong breed from Galloway, an area in SW Scotland; a small horse. **2.** an animal of a breed of cattle from Galloway.

gallows /ˈgæləʊz/ *n. pl.* (usu. treated as *sing.*) a structure, usually of two uprights and a cross-piece, for the hanging of criminals. [f. ON]

gallstone /ˈgɔːlstəʊn/ *n.* a small hard stony mass formed in the gall-bladder. [f. GALL¹ + STONE]

Gallup poll /ˈgæləp/ an assessment of public opinion by the questioning of a representative sample, especially as the basis of forecasts of voting etc. [f. G. H. *Gallup*, American statistician (1901-84) who devised such assessment]

Galois /ˈgælwɑː/, Évariste (1811-32), French mathematician, whose name is used to designate various concepts in algebra that arose out of his work. His bids for recognition were dogged by lost and rejected manuscripts; his memoir on the conditions for solubility of polynomial equations was highly innovative and unappreciated by his contemporaries, and was not published until fourteen years after his death. Having made fundamental discoveries in mathematics at the age of 18, he was imprisoned for his republican activities aged 19, and died aged 20 of wounds received in a mysterious early-morning duel.

galop /ˈgæləp/ *n.* a lively dance in duple time; the music for this. [F, = GALLOP]

galore /gəˈlɔː(r)/ *adv.* in plenty. [f. Ir.]

galosh /gəˈlɒʃ/ *n.* a waterproof overshoe. [f. OF f. L *gallicula* small Gallic shoe]

Galsworthy /ˈgɔːlzwɜːðɪ/, John (1867-1933), English novelist and dramatist. A severe and humourless writer, he wrote several plays on social and moral themes, notably *The Silver Box* (1906) and *Strife* (1909), but is remembered chiefly for his sequence of novels known collectively as *The Forsyte Saga* (1922), tracing the declining fortunes of an affluent Victorian middle-class family. Galsworthy was caricatured by his contemporaries for his superficial and limited vision of social phenomena, but the Forsyte novels

have a history of continuing success. He was awarded the Nobel Prize for literature in 1932.

Galton /ˈgɔːlt(ə)n/, Sir Francis (1822-1911), English scientist. A man of wide interests and a cousin of Charles Darwin, he is remembered chiefly for his advocacy of eugenics (a word coined by him) as a method of improving the human race as a whole. To this end he introduced methods of measuring human mental and physical abilities, and developed statistical techniques to analyse his data. Galton also carried out important work in meteorology and pioneered the use of fingerprints as a means of identification. Eugenics, a widely supported idea in the early decades of the 20th c., fell into disfavour after the perversion of its doctrines by the Nazis.

galumph /gəˈlʌmf/ *v.i.* (*colloq.*) to go prancing in triumph; to move noisily or clumsily. [coined by Lewis Carroll in *Through the Looking-glass*, perh. f. GALLOP, TRIUMPH]

Galvani /gælˈvɑːnɪ/, Luigi (1737-98), Italian anatomist. He studied the structure of the kidneys and ears of birds, the irritability of tissue, and the physiology of muscles and nerves, but he is best remembered for his chance discovery in the 1780s of the twitching of frogs' legs in an electric field produced by his electrostatic generator. He concluded that these convulsions were caused by 'animal electricity' found in the body. This was disputed by Volta who, in the course of this argument, invented his electrochemical cell. The current produced by this device was, for many years, called 'galvanic electricity', and the terms *galvanize* and *galvanometer* embody his name.

galvanic /gælˈvænɪk/ *adj.* **1.** producing an electric current by chemical action; (of electricity) produced by chemical action. **2.** stimulating, full of energy; sudden and remarkable. —**galvanically** *adv.* [f. prec.]

galvanize /ˈgælvənaɪz/ *v.t.* **1.** to stimulate by or as by electricity *into* activity. **2.** to coat (iron) with zinc to protect from rust. —**galvanization** /-ˈzeɪʃ(ə)n/ *n.* [f. GALVANI]

galvanometer /gælvəˈnɒmɪtə(r)/ *n.* an instrument for measuring small electric currents. [as prec. + -METER]

Gama /ˈgɑːmə/, Vasco da (*c.*1469-1524), Portuguese explorer. Da Gama led a Portuguese expedition round the Cape of Good Hope in 1497-9 (the first European to do so), crossing the Indian Ocean to Calicut. Ennobled on his return, he led a second expedition in 1502-3, forcing the Raja of Calicut (who had massacred settlers left behind earlier) to make peace and establishing colonies at Mozambique and Sofala. After 20 years in retirement, da Gama was sent east again to restore Portuguese authority in the East Indies but died soon after his arrival.

Gambia /ˈgæmbɪə/ (also **the Gambia**) a picturesque but poor country of West Africa, consisting of a narrow strip on either side of the River Gambia upstream from its mouth, forming an enclave in Senegal; pop. (1983) approx. 700,000; official language, English; capital, Banjul. A British trading-post from the 17th c., Gambia was created a colony in 1843. It became an independent member of the Commonwealth in 1965, and a republic in 1970. The economy is mainly agricultural, the chief product being ground-nuts. —**Gambian** *adj. & n.*

gambit /ˈgæmbɪt/ *n.* **1.** a chess opening in which a player sacrifices a pawn or piece for the sake of later advantage. **2.** an opening move in a discussion etc.; a trick, a device. [It. *gambetto* tripping up]

gamble *v.t./i.* to play games of chance for money; to risk much in hope of great gain. —*n.* gambling; a risky undertaking. —**gamble away,** to lose by gambling. **gamble on,** to act in the hope of (an event). [f. obs. *gamel* to sport (as GAME¹)]

gambler *n.* one who gambles, esp. habitually. [f. prec.]

gamboge /gæmˈbuːʒ, -bəʊʒ/ *n.* a gum resin used as a yellow pigment and as a purgative. [f. *Cambodia*, where the substance is obtained]

gambol /ˈgæmb(ə)l/ *v.i.* (**-ll-**) to jump about playfully. —*n.* a gambolling movement. [f. *gambade* leap f. It. (*gamba* leg)]

game¹ *n.* **1.** a form of play or sport, especially a competitive one organized with rules, penalties, etc. **2.** a portion of play forming a scoring unit e.g. in bridge or tennis; the winning score in a game; the state of the score. **3.** (in *pl.*) a series of athletic etc. contests. **4.** a scheme, undertaking, etc. **5.** wild animals or birds hunted for sport or food; their flesh as food. —*adj.* spirited, eager and willing. —*v.i.* to gamble for money stakes. —**the game is up,** the scheme is revealed or foiled. **game theory,** the branch of mathematics that deals with the selection of best strategies for participants in conflict. The theory was founded by John von Neumann in 1928 and was expanded in collaboration with Oskar Morgenstern in their book *Theory of games and economic behavior* (1944). **give the game away,** to reveal intentions or a secret. **make game of,** to ridicule. **on the game,** (*slang*) involved in prostitution or thieving. —**gamely** *adv.*, **gameness** *n.* [OE]

game² *adj.* (of a leg, arm, etc.) crippled. [orig. unkn.]

gamecock *n.* a cock bred and trained for cock-fighting.

gamekeeper *n.* a person employed to breed and protect game.

gamelan /ˈgæmələn/ *n.* the standard instrumental ensemble of Indonesia, comprising sets of tuned gongs, gong-chimes, and other percussion instruments as well as string and wood-wind instruments. Sir Francis Drake heard the 'pleasant and delightful' sound of the gamelan during his visit to Java in 1580, and in 1889 a Javanese gamelan formed one of the attractions of the Paris World Exhibition, where it was heard by Debussy and had a marked influence on his music. [Javanese]

gamesmanship *n.* the art of winning games by gaining a psychological advantage over an opponent, first described by Stephen Potter (1947). [f. GAME¹, after *sportsmanship*]

gamesome /ˈgeɪmsəm/ *adj.* playful, sportive. [f. GAME + -SOME]

gamester /ˈgeɪmstə(r)/ *n.* a gambler.

gamete /ˈgæmiːt/ *n.* a mature germ-cell which unites with another in sexual reproduction. —**gametic** /gəˈmetɪk/ *adj.* [f. Gk, = wife (*gamos* marriage)]

gamin /ˈgæmɪn/ *n.* a street urchin; an impudent child. [F]

gamine /gəˈmiːn/ *n.* a girl with mischievous charm. [F (fem. of prec.)]

gamma /ˈgæmə/ *n.* 1. the third letter of the Greek alphabet, = g. 2. a third-class mark in an examination. 3. a designation of the third-brightest star in a constellation, or sometimes the star's position in a group. —**gamma radiation** *or* **rays,** X-rays of very short wavelength emitted by radio-active substances. [Gk]

gammon /ˈgæmən/ *n.* the bottom piece of a flitch of bacon including a hind leg; pig's ham cured like bacon. [f. OF *gambon* (*gambe* leg)]

gammy *adj.* (*slang*) game (GAME²). [f. dial. form of GAME²]

gamut /ˈgæmət/ *n.* 1. the lowest note in the medieval sequence of hexachords, = modern G on the lowest line of the bass staff. 2. the whole series of notes used in medieval or modern music; the major diatonic scale; the compass of a voice or instrument. 3. the entire series or range. [f. L *gamma ut* (GAMMA taken as name for note one tone lower than A of classical scale, *ut* first of six arbitrary names of notes forming hexachord, being italicized syllables of a 7th-c. Latin hymn: *Ut queant laxis resonare fibris Mira gestorum famuli tuorum, Solve polluti labii reatum, Sancte Ioannes*]

gamy /ˈgeɪmɪ/ *adj.* smelling or tasting like high game. [f. GAME¹]

Ganapati /ˈgənəpəti/ = GANESHA. [as GANESHA]

gander *n.* 1. a male goose. 2. (*slang*) a look, a glance. [OE]

Gandhi¹ /ˈgɑːndi/, Indira (1917-84), Indian stateswoman, who sought to establish a secular State and to lead her country out of poverty. Daughter of an independent India's first prime minister, Jawaharlal Nehru, she was herself prime minister 1966-77 and again from 1980, dominating Indian politics for nearly twenty years before her assassination.

Gandhi² /ˈgɑːndi/, Mohandas Karamchand, called 'Mahatma' (1869-1948), Indian statesman. After early civil rights activities as a lawyer in South Africa, Gandhi returned to India in 1914 and after 1918 began to take an increasingly important part in the opposition to British rule, utilizing policies of passive resistance and civil disobedience. President of the Indian National Congress 1925-34, Gandhi was at once the leader and the symbol of the nationalist movement. He was assassinated by a Hindu fanatic at the very time when independence had finally been achieved.

Ganesha /gəˈneɪʃə/ (*Hinduism*) an elephant-headed deity, also called Ganapati, son of Siva and Parvati. Worshipped as the remover of obstacles and patron of learning, he is invoked at the beginning of literary works, rituals, or any new undertaking. He is usually depicted coloured red, with a pot belly and one broken tusk, riding a rat. [Skr., = lord of ganas, Siva's attendants]

gang¹ *n.* 1. a band of persons associating for some (usu. criminal) purpose. 2. a set of workers, slaves, or prisoners. 3. a set of tools working in co-ordination. —*v.t.* to arrange (tools etc.) to work in co-ordination. —**gang up,** to act in concert (*with*). **gang up on,** (*colloq.*) to combine against. [f. ON, = GOING]

gang² *v.i.* (*Sc.*) to go. —**gang agley,** (of a plan etc.) to go wrong. [OE (as prec.; cf. GO)]

ganger *n.* the foreman of a gang of workers. [f. GANG¹]

Ganges /ˈgændʒiːz/ a river in the north of India, held sacred by the Hindus who seek to wash away their sins in its waters. It flows some 2,700 km (1,678 miles) from the Himalayas south-east to Bangladesh, where it reaches the Bay of Bengal in the world's largest delta.

gangling /ˈgæŋglɪŋ/ *adj.* (of a person) loosely built, lanky. [frequent. of GANG²]

ganglion /ˈgæŋglɪən/ *n* (*pl.* **-ia**) 1. an enlargement or knot on a nerve forming a centre for the reception and transmission of impulses. 2. a centre of activity etc. —**ganglionic** /-ˈɒnɪk/ *adj.* [Gk]

gangplank *n.* a movable plank for walking into and out of a boat etc. [f. GANG¹ + PLANK]

gangrene /ˈgæŋgriːn/ *n.* 1. death of body tissue, usually caused by obstructed blood-circulation. 2. moral corruption. —*v.t./i.* to affect or become affected with gangrene. —**gangrenous** /-grɪnəs/ *adj.* [f. F f. L f. Gk]

gangster *n.* a member of a gang of violent criminals. [f. GANG¹]

gangue /gæŋ/ *n.* valueless earth etc. in which ore is found. [F, f. G *gang* lode (= GANG¹)]

gangway *n.* 1. a passage, especially between rows of seats. 2. the opening in a ship's bulwarks; a bridge from this to the shore. [f. GANG¹ + WAY]

gannet /ˈgænɪt/ *n.* a large sea-bird of the genus *Sula*. [OE, cogn. with GANDER]

gantlet /ˈgæntlɪt/ *n.* *US* var. of GAUNTLET.

gantry /ˈgæntrɪ/ *n.* a structure supporting a travelling crane, railway signals, equipment for a rocket-launch, etc. [prob. f. dial. form of GALLON + TREE]

Ganymede /ˈgænɪmiːd/ 1. (*Gk myth.*) a Trojan youth who was so beautiful that he was carried off (in one version, by an eagle) to be Zeus' cup-bearer. 2. (*Astron.*) the largest satellite of the planet Jupiter.

gaol /dʒeɪl/ *n.* a public prison; confinement in this. —*v.t.* to put in gaol. [= JAIL; f. OF *jaiole* f. Rom. dim. of L *cavea* cage]

gaolbird *n.* a habitual criminal; a prisoner.

gaolbreak *n.* an escape from gaol.

gaoler *n.* a person in charge of a gaol or the prisoners in it. [f. GAOL]

gap *n.* 1. a breach in a hedge, fence, or wall. 2. an empty space; an interval. 3. a deficiency. 4. a wide divergence in views etc. 5. a gorge or pass. —**gappy** *adj.* [f. ON, = chasm (rel. to foll.)]

gape *v.i.* to open the mouth wide; (of the mouth etc.) to open or be open wide; to stare *at*; to yawn. —*n.* an open-mouthed stare; a yawn; an open mouth. [f. ON]

garage /ˈgærɑːdʒ, -ɑːʒ, -ɪdʒ/ *n.* 1. a building for housing a motor vehicle or vehicles. 2. an establishment repairing and selling motor vehicles. —*v.t.* to put or keep (a vehicle) in a garage. [F (*garer* shelter)]

garb *n.* clothing, especially of a distinctive kind. —*v.t.* (usu. in *pass* or *refl.*) to dress, especially in distinctive clothes. [f. F f. It. f. Gmc (as GEAR)]

garbage /ˈgɑːbɪdʒ/ *n.* rubbish or refuse of any kind; domestic waste. [f. AF]

garble *v.t.* to distort or confuse (facts, messages, etc.). [f. It. f. Arab. *garbala* sift (cf. L *cribrum* sieve)]

Garbo /ˈgɑːbəʊ/, Greta (1905-), real name Greta Gustafsson, Swedish film actress. Her first important Swedish film, *Gösta Berlings Saga* (1924), led to a Hollywood contract, and her beauty and compelling screen presence received instant recognition in *The Torrent* (1925). After a number of silent films she made a successful transition to sound in *Anna Christie* (1930). She played a number of tragic heroines including Queen Christina (1934), Anna Karenina (1935), and Camille (1936), and in 1939 made her first comedy, *Ninotchka*. After another comedy, *Two Faced Woman* (1941), she abruptly announced her retirement. She is considered by many the greatest of all film actresses.

García Lorca see LORCA.

garden /ˈgɑːd(ə)n/ *n.* 1. a piece of ground for growing flowers, fruit, or vegetables. **2.** (*attrib.*) cultivated. **3.** (esp. in *pl.*) grounds laid out for public enjoyment. —*v.i.* to cultivate a garden. —**garden centre,** an establishment selling garden plants and equipment. **garden city,** a town laid out with many open spaces and trees. **garden party,** a party held in a garden. [f. OF *gardin* (F *jardin*) (as YARD²)]

gardener /ˈgɑːdnə(r)/ *n.* a person who gardens; a person employed to tend a garden. [f. prec.]

gardenia /gɑːˈdiːnɪə/ *n.* a tree or shrub of the genus *Gardenia*, with large fragrant white or yellow flowers; its flower. [f. Dr A. *Garden*, Scottish naturalist (d. 1791)]

garderobe /ˈgɑːdrəʊb/ *n.* (*hist.*) **1.** a store-room or wardrobe. **2.** a lavatory. [F (*garder* keep, ROBE)]

garfish /ˈgɑːfɪʃ/ *n.* (*pl.* same) a fish with a long spearlike snout. [f. OE *gar* spear + FISH]

gargantuan /gɑːˈgæntjʊən/ *adj.* gigantic. [f. *Gargantua* giant in book by Rabelais]

gargle *v.t.* to wash (the throat) with a liquid held there and kept in motion by the breath (or *abs.*). —*n.* a liquid so used. [f. F (as foll.)]

gargoyle /ˈgɑːgɔɪl/ *n.* a grotesque carved face or figure as a spout from the gutter of a building. [f. OF *gargouille* throat]

Garibaldi /ˌgærɪˈbɔːldɪ/, Giuseppe (1807–82), Italian patriot and military leader, one of the heroes of the Risorgimento. After involvement in the early struggles against Austrian rule in the 1830s and 1840s he commanded a volunteer force on the Sardinian side in the campaign of 1859, and successfully led his 'Red Shirts' to victory in Sicily and southern Italy in 1860–1, thus playing a vital part in the establishment of a united kingdom of Italy. Subsequent independent attempts to conquer the papal territories around French-held Rome failed in 1862 and 1867, and Garibaldi proved no more successful in French service during the Franco-Prussian War in 1870–1. In the last years of his life, his health ruined by years of soldiering, he served as a Deputy in the Italian Parliament.

garibaldi /ˌgærɪˈbɔːldɪ/ *n.* a biscuit containing a layer of currants. [f. prec.]

garish /ˈgeərɪʃ/ *adj.* obtrusively bright, showy, gaudy. [app. f. obs. *gaure* stare]

garland /ˈgɑːlənd/ *n.* a wreath, usually of flowers, worn on the head or hung on an object as a decoration. —*v.t.* to deck with garlands; to crown with a garland. [f. OF]

garlic /ˈgɑːlɪk/ *n.* a plant of the genus *Allium* (usually *A. sativum*) with a pungent strong-smelling bulb used in cookery. —**garlicky** /ˈgɑːlɪkɪ/ *adj.* [OE (*gar* spear, LEEK)]

garment /ˈgɑːmənt/ *n.* an article of dress; an outward covering. [f. OF (as GARNISH)]

garner /ˈgɑːnə(r)/ *v.t.* to store; to collect. —*n.* (*literary*) a storehouse, a granary (*lit.* or *fig.*). [f. OF f. L, = GRANARY]

garnet /ˈgɑːnɪt/ *n.* a vitreous silicate mineral, especially a red kind used as a gem. [f. OF f. L *granatum* pomegranate]

garnish /ˈgɑːnɪʃ/ *v.t.* to decorate (esp. a dish for the table). —*n.* a decorative addition. —**garnishment** *n.* [f. OF *garnir*]

garotte var. of GARROTTE.

garret /ˈgærɪt/ *n.* an attic or room in the roof, especially a dismal one. [f. OF *garite* watch-tower (as GARRISON)]

Garrick /ˈgærɪk/, David (1717–79), one of the greatest English actors, who replaced formal declamation with an easy natural manner of speech, of whom Burke said that 'he raised the character of his profession to the rank of a liberal art'. In 1747 he became involved in the management, later becoming sole manager, of Drury Lane theatre. Unsurpassed as the tragic heroes of contemporary works as well as Hamlet, Macbeth, and Lear, he proved his versatility with successes in comedy roles such as Benedick in *Much Ado About Nothing* and Abel Drugger in Jonson's *The Alchemist*, and was also a prolific dramatist. He is buried in Westminster Abbey.

garrison /ˈgærɪs(ə)n/ *n.* troops stationed in a town etc. to defend it. —*v.t.* to provide with or occupy as a garrison. [f. OF (*garir* defend)]

garrotte /gəˈrɒt/ *n.* **1.** a Spanish method of capital punishment by strangulation with a metal collar; the apparatus for this. **2.** a cord or wire used to strangle a victim. —*v.t.* to execute or strangle with a garrotte. [f. F or Sp. (*garrote* cudgel)]

garrulous /ˈgærʊləs/ *adj.* talkative. —**garrulity** /gəˈruːlɪtɪ/ *n.*, **garrulously** *adv.*, **garrulousness** *n.* [f. L (*garrire* chatter)]

garter *n.* **1.** a band worn near the knee to keep up a sock etc. **2. the Garter,** the highest order of English knighthood

(see below); the badge or membership of this. —**garter stitch,** rows of plain stitch in knitting. [f. OF *gartier* (*garet* bend of knee)]

The Order of the Garter was founded by Edward III *c.*1344. The traditional story of the order's founding is that the garter was that of the Countess of Salisbury, which the king placed on his own leg after it fell off while she was dancing with him. The king's comment to those present, 'Honi soit qui mal y pense', became the motto of the order, which became the highest in English knighthood and the model for others founded by other late medieval kings. The Garter as the badge of the order is a ribbon of dark-blue velvet, edged and buckled with gold, bearing the motto embroidered in gold, and is worn below the left knee; garters also form part of the ornament of the collar worn by the Knights.

garth *n.* **1.** (*archaic*) a close or yard, a garden or paddock. **2.** an open space within cloisters (ill. CHURCH). [f. ON (cf. YARD)]

garuda /ˈgɑːrʊdə/ *n.* **1.** (*Indian myth.*) a bird (half eagle, half man) ridden by the god Vishnu. **2.** the eagle in the official seal of Indonesia. [f. Skr.]

gas *n.* (*pl.* **gases** /ˈgæsɪz/) **1.** any substance which is compressible, expands to fill any space in which it is enclosed, and consists of molecules which are not bound together but move about relatively independently (see below, and cf. KINETIC THEORY); a substance which is a gas at normal temperatures and pressures; a gas which at a given temperature cannot be liquefied by pressure alone (other gases generally being known as 'vapours' in this context). **2.** such a substance (especially coal gas or natural gas) used for heating, lighting, or cooking (see below). **3.** nitrous oxide or other gas used as an anaesthetic. **4.** a poisonous gas used to disable an enemy in war. **5.** (*US colloq.*) petrol, gasoline. **6.** (*colloq.*) idle talk, boasting. —*v.t./i.* (**-ss-**) **1.** to expose to gas; to poison or injure by gas. **2.** (*colloq.*) to talk idly or boastfully. —**gas chamber,** an enclosed space that can be filled with poisonous gas to kill animals or people. **gas fire,** a domestic heater burning gas. **gas-fired** *adj.* using gas as a fuel. **gas mask,** a device worn over the face as protection against poison gas. **gas ring,** a hollow perforated ring fed with gas for cooking etc. **gas turbine,** one driven by a flow of gas or by gas from combustion. **step on the gas,** (*colloq.*) to accelerate a motor vehicle. [word invented by J. B. van Helmont, Dutch chemist (d. 1644), after Gk *khaos* chaos]

Different 'airs', vapours, and exhalations were recognized in antiquity and classified with the element 'air', distinguishing them from the other Aristotelian elements earth, water, and fire. It was not until the second half of the 18th c. that different chemical species of gases were clearly distinguished and identified, and recognized as elements in their own right. During the same period the four Aristotelian elements were definitively replaced by three states of matter—solid, liquid, and gas.

The technical founder of the modern gas industry was William Murdock, a Scotsman, who experimented with the distillation of gas from coal (as an Irish clergyman named Clayton had done, for frivolous purposes, nearly a century before him), and in 1792 succeeded in lighting his office with the new gas. In 1807 the first street in London was lighted with it, and the Gas Light and Coke Company came into being three years later. In the early years rival companies competed for business, but soon after 1850 many amalgamated and 'zoning' arrangements were established whereby a single company was responsible for supplies in an allotted district. Gas for lighting was followed by the use of gas for cooking and (from 1863) for heating water. The British gas industry was nationalized in 1949 and there are now plans for denationalization (1986). Early in the 1960s oil began to replace coal as the primary raw material, but from 1965 great natural gas deposits were discovered under the North Sea, creating a rapidly expanding market for gas in western Europe. Natural gas reserves are found also in the USSR (which supplies Eastern Europe), the USA, Algeria, Iran, the Netherlands, Saudi Arabia, and Kuwait.

gasbag *n.* **1.** a container of gas. **2.** (*slang*) an idle talker.

gaseous /ˈgæsɪəs, ˈgeɪ-/ *adj.* of or like gas. [f. GAS]

gash *n.* a long deep cut, wound, or cleft. —*v.t.* to make a gash in, to cut. [var. of earlier *garce* f. OF (*garcer* wound)]

gasholder /ˈgæshəʊldə(r)/ *n.* a large receptacle for storing gas, a gasometer.

gasify /ˈgæsɪfaɪ/ *v.t.* to convert into a gas. —**gasification** /-fɪˈkeɪʃ(ə)n/ *n.* [f. GAS]

Gaskell /ˈgæsk(ə)l/, Mrs Elizabeth Cleghorn (1810–65),

English novelist, whose father and husband were Unitarian ministers. Her first novel, *Mary Barton* (1848), was admired by Dickens, and much of her subsequent works appeared in his *Household Words*, including *Cranford* (1851-3), drawn from childhood experiences in Cheshire. Mrs Gaskell was an active humanitarian; the message in several of her novels is the need for social reconciliation, notably in *North and South* (1855); she also wrote a celebrated biography of her friend Charlotte Brontë (1857).

gasket /'gæskɪt/ *n*. **1**. a sheet or ring of rubber etc. to seal a junction of metal surfaces. **2**. a small cord securing a furled sail to a yard. [perh. f. F *garcette* little girl, thin rope]

gaskin /'gæskɪn/ *n*. the hinder part of a horse's thigh (ill. HORSE). [perh. erron. f. *galligaskins* wide hose of 16th-17th c.]

gaslight *n*. the light given by burning gas.

gasoline /'gæsəliːn/ *n*. (*US*) petrol. [f. GAS]

gasometer /gæ'sɒmɪtə(r)/ *n*. a large tank from which gas is distributed by pipes. [f. F *gazomètre* (as GAS, -METER)]

gasp /gɑːsp/ *v.t./i*. to catch the breath with an open mouth as in exhaustion or surprise; to utter with gasps. —*n*. a convulsive catching of the breath. —**at one's last gasp**, at the point of death, exhausted. [f. ON]

gassy *adj*. **1**. of, like, or full of gas. **2**. verbose. [f. GAS]

gastric /'gæstrɪk/ *adj*. of the stomach. —**gastric flu**, (*colloq*.) sickness and diarrhoea of unknown cause. **gastric juice**, the digestive fluid secreted by the stomach glands. [f. Gk (*gastēr* stomach)]

gastro- /gæstrəʊ-/ *in comb*. stomach. [f. Gk (as prec.)]

gastro-enteritis /gæstrəʊentə'raɪtɪs/ *n*. inflammation of the stomach and intestine.

gastronome /'gæstrənəʊm/ *n*. a connoisseur of eating and drinking. [F (as foll.)]

gastronomy /gæ'strɒnəmɪ/ *n*. the science of good eating and drinking. —**gastronomic** /-'nɒmɪk/ *adj*. [f. F f. Gk (GASTRO-, -*nomia* f. *nomos* law]

gastropod /'gæstrəpɒd/ *n*. a mollusc, such as a snail or limpet, of the class Gastropoda, moving by means of a muscular ventral organ and possessing both tentacles and eyes. [f. F (GASTRO-, Gk *pous podos* foot)]

gastroscope /'gæstrəskəʊp/ *n*. an instrument that can be passed down the throat for looking inside the stomach. [f. GASTRO- + -SCOPE]

gasworks *n.pl*. a place where gas for lighting and heating is manufactured.

gate *n*. **1**. a barrier, usually hinged, used to close an opening made for entrance and exit through a wall, fence, etc. **2**. such an opening; a means of entrance or exit; a numbered place of access to an aircraft at an airport. **3**. a device regulating the passage of water in a lock etc. **4**. the number entering by payment at gates to see a football match etc.; the amount of money thus taken. —*v.t*. to confine to a college or school, especially after a fixed hour. —**gate-leg** *adj*., **gate-legged** *adj*. (of a table) with the legs in a gatelike frame which swings back to allow the top to fold down. [OE]

gateau /'gætəʊ/ *n*. a large rich cake often filled with cream, or cream and fruit, and highly decorated. [f. F *gâteau* cake]

gatecrash *v.t./i*. to go to (a private party etc.) without having been invited. —**gatecrasher** *n*.

gatehouse *n*. the lodge of a park etc.; the entrance building of a castle.

gateway *n*. an opening which can be closed with a gate; a means of access (*lit. or fig*.).

gather /'gæðə(r)/ *v.t./i*. **1**. to bring or come together. **2**. to collect, to obtain gradually; to summon up (energy etc.). **3**. to infer or deduce. **4**. to pluck, to collect as harvest. **5**. to increase (speed etc.) gradually. **6**. to draw together in folds or wrinkles. **7**. to develop a purulent swelling. —*n*. (usu. in *pl*.) to fold or pleat. —**gather up**, to bring together; to pick up from the ground; to draw into a small compass. [OE]

gathering *n*. **1**. an assembly. **2**. a purulent swelling. **3**. a group of leaves taken together in bookbinding. [f. prec.]

GATT /gæt/ *abbr*. General Agreement on Tariffs and Trade (a treaty to which more than 80 countries are parties, in operation since 1948, to promote trade and economic development).

gauche /gəʊʃ/ *adj*. lacking in ease and grace of manner, awkward and tactless. [F, lit. = left(-handed)]

gaucherie /'gəʊʃəriː/ *n*. gauche manners, a gauche act. [F (as prec.)]

gaucho /'gaʊtʃəʊ/ *n*. (*pl*. **-os**) a mounted herdsman in the South American pampas. [Sp., f. Quechua]

gaudy[1] /'gɔːdɪ/ *adj*. tastelessly showy or bright. —**gaudily** *adv*., **gaudiness** *n*. [prob. f. OF f. L *gaudēre* rejoice]

gaudy[2] /'gɔːdɪ/ *n*. an annual entertainment, especially a college dinner for old members etc. [f. L *gaudium* joy (cf. prec.)]

gauge /geɪdʒ/ *n*. **1**. a standard measure especially of the capacity or contents of a barrel, fineness of textile, diameter of a bullet, or thickness of sheet metal; the distance between rails or opposite wheels. **2**. a graduated instrument used as a measuring device; a device for measuring the dimensions of tools, wire, etc.; a carpenter's adjustable tool for marking parallel lines. **3**. capacity, extent. **4**. a means of estimating, a criterion, a test. **5**. (*Naut*.) relative position with respect to the wind. —*v.t*. **1**. to measure exactly; to measure the content or capacity of (a cask etc.). **2**. to estimate (a person or character). [f. OF; orig. unkn.]

Gauguin /'gəʊgæ̃/, Paul (1848-1903), French painter, son of a French father and a Peruvian Creole mother, who was a stockbroker, collector, and amateur artist before becoming a professional artist in 1883. In 1891 he left France for Tahiti, and remained in the tropics until his death, apart from two years in Europe in 1893-5. Gauguin yearned for the simple life of nature and regarded civilization as a disease; he found inspiration in primitive art (e.g. pre-Columbian Peruvian pottery). Reacting against the realism of the impressionists, he freed colour from its representational function, using it in flat contrasting areas to emphasize its decorative or emotional effect, and introduced emphatic outlines, suggestive of Japanese prints or stained glass. Both the Nabis and the Symbolist movements were formed under the inspiration of Gauguin's ideas.

Gaul /gɔːl/ an ancient region of Europe, divided by the Romans into Cisalpine Gaul (northern Italy, = 'Gaul on this side of the Alps') and Transalpine Gaul (= 'Gaul beyond the Alps'), an area corresponding roughly to modern France and Belgium. Tribal groups of Celts had spread from across the Rhine over Transalpine Gaul perhaps as early as 900 BC. From *c*.400 BC some migrated south of the Alps in successive waves, gradually ousting the Etruscans, and waging long and ultimately unsuccessful wars against Rome; before 100 BC the area had been made into a Roman province. Transalpine Gaul was conquered by Julius Caesar in 58-51 BC and remained under Roman rule, extensively romanized, until the withdrawal of the garrisons in the 5th c. AD. —*n*. an inhabitant of Gaul. —**Gaulish** *adj*. & *n*. [f. F f. Gmc, = foreigners]

Gaulle /gəʊl/, Charles Joseph de (1890-1970), French general and statesman. A career soldier with extensive service in the First World War behind him, de Gaulle became the leading French advocate of mechanized warfare in the 1920s and 1930s and commanded a French armoured division in the early days of the Second World War. In Britain at the time of France's surrender, he refused to recognize the capitulation and organized the Free French forces to fight alongside the Allies. After the war he became interim President of the new French Republic, but resigned after he was refused wide presidential powers and retired to his country home to await the recall he was sure must come. He returned as President in 1959 and extracted France from the Algerian crisis, going on to stamp his own highly individualistic mark on the government, withdrawing French forces from NATO command, and blocking British entry into the EEC. He resigned in 1969 after proposed political reforms had been rejected by a referendum, and died suddenly shortly afterwards.

gaunt /gɔːnt/ *adj*. **1**. lean, haggard. **2**. grim, desolate. —**gauntness** *n*. [orig. unkn.]

gauntlet[1] /'gɔːntlɪt/ *n*. **1**. a glove with a long loose wrist. **2**. (*hist*.) an armoured glove (ill. ARMOUR). —**pick up the gauntlet**, to accept a challenge. **throw down the gauntlet**, to issue a challenge. [f. OF (*gant* glove)]

gauntlet[2] /'gɔːntlɪt/ *n*. **run the gauntlet**, to pass between rows of persons who strike one with sticks etc., orig. as a naval or military punishment; to undergo criticism etc. [f. Sw. *gattlopp* (*gata* lane, *lopp* course)]

Gauss /gaʊs/, Karl Friedrich (1777-1855), German mathematician, astronomer, and physicist. Regarded as the 'prince of mathematics', he laid the foundations of number theory, producing the first major book on this subject in 1801. In the same year he rediscovered the lost asteroid, Ceres, using computational techniques too advanced for most astronomers. He contributed to many areas of mathematics (his name is attached to a number of important results), and refused to distinguish between pure and applied mathematics, applying his rigorous mathematical analysis to such subjects as geometry, geodesy, electrostatics, and electromagnetism. He was involved in the first world-wide survey of the earth's magnetic field. Two of Gauss's most interesting discoveries, which he did not pursue, were non-Euclidean geometry and quaternions (a kind of complex number later developed by the mathematician W. R. Hamilton, 1805-65).

gauss /gaʊs/ n. (pl. same) an electromagnetic unit of magnetic induction. [f. prec.]

Gautama /ˈɡaʊtəmə/ the family name of the Buddha. [Skr.]

gauze /ɡɔːz/ n. a thin transparent fabric of silk, cotton, wire, etc. —**gauzy** adj. [f. F f. Gaza in Palestine]

gave past of GIVE.

gavel /ˈɡæv(ə)l/ n. a hammer used for calling attention by an auctioneer or chairman or judge. [orig. unkn.]

gavotte /ɡəˈvɒt/ n. a medium-paced dance in common time; the music for this. [F f. Prov. (Gavot native of region in Alps)]

gawk v.i. (colloq.) to stare stupidly. —n. an awkward or bashful person. [rel. to obs. gaw gaze]

gawky adj. awkward, ungainly. —**gawkily** adv., **gawkiness** n. [as prec.]

gawp v.i. (colloq.) to gawk. [f. obs. galpen yawn (as YELP)]

Gay, John (1685-1732), English poet and dramatist, who achieved success with his Fables (1727) but is now best known for The Beggar's Opera (1728), a ballad opera dealing with life in low society, adapted by Brecht in The Threepenny Opera (1928). This with its sequel Polly (1729) contained some of his best-known ballads. In 'Mr Pope's Welcome from Greece' (1776) he vividly portrays members of the Scriblerus Club, including Pope and Arbuthnot with whom he collaborated in Three Hours after Marriage (1717).

gay adj. 1. light-hearted and cheerful, happy and full of fun. 2. brightly-coloured, dressed or decorated in bright colours. 3. (colloq.) homosexual; of or for homosexuals. —n. (colloq.) a homosexual person. —**gayness** n. [f. OF gai; etym. unkn.]

Gay-Lussac /ɡeɪˈluːsæk/, Joseph Louis (1778-1850), French chemist and physicist, best known for his careful work on gases. In 1802 he re-established a law of gas expansion suggested c.1787 by Jacques Charles (1746-1823): at constant pressure the volume of a gas is proportional to the temperature. Six years later he formulated the law usually known by his name, that gases which combine chemically do so in volumes which are in a simple ratio to each other. His discovery was an important step towards an understanding of the nature of molecules. He developed techniques of quantitative chemical analysis, notably that of titration, identified iodine as an element and the gas, cyanogen, improved the process for manufacturing sulphuric acid, prepared with the chemist Louis-Jacques Thenard (1777-1857) potassium and boron, and made two balloon ascents in 1804 to study the composition of air, atmospheric electricity, and terrestrial magnetism at high altitudes.

Gaza Strip /ˈɡɑːzə/ a strip of coastal territory in the SE Mediterranean, including the town of Gaza. Administered by Egypt from 1949, it was occupied by Israel in 1967.

gaze v.i. to look long and steadily. —n. a long steady look. [orig. unkn.]

gazebo /ɡəˈziːbəʊ/ n. (pl. -os) a summer-house, turret, etc., with a wide view. [perh. joc. f. prec.]

gazelle /ɡəˈzel/ n. a small graceful antelope, especially of the genus Gazella. [F, prob. f. Sp. f. Arab.]

gazette /ɡəˈzet/ n. 1. (used in titles) a newspaper. 2. an official publication with announcements etc. —v.t. to publish, or announce the appointment of (a person), in an official gazette. [F f. It.]

gazetteer /ɡæzɪˈtɪə(r)/ n. a geographical index. [f. F f. It. (as prec.)]

gazump /ɡəˈzʌmp/ v.t. (slang) to raise a price after accepting an offer from (a buyer); (slang) to swindle. [orig. unkn.]

GB abbr. Great Britain.

GC abbr. George Cross.

GCE abbr. General Certificate of Education.

GCSE abbr. General Certificate of Secondary Education.

Gd symbol gadolinium.

GDP abbr. gross domestic product.

GDR abbr. German Democratic Republic.

Ge /ɡeɪ/ (Gk myth.) a personification of the Earth, wife of Uranus and mother of the Titans. [Gk, = earth]

Ge symbol germanium.

gear /ɡɪə(r)/ n. 1. (often in pl.) a set of toothed wheels working on one another to transmit rotational motion from one shaft to another, especially those connecting a vehicle's engine to its road wheels; a particular setting of these (high with faster revolutions of the driven part relative to the driving part, low with slower). 2. equipment, apparatus, etc. 3. (colloq.) clothing; rigging. —v.t. 1. to put in gear, to provide with gear(s). 2. to adjust or adapt to. 3. to harness (up). —**gear-lever** n. a lever used to engage or change a gear. **gear-shift** n. (US) a gear-lever. **in gear**, with a gear engaged. **out of gear**, with the gears disengaged; not proceeding or produced uniformly (with). [f. ON f. Gmc, = prepare]

gearbox n. a case enclosing the gears of a vehicle or other machine.

gearing n. a set or arrangement of gears. [f. GEAR]

gearwheel n. a toothed wheel in a set of gears.

gecko /ˈɡekəʊ/ n. (pl. -os) a tropical house-lizard of the family Geckonidae. [Malay, imit. its cry]

gee¹ int. (also **gee whiz**) expressing surprise etc. [perh. abbr. of JESUS]

gee² int. (usu. with up) a command to a horse etc. to start or go faster. [orig. unkn.]

gee-gee /ˈdʒiːdʒiː/ n. (colloq.) a horse. [orig. a child's word, f. prec.]

geese pl. of GOOSE.

Ge'ez /ˈɡiːez/ n. the classical literary language of Ethiopia, a Semitic language thought to have been introduced from Arabia in the 1st c. BC. It is the ancestor of all the modern Ethiopian languages such as Amharic, and survives in the liturgical language of the Coptic Church in Ethiopia. [Ethiopic]

geezer /ˈɡiːzə(r)/ n. (slang) a person, especially an old man. [dial. pronunc. of guiser mummer, f. GUISE]

Gehenna /ɡɪˈhenə/ n. Hell, a place of burning, torment, or misery. [L f. Gk f. Heb., orig. name of valley of Hinnom, near Jerusalem, where children were burnt in ancient times in sacrifice to pagan gods]

Geiger /ˈɡaɪɡə(r)/, Hans (Johann) Wilhelm (1882-1945), German nuclear physicist who developed the first radiation counter. He worked with Rutherford at Manchester on radioactivity, and in 1908 developed his prototype counter for detecting alpha particles. In 1925 he was appointed professor of physics at Kiel, where he improved the sensitivity of his device with Walther Müller (hence, it is often referred to as the 'Geiger-Müller counter'), and it was used for measuring all kinds of radiation, including cosmic ray showers for the first time in 1928.

geisha /ˈɡeɪʃə/ n. a Japanese woman trained to entertain men. [Jap.]

gel /dʒel/ n. a semi-solid colloidal solution or jelly. [abbr. of foll.]

gelatine /ˈdʒelətiːn/ n. (also **gelatin** /-tɪn/) a transparent tasteless substance got from skins, tendons, etc., and used in cookery, photography, etc. [f. F f. It. (as JELLY)]

gelatinize /dʒɪˈlætɪnaɪz/ v.t./i. to make or become gelatinous; to coat or treat with gelatine. —**gelatinization** /-ˈzeɪʃ(ə)n/ n. [f. prec.]

gelatinous /dʒɪˈlætɪnəs/ adj. like jelly, especially in consistency. [f. GELATINE]

geld /ɡeld/ v.t. to deprive (usu. a male animal) of reproductive ability, to castrate. [f. ON (geldr barren)]

gelding /ˈɡeldɪŋ/ n. a gelded animal, especially a male horse. [as prec.]

gelignite /ˈdʒelɪɡnaɪt/ n. a plastic high explosive (also known as gelatine dynamite) consisting of nitro-glycerine which is at least partially gelatinized by means of gun cotton. It is favoured for its good handling properties, water resistance, and low fume emission, and is a preferred explosive for rock-blasting under wet conditions. [f. GELATINE + L ignis fire]

gem n. 1. (also **gemstone**) a precious stone, especially cut and polished or engraved. 2. a thing of great beauty or worth. —v.t. (-mm-) to adorn with or as with gems. [f. OF f L gemma bud, jewel]

Gemara /ɡɪˈmɑːrə/ n. a Rabbinical commentary on the Mishnah, written in Aramaic and forming the second part of the Talmud. [f. Aram., = completion]

geminate /ˈdʒemɪneɪt/ v.t. to double, to repeat; to arrange in pairs. —/also -ət/ *adj.* combined in pairs. —**gemination** /-ˈneɪʃ(ə)n/ *n.* [f. L *geminare* (as foll.)]

Gemini /ˈdʒemɪnaɪ, -nɪ/ a constellation and the third sign of the zodiac, the Twins (see DIOSCURI), which the sun enters about 21 May. [L, = twins]

gemma /ˈdʒemə/ *n.* (*pl.* **-ae**) (in cryptogams) the small cellular body that separates from the mother-plant and starts a new one. [L, = gem]

gemmation /dʒeˈmeɪʃ(ə)n/ *n.* reproduction by gemmae. [F (as prec.)]

gen /dʒen/ *n.* (*slang*) information. —*v.t./i.* (**-nn-**) (*slang*, with *up*) to gain or give information (to). [perh. f. *general information*]

-gen /-dʒ(ə)n/ *suffix* forming nouns in the sense 'that which produces' (*hydrogen*). [f. F f. Gk -*genēs* -born, of a specified kind (as GENESIS)]

Gen. *abbr.* General.

gendarme /ˈʒɒndɑːm/ *n.* a soldier employed in police duties, especially in France. [F, f. *gens d'arme* men of arms]

gender /ˈdʒendə(r)/ *n.* **1.** a grammatical classification of words, found mainly in Indo-European and Semitic languages, by which words are classed as masculine, feminine, and sometimes also neuter and common; any of these classes, the property of belonging to such a class; (of adjectives) the appropriate form for accompanying a noun of one such class. **2.** (*colloq.*) a person's sex. [f. OF f. L GENUS]

gene /dʒiːn/ *n.* each of the units of heredity in an organism. The word has been defined in a number of ways since its coinage (in German) in 1909; genes were originally regarded as inherited factors each controlling one feature (e.g. eye colour) of an organism, but are now usually regarded as lengths of DNA (or in certain viruses RNA) which determine the synthesis of protein molecules needed by living cells (see DNA). [f. G *gen* (cf. -GEN)]

genealogy /dʒiːnɪˈælədʒɪ/ *n.* descent traced continuously from an ancestor, a pedigree; the study of pedigrees; a plant's or animal's line of development from earlier forms. —**genealogical** /-ˈlɒdʒɪk(ə)l/ *adj.*, **genealogist** *n.* [f. OF f. L f. Gk (*genea* race, -LOGY)]

genera *pl.* of GENUS.

general /ˈdʒenər(ə)l/ *adj.* **1.** including or affecting all or most parts, cases, or things; not partial or local or particular. **2.** not restricted or specialized; applying to all or most cases. **3.** involving only main features, not detailed. **4.** usual, prevalent. **5.** chief, head; with unrestricted authority. —*n.* **1.** an army officer next below Field Marshal; a lieutenant-general or major-general; the commander of an army. **2.** a strategist. **3.** the chief of a religious order (e.g. of the Jesuits). —**general election,** an election of representatives to Parliament etc. from the whole country. **general practitioner,** a doctor treating cases of all kinds in the first instance. **general staff,** the officers assisting a military commander at headquarters. **general strike,** a strike of workers in all or most trades. That in Britain lasted from 3 to 12 May 1926. **in general,** as a normal rule, usually, for the most part. —**generalship** *n.* [f. OF f. L (as GENUS)]

generalissimo /dʒenərəˈlɪsɪməʊ/ *n.* (*pl.* **-os**) a commander of combined military and naval and air forces, or of several armies. [It., superl. of *generale* (as prec.)]

generality /dʒenəˈrælɪtɪ/ *n.* **1.** a general statement or rule. **2.** general applicability, indefiniteness. **3.** the majority or bulk of. [f. F f. L (as GENERAL)]

generalize /ˈdʒenərəlaɪz/ *v.t./i.* **1.** to speak in general or indefinite terms; to form general notions; to reduce to a general statement. **2.** to infer (a rule etc.) from particular cases. **3.** to bring into general use. —**generalization** /-ˈzeɪʃ(ə)n/ *n.* [f. F (as GENERAL)]

generally *adv.* in a general sense, without regard to particulars or exceptions; in most respects or cases. [f. GENERAL]

generate /ˈdʒenəreɪt/ *v.t.* to bring into existence, to produce. [f. L *generare* (as GENUS)]

generation /dʒenəˈreɪʃ(ə)n/ *n.* **1.** procreation. **2.** production, especially of electricity. **3.** a step in a pedigree; all persons born about the same time; the average time in which children are ready to take the place of their parents (about 30 years). —**generation gap,** differences of opinion or attitude between different generations. [f. OF f. L (as prec.)]

generative /ˈdʒenərətɪv/ *adj.* **1.** of procreation. **2.** productive. —**generative grammar,** see GRAMMAR. [f. OF or L (as prec.)]

generator /ˈdʒenəreɪtə(r)/ *n.* **1.** a machine for converting mechanical into electrical energy (ill. ELECTRICAL POWER). **2.** an apparatus for producing gas, steam, etc. **3.** an originator. [f. GENERATE]

generic /dʒɪˈnerɪk/ *adj.* characteristic of or applied to a genus or class; not specific or special. —**generically** *adv.* [f. F f. L (as GENUS)]

generous /ˈdʒenərəs/ *adj.* **1.** giving freely. **2.** not petty in feelings or conduct, free from prejudice. **3.** given freely, plentiful. —**generosity** /-ˈrɒsɪtɪ/ *n.*, **generously** *adv.* [f. OF f. L *generosus* (as GENUS)]

Genesis /ˈdʒenɪsɪs/ the first book of the Old Testament, containing an account of the creation of the universe and the early history of mankind. (See PENTATEUCH.) [= foll.]

genesis /ˈdʒenɪsɪs/ *n.* origin; mode of formation or generation. [L f. Gk, = origin]

genet /ˈdʒenɪt/ *n.* a kind of civet-cat (*Genetta vulgaris*); its fur. [f. OF f. Arab.]

genetic /dʒɪˈnetɪk/ *adj.* **1.** of genetics or genes. **2.** of or in origin. —**genetic code,** the system by which DNA and RNA molecules carry genetic information. Particular sequences of bases in these molecules represent particular sequences of amino acids (the building blocks of proteins) and thereby embody 'instructions' for the making of individual types of proteins (see DNA). **genetic engineering,** the deliberate modification of hereditary features by transferring fragments of DNA containing particular genes from one organism to another. —**genetically** *adv.* [f. GENESIS]

genetics *n.* the study of heredity and variation in animals and plants (see ill. pp. 336-7). —**geneticist** *n.* [f. prec.]

Geneva /dʒɪˈniːvə/ a city of SW Switzerland, on the Lake of Geneva; pop. (1982) 161,000. In the 16th c. it was a stronghold of John Calvin, who re-wrote its laws and constitution. More recently it has become the headquarters of international bodies such as the Red Cross, the League of Nations (1920-46), and the World Health Organization. —**Geneva Bible,** an English translation of the Bible prepared by Protestant exiles at Geneva and printed there in 1560, the 'Breeches Bible'. **Geneva Conventions,** a series of international agreements concluded at Geneva between 1846 and 1949 with the object of mitigating the harm done by war to both service personnel and civilians. They govern the status of hospitals, ambulances, the wounded, etc.

Genghis Khan /dʒeŋgɪs ˈkɑːn/ (1162-1227), founder of the Mongol empire, one of the greatest conquerors in history. Originally named Temujin, he took the name Genghis Khan (= ruler of all) in 1206 after uniting the nomadic Mongol tribes under his command and becoming master of both eastern and western Mongolia. He then attacked China, and captured Peking in 1215. By the time of his death his empire extended from the shores of the Pacific to the northern shores of the Black Sea, won through brilliant generalship, iron discipline, and unimaginable cruelty particularly towards conquered peoples. A good administrator, he organized his empire into States. His grandson Kublai Khan carried on his empire and completed the conquest of China.

genial /ˈdʒiːnɪəl/ *adj.* **1.** jovial, kindly, sociable. **2.** (of climate etc.) mild, warm, conducive to growth; cheering. —**geniality** /-ˈælɪtɪ/ *n.*, **genially** *adv.* [f. L *genialis* (as GENIUS)]

-genic /-dʒenɪk/ *suffix* forming adjectives in the sense (1) 'producing' (*pathogenic*), (2) 'well suited to' (*photogenic*), (3) 'produced by' (*iatrogenic*). [f. -GEN]

genie /ˈdʒiːnɪ/ *n.* (*pl.* **genii** /-nɪaɪ/) a jinnee, a sprite or goblin of Arabian tales. [f. F *génie* f. L GENIUS]

genista /dʒɪˈnɪstə/ *n.* a kind of flowering shrub of the genus *Genista*, e.g. dyer's broom, *G. tinctoria*. [L]

genital /ˈdʒenɪt(ə)l/ *adj.* of animal reproduction. —*n.* (in *pl.*; also **genitalia** /-ˈteɪlɪə/) the external genital organs. [f. OF or L (*gignere genit-* beget)]

genitive /ˈdʒenɪtɪv/ *adj.* (*Gram.*, of a case) corresponding to *of*, *from*, etc., with a noun representing a possessor, source, etc. —*n.* the genitive case. [as prec.]

genius /ˈdʒiːnɪəs/ *n.* (*pl.* **geniuses**) **1.** an exceptional intellectual or creative power or other natural ability or tendency; a person having this. **2.** the tutelary spirit of a person, place, etc.; a person or spirit influencing a person powerfully for good or evil. **3.** the prevalent feeling or association etc. (*of* a people, place, or age). [L, f. *gignere genit-* beget]

genizah /geˈniːzə/ *n.* a store-room or repository attached to a synagogue, housing damaged, discarded, or heretical

Genetics

Genes, chromosomes, and heredity

Nuclei of male and female cells of a fruit-fly (*Drosophila melanogaster*) showing the four chromosome pairs (fruit-flies are commonly used in studies of heredity).

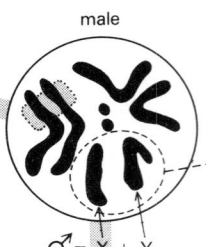

male

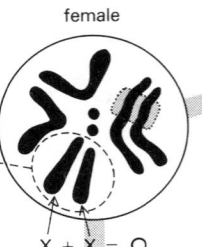

female

pairs of sex
- - - chromosomes - - -
(one pair in each nucleus)

♂ = X + Y

X + X = ♀

The fate of the chromosomes during the reproductive cycle

The nucleus and its chromosome pairs divide (meiosis) to produce two reproductive cells (gametes).

The fate of an individual gene

g = gene producing grey colouring, the dominant characteristic

♂

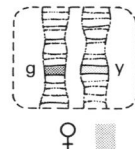

y = gene producing yellow colouring, the recessive characteristic

♀

Close-ups of pairs of chromosomes showing the location of corresponding pairs of genes (in this instance controlling colour). In this example each parent has one dominant and one recessive gene, and so both are grey in appearance.

sperm
(in male)

ovum
(in female)

X   Y   X   X

50% of sperm carry an X- and 50% carry a Y-chromosome

all ova carry an X-chromosome

meiosis

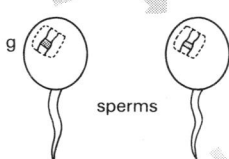

g   y   g   y

sperms   ova

On fertilization, the nuclei of the male and female gametes fuse to produce a new cell (a zygote) which can be either male or female — female if it combines an X- with an X- and male if an X- with a Y-chromosome. This is also true of man.

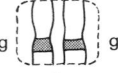   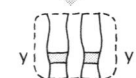

g   g   g   y   y   g   y   y

close-ups of chromosome pairs in zygotes formed after fertilization

X + X
female zygote

Y + X
male zygote

grey adult   grey adult   grey adult   yellow adult

The dominant gene controls the characteristic. Mendel's laws state that when both parents have one dominant and one recessive gene, on average three out of four of the offspring will show the dominant characteristic, as here.

Genetic engineering

Genes are made of DNA (deoxyribonucleic acid). The construction of a DNA molecule defines the nature of an organism, each cell containing the complete genetic plan for that organism. Artificial insertion of fragments of DNA from one organism into the genetic material of another has important medical applications — for example, producing bacteria to make insulin.

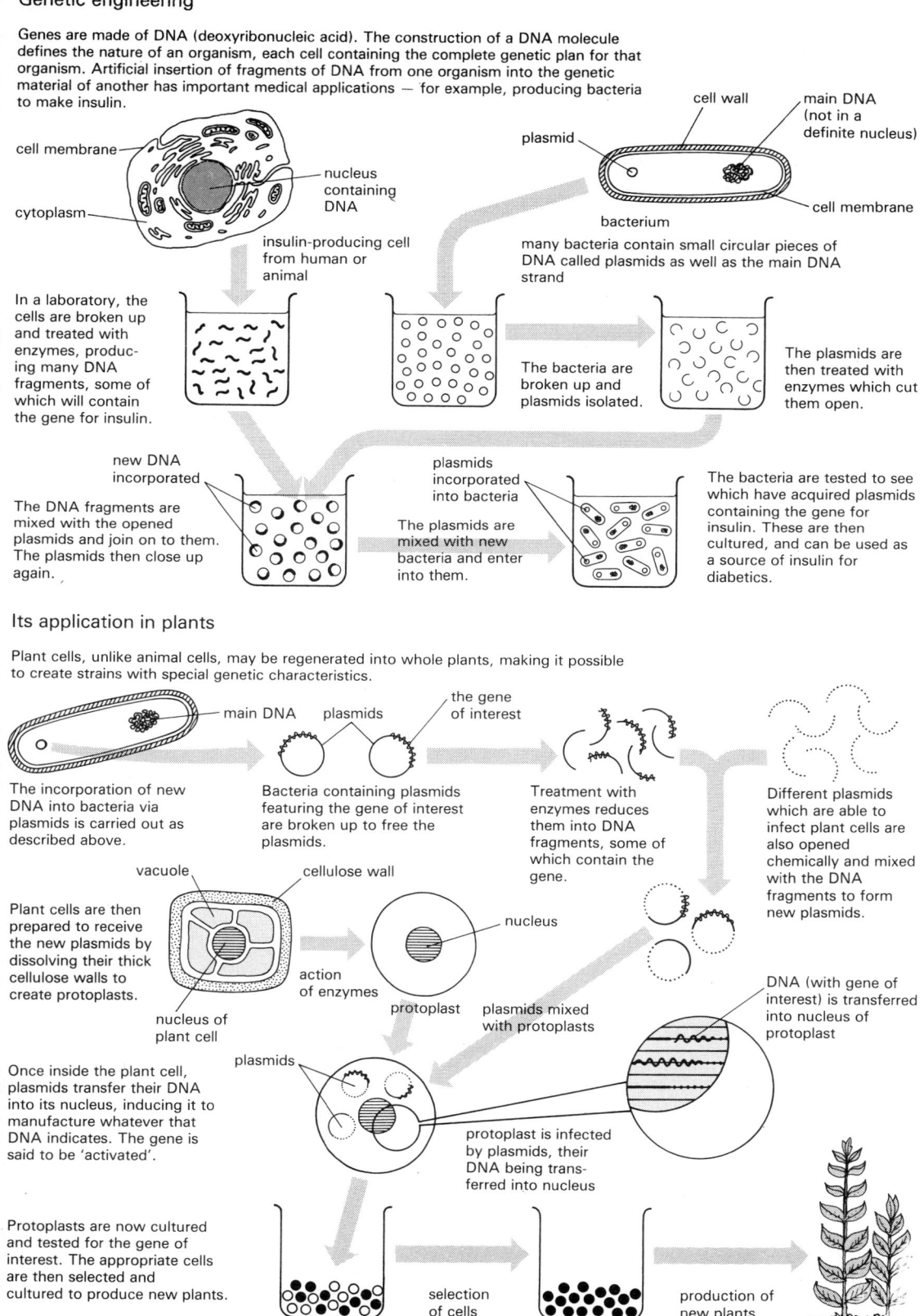

cell membrane

cytoplasm

nucleus containing DNA

insulin-producing cell from human or animal

cell wall

main DNA (not in a definite nucleus)

plasmid

cell membrane

bacterium

many bacteria contain small circular pieces of DNA called plasmids as well as the main DNA strand

In a laboratory, the cells are broken up and treated with enzymes, producing many DNA fragments, some of which will contain the gene for insulin.

The bacteria are broken up and plasmids isolated.

The plasmids are then treated with enzymes which cut them open.

new DNA incorporated

The DNA fragments are mixed with the opened plasmids and join on to them. The plasmids then close up again.

plasmids incorporated into bacteria

The plasmids are mixed with new bacteria and enter into them.

The bacteria are tested to see which have acquired plasmids containing the gene for insulin. These are then cultured, and can be used as a source of insulin for diabetics.

Its application in plants

Plant cells, unlike animal cells, may be regenerated into whole plants, making it possible to create strains with special genetic characteristics.

main DNA   plasmids   the gene of interest

The incorporation of new DNA into bacteria via plasmids is carried out as described above.

Bacteria containing plasmids featuring the gene of interest are broken up to free the plasmids.

Treatment with enzymes reduces them into DNA fragments, some of which contain the gene.

Different plasmids which are able to infect plant cells are also opened chemically and mixed with the DNA fragments to form new plasmids.

vacuole   cellulose wall

nucleus

Plant cells are then prepared to receive the new plasmids by dissolving their thick cellulose walls to create protoplasts.

action of enzymes

nucleus of plant cell

protoplast   plasmids mixed with protoplasts

DNA (with gene of interest) is transferred into nucleus of protoplast

plasmids

Once inside the plant cell, plasmids transfer their DNA into its nucleus, inducing it to manufacture whatever that DNA indicates. The gene is said to be 'activated'.

protoplast is infected by plasmids, their DNA being transferred into nucleus

Protoplasts are now cultured and tested for the gene of interest. The appropriate cells are then selected and cultured to produce new plants.

selection of cells

production of new plants

books etc. and sacred relics; its contents. [Heb., = hiding-place (*gānaz* hide, set aside)]

Genoa /ˈdʒenəʊə/ a city and seaport of NW Italy. —**Genoese** /dʒenəʊˈiːz/ adj. & n.

genocide /ˈdʒenəsaɪd/ n. deliberate extermination of a people or nation. —**genocidal** /-ˈsaɪd(ə)l/ adj. [f. Gk *genos* race + -CIDE]

genotype /ˈdʒenəʊtaɪp/ n. the genetic constitution of an individual. [f. G *genotypus* (as GENE, TYPE)]

-genous /-dʒənəs/ suffix forming adjectives in the sense 'produced' (*endogenous*). [as -GEN]

genre /ʒãr/ n. 1. a kind or style of art, literature, etc. 2. (also **genre-painting**) portrayal of scenes etc. from ordinary life, especially the type of subject-matter favoured by Dutch artists of the 17th c. (e.g. Pieter Bruegel the Elder and Vermeer). [F (as GENDER)]

gent n. (*colloq.*) gentleman; (in *pl.*, in shops) men. —**the Gents**, (*colloq.*) a men's public lavatory. [abbr. of GENTLEMAN]

genteel /dʒenˈtiːl/ adj. affectedly stylish or refined; upper--class. —**genteelly** adv. [f. *gentil* (as GENTLE)]

genteelism n. a word used because thought to be less vulgar than the usual word (e.g. *perspire* for *sweat*). [f. prec.]

gentian /ˈdʒenʃ(ə)n/ n. a plant of the genus *Gentiana* or *Gentianella*, especially one of the blue-flowered mountain kinds. —**gentian violet**, a purple dye with various uses, e.g. as an antiseptic. [OE f. L (acc. to Pliny, f. *Gentius* king of Illyria)]

gentile /ˈdʒentaɪl/ adj. not Jewish; heathen. —n. a non-Jewish person. [f. L (*gens* race, family)]

gentility /dʒenˈtɪlɪtɪ/ n. social superiority; good manners and elegance, upper-class habits. [f. OF (as foll.)]

gentle adj. 1. not rough or severe; mild, moderate; quiet, requiring patience. 2. (of birth etc.) of good family. —**gently** adv., **gentleness** n. [f. OF *gentil* (as GENTILE)]

gentlefolk n.pl. people of good family.

gentleman n. (*pl.* **-men**) 1. (in polite or formal use) a man. 2. a chivalrous well-bred man; a man of good social position or of wealth and leisure. 3. a man of gentle birth attached to a royal household. —**gentleman-at-arms** n. one of the sovereign's bodyguard. **gentleman's** (*or* **-men's**) **agreement**, an agreement binding in honour but not enforceable. —**gentlemanly** adj.

gentlewoman n. (*pl.* **-women**) (*archaic*) a woman of good birth or breeding.

gentry /ˈdʒentrɪ/ n.pl. 1. people next below the nobility. 2. (*derog.*) people. [f. OF (as GENTLE)]

genuflect /ˈdʒenjuːflekt/ v.i. to bend the knee, especially in worship. —**genuflexion** /-ˈflekʃ(ə)n/ n. [f. L (*genu* knee, *flectere* bend)]

genuine /ˈdʒenjuːɪn/ adj. 1. really coming from its reputed source etc.; not sham. 2. properly so called; pure-bred. —**genuinely** adv., **genuineness** n. [f. L (*genu* knee, because a father acknowledged a new-born child by placing it on his knee)]

genus /ˈdʒiːnəs/ n. (*pl.* **genera** /ˈdʒenərə/) 1. a group of animals or plants with common structural characteristics, usually containing several species. 2. (in logic) kinds of things including subordinate kinds or species. 3. (*colloq.*) a kind, a class. [L, = race, stock]

geo- /dʒiːəʊ/ in comb. earth. [f. Gk (*gē* earth)]

geocentric /dʒiːəʊˈsentrɪk/ adj. 1. considered as viewed from the earth's centre. 2. having the earth as the centre. —**geocentrically** adv. [f. GEO- + CENTRIC]

geochemistry /dʒiːəʊˈkemɪstrɪ/ n. the study of the chemistry of the earth, especially the principles governing the geological distribution of individual elements.

geochronology /dʒiːəʊkrəˈnɒlədʒɪ/ n. the chronology of the earth; the measurement of geological time and the ordering of past geological events.

geode /ˈdʒiːəʊd/ n. a small cavity lined with crystals; a rock containing this. [f. Gk *geōdēs* earthy (*gē* earth)]

geodesic /dʒiːəʊˈdiːsɪk, -desɪk/ adj. (also **geodetic**) of geodesy. —**geodesic** (*or* **geodetic**) **dome**, a dome built of short struts holding flat triangular or polygonal pieces fitted together to form a rough hemisphere. **geodesic line**, the shortest possible line on a curved surface between two points.[f. foll.]

geodesy /dʒiːˈɒdɪsɪ/ n. the study of the shape and area of the earth. [f. Gk *geōdaisia* (GEO-, *daiō* divide)]

Geoffrey of Monmouth /ˈdʒefrɪ, ˈmɒnməθ/ (1100?-1155), British chronicler. His *Historia Regum Britanniae*

(first printed in 1508), a purported account, in Latin, of the kings of Britain, is highly suspect as history but was a major source of Arthurian legend.

geographical /dʒiːəˈgræfɪk(ə)l/ adj. (also **geographic**) of geography. —**geographical mile**, 1 minute of latitude, about 1.85 km. —**geographically** adv. [as foll.]

geography /dʒɪˈɒgrəfɪ/ n. 1. the science of the earth's form, physical features, climate, population, etc. 2. the features or arrangement of a place. —**geographer** n. [f. F or L f. Gk (as GEO-, -GRAPHY)]

geology /dʒɪˈɒlədʒɪ/ n. 1. the study of the composition, structure, and history of the earth, and the processes occurring within it (see below and ill. pp. 340-1); the study of the rocks of the earth's crust; the corresponding study of other planets. 2. the geological features of a district. —**geological** /-ˈlɒdʒɪk(ə)l/ adj., **geologically** adv., **geologist** n. [f. GEO- + -LOGY.]

The medieval Latin word *geologia* was used by Bishop Richard de Bury (14th c.) in the sense of 'science of earthly things', applied to the study of law as distinguished from the arts and sciences which are concerned with the works of God. Use of the term *geology* to mean study of the earth, and specifically of its crust, dates from the 18th c. in English.

geomagnetism /dʒiːəʊˈmægnɪtɪz(ə)m/ n. study of the earth's magnetic properties. —**geomagnetic** /-ˈnetɪk/ adj.

geometric /dʒiːəˈmetrɪk/ adj. (also **geometrical**) of geometry. —**geometric progression**, a progression with a constant ratio between successive quantities, e.g. 1, 3, 9, 27. —**geometrically** adv. [f. F (as foll.)]

geometry /dʒɪˈɒmɪtrɪ/ n. the branch of mathematics that deals with space and the properties of such entities as points, lines, curves, planes, curved surfaces. For 2,000 years geometry was based on the teachings of the thirteen books of Euclid but since the early 19th c. mathematics has embraced successful theories describing non-euclidean geometry, higher dimensional geometry, and many other related topics. —**geometer** n., **geometrician** /-ˈtrɪʃ(ə)n/ n. [f. OF f. L f. Gk (as GEO-, -METRY)]

geomorphology /dʒiːəʊmɔːˈfɒlədʒɪ/ n. the study of the physical features of the earth's (or other planet's) surface and their relation to its geological structures.

geophysics /dʒiːəʊˈfɪzɪks/ n. the study of the physical properties of the earth, especially of its crust; the application of the principles, methods, and techniques of physics to the study of the earth. —**geophysical** adj., **geophysicist** n.

geopolitics /dʒiːəʊˈpɒlɪtɪks/ n. the influence of geographical features on the political character, history, and institutions etc. of States; the study of this.

Geordie /ˈdʒɔːdɪ/ n. a native of Tyneside. [f. name *George*]

George¹ /dʒɔːdʒ/ the name of six kings of Great Britain and Ireland.

George I (1660-1727), great-grandson of James I, reigned 1714-27. Elector of Hanover from 1698, George succeeded to the British throne on the death of Anne, as a result of the Act of Settlement. Unpopular in England, the language of which he never learnt, he left the administration of his new kingdom to his ministers and devoted himself to diplomacy and the interests of Hanover, but despite all this the relatively easy suppression of the Jacobite uprisings of 1715 and 1719 demonstrated that he was generally preferred to the Catholic Old Pretender.

George II (1683-1760), son of George I, reigned 1727-60. While Prince of Wales, George quarrelled openly with his father and became the centre of opposition to the administration. Like George I, he depended heavily on his ministers, but took an active part in Britain's entry into the War of Austrian Succession and successfully led his army against the French at Dettingen in 1743, the last occasion on which a British king was present on the field of battle. In the latter years of his reign, George largely withdrew from active politics, allowing advances in the development of constitutional monarchy which his successor George III was unable permanently to reverse.

George III (1738-1820), grandson of George II, reigned 1760-1820. Unlike his two predecessors George III took great interest in domestic politics and attempted to exercise royal control of government to the fullest possible extent. His determination to suppress the American Revolution dominated British war policy 1775-83, but in 1788 he suffered a serious bout of insanity and thereafter his political influence declined. This insanity became permanently incapacitating in 1811 and his son, later George IV, was made regent.

George IV (1762–1830), son of George III, reigned 1820–30, known as 'the First Gentleman of Europe'. As Prince of Wales, George IV was prince regent during his father's final bout of insanity (1811–20), by which time his dissolute lifestyle had already gained him an unsavoury reputation. His attempt to divorce his estranged wife Caroline of Brunswick just after coming to the throne caused a great scandal and further damaged his reputation.

George V (1865–1936), son of Edward VII, reigned 1910–36. He proved to be one of Britain's most popular sovereigns, winning great respect for his punctilious attitude towards royal duties and responsibilities, especially during the First World War. He exercised restrained but none the less important influence over British politics, playing an especially significant role in the formation of the National Government in 1931.

George VI (1894–1952), son of George V, reigned 1936–52. He came to the throne on the abdication of his elder brother Edward VIII, and despite a retiring disposition became a popular and respected monarch, playing an important part in the Second World War as a symbol of the nation's determination to resist Nazi aggression.

George² /dʒɔːdʒ/, St, patron saint of England. Little is known of his life, but his historical existence is now generally accepted. He may have been martyred near Lydda in Palestine some time before the reign of Constantine (d. 337), but his cult did not become popular until the 6th c. and the slaying of the dragon (possibly derived from the legend of Perseus) was not attributed to him until the 12th c. His rank as patron saint of England (in place of Edward the Confessor) probably dates from the reign of Edward III, who founded the Order of the Garter (c.1344) under the patronage of St George who by that time was honoured as the ideal of chivalry.

George Cross, George Medal decorations for gallantry, chiefly in civilian life, instituted in 1940 by King George VI.

Georgetown /ˈdʒɔːdʒtaʊn/ the capital of Guyana at the mouth of the Demerara River; pop. (est.) 185,000.

georgette /dʒɔːˈdʒet/ n. a thin dress-material made from highly twisted yarn. [f. *Georgette* de la Plante, French dressmaker]

Georgia¹ /ˈdʒɔːdʒɪə/ a district of the Caucasus that was an independent kingdom in medieval times until divided between Persia and Turkey in 1555 and acquired by the Russian Empire in the 19th c. It is now the Georgian SSR, a constituent republic of the USSR; capital, Tbilisi (Tiflis).

Georgia² /ˈdʒɔːdʒɪə/ a State of the south-eastern USA, bordering on the Atlantic. Originally an English colony, founded in 1733 and named after George II, it was one of the original 13 States of the USA (1788); capital, Atlanta.

Georgian¹ /ˈdʒɔːdʒɪən/ adj. belonging to the characteristic of the reigns of the first four Kings George (1714–1830) or of Kings George V and VI (1910–52), especially of literature of 1910–20. [f. GEORGE¹]

Georgian² /ˈdʒɔːdʒɪən/ adj. of Georgia in the Caucasus or its people or language. —n. **1.** a native or inhabitant of Georgia. **2.** the language of Georgia, a Caucasian language spoken by some 3 million people. The origin of the characteristic Georgian alphabet is obscure but it is known to have been invented in the 5th c. AD. [f. GEORGIA¹]

Georgian³ /ˈdʒɔːdʒɪən/ adj. of Georgia in the USA. —n. a native or inhabitant of Georgia. [f. GEORGIA²]

geothermal /dʒiːəʊˈθɜːm(ə)l/ adj. of or using the heat produced in the earth's interor.

geranium /dʒəˈreɪnɪəm/ n. a herb or shrub of the genus *Geranium*, bearing fruit shaped like a crane's bill; (pop.) the cultivated pelargonium. [L f. Gk (*geranos* crane)]

gerbil /ˈdʒɜːbɪl/ n. a mouselike rodent of the subfamily Gerbillinae, with long hind legs. [f. F (as JERBOA)]

geriatrics /dʒerɪˈætrɪks/ n.pl. (usu. treated as *sing.*) the branch of medical science dealing with old age and its diseases. —**geriatric** adj., **geriatrician** /-ˈtrɪʃ(ə)n/ n. [f. Gk *gēras* old age + *iatros* physician]

germ n. **1.** a micro-organism or microbe, especially one causing disease. **2.** a portion of an organism capable of becoming a new one; a rudiment of an animal or plant; the embryo of a seed. **3.** a thing that may develop, an elementary principle. —**germ warfare,** the use of germs to spread disease in war. [F f. L *germen* sprout]

German /ˈdʒɜːmən/ adj. of Germany or its people or language. —n. **1.** a native of Germany. **2.** the language of Germany, a Germanic language spoken by some 100 million

people mainly in Germany, Austria, and Switzerland, although there are large German-speaking communities in the USA. It is the official language of East and West Germany and of Austria, and one of the official languages of Switzerland. —**German measles,** a disease like mild measles. **German shepherd dog,** an Alsatian. **High German,** the variety of Teutonic speech, originally confined to 'High' or southern Germany, now accepted as the literary language of the whole country. Its chief distinctive characteristic is that certain consonants have been altered from their original Teutonic sounds which the other dialects in the main preserve. The spread of this form of the language owes much to the biblical translations of Martin Luther in the 16th c. **Low German,** the general name for the dialects of Germany which are not High German. It is spoken in the lowland areas of northern Germany, and is most closely related to Dutch and Friesian. [f. L *Germanus*]

german /ˈdʒɜːmən/ adj. (placed after *brother, sister, cousin*) having a full relationship, not a half-brother etc. [f. OF f. L *germanus* genuine, of same parents]

germander /dʒɜːˈmændə(r)/ n. a plant of the genus *Teucrium*. —**germander speedwell,** a speedwell with leaves like a germander. [f. L, ult. f Gk *chamaedrys* ground-oak]

germane /dʒɜːˈmeɪn/ adj. relevant *to* a subject. [var. of GERMAN]

Germanic /dʒɜːˈmænɪk/ adj. **1.** of Germanic (see below). **2.** of the Scandinavians, Anglo-Saxons, or Germans. **3.** having German characteristics. **4.** (*hist.*) of the Germans. —n. the primitive (unrecorded) language of the Germanic peoples; a branch of the Indo-European family of languages, including English, German, Dutch, and the Scandinavian languages. These different languages reflect an original dialectal split into West Germanic (English and German), North Germanic (the Scandinavian languages for which the oldest evidence is that of Old Norse), and East Germanic, which has died out but for which Gothic provided the oldest evidence. [f. L (as GERMAN)]

germanium /dʒɜːˈmeɪnɪəm/ n. a brittle greyish-white semi-metallic element, symbol Ge, atomic number 32. A rare element, first isolated in 1886, germanium became very important after the Second World War in the making of transistors and other semiconductor devices, but more recently it has been largely displaced by silicon for this purpose. [f. L *Germanus* German]

Germano- /dʒɜːmənəʊ-/ in comb. German.

Germany /ˈdʒɜːmənɪ/ a country in central Europe, divided since the Second World War into the Federal Republic of Germany (West Germany; pop. (1983) 61,333,000; capital, Bonn) and the German Democratic Republic (East Germany; pop. (1980) 16,740,000; seat of government, East Berlin); the official language of both States is German. German tribes came repeatedly into conflict with the Romans, and after the collapse of the Roman Empire they overran the Rhine which had been its northern frontier. Loosely unified under the Holy Roman Empire during the Middle Ages, the multiplicity of small German States achieved real unity only with the rise of Prussia and the formation of the German empire in the mid-19th c. Defeated in the First World War, in the 1930s Germany was taken over by the Nazi dictatorship which led her into a policy of expansionism and eventually complete defeat in the Second World War. Since the partition of Germany, the West has emerged as a European industrial power incorporated within the western defence and economic community, while the East has remained to a considerable extent under Russian domination, but has also become a major industrial power, albeit with a lower general standard of living than her western neighbour.

germicide /ˈdʒɜːmɪsaɪd/ n. a substance that destroys germs. —**germicidal** adj. [f. GERM + -CIDE]

germinal /ˈdʒɜːmɪn(ə)l/ adj. **1.** of germs. **2.** in the earliest stage of development. **3.** productive of new ideas etc. —**germinally** adv. [as GERM]

germinate /ˈdʒɜːmɪneɪt/ v.t./i. to sprout or bud (*lit.* or *fig.*); to cause to do this. —**germination** /-ˈneɪʃ(ə)n/ n., **germinative** adj. [f. L *germinare* (as GERM)]

gerontology /dʒerɒnˈtɒlədʒɪ/ n. the study of old age and the process of ageing. [f. Gk *gerōn* old man + -LOGY]

gerrymander /ˈdʒerɪmændə(r)/ v.t./i. to manipulate the boundaries of (a constituency etc.) so as to give undue influence to some party or class in an election. —n. this practice. [f. Governor *Gerry* of Massachusetts (who rearranged boundaries for this purpose in 1812), after *salamander*]

Geology

Cross-section of the earth

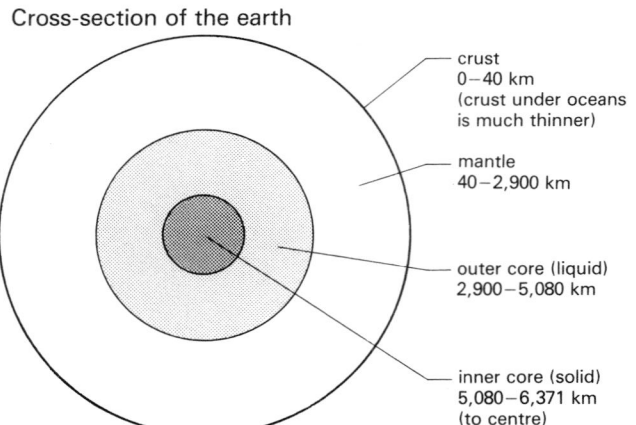

crust
0–40 km
(crust under oceans
is much thinner)

mantle
40–2,900 km

outer core (liquid)
2,900–5,080 km

inner core (solid)
5,080–6,371 km
(to centre)

Positions of the continents
c.200 million years ago

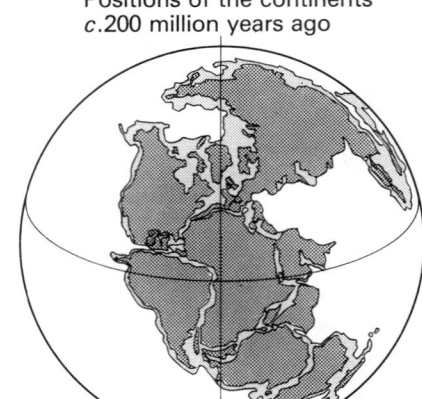

Plates of the earth's crust

the slow but continuous motion of these plates (arrowed) leads to earthquakes, volcanic activity, and continental drift

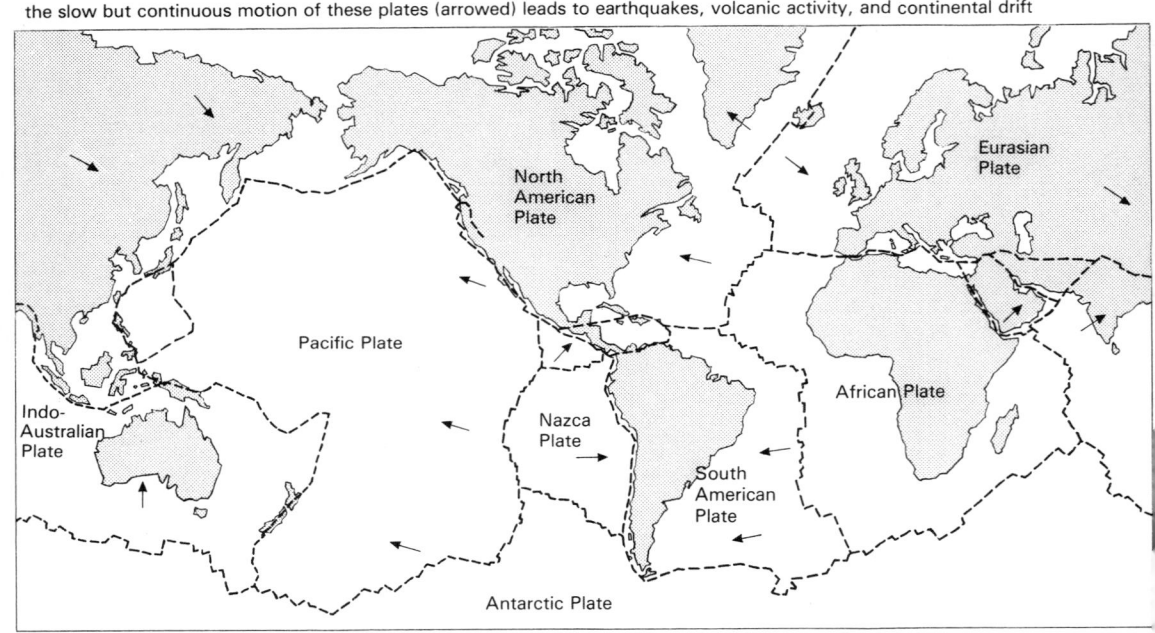

Eurasian
Plate

North
American
Plate

Pacific Plate

Indo-
Australian
Plate

Nazca
Plate

African Plate

South
American
Plate

Antarctic Plate

Some features of rock strata

folds

anticline

syncline

thrust plane

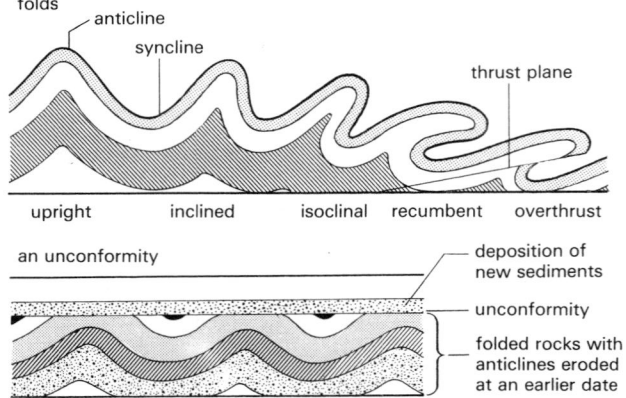

upright   inclined   isoclinal   recumbent   overthrust

an unconformity

deposition of
new sediments

unconformity

folded rocks with
anticlines eroded
at an earlier date

faults

horst or
block mountain

graben or
rift valley

compression

tension

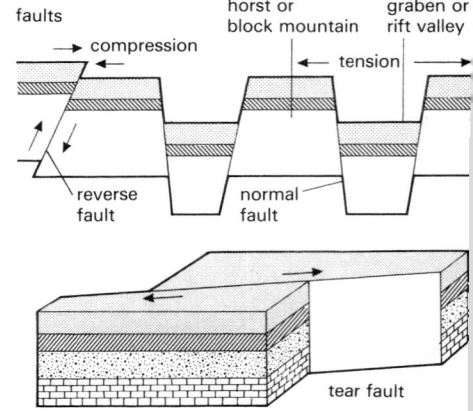

reverse
fault

normal
fault

tear fault

Fossil history

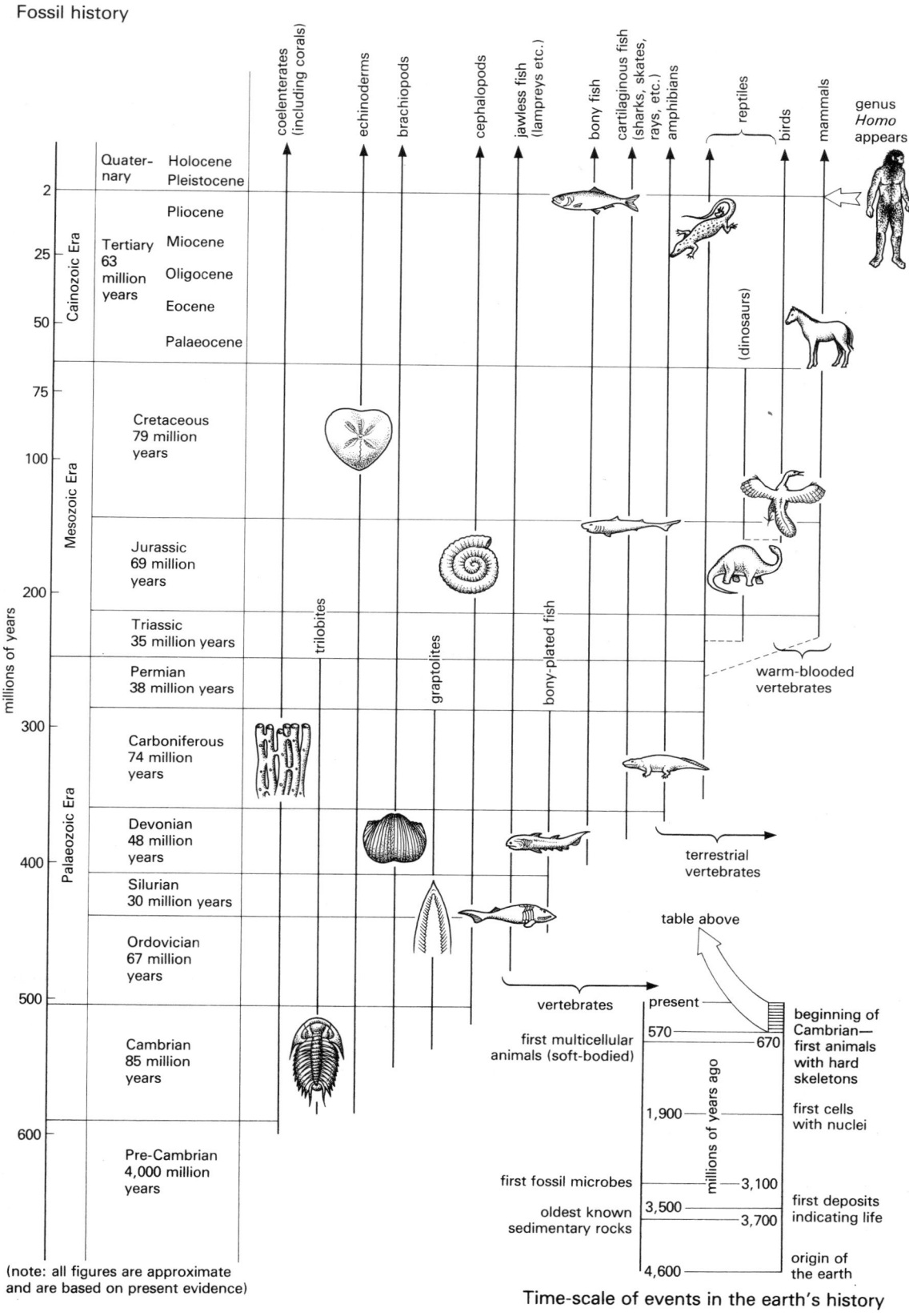

Time-scale of events in the earth's history

(note: all figures are approximate and are based on present evidence)

Gershwin /ˈɡɜːʃwɪn/, George (1898-1937), American composer and pianist, of Russian-Jewish family (Gershovitz). He had early experience of popular music, gained from working in Tin Pan Alley, but no formal musical training. His works made an immediate impact in the USA. Gershwin composed many popular songs, mainly with lyrics by his elder brother Ira (Israel, d. 1983), the opera *Porgy and Bess*, and works for piano and orchestra, including *Rhapsody in Blue* and *Concerto in F*. His mixture of the primitive and sophisticated gives his works individuality and an appeal which shows no sign of diminishing.

gerund /ˈdʒerənd/ n. a verbal noun, in English ending in -*ing*. —**gerundial** adj. [f. L (*gerundum* gerund of *gerere* carry on)]

gerundive /dʒəˈrʌndɪv/ n. a Latin form of the verb functioning as an adjective with the sense 'that should be done' etc. [as prec.]

gesso /ˈdʒesəʊ/ n. (pl. **-oes**) gypsum as used in painting or sculpture. [It., = GYPSUM]

Gestalt /ɡəˈʃtaːlt/ n. a perceived organized whole that is more than the sum of its parts, e.g. a melody as distinct from its separate notes. —**Gestalt psychology,** a movement in psychology founded in 1912 by three German psychologists, Wertheimer, Köhler, and Koffka, as a reaction to the analytic approach of Wundt's structuralism. Its essential tenet was that perceptions, reactions, etc., are Gestalts. The job of the psychologist is then to analyse the conditions under which the Gestalt is experienced and understood. [G, = form, shape]

Gestapo /ɡeˈstɑːpəʊ/ n. the Nazi secret police; any comparable organization. [G, = *Geheime Staatspolizei*]

gestation /dʒeˈsteɪʃ(ə)n/ n. **1.** carrying in the womb; the period of this, between conception and birth. **2.** the development of an idea etc. [f. L (*gestare* carry)]

gesticulate /dʒeˈstɪkjʊleɪt/ v.t./i. to use gestures instead of or to reinforce speech; to express thus. —**gesticulation** /-ˈleɪʃ(ə)n/ n. [f. L *gesticulari* (*gesticulus* dim. of *gestus*, as foll.)]

gesture /ˈdʒestʃə(r)/ n. **1.** a movement of a limb or the body conveying meaning; the use of such movements. **2.** an action to evoke a response or convey an intention. —v.t./i. to gesticulate. —**gestural** adj. [f. L (*gerere* wield)]

get /ɡet/ v.t./i. (**-tt-**; past **got**; p.p. **got** or (archaic & US) **gotten**) **1.** to come into possession of, to obtain or receive. **2.** to fetch or procure; to go to reach or catch (a train, bus, etc.). **3.** to prepare (a meal). **4.** to receive (a broadcast signal); to establish communication by telephone etc. with. **5.** to experience or suffer; to contract (an illness); to establish (an idea etc.) in one's mind. **6.** to bring or come into a specified condition; to induce. **7.** to come or go or arrive; to cause to do this. **8.** (in perf.) to possess, to have, to be bound *to do* or *be*. **9.** (colloq.) to understand. **10.** (colloq.) to attract, obsess, or irritate. **11.** (colloq.) to harm, injure, or kill, especially in retaliation. **12.** to develop an inclination (with *infin.*). **13.** (usu. of animals) to beget. —**get across,** (colloq.) to be or make effective or acceptable; (slang) to annoy. **get along,** to get on. **get at,** to reach; (colloq.) to mean, to imply; (slang) to imply a criticism of; (slang) to tamper with, to bribe. **get away,** to escape; to depart on a journey etc. **get away with,** to escape blame, punishment, or misfortune deserved for (an action). **get by,** (colloq.) to manage; to be acceptable. **get down,** to record in writing; to swallow; to make dejected. **get down to,** to begin working on. **get going,** (colloq.) to begin moving or acting. **get off,** to be or cause to be acquitted; to escape with little or no punishment; to start; to alight from (a bus etc.); (colloq.) to achieve an amorous or sexual relationship *with*. **get on,** to manage; to make progress; to be on friendly or harmonious terms. **get on!** (colloq.) an expression of incredulity. **get one's own back,** (colloq.) to have one's revenge. **get-out** n. a means of avoiding something. **get out of,** to avoid or escape (a duty etc.). **get over,** to get across; to recover from (an illness or shock etc.). **get round,** to evade (a rule or law); to coax or cajole (a person), especially to secure a favour. **get round to,** to deal with (a task etc.) in due course. **get somewhere,** to make progress, to be successful. **get there,** to reach one's goal; (slang) to succeed, to understand what is meant. **get through,** to pass (an examination etc.); to finish or use up; to make contact by telephone. **get through to,** (colloq.) to succeed in making (a person) understand. **get-together** n. (colloq.) a social gathering. **get up,** to rise from sitting etc., or from bed after sleeping; to prepare or organize; to work up (anger etc., a subject for an examination etc.); to dress or arrange elaborately. **get-up** n. (colloq.) a style or arrangement of dress etc. **get up to,** to become involved in (mischief etc.). [f. ON *geta* obtain, beget, guess]

get-at-able /ɡetˈætəb(ə)l/ adj. accessible.

getaway n. an escape, especially after a crime.

Gettysburg /ˈɡetɪzbɜːɡ/ a small town in Pennsylvania, scene of a decisive battle of the American Civil War, fought in the first three days of July 1863. The Confederate Army of Northern Virginia, commanded by General Lee, was repulsed in a bloody engagement by the Union Army of the Potomac, commanded by General Meade, forcing Lee to abandon his invasion of the north. —**Gettysburg address,** a speech delivered on 18 Nov. 1863 by President Abraham Lincoln at the dedication of the national cemetery on the battlefield.

geum /ˈdʒiːəm/ n. a perennial rosaceous plant of the genus *Geum* (which includes herb bennet), with red, orange, yellow, or white flowers. [var. of L *gaeum*]

gewgaw /ˈɡjuːɡɔː/ n. a gaudy plaything or ornament; a showy trifle. [orig. unkn.]

geyser /ˈɡaɪzə(r), ˈɡiː-, ˈɡeɪ-/ n. **1.** an intermittently erupting hot spring. **2.** /ˈɡiːzə(r)/ an apparatus for heating water for use in baths, sinks, etc. [f. Icel. *Geysir* name of a spring (*geysa* gush)]

Ghana /ˈɡɑːnə/ a country of West Africa, with its southern coastline bordering on the Atlantic Ocean; pop. (est. 1980) 11,542,300; official language, English; capital, Accra. The country's principal crop is cocoa, of which it is the world's chief producer. In the 15th c. it was visited by Portuguese and other European traders, who called it the Gold Coast, and it became a centre of the slave trade until the 19th c. Britain established control over the area and it became the British colony of Gold Coast in 1874. In 1957 it gained independence as a member State of the Commonwealth, the first British colony to do so, under the leadership of Dr Kwame Nkrumah, taking the name of Ghana from an important kingdom (said to date from the 4th c.) that had flourished in that region in medieval times. Ghana became a republic in 1960. —**Ghanaian** /ɡɑːˈneɪən/ adj. & n.

ghastly /ˈɡɑːstlɪ/ adj. **1.** horrible, frightful; (colloq.) objectionable. **2.** deathlike, pallid. **3.** (of a smile etc.) forced, grim. —adv. ghastlily (pale etc.). —**ghastlily** adv., **ghastliness** n. [f. obs. *gast* terrify]

ghat /ɡɔːt/ n. (also **ghaut**) (in India), steps leading to a river, a landing-place. —**burning-ghat** n. a level area at the top of a river ghat where Hindus burn their dead. **Eastern Ghats, Western Ghats,** mountain chains parallel to the east and west coasts in southern India. [f. Hindi]

ghee /ɡiː/ n. Indian clarified butter made from the milk of a buffalo or cow. [f. Hindi f. Skr., = sprinkled]

gherkin /ˈɡɜːkɪn/ n. a small cucumber for pickling. [f. Du.]

ghetto /ˈɡetəʊ/ n. (pl. **-os**) a part of a city occupied by a minority group (hist., the Jewish quarter in a city); a segregated group or area. [perh. f. It. *getto* foundry, as the first ghetto founded in Venice in 1516 was on the site of a foundry]

Ghibelline /ˈɡɪbɪlaɪn/ n. a member of one of the two great political factions in Italian medieval politics, traditionally supporting the Holy Roman Emperor against the pope and his supporters, the Guelphs, during the long struggle between the papacy and the Empire. [It., perh. f. G *Waiblingen* estate belonging to Hohenstaufen emperors]

Ghiberti /ɡɪˈbeətɪ/, Lorenzo (1378-1455), Florentine sculptor, who spent most of his career working on two successive pairs of bronze doors for the Baptistery of Florence. The second, more famous, pair (1425-52), dubbed by Michelangelo the 'Gates of Paradise', represent episodes from the Old Testament laid out on carefully constructed perspective stages.

ghost /ɡəʊst/ n. **1.** an apparition of a dead person or animal, a disembodied spirit. **2.** an emaciated or pale person. **3.** a shadow or semblance. **4.** a secondary or duplicated image in a defective telescope or television-picture. —v.t./i. to act as a ghost writer (of). —**ghost town,** a town with few or no remaining inhabitants. **ghost writer,** a writer doing work for which the employer takes credit. **give up the ghost,** to die. —**ghostliness** n., **ghostly** adj. [OE]

ghoul /ɡuːl/ n. **1.** a person morbidly interested in death etc. **2.** (in Muslim folklore) a spirit preying on corpses. —**ghoulish** adj., **ghoulishly** adv. [f. Arab., = protean desert demon]

GHQ abbr. General Headquarters.

ghyll var. of GILL[3].

GI /dʒi:'aɪ/ *n.* a private soldier in the US army. —*adj.* of or for US servicemen. [abbr. of *government* (or *general*) *issue*]

giant /'dʒaɪənt/ *n.* **1.** an imaginary or mythical being of human form but superhuman size; **Giants,** (*Gk myth.*) a race of monstrous appearance and great strength, sons of Ge (Earth) who tried to overthrow the Olympian gods and were defeated with the help of Hercules. **2.** a person of great size, ability, strength, etc.; an abnormally tall animal or plant. **3.** a star of relatively great luminosity arising from either high surface temperatures (**blue giants,** young massive stars with a high rate of consumption of hydrogen at their centres) or very extended atmospheres (**red giants,** whose energy is generated by nuclear reactions in regions of the star outside its centre). —*adj.* gigantic; of a very large kind. —**giantess** *n.fem.* [f. OF f. L f. Gk *gigas gigantos*]

Giant's Causeway a formation of basalt columns dating from the Tertiary period on the coast of Antrim, Northern Ireland. It was once believed to be the end of a road made by a legendary giant to Staffa in the Inner Hebrides, where there is a similar formation.

gibber /'dʒɪbə(r)/ *v.i.* to jabber inarticulately. [imit.]

gibberish /'dʒɪbərɪʃ/ *n.* unintelligible speech, meaningless sounds. [perh. f. prec.]

gibbet /'dʒɪbɪt/ *n.* (*hist.*) a gallows, a post with an arm on which an executed criminal was hung. —*v.t.* **1.** to put to death by hanging; to expose or hang up on a gibbet. **2.** to hold up to contempt. [f. OF *gibet,* dim. of *gibe* club]

Gibbon /'gɪbən/, Edward (1737-94), English historian. He became a Catholic convert at 16, was sent to Lausanne and soon reconverted to Protestantism. In Rome in 1764, while musing amid the ruins of the Capitol, he formed the plan for his *The History of the Decline and Fall of the Roman Empire* (1776-88), the greatest historical work in English literature, marked by its eloquent prose and sustained by a lively dramatic style. His remarkable *Memoirs* (1796) reveal Gibbon's sense of vocation as a historian; anti-clerical, rational, he was one of the last great Augustans.

gibbon /'gɪbən/ *n.* a long-armed SE Asian anthropoid ape of the genus *Hylobates* (ill. MAMMALS). [F, f. aboriginal name]

Gibbons /'gɪbənz/, Grinling (1648-1721), English sculptor, born in Rotterdam, famous for his decorative carvings (chiefly in wood) of fruit and flowers, small animals, and cherubs' heads. Examples may be seen at Windsor, Hampton Court, and in the choir stalls of St Paul's Cathedral.

gibbous /'gɪbəs/ *adj.* convex; (ofthe moon or a planet) having the bright part greater than a semicircle but less than a circle; hump-backed. [f. L (*gibbus* hump)]

Gibbs, James (1682-1754), Scottish architect who settled in London in 1709. An admirer of Wren, he developed the ideas of Wren's city churches, especially in his masterpiece St Martin's-in-the-Fields (1722-6); its combination of steeple and portico was very influential.

gibe /dʒaɪb/ *v.t./i.* to jeer or mock (at). —*n.* a jeering remark, a taunt. [perh. f. OF *giber* handle roughly]

giblets /'dʒɪblɪts/ *n.pl.* the edible organs etc. of a bird, taken out and usually cooked separately. [f. OF *gibelet* game stew (*gibier* game)]

Gibraltar /dʒɪ'brɔːltə(r)/ a fortified town and rocky headland (the Rock of Gibraltar) at the southern tip of Spain on the Strait of Gibraltar that forms the only outlet of the Mediterranean Sea to the Atlantic. It is a British naval and air base of great strategic importance; pop. (1981) 28,719; official languages, English and Spanish. The site has been in British hands since it was captured during the War of the Spanish Succession in 1704 and formally ceded to Britain by the Treaty of Utrecht (1713), and is now a British dependency with Britain responsible for defence, external affairs, and internal security. Since the Second World War Spain has forcefully urged her claim to the territory. Remains of what was later called Neanderthal man were first discovered in Gibraltar in 1848, but were not recognized to be of this species until the discovery of other remains in the Neander Valley in 1857. —**Gibraltarian** /-'teərɪən/ *adj.* & *n.* [f. Arab. *gebel-al-Tarik* hill of Tarik (8th-c. Saracen commander)]

giddy /'gɪdɪ/ *adj.* **1.** dizzy, tending to fall or stagger. **2.** causing dizziness. **3.** mentally intoxicated, frivolous; flighty. —**giddily** *adv.,* **giddiness** *n.* [OE, = insane, lit. 'possessed by a god' (f. GOD)]

Gide /ʒiːd/, André (1869-1951), French novelist and critic, whose early works were influenced by symbolism. After a visit to Algeria in the mid-1890s Gide reacted against the restraints of his Protestant upbringing and *Les Nourritures terrestres* (*Fruits of the Earth,* 1897) reflects his subsequent emancipation. Homosexuality, and the conflict between desire and strict morality, are recurrent themes in his works, notably in the autobiographical *Si le grain ne meurt* (1926). Gide experimented in many literary genres but is best known for his two short works *l'Immoraliste* (1902) and *La Porte étroite* (*Strait is the Gate,* 1909), for which his cousin Madeleine Rondeaux, whom he married in 1895, was the inspiration, for the longer *Les Caves du Vatican* (1914), and for his novel *Les Faux-Monnayeurs* (*The Counterfeiters,* 1926). In his works, and as co-founder of the literary journal *Nouvelle Revue française,* he influenced the aesthetic and moral values of the inter-war generation. He was awarded the Nobel Prize for literature in 1947.

Gideon /'gɪdɪən/ **1.** an Israelite leader (see Judges 6: 11 ff.). **2.** a member of a Christian organization of American commercial travellers, founded in 1899. —**Gideon Bible,** a Bible purchased by this organization and placed in a hotel room etc.

Gielgud /'giːlgʊd/, Sir (Arthur) John (1904-), English actor, famous for his Shakespearian roles, especially for his interpretation of Hamlet.

gift /gɪft/ *n.* **1.** a thing given, a present; a natural ability or talent. **2.** giving. **3.** (*colloq.*) an easy task. —*v.t.* to endow with gifts; to present *with* as a gift; to bestow as a gift. —**gift token** or **voucher,** a voucher used as a gift and exchangeable for goods. **gift-wrap** *v.t.* to wrap attractively (as a gift). **in a person's gift,** his to bestow. [f. ON (as GIVE)]

gifted *adj.* talented. [f. GIFT]

gig[1] /gɪg/ *n.* **1.** a light two-wheeled one-horse carriage. **2.** a light ship's-boat for rowing or sailing. **3.** a rowing-boat chiefly used for racing. [prob. imit.]

gig[2] /gɪg/ *n.* (*colloq.*) an engagement to play jazz etc., especially for one night. [orig. unkn.]

giga- /gɪgə-, gaɪgə-/ *in comb.* one thousand million. [f. Gk *gigas* giant]

gigantic /dʒaɪ'gæntɪk/ *adj.* giant-like, huge. —**gigantically** *adv.* [f. L *gigas gigantis* giant]

Gigantopithecus /dʒaɪgæntə'pɪθɪkəs/ *n.* a genus of large fossil primates, sometimes considered hominids, known from bones found in China. [f. Gk *gigas* giant + *pithēkos* ape]

giggle *v.i.* to laugh in small half-suppressed bursts. —*n.* such a laugh; (*colloq.*) an amusing person or thing, a joke. —**giggly** *adj.* [imit.]

gigolo /'ʒɪgələʊ/ *n.* (*pl.* **-os**) a young man paid by an older woman to be an escort or lover. [F, as masc. of *gigole* dance-hall woman]

Gila /'hiːlə/ *n.* (in full **Gila monster**) a large venomous lizard, *Heloderma suspectum,* found in the southwestern USA. [name of river in New Mexico and Arizona]

Gilbert[1] /'gɪlbət/, Sir Humphrey (*c.*1537-83), English explorer. After an active and distinguished career as a soldier in Ireland and the Netherlands Gilbert led an unsuccessful attempt to colonize the New World in 1578-9. On a second such voyage in 1583 he claimed Newfoundland for Elizabeth I and established a colony at St John's, but was lost on the trip homewards when his tiny vessel *The Squirrel* foundered in a storm off Nova Scotia.

Gilbert[2] /'gɪlbət/, Sir William Schwenck (1836-1911), English comic dramatist. He excelled as a writer of humorous verse, and his *Bab Ballads* (1866-73) were extremely popular. Between 1871 and 1896 he collaborated with the composer Sir Arthur Sullivan, writing the libretti for 14 comic operas.

gild[1] /gɪld/ *v.t.* (*p.p.* sometimes GILT[1] as adj. in lit. sense, otherwise **gilded**) to cover thinly with gold; to tinge with golden colour. —**gild the lily,** to try to improve what is already satisfactory. [OE (as GOLD)]

gild[2] var. of GUILD.

Gilgamesh /'gɪlgəmeʃ/ a legendary king of the Sumerian city-state of Uruk in southern Mesopotamia some time during the first half of the 3rd millennium BC, and hero of the Gilgamesh epic, one of the best-known works of ancient literature. This epic, the latest version of which is mostly preserved on twelve tablets, inscribed in Akkadian, from the library of Ashurbanipal at Nineveh, recounts Gilgamesh's exploits in his ultimately unsuccessful quest for immortality. It contains an account of a flood that has close parallels with the biblical story of Noah.

gill[1] /gɪl/ n. (usu. in pl.) **1.** a respiratory organ in a fish etc. (ill. FISH). **2.** a vertical radial plate on the underside of a mushroom etc. **3.** the flesh below a person's jaws and ears. [f. ON]

gill[2] /dʒɪl/ n. a unit of liquid measure, equal to ¼ pint. In many districts the gill is equal to ½ pint, the ¼ pint being called a *jack*. [f. OF f. L *gillo* water-pot]

gill[3] /gɪl/ n. **1.** a deep ravine, usually wooded. **2.** a narrow mountain torrent. [f. ON]

Gillespie /gɪˈlespɪ/, John Birks ('Dizzy') (1917–), American jazz trumpet-player, a leading exponent of the 'bop' style. After working with various other groups he formed his own in New York in 1944.

gillie /ˈgɪlɪ/ n. a man or boy attending a sportsman in Scotland. [f. Gael. *gille* lad, servant]

gillyflower /ˈdʒɪlɪflaʊə(r)/ n. a clove-scented flower, e.g. the wallflower; the clove-scented pink (*Dianthus carophyllus*). [f. OF *gilofre*, *girofle* f. L f. Gk *karuophullon* clove-tree]

gilt[1] /gɪlt/ adj. covered thinly with gold; gold-coloured. —n. **1.** gilding. **2.** a gilt-edged security. —**gilt-edged** adj. (of securities, stocks, etc.) having a high degree of reliability. [f. GILD[1]]

gilt[2] /gɪlt/ n. a young sow. [f. ON]

gimbals /ˈdʒɪmb(ə)lz/ n.pl. a contrivance of rings and pivots for keeping instruments horizontal at sea. [f. OF *gemel* double finger-ring f. L *gemellus* twin]

gimcrack /ˈdʒɪmkræk/ adj. showy but flimsy and worthless. —n. a showy ornament etc., a knick-knack. [f. earlier *gibecrake* (?inlaid work), of unkn. orig.]

gimlet /ˈgɪmlɪt/ n. a small tool with a screw-tip for boring holes (ill. CARPENTRY). —**gimlet eye,** an eye with a piercing glance. [f. OF *guimbelet*]

gimmick /ˈgɪmɪk/ n. a trick or device, especially to attract attention or publicity. —**gimmickry** n., **gimmicky** adj. [orig. US; etym. unkn.]

gimp /gɪmp/ n. a twist of silk etc. with a cord or wire running through it; a fishing-line of silk etc. bound with wire. [f. Du.]

gin[1] /dʒɪn/ n. a spirit made from grain or malt and flavoured with juniper berries (see below). —**gin rummy,** a form of the card-game rummy. **gin sling,** (*US*) a cold drink of gin flavoured and sweetened. [abbr. of *geneva* f. Du. f. OF *genevre*, = JUNIPER]
  The origin of gin is attributed to a professor of medicine, François de la Boë (d. 1672), at the university of Leyden in Holland: he distilled the juniper berry with spirits to produce a cheap diuretic medicine. The beverage became popular, and was brought to Britain by soldiers returning from the Low Countries. By the late 18th c. its excessive consumption had made it the scourge of the poor in London, until heavy taxation removed it from what they could afford. Netherlands gin has a strong grain flavour; English and US gins are based on spirit that is almost without flavour or aroma, to which flavouring agents are added.

gin[2] /dʒɪn/ n. **1.** a snare, a trap. **2.** a machine separating cotton from its seeds, first devised by the American inventor Eli Whitney in 1792. **3.** a kind of crane and windlass. —v.t. (**-nn-**) **1.** to treat (cotton) in a gin. **2.** to trap. [f. OF *engin* engine]

ginger /ˈdʒɪndʒə(r)/ n. **1.** a hot spicy root used in cooking and medicine and preserved in syrup or candied; the plant from which this comes (*Zingiber officinale*). **2.** light reddish yellow. **3.** mettle, spirit; stimulation. —v.t. **1.** to flavour with ginger. **2.** to liven *up*. —**ginger-ale, -beer** ns. kinds of aerated ginger-flavoured drink. **ginger group,** a group urging a party or movement to more decided action. **ginger-nut** n. a ginger-flavoured biscuit. **ginger-snap** n. a thin brittle ginger-flavoured biscuit. —**gingery** adj. [f. OE & OF f. L *zingiber* f. Gk f. Skr.]

gingerbread n. ginger-flavoured treacle cake. —adj. gaudy, tawdry.

gingerly /ˈdʒɪndʒəlɪ/ adj. showing great care or caution. —adv. in a gingerly manner. [perh. f. OF *gensor* delicate]

gingham /ˈgɪŋəm/ n. a plain-woven cotton cloth often striped or checked. [f. Du. f. Malay, = striped]

gingivitis /dʒɪndʒɪˈvaɪtɪs/ n. inflammation of the gums. [f. L *gingiva* gum + -ITIS]

ginkgo /ˈgɪŋkəʊ/ n. (pl. **-os**) a tree (*Gingko biloba*) with fan-shaped leaves and yellow flowers, originally from China and Japan. [f. Jap. f. Chin., = silver apricot]

ginseng /ˈdʒɪnseŋ/ n. a medicinal plant of the genus *Panax* found in eastern Asia and North America; the root of this. [f. Chin., perh. = man-image, alluding to forked root]

Giorgione /dʒɔːˈdʒɪˈəʊnɪ/, Giorgio Barbarelli or Giorgio del Castelfranco (*c.*1478-1510), Venetian painter, a pivotal figure in the Renaissance in Venice, though the definite details of his life and work are tantalizingly few. According to Vasari he developed a new method of painting, without preliminary drawing; many of his works were easel pictures for private collectors, enigmatic in subject and mood. His pupils included Titian and Sebastiano del Piombo, who are said to have completed some of his works when he died suddenly, of plague, in 1510. Many 'Giorgionesque' paintings were produced after his death, as a result of the unsatisfied demand for his work, and there is now a great discrepancy between the many paintings attributed to him and the few that are undoubtedly of his hand.

Giotto di Bondone /ˈdʒɒtəʊ dɪ bɒnˈdəʊnɪ/ (*c.*1267-1337), Florentine painter, an important figure in the birth of modern painting, since he moved away from the stylized two-dimensional stereotypes of Italo-Byzantine art in the direction of naturalism and human expression. The frescos of the *Life of St Francis* in Assisi (1297-*c.*1305), long thought to be by Giotto, are now considered of doubtful attribution, but the cycle in the Arena Chapel, Padua (1305-8), with its revolutionary rejection of medieval formulae in composition, is unchallenged. Giotto was famous in his own day, was court painter in Naples 1329-33, and in 1334 was made overseer of works for the cathedral in Florence.

gippy tummy /ˈdʒɪpɪ/ (*colloq.*) diarrhoea affecting visitors to hot countries. [f. EGYPTIAN]

gipsy var. of GYPSY.

giraffe /dʒɪˈrɑːf/ n. a large four-legged African animal (*Giraffa camelopardalis*) with a long neck and forelegs (ill. MAMMALS). [f. F ult. f. Arab.]

gird /gɜːd/ v.t. (*past & p.p.* **girded** or **girt**) to encircle or attach or secure with a belt or band; to put (a cord) *round*; to enclose or encircle. —**gird up one's loins,** to prepare for action. [OE]

girder n. an iron or steel beam or compound structure for a bridge-span etc. (ill. BRIDGES); a beam supporting joists. [f. GIRD]

girdle[1] /ˈgɜːd(ə)l/ n. **1.** a belt or cord used to gird the waist. **2.** an elasticated corset not extending above the waist. **3.** a thing that surrounds. **4.** the bony support of a limb. —v.t. to surround with a girdle. [OE (as GIRD)]

girdle[2] /ˈgɜːd(ə)l/ n. (esp. *Sc.*) a round iron plate set over a fire or otherwise heated for baking etc. [var. of GRIDDLE]

girl /gɜːl/ n. **1.** a female child. **2.** a young woman. **3.** a woman working in an office, factory, etc.; a female servant. **4.** a man's girl-friend. —**girl Friday,** see FRIDAY. **girl-friend** n. a regular female companion. —**girlhood** n., **girlish** adj. **girlishly** adv., **girlishness** n. [perh. cogn. with LG *gör* child]

girlie n. a little girl (as a term of endearment). —adj. (of a publication etc.) depicting young women in erotic poses. [f. GIRL]

giro /ˈdʒaɪrəʊ/ n. (pl. **-os**) a system of credit transfer between banks, post offices, etc. [G f. It., = circulation (of money)]

girt see GIRD.

girth /gɜːθ/ n. **1.** the distance round a thing. **2.** a strap round the body of a horse etc. securing the saddle etc. (ill. HORSE). [f. ON (as GIRD)]

gist /dʒɪst/ n. the main substance or essence *of* a matter. [OF (*gesir* lie f. L *jacēre*)]

git /gɪt/ n. (*slang*) a silly or contemptible person. [var. of *get* fool]

give /gɪv/ v.t./i. (*past* **gave**; *p.p.* **given** /ˈgɪv(ə)n/) **1.** to transfer the possession of gratuitously; to cause to receive or have; to supply. **2.** to deliver (a message); to render (a benefit); to assign; to pledge (one's word etc.); to cause to undergo or experience. **3.** to make over in exchange or payment. **4.** to devote, to dedicate. **5.** to utter; to declare (judgement etc.) authoritatively; (*colloq.*) to tell what one knows. **6.** to perform (an action or effort); to affect with this. **7.** to provide (a meal etc.) as host. **8.** to present or offer (news, a sign, etc.); to perform (a play or lecture etc.) in public; (usu. in *p.p.*) to grant or specify. **9.** to yield as a product or result. **10.** to be the source of. **11.** (of a window or road etc.) to look or lead (*on to, into,* etc.). **12.** to lose firmness, to be flexible, to yield when pressed or pulled. —**give and take,** exchange of talk or ideas; willingness to make concessions. **give away,** to transfer as a gift; to hand over (the bride) to the bridegroom at a wedding; to reveal (a secret etc.) unintentionally. **give-away** n. (*colloq.*) a thing given as a gift or at a low price; an unintentional disclosure.

give in, to yield, to acknowledge defeat; to hand in (a document etc.) to the proper official. **give it to,** (*colloq.*) to scold or punish (a person). **give me,** (in *imper.*) I prefer or admire. **given name,** (*US*) a first or Christian name. **give off,** to emit (fumes etc.). **give or take,** (*colloq.*) to accept as a margin of error in estimating. **give out,** to distribute; to announce, to emit; to be exhausted, to run short. **give over,** to devote, to hand over; (*colloq.*) to stop or desist. **give to understand,** to inform or assure. **give tongue,** to speak one's thoughts; (of hounds) to bark, especially on tracing a scent. **give up,** to cease from effort or activity; to part with; to resign or surrender; to renounce hope (of); to pronounce incurable or insoluble; to deliver (a fugitive etc.) to pursuers etc.; to abandon or addict (*oneself to*). **give way,** to yield under pressure; to give precedence. —**giver** *n.* [OE]

Giza /ˈgiːzə/, **El** a city SW of Cairo in northern Egypt, on the west bank of the Nile, site of the pyramids of Khufu, Khephren, and Menkaure, and of the great sphinx.

gizzard /ˈgɪzəd/ *n.* a bird's second stomach for grinding food; the muscular stomach of some fish, insects, molluscs, etc. [f. OF f. L *gigeria* cooked entrails of fowl]

glacé /ˈglæseɪ/ *adj.* **1.** (of fruit) iced or sugared. **2.** (of cloth etc.) smooth, polished. —**glacé icing,** icing made from icing sugar and water. [F, = iced (as foll.)]

glacial /ˈgleɪʃ(ə)l/ *adj.* **1.** of ice; characterized or produced by ice. **2.** cold and forbidding. —**glacially** *adv.* [F, or f. L (*glacies* ice)]

glacial period a period in the earth's history characterized by an unusual extension of polar and mountain ice-sheets over the earth's surface. The Pleistocene and the preceding Pliocene epoch included a number of such periods, interrupted by warmer phases called interglacials, and it may be that the climate of the present day represents such a warm phase and that another ice age is to follow. During the coldest time, about 18,000 years ago, extensive ice-sheets covered much of Europe, North America, and Asia, and sea-levels were up to 200 metres lower than they are today. In the southern hemisphere glaciation was less extensive owing to the isolation of the Antarctic ice-sheet from the other southern continents. Although the glacial periods of the Pleistocene epoch are the most important in terms of their effect upon present-day topography, there is evidence of earlier glaciations in Palaeozoic and Precambrian times. Their causes are not fully understood but it is thought that their onset may be affected by the position of the continents relative to the pole and by small variations in the brightness of the sun.

glaciated /ˈgleɪsɪeɪtɪd/ *adj.* covered with glaciers or an ice-sheet; affected by the friction of moving ice. —**glaciation** /-ˈeɪʃ(ə)n/ *n.* [f. L *glaciare* freeze (as GLACIAL)]

glacier /ˈglæsɪə(r)/ *n.* a slowly moving river or mass of ice formed by an accumulation of snow on higher ground (ill. MOUNTAINS). [F (as GLACIAL)]

glad *adj.* **1.** pleased (usu. *predic.*); expressing or causing pleasure. **2.** ready and willing. —**be glad of,** to find useful. **glad eye,** (*slang*) an amorous glance. **glad hand,** (*colloq.*) a hearty welcome. **glad rags,** (*colloq.*) best clothes. —**gladly** *adv.*, **gladness** *n.* [OE]

gladden /ˈglæd(ə)n/ *v.t.* to make glad. [f. prec.]

glade *n.* an open space in a forest. [orig. unkn.]

gladiator /ˈglædɪeɪtə(r)/ *n.* a trained fighter in ancient Roman shows. —**gladiatorial** /-əˈtɔːrɪəl/ *adj.* [L (*gladius* sword)]

gladiolus /glædɪˈəʊləs/ *n.* (*pl.* **-li** /-laɪ/) a plant of the genus *Gladiolus,* with spikes of flowers and sword-shaped leaves. [L., dim. of *gladius* sword]

gladsome *adj.* (*poetic*) cheerful, joyous. [f. GLAD + -SOME]

Gladstone /ˈglædst(ə)n/, William Ewart (1809-98), British statesman. After an early career as a Conservative minister, Gladstone joined the Liberal Party and succeeded Russell as its leader in 1867. Prime Minister on four separate occasions (1868-74, 1880-5, 1886, and 1892-4), Gladstone dominated British political life in the second half of the 19th c. His career was particularly notable for his rivalry with his Conservative opposite number, Disraeli, the long series of social and political reforms he was responsible for introducing (of which Cardwell's army reforms, the Irish Land Acts, and the third Reform Act are important examples) and for his conversion to Home Rule for Ireland, which led to the defection of the Unionists from the Liberal Party.

Gladstone bag a case for clothes etc. hinged so that it opens flat into two approximately equal compartments. [f. prec.]

Glagolitic /glægəˈlɪtɪk/ *adj.* of an alphabet, based largely on Greek minuscules, formerly used in writing some Slavonic languages. It was introduced about the same time as Cyrillic (9th c.), and may have been devised by St Cyril, but its origin is obscure. [ult. f. Old Slavonic *glagol* word]

glair *n.* white of egg; a viscous substance made from or resembling this. [f. OF, ult. f. L *clarus* clear]

glamorize /ˈglæməraɪz/ *v.t.* to make glamorous or attractive. [f. foll.]

glamour /ˈglæmə(r)/ *n.* **1.** alluring beauty. **2.** attractive and exciting qualities. —**glamorous** *adj.* [var. of GRAMMAR in obs. sense 'magic']

glance /glɑːns/ *v.t./i.* **1.** to look briefly. **2.** to strike at an angle and glide *off* an object. **3.** (usu. *with at*) to refer briefly or indirectly to (a subject). **4.** (of a light etc.) to flash or dart. —*n.* **1.** a brief look. **2.** a flash or gleam. **3.** a glancing stroke in cricket. [prob. f. OF *glacier* to slip (as GLACIER)]

gland *n.* an organ secreting substances that are to be used in the body or expelled from it; a similar organ in a plant. [f. F f. L *glandulae* gland]

glanders /ˈglændəz/ *n.pl.* a contagious disease of horses and related animals. [f. OF *glandre* (as GLAND)]

glandular /ˈglændjʊlə(r)/ *adj.* of a gland or glands. —**glandular fever,** an infectious disease with swelling of the lymph-glands. [f. F (as GLAND)]

glare /gleə(r)/ *v.i.* **1.** to look fiercely or fixedly. **2.** to shine oppressively. —*n.* **1.** a fierce or fixed look. **2.** an oppressive light; tawdry brilliance. [f. MDu. or MLG]

glaring *adj.* **1.** shining oppressively. **2.** obvious or conspicuous. —**glaringly** *adv.* [f. prec.]

glass /glɑːs/ *n.* **1.** a hard usually brittle and transparent substance made by fusing sand with soda or potash and other ingredients (see below); a substance of similar properties, e.g. fibreglass. **2.** glass utensils, ornaments, windows, greenhouses, etc. **3.** an object made (partly) of glass; a glass drinking-vessel or its contents; a mirror; a lens; a barometer. **4.** (in *pl.*) spectacles, binoculars. —*v.t.* to fit with glass. —**crown glass,** which contains no lead or iron, was formerly used in windows and is now used as an optical glass of low refractive index. **flint glass,** pure and lustrous, was originally made with flint, and was invented in 1674 by George Ravenscroft. **glass-blowing** *n.* shaping semi-molten glass by blowing air into it through a tube. **glass-cloth** *n.* a cloth for drying glasses. **glass fibre,** a fabric made from or plastic reinforced by glass filaments. **glass-paper** *n.* paper coated with glass particles, for smoothing or polishing. **glass wool,** a mass of fine glass fibres for packing and insulation. **plate glass,** used for shop windows, was cast in plates, rolled through heated rollers, then ground and polished, until about 1959 when the float process was introduced (saving labour and space but introducing a rich variety of technological and scientific problems), in which the glass is drawn in a continuous sheet from the melting-tank and made to float on the surface of molten metal while it hardens. Its surface has a brilliant finish and is perfectly true because it has not been in contact, when soft, with anything but a liquid. [OE]

Glass has the property of being smoothly and reversibly converted to a liquid by the application of heat. The art of producing a vitreous surface on stone or clay was known in ancient Egypt. Objects composed entirely of glass paste begin to appear there *c.*1500 BC, when two allied processes seem to have been in use: modelling molten glass about a removable core of sand, and pressing it into an open mould. The invention of glass-blowing in the 1st c. BC (probably in Syria) wrought a profound change in the glass industry which, hitherto limited to luxury articles, now became capable of cheap mass production. Window glass, made by a primitive process of rolling, was known at Pompeii and later became common. Because of its special properties of transparency and resistance to corrosion glass has found widespread uses for windows, food containers, chemical apparatus, and optical lenses.

glasshouse *n.* **1.** a greenhouse. **2.** (*slang*) a military prison.

glassware *n.* articles made of glass.

glassy *adj.* **1.** like glass. **2.** (of the eye or expression) dull and fixed. —**glassily** *adv.*, **glassiness** *n.* [f. GLASS]

Glastonbury /ˈglæst(ə)nbəri/ the site in Somerset of the abbey supposed to have been founded by Joseph of Arimathea, and of the legendary resting-place of King Arthur and his queen Guinevere. It was also identified in medieval times with the legendary Avalon.

Glaswegian /glæz'wi:dʒ(ə)n/ *adj.* of Glasgow, a city in western Scotland. —*n.* a native of Glasgow. [f. *Glasgow* after *Norwegian*]

glaucoma /glɔ:'kəʊmə/ *n.* a condition caused by increased pressure of the fluid within the eyeball, causing weakening or loss of sight. [L f. Gk (*glaukos* greyish-blue)]

glaze *v.t./i.* **1.** to fit or cover with glass. **2.** to coat with a glossy surface. **3.** to cover (the eye) with a film. **4.** to become glassy. —*n.* **1.** a vitreous substance for glazing pottery. **2.** a smooth shiny coating on materials or food. **3.** a coat of transparent paint to modify an underlying tone. **4.** a surface formed by glazing. [f. GLASS]

glazier /'gleɪzɪə(r)/ *n.* a person who glazes windows etc. professionally. [f. prec.]

GLC *abbr.* Greater London Council (1963–86).

gleam *n.* **1.** a subdued or transient light. **2.** a faint or momentary show (*of* humour, hope, etc.). —*v.i.* to emit gleams. [OE]

glean *v.t./i.* **1.** to acquire (facts etc.) in small amounts. **2.** to gather (corn left by reapers). —**gleaner** *n.* [f. OF *glener*, prob. f. Celtic]

gleanings *n.pl.* things gleaned. [f. prec.]

glebe /gli:b/ *n.* a portion of land going with a benefice and providing revenue. [f. L *gl(a)eba* clod, soil]

glee *n.* **1.** lively or triumphant joy. **2.** a part-song for three or more (usu. male) voices. —**glee club**, a society for singing part-songs. [OE]

gleeful *adj.* joyful. —**gleefully** *adv.* [f. GLEE + -FUL]

glen *n.* a narrow valley. [f. Gaelic & Ir.]

Glencoe /glen'kəʊ/ a glen in the Scottish Highlands, scene of the massacre in 1692 of Jacobite MacDonald clansmen by Campbell soldiers acting for the government of William III. While this massacre has often been considered a particularly foul violation of the rules of Highland hospitality in continuation of the long-standing feud between the Campbells and the MacDonalds, it was in fact a deliberate government attempt to make an example of one of the most notorious Jacobite clans, badly botched by the men on the spot (who killed less than a third of about 140 intended victims).

Glendower /glen'daʊə(r)/, Owen (*c.*1355–*c.*1417), the last independent prince of Wales. Leader first of guerrilla resistance to English overlordship and then of a national uprising against Henry IV, which by 1404 had progressed sufficiently for him to hold his own parliament, Glendower benefited considerably from supporting Henry's English opponents, notably the Percy family. Although Welsh independence collapsed soon after Glendower's death, he rapidly became a legendary symbol of Welsh nationalism.

glengarry /glen'gærɪ/ *n.* a kind of Highland cap with a pointed front. [f. *Glengarry* in Highland]

glib *adj.* fluent but insincere. —**glibly** *adv.*, **glibness** *n.* [rel. to obs. *glibbery* slippery, perh. imit.]

glide *v.t./i.* **1.** to move smoothly and continuously; to pass gradually or imperceptibly. **2.** to fly in a glider or (of aircraft) without engine-power. —*n.* a gliding movement. —**glide path**, an aircraft's line of descent to land, especially as indicated by ground radar. [OE]

glider /'glaɪdə(r)/ *n.* a fixed-wing aircraft that is not power-driven when in flight. It is launched by being towed from an aircraft, winch, or car, or by catapult; some gliders are fitted with a small retractable engine and propeller to enable them to be self-launched and dispense with this. The first glider to fly in free flight was devised by Sir George Cayley (see entry). [f. GLIDE]

glimmer *n.* **1.** a faint or intermittent light. **2.** (also **glimmering**) a gleam (*of* hope etc.). —*v.i.* to shine faintly or intermittently. [prob. f. Scand. (as GLEAM)]

glimpse *n.* a brief view (*of*); a faint transient appearance. —*v.t.* to have a brief view of. [corresp. to MHG *glimsen* (as prec.)]

glint *v.i.* to flash, to glitter. —*n.* a brief flash of light. [prob. f. Scand.]

glissade /glɪ'sɑ:d, -'seɪd/ *v.i.* **1.** to make a controlled slide down a snow slope in mountaineering. **2.** to make a gliding step in a dance. —*n.* a glissading movement or step. [F (*glisser* slide, slip)]

glisten /'glɪs(ə)n/ *v.i.* to shine like a wet or polished surface; to glitter, to sparkle. —*n.* glistening. [OE]

glitter *v.i.* **1.** to sparkle. **2.** to be showy or splendid. —*n.* a sparkle. [f. ON]

gloaming *n.* the evening twilight. [OE, rel. to GLOW]

gloat *v.i.* to look or ponder with greedy or malicious pleasure (*over* etc.). —*n.* the act of gloating. [perh. rel. to ON *glotta* grin]

global /'gləʊb(ə)l/ *adj.* **1.** world-wide. **2.** all-embracing. —**globally** *adv.* [F (as foll.)]

globe *n.* a spherical object, especially *the* earth, or a representation of it with a map on its surface; a thing shaped like this, e.g. a lamp-shade or a fish-bowl. —**globe-fish** *n.* a fish of the family Tetraodontidae, that inflates itself into a globe form. **globe-flower** *n.* a plant of the genus *Trollius*, with spherical usually yellow flowers. **globe-trotter** *n.* one who travels widely. **globe-trotting** *n.* such travel. [F, or f. L *globus*]

Globe Theatre the Burbages' theatre at Bankside in Southwark, London, erected in 1599 with materials from the old Theatre on the north side of the river. It was a large thatched circular building, with the centre open to the sky, and was used only during the summer months. The thatch caught fire in 1613 from a discharge of stage gunfire during a play, and the whole building was destroyed. It was rebuilt in 1614 and was in constant use until all the London theatres were closed on the outbreak of the Civil War in 1642. Shakespeare had a share in the theatre and acted there.

globular /'glɒbjʊlə(r)/ *adj.* **1.** globe-shaped. **2.** composed of globules. [f. foll.]

globule /'glɒbju:l/ *n.* a small globe or round particle, a drop. [F, or f. L *globulus* (as GLOBE)]

globulin /'glɒbjʊlɪn/ *n.* a protein found usually associated with albumin in animal and plant tissues. [f. prec.]

glockenspiel /'glɒkənspi:l/ *n.* a percussion instrument formed from a set of tuned metal bars each supported at two points but with both ends free and struck in the centre with small hand-held hammers. It has a range of about two-and-a-half octaves, and became a fairly regular member of the orchestra in the 19th c. [G, = bell-play]

gloom *n.* **1.** semi-darkness. **2.** a feeling of sadness and depression. —*v.t./i.* to make, look, or be gloomy. [orig. unkn.; cf. GLUM]

gloomy *adj.* **1.** dark or dim. **2.** depressed; depressing. —**gloomily** *adv.*, **gloominess** *n.* [f. obs. *gloom* a frown f. prec.]

Gloriana /glɔ:rɪ'ɑ:nə/ the nickname of Elizabeth I of England.

glorify /'glɔ:rɪfaɪ/ *v.t.* **1.** to praise highly. **2.** to worship with adoration and praise. **3.** to make seem more splendid than it is. —**glorification** /-'keɪʃ(ə)n/ *n.* [f. OF f. L (as GLORY)]

glorious /'glɔ:rɪəs/ *adj.* **1.** possessing or conferring glory. **2.** splendid, illustrious; excellent (often *iron.*). —**Glorious Revolution**, the events that led to the removal of James II from the English throne and his replacement by his daughter Mary and her husband William of Orange (1688), with their acceptance of the conditions laid down in the Bill of Rights. —**gloriously** *adv.* [f. AF (as foll.)]

glory /'glɔ:rɪ/ *n.* **1.** fame and honour. **2.** adoration and praise in worship. **3.** resplendent beauty, magnificence, etc.; an exalted or prosperous state. **4.** a thing that brings renown, a special distinction. **5.** the halo of a saint etc. —*v.i.* to take great pride (*in*). —**glory-hole** *n.* (*slang*) an untidy room or cupboard etc. **go to glory**, (*slang*) to die, to be destroyed. [f. OF f. L *gloria*]

Glos. *abbr.* Gloucestershire.

gloss[1] *n.* **1.** the lustre of a surface. **2.** a deceptively attractive appearance. —*v.t.* to make glossy. —**gloss over**, to seek to conceal. **gloss paint**, paint giving a glossy finish. [orig. unkn.]

gloss[2] *n.* an explanatory comment added to a text, e.g. in the margin; a comment or paraphrase. —*v.t./i.* to make such a comment; to add a comment to (a text or word etc.). [f. OF f. L *glossa* f. Gk (as GLOTTIS)]

glossary /'glɒsərɪ/ *n.* a dictionary or list of technical or special words; a collection of glosses. [f. L (as GLOSS[2])]

glossy *adj.* having a gloss, shiny. —**glossily** *adv.*, **glossiness** *n.* [f. GLOSS[1]]

glottal /'glɒt(ə)l/ *adj.* of the glottis. —**glottal stop**, the sound produced by the sudden opening or shutting of the glottis. [f. foll.]

glottis /'glɒtɪs/ *n.* the opening at the upper end of the windpipe between the vocal cords. [f. Gk *glōtta* var. of *glōssa* tongue]

Gloucester /'glɒstə(r)/ n. a cheese made in Gloucestershire (now usu. **double Gloucester,** originally a richer kind). [f. *Gloucester* city in SW England]

Gloucestershire /'glɒstəʃɪə(r)/ a county of SW England.

glove /glʌv/ n. a hand-covering, usually with separate fingers, for protection, warmth, etc.; a boxing-glove. *v.t.* to cover or provide with a glove or gloves. —**with the gloves off,** arguing or contending in earnest. [OE]

glover /'glʌvə(r)/ n. a glove-maker. [f. prec.]

glow /gləʊ/ v.i. 1. to emit light and heat without flame. 2. to shine like a thing intensely heated; to show a warm colour. 3. to burn *with* or indicate bodily heat or fervour. —n. a glowing state; warmth of colour; ardour. —**glow-worm** n. a beetle (*Lampyris noctiluca*) whose wingless female emits light from the end of the abdomen. [OE]

glower /'glaʊə(r)/ v.i. to look angrily (*at*). [orig. unkn.]

gloxinia /glɒk'sɪnɪə/ n. an American tropical plant of the genus *Gloxinia,* with bell-shaped flowers. [f. B. P. *Gloxin,* 18th-c. German botanist]

Gluck /glʊk/, Christoph Willibald von (1714–87), composer who was born in Germany and died in Vienna, having travelled widely. From early operas in the Italian style he went on to seek a balance of music and drama in his 'reform' operas, discarding the claims of the star singer and attempting a continuous musical unfolding of the narrative. He had a lyrical gift which can be seen at its best in his operas, and the simplicity and sublimity of his melodies, supported by a vivid dramatic sense, have ensured the survival of a large proportion of his music.

glucose /'glu:kəʊs, -əʊz/ n. a sugar found in the blood or in fruit-juice etc. [F, f. Gk *gleukos* sweet wine (*glukus* sweet)]

glue /glu:/ n. a sticky substance used as an adhesive. —v.t. 1. to attach with glue. 2. to hold closely. —**glue-sniffer** n. one who inhales the fumes of plastic glue as a narcotic. **glue-sniffing** n. —**gluey** adj. [f. OF f. L *gluten*]

glum adj. dejected, sullen. —**glumly** adv., **glumness** n. [rel. to dial. *glum* v. frown, var. of GLOOM]

glut v.t. (**-tt-**) 1. to satisfy fully with food; to sate. 2. to overstock (a market). —n. an excessive supply. [prob. f. OF *gloutir* swallow f. L (as GLUTTON)]

glutamate /'glu:təmeɪt/ n. a salt or ester of glutamic acid, especially the sodium salt used to flavour food. [f. foll.]

glutamic acid /glu:'tæmɪk/ an amino acid normally found in proteins. [f. foll. + AMINE]

gluten /'glu:t(ə)n/ n. 1. the viscous part of flour left when the starch is removed. 2. a viscous animal secretion. [F f. L, = glue]

glutinous /'glu:tɪnəs/ adj. sticky, gluelike, viscous. [f. F or L (as prec.)]

glutton /'glʌt(ə)n/ n. 1. an excessive eater; a person insatiably eager (*for* work etc.). 2. the wolverine (see entry). —**gluttonous** adj. [f. OF f. L (*gluttire* swallow)]

gluttony /'glʌtənɪ/ n. the character or conduct of a glutton. [f. prec.]

glyceride /'glɪsəraɪd/ n. a compound ester of glycerine. [f. foll.]

glycerine /'glɪsəri:n/ n. (also **glycerol**) a colourless sweet viscous liquid obtained from fats, used as an ointment etc. and in explosives. [f. F f. Gk *glukeros* sweet]

Glyndebourne /'glaɪndbɔːn/ an estate near Lewes in Sussex, England, where an annual festival of opera is held. The opera house was built by the owner of the estate, John Christie (d. 1962), who founded the festival in 1934 to stage ideal performances in a beautiful setting. The inspiration for the enterprise was his wife, the soprano Audrey Mildmay.

gm abbr. gram(s).

G-man /'dʒiːmæn/ n. (*US slang*) a federal criminal-investigation officer. [f. Government + MAN]

GMT abbr. Greenwich Mean Time.

gnarled /nɑːld/ adj. (of a tree, hands, etc.) knobbly, rugged, twisted. [rel. to KNURL]

gnash /næʃ/ v.t./i. to grind (one's teeth); (of the teeth) to strike together. [f. ON (imit.)]

gnat /næt/ n. a small two-winged biting fly of the genus *Culex.* [OE]

gnaw /nɔː/ v.t./i. (p.t. **gnawed** or **gnawn**) 1. to bite persistently. 2. (of a destructive agent) to corrode or consume. 3. (of pain etc.) to hurt continuously. [OE]

gneiss /naɪs, gnaɪs/ n. a coarse-grained metamorphic rock of quartz, feldspar, and mica. [G]

gnome /nəʊm/ n. 1. a kind of dwarf in fairy-tales, living underground and guarding the treasures of the earth. 2. a figure of such a dwarf as a garden ornament. 3. (in *pl.*) persons (esp. financiers) with secret influence. [F, f. L *gnomus* (word invented by Paracelsus)]

gnomic /'nəʊmɪk/ adj. of maxims, sententious. [f. Gk (*gnōmē* opinion)]

gnomon /'nəʊmən/ n. the rod or pin etc. of a sundial, showing the time by its shadow (ill. TIME). [F, or f. L f. Gk, = indicator]

gnostic /'nɒstɪk/ adj. 1. of knowledge. 2. having special mystical knowledge. 3. **Gnostic,** of the Gnostics or Gnosticism. —n. **Gnostic,** an adherent of Gnosticism (see foll.). [f. L f. Gk (*gnōsis* knowledge)]

Gnosticism /'nɒstɪsɪz(ə)m/ n. a movement, in part at least of pre-Christian origin and with ideas drawn from Greek philosophy and other pagan sources, prominent in the Christian Church in the 2nd c. It took many different forms, some of which are wild amalgams of mythology and magical rites with only an admixture of Christian terminology. Gnostics emphasized the power of *gnosis,* the supposed revealed knowledge of God, to redeem the spiritual element in man; they contrasted the supreme remote Divine Being with the 'Demiurge' or 'creator god', who controlled the world and was antagonistic to all that was purely spiritual. Christ came as an emissary from the supreme god, bringing *gnosis.* Gnostic teaching for long was known only from anti-heretical writers, such as Irenaeus and Tertullian, until in 1945–6 a collection of Gnostic texts was found at Nag Hammadi in Upper Egypt. [as prec.]

GNP abbr. gross national product.

gnu /nuː/ n. an oxlike antelope of the genus *Connochaetes,* also called a wildebeest. [ult. f. Kaffir]

go¹ /gəʊ/ v.i. (past **went**; p.p. **gone** /gɒn/; partic. **going**) 1. to begin to move, to be moving from one position or point in time to another; (with *partic.*) to make a trip for (a specified purpose). 2. to lie or extend in a certain direction. 3. to be functioning, moving, etc. 4. to make a specified motion or sound. 5. to be in a specified state, habitually or for a time; to pass into a specified condition, to escape *free, unnoticed,* etc. 6. (of time or a distance) to pass, to be traversed. 7. to be regularly kept or put, to belong; to fit, to be able to be put. 8. (of a number) to be contained in another, especially without a remainder. 9. to be current; to be on the average. 10. to fare, (of events) to turn out; to take a certain course or views. 11. to have a specified form or wording. 12. to be successful; (*colloq.*) to be acceptable or permitted, to be accepted without question. 13. to be sold. 14. (of money or supplies etc.) to be spent or used up. 15. to be relinquished or abolished. 16. to fail or decline; to give way, to collapse. 17. to die. 18. to be allotted or awarded. 19. to contribute, to tend, to extend, to reach. 20. to carry an action or commitment to a certain point. 21. (in *imper., colloq.* or *US*) to proceed to. —n. 1. animation, dash. 2. a turn or try; an attack *of* an illness; a portion served at one time. 3. a success. 4. (*colloq.*) vigorous activity. 5. (*colloq.*) a state of affairs. —adj. (*colloq.*) functioning properly. —**go ahead,** to proceed immediately. **go-ahead** n. permission to proceed; (*adj.*) enterprising. **go along with,** to agree with. **go and,** (*colloq.*) to be so unwise etc. as to. **go back on,** to fail to keep (a promise etc.). **go-between** n. an intermediary. **go by,** to be dependent on; to be guided by. **go-cart** n. a simple four-wheeled structure for a child to play on. **go down,** to descend or sink; to be swallowed; to be written down; to leave university; to find acceptance (*with*); to become ill (*with* a disease). **go for,** to like, to prefer, to choose; to pass or be accounted as (*little* etc.); (*slang*) to attack. **go-getter** n. (*colloq.*) a pushful enterprising person. **go-go** adj. (*colloq.*) very active or energetic. **go-go dancer,** a performer of lively erotic dances at a night-club etc. **go in for,** to compete or engage in. **go into,** to become a member of (a profession etc.) or a patient in (a hospital etc.); to investigate (a matter). **go a long way,** to have much effect *towards*; (of supplies) to last long; (of money) to buy much. **go off,** to explode; to deteriorate; to fall asleep; (of an event) to proceed *well* etc.; to begin to dislike. **go on,** to continue (*doing*); to persevere (*with*); to proceed next to *do*; (*colloq.*) to nag (*at*). **go on** or **upon,** to judge by, to base conclusions on. **go out,** to be extinguished; to go to social functions; to be broadcast; to cease to be fashionable; (*US colloq.*) to lose consciousness; (of the heart etc.) to feel sympathy. **go round,** to be large enough or sufficient. **go slow,** to work at a deliberately slow pace as an industrial protest. **go-slow** n. such action. **go through,** to examine or revise; to perform or undergo;

to spend or use up (money or supplies). **go through with,** to complete (an undertaking). **go to,** to attend (a school, church, etc.). **go under,** to succumb, to fail. **go up,** to rise in price; to explode, to burn; to enter university. **go with,** to match or suit, to harmonize or belong with. **go without,** to abstain from, to tolerate the lack (of). **on the go,** (*colloq.*) in constant motion, active. [OE; *went* orig. past of WEND]

go² /gəʊ/ *n.* a Japanese board-game of territorial possession, played on a board of 18 × 18 squares, each player having about 200 pieces. [Jap.]

Goa /'gəʊə/ a district on the west coast of India, formerly a Portuguese territory. It was seized by India in 1961 and now, together with two other former Portuguese territories, Daman and Diu, forms a Union Territory of India (capital, Panaji). —**Goan** *adj.* & *n.*, **Goanese** /-'niːz/ *adj.* & *n.*

goad *n.* **1.** a spiked stick for urging cattle. **2.** a thing that torments or incites. —*v.t.* **1.** to urge with a goad. **2.** to irritate; to drive or stimulate (*into* action etc.). [OE]

goal *n.* **1.** a structure into or through which a ball is to be driven in certain games. **2.** a point or points scored thus. **3.** an objective; a destination; the point where a race ends. —**goal-line** *n.* a line forming the end boundary of a field of play. **goal-post** *n.* either of the pair of posts marking the limits of a goal. [perh. = obs. *gol* boundary]

goalie /'gəʊlɪ/ *n.* (*colloq.*) a goalkeeper. [f. GOAL]

goalkeeper *n.* a player defending the goal.

goat *n.* **1.** a small horned ruminant of the genus *Capra*. **2. the Goat,** the constellation or sign of the zodiac Capricorn. **3.** a licentious man. **4.** (*colloq.*) a foolish person. —**get a person's goat,** (*slang*) to annoy him. [OE]

goatee /gəʊ'tiː/ *n.* a small pointed beard like a goat's. [f. prec.]

goatherd *n.* one who tends goats.

goatsucker *n.* the nightjar.

gob¹ *n.* (*slang*) the mouth. —**gob-stopper** *n.* a large hard sweet for sucking. [perh. f. Gael. & Ir., = beak, mouth]

gob² *n.* (*vulgar*) a clot of a slimy substance. [f. OF *go(u)be* mouthful]

gobbet /'gɒbɪt/ *n.* an extract from a text, set for translation or comment. [f. OF *gobet* (as prec.)]

gobble¹ *v.t./i.* to eat hurriedly and noisily. [prob. f. GOB²]

gobble² *v.i.* **1.** (of a turkey-cock) to make a gurgling sound in the throat. **2.** to speak thus. [imit.]

gobbledegook /'gɒb(ə)ldɪguːk/ *n.* (*slang*) pompous or unintelligible official or professional jargon. [imit. of turkey-cock]

Gobelins /'gəʊbəlɪnz, 'gɒblæ̃/ the most important tapestry factory of the late 17th and early 18th c., producing work of unrivalled excellence. It originated as a family dyeing workshop *c.*1440, and was taken over by the French Crown in 1662; in the 18th c. leading French painters provided cartoons, and tapestry panels became an alternative to oil painting. The leaders of the Revolution condemned its productions as frivolous, but it was revived by Napoleon. The factory still exists, and now works exclusively for the State.

Gobi Desert /'gəʊbɪ/ a barren plateau of southern Mongolia and northern China.

goblet /'gɒblɪt/ *n.* a drinking-vessel, especially of glass, with a foot and stem. [f. OF *gobel* cup)]

goblin /'gɒblɪn/ *n.* a mischievous ugly demon in folklore. [f. L *Gobelinus* name of spirit, rel. to G *kobold* demon in mines]

goby /'gəʊbɪ/ *n.* a small fish of the genus *Gobius*, with the ventral fins joined to form a disc or sucker. [f. L *gōbius* f. Gk *kōbios*, = GUDGEON]

god *n.* **1.** a superhuman being worshipped as having power over nature and human affairs. **2. God,** the supreme being, creator and ruler of the universe in the Christian and other monotheistic religions. **3.** an image of a god, an idol. **4.** a person or thing greatly admired or adored. —**the gods,** (*colloq.*) the gallery of a theatre. **God-fearing** *adj.* earnestly religious. **God forbid,** may it not be so. **God-forsaken** *adj.* dismal, wretched. **God knows,** we (or I) cannot know. **God Save the King** or **Queen,** the British national anthem. The origins of both words and tune are obscure. The phrase 'God save the king' occurs in various passages in the Old Testament, while as early as 1545 it was a watchword in the Navy, with 'long to reign over us' as a counter-sign. The anthem probably arose from a series of common loyal phrases being gradually combined into one national hymn,

and evidence points to the 17th c. for both the words and the tune of this. **God willing,** if circumstances allow. [OE]

godchild *n.* a child or person in relation to a godparent or godparents.

god-daughter *n.* a female godchild.

goddess /'gɒdɪs/ *n.fem.* **1.** a female deity. **2.** an adored woman. [f. GOD]

Gödel /'gɜːd(ə)l/, Kurt (1906–78), Austrian mathematician who emigrated to the USA in 1938. He made several contributions to mathematical logic, the greatest of which is his incompleteness theorem (1931): that in any sufficiently powerful, logically consistent formulation of the logic of mathematics there must be true formulas which are neither provable nor disprovable, thus making mathematics essentially incomplete, and also the corollary that the consistency of such a system as arithmetic cannot be proved within that system.

godetia /gə'diːʃə/ *n.* a showy-flowered hardy annual of the genus *Godetia*. [f. C. H. *Godet,* Swiss botanist (d. 1879)]

godfather *n.* **1.** a male godparent. **2.** a person directing an illegal organization.

godhead *n.* **1.** divine nature, deity. **2. the Godhead,** God. [f. GOD + -HEAD]

Godiva /gə'daɪvə/ the wife of an 11th-c. Earl of Mercia, who (according to a 13th-c. legend) agreed to her husband's proposition that he would remit some particularly unpopular taxes only if she rode naked on horseback through Coventry.

godless *adj.* not believing in God or a god; impious, wicked. —**godlessly** *adv.*, **godlessness** *n.* [f. GOD + -LESS]

godlike *adj.* like God or a god.

godly *adj.* pious, devout. —**godliness** *n.* [f. GOD]

godmother *n.* a female godparent.

godown /gə'daʊn/ *n.* a warehouse in eastern Asia, especially in India. [f. Port. f. Malay]

godparent *n.* a person who sponsors another (especially a child) at baptism.

godsend *n.* a piece of unexpected good luck having a decisive effect, a useful or effective acquisition.

godson *n.* a male godchild.

Godspeed *n.* an expression of good wishes to a person starting a journey.

Godunov /'gɒdʊnɒf/, Boris (1550–1605), tsar of Russia 1598–1605. A noble of Tartar descent, Boris Godunov rose to prominence as a counsellor of Ivan the Terrible and eventually succeeded Ivan's son as tsar. His brief reign was overshadowed by famine, doubts over his involvement in the earlier death of Ivan's eldest son, and the appearance of a pretender, the so-called False Dmitry. His position was seriously undermined by the intrigues of several influential noble families (notably the Romanovs who were later to gain the throne), and Boris died suddenly at a time when his army was trying to defeat an invasion by the Pretender. His family was murdered during the period of anarchy that followed, thus bringing the Ruril dynasty to an end. He was the subject of a play by Pushkin and an opera (based on this) by Mussorgsky.

Godwin /'gɒdwɪn/, William (1756–1836), English philosopher and novelist, who began as a dissenting minister but became an atheist and anarchical philosopher. His propagandist novel *Caleb Williams* (1794), which exposes the perfidiousness of the ruling classes, was an early example of the crime and detection novel. Godwin married Mary Wollstonecraft (1759–97), author of *A Vindication of the Rights of Women* (1792); their daughter, Mary, married the poet Shelley.

Godwin-Austen /gɒdwɪn 'ɔːstɪn/, **Mount** see K2.

godwit *n.* a wading bird of the genus *Limosa*, like the curlew but with a straight or slightly upcurved bill. [orig. unkn.]

goer /'gəʊə(r)/ *n.* **1.** a person or thing that goes. **2.** a lively or persevering person. **3.** (*in comb.*) a regular attender. [f. GO¹]

Goes /guːs/, Hugo van der (active *c.*1467–82), Flemish painter, born in Ghent and mainly working there, though his best-known work is the large-scale *Portinari Altarpiece* commissioned for a church in Florence.

Goethe /'gɜːtə/, Johann Wolfgang von (1749–1832), German writer, scholar, and statesman who spent most of his life at the court of the Duke of Saxe-Weimar where he was Prime Minister until 1785 as well as being director of the

Weimar court theatre from 1791 and head of various scientific institutions, for his wide-ranging interests included not only philosophy but physics, biology, and astrology. He was raised to the nobility in 1782. Goethe's literary achievements cover many forms and closely relate to the social and emotional events of his life. His first important work was an epic drama *Götz von Berlichingen* (1773), inspired by his discovery of Shakespeare. *The Sorrows of Young Werther* (1774), an epistolary novel ending in the hero's death, caused a European sensation. After a visit to Italy, recorded in *Italian Journey* (1816–17), Goethe turned to the classicism which is demonstrated in his dramas *Iphigenia in Tauris* (1787) and *Tasso* (1790). His 'Wilhelm Meister' novels are the prototype of the German *Bildungsroman*. Goethe was a poet of great genius but outside Germany is celebrated for his major work, *Faust* (1808–32). Among his friends was the dramatist Schiller. He has emerged as the major force that created a national literature of Germany.

Gog and Magog /ˈmeɪgɒg/ **1.** the names of various people and lands in the Old Testament. **2.** nations under the dominion of Satan (Rev. 20: 8), opposed to the people of God. **3.** (in medieval legend) opponents of Alexander the Great, living north of the Caucasus. **4.** the names given to two giant statues standing in Guildhall, London, from the time of Henry V (destroyed in 1666 and 1940; replaced in 1953), either (according to Caxton) the last two survivors of a race of giants inhabiting Britain before Roman times, or (in another account) Gogmagog, chief of the giants, and Corineus, a Roman invader.

goggle *v.t./i.* **1.** to look with wide-open eyes. **2.** (of the eyes) to be rolled, to project. **3.** to roll (the eyes). —*adj.* (of the eyes) protuberant, rolling. —*n.* (in *pl.*) enclosed transparent shields for protecting the eyes from glare, dust, etc. [prob. imit. (cf. JOG)]

Gogh /gɒf/, Vincent Willem van, see VAN GOGH.

Gogol /ˈgɒgɒl/, Nikolai Vasilievich (1809–52), Russian writer, born in the Ukraine, which provided the background for his early writings. His play *The Inspector General* (1836) is a savagely satirical picture of life in a provincial Russian town. His St Petersburg stories (including *Notes of a Madman*, 1835; *The Portrait*, 1835; and *The Greatcoat*, 1842) are set in a mad city where nothing is what it seems. Living mainly abroad from 1836 to 1848, mostly in Rome, he produced his masterpiece, the comic epic *Dead Souls* (1842), but after a spiritual crisis burnt the manuscript of the second part. His fictional world is unique and fantastic, and his prose is marked by an intense imaginative power and linguistic originality.

Goidel /ˈgɔɪd(ə)l/ *n.* a member of the Gaelic people that comprise the Scots, Irish, and Manx Celts. —**Goidelic** /-ˈdelɪk/ *adj. & n.* [f. OIr.]

going /ˈgəʊɪŋ/ *n.* **1.** the state of the ground for walking or riding on. **2.** rate of progress. —*adj.* in action; existing, functioning, available; currently valid. —**get going,** to begin, to start. **going on (for),** approaching (a time, age, etc.). **going-over** *n.* (*colloq.*) an inspection or overhaul, (*slang*) a beating. **goings-on** *n.pl.* strange behaviour or events. **going to,** about to, intending or likely to. **to be going on with,** to start with, for present needs. **while the going is good,** while circumstances are favourable. [f. GO¹]

goitre /ˈgɔɪtə(r)/ *n.* abnormal enlargement of the thyroid glands. [F, ult. f. L *guttur* throat]

go-kart *n.* = KART.

gold /gəʊld/ *n.* **1.** a precious yellow malleable ductile metallic element of high density (see below), symbol Au, atomic number 79. **2.** its yellow colour. **3.** coins or articles made of gold, wealth; a gold medal, usually given as a first prize. **4.** the bull's-eye of an archery target; a shot that strikes this. **5.** something very good or precious. —*adj.* of or coloured like gold. —**gold-digger** *n.* (*slang*) a woman who uses her attractions to wheedle money out of men. **gold-dust** *n.* gold in fine particles as often found naturally. **gold-field** *n.* an area where gold is found. **gold mine,** a place where gold is mined; a source of wealth. **gold plate,** vessels of gold; material plated with gold. **gold-plate** *v.t.* to plate with gold. **gold reserve,** gold held by a central bank to guarantee the value of a country's currency. **gold-rush** *n.* a rush to a newly discovered gold-field, especially the transcontinental journey to California after the discovery of gold there in 1848. **gold standard,** a system by which the value of money is based on that of gold. Most countries held to this from 1900 until it was suspended during the First World War. It was reintroduced in 1925 but abandoned in 1931. **Gold Stick,** the bearer of a gilt rod carried on State occasions. [OE]

Gold is quite widely distributed in nature. It occurs in minute quantities in almost all rocks and in seawater, but its extraction from these is not economically feasible and most gold is collected from lodes or rock veins and the alluvial deposits that represent the disintegration of auriferous rocks; it exists in association with most copper and lead deposits, and some gold is recovered in the refining of these. It occurs naturally in the metallic state, never quite pure but alloyed with silver, copper, platinum, or certain other elements; in world production of gold South Africa is dominant, while Russia has considerable resources. Gold has been known from ancient times and valued for its colour and brightness, rareness, and durability; in normal conditions it does not corrode or tarnish. Its most important uses are for jewellery and other decorative purposes and as currency or to guarantee its value; it is also used in electrical contacts and (in some countries) as a filling for teeth. The relative purity of gold is measured in carats (see ill. HALLMARKS).

Gold Coast the name given by European traders to a coastal area of West Africa, on the Gulf of Guinea, that was an important source of gold. (See GHANA.)

goldcrest *n.* a very small bird (*Regulus regulus*) with a golden crest.

golden *adj.* **1.** made of gold. **2.** yielding gold. **3.** coloured or shining like gold. **4.** precious, excellent. —**golden age,** a period of great prosperity or cultural achievement. **golden eagle,** a large eagle (*Aquila chrysaetos*) with yellow-tipped head-feathers. **Golden Fleece,** (Gk legend) the fleece of gold taken from the ram, given by Hermes, that bore Phrixus through the air to Colchis. It was guarded by a sleepless dragon until secured by Jason with the help of Medea. (See ARGONAUTS.) **Golden Gate,** a deep channel connecting San Francisco Bay with the Pacific Ocean, spanned by a suspension bridge (1937). **golden handshake,** a gratuity as compensation for dismissal or early retirement. **Golden Horde,** a Mongol tribe which overran Asia in the 13th c., and maintained an empire of varying size in the centre of the continent until the end of the 15th c. **Golden Horn,** a curved inlet of the Bosporus, forming the harbour of Istanbul. **golden jubilee,** a 50th anniversary. **golden mean,** neither too much nor too little. **golden rod,** a plant of the genus *Solidago*, with yellow flower-spikes. **golden rule,** a basic principle of action. **golden section,** the name given in the 19th c. to the proportion (derived from a Euclidean line-division) in which the third term is the sum of the first and second (A : B = B : A + B). (See ill. SHAPES.) **golden syrup,** pale treacle. **golden wedding,** the 50th anniversary of a wedding. [f. GOLD]

Golden Hind /haɪnd/ the ship in which, in 1577–80, Francis Drake circumnavigated the globe and was knighted on his return. She was originally the *Pelican*, but Drake changed the name en route in honour of his patron, Sir Christopher Hatton, whose crest was a golden hind.

goldfinch *n.* a songbird (*Carduelis carduelis*) with a yellow band across each wing.

goldfish *n.* a small reddish Chinese carp (*Carassius auratus*), often kept as an ornamental fish.

Golding /ˈgəʊldɪŋ/, William Gerald (1911–), English novelist, who achieved literary success with his first novel *Lord of the Flies* (1954) about a group of boys who revert to savagery when stranded on a desert island. The intrinsic cruelty of man is at the heart of many of his novels, including *The Inheritors* (1955) and *Rites of Passage* (1980). In presenting man in his basic condition, in extreme situations, and 'gripped by original sin', Golding creates the quality of a fable. He was awarded the Nobel Prize for literature in 1983.

Goldsmith /ˈgəʊldsmɪθ/, Oliver (?1730–74), Anglo-Irish novelist, poet, essayist, and dramatist. After studying medicine at Edinburgh and Leyden and wandering on the Continent he arrived destitute in London in 1756 where he practised as a physician and began his literary career as a reviewer and hack-writer. His first substantial work was *An Enquiry into the Present State of Polite Learning* (1759). His masterpieces are *The Citizen of the World* (1762), a collection of satirical letters written by an imaginary Chinese philosopher, his novel *The Vicar of Wakefield* (1766), and his poem *The Deserted Village* (1770). His most successful plays were *She Stoops to Conquer* (1773) and *The Good-Natur'd*

Man (1768). Goldsmith was admired by Samuel Johnson for the charm and elegance of his writing.

goldsmith *n.* one who works in gold.

Goldwyn /'gəʊldwɪn/, Samuel (1882–1974), real name Samuel Goldfish, American film producer. He became independent by 1925, producing films of high quality in his own studio, including *Wuthering Heights* (1939), *The Little Foxes* (1941), and *The Best Years of Our Lives* (1946). He also produced some notable musicals, such as *Guys and Dolls* (1955), and the opera *Porgy and Bess* (1959). Goldwynisms such as 'Include me out' became common usage.

golf /gɒlf/ *n.* a game in which a small hard ball is struck with various clubs into a series of small cylindrical holes (now usually 18 or 9) on smooth greens at varying distances apart and separated by fairways, rough ground, hazards, etc. The aim is to drive the ball into any one hole, or into all the holes successively, with the fewest possible strokes, with two persons or two couples playing against each other. (See below.) —*v.i.* to play golf. —**golf ball**, a ball used in golf; a spherical unit carrying the type in some electric typewriters. —**golf-course** *or* **-links** *n.* an area of land on which golf is played. —**golfer** *n.* [Sc.; orig. unkn.]

The game of golf is of considerable antiquity in Scotland (the word is attested in the 15th c.) and in Holland. James II banned the game in 1457 because (like football) it interfered with the practice of archery, but royal patronage after the peace treaty of 1502 stimulated the growth of the game, and James VI of Scotland brought it south with him when he succeeded to the English throne. In early days it was played on the common links east bordering the sea.

Golgi /'gɒldʒɪ/, Camillo (1844–1926), Italian anatomist noted for his study of the minute structure of the nervous system. He devised a method of staining tissue with silver salts which revealed details of the cells and enabled individual nerve fibres to be traced, classified types of nerve cell, and described a complex structure in the cytoplasm of most cells, the 'Golgi apparatus', that is now believed to be involved in secretion. Golgi was awarded the Nobel Prize for medicine, jointly with Ramón y Cajal, in 1906.

Golgotha /'gɒlgəθə/ the Aramaic name of Calvary (Mark 15: 22). [f. Heb., = skull]

golliwog /'gɒlɪwɒg/ *n.* a black-faced soft male doll with bright clothes and fuzzy hair. [perh. f. GOLLY¹ + dial. *polliwog* tadpole]

Goliath /gə'laɪəθ/ a Philistine giant, according to legend slain by David (1 Sam. 17), but according to another tradition slain by Elhanan (2 Sam. 21: 19).

golly¹ *int.* expressing surprise. [euphem. for *God*]

golly² *n.* a golliwog. [abbr.]

golosh var. of GALOSH.

Gomorrah /gə'mɒrə/ a town of ancient Palestine, probably south of the Dead Sea, destroyed by fire from heaven (according to Genesis 19:24), along with Sodom, for the wickedness of its inhabitants.

gonad /'gəʊnæd/ *n.* an animal organ producing gametes, e.g. a testis or ovary. [f. Gk *gonē*, *gonos*, generation, seed]

Goncourt /'gɔ̃kuːr/, Edmond and Jules de (1822–96 and 1830–70), French authors, brothers, who wrote in close collaboration. Their early work included art criticism and social history. *Soeur Philomène* (1861), *Germinie Lacerteux* (1864), and *Madame Gervaisais* (1869) are among their painstakingly documented novels often cited as examples of 19th-c. realism and naturalism. The *Journal des Goncourt* is their detailed record of literary and artistic life in Paris between 1851 and 1896. The Académie Goncourt which awards the annual *Prix Goncourt* for imaginative prose was founded under the will of Edmond de Goncourt.

gondola /'gɒndələ/ *n.* 1. a light pleasure-boat, much ornamented, with a high rising and curving stem and stern-post, used on the canals of Venice and propelled by one man with a single oar, standing near the stern. Its origin is unknown but it is mentioned as early as 1094. 2. an elongated car attached to the under side of a dirigible balloon or airship (ill. FLIGHT). [It. f. dial., = rock, roll]

gondolier /gɒndə'lɪə(r)/ *n.* a rower of a gondola. [F f. It. (as prec.)]

Gondwana /gɒn'dwɑːnə/ (also **Gondwanaland**) a vast continental land area thought to have once existed in the southern hemisphere and to have broken up in Mesozoic or late Palaeozoic times to form Arabia, Africa, South America, Antarctica, Australia, and the peninsula of India. [f. *Gondwana* land of the Gonds, a Dravidian people of central India]

gone *p.p.* of GO¹.

goner /'gɒnə(r)/ *n.* (*slang*) a person or thing that is dead, ruined, or irretrievably lost. [f. prec.]

gonfalon /'gɒnfələn/ *n.* a banner, often with streamers, hung from a crossbar. [f. It. f. Gmc]

gong *n.* 1. a large metal disc with a turned rim giving a resonant note when struck, especially one used as a signal for meals. 2. a percussion instrument which exists in widely varying shapes and sizes, generally comprising a large hanging bronze disc with a bossed centre which is struck in the middle with a soft-headed drumstick. Today the name 'tam-tam' refers to a gong of indefinite pitch, and 'gong' to one which may be tuned to a specific pitch. The ancient gong dates from at least the 6th c. AD in an area extending from Tibet to Indonesia (in the latter, for example, forming an important part of the gamelan); in the West it began to appear in orchestral music towards the end of the 19th c. 3. a saucer-shaped bell. 4. (*slang*) a medal. [f. Malay (imit.)]

goniometer /gəʊnɪ'ɒmɪtə(r)/ *n.* an instrument for measuring angles. [f. F f. Gk *gōnia* angle + -METER]

gonorrhoea /gɒnə'riːə/ *n.* a venereal disease with an inflammatory discharge from the urethra or vagina. [L f. Gk (*gonos* semen, *rhoia* flux)]

goo *n.* (*slang*) 1. a viscous or sticky substance. 2. sickly sentiment. [perh. f. slang *burgoo* porridge]

good /gʊd/ *adj.* (*compar.* BETTER; *superl.* BEST) 1. having the right or desirable qualities, satisfactory. 2. right, proper, expedient. 3. commendable, worthy (esp. in *my good man* etc.). 4. morally correct, virtuous; (of a child) well-behaved. 5. agreeable, enjoyable. 6. suitable, efficient, competent. 7. thorough, considerable. 8. valid, genuine; financially sound. 9. not less than. 10. used in exclamations (*good God!*, *gracious!*, etc.). —*adv.* (*US colloq.*) well. —*n.* 1. a good quality or circumstance, especially what is beneficial or morally right. 2. (in *pl.*) movable property or merchandise; things to be transported or supplied. —**the good,** (*pl.*) good people. **all in good time,** in due course but without haste. **as good as,** practically. **for good (and all),** finally, permanently. **good afternoon, day,** etc., forms used in greeting or parting. **good faith,** an honest or sincere intention. **good for,** beneficial to, having a good effect on; able to undertake or pay. **good-for-nothing** *adj.* worthless; (*n.*) a worthless person. **Good Friday,** the Friday before Easter Sunday, commemorating the Crucifixion. **good-looking** *adj.* having a pleasing appearance. **in good time,** with no risk of being late. **good will,** an intention that good shall result (see also GOODWILL). **to the good,** having as a profit or benefit. [OE]

goodbye /gʊd'baɪ/, *int.* farewell (expressing good wishes on parting, ending a telephone conversation, etc.). —*n.* a parting, a farewell. [contr. of *God be with you*]

goodly /'gʊdlɪ/ *adj.* 1. handsome. 2. of imposing size etc. —**goodliness** *n.* [OE (as GOOD)]

Goodman /'gʊdmən/, Benjamin David ('Benny') (1909–), American clarinettist and jazz musician, who formed his own band in 1933. He was known as the 'King of Swing' and his style started a new era in the history of jazz. His skill as a clarinettist was not confined to jazz: Bartók, Hindemith, and Copland all composed solo works for him, and he also gave distinguished performances of classical works.

goodness *n.* 1. virtue, excellence; kindness. 2. used instead of 'God' in exclamations. [OE (as GOOD)]

goodwill *n.* 1. kindly feeling. 2. the established reputation of a business etc. as enhancing its value.

goody *n.* 1. something good or attractive, especially to eat. 2. (*colloq.*) a good or favoured person. —*int.* expressing childish delight. [f. GOOD]

goody-goody *adj.* obtrusively or smugly virtuous. —*n.* a goody-goody person. [f. GOOD]

gooey *adj.* (*slang*) 1. viscous or sticky. 2. sentimental. [f. GOO]

goof *n.* (*slang*) 1. a foolish or stupid person. 2. a mistake. —*v.t./i.* (*slang*) 1. to blunder, to bungle. 2. to idle. —**goofy** *adj.* [f. F f. It. f. L *gufus* coarse]

googly /'guːglɪ/ *n.* a ball in cricket bowled so as to bounce in an unexpected direction. [orig. unkn.]

goon *n.* (*slang*) 1. a stupid person. 2. a hired ruffian. [perh. f. dial. *gooney* booby; influenced by subhuman cartoon character 'Alice the *Goon*']

goosander /guː'sændə(r)/ *n.* a duck (*Mergus merganser*) with a sharp serrated bill. [app. f. foll.]

goose *n.* (*pl.* **geese**) **1.** a web-footed bird of the genus *Anser* or subfamily Anserinae, between a duck and a swan in size; the female of this (cf. GANDER); the flesh of the goose as food. **2.** a simpleton. **3.** (*pl.* **gooses**) a tailor's smoothing-iron (with a handle like a goose's neck). —**goose-flesh** *or* -**pimples** *ns.* a bristling state of the skin due to cold or fright. **goose-neck** *n.* a thing shaped like the neck of a goose. **goose-step** *n.* a parade-step of marching soldiers with the legs kept straight. [OE]

gooseberry /ˈɡʊzbəri/ *n.* a small green sour berry; the thorny shrub bearing it (*Ribes grossularia*). —**play gooseberry**, to be an unwanted extra person. [perh. f. prec.]

gopher /ˈɡəʊfə(r)/ *n.* **1.** an American burrowing rodent of the genus *Geomys* or *Thomomys*. **2.** a ground-squirrel of the genus *Citellus*. **3.** a burrowing tortoise (*Testudo carolina*). [perh. f. Canadian F *gaufre* honeycomb]

Gorbachov /ˈɡɔːbətʃɒf/, Mikhail Sergeevich (1931–), Russian statesman, General Secretary of the Communist Party of the USSR 1985–.

Gordian /ˈɡɔːdiən/ *adj.* **cut the Gordian knot,** to solve a problem forcefully. [f. *Gordius*, king of ancient Phrygia, who tied an intricate knot that was later cut, rather than untied, by Alexander the Great]

Gordon /ˈɡɔːd(ə)n/, Charles George (1833–85), British general and colonial administrator, known as 'Chinese Gordon' after service against the Taiping rebels in 1863–4. Sent to rescue the Egyptian garrisons in the Sudan from the Dervishes, he was trapped at Khartoum and killed before a relieving force could reach him.

Gordon riots /ˈɡɔːd(ə)n/ a series of anti-Catholic riots in London on 2–9 June 1780, in which about 300 people were killed. The riots were provoked by a petition presented to Parliament by Lord George Gordon against the relaxation of restrictions on the holding of landed property by Roman Catholics.

gore[1] *n.* blood shed and clotted. [OE, = dirt]

gore[2] *v.t.* to pierce with a horn, tusk, etc. [orig. unkn.]

gore[3] *n.* a wedge-shaped piece in a garment; a triangular or tapering piece in an umbrella etc. —*v.t.* to shape with a gore. [OE, = triangle of land]

gorge *n.* **1.** a narrow opening between hills (ill. RIVERS). **2.** gorging, a surfeit. **3.** the contents of the stomach. —*v.t./i.* **1.** to feed or devour greedily. **2.** to satiate; to choke up. —**one's gorge rises at,** one is sickened by. [f. OF, = throat]

gorgeous /ˈɡɔːdʒəs/ *adj.* richly coloured, sumptuous; (*colloq.*) strikingly beautiful; (*colloq.*) very pleasant, splendid. —**gorgeously** *adv.*, **gorgeousness** *n.* [f. OF *gorgias* elegant]

gorgon /ˈɡɔːɡən/ *n.* **1.** a frightening woman. **2.** **Gorgon,** (*Gk myth.*) any of three sisters, Stheno, Euryale, and Medusa (the only mortal one), with snakes for hair, whose look turned the beholder to stone. [f. L f. Gk *Gorgō* (*gorgos* terrible)]

Gorgonzola /ɡɔːɡənˈzəʊlə/ *n.* a kind of rich blue-veined cheese. [f. *Gorgonzola* in N. Italy]

gorilla /ɡəˈrɪlə/ *n.* a large powerful anthropoid ape. [perh. Afr. = wild man, in Gk account of Hanno's voyage (5th or 6th c. BC), adapted as specific name 1847]

Gorky /ˈɡɔːkɪ/, Maxim (pseudonym of Alexei Maximovich Peshkov, 1868–1936) Russian novelist, playwright, and revolutionary, who was largely self-educated, being obliged to earn his living from the age of eight. His childhood experiences of wanderings all over Russia are related in his autobiographical masterpiece *Childhood* (1913), *Among People* (1915), and *My Universities* (1923). Gorky became famous for the short realistic stories that he published in 1895–1900, and followed these with novels and plays including *The Mother* (1906–7, the story of the radicalization of an uneducated woman, which became a model for the socialist-realist novel), and *The Lower Depths* (1902), but suffered for his radical views. From 1906 to 1913 and again from 1921 to 1928 he lived abroad, then returning to Russia as an enthusiastic supporter of the government and Stalinism. Officially lionized as the father of the new socialist art, he was partly responsible for the doctrine of socialist realism, and became president of the Union of Soviet Writers in 1934. His last years and the circumstances of his death are shrouded in mystery.

gormandize /ˈɡɔːməndaɪz/ *v.t./i.* to eat greedily. —**gormandizer** *n.* [f. GOURMAND]

gormless /ˈɡɔːmlɪs/ *adj.* (*colloq.*) foolish, lacking sense. [f. dial. *gaum* understanding]

gorse *n.* furze. —**gorsy** *adj.* [OE]

Gorsedd /ˈɡɔːseð/ *n.* a meeting of Welsh etc. bards and druids (especially as the preliminary to an eisteddfod). [Welsh, lit. 'throne']

gory /ˈɡɔːrɪ/ *adj.* covered with blood; involving bloodshed. —**gorily** *adv.*, **goriness** *n.* [f. GORE[1]]

gosh *int.* expressing surprise. [euphem. for *God*]

goshawk /ˈɡɒshɔːk/ *n.* a large hawk (*Accipiter gentilis*) with short wings. [OE (as GOOSE, HAWK[1])]

gosling /ˈɡɒzlɪŋ/ *n.* a young goose. [dim. of GOOSE]

gospel /ˈɡɒspəl/ *n.* **1.** the tidings of redemption preached by Christ. **2. Gospel,** each of the four books in which this was set forth (the use probably originated from the occurrence of the word in the opening sentence at Mark 1: 1), attributed to Matthew, Mark, Luke, and John. **3.** a thing that may safely be believed; a principle one acts upon or advocates. [OE (as GOOD, SPELL[1] = news)]

gossamer /ˈɡɒsəmə(r)/ *n.* **1.** the filmy substance of small spiders' webs. **2.** delicate flimsy material. —*adj.* light and flimsy as gossamer. [app. f. GOOSE + SUMMER, (*goose summer*, St Martin's summer, i.e. early November)]

gossip /ˈɡɒsɪp/ *n.* **1.** casual talk or writing, especially about persons or social incidents. **2.** a person indulging in gossip. —*v.i.* to talk or write gossip. —**gossip column,** a section of a newspaper devoted to gossip about well-known people. —**gossipy** *adj.* [OE, orig. = godparent (GOD, SIB)]

got *past* & *p.p.* of GET.

Goth /ɡɒθ/ *n.* a member of a Germanic tribe which invaded the Roman Empire from the east between the 3rd and 5th centuries. The eastern half of the tribe, the Ostrogoths, eventually founded a kingdom in Italy, while the Visigoths, their western cousins, went on to found one in Spain. [f. L *Gothi* f. Gk f. Gothic]

Gothic /ˈɡɒθɪk/ *adj.* **1.** of the Goths. **2.** in the style of architecture prevalent in western Europe in the 12th–16th c., characterized by pointed arches. **3.** (*Print.*) of an old-fashioned German style of type, also known as 'black letter'. —*n.* **1.** Gothic architecture or type. **2.** the Gothic language, which constitutes the oldest manuscript evidence for the Germanic language group. It belongs to the East Germanic group and was spoken in the area to the north and west of the Black Sea. The evidence is fragmentary, the main text being part of a Gothic translation of the Greek Bible written in the 4th c. by Bishop Wulfila. **3.** Gothic type. —**Gothic novel** etc., an English genre of fiction, popular in the 18th–early 19th c., characterized by an atmosphere of mystery and horror and with a pseudo-medieval ('Gothic') setting. Examples include Horace Walpole's *Castle of Otranto* (1765) and Ann Radcliffe's *The Mysteries of Udolpho* (1794). **Gothic revival,** the reintroduction in England of Gothic architecture towards the middle of the 19th c. [f. F or L (as GOTH)]

gotten see GET.

Götterdämmerung /ɡɜːtəˈdemərʊŋ/ *n.* the twilight of the gods (see TWILIGHT), the complete downfall of a regime etc. [G, esp. as title of opera by Wagner]

gouache /ɡuːˈɑːʃ/ *n.* painting with opaque pigments ground in water and thickened with gum and honey; these pigments. [F, f. It. *guazzo*]

Gouda /ˈɡaʊdə/ *n.* a flat round cheese with yellow rind, originally made at Gouda in Holland.

gouge /ɡaʊdʒ/ *n.* a chisel with a concave blade. —*v.t.* **1.** to cut with or as with a gouge. **2.** to scoop or force *out*. [F, f. L. *gubia*, perh. f. Celtic]

goulash /ˈɡuːlæʃ/ *n.* a stew of meat and vegetables highly seasoned with paprika. [f. Magyar, = herdsman's meat]

Gounod /ˈɡuːnəʊ/, Charles François (1818–93), French composer, conductor, and organist, a Parisian born and bred. He wrote his first opera in 1851 but did not achieve success in the opera house until 1859 with *Faust*, a grand opera in the French tradition but with a lyrical grace and an easy naturalism quite new to the genre. Gounod's later operas have not maintained their popularity to the extent that *Faust*—translated into over 25 languages—has, but *Roméo et Juliette* (1867) is still heard and several of his songs remain in the French repertory.

gourd /ɡʊəd/ *n.* **1.** the fleshy usually large fruit of a trailing or climbing plant of the family Cucurbitaceae. **2.** the dried rind of this fruit used as a bottle. [f. AF, ult. f. L *cucurbita*]

gourmand /ˈɡʊəmənd/ *n.* **1.** a glutton. **2.** a gourmet. [f. OF; orig. unkn.]

gourmandise /ˈɡʊəmɑ̃diːz/ *n.* gluttony. [F (as prec.)]

gourmet /ˈɡʊəmeɪ/ n. a connoisseur of good or delicate food. [F, = wine-taster]

gout n. a disease with inflammation of the joints, especially of the big toe. —**gouty** adj. [f. OF f. L gutta drop]

govern /ˈɡʌv(ə)n/ v.t. **1.** to rule or control with authority, to conduct the policy and affairs of. **2.** to influence or determine (a person or course of action etc.). **3.** to restrain or control. **4.** (Gram., esp. of a verb or preposition) to have (a noun or its case) depending on it. [f. OF f. L gubernare f. Gk kubernaō steer]

governance /ˈɡʌvənəns/ n. the act, manner, or function of governing. [f. OF (as prec.)]

governess /ˈɡʌv(ə)nɪs/ n. fem. a woman employed to teach children in a private household. [f. OF (as GOVERNOR)]

government /ˈɡʌvənmənt/ n. **1.** governing; the manner or system of this; the form of organization of a State. **2.** the group of persons governing a State. **3.** the State as an agent. —**governmental** /-ˈment(ə)l/ adj. [f. OF (as GOVERN)]

governor /ˈɡʌv(ə)nə(r)/ n. **1.** a ruler; an official governing a province, town, etc., or representing the Crown in a colony. **2.** the executive head of each State of the USA. **3.** an officer commanding a fortress etc. **4.** the head, or a member of the governing body, of an institution; the official in charge of a prison; (slang) one's employer or father. **5.** an automatic regulator controlling the speed of an engine, etc. —**Governor-General** n. a representative of the Crown in a Commonwealth country that regards the Queen as the Head of State. [f. AF f. L gubernator (as GOVERN)]

gown n. **1.** a loose flowing garment, especially a long dress worn by a woman. **2.** the loose flowing outer garment that is the official or uniform robe of a lawyer, judge, member of a university, etc. **3.** a surgeon's overall. [f. OF f. L gunna fur garment]

goy n. (pl. **goyim** or **goys**) the Jewish name for a non-Jew. [f. Heb. goy people]

Goya y Lucientes /ˈɡɔɪə iː luːˈθɪˈentiz/, Francisco José de (1746–1828), Spanish painter and etcher, whose early tapestry cartoons (1776–91) presented idyllic and everyday scenes with rococo lightness and charm, contributing to his appointment as court painter in 1789. An illness, 1792–4, left him stone deaf, and from this time darker themes of fantasy, terror, and menace predominate. In his day, Goya was celebrated for his portraits, such as *The Family of Charles IV* (1800), which reveals the weaknesses of the royal family with unsparing realism. Most admired today, however, are the works which express his reaction to the French occupation of Spain 1808–14: *The Shootings of May 3rd 1808* (1814), and the set of 65 etchings *Los Desastres de la Guerra* (1810–14), a savage nightmarish attack on the cruelty and horror of war. In 1824 he settled in Bordeaux, where he took up the new medium of lithography. His work was an important influence on the impressionists, especially Manet.

GP abbr. general practitioner.

GPO abbr. General Post Office.

gr. abbr. **1.** gram(s). **2.** grain(s). **3.** gross.

Graafian follicle or **vesicle** /ˈɡrɑːfɪən/ each of the small sacs in the mammal ovary in which ova are matured. [f. R. de Graaf, Dutch anatomist (d. 1673)]

grab v.t./i. (**-bb-**) **1.** to grasp suddenly; to snatch at. **2.** to take greedily; to appropriate. **3.** (of brakes) to act harshly or jerkily. **4.** (slang) to attract the attention of, to impress. —n. **1.** a sudden clutch or attempt to seize. **2.** a mechanical device for gripping things and lifting them. [f. MLG or MDu.; cf. GRIP]

graben /ˈɡrɑːbən/ n. a depression of the earth's surface between faults (ill. GEOLOGY). [G, orig. = ditch]

Gracchus /ˈɡrækəs/, Tiberius Sempronius (d. 133 BC), the elder of two aristocratic Roman brothers who, as tribunes of the people, pushed through revolutionary social and economic legislation against the wishes of the senatorial class. He was killed by his opponents after the passing of his agrarian bill (133 BC) which aimed at a redistribution of land by limiting the amount that could be held and dividing the surplus amongst poorer citizens. Gaius Sempronius Gracchus continued his brother's programme and instituted other reforms to relieve poverty, but was killed in a riot in 121 BC over the proposal to grant Roman citizenship to the people of Latium.

Grace /ɡreɪs/, Dr William Gilbert (1848–1915), English cricketer, the best-known of all in the history of the game, who was supreme amongst his contemporaries. He began

playing at the highest level while still a youth, and played in his last test match at the age of 50.

grace n. **1.** attractiveness, especially in design, manner, or movement. **2.** becoming courtesy. **3.** manner, bearing; an attractive feature, an accomplishment. **4.** (in Christian theology) the supernatural assistance of God bestowed upon a rational being with a view to his salvation. The nature and conditions of divine grace were a subject of controversy between St Augustine and the adherents of Pelagianism, and between Calvin and his opponents at the Reformation. **5.** goodwill, favour; a delay granted as a favour. **6.** a prayer of thanksgiving before or after a meal. —v.t. to add grace to; to bestow honour on. —**grace-and-favour house** etc., a house etc. occupied by permission of a sovereign. **grace-note** n. a note embellishing a melody or harmony but not essential to it. **His, Her, Your**, etc., **Grace**, a title used in addressing or referring to a duke, duchess, or archbishop. **in a person's good graces**, in his favour. **with a good** (or **bad**) **grace**, as if willingly (or reluctantly). **year of grace**, a year of the Christian era. [f. OF f. L gratia (gratus pleasing)]

graceful adj. having or showing grace or elegance. —**gracefully** adv., **gracefulness**. n. [f. GRACE + -FUL]

graceless adj. lacking grace, inelegant, ungracious. [f. GRACE + -LESS]

Graces /ˈɡreɪsɪz/ n.pl. (Gk myth.) beautiful goddesses, usually three (Aglaia, Thalia, Euphrosyne), daughters of Zeus, personifying charm, grace, and beauty, which they bestowed as physical, intellectual, artistic, and moral qualities.

gracious /ˈɡreɪʃəs/ adj. kind, indulgent and beneficent to inferiors; (of God) merciful, benign. —int. expressing surprise. —**gracious living**, an elegant way of life. —**graciously** adv., **graciousness** n. [f. OF f. L (as GRACE)]

gradate /ɡrəˈdeɪt/ v.t./i. to pass or cause to pass by gradations from one shade to another; to arrange in gradations. [back-formation f. foll.]

gradation /ɡrəˈdeɪʃ(ə)n/ n. **1.** (usu. in pl.) a stage of transition or advance. **2.** a degree in rank, merit, intensity, etc.; arrangement in such degrees. **3.** gradual passing from one shade or tone etc. to another. —**gradational** adj. [f. L gradatio (as foll.)]

grade n. **1.** a step, stage, or degree in rank, quality, proficiency, etc. **2.** a class of persons or things of the same grade. **3.** a mark indicating the quality of a student's work. **4.** a slope. **5.** (US) a class or form in a school. —v.t./i. **1.** to arrange in grades. **2.** to give a grade to (a student). **3.** to reduce (a road etc.) to easy gradients. **4.** to pass gradually between grades or into a grade. —**grade school**, (US) an elementary school. **make the grade**, to succeed. [F, or f. L gradus step]

gradient /ˈɡreɪdɪənt/ n. the amount of slope in a road, railway, etc.; a sloping road etc. [prob. f. prec., after salient]

gradual /ˈɡrædjʊəl/ adj. occurring by degrees, not rapid or steep or abrupt. —**gradually** adv. [f. L (as GRADE)]

gradualism n. a policy of gradual change. [f. prec.]

graduate /ˈɡrædjʊət/ n. the holder of an academic degree. —/-eɪt/ v.t./i. **1.** to take an academic degree. **2.** to move up to (a higher grade of activity etc.). **3.** to mark out in degrees or parts; to arrange in gradations; to apportion (tax) according to a scale. —**graduation** /-ˈeɪʃ(ə)n/ n. [f. L graduari take degree (as GRADE)]

Graeco-Roman /ˈɡriːkəʊˈrəʊmən/ adj. of the Greeks and Romans. [f. L Graecus Greek + ROMAN]

graffito /ɡrəˈfiːtəʊ/ n. (pl. **-ti** /-tiː/) writing or a drawing scribbled or scratched on a wall etc. [It. (graffio scratching)]

graft[1] /ɡrɑːft/ n. **1.** a shoot or scion from one plant or tree planted in a slit made in another. **2.** a piece of living tissue transplanted surgically. **3.** the process of grafting. **4.** (slang) hard work. —v.t./i. **1.** to insert (a graft) in or on; to transplant (living tissue). **2.** to fix or join (a thing) permanently to another. **3.** (slang) to work hard. [f. OF grafe f. L f. Gk graphion stylus]

graft[2] /ɡrɑːft/ n. (colloq.) practices, especially bribery, used to secure illicit gains in politics or business; such gains. —v.i. to seek or make such gains. [orig. unkn.]

Grail /ɡreɪl/ n. **the Holy Grail**, an object of quest in medieval legend, conferring mystical benefits. Its origin, nature, and significance are unknown. From the late 12th c. onwards it was given a Christian significance (though no church authority has ever recognized the legend), and was supposed to be the vessel from which Christ drank at the Last Supper and in which Joseph of Arimathea, who acquired it and brought it to England, had caught some of the blood of the crucified Christ; in other legends it was the dish used at the Last Supper. By the early 13th c. it had become attached to the Arthurian cycle of legends as a symbol of perfection sought by the knights of the Round Table. The three principal ways of explaining its origin and motivation are (1) as a Christian legend, which altered only in detail through its history; (2) as an ancient pagan fertility ritual, 'the horn of plenty'; (3) as a Celtic story, already mythological in its origins in Irish, transmitted through Welsh and Breton to the French romance tradition and gradually Christianized. [f. F f. L *gradalis* dish]

grain *n.* **1.** the fruit or a seed of a cereal; (*collect.*) wheat or an allied food-grass, its fruit, corn. **2.** a small hard particle of salt, sand, etc. **3.** the smallest unit of weight in some systems, 0.0648 gram; the least possible amount. **4.** granular texture, roughness of a surface; the texture produced by the particles in skin, wood, stone, etc.; the pattern of the lines of fibre in wood or paper, the lamination in stone, etc. —*v.t./i.* **1.** to paint in imitation of the grain of wood etc. **2.** to give a granular surface to. **3.** to dye in the grain. **4.** to form into grains. —**against the grain,** contrary to one's natural inclination or feeling. —**grainy** *adj.* [f. OF f. L *granum*]

grallatorial /ˌgrælə'tɔːrɪəl/ *adj.* of the long-legged wading birds. [f. L *grallator* stilt-walker (*grallae* stilts)]

Gram /græm/, Hans Christian Joachim (1853–1938), Danish physician and bacteriologist, who invented a technique of staining bacteria and discovered that certain species (called gram-positive) retained the colour, while others lost it (gram-negative). This became a useful technique for classifying micro-organisms.

gram *n.* the metric unit of mass, 0.001 kilogram, originally defined as the mass of 1 cc of pure water at its maximum density. [f. F *gramme* f. Gk *gramma* small weight]

-gram *suffix* forming nouns denoting a thing (so) written or recorded (*diagram, monogram, telegram*); cf. -GRAPH. [f. Gk *gramma* thing written (*graphō* write)]

graminaceous /ˌgræmɪ'neɪʃəs/ *adj.* of or like grass. [f. L *gramen* grass]

graminivorous /ˌgræmɪ'nɪvərəs/ *adj.* feeding on grass, cereals, etc. [as prec. + L *vorare* devour]

grammar /'græmə(r)/ *n.* **1.** the study of the main elements of a language, including its sounds, inflections or other means of showing the relation between words as used in speech or writing, and the established rules for using these (often limited to phonology, morphology, and syntax, and excluding vocabulary, stylistics, etc.; see LINGUISTICS). **2.** the elements themselves. **3.** a treatise or book on grammar. **4.** a person's manner of using grammatical forms; speech or writing regarded as good or bad by the rules of grammar. **5.** the elements of an art or science. —**generative grammar,** a theory which aims at formulating for each language a set of rules capable of 'generating' all the infinite sentences of that language and providing them with the correct structural description. The theory, which was obviously influenced by mathematics, is best known in the many versions which it had in the USA from the 1960s onwards. **grammar school,** see separate entry. **transformational grammar,** a form of generative grammar which makes use of operations called 'transformations' which systematically indicate the links between various types of sentences (e.g. declarative and interrogative, active and passive) and derive one type from the other. The use of transformations in linguistics started with the American linguist Z. S. Harris (1909–), but transformational grammar is more commonly associated with the name of N. Chomsky. [f. AF f. L f. Gk *grammatikē* (*tekhnē* art) of letters of the alphabet]

grammarian /grə'meərɪən/ *n.* an expert in grammar or linguistics. [f. OF (as prec.)]

grammar school any of a class of (usually endowed) schools founded in the 16th c. or earlier for teaching Latin, with some instruction also in literature and elementary mathematics. By the end of the 19th c. they had become secondary schools with a curriculum including languages, literature, history, and science, and under the Education Act of 1947 offered a similar curriculum for pupils with academic ability. Since 1965 many have been absorbed into or replaced by comprehensive schools.

grammatical /grə'mætɪk(ə)l/ *adj.* of or according to grammar. —**grammatically** *adv.* [F, or f. L f. Gk (as GRAMMAR)]

gramme var. of GRAM.

gramophone /'græməfəʊn/ *n.* an instrument for reproducing recorded sounds such as music or speech. The sound-wave is defined by a pattern of lateral waves moulded into a fine spiral groove in a thin plastic disc, the 'record'. A fine stylus is used under a pickup to sense the lateral vibrations as the disc is rotated about its centre at a steady speed of revolution. Formerly the stylus acted directly on a diaphragm, creating sound-waves which were amplified by a divergent horn, but modern pick-ups use a variable magnetic circuit and coil to induce a varying voltage, which is amplified electronically and passed to a loudspeaker. The gramophone evolved from the earlier phonograph, invented by Thomas Edison in 1877, which used a rotating wax cylinder to record and reproduce sound waves. The flat gramophone disc, with a needle moving in a groove, was the invention of the German-American Emile Berliner (1851–1929) in 1888. [inversion of PHONOGRAM]

Grampian /'græmpɪən/ a local government region in NE Scotland.

grampus /'græmpəs/ *n.* a sea-animal (*Grampus griseus*) resembling the dolphin and famous for blowing. [f. OF f. L (*crassus piscis* fat fish)]

gran *n.* (*colloq.*) a grandmother. [abbr.]

granadilla /ˌgrænə'dɪlə/ *n.* a passion-fruit. [Sp., dim. of *granada* pomegranate]

granary /'grænərɪ/ *n.* **1.** a storehouse for threshed grain. **2.** a region producing, and especially exporting, much corn. [f. L *granarium* (as GRAIN)]

grand *adj.* **1.** splendid, magnificent, imposing, dignified. **2.** main, of chief importance; of the highest rank. **3.** (*colloq.*) excellent, enjoyable. —*n.* **1.** a grand piano. **2.** (*slang*) a thousand pounds, dollars, etc. —**grand jury,** (*US*) a jury convened to decide whether the evidence against an accused justifies a trial. **grand opera,** an opera on a serious theme, or in which the entire libretto is sung and there are no spoken parts. **grand piano,** a large full-toned piano with horizontal strings. **grand slam,** see SLAM². **grand total,** the sum of other totals. **grand tour,** (*hist.*) a tour of the chief cities etc. of Europe, completing a person's education; an extensive tour. —**grandly** *adv.*, **grandness** *n.* [f. OF f. L *grandis* full-grown)]

grand- *in comb.* denoting the second degree of ascent or descent in relationships. [= prec.]

grandad *n.* (*colloq.*) a grandfather; an elderly man. [f. GRAND- + DAD]

grandam /'grændæm/ *n.* (*archaic*) a grandmother; an elderly woman. [f. AF (as GRAND, DAME)]

Grand Canyon a deep gorge about 350 km (217 miles) long, formed by the Colorado River in Arizona, USA. It is 8–24 km (5–15 miles) wide and, in places, 1,800 m (6,000 ft.) deep.

grandchild *n.* a person's child's child. [f. GRAND- + CHILD]

grand-dad var. of GRANDAD.

granddaughter *n.* a female grandchild. [f. GRAND- + DAUGHTER]

grandee /græn'diː/ *n.* a Spanish or Portuguese noble of high rank; a great personage. [f. Sp. & Port. *grande* (as GRAND)]

grandeur /'grændjə(r), -ndʒə(r)/ *n.* splendour, magnificence, grandness; high rank, eminence; nobility of character. [F (as GRAND)]

grandfather *n.* a male grandparent. —**grandfather clock,** a clock in a tall wooden case, worked by weights. [f. GRAND- + FATHER]

Grand Guignol see GUIGNOL.

grandiloquent /græn'dɪləkwənt/ *adj.* pompous or inflated in language. —**grandiloquence** *n.*, **grandiloquently** *adv.* [f. L *grandiloquus* (as GRAND, *loqui* speak)]

grandiose /'grændɪəʊs/ *adj.* producing or meant to produce an imposing effect; planned on a large scale. —**grandiosity** /-'ɒsɪtɪ/ *n.* [F f. It. (as GRAND)]

grandma /'grænmɑː/ *n.* (*colloq.*) a grandmother. [f. GRAND- + MA]

grand mal /grɑ̃ mæl/ epilepsy with loss of consciousness. [F, = great sickness]

grandmaster *n.* a chess-player of the highest class.

grandmother *n.* a female grandparent. [f. GRAND- + MOTHER]

Grand National a steeplechase established in 1839, run annually over a course of 4 miles 856 yds (about 7,200 metres) with 30 jumps at Aintree, Liverpool, in the first week of the flat-racing season.

Grand Prix /grɑ̃ 'priː/ **1.** (in full **Grand Prix de Paris**) an international horse-race for three-year-olds, founded in 1863 and run annually in June at Longchamp near Paris.

2. any of various important motor-racing contests, governed by international rules. [F, = great or chief prize]

grandsire *n.* (*archaic*) a grandfather. [f. GRAND- + SIRE]

grandson *n.* a male grandchild. [f. GRAND- + SON]

grandstand *n.* the main stand for spectators at a racecourse etc. —**grandstand finish,** a close and exciting finish to a race, etc.

grange /greɪndʒ/ *n.* a country house with farm-buildings. [f. AF f. L *granica* (as GRAIN)]

graniferous /grəˈnɪfərəs/ *adj.* producing grain or grainlike seed. [as GRAIN + L *ferre* bear]

granite /ˈgrænɪt/ *n.* a granular crystalline plutonic rock consisting mainly of quartz, feldspar, and (commonly) mica, used for building. —**granitic** /-ˈnɪtɪk/ *adj.* [f. It. *granito* grained (L *granum* grain)]

granivorous /grəˈnɪvərəs/ *adj.* feeding on grains. [as GRAIN + L *vorare* devour]

granny *n.* (*colloq.*) (also **grannie**) a grandmother. —**granny flat,** a part of a house, made into self-contained accommodation for a relative. **granny knot,** a reef-knot crossed the wrong way and therefore insecure. [dim. of obs. *grannam* for GRANDAM]

Grant /grɑːnt/, Ulysses Simpson (1822–85), Union general and later President of the USA (1869–77). Having made his reputation through a series of victories in the western theatre of the American Civil War (most notably the capture of Vicksburg in 1863), Grant was made supreme commander of the northern armies. By pursuing a policy of attrition he was eventually able to wear down the Confederate Army of Northern Virginia and bring the war to an end. He was elected President in 1868 but proved unequal to the post and was unable to check widespread political corruption and inefficiency.

grant /grɑːnt/ *v.t.* **1.** to consent to fulfil (a request etc.). **2.** to give formally, to transfer (property) legally. **3.** to admit as true; to concede, to allow. —*n.* **1.** something granted, especially a sum of money. **2.** granting; formal conferment. —**take for granted,** to assume to be true or valid; to cease to appreciate through familiarity. [f. OF *gr(e)anter* ult. f. L *credere* entrust]

Granth /grʌnt/ = ADI GRANTH.

Grantha /ˈgrʌntə/ *n.* a South Indian alphabet dating from the 5th c. AD, used by the Tamil brahmins for the Sanskrit transcriptions of their sacred books. [Skr., = tying, literary composition]

grantor /grɑːnˈtɔː(r)/ *n.* a person by whom property etc. is legally transferred. [f. GRANT]

granular /ˈgrænjʊlə(r)/ *adj.* of or like grains or granules. —**granularity** /-ˈlærɪtɪ/ *n.* [f. L (as GRANULE)]

granulate /ˈgrænjʊleɪt/ *v.t./i.* **1.** to form into grains. **2.** to roughen the surface of. **3.** (of a wound etc.) to form small prominences as the beginning of healing or junction. —**granulation** /-ˈleɪʃ(ə)n/ *n.* [as prec.]

granule /ˈgrænjuːl/ *n.* a small grain. [f. L *granulum* dim. of *granum* grain]

grape *n.* a berry (usually green or purple) growing in clusters on a vine, used as a fruit and in making wine. —**grape hyacinth,** a small plant of the genus *Muscari* with a cluster of flowers, usually blue. (*hist.*) small balls as a scattering charge for cannon. **grape-vine** *n.* a vine; a means of transmission of rumour. [f. OF, = bunch of grapes]

grapefruit *n.* (*pl.* same) a large round yellow citrus fruit (that of *Citrus paradisi*) with an acid juicy pulp.

graph /grɑːf/ *n.* a diagram showing the relation of two variable quantities each measured along one of a pair of axes. —*v.t.* to plot or trace on a graph. —**graph paper,** paper ruled with a grid of lines as a help in drawing graphs. [abbr. of *graphic formula*]

-graph /grɑːf/ *suffix* forming nouns denoting a thing written or drawn etc. in a specified way (*holograph*, *photograph*), an instrument that records (*telegraph*), or the corresponding verbs. [f. F f. L f. Gk (*graphō* write)]

graphic /ˈgræfɪk/ *adj.* **1.** of writing, drawing, etching, etc. **2.** vividly descriptive. —**graphically** *adv.* [f. L f. Gk (*graphē* writing)]

-graphic /-ˈgræfɪk/ *suffix* (also **-graphical**) forming adjectives from nouns in -*graph* or -*graphy*. [f. Gk (as prec.)]

graphics /ˈgræfɪks/ *n.pl.* **1.** the products of the graphic arts. **2.** (usu. treated as sing.) the use of diagrams in calculation and design. [f. GRAPHIC]

graphite /ˈgræfaɪt/ *n.* a crystalline allotropic electrically-conducting form of carbon used in pencils (see LEAD[2] 2) as

a lubricant, in various electrical devices, as a moderator in nuclear reactors, etc. —**graphitic** /-ˈɪtɪk/ *adj.* [f. G f. Gk *graphō* write]

graphology /grəˈfɒlədʒɪ/ *n.* the study of handwriting, especially as a guide to character. —**graphological** /-ˈlɒdʒɪk(ə)l/ *adj.*, **graphologist** *n.* [as GRAPHIC + -LOGY]

-graphy *suffix* forming nouns denoting a descriptive science (*geography*) or a style or method of writing etc. (*calligraphy*, *stenography*). [ult. f. Gk *graphia* writing]

grapnel /ˈgræpn(ə)l/ *n.* an instrument with iron claws, for dragging or grasping things; a small anchor with several flukes. [f. OF *grapon*]

grapple *v.t./i.* **1.** to seize or hold firmly. **2.** to struggle at close quarters (*with*). **3.** to try to deal *with* (a problem). **4.** to seize (as) with a grapnel. —*n.* **1.** a hold (as) in wrestling. **2.** a close contest. **3.** a clutching-instrument, a grapnel. —**grappling-iron** *n.* a grapnel. [f. OF f. Prov. (*grapa* hook, as GRAPNEL)]

grasp /grɑːsp/ *v.t./i.* **1.** to seize or hold firmly, especially with the hands or arms; to seize eagerly or greedily. **2.** to understand or realize. —*n.* **1.** a firm hold, a grip. **2.** mastery, control. **3.** a mental hold, understanding. —**grasp at,** to try to seize; to accept eagerly. **grasp the nettle,** to tackle a difficulty boldly. [for earlier *grapse*, rel. to GROPE]

grasping *adj.* greedy for money or possessions. [f. GRASP]

grass /grɑːs/ *n.* **1.** any of a group of wild low-lying plants with green blades that are eaten by animals; any species of this (*Bot.* including cereals, reeds, and bamboos). **2.** pasture land; grass-covered ground, a lawn; grazing. **3.** (*slang*) marijuana. **4.** (*slang*) a person who 'grasses', an informer. —*v.t./i.* **1.** to cover with turf. **2.** (*US*) to provide with pasture. **3.** (*slang*) to betray, to inform the police. —**grass roots,** the fundamental level or source; ordinary people; the rank and file of a political party etc. **grass snake,** a small non-poisonous snake (*Natrix natrix*). **grass widow,** a woman whose husband is away for a prolonged period. —**grassy** *adj.* [OE, rel. to GREEN]

grasshopper *n.* a jumping insect of the sub-order Saltatoria, with a loud chirping sound (ill. INSECTS).

grassland *n.* a large open area covered with grass, especially used for pasture.

grate[1] *v.t./i.* **1.** to reduce to small particles by rubbing on a rough surface. **2.** to rub with a harsh noise; to grind (the teeth); to sound harshly. **3.** to have an irritating effect (*on* a person or the nerves). [f. OF *grater*]

grate[2] *n.* a metal framework that keeps fuel in a fireplace; the fireplace itself. [orig. = grating; f. OF f. L *cratis* hurdle]

grateful /ˈgreɪtfʊl/ *adj.* **1.** thankful, feeling or showing gratitude. **2.** pleasant, acceptable. —**gratefully** *adv.* [f. obs. *grate* adj. f. L *gratus* thankful, pleasing]

gratify /ˈgrætɪfaɪ/ *v.t.* to please, to delight; to please by compliance; to yield to (a desire). —**gratification** /-fɪˈkeɪʃ(ə)n/ *n.* [f. F or L *gratificari* (as prec.)]

grating /ˈgreɪtɪŋ/ *n.* a framework of parallel or crossed bars, wires, lines ruled on glass, etc. [f. GRATE[2]]

gratis /ˈgreɪtɪs, ˈgrɑː-/ *adj.* & *adv.* free, without charge. [L (*gratia* thanks)]

gratitude /ˈgrætɪtjuːd/ *n.* being thankful, feeling or showing that one values a kindness or benefit received. [f. F or L (as GRATEFUL)]

gratuitous /grəˈtjuːɪtəs/ *adj.* **1.** given or done gratis. **2.** uncalled for, lacking good reason. —**gratuitously** *adv.* [f. L (as GRATIS)]

gratuity /grəˈtjuːɪtɪ/ *n.* money given in recognition of services. [f. OF or L (as GRATEFUL)]

gravamen /grəˈveɪmen/ *n.* (*pl.* **-s**) **1.** the essence or most serious part (*of* an accusation). **2.** a grievance. [L (*gravare* to load f. *gravis* heavy)]

grave[1] *n.* **1.** a hole dug for the burial of a corpse; a mound or monument over this. **2.** death. [OE (as GRAVE[3])]

grave[2] *adj.* **1.** serious, weighty, important; dignified, solemn; sombre. **2.** (of a sound) low-pitched, not acute. —**gravely** *adv.* [F, or f. L *gravis* heavy]

grave[3] *v.t.* (*p.p.* **graven**, **graved**) **1.** to fix indelibly (*in* or *on* one's memory etc.). **2.** (*archaic*) to engrave, to carve. —**graven image,** an idol. [OE]

grave[4] /grɑːv, greɪv/ *n.* an accent (`) over a vowel to show its quality or length. [f. GRAVE[2]]

grave[5] *v.t.* to clean (a ship's bottom) by burning and tarring. —**graving dock,** a dry dock. [perh. f. F *grave*, *grève* shore]

gravel /ˈgræv(ə)l/ *n.* **1.** coarse sand and small stones, used for paths etc. **2.** crystals formed in the bladder. —*v.t.* (**-ll-**) **1.** to lay with gravel. **2.** to perplex. [f. OF, dim. of *grave* (as GRAVE⁵)]

gravelly *adj.* **1.** like gravel; consisting of gravel. **2.** (of the voice) deep and rough-sounding. [f. prec.]

graven see GRAVE³.

Graves¹ /graːv/ *n.* a wine (esp. white) from the Graves district of the Bordeaux region in France.

Graves² /greɪvz/, Robert (Ranke) (1895–1985), English poet, who has also written unconventional historical novels such as *I, Claudius* (1934), an autobiography *Good-bye to all That* (1929), recounting his experiences in the trenches, and an idiosyncratic mythological study *The White Goddess* (1948). All his work is strongly individualistic and often drily humorous.

gravestone *n.* a stone (usually inscribed) marking a grave.

Gravettian /grəˈvetɪən/ *adj.* of an upper palaeolithic industry in Europe, following the Aurignacian, named after the type-site at La Gravette in the Dordogne, France. —*n.* this industry.]

graveyard *n.* a burial-ground.

gravid /ˈgrævɪd/ *adj.* pregnant. [f. L *gravidus* (*gravis* heavy)]

gravimeter /grəˈvɪmɪtə(r)/ *n.* an instrument measuring the difference in the force of gravity between two places. [f. F (L *gravis* heavy, -METER)]

gravitate /ˈgrævɪteɪt/ *v.t./i.* **1.** to move or be attracted (*to* or *towards*). **2.** to move or tend by the force of gravity (*towards*); to sink by or as by gravity. [as GRAVITY]

gravitation /grævɪˈteɪʃ(ə)n/ *n.* **1.** gravitating. **2.** the attraction exercised by every particle of matter on every other; the movement or tendency produced by this; the falling of bodies to earth (see below). —**gravitational** *adj.* [as prec.]   In Plato's cosmology gravity was a tendency of like bodies to cluster together. In Aristotle's theory it was a self-propelling force which urged a body towards the centre of the universe, which coincided with the centre of the earth. In Newton's theory all bodies in the universe attract each other gravitationally with a force which depends directly on the mass of each body and which is also inversely proportional to the square of the distance between both bodies. Long thought to be conclusively established, Newton's theory gave way to Einstein's after 1916, when the latter's theory of gravity, also called the general theory of relativity (see RELATIVITY), was published, according to which gravitational force is the consequence of space-time being 'curved' in the vicinity of matter. For most terrestrial events the predictions of the Newtonian theory and that of Einstein do not differ significantly, but evidence in support of the latter has come from a number of astronomical observations.

gravity /ˈgrævɪtɪ/ *n.* **1.** the force that attracts a body to the centre of the earth etc. (see prec.); the intensity of this. **2.** weight. **3.** importance, seriousness; solemnity. —**gravity feed,** the supply of material by its fall under gravity. [f. F or L *gravitas* heaviness (as GRAVE²)]

gravy /ˈgreɪvɪ/ *n.* **1.** the juices exuding from meat in and after cooking; a dressing for food, made of these. **2.** (*slang*) unearned or unexpected money. —**gravy-boat** *n.* a boat-shaped vessel for gravy. [perh. f. OF *grané* (as GRAIN), misread as *gravé*]

Gray, Thomas (1716–71), English poet, who spent most of his life in Cambridge. The popularity of his first major poem *Elegy Written in a Country Church-Yard* (1751) led to the general recognition of Gray as the foremost poet of the day and (in 1757) to the offer of the laureateship—which he declined. Two Pindaric odes, *The Bard* (1757) and *The Progress of Poesy* (1757), published by his friend Horace Walpole, mark a clear transition from neo-classical lucidity towards the obscure and the sublime. His letters reveal his character and humorous spirit.

grayling *n.* a silver-grey freshwater fish of the genus *Thymallus*. [f. GREY]

graze¹ *v.t./i.* to suffer or cause a slight abrasion of (a part of the body); to touch lightly in passing; to move (*against*, *along*, etc.) with such a contact. —*n.* an abrasion. [perh. by transference f. foll. 'take off the grass close to the ground']

graze² *v.t./i.* **1.** (of cattle etc.) to eat growing grass; to feed on (grass). **2.** to feed (cattle etc.) on growing grass; to pasture cattle. [OE (as GRASS)]

grazier /ˈgreɪzɪə(r)/ *n.* **1.** one who feeds cattle for market. **2.** (*Austral.*) a sheep-farmer. [f. GRASS]

grazing *n.* grassland suitable for pasturage. [f. GRAZE²]

grease /griːs/ *n.* oily or fatty matter, especially as a lubricant; the melted fat of a dead animal. —/also griːz/ *v.t.* to smear or lubricate with grease. —**grease-paint** *n.* the make-up used by actors etc. **grease the palm of,** (*colloq.*) to bribe. [f. OF *graisse* f. L *crassus* fat]

greasy *adj.* **1.** of or like grease. **2.** smeared or covered with grease; having much or too much grease; slippery. **3.** (of a person or manner) too unctuous. —**greasily** *adv.*, **greasiness** *n.* [f. prec.]

great /greɪt/ *adj.* **1.** of a size, amount, extent, or intensity much above the normal or average (also *contemptuously*). **2.** important, pre-eminent. **3.** remarkable in ability, character, etc. **4.** (also **greater**) the larger of the name. **5.** fully deserving the name of; doing a thing much or on a large scale. **6.** (*colloq.*) very enjoyable or satisfactory. **7.** competent *at*; well-informed *on.* —*n.* a great person or thing. —**great circle,** a circle whose plane passes through the centre of the sphere on which the circle lies (ill SHAPES). **Greats,** the Oxford BA course in classics and philosophy; the final examinations in this. —**greatness** *n.* [OE]

great- *in comb.* (of family relationships) one degree more remote (*great-aunt*, *great-grandfather*; *great-great-grandfather*). [= prec.]

Great Australian Bight a wide bay (part of the Indian Ocean) on the south coast of Australia.

Great Barrier Reef the largest coral reef in the world, stretching for about 2,000 km (1,250 miles) roughly parallel to the NE coast of Australia.

Great Bear the constellation Ursa Major.

Great Bible the edition of the English Bible which Thomas Cromwell ordered in 1538 to be set up in every parish church. It was the work of Martin Coverdale, and was first issued in 1539.

Great Britain England, Wales, and Scotland considered as a unit (see BRITAIN). Wales was politically incorporated with England in the 16th c., and the Act of Union formally united Scotland with England in 1707. (See ENGLAND, SCOTLAND, WALES.) Constitutional monarchy was established by the 'Glorious Revolution' of 1688, with parliamentary supremacy guaranteed by the passing of the Bill of Rights (1689). Although the American colonies broke away in 1783, in the 18th c. Britain was the leading naval and colonial power in the world, while the Industrial Revolution which was then beginning made it the first industrialized country, with improvements also in agriculture and communications (see INDUSTRIAL REVOLUTION). During Queen Victoria's long reign the monarchy regained the esteem and affection of the people, and the last quarter of the 19th c. saw a new wave of imperial expansion. The Commonwealth system replaced the Empire in the 20th c., and one country after another gained independence. After the Second World War the newly elected Labour government initiated a programme of nationalization, established a National Health Service, and laid the foundations of the Welfare State. In the following decades immigration from Commonwealth countries made Britain a multiracial society. Manufacturing is the largest industry, though most of the raw materials needed must be imported. New methods of farming have greatly reduced the numbers employed in this, but productivity has increased. Coal (which was of crucial importance during the Industrial Revolution) is mined in large quantities, and the revenue from North Sea oil wells, where production began in 1975, is an important factor in the economy.

greatcoat *n.* a heavy overcoat.

Great Dane see DANE.

Great Dividing Range the crest of the eastern highlands of Australia, curving roughly parallel to the coast for almost its entire north–south length.

Great Elector Frederick William, Elector of Brandenburg (1620–88).

Greater London an administrative area comprising London and the surrounding regions.

Greater Manchester a metropolitan county of NW England.

Great Exhibition the first international exhibition of the products of industry, promoted by Prince Albert and held in the Crystal Palace in London in 1851.

Great Fire (of London) the fire which destroyed some 13,000 houses over 400 acres in London between 2 and 6 Sept. 1666 after starting in a bakery in Pudding Lane east of the City of London.

Great Lakes five large interconnected lakes (Superior,

Michigan, Huron, Erie, and Ontario) in North America. Except for Lake Michigan, which is wholly within the USA, they lie on the Canada–US border. They are connected to the Atlantic Ocean by the St Lawrence Seaway and form an important commercial waterway.

greatly *adv.* by a considerable amount, much. [f. GREAT]

Great Plains a vast area of plains in Canada and the USA, between the Rocky Mountains and the Mississippi valley.

Great Rebellion the Royalist name for the English Civil War of 1642–51.

Great Rift Valley the most extensive rift valley system in the earth's surface, running from the Jordan valley in Syria, along the Red Sea into Ethiopia, and through Kenya, Tanzania, and Malawi into Mozambique. It is marked by a chain of steep-sided lakes and a series of volcanoes, including Mount Kilimanjaro.

Great Russian a member or the language of the principal ethnic group in the USSR.

Great Salt Lake a heavily saline lake in northern Utah.

Great Sandy Desert a large tract of waterless country in north-central Western Australia.

Great Schism 1. the breach between the Eastern and the Western Church, traditionally dated 1054, when, in an attempt to assert the primacy of the papacy, Cardinal Humbert excommunicated the Patriarch of Constantinople and the latter excommunicated the Western legates. (See also FILIOQUE.) Negotiations to restore unity continued over a long period but the breach became final in 1472. 2. the period 1378–1417, when the Western Church was divided by the creation of antipopes. The Council of Constance ended the schism by the election of Martin V in 1417.

Great Seal a seal used to authenticate important documents issued in the name of the sovereign or highest executive authority. In Britain the Great Seal is held by the Lord Chancellor, who was formerly sometimes also referred to as the Lord Keeper (of the Seal); the analogous Great Seal of the USA is held by the Secretary of State.

Great Trek the northward migration in 1835–7 of large numbers of Boers, discontented with British rule in the Cape, to the areas where they eventually founded the Transvaal Republic and the Orange Free State.

Great Victoria Desert a vast arid region straddling the boundary between Western Australia and South Australia.

Great Wall of China a defensive wall in northern China, extending some 2,400 km (1,500 miles) from Kansu province to the Yellow Sea north of Peking. Its origin dates from c.210 BC when the country was unified under one ruler, and the northern walls of existing rival States were linked to form a continuous protection against nomad invaders. It was rebuilt in medieval times largely against the Mongols, and the present wall dates from the Ming dynasty. Although principally a defensive wall it served also as a means of communication: for most of its length it was wide enough to allow five horses to travel abreast. It has the distinction of being the only structure on earth that is visible from the moon.

Great War the First World War.

Great White Way Broadway in New York City, in reference to its brilliant street illuminations.

Great Zimbabwe see ZIMBABWE.

greave *n.* (usu. in *pl.*) armour for the shin (ill. ARMOUR). [f. OF, = shin]

grebe /griːb/ *n.* any of various short-bodied almost tailless diving birds of the family Podicipedidae, especially of the genus *Podiceps*. [f. F]

Grecian /ˈgriːʃ(ə)n/ *adj.* (of architecture or facial outline) Greek. —**Grecian nose,** a straight nose that continues the line of the forehead without a dip. [f. OF or L (*Graecia* Greece)]

Greece /griːs/ a country in SE Europe comprising a peninsula bounded by the Ionian, Mediterranean, and Aegean Seas, and numerous outlying islands; pop. (1981) 9,740,417; official language, Greek; capital, Athens. Agriculture remains important to the economy, though there has been a substantial increase in industrialization; tobacco, fresh fruit, and currants are among the main exports. The chief industries include textiles, chemicals, metallurgy, and electrical equipment. Greece became a full member of the EEC in 1981.

The country was invaded by Greek-speaking peoples c.2000–1700 BC, and thereafter enjoyed settled conditions which allowed the Mycenaean civilization to develop and flourish until the arrival in the 12th c. of the Dorians (see DARK AGE). Village settlements developed into city-states, of which the most prominent were Athens and Sparta, and rising populations and expanding trade led to overseas colonization, especially in Ionia. Although the city-states showed themselves able to combine in a crisis, as against the Persian expeditionary force which they unexpectedly defeated in 480 BC, they were weakened by rivalries and conflicts with each other and by internal political turmoil. In 338 BC they fell to the superior military power of Philip II of Macedon, and formed part of the empire of his successor Alexander the Great. Towards the end of the 3rd c. BC Macedonia came into conflict with the expanding power of Rome, and in 146 BC Greece was made a Roman province; the liberties of the Greek city-states were at an end.

In AD 395 the Roman Empire was divided and Greece became part of the Eastern Empire, centred on Constantinople. It was conquered by the Ottoman Turks (1466) and remained under Turkish rule until the successful war of independence (1821–30), after which it became a monarchy and then in 1973 a republic.

greed *n.* an excessive desire especially for food or wealth. [back-formation f. foll.]

greedy *adj.* showing greed, wanting or taking in excess; gluttonous; very eager (*to do* a thing). —**greedily** *adv.*, **greediness** *n.* [OE]

Greek *adj.* of Greece or its people or language. —*n.* a native or the language of Greece (see below). —**Greek cross,** a cross with four equal arms (ill. VESTMENTS). **Greek fire,** a combustible composition for setting fire to an enemy's ships, works, etc., emitted by a flame-throwing weapon, so called from being first used by the Greeks besieged in Constantinople (673–8). **Greek to me,** incomprehensible to me. [OE f. L *Graecus* f. Gk]

Greek belongs to the Indo-European family of languages. Its ancient form was spoken in the Balkan peninsula from the 2nd millennium BC; the earliest evidence is to be found in the Linear B tablets dating from 1500 BC. Like Latin, it was a highly inflected language with strict rules and rather complicated grammar. The alphabet normally used was adapted from the Phoenician c.1000 BC; the capitals have remained unaltered, and the lower-case letters have developed from them. There were four main dialects, but with the rise of Athens the dialect of that city (Attic) predominated and formed the basis of the koine which became the standard dialect from the 3rd c. BC onwards. It was the official language of the Byzantine empire, but in the four centuries when Greece was under Turkish rule oral speech and dialects developed unchallenged. Today Greek is spoken by some 10 million people in mainland Greece and the Aegean archipelago, and is the official language of Greece. Modern Greek has changed from ancient Greek in various ways: some vowels, diphthongs, and consonants have changed or modified their sounds, there are fewer grammatical forms, and the structure is simpler. Two forms of the language are in use: demotic, the common language, and *katharevousa*, an imitation of classical Greek which has been revived for literary purposes. Demotic is gaining ground not only for conversation but also in literature.

green *adj.* 1. of a colour between blue and yellow, like that of grass. 2. covered with leaves or grass. 3. (of fruit etc. or wood) unripe or unseasoned; not dried, smoked, or tanned. 4. inexperienced, gullible. 5. sickly-hued; jealous, envious. 6. young, flourishing; not withered or worn out. —*n.* 1. green colour or pigment; green clothes or material. 2. a piece of grassy public land; a grassy area for a special purpose. 3. (in *pl.*) green vegetables. 4. vigour, youth. —*v.t./i.* to make or become green. —**green belt,** an area of open land for preservation round a city. **green card,** a motorist's international insurance document. **green-eyed** *adj.* jealous. **green fingers,** skill in growing plants. **green light,** a signal to proceed on a road etc., (*colloq.*) permission to go ahead with a project. **Green Paper,** a preliminary report of government proposals, for discussion. **green party,** a political party of environmentalists and ecologists. **green pound,** the agreed value of the £ according to which payments to agricultural producers are reckoned in the EEC. **green revolution,** greatly increased crop production in the developing countries by improvement of soil fertility, pest control, increased mechanization, etc. **green-room** *n.* a room behind the stage, probably so called because it was originally painted green, for the use of actors and actresses when not required on stage. It has almost disappeared from the modern English theatre. **Greens** *n.pl.* (*colloq.*) = green party. **green-stick fracture**, a fracture, especially in children, in which one side of a bone is broken and one only bent (ill. BODY 1). **green tea**, tea made from steam-dried leaves. —**greenish** *adj.*, **greenly** *adv.*, **greenness** *n.* [OE]

Greenaway /ˈgriːnəweɪ/, Catherine ('Kate') (1846–1901), English artist, known especially for her book-illustrations of children in early 19th-c. dress.

Greene /griːn/, (Henry) Graham (1904–), English novelist. He became a Roman Catholic in 1926, and from 1930 was a full-time writer. Among his major novels are *The Power and the Glory* (1940), set in Mexico, which combines a conspicuous religious theme with elements of a thriller, *The Heart of the Matter* (1948), and *The End of the Affair* (1951). Other fictional works classed as 'entertainments' include *Brighton Rock* (1938) which paradoxically introduced a strong Catholic message foreshadowing the religious complexity and ambiguities of his later work, and *The Third Man* (1950), originally written as a screenplay and filmed by Carol Reed in 1949. He has also written plays, travel books, essays, and two volumes of autobiography. His skilful variations of popular forms (e.g. the thriller, the detective story), his preoccupations with moral dilemmas (personal, religious, and political), and his choice of seedy locations give his work a highly distinctive quality.

greenery *n.* green foliage or growing plants. [f. GREEN]

greenfinch *n.* a finch (*Carduelis chloris*) with green and yellow plumage.

greenfly *n.* a green aphid; such insects collectively.

greengage *n.* a round green plum. [f. GREEN + Sir W. Gage (c. 1725)]

greengrocer *n.* a retailer of fruit and vegetables. —**greengrocery** *n.*

greenhorn *n.* an inexperienced person, a new recruit. [orig. of animals with 'green' or young horns]

greenhouse *n.* a light structure with the sides and roof mainly of glass, for rearing plants. —**greenhouse effect**, the phenomenon whereby the surface and the lower atmosphere of a planet are maintained at a relatively high temperature owing to the greater transparency of the atmosphere to visible radiation from the sun than to infra-red radiation from the planet.

Greenland /ˈgriːnlənd/ an island, the largest in the world, lying to the NE of North America and mostly within the Arctic Circle. It was discovered and named by the Norse explorer Eric the Red in 986 and settled by Norse colonists. From 1721 onwards it was resettled by the Danes, and became part of Denmark in 1953, with internal autonomy from 1979; it withdrew from the EEC in 1985; pop. (1976) 49,666, mostly Eskimos; capital, Godthaab. —**Greenlander** *n.*

greensand *n.* a green sandstone.

greenstone *n.* **1.** a green eruptive rock containing feldspar and hornblende. **2.** (*NZ*) a kind of jade.

greenstuff *n.* vegetation, green vegetables.

greensward *n.* an expanse of grassy turf.

Greenwich /ˈgrenɪtʃ/ a London borough, site of the Royal Observatory, founded in 1675 by Charles II, in a building designed by Sir Christopher Wren. Soon after the Second World War, the observatory was moved to Herstmonceux in East Sussex; to preserve its links with the past, it is called the Royal Greenwich Observatory. The buildings at Greenwich itself, together with many of the old instruments, now form part of the National Maritime Museum. The Greenwich Meridian, which was defined to pass through the Airy Transit Circle at Greenwich, was adopted internationally as the zero of longitude at a conference in Washington in 1884. Its acceptance was facilitated by the overwhelming use of the Greenwich Meridian in navigation and the adoption, in the USA and Canada, of time zones based on Greenwich. Originally, different towns in Great Britain kept their own local time, varying according to longitude. In the mid-19th c. Greenwich time was adopted by railways throughout Britain for the sake of uniformity. However, it was only in 1880 that Greenwich Mean Time, mean solar time on the Greenwich Meridian, became the legal time throughout Great Britain. The international reference time-scale for civil use is now based on atomic clocks but is subject to step adjustments (leap seconds) to keep it close to mean solar time on the Greenwich meridian. The formal name of this time-scale is UTC (a language-independent abbreviation

of co-ordinated universal time) but it is still widely known as Greenwich Mean Time.

greenwood *n.* woodlands in summer.

greet[1] *v.t.* **1.** to address politely on meeting or arrival. **2.** to salute, to receive (a person, news, etc., *with* a reaction). **3.** (of a sight, sound, etc.) to meet (the eye, ear, etc.). [OE]

greet[2] *v.i.* (*Sc.*) to weep. [OE]

greeting *n.* words, gestures, etc., used to greet a person; (often in *pl.*) an expression of goodwill. —**greetings card**, a decorative card sent to convey greetings. [f. GREET[1]]

gregarious /grɪˈgeərɪəs/ *adj.* **1.** fond of company. **2.** living in flocks or communities. —**gregariously** *adv.*, **gregariousness** *n.* [f. L (*grex* flock)]

Gregorian /grɪˈgɔːrɪən/ *adj.* of the plainchant ritual music named after Gregory the Great (see PLAINSONG). [f. GREGORY[3]]

Gregorian calendar the modified calendar, also known as the 'New Style', introduced by Pope Gregory XIII in 1582, adopted in Great Britain in 1752, and now in use throughout most of the Christian world. It is a modification of the Julian calendar, which was adapted to bring it into closer conformity with astronomical data and in order to correct errors which had accumulated because the Julian year of 365¼ days was 11 min. 10 sec. too long, 10 days were suppressed in 1582 and in Great Britain 11 in 1752, and to prevent further displacement Gregory provided that of the centenary years (1600, 1700, etc.) only those exactly divisible by 400 should be counted as leap years.

Gregory[1] /ˈgregərɪ/, St (329–89), Doctor of the Church, born at Nazianzus in Cappadocia. With St Basil and Gregory of Nyssa he was an upholder of orthodoxy against the Arian and Apollinarian heresies, and influential in restoring the Nicene faith. Feast day, 2 Jan.

Gregory[2] /ˈgregərɪ/, St (c.330–c.395), Doctor of the Church, bishop of Nyssa in Cappadocia, brother of St Basil, and an orthodox follower of Origen. (See GREGORY[1].) Feast day, 9 March.

Gregory[3] /ˈgregərɪ/, St, 'the Great' (c. 540–604), pope from 590 and Doctor of the Church. When he became pope Italy was in an alarming state, devastated by floods, famine, and the Lombard invasions, and the position of the Church was threatened by the imperial power at Constantinople; it was owing to Gregory that many of these evils were conquered. He made a separate peace with the Lombards in 592–3, and (acting independently of the imperial authorities) appointed governors to the Italian cities, thus establishing the temporal power of the papacy. One of his great achievements was the conversion of England, for which he selected St Augustine as head of the mission. He was a prolific author, promoted monasticism, made important changes in the liturgy and fostered the development of liturgical music, and is credited with the invention of Gregorian chant (see PLAINSONG). Feast day, 12 March.

Gregory of Tours /ˈgregərɪ, tʊə(r)/, St (c.540–94), bishop of Tours, whose writings are our chief authority for the early Merovingian period of French history.

gremlin /ˈgremlɪn/ *n.* (*slang*) a mischievous sprite said to interfere with machinery etc. [orig. unkn., but prob. formed by analogy with GOBLIN]

Grenada /greˈneɪdə/ a State in the West Indies, consisting of the island of Grenada (the southernmost of the Windward Islands) and the southern Grenadines; pop. (est. 1982) 110,410; official language, English; capital, St George's. The island was sighted in 1498 by Columbus on 15 Aug., which is now Grenada's national day. Colonized by the French, it was ceded to Britain, 1763, recaptured by the French, and restored to Britain in 1783. It became an independent State within the Commonwealth in 1974. —**Grenadian** *adj.* & *n.*

grenade /grɪˈneɪd/ *n.* a small bomb thrown by hand or shot from a rifle. [F, f. OF & Sp., = pomegranate]

grenadier /grenəˈdɪə(r)/ *n.* (*hist.*) a soldier armed with grenades. —**Grenadiers** or **Grenadier Guards**, the first regiment of the royal household infantry. [F (as prec.)]

Grenadine Islands /ˈgrenədiːn/ (also **Grenadines**) a chain of small islands in the West Indies, divided between St Vincent and Grenada.

Gresham /ˈgreʃəm/, Sir Thomas (c.1519–79), English financier who founded the Royal Exchange in 1566 and served as the chief financial adviser to the Elizabethan government. —**Gresham's law**, the tendency for money of lower intrinsic value to circulate more freely than money of higher intrinsic and equal nominal value (pithily expressed as 'Bad money drives out good'). Formulation of this principle is attributed to Gresham.

Gretna Green /ˈgretnə/ a village just north of the Scottish/English border near Carlisle, formerly a popular place for runaway couples from England to be married according to Scots law without the parental consent required in England for those who had not attained their majority. A valid marriage could be contracted in Scotland merely by a declaration of consent by the two parties before a witness (traditionally the village blacksmith, who also read the marriage service to couples for sentiment's sake). The practice began after 1753, when English law made it impossible to conduct a marriage clandestinely, and lapsed after 1857 when Scots law prescribed certain conditions for 'irregular' marriages, though it recognized such marriages until 1939.

grew *past* of GROW.

Grey /greɪ/, Lady Jane (1537-54), queen of England for nine days. The granddaughter of Henry VIII's sister, Jane fell victim to the dynastic ambitions of the Duke of Northumberland, who, in 1553, married her against her will to his son and then persuaded the dying Edward VI to name her as his successor. Jane was deposed after nine days on the throne by forces loyal to Edward's elder sister Mary. She was initially spared, but after Wyatt's Rebellion in 1554 was executed because she was seen as a potential focal point for Protestant opposition to Mary's Catholic regime.

grey /greɪ/ *adj.* **1.** of a colour between black and white. **2.** dull, dismal. **3.** (of the hair) turning white; (of a person) with grey hair. **4.** aged, experienced, mature, ancient. **5.** anonymous, unidentifiable. —*n.* **1.** grey colour or pigment; grey clothes or material. **2.** a grey horse. —*v.t./i.* to become or make grey. —**grey area,** that part of a matter where there are no exact rules about right and wrong etc. **Grey Friars,** Franciscan friars, so called from their grey cloaks. **grey matter,** the parts of the brain, consisting of nerve-cell bodies, that are grey in appearance; (*colloq.*) intelligence. **grey squirrel,** a common squirrel of the USA (*Sciurus carolinensis*) which was introduced into Europe in the late 19th c. —**greyish** *adj.*, **greyness** *n.* [OE]

greyhound *n.* a slender dog noted for swiftness and used in racing and coursing. Dogs of greyhound type are depicted on murals of ancient Egypt dating from the 2nd millennium BC and were valued in the east for hunting in deserts and plains, where speed is crucial. In England greyhounds were used to hunt small game, especially hares, and in the Middle Ages ownership was restricted by law to the aristocracy. By the early 19th c. hare-coursing had become an organized sport, and the sport of dog-racing, with an electrically propelled lure, developed from this in the early 20th c., originally in the USA. [OE, = bitch-hound]

greylag *n.* the European wild goose, *Anser anser*. [f. GREY + *lag* (perh. = obs. *lag* goose, of imit. origin)]

grid *n.* **1.** a grating. **2.** a system of numbered squares printed on a map and forming the basis of map references. **3.** a network of lines, electric-power connections, gas-supply lines, etc. **4.** a pattern of lines marking the starting-places on a car-racing track. **5.** a wire network between the filament and anode of a thermionic valve. **6.** an arrangement of town streets in a rectangular pattern. **7.** a gridiron. [f. GRIDIRON]

griddle *n.* = GIRDLE². [f. OF f. L *craticula* (*cratis* hurdle)]

gridiron /ˈgrɪdaɪən/ *n.* a cooking utensil of metal bars for broiling or grilling. [as GRIDDLE]

grief /griːf/ *n.* deep or intense sorrow; a cause of this. —**come to grief,** to meet with disaster. [f. OF (as GRIEVE)]

Grieg /griːg/, Edvard (1843-1907), Norwegian composer, conductor, and violinist. He married his cousin, the soprano Nina Hagerup, in 1867, she being the inspiration and interpreter of many of his songs. His compositions earned the admiration of Liszt, whom he met in Rome (1870) where Liszt played the piano concerto, from manuscript, at sight. In 1874 he was asked by Ibsen to write the incidental music to *Peer Gynt*, and its performance (1876) made Grieg a national figure. His music eschews the larger forms of opera and symphony, but within his chosen scale it is deeply poetic, superbly fashioned, and (in the songs especially) emotionally passionate. His nationalist idiom transcends local boundaries by reason of the strong individuality of his work.

grievance /ˈgriːvəns/ *n.* a real or fancied ground of complaint. [f. OF (as GRIEF)]

grieve /griːv/ *v.t./i.* to cause grief to; to feel grief. [f. OF f. L *gravare* (*gravis* heavy)]

grievous /ˈgriːvəs/ *adj.* (of pain etc.) severe; causing grief;

injurious; flagrant, heinous. —**grievous bodily harm,** (*Law*) serious injury. —**grievously** *adv.* [f. OF (as prec.)]

griffin /ˈgrɪfɪn/ *n.* a fabulous creature with an eagle's head and wings and a lion's body (ill. HERALDRY). [f. OF f. L *gryphus* f. Gk]

Griffith, D(avid) W(ark) (1875-1948), American film director, one of the most significant figures in the history of film. He began to discover the elements of cinematic expression in his early one-reel films, and he is responsible for introducing the techniques of flashback and fade-out. His most memorable films included his epic of the American Civil War *The Birth of a Nation* (1915), *Intolerance* (1916), which incorporated four separate stories to illustrate the theme, and *Broken Blossoms* (1919). He made only two sound films, in 1930 and 1931, and then had a long and lonely retirement virtually forgotten.

griffon /ˈgrɪf(ə)n/ *n.* **1.** a terrier-like dog with coarse hair. **2.** a large vulture of the genus *Gyps*. **3.** a griffin. [var. of GRIFFIN]

grill *n.* **1.** a device on a cooker for radiating heat downwards. **2.** a gridiron. **3.** grilled food. **4.** a grill-room. **5.** a grille. —*v.t.* **1.** to cook on a gridiron or under a grill. **2.** to subject to or undergo torture or great heat; to subject to severe questioning, especially by the police. —**grill-room** *n.* a small restaurant serving grills etc. [var. of foll.]

grille /grɪl/ *n.* **1.** a grating or latticed screen, especially in a door; (in real tennis) a square opening in the wall at the end of the hazard side (a ball entering it scores a point). **2.** a metal grid protecting the radiator of a motor vehicle. [F f. L (as GRIDDLE)]

grilse *n.* a young salmon that has been only once to the sea. [orig. unkn.]

grim *adj.* **1.** of harsh or forbidding appearance; stern, merciless. **2.** ghastly, joyless; unpleasant, unattractive. —**grimly** *adv.*, **grimness** *n.* [OE]

grimace /grɪˈmeɪs/ *n.* a distortion of the face in disgust etc., or to amuse. —*v.i.* to make a grimace. [F f. Sp. *grimazo* (*grima* fright)]

Grimaldi¹ /grɪˈmældɪ/, Francesco Maria (1618-63), Italian Jesuit physicist and astronomer, who discovered the diffraction of light. He verified Galileo's law of falling bodies, drew a detailed map of the moon, based on many telescopic observations, and began the practice of naming lunar regions after astronomers and physicists.

Grimaldi² /grɪˈmældɪ/, Joseph (1779-1837), English actor, the creator of the English clown, in whose honour all later clowns were nicknamed Joey. He performed at Covent Garden from 1806 until his retirement in 1823. His inventive comic genius could make a man out of vegetables and a coach out of four cheeses, and he designed a number of trick scenes. Making Clown a rustic booby, Grimaldi gave him his traditional costume. His acrobatics were characterized by dynamic energy which finally wore him out.

grime *n.* soot or dirt ingrained in a surface, especially the skin. —*v.t.* to blacken with grime. —**grimy** *adj.*, **griminess** *n.* [f. MLG or MDu.]

Grimm, Jacob Ludwig Carl (1785-1863) and Wilhelm Carl (1786-1859), German linguistics scholars. Jacob produced a historical and descriptive German grammar (1819, 1822) and the brothers jointly inaugurated a dictionary of German on historical principles; begun in 1852, it was continued by other scholars and completed in 1960. They are remembered also for the anthology of German fairy-tales which they compiled. —**Grimm's law,** a statement of the regular consonantal differences between related words in the different Indo-European languages, first fully formulated by Jacob Grimm in the second edition of his German grammar (1822).

grin *v.t./i.* (**-nn-**) to smile broadly, showing the teeth; to make a forced, unrestrained or stupid smile; to express by grinning. —*n.* an act or the action of grinning. —**grin and bear it,** to take pain etc. stoically. [OE]

grind /graɪnd/ *v.t./i.* (*past & p.p.* **ground**) **1.** to crush to small particles; to produce (flour) thus. **2.** to oppress, to harass with exorbitant demands. **3.** to sharpen or smooth by friction. **4.** to rub together gratingly. **5.** to study hard, to toil. **6.** to produce or bring *out* with effort. **7.** to turn the handle of (a barrel-organ). —*n.* **1.** grinding. **2.** hard dull work. **3.** the size of ground particles. —**grind to a halt,** to stop laboriously with the sound of grating. **ground glass,** glass made opaque by grinding. [OE]

grinder /ˈgraɪndə(r)/ *n.* **1.** a person or thing (especially a machine) that grinds. **2.** a molar tooth. [f. prec.]

grindstone *n.* a thick revolving disc used for grinding, sharpening, and polishing; the kind of stone used for this. —**keep one's nose to the grindstone,** to work hard and continuously.

grip *v.t./i.* (**-pp-**) **1.** to grasp tightly; to take a firm hold, especially by friction. **2.** to compel the attention of. —*n.* **1.** a firm hold, a grasp. **2.** grasping power; way of clasping the hands or of grasping or holding. **3.** mastery, intellectual hold. **4.** a gripping part of a machine etc.; the part of a weapon etc. that is held. **5.** a hair-grip. **6.** (*US*) a suitcase, a travelling-bag. —**come** or **get to grips with,** to approach purposefully, to begin to deal with. [OE (as GRIPE)]

gripe *v.t./i.* **1.** to cause colic; to affect with colic. **2.** (*slang*) to complain. **3.** to clutch, to grip. **4.** to oppress. —*n.* **1.** (usu. in *pl.*) colic. **2.** (*slang*) a complaint. —**gripe-water** *n.* a medicine to cure colic in babies. [OE]

grisaille /grɪˈzeɪl, -ˈzaɪ/ *n.* a method of decorative painting in grey monochrome representing figures and objects in relief; a stained-glass window of this kind. [F (*gris* grey)]

grisly /ˈgrɪzlɪ/ *adj.* causing horror, disgust, or fear. —**grisliness** *n.* [OE]

grist *n.* corn to grind. —**grist to the mill,** a source of profit or advantage. [OE (as GRIND)]

gristle /ˈgrɪs(ə)l/ *n.* tough flexible tissue, cartilage, especially in meat. —**gristly** *adj.* [OE]

grit *n.* **1.** particles of stone or sand, especially as causing discomfort, clogging machinery, etc. **2.** coarse sandstone. **3.** (*colloq.*) courage, endurance. —*v.t./i.* (**-tt-**) **1.** to spread grit on (icy roads etc.). **2.** to clench (the teeth), especially in enduring pain or trouble. **3.** to make a grating sound. —**gritty** *adj.*, **grittiness** *n.* [OE]

grits *n.pl.* coarsely ground grain, especially oatmeal; oats that have been husked but not ground. [OE]

grizzle *v.i.* (*colloq.*, esp. of a child) to cry fretfully. —**grizzler** *n.* [orig. unkn.]

grizzled /ˈgrɪz(ə)ld/ *adj.* grey-haired or partly so. [f. *grizzle* grey f. OF *grisel* (*gris* grey)]

grizzly *adj.* grey, grey-haired. —*n.* a grizzly bear. —**grizzly bear,** a large fierce bear (*Ursus horribilis*) of North America. [as prec.]

groan *v.t./i.* **1.** to make a deep sound expressing pain, grief, or disapproval; to utter with groans. **2.** to be loaded or oppressed. —*n.* the sound made in groaning. [OE]

groat *n.* **1.** a silver coin recognized from the 13th c. in various countries of Europe; an English coin issued 1351-1662. **2.** a fourpenny piece 1836-56. [f. MDu., = great]

groats *n.pl.* hulled or crushed grain, especially oats. [OE (rel. to GRIT, GRITS)]

grocer /ˈgrəʊsə(r)/ *n.* a dealer in food and household provisions. [f. AF *grosser* f. L (as GROSS); orig. one who sells in the gross]

grocery *n.* a grocer's trade or shop; (in *pl.*) grocer's provisions. [f. prec.]

grog *n.* a drink of spirit (originally rum) and water. [perh. f. *Grogram* nickname of Admiral Vernon, who in 1740 first had grog served to sailors instead of neat rum]

groggy *adj.* unsteady, tottering. —**groggily** *adv.*, **grogginess** *n.* [f. prec.]

grogram /ˈgrɒgrəm/ *n.* a coarse fabric of silk, mohair, etc. [f. *gros grain* coarse grain]

groin *n.* **1.** the depression between the belly and the thigh. **2.** the edge formed by vaults intersecting in a roof; an arch supporting a vault. —*v.t.* to build with groins. [perh. f. OE *grynde* depression]

Gromyko /grəˈmiːkəʊ/, Andrei Andreievich (1909-), Russian statesman, Foreign Minister 1957-85, President of the USSR (Chairman of the Presidium of the Supreme Soviet) 1985-.

groom *n.* **1.** a person employed to take care of horses. **2.** a bridegroom. **3.** any of certain officers of the Royal Household. —*v.t.* **1.** to curry or tend (a horse). **2.** to give a neat appearance to (a person etc.). **3.** to prepare (a person) *as* a political candidate, *for* a career, etc. [orig. = 'boy', etym. unkn.]

groove *n.* **1.** a channel or hollow, especially one made to guide motion or receive a ridge; a spiral cut in a gramophone record for the stylus. **2.** a piece of routine, a habit. **3.** (*slang*) something excellent. —*v.t./i.* to make a groove or grooves in. [f. Du.; cf. GRAVE¹]

groovy *adj.* **1.** of or like a groove. **2.** (*slang*) excellent. [f. prec.]

grope *v.t./i.* to feel about as in the dark; to search blindly (*lit.* or *fig.*). —**grope one's way,** to proceed tentatively. [OE, rel. to GRIP]

Gropius /ˈgrəʊpɪəs/, Walter (1883-1969), German architect, director of the Bauhaus School of Design 1919-28, one of the leading personalities in modern architecture, both as teacher and as designer. His special contribution was to bring architecture into closer relationship firstly with social needs and secondly with the industrial techniques on which it was increasingly coming to rely. In 1934, finding his ideas unpalatable to the Nazi regime, he came to England, and in 1938 moved to Harvard University, where he was an influential teacher.

grosbeak /ˈgrɒsbiːk/ *n.* any of various large finches, e.g. the pine grosbeak *Pinicola enucleator*. [f. F *grosbec*, = large beak]

grosgrain /ˈgrəʊgreɪn/ *n.* a corded fabric of silk etc. [F, = coarse grain]

gros point /grəʊ ˈpwæ̃/ cross-stitch embroidery on canvas. [F (as GROSS, POINT)]

gross /grəʊs/ *adj.* **1.** flagrant, outrageous. **2.** total, without deductions, not net. **3.** not refined, indecent, vulgar. **4.** thick, solid. **5.** overfed, bloated, repulsively fat; (of vegetation) luxuriant, rank. **6.** (of the senses etc.) dull. —*n.* (*pl.* same) twelve dozen. —*v.t.* to produce as gross profit. —**gross domestic product,** the total value of goods produced and services provided in a country in one year. **gross national product,** the gross domestic product plus the total of net income from abroad. —**grossly** *adv.* [f. OF f. L *grossus* big]

grotesque /grəʊˈtesk/ *adj.* comically or repulsively distorted; incongruous, absurd. —*n.* **1.** a decoration interweaving human and animal forms with foliage. **2.** a comically distorted figure or design. —**grotesquely** *adv.*, **grotesqueness** *n.* [f. F f. It. (as foll.)]

Grotius /ˈgrəʊʃəs/, Hugo (1583-1645), Dutch jurist. He led an interesting life, serving as a diplomat, escaping from life imprisonment in Holland, and eventually dying in the service of Queen Christina of Sweden, but his fame rests on the legal treatise *De Jure Belli et Pacis*, written in exile in Paris and published in 1625, which established the basis of modern international law.

grotto /ˈgrɒtəʊ/ *n.* (*pl.* **-oes**) a picturesque cave; an artificial or simulated cave. [f. It. *grotta* f. L (as CRYPT)]

grotty *adj.* (*slang*) unpleasant, dirty, ugly, useless. [f. GROTESQUE]

grouch *v.i.* (*colloq.*) to grumble. —*n.* (*colloq.*) a discontented person; a fit of grumbling or the sulks. —**groucher** *n.*, **grouchy** *adj.* [as GRUDGE]

ground¹ *n.* **1.** the surface of the earth, especially as contrasted with the air around it; a part of this specified in some way; a position or area on the earth's surface. **2.** a foundation or motive. **3.** an area of a special kind or use. **4.** the surface worked upon in painting etc.; the predominant colour. **5.** (in *pl.*) enclosed land attached to a house. **6.** (in *pl.*) dregs, especially of coffee. **7.** an electrical earth. **8.** the bottom of the sea. **9.** the floor of a room etc. —*attrib.* (in the names of birds) terrestrial; (of animals) burrowing, living on the ground; (of plants) dwarfish, trailing. —*v.t./i.* **1.** to run aground, to strand. **2.** to refuse authority for (an airman or aircraft) to fly. **3.** to instruct thoroughly (*in* a subject). **4.** to base (a principle or conclusion *on* a fact etc.). **5.** to connect with the earth as a conductor. **6.** to alight on the ground. **7.** to place or lay (esp. weapons) on the ground. —**break new ground,** to treat a subject previously not dealt with. **cover the ground,** to deal adequately with a subject. **fall to the ground,** (of a plan etc.) to fail. **get off the ground,** to make a successful start. **give** or **lose ground,** to retreat, to decline. **go to ground,** (of a fox etc.) to enter an earth etc.; (of a person) to withdraw from public notice. **ground bass,** a short theme constantly repeated in the bass with the upper parts of the music varied. **ground frost,** frost on the surface of the ground or in the top layer of soil. **ground-nut** *n.* a peanut; a wild bean (*Apios tuberosa*), originally from North America, with an edible tuber. **ground-plan** *n.* a plan of a building at ground level, the general outline of a scheme. **ground-rent** *n.* the rent for land leased for building. **ground speed,** aircraft speed relative to the ground. **ground swell,** a heavy sea due to a distant or past storm or earthquake. **ground water,** the water found in the surface soil. **hold one's ground,** not to retreat. [OE]

ground² *past* & *p.p.* of GRIND.

groundhog *n.* the North American marmot, the wood-chuck. —**Groundhog Day,** (*US*) 2 Feb., when the ground-hog is said to come out of his hole at the end of hibernation. (If he sees his shadow—i.e. if the weather is sunny—there are supposed to be six weeks more of winter weather.)

grounding *n.* basic training or instruction in a subject. [f. GROUND¹]

groundless *adj.* without motive or foundation. —**groundlessly** *adv.* [f. GROUND¹ + -LESS]

groundsel /ˈgraʊns(ə)l/ *n.* a plant of the genus *Senecio*, of which the commonest species, a garden weed, is used as a food for cage-birds. [OE]

groundsheet *n.* a waterproof sheet for spreading on the ground.

groundsman *n.* (*pl.* **-men**) a person who maintains a sports ground.

groundwork *n.* preliminary or basic work.

group /gruːp/ *n.* **1.** a number of persons or things close together, or belonging or classed together. **2.** a number of commercial companies under a single ownership. **3.** a pop group. **4.** a division of an air force. **5.** (*Math.*) a set of elements with an operation for combining any pair to give another element in the set. —*v.t.* to form into a group; to place in a group or groups. —**group captain,** an RAF officer next below air commodore. **group therapy,** therapy in which similarly affected patients are brought together to assist one another. [f. F f. It. *gruppo*]

grouse¹ /graʊs/ *n.* (*pl.* same) a game-bird of the family Tetraonidae with feathered feet; its flesh as food. [orig. unkn.]

grouse² /graʊs/ *v.i.* (*colloq.*) to grumble, to complain. —*n.* (*colloq.*) a grumble. —**grouser** *n.* [orig. unkn.]

grout *n.* thin fluid mortar. —*v.t.* to apply grout to. [cf. dial. F *grouter* grout a wall.]

grove *n.* a small wood, a group of trees. [OE]

grovel /ˈgrɒv(ə)l/ *v.i.* (**-ll-**) to lie prone in abject humility; to humble oneself. [f. foll.]

grovelling *adj.* abject, base; prone. [f. obs. *grufe* face down f. ON]

grow /grəʊ/ *v.t./i.* (*past* **grew**; *p.p.* **grown**) **1.** to increase in size, height, amount, intensity, etc. **2.** to develop or exist as a living plant or natural product. **3.** to become gradually. **4.** to produce by cultivation; to let (a beard etc.) develop; (*in pass.*) to be covered (*over* etc.) with growth. —**growing pains,** neuralgic pain in children's legs due to fatigue etc.; early difficulties in the development of a project etc. **grown-up** *adj.* adult; (*n.*) an adult. **grow on,** to have an increasing charm etc. for. **grow out of,** to become too large to wear (a garment); to become too mature to retain (a habit etc.); to develop from. **grow up,** to advance to maturity; (of a custom) to arise. [OE]

grower *n.* **1.** a person growing produce, especially fruit. **2.** a plant that grows in a specified way. [f. GROW]

growl /graʊl/ *n.* a guttural sound of anger; a rumble; an angry murmur, a complaint. —*v.t./i.* to make a growl; to utter with a growl. [imit.]

grown *p.p.* of GROW.

growth /grəʊθ/ *n.* **1.** growing, development. **2.** increase in size or value. **3.** what has grown or is growing. **4.** a tumour. —**growth industry,** an industry developing faster than most others. [f. GROW]

groyne /grɔɪn/ *n.* a structure of wood, stone, or concrete projecting towards the sea, preventing sand and pebbles from being washed away by the current (ill. COASTS). —*v.t.* to protect with groynes. [f. dial. *groin* snout f. OF f. L (*grunnire* grunt)]

grub *n.* **1.** the larva of an insect; a maggot. **2.** (*slang*) food. —*v.t./i.* (**-bb-**) **1.** to dig superficially. **2.** to clear (ground) of roots etc.; to clear away (roots etc.); to fetch *up* or *out* by digging (*lit.* or *fig.* in books etc.); to rummage. —**grub-screw** *n.* a headless screw. [perh. as GRAVE³]

grubby *adj.* **1.** dirty. **2.** full of grubs. —**grubbily** *adv.*, **grubbiness** *n.* [f. GRUB]

Grub Street a street in London (later Milton Street, Moorgate) associated in the 17th-18th c. with small-time professional writers. The term is used allusively of literary hacks or hack-work.

grudge *v.t.* to be resentfully unwilling to give or allow. —*n.* a feeling of resentment or ill will. —**grudging** *adj.*, **grudgingly** *adv.* [f. OF *grouc(h)ier* murmur]

gruel /ˈgruːəl/ *n.* a liquid food of oatmeal etc. boiled in milk or water. [f. OF]

gruelling /ˈgruːəlɪŋ/ *adj.* exhausting. [f. prec.]

gruesome /ˈgruːsəm/ *adj.* horrible, grisly, disgusting. [f. Sc. *grue* to shudder]

gruff *adj.* (of the voice) low and harsh; having a gruff voice; surly. —**gruffly** *adv.*, **gruffness** *n.* [f. Du. or MLG *grof* coarse]

grumble *v.t./i.* **1.** to complain peevishly; to be discontented. **2.** to make a rumbling sound. —*n.* an act or sound of grumbling. —**grumbler** *n.* [cf. MDu. *grommen*]

grummet /ˈgrʌmɪt/ *n.* **1.** an insulating washer placed round an electric conductor where it passes through a hole in metal. **2.** (*Naut.*) a ring usually of twisted rope as a fastening etc. [f. F (*gourmer* to curb)]

grumpy *adj.* morose and irritable, surly. —**grumpily** *adv.*, **grumpiness** *n.* [imit.]

Grundy /ˈgrʌndɪ/, **Mrs** a person embodying conventional propriety and prudery. [neighbour who never appears but is constantly referred to ('What will Mrs Grundy say?') in T. Morton's play *Speed the Plough* (1798)]

Grünewald /ˈgruːnvɑːlt/, Mathias, properly Mathis Neithart, called Gothart (*c.*1460-1528), German painter. His early life is obscure, but he may have been apprenticed in Augsburg since his style resembles that of the elder Holbein. In 1501-25 he worked near Frankfurt, from 1511 for successive archbishops of Mainz, but lost their patronage because of his sympathy for the doctrines of Luther and involvement in the Peasants' Rising of 1525. His masterpiece, the *Isenheim Altar*, is an intensely moving work and exemplifies his characteristic style: twisted limbs, contorted postures, and highly expressive heads, painted in glowing colour against a dark background. He was the subject of a symphony and of an opera (*Mathis der Maler*, 1933-8) by Hindemith, in which an artist leads a rebellion against authority—a theme unpopular with the Nazi regime.

grunt *n.* the low guttural sound characteristic of the pig. —*v.t./i.* **1.** to utter a grunt. **2.** to speak or say with a grunt. **3.** to grumble. [OE (imit.)]

gruyère /ˈgruːjeə(r)/ *n.* a kind of cheese, originally Swiss, with many holes. [f. *Gruyère* in Switzerland]

gryphon var. of GRIFFIN.

G-string /ˈdʒiːstrɪŋ/ *n.* **1.** a narrow strip of cloth etc. covering the genitals, attached to a string round the waist. **2.** the string on a violin etc. sounding the note G.

GT *n.* a high-performance car. [abbr. of It. *gran turismo* great touring]

guano /ˈgwɑːnəʊ/ *n.* (*pl.* **-os**) **1.** excrement of sea-fowl, used as manure. **2.** artificial manure, especially that made from fish. [Sp. f. Quechua]

Guarani /ˈgwɑːrənɪ/ *n.* a member or the language of a South American ethnic group. —*adj.* of this group or their language. [Sp.]

guarantee /gærənˈtiː/ *n.* **1.** a formal promise or assurance, especially that a thing is of a specified quality and durability. **2.** a guarantor. **3.** a guaranty; a thing serving as a security. —*v.t.* to give or serve as a guarantee for; to provide with a guarantee; to give one's word; to secure (a thing *to* a person). [earlier *garante*, perh. f. Sp. and F (as WARRANT)]

guarantor /ˈgærəntə(r), -ˈtɔː(r)/ *n.* the giver of a guaranty or security. [f. prec.]

guaranty /ˈgærəntɪ/ *n.* an undertaking, usually written, to answer for the payment of a debt or the performance of an obligation by the person primarily liable; the ground of a security. [f. OF *guarantie*, var. of *warantie* warranty]

guard /gɑːd/ *v.t./i.* **1.** to watch over and defend or protect. **2.** to supervise (prisoners etc.) and prevent from escaping. **3.** to keep (thoughts or speech) in check. **4.** to take precautions (*against*). —*n.* **1.** a state of vigilance or watchfulness. **2.** a protector, a sentry; (*US*) a prison warder. **3.** a railway official in charge of a train. **4.** soldiers protecting a place or person; an escort; a separate portion of an army. **5.** a device to prevent injury or accident. **6.** a defensive posture or motion in boxing, fencing, etc. **7.** (*in pl.*, usu. **Guards**) the Household troops. —**on** (or **off**) **one's guard,** ready (or not ready) against an attack or challenge. **stand guard,** to act as a sentry or guard (*over*). [f. OF *garder* (as WARD)]

guardant /ˈgɑːd(ə)nt/ *adj.* (in heraldry) depicted with the body sideways but the face towards the spectator (ill. HERALDRY). [f. prec.]

guarded /ˈgɑːdɪd/ *adj.* (of remarks) cautious. [f. GUARD]

guardhouse *n.* a building accommodating a military guard or securing prisoners.

Guardi /ˈgwɑːdɪ/ a family of Venetian painters. Giacomo

(1678-1716) founded the workshop, and was followed by his sons, Gianantonio (1699-1760) and Francesco (1712-93). Francesco is famous as a painter of views, but was never as successful as his contemporary, Canaletto, and was not elected to the Venetian Academy until 1784, in spite of being brother-in-law to its first president, Tiepolo. His reputation has risen in the 20th c., and his broken touch and feeling for light and atmosphere now appear to anticipate the impressionists.

guardian /ˈgɑːdɪən/ n. **1.** a protector, a keeper. **2.** a person having legal custody of one incapable of managing his own affairs, or of his property. —**guardianship** n. [f. AF (as GUARD, WARDEN)]

guardroom n. a room accommodating a military guard or securing prisoners.

guardsman n. (pl. **-men**) a soldier belonging to a guard or the Guards.

Guarneri 'del Gesù' /gwɑːˈneərɪ del ˈjeɪsuː/, Giuseppe (1687-1744), the most celebrated of a family of violin-makers based in Cremona, noted for the attention he gave to the tone quality of his instruments, which do not conform to any standard details of shape or size. Paganini owned a 'del Gesù', which he bequeathed to his native city, Genoa.

Guatemala /gwætɪˈmɑːlə/ a country in the north of Central America, bordering on the Pacific Ocean and with a short coastline on the Caribbean Sea; pop. (est.) 7,500,000; official language, Spanish; capital, Guatemala City (pop. 1,500,000). The land is fertile, with numerous rivers, but is subject to frequent earthquakes. The principal export is coffee; oil was discovered in the 1970s. A former centre of Mayan civilization, Guatemala was conquered by the Spanish in 1523-4. After independence it formed the core of the short-lived Central American Federation (1828-38) before becoming an independent republic in its own right. Its history since then has frequently been characterized by dictatorship and revolution, and in modern times it has not escaped the unrest and guerrilla activity which paralyses the general area. Guatemala still claims the territory on its NE frontier, despite the establishment of this as the independent republic of Belize in 1981. —**Guatemalan** adj. & n.

guava /ˈgwɑːvə/ n. a tropical American tree (Psidium guajava,); its edible orange acid fruit. [f. Sp. guayaba prob. f. S. Amer. name]

gubernatorial /gjuːbənəˈtɔːrɪəl/ adj. (US) of a governor. [f. L gubernator governor]

gudgeon¹ /ˈgʌdʒ(ə)n/ n. **1.** a small freshwater fish (Gobio gobio) used as bait. **2.** a credulous person. [f. OF f. L gobio goby]

gudgeon² /ˈgʌdʒ(ə)n/ n. a kind of pivot or metal pin; a socket for a rudder. [f. OF goujon (as GOUGE)]

guelder rose /ˈgeldə(r)/ a shrub (Viburnum opulus) with bunches of round white flowers. [f. Du. (Gelderland in Holland)]

Guelph /gwelf/ n. **1.** a member of one of the two great factions in Italian medieval politics (see GHIBELLINE). **2.** a member of a princely family of Swabian origin from which the British royal house is descended through George I (the name is often given as the surname of the House of Hanover, although D'Este is equally accurate). [f. It. f. MHG Welf name of German noble family]

Guernsey /ˈgɜːnzɪ/ the second largest of the Channel Islands; pop. (1981) 54,380; capital, St Peter Port. —n. a breed of dairy cattle from Guernsey; an animal of this breed. —**Guernsey lily**, a kind of amaryllis (Nerine sarniensis).

guernsey /ˈgɜːnzɪ/ n. **1.** a thick knitted woollen (usually blue) outer tunic or jersey. **2.** (Austral.) a football shirt. [f. prec.]

guerrilla /gəˈrɪlə/ n. a person taking part in irregular fighting by small groups acting independently. [f. Sp. (dim. of guerra war)]

guess /ges/ v.t./i. **1.** to estimate without measurement or detailed calculation. **2.** to form an opinion; to form a hypothesis about; to think likely. **3.** to conjecture (the answer to a riddle etc.) correctly. —n. a rough estimate; a conjecture. —**guess at**, to make a guess concerning. **I guess**, (US) I think it likely, I suppose. —**guesser** n. [orig. unkn.]

guesswork n. guessing; procedure based on this.

guest /gest/ n. **1.** a person invited to visit one's house or have a meal etc. at one's expense. **2.** a person lodging at a hotel etc. **3.** a performer not belonging to the regular

company. —**guest-house** n. a superior boarding-house. [f. ON]

guff n. (slang) empty talk. [imit.]

guffaw /gʌˈfɔː/ n. a boisterous laugh. —v.i. to utter a guffaw. [imit.]

guidance /ˈgaɪd(ə)ns/ n. guiding, being guided; advice on problems. [f. foll.]

guide /gaɪd/ n. **1.** one who shows the way. **2.** a hired conductor for tourists. **3.** a person or thing by which others regulate their movements. **4. Guide** (formerly **Girl Guide**) a member of a girls' organization, established in 1910, corresponding to the Scout Association. **5.** an adviser; a directing principle. **6.** a book of rudiments; a guidebook. **7.** a rod etc. directing motion. **8.** a thing marking a position or guiding the eye. —v.t. **1.** to act as a guide to. **2.** to be the principle or motive of. **3.** to arrange the course of (events). —**guided missile**, a missile under remote control or directed by equipment within itself. **guide-dog** n. a dog trained to guide a blind person. **guided tour**, a tour accompanied by a guide. **guide-line** n. a directing principle. [f. OF]

guidebook n. a book of information for tourists.

Guider n. an adult leader of Guides. [f. GUIDE]

Guignol /giːˈnjɒl/ the chief character in a French puppet-show of that name, similar to 'Punch and Judy'. The term is also used for the theatre where the show is performed. —**Grand Guignol** /grɑ̃/, a theatre presenting a succession of short plays of gruesome character (in this respect resembling 'Punch and Judy').

guild /gɪld/ n. an association formed for the mutual aid and protection of its members, or for some common purpose. Such associations are first recorded in England in pre-Conquest times and resembled the later burial and benefit societies which were convivial. Merchant guilds were formed from the 11th c. (earlier on the Continent), and many became powerful in local government. Trade guilds (associations of persons exercising the same craft) came into prominence in England in the 14th c. and were powerful there and elsewhere in medieval Europe, effectively controlling trade and commerce in many countries, particularly in large cities. Their monopolistic policies generally brought them into conflict with strengthening central governments and their powers were gradually curtailed. [prob. f. G and Du., rel. to OE gi(e)ld payment, guild]

guilder /ˈgɪldə(r)/ n. **1.** a currency unit of the Netherlands, a florin. **2.** (hist.) a gold coin of the Netherlands and Germany. [alt. of Du. gulden]

guild-hall n. **1.** a hall in which a medieval guild met. **2.** a town hall. —**Guildhall**, the hall of the Corporation of the City of London, used for State banquets etc.

guile /gaɪl/ n. treachery, deceit; cunning, craftiness. —**guileful** adj., **guileless** adj., **guilelessness** n. [f. OF]

guillemot /ˈgɪlɪmɒt/ n. an auk of the genus Uria or Cepphus. [F, f. Guillaume William]

guillotine /ˈgɪlətiːn, -ˈtiːn/ n. **1.** a machine with a blade sliding in grooves, used for beheading criminals. **2.** a machine for cutting paper, metal, etc. **3.** a method of preventing a delay in Parliament by fixing the times for voting on parts of a bill. —v.t. to use a guillotine on. [F, f. J.-I. Guillotin, physician who suggested its use in 1789]

guilt /gɪlt/ n. the fact of having committed a specified or implied offence; culpability; a feeling that one is to blame. [OE]

guiltless adj. **1.** innocent. **2.** not having knowledge or possession of. [f. GUILT + -LESS]

guilty adj. **1.** having, showing, or due to guilt. **2.** having committed the offence (of). —**guiltily** adv., **guiltiness** n. [f. GUILT]

Guinea /ˈgɪnɪ/ a country on the west coast of Africa; pop. (est. 1981) 5,144,000; official language, French; capital, Conakry. Formerly part of French West Africa, Guinea became an independent republic in 1958. The economy is chiefly agricultural; bauxite and iron-ore are extensively mined, and alumina is the principal export. —**Gulf of Guinea**, a large inlet of the Atlantic Ocean bordering on the coast of Guinea.

guinea /ˈgɪnɪ/ n. **1.** a former British gold coin worth 21 shillings (£1.05), first coined for the African trade (whence its name). **2.** this sum of money, used in stating professional fees etc. —**guinea-fowl** n. a domestic fowl of the genus Numida (especially N. meleagris) with grey plumage spotted with white. Its name was given when it was brought by the

Portuguese from Guinea in West Africa. **guinea-pig** *n.* a South American rodent of the genus *Cavia* kept as a pet or for research in biology; a person used as a subject for experiment. [f. prec.]

Guinea-Bissau /gɪnɪbɪˈsaʊ/ a country on the west coast of Africa, between Senegal and Guinea; pop. (est. 1979) 760,000; official language, Portuguese; capital, Bissau. The area was explored by the Portuguese in the 15th c. and became a colony in 1879. It gained independence, as a republic, in 1974. The economy is chiefly agricultural, groundnuts being the principal crop.

Guinevere /ˈgwɪnɪvɪə(r)/ (in Arthurian legend) the wife of King Arthur and mistress of Lancelot.

guipure /ˈgiːpʊə(r)/ *n.* a heavy lace of linen pieces joined by embroidery. [F (*guiper* cover with silk etc.)]

guise /gaɪz/ *n.* an assumed appearance, a pretence; external appearance. [f. OF (as WISE[2])]

guitar /gɪˈtɑː(r)/ *n.* a plucked string instrument with frets, played either with the fingers or with a plectrum or finger-pick. The characteristic form of the instrument, probably of Spanish origin, came in at the end of the 15th c., although there have been from pre-Christian times stringed instruments played with a plectrum; the strings or courses (two or more strings to a note) then numbered four, the present six strings dating from the 1790s. 'Acoustic' (i.e. non-electric) guitars include the Spanish, or classical, with nylon strings; the 'country-and-western', or 'folk', with steel strings; and the Hawaiian guitar, which is played with the strings stopped by a small metal bar. The electric guitar (with built-in microphone) dates back to the 1930s. (See ill. MUSICAL NOTATION.) —**guitarist** *n.* [f. F or Sp. f. Gk *kithara*]

Gujarat /guːdʒəˈrɑːt/ a State in western India formed from the north part of the former Bombay State; capital, Gandhinagar.

Gujarati /guːdʒəˈrɑːtɪ/ *n.* **1.** a native of the State of Gujarat. **2.** a language descended from Sanskrit and so belonging to the Indo-Iranian language group, spoken by some 25 million people mainly in the State of Gujarat. It is written in a form of the Devanagari script. [Hindi]

gulch *n.* (*US*) a ravine, especially containing a torrent. [perh. f. dial. *gulch* to swallow]

gules /gjuːlz/ *n. & adj.* (in heraldry) red. [f. OF *go(u)les* (pl. of *gole* throat) red-dyed fur neck-ornaments]

gulf *n.* **1.** a large area of sea partly surrounded by land. **2.** a deep hollow, a chasm. **3.** a wide difference of opinion etc. [f. OF f. It. f. Gk *kolpos* bosom, gulf]

Gulf Stream a warm ocean current which flows from the Gulf of Mexico parallel with the American coast towards Newfoundland, continuing (as the North Atlantic Drift) across the Atlantic Ocean and along the coast of NW Europe, where it has a significant effect upon the climate.

Gulf War the war between Iraq and Iran, in the general area of the Persian Gulf, which broke out in 1980.

gull[1] *n.* a large sea-bird of the family Laridae, with webbed feet and long wings. [prob. f. Welsh *gwylan*]

gull[2] *n.* (*archaic*) a fool, a dupe. —*v.t.* (*archaic*) to cheat, to fool. [perh. f. obs. *gull* yellow f. ON]

gullet /ˈgʌlɪt/ *n.* the passage for food, extending from the mouth to the stomach. [f. OF dim. (*goule* throat f. L *gula*)]

gullible /ˈgʌlɪb(ə)l/ *adj.* easily persuaded or deceived. —**gullibility** /-ˈbɪlɪtɪ/ *n.* [f. GULL[2]]

gully *n.* **1.** a channel or ravine cut by water. **2.** a gutter, a drain. **3.** a fielding-position in cricket between point and slips (ill. SPORTS). [f. F *goulet* bottle-neck (as GULLET)]

gulp *v.t./i.* **1.** to swallow (*down*) hastily, greedily, or with effort. **2.** to keep (sobs etc.) *back* or *down* with difficulty. **3.** to make a swallowing action with effort, to choke. —*n.* **1.** the act of gulping. **2.** a large mouthful of liquid. [f. MDu. *gulpen* (imit.)]

gulper *n.* a deep-sea fish with a soft tapered body, long tail, and greatly expandable stomach that can accommodate large prey. In those of the family Eupharyngidae (ill. SEA) the mouth is larger than the body. [f. GULP]

gum[1] *n.* **1.** a sticky substance secreted by some trees and shrubs, used especially for sticking paper etc. together. **2.** chewing-gum. **3.** a gum-drop. **4.** gum arabic. **5.** a gum tree. —*v.t.* (**-mm-**) to fasten with gum; to apply gum to. —**gum arabic,** a gum exuded by some kinds of acacia. **gum-drop** *n.* a hard transparent sweet made of gelatine etc. **gum-tree** *n.* a tree that exudes gum, especially a eucalyptus (*up a gum-tree*, in great difficulty). **gum up,**

(*colloq.*) to interfere with, to spoil. [f. OF f. L *gummi, cummi* f. Gk f. Egyptian]

gum[2] *n.* (often in *pl.*) the firm flesh around the roots of the teeth. [OE]

gum[3] *n.* **by gum!**, (*slang*) by God! [corruption of *God*]

gumboil *n.* a small abscess on the gum.

gumboot *n.* a rubber boot.

gummy[1] *adj.* sticky, exuding gum. —**gumminess** *n.* [f. GUM[1]]

gummy[2] *adj.* toothless. [f. GUM[2]]

gumption /ˈgʌmpʃ(ə)n/ *n.* (*colloq.*) common sense; resource, initiative. [orig. unkn.]

gun *n.* **1.** any kind of weapon consisting of a metal tube for throwing missiles with an explosive propellant. **2.** a starting-pistol. **3.** a device for discharging grease etc. on to a desired point. **4.** a person using a sporting gun as a member of a shooting-party. **5.** (*US*) a gunman. —*v.t./i.* (**-nn-**) **1.** to shoot at or *down*. **2.** (*colloq.*) to accelerate (an engine etc.). **3.** to go shooting. —**at gunpoint,** threatened by a gun. **be gunning for,** to seek to attack or rebuke. **going great guns,** acting vigorously and near success. **gun-carriage** *n.* a wheeled support for a gun. **gun cotton,** an explosive of cellulose steeped in acid. **gun dog,** a dog trained to retrieve game in a shoot. **gun-fight** *n.* (*US*) a fight with firearms. **gun-metal** *n.* an alloy formerly used for guns; its bluish-grey colour. **gun-runner** *n.* a person involved in gun-running. **gun-running** *n.* the systematic smuggling of guns and ammunition into a country. **stick to one's guns,** to maintain one's position. [perh. f. Scand. *Gunnhildr* woman's name]

gunboat *n.* a small warship with relatively heavy guns. —**gunboat diplomacy,** diplomacy backed by the threat of force.

gunfire *n.* the firing of guns.

gunman *n.* (*pl.* **-men**) a man armed with a gun, especially in committing a crime.

Gunn, Thomson William ('Thom') (1929–), English poet who settled permanently in California. His volumes of verse include *Fighting Terms* (1954), *The Sense of Movement* (1959), *My Sad Captains* (1961), *Moly* (1971), and *Jack Straw's Castle* (1976). His works combine a celebration of men of action, a fascination for violence, and a gallery of heroes (ranging from Elvis Presley to Caravaggio), with a low-key, rational, laconic, colloquial manner.

gunnel var. of GUNWALE.

gunner *n.* **1.** an artillery soldier especially as the official term for a private. **2.** a naval warrant officer in charge of a battery, magazine, etc. **3.** an airman who operates a gun. **4.** a game-shooter. [f. GUN]

gunnery *n.* **1.** the construction and management of large guns. **2.** the firing of guns. [f. GUN]

gunny *n.* a coarse sacking usually of jute fibre; a sack made of this. [f. Hindi & Marathi f. Skr.]

gunpowder *n.* the earliest known propellant explosive, a mixture of potassium nitrate, charcoal, and sulphur. It was made by Roger Bacon *c.*1250, though probably discovered much earlier. By the mid-14th c. its military uses were well established (it was used in the battle of Crécy, 1346), and it remained the foremost military explosive for five centuries, having a profound effect on weapons and warfare.

Gunpowder Plot a conspiracy by a small group of extremist Catholics to blow up James I and his Parliament on 5 Nov. 1605, uncovered when a Catholic MP was sent an anonymous letter telling him to stay away from the House on the appointed day. Guy Fawkes was arrested in the cellars of the Houses of Parliament the day before the scheduled attack and betrayed his colleagues under torture. The leader of the plot, Robert Catesby, was killed resisting arrest and the rest of the conspirators were captured and executed. Controversy continues about whether the episode was a contrived plot against the Catholics (who looked as if they were about to regain power), with Fawkes and others 'framed' to discredit them. The plot is commemorated by the traditional searching of the vaults by the Yeomen of the Guard before the opening of each session of Parliament, and by bonfires and fireworks, with the burning of a 'guy', annually on 5 Nov.

gunroom *n.* **1.** a room in a warship for junior officers. **2.** a room for sporting-guns etc. in a house.

gunshot *n.* **1.** a shot from a gun. **2.** the range of a gun.

gunsmith *n.* a maker and repairer of small firearms.

Gunter /ˈgʌntə(r)/, Edmund (1581–1626), English mathematician who invented or improved several mathematical instruments. —**Gunter's chain,** a measuring instrument 66 ft. long (80 chains = 1 mile), subdivided into 100 links (1 rod or perch = 25 links; each link was a short section of wire connected to the next link by a loop). It was long used for land-surveying in the English-speaking countries and elsewhere, but has now been superseded by the steel tape and electronic equipment.

Gunther /ˈɡʊntə(r)/ (in the Nibelungenlied) husband of Brunhild and brother of Kriemhild, by whom he was beheaded in revenge for Siegfried's murder.

gunwale /ˈɡʌn(ə)l/ n. the upper edge of a ship's or boat's side. [f. GUN + WALE (because formerly used to support guns)]

guppy /ˈɡʌpɪ/ n. a small West Indian fish (*Lebistes reticulatus*). [f. R. J. L. *Guppy*, who sent the first specimen to the British Museum]

Gupta /ˈɡʊptə/ the name of a Hindu dynasty established in 320 by Chandra Gupta I in Bihar. The Gupta empire eventually stretched across most of northern India, but began to disintegrate towards the end of the 5th c., only North Bengal being left by the middle of the 6th c. —**Guptan** adj.

gurdwara /ɡɜːˈdwɑːrə/ n. a Sikh place of worship, containing a copy of the Adi Granth. [Punjabi, f. Skr. *guru* teacher, *dvara* door]

gurgle n. a bubbling sound as of water from a bottle. — v.t./i. to make gurgles; to utter with gurgles. [prob. imit.]

Gurkha /ˈɡɜːkə/ n. **1.** a member of a military people of Hindu descent and Sanskritic speech, who settled in the province of Gurkha, Nepal, in the 18th c. and made themselves supreme. **2.** a member of one of the Gurkha regiments (orig. specifically for Nepalese soldiers) in the British Army. [native name, f. Skr. *gāus* cow, *raksh* protect]

gurnard /ˈɡɜːnəd/ n. a sea-fish of the family Triglidae, with a large head, mailed cheeks, and finger-like pectoral rays. [f. OF]

guru /ˈɡʊruː/ n. **1.** a Hindu spiritual teacher or head of a religious sect. **2.** an influential or revered teacher. [f. Hindi, f. Skr. *gurús* dignified]

gush n. **1.** a sudden or copious stream. **2.** effusiveness. —v.t./i. **1.** to flow (*out* etc.) with a gush; to emit a gush of (water etc.). **2.** to speak or behave effusively. [prob. imit.]

gusher n. **1.** an oil-well emitting unpumped oil. **2.** an effusive person. [f. GUSH]

gusset /ˈɡʌsɪt/ n. **1.** a piece let into a garment etc. to strengthen or enlarge it. **2.** a strengthening iron bracket. [f. OF *gousset* flexible piece filling up a joint in armour]

gust n. a sudden violent rush of wind; a burst of rain, smoke, anger, etc. —v.i. to blow in gusts. —**gusty** adj., **gustily** adv. [f. ON]

gustatory /ˈɡʌstətərɪ/ adj. connected with the sense of taste. [f. L (*gustare* f. *gustus* taste)]

Gustavus Adolphus /ɡʊˈstɑːvəs əˈdɒlfəs/ (1594–1632), king of Sweden 1611–32. One of the greatest soldiers of his day, Gustavus raised Sweden to the status of a European power by his victories against Denmark, Poland, and Russia in the first decade and a half of his reign. In 1630 he intervened on the Protestant side in the Thirty Years War, revitalizing the anti-Imperialist cause with several brilliant victories and earning himself the title of 'Lion of the North'. His motives are debated, but his own assertion, that he sought security for the Swedish State and Church, was probably part if not the whole of the truth. At home he instituted creative reforms in administration, economic development, and education, laying the foundation of the modern State.

gusto /ˈɡʌstəʊ/ n. zest, enjoyment in doing a thing. [It. (as prec.)]

gut n. **1.** the intestine; (in pl.) the bowels or entrails. **2.** (in pl., colloq.) pluck, force of character; staying power. **3.** material for violin etc. strings or surgical use made from the intestines of animals; material for fishing-lines made from the intestines of the silk-worm. **4.** (in pl.) the contents or fittings; a thing's essence. **5.** a narrow passage or water-passage. —adj. instinctive; fundamental. —v.t. (**-tt-**) **1.** to remove the guts of (a fish). **2.** to remove or destroy the internal fittings of (a building). **3.** to extract the essence of (a book etc.). —**hate a person's guts,** to dislike him intensely. [OE]

Gutenberg /ˈɡuːt(ə)nbɑːɡ/, Johann (c.1400–68), German inventor of printing using movable type, i.e. individual letters arranged to form words and lines of type (rather than using a solid block for each page), achieving the high degree of accuracy in casting the type which this method of printing requires. By c.1456 an edition of the Bible had been produced, probably the first book to be printed in Europe, with double columns and 42 lines to the page. It was known as the Mazarin Bible because the copy which first attracted the attention of bibliographers was discovered in the library of Cardinal Mazarin (17th c.).

gutless adj. (colloq.) lacking energy or courage. [f. GUT + -LESS]

gutsy adj. **1.** (colloq.) courageous. **2.** (slang) greedy. [f. GUT]

gutta-percha /ɡʌtəˈpɜːtʃə/ n. a tough plastic substance from the latex of various Malayan trees. [f. Malay]

gutter n. a shallow trough below the eaves, or a channel at the side of a street, for carrying off rain-water; a channel, a groove. —v.i. (of a candle) to burn unsteadily and melt away rapidly. —**the gutter,** a place of low breeding or vulgar behaviour. **gutter press,** sensational journalism. [f. AF f. L *gutta* drop]

guttering n. material for gutters. [f. prec.]

guttersnipe n. a street urchin.

guttural /ˈɡʌtər(ə)l/ adj. **1.** throaty, harsh-sounding. **2.** (of consonants) produced in the throat or by the back of the tongue and palate. **3.** of the throat. —n. a guttural consonant (as g, k). —**gutturally** adv. [F, or f. L (*guttur* throat)]

guv n. an informal form of address to a superior. [abbr.]

guy[1] /ɡaɪ/ n. **1.** an effigy of Guy Fawkes burnt on 5 Nov. **2.** (slang) a man. **3.** a grotesquely-dressed person. —v.t. to ridicule. [f. Guy FAWKES]

guy[2] /ɡaɪ/ n. a rope or chain to secure a tent or steady a crane-load etc. —v.t. to secure with guys. [prob. f. LG]

Guyana /ɡaɪˈænə/ a country on the NE coast of South America; pop. (est. 1981) 904,000; official language, English; capital, Georgetown. The Spaniards explored the area in 1499, and the Dutch settled there in the 17th c. It was occupied by the British from 1796 and established, with adjacent areas, as the colony of British Guiana in 1831. In 1966 it gained independence as Guyana (the name is taken from an American Indian word meaning 'land of waters'), and became a Co-operative Republic within the Commonwealth in 1970. Much of the country is covered with dense rain-forest. Its economy is dominated by the sugar industry (the province of Demerara has given its name to a type of sugar that originated there), but bauxite-mining is becoming increasingly important. —**Guyanese** /ɡaɪəˈniːz/ adj. & n.

guzzle v.t./i. to eat or drink greedily. [prob. f. OF *gosiller* (*gosier* throat)]

Gwent /ɡwent/ a county of SE Wales.

Gwynedd /ˈɡwɪnəð/ a county of NW Wales.

Gwynn /ɡwɪn/, Nell (1650–87), an actress who became one of Charles II's many mistresses, one of her sons later being created Duke of St Albans.

gybe /dʒaɪb/ v.t./i. (of a fore-and-aft sail or boom) to swing to the other side (ill. SAILING-SHIPS); to make (a sail) gybe; (of a boat etc.) to change course thus. [f. obs. Du. *gibjen*]

gym /dʒɪm/ n. (colloq.) **1.** a gymnasium. **2.** gymnastics. —**gym-slip** n. a sleeveless tunic, usually belted, worn by schoolgirls. [abbr.]

gymkhana /dʒɪmˈkɑːnə/ n. a meeting for competition in a sport, especially horse-riding. [f. Hindi *gendkhāna* ball-house, assim. to foll.]

gymnasium /dʒɪmˈneɪzɪəm/ n. (pl. **-ums**) a room etc. equipped for gymnastics. [L f. Gk (*gumnos* naked)]

gymnast /ˈdʒɪmnæst/ n. an expert in gymnastics. [f. F or Gk (as prec.)]

gymnastic /dʒɪmˈnæstɪk/ adj. of gymnastics. —**gymnastically** adv. [f. L f. Gk (as GYMNASIUM)]

gymnastics n.pl. (occas. treated as sing.) exercises to develop the muscles or demonstrate agility (also fig.). [f. prec.]

gymnosperm /ˈdʒɪmnəspɜːm/ n. a member of the group of plants (mainly trees) that bear seeds 'naked', i.e. not enclosed in an ovary (opp. ANGIOSPERM). [f. Gk *gumnos* naked]

gymp var. of GIMP.

gynaecology /ɡaɪnɪˈkɒlədʒɪ/ n. the science of the physiological functions and diseases of women. —**gynaecological** /-kəˈlɒdʒɪk(ə)l/ adj., **gynaecologist** n. [f. Gk *gunē* woman + -LOGY]

gyp /dʒɪp/ n. **give a person gyp,** (colloq.) to punish severely or hurt him. [perh. f. *gee up* (GEE[2])]

gypsum /ˈdʒɪpsəm/ *n.* a mineral (calcium sulphate) used to make plaster of Paris or as a fertilizer. —**gypseous** *adj.* [L f. Gk *gupsos*]

gypsy /ˈdʒɪpsɪ/ *n.* a member of a travelling people with dark skin and hair, speaking a language related to Hindi (see ROMANY) and usually living by seasonal work, itinerant trade, and fortune-telling (see below). —**gypsy moth,** a kind of tussock-moth very destructive to foliage. **gypsy's warning,** a cryptic or sinister warning. [earlier *gipcyan*, *gipsen*, f. EGYPTIAN, reflecting their supposed origin when they appeared in England about the beginning of the 16th c.]

Gypsies, who now number approximately one million, are found on most continents. Their primary identifying cultural characteristic is their distinctive language, and it is generally agreed that their original homeland was the Indian subcontinent which they probably left in three separate migrations. With their distinctive language and customs the gypsies continue to resist assimilation and their dispersion has been accelerated in modern times by prejudice and by persecution. The English began a policy of transportation in 1544 and sent them to the West Indies, the American colonies, and later to Australia. Similar forced migration was practised by the Portuguese (to Brazil and Angola), the Dutch, Germans, etc.; Nazi extermination campaigns directed against the gypsies reduced their numbers in Europe by 250,000 between 1939 and 1945.

gyrate /dʒaɪˈreɪt/ *v.i.* to move in a circle or spiral. —**gyration** *n.*, **gyratory** /ˈdʒaɪrətərɪ/ *adj.* [f. L *gyrare* (as GYRO-)]

gyrfalcon /ˈdʒɜːfɔːlkən/ *n.* a large northern falcon (*Falco rusticolus*). [f. OF f. ON]

gyro- /gaɪrəʊ-/ *in comb.* rotation; gyroscopic. [f. Gk *guros* ring]

gyro /ˈdʒaɪrəʊ/ *n.* (*colloq.*) a gyroscope. [abbr.]

gyro-compass *n.* a compass giving the true north and bearings from it relative to the earth's rotation and depending on the properties of a gyroscope, independent of earth's magnetism. It is used in ships and provided that the speed of the vessel is comparatively low the axis of the gyroscope, which remains horizontal, aligns itself north/south under the influence of the earth's rotation. The high speed of aircraft renders the gyro-compass less suitable for use in flight.

gyroscope /ˈdʒaɪrəskəʊp/ *n.* a rotating wheel whose axis is free to change its direction but maintains a fixed direction in the absence of perturbing forces. The most familiar example is the spinning-top, whose axis remains vertical as it spins, but in most of its practical uses the wheel is spun by electric motors. The gyroscope is used in automatic pilots in aircraft and in gyro-compasses. —**gyroscopic** /-ˈskɒpɪk/ *adj.* [F (as GYRO-, -SCOPE)]

H

H, h /eɪtʃ/ n. (pl. **Hs, H's**) the eighth letter of the alphabet.
H abbr. hard (pencil-lead).
H symbol hydrogen.
h. abbr. **1.** hecto-. **2.** hot. **3.** hour(s).
Ha symbol hahnium.
ha /hɑː/ int. expressing surprise, suspicion, triumph, etc.
ha. abbr. hectare(s).
Habakkuk /ˈhæbəkək, həˈbæ-/ **1.** a Hebrew minor prophet probably of the 7th c. BC. **2.** a book of the Old Testament bearing his name.
habeas corpus /ˈheɪbɪəs ˈkɔːpəs/ a writ requiring a person under arrest to be brought before a judge or into court, especially to investigate the lawfulness of his restraint, thus ensuring that imprisonment cannot take place without a legal hearing. The right to sue for such a writ was an old common-law right; formulations of it look back to a phrase in Magna Carta, but the right may predate this. It was not actually passed as an Act of Parliament until 1679 and before that date was frequently disregarded. A similar right is recognized in the legal system of the USA. [L, = you must have the body]
haberdasher /ˈhæbədæʃə(r)/ n. a dealer in accessories of dress and in sewing-goods. —**haberdashery** n. [orig. unkn.]
habiliments /həˈbɪlɪmənts/ n.pl. clothing, attire. [f. OF (habiller fit out, f. habile able)]
habit /ˈhæbɪt/ n. **1.** a settled or regular tendency or practice; a practice that is hard to give up. **2.** mental constitution. **3.** dress, especially of a religious order. —**habit-forming** adj. causing addiction. [f. OF f. L habitus (habēre have)]
habitable adj. suitable for living in. —**habitability** /-ˈbɪlɪtɪ/ n. [f. OF f. L (habitare inhabit)]
habitat /ˈhæbɪtæt/ n. the natural home of an animal or plant. [L, = it inhabits]
habitation /hæbɪˈteɪʃ(ə)n/ n. **1.** a house or home. **2.** inhabiting. [f. OF f. L (as HABITABLE)]
habitual /həˈbɪtjʊəl/ adj. **1.** done constantly or as a habit; regular, usual. **2.** given to a habit. —**habitually** adv. [f. L (as HABIT)]
habituate /həˈbɪtjʊeɪt/ v.t. to accustom (to). —**habituation** /-ˈeɪʃ(ə)n/ n. [f. L (as HABIT)]
habitué /həˈbɪtjʊeɪ/ n. a resident or frequent visitor (of). [F(as prec.)]
hachures /hæˈʃʊə(r)z/ n.pl. parallel lines used on maps to indicate the degree of slope in hills. [F (as HATCH³)]
hacienda /hæsɪˈendə/ n. (in a Spanish-speaking country) a large estate etc. with a dwelling-house. [Sp., f. L facienda things to be done]
hack¹ v.t./i. **1.** to cut or chop roughly. **2.** to kick the shin of (an opponent at football); to deal chopping blows (at). **3.** (colloq.) to gain unauthorized access to (computer files); (in partic.) to use a computer for the satisfaction that it gives. —n. **1.** a kick with the toe of a boot etc.; a wound from this. **2.** a mattock. **3.** a miner's pick. —**hacking cough**, a short dry frequent cough. **hack-saw** n. a saw with a narrow blade set in a frame, for cutting metal. —**hacker** n. [OE]
hack² n. **1.** a horse for ordinary riding; a horse let out for hire. **2.** a person hired to do dull routine work, especially as a writer. —v.i. to ride on horseback at an ordinary pace. —adj. used as a hack; commonplace. [abbr. of HACKNEY]
hackle n. **1.** the long feather(s) on the neck of the domestic cock etc. **2.** a steel comb for dressing flax etc. —**make a person's hackles rise,** to make him very angry. **with his hackles up,** angry, ready to fight. [rel. to HOOK]
hackney /ˈhæknɪ/ n. a horse for ordinary riding. —**hackney carriage**, a taxi. Hackney coaches began to ply in London in 1625, and were only 20 in number, but ten years later there were so many that Charles I issued an order restricting them. By the reign of George III the number had been increased to 1,000, operating by licence and paying duty of five shillings a week to the king. Drivers of hackney coaches were required to give way to persons of quality and gentlemen's coaches. [perh. f. Hackney in London]
hackneyed /ˈhæknɪd/ adj. (of a phrase etc.) made commonplace or trite by long over-use. [f. prec.]
had past & p.p. of HAVE.
haddock /ˈhædək/ n. (pl. same) a sea-fish (Melanogrammus aeglefinus) related to the cod, used for food. [prob. f. AF]
Hades /ˈheɪdiːz/ (Gk myth.) one of the sons of Cronus, lord of the lower world (which is known as 'the House of Hades'). In classical Greek the name is always that of a person, not of a place, but later it was transferred to his kingdom. He is represented as grim and unpitying, never as evil (Greek mythology has no Satan). One of his titles is Pluto. —n. hell. [Gk, = unseen]
Hadith /ˈhædɪθ/ n. any of a number of collections of traditions rendering the sayings of the Prophet Muhammad and, with accounts of his daily practice (see SUNNA), constituting the major source of guidance for Muslims after the Koran. [f. Arab., = tradition]
hadj /hædʒ/ n. pilgrimage to Mecca, a duty of Muslims. [f. Arab., = pilgrimage]
hadji /ˈhædʒɪ/ n. (also **hajji**) a Muslim who has been to Mecca as a pilgrim. [f. Pers. & Turk., = pilgrim (as prec.)]
hadn't (colloq.) had not.
Hadrian /ˈheɪdrɪən/ (Publius Aelius Hadrianus, 76–138) Roman emperor 117–38, born in Spain, the adopted successor of Trajan. He spent much of his reign touring the provinces of the empire, promoting good government and loyalty to Rome, and securing the frontiers. An admirer of Greek culture, he was both practitioner and patron of the arts, and erected many buildings in Rome (including the Pantheon) and Athens.
Hadrian's Wall a Roman defensive wall across northern England from the Solway Firth in the west to the mouth of the River Tyne in the east (about 120 km, 74 miles). It was begun in AD 122, after the emperor Hadrian's visit, to defend the province of Britain against invasions of tribes from the north. There were forts and fortified posts at intervals, a ditch on the north and a wider ditch on the south, and the wall itself (2.5–3 m thick) was eventually built of stone throughout its length. After Hadrian's death the frontier was advanced to the Antonine Wall, which the Romans proved unable to hold; after being overrun and restored several times Hadrian's Wall was abandoned c. AD 410.
hadron /ˈhædrɒn/ n. any strongly interacting sub-atomic particle. [f. Gk hadros thick, bulky]
Haeckel /ˈhek(ə)l/, Ernst Heinrich (1834–1919) German biologist and firm supporter of Darwin's theories. His vivid popularizations of Darwinism were best-sellers, and through his works many millions first encountered the theory that man was descended from the ape. For Haeckel the implications of evolution were that Roman Catholicism promoted superstition and that the German empire was the highest evolved form of civilized nation. He upheld the essential unity of mind, organic life, and inorganic matter, and compared crystals to simple nerve-cells. By careful studies of the earliest stages of embryos he developed his 'recapitulation' theory—that the development of the individual organism reflects the evolutionary history of the species—a theory now discredited.
haemal /ˈhiːm(ə)l/ adj. of the blood. [f. Gk haima blood]
haematic /hiːˈmætɪk/ adj. of or containing blood. [as prec.]
haematite /ˈhiːmətaɪt/ n. ferric oxide as ore. [f. L f. Gk, = bloodlike stone (as HAEMAL)]
haematology /hiːməˈtɒlədʒɪ/ n. the study of the physiology of the blood. [as HAEMAL + -LOGY]
haemoglobin /hiːməˈɡləʊbɪn/ n. the oxygen-carrying substance in the red blood-cells of vertebrates. [f. haematin constituent of haemoglobin (as HAEMAL) + GLOBULIN]
haemophilia /hiːməˈfɪlɪə/ n. a constitutional, usually hereditary, tendency to bleed severely from even a slight injury, through failure of the blood to clot normally. —**haemophilic** adj. [f. Gk haima blood + philia loving]

haemophiliac/hiːməˈfɪlɪæk/ *n.* a person suffering from haemophilia. [f. prec.]

haemorrhage /ˈhemərɪdʒ/ *n.* an escape of blood from a blood-vessel, especially when profuse. —*v.i.* to undergo haemorrhage. [f. F f. L f. Gk (*haima* blood, *rhēgnumi* burst)]

haemorrhoid /ˈhemərɔɪd/ *n.* (usu. in *pl.*) a swollen vein at or near the anus. [f. OF or L f. Gk (*haima* blood, *-rhoos* -flowing)]

hafnium /ˈhæfnɪəm/ *n.* a metallic element with a silver lustre, symbol Hf, atomic number 72, chemically similar to zirconium and usually found associated with it. It was discovered in 1923 and is used in control rods of nuclear reactors because of its capacity to absorb neutrons, its resistance to corrosion in hot water, and its adequate strength at the operating temperature of reactors. [f. *Hafnia* Latinized name of Copenhagen (Da. *havn* harbour)]

haft /hɑːft/ *n.* a handle (of a dagger, knife, etc.). —*v.t.* to furnish with a haft. [OE]

hag *n.* an ugly old woman; a witch. —**haggish** *adj.* [OE]

Haggai /ˈhægɪaɪ/ **1.** a Hebrew minor prophet of the 6th c. BC. **2.** a book of the Old Testament containing his prophecies of a glorious future in the Messianic age.

Haggard /ˈhægəd/, Sir Henry Rider (1856–1925), English writer, a close friend of Kipling, famous for his 34 adventure novels which have been continuously popular (several have been filmed). The most celebrated of these are *King Solomon's Mines* (1886) and *She* (1889), both set in Africa, which vividly convey the author's fascination with the life, landscape, and history of that continent.

haggard /ˈhægəd/ *adj.* looking exhausted and distraught from prolonged worry etc. —*n.* a hawk caught when full-grown. [f. F]

haggis /ˈhægɪs/ *n.* a Scottish dish of offal boiled in a bag with suet, oatmeal, etc. [orig. unkn.]

haggle *v.i.* to dispute or argue (esp. *about* or *over* a price or terms). —*n.* haggling. [orig. = 'to hack', f. ON]

hagio- /ˈhægɪəʊ-/ *in comb.* of saints. [f. Gk *hagios* holy]

hagiography /hægɪˈɒgrəfɪ/ *n.* the writing of saints' lives. —**hagiographer** *n.* [f. HAGIO- + -GRAPHY]

hagiology /hægɪˈɒlədʒɪ/ *n.* the literature of the lives and legends of saints. [f. HAGIO- + -LOGY]

hagridden *adj.* afflicted by nightmares or fears. [f. HAG + *ridden* p.p. of RIDE]

Hague /heɪg/, **The** the seat of government and administrative centre of the Netherlands, on the North Sea coast in southern Holland; pop. 449,364. The International Court of Justice is based at The Hague.

ha ha /hɑː ˈhɑː/ repr. laughter. [OE]

ha-ha /ˈhɑːhɑː/ *n.* a ditch with a wall on the inner side, forming the boundary to a park or garden without interrupting the view. [F, perh. f. cry of surprise at discovering an obstacle]

Hahn /hɑːn/, Otto (1879–1968), German chemist, co-discoverer of nuclear fission, for which he shared the 1944 Nobel Prize for chemistry with Fritz Strassmann (1902–). He started the study of radiochemistry during a brief work period outside Germany to study English, first with Sir William Ramsey in London and then with Rutherford in Manchester, identifying various radioactive isotopes of thorium. His fruitful partnership with Lise Meitner (1878–1968) began shortly after his return to Germany and ended when she, a Jew, fled from the Nazis in 1938. They discovered the new element protoactinium in 1917, but the culmination of their collaboration occurred in 1938 when, with Strassmann, they discovered nuclear fission, so named by Meitner's nephew, the physicist Otto Robert Frisch (1904–79).

hahnium /ˈhɑːnɪəm/ *n.* the US name for the chemical element of atomic number 105, a short-lived artificially produced transuranic element (cf. NIELSBOHRIUM). [f. HAHN]

Haig /heɪg/, Douglas, 1st Earl Haig of Bemersyde (1861–1928), commander of British armies in France 1915–18. Firmly believing that the war could be won only by defeating the German army on the Western Front, he maintained a policy of attrition throughout his period of command, despite political pressure to reduce casualties. Although frequently dismissed as a butcher, Haig was among the most competent soldiers of his day, and did at last succeed in winning the war in the way he said he would, by breaking the strength of the main enemy army in the field, albeit at a dreadful cost in British lives. After the war he established the (Royal) British Legion, and organized Poppy Day.

haiku /ˈhaɪkʊ/ *n.* (*pl.* same) a Japanese lyric form of 17 syllables in lines of 5, 7, 5, syllables. It emerged in the 16th c. and flourished from the 17th c. to the 19th c., and dealt traditionally with images of the natural world; in the 20th c. it has been much imitated in Western literature. [Jap.]

hail[1] *n.* **1.** pellets of frozen rain falling in a shower. **2.** a shower *of* blows, missiles, questions, etc. —*v.t./i.* to fall or send down as or like hail. [OE]

hail[2] *int.* of greeting. —*v.t./i.* **1.** to salute; to greet *as.* **2.** to call to (a person or ship) in order to attract attention; to signal to (a taxi etc.) to stop. **3.** to originate, to have come. —*n.* hailing. —**be hail-fellow-well-met,** to be very friendly or too friendly (*with* strangers etc.). **Hail Mary,** an Ave Maria (see AVE). [f. ON *heill* whole, sound (cf. HALE)]

Haile Selassie /ˈhaɪlɪ səˈlæsɪ/ (1891–1975), emperor of Ethiopia 1930–74. He became an internationally known figure during his country's heroic but unsuccessful resistance to Italian invasion. After living in exile in Britain during the Italian occupation (1936–41) he returned to his throne, eventually being deposed in a Communist military coup in 1974.

hailstone *n.* a pellet of hail.

hailstorm *n.* a prolonged period of heavy hail.

hair *n.* **1.** any of the fine threadlike strands growing from the skin of animals, especially from the human head; these collectively; an elongated cell growing from the surface of a plant. **2.** a thing resembling a hair. **3.** a very small quantity. —**get in a person's hair,** to encumber or annoy him. **hair-do** *n.* (*pl.* **-dos**) (*colloq.*) a hair-style; the process of a woman's hairdressing. **hair-grip** *n.* a flat hairpin with the prongs closing tightly together. **hair-line** *n.* the edge of a person's hair on the forehead etc.; a very narrow crack or line. **hair-net** *n.* a net worn to hold the hair in place. **hair-piece** *n.* a quantity of false hair worn to augment a person's natural hair. **hair-raising** *adj.* terrifying. **hair's breadth,** a minute distance. **hair shirt,** a shirt of haircloth worn by penitents or ascetics. **hair-slide** *n.* a clip for keeping the hair in position. **hair-splitting** *adj.* splitting hairs (see below). **hair-style** *n.* a particular way of arranging the hair. **hair-trigger** *n.* a trigger set for release at the slightest pressure. **keep one's hair on,** (*slang*) to remain calm and not get angry. **let one's hair down,** (*colloq.*) to abandon restraint, to behave wildly; to become confidential. **make one's hair stand on end,** to horrify one. **not to turn a hair,** to remain unmoved or unaffected. **split hairs,** to make small and insignificant distinctions. [OE]

hairbrush *n.* a brush for arranging the hair.

haircloth *n.* cloth woven from hair.

haircut *n.* cutting the hair; a style of doing this.

hairdresser *n.* one whose business is to arrange and cut hair.

hairpin *n.* a U-shaped pin for fastening the hair. —**hairpin bend,** a sharp U-shaped bend in a road.

hairspring *n.* a fine spring regulating the balance-wheel in a watch.

hairy *adj.* **1.** having much hair; made of hair. **2.** (*slang*) hair-raising, unpleasant, difficult. —**hairiness** *n.* [f. HAIR]

Haiti /ˈheɪtɪ/ a country in the Caribbean, the French-speaking western portion of the island of Hispaniola; pop. 6,000,000; official language, French; capital, Port-au-Prince. In 1492 Columbus discovered the island that now comprises Haiti and the Dominican Republic, and named it La Isla Española (the Spanish Island). The native inhabitants were quickly enslaved or killed by the Spaniards, who established some not very successful settlements at the east end of the island, while French pirates were more successful in establishing plantations in the west. In 1697 the eastern area was ceded to the French, who introduced large numbers of slaves from West Africa to work in the sugar-plantations. In 1791 the slaves rose in rebellion; they swept to victory under Black leaders such as Toussaint L'Ouverture and in 1804 the colony was proclaimed an independent State, under the name of Haiti, the first country in the Americas (after the USA) to achieve freedom from colonial rule. Haiti's West African heritage is shown by the great preponderance of pure Blacks in the population (in contrast to the largely mulatto Dominican Republic) and the practice of voodoo rites. —**Haitian** *adj.* & *n.*

hake *n.* a sea-fish of the genus *Merluccius*, resembling the cod, used as food. [perh. f. dial. *hake* hook]

Hakluyt /ˈhæklʊːt/, Richard (*c.*1552–1616), English geographer. A distinguished scholar and cleric, he was lecturer in geography at Oxford University and Archdeacon of

Westminster. His fame, however, is due to his writings on exploration, his most famous work *Principall Navigations* (1589) being a compilation of accounts of famous voyages of discovery up to his time of writing, which brought to light the hitherto obscure achievements of English navigators and gave great impetus to discovery and colonization.

Halafian /hæ'læfɪən/ *adj.* of a chalcolithic culture (*c.*5000-4500 BC) identified primarily by the use of polychrome pottery (Halaf ware) which was first noted during excavations at Tell Halaf in NE Syria. Its distribution extends to the Mediterranean coast and the region of Lake Van in eastern Turkey. —*n.* this culture.

halal /hɑː'lɑːl/ *v.t.* to kill (an animal for meat) as prescribed by Muslim law. —*n.* meat prepared thus. [f. Arab., = lawful]

halberd /'hælbəd/ *n.* (*hist.*) a combined spear and battle-axe. [f. F f. It. f. MHG *helmbarde*]

halcyon /'hælsɪən/ *adj.* calm and peaceful; (of a period) happy, prosperous. [f. L f. Gk, = kingfisher, reputed to calm the sea at midwinter]

Haldane /'hɔːldeɪn/, John Burdon Sanderson (1892-1964), Scottish mathematical biologist who helped to lay the foundations of population genetics (the genetics of breeding groups of organisms). He also carried out experimental work in biochemistry and on the effects of diving on human physiology. Haldane became well known as a popularizer of science and for his outspoken Marxist political views. He was the brother of the novelist Naomi Mitchison.

hale[1] *adj.* strong and healthy. [northern var. of WHOLE]

hale[2] *v.t.* (*archaic*) to drag or draw forcibly. [f. OF f. ON]

half /hɑːf/ *n.* (*pl.* **halves** /hɑːvz/) **1.** either of two equal or corresponding parts into which a thing is or might be divided; either of two equal periods of play in sports. **2.** a half-price ticket, especially for a child. **3.** a school term. **4.** (*colloq.*) a half-back. **5.** (*colloq.*) a half-pint. —*adj.* amounting to half; forming a half. —*adv.* to the extent of half; (*loosely*) to some extent. —**at half cock,** when only half-ready. **by half,** excessively. **by halves,** without complete commitment (usu. after *neg.*). **go halves,** to share equally (*with*). **half-and-half** *adj.* being half one thing and half another. **half-back** *n.* a player between the forwards and the full-back in football, hockey, etc. **half-baked** *adj.* not thoroughly thought out, foolish. **half-binding** *n.* the binding of a book with leather on the spine and corners. **half-breed, -caste** *ns.* a person of mixed race. **half-brother, -sister** *ns.* a brother or sister with only one parent in common. **half-crown, half a crown,** (*hist.*) a coin or amount of 2*s.* 6*d.* **half-hearted** *adj.* lacking enthusiasm. **half hitch,** a knot formed by passing the end of a rope round its standing part and then through the bight. **half-landing** *n.* a landing half-way up a flight of stairs (ill. HOUSES). **half-mast** *n.* the position of a flag half-way up a mast, as a mark of respect for a dead person. **half measures,** measures lacking thoroughness. **half moon,** the moon when only half its disc is illuminated; the time when this occurs; a semicircular object. **half nelson,** a hold in wrestling with the arm under an opponent's arm and behind his back. **half-term** *n.* the period about half-way through a school term, usually with a short holiday. **half-timbered** *adj.* having walls with a timber frame and brick or plaster filling, a structural style common in England in the 15th-16th c. **half-time** *n.* the time at which half of a game or contest is completed, the interval then occurring. **half-title** *n.* the title or short title of a book usually printed on the recto of the leaf preceding the title-leaf. **half-tone** *n.* a black-and-white photographic illustration in which the light and dark shades are reproduced by small and large dots. **half-track** *n.* a propulsion system with wheels at the front and an endless driven belt at the back; a vehicle having this. **half-truth** *n.* a statement conveying only part of the truth. **half-volley** *n.* a return of the ball in tennis as soon as it has touched the ground, a ball in cricket so pitched that the batsman may hit it as it bounces; a hit so made. **half-way** *adj.* & *adv.* at a point equidistant between two others (*half-way house*, a compromise). **not half,** by no means; (*colloq.*) not at all; (*slang*) extremely, violently. [OE]

half-life *n.* the time taken for half of any sample of a particular radioactive isotope to decay into other materials. (The term is also used in other contexts, e.g. to describe the persistence of a drug in the body after administration.) Half-lives of radioactive isotopes vary enormously from minute fractions of a second to periods longer than the age of the universe. Each isotope, however, has a characteristic half-life which is independent of its physical and chemical

environment. Knowledge of the half-lives of radio-carbon and other naturally occurring isotopes forms the basis of their use for dating purposes. For a given initial level of radioactivity, isotopes with long half-lives are more dangerous because their radioactivity persists longer.

halfpenny /'heɪpnɪ/ *n.* (*pl.* as PENNY) (*hist.*) half a penny, a coin of this value (legal tender until 1984). —**halfpennyworth** *n.*

half-wit *n.* a stupid or foolish person —**half-witted** *adj.*

halibut /'hælɪbət/ *n.* a large flat-fish (*Hippoglossus vulgaris*) used for food. [f. *haly* holy + *butt* flat-fish, perh. because eaten on holy days]

Halicarnassus /hælɪkɑː'næsəs/ an ancient Greek city on the SW coast of Asia Minor, birthplace of the historian Herodotus and site of the Mausoleum, tomb of the local dynast Mausolus (d. 353 BC), which was one of the Seven Wonders of the World.

halitosis /hælɪ'təʊsɪs/ *n.* unpleasant-smelling breath. [f. L *halitus* breath]

hall /hɔːl/ *n.* **1.** a space or passage into which the front entrance of a house etc. opens. **2.** a large room or building for meetings, meals, concerts, etc. **3.** a large country house, especially with a landed estate; a university building used for the residence or instruction of students; (in college etc.) a common dining-room. **4.** a large public room in a palace etc.; the principal living-room of a medieval house. **5.** the building of a guild. [OE]

hallelujah var. of ALLELUIA.

Halley /'hælɪ, 'hɔːlɪ/, Edmond (1656-1742), English astronomer and mathematician, an influential Fellow of the Royal Society and friend of Newton, the publication of whose *Principia* was due largely to him. He became Professor of Geometry at Oxford University in 1703 (he was refused the chair of astronomy owing to a suspicion, which he vainly tried to combat, of his holding materialistic views), and was appointed Astronomer Royal in 1720. Halley was involved in most of the weighty astronomical problems of his day, realizing in particular that the nebulae were clouds of luminous gas among the stars and that the aurora was a phenomenon connected with the earth's magnetism. He is best known for the prediction, published in 1705, that a bright comet seen in 1531, 1607, and 1682 would reappear in 1758.

Halley's comet a bright comet whose reappearance in 1758 was predicted by Halley (see prec.). Its orbital period is about 76 years (varying slightly, depending on gravitational perturbations by the planet Jupiter), and earlier appearances can be traced in historical documents. It is first recorded in 240 BC; a representation of its appearance in 1066 is visible on the Bayeux Tapestry.

halliard var. of HALYARD.

hallmark *n.* **1.** a mark used at Goldsmiths' Hall (and by UK assay offices) for indicating the standard of gold, silver, and (since 1975) platinum (see below). **2.** a distinctive feature —*v.t.* to stamp with a hallmark.
In the UK hallmarking dates from a statute of 1300, in the reign of Edward I. The Worshipful Company of Goldsmiths has been responsible for the assaying and marking of plate in London since then, and there are assay offices in certain other towns also. With certain exceptions, all gold, silver, and platinum articles are required by law to be hallmarked before they are offered for sale. The marks impressed include a number of symbols indicating the maker, standard, date, and office. Many countries outside the UK have a system of plate marks. In the USA there is no hallmarking; local regulations existed in the 18th and 19th c., but there is no consistent system of symbols. The illustration on p. 368 shows some of the hallmarks that are or were used in Britain; imported articles have special markings. Signatory countries of the International Convention—the UK, Austria, Finland, Ireland, Portugal, Norway, Sweden, and Switzerland—recognize equivalents to their own hallmarks applied in the others.

hallo /hə'ləʊ/ *int.* used in greeting, or to call attention or express surprise. —*n.* (*pl.* **-os**) the cry 'hallo'. [var. of earlier *hollo*]

halloo /hə'luː/ *int.* & *n.* a cry used to urge on hounds, or to attract attention. —*v.t./i.* to shout 'halloo' (to). [perh. f. *hallow* pursue with shouts f. OF (imit.)]

hallow /'hæləʊ/ *v.t.* to make or honour as holy. [OE (as HOLY]

Hallowe'en /hæləʊ'iːn/ *n.* 31 Oct., the eve of All Saints' Day. [f. *hallow* holy person + EVEN[2]]

Hallmarks

All marks shown relate to silver
except where otherwise indicated

A hallmark

maker's mark   standard mark   Assay Office mark   date letter

Maker's mark (from 1363)

originally symbols, now initials

 symbol

 symbol and initials

  initials

Assay Office mark (from 1300)

now only London, Birmingham, Sheffield, and Edinburgh

London

gold and silver (leopard's head uncrowned from 1821; mark includes platinum from 1975)   Britannia silver (prior to 1975)

Edinburgh

gold and silver (also platinum from 1975)

Birmingham

gold (also platinum from 1975)   silver

Sheffield

silver (prior to 1975)   gold (also silver and platinum from 1975)

Some earlier Assay Office marks (with dates of closure)

Norwich (1702)   York (1856)   Exeter (1883)   Newcastle (1884)   Chester (1962)   Glasgow (1964)

Standard mark (from 1544)

Marks guaranteeing pure metal content of the percentage shown

sterling silver 92.5%

 marked in England

 marked in Scotland (from 1975)

 marked in Scotland (prior to 1975)

Britannia standard silver (1697–1720, also occasional use since) 95.8%

gold (crown followed by millesimal figure of the standard)

 750 i.e. 18 carat 75%

916 22 carat 91.6%

585 14 carat 58.5%

375 9 carat 37.5%

(prior to 1975 marks incorporated the carat figure, and Scottish 18 and 22 carat gold bore a thistle mark instead of the crown)

Date letter (from 1478)

one letter per year before changing to next style of letter and/or shield

cycles vary between Assay Offices

London date letters (A-U used, excluding J) showing style of first letter and years of cycle

	1498–1518[1]		1598–1618		1697[3]–1716		1796–1816		1896–1916
	1518–1538		1618–1638		1716–1736		1816–1836		1916–1936
	1538–1558		1638–1658		1736–1756		1836–1856		1936–1956
	1558–1578		1658–1678		1756–1776		1856–1876		1956–1974[2]
	1578–1598		1678–1697[2]		1776–1796		1876–1896		1975[4] –

Notes   1. Letter changed on 19 May until 1697
       2. No U used in these cycles
       3. A from 27 March–28 May 1697; year letters then changed on 29 May until 1975
       4. Year letter changed with each calendar year; from 1975 all UK Offices use the same date letters and shield shape

Hallstatt /'hɑːlʃtɑːt/ *adj.* of a phase of the late Bronze–early Iron Age, (*c*.700–500 BC), preceding the La Tène, named after a village in Austria, site of an ancient necropolis, where remains of the period were found.

hallucinate /hə'luːsɪneɪt/ *v.t./i.* to experience or cause to experience hallucinations. —**hallucinant** *adj.* & *n.* [f. L, = wander in mind f. Gk *alussō* be uneasy]

hallucination /həluː:sɪ'neɪʃ(ə)n/ *n.* an illusion of seeing or hearing an external object not actually present. —**hallucinatory** /hə'luːsɪnətərɪ/ *adj.* [as prec.]

hallucinogen /hə'luːsɪnədʒen/ *n.* a drug causing hallucinations. —**hallucinogenic** /-'dʒenɪk/ *adj.* [f. prec. + -GEN]

halma /'hælmə/ *n.* a game for two or four persons, played on a board of 256 squares, with men that are moved by leaping over others into the vacant squares beyond, from one corner to the opposite corner. It dates from *c*.1880. [Gk, = leap]

halo /'heɪləʊ/ *n.* (*pl.* -**oes**) **1.** a disc or ring of light shown round the head of a sacred figure. **2.** a glory round an idealized person etc. **3.** a disc of light seen round a luminous body, especially the sun or moon, caused by the refraction of light through vapour. —*v.t.* to surround with a halo. [f. L f. Gk *halōs* threshing-floor, disc of sun or moon]

halogen /'hælədʒ(ə)n/ *n.* any of the five chemically related non-metallic elements fluorine, chlorine, bromine, iodine, and astatine. Only iodine and astatine are solids at room temperature. All the halogens display a valency of 1 and form simple salts, such as common salt, with alkali metals. Being very reactive, they are not found in the free state in nature. [f. Gk. *hals halos* salt + -GEN]

Hals /hæls/, Frans (1581/5–1666), Dutch painter who spent his life in Haarlem, specializing in portraits. His early life is obscure, but in 1616 his *Banquet of the Officers of the St George Militia Company* shattered well-established traditions with its unprecedentedly vigorous characterization. By exploiting facial expression and using bold brushwork Hals sought in his portraits to capture the character and vitality of the individual rather than producing a map-like record of the features. His genre pictures, which reflect the influence of the Dutch followers of Caravaggio, also have a portrait-like quality. A late phase of sober restraint culminated in the group portraits of the *Regents* and *Regentesses of the Old Men's Alms House* (Haarlem, 1664) which are among the most moving portraits ever painted. Two of Hals' brothers, Dirk and Joost, and five of his sons, were also artists, but none approached his level.

halt¹ /hɔːlt, hɒlt/ *n.* **1.** a stop (usually temporary); an interruption to progress. **2.** a railway stopping-place for local services, without station buildings. —*v.t./i.* to come or bring to a halt, —**call a halt,** to decide to stop. [f. G (*halt* hold)]

halt² /hɔːlt, hɒlt/ *v.i.* **1.** to walk hesitatingly; (*archaic*) to be lame. **2.** to waver. **3.** (esp. of reasoning, verse, etc.) to falter, to be defective. —**the halt,** (*archaic*) lame or crippled people. [OE; orig. in phr. *make halt* f. G (*halt* hold)]

halter /'hɔːltə(r)/ *n.* **1.** a rope or strap with a headstall, used for leading or tying up a horse. **2.** a style of dress-top held up by a strap passing round the back of the neck. —*v.t.* to put a halter on (a horse). [OE]

halve /hɑːv/ *v.t.* **1.** to divide into two halves or parts. **2.** to reduce by half. **3.** (in golf) to draw (a hole or match) with an opponent. **4.** to fit (crossing timbers) together by cutting out half the thickness of each (ill. CARPENTRY). [f. HALF]

halves *pl.* of HALF.

halyard /'hæljəd/ *n.* a rope for raising or lowering a sail, yard, etc. (ill. SAILING-SHIPS). [f. HALE²]

Ham a son of Noah (Gen. 10: 1), traditional ancestor of the Hamites.

ham *n.* **1.** the upper part of a pig's leg salted and dried or smoked for food; meat from this. **2.** the back of the thigh, the thigh and buttock. **3.** (*slang*) an inexpert performer or actor. **4.** (*colloq.*) the operator of an amateur radio station. —*v.t./i.* (-**mm**-) to overact, to exaggerate one's actions. —**ham-fisted** *adj.*, **ham-handed** *adj.* (*slang*) clumsy. [OE]

hamburger /'hæmbɜːgə(r)/ *n.* a flat round cake of minced beef served fried, often eaten in a soft bread roll. [G (f. city of *Hamburg*)]

Hamilcar /'hæmɪlkɑː(r)/, (d. 229/8 BC) Carthaginian general and father of Hannibal, who fought Rome in the First Punic War and negotiated terms of peace after the Carthaginian defeat of 241, which led to the loss of Sicily to the Romans. From 237 BC he and Hannibal were engaged in the conquest of Spain.

Hamite /'hæmaɪt/ *n.* a member of a group of North African peoples, including the ancient Egyptians and Berbers, supposedly descended from Ham.

Hamitic /hə'mɪtɪk/ *adj.* **1.** of the Hamites. **2.** of a group of African languages including ancient Egyptian, Berber, and Cushitic, probably related in the past to the Semitic languages [f. prec.]

Hamito-Semitic /ˌhæmɪtəʊsɪ'mɪtɪk/ *adj.* of a family of languages (also known as *Afro-Asiatic*) spoken in the Middle East and in northern Africa. They can be divided into five groups: Semitic, Berber, Cushitic (spoken mainly in Ethiopia and Somalia), Chadic (which includes Hausa), and Egyptian. [f. prec.]

Hamlet /'hæmlɪt/ a legendary prince of Denmark, hero of a tragedy by Shakespeare. —**Hamlet without the Prince,** an entertainment etc. from which the chief personage is absent.

hamlet /'hæmlɪt/ *n.* a small village, especially one without a church. [f. AF dim. *hamelet* ult.f. MLG *hamm*]

hammer *n.* **1.** a tool with a heavy metal head at right angles to the handle, used for breaking, driving nails, etc. (ill. CARPENTRY). **2.** a similar contrivance, as for exploding the charge in a gun, striking the strings of a piano (ill. MUSICAL NOTATION), etc.; an auctioneer's mallet indicating by a rap that an article is sold. **3.** a metal ball attached to a wire for throwing as an athletic contest (ill. SPORTS). —*v.t./i.* **1.** to hit or beat (as) with a hammer; to strike loudly. **2.** to defeat utterly. —**come under the hammer,** to be sold at an auction. **hammer and sickle,** the symbols of the industrial worker and the peasant, used as the emblem of the USSR. **hammer and tongs,** with great vigour and commotion. **hammer-beam** *n.* a beam that projects into a room etc. from the foot of one of the roof's principal rafters (ill. CHURCH). **hammer-head** *n.* a shark of the family Sphyrnidae, with lateral extensions of the head bearing the eyes. **hammer out,** to devise (a plan) with great effort. **hammer-toe** *n.* a toe bent permanently downwards. [OE]

Hammerstein /'hæməstaɪn/, Oscar (1895–1960), American librettist and song-writer, who collaborated with the composer Richard Rodgers.

hammock /'hæmək/ *n.* a bed of canvas or rope network, suspended by cords at the ends, used especially on board ship. [f. earlier *hamaca* f. Sp. f. Carib]

Hammurabi /ˌhæmjʊə'rɑːbɪ/ (d. 1750 BC), the sixth king of the first dynasty of Babylonia. He is best known for his code of laws, drawn up late in his reign, and inscribed in Akkadian on an upright slab (now in the Louvre) originally set up in the temple of the god Marduk in Babylon. The code, in the form of 282 case laws, deals with economic provisions and with family, criminal, and civil law, providing crucial insight into the contemporary social organization.

hamper¹ *n.* a large basket usually with a hinged lid, especially with contents of food. [f. OF *hanapier* case for goblet (*hanap* goblet)]

hamper² *v.t.* to prevent the free movement or activity of; to hinder. [orig. unkn.]

Hampshire /'hæmpʃɪə(r)/ a county of southern England.

Hampton Court a palace on the north bank of the Thames in the borough of Richmond, London. It was built by Cardinal Wolsey as his private residence but later presented by him to Henry VIII, and was a favourite royal residence until the reign of George II. William III had part rebuilt by Sir Christopher Wren and the gardens laid out in formal Dutch style.

hamster *n.* a small ratlike rodent of the genus *Cricetus* etc., with cheek-pouches for carrying grain. [G]

hamstring *n.* any of the five tendons at the back of the human knee; the great tendon at the back of the quadruped's hock. —*v.t.* (*past* & *p.p.* -**stringed** or -**strung**). **1.** to cripple (a person, an animal) by cutting the hamstring or hamstrings. **2.** to impair the activity or efficiency of.

hand *n.* **1.** the end part of the human arm beyond the wrist (ill. BODY 1); the similar member of a monkey. **2.** control, custody, disposal; a share in an action, active support; agency. **3.** a thing like a hand, especially the pointer of a clock or watch. **4.** the right or left side or direction relative to a person or thing. **5.** a pledge of marriage. **6.** skill; a person with reference to a skill. **7.** style of writing; a signature. **8.** a person who does or makes something; a person etc. as a source. **9.** a manual worker in a factory, farm, etc. **10.** the playing-cards dealt to a player; such a player; a round of play. **11.** (*colloq.*) applause. **12.** a forefoot of a quadruped; a forehock of pork. **13.** the measure of a horse's height, = 4 in. —*attrib.* operated by hand; held or carried by hand; done by hand not by machine. —*v.t.* to deliver, to transfer by hand or otherwise (*down, in, over,* etc.); to serve or distribute *round.* —**all hands,** the entire crew of a ship. **at hand,** close by; about to happen. **by hand,** by a person not a machine; delivered by messenger not by post. **from hand to mouth,** with only one's immediate needs. **get** *or* **have** *or* **keep one's hand in,** to become or be in practice. **hand and** *or* **in glove,** in collusion or association (*with*). **hand-axe** *n.* a prehistoric stone implement, normally oval or pear-shaped and bi-facially worked, used for cutting and scraping things as well as for chopping (ill. ARCHAEOLOGY). **hand down,** to transmit (a decision) from a higher court etc. **hand it to,** (*colloq.*) to award deserved praise to. **hand-me-down** *n.* clothing etc. passed on from someone else. **hand-out** *n.* something given free to a needy person; a statement given to the press etc. **hand-over-fist,** (*colloq.*) with rapid progess. **hand-picked** *adj.* carefully chosen. **hands down,** with no difficulty. **hand to hand,** (of fighting) at close quarters. **have one's hands full,** to be fully occupied. **in hand,** at one's disposal, under one's control, receiving attention. **off one's hands,** no longer one's responsibility. **on hand,** available. **on one's hands,** resting on one as a responsibility. **on the one** (*or* **on the other**) **hand,** as one (or another) point of view. **out of hand,** out of control, peremptorily. **put** *or* **set** *or* **turn one's hand to,** to start work on, to engage in. **to hand,** within reach; available. [OE]

handbag *n.* a small bag for holding a purse and small personal articles, carried especially by women.

handball *n.* **1.** a ball for throwing with the hand. **2.** a game played with this. Various handball games were played in ancient times (one is mentioned in the *Odyssey*), but the term is now usually applied to one played between two goals or in a walled court. An annual contest, usually on a holiday in spring, is an ancient institution in towns, villages, and parishes in southern Scotland.

handbell *n.* a small bell rung by hand.

handbill *n.* a printed notice circulated by hand.

handbook *n.* a short manual or guidebook.

handbrake *n.* a brake operated by hand.

h. & c. *abbr.* hot and cold (water).

handcart *n.* a small cart pushed or drawn by hand.

handclap *n.* a clapping of the hands.

handcuff *v.t.* to put handcuffs on. —*n.* (in *pl.*) a pair of lockable linked metal rings for securing a prisoner's wrists.

Handel /ˈhænd(ə)l/, George Frederick (1685-1759), German-born composer, who settled in London in 1712 and became English by naturalization. His patrons in England included George I, for whom he composed the *Water Music* suite (*c.*1717). Handel stands in complete contrast to his great contemporary, Bach: his way of life was cosmopolitan, he had a natural feeling for the dramatic and the personal in music, and he was in touch with all the modern styles and developments. Like Bach he was a superb organist; most of his works for that instrument are organ concertos, a form invented by him and intended to be performed between the acts of his own oratorios. Superb as are his instrumental compositions it is in the operas and oratorios that the nobility, expressiveness, and captivation of his art are found at their highest degree of development. Handel's English oratorios, perhaps his most original contribution to the art of music, became and have remained an institution in this country. The *Messiah* (1742), by which his name is known throughout the world, takes words directly from the Bible and is without a plot in the usual sense, but more typical of his concept of oratorio as biblical stories expressed in musical drama are *Alexander's Feast* (1736), *Saul* (1739), *Belshazzar* (1745), and *Judas Maccabaeus* (1747). For the last seven years of his life Handel was blind, but he continued to conduct oratorio performances and to revise his scores. The popularity of his work dominated English music for nearly 150 years. He died a national figure, and so has remained; he is buried in Westminster Abbey.

handful *n.* **1.** a quantity that fills the hand. **2.** a small number (*of* people or things). **3.** (*colloq.*) a troublesome person or task. [f. HAND + -FUL]

handicap /ˈhændɪkæp/ *n.* **1.** a disadvantage imposed on a superior competitor or competitors in order to make the chances more equal; a race or contest in which this is imposed. **2.** the number of strokes by which a golfer

normally exceeds par for the course. **3.** a thing that makes progress or success difficult. **4.** a physical or mental disability. —*v.t.* (-**pp**-) to impose a handicap on; to place (a person) at a disadvantage. [app. f. phr. *hand i'* (= in) *cap* describing a kind of sporting lottery]

handicapped *adj.* suffering from a physical or mental disability. [f. prec.]

handicraft /ˈhændɪkrɑːft/ *n.* work that requires both manual and artistic skill. [f. earlier *handcraft*]

handiwork /ˈhændɪwɜːk/ *n.* work done or a thing made by the hands, or by a particular person. [OE *handgeweorc* (as HAND, WORK)]

handkerchief /ˈhæŋkətʃɪf, -tʃiːf/ *n.* (*pl.* -**chiefs,** -**chieves** /-tʃiːvz/) a square of linen, cotton, etc., usually carried in a pocket for wiping the nose etc. [f. HAND + KERCHIEF]

handle *n.* **1.** the part by which a thing is held, carried, or controlled. **2.** a fact that may be taken advantage of. **3.** (*colloq.*) a personal title. —*v.t./i.* **1.** to touch, to feel, or move with the hands. **2.** to manage or deal with; to deal in (goods); to discuss or write about (a subject). —**fly off the handle,** (*colloq.*) to lose one's self-control. [OE (as HAND)]

handlebar *n.* (often in *pl.*) the steering-bar of a bicycle etc., with a hand-grip at each end. —**handlebar moustache,** a thick moustache with curved ends.

handler *n.* a person who handles things; a person who handles animals, especially one in charge of a trained police-dog etc. [f. prec.]

handmade *adj.* made by hand not machine.

handmaid *n.* (also -**maiden**) (*archaic*) a female servant.

handrail *n.* a narrow rail for holding as a support on stairs etc.

handset *n.* a telephone mouthpiece and ear-piece as one unit.

handshake *n.* a shaking of a person's hand with one's own as a greeting etc.

handsome /ˈhænsəm/ *adj.* **1.** good-looking. **2.** generous; (of a price, fortune, etc.) considerable. —**handsomely** *adv.*, **handsomeness** *n.* [f. HAND; orig. = 'easily handled']

handspring *n.* a somersault in which one lands first on the hands and then on the feet.

handstand *n.* the acrobatic feat of supporting one's body on one's hands with feet in the air or against a wall.

handwriting *n.* writing with a pen, pencil, etc.; a person's particular style of this. —**handwritten** *adj.*

handy *adj.* **1.** convenient to handle or use; ready to hand. **2.** clever with the hands. —**handily** *adj.*, **handiness** *n.* [f. HAND]

handyman *n.* (*pl.* -**men**) a person who is good at doing household repairs etc. or who is employed to do odd jobs.

hang *v.t./i.* (*past & p.p.* **hung** except in sense 6) **1.** to cause a thing to be supported from above, especially with the lower part free. **2.** to set up (a door) on hinges. **3.** to place (a picture) on a wall or in an exhibition. **4.** to attach (wallpaper) to a wall. **5.** to decorate (a room etc.) *with* pictures, ornaments, etc. **6.** (*past & p.p.* **hanged**) to execute or kill by suspending from a rope round the neck. **7.** (*colloq.*, as an imprecation) damn, be damned. **8.** to let droop; to be or remain hung (in various senses); to be hanged. —*n.* the way a thing hangs. —**get the hang of,** (*colloq.*) to get the knack of, to understand. **hang about** *or* **around,** to loiter, not to move away. **hang back,** to show reluctance. **hang fire,** to be slow in taking action or in progressing. **hang heavily** *or* **heavy,** (of time) to pass slowly. **hang on,** to stick or hold closely (*to*); to depend on (a circumstance); to remain in office or doing one's duty etc.; to attend closely to; (*colloq.*) not to ring off in telephoning; (*slang*) to wait for a short time. **hang out,** to lean out (*of* a window etc.); to put on a clothes-line etc. **hang over,** to threaten. **hang together,** to be coherent; to remain associated. **hang up,** to hang from a hook etc.; to put aside; to end a telephone conversation; to cause delay to. **hang-up** *n.* (*slang*) an emotional inhibition or problem. **hung parliament,** one in which no party has a clear majority. **not care** *or* **give a hang,** (*colloq.*) not to care at all. [OE]

hangar /ˈhæŋə(r), -ŋgə(r)/ *n.* a shed for housing aircraft etc. [F]

hangdog *adj.* shame-faced.

hanger *n.* **1.** a person or thing that hangs. **2.** a shaped piece of wood etc. from which clothes may be hung. **3.** a loop etc. by which a thing may be hung. —**hanger-on** *n.* (*pl.* **hangers-on**) a follower or dependant, especially an unwelcome one.

hang-glider *n.* the frame used in hang-gliding (ill. FLIGHT).

hang-gliding *n.* the sport of gliding while being suspended from an airborne frame controlled by one's movements.

hanging *n.* **1.** execution by being hanged. **2.** (in *pl.*) draperies hung on a wall etc. —*adj.* that hangs. —**Hanging Gardens of Babylon,** terraced gardens at Babylon, watered by pumps from the Euphrates, ascribed to Nebuchadnezzar II (*c.*600 BC). They were one of the Seven Wonders of the World. **hanging valley** etc., one ending in an abrupt descent to another valley or to the sea (ill. MOUNTAINS). [f. HANG]

hangman *n.* (*pl.* **-men**) an executioner who hangs condemned persons.

hangnail *n.* an agnail. [corrupt.]

hangover *n.* **1.** a severe headache or other after-effects caused by an excess of alcohol. **2.** something left over from an earlier time.

hank *n.* a coil or length of wool or thread etc. [f. ON]

hanker *v.i.* to long *for,* to crave *after.* [f. obs. *hank*]

hanky *n.* (*colloq.*) a handkerchief. [abbr.]

hanky-panky *n.* (*slang*) dishonest dealing, trickery; naughtiness. [arbitrary]

Hannibal /ˈhænɪb(ə)l/ (247–183/2 BC), Carthaginian general, one of the world's greatest soldiers, with extraordinary tactical skill, a bold conception of strategy, and a capacity for leadership which commanded the loyalty of mercenary troops amid danger and defeat. He precipitated the Second Punic War by attacking Rome's ally Saguntum in Spain. In 218 BC by a pre-emptive move he led an army of about 30,000 over the Alps into Italy; the perennial problem of his exact route remains unsolved but the achievement still rouses admiration. There he inflicted a series of defeats on the Romans, campaigning for sixteen years undefeated but failing to take Rome itself. Finally recalled to Africa he was defeated at Zama by Scipio in 202 BC, escaped to Carthage, and counselled peace. After a further career as statesman in Carthage he committed suicide in exile in Bithynia to avoid a Roman extradition order.

Hanoi /hæˈnɔɪ/ the capital of Vietnam, and formerly of North Vietnam before the reunification of North and South Vietnam; pop. (1984) 925,000.

Hanover /ˈhænəvə(r)/ **1.** a North German town (pop. (est. 1981) 527,500), capital of Lower Saxony and formerly capital of the State of Hanover. **2.** a North German State, an electorate of the Empire ruled by the Guelph dynasty, and subsequently a province of Prussia. In 1714 the Elector of Hanover succeeded to the British throne as George I, and from then until 1837 the same monarch ruled both Britain and Hanover. With the accession of Victoria to the British throne, however, Hanover passed to her uncle, Ernest, Duke of Cumberland, the Hanoverian succession being denied to a woman as long as a male member of the Guelph family survived. **3.** the name of the British royal house from 1714 to the death of Queen Victoria in 1901. —**Hanoverian** /-ˈvɪərɪən/ *adj. & n.*

Hansard /ˈhænsɑːd/ the official reports of the proceedings of the Houses of Parliament, colloquially so called because for most of the 19th c. they were published by Messrs Hansard. The name disappeared from the title-page in 1892 and was restored in the reports on the session of 1942–3; since 1909 publication has been by HMSO.

Hanseatic League /hænsɪˈætɪk/ a medieval association of north German cities, formed in 1241 as a commercial alliance for trade between the eastern and western sides of northern Europe. In the later Middle Ages the League, with about 100 member towns, functioned as an independent political power, with its own army and navy, but it began to collapse in the early 17th c. and only three major cities (Hamburg, Bremen, and Lübeck) remained until it was finally broken up in the 19th c. [f. G f. Gothic *hansa* company]

Hansen's disease /ˈhæns(ə)nz/ leprosy. [f. G. H. A. *Hansen,* Norwegian physician (d. 1912), discoverer of the leprosy bacillus]

hansom /ˈhænsəm/ *n.* (*hist.*) (in full **hansom cab**) a two-wheeled horse-drawn cab for two inside, with the driver seated behind. [f. J. A. *Hansom,* English architect (d. 1882)]

Hants *abbr.* Hampshire.

Hanukka /ˈhɑːnəkə/ *n.* an eight-day Jewish festival of lights, beginning in December, commemorating the re-

dedication of the Temple in 165 BC after its desecration by the Syrian king. [f. Heb., = consecration]

hanuman /hənuːˈmɑːn/ *n.* **1.** an Indian langur venerated by Hindus. **2. Hanuman,** (*Hinduism*) a semi-divine monkey-like creature to whom extraordinary powers were attributed, whose exploits are described in the Ramayana. [Hindi f. Skr., = (large-)jawed]

hap *n.* (*archaic*) change, luck; a chance occurrence. —*v.i.* (**-pp-**) (*archaic*) to come about by chance. [f. ON]

haphazard /hæpˈhæzəd/ *adj.* done etc. by chance, random. —*adv.* at random. —**haphazardly** *adv.* [f. HAP + HAZARD]

hapless *adj.* unlucky. [f. HAP + -LESS]

haploid /ˈhæplɔɪd/ *adj.* having a single set of unpaired chromosomes; having this in somatic cells. —*n.* a haploid cell or organism. [G, f. Gk *haplous* single + *eidos* form]

ha'p'orth /ˈheɪpəθ/ *n.* a halfpennyworth. [contr.]

happen *v.i.* **1.** to occur (by chance or otherwise). **2.** to have the (good or bad) fortune (*to do* a thing). **3.** to be the fate or experience of. —**happen on** or **upon,** to find by chance. [f. HAP]

happening *n.* **1.** an event. **2.** an improvised or spontaneous theatrical etc. performance. [f. prec.]

happy *adj.* **1.** feeling or showing pleasure or contentment. **2.** fortunate. **3.** (of words or behaviour) apt, pleasing. —**happy event,** the birth of a child. **happy-go-lucky** *adj.* cheerfully casual. **happy medium,** a means of satisfactory avoidance of extremes. —**happily** *adv.,* **happiness** *n.* [f. HAP]

Hapsburg /ˈhæpsbɜːg/ the name, taken from Castle Hapsburg in Switzerland, of a German family to which belonged rulers of various countries of Europe from 1273, when they first became kings of Germany, until 1918, and various Holy Roman Emperors from 1483. A branch of the family ruled in Spain 1504–1700.

hara-kiri /hærəˈkɪrɪ/ *n.* ritual suicide involving disembowelment with the sword, formerly practised by samurai to avoid dishonour. [Jap *hara* belly, *kiri* cutting)]

harangue /həˈræŋ/ *n.* a lengthy and earnest speech. —*v.t./i.* to make a harangue to. [f. OF f. L]

Harappa /həˈræpə/ an ancient city of the Indus Valley civilization, in NW Pakistan.

Harare /hɑːˈrɑːrɪ/ (formerly *Salisbury*) the capital of Zimbabwe; pop. (est. 1982) 656,000.

harass /ˈhærəs/ *v.t.* to trouble and annoy continually; to make repeated attacks on (an enemy). —**harassment** /ˈhærəsmənt/ *n.* [f. F f. OF *harer* set dog on]

harbinger /ˈhɑːbɪndʒə(r)/ *n.* a person or thing that announces or signals the approach of another; a forerunner. [f. OF (*herberge* lodging, as foll.), formerly = one sent on ahead to purvey lodgings for army etc.]

harbour /ˈhɑːbə(r)/ *n.* a place of shelter for ships; shelter. —*v.t.* **1.** to give shelter to (a criminal etc.). **2.** to keep in one's mind (an unfriendly thought etc.). —**harbour-master** *n.* the officer in charge of a harbour. [OE or f. ON, = army shelter]

hard *adj.* **1.** firm, not yielding to pressure; solid, not easily cut. **2.** difficult to understand or do or answer. **3.** causing unhappiness, difficult to bear; harsh, unpleasant; unsympathetic; (of a season or weather) severe, frosty; (of a bargain) without concessions. **4.** strenuous, enthusiastic. **5.** (of liquor) strongly alcoholic. **6.** (of a drug) potent and addictive. **7.** (of water) containing mineral salts that prevent soap from lathering freely and cause a hard coating to form inside kettles, water, tanks, etc. **8.** (of facts etc.) established, not to be disputed. **9.** (of currency or prices) not likely to fall suddenly in value. **10.** (of pornography) highly obscene. **11.** (of consonants) guttural (as *c* in *cat, g* in *go*). —*adv.* strenuously, intensively; copiously. —**hard and fast,** (of a rule or distinction) definite, unalterable. **hard-boiled** *adj.* (of an egg) boiled until the white and yolk are solid; (of a person) callous. **hard by,** close by. **hard case,** an intractable person; a case of hardship. **hard cash,** coins and banknotes, not cheques or credit. **hard copy,** printed material produced by computer, suitable for ordinary reading. **hard core,** an irreducible nucleus; heavy material as a road-foundation. **hard-headed** *adj.* practical, not sentimental. **hard-hearted** *adj.* unsympathetic. **hard labour,** heavy manual work (e.g. stone-breaking) formerly imposed on persons convicted of serious crimes. **hard line,** unyielding adherence to a firm policy. **hard of hearing,** somewhat deaf. **hard on** or **upon,** close to in pursuit or sequence. **hard pad,** a form of distemper in dogs etc. **hard**

palate, the front part of the palate. **hard-pressed** *adj.* closely pursued; burdened with urgent business. **hard put to it,** in difficulty. **hard sell,** aggressive salesmanship. **hard shoulder,** a hardened strip alongside a motorway for stopping on in an emergency. **hard up,** short of money; at a loss *for.* **hard-wearing** *adj.* able to stand much wear. —**hardness** *n.* [OE]

hardback *adj.* bound in stiff covers. —*n.* a hardback book.

hardbitten *adj.* tough and tenacious.

hardboard *n.* stiff board made of compressed and treated wood-pulp.

harden *v.t./i.* to make or become hard or harder, or (of an attitude etc.) unyielding. [f. HARD]

Hardie /ˈhɑːdɪ/, James Keir (1856-1915), Scottish labour leader and politician, first chairman of the Labour Party (1906).

hardihood /ˈhɑːdɪhʊd/ *n.* boldness, daring. [f. HARDY]

hardly *adv.* **1.** only with difficulty. **2.** scarcely, only just. **3.** harshly. [f. HARD]

hardship *n.* severe discomfort or lack of the necessaries of life; a circumstance causing this. [f. HARD + -SHIP]

hardware *n.* **1.** tools and household articles of metal etc. **2.** heavy machinery or weaponry. **3.** the mechanical and electronic components of a computer etc.

hardwood *n.* the hard heavy wood from deciduous trees.

Hardy /ˈhɑːdɪ/, Thomas (1840-1928), English novelist and poet, born in Dorset (the son of a stonemason), where he spent most his life, working as an architect until his literary reputation became established. His most popular novels are those set in 'Wessex' (Dorset) with which Hardy is so closely identified, among them *Under the Greenwood Tree* (1872), *Far from the Madding Crowd* (1874), *The Mayor of Casterbridge* (1886), *Tess of the D'Urbervilles* (1891), and *Jude the Obscure* (1896), his most pessimistic. Hardy then turned to poetry and produced eight volumes of poems of great variety and distinction. In all his works, including his epic drama *The Dynasts* (1904-8), the underlying theme is man's struggle against the indifferent force that inflicts the sufferings and ironies of life and love, though there is sharp humour in his rustic characters.

hardy /ˈhɑːdɪ/ *adj.* robust, capable of enduring difficult conditions; (of a plant) able to grow in the open air all the year. —**hardy annual,** an annual plant that may be sown in the open; a subject that comes up at regular intervals. —**hardiness** *n.* [f. OF *hardi* (*hardir* become bold, as HARD)]

Hare /heə(r)/, William, see BURKE[4].

hare *n.* a field mammal of the genus *Lepus* like a rabbit, with long ears, a short tail, hind legs longer than the forelegs, and a divided upper lip. —*v.i.* to run rapidly. —**hare-brained** *adj.* wild and foolish, rash. [OE]

harebell *n.* a plant (*Campanula rotundifolia*) with pale-blue bell-shaped flowers.

Hare Krishna /ˌhɑːreɪ ˈkrɪʃnə/ the title of a love-chant or mantra based on the name of the Hindu deity Vishnu, used as an incantation by members of a religious cult in the USA and elsewhere. The International Society for Krishna Consciousness was founded in New York in 1966; its principles include strict vegetarianism and prohibit gambling, drugs, and extramarital sex. Members dress in saffron robes, the men have shaved heads, and daily ritual includes dance-marching through the streets to the accompaniment of Oriental instruments and chanting of the Hare Krishna mantra. [f. Hindi *hare* O God, KRISHNA]

harelip *n.* a congenital fissure of the upper lip.

harem /ˈhɑːriːm, -ˈriːm/ *n.* the women of a Muslim household, living in a separate part of the house; their quarters. [f. Arab., = prohibited]

Hargreaves /ˈhɑːgriːvz/, James (1720-78), English inventor, one of the great pioneers of the cotton industry in Lancashire. He was employed by Robert Peel (grandfather of the statesman) to construct an improved carding-machine (*c.*1760), and produced one using a roller with multiple pins to comb out the cotton fibres, but is best known for the 'spinning jenny' (the reason for its name is not known) which he patented in 1770. This was the first machine with multiple spindles, enabling one man to work 8 or even 16 spindles simultaneously. The invention was greatly needed: improvements in weaving following the invention of the flying shuttle (1733) meant that the weavers were working more quickly and the spinners could no longer keep pace with them. Unfortunately Hargreaves's success in speeding up the spinning process caused opposition; spinners on the old-fashioned wheels were alarmed at the threat to their

employment, and in 1768 a mob broke into his house and destroyed it and the machinery. He failed commercially, though Arkwright later developed the machine successfully and Crompton improved upon it with his 'mule'.

haricot /ˈhærɪkəʊ/ *n.* (in full **haricot bean**) the white dried seed of a variety of bean (*Phaseolus vulgaris*). [F]

hark *v.i.* to listen attentively. —**hark back,** to revert *to* a subject. [as HEARKEN]

Harlequin /ˈhɑːlɪkwɪn/ originally a stock character in Italian comedy, a witty servant, always in love, always in trouble, easily despairing, easily consoled. In English pantomime he is a mute character supposed to be invisible to the clown and pantaloon, the clown's rival in the affections of Columbine, usually wearing a mask and particoloured tights. [F, f. *Herlequin* leader of a legendary nocturnal troop of demon horsemen]

harlequin /ˈhɑːlɪkwɪn/ *adj.* in varied colours. [f. prec.]

harlequinade /ˌhɑːlɪkwɪˈneɪd/ *n.* **1.** a play or section of a pantomime in which Harlequin plays the leading role (see below). **2.** a piece of buffoonery. [f. F (see HARLEQUIN)]

Harlequinade was an important element, originating in Italy, in the development of the English pantomime. It originally consisted of story-telling dances in which Harlequin, a magical character, played the leading role. In the 19th c. Grimaldi made the purely English character Clown into the chief personage, and to ease the burden on the dancers the harlequinade was preceded by a fairy-tale. As Harlequin's importance lessened and the fairy-tales became longer and more popular, the harlequinade dwindled into a short epilogue to what became the present English pantomime (see entry). It was finally abandoned completely.

Harley Street /ˈhɑːlɪ/ a street in London long associated with the premises of eminent physicians and surgeons, whence the allusive use of its name to refer to medical specialists.

harlot /ˈhɑːlət/ *n.* (*archaic*) a prostitute. —**harlotry** *n.* [f. OF, = lad, knave]

harm *n.* damage, injury. —*v.t.* to cause harm to. —**out of harm's way,** in safety. [OE]

harmattan /hɑːməˈtæn/ *n.* a dry dusty wind that blows on the coast of West Africa from December to February. [f. Afr. dialect *haramata*]

harmful *adj.* causing harm. —**harmfully** *adv.* [f. HARM + -FUL]

harmless *adj.* not able or likely to cause harm; inoffensive. —**harmlessly** *adv.*, **harmlessness** *n.* [f. HARM + -LESS]

harmonic /hɑːˈmɒnɪk/ *adj.* **1.** (*Mus.*) of or relating to harmony; (of tones) produced by the vibration of a sting etc. in any of certain fractions (half, third, quarter, fifth, etc.) of its length. **2.** harmonious. —*n.* a harmonic tone, an overtone. —**harmonic series,** (*Mus.*) the series of overtones that make up the natural components of a single sound. —**harmonically** *adv.* [f. L f. Gk (as HARMONY)]

harmonica *n.* a mouth-organ. [L (as prec.)]

harmonious /hɑːˈməʊnɪəs/ *adj.* **1.** sweet-sounding. **2.** forming a pleasing or consistent whole. **3.** free from disagreement or dissent. —**harmoniously** *adv.* [f. HARMONY]

harmonium /hɑːˈməʊnɪəm/ *n.* a keyboard musical instrument in which the notes are produced by air driven through metal reeds by bellows operated by the feet. [F f. L (as HARMONY)]

harmonize /ˈhɑːmənaɪz/ *v.t./i.* **1.** to add notes to a melody to provide a harmonic accompaniment to it. **2.** to bring into or be in harmony (*with*). —**harmonization** /-ˈzeɪʃ(ə)n/ *n.* [f. F (as foll.)]

harmony /ˈhɑːmənɪ/ *n.* **1.** a combination of simultaneously sounded musical notes to form chords and chord progressions (see below); the study of this. **2.** a pleasing effect of the apt arrangement of parts. **3.** agreement, concord. —**in harmony (with),** in agreement (with). [f. OF f. L f. Gk *harmonia* joining (*harmos* joint)]

Harmony gives what is known as 'vertical' music, contrasted with the 'horizontal' music of melody. Chords and chord progressions play an important role, and one melody is usually given prominence, whereas in counterpoint several strands of melody are given equal prominence. The traditional system of harmony became the dominating force in Western music towards the beginning of the 17th c., and the principle of melody and accompaniment has underpinned much music since. Chromatic harmony was always a means of creating particularly expressive passages, but in the 19th c. it became so pervasive that often the tonal organization of a piece seems lost in dense ambiguous texture. Schoenberg's early music is of this kind, and he was one of the first composers to tip the scales away from tonal thinking towards atonality (called by him 'pan-tonality') and from there into serial composition.

harness /'hɑːnɪs/ *n.* the equipment of straps and fittings by which a horse is fastened to a cart etc. and controlled; a similar arrangement for fastening a thing to a person. —*v.t.* **1.** to put a harness on (a horse); to attach by a harness (*to*). **2.** to utilize (a river or other natural force) to produce electrical power etc. —**harness racing**, see TROTTING. **in harness,** in the routine of daily work. [f. OF, = military equipment]

Harold /'hær(ə)ld/ the name of two kings of England:
  Harold I 'Harefoot' (d. 1040), reigned 1035–40. An illegitimate son of Cnut, Harold first came to the throne when Cnut's legitimate son was absent in Denmark at the time of his father's death. When the other royal claimant, Alfred the Aetheling, was murdered a year later, Harold was formally recognized as king, although Cnut's legitimate son Harthacnut returned to the kingdom when Harold himself died in 1040.
  Harold II (*c.*1019–66), reigned 1066, the last Anglo-Saxon king of England. He succeeded Edward the Confessor, having dominated the court in the last two years of his predecessor's reign, but was faced with two invasions within months of his accession. He defeated and killed his half-brother Tostig and the Norse king Harald Hardrada at Stamford Bridge, but was himself slain at Hastings by William, Duke of Normandy, who took the throne as William I.

harp *n.* a large very ancient instrument comprising a set of strings placed over an open frame so that they can be plucked or swept with the fingers from both sides (ill. ORCHESTRA). The standard orchestral harp has a range of about six-and-a-half octaves, but has only seven notes to each octave, further notes being obtained by use of the pedals. The harp may be the oldest stringed instrument: it is depicted in various forms in pre-Christian times, is mentioned in the Old Testament (Gk *psalterion*), and appears in Ireland, Scotland, and France in the 9th and 10th centuries. —*v.i.* to dwell tediously *on* (a subject). —**harpist** *n.* [OE]

Harpocrates /hɑːˈpɒkrəti:z/ see HORUS.

harpoon /hɑːˈpuːn/ *n.* a barbed spear-like missile with a rope attached, for catching whales etc. —*v.t.* to spear with a harpoon. [f. F *harpoon* f. L f. Gk *harpē* sickle]

harp-seal *n.* a Greenland seal with a dark harp-shaped mark on its back.

harpsichord /'hɑːpsɪkɔːd/ *n.* a wing-shaped keyboard instrument which differs from clavichord and piano in that the strings are plucked by a small leather or quill plectrum. Other instruments of the harpsichord type are the spinet and the oblong-shaped virginal, but the terms were sometimes used interchangeably. The first full description of an instrument of this kind is found in the mid-15th c., and an upright harpsichord (or *clavicytherium*) survives from the same period, but the heyday of the harpsichord was from the late 16th–mid-18th c. Its tone is crisp and clear, but it is unable to make a gradual progression between loud and soft sounds by pressure on the keys. It was overtaken in popularity by the piano, which can do this, at the end of the 18th c., but enjoyed a revival in the 20th c. —**harpsichordist** *n.* [f. F f. *harpa* harp + *chorda* string]

harpy /'hɑːpɪ/ *n.* **1.** (*Gk myth.*) any of the winged beings, apparently winds in origin, who carry off various persons and things. Their names are Aello, Ocypete, and Celoeno. In ancient art they are shown as winged women; Virgil, however, describes them as birds with women's faces, and they were later portrayed in this form. **2.** a grasping unscrupulous person. [f. F or L f. Gk *harpuiai* snatchers (*harpazō* snatch)]

harquebus /'hɑːkwɪbəs/ *n.* (*hist.*) a portable gun supported on a tripod or forked rest. [f. F ult. f. G (*haken* hook, *busse* gun)]

harridan /'hærɪd(ə)n/ *n.* a bad-tempered old woman. [perh. f. F *haridelle* old horse]

harrier /'hærɪə(r)/ *n.* **1.** a hound used for hunting hares. **2.** (in *pl.*) cross-country runners. **3.** a falcon of the genus *Circus*. [f. HARE or HARROW]

Harrow /'hærəʊ/ (short for **Harrow School**) a public school at Harrow-on-the-Hill, Middlesex, and traditional rival of Eton College. It was founded and endowed by John Lyon under a charter (1572) granted by Queen Elizabeth I.

harrow /'hærəʊ/ *n.* a heavy frame with iron teeth dragged over ploughed land to break up clods, cover seed, etc. —*v.t.* **1.** to draw a harrow over (land). **2.** to distress greatly. [f. ON]

Harrowing of Hell the medieval term of the defeat of the powers of evil, and the release of its victims, by the descent of Christ into Hell after his death. It is mentioned in the Epistle to the Ephesians 4: 9 and included in certain early creeds (but not the Nicene Creed). In art, it was depicted mainly in the Greek Church, where it superseded the Resurrection; examples in the West are usually those under Greek influence. It was also a subject of medieval mystery plays.

harry /'hærɪ/ *v.t.* to ravage or despoil; to harass. [OE]

harsh *adj.* unpleasantly rough or sharp, especially to the senses; severe, cruel. —**harshly** *adv.*, **harshness** *n.* [f. MLG (as HAIR)]

hart *n.* the male of the (red) deer, especially after the 5th year. [OE]

Harte /hɑːt/, Francis Bret (1836–1902), American writer, remembered chiefly for his short stories about low-life in a gold-mining settlement, inspired by his own brief experience in mining, collected in *The Luck of Roaring Camp* (1870). His humorous-pathetic verse included 'Plain Language from Truthful James' (1870), often referred to as 'The Heathen Chinee'.

hartebeest /'hɑːtɪbiːst/ *n.* a large African antelope of the genus *Alcelaphus*, with curving horns. [Afrik. f. Du. (as HART + BEAST)]

Hartley /'hɑːtlɪ/, Leslie Poles (1895–1972), English novelist. After years as a fiction reviewer and writer of short stories he published his trilogy *The Shrimp and the Anemone* (1944), *The Sixth Heaven* (1946), and *Eustace and Hilda* (1947), a vivid evocation of childhood and young manhood. His most successful novel *The Go-Between* (1953) records the events of the hot summer of 1900 and gives a spirited account of leisurely Edwardian England.

harum-scarum /heərəm ˈskeərəm/ *adj.* wild and reckless. —*n.* such a person. [rhyming formation on HARE, SCARE]

Harvard /'hɑːvəd/ the oldest American university, founded in 1636 at Cambridge, Massachusetts. It is named after John Harvard (d. 1638), an English settler who bequeathed to it his library and half his estate.

harvest /'hɑːvɪst/ *n.* the gathering in of crops etc., the season of this; the season's yield; the product of any action. —*v.t./i.* to gather as a harvest, to reap. —**harvest festival,** a thanksgiving festival in church for the harvest. **harvest moon,** the full moon nearest to the autumn equinox (22 or 23 Sept.). **harvest mouse,** a very small mouse (*Micromys minutus*) nesting in the stalks of standing corn. [OE]

harvester *n.* **1.** a reaper. **2.** a reaping-machine. [f. prec.]

Harvey /'hɑːvɪ/, William (1578–1657), English discoverer of the circulation of the blood, and physician to James I and Charles I. Harvey set himself to provide, on the basis of the Aristotelian technique of sensory observation, a satisfactory account of the motion of the heart, and concluded that it forcibly expelled blood in contraction. He emphasized the quantity of blood emerging from the heart into the arteries, and finding that this quanitity was too great to be absorbed by the body as food, as contemporary theory held, noted that it must therefore pass through the flesh and enter the veins, returning once more to the heart. Harvey also applied his Aristotelianism to a study of insects, the motions of animals, and animal reproduction.

Haryana /hʌrɪˈɑːnə/ a State of India, formed in 1966 mostly from the Hindi-speaking part of the former State of Punjab.

has see HAVE. —**has-been** *n.* a person or thing that is no longer as famous or successful etc. as formerly.

hash¹ *n.* **1.** a dish of cooked meat cut into small pieces and recooked. **2.** a mixture, a jumble. **3.** re-used material. —*v.t.* to make (meat) into a hash. —**make a hash of,** (*colloq.*) to make a mess of, to bungle. **settle a person's hash,** (*colloq.*) to deal with and subdue him. [f. F *hacher* (*hache* hatchet)]

hash² *n.* (*colloq.*) hashish. [abbr.]

Hashemite /'hæʃɪmaɪt/ *adj.* of an Arab princely family related to Muhammad. [f. *Hashim* great-grandfather of Muhammad]

hashish /'hæʃiːʃ/ *n.* the top leaves and tender parts of hemp, dried for smoking or chewing as a narcotic. [f. Arab.]

Hasmonean /hæzməˈnɪən/ *adj.* of a Jewish dynasty or

family to which the Maccabees belonged. —*n.* a member of this dynasty. [f. Gk f. name of reputed ancestor]

hasn't /'hæz(ə)nt/ (*colloq.*) has not.

hasp /hɑːsp/ *n.* a hinged metal clasp that fits over a staple and is secured by a padlock. [OE]

hassle *n.* (*colloq.*) a quarrel, a struggle; a difficulty. —*v.t./i.* (*colloq.*) to quarrel; to harass. [dial.]

hassock /'hæsək/ *n.* **1.** a thick firm cushion for kneeling on. **2.** a tuft of grass. [OE]

hastate /'hæsteɪt/ *adj.* (esp. of leaves) triangular like a spearhead (ill. PLANTS). [f. L (*hasta* spear)]

haste /heɪst/ *n.* urgency of movement or action, hurry. —*v.i.* to hasten. —**in haste,** quickly, hurriedly. **make haste,** to be quick. [f. OF]

hasten /'heɪs(ə)n/ *v.t./i.* **1.** to make haste, to hurry. **2.** to cause to occur or be ready or be done sooner. [f. prec.]

Hastings[1] /'heɪstɪŋz/ a town on the coast of East Sussex, scene of William the Conqueror's victory over the Anglo-Saxon king Harold II in 1066. Having invaded England to enforce his claim to the throne, William, Duke of Normandy was confronted by Harold's army drawn up on a hill. The English shield wall withstood Norman attacks through most of the day, but eventually broke after the less disciplined parts of the army had been lured off the hill and destroyed. Harold, along with most of his good fighting men, died in the battle, and William subsequently seized London and the vacant throne.

Hastings[2] /'heɪstɪŋz/, Warren (1732–1818), British colonial administrator who rose from being a clerk in the East India Company to become India's first Governor-General in 1774, and, while holding that post, introduced many of the administrative reforms vital to the successful maintenance of British rule in India, while also overseeing the defence of his territories against invasion. On his return to England in 1785 he was accused, not completely unjustly, of high-handedness and corruption, and was eventually impeached on the latter charge. After a seven-year trial before the House of Lords, he was acquitted in 1795 and retired to private life.

hasty /'heɪstɪ/ *adj.* **1.** hurried, acting too quickly. **2.** said, made, or done too quickly or too soon. —**hastily** *adv.*, **hastiness** *n.* [f. OF]

hat *n.* a covering for the head, especially worn out of doors. —**hat trick,** the taking of three wickets at cricket by the same bowler with three successive balls; the scoring of three goals or winning of three victories by one person. **keep it under one's hat,** to keep it secret. **out of a hat,** by random selection. **pass the hat round,** to collect contributions of money. **take off one's hat,** to applaud. **talk through one's hat,** (*slang*) to talk wildly or ignorantly. [OE]

hatband *n.* a band of ribbon etc. round a hat above the brim.

hatch[1] *n.* **1.** an opening in a floor or wall etc.; an opening or door in an aircraft etc. **2.** a cover for a hatchway. [OE]

hatch[2] *v.t./i.* **1.** (of a young bird or fish etc.) to emerge from the egg; (of an egg) to produce a young animal; to incubate (an egg). **2.** to devise (a plot etc.). —*n.* hatching; a brood hatched. [rel. to MHG *hecken* etc.]

hatch[3] *v.t.* to mark with close parallel lines. —**hatching** *n.* [f. F *hacher* (as HASH[1])]

hatchback *n.* a car with a sloping back hinged at the top to form a door.

hatchet /'hætʃɪt/ *n.* a light short-handled axe. —**hatchet man,** a hired killer, a person employed to make personal attacks. [f. OF *hachette* (*hache* axe)]

hatchway *n.* an opening in a ship's deck for lowering cargo.

hate *n.* **1.** hatred. **2.** (*colloq.*) a hated person or thing. —*v.t.* to feel hatred towards; to dislike greatly; (*colloq.*) to be reluctant. —**hater** *n.* [OE]

hateful *adj.* arousing hatred. [f. HATE + -FUL]

Hathaway /'hæθəweɪ/, Anne (?1557–1623), the wife of Shakespeare, whom she married in 1582.They had three children, a daughter (Susannah) and a twin daughter and son (Judith and Hamnet).

Hathor /'hæːθɔ:(r), 'hæthɔː(r)/ (*Egyptian myth.*) a sky and cow goddess, the patron of love and joy, represented as a cow or with a cow's head or ears, or with a solar disc between a cow's horns. Her name means 'House of Horus' (= the sky, in which Horus (the sun) rises and sets).

hatred /'heɪtrɪd/ *n.* intense dislike or ill will. [f. HATE + -*red* f. OE *ræden* condition]

Hatshepsut /hæt'ʃepsʊt/ a queen of Egypt (c.1473–1458 BC) of the 18th Dynasty, widow of Tuthmosis II. Initially ruler under her nephew Tuthmosis III, she proclaimed herself co-ruler and dominated the partnership until her death, after which she was vilified by Tuthmosis who defaced her monuments.

hatter *n.* a maker or seller of hats. [f. HAT]

Hattusas /'hætu:sæs/ the capital of the Hittite empire, situated in central Turkey about 35 km (22 miles) east of Ankara.

haughty /'hɔːtɪ/ *adj.* arrogantly proud of oneself and looking down on others. —**haughtily** *adv.*, **haughtiness** *n.* [f. OF *haut* high f. L *altus*]

haul /hɔːl/ *v.t./i.* **1.** to pull or drag forcibly. **2.** to transport by lorry or cart etc. **3.** to turn a ship's course. **4.** (*colloq.*) to bring (*up*) for reprimand or trial. —*n.* **1.** hauling. **2.** an amount gained or acquired. **3.** a distance to be traversed. [var. of HALE[2]]

haulage /'hɔːlɪdʒ/ *n.* transport of goods; the charge for this. [f. HAUL]

haulier /'hɔːlɪə(r)/ *n.* a firm or person engaged in the transport of goods by road. [f. HAUL]

haulm /hɔːm/ *n.* a stalk or stem; (*collect.*) the stems of potatoes, peas, beans, etc. [OE]

haunch /hɔːntʃ/ *n.* the fleshy part of the buttock and thigh; a leg and loin of deer etc. as food. [f. OF *hanche*]

haunt /hɔːnt/ *v.t.* **1.** (of a ghost) to be frequently in (a place), especially with reputed manifestations of its presence. **2.** to be persistently in (a place). **3.** (of a memory etc.) to linger in the mind of. —*n.* a place frequented by a person. [f. OF *hanter* (rel. to HOME)]

Hauptmann /'haʊptmæn/, Gerhart (1862–1946), German dramatist, who studied sculpture before turning to literature. His first play *Vor Sonnenaufgang* (*Before Sunrise*, 1889), and *Die Weber* (*The Weavers*, 1892) are important examples of German naturalism, but *Hanneles Himmelfahrt* (*The Ascension of Joan*, 1893), with its visionary elements, deviated towards a new symbolism. Though he frequently returned to more realistic drama during his productive career, Hauptmann's reputation rests on his earlier works which significantly influenced German literature by introducing to the theatre the most uncompromising material of daily life. He was awarded the Nobel Prize for literature in 1912.

Hausa /'haʊsə/ *n.* (*pl.* same or **-s**) **1.** a member of a wide-spread Negroid people of the Sudan and northern Nigeria, of the Bantu family with some Hamitic mixture. **2.** their language, the most important in West Africa, spoken by some 25 million people mainly in Nigeria and Niger. It belongs to the Chadic branch of the Afro-Asiatic language group. [native name]

hautboy /'ɔʊbɔɪ/ *n.* obs. name of the OBOE. [f. F, = high wood]

haute couture /əʊt ku:'tjʊə(r)/ high fashion; the leading fashion houses collectively, or their products. [F]

haute cuisine /əʊt kwɪ'zi:n/ high-class cookery. [F]

hauteur /əʊ'tɜ:(r)/ *n.* haughtiness of manner. [F (*haut* high)]

Havana /hə'vænə/ the capital of Cuba and chief port of the West Indies, famous for its cigars; pop. (est. 1981) 1,924,886. —*n.* a cigar made at Havana or elsewhere in Cuba.

have[1] /həv, *emphat.* hæv/ *v.t.* (3 sing. pres. **has** /həz, *emphat.* hæz/; *past & p.p.* **had** /həd, *emphat.* hæd/; *partic.* **having**) **1.** to be in possession of; to possess in a certain relationship. **2.** to contain as a part or quality. **3.** to experience, to undergo. **4.** to engage in (an activity). **5.** to give birth to (a baby). **6.** to form (an idea etc.) in the mind; to know (a language). **7.** to receive; to eat or drink. **8.** to be burdened with or committed to. **9.** to be provided with. **10.** to cause or instruct to be or do or be done etc.; to accept or tolerate; (usu. *neg.*) to permit to. **11.** to let (a feeling etc.) be present in the mind; to be influenced by (a quality, as mercy etc.). **12.** (*colloq.*) to have sexual intercourse with. **13.** (*colloq.*) to deceive; to get the better of. —*v.aux.* with p.p. of verbs forming past tenses (*I have, had, shall have, seen; had I known I would have gone*). **have had it,** (*colloq.*) to have missed one's chance, to have passed one's prime, to have been killed. **have it,** to express the view *that*; to win a discussion; (*colloq.*) to have found the answer; to possess an advantage. **have it in for,** (*colloq.*) to be hostile or ill-disposed to. **have it off**, (*slang*) to have sexual intercourse. **have it out**, to settle a dispute by argument (*with*). **have on**, to wear (clothes); to have (an engagement); to tease or hoax. **have to**, (*colloq.*) to have got to, to be obliged to, must. **have up**, to bring before a court of justice or to be interviewed. [OE]

have² /hæv/ *n*. **1.** one who has (especially wealth or resources). **2.** (*slang*) a swindle. —**haves and have-nots**, the rich and the poor. [= prec.]

haven /ˈheɪv(ə)n/ *n*. a refuge; a harbour; a port. [OE]

haven't /ˈhæv(ə)nt/ (*colloq.*) have not.

haver /ˈheɪvə(r)/ *v.i.* **1.** to hesitate, to vacillate. **2.** to talk foolishly. [orig. unkn.]

haversack /ˈhævəsæk/ *n*. a strong canvas etc. bag carried on the back or over the shoulder. [f. F f. G, = oats-sack]

havoc /ˈhævək/ *n*. widespread destruction, great disorder. [f. AF f. OF *havo(t)*]

haw¹ *n*. a hawthorn berry [OE; cf. HEDGE]

haw² see HUM.

Hawaii /həˈwaɪɪ/ a State of the USA comprising a chain of islands (including Hawaii) in the North Pacific, discovered by Captain Cook in 1778. Annexed by the USA in 1898, it became the 50th State in 1959; capital, Honolulu. —**Hawaiian** *adj.* & *n*.

hawfinch *n*. a large finch (*Coccothraustes coccothraustes*) with a powerful beak. [f. HAW¹ + FINCH]

hawk¹ *n*. **1.** a bird of prey of the family Accipitridae, with rounded wings shorter than a falcon's. **2.** a person who advocates an aggressive policy. —*v.t./i.* to hunt with a hawk —**hawk-eyed** *adj.* keen-sighted. **hawk-moth** *n*. a large hovering and darting moth of the family Sphingidae. [OE]

hawk² *v.t./i.* to clear the throat of phlegm noisily; to bring up (phlegm) thus. [prob. imit.]

hawk³ *v.t.* to carry (goods) about for sale. [f. foll.]

hawker *n*. one who hawks goods about. [prob. f. LDu.; cf. HUCKSTER]

Hawkins /ˈhɔːkɪnz/, Sir John (1532–95), Elizabethan sailor. A former slave-trader (associated with his cousin Sir Francis Drake), Hawkins was involved in the early privateering raids on the Spanish West Indies in the 1560s and 1570s. As first Treasurer and then Comptroller of the Elizabethan navy he played an important part in building up the fleet which defeated the Spanish Armada in 1588, during which time he was third in command of the English forces. Like Drake, he died at sea on an unsuccessful expedition to the West Indies in 1595.

Hawksmoor /ˈhɔːksmʊə(r)/, Nicholas (1661–1736), English architect who worked with Wren and with Vanbrugh. His most distinguished works are the six London churches designed under the commission of 1711.

hawser /ˈhɔːzə(r)/ *n*. a thick rope or cable for mooring or towing a ship. [f. OF *haucier* hoist f. L *altus* high]

hawthorn *n*. a thorny shrub of the genus *Crataegus* with small dark red berries. [f. HAW¹ and THORN]

Hawthorne /ˈhɔːθɔːn/, Nathaniel (1804–64), American novelist, best known as the author of *The Scarlet Letter* (1850), an inquiry into the nature of American Puritanism and the New England conscience, and *The House of Seven Gables* (1851), dealing with hereditary guilt and emulation. He was in England as consul in Liverpool 1853–7, then spent two years in Italy which inspired *The Marble Faun* (1860). Hawthorne is recognized as one of the greatest of American writers, a moralist much preoccupied with the 'transmitted vices of society', reflecting his own sensitivity about his Puritan ancestry.

hay *n*. grass mown and dried for fodder. —**hay fever**, an allergic disorder caused by pollen or dust. **hit the hay**, (*slang*) to go to bed. **make hay of**, to throw into confusion. **make hay while the sun shines**, to seize opportunities for profit. [OE]

Haydn /ˈhaɪd(ə)n/, Franz Joseph (1732–1809), Austrian-born composer, of German parentage. He has long been regarded as the 'father of the symphony', and although the paternity of that form must remain in doubt his position in musical history is assured by the number and magnitude of his masterpieces. His oratorios *The Creation* (1796–8) and *The Seasons* (1799–1801), with their vivid pictorialism and expansive choruses, have long been favourites with the musical public, but his humour, vitality, and sophisticated strength are equally at home in his vast output of over 100 symphonies, 68 string quartets, 47 firmly attributable keyboard sonatas, and the six great Masses composed in

Vienna 1796–1802. Haydn spent 30 years with the Esterházy household, mostly in Hungary, and this enforced isolation from the musical world meant that, in his own words, he was 'forced to become original'. He became a friend of Mozart, whom he greatly admired, and his later years were crowded with invitations to conduct and compose abroad; when he visited England in 1791–2 and 1794–5 he was fêted, lionized, and entertained by royalty. On his return to Vienna he accepted Beethoven as a pupil, an uneasy relationship for them both. From about 1801 his health began to fail and he died during the French occupation of Vienna.

haymaking *n*. mowing grass and spreading it to dry. —**haymaker** *n*.

haystack *n*. (also **hayrick**) a packed pile of hay with a pointed or ridged top.

haywire *adj.* (*colloq.*) badly disorganized, out of control. [f. use of hay-baling wire in makeshift repairs]

hazard /ˈhæzəd/ *n*. **1.** a danger or risk; a source of this. **2.** an obstacle on a golf-course. —*v.t.* to risk; to venture (an action or suggestion etc.). [f. F f. Sp. f. Arab., = chance, luck]

hazardous *adj.* risky. —**hazardously** *adv.* [f. prec.]

haze *n*. **1.** thin atmospheric vapour. **2.** mental confusion or obscurity. [f. HAZY]

hazel /ˈheɪz(ə)l/ *n*. **1.** a bush or small tree of the genus *Corylus* bearing small edible nuts. **2.** a light brown colour. —**hazel-nut** *n*. [OE]

Hazlitt /ˈhæzlɪt/, William (1778–1830), British essayist and critic, the son of a Unitarian minister whose radical views he inherited. Hazlitt began as a painter but, encouraged by Coleridge, chose a literary career. He became a prominent journalist, lecturer, and critic, contributing articles on diverse subjects to many periodicals; some of his best essays are collected in *Table Talk* (1821–2) and *The Plain Speaker* (1826). Among his important critical works are *Lectures on the English Poets* (1818) and *The Spirit of the Age* (1825). His style, marked by clarity and conviction, brought a new vigour to English prose writing.

hazy *adj.* **1.** misty; vague, indistinct. **2.** confused, uncertain. —**hazily** *adv.*, **haziness** *n*. [orig. unkn.]

HB *abbr.* hard black (pencil-lead).

H-bomb /ˈeɪtʃbɒm/ *n*. a hydrogen bomb. [f. H (for HYDROGEN) + BOMB]

HCF *abbr.* highest common factor.

HE *abbr.* **1.** high explosive. **2.** His Eminence. **3.** His or Her Excellency.

He *symbol* helium.

he /hiː/ *pron.* (*obj.* HIM; *poss.* HIS; *pl.* THEY) **1.** the man, boy, or male animal previously named or in question. **2.** a person etc. of unspecified sex. —*n*. a male, a man. —*adj.* (usu. with hyphen) male (*he-goat*). —**he-man** *n*. a masterful or virile man. [OE]

head /hed/ *n*. **1.** the upper part of the human body, or the foremost part of an animal's body, containing the mouth, sense-organs, and brain. **2.** the seat of the intellect and the imagination; mental aptitude. **3.** (*colloq.*) a headache. **4.** a person, an individual; an individual animal; (*collect.*) animals. **5.** an image of the head on one side of a coin; (usu. in *pl.*) this side turning up in the toss of a coin. **6.** the height or length of the head as a measure. **7.** a thing like a head in form or position, e.g. the striking part of a tool, the flattened top of a nail, the mass of leaves or flowers at the top of a stem, the flat end of a drum; the foam on top of beer etc.; the closed end of the cylinder in a pump or engine; the component on a tape-recorder that touches the moving tape in play and converts the signals. **8.** the upper end (of a table, occupied by the host; of a lake, at which a river enters; of a bed etc., for one's head); the front (of a procession etc.); the bows of a ship. **9.** the top or highest part (of stairs, a list, page, mast, etc.). **10.** a chief person or ruler; a master etc. of a college; a headmaster or headmistress; (*attrib.*) highest in authority. **11.** a position of command. **12.** a confined body of water or steam; the pressure exerted by this. **13.** a promontory (esp. in place-names). **14.** a division in a discourse; a category. **15.** a culmination, a climax or crisis. **16.** the fully developed top of a boil etc. —*v.t./i.* **1.** to be at the head of or in charge of. **2.** to strike (the ball) with the head in football. **3.** to provide with a head or heading. **4.** to face or move (in a specified direction). **5.** to direct the course (of). —**give a person his head**, to let him move or act freely. **go to one's head**, (of liquor) to make one dizzy or slightly drunk; (of success) to make one conceited. **head-dress** *n.* an ornamental covering or band for head. **head first,** (of a plunge etc.) with the head foremost; (*fig.*) precipitately. **head for,** to be moving towards (a place, or (*fig.*) trouble). **head off,** to get ahead so as to intercept; to forestall. **head-on** *adj.* & *adv.* (of a collision etc.) head to head or front to front. **head over heels,** rolling the body over in a forward direction; topsy-turvy. **head-shrinker** *n.* (*slang*) a psychiatrist. **head start,** an advantage granted or gained at an early stage. **head wind,** a wind blowing from directly in front. **keep** (*or* **lose**) **one's head,** to keep (or lose) calm or self-control. **make head or tail of** (usu. *neg.*), to understand. **off one's head,** (*colloq.*) crazy. **off the top of one's head,** (*colloq.*) impromptu, at random. **on one's** (**own**) **head,** being one's responsibility. **over a person's head,** beyond his understanding; to a position or authority higher than his. **put heads together,** to consult together. **turn a person's head,** to make him conceited. [OE]

headache *n.* **1.** a continuous pain in the head. **2.** (*colloq.*) a worrying problem.

headboard *n.* an upright panel along the head of a bed.

header *n.* **1.** a heading of the ball in football. **2.** (*colloq.*) a dive or plunge with the head first. **3.** a brick etc. laid at right angles to the face of a wall. (ill. BUILDING). [f. HEAD]

headgear *n.* a hat or head-dress.

heading *n.* **1.** a title at the head of a page or section of a book etc. **2.** a horizontal passage in a mine. [f. HEAD]

headlamp *n.* a headlight.

headland *n.* a promontory.

headlight *n.* a powerful light at the front of a motor vehicle or railway engine; the beam from this.

headline *n.* a heading at the top of an article or page, especially in a newspaper; (in *pl.*) a summary of the most important items in a broadcast news bulletin.

headlong *adj.* & *adv.* with the head foremost; in a rush.

headman *n.* (*pl.* **-men**) the chief man of a tribe etc.

headmaster *n.* the principal master of a school, responsible for organizing it. —**headmistress** *n.fem.*

headphones *n.pl.* earphones held in position by a band fitting over the head.

headquarters *n.* (as *sing.* or *pl.*) the place where a military or other organization is centred.

headroom *n.* the space or clearance above a vehicle etc.

headship *n.* the position of chief or leader, especially of a headmaster or headmistress.

headstall *n.* the part of a bridle or halter fitting round a horse's head.

headstone *n.* a stone set up at the head of a grave.

headstrong *adj.* self-willed and obstinate.

headwaters *n.pl.* the streams formed from the sources of a river.

headway *n.* **1.** progress; the rate of progress of a ship. **2.** headroom.

headword *n.* a word forming a heading.

heady *adj.* **1.** (of liquor) strong, likely to cause intoxication. **2.** (of success etc.) likely to cause conceit. **3.** impetuous. —**headily** *adv.*, **headiness** *n.* [f. HEAD]

heal *v.t./i.* **1.** (of sore or wounded parts) to form healthy flesh again; to unite after being cut or broken. **2.** to cause to do this. **3.** to put right (differences etc.). **4.** to alleviate (sorrow etc.). **4.** (*archaic*) to cure. —**healer** *n.* [OE]

health /helθ/ *n.* the state of being well in body or mind; a person's mental or physical condition. —**health centre,** the headquarters of a group of local medical services. **health food,** natural food thought to have health-giving qualities. **health service,** a public service providing medical care. **health visitor,** a trained person visiting babies or sick or elderly people at their homes. [OE (as WHOLE)]

healthful *adj.* conducive to good health, beneficial. —**healthfully** *adv.*, **healthfulness** *n.* [f. prec. + -FUL]

healthy *adj.* **1.** having, showing, or producing good health. **2.** beneficial; functioning well. —**healthily** *adv.*, **healthiness** *n.* [f. HEALTH]

heap *n.* **1.** a number of things or particles lying irregularly upon one another. **2.** (*colloq.*, esp. in *pl.*) a large number or amount. —*v.t./i.* **1.** to pile or become piled (*up*) in a heap. **2.** to load with large quantities; to give large numbers of. [OE]

hear *v.t./i.* (*past* & *p.p.* **heard** /hɜ:d/) **1.** to perceive with the ear. **2.** to listen or pay attention to; to listen to and try (a case) in a lawcourt. **3.** to be informed (*that*); to be told

(*about*). **4.** to grant (a prayer); to obey (an order). —**hear from,** to receive a letter etc. from. **hear! hear!** an expression of agreement or applause. **hear of,** to be told about; (with *neg.*) to consider, to allow. [OE]

hearer *n.* one who hears, especially as a member of an audience. [f. HEAR]

hearing *n.* **1.** the faculty of perceiving sounds by the response of the brain to the action of sound upon the ear. **2.** the range within which sounds may be heard; presence. **3.** an opportunity to be heard; trial of a case in a lawcourt, especially before a judge without a jury. —**hearing-aid** *n.* a small sound-amplifier worn by a deaf person. [f. HEAR]

hearken /ˈhɑ:kən/ *v.i.* (*archaic*) to listen (*to*). [OE]

hearsay *n.* rumour, gossip [f. *hear say*]

hearse /hɜ:s/ *n.* a vehicle for conveying the coffin at a funeral. [f. OF *herse* harrow f. L (*h*)*irpex* large rake f. Samnite (*h*)*irpus* wolf, w. ref. to its teeth]

heart /hɑ:t/ *n.* **1.** the hollow muscular organ maintaining the circulation of blood in the vascular system by rhythmic contraction and dilation (see below; ill. BODY 3). **2.** the region of the heart, the breast. **3.** the centre of thought, feeling, and emotion (especially love); capacity for feeling emotion; courage, enthusiasm. **4.** the central or innermost part, the essence; the compact head of a cabbage etc. **5.** a symmetrical figure conventionally representing a heart; a playing-card of the suit (**hearts**) marked with red designs of this shape. —**at heart,** in one's innermost feelings; basically. **break a person's heart,** to distress him or her overwhelmingly. **by heart,** in or from memory. **change of heart,** a change in one's feeling about something. **give** (*or* **lose**) **one's heart to,** to fall in love with. **have the heart to,** (usu. with *neg.*) to be insensitive or hard-hearted enough to do a thing. **heart attack,** a sudden occurrence of heart failure. **heart-break** *n.* overwhelming distress. **heart-breaking, -broken** *adjs.* causing or affected by this. **heart failure,** a failure of the heart to function properly. **heart-lung machine,** a machine which can temporarily take over the functions of the heart and lungs. **heart-rending** *adj.* very distressing. **heart-searching** *n.* an examination of one's own feelings and motives. **heart-strings** *n.* one's deepest feelings. **heart-throb** *n.* the beating of the heart; (*colloq.*) an object of romantic affections. **heart-to-heart** *adj.* frank and personal. **heart-warming** *adj.* emotionally rewarding or uplifting. **set one's heart on,** to want eagerly. **take to heart,** to be much affected by. **with all one's heart,** sincerely, with all goodwill. [OE]

The heart is a four-chambered double-barrelled muscular pump whose function is to drive arterial blood through the body and venous blood through the lungs. The two sides of the heart are quite separate, each consisting of a receiving chamber or atrium and a pumping chamber or ventricle. Venous blood from the body, laden with carbon dioxide, flows into the right atrium, is drawn into the right ventricle, ejected by each contraction or beat of the ventricle into the pulmonary artery, and so to the lungs. Oxygenated blood from the lungs flows into the left atrium, passes to the left ventricle, and is pumped into the large artery (the aorta) and so to all arteries of the body. The heartbeat begins as the spontaneous electrical discharge of clusters of cells in the right atrium, known collectively as the pace-maker. Brief electrical impulses are transmitted to both atria and then to the ventricles, causing these to contract and force the blood to the next stage in its journey round the body; flap valves at the openings between atria and ventricles open to allow its passage and close to prevent it from flowing back. The heart is controlled by two sets of nerves which can make it beat more or less often according to circumstances (during exercise, for example, the tissues need more blood and the heartbeat becomes faster).

The heart has been regarded as the seat of feeling, understanding, and thought (whence phrases such as *a warm heart, knew in his heart*), as the seat of the emotions and distinguished from the intellectual nature (placed in the *head*), or of courage (as in *stout-hearted*). (Cf. LIVER.)

heartache *n.* mental anguish.

heartbeat *n.* the pulsation of the heart.

heartburn *n.* a burning sensation in the chest.

hearten *v.t./i.* to make or become more cheerful. [f. HEART]

heartfelt *adj.* sincere, deeply felt.

hearth /hɑ:θ/ *n.* **1.** the floor of a fireplace; the area in front of this. **2.** the fireside as the symbol of domestic comfort. **3.** the bottom of a blast furnace; a fire for heating metal for forging etc. [OE]

heartily *adv.* in a hearty manner; very. [f. HEARTY]

heartland *n.* the central part of a homogeneous geographical, political, industrial, etc., area.

heartless *adj.* unfeeling, pitiless. —**heartlessly** *adv.*, **heartlessness** *n.* [f. HEART + -LESS]

heartsick *adj.* despondent.

heartwood *n.* the dense inner part of a tree-trunk, yielding the hardest timber (ill. TREES).

hearty /ˈhɑːtɪ/ *adj.* 1. strong, vigorous. 2. (of a meal or appetite) copious. 3. showing warmth of feeling, enthusiastic. —**heartiness** *n.* [f. HEART]

heat *n.* 1. a form of energy arising from the random motion of the molecules of bodies, capable of transmission by conduction, convection, or radiation (see below and ill. p. 378). 2. being hot; the sensation or perception of this; temperature; a high temperature. 3. hot weather. 4. an intense feeling, especially of anger; tension; the most vigorous stage of a discussion etc. 5. a preliminary or trial round in a race or contest, of which winners take part in a further round or in the final. 6. the receptive period of the sexual cycle, especially in female mammals. 7. redness of the skin with a sensation of heat. —*v.t./i.* to make or become hot; to inflame. —**heat capacity,** thermal capacity. **heat-engine** *n.* an engine using heat to produce mechanical energy (e.g. a steam-engine, internal-combustion engine, gas turbine). **heat pump,** see separate entry. **heat-shield** *n.* a device to protect (esp. a spacecraft) from excessive heat. **heat-stroke** *n.* an illness caused by excessive heat. **heat treatment,** the use of heat to modify the physical properties of metal etc. **heat wave,** a period of very hot weather. [OE (as HOT)]
The scientific concept of heat is a development of the ordinary understanding of heat as that which passes into a cold body from a hot body in contact with it. In the late 18th and early 19th c. heat was widely believed to be a kind of fluid substance, called caloric. It is now well established, however, that heat is a form of energy consisting of the motions of the individual molecules that make up all solids, liquids, and gases; temperature is a measure of the average kinetic energy of the molecules in a body.
Addition of heat to a body does not always lead to an increase in temperature, because the body may change state (from solid to liquid, or liquid to gas). Heat can be transmitted by conduction, convection, or radiation.

heated *adj.* (of a person or discussion etc.) angry, inflamed with passion or excitement. —**heatedly** *adj.* [f. HEAT]

heater *n.* a stove or other heating device. [f. HEAT]

heath *n.* 1. an area of flat uncultivated land covered with heather and related plants. 2. a plant growing on such land, especially of the genus *Erica* or *Calluna*. [OE]

heathen /ˈhiːð(ə)n/ *n.* one who is not a member of a widely-held religion, especially not a Christian, Jew, or Muslim. —*adj.* of heathens; having no religion. —**the heathen,** heathen people. [OE (as prec., perh. rendering L *paganus* pagan)]

heather /ˈheðə(r)/ *n.* a low shrub (*Calluna vulgaris*) with small usually purple bell-shaped flowers. [orig. unkn.]

Heath Robinson /hiːθ ˈrɒbɪns(ə)n/ absurdly ingenious and impractical. [f. W. *Heath Robinson* English cartoonist (d. 1944)]

heat pump an engine which (operating as a heat-engine in reverse) uses mechanical energy to extract heat from a source (e.g. river water, the earth, or even the air) that is at a slightly lower temperature than its surroundings and transfer a higher level of heat (e.g. to a hot-water system). Its mechanical arrangement, and the principle upon which it works, are exactly those of a large refrigerator. The idea of a heat pump was suggested by Lord Kelvin in 1852, but was not a practical proposition in the 19th c. when fuel (coal) was cheap and the cost of machinery and repairs was expensive.

heave *v.t./i.* (*past* **heaved** or (*Naut.*) **hove**) 1. to lift or haul (a heavy thing) with great effort. 2. to utter with effort. 3. (*colloq.*) to throw. 4. (*Naut.*) to haul by rope. 5. to rise and fall alternately like waves at sea. 6. to pant, to retch. —*n.* heaving. —**heave in sight,** to come into view. **heave to,** to bring (a ship) or come to a standstill with the ship's head to the wind. —**heaver** *n.* [OE]

heaven /ˈhev(ə)n/ *n.* 1. (in Christian, Jewish, and Islamic theology) a place believed to be the abode of God and of the righteous after death. Analogous concepts are found in other major religions. 2. (usu. **Heaven**) God, Providence. 3. a place or state of supreme bliss; something delightful. —**the heavens,** the sky as seen from the earth, in which the sun, moon, and stars appear. **heaven-sent** *adj.* providential. [OE]

heavenly *adj.* 1. of heaven, divine; 2. of the heavens or sky. 3. (*colloq.*) very pleasing. —**heavenly bodies,** the sun, stars, etc. [f. prec.]

Heaviside /ˈhevɪsaɪd/, Oliver (1850-1925), English physicist and electrical engineer. Largely self-taught, he began as a telegraph operator, but was forced to retire through deafness. His contributions to telegraphy theory not only improved long-distance telephone communication, but had much broader significance to both cable and wireless telegraphy. He studied inductance, and introduced the concept of impedance and of operational calculus for dealing with transient currents in electrical networks. He suggested in 1902, independently of A. E. Kennelly (1861-1939) of Harvard University, the existence of a layer in the atmosphere responsible for reflecting radio waves back to earth. The Kennelly-Heaviside (or E) Layer was later found by Appleton and others in the ionosphere.

heavy /ˈhevɪ/ *adj.* 1. of great weight or density, difficult to lift or carry or move; abundant; laden *with*; (of machinery, artillery, etc.) very large of its kind, large in calibre etc. 2. (*Phys.*, esp. of isotopes and compounds containing them) having a greater than the usual mass. 3. severe, intense, extensive; doing a thing to excess; needing much physical effort. 4. striking or falling with force; (*colloq.*) using brutal methods. 5. (of ground) difficult to traverse, clinging; (of mist or fog) dense; (of bread etc.) dense from not having risen; (of food or *fig.* of writings) stodgy, hard to digest. 6. (of the sky) overcast, gloomy. 7. clumsy or ungraceful in appearance or effect; unwieldy; tedious; serious or sombre in attitude or tone; stern. 8. oppressive, hard to endure. —*n.* 1. a villainous or tragic role or actor in a play etc. 2. (usu. in *pl.*) a serious newspaper; a heavy vehicle. —*adv.* (esp. *in comb.*) heavily. —**heavier-than-air** *adj.* (of an aircraft) weighing more than the air it displaces. **heavy-duty** *adj.* intended to withstand hard use. **heavy going,** slow or difficult progress. **heavy-handed** *adj.* clumsy, oppressive. **heavy-hearted** *adj.* sad, doleful. **heavy hydrogen,** deuterium. **heavy industry,** that producing metal, machinery, etc. **heavy metal,** heavy guns; metal of high density. **heavy water,** deuterium oxide, used as a moderator and coolant in some nuclear reactors. **make heavy weather of,** to exaggerate a difficulty or burden presented by a problem etc. —**heavily** *adv.*, **heaviness** *n.* [OE (rel. to HEAVE)]

heavyweight *n.* 1. the heaviest boxing-weight, with no upper limit (see BOXING-WEIGHT). 2. a person of above average weight. 3. a person of influence or importance —**light heavyweight,** the boxing-weight between middle-weight and heavyweight.

hebdomadal /hebˈdɒməd(ə)l/ *adj.* weekly. [f. L f. Gk *hebdomas* week (*hepta* seven)]

Hebe /ˈhiːbɪ/ 1. (*Gk myth.*) daughter of Hera and Zeus, and cup-bearer of the gods. 2. (*Astron.*) the sixth of the minor planets, discovered in 1847. [Gk, = youthful beauty]

Hebraic /hiːˈbreɪk/ *adj.* of Hebrew or the Hebrews. [f. L f. Gk (as HEBREW)]

Hebraist /ˈhiːbreɪɪst/ *n.* an expert in Hebrew. [f. foll.]

Hebrew /ˈhiːbruː/ *n.* 1. a member of a Semitic people living in ancient Palestine, traditionally from the middle Bronze Age (mid-18th c. BC); an Israelite, a Jew. 2. their Semitic language or a modern form of this (see below). —*adj.* 1. of Hebrew. 2. of the Hebrews or Jews. —**(Epistle to the) Hebrews,** a book of the New Testament, traditionally included among the letters of St Paul but now generally held to be non-Pauline. [f. OF, ult. f. Aramaic f. Heb., = one from the other side (of the river)]
Hebrew was spoken and written in ancient Palestine for more than a thousand years. It is written from right to left in an alphabet consisting of 22 letters, all consonants; not until the 6th c. AD were vowel signs added to the Hebrew text of the Old Testament to facilitate reading. By c.500 BC it had come greatly under the influence of Aramaic, which largely replaced it as a spoken language by c.200 AD, but it continued as the religious language of the Jewish people. It was revived as a spoken language in the 19th c., with the modern form having its roots in the ancient language but drawing words from the vocabularies of European languages, and is now the official language of the State of Israel.

Hebrides /ˈhebrɪdiːz/ a group of about 500 islands off the NW coast of Scotland. Until near the end of the 13th c. 'The Hebrides' included also Scottish islands in the Firth of Clyde, the peninsula of Kintyre in SW Scotland, the Isle of Man, and the (Irish) Isle of Rathlin; they formed part

Heat

Change of state

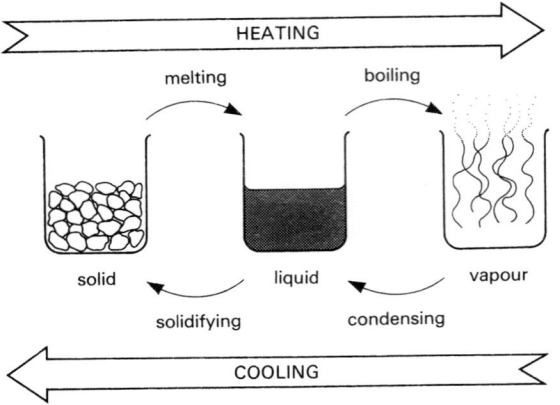

HEATING

melting   boiling

solid   liquid   vapour

solidifying   condensing

COOLING

Transfer of heat

1 conduction

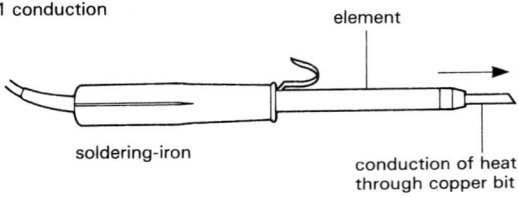

element

soldering-iron

conduction of heat
through copper bit

2 convection

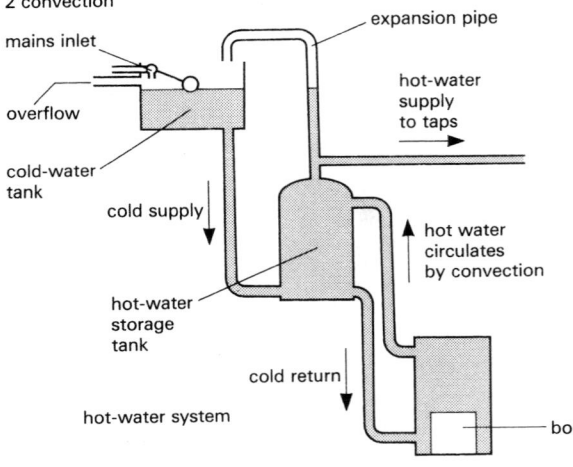

expansion pipe

mains inlet

overflow

cold-water
tank

cold supply

hot-water
storage
tank

cold return

hot-water system

hot-water
supply
to taps

hot water
circulates
by convection

boiler

3 radiation

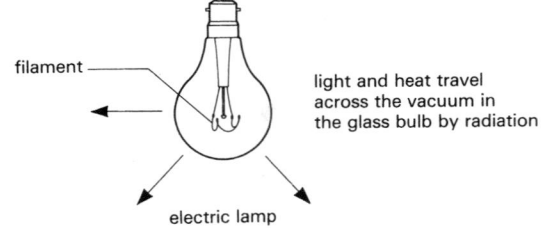

filament

light and heat travel
across the vacuum in
the glass bulb by radiation

electric lamp

Temperature measurement/thermometer

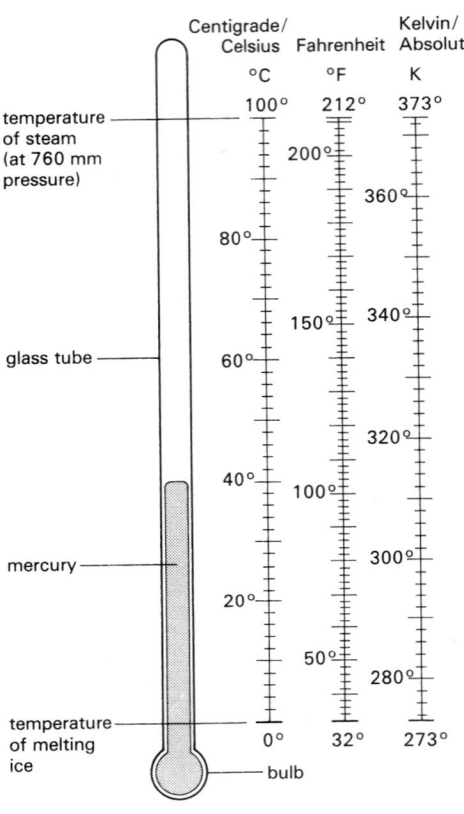

	Centigrade/ Celsius	Fahrenheit	Kelvin/ Absolute
	°C	°F	K

temperature
of steam
(at 760 mm
pressure) — 100°   212°   373°

200°

360°

80°

150°   340°

glass tube — 60°

320°

40°   100°

300°

mercury —

20°

50°

280°

temperature
of melting
ice — 0°   32°   273°

bulb

Insulation

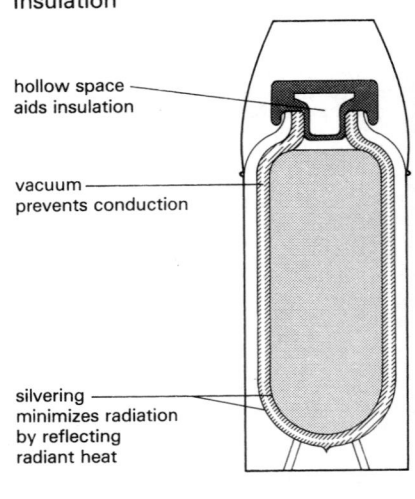

hollow space
aids insulation

vacuum
prevents conduction

silvering
minimizes radiation
by reflecting
radiant heat

vacuum flask

of the kingdom of Scotland from 1266, when they were ceded to the Scottish king Alexander III by Magnus of Norway. Norse occupation has influenced the language, customs, and place-names of the islands. The main occupations are farming, fishing, and the manufacture of textiles and woollens. —**Hebridean** /-'dɪ:ən/ adj. & n.

Hecate /'hekətɪ/ (Gk myth.) a goddess, probably of Carian origin, frequently confused with Artemis and also with Selene. She was a powerful and formidable figure, associated with uncanny things, the ghost-world, and sorcery, and was worshipped at road-junctions, which seem to be haunted the world over.

heck n. (colloq.) (in oaths) hell. [alt. of HELL]

heckle v.t. to interrupt and harass (a public speaker). —**heckler** n. [var. of HACKLE]

hectare /'hekta:(r)/ n. a metric unit of square measure, 100 ares (2.471 acres). —**hectarage** n. [f. (as HECTO- + ARE²)]

hectic adj. busy and confused, excited; feverish. —**hectically** adv. [f. OF f. L f. Gk (hexis habit)]

hecto- /hektə-/ in comb. one hundred. [F f. Gk hekaton a hundred]

hectogram /'hektəgræm/ n. a metric unit of mass, equal to 100 grams. [f. HECTO- + GRAM]

Hector /'hektə(r)/ (Gk legend) a Trojan warrior, son of Priam and Hecuba and husband of Andromache. He was killed by Achilles, who dragged his body at the wheels of his chariot three times round the walls of Troy.

hector /'hektə(r)/ v.t. to bully, to intimidate. —n. a bully. [f. prec.]

Hecuba /'hekjʊbə/ (Gk legend) wife of Priam, mother of Hector and eighteen others of Priam's fifty sons. The legends about her are many and varied.

hedge n. 1. a fence or boundary formed by closely planted bushes or shrubs. 2. a protection against possible loss. —v.t./i. 1. to surround or bound with a hedge; to surround and restrict the movement of. 2. to make or trim hedges. 3. to reduce one's risk of loss on (a bet etc.) by compensating transactions on the other side. 4. to avoid committing oneself. —**hedge-hop** v.i. to fly at a very low altitude. **hedge-sparrow** n. a common brown-backed bird, the dunnock (Prunella modularis). —**hedger** n. [OE]

hedgehog n. a small insect-eating mammal of the genus Erinaceus with a piglike snout and a thick coat of spines, rolling itself up into a ball when attacked.

hedgerow n. a row of bushes etc. forming a hedge.

hedonic /hi:'dɒnɪk/ adj. of pleasure. [f. Gk (as foll.)]

hedonism /'hi:d(ə)nɪz(ə)m/ n. the theory that pleasure is the chief good or the proper aim; behaviour based on this. —**hedonist** n., **hedonistic** /-'nɪstɪk/ adj. [f. Gk hēdonē pleasure]

heebie-jeebies /'hi:bɪdʒi:bɪz/ n.pl. (slang) nervous depression or anxiety. [orig. unkn.]

heed v.t./i. to attend to, to take notice of. —n. careful attention. [OE]

heedless adj. not taking heed. —**heedlessly** adv., **heedlessness** n. [f. HEED + -LESS]

hee-haw n. the bray of a donkey. —v.i. to bray like a donkey. [imit.]

heel¹ n. 1. the back part of the human foot below the ankle; the corresponding part of the hind limb in a quadruped, often raised above the ground; the hinder part of a hoof (ill. HORSE); (in pl.) hind feet. 2. the part of a stocking or sock covering the heel; the part of a shoe etc. supporting the heel. 3. a thing like a heel in form or position, e.g. the part of the palm next to the wrist, the handle-end of a violin bow. 4. (slang) a dishonourable person. —v.t./i. 1. to fit or renew the heel on (a shoe etc.). 2. to touch the ground with the heel, as in dancing. 3. to pass the ball with the heel in Rugby football. —**at** or **to heel**, (of a dog or fig.) close behind, under control. **at** or **on the heels of**, following closely after. **cool** or **kick one's heels**, to be kept waiting. **down at heel**, (of a shoe) with the heel worn down; (of a person) shabby. **take to one's heels**, to run away. **well-heeled** adj. wealthy. [OE]

heel² v.t./i. (of a ship) to tilt temporarily to one side; to cause (a ship) to do this. —n. an act or the amount of heeling. [prob. f. obs. heeld incline, f. OE]

heel³ var. of HELE.

heelball n. a mixture of hard wax and lampblack used by shoemakers for polishing; this or a similar mixture used in brass-rubbing.

hefty adj. (of a person) big and strong; (of thing) large, heavy, powerful. —**heftily** adv., **heftiness** n. [f. dial. heft weight (as HEAVE)]

Hegel /'heɪg(ə)l/, Georg Wilhelm Friedrich (1770–1831), German idealist philosopher. Kant's philosophy had left an essential dualism: nature opposed to spirit, object to subject, the outer world composed of isolated unrelated substances. Hegel sought to bridge this gulf, to reduce duality to unity, by finding more reality (and more value) in a whole than in its parts; the apparently separate things of which the world is composed each have a reality which consists in an aspect of the whole. Among his major works is his Philosophy of History, which can be interpreted in different ways. Hegel himself states his view of the direction and destination of human history as 'the development of the idea of freedom', reaching its consummation in the Germanic world of his own time. His influence was greatest in the 1880s and 1890s; his doctrine was broad enough (or contained sufficient ambiguity) to encourage great diversity in its application, having attractions for political thinkers of both right and left (Marx, in his youth, was a disciple of Hegel), and some theologians developed the more spiritualistic aspects of his teaching. —**Hegelian** /hɪ'geɪlɪən/ adj. & n.

hegemony /hɪ'geməni/ n. leadership, especially by one State of a confederacy. [f. Gk (hēgemōn leader)]

Hegira /'hedʒɪrə/ n. Muhammad's flight from Mecca to Medina in AD 622, which made possible the consolidation of the first Muslim community. The departure was made necessary by the opposition of the merchant community in Mecca to both Muhammad's preaching and his attempt to achieve a social solidarity that was not tribally based. Its significance to the history of Islam is indicated by the fact that the Islamic calendar (which is based on lunar months) is dated from AD 622 (= 1 AH). [L f. Arab., = departure from one's country]

Heidegger /'haɪdegə(r)/, Martin (1889–1976), German philosopher, a professor at Freiburg for much of his life and probably the leading Continental philosopher of the 20th c. His early existentialist work (though he did not regard himself as an existentialist) Being and Time (1927) examines the setting of human existence in the world. His picture of mankind's place in nature is a gloomy one: Angst (dread) is a fundamental part of their consciousness, a symptom of the gravity of their situation with its radical freedom of choice and its horizon of death. Consequently we are continually in flight from our destiny, disguising it and distracting our attention from its inevitability. Heidegger's later work addresses the question of Being: human destiny is to seek and be 'the shepherd' of Being through the almost mystical power of language, yet the mediocrity of modern life falls far short of this. His early flirtation with Nazism casts a shadow, in the eyes of some critics, over his entire philosophy.

heifer /'hefə(r)/ n. a young cow, especially one that has not had a calf. [OE]

heigh /heɪ/ int. expressing surprise or curiosity. [var. of heh, imit.]

height /haɪt/ n. 1. the measurement from the base to the top or (of a standing person) from the head to the foot. 2. the distance (of an object or position) above ground or sea level. 3. a high place or area. 4. the top; the highest point, the utmost degree. [OE (as HIGH)]

heighten v.t./i. to make or become higher or more intense [f. prec.]

Heine /'haɪnə/, Heinrich (1797–1856), German poet, born in Düsseldorf of Jewish parents. His reputation rests on his lyrics which combine a self-indulgent emotion with sharp self-criticism and deflated irony. The Buch der Lieder (Book of Songs, 1827) is one of the most influential volumes of poetry in Germany (many of these poems were set to music by Schumann and Schubert). Reisebilder (Travel Pictures, 1826–31) contains the satirical-idyllic prose book Die Harzreise. After the expulsion of Napoleon, Heine emigrated to Paris in 1830, where his works became more political; they include Zur Geschichte der Religion und Philosophie in Deutschland (1834), a witty and savage attack on German thought and literature, and his two masterpieces of verse satire Atta Troll (1843) and Deutschland (1844).

heinous /'heɪnəs/ adj. utterly odious or wicked. [f. OF (haine hatred)]

heir /eə(r)/ n. a person entitled to property or rank as the legal successor of its former owner. —**heir apparent,** an heir whose claim cannot be set aside by the birth of another

heir. heir presumptive, one whose claim may be set aside thus. —**heiress** n.fem. [f. OF f. L heres]

heirloom n. a piece of personal property that has been in a family for several generations; a piece of property as part of an inheritance. [f. HEIR + LOOM¹ in sense 'tool']

Heisenberg /'haɪz(ə)nbɜːg/, Werner Karl (1901-76), German mathematical physicist and philosopher, who developed a system of quantum mechanics based on matrix algebra. For this and his discovery of the allotropic forms of hydrogen he was awarded the 1932 Nobel Prize for physics. He announced his famous uncertainty principle (also known as the interdeterminacy principle) in 1927, which overthrew classical physics and has found applications in many other fields of study. According to this, at the atomic level, the position and momentum of a particle cannot be determined with limitless accuracy simultaneously, and follows from the wave property of matter. During the Second World War he was involved with the German atomic energy programme.

held past & p.p. of HOLD.

hele v.t. to set (a plant) in the ground and cover its roots in. [OE, rel. to HELL]

Helen /'helɪn/ (Gk legend) daughter of Zeus and Leda, born from an egg. She has a non-Greek name and is probably an ancient pre-Hellenic goddess connected with vegetation and fertility. In the Homeric poems she is the (human) wife of Menelaus, and her abduction by Paris (to whom she had been promised, as a bribe, by Aphrodite; see PARIS¹) led to the Trojan War.

Helena /'helɪnə/, St (c.255-c.330), mother of Constantine and a zealous supporter of Christianity. In 326 she visited the Holy Land and founded basilicas on the Mount of Olives and at Bethlehem; later tradition ascribes to her the finding of the Cross on which Christ was crucified.

heliacal /hɪ'laɪək(ə)l/ adj. of or near the sun. —**heliacal rising** (or **setting**), the first rising of a star after (or its last setting before) a period of invisibility due to its conjunction with the sun. [f. L f. Gk (hēlios sun)]

helical /'helɪk(ə)l/ adj. having the form of a helix. [as HELIX]

Helicon /'helɪkən/ a mountain in Boeotia, sacred to the Muses. The spring Hippocrene (see entry) rises there.

helicopter /'helɪkɒptə(r)/ n. an aircraft which derives both its lift and its control from one or more powered rotors which rotate about a vertical or near-vertical axis (ill. FLIGHT). Additional directional control may sometimes be provided by a tail-rotor. It differs from an autogiro which, since its rotors were not powered, could not take off vertically. Leonardo da Vinci drew and described an aircraft using its principle of flight. A design was patented in 1861, and the Wright brothers built and tested flying machines of this kind in the early 20th c., but the name chiefly associated with its development is that of Igor Sikorski. [f. F f. Gk HELIX + pteron wing]

helio- /hiːlɪə-/ in comb. sun. [f. Gk hēlios sun]

heliocentric /hiːlɪə'sentrɪk/ adj. **1.** considered as viewed from the sun's centre. **2.** regarding the sun as the centre.

Heliogabalus /hiːlɪə'gæbələs/ var. of ELAGABALUS.

heliograph /'hiːlɪəgrɑːf/ n. a signalling device reflecting the sun's rays in flashes; a message sent by this. —v.t. to send (a message) thus. [f. HELIO- + -GRAPH]

Helios /'hiːlɪɒs/ (Gk myth.) the sun-god, father of Phaethon. [Gk, = sun]

heliotrope /'hiːlɪətrəʊp/ n. **1.** a plant of the genus Heliotropium with small fragrant purple flowers. **2.** a light purple colour. [f. L f. Gk, = plant turning its flowers to the sun (as HELIO-, trepō turn)]

heliport /'helɪpɔːt/ n. a place where helicopters take off and land. [f. HELICOPTER, after airport]

helium /'hiːlɪəm/ n. a colourless odourless element, the lightest of the noble gases, symbol He, atomic number 2. Before it was discovered on earth, helium was detected spectroscopically in the sun (1868), where it is present as the main product of the thermonuclear fusion of hydrogen. On earth it is found most abundantly in natural gas deposits, especially in the USA. Because helium is light and chemically inert it is a particularly suitable lifting gas for balloons and airships, and is now used for this purpose and as a coolant. In the 1930s the USA had a monopoly of the manufacture of helium, which they would not sell to Germany lest this should bring America within the range of bombing raids by German airships. This embargo gave rise to the Hindenburg disaster since the airship, designed to use helium, was obliged to substitute hydrogen (which

is inflammable), with tragic consequences. [f. Gk hēlios sun]

helix /'hiːlɪks/ n. (pl. **helices** /-lisiːz/) a spiral (like a corkscrew, or in one plane like a watch-spring). —**double helix,** a pair of parallel helices with a common axis, especially in the structure of the DNA molecule. [L f. Gk]

hell n. **1.** the place or state of punishment for the wicked after death, the abode of devils. The popular idea of hell as a dark and fiery pit is derived from texts such as Matt. 25: 41 and Rev. 19: 20. **2.** a place or state of misery or wickedness. **3.** (colloq.) an exclamation of surprise or annoyance. —**beat** or **knock hell out of,** to pound heavily. **come hell or high water,** no matter what the obstacles. **for the hell of it,** just for fun. **get hell,** (colloq.) to be scolded or punished. **give a person hell,** (colloq.) to scold or punish him. **hell-bent** adj. recklessly determined (on). **hell-fire** n. the fire(s) of hell. **hell for leather,** at full speed. **Hell's Angel,** see separate entry. [OE f. Gmc, = cover, conceal]

Helladic /he'lædɪk/ adj. of the Bronze Age culture of mainland Greece (c.3000-1050 BC), of which the latest period is equivalent to Mycenaean. —n. this culture. [f. Gk (Hellas Greece)]

Hellas /'helæs/ the ancient and modern Greek name for Greece. [cf. HELLENE]

hellebore /'helɪbɔː(r)/ n. a plant with white or greenish flowers, of the genus Helleborus including the Christmas rose. [f. OF or L f. Gk]

Hellene /'heliːn/ n. a Greek person; an ancient Greek of genuine Greek descent. —**Hellenic** /-'liːnɪk/ adj. [f. Gk Hellēn eponymous ancestor, son or brother of Deucalion]

Hellenism /'helɪnɪz(ə)m/ n. Greek character or culture (especially of ancient Greece). —**Hellenist** n. [f. Gk (as prec.)]

Hellenistic /helɪ'nɪstɪk/ adj. of the Greek world from the death of Alexander the Great in 323 BC until the defeat of Mark Antony and Cleopatra by Roman forces under Octavian at the battle of Actium in 31 BC. [as prec.]

Heller /'helə(r)/, Joseph (1923-), American novelist. His experiences in the air force during the Second World War inspired his first novel Catch 22 (1961). This grotesque and comic tale of an American bombardier's resistance to his fanatic commander's ambition for promotion at the expense of his squadron satirizes military illogicality. It became enormously popular, particularly among younger readers during the Vietnam era, and its title passed into the language. His subsequent novels include Something Happened (1964) and Good as Gold (1979).

Hellespont /'helɪspɒnt/ the ancient name for the Dardanelles, named after the legendary Helle who, with her brother Phrixus, fell into the strait and was drowned while escaping from their stepmother, Ino, on a golden-fleeced ram (see ARGONAUTS). [f. Gk Hellēspontos sea of Helle]

hellish adj. of or like hell; extremely unpleasant. [f. HELL]

hello var. of HALLO.

Hell's Angel a member of a group of lawless usually leather-jacketed motor-cyclists in California in the 1950s, notorious for their disturbances of civil order there, or of a similar group elsewhere. Their culture revolves round the motor cycle, and the winged death's-head is their symbol.

helm¹ n. the tiller or wheel by which a ship's rudder is controlled. —**at the helm,** at the head of an organization etc., in control. [OE, prob. rel. to HELVE]

helm² n. (archaic) a helmet. [OE, cf. foll.].

helmet n. a protective head-covering worn by a policeman, fireman, diver, motor-cyclist, etc., or as part of armour (ill. ARMOUR). [f. OF, dim. of helme, f. Gmc]

Helmholtz /'helmhɔːlts/, Hermann Ludwig Ferdinand von (1821-94), German physiologist and physicist, one of the greatest scientists and teachers of his age, who made fundamental contributions to all the fields he studied. His investigation of animal heat led to his formulation of the principle of the conservation of energy in 1847, central to the subsequent development of thermodynamics. He produced two monumental studies on sense perception: the first dealt with physiological optics (in the course of which he invented the ophthalmoscope), and the second with physiological acoustics, for which he devised the Helmholtz resonators for the analysis of complex sounds in 1856. Other achievements include his attemtps to measure the speed of nerve impulses, and his study of vortex motion in hydrodynamics; he also contributed to non-Euclidean geometry. His research into the properties of oscillating electric currents was continued by his assistant, Heinrich Hertz.

helmsman /'helmzmən/ n. (pl. **-men**) one who steers a ship. [f. HELM¹]

Héloïse /'eɪləʊi:z/ see ABELARD.

helot /'helət/ n. a member of the class of serfs in ancient Sparta, owned by the State and employed in the service of the Spartans, whom they greatly outnumbered. [f. L f. Gk]

help v.t. **1.** to make it easier for (a person) to do something or for (a thing) to happen, to do part of the work of (a person) for him. **2.** to be of use or service; to do something for the benefit of (one in need); to contribute to alleviating (a pain or difficulty). **3.** to prevent, to remedy. **4.** (with neg.) to refrain from. —n. **1.** the act of helping or being helped. **2.** a person or thing that helps. **3.** a domestic servant or servants; an employee or employees. **4.** a remedy etc. —**cannot help oneself**, cannot avoid an undesired action. **help oneself (to)**, to take without seeking help or permission. **help out**, to give help, especially in difficulty. **help a person to**, to serve him with (food at a meal). —**helper** n. [OE]

helpful adj. giving help, useful. —**helpfully** adv., **helpfulness** n. [f. HELP + -FUL]

helping n. a portion of food at a meal. [f. HELP]

helpless adj. **1.** lacking help, defenceless. **2.** having or showing an inability to act without help; unable to help oneself. —**helplessly** adv., **helplessness** n. [f. HELP + -LESS]

Helpmann /'helpmən/, Sir Robert Murray (1909-), Australian dancer, choreographer, director, and actor. Having studied with the Pavlova company he came to England in 1933 and joined the Vic-Wells (later Saddler's Wells, now the Royal) Ballet. He partnered Alicia Markova in de Valois's *Haunted Ballroom* (1934), and became the regular partner of Margot Fonteyn; their partnership contributed to the success of the company. Helpmann was noted for his dramatic ability and for his strongly theatrical choreography.

helpmate n. a helpful companion or partner.

Helsinki /hel'sɪŋkɪ/ the capital of Finland; pop. (1981) 482,800.

helter-skelter /heltə 'skeltə(r)/ adv. in disorderly haste. —n. a tall structure with an external spiral track for sliding down. [imit., perh. f. obs. *skelte* hasten]

helve n. the handle of a weapon or tool. [OE]

Helvetian /hel'vi:ʃ(ə)n/ adj. Swiss. —n. a Swiss person. [f. L *Helvetia* Switzerland (*Helvetii* Celtic tribe living there)].

hem¹ n. the border of cloth where the edge is turned under and sewn down. —v.t. (**-mm-**) to turn down and sew in the edge of (cloth etc.). —**hem in**, to surround and restrict the movement of. **hem-stitch** n. an ornamental stitch; (v.t.) to hem with this. —**hemmer** n. [OE]

hem² int. calling attention or expressing hesitation by a slight cough. —n. an utterance of this. —v.i. (**-mm-**) to say *hem*, to hesitate in speech. [imit.]

hemi- /hemɪ-/ prefix half. [f. Gk *hēmi-* = L *semi-*]

Hemingway /'hemɪŋweɪ/, Ernest Miller (1899-1961), American novelist, who settled in Paris among an American expatriate literary group which included Gertrude Stein and Ezra Pound. He achieved success with *The Sun Also Rises* (1926) which catches the post-war mood of disillusion of the 'lost generation', and *A Farewell to Arms* (1929), the story of a love affair between an American lieutenant and an English nurse, confirmed his position as one of the most influential writers of the time. *Death in the Afternoon* (1932), about bull-fighting, shows his deliberate cultivation of the brutal and primitive which grew from his dissatisfaction with contemporary culture. Hemingway actively supported the Republicans in the Spanish Civil War and *For Whom the Bell Tolls* (1940) is set against its background. In his later years he lived mostly in Cuba where his passion for deep-sea fishing provided the background for *The Old Man and the Sea* (1952) about man's struggle against nature. His fine short stories appeared in *Men without Women* (1927), *Winner Take Nothing*, and other volumes. In 1954 he was awarded the Nobel Prize for literature. He committed suicide after a period of serious illness.

hemipterous /he'mɪptərəs/ adj. of the insect order including aphids, bugs, and cicadas, with the base of the front wings thickened. [f. HEMI- + Gk *pteron* wing]

hemisphere /'hemɪsfɪə(r)/ n. half a sphere; any half of the earth, especially as divided by the equator or by a line passing through the poles. —**hemispherical** /-'sferɪk(ə)l/ adj. [f. OF & L f. Gk (as HEMI-, SPHERE)]

hemline n. the lower edge of a skirt or dress.

hemlock /'hemlɒk/ n. a poisonous plant (*Conium maculatum*) with small white flowers; the poison made from it. [OE]

hemp n. **1.** an Asian herbaceous plant (*Cannabis sativa*); its fibre, used to make rope and coarse fabrics. **2.** any of several narcotic drugs made from the hemp plant. —**hempen** adj. [OE]

hen n. the female bird, especially of the common domestic fowl. —**hen-party** n. (colloq.) a social gathering of women only. [OE]

henbane n. a poisonous plant (*Hyoscyamus niger*) with an unpleasant smell.

hence adv. **1.** from this time. **2.** for this reason. **3.** (archaic) from here. [OE (f. root of HE)]

henceforth /hens'fɔ:θ/ adv. (also **henceforward**) from this time onwards.

henchman n. (pl. **-men**) a trusty supporter. [f. OE *heng(e)st* male horse + MAN]

henge /hendʒ/ n. a monument of wood or stone resembling the circle of stones at Stonehenge. Such monuments are found only in the British Isles and are believed to have served a ritual function. [f. STONEHENGE]

Hengist /'hengɪst/ the reputed leader, along with his brother Horsa, of the Jutes who came to Britain at the invitation of the British King Vortigern in 449 and later revolted and established an independent Anglo-Saxon kingdom in Kent. The historicity of the brothers has been questioned, and they may have been mythological figures (their names mean 'gelding' and 'horse').

Henley /'henlɪ/ Henley Royal Regatta, the oldest rowing regatta in Europe, inaugurated in 1839 at Henley-on-Thames, Oxfordshire, as a direct result of the interest aroused locally by the first Oxford and Cambridge boat race which took place at Henley in 1829. It is held annually in the first week in July.

henna n. **1.** a tropical shrub (*Lawsonia inermis*). **2.** the reddish dye made from it, used especially on the hair. [f. Arab.]

henpeck v.t. (of a wife) to domineer over (a husband).

Henry¹ /'henrɪ/ the name of eight kings of England:

Henry I (1068-1135), youngest son of William I, reigned 1100-35. On the death of his brother William II, Henry was able to seize the throne in the absence of his other brother Robert on crusade. He campaigned successfully in France (1111-13 and 1116-20) after conquering Normandy in 1105. At home his reign was characterized by the development of the royal administration and the restraint of baronial power, but after his only son William drowned in 1120 there were problems with the succession, and although Henry extracted an oath of loyalty to his daughter Matilda from the barons in 1127, his death eight years later was followed almost immediately by the outbreak of civil war.

Henry II (1133-89), son of Matilda, reigned 1154-89. The first Angevin king, Henry restored order after the anarchy of the disputed reigns of Stephen and Matilda, added Anjou and Aquitaine to the English possessions in France, established his rule in Ireland, and forced the king of Scotland to acknowledge him overlord of that kingdom. These successes were overshadowed by his feud with Thomas à Becket, who disagreed with him over the relative rights of Church and Crown and was eventually murdered by some of Henry's knights. In the last years of his reign much trouble was caused by his four sons who intrigued with France in particular to raise rebellion against him.

Henry III (1207-72), son of John, reigned 1216-72. Until Henry declared himself of age to rule personally in 1227, his regent the Earl of Pembroke kept the rebellious barony in check, but afterwards the King's ineffectual government, characterized by financial mismanagement and a dependence on unpopular foreign favourites, caused widespread discontent, ending in de Montfort's defeat and capture of the King at Lewes in 1264. Although Henry was restored following the defeat of the rebels a year later at Evesham, he was by this time little more than a figurehead, real power resting with his son who eventually succeeded him as Edward I.

Henry IV (1367-1413), known as Henry Bolingbroke, son of John of Gaunt, reigned 1399-1413. One of the Lords Appellant who opposed Richard II, Henry returned from exile in 1399 to overthrow Richard and establish the Lancastrian dynasty. His reign was scarred by rebellion, both in Wales where Owen Glendower was briefly successful in establishing Welsh independence, and in the north where the powerful Percy family raised several dangerous uprisings. Although Henry defeated and killed Hotspur (Sir Henry Percy) at Shrewsbury in 1403, the Percy threat did not abate until the head of the family was killed at Bramham Moor in 1408.

Henry V (1387-1422), son of Henry IV, reigned 1413-22. Having shown early military prowess in his father's wars against the Percy family and the Welsh, Henry V renewed the Hundred Years War soon after coming to the throne and won a resounding victory over the French at Agincourt in 1415. By the Treaty of Troyes (1420) Henry was named successor to Charles VI of France and betrothed to his daughter Catherine of Valois. When the Dauphin repudiated the treaty Henry took the field against him but died of dysentery, leaving a difficult inheritance to his infant son Henry VI.

Henry VI (1421-71), son of Henry V, reigned 1422-61 and 1470-1. Succeeding his father while still an infant, Henry VI proved scholarly and kindly but prone to bouts of madness and unfit to rule effectively on his own. During his reign the Hundred Years War with France was finally lost, and the royal government, in the hands of a series of regents and noble favourites, became increasingly unpopular through corruption and inefficiency. In the 1450s opposition coalesced round the House of York, and, after intermittent civil war (see Wars of the Roses), Henry was deposed in 1461 by Edward IV. He regained his throne briefly in 1470-1 following a Lancastrian uprising, but was deposed once again following Edward's victories at Barnet and Tewkesbury, and died within days of his deposition, almost certainly murdered by the victorious Edward IV.

Henry VII (1457-1509), the first Tudor king, son of Edmund Tudor, Earl of Richmond, reigned 1485-1509. He inherited the Lancastrian claim to the throne through his grandfather's marriage to the widow of Henry V. After growing up in exile in France and Brittany, Henry eventually returned to England in 1485 and, after defeating and killing the Yorkist king Richard III at Bosworth, ascended the throne as Henry VII. Threatened in the early years of his reign by a series of Yorkist plots, Henry eventually established an unchallenged Tudor dynasty, dealing ruthlessly with other claimants to the throne. As king he continued the modernization and strengthening of royal government commenced by his Yorkist predecessors, although his attempts to increase royal revenues made him increasingly unpopular.

Henry VIII (1491-1547), son of Henry VII, reigned 1509-47. Although most widely known for his six wives, two of whom he had executed and two of whom he divorced, Henry was responsible for some of the most dramatic changes in post-medieval English society. His efforts to divorce his first wife, Catherine of Aragon, led to England's break with the Roman Church and less directly to the establishment of Protestantism. The dissolution of the monasteries, masterminded by his chief minister Thomas Cromwell, not only destroyed most of the remaining vestiges of the old religious establishment but also changed the pattern of land ownership. Though Henry's reign began in a burst of Renaissance splendour, costly wars, internal rebellion, and general mismanagement in his last years left England in a weak and uncertain condition.

Henry² /'henrɪ/ (Fr. *Henri*), the name of four kings of France:

Henry IV of Navarre (1553-1610), reigned 1589-1610. As king of Navarre, Henry was the leader of Huguenot forces in the latter stages of the French Wars of Religion, but upon succeeding the Catholic Henry III he turned Catholic himself in order to guarantee peace. The founder of the Bourbon dynasty, Henry established religious freedom with the Edict of Nantes (1598) and became nationally popular, restoring normalcy in a country long plagued by civil war. He was eventually assassinated by a Catholic fanatic in Paris in 1610.

Henry³ /'henrɪ/ (1394-1460), 'the Navigator', Portuguese prince. The third son of John I of Portugal, despite his title he never undertook any explorations himself but was a notable patron of such voyages. He established a school of navigation at Cape St Vincent and spent his life organizing and funding voyages of discovery, most notably south along the African coast. The efforts of his captains, who reached as far south as Cape Verde and the Azores, laid the groundwork for later Portuguese imperial expansion southeast round Africa to the Far East.

henry /'henrɪ/ n. (*pl.* **-ries**) a unit of inductance which gives an e.m.f. of one volt in a closed circuit with rate of change of current one ampere per second. [f. J. *Henry*, American physicist (d. 1878)]

Henze /'hentsə/, Hans Werner (1926-), German composer and conductor. A committed socialist, his musical style is bewilderingly diverse, reflecting his fertile imaginative gifts and his refusal to be 'tied down' by formulae. Sensuous lyricisim, rich and delicate tone-colours, and easy mastery of choral writing are among the principal features of his works.

hep adj. (slang) aware of the latest trends and styles. [orig. unkn.]

hepatic /hɪ'pætɪk/ adj. of the liver [f. L f. Gk (*hēpar* liver)]

hepatitis /hepə'taɪtɪs/ n. inflammation of the liver. [as prec. + -ITIS]

Hephaestus /hɪ'fiːstəs/ (*Gk myth.*) the god of fire (especially the smithy fire), a craftsman's god and himself a divine craftsman, called Vulcan by the Romans.

Hepplewhite /'hep(ə)lwaɪt/ n. a light and graceful style of furniture made by George Hepplewhite, English cabinet-maker (d. 1786), or according to his designs.

hepta- in comb. seven. [f. Gk *hepta* seven]

heptagon /'heptəgən/ n. plane figure with seven sides and angles. —**heptagonal** /-'tægən(ə)l/ adj. [f. Gk (HEPTA-, -*gōnos* -angled)]

Hepworth /'hepwəθ/, Dame Jocelyn Barbara (1903-75) English sculptor, winner of international awards for works such as *The Unknown Political Prisoner* (1953), married to the painter Ben Nicholson from 1933 to 1951. She professed an emotional affinity with nature, but from the 1930s her work was entirely abstract, characterized by simple shapes such as the sphere, cylinder, and ovoid. From the 1950s onwards she gave greater attention to bronze, using this medium to express essentially the same structural principles as in her carved sculpture, seeking 'to infuse the formal perfection of geometry with the vital grace of nature'.

her pron. obj. case of SHE; (*colloq.*) she. —poss. adj. **1.** of or belonging to her. **2.** (in titles) that she is (*Her Majesty*). [OE dat. & gen. of SHE]

Hera /'hɪərə/ (*Gk myth.*) an ancient pre-Hellenic goddess. The Greeks made her the wife and sister of Zeus, and the daughter of Cronus and Rhea. She was worshipped as the queen of heaven and as a marriage-goddess, and was identified by the Romans with Juno. [Gk, = lady]

Heracles /'herəkliːz/ the Greek form of HERCULES.

Heraclitus¹ /hɪərə'klaɪtəs/ (*c.*500 BC) Greek philosopher from Ephesus, noted for the oracular obscurity of his writings. He regarded the universe as a ceaselessly changing conflict of opposites, all things being in a state of flux, coming into being and passing away, and held that fire, the type of this constant change, is their origin. From the passing impressions of experience the mind derives a false idea of the permanence of the external world, which is really in a harmonious process of constant change; for his melancholy view of the changing and fleeting character of life he was known as the 'weeping philosopher'.

Heraclitus² /hɪərə'klaɪtəs/ (4th c. BC) Greek poet of Halicarnassus, a friend of the poet Callimachus whose epigram on Heraclitus' death was translated by the Victorian schoolmaster W. J. Cory (1823-92), 'They told me, Heraclitus, they told me you were dead'.

herald /'her(ə)ld/ n. **1.** a forerunner; a messenger, a bringer of news (often as the title of a newpaper). **2.** (*hist.*) an officer who made State proclamations and bore messages between princes, officiated in the tournament, arranged various State ceremonials, regulated the use of armorial bearings, settled questions of precedence, or recorded the names and pedigrees of those entitled to armorial bearings. **3.** an official of the Heralds' College. —v.t. to proclaim the approach of, to usher in. —**Heralds' College**, the College of Arms (see entry). —**heraldic** /-'rældɪk/ adj. [f. OF f. Gmc]

heraldry /'herəldrɪ/ n. the science or art of a herald, especially in blazoning armorial bearings and settling the right of persons to bear arms. Bearings probably originated as designs on shields at a time when chain-mail was worn and a bold, simple identification device was needed. Such designs are found in western Europe from the 12th c.; Japan is the only country outside this area where a similar system (dating also from the 12th c.) occurs. When such devices were no longer needed in war their design became more intricate and developed into a complex system. The designs were associated originally with the higher social classes, a link which still persists. Armorial bearings are hereditary, and strictly belong to the head of a family, other members being entitled to use them only with some mark of cadency. The use of heraldic devices is now widespread, and they are sought by corporate bodies for reasons of prestige and identification. (See ill. pp. 384-5.)

herb *n*. a plant whose stem is soft and dies to the ground after flowering; a plant whose leaves or seeds etc. are used for flavouring, food, medicine, scent, etc. —**herb bennet,** the common yellow-flowered avens (*Geum urbanum*; ill. FLOWERS) [prob. f. L *herba benedicta* blessed herb, as having expelled the Devil]. —**herby** *adj*. [f. OF f. L *herba* grass, herb]

herbaceous /hɜːˈbeɪʃəs/ *adj*. of or like herbs. —**herbaceous border,** a garden border containing especially perennial flowering plants. [f. L (as prec.)]

herbage *n*. herb collectively, especially as pasture. [f. OF f. L (as HERB)]

herbal *adj*. of herbs in medicinal and culinary use. —*n*. a manual describing these. [f. L (as HERB)]

herbalist *n*. a dealer in medicinal herbs; a writer on herbs. [f. prec.]

herbarium /hɜːˈbeərɪəm/ *n*. (*pl.* **-ia**) a systematic collection of dried plants; a book, case, or room for these. [f. L (as HERB)]

Herbert[1] /ˈhɜːbət/, Sir Alan Patrick (1890-1970), English writer of great versatility and humour, who contributed to *Punch* for many years. He campaigned for several causes such as divorce law reform (expressed in *Holy Deadlock*, 1934) and reform in English spelling (in *What a Word*, 1935). *Independent Member* (1950) describes his experiences as MP for Oxford University (1935-50), and *My Life and Times* (1970) is his autobiography.

Herbert[2] /ˈhɜːbət/, George (1593-1633), English poet. Renouncing worldly ambition, he became the saintly vicar of Bemerton, near Salisbury. His devout trustful religious verse is marked by metrical versatility and homely, if at times far-fetched imagery. An account of his life was written by Izaak Walton (1670).

herbicide /ˈhɜːbɪsaɪd/ *n*. a toxic substance used to destroy unwanted vegetation. [f. HERB + -CIDE]

herbivore /ˈhɜːbɪvɔː(r)/ *n*. a herbivorous animal. [as foll.]

herbivorous /hɜːˈbɪvərəs/ *adj*. feeding on plants. [as HERB + L *vorare* devour]

Herculaneum /hɜːkjʊˈleɪnɪəm/ a small but luxurious ancient Roman town on the lower slopes of Vesuvius, whose eruption in AD 79 buried it and thus largely preserved it for modern excavators.

herculean /hɜːkjʊˈliːən/ *adj*. **1.** extremely strong. **2.** (of a task) requiring great strength. [f. foll.]

Hercules /ˈhɜːkjʊliːz/ **1.** (*Gk & Rom. myth.*) a hero (occasionally worshipped as a god) of prodigious strength and courage who performed twelve immense tasks or labours imposed on him by Eurystheus king of Argos. He is usually shown in art with a lion-skin, club, and bow. **2.** (*Astron.*) a northern constellation, figured as a man kneeling on his right knee. —**Pillars of Hercules,** the name given in ancient times to two mountains (Calpe and Abyla) opposite one another at the eastern end of the Strait of Gibraltar, marking the limit of the known world. They are identified as the Rock of Gibraltar and Mount Acho, just south of Ceuta in North Africa, said to have been parted by the arm of Hercules. [f. Gk, = Hera's glory]

herd *n*. **1.** a number of cattle or other animals feeding or staying together. **2.** a large number of people, a mob. —*v.t./i.* **1.** to collect, go, or drive in a herd. **2.** to tend (sheep or cattle). —**herd instinct,** the tendency to remain or conform with the majority. [OE]

herdsman *n*. (*pl.* **-men**) a person who tends a herd of animals.

here /hɪə(r)/ *adv*. **1.** in, at, or to this place or position. **2.** at this point (in a speech, performance, writing, etc.). —*int.* calling attention or as a command; as a reply (= I am present) in a roll-call. —*n*. this place. **here and there,** in or to various places. **here goes,** I am ready to begin. **here's to,** I drink to the health of. **neither here nor there,** of no importance. [OE]

hereabouts /hɪərəˈbaʊts/ *adv*. (also **hereabout**) near this place.

hereafter /hɪərˈɑːftə(r)/ *adv*. in future, from now on. —*n*. the future; life after death.

hereby /hɪəˈbaɪ/ *adv*. by this means, as a result of this.

hereditable /hɪˈredɪtəb(ə)l/ *adj*. that may be inherited. [f. obs. F or L (*hereditare* inherit f. *heres* heir)]

hereditary /hɪˈredɪtərɪ/ *adj*. **1.** descending by inheritance. **2.** that may be transmitted from one generation to another. **3.** holding a hereditary office. [f. L (as prec.)]

heredity /hɪˈredɪtɪ/ *n*. the property of organic beings by which offspring have the nature and characteristics of their parents or ancestors (see below); the sum of these characteristics; genetic constitution. [f. F or L *hereditas* heirship (as HEIR)]

That 'like begets like' has been recognized since ancient times, but a real understanding of the nature of heredity came slowly and had to await the discovery of the sex cells (gametes), the phenomenon of fertilization, and the existence of genes. Lamarck proposed that characteristics acquired by parents during life could be passed on to their offspring, and Darwin too believed that this was possible, although it is now known not to be the case. It was also widely believed in the 19th c. that sexual reproduction involved 'blending' of the characteristics of the two parents in the offspring, a view which appeared to cause difficulties for the theory of natural selection since it seemed that advantageous variations in one parent would inevitably be 'diluted' in the progeny. It was Mendel who first demonstrated that, on the contrary, the hereditary material consists of discrete hereditary factors now known as genes (see MENDELISM).

Hereford /ˈherɪfəd/ *n*. a breed of red and white beef cattle; an animal of this breed. [f. *Hereford* in England]

Hereford and Worcester /ˈherɪfəd, ˈwʊstə(r)/ a west midland county of England, bordering on Wales.

herein /hɪərˈɪn/ *adv*. (*formal*) in this place, document, etc.

hereinafter /hɪərɪnˈɑːftə(r)/ *adv*. (*formal*) in a later part of this document etc.

hereof /hɪərˈɒv/ *adv*. (*archaic*) of this.

heresy /ˈherɪsɪ/ *n*. an opinion contrary to the doctrine of the Christian Church, or to the accepted doctrine on any subject. [f. OF f. L *haeresis* school of thought f. Gk *hairesis* choice, sect (*haireomai* choose)]

heretic /ˈherɪtɪk/ *n*. one advocating a heresy (especially in religion). —**heretical** /hɪˈretɪk(ə)l/ *adj*. [f. OF f. L f. Gk *hairetikos* able to choose (as prec.)]

hereto /hɪəˈtuː/ *adv*. (*archaic*) to this.

heretofore /hɪətuˈfɔː(r)/ *adv*. (*formal*) formerly.

hereupon /hɪərəˈpɒn/ *adv*. after or in consequence of this.

Hereward the Wake /ˈherɪwəd/ a semi-legendary leader of Anglo-Saxon resistance to William the Conqueror. Although little is known of Hereward's life beyond what can be found in unreliable literary accounts, he was apparently responsible for a rising at Ely in 1070 which caused some trouble for William I's new Norman regime.

herewith /hɪəˈwɪð/ *adv*. with this (especially of an enclosure in a letter etc.).

heritable /ˈherɪtəb(ə)l/ *adj*. **1.** that may be inherited; transmissible from parent to offspring. **2.** capable of inheriting. [f. OF *heriter* (as HEREDITABLE)]

heritage /ˈherɪtɪdʒ/ *n*. what is or may be inherited; inherited circumstances or benefits etc.; one's portion or lot. [f. OF (as prec.)]

hermaphrodite /hɜːˈmæfrədaɪt/ *n*. a person or animal having the characteristics or organs of both sexes; a plant in which the same flower has stamens and a pistil. —*adj*. having such characteristics. —**hermaphroditic** /-ˈdɪtɪk/ *adj*. [f. L f. Gk, orig. name of son of Hermes and Aphrodite, who became joined in one body with the nymph Salmacis]

Hermes /ˈhɜːmiːz/ **1.** (*Gk myth.*) son of Zeus and Maia. He was the messenger of the gods, god of merchants, thieves, oratory, etc.; identified by the Romans with Mercury, he was represented in human form as a herald equipped for travelling, with broad-brimmed hat, winged shoes, and a winged rod. But he was also associated with fertility, and from early times is shown as a mere stock or stone (*herm*) having generally a human head carved at the top and a phallus half way up it. **2. Hermes Trismegistus** (= thrice greatest), a clumsy translation of the Egyptian 'Thoth the very great', regarded by Neoplatonists and others as the author of certain works on astrology, magic, and alchemy. [prob. f. Gk *herma* heap of stones]

hermetic /hɜːˈmetɪk/ *adj*. **1.** with an airtight closure. **2.** of alchemy or other occult science; esoteric. —**hermetically** *adv*. [f. HERMES, regarded as founder of alchemy (see prec., sense 2)]

hermit /ˈhɜːmɪt/ *n*. a person (especially an early Christian) living in solitude. —**hermit-crab** *n*. a crab of the family

Heraldry

Points of the shield

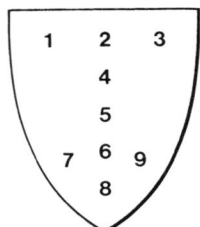

1. dexter chief
2. middle chief
3. sinister chief
4. honour point
5. fess point
6. nombril point
7. dexter base
8. middle base
9. sinister base

Armorial bearings

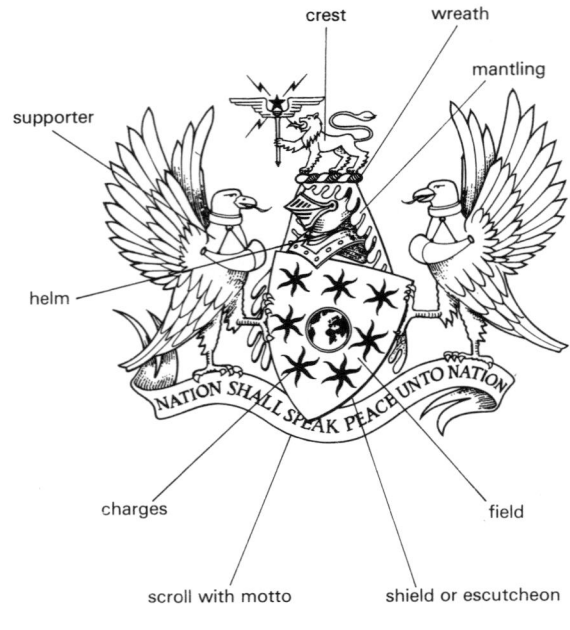

crest

wreath

mantling

supporter

helm

charges

scroll with motto

field

shield or escutcheon

NATION SHALL SPEAK PEACE UNTO NATION

Marshalling

impalement

quartering

dimidiation

in pretence

Helms

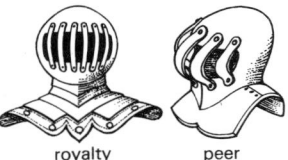

royalty

peer

knight or baronet

gentleman, esquire, or corporate body

Coronets

duke

marquis

earl

viscount

baron

Tinctures

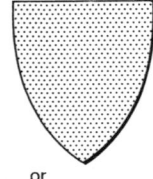  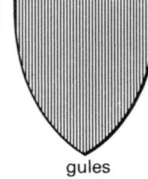 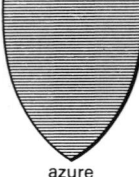 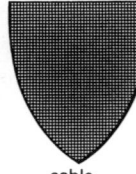  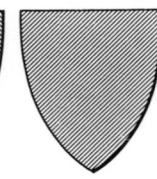

| or (gold/yellow) | argent (silver/white) | gules (red) | azure (blue) | sable (black) | vert (green) | purpure (purple) |

Furs

 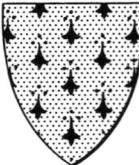 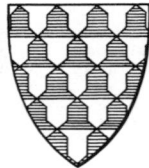 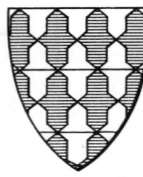 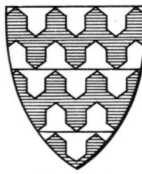  

| ermine | erminois | vair | counter-vair | vair en point | potent | fleury or flory |

Some ordinaries

   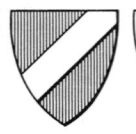    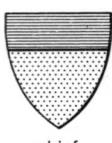

| fess | bar | chevron | bend | bend sinister | pale | cross | saltire | chief |

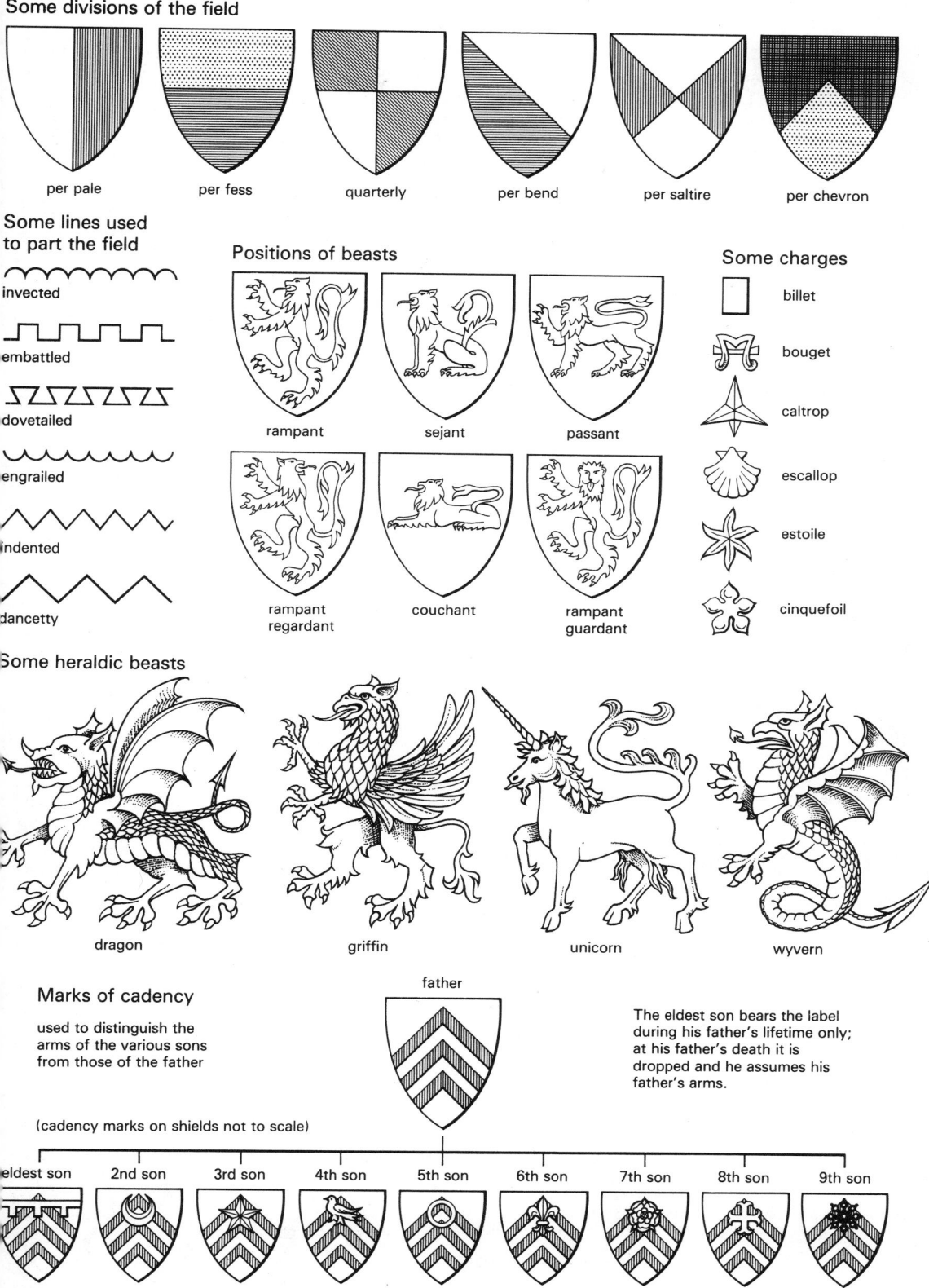

Some divisions of the field

per pale   per fess   quarterly   per bend   per saltire   per chevron

Some lines used to part the field

invected

embattled

dovetailed

engrailed

indented

dancetty

Positions of beasts

rampant   sejant   passant

rampant regardant   couchant   rampant guardant

Some charges

billet

bouget

caltrop

escallop

estoile

cinquefoil

Some heraldic beasts

dragon   griffin   unicorn   wyvern

Marks of cadency

used to distinguish the arms of the various sons from those of the father

father

The eldest son bears the label during his father's lifetime only; at his father's death it is dropped and he assumes his father's arms.

(cadency marks on shields not to scale)

eldest son   2nd son   3rd son   4th son   5th son   6th son   7th son   8th son   9th son

label   crescent   mullet   martlet   annulet   fleur-de-lis   rose   cross moline   double quatrefoil

Paguridae, that lives in a mollusc's cast-off shell. [f. OF or L f. Gk *erēmitēs* (*erēmos* solitary)]

Hermitage /'hɜːmɪtɪdʒ/, **the** a leading art museum in Leningrad, containing the collections begun by Catherine the Great, one of the most voracious collectors of all time. It derives its name from the 'retreat' in which she displayed them to her friends.

hermitage /'hɜːmɪtɪdʒ/ *n.* the place of a hermit's retreat; a secluded dwelling. [as HERMIT]

hernia /'hɜːnɪə/ *n.* a protrusion of part of an organ through an aperture in the enclosing membrane etc., especially of the abdomen. [L]

Hero[1] /'hɪərəʊ/ (*Gk legend*) a beautiful priestess of Aphrodite at Sestos on the European shore of the Hellespont, whose lover Leander, a youth of Abydos on the opposite shore, swam the strait nightly to visit her until one stormy night he was drowned and Hero in grief threw herself into the sea.

Hero[2] /'hɪərəʊ/ of Alexandria (1st c.), Greek mathematician and inventor, whose surviving works are important as a source for ancient practical mathematics and mechanics. He describes a number of hydraulic, pneumatic, and other mechanical devices, designed both for utility and amusement, including elementary applications of the power of steam.

hero /'hɪərəʊ/ *n.* (*pl.* **-oes**) **1.** a man admired for great deeds and noble qualities. **2.** the chief male character in a poem, play, or story. —**hero-worship** *n.* excessive devotion to an admired person. [f. L f. Gk *hērōs*]

Herod /'herəd/ the name of 4 rulers in ancient Palestine:
Herod the Great (d. 4 BC), ruled for 37 years; Christ was born during his reign. He rebuilt the Temple, and was an effective and able ruler until illness and mental instability marred the last years of his reign.
Herod Antipas son of Herod the Great, governor (tetrarch) of Galilee and Peraea 4 BC–AD 39. He married Herodias and was responsible for the beheading of John the Baptist.
Herod Agrippa I (called 'Herod' in Acts) grandson of Herod the Great, king of the Jews AD 41–4; he put St James the Apostle to death.
Herod Agrippa II son of Herod Agrippa I, was king of various territories in northern Palestine AD 50–*c*.93; St Paul appeared before him (Acts 25: 13 ff.).

Herodotus /hɪˈrɒdətəs/ (5th c. BC) Greek historian from Halicarnassus in Asia Minor, the 'Father of History'. His *History* tells of the wars between Greece and Persia in the early 5th c. BC, with an account of the earlier history of the Persian Empire and its relations with the Greeks in order to explain the origins of those wars. He professes to record what he had seen and heard (some on his own extensive travels), and this is supplemented by reading, verified by inquiry, and criticized by common sense, with moral honesty. Explorer, observer, and listener, he combines encyclopaedic interest and curiosity with humane sympathy and goodwill, loves wonders and secrets, enjoys a tale and a joke, and tells them vividly. Devoid of race-prejudice and intolerance he venerates antiquity, without military insight he has recorded a great war, and his narrative is constructed to the rules of literary art.

heroic /hɪˈrəʊɪk/ *adj.* having the characteristics of or suited to a hero, very brave. —*n.* (in *pl.*) **1.** over-dramatic talk or behaviour. **2.** heroic verse. —**heroic verse,** a form used in epic poetry, e.g. the iambic pentameter. —**heroically** *adv.* [f. F or L f. Gk (as prec.)]

heroin /'herəʊɪn/ *n.* a powerful sedative addictive drug prepared from morphine. [G, perh. as HERO (from its effects on the user's opinion of himself)]

heroine /'herəʊɪn/ *n.fem.* a female hero. [f. F or L f. Gk (as HERO)]

heroism /'herəʊɪz(ə)m/ *n.* heroic conduct or qualities. [f. F (as HERO)]

heron /'herən/ *n.* a wading bird of the genus *Ardea* with a long neck and long legs. [f. OF *hairon*]

heronry *n.* a place where herons breed. [f. prec.]

herpes /'hɜːpiːz/ *n.* a virus disease causing blisters on the skin. [f. L f. Gk, = shingles (*herpō* creep)]

herpetology /hɜːpɪˈtɒlədʒɪ/ *n.* the study of reptiles. —**herpetologist** *n.* [f. Gk *herpeton* reptile (*herpō* creep) + -LOGY]

Herr /heə(r)/ *n.* (*pl.* **Herren**) a German man; the title of a German man, = Mr. [G]

Herrick /'herɪk/, Robert (1591–1674), English poet, who

graduated from Cambridge and was ordained priest in 1617. In London he was part of Jonson's literary circle. He was incumbent of Dean Prior in Devon during 1630–47, and again after the Restoration. His poems *Hesperides* (1648) were published together with his religious poems, *Noble Numbers*; the latter are often derided as naïve. His secular poems, which treat such subjects as country rituals, Christian festivals, folklore, and love, are marked with gaiety and grace and show a clear debt to the classical poets, particularly Horace and Catullus.

herring /'herɪŋ/ *n.* an Atlantic fish (*Clupea harengus*) used for food. —**herring-bone** *n.* a stitch or weave suggesting the bones of a herring; a zigzag pattern. **herring gull,** a large gull (*Larus argentatus*) with dark wing-tips. [OE]

hers /hɜːz/ *poss.pron.* of or belonging to her; the thing(s) belonging to her. [f. HER]

Herschel /'hɜːʃ(ə)l/, Sir William (1738–1822), German-born astronomer who settled in England and became court astronomer to George III. He is often called the Father of Stellar Astronomy, and was a first-rate observer whose painstaking cataloguing of the skies was rewarded in 1781 by the discovery of the planet Uranus. A skilful telescope maker, his unsuccessful attempts to measure the distances of the stars convinced him of their remoteness, while his mapping of stellar distributions suggested to him that the sun was a member of a great star system forming the disc of the Milky Way. Elected first President of the Royal Astronomical Society in 1820, in his work he was greatly helped by his sister Caroline (1750–1848) who was also an able and careful observer. The family's domination of the science of astronomy was continued into the next generation by his son John (1792–1871).

herself /hɜːˈself/ *pron.* emphat. & refl. form of SHE and HER. —**be herself,** to behave in her normal manner, to be in her normal health and spirits. [OE (as HER, SELF)]

Hertfordshire /'hɑːfədʃɪə(r)/ one of the Home Counties of England.

Herts. *abbr.* Hertfordshire.

Hertz /hɜːts/, Heinrich Rudolph (1857–94), German physicist and a pioneer of radio communication, who worked for a time as Helmholtz's assistant in Berlin. He began his world-famous study of electromagnetic waves in 1886. Maxwell had predicted the existence of these waves in his electromagnetic theory; Hertz demonstrated this experimentally, and also the fact that these waves behaved like light and radiant heat, thus proving that these phenomena, too, were electromagnetic. In 1889 he was appointed professor of physics at Bonn, where he had more time for research, but he died of blood poisoning at the early age of 37.

hertz *n.* (*pl.* same) a unit of frequency, equal to one cycle per second. [f. prec.]

Hertzian /'hɜːtsɪən/ *adj.* **Hertzian waves,** electromagnetic waves of length suitable for use in radio. [f. HERTZ]

Hertzsprung-Russell diagram /'hɜːtspruŋ 'rʌs(ə)l/ a two-dimensional graph, discovered independently by the Danish astronomer E. Hertzsprung (1911) and the American astronomer H. N. Russell (1913), in which the spectral types and absolute magnitudes of stars may be plotted as points. Stars are found to occupy only certain regions of this diagram, depending on their mass and the stage of their life-cycle which they occupy. Most stars fall on a line known as the *main sequence,* which represents a well-defined relationship between the physical properties of a star which is still relying on hydrogen as its energy source; when a star has exhausted its hydrogen and begun to consume other elements, it will occupy a different position on the diagram.

Herzl /'hɜːts(ə)l/, Theodor (1860–1904), Zionist writer, a Hungarian-born Jew. He worked for most of his life as a writer and journalist in Vienna, advocating the establishment of a Jewish State in Palestine and building up the Zionist movement of which he was the most influential statesman.

Hesiod /'hiːsɪəd/ (*c.*700 BC), one of the oldest known Greek poets, often coupled or contrasted with Homer as the other main representative of early epic. His hexameter poem the *Theogony* deals with the origin and genealogies of the gods; his *Works and Days* contains moral and practical advice for living an honest life of (chiefly agricultural) work, and was the chief model for later ancient didactic poetry. Both bear the marks of a distinct personality: a surly conservative countryman, given to reflection, no lover of women or of life, who felt the gods' presence heavy about him.

hesitant /'hezɪtənt/ *adj.* irresolute, hesitating. —**hesitancy** *n.*, **hesitantly** *adv.* [as foll.]

hesitate /'hezɪteɪt/ *v.i.* to feel or show uncertainty or reluctance, to pause in doubt; to be reluctant. —**hesitation** /-'teɪʃ(ə)n/ *n.*, **hesitator** *n.* [f. L *haesitare* (*haerēre* stick fast)]

Hesperides /he'sperɪdi:z/ (*Gk myth.*) three, four, or seven nymphs, daughters of Hesperus (or, in earlier versions, of Night and Hades). They were guardians, with the aid of a watchful dragon, of a tree of golden apples in a garden popularly located beyond the Atlas mountains at the western border of Oceanus, the river encircling the world.

Hess, Victor Franz (Francis) (1883-1964), Austrian-born American physicist who divided his academic career between Austria and the USA. His research interests in atmospheric electricity and radioactivity culminated in the discovery of cosmic rays, which led to the discovery of the positively-charged electron or positron by the American physicist C. D. Anderson (1905-). They shared the 1936 Nobel Prize for physics.

hessian /'hesɪən/ *n.* a strong coarse fabric of hemp or jute, sack-cloth. [f. *Hesse* in Germany]

het *adj.* **het up**, (*slang*) excited, overwrought. [dial. *p.p.* of HEAT]

hetaera /hɪ'tɪərə/ *n.* (*pl.* **-rae**) a courtesan, especially in ancient Greece. [Gk, lit. = 'female companion']

hetero- /hetərə-/ *in comb.* other, different. [f. Gk *heteros* other]

heterodox /'hetərədɒks/ *adj.* not orthodox. —**heterodoxy** *n.* [f. HETERO- + Gk *doxa* opinion]

heterodyne /'hetərədaɪn/ *adj.* relating to the production of a lower radio frequency from a combination of two high frequencies.

heterogeneous /hetərə'dʒi:nɪəs/ *adj.* diverse in character; varied in content. —**heterogeneity** /-dʒɪ'ni:ɪtɪ/ *n.* [f. L f. Gk (HETERO-, *genos* kind)]

heteromorphic /hetərə'mɔ:fɪk/ *adj.* of dissimilar forms. —**heteromorphism** *n.* [f. HETERO- + Gk *morphē* form]

heterosexual /hetərə'seksjʊəl/ *adj.* characterized by attraction to the opposite sex. —*n.* a heterosexual person. —**heterosexuality** /-'ælɪtɪ/ *n.*

heuristic /hjʊə'rɪstɪk/ *adj.* serving or helping to find out or discover; proceeding by trial and error. [f. Gk *heuriskō* find]

hew *v.t./i.* (*p.p.* **hewed** or **hewn**) to chop or cut with an axe, sword, etc.; to cut into shape. [OE]

hexa- /heksə/ *in comb.* six. [f. Gk (*hex* six)]

hexagon /'heksəgən/ *n.* a plane figure with six sides and angles (ill. SHAPES). —**hexagonal** /-'ægən(ə)l/ *adj.* [f. L f. Gk (HEXA-, *-gōnos* -angled)]

hexagram /'heksəgræm/ *n.* a six-pointed star formed by two intersecting equilateral triangles. [f. HEXA- + -GRAM]

hexameter /hek'sæmɪtə(r)/ *n.* a line of six metrical feet, especially (**dactylic hexameter**) one with five dactyls and a trochee or spondee, any of the first four feet (and rarely the fifth) being replaceable by a spondee. [f. L f. Gk (HEXA-, *metron* measure)]

hey /heɪ/ *int.* calling attention or expressing surprise or inquiry. —**hey presto!** a conjuror's formula in performing a trick. [cf. OF *hay*, *hey*]

heyday /'heɪdeɪ/ *n.* the time of greatest success or prosperity. [f. LG *heidi*, *heida* excl. of joy]

HF *abbr.* high frequency.

Hf *symbol* hafnium.

Hg *symbol* mercury.

hg *abbr.* hectogram(s).

HGV *abbr.* heavy goods vehicle.

HH *abbr.* double-hard (pencil-lead).

hi /haɪ/ *int.* calling attention or as a greeting. [parallel form to HEY]

hiatus /haɪ'eɪtəs/ *n.* a break or gap in a sequence or series; a break between two vowels coming together but not in the same syllable. [L, = gaping (*hiare* gape)]

hibernate /'haɪbəneɪt/ *v.i.* (of an animal) to spend the winter in a dormant state. —**hibernation** /-'neɪʃ(ə)n/ *n.* [f. L *hibernare* (*hibernus* of winter)]

Hibernian /haɪ'bɜ:nɪən/ *adj.* of Ireland. —*n.* a native of Ireland. [f. L *Hibernia* Ireland f. Gk *Iernē*]

hibiscus /hɪ'bɪskəs/ *n.* a cultivated shrub of the genus *Hibiscus*, with large bright-coloured flowers. [L f. Gk, = marsh-mallow]

hiccup /'hɪkʌp/ *n.* (also **hiccough**) an involuntary spasm of the respiratory organs with an abrupt cough-like sound —*v.i.* to make a hiccup. [imit.]

hick *n.* (*US colloq.*) a country bumpkin. [familiar form of *Richard*]

hickory /'hɪkərɪ/ *n.* a North American tree of the genus *Carya*, related to the walnut; its hard wood. —**Old Hickory**, the nickname of US President Andrew Jackson. [f. Virginian Indian *pohickery*]

hid *past* of HIDE[1].

hidalgo /hɪ'dælgəʊ/ *n.* (*pl.* **-os**) a member of the lower nobility in Spain. [Sp. (*hijo dalgo* son of something)]

hidden *p.p.* of HIDE[1].

hide[1] *v.t./i.* (*past* **hid**; *p.p.* **hidden**) **1.** to put or keep out of sight; to prevent from being seen. **2.** to keep (a fact etc.) secret (*from*). **3.** to conceal oneself. —*n.* a concealed place for observing wildlife. —**hide-and-seek** *n.* a children's game in which a player hides and is sought by others. **hide-out** *n.* (*colloq.*) a hiding-place. [OE]

hide[2] *n.* an animal's skin, raw or dressed; (*colloq.*) the human skin. [OE]

hidebound *adj.* rigidly conventional, narrow-minded.

hideous /'hɪdɪəs/ *adj.* very ugly, revolting. —**hideously** *adv.*, **hideousness** *n.* [f. AF (OF *hisde* horror)]

hiding[1] /'haɪdɪŋ/ *n.* the state of remaining hidden. —**hiding-place** *n.* a place in which one hides or where something is hidden. [f. HIDE[1]]

hiding[2] /'haɪdɪŋ/ *n.* (*colloq.*) a thrashing. [f. HIDE[2]]

hie /haɪ/ *v.i.* & *refl.* (*archaic* or *poetic*) to go quickly. [OE *higian* strive, pant]

hierarchy /'haɪərɑ:kɪ/ *n.* a system in which grades of status or authority rank one above another. —**hierarchical** /-'rɑ:kɪk(ə)l/ *adj.* [f. OF f. L f. Gk (*hieros* sacred, *arkhō* rule)]

hieratic /haɪə'rætɪk/ *adj.* of the priests, priestly. —*n.* hieratic script, a form of cursive hieroglyphs used from early times in ancient Egypt, originally for religious texts, and eventually superseded by demotic. [f. L f. Gk (*hiereus* priest)]

hieroglyph /'haɪərəglɪf/ *n.* **1.** a picture of an object used to represent a word, sound, or syllable in any of the pictorial systems of writing, especially the ancient Egyptian (see below and ill. ALPHABETS). **2.** a secret or enigmatic symbol. **3.** (in *pl.*, *joc.*) writing that is difficult to make out. [f. foll.] Hieroglyphs were used in ancient Egypt for monumental inscriptions from the end of the 4th millennium BC until the 4th c. AD. Monumental hieroglyphs were an art form; there was no separation between words or phrases, and the direction of the writing varied (vertical, right to left, or left to right), with the purely decorative aspect sometimes having priority. In the classic period there were about 700 signs, but signs were continually invented and modified and became innumerable. Hieroglyphs remained undeciphered until the discovery of Rosetta stone (see entry).

hieroglyphic /haɪərə'glɪfɪk/ *adj.* of or written in hieroglyphs. —*n.* (in *pl.*) hieroglyphs, hieroglyphic writing. [f. F or L f. Gk (*hieros* sacred, *gluphē* carving)]

hi-fi /'haɪfaɪ/ *adj.* (*colloq.*) high-fidelity. —/also -'faɪ/ *n.* (*colloq.*) high-fidelity equipment. [abbr.]

higgledy-piggledy /hɪg(ə)ldɪ'pɪg(ə)ldɪ/ *adj.* & *adv.* disordered, in confusion. [rhyming jingle, perh. ref. to irregular herding together of pigs]

high /haɪ/ *adj.* **1.** extending far upwards; extending above the normal or average level. **2.** situated far above the ground or above sea level. **3.** measuring a specified distance in upward extent. **4.** ranking above others in importance or quality; luxurious. **5.** extreme, intense, greater than the normal or average; (of opinion) very favourable. **6.** (of time) far advanced; fully reached; (of a period) at its peak of development. **7.** (of sound) having rapid vibrations, not deep or low. **8.** (of meat etc.) beginning to go bad; (of game) hung until slightly decomposed and ready to cook. **9.** (*colloq.*) intoxicated by or *on* alcohol or drugs. **10.** (of animals or plants etc.) of complex structure, highly developed. —*n.* **1.** a high or the highest level or number. **2.** an area of high pressure. **3.** (*slang*) a euphoric state caused by a drug. —*adv.* **1.** far up, aloft. **2.** in or to a high degree. **3.** at a high price. **4.** (of sound) at or to a high pitch. —**high and dry**, aground, stranded. **high and low**, everywhere. **high and mighty**, (*colloq.*) pompous, arrogant. **high chair**, a young child's chair for meals, with long legs and usually an attached tray. **High Church**, the section of the Church of England which stresses historical continuity with Catholic Christianity and attaches 'high' importance to the authority of the episcopate and the saving grace of the Sacraments.

In its modern sense the term dates back to the Oxford Movement. **High Commission,** an embassy from one Commonwealth country to another. **High Commissioner,** the head of this. **High Court (of Justice),** the supreme court for civil cases. **higher education,** education at university etc. **high explosive,** an explosive with a violent shattering effect. **high-falutin(g)** adj. (colloq.) bombastic, pretentious. **high fidelity,** reproduction of sound with little distortion, giving a result very similar to the original. In order to achieve this the system must be able to record all frequencies and their respective intensities within the audible frequency and volume range, and the reverberation and spatial sound-pattern of the original must be reproduced too. **high-flown** adj. (of language etc.) extravagant, bombastic. **high-flyer, high-flier** n. an ambitious person; a person or thing with the potential for great achievements. **high-flying** adj. ambitious. **high frequency,** (in radio) 3–30 megahertz. **high-handed** adj. overbearing. **high hat,** a tall hat; = HI-HAT. **high jump,** an athletic contest of jumping over a high horizontal bar; *be for the high jump,* to be likely to receive a severe punishment (the reference is to being hanged). **high-level** adj. (of discussions etc.) conducted by persons of the highest rank. **high-level language,** a computer language close to ordinary language and usually not machine-readable. **high-minded** adj. having high moral principles. **high-pitched** adj. (of a sound or voice) shrill; (of a roof) steep. **high-powered** adj. having or using great power, important or influential. **high pressure,** a high degree of activity or exertion; a condition of the atmosphere with the pressure above average. **high priest,** a chief priest, a head of a cult. **high-rise** adj. (of a building) having many storeys. **high road,** a main road. **high school,** a secondary (especially a grammar) school. **high seas,** the open seas not under any country's jurisdiction. **high season,** the regular period of the greatest number of visitors at a resort etc. **high-spirited** adj. in high spirits, cheerful. **high spot,** (colloq.) the most important place or feature. **high street,** the principal street of a town etc. **high table,** an elevated table at a public dinner or in a college etc., for the most important guests or members. **high tea,** an evening meal of tea and cooked food. **high-tech** adj. (colloq.) characterized by high technology; (of interior design etc.) imitating styles more usual in industry etc. **high technology,** a state of advanced technological development. **high tension,** high voltage. **high tide,** a tide at the highest level; the time of this. **high treason,** treason against one's ruler or country. **high-up** n. (colloq.) a person of high rank. **high water,** high tide. **high-water mark,** the level reached at high water; the highest recorded point or value. **high wire,** a high tightrope. **on high,** in or to a high place or heaven. [OE]

highball n. (US) a drink of spirits and soda etc. served with ice in a tall glass.

highbrow adj. (colloq.) intellectual or highly cultural in interest or appeal. —n. (colloq.) a highbrow person.

Highland /ˈhaɪlənd/ a local government region of northern Scotland.

highland n. (usu. in pl.) mountainous country, especially (**Highlands**) of northern Scotland. —adj. of the highland or the Scottish Highlands. —**Highland cattle,** a breed with shaggy hair and long curved horns.

highlander n. a native or inhabitant of highlands or (**Highlander**) of the Scottish Highlands.

highlight n. 1. a moment or detail of vivid interest; an outstanding feature. 2. the bright part of a picture, etc. —v.t. to bring into prominence.

highly adv. in a high degree; favourably. —**highly-strung** adj. very sensitive and nervous. [f. HIGH]

highness n. 1. the title used in addressing or referring to a prince or princess. 2. the state of being high (esp. fig.).

highway n. 1. a public road. 2. a main route. 3. a conductor transmitting signals in a computer. —**Highway Code,** the set of rules issued officially for the guidance of road-users. **King's** or **Queen's highway,** a public road regarded as protected by royal power.

highwayman n. (pl. **-men**) (hist.) a man, usually on horseback, who held up and robbed travellers on the highway.

hi-hat /haɪˈhæt/ n. (also **high hat**) a pair of cymbals worked by the foot (ill. MUSICAL NOTATION). [abbr. HIGH + HAT]

hijack /ˈhaɪdʒæk/ v.t. to seize control of (a vehicle or aircraft), especially to force it to a new destination; to seize (goods in transit). —n. a hijacking. —**hijacker** n. [orig. unkn.]

hike n. a long walk, especially across country. —v.i. to go for a hike; to walk laboriously. —**hiker** n. [dial.; orig. unkn.]

hilarious /hɪˈleərɪəs/ adj. 1. boisterously merry. 2. extremely funny. —**hilariously** adv., **hilarity** /hɪˈlærɪtɪ/ n. [f. L. f. Gk hilaros cheerful]

Hilary /ˈhɪlərɪ/, St (c.315–c.367), bishop of Poitiers, champion of orthodoxy against Arianism, and the leading Latin theologian of his age. His feast day (13 Jan. in the Anglican Church, 14 Jan. in the RC calendar) gives its name to the university and law terms that begin in January.

Hilbert, /ˈhɪlbət/, David (1862–1943), German mathematician who epitomizes, and did more than anyone else to produce, the changes in mathematics that occurred around the turn of the century. He proved fundamental theorems about rings and their ideals, he collected, systematized, and extended all that was then known about algebraic numbers, he reorganized the axiomatic foundations of geometry, he set potential theory and the theory of integral equations on its modern course with his invention of Hilbert space (an infinite-dimensional analogue of Euclidean space), and he formulated the formalist philosophy of mathematics and mathematical logic. At the International Congress of Mathematicians in Paris in 1900 Hilbert proposed 23 problems which, as he had hoped, crystallized mathematical thinking for the next few decades.

hill n. 1. a natural elevation of the ground, not as high as a mountain. 2. a sloping piece of road. 3. a heap or mound. —**hill figure,** a design (usually either a horse or a human figure) cut into the chalk or limestone hills of southern England and standing out white against the green turf. The oldest of these (the White Horse at Uffington, Oxon.) dates back to the Iron Age (1st or 2nd c. BC), and probably had a religious function. **hill-fort** n. a fortified place built on a hill-top, with ramparts and ditches, occurring in western Europe from the late Bronze Age until the Roman period. [OE]

Hillary /ˈhɪlərɪ/, Sir Edmund (1919–), New Zealand mountaineer and explorer who, with Sherpa Tenzing Norgay, was the first to reach the summit of Mount Everest (1953).

hill-billy /ˈhɪlbɪlɪ/ n. 1. folk music like that of the southern USA. 2. (US colloq., often derog.) a person from a remote rural area in a southern State. [f. HILL + billy fellow]

hillock /ˈhɪlək/ n. a small hill, a mound. [f. HILL]

hillside n. the sloping side of a hill.

hilly adj. having many hills. —**hilliness** n. [f. HILL]

hilt n. the handle of a sword, dagger, etc. —**up to the hilt,** completely. [OE]

him pron. obj. case of HE; (colloq.) he. [OE, dat. of HE]

Himachal Pradesh /hɪˈmaːtʃ(ə)l prəˈdeʃ/ a State in northern India; capital, Simla.

Himalayas /hɪməˈleɪəz/ a system of high mountains which stretches for over 1,600 km (1,000 miles) and forms the NE boundary of the Indian subcontinent. It includes the highest summits in the world with several peaks rising to over 7,700 (25,000 ft.). —**Himalayan** adj.

himself /hɪmˈself/ pron. emphat. & refl. form of HE and HIM (cf. HERSELF). [OE (as HIM, SELF)]

Hinayana /hiːnəˈjɑːnə/ n. a derogatory name given by the followers of Mahayana Buddhism to denote the other major division of early Buddhism. It died out in India by the 7th c. AD but survived in Ceylon (see THERAVADA) and was taken from there to Burma, Thailand, and other regions of SE Asia. Hinayana was the pristine form of the faith, while Mahayana represents the general one, of the majority of followers. [Skr., = lesser vehicle]

hind[1] /haɪnd/ adj. situated at the back. [perh. shortened f. OE bihindan behind]

hind[2] /haɪnd/ n. the female of the (esp. red) deer, especially in and after the third year. [OE]

Hindemith /ˈhɪndəmɪt/, Paul (1895–1963), a successful composer, conductor, and teacher in Germany until the 1930s, when criticisms of his music by the Nazis led him to leave the country and settle in the USA, becoming an American citizen in 1946. He is invariably associated with *Gebrauchsmusik* ('music for use'), a term used in the 1920s to describe music with a social purpose; his attitude was that audiences should participate as well as listen. His harmonic idiom was based on well-controlled dissonant tensions, but he remained firmly committed to tonality. The severe reaction against his music eventually slackened, and the best of his prolific works (which include operas, concertos, and orchestral and chamber music) occupy an important place in the history of 20th-c. composition.

hinder[1] /ˈhɪndə(r)/ *v.t.* to keep (a person or thing) back by delaying progress. [OE, rel. to HIND[1]]

hinder[2] /ˈhaɪndə(r)/ *adj.* hind (HIND[1]). [perh. f. OE (as HIND[1])]

Hindi /ˈhɪndɪ/ *n.* **1.** a literary form of Hindustani with vocabulary based on Sanskrit, written in the Devanagari script, an official language of India. Hindi is the most widely spoken language in India, with some 180 million speakers. **2.** a group of spoken dialects of northern India, belonging to the Indo-European family of languages and related to Urdu. —*adj.* of Hindi. [f. Urdu (*hind* India)]

hindmost /ˈhaɪndməʊst/ *adj.* furthest behind. [f. HIND[1] +-MOST]

hindquarters /haɪndˈkwɔːtəz/ *n.pl.* the hind legs and adjoining parts of a quadruped (ill. HORSE).

hindrance /ˈhɪndrəns/ *n.* **1.** a thing that hinders. **2.** hindering, being hindered. [f. HINDER[1]]

hindsight /ˈhaɪndsaɪt/ *n.* wisdom after the event.

Hindu /hɪnˈduː, ˈhɪ-/ *n.* an adherent of Hinduism. —*adj.* of the Hindus. [Urdu, f. Pers. (*Hind* India)]

Hinduism /ˈhɪnduːɪz(ə)m/ *n.* a system of religious beliefs and social customs, with adherents especially in India, both a way of life and a rigorous system of religious law, developed over a period of about fifty centuries. Unlike most religions, Hinduism requires no one belief concerning the nature of god: it embraces polytheism, monotheism, and monism. More important are the beliefs concerning the nature of the universe and the structure of society. The former is described by the key concepts of *dharma*, the eternal law underlying the whole of existence; *karma*, the law of action by which each cause has its effect in an endless chain reaching from one life to the next; and *moksha*, liberation from this chain of birth, death, and rebirth. The latter is prescribed by the ideals of *varna*, the division of mankind into four classes or types, the forerunner of caste; *ashrama*, the four stages of life; and personal dharma, according to which one's religious duty is defined by birth and circumstance. [f. prec.]

Hindu Kush /hɪndu ˈkuːʃ, ˈkʊʃ/ a range of high mountains in northern Pakistan and Afghanistan which forms a westward continuation of the Himalayas. Several peaks exceed 6,150m (20,000 ft.).

Hindustan /hɪndʊˈstɑːn/ (lit. 'the country of the Hindus') (*hist.*) northern India; the Indian subcontinent. [f. HINDU + -*stan* country]

Hindustani /hɪndəˈstɑːnɪ/ *n.* a language based on the Western Hindi dialect of the Delhi region with an admixture of Arabic, Persian, etc., current as the standard language and lingua franca in much of northern India and (as colloquial Urdu) Pakistan. —*adj.* of Hindustani. [Urdu f. Pers. (as prec.)]

hinge /hɪndʒ/ *n.* **1.** a movable joint on which a door, lid, etc. turns or swings. **2.** a principle on which all depends. —*v.t./i.* **1.** to attach or be attached by a hinge. **2.** to depend *on*. [rel. to HANG]

hinny *n.* the offspring of a she-ass and a stallion. [f. L *hinnus* f. Gk]

hint *n.* **1.** a slight or indirect indication or suggestion. **2.** a small piece of practical information. **3.** a small amount, a trace. —*v.t./i.* to suggest slightly or indirectly. —**hint at**, to refer indirectly to. **take a hint**, to act upon a hint. [f. obs. *hent* grasp]

hinterland /ˈhɪntəlænd/ *n.* the district behind a coast or a river's banks; an area served by a port or other centre. [G (*hinter* behind, as LAND)]

hip[1] *n.* **1.** the projection formed by the pelvis and upper part of the thigh-bone. **2.** the arris of a roof from ridge to eaves (ill. HOUSES). —**hip-bath** *n.* a portable bath in which one sits immersed to the hips. **hip-bone** *n.* the bone forming the hip. **hip-flask** *n.* a flattish flask for spirits, carried in the hip-pocket. **hip-pocket** *n.* a trouser-pocket just behind the hip. [OE]

hip[2] *n.* the fruit of the (esp. wild) rose. [OE]

hip[3] *int.* used in cheering (*hip, hip, hurray*). [orig. unkn.]

hip[4] *adj.* (*slang*) var. of HEP.

Hipparchus /hɪˈpɑːkəs/ (*c.*190- after 126 BC) Greek astronomer, working in Rhodes. His major works are lost, but his astronomical observations were preserved and developed by Ptolemy. He constructed the celestial co-ordinates of some 800 stars, indicating their relative brightness, but rejected Aristarchus' hypothesis that the sun is the centre of the planetary system. Hipparchus is best known for his discovery of the precession of the equinoxes. His geographical work was a polemic against that of Eratosthenes, criticising descriptive and mathematical data.

hippeastrum /hɪpɪˈæstrəm/ *n.* a South American plant of the genus *Hippeastrum* with showy red or white flowers. [f. Gk *hippeus* horseman (the leaves appearing to ride on one another) + *astron* star (from the flower-shape)]

hippie /ˈhɪpɪ/ *n.* a young person who rejects conventional ideas and society and adopts an unusual style of dress, living habits, etc. [f. HIP[4]]

hippo /ˈhɪpəʊ/ *n.* (*pl.* -**os**) (*colloq.*) a hippopotamus. [abbr.]

Hippocrates /hɪˈpɒkrətiːz/ (*c.*460-357 BC), the most famous of all physicians, of whom almost nothing is known. Referred to briefly and historically by Plato, his name was attached, probably by later Alexandrian historians, to a body of ancient Greek medical writings of which probably none was written by Hippocrates. This collection is so various in style and content that all subsequent physicians have been able to find within it notions that agreed with their own of what medicine and doctors should be: 'Hippocrates' is a synthesis of history. Thus the Hippocratic oath is Pythagorean in origin, but exerted great influence in medical ethics; Galen, the greatest commentator upon Hippocrates, made his subject an Aristotelian rationalist; and numberless others have found 'true Hippocratism' in an anti-philosophical and observational accumulation of medical data. If there are common features of an agreed Hippocratism, they might be that nature has an innate power of healing, and that diseases are closely linked to the physical environment.

Hippocratic oath /hɪpəˈkrætɪk/ an oath stating the obligations and proper conduct of physicians, formerly taken by those beginning medical practice. [f. prec.]

Hippocrene /ˈhɪpəkriːn/ a spring on Mount Helicon, the inspiration of poets. It was fabled to have been produced by a stroke from the hoof of Pegasus. [Gk, = fountain of the horse]

hippodrome /ˈhɪpədrəʊm/ *n.* **1.** a music-hall or dance-hall. **2.** (in classical antiquity) a course for chariot races etc. [F, or f. L f. Gk (*hippos* horse, *dromos* race-course]

hippopotamus /hɪpəˈpɒtəməs/ *n.* (*pl.* -**muses**) a large African mammal (*Hippopotamus amphibius*) with short legs and a thick skin, inhabiting rivers etc. [f. L f. Gk (*hippos* horse, *potamos* river)]

hipster /ˈhɪpstə(r)/ *adj.* (of a garment) hanging from the hips rather than the waist. [f. HIP[1]]

hire *v.t.* to obtain the use of (a thing) or the services of (a person) temporarily, for payment; (often with *out*) to grant the use of thus. —**for** or **on hire**, ready to be hired. **hire-purchase** *n.* a system by which a thing becomes the hirer's after a number of payments. The system was introduced in the USA in the 19th c. for the purchase of sewing-machines (see entry). —**hirer** *n.* [OE]

hireable /ˈhaɪ(ə)rəb(ə)l/ *adj.* that may be hired. [f. HIRE]

hireling /ˈhaɪəlɪŋ/ *n.* (usu. *derog.*) a person who works for hire. [OE, as HIRE, -LING]

Hirohito /hɪrəˈhiːtəʊ/ (1901-), emperor of Japan from 1926. Supposedly divine and all-powerful, he was venerated but in fact had little authority. He did, however, influence his government to agree to the unconditional surrender which ended the Second World War. Afterwards he renounced his divinity and, as a constitutional monarch, has lived to see his country recover and prosper.

Hiroshima /hɪˈrɒʃɪmə/ Japanese city, target of the first atomic bomb on 6 Aug. 1945, which resulted in the deaths of about one third of the city's population of 300,000, and, together with a second attack on Nagasaki three days later, led directly to Japan's surrender and the end of the Second World War.

hirsute /ˈhɜːsjuːt/ *adj.* hairy, shaggy. [f. L *hirsutus*]

his /hɪz/ *poss. pron.* & *adj.* **1.** of or belonging to him, the thing(s) belonging to him. **2.** (in titles) that he is (*His Majesty*). [OE, gen. of HE]

Hispanic /hɪsˈpænɪk/ *adj.* of Spain (and Portugal); of Spain and other Spanish-speaking countries. —*n.* a Hispanic person. [f. L (*Hispania* Spain)]

Hispaniola /hɪspænˈjəʊlə/ an island of the Greater Antilles in the West Indies, divided between the States of Haiti and the Dominican Republic. [f. Sp. *La Isla Española* (the Spanish island), so named by Columbus who discovered it in 1492]

hiss *n.* a sharp sibilant sound, as of the letter *s*. —*v.t./i.* to make a hiss; to express disapproval (of) by hisses; to utter with an angry hiss. [OE]

histamine /ˈhɪstəmɪn, -iːn/ *n.* a chemical compound in the body tissues, causing some allergic reactions. [as HISTOLOGY + AMINE]

histogram /'hɪstəgræm/ n. a statistical diagram in which the frequency of the values of a quantity is shown by columns. [f. Gk. *histos* mast + -GRAM]

histology /hɪs'tɒlədʒɪ/ n. the science of organic tissues. —**histological** /hɪstə'lɒdʒɪk(ə)l/ adj. [f. Gk. *histos* web + -LOGY]

historian /hɪ'stɔːrɪən/ n. a writer of history; a person learned in history. [f. F f. L (as HISTORY)]

historic /hɪ'stɒrɪk/ adj. 1. famous or important in history or potentially so. 2. (*Gram.*, of a tense) normally used of past events. [f. L f. Gk (as HISTORY)]

historical adj. 1. of or concerning history or facts in history. 2. having occurred in fact not legend or rumour. 3. (of a novel etc.) dealing with a past period. 4. (of the study of a subject) showing the development over a period of time. —**historically** adv. [as prec.]

historicism /hɪ'stɒrɪsɪz(ə)m/ n. 1. the belief that historical events are governed by laws. 2. a tendency to stress historical development and the influence of the past etc. [f. HISTORIC]

historicity /hɪstə'rɪsɪtɪ/ n. historical truth or authenticity. [as prec.]

historiography /hɪstɒrɪ'ɒgrəfɪ/ n. the writing of history; the study of this. —**historiographer** n. [f. Gk (as foll.)]

history /'hɪstərɪ/ n. 1. a continuous record of important or public events. 2. the study of past events, especially of human affairs. 3. past events; those connected with a person or thing. 4. an interesting or eventful past. —**history painting**, pictorial representation of an event or series of events. **make history**, to do something memorable; to be the first to do something. [f. L f. Gk *historia* finding out by enquiry, narrative]

histrionic /hɪstrɪ'ɒnɪk/ adj. of acting; dramatic or theatrical in manner. —n. (in *pl.*) theatricals; dramatic behaviour intended to impress others. [f. L (*histrio* actor)]

hit v.t./i. (-tt-; past & p.p. **hit**) 1. to strike with a blow or missile; to aim a blow *at*; to come against (a thing) with force. 2. to have an effect on (a person), to cause to suffer. 3. to propel (a ball etc.) with a bat or club; to score runs or points thus. 4. (*colloq.*) to encounter, to reach. 5. (*slang*) to attack; to raid. —n. 1. a blow, a stroke. 2. a shot that reaches its target. 3. a success, especially in popularity. —**hit-and-run** adj. causing damage or injury and fleeing immediately. **hit back**, to retaliate. **hit in the eye**, to be glaringly obviously to. **hit it off**, to get on well (*with* a person). **hit list**, (*slang*) a list of people to be killed or eliminated etc. **hit man**, (*slang*) a hired assassin. **hit the nail on the head**, to guess or explain precisely. **hit on**, to find (a solution etc., especially by chance). **hit-or-miss** adj. aimed or done carelessly. **hit out**, to deal vigorous blows (*lit.* or *fig.*). **hit parade**, a list of the best-selling records of popular music. **hit the road**, (*slang*) to depart. [OE f. ON, = meet with]

hitch v.t./i. 1. to move (a thing) with a slight jerk. 2. to fasten or be fastened with a loop or hook etc. 3. to hitch-hike; to obtain (a lift) in this way. —n. 1. a temporary difficulty, a snag. 2. a slight jerk. 3. any of various kinds of noose or knot. —**get hitched**, (*slang*) to get married. [orig. unkn.]

Hitchcock /'hɪtʃkɒk/, Sir Alfred Joseph (1899–1980), British film director, master of the suspense thriller. He established his reputation in Britain in the 1930s with *The Man Who Knew Too Much* (1934; remade in 1956), *The Thirty-Nine Steps* (1935), and *The Lady Vanishes* (1938). In 1939 he moved to Hollywood, where his first film was *Rebecca* (1940). His numerous later works include *Strangers on a Train* (1951), *Psycho* (1960), and *The Birds* (1963). He could show great technical ingenuity: *Lifeboat* (1944) was shot entirely within the boat; *Rope* (1948) was filmed in one room in one continuous shot. Of Irish-Catholic background in London, son of a greengrocer, Hitchcock was an unhappy, disturbed, and permanently insecure man (almost anyone who crossed him was rejected or humiliated), yet one of the authentic geniuses of the popular cinema, intuitively aware of the extent to which his private fantasies were universally shared.

hitch-hike v.i. to travel by seeking free rides in passing vehicles. —**hitch-hiker** n.

hither /'hɪðə(r)/ adv. to or towards this place. —adj. situated on this side; the nearer (of two). —**hither and thither**, to and fro. [OE]

hitherto /hɪðə'tuː/ adv. until this time, up to now.

Hitler /'hɪtlə(r)/, Adolf (1889–1945), German dictator.

An Austrian by birth, Hitler served in the German Army during the First World War before becoming involved in right-wing politics. An attempted *putsch* in 1923 failed and earned him a spell in prison (during which he wrote *Mein Kampf*, an exposition of his political ideas), but after his release his powers as an orator soon won prominence for him and his National Socialist (Nazi) party, and with his appointment as Chancellor in 1933 he was able to overthrow the Weimar Republic and establish a Nazi dictatorship. Hitler succeeded in rescuing the German economy from collapse, but his expansionist foreign policy led eventually to the Second World War, while his racist ideas launched Germany on an attempt to wipe out European Jewry and establish a German super-State. After a series of overwhelming early successes, Germany was eventually defeated by the combined strengths of the Allied powers, and Hitler committed suicide in his Berlin headquarters just as Russian troops were storming the city.

Hittite /'hɪtaɪt/ n. 1. a member of a powerful and widespread ancient (non-Semitic) people whose history can be traced from *c.*1900–700 BC in Asia Minor and Syria (see below); a subject of the Hittite empire. 2. their Indo-European language, written in cuneiform and hieroglyphs, deciphered in 1916. 3. (in the Bible) a member of a Canaanite or Syrian tribe, perhaps an offshoot of the peoples described above. [f. Heb.]

The Hittites gained political control of central Anatolia *c.*1800–1200 BC and reached the zenith of their power under the totalitarian rule of Suppiluliuma I (*c.*1380 BC), whose political influence extended from the capital, Hattusas, situated at Boğazkale (about 35 km (22 miles) east of Ankara) west to the Mediterranean coast and SE into northern Syria. In their struggle for power over Syria and Palestine they clashed with the troops of Rameses II of Egypt in a battle (1285 BC) at Kadesh on the River Orontes which seems to have ended indecisively. The subsequent decline of Hittite power resulted from internal and external dissension, probably following an outbreak of famine.

hive /haɪv/ n. 1. a box etc. for housing bees. 2. the bees occupying a hive. 3. a scene of busy activity. —v.t./i. place (bees) in a hive; to store (as) in a hive. —**hive off**, to separate from a larger group. [OE]

hives n.pl. a skin eruption, especially nettle-rash. [orig. Sc.; etym. unkn.]

HM abbr. Her or His Majesty('s).

HMS abbr. Her or His Majesty's Ship.

HMSO abbr. Her or His Majesty's Stationery Office.

HNC abbr. Higher National Certificate.

HND abbr. Higher National Diploma.

Ho symbol holmium.

ho /həʊ/ int. expressing triumph or scorn, or calling attention. [natural excl.]

hoar-frost n. frozen water vapour on lawns etc. [OE *hār* + FROST]

hoard n. a carefully kept store of money etc. —v.t./i. to amass and store in a hoard. —**hoarder** n. [OE]

hoarding n. 1. a temporary fence of light boards round a building; a structure erected to carry advertisements etc. [f. obs. *hoard* f. AF, rel. to HURDLE]

hoarse adj. 1. (of the voice) rough and deep-sounding, husky, croaking. 2. having a hoarse voice. —**hoarsely** adv., **hoarseness** n. [f. ON & OE]

hoary adj. 1. (of the hair) white or grey with age; having such hair, aged. 2. (of a joke etc.) old. [f. HOAR]

hoax v.t. to deceive, especially by way of a joke. —n. a humorous or mischievous deception. —**hoaxer** n. [prob. contr. of *hocus* (HOCUS-POCUS)]

hob n. a flat metal shelf at the side of a fireplace, where a kettle, pan, etc., can be kept hot; a flat heating surface on a cooker. [perh. var. of HUB]

Hobbema /'hɒbɪmə/, Meindert (1638–1709), the last of the great 17th-c. Dutch painters of landscape, a native of Amsterdam, friend and pupil of Jacob van Ruisdael. He painted a narrow range of favourite subject-matter—watermills and trees round a pool—over and over again. By the later 1660s, the demand in Holland for this type of landscape had much diminished, and he took up a clerical appointment at the age of 30 and practically ceased to paint. His *Avenue at Middelharnis* (1689) ranks among the best-known achievements of Dutch art.

Hobbes /hɒbz/, Thomas (1588–1679), English philosopher. His philosophy arose from a systematic project of investigating in turn the nature of matter, of man, and of society. He thought that the method of science should be the axiomatic method of geometry. There were two key components in his conception of man: he was fiercely materialist, claiming that there was no more to the mind than the physical motions discovered by science, and he thought that human action was motivated entirely by selfish concerns, notably fear of death. His view of society was expressed in his most famous work, *Leviathan* (1651), in which he argued, by means of a version of a social contract theory, that given his view of human motivation, simple rationality made social institutions and even absolute monarchy inevitable. His adherence to the axiomatic method led him to give great weight to definition, and this in turn led him to locate philosophical confusions in the misuse of words. In all these respects he was a peculiarly forthright exponent of a distinctive tendency in British philosophy.

hobbit /'hɒbɪt/ *n.* any of the imaginary dwarfish creatures in stories by J. R. R. Tolkien. [invented by Tolkien and said by him to mean 'hole-builder']

hobble *v.t./i.* **1.** to walk lamely; to cause to do this. **2.** to tie the legs of (a horse etc.) to limit its movement. —*n.* **1.** a hobbling walk. **2.** a rope etc. for hobbling a horse. [prob. f. LG]

Hobbs, Sir John Berry (1882-1963), English cricketer, a batsman whose career extended from 1905 to 1934.

hobby *n.* an occupation or activity pursued for pleasure, not as a livelihood. [as foll.]

hobby-horse *n.* **1.** a stick with a horse's head, used as a toy; a figure of a horse used in the morris dance etc. **2.** a favourite subject or idea. [f. *Hobby* pet-form of name Robin + HORSE]

hobgoblin /'hɒbgɒblɪn/ *n.* a mischievous or evil spirit; a bugbear. [f. *Hob* pet-form of Robin (Goodfellow) + GOBLIN]

hobnail *n.* a heavy-headed nail for boot-soles.

hob-nob *v.i.* (**-bb-**) to associate or spend time (*with*). [f. *hob or nob* give or take, of alternate drinking]

hobo /'həʊbəʊ/ *n.* (*pl.* **-os**) (*US*) a wandering workman or tramp. [orig. unkn.]

Hobson's choice /'hɒbs(ə)nz/ the option of taking what is offered or nothing. [f. T. *Hobson* (d. 1831) Cambridge carrier who hired horses on this basis, customers being obliged to take the one nearest to the stable door]

Ho Chi Minh /həʊ tʃɪ 'mɪn/ (Nguyen That Thanh, 1890-1969), Vietnamese Communist statesman, who led his country in its struggle for independence from French rule. A founder of what became the Indo-Chinese Communist Party, in 1945, when the Japanese, who had overrun Indo-China, had surrendered to the West, having entered Hanoi with a guerrilla force he proclaimed Vietnamese independence (Viet Minh). Years of guerrilla warfare ended in victory in May 1954, and Vietnam was divided along the 17th parallel into North Vietnam, of which Ho became president, and South Vietnam. His aim of Vietnamese unification was achieved after his death, with victory not only over the French but over the forces of the USA.

Ho Chi Minh City (formerly *Saigon*) a city in southern Vietnam (pop. 3,500,000).

hock¹ *n.* the joint of a quadruped's hind leg between the knee and the fetlock (ill. HORSE). [f. obs. *hockshin* f. OE (as HOUGH)]

hock² *n.* a German white wine, properly that of Hochheim on the River Main. [abbr. of obs. *hockamore* f. G *Hochheimer* (German name of the wine)]

hock³ *v.t.* (*slang*) to pawn. —**in hock**, in pawn; in prison; in debt. [f. Du. *hok* hutch, prison]

hockey¹ /'hɒkɪ/ *n.* a game played with a ball on a field or by skaters with a puck on ice (when it is also called **ice hockey**) with hooked sticks, between two goals. The word *hockie* dates from the 16th c. in an isolated example, but the game has descended from early civilizations (it is depicted on an ancient Egyptian tomb). Forms of it are at least 4,000 years old, but it was not an organized sport until the end of the 19th c. [orig. unkn.; the name probably belonged originally to the hooked stick]

hockey² /'hɒkɪ/ *n.* (in the game of darts) the line from which the player throws. [orig. unkn.]

Hockney /'hɒknɪ/, David (1937-   ), English painter and draughtsman, often classified as a pop artist (though he himself dislikes the label) who won international success, while still a student, with a set of 16 etchings, *A Rake's Progress*, inspired by a visit to New York in 1961.

Hocktide /'hɒktaɪd/ *n.* the time of hock-days (Hock Mon-

day and Hock Tuesday), the second Monday and Tuesday after Easter Day, on which in pre-Reformation times money was collected for church and parish purposes, and various sports and amusements took place. The merrymaking at this season survived in some places until the 19th c. [orig. unkn.]

hocus-pocus /ˌhəʊkəs 'pəʊkəs/ *n.* trickery. [sham L]

hod *n.* **1.** a builder's light trough on a pole for carrying bricks etc. **2.** a container for shovelling and holding coal. [prob. f. OF *hotte* pannier]

hodgepodge /'hɒdʒpɒdʒ/ var. of HOTCHPOTCH.

Hoe /həʊ/, Richard March (1812-86), American inventor, the first printer to develop a successful rotary press (in 1846). This greatly increased the speed of printing over that of a flat-bed press; by 1857 *The Times* had a Hoe press printing 20,000 impressions an hour. This machine had still to be fed with individual cut sheets, but by 1871 Hoe had developed a machine fed from a continuous roll.

hoe *n.* a long-handled tool with a blade, used for loosening the soil or scraping up weeds etc. —*v.t./i.* (*partic.* **hoeing**) to weed (crops), to loosen (ground), to dig up (weeds), with a hoe. [f. OF *houe* (as HEW)]

Hoffmann /'hɒfmən/, Ernst Theodor (1776-1882), German writer and music critic, whose stories and his wild unhappy life provided the inspiration for Offenbach's *Tales of Hoffmann*. His works include the extravagantly fantastic *Phantasiestücke* (1814-15) and *Elixire des Teufels* (*The Devil's Elixir*, 1815-16).

Hofmannsthal /'hɒfmænstɑːl/, Hugo von (1874-1929), Austrian dramatist and poet. He wrote the libretti for Strauss's operas *Elektra* (1909), *Der Rosenkavalier* (1911), *Ariadne auf Naxos* (1912), and *Arabella* (1933); his correspondence with Strauss is of literary and musical interest. With Max Reinhardt, they founded the Salzburg Festival; *Jedermann* (*Everyman*, 1912; a modernization of the morality play) was first performed at the opening of the Festival in 1920. This work inaugurated his development away from the aestheticism of the *fin de siècle* towards a social and religious literature completed in his last play *Der Turm* (*The Tower*, 1925).

hog *n.* **1.** a castrated male pig. **2.** (*colloq.*) a greedy person. —*v.t./i.* (**-gg-**) to take greedily; to hoard selfishly.—**go the whole hog**, (*slang*) to do a thing thoroughly. **hog's back**, a steep-sided hill-ridge. —**hoggish** *adj.* [OE]

Hogarth /'həʊgɑːθ/, William (1697-1764), English painter and engraver. An important figure in the development of an English school of painting, Hogarth railed against the taste of his time for foreign artists and blackened Old Masters, and was instrumental in the moves to found art institutions in England which culminated after his death in the foundation of the Royal Academy (1769). Many of his works were engraved, most notably the 'modern moral subjects' such as *Marriage à la Mode*, which vividly satirized the vices of both high and low life in 18th-c. England. He was much influenced by the French rococo, despite his pugnacious pride in his nationality. Hogarth attempted history painting, in accordance with the contemporary emphasis about to 'high art', but was at his best in spontaneous sketches such as *A Shrimp Girl*.

Hogg, James (1770-1835), Scottish poet, a shepherd in the Ettrick Forest until his poetic talent was recognized by Scott (whence his nickname 'the Ettrick Shepherd'). He made his reputation as a poet with *The Queen's Wake* (1813) but is better known today for his prose work *The Confessions of a Justified Sinner* (1824).

hogmanay /'hɒgməneɪ/ *n.* (*Sc.*) New Year's Eve. [cf. OF *aguillanneuf*]

hogshead *n.* a large cask; a liquid or dry measure, usually about 50 gallons.

hogwash *n.* nonsense, rubbish.

hogweed *n.* a tall plant of the genus *Heracleum*, with thick hollow stems and umbrella-like clusters of white or pinkish flowers, liable to be eaten by animals.

Hohenstaufen /həʊɪn'ʃtaʊf(ə)n/ the name of a German princely family from which came Holy Roman Emperors from 1138 to 1254.

Hohenzollern /həʊɪn'zɒlən/ the name of a German princely family from which came the kings of Prussia from 1701 to 1918 and German emperors from 1871 to 1918.

ho-ho /həʊ'həʊ/ *int.* expressing surprise, triumph, or derision. [redupl. of HO]

hoick *v.t.* (*slang*) to lift or bring (*out*), especially with a jerk. [perh. var. of HIKE]

hoi polloi /ˌhɔɪ pəˈlɔɪ/ the masses, the common people. [Gk, = the many]

hoist *v.t.* to raise or haul up; to lift with ropes and pulleys etc.—*n.* **1.** an apparatus for hoisting things. **2.** hoisting. —**hoist with one's own petard**, caught by one's own trick etc. [alt. of *hoise*, prob. f. LG]

hoity-toity /ˌhɔɪtɪˈtɔɪtɪ/ *adj.* haughty. [f. obs. *hoit* indulge in riotous mirth]

hokum /ˈhəʊkəm/ *n.* (*slang*) **1.** a speech, action, or properties etc. used in a play or film to make a sentimental or melodramatic appeal to an audience. **2.** bunkum. [orig. unkn.]

Holbein /ˈhɒlbaɪn/, Hans (1497/8–1543), German painter who worked in Basle 1514–26, where he executed a series of woodcuts, the *Dance of Death* (*c.*1523–6). In 1526, finding his patronage reduced as a result of the Reformation, he came to England, with an introduction (from Erasmus) to Sir Thomas More. His group portrait of the More family is the first picture to be painted of full-length figures in their own home. By 1536 he had gained the patronage of Henry VIII, but was disappointed by the English court's almost exclusive interest in portraits. His late portraits (*The Ambassadors*, 1533, and *Christina, Duchess of Milan*, 1538) became increasingly detailed, frozen, and spaceless, perhaps in connection with an interest in miniature painting.

hold[1] /həʊld/ *v.t./i.* (past & *p.p.* **held**) **1.** to take and keep in one's hand(s), arms, teeth, etc.; to grasp. **2.** to keep in a particular position or condition; to grasp so as to control; to detain in custody; to keep (a person) *to* (a promise etc.). **3.** to be able to contain. **4.** to have in one's possession; to have gained (a qualification or achievement); to have the position of, to occupy (a job or office). **5.** to occupy militarily; to keep possession of (a place) against attack; to keep the attention of; to dominate (the stage etc.). **6.** to conduct or celebrate (a conversation, meeting, festival, etc.). **7.** to remain unbroken under pressure etc.; (of weather) to continue fine; (of a circumstance or condition) to remain. **8.** to believe, to consider; to assert. **9.** to restrain; (*colloq.*) to cause to cease action or movement.—*n.* **1.** the act or manner of holding something; grasp (*lit.* or *fig.*). **2.** a means of exerting influence. —**hold back**, to restrain; to hesitate, to refrain *from*. **hold down**, to repress; (*colloq.*) to be competent enough to keep (one's job). **hold forth**, to speak at length or tediously. **hold it!** cease action etc. **hold the line**, not to ring off (on the telephone). **hold off**, to delay; to keep one's distance; not to begin. **hold on**, to maintain one's grasp; to wait a moment; not to ring off (on the telephone). **hold one's own**, to maintain one's position, not to be beaten. **hold out**, to offer (an inducement etc.); (of supplies etc.) to last; to maintain resistance; to continue to make a demand *for*. **hold out on**, (*colloq.*) to refuse something to (a person). **hold over**, to postpone. **hold up**, to hinder or obstruct; to support or sustain; to stop with force and rob. **hold-up** *n.* a stoppage or delay; a robbery by force. **hold water**, (of reasoning) to be sound, to bear examination. **hold with** (usu. with *neg.*), to approve of. **no holds barred**, with all restrictions on methods etc. relaxed. **take hold**, (of a custom or habit) to become established. —**holder** *n.* [OE]

hold[2] /həʊld/ *n.* a cavity below the deck of a ship for cargo. [OE (rel. to HOLLOW)]

holdall *n.* a large soft travelling bag.

Hölderlin /ˈhœldəlɪn/, Johann Christian Friedrich (1770–1843), German poet who studied for the Church. His early poetry was full of political idealism fostered by the French Revolution, but most of his poems express a hopeless romantic yearning for ancient Greek harmony with nature and beauty. While working as a tutor he fell in love with his employer's wife, who is portrayed in his novel *Hyperion* (1797–9); and after her death in 1802 he drifted into insanity.

holdfast *n.* a clamp securing an object to a wall etc.

holding *n.* the tenure of land; land or stocks held. —**holding company**, one formed to hold the shares of other companies, which it then controls. [f. HOLD[1]]

hole *n.* **1.** an empty place in a solid body or mass; a sunken place on a surface; an opening through something. **2.** an animal's burrow. **3.** a small or gloomy place. **4.** (*slang*) an awkward situation. **5.** a hollow or cavity into which the ball etc. must be got in various games; (in golf) a section of a course between the tee and the hole. —*v.t./i.* **1.** to make a hole or holes in; to pierce the side of (a ship). **2.** to put into a hole. —**hole-and-corner** *adj.* underhand. **hole in the heart**, a congenital defect in the heart membrane. **hole up**, (*US slang*) to hide oneself. **make a hole in**, to use a large

amount of (one's supply). **pick holes in**, to find fault with. —**holey** *adj.* [OE]

Holi /ˈhəʊliː/ *n.* a Hindu spring festival celebrated in February or March in honour of Krishna the amorous cowherd. [Hindi f. Skr.]

holiday /ˈhɒlɪdeɪ/ *n.* **1.** a day of break from one's normal work, especially for recreation or festivity; (also in *pl.*) a period of this, a period of recreation away from home. **2.** a religious festival. —*v.i.* to spend a holiday. [OE (as HOLY, DAY)]

holiness /ˈhəʊlɪnɪs/ *n.* being holy or sacred. —**His Holiness**, the title of the Pope. [OE, as HOLY]

holistic /hɒˈlɪstɪk/ *adj.* of or involving the whole. —**holistic medicine**, a form of medical treatment that attempts to deal with the whole person and not merely with his or her physical condition. [f. Gk *holos* whole]

Holland /ˈhɒlənd/ a former province of the Netherlands, now divided into North and South Holland. Its name is often used interchangeably with the Netherlands as the name of the country. [Du., earlier *Holtlant* f. *Holt* wood + *-lant* land, describing Dordrecht district]

holland /ˈhɒlənd/ *n.* a smooth hard-wearing linen fabric. —**brown holland**, this fabric unbleached. [f. prec.]

holler *v.t./i.* (*US colloq.*) to shout. —*n.* a shout. [f. *hollo* (as HALLO)]

Hollerith /ˈhɒlərɪθ/, Herman (1860–1929), American inventor of a tabulating machine that was an important precursor of the electronic computer.

hollow /ˈhɒləʊ/ *adj.* **1.** having a space or cavity inside, not solid. **2.** having a sunken area. **3.** hungry. **4.** (of a sound) echoing, as if made in or on a hollow container. **5.** without validity, worthless. **6.** cynical, insincere. —*n.* a hollow or sunken place, a hole; a valley. —*adv.* completely. —*v.t./i.* (often with *out*) to make or become hollow. —**hollowly** *adv.* [f. OE *holh* cave (as HOLE)]

holly *n.* an evergreen shrub of the genus *Ilex* with prickly leaves and red berries, used to decorate houses and churches at Christmas (ill. TREES). [OE]

hollyhock /ˈhɒlɪhɒk/ *n.* a tall plant (*Althaea rosea*) with showy flowers. [orig. = marsh mallow, f. HOLY + obs. *hock* mallow]

Hollywood /ˈhɒlɪwʊd/ a district of Los Angeles. American film-making was originally based on New York, but Southern California, with its sunshine and scenic variety, appealed to film-makers from as early as 1907. In 1911 the first studio was established in Hollywood and 15 others followed in the same year. The Hollywood studio system reached its peak in the 1930s, but by 1950 television had become a serious competitor, and many films are now made for that medium.

Holmes[1] /həʊmz/, Oliver Wendell (1809–94), American physician, poet, and essayist, professor and dean of the medical school at Harvard, and father of the eminent Supreme Court Justice of the same name (1841–1935). His example was much prized among medical men as showing an ability to combine scientific and literary interests. In medicine his main contribution was an essay (1843) on contagion as one cause of puerperal fever. As a member of a literary circle in Boston, Holmes published novels, volumes of verse, and a series of 'table talks', beginning with 'The Autocrat of the Breakfast Table' (1857–8). Holmes's opinions were in general more conventional than is implied by many of the much-loved quotations from his writings.

Holmes[2] /həʊmz/, Sherlock. A private detective, the central figure in a number of detective stories by Conan Doyle. The character was in part based on an eminent Edinburgh surgeon, Dr Joseph Bell, under whom Doyle studied medicine. Holmes was so credited by readers that requests for his help are still received at his fictional address in Baker Street, London.

holmium /ˈhəʊlmɪəm/ *n.* a silvery soft metallic element of the lanthanide series, symbol Ho, atomic number 67, first discovered in 1878. It has few uses at present. [f. *Holmia* Stockholm, native city of its discoverer (P. T. Cleve)]

holm-oak /ˈhəʊməʊk/ *n.* an evergreen oak (*Quercus ilex*) with holly-like leaves, the ilex. [f. dial. *holm* holly]

holocaust /ˈhɒləkɔːst/ *n.* large-scale destruction, especially by fire. —**the Holocaust**, the mass murder of Jews by the Nazis in 1939–45. [f. OF f. L f. Gk (*holos* whole, *kaustos* burnt)]

Holocene /ˈhɒləsiːn/ *adj.* (also called *Recent*) of the second of the two epochs of the Quaternary period, following the Pleistocene and lasting from about 10,000 years ago to the present. The epoch has seen a rise in world temperatures after the last of the Pleistocene ice ages, and coincides with the development of human agricultural settlement and civilization. —*n.* this epoch. [f. Gk *holos* whole + *kainos* new]

Holofernes /hɒləˈfɜːniːz/ the Assyrian general of Nebu-chadnezzar's forces who was killed by Judith (Judith 4: 1 etc.).

hologram /ˈhɒləgræm/ *n.* a photograph of the pattern produced by interference between a coherent light-beam and light diffracted, reflected, or transmitted from the same beam by an object. When suitably illuminated such a photograph produces a two- or three-dimensional image of the object. [f. Gk *holos* whole + -GRAM]

holograph[1] /ˈhɒləgrɑːf/ *v.t.* to record as a hologram. —**holographic** /-ˈgræfɪk/ *adj.*, **holography** /-ˈlɒgrəfɪ/ *n.* [f. prec., after *telegraph*]

holograph[2] /ˈhɒləgrɑːf/ *adj.* wholly written by the person named as the author. —*n.* a holograph document. [f. F or L f. Gk (*holos* whole, -GRAPH)]

Holst /hɒlst/, Gustav (1874-1934), English-born com-poser of mixed Swedish and Russian descent. Like his friend and contemporary, Vaughan Williams, Holst was deeply interested in English folk-song, but while still a student he took lessons in Hindi, making his own translation of Sanskrit verses from the *Rig-Veda* and writing several works on Indian subjects. Much of his music has a timeless quality which was unfamiliar in English ears of the time, and Vaughan Williams said of his *Choral Symphony* (1923-4) that he felt for it only a 'cold admiration'. Holst was bewildered by the immediate popularity of *The Planets* (first performed in 1919), but here the essence of his style is plainly seen, combining a love for tight rhythmic control with a visionary quality perfectly expressed. He was also an inspiring teacher, with great feeling for the community spirit engendered by music, and played an outstanding part in music-making in the early 20th c.

holster /ˈhəʊlstə(r)/ *n.* a leather case for a pistol or revolver, usually fixed to a saddle or belt. [= Du. *holster*]

holy /ˈhəʊlɪ/ *adj.* **1.** of God and therefore regarded with reverence; associated with God or religion. **2.** consecrated, sacred. **3.** devoted to the service of God. —**holier-than-thou** *adj.* (*colloq.*) self-righteous. **Holy Communion,** see COMMUNION. **Holy Father,** the title of the pope. **Holy Ghost,** the Holy Spirit. **Holy Grail,** see GRAIL. **holy of holies,** the sacred inner chamber of a Jewish temple; any place or retreat regarded as most sacred. **holy orders,** see ORDER. **Holy Spirit,** the third Person of the Trinity, God acting spiritually. **Holy Week,** the week before Easter Sunday. **Holy Writ,** holy writing especially the Bible. [OE (rel. to WHOLE)]

Holy Island see LINDISFARNE.

Holy Land the western part of Palestine.

Holy Office an ecclesiastical court established in 1542 (see INQUISITION) as the final court of appeal in trials of heresy. In 1965 it was renamed the Sacred Congregation for the Doctrine of the Faith; its function is to promote as well as to safeguard sound doctrine in the Roman Catholic Church.

Holy Roman Empire the empire set up in the West following the coronation of Charlemagne as emperor, in the year 800. Of the emperors after 1250 only five were crowned as such; the dignity was abolished by Napoleon in 1806. In true apocalyptic style the Empire lasted about 1,000 years. The creation of the medieval popes, it has been called their greatest mistake; for whereas their intention was to appoint a powerful secular deputy to rule Christendom, in fact they generated a rival. The Emperor never ruled the whole of Christendom, nor was there any substantial machinery of imperial government. From Otto I's coro-nation (962) the Empire was always associated with the German Crown, even after it became a Hapsburg/Austrian preserve in the 15th c. Its somewhat mystical ideal was formal unity of government, based on coronation in Rome, memories of the old Roman Empire as well as Charlemagne, and devotion to the Roman Church. Perhaps for the very reason that this was generally at odds with the facts of political fragmentation within imperial territories, its ideo-logical appeal remained astonishingly persistent, although as the supposed embodiment of a united Christendom it took a blow in the Reformation.

Holy See the papacy or papal court; those associated with the pope in the government of the Roman Catholic Church at its headquarters in Rome (see VATICAN).

Holy Shroud a relic, preserved at Turin in Italy since 1578, venerated as the winding-sheet in which Christ's body was wrapped for burial. It bears the imprint of the front and back of a human body marked with the traditional stigmata. Its history has not been traced back beyond the mid-14th c.

holystone /ˈhəʊlɪstəʊn/ *n.* a soft sandstone formerly used for scouring the decks of ships. —*v.t.* to scour with this. [prob. f. HOLY + STONE; the stones were called *bibles* etc., perh. because used while kneeling]

homage /ˈhɒmɪdʒ/ *n.* a tribute, an expression of reverence; (in feudal law) a formal expression of allegiance. [f. OF f. L *hominaticum* (*homo* man)]

Homburg /ˈhɒmbɜːg/ *n.* a man's hat with a curled brim and a lengthwise dent in the crown. [f. *Homburg* in West Germany, where first worn]

home *n.* **1.** the place where one lives; the fixed residence of a family or household. **2.** one's native land; the district where one was born or has lived for a long time, or to which one feels attached. **3.** a dwelling-house or flat. **4.** an institution where those needing care or rest etc. may live. **5.** the place where a thing originates or is most common; the natural environment of a plant or animal. **6.** the finishing point in a race etc. **7.** (in games) a home match or win. —*adj.* **1.** of or connected with one's home or country; carried on, done, or produced there. **2.** (of a game or team) played or playing on one's own ground etc. —*adv.* **1.** to or at one's home. **2.** to the point aimed at; as far as possible. —*v.t./i.* **1.** (of a pigeon etc.) to make its way home. **2.** (of a vessel, missile, etc.), to be guided (*in*) to a destination or on a target. —**at home,** in one's own house etc.; at ease; familiar or well-informed (*in, on, with,* a subject); available to callers. **at-home** *n.* a reception of visitors within certain hours. **bring home to,** to cause to realize fully. **home and dry,** having achieved one's aim. **home-brew** *n.* beer brewed at home. **Home Counties,** the counties closest to London. **home economics,** the study of household management. **home farm,** a farm worked by the owner of an estate containing other farms. **Home Guard,** the British volunteer army organized for defence in 1940. **home help,** a person who helps with housework etc., especially in a service organized by a local authority. **home-made** *adj.* made at home. **Home Office,** the government department dealing with law and order etc. in England and Wales. **Home Rule,** see separate entry. **Home Secretary,** the government minister in charge of the Home Office. **home truth,** a (usu. unwelcome) truth about oneself heard from another. [OE]

homeland *n.* **1.** one's native land. **2.** (in the Republic of South Africa) an area reserved for African Blacks, 1948- .

homeless *adj.* lacking a dwelling-place. [f. HOME + -LESS]

homely *adj.* **1.** simple and informal, unpretentious. **2.** (*US,* of a person's appearance) plain, not beautiful. —**homeliness** *n.* [f. HOME]

Homer /ˈhəʊmə(r)/ (? *c.*700 BC) Greek epic poet, tradition-ally the author of the *Iliad* and the *Odyssey*. Various cities in Ionia claimed him as a son, and he is said to have been blind. Modern scholarship has fully revealed the nature of the Homeric poems as the product of a pre-literate oral tradition, in which a succession of bards elaborated the traditional stories of the heroic age (historically to be placed at the end of the Mycenaean period) in formulaic language in hexameter verse; questions of authorship are thus very difficult to answer. In later antiquity Homer was regarded as the greatest and unsurpassable poet, and his poems were constantly used as a model and source by others.

homer /ˈhəʊmə(r)/ *n.* a homing pigeon. [f. HOME]

Homeric /həʊˈmerɪk/ *adj.* of the writings of Homer; of Bronze Age Greece as described in them. [f. L f. Gk]

Home Rule government of a country or region by its own citizens, especially in a movement campaigning for autonomy for Ireland under the British Crown, 1870-1914. The campaign was one of the dominant forces in British politics in the late 19th and early 20th c., particularly in that the Irish nationalists, under Parnell and later Redmond, frequently held the balance of power in the House of Commons. After Gladstone's conversion in 1885 the Lib-eral Party supported Home Rule, but the Conservatives, joined by the Unionists, continued to oppose it. The situation was complicated by the opposition to Home Rule of the Ulster Unionists on one side and Sinn Fein on the other. Although a Home Rule Act was finally passed in 1914 it was suspended because of the First World War, the onset of which probably prevented, as least for a time, civil war breaking out in Ireland.

homesick adj. depressed by absence from home. —**homesickness** n.

homespun adj. **1.** made of yarn spun at home. **2.** plain, simple. —n. a homespun fabric.

homestead /ˈhəʊmsted/ n. **1.** a house with its adjoining land and outbuildings, a farm. **2.** (*Austral. & NZ*) the owner's residence on a sheep or cattle station. [OE, as HOME, STEAD]

homeward /ˈhəʊmwəd/ adv. (also **homewards**) towards home. —adj. going towards home. [OE (as HOME, -WARD)]

homework n. work to be done at home by a school pupil; preparatory work or study.

homicide /ˈhɒmɪsaɪd/ n. **1.** the killing of one person by another. **2.** a person who kills another. —**homicidal** /-ˈsaɪd(ə)l/ adj. [f. OF f. L (*homo* man, -CIDE)]

homily /ˈhɒmɪlɪ/ n. a sermon, a moralizing lecture. —**homiletic** /-ˈletɪk/ adj. [f. L f. Gk *homilia* (*homilos* crowd)]

homing adj. **1.** (of a pigeon) trained to fly home from a distance. **2.** (of a device) for guiding to a target etc. [f. HOME]

hominid /ˈhɒmɪnɪd/ adj. of the zoological family Hominidae that includes existing and fossil man. —n. a member of this family. [f. L *homo* man]

hominoid /ˈhɒmɪnɔɪd/ adj. manlike. —n. an animal resembling man. [as prec.]

Homo /ˈhəʊməʊ/ n. the genus of which we (*Homo sapiens sapiens*) are the modern representatives. The genus *Homo* has now been in existence for *c.*2 million years, while our species, including the archaic *H. sapiens*, has occupied only the last 80,000 years or so, *H. habilis* 2.1/1.7-*c.*1.5 million years, *H. erectus* 1.5 million years to *c.*80,000 years BP, and *H. sapiens c.*80,000 years BP to the present. The genus appears to have begun in East Africa with the advent of *H. habilis*, from Olduvai Gorge, Tanzania, and an as yet undifferentiated species from Koobi Fora, Kenya. It is believed that this or some other early species of *Homo* diverged from the Australopithecines more than two million years ago. This divergence is most readily seen in the fossil record where significant differences in the cranial and post-cranial skeleton can be observed. What is not so easily seen, though of equal significance, is the emergence and/or further development of social and cultural traits that we commonly view as human. With respect to material culture, only members of the genus *Homo* can be confidently shown to have made and used stone and bone tools and to have the controlled use of fire. These extra-personal aids enabled *Homo* (*H. erectus*) to radiate out from East Africa to the more varied environments of the remainder of the Old World to produce a distribution of individuals far greater than that of the earlier Australopithecines. The principal trends within the genus *Homo* through time can be summarized thus: an increase in brain size and complexity, an increase in the complexity of culture and social relationships, and the increasing ability to modify the environment.

homo /ˈhəʊməʊ/ n. (*pl.* -**os**) (*colloq.*) a homosexual. [abbr.]

homo- in comb. same. [f. Gk *homos* same]

homoeopathy /həʊmɪˈɒpəθɪ/ n. treatment of disease by substances, usually in minute doses, that in a healthy person would produce symptoms like those of the disease. The practice is based on the theory that 'like cures like', an idea known to the Greeks and Romans but first given definite expression by Samuel Hahnemann (1755-1843), a German physician and chemist who had become dissatisfied with orthodox medical teaching. He explained the success of his method by affirming that the drug induced a condition which displaced the disease; some of his followers maintained that the drugs stimulated the body's protective responses to the disease and thereby quickened its natural healing power. Homoeopathy made converts throughout Europe in the early 19th c. and was introduced into America, but with advances in medicine and related sciences its influence diminished, though the practice still has its supporters. —**homoeopathic** /-ˈpæθɪk/ adj., **homoeopathist** n. [f. G f. Gk *homoios* like + -PATHY]

homogeneous /hɒməˈdʒiːnɪəs/ adj. of the same kind; consisting of parts all of the same kind. —**homogeneity** /-dʒɪˈniːɪtɪ/ n. [f. L f. (HOMO-, *genos* kind)]

homogenize /həˈmɒdʒɪnaɪz/ v.t. **1.** to make homogeneous. **2.** to treat (milk) so that fat droplets are emulsified and cream does not separate. —**homogenization** /-ˈzeɪʃ(ə)n/ n. [f. prec.]

homograph /ˈhɒməgrɑːf/ n. a word spelt like another, but of different meaning or origin, e.g. BAT¹, BAT². [f. HOMO- + -GRAPH]

homologous /həˈmɒləgəs/ adj. having the same relation or relative position; corresponding; (*Biol.*) similar in position and structure but not necessarily in function; (*Chem.*) forming a series with constant successive differences of composition. [f. L f. Gk (HOMO-, *logos* ratio)]

homologue /ˈhɒməlɒg/ n. a homologous thing. [F f. Gk (as prec.)]

homology /həˈmɒlədʒɪ/ n. a homologous state or relation. —**homological** /-ˈlɒdʒɪk(ə)l/ adj. [f. HOMOLOGOUS]

homonym /ˈhɒmənɪm/ n. **1.** a word of the same spelling or sound as another but with a different meaning, e.g. POLE¹, POLE²; THEIR, THERE. **2.** a namesake. [f. L f. Gk (HOMO-, *onoma* name)]

homophone /ˈhɒməfəʊn/ n. a word having the same sound as another, but of different meaning or origin, e.g. SON, SUN. [f. Gk (HOMO-, *phōnē* sound)]

homosexual /həʊməʊˈseksjʊəl, hɒm-/ adj. feeling sexually attracted to people of the same sex. —n. a homosexual person. —**homosexuality** /-ˈælɪtɪ/ n. [f. HOMO- + SEXUAL]

Hon. abbr. **1.** Honorary. **2.** Honourable.

Honduras /hɒnˈdjuːrəs/ a country of Central America, between Guatemala and Nicaragua; pop. (est. 1982) 3,600,000; official language, Spanish; capital, Tegucigalpa. Discovered by Columbus in 1502, for nearly three centuries until the proclamation of independence in 1821 Honduras was a dependency of Spain. Much of the country is mountainous and there are extensive pine-forests; its principal exports are bananas and coffee. —**Honduran** adj. & n.

hone /həʊn/ n. a whetstone for sharpening razors and tools. —v.t. to sharpen (as) on a hone (*lit. & fig.*). [OE, = stone]

Honegger /ˈɒnegə(r)/, Arthur (1892-1955), Swiss composer who lived and worked in Paris, a somewhat uneasy member of the group of advanced composers know as Les Six, since he was influenced as much by the German Romantics as by Satie and Cocteau. His representation of a steam-engine in *Pacific 231* (1923) brought him his first major success, and his dramatic oratorio *Jeanne d'Arc au bûcher* (1934-5) achieves strong emotional power through its combination of speech and song.

honest /ˈɒnɪst/ adj. **1.** truthful, trustworthy. **2.** fairly earned. **3.** sincere but undistinguished. [f. OF f. L *honestus* (*honos* honour)]

honestly adv. **1.** in an honest way. **2.** really. [f. prec.]

honesty n. **1.** being honest; truthfulness. **2.** a plant of the genus *Lunaria*, with purple flowers and flat round semi-transparent seed-pods. [f. OF f. L *honestas* (as HONEST)]

honey /ˈhʌnɪ/ n. **1.** the sweet sticky fluid made by bees from nectar collected from flowers. **2.** its yellowish colour. **3.** sweetness; a sweet thing, **4.** an excellent person or thing; darling (esp. as a form of address). —**honey-bee** n. the common hive-bee (*Apis mellifera*). —**honeyed** adj. [OE]

honeycomb n. **1.** the bees' wax structure of hexagonal cells for honey and eggs. **2.** a pattern arranged hexagonally. —v.t. to fill with cavities or tunnels; to mark with a honeycomb pattern.

honeydew n. **1.** a sweet sticky substance found on leaves and stems, excreted by aphids. **2.** a variety of melon with a smooth pale skin and green flesh.

honeymoon n. **1.** the holiday spent together by a newly-married couple. **2.** an initial period of enthusiasm or goodwill. —v.i. to spend a honeymoon. [f. HONEY + MOON, orig. with ref. to waning affection, not to period of a month]

honeysuckle n. a climbing shrub of the genus *Lonicera* with fragrant yellow and pink flowers.

Hong Kong /hɒŋ ˈkɒŋ/ a British dependency on the SE coast of China; pop. (est. 1984) 5,397,000; official languages, English and Chinese. It comprises Hong Kong island, ceded by China in 1841, the Kowloon peninsula, ceded in 1860, and the New Territories, additional areas of the mainland, leased for 99 years in 1898. By an agreement between the British and Chinese governments (signed in 1984), in 1997 China will resume sovereignty over Hong Kong which will then become a Special Administrative Region whose basic law will guarantee present systems and life-styles for a period of 50 years. Hong Kong is a major financial and manufacturing centre. Its container port is the third largest in the world.

honk n. **1.** the hooting cry of the wild goose. **2.** the sound of a vehicle's horn. —*v.t./i.* to make a honk; to sound (a horn). [imit.]

honky-tonk /ˈhɒŋkɪtɒŋk/ *n.* (*colloq.*) **1.** ragtime piano music. **2.** a cheap or disreputable night-club. [orig. unkn.]

honorarium /ɒnəˈreərɪəm/ *n.* (*pl.* **-iums**) a voluntary payment for services without the normal fee. [L (as foll.)]

honorary /ˈɒnərərɪ/ *adj.* **1.** conferred as an honour. **2.** (of an office or its holder) unpaid. [f. L *honorarius* (as HONOUR)]

honorific /ɒnəˈrɪfɪk/ *adj.* conferring honour; implying respect. [f. L *honorificus* (as HONOUR + *-fic* f. *facere* make)]

honour /ˈɒnə(r)/ *n.* **1.** great respect, high public regard. **2.** a mark of this; an official award for bravery or achievement; a privilege given or received. **3.** a person or thing that brings honour. **4.** adherence to what is right or to an accepted standard of conduct; (of a woman) chastity, a reputation for this. **5.** exalted position; a title of respect to certain judges and other important persons. **6.** (in *pl.*) a specialized degree-course or special distinction in an examination. **7.** (in card-games) the four or five highest-ranking cards. —*v.t.* **1.** to respect highly; to confer honour on. **2.** to accept or pay (a bill or cheque) when due; to observe the terms of (an agreement). —**do the honours,** to perform the duties of a host to guests etc. **on one's honour,** under a moral obligation (*to do* a thing). [f. OF f. L *honor*]

honourable /ˈɒnərəb(ə)l/ *adj.* **1.** deserving, bringing, or showing honour. **2. Honourable,** the courtesy title of certain high officials and judges, also of the children of viscounts and barons, the younger sons of earls, and used during debates by MPs to one another. —**Right Honourable,** see RIGHT. —**honourably** *adv.* [f. OF f. L (as prec.)]

hooch /huːtʃ/ *n.* (*US colloq.*) alcoholic liquor, especially inferior or illicit whisky. [abbr. of Alaskan *hoochinoo* liquor-making tribe]

hood¹ /hʊd/ *n.* **1.** a covering for the head and neck, often forming part of a garment. **2.** a separate hoodlike garment worn as a part of academic dress. **3.** a thing resembling a hood, e.g. a folding soft roof over a car. **4.** (*US*) the bonnet of a car. **5.** a canopy to protect the user of machinery or to remove fumes etc. (ill. HOUSES). —*v.t.* to cover with a hood [OE]

hood² /hʊd/ *n.* (*US slang*) a gangster, a gunman. [abbr. of HOODLUM]

-hood /-hʊd/ *suffix* forming nouns of condition, quality, or grouping (*childhood, falsehood, sisterhood*). [OE (orig. a separate word *hād* person, condition, quality)]

hooded *adj.* having a hood; (of an animal) having a hoodlike part. [f. HOOD¹]

hoodlum /ˈhuːdləm/ *n.* a hooligan, a young thug; a gangster. [orig. unkn.]

hoodoo /ˈhuːduː/ *n.* (*US*) **1.** bad luck; a thing that brings or causes this. **2.** voodoo. —*v.t.* (*US*) to make unlucky, to bewitch. [alt. of VOODOO]

hoodwink /ˈhʊdwɪŋk/ *v.t.* to deceive, to delude. [f. HOOD¹ + WINK]

hooey /ˈhuːɪ/ *n.* & *int.* (*slang*) nonsense. [orig. unkn.]

hoof /huːf/ *n.* (*pl.* **hoofs, hooves**) the horny part of the foot of a horse etc. (ill. HORSE). —*v.i.* (usu. as **hoof it**) (*slang*) to go on foot. [OE]

hoo-ha /ˈhuːhɑː/ *n.* (*slang*) a commotion. [orig. unkn.]

hook /hʊk/ *n.* **1.** a bent or curved piece of wire or metal etc. for catching hold or for hanging things on. **2.** a curved cutting instrument. **3.** a hooklike thing or formation of land, a bend in a river etc. **4.** a hooking stroke; a short swinging blow in boxing. —*v.t./i.* **1.** to grasp or secure with a hook or hooks. **2.** to catch with a hook or (*fig.*) as if with a hook; (*slang*) to steal. **3.** (in sports) to send (the ball) in a curving or deviating path; (in a Rugby football scrum) to secure and pass (the ball) backward with the foot. —**be hooked on,** (*slang*) to be addicted to or captivated by. **by hook or by crook,** by one means or another. **hook and eye,** a small metal hook and loop as a dress-fastener. **hook, line, and sinker,** entirely. **hook it,** (*slang*) to make off. **hook-up** *n.* a connection, especially an interconnection in a broadcast transmission. **off the hook,** (*colloq.*) out of difficulty or trouble. [OE]

hookah /ˈhʊkə/ *n.* an oriental tobacco-pipe with a long tube passing through water for cooling the smoke as it is drawn through. [Urdu f. Arab., = casket]

Hooke /hʊk/, Robert (1635-1703), English scientist, one of the most versatile of his age. In 1655 he became Boyle's assistant, and devised an improved air-pump for him. In 1662 he became the first curator of experiments of the recently founded Royal Society; after the Fire of London in 1666 he was made one of the surveyors to the City and also designed several of London's prominent buildings. His scientific achievements are many: he proposed an undulating theory of light, formulated the law of elasticity (Hooke's Law), contributed to the study of fossils, introduced the term 'cell' to biology, postulated elliptical orbits for the earth and moon, and proposed the inverse-square of gravitation attraction which helped Newton to formulate his theory of universal gravitation applied to planetary motion. He improved and invented many scientific instruments. He stimulated the improvement of the compound microscope and reflecting telescope and invented, among other things, the wheel barometer, the balance-spring for watches, the universal or Hooke joint, a sounding instrument and sea-water sampler, and several meteorological instruments.

hooked *adj.* in the shape of a hook. [f. HOOK]

Hooker /ˈhʊkə(r)/, Sir Joseph Dalton (1817-1911), English botanist who travelled widely and was a pioneer in plant geography. In 1839-43 he joined a voyage to the Antarctic, and concluded that the distribution of plants indicated an ancient joining of land between Australia and South America. From 1847 he spent three years in NE India, from which area he sent home a collection of rhododendrons and (through Kew Gardens) introduced their cultivation. Hooker was a firm friend and admirer of Charles Darwin, whose theories he supported and applied to the development of plants. His many works include *Genera Plantarum* (1862-83), a classification of plants devised jointly with George Bentham. In 1865 he became Director of the Botanic Gardens at Kew near London, succeeding his father Sir William Jackson Hooker (1785-1865), who had greatly extended the royal gardens there, founded a museum, and opened the gardens to the public.

hooker¹ *n.* **1.** a player in the front row of the scrum in Rugby football, who tries to hook the ball. **2.** (*US slang*) a prostitute. [f. HOOK]

hooker² *n.* a small Dutch or Irish fishing-vessel. [f. Du. *hoeker* (as HOOK)]

hookey *n.* **play hookey** (*US slang*) to play truant. [orig. unkn.]

hookworm *n.* a worm of the family Ancylostomatidae, the male of which has hooklike spines, infesting humans and animals.

hooligan /ˈhuːlɪgən/ *n.* a young ruffian. —**hooliganism** *n.* [perh. orig. name of Irish family of ruffians in SE London]

hoop /huːp/ *n.* **1.** a circular band of metal or wood etc. for binding a cask etc., or forming part of a framework. **2.** a large ring of wood etc., bowled along by a child, or for circus performers to jump through. **3.** an iron etc. arch used in croquet. —*v.t.* to bind or encircle with a hoop or hoops. —**be put** or **go through the hoop,** to undergo an ordeal. [OE]

hoop-la /ˈhuːplɑː/ *n.* a game in which rings are thrown in an attempt to encircle a prize. [f. HOOP + *la* int.]

hoopoe /ˈhuːpuː/ *n.* a bird, especially *Upupa epops*, with a fanlike crest and striped wings and tail. [f. OF f. L *upupa*, imit. of its cry]

hooray /hʊˈreɪ/ var. of HURRAH.

hoot /huːt/ *n.* **1.** an owl's cry. **2.** the sound made by a vehicle's horn or a steam whistle. **3.** a shout expressing scorn or disapproval. **4.** (*colloq.*) laughter; a cause of this. —*v.t./i.* to make a hoot or hoots; to sound (a horn). —**not care** or **give** etc. **a hoot,** (*slang*) not to care at all. [perh. imit.]

hooter /ˈhuːtə(r)/ *n.* **1.** a siren, a steam whistle, especially as a signal for work to begin or cease. **2.** a vehicle's horn. **3.** (*slang*) the nose. [f. HOOT]

Hoover /ˈhuːvə(r)/ *n.* [P] a type of vacuum cleaner. —**hoover** *v.t.* to clean with a vacuum cleaner.

hooves *pl.* of HOOF.

hop¹ *v.t./i.* (**-pp-**) **1.** (of a bird or animal) to spring with two or all feet at once. **2.** (of a person) to jump on one foot. **3.** to cross (a ditch etc.) —*n.* **1.** a hopping movement. **2.** an informal dance. **3.** a short flight in an aircraft. —**hop in** (or **out**), (*colloq.*) to get into (or out of) a car. **hop it!** (*slang*) go away! **hopping mad,** (*colloq.*) very angry. **on the hop,** unprepared. [OE]

hop² *n.* a climbing plant (*Humulus lupulus*) bearing cones; (in *pl.*) its ripe cones used to flavour beer. —*v.t.* (**-pp-**) to flavour with hops. —**hop-bind** or **hop-bine** *n.* the climbing stem of the hop. [f. MLG or MDu.]

hope *n.* **1.** expectation and desire, e.g. for a certain event to occur. **2.** a person, thing, or circumstance that encourages

The Horse

Anatomy

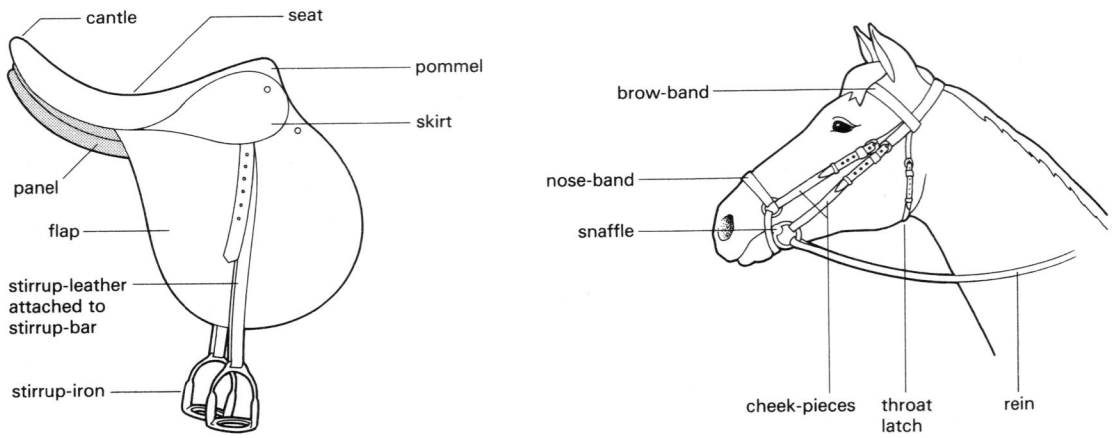

crest
poll
mane
withers
forelock
dock croup loin
muzzle
girth
shoulder
gaskin
elbow
forearm
point of hock
sheath
chestnut
knee
chestnut
stifle
cannon-bone
hock
splint-bone
tendons
ergot
fetlock
pastern
hoof
heel
coronet

Tack

saddle

snaffle bridle and drop nose-band

cantle
seat
pommel
skirt
panel
flap
brow-band
nose-band
snaffle
stirrup-leather
attached to
stirrup-bar
stirrup-iron

cheek-pieces   throat
latch
rein

Paces

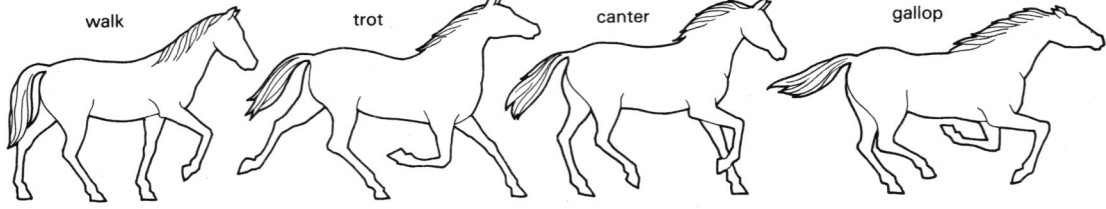

walk   trot   canter   gallop

hope. **3.** what is hoped for. —*v.t./i.* to feel hope; to expect and desire; to feel fairly confident. —**hope against hope,** to cling to a mere possibility. [OE]

hopeful *adj.* feeling or causing hope; likely to succeed. —*n.* a person who hopes or seems likely to succeed. [f. HOPE + -FUL]

hopefully *adv.* **1.** in a hopeful manner. **2.** (**D**) it is to be hoped. [f. prec.]

hopeless *adj.* **1.** feeling or admitting no hope. **2.** inadequate, incompetent. —**hopelessly** *adv.*, **hopelessness** *n.* [f. HOPE + -LESS]

Hopkins[1] /ˈhɒpkɪnz/, Sir Frederick Gowland (1861–1947), English biochemist, who in 1912 published an important paper giving precision to ideas about the existence of certain substances (now called vitamins) which are essential to the diet. For his work in the development of this concept he shared the Nobel Prize for medicine in 1929.

Hopkins[2] /ˈhɒpkɪnz/, Gerard Manley (1844–89), English poet. At Oxford he became influenced by Newman, was converted to Roman Catholicism in 1866, became a Jesuit, and renounced poetry until 1876. His most ambitious work 'The Wreck of the Deutschland', with 'Windhover' and 'Pied Beauty', is among his best-known poems. Hopkins developed his theories of natural beauty, using the terms 'inscape' (the individual or essential quality of the object) and 'instress' (the force of 'inscape' on the mind of the observer). A skilful innovator, he sought to unite the rhythm of his verse with the flow and varying emphasis of spoken language by using 'sprung rhythm' (a combination of regularity of stress patterns with freely varying numbers of syllables). His *Poems* were all published posthumously by his friend Robert Bridges in 1918. The great impact of his work on 20th-c. poets inspired a revival of poetic energy, seriousness, and originality.

hoplite /ˈhɒplaɪt/ *n.* a heavy-armed infantry soldier in ancient Greece (ill. ARMOUR). [f. Gk (*hoplon* weapon)]

hopper[1] *n.* **1.** one who hops; a hopping insect. **2.** a container tapering to the base, with an opening at the base for discharging the contents. [f. HOP[1]]

hopper[2] *n.* a hop-picker. [f. HOP[2]]

hopsack *n.* a kind of loosely-woven fabric. [f. HOP[2] + SACK]

hopscotch *n.* a children's game of hopping over squares marked on the ground to retrieve a stone tossed into these. [f. HOP[1] + SCOTCH[2]]

Horace /ˈhɒrəs/ (Quintus Horatius Flaccus, 65–8 BC), Roman poet born in southern Italy, the son of a freedman. Educated in Rome and Athens, he was pardoned after fighting for Brutus at the battle of Philippi, and was subsequently a star in the poetic circle of Maecenas. His works, frequently with an autobiographical element, include two books of hexameter *Satires* presenting the poet's reflections on life, literature, and morality, four books of *Odes* (short lyric poems in a variety of metres), two books of hexameter *Epistles*, essays in a conversational letter form, one book of *Epodes*, and a hexameter didactic, the *Art of Poetry* (*Ars Poetica*).

horde /hɔːd/ *n.* **1.** a large group, a gang. **2.** a troop of Tartar or other nomads. [f. Pol. f. Turki *ordī, ordū* camp; cf. URDU]

horehound /ˈhɔːhaʊnd/ *n.* a herb (*Marrubium vulgare*) producing a bitter juice used against coughs. [OE (as HOAR, *hune* a plant)]

horizon /həˈraɪz(ə)n/ *n.* **1.** the line at which earth and sky appear to meet. **2.** the limit of mental perception, experience, interest, etc. —**on the horizon,** imminent, becoming apparent. [f. OF f. L f. Gk (*horizō* bound)]

horizontal /hɒrɪˈzɒnt(ə)l/ *adj.* **1.** parallel to the plane of the horizon; at right angles to the vertical. **2.** at or concerned with the same status, work, etc. —*n.* a horizontal line etc. —**horizontally** *adv.* [as prec.]

hormone /ˈhɔːməʊn/ *n.* any of numerous organic compounds secreted internally (esp. into the bloodstream) by a specific group of cells, and regulating a specific physiological activity of other cells, or produced by plants whose growth and other physiological activities they regulate; a similar synthetic substance. —**hormonal** /-ˈməʊn(ə)l/ *adj.* [f. Gk (*hormaō* impel)]

Hormuz /ˈhɔːmʊz/ an ancient city on an island at the mouth of the Persian Gulf, an important centre of commerce in the Middle Ages. —**Strait of Hormuz,** a strait separating Iran from the Arabian peninsula and linking the Persian Gulf with the Gulf of Oman which leads to the Arabian Sea, of strategic and economic importance as a waterway through which sea traffic to and from the oil-rich States of the Persian Gulf must pass.

horn *n.* **1.** a hard outgrowth, often curved and pointed, from the head of an animal; each of the two branched appendages on the head of (esp. male) deer. **2.** a hornlike projection on other animals, e.g. a snail's tentacle. **3.** the substance of which horns are made. **4.** a wind instrument, originally made of horn, now usually brass (see below). **5.** an instrument for sounding a warning. **6.** a receptacle or instrument made of horn. **7.** a horn-shaped projection; an extremity of the moon or other crescent, an arm of a river etc. **8.** either alternative of a dilemma. —*v.t.* **1.** to furnish with horns. **2.** to gore with the horns. —**the Horn,** Cape Horn. **horn in,** (*slang*) to intrude, to interfere. **Horn of Africa,** the peninsula of NE Africa separating the Gulf of Aden from the main part of the Indian Ocean. It is also called the Somali Peninsula and comprises Somalia and parts of Ethiopia. **horn of plenty,** a cornucopia. [OE, cogn. w. L *cornu*]

The horn of domesticated cattle, with the tip cut off (or, in Africa, with a central orifice cut) to leave a hole for blowing, has been used by herdsmen, watchmen, and huntsmen from time immemorial. Instruments of this kind were also made of bronze, ivory, and brass. In written music and among musicians the term 'horn' denotes the French horn (see FRENCH).

hornbeam *n.* a tree (*Carpinus betulus*) with hard tough wood.

hornbill *n.* a tropical bird of the family Bucerotidae with a hornlike excrescence on the bill.

hornblende /ˈhɔːnblend/ *n.* a black or green or dark brown mineral, a constituent of granite etc. [G (as HORN, BLENDE)]

hornet /ˈhɔːnɪt/ *n.* a large kind of wasp (especially *Vespa crabro*). —**hornet-moth,** a kind of moth (*Sesia apiformis*) resembling the hornet (ill. INSECTS). **stir up a hornet's nest,** to cause an angry outburst. [prob. f. MLG or MDu.]

hornpipe *n.* a lively dance, usually for one person; the music for this. Its traditional association with British seamen seems to date from the late 18th *c.*

Hornung /ˈhɔːnʌŋ/, Ernest William (1866–1921), English novelist and writer of short stories, brother-in-law of Sir Arthur Conan Doyle. He is remembered as the creator of the gentleman burglar Raffles.

horny *adj.* **1.** of or like horn; hard like horn, calloused. **2.** (*slang*) lecherous. [f. HORN]

horology /həˈrɒlədʒɪ/ *n.* the art of measuring time or making clocks, watches, etc. —**horological** /hɒrəˈlɒdʒɪk(ə)l/ *adj.* [f. Gk *hōra* time + -LOGY]

horoscope /ˈhɒrəskəʊp/ *n.* a forecast of a person's future from a diagram showing the relative positions of the planets etc. at a particular time; this diagram. [F f. L f. Gk (as prec., *skopos* observer)]

horrendous /həˈrendəs/ *adj.* horrifying. [f. gerundive of L *horrēre* (as foll.)]

horrible /ˈhɒrɪb(ə)l/ *adj.* causing or exciting horror; (*colloq.*) unpleasant. —**horribly** *adv.* [f. L *horribilis* (*horrēre* bristle, shudder)]

horrid /ˈhɒrɪd/ *adj.* horrible, revolting; (*colloq.*) unpleasant. —**horridly** *adv.* [f. L *horridus* (as prec.)]

horrific /həˈrɪfɪk/ *adj.* horrifying. —**horrifically** *adv.* [f. F or L (as HORRIBLE)]

horrify /ˈhɒrɪfaɪ/ *v.t.* to arouse horror in, to shock. [f. L (as prec.)]

horror /ˈhɒrə(r)/ *n.* **1.** an intense feeling of loathing and fear; intense dislike or dismay. **2.** a person or thing causing horror; (*colloq.*) a bad or mischievous person etc. —**the horrors,** a fit of depression or nervousness etc. [f. OF f. L (as HORRIBLE)]

Horsa /ˈhɔːsə/ see HENGIST.

hors d'œuvre /ɔːˈdɜːvr/ *n.* an appetizer served at the beginning of a meal. [F, = outside the work]

horse *n.* **1.** a large four-legged animal (*Equus caballus*) with a long mane and tail, used for riding or to carry or pull loads (see below and ill. p. 396); an adult male horse, a stallion. **2.** (*collect.*, as *sing.*) cavalry. **3.** a gymnastic vaulting-block. **4.** a supporting frame. —*v.i.* (*colloq.*) to fool around. —**from the horse's mouth,** (of information etc.) from the original or an authoritative source. **horse-box** *n.* a closed vehicle for transporting a horse or horses. **horse-chestnut** *n.* a tree of the genus *Aesculus* with conical clusters of white or pink flowers (ill. TREES); its dark brown fruit. **horse-fly** *n.* any of various insects troublesome to horses and cattle. **Horse Guards,** a cavalry brigade of

household troops; its headquarters in Whitehall, London. **horse latitudes**, a belt of calms at the northern edge of the NE trade winds. The origin of the name is uncertain; some hold that it arose from the alleged practice of throwing overboard horses, which were being transported to America or the West Indies, when the ship's passage was unduly prolonged by lack of a favourable wind. **horse laugh**, a loud coarse laugh. **horse-radish** *n.* a plant (*Armoracia rusticana*) with a pungent root used to make a sauce. **horse sense**, (*colloq.*) plain common sense. **horse-tail** *n.* the tail of a horse; a plant of the genus *Equisetum* resembling it. **horse-trading** *n.* (*US*) dealing in horses; shrewd bargaining. **on one's high horse**, (*colloq.*) acting haughtily. **on horseback**, mounted on a horse. [OE]
The horse family is thought to have evolved in North America and spread to Asia and into Africa. During the ice age these animals provided human populations in Europe with an abundant source of food, but the effective domestication of horses there did not take place before the Bronze Age, by which time, paradoxically, they had become extinct in their country of origin until reintroduced by European settlers. There is some evidence that the horse was used for riding from *c*.4000 BC in the lands north of the Black Sea, but its most important use from *c*.19th c. BC was to draw the war chariots which gave mounted archers superiority over infantry bowmen. The use of cavalry dates from the Iron Age, when larger breeds of horses, capable of carrying mounted warriors, became available; spurs, and cheek-pieces attached to the bit, were introduced in this period and used to control the speed and direction of horses ridden in combat; stirrups reached Europe in the 6th-8th c. AD, having been known earlier in China and India. The new breeds of heavy horses found a use also in traction, and in medieval times became of economic as well as military importance, very gradually replacing the ox at cart and plough; from the 17th c. they were used to draw public conveyances. These animals were the heavy 'working' horses; introduction of Arab and Barbary blood for race-horses and hunters in the Stuart period changed the appearance of horses in Britain, and royal patronage of Newmarket greatly increased the popularity of horse-racing.

horseflesh *n.* **1.** the flesh of the horse as food. **2.** horses collectively.

horsehair *n.* hair from the mane or tail of a horse, used for padding etc.

horseman *n.* (*pl.* **-men**) a rider on horseback; a skilled rider. —**horsemanship** *n.*, **horsewoman** *n.fem.* (*pl.* **-women**).

horseplay *n.* boisterous play.

horsepower *n.* (*pl.* same) a unit for measuring the power of an engine, about 750 watts. The term was introduced by James Watt, who modified Savery's method of estimating engine-power in terms of equivalent work done by horses.

horse-racing *n.* the sport of conducting races between horses with riders. Its origin is lost in time; racing is attested in ancient Assyria by *c*.1500 BC. The first permanent racecourse with an annual fixture was established at Chester in 1540; by 1660 Charles II made Newmarket the headquarters, and 'Newmarket's glory rose, as Britain's fell'.

horseshoe *n.* a U-shaped iron shoe for a horse; a thing of this shape.

horsewhip *n.* a whip for driving horses. —*v.t.* (**-pp-**) to beat (a person) with a horsewhip.

horst *n.* a long plateau with a geological fault on each side (ill. GEOLOGY). [G = heap]

horsy *adj.* **1.** of or like a horse. **2.** concerned with or devoted to horses; showing this in dress, conversation, etc. [f. HORSE]

hortative /ˈhɔːtətɪv/ *adj.* (also **hortatory** /ˈhɔːtətərɪ/) tending or serving to exhort. [f. L (*hortari* exhort)]

horticulture /ˈhɔːtɪkʌltʃə/ *n.* the art of garden cultivation. —**horticultural** /-ˈkʌltʃər(ə)l/ *adj.*, **horticulturist** *n.* [f. L *hortus* garden, after *agriculture*]

Horus /ˈhɔːrəs/ (*Egyptian myth.*) originally a sky god (his eyes were the sun and the moon) whose symbol was the hawk ('Horus the Elder'). From early dynastic times he was regarded as the protector of the king and of the monarchy; his name is often added to the royal titles. He is usually depicted as a falcon-headed man. Horus assumed various aspects in different theologies: in the myth of Isis and Osiris he was the posthumous son of the latter, whose murder he avenged, and in this aspect was known to the Greeks as Harpocrates (= 'Horus the Child'), most often represented as a chubby infant with a finger held to his mouth.

hosanna /həʊˈzænə/ *n.* a shout of adoration. [f. L f. Gk f. Heb., = save now]

hose /həʊz/ *n.* **1.** (also **hose-pipe**) a flexible tube for conveying water. **2.** (*collect.* as *pl.*, esp. in trade use) stockings and socks. **3.** (*hist.*) breeches (ill. DRESS). —*v.t.* to water or spray with a hose. [OE]

Hosea /həʊˈzɪə/ **1.** a Hebrew minor prophet of the 8th c. BC. **2.** a book of the Old Testament containing his prophecies.

hosier /ˈhəʊzɪə(r)/ *n.* a dealer in stockings and socks. [f. HOSE]

hosiery *n.* (esp. in trade use) stockings and socks; knitted or woven underwear. [f. prec.]

hospice /ˈhɒspɪs/ *n.* **1.** a lodging for travellers, especially one kept by a religious order. **2.** a home for destitute or (esp. terminally) ill people. [F, f. L *hospitium* (as HOST²)]

hospitable /hɒsˈpɪtəb(ə)l/ *adj.* giving or disposed to give hospitality. —**hospitably** *adv.* [F, f. L *hospitare* entertain (as HOST²)]

hospital /ˈhɒspɪt(ə)l/ *n.* **1.** an institution providing medical and surgical treatment and nursing care for ill or injured people. **2.** (*hist.*) a charitable institution, a hospice. [f. OF f. L *hospitale* (as HOST²)]

hospitality /hɒspɪˈtælɪtɪ/ *n.* friendly and generous reception and entertainment of guests or strangers. [as prec.]

hospitalize /ˈhɒspɪtəlaɪz/ *v.t.* to send or admit (a patient) to hospital. —**hospitalization** /-ˈzeɪʃ(ə)n/ *n.* [f. HOSPITAL]

hospitaller /ˈhɒspɪt(ə)lə(r)/ *n.* a member of certain charitable religious orders. (See KNIGHTS HOSPITALLERS.) [as HOSPITAL]

host¹ /həʊst/ *n.* a large number of people or things; (*archaic*) an army. [f. OF f. L *hostis* enemy, army]

host² /həʊst/ *n.* **1.** one who receives or entertains another as his guest; the landlord of an inn. **2.** an animal or plant having a parasite. —*v.t.* to act as host to (a person) or at (an event). [f. OF f. L *hospes* host, guest]

host³ /həʊst/ *n.* the bread consecrated in the Eucharist. [f. OF f. L *hostia* sacrificial victim]

hostage /ˈhɒstɪdʒ/ *n.* a person seized or held as security for the fulfilment of a condition or conditions. [f. OF f. L *obses*]

hostel /ˈhɒst(ə)l/ *n.* a house of residence or lodging for students or other special groups. [f. OF f. L (as HOSPITAL)]

hostelry /ˈhɒst(ə)lrɪ/ *n.* (*archaic*) an inn. [f. OF (h)*ostelier* innkeeper (as prec.)]

hostess /ˈhəʊstɪs/ *n.fem.* a woman host; a woman employed to entertain guests in a night-club etc. [f. HOST²]

hostile /ˈhɒstaɪl/ *adj.* **1.** of an enemy. **2.** unfriendly, opposed (*to*). —**hostilely** *adv.* [F, or f. L (as HOST¹)]

hostility /hɒˈstɪlɪtɪ/ *n.* being hostile, enmity; a state of warfare; (in *pl.*) acts of warfare. [f. F or L (as prec.)]

hot *adj.* **1.** having a relatively or noticeably high temperature; causing a sensation of heat; feeling heat. **2.** (of pepper, spices, etc.) producing a burning sensation to the taste. **3.** eager, excited; having intense feeling, angry or upset. **4.** (of news etc.) fresh, recent; (of a scent in hunting) strong. **5.** (of a competitor, performer, feat) skilful, formidable. **6.** (of music) strongly rhythmical and emotional. **7.** (*slang*) (of goods) stolen, especially if difficult to dispose of. **8.** (*slang*) radioactive. —*v.t./i.* (**-tt-**) (*colloq.*, often with *up*) **1.** to make or become hot. **2.** to become active or exciting. —**hot air**, (*slang*) empty or boastful talk. **hot-blooded** *adj.* ardent, passionate. **hot cross bun**, a bun marked with a cross and eaten on Good Friday. **hot dog**, (*colloq.*) a hot sausage sandwiched in a soft roll. **hot gospeller**, (*colloq.*) an eager preacher of the gospel. **hot line**, a direct exclusive line of communication especially for an emergency. **hot money**, capital frequently transferred. **hot potato**, (*colloq.*) a controversial or awkward matter or situation. **hot rod**, a motor vehicle modified to have extra power and speed. **hot seat**, (*slang*) a position of difficult responsibility; the electric chair. **hot stuff**, (*colloq.*) a formidably capable person; an important person or thing; a sexually attractive person. **hot-tempered** *adj.* impulsively angry. **hot water**, (*colloq.*) difficulty or trouble. **hot-water bottle**, a rubber, metal, of earthenware container filled with hot water to warm a bed etc. —**hotly** *adv.*, **hotness** *n.* [OE]

hotbed *n.* **1.** a bed of earth heated by fermenting manure. **2.** a place promoting the growth of something (esp. unwelcome).

hotchpotch /ˈhɒtʃpɒtʃ/ *n.* a confused mixture, a jumble; a mixed broth or stew. [f. OF *hochepot* (*hocher* shake, as POT)]

hotel /həʊ'tel/ *n.* an establishment providing meals and accommodation for payment. [f. F (as HOSTEL)]

hotelier /həʊ'telɪə(r)/ *n.* a hotel-keeper. [f. F f. OF (see HOSTELRY)]

hotfoot *adv.* in eager haste. —*v.i.* (usu. with *it*) to hurry eagerly.

hothead *n.* an impetuous person. —**hotheaded** *adj.*

hothouse *n.* a heated building, usually largely of glass, for rearing plants.

hotplate *n.* a heated metal plate etc. (or a set of these) for cooking food or keeping it hot.

hotpot *n.* meat and vegetables cooked in an oven in a closed pot.

Hottentot /'hɒt(ə)ntɒt/ *n.* (*pl.* same or **-s**) **1.** a member of a people now found chiefly in SW Africa, characterized by short stature, yellow-brown skin colour, and tightly curled hair, related to the Bushmen. They formerly occupied the region near the Cape but were largely dispossessed by Dutch settlers. **2.** their language (also known as *Nama*), spoken in Namibia by about 50,000 people. It is characterized by a series of 'click' consonants made by drawing air into the mouth and clicking the tongue. [Afrik., perh. = stutterer, from their mode of pronunciation]

Houdini /huː'diːnɪ/, Harry (real name Eric Weiss, 1874–1926), American escapologist.

hound *n.* **1.** a dog used in hunting, a foxhound. **2.** a contemptible man. —*v.t.* to harass or pursue; to urge or incite. [OE]

hour /aʊə(r)/ *n.* **1.** a twenty-fourth part of a day and night, 60 minutes. **2.** a time of day; a point in time; (in *pl.* with preceding numerals in the form *18.00, 20.30, etc.*) this number of hours and minutes past midnight on the 24-hour clock. **3.** a period set aside for some purpose; (in *pl.*) a fixed period of time for work, the use of a building, etc. **4.** a short, indefinite period of time. **5.** *the* present time; a time for action etc. **6.** the distance traversed in an hour. **7.** (in the RC Church) prayers said at one of seven fixed times of the day. —**the hour,** the time o'clock; the time of a whole number of hours. **after hours,** after normal business etc. hours. [f. AF f. L *hora* f. Gk]

hourglass *n.* a sand-glass that runs for an hour.

houri /'hʊərɪ/ *n.* a beautiful young woman of the Muslim paradise. [F f. Pers. f. Arab., = gazelle-like]

hourly /'aʊəlɪ/ *adj.* done or occurring every hour; frequent. —*adv.* every hour; frequently. [f. HOUR]

house /haʊs/ *n.* (*pl.* **houses** /'haʊzɪz/) **1.** a building for human habitation (see ill. pp. 400–1). **2.** a building for a special purpose or for keeping animals or goods. **3.** a residential establishment, especially of a religious order, university college, section of a boarding-school, etc. **4.** a division of a day-school for games, competitions, etc. **5.** a royal family or dynasty. **6.** a firm or institution; its place of business. **7.** a legislative etc. assembly; the building where it meets. **8.** an audience or performance in a theatre etc. **9.** a twelfth part of the heavens in astrology. —/haʊz/ *v.t.* **1.** to provide a house or accommodation for; to store (goods etc.). **2.** to enclose or encase (a part or fitting). —**house-agent** *n.* an agent for the sale and letting of houses. **house arrest,** detention in one's own house, not prison. **house-bound** *adj.* unable to leave one's house. **house-dog** *n.* a dog kept to guard a house. **house-fly** *n.* the common fly (*Musca domestica*) found in and around houses. **house martin,** a bird (*Delichon urbica*) that builds a mud nest on house walls. **house of cards,** an insecure scheme etc. **House of Commons,** the lower house of the British Parliament; its buildings. (See PARLIAMENT.) **House of Keys,** the elective branch of the legislature of the Isle of Man, with 24 members. **House of Lords,** the upper house of the British Parliament; its buildings. (See PARLIAMENT.) **House of Representatives,** see CONGRESS. **house party,** a group of guests staying at a country house etc. **house-proud** *adj.* attentive to the care and appearance of the home. **house-room** *n.* space or provision in one's house (*would not give it house-room*, would not have it in any circumstances). **house-trained** *adj.* (of animals) trained to be clean in the house; (*colloq.*) well-mannered. **house-warming** *n.* a party celebrating a move to a new home. **keep house,** to provide for a household. **like a house on fire,** vigorously, successfully. **on the house,** at the management's expense, free. **put** *or* **set one's house in order,** to make needed reforms. [OE]

houseboat *n.* a boat fitted up for living in.

housebreaking *n.* the act of breaking into a building,

especially in daytime, to commit a crime. (In 1968 the term was replaced, in English law, by *burglary*.)

housecoat *n.* a woman's long dresslike garment for informal wear in the house.

household *n.* **1.** the occupants of a house regarded as a unit. **2.** a house and its affairs. —**Household troops,** troops nominally employed to guard the sovereign. **household word,** a familiar saying or name.

householder *n.* **1.** a person owning or renting a house. **2.** the head of a household.

housekeeper *n.* a person employed to manage a household.

housekeeping *n.* **1.** management of household affairs. **2.** money allowed for this.

houseleek *n.* a plant (*Sempervivum tectorum*) with pink flowers, growing on walls and roofs.

housemaid *n.* a woman servant in a house. —**housemaid's knee,** inflammation of the kneecap.

houseman *n.* (*pl.* **-men**) a resident doctor at a hospital etc.

housemaster *n.* a teacher in charge of a house at a boarding-school. —**housemistress** *n.fem.*

housewife *n.* a woman managing a household. —**housewifely** *adj.* [f. HOUSE + WIFE = woman (not 'married woman')]

housework *n.* the cleaning and cooking etc. done in housekeeping.

housing /'haʊzɪŋ/ *n.* **1.** dwelling-houses collectively; provision of these; shelter, lodging. **2.** a rigid casing enclosing machinery etc. **3.** a shallow trench or groove cut across the grain in a piece of wood to receive an insertion (ill. CARPENTRY). —**housing estate,** a residential area planned as a unit. [f. HOUSE]

Housman /'haʊsmən/, Alfred Edward (1859–1936), English poet and classical scholar. Having failed at Oxford and spent ten years in obscurity as a clerk in the Civil Service, he afterwards became Professor of Latin at London University and then at Cambridge. His best poems are found in *A Shropshire Lad* (1896), a series of spare nostalgic verses largely based on ballad forms, and *Last Poems* (1922), in which he combines a classical simplicity with an underlying mood of pessimism and melancholy.

Houston /'hjuːst(ə)n/ an inland port of Texas, linked to the Gulf of Mexico by the Houston Ship Canal. Since 1961 it has been an important centre for space research and manned space-flight.

hove see HEAVE.

hovel /'hɒv(ə)l/ *n.* a small miserable dwelling. [orig. unkn.]

hover /'hɒvə(r)/ *v.i.* **1.** (of a bird etc.) to remain in one place in the air. **2.** to wait (*about, round*); to wait close at hand. —*n.* **1.** hovering. **2.** a state of suspense. [f. obs. *hove* hover, linger]

hovercraft *n.* a vehicle that travels over land or water on a cushion of air provided by a downward blast (ill. FLIGHT). A design was first patented by the English boat-designer, Christopher Cockerell, in 1955.

how *adv.* **1.** in what way, by what means. **2.** in what condition (esp. of health); to what extent. **3.** in whatever way, as. **4.** (*colloq.*) = that. —**how about,** what do you think of; would you like. **how do you do,** a formal greeting. **how-do-you-do** *n.* (*colloq.*) an awkward situation. **how many,** what number of. **how much,** what amount; what price. **how's that?** how do you regard or explain that?; (said to an umpire in cricket) is the batsman out or not? [OE (as WHO)]

Howard[1] /'haʊəd/, Catherine (d. 1542), fifth wife of Henry VIII. Thrust on the ailing and increasingly despotic king by her ambitious Howard relatives, Catherine, a flirtatious girl of nineteen, was soon in trouble over alleged infidelities. She went to the block in 1542 after only two years of marriage.

Howard[2] /'haʊəd/, John (?1726–90), English philanthropist and prison reformer, who travelled all over the country unearthing abuses and scandals in the prison system, and extended his tours to Ireland and the Continent. His great work on the *State of Prisons in England and Wales* (1777) gave the initial impetus to the movement for improvement in the building and management of prisons.

howbeit /haʊ'biːɪt/ *adv.* (*archaic*) nevertheless.

howdah /'haʊdə/ *n.* a seat, usually with a canopy, for riding on the back of an elephant or camel. [f. Urdu f. Arab., = litter]

Houses

Norman manor house c.1200
(central window 15th century)

cruck house
14th – 15th century

hip

studding

timber-framed house c.1500

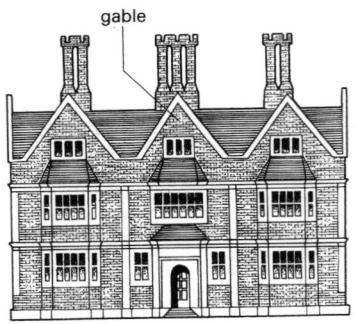

gable

late Tudor brick house c.1600
(plaster used to simulate stone)

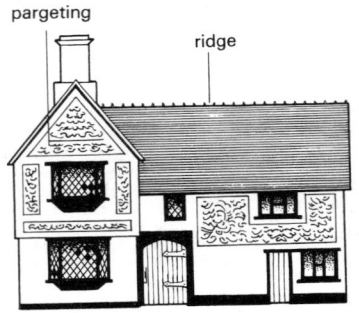

pargeting

ridge

17th-century pargeting
on a 15th-century house

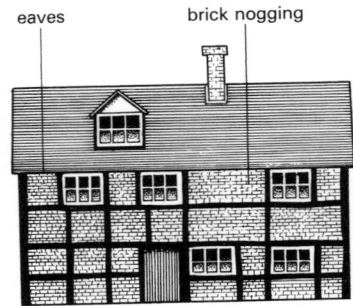

eaves

brick nogging

17th-century square-framed
house with brick infilling

Cruck frame

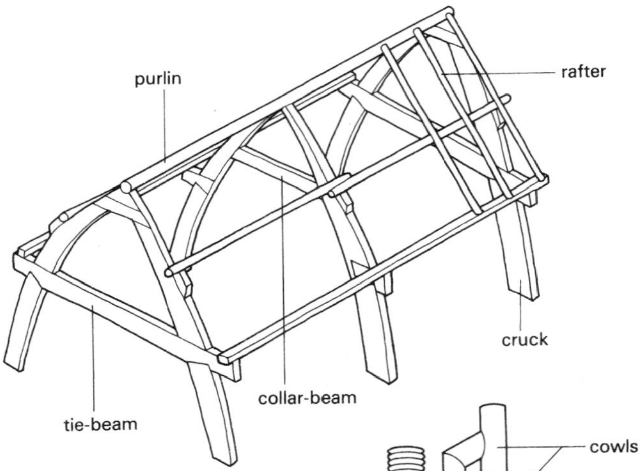

purlin

rafter

cruck

tie-beam

collar-beam

Stairs

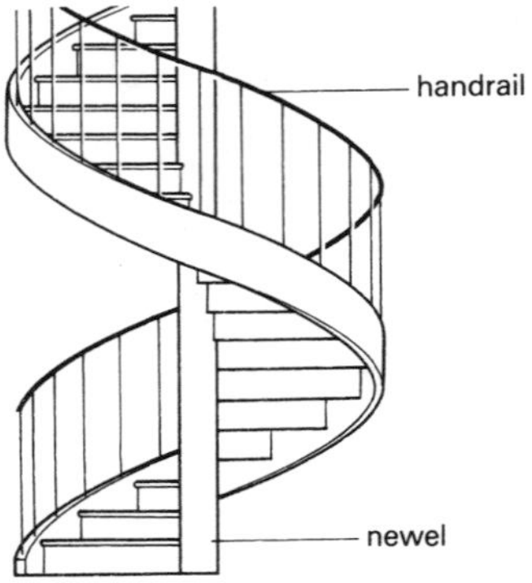

handrail

newel

spiral staircase

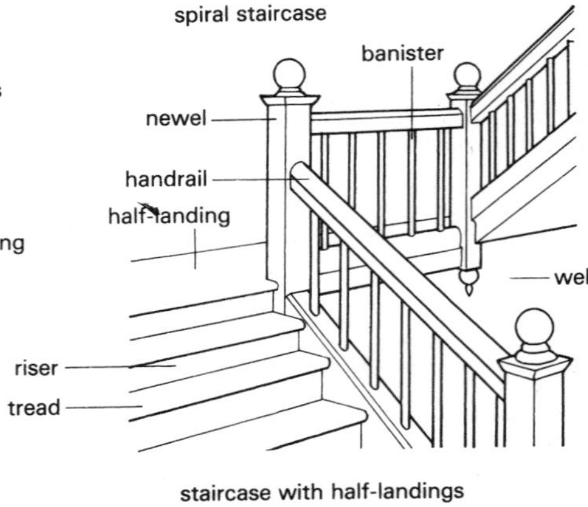

banister

newel

handrail

half-landing

well

Chimney

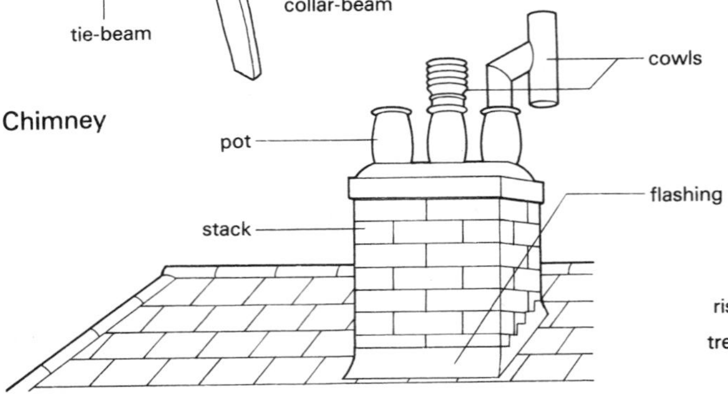

cowls

pot

flashing

stack

riser

tread

staircase with half-landings

stone-built house *c*.1640

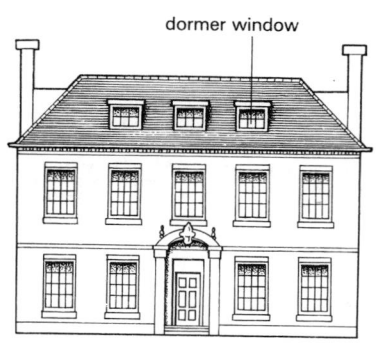
dormer window

Queen Anne house *c*.1700

mansard roof

a Georgian terrace, 18th century

19th-century Regency houses

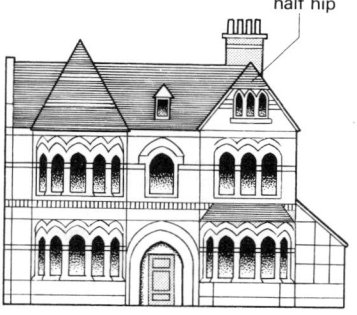
half hip

Victorian Gothic Revival house, 1867

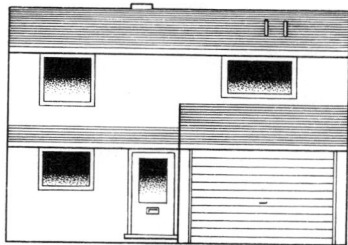
1970s terrace house

Door
(early 18th century)

pilaster

stile

rail

architrave

panel

Windows

oriel

mullion

transom

mullion

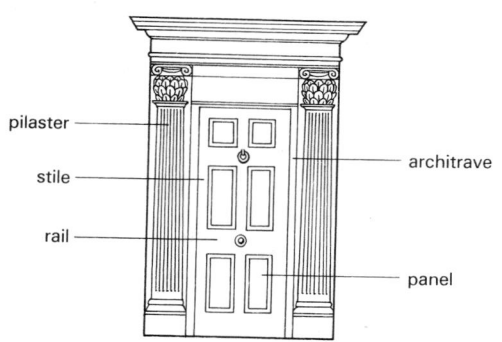

Fireplaces

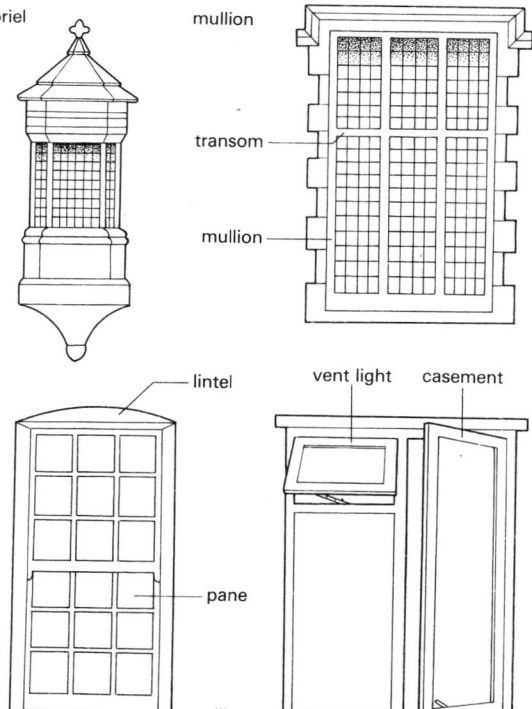

hood

overmantel

mantel

andiron
or firedog

fire-basket

medieval

early 18th century

lintel

pane

sill

sash

vent light   casement

casement

however /haʊˈevə(r)/ adv. 1. in whatever way, to whatever extent. 2. nevertheless.

howitzer /ˈhaʊɪtsə(r)/ n. a short gun for the high-angle firing of shells. [f. Du. f. G f. Czech, = catapult]

howl n. 1. the long doleful cry of a dog etc.; a similar noise, e.g. that made by a strong wind. 2. a loud cry of pain, rage, derision, or laughter. —v.t./i. 1. to make a howl. 2. to weep loudly. 3. to utter with a howl. —**howl down,** to prevent (a speaker) from being heard by howling derision. [= MLG, MDu. *hulen* (imit.)]

howler n. 1. a South American monkey of the genus *Alouatta*, with a howling cry. 2. (*colloq.*) a glaring mistake. [f. HOWL]

howsoever /haʊsəʊˈevə(r)/ adv. in whatsoever way, to whatever extent.

hoy int. used to call attention. [natural cry]

hoyden /ˈhɔɪd(ə)n/ n. a girl who behaves boisterously. —**hoydenish** adj. [prob. f. MDu. *heiden* (as HEATHEN)]

HP abbr. 1. hire-purchase. 2. (also **hp**) horsepower. 3. (also **h.p.**) high pressure.

HQ abbr. headquarters.

HRH abbr. Her or His Royal Highness.

hr(s). abbr. hour(s).

HT abbr. high tension.

hub n. 1. the central part of a wheel, from which the spokes radiate. 2. a central point of interest, activity, etc. [orig. unkn.]

Hubble /ˈhʌb(ə)l/, Edwin Powell (1889–1953), American astronomer, who in 1929 demonstrated the statement (known as Hubble's law) that the distance to a distant galaxy is directly proportional to its observed velocity of recession from us. Such a result is a natural consequence of a uniformly expanding universe, as predicted by the 'big bang' theory of cosmology, and implies that the age of the universe is inversely proportional to the constant of proportionality in the mathematical expression of the law. This constant (Hubble's constant) is uncertain to a factor of two, suggesting an age for the universe of between ten and twenty thousand million years.

hubble-bubble /ˈhʌb(ə)l bʌb(ə)l/ n. 1. a simple form of hookah. 2. a bubbling sound; confused talk. [redupl. of BUBBLE; imit.]

hubbub /ˈhʌbʌb/ n. a confused noise; a disturbance. [perh. of Ir. orig.]

hubby n. (*colloq.*) a husband. [abbr.]

hubris /ˈhjuːbrɪs/ n. arrogant pride or presumption. —**hubristic** /hjuːˈbrɪstɪk/ adj. [Gk]

huckaback /ˈhʌkəbæk/ n. a strong linen or cotton fabric with a rough surface, used for towels. [orig. unkn.]

huckleberry /ˈhʌk(ə)lbərɪ/ n. a low shrub of the genus *Gaylussacia* common in North America; its blue or black fruit. [perh. alt. of *hurtleberry* = WHORTLEBERRY]

huckster n. 1. a hawker. 2. a mercenary person. —v.i. 1. to haggle. 2. to be a hawker. [prob. f. LG; rel. to HAWKER]

huddle v.t./i. 1. to heap or crowd together. 2. to nestle closely; to curl one's body into a small space. —n. a confused mass. —**go into a huddle,** to hold a close or secret conference. [perh. f. LG]

Hudson /ˈhʌds(ə)n/, Henry (d. 1611), English explorer, discoverer of the North American bay, river, and strait which bear his name. He conducted two voyages in 1607–8 for the English Muscovy Company in search of the Northeast Passage to Asia, reaching Greenland and Spitzbergen on the first and Novaya Zemlya on the second. In 1609 he explored the NE coast of America for the Dutch East Indies Company, sailing 240 km (150 miles) up the Hudson River to Albany. In 1610 he set out on his last voyage, again under English colours, and reached Hudson('s) Bay in the north of Canada. He attempted to winter in the Bay, but when food ran out his men mutinied and set him adrift in a small boat with a few companions—none of them were ever seen again.

Hudson's Bay Company a British colonial trading company. Created by Royal Charter in 1670, it was granted the lands draining into Hudson's Bay in northern Canada for purposes of commercial exploitation. The Company continued to control these lands, amalgamating with the rival North-West Company in 1821, for two centuries, finally handing them over to the new Canadian government in 1869.

hue[1] /hjuː/ n. a colour, a tint; a variety or shade of a colour. —**hued** adj. [OE]

hue[2] n. **hue and cry,** a loud outcry (*against*), a clamour; (*hist.*) a proclamation for the pursuit and capture of a criminal. In former English law, such an outcry had to be raised by the inhabitants of a hundred in which a robbery had been committed, if they were not to become liable for the damages suffered by the victim. [f. OF, = outcry (imit.). There is some ground for thinking that *hue* (as distinct from *cry*) originally meant inarticulate sound, including that of a horn or trumpet as well as of the voice.]

huff n. a fit of petty annoyance. —v.t./i. 1. to blow. 2. to remove (an opponent's piece) as a forfeit in draughts. —**in a huff,** annoyed and offended. [imit. of blowing]

huffy adj. apt to take offence; offended. [f. HUFF]

hug v.t. (**-gg-**) 1. to squeeze tightly in one's arms, usually with affection. 2. (of a bear) to squeeze between the forelegs. 3. to keep close to. —n. a strong clasp with the arms; a grip in wrestling. [prob. f. Scand.]

huge /hjuːdʒ/ adj. extremely large, enormous; (of an abstract thing) very great. —**hugeness** n. [f. OF *ahuge*]

hugely adv. very much. [f. HUGE]

hugger-mugger /ˈhʌgəmʌgə(r)/ adj. & adv. 1. secret(ly). 2. confused, in confusion. —n. 1. confusion. 2. secrecy. [perh. rel. to obs. *hoder* huddle, *mokere* conceal]

Hughes /hjuːz/, Ted (1930–), English poet, whose wife was the American poet Sylvia Plath, whom he met at Cambridge University. His obsession with animals and his sense of the beauty and violence of the natural world appear in his first volume, *The Hawk in the Rain* (1957). In *Crow* (1970) Hughes retells the legends of creation and birth through the dark vision of the predatory, mocking, indestructible crow. His style is rough and forceful; his poetry is vital, original, at times excessively brutal with a stress on the physical and animal. He was appointed Poet Laureate in 1984.

Hugo /ˈhjuːgəʊ/, Victor-Marie (1802–85), the greatest French poet of the 19th c., novelist, and dramatist, the central figure of the Romantic movement in France. He spent the years 1851–70 in exile, mainly in Guernsey where he wrote his violent satire against Napoleon (*Les Châtiments*, 1853); after his return to Paris he became a senator of the Third Republic. Hugo brought a new freedom of subject, diction, and versification to French poetry; among his many collections are the spiritual and cosmic *Les Contemplations* (1856), *Les Orientales* (1829), and *Les Chants du crépuscule* (1835). Of his plays, the Preface of *Cromwell* (1827) became a manifesto of the Romantic movement, *Hernani* (1830) broke with dramatic conventions and won the day for the Romantics, and *Ruy Blas* (1838) continued his success in verse drama. *Notre Dame de Paris* (1831) and *Les Misérables* (1862) are among his best-known novels. National recognition came to him in the last years of his life, and he was buried in the Panthéon in Paris.

Huguenot /ˈhjuːgənəʊ/ n. a member of the Calvinist French Protestants c.1560, who were involved in almost continuous civil war with the Catholic majority and were a disruptive element even after full freedom of worship was granted by the Edict of Nantes (1598). When the edict was revoked in 1685 many Huguenots were forced to apostatize or flee from France. [F, assim. of *eiguenot* (= confederate) to name of Geneva burgomaster Hugues]

huh /hʌ/ int. expressing disgust, surprise, etc. [imit.]

hula /ˈhuːlə/ n. a Hawaian woman's dance with flowing movements of the arms. —**hula hoop,** a large hoop for spinning round the body. [Hawaiian]

hulk n. 1. the body of a dismantled ship; (*hist.*, in *pl.*) used as a prison. 2. a large clumsy-looking person or thing. [OE]

hulking adj. (*colloq.*) bulky, clumsy. [f. HULK]

hull[1] n. the body of a ship, airship, etc. [perh. rel. to HOLD[2]]

hull[2] n. the pod of peas or beans, the husk of certain seeds or fruits, the calyx of a ripe strawberry, raspberry, etc. —v.t. to remove the hulls of (strawberries etc.). [OE]

hullabaloo /hʌləbəˈluː/ n. an uproar. [redupl. of *hallo, hullo,* etc.]

hullo var. of HALLO.

hum v.t./i. (**-mm-**) 1. to make a low steady continuous sound like that of a bee. 2. to sing with closed lips and without words. 3. to utter a slight inarticulate sound, especially of hesitation. 4. (*colloq.*) to be in an active state. 5. (*slang*) to smell unpleasantly. —n. 1. a humming sound. 2. an exclamation of hesitation. 3. (*slang*) a bad smell. —**hum and ha** or **haw,** to hesitate. [imit.]

human /ˈhjuːmən/ adj. 1. of or belonging to mankind. 2.

having the qualities that distinguish mankind, not divine or animal or mechanical; showing mankind's better qualities (as kindness, pity, etc.). —*n.* a human being. —**human being,** see MAN¹. **human rights,** the rights held to be claimable by any living person. [f. OF f. L *humanus* (*homo* man)]

humane /hjʊˈmeɪn/ *adj.* benevolent, compassionate, merciful; (of learning), tending to civilize. —**humane killer,** an implement for the painless slaughter of animals. —**humanely** *adv.* [var. of prec.]

humanism /ˈhjuːmənɪz(ə)m/ *n.* **1.** literary culture, especially the cultural movement of the Renaissance which turned away from medieval scholasticism (with its theological bias) to value the human achievement of the language, literature, and antiquities of ancient Rome (later of Greece). **2.** humanitarianism. **3.** any system of thought or action which is concerned with human (not divine or religious) interests, or with the human race (not the individual), or with man as a responsible intellectual being. **4.** a pragmatic system of thought, introduced by F. C. S. Schiller and William James, which emphasizes that man can comprehend and investigate only with the resources of the human mind, and discounts abstract theorizing; the futher theory that technological advance must be guided by awareness of widely understood human needs. —**humanist** *n.*, **humanistic** /-ˈnɪstɪk/ *adj.* [f. F f. It. (as HUMAN)]

humanitarian /hjuːmænɪˈteərɪən/ *adj.* concerned with promoting human welfare. —*n.* a humanitarian person. —**humanitarianism** *n.* [f. foll.]

humanity /hjuːˈmænɪtɪ/ *n.* **1.** human nature or (in *pl.*) qualities. **2.** the human race, people. **3.** being humane, kind-heartedness. **4.** (in *pl.*) learning or literature concerned with human culture, formerly especially the Greek and Latin classics. [as HUMAN]

humanize /ˈhjuːmənaɪz/ *v.t.* to make human or humane. —**humanization** /-ˈzeɪʃ(ə)n/ *n.* [f. F (as HUMAN)]

humanly /ˈhjuːmənlɪ/ *adv.* in a human manner; by human means, within human limitations. [f. HUMAN]

Humberside /ˈhʌmbəsaɪd/ a county of NE England.

humble *adj.* **1.** having orshowing a low estimate of one's own importance. **2.** of a low social or political rank. **3.** (of a thing) not large or elaborate. —*v.t.* to make humble, to lower the rank or self-importance of. —**eat humble pie,** to make a humble apology [f. *umbles* edible offal of deer]. —**humbleness** *n.*, **humbly** *adv.* [f. OF f. L *humilis* lowly (*humus* ground)]

Humboldt /ˈhʌmbəʊlt/, Friedrich Heinrich Alexander, Baron von (1769-1859), German explorer and scientist who travelled for five years in Central and South America (1799-1804) and wrote extensively on natural history, meteorology, and physical geography, financing his expeditions and scientific work out of his own pocket. During his travels in South America, accompanied by the French botanist Bonpland, he proved that the Amazon and Orinoco river systems are connected and ascended to 5,877 metres (19,280 ft.) in the Andes, the highest ascent ever made at that time. Returning to Europe in 1804, he settled in Paris and spent the next 20 years writing up the results of the collections and observations made during his travels. By 1827 Humboldt's private funds had almost run out and he returned to his birthplace, Berlin, serving in various capacities at the Prussian court. Towards the end of his life he wrote a popular work in several volumes, *Kosmos* (1845-62) describing the structure of the universe as it was then known. A kindly and liberal-minded man, Humboldt gave encouragement and financial assistance to students and young scientists and was also an early advocate of international scientific co-operation.

humbug /ˈhʌmbʌg/ *n.* **1.** deceptive or false talk or behaviour. **2.** an impostor. **3.** a hard-boiled sweet usually flavoured with peppermint. —*v.t./i.* (**-gg-**) to be or behave like an impostor; to deceive. [orig. unkn.]

humdinger /ˈhʌmdɪŋə(r)/ *n.* (*slang*) a remarkable person or thing. [orig. unkn.]

humdrum /ˈhʌmdrʌm/ *adj.* dull, commonplace, monotonous. [prob. redupl. f. HUM]

Hume /hjuːm/, David (1711-76), Scottish philosopher and historian. His chief work *A Treatise of Human Nature* (1739/40) was followed by a number of essays and a *History of Great Britain* (1754-61) which was, in spite of its faults, the first great English history, written while he was librarian of the Advocates' Library in Edinburgh. He obtained a literary reputation and, because of that, some well-paid diplomatic appointments, including one in Paris in 1763-5.

There he was well received by court and literary society, and befriended and brought back Rousseau to England, but the latter's suspicious and ungrateful nature led to a quarrel. For the rest of his life Hume lived in his native Edinburgh. Hume developed the empirical philosophy of Locke and Berkeley to its logical conclusion, and thereby made it incredible. He rejected the possibility of certainty in knowledge, finding in the mind only a series of sensations ('impressions'), and discounted the existing notion of causation: we are aware of things in pairs, but although we can observe that one constantly follows another we can never be certain that it must follow. A similar scepticism is apparent in his writings on religion.

humerus /ˈhjuːmərəs/ *n.* the bone of the upper arm (ill. BODY 1). —**humeral** *adj.* [L, = shoulder]

humid /ˈhjuːmɪd/ *adj.* (of the air or a climate) damp. [f. F or L ((*h*)*umēre* be moist)]

humidifier /hjuːˈmɪdɪfaɪə(r)/ *n.* a device for keeping the air moist in a room etc. [f. foll.]

humidify /hjuːˈmɪdɪfaɪ/ *v.t.* to make humid. [f. HUMID]

humidity /hjuːˈmɪdɪtɪ/ *n.* dampness; degree of moisture, especially in the atmosphere. [f. OF or L (as HUMID)]

humiliate /hjuːˈmɪlɪeɪt/ *v.t.* to harm the dignity or self-respect of. —**humiliation** /-ˈeɪʃ(ə)n/ *n.* [f. L *humiliare* (as HUMBLE)]

humility /hjuːˈmɪlɪtɪ/ *n.* a humble attitude of mind; humbleness. [f. OF f. L (as HUMBLE)]

humming-bird *n.* a small tropical bird of the family Trochilidae, that makes a humming sound with its wings.

hummock /ˈhʌmək/ *n.* a low hill or hump. [orig. unkn.]

hummus /ˈhʊməs/ *n.* an hors d'œuvre made from ground chick-peas and sesame oil flavoured with lemon and garlic. [f. Turk.]

humoresque /hjuːməˈresk/ *n.* a light and lively musical composition. [f. G. *humoreske* (as HUMOUR)]

humorist /ˈhjuːmərɪst/ *n.* a writer or speaker noted for humour. [f. HUMOUR]

humorous /ˈhjuːmərəs/ *adj.* full of humour, amusing. —**humorously** *adv.* [f. foll.]

humour /ˈhjuːmə(r)/ *n.* **1.** the quality of being amusing. **2.** the ability to enjoy what is comic or amusing. **3.** a state of mind. **4.** each of the four fluids (blood, phlegm, choler, and melancholy) formerly (in Galen's theory) held to determine a person's physical and mental qualities. —*v.t.* to keep (a person) contented by indulging his wishes. —**aqueous humour,** the transparent substance between the lens of the eye and the cornea. **vitreous humour,** that filling the eyeball (ill. BODY 4). [f. OF f. L (*h*)*umor* moisture (as HUMID)]

hump *n.* **1.** the rounded protuberance on the back of a camel etc., or as an abnormality on a person's' back. **2.** a rounded raised mass of earth etc. **3.** (*slang*) a fit of depression or annoyance. —*v.t.* **1.** to form into a hump. **2.** to hoist or shoulder (one's pack etc.). [perh. f. LG or Du.]

humpback *n.* a deformed back with a hump; a person with this. —**humpback bridge,** a small bridge with a steep ascent and descent. —**humpbacked** *adj.*

humph /hʌmf/ *int. & n.* an inarticulate sound expressing doubt or dissatisfaction. [imit.]

humus /ˈhjuːməs/ *n.* a rich dark organic material formed by the decay of dead leaves and plants etc., and essential to the fertility of soil. [L, = ground]

Hun *n.* **1.** (usu. *derog.*) a German. **2.** an Asiatic people who ravaged Europe in the 4th-5th c. [OE, ult. f. Turki *Hun-yü*]

hunch *v.t./i.* to bend or arch into a hump. —*n.* **1.** a hump, a hunk. **2.** an intuitive feeling. [orig. unkn.]

hunchback *n.* a humpback. —**hunchbacked** *adj.*

hundred /ˈhʌndrəd/ *adj. & n.* **1.** (*sing.* form is used, with plural verb, when qualified by a preceding word) ten times ten; the symbol for this (100, c, C). **2.** (in *pl.*) very many. **3.** (*hist.*) a subdivision of a county or shire with its own court. —**hundreds and thousands,** tiny coloured sweets for decorating a cake etc. —**hundredth** *adj. & n.* [OE]

hundredfold *adj. & adv.* **1.** a hundred times as much or as many. **2.** consisting of a hundred parts. [f. prec. + -FOLD)]

hundredweight *n.* (*pl.* same) a measure of weight, 112 lb. —**metric hundredweight,** 50 kg. **short hundredweight,** (*US*) 100 lb.

Hundred Years War a war between France and England which stretched over more than a century between the

1340s and the 1450s, not as one continuous conflict but rather a series of attempts by English kings to dominate France. Edward III began the war by claiming the throne of France following the death of the last Capetian king (a brother of his mother), but despite an early string of military successes, most notably Crécy and Poitiers, and the occupation of a large part of France, the House of Valois retained its new position on the French throne. The French gradually improved their position, and in the reign of Edward's son Richard II hostilities ceased almost completely. The English claim was revived by the Lancastrian king Henry V, who renewed hostilities in 1415 with a crushing victory at Agincourt and occupied much of northern France. England once again proved unable to consolidate her advantage, however, and following Henry V's early death the regents of his ineffectual son Henry VI gradually lost control of conquered territory to French forces, revitalized in the first instance by Joan of Arc. With the exception of Calais, which did not fall for another century, all English conquests had been lost by 1453 when the war finally ended.

hung see HANG.

Hungarian /hʌnˈgeərɪən/ *adj.* of Hungary or its people or language. —*n.* **1.** a native or inhabitant of Hungary. **2.** the official language of Hungary, one of the Finno-Ugric languages, spoken by some 11 million people in Hungary and Romania, the only major language of the Ugric branch. [f. L (*Hungari* Magyar nation)]

Hungary /ˈhʌngərɪ/ a country in central Europe, bordering on Czechoslovakia in the north and Yugoslavia in the south; pop. (1980) 10,710,000; official language, Hungarian; capital, Budapest. Settled by the Magyars in the 9th c., Hungary emerged as the centre of a strong Magyar kingdom in the late Middle Ages, but was conquered first by the Turks in the 16th c. and then by the Hapsburgs in the 17th c., being incorporated into the Austrian empire thereafter. Nationalist pressure resulted in increased Hungarian power and autonomy within the empire in the 19th c., and following the collapse of Hapsburg power in 1918 Hungary finally achieved independence. After participation in the Second World War on the Axis side, Hungary was occupied by the Russians and became a Communist State under strong Soviet influence, a liberal reform movement being crushed by Soviet troops in 1956. In recent years the traditionally agricultural Hungarian economy has been progressively industrialized, but trade links remain largely restricted to eastern Europe and the USSR.

hunger /ˈhʌngə(r)/ *n.* **1.** need for food, the discomfort felt when one has not eaten for some time. **2.** strong desire. —*v.i.* to feel hunger. —**hunger march,** any of the demonstrations launched by unemployed workers in Britain between the two World Wars, particularly after the economic collapse of 1929, which took the form of marches from various cities to London. The first took place in 1922 from Glasgow, the most famous from Jarrow in 1936. **hunger strike,** refusal of food (esp. by a prisoner) as a form of protest. [OE]

hungry /ˈhʌngrɪ/ *adj.* feeling or showing hunger; inducing hunger. —**hungrily** *adv.* [OE (as prec.)]

hunk *n.* a large piece cut off. [prob. f. LDu.]

hunkers *n.pl.* the haunches. [orig. Sc. (*hunker* to squat)]

Hunt, William Holman (1827–1910), English painter, co-founder of the Pre-Raphaelite Brotherhood in 1848, who remained true to its aims, which he summarized as seriousness, direct study from nature, and the attempt to envisage events as they must have happened. Many of his works have a didactic emphasis on moral or religious symbolism (e.g. *The Awakening Conscience,* 1852; *The Light of the World,* 1852). From 1854, Hunt made several journeys to Egypt and Palestine and painted biblical scenes with attention to accuracy of local detail. His painting from nature is characterized by minute precision and bright colour.

hunt *v.t./i.* **1.** to pursue (wild animals or game, or *absol.*) for sport or food; (of an animal) to pursue its prey. **2.** to pursue with hostility. **3.** to search for; to make a search (*for*); to search (a district) for game. **4.** to use (a horse or hounds) for hunting. **5.** (of an engine) to run alternately too fast and too slow. —*n.* **1.** hunting. **2.** an association of people hunting; the district where they hunt. [OE (*hentan* seize)]

Hunter /ˈhʌntə(r)/, John (1728–93), Scottish anatomist, who is regarded as a founder of scientific surgery and made valuable investigations in pathology, physiology, and biology. His elder brother William (1718–83), under whom he studied, became one of London's foremost obstetricians.

hunter *n.* **1.** one who hunts. **2.** a horse ridden for hunting. **3.** a watch with a hinged metal cover protecting the glass. —**hunter's moon,** the first full moon after the harvest moon. [f. HUNT]

Huntingdon /ˈhʌntɪŋd(ə)n/, Selina, Countess of (1707–91). Selina Hastings, foundress of the body of Calvinistic Methodists known as 'the Countess of Huntingdon's Connexion'. On her husband's death in 1746 she gave herself wholly to religious and social work, making herself the chief medium for introducing Methodism to the upper classes.

huntsman *n.* (*pl.* **-men**) a hunter; a person in charge of hounds.

hurdle *n.* **1.** a portable rectangular frame with bars, for a temporary fence etc. **2.** each of a series of upright frames to be jumped over in a race (ill. SPORTS); (in *pl.*) a race with such jumps. **3.** an obstacle; a difficulty. —*v.t./i.* **1.** to fence off with hurdles. **2.** to run in a hurdle-race. [OE]

hurdler *n.* **1.** one who runs in hurdle-races. **2.** one who makes hurdles. [f. prec.]

hurdy-gurdy /ˈhɜːdɪgɜːdɪ/ *n.* **1.** a stringed instrument with the bowing action replaced by a resined wheel cranked by a handle, the strings being brought into play by means of slide-keys projecting from a key-box. The instrument, called 'organistrum', was known in Europe from the early 12th c., used at first in choir schools; today it is mainly heard as a folk instrument, especially in France. **2.** (*colloq.*) a barrel-organ. [prob. imit.]

hurl *v.t.* **1.** to throw with great force. **2.** to utter vehemently. —*n.* a forceful throw. [prob. imit.; cf. LG *hurreln*]

hurling *n.* the game of **hurley,** an Irish form of hockey played with broad sticks. It is the national game of Ireland, mentioned in folk tales, in the Irish Annals (relating events of *c.*1272 BC), and in an Irish legal code dating from centuries BC. [f. HURL]

hurly-burly /ˈhɜːlɪbɜːlɪ/ *n.* boisterous activity, a commotion. [redupl. f. HURL]

Huron /ˈhjʊərən/ *n.* **1.** a confederation of five Iroquoian tribes formerly inhabiting a region adjacent to Lake Huron; a member of these tribes. **2.** their language. —**Lake Huron,** one of the five Great Lakes of North America.

hurrah /hʊˈrɑː/ *int.* & *n.* (also **hurray** /-ˈreɪ/) an exclamation of joy or approval. [alt. of earlier *huzza* (perh. orig. sailor's cry)]

Hurrian /ˈhʌrɪən/ *n.* **1.** a member of a widespread non-Semitic people in the Middle East during the 3rd–2nd millennium BC (see MITANNI), sometimes identified with the Horites of the Bible. **2.** their language, written in cuneiform, of unknown derivation (it is neither Semitic nor Indo-European). —*adj.* of the Hurrians or their language. [f. Hittite & Assyrian]

hurricane /ˈhʌrɪkən/ *n.* a storm with a violent wind, especially a West Indian cyclone; a wind of 73 m.p.h. or more. —**hurricane lamp,** a lamp with the flame protected from violent wind. [f. Sp. & Port. f. Carib]

hurry /ˈhʌrɪ/ *n.* great haste; eagerness, urgency; the need for haste. —*v.t./i.* **1.** to move or act with eager or excessive haste. **2.** to cause to move or proceed in this way. **3.** (in *p.p.*) hasty, done rapidly. —**hurry up,** (*colloq.*) to make haste. **in a hurry,** hurrying; easily or readily. [imit.]

hurry-scurry /ˈhʌrɪˈskʌrɪ/ *n.* disorderly haste. —*adj.* & *adv.* in confusion. [redupl. f. prec.]

hurt *v.t./i.* (*past* & *p.p.* **hurt**) **1.** to cause pain, injury, or damage to; to cause pain or harm. **2.** to cause mental pain or distress to. **3.** to feel pain. —*n.* an injury, harm. [f. OF *hurter*]

hurtful *adj.* causing (esp. mental) hurt. —**hurtfully** *adv.* [f. HURT + -FUL]

hurtle *v.t./i.* to move or hurl rapidly or with a clattering sound; to come with a crash. [f. HURT in obs. sense 'strike forcibly']

husband /ˈhʌzbənd/ *n.* a married man in relation to his wife. —*v.t.* to use economically. [OE f. ON, = house-dweller]

husbandry *n.* **1.** farming. **2.** the management of resources. [f. prec. in archaic use = manager of affairs]

hush *v.t./i.* to make or become silent or quiet. —*n.* silence. —**hush-hush** *adj.* (*colloq.*) highly confidential, very secret. **hush-money** *n.* money paid to prevent the disclosure of a discreditable affair. **hush up,** to suppress public mention of (an affair). [f. obs. *husht* imit. int. taken as *p.p.*]

husk *n.* **1.** the dry outer covering of certain seeds and fruits. **2.** the worthless outside part of anything. —*v.t.* to remove the husk(s) from. [f. LG, = sheath (as HOUSE)]

husky[1] *adj.* **1.** full of or dry as husks. **2.** (of a person or voice) dry in the throat, hoarse. **3.** big and strong. —**huskily** *adv.*, **huskiness** *n.* [f. prec.]

husky[2] *n.* a dog of a powerful breed used in the Arctic for pulling sledges. [perh. contr. f. ESKIMO]

Huss /hʌs/, John (c.1372-1415), Bohemian reformer. A preacher in Prague and enthusiastic supporter of Wyclif's views, he aroused the hostility of the Church, was excommunicated (1411), tried (1414), and burnt at the stake. By his death he became a national hero and was declared a martyr by the university of Prague. His followers took up arms against the Holy Roman Empire, and, through a combination of religious fervour and innovative military methods, inflicted a dramatic series of defeats on imperialist forces. —**Hussite** *adj.* & *n.*

hussar /hʊˈzɑː(r)/ *n.* a soldier of a light cavalry regiment. [f. Magyar ult. f. It. (as CORSAIR)]

Husserl /ˈhʊsɜːl/, Edmund (1859-1938), German philosopher. Having originally trained as a mathematician he turned to philosophy and taught in German universities, latterly coming under pressure because of his Jewish ancestry. In his philosophy he sought the clarity and certainty belonging to mathematics and science, and became the leading figure in the movement known as phenomenology. He rejected metaphysical assumptions about what actually exists, and explanations of why it exists, in favour of pure subjective consciousness as the condition for all experience, with the world as the object of this consciousness; the task of philosophy was to describe the fundamental structures of the world which make experience and consciousness possible. Among his pupils was Heidegger, who succeeded him as professor at Freiburg in 1928.

hussy *n.* a saucy girl; an immoral woman. [contr. of HOUSEWIFE]

hustings *n.* **1.** parliamentary election proceedings. **2.** (*hist.*) a platform from which (before 1872) candidates for Parliament were nominated and addressed electors. [pl. of *husting*, OE, f. ON, = house of assembly (as HOUSE, THING)]

hustle /ˈhʌs(ə)l/ *v.t./i.* **1.** to jostle, to push roughly. **2.** to hurry. **3.** to bustle; to cause to act quickly and without time to consider things. **4.** (*slang*) to swindle; to obtain by force. —*n.* hustling, bustle. —**hustler**. *n.* [f. MDu *husselen* shake]

hut *n.* a small simple or crude house or shelter; a temporary housing for troops. —*v.t.* (**-tt-**) **1.** to place (troops etc.) in huts. **2.** to furnish with huts. [f. F *hutte* f. MHG]

hutch *n.* a boxlike pen for rabbits etc. [orig. = coffer, f. OF *huche* f. L]

Hutton /ˈhʌt(ə)n/, James (1726-97), Scottish geologist who put forward certain views, controversial at the time, that became accepted tenets of modern geology. In opposition to Werner's Neptunian theory he emphasized heat as the principal agent in the formation of land masses, and held that rocks such as granite were igneous in origin. He described the processes of deposition and denudation and proposed that such phenomena, operating with roughly equal intensity over millions of years, would account for the present configuration of the earth's surface; it therefore followed that the earth was very much older than was generally believed at the time. These conclusions were presented in his *Theory of the Earth* (1785), and met with the hostility of those who accepted the biblical account of the creation of the world. Hutton's writing style was poor, however, and his views did not become widely known until a concise account of them was published by his friend Playfair in 1802.

Huxley[1] /ˈhʌkslɪ/, Aldous Leonard (1894-1963), English novelist and essayist. During the 1920s and 1930s he lived in Italy and France, and there wrote much of his best fiction, notably *Brave New World* (1932) and *Eyeless in Gaza* (1936). Disillusioned with Europe he left for California in 1937, in search of new spiritual direction. There he became interested in mysticism and parapsychology; *The Doors of Perception* (1954) describes his experiments with mescalin. His works, often pessimistic, combine satire and earnestness, brutality and humanity, and shed light on unexplored territory.

Huxley[2] /ˈhʌkslɪ/, Sir Julian (1887-1975), English biologist, grandson of T. H. Huxley. He contributed to the early development of the study of animal behaviour, was an outstanding interpreter of science to the public through writing and broadcasting, and became the first director-general of UNESCO (1946-8).

Huxley[3] /ˈhʌkslɪ/, Thomas Henry (1825-95), English bio-

logist. A qualified surgeon and self-taught naturalist, he made his reputation as a marine biologist during service as ship's surgeon on HMS *Rattlesnake*, reporting his studies of marine species off the coast of northern Australia. Later he studied fossils, especially of fishes and reptiles, and became a firm supporter of Darwin, although he did not accept his theories without qualification. On the basis of a detailed study in anthropology he wrote *Man's Place in Nature* (1863), and coined the word 'agnostic' to describe his position in the face of religious orthodoxy, taking it from St Paul's mention of the altar 'to the Unknown God'. A liberal-minded man, Huxley was a supporter of education for the less privileged and argued for the inclusion of science in the school curriculum.

Huygens /ˈhaɪɡənz/, Christiaan (1629-95), Dutch physicist, mathematician, and astronomer, best known for his pendulum-regulated clock invented in 1656. He improved the lenses of his telescope, discovered a satellite of Saturn, and also the latter's rings, which had foxed Galileo. In dynamics he studied such topics as centrifugal force and the problem of colliding bodies, but his greatest contribution was his wave theory of light, made public in 1678. He formulated what has become known as 'Huygen's principle', that every point on a wave front is the centre of a new wave, and this allowed him to explain the reflection and refraction of light, including its double refraction in Iceland spar.

hyacinth /ˈhaɪəsɪnθ/ *n.* **1.** a plant of the genus *Hyacinthus* with fragrant bell-shaped (esp. purplish-blue) flowers. **2.** purplish-blue. —**wild hyacinth**, the bluebell. [f. F f. L f. Gk *huakinthos* flower and gem, also name of youth loved by Apollo (see foll.)]

Hyacinthus /haɪəˈsɪnθəs/ (*Gk myth.*) a pre-Hellenic god whose cult, in historical times, was subordinate to that of Apollo. He is said to have been a beautiful boy whom the god loved but killed accidentally with a discus. From his blood Apollo caused the flower that bears his name to spring up.

Hyades /ˈhaɪədiːz/ *n.pl.* a group of stars in Taurus near the Pleiades, whose heliacal rising was thought to foretell rain. [f. Gk *Huades* (acc. to pop. etym. f. *huō* rain, but perh. f. *hus* pig, the Latin name being *suculae* little pigs)]

hybrid /ˈhaɪbrɪd/ *n.* **1.** the offspring of two animals or plants of different species or varieties. **2.** a thing composed of diverse elements; a word with parts from different languages. —*adj.* bred or produced as a hybrid; cross-bred. —**hybridism** *n.*, **hybridity** /-ˈbɪdɪtɪ/ *n.* [f. L *hybrida* orig. = offspring of tame sow and wild boar]

hybridize *v.t./i.* to subject (a species etc.) to cross-breeding; to produce hybrids; (of an animal or plant) to interbreed. —**hybridization** /-ˈzeɪʃ(ə)n/ *n.* [f. prec.]

Hyde[1] /haɪd/, Edward, see CLARENDON.

Hyde[2] /haɪd/, Edward, see JEKYLL.

Hydra /ˈhaɪdrə/ **1.** (*Gk myth.*) a many-headed snake of the marshes of Lerna in the Peloponnese, whose heads grew again as they were cut off, killed by Hercules. **2.** (*Astron.*) a southern constellation represented as a water-snake or sea-serpent. [Gk, = water-snake]

hydra /ˈhaɪdrə/ *n.* **1.** a thing hard to extirpate (see prec. sense 1). **2.** a water-snake. **3.** a freshwater polyp of the genus *Hydra*, with a tubular body and tentacles around the mouth. [f. prec.]

hydrangea /haɪˈdreɪndʒə/ *n.* a shrub of the genus *Hydrangea*, with globular clusters of white, pink, or blue flowers. [f. Gk *hudōr* water + *aggos* vessel (from shape of seed-capsules)]

hydrant /ˈhaɪdrənt/ *n.* a pipe (especially in a street) with a nozzle for a hose, for drawing water from a main. [as HYDRO-]

hydrate /ˈhaɪdreɪt/ *n.* a chemical compound of water with another compound or an element. —*v.t.* to combine chemically with water; to cause to absorb water. —**hydration** /-ˈdreɪʃ(ə)n/ *n.* [F (as HYDRO-)]

hydraulic /haɪˈdrɔːlɪk/ *adj.* **1.** (of water etc.) conveyed through pipes or channels. **2.** operated by the movement of liquid. —**hydraulically** *adj.* [f. L F. Gk (*hudōr* water, *aulos* pipe)]

hydraulics *n.pl.* (usu. treated as *sing.*) the science of the conveyance of liquids through pipes etc., especially as motive power. [f. prec.]

hydride /ˈhaɪdraɪd/ *n.* a compound of hydrogen especially with a metal. [f. HYDROGEN]

hydro /ˈhaɪdrəʊ/ *n.* (*pl.* **-os**) (*colloq.*) **1.** a hotel etc. providing hydropathic treatment. **2.** a hydroelectric power plant. [abbr.]

hydro- /'haɪdrə(ʊ)-/ *in comb.* **1.** water, liquid. **2.** combined with hydrogen. [f. Gk (*hudōr* water)]

hydrocarbon /haɪdrəʊ'kɑːbən/ *n.* a compound consisting only of hydrogen and carbon (e.g. methane, benzene).

hydrocephalus /haɪdrəʊ'sefələs/ *n.* a condition (especially in young children) with an accumulation of fluid in the cavity of the cranium, which can impair the mental faculties. **—hydrocephalic** /-sɪ'fælɪk/ *adj.* [f. HYDRO- + Gk *kephalē* head]

hydrochloric /haɪdrəʊ'klɔːrɪk/ *adj.* containing hydrogen and chlorine.

hydrochloride /haɪdrəʊ'klɔːraɪd/ *n.* a compound of an organic base with hydrochloric acid.

hydrocyanic /haɪdrəʊsaɪ'ænɪk/ *adj.* containing hydrogen and cyanogen.

hydrodynamics /haɪdrəʊdaɪ'næmɪks/ *n.pl.* (usu. treated as *sing.*) the science of the forces acting on or exerted by liquids (esp. water). **—hydrodynamic** *adj.*

hydroelectric /haɪdrəʊɪ'lektrɪk/ *adj.* developing electricity by the utilization of water-power; (of electricity) produced thus (see ill. ELECTRICAL POWER). The first public supply of electricity to be generated by water-power was that at Godalming in Surrey (see ELECTRICITY). **—hydroelectricity** /-'trɪsɪtɪ/ *n.*

hydrofining /'haɪdrəʊfaɪnɪŋ/ *n.* a catalytic process in which a petroleum product is stabilized and its sulphur content reduced by treatment with gaseous hydrogen under relatively mild conditions, so that unsaturated hydrocarbons and sulphur compounds undergo selective hydrogenation. **—hydrofined** *adj.* [f. HYDRO- + REFINING]

hydrofoil /'haɪdrəfɔɪl/ *n.* a boat equipped with a device for raising the hull out of the water to enable rapid motion; this device, which provides lift in much the same way as an aerofoil. The first true hydrofoil was probably built by an Italian inventor, Enrico Forlamini, in 1898-1905, but such craft were not widely used until the 1950s. [f. HYDRO-, after *aerofoil*]

hydrogen /'haɪdrədʒ(ə)n/ *n.* a gaseous element, the lightest of all the elements, symbol H, atomic number 1, first recognized by Cavendish in 1766 and named by Lavoisier. Its chief isotope has a nucleus consisting of a single proton. Hydrogen is by far the commonest element in the universe (although not on the earth). It combines with oxygen to form water, and is a constituent of nearly all organic compounds. **—hydrogen bomb,** an immensely powerful bomb utilizing the explosive fusion of hydrogen nuclei. **hydrogen sulphide,** an unpleasant-smelling poisonous gas formed by rotting animal matter. **—hydrogenous** /-'drɒdʒɪnəs/ *adj.* [f. F (as HYDRO-, -GEN)]

hydrogenate /haɪ'drɒdʒɪneɪt/ *v.t.* to charge with or cause to combine with hydrogen. **—hydrogenation** /-'neɪʃ(ə)n/ *n.* [f. prec.]

hydrography /haɪ'drɒgrəfɪ/ *n.* the scientific study of seas, lakes, rivers, etc. **—hydrographer** *n.,* **hydrographic** /-'græfɪk/ *adj.* [f. HYDRO- + -GRAPHY]

hydrology /haɪ'drɒlədʒɪ/ *n.* the science of the properties of water, especially of its movement in relation to the land. **—hydrological** /haɪdrə'lɒdʒɪk(ə)l/ *adj.* [f. HYDRO- + -LOGY]

hydrolyse /'haɪdrəlaɪz/ *v.t.* to decompose by hydrolysis. [as foll.]

hydrolysis /haɪ'drɒlɪsɪs/ *n.* the decomposition of a substance by the chemical action of water. [f. HYDRO- + Gk *lusis* dissolving]

hydrometer /haɪ'drɒmɪtə(r)/ *n.* an instrument for measuring the density of liquids. [f. HYDRO- + -METER]

hydropathy /haɪ'drɒpəθɪ/ *n.* medical treatment by external and internal application of water. **—hydropathic** /-'pæθɪk/ *adj.* [f. HYDRO-, after *homoeopathy* etc.]

hydrophilic /haɪdrə'fɪlɪk/ *adj.* having an affinity for water; able to be wetted by water. [f. HYDRO- + Gk *philos* loving]

hydrophobia /haɪdrə'fəʊbɪə/ *n.* aversion to water, especially as a symptom of rabies in man; rabies, especially in man. **—hydrophobic** *adj.* [f. L f. Gk (as HYDRO-, -PHOBIA)]

hydroplane /'haɪdrəpleɪn/ *n.* **1.** a light fast motor boat designed to skim over the surface of the water. **2.** a finlike device on a submarine enabling it to rise or descend. [f. HYDRO-, after *aeroplane*]

hydroponics /haɪdrə'pɒnɪks/ *n.* the art of growing plants without soil, in sand etc. or liquid with added nutrients. [f. HYDRO- + Gk *ponos* labour]

hydrosphere /'haɪdrəsfɪə(r)/ *n.* the waters of the earth's surface.

hydrostatic /haɪdrəʊ'stætɪk/ *adj.* of the equilibrium of liquids and the pressure exerted by liquids at rest. [f. Gk *hudrostatēs* hydrostatic balance (as HYDRO-, STATIC)]

hydrostatics /n.pl./ (usu. treated as *sing.*) the branch of mechanics concerned with the hydrostatic properties of liquids. [f. prec.]

hydrous /'haɪdrəs/ *adj.* (of substances) containing water. [as HYDRO-]

hydroxide /haɪ'drɒksaɪd/ *n.* a compound of an element or radical with a hydroxyl. [f. HYDRO- + OXIDE]

hydroxyl /haɪ'drɒksɪl/ *n.* a radical containing hydrogen and oxygen. [f. HYDRO- + OXYGEN]

hyena /haɪ'iːnə/ *n.* a carnivorous mammal of the order Hyaenidae of Africa and Asia, with a shrill cry resembling laughter. [f. OF & L f. Gk *huaina*]

hygiene /'haɪdʒiːn/ *n.* the principles of maintaining health, especially by cleanliness; sanitary science. **—hygienic** /-'dʒiːnɪk/ *adj.,* **hygienically** *adv.,* **hygienist** *n.* [f. F f. Gk *hugieine* (*tekhne*) (*hugies* healthy)]

hygrometer /haɪ'grɒmɪtə(r)/ *n.* an instrument for measuring the humidity of the air or a gas. [f. Gk *hugros* wet + -METER]

hygroscope /'haɪgrəskəʊp/ *n.* an instrument indicating but not measuring the humidity of the air. [as prec. + -SCOPE]

hygroscopic /haɪgrə'skɒpɪk/ *adj.* **1.** of the hygroscope. **2.** (of a substance) tending to absorb moisture from the air. [as prec.]

Hyksos /'hɪksɒs/ *n.pl.* a people of mixed Semitic-Asiatic stock who settled in the Nile delta *c.*1640 BC. They formed the 15th and 16th Dynasties of Egypt, and ruled a large part of the country until driven out by the powerful 18th Dynasty *c.*1532 BC. Described as oppressors by later Egyptians they nevertheless upheld many Egyptian traditions. During their reign the composite bow, the horse and chariot, and new military techniques were introduced into Egypt. [f. Gk f. Egyptian, = rulers of foreign lands; interpreted by Manetho as 'shepherd kings' or 'captive shepherds']

Hymen /'haɪmen/ *int.* a cry (*Hymen Hymenaie*) used at ancient Greek weddings, and understood (rightly or wrongly) as an invocation of a being of that name. Various stories were invented of him, all to the effect that he was a very handsome young man who had either married happily or had something happen to him on his wedding-day.

hymen /'haɪmen/ *n.* the membrane partially closing the external opening of the vagina of a virgin. [L f. Gk *humēn* membrane]

hymenopterous /haɪmə'nɒptərəs/ *adj.* of the order of insects including the ant, bee, wasp, etc., with four membranous wings. [f. Gk (as prec. + *pteron* wing)]

hymn /hɪm/ *n.* a song of praise, especially to God. **—v.t.** to praise or celebrate in hymns. [f. OF f. L f. Gk *humnos*]

hymnal /'hɪmn(ə)l/ *n.* a book of hymns. [f. L (as prec.)]

hymnology /hɪm'nɒlədʒɪ/ *n.* the composition or study of hymns. **—hymnologist** *n.* [f. HYMN + -LOGY]

hyoscine /'haɪəsiːn/ *n.* a poisonous alkaloid from which a sedative is made, found in plants of the nightshade family. [f. foll.]

hyoscyamine /haɪə'saɪəmiːn/ *n.* a poisonous alkaloid used as a sedative, got from henbane. [f. Gk *huoskuamos* henbane (*hus* pig, *kuamos* bean)]

hyper- /haɪpə(r)-/ *prefix* in the senses 'over', 'above', 'too'. [f. Gk (*huper* over)]

hyperactive /haɪpə'ræktɪv/ *adj.* (of a person) abnormally active.

hyperbola /haɪ'pɜːbələ/ *n.* the plane curve produced when a cone is cut by a plane that makes a larger angle with the base than the side of the cone makes (ill. SHAPES). **—hyperbolic** /-'bɒlɪk/ *adj.* [as foll.]

hyperbole /haɪ'pɜːbəlɪ/ *n.* a statement exaggerated for special effect. **—hyperbolical** /-'bɒlɪk(ə)l/ *adj.* [L f. Gk, = excess (as HYPER-, *ballō* throw)]

Hyperborean /haɪpəbə'riːən, -'bɔːrɪən/ *n.* (*Gk myth.*) a member of a race who worshipped Apollo and lived in a land of sunshine and plenty beyond the north wind. **—adj.** of this race. [f. L f. Gk (HYPER-, *Boreas* god of north wind)]

hypercritical /haɪpə'krɪtɪk(ə)l/ *adj.* excessively critical. **—hypercritically** *adv.*

hypermarket /'haɪpəmɑːkɪt/ *n.* a very large self-service store usually outside a town. [f. F *hypermarché* (as HYPER-, MARKET)]

hyperon /ˈhaɪpərɒn/ *n.* an unstable baryon. [f. HYPER-]

hypersensitive /haɪpəˈsensɪtɪv/ *adj.* excessively sensitive. —**hypersensitivity** /-ˈtɪvɪtɪ/ *n.*

hypersonic /haɪpəˈsɒnɪk/ *adj.* **1.** of speeds more than about five times that of sound. **2.** of sound frequencies above about 1,000 megahertz. [f. HYPER-, after *supersonic*]

hypertension /haɪpəˈtenʃ(ə)n/ *n.* **1.** abnormally high blood pressure. **2.** great emotional tension.

hypertrophy /haɪˈpɜːtrəfɪ/ *n.* enlargement of an organ etc. due to excessive nutrition. —**hypertrophic** /-pəˈtrɒːfɪk/ *adj.* [f. HYPER- + Gk *trophē* nourishment]

hyphen /ˈhaɪf(ə)n/ *n.* the sign (-) used to join words together (e.g. *fruit-tree*, *pick-me-up*), to mark the division of a word at the end of a line, to divide a word into parts, etc. —*v.t.* to join (words) with a hyphen; to write (a word or words) with a hyphen. [L f. Gk *huphen* together (as HYPO-, *hen* one)]

hyphenate /ˈhaɪfəneɪt/ *v.t.* to hyphen. —**hyphenation** /-ˈneɪʃ(ə)n/ *n.* [f. prec.]

Hypnos /ˈhɪpnɒs/ (*Gk myth.*) the god of sleep, son of Night. [Gk, = sleep]

hypnosis /hɪpˈnəʊsɪs/ *n.* (*pl.* -**oses** /-əʊsiːz/) a state like sleep in which the subject acts only on external suggestion; an artificially produced sleep. Hypnotic techniques were used in ancient times, but it was the experiments of Mesmer in the 18th c. that led to its introduction into Europe; the word 'hypnotism' was first applied by the Scottish surgeon James Braid in 1842. In France the process was used by the physiologist J.-M. Charcot (1825–93), and one of his students was Sigmund Freud, who from his study of hypnosis began his exploration of the unconscious mind, which he elaborated into his theory of psychoanalysis. Some subjects under hypnosis seem able to recall memories (e.g. of childhood or other experiences) that have been forgotten by the conscious mind. Hypnosis has always been regarded with suspicion arising from its use as a form of stage entertainment, from recognition that the process is not fully understood, and from unwillingness to allow one person to control another's actions in this way. [f. Gk *hupnos* sleep]

hypnotic /hɪpˈnɒtɪk/ *adj.* of or producing hypnosis. —*n.* a hypnotic drug or influence. —**hypnotically** *adv.* [f. F f. L f. Gk (*hupnoō* put to sleep)]

hypnotism /ˈhɪpnətɪz(ə)m/ *n.* the production or process of hypnosis. —**hypnotist** *n.* [f. prec.]

hypnotize *v.t.* to produce hypnosis in; to fascinate, to capture the mind of (a person). [f. HYPNOTIC]

hypo[1] /ˈhaɪpəʊ/ *n.* sodium thiosulphate (incorrectly called hyposulphite) used in photographic fixing. [abbr.]

hypo[2] /ˈhaɪpəʊ/ *n.* (*pl.* -os) (*slang*) a hypodermic. [abbr.]

hypo- /haɪpə(ʊ)-/ *prefix* in the senses 'under', 'below', 'slightly'. [f. Gk (*hupo* under)]

hypocaust /ˈhaɪpəkɔːst/ *n.* a hollow space under a floor into which hot air from a furnace was sent for heating an ancient Roman house or baths. [f. L f. Gk (as HYPO-, *kaiō* burn)]

hypochondria /haɪpəˈkɒndrɪə/ *n.* abnormal anxiety about one's health. [L f. Gk, = parts of body below ribs (whence melancholy was thought to arise)]

hypochondriac *n.* a person suffering from hypochondria. —*adj.* of hypochondria. [f. prec.]

hypocrisy /hɪˈpɒkrɪsɪ/ *n.* simulation of virtue or goodness, insincerity. [f. OF f. L f. Gk, = acting of a part]

hypocrite /ˈhɪpəkrɪt/ *n.* a person guilty of hypocrisy. —**hypocritical** /-ˈkrɪtɪk(ə)l/ *adj.*, **hypocritically** *adv.* [as prec.]

hypodermic /haɪpəˈdɜːmɪk/ *adj.* **1.** of the area beneath the skin. **2.** injected there; used for such injection. —*n.* a hypodermic injection or syringe. —**hypodermic syringe,** a syringe with a hollow needle for injection beneath the skin. —**hypodermically** *adv.* [f. HYPO- + Gk *derma* skin]

hypostasis /haɪˈpɒstəsɪs/ *n.* (*pl.* -**ses** = /siːz/) **1.** the underlying substance of a thing as distinct from its attributes. **2.** any of the three persons of the Trinity. [L f. Gk (as HYPO-, *stasis* standing)]

hypostatic /haɪpəˈstætɪk/ *adj.* of or involving hypostasis. —**hypostatic union,** the union of divine and human natures in Christ, a doctrine formally accepted by the Church in 451. [as prec.]

hypotension /haɪpəˈtenʃ(ə)n/ *n.* abnormally low blood pressure.

hypotenuse /haɪˈpɒtənjuːz/ *n.* the side opposite the right angle of a right-angled triangle (ill. SHAPES). [f. L f. Gk, = subtending line]

hypothalamus /haɪpəʊˈθæləməs/ *n.* a part of the brain, controlling body-temperature etc. (ill. BODY 4). [f. HYPO- + Gk *thalamos* room]

hypothecate /haɪˈpɒθɪkeɪt/ *v.t.* to pledge, to mortgage. —**hypothecation** /-ˈkeɪʃ(ə)n/ *n.* [f. L f. Gk *hupothécē* deposit (as HYPO-, *tithēmi* place)]

hypothermia /haɪpəˈθɜːmɪə/ *n.* the condition of having an abnormally low body-temperature. [f. HYPO- + Gk *thermē* heat]

hypothesis /haɪˈpɒθɪsɪs/ *n.* (*pl.* -**ses** /-siːz/) a proposition or supposition made from known facts as the basis for reasoning or investigation. [L f. Gk, = foundation]

hypothesize /haɪˈpɒθɪsaɪz/ *v.t./i.* to form a hypothesis; to assume as a hypothesis. [f. prec.]

hypothetical /haɪpəˈθetɪk(ə)l/ *adj.* of or based on a hypothesis; supposed but not necessarily real or true. —**hypothetically** *adv.* [f. HYPOTHESIS]

hyssop /ˈhɪsəp/ *n.* **1.** a small bushy aromatic herb of the genus *Hyssopus* formerly used medicinally. **2.** a plant used for sprinkling in ancient Jewish rites. [OE, ult. f. Gk f. Semitic]

hysterectomy /hɪstəˈrektəmɪ/ *n.* a surgical removal of the womb. [f. Gk *hustera* womb + -ECTOMY]

hysteresis /hɪstəˈriːsɪs/ *n.* (*pl.* **hystereses** /-siːz/) the lagging of an effect when the cause varies in amount, especially of magnetic induction lagging behind the magnetizing force. [f. Gk (*husteros* coming after)]

hysteria /hɪˈstɪərɪə/ *n.* **1.** wild uncontrollable emotion or excitement. **2.** a functional disturbance of the nervous system, of psychoneurotic origin. [as foll.]

hysteric /hɪˈsterɪk/ *n.* **1.** a hysterical person. **2.** (in *pl.*) a fit of hysteria. [f. L f. Gk (*hustera* womb), hysteria being thought to affect women more than men]

hysterical *adj.* of or caused by hysteria; suffering from hysteria. —**hysterically** *adv.* [f. prec.]

Hz *abbr.* hertz.

I

I, i /aɪ/ n. (pl. **Is, I's**) **1.** the ninth letter of the alphabet. **2.** (as a Roman numeral) 1.

I symbol iodine.

I /aɪ/ pron. (obj. ME[1]; poss. MY, MINE[1]; pl. WE etc.) the person who is speaking and referring to himself. [OE]

I. abbr. Island(s); Isle(s).

iambic /aɪˈæmbɪk/ adj. of or using iambuses. —n. (usu. in pl.) iambic verse. [f. F f. L f. Gk (as foll.)]

iambus /aɪˈæmbəs/ n. (pl. **-uses**) a metrical foot with one long or stressed syllable followed by one short or unstressed syllable. [L f. Gk (iaptō assail in words, f. its use in lampoons)]

IBA abbr. Independent Broadcasting Authority.

Iban /ˈiːbæn/ n. (pl. same) **1.** a member of a group of non-Muslim indigenous peoples from the island of Borneo; a member of the Sea Dyaks. (See DYAK.) **2.** their language, spoken by about 303,000 people, belonging to the Indonesian section of the Malayo-Polynesian group of languages. —adj. of the Iban or their language. [native name]

Iberia /aɪˈbɪərɪə/ the ancient name for the country now comprising Spain and Portugal, forming the extreme SW peninsula of Europe. —**Iberian** adj. & n.

ibex /ˈaɪbeks/ n. a wild goat (genus Capra) of the Alps etc., with large recurved horns. [L]

ibid. abbr. in the same book or passage etc. [L ibidem in the same place]

ibis /ˈaɪbɪs/ n. a wading bird of the family Threskiornithidae, with a down-curved bill. —**sacred ibis**, the white ibis, common in the Nile valley, venerated by the ancient Egyptians. [f. L f. Gk]

Ibiza /ɪˈbiːθə/ the westernmost of the Balearic Islands, pop. (1970) 45,075; its capital.

-ible suffix forming adjectives with senses as -ABLE (terrible, defensible, forcible, possible). [F, or f. L -ibilis]

Ibn Batuta /ˈɪbən bɑːˈtuːtɑː/ (c.1304-68), Arab explorer who spent 24 years on journeys through North and West Africa, Asia, India, and China, and wrote a vivid description of his travels (the Rihlah).

Ibo /ˈiːbəʊ/ n. (pl. same or **-os**) **1.** a member of a Black people of SE Nigeria. **2.** their language, which belongs to the Niger-Congo language group and is spoken by some 8 million people, one of the major languages of Nigeria. —adj. of the Ibo or their language. [native name]

Ibsen /ˈɪbs(ə)n/, Henrik (1828-1906), Norwegian dramatist, generally acknowledged as the founder of modern prose drama, who came to fame at a time when the theatre in Europe was at a low ebb. He gave vent to his despondency at his country's attitude to the Danish-German War in two great lyrical dramas, Brand (1866) and Peer Gynt (1867). A series of problem plays followed, dealing mainly with the relation of the individual to his social environment, and particularly the case of woman in marriage; these include A Doll's House (1879), Ghosts (1881), Rosmersholm (1886), and Hedda Gabler (1890) which influenced Shaw who introduced Ibsen's work to English theatre. Ibsen's later works, such as The Master Builder (1892) and When we Dead Awake (1900), deal increasingly with the forces of the unconscious and were of great interest to Freud. The quality of Ibsen's dialogue and his disregarding of traditional theatrical effects demanded a new style of performance.

Icarus /ˈɪkərəs/ (Gk legend) son of Daedalus (see entry).

ice /aɪs/ n. **1.** frozen water; a sheet of this on the surface of water. **2.** a portion of ice-cream or water-ice. —v.t./i. **1.** to become covered with ice; to freeze. **2.** to cover or mix with ice; to cool in ice. **3.** to cover (a cake etc.) with icing. —**break the ice**, to make a start; to overcome formality. **ice age**, a glacial period (see GLACIAL), especially that in the Pleistocene epoch which ended about 10,000 years ago. **ice-blue** adj. very pale blue. **ice-breaker** n. a ship designed to break through ice. **ice-cap** n. a permanent covering of ice, e.g. in polar lands. **ice-cream** n. a sweet creamy frozen food. **ice-field** n. a large expanse of floating ice. **ice hockey**, a form of hockey played on ice with a puck instead

of a ball (see HOCKEY). **ice lolly**, a kind of water-ice on a stick. **on ice**, (colloq.) held in a state of temporary suspension, or in reserve; quite certain. **on thin ice**, in a risky situation. [OE]

iceberg /ˈaɪsbɜːg/ n. a huge floating mass of ice. [prob. f. Du.]

icebox n. a compartment in a refrigerator for making or storing ice; (US) a refrigerator.

Iceland /ˈaɪslənd/ a volcanic island country in the North Atlantic, just south of the Arctic Circle; pop. (1983) 237,894; official language, Icelandic; capital, Reykjavik. First settled by Norse colonists in the 9th c., Iceland was under Norwegian rule from 1262 to 1380 when it passed to Denmark. Granted internal self-government in 1874, it became a fully fledged independent republic in 1944. The Icelandic economy is dominated by fishing, and since the late 1950s there have been periodic disputes with Great Britain over fishing rights around the island. —**Iceland spar**, a transparent variety of calcite with strong double refraction. —**Icelander** n.

Icelandic /aɪsˈlændɪk/ adj. of Iceland or its language. —n. the official language of Iceland, spoken by its 200,000 inhabitants, a Scandinavian language which is the purest descendant of Old Norse. Its purity is due partly to the geographical position of Iceland but also to a policy of avoiding the use of loan-words. [f. prec.]

I Ching /iː ˈtʃɪŋ/ an ancient Chinese manual with symbols known as the eight trigrams and sixty-four hexagrams that were symbolically interpreted in terms of the principles of yin and yang. Originally used for divination, it was later included as one of the 'five classics' of Confucianism. [Chinese, = book of changes]

ichneumon /ɪkˈnjuːmən/ n. **1.** a mongoose (Herpestes ichneumon) of North Africa etc., noted for destroying crocodiles' eggs. **2.** an ichneumon fly. —**ichneumon fly**, an insect of the family Ichneumonidae, that deposits its eggs in or on the larva of another egg. [L f. Gk (ikhneuō track)]

ichthyology /ɪkθɪˈɒlədʒɪ/ n. the study of fishes. [f. Gk ikhthus fish + -LOGY]

ichthyosaurus /ɪkθɪəˈsɔːrəs/ n. (pl. **-uses**) an extinct marine animal of the order Ichthyosauria, with a long head, tapering body, four paddles, and a large tail. [f. Gk ikhthus fish + sauros lizard]

ICI abbr. Imperial Chemical Industries.

icicle /ˈaɪsɪk(ə)l/ n. a tapering, hanging spike of ice formed from dripping water. [f. ICE + dial. ickle icicle]

icing /ˈaɪsɪŋ/ n. **1.** a coating of sugar etc. on a cake or biscuit. **2.** the formation of ice on an aircraft. —**icing sugar**, finely powdered sugar used for making icing. [f. ICE]

Icknield Way /ˈɪkniːld/ an ancient pre-Roman track crossing England in a wide curve from Wiltshire to Norfolk.

icon /ˈaɪkɒn/ n. an image or statue; (in the Orthodox Church) a painting or mosaic of a sacred person, itself regarded as sacred. [L f. Gk eikōn image]

iconoclast /aɪˈkɒnəklæst/ n. **1.** a breaker of images, especially one who took part in a movement in the 8th-9th c. against the use of images in religious worship in churches in the Eastern Roman Empire, or a Puritan of the 16th-17th c. **2.** one who attacks cherished beliefs. —**iconoclasm** n., **iconoclastic** /-ˈklæstɪk/ adj. [f. L f. Gk (eikōn image, klaō break)]

iconography /aɪkəˈnɒgrəfɪ/ n. **1.** the illustration of a subject by drawings etc. **2.** the study of portraits especially of one person. [f. Gk, = sketch (as ICON, -GRAPHY)]

icosahedron /aɪkɒsəˈhiːdrən/ n. a solid figure with twenty faces (ill. SHAPES). [f. L f. Gk (eikosi twenty, hedra base)]

Ictinus /ɪkˈtiːnəs/ (5th c. BC) Greek architect. His most famous building was the Parthenon at Athens which he designed with his colleague Callicrates and the sculptor Phidias between 448 and 437 BC.

ictus /ˈɪktəs/ n. a rhythmical or metrical stress. [L, = a blow (icere strike)]

icy /ˈaɪsɪ/ adj. **1.** very cold. **2.** covered with or abounding in ice. **3.** (of tone or manner) unfriendly, hostile. —**icily** *adv.*, **iciness** *n.* [f. ICE]

id *n.* a person's inherited psychological impulses as part of the unconscious. [L, = that]

Idaho /ˈaɪdəhəʊ/ a State in the north-western USA, bordering on British Columbia and containing part of the Rocky Mountains. It became the 43rd State of the USA in 1890; capital, Boise.

idea /aɪˈdɪə/ *n.* **1.** a plan or scheme formed in the mind by thinking. **2.** a mental impression or conception. **3.** an opinion or belief; a vague notion, a fancy. **4.** an ambition or aspiration. **5.** an archetype, a pattern. —**have no idea**, (*colloq.*) to be ignorant or incompetent. [L f. Gk, = look, form, kind]

ideal /aɪˈdɪəl/ *adj.* **1.** satisfying one's idea of what is perfect. **2.** existing only in an idea, visionary. —*n.* a person or thing regarded as perfect or as a standard for attainment or imitation; a conception of this. [f. F f. L (as prec.)]

idealism /aɪˈdɪəlɪz(ə)m/ *n.* (usu. opp. REALISM) **1.** the representation of things in an ideal or idealized form; imaginative treatment; the practice of forming or following after ideals. **2.** a system of thought in which the object of external perception is held to consist of ideas. —**idealist** *n.*, **idealistic** /-ˈlɪstɪk/ *adj.* [f. F or G (as prec.)]

idealize /aɪˈdɪəlaɪz/ *v.t.* to regard or represent as ideal or perfect. —**idealization** /-ˈzeɪʃ(ə)n/ *n.* [f. IDEAL]

ideally /aɪˈdɪəlɪ/ *adv.* according to an ideal; in ideal circumstances. [f. IDEAL]

idée fixe /iːdeɪ ˈfiːks/ a recurrent or dominating idea. [F, = fixed idea]

identical /aɪˈdentɪk(ə)l/ *adj.* **1.** one and the same. **2.** agreeing in all details. **3.** (of twins) developed from a single fertilized ovum and thus of the same sex and very similar in appearance. —**identically** *adv.* [f. L (as IDENTITY)]

identifiable /aɪˈdentɪfaɪəb(ə)l/ *adj.* that may be identified. [f. IDENTIFY]

identification /aɪdentɪfɪˈkeɪʃ(ə)n/ *n.* identifying; a means of identifying. —**identification parade**, an assembly of persons from whom a suspect is to be identified. [f. foll.]

identify /aɪˈdentɪfaɪ/ *v.t./i.* **1.** to establish the identity of, to recognize. **2.** to treat as identical (*with*). **3.** to associate (a person, *oneself*) closely (*with* a party, policy, etc.); to associate oneself *with*; to regard oneself as sharing characteristics *with* another person. **4.** to select by consideration. [f. L *identificare* (as IDENTITY)]

Identikit /aɪˈdentɪkɪt/ *n.* [P] a composite picture made from drawings of separate features, assembled from descriptions, put together to form a likeness, especially of a person sought by the police. [f. foll. + KIT]

identity /aɪˈdentɪtɪ/ *n.* **1.** the condition of being a specified person or thing. **2.** the state of being identical, absolute sameness. **3.** individuality, personality. **4.** equality of two algebraic expressions for all values of quantities, the expression of this. [f. L *identitas* (*idem* same)]

ideogram /ˈɪdɪəgræm/ *n.* a character or symbol indicating the idea of a thing without expressing the sounds in its name. [f. IDEA + -GRAM]

ideograph /ˈɪdɪəɡrɑːf/ *n.* an ideogram. —**ideographic** /-ˈgræfɪk/ *adj.*, **ideography** /-ˈɒɡrəfɪ/ *n.* [f. IDEA + -GRAPH]

ideologue /ˈaɪdɪəlɒɡ/ *n.* an adherent of an ideology. [as foll.]

ideology /aɪdɪˈɒlədʒɪ/ *n.* the ideas at the basis of an economic or political theory or system, or characteristic of some class etc. —**ideological** /-ˈlɒdʒɪk(ə)l/ *adj.*, **ideologist** *n.* [f. F (as IDEA, -LOGY)]

ides /aɪdz/ *n.pl.* the 15th day of March, May, July, October, the 13th of other months, in the ancient Roman calendar. [f. OF f. L *idus*]

idiocy /ˈɪdɪəsɪ/ *n.* **1.** the state of being an idiot. **2.** extreme stupidity; stupid behaviour or action. [f. IDIOT]

idiom /ˈɪdɪəm/ *n.* **1.** a form of expression or usage peculiar to a language, especially one whose meaning is not given by those of its separate words. **2.** the language of a people. **3.** a characteristic mode of expression in art etc. [f. F or L f. Gk *idiōma* (*idios* own, private)]

idiomatic /ɪdɪəˈmætɪk/ *adj.* relating or conforming to an idiom; characteristic of a language. —**idiomatically** *adv.* [f. Gk (as prec.)]

idiosyncrasy /ɪdɪəˈsɪŋkrəsɪ/ *n.* an attitude, form of behaviour, or mental or physical constitution, peculiar to a person. —**idiosyncratic** /-ˈkrætɪk/ *adj.* [f. Gk (*idios* own, *sun* together, *krasis* mixture)]

idiot /ˈɪdɪət/ *n.* **1.** a mentally deficient person who is permanently incapable of rational conduct. **2.** (*colloq.*) a stupid person. —**idiotic** /-ˈɒtɪk/ *adj.*, **idiotically** /-ˈɒtɪk(ə)lɪ/ *adv.* [f. OF f. L f. Gk, = private citizen, layman]

idle /ˈaɪd(ə)l/ *adj.* **1.** doing no work, not employed; not active or in use. **2.** avoiding work, lazy. **3.** (of time) unoccupied. **4.** useless; having no special purpose; groundless. —*v.t./i.* **1.** (of an engine) to run slowly without doing work. **2.** to pass (time etc.) in idleness. —**idleness** *n.*, **idler** *n.*, **idly** *adv.* [OE]

idol /ˈaɪd(ə)l/ *n.* **1.** an image of a deity as an object of worship. **2.** an object of excessive or supreme devotion. [f. OF f. L f. Gk *eidōlon* (*eidos* form)]

idolater /aɪˈdɒlətə(r)/ *n.* one who worships idols; a devout admirer. —**idolatrous** *adj.*, **idolatry** *n.* [f. OF f. L f. Gk (as prec., *latreuō* worship)]

idolize /ˈaɪdəlaɪz/ *v.t.* to venerate or love excessively; to treat as an idol. —**idolization** /-ˈzeɪʃ(ə)n/ *n.* [f. IDOL]

idyll /ˈɪdɪl/ *n.* a short description usually in verse of a picturesque scene or incident especially in rustic life; such a scene or incident. [f. L f. Gk *eidullion* (*eidos* form)]

idyllic /ɪˈdɪlɪk/ *adj.* of or like an idyll; peaceful and happy. —**idyllically** *adv.* [f. prec.]

i.e. *abbr.* that is to say. [L *id est*]

if *conj.* **1.** on the condition or supposition that; in the event that; supposing or granting that. **2.** even though. **3.** whenever. **4.** whether. **5.** expressing a wish or surprise. —*n.* a condition or supposition. —**as if**, as the case would be if. [OE]

igloo /ˈɪɡluː/ *n.* an Eskimo dome-shaped hut, especially one built of snow. [Eskimo, = house]

Ignatius Loyola /ɪɡˈneɪʃəs ˈlɔɪələ/, St (1491 or 1495–1556), Spanish theologian, founder of the Jesuits and their first superior general. Of noble birth, he entered on a military career, but after reading a Life of Christ and biographies of the saints while convalescing from a wound decided to change his life and become a soldier of Christ, hung up his sword at the altar of Our Lady, and devoted himself to a life of prayer and extreme mortification. His greatest work is the *Spiritual Exercises*, an ordered scheme of meditations on the life of Christ and the truths of the Christian faith, manifesting considerable psychological insight, aimed at bringing the individual to a firm commitment to God and the Church.

igneous /ˈɪɡnɪəs/ *adj.* **1.** of fire, fiery. **2.** (of rocks) formed by solidification of magma (cf. METAMORPHIC, SEDIMENTARY). Igneous rocks are commonly divided into *volcanic* (those which solidified at the earth's surface) and *plutonic* (which solidified below it); they constitute 95 per cent of the known crust of the earth. [f. L *igneus* (*ignis* fire)]

ignite /ɪɡˈnaɪt/ *v.t./i.* to set fire to; to catch fire; to make intensely hot. [f. L *ignire* (as prec.)]

ignition /ɪɡˈnɪʃ(ə)n/ *n.* **1.** igniting. **2.** the mechanism for or act of starting combustion in the cylinder of an internal-combustion engine. [F or f. L (as prec.)]

ignoble /ɪɡˈnəʊb(ə)l/ *adj.* **1.** dishonourable, not noble in character, aims, or purpose. **2.** of lowly birth or position. —**ignobly** *adv.* [F or f. L (as IN-², NOBLE)]

ignominious /ɪɡnəˈmɪnɪəs/ *adj.* bringing contempt or disgrace, humiliating. —**ignominiously** *adv.* [f. F or L (as foll.)]

ignominy /ˈɪɡnəmɪnɪ/ *n.* disgrace, humiliation. [f. F or L (as IN-², *nomen* name)]

ignoramus /ɪɡnəˈreɪməs/ *n.* an ignorant person. [L, = we do not know (as IGNORE)]

ignorant /ˈɪɡnərənt/ *adj.* lacking knowledge; uninformed; uncouth through lack of knowledge. —**ignorance** *n.*, **ignorantly** *adv.* [f. OF f. L (as foll.)]

ignore /ɪɡˈnɔː(r)/ *v.t.* to refuse to take notice of; to disregard intentionally. [f. F or L *ignorare* not know]

iguana /ɪɡˈwɑːnə/ *n.* a large tree lizard (of the family Iguanidae) of the West Indies and South America. [Sp. f. Carib]

iguanodon /ɪɡˈwɑːnədɒn/ *n.* a large herbivorous dinosaur. [f. prec., after *mastodon*]

il-¹,² see IN-¹,².

ileum /ˈɪlɪəm/ *n.* (*pl.* ilea) the third and last portion of the small intestine (ill. BODY 2). [var. of L *ilium*]

ilex /ˈaɪleks/ *n.* **1.** the holm-oak. **2.** a plant of the genus *Ilex*, including holly. [f. L]

iliac /ˈɪlɪæk/ *adj.* of the flank. [f. L *ilia* flanks]

Iliad /ˈɪlɪəd/ a Greek hexameter epic poem in 24 books,

traditionally ascribed to Homer. It tells of the climax of the war at Troy (Ilium) between Greeks and Trojans: the greatest of the Greek heroes, Achilles, retires to his tent enraged at Agamemnon's abduction of his mistress, the captive Briseis; in his absence the Trojan forces under Hector push the Greeks back on their ships; Achilles' close companion Patroclus fights and is killed by Hector; the grief-stricken Achilles takes the field and kills Hector under the walls of Troy.

Ilium /'ɪlɪəm/ the Homeric city of Troy, or a Greek foundation of the 7th c. BC on the same site.

ilk *n.* **of that ilk**, (*Sc.*) of the ancestral estate with the same name as a family; (*colloq.*) of that kind. [OE, = same]

ill *adj.* **1.** physically or mentally unwell; (of health) unsound, not good. **2.** harmful. **3.** wretched, disastrous; hostile, unfavourable. **4.** irritable. **5.** improper, deficient. —*adv.* **1.** badly, wrongly. **2.** unfavourably. **3.** imperfectly, scarcely. —*n.* injury, harm, evil; (in *pl.*) misfortunes. **—ill-advised** *adj.* (of an action) unwise. **ill at ease**, embarrassed, uncomfortable. **ill-bred** *adj.* badly brought up, rude. **ill-fated** *adj.* unlucky. **ill-favoured** *adj.* unattractive. **ill-gotten** *adj.* acquired by evil or unlawful means. **ill-mannered** *adj.* having bad manners. **ill-natured** *adj.* churlish, unkind. **ill-starred** *adj.* unlucky. **ill-tempered** *adj.* morose, irritable. **ill-timed** *adj.* done or occurring at an unsuitable time. **ill-treat** *v.t.*, **ill-use** *v.t.* to treat badly or cruelly. **ill will**, hostility, unkind feeling. [f. ON]

illegal /ɪ'li:g(ə)l/ *adj.* not legal, contrary to the law. **—illegality** /ɪlɪ'gælɪtɪ/ *n.*, **illegally** *adv.* [f. F or L (as IL-², LEGAL)]

illegible /ɪ'ledʒɪb(ə)l/ *adj.* not legible. **—illegibility** /-'bɪlɪtɪ/ *n.*, **illegibly** *adv.* [f. IL-² + LEGIBLE]

illegitimate /ɪlɪ'dʒɪtɪmət/ *adj.* **1.** (of a child) born of parents who are not married to each other. **2.** not authorized by law or by rules. **3.** illogical, wrongly inferred. **—illegitimacy** *n.*, **illegitimately** *adv.* [f. L (as IL-², LEGITIMATE)]

illiberal /ɪ'lɪbər(ə)l/ *adj.* **1.** intolerant, narrow-minded. **2.** without liberal culture, sordid. **3.** stingy. **—illiberality** /-'rælɪtɪ/ *n.*, **illiberally** *adv.* [f. F (as IL-², LIBERAL)]

illicit /ɪ'lɪsɪt/ *adj.* unlawful, forbidden. **—illicitly** *adv.* [f. F or L (as IL-², LICIT)]

Illinois /ɪlɪ'nɔɪ/ a State in the Middle West of the USA, ceded to Britain by the French in 1763 and acquired by the USA in 1783. It became the 21st State in 1818; capital, Springfield.

illiterate /ɪ'lɪtərət/ *adj.* unable to read; uneducated. —*n.* an illiterate person. **—illiteracy** *n.* [f. L (as IL-², LITERATE)]

illness *n.* **1.** ill health, the state of being ill. **2.** a disease. [f. ILL]

illogical /ɪ'lɒdʒɪk(ə)l/ *adj.* contrary to or devoid of logic. **—illogicality** /-kælɪtɪ/ *n.*, **illogically** *adv.* [f. IL-² + LOGICAL]

illuminant /ɪ'lu:mɪnənt/ *n.* a means of illumination. —*adj.* serving to illuminate. [f. L (as foll.)]

illuminate /ɪ'lu:mɪneɪt/ *v.t.* **1.** to light up, to make bright. **2.** to enlighten spiritually or intellectually; to help to explain (a subject); to shed lustre on. **3.** to decorate with lights as a sign of festivity. **4.** to decorate (a manuscript, initial letter, etc.) with gold or other bright colours. **—illumination** /-'neɪʃ(ə)n/ *n.*, **illuminative** *adj.* [f. L *illuminare* (IL-¹, *lumen* light)]

illumine /ɪ'lju:mɪn/ *v.t.* (*literary*) to light up; to enlighten spiritually. [f. OF f. L (as prec.)]

illusion /ɪ'lu:ʒ(ə)n, ɪ'lju:-/ *n.* **1.** a false belief; something wrongly believed to exist. **2.** deceptive appearances. **—illusive** *adj.*, **illusory** *adj.* [f. F f. L (*iludere* mock)]

illusionist *n.* a producer of illusions, a conjuror. [f. prec.]

illustrate /'ɪləstreɪt/ *v.t.* **1.** to provide (a book, newspaper, etc.) with pictures. **2.** to make clear, especially by examples or drawings. **3.** to serve as an example of. **—illustrator** *n.* [f. L *illustrare* (IL-¹, *lustrare* light up)]

illustration /ɪlə'streɪʃ(ə)n/ *n.* **1.** illustrating. **2.** a picture or drawing in a book etc. **3.** an explanatory example. [f. OF f. L (as prec.)]

illustrative /'ɪləstrətɪv/ *adj.* illustrating, explanatory (*of*). [f. ILLUSTRATE]

illustrious /ɪ'lʌstrɪəs/ *adj.* distinguished, renowned. [f. L *illustris* (as ILLUSTRATE)]

Illyria /ɪ'lɪrɪə/ the country of an ancient Indo-European people, the Illyrians, along the coast of the Adriatic Sea in what is now Yugoslavia and part of Albania. It was subsequently the Roman province of Illyricum. **—Illyrian** *adj. & n.*

im-¹,² see IN-¹,².

image /'ɪmɪdʒ/ *n.* **1.** a representation of an object's external form, e.g. a statue (especially as an object of worship). **2.** reputation, the general impression of a person or thing as perceived by the public. **3.** a simile, a metaphor. **4.** a mental representation. **5.** an optical counterpart produced by rays of light reflected from a mirror etc. **6.** a counterpart in appearance. **7.** an idea, a conception. —*v.t.* **1.** to describe or imagine vividly. **2.** to make an image of, to portray. **3.** to reflect, to mirror. [f. OF f. L *imago*]

imagery *n.* **1.** figurative illustration; use of images in literature etc. **2.** images, statuary; carving. [as prec.]

imaginable /ɪ'mædʒɪnəb(ə)l/ *adj.* able to be imagined. [f. foll.]

imaginary /ɪ'mædʒɪnərɪ/ *adj.* existing only in the imagination. [f. L (as foll.)]

imagination /ɪmædʒɪ'neɪʃ(ə)n/ *n.* the mental faculty forming images or concepts of objects not existent or present, the creative faculty of the mind. [f. OF f. L (as IMAGINE)]

imaginative /ɪ'mædʒɪnətɪv/ *adj.* having or showing a high degree of imagination. **—imaginatively** *adv.* [as foll.]

imagine /ɪ'mædʒɪn/ *v.t.* **1.** to form a mental image of, to picture in one's mind. **2.** to think or believe; to guess; (*colloq.*) to suppose. [f. OF f. L (as IMAGE)]

imagist /'ɪmədʒɪst/ *n.* a member of a group of English and American poets who, in a revolt against romanticism (*c.*1910–17), sought clarity of expression through the use of precise images. The movement derived in part from the aesthetic philosophy of T. E. Hulme and involved Ezra Pound, James Joyce, Amy Lowell, and others. **—imagism** *n.* [f. IMAGE]

imago /ɪ'meɪgəʊ/ *n.* (*pl.* **imagines** /-dʒɪni:z/) the fully developed stage of an insect, e.g. a butterfly. [L (as IMAGE)]

imam /ɪ'mɑ:m/ *n.* **1.** the leader of prayers in a mosque. **2.** the title of various Muslim leaders, especially of one succeeding Muhammad as leader of Islam. **—imamate** *n.* [f. Arab., = leader ('*amma* precede)]

imbalance /ɪm'bæləns/ *n.* lack of balance; disproportion. [f. IM-² + BALANCE]

imbecile /'ɪmbɪsi:l/ *n.* **1.** a mentally deficient person; an adult whose intelligence is equal to that of an average five-year-old child. **2.** a stupid person. —*adj.* idiotic. **—imbecility** /-'sɪlɪtɪ/ *n.* [f. F f. L *imbecillus* weak]

imbibe /ɪm'baɪb/ *v.t.* **1.** to drink (esp. alcoholic liquor). **2.** to absorb (ideas, moisture, etc.). **3.** to inhale (air etc.). [f. L *imbibere* (IM-¹, *bibere* drink)]

imbroglio /ɪm'brəʊljəʊ/ *n.* (*pl.* **-os**) **1.** a complicated or confused situation. **2.** a confused heap. [It. (as EMBROIL)]

imbue /ɪm'bju:/ *v.t.* **1.** to inspire or permeate (*with* feelings, opinions, or qualities). **2.** to saturate or dye (*with*). [f. F or L *imbuere* moisten]

IMF *abbr.* International Monetary Fund.

Imhotep /ɪm'həʊtep/ an ancient Egyptian architect and scholar, the probable designer of the step pyramid built at Saqqara for the 3rd-Dynasty pharaoh Djoser (early 3rd millennium BC) and said by Manetho to be the inventor of building in hewn stone. He was later deified: his cult was widespread in Egypt during the Graeco-Roman period, when he was regarded as the patron of architects, scribes, and doctors; the Greeks identified him with Asclepius. Imhotep is represented with a shaven head and seated, with a roll of papyrus on his knees.

imitable /'ɪmɪtəb(ə)l/ *adj.* able to be imitated. [f. foll.]

imitate /'ɪmɪteɪt/ *v.t.* to follow the example of; to mimic; to make a copy of; to be like. **—imitator** *n.* [f. L (rel. to IMAGE)]

imitation /ɪmɪ'teɪʃ(ə)n/ *n.* **1.** imitating. **2.** a copy, a counterfeit (often *attrib.*). [f. F f. L (as prec.)]

imitative /'ɪmɪtətɪv/ *adj.* imitating. [f. L (as IMITATE)]

immaculate /ɪ'mækjʊlət/ *adj.* pure, spotless; faultless, innocent. **—immaculacy** *n.*, **immaculately** *adv.* [f. L *immaculatus* (IM-², *macula* spot)]

Immaculate Conception the doctrine that the Virgin Mary was conceived, and remained, free from all stain of original sin. The belief, which sought biblical support from Gen. 3: 15 and Luke 1: 28, was much disputed in the Middle Ages, but was generally accepted by Roman Catholics from the 16th c.; it was defined as a dogma of the RC Church in 1854. The feast is kept on 8 Dec.

immanent /'ɪmənənt/ *adj.* inherent; (of God) permanently pervading the universe. —**immanence** n. [f. L immanēre (IM-¹, manēre remain)]

Immanuel /ɪˈmænjʊəl/ the name given to Christ as the deliverer of Judah prophesied by Isaiah (Isa. 7: 14, 8: 8; Matt. 1: 23). [Heb., = God with us]

immaterial /ɪməˈtɪərɪəl/ adj. not material, not corporeal; unimportant, irrelevant. —**immateriality** /-ˈælɪtɪ/ n. [f. L (as IM-², MATERIAL)]

immature /ɪməˈtjʊə(r)/ adj. not mature; unripe. —**immaturity** n. [f. L (as IM-², MATURE)]

immeasurable /ɪˈmeʒərəb(ə)l/ adj. not measurable; immense. —**immeasurably** adv. [f. IM-² + MEASURABLE]

immediate /ɪˈmiːdɪət/ adj. 1. occurring at once. 2. without an intervening medium; direct, nearest; not separated by others. —**immediacy** n. [f. F or L (as IM-², MEDIATE)]

immediately adv. 1. without pause or delay. 2. without an intermediary. —conj. (colloq.) as soon as. [f. prec.]

immemorial /ɪmɪˈmɔːrɪəl/ adj. ancient beyond memory or record; very old. [f. L (as IM-², MEMORIAL)]

immense /ɪˈmens/ adj. exceedingly large; (colloq.) great. —**immensely** adv., **immensity** n. [f. F f. L immensus (IM-², p.p. of metiri measure)]

immerse /ɪˈmɜːs/ v.t. 1. to put completely in water or other liquid. 2. to absorb or involve deeply in thought, business, etc. 3. to embed. [f. L immergere (IM-¹, mergere mers- dip)]

immersion /ɪˈmɜːʃ(ə)n/ n. immersing, being immersed. —**immersion heater**, an electric heater designed to be immersed in the liquid to be heated, especially as a fixture in a hot-water tank. [as prec.]

immigrant /ˈɪmɪgrənt/ n. one who immigrates; a descendant of recent immigrants. —adj. immigrating; of immigrants. [as foll.]

immigrate /ˈɪmɪgreɪt/ v.i. to come into a foreign country as a settler. —**immigration** /-ˈgreɪʃ(ə)n/ n. [f. L immigrare (as IM-¹, MIGRATE)]

imminent /ˈɪmɪnənt/ adj. (of an event, esp. danger) about to happen. —**imminence** n. [f. L imminēre overhang]

immiscible /ɪˈmɪsɪb(ə)l/ adj. that cannot be mixed (with another substance). —**immiscibility** /-ˈbɪlɪtɪ/ n. [f. L (as IM-², MISCIBLE)]

immobile /ɪˈməʊbaɪl/ adj. immovable; not mobile; motionless. —**immobility** /ɪməˈbɪlɪtɪ/ n. [f. OF f. L (as IM-², MOBILE)]

immobilize /ɪˈməʊbɪlaɪz/ v.t. to make or keep immobile; to keep (a limb or patient) still for healing purposes. —**immobilization** /-ˈzeɪʃ(ə)n/ n. [f. (as prec.)]

immoderate /ɪˈmɒdərət/ adj. excessive, lacking moderation. —**immoderately** adv. [f. L (as IM-², MODERATE)]

immodest /ɪˈmɒdɪst/ adj. 1. lacking in modesty, indecent. 2. conceited. —**immodestly** adv., **immodesty** n. [f. F or L (as IM-², MODEST)]

immolate /ˈɪməleɪt/ v.t. to kill as a sacrifice. —**immolation** /-ˈleɪʃ(ə)n/ n. [f. L immolare, orig. = sprinkle with meal (mola)]

immoral /ɪˈmɒr(ə)l/ adj. not conforming to the accepted rules of morality, morally wrong (especially in sexual matters). —**immorality** /ɪməˈrælɪtɪ/ n., **immorally** adv. [f. IM-² + MORAL]

immortal /ɪˈmɔːt(ə)l/ adj. 1. not mortal, living for ever. 2. famous for all time. —n. an immortal being or person. —**immortality** /-ˈtælɪtɪ/ n., **immortally** adv. [f. L (as IM-², MORTAL)]

immortalize /ɪˈmɔːtəlaɪz/ v.t. to make immortal. [f. prec.]

immovable /ɪˈmuːvəb(ə)l/ adj. 1. unable to be moved; motionless. 2. steadfast, unyielding, not changing in one's purpose; not moved emotionally. 3. (of property) consisting of land, houses, etc. —**immovability** /-ˈbɪlɪtɪ/ n., **immovably** adv. [f. IM-² + MOVABLE]

immune /ɪˈmjuːn/ adj. having immunity (from punishment or taxation; against infection or poison; to criticism). [f. L immunis exempt from public service]

immunity /ɪˈmjuːnɪtɪ/ n. 1. the ability of an organism to resist and overcome infection. 2. freedom or exemption (from). [as prec.]

immunize /ˈɪmjʊnaɪz/ v.t. to make immune, especially against infection. —**immunization** /-ˈzeɪʃ(ə)n/ n. [f. IMMUNE]

immunology /ɪmjʊˈnɒlədʒɪ/ n. the study of resistance to infection. [f. IMMUNITY + -LOGY]

immure /ɪˈmjʊə(r)/ v.t. to imprison; to shut in. [f. F or L immurare (IM-¹, murus wall)]

immutable /ɪˈmjuːtəb(ə)l/ adj. unchangeable. —**immutability** /-ˈbɪlɪtɪ/ n., **immutably** adv. [f. L (as IM-², MUTABLE)]

imp n. 1. a small devil. 2. a mischievous child. [OE, = young shoot]

impact /ˈɪmpækt/ n. 1. a collision; the force of a collision. 2. strong effect or influence, especially of something new. —/ɪmˈpækt/ v.t. 1. to press or fix firmly. 2. (in p.p., of a tooth) wedged between another tooth and the jaw, (of a fractured bone) with the parts pushed together (ill. BODY 1). —**impaction** /-ˈpækʃ(ə)n/ n. [f. L (as IMPINGE)]

impair /ɪmˈpeə(r)/ v.t. to damage, to weaken. —**impairment** n. [f. OF f. L (IM-¹, pejorare f. pejor worse)]

impala /ɪmˈpɑːlə/ n. (pl. same) a small African antelope (Aepyceros melampus). [Zulu]

impale /ɪmˈpeɪl/ v.t. 1. to fix or pierce with a pointed stake etc. 2. (in heraldry) to combine (two coats of arms) by placing side by side on one shield separated by a vertical line down the middle (ill. HERALDRY). —**impalement** n. [f. F or L impalare (IM-¹, palus stake)]

impalpable /ɪmˈpælpəb(ə)l/ adj. 1. not palpable. 2. not easily grasped by the mind, intangible. 3. (of a powder) very fine. —**impalpability** /-ˈbɪlɪtɪ/ n., **impalpably** adv. [F or f. L (as IM-², PALPABLE)]

impart /ɪmˈpɑːt/ v.t. 1. to give a share of. 2. to communicate (news etc. to). [f. OF f. L impartire (IM-¹, pars part)]

impartial /ɪmˈpɑːʃ(ə)l/ adj. not favouring one side more than another. —**impartiality** /-ʃɪˈælɪtɪ/ n., **impartially** adv. [f. IM-² + PARTIAL]

impassable /ɪmˈpɑːsəb(ə)l/ adj. that cannot be traversed. —**impassability** /-ˈbɪlɪtɪ/ n., **impassably** adv. [f. IM-² + PASSABLE]

impasse /ˈæmpɑːs/ n. deadlock; a position from which there is no escape. [F (as IM-², PASS¹)]

impassible /ɪmˈpæsɪb(ə)l/ adj. not liable to pain or injury; impassive. —**impassibility** /-bɪlɪtɪ/ n., **impassibly** adv. [f. OF f. L (IM-², passibilis capable of suffering, as PASSION)]

impassioned /ɪmˈpæʃ(ə)nd/ adj. deeply moved, ardent [f. It. impassionato (as IM-¹, PASSION)]

impassive /ɪmˈpæsɪv/ adj. not feeling or showing emotion; serene. —**impassively** adv., **impassivity** /-ˈsɪvɪtɪ/ n. [f. IM-² + PASSIVE]

impasto /ɪmˈpæstəʊ/ n. the laying on of paint thickly so that it projects from the picture surface and gives a textured quality, catching and reflecting light and throwing its own shadow. [It. (as IM-¹, pasta paste)]

impatient /ɪmˈpeɪʃ(ə)nt/ adj. 1. unable to wait patiently; eager. 2. showing a lack of patience. 3. intolerant (of). —**impatience** n., **impatiently** adv. [f. OF f. L (as IM-², PATIENT)]

impeach /ɪmˈpiːtʃ/ v.t. 1. to accuse of treason or other serious crime before a competent tribunal. 2. to call in question, to disparage. —**impeachment** n. [f. OF empecher f. L (IM-¹, pedica fetter)]

impeccable /ɪmˈpekəb(ə)l/ adj. faultless; not liable to sin. —**impeccability** /-ˈbɪlɪtɪ/ n., **impeccably** adv. [f. L (IM-², peccare sin)]

impecunious /ɪmpɪˈkjuːnɪəs/ adj. having little or no money. —**impecuniosity** /-ˈɒsɪtɪ/ n. [f. IM-² + L pecuniosus (pecunia money)]

impedance /ɪmˈpiːdəns/ n. 1. the total effective resistance of an electric circuit etc. to the flow of alternating current. 2. a similar mechanical property. [f. foll.]

impede /ɪmˈpiːd/ v.t. to retard by obstructing, to hinder. [f. L impedire, lit. = shackle the feet of (IM-¹, pes foot)]

impediment /ɪmˈpedɪmənt/ n. 1. a hindrance. 2. a defect in speech, especially a lisp or stammer. [f. L (as prec.)]

impedimenta /ɪmpedɪˈmentə/ n.pl. encumbrances; baggage, especially of the army. [L, = prec.]

impel /ɪmˈpel/ v.t. (-ll-) 1. to urge or drive to do something. 2. to send or drive forward, to propel. [f. L impellere (IM-¹, pellere puls- drive)]

impend /ɪmˈpend/ v.i. (of an event or danger) to be imminent; to hang (over). [f. L impendēre (IM-¹, pendēre hang)]

impenetrable /ɪmˈpenɪtrəb(ə)l/ adj. 1. not penetrable. 2. inscrutable. 3. impervious (to or by ideas etc.). —**impenetrability** /-ˈbɪlɪtɪ/ n., **impenetrably** adv. [f. F f. L (as IM-², PENETRABLE)]

impenitent /ɪmˈpenɪt(ə)nt/ adj. not penitent. —**impenitence** n. [f. L (as IM-², PENITENT)]

imperative /ɪmˈperətɪv/ adj. 1. essential, urgently needed. 2. (Gram.) of the mood expressing command. 3.

peremptory. —*n.* (*Gram.*) the imperative mood. [f. L (*imperare* command)]

imperceptible /ɪmpə'septɪb(ə)l/ *adj.* not perceptible, very slight or gradual. —**imperceptibly** *adv.* [f. F or L (as IM-², PERCEPTIBLE)]

imperfect /ɪm'pɜːfɪkt/ *adj.* **1.** not perfect, incomplete, faulty. **2.** (*Gram.*) of a tense denoting action going on but not completed (esp. in the past, e.g. *was doing*). —*n.* (*Gram.*) the imperfect tense. —**imperfectly** *adv.* [f. OF f. L (as IM-², PERFECT)]

imperfection /ɪmpə'fekʃ(ə)n/ *n.* **1.** being imperfect. **2.** a fault, a blemish. [as prec.]

imperial /ɪm'pɪərɪəl/ *adj.* **1.** of or characteristic of an empire or similar sovereign State; of an emperor or empress. **2.** majestic. **3.** (of weights and measures) used (now or formerly) by statute in the UK (see below). —**imperially** *adv.* [f. OF f. L (*imperium* supreme power)]

Imperial measures are often of great antiquity, but until defined by Parliament they often varied from place to place. Units of length are the mile and the yard; area of land is measured in acres. The basic unit of capacity is the gallon, divided into 8 pints; 8 gallons = 1 bushel; these units are larger than their counterparts in US measures. The basic unit of weight is the pound, divided into 16 ounces; the hundredweight is 112 pounds, and the ton is 20 hundredweight. A unit peculiar to Britain is the stone (14 pounds).

imperialism *n.* **1.** imperial rule; an imperial system. **2.** (usu. *derog.*) the policy of extending a country's influence over less powerful, less developed countries by acquiring dependencies or through trade, diplomacy, etc. —**imperialist** *n.*, **imperialistic** /-'lɪstɪk/ *adj.* [f. prec.]

imperil /ɪm'perɪl/ *v.t.* (-**ll**-) to endanger. [f. IM-¹ + PERIL]

imperious /ɪm'pɪərɪəs/ *adj.* **1.** domineering. **2.** urgent. —**imperiously** *adv.* [f. L (as IMPERIAL)]

imperishable /ɪm'perɪʃəb(ə)l/ *adj.* that cannot perish. [f. IM-² + PERISHABLE]

impermanent /ɪm'pɜːmənənt/ *adj.* not permanent. —**impermanence** *n.*, **impermanency** *n.* [f. IM-² + PERMANENT]

impermeable /ɪm'pɜːmɪəb(ə)l/ *adj.* not permeable. —**impermeability** /-'bɪlɪtɪ/ *n.* [f. F or L (as IM-², PERMEABLE)]

impersonal /ɪm'pɜːsən(ə)l/ *adj.* **1.** not influenced by personal feeling; showing no emotion. **2.** not referring to any particular person. **3.** having no existence as a person. **4.** (of a verb) used without a definite subject (e.g. *it is raining*); (of a pronoun) indefinite. —**impersonality** /-'nælɪtɪ/ *n.*, **impersonally** *adv.* [f. L (as IM-², PERSONAL)]

impersonate /ɪm'pɜːsəneɪt/ *v.t.* to pretend to be (another person); to play the part of. —**impersonation** /-'neɪʃ(ə)n/ *n.*, **impersonator** *n.* [as IM-¹ + PERSONATE]

impertinent /ɪm'pɜːtɪnənt/ *adj.* **1.** insolent, not showing proper respect. **2.** irrelevant. —**impertinence** *n.*, **impertinently** *adv.* [f. OF or L (as IM-², PERTINENT)]

imperturbable /ɪmpə'tɜːbəb(ə)l/ *adj.* not excitable, calm. —**imperturbability** /-'bɪlɪtɪ/ *n.*, **imperturbably** *adv.* [f. L (as IM-², PERTURB)]

impervious /ɪm'pɜːvɪəs/ *adj.* **1.** not able to be penetrated, not affording passage *to* water etc. **2.** not responsive (*to* an argument etc.). [f. L (as IM-², PERVIOUS)]

impetigo /ɪmpɪ'taɪɡəʊ/ *n.* a contagious skin disease causing blisters or pimples. [f. L (*impetere* assail)]

impetuous /ɪm'petjuːəs/ *adj.* acting or done rashly or on impulse or with sudden energy; moving violently or fast. —**impetuosity** /-'ɒsɪtɪ/ *n.*, **impetuously** *adv.* [f. OF f. L (as foll.)]

impetus /'ɪmpɪtəs/ *n.* the force or energy with which a body moves; an impulse, a driving force. [L, = assault (as IMPETIGO)]

impiety /ɪm'paɪətɪ/ *n.* lack of piety or reverence. [f. OF or L (as IMPIOUS)]

impinge /ɪm'pɪndʒ/ *v.i.* to make an impact; to encroach. —**impingement** *n.* [f. L *impingere* (IM-¹, *pangere* fix, drive)]

impious /'ɪmpɪəs/ *adj.* not pious; wicked. —**impiously** *adv.* [f. L (as IM-², PIOUS)]

impish *adj.* of or like an imp; mischievous. —**impishly** *adv.*, **impishness** *n.* [f. IMP]

implacable /ɪm'plækəb(ə)l/ *adj.* not able to be placated, relentless. —**implacability** /-'bɪlɪtɪ/ *n.*, **implacably** *adv.* [f. F or L (as IM-², PLACABLE)]

implant /ɪm'plɑːnt/ *v.t.* **1.** to plant, to insert or fix (*in*). **2.** to instil (an idea etc.) *in* a person's mind. **3.** to insert (tissue etc.) in a living body. —/'ɪmplɑːnt/ *n.* a thing implanted,

especially a piece of tissue. —**implantation** /-'teɪʃ(ə)n/ *n.* [f. F or L (as IM-¹, PLANT)]

implausible /ɪm'plɔːzɪb(ə)l/ *adj.* not plausible. —**implausibility** /-'bɪlɪtɪ/ *n.*, **implausibly** *adv.* [f. IM-² + PLAUSIBLE]

implement /'ɪmplɪmənt/ *n.* a tool, an instrument, a utensil. —/also -ment/ *v.t.* to put (a contract, decision, promise, etc.) into effect. —**implementation** /-'teɪʃ(ə)n/ *n.* [f. L (*implēre* fill up)]

implicate /'ɪmplɪkeɪt/ *v.t.* **1.** to show (a person) to be concerned (*in* a charge, crime, etc.). **2.** to lead to as a consequence or inference. [f. L *implicare* (IM-¹, *plicare* fold)]

implication /ɪmplɪ'keɪʃ(ə)n/ *n.* **1.** implying; implicating. **2.** a thing implied. [f. prec.]

implicit /ɪm'plɪsɪt/ *adj.* **1.** implied though not expressed. **2.** absolute, unquestioning. —**implicitly** *adv.* [f. F or L (as IMPLICATE)]

implode /ɪm'pləʊd/ *v.t./i.* to burst or cause to burst inwards. —**implosion** /-'pləʊʒ(ə)n/ *n.* [f. IM-¹ + L -*plodere* (after EXPLODE)]

implore /ɪm'plɔː(r)/ *v.t.* to entreat, to request earnestly. —**imploringly** *adv.* [f. F or L *implorare* (IM-¹, *plorare* lament)]

imply /ɪm'plaɪ/ *v.t.* **1.** to indicate or suggest without stating directly. **2.** to involve the truth or existence of. **3.** to mean. [f. OF f. L, = IMPLICATE]

impolite /ɪmpə'laɪt/ *adj.* not polite. —**impolitely** *adv.* [f. L (as IM-², POLITE)]

impolitic /ɪm'pɒlɪtɪk/ *adj.* inexpedient, unwise. [f. IM-² + POLITIC]

imponderable /ɪm'pɒndərəb(ə)l/ *adj.* **1.** that cannot be estimated. **2.** weightless, very light. —*n.* an imponderable thing. —**imponderably** *adv.* [f. IM-² + PONDERABLE]

import /ɪm'pɔːt/ *v.t.* **1.** to bring (goods etc.) into a country from abroad; to bring in from an outside source. **2.** to imply, to indicate. —/'ɪmpɔːt/ *n.* **1.** the importing of goods etc. **2.** something imported. **3.** meaning. **4.** importance. —**importation** /-'teɪʃ(ə)n/ *n.*, **importer** *n.* [f. L *importare* (IM-¹, *portare* carry)]

important /ɪm'pɔːt(ə)nt/ *adj.* **1.** having or able to have a great effect. **2.** (of a person) having high rank or great authority or influence. **3.** pompous. —**importance** *n.*, **importantly** *adv.* [f. F f. L (as prec.)]

importunate /ɪm'pɔːtʊnət/ *adj.* making persistent or pressing requests. —**importunity** /ɪmpɔː'tjuːnɪtɪ/ *n.* [f. L *importunus* inconvenient, orig. = harbourless (IM-², *portus* harbour)]

importune /ɪm'pɔːtjuːn, -'tjuːn/ *v.t.* **1.** to make insistent requests (to). **2.** to solicit for an immoral purpose. [f. F or L (as prec.)]

impose /ɪm'pəʊz/ *v.t./i.* **1.** to lay (a tax, duty, etc., *on* or *upon*). **2.** to enforce compliance with. **3.** to inflict; to palm off (a thing *upon* a person). **4.** to lay (pages of type) in proper order. —**impose on** or **upon,** to take advantage of (a person, his good nature etc.); to deceive, to impress, to overawe. [f. F f. L *imponere* (IM-¹, *ponere* put)]

imposing *adj.* impressive, formidable, especially in appearance. [f. prec.]

imposition /ɪmpə'zɪʃ(ə)n/ *n.* **1.** an unfair demand or burden. **2.** a tax, a duty. **3.** work set as a punishment at school. **4.** the laying on of hands in blessing etc. **5.** an act of deception or taking advantage. [f. OF or L (as IMPOSE)]

impossible /ɪm'pɒsɪb(ə)l/ *adj.* **1.** not possible, unable to be done or to exist; (*loosely*) not easy, inconvenient, incredible. **2.** (*colloq.*) outrageous, intolerable. —**impossibility** /-'bɪlɪtɪ/ *n.*, **impossibly** *adv.* [f. OF or L (as IM-², POSSIBLE)]

impost¹ /'ɪmpəʊst/ *n.* a tax or duty. [F f. L (as IMPOSE)]

impost² /'ɪmpəʊst/ *n.* the upper course of a pillar, carrying the arch. [f. F or It. *imposta* f. L (as IMPOSE)]

impostor /ɪm'pɒstə(r)/ *n.* one who assumes a false character or personality; a swindler. [f. L (as IMPOSE)]

imposture /ɪm'pɒstʃə(r)/ *n.* a deception, a sham. [F f. L (as IMPOST¹)]

impotent /'ɪmpət(ə)nt/ *adj.* **1.** powerless, unable to take action. **2.** (of a male) unable to copulate or reach orgasm; unable to procreate. —**impotence** *n.*, **impotently** *adv.* [f. OF f. L (as IM-², POTENT)]

impound /ɪm'paʊnd/ *v.t.* **1.** to confiscate; to take legal possession of. **2.** to shut up (cattle etc.) in a pound. [f. IM-¹ + POUND³]

impoverish /ɪm'pɒvərɪʃ/ *v.t.* **1.** to make poor. **2.** to exhaust the vitality or fertility of. —**impoverishment** *n.* [f. OF (as IM-¹, *poverir* f. *povre* poor)]

impracticable /ɪmˈpræktɪkəb(ə)l/ adj. not practicable. —**impracticability** /-ˈbɪlɪtɪ/ n., **impracticably** adv. [f. IM-² + PRACTICABLE]

impractical /ɪmˈpræktɪk(ə)l/ adj. 1. not practical. 2. not practicable. —**impracticality** /-ˈkælɪtɪ/ n. [f. IM-² + PRACTICAL]

imprecate /ˈɪmprɪkeɪt/ v.t. to invoke (evil upon). —**imprecation** /-ˈkeɪʃ(ə)n/ n. [f. L (IM-¹, precari pray)]

imprecatory /ˈɪmprɪkeɪtərɪ/ adj. making an imprecation. [f. prec.]

imprecise /ɪmprɪˈsaɪs/ adj. not precise. —**imprecision** /-ˈsɪʒ(ə)n/ n. [f. IM-² + PRECISE]

impregnable /ɪmˈpregnəb(ə)l/ adj. (of a fortress etc. or fig.) proof against attack. —**impregnability** /-ˈbɪlɪtɪ/ n., **impregnably** adv. [f. OF imprenable (IM-², prendre take)]

impregnate /ˈɪmpregneɪt/ v.t. 1. to fill or saturate (with). 2. to imbue (with). 3. to make (a female) pregnant; to fertilize (an ovum). —**impregnatable** adj., **impregnation** /-ˈneɪʃ(ə)n/ n. [f. L (IM-¹, praegnare be pregnant)]

impresario /ɪmprɪˈsɑːrɪəʊ/ n. (pl. -os) an organizer of public entertainment, especially an opera or concert. [It. (impresa undertaking)]

impress¹ /ɪmˈpres/ v.t. 1. to cause to form a strong (usually favourable) opinion. 2. to fix or imprint (an idea etc. on a person). 3. to imprint or stamp (a mark etc. on a thing, a thing with a mark). —/ˈɪmpres/ n. 1. a mark impressed. 2. a characteristic quality. —**impressible** adj. [f. OF (as IM-¹, PRESS¹)]

impress² /ɪmˈpres/ v.t. (hist.) to force to serve in the army or navy. —**impressment** n. [f. IM-¹ + PRESS²]

impression /ɪmˈpreʃ(ə)n/ n. 1. an effect, especially on the mind or feelings. 2. an uncertain idea, belief, or remembrance. 3. an imitation of a person or sound, done to entertain. 4. impressing; a mark impressed. 5. an unaltered reprint from standing type or plates; the copies forming one issue of a book, newspaper, etc. 6. a print made from type or from an engraving. [f. OF f. L (as IMPRESS¹)]

impressionable adj. easily influenced. —**impressionability** /-ˈbɪlɪtɪ/ n., **impressionably** adv. [f. F (as prec.)]

impressionism n. a style of painting so as to give a general tone and effect without elaborate finish or detail (see below); an analogous style in music or literature. —**impressionist** n., **impressionistic** /-ˈnɪstɪk/ adj. [f. F (as IMPRESSION)]

The name and reputation of this French art movement of the late 19th c. derive from eight exhibitions held in Paris in 1874–86. The title of one of Monet's paintings—*Impression: soleil levant*—prompted the critic Leroy to dub the whole group 'impressionists'. The term was coined in derision but was accepted by the artists as an adequate indicator of at least one significant aspect of their aims. It refers to their free loose brushwork, lack of interest in precise academic draughtsmanship, and the immediacy of the resultant image, the picture's 'unfinished' quality. They painted chiefly out of doors, and the ability to treat nature as light, and light as colour, resulted in a freshness and luminosity, enhanced by the use of bright colours and white grounds. Among the principal members of the group were Monet, Renoir, Pissarro, Cézanne, Degas, and Sisley. In music, the term is applied to a style of composition originating in the 1880s with Debussy, departing from the strong direct structure and themes of the Romantic composers, and also to a type of jazz with similar 'atmospheric' characteristics.

impressive /ɪmˈpresɪv/ adj. able to excite deep feeling, especially of approval or admiration. —**impressively** adv. [f. IMPRESS¹]

imprimatur /ɪmprɪˈmeɪtə(r)/ n. a licence to print, usually from the Roman Catholic Church; authoritative permission. [L, = let it be printed]

imprint /ɪmˈprɪnt/ v.t. 1. to set firmly (a mark on, an idea etc. on or in the mind). 2. to stamp (with a figure). 3. to make or become recognized by (a young bird or animal in the first hours of its life) as an object of trust etc. This type of behaviour was first described by the Austrian zoologist Konrad Lorenz in 1937. —/ˈɪmprɪnt/ n. 1. a mark made by pressing or stamping a surface. 2. a publisher's name etc. on the title-page of a book. [f. OF f. L (as IMPRESS¹)]

imprison /ɪmˈprɪz(ə)n/ v.t. to put into prison; to confine. —**imprisonment** n. [f. OF (as IM-¹, PRISON)]

improbable /ɪmˈprɒbəb(ə)l/ adj. not likely. —**improbability** /-ˈbɪlɪtɪ/ n., **improbably** adv. [F or f. L (as IM-², PROBABLE)]

improbity /ɪmˈprəʊbɪtɪ/ n. wickedness, dishonesty. [f. L (as IM-², PROBITY)]

impromptu /ɪmˈprɒmptjuː/ adj. & adv. unrehearsed. —n. 1. a musical composition resembling an improvisation. 2. an extempore performance. [F f. L in promptu in readiness (as PROMPT)]

improper /ɪmˈprɒpə(r)/ adj. 1. not conforming to the rules of social or lawful conduct; indecent. 2. wrong, incorrect. —**improper fraction**, a fraction with the numerator greater than the denominator. —**improperly** adv. [f. F or L (as IM-², PROPER)]

impropriety /ɪmprəˈpraɪɪtɪ/ n. being improper; an improper act or remark etc. [as prec.]

improvable /ɪmˈpruːvəb(ə)l/ adj. able to be improved. [f. foll.]

improve /ɪmˈpruːv/ v.t./i. 1. to make or become better. 2. to make good use of (an occasion, opportunities). —**improve on** or **upon,** to produce something better than. —**improvement** n. [f. AF emprower (EM-, OF prou profit)]

improver n. 1. a person who works at a trade for little or no payment in order to improve his skill. 2. a substance added to food by a manufacturer or processor in order to improve its texture, keeping quality, etc. [f. prec.]

improvident /ɪmˈprɒvɪdənt/ adj. lacking foresight or care for the future, wasting one's resources. —**improvidence** n., **improvidently** adv. [f. IM-², PROVIDENT)]

improvise /ˈɪmprəvaɪz/ v.t. 1. to compose (verse, music, etc.) extempore. 2. to construct from materials not intended for the purpose. —**improvisation** /-ˈzeɪʃ(ə)n/ n., **improviser** n. [f. F or It. (improvviso extempore)]

imprudent /ɪmˈpruːdənt/ adj. unwise, rash. —**imprudence** n., **imprudently** adv. [f. L (as IM-², PRUDENT)]

impudent /ˈɪmpjʊdənt/ adj. impertinent, cheeky. —**impudence** n., **impudently** adv. [f. L impudens (IM-², pudēre be ashamed)]

impugn /ɪmˈpjuːn/ v.t. to express doubts about the truth or honesty of, to try to discredit. —**impugnment** n. [f. L impugnare assail (IM-¹, pugnare fight)]

impulse /ˈɪmpʌls/ n. 1. impelling; a push or thrust, impetus; a sharp force producing change of momentum; this change. 2. a stimulating force in a nerve. 3. a sudden inclination to act, without thought for the consequences. [f. L (as IMPEL)]

impulsion /ɪmˈpʌlʃ(ə)n/ n. 1. impelling, a push; impetus. 2. a mental impulse. [f. OF f. L (as prec.)]

impulsive /ɪmˈpʌlsɪv/ adj. 1. tending to act on impulse; done on impulse. 2. tending to impel. —**impulsively** adv., **impulsiveness** n. [f. F or L (as IMPEL)]

impunity /ɪmˈpjuːnɪtɪ/ n. exemption from punishment or injurious consequences. [f. L (IM-², poena penalty)]

impure /ɪmˈpjʊə(r)/ adj. not pure. [f. L (as IM-², purus pure)]

impurity /ɪmˈpjʊərɪtɪ/ n. 1. being impure. 2. a substance that makes another impure by being present in it. [f. prec.]

impute /ɪmˈpjuːt/ v.t. to attribute (a fault etc.) to. —**imputation** /-ˈteɪʃ(ə)n/ n. [f. OF f. L imputare, orig. = enter in an account]

In symbol indium.

in prep. 1. expressing inclusion or a position within the limits of space, time, circumstances, surroundings, etc. 2. expressing quantity, proportion (packed in tens), form or arrangement (written in French; hanging in folds), material, dress, or colour (in shades of blue), influence or respect (spoke in anger; lacking in courage). 3. expressing activity, occupation, or membership (he is in the army). 4. within the ability of. 5. (of a female animal) pregnant with (in calf). 6. (with verbs of motion or change) into (put it in your pocket). 7. introducing an indirect object after a verb (believe in; share in). 8. forming adverbial phrases (in any case; in vain). —adv. 1. expressing position bounded by certain limits, or to a point enclosed by these. 2. into a room, house, etc. 3. at home. 4. on or towards the inside. 5. in fashion, season, or office; elected; in effective or favourable action; (of the tide) high; (in cricket and baseball) batting. 6. (of a domestic fire) burning. 7. having arrived or been gathered or received. —adj. 1. internal; living etc. in, inside. 2. fashionable. —**in for,** about to undergo; competing in or for. **in on,** sharing in, privy to. **ins and outs,** all the details of an activity or procedure. **in shore,** on the water near or nearer to the shore. **in that,** because; in so far as. **in with,** on good terms with; sharing or co-operating with. **nothing**

(*or* **not much**) **in it**, no (or little) advantage to be seen in one possibility over another. [OE]

in-[1] *prefix* (**il-** before *l*; **im-** before *b*, *m*, *p*; **ir-** before *r*) in, on, into, towards, within. [f. prec. or L *in* in, into]

in-[2] *prefix* (**il-** etc. as prec.) added to adjectives in sense 'not', and to nouns in sense 'without', 'lacking'. [L]

in. *abbr.* inch(es).

inability /ɪnəˈbɪlɪtɪ/ *n.* being unable [f. IN-[2] + ABILITY]

in absentia /ɪn æbˈsentɪə/ in (his or her or their) absence. [L]

inaccessible /ɪnəkˈsesɪb(ə)l/ *adj.* not accessible; (of a person) unapproachable. —**inaccessibility** /-ˈbɪlɪtɪ/ *n.*, **inaccessibly** *adv.* [f. F or L (as IN-[2], ACCESSIBLE)]

inaccurate /ɪnˈækjʊrət/ *adj.* not accurate. —**inaccuracy** *n.*, **inaccurately** *adv.* [f. IN-[2] + ACCURATE]

inaction /ɪnˈækʃ(ə)n/ *n.* lack of action, doing nothing. [f. IN-[2] + ACTION]

inactive /ɪnˈæktɪv/ *adj.* not active, showing no activity. —**inactively** *adv.*, **inactivity** /-ˈtɪvɪtɪ/ *n.* [f. IN-[2] + ACTIVE]

inadmissible /ɪnədˈmɪsɪb(ə)l/ *adj.* not allowable. —**inadmissibility** /-ˈbɪlɪtɪ/ *n.*, **inadmissibly** *adv.* [f. IN-[2] + ADMISSIBLE]

inadvertent /ɪnədˈvɜːtənt/ *adj.* **1.** unintentional. **2.** negligent, inattentive. —**inadvertence** *n.*, **inadvertency** *n.*, **inadvertently** *adv.* [f. IN-[2] + ADVERT[2]]

inadvisable /ɪnədˈvaɪzəb(ə)l/ *adj.* not advisable. [f. IN-[2] + ADVISABLE]

inalienable /ɪnˈeɪlɪənəb(ə)l/ *adj.* not able to be given or taken away. —**inalienability** /-ˈbɪlɪtɪ/ *n.*, **inalienably** *adv.* [f. IN-[2] + ALIENABLE]

inamorato /ɪnæməˈrɑːtəʊ/ *n.* (*fem.* **inamorata** /-tə/) a lover. [It. as ENAMOUR)]

inane /ɪˈneɪn/ *adj.* silly, senseless; empty, void. —**inanely** *adv.*, **inanity** /ɪˈnænɪtɪ/ *n.* [f. L *inanis* empty]

inanimate /ɪnˈænɪmət/ *adj.* **1.** not endowed with life; lacking animal life. **2.** showing no sign of life. **3.** spiritless, dull. —**inanimation** /-ˈmeɪʃ(ə)n/ *n.* [f. L (as IN-[2], ANIMATE)]

inanition /ɪnəˈnɪʃ(ə)n/ *n.* emptiness, especially from lack of nourishment. [f. L (*inanire* make empty, as INANE)]

inapplicable /ɪnˈæplɪkəb(ə)l/ *adj.* not applicable. [f. IN-[2] + APPLICABLE]

inapposite /ɪnˈæpəzɪt/ *adj.* not apposite, out of place. [f. IN-[2] + APPOSITE]

inapprehensible /ɪnæprɪˈhensɪb(ə)l/ *adj.* that cannot be grasped by the mind or perceived by the senses. [f. IN-[2] + APPREHENSIBLE]

inappropriate /ɪnəˈprəʊprɪət/ *adj.* unsuitable. —**inappropriately** *adv.* [f. IN-[2] + APPROPRIATE]

inapt /ɪnˈæpt/ *adj.* **1.** unsuitable. **2.** unskilful. —**inaptitude** *n.*, **inaptly** *adv.* **inaptness** *n.* [f. IN-[2] + APT]

inarticulate /ɪnɑːˈtɪkjʊlət/ *adj.* **1.** unable to speak distinctly or express oneself clearly. **2.** not expressed in words; indistinctly pronounced. **3.** dumb. **4.** not jointed. —**inarticulately** *adv.* [f. L (as IN-[2], ARTICULATE)]

inartistic /ɪnɑːˈtɪstɪk/ *adj.* not artistic. —**inartistically** *adv.* [f. IN-[2] + ARTISTIC]

inasmuch /ɪnəzˈmʌtʃ/ *adv.* **inasmuch as**, since, because; (*archaic*) in so far as. [f. *in as much*]

inattention /ɪnəˈtenʃ(ə)n/ *n.* lack of attention; neglect. [f. IN-[2] + ATTENTION]

inattentive /ɪnəˈtentɪv/ *adj.* not paying attention; neglecting to show courtesy. —**inattentively** *adv.*, **inattentiveness** *n.* [f. IN-[2] + ATTENTIVE]

inaudible /ɪnˈɔːdɪb(ə)l/ *adj.* not audible, unable to be heard. —**inaudibility** /-ˈbɪlɪtɪ/ *n.*, **inaudibly** *adv.* [f. IN-[2] + AUDIBLE]

inaugural /ɪˈnɔːgjʊr(ə)l/ *adj.* of an inauguration. —*n.* an inaugural speech or lecture. [F (as foll.)]

inaugurate /ɪˈnɔːgjʊreɪt/ *v.t.* **1.** to admit formally to office. **2.** to begin (an undertaking) ceremonially; to initiate the public use of (a building etc.) with a ceremony. **3.** to begin, to introduce. —**inauguration** /-ˈreɪʃ(ə)n/ *n.*, **inaugurator** *n.* [f. L (as IN-[1], AUGUR)]

inauspicious /ɪnɔːˈspɪʃəs/ *adj.* not auspicious. —**inauspiciously** *adv.*, **inauspiciousness** *n.* [f. IN-[2] + AUSPICIOUS]

inboard /ˈɪnbɔːd/ *adv.* within the sides or towards the centre of a ship, aircraft, or vehicle. —*adj.* situated inboard. [f. IN + BOARD]

inborn *adj.* naturally inherent, innate. [f. IN + BORN]

inbred *adj.* **1.** inborn. **2.** produced by inbreeding. [f. IN + BRED]

inbreeding *n.* breeding from closely related animals or persons. [f. IN + BREEDING]

in-built *adj.* built-in.

Inc. *abbr.* (*US*) Incorporated.

Inca /ˈɪŋkə/ *n.* (*pl.* same or **-s**) a member of an American Indian people of the central Andes before the Spanish conquest. The Inca arrived in the valley of Cuzco *c.*1250. Their origin and early history are uncertain, but in the first part of the 15th c. they began a series of rapid conquests and a century later their power extended over most of modern Ecuador and Peru, large areas of Bolivia, and parts of Argentina and Chile. Their empire was highly centralized and governed by a despotic monarchy supported by an aristocratic bureaucracy, with Cuzco as its capital city and religious centre. They were skilled engineers, and built a network of roads; technology and architecture were highly developed despite the absence of wheeled vehicles and a system of writing, and many of their palaces, temples, fortifications, and irrigation systems still survive. The empire was weakened by civil war in the early 16th c., and fell to the invading Spaniards in 1532. [Quechua, = lord, royal person]

incalculable /ɪnˈkælkjʊləb(ə)l/ *adj.* too great for calculation; not calculable beforehand, uncertain. —**incalculability** /-ˈbɪlɪtɪ/ *n.*, **incalculably** *adv.* [f. IN-[2] + CALCULABLE]

incandesce /ɪnkænˈdes/ *v.t./i.* to glow with heat; to cause to do this [f. foll.]

incandescent /ɪnkænˈdes(ə)nt/ *adj.* glowing with heat; shining; (of artificial light) produced by a glowing filament etc. —**incandescence** *n.* [F f. L *incandescere* (IN-[1], *candēre* be white)]

incantation /ɪnkænˈteɪʃ(ə)n/ *n.* a magical formula, a spell or charm. —**incantatory** *adj.* [f. OF f. L (IN-[1], *cantare* sing)]

incapable /ɪnˈkeɪpəb(ə)l/ *adj.* not capable; not capable of rational conduct. —**incapability** /-ˈbɪlɪtɪ/ *n.*, **incapably** *adv.* [F or f. L (as IN-[2], CAPABLE)]

incapacitate /ɪnkəˈpæsɪteɪt/ *v.t.* to make incapable or unfit. —**incapacitation** /-ˈteɪʃ(ə)n/ *n.* [f. foll.]

incapacity /ɪnkəˈpæsɪtɪ/ *n.* inability, lack of power; legal disqualification. [f. F or L (as IN-[2], CAPACITY)]

incarcerate /ɪnˈkɑːsəreɪt/ *v.t.* to imprison. —**incarceration** /-ˈreɪʃ(ə)n/ *n.* [f. L *incarcerāre* (IN-[1], *carcer* prison)]

incarnate /ɪnˈkɑːneɪt/ *adj.* (*also* -ət) embodied in flesh, especially in human form. —*v.t.* **1.** to embody in flesh. **2.** to put (an idea etc.) into concrete form. **3.** to be a living embodiment of (a quality etc.) [f. L *incarnare* (IN-[1], *caro* flesh)]

incarnation /ɪnkɑːˈneɪʃ(ə)n/ *n.* **1.** embodiment in flesh, especially in human form. **2.** a living type (*of* a quality). —**the Incarnation**, the embodiment of God in human form as Jesus Christ. [f. OF f. L (as prec.)]

incautious /ɪnˈkɔːʃəs/ *adj.* not cautious, rash. —**incautiously** *adv.*, **incautiousness** *n.* [f. IN-[2] + CAUTIOUS]

incendiarism /ɪnˈsendɪərɪz(ə)m/ *n.* an act or acts of arson. [f. foll.]

incendiary /ɪnˈsendɪərɪ/ *adj.* **1.** (of a bomb) filled with material for causing fires. **2.** tending to stir up strife, inflammatory. **3.** of arson; guilty of arson. —*n.* **1.** an incendiary bomb. **2.** an arsonist. **3.** a person who stirs up strife. [f. L *incendere* set fire to)]

incense[1] /ˈɪnsens/ *n.* a gum or spice giving a sweet smell when burning; the smoke of this, especially in religious ceremonial. —*v.t.* to burn incense to; to perfume or fumigate (as) with incense. [f. OF f. L *incensum* (as prec.)]

incense[2] /ɪnˈsens/ *v.t.* to make angry. [f. OF f. L *incendere* (as INCENDIARY)]

incentive /ɪnˈsentɪv/ *n.* a motive or incitement; a payment or concession encouraging an effort in work. —*adj.* inciting. [f. L, = setting the tune (IN-[1], *canere* sing)]

inception /ɪnˈsepʃ(ə)n/ *n.* beginning. [f. OF or L (*incipere* begin)]

inceptive /ɪnˈseptɪv/ *adj.* beginning; initial; (of a verb) denoting the beginning of action. [f. L (as prec.)]

incertitude /ɪnˈsɜːtɪtjuːd/ *n.* uncertainty. [F or f. L (as IN-[2], CERTITUDE)]

incessant[†] /ɪnˈses(ə)nt/ *adj.* continual, repeated; unceasing. —**incessantly** *adv.* [F or f. L (as IN-[2], CEASE)]

incest /ˈɪnsest/ *n.* sexual intercourse of near relations. [f. L (IN-[2], *castus* chaste)]

incestuous /ɪnˈsestjʊəs/ *adj.* of incest; guilty of incest. [as prec.]

inch *n.* **1.** a twelfth of a (linear) foot, 2.54 cm; this used as a unit of rainfall (= 1 inch depth of water) or as a unit of map-scale (= 1 inch to 1 mile). **2.** a small amount. —*v.t./i.* to move gradually. —**every inch,** thoroughly. **within an inch of his life,** almost to death. [OE, f. L *uncia* twelfth part]

inchoate /ˈɪnkəʊət/ *adj.* undeveloped; just begun. —**inchoation** /-ˈeɪʃ(ə)n/ *n.* [f. L *inchoare, incohare* begin]

incidence /ˈɪnsɪdəns/ *n.* **1.** falling on or contact with a thing. **2.** the range, scope, extent, or rate of occurrence or influence (*of* a disease, tax, etc.). **3.** the falling of a line, ray, particles, etc., on a surface. [f. OF or L (as foll.)]

incident /ˈɪnsɪdənt/ *n.* **1.** an event or occurrence, especially a minor one. **2.** a clash of armed forces. **3.** a public disturbance. **4.** a distinct piece of action in a film, play, etc. —*adj.* **1.** apt to occur; naturally attaching (*to*). **2.** (of rays etc.) falling (*on* or *upon*). [f. F or L *incidere* fall on (IN-1, *cadere* fall)]

incidental /ɪnsɪˈdent(ə)l/ *adj.* having a minor role in relation to a more important thing or event etc., not essential. —**incidental music,** music played during or between the scenes of a play, film, etc. [f. prec.]

incidentally *adv.* **1.** as an unconnected remark. **2.** in an incidental way. [f. prec.]

incinerate /ɪnˈsɪnəreɪt/ *v.t.* to consume by fire. —**incineration** /-ˈreɪʃ(ə)n/ *n.* [f. L *incinerare* (IN-1, *cinis* ashes)]

incinerator /ɪnˈsɪnəreɪtə(r)/ *n.* a furnace or device for incinerating things. [f. prec.]

incipient /ɪnˈsɪpɪənt/ *adj.* beginning, in its early stages. [f. L (as INCEPTION)]

incise /ɪnˈsaɪz/ *v.t.* to make a cut in; to engrave. —**incision** /ɪnˈsɪʒ(ə)n/ *n.* [f. F f. L *incidere* (IN-1, *caedere* cut)]

incisive /ɪnˈsaɪsɪv/ *adj.* sharp; clear and effective. —**incisively** *adv.,* **incisiveness** *n.* [f. L (as prec.)]

incisor /ɪnˈsaɪzə(r)/ *n.* any of the teeth between the canine teeth (ill. BODY 1 and MAMMALS). [L, = cutter (as INCISE)]

incite /ɪnˈsaɪt/ *v.t.* to urge or stir up (*to* action). —**incitement** *n.* [f. F f. L *incitare* (IN-1, *citare* rouse)]

incivility /ɪnsɪˈvɪlɪtɪ/ *n.* rudeness; an impolite act. [f. F or L (as IN-2, CIVILITY)]

inclement /ɪnˈklemənt/ *adj.* (of weather) severe or stormy. —**inclemency** *n.* [f. F or L (as IN-2, CLEMENT)]

inclination /ɪnklɪˈneɪʃ(ə)n/ *n.* **1.** a tendency. **2.** a liking or preference. **3.** the slope or slant (*of* a line from the vertical, *to* another line); the angle between the lines. **4.** a leaning or bending movement; the dip of a magnetic needle. [f. OF or L (as foll.)]

incline /ɪnˈklaɪn/ *v.t./i.* **1.** to lean or cause to lean, usually from the vertical; to bend forward or downward. **2.** to dispose or influence. **3.** to have a certain tendency. —/ˈɪnklaɪn/ *n.* a slope; an inclined plane. —**inclined plane,** a sloping plane used e.g. to raise a load with less force. **incline one's ear,** to listen favourably. [f. OF f. L *inclinare* bend]

include /ɪnˈkluːd/ *v.t.* **1.** to have, regard, or treat as part of a whole. **2.** to put into a certain category etc. —**inclusion** *n.* [f. L *includere* enclose (IN-1, *claudere* shut)]

inclusive /ɪnˈkluːsɪv/ *adj.* including (with *of*); including the limits stated; including all or much. —**inclusively** *adv.* [f. L (as prec.)]

incognito /ɪnkɒgˈniːtəʊ, ɪnˈkɒgnɪtəʊ/ *adv.* under a false name, with one's identity concealed. —*adj.* acting incognito. —*n.* (*pl.* **-os**) a pretended identity; a person who is incognito. [It., = unknown (as foll.)]

incognizant /ɪnˈkɒgnɪz(ə)nt/ *adj.* unaware. —**incognizance** *n.* [f. IN-2 + COGNIZANT]

incoherent /ɪnkəʊˈhɪərənt/ *adj.* rambling in speech or reasoning. —**incoherence** *n.,* **incoherently** *adv.* [f. IN-2 + COHERENT]

incombustible /ɪnkəmˈbʌstɪb(ə)l/ *adj.* not able to be burnt by fire. [f. L (as IN-2, COMBUSTIBLE)]

income /ˈɪnkʌm/ *n.* money received, especially periodically or in a year, from one's work, lands, investments, etc. —**income tax,** a tax levied on income, first introduced in Britain in 1799 to help pay for the war against Revolutionary France. Through most of the 19th c. it was regarded as a temporary measure to meet extraordinary expenses, and the rate was generally kept below two shillings in the pound. By the end of the century, however, it had become the major source of revenue. The rate of taxation rose dramatically during the two World Wars, and during the Second (1944) the pay-as-you-earn system, deducting tax at the source of income, was introduced. [f. IN + COME]

incoming /ˈɪnkʌmɪŋ/ *adj.* coming in; succeeding another person or thing. [f. IN + *coming* (COME)]

incommensurable /ɪnkəˈmenʃərəb(ə)l/ *adj.* not commensurable; having no common measure integral or fractional (*with*). —**incommensurability** /-ˈbɪlɪtɪ/. [f. L (as IN-2, COMMENSURABLE)]

incommensurate /ɪnkəˈmenʃərət/ *adj.* disproportionate, inadequate (*to*); incommensurable. [f. IN-2 + COMMENSURATE]

incommode /ɪnkəˈməʊd/ *v.t.* to inconvenience; to annoy; to impede. [f. F or L *incommodare* (IN-2, *commodus* convenient)]

incommodious /ɪnkəˈməʊdɪəs/ *adj.* not providing comfort, inconvenient. [f. IN-2 + COMMODIOUS]

incommunicable /ɪnkəˈmjuːnɪkəb(ə)l/ *adj.* that cannot be shared or told. [f. L (as IN-2, COMMUNICABLE)]

incommunicado /ɪnkəˌmjuːnɪˈkɑːdəʊ/ *adj.* without means of communication; (of a prisoner) in solitary confinement. [f. Sp. (*incomunicar* deprive of communication)]

incommunicative /ɪnkəˈmjuːnɪkətɪv/ *adj.* not communicative, taciturn. [f. IN-2 + COMMUNICATIVE]

incomparable /ɪnˈkɒmpərəb(ə)l/ *adj.* without an equal, matchless. —**incomparability** /-ˈbɪlɪtɪ/ *n.,* **incomparably** *adv.* [f. OF f. L (as IN-2, COMPARABLE)]

incompatible /ɪnkəmˈpætɪb(ə)l/ *adj.* not compatible; inconsistent. —**incompatibility** /-ˈbɪlɪtɪ/ *n.,* **incompatibly** *adv.* [f. L (as IN-2, COMPATIBLE)]

incompetent /ɪnˈkɒmpɪt(ə)nt/ *adj.* not qualified or able; not able to function; not legally qualified. —*n.* an incompetent person. —**incompetence** *n.,* **incompetently** *adv.* [f. F or L (as IN-2, COMPETENT)]

incomplete /ɪnkəmˈpliːt/ *adj.* not complete. —**incompletely** *adv.,* **incompleteness** *n.* [f. L (as IN-2, COMPLETE)]

incomprehensible /ɪnkɒmprɪˈhensɪb(ə)l/ *adj.* not able to be understood. —**incomprehensibility** /-ˈbɪlɪtɪ/ *n.,* **incomprehensibly** *adv.* [f. L (as IN-2, COMPREHENSIBLE)]

incomprehension /ɪnkɒmprɪˈhenʃ(ə)n/ *n.* failure to understand. [f. IN-2 + COMPREHENSION]

inconceivable /ɪnkənˈsiːvəb(ə)l/ *adj.* that cannot be imagined; (*colloq.*) most unlikely. —**inconceivably** *adv.* [f. IN-2 + CONCEIVABLE]

inconclusive /ɪnkənˈkluːsɪv/ *adj.* (of evidence or an argument etc.) not fully convincing, not decisive. —**inconclusively** *adv.* [f. IN-2 + CONCLUSIVE]

incongruous /ɪnˈkɒŋgrʊəs/ *adj.* out of place, absurd; out of keeping (*with*). —**incongruity** /-ˈuːɪtɪ/ *n.,* **incongruously** *adv.* [f. L (as IN-2, CONGRUOUS)]

inconsequent /ɪnˈkɒnsɪkwənt/ *adj.* irrelevant; disconnected; not following logically. —**inconsequence** *n.,* **inconsequently** *adv.* [f. L (as IN-2, CONSEQUENT)]

inconsequential /ɪnkɒnsɪˈkwenʃ(ə)l/ *adj.* unimportant; inconsequent. —**inconsequentially** *adv.* [f. IN-2 + CONSEQUENTIAL]

inconsiderable /ɪnkənˈsɪdərəb(ə)l/ *adj.* not worth considering; of small size, amount, or value. —**inconsiderably** *adv.* [f. obs. F or L (as IN-2, CONSIDERABLE)]

inconsiderate /ɪnkənˈsɪdərət/ *adj.* (of a person or action) lacking in regard for others' feelings, thoughtless. —**inconsiderately** *adv.* [f. L (as IN-2, CONSIDERATE)]

inconsistent /ɪnkənˈsɪstənt/ *adj.* not consistent. —**inconsistency** *n.,* **inconsistently** *adv.* [f. IN-2 + CONSISTENT]

inconsolable /ɪnkənˈsəʊləb(ə)l/ *adj.* unable to be consoled. —**inconsolability** /-ˈbɪlɪtɪ/ *n.,* **inconsolably** *adv.* [F or f. L (as IN-2, CONSOLE1)]

inconsonant /ɪnˈkɒnsənənt/ *adj.* not consistent, not harmonious. [f. IN-2 + CONSONANT]

inconspicuous /ɪnkənˈspɪkjʊəs/ *adj.* not conspicuous. —**inconspicuously** *adv.,* **inconspicuousness** *n.* [f. L (as IN-2, CONSPICUOUS)]

inconstant /ɪnˈkɒnst(ə)nt/ *adj.* fickle; variable. —**inconstancy** *n.* [f. OF f. L (as IN-2, CONSTANT)]

incontestable /ɪnkənˈtestəb(ə)l/ *adj.* that cannot be disputed. —**incontestably** *adv.* [F or f. L (as IN-2, CONTEST)]

incontinent /ɪnˈkɒntɪnənt/ *adj.* unable to control excretions voluntarily; lacking self-restraint (especially in sexual desire). —**incontinence** *n.* [f. OF or L (as IN-2, CONTINENT)]

incontrovertible /ɪnkɒntrəˈvɜːtɪb(ə)l/ *adj.* indisputable, undeniable. —**incontrovertibility** /-'bɪlɪtɪ/ *n.*, **incontrovertibly** *adv.* [f. IN-² + *controvertible* (f. CONTROVERT)]

inconvenience /ɪnkən'viːnɪəns/ *n.* being inconvenient; a cause or instance of this. —*v.t.* to cause inconvenience to. [f. OF f. L (as foll.)]

inconvenient /ɪnkən'viːnɪənt/ *adj.* not convenient, not suiting one's needs or requirements; slightly troublesome. —**inconveniently** *adv.* [f. OF f. L (as IN-², CONVENIENT)]

incorporate /ɪn'kɔːpəreɪt/ *v.t./i.* 1. to include as a part or ingredient; to unite. 2. to form into a corporation; to admit as a member of a company etc. —/-ət/ *adj.* incorporated. —**incorporation** /-'reɪʃ(ə)n/ *n.* [f. L *incorporare* (IN-¹, *corpus* body)]

incorporeal /ɪnkɔː'pɔːrɪəl/ *adj.* without substance or material existence. —**incorporeally** *adv.*, **incorporeity** /-'riːɪtɪ/ *n.* [f. L *incorporeus* (IN-², *corpus* body)]

incorrect /ɪnkə'rekt/ *adj.* not correct. —**incorrectly** *adv.*, **incorrectness** *n.* [f. OF or L (as IN-², CORRECT)]

incorrigible /ɪn'kɒrɪdʒɪb(ə)l/ *adj.* (of a person or habit) incurably bad. —**incorrigibility** /-'bɪlɪtɪ/ *n.*, **incorrigibly** *adv.* [f. OF or L (as IN-², CORRIGIBLE)]

incorruptible /ɪnkə'rʌptɪb(ə)l/ *adj.* that cannot decay or be corrupted (especially by bribery). —**incorruptibility** /-'bɪlɪtɪ/ *n.*, **incorruptibly** *adv.* [f. OF or L (as IN-², CORRUPTIBLE)]

increase /ɪn'kriːs/ *v.t./i.* 1. to make or become greater or more numerous. 2. to advance (*in* power etc.). —/'ɪnkriːs/ *n.* 1. growth, enlargement; the amount of this. 2. (of people, animals, or plants) multiplication. —**on the increase**, increasing. —**increasingly** *adv.* [f. OF f. L *increscere* (IN-¹, *crescere* grow)]

incredible /ɪn'kredɪb(ə)l/ *adj.* that cannot be believed; (*colloq.*) surprising. —**incredibility** /-'bɪlɪtɪ/ *n.*, **incredibly** *adv.* [f. L (as IN-², CREDIBLE)]

incredulous /ɪn'kredjʊləs/ *adj.* unwilling to believe. —**incredulity** /ɪnkrɪ'djuːlɪtɪ/ *n.*, **incredulously** *adv.* [f. L (as IN-², CREDULOUS)]

increment /'ɪnkrɪmənt/ *n.* an increase, an added amount; profit. —**incremental** /-'ment(ə)l/ *adj.* [f. L *incrementum* (as INCREASE)]

incriminate /ɪn'krɪmɪneɪt/ *v.t.* to indicate as involved in a crime. —**incrimination** /-'neɪʃ(ə)n/ *n.*, **incriminatory** *adj.* [f. L *incriminare* (IN-¹, *crimen* accusation)]

incrustation /ɪnkrʌs'teɪʃ(ə)n/ *n.* 1. encrusting. 2. a crust, a hard coating; a deposit on a surface. [F or f. L (as ENCRUST)]

incubate /'ɪnkjʊbeɪt/ *v.t./i.* 1. to hatch (eggs) by sitting on them or by artificial heat; to sit on eggs. 2. to cause (bacteria etc.) to develop. [f. L *incubare* (IN-¹, *cubare* lie)]

incubation /ɪnkjʊ'beɪʃ(ə)n/ *n.* incubating; the development of disease germs before the first symptoms appear. [as prec.]

incubator /'ɪnkjʊbeɪtə(r)/ *n.* 1. an apparatus with artificial warmth for hatching eggs or developing bacteria. 2. an apparatus in which babies born prematurely can be kept in a constant controlled heat and supplied with oxygen etc. [f. INCUBATE]

incubus /'ɪŋkjʊbəs/ *n.* (*pl.* **-uses**) 1. an oppressive person or thing. 2. an evil spirit visiting a sleeper; a nightmare. [L, = nightmare (as INCUBATE)]

inculcate /'ɪnkʌlkeɪt/ *v.t.* to implant (a habit or idea) by persistent urging. —**inculcation** /-'keɪʃ(ə)n/ *n.* [f. L *inculcare* (IN-¹, *calcare* tread)]

inculpate /'ɪnkʌlpeɪt/ *v.t.* to incriminate; to accuse, to blame. —**inculpation** /-'peɪʃ(ə)n/ *n.*, **inculpatory** /ɪn'kʌlpətərɪ/ *adj.* [f. L *inculpare* (IN-¹, *culpare* blame)]

incumbency /ɪn'kʌmbənsɪ/ *n.* the office or tenure of an incumbent. [as foll.]

incumbent /ɪn'kʌmbənt/ *adj.* 1. forming an obligation or duty. 2. lying or resting (*on*). —*n.* the holder of an office, especially a benefice. [f. L *incumbere* lie on]

incunabulum /ɪnkju:'næbjʊləm/ *n.* (*pl.* **-la**) 1. an early printed book, especially from before 1501. 2. (in *pl.*) the early stages of a thing [L (in *pl.*), = swaddling-clothes]

incur /ɪn'kɜː(r)/ *v.t.* (**-rr-**) to bring on oneself (danger, blame, loss, etc.). [f. L *incurrere* (IN-¹, *currere* run)]

incurable /ɪn'kjʊərəb(ə)l/ *adj.* that cannot be cured. —*n.* an incurable person. —**incurability** /-'bɪlɪtɪ/ *n.*, **incurably** *adv.* [f. OF or L (as IN-², CURABLE)]

incurious /ɪn'kjʊərɪəs/ *adj.* feeling or showing no curiosity about something. —**incuriously** *adv.* [f. L (as IN-², CURIOUS)]

incursion /ɪn'kɜːʃ(ə)n/ *n.* an invasion or attack, especially sudden or brief. —**incursive** *adj.* [f. L (as INCUR)]

incurve /ɪn'kɜːv/ *v.t.* to bend into a curve; (esp. in *p.p.*) to curve inwards. —**incurvation** /-'veɪʃ(ə)n/ *n.* [f. L *incurvare* (as IN-¹, CURVE)]

indebted /ɪn'detɪd/ *adj.* under a debt or obligation (to). —**indebtedness** *n.* [f. OF *endetté* (as IN-¹, DEBT)]

indecent /ɪn'diːsənt/ *adj.* offending against decency; unseemly. —**indecent assault**, a sexual attack not involving rape. —**indecency** *n.*, **indecently** *adv.* [f. F or L (as IN-², DECENT)]

indecipherable /ɪndɪ'saɪfərəb(ə)l/ *adj.* that cannot be deciphered. [f. IN-² + DECIPHERABLE]

indecision /ɪndɪ'sɪʒ(ə)n/ *n.* lack of decision, hesitation. [f. F (as IN-², DECISION)]

indecisive /ɪndɪ'saɪsɪv/ *adj.* not decisive. —**indecisively** *adv.*, **indecisiveness** *n.* [f. IN-² + DECISIVE]

indeclinable /ɪndɪ'klaɪnəb(ə)l/ *adj.* (of words) having no inflexions. [f. F f. L (as IN-², DECLINE)]

indecorous /ɪn'dekərəs/ *adj.* improper, not in good taste. —**indecorously** *adv.* [f. L (as IN-², DECOROUS)]

indeed /ɪn'diːd/ *adv.* 1. in truth, really. 2. admittedly. —*int.* expressing incredulity, surprise, etc. [f. IN + DEED]

indefatigable /ɪndɪ'fætɪgəb(ə)l/ *adj.* not becoming tired; unremitting. —**indefatigably** *adv.* [f. obs. F or L (as IN-², *defatigare* tire out)]

indefeasible /ɪndɪ'fiːzɪb(ə)l/ *adj.* (of a right, possession, etc.) that cannot be forfeited or annulled. —**indefeasibly** *adv.* [f. IN-² + *defeasible* (AF f. OF *defaire* undo)]

indefensible /ɪndɪ'fensɪb(ə)l/ *adj.* that cannot be defended or justified. —**indefensibility** /-'bɪlɪtɪ/ *n.*, **indefensibly** *adv.* [f. IN-² + DEFENSIBLE]

indefinable /ɪndɪ'faɪnəb(ə)l/ *adj.* that cannot be defined or described clearly. —**indefinably** *adv.* [f. IN-² + DEFINABLE]

indefinite /ɪn'defɪnɪt/ *adj.* 1. not clearly defined, stated, or decided; unlimited. 2. (of adjectives, adverbs, and pronouns) not determining the person etc. referred to (e.g. *some, someone, anyhow*). —**indefinite article**, see ARTICLE. —**indefinitely** *adv.* [f. L (as IN-², DEFINITE)]

indelible /ɪn'delɪb(ə)l/ *adj.* that cannot be rubbed out; that makes indelible marks. —**indelibly** *adv.* [f. F or L (IN-², *delēre* efface)]

indelicate /ɪn'delɪkət/ *adj.* 1. slightly indecent; not refined. 2. tactless. —**indelicacy** *n.*, **indelicately** *adv.* [f. IN-² + DELICATE]

indemnify /ɪn'demnɪfaɪ/ *v.t.* 1. to protect or insure (a person *from* or *against* loss); to exempt from a penalty (*for* actions). 2. to compensate. —**indemnification** /-'keɪʃ(ə)n/ *n.* [f. L *indemnis* free from loss]

indemnity /ɪn'demnɪtɪ/ *n.* 1. protection or insurance against damage or loss; exemption from a penalty. 2. compensation for damage. [f. F f. L (as prec.)]

indent /ɪn'dent/ *v.t./i.* 1. to make notches, dents, or recesses in. 2. to start (a line of print or writing) further from the margin than the others. 3. to place an indent for goods; to order (goods) by an indent. 4. to draw up (a document) in duplicate. —/'ɪndent/ *n.* 1. an official order for goods. 2. an indentation. 3. an indenture. [f. AF f. L (IN-¹, *dens* tooth)]

indentation /ɪnden'teɪʃ(ə)n/ *n.* 1. indenting. 2. a notch; a deep recess. [f. prec.]

indention /ɪn'denʃ(ə)n/ *n.* indenting, especially in printing; a notch. [f. INDENT]

indenture /ɪn'dentʃə(r)/ *n.* 1. a formal sealed agreement, especially (usu. in *pl.*) one binding an apprentice to a master. 2. a formal list, certificate, etc. —*v.t.* to bind by indentures. [f. AF (as INDENT)]

independence /ɪndɪ'pend(ə)ns/ *n.* being independent. —**Independence Day**, 4 July, celebrated in the USA as the anniversary of the date in 1776 when the American colonies formally declared themselves free and independent of Britain; a similar festival elsewhere. [f. foll.]

independent /ɪndɪ'pend(ə)nt/ *adj.* 1. not depending on the authority or control (*of*, or abs.); self-governing. 2. not depending on another thing for validity etc., or on another person for one's opinion or livelihood. 3. (of broadcasting, a school, etc.) not supported from public funds. 4. (of an income or resources) making it unnecessary to earn one's living. 5. unwilling to be under obligation to others. 6. acting independently of any political party. —*n.* a person who is politically independent. —**independently** *adv.* [f. IN-² + DEPENDENT]

indescribable /ɪndɪ'skraɪbəb(ə)l/ *adj.* too unusual to be described; vague. —**indescribably** *adv.* [f. IN-² + *describable* (f. DESCRIBE)]

indestructible /ɪndɪ'strʌktɪb(ə)l/ *adj.* that cannot be destroyed. —**indestructibility** /-'bɪlɪtɪ/ *n.*, **indestructibly** *adv.* [f. IN-² + *destructible* (f. DESTROY)]

indeterminable /ɪndɪ'tɜːmɪnəb(ə)l/ *adj.* that cannot be ascertained or settled. —**indeterminably** *adv.* [f. L (as IN-², DETERMINE)]

indeterminate /ɪndɪ'tɜːmɪnət/ *adj.* not fixed in extent, character, etc.; left doubtful. —**indeterminate vowel,** the vowel /ə/ heard in '*a moment ago*'. —**indeterminacy** *n.*, **indeterminately** *adv.*, **indeterminateness** *n.* [f. L (as IN-², DETERMINATE)]

indetermination /ɪndɪtɜːmɪ'neɪʃ(ə)n/ *n.* lack of determination. [f. prec.]

Index short for *Index Librorum Prohibitorum* (L, = list of prohibited books) a list of books forbidden to Roman Catholics (or to be read only in expurgated editions) as contrary to their faith or morals. The first Index was issued in 1557; it was revised at intervals until abolished in 1966.

index /'ɪndeks/ *n.* (*pl.* **indexes** or **indices** /-ɪsiːz/) **1.** an alphabetical list of subjects etc. with references, usually at the end of a book. **2.** a number indicating the level of prices or wages as compared with some standard value. **3.** the exponent of a number. **4.** a pointer (*lit.* or *fig.*). —*v.t.* **1.** to furnish (a book) with an index; to enter in an index. **2.** to relate (wages etc.) to the value of a price index. —**index finger,** the forefinger. **index-linked** *adj.* related to the value of a price index. [L, = forefinger, informer]

indexation /ɪndek'seɪʃ(ə)n/ *n.* making wages etc. index-linked. [f. prec.]

India /'ɪndɪə/ a country in South Asia, a member State of the Commonwealth, occupying the greater part of the Indian subcontinent, a peninsula bounded by the Arabian Sea and the Bay of Bengal and on the north by the Himalayas; pop. (1981) 683,880,051; official languages, Hindi and English (another 14 are also recognized by the constitution); capital, New Delhi. India comprises 22 States and 9 Union Territories and is inhabited by brown-skinned peoples following the Hindu, Muslim, and other religions and speaking over 200 languages and dialects, with Hindi being the most widespread in the north and Tamil and Telugu in the south. The economy is heavily dependent on agriculture, but since 1947 the country has built up a substantial industrial base. The textile and jute industries are important; other major industries are based on the exploitation of the country's mineral resources, chiefly coal, oil, and iron. The second most populous country in the world, India faces serious problems arising from poverty and a high rate of illiteracy.

Its history began in the 3rd millennium BC, when the Indus valley was the site of a fully developed civilization. This collapsed *c.*1760 BC when the invading Aryans spread from the west through the northern part of the country. Consolidated first within the Buddhist empire of Asoka and then the Hindu empire of the Gupta dynasty, much of India was united under a Muslim sultanate based on Delhi from the 12th c. until incorporated in the Mogul empire by Babur and Akbar the Great in the 16th c. The decline of Mogul power in the late 17th and early 18th c. coincided with increasing European penetration, with Britain eventually triumphing over her colonial rivals. British interest had begun in the 17th c. with the formation of the East India Company, which in 1765 acquired the right to administer Bengal and afterwards other parts; in 1858, after the Indian Mutiny, the Crown took over the Company's authority, and in 1877 Queen Victoria was proclaimed Empress of India. Rising nationalism, with Mahatma Gandhi a notable leader, resulted in independence and partition in 1947, but the new States of India and Pakistan did not prove good neighbours, going to war several times (most recently in 1971) over the disputed territory of Kashmir and the Pakistani enclave (now Bangladesh) in the north-east.

India ink (*US*) Indian ink.

Indiaman /'ɪndɪəmən/ *n.* (*pl.* **-men**) (*hist.*) a ship engaged in trade with India or the East Indies.

Indian /'ɪndɪən/ *adj.* **1.** of India; of the subcontinent comprising India, Pakistan, and Bangladesh. **2.** of the original inhabitants (other than Eskimo) of America and the West Indies. —*n.* **1.** a native of India. **2.** an original inhabitant (other than an Eskimo) of America or the West Indies; a Red Indian (see RED). —**Indian clubs,** a pair of bottle-shaped clubs swung to exercise the arms. **Indian corn,** maize. **Indian file,** single file. **Indian ink,** a black

pigment. **Indian summer,** a calm dry period in late autumn; (*fig.*) a tranquil late period. [f. INDIA]

Indiana /ɪndɪ'ænə/ a State in the Middle West of the USA, ceded to Britain by the French in 1763 and to the USA in 1783. It became the 19th State in 1816; capital, Indianapolis.

Indian Mutiny a revolt of Indians against British rule, 1857-8. At a time when the number of British troops in India had reached a low point and the ruling East India Company was almost totally dependent on native soldiers (sepoys), discontent with British administration finally resulted in widespread mutinies in British garrison towns with accompanying massacres of white soldiers and inhabitants. After a series of sieges (most notably that of Lucknow) and battles in which British training and discipline triumphed over Indian numbers, order was finally restored. The most important of the reforms enacted in the wake of the mutiny was the institution of direct rule by the British Crown in place of the East India Company administration.

Indian Ocean the ocean to the south of India, extending from the east coast of Africa to the East Indies and Australia.

India paper thin tough opaque paper used for printing.

indiarubber /ɪndɪə'rʌbə(r)/ *n.* a rubber, especially for rubbing out pencil marks etc.

Indic /'ɪndɪk/ *adj.* Indo-Aryan. [f. L f. Gk *Indikos* Indian]

indicate /'ɪndɪkeɪt/ *v.t.* **1.** to point out, to make known. **2.** to be a sign of, to show the presence of. **3.** to show the need of, to require. **4.** to state briefly. —**indication** /-'keɪʃ(ə)n/ *n.* [f. L *indicare* point out (as INDEX)]

indicative /ɪn'dɪkətɪv/ *adj.* **1.** suggestive *of*, giving an indication. **2.** (*Gram.*, of a mood) expressing a statement not a command, wish, etc. —*n.* (*Gram.*) the indicative mood or form. [f. F f. L (as prec.)]

indicator /'ɪndɪkeɪtə(r)/ *n.* **1.** a person or thing that indicates or points to something. **2.** a device indicating the condition of a machine etc. **3.** a board giving current information. **4.** a device to show the direction of an intended turn by a vehicle. [f. INDICATE]

indicatory /ɪn'dɪkətərɪ/ *adj.* indicative (*of*). [as prec.]

indices see INDEX.

indict /ɪn'daɪt/ *v.t.* to accuse formally by legal process. [f. AF (as DICTATE)]

indictable /ɪn'daɪtəb(ə)l/ *adj.* (of an offence) making the doer liable to be charged with a crime; (of a person) so liable. [f. prec.]

indictment /ɪn'daɪtmənt/ *n.* a document stating alleged crimes; an accusation. [f. AF (as INDICT)]

Indies /'ɪndiːz/ *n.pl.* **the Indies,** (*archaic*) India and adjacent regions. **East Indies, West Indies,** see separate entries. [pl. of obs. *Indy* India]

indifference /ɪn'dɪfərəns/ *n.* **1.** lack of interest or attention. **2.** unimportance. [f. L (as foll.)]

indifferent /ɪn'dɪfərənt/ *adj.* **1.** showing indifference or lack of interest. **2.** neither good nor bad. **3.** of poor quality or ability. **4.** unimportant. —**indifferently** *adv.* [f. OF or L (as IN-², DIFFERENT)]

indigenous /ɪn'dɪdʒɪnəs/ *adj.* native or belonging naturally (*to* a place). [f. L *indigena* (*indi-* = IN¹, *gen-* be born)]

indigent /'ɪndɪdʒ(ə)nt/ *adj.* needy, poor. —**indigence** *n.* [f. OF f. L *indigēre* (*indi-* = IN-¹, *egēre* need)]

indigestible /ɪndɪ'dʒestɪb(ə)l/ *adj.* difficult or impossible to digest. —**indigestibility** /-'bɪlɪtɪ/ *n.* [F or f. L (as IN-², DIGESTIBLE)]

indigestion /ɪndɪ'dʒestʃ(ə)n/ *n.* difficulty in digesting food; pain caused by this. [f. OF or L (as IN-², DIGESTION)]

indignant /ɪn'dɪgnənt/ *adj.* feeling or showing indignation. —**indignantly** *adv.* [f. L *indignari* regard as unworthy (IN-², *dignus* worthy)]

indignation /ɪndɪg'neɪʃ(ə)n/ *n.* scornful anger at supposed injustice, wickedness, etc. [f. OF or L (as prec.)]

indignity /ɪn'dɪgnɪtɪ/ *n.* humiliating treatment, an insult; humiliating quality. [f. F or L *indignitas* (as INDIGNANT)]

indigo /'ɪndɪgəʊ/ *n.* (*pl.* **-os**) deep violet-blue; a dye of this colour. [Sp. or Port. f. L f. Gk, = Indian dye]

indirect /ɪndɪ'rekt, -daɪ-/ *adj.* not direct. —**indirect object,** a person or thing affected by verbal action but not primarily acted on (e.g. *him* in *give him the book*). **indirect question,** a question in indirect speech. **indirect speech,** reported speech. **indirect tax,** a tax paid in the form of an increased price for taxed goods. —**indirectly** *adv.* [f. OF or L (as IN-², DIRECT)]

indiscernible /ɪndɪˈsɜːnɪb(ə)l/ adj. that cannot be discerned. —**indiscernibly** adv. [f. IN-² + DISCERNIBLE]

indiscipline /ɪnˈdɪsɪplɪn/ n. lack of discipline. [f. IN-² + DISCIPLINE]

indiscreet /ɪndɪsˈkriːt/ adj. **1.** not discreet, revealing secrets. **2.** incautious, unwary. —**indiscreetly** adv. [f. L indiscretus (as IN-², DISCREET)]

indiscretion /ɪndɪsˈkreʃ(ə)n/ n. indiscreet conduct or action. [f. OF or L (as IN-², DISCRETION)]

indiscriminate /ɪndɪsˈkrɪmɪnət/ adj. done or acting without judgement or discrimination. —**indiscriminately** adv., **indiscrimination** /-ˈneɪʃ(ə)n/ n. [f. IN-² + discriminate adj. (as DISCRIMINATE)]

indispensable /ɪndɪˈspensəb(ə)l/ adj. that cannot be dispensed with, necessary to or for. —**indispensability** /-ˈbɪlɪtɪ/ n., **indispensably** adv. [f. L (as IN-², DISPENSABLE)]

indisposed /ɪndɪˈspəʊzd/ adj. **1.** slightly unwell. **2.** averse or unwilling. —**indisposition** /-spəˈzɪʃ(ə)n/ n. [f. IN-² + DISPOSE]

indisputable /ɪndɪˈspjuːtəb(ə)l/ adj. not able to be disputed, undeniable. —**indisputability** /-ˈbɪlɪtɪ/ n., **indisputably** adv. [f. L (as IN-², DISPUTE)]

indissoluble /ɪndɪˈsɒljʊb(ə)l/ adj. that cannot be dissolved or destroyed, firm and lasting. —**indissolubly** adv. [f. L (as IN-², DISSOLUBLE)]

indistinct /ɪndɪˈstɪŋkt/ adj. not distinct; confused, obscure. —**indistinctness** n. [f. L (as IN-², DISTINCT)]

indistinguishable /ɪndɪˈstɪŋgwɪʃəb(ə)l/ adj. that cannot be distinguished. —**indistinguishably** adv. [f. IN-² + DISTINGUISHABLE]

indite /ɪnˈdaɪt/ v.t. to put into words; to write (a letter etc.). [f. OF (as INDICT)]

indium /ˈɪndɪəm/ n. a rare silver-white soft metallic element, symbol In, atomic number 49, first discovered by spectrum analysis in 1863, that occurs in association with zinc and other metals. It is used in semiconductor devices and in alloys of low melting-point. [f. L indicum indigo, with ref. to the two indigo lines which form its characteristic spectrum]

individual /ɪndɪˈvɪdjʊəl/ adj. **1.** single, separate; of or for one person. **2.** having a distinct character; characteristic of a particular person or thing. —n. a single member of a class; a single human being; (colloq.) a person. —**individually** adv. [orig. = indivisible, f. L individuus (as IN-², DIVIDE)]

individualism n. **1.** self-reliant action by an individual. **2.** a social theory favouring free action by individuals. **3.** egotism. —**individualist** n., **individualistic** /-ˈlɪstɪk/ adj. [f. prec.]

individuality /ɪndɪvɪdjʊˈælɪtɪ/ n. **1.** separate existence. **2.** individual character, especially when strongly marked. [f. INDIVIDUAL]

individualize v.t. to give an individual character to. [as prec.]

indivisible /ɪndɪˈvɪzɪb(ə)l/ adj. not divisible. —**indivisibility** /-ˈbɪlɪtɪ/ n., **indivisibly** adv. [f. L (as IN-², DIVISIBLE)]

Indo- /ˈɪndəʊ-/ in comb. Indian (and).

Indo-Aryan adj. of the group of Indo-European languages comprising Sanskrit and the modern Indian languages which are its descendants. —n. **1.** this language group. **2.** its speakers.

Indo-China 1. the peninsula of SE Asia containing Burma, Thailand, Malaya, Laos, Kampuchea, and Vietnam. **2.** (hist.) the region that now consists of Laos, Kampuchea, and Vietnam. It was formerly a French dependency (French Indo-China). —**Indo-Chinese** adj. & n.

indoctrinate /ɪnˈdɒktrɪneɪt/ v.t. to imbue with a doctrine or opinion; to teach, to instruct. —**indoctrination** /-ˈneɪʃ(ə)n/ n. [f. IN-¹ + DOCTRINE]

Indo-European adj. of the family of languages (also called Indo-Germanic or Aryan) spoken for at least the last 3,000 years over the greater part of Europe and extending into Asia as far as northern India. —n. **1.** this family of languages. **2.** a speaker of any of these.
 The name has become established as a technical term, but it must not be supposed to include all the languages of India and Europe, some of which (e.g. the Dravidian languages, Finnish, and Hungarian) belong to quite different families. Considerably before 2000 BC there must have existed a relatively small tribe speaking a language which we may call 'Proto-Indo-European'. No records of it survive, nor is there any evidence that it could ever have been written, but its existence can be inferred from a

comparison of its daughter languages, and most of its phonology and morphology and some of its vocabulary can be reconstructed with some degree of certainty. The main divisions into which it split up, in the course of time, are the Indo-Iranian or Aryan group, the Hellenic group or Greek, the Italic group (of which the most important member is Latin, together with its daughter languages French and the other Romance languages), the Germanic languages (to which English belongs), the Celtic group, the Baltic languages and the closely related Slavonic languages. In addition to these, Albanian forms a distinct member of the family and so does Armenian. Two important discoveries of the 20th c. have added to the family the ancient Anatolian languages (from the 2nd millennium BC: Hittite is the oldest attested Indo-European language), and Tocharian, which flourished in Chinese Turkestan more than 1,000 years ago.
 Recognition of the breadth of this language family is only relatively recent and was first reached when a number of European scholars started studying Sanskrit in the late 18th and early 19th c. In 1786 the English orientalist Sir William Jones pointed out the strong affinity that Sanskrit bore to Greek and Latin, and spoke of a common origin for these languages, but most of the research on which the language groupings and the reconstruction of the parent language are based was the work of German scholars in the 19th c.

Indo-Germanic adj. & n. Indo-European.

Indo-Iranian adj. of the large group of Indo-European languages spoken chiefly in northern India and Iran. It can be divided into the Indo-Aryan (or Indic) group and the Iranian.

indolent /ˈɪndələnt/ adj. lazy, averse to exertion. —**indolence** n., **indolently** adv. [f. L (IN-², dolere suffer pain)]

indomitable /ɪnˈdɒmɪtəb(ə)l/ adj. unyielding, stubbornly persistent. —**indomitably** adv. [f. L (IN-², domitare tame)]

Indonesia /ɪndəˈniːʃə/ a large island group in SE Asia, formerly the Dutch East Indies, composed of Java, Sumatra, South Borneo, West New Guinea, the Moluccas, Sulawesi, and a host of minor islands; pop. approx. 153,000,000; official language, Indonesian; capital (on Java) Jakarta. Most of the population is engaged in agriculture and the industries based on its products; timber is the second most important export, after oil. Economic and political power is largely centred in Java. Colonized, largely by the Dutch, in the early 17th c., the area was conquered by the Japanese in 1942 and upon liberation was proclaimed a republic by local nationalists. Sovereignty passed formally to the new Indonesian government in 1949 and the last Dutch enclave in the area was finally handed over in 1963.

Indonesian /ɪndəˈniːʃ(ə)n/ adj. of Indonesia or its people or language. —n. **1.** a native or inhabitant of Indonesia. **2.** the official language of the Republic of Indonesia, although it is virtually the same language as Malay; the apparent differences are mainly due to the different spelling systems, the Indonesian one having been developed by the Dutch and the Malay by the British. [f. prec.]

indoor adj. of or done or for use in a building or under cover. [for earlier within-door]

indoors /ɪnˈdɔːz/ adv. in(to) a building; under a roof. [earlier within doors]

Indra /ˈɪndrə/ (Hinduism) the most popular deity of the Rig-Veda, warrior-king of the heavens, god of war and storm. His weapons are the thunderbolt and lightning, his helpers are the Maruts. His role in later Hinduism is small. [Skr., = lord]

indrawn /ˈɪndrɔːn/ adj. **1.** drawn in. **2.** aloof. [f. IN + DRAW]

indubitable /ɪnˈdjuːbɪtəb(ə)l/ adj. that cannot be doubted. —**indubitably** adv. [F or f. L (IN-², dubitare doubt)]

induce /ɪnˈdjuːs/ v.t. **1.** to persuade. **2.** to produce or cause; to bring on (labour in childbirth) artificially. **3.** to produce by induction; to infer as an induction. [f. L inducere (IN-¹, ducere lead)]

inducement n. a thing that induces; an attraction, a motive. [f. prec.]

inducible adj. that may be induced. [f. INDUCE]

induct /ɪnˈdʌkt/ v.t. to install or initiate (into a benefice or office etc.). [as INDUCE]

inductance /ɪnˈdʌkt(ə)ns/ n. the amount of induction of an electric current. [f. prec.]

induction /ɪnˈdʌkʃ(ə)n/ n. **1.** inducting. **2.** inducing. **3.** the inferring of a general law from particular instances. **4.** the production of an electric or magnetic state by the proximity (without contact) of an electrified or magnetized body; the quantity giving the measure of such an influence; the production of an electric current by a change of magnetic field. **5.** the drawing of a fuel mixture into the cylinder(s) of an internal-combustion engine. [f. OF or L (as INDUCE)]

inductive /ɪnˈdʌktɪv/ adj. **1.** (of reasoning etc.) based on or using induction. **2.** of electric or magnetic induction. [f. L (as INDUCE)]

indulge /ɪnˈdʌldʒ/ v.t./i. **1.** to take pleasure freely (*in* an activity etc.). **2.** to yield freely to (a desire etc.). **3.** to gratify by compliance with wishes. [f. L *indulgēre*]

indulgence /ɪnˈdʌldʒ(ə)ns/ n. **1.** indulging. **2.** a privilege granted. **3.** remission of the temporal punishment still due for sins even after sacramental absolution. The later Middle Ages saw the growth of considerable abuses, such as the unrestricted sale of indulgences by professional 'pardoners', which were an immediate occasion of the Reformation. In the Roman Catholic Church the granting of indulgences is now ordinarily confined to the pope. [f. OF f. L (as prec.)]

indulgent adj. indulging; lenient, willing to overlook faults etc.; too lenient. —**indulgently** adv. [F or f. L (as INDULGE)]

indurate /ˈɪndjʊəreɪt/ v.t./i. to make or become hard; to make callous. —**induration** /-ˈreɪʃ(ə)n/ n., **indurative** adj. [f. L *indurare* (IN-¹, *durus* hard)]

Indus /ˈɪndəs/ a river of southern Asia, about 2,900 km (1,800 miles) in length, flowing from Tibet through Kashmir and Pakistan to the Arabian Sea. Along its valley an early culture flourished from c.2600 to 1760 BC, with important centres at Mohenjo-Daro and Harappa, characterized by towns built to a grid-like plan with granaries, drainage systems, and public buildings, copper-bronze technology, a standard system of weights and measures, and steatite seals with (undeciphered) hieroglyphic inscriptions. Its economic wealth was derived from well-attested sea and land trade with the Indian subcontinent, Afghanistan, the Gulf, Iran, and Mesopotamia. In the early 2nd millennium its power declined, probably because of incursions by the Aryans.

industrial /ɪnˈdʌstrɪəl/ adj. of, engaged in, for use in, or serving the needs of industries; (of a nation etc.) having highly developed industries. —**industrial action,** a strike or other disruptive action used in an industrial dispute. **industrial relations,** the relations between management and workers in industries. —**industrially** adv. [f. INDUSTRY]

industrialism n. a system involving the prevalence of industries. [f. prec.]

industrialist n. a person engaged in the management of industry. [f. INDUSTRIAL]

industrialize v.t. to make (a nation or area etc.) industrial. —**industrialization** /-ˈzeɪʃ(ə)n/ n. [as prec.]

Industrial Revolution the transformation of society, occurring first in Britain in the second half of the 18th c. and the first half of the 19th c., in which the bulk of the working population changed from agriculture to industry. Preceded by major changes in agriculture in which machines replaced manual labour and so freed workers for the factories, it was caused by the rise of modern industrial methods, with steam-power replacing the use of muscle, wind, and water, the growth of factories, and the mass production of manufactured goods. The textile industry was the prime example of industrialization, and created a demand for machines, and for tools for their manufacture, which stimulated further mechanization. Improved transport was needed, provided by canals, roads, railways, and steamships; construction of these required a large labour force, and the skills acquired were exported to other countries. It made Britain the most powerful industrial country in the world but radically changed the face of British society, throwing up large cities (particularly in the Midlands) as the population shifted from the countryside, and causing a series of profound social and economic problems, the solution of which dominated domestic politics for more than a century.

industrious /ɪnˈdʌstrɪəs/ adj. hard-working. —**industriously** adv. [f. F or L (as foll.)]

industry /ˈɪndəstrɪ/ n. **1.** trade or manufacture; a branch of this; any business activity. **2.** diligence. [f. F or L *industria*]

indwelling adj. permanently present in something. [f. IN-¹ + DWELL]

Ine /ˈiːnə/ king of Wessex 688–726. The strongest king of the West Saxons before Alfred, Ine greatly extended the prestige and power of the throne, developing the most

extensive legal code of the age. He abdicated in 726 at an advanced age and retired to Rome.

inebriate /ɪˈniːbrɪət/ adj. drunken. —n. a drunkard. —/-eɪt/ v.t. to make drunk. —**inebriation** /-ˈeɪʃ(ə)n/ n., **inebriety** /-ˈbraɪətɪ/ n. [f. L *inebriare* (IN-¹, *ebrius* drunk)]

inedible /ɪnˈedɪb(ə)l/ adj. not edible (because of its nature). [f. IN-² + EDIBLE]

ineducable /ɪnˈedjʊkəb(ə)l/ adj. incapable of being educated, especially through mental retardation. [f. IN-² + EDUCABLE]

ineffable /ɪnˈefəb(ə)l/ adj. **1.** too great for description in words. **2.** that must not be uttered. —**ineffably** adv. [f. OF or L (IN-², *effari* speak out)]

ineffaceable /ɪnɪˈfeɪsəb(ə)l/ adj. not able to be effaced. [f. IN-² + EFFACE]

ineffective /ɪnɪˈfektɪv/ adj. not effective; (of a person) inefficient. —**ineffectively** adv. [f. IN-² + EFFECTIVE]

ineffectual /ɪnɪˈfektjʊəl/ adj. not effectual. —**ineffectually** adv. [f. L (as IN-², EFFECTUAL)]

inefficacious /ɪnefɪˈkeɪʃəs/ adj. (of a remedy etc.) not efficacious. [f. IN-² + EFFICACIOUS]

inefficient /ɪnɪˈfɪʃ(ə)nt/ adj. not efficient. —**inefficiency** n., **inefficiently** adv. [f. IN-² + EFFICIENT]

inelastic /ɪnɪˈlæstɪk/ adj. not elastic, not adaptable. [f. IN-² + ELASTIC]

inelegant /ɪnˈelɪɡənt/ adj. not elegant. —**inelegance** n., **inelegantly** adv. [f. F F f. L (as IN-², ELEGANT)]

ineluctable /ɪnɪˈlʌktəb(ə)l/ adj. against which it is useless to struggle. [f. L (IN-², *eluctari* struggle clear)]

inept /ɪˈnept/ adj. **1.** unskilful. **2.** unsuitable, absurd. —**ineptitude** n., **ineptly** adv. [f. L *ineptus* (as IN-², APT)]

inequable /ɪnˈekwəb(ə)l/ adj. **1.** unfair. **2.** not uniform. [f. L (as IN-², EQUABLE)]

inequality /ɪnɪˈkwɒlɪtɪ/ n. lack of equality in any respect, variableness; unevenness of surface. [f. OF or L (as IN-², EQUALITY)]

inequitable /ɪnˈekwɪtəb(ə)l/ adj. unfair, unjust. [f. IN-² + EQUITABLE]

inequity /ɪnˈekwɪtɪ/ n. unfairness, bias. [f. IN-² + EQUITY]

ineradicable /ɪnɪˈrædɪkəb(ə)l/ adj. that cannot be eradicated. [f. IN-² + ERADICABLE]

inert /ɪˈnɜːt/ adj. **1.** without an inherent power of action, reaction, motion, or resistance. **2.** sluggish, slow. —**inert gas,** a noble gas (see NOBLE). —**inertly** adv., **inertness** n. [f. L *iners* (as IN-², ART)]

inertia /ɪˈnɜːʃə/ n. **1.** inertness. **2.** the property by which matter continues in its existing state of rest or uniform motion in a straight line unless that state is changed by an external force. —**inertia reel,** a reel allowing the automatic adjustment of a safety-belt rolled round it. **inertia selling,** the sending of goods not ordered in the hope that they will not be refused. [L (as prec.)]

inertial /ɪˈnɜːʃ(ə)l/ adj. of or involving inertia; (of navigation) in which the course of a vehicle or vessel is calculated or controlled automatically, by a computer, from its acceleration at each successive moment (ill. NAVIGATION). [f. prec.]

inescapable /ɪnɪˈskeɪpəb(ə)l/ adj. that cannot be escaped or avoided. —**inescapably** adv. [f. IN-² + ESCAPE]

inescutcheon /ɪnɪˈskʌtʃ(ə)n/ n. (in heraldry) a small escutcheon placed on a larger one. [f. IN-¹ + ESCUTCHEON]

inessential /ɪnɪˈsenʃ(ə)l/ adj. not essential. —n. an inessential thing. [f. IN-² + ESSENTIAL]

inestimable /ɪnˈestɪməb(ə)l/ adj. too good, great, etc. to be estimated. —**inestimably** adv. [f. OF f. L (as IN-², ESTIMABLE)]

inevitable /ɪnˈevɪtəb(ə)l/ adj. unavoidable, bound to happen or appear; (colloq.) tiresomely familiar. —**inevitability** /-ˈbɪlɪtɪ/ n., **inevitably** adv. [f. L (IN-², *evitare* avoid)]

inexact /ɪnɪɡˈzækt/ adj. not exact. —**inexactitude** n., **inexactly** adv. [f. IN-² + EXACT]

inexcusable /ɪnɪkˈskjuːzəb(ə)l/ adj. that cannot be excused or justified. —**inexcusably** adv. [f. L (as IN-², EXCUSE)]

inexhaustible /ɪnɪɡˈzɔːstɪb(ə)l/ adj. that cannot be totally used up, available in unlimited quantity. [f. IN-² + EXHAUSTIBLE]

inexorable /ɪnˈeksərəb(ə)l/ adj. relentless; that cannot be persuaded by entreaty. —**inexorably** adv. [F or f. L (IN-², *exorare* move by entreaty)]

inexpedient /ɪnɪkˈspiːdɪənt/ adj. not expedient. —**inexpediency** n. [f. IN-² + EXPEDIENT]

inexpensive /ɪnɪkˈspensɪv/ adj. not expensive, offering

good value for the price. —**inexpensively** adv. [f. IN-² + EXPENSIVE]

inexperience /ɪnɪk'spɪərɪəns/ n. lack of experience or of knowledge or skill arising from experience. —**inexperienced** adj. [f. F f. L (as IN-², EXPERIENCE)]

inexpert /ɪn'ekspɜːt/ adj. unskilful, lacking expertise. —**inexpertly** adv. [f. OF f. L (as IN-², EXPERT)]

inexpiable /ɪn'ekspɪəb(ə)l/ adj. that cannot be expiated or appeased. [f. L (as IN-², EXPIATE)]

inexplicable /ɪn'eksplɪkəb(ə)l, ɪnɪk'splɪk-/ adj. that cannot be explained. —**inexplicably** adv. [F or f. L (as IN-², EXPLICABLE)]

inexpressible /ɪnɪk'spresɪb(ə)l/ adj. that cannot be expressed in words. —**inexpressibly** adv. [f. IN-² + EXPRESSIBLE]

in extenso /ɪn eks'tensəʊ/ at full length. [L]

in extremis /ɪn eks'triːmɪs/ 1. at the point of death. 2. in great difficulties. [L]

inextricable /ɪn'ekstrɪkəb(ə)l/ adj. 1. that cannot be resolved or escaped from. 2. that cannot be loosened. —**inextricably** adv. [f. L (as IN-², EXTRICATE)]

infallible /ɪn'fælɪb(ə)l/ adj. 1. incapable of making a mistake or being wrong. 2. never failing in its effect. —**infallibility** /-'bɪlɪtɪ/ n., **infallibly** adv. [f. F or L (as IN-², FALLIBLE)]

infamous /'ɪnfəməs/ adj. having or deserving a very bad reputation, abominable. —**infamy** /'ɪnfəmɪ/ n. [f. L (as IN-², FAME)]

infant /'ɪnf(ə)nt/ n. 1. a child during the earliest period of life; (Law) a person under the age of 18. 2. a thing in an early stage of development. —**infancy** n. [f. OF f. L (IN-², fari speak), lit. = one unable to speak]

infanta /ɪn'fæntə/ n. (hist.) a daughter of the Spanish or Portuguese king. [Sp. & Port. f. L (as prec.)]

infanticide /ɪn'fæntɪsaɪd/ n. the killing of an infant soon after birth; one who is guilty of this. [F f. L (as INFANT, -CIDE)]

infantile /'ɪnfəntaɪl/ adj./ of or like infants. —**infantile paralysis,** poliomyelitis. [F or f. L (as INFANT)]

infantry /'ɪnfəntrɪ/ n. soldiers marching and fighting on foot. [f. F f. It. (infante youth, as INFANT)]

infantryman n. (pl. -men) a soldier of an infantry regiment.

infatuate /ɪn'fætjʊeɪt/ v.t. to inspire with intense fondness and admiration. —**infatuation** /-'eɪʃ(ə)n/ n. [f. L infatuare (IN-¹, fatuus foolish)]

infect /ɪn'fekt/ v.t. 1. to affect or contaminate with a germ or virus or the consequent disease. 2. to imbue with an opinion or feeling etc. [f. L inficere taint]

infection /ɪn'fekʃ(ə)n/ n. infecting, being infected; an instance of this; a disease; the communication of disease, especially by the agency of air, water, etc. [f. OF or L (as prec.)]

infectious /ɪn'fekʃəs/ adj. 1. infecting others. 2. able to be transmitted by infection. —**infectiousness** n. [f. prec.]

infelicitous /ɪnfɪ'lɪsɪtəs/ adj. not felicitous, unfortunate. —**infelicitously** adv. [f. IN-² + FELICITOUS]

infelicity /ɪnfɪ'lɪsɪtɪ/ n. 1. unhappiness. 2. an infelicitous expression or detail. [f. L (as IN-², FELICITY)]

infer /ɪn'fɜː(r)/ v.t. (-rr-) 1. to deduce or conclude. 2. (D) to imply, to suggest. [f. L inferre (IN-¹, ferre bring)]

inferable adj. that may be inferred. [f. prec.]

inference /'ɪnfərəns/ n. 1. inferring. 2. a thing inferred. —**inferential** /-'renʃ(ə)l/ adj. [f. L (as INFER)]

inferior /ɪn'fɪərɪə(r)/ adj. 1. lower in rank or quality etc. (to); of poor quality. 2. situated below; written or printed below the line. —n. a person inferior to another especially in rank. [f. compar. of L inferus that is below]

inferiority /ɪnfɪərɪ'ɒrɪtɪ/ n. being inferior. —**inferiority complex,** an unconscious feeling of inferiority to others, sometimes manifested in aggressive behaviour (first described by the Austrian psychiatrist Alfred Adler); (colloq.) a feeling of inferiority. [f. prec.]

infernal /ɪn'fɜːn(ə)l/ adj. 1. of hell; hellish. 2. (colloq.) detestable, annoying. —**infernally** adv. [f. OF f. L (infernus situated below)]

inferno /ɪn'fɜːnəʊ/ n. (pl. -os) a raging fire; a scene of horror or distress; hell. [It., = hell (with reference to Dante's Divine Comedy), f. L (as prec.)]

infertile /ɪn'fɜːtaɪl/ adj. not fertile. —**infertility** /-'tɪlɪtɪ/ n. [F or f. L (as IN-², FERTILE)]

infest /ɪn'fest/ v.t. (of harmful persons or things, esp. vermin) to overrun (a place) in large numbers. —**infestation** /-'teɪʃ(ə)n/ n. [f. F or L infestare assail (infestus hostile)]

infibulation /ɪnfɪbju:'leɪʃ(ə)n/ n. fastening with a clasp; fastening of the genitals thus or surgically to prevent sexual intercourse. [f. L infibulare (IN-¹, FIBULA)]

infidel /'ɪnfɪd(ə)l/ n. a disbeliever in religion or in a specified religion. —adj. unbelieving; of infidels. [f. F or L infidelis (IN-², fidelis faithful)]

infidelity /ɪnfɪ'delɪtɪ/ n. disloyalty, especially to one's husband or wife. [f. F or L (as prec.)]

infield n. (in cricket) the part of the ground near the wicket.

infighting n. 1. hidden conflict in an organization. 2. boxing within arm's length.

infilling n. the placing of buildings in the gaps between others.

infiltrate /'ɪnfɪltreɪt/ v.t./i. 1. to enter (a territory, political party, etc.) gradually and imperceptibly; to cause (troops etc.) to do this. 2. to pass (fluid) by filtration (into); to permeate by filtration. —**infiltration** /-'treɪʃ(ə)n/ n., **infiltrator** n. [f. IN-¹ + FILTRATE]

infinite /'ɪnfɪnɪt/ adj. 1. having no limit, endless. 2. very great; very many. 3. (Math.) greater than any assignable quantity or countable number; (of a series) that may be continued indefinitely. —**the Infinite,** God. **the infinite,** infinite space. —**infinitely** adv. [f. L (as IN-², FINITE)]

infinitesimal /ɪnfɪnɪ'tesɪm(ə)l/ adj. infinitely or very small. —**infinitesimal calculus,** that dealing with very small quantities. —**infinitesimally** adv. [f. prec.]

infinitive /ɪn'fɪnɪtɪv/ n. a verb form expressing the verbal notion without a particular subject, tense, etc. (often with to; e.g. see in we came to see, let him see). —adj. having this form. —**infinitival** /-'taɪv(ə)l/ adj. [f. L (IN-², finitivus definite)]

infinitude /ɪn'fɪnɪtjuːd/ n. infinity, being infinite. [as INFINITE]

infinity /ɪn'fɪnɪtɪ/ n. 1. an infinite number, extent, or time. 2. being infinite. [f. OF f. L (as INFINITE)]

infirm /ɪn'fɜːm/ adj. 1. physically weak, especially from age. 2. weak, irresolute. [f. L (as IN-², FIRM¹)]

infirmary n. a hospital; the sick-quarters in a monastery, school, etc. [as prec.]

infirmity n. 1. being infirm. 2. a particular physical weakness. [f. INFIRM]

infix /ɪn'fɪks/ v.t. to fasten or fix in. [f. IN-¹ + FIX]

in flagrante delicto /ɪn flæ'græntɪ de'lɪktəʊ/ in the very act of committing an offence. [L, = in blazing crime]

inflame /ɪn'fleɪm/ v.t./i. 1. to provoke to strong feeling; to arouse anger in. 2. to cause inflammation in. 3. to catch fire, to cause to do this; to light up with or as with a flame; to make hot. [f. OF f. L inflammare (as IN-¹, FLAME)]

inflammable /ɪn'flæməb(ə)l/ adj. easily set on fire or excited. —**inflammably** adv. [f. prec.]

inflammation /ɪnflə'meɪʃ(ə)n/ n. 1. inflaming (lit. or fig.). 2. a condition of a part of the body with heat, swelling, redness, and usually pain. [f. L (as INFLAME)]

inflammatory /ɪn'flæmətərɪ/ adj. 1. tending to arouse anger or strong feeling. 2. of inflammation. [as prec.]

inflatable /ɪn'fleɪtəb(ə)l/ adj. that may be inflated. [f. foll.]

inflate /ɪn'fleɪt/ v.t. 1. to distend or become distended with air or gas. 2. to puff up (with pride etc.). 3. to increase (a price etc.) artificially. 4. to resort to the inflation of (currency). [f. L inflare (IN-¹, flare blow)]

inflation /ɪn'fleɪʃ(ə)n/ n. 1. inflating, being inflated. 2. a general rise in prices and fall in the purchasing power of money; an increase in the supply of money, regarded as the cause of such a rise. [as prec.]

inflationary adj. causing inflation. [f. prec.]

inflect /ɪn'flekt/ v.t. 1. to change the pitch of (the voice). 2. to modify (a word) to express grammatical relation. 3. to bend, to curve. [f. L inflectere (IN-¹, flectere bend)]

inflective /ɪn'flektɪv/ adj. of grammatical inflexion. [f. prec.]

inflexible /ɪn'fleksɪb(ə)l/ adj. 1. not flexible, that cannot be bent. 2. that cannot be altered. 3. refusing to alter one's demands etc., unyielding. —**inflexibility** /-'bɪlɪtɪ/ n., **inflexibly** adv. [f. L (as IN-², FLEXIBLE)]

inflexion /ɪn'flekʃ(ə)n/ n. 1. a modulation of the voice. 2. an inflected word; a suffix etc. used to inflect. 3. inflecting. —**inflexional** adj. [F or f. L (as INFLECT)]

inflict /ɪnˈflɪkt/ *v.t.* **1.** to deal (a blow etc.) *on*. **2.** to impose or deliver forcibly. —**infliction** *n.*, **inflictor** *n.* [f. L *infligere* (IN-¹, *fligere* strike)]

inflorescence /ɪnfləˈres(ə)ns/ *n.* **1.** the arrangement of the flowers of a plant in relation to the axis and to each other (ill. PLANTS). **2.** the flower(s) of a plant. **3.** flowering (*lit.* or *fig.*). [f. L *inflorescere* (as IN-¹, FLORESCENCE)]

inflow *n.* **1.** flowing in. **2.** that which flows in. [f. IN + FLOW]

influence /ˈɪnfluəns/ *n.* **1.** the power to produce an effect. **2.** the ability to affect a person's character, beliefs, or actions. **3.** a thing or person with this ability. —*v.t.* to exert an influence on, to affect. —**under the influence**, (*colloq.*) drunk. [f. OF or L *influentia* (IN-¹, *fluere* flow)]

influential /ɪnfluˈenʃ(ə)l/ *adj.* having great influence. —**influentially** *adv.* [f. L (as prec.)]

influenza /ɪnfluˈenzə/ *n.* an acute virus disease usually with fever and severe aching and catarrh, occurring in epidemics. [It. f. L (as INFLUENCE)]

influx /ˈɪnflʌks/ *n.* a flowing in, especially of persons or things into a place. [F or f. L *influxus* (as INFLUENCE)]

inform /ɪnˈfɔːm/ *v.t./i.* **1.** to give information to. **2.** to bring a charge or complaint (*against* or *on*). **3.** (in *p.p.*) knowing the facts, enlightened. [f. OF f. L, orig. = give shape to (as IN-¹, FORM)]

informal /ɪnˈfɔːm(ə)l/ *adj.* not formal; without formality. —**informality** /-ˈmælɪtɪ/ *n.*, **informally** *adv.* [f. IN-² + FORMAL]

informant /ɪnˈfɔːmənt/ *n.* a giver of information. [f. L (as INFORM)]

information /ɪnfəˈmeɪʃ(ə)n/ *n.* **1.** facts told, heard, or discovered. **2.** a charge or complaint lodged with a court etc. **3.** facts fed into a computer etc. **4.** the process of informing. —**information technology**, a wide range of modern technologies based on the widespread availability of computing power for recording, transmitting, and disseminating information, and including computing science, telecommunications, printing, and broadcasting. [f. OF f. L (as INFORM)]

informative /ɪnˈfɔːmətɪv/ *adj.* giving information, instructive. [f. L (as INFORM)]

informer *n.* one who informs against others. [f. INFORM]

infra /ˈɪnfrə/ *adv.* below or further on in a book etc. [L, = below]

infra- /ɪnfrə-/ *prefix* below. [L (as prec.)]

infraction /ɪnˈfrækʃ(ə)n/ *n.* infringement. [f. L (as INFRINGE)]

infra dig (*colloq.*) beneath one's dignity. [abbr. of L *infra dignitatem*]

infra-red /ɪnfrəˈred/ *adj.* of or using rays with a wavelength just below the red end of the visible spectrum.

infrastructure /ˈɪnfrəstrʌktʃə(r)/ *n.* the subordinate parts of an undertaking, especially permanent installations forming a basis of defence. [F as INFRA-, STRUCTURE)]

infrequent /ɪnˈfriːkwənt/ *adj.* not frequent. —**infrequency** *n.*, **infrequently** *adv.* [f. L (as IN-², FREQUENT)]

infringe /ɪnˈfrɪndʒ/ *v.t./i.* **1.** to act contrary to (a law, another's rights, etc.). **2.** to encroach or trespass (*on*). —**infringement** *n.* [f. L *infringere* (IN-¹, *frangere* break)]

infuriate /ɪnˈfjʊərɪeɪt/ *v.t.* to make furious. [f. L *infuriare* (as IN-¹, FURY)]

infuse /ɪnˈfjuːz/ *v.t./i.* **1.** to cause to be saturated or filled *with* a quality. **2.** to instil (life, a quality, etc., *into*). **3.** to steep (tea etc.) in a liquid to extract the constituents; (of tea etc.) to be steeped thus. [f. L *infundere* (IN-¹, *fundere* pour)]

infusible /ɪnˈfjuːzɪb(ə)l/ *adj.* that cannot be melted. —**infusibility** /-ˈbɪlɪtɪ/ *n.* [f. IN-² + FUSIBLE]

infusion /ɪnˈfjuːʒ(ə)n/ *n.* **1.** infusing. **2.** a liquid extract so obtained. **3.** an infused element. [f. F or L (as INFUSE)]

ingenious /ɪnˈdʒiːnɪəs/ *adj.* **1.** clever at inventing things or methods. **2.** cleverly contrived. —**ingeniously** *adv.* [f. F or L *ingeniosus* (*ingenium* cleverness)]

ingénue /ˈæ̃ʒeɪnjuː/ *n.* an artless young woman, especially as a stage role. [F (as INGENUOUS)]

ingenuity /ɪndʒɪˈnjuːɪtɪ/ *n.* ingeniousness. [f. L, = ingenuousness; assoc. in Eng. with INGENIOUS]

ingenuous /ɪnˈdʒenjʊəs/ *adj.* artless; frank. —**ingenuously** *adv.*, **ingenuousness** *n.* [f. L *ingenuus* free-born, frank (IN-¹, *gignere* beget)]

ingest /ɪnˈdʒest/ *v.t.* to take in by swallowing or absorbing. —**ingestion** *n.* [f. L *ingerere* (IN-¹, *gerere* carry)]

ingle-nook /ˈɪŋɡ(ə)lnʊk/ *n.* a nook providing a seat beside a recessed fireplace. [f. *ingle* fire in hearth (orig. Sc., perh. f. Gael.) + NOOK]

inglorious /ɪnˈɡlɔːrɪəs/ *adj.* **1.** ignominious. **2.** not famous. [f. L (as IN-², GLORY)]

ingoing *adj.* going in.

ingot /ˈɪŋɡət/ *n.* a mass, usually oblong, of cast metal, especially gold, silver, or steel. [perh. f. IN + *p.p.* of OE *geotan* cast]

ingrained /ɪnˈɡreɪnd, *attrib.* ˈɪn-/ *adj.* **1.** (of habits, feelings, or tendencies) deeply rooted, inveterate. **2.** (of dirt etc.) deeply embedded. [f. OF *engrainer* dye thoroughly (as EN-, GRAIN)]

ingratiate /ɪnˈɡreɪʃɪeɪt/ *v.t.* to bring *oneself* into favour (*with*). [f. L *in gratiam* into favour]

ingratitude /ɪnˈɡrætɪtjuːd/ *n.* lack of due gratitude. [f. OF or L (as IN-², GRATITUDE)]

ingredient /ɪnˈɡriːdɪənt/ *n.* a component part in a mixture. [f. L *ingredi* enter into]

Ingres /ˈæ̃ɡrə/, Jean Auguste Dominique (1780–1867), French painter, David's pupil and successor, the most generally admired of his day, rival of Delacroix, and upholder of classicism. He was a doctrinaire teacher, who forbade his students to look at the works of Rubens, and was fully accepted by the Establishment, becoming a Senator in 1862. Ingres is a puzzling artist: his portraits are sentimental, his nudes have a strong almost cruelly sensuous quality, but as a draughtsman he is supreme. In his feeling for pure form his true heirs are Degas, Matisse, and Picasso.

ingress /ˈɪnɡres/ *n.* going in; the right to go in. [f. L *ingressus* (as INGREDIENT)]

ingrowing *adj.* (of a nail) growing into the flesh.

inguinal /ˈɪŋɡwɪn(ə)l/ *adj.* of the groin. [f. L (*inguen* groin)]

inhabit /ɪnˈhæbɪt/ *v.t.* to live in (a place) as one's home or dwelling-place. [f. OF or L *inhabitare* (IN-¹, *habitare* dwell)]

inhabitable *adj.* suitable for inhabiting. [f. prec.]

inhabitant *n.* a person etc. who inhabits a place. [f. OF f. L (as prec.)]

inhalant /ɪnˈheɪlənt/ *n.* a medicinal substance for inhaling. [f. L (as foll.)]

inhale /ɪnˈheɪl/ *v.t./i.* to breathe in (air, gas, etc.); to take (tobacco-smoke etc.) into the lungs. —**inhalation** /ɪnhəˈleɪʃ(ə)n/ *n.* [f. L *inhalare* (IN-¹, *halare* breathe)]

inhaler *n.* an inhaling-apparatus, especially a device for sending out vapour for inhaling. [f. prec.]

inharmonious /ɪnhɑːˈməʊnɪəs/ *adj.* not harmonious. [f. IN-² + HARMONIOUS]

inhere /ɪnˈhɪə(r)/ *v.i.* to be inherent. [f. L *inhaerēre* (IN-¹, *haerēre* stick)]

inherent /ɪnˈhɪərənt/ *adj.* existing or abiding in something as an essential quality or characteristic. —**inherence** *n.*, **inherently** *adv.* [f. L (as prec.)]

inherit /ɪnˈherɪt/ *v.t.* to receive (property or rank) as an heir; to derive (qualities, problems, etc.) from parents, a predecessor, etc. —**inheritor** *n.* [f. OF f. L *inhereditare* (IN-¹, *heres* heir)]

inheritance *n.* **1.** what is inherited. **2.** inheriting. [f. AF (as prec.)]

inhibit /ɪnˈhɪbɪt/ *v.t.* **1.** to restrain, to prevent. **2.** to hinder the impulses of; to cause inhibitions in. —**inhibitory** *adj.* [f. L *inhibēre* (IN-¹, *habēre* hold)]

inhibition /ɪnhɪˈbɪʃ(ə)n/ *n.* **1.** inhibiting, being inhibited. **2.** the restraint of a direct expression of instinct; (*colloq.*) an emotional resistance to a thought or action. [f. OF or L (as prec.)]

inhospitable /ɪnˈhɒspɪtəb(ə)l, -ˈpɪt-/ *adj.* not hospitable; (of a place or climate) not giving shelter or favourable conditions. —**inhospitably** *adv.* [f. obs. F (as IN-², HOSPITABLE)]

in-house *adv.* within an institution. —*adj.* done or existing in-house.

inhuman /ɪnˈhjuːmən/ *adj.* brutal, lacking the human qualities of kindness, pity, etc. —**inhumanity** /-ˈmænɪtɪ/ *n.* [f. L (as IN-², HUMAN)]

inhumane /ɪnhjuːˈmeɪn/ *adj.* not humane. [f. IN-² + HUMANE]

inimical /ɪˈnɪmɪk(ə)l/ *adj.* hostile, harmful. —**inimically** *adv.* [f. L *inimicus* enemy]

inimitable /ɪˈnɪmɪtəb(ə)l/ adj. that cannot be imitated. —**inimitably** adv. [F or f. L (as IN-², IMITABLE)]

iniquity /ɪˈnɪkwɪtɪ/ n. **1.** wickedness. **2.** gross injustice. —**iniquitous** adj. [f. OF f. L (as IN-², EQUITY)]

initial /ɪˈnɪʃ(ə)l/ adj. of or at the beginning; (of a letter) at the beginning of a word. —n. an initial letter, especially (in pl.) those of a person's names. —v.t. (-ll-) to mark or sign with initials. —**initially** adv. [f. L (initium beginning)]

initiate /ɪˈnɪʃɪeɪt/ v.t. **1.** to originate, to begin, to set going. **2.** to admit (a person) into a society, office, etc. **3.** to instruct, especially in rites or forms. —/-ət/ n. an initiated person. —**initiation** /-ˈeɪʃ(ə)n/ n., **initiator** n., **initiatory** adj. [f. L initiare (as prec.)]

initiative /ɪˈnɪʃɪətɪv/ n. **1.** the ability to initiate things, enterprise. **2.** the first step. **3.** the power or right to begin. [F (as prec.)]

inject /ɪnˈdʒekt/ v.t. **1.** to force (a fluid, medicine, etc., into a cavity etc.) by or as by a syringe; to fill with fluid etc. thus; to administer medicine etc. to (a person) thus. **2.** to introduce (a new element or quality etc.). —**injection** n., **injector** n. [f. L injicere (IN-¹, jacere throw)]

injudicious /ɪndʒʊˈdɪʃəs/ adj. unwise, ill-judged. —**injudiciously** adv., **injudiciousness** n. [f. IN-² + JUDICIOUS]

injunction /ɪnˈdʒʌŋkʃ(ə)n/ n. an authoritative order; a judicial process restraining a person from a specified act, compelling restitution, etc. [f. L (as ENJOIN)]

injure /ˈɪndʒə(r)/ v.t. to cause harm, damage, or hurt to; to do wrong to. [f. INJURY]

injurious /ɪnˈdʒʊərɪəs/ adj. causing or likely to cause injury. [f. F or L (as foll.)]

injury /ˈɪndʒərɪ/ n. **1.** harm, damage; a particular form of this. **2.** an unjust action. [f. AF f. L injuria (IN-², jus right)]

injustice /ɪnˈdʒʌstɪs/ n. lack of justice, unfairness; an unjust action. —**do a person an injustice,** to judge him unfairly. [f. OF f. L (as IN-², JUSTICE)]

ink n. **1.** a black or coloured fluid used for writing, printing, etc. (see below). **2.** a black liquid ejected by cuttlefish etc. —v.t. to mark (in, over, etc.) with ink. —**ink out,** to obliterate with ink. **ink-well** n. a pot for holding ink, fitted into a hole in a desk. [f. OF f. L f. Gk egkauston Roman emperors' purple ink (as ENCAUSTIC)]

The ancient Egyptians and Chinese made ink from lamp-black mixed with gum or glue; such inks continued in use in medieval Europe. Plant juices and other substances were also used as colouring-matter, especially an extract of tannin with a soluble iron salt. Oil-based printing inks were developed in the mid-15th c. and used for over three hundred years. Synthetic dyes, developed in the 1860s, provided a better colouring-matter, chemical drying-agents appeared, and by the early 20th c. ink-making for various purposes had become a complicated industrial process. Ball-point pens use an oil-based ink that dries almost instantly.

inkling /ˈɪŋklɪŋ/ n. a hint, slight knowledge or suspicion (of). [f. obs. inkle utter in an undertone]

inkstand n. a stand for one or more ink-bottles.

inky adj. **1.** of ink; stained with ink. **2.** very black. —**inkiness** n. [f. INK]

inland /ˈɪnlənd, -lænd/ adj. **1.** in the interior of a country, remote from the sea or a border. **2.** within a country. —/usu. -ˈlænd/ adv. in or towards the interior of a country. —n. the interior of a country. —**inland revenue,** revenue from taxes and inland duties.

in-laws n.pl. (colloq.) relatives by marriage. [f. IN + LAW (as in father-in-law)]

inlay /ɪnˈleɪ/ v.t. (past & p.p. **inlaid**) to set or embed (pieces of wood or metal etc.) in another material so that the surfaces are level, forming a design; to decorate thus. —/ˈɪnleɪ/ n. **1.** inlaid material or work. **2.** a filling shaped to fit a tooth-cavity. [f. IN- + LAY¹]

inlet /ˈɪnlet/ n. **1.** a small arm of a sea, lake, or river. **2.** a piece inserted. **3.** a way in. [f. IN + LET¹]

in loco parentis /ɪn ləʊkəʊ pəˈrentɪs/ in the place of a parent. [L]

inmate /ˈɪnmeɪt/ n. any of the occupants of a house, hospital, prison, etc. [prob. orig. f. INN + MATE¹]

in memoriam /ɪn mɪˈmɔːrɪæm/ in memory of. [L]

inmost adj. most inward. [OE (as IN, -MOST)]

inn /ɪn/ n. a house providing lodgings etc. for payment, especially for travellers; a house providing alcoholic liquor. —**Inn of Court,** any of the four law societies in London with the exclusive right of admitting people to practise as barristers in England; a similar society in Ireland. Originally there were a number of these societies, the chief being the ones now remaining—Lincoln's Inn, the Inner Temple, the Middle Temple, and Gray's Inn; subordinate to them were a number of Inns of Chancery, all of which have ceased to exist. [OE (as IN)]

innards /ˈɪnədz/ n.pl. (colloq.) inner parts, especially entrails. [f. dial. pronunc. of INWARD]

innate /ɪˈneɪt, ˈɪn-/ adj. inborn, natural. [f. L innatus (IN-¹, nasci be born)]

inner adj. nearer to the centre or inside, interior, internal. —n. the division of a target next outside the bull's-eye; a shot striking this. —**inner city,** the central area of a city, usually with overcrowding and poverty. **inner man** or **woman,** the soul, the mind; the stomach. **inner tube,** a separate inflatable tube in a pneumatic tyre. —**innermost** adj. [OE (compar. of IN)]

innings /ˈɪnɪŋz/ n. (pl. same) **1.** the part of a game of cricket etc. in which one side or player is batting. **2.** the time of power etc. of a political party etc.; the period of a person's chance to achieve something. [f. in v. go in]

innkeeper n. the keeper of an inn.

innocent /ˈɪnəs(ə)nt/ adj. **1.** not guilty of a particular crime etc. **2.** free of all evil or wrongdoing. **3.** harmless, without guile; affectedly so. —n. an innocent person, especially a child. —**innocence** n., **innocently** adv. [f. OF or L (IN-², nocēre do harm)]

innocuous /ɪˈnɒkjʊəs/ adj. harmless. [f. L innocuus (as prec.)]

innovate /ˈɪnəveɪt/ v.i. to bring in new methods, ideas, etc.; to make changes in. —**innovation** /-ˈveɪʃ(ə)n/ n., **innovative** adj., **innovator** n., **innovatory** adj. [f. L innovare (IN-¹, novus new)]

innuendo /ɪnjuːˈendəʊ/ n. (pl. -oes) an allusive remark or hint, usually disparaging. [L, = by nodding at (IN-¹, nuere nod)]

innumerable /ɪˈnjuːmərəb(ə)l/ adj. too many to be counted. —**innumerably** adv. [f. L (IN-², numerare count)]

innumerate /ɪˈnjuːmərət/ adj. not knowing basic mathematics and science. —**innumeracy** n. [f. IN-² + NUMERATE]

inoculate /ɪˈnɒkjʊleɪt/ v.t. to treat (a person or animal) with a vaccine or serum, especially as a protection against disease. —**inoculation** /-ˈleɪʃ(ə)n/ n. [f. L inoculare engraft (IN-¹, oculus eye, bud)]

inoffensive /ɪnəˈfensɪv/ adj. not offensive, harmless, not objectionable. [f. IN-² + OFFENSIVE]

inoperable /ɪnˈɒpərəb(ə)l/ adj. that cannot be cured by surgical operation. [f. IN-² + OPERABLE]

inoperative /ɪnˈɒpərətɪv/ adj. not working or taking effect. [f. IN-² + OPERATIVE]

inopportune /ɪnˈɒpətjuːn/ adj. not opportune, coming or happening at an unsuitable time. —**inopportunely** adv. [f. L (as IN-², OPPORTUNE)]

inordinate /ɪnˈɔːdɪnət/ adj. excessive. —**inordinately** adv. [f. L (as IN-², ORDAIN)]

inorganic /ɪnɔːˈgænɪk/ adj. **1.** (of a chemical compound etc.) mineral not organic. **2.** without an organized physical structure. **3.** extraneous. —**inorganic chemistry,** the chemistry of inorganic substances (see CHEMISTRY). [f. IN-² + ORGANIC]

in-patient n. a patient residing in hospital during treatment.

input /ˈɪnpʊt/ n. **1.** what is put in. **2.** the place of entry of energy, information, etc. —v.t. (-tt-; past & p.p. **input**, **inputted**) to put in or into; to supply (data, programs, etc., to a computer).

inquest /ˈɪnkwest/ n. **1.** an inquiry held by a coroner into the cause of death. **2.** a prolonged discussion after misfortune, failure, etc. [as INQUIRE]

inquietude /ɪnˈkwaɪɪtjuːd/ n. uneasiness. [f. OF or L (as IN-², QUIET)]

inquire /ɪnˈkwaɪə(r)/ v.i. to undertake a formal investigation (into). [f. OF f. L inquirere (quaerere seek)]

inquiry /ɪnˈkwaɪərɪ/ n. an investigation, especially an official one. [f. prec.]

Inquisition n. an ecclesiastical court established c.1232 for the detection and punishment of heretics, at a time when certain heretical groups threatened not only religion but the institutions of contemporary society. Its officials were chiefly Dominicans and Franciscans, and it became notorious for the use of torture (though at the time this was part of accepted judicial procedure); in grave cases the penalties included death at the stake. The 'Spanish Inquisition' was a separate body, established in 1479 by the Spanish monarchy (with papal approval), and was a political instrument, directed originally against converts from Judaism and Islam but later also against Protestants, operating with great severity especially under its first inquisitor, Torquemada; it was finally suppressed in 1820. In 1542 the medieval Inquisition was assigned by Pope Paul III to a Church department, the Congregation of the Inquisition or Holy Office. Originally established to combat Protestantism, which threatened Italian religious unity, it became an organ of papal government. [= foll.]

inquisition /ɪŋkwɪ'zɪʃ(ə)n/ n. an intensive investigation or inquiry. —**inquisitional** adj. [as INQUIRE]

inquisitive /ɪn'kwɪzɪtɪv/ adj. seeking knowledge; unduly curious, prying. —**inquisitively** adv. [as INQUIRE]

inquisitor /ɪn'kwɪzɪtə(r)/ n. one who questions searchingly; an official investigator; an officer of the Inquisition. [f. F f. L (as INQUIRE)]

inquisitorial /ɪnkwɪzɪ'tɔːrɪəl/ adj. of or like an inquisitor; prying. —**inquisitorially** adv. [f. L (as prec.)]

in re /ɪn riː/ =RE¹. [L, = in the matter (of)]

INRI abbr. Jesus of Nazareth, king of the Jews. [f. L Iesus Nazarenus Rex Iudaeorum]

inroad n. 1. a hostile incursion. 2. (often in pl.) an encroachment; the using up of resources etc. [f. IN + ROAD (in sense 'riding')]

inrush n. a violent influx.

insalubrious /ɪnsə'luːbrɪəs/ adj. (of a place or climate etc.) unhealthy. [f. L (as IN-², SALUBRIOUS)]

insane /ɪn'seɪn/ adj. 1. not sane, mad. 2. very foolish. —**insanely** adv., **insanity** /-'sænɪtɪ/ n. [f. L (as IN-², SANE)]

insanitary /ɪn'sænɪtərɪ/ adj. unclean and likely to be harmful to health. [f. IN-² + SANITARY]

insatiable /ɪn'seɪʃəb(ə)l/ adj. that cannot be satisfied, very greedy. —**insatiability** /-'bɪlɪtɪ/ n., **insatiably** adv. [f. OF or L (as IN-², SATIABLE)]

insatiate /ɪn'seɪʃɪət/ adj. never satisfied. [f. L (as IN-², SATIATE)]

inscribe /ɪn'skraɪb/ v.t. 1. to write (words etc. in or on a surface); to mark (a surface with characters). 2. to draw (a geometrical figure) within another so that points of it lie on the other's boundary. 3. to enter (a name) on a list or in a book. 4. to place an informal dedication in or on (a book etc.). [f. L inscribere (IN-¹, scribere write)]

inscription /ɪn'skrɪpʃ(ə)n/ n. 1. words inscribed. 2. inscribing. —**inscriptional** adj. [f. L (as prec.)]

inscrutable /ɪn'skruːtəb(ə)l/ adj. baffling, impossible to understand or interpret. —**inscrutability** /-'bɪlɪtɪ/ n., **inscrutably** adv. [f. L (IN-², scrutari search)]

insect /'ɪnsekt/ n. any of a class of small invertebrate animals of the phylum Arthropoda, typically having six legs, two or four wings, and a body divided into three sections: head, thorax, and abdomen. Insects, of which there are over a million species, are abundant on land and in fresh water, but are almost absent from the sea. They display great diversity of form (see ill., pp. 424-5) and have a number of roles in nature: some are important in the pollination of crops, some produce useful substances such as honey, beeswax, and silk, others are harmful to plants and animals, and some are carriers of disease. [f. L insectum notched (animal) (IN-¹, secare cut)]

insecticide /ɪn'sektɪsaɪd/ n. a substance for killing insects. [f. prec. + -CIDE]

insectivore /ɪn'sektɪvɔː(r)/ n. an animal that feeds on insects and other small creatures; a plant that traps and absorbs insects. —**insectivorous** /-'tɪvərəs/ adj. [F (as INSECT, L vorare devour)]

insecure /ɪnsɪ'kjʊə(r)/ adj. 1. not secure or safe or dependable. 2. feeling a lack of security, constantly anxious. —**insecurely** adv., **insecurity** n. [f. L (as IN-², SECURE)]

inseminate /ɪn'semɪneɪt/ v.t. 1. to impregnate with semen. 2. to sow (a seed etc., lit. & fig., in). —**insemination** /-'neɪʃ(ə)n/ n. [f. L inseminare (IN-¹, SEMEN)]

insensate /ɪn'senseɪt/ adj. 1. without sensibility, unfeeling. 2. stupid. 3. without physical sensation. [f. L (as IN-², SENSE)]

insensible /ɪn'sensɪb(ə)l/ adj. 1. unconscious. 2. unaware (of, to, how). 3. callous. 4. too small or gradual to be perceived. —**insensibility** /-'bɪlɪtɪ/ n., **insensibly** adv. [f. OF or L (as IN-², SENSIBLE)]

insensitive /ɪn'sensɪtɪv/ adj. not sensitive. —**insensitively** adv., **insensitivity** /-'tɪvɪtɪ/ n. [f. IN-² + SENSITIVE]

insentient /ɪn'senʃ(ə)nt/ adj. not sentient. [f. IN-² + SENTIENT]

inseparable /ɪn'sepərəb(ə)l/ adj. 1. that cannot be separated. 2. liking to be constantly together. —n. (usu. in pl.) an inseparable person or thing, especially a friend. —**inseparability** /-'bɪlɪtɪ/ n., **inseparably** adv. [f. L (as IN-², SEPARABLE)]

insert /ɪn'sɜːt/ v.t. to place or put (one thing into another). —/'ɪnsɜːt/ n. the thing inserted. [f. L inserere (IN-¹, serere join)]

insertion /ɪn'sɜːʃ(ə)n/ n. 1. inserting. 2. a thing inserted. [f. L (as prec.)]

inset /'ɪnset/ n. an extra piece inserted in a book, garment, etc.; a small map etc. within the border of a larger one. —/ɪn'set/ v.t. (-tt-; past & p.p. **inset** or **insetted**) to put in as an inset; to decorate with an inset.

inshore adj. & adv. near the shore.

inside n. 1. the inner side, surface, or part. 2. a position on the inner side. 3. (in sing. or pl., colloq.) the stomach and bowels. 4. (of a path) the side away from the road. —adj. of or on or in the inside; nearer to the centre of a games field. —adv. 1. on, to, or in the inside. 2. (slang) in prison. —prep. 1. within, on the inside of. 2. in less than. —**inside information**, information not accessible to outsiders. **inside job**, (colloq.) a burglary etc. by one living or working on the premises. **inside out**, turned so that the inner side becomes the outer.

insider n. a person within a group or a society etc.; one who is in the secret. [f. prec.]

insidious /ɪn'sɪdɪəs/ adj. 1. proceeding inconspicuously but harmfully. 2. crafty. —**insidiously** adv., **insidiousness** n. [f. L, = cunning (insidiae ambush)]

insight n. 1. the ability to perceive and understand a thing's true nature; mental penetration. 2. a piece of knowledge obtained by this.

insignia /ɪn'sɪgnɪə/ n.pl. badges or emblems of rank, office, etc. [L (insignis distinguished)]

insignificant /ɪnsɪg'nɪfɪkənt/ adj. of no importance or meaning; worthless, trivial. —**insignificance** n., **insignificantly** adv. [f. IN-² + SIGNIFICANT]

insincere /ɪnsɪn'sɪə(r)/ adj. not sincere or candid. —**insincerely** adv., **insincerity** /-'serɪtɪ/ n. [f. L (as IN-², SINCERE)]

insinuate /ɪn'sɪnjʊeɪt/ v.t. 1. to hint obliquely or unpleasantly. 2. to insert gradually or stealthily. —**insinuation** /-'eɪʃ(ə)n/ n. [f. L insinuare (IN-¹, sinuare curve)]

insipid /ɪn'sɪpɪd/ adj. 1. lacking in flavour. 2. dull, without liveliness. —**insipidity** /-'pɪdɪtɪ/ n., **insipidly** adv. [f. F or L (as IN-², SAPID)]

insist /ɪn'sɪst/ v.t./i. to demand or declare emphatically. [f. L insistere (IN-¹, sistere stand)]

insistent adj. 1. insisting. 2. forcing itself upon the attention. —**insistence** n., **insistently** adv. [f. prec.]

in situ /ɪn 'sɪtjuː/ in its original place. [L]

insobriety /ɪnsə'braɪətɪ/ n. intemperance, especially in drinking. [f. IN-² + SOBRIETY]

insofar /ɪnsəʊ'fɑː(r)/ adv. in so far (see FAR).

insolation /ɪnsə'leɪʃ(ə)n/ n. exposure to the sun's rays. [f. L insolare (IN-¹, sol sun)]

insole /'ɪnsəʊl/ n. the inner sole of a boot or shoe; a removable inner sole for use in a shoe. [f. IN + SOLE¹]

insolent /'ɪnsələnt/ adj. impertinently insulting. —**insolence** n., **insolently** adv. [f. L, = unaccustomed, immoderate (IN-², solēre be accustomed)]

insoluble /ɪn'sɒljʊb(ə)l/ adj. that cannot be dissolved or solved. —**insolubility** /-'bɪlɪtɪ/ n., **insolubly** adv. [f. OF or L (as IN-², SOLUBLE)]

insolvent /ɪn'sɒlv(ə)nt/ adj. unable to pay debts. —n. an insolvent debtor. —**insolvency** n. [f. IN-² + SOLVENT]

insomnia /ɪn'sɒmnɪə/ n. habitual sleeplessness. [L (IN-², somnus sleep)]

insomniac /ɪn'sɒmnɪæk/ n. a person suffering from insomnia. [f. prec.]

insomuch /ɪnsəʊ'mʌtʃ/ adv. to such an extent that; inasmuch as. [orig. in so much]

insouciant /ɪn'suːsɪənt/ adj. carefree, unconcerned. —**insouciance** n. [F (IN-², soucier care)]

inspan /ɪn'spæn/ v.t. (-nn-) (S.Afr.) to yoke (oxen etc.) in

Insects

Life cycles

incomplete metamorphosis

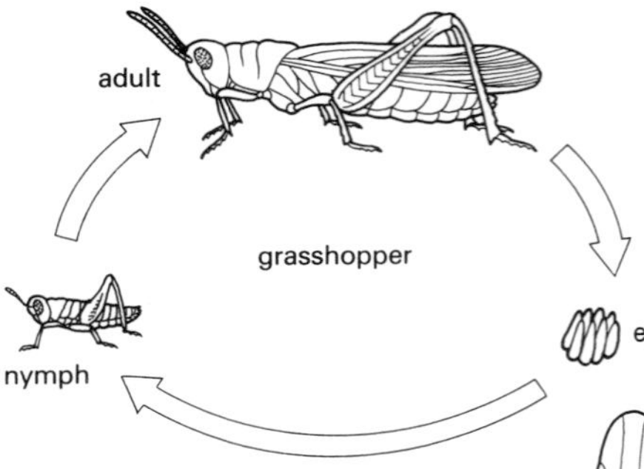

adult

grasshopper

nymph

eggs

complete metamorphosis

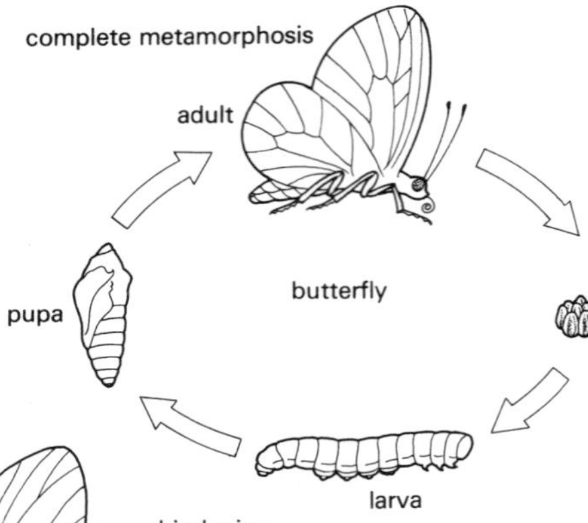

adult

pupa

butterfly

eggs

larva

forewing — hind wing

Anatomy

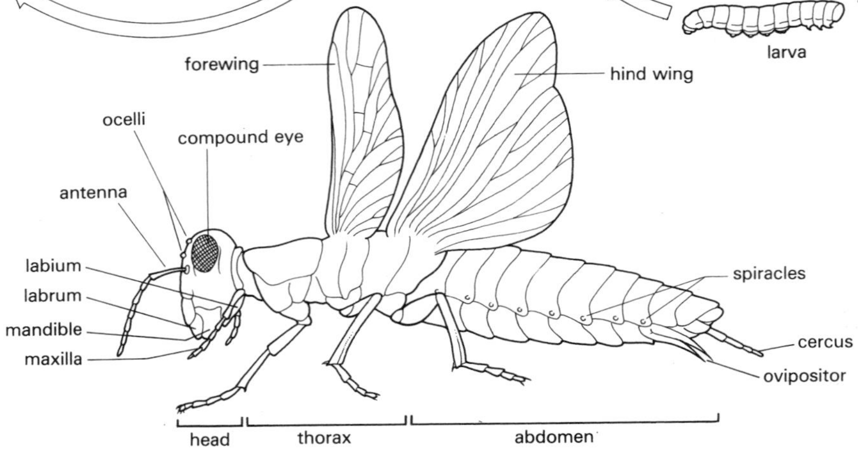

ocelli

compound eye

antenna

labium

labrum

mandible

maxilla

spiracles

cercus

ovipositor

head | thorax | abdomen

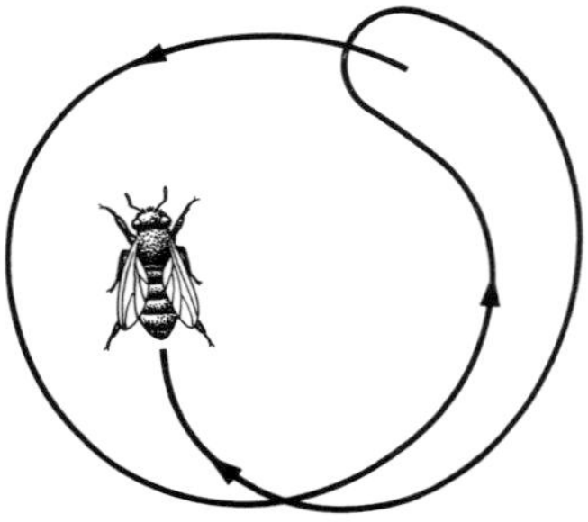

Communication: bee dances

The round dance (often performed near the hive entrance) is thought to show other bees the location of food sources close to the hive, the waggle dance (usually performed on the comb) those further afield. The latter indicates direction (in relation to the vertical comb) and distance (conveyed by rate and degree of waggle).

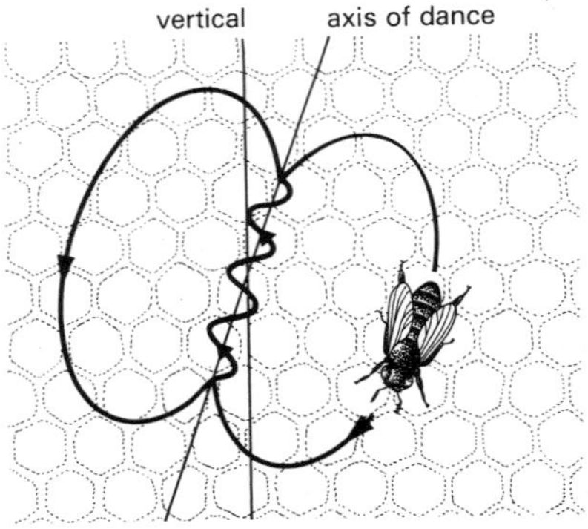

round dance

vertical   axis of dance

waggle dance

Representatives of some of the principal insect orders

(figures indicate approximate number of known species in each order)

Apterygota (wingless) incomplete metamorphosis

Pterygota (usually winged) orders with incomplete metamorphosis

several orders of primitive form, including silver-fish and bristletails (1970)

stone-flies (1,500)

grasshoppers, locusts, crickets (10,000)

stick-and leaf-insects (2,000)

bugs (55,000)

thrips (3,100)

mayflies (1,500)

biting-lice (2,800)

sucking-lice (300)

termites (1,900)

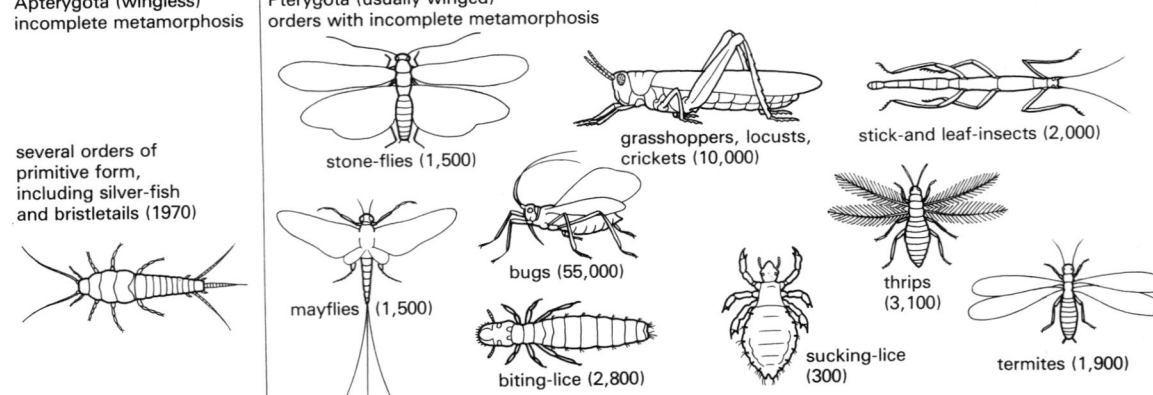

Survival

camouflage

cryptic coloration

darker underside

the larva of the eyed hawk-moth resembles the colour and vein pattern of the leaves on which it feeds; by clinging upside-down with its darker underside presented to the light it also avoids the effect of a conspicuous shadow

shadow covers lighter part

the stick-insect escapes notice by resembling a leafless twig

using a tool

aggression and defence

the male stag-beetle rears on its hind legs and opens its jaws

the sand-wasp uses a pebble to beat down sand on the nesting-hole containing its egg and the caterpillar on which the larva will feed

mimicry

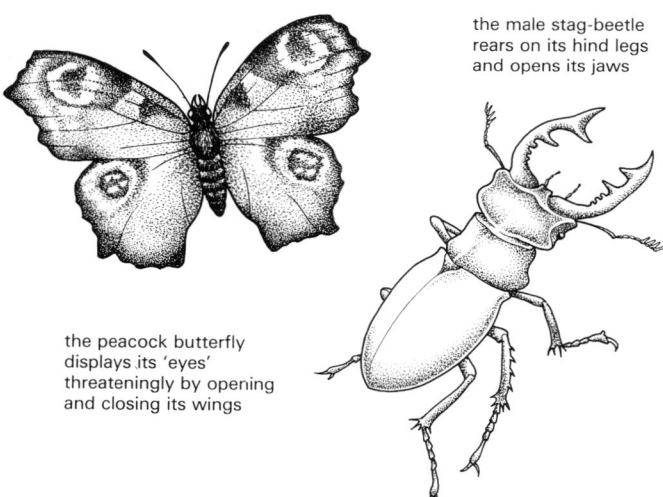

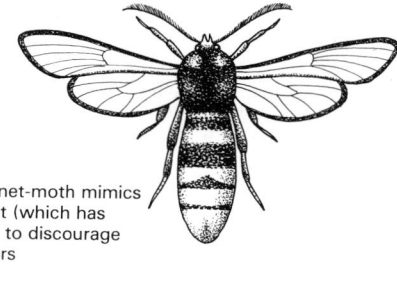

the peacock butterfly displays its 'eyes' threateningly by opening and closing its wings

the hornet-moth mimics a hornet (which has a sting) to discourage predators

orders with complete metamorphosis

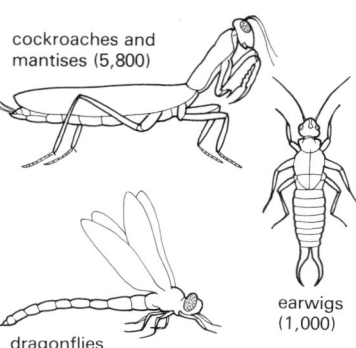

cockroaches and mantises (5,800)

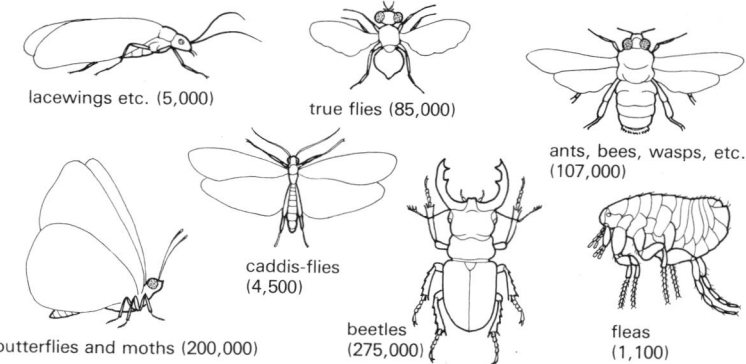

lacewings etc. (5,000)

true flies (85,000)

ants, bees, wasps, etc. (107,000)

earwigs (1,000)

caddis-flies (4,500)

dragonflies and damselflies (5,000)

butterflies and moths (200,000)

beetles (275,000)

fleas (1,100)

a team to a vehicle; to harness animals to (a wagon). [f. Du. (as IN-¹, SPAN¹)]

inspect /ɪnˈspekt/ v.t. to examine carefully and critically, especially looking for faults; to examine officially; to visit in order to see that rules and standards are being observed. —**inspection** n. [f. L inspicere (IN-¹, specere look at)]

inspector n. **1.** a person employed to inspect or supervise. **2.** a police officer next above sergeant. —**inspector of taxes**, an official assessing income tax payable. [as prec.]

inspiration /ɪnspɪˈreɪʃ(ə)n/ n. **1.** inspiring. **2.** a sudden brilliant idea. **3.** a source of inspiring influence. [as foll.]

inspire /ɪnˈspaɪə(r)/ v.t. **1.** to stimulate (a person) to creative or other activity. **2.** to animate (a person etc. with a feeling); to instil thought or feeling into (a person). **3.** to breathe (air etc.) in. [f. OF f. L inspirare (IN-¹, spirare breathe)]

inspirit /ɪnˈspɪrɪt/ v.t. to put life into, to animate; to encourage. —**inspiriting** adj. [f. IN-¹ + SPIRIT]

inst. abbr. instant (= of the current month, the 6th inst.).

instability /ɪnstəˈbɪlɪtɪ/ n. lack of stability or firmness. [f. F f. L (as IN-², STABILITY)]

install /ɪnˈstɔːl/ v.t. **1.** to place (a person) formally or ceremonially in office. **2.** to fix or establish (a person, equipment, etc.). —**installation** /ɪnstəˈleɪʃ(ə)n/ n. [f. L installare (as IN-¹, STALL)]

instalment /ɪnˈstɔːlmənt/ n. any of the successive parts in which a sum is (to be) paid; any of the parts of a whole successively delivered, published, etc. [f. AF estalement (estaler fix)]

instance /ˈɪnst(ə)ns/ n. an example, an illustration of a general truth; a particular case. —v.t. to cite as an instance. —**in the first instance**, as the first stage (in a process). [f. OF f. L (as foll.)]

instant /ˈɪnst(ə)nt/ adj. **1.** immediate. **2.** (of food) that can be prepared easily for immediate use. **3.** of the current month. —n. **1.** a precise moment. **2.** a short time, a moment. [f. F f. L instare be urgent]

instantaneous /ɪnstənˈteɪnɪəs/ adj. occurring or done in an instant. —**instantaneously** adv. [f. L (as prec.)]

instantly adv. immediately. [f. INSTANT]

instead /ɪnˈsted/ adv. as an alternative or substitute. [f. IN + STEAD]

instep /ˈɪnstep/ n. the top of the foot between the toes and the ankle; the part of a shoe etc. over or under this. [ult. as IN-¹ + STEP]

instigate /ˈɪnstɪgeɪt/ v.t. to incite or persuade; to bring about thus. —**instigation** /-ˈgeɪʃ(ə)n/ n., **instigator** n. [f. L instigare (IN-¹, stigare prick)]

instil /ɪnˈstɪl/ v.t. (-ll-) **1.** to put (ideas etc. into the mind etc.) gradually. **2.** to put into by drops. —**instillation** /-ˈleɪʃ(ə)n/ n., **instilment** n. [f. L instillare (IN-¹, stilla drop)]

instinct /ˈɪnstɪŋkt/ n. an innate propensity, especially in lower animals, to seemingly rational acts; an innate impulse or behaviour; intuition. —/ɪnˈstɪŋkt/ adj. filled or charged (with life, energy, etc.). —**instinctive** /ɪnˈstɪŋktɪv/ adj., **instinctively** adv., **instinctual** /ɪnˈstɪŋktjʊəl/ adj., **instinctually** adv. [f. L instinctus (IN-¹, stinguere prick)]

institute /ˈɪnstɪtjuːt/ n. **1.** an organized body for the promotion of an educational, scientific, or similar object. **2.** its building. —v.t. **1.** to establish, to found. **2.** to initiate (an inquiry etc.). **3.** to appoint (a person to or into a benefice). —**institutor** n. [f. L instituere (IN-¹, statuere set up)]

institution /ɪnstɪˈtjuːʃ(ə)n/ n. **1.** instituting, being instituted. **2.** an organized body, especially with a charitable purpose. **3.** an established law, custom, or practice. **4.** (colloq.) a person who has become a familiar figure in some activity. [f. OF f. L (as prec.)]

institutional adj. of or like an institution; typical of charitable institutions. —**institutionally** adv. [f. prec.]

institutionalize v.t. to make institutional; to place or keep (a person needing care) in an institution. [f. prec.]

instruct /ɪnˈstrʌkt/ v.t. **1.** to give instruction to (a person in a subject or skill). **2.** to inform. **3.** to give instructions to. **4.** to authorize (a solicitor or counsel) to act on one's behalf. —**instructor** n., **instructress** n.fem. [f. L instruere furnish, teach (as IN-¹, STRUCTURE)]

instruction /ɪnˈstrʌkʃ(ə)n/ n. **1.** the process of teaching. **2.** knowledge or teaching imparted. **3.** (usu. in pl.) statements making known to a person what he is required to do; orders. —**instructional** adj. [f. OF f. L (as prec.)]

instructive /ɪnˈstrʌktɪv/ adj. tending to instruct, enlightening. [f. INSTRUCT]

instrument /ˈɪnstrʊmənt/ n. **1.** a tool or implement, es-

pecially for delicate or scientific work. **2.** a device for measuring or controlling the function of a machine or aircraft etc. **3.** a device for giving controlled musical sounds. **4.** a thing used in an action; a person used and controlled by another to perform an action. **5.** a formal or legal document. [f. OF or L (as INSTRUCT)]

instrumental /ɪnstrʊˈment(ə)l/ adj. **1.** serving as an instrument or means. **2.** (of music) performed on instruments. **3.** of or due to an instrument. **4.** (Gram., of a case) denoting the means. [f. F f. L (as prec.)]

instrumentalist n. a performer on a musical instrument. [f. prec.]

instrumentality /ɪnstrʊmenˈtælɪtɪ/ n. agency or means. [f. INSTRUMENTAL]

instrumentation /ɪnstrʊmenˈteɪʃ(ə)n/ n. **1.** the arrangement of music for instruments. **2.** the provision or use of mechanical or scientific instruments. [F, as INSTRUMENT]

insubordinate /ɪnsəˈbɔːdɪnət/ adj. disobedient, rebellious. —**insubordination** /-ˈneɪʃ(ə)n/ n. [f. IN-² + SUBORDINATE]

insubstantial /ɪnsəbˈstænʃ(ə)l/ adj. **1.** not existing in reality. **2.** not strongly made, lacking solidity. [f. L (as IN-², SUBSTANTIAL)]

insufferable /ɪnˈsʌfərəb(ə)l/ adj. **1.** intolerable. **2.** unbearably conceited or arrogant. —**insufferably** adv. [f. IN-² + SUFFERABLE]

insufficient /ɪnsəˈfɪʃ(ə)nt/ adj. not sufficient. —**insufficiency** n., **insufficiently** adv. [f. OF f. L (as IN-², SUFFICIENT)]

insufflate /ˈɪnsʌfleɪt/ v.t. to blow or breathe (air, gas, powder, etc.) into a cavity of the body; to treat thus. —**insufflation** /-ˈfleɪʃ(ə)n/ n., **insufflator** n. [f. L insufflare (IN-¹, sufflare blow upon)]

insular /ˈɪnsjʊlə(r)/ adj. **1.** of or on an island; forming an island. **2.** of or like islanders; unable or unwilling to take a broad mental view. —**insularity** /-ˈlærɪtɪ/ n. [as foll.]

insulate /ˈɪnsjʊleɪt/ v.t. to isolate, especially with a substance or device preventing the passage of electricity, heat, or sound. —**insulation** /-ˈleɪʃ(ə)n/ n., **insulator** n. [f. L insula island]

insulin /ˈɪnsjʊlɪn/ n. a hormone concerned with carbohydrate metabolism in man and some other vertebrates, produced in the pancreas and having effects that include the removal of sugar from the blood (so that a deficiency of insulin causes diabetes mellitus) and the promotion of protein synthesis and fat storage. (See BANTING¹.) [f. L insula island (because it is produced by the islets of Langerhans)]

insult /ɪnˈsʌlt/ v.t. **1.** to abuse scornfully. **2.** to offend the self-respect or modesty of. **3.** to affect and damage (an organ etc. of the body). —/ˈɪnsʌlt/ n. **1.** an insulting remark or action. **2.** damage to the body; a substance causing this. [f. L insultare leap upon, assail]

insuperable /ɪnˈsuːpərəb(ə)l/ adj. (of a barrier, difficulty, etc.) that cannot be surmounted or overcome. —**insuperability** /-ˈbɪlɪtɪ/ n., **insuperably** adv. [f. OF or L (IN-², superare overcome)]

insupportable /ɪnsəˈpɔːtəb(ə)l/ adj. unbearable; unjustifiable. —**insupportably** adv. [F (as IN-², SUPPORT)]

insurable /ɪnˈʃʊərəb(ə)l/ adj. that may be insured. [f. INSURE]

insurance /ɪnˈʃʊərəns/ n. **1.** a procedure or contract securing compensation for loss, damage, or injury, etc., especially in return for a premium paid in advance (see below). **2.** the business of providing this. **3.** the sum paid to effect such a contract, a premium. **4.** the amount paid in compensation. [f. OF (as ENSURE)]

Insurance was known in ancient Greece and among the maritime peoples with whom they traded. It developed first as a means of spreading the huge risks attendant on early maritime enterprises, and dates as a distinct contract from the 14th c., when it evolved in the commercial cities of Italy. It is found in the Admiralty Court in England in the 16th c.; life and fire insurance developed later. Lloyd's of London began in the 17th c., and the first US company was organized by Benjamin Franklin in 1752. Since the mid-19th c. insurance against other kinds of risk has developed greatly.

insure /ɪnˈʃʊə(r)/ v.t. to effect insurance against or with respect to. —**insurer** n. [var. of ENSURE]

insurgent /ɪnˈsɜːdʒ(ə)nt/ n. a rebel. —adj. in revolt, rebellious. —**insurgence** n., **insurgency** n. [F f. L (IN-¹, surgere rise)]

insurmountable /ɪnsəˈmaʊntəb(ə)l/ *adj.* unable to be surmounted, insuperable. [f. IN-² + SURMOUNTABLE]

insurrection /ɪnsəˈrekʃ(ə)n/ *n.* a rising in open resistance to established authority, an incipient rebellion. —**insurrectionist** *n.* [f. OF f. L (as INSURGENT)]

insusceptible /ɪnsəˈseptɪb(ə)l/ *adj.* not susceptible. [f. IN-² + SUSCEPTIBLE]

intact /ɪnˈtækt/ *adj.* **1.** undamaged, unimpaired. **2.** entire. **3.** untouched. [f. L (IN-², *tangere* touch)]

intaglio /ɪnˈtɑːlɪəʊ/ *n.* (*pl.* **-os**) an engraved design; a gem with an incised design. [It. (IN-¹, *tagliare* cut)]

intake /ˈɪnteɪk/ *n.* **1.** the action of taking in. **2.** the place where water is taken into a pipe, fuel or air into an engine etc. **3.** the persons, things, or quantity taken in or received.

intangible /ɪnˈtændʒɪb(ə)l/ *adj.* that cannot be touched or mentally grasped. —**intangibly** *adv.* [F or f. L (as IN-², TANGIBLE)]

integer /ˈɪntɪdʒə(r)/ *n.* a whole number. [L, = untouched, whole]

integral /ˈɪntɪgr(ə)l/ *adj.* **1.** of or necessary to a whole. **2.** complete, forming a whole. **3.** of or denoted by an integer. —*n.* (*Math.*) a quantity of which a given function is a derivative. —**integral calculus**, the branch of calculus concerned with finding integrals, their properties, etc. (see NEWTON). —**integrally** *adv.* [f. L (as prec.)]

integrate /ˈɪntɪgreɪt/ *v.t./i.* **1.** to combine (parts) into a whole. **2.** to bring or come into equal membership of a community; to end racial segregation (of or at). **3.** to complete by the addition of parts. **4.** (*Math.*) to find the integral of. —**integrated circuit**, a small piece of material replacing a conventional electric circuit of many components. —**integration** /-ˈreɪʃ(ə)n/ *n.* [f. L *integrare* make whole (as INTEGER)]

integrity /ɪnˈtegrɪtɪ/ *n.* **1.** honesty. **2.** wholeness; soundness. [f. F or L (as INTEGER)]

integument /ɪnˈtegjʊmənt/ *n.* a skin, husk, rind, or other covering. [L (*integere* cover)]

intellect /ˈɪntɪlekt/ *n.* **1.** the faculty of knowing and reasoning. **2.** ability to use this well; a person with such ability. [f. OF f. L (as INTELLIGENT)]

intellectual /ɪntɪˈlektjʊəl/ *adj.* of, requiring, or using the intellect; having a highly developed intellect. —*n.* an intellectual person. —**intellectuality** /-ˈælɪtɪ/ *n.*, **intellectually** *adv.* [f. L (as prec.)]

intellectualism *n.* **1.** (esp. excessive) exercise of the intellect alone. **2.** the theory that knowledge is wholly or mainly derived from pure intellect. —**intellectualist** *n.* [f. prec.]

intelligence /ɪnˈtelɪdʒ(ə)ns/ *n.* **1.** mental ability, the power of learning; quickness of understanding. **2.** information, news; the collection of this, especially for military purposes; persons engaged in such collection. —**intelligence quotient**, the ratio of a given person's intelligence to the normal or average. **intelligence test**, a test designed to measure intelligence rather than acquired knowledge (see BINET). [f. OF f. L (as foll.)]

intelligent /ɪnˈtelɪdʒ(ə)nt/ *adj.* having or showing great intelligence, clever. —**intelligently** *adv.* [f. L *intellegere* understand]

intelligentsia /ɪntelɪˈdʒentsɪə/ *n.* intellectuals as a class, especially those regarded as cultured and politically enterprising. [Russ. f. Polish f. L (as INTELLIGENCE)]

intelligible /ɪnˈtelɪdʒɪb(ə)l/ *adj.* that can be understood. —**intelligibility** /-ˈbɪlɪtɪ/ *n.*, **intelligibly** *adv.* [as INTELLIGENT]

intemperate /ɪnˈtempərət/ *adj.* **1.** lacking moderation. **2.** excessive in indulging the appetite; addicted to drinking. —**intemperance** *n.*, **intemperately** *adv.* [f. L (as IN-², TEMPERATE)]

intend /ɪnˈtend/ *v.t.* **1.** to have as one's purpose or wish. **2.** to plan or destine (a person or thing *for* a purpose, *as* something, *to do*). [f. L *intendere* (IN-¹, *tendere* stretch, tend)]

intended *adj.* done on purpose. —*n.* (*colloq.*) a fiancé(e). [f. prec.]

intense /ɪnˈtens/ *adj.* **1.** strong in quality or degree, violent, vehement; having a quality strongly. **2.** eager, ardent, strenuous. **3.** feeling or apt to feel emotion strongly. —**intensely** *adv.*, **intenseness** *n.* [f. OF or L (as INTEND)]

intensify /ɪnˈtensɪfaɪ/ *v.t./i.* to make or become intense or more intense. —**intensification** /-fɪˈkeɪʃ(ə)n/ *n.* [f. prec.]

intensity /ɪnˈtensɪtɪ/ *n.* **1.** intenseness. **2.** amount of force, brightness, etc. [f. prec.]

intensive /ɪnˈtensɪv/ *adj.* **1.** employing much effort, concentrated. **2.** (of words) giving emphasis. **3.** (as *suffix*) making much use of (*labour-intensive*). —**intensive care**, medical treatment with constant supervision of the patient. —**intensively** *adv.* [f. F or L (as INTEND)]

intent /ɪnˈtent/ *n.* intention. —*adj.* **1.** with one's mind or intention fixed on a purpose. **2.** with one's attention concentrated (*on*); earnest, eager. —**to all intents and purposes**, virtually, practically. —**intently** *adv.*, **intentness** *n.* [f. OF or L (as INTEND)]

intention /ɪnˈtenʃ(ə)n/ *n.* **1.** a thing intended, a purpose. **2.** intending. [f. OF f. L (as INTEND)]

intentional *adj.* done on purpose, intended. —**intentionally** *adv.* [f. prec.]

inter /ɪnˈtɜː(r)/ *v.t.* (**-rr-**) to place (a corpse etc.) in the earth or a tomb, to bury. [f. OF *enterrer* f. L *terra* earth]

inter- *prefix* between, among, mutually, reciprocally. [f. OF *entre-* or L *inter-*]

interact /ɪntərˈækt/ *v.i.* to act on each other. —**interaction** *n.*, **interactive** *adj.*

inter alia /ɪntə(r) ˈeɪlɪə/ among other things. [L]

interbreed /ɪntəˈbriːd/ *v.t./i.* to breed with each other; to cause animals to do this; to produce (a hybrid individual).

intercalary /ɪntəˈkælərɪ/ *adj.* (of a day or days of a month) inserted to harmonize the calendar with the solar year; (of a year) having such additions; interpolated. [f. L (as foll.)]

intercalate /ɪnˈtɜːkəleɪt/ *v.t.* to interpose; to insert (an intercalary day etc.). —**intercalation** /-ˈleɪʃ(ə)n/ *n.* [f. L *intercalare* (INTER-, *calare* proclaim)]

intercede /ɪntəˈsiːd/ *v.i.* to interpose on another's behalf, to mediate; to plead (*with* a person *for* another). [f. F or L *intercedere* (INTER-, *cedere* go)]

intercept /ɪntəˈsept/ *v.t.* to seize, catch, or stop in transit or progress; to cut off (light etc. *from*). —/ˈɪntəsept/ *n.* **1.** a message or conversation picked up by intercepting a letter or a telephone or radio conversation. **2.** a device for performing such interception. —**interception** *n.*, **interceptive** *adj.*, **interceptor** *n.* [f. L *intercipere* (INTER-, *capere* catch)]

intercession /ɪntəˈseʃ(ə)n/ *n.* interceding. —**intercessor** *n.* [F or f. L (as INTERCEDE)]

interchange /ɪntəˈtʃeɪndʒ/ *v.t.* **1.** to put (things) in each other's place. **2.** (of two persons) to exchange (things) with each other. **3.** to alternate. —/ˈɪntətʃeɪndʒ/ *n.* **1.** an exchange (*of* things) between persons etc. **2.** alternation. **3.** a junction of roads on different levels. —**interchangeability** /-ə'bɪlɪtɪ/ *n.*, **interchangeable** *adj.*

inter-city /ɪntəˈsɪtɪ/ *adj.* existing or travelling between cities.

intercom /ˈɪntəkɒm/ *n.* (*colloq.*) a system of inter-communication operating like a telephone. [abbr.]

intercommunicate /ɪntəkəˈmjuːnɪkeɪt/ *v.i.* to communicate mutually; to have free passage into each other. —**intercommunication** /-ˈkeɪʃ(ə)n/ *n.*

intercommunion /ɪntəkəˈmjuːnɪən/ *n.* mutual communion, especially between Christian denominations.

interconnect /ɪntəkəˈnekt/ *v.t./i.* to connect with each other. —**interconnection** *n.*

intercontinental /ɪntəkɒntɪˈnent(ə)l/ *adj.* connecting or travelling between continents.

intercourse /ˈɪntəkɔːs/ *n.* **1.** social communication between individuals. **2.** communication between countries etc., especially in trade. **3.** sexual intercourse (see SEXUAL).

interdenominational /ɪntədɪnɒmɪˈneɪʃən(ə)l/ *adj.* of or involving more than one Christian denomination.

interdepartmental /ɪntədiːpɑːtˈment(ə)l/ *adj.* of more than one department.

interdependent /ɪntədɪˈpend(ə)nt/ *adj.* dependent on each other. —**interdependence** *n.*, **interdependency** *n.*

interdict /ɪntəˈdɪkt/ *v.t.* to prohibit or forbid authoritatively. —/ˈɪntədɪkt/ *n.* an authoritative prohibition; (*RC Church*) a sentence debarring a person or place from ecclesiastical functions etc. —**interdiction** /-ˈdɪkʃ(ə)n/ *n.*, **interdictory** /-ˈdɪktərɪ/ *adj.* [f. OF f. L (INTER-, *dicere* say)]

interdisciplinary /ɪntədɪsɪˈplɪnərɪ/ *adj.* of or involving different branches of learning.

interest /ˈɪntrəst/ *n.* **1.** a feeling of curiosity or concern; a quality causing this; the thing towards which one feels it. **2.** advantage, benefit. **3.** money paid for the use of a loan of money. **4.** a legal concern, title, or right (*in* property); a money stake (*in* a business); a thing in which one has a stake or concern. —*v.t.* to arouse the interest of; to cause to be interested or involved (*in*). —**compound interest,** interest (on a loan) reckoned on the principal and accumulations of interest. **simple interest,** interest reckoned on the principal only and paid at fixed intervals. [f. AF f. L, = it matters]

interested *adj.* **1.** feeling interest or curiosity. **2.** having a private interest, not impartial. [f. prec.]

interesting *adj.* causing curiosity, holding the attention. [f. INTEREST]

interface *n.* **1.** a surface forming the common boundary of two regions. **2.** a place or piece of equipment where interaction occurs between two systems etc.

interfere /ɪntə'fɪə(r)/ *v.i.* **1.** to take part in dealing with others' affairs without right or invitation. **2.** to obstruct wholly or partially. [f. OF, = strike one another (f. L INTER-, *ferire* strike)]

interference *n.* **1.** interfering. **2.** the fading of received radio signals because of atmospherics or unwanted signals. [f. prec.]

interferon /ɪntə'fɪərɒn/ *n.* a protein released by an animal cell, usually in response to the entry of a virus, which has the property of inhibiting further development of viruses of any kind in the animal or in others of the same species. Its discovery by the virologists A. Isaacs and J. Lindenmann was announced in 1957. [f. INTERFERE]

interfuse /ɪntə'fjuːz/ *v.t./i.* to intersperse; to blend. — **interfusion** *n.* [f. L *interfundere* (INTER-, *fundere* pour)]

interglacial /ɪntə'gleɪʃ(ə)l/ *n.* a period of milder climate between glacial periods.

interim /'ɪntərɪm/ *n.* the intervening time. —*adj.* temporary, provisional. [L, = meanwhile]

interior /ɪn'tɪərɪə(r)/ *n.* **1.** the inner part, the inside. **2.** an inland region. **3.** the inside of a room etc.; a picture of this. **4.** the home affairs of a country. —*adj.* **1.** situated or coming from within. **2.** further in. **3.** inland. **4.** internal, domestic. **5.** existing in the mind. [L, compar. of *inter* among]

interject /ɪntə'dʒekt/ *v.t.* to put in (words) abruptly or parenthetically. [f. L *interjicere* (INTER-, *jacere* throw)]

interjection /ɪntə'dʒekʃ(ə)n/ *n.* an exclamation, especially as a part of speech (e.g. *ah*, *whew*). [f. OF f. L (as prec.)]

interlace /ɪntə'leɪs/ *v.t./i.* to bind intricately together, to interweave; to cross each other intricately. —**interlacement** *n.*

interlard /ɪntə'lɑːd/ *v.t.* to mix (writing or speech *with* unusual words or phrases).

interleave /ɪntə'liːv/ *v.t.* to insert leaves, usually blank, between the leaves of (a book). [f. INTER- + LEAF]

interlinear /ɪntə'lɪnɪə(r)/ *adj.* written or printed between the lines of a text.

interlink /ɪntə'lɪŋk/ *v.t./i.* to link together.

interlock /ɪntə'lɒk/ *v.t./i.* to engage with each other by overlapping; to lock or clasp in each other. —*adj.* (of a fabric) knitted with closely interlocking stitches. —*n.* such a fabric. [f. INTER- + LOCK¹]

interlocutor /ɪntə'lɒkjʊtə(r)/ *n.* one who takes part in a conversation. [f. L (INTER-, *loqui* speak)]

interlocutory /ɪntə'lɒkʊtərɪ/ *adj.* **1.** of dialogue. **2.** (of a decree etc.) given in the course of a legal action. [f. L (as prec.)]

interloper /'ɪntələʊpə(r)/ *n.* an intruder, one who thrusts himself into others' affairs, especially for profit. [f. INTER- + *loper* (as in *landloper* vagabond, f. Du.)]

interlude /'ɪntəluːd/ *n.* **1.** a pause between the parts of a play etc.; something performed during this. **2.** an intervening time or event of a different character. **3.** a piece of music played between the verses of a hymn etc. [f. L *interludium* (INTER-, *ludus* play)]

intermarry /ɪntə'mærɪ/ *v.i.* (of tribes, nations, families, etc.) to become connected by marriage. —**intermarriage** *n.*

intermediary /ɪntə'miːdɪərɪ/ *n.* **1.** a mediator. **2.** an intermediate thing. —*adj.* **1.** acting as a mediator. **2.** intermediate. [f. F ult. f. L *intermedius* (INTER-, *medius* middle)]

intermediate /ɪntə'miːdɪət/ *adj.* coming between two things in time, place, character, etc. —*n.* **1.** an intermediate thing. **2.** a chemical compound formed by one reaction and then taking part in another. [f. L (as prec.)]

interment /ɪn'tɜːmənt/ *n.* a burial. [f. INTER]

intermezzo /ɪntə'metsəʊ/ *n.* (*pl.* -**zzi** /-tsiː/) **1.** a short connecting movement in a musical work, or a similar but independent piece. **2.** a short light dramatic or other

performance between the acts of a play or opera. [It. (as INTERMEDIARY)]

interminable /ɪn'tɜːmɪnəb(ə)l/ *adj.* tediously long; endless. —**interminably** *adv.* [f. L (as IN-², TERMINABLE)]

intermingle /ɪntə'mɪŋg(ə)l/ *v.t./i.* to mix together, to mingle.

intermission /ɪntə'mɪʃ(ə)n/ *n.* an interval, a pause in work or action. [F or f. L (as foll.)]

intermittent /ɪntə'mɪt(ə)nt/ *adj.* occurring at intervals, not continuous. —**intermittently** *adv.* [f. L (INTER-, *mittere* let go)]

intermix /ɪntə'mɪks/ *v.t./i.* to mix together.

intern /ɪn'tɜːn/ *v.t.* to oblige (a prisoner, alien, etc.) to live within prescribed limits. —/'ɪntɜːn/ *n.* (*US*) a recent graduate or advanced student living in a hospital and acting as an assistant physician or surgeon. —**internment** *n.* [f. F (as foll.)]

internal /ɪn'tɜːn(ə)l/ *adj.* **1.** of or in the inside or invisible part. **2.** relating or applied to the interior of the body. **3.** of a country's domestic affairs. **4.** of students attending a university as well as taking its examinations. **5.** used or applying within an organization. **6.** intrinsic. **7.** of the mind or soul. —**internal evidence,** evidence derived from the contents of the thing discussed. —**internality** /-'nælɪtɪ/ *n.*, **internally** *adv.* [f. L *internus*]

internal-combustion engine a form of heat-engine in which fuel is burnt inside the cylinder of the engine instead of in a separate boiler (as used in a steam-engine). The gases produced attain high values of pressure and temperature, driving the piston outwards as they expand. The exhaust gases are then released and a fresh supply of air (in a diesel engine) or a mixture of air and fuel (in a spark-ignition engine) is admitted and compressed before combustion again takes place. Most engines work on a four-stroke cycle (see OTTO), with four piston-strokes for each explosion, but two-stroke engines are used where lower power is sufficient. The advantage of internal-combustion engines over external combustion is their compactness, with all processes taking place in a single mechanism, giving a high output of power for a low weight, thus making them very suitable for transport purposes; their disadvantage is the need for very specific types of liquid or gaseous fuels, while external-combustion engines can use coal or any other fuel. (See ill. CAR.)

Internal-combustion engines originated in the early 19th c. The first reliable one was that of J. J. É. Lenoir in Paris in 1859. It ran slowly, lacked power, and consumed large quantities of fuel, but was the first real challenge to the dominance of steam. In 1862 a French engineer, Alphonse de Rochas, described a four-stroke cycle, but his work remained theoretical and he never made an engine; the principle was re-invented by Otto.

International *n.* an international Socialist organization. The First International was formed by Karl Marx in London in 1864 as an international working men's association and was dissolved twelve years later after internal wrangling between Marxists and Anarchists. The Second International was formed in Paris in 1889 and, although gravely weakened by the First World War, still survives as a loose association of Social Democrats. The Third International, also known as the Comintern, was formed by the Bolsheviks in 1919 to further the cause of the world revolution. Active if seldom effective between the wars, it was abolished in 1943 as a gesture towards Russia's allies. The Fourth International, a body of Trotskyist organizations, was formed in 1938 in opposition to the policies of the Stalin-dominated Third International. [= foll.]

international /ɪntə'næʃən(ə)l/ *adj.* existing or carried on between nations; agreed on or used by all or many nations. —*n.* **1.** a contest, usually in sport, between representatives of different nations. **2.** such a representative. —**internationality** /-'nælɪtɪ/ *n.*, **internationally** *adv.*

International Court of Justice a judicial court of the United Nations which replaced the Cour Permanente de Justice in 1945 and meets at The Hague.

Internationale /ɪntənæʃ(ə)'nɑːl/ *n.* **1.** a revolutionary hymn composed by P. Degeyter (d. 1932) to words by Eugène Pottier, a Lisle woodworker, in 1871. It was adopted by French socialists and subsequently by others, and was the official anthem of Communist Russia until 1 Jan. 1944. **2.** the International. [F, = international (sc. *chanson* song)]

internationalism *n.* **1.** advocacy of the community of interests among nations. **2.** support of an International. —**internationalist** *n.* [f. INTERNATIONAL]

internationalize *v.t.* to make international; to bring under the protection or control of two or more nations. [f. INTERNATIONAL]

International Monetary Fund an international organization affiliated to the UN, with headquarters in Washington, DC. Established in 1945, it exists to promote international trade and monetary co-operation, and the stabilization of exchange rates. Member countries contribute in gold and in their own currencies to provide a reserve on which they may draw (on certain conditions) to meet foreign obligations during periods of deficit in their international balance of payments.

International Phonetic Alphabet a set of phonetic symbols for international use, introduced in the late 19th c. by the International Phonetic Association, based on the Roman and Greek alphabets with the addition of some special symbols and diacritical marks.

international style an architectural style of the 20th c., associated especially with Gropius, Wright, and Le Corbusier, so called because it breached national and cultural barriers. It is characterized by the use of new building materials (especially steel and reinforced concrete), wide windows, uninterrupted interior spaces, simple lines, and strict geometric forms.

International System (of Units) see SI.

internecine /ɪntəˈniːsaɪn/ *adj.* mutually destructive. [orig. = deadly, murderous; f. L (INTER-, *necare* kill)]

internee /ɪntɜːˈniː/ *n.* a person interned. [f. INTERN]

internist /ɪnˈtɜːnɪst/ *n.* a specialist in internal diseases; (*US*) a general practitioner. [f. INTERNAL]

interpenetrate /ɪntəˈpenɪtreɪt/ *v.t./i.* to penetrate each other; to pervade. —**interpenetration** /-ˈtreɪʃ(ə)n/ *n.*

interpersonal /ɪntəˈpɜːs(ə)n(ə)l/ *adj.* between persons.

interplanetary /ɪntəˈplænɪtərɪ/ *adj.* between planets; of travel between planets.

interplay /ˈɪntəpleɪ/ *n.* interaction.

Interpol /ˈɪntəpɒl/ *n.* International Criminal Police Commission, an organization (founded in 1923, with headquarters in Paris) that co-ordinates investigations made by the police forces of member countries into crimes with an international basis. [abbr. *International police*]

interpolate /ɪnˈtɜːpəleɪt/ *v.t.* **1.** to interject. **2.** to insert (new material) misleadingly into a book etc.; to make such insertions in (a book). **3.** to insert (terms) in a mathematical series; to estimate (values) from known ones in the same range. —**interpolation** /-ˈleɪʃ(ə)n/ *n.*, **interpolator** *n.* [f. L *interpolare* furbish up (INTER-, *-polare* rel. to *polire* polish)]

interpose /ɪntəˈpəʊz/ *v.t./i.* **1.** to insert (a thing *between* others). **2.** to say (words) as an interruption; to speak thus. **3.** to exercise or advance (a veto or objection) so as to interfere. **4.** to intervene (*between* parties). —**interposition** /-pəˈzɪʃ(ə)n/ *n.* [f. F (INTER-, *ponere* put)]

interpret /ɪnˈtɜːprɪt/ *v.t./i.* **1.** to explain the meaning of. **2.** to understand in a specified way. **3.** to act as interpreter. —**interpretation** /-ˈteɪʃ(ə)n/ *n.*, **interpretative** *adj.*, **interpretive** *adj.* [f. OF or L (*interpres* one who explains)]

interpreter *n.* one who interprets, especially one who orally translates the words of persons speaking different languages. [f. prec.]

interregnum /ɪntəˈregnəm/ *n.* (*pl.* **-ums**) **1.** an interval when usual government is suspended, especially between successive reigns. **2.** an interval, a pause. [L (INTER-, *regnum* reign)]

interrelated /ɪntərɪˈleɪtɪd/ *adj.* related to each other. —**interrelation** *n.*

interrogate /ɪnˈterəgeɪt/ *v.t.* to question closely or formally. —**interrogation** /-ˈgeɪʃ(ə)n/ *n.*, **interrogator** *n.* [f. L *interrogare* (INTER-, *rogare* ask)]

interrogative /ɪntəˈrɒgətɪv/ *adj.* of or like or used in questions. —*n.* an interrogative word (e.g. *who?*). —**interrogatively** *adv.* [as prec.]

interrogatory /ɪntəˈrɒgətərɪ/ *adj.* questioning. —*n.* a formal set of questions. [as INTERROGATE]

interrupt /ɪntəˈrʌpt/ *v.t.* **1.** to break the continuity of. **2.** to break the flow of (a speech or speaker etc.) by inserting a remark. **3.** to obstruct (a view etc.). —**interrupter** *n.*, **interruption** *n.* [f. L *interrumpere* (INTER-, *rumpere* break)]

intersect /ɪntəˈsekt/ *v.t./i.* **1.** to divide (a thing) by passing or lying across it. **2.** (of lines, roads, etc.) to cross each other. [f. L *intersecare* (INTER-, *secare* cut)]

intersection *n.* **1.** a place where two roads intersect. **2.**

the point or line common to lines or planes that intersect. **3.** intersecting. [as prec.]

interspace /ˈɪntəspeɪs/ *n.* an intervening space. —/ɪntəˈspeɪs/ *v.t.* to put a space or spaces between.

intersperse /ɪntəˈspɜːs/ *v.t.* to insert contrasting material here and there in (a thing); to scatter (material) thus. [f. L *interspergere* (INTER-, *spargere* scatter)]

interstate /ˈɪntəsteɪt/ *adj.* existing or carried on between States especially of the USA.

interstellar /ɪntəˈstelə(r)/ *adj.* between stars. [f. INTER- + L *stella* star]

interstice /ɪnˈtɜːstɪs/ *n.* an intervening space; a chink, a crevice. [f. L *interstitium* (INTER-, *sistere* stand)]

interstitial /ɪntəˈstɪʃ(ə)l/ *adj.* of or in or forming interstices. —**interstitially** *adv.* [as prec.]

intertwine /ɪntəˈtwaɪn/ *v.t./i.* to twine closely together.

interval /ˈɪntəv(ə)l/ *n.* **1.** an intervening time or space. **2.** a pause, a break, especially between parts of a performance. **3.** the difference of pitch between two sounds. —**at intervals,** here and there, now and then. [f. L, = space between ramparts (INTER-, *vallum* rampart)]

intervene /ɪntəˈviːn/ *v.i.* **1.** to occur in time between events. **2.** to cause hindrance by occurring; to enter a discussion or dispute etc. in order to change its course or resolve it. **3.** to come in as an extraneous thing. **4.** to be situated *between* others. [f. L *intervenire* (INTER-, *venire* come)]

intervention /ɪntəˈvenʃ(ə)n/ *n.* intervening, interference, especially by the State; mediation. [f. prec.]

interventionist *n.* one who favours intervention. [f. prec.]

interview /ˈɪntəvjuː/ *n.* **1.** a conversation between a reporter and a person whose views he wishes to publish or broadcast. **2.** an oral examination of an applicant. **3.** a meeting of persons face to face, especially for consultation. —*v.t.* to have an interview with. —**interviewee** /-vjuːˈiː/ *n.*, **interviewer** *n.* [f. F *entrevue* (INTER-, VIEW)]

inter-war /ɪntəˈwɔː(r)/ *adj.* existing in the period between two wars.

interweave /ɪntəˈwiːv/ *v.t.* to weave together; to blend intimately.

intestate /ɪnˈtesteɪt/ *adj.* not having made a will before death. —*n.* a person who has died intestate. —**intestacy** /ɪnˈtestəsɪ/ *n.* [f. L (IN-², *testari* make a will)]

intestine /ɪnˈtestɪn/ *n.* (in *sing.* or *pl.*) the lower part of the alimentary canal. —**intestinal** *adj.* [f. L (*intestinus* internal)]

intimacy /ˈɪntɪməsɪ/ *n.* **1.** being intimate. **2.** an intimate act; sexual intercourse. [f. foll.]

intimate /ˈɪntɪmət/ *adj.* **1.** closely acquainted, familiar. **2.** private and personal. **3.** having sexual relations (*with*). **4.** (of knowledge) detailed, thorough. **5.** (of relations between things) close. —*n.* an intimate friend. —/-eɪt/ *v.t.* to state or make known; to imply, to hint. —**intimately** *adv.*, **intimation** /-ˈmeɪʃ(ə)n/ *n.* [f. L (*intimus* inmost)]

intimidate /ɪnˈtɪmɪdeɪt/ *v.t.* to frighten, especially in order to subdue or influence. —**intimidation** /-ˈdeɪʃ(ə)n/ *n.*, **intimidator** *n.* [f. L *intimidare* (IN-¹, *timidus* timid)]

into /ˈɪntʊ, -tə/ *prep.* **1.** expressing motion or direction to a point on or within. **2.** expressing a change of state. **3.** (*colloq.*) interested and involved in. [OE (as IN, TO)]

intolerable /ɪnˈtɒlərəb(ə)l/ *adj.* that cannot be endured. —**intolerableness** *n.*, **intolerably** *adv.* [f. OF or L (as IN-², TOLERABLE)]

intolerant /ɪnˈtɒlərənt/ *adj.* not tolerant, especially of views or beliefs differing from one's own. —**intolerance** *n.*, **intolerantly** *adv.* [f. L (as IN-², TOLERANT)]

intonation /ɪntəˈneɪʃ(ə)n/ *n.* **1.** intoning. **2.** a modulation of the voice, a slight accent. [f. L (as foll.)]

intone /ɪnˈtəʊn/ *v.t.* **1.** to recite (prayers etc.) with prolonged sounds, especially in a monotone. **2.** to utter with a particular tone. [f. L *intonare* (IN-¹, *tonus* tone)]

in toto /ɪn ˈtəʊtəʊ/ completely. [L]

intoxicant /ɪnˈtɒksɪkənt/ *adj.* intoxicating. —*n.* an intoxicant drink or substance. [as foll.]

intoxicate /ɪnˈtɒksɪkeɪt/ *v.t.* to make drunk; to excite or elate beyond self-control. —**intoxication** /-ˈkeɪʃ(ə)n/ *n.* [f. L *intoxicare* poison (IN-¹, *toxicum* poison)]

intra- *prefix* within, on the inside. [f. L *intra* inside]

intractable /ɪnˈtræktəb(ə)l/ *adj.* hard to control or deal with; difficult, stubborn. —**intractability** /-ˈbɪlɪtɪ/ *n.*, **intractably** *adv.* [f. L (as IN-², TRACTABLE)]

intramural /ɪntrəˈmjʊər(ə)l/ *adj.* **1.** situated or done within walls. **2.** forming part of ordinary university work. —**intramurally** *adv.* [f. INTRA- + L *murus* wall]

intransigent /ɪnˈtrænsɪdʒ(ə)nt/ *adj.* uncompromising, stubborn. —*n.* an intransigent person. —**intransigence** *n.* [f. F f. Sp. *los intransigentes* extreme republicans (as IN-², TRANSACT)]

intransitive /ɪnˈtrænsɪtɪv/ *adj.* (of a verb) not taking a direct object. —**intransitively** *adv.* [f. L (as IN-², TRANSITIVE)]

intra-uterine /ɪntrəˈjuːtəraɪn, -rɪn/ *adj.* within the womb.

intravenous /ɪntrəˈviːnəs/ *adj.* in or into a vein or veins. —**intravenously** *adv.* [f. INTRA- + L *vena* vein]

in-tray *n.* a tray for incoming documents.

intrepid /ɪnˈtrepɪd/ *adj.* fearless, brave. —**intrepidity** /ɪntrɪˈpɪdɪtɪ/ *n.*, **intrepidly** *adv.* [f. F or L (IN-², *trepidus* alarmed)]

intricate /ˈɪntrɪkət/ *adj.* very complicated. —**intricacy** /ˈɪntrɪkəsɪ/ *n.*, **intricately** *adv.* [f. L (IN-¹, *tricae* tricks, perplexities)]

intrigue /ɪnˈtriːg/ *v.t./i.* **1.** to plot in an underhand way; to use secret influence. **2.** to rouse the interest or curiosity of. —*also* ˈɪn-/ *n.* **1.** underhand plotting or plot. **2.** (*archaic*) a secret love affair. [f. F f. It. (as prec.)]

intrinsic /ɪnˈtrɪnsɪk/ *adj.* inherent, essential. —**intrinsically** *adv.* [f. F f. L *intrinsecus* inwardly]

intro- *prefix* into, inwards. [f. L, = to the inside]

introduce /ɪntrəˈdjuːs/ *v.t.* **1.** to make known by name *to* another. **2.** to announce or present to an audience. **3.** to bring (a bill) before Parliament. **4.** to cause to become acquainted with a subject. **5.** to bring (a custom or idea etc.) into use or into a system. **6.** to bring or put in. [f. L *introducere* (INTRO-, *ducere* lead)]

introduction /ɪntrəˈdʌkʃ(ə)n/ *n.* **1.** introducing. **2.** a formal presentation of a person to another. **3.** an explanatory section at the beginning of a book etc. **4.** an introductory treatise. **5.** a thing introduced. [f. OF or L (as prec.)]

introductory /ɪntrəˈdʌktərɪ/ *adj.* that introduces; preliminary. [f. L (as INTRODUCE)]

introit /ˈɪntrɔɪt/ *n.* a psalm or antiphon sung or said while a priest approaches the altar for Eucharist. [f. OF f. L *introitus* entrance]

introspection /ɪntrəˈspekʃ(ə)n/ *n.* examining one's own thoughts. —**introspective** *adj.* [f. L (INTRO-, *specere* look)]

introvert /ˈɪntrəvɜːt/ *n.* an introverted person. [f. foll.]

introverted /ˈɪntrəvɜːtɪd/ *adj.* principally interested in one's own thoughts; reserved, shy. —**introversion** /-ˈvɜːʃ(ə)n/ *n.* [f. INTRO- + L *vertere* turn]

intrude /ɪnˈtruːd/ *v.t./i.* to force or come uninvited or unwanted. [f. L *intrudere* (IN-¹, *trudere* thrust)]

intruder *n.* one who intrudes; a burglar; a raiding aircraft. [f. prec.]

intrusion /ɪnˈtruːʒ(ə)n/ *n.* **1.** intruding. **2.** an influx of molten rock between strata etc. —**intrusive** *adj.* [f. OF or L (as prec.)]

intuition /ɪntjuːˈɪʃ(ə)n/ *n.* immediate apprehension by the mind without reasoning; immediate apprehension by a sense. —**intuitional** *adj.* [f. L (IN-¹, *tuēri* look)]

intuitionism /ɪntjuːˈɪʃ(ə)nɪz(ə)m/ *n.* the theory that the perception of truth is by intuition; the theory that in perception objects are known immediately by intuition; the theory that ethical principles are matters of intuition. [f. prec.]

intuitive /ɪnˈtjuːɪtɪv/ *adj.* of, having, or perceived by intuition. —**intuitively** *adv.* [f. L (as INTUITION)]

inundate /ˈɪnʌndeɪt/ *v.t.* to flood or overwhelm (*with*). —**inundation** /-ˈdeɪʃ(ə)n/ *n.* [f. L *inundare* flow (IN-¹, *unda* wave)]

inure /ɪˈnjʊə(r)/ *v.t./i.* **1.** to accustom (*to* a difficulty etc.). **2.** (*Law*) to take effect. —**inurement** *n.* [f. OF *euvre* work f. L *opera*]

in vacuo /ɪn ˈvækjuːəʊ/ in a vacuum. [L]

invade /ɪnˈveɪd/ *v.t.* **1.** to enter (a country) with armed forces to control or subdue it. **2.** to swarm into. **3.** (of a disease etc.) to attack. **4.** to encroach on (rights, esp. privacy). —**invader** *n.* [f. L *invadere* (IN-¹, *vadere* go)]

invalid¹ /ˈɪnvəliːd/ *n.* a person enfeebled or disabled by illness or injury. —*adj.* of or for invalids; being an invalid. —*v.t.* **1.** to remove from active service or send away (*home* etc.) as an invalid. **2.** to disable by illness. —**invalidism** *n.* [f. L (IN-², *validus* strong); = INVALID², with F pronunc.]

invalid² /ɪnˈvælɪd/ *adj.* not valid. [f. L (as IN-², VALID)]

invalidate /ɪnˈvælɪdeɪt/ *v.t.* to make (an argument, con-

tract, etc.) invalid. —**invalidation** /-ˈdeɪʃ(ə)n/ *n.* [f. L (as prec.)]

invalidity /ɪnvəˈlɪdɪtɪ/ *n.* **1.** lack of validity. **2.** being an invalid. [f. F or L (as INVALID¹,²)]

invaluable /ɪnˈvæljuːəb(ə)l/ *adj.* having a value that is too great to be measured. —**invaluably** *adv.* [f. IN-² VALUABLE]

invariable /ɪnˈveərɪəb(ə)l/ *adj.* not variable, always the same. —**invariably** *adv.* [F or f. L (as IN-², VARIABLE)]

invasion /ɪnˈveɪʒ(ə)n/ *n.* invading, being invaded. —**invasive** *adj.* [F or f. L (as INVADE)]

invected /ɪnˈvektɪd/ *adj.* (in heraldry) bordered by or consisting of a series of small convex lobes (ill. HERALDRY). [as INVEIGH]

invective /ɪnˈvektɪv/ *n.* a strong verbal attack; abusive language. [f. OF f. L (as foll.)]

inveigh /ɪnˈveɪ/ *v.i.* to speak or write with strong hostility (*against*). [f. L *invehi* ride into, assail]

inveigle /ɪnˈveɪg(ə)l/ *v.t.* to entice, to persuade by guile (*into*). —**inveiglement** *n.* [f. OF *aveugler* to blind]

invent /ɪnˈvent/ *v.t.* **1.** to create by thought, to make or design (something that did not exist before). **2.** to concoct (a false or fictional story). —**inventor** *n.* [f. L *invenire* discover]

invention /ɪnˈvenʃ(ə)n/ *n.* **1.** inventing. **2.** a thing invented; a fictitious story. **3.** inventiveness. [f. L (as prec.)]

inventive /ɪnˈventɪv/ *adj.* able to invent. —**inventiveness** *n.* [f. F or L (as INVENT)]

inventory /ˈɪnvəntərɪ/ *n.* a detailed list (of goods etc.); goods in this. —*v.t.* to make an inventory of; to enter (goods) in an inventory. [f. L *inventorium* (as INVENT)]

inverse /ɪnˈvɜːs, ˈɪn-/ *adj.* **1.** inverted in position or order or relation. **2.** (of a proportion or ratio) between two quantities one of which increases in proportion as the other decreases. —*n.* **1.** an inverted state. **2.** a thing that is the direct opposite (*of* another). —**inversely** *adv.* [f. L (as INVERT)]

inversion /ɪnˈvɜːʃ(ə)n/ *n.* turning upside down; reversal of normal order, position, or relation. —**inversive** *adj.* [as foll.]

invert /ɪnˈvɜːt/ *v.t.* to turn upside down; to reverse the position, order, or relation of. —/ˈɪnvɜːt/ *n.* a homosexual. —**inverted commas**, quotation marks. [f. L *invertere* (IN-¹, *vertere* turn)]

invertebrate /ɪnˈvɜːtɪbrət/ *adj.* without a backbone or spinal column. —*n.* an invertebrate animal. [f. IN-² VERTEBRATE]

invest /ɪnˈvest/ *v.t./i.* **1.** to use (money) to buy stocks, shares, or property, etc. so as to earn interest or bring profit; to spend money, time, or effort *in* obtaining stocks etc. or something useful. **2.** to end *with* qualities, insignia, or rank. **3.** to clothe, to cover (as) with a garment. **4.** to lay siege to. [f. F or L *investire* (IN-¹, *vestire* clothe)]

investigate /ɪnˈvestɪgeɪt/ *v.t./i.* to make a careful study of (a thing) in order to discover the facts about it; to make a systematic inquiry. —**investigation** /-ˈgeɪʃ(ə)n/ *n.*, **investigative** *adj.*, **investigator** *n.*, **investigatory** *adj.* [f. L *investigare* (IN-¹, *vestigare* track)]

investiture /ɪnˈvestɪtʃə(r)/ *n.* the process of investing a person with rank or office, etc.; a ceremony at which the sovereign confers honours. [f. L (as INVEST)]

investment *n.* **1.** investing. **2.** money invested. **3.** something in which money, time, or effort is invested. [f. INVEST]

investor *n.* one who invests money. [as prec.]

inveterate /ɪnˈvetərət/ *adj.* (of a habit etc.) deep-rooted; (of a person) confirmed in a habit etc. —**inveteracy** *n.* [f. L *inveterare* (IN-¹, *vetus* old)]

invidious /ɪnˈvɪdɪəs/ *adj.* likely to excite ill-will or indignation against the performer, possessor, etc. —**invidiously** *adv.* [f. L (*invidia* envy)]

invigilate /ɪnˈvɪdʒɪleɪt/ *v.i.* to supervise candidates at an examination. —**invigilation** /-ˈleɪʃ(ə)n/ *n.*, **invigilator** *n.* [f. L *invigilare* (IN-¹, *vigilare* keep watch)]

invigorate /ɪnˈvɪgəreɪt/ *v.t.* to give vigour or strength to. [f. L (IN-¹, *vigorare* make strong)]

invincible /ɪnˈvɪnsɪb(ə)l/ *adj.* unconquerable. —**invincibility** /-ˈbɪlɪtɪ/ *n.*, **invincibly** *adv.* [f. OF f. L (IN-², *vincere* conquer)]

inviolable /ɪnˈvaɪələb(ə)l/ *adj.* not to be violated or profaned. —**inviolability** /-ˈbɪlɪtɪ/ *n.*, **inviolably** *adv.* [F or f. L (as IN-², VIOLABLE)]

inviolate /ɪnˈvaɪələt/ adj. not violated. —**inviolacy** n. [f. L (as IN-², VIOLATE)]

invisible /ɪnˈvɪzɪb(ə)l/ adj. that cannot be seen. —**invisible exports, imports**, items for which payment is made by or to another country but which are not goods. —**invisibility** /-ˈbɪlɪti/ n., **invisibly** adv. [f. OF or L (as IN-², VISIBLE)]

invitation /ɪnvɪˈteɪʃ(ə)n/ n. 1. inviting, being invited. 2. a letter or card etc. used to invite someone. 3. a thing that invites (unintentional) consequences. [f. foll.]

invite /ɪnˈvaɪt/ v.t. 1. to ask courteously to come to one's house or to a function etc. 2. to ask for (suggestions etc.). 3. to tend to call forth (criticism etc.), to act so as to be likely to cause (a thing) unintentionally. 4. to attract, to tempt. —/ˈɪnvaɪt/ n. (colloq.) an invitation. [f. F or L invitare]

inviting adj. attractive, tempting. [f. prec.]

invocation /ɪnvəˈkeɪʃ(ə)n/ n. 1. invoking. 2. an appeal to a Muse for inspiration. 3. a preacher's prefatory words 'In the name of the Father' etc. —**invocatory** /ɪnˈvɒkətəri/ adj. [f. OF f. L (as INVOKE)]

invoice /ˈɪnvɔɪs/ n. a list of goods shipped or sent, or services rendered, with prices. —v.t. to make an invoice of; to send an invoice to. [app. f. OF envoy dispatch of goods (envoyer send)]

invoke /ɪnˈvəʊk/ v.t. 1. to call on (a deity etc.) in prayer or as a witness. 2. to appeal to (a law, authority, etc.) for protection or help. 3. to summon (a spirit) by charms. 4. to ask earnestly for (vengeance etc.). [f. F f. L invocare (IN-¹, vocare call)]

involuntary /ɪnˈvɒləntəri/ adj. done without exercise of the will; not controlled by the will. —**involuntarily** adv., **involuntariness** n. [f. L (as IN-², VOLUNTARY)]

involute /ˈɪnvəluːt, -ljuːt/ adj. involved, intricate. 2. spirally curved. —n. the locus of a point fixed on a straight line that rolls without sliding on a curve and is in the plane of that curve (cf. EVOLUTE; ill. SHAPES). [f. L (as INVOLVE)]

involuted /ˈɪnvəluːtɪd/ adj. complicated, abstruse. [f. prec.]

involution /ɪnvəˈluːʃ(ə)n/ n. 1. involving; intricacy; entanglement. 2. curling inwards; a part so curled. [as foll.]

involve /ɪnˈvɒlv/ v.t. 1. to cause to share (in) an experience or effect; to include or affect in its operation. 2. to contain within itself, to make necessary as a condition or result. 3. to implicate. 4. (in p.p.) concerned (in); complicated in thought or form. —**involvement** n. [f. L involvere (IN-¹, volvere roll)]

invulnerable /ɪnˈvʌlnərəb(ə)l/ adj. that cannot be wounded or hurt (esp. fig.). —**invulnerability** /-ˈbɪlɪti/ n., **invulnerably** adv. [f. L (as IN-², VULNERABLE)]

inward /ˈɪnwəd/ adj. 1. directed towards the inside, going in. 2. situated within. 3. mental, spiritual. —adv. (also **inwards**) 1. towards the inside. 2. within the mind or spirit. [OE (as IN, -WARD)]

inwardly adv. 1. on the inside. 2. not aloud. 3. in the mind or spirit. [OE (as prec.)]

inwardness n. inner nature; spirituality. [f. INWARD]

inwrought /ɪnˈrɔːt, attrib. ˈɪn-/ adj. (of fabric) decorated (with a pattern); (of a pattern) wrought (in or on fabric). [f. IN + WROUGHT]

Io /ˈaɪəʊ/ 1. (Gk myth.) priestess of Hera, loved by Zeus who, trying to protect her from the jealousy of Hera, turned her into a beautiful heifer. 2. (Astron.) a satellite of the planet Jupiter.

iodide /ˈaɪədaɪd/ n. a binary compound of iodine. [f. foll.]

iodine /ˈaɪədiːn, -ɪn/ n. a non-metallic element of the halogen group, symbol I, atomic number 53, forming black crystals and a violet vapour, resembling chlorine and bromine in its chemical properties; a solution of this in alcohol, used as an antiseptic. Identified as an element by Gay-Lussac in 1811, iodine has a number of uses in chemistry; potassium iodide is used in photography. As a constituent of thyroid hormones iodine is required in small amounts in the body, and deficiency can lead to goitre. [f. F f. Gk iōdēs violet-like (ion violet)]

iodize /ˈaɪədaɪz/ v.t. to impregnate with iodine. [f. prec.]

IOM abbr. Isle of Man.

ion /ˈaɪən/ n. any of the electrically charged particles into which the atoms or molecules of certain substances are dissociated by solution in water, making the solution a conductor of electricity; a similarly charged molecule of gas e.g. in air exposed to X-rays. [Gk, partic. of eimi go]

Iona /aɪˈəʊnə/ an island in the Inner Hebrides, site of a monastery founded by St Columba c.563 which became a centre for Celtic Christian missions to Scotland.

Ionesco /jɒˈneskəʊ/, Eugene (1912–), French dramatist of Romanian birth, who settled permanently in France in 1938. He was a leading exponent of the Theatre of the Absurd which he demonstrated in his first play La Cantatrice Chauve (The Bald Prima Donna, 1950) and continued in La Leçon (1951), Les Chaises (1952), and Le Roi se meurt (1962). By employing visual imagery, verbal rhythm, and balletic movement he achieves surrealistic effects and presents a disturbing world where grotesque events or objects symbolize man's condition.

Ionia /aɪˈəʊnɪə/ the ancient Greek name for the central part of the west coast of Asia Minor. Tribes speaking the Ionic dialect of Greek left the mainland in the 11th c. BC, according to early tradition, settling in the Aegean islands and in the coastal area of Asia Minor, later known as Ionia, which was colonized by the Greeks from about the 8th c. BC. They retained their distinctive dialect, also spoken in Athens, and are noted for their contributions in science, poetry, and architecture. Throughout the eastern Mediterranean 'Yawani' (= Ionians) became the generic word for 'Greek'. —**Ionian** adj. & n.

Ionian Islands /aɪˈəʊnɪən/ a chain of islands off the western coast of Greece, of which the largest are Corfu and Cephalonia.

Ionic /aɪˈɒnɪk/ adj. of an order of Greek architecture characterized by columns with scroll-shapes on either side of the capital (ill. TEMPLES). [f. L f. Gk]

ionic /aɪˈɒnɪk/ adj. of or using ions. —**ionically** adv. [f. ION]

ionize /ˈaɪənaɪz/ v.t. to convert or be converted into an ion or ions. —**ionization** /-ˈzeɪʃ(ə)n/ n. [f. ION]

ionosphere /aɪˈɒnəsfɪə(r)/ n. an ionized region of the upper atmosphere reflecting radio-waves. —**ionospheric** /-ˈferɪk/ adj. [f. ION + SPHERE]

iota /aɪˈəʊtə/ n. 1. the ninth letter of the Greek alphabet, = i. 2. the smallest possible amount, a jot. [Gk iōta]

IOU /aɪəʊˈjuː/ n. a signed document acknowledging a debt. [= I owe you]

IOW abbr. Isle of Wight.

Iowa /ˈaɪəwə/ a State in the Middle West of the USA, acquired as part of the Louisiana Purchase in 1803. It became the 29th State of the USA in 1846; capital, Des Moines.

IPA abbr. International Phonetic Alphabet.

ipecacuanha /ɪpɪkækjʊˈɑːnə/ n. the root of a South American plant (Cephaëlis ipecacuanha), used as an emetic or purgative. [f. Port. f. Tupi-Guarani, = emetic creeper]

Iphigenia /ɪfɪdʒɪˈnaɪə/ (Gk legend) daughter of Agamemnon, who was obliged to offer her as a sacrifice to Artemis when the Greek fleet was becalmed at Aulis (on the coast of Greece) on its way to the Trojan War. The goddess snatched her away to Tauris in the Crimea, where she became a priestess until rescued by Orestes.

ipso facto /ˈɪpsəʊ ˈfæktəʊ/ by that very fact. [L]

IQ abbr. intelligence quotient.

Ir symbol iridium.

ir-¹,² see IN-¹,².

IRA abbr. Irish Republican Army.

Iran /ɪˈrɑːn/ a country in the Middle East lying between the Caspian Sea and the Persian Gulf; pop. (est. 1982) 39,190,000; official language, Persian (Farsi); capital, Tehran. Oil is the chief source of revenue, otherwise the country is largely agricultural; the developing industrial output was largely curtailed by the 1979 revolution. (For its early history, see PERSIA.) The country was successively the centre of the Persian, Seleucid, Parthian, and Sassanian empires. Following the Muslim conquest in the 7th c. it was part of various Turkish, Persian, Tartar, and Mongol empires. A coup in 1925 brought the Pahlavi family to the throne, but following the overthrow of the Shah in 1979 Iran became an Islamic fundamentalist State. Since 1980 Iran has been involved in war with her neighbour Iraq.

Iranian /ɪˈreɪnɪən/ adj. 1. of Iran or its people. 2. of the group of Indo-European languages that includes Persian (Farsi), Pashto, Avestan, and Kurdish. —n. 1. a native of Iran. 2. the Iranian language group. [f. IRAN]

Iraq /ɪˈrɑːk/ a country in the Middle East bordering on the Persian Gulf, traversed by the Tigris and Euphrates Rivers and corresponding roughly to ancient Mesopotamia; pop. (1977) 12,171,480; official language, Arabic; capital, Baghdad.

Oil is the principal source of revenue, but agriculture makes a considerable contribution. The Tigris-Euphrates valley was the site of an early civilization (see MESOPOTAMIA). It was conquered by Arabia in the 7th c. and from 1534 formed part of the Ottoman empire, becoming an independent State after the First World War when the Turks were expelled. Since then the country's history has been characterized by political instability and involvement in Middle Eastern wars, most recently (from 1980) with her eastern neighbour Iran. —**Iraqi** *adj. & n.*

irascible /ɪˈræsɪb(ə)l/ *adj.* irritable, hot-tempered. —**irascibility** /-ˈbɪlɪtɪ/ *n.*, **irascibly** *adv.* [f. L (*irasci* grow angry, f. *ira* anger)]

irate /aɪˈreɪt/ *adj.* angry, enraged. [f. L *iratus* (as prec.)]

ire /ˈaɪə(r)/ *n.* (*literary*) anger. [f. OF f. L *ira* anger]

Ireland /ˈaɪələnd/ an island of the British Isles, lying west of Great Britain. Four-fifths of it is occupied by the Republic of Ireland (pop. (1981) 3,443,405; official languages, Irish and English; capital Dublin), and the remainder by Northern Ireland. The soil is fertile and the pasturage lush, swept by warm damp winds from the Atlantic; the economy relies heavily on agriculture, especially beef production and dairy farming. Settled by the Celts, the country became divided into independent tribal territories over which the lords of Tara exercised nominal suzerainty. Christianity reached Ireland, probably by the 4th c., to be consolidated by the work of St Patrick, and after the break-up of the Roman Empire the country became for a time a leading cultural centre, with the monasteries fostering learning and missionary work. English invasions began in the 12th c. under Henry II, but the authority that he established was never secure and by the 16th c. was confined to an area round Dublin (the English Pale) until the Tudors succeeded in extending it over the whole of the island. Revolts against English rule, and against the imposition of Protestantism (which met with unexpectedly stubborn resistance), resulted in the 'plantation' of Ireland by English (and later Scottish) families on confiscated land in an attempt to anglicize the country and secure its allegiance; in Ulster particularly the descendants of such settlers retained a distinctive identity. After an unsuccessful rebellion in 1798, union of Britain and Ireland followed in 1801. In spite of genuine efforts towards its success Ireland sank deeper into destitution. A share of Britain's industrial prosperity reached Protestant Ulster, but the rest of the island found its agricultural produce and assets dropping in value, and at the failure of the potato crop (Ireland's staple) in the 1840s thousands died in the famine, thousands more fled abroad. The Home Rule movement, led by Parnell, failed to achieve its aims in the 19th c. and implementation of a bill passed in 1910 was delayed by the outbreak of the First World War. An Act of 1920 divided Ireland into two parts: Southern Ireland, later recognized as an independent State (called the Irish Free State 1921-37, Eire 1937-49, the Republic of Ireland 1949-), and Northern Ireland (see separate entry).

Irenaeus /aɪrɪˈniːəs/, St (*c.*130-*c.*200), the leading Greek theologian of the 2nd c., bishop of Lyons in Gaul from 177, and author of a detailed attack on Gnosticism. Feast day, (in the East) 23 Aug., (in the West) 28 June.

iridaceous /ɪrɪˈdeɪʃəs/ *adj.* of the iris family (Iridaceae). [as IRIS]

iridescent /ɪrɪˈdes(ə)nt/ *adj.* showing rainbow-like colours; changing colour with position. —**iridescence** *n.* [f. L *iris* (see IRIS)]

iridium /ɪˈrɪdɪəm/ *n.* a rare hard white metallic element, symbol Ir, atomic number 77, related to platinum and resembling polished steel. One of the densest metals known, iridium has limited uses in its pure state, but alloyed with platinum it is used in jewellery, electrical contacts, and other situations where hardness and resistance to corrosion are important. It was discovered in 1803. [f. L *iris* rainbow, from its highly coloured salts]

Iris /ˈaɪərɪs/ (*Gk myth.*) goddess of the rainbow. When thought of in human form she acts as messenger of the gods, presumably because the rainbow seems to touch both earth and sky.

iris /ˈaɪərɪs/ *n.* **1.** the circular coloured membrane behind the cornea of the eye, with a circular opening (the pupil) in the centre (ill. BODY 4). **2.** a perennial herbaceous plant of the genus *Iris* usually with tuberous roots, sword-shaped leaves, and showy flowers. **3.** a diaphragm with a hole of variable size. [f. L f. Gk, = rainbow]

Irish /ˈaɪərɪʃ/ *adj.* of Ireland; of or like its people. —*n.* the Celtic language of Ireland (see below). —**the Irish,** the people of Ireland. **Irish stew** a stew of mutton, potato, and onion. [f. OE]

Irish (or Erse) belongs to the Celtic family of languages and is a distinct variety of Gaelic. It was brought to Ireland by Celtic invaders *c.*1000 BC, and down to the end of the 18th c. was spoken by the great majority of the people especially in areas other than the cities. Its earliest attestation is in inscriptions from the 4th c. AD, written in the Ogham script, and there has been a tradition of literature since the 6th c., with a mass of material from the 9th to 19th c. In the 19th c. English gained ground rapidly and Irish is now spoken regularly only in certain areas in the west of Ireland. Since 1922 the Irish government has organized its revival, and it is now taught in all the schools, but despite this active support and the establishment of Irish as an official language there are probably fewer than 60,000 native speakers. It is the first official language of the Irish Republic (the second is English). A few English words are derived from Irish, e.g. *banshee, blarney, galore, leprechaun,* and *Tory.*

Irishman *n.* (*pl.* **-men**) a man of Irish birth or descent. —**Irishwoman** *n.fem.* (*pl.* **-women**)

Irish Republican Army the military arm of Sinn Fein, formed during the struggle for independence from Britain in 1916-21, which continues to attempt to achieve union between the Republic of Ireland and Northern Ireland in the present day. Having maintained a relatively low level of armed activity up until the late 1960s the IRA split in 1969, and the radical minority, known as the Provisional IRA, stepped up the level of violence against British security forces and those associated with the Protestant Establishment in Northern Ireland.

Irish Sea the sea separating Ireland from England and Wales.

Irish Sweep(stake) a sweepstake on the results of certain major horse-races (especially the Derby and the Grand National), authorized since 1930 by the government of the Republic of Ireland in order to benefit Irish hospitals, which receive most of the profits. It is the largest international lottery. Most of its revenue is derived from the USA, though the buying and selling of sweepstake tickets is illegal there and they have to be smuggled into the country.

irk *v.t.* to annoy, to be tiresome to. [orig. unkn.]

irksome /ˈɜːksəm/ *adj.* tiresome, annoying. [f. IRK + -SOME]

iron /ˈaɪən/ *n.* **1.** an abundant metallic element of great strength (see below), atomic number 26, symbol Fe. **2.** a tool or implement made of iron; an implement (orig. of iron) with a flat base that is heated for smoothing cloth or clothes etc.; a golf-club with an iron or steel head and a sloping face; (in *pl.*) fetters, stirrups; (often in *pl.*) a leg-support to rectify malformations etc. **3.** a preparation of iron as a tonic. —*adj.* **1.** of iron. **2.** very robust. **3.** unyielding, merciless. —*v.t.* to smooth (cloth or clothes etc.) with an iron. —**Iron Chancellor,** Bismarck. **Iron Cross,** a German military decoration. **Iron Duke,** the first Duke of Wellington. **iron-grey** *adj. & n.* grey like the colour of freshly broken iron. **ironing-board** *n.* a narrow flat stand on which clothes etc. are ironed. **iron lung,** a rigid case over a patient's body for prolonged artificial respiration. Such an apparatus was first devised in the USA in 1929. **iron out,** to remove (difficulties etc.). **iron ration,** a small supply of tinned food etc. for use in an emergency. **many irons in the fire,** many undertakings or resources. **strike while the iron is hot,** to act promptly at a good opportunity. [OE]

Iron is one of the most abundant elements, widely distributed throughout the earth's crust in the form of ores, which are easily reduced to the metal, found in its free state only in meteorites, and essential to many types of animal life as a constituent of haemoglobin. Silver-white in colour, it is strong and ductile, with magnetic susceptibility, and is the most extensively used of all metals because of its many properties. Iron was known in Egypt *c.*3000 BC and was used in Europe *c.*1000 BC (see IRON AGE). When purified and alloyed with small quantities of other materials it is known as steel.

Cast iron is obtained by smelting from ores. It is silvery-grey when clean, hard, brittle, crystalline in structure, and contains 2-5% of carbon and smaller quantities of sulphur, phosphorus, and silicon. **Pig-iron** is cast iron as first obtained from the smelting furnace, cast in long blocks (pigs) for convenience. **Wrought iron,** which is highly malleable, is obtained by puddling (= stirring) pig-iron when molten, nearly pure but always containing some slag in the form of filaments and thus showing a fibrous structure.

Iron Age the third stage in the classification of prehistoric periods (see PREHISTORY), when weapons and tools were made of iron. The Hittites in Anatolia were working iron by *c.*1400 BC, but on a small scale and the technique was not fully understood. By the 12th c. BC its use had spread more widely; the Hebrews and Greeks knew it by 1000 BC, but it was not in use on a large scale until two centuries later. The application of the term ends, in Europe, at the Roman period.

ironclad *adj.* covered in or protected with iron. —*n.* (*hist.*) a ship cased with plates of iron.

Iron Curtain a barrier to the passage of persons and information at the limit of the Soviet sphere of influence. The first 'iron curtain' dates from the rebuilding of Drury Lane Theatre in 1794, after its destruction by a fire which started on the stage, and was designed for lowering as a protection. The figurative sense (= an impenetrable barrier) is found from about 25 years later. The first reference to such a barrier in connection with Russia dates from 1920. In 1945 the phrase occurs in its current application, and its use by W. S. Churchill in 1946 fixed it in the language.

ironic /aɪˈrɒnɪk/ *adj.* (also **ironical**) using or displaying irony. —**ironically** *adv.* [f. F or L f. Gk *eirōnikos* dissembling (as IRONY)]

ironmaster *n.* a manufacturer of iron.

ironmonger /ˈaɪənmʌŋgə(r)/ *n.* a dealer in hardware etc. —**ironmongery** *n.*

Ironsides /ˈaɪənsaɪdz/ *n.* **1.** a man of great bravery. **2.** (as *pl.*) Cromwell's cavalry troopers during the English Civil War, so called by their Royalist opponents in allusion to their hardiness in battle.

ironstone *n.* **1.** hard iron-ore. **2.** a kind of hard white pottery.

ironware *n.* things made of iron.

ironwork *n.* work in iron; things made of iron.

ironworks *n.pl.* (often treated as *sing.*) a place where iron is smelted or where heavy iron goods are made.

irony /ˈaɪərənɪ/ *n.* **1.** the expression of one's meaning by language of the opposite or a different tendency, e.g. adoption of a laudatory tone for the purpose of ridicule. **2.** the ill-timed or perverse occurrence of an event or circumstance that would in itself be desirable. —**dramatic** *or* **tragic irony,** (orig. in Greek tragedy) the use of statements etc. whose implications are understood by the audience but not by the person(s) addressed or concerned (occas. including the speaker). **Socratic irony,** a pose of ignorance assumed in order to confute others by enticing them into a display of supposed knowledge. [f. L f. Gk, = simulated ignorance (*eirōn* dissembler)]

Iroquois /ˈɪrəkwɔɪ/ *n.* (*pl.* same) an American Indian of the NE woodlands of North America (see below). —**Iroquoian** /-ˈɔɪən/ *adj.* & *n.* [f. F f. Algonquin]
Iroquois is the collective designation of the League of Five (later Six) Nations of American Indian tribes (i.e. Huron, Mohawk, Oneida, Seneca, Onondaga, and Cayuga), speaking Iroquoian languages, which joined in a confederacy *c.*1570 by the efforts of the Huron prophet Deganawida and his disciple Hiawatha. A powerful force in early colonial history, the divisions in the confederacy occasioned by conflicting support of the various contestants in the American Revolution saw the rapid decline of the Six Nations in the late 18th c., with half the League (i.e. the Cayugas, Mohawks, and Senecas) migrating north to Canada, where they accepted grants of land as allies of the defeated Loyalists and where they continue to live today. Traditional Iroquois society revolved around matrilineal residential and social organization.

irradiate /ɪˈreɪdɪeɪt/ *v.t.* **1.** to subject to radiation; to shine upon, to light up. **2.** to throw light on (a subject). —**irradiation** /-ˈeɪʃ(ə)n/ *n.* [f. L *irradiare* (IN-¹, *radius* ray)]

irrational /ɪˈræʃən(ə)l/ *adj.* **1.** unreasonable, illogical. **2.** not endowed with reason. **3.** not commensurable with natural numbers. —**irrationality** /-ˈnælɪtɪ/ *n.*, **irrationally** *adv.* [f. L (as IR-², RATIONAL)]

Irrawaddy /ɪrəˈwɒdɪ/ the principal river of Burma, 2,090 km (1,300 miles) long. It flows in a large delta into the eastern part of the Bay of Bengal.

irreconcilable /ɪˈrekənsaɪləb(ə)l/ *adj.* **1.** implacably hostile. **2.** incompatible. —**irreconcilability** /-ˈbɪlɪtɪ/ *n.*, **irreconcilably** *adv.* [f. IR-² + RECONCILABLE]

irrecoverable /ɪrɪˈkʌvərəb(ə)l/ *adj.* that cannot be recovered or remedied. —**irrecoverably** *adv.* [f. IR-² + RECOVERABLE]

irredeemable /ɪrɪˈdiːməb(ə)l/ *adj.* that cannot be redeemed; hopeless. —**irredeemably** *adv.* [f. IR-² + REDEEMABLE]

Irredentist /ɪrɪˈdentɪst/ *n.* an Italian nationalist of the late 19th c. advocating the return to Italy of the Italian-speaking districts of the Austro-Hungarian empire; a person holding similar views of other areas. [f. It. (*Italia*) *irredenta* unredeemed (Italy)]

irreducible /ɪrɪˈdjuːsɪb(ə)l/ *adj.* that cannot be reduced or simplified. —**irreducibly** *adv.* [f. IR-² + REDUCIBLE]

irrefutable /ɪˈrefjʊtəb(ə)l, ɪrɪˈfjuː-/ *adj.* that cannot be refuted. —**irrefutably** *adv.* [f. L (as IR-², REFUTABLE)]

irregular /ɪˈregjʊlə(r)/ *adj.* **1.** not regular; unsymmetrical, uneven, varying. **2.** contrary to a rule, principle, or custom. **3.** (of troops) not in the regular army. **4.** abnormal. **5.** (of a verb, noun, etc.) not inflected normally. **6.** disorderly. —*n.* (in *pl.*) irregular troops. —**irregularity** /-ˈlærɪtɪ/ *n.*, **irregularly** *adv.* [f. OF f. L (as IR-², REGULAR)]

irrelevant /ɪˈrelɪv(ə)nt/ *adj.* not relevant. —**irrelevance** *n.*, **irrelevancy** *n.*, **irrelevantly** *adv.* [f. IR-² + RELEVANT]

irreligious /ɪrɪˈlɪdʒəs/ *adj.* lacking or hostile to religion. [f. L (as IR-², RELIGIOUS)]

irremediable /ɪrɪˈmiːdɪəb(ə)l/ *adj.* that cannot be remedied. —**irremediably** *adv.* [f. L (as IR-², REMEDIABLE)]

irremovable /ɪrɪˈmuːvəb(ə)l/ *adj.* that cannot be removed, especially from office. —**irremovably** *adv.* [f. IR-² + REMOVABLE]

irreparable /ɪˈrepərəb(ə)l/ *adj.* that cannot be rectified or made good. —**irreparably** *adv.* [f. OF f. L (as IR-², REPARABLE)]

irreplaceable /ɪrɪˈpleɪsəb(ə)l/ *adj.* that cannot be replaced. —**irreplaceability** /-ˈbɪlɪtɪ/ *n.*, **irreplaceably** *adv.* [f. IR-² + REPLACEABLE]

irrepressible /ɪrɪˈpresɪb(ə)l/ *adj.* that cannot be repressed or restrained. —**irrepressibly** *adv.* [f. IR-² + REPRESS]

irreproachable /ɪrɪˈprəʊtʃəb(ə)l/ *adj.* faultless, blameless. —**irreproachably** *adv.* [f. F (as IR-², REPROACH)]

irresistible /ɪrɪˈzɪstɪb(ə)l/ *adj.* too strong or delightful or convincing to be resisted. —**irresistibly** *adv.* [f. L (as IR-², RESISTIBLE)]

irresolute /ɪˈrezəluːt/ *adj.* feeling or showing uncertainty, hesitating. —**irresolutely** *adv.*, **irresoluteness** *n.*, **irresolution** /-ˈluːʃ(ə)n/ *n.* [f. IR-² + RESOLUTE]

irrespective /ɪrɪˈspektɪv/ *adj.* not taking account *of*, regardless *of*. [f. IR-² + RESPECTIVE]

irresponsible /ɪrɪˈspɒnsɪb(ə)l/ *adj.* acting or done without due sense of responsibility; not responsible for one's conduct. —**irresponsibility** /-ˈbɪlɪtɪ/ *n.*, **irresponsibly** *adv.* [f. IR-² + RESPONSIBLE]

irretrievable /ɪrɪˈtriːvəb(ə)l/ *adj.* that cannot be retrieved or recovered. —**irretrievably** *adv.* [f. IR-² + RETRIEVABLE]

irreverent /ɪˈrevərənt/ *adj.* lacking reverence. —**irreverence** *n.*, **irreverently** *adv.* [f. L (as IR-², REVERENT)]

irreversible /ɪrɪˈvɜːsɪb(ə)l/ *adj.* not reversible or alterable. —**irreversibly** *adv.* [f. IR-² + REVERSIBLE]

irrevocable /ɪˈrevəkəb(ə)l/ *adj.* unable to be revoked, unalterable; gone beyond recall. —**irrevocably** *adv.* [f. L (as IR-², REVOCABLE)]

irrigate /ˈɪrɪgeɪt/ *v.t.* **1.** to supply (land or crops) with water by means of streams, channels, pipes, etc. **2.** to wash (a wound) with a constant flow of liquid. —**irrigation** /-ˈgeɪʃ(ə)n/ *n.*, **irrigator** *n.* [f. L *irrigare* (IR-¹, *rigare* moisten)]

irritable /ˈɪrɪtəb(ə)l/ *adj.* **1.** easily annoyed, bad-tempered. **2.** (of an organ etc.) sensitive. —**irritability** /-ˈbɪlɪtɪ/ *n.*, **irritably** *adv.* [f. L (as IRRITATE)]

irritant /ˈɪrɪt(ə)nt/ *adj.* causing irritation. —*n.* an irritant substance. [f. foll.]

irritate /ˈɪrɪteɪt/ *v.t.* **1.** to annoy, to rouse slight anger or impatience in. **2.** to cause itching in (a part of the body). **3.** to stimulate (an organ) to action. —**irritation** /-ˈteɪʃ(ə)n/ *n.*, **irritative** *adj.* [f. L *irritare*]

irrupt /ɪˈrʌpt/ *v.i.* to enter forcibly or violently (*into*). —**irruption** *n.* [f. L *irrumpere* (IR-¹, *rumpere* break)]

Irving¹ /ˈɜːvɪŋ/, Sir Henry (1838–1905), real name Henry Brodribb, English actor-manager. In 1871 his appearance at the Lyceum Theatre in the melodrama *The Bells* brought him immediate fame, and he was to dominate the London stage during the next 30 years. In 1874 he first played

Hamlet, inaugurating his own management of the Lyceum in the same role in 1878. His tenancy (in association with Miss Ellen Terry) is mainly remembered for his productions of Shakespeare, from *The Merchant of Venice* in 1879 to *Cymbeline* in 1896. He was a good manager and his acting, in spite of mannerisms and a not particularly melodious voice, had enormous power.

Irving[2] /ˈɜːvɪŋ/, Washington (1783-1859), American writer who first came into literary repute with his burlesque *A History of New York* (1809) by 'Diedrich Knickerbocker'. He visited England where he met Sir Walter Scott, who encouraged him to write his celebrated *The Sketch Book* (1820) which contains his best tales, including 'Rip Van Winkle' and 'The Legend of Sleepy Hollow'. He later held diplomatic posts in Spain and London, and on his return to America was enthusiastically received as the first American author to have achieved international fame. His later works include a life of George Washington (1855-9).

is see BE.

Isaac /ˈaɪzək/ Hebrew patriarch, son of Abraham and Sarah and father of Jacob and Esau (Gen. 21: 3 etc.).

Isaiah /aɪˈzaɪə/ **1.** a Hebrew major prophet of Judah in the 8th c. BC, teaching the supremacy of the God of Israel and emphasizing the moral demands upon worshippers. His expectations for the future centred on his belief in the permanence of the Davidic throne, and the 'Messianic' passages in the prophecies ascribed to him were frequently referred by Christian writers to Jesus Christ. **2.** a book of the Old Testament ascribed to him but now generally agreed to fall into three portions, of which chapters 36-66, and portions of the earlier chapters, have no real claim to be his.

-isation, -ise variants of -IZATION, -IZE.

ISBN *abbr.* international standard book number.

Iseult /ɪˈzuːlt, ɪˈzuːlt/ (in medieval legend) the sister or daughter of the king of Ireland, and wife of King Mark of Cornwall, loved by Tristram; (in another account) the daughter of the king of Brittany, and wife of Tristram.

-ish *suffix* forming adjectives (1) from nouns, in the senses 'having the qualities of' (*knavish*), 'of the nationality of' (*Danish*); (2) from adjectives, in the sense of 'somewhat' (*thickish*); (3) (*colloq.*) of an approximate age or time (*forty-ish*). [OE]

Isherwood /ˈɪʃəwʊd/, Christopher William Bradshaw (1904-86), English novelist. His novels, *Mr. Norris Changes Trains* (1935), about the adventures in the criminal and political underworld of double-agent Arthur Norris, and *Goodbye to Berlin* (1939), about eccentric witty cabaret artist Sally Bowles (dramatized as *I am a Camera*, 1951; as a musical, *Cabaret*, 1968), vividly portray Germany on the eve of Hitler's rise to power and reflect Isherwood's experiences in Berlin during 1929-33. He collaborated with Auden in several plays and with him left for America in 1939, becoming a US citizen in 1946. After settling in Hollywood he developed an interest in Hindu philosophy and Vedanta and translated several Hindu classics, notably the *Bhagavadgita* (1944). His later novels include *Down there on a Visit* (1962) and *Christopher and his Kind* (1976), a frank account of the homosexual affairs of his young manhood.

Ishmael /ˈɪʃmeɪl/ a son of Abraham and Hagar, of whom it was prophesied 'his hand will be against every man, and every man's hand against him' (Gen. 16: 12); hence, an outcast, one at war with society. —**Ishmaelite** *n.*

Ishtar /ˈɪʃtɑː(r)/ a Babylonian and Assyrian goddess whose name and functions correspond to those of Astarte.

Isidore[1] /ˈɪzɪdɔː(r)/ (6th c.) Greek mathematician and engineer, of Miletus in Ionia, co-architect (with Anthemius of Tralles) of Santa Sophia in Constantinople, and author of a fifteenth book of Euclid's *Elements*.

Isidore[2] /ˈɪzɪdɔː(r)/, St (*c.*560-636), archbishop of Seville and Doctor of the Church, an encyclopaedic writer whose works became a storehouse of knowledge freely used by innumerable medieval authors. Feast day, 4 April.

isinglass /ˈaɪzɪŋglɑːs/ *n.* **1.** a kind of gelatin obtained from fish, especially the sturgeon, and used for jellies, glue, etc. **2.** mica. [f. obs. Du. *huisenblas* sturgeon's bladder]

Isis /ˈaɪsɪs/ (*Egyptian myth.*) a nature-goddess, wife of Osiris and mother of Horus. Her worship spread to Western Asia, Greece, and Rome, where she was identified with many and varied local goddesses, and became one of the major mystery religions, involving enactment of the myth of the death and resurrection of Osiris.

Islam /ˈɪzlɑːm, -ˈlɑːm/ *n.* the religion of Muslims, revealed through Muhammad as Prophet of Allah (see below); the Muslim world. —**Islamic** /-ˈlæmɪk/ *adj.* [f. Arab., = submission (to God), f. *aslama* resign oneself]

The monotheistic religion founded by the Prophet Muhammad in the Arabian Peninsula in the 7th c. AD is now the professed faith of over seven million people world wide. To become a Muslim means both to accept and affirm an individual surrender to God, and to live as a member of a social community. The Muslim performs prescribed acts of worship and strives to fulfil good works within the group; the 'Pillars of Islam' include profession of the faith in a prescribed form, observance of ritual prayer (five obligatory prayer sequences each day as well as non-obligatory prayers), giving alms to the poor, fasting during the month of Ramadan, and performing the pilgrimage to Mecca. These ritual observances, as well as a code governing social behaviour, were given to Muhammad as a series of revelations, codified in the Koran and supplemented by the deeds and discourse of the Prophet (see SUNNA, HADITH). Islam is regarded by its adherents as the last of the revealed religions (following Judaism and Christianity), and Muhammad is seen as the Seal of the Prophets, building upon and perfecting the examples and teachings of Abraham, Moses, and Jesus. The term Islam carries three interrelated significations: the personal individual submission to Allah; the 'world of Islam' as a concrete historical reality comprising a variety of communities which, however, share not only a common religious outlook but also a common fund of cultural legacies; and finally, the concept of an 'ideal Muslim community' as set forth in the Koran and supporting sources.

Islamabad /ɪzˈlɑːməbɑːd/ the capital, since 1967, of Pakistan, replacing Karachi; pop. 250,000.

island /ˈaɪlənd/ *n.* **1.** a piece of land surrounded by water. **2.** a detached or isolated thing; a traffic island. —**islands area**, an administrative area in Scotland, consisting of a number of islands. **Islands of the Blessed**, a mythical abode, often located in the west, near where the sun sets, to which, in the belief of many ancient peoples, the souls of the good were conveyed to a life of bliss. [OE, orig. *igland*; -*s*- after ISLE]

islander *n.* an inhabitant of an island. [f. prec.]

isle /aɪl/ *n.* (chiefly *poetic* and in names) an island, especially a small one. [f. OF f. L *insula*]

Isle of Man an island in the Irish Sea which is a British Crown possession enjoying home rule, with its own legislature (the *Tynwald*) and judicial system; pop. (1981) 64,679; capital, Douglas. The island was part of the Norse kingdom of the Hebrides in the Middle Ages, passing into Scottish hands in 1266 for a time, until the English gained control in the early 15th c. Its ancient language, Manx, is still used for ceremonial purposes.

Isle of Wight /waɪt/ an island off the south coast of England, a county since 1974; pop. (1981) 115,400.

islet /ˈaɪlɪt/ *n.* **1.** a small island. **2.** a detached portion of tissue. —**islets of Langerhans**, groups of pancreatic cells secreting insulin. [OF, dim. of *isle* (as prec.)]

ism /ɪz(ə)m/ *n.* (usu. *derog.*) any distinctive doctrine or practice. [f. foll.]

-ism /-ɪz(ə)m/ *n. suffix* forming nouns, especially a system or principle (*Conservatism, jingoism*), a state or quality (*barbarism, heroism*), or a peculiarity in language (*Americanism*). [f. F f. L f. Gk (as -IZE)]

Ismaili /ɪzˈmaɪlɪ/ *n.* a member of a Shiite Muslim sect that seceded from the main group in the 8th c. over the question of succession to the position of imam. They regarded Ismail, eldest son of the sixth imam, as the seventh and final imam, while the rest of the Shiites supported the second son, Musa al-Kazim. The Ismaili movement (which consisted of several groups rather than one unified body) represented a revolutionary political force in its early stages, and its adherents developed an elaborate esoteric doctrine (diverging considerably from the rest of Islam) concerning the believer's place in the cosmos and the highly structured path to spiritual fulfilment. Initiation into the group's doctrines was a long process to which only a few were admitted, and the organization tended to be that of a very hierarchical secret society. It eventually split into many sub-sects, of which the best known is that headed by the Aga Khan. Today Ismailis are found especially in India, Pakistan, and East Africa, with smaller groups in Syria, Iran, and other predominantly Muslim countries.

isn't /ˈɪz(ə)nt/ (*colloq.*) is not.

iso- /aɪsəʊ-/ *in comb.* equal. [f. Gk *isos* equal]

isobar /ˈaɪsəbɑː(r)/ *n.* a line on a map connecting places with the same atmospheric pressure. —**isobaric** /-ˈbærɪk/ *adj.* [f. Gk (ISO-, *baros* weight)]

isochronous /aɪˈsɒkrənəs/ *adj.* **1.** occupying an equal time. **2.** occurring at the same time. [f. Gk (ISO-, *khronos* time)]

isoclinal /aɪsəʊˈklaɪn(ə)l/ *adj.* **1.** corresponding to equal values of magnetic dip. **2.** (*Geol.*, of a fold) with the parts of each side parallel to each other (ill. GEOLOGY). [f. ISO- + Gk *klinō* slope]

Isocrates /aɪˈsɒkrəti:z/ (436–338 BC) Athenian orator. His written speeches were vehicles for his political ideals, the union of Greeks under the shared hegemony of Athens and Sparta, and later under the championship of Philip II of Macedon; he also advocated a Panhellenic crusade against Persia. His style is elaborate and studied. His influential educational system provided a combination of philosophical and rhetorical instruction.

isolate /ˈaɪsəleɪt/ *v.t.* **1.** to place apart or alone. **2.** to separate (a patient with a contagious or infectious disease) from others. **3.** to separate (a substance) from a compound. **4.** to insulate (electrical apparatus). —**isolation** /-ˈleɪʃ(ə)n/ *n.* [f. F f. It. f. L *insulatus* (as ISLE)]

isolationism *n.* the policy of holding aloof from affairs of other countries or groups. —**isolationist** *n.* [f. ISOLATION]

isomer /ˈaɪsəmɜː(r)/ *n.* any of two or more substances whose molecules have the same atoms in different arrangements. —**isomeric** /-ˈmerɪk/ *adj.*, **isomerism** /aɪˈsɒmərɪz(ə)m/ *n.* [G f. Gk (ISO-, *meros* portion)]

isometric /aɪsəˈmetrɪk/ *adj.* **1.** (of muscle action) developing tension while the muscle is prevented from contracting. **2.** (of a drawing or projection) with the plane of projection at equal angles to the three principal axes of the object shown. **3.** of equal measure. [f. Gk *isometria* equality of measure]

isometrics *n.pl.* a system of physical exercises in which muscles are caused to act against each other or against a fixed object. [f. prec.]

isomorph /ˈaɪsəmɔːf/ *n.* a substance having the same form as another. —**isomorphic** *adj.*, **isomorphous** *adj.* [f. ISO- + Gk *morphē* form]

isosceles /aɪˈsɒsɪliːz/ *adj.* (of a triangle) having two sides equal. [L f. Gk (ISO-, *skelos* leg)]

isotherm /ˈaɪsəθɜːm/ *n.* a line on a map connecting places with the same temperature. —**isothermal** /-ˈθɜːm(ə)l/ *adj.* [f. F (as ISO- + Gk *thermē* heat)]

isotope /ˈaɪsətəʊp/ *n.* any of two or more types of atom of the same element that contain equal numbers of protons but different numbers of neutrons in their nuclei, and hence differ in atomic weight but not in chemical properties. The term was coined in 1913 by F. Soddy. Most elements consist of one stable (non-radioactive) isotope; there are also numerous radioactive isotopes, the majority of them artificially created. —**isotopic** /-ˈtɒpɪk/ *adj.* [f. ISO- + Gk *topos* place (i.e. in the periodic table of elements)]

isotropic /aɪsəˈtrɒpɪk/ *adj.* having the same physical properties in all directions. —**isotropy** /aɪˈsɒtrəpɪ/ *n.* [f. ISO- + Gk *tropos* turn]

Israel[1] /ˈɪzreɪ(ə)l/ **1.** (also **children of Israel**) the Hebrew nation or people traditionally descended from the patriarch Jacob (his alternative name was 'Israel'), whose 12 sons became founders of the 12 tribes. **2.** the northern kingdom of the Hebrews (*c*.930–721 BC, in contrast to Judah), whose inhabitants were carried away to captivity in Assyria. The name 'Israel' is first found on the Moabite Stone (*c*.850 BC) commemorating the successes of the king of Moab against Israel. —**Israelite** /ˈɪzrəlaɪt/ *adj.* & *n.* [f. Heb., = he that strives with God; see Gen. 32: 28]

Israel[2] /ˈɪzreɪl/ a country in SW Asia, with the River Jordan forming part of its eastern border and with a coastline on the Mediterranean Sea; pop. (est. 1980) 3,921,700; official language, Hebrew; capital (not recognized as such by the UN), Jerusalem. Much of the country is very fertile, and since 1948 massive irrigation programmes have brought large areas of former desert under cultivation. The 'Holy Land' of Jews and Christians, and with Jerusalem sacred also to Muslims, it contains numerous sites that attract both pilgrims and tourists. Remains of early man were found in caves on Mount Carmel, and the country is rich in archaeological remains of all periods. Although it is the ancient and traditional home of the Jewish people, for most of its history it was controlled by one or other of the powerful nations of each succeeding era (see prec. and PALESTINE), until following the surrender of the British

mandate at the end of the Second World War the independent Jewish State of Israel was proclaimed in 1948. Conflict with the surrounding Arab States has led to war in 1948, 1956, 1967, and 1973, and resulted in Israel's expansion to her present boundaries. Continuing problems with the Arab States and the native Palestinian peoples of the area keep the international situation in an unstable state, but Israel has emerged as the strongest military power in the Middle East, and despite a high inflation rate, the development of the economy has made it the most industrialized country in the region. —**Israeli** /ɪzˈreɪlɪ/ *adj.* & *n.*

Israfel /ˈɪzrəfel/ (in Muslim tradition) the angel of music, who will sound the trumpet on the Day of Judgement.

Issachar /ˈɪsəkə(r)/ **1.** Hebrew patriarch, son of Jacob and Leah (Gen. 30: 18). **2.** the tribe of Israel traditionally descended from him.

issue /ˈɪʃuː, ˈɪsjuː/ *n.* **1.** an outgoing or outflow. **2.** the issuing of things for use or for sale; the number or quantity issued. **3.** any set of publications in a series issued regularly. **4.** a result, an outcome. **5.** the point in question, an important topic of discussion or litigation. **6.** a way out; a place of emergence of a stream etc. **7.** (*Law*) progeny, children. —*v.t./i.* **1.** to go or come or flow out. **2.** to put out for sale or as information etc., to publish; to send out (orders etc.). **3.** to supply or distribute for use. **4.** to result; to originate. —**at issue**, in dispute, under discussion. **join** or **take issue**, to proceed to argue. [f. OF f. L *exitus* (as EXIT)]

-ist *suffix* forming personal nouns expressing an adherent of a creed etc. in -*ism* (*Marxist, fatalist*), a person concerned with something (*pathologist, tobacconist*), a person who uses a thing (*violinist, motorist*), or a person who does a thing expressed by a verb in -*ize* (*plagiarist*). [F & L f. Gk]

Istanbul /ɪstænˈbʊl/ a port and the former capital (until 1923) of Turkey, situated on the Bosporus and partly in Europe, partly in Asia, to which it is linked by a suspension bridge; pop. 4,870,747. It was formerly the Roman city of Constantinople, ancient Byzantium; most of its characteristic buildings date from the Ottoman era (1453–1923).

isthmus /ˈɪsməs/ *n.* a narrow piece of land connecting two larger bodies of land; a narrow connecting part. —**isthmian** *adj.* [L f. Gk]

it[1] *pron.* (*pl.* THEY) **1.** the thing (or occas. animal or child) previously named or in question; the person in question. **2.** as the subject of an impersonal verb making a general statement about the weather or about circumstances etc., or as an indefinite object. **3.** as a substitute for a deferred subject or object; as the antecedent to a relative pronoun. **4.** exactly what is needed. **5.** the extreme limit of achievement etc. **6.** (*colloq.*) sexual intercourse; sex appeal. **7.** (in children's games) the player who has to catch others. [OE]

it[2] *n.* (*colloq.*) Italian vermouth. [abbr.]

Italian /ɪˈtælɪən/ *adj.* of Italy or its people or language. —*n.* **1.** a native or inhabitant of Italy. **2.** the official language of Italy, a Romance language which in many ways has remained closer to Latin than have the others of this group. It is spoken by some 60 million people in Italy and Switzerland, and by large numbers of speakers in the USA and South America. —**Italian vermouth,** sweet vermouth. [f. It. (*Italia* Italy)]

Italianate /ɪˈtælɪəneɪt/ *adj.* of Italian style or appearance. [f. It. *Italianato*]

Italic /ɪˈtælɪk/ *adj.* of ancient Italy. —**Italic languages,** the Italic branch of the Indo-European family of languages, comprising Latin, Oscan, Umbrian, and the dialects of various mountain tribes of central Italy. The term is more often confined to Oscan and Umbrian, the two chief non-Latin dialects of the group. [f. L f. Gk (as ITALIAN)]

italic /ɪˈtælɪk/ *adj.* **1.** (of printed letters) of a sloping kind now used especially for emphasis and in foreign words. **2.** (of handwriting) compact and pointed like early Italian handwriting. —*n.* **1.** a letter in italic type; such type. **2.** of a form of handwriting (developed in Italy) somewhat resembling this, or a modern adaptation of such a form. [= prec.]

italicize /ɪˈtælɪsaɪz/ *v.t.* to print in italics. [f. prec.]

Italy /ˈɪtəlɪ/ a country in southern Europe comprising a peninsula that juts south into the Mediterranean Sea, and a number of offshore islands of which the largest are Sicily and Sardinia; pop. (1981) 56,830,000; official language, Italian; capital, Rome. The centre of the Roman Empire, Italy was dominated by the city-states and the papacy in the Middle Ages, but fell under Spanish and Austrian rule in the 16th–17th c. Modern Italy was created by the nationalist movement of the mid-19th c., led by Garibaldi and the kingdom of Sardinia, the monarch of the latter country becoming king of Italy in 1861. Italy entered the First World War on the Allied side in 1915, but after the war the country was taken over by the Fascist dictator Mussolini; participation in the Second World War resulted in defeat and much devastation. A republic was established by popular vote in 1946. The country is divided between the industrialized north and the agricultural south, and by European standards has experienced a considerable degree of political instability in recent decades.

itch *n.* **1.** an irritation in the skin; a contagious disease accompanied by this. **2.** an impatient desire. —*v.i.* to feel an itch. —**itching palm,** avarice. [OE]

itchy *adj.* having or causing an itch. —**itchiness** *n.* [f. ITCH]

item /ˈaɪtəm/ *n.* any one of enumerated things; a detached piece of news etc. [L, = in like manner, also]

itemize /ˈaɪtəmaɪz/ *v.t.* to state by items. —**itemization** /-ˈzeɪʃ(ə)n/ *n.* [f. ITEM]

iterate /ˈɪtəreɪt/ *v.t.* to repeat, to state repeatedly. —**iteration** /-ˈreɪʃ(ə)n/ *n.*, **iterative** /-rətɪv/ *adj.* [f. L *iterare* (*iterum* again)]

Ithaca /ˈɪθəkə/ an island off the western coast of Greece, the legendary home of Odysseus.

itinerant /aɪˈtɪnərənt, ɪ-/ *adj.* travelling from place to place. —*n.* an itinerant person. [f. L *itinerare* (*iter* journey)]

itinerary /aɪˈtɪnərəri, ɪ-/ *n.* a route, a list of places to be visited on a journey. [f. L (as prec.)]

-itis /-aɪtɪs/ *suffix* forming nouns, especially names of inflammatory diseases (*appendicitis*) or (*colloq.*) of mental states fancifully regarded as diseases (*electionitis*). [Gk]

its *poss. pron. & adj.* of it, of itself. [f. IT¹]

it's (*colloq.*) it has, it is.

itself /ɪtˈself/ *pron.* emphat. and refl. form of IT¹. —**by itself,** apart from its surroundings, automatically. **in itself,** viewed in its essential qualities. [OE (IT¹, SELF)]

ITV *abbr.* independent television.

IUD *abbr.* intra-uterine (contraceptive) device.

Ivan /ˈaɪv(ə)n/ the name of several rulers of Russia:

Ivan I (*c.*1304–41), grand duke of Muscovy 1328–40. He strengthened and enlarged the duchy, making Moscow the ecclesiastical capital.

Ivan III 'the Great' (1440–1505), grand duke of Muscovy 1462–1505. He consolidated and enlarged his territory, defending it against a Tatar invasion in 1480, and established autocratic government.

Ivan IV 'the Terrible' (1530–84), first tsar of Muscovy 1533–84. Although an energetic and intelligent ruler Ivan was prone to bouts of paranoiac violence, being particularly suspicious of his own nobles, the Boyars. In the early years

following the end of the regency in 1547 Ivan carried out some important administrative reforms and pursued a successful expansionist foreign policy, but in later life his rule became disastrously despotic, and he was subject to fits of rage, in one of which he killed his son. Periodic pogroms, most notably those at Novgorod in 1567 and Moscow in 1572, left Russia weak and divided, while most of his foreign conquests were eventually lost to the Poles.

Ives /aɪvz/, Charles (1874–1954), American highly original composer, strongly influenced by popular music and the sounds of everyday life and at the same time innovative and forward-looking, developing from the experiments of his father, a town bandmaster, the use of polyrhythm, polytonality, quartertones, note-clusters, and aleatory techniques. In the two pieces for small orchestra *The Unanswered Question* and *Central Park in the Dark* (both 1906) two orchestras, each with its own conductor, play independently, never synchronizing, an effect dating back to his memories of two bands playing different marches in different streets in his home town.

ivory /ˈaɪvəri/ *n.* **1.** the hard substance of the tusks of the elephant etc. **2.** the creamy-white colour of this. **3.** (usu. in *pl.*) an article made of ivory. **4.** (usu. in *pl.*, *slang*) a dice; a billiard-ball; a piano-key; a tooth. —**ivory tower,** seclusion or withdrawal from harsh realities. [f. OF f. L *ebur*]

Ivory Coast a country in West Africa on the Gulf of Guinea, between Liberia and Ghana; pop. (est. 1981) 8,574,800; official language, French; capital, Abidjan. The area was explored by the Portuguese in the late 15th c., and subsequently disputed by traders from various European countries who sought the ivory from which the country takes its name, and slaves. It was made a French protectorate in 1842, and became an autonomous republic within the French Community in 1958 and a fully independent republic outside it in 1960. One of the more developed of African economies, it is noted for its forest resources which make it the leading African exporter of tropical wood.

ivy /ˈaɪvi/ *n.* a climbing evergreen (*Hedera helix*) with shining usually five-pointed leaves. [OE]

Ivy League a name applied to a group of long-established eastern US universities of high academic and social prestige, including Harvard, Yale, Princeton, and Columbia.

ixia /ˈɪksɪə/ *n.* a South African iridaceous plant of the genus *Ixia* with large showy flowers. [L f. Gk, = kind of thistle]

Ixion /ˈɪksɪən/ (*Gk myth.*) the Greek Cain, the first to murder one of his kin. He was purified by Zeus, but tried to seduce Hera, and was first deceived with a cloud-image of her (on which he begat the Centaurs) and afterwards was punished by being pinned to a fiery wheel that revolved unceasingly through the underworld.

J

J, j /dʒeɪ/ *n.* (*pl.* **Js, J's**) the tenth letter of the alphabet.

J *abbr.* joule(s).

jab *v.t.* (**-bb-**) to poke roughly; to thrust abruptly (a thing *into*). —*n.* **1.** an abrupt blow with a pointed thing or with the fist. **2.** (*colloq.*) a hypodermic injection. [var. of *job* prod]

jabber *v.t./i.* to chatter volubly; to utter (words) fast and indistinctly. —*n.* chatter, gabble. [imit.]

jabot /ˈʒæbəʊ/ *n.* an ornamental frill or ruffle of lace etc. worn on the front of a shirt or blouse. [F, orig. = crop of bird]

jacaranda /dʒækəˈrændə/ *n.* a tropical American tree of the genus *Dalbergia* etc. with hard scented wood, or one of the genus *Jacaranda* with blue flowers. [Tupi-Guarani]

jacinth /ˈdʒæsɪnθ/ *n.* a reddish-orange gem, a variety of zircon. [f. OF or L, = HYACINTH]

jack *n.* **1.** a device for lifting heavy objects, especially one for raising the axle of a motor vehicle so that a wheel may be changed. **2.** a court-card with a picture of a soldier or page. **3.** a ship's flag, especially one flown from the bow and showing nationality. **4.** a device using a single plug to connect an electrical circuit. **5.** a device for turning a spit. **6.** a type of the common man. **7.** (*slang*) a policeman, a detective. **8.** a small white ball in bowls for the players to aim at. **9.** a pike, especially a young one. **10.** the male of various animals. —*v.t.* (often with *up*) to raise with or as with a jack. —**Jack Frost,** frost personified. **jack in** *or* **up,** (*slang*) to abandon (an attempt etc.). **jack-in-the-box** *n.* a toy figure that springs out of a box when the lid is lifted. **jack-in-office** *n.* a self-important official. **jack of all trades,** a person who can do many different kinds of work. **jack-rabbit,** (*US*) a large prairie hare (*Lepus townsendii,* etc.) with very long ears. **Jack tar,** a sailor. [f. *Jack,* pet-name for JOHN]

jackal /ˈdʒækɔːl, -(ə)l/ *n.* **1.** any of several members of the dog family found wild in Asia and Africa, living on carrion and small animals. The jackal was formerly supposed to find prey for the lion. **2.** one who does the preliminary drudgery etc. for another. [f. Turk. f. Pers.]

jackanapes /ˈdʒækəneɪps/ *n.* a pert or insolent fellow. [f. *Jack Napes* nickname (1450) of Duke of Suffolk whose badge was an ape's clog and chain]

jackass /ˈdjækæs/ *n.* **1.** a male ass. **2.** a stupid person. —**laughing jackass,** the kookaburra. [f. JACK + ASS]

jackboot *n.* **1.** a large boot reaching above the knee. **2.** military oppression, bullying behaviour.

jackdaw *n.* a bird (*Corvus monedula*) of the crow family, with a chuckling call. [f. JACK + DAW]

jacket /ˈdʒækɪt/ *n.* **1.** a short coat, usually reaching to the hips. **2.** a thing worn similarly. **3.** an outer covering round a boiler etc. to reduce loss of heat. **4.** a dust jacket. **5.** the skin of a potato. **6.** an animal's coat. —**jacketed** *adj.* [f. OF *ja(c)quet*]

jackknife *n.* **1.** a large clasp-knife. **2.** a dive in which the body is first bent at the waist and then straightened. —*v.i.* (of an articulated vehicle) to fold against itself in an accidental skidding movement.

jackpot *n.* the accumulated prize or stakes in a lottery, the game of poker, etc. —**hit the jackpot,** to win remarkable luck or success.

Jackson[1] /ˈdʒæks(ə)n/, Andrew (1767-1845), 7th President of the USA, 1829-37, known as 'Old Hickory'. After an active early career in which he defeated a British Army at New Orleans (1815), successfully invaded Florida (1818), and waged several campaigns against the Indians, as well as serving as a Congressman, Senator, and State judge and earning a reputation as a duellist, Jackson was elected President in 1829 and initiated the spoils system while generally strengthening presidential powers. He retired in 1837 and lived out his life at his home in Tennessee.

Jackson[2], Thomas Jonathan ('Stonewall') (1824-63), Confederate general of the American Civil War, who made his mark as a brigade commander at the first battle of Bull Run in 1861 (where a successful defensive stand earned him his nickname). As the trusted deputy of R. E. Lee he played a crucial part in the Confederate victories in Virginia in the first two years of the war. Jackson died after being mistakenly shot by his own troops at the battle of Chancellorsville.

Jack the Ripper a notorious Victorian murderer, never identified, who carried out a series of grisly murders of prostitutes in the East End of London in 1888-9. In each case the body was mutilated in a way that indicated a knowledge of anatomy. The authorities received taunting notes from a person calling himself Jack the Ripper and claiming to be the murderer, but the case remains unsolved.

Jacob /ˈdʒeɪkəb/ a Hebrew patriarch (see ISRAEL). —**Jacob's ladder,** a ladder between earth and heaven, with angels ascending and descending, which Jacob saw in a dream at Bethel (Gen. 28: 12). [f. Heb., = supplanter]

Jacobean /dʒækəˈbiːən/ *adj.* of James I's reign. [f. L *Jacobus* James f. Gk *Iakōbos* Jacob (see prec.)]

Jacobin /ˈdʒækəbɪn/ *n.* **1.** see DOMINICAN. **2.** a member of an extreme political party during the French Revolution. Taking their name from the old Jacobin convent where they held their first meetings in 1789, the Jacobins were the most radical of the large political groups formed in the wake of the revolution of 1789, advocating complete equality and democracy and willing to undertake extreme actions to realize their goals. [f. F f. L (as prec.)]

Jacobite[1] /ˈdʒækəbaɪt/ *n.* a follower of Jacobus Bardaeus (6th-c. Syrian monophysite monk). The Jacobites (not so called until 787) became the national Church of Syria; a small membership still exists. [f. *Jacobus* (see JACOBEAN)]

Jacobite[2] /ˈdʒækəbaɪt/ *n.* an adherent of the deposed James II, or of his descendants, or of the Stuarts after the Revolution of 1688, in their claim to the British throne. The Jacobites drew most of their support from Catholic clans of the Scottish Highlands, backed by France only when it suited her political convenience. Three serious attempts were launched to regain the throne in 1689-90, 1715, and 1745-6, but support finally collapsed when the clans were suppressed after the battle of Culloden. [as prec.]

Jacquard /ˈdʒækɑːd/ *n.* **1.** an apparatus with perforated cards, fitted to a loom to facilitate the weaving of figured fabrics. **2.** a fabric made thus. [f. J.M. *Jacquard* of Lyons (d.1834), the inventor]

Jacuzzi /dʒəˈkuːzɪ/ *n.* [P] a large bath with underwater jets of water to massage the body. [f. name of inventor and manufacturer]

jade[1] *n.* **1.** a hard green, blue, or white stone, a silicate of calcium and magnesium. **2.** its green colour. [F, f. Sp. (*piedra de*) *ijada* (stone of) the colic f. L. *ilia* flanks]

jade[2] *n.* **1.** a poor worn-out horse. **2.** a hussy. [orig. unkn.]

jaded /ˈdʒeɪdɪd/ *adj.* tired and bored; (of the appetite) dulled, lacking zest for food. [f. prec.]

jadeite /ˈdʒeɪdaɪt/ *n.* a jadelike silicate of sodium and aluminium. [f. JADE[1]]

Jaffa /ˈdʒæfə/ *n.* (also **Jaffa orange**) a large oval thick-skinned variety of orange. [f. *Jaffa* port in Israel, near which it was first grown]

jag[1] *n.* a sharp projection of rock etc. —*v.t.* (**-gg-**) to cut or tear unevenly; to make indentations in. [prob. imit.]

jag[2] *n.* (*slang*) a drinking bout; a period of indulgence in an activity, emotion, etc. [orig. = load for one horse; orig. unkn.]

Jagannatha /dʒægəˈnɑːθə/ (*Hinduism*) the form of Krishna worshipped in Puri, Orissa. In the annual festival held in June or July his image is carried through the streets in a heavy chariot dragged along by devotees; some devotees are said to have thrown themselves under its wheels. [Skr., = lord of the world]

jagged /ˈdʒægɪd/ *adj.* with an unevenly cut or torn edge. [f. JAG[1]]

jaguar /ˈdʒægjʊə(r)/ *n.* a large American carnivorous spotted animal (*Panthera onca*) of the cat family. [f. Tupi-Guarani]

jail, jailer var. of GAOL, GAOLER.

Jain /dʒaɪn/ *n.* an adherent of Jainism. —*adj.* of Jainism. [Hindi f. Skr. *jainas* of the conquerors (*ji* conquer)]

Jainism /'dʒaɪnɪz(ə)m/ *n.* a non-theistic religion founded in India in the 6th c. BC by Vardhamana Mahavira as a reaction against the teachings of orthodox Brahminism. Its central doctrine is non-injury to living creatures. Salvation is attained by perfection of the soul through successive lives (see KARMA). Unlike Buddhism, Jainism survives in India today but never spread outside it. There are two major sects: the white-robed Svetambaras and the naked Digambaras. —**Jainist** *n.* [f. prec.]

Jakarta /dʒə'kɑːtə/ the capital of Indonesia, situated in NW Java; pop. (1980) 6,503,400.

jalap /'dʒæləp/ *n.* a purgative drug from the tubers of a Mexican plant (*Exogonium purga*). [F f. Sp. (*Jalapa, Xalapa* Mexican city)]

jalopy /dʒə'lɒpɪ/ *n.* (*colloq.*) a dilapidated old motor vehicle. [orig. unkn.]

jalousie /'ʒæluːziː/ *n.* a slatted blind or shutter to admit air and light but not rain etc. [F, = JEALOUSY]

jam[1] *v.t./i.* (**-mm-**) **1.** to squeeze or wedge (*into* a space); to become wedged. **2.** to cause (machinery) to become wedged etc. so that it cannot work; to become thus wedged. **3.** to force or thrust violently. **4.** to push or cram together in a compact mass; to block (a passage, road, etc.) by crowding. **5.** to make (a radio transmission) unintelligible by causing interference. **6.** (*colloq.*, in jazz etc.) to extemporize with other musicians. —*n.* **1.** a squeeze, a crush; a stoppage (of a machine etc.) due to jamming. **2.** a crowded mass. **3.** (*colloq.*) an awkward position, a fix. **4.** (*colloq.*) improvised playing by a group of jazz musicians. —**jam-packed** *adj.* (*colloq.*) very full. [imit.]

jam[2] *n.* **1.** a sweet substance made of fruit and sugar boiled until thick. **2.** (*colloq.*) something easy or pleasant. —**jam tomorrow**, a pleasant thing continually promised but usually never produced. [perh. = prec.]

Jamaica /dʒə'meɪkə/ an island country in the Caribbean Sea SE of Cuba, a member State of the Commonwealth; pop. (est. 1982) 2,265,400; official language, English; capital, Kingston. The economy is based on both agriculture and industry, in the latter respect particularly upon bauxite and aluminium, but chronic unemployment has continued to cause serious social problems. Discovered by Columbus in 1494, Jamaica remained a Spanish colony until conquered by the British in 1655. British colonial rule was threatened by popular violence in the mid-19th c. which led to the suspension of representative government for two decades, but self-government was granted in 1944, and in 1962 Jamaica became an independent Commonwealth State. —**Jamaican** *adj. & n.*

jamb /dʒæm/ *n.* a side post or side of a doorway, window, or fireplace. [f. OF *jambe* leg f. L]

jamboree /dʒæmbə'riː/ *n.* **1.** a celebration, merry-making. **2.** a large rally of Scouts. [orig. unkn.]

James[1] /dʒeɪmz/ the name of seven Stuart kings of Scotland: **James I** (1394–1437), son of Robert III, reigned 1406–37. Captured by the English while a child, James remained a captive until he was able to buy his freedom in 1424. He returned to a land riven by nobles' feuds, and managed to restore some measure of royal authority, but only at the cost of making powerful enemies, some of whom eventually murdered him in Perth. **James II** (1430–60), son of James I, reigned 1437–60. Coming to the throne as a minor after his father's murder, James II eventually broke free from the domination of his regents and considerably strengthened the position of the Crown by crushing the Black Douglases, the most powerful noble house in the country. He was killed by the accidental explosion of a cannon at the siege of Roxburgh Castle. **James III** (1451–88), son of James II, reigned 1460–88. A weaker man than either his father or grandfather, James III proved increasingly unable to control his nobles who eventually raised an army against him, using his son (the future James IV) as a figurehead. The king was defeated at Sauchieburn near Stirling and killed by an unknown hand while fleeing the field. **James IV** (1473–1513), son of James III, reigned 1488–1513. Strongest of the Stuart kings of Scotland, James IV re-established royal power throughout the realm, most notably in the turbulent Highlands. He took an active part in European alliance politics, forging a dynastic link with England through his marriage to the daughter of Henry VII, and revitalizing the traditional pact with France. When England and France went to war in 1513, he supported the

latter and invaded England at the head of a large army. He died along with many of his nobles when this army was defeated by the Earl of Surrey at Flodden. **James V** (1512–42), son of James IV, reigned 1513–42. Both during his long minority and after his marriage to Mary of Guise, the Scotland of James V was dominated by French interests. The later years of his reign were marred by the return of nobles' discontent, rising Protestant agitation, and trouble with Henry VIII's England. He died young, leaving only an infant daughter. **James VI, VII** see JAMES[2].

James[2] the name of two kings of England and Scotland: **James I** (James VI of Scotland, 1566–1625), son of Mary Queen of Scots, king of Scotland 1567–1625 and of England 1603–25. Having survived a long and difficult minority, James had largely succeeded in restoring royal authority in Scotland before inheriting the throne of England on the extinction of the Tudor line. He was a difficult and at times erratic monarch, and although he managed to avoid serious trouble in the deepening constitutional and religious crisis in his new kingdom, his lack of decisiveness and the fecklessness of his declining years, when government was effectively in the hands of his favourite the Duke of Buckingham, left his son Charles I a difficult and potentially explosive legacy. **James II** (James VII of Scotland, 1633–1701), younger son of Charles I, reigned 1685–8. James was an accomplished soldier and sailor in the reign of his elder brother Charles II, but lost the support of many of his subjects soon after his accession as a result of his strong Catholic views and his attempts to reassert royal absolutism. Although he put down the rebellion of the Duke of Monmouth in 1685 he was deposed three years later in favour of William and Mary, and failed to regain his throne despite military action in Ireland and Scotland in 1689–90. He died in exile in France, leaving the Jacobite claim to the throne in the hands of his son James, the Old Pretender.

James[3] /dʒeɪmz/, Henry (1843–1916), American novelist and critic, younger brother of the philosopher William James. Educated in New York and Europe, he moved to Paris (1875) where he became influenced by Turgenev, Flaubert, Zola, and others; from 1876 he lived in England. His early novels, which deal predominantly with the impact of the older European civilizations on American life, include *Roderick Hudson* (1875) and *Portrait of a Lady* (1881). To this period belong *The Bostonians* (1886), about American society, *What Maisie knew* (1897), concerning English life, and the ghost story *The Turn of the Screw* (1898). International themes are revived in his mature though stylistically obscure works *The Wings of the Dove* (1902), *The Ambassadors* (1903), and *The Golden Bowl* (1904). James was the first important writer in English to give systematic criticism to the art of the novel, and, by his own example, demonstrated the scope of psychological and aesthetic considerations that the form could encompass. His critical essays are collected in *The House of Fiction* (1957).

James[4] /dʒeɪmz/, St **1.** 'the Great', an Apostle, elder brother of St John, martyred in AD 44. According to an old Spanish tradition his body was translated to Santiago de Compostela. Feast day, 25 July. **2.** 'the Less', an Apostle, son of Alphaeus. Feast day, 1 May. **3.** a person described as 'the Lord's brother', a leader of the Church at Jerusalem until put to death by the Sanhedrin in AD 62; **Epistle of St James**, a book of the New Testament traditionally ascribed to him. —**St James's Palace**, see separate entry.

James[5] /dʒeɪmz/, William (1842–1910), American philosopher and psychologist. Belonging to a family of Irish Calvinist stock he taught at Harvard where his philosophical work was bound up with an interest in psychology and physiology. Influenced by Peirce, James was a leading exponent of pragmatism. Its central theme is a functional definition of truth as that which we must take account of in order to survive and prosper; truth is what works for us rather than a depiction of some structural relation between ideas and reality. A similar approach to religious and moral beliefs is found in *The Varieties of Religious Experience* (1902) and *The Meaning of Truth* (1909). In psychology he introduced the concept of the 'stream of consciousness', which was influential also in philosophy and in literature. The novelist Henry James was his brother.

Jameson Raid /'dʒeɪmsn(ə)n/ an abortive raid made into Boer territory by pro-British extremists led by Dr L. S. Jameson in 1895 in an attempt to incite an uprising among recent, non-Boer immigrants. The raid seriously heightened tension in South Africa and contributed to the eventual outbreak of the Second Boer War.

Jamestown /'dʒeɪmstaʊn/ the site of an English colony established in Virginia in 1607 during the reign of James I. Built on a marshy and unhealthy site, the town suffered badly at the hands of fire, disease, and Indians, and was finally abandoned when the colony's capital was moved to Williamsburg at the end of the 17th c.

Jammu and Kashmir /'dʒʌmu:, kæʃ'mɪə(r)/ a State in NW India; capitals, Srinagar (in summer) and Jammu (in winter). (See KASHMIR.)

jammy *adj.* **1.** covered with jam. **2.** (*colloq.*) lucky, profitable. [f. JAM²]

Jamshid /dʒæm'ʃiːd/ (*Persian myth.*) a legendary early king of Persia, reputed inventor of the arts of medicine, navigation, iron-working, etc. He was king of the peris, condemned to assume human form for boasting of his immortality, and ruled Persia for 700 years.

Jan. *abbr.* January.

Janáček /'jænətʃek/, Leoš (1854-1928), Czech composer and conductor, who combined a sense of Czech nationalism with a powerful modernity, expressed not so much by breaking away from traditional forms and harmonic thinking as by the juxtaposition of conflicting elements: romantic melodic writing side by side with stark dissonant passages, lush orchestration offset by harsh widely spaced sonorities. In his operas emotions are portrayed with unflinching clarity, enhanced by their unusual settings.

jangle *v.t./i.* **1.** to make or cause to make a harsh metallic sound. **2.** to cause irritation to (nerves etc.). —*n.* a jangling sound. [OF *jangler*]

janitor /'dʒænɪtə(r)/ *n.* a door-keeper; the caretaker of a building. —**janitorial** /-'tɔːrɪəl/ *adj.* [L (*janua* door)]

janissary /'dʒænɪsərɪ/ *n.* a Turkish soldier; (*hist.*) a member of an elite and powerful body of Turkish infantry forming the sultan's guard and the main fighting force of the Turkish army from the late 14th to early 19th c. [f. Turk., = new troops]

Jansen /'dʒæns(ə)n/, Cornelius (1585-1638), Dutch Roman Catholic theologian, bishop of Ypres in Flanders and founder of Jansenism. Jansen held that the natural human will is perverse and incapable of doing good.

Jansenism /'dʒæns(ə)nɪzm/ *n.* a religious movement of the 17th and 18th c., based on the writings of Jansen and characterized by general harshness and moral rigour. Its most famous exponent was Pascal. The movement received papal condemnation and its adherents were persecuted in France (though tolerated in the Netherlands) during most of the 18th c. —**Jansenist** *n.* [f. prec.]

Janssens /'dʒæns(ə)nz/, Abraham (1575-1632), Flemish painter. He worked at first in the mannerist and later in the classical baroque style; in his *Lamentation* and *Crucifixion* balance and harmony are combined with decorative beauty and detail. The influence of Rubens is apparent in his later works.

January /'dʒænjʊərɪ/ the first month of the year. [L (*mensis*) *Januarius* (month) of Janus]

Janus /'dʒeɪnəs/ **1.** (*Rom. myth.*) an ancient Italian deity, guardian of doorways, gates, and beginnings, and protector of the State in time of war. He is usually represented with two faces, one at the front and one at the back of his head, so that he looks both forwards and backwards. **2.** (*Astron.*) a satellite of the planet Saturn, discovered in 1966.

Jap *adj. & n.* (*colloq.*) Japanese. [abbr.]

Japan /dʒə'pæn/ a country in eastern Asia, occupying a festoon of islands in the Pacific roughly parallel with the east coast of the Asiatic mainland; pop. (1982) 118,390,000; official language, Japanese; capital, Tokyo. Japan is now the leading economic power in SE Asia and the most highly industrialized country in that region, with a range of manufacturing industries that includes electrical goods, motor vehicles, chemicals, and shipping. According to Japanese tradition, the empire was founded in 660 BC by the emperor Jimmu, a descendant of the sun goddess. After a long period of courtly rule centred on Kyoto, from the 12th c. onwards the country was dominated by succeeding clans of military warriors. With the restoration of direct Imperial rule in 1868 it entered the modernizing process, which was accelerated by wars against China (1894-5) and Russia (1904-5), but Japan did not become a major world power until the 20th c. Its occupation of the Chinese province of Manchuria in 1931 was followed by full-scale invasion of China in 1937. In 1936 an alliance was formed

with Germany and later with Italy. After attacking Pearl Harbor (1941) the Japanese invaded Malaya and captured Hong Kong, Manila and Singapore. Their advance was halted by a series of US air and naval victories in 1942-4, and Japan surrendered in 1945 after the dropping of atomic bombs on Hiroshima and Nagasaki; a constitutional monarchy was established in 1947. —**Sea of Japan**, the sea between Japan and the mainland of Asia. [Chinese *Riben* sunrise (*ri* sun, *ben* origin)]

japan /dʒə'pæn/ *n.* a hard usually black varnish, especially a kind brought originally from Japan. —*v.t.* (-**nn**-) to coat with japan. [f. prec.]

Japanese /dʒæpə'niːz/ *adj.* of Japan or its people or language. —*n.* **1.** a Japanese person. **2.** the official language of Japan, spoken by virtually the whole population of that country. An agglutinative language, it contains many Chinese loan-words and has no genders, no article, and no number in nouns or verbs. It is written vertically, in a system that is partly ideographic and partly syllabic. The ideographs (known as *kanji*) were adopted from the Chinese in the early centuries of the Christian era and designate the chief meaningful elements of the language. They are supplemented by two groups of syllabic characters (*kana*), known as *hiragana* and *katakana*, for the agglutinative and inflexional endings. Attempts have been made to abolish characters altogether, but this is unsatisfactory since many words look exactly alike when written in Roman letters. There is no definite link between Japanese and any other language, although it may be related to Korean. [f. JAPAN]

Japheth /'dʒeɪfeθ/ a son of Noah (Gen. 10: 1); traditional ancestor of the peoples living round the Mediterranean. His name is probably to be connected with that of Iapetus, ancestor of the human race in Greek mythology.

japonica /dʒə'pɒnɪkə/ *n.* an ornamental variety of quince bearing red flowers in spring. [L *Japonicus* Japanese]

jar¹ *v.t./i.* (-**rr**-) **1.** to jolt. **2.** to sound with a harsh or unpleasant effect. **3.** to shock. —*n.* a jarring movement or effect. [prob. imit.]

jar² *n.* **1.** a glass or ceramic container with or without handle(s) and usually cylindrical. **2.** its contents. **3.** (*colloq.*) a glass (of beer etc.). [f. F. f. Arab. *jarra*]

jardinière /ʒɑːdɪ'njeə(r)/ *n.* a large ornamental pot for holding indoor plants. [F]

jargon /'dʒɑːgən/ *n.* words or expressions developed for use within a particular group or profession, sounding ugly and unintelligible to outsiders. [OF, = chatter]

Jarrow /'dʒærəʊ/ a town in north-east England on the Tyne estuary. It was the cultural jewel in the Northumbrian crown until the Viking invasions; the Venerable Bede lived and worked in its monastery. Its name is now associated with the hunger-marches to London that epitomised the despair of the economic depression of the 1930s.

Jarry /'dʒærɪ/, Alfred (1873-1907), French dramatist, remembered chiefly for his satirical farce *Ubu Roi* (*Ubu the King*, 1896). Jarry became a legendary character, adopting Ubu's grotesque absurdities and living a life of dissipation. He is regarded as a precursor of surrealism and the Theatre of the Absurd.

jasmine /'dʒæzmɪn/ *n.* a shrub of the genus *Jasminum* with white or yellow flowers, especially **common** or **white jasmine**, a climbing shrub (*J. officinale*) with fragrant flowers. **red jasmine**, a red-flowered frangipani (*Plumeria rubra*). **winter jasmine**, (*J. nudiflorum*) with yellow flowers. [f. F, ult. f. Pers. *yāsamīn*]

Jason /'dʒeɪs(ə)n/ (*Gk legend*) son of the king of Iolcos in Thessaly, and leader of the Argonauts in the quest for the Golden Fleece.

jasper /'dʒæspə(r)/ *n.* an opaque variety of quartz, usually red, yellow, or brown. [f. OF f. L f. Gk *iaspis*, of oriental orig.]

Jat /dʒɑːt/ *n.* a member of an Indian tribe widely distributed in NW India. [f. Hindi]

Jataka /'dʒɑːtəkə/ *n.* any of the various stories of the former lives of the Buddha found in Buddhist literature. [Skr., f. *jata* born]

jaundice /'dʒɔːndɪs/ *n.* **1.** a condition caused by obstruction of the bile or by infective hepatitis and other diseases, and marked by yellowness of the skin, fluids, and tissues and occasionally by disordered vision. **2.** disordered mental vision; resentment, jealousy. —*v.t.* **1.** to affect with jaundice. **2.** to fill with resentment or jealousy. [f. OF *jaunice* yellowness (*jaune* yellow)]

jaunt *n.* an excursion or journey, especially for pleasure.

—v.i. to take a jaunt. **—jaunting car,** a two-wheeled horse-drawn vehicle formerly common in Ireland. [orig. unkn.]

jaunty *adj.* **1.** cheerful and self-confident. **2.** (of clothes) stylish and cheerful. **—jauntily** *adv.*, **jauntiness** *n.* [f. F *gentil* (see GENTLE)]

Java /ˈdʒɑːvə/ a large island of the Malay Archipelago, chiefly under Dutch rule from the 17th c. until it was occupied by Japanese troops in 1942; it has formed part of Indonesia since 1950. **—Java man,** the fossil hominid, whose remains were first found in Java in 1891 (see PITHECANTHROPUS).

Javanese /dʒɑːvəˈniːz/ *adj.* of Java or its people or language. *—n.* (*pl.* same) **1.** a native or inhabitant of Java. **2.** the language of Java, which belongs to the Malayo-Polynesian group of languages and is spoken by about 45 million people. [f. JAVA]

javelin /ˈdʒæv(ə)lɪn/ *n.* a light spear thrown by hand as a weapon or in athletics (ill. SPORTS). [f. F]

jaw *n.* **1.** the bone(s) forming the framework of the mouth and (in vertebrates) carrying the teeth; the lower of these, the part of the face covering it; (in *pl.*) the mouth, its bones and teeth. **2.** (in *pl.*) something resembling or gripping like jaws. **3.** (*colloq.*) talkativeness, a lecture, a gossiping talk. *—v.t./i.* (*slang*) to talk long and boringly, to gossip. **—jaw-bone** *n.* a bone of the jaws, especially the lower jaw. **jaw-breaker** *n.* a word that is very long, or hard to pronounce. [f. OF *joe* cheek, jaw]

jay *n.* a bird of the crow family, especially the noisy chattering European bird *Garrulus glandarius* which has pinkish-brown plumage, a black tail, and a small blue barred patch on each wing. [f. OF f. L *gaius*, perh. f. name *Gaius*]

jay-walk *v.i.* to cross or walk in a road carelessly without regard for traffic or signals. **—jay-walker** *n.* [f. JAY = stupid person]

jazz *n.* **1.** a type of 20th-c., music (see below). **2.** pretentious talk or behaviour. *—adj.* of, in or like jazz. *—v.t./i.* **1.** to play or arrange as jazz. **2.** to brighten or liven *up.* [perh. orig. = copulation]
Jazz was developed in the southern USA early in the 20th c., blending West African rhythms with elements from ragtime, brass bands, spirituals, blues, and work-songs. Its characteristic features are improvisation, syncopation, and strong rhythm. In its earliest form—'Dixieland'—jazz was played by small groups. During the 1920s bands became larger, leading to the 'swing' of the 1930s emphasizing pre-arranged orchestrations. 'Be-bop' in the early 1940s marked a return to smaller groups, playing complex melodies with extreme syncopation. Later developments have included modal and atonal experiments, and attempts to fuse jazz with classical or rock music.

jazzy *adj.* **1.** of or like jazz. **2.** vividly coloured, showy. [f. JAZZ]

jealous /ˈdʒeləs/ *adj.* **1.** resentful of a rival or a person's advantages etc. **2.** watchfully tenacious (*of* rights etc.). **3.** (of God) intolerant of disloyalty. **—jealously** *adv.*, **jealousy** *n.* [f. OF f. L *zelosus* (as ZEAL)]

Jeanneret /ˈdʒenəreɪ/, Charles Edouard, see LE CORBUSIER.

Jean Paul /ʒɑ̃ː ˈpɔːl/ Johann Paul Friedrich Richter (1763-1825), German Romantic novelist. The humble village surroundings of his childhood are idyllically represented in his works. His best-known novels include *Hesperus* (1795), *Quintus Fixlein* (1796), and *Siebenkäs* (1796), which combine humour and sentiment with mystic idealism.

jean /dʒiːn/ *n.* **1.** a kind of twilled cotton cloth. **2.** (in *pl.*) trousers made of jean or of denim. [f. OF f. L *Janua* Genoa]

Jeans /dʒiːnz/, Sir James Hopwood (1877-1946), English physicist, mathematician, and writer on astronomy. He was the first to propose (in 1928) that matter is continuously created throughout the universe.

Jedburgh /ˈdʒedbərə/ a town in southern Scotland near the English border, where disputes frequently arose between border peoples, giving its name to **Jedburgh justice,** a summary procedure whereby a person is sentenced first and tried later.

Jeep *n.* [P] a small sturdy motor vehicle with four-wheel drive. [f. *GP* = general purposes, influenced by 'Eugene the *Jeep*', animal in a comic strip]

jeer *v.t./i.* to laugh or shout (*at*) rudely or scornfully. *—n.* a jeering remark or shout. [orig. unkn.]

Jeeves /dʒiːvz/, Reginald. Bertie Wooster's resourceful and omniscient valet in the novels of P. G. Wodehouse.

Jefferies /ˈdʒefrɪz/, John Richard (1848-87), English writer with a remarkable power of observing nature and representing it in combination with a strain of poetry and philosophy. He is probably best known for the boys' book *Bevis* (1882) and his autobiography *The Story of my Heart* (1883).

Jefferson /ˈdʒefəs(ə)n/, Thomas (1743-1826), 3rd President of the USA 1801-9. As a delegate to the Continental Congress (1775-6), Jefferson drafted the Declaration of Independence and thereafter played a key role in the American leadership during the Revolution. After serving in several important government posts he was chosen as President by the House of Representatives after tying with his opponent in electoral votes. Very much a philosopher-statesman in the mould of the Enlightenment, Jefferson advocated decentralization and the restrained use of presidential power. After his retirement he founded the University of Virginia and actively fostered the growth of culture in what was still a relatively young country.

Jehovah /dʒɪˈhəʊvə/ God, the name of God used in the Old Testament. [f. L *IeHoVa(H)*, erroneously formed f. YHVH (the ineffable name of God) and the vowels of *adonai* (Heb., = my lord) which was substituted for it in reading the Hebrew Bible]

Jehovah's Witnesses a sect of American origin, the Watch Tower Bible and Tract Society, founded c.1879 by Charles Taze Russell (1852-1916) of Pittsburgh, Pennsylvania, denying most of the fundamental Christian doctrines and refusing to acknowledge the claims of the State when these conflict with the sect's principles.

Jehu /ˈdʒiːhjuː/ king of Israel (9th c. BC), famous for driving his chariot furiously (2 Kings 9).

jejune /dʒɪˈdʒuːn/ *adj.* **1.** insipid, unsatisfying to the mind. **2.** deficient in nourishing qualities, barren. [L *jejunus* fasting]

jejunum /dʒɪˈdʒuːnəm/ *n.* the part of the small intestine between the duodenum and the ileum (ill. BODY 2). [L, as prec.]

Jekyll and Hyde /ˈdʒekɪl, ˈdʒiː-/ a single person in whom two personalities (one good, one evil) alternate. [f. R. L. Stevenson's story *The Strange Case of Dr Jekyll and Mr Hyde*, in which the respected Dr Jekyll could transform himself by means of a potion into the evil Mr Hyde, in whom was embodied only the evil side of Jekyll]

jell *v.i.* (*colloq.*) **1.** to set as jelly. **2.** to take definite form. [f. JELLY]

jellaba /ˈdʒeləbə/ *n.* a loose hooded cloak worn by Arab men in some countries. [Arab.]

Jellicoe /ˈdʒelɪkəʊ/ John Rushworth, 1st Earl (1859-1935), British admiral, commander of the Grand Fleet at the battle of Jutland.

jelly[1] *n.* **1.** a soft solid semitransparent food made of or with gelatine. **2.** a substance of similar consistency. **3.** a kind of jam made of strained fruit-juice and sugar. *—v.t./i.* **1.** to set or cause to set as jelly, to congeal. **2.** to set (food) in jelly. **—jelly baby,** a gelatinous sweet in the shape of a baby. [f. OF *gelee* frost, jelly, f. L *gelare* freeze (*gelu* frost)]

jelly[2] *n.* (*slang*) gelignite. [f. GELIGNITE]

jellyfish *n.* (*pl.* **-fish**) a coelenterate (usually marine) animal with a saucer-shaped gelatinous body and stinging tentacles, = MEDUSA.

jemmy *n.* a burglar's crowbar for forcing doors, windows, etc. [pet-form of *James*]

Jena /ˈjeɪnə/ a university town in East Germany scene of a battle (1806) in which Napoleon defeated the Prussians.

Jenkins's Ear, War of a war between England and Spain (1739). Robert Jenkins, a British sea captain, appeared before the Commons in 1738 to produce what he claimed was his ear, cut off by the Spanish in the West Indies while carrying out a search of his ship. His story was probably at least partially fabricated, but it caused great popular indignation and precipitated a naval war with Spain (a war already much sought after in many circles) in the following year.

Jenner /ˈdʒenə(r)/, Edward (1749-1823), English physician, the pioneer of vaccination. His home was at Berkeley in Gloucestershire where there was a local belief that dairymaids who had had cowpox did not catch smallpox, which was then a very common epidemic disease in all ranks of society. This led Jenner to the idea of deliberately infecting people with cowpox in order to protect them from the more serious disease, a practice which was eventually accepted throughout the world and led to the extermination of smallpox. In the intervals of medical practice he indulged his keen interest in natural history, and in 1787 wrote a paper on the habits of the cuckoo.

jeopardize /ˈdʒepədaɪz/ *v.t.* to endanger. [f. foll.]

jeopardy /ˈdʒepədɪ/ *n.* danger. [f. OF *ieu parti* divided (i.e. even) game f. L *jocus* game, *partiri* divide]

Jephthah /ˈdʒefθə/ a judge of Israel who sacrificed his daughter in consequence of a vow that if victorious against the Ammonites he would sacrifice the first living thing that met him on his return (Judges 11, 12). A similar rash promise was made by Idomeneus in Greek legend.

jerboa /dʒɜːˈbəʊə/ *n.* **1.** a small African desert rodent of the family Dipodidae, with long hind legs and tail. **2.** any of various Australian animals resembling this. [L, f. Arab. *yarbū'* flesh of loins, jerboa]

jeremiad /dʒerɪˈmaɪəd/ *n.* a long mournful complaint about one's troubles. [f. F f. foll.]

Jeremiah /dʒerɪˈmaɪə/ **1.** a Hebrew major prophet (c. 650 –c.585 BC) who saw the fall of Assyria, the conquest of his country by Egypt and then by Babylon, and the destruction of Jerusalem. **2.** a book of the Old Testament containing his prophecies. —*n.* a pessimistic person.

Jerez /ˈhereθ/ (also **Jerez de la Frontera**) a town in Andalusia, Spain, centre of the sherry-making industry.

Jericho /ˈdʒerɪkəʊ/ an ancient city north of the Dead Sea, now in Israel, occupied from c.9000 BC and one of the oldest continuously inhabited cities in the world. Little remains of the late Bronze Age period, the probable date of its destruction by Joshua recorded in the Old Testament.

jerk[1] *n.* **1.** a sudden sharp pull, push, twist, start, etc. **2.** a movement caused by involuntary contraction of a muscle. —*v.t./i.* to move with a jerk; to throw with suddenly arrested motion. —**jerky** *adj.*, **jerkily** *adv.*, **jerkiness** *n.* [perh. imit.]

jerk[2] *v.t.* to cure (beef etc.) by cutting it into long slices and drying it in the sun. [f. Amer. Sp. f. Quechua *echarqui* dried flesh]

jerkin *n.* **1.** a sleeveless jacket. **2.** (*hist.*) a man's close-fitting jacket, often of leather (ill. DRESS). [orig. unkn.]

jeroboam /dʒerəˈbəʊəm/ *n.* a wine-bottle of 6–12 times the ordinary size. [named after *Jeroboam*, a 'mighty man of valour', king of Israel, 10th c. BC (1 Kings 11: 28)]

Jerome[1] /dʒəˈrəʊm/, Jerome Klapka (1859–1927), English novelist and playwright, author of the humorous novel *Three Men in a Boat* (1889) and the play *The Passing of the Third Floor Back* (1908).

Jerome[2] /dʒəˈrəʊm/, St (Latin name *Eusebius Hieronymus*; c.342–420), Doctor of the Church, born in Dalmatia. He was a scholar, traditionalist, and monastic figure, who acted as secretary to Pope Damasus in Rome from 382 to 385, and finally settled at Bethlehem where he ruled a newly-founded monastery and devoted his life to study. His greatest achievement was the translation of most of the Bible from the original Hebrew and Greek into the language (Latin) of the people of his time (see VULGATE). Since the 13th c. he has often been depicted in art with a red hat, on the supposition that Damasus created him a cardinal; he is also often shown with a lion at his feet. Feast day, 30 Sept.

Jerry *n.* (*colloq.*) a German; Germans collectively. [f. GERMAN]

jerry *n.* (*slang*) a chamber-pot. [prob. f. *Jeroboam*]

jerry-built *adj.* built badly and with poor materials —**jerry-builder** *n.*, **jerry-building** *n.* [prob. orig. dial.]

jerrycan /ˈdʒerɪkæn/ *n.* a kind of 5-gallon can for petrol or water, used by the Germans and named and later adopted by the Allied forces in the war of 1939–45.

Jersey /ˈdʒɜːzɪ/ the largest of the Channel Islands; pop. (1981) 76,050; capital, St Helier. —*n.* a breed of light-brown dairy cattle that originated in Jersey, producing milk with a high fat content; an animal of this breed.

jersey /ˈdʒɜːzɪ/ *n.* **1.** a pullover with sleeves. **2.** machine-knitted fabric used for making clothes. [f. prec.]

Jerusalem /dʒəˈruːsələm/ the holy city of the Jews, sacred also to Christians and Muslims, lying in the Judaean hills about 30 km (20 miles) from the Jordan River, proclaimed by the State of Israel as its capital; pop. (1980) 448,200. It was a Canaanite stronghold, captured by David (c.1000 BC) who made it the capital of the national State; after the building of the Temple by Solomon it became a religious as well as a political capital. Since then it has shared the troubled history of its area — destroyed by the Babylonians in 586 BC and by the Romans in AD 70, refounded by Hadrian as a gentile city (AD 135) under the name of Aelia

Capitolina, destroyed again by the Persians in 614, and fought over by Saracens and Crusaders in the Middle Ages; Suleiman the Magnificent rebuilt its walls (1542). From 1947 the city was divided between the States of Israel and Jordan until the Israelis occupied the whole city in June 1967. Its Christian history begins with the short ministry of Christ, culminating in his crucifixion. For Muslims Jerusalem is the holiest city after Mecca and Medina, containing the Dome of the Rock, one of Islam's most sacred sites. —**the New Jerusalem,** the abode of the blessed in heaven. **New Jerusalem Church,** the followers of Swedenborg.

Jespersen /ˈjespəs(ə)n/, Jens Otto Harry (1860–1943), Danish philologist and writer on grammar and linguistics. His great work was *Modern English Grammar* (1909–49).

jess *n.* a short strap put round the leg of a hawk used in falconry. [f. OF *ges*, f. L *jactus* throw]

jessamine /ˈdʒesəmɪn/ *n.* = JASMINE.

Jesse /ˈdʒesɪ/ father of David (1 Sam. 16), hence represented as the first in the genealogy of Jesus Christ. —**Jesse window,** a church window showing Christ's descent from Jesse, usually in the form of a **tree of Jesse,** a tree springing from Jesse and ending in Jesus or the Virgin and Holy Child, with the intermediate descendants placed on scrolls of foliage branching out of each other.

jest *n.* a joke. —*v.i.* to joke. —**in jest,** jokingly. [orig. = exploit, f. OF *geste* f. L *gesta* (*gerere* do)]

jester *n.* **1.** a professional entertainer employed at a king's court or in a noble household in the Middle Ages. **2.** a person who makes jests. [f. JEST]

Jesu /ˈdʒiːzjuː/ (*archaic*, *vocative*) Jesus.

Jesuit /ˈdʒezjʊɪt/ *n.* a member of the Society of Jesus, an order of priests founded in 1534 in Paris by Ignatius Loyola, Francis Xavier, and others. The Society became the spearhead of the Counter-Reformation, though originally intended as a missionary order. Its genius is found in Ignatius' *Spiritual Exercises* (see IGNATIUS LOYOLA). The success of the Jesuits as missionaries, teachers, scholars, and spiritual directors—as well as the fear they have inspired—manifests how close they have been to their ideal of a disciplined force, effective in the cause of the Roman Church. [f. JESUS]

Jesuitical /dʒezjʊˈɪtɪk(ə)l/ *adj.* **1.** of or like Jesuits. **2.** (*derog.*) dissembling, equivocating. The Jesuits were accused by their enemies of using clever but false reasoning, and this suspicion gave rise to an offensive sense of *Jesuitical*. [f. prec.]

Jesus /ˈdʒiːzəs/ (also **Jesus Christ**) the central figure of the Christian religion. Jesus was a Jew living in Palestine at the beginning of the 1st c. AD, who in about AD 28–30 conducted a mission of preaching and healing (with reported miracles), which is described in the New Testament. He was arrested and put to death by crucifixion. Belief in his resurrection from the dead spread among his followers who saw in this proof that he was the Christ or Messiah, the fulfilment of the hopes of Israel, and indeed of all men. Further beliefs arose—about his virgin birth, and that he is the living Son of God, who has the power to grant eternal life to all who believe in him.

jet[1] *n.* **1.** a stream of water, gas(es), or flame etc. ejected, usually from a small opening. **2.** a spout or opening from which this comes; a burner on a gas cooker. **3.** a jet-propelled aircraft; a jet engine. —*v.t./i.* (**-tt-**) **1.** to spurt in jets. **2.** to travel or convey by jet-propelled aircraft. **3.** to jut. —**jet engine,** an engine utilizing jet propulsion to provide forward thrust, especially an aircraft engine that takes in air and ejects hot compressed air and exhaust gases (see TURBO-JET and ill. FLIGHT). **jet-foil** *n.* a vessel that travels above the surface of the water on struts attached to underwater foils. **jet lag,** delayed physical effects of tiredness etc. felt after a long flight by jet aircraft, especially owing to the difference of local time. **jet-propelled** *adj.* using jet propulsion. **jet propulsion,** see separate entry. **jet set,** the wealthy élite making frequent air journeys between social or business events. **jet stream,** a fast-moving relatively narrow stream of fluid that is present as a current in an atmosphere or ocean, especially a strong wind in the upper troposphere at middle latitudes that blows in an approximately horizontal direction, predominantly from west to east. [f. F *jeter* throw f. L *jactare* frequent. of *jacere* throw]

jet[2] *n.* **1.** hard black lignite that takes a brilliant polish. **2.** its colour, deep glossy black. —*adj.* of this colour. —**jet-black** *adj.* & *n.* [f. Gk *Gagai*, town in Asia Minor]

jet propulsion ejection of a usually high-speed jet of gas (or liquid) as a source of propulsive power, especially for aircraft. Simple examples are the movement of a balloon suddenly released after being inflated, and of the cuttlefish which propels itself by exuding spurts of its 'ink'. The principle of jet propulsion for aircraft was discussed in the 1860s, but its successful application awaited the development of the turbo-jet engine (see TURBO-JET).

jetsam *n.* goods thrown overboard from a ship in distress to lighten it, especially those that are washed ashore. [f. foll.]

jettison /ˈdʒetɪs(ə)n/ *v.t.* **1.** to throw (goods) overboard; to release or drop from an aircraft or spacecraft in flight. **2.** to discard as unwanted. [f. AF & OF f. L (as JET¹)]

jetty *n.* a breakwater or landing-stage. [f. OF (as JET¹)]

Jew *n.* a person of Hebrew descent; one whose religion is Judaism. European Jews were traditionally the subject of persecution by the Christian majority, partly as a result of religious prejudice but also because of jealousy of Jewish commercial success and because the Jewish community tended to maintain a separate and highly distinct identity. Anti-Semitism was a feature of European life from the Middle Ages, the killing of Jews being a common response to economic or social crisis, and in the modern age anti-Semitism became a central part of many right-wing political philosophies, most notably Nazism. In medieval England, Jews were particularly familiar as money-lenders, their activities being publicly regulated for them by the Crown, whose protégés they were. (In private, Christians also practised money-lending, though forbidden to do so by Canon Law.) Thus the name of Jew came to be associated in the popular mind with usury and any extortionate practices that might be supposed to accompany it, and gained an offensive sense in some contexts. [f. F, ult. f. Heb. *yehudi*, member of the tribe of Judah]

jewel /ˈdʒuːəl/ *n.* **1.** a precious stone worn as an ornament, a jewelled ornament. **2.** a highly valued person or thing. [f. AF, perh. f. L *jocus* jest]

jewelled /ˈdʒuːəld/ *adj.* **1.** set with jewels. **2.** (of a watch) fitted with jewels for the pivot-holes on account of their resistance to wear. [f. prec.]

jeweller /ˈdʒuːələ(r)/ *n.* a person who deals in or makes jewellery or jewels. [f. JEWEL]

jewellery /ˈdʒuːəlrɪ/ *n.* jewels or similar ornaments to be worn. [as prec.]

Jewess *n.* a female Jew. [f. JEW]

Jewish *adj.* of Jews. —**Jewish calendar,** a complex ancient calendar in use among Jews. It is a lunar calendar adapted to the solar year, having normally 12 months, but 13 months in leap years which occur 7 times in every cycle of 19 years. The years are reckoned from the Creation (3761 BC): the months are Nisan (normally March–April), Iyar (April–May), Sivan (May–June), Tammuz (June–July), Ab (July–Aug.), Elul (Aug.–Sept.), Tishri (Sept.–Oct.), Cheshvan (Oct.–Nov.), Kislev (Nov.–Dec.), Teveth (Dec.–Jan.), Shebat (Jan.-Feb.), Adar (Feb.-Mar.), 2nd Adar (intercalary month). The ecclesiastical year begins with Nisan and ends with Tishri. [f. JEW]

Jewry *n.* the Jewish people. [f. JEW]

Jew's harp a musical instrument consisting of a small U-shaped metal frame held in the teeth while a springy metal clip joining its ends is twanged with a finger. The strip can produce only one note but the harmonics of this note are produced by resonance by altering the shape of the mouth-cavity. [f. JEW; the name of the instrument is an ancient one, but no connection with Jews has been established with certainty]

Jezebel /ˈdʒezəb(ə)l/ (9th c. BC) Phoenician princess, daughter of Ethbaal king of Sidon and according to ancient tradition great-aunt of the legendary Dido (Elissa), queen of Carthage. She became the wife of Ahab king of Israel (I Kings 16: 31), and was denounced by Elijah for introducing the worship of Baal into Israel; she was killed when Jehu triumphed over Ahab. Puritan England was shocked by the fact that she 'painted her face', a practice which would have caused no surprise to her contemporaries since the use of cosmetics was widespread at that time.

jib¹ *n.* **1.** a triangular stay-sail from the outer end of the jib-boom to the head of the fore-topmast in large ships or from bowsprit to masthead in smaller ones (ill. SAILING-SHIPS). **2.** the projecting arm of a crane. —*v.t.* (**-bb-**) = GYBE 1,2. —**cut of a person's jib,** his general appearance or manner. **jib-boom** *n.* a spar run out from the end of a bowsprit. [orig. unkn.]

jib² *v.i.* (**-bb-**) **1.** to refuse to proceed in some action. **2.** (of a horse) to stop suddenly and refuse to go forwards. —**jib at,** to show unwillingness or dislike for. [orig. unkn.]

jibbah /ˈdʒɪbə/ *n.* a long coat worn by Muslim men in some countries. [Arab.]

jibe /dʒaɪb/ *v.t./i.* & *n.* = GIBE.

Jibuti /dʒɪˈbuːtɪ/ a country on the NE coast of Africa, formerly known as French Somaliland and then as the French Territory of the Afars and Issas, becoming independent in 1977; pop. (est. 1980) 315,000; official languages, French and Arabic; capital, Jibuti (pop. (est.) 150,000). —**Jibutian** *adj.* & *n.*

jiff *n.* (also **jiffy**) (*colloq.*) a short time. [orig. unkn.]

jig *n.* **1.** a lively jumping dance; the music for this. **2.** a device that holds a piece of work and guides the tools operating upon it. **3.** a template. —*v.t./i.* (**-gg-**) to move up and down rapidly and jerkily. [orig. unkn.]

jigger¹ *n.* **1.** a measure of spirits etc.; a small glass holding this amount. **2.** (*slang*) a cue-rest used in billiards. [partly f. JIG]

jigger² *n.* **1.** = CHIGGER. **2.** = CHIGOE. [corrupt. of these words]

jiggered /ˈdʒɪgəd/ *adj.* (*colloq.*, in a mild oath) damned. [euphem.]

jiggery-pokery /ˈdʒɪgərɪ ˈpəʊkərɪ/ *n.* (*colloq.*) trickery, underhand dealing. [Sc. *jouk* dodge, skulk]

jiggle *v.t./i.* to rock or jerk lightly. [f. JIG or JOGGLE]

jigsaw /ˈdʒɪgsɔː/ *n.* **1.** a mechanically operated fretsaw (ill. CARPENTRY). **2.** (also **jigsaw puzzle**) a picture on wood or cardboard etc. cut into irregular pieces which can be shuffled and reassembled for amusement. The first jigsaw puzzles (18th c.) were maps, mounted on wood and cut into oddly-shaped pieces. [f. JIG + SAW¹]

jihad /dʒɪˈhɑːd/ *n.* (in Islam) a holy war. One of the basic duties of a Muslim, prescribed as a religious duty by the Koran and by tradition, is to struggle against external threats to the vigour of the Islamic community and also against personal resistance to the rule of divine law within oneself. [Arab., = fight, struggle]

jilt *v.t.* to reject or abandon (a person) after having courted or promised to marry him or her. [orig. unkn.]

Jim Crow /krəʊ/ the policy of segregating and discriminating against Blacks, especially by laws passed in the southern States of the USA in the late 19th c. [from the refrain ('jump Jim Crow') of a plantation song]

Jimmu /ˈdʒɪmuː/ the legendary first emperor of Japan (660 BC), descendant of the sun goddess and founder of the imperial dynasty.

jingle *v.t./i.* to make or cause to make a metallic ringing or clinking sound. —*n.* **1.** a jingling sound. **2.** verse or words with simple catchy rhymes or repetitive sounds. [imit.]

jingo *n.* (*pl.* **-oes**) an aggressive fanatical patriot. —**jingoism** *n.*, **jingoist** *n.*, **jingoistic** *adj.* [orig. a nickname for a supporter of Disraeli in sending the British fleet into Turkish waters in 1878 to resist the advance of Russia, f. use of *by jingo* (= by God) in a popular music-hall refrain of 1878: 'We don't want to fight, yet by Jingo! if we do, We've got the ships, we've got the men, and got the money too'.]

jink *v.i.* to move with sudden quick turns, especially in dodging —*n.* an act of jinking. —**high jinks,** boisterous fun. [orig. Sc., prob. imit. of nimble motion]

Jinnah /ˈdʒɪnə/, Muhammad Ali (1876–1948), founder of Pakistan. An influential member of the Muslim League (the chief Muslim political party in British India), he led it in its struggle with the Hindu-dominated Indian National Congress, and from 1928 onwards, at conferences on Indian independence, championed the rights of the Muslim minority. After 1935, when self-governing Hindu provinces began to be formed, his fear that Muslims would be excluded from office led him to campaign for a separate Muslim State. When the State of Pakistan was finally set up under the India Independence Act of 1947, he was its first Governor-General.

jinnee /dʒɪˈniː/ *n.* (*pl.* **jinn** also used as *sing.*) (*Islamic myth.*) any of the supernatural beings, similar to but distinguished from angels, able to appear in human and animal form, and to help or hinder human beings according to their prescribed rule in the cosmos. [Arab.]

jinx *n.* (*colloq.*) a person or thing that seems to bring bad luck. [perh. var. of *jynx* the wryneck, a bird used in witchcraft]

jitter *v.i.* (*colloq.*) to be nervous, to behave nervously. —*n.* (in *pl.*, *colloq.*) nervousness. —**jittery** *adj.* [orig. unkn.]

jitterbug *n.* **1.** a nervous person. **2.** a dance performed chiefly to boogie-woogie and swing music, popular in the early 1940s. —*v.i.* (**-gg-**) to dance the jitterbug. [f. prec.]

jive *n.* a type of fast lively jazz music; a dance done to this. —*v.i.* to dance to or play jive. [orig. unkn.]

Jnr. *abbrev.* Junior.

Joachim /ˈdʒəʊəkɪm/, St, the husband of St Anne and father of the Virgin Mary. He is first mentioned in an apocryphal work of the 2nd c., and then rarely referred to until much later times.

Joan of Arc, St (1412-31), a French peasant girl who became a national heroine. Inspired by 'voices' of St Catherine and St Michael, she led the French armies against the English, relieved Orleans, and stood beside the French king Charles VII at his coronation. Captured by the Burgundians, she was handed over to the English, tried, condemned for heresy, and burnt at the stake in Rouen. She was canonized in 1920. Feast day, 30 May.

Job /dʒəʊb/ **1.** a book of the Old Testament, variously dated 5th-2nd c. BC. **2.** its hero, a wealthy and prosperous man whose patience and exemplary piety are tried by dire and undeserved misfortunes, and who, in spite of his bitter lamentations, remains finally confident in the goodness and justice of God. —**Job's comforter**, a person who aggravates the distress of the person he is supposed to be comforting.

job *n.* **1.** a piece of work. **2.** a position in paid employment. **3.** a difficult task. —*v.t./i.* (**-bb-**) **1.** to do jobs, to do piece-work. **2.** to hire or let out for a definite time or job. **3.** to buy and sell (stock or goods) as a middleman. —**bad** (*or* **good**) **job**, an unsatisfactory (or satisfactory) state of affairs. **job lot**, a collection of miscellaneous articles. **just the job**, (*slang*) precisely what is wanted. **make a (good) job of**, to do thoroughly or successfully. [orig. unkn.]

jobber *n.* **1.** a stockjobber. **2.** one who jobs. [f. JOB]

jobbery /ˈdʒɒbərɪ/ *n.* corrupt dealing. [f. JOB]

jobcentre *n.* a government office displaying information about available jobs.

jobless *adj.* unemployed. [f. JOB + -LESS]

Jocasta /dʒəˈkæstə/ (*Gk legend*) the mother and wife of Oedipus.

Jock *n.* a nickname for a Scotsman. [Sc. form of *Jack*]

jockey *n.* a person who rides in horse-races, especially a professional. —*v.t./i.* to manœuvre in order to gain an advantage. [f. Sc. *Jock* Jack]

Jockey Club a club whose stewards are the central authority for the administration and control of horse-racing in England. It was founded in 1750.

jock-strap *n.* a support or protection for the male genitals, worn especially by sportsmen. [f. vulg. *jock* genitals]

jocose /dʒəˈkəʊs/ *adj.* joking. —**jocosely** *adv.*, **jocoseness** *n.*, **jocosity** /-ˈkɒsɪtɪ/ *n.* [f. L (*jocus* jest)]

jocular /ˈdʒɒkjʊlə(r)/ *adj.* joking, humorous. **jocularly** *adv.*, **jocularity** /-ˈlærɪtɪ/ *n.* [as prec.]

jocund /ˈdʒɒkənd/ *adj.* (*literary*) merry, cheerful. —**jocundity** /dʒəˈkʌndɪtɪ/ *n.* [f. OF f. L *jocundus* pleasant]

jodhpurs /ˈdʒɒdpəz/ *n.pl.* riding-breeches reaching to the ankle, fitting closely below the knee and loosely above it. [f. *Jodhpur*, city and former State of India]

Jodrell Bank /ˈdʒɒdr(ə)l/ the site in Cheshire of the Nuffield Radio Astronomy Laboratory of Manchester University. It has one of the world's largest radio telescopes, with a giant reflector, 76m (250 ft.) in diameter, that can be tilted in any direction.

Joel /ˈdʒəʊ(ə)l/ **1.** a Hebrew minor prophet of the 5th or possibly 9th c. BC. **2.** a book of the Old Testament containing his prophecies.

joey *n.* (*Austral.*) **1.** a young kangaroo. **2.** a young animal. [Aboriginal *joè*]

jog *v.t./i.* (**-gg-**) **1.** to shake with a push or jerk, to nudge. **2.** to rouse or stimulate (memory). **3.** to move up and down with an unsteady motion. **4.** to move at a jogtrot, to run at a leisurely pace with short strides as a form of exercise. —*n.* **1.** a slight shake or push, a nudge. **2.** a slow walk, run, or trot. —**jog on** *or* **along**, to proceed slowly or laboriously. —**jogger** *n.* [imit.]

joggle *v.t./i.* to shake slightly, to move by slight jerks. —*n.* a slight shake, a joggling movement. [f. JOG]

jogtrot *n.* a slow regular trot.

Johannesburg /dʒəʊˈhænɪsbɜːg/ a city of Transvaal, the largest city of the Republic of South Africa and the centre of its gold-mining industry; pop. (1980) 1,536,457.

John¹ /dʒɒn/ (1165-1216), son of Henry II, king of England 1199-1216, nicknamed John Lackland because, unlike his elder brothers, he did not receive a large fief from his father. On his accession he was recognized by both England and Normandy, but lost Normandy and other areas of France by 1205. At home, his despotic inclinations caused him to fall foul of both the Church and the barons. His refusal to accept the papal nominee Stephen Langton as Archbishop of Canterbury led to England's being placed under an interdict in 1208, and to his own excommunication. His character, a mixture of brutality, cowardice, and sloth, caused him to be generally hated and despised. The English barons opposed his high-handed methods of raising money and forced him to sign Magna Carta in 1215; when John ignored its provisions civil war broke out, and he died on campaign.

John² /dʒɒn/ the name of six kings of Portugal:

John I 'the Great' (1357-1433), reigned 1385-1433. Regent from 1383, John defeated a Castilian attempt to seize the throne, and, after being chosen king, won a final decisive victory over the Castilians at Aljubarrota in 1385 with English help. He established an English alliance, married a daughter of John of Gaunt, and presided over a long period of peace and prosperity notable for his encouragement of voyages of discovery.

John IV 'the Fortunate' (1605-1656), reigned 1640-56. The founder of the Braganza dynasty, he expelled a Spanish usurper and proclaimed himself king in 1640. He defeated the Spanish at Montijo in 1644, drove the Dutch out of Brazil in 1654, and generally restored Portugal's international position.

John³ /dʒɒn/, Augustus (1878-1961), British painter, born in Wales, who studied at the Slade School in London and began to exhibit at the New English Art Club in 1903. His '*Smiling Woman*' (1910), a portrait of his wife, is considered one of his masterpieces. Other portraits include those of Hardy, Shaw, Yeats, Joyce, and Dylan Thomas, indicating the literary and artistic milieu of which he was part. He was a fine draughtsman, and his modified Post-Impressionist approach lent an individual vitality and colour to his landscapes and drawings which set him apart. John was seen as a notorious rebel, a leader of independent thought in English art.

John⁴ /dʒɒn/, Don (*c.*1545-78) of Austria, Spanish soldier. The illegitimate son of the Emperor Charles V, John led the Christian fleet to victory over the Turks at Lepanto in 1571, but afterwards, as Governor-General of the Netherlands, fell foul of his half-brother Philip II and was deposed.

John⁵ /dʒɒn/, Gwen (Gwendolen Mary), (1876-1939), British painter, sister of Augustus John, who took lessons, in Paris, from Whistler. The influence of his grey tonality can be seen in her works, which are largely figures of girls or nuns in interior settings, water-colour genre scenes, and landscapes. From 1904 she worked as Rodin's model, and was his devoted friend and mistress. After 1898 she lived in France and became a devout Roman Catholic and a recluse.

John⁶ /dʒɒn/, St **1.** an Apostle (called also St John the Evangelist or St John the Divine), son of a Galilean fisherman and brother of St James. He was credited since very early times (probably erroneously) with the authorship of the fourth Gospel, the Apocalypse, and three epistles of the New Testament. Feast day, 27 Dec. **2.** the fourth Gospel. **3.** any of the three epistles attributed to St John.

John Bull /bʊl/ a personification of the English nation, a typical Englishman, represented as a stout red-faced farmer-like man in a top hat and high boots. It was originally the name of a character representing the English nation in J. Arbuthnot's satire 'Law is a Bottomless Pit' (1712).

johnny /ˈdʒɒnɪ/ *n.* (*colloq.*) a fellow, a man. —**johnny-come-lately** *n.* a newcomer, an upstart. [dim. of forename *John*]

John of the Cross, St (1542-91), Spanish mystic and poet, joint founder, with St Teresa, of the 'Discalced' (i.e. reformed) Carmelite order. His extensive treatises on the mystical life include accounts of the purgation and purification of the soul which are regarded as amongst the finest mystical literature. He was declared Doctor of the Church in 1926.

John o'Groats /dʒɒn ə ˈgrəʊts/ a village on the extreme NE point of the Scottish mainland. It is the reputed site of a house built in the 16th c. by a Dutchman, John Groot. (See LAND'S END.)

John Sobieski /sou'bjeskɪ/ (1624-96), king of Poland 1674-96. Sobieski was elected king of Poland, as John III, in 1674 after a distinguished early career as a soldier. In 1683 he relieved Vienna when it was besieged by the Turks, thereby becoming the hero of the Christian world, but at home his rule was not particularly distinguished and failed to improve Poland's bad political situation.

Johnson[1] /'dʒɒns(ə)n/, Amy (1903-41), English aviator who established several long-distance records with her solo flights to Australia (1930), Tokyo (1932), and to and from the Cape of Good Hope (1936).

Johnson[2] /'dʒɒns(ə)n/, Cornelius (also Jonson Van Ceulen), (1593-1661), portrait painter, born in London of Dutch parents. Probably trained in Holland, from 1619-43 he painted many portraits in England before going to live in Holland. His style is best exemplified by sensitive individual portrait heads. He painted for Charles I and also widely outside court circles.

Johnson[3] /'dʒɒns(ə)n/, Samuel (1709-84), English poet, critic, and lexicographer. He suffered from impaired eyesight, depression, and poverty, and he left Oxford without a degree. After a period as a teacher, and his marriage to Mrs Porter (a widow twice his age), he left for London (1737) and began writing for *The Gentleman's Magazine*. He produced his own journal, *The Rambler* (1750-2), written almost entirely by himself. His best poetic works include *London* (1738) and *The Vanity of Human Wishes* (1749); these and his didactic romance *Rasselas* (1759) showed his strength as a moralist. After nine years of labour he published his *Dictionary* (1755) which earned him an Oxford degree (see DICTIONARY). In 1763 Johnson met his biographer, Boswell, while Burke, Goldsmith, Reynolds, and others, were friends as well as members of his literary club. His finest critical works are his Preface to his edition of Shakespeare (1765), and *The Lives of the English Poets* (1779-81). Johnson's reputation rests partly on Boswell's evocation of his humanity, his brilliant conversation, and his surges of eloquence whose effect was increased by the rollings of his huge form.

John the Baptist, St, a preacher who appeared *c.* AD 27 on the banks of the Jordan, demanding repentance and baptism from his hearers in view of the approach of the Kingdom of God. Among those whom he baptized was Christ. Later, his denunciation of Herod Antipas for his marriage led to his imprisonment and subsequent beheading (Matt. 14: 1-12).

joie de vivre /ʒwɑː də 'viːvr/ a feeling of exuberant enjoyment of life; high spirits. [F, = joy of living]

join *v.t./i.* **1.** to put together, to fasten, to unite. **2.** to connect (points) by a line etc. **3.** to become a member of (a club, army, etc.); to take one's place with or in (a company, procession, etc.); to take part with others (*in an activity* etc.). **4.** to unite (persons, or one *with* or *to* another); to be united in marriage, an alliance, etc. **5.** (of a river, road, etc.) to become continuous or connected with (another). —*n.* the point, line, or surface where things join. —**join battle,** to begin fighting. **join forces,** to combine efforts. **join up,** to enlist in an army etc. [f. OF *joindre* f. L *jungere*]

joiner *n.* a maker of furniture and light woodwork. —**joinery** *n.* [f. AF & OF (as JOIN)]

joint *n.* **1.** a place where two things are joined. **2.** a means or device for joining parts of a structure; a structure by which bones fit together. **3.** a section of an animal's carcass used for food. **4.** a fissure in a mass of rock. **5.** (*slang*) a place of meeting for drinking etc. **6.** (*slang*) a marijuana cigarette. —*adj.* belonging to or done by two or more persons etc. in common; sharing in possession etc. —*v.t.* **1.** to connect by a joint or joints. **2.** to divide (a carcass) into joints or at a joint. —**joint-stock company,** a company with the capital held jointly by the shareholders. **out of joint,** dislocated; (*fig.*) out of order. —**jointly** *adv.* [f. OF (as JOIN)]

jointure /'dʒɔɪntʃə(r)/ *n.* an estate settled on a wife for the period during which she survives her husband. —*v.t.* to provide with a jointure. [f. OF f. L (as JOIN)]

joist *n.* one of the parallel timbers stretched from wall to wall to carry floorboards or a ceiling. [f. OF *giste* f. L *jacēre* lie]

joke *n.* **1.** a thing said or done to excite laughter. **2.** a ridiculous circumstance, person, etc. —*v.i.* to make jokes. —**no joke,** a serious matter. [perh. f. L *jocus* jest]

joker *n.* **1.** one who jokes. **2.** an extra playing-card used in some games. **3.** (*slang*) a person. [f. JOKE]

jokey /'dʒəʊkɪ/ *adj.* joking, not serious. [f. JOKE]

Joliot /'ʒɒljəʊ/, Jean-Frédéric (1900-58), French nuclear physicist. He gave up a career in engineering to study radioactivity and in 1925 became Madame Curie's assistant at the Radium Institute. There, he worked with her daughter Irène, whom he married, and took the name Joliot-Curie; their joint discovery of artificial radioactivity earned them the 1935 Nobel Prize for chemistry. This research allowed Sir James Chadwick to discover the neutron when he reviewed their experiments in Cambridge. Shortly before the Second World War Joliot demonstrated that a nuclear chain reaction was possible, and after the war both he and his wife became involved with the development of nuclear energy and the establishment of the French atomic energy commission, but were removed from this government body because of their communism. Irène, like her mother, died of leukaemia.

jollify /'dʒɒlɪfaɪ/ *v.t./i.* to make or be merry. —**jollification** /-fɪ'keɪʃ(ə)n/ *n.* [f. JOLLY]

jollity /'dʒɒlɪtɪ/ *n.* being jolly; merry-making. [f. OF *joliveté* (as foll.)]

jolly *adj.* **1.** full of high spirits, cheerful, merry. **2.** slightly drunk. **3.** (*colloq.*, of a person or thing) pleasant, delightful (also *iron.*). —*adv.* (*colloq.*) very. —*v.t.* to coax or humour (a person) in a friendly way. —**Jolly Roger,** a black flag, usually with a white skull and cross-bones, popularly associated with pirates (though in fact gangs of robbers at sea generally flew a proper national flag to avoid causing suspicion). [f. OF *jolif* gay, pretty (perh. as YULE)]

jolly-boat *n.* a clinker-built ship's boat, smaller than a cutter. [orig. unkn.]

jolt /dʒəʊlt/ *v.t./i.* **1.** to shake or dislodge with a jerk. **2.** to move along jerkily, as on a rough road. **3.** to give a mental shock to. —*n.* **1.** a jolting movement. **2.** a surprise or shock. [orig. unkn.]

Jomon /'dʒəʊmən/ *adj.* of a kind of very early hand-made pottery of Japan, decorated with a characteristic cord-pattern (*jomon*), or the early neolithic or pre-neolithic culture (*c.*3000 BC) characterized by this pottery. [Jap.]

Jonah /'dʒəʊnə/ **1.** a Hebrew minor prophet. **2.** a book of the Old Testament bearing his name, telling of God's call to him to go to Nineveh and preach repentance, his disobedience and attempted escape by sea, his punishment of being thrown overboard and swallowed by a great fish, his deliverance, and the final success of his mission. —*n.* a person who is believed to bring bad luck.

Jonathan /'dʒɒnəθən/ son of Saul and friend of David, killed at the battle of Mount Gilboa (1 Sam. 13ff.).

Jones[1] /dʒəʊnz/, Daniel (1881-1967), British linguistics scholar, one of the founders of modern phonetic studies in Britain. He was responsible for describing, and setting out in his *English Pronouncing Dictionary*, the educated speech used in southern England by those influenced by attendance at the great public schools, a style of pronunciation which by the 19th c. had become characteristic of the upper classes throughout the country. He also invented a system of cardinal vowels, making it possible for variations of vowel-sounds to be described by reference to these.

Jones[2] /dʒəʊnz/, Inigo (1573-1652), English architect and stage designer about whose early life little is known. He was greatly impressed by Palladian architecture while on a visit to Italy (*c.*1600). He introduced movable stage scenery and was for many years involved with costume design for court masques. His two best-known architectural works, Queen's House, Greenwich, 1616-35 (an Italian villa design), and the Banqueting House, Whitehall, 1619-21 (an Italian palace design), were built after he became Surveyor to the Crown (1614). His works reflect, in a more subdued form, his debt to Palladio and the High Renaissance, and he was instrumental in introducing this Italian style into England.

Jones[3] /dʒəʊnz/, Robert Tyre ('Bobby') (1902-), American amateur golfer, probably the greatest player the game has known. In a career spanning only 8 years of serious golf, during which he played only intermittently between studying for degree courses in law, English literature, and engineering, he entered for 27 major championships and won 13 of them, retiring from competitive golf at the end of 1930. He later inaugurated the Masters tournament.

jonquil /'dʒɒŋkwɪl/ *n.* a species of narcissus (*Narcissus jonquilla*) with white or yellow fragrant flowers. [f. F f. Sp. f. L *juncus* rush; so called f. its rushlike leaves]

Jonson /'dʒɒns(ə)n/, Ben(jamin) (1572/3-1637), English dramatist and poet. His first important play *Every Man in his Humour* (1598) established his 'comedy of humours' whereby each character is dominated by a particular obsession. *Sejanus* (1603) and *Catiline* (1611) are his only tragedies, both on Roman themes. These closely follow classical models, as do his many court masques (with scenery by Inigo Jones) in which he embodied the 'antimasque', as a deliberate foil to the principal masque. His vigorous even savage humour and his originality are best manifested in his greatest comedies *Volpone* (1605/6), *The Alchemist* (1612), and *Bartholomew Fayre* (1614). His prestige and influence remained unrivalled in the 17th c. (he was ranked above Shakespeare). He presided over a literary circle which met at the Mermaid Tavern and his friends included Shakespeare, Bacon, and Donne, and younger writers known as 'the tribe of Ben'. Jonson is buried in Westminster Abbey.

Jordaens /jɔː'dɑːns/, Jacob (1593-1678), Flemish painter of religious, genre, and mythological subjects, best known for his peasant scenes using a technique of thick impasto. He was influenced by Caravaggio and Rubens, his contemporary. He was commissioned in 1660, along with Rembrandt and Lievens, to make paintings for the Town Hall in Amsterdam, an indication of his standing.

Jordan /'dʒɔːd(ə)n/ **1.** a river flowing southward from the Anti-Lebanon mountains through the Sea of Galilee into the Dead Sea. **2.** the Hashemite Kingdom of the Jordan, an Arab State east of the River Jordan, bordered by Syria, Israel, Saudi Arabia, and Iraq; pop. (est.) 2,400,000; official language, Arabic; capital, Amman. Romans, Arabs, and Crusaders dominated the area successively until it fell under Turkish rule in the 16th c. In 1916 the land east of the River Jordan was made a British protectorate, the Amirate of Transjordan; this became independent in 1946 and changed its name to the Hashemite Kingdom of Jordan in 1949. During the Arab-Israeli war of 1948-9 the Jordanians overran a large area on the west bank of the river, but were driven from this by Israel in the Six-Day War of 1967. Its natural resources are meagre, and its only outlet to the sea is the port of Aqaba at the NE end of the Red Sea. —**Jordanian** /-'deɪnɪən/ *adj.* & *n.*

Joseph[1] /'dʒəʊsɪf/ Hebrew patriarch, son of Jacob and Rachel, sold by his brothers into captivity in Egypt, where he attained high office (Gen. 30-50).

Joseph[2] /'dʒəʊsɪf/, St, a carpenter of Nazareth, husband of the Virgin Mary, to whom she was betrothed at the time of the Annunciation. Feast day, 19 March.

Josephine /'dʒəʊzɪfiːn/ (Marie Rose Joséphine Tascher de la Pagerie) (1763-1814), Empress of France. A West Indian by birth, Josephine, who had previously been married to the Viscount de Beauharnais, married Napoleon in 1796. Her failure to give the Emperor the heir he desired led to a breakdown of the marriage, and in 1809 Napoleon divorced her in order to marry the Austrian princess Marie-Louise.

Joseph of Arimathea /ærɪmə'θiːə/ a member of the Council at Jerusalem who, after the Crucifixion, asked Pilate for Christ's body, which he buried. The story that he came to England with the Holy Grail and built the first church at Glastonbury is not found before the 13th c.

Josephus /dʒəʊ'siːfəs/, Flavius (c.37-c.100), Jewish priest of aristocratic descent, native of Palestine, Pharisee, and Jewish historian. A zealous defender of Jewish religion and culture, he was politically pro-Roman and without sympathy for extreme Jewish nationalism. Captured in 67 during the revolt against the Romans, he saved his life by prophesying that Vespasian would become emperor, and during the siege of Jerusalem acted as interpreter to Titus. He returned with Titus to Rome, received Roman citizenship and a pension, and devoted himself to literary work; his *Jewish War* included an eye-witness account of the events that led to its outbreak.

josh *v.t./i.* (*US slang*) to make fun of; to hoax; to indulge in ridicule. —*n.* (*US slang*) a good-natured joke. [orig. unkn.]

Joshua /'dʒɒʃʊə/ **1.** the Israelite leader (probably 13th c. BC) who succeeded Moses and led his people into the Promised Land. **2.** the sixth book of the Old Testament, telling of the conquest of Canaan and its division among the twelve tribes of Israel.

Josquin Des Prés see Des Prés.

joss *n.* a Chinese idol. —**joss-house** *n.* a temple. **joss-stick** *n.* a stick of fragrant tinder and clay for incense. [perh. ult. f. Port. *deos* f. L *deus* god]

jostle *v.t./i.* to push roughly, especially when in a crowd; to struggle. —*n.* jostling. [f. JOUST]

jot *n.* a small amount, a whit. —*v.t.* (-tt-) to write (usu. *down*) briefly. [f. L f. Gk IOTA]

Jötun /'jəʊtʊn/ *n.pl.* (*Scand. myth.*) giants, enemies of the gods.

jotter *n.* a small notebook or note-pad. [f. JOT]

jottings *n.pl.* jotted notes. [f. JOT]

Joule /dʒuːl/, James Prescott (1818-89), English physicist from a wealthy brewing family, who experimented in his private laboratory and at the brewery. He was taught privately by Dalton, then an old man, and established that all forms of energy (heat, mechanical, or electrical) were basically the same and interchangeable. This was the basis of what is now called the first law of thermodynamics. He demonstrated this by means of very careful measurements, for instance, of the thermal effects of an electric current caused by the resistance of the wire, now known as Joule's Law. In 1852 he and Thomson, later Lord Kelvin, discovered the fall in temperature when gases expand (the Joule-Thomson effect), which led to the development of the refrigerator and to a new branch of science, cryogenics. The joule (see foll.) is named after him.

joule /dʒuːl/ *n.* a unit of work or energy, the work done by a force of 1 newton when its point of application moves 1 metre in the direction of action of the force, work done or heat generated by a current of 1 ampere flowing for 1 second against a resistance of 1 ohm. [f. prec.]

jounce *v.t./i.* to bump, to bounce, to jolt. [orig. unkn.]

journal /'dʒɜːn(ə)l/ *n.* **1.** a daily record of events or of business transactions and accounts. **2.** a periodical (orig. a daily newspaper). **3.** the part of a shaft or axle that rests on the bearings. [f. OF f. L, = DIURNAL]

journalese /dʒɜːnə'liːz/ *n.* a hackneyed style of language characteristic of some newspaper writing. [f. prec.]

journalist /'dʒɜːn(ə)lɪst/ *n.* a person employed to write for a journal or newspaper. —**journalism** *n.*, **journalistic** /-'lɪstɪk/ *adj.* [f. JOURNAL]

journey /'dʒɜːnɪ/ *n.* an act of going from one place to another, especially at a long distance; the distance travelled in a specified time. —*v.i.* to make a journey. [f. OF, = day's work or travel, f. L *diurnus* daily]

journeyman *n.* (*pl.* -men) **1.** a qualified mechanic or artisan working for another. **2.** a sound but undistinguished workman.

joust /dʒaʊst/ *n.* a combat with lances between two mounted knights or men-at-arms. —*v.i.* to engage in a joust. [f. OF *juster* bring together f. L *juxta* beside]

Jove /dʒəʊv/ Jupiter. —**by Jove!**, an exclamation of surprise or approval. —**Jovian** *adj.* [f. L *Jovis* used as genitive of *Jupiter*]

jovial /'dʒəʊvɪ(ə)l/ *adj.* full of cheerful good humour. —**joviality** /-'ælɪtɪ/ *n.*, **jovially** *adv.* [F f. L (as prec.); orig. ref. to influence of planet Jupiter]

jowl *n.* **1.** the jaw or jawbone; the cheek. **2.** loose skin on the throat, a dewlap. [OE]

joy *n.* gladness, deep pleasure; a cause of this. —**no joy**, (*colloq.*) no satisfaction or success. —**joyous** *adj.*, **joyously** *adv.* [f. OF *joie* f. L *gaudia* (*gaudēre* rejoice)]

Joyce /dʒɔɪs/, James Augustine Aloysius (1882-1941), Irish novelist and poet. Renouncing Irish Catholicism he left Ireland permanently in 1904 with Nora Barnacle (whom he later married) and thereafter lived in Trieste, Zürich, and Paris. His first important work *Dubliners* (1914; short stories) depicts Dublin as 'the centre of paralysis'. His autobiographical novel *A Portrait of the Artist as a Young Man* (1916) introduced Stephen Dedalus, who reappears in *Ulysses* (1922), his greatest novel. *Ulysses* and his second important work *Finnegan's Wake* (1939) revolutionized the form and structure of the novel and influenced the development of the 'stream of consciousness', while pushing linguistic experiment to the extreme limits of communication.

joyful *adj.* full of joy. —**joyfully** *adv.*, **joyfulness** *n.* [f. JOY + -FUL]

joyless *adj.* without joy. [f. JOY + -LESS]

joy-ride *n.* a ride for pleasure in a car etc., usually unauthorized. —**joy-rider** *n.*, **joy-riding** *n.*

joystick *n.* the control-lever of an aeroplane.

JP *abbr.* Justice of the Peace.

Jr. *abbr.* Junior.

jubilant /'dʒuːbɪlənt/ *adj.* exultant, rejoicing. **—jubilance** *n.*, **jubilantly** *adv.* [f. L (*jubilare* shout for joy)]

jubilation /dʒuːbɪ'leɪʃ(ə)n/ *n.* exultation, rejoicing. [as prec.]

jubilee /'dʒuːbɪliː/ *n.* **1.** an anniversary (especially the 50th). **2.** a time of rejoicing. [f. OF f. L ult. f. Heb. *yobel* ram's-horn trumpet; assoc. with L *jubilare* (see JUBILANT)]

Judaea /dʒuː'diːə/ the name in Graeco-Roman times for the southern district of ancient Palestine, west of the Jordan, which was the region occupied by the Jews from 537 BC after their return from the Babylonian Captivity. **—Judaean** *adj.*

Judah /'dʒuːdə/ the most powerful of the twelve tribes of Israel. After the reign of Solomon it formed a separate kingdom, with Benjamin, which outlasted that of the northern tribes (see ISRAEL[1]).

Judaic /dʒuː'deɪɪk/ *adj.* of or characteristic of the Jews. [f. L f. Gk (as JEW)]

Judaism /'dʒuːdeɪɪz(ə)m/ *n.* **1.** the religion of the Jews (see below). **2.** Jews collectively. [as prec.]
  The Jews were a race called to reject polytheism and worship the one God, the Creator. This monotheism, inherited by both Christianity and Islam, is the heart of the Jewish experience. But it is more than a speculative belief: the decisive events of their history, such as the call of Abraham, the Exodus, the witness of the prophets and the Exile, all draw out its radical moral character of abandonment to God and his often mysterious purposes, with rejection of any human self-reliance.

Judaize /'dʒuːdeɪaɪz/ *v.t./i.* to make Jewish; to follow Jewish customs. [as JUDAIC]

Judas /'dʒuːdəs/ *n.* an infamous traitor. [f. foll.]

Judas Iscariot /ɪ'skærɪət/ the Apostle who betrayed Christ to the Jewish authorities—the Gospels leave his motive uncertain. He later committed suicide.

Judas Maccabaeus see MACCABEES.

judder *v.i.* to shake noisily or violently. *—n.* a juddering movement or sound. [imit., cf. *shudder*]

Jude /dʒuːd/ St, an Apostle, also called Judas, generally identified with Jude the brother of James (*Jude* 1), martyred in Persia with St Simon. The last epistle of the New Testament is traditionally ascribed to him. Feast day (with St Simon) 28 Oct.

judge /dʒʌdʒ/ *n.* **1.** a public officer appointed to try causes in a court of justice. **2.** a person appointed to decide a dispute or contest. **3.** a person fit to decide on the merits of a thing or question. **4.** (in ancient Israel) any of the leaders with temporary authority in the period between Joshua and the kings (*c.*13th-11th c. BC). **5. Judges,** the seventh book of the Old Testament, describing the gradual conquest of Canaan under various leaders (*judges*) in an account that is parallel to that of the Book of Joshua and probably gives a truer picture. *—v.t./i.* **1.** to try (a cause) in a court of justice. **2.** to pronounce sentence on. **3.** to decide (a contest or question). **4.** to form an opinion about; to estimate; to conclude or consider. **5.** to act as judge (of). **—Judges' Rules,** a set of rules about the mode of questioning of suspects by police. Although the rules have no force in law, if they are not observed a court may decline to admit an accused person's statements in evidence. [f. OF f. L *judex*]

judgement /'dʒʌdʒmənt/ *n.* (in Law also **judgment**) **1.** judging, being judged. **2.** ability to judge; good sense. **3.** the decision of a judge etc. in a court of justice. **4.** the judging of mankind by God. **5.** a misfortune as a sign of divine displeasure. **—Judgement Day** or **Day of Judgement,** the day of the Last Judgement when God will judge all mankind. [as prec.]

judicature /'dʒuːdɪkətʃə(r)/ *n.* **1.** the administration of justice. **2.** a judge's office. **3.** a body of judges. [f. L (*judicare* to judge)]

judicial /dʒuː'dɪʃ(ə)l/ *adj.* **1.** of or by a court of law. **2.** having the function of judgement. **3.** of or proper to a judge. **4.** expressing a judgement. **5.** able to judge wisely, impartial. **—judicially** *adv.* [f. L (*judicium* court, judgement)]

judiciary /dʒuː'dɪʃərɪ/ *n.* the judges of a State collectively [as prec.]

judicious /dʒuː'dɪʃəs/ *adj.* judging wisely, showing good sense **—judiciously** *adv.* [f. F f. L (as JUDICIAL)]

Judith /'dʒuːdɪθ/ a book of the Apocrypha recounting the story of Judith, a rich Israelite widow who saved the town of Bethulia from Nebuchadnezzar's army by captivating the besieging general Holofernes and cutting off his head while he slept.

judo /'dʒuːdəʊ/ *n.* a sport of unarmed combat that developed from ju-jitsu primarily in Japan, founded by Dr Jigoro Kano (1860-1938). Its aim is to train the body and cultivate the mind through practice of the methods of attack and defence. [Jap. *jū* gentle, *dō* way]

judoist /'dʒuːdəʊɪst/ *n.* a student of or an expert in judo. [f. JUDO]

Judy /'dʒuːdɪ/ see PUNCH.

jug *n.* **1.** a deep vessel for liquids, with a handle and often a shaped lip. **2.** (*slang*) prison. *—v.t.* (**-gg-**) to stew (a hare) in a covered vessel. [perh. f. *Jug,* pet-form of *Joan*]

Juggernaut /'dʒʌgənɔːt/ = JAGANNATHA.

juggernaut /'dʒʌgənɔːt/ *n.* **1.** a large heavy vehicle. **2.** an overpowering force or object. [f. prec.]

juggins /'dʒʌgɪnz/ *n.* (*slang*) a simpleton. [perh. f. surname *Juggins*]

juggle *v.t./i.* **1.** to perform feats of dexterity (*with* objects), especially by tossing and catching them, keeping several in the air at once. **2.** to manipulate or arrange (facts, figures, etc.) to suit a purpose. *—n.* a trick, a deception. [f. OF *jogler* f. L *joculari* jest (as JOKE)]

juggler *n.* one who juggles, especially to entertain. [f. OF f. L *joculator* (as prec.)]

jugular /'dʒʌgjʊlə(r)/ *adj.* of the neck or throat. *—n.* the jugular vein. **—jugular vein,** either of the two large veins in the neck, conveying the blood from the head. [f. L (*jugulum* collar-bone, throat)]

Jugurtha /dʒə'gɜːθə/ (d. 104 BC) joint ruler of Numidia from 118 BC. His attacks on his royal partners prompted intervention by Rome and led to the outbreak of the Jugurthine War (described by the historian Sallust). He was eventually captured by Marius and executed in Rome.

juice /dʒuːs/ *n.* **1.** the liquid content of fruits, vegetables, or meat. **2.** a liquid bodily secretion. **3.** (*slang*) electricity. **4.** (*slang*) petrol used in an engine etc. [f. OF f. L *jus* broth]

juicy *adj.* **1.** full of juice. **2.** (*colloq.*) interesting, especially because scandalous. **—juicily** *adv.*, **juiciness** *n.* [f. prec.]

ju-jitsu /dʒuː'dʒɪtsuː/ *n.* a Japanese method of self-defence using throws, punches, kicks, arm-locks, etc. and seeking to utilize the opponent's strength and weight to his disadvantage. It began to take on a systematized form in the latter half of the 16th c. and many schools developed, each distinguished by its individual features. It fell into disrepute for various reasons (including its ruthlessness), and the expansion of judo further reduced its popularity. [f. Jap. (*jū* gentle, *jutsu* skill)]

ju-ju /'dʒuːdʒuː/ *n.* an object venerated in West Africa as a charm or fetish; the magic attributed to this. [perh. f. F *joujou* toy]

jujube /'dʒuːdʒuːb/ *n.* a sweet fruit-flavoured lozenge of gelatin etc. [F or f. L ult. f. Gk *zizuphon* edible fruit of species of plant *zizyphus,* orig. used to flavour jujubes]

juke-box /'dʒuːkbɒks/ *n.* a machine that automatically plays a selected gramophone record when a coin is inserted. [f. *juke* cheap roadhouse providing music for dancing, f. Negro dialect (of West African origin) in the south-western USA + BOX[1]]

Jul. *abbr.* July.

julep /'dʒuːlep/ *n.* **1.** a sweet drink, especially as a vehicle for medicine; a medicated drink. **2.** (*US*) iced and flavoured spirit and water, especially *mint julep.* [f. OF f. Arab. f. Pers., = rose-water]

Julian¹ /'dʒuːlɪən/ *adj.* of Julius Caesar. **—Julian calendar,** the calendar introduced by him in 46 BC and slightly modified under Augustus (see MONTH), in which the ordinary year has 365 days, and every fourth year is a leap year of 366 days (see also GREGORIAN CALENDAR). [f. L *Julianus* f. JULIUS]

Julian² /'dʒuːlɪən/ 'the Apostate' (Flavius Claudius Julianus, 332-63), Roman emperor 360-3, nephew of Constantine. He restored paganism as the State cult in place of Christianity, but this move was reversed after his death on campaign against the Persians. His own religious belief was based on a Neoplatonist monotheism; several of his works (in Greek) survive, including a prose *Hymn to the Sun.*

julienne /dʒuː'lɪ'en/ *n.* a clear meat soup containing vegetables cut into thin strips; such vegetables. *—adj.* cut into thin strips. [F, f. names *Jules* or *Julien*]

Juliet cap /'dʒuːlɪət/ a small network skull-cap, usually ornamented with pearls. [f. name of heroine of Shakespeare's romantic tragedy 'Romeo and Juliet']

Julius Caesar /dʒuːlɪəs ˈsiːzə(r)/, Gaius (100-44 BC), Roman general and statesman, of formidable intellect and physical energy. A member of the so-called First Triumvirate of 60 BC with Pompey and Crassus, from 58 to 51 BC he was engaged in the wars which completed the Roman conquest of Gaul, during which he mounted raids on Britain (55 and 54 BC). He was not popular as a person, but the victories achieved under his leadership assured him of the devotion of his soldiers, as well as enhancing his prestige, so that when disagreement with Pompey led to civil war he was sufficiently confident of his role to cross the River Rubicon (49 BC), defeating Pompey at Pharsalus in the following year. Now the undisputed first man in Rome, he carried through a series of reforms (including that of the calendar), and received extraordinary offices and honours; his monarchical tendencies were cut short by his murder on the Ides (15th) of March 44 BC in a conspiracy led by Brutus and Cassius. He was deified after his death. Of his writings there survive commentaries on the Gallic and Civil Wars, written in a spare style.

July /dʒuːˈlaɪ/ n. the seventh month of the year. [f. AF f. L *Julius* (*mensis*), named after Julius Caesar]

jumble v.t. to mix up, to confuse. —n. **1.** a confused pile etc., a muddle. **2.** articles for a jumble sale. —**jumble sale,** a sale of miscellaneous articles, usually second-hand, to raise funds for charity etc. [prob. imit.]

jumbo /ˈdʒʌmbəʊ/ n. (pl. -os) **1.** a person, animal, or thing that is very large of its kind. **2.** an elephant. **3.** a jumbo jet. —adj. very large of its kind. —**jumbo jet,** a very large jet aircraft able to carry several hundred passengers. [prob. f. MUMBO-JUMBO]

Jumna /ˈdʒʌmnə/ a river of northern India, rising in the Himalayas and flowing into the Ganges below Allahabad.

jump v.t./i. **1.** to move up off the ground etc. by bending and then extending the legs or (of fish) by a movement of the tail. **2.** to move suddenly with a jump or bound; to rise suddenly from a seat etc.; to give a sudden movement from shock or excitement etc. **3.** to pass over by jumping; to cause (a horse etc.) to jump. **4.** to pass over (a thing) to a point beyond; to skip (part of a book etc.) in reading or studying. **5.** to come *to* (a conclusion) hastily. **6.** (of a train etc.) to leave (the rails). **7.** to ignore and pass (a red traffic-light etc.). **8.** to abscond from. **9.** to pounce upon or attack (a person etc.). **10.** to take summary possession of (a claim allegedly forfeit etc.). —n. **1.** an act of jumping. **2.** an abrupt rise in a price etc. **3.** an obstacle to be jumped, especially by a horse. **4.** a sudden transition. **5.** a sudden movement caused by shock, excitement, etc. —**have the jump on,** (slang) to have an advantage over. **jump at,** to accept eagerly. **jump down a person's throat,** to reprimand or contradict him severely. **jumped-up** adj. upstart. **jump the gun,** (colloq.) to begin before the signal is given, or prematurely. **jump-jet** n. a jet aircraft that can take off and land vertically. **jump-lead** n. a cable for conveying current from one battery through another. **jump-off** n. a deciding round in show-jumping. **jump on,** to attack or criticize crushingly. **jump the queue,** to take unfair precedence. **jump suit,** a one-piece garment for the whole body. **jump to it,** to act promptly and energetically. **one jump ahead,** one stage ahead of a rival etc. [prob. imit.]

jumper[1] n. **1.** a person or animal that jumps. **2.** a short wire used to make or break an electrical circuit. [f. JUMP]

jumper[2] n. **1.** a woman's knitted garment for the upper part of the body. **2.** a loose outer jacket worn by sailors. [perh. f. dial. *jump* short coat]

jumpy adj. nervous, easily startled; making sudden movements. —**jumpily** adv., **jumpiness** n. [f. JUMP]

Jun. abbr. **1.** Junior. **2.** June.

junction /ˈdʒʌŋkʃ(ə)n/ n. **1.** joining. **2.** a place where things join. **3.** a place where railway lines or roads meet. —**junction box,** a box containing a junction of electric cables etc. [f. L (as JOIN)]

juncture /ˈdʒʌŋktʃə(r)/ n. **1.** a critical convergence of events; a point of time. **2.** joining. **3.** a place where things join. [f. L (as JOIN)]

June /dʒuːn/ n. the sixth month of the year. [f. OF & L *Junius* (goddess *Juno*)]

Jung /jʊŋ/, Carl Gustav (1875-1961), Swiss psychologist, collaborator with Freud in the development of the psychoanalytic theory of personality, though he later divorced himself from Freud's viewpoint because of its preoccu-

pation with sexuality as the determinant of personality. Jung originated the concept of two types of personality, introvert and extrovert, and four psychological functions (sensation, intuition, thinking, and feeling), of which one or more are held to predominate in any one person. His most novel proposition, expressed in his major work *The Psychology of the Unconscious* (1912) was the existence of a 'collective unconscious' (see COLLECTIVE), a conception which he combined with a theory of archetypes that he believed were of importance for study of the history and psychology of religion.

Jungfrau /ˈjʊŋfraʊ/ a mountain in the Swiss Alps, 4,158 m (13,642 ft.) high.

jungle n. **1.** land overgrown with tangled vegetation, especially in the tropics; an area of such land. **2.** a tangled mass. **3.** a place of bewildering complexity or confusion, or of ruthless struggle. —**jungly** adj. [f. Hindi f. Skr.]

junior /ˈdʒuːnɪə(r)/ adj. **1.** the younger (esp. appended to a name for distinction between two persons of the same name). **2.** younger in age; lower in rank or authority. **3.** of a low or the lowest position. **4.** for younger children. —n. **1.** a junior person. **2.** a person acting or working in a junior capacity. [L, compar. of *juvenis* young]

juniper /ˈdʒuːnɪpə(r)/ n. an evergreen shrub or tree of the genus *Juniperus*, especially one with purple berrylike cones yielding an oil used for flavouring gin and in medicine. [f. L *juniperus*]

junk[1] n. **1.** discarded articles, rubbish; anything regarded as of little value. **2.** (slang) a narcotic drug, especially heroin. —**junk food,** food which is not nutritious. **junk shop,** a shop selling miscellaneous cheap second-hand goods. [orig. unkn.]

junk[2] n. a flat-bottomed sailing vessel in the China seas. [f. F, Port. or Du., f. Javanese]

junket /ˈdʒʌŋkɪt/ n. **1.** a dish of milk curdled by rennet and sweetened and flavoured. **2.** a feast. **3.** (US) a pleasure outing. **4.** (US) an official's tour at public expense. —v.i. **1.** to feast, to make merry. **2.** (US) to hold a picnic or outing. —**junketing** n. [f. OF *jonquette* rush-basket (used for junket) f. L *juncus* rush]

junkie /ˈdʒʌŋkɪ/ n. (slang) a drug addict. [f. JUNK[1]]

Juno /ˈdʒuːnəʊ/ **1.** (Rom. myth.) an early and very important Italian goddess, in functions resembling Hera with whom she was anciently identified, and a great goddess of the Roman State. **2.** (Astron.) one of the minor planets, discovered in 1804.

Junoesque /dʒuːnəʊˈesk/ adj. resembling the goddess Juno in stately beauty. [f. JUNO]

junta /ˈdʒʌntə/ n. a political clique or faction, especially one holding power after a revolution. [Sp. & Port. f. L (as JOIN)]

Jupiter /ˈdʒuːpɪtə(r)/ **1.** (Rom. myth.) originally a sky-god, associated with lightning and the thunderbolt; later, the chief of the gods, giver of victory, identified with Zeus. **2.** (Astron.) a planet revolving in orbit between the orbits of Mars and Saturn. It is the largest planet of the solar system, with an equatorial diameter of 143,800 km, a massive atmosphere (its major component is hydrogen) with swirling clouds of ammonia and methane, a thin system of encircling rings, and a retinue of at least thirteen moons. A familiar planet to the ancients, Jupiter appears as one of the brightest objects in the night sky. Seen through a small telescope, coloured bands on its surface are obvious; these we now know to be due to atmospheric circulation, as is the Great Red Spot, a cyclonic weather system in the southern hemisphere extending over 10,000 km which has persisted at least since the beginning of telescopic observations. [L, = father of the bright heaven]

Jura /ˈdʒʊərə/ a system of mountain ranges, on the border of France and Switzerland, which has given its name to the Jurassic period when most of its rocks were laid down.

jural /ˈdʒʊər(ə)l/ adj. of the law; of (moral) rights and obligations. [f. L *jus* law, right]

Jurassic /dʒʊəˈræsɪk/ adj. of the second period of the Mesozoic era, following the Triassic and preceding the Cretaceous, lasting from about 213 to 144 million years ago. During this period dinosaurs and other reptiles attained their maximum size and were found on land, in the sea, and in the air. The first birds appeared towards the end of the period. —n. this period. [f. F *jurassique* f. JURA]

juridical /dʒʊəˈrɪdɪk(ə)l/ adj. of judicial proceedings; relating to the law. —**juridically** adv. [f. L *juridicus* (*jus* law, *dicere* say)]

jurisdiction /dʒʊərɪsˈdɪkʃ(ə)n/ n. **1.** authority to interpret and apply the law. **2.** official power exercised within a particular sphere of activity. **3.** the extent or territory over which legal or other power extends. [f. OF & L (as prec.)]

jurisprudence /dʒʊərɪsˈpruːd(ə)ns/ n. the science or philosophy of law. —**jurisprudential** /-ˈdenʃ(ə)l/ adj. [f. L (as prec. + PRUDENCE)]

jurist /ˈdʒʊərɪst/ n. one who is skilled in the law. —**juristic** /-ˈrɪstɪk/ adj., **juristical** adj., **juristically** adv. [f. F or L (jus law)]

juror /ˈdʒʊərə(r)/ n. **1.** a member of a jury. **2.** a person taking an oath. [f. AF f. L jurator (jurare swear)]

jury /ˈdʒʊərɪ/ n. **1.** a body of persons sworn to render a verdict in a court of justice or a coroner's court. **2.** a body of persons selected to award the prizes in a competition. —**jury-box** n. an enclosure for the jury in a court. **grand jury,** see GRAND. **petty** or **trial jury,** a jury of twelve persons who try the final issue of fact in civil or criminal cases and pronounce the verdict. —**juryman** n. (pl. **-men**), **jurywoman** n.fem. (pl. **-women**) [f. AF jurée oath, inquiry (as prec.)]

jury-mast /ˈdʒʊərɪmɑːst/ n. a temporary mast replacing one broken or lost. [perh. f. OF ajurie aid + MAST¹]

jury-rigged /ˈdʒʊərɪrɪgd/ adj. makeshift. [as prec.]

Jussieu /ˈʒuːsɪə/, Antoine Laurent de (1748-1836), a member of a French family of botanists whose home was a centre for plant collection and research. From extensive observation he grouped plants into families on the basis of common essential properties, and in Genera Plantarum (1789) developed the system on which modern classification of plants is based.

just adj. **1.** giving proper consideration to the claims of everyone concerned. **2.** deserved, right in amount etc. **3.** well-grounded in fact. —adv. **1.** exactly. **2.** barely, no more than; by only a short distance etc. **3.** at this or that moment, only a little time ago. **4.** (colloq.) simply, merely. **5.** positively, quite. **6.** (slang) really, indeed. —**just about,** (colloq.) almost exactly; almost completely. **just in case,** as a precaution. **just now,** at this moment; only a little time ago. **just so,** exactly arranged; exactly as you say. —**justly** adv., **justness** n. [f. OF f. L justus (jus law, right)]

justice /ˈdʒʌstɪs/ n. **1.** justness, fairness; the exercise of authority in the maintenance of right. **2.** judicial proceedings. **3.** a judge or magistrate. —**do justice to,** to treat fairly; to appreciate duly. **do oneself justice,** to perform in a manner worthy of one's abilities. **Justice of the Peace,** an unpaid lay magistrate appointed to hear minor cases. **Mr** (or **Mrs**) **Justice —,** the title of a High Court judge. [f. OF f. L justitia (as prec.)]

justiciary /dʒʌˈstɪʃərɪ/ n. an administrator of justice. —**Court of Justiciary,** the supreme criminal court in Scotland. [f. L (as prec.)]

justifiable /ˈdʒʌstɪfaɪəb(ə)l/ adj. that can be justified or defended. —**justifiably** adv. [F (as foll.)]

justify /ˈdʒʌstɪfaɪ/ v.t. **1.** to show the justice or truth of. **2.** (of circumstances) to be an adequate ground for, to warrant. **3.** (Theol.) to declare (a person) free from the penalty of sin (in Protestant theology on the ground of Christ's righteousness, according to Luther in response to faith alone; according to Aquinas by infusion of grace). **4.** to adjust (a line of type) to fill the space evenly. —**justification**

/-fɪˈkeɪʃ(ə)n/ n., **justificatory** /-fɪˈkeɪtərɪ/ adj. [f. F f. L justificare (as JUST)]

Justinian /dʒʌˈstɪnɪən/ (Flavius Petrus Sabbatius Justinianus, 483-565) Roman emperor from 527. He had a deep sense of the past greatness of the Roman Empire and was determined to restore it, by recovering the lost provinces of the West, by reforming its administrative abuses, and by codifying and rationalizing its legal system, making it his aim to restore religious and political unity. Under his general Belisarius Africa was reconquered from the Vandals (533) and Italy from the Ostrogoths (533-40); in 551 part of Spain was conquered from the Visigoths. His codification of the law produced an authoritative and ordered statement; the insistence that the monarch's will was supreme legitimized the State's control over ecclesiastical affairs which characterized the subsequent history of the Byzantine Church. Justinian carried out an active building programme throughout the Empire, erecting fortresses and churches and restoring aqueducts and other public buildings. His supreme achievement was Santa Sophia at Constantinople.

jut v.i. (**-tt-**) to project. —n. a projection. [var. of JET¹]

Jute /dʒuːt/ n. a member of a Low German tribe that invaded southern England (according to legend under Horsa and Hengist) in the 5th c. and set up a kingdom in Kent. [OE (cf. Icel. Iatar people of Jutland in Denmark)]

jute /djuːt/ n. fibre from the bark of tropical plants of the genus Corchorus, used for sacking, mats, etc. [f. Bengali f. Skr.]

Jutland /ˈdʒʌtlənd/ a peninsula which forms the continental part of Denmark. —**Battle of Jutland,** a major naval battle in which the British Grand Fleet under Admiral Jellicoe and the German High Seas Fleet under Admiral Scheer fought the only full fleet action of the First World War in the North Sea west of Jutland on 31 May 1916. Although the Germans had the better of the early part of the engagement, they eventually escaped from superior British firepower only as a result of poor British communications and the advent of darkness. Jellicoe was criticized for not winning a decisive victory, but in fact the German fleet never again sought a full-scale engagement, and British control of the North Sea remained unshaken.

Juvenal /ˈdʒuːvən(ə)l/ (Decimus Junius Juvenalis, c.60-c.130) Roman satirist. His sixteen hexameter satires, written, he says, out of a sense of indignation, present a savage attack on the vice and folly of Roman society. His anger was fuelled by the poverty which made him an unwilling dependent of the rich, and by his bitterness towards the emperor Domitian.

juvenile /ˈdʒuːvənaɪl/ adj. youthful; of or for young persons. —n. a young person; an actor playing such a part. —**juvenile delinquency,** violation of the law by persons below the age of legal responsibility. **juvenile delinquent,** such an offender. [f. L (juvenis young person)]

juvenilia /dʒuːvəˈnɪlɪə/ n.pl. the works produced by an author or artist in his youth. [L (as prec.)]

juvenility /dʒuːvəˈnɪlɪtɪ/ n. youthfulness; a youthful manner etc. [f. JUVENILE]

juxtapose /dʒʌkstəˈpəʊz/ v.t. to put side by side. —**juxtaposition** /-pəˈzɪʃ(ə)n/ n. [f. F f. L (juxta next, ponere put)]

K

K, k /keɪ/ *n.* (*pl.* **Ks, K's**) the eleventh letter of the alphabet.

K *abbr.* **1.** kelvin. **2.** king (in chess). **3.** the unit of core-memory size in computers, = 1,024 (often taken as 1,000) words.

K *symbol* potassium. [f. modern L *kalium* (as ALKALI)]

K. *abbr.* **1.** carat. **2.** King('s). **3.** Köchel (catalogue of Mozart's works).

k *abbr.* kilo-.

K2 the second highest peak in the world (8,611 m, 28,250 ft.), in the western Himalayas. Discovered in 1856, it was named K2 because it was the second peak measured in the Karakoram range. It has also been known as Mount Godwin-Austen, after Col. H. H. Godwin-Austen, its first surveyor.

ka /kɑ:/ *n.* the ancient Egyptian name for the lasting part of the individual human being or god, which survived (with the soul) after death and could reside in a statue of the dead person.

Kaaba /ˈkɑ:əbə/ *n.* a building at Mecca, the Muslim Holy of Holies, containing a sacred black stone. It is a pre-Islamic granite and marble shrine shaped like an irregular cube of about 12 × 10 × 15 metres (40 × 33 × 50 ft.), said to have been constructed by Abraham upon divine command (some say it was built by Adam). It is considered by Muslims as the 'navel' of the earth and indeed as the centre of the cosmos, the point where communications with heaven and the underworld of the spirits is easiest. Now surrounded by the Great Mosque, the Kaaba—or rather its northwest wall—replaced Jerusalem during Muhammad's lifetime as the point which all Muslims face in ritual prayer. The entire cube is covered by a black cloth covering (*kiswa*) around which the *shahāda*, or witness of the faith, is woven in gold. The Egyptian government traditionally provides a new kiswa each year. The Kaaba is the focal point of the first ritual devotions of the pilgrims (see HADJ) who circumambulate it seven times, touching or kissing the sacred black stone. This is a stone of basalt, originally about 30 cm (12 inches) in diameter, lodged in the eastern corner of the shrine, said to have been conveyed to Abraham by the angel Gabriel and originally white in colour, its present black colour being due to contact with the sin of the pre-Islamic period. It is thought that on Judgement Day the stone will speak as witness to the sins of humanity. [f. Arab., = cube]

kabaddi /kəˈbɑ:dɪ/ *n.* a game popular in northern India and Pakistan, played between two teams of 9 boys or young men. It is a traditional team pursuit game, requiring the players to run and hold their breath for a long time. [Tamil]

kabuki /kəˈbu:kɪ/ *n.* a form of classical Japanese theatre. It originated in narrative dances performed by women in the early 17th c. but by the end of that century was part danced, part acted, and performed by men, who until the 19th c. specialized in male or female roles. Unashamedly commercial, it adopted from other theatre forms. Kabuki actors used their whole bodies to express complex emotions through stylized and exaggerated techniques. The plays were divided mainly into historical plays, domestic dramas, and dance pieces, a programme consisting of scenes or acts from several different plays. The kabuki theatre still flourishes. [Jap. (*ka* song, *bu* dance, *ki* art)]

Kabul /ˈkɑ:bʊl/ the capital of Afghanistan; pop. approx. 1,500,000.

Kaddish /ˈkædɪʃ/ *n.* a Jewish prayer recited as a doxology in the synagogue service and as a prayer of mourning. [f. Aram., = holy]

Kaffir /ˈkæfə(r)/ *n.* a member or language of a South African people of the Bantu family. [f. Arab., = infidel]

Kafka /ˈkæfkə/, Franz (1883-1924), German-speaking Jewish novelist, born in Prague. His short stories, *The Judgement* (1916) and *The Metamorphosis* (1917) were among the few works published in his lifetime. His novels *The Trial* (1925), *The Castle* (1926), and the unfinished *America* (1927) were published posthumously by his friend Max Brod, against Kafka's testamentary directions. Guilt is one of his major themes, and his work is characterized by its lack of scenic description and its portrayal of an enigmatic

reality where the individual is seen as lonely, perplexed, and threatened. The term 'Kafkaesque' is used to describe work which employs similar narrative techniques and evokes a similarly uneasy response.

Kaiser /ˈkaɪzə(r)/, Georg (1878-1945), German dramatist, the prolific and inventive author of some sixty plays, of which *Die Bürger von Calais* (1914) was his masterpiece. *Die Koralle* (1917), *Gas I* (1918), and *Gas II* (1920) make up the so-called *Gas-Trilogie*, a gruesome interpretation of futuristic science which ends with extinction of all life by poisonous gas. These works were leading examples of German expressionist theatre.

kaiser /ˈkaɪzə(r)/ *n.* (*hist.*) an emperor, especially of Germany, Austria, or the Holy Roman Empire. [f. G f. L, = CAESAR]

kakemono /kækɪˈməʊnəʊ/ *n.* (*pl.* **-os**) a Japanese wall-picture, usually painted or inscribed on paper or silk and mounted on rollers. [Jap.(*kake-* hang, *mono* thing)]

Kalahari Desert /kæləˈhɑ:rɪ/ a high barren plateau in southern Africa north of the Orange River, mainly in Botswana.

kale *n.* a hardy variety of cabbage with wrinkled leaves. [northern form of COLE]

Kalevala /ˈkɑ:lɪvɑ:lə/ the Finnish national epic poem, compiled from popular lays of great antiquity transmitted orally until the 19th c., concerned with the myths of Finland and the conflicts of the Finns with the Lapps. [Finnish, = land of heroes]

kaleidoscope /kəˈlaɪdəskəʊp/ *n.* a tube containing mirrors and pieces of coloured glass whose reflections produce patterns when the tube is rotated. —**kaleidoscopic** /-ˈskɒpɪk/ *adj.*, **kaleidoscopically** /-ˈskɒpɪkəlɪ/ *adv.* [f. Gk *kalos* beautiful + *eidos* form + -SCOPE]

kaleyard /ˈkeɪljɑ:d/ *n.* (*Sc.*) a kitchen garden.

Kali /ˈkɑ:lɪ/ (*Hinduism*) the most terrifying goddess, wife of Siva (see PARVATI), often identified with Durga. She is usually depicted as black, naked, old, and hideous, with a necklace of skulls, a belt of severed hands, and a protruding blood-stained tongue. The infamous thugs (see entry) were her devotees. [Skr., = black]

Kalidasa /kælɪˈdɑ:sə/ (3rd c.) Indian poet and dramatist. Little is known of his life and he is best known for his celebrated drama *Sakuntala*, the story of King Dushyanta's love and courtship of the maiden Sakuntala, whom he first observed while hunting in the forest.

Kalmuck /ˈkælmʌk/ *n.* **1.** a member of a Buddhist Mongol people of central Asia who invaded Russia in the 17th-18th c. and settled along the lower Volga. Many migrated to Chinese Turkestan in the 18th c. **2.** their language, of the Ural-Altaic family. [f. Russ.]

Kama /ˈkɑ:mə/ (*Hinduism*) the god of sexual love, usually presented as a beautiful youth with a bow of sugar-cane, a bowstring of bees, and arrows of flowers. [Skr., = love]

Kama Sutra /kɑ:mə ˈsu:trə/ an ancient Sanskrit treatise on the art of love and sexual technique. [Skr., = love-treatise]

Kamerlingh Onnes /ˈkæməlɪŋ ˈɒnɪs/, Heike (1853-1926), Dutch physicist who studied cryogenic phenomena. Onnes succeeded in liquefying first oxygen (1906) and then helium (1908). He discovered the phenomenon of superconductivity in 1911 and was awarded the Nobel Prize for physics two years later.

kamikaze /kæmɪˈkɑ:zɪ/ *n.* (in the Second World War) a Japanese aircraft laden with explosives and suicidally crashed on a target by the pilot; the pilot of this. [Jap. (*kami* divinity, *kaze* wind)]

Kampala /kæmˈpɑ:lə/ the capital of Uganda, on Victoria Nyanza (Lake Victoria); pop. (est.1980) 458,000.

Kampuchea /kæmpʊˈtʃɪə/ a country in SE Asia between Thailand and the south of Vietnam; pop. (1981) approx. 6,000,000; official language, Khmer; capital, Phnomh Penh. The economy is chiefly agricultural, with rice as the staple crop; there is little industry. Formerly part of the Khmer empire (see KHMER), the country, known until 1976 as Cambodia, was made a French protectorate in 1863 and remained under French influence until it became fully independent in 1953. Civil war in 1970-5 undermined and finally overthrew the government, but the victorious Communist Khmer Rouge regime was itself toppled by a Vietnamese invasion in 1979. The country is still plagued by intermittent guerrilla activity. —**Kampuchean** *adj.* & *n.*

kana /ˈkɑːnə/ *n.* Japanese syllabic writing. [Jap.]

Kanarese /kænəˈriːz/ *adj.* of Kanara, a district in SW India, or its people or language. —*n.* **1.** a native of Kanara. **2.** the language spoken there (now generally and officially called **Kannada**), a member of the Dravidian language group, closely allied to Telugu, with about 22 million speakers. Its alphabet is similar to that of Telugu, developed from the Grantha script. [f. *Kanara* in India]

Kandinsky /kænˈdɪnski/, Wassily (1866-1944), Russian painter and theorist, usually considered the initiator of abstraction or non-objectivity in painting. Born in Moscow, he studied law and political economics, but in 1896 settled in Munich to study art. Kandinsky's paintings at first belonged to the mainstream of German expressionism, but by 1910-11 his rich colour and simplified rather crude forms had begun to take on an independent meaning and life of their own. His booklet *Concerning the Spiritual in Art* (1910) provided the theoretical basis for these experiments. Deeply influenced by the theosophy of Mme Blavatsky and Steiner, he evolved principles of transcendental meaning in colour and form; it is a matter of contention whether Kandinsky in Munich or Delaunay in Paris produced the first non-objective painting. He edited the *Blaue Reiter* almanac with Franz Marc, and the attention given there to Schoenberg's exactly contemporary principles of atonality in music is worthy of note. In 1914 Kandinsky returned to Russia, where he supported the revolution. Although receiving several State appointments after 1917, he felt obliged to leave Russia when social realism was applied as the official style. Settling in Germany, he was appointed to the staff of the Bauhaus in 1922, and remained there until obliged to leave, for Paris, in 1933. His abstract work of this period adopted a new geometric rigidity, his ideas being published in his booklet *Point and Line to Plane* of 1926.

kangaroo /kæŋgəˈruː/ *n.* an Australian marsupial of the genus *Macropus* with hindquarters strongly developed for jumping (ill. MAMMALS). —**kangaroo court**, an illegal court held by strikers, prisoners, etc. [perh. f. Aboriginal name; the assertion that it really means 'I don't understand' (the supposed reply of the native to his questioner) lacks confirmation]

Kangchenjunga /kæŋtʃenˈdʒʊŋgə/ the third highest peak in the world (8,586 m, 28,168 ft.) situated 113 km (70 miles) east of Mount Everest in the Himalayas.

Kannada /ˈkænədə/ *n.* the Kanarese language. [Kanarese *Kannada*]

Kansas /ˈkænsəs/ a State in the Middle West of the USA acquired as part of the Louisiana Purchase in 1803. It became the 34th State of the USA in 1861; capital, Topeka.

Kant /kɑːnt/, Immanuel (1724-1804), German philosopher, who never travelled more than 40 miles from his native town, Königsberg, where he was a professor at the university from 1770 to 1797. His most important book is the *Critique of Pure Reason* (1781, 1787). According to Kant, the world of which we are aware is constructed out of the given material by our ways of classifying it. The human mind can never grasp the ultimate nature of reality, of 'things-in-themselves'; these can neither be confirmed, denied, nor scientifically demonstrated. What it can know are the objects of experience, 'phenomena', which it interprets by imposing upon them its built-in notions of space and time and ordering the sense-data according to its a priori concepts, the twelve 'categories' of thought which he grouped into those of quantity, quality, reason, and modality. His *Critique of Practical Reason* (1788) deals with ethics. Kant held that there is an absolute moral law, the 'categorical imperative' whose motivation is reason and a requirement of consistency ('act as if the principle by which you act were about to be turned into a universal law of nature'). Towards the end of his life in his work *Perpetual Peace* (1795) he advocated a federation of free States, bound by a covenant forbidding war.

kaolin /ˈkeɪəlɪn/ *n.* a fine white clay used for porcelain and in medicine. [F f. Chinese *kao-ling* name of mountain]

kapok /ˈkeɪpɒk/ *n.* a fine cotton-like material from a tropical tree (*Ceiba pentandra*) used as padding. [f. Malay]

kappa /ˈkæpə/ *n.* the tenth letter of the Greek alphabet, = k. [Gk]

kaput /kæˈpʊt/ *adj.* (*slang*) broken, ruined, done for. [f. G]

Karachi /kəˈrɑːtʃɪ/ a seaport and former capital (1947-9) of Pakistan, on an inlet of the Arabian Sea; pop. 5,500,000.

Karadzić /kəˈrɑːʒɪtʃ/, Vuk Stefanović (1787-1864), Serbian author, grammarian, and lexicographer, the 'father' of modern Serbian literature.

Karaite /ˈkeərəaɪt/ *n.* a member of a Jewish sect chiefly in the Crimea etc., founded in the 8th c., rejecting rabbinical tradition and basing its tenets on a literal interpretation of the Scriptures. [f. Heb., = scripturalists]

Karakoram /kærəˈkɔːrəm/ a great chain of mountains lying to the north of the west end of the Himalayas.

karakul /ˈkærəkʊl/ *n.* **1.** an Asian sheep whose lambs have a dark curled fleece. **2.** a fur made from or resembling this. [Russ.]

karate /kəˈrɑːtɪ/ *n.* a Japanese system of unarmed combat using the hands, feet, etc., as weapons. It involves a training of the mind as well as the body, and seeks to concentrate the body's power at the point of impact. Modern karate is a product of the 20th c., but its roots can be traced back to before the time of Christ, and Okinawa, China, and India have all contributed to its development. (See ill. SPORTS.) [Jap. (*kara* empty, *te* hand)]

karma /ˈkɑːmə/ *n.* (*Buddhism & Hinduism*) the law of action according to which good or appropriate acts give rise to good effects, bad or inappropriate ones to bad effects, impelling a chain of successive births by transmigration, each life's condition being explained by actions in a previous life. [Skr., = action, fate]

Karnak /ˈkɑːnæk/ a village in Egypt, site of the northern complex of monuments of ancient Thebes, including the great temple of Amun.

Karnataka /kəˈnɑːtəkə/ a State in southern India, formerly called Mysore; capital, Bangalore.

karoo /kəˈruː/ *n.* (also **karroo**) a high plateau in South Africa, waterless in the dry season. [Hottentot]

karst *n.* a limestone region with underground streams and many cavities caused by dissolution of the rock. [name of such a region in Yugoslavia]

kart *n.* a miniature wheeled vehicle usually consisting of a tubular frame with a small rear-mounted engine and a seat for the driver. It is used for a motor-racing sport (**karting**), and is an American invention dating from 1956. The first vehicles incorporated surplus 750 cc engines that had been intended to power rotary lawnmowers whose manufacture was abandoned when the mowers proved unreliable. [commercial alteration of *cart*]

kasbah /ˈkæzbɑː/ *n.* **1.** the citadel of an Arab city in North Africa. **2.** the old crowded part near this, especially in Algiers. [f. F f. Arab., = citadel]

Kashmir /kæʃˈmɪə(r)/ a former State on the border of India, since 1947 disputed between India and Pakistan. It was partitioned in 1949, the NW area becoming Azad Kashmir (= Free Kashmir), controlled by Pakistan, and the remainder being incorporated into India as the State of Jammu and Kashmir (see entry). Sporadic fighting continued until 1972.

Kassite /ˈkæsaɪt/ *n.* **1.** a member of an Elamite people from the Zagros mountains in western Iran, who ruled Babylonia from the 18th to the 12th c. BC until overthrown by Assyria. **2.** their language. —*adj.* of the Kassites or their language. [native name]

Kathmandu /kætmænˈduː/ the capital of Nepal, situated in the Himalayas at 1,370 m (c.4,500 ft.); pop. (1981) 235,000.

katydid /ˈkeɪtɪdɪd/ *n.* a large green grasshopper (family Tettigoniidae) of the USA. [imit. of its sound]

Kauffmann /ˈkaʊfmæn/, Angelica (1740-1807), Swiss painter who as a young woman travelled widely in Europe. In Rome she was introduced into the neo-classical circle, and in 1764 painted her famous portrait of Winckelmann. In London 1766, she was a friend of Reynolds and a foundation member of the Royal Academy. Her work was greatly admired, and although she painted large canvases of classical subjects she is best represented in her small-scale decorative panels for ceilings, walls, and furniture, as commissioned by the Adam Brothers for houses they designed. She left England and settled in Rome in 1782, with her second husband Antonio Zucchi, also a decorative painter. She is a rare example of a female artist who achieved professional status in the 18th c.

kauri /ˈkaʊrɪ/ *n.* a coniferous New Zealand timber-tree (*Agathis australis*) yielding a gum. [Maori]

kayak /ˈkaɪæk/ *n.* **1.** a light covered-in canoe-type boat consisting of a wooden framework covered with sealskins, in which the paddler sits facing forward and using a double-bladed paddle, used by the Eskimo for fishing. **2.** a boat developed from this, used for touring and sport. [Eskimo]

Kazakhstan /ˌkæzɑːkˈstɑːn/ the Kazakh SSR, the second largest constituent republic of the USSR, extending from the Caspian Sea east to the Altai mountains and Mongolia; capital, Alma-Ata.

KBE *abbr.* Knight Commander of the Order of the British Empire.

KCB *abbr.* Knight Commander of the Order of the Bath.

KCMG *abbr.* Knight Commander of the Order of St Michael and St George.

kc/s *abbr.* kilocycles per second.

kea /ˈkeɪə/ *n.* a green New Zealand parrot (*Nestor notabilis*) said to attack sheep. [Maori, imit.]

Kean, Edmund (1787–1833), English actor, with a reputation as the greatest tragic actor of his day. After a wild and uncared-for childhood, from 1814, when he played Shylock in London, his place on the stage was assured. Although less good in any character that called for virtue or sustained nobility, as Macbeth, Shylock, or Iago he was unmatchable. His life was as fierce as much of his playing : he drank to excess, and was often absent from the theatre. His last role was as Othello to his son's Iago; he collapsed during the performance and died a few weeks later.

Keaton /ˈkiːt(ə)n/, Buster (Joseph Francis) (1895–1966), American comic silent-film actor and director, noted for his presentation of emotional restraint which established an essential calm in the midst of the wildest events. In his mastery of screen comedy he is rivalled only by Chaplin.

Keats, John (1795–1821), English poet who was apprenticed to an apothecary-surgeon but with encouragement from the poet Leigh Hunt turned to literature. His *Poems* (1817) and *Endymion* (1818) received harsh criticism. In 1818 he fell in love with Fanny Brawne, and the following year wrote his greatest poems, including 'Hyperion', 'Ode on a Grecian Urn', 'Ode to Melancholy', and 'Ode to a Nightingale', all published in 1820. By now he was ill with tuberculosis and he died in Rome in the following year. A principal figure of the Romantic movement, Keats was commended by Arnold for his 'intellectual and spiritual passion' for beauty. His *Letters* (1848, 1878) reveal his profoundest thoughts on love, poetry, and the nature of man.

kebab /kɪˈbæb/ *n.* (usu. in *pl.*) small pieces of meat, vegetables, etc., grilled on a skewer. [f. Urdu f. Arab.]

Keble /ˈkiːb(ə)l/, John (1792–1866), a leader of the Oxford Movement. His assize sermon on *National Apostasy* (1833), preached while he was Professor of Poetry at Oxford, challenged the masses to take stock of their weakening Christian faith, and is usually regarded as the beginning of the movement. The aim of the sermon was political rather than theological, directed at the new idea that the law of the land need not coincide with the Church's teaching. In this it ultimately failed, but the work of his followers was victorious in reviving traditional Catholic teaching, and did much to define and mould the Church of England.

kedge *v.t./i.* to move (a ship) by a hawser attached to a small anchor. —*n.* a small anchor for this purpose. [perh. var. of dial. *cadge* bind]

kedgeree /ˈkedʒəriː, -ˈriː/ *n.* **1.** a European dish of fish, rice, hard-boiled eggs, etc. **2.** an Indian dish of rice, pulse, onions, eggs, etc. [f. Hindi]

keel *n.* **1.** the lengthwise timber or steel structure along the base of a ship, from which the framework is built up (ill. SAILING-SHIPS). **2.** a structure resembling this; a ridge along the breastbone of many birds. —*v.t./i.* to turn keel upwards. —**keel over,** to overturn; to fall or collapse. **on an even keel,** level, steady. [f. ON]

keelhaul *v.t.* **1.** to haul (a person) under a keel as a punishment. **2.** to rebuke severely.

keelson var. of KELSON.

keen[1] *adj.* **1.** showing or feeling intense interest or desire; (of desire etc.) intense. **2.** perceiving things very distinctly; intellectually acute. **3.** sharp, having a sharp edge or point. **4.** (of sound or light etc.) acute, penetrating; (of wind etc.) piercingly cold; (of pain) acute. **5.** (of a price) competitively low. —**keen on,** (*colloq.*) much attracted by. —**keenly** *adv.*, **keenness** *n.* [OE]

keen[2] *n.* an Irish funeral song accompanied by wailing. —*v.t./i.* to utter the keen; to bewail (a person) thus. [f. Ir. *caoine*]

Keene /kiːn/, Charles Samuel (1823–91), English caricatur-

ist, self-taught and noted for his spontaneity of execution and subtle characterizations. He was associated with the weekly journal *Punch* from 1851.

keep *v.t./i.* (*past & p.p.* **kept**) **1.** to have continuous charge of; to retain possession of; to reserve (*for* a future time etc.). **2.** to remain or cause to remain in a specified condition, position, course, etc. **3.** to restrain, to hold back *from*; to detain. **4.** to observe, to pay due regard to (a law, promise, appointment, etc.). **5.** to refrain from disclosing (a secret etc.). **6.** to own and look after (animals etc.); to maintain in return for sexual favours. **7.** to guard or protect (a person, place, goal at football, etc.). **8.** to maintain (a house etc.) in proper order; to manage (a shop etc.); to maintain (a diary, account-books, etc.) by making the requisite entries. **9.** to preserve in being; to continue to have or do. **10.** (of food etc.) to remain in good condition; to be able to be put aside until later. **11.** to have (a commodity) regularly on sale. **12.** to celebrate (a feast or ceremony). —*n.* **1.** maintenance, food. **2.** the central tower or other strongly fortified structure in a castle etc. —**for keeps,** (*colloq.*) permanently. **keep on,** to continue; to nag *at.* **keep to oneself,** to avoid contact with others; to keep (a thing) a secret. **keep under,** to repress. **keep up,** to maintain; to prevent from sinking (especially one's spirits etc.). **keep up with,** to achieve the same pace as. **keep up with the Joneses,** to strive to remain on terms of obvious social equality with one's neighbours. [OE]

keeper *n.* a person who keeps or looks after something; a custodian of a museum or art gallery or forest; a wicketkeeper. [f. KEEP]

keeping *n.* **1.** custody, charge. **2.** harmony, conformity. [f. KEEP]

keepsake *n.* a thing kept in memory of its giver.

keg *n.* a small cask or barrel. —**keg beer,** beer supplied from a sealed metal container. [f. ON]

Kekulé /ˈkekjʊleɪ/, Friedrich August, von Stradonitz (1829–96), German chemist, one of the founders of structural organic chemistry. His training as an architect may have aided him in visualizing the structure of molecules. He concentrated on carbon compounds and in 1858 suggested that carbon was quadrivalent, that is that each carbon atom could combine with four other atoms; furthermore, they could combine with other carbon atoms and form complex chains. However, Kekulé is best known for discovering the ring structure of benzene, which came to him in a waking dream as a chain of six carbon atoms whirling round, like a snake biting its own tail. A new generation of chemists could now assign such structures to other organic compounds.

Keller /ˈkelə(r)/, Helen Adams (1880–1968), American author who, although she became blind and deaf before she was two years old, graduated in 1904 and became a prominent social reformer, raising money for the education of handicapped people. Her books include *The Story of My Life* (1902).

Kellogg Pact /ˈkelɒg/ a treaty renouncing war as an instrument of national policy, signed in Paris in 1928 by representatives of 15 nations. [f. F. B. *Kellogg* (d. 1937), US Secretary of State 1924–9]

Kells, Book of an illuminated manuscript of the gospels, perhaps made by Irish monks in Iona in the 8th or early 9th c., now kept at Trinity College, Dublin. [f. *Kells*, town in Co. Meath, Ireland, where formerly kept]

kelp *n.* a large brown seaweed; the calcined ashes of this yielding iodine etc. [orig. unkn.]

kelpie *n.* (*Sc.*) **1.** a malevolent water-spirit usually in the form of a horse. **2.** an Australian sheepdog of Scottish origin. [orig. unkn.]

kelson /ˈkels(ə)n/ *n.* the line of timber fixing a ship's floor-timbers to the keel. [perh. f. LG (as KEEL, SWINE as name of timber)]

kelt *n.* a salmon or sea trout after spawning. [orig. unkn.]

Kelvin /ˈkelvɪn/, William Thomson, 1st Baron (1824–1907), British physicist, born in Belfast, who was appointed professor of natural philosophy at Glasgow in 1846 and did not retire until 1895. He worked on a great range of scientific problems. Amongst his greatest successes was his formulation in 1850 of the second law of thermodynamics (according to which heat cannot pass from a hotter to a colder body without work being done, in other words, perpetual motion is an impossibility). He introduced an absolute temperature scale, the unit of which is named the kelvin in his honour. His concept of an electromagnetic field was derived from his own extensive researches into magnetism and electricity and those of Faraday before him, and in turn influenced

Maxwell's electromagnetic theory of light, which Kelvin never accepted. He became best known to the general public for his involvement in the laying of the first Atlantic cable, for which he invented the siphon recorder and a sensitive mirror galvanometer. Indeed, he devised many scientific instruments, including electrometers, galvanometers, deep-sea sounding gear, a mariner's compass, and an electric clock. His calculation of the age of the earth in 1862, based on its rate of cooling, was a gross underestimate and was controversial, but showed that physics (or geophysics) could be useful in helping to establish a geological time-scale. He is buried in Westminster Abbey.

kelvin /ˈkelvɪn/ n. the base unit of thermodynamic temperature (symbol K; adopted in 1954 and 1967 for international use), the fraction 1/273.16 of the thermodynamic temperature of the triple point of water; a degree (equal to a Celsius degree) of the Kelvin scale. —**Kelvin scale**, a scale of temperature with zero at absolute zero. [f. prec.]

Kemal Pasha /keˈmɑːl ˈpɑːʃə/ see ATATÜRK.

ken v.t. (**-nn-**) (Sc.) to know. —n. the range of knowledge or sight. [OE (as CAN¹)]

kendo /ˈkendəʊ/ n. the Japanese sport of fencing with two-handed bamboo swords. Its origins go back more than 1,500 years, developing from the need for non-lethal practice in the art of swordsmanship which was an essential skill for the samurai of medieval Japan, and changing from training for battle to a sport. [Jap., = sword-way]

Kennedy /ˈkenədɪ/, John Fitzgerald (1917-63), 35th President of the USA, 1961-3. A national war hero during the Second World War, Kennedy served successively as Congressman and Senator for Massachusetts between 1947 and 1960 before becoming at 43 the youngest man (and also the first Catholic) to be elected President. Kennedy gained a popular reputation as an advocate of civil rights and as an opponent of Communist Russia (particularly during the Cuban Missile Crisis of 1962), but was assassinated in Dallas, Texas, in November 1963.

kennel /ˈken(ə)l/ n. **1.** a small shelter for a dog. **2.** (in pl.) a place where dogs are bred or boarded. **3.** a pack of dogs. —v.t. (**-ll-**) to put or keep in a kennel. [f. OF chenil f. L canis dog]

Kenneth /ˈkenɪθ/ the name of two Scottish kings, Kenneth I MacAlpin (d. c.860), traditional founder of the kingdom of Scotland, and Kenneth II (d. 995).

Kent¹ a county of SE England.

Kent² William (1685-1748), English architect, landscape designer, and decorative painter. Assisted by local patrons he travelled to Italy in 1709, where he studied and became a guide and agent for English noblemen on tour. He met Lord Burlington, returned to England with him in 1719, and enjoyed his friendship and patronage for the rest of his life. With Burlington he promoted the development of a neo-Palladian style which re-interpreted the classicism of the 16th-c. architect Andrea Palladio. His major works include Lord Leicester's Holkham Hall, garden designs for Burlington's own Chiswick villa, Rousham, and Stowe. Kent's principles of landscape design broke down the formality of existing taste, opening the way for the innovations of Capability Brown.

Kentucky /kenˈtʌkɪ/ a State in the central south-eastern USA. It became the 15th State of the USA in 1792; capital, Frankfort.

Kentucky Derby an annual horse-race for 3-year-olds at Louisville, Kentucky, founded in 1875.

Kenya /ˈkenjə/ a country in East Africa, a member State of the Commonwealth, bisected by the equator and with a coastline on the Indian Ocean; pop. (est.) 17,000,000; official language, Swahili (also English); capital, Nairobi. Largely populated by Bantu peoples, Kenya was not exposed to European influence until the arrival of the British in the late 19th c. After the opening up of the interior it became a Crown Colony in 1920 and attracted a large number of white settlers. The demands these made on land caused increasingly severe problems with the native population and resulted in the Mau Mau rebellion of 1952-4. The admission of native Kenyans into government eventually defused the situation and the country was granted independence in 1963, becoming a republic in 1964 and a one-party State in 1982. The economy is based on agriculture, the tea crop being particularly important. Kenya is now one of the most stable and prosperous of African nations, wealth being largely concentrated in the temperate agricultural south. Tourism is also important, the main attraction being the wildlife reserves. —**Kenyan** adj. & n.

Kenyatta /kenˈjætə/, Jomo (c.1894-1978), Kenyan statesman. After spending a long period in prison through involvement with the Mau Mau, Kenyatta led his country to independence in 1963 and served as its first President from 1964 until his death in 1978.

kepi /ˈkepɪ, ˈkeɪpɪ/ n. a French military cap with a horizontal peak. [f. F f. Swiss G]

Kepler /ˈkeplə(r)/, Johannes (1571-1630), German astronomer and court mathematician to Rudolph II of Prague. He studied theology at Tübingen, where he became acquainted with the Copernican system, and fled to Prague after the expulsion of the Protestants, becoming Tycho Brahe's assistant and, later, successor. His studies of the positions of Mars led to the formulation of his first two laws of motion, which recognized the elliptical orbits of the planets about the sun. In 1620, his book Harmonices Mundi expounded the Third Law of planetary dynamics, relating the distances of the planets from the sun to their orbital periods. Although his work accounted concisely and mathematically for the detailed planetary observations of Tycho, and his analysis foreshadowed the general application of the scientific method to astronomy, Kepler remained influenced by the astrological notions of his day, and sought an inner relationship between the planets that would express the 'music of the spheres'. His exposition of the ratios between planetary orbits as just those which would allow the crystal spheres which carried the planets to accommodate the five perfect Platonic solids is but one example of the medieval approach to cosmology which he retained.

kept past & p.p. of KEEP.

Kerala /ˈkerələ/ a State in SW India, constituted in 1956; capital, Trivandrum. —**Keralite** /-laɪt/ adj. & n.

kerb n. a stone edging to a pavement or raised path. [var. of CURB]

kerbstone n. each of the stones forming a kerb.

kerchief /ˈkɜːtʃɪf/ n. **1.** a square cloth used to cover the head. **2.** a handkerchief. [f. OF couvrechief (as COVER, chief head)]

kerfuffle /kəˈfʌf(ə)l/ n. (colloq.) a fuss, a commotion. [orig. Sc.]

kermes /ˈkɜːmɪz/ n. the female of an insect (Kermes ilicis), formerly taken to be a berry, that feeds on an evergreen oak (Quercus coccinea); a red dye made from the dried bodies of these. [f. F f. Arab. & Pers.; rel. to CRIMSON]

Kern, Jerome (1885-1945), American composer of popular melodies and songs, several of which were featured in films, including 'Ol' Man River' (first sung by Paul Robeson) and 'Smoke gets in your Eyes'.

kernel /ˈkɜːn(ə)l/ n. **1.** the softer part within the hard shell of a nut or stone-fruit. **2.** a seed within a husk etc., e.g. a grain of wheat. **3.** the central or essential part of a thing. [OE, dim. of CORN¹]

kerosene /ˈkerəsiːn/ n. a fuel-oil distilled from petroleum or from coal or bituminous shale, paraffin oil. [f. Gk kēros wax]

kestrel /ˈkestr(ə)l/ n. a kind of small falcon (esp. Falco tinnunculus) that often hovers in the air with its head to the wind. [perh. f. F casserelle, créc(er)elle]

Ketch, Jack (d. 1686), English hangman, public executioner in England 1663-86.

ketch n. a small sailing vessel with two masts (ill. SAILING-SHIPS). [prob. f. CATCH]

ketchup /ˈketʃəp/ n. a thick spicy sauce made from tomatoes, mushrooms, etc. [f. Chinese, = pickled-fish brine]

ketone /ˈkiːtəʊn/ n. one of a class of organic compounds including acetone. [f. G keton alt. of aketon acetone]

Kettering /ˈketərɪŋ/, Charles Franklin (1876-1958), American engineer responsible for many significant developments in automobile engineering, beginning with the electric starter (1912) which opened the way to women drivers. He joined the General Motors Corporation in 1919 and was leader of research there until he retired in 1947. During this time he led the team which discovered tetra-ethyl lead as a powerful anti-knock agent and went on to define the 'octane number' method of rating the anti-knock properties of fuels. After an unsuccessful attempt to produce air-cooled engines he turned to the development of 2-stroke diesel engines which came into widespread use for railway locomotives and long-distance road coaches. He was also responsible for the development first of synchromesh gearboxes then of fully-automatic transmissions, also of power steering. For the refrigerator division he was involved in the development of a range of safe refrigerants.

kettle *n.* a vessel, usually of metal with a spout and handle, for boiling water. —**a fine** *or* **pretty** etc. **kettle of fish,** an awkward state of affairs. [f. ON ult. f. L *catillus*]

kettledrum *n.* a large drum consisting of an inverted metal bowl over which an adjustable membrane is stretched, enabling it to be tuned to a definite note; (in *pl.*) the timpani of an orchestra.

Kew Gardens the Royal Botanic Gardens at Kew near Richmond upon Thames, Surrey. Originally the garden of Kew House, it was developed as a botanic garden by the mother of George III from 1761, with the aid of Sir Joseph Banks, and was presented to the nation in 1841.

key[1] /kiː/ *n.* **1.** an instrument, usually of metal, for moving the bolt of a lock so that it locks or unlocks. **2.** a similar implement for operating a switch in the form of a lock, winding a clock etc., or grasping a screw, nut, etc. **3.** each of a set of levers or buttons pressed by the finger in a musical instrument, typewriter, etc. **4.** (*Mus.*) a system of notes based on material in a particular scale; (*fig.*) the general tone or style of thought or expression. **5.** a solution to a problem, an explanation, a word or system for solving a cipher or code. **6.** a thing or factor governing an opportunity for or access to something; (*attrib.*) essential, of vital importance. **7.** a piece of wood or metal inserted between others to secure them. **8.** a mechanical device for making or breaking an electric circuit. **9.** the winged fruit of the sycamore, ash, etc. **10.** roughness of surface to help adhesion of plaster etc. —*v.t./i.* **1.** to fasten with a pin, wedge, bolt, etc. **2.** to roughen (a surface) to help the adhesion of plaster etc. **3.** to align or link (*to*). **key in,** to enter (data) by means of a keyboard. **key money,** a payment required from an incoming tenant nominally for the provision of the key to a premises. **keypad** *n.* a miniature keyboard for holding in the hand. **keyring** *n.* a ring for keeping keys on. **key up,** to stimulate or excite (a person). [OE]

key[2] /kiː/ *n.* a reef, a low island. [f. Sp. *cayo*]

keyboard *n.* a set of keys on a typewriter, piano, etc.

keyhole *n.* the hole by which a key is put into a lock.

Keynes /keɪnz/, John Maynard, 1st Baron (1883–1946), English economist, advocate of the planned economy and of the view that full employment is not a natural condition and requires positive intervention by the State, with government spending in excess of revenue by borrowing to finance the resultant deficit. Keynes served as an adviser to the Treasury during both World Wars and represented that department at the Versailles Peace Conference, subsequently becoming one of the most influential critics of the Treaty. He was an outspoken opponent of the orthodox economic policies of the British government during the inter-war depression, and his theories influenced Roosevelt's decision to introduce the American 'New Deal'. His most important works include *The Economic Consequences of the Peace* (1919), *A Treatise on Money* (1930), and *The General Theory of Employment, Interest and Money* (1936). —**Keynesian** *adj. & n.*

keynote *n.* **1.** the prevailing idea or tone in a speech etc. **2.** the lowest note in a scale on which a musical key is based.

Keys, House of see HOUSE OF KEYS.

keystone *n.* **1.** the central locking stone in an arch (ill. BUILDING TECHNIQUES). **2.** a central principle.

keyword *n.* the key to a cipher.

KG *abbr.* Knight of the Order of the Garter.

kg *abbr.* kilogram(s).

KGB the secret police of the USSR since 1953. [Russ. abbr., = State security committee]

khaki /ˈkɑːkɪ/ *adj.* dull brownish-yellow. —*n.* khaki cloth or uniform. [f. Urdu, = dust-coloured]

khan /kɑːn/ *n.* the title of rulers and officials in Central Asia, Afghanistan, etc.; the supreme ruler of Turkish, Tartar, and Mongol tribes, and emperor of China, in the Middle Ages. [f. Turki, = lord]

Khartoum /kɑːˈtuːm/ the capital of Sudan, situated at the junction of the Blue Nile and the White Nile; pop. (est.) 194,000.

Khedive /kɪˈdiːv/ *n.* (*hist.*) the title of the viceroy of Egypt under Turkish rule, 1867–1914. [f. F ult. f. Pers., = prince]

Khmer /kmeə(r)/ *n.* **1.** a native or inhabitant of the ancient kingdom of Khmer in SE Asia, which reached the peak of its power in the 11th c., ruling over the entire Mekong valley from the capital at Angkor, and was destroyed by Siamese conquests in the 12th and 14th c. **2.** the monosyllabic language of this people, belonging to the Mon-Khmer group of the Austro-Asiatic family. The official language of Kam-

puchea, spoken by most of its population (some 6 million people), it is the most important member of the Mon-Khmer group. **3.** a native or inhabitant of the Khmer Republic (the official name in 1970–5 of what is now Kampuchea). —*adj.* of the Khmers or their language. —**Khmer Rouge** /ruːʒ/, the Communist guerrilla organization prominent in the wars in the region in the 1960s and 1970s, holding power 1975–9 (see KAMPUCHEA). [native name]

Khomeini /xɒˈmeɪnɪ/, Ruhollah (1900–), known as Ayatollah Khomeini, Iranian Shiite Muslim leader who returned to Iran in 1979, after 16 years in exile, and established an overtly Islamic constitution, with strict authoritarian rule, in the revolt against westernization that accompanied the overthrow of the Shah.

Khonsu /ˈkɒnsuː/ (*Egyptian myth.*) a moon god, whose principal cult centre was at Thebes, a member of the Theban triad as the divine son of Amun and Mut. His name means 'he who crosses'.

Khrushchev /ˈkruːʃtʃɒf/, Nikita Sergevich (1894–1971), Russian statesman. The first strong leader to emerge in Russia after the death of Stalin, Khrushchev became leader after succeeding Bulganin as Premier in 1958, having already played a prominent part in the 'de-Stalinization' programme. The most flamboyant of Soviet leaders, Khrushchev exacerbated the poor state of relations with the West and the USA in particular, but was eventually forced to back down in the Cuban missile crisis of 1962. He was deposed two years later by Kosygin and Brezhnev.

Khufu /ˈkuːfuː/ (also known as *Cheops, c.*2551–2528 BC) a pharaoh of the 4th Dynasty in ancient Egypt, who commissioned the building of the great pyramid at Giza.

Khyber Pass /ˈkaɪbə(r)/ the major mountain pass on the border between northern Pakistan and Afghanistan. The pass was for long of great commercial and strategic importance, the route by which successive invaders entered India, and was garrisoned by the British intermittently between 1839 and 1947.

kHz *abbr.* kilohertz.

kibbutz /kɪˈbuːts/ *n.* (*pl.* **-tzim** /-ˈtsiːm/) a communal settlement in Israel. [f. Heb., = gathering]

kibosh /ˈkaɪbɒʃ/ *n.* (*slang*) nonsense. —**put the kibosh on,** (*slang*) to put an end to. [orig. unkn.]

kick *v.t./i.* **1.** to thrust, strike, or propel forcibly with the foot or hoof. **2.** to score (a goal) by a kick. **3.** to protest, to show dislike. **4.** (*slang*) to abandon (a habit). —*n.* **1.** a kicking action or blow. **2.** the recoil of a gun when fired. **3.** (*colloq.*) resilience. **4.** (*colloq.*) a temporary interest or enthusiasm; a sharp stimulant effect, (usu. in *pl.*) a thrill. —**kick about** *or* **around,** to treat roughly; to move idly from place to place; to be unused or unwanted. **kick off,** to begin a football match; (*colloq.*) to make a start. **kick-off** *n.* a start, especially of a football match. **kick out,** (*colloq.*) to expel forcibly, to dismiss. **kick up,** (*colloq.*) to create or cause (a fuss, trouble, etc.). **kick upstairs,** to promote (a person) to an ostensibly higher position to remove him from the scene of real influence. —**kicker** *n.* [orig. unkn.]

kickback *n.* **1.** a recoil. **2.** (*colloq.*) a payment for help in making a profit or for showing favour etc.

kick-start *n.* (also **kick-starter**) a device to start the engine of a motorcycle etc. by a downward thrust of a pedal. —*v.t.* to start (a motorcycle etc.) thus.

kid *n.* **1.** a young goat. **2.** the leather made from its skin. **3.** (*slang*) a child. —*v.t./i* (**-dd-**) **1.** to give birth to a young goat. **2.** (*slang*) to deceive or hoax. —**handle** *or* **treat** etc. **with kid gloves,** to treat tactfully. [f. ON]

Kidd /kɪd/, Captain William (1645–1701), British pirate. Sent to the Indies in 1695 in command of an anti-pirate expedition, Kidd turned pirate himself, but was eventually arrested in New York (where he had gone in hope of getting a pardon) and sent back to London where he was hanged. His supposed buried treasure has become the subject of legend and is still being searched for today.

kidnap /ˈkɪdnæp/ *v.t.* (**-pp-**) to carry off (a person) illegally especially to obtain a ransom; to steal (a child). —**kidnapper** *n.* [f. KID + *nap* var. of NAB]

kidney /ˈkɪdnɪ/ *n.* **1.** either of the pair of glandular organs in the abdominal cavity of mammals, birds, and reptiles, serving to remove waste products from the blood and secrete urine (ill. BODY 3); an animal's kidney as food. **2.** nature, kind, temperament. —**kidney bean,** a kidney-shaped dwarf French bean, a scarlet runner bean. **kidney dish,** an oval dish indented at one side. **kidney machine,** a machine able to take over the functions of a kidney. The first 'artificial kidney' was demonstrated (on an animal) in 1913. [orig. unkn.]

Kiel Canal /kiːl/ a canal connecting the North Sea with the Baltic. It runs from the German naval port of Kiel on the Baltic to Brunsbüttel at the mouth of the Elbe, and was opened in 1895.

Kierkegaard /ˈkɪərkəgɑːd/, Søren (1813–55), Danish philosopher, of a wealthy Lutheran family. To the prevailing Hegelian philosophy he opposed his own 'existential' dialectics, pointing out what was involved in the position of man 'existing before God', i.e. relating only to God. His oft-repeated statement 'truth is subjectivity' links truth with the existing subject instead of with its object, and so, in the last resort, makes its communication to other subjects impossible. Kierkegaard drew the theological consequences from this position by denying the possibility of an objective system of doctrinal truths, but his religious works have aroused less interest than his philosophical writings. His influence on contemporary thought has been considerable.

Kigali /kɪˈgɑːlɪ/ the capital of Rwanda; pop. approx. 7,000.

Kilimanjaro /ˌkɪlɪmənˈdʒɑːrəʊ/ an extinct volcano in Tanzania. It has twin peaks, the higher of which, Kibo (5,895 m, 19,340 ft.), is the highest mountain in Africa.

Kilkenny /kɪlˈkenɪ/ the county town of Co. Kilkenny, S. Ireland; pop. (1971) 9,838. —**Kilkenny cats,** cats proverbially said to have fought until only the tails remained.

kill v.t. 1. to deprive of life or vitality, to cause the death of. 2. to put an end to; to render ineffective; to switch off (a light, engine, etc.). 3. (colloq.) to cause severe pain to; to overwhelm with amusement. 4. to spend (time) unprofitably while waiting for something. —n. 1. the act of killing. 2. the animal(s) killed, especially in sport. —**dressed to kill,** dressed showily or alluringly. **in at the kill,** present at the time of victory. **kill off,** to get rid of by killing. **make a killing,** to have a great financial success. —**killer** n. [perh. rel. to QUELL]

killjoy n. a person who spoils or questions others' enjoyment.

kiln n. a furnace or oven for burning, baking, or drying, especially for calcining lime or firing pottery etc. [OE f. L culina kitchen]

kilo /ˈkiːləʊ/ n. (pl. -os) 1. a kilogram. 2. a kilometre. [F, abbr.]

kilo- /kɪlə-/ in comb. thousand. [F f. Gk khilioi]

kilocycle /ˈkɪləsaɪk(ə)l/ n. a kilohertz.

kilogram /ˈkɪləgræm/ n. the base unit of mass (symbol kg; established in 1889 for international use) equal to that of the international prototype, made of platinum–iridium, kept at Sèvres near Paris, approx. 2.205 lb.

kilohertz /ˈkɪləhɜːts/ n. a unit of frequency of electromagnetic waves, = 1,000 cycles per second.

kilolitre /ˈkɪlɪliːtə(r)/ n. a metric unit of capacity, 1,000 litres or approx. 35.31 cu. ft.

kilometre /ˈkɪləmiːtə(r), (D) kɪˈlɒmɪtə(r)/ n. a metric unit of length, 1,000 metres or approx. 0.62 mile.

kiloton /ˈkɪlətʌn/ n. a unit of explosive force equal to 1,000 tons of TNT.

kilotonne /ˈkɪlətʌn/ n. a metric unit equivalent to the kiloton.

kilowatt /ˈkɪləwɒt/ n. a unit of electrical power, equal to 1,000 watts. —**kilowatt-hour** n. the energy equal to one kilowatt working for one hour.

Kilroy /ˈkɪlrɔɪ/ the name of a mythical person, popularized by American servicemen in the Second World War, who left such inscriptions as 'Kilroy was here' on walls etc. all over the world. There are many unverifiable accounts of the origin of the name.

kilt n. a pleated usually tartan skirt reaching from the waist to the knee, especially worn by a Highland man. —v.t. 1. to tuck up (skirts) round the body. 2. to gather in vertical pleats. [f. Scand., cf. Da. kilte tuck]

kilted adj. wearing a kilt. [f. KILT]

kimono /kɪˈməʊnəʊ/ n. (pl. -os) 1. a long loose Japanese robe with wide sleeves, worn with a sash. 2. a European dressing-gown modelled on this. [Jap.]

kin n. one's relatives or family. —predic. adj. related. —**kinship** n. [OE]

-kin suffix forming diminutive nouns (catkin, lambkin). [f. MDu. -kijn, -ken, OHG -chin]

Kinchinjunga /ˌkɪntʃɪnˈdʒʌŋgə/ a mountain in the Himalayas on the border between Nepal and Sikkim, height 8,586 m. (28,168 ft.), the world's third-highest mountain. Its summit is split into five separate peaks, whence its name, which in Tibetan means 'the five treasures of the snows'.

kind[1] /kaɪnd/ n. a class of similar or related things or animals. —**a kind of,** something resembling or belonging approximately to (the class named). **in kind,** (of payment) in goods or produce, not money; (of repayment, esp. fig.) in the same form as that received. **kind of,** (colloq.) somewhat. [OE (as KIN)]

kind[2] /kaɪnd/ adj. gentle or considerate in conduct or manner towards others. —**kind-hearted** adj., **kindness** n. [as prec.; orig. = natural, native]

kindergarten /ˈkɪndəgɑːt(ə)n/ n. a school for very young children (see FROEBEL). [G, = children's garden]

kindle v.t./i. 1. to set on fire; to cause (a fire) to begin burning. 2. to arouse or stimulate (a feeling etc.). 3. to become kindled. [f. ON, rel. to kindill candle, torch]

kindling /ˈkɪndlɪŋ/ n. small sticks etc. for lighting a fire. [f. prec.]

kindly /ˈkaɪndlɪ/ adj. 1. kind. 2. (of a climate) pleasant, genial. —adv. 1. in a kind way. 2. (in a polite request or iron. command) please. —**not take kindly to,** to be displeased by. —**kindliness** n. [f. KIND[2]]

kindred /ˈkɪndrɪd/ n. 1. blood relationship. 2. one's relatives. 3. resemblance in character. —adj. related, of similar kind. —**kindred spirit,** a person whose tastes are similar to one's own. [f. KIN + OE ræden condition]

kine /kaɪn/ archaic pl. of COW[1].

kinematic /kɪnɪˈmætɪk/ adj. of motion considered abstractly without reference to force or mass. [f. Gk kinēma motion (as KINETIC)]

kinematics /kɪnɪˈmætɪks/ n.pl. the science of pure motion. [f. prec.]

kinetic /kɪˈnetɪk, kaɪ-/ adj. of or due to motion. —**kinetic art,** a form of visual art depending on moving components for its effect. **kinetic energy,** a body's ability to do work by virtue of its motion. [f. Gk kinētikos (kineō move)]

kinetics /kɪˈnetɪks, kaɪ-/ n.pl. (usu. treated as sing.) 1. the science of the relations between the motions of bodies and the forces acting upon them. 2. the study of the mechanisms and rates of chemical reactions or other processes. [f. prec.]

kinetic theory a theory that attempts to explain many of the observed properties of matter (e.g. heat, the melting of solids, the evaporation of liquids) as due to the continual motion of the discrete particles (atoms and molecules) of which they consist. In solids the particles vibrate about a fixed point; in liquids they 'slide over' one another but remain in close contact; in gases they move freely and independently. According to the kinetic theory the temperature of a solid, liquid, or gas is due to the mean kinetic energy distributed among its particles; evaporation from a liquid is due to the escape of the more rapidly moving molecules. The theory has existed in a rudimentary form from antiquity but it was not until the 19th c. that it acquired its present form, mainly through the investigations of Rudolf Clausius, James Clerk Maxwell, and Ludwig Boltzmann. It has successfully explained and predicted many other physical and chemical properties of matter, and is a powerful and well established instrument of scientific method today.

King, Martin Luther (1929–68), Black Baptist minister and American civil rights leader, an outstanding orator, who opposed discrimination against Blacks by organizing non-violent mass demonstrations. He was awarded the Nobel Peace Prize in 1964, and was assassinated in 1968.

king n. 1. a male sovereign (esp. hereditary) ruler of an independent State. 2. a male person or a thing regarded as pre-eminent in a specified field or class. 3. (attrib.) the large or largest kind of. 4. the piece in chess that has to be protected from checkmate. 5. a crowned piece in draughts. 6. a court-card with a picture of a king. 7. **Kings,** either of two books of the Old Testament recording Jewish history from the accession of Solomon to the destruction of the Temple in 586 BC. —**King James version,** the Authorized Version of the Bible. **King Log, King Stork,** rulers going respectively to extremes of laissez-faire and active oppression. The allusion is to the fable in which the frogs, dissatisfied with their inert King Log, appealed to Jupiter, who sent them King Stork who gobbled them all up. **King of Arms,** a chief herald (at the College of Arms, Garter, Clarenceaux, and Norroy & Ulster; in Scotland, Lyon). **king of beasts,** the lion. **king of birds,** the eagle. **king-post** n. an upright post from a tie-beam to the top of a rafter (ill. BUILDING TECHNIQUES). **king's evil,** scrofula, formerly held to be curable by the royal touch. **king-size, king-sized** *adjs.* larger than normal, very large. —**kingly** *adj.*, **kingship** *n.* [OE]

kingcup *n.* the marsh marigold.

kingdom /'kɪŋdəm/ *n.* **1.** a territory or State ruled by a king or queen; a domain. **2.** the most inclusive taxonomic category, consisting of a number of phyla (in zoology) or divisions (in botany). —**kingdom-come** *n.* (*slang*) the next world. [OE, as KING]

kingfisher *n.* a small land-bird of the family Alcedinidae with brilliant plumage, which dives for fish.

King Kong an ape-like monster featured in a film of that name (1933).

kingpin *n.* **1.** a vertical bolt used as a pivot. **2.** an essential person or thing.

Kingsley /'kɪŋzlɪ/, Charles (1819–75), English novelist and clergyman, professor of modern history at Cambridge (1860–9). His concern for the injustices suffered by the working classes is expressed in his novels *Yeast* (1850) and *Alton Locke* (1850). His historical novel *Westward Ho!* (1855) and his classic children's book *The Water-Babies* (1863) are characteristically didactic.

Kingston /'kɪŋst(ə)n/ the capital and chief port of Jamaica; pop. (est. 1980) 671,000.

kink *n.* **1.** a sudden bend or twist in something straight or smoothly curved. **2.** a mental peculiarity or twist. —*v.t./i.* to form or cause to form a kink. [f. MLG]

kinky *adj.* **1.** having kinks. **2.** (*colloq.*) bizarre, perverted (esp. sexually). —**kinkily** *adv.*, **kinkiness** *n.* [f. prec.]

kinsfolk /'kɪnzfəʊk/ *n.* one's blood relations.

Kinshasa /kɪn'ʃɑːsə/ (formerly *Leopoldville*) the capital of Zaïre, founded in 1881 by the explorer H. M. Stanley; pop. (est. 1980) 2,500,000.

kinsman /'kɪnzmən/ *n.* (*pl.* **-men**) a (male) blood relation. —**kinswoman** *n.fem.* (*pl.* **-women**).

kiosk /'kiːɒsk/ *n.* **1.** a light usually outdoor structure for the sale of newspapers, food, etc. **2.** a box-like structure in the street etc. for a public telephone. [f. F f. Turk. f. Pers., = pavilion]

kip *n.* (*slang*) **1.** a sleep. **2.** a place to sleep, a bed. —*v.i.* (**-pp-**) (*slang*) to sleep. [cf. Da. *kippe* mean hut]

Kipling /'kɪplɪŋ/, Rudyard (1865–1936), English writer and poet, born in Bombay. His education in England is depicted in his schoolboy tales *Stalky & Co.* (1899). Working as a journalist in India (1882–9) he published poems and short stories, and received celebrity with *Barrack-Room Ballads* (1892). Kipling's output was vast and varied. His fluent versification with its echoes of hymns and ballads, and his use of colloquial speech, in prose and verse, has been variously judged; his belief in duty, responsibility, and personal honour has given his works a powerful moral force. His most durable achievements were his tales for children, notably *The Jungle Book* (1894), *Just So Stories* (1902), and his picaresque novel of India *Kim* (1901). He was the first English writer to be awarded the Nobel Prize for literature (1907).

kipper *n.* **1.** a kippered fish, especially a herring. **2.** a male salmon in the spawning season. —*v.t.* to cure (a herring etc.) by splitting open, salting, drying, and smoking. [orig. unkn.]

Kirchhoff /'kɪrxhɒf/, Gustav Robert (1824–87), German physicist who, working with Bunsen, developed a technique of spectrum analysis and, using this, discovered the elements caesium and rubidium (1860–1). He also worked on electrical circuits and the flow of currents.

Kirghizia /kɑː'gɪːzɪə/ the Kirghiz SSR, a constituent republic of the USSR, on the Chinese frontier; capital, Frunze.

Kiribati /kɪrɪ'bæs/ a small country in the SW Pacific, consisting of groups of islands including the former Gilbert Islands; pop. (est. 1982) 60,000; official languages, English and local dialect; capital, Bairiki. First sighted by the Spaniards in the mid-16th c., the islands were visited by the British in the 18th c. and named after Thomas Gilbert, an English adventurer who arrived there in 1788; they became a favourite centre for the hunting of sperm whales. Britain declared a protectorate over the Gilbert and Ellice Islands in 1892, and they became a colony in 1915. Links with the Ellice Islands (now Tuvalu) ended in 1975, and in 1979 Kiribati became an independent republic within the Commonwealth. The phosphate deposits which were formerly a main source of revenue are almost exhausted, and the principal exports are copra and fish; budgetary assistance is provided by aid from the UK.

kirk *n.* (*Sc. & N. Engl.*) a church. —**kirk-session** *n.* the lowest court in the Church of Scotland and (*hist.*) other Presbyterian Churches, composed of ministers and elders. **the Kirk (of Scotland)**, the Church of Scotland as opposed to the Church of England or to the Episcopal Church in Scotland. [f. ON f. OE, = CHURCH]

Kirundi /kɪ'rʊndɪ/ *n.* a Bantu language, the official language of Burundi.

kismet /'kɪsmet, 'kɪz-/ *n.* destiny, fate. [Turk., f. Arab.]

kiss *n.* a touch given with the lips. —*v.t.* **1.** to touch with the lips, especially as a sign of love, affection, greeting, or reverence; (absol., of two persons) to touch each other's lips thus. **2.** to touch gently. —**kiss-curl** *n.* a small curl of hair arranged on the face or at the nape. **kiss hands**, to greet a sovereign thus. **kiss of death**, an apparently friendly act causing ruin. **kiss of life**, the mouth-to-mouth method of artificial respiration. [OE]

kisser *n.* (*slang*) the mouth or face. [f. KISS]

Kiswahili /kɪswɑː'hiːlɪ/ *n.* the Swahili language. [native name, f. *ki-* object + SWAHILI]

kit *n.* **1.** the equipment or clothing required for a particular activity or situation. **2.** a soldier's or traveller's pack or equipment. **3.** a set of parts sold together from which a whole thing can be made. —*v.t./i.* (**-tt-**) to equip, to fit *out* or *up* with a kit. [f. MDu., = wooden vessel]

kitbag *n.* a large usually cylindrical bag for a soldier's or traveller's kit.

Kit-cat Club a club founded in the early part of the 18th c. by leading Whigs, including (according to Pope) Steele, Addison, Congreve, and Vanbrugh.

kitchen /'kɪtʃɪn/ *n.* a place where food is prepared and cooked. —**kitchen cabinet**, a group of unofficial advisers (orig. of the President of the USA) popularly believed to have greater influence than the official Cabinet or other elected group. **kitchen garden**, a garden for growing fruit and vegetables. **kitchen-sink drama**, a term applied in the British theatre after John Osborne's *Look Back in Anger* (1956) and Arnold Wesker's plays such as *Roots* (1959) to plays using working-class settings rather than the drawing-rooms of conventional middle-class drama. **kitchen-sink school**, a group of British painters who, in the late 1940s and early 1950s, chose drab and sordid themes and aggressive techniques expressive of the post-war mood of dissatisfaction with the current state of affairs. [OE, ult. f. L *coquina* (*coquere* cook)]

Kitchener /'kɪtʃɪnə(r)/, Horatio Herbert, Earl Kitchener of Khartoum (1850–1916), British soldier and statesman who became a national hero following his defeat of the Dervishes at Omdurman and reconquest of the Sudan in 1898. He served as Roberts's chief of staff in the Boer War, and then successively as commander-in-chief, India, and consul-general, Egypt, before being made Secretary of State for War at the outbreak of the First World War. Kitchener was among the first to recognize that the war would be a long one, and was responsible for organizing the large volunteer army which eventually fought the war on the Western Front. As the war progressed, however, he proved unequal to the demands of his post and gradually lost influence, although he kept his Cabinet post until he was drowned when HMS *Hampshire* struck a mine while carrying him on a mission to Russia.

kitchenette /kɪtʃɪ'net/ *n.* a small room or alcove used as a kitchen. [f. KITCHEN + -ETTE]

kite *n.* **1.** a toy consisting of a light framework with paper etc. stretched over it and flown in the wind at the end of a long string. **2.** a bird of prey of the hawk family (esp. *Milvus milvus*). —**fly a kite**, (*colloq.*) to sound out public opinion. [OE]

Kitemark *n.* the official kite-shaped mark on goods approved by the British Standards Institution.

kith /kɪθ/ *n.* **kith and kin**, friends and relations. [OE, orig. = knowledge (as UNCOUTH)]

kitsch /kɪtʃ/ *n.* worthless pretentiousness or bad taste in art; art of this type. —**kitschy** *adj.* [G]

kitten /'kɪt(ə)n/ *n.* the young of a cat, ferret, etc. —*v.t./i.* to give birth to (kittens). —**have kittens**, (*colloq.*) to be very upset or nervous. —**kittenish** *adj.* [f. OF *chitoun* dim. of *chat* cat]

kittiwake /'kɪtɪweɪk/ *n.* a kind of small seagull (*Rissa tridactyla*). [imit. of its cry]

kitty *n.* a fund of money for communal use; the pool in some card-games. [orig. unkn.]

kiwi /'kiːwiː/ *n.* **1.** a flightless New Zealand bird of the genus

Apteryx, with rudimentary wings and no tail. **2. Kiwi,** (*colloq.*) a New Zealander. —**kiwi fruit,** the fruit of a deciduous fruiting vine (*Actinidia chinensis*), also called Chinese gooseberry. [Maori]

kl *abbr.* kilolitre(s).

Klaproth /'klæprəʊt/, Martin Heinrich (1743-1817), German chemist, one of the founders of chemical analysis. He discovered the elements zirconium and uranium (actually, the oxide) in 1789, rediscovered and named titanium in 1795, and recognized chromium in 1797, tellurium in 1798, and cerium in 1803. Several of these were also discovered independently by other chemists. A follower of Lavoisier, he helped to introduce the latter's new system of chemistry into Germany.

Klaxon /'klæks(ə)n/ *n.* [P] a powerful electric horn. [f. name of manufacturer]

Klee /kleɪ/, Paul (1879-1940), Swiss painter who trained in Munich, where he settled in 1906. He began as a graphic artist and was influenced by Blake, Goya, Beardsley, Ensor, and Toulouse-Lautrec, and exhibited with Kandinsky, whose interest in music, poetry, and eastern philosophy he shared. In 1920 Klee was appointed to the staff of the Bauhaus and taught there until 1933, when he left Germany for Switzerland. He developed an international reputation as a modernist, after 1920, and it is interesting that seventeen of his works appeared in the Degenerate Art exhibition mounted by the Nazi régime in Munich in 1937.

Klein bottle /klaɪn/ a closed surface with only one side, formed by passing the neck of a bottle through the side of the bottle to join a hole in the base. [f. C. F. *Klein*, German mathematician (d. 1925)]

kleptomania /kleptə'meɪnɪə/ *n.* a tendency to steal, without regard for need or profit. —**kleptomaniac** *n. & adj.* [f. Gk *kleptēs* thief + -MANIA]

Klondike /'klɒndaɪk/ a river and district in Yukon, Canada. The discovery of gold there in 1896 led to a spectacular gold-rush.

kloof *n.* (*S.Afr.*) a ravine or valley. [Du., = cleft]

km *abbr.* kilometre(s).

knack /næk/ *n.* **1.** an acquired or intuitive ability to do something skilfully. **2.** a habit. [prob. = *knack* sharp blow, f. LG]

knacker /'nækə(r)/ *n.* a buyer of useless horses for slaughter, or of old houses etc. for their materials. —*v.t.* (esp. in *p.p.*) (*slang*) to exhaust, to wear out. [orig. unkn.]

knapsack /'næpsæk/ *n.* a soldier's or traveller's bag, usually of canvas, strapped to the back. [MLG (prob. f. *knapp* food, SACK)]

knapweed /'næpwi:d/ *n.* a plant of the genus *Centaurea*, with purple flowers in a globular head. [f. earlier *knopweed* (KNOP, WEED)]

knave /neɪv/ *n.* **1.** an unprincipled or dishonest person, a rogue. **2.** the jack in playing-cards. —**knavish** *adj.* [OE, = boy, servant]

knavery *n.* the conduct of a knave. [f. prec.]

knead /ni:d/ *v.t.* **1.** to work (moist flour, clay, etc.) into dough by pressing with the hands; to make (bread, pottery) thus. **2.** to operate on using such motions (in massaging etc.). [OE]

knee /ni:/ *n.* **1.** the joint between the thigh and the lower leg in man. **2.** the corresponding joint in an animal. **3.** the upper surface of the thigh of a sitting person. **4.** the part of a garment covering the knee. —*v.t.* to touch or strike with the knee. —**bring a person to his knees,** to reduce him to submission. **knee-breeches** *n.pl.* breeches reaching to or just below the knee. **knee-deep** *adj.* immersed up to the knees; deeply involved; so deep as to reach the knees. **knee-high** *adj.* so high as to reach the knees. **knee-hole** *n.* a space for the knees, especially between columns of drawers at each side of a desk etc. **knee-jerk** *n.* a sudden involuntary kick caused by a blow on the tendon below the knee. **knees-up** *n.* (*colloq.*) a lively party with dancing. [OE]

kneecap *n.* **1.** the convex bone in the front of the knee-joint. **2.** a protective covering for the knee.

kneecapping *n.* shooting in the legs to lame a person as a punishment.

kneel /ni:l/ *v.i.* (*past & p.p.* **knelt** or (*US*) **kneeled**) to take or be in a position where the body is supported on the knee(s) with the lower part of the leg(s) bent back, especially in prayer or reverence. [OE (as KNEE)]

kneeler *n.* a hassock etc. for kneeling on. [f. prec.]

knell /nel/ *n.* **1.** the sound of a bell, especially after a death or at a funeral. **2.** an omen of death or extinction. [OE]

Kneller /'nelə(r)/, Sir Godfrey (1649-1723), German-born portrait painter who established a prolific workshop in London from 1674. He was a dominant court and society painter, executing commissions for Charles II and James II, and becoming principal painter to William and Mary at their accession. His best work captures the sitter's personality, and is more than a mere visual record. Although Kneller always painted the faces the work of many assistants can often be seen in backgrounds and details. Knighted in 1692 and created a baronet in 1715, he was the most socially eminent and successful English artist of his age.

knelt *past & p.p.* of KNEEL.

Knesset /'knesɪt/ *n.* the parliament of the State of Israel. [Heb., = gathering]

knew *past* of KNOW.

knickerbockers /'nɪkəbɒkəz/ *n.pl.* loose-fitting breeches gathered in at the knee. [f. Diedrich *Knickerbocker*, pretended author of Washington Irving's *History of New York* (1809)]

knickers /'nɪkəz/ *n.pl.* a woman's or girl's undergarment covering the body below the waist and having separate legs or leg-holes. [abbr. of prec.]

knick-knack /'nɪknæk/ *n.* a trinket or small ornament. [redupl. of *knack* in obs. sense 'trinket']

knife /naɪf/ *n.* (*pl.* **knives**) a cutting instrument or weapon consisting of a metal blade with a long sharpened edge fixed in a handle; a cutting-blade in a machine. —*v.t.* to cut or stab with a knife. —**at knife-point,** threatened by a knife. **the knife,** (*colloq.*) surgery. **have got one's knife into,** to be persistently malicious or vindictive towards. **knife-edge** *n.* the sharp edge of a knife, a position of tense uncertainty about an outcome. **knife-pleat** *n.* a narrow flat pleat in an overlapping series. **night of the long knives,** see LONG[1]. [OE f. ON]

knight /naɪt/ *n.* **1.** a man raised to the rank below the baronetcy as a reward for personal merit or services to Crown or country, entitling the holder to the prefix *Sir*. **2.** (*hist.*) a man raised to an honourable military rank by a king etc. **3.** (*hist.*) a military follower, especially one devoted to the service of a lady as her attendant or champion in a war or tournament. **4.** a chess piece usually with the shape of a horse's head. —*v.t.* to confer a knighthood on. —**knight errant,** a medieval knight wandering in search of chivalrous adventures; a man of such a spirit. **knight-errantry** *n.* [OE, = boy, youth]

knighthood *n.* the rank or dignity of a knight. [f. prec. + -HOOD]

knightly *adj.* of or like a knight; chivalrous. [f. KNIGHT]

Knights Hospitallers /hɒs'pɪt(ə)l(ə)rz/ a military religious order founded as the Knights of the Hospital of St John at Jerusalem in the 11th c. Their headquarters were later at Rhodes (1309-1522), then Malta (1530-1798). Originally protectors of pilgrims, they also undertook the care of the sick and became a powerful and wealthy military force, with foundations in various European countries, and valiant fighters against the Turks. Gradually there was a decline in morals and discipline, and their military power ended when Malta was surrendered to Napoleon (1798). In England their property was sequestered in 1540, and the order remained dormant until revived on a mainly Anglican basis in 1831, and constituted an order of chivalry in 1888. It was responsible for the foundation of the St John Ambulance Association in 1878 and the St John Ambulance Brigade in 1888 (now St John Ambulance).

Knights Templars the 'Poor Knights of Christ and of the Temple of Solomon', a military order founded in 1118 to protect pilgrims from bandits in the Holy Land, where they were given quarters on the site of Solomon's temple in Jerusalem. The order became powerful and wealthy, particularly in the 13th c. Their wealth was deposited in 'temples' in Paris and London and they became trusted bankers. Their arrogance towards rulers, their wealth, and their rivalry with the Knights Hospitallers, led to their downfall. Philip IV of France coveted their wealth and brought false charges of sodomy, blasphemy, and heresy against the order. It was suppressed in 1312, and many of its possessions were given to the Hospitallers. The Inner and Middle Temple in London are on the site of the Templars' English headquarters.

knit /nɪt/ *v.t./i.* (**-tt-**; *past & p.p.* **knitted** or (esp. *fig.*) **knit**) **1.** to make (a garment etc. or *absol.*) by interlocking loops of yarn or thread. **2.** to form (yarn) into a fabric etc. in this way. **3.** to make (a plain stitch) in knitting. **4.** to wrinkle (the brow). **5.** to make or become close or compact, to grow together. —**knitter** *n.* [OE (as KNOT)]

knitting *n.* work being knitted. —**knitting-needle** *n.* each of a pair of slender pointed rods used in knitting by hand. [f. KNIT]

knitwear *n.* knitted garments.

knob /nɒb/ *n.* **1.** a rounded protuberance, especially at an end or on a surface of a thing, e.g. a handle of a door, drawer, etc. or for adjusting a radio etc. **2.** a small lump (of butter etc.). —**with knobs on,** (*slang*) that and more (often as an emphatic or ironical agreement). —**knobbly** *adj.* [f. MLG; cf. KNOP]

knobkerrie /ˈnɒbkerɪ/ *n.* a short stick with a knob at the end as a weapon of South African tribes. [f. Afrik. *knopkierie*]

knobbly /ˈnɒblɪ/ *adj.* hard and lumpy. [f. *knobble* dim. of KNOB]

knock /nɒk/ *v.t./i.* **1.** to strike with an audible sharp blow. **2.** to make a noise by striking a door etc. to summon a person or gain admittance. **3.** to drive or make by striking. **4.** (of an engine) to make a thumping or rattling noise, to pink. **5.** to criticize or insult. —*n.* an act or sound of knocking; a sharp blow. —**knock about** or **around,** to treat roughly, to strike repeatedly; to wander about aimlessly. **knock back,** (*slang*) to eat or drink, esp. hastily; to disconcert. **knock down,** to strike (a person) to the ground; to demolish; to dispose of (an article *to* a bidder) by the knock of the hammer at an auction. **knock-down** *adj.* (of a price) very low; (of furniture etc.) easily dismantled and reassembled; overwhelming. **knock-for-knock** *adj.* (of insurance terms) with each company paying its policy-holder in a claim, regardless of liability. **knocking-shop** *n.* (*slang*) a brothel. **knock knees,** an abnormal inward curving of the legs at the knees. **knock-kneed** *adj.* having this. **knock off,** (*colloq.*) to cease work; to complete (a piece of work etc.) quickly; to deduct (a sum from a total); (*slang*) to steal or kill. **knock-on effect,** the effect of an alteration that causes similar alterations elsewhere. **knock out,** to render unconscious, especially by a blow to the head; to disable (a boxer) so that he is unable to recover in the required time; to defeat in a knock-out competition; to exhaust or disable. **knock spots off,** (*colloq.*) to surpass easily. **knock up,** to make or arrange hastily; to arouse by knocking at the door; to score (runs) at cricket, (*US slang*) to make pregnant. **knock-up** *n.* a practice game etc. [OE]

knockabout *adj.* rough, boisterous.

knocker *n.* a hinged metal device on a door for knocking to call attention. [f. KNOCK]

knock-out *adj.* **1.** that knocks a boxer etc. out. **2.** (of a competition) in which the loser of each round is eliminated. —*n.* **1.** a knock-out blow. **2.** (*slang*) an outstanding person or thing.

knoll /nəʊl/ *n.* a hillock, a mound. [OE]

knop /nɒp/ *n.* **1.** an ornamental knob. **2.** a loop, a tuft in a yarn. [f. MLG or MDu.]

Knossos /ˈknɒsɒs/ the principal city of Minoan Crete, near the port of Heraklion. It was occupied from neolithic times until *c.*1200 BC. Excavations by Sir Arthur Evans from 1900 onwards revealed remains of a luxurious and spectacularly decorated complex of buildings which he named the Palace of Minos, with frescoes of landscapes, animal life, and the sport of bull-leaping. In *c.*1450 BC Crete was overrun by the Mycenaeans, but the palace was not finally destroyed until the 14th or early 13th c. BC.

knot[1] /nɒt/ *n.* **1.** an intertwining of one or more pieces of rope, string, etc., to fasten them together. **2.** a tangle. **3.** a ribbon etc. tied with a knot for ornament etc. **4.** a group or cluster. **5.** a hard mass formed in a tree-trunk where a branch once grew out; a corresponding cross-grained piece in a board. **6.** a difficulty or problem. **7.** that which forms or maintains a union, especially a marriage. **8.** the unit of a ship's or aircraft's speed equal to one nautical mile per hour (1 knot = 1.85 k.p.h. = 1.15 m.p.h.). It was originally measured by a series of knots on a string fastened to the log-line; the number of knots that ran out while the sand-glass was running indicated the ship's speed in nautical miles per hour. —*v.t./i.* (**-tt-**) **1.** to tie in or with a knot or knots. **2.** to make a (fringe) by knotting threads. **3.** to entangle. **4.** to unite closely or intricately. —**at a rate of knots,** (*colloq.*) very fast. **knot-grass** *n.* a weed (*Polygonum aviculare*) with intricate creeping stems and pink flowers. **knot-hole** *n.* a hole in a wooden board, where a knot has fallen out. **tie in knots,** to make (a person) confused or baffled. [OE]

knot[2] /nɒt/ *n.* a small wading bird (*Calidris canutus*) of the sandpiper family. [orig. unkn.; the conjecture that the bird was named after King Cnut (Canute), because believed to be a visitor from Denmark, is without foundation]

knotty *adj.* **1.** full of knots. **2.** puzzling, difficult. [f. KNOT[1]]

know /nəʊ/ *v.t./i.* (*past* **knew** /njuː/, *p.p.* **known** /nəʊn/) **1.** to have in the mind or memory as the result of experience, learning, or information. **2.** to feel certain. **3.** to be acquainted or have regular social contact with (a person). **4.** to recognize or identify. **5.** to understand and be able to use (a language, subject, or skill). **6.** to have personal experience of (fear etc.). **7.** to be subject to (limits etc.). —*n.* (*colloq.*) **in the know,** knowing secret or inside information. —**know-all** *n.* (*derog.*) a person who claims to know much. **know-how** *n.* practical knowledge or skill. **know one's own mind,** to know one's intentions firmly. **you never know,** it is always possible. [OE]

knowable *adj.* that may be known. [f. KNOW]

knowing *adj.* having or showing knowledge or awareness; shrewd, clever. —**knowingly** *adv.* [f. KNOW]

knowledge /ˈnɒlɪdʒ/ *n.* **1.** knowing. **2.** all that a person knows. **3.** the sum of what is known to mankind. —**to my knowledge,** as far as I know. [f. KNOW]

knowledgeable /ˈnɒlɪdʒəb(ə)l/ *adj.* having much knowledge, well-informed. [f. prec.]

known *p.p.* of KNOW.

Knox[1] /nɒks/, John (*c.*1505–72), Scottish Protestant reformer. After early involvement in the Scottish Reformation, and more than a decade spent preaching in various parts of Protestant Europe, Knox returned to his homeland in 1559 and played a central part in the overthrow of the French regency and the establishment of a Scottish Protestant State. During the brief reign of the Catholic queen Mary Queen of Scots he was the spokesman of the religious interests opposed to her. A fiery orator, Knox was very much a radical in his own day, but considerably more moderate than many of his 17th-c. successors.

Knox[2] /nɒks/, Ronald Arbuthnott (1888–1957), British Roman Catholic priest whose translation of the Bible from the Vulgate (1945–9) was accepted for use in the Roman Catholic Church. He also wrote detective stories and various works of humour.

knuckle /ˈnʌk(ə)l/ *n.* **1.** the bone at the finger-joint, especially at the root of the finger. **2.** the knee- or ankle-joint of an animal, especially with the adjacent parts as a joint of meat. —*v.t./i.* to strike, press, or rub with the knuckles. —**knuckle down,** to apply oneself earnestly (*to* work etc.). **knuckle-duster** *n.* a metal guard worn over the knuckles in fist-fighting especially to increase the violence of a blow. **knuckle under,** to give in, to submit. **near the knuckle,** (*colloq.*) verging on indecency. [f. MLG or MDu. (dim. of *knoke* bone)]

knurl /nɜːl/ *n.* a small projecting ridge etc. [cf. *knur* knot, swelling, f. MDu. or MLG]

KO *abbr.* knock-out.

koala /kəʊˈɑːlə/ *n.* an Australian arboreal marsupial (*Phascolarctos cinereus*) with thick grey fur and large ears. [f. Aboriginal *kūl(l)a*]

kobold /ˈkəʊbɒld/ *n.* (*Germanic myth.*) a familiar spirit; an underground spirit in mines etc. [G]

Koch /kɒx/, Robert (1843–1910), German bacteriologist. As a young country doctor he studied an outbreak of anthrax in local cattle, and successfully identified and cultured the bacillus causing this. He devised new and better methods for obtaining pure cultures, and identified first the tuberculosis bacillus (his greatest discovery) and then the organism that causes cholera. He also studied typhoid fever, malaria, and other tropical diseases, and formulated rules as to the conditions which must be satisfied before a disease can be ascribed to a specific microorganism. The techniques that he devised are the basis of modern methods. Koch was awarded the Nobel Prize for medicine in 1905.

Kodály /ˈkəʊdaɪ/, Zoltán (1882–1967), Hungarian composer whose works include operas and orchestral and choral music. He attached equal importance to his work in collecting and publishing folk-songs and his long composing career which spanned 70 years. He heard and was influenced by Debussy's music while in Paris, but his main source of inspiration was his native land, and Bartók described his music as 'the most perfect embodiment of the Hungarian spirit'.

Koestler /ˈkɜːstlə(r)/, Arthur (1905–83), Hungarian-born essayist and novelist, in his youth a science correspondent. His best-known novel *Darkness at Noon* (1940) exposed the

Stalinist purges of the 1930s. In *The Sleepwalkers* (1959) and other late works he questioned some of the common assumptions of science, and left money in his will for research into the paranormal. He and his wife committed suicide together.

Koh-i-noor /ˈkəʊɪnʊə(r)/ *n.* an Indian diamond, famous for its size, one of the treasures of Aurangzeb, with a history going back to the 14th c. It became one of the British Crown jewels on the annexation of the Punjab in 1849. [f. Pers., = mountain of light]

kohl /kəʊl/ *n.* a powder used (especially in eastern countries) to darken the eyelids etc. [f. Arab.]

kohlrabi /kəʊlˈrɑːbɪ/ *n.* a cabbage with a turnip-like edible stem. [G f. It. f. L *caulorapa* (as COLE, RAPE²)]

koine /ˈkɔɪnɪ/ *n.* **1.** the common language of the Greeks from the close of the classical period to the Byzantine era. **2.** a common language shared by various peoples, a lingua franca. [f. Gk, = common (language)]

kolinsky /kəˈlɪnskɪ/ *n.* the Siberian mink (*Mustela sibirica*); its fur. [f. Russ. (*Kola* in NW Russia)]

kolkhoz /ˈkɒlkɒz/ *n.* a collective farm in the USSR. [Russ.]

koodoo var. of KUDU.

kook /kuːk/ *n.* (*US slang*) a crazy or eccentric person. —**kooky** *adj.* [prob. f. CUCKOO]

kookaburra /ˈkʊkəbʌrə/ *n.* a large Australian kingfisher (*Dacelo novaeguineae*) with a loud discordant cry. [Abor.]

kopje /ˈkɒpɪ/ *n.* (also **koppie**) (*S. Afr.*) a small hill. [Du. & Afrik., dim. of *kop* head]

Koran /kɔːˈrɑːn, kə-/ *n.* **the** holy book of Islam, composed of the revelations which came to the Prophet Muhammad during his lifetime, from *c.*610 to his death in AD 632. Written in Arabic, the revelations are grouped into 114 units of varying sizes which are known as suras; the first sura is said as part of the ritual prayer. The traditional arrangement of the suras is not chronological but rather according to length, from the longest. The revelations touch upon all aspects of human existence, from the doctrinally focused revelations of Muhammad's early career in Mecca to those concerning social organization and legislation, which were communicated while the Muslim community was based in Medina (622–30). Considered to be the direct and inimitable word of God, which is applicable for all time and in all circumstances to the regulation and religious expression of human society, the Koran is held by Muslims to be untranslatable, although versions or interpretations in many other languages are available. The Koran is regarded as the ultimate exemplar of Arabic linguistic and literary prowess and the supreme and perfect guide to Arabic grammar and stylistics. Its memorization forms the basis of a traditional Islamic elementary education in a 'Koran school'. —**Koranic** /-ˈrɑːnɪk, -ˈræ-/ *adj.* [f. Arab., = recitation (*kara'a* read)]

Korda /ˈkɔːdə/ Sir Alexander (1893–1956), real name Sándor Kellner, Hungarian-born film producer and director, who settled in England and in 1932 formed London Film Productions. His extravagant films, which achieved international recognition, included *The Private Life of Henry VIII* (1933), *Rembrandt* (1936), both of which he directed himself, *Catherine the Great*, *The Scarlet Pimpernel* (both 1934), *Sanders of the River*, *The Ghost Goes West* (both 1935), *Things to Come*, and *Elephant Boy* (both 1936). By 1939 he had over-extended himself and lost Denham Studios, which he had built, and though he later refloated London Films he never regained his earlier eminence.

Korea /kəˈriːə/ a country in eastern Asia situated on a peninsula between the Sea of Japan and the Yellow Sea, now divided along the 38th parallel into the People's Democratic Republic of Korea (North Korea; pop. (1982) approx. 18,000,000; capital, Pyongyang) and the Republic of Korea (South Korea; pop. approx. 39,000,000; capital, Seoul); the official language of both countries is Korean. Possessed of a distinct national and cultural identity and ruled from the 14th c. by the Korean Yi Dynasty, Korea has suffered as a result of its position between Chinese and Japanese spheres of influence. Chinese domination was ended by the Sino-Japanese War (1894–5) and after the Russo-Japanese War a decade later the country was finally annexed by Japan in 1910. After the Japanese surrender at the end of the Second World War, the northern half of the country was occupied by the Russians and the southern half by the Americans. Separate countries were created in 1948 and two years later the Northern invasion of the South resulted in the Korean War (1950–3). The borders were restored at the end of the war but both countries were some time in recovering from the devastation caused by military operations. Each is now

prospering, particularly the South which is now the most rapidly growing industrial nation in the world.

Korean /kəˈrɪən/ *adj.* of Korea or its people or language. —*n.* **1.** a native or inhabitant of Korea. **2.** the language of North and South Korea, spoken by about 50 million people. Its linguistic affiliations are uncertain although it seems most similar to Japanese. Its vocabulary and orthography has been heavily influenced by Chinese. The Korean alphabet is the only true alphabetical script native to the Far East. [f. prec.]

Kosciusko /kɒsɪˈtʃʊʃkəʊ/, Thaddeus (1746–1817), Polish soldier and patriot. A trained soldier, he offered his services to the American rebels during the War of Independence and was made Colonel of Engineers in 1776. He returned to Poland after the war and led the rebellion against foreign rule in 1794. Captured and imprisoned by the Russians (1794–6), he eventually moved to France, where he devoted the rest of his life to the cause of Polish independence.

kosher /ˈkəʊʃə(r)/ *adj.* **1.** (of food or a foodshop) fulfilling the requirements of Jewish law. **2.** (*colloq.*) correct, genuine, legitimate. —*n.* kosher food; a kosher shop. [f. Heb., = proper]

Kossuth /ˈkɒsuːθ/, Lajos (1802–94), Hungarian statesman and patriot. After an early career as an opponent of Hapsburg domination of Hungary, he led the 1848 insurrection and was appointed governor of the country during the brief period of independence. The uprising was crushed in 1849, and he fled into exile where he spent the rest of his life.

Kosygin /kɒˈsiːgɪn/, Alexsei Nikolayevich (1904–80), Russian statesman. Mayor of Leningrad in 1938–9, he became a Central Committee member in 1939 and went on to hold a series of ministerial posts, mostly concerned with finance and industry. He succeeded Khrushchev as Prime Minister in 1964, but devoted most of his attention to internal economic affairs, being gradually eased out of the leadership by Brezhnev.

Kotzebue /ˈkɒtsəbuːeɪ/, August von (1761–1819), German dramatist whose many sentimental plays were very popular in their day, notably *Die deutschen Kleinstädter* (1803), and *Das Kind der Liebe* (1790), adapted as *Lovers' Vows* and made famous by Jane Austen's *Mansfield Park*. He was a political informant to Tsar Alexander I and was assassinated by the Germans. His son, Otto von Kotzebue (1787–1846), was a navigator and explorer, discoverer of an inlet of NW Alaska (Kotzebue Sound) now named after him.

kowtow /kaʊˈtaʊ/ *v.i.* **1.** to behave obsequiously. **2.** to perform the kowtow. —*n.* the Chinese custom of touching the ground with the head as a sign of worship or submission. [f. Chin., = knock the head]

k.p.h. *abbr.* kilometres per hour.

Kr *symbol* krypton.

kraal /krɑːl/ *n.* (*S. Afr.*) **1.** a village of huts enclosed by a fence. **2.** an enclosure for sheep or cattle. [Afrik. f. Port. *curral*, of Hottentot orig.]

Krafft-Ebing /krʌftˈeɪbɪŋ/, Richard von (1840–1902), German physician and psychologist. He is best known for having established the relationship between syphilis and general paralysis, and for his *Psychopathia Sexualis* (1886), a pioneer examination of sexual aberrations.

Krakatoa /krækəˈtəʊə/ a small volcanic island in Indonesia, lying between Java and Sumatra, scene of a great eruption in 1883.

kraken /ˈkrɑːkən/ *n.* a mythical sea-monster said to appear off the coast of Norway. [Norw.]

Kraut /kraʊt/ *n.* (*slang, derog.*) a German. [f. SAUERKRAUT]

Krebs /krebz/, Sir Hans Adolf (1900–81), British biochemist, born in Germany, who (while in Germany) discovered the cycle of reactions by which urea is synthesized by the liver. After moving to Britain in 1933 came his greatest discovery (1937), the **Krebs cycle,** a series of biochemical reactions which constitutes a major part of the process of respiration in most living cells.

kremlin /ˈkremlɪn/ *n.* a citadel within a Russian town, especially that of Moscow, traditionally the centre of administration as well as the last bastion of defence. —**the Kremlin,** the government of the USSR. [F f. Russ.]

Kriemhild /ˈkriːmhɪlt/ (in the Nibelungenlied) a Burgundian princess, wife of Siegfried and later of Etzel (Attila), whom she marries in order to be revenged on her brothers for Siegfried's murder.

krill *n.* small shrimp-like crustaceans of the order Euphausiacea; a large group of these animals forming food for fishes and whales. [f. Norw. *krill* tiny fish]

kris /kri:s, krɪs/ *n*. a Malay dagger with a wavy blade. [ult. f. Malay]

Krishna /ˈkrɪʃnə/ (*Hinduism*) one of the most popular gods, the eighth and most important avatar of Vishnu. He is worshipped in several forms; as the child god whose miracles and pranks are extolled in the Puranas; as the divine cowherd whose erotic exploits, especially with his favourite, Radha, have produced both romantic and religious literature; and as the divine charioteer who preaches to Arjuna on the battlefield in the Bhagavadgita. [Skr., = black]

kromesky /krəˈmeskɪ/ *n*. minced meat or fish rolled in bacon and fried. [app. f. Polish *kromeczka* small slice]

krona /ˈkrəʊnə/ *n*. the currency unit of Sweden (*pl.* **kronor**) and of Iceland (*pl.* **kronur**). [Sw. & Icel., = CROWN]

krone /ˈkrəʊnə/ *n*. (*pl.* **kroner**) the currency unit of Denmark and of Norway. [Da. & Norwegian, = CROWN]

Kronos /ˈkrɒnəs/ = CRONUS.

Kroo /kru:/ *n*. a member of a Black people on the coast of Liberia, skilful as seamen. [W. Afr.]

Kropotkin /krəˈpɒtkɪn/, Peter Alexeevich, Prince (1842–1921), Russian anarchist. A geographer of some distinction, he carried out important explorations of Siberia, Finland, and Manchuria before devoting his life to political activities, in particular the espousal of anarchism, of which he was one of the most influential exponents. Arrested in 1874, he escaped abroad two years later and only returned to Russia after the Russian Revolution in 1917.

Kruger /ˈkru:gə(r)/, Stephanus Johannes Paulus, (1825–1904), 'Oom Paul', South African soldier and statesman. Kruger led the Afrikaners to victory in the First Boer War in 1881 and afterwards served as President of the Transvaal from 1883 to 1899. His refusal to allow equal rights to non-Boer immigrants was one of the causes of the Second Boer War, during which Kruger was forced to flee the country. He died in exile in Switzerland in 1904.

krugerrand /ˈkru:gərænt/ *n*. a South African gold coin bearing a portrait of Kruger. [f. prec. + RAND]

krummhorn /ˈkrʌmhɔ:n/ *n*. a medieval wind instrument with a double reed and curved end. It had seven finger-holes with three extension keys for low notes. [G (*krumm* crooked, *horn* horn)]

Krupp /krɒp/, Alfred (1812–87), German arms manufacturer, who in the 1840s began to manufacture ordnance in the ironworks founded in Essen by his father, and built up the works to be the largest such firm on the Continent of Europe. Under the management of successive members of the family the Krupp Works continued to play a pre-eminent part in German arms production through to the end of the Second World War.

krypton /ˈkrɪptɒn/ *n*. a rare colourless odourless element of the noble gas group, symbol Kr, atomic number 36, discovered in 1898 by Sir William Ramsay and M. W. Travers (1872–1961) by distillation of liquid air. It is used in various types of electric lamps and bulbs. Although chemically almost inert, it can be made to combine with fluorine. The metre is defined in terms of a transition of one of its isotopes. [f. Gk *krupton* hidden]

Kshatriya /ˈkʃɑ:trɪjə/ *n*. a member of the second of the four great Hindu castes, the warrior or baronial caste. His function is to protect society, to fight in wartime and govern in peacetime. [Skr. (*kshatra* rule)]

Kt. *abbr*. Knight.

Kuala Lumpur /ˈkwɑːlə ˈlʊmpʊə(r)/ the capital of the Federation of Malaysia, proclaimed Federal Territory in 1974; pop. (1980) 997,100.

Kuan Yin /kwɑːn/ (in Chinese Buddhism) the goddess of compassion.

Kublai Khan /ku:blaɪ ˈkɑːn/ (1216–94), Mongol emperor of China, grandson of Genghis Khan. With his brother Mangu, then Mongol Khan, Kublai conquered southern China in 1252–9. On Mangu's death in 1259 he was elected Khan himself, completing the pacification of China and adopting the name Yuan for the dynasty. He successfully invaded Korea and Burma, but failed in attacks on Java and Japan. His reign was notable for his policy of religious toleration and his humane treatment of conquered peoples.

kudos /ˈkju:dɒs/ *n*. (*colloq.*) renown, glory. [Gk]

kudu /ˈku:du:/ *n*. a large white-striped, spiral-horned African antelope of the genus *Strepsiceros*. [f. Xhosa-Kaffir]

kufic /ˈkju:fɪk/ *n*. an early form of the Arabic alphabet, found especially in inscriptions. —*adj*. of or in this script. [f. *Kufa* ancient city S. of Baghdad]

Ku-Klux-Klan /ˌku:klʌksˈklæn/ an American secret society, founded in the southern States in the wake of the Civil War. Although originally intended to defend the southern way of life against northern attempts to change it, the society rapidly became devoted to keeping the Black population from attaining equality, and adopted terrorism and murder as means to that end. Although the original Klan was outlawed by Congress in 1871, a similar organization exists to this day. [perh. f. Gk *kuklos* circle + CLAN]

kukri /ˈkʊkrɪ/ *n*. a heavy curved knife, broadening towards the point, used by Gurkhas as a weapon. [f. Hindi]

Kulturkampf /ˈkʊltʊəkæmpf/ *n*. the conflict between the German government (headed by Bismarck) and the papacy for the control of schools and Church appointments (1872–87). This attempt to break the authority and influence of the Catholic Church in the new German empire failed in its long-term aims and was to a considerable extent responsible for delaying the integration of traditionally Catholic areas of Germany. [G, *kultur* culture, *kampf* conflict]

kümmel /ˈkʊm(ə)l/ *n*. a liqueur flavoured with caraway and cumin seeds. [G (as CUMIN)]

kumquat /ˈkʌmkwɒt/ *n*. a plum-sized orange-like fruit of the genus *Fortunella* used in preserves. [dial. form of Chin. *kin kü* golden orange]

kung fu /kʌŋ ˈfu:/ a Chinese form of karate. [Chin.]

Kuomintang /ˌkwəʊmɪnˈtæŋ/ *n*. a nationalist radical party founded in China under Sun Yat-sen in 1912 and led, after his death in 1925, by Chiang Kai-Shek, constituting the government before the Communist Party took power in October 1949, and subsequently forming the central administration of Taiwan. [Chinese, = national people's party]

kurchatovium /ˌkɜ:ʃəˈtəʊvɪəm/ *n*. the Russian name for the element of atomic number 104, a short-lived artificially produced radioactive transuranic element (cf. RUTHERFORDIUM). [f. I. G. *Kurchatov* (d. 1960), Russian nuclear physicist]

Kurd /kɜ:d/ *n*. a member of a tall pastoral people in Kurdistan etc. [native name]

Kurdish /ˈkɜ:dɪʃ/ *adj*. of the Kurds or their language. —*n*. a language spoken by some 5 million people in the region of Kurdistan. It belongs to the Indo-Iranian language group and is generally written in an Arabic script.

Kurdistan /ˌkɜ:dɪˈstɑːn/ a region inhabited by the Kurds, covering parts of Turkey, Iraq, Iran, Syria, and the USSR.

Kurosawa /ˌkʊərəˈsɑːwə/, Akira (1910–), Japanese film director, a stylist who bases most of his films on his own ideas. He was introduced to the West by *Rashomon* (1950), and his continuing popularity there is founded on his 'sword-fight' films such as *The Seven Samurai* (1954). He also treats modern themes, mainly of social injustice, including *Living* (1952) and *Red Beard* (1965), and has made adaptations of Dostoevsky (*The Idiot*, 1951), Gorky (*The Lower Depths*, 1957), and Shakespeare (*The Throne of Blood*, 1957, from *Macbeth*).

Kuwait /kuˈweɪt/ an Arab sheikdom on the NW coast of the Persian Gulf, one of the world's leading oil-producing countries; pop. (est. 1984) 1,786,616; official language, Arabic; capital, Kuwait, pop. 400,000. Kuwait was an autonomous sheikdom from the 18th c. It became a British protectorate from 1897, and fully independent again in 1961. —**Kuwaiti** *adj*. & *n*.

kV *abbr*. kilovolt(s).

kW *abbr*. kilowatt(s).

kWh *abbr*. kilowatt-hour(s).

Kyd /kɪd/, Thomas (1558–94), English dramatist, a friend of Marlowe. His anonymously published *Spanish Tragedy* (1592) was an exceptionally popular play on the Elizabethan stage, and an early example of revenge tragedy. The only work published under his name was a translation of Robert Garnier's *Cornelia* (1594; re-issued as *Pompey the Great*, 1595). Other works attributed to Kyd are *The Tragedye of Solyman and Perseda* (1592) and a lost pre-Shakespearian play on Hamlet.

kyle /kaɪl/ *n*. a narrow channel between an island and the mainland (or another island) in western Scotland. [f. Gael.]

Kyoto /kɪˈəʊtəʊ/ a city of Japan, the imperial capital 794–1868; pop. 1,472,993.

Kyrie /ˈkɪərɪeɪ/ *n*. (also **Kyrie eleison** /ɪˈleɪs(ə)n/) **1**. a short petition, beginning thus, used in the Roman and Orthodox Churches, especially at the beginning of Mass; a musical setting of this. **2**. a response to each of the Commandments, sometimes used in the Anglican Communion Service. [f. L f. Gk, = Lord have mercy]

L

L, 1 /el/ n. (pl. **Ls**, **L's**) **1.** the twelfth letter of the alphabet. **2.** an L-shaped thing. **3.** (as a Roman numeral) 50.

L abbr. learner (driver).

L. abbr. **1.** Lake. **2.** Liberal. **3.** Licentiate of.

£ abbr. pound (money). [f. L libra]

l. abbr. **1.** left. **2.** line. **3.** litre(s).

LA abbr. Los Angeles.

La symbol lanthanum.

la var. of LAH.

lab n. (colloq.) laboratory. [abbr.]

Lab. abbr. Labour.

Laban /'leɪbən/, Rudolf von (1879-1958), real name R. L. de Varaljan, Hungarian dancer, choreographer, ballet master, and dance theoretician. He was the leader of the Central European school of modern dance, of far greater importance as an intellectual and theoretician than as a choreographer. His greatest contribution was Kinetographie Laban, his system of dance notation, further developed by his pupils. After emigrating to England in 1938 he concentrated on modern educational dance and on research into movement and movement notation in industrial processes.

labarum /'læbərəm/ n. a standard, said to have been devised by Constantine the Great in 312 after a vision, consisting of a spear converted by a transverse bar into a cross and surmounted by a wreath enclosing the Christian monogram of the first two letters (chi rho) of Christos (Gk, = Christ); any of several variants of this. [L, orig. unkn.]

label /'leɪb(ə)l/ n. **1.** a slip of paper etc. attached to an object to give some information about it. **2.** a general classifying phrase applied to persons etc. **3.** (in heraldry) the mark of the eldest son, consisting of a horizontal bar with (usually three) downward projections (ill. HERALDRY). —v.t. (-ll-) **1.** to attach a label to. **2.** to assign to a category. **3.** to make (a substance, molecule, or constituent atom) recognizable, for identification in an experiment. [f. OF, = ribbon]

labial /'leɪbɪəl/ adj. **1.** of the lips. **2.** of the nature of a lip. **3.** pronounced with partially or completely closed lips. —n. a labial sound (e.g. p, m, v). [f. L (labia lips)]

labium /'leɪbɪəm/ n. (pl. **-ia**) **1.** (usu. in pl.) the lip of the female genitals (ill. BODY 2). **2.** the lower part of the mouth of an insect, crustacean, etc. (ill. INSECTS). —**labia majora**, the outer folds of the genital labia. **labia minora**, the inner folds. [L, = lip]

laboratory /lə'bɒrətərɪ/ n. a room or building used for scientific experiments and research. [f. L (laborare toil, as LABOUR)]

laborious /lə'bɔ:rɪəs/ adj. **1.** needing much work or perseverance. **2.** showing signs of effort. **3.** hard-working. —**laboriously** adv. [f. OF f. L (as foll.)]

labour /'leɪbə(r)/ n. **1.** bodily or mental work, exertion. **2.** a task. **3.** the body of those doing (esp. manual or non-managerial) work; such a body as a political force. **4. Labour**, the Labour Party. **5.** the pains of childbirth; the process of giving birth. —v.t./i. **1.** to exert oneself, to work hard. **2.** to have to make a great effort, to operate or progress only with difficulty. **3.** to treat (a point etc.) at great length or in excessive detail. **4.** to suffer under (a delusion etc.). —**labour camp**, a place where prisoners must work as labourers. **Labour Day**, a day celebrated in honour of workers (often 1 May); in the USA a public holiday on the first Monday in September. **Labour Exchange**, (colloq. or hist.) an employment exchange. **labour-saving** adj. designed to reduce or eliminate work. [f. OF f. L labor]

laboured adj. showing signs of great effort, not spontaneous. [f. prec.]

labourer n. a person who labours, especially one employed to do unskilled manual work. [f. LABOUR]

Labour Party a British political party representing the interests especially of workers, and in its heyday enjoying the support of the industrial working class and those members of the middle and professional classes whose views were socialist or reformist. It had its roots in the trade union movement which, in 1900, combined with the small Independent Labour Party, the Social Democratic Federation, and the Fabian Society to form the Labour Representation Committee, which changed its name to the Labour Party after electoral successes in 1906. After the First World War, Labour was reorganized as a true national party and replaced the Liberals as the country's second major political party. Having formed minority governments in 1924 and 1929-31, the Labour Party entered Churchill's wartime coalition before forming its first majority government under Attlee (1945-51).

Labrador¹ /'læbrədɔ:(r)/ **1.** (in a broad sense, in full **Labrador-Ungava**) the NE peninsula of Canada, from Hudson Bay to the mouth of the St Lawrence. It has been the subject of much dispute between Newfoundland and Quebec; in 1927 the eastern seaboard was awarded to Newfoundland. **2.** (in a restricted sense) the part of the peninsula belonging to Newfoundland, which since 1949 has formed the mainland section of Newfoundland and Labrador province; chief town, Battle Harbour. —**Labrador Current**, a cold ocean current moving southwards from the Arctic Ocean along part of the east coast of North America.

Labrador² /'læbrədɔ:(r)/ n. a retriever dog of a breed with a smooth black or golden coat. [f. prec.]

labrum /'leɪbrəm/ n. (pl. **-a**) the upper lip of an insect. [L, = lip (cogn. w. LABIUM)]

La Bruyère /lɑ: bru:'jeə(r)/, Jean de (1645-96), French moralist, who studied law and entered the service of Louis II, 'le Grand Condé'. His famous Caractères, on the model of Theophrastus, are portrait sketches (often of living people with disguised names) exposing the vanity and corruption of human behaviour and giving a vivid satirical picture of Parisian society.

laburnum /lə'bɜ:nəm/ n. an ornamental tree of the genus Laburnum (esp. L. anagyroides), with drooping yellow flowers. [L]

labyrinth /'læbərɪnθ/ n. **1.** a complicated or confusing network of passages. The term was first used of the building constructed by Daedalus for King Minos of Crete, from which nobody could escape; the Minotaur live there in. **2.** a tangled or intricate arrangement. **3.** the complex cavity of the inner ear. —**labyrinthine** /læbə'rɪnθaɪn/ adj. [f. F or L f. Gk]

lac /læk/ n. a resinous substance secreted by a SE Asian insect as a protective covering. [ult. f. Hindi f. Skr.]

Laccadive Islands /'lækədɪv/ see LAKSHADWEEP.

lace n. **1.** a cord or narrow strip threaded through holes or hooks for fastening or tightening shoes etc. **2.** a fabric or trimming in an ornamental openwork design. —v.t. **1.** to fasten or tighten with a lace or laces; to pass (a cord etc.) through. **2.** to trim with lace. **3.** to add a dash of spirits etc. to (a drink). **4.** to beat, to lash. [f. OF f. L laqueus noose]

lacerate /'læsəreɪt/ v.t. to tear (flesh etc.) roughly; to wound (the feelings). —**laceration** /-'reɪʃ(ə)n/ n. [f. L lacerare (lacer torn)]

lacewing n. a neuropterous fly.

Lachesis /'lækɪsɪs/ (Gk myth.) one of the three Fates (see FATES). [Gk, = getting by lot]

lachrymal /'lækrɪm(ə)l/ adj. of tears. [f. L (lacrima tear)]

lachrymose /'lækrɪməʊs/ adj. tearful, given to weeping. [as prec.]

lack n. the state or fact of not having something.—v.t. not to have when needed, to be without. —**be lacking**, to be undesirably absent or deficient. [rel. to MDu., MLG lak deficiency]

lackadaisical /lækə'deɪzɪk(ə)l/ adj. lacking vigour or determination, unenthusiastic. —**lackadaisically** adv. [f. archaic lackaday, lackadaisy int. (as ALACK)]

lackey /'lækɪ/ n. an obsequious follower; a humble servant. —v.t. to play lackey to. [f. F. f. Catalan = Sp. alcalde]

Lackland /'læklænd/ see JOHN¹.

lacklustre /'læklʌstə(r)/ adj. without lustre, dull.

Laconia /lə'kəʊnɪə/ an ancient territory of SW Greece, now a department, its ancient capital, Sparta, being still the administrative centre. —**Laconian** *adj.* & *n.*

laconic /ləˈkɒnɪk/ *adj.* terse, using few words. —**laconically** *adv.* [f. L f. Gk (*Lakōn* Spartan), the Spartans being proverbially terse]

lacquer /ˈlækə(r)/ *n.* **1.** a hard shiny shellac or synthetic varnish. **2.** a substance sprayed on the hair to keep it in place. —*v.t.* to coat with lacquer. [f. obs. F *lacre* sealing-wax f. Port. (as LAC)]

lacrosse /ləˈkrɒs/ *n.* a field game played with a netted stick with which a ball is driven or thrown, caught, and carried, and scoring is by goals. It is said that lacrosse was born of the North American Indian, christened by the French, but adopted and raised by the Canadians. The game was played by Indians in southern Canada and parts of the USA in the 17th c. or earlier; called *baggataway*, it had a religious significance and was also a means of training tribal warriors. The form of the stick or racket used vaguely resembled a bishop's crozier (Fr. *crosse*). By the mid-19th c. white men were playing the game, and it spread from America and Canada to Britain. [F. (*la* the, *crosse* crozier)]

lactate /lækˈteɪt/ *v.i.* to secrete milk. —/ˈlækteɪt/ *n.* a salt or ester of lactic acid. [f. L. *lactare* suckle (*lac* milk)]

lactation /lækˈteɪʃ(ə)n/ *n.* suckling, the secretion of milk [as prec.]

lactic *adj.* of milk. —**lactic acid,** the acid found in sour milk. [f. L *lac* milk]

lactose /ˈlæktəʊs/ *n.* a sugar present in milk. [f. L *lac* milk]

lacuna /ləˈkjuːnə/ *n.* (*pl.* **-as, -ae** /-iː/) a gap or missing part, especially in a manuscript. [L, orig. = pool (as LAKE¹)]

lacy /ˈleɪsɪ/ *adj.* like lace fabrics, especially in fineness. [f. LACE]

lad *n.* a boy, a young fellow; (*colloq.*) a man. [orig. unkn.]

ladder *n.* **1.** a series of horizontal bars fixed between a pair of long uprights, used for climbing up or down. **2.** a vertical ladderlike flaw in stockings etc. **3.** a means of progress in a career etc. —*v.t./i.* to cause a ladder in (a stocking etc.); to develop a ladder. —**ladder-back** *n.* a chair with the back made of horizontal bars between uprights. [OE (as LEAN¹)]

lade *v.t.* (*p.p.* **laden**) to load (a ship), to ship (goods); (in *p.p.*) loaded or burdened (*with*). —**bill of lading,** a detailed list of a ship's cargo. [OE]

la-di-da /lɑːdɪːˈdɑː/ *adj.* (*colloq.*) pretentious or affected in manner or speech. [imit. of pronunc. used]

Ladino /ləˈdiːnəʊ/ *n.* (*pl.* **-os**) **1.** the Spanish dialect of Sephardic Jews. **2.** a mestizo or white person in Central America. [Sp., orig. = Latin]

Ladislaus /ˈlædɪslaʊs/ the name of several kings of Hungary:

Ladislaus I (*c.*1040-95), reigned 1077-95, conquered Croatia and Bosnia and extended Hungarian power into Transylvania, as well as establishing order in his kingdom and advancing the spread of Christianity. He supported Pope Gregory VII in his confrontation with the Emperor Henry VI and was canonized in 1192.

Ladislaus II (1262-90), reigned 1272-90, was killed after two years of civil war following the declaration of a crusade against him by Pope Nicholas IV.

ladle /ˈleɪd(ə)l/ *n.* a deep long-handled spoon for transferring liquids. —*v.t.* to transfer with a ladle. [OE (as LADE)]

Ladoga /ˈlɑːdəgə/ the largest European lake, in the USSR, near the Finnish border.

lady /ˈleɪdɪ/ *n.* **1.** a woman of good social standing; (as a polite term) any woman; a woman of polite or refined disposition. **2. Lady,** the titled used as a less formal prefix to the name of a peeress below a duchess, or to the Christian name of a daughter of a duke, marquis, or earl, or to the surname of the wife or widow of a baronet or knight. **3.** the woman with the authority in a household. **4.** (*archaic*) a wife. **5.** (*attrib.*) female. —**the Ladies,** (as *sing.*) a women's public lavatory. **ladies' man,** a man fond of women's company. **Lady Chapel,** a chapel dedicated to the Virgin Mary. **Lady Day,** the feast of the Annunciation, 25 March. **lady-in-waiting** *n.* a lady attending a royal lady. **lady-killer** *n.* a man given to making amorous conquests of women. **Lady of the Lamp,** Florence Nightingale (see entry). **lady's-maid** *n.* the personal maidservant of a lady. **lady's slipper,** a flower of the genus *Cypripedium* of the orchid family, with the flowers shaped like a slipper or pouch. **Our Lady,** the Virgin Mary. [OE, = loaf-kneader]

ladybird *n.* a small round beetle of the family Coccinellidae, often reddish-brown with black spots.

ladylike *adj.* like or appropriate to a lady.

ladyship *n.* the title used in addressing or referring to a woman with the rank of Lady. [f. LADY + -SHIP]

Ladysmith /ˈleɪdɪsmɪθ/ a town in Natal, beseiged by Boers 2 Nov. 1899-28 Feb. 1900, relieved by Sir R. H. Buller (d. 1908).

La Fayette /lɑː faɪˈet/ Marie Joseph Paul Yves Roch Gilbert du Motier, Marquis de (1757-1834), French soldier and liberal statesman. As a young man, La Fayette was one of the leaders of the French expeditionary force which fought alongside the Americans in the second half of the War of Independence. He played a crucial part in the early phase of the French Revolution, commanding the National Guard and advocating moderate policies, but was subsequently forced from the scene by more radical opponents.

La Fontaine /lɑː fɒnˈteɪn/, Jean de (1621-95), French poet, author of *Fables* drawn from oriental, classical, and modern sources. They include such tales as 'The Cicada and the Ant' and 'The Crow and the Fox' which have enjoyed wide popularity. His bawdy verse tales *Contes et Nouvelles* (1664-74) were drawn from Ariosto, Boccaccio, and others; many of them were censured for their immorality and La Fontaine is said to have publicly disavowed them after his religious conversion in 1692.

lag¹ *v.i.* (**-gg-**) to go too slow, to fail to keep up with the others. —*n.* lagging, a delay. —**lagger** *n.* [orig. = hindmost person; perh. f. distortion of LAST¹ in children's game]

lag² *v.t.* (**-gg-**) to enclose (a boiler etc.) with a heat-insulating material. —*n.* such a material; an insulating cover. —**lagger** *n.* [prob. f. Scand.]

lag³ *n.* a convict (esp. in *old lag*). [orig. unkn.]

lager /ˈlɑːgə(r)/ *n.* a kind of light beer. [f. G *lager-bier* beer brewed for keeping (*lager* store)]

Lagerlöf /ˈlɑːgələf/, Selma (Ottiliana Lovisa) (1858-1940), Swedish writer of fiction, who made her name with *Gösta Berlings Saga* (1891). Romantic in mood, her work was inspired by local legends and traditions. She was awarded the Nobel Prize for literature in 1909, the first woman to win a Nobel Prize in any field.

laggard /ˈlægəd/ *n.* a person who lags behind, a procrastinator. [f. LAG¹]

lagging¹ *n.* a material used to lag a boiler etc. [f. LAG²]

lagging² *n.* a term of imprisonment. [as LAG³]

lagoon /ləˈguːn/ *n.* a salt-water lake separated from the sea by a sandbank or coral reef etc. (ill. COASTS). [f. F or It. & Sp. f. L, = LACUNA]

Lagos /ˈleɪgɒs/ the capital and chief port of Nigeria; pop. (est. 1990) 4,100,000.

Lagrange /lɑːˈgrɑ̃ʒ/, Joseph Louis, Comte de (1736-1813), mathematician, born in Italy of French parents. He is remembered for his proof that every positive integer can be expressed as a sum of at most four squares and for his study of the solution of algebraic equations which, many years later, provided the inspiration for the founding of the theory of groups and Galois theory. But his greatest and most influential work was the *Traité de mécanique analytique* (1788) which was the culmination of his extensive work on mechanics and its application to the description of planetary and lunar motion.

lah /lɑː/ *n.* (*Mus.*) the sixth note of the major scale in tonic sol-fa (see entry). [f. *labii* (see GAMUT)]

laicize /ˈleɪɪsaɪz/ *v.t.* to make secular. —**laicization** /-ˈzeɪʃ(ə)n/ *n.* [f. *laic* lay, f. L f. Gk (as LAY²)]

laid *past* & *p.p.* of LAY¹

lain *p.p.* of LIE¹.

lair *n.* **1.** a sheltered place where a wild animal habitually rests or eats. **2.** a person's hiding-place. [OE (rel. to LIE¹)]

laird *n.* a landowner in Scotland. [Sc. form of LORD]

laissez-faire /leɪseɪˈfeə(r)/ *n.* (also **laisser-faire**) a policy of non-interference. [F, = let act]

laity /ˈleɪɪtɪ/ *n.* a body of laymen, especially in a Church. [f. LAY¹]

lake¹ *n.* a large expanse of water surrounded by land. —**Lake District** *or* **the Lakes,** the region round the lakes in Cumbria in NW England. **lake-dwelling** *n.* a prehistoric dwelling built on piles driven into the bed or shore of a lake. Such dwellings occur in Switzerland and northern Italy from neolithic to Iron Age periods (4th-1st millennium BC) and in other parts of temperate Europe in the Iron Age (7th-1st c. BC). **Lake Poets** *or* **Lake School,** the poets Coleridge, Southey, and Wordsworth, who lived in the Lake District. [f. OF f. L *lacus*]

lake[2] *n.* a pigment made from a dye and a mordant; a reddish pigment, originally made from lac. [var. of LAC]

lakh /læk/ *n.* (in India) 100,000 (esp. in *a lakh of rupees*). [f. Hindustani f. Skr.]

Lakshadweep /lækʃæˈdwiːp/ a Union Territory of India, formerly the Laccadive, Minicoy, and Amindivi Islands, off the coast of Malabar; capital, Kavaratti.

Lakshmi /ˈlʌkʃmɪ/ (*Hinduism*) the goddess of prosperity, and consort of Vishnu. She assumes different forms in order to accompany her husband in his incarnations (e.g. Sita, Radha). [Skr., = prosperity]

Lallan /ˈlælən/ *adj.* (*Sc.*) of the Lowlands of Scotland. —*n.* (*Sc.*; also **Lallans**) Lowland Scots dialect, especially as a literary language. [var. of LOWLAND]

lam *v.t.* (**-mm-**) (*slang*) to hit hard, to thrash. [perh. f. Scand., as LAME]

lama /ˈlɑːmə/ *n.* an honorific applied to a spiritual leader in Tibetan Buddhism, whether a reincarnate lama (e.g. the Dalai Lama; see entry) or one who has earned the title in this life; any Tibetan Buddhist monk. [f. Tibetan *blama* superior one]

lamaism /ˈlɑːmɑɪz(ə)m/ *n.* a common but (strictly) incorrect term for Tibetan Buddhism. [f. prec.]

Lamarck /læˈmɑːk/, Jean Baptiste de (1744–1829), French botanist and zoologist who among others anticipated Darwin's concept of organic evolution. He suggested that species could have evolved from each other by small changes in their structure, and the mechanism of this change was that characteristics acquired in order to survive could be passed on to offspring. His theory found little favour in his lifetime (it was criticized notably by Cuvier), and he died in poverty, but the concept of inheritance of acquired characteristics was revived by those who did not accept Darwin's later theory of natural selection as explaining evolution.

Lamartine /lɑːmɑːrˈtiːn/, Alphonse de (1790–1869), French poet. A diplomat in Italy from 1820, he turned to politics during the Revolution of 1830 and was Foreign Minister during that of 1848. His speeches in the cause of liberty and justice aroused the imagination of his countrymen, and *Méditations poétiques* (1820) established him as a leading figure of the French Romantic movement. In these plaintive melodious verses, some inspired by his love for the 'Elvire' of many of his poems, he used Nature to reflect the poet's moods, and brought a fresh lyricism to French poetry. His other works include *Jocelyn* (1836) and *La Chute d'un ange* (1838), fragments of a projected epic poem, and biographical, historical, political, and travel works.

lamasery /ləˈmɑːsərɪ/ *n.* a common but strictly incorrect term for a Tibetan Buddhist monastery. [f. LAMA]

Lamb /læm/, Charles (1775–1834), English essayist and critic. He devoted much of his life to caring for his sister Mary, who had killed their mother during one of her recurrent bouts of insanity; together they wrote *Tales from Shakespear* (1807) for children. His *Specimens of English Dramatic Poets* (1808) is an anthology of scenes and speeches from Elizabethan and Jacobean dramatists which drew the attention of his contemporaries to that period of drama. Lamb's essays were published in the important periodicals of his day, including his most famous series, *The Essays of Elia* (1820–3); Lamb adopted the name 'Elia' to save the susceptibilities of his brother John, then a clerk in the South-Sea House (the subject of the first Essay). The semi-autobiographical essays, dealing with mankind at large, are presented with wit and pathos in a literary and archaic style; the character of the narrator, 'a bundle of prejudices' much attracted to the whimsical and eccentric, is maintained throughout the series.

lamb /læm/ *n.* **1.** a young sheep. **2.** its flesh as food. **3.** a gentle, endearing, or vulnerable person. —*v.t./i.* **1.** to give birth to a lamb; (in *pass.*, of a lamb) to be born. **2.** to tend (lambing ewes). —**Lamb (of God)**, Christ. **lamb's-wool** *n.* soft fine wool. [OE]

lambaste /læmˈbeɪst/ *v.t.* (*colloq.*) to thrash, to beat. [f. LAM + BASTE[1]]

lambda /ˈlæmdə/ *n.* the eleventh letter of the Greek alphabet, = l. [Gk]

lambent /ˈlæmbənt/ *adj.* (of a flame or light) playing about a surface; (of the eyes, wit, etc.) gently brilliant. —**lambency** *n.* [f. L *lambere* lick]

Lambeth Palace /ˈlæmbəθ/ a palace in the London borough of Lambeth, south of the Thames, that since 1197 has been the residence of the archbishop of Canterbury.

lame *adj.* **1.** (of a person or limb) disabled or unable to

walk normally, especially by an injury or defect in the foot or leg. **2.** (of an excuse etc.) unconvincing. **3.** (of a metre) halting. —*v.t.* to make lame, to disable. —**lame duck,** a person or firm unable to cope without help. —**lamely** *adv.*, **lameness** *n.* [OE]

lamé /ˈlɑːmeɪ/ *n.* a fabric with gold or silver thread interwoven. [F]

lament /ləˈment/ *n.* a passionate expression of grief; an elegy. —*v.t./i.* to feel or express grief for or about; to utter a lament; (in *p.p.*) mourned for. [f. L *lamentum*, F or L *lamentari*]

lamentable /ˈlæməntəb(ə)l/ *adj.* deplorable, regrettable. —**lamentably** *adv.* [f. prec.]

lamentation /læmenˈteɪʃ(ə)n/ *n.* **1.** a lament. **2.** lamenting. **3. Lamentations,** a book of the Old Testament traditionally ascribed to Jeremiah but probably of a later period, telling the desolation of Judah after the destruction of Jerusalem in 586 BC. [f. LAMENT]

lamina /ˈlæmɪnə/ *n.* (*pl.* **-ae** /-iː/) a thin plate, scale, or layer. —**laminar** *adj.* [L]

laminate /ˈlæmɪneɪt/ *v.t./i.* **1.** to beat or roll into laminae; to split into layers. **2.** to overlay with metal plates, a plastic layer, etc. —/-ət/ *n.* a laminated structure, especially of layers fixed together. —/-ət/ *adj.* in the form of a lamina or laminae. —**lamination** /-ˈneɪʃ(ə)n/ *n.* [f. prec.]

Lammas /ˈlæməs/ *n.* 1 August, formerly observed as an English harvest festival at which loaves made from the first ripe corn were consecrated; in Scotland, one of the quarter-days. [f. OE *hlafmæsse* (LOAF[1], MASS[2])]

lamp *n.* a device or vessel for giving light or rays by the use of electricity (ill. HEAT) or gas or by burning oil or spirit. [f. OF f. L f. Gk *lampas* torch]

lampblack *n.* a pigment made from soot.

lamplight *n.* the light given by a lamp.

lamplighter *n.* (usu. *hist.*) a man who lights street lamps.

lampoon /læmˈpuːn/ *n.* a piece of virulent or scurrilous satire on a person. —*v.t.* to write a lampoon against. —**lampoonist** *n.* [f. F *lampon*]

lamppost *n.* a tall post supporting a street lamp.

lamprey /ˈlæmprɪ/ *n.* an eel-like aquatic animal (genera *Lampetra* and *Petromyzon*) with a sucker mouth. [f. OF f. L *lampetra* (perh. *lambere* lick, *petra* stone)]

lampshade *n.* a shade placed over a lamp.

Lancashire /ˈlæŋkəʃɪə(r)/ a county of NW England.

Lancaster /ˈlæŋkæstə(r)/ the name of the English royal house descended from John of Gaunt, Duke of Lancaster (4th son of Edward III), which ruled England from 1399 (Henry IV) until the death of Henry VI (1471).

Lancastrian /læŋˈkæstrɪən/ *adj.* **1.** of Lancashire or Lancaster. **2.** of the family descended from John of Gaunt, Duke of Lancaster (see prec.), or of the Red Rose party supporting it in the Wars of the Roses (cf. YORKIST). —*n.* **1.** a native or inhabitant of Lancashire or Lancaster. **2.** a member or adherent of the Lancastrian family. [f. prec.]

lance /lɑːns/ *n.* a long spear, especially one used by a horseman. —*v.t.* **1.** to pierce with a lance. **2.** to prick or cut open with a surgical lancet. —**lance-corporal** *n.* an NCO below a corporal. [f. OF f. L *lancea*]

Lancelot /ˈlɑːnsələt/ (in Arthurian legend) the most famous of Arthur's knights, lover of Queen Guinevere.

lanceolate /ˈlænsɪələt/ *adj.* shaped like a spearhead, tapering to each end (ill. PLANTS). [f. L (*lanceola* dim. of *lancea* lance)]

lancer /ˈlɑːnsə(r)/ *n.* **1.** a soldier of a cavalry regiment originally armed with lances. **2.** (in *pl.*) a kind of quadrille; the music for this. [f. F (as LANCE)]

lancet /ˈlɑːnsɪt/ *n.* **1.** a surgical instrument with a point and two edges for small incisions. **2.** a narrow pointed arch or window (ill. CHURCH). [f. OF (as LANCE)]

Lancs. *abbr.* Lancashire.

land *n.* **1.** the solid part of the earth's surface, not covered by water. **2.** the ground, the soil, an expanse of country; this as a basis for agriculture, building, etc. **3.** landed property; (in *pl.*) estates. **4.** a country or State. —*v.t./i.* **1.** to set or go ashore from a ship etc. **2.** to bring (an aircraft) to the ground or other surface; to come down thus. **3.** to alight after a jump etc. **4.** to reach or find oneself in a certain place or situation; to cause to do this. **5.** to deliver (a person a blow etc.). **6.** to present (a person *with* a problem etc.). **7.** to bring (a fish) to land; to win (a prize); to secure (an appointment etc.). —**how the land lies,** what is the state of affairs. **land-agent** *n.* a steward of an estate; a dealer in estates. **land-girl** *n.* a woman doing farm work, especially in wartime. **land-line** *n.* a means of telegraphic communication over land. **land-locked** *adj.* almost or entirely surrounded by land. **land mass,** a large area of land. **land-mine** *n.* an explosive mine laid in or on the ground. [OE]

landau /ˈlændɔː/ *n.* a four-wheeled horse-drawn carriage with a top of which the front and back halves can be raised and lowered independently. [f. *Landau* near Karlsruhe in W. Germany, where first made]

landed *adj.* **1.** owning much land. **2.** consisting of land. [f. LAND]

landfall *n.* an approach to land after a sea or air journey.

landing *n.* **1.** the process of coming or bringing to land. **2.** a place for disembarking. **3.** the area at the top of a flight of stairs or between flights. —**landing-craft** *n.* a naval craft for putting ashore troops and equipment. **landing-gear** *n.* the undercarriage of an aircraft. **landing-stage** *n.* a platform for disembarking passengers and goods. [f. LAND]

landlady *n.* a woman landlord.

landless *adj.* holding no land. [f. LAND + -LESS]

landlord *n.* a person who lets rooms or keeps a boarding house, a public-house, etc.

landlubber *n.* a person with little or no experience of ships and the sea.

landmark *n.* **1.** a conspicuous and easily recognized feature of the landscape. **2.** an event marking an important stage in a process or history.

Landor /ˈlændə(r)/, Walter Savage (1775-1864), English writer. His exotic oriental tale *Gebir: A Poem in seven Books* (1798) won him the admiration and friendship of Southey. During his long residence in Italy he wrote his best-known prose work *Imaginary Conversations of Literary Men and Statesmen* (1824-8). In verse and prose his elaborate and highly polished style shows a clear debt to classical forms and themes.

landowner *n.* one who owns land, especially a large area.

landscape /ˈlændskeɪp/ *n.* **1.** the features of a land area as seen in broad view. **2.** a picture of this. —*v.t./i.* to lay out or enhance (an area of land) with natural features. —**landscape gardening,** the laying-out of grounds to imitate natural scenery. [f. Du. (as LAND, -SHIP)]

Landseer /ˈlændsɪə(r)/, Sir Edwin (1802-73), English painter and occasional sculptor, known best for his animal subjects. He was Queen Victoria's favourite painter, and engravings of his works spread his popularity far and wide, their often sentimental manner appealing greatly to contemporary taste, and were instrumental in establishing the Victorian liking for Highland hunting genre. As a sculptor he is best known for the bronze lions which he modelled in 1867 for the base of Nelson's Column in Trafalgar Square, London.

Land's End a rocky promontory in Cornwall forming the SW extremity of England. It is approximately 1,400 km (876 miles) by road from John o' Groats.

landslide *n.* **1.** a landslip. **2.** an overwhelming majority for one side in an election.

landslip *n.* the sliding down of a mass of land on a slope or mountain.

Landsteiner /ˈlændstaɪnə(r)/, Karl (1868-1943), Austrian physician whose work covered many fields but whose main interest was in immunology. In 1930 he was awarded a Nobel Prize for his work on blood groups; the classification system of the four main groups, which he devised in the first decade of the 20th c., has remained in use and made it possible for blood transfusions to be carried out successfully. Landsteiner was the first to describe the rhesus factor in blood (1940).

landward /ˈlændwəd/ *adv.* (also **landwards**) towards the land. —*adj.* going or facing towards the land. [f. LAND + -WARD]

lane *n.* **1.** a narrow road or street. **2.** a passage between rows of people. **3.** a strip of road for one line of traffic. **4.** a strip of track or water for a competitor in a race. **5.** a regular course followed by or prescribed for ships or aircraft. [OE]

Langland /ˈlæŋlənd/, William (c.1330-c.1386), English poet. Little is known of his life and identity but he was probably in minor orders and possibly lived in the Malvern district and London. He was the author of *Piers Plowman* (c.1367-70), the greatest allegorical poem of the Middle English alliterative revival, in the form of a spiritual pilgrimage guided by the Plowman on a journey in search of Truth.

The author expresses concretely his concern with the corruption of the Church and the suffering of the poor.

Langley /ˈlæŋlɪ/, Samuel Pierpoint (1834-1906), American astronomer and aviation pioneer. His work on aerodynamics contributed to the design of early aeroplanes.

Langton /ˈlæŋt(ə)n/, Stephen (d. 1228), Archbishop of Canterbury who defended the Church's interests against King John with some success, was intermediary during the negotiations leading to the signing of Magna Carta, and protected the young Henry III against baronial domination. His reputation as perhaps England's greatest medieval archbishop rests mainly on his promotion of the interests of the English Church in the face of conflicting pressures from the papacy and the English throne.

language /ˈlæŋgwɪdʒ/ *n.* **1.** words and their use; the faculty of speech. **2.** a system of words prevalent in one or more countries or in a profession etc. **3.** a method or style of expression. **4.** a system of symbols and rules for computer programs. —**language laboratory,** a room with tape-recorders etc. for learning foreign languages. [f. OF f. L *lingua* tongue]

languid /ˈlæŋgwɪd/ *adj.* **1.** lacking vigour, not inclined to exert oneself. **2.** (of a stream etc., or *fig.*) slow-moving, slack. —**languidly** *adv.* [f. F or L (as foll.)]

languish /ˈlæŋgwɪʃ/ *v.i.* **1.** to lose or lack vitality. **2.** to live *under* depressing conditions; to be neglected. **3.** to pine (*for*). [f. OF f. L *languēre*]

languor /ˈlæŋgə(r)/ *n.* **1.** a languid state, listlessness. **2.** a soft or tender mood or effect. **3.** an oppressive stillness of the air. —**languorous** *adj.* [as prec.]

lank *adj.* **1.** tall and lean. **2.** (of grass, hair, etc.) long and limp. [OE]

lanky *adj.* ungracefully lean and tall or long. —**lankiness** *n.* [f. LANK]

lanolin /ˈlænəlɪn/ *n.* a fat extracted from sheep's wool and used in ointments. [G f. L (*lana* wool, *oleum* oil)]

lantern /ˈlæntən/ *n.* **1.** a transparent case holding a light and shielding it from wind etc. **2.** the light-chamber of a lighthouse. **3.** an erection on top of a dome or room, with glazed sides. —**lantern jaws,** long thin jaws giving the face a hollow look. [f. OF f. L *lanterna* f. Gk]

lanthanide /ˈlænθənaɪd/ *n.* any of the series of 15 rare earth elements from lanthanum to lutetium (atomic numbers 57-71); the same series excluding lanthanum itself. [f. G. *lanthanid* (as foll.)]

lanthanum /ˈlænθənəm/ *n.* a soft silvery-white metallic element of the lanthanide series, symbol La, atomic number 57, first discovered (as the oxide) in 1839. Purified lanthanum metal has few uses, but it is a component of certain alloys, and the oxide is used in the manufacture of specialized types of glass. [f. Gk *lanthanō* escape notice, from having remained undetected in cerium oxide]

lanyard /ˈlænjəd/ *n.* **1.** a short rope used on a ship for securing or fastening. **2.** a cord worn round the neck or on the shoulder to which a knife etc. may be attached. [f. OF *lanière*, assim. to YARD[1]]

Laocoon /leɪˈɒkəʊɒn/ (*Gk legend*) a Trojan priest who, with his two sons, was crushed to death by two great sea-serpents as a penalty for warning the Trojans against drawing the wooden horse of the Greeks into Troy. The incident is the subject of one of the most famous examples of ancient sculpture, now in the Vatican Museum. This masterpiece, probably of the Pergamene school (2nd c. BC), in Pliny's time stood in the palace of the emperor Titus in Rome, but later disappeared and was dramatically rediscovered in 1506, when it made a great impression, especially on Michelangelo.

Laos /ˈlaːɒs/ a small landlocked country of SE Asia, formerly part of French Indochina; pop. (est. 1976) 3,000,000; official language, Laotian; capital, Vientiane. Laos became independent of France in 1949, but for most of the next 25 years was torn by strife and civil war between the Communist Pathet Lao movement (latterly aided by the North Vietnamese) and government supporters (aided by the USA and Thai mercenaries). In 1975 the Pathet Lao achieved total control of the country, the king abdicated, and Laos was proclaimed a People's Democratic Republic. —**Laotian** /ˈlaʊʃɪən/ *adj. & n.*

Lao-tzu /laːəʊˈtsuː/ **1.** the legendary founder of Taoism and traditonal author of the *Tao-te-Ching*, its most sacred scripture. **2.** this scripture. [Chinese, = Lao the Master]

lap[1] *n.* **1.** the flat area formed by the front of the thighs of a seated person; the part of a dress etc. covering this. **2.** one circuit of a race-track etc. **3.** a section of a journey etc. **4.** the amount of overlap; an overlapping part. **5.** a single turn of thread etc. round a reel etc. —*v.t./i.* (**-pp-**) **1.** to be ahead of (a competitor in a race) by one or more laps. **2.** to fold or wrap (*about* or *round*); to enfold (*in* wraps); (esp. in *pass.*) to enfold caressingly. **3.** to cause to overlap. —**in the lap of the gods,** beyond human control. **in the lap of luxury,** in great luxury. **in a person's lap,** as his responsibility. **lap-dog** *n.* a small pet dog. **lap of honour,** a ceremonial circuit of a race-track etc. by the winner(s). **lap over,** to extend beyond (a limit). [OE]

lap[2] *v.t./i.* (**-pp-**) **1.** to drink by scooping liquid with movements of the tongue. **2.** (usu. with *up*) to take in (facts etc.) eagerly. **3.** to flow (against) in ripples making a gentle splashing sound. —*n.* an act or sound of lapping. [OE]

laparotomy /læpəˈrɒtəmɪ/ *n.* surgical cutting through the abdominal wall for access to the internal organs etc. in the abdomen. [f. Gk *lapara* flank (*laparos* soft) + -TOMY]

La Paz /lɑː ˈpæz/ the seat of government of Bolivia; pop. (1979) 696,800.

lapel /ləˈpel/ *n.* the part of either side of a coat-front etc. folded back against the outer surface. —**lapelled** *adj.* [f. LAP[1]]

lapidary /ˈlæpɪdərɪ/ *adj.* **1.** concerned with stones. **2.** engraved on stone. —*n.* a cutter, polisher, or engraver of gems. [f. L (*lapis* stone)]

lapis lazuli /ˈlæpɪs ˈlæzjuːlɪ/ a bright blue gem, mineral, colour, and pigment. [f. L (*lapis* stone, *lazulum* f. Pers., as AZURE)]

Lapith /ˈlæpɪθ/ *n.* (*Gk myth.*) a member of a Thessalian people who fought and defeated the Centaurs.

Laplace /lɑːˈplɑːs/, Pierre Simon, Marquis de (1749–1827), French applied mathematician and theoretical physicist. Like his near-contemporary Lagrange, he devoted his greatest work, the *Traité de mécanique céleste* (1799–1825), to an extensive mathematical analysis of geophysical matters and of planetary and lunar motion. He is known for his innovative work on partial differential equations, for his contributions to probability theory, and for various other mathematical discoveries, but his reputation is mixed: he is also known for his sycophantic relationship to Napoleon Bonaparte and for phrases such as 'il est aisé de voir' which occur frequently but inaccurately in his writings.

Lapland /ˈlæplænd/ the region inhabited by Lapps, the most northerly part of Scandinavia, stretching from the Norwegian coast to the White Sea. —**Laplander** *n.*

Lapp *n.* **1.** a member of the indigenous population of the extreme north of Scandinavia. **2.** their language. (See below.) —*adj.* of the Lapps or their language. —**Lappish** *adj.* [f. Sw. *Lapp*, perh. orig. a term of contempt; cf. MHG *lappe* simpleton]

Originating in the region of Lake Onega in Russia the Lapps moved westward 10,000 years ago. Although nominally under Swedish and Norwegian control since the Middle Ages, their Christianization was not completed until the 18th c. The Lappish language, of which there are several mutually unintelligible dialects, is related to Finnish. Today the majority of Lapps live in Norway and Sweden with small communities in Finland and the USSR. Traditionally associated with the domestication and herding of reindeer, few Lapps continue the nomadic herding of the animals. Approximately 50 per cent of the Lapps now live in permanent settlements with year-round pasture, and another 40 per cent live on the coasts and derive their livelihood from a combination of fishing, hunting, trapping, and farming. Scandinavian industrialization—particularly hydroelectric schemes, mining, and new roads—has severely disrupted the Lapps' traditional life-style.

lappet /ˈlæpɪt/ *n.* **1.** a flap or fold of a garment etc. or of flesh. **2.** a kind of large moth whose caterpillars have side lobes. [f. LAP[1]]

lapse *n.* **1.** a slight mistake, a slip of the memory etc. **2.** a weak or careless decline to an inferior state. **3.** the passage *of* time. —*v.i.* **1.** to fail to maintain a position or standard; to fall back (*into* an inferior or previous state). **2.** (of a right etc.) to become no longer valid because not used or claimed or renewed. **3.** (in *p.p.*) that has lapsed. [f. L *lapsus* (*labi* slip, fall)]

lapwing /ˈlæpwɪŋ/ *n.* the peewit. [OE (as LEAP, WINK), f. mode of flight]

larboard /lɑːbəd/ *n.* & *adj.* = PORT[3]. [orig. *ladboard*, perh. 'side on which cargo is taken in' (f. LADE + BOARD)]

larceny /ˈlɑːsənɪ/ *n.* theft of personal goods. —**larcenous** *adj.* [f. OF f. L *latrocinium* (*latro* robber)]

larch *n.* a deciduous coniferous tree of the genus *Larix*, with bright foliage (ill. TREES); its wood. [f. MHG f. L *larix*]

lard *n.* pig fat prepared for use in cooking etc. —*v.t.* **1.** to insert strips of bacon in (meat etc.) before cooking. **2.** to garnish (talk etc.) *with* strange terms etc. [f. OF, = bacon, f. L *lardum*]

larder *n.* a room or cupboard for storing food. [f. AF (as prec.)]

lardy *adj.* like lard. —**lardy-cake** *n.* cake made with lard, currants, etc. [f. LARD]

Lares /ˈlɑːriːz/ *n.pl.* gods worshipped, together with the Penates, by households in ancient Rome. They are probably originally deities of the farm-land.

large /lɑːdʒ/ *adj.* **1.** of considerable or relatively great size or extent. **2.** of the larger kind. **3.** of wide range, comprehensive. **4.** doing a thing on a large scale. —**at large,** at liberty; as a body or whole; with all details; without a specific aim. —**large-scale** *adj.* made or occurring on a large scale or in large amounts. —**largeness** *n.* [f. OF f. L *largus* copious]

largely *adv.* to a great or preponderating extent. [f. prec.]

largess /lɑːˈdʒes/ *n.* (also **largesse**) money or gifts freely given, especially on an occasion of rejoicing. [f. OF f. L (as LARGE)]

largo /ˈlɑːgəʊ/ *adv.* (*Mus.*) in a slow tempo with a broad dignified treatment. —*n.* (*pl.* **-os**) a movement to be played in this way. [It., = broad]

lariat /ˈlærɪət/ *n.* a lasso, a rope used to catch or tether a horse etc. [f. Sp. *la reata* (*reatar* tie again)]

lark[1] *n.* a kind of small songbird, of the family Alaudidae, especially the skylark. —**get up with the lark,** to get up early. [OE]

lark[2] *n.* (*colloq.*) **1.** a frolic or spree; an amusing incident. **2.** an affair, a type of activity etc. —*v.i.* (*colloq.*) to play (*about*). [orig. unkn.]

Larkin /ˈlɑːkɪn/, Philip Arthur (1922–85), English poet and novelist. His early poems were influenced by Yeats, including those collected in *The North Ship* (1945). Larkin's own poetic voice became distinct in *The Less Deceived* (1955) where the colloquial bravura of poems such as 'Toads' is offset by the half-tones and bitter lyricism of other pieces. *The Whitsun Weddings* (1964) adds a range of melancholy urban and suburban landscapes, and a stoic wit, while many of the poems in *High Windows* (1974) show a preoccupation with death and transience. The adaptation of contemporary speech rhythms and vocabulary to an unobtrusive elegance distinguishes much of his work. His novels include *Jill* (1946) and *A Girl in Winter* (1947).

larkspur *n.* a plant of the genus *Delphinium* with a spur-shaped calyx.

larn *v.t./i.* joc. or *vulgar var.* of LEARN; (*colloq.*) to teach. [dial. form of LEARN]

La Rochefoucauld /lɑːrɒʃfuːˈkəʊ/, François de Marsillac, Duc de (1613–80), French moralist, active in abortive intrigues against Richelieu and Mazarin, related in his *Mémoires* (1662). His chief work, the *Maximes* (1665), consists of 504 brief reflections, in a highly polished style, analysing the motives of human conduct embodying a cynical philosophy that finds in self-love the prime motive of all action.

Larousse /lɑːˈruːs/, Pierre (1817–75), French lexicographer and encyclopaedist, who edited the *Grand Dictionnaire universel du XIXe siècle* (1866–76), which aimed to comprehend every department of human knowledge. In 1852 he founded, with Augustin Boyer, the publishing house of Larousse, which continues to issue the dictionaries and reference works that bear its name.

larrikin /ˈlærɪkɪn/ *n.* (*Austral.*) a hooligan. [perh. f. *Larry* pet-form of name *Lawrence*]

larva *n.* (*pl.* **-vae** /-viː/) an insect in the stage between egg and pupa (e.g. a caterpillar; ill. INSECTS). —**larval** *adj.* [L, = ghost, mask]

laryngeal /ləˈrɪndʒɪəl/ *adj.* of the larynx. [f. LARYNX]

laryngitis /lærɪnˈdʒaɪtɪs/ *n.* inflammation of the larynx. [f. foll. + -ITIS]

larynx /ˈlærɪŋks/ *n.* the cavity in the throat holding the vocal cords. [f. Gk]

lasagne /ləˈsænjɛ/ *n.* pasta in a wide ribbon form, especially as served with minced meat and a sauce. [It. pl., f. L *lasanum* cooking-pot]

La Salle /lɑː ˈsɑːl/, Robert Cavalier, Sieur de (1643–87), French explorer. A settler in French Canada, La Salle sailed down the Ohio and Mississippi Rivers to the Gulf of Mexico in 1682, naming the valley of the latter river Louisiana in honour of Louis XIV. He returned to France and was appointed Viceroy of North America, returning in 1684 with a colonizing expedition. This venture went disastrously wrong, landing in Texas by mistake and squandering time and resources in fruitless attempts to get back to the Mississippi. Eventually La Salle's followers, embittered by their wanderings and his harsh discipline, mutinied and killed their leader.

Lascar /ˈlæskə(r)/ n. an East Indian seaman. [ult. f. Urdu & Pers., = army (Arab. *al-ʿaskari* the soldier)]

lascivious /ləˈsɪvɪəs/ adj. lustful; inciting to lust. —**lasciviously** adv., **lasciviousness** n. [f. L (*lascivus* sportive, wanton)]

laser /ˈleɪzə(r)/ n. any device that is capable of emitting a very narrow parallel beam of highly monochromatic and coherent light (or other electromagnetic radiation), either continuously or in pulses, and operates by using light to stimulate the emission of more light of the same wavelength and phase by atoms or molecules that have been excited by some means. The light is reflected back and forth between mirrors, building up into an intense beam. The power and pinpoint accuracy of laser beams finds applications in industry, medicine, and research, e.g. in drilling holes in metal and diamonds, providing standards of straightness in engineering, undertaking surgery on the retina, and in holography. The first laser was built in 1960 in the USA by the American physicist T. H. Maiman; the term now includes devices emitting radiation other than light. [f. *light amplification by stimulated emission of radiation*]

lash v.t./i. 1. to move in a sudden whiplike movement. 2. to strike with a whip; to beat or strike violently. 3. to attack violently in words. 4. to urge as with a lash. 5. to fasten or secure with cord etc. —n. 1. a stroke with a whip etc. (*lit.* or *fig.*). 2. the flexible part of a whip. 3. an eyelash. —**lash out**, to hit or speak out angrily; to spend lavishly. [prob. imit.]

lashings n.pl. (slang) a lot (*of*). [f. LASH]

lass /læs/ n. (also dim. **lassie**) (esp. *Sc.*, *N.Engl.*, or *poetic*) a girl. [f. ON, = unmarried]

Lassa fever /ˈlæsə/ an acute virus disease, with fever, of tropical Africa. It was first reported at the village of Lassa in Nigeria in 1969, and has a high mortality rate.

lassitude /ˈlæsɪtjuːd/ n. tiredness, listlessness. [F or f. L (*lassus* tired)]

lasso /læˈsuː/ n. (pl. **-os**) a rope with a running noose, especially for catching cattle. —v.t. to catch with a lasso. [f. Sp. *lazo*, = LACE]

Lassus /ˈlæsʊs/, Orlande de (c.1532–94), Flemish composer, who entered the service of Duke Albrecht V in Munich and built up one of the most celebrated centres of music in Europe. One of the great polyphonic masters of the 16th c., he reveals something of the melancholia from which he suffered in later years in music of expressive intensity such as the settings he made of the seven Penitential Psalms.

last[1] /lɑːst/ adj. 1. after all the others in position or time, coming or belonging at the end. 2. most recent; next before a specified time. 3. only remaining. 4. least likely, least suitable. —adv. 1. (esp. *in comb.*) after all the others. 2. on the last occasion before the present. 3. lastly. —n. 1. a person or thing that is last. 2. the last mention or sight. 3. the last performance of certain actions; the end or last moment, death. —**at (long) last**, in the end, after much delay. **have the last laugh**, to be ultimately the victor. **last ditch**, a place of final desperate defence. **last minute** *or* **moment**, the time just before a decisive event. **last name**, a surname. **last rites**, rites for a dying person. **last straw**, an addition to a burden or difficulty that makes it finally unbearable. **last word**, a final or definitive statement; the latest fashion. [OE, = *latest* (LATE)]

last[2] /lɑːst/ v.t./i. to remain unexhausted, adequate, or alive for a specified or long time; to continue for a specified time. —**last out**, to be strong enough or sufficient to last. [OE]

last[3] /lɑːst/ n. a shoemaker's model for shaping a shoe etc. on. [OE]

lasting adj. permanent, durable. [f. LAST[2]]

lastly adv. finally, in the last place. [f. LAST[1]]

lat. abbr. latitude.

latch n. 1. a bar with a catch and lever as the fastening of a gate etc. 2. a spring-lock preventing a door from being opened from the outside without the key after being shut. —v.t./i. to fasten with a latch. —**latch on to**, (*colloq.*) to attach oneself to; to understand. **on the latch**, fastened by the latch only. [prob. f. dial. *latch* v. seize, f. OE]

latchkey n. a key of an outer door.

late adj. (compar. **later**, LATTER; superl. **latest**, LAST[1]) 1. after the due or usual time; occurring or done etc. thus. 2. far on in the day or night or in a time, period, or development. 3. flowering or ripening towards the end of the season. 4. no longer alive or having a specified status. 5. of recent date. —adv. 1. after the due or usual time. 2. far on in time, at or until a late hour. 3. at a late stage of development. 4. formerly but not now. —**late in the day**, (*colloq.*) at a late stage in the proceedings. **of late**, recently. —**lateness** n. [OE]

lateen /ləˈtiːn/ adj. (of a sail) triangular and on a long yard at an angle of 45° to the mast. —**lateen-rigged** adj. rigged with such a sail (ill. SAILING-SHIPS). [f. F (*voile*) *latine* Latin sail (because common in the Mediterranean)]

lately adv. in recent times, not long ago. [OE (as LATE)]

La Tène /lɑː ˈtɛn/ the second phase of the European Iron Age, named after the type-site at the east end of Lake Neuchâtel, Switzerland, and dating from the mid-5th c. BC until the Roman conquest. The culture of this period (which follows the Hallstatt) represents the height of early Celtic achievement. It is characterized by hill-forts, developments in agriculture (see CELT), rich and elaborate burials, and artefacts of excellent craftsmanship and artistic design, ornamented with the very idiosyncratic Celtic style of swinging swelling lines, lively and yet restful.

latent /ˈleɪtənt/ adj. concealed, dormant, existing but not developed or manifest. —**latent heat**, the amount of heat lost or gained by a substance changing from a solid to a liquid or from a liquid to a vapour, without change of temperature. —**latency** n. [f. L *latēre* be hidden]

lateral /ˈlætər(ə)l/ adj. 1. of, at, towards, or from the side(s). 2. descended from a brother or sister of a person in the direct line. —n. a lateral shoot or branch. —**lateral line**, a longitudinal line of pores opening into sensory organs along each side of many fishes and amphibians (ill. FISH). **lateral thinking**, seeking to solve problems by indirect or unexpected methods. —**laterally** adv. [f. L (*latus* side)]

Lateran /ˈlætərən/ the site in Rome containing the basilica of St John the Baptist (St John Lateran) which is the cathedral church of Rome, and the Lateran Palace where the popes resided until the 14th c. Five general ecclesiastical councils of the Western Church were held in the basilica (1123, 1139, 1179, 1215, 1512–17). —**Lateran treaty**, a treaty signed in 1929 in the Lateran Palace, a concordat between the kingdom of Italy and the Holy See, recognizing as fully sovereign and independent a new (papal) State called Vatican City.

latex /ˈleɪteks/ n. 1. a milky fluid exuded from the cut surface of certain plants, e.g. the rubber plant. 2. a synthetic substance resembling this. [L, = liquid]

lath /lɑːθ/ n. (pl. /lɑːðz/) a thin narrow strip of wood. [OE]

lathe /leɪð/ n. a machine for shaping wood, metal, etc., by rotating the article against cutting tools. [prob. rel. to ODa. *lad* structure, frame]

lather /ˈlɑːðə(r)/ n. 1. the froth produced by soap etc. mixed with water. 2. frothy sweat, especially of a horse. 3. a state of agitation. —v.t./i. 1. to form a lather. 2. to cover with a lather. 3. to thrash. [OE]

Latimer /ˈlætɪmə(r)/, Hugh (c.1485–1555), English reformer and martyr, a priest and influential preacher, noted for his homely style, ready wit, extreme Protestant doctrines, and denunciation of social wrongs. When Henry VIII formally broke with the papacy in 1534 Latimer became one of the King's chief advisers, and was made bishop of Worcester in 1535, but opposed Henry's 'Six Articles' aimed at preventing the spread of Reformation doctrines and practices and was obliged to resign his see. Under Edward VI he returned to favour, but on Mary's accession he was imprisoned, refused to accept certain Catholic doctrines, and was burnt at the stake with Ridley at Oxford.

Latin /ˈlætɪn/ n. the language of ancient Rome and its empire (see below). —adj. 1. of or in Latin. 2. of the countries or peoples (e.g. France, Spain) using the languages developed from Latin. 3. of the Roman Catholic Church. —**Latin America**, the parts of Central and South America where Spanish or Portuguese is the main language.

Latin Church, the Western Church. **Latin cross,** a plain cross with the lowest arm longer than the other three (ill. VESTMENTS). [f. OF or L *Latinus* (*Latium* district of Italy including Rome)]

Latin is an Indo-European language, inflected and with complex syntax, the ancestor of all the Romance languages. It was originally the dialect of the people of Latium (*Latini*), a district of Italy lying south of the Apennines and east of the Tiber, and the rise of Rome led to its spread as the official and literary language of the Roman Empire. In the Middle Ages it remained the international medium of communication in western Europe, the language of law, the sciences, and in particular of liturgy; it was the official language of the Roman Catholic Church until the mid-20th c. Latin of the post-classical period is distinguished chronologically as Late Latin (*c.*AD 200–600) and Medieval Latin (*c.*600–1500); Silver Latin is the literary language and style of the century following the death of Augustus in AD 14; the term Vulgar Latin is applied to popular and provincial forms of Latin, especially those from which the Romance languages developed.

Latinate /ˈlætɪneɪt/ *adj.* like or having the character of Latin. [f. prec.]

latish /ˈleɪtɪʃ/ *adj.* fairly late. [f. LATE]

latitude /ˈlætɪtjuːd/ *n.* **1.** angular distance on a meridian; a place's angular distance north or south of the equator; (usu. in *pl.*) regions with reference to their distance from the equator. (See ill. NAVIGATION.) **2.** freedom from restriction in action or opinion. [f. L, = breadth (*latus* broad)]

Latitudinarian /ˌlætɪtjuːdɪˈnɛərɪən/ *n.* one who tolerates laxity of belief on religious questions. The term was opprobriously applied in the 17th c. to Anglican divines who, while remaining in the Church of England, attached relatively little importance to matters of dogmatic truth, ecclesiastical organization, and liturgical practice, and deprecated quarrels over these, regarding personal piety and morality as of more consequence. [as prec.]

latitudinarian /ˌlætɪtjuːdɪˈnɛərɪən/ *adj.* liberal, especially in religion. —*n.* a latitudinarian person. [as prec.]

Latona /ləˈtəʊnə/ (*Rom. myth.*) = LETO.

latrine /ləˈtriːn/ *n.* a lavatory in a camp or barracks etc.; a trench or pit for human excreta where there are no sewers. [F f. L (*lavare* wash)]

latter *adj.* **1.** second-mentioned of two; last-mentioned of three or more. **2.** nearer to the end; recent; belonging to the end of a period, the world, etc. —**the latter,** the latter person or thing. **latter-day** *adj.* modern, newfangled. **Latter-day Saints,** the Mormons' name for themselves. [OE = *later* (LATE)]

latterly *adv.* in the later part of life or of a period; of late. [f. prec.]

lattice /ˈlætɪs/ *n.* **1.** a structure of crossed laths or bars with spaces between, used as a screen, fence, etc. **2.** a regular arrangement of atoms or molecules. —**lattice window,** a window with small panes set in diagonally crossing strips of lead. [f. OF *lattis* (*latte* lath)]

Latvia /ˈlætvɪə/ an area on the shores of the Baltic Sea and the Gulf of Riga, a Baltic province of the Russian Empire after having been under Polish and then Swedish rule. It was proclaimed an independent republic in 1918 but in 1940 was incorporated in the USSR as a constituent republic, the Latvian SSR; capital, Riga.

Latvian /ˈlætvɪən/ *adj.* of Latvia or its people or language. —*n.* **1.** a native or inhabitant of Latvia. **2.** (also *Lettish*) the language of Latvia, spoken by some 1,500,000 people, most closely related to Lithuanian with which it constitutes the Baltic language group.

Laud /lɔːd/, William (1573–1645), English cleric, Archbishop of Canterbury from 1633. Although Protestant he opposed the prevailing Calvinism and attempted to impose liturgical uniformity on both Roman Catholics and Puritans by restoring pre-Reformation practices, arousing the bitter hostility of both parties. His attempt to impose these reforms in Scotland led to war and his downfall, and he was impeached, imprisoned, and executed for treason in a trial generally agreed to have been without regard for justice. His apparent failure arose from his inability to understand the popular leaning towards Puritanism and the hatred aroused by his violent measures against those who did not share his views on ritual.

laud /lɔːd/ *v.t.* to praise. —*n.* **1.** praise, a hymn of praise. **2.** (in *pl.*) the first religious service of the day in the Western (Roman Catholic) Church. In the Book of Common Prayer

parts of Lauds and Matins were combined to form the service of Morning Prayer. [f. L *laudare* (*laus* praise)]

laudable *adj.* commendable. —**laudability** /-ˈbɪlɪtɪ/ *n.,* **laudably** *adv.* [f. LAUD]

laudanum /ˈlɔːdnəm, ˈlɒd-/ *n.* tincture of opium. [orig. name of a costly medicament prescribed by Paracelsus]

laudatory /ˈlɔːdətərɪ/ *adj.* praising. [f. LAUD]

laugh /lɑːf/ *v.t./i.* to make the sounds and movements usual in expressing lively amusement, scorn etc.; to utter with a laugh. —*n.* **1.** a sound, act, or manner of laughing. **2.** (*colloq.*) a comical thing. —**laugh at,** to ridicule. **laugh in** or **up one's sleeve,** to laugh secretly. **laugh off,** to get rid of (embarrassment or humiliation) with a jest. [OE (imit.)]

laughable *adj.* ridiculous, causing amusement. —**laughably** *adv.* [f. prec.]

laughing *n.* laughter. —**laughing-gas** *n.* nitrous oxide as an anaesthetic, with an exhilarating effect when inhaled. **laughing-stock** *n.* a person or thing generally ridiculed. **no laughing matter,** a serious thing. [f. LAUGH]

laughter /ˈlɑːftə(r)/ *n.* the act or sound of laughing. [OE (as LAUGH)]

launch[1] /lɔːntʃ/ *v.t./i.* **1.** to cause (a ship) to move or slide from land into the water. **2.** to send forth by hurling or thrusting; to send on its course. **3.** to put into action; to enter boldly or freely on a course of action. —*n.* the launching of a ship or spacecraft etc., or of an enterprise. —**launch out,** to spend money freely; to burst out into strong language; to start on an ambitious enterprise. —**launcher** *n.* [f. AF *launcher* (as LANCE)]

launch[2] /lɔːntʃ/ *n.* **1.** a large motor boat. **2.** a warship's largest boat. [f. Sp. *lancha,* perh. f. Malay]

launder /ˈlɔːndə(r)/ **1.** to wash and iron (clothes etc.). **2.** to transfer (funds) so as to conceal their illegal origin. [f. OF *lavandier* washer of linen f. L *lavanda* things to be washed (*lavare* wash)]

launderette /lɔːnˈdret/ *n.* an establishment with coin-operated automatic washing-machines for public use. [f. prec. + -ETTE]

laundress /ˈlɔːndrɪs/ *n.* a woman whose job is to launder things. [f. LAUNDER]

laundry *n.* **1.** a place for washing clothes. **2.** a batch of clothes to be laundered. [f. OF *lavanderie* (as LAUNDER)]

Laurasia /lɔːˈreɪʃə/ a vast continental area thought to have once existed in the northern hemisphere and to have broken up in Mesozoic or late Palaeozoic times, forming North America, Greenland, Europe, and most of Asia north of the Himalayas. [f. *Laurentia,* name given to the ancient forerunner of N. America + Eur*asia*]

laureate /ˈlɒrɪət/ *adj.* wreathed with laurel as an honour. —*n.* a Poet Laureate (see below). —**laureateship** *n.* [f. L *laureatus* (*laurea* laurel-wreath, as foll.)]

In early use the title 'laureate' (implying 'worthy of the Muses' crown') was given generally to eminent poets, and sometimes conferred by certain universities. In modern use it is given to a poet who is appointed to write poems for State occasions and who receives a stipend as an officer of the Royal Household. The first Poet Laureate in the modern sense was Ben Jonson, but the title seems to have been first held by his successor Davenant (appointed in 1638). There is no official evidence for the tradition that Samuel Daniel (1599), or Spenser before him, held the title, though Daniel was often at court in James I's reign and Spenser had received a pension from the Queen. Dryden, Wordsworth, and Tennyson are among later holders of the title, which at present is held by Ted Hughes.

laurel /ˈlɒr(ə)l/ *n.* **1.** an evergreen shrub (*Prunus laurocerasus*) with dark glossy leaves. **2.** (in *sing.* or *pl.*) a wreath of bay-leaves (*Laurus nobilis*) as an emblem of victory or poetic merit. —**look to one's laurels,** to take care not to lose pre-eminence. **rest on one's laurels,** not to seek further success. [f. OF f. Prov. f. L *laurus* bay-tree]

Laurence /ˈlɒrəns/, St (d. 258), deacon of Rome, and martyr. According to tradition (widely rejected by modern scholars) when asked by the Prefect of Rome to deliver up the treasure of the Church he assembled and presented the poor; he was punished by being roasted on the famous but unhistorical gridiron (he was probably beheaded).

lav *n.* (*colloq.*) a lavatory. [abbr.]

lava /ˈlɑːvə/ *n.* matter flowing from a volcano and solidifying as it cools. [It. (*lavare* wash f. L)]

lavatory /ˈlævətərɪ, -trɪ/ *n.* a pan (usually a fixture) into which urine and faeces may be discharged for hygienic disposal; a room, building, or compartment with this. [f. L (*lavare* wash)]

lave *v.t.* (*literary*) to wash or bathe; (of water) to wash against, to flow along. [f. OF f. L *lavare* (as prec.)]

lavender /ˈlævɪndə(r)/ *n.* **1.** a shrub of the genus *Lavandula* with fragrant light purple flowers; these dried and used to scent linen etc. **2.** a light purple colour. —**lavender-water** *n.* a light perfume made from lavender. [f. AF f. L *lavandula*]

laver /ˈleɪvə(r), ˈlɑː-/ *n.* edible seaweed. [L (orig. an unidentified water-plant, not a seaweed)]

Lavery /ˈleɪvərɪ/, Sir John (1856–1941), British painter, born in Belfast. His early work was influenced by Whistler and the impressionists, and held a promise which was not fulfilled as in later life he succumbed to the facile lures of a society portrait painter.

lavish /ˈlævɪʃ/ *v.t.* to bestow or spend (money, effort, praise etc.) abundantly. —*adj.* giving or producing in large quantities. —**lavishly** *adv.*, **lavishness** *n.* [orig. = profusion, f. OF *lavasse* deluge of rain (as LAVE)]

Lavoisier /laˈvwɑːzɪeɪ/, Antoine Laurent (1743–94), French scientist, regarded as the father of modern chemistry. He followed the family tradition of studying law, but his first love was science which, apart from chemistry, included for him agriculture, geology, and experimental physics. The chemical revolution which he caused was to describe the true nature of combustion, to introduce rigorous methods of analysis, and to develop a new rational chemical nomenclature, published in 1789. He realized in 1774 that it was Priestley's 'dephlogisticated air' that combined with substances during burning, renamed this gas 'oxygen' in 1779, because he thought it a constituent of all acids and, in 1783, suggested that water was made up of the gases of oxygen and hydrogen; but in this he was anticipated by Cavendish. The holder of a number of important public offices, he supplemented his private income by becoming a member of a consortium that gathered the indirect taxes for the government, and it was this position that led to his death by guillotine during the Reign of Terror of the French Revolution.

law *n.* **1.** a rule established in a community by authority or custom; a body of such rules; the controlling influence of or obedience to this; the subject or study of such rules. **2.** the legal profession. **3.** (*colloq.*) the police. **4.** a judicial remedy; the lawcourts providing it. **5.** a divine commandment; **the Law**, the Jewish name for the Pentateuch. **6.** something that must be obeyed. **7.** a factual statement of what always happens in certain circumstances; a regularity in natural occurrences. —**be a law unto oneself**, to disregard custom. **law-abiding** *adj.* obedient to the laws. **Law Lord**, a member of the House of Lords qualified to perform its legal work (see LORDS TEMPORAL). **take the law into one's own hands**, to redress a grievance by one's own means, especially by force. [OE f. ON *lag* something 'laid down' or fixed]

lawcourt *n.* a court of law (see COURT).

lawful *adj.* conforming with or recognized by law; not illegal; (of a child) legitimate. —**lawfully** *adv.*, **lawfulness** *n.* [f. LAW + -FUL]

lawgiver *n.* one who codifies a body of laws.

lawless *adj.* **1.** having no laws or no enforcement of them. **2.** disregarding laws, uncontrolled. —**lawlessly** *adv.*, **lawlessness** *n.* [f. LAW + -FUL]

lawmaker *n.* a legislator.

lawn[1] *n.* a piece of grass kept mown and smooth in a garden etc. —**lawn-mower** *n.* a machine for cutting the grass of lawns. **lawn tennis**, a game that was originally a modification of tennis (see entry) played by two persons (*singles*) or four (*doubles*) with a soft ball on an outdoor grass or hard court without walls (ill. SPORTS). It became popular in Victorian times as a diversion for the middle classes ('real' tennis was always an aristocratic sport), a perfect game for large gardens and a leisured society. [f. obs. *laund* glade f. OF (as LAND)]

lawn[2] *n.* fine woven cotton or synthetic material. [prob. f. *Laon* in France]

Lawrence[1] /ˈlɒrəns/, David Herbert (1885–1930), English novelist, poet, critic, and painter, son of a Nottinghamshire miner and an ex-schoolteacher who encouraged Lawrence to become a teacher. In 1911 he published his first novel, and achieved success with his closely autobiographical *Sons and Lovers* (1913). In 1912 he eloped with the German wife of a Nottingham professor, subsequently travelling extensively with her: *Kangaroo* (1923) was written in Aus-

tralia and *The Plumed Serpent* (1926) in New Mexico, where he became seriously ill. Lawrence is remembered most for his exploration of marital and sexual relations: *The Rainbow* (1915) was declared obscene, and *Women in Love* (1920) was described as an 'analytical study of sexual depravity'. In 1925 he returned to Europe, living mainly in Italy until he finished *Lady Chatterley's Lover* (1928) not published in Britain in its unexpurgated form until 1960. Its publishers were then prosecuted under the Obscene Publications Act and acquitted after a celebrated trial which influenced writing and publishing thereafter. Lawrence was a moralist and believed that modern man was becoming divorced from his natural feelings. By illuminating areas of human experience not previously explored in fiction he shocked the reading public. His verse, collected in *Complete Poems* (1957), had the immediacy and personal quality of his prose.

Lawrence[2] /ˈlɒrəns/, Sir Thomas (1769–1830), English painter, self-taught, whose portrait of Queen Charlotte, painted in 1789 and exhibited the following year at the Royal Academy, brought his first success. Many portrait commissions followed, displaying fine draughtsmanship if often with exaggerated surface effects. By 1810, his style now more subdued, he was recognized as the leading portrait painter of his time and was sent by the Prince Regent, in 1818, to paint the portraits of heads of State and military leaders after the allied victory over Napoleon. Lawrence, as well as being a painter and public figure, was a connoisseur with, perhaps the finest collection ever made of old master drawings.

Lawrence[3] /ˈlɒrəns/, Thomas Edward (1888–1935), English soldier and writer, known as 'Lawrence of Arabia', who helped to organize and lead the Arab revolt against the Turks in the Middle East during the second half of the First World War. His guerrilla activities behind Turkish lines drew thousands of enemy soldiers away from the front and contributed to Allenby's eventual victory in Palestine; they are described in his powerful classic *Seven Pillars of Wisdom* (1926), important as a document of military history and as a revelation of the author's complex personality. After the war Lawrence became disillusioned with his public life. He enlisted in the RAF under a pseudonym ('J. H. Ross') to avoid attention and joined the tank corps as 'T. E. Shaw', later returning to the RAF; this period is reflected in his posthumously-published *The Mint*. Shortly after retiring he was killed in a motor-cycle accident near his Dorset home. His multiple roles—man of action, poet, ascetic, leader of men—have fascinated the public and his many biographers.

lawrencium /ləˈrensɪəm/ *n.* an artificially made transuranic radioactive metallic element, symbol Lr, atomic number 103, first obtained in 1961 by bombarding californium with boron ions. [f. E. O. *Lawrence*, Amer. physicist (d. 1958)]

lawsuit *n.* a prosecution of a claim in a lawcourt.

lawyer /ˈlɔːjə(r), ˈlɔɪə(r)/ *n.* a person pursuing law as a profession; a solicitor; an expert at law. [f. LAW]

lax *adj.* not strict, careless, slack. —**laxity** *n.*, **laxly** *adv.* [f. L *laxus*, rel. to SLACK]

laxative /ˈlæksətɪv/ *adj.* tending to cause or facilitate evacuation of the bowels. —*n.* a medicine for this. [f. OF or L (*laxare* loosen, as prec.)]

lay[1] *v.t./i.* (*past & p.p.* **laid**) **1.** to place on a surface or in a certain position; to place or arrange in a horizontal position, to put into place; to locate (a scene). **2.** to apply or impose; to assign. **3.** to present or put forward for consideration. **4.** (of a hen bird) to produce (an egg, or *absol.*). **5.** to cause to subside or lie flat. **6.** to stake as a wager, to bet. **7.** to prepare (a plan or trap). **8.** to prepare (a table) for a meal; to arrange fuel for (a fire). **9.** to coat or strew *with*. **10.** (*slang*) to have sexual intercourse with (a woman). —*n.* **1.** the way, position, or direction in which something lies. **2.** (*slang*) a woman partner in sexual intercourse. —**in lay**, (of a hen) laying eggs regularly. **laid paper**, paper with the surface marked in fine ribs. **lay about one**, to hit out on all sides. **lay bare**, to reveal. **lay down**, to put on the ground etc.; to give up (office); to establish as a rule or instruction; to store (wine) in a cellar for future use; to sacrifice (one's life). **lay down the law**, to talk authoritatively or as if sure of being right. **lay hands on**, to seize or attack. **lay one's hands on**, to obtain; to be able to find. **lay hold of**, to seize or grasp. **lay in**, to provide oneself with a stock of. **lay into**, (*slang*) to punish or scold harshly. **lay it on thick** *or* **with a trowel**, (*slang*) to exaggerate greatly. **lay low**, to overthrow; to humble; to incapacitate. **lay off**, to discharge (workers) temporarily through shortage of work; (*colloq.*) to cease, especially from causing trouble or annoyance. **lay-off** *n.* a temporary discharge of workers. **lay on**, to inflict blows forcibly; to provide; to spread (paint etc.). **lay open**, to break the skin of; to expose *oneself* (to criticism etc.). **lay out**, to arrange according to a plan; to prepare (a body) for burial; to spend (money) for a purpose; (*colloq.*) to knock unconscious; to cause (oneself) to make every effort. **lay up**, to store or save; to cause (a person) to be confined to bed or unfit for work etc. **lay waste**, to destroy the crops and buildings of. [OE, (rel. to LIE¹)]

lay² *adj.* **1.** non-clerical; not ordained into the clergy. **2.** not professionally qualified, especially in law or medicine; of or done by such persons. —**lay reader**, a layman licensed to conduct some religious services. [f. F f. L f. Gk *laïkos* (*laos* people)]

lay³ *n.* a minstrel's song, a ballad. [f. OF or Prov.]

lay⁴ *past* of LIE¹.

layabout *n.* a habitual loafer or idler.

Layamon /ˈlaɪəmən/ (late 12th c.) English poet and priest, author of the verse chronicle, the *Brut*, a history of England from the arrival of the legendary Brutus to Cadwallader (AD 689). One of the earliest major works in Middle English, it introduces for the first time in English the story of King Arthur, Lear, and other figures prominent in later English literature.

lay-by *n.* (*pl.* **lay-bys**) an extra strip at the side of the open road for vehicles to stop temporarily.

layer *n.* **1.** a thickness of matter, especially one of several, spread over a surface. **2.** a person etc. that lays. **3.** a shoot fastened down to take root while attached to the parent plant. —*v.t.* **1.** to arrange or cut (hair) in layers. **2.** to propagate (a plant) by fastening down an attached shoot to take root. [f. LAY¹]

layette /leɪˈet/ *n.* the clothes etc. prepared for a new-born child. [F, dim. of OF *laie* drawer f. MDu.]

lay figure 1. a jointed figure of the human body used by artists for arranging drapery on etc. **2.** an unreal character in a novel etc. **3.** a person lacking in individuality. [*lay* f. obs. *layman* lay figure f. Du. (*led* joint]

layman *n.* (*pl.* **-men**) **1.** a person not in holy orders. **2.** a person without professional or special knowledge. [f. LAY² + MAN]

layout *n.* the disposing or arrangement of ground, printed matter, etc.; a thing arranged thus.

layshaft *n.* a second or intermediate transmission-shaft in a machine.

laze *v.i.* (*colloq.*) to spend time doing nothing or relaxing. —*n.* a spell of lazing. [back-formation f. LAZY]

lazy /ˈleɪzɪ/ *adj.* **1.** disinclined to work, doing little work. **2.** of or inducing idleness. —**lazy-bones** *n.* a lazy person. —**lazily** *adv.*, **laziness** *n.* [perh. f. LG]

lb *abbr.* pound(s) weight. [f. L *libra*]

l.b.w. *abbr.* leg before wicket.

l.c. *abbr.* **1.** in the passage etc. cited. [f. L *loco citato*]. **2.** lower case.

LCM *abbr.* lowest common multiple.

LEA *abbr.* Local Education Authority.

lea *n.* (poetic) a piece of meadow or pasture or arable land. [OE]

leach *v.t.* to make (liquid) percolate through some material; to subject (bark, ore, ash, soil) to the action of a percolating fluid; (with *away* or *out*) to remove or be removed thus. [prob. f. OE *leccan* to water]

lead¹ /liːd/ *v.t./i.* (*past & p.p.* **led**) **1.** to cause to go with one, to guide or help to go, especially by going in front or by taking a person's hand or an animal's halter etc. **2.** to influence the actions or opinions of, to guide by persuasion, example, or argument. **3.** to provide access; (with *to*) to have as its result. **4.** to make (a rope, water, etc.) go in a certain course. **5.** to live or go through (a life etc. of a specified kind). **6.** to have the first place in; to go first; to be first in a race or game. **7.** to be in charge of; to be pre-eminent in some field. **8.** (in card-games) to play as one's first card; to be the first player in a trick. —*n.* **1.** guidance given by going in front; an example; a clue. **2.** the leader's place; the amount by which a competitor is ahead of the others. **3.** a strip of leather or cord for leading a dog etc. **4.** a conductor (usually a wire) conveying an electric current to the place of use. **5.** the chief part in a play etc.; its player. **6.** (in card-games) the act or right of playing first; a card so played. —**lead by the nose**, to control the

actions of (a person) completely. **lead off**, to begin. **lead on**, to entice. **lead up the garden path**, to mislead. **lead up to**, to form the preparation for or introduction to; to direct a conversation towards. [OE]

lead² /led/ *n.* **1.** a heavy soft grey metallic element (see below), symbol Pb, atomic number 82. **2.** (also called 'black lead'; the name was applied before the composition of the substance was known) the graphite used in pencils; a stick of this. **3.** a lump of lead used for taking soundings in water. **4.** (in *pl.*) strips of lead covering a roof; a piece of lead-covered roof; the lead frames holding the glass of a lattice etc. **5.** a metal strip in printing to give a space between lines. **6.** (*attrib.*) made of lead. —*v.t.* to cover, weight, frame, or space with lead(s). —**lead pencil**, a pencil of graphite enclosed in wood. —**leaded** *adj.* [OE]

Lead was known to the ancient Egyptians and Babylonians, and was used by the Romans for making water-pipes. It is durable, resistant to corrosion, and a poor conductor of electricity; it has been used in roofing, ammunition, damping sound and vibration, storage batteries, cable sheathing, and shielding radioactive material. Lead compounds have been used in crystal glass, as an antiknock agent in petrol, and were formerly used extensively in paints. Lead and its compounds can accumulate in the body as poisons.

leaden /ˈledən/ *adj.* **1.** of or like lead, heavy or slow. **2.** lead-coloured. [f. LEAD²]

leader /ˈliːdə(r)/ *n.* **1.** a person or thing that leads; a person followed by others. **2.** the principal first violin in an orchestra, or the first violin in a quartet etc. **3.** a leading article. —**Leader of the House**, a member of the government in the House of Commons or Lords who arranges and announces the business of the House. —**leadership** *n.* [f. LEAD¹]

leading¹ /ˈliːdɪŋ/ *adj.* direct, most important. —**leading aircraftman**, one ranking above aircraftman. **leading article**, a newspaper-article giving the editorial opinion. **leading light**, a prominent and influential person. **leading note**, the seventh note of the diatonic scale. **leading question**, one prompting the desired answer. [f. LEAD¹]

leading² /ˈledɪŋ/ *n.* a covering or framework of lead. [f. LEAD²]

leaf *n.* (*pl.* **leaves**) **1.** a broad flat usually green part of a plant, often on a stem (ill. PLANTS); (*collect.*) leaves. **2.** the state of having leaves out. **3.** a single thickness of paper, especially in a book with each side forming a page. **4.** a very thin sheet of metal etc. **5.** a hinged flap of a table etc.; an extra section inserted to extend a table. —*v.i.* to put forth leaves. —**leaf-insect** *n.* an insect of the family Phyllidae with wings like a plant-leaf. **leaf-mould** *n.* soil chiefly of decaying leaves. **leaf through**, to turn over the pages of (a book etc.). —**leafy** *adj.* [OE]

leafage *n.* the leaves of plants. [f. LEAF]

leaflet *n.* **1.** a division of a compound leaf; a young leaf. **2.** a sheet of paper (sometimes folded but not stitched) giving information, especially for free distribution. [f. LEAF + -LET]

league¹ /liːg/ *n.* **1.** a group of people or countries etc. combining for a particular purpose. **2.** an agreement to combine in this way. **3.** a group of sports clubs which compete against each other for a championship. **4.** a class of contestants. —*v.t./i.* to join in a league. —**in league**, allied, conspiring. **league table**, a list of contestants etc. in order of merit. [f. F or It. (*legare* bind f. L, as LIGATURE)]

league² /liːg/ *n.* (*archaic*) a varying measure of travelling-distance, usually about 3 miles. [ult. f. L *leuga*, f. Gaulish]

League of Nations an association of self-governing States, dominions, and colonies established in 1919 by the Treaty of Versailles, at the instigation of the US President Woodrow Wilson, 'to promote international co-operation and to achieve international peace and security'. Although the League accomplished much of value in post-war economic reconstruction, it failed in its prime purpose through the refusal of member nations to put international interests before national ones, and was powerless in the face of Italian, German, and Japanese expansionism. By the outbreak of the Second World War the League of Nations was little more than a helpless spectator, and the war itself destroyed it entirely. (See UNITED NATIONS.)

leak *n.* **1.** a hole or crack etc. through which liquid or gas passes wrongly in or out. **2.** the liquid or gas passing through this. **3.** a similar escape of an electric charge; the charge that escapes. **4.** a disclosure of secret information. —*v.t./i.* **1.** to escape wrongly through an opening. **2.** (of a container) to allow such escape; to let out (liquid or gas) wrongly. **3.**

to disclose (a secret). —**leak out,** (of a secret) to become known. —**leaky** *adj.* [prob. f. LG]

leakage *n.* **1.** leaking. **2.** that which has leaked out. [f. LEAK]

lean[1] *v.t.* (*past & p.p.* **leaned** or **leant** /lent/) **1.** to be or put in a sloping position; to incline from the perpendicular. **2.** to rest *against, on,* or *upon* for support. **3.** to rely *on* or *upon* for help. **4.** to be inclined or have a leaning *to* or *towards.* —*n.* a deviation from the perpendicular, an inclination. —**lean on,** (*slang*) to put pressure on (a person) to make him co-operate. **lean-to** *n.* a building with the roof resting against a larger building or wall. [OE]

lean[2] *adj.* **1.** (of a person or animal) without much flesh, having no superfluous fat. **2.** (of meat) containing little fat. **3.** meagre. —*n.* the lean part of meat (opp. *fat*). —**lean years,** a period of scarcity. —**leanness** *n.* [OE]

Leander /li'ændə(r)/ **1.** (*Gk legend*) the lover of Hero (see entry). **2.** (in full **Leander Club**) the oldest amateur rowing club in the world, founded early in the 19th c. Membership is a mark of distinction in the rowing world, and a large proportion of its members are former Oxford and Cambridge oarsmen.

leaning *n.* a tendency or partiality. [f. LEAN[1]]

leap *v.t./i.* (*past & p.p.* **leaped** /li:pt, lept/ or **leapt** /lept/) to jump or spring vigorously. —*n.* a vigorous jump. —**by leaps and bounds,** with startlingly rapid progress. **leap in the dark,** a rash step or enterprise. **leap year,** a year with 366 days (including 29 Feb. as an intercalary day). [OE]

leap-frog *n.* a game in which the players in turn vault with parted legs over another who is bending down. —*v.t./i.* (-**gg**-) **1.** to perform such a vault (over). **2.** to overtake alternately.

Lear /'lɪə(r)/, Edward (1812–88), English artist and poet, the twentieth child of a stockbroker of Danish descent. At the age of 15 he was obliged to earn his own living, and began his artistic career by making tinted drawings of birds; in 1831 he became employed as a draughtsman in the gardens of the Zoological Society. Lear came under the patronage of the Earl of Derby, for whose grandchildren he wrote *A Book of Nonsense* (1845) with his own limericks and illustrations, the first of his series of nonsense verses in which he combines linguistic fantasies and inventiveness with touches of underlying melancholy. His reputation as a water-colourist has risen steadily since his death.

learn /lɜ:n/ *v.t./i.* (*past & p.p.* **learned** /lɜ:nt/, **learnt**) **1.** to gain knowledge of or skill in by study, experience, or being taught. **2.** to commit to memory. **3.** to receive instruction; to become aware *of* by information or observation. **4.** (*archaic, vulgar,* or *joc.*) to teach. [OE]

learned /'lɜ:nɪd/ *adj.* **1.** having much knowledge acquired by study; showing or requiring learning. **2.** concerned with the interests of learned persons. —**learnedly** *adv.* [f. prec.]

learner *n.* one who is learning a subject or skill. —**learner driver,** one who is learning to drive a motor vehicle but has not yet passed a driving test. [f. LEARN]

learning *n.* knowledge acquired by study. [as prec.]

lease /li:s/ *n.* a contract by which the owner of a building or land allows another to use it for a specified time, usually in return for payment. —*v.t.* to grant or take on lease. —**a new lease of** or (*US*) **on life,** an improved prospect of living or of use after repair. [f. AF *les* (*lesser* let f. L *laxare* loosen)]

leasehold *n.* the holding of property by lease; property held thus. —**leaseholder** *n.*

Lease-Lend *n.* = LEND-LEASE.

leash *n.* a thong for holding hounds etc. under restraint; a dog's lead. —*v.t.* to put a leash on; to hold in a leash. —**straining at the leash,** eager to begin. [f. OF (*laisser* let run on slack lead, as LEASE)]

least *adj.* **1.** smallest in amount or degree; of a very small species etc. **2.** lowest in rank or importance. —*n.* the least amount. —*adv.* in the least degree. —**at least,** at all events, anyway; not less than. **(in) the least,** at all. **to say the least (of it),** putting the case moderately. [OE, superl. of LESS]

leather /'leðə(r)/ *n.* **1.** material made from animal skins by tanning or a similar process. **2.** the leather part(s) of something. **3.** a piece of leather for polishing with. **4.** (in *pl.*) leggings, breeches. —*v.t.* **1.** to cover with leather. **2.** to polish or wipe with a leather. **3.** to beat, to thrash. —**leather-back** *n.* the largest existing turtle (*Sphargis*

coriacea), with a flexible shell. **leather-jacket** *n.* a crane-fly grub, which has a tough skin. [OE]

leatherette /leðə'ret/ *n.* an imitation leather. [f. prec. + -ETTE]

leathery *adj.* like leather; tough. —**leatheriness** *n.* [f. LEATHER]

leave[1] *v.t./i.* (*past & p.p.* **left**) **1.** to go away (from); to go away finally or permanently; to abandon, to desert. **2.** to cease to reside at or belong to or work for. **3.** to cause or allow to remain; to depart without taking. **4.** to have remaining after one's death. **5.** to give as a legacy. **6.** to allow to stay or proceed without interference. **7.** to commit or refer *to* another person; to depute (a person) to perform a function in one's absence. **8.** to refrain from consuming or dealing with. **9.** to deposit for collection or transmission. —**leave alone,** to refrain from disturbing; not to interfere with. **leave off,** to discontinue; to come to or make an end. **leave out,** to omit. **left luggage,** luggage deposited for later retrieval. **left-overs** *n.pl.* items (especially food) remaining after the rest has been used. [OE]

leave[2] *n.* **1.** permission. **2.** permission to be absent from duty; the period for which this lasts. —**on leave,** legitimately absent from duty. **take (one's) leave (of),** to bid farewell (to). **take leave of one's senses,** to go mad. [OE]

leaved *adj.* having leaves; having a specified number of leaves. [f. LEAF]

leaven /'lev(ə)n/ *n.* **1.** a substance (esp. yeast) used to make dough ferment and rise. **2.** a pervasive transforming influence; an admixture of some quality. —*v.t.* **1.** to ferment (dough) with leaven. **2.** to permeate and transform; to modify *with* a tempering element. [f. OF f. L *levamen* (*levare* lift)]

leaves *pl.* of LEAF.

leavings *n.pl.* things left over, especially as worthless. [f. LEAVE[1]]

Lebanon /'lebənən/ a country in SW Asia with a coastline on the Mediterranean Sea; pop. (1974) 2,780,000; official language, Arabic; capital, Beirut. The country was once heavily forested, but little remains of the famous cedars of Lebanon, imported by the pharaohs of ancient Egypt for coffins and for buildings and by Solomon for his temple. Until the mid-1970s the country's main sources of income were based on international trade and commerce, with Beirut the commercial capital of the Middle East. Lebanon has a number of archaeological sites, with Baalbek as its showpiece and Byblos one of the oldest continuously inhabited cities in the world. Part of the Ottoman empire from the 16th c., it became a French mandate after the First World War and achieved independence after the defeat of the Vichy garrison by the Allies during the Second World War. For a generation the Christian community dominated the country, but friction between these and the Muslims, the influx of Palestinian refugees, and repeated Middle Eastern wars, have continually destabilized the country, leading to intermittent (later continuous) civil war and military intervention by her neighbours and making Lebanon one of the most troubled areas in the world. —**Lebanese** /-'ni:z/ *adj.* & *n.*

Leblanc /lə'blɑ̃/, Nicolas (1742–1806), French surgeon and chemist, who became interested in the large-scale manufacture of soda because of a prize offered by the Académie Royale des Sciences. In 1789 he developed the process that bears his name for making soda ash (sodium carbonate) from sodium chloride (common salt), which made possible the large-scale manufacture of glass, soaps, paper, and other chemicals, but by then it was too late for him to be awarded the prize. The factory he set up with others was confiscated during the French Revolution, the eventual compensation was insufficient to start the business, and he committed suicide.

Lebrun /lə'brœ̃/, Charles (1619–90), French painter, designer, and decorator, who was influenced by Raphael and especially Poussin and in 1848 was a prominent figure in the foundation of the Académie Royale de Peinture et Sculpture. His importance in the history of French art is twofold. First, in the employ of Louis XIV from 1661, he executed works which reflected the power and splendour of the Sun King's court and established himself as a leading exponent of 17th-c. French classicism; his decorative scenes at Versailles, including painting, furniture, garden sculpture, and tapestry design (in 1663 he was appointed director of the Gobelins factory) must be seen as a highlight in his *œuvre*. Secondly, as director of the Académie from 1663 he turned it into a channel for imposing a codified system of orthodoxy in matters of art, laying the basis of academicism.

Le Carré /lə ˈkæreɪ/, John (pseudonym of David John Moore Cornwell, 1931-), English novelist, who served in the Foreign Service in the early 1960s. His first thriller *Call for the Dead* (1961) introduces mastermind and secret agent George Smiley, who reappears in many of his later books. *The Spy Who Came in from the Cold* (1963), a cold-war thriller inspired by the Berlin wall, brought him immediate fame, and with *The Looking Glass War* (1965), *Tinker, Tailor, Soldier, Spy* (1974), *Smiley's People* (1980), *The Little Drummer Girl* (1983), and many others, he has confirmed his reputation for realistic fictional studies of espionage.

lecher /ˈletʃə(r)/ *n.* a lecherous man, a debauchee. [f. OF (*lechier* live in debauchery or gluttony, rel. to LICK)]

lecherous /ˈletʃərəs/ *adj.* lustful, having strong or excessive sexual desire. [f. prec.]

lechery /ˈletʃərɪ/ *n.* unrestrained indulgence of sexual desire. [f. LECHER]

Leclanché /ləˈklɑ̃ʃeɪ/, Georges (1839-82), French chemist, inventor of a primary cell (named after him) that has a zinc cathode in contact with zinc chloride, ammonium chloride (solution or paste) as the electrolyte, and a carbon anode in contact with a mixture of manganese dioxide and carbon powder.

Leconte de Lisle /ləkɔ̃t də ˈliːl/ Charles-Marie-René (1818-94), French poet, whose inspiration was drawn from Greek, Egyptian, and Nordic mythology, biblical history, exotic eastern scenery, and archaeological beauty. His poetry is marked by a formal perfection and static visual quality, though his choice of subject was often directed by his pessimistic and atheistic view of life.

Le Corbusier /lə kɔːˈbjuːzɪeɪ/ (1887-1965), real name Charles-Edouard Jeanneret, French architect of Swiss parentage, who began as a painter of semi-abstract compositions and became a great influence on modern architecture through his designs, buildings, and writings, and his use of steel and raw concrete. He began architectural practice in 1922 with his cousin Pierre Jeanneret, and their early buildings already showed Le Corbusier's genius for subtle manipulation of pure geometrical forms as well as his imaginative application of new technical ideas. Their most important buildings include the Centrosoyons (co-operative) building in Moscow (1928), and the hostel for Swiss students in Paris (1931-3) with Le Corbusier's characteristic use of *pilotis* to raise the building off the ground. His visit to Brazil in 1936 greatly influenced the modern architectural movement in that country. The UN Secretariat building in New York (1951) owes its basic conception and clarity of form to his ideas. He was involved also in the planning of functional cities (e.g. Chandigarh in India).

lectern /ˈlektɜːn/ *n.* a desk for holding a bible or hymn-book in church (ill. VESTMENTS); a similar desk for a lecturer etc. [f. OF f. L *lectrum* (*legere* read)]

lectionary /ˈlekʃənərɪ/ *n.* a list of portions of Scripture apppointed to be read in churches. [f. L (*lectio* reading, as prec.)]

lecture /ˈlektʃə(r)/ *n.* a discourse giving information about a subject to a class or other audience; a long serious speech, especially as a scolding or reprimand. —*v.t./i.* to deliver a lecture or lectures; to talk seriously or reprovingly to. —**lecturer** *n.* [f. OF or L (as prec.)]

lectureship *n.* the official position of lecturer, especially at a university etc.

led *past & p.p.* of LEAD[1].

Leda /ˈliːdə/ (*Gk myth.*) wife of Tyndareus king of Sparta. She was loved by Zeus who visited her in the form of a swan; among their children were the Dioscuri, Helen, and Clytemnestra.

ledge *n.* a narrow horizontal projection or shelf. [perh. rel. to LAY[1]]

ledger *n.* a tall narrow book in which a firm's accounts are kept. [= Du. *ligger, legger* (as LIE[1], LAY[1])]

Lee, Robert Edward (1807-70), Confederate general, commander of the army of Northern Virginia. Widely acclaimed as the greatest military leader of the American Civil War, Lee led the main Confederate army in the eastern theatre for most of the war. Revered by his own men and respected by his opponents, he did more than any other individual to prolong Confederate resistance against the Union's greater manpower and industrial might.

lee *n.* 1. the shelter given by a neighbouring object. 2. (in full **lee side**) the sheltered side, the side away from the wind. —**lee shore**, the shore to leeward of a ship. [OE]

leech[1] *n.* 1. a blood-sucking worm (*Hirudo medicinalis*) formerly used medicinally for bleeding. 2. a person who sponges on another. [OE]

leech[2] *n.* a verticle side of a square sail; the after side of a fore-and-aft sail (ill. SAILING-SHIPS). [perh. rel. to ON *lik*, nautical term of uncertain meaning]

leek *n.* a vegetable (*Allium porrum*) of the onion family with a cylindrical white bulb; this as the Welsh national emblem. [OE]

leer *v.i.* to look slyly or lasciviously or maliciously. —*n.* a leering look. [perh. f. obs. *leer* cheek f. OE, as though 'to glance over one's cheek']

leery *adj.* knowing, sly, wary *of*. [perh. f. obs. *leer* looking askance (as prec.)]

lees /liːz/ *n.pl.* the sediment of wine etc.; the dregs. [f. OF *lie*]

Leeuwenhoek /ˈleɪvənhuːk/, Antoni van (1632-1723), Dutch naturalist. Apprenticed to a Delft cloth-merchant, he developed a lens for scientific purposes from those used to inspect cloth, and was the first to observe bacteria, protozoa, and yeast. He accurately described red blood corpuscles, capillaries, striated muscle fibres, spermatozoa, and the crystalline lens of the eye. Being without Latin he was out of touch with the scientific community and his very original work on micro-organisms became known through the Royal Society's translation and publication of his letters.

leeward /ˈliːwəd, (*Naut.*) ˈluːəd/ *adj. & adv.* on or towards the sheltered side. —*n.* the leeward side or region. [f. LEE + -WARD]

Leeward Islands /ˈliːwəd/ a group of islands in the eastern Caribbean which constitute the northern part of the Lesser Antilles. The largest are Guadeloupe, Antigua, St Kitts, and Montserrat. Their name refers to the fact that they are further from the direction of prevailing winds, which are easterly, than are the Windward Islands.

leeway *n.* 1. a ship's sideways drift leeward of a desired course. 2. an allowable deviation or freedom of action.

Le Fanu /ˈlefənjuː, ləˈfɑːnuː/, Joseph Sheridan (1814-73), Irish novelist who achieved recognition as a writer of stories of mystery, suspense, and the supernatural. His best-known works include, *The House by the Churchyard* (1861), *Uncle Silas* (1864), and the collection of ghost stories *In a Glass Darkly* (1872).

left[1] *adj.* 1. on or towards the side of the human body which in the majority of persons has the less-used hand and on which the heart lies; on or towards the analogous part of a thing. 2. politically to the left (see sense 3 below). —*adv.* on or to the left side. —*n.* 1. the left-hand part, region, or direction. 2. the left hand; a blow with this; (in marching) the left foot. 3. (often **Left**) a political group or section favouring radical socialism; such radicals collectively; the more advanced or innovative section of any group. —**have two left feet**, to be clumsy. **left bank**, the bank of a river on the left as one faces downstream. **left-hand** *adj.* of, on, or towards the left side of a person or thing. **left-handed** *adj.* using the left hand by preference as more serviceable; made by or for the left hand; turning to the left; awkward or clumsy; (of a compliment) ambiguous, of doubtful sincerity. **left-hander** *n.* a left-handed person or blow. **left wing**, the left side of a football etc. team on the field; a player in this position; the left section of a political party (see sense 3 above). **left-winger** *n.* a person on the left wing. [orig. = weak, worthless; cf. OE *lyft-adl* paralysis]

left[2] *past & p.p.* of LEAVE[1].

leftism *n.* radical socialism. —**leftist** *n.* [f. LEFT[1]]

leftward /ˈleftwəd/ *adv.* (also **leftwards**) towards the left. —*adj.* going towards or facing the left. [f. LEFT[1] + -WARD]

lefty *n.* (*colloq.*) 1. a left-winger in politics. 2. a left-handed person. [f. LEFT[1]]

leg *n.* 1. each of the projecting parts of an animal's body, on which it stands or moves; either of the two lower limbs of the human body; an artificial replacement of this. 2. the part of a garment covering the leg. 3. any of the projecting supports beneath a chair or other piece of furniture. 4. the part of a cricket field on the side where the batsman places his feet. 5. one section of a journey. 6. each of several stages in a competition etc. 7. one branch of a forked object. 8. (*Naut.*) a run made on a single tack. —**give a person a leg up,** to help him to mount a horse etc. or get over an obstacle or difficulty. **leg before wicket,** (of a batsman) out because of an illegal obstruction of the ball with a part of the body other than the hand. **leg it,** to walk or run hard. **leg-pull** *n.* a hoax. **not have a leg to stand on,** to be unable to support an argument by facts or sound reasons. **on one's last legs,** near death or the end of usefulness etc. —**legged** /legd, ˈlegɪd/ *adj.* [f. ON]

legacy /ˈlegəsɪ/ *n.* **1.** money or an article given by will to a survivor. **2.** something handed down by a predecessor. [f. OF f. L (*legare* bequeath, commit)]

legal /ˈliːg(ə)l/ *adj.* of or based on law; concerned with, appointed, required, or permitted by law. —**legal aid,** a payment from public funds for legal advice or proceedings. **legal tender,** currency that cannot legally be refused in payment of a debt. —**legality** /lɪˈgælɪtɪ/ *n.,* **legally** /ˈliːgəlɪ/ *adv.* [f. F or L (*lex* law)]

legalism *n.* excessive adherence to a law or formula. —**legalist** *n.,* **legalistic** /-ˈlɪstɪk/ *adj.* [f. prec.]

legalize *v.t.* to make lawful; to bring into harmony with the law. —**legalization** /-ˈzeɪʃ(ə)n/ *n.* [f. LEGAL]

legate /ˈlegət/ *n.* an ambassador (now only one representing the pope). [f. OF f. L (*legare* commission)]

legatee /legəˈtiː/ *n.* a recipient of a legacy. [f. L *legare* bequeath]

legation /lɪˈgeɪʃ(ə)n/ *n.* **1.** a body of deputies. **2.** a diplomatic minister (especially below ambassadorial rank) and his staff. **3.** a diplomatic minister's residence. **4.** a legateship. [f. OF or L (as LEGATE)]

legato /lɪˈgɑːtəʊ/ *adv. & adj.* (*Mus.*) in a smooth manner. —*n.* (*pl.* **-os**) (*Mus.*) smooth playing; a passage played smoothly. [It., = bound, f. L *ligare* bind]

legend /ˈledʒ(ə)nd/ *n.* **1.** a story (true or invented) handed down from the past; such stories collectively. **2.** an inscription on a coin or medal. **3.** a caption. **4.** an explanation on a map etc. of the symbols used. [f. OF f. L *legenda* what is to be read (*legere* read)]

legendary /ˈledʒ(ə)ndərɪ/ *adj.* **1.** of or based on legends, described in a legend. **2.** (*colloq.*) famous, often talked about. [f. L (as prec.)]

legerdemain /ledʒədəˈmeɪn/ *n.* sleight of hand, juggling; trickery, sophistry. [f. F, = light of hand]

leger line /ˈledʒə(r)/ a short line added in a musical score for notes above or below the range of the staff. [var. of LEDGER]

legging *n.* (usu. in *pl.*) a protective outer covering of leather etc. for the leg from the knee to the ankle. [f. LEG]

leggy *adj.* long-legged. —**legginess** *n.* [f. LEG]

leghorn /ˈleghɔːn, lɪˈgɔːn/ *n.* **1.** fine plaited straw; a hat of this. **2. Leghorn,** one of a small hardy breed of domestic fowl. [f. *Leghorn* (*Livorno*) in Italy]

legible /ˈledʒɪb(ə)l/ *adj.* clear enough to be deciphered, readable. —**legibility** /-ˈbɪlɪtɪ/ *n.,* **legibly** *adv.* [f. L (*legere* read)]

legion /ˈliːdʒ(ə)n/ *n.* **1.** a division of 3,000–6,000 men in the ancient Roman army. **2.** a vast group, a multitude. —**American Legion,** an American association similar to the Royal British Legion. **Foreign Legion,** see separate entry. **Legion of Honour,** (F *légion d'honneur*) a French order of distinction conferred for civil or military services, founded by Napoleon I in 1802. **Royal British Legion,** an association of British ex-service men and women. [f. OF f. L *legere* choose)]

legionary *adj.* of a legion or legions. —*n.* a member of a legion; a legionary soldier in the ancient Roman army (ill. ARMOUR). [f. L (as prec.)]

legionnaire /liːdʒəˈneə(r)/ *n.* a member of the foreign legion or of the American or Royal British Legion. —**legionnaires' disease,** a form of bacterial pneumonia first identified after an outbreak at an American Legion meeting in 1976. [f. F (as LEGION)]

legislate /ˈledʒɪsleɪt/ *v.i.* to make laws. —**legislator** *n.* [as foll.]

legislation /ledʒɪsˈleɪʃ(ə)n/ *n.* law-making; the laws made. [f. L (*lex legis* law, *latio* proposing)]

legislative /ˈledʒɪslətɪv/ of or empowered to make legislation. [f. prec.]

legislature /ˈledʒɪsleɪtʃə(r)/ *n.* the legislative body of a State. [f. prec.]

legitimate /lɪˈdʒɪtɪmət/ *adj.* **1.** in accordance with the law or rules. **2.** (of a child) born of parents married to each other. **3.** logically acceptable, justifiable, —**legitimate drama** *or* **theatre,** plays of recognized merit, normal comedy and

tragedy as distinct from musical comedy, farce, revue, etc. The term arose in the 18th c. during the struggle of the patent theatres, Covent Garden and Drury Lane, against the illegitimate theatres springing up all over London. It covered plays dependent entirely on acting, with little or no singing, dancing, or spectacle. —**legitimacy** *n.,* **legitimately** *adv.* [f. L (*legitimus* lawful, f. *lex legis* law)]

legitimatize /lɪˈdʒɪtɪmətaɪz/ *v.t.* to legitimize. [f. prec.]

legitimize /lɪˈdʒɪtɪmaɪz/ *v.t.* to make legitimate; to serve as a justification for. —**legitimization** /-ˈzeɪʃ(ə)n/ *n.* [as LEGITIMATE]

legume /legjuːm/ *n.* a leguminous plant; a fruit or edible part or pod of this. [f. F f. L *legumen* (*legere* pick), because pickable by hand]

leguminous /lɪˈgjuːmɪnəs/ *adj.* of the family of plants Leguminosae, with seeds in pods (e.g. peas, beans). [as prec.]

lei /ˈleɪiː/ *n.* a Polynesian garland of flowers. [Hawaiian]

Leibniz /ˈlaɪbnɪts/, Gottfried Wilhelm (1646–1716), German rationalist philosopher. A man of wide-ranging expertise, who served at the court of the Duke of Brunswick-Lüneburg, he worked on the problem of the continuum and the laws of motion, and discovered the infinitesimal calculus independently of Newton, which made his disputes with Newton's followers acrimonious. He believed that the world is fundamentally harmonious and good. In his philosophical writings he argued that it is composed of single units (monads) which are simple yet each in its own way mirrors the whole universe; each is self-contained, but acts in harmony with every other, and they form a continuously ascending series from the lowest (which is next to nothing) to the highest (which is God; though in some places he speaks as though God were outside the series). Their pre-established harmony is ordained by God who, Leibniz argued, never acted except for a reason that required it, and so the world that he had created was the best of all possible worlds (a view satirized in Voltaire's *Candide*). Throughout his life Leibniz was ardently devoted to the cause of international peace.

Leicestershire /ˈlestəʃɪə(r)/ a midland county of England.

Leichhardt /ˈlaɪkhɑːt/, Friedrich Wilhelm Ludwig (1813–48), German-born explorer of Australia. Having emigrated to Australia in 1841, Leichhardt began a series of geological surveys of that continent, crossing from Moreton Bay to Port Esslington in 1843–5, but disappearing without trace in the area of the Cogoon River on another attempt at an east–west crossing in 1848.

Leics. *abbr.* Leicestershire.

Leighton /ˈleɪt(ə)n/, Frederic, Lord (1830–96), English painter and sculptor who was the leading exponent of Victorian neo-classicism. He studied painting in Italy, Germany, and Paris, and first gained renown with his work *Cimabue's Madonna carried in procession through the streets of Florence,* exhibited at the Royal Academy in 1855 and bought by Queen Victoria. He was chiefly a painter of large-scale mythological and genre scenes, and he dominated the London art world in his day. Made a baronet, President of the Royal Academy, and, in 1895, a peer, he enjoyed great success, building Leighton House in London, famous for its Arab Hall, decorated with objects collected on trips to the East.

Leipzig /ˈlaɪpzɪg/ a city in the south of East Germany, a centre of the publishing and music trade. An annual fair has been held there since the 12th c.

leisure /ˈleʒə(r)/ *n.* free time, time at one's disposal; the enjoyment of this. —**at leisure,** not occupied; in an unhurried manner. **at one's leisure,** when one has time. [f. AF f. L *licēre* be allowed]

leisured *adj.* having ample leisure. [f. prec.]

leisurely *adj.* unhurried, relaxed. —*adv.* without hurry. —**leisureliness** *n.* [f. LEISURE]

leitmotiv /ˈlaɪtməʊtiːf/ *n.* (also **leitmotif**) a theme associated throughout a musical etc. composition with a particular person or idea. [G (as LEAD[1], MOTIVE)]

Lely /ˈliːlɪ/, Sir Peter (1618–80), portrait painter, born in Germany of Dutch parents and trained at Haarlem in the Netherlands before coming to London in 1643, where he had a large practice by 1650. He became principal court painter to Charles II and attained a high social standing, being knighted in 1680. Many works survive, his early portraits imbued with a Dutch solidity. Less fluent than Van Dyck, he was a flattering if repetitious portraitist whose works mirror the external trappings of royal court life, but with little evidence of psychological insight. He consolidated the tradition of society portrait painting.

lemming /ˈlemɪŋ/ *n.* a small arctic rodent of the genus *Lemmus* etc., of which one species migrates in large numbers and has been reputed to continue headlong into the sea and drown. [Norw.]

lemon[1] /ˈlemən/ *n.* **1.** a pale-yellow oval fruit with acid juice; the tree bearing it (*Citrus limon*). **2.** pale yellow colour. **3.** (*slang*) a simpleton; something disappointing or unsuccessful. —**lemon cheese** or **curd,** a thick creamy spread made from lemons. —**lemony** *adj.* [f. OF f. Arab. (as LIME[2])]

lemon[2] /ˈlemən/ *n.* (in full **lemon sole**) a kind of plaice (*Microstomus kitt*). [f. F *limande*]

lemonade /leməˈneɪd/ *n.* a drink made from lemon-juice or a synthetic substitute with similar flavour. [f. LEMON[1]]

lemur /ˈliːmə(r)/ *n.* a nocturnal mammal of Madagascar of the genus *Lemur*, allied to the monkeys. [f. L *lemures* spirits of the dead, f. its spectre-like face]

Lena /ˈliːnə/ a river rising west of Lake Baikal, the most easterly of the three great Siberian rivers flowing to the Arctic Ocean, famous for the gold-fields in its basin.

Lenclos /lɑ̃ˈkloʊ/, Anne de (known as Ninon de Lenclos) (1620-1705), a famous French beauty, who retained her physical attractiveness until an advanced age, numbered many of the great Frenchmen of the day among her lovers, and presided over one of the most distinguished literary salons of the age.

lend *v.t.* (*past* & *p.p.* **lent**) **1.** to give or allow the use of (a thing) temporarily on the understanding that it or its equivalent will be returned. **2.** to provide (money) temporarily in return for payment of interest. **3.** to contribute as a temporary help or effect etc. —**lend an ear,** to listen. **lend a hand,** to help. **lend itself to,** to be suitable for. **lend oneself to,** to accommodate oneself to. —**lender** *n.* [OE (as LOAN)]

Lend-Lease *n.* an arrangement (1941) whereby the USA supplied equipment etc. to the UK and her allies in the Second World War, originally as a loan in return for the use of British-owned military bases.

length /leŋθ/ *n.* **1.** measurement or extent from end to end, especially along a thing's greatest dimension. **2.** the amount of time occupied by something. **3.** the distance a thing extends used as a unit of measurement; the length of a horse, boat, etc., as a measure of the lead in a race. **4.** the degree of thoroughness in an action. **5.** a piece of cloth etc. cut from a longer one; a piece of a certain length. **6.** the quantity of a vowel or syllable. **7.** (in cricket) the distance from the batsman at which the ball pitches; the proper amount of this. —**at length,** after a long time; taking a long time, in detail. [OE (as LONG[1])]

lengthen /ˈleŋθ(ə)n/ *v.t./i.* to make or become longer. [f. prec.]

lengthways *adv.* (also **lengthwise**) in a direction parallel with a thing's length.

lengthy *adj.* of unusual length; long and tedious. —**lengthily** *adv.*, **lengthiness** *n.* [f. LENGTH]

lenient /ˈliːnɪənt/ *adj.* merciful, not severe, mild. —**lenience** *n.* **leniency** *n.*, **leniently** *adv.* [f. L *lenire* soothe (*lenis* gentle)]

Lenin /ˈlenɪn/, Nicolai, the assumed name of Vladimir Ilyich Ulyanov (1870-1924), Russian revolutionary statesman. A lawyer by training, Lenin was arrested in 1895 for socialist agitation and was subsequently exiled to Siberia. Living in Switzerland from 1900, he became the leader of the Bolshevik party and took a prominent part in socialist organization and propaganda in the years preceding the First World War. He returned to Russia after the overthrow of the Tsar in 1917 and quickly established Bolshevik control over the revolution, emerging as Premier and virtual dictator of the new communist State. He took Russia out of the war and successfully resisted counter-revolutionary forces in the Russian Civil War (1918-21), but was forced to moderate his socio-economic policies to give the country a chance to recover from the dislocation caused by war and revolution. In 1918 he was severely injured by a would-be assassin, and died in 1924 before he had completed the reconstruction of the Marxist State. —**Leninist** *n.*

Leningrad /ˈlenɪngræd/ a city of the USSR on an inlet of the Gulf of Finland; pop. (1984) 4,832,000. It was founded in 1703 by Peter the Great as his 'Window on the West',

under the name St Petersburg, and was the capital of Russia from then until 1918. It was called Petrograd from 1914 until 1924, when it was renamed after Lenin. During the Second World War it was subjected to a 900-day siege which began in 1941.

Le Nôtre /lə ˈnəʊtr/, André (1613-1700), French landscape gardener who from the 1630s was engaged in design of the grounds of many châteaux and town houses. He designed some of the best examples of formal French gardens, including the parks of Vaux-le-Vicomte and Versailles, begun in 1655 and 1662 respectively. These incorporated his ideas on architecturally conceived garden schemes: geometric formality and perfect equilibrium of all the individual elements—sculpture, fountains, parterres, and open spaces. Le Nôtre's gardens became a part of the architecture, an extension of the châteaux themselves. His influence was felt throughout the Continent and in England, where his style was imitated.

lens /lenz/ *n.* **1.** a piece of a transparent substance with one or both sides curved for concentrating or dispersing light-rays in optical instruments. **2.** a combination of lenses in photography. **3.** the transparent substance behind the iris of the eye (ill. BODY 4). [L, = lentil (from its shape)]

Lent *n.* the period from Ash Wednesday to Easter Eve of which the 40 weekdays are devoted to fasting and penitence in commemoration of Christ's fasting in the wilderness. —**Lenten** *adj.* [f. *Lenten*, orig. as *n.* = spring, f. OE]

lent *past* & *p.p.* of LEND.

lentil /ˈlentɪl/ *n.* a kind of leguminous plant (*Lens esculenta*); its edible seed. [f. OF f. L *lenticula* (as LENS)]

lento /ˈlentəʊ/ *adj.* & *adv.* (*Mus.*) slow, slowly. [It.]

Leo[1] /ˈliːəʊ/ a sickle-shaped constellation, the Lion, fifth sign of the zodiac, which the sun enters about 21 July. A rich swarm of meteors (the Leonids) is associated with the constellation when dust from the disintegration of a comet of 1866, which had an orbital period of 33 years, collides with the atmosphere three times a century. [OE f. L, = lion]

Leo[2] /ˈliːəʊ/ the name of 13 popes:
Leo I, St, 'the Great' (d. 461), pope from 440 and Doctor of the Church. His statement of the doctrine of the Incarnation was accepted at the Council of Chalcedon (451). His greatest achievement was the extension and consolidation of the power of the Roman see, claiming jurisdiction in Africa, Spain, and Gaul. He persuaded the Huns to retire beyond the Danube, and secured concessions from the Vandals when they captured Rome.
Leo X (Giovanni de' Medici, 1475-1521) pope from 1513, who excommunicated Luther and bestowed on Henry VIII of England the title of 'Defender of the Faith'.

Leo[3] /ˈliːəʊ/ the name of 6 Byzantine emperors:
Leo I 'the Great', emperor 457-74.
Leo III (*c*.680-741), emperor 717-41. Known as 'the Isaurian' after the dynasty which he founded, Leo came to prominence as a soldier before overthrowing Theodosius III and seizing the throne. He threw back several Muslim invasions and carried out an extensive series of financial, legal, administrative, and military reforms, but his iconoclastic policies caused severe problems and led to a complete rupture with the papacy.

Leonardo da Vinci /liːəˈnɑːdəʊ dɑː ˈvɪntʃɪ/ (1452-1519), Italian painter and designer, a supreme example of a Renaissance genius, born at Vinci in Tuscany, the illegitimate son of a Florentine notary. He devoted his restlessly curious mind and indefatigable mental energy to a variety of theoretical and practical problems, making studies of flowers, clouds, skeletons, etc., from nature, drawing up plans for a type of aircraft (see HELICOPTER) and a submarine, and anticipating many of the machines and methods of modern mechanical engineering, and though not always able to see things through to a successful practical conclusion emerged as the most divergent thinker of his period. The most tangible examples of his creative energies are his paintings, although it is unlikely that he saw himself as a full-time artist. A period in Milan (1482-99) saw the execution of three of his great works, the *Virgin of the Rocks*, the *Sforza Monument* (never completed), and the *Last Supper* fresco in the refectory of Sta Maria delle Grazie. He painted the *Mona Lisa* in Florence (*c*.1504-5), and his last work was *St John* (*c*.1515) an even more enigmatic work than the better-known portrait. He died at Cloux (now Clos-Lucé) in France, having left Italy in 1516 at the invitation of Francis I. The nineteen known sketchbooks and notebooks of Leonardo's work reveal his wide range of interests and bear witness to his place as one who helped to usher in the High Renaissance.

leonine /ˈliːənaɪn/ adj. of or like a lion. [f. OF or L (leo lion)]

leopard /ˈlepəd/ n. **1.** a large African and South Asian carnivorous animal (*Panthera pardus*) of the cat family, with a dark-spotted yellowish-fawn or black coat, a panther. The name was originally given to the animal now called a cheetah (the 'hunting-leopard') which was thought to be a cross between the lion and a 'pard' or panther (formerly supposed to be a more powerful leopard). The animal varies greatly in size and markings. The black form is widely known as the 'black panther'. **2.** any of various similar animals. **3.** (in heraldry) a lion passant guardant as in the arms of England. —**leopardess** n. fem. [f. OF f. L (as LEO, pardus panther)]

Leopold I /ˈlɪəpəʊld/ (1790–1865), king of Belgium 1831–65. The fourth son of the Duke of Saxe-Coburg-Saalfield, Leopold was an uncle of Queen Victoria. In 1830 he refused the throne of Greece, but a year later accepted that of newly independent Belgium, reigning peacefully thereafter.

leotard /ˈliːətɑːd/ n. a close-fitting one-piece garment worn by dancers etc. [f. J. *Léotard*, French trapeze artist (d. 1870)]

Lepanto /ləˈpæntəʊ/ a strait at the entrance to the Gulf of Corinth, scene of a naval battle (1571) in which the fleet of the Holy League (the papacy, Venice, and Spain) under the command of Don John of Austria defeated a large Turkish fleet, ending for the time being the Turkish naval threat in the Mediterranean.

leper /ˈlepə(r)/ n. **1.** a person with leprosy. **2.** a person shunned on moral grounds. [orig.=leprosy, f. OF f. L f. Gk *lepra* (*lepros* scaly)]

lepidopterous /lepɪˈdɒptərəs/ adj. of the Lepidoptera or insects with four scale-covered wings, including moths and butterflies. —**lepidopterist** n. [f. Gk *lepis* scale + *pteron* wing]

leprechaun /ˈleprəkɔːn/ n. a small mischievous sprite in Irish folklore. [f. OIr. *luchorpán* (*lu* small, *corp* body)]

leprosy /ˈleprəsɪ/ n. a chronic infectious bacterial disease affecting the nerves, skin, and certain other tissues of the human body, resulting in mutilations and deformities. It is caused by the presence of the bacillus *Mycobacterium leprae*, first demonstrated by the Norwegian Gerhard Hansen (1841–1912; whence its alternative name *Hansen's disease*) and is now almost entirely a tropical disease, with many millions of sufferers in Africa and Asia. Common in medieval Europe, it was gradually stamped out by strict isolation and improved hygiene. The disease takes two main forms, of which the more acute malignant type is sometimes fatal. To the layman it was always a disease that created both fear and superstition, but modern methods of treatment are effective if applied in the early stages. Among those who have worked heroically among sufferers are the missionary Father Damien (1840–89) and Albert Schweitzer. [f. foll.]

leprous /ˈleprəs/ adj. of leprosy; having or resembling leprosy. [f. OF f. L (as LEPER)]

lesbian /ˈlezbɪən/ n. a homosexual woman. —adj. of lesbians; of homosexuality in women. —**lesbianism** n. [f. foll.]

Lesbos /ˈlezbɒs/ the largest of the Greek islands, lying off the western coast of Turkey, whose artistic Golden Age of the late 7th and early 6th c. BC produced the poets Alcaeus and Sappho.

lèse-majesté /leɪzˈmæʒesteɪ/ n. (also **lese-majesty** /liːzˈmædʒɪstɪ/) **1.** treason; an insult to a sovereign or ruler. **2.** presumptuous conduct. [f. F *lèse-majesté* f. L (as foll., MAJESTY)]

lesion /ˈliːʒ(ə)n/ n. **1.** damage, injury. **2.** a harmful change in the functioning or texture of an organ of the body. [f. OF f. L *laesio* (*laedere* injure)]

Lesotho /ləˈsuːtuː/ a landlocked mountainous country, a member State of the Commonwealth with few natural resources (though diamonds are found), forming an enclave in the republic of South Africa; pop. (est. 1981) 1,204,000; official languages, Sesotho and English; capital, Maseru. The country came under British protection (as Basutoland) in 1868, and became an independent kingdom in 1966, changing its name to Lesotho.

less adj. **1.** smaller in size, degree, duration, number, etc. **2.** of smaller quantity, not so much. **3.** (D) fewer. —adv. to a smaller extent, in a lower degree. —n. a smaller amount, quantity, or number. —prep. minus, deducting. [OE]

-less /-lɪs/ suffix forming adjectives and adverbs from nouns,

in the sense 'not having, without, free from' (*doubtless*, *powerless*), and from verbs, in the sense 'unable to be —ed', 'not —ing' (*fathomless*, *tireless*). [OE]

lessee /leˈsiː/ n. a person holding property by lease, a tenant. [f. AF (as LEASE)]

lessen v.t./i. to make or become less, to diminish. [f. LESS]

Lesseps /leˈseps/, Ferdinand Marie, Vicomte de (1805–94), French diplomat, best known for his work on the Suez Canal. He spent several years in Egypt in the French consular service, and becoming aware of plans to join the Mediterranean and Red Seas by means of a sea-level canal without locks, from 1854 onwards devoted his skills to the project. Digging by Egyptian labourers began in 1859 but was slow until 1863 when machine dredgers were brought into use and enabled the canal to be opened with great ceremony in 1869. Ten years later he became involved in the building of the Panama Canal, but not being an engineer he did not realize the difficulties of this very different enterprise, which involves raising the level of the canal by huge locks to cross the mountainous isthmus. This and the incidence of yellow fever caused abandonment of the project in 1888 and the Panama Canal was not built until 1912, well after de Lesseps' death.

lesser adj. (usu. attrib.) not so great as the other or the rest. [compar. of LESS]

Lessing[1] /ˈlesɪŋ/, Doris (May) (1919-), English novelist and short-story writer, brought up in Southern Rhodesia (now Zimbabwe). Her most substantial work, the novel sequence *Children of Darkness* (1952–69), reflects her preoccupation with feminism and left-wing politics.

Lessing[2] /ˈlesɪŋ/, Gotthold Ephraim (1729–81), German dramatist and critic. His principal dramatic works were the tragedies *Emilia Galotti* (1772) and *Miss Sara Sampson* (1755), the first significant domestic tragedy in German, the serious comedy *Minna von Barnhelm* (1767), and *Nathan der Weise* (1779), a plea for religious toleration. In his critical works, such as *Briefe die neueste Litteratur betreffend* (1759–65) and *Laokoon* (1766), he emancipated German literature from the narrow conventions of the French classical school. Lessing won the admiration of many 19th-c. English writers for his mundane and liberal beliefs and the clarity of his prose.

lesson /ˈles(ə)n/ n. **1.** a spell of teaching. **2.** (in pl.) systematic instruction in a subject. **3.** a thing to be learnt by a pupil. **4.** an experience that serves to warn or encourage. **5.** a passage from the Bible read aloud during a church service. [f. OF *leçon* f. L *lectio* (*legere* read)]

lessor /leˈsɔː(r)/ n. a person who lets a property by lease. [AF (as LEASE)]

lest conj. **1.** in order that not, for fear that. **2.** that. [OE, = whereby less that]

let[1] v.t./i. (**-tt-**; past & p.p. **let**) **1.** to allow, enable, or cause to, not to prevent or forbid. **2.** to allow or cause to come, go, or pass. **3.** to grant the use of (rooms, land, etc.) for rent or hire. **4.** as an auxiliary verb (with 1st and 3rd persons) expressing commands, appeals, etc. —n. the letting of rooms, land, etc. —**let alone**, to refrain from interfering with or doing; apart from, far less or more than, let be, to refrain from interfering with or doing. **let down**, to lower; to let out air from (an inflated tyre etc.); to fail to support or satisfy, to disappoint; to lengthen (a garment); to treat (gently etc.). **let-down** n. a disappointment. **let go**, to release, to loose one's hold (*of*). **let oneself go**, to abandon self-restraint. **let in for**, to involve in (loss or difficulty). **let loose**, to release. **let off**, to fire (a gun), to explode (a bomb); to ignite (a firework); to excuse from (duties etc.); to give little or no punishment to. **let off steam**, to allow steam to escape; to release pent-up energy or feeling. **let on**, (colloq.) to reveal a secret. **let out**, to release from restraint or obligation; to reveal (a secret etc.), to make (a garment) looser; to put out to rent or to contract. **let-out** n. an opportunity to escape. **let up**, (colloq.) to become less intense or severe, to relax one's efforts. **let-up** n. a reduction in intensity, a relaxation of effort. **to let**, available to rent. [OE]

let[2] n. an obstruction of the ball or a player in tennis etc., requiring the ball to be served again. —v.t. (**-tt-**; past & p.p. **letted** or **let**) (archaic) to hinder, to obstruct. —**without let or hindrance** unimpeded. [OE]

-let /-lɪt/ suffix forming nouns usu. diminutive (*flatlet*) or denoting articles of ornament or dress (*anklet*). [orig. f. OF, wrongly understood as dim. suffix]

lethal /ˈliːθ(ə)l/ adj. causing or sufficient to cause death.

—lethality /-ˈælɪtɪ/ *n.*, **lethally** *adv.* [f. L *let(h)alis* (*letum* death)]

lethargy /ˈleθədʒɪ/ *n.* lack of energy or vitality; abnormal drowsiness. **—lethargic** /lɪˈθɑːdʒɪk/ *adj.*, **lethargically** *adv.* [f. OF f. L f. Gk (*lēthargos* forgetful)]

Lethe /ˈliːθɪ/ (*Gk myth.*) one of the rivers of the underworld, whose water when drunk made the souls of the dead forget their life on earth. [Gk, = oblivion]

Leto /ˈliːtəʊ/ (*Gk myth.*) daughter of a Titan, mother (by Zeus) of Artemis and Apollo.

Lett *n.* a member of a people living near the Baltic, mainly in Latvia. [f. G f. Lettish *Latvi*]

letter /ˈletə(r)/ *n.* **1.** any of the characters, representing one or more of the simple or compound sounds used in speech, of which written words are composed; an alphabetic symbol. **2.** a written or printed communication, usually sent by post or messenger; (in *pl.*) an addressed legal or formal document. **3.** the precise terms of a statement, strict verbal interpretation. **4.** (in *pl.*) literature; acquaintance with books; erudition. —*v.t.* **1.** to inscribe letters on. **2.** to classify with letters. **—letter-bomb** *n.* a terrorist explosive device in the form of a letter sent through the post. **letter-box** *n.* a slit in a door, with a hinged flap, through which letters are delivered; a post-box. **letter of credit,** a letter from a bank authorizing the bearer to draw money from another bank. **man of letters,** a scholar or author. **to the letter,** with adherence to every detail. [f. OF f. L *littera*]

lettered *adj.* well-read, well-educated. [f. prec.]

letterhead *n.* a printed heading on stationery; stationery with this.

letterpress *n.* **1.** the printed words in an illustrated book. **2.** printing from raised type.

Lettish /ˈletɪʃ/ *adj.* of the Letts. —*n.* the language of the Letts, Latvian. [f. LETT]

lettuce /ˈletɪs/ *n.* a garden plant (*Lactuca sativa*) with crisp leaves used as salad. [f. OF f. L *lactuca* (*lac* milk, f. its milky juice)]

leuco- /ˈluːkəʊ-/ *in comb.* white. [f. Gk *leukos* white]

leucocyte /ˈluːkəʊsaɪt/ *n.* a white or colourless corpuscle in the blood. [f. LEUCO- + -CYTE]

leucotomy /luːˈkɒtəmɪ/ *n.* surgical incision into the white tissue of the frontal lobe of the brain to relieve some cases of mental disorder. [f. LEUCO- + -TOMY]

leukaemia /luːˈkiːmɪə/ *n.* a progressive disease with an abnormal accumulation of white corpuscles in the tissues and usually in the blood. [G f. Gk (*leukos* white, *haima* blood)]

Levalloisean /ləvælˈwɑːzɪən/ *adj.* of a flint-working technique first employed in the late Acheulian period in western Europe and associated with numerous Mousterian industries throughout the world, named after the type-site of Levallois in northern France, NW of Paris. The technique involves trimming a piece of flint and then striking the required flake from it; the flake produced has one face trimmed and the other plane, and the residual core is tortoise-shaped, domed with one face plane. —*n.* this industry. [f. *Levallois*]

Levant /lɪˈvænt/ the eastern part of the Mediterranean together with its islands and neighbouring countries. **—Levantine** /lɪˈvæntaɪn, ˈlev(ə)n-/ *adj.* & *n.* [F, = point of sunrise, east (*lever* rise)]

levee[1] /ˈlevɪ/ *n.* (*archaic*) an assembly of visitors or guests, especially at a formal reception; (*hist.*) a sovereign's assembly for men only. [f. F *levé* var. of *lever* rising (as LEVY)]

levee[2] /ˈlevɪ/ *n.* **1.** an embankment against river floods; a river's natural embankment (ill. RIVERS). **2.** a landing-place. [f. F *levée* (*lever* raise, as LEVY)]

level /ˈlev(ə)l/ *n.* **1.** a horizontal line or plane, one joining points of equal height. **2.** a measured height or value etc., a position on a scale; social, moral, or intellectual standard. **3.** a plane of rank or authority. **4.** an instrument for giving or testing a horizontal line or plane. **5.** a more or less flat surface or area. —*adj.* **1.** horizontal. **2.** on a level or equality (with); at the same height, rank, or position on a scale. **3.** (of ground) flat, without hills or hollows. **4.** steady, even, uniform. **5.** equable or well-balanced in quality, style, temper, judgement, etc. —*v.t./i.* (**-ll-**) **1.** to make or become level, even, or uniform. **2.** to place on the same level; to bring *up* or *down* to a standard. **3.** to raze or demolish. **4.** to aim (a missile or gun). **5.** to direct (an accusation etc., or *absol.*, *at* or *against*). **do one's level best,** (*colloq.*) to do one's utmost. **find one's level,** to reach the social or intellectual level etc. that is most suitable for oneself. **level**

crossing, a crossing of a railway and road, or two railways, at the same level. **level-headed** *adj.* mentally well-balanced, sensible. **level pegging,** equality of scores or achievements. **on the level,** (*colloq.*) honest, honestly, without deception. **on a level with,** in the same horizontal plane, as, equal with. —**leveller** *n.* [f. OF f. L *libella* (*libra* scales, balance)]

lever /ˈliːvə(r)/ *n.* **1.** a bar resting on a pivot and used to raise a heavy or firmly fixed object. **2.** a device consisting of a straight bar or other rigid structure of which one point (the *fulcrum*) is fixed, another is connected with the force (*weight*) to be resisted or acted upon, and a third is connected with the force (*power*) applied. It is the simplest, oldest, and most adaptable of mechanisms. **3.** a projecting handle moved to operate mechanism. **4.** a means of exerting moral pressure. —*v.t./i.* to use a lever; to lift or move etc. by means of a lever. [f. AF (*lever* raise f. L *levare*)]

leverage /ˈliːvərɪdʒ/ *n.* **1.** the action or power of a lever. **2.** the means of accomplishing a purpose; power, influence. [f. prec.]

leveret /ˈlevərɪt/ *n.* a young hare, especially in the first year. [f. AF dim. of *levre* hare f. L *lepus*]

Le Verrier /lə ˈverjeɪ/, Urbain (1811–77), French mathematician whose analysis of the motions of the planets suggested that an unknown body was perturbing the orbit of Uranus (the same conclusion was reached almost simultaneously by the English mathematician John Couch Adams). Under the prompting of Le Verrier, the German astronomer Galle searched the region of the sky in which the mysterious perturber was predicted to lie, and discovered the planet Neptune on 23 Sept. 1846.

Levi /ˈliːvaɪ/ **1.** Hebrew patriarch, son of Jacob and Leah (Gen. 29: 34). **2.** the tribe of Israel traditionally descended from him.

leviathan /lɪˈvaɪəθ(ə)n/ *n.* **1.** (in the Bible) a sea monster. **2.** anything very large or powerful. [f. L f. Heb.]

Levis /ˈliːvaɪz/ *n.pl.* [P] a type of (usually blue) denim jeans or overalls reinforced with rivets. [f. *Levi* Strauss, orig. US manufacturer in 1860s]

levitate /ˈlevɪteɪt/ *v.t./i.* to rise and float in the air, to cause to do this (esp. with reference to spiritualism). **—levitation** /-ˈteɪʃ(ə)n/ *n.* [f. L *levis* light, after *gravitate*]

Levite /ˈliːvaɪt/ *n.* a member of the Hebrew tribe of Levi, from which priests were drawn until after the Exile, when Levites were allotted only inferior duties in the Temple. [f. L f. Gk f. *Levi*, son of Jacob]

Leviticus /lɪˈvɪtɪkəs/ *n.* the third book of the Old Testament, containing details of laws and ritual. [L, = (book) of the Levites]

levity /ˈlevɪtɪ/ *n.* a disposition to make light of weighty matters, frivolity, lack of serious thought. [f. L *levitas* (*levis* light)]

levy /ˈlevɪ/ *v.t.* **1.** to impose or collect (a payment etc.) compulsorily. **2.** to enrol (troops etc.). **3.** to wage (war). —*n.* **1.** levying. **2.** a payment etc. levied. **3.** (in *pl.*) troops levied. [f. OF *levée* (*lever* raise f. L *levare*)]

lewd /ljuːd/ *adj.* lascivious; indecent; treating sexual matters in a vulgar way. **—lewdly** *adv.*, **lewdness** *n.* [OE, = lay (LAY[2])]

Lewis[1] /ˈluːɪs/, Clive Staples (1898–1963), English literary scholar who taught at Oxford University from 1925 to 1954 and then held a chair of English at Cambridge until 1963. His works include science fiction, and he became celebrated for his books of popular Christian apologetics, including *The Screwtape Letters* (1942), and his series of fantasies for children about the imaginary country of 'Narnia'.

Lewis[2] /ˈluːɪs/, Meriwether (1774–1809), American explorer. Formerly private secretary to President Jefferson, he was named by the President to lead an expedition to explore the newly acquired Louisiana Purchase, and chose William Clark as co-leader. Between 1804 and 1806 the Lewis and Clark Expedition successfully crossed America from St Louis to the mouth of the Columbia River and returned (once again by land). During the last two years of his life (1807–9) Lewis served as Governor of the Louisiana Territory.

Lewis[3] /ˈluːɪs/, Percy Wyndham (1882–1957), British novelist and painter, a leader of the vorticist movement, who with Ezra Pound edited the journal *Blast* (1914–15). His satirical novels and polemical works include *The Apes of God* (1930), *The Revenge for Love* (1937), and *The Human Age* (1928–55, unfinished). He expounds his philosophical ideas in *Time and the Western World* (1927) and in his two autobiographies (1937, 1950). Critical of the increasing mechanization and hollowness of 20th-c. civilization, his savage satirical attacks on his contemporaries (especially the Bloomsbury Group), and his sympathies with Fascism and Hitler, alienated him from the literary world.

Lewis[4] /ˈluːɪs/, (Harry) Sinclair (1885-1951), American novelist, who became highly successful with *Main Street* (1920), a social satire on dull small-town Mid-West life. He strengthened his reputation with *Babitt* (1922), about a Mid-West house agent who questions conventions in middle-class society, *Arrowsmith* (1925), describing the career of a bacteriologist, *Elmer Gantry* (1927), a satiric view of Mid-West religious evangelism, and *Dodsworth* (1929). He was awarded the Nobel Prize for literature in 1930, the first American writer to achieve this.

lexical /ˈleksɪk(ə)l/ *adj.* **1.** of the words of a language. **2.** of a lexicon or dictionary. [f. Gk (as LEXICON)]

lexicography /leksɪˈkɒɡrəfɪ/ *n.* the compilation of dictionaries. —**lexicographer** *n.*, **lexicographical** /-ˈɡræfɪk(ə)l/ *adj.* [f. foll. + -GRAPHY]

lexicology /leksɪˈkɒlədʒɪ/ *n.* the study of words and their form, history, and meaning. [f. foll. + -GRAPHY]

lexicon /ˈleksɪk(ə)n/ *n.* **1.** a dictionary, especially of Greek, Hebrew, Syriac, or Arabic. Until the 19th c. dictionaries of these languages were usually in Latin and entitled *lexicon* rather than *dictionarius*. **2.** the vocabulary of a person, language, branch of knowledge, etc. [f. Gk *lexicon* (*biblion* book), f. *lexis* word (*legō* speak)]

lexis /ˈleksɪs/ *n.* words, vocabulary; a total stock of words. [Gk (see prec.)]

ley[1] /leɪ/ *n.* land temporarily under grass. [f. *ley, lea* adj. fallow (as LAY[1], LIE[1])]

ley[2] /liː, leɪ/ *n.* the supposed straight line of a prehistoric track, usually between hilltops, with identifying points such as ponds, mounds, etc., marking its route. [var. of LEA]

Leyden jar /ˈleɪd(ə)n/ a kind of electrical condenser with a glass jar as a dielectric between sheets of tin foil, invented in 1745 at Leyden University. [f. *Leyden* (now *Leiden*) in Holland]

LF *abbr.* low frequency.

l.h. left hand.

Lhasa /ˈlɑːsə/ the capital of the Autonomous Region of Tibet in SW China, situated in the Himalayas at 3,600 m (*c.*11,800 ft.); pop. (est. 1970) 175,000. Its inaccessibility and the hostility of the Tibetan Buddhist priests to foreign visitors earned it the title of the Forbidden City. It was the spiritual centre of Lamaism and the seat (until 1959) of the Dalai Lama.

Li *symbol* lithium.

liability /laɪəˈbɪlɪtɪ/ *n.* **1.** being liable. **2.** a troublesome person, a handicap. **3.** (in *pl.*) debts etc. for which one is liable. [f. foll.]

liable /ˈlaɪəb(ə)l/ *predic. adj.* **1.** legally obliged; subject or under an obligation *to*. **2.** exposed or open *to* (something undesirable); apt or likely *to*. **3.** answerable (*for*). [perh. f. OF *lier* bind f. L *ligare*]

liaise /lɪˈeɪz/ *v.i.* (*colloq.*) to act as a liaison or go-between. [back-formation f. foll.]

liaison /lɪˈeɪz(ə)n/ *n.* **1.** communication and co-operation between units of an organization; a person effecting this. **2.** an illicit sexual relationship. [F (*lier* bind, as LIABLE)]

liana /lɪˈɑːnə/ *n.* a climbing and twining plant in tropical forests.[f. F *liane, lierne* clematis]

liar /ˈlaɪə(r)/ *n.* a person who tells lies. [f. LIE[2]]

lias /ˈlaɪəs/ *n.* a blue limestone rich in fossils. —**liassic** /lɪˈæsɪk/ *adj.* [f. OF *liois*]

Lib. *abbr.* **1.** Liberal. **2.** (*colloq.*) liberation.

libation /laɪˈbeɪʃ(ə)n/ *n.* the pouring of a drink-offering to a god; such a drink-offering. [f. L (*libare* pour as an offering)]

libel /ˈlaɪb(ə)l/ *n.* **1.** a published false statement that is damaging to a person's reputation; the act of publishing it. **2.** a false defamatory statement or representation.—*v.t.* (**-ll-**) to utter or publish a libel against. —**be a libel on**, do injustice to. —**libellous** *adj.* [f. OF f. L *libellus* dim. of *liber* book]

liberal /ˈlɪbər(ə)l/ *adj.* **1.** given or giving freely; abundant. **2.** open-minded, not prejudiced; not strict or rigorous; (of studies etc.) for general broadening of the mind. **3.** favouring moderate political and social reform; **Liberal**, of the Liberal Party. —*n.* **1.** a person of liberal views. **2. Liberal**, a member or supporter of the Liberal Party. —**liberalism** *n.*,

liberality /-ˈrælɪtɪ/ *n.*, **liberally** *adv.* [orig. = befitting a free man, f. OF f. L (*liber* free)]

liberalize /ˈlɪbərəlaɪz/ *v.t.* to make more liberal or less strict. —**liberalization** /-ˈzeɪʃ(ə)n/ *n.* [f. prec.]

Liberal Party a British political party which emerged in the 1860s from the old Whig party, encompassing not only former Whigs but also Radicals and former Peelite Conservatives. Dominated by Gladstone until the 1890s, the Liberal party advocated free trade, political reform, and a restrained foreign policy. With Gladstone's conversion to Home Rule, the party was weakened by the defection of the Unionists and only returned to a position of strength under Campbell-Bannerman and Asquith in the decade before the First World War. Lloyd George's revolt against Asquith's wartime administration fatally weakened the Liberals and after the war they lost their position as one of the two major parties to Labour. In recent years the Liberals have enjoyed a revival but have not yet regained their former position of eminence.

liberate /ˈlɪbəreɪt/ *v.t.* **1.** to set free. **2.** to free (a country) from an oppressor or enemy occupation. **3.** to free from rigid social conventions. —**liberation** /-ˈreɪʃ(ə)n/ *n.*, **liberator** *n.* [f. L *liberare* (as LIBERAL)]

Liberia /laɪˈbɪərɪə/ a country in West Africa, bordering on the Atlantic, between the Ivory Coast and Sierra Leone; pop. (est. 1981) 1,926,000; official language, English; capital, Monrovia. Liberia is the oldest republic in the continent of Africa, and the only one never to have known colonial status. Founded in 1822 as a settlement for freed Black slaves from the USA, with which country it maintains a traditional friendship, it was proclaimed independent in 1847. The country's rich mineral resources form the basis of its economy, and it is a major producer of iron ore. —**Liberian** *adj.* & *n.* [f. L *liber* free]

libertine /ˈlɪbətiːn/ *n.* a dissolute or licentious man. —*adj.* licentious. [f. L, = freedman (*liber* free)]

liberty /ˈlɪbətɪ/ *n.* **1.** freedom from captivity, slavery, imprisonment, or despotic control. **2.** the right or power to do as one pleases. **3.** a right or privilege granted by authority. —**at liberty**, free, not imprisoned; allowed. **take liberties**, to behave in an unduly familiar manner; to interpret facts etc. too freely. [f. OF f. L *libertas* (*liber* free)]

Liberty, Statue of a statue on an island at the entrance to New York harbour, a symbol of welcome to immigrants, representing a draped female figure carrying a book of laws in her left hand and holding aloft a torch in her right. Dedicated in 1886, it was the work of the French sculptor F. A. Bartholdi (who used his mother as a model) and was the gift of the French to the American people, commemorating the alliance of France and the USA during the War of American Independence and marking its centenary.

libidinous /lɪˈbɪdɪnəs/ *adj.* lustful. [f. L (as foll.)]

libido /lɪˈbiːdəʊ/ *n.* (*pl.* **-os**) a psychic impulse or drive, especially that associated with sexual desire. —**libidinal** /lɪˈbɪdɪn(ə)l/ *adj.* [L, = lust]

Libra /ˈliːbrə/ a constellation and the seventh sign of the zodiac, the Scales, which the sun enters at the autumnal equinox. [L, = scales, balance]

librarian /laɪˈbreərɪən/ *n.* a person in charge of or assisting in a library. —**librarianship** *n.* [f. L (as foll.)]

library /ˈlaɪbrərɪ/ *n.* **1.** a collection of books for reading or borrowing. **2.** a room or building where these are kept. **3.** a similar collection of films, records, computer routines, etc.; the place where they are kept. **4.** a series of books issued in similar bindings as a set. [f. OF f. L (*liber* book)]

libretto /lɪˈbretəʊ/ *n.* (*pl.* **-ti** /-tɪ/, **-tos**) the text of an opera or other long musical vocal work. —**librettist** *n.* [It., dim. of *libro* book f. L *liber*]

Libreville /ˈliːbrəviːl/ the capital of Gabon; pop. 251,000.

Libya /ˈlɪbɪə/ a country in North Africa consisting chiefly of desert, with a narrow coastal plain bordering on the Mediterranean Sea; pop. (est. 1981) 3,100,000; official language, Arabic; capital, Tripoli. The country has major deposits of oil, now the main source of revenue. Having formed part of the Roman Empire, Libya was conquered by the Arabs, finally brought under Turkish domination in the 16th c., and annexed by Italy in 1912 and partially colonized. During the Second World War it was the scene of heavy fighting, and, after a brief period of French and British administration, achieved full independence in 1951. After prolonged political disturbances the country has emerged with a radical revolutionary leadership and an economy bolstered by its large oil exports. Relations with neighbouring countries are very difficult. —**Libyan** *adj. & n.*

lice *pl.* of LOUSE.

licence /ˈlaɪsəns/ *n.* **1.** a permit from the government etc. to own or do something or carry on some trade. **2.** leave, permission. **3.** excessive liberty of action. **4.** disregard of law, rules, or custom; a writer's or artist's transgression of established rules for effect. [f. OF f. L (*licēre* be allowed)]

license /ˈlaɪsəns/ *v.t.* **1.** to grant a licence to or for. **2.** to authorize the use of (premises) for a certain purpose, especially the sale of alcoholic liquor. [f. prec.]

licensee /laɪsənˈsiː/ *n.* a holder of a licence, especially to sell alcoholic liquor. [f. prec.]

licentiate /laɪˈsenʃɪət/ *n.* a holder of a certificate of competence to practise a certain profession. [f. L (as LICENCE)]

licentious /laɪˈsenʃəs/ *adj.* disregarding the rules of conduct, especially in sexual matters. —**licentiousness** *n.* [f. L (as LICENCE)]

lichee var. of LITCHI.

lichen /ˈlaɪkən, ˈlɪtʃən/ *n.* a plant organism of the group Lichenes, composed of a fungus and an alga in association, usually of grey green, or yellow tint growing on and colouring rocks, tree-trunks, walls, roofs, etc. There are encrusting, leaflike, and branching forms (ill. PLANTS). The alga provides nutrients for the fungus, and the fungus presumably supplies a suitable protective environment. Classification is complicated because many types were named before their symbiotic nature was realized; they are now classified mainly by their fungal component. Lichens are small, slow-growing, very hardy, and are distributed world-wide, often growing on bare rock surfaces and in polar regions where other plants cannot survive, forming an important source of food for browsing animals in tundra regions. Their economic uses include the production of dyes, and they are also used as pollution indicators. —**lichenous** *adj.* [L, f. Gk *leikhēn*]

lich-gate *n.* a roofed gateway to a churchyard, where a coffin awaits the clergyman's arrival. [OE *lic* corpse + GATE]

licit /ˈlɪsɪt/ *adj.* not forbidden. —**licitly** *adv.* [f. L *licitus* (as LICENCE)]

lick *v.t./i.* **1.** to pass the tongue over; to take *up* or *off* or make *clean* by doing this. **2.** (of a flame or waves etc.) to move like a tongue, to touch lightly. **3.** (*slang*) to thrash. **4.** (*slang*) defeat; to excel. —*n.* **1.** an act of licking with the tongue. **2.** a blow with a stick etc. **3.** (*slang*) a (fast) pace. — **a lick and a promise,** (*colloq.*) a slight and hasty wash. **lick into shape,** to make presentable or efficient. **lick one's chops** *or* **lips,** to look forward with relish. **lick one's wounds,** to be in retirement trying to recover after a defeat. **lick a person's boots,** to be servile towards him or her. [OE]

lid *n.* **1.** a hinged or removable cover, especially at the top of a container. **2.** an eyelid. **3.** (*slang*) a hat. —**put the lid on,** (*slang*) to be the culmination of; to put a stop to. —**lidded** *adj.* [OE]

lido /ˈliːdəʊ/ *n.* (*pl.* -os) a public open-air swimming-pool or bathing-beach. [It., name of beach near Venice]

lie[1] /laɪ/ *v.i.* (*past* lay; *p.p.* lain; *partic.* lying) **1.** to be in or assume a horizontal position on a supporting surface. **2.** to be resting on a surface. **3.** to be or be kept or remain in a specified state or place; to be situated; (of troops) to be encamped. **4.** (of an abstract thing) to exist or be found. **5.** to be spread out to view. **6.** (*Law*) to be admissible or able to be upheld. —*n.* the way, direction, or position in which a thing lies. —**lie down,** to assume a lying position; to have a short rest. **lie-down** *n.* a short rest. **lie down under,** to accept (an insult etc.) without protest. **lie in,** to remain in bed in the morning; to be brought to bed in childbirth. **lie-in** *n.* remaining in bed in the morning. **lie low,** to keep quiet or unseen; to be discreet about one's intentions. **lie of the land,** the state of affairs. **lie with,** to be the responsibility of. **take lying down,** to accept (an insult etc.) without protest. [OE]

lie[2] *n.* **1.** an intentionally false statement. **2.** an imposture, a thing that deceives. —*v.i.* (*partic.* lying) to tell lies; (of a thing) to be deceptive. —**give the lie to,** to serve to show the falsity of (a supposition etc.). **lie-detector** *n.* an instrument for determining whether a person is telling the truth by measuring physiological changes. The first instrument so used was devised by J. A. Larson in Berkeley, California, in 1921. [OE]

Liebig /ˈliːbɪx/, Baron Justus von (1803–73), German chem-

ist and outstanding teacher. With the German chemist Friedrich Wöhler (1800–82), famous for his synthesis of urea, he discovered in 1831 the 'benzoyl radical' (now known as the benzoyl group), and demonstrated that such radicals were groups of atoms that remained unchanged in many chemical reactions. He applied chemistry to physiology and to agriculture (which inspired the founding of the Rothamsted Agricultural Research Station), stressed the importance of artificial manures (fertilizers), and developed techniques for organic quantitative analysis.

Liechtenstein /ˈlɪkt(ə)nstaɪn/ a small independent principality (created in 1719) in the Rhine valley between Switzerland and Austria; pop. (1983) 26,512; official language, German; capital, Vaduz. —**Liechtensteiner** *n.*

lied /liːt/ *n.* (*pl.* **lieder** /ˈliːdə(r)/) a German song, especially of the Romantic period, e.g. one composed by Schubert, Schumann, Brahms, Wolf. [G]

lief /liːf/ *adv.* (*archaic*) gladly, willingly (usu. *had* or *would lief*). [orig. adj., f. OE, = dear]

liege /liːdʒ/ *adj.* (usu. *hist.*) entitled to receive or bound to give feudal service or allegiance. —*n.* **1.** a liege lord. **2.** (usu. in *pl.*) a vassal, a subject. —**liege lord,** a feudal superior, a sovereign. [f. OF f. L *laeticus*]

lien /ˈliːən/ *n.* the right to hold another's property until a debt on it is paid. [f. OF f. L *ligamen* bond (*ligare* bind)]

lieu /ljuː/ *n.* **in lieu,** instead or in the place (*of*). [f. F f. L *locus* place]

Lieut. *abbr.* Lieutenant.

lieutenant /lefˈtenənt/ *n.* **1.** a deputy or substitute acting for a superior. **2.** an army officer of the rank next below captain. **3.** a naval officer of the rank next below lieutenant-commander. —**lieutenant-colonel, commander, -general** *ns.* an officer ranking next below colonel etc. —**lieutenancy** *n.* [f. OF (as LIEU, TENANT).]

life *n.* (*pl.* **lives**) **1.** being alive, the functional activity and continual change that is peculiar to animals and plants (before their death) and is not found in rocks and synthetic substances; state of existence as a living individual. **2.** a living person; living things and their activity. **3.** the period during which life lasts; the period from birth to the present time or from the present time to death. **4.** an individual's actions and fortunes; a manner of existence or a particular aspect etc. of this. **5.** energy, liveliness, animation. **6.** the active part of existence; the business, pleasures, and social activities of the world. **7.** a biography. **8.** the time for which a thing exists or continues to function; period of use. **9.** spiritual salvation, regenerate condition. **10.** (*colloq.*) a sentence of imprisonment for life. —**as large as life,** life-size; (*joc.*) in person. **for dear life,** to escape death or as if to do this. **for life,** for the rest of one's life. **life-blood** *n.* the blood necessary to life; a vital factor or influence. **life cycle,** the cyclic series of changes undergone by an organism. **life-guard** *n.* an expert swimmer employed to rescue bathers from drowning; a bodyguard of soldiers. **Life Guards,** a regiment of the Household cavalry. **life-jacket** *n.* a jacket of buoyant material for supporting a person in the water. **life peer,** a peer whose title lapses on his or her death. **life-preserver** *n.* a short stick with a heavily leaded end; a life-jacket etc. **life sciences,** biology and related subjects. **life-size(d)** *adj.* of the same size as the person or thing represented. **life-style** *n.* an individual's way of life. **matter of life and death,** an issue on which a person's living or dying depends; a matter of great importance. **this life,** earthly life. [OE (as LIVE[1])]

lifebelt *n.* a belt of buoyant or inflatable material for supporting a person in the water.

lifeboat *n.* a specially constructed boat for rescuing those in distress at sea, launched from the land; a ship's small boat for use in an emergency. In 1785 a patent was granted to Lionel Lukin for an 'insubmergible boat'. He converted a flat-bottomed fishing-boat by adding buoyancy chambers at bow and stern, a false keel, and a projecting gunwale to serve as a fender. It was used for rescuing those in danger in the sea off the coast of NE England.

lifebuoy *n.* a buoyant support for a person in the water.

lifeless *adj.* **1.** lacking life, dead. **2.** lacking movement or vitality. —**lifelessness** *n.* [f. LIFE + -LESS]

lifelike *adj.* closely resembling the person or thing represented.

lifeline *n.* **1.** a rope used for life-saving, e.g. that attached to a lifebuoy. **2.** a diver's signalling line. **3.** a sole means of communication or transport.

lifelong *adj.* lasting a lifetime.

lifer n. (slang) **1.** a person sentenced to imprisonment for life. **2.** such a sentence. [f. LIFE]

lifetime n. the duration of a person's life.

lift v.t./i. **1.** to raise to a higher level or position; to give an upward direction to (the eyes or face). **2.** to take up from the ground or from its resting-place; to dig up (potatoes at harvest, plants for storing etc.). **3.** to go up, to rise; (of fog etc.) to disperse. **4.** to steal; to copy from another source. **5.** to remove (a barrier or restriction). —n. **1.** lifting, being lifted. **2.** a ride as a passenger in a vehicle without payment. **3.** an apparatus for raising and lowering persons or things from one floor to another in a building (see below); an apparatus for carrying persons up or down a mountain etc. **4.** the upward pressure that air exerts on an aircraft in flight (ill. FLIGHT). **5.** an air-lift of goods etc.; the quantity thus transported. **6.** a supporting or elating influence; a feeling of elation. —**lift-off** n. the vertical take-off of a spacecraft or rocket. [f. ON]

Stationary engines were used from the early 19th c. to raise and lower a rope-supported platform bearing miners up and down a mineshaft, replacing the earlier windlass or horse-operated revolving drum which had served the same purpose. The American inventor James Borgardus proposed a steam passenger elevator for the New York World's Fair in 1853. In the same year E. G. Otis displayed the first efficient elevator with a safety device, and installed one in a New York department store in 1857. The first lift in Europe was built at the Paris Exhibition of 1867; it was operated hydraulically. The electric lift did not come until near the end of the century. Its invention was doubly important for the skyscraper: without it such a building would not have been feasible, and the economic height of the skyscraper is limited by the fact that beyond a certain point so many lifts are required to serve its offices or flats that they occupy too large a proportion of the floor-space.

ligament /'lɪgəmənt/ n. a band of tough fibrous tissue binding bones together (ill. BODY 2). [f. L (ligare bind)]

ligature /'lɪgətʃə(r)/ n. **1.** a thing used in tying, especially a band or cord used in surgery. **2.** the process of tying. **3.** (Mus.) a slur, a tie. **4.** two or more letters joined (as æ). **5.** a bond, a thing that unites. —v.t. to bind with a ligature. [f. L (as prec.)]

Ligeti /'lɪgeti/, György (1923–), Hungarian composer. His early works employ electronic means, but from 1958 he has returned to traditional forces to express his complex and mathematically worked out musical thought. The wit of his *Aventures* (1962), for three singers and seven instrumentalists, was developed into satire in his opera *Le grand Macabre* (1978).

light[1] /laɪt/ n. **1.** the natural agent that stimulates the sense of sight; visible or other electromagnetic radiation from the sun, a fire, a lamp, etc. (see below and ill. pp. 478–9). **2.** the medium or condition of space in which this is present and therefore sight is possible (opp. *darkness*). **3.** an appearance of brightness; the amount of this. **4.** an object from which brightness emanates; a lamp lighthouse, traffic-light, etc. **5.** a flame or spark serving to ignite something; a device producing this. **6.** a thing's aspect, the way it appears to the mind. **7.** enlightenment, elucidation. **8.** spiritual illumination by divine truth. **9.** vivacity, enthusiasm, or inspiration in a person's face, especially in the eyes. **10.** (in *pl.*) one's mental attitude. **11.** an eminent person. **12.** the bright parts of a picture etc. **13.** a window or opening in a wall to let in light (ill. HOUSES). **14.** (in a crossword etc.) a word to be deduced from clues. —adj. **1.** well provided with light, not dark. **2.** pale. —v.t./i. (past **lit** or (esp. as attrib. adj.) **lighted**) **1.** to set burning; to begin to burn. **2.** (often with *up*) to provide (a room etc.) with light; to show (a person) the way or the surroundings with a light. **3.** to brighten with animation. —**bring** (*or* **come**) **to light**, to reveal (or be revealed). **in a good** (*or* **bad**) **light**, easily (or barely) visible; giving a favourable (or unfavourable) impression. **in the light of**, drawing information from; with the help given by. **lighting-up time**, the time after which vehicles on the road must show prescribed lights. **light meter**, an instrument for measuring the intensity of light, especially to assess the correct photographic exposure. **light pen**, a penlike photosensitive device held to the screen of a computer terminal for passing information on to it. **light up**, to begin to smoke a cigarette etc.; to switch on lights. **light-year** n. a unit of distance employed by astronomers, representing the distance travelled by a ray of light in a vacuum during one year, and equal to 9.46 million km (5.9 million million miles). **lit up**, (slang) drunk. **strike a light**, to produce a spark or flame with matches etc. [OE]

Light is any electromagnetic radiation (see RADIATION) whose wavelengths fall within the range to which the human retina responds. This wavelength range lies between about 400 nanometres (violet light) and 750 nanometres (red light). White light consists of a roughly equal mixture of all visible wavelengths, which can be separated to yield the colours of the spectrum, as was first demonstrated conclusively by Newton. The nature of light has been a subject of dispute since ancient times. The speed of light was shown to be finite in the 17th c., and at about the same time two rival theories of its nature, a corpuscular (particle) theory and a wave theory, were proposed. The former, advocated by Newton, predominated until about 1800, when experiments showed that light could be made to produce the interference patterns characteristic of waves. Following the work of J. C. Maxwell later in the century it became clear that light was a form of electromagnetic radiation. Although the wave theory seemed well established, in the 20th c. it has become apparent that light consists of energy quanta called 'photons' which behave partly like waves and partly like particles. The velocity of light is 299,792 km per second.

light[2] /laɪt/ adj. **1.** of little weight, not heavy; easy to lift, carry, or move. **2.** relatively low in weight, amount, density, strength, etc.; deficient in weight. **3.** carrying or suitable for small loads; (of a ship) unladen; carrying only light arms, armaments, etc. **4.** (of food) easy to digest. **5.** easily borne or done. **6.** intended only as entertainment, not profound. **7.** (of sleep) easily disturbed. **8.** free from sorrow, cheerful. **9.** giddy. **10.** nimble, quick-moving. **11.** unchaste, wanton. **12** (of a building) elegant, graceful. —adv. **1.** in a light manner. **2.** with a minimum load. —v.i. (past & p.p. **lit** or **lighted**) to come by chance *on* or *upon*. —**lighter-than-air** adj. (of an aircraft) weighing less than the air it displaces. **light-fingered** adj. given to stealing. **light-headed** adj. giddy; frivolous; delirious. **light-hearted** adj. cheerful; (unduly) casual. **light industry**, that producing small or light articles. **light into**, to attack. **light out**, to depart. **make light of**, to treat as unimportant. —**lightly** adv., **lightness** n. [OE]

lighten[1] /'laɪt(ə)n/ v.t./i. **1.** to shed light on; to make or become brighter. **2.** to emit lightning. [f. LIGHT[1]]

lighten[2] /'laɪt(ə)n/ v.t./i. **1.** to make or become lighter in weight. **2.** to reduce the weight or load of. **3.** to bring relief to (the heart, mind, etc.). **4.** to mitigate (a penalty). [f. LIGHT[2]]

lighter[1] n. a device for lighting cigarettes etc. [f. LIGHT[1]]

lighter[2] n. a boat, usually flat-bottomed, for transporting goods between a ship and a wharf etc. [f. MDu. (as LIGHT[2] v. in sense 'unload')]

lighthouse n. a tower or other structure containing a powerful light to warn or guide ships at sea. One of the earliest was the Pharos off Alexandria, one of the Seven Wonders of the World, which used a fire of burning wood, as did later lighthouses until first oil lamps and then electric lamps came into use, giving greatly increased power. The intensity of the light is increased by the use of mirrors and lenses to concentrate the light into a narrow beam which usually sweeps round in a horizontal circle at a fixed speed. Nowadays lighthouses are equipped also with radio beacons, and each has a characteristic pattern of light or radio signals which enables it to be identified.

lighting n. the equipment in a room or street etc. for producing light; an arrangement or effect of lights. [f. LIGHT[1]]

lightning /'laɪtnɪŋ/ n. a flash of bright light produced by an electric discharge between clouds or cloud and the ground. —adj. very quick. —**lightning conductor** or (US) **rod**, a metal rod or wire fixed to an exposed part of a building or to a mast to divert lightning into the earth or sea. Its invention is associated with the work of Benjamin Franklin. **like (greased) lightning**, (colloq.) with great speed. [f. LIGHTEN[2]]

lights n.pl. the lungs of sheep, pigs, etc., used as food especially for pets. [f. LIGHT[2] used as noun]

lightship n. a moored or anchored ship with a beacon light.

lightsome /'laɪtsəm/ adj. gracefully light, agile, merry. [f. LIGHT[2]]

lightweight adj. **1.** below average weight. **2.** of little importance or influence. —n. **1.** a lightweight person or thing. **2.** a boxing-weight between featherweight and welterweight (see BOXING-WEIGHT).

ligneous /'lɪgnɪəs/ adj. of the nature of wood; (of plants) woody. [f. L (lignum wood)]

Light and Optics

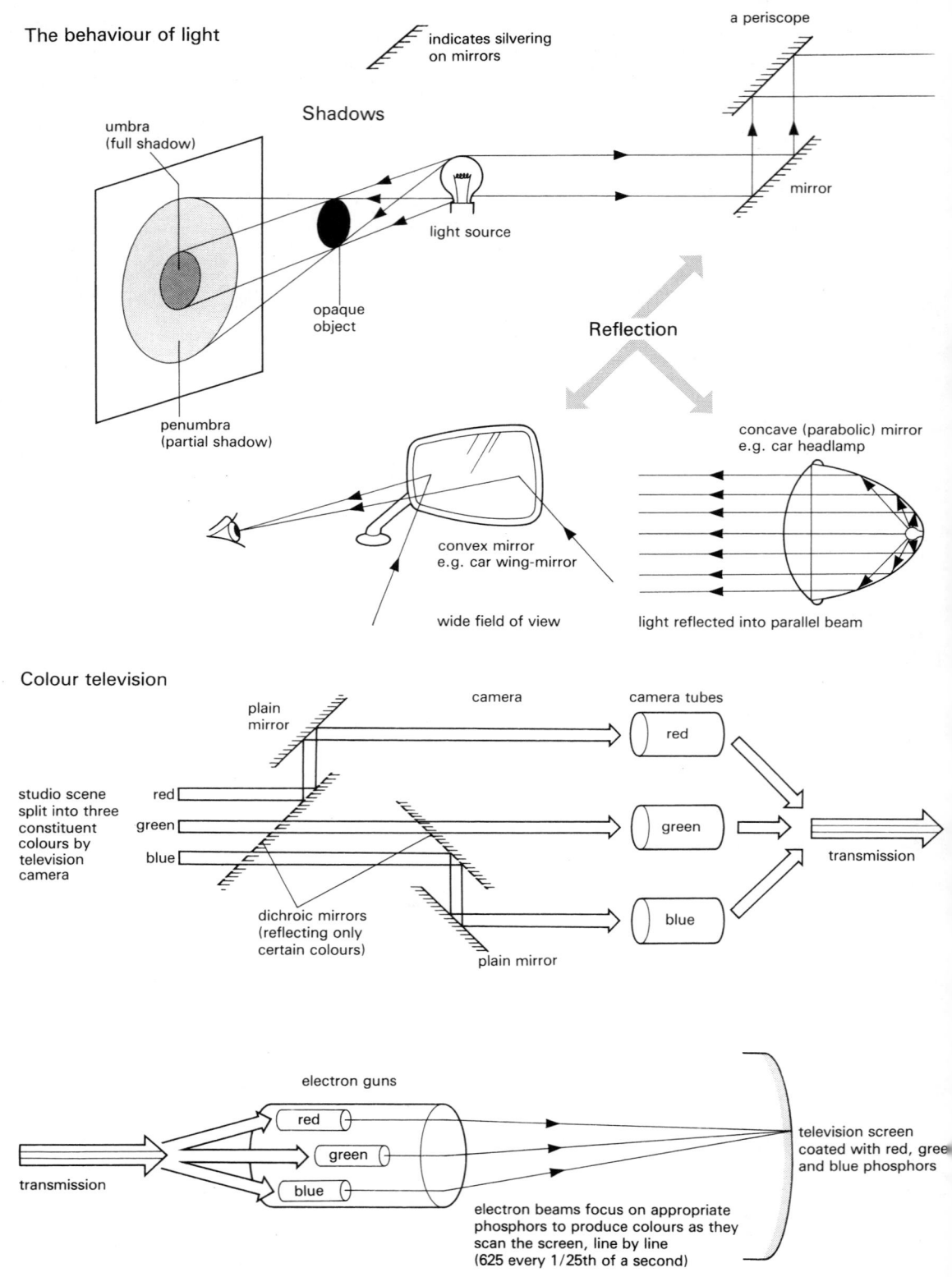

The behaviour of light

indicates silvering on mirrors

a periscope

mirror

Shadows

umbra (full shadow)

opaque object

light source

penumbra (partial shadow)

Reflection

convex mirror e.g. car wing-mirror

wide field of view

concave (parabolic) mirror e.g. car headlamp

light reflected into parallel beam

Colour television

plain mirror

camera

camera tubes

red

studio scene split into three constituent colours by television camera

red
green
blue

green

transmission

dichroic mirrors (reflecting only certain colours)

plain mirror

blue

electron guns

red
green
blue

transmission

television screen coated with red, green and blue phosphors

electron beams focus on appropriate phosphors to produce colours as they scan the screen, line by line (625 every 1/25th of a second)

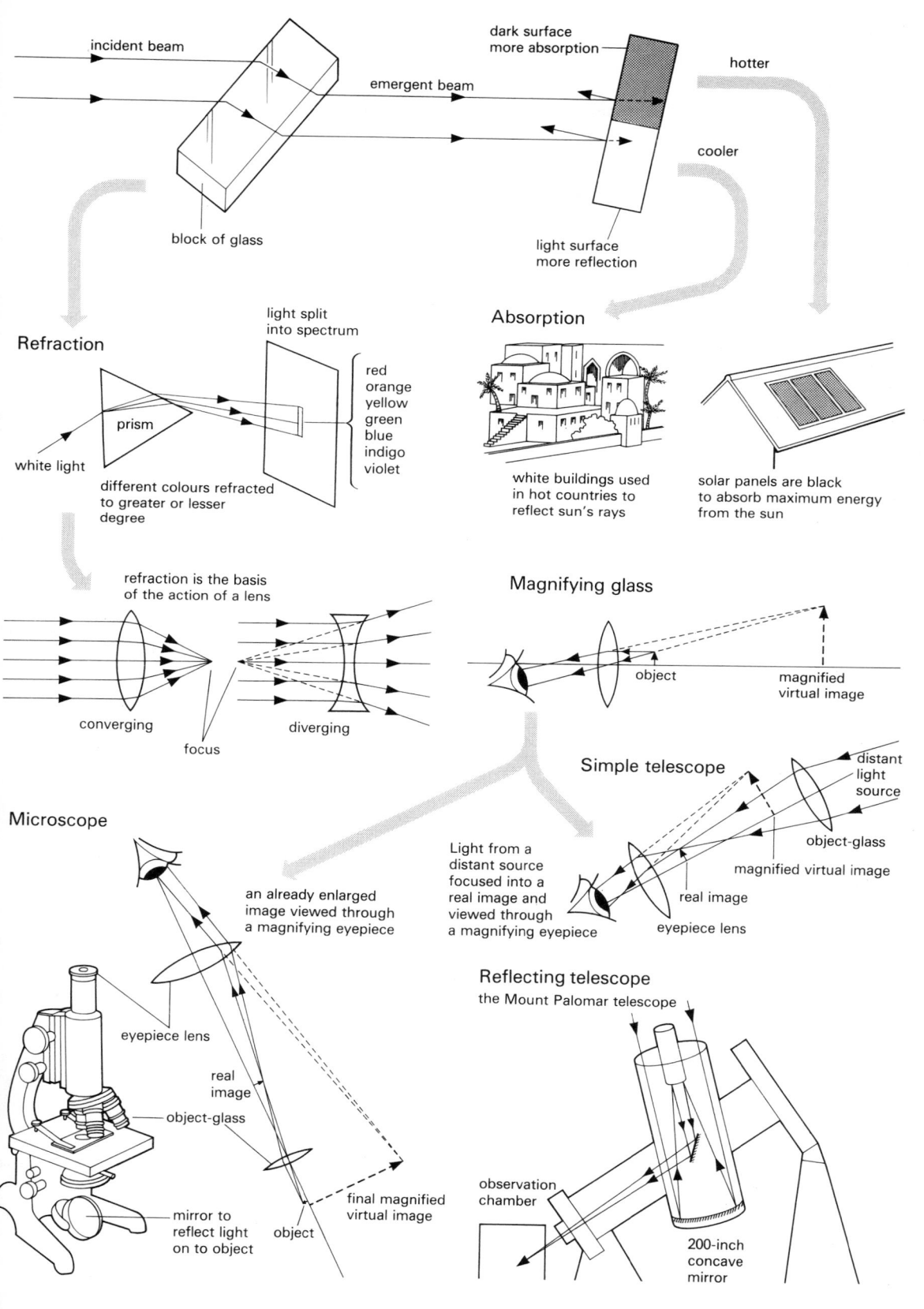

incident beam

emergent beam

block of glass

dark surface
more absorption

hotter

cooler

light surface
more reflection

Refraction

light split
into spectrum

prism

red
orange
yellow
green
blue
indigo
violet

white light

different colours refracted
to greater or lesser
degree

Absorption

white buildings used
in hot countries to
reflect sun's rays

solar panels are black
to absorb maximum energy
from the sun

refraction is the basis
of the action of a lens

converging

focus

diverging

Magnifying glass

object

magnified
virtual image

Simple telescope

distant
light
source

object-glass

magnified virtual image

real image

eyepiece lens

Microscope

an already enlarged
image viewed through
a magnifying eyepiece

Light from a
distant source
focused into a
real image and
viewed through
a magnifying eyepiece

eyepiece lens

real
image

object-glass

mirror to
reflect light
on to object

object

final magnified
virtual image

Reflecting telescope

the Mount Palomar telescope

observation
chamber

200-inch
concave
mirror

lignite /ˈlɪgnaɪt/ n. a brown coal of woody texture. [as prec.]

lignum vitae /ˈlɪgnəm ˈvaɪtiː, ˈviːtaɪ/ a hard-wooded tree of the genus *Guaiacum*. [L, = wood of life]

Liguria /laɪˈdʒʊərɪə/ 1. a territorial division of northern Italy, once forming the republic of Genoa or Ligurian Republic, formed in 1797 after Napoleon's Italian campaign, annexed to France in 1805, and subsequently merged in the kingdom of Italy. 2. the more extensive region inhabited by the ancient Ligurians. [f. foll.]

Ligurian /laɪˈdʒʊərɪən/ adj. 1. of Liguria or its people or language. 2. of an ancient people (the *Ligures*) inhabiting NW Italy, Switzerland, and SE Gaul and speaking a pre-Italic Indo-European language. —n. 1. a native or inhabitant of Liguria. 2. the language of the ancient Ligurians. —**Ligurian Republic**, see prec. **Ligurian Sea**, the part of the Mediterranean between Corsica and the NW coast of Italy round Genoa. [f. L F. Gk]

like[1] adj. 1. having some or all of the qualities or appearance etc. of; similar. 2. characteristic of. 3. such as, for example. 4. in a suitable state or mood for. 5. (*archaic* or *colloq.*) likely. —prep. in the manner of, to the same degree as. —adv. 1. (*archaic*) in the same manner as. 2. (*vulgar*) so to speak. —conj. 1. (*colloq.*, D) as. 2. (*US*) as if. —n. one that is like another, a similar thing. —**like anything** or **blazes** etc., (*colloq.*) very much; vigorously. **like hell**, recklessly; (*iron.*) not at all. **like-minded** adj. having the same tastes, opinions, etc. **what is he** (or **it** etc.) **like?** what sort of person is he (or thing is it etc.)? [OE]

like[2] v.t. 1. to find agreeable or pleasant (also *iron.*). 2. to choose to have, to prefer; to wish or be inclined *to*. —n. (usu. in *pl.*) a thing one likes or prefers. [OE]

-like /-laɪk/ suffix forming adjectives from nouns in the sense 'similar to', 'characteristic of'. [f. LIKE[1]]

likeable adj. pleasant, easy to like. —**likeably** adv. [f. LIKE[2]]

likelihood /ˈlaɪklɪhʊd/ n. probability. —**in all likelihood**, very probably. [f. foll.]

likely /ˈlaɪklɪ/ adj. 1. such as may reasonably be expected to happen or be true etc. 2. apparently suitable. 3. showing promise of being successful. —adv. probably. —**not likely**, (*colloq.*) certainly not, I refuse. [f. ON (as LIKE[1])]

liken v.t. to indicate or find a resemblance of (one person or thing to another). [f. LIKE[1]]

likeness n. 1. being like, a resemblance. 2. a semblance or guise. 3. a portrait, a representation. [f. LIKE[1]]

likewise adv. 1. also, moreover. 2. similarly. [f. LIKE[1] + -WISE]

liking n. 1. what one likes, one's taste. 2. one's feeling that one likes something. [OE (as LIKE[2])]

lilac /ˈlaɪlək/ n. 1. a shrub of the genus *Syringa* (esp. *S. vulgaris*), with fragrant pale pinkish-violet or white blossoms. 2. a pale pinkish-violet colour. —adj. of lilac colour. [obs. F, ult. f. Pers. (*nīl* blue)]

liliaceous /lɪlɪˈeɪʃəs/ adj. of the lily family. [f. L (as LILY)]

Lilienthal /ˈliːlɪəntɑːl/, Otto (1848–96), German pioneer in the design and flying of gliders. Trained as an engineer, he invented a light steam motor and received a medal for his work on marine signals. In his flying experiments he constructed wings connected to a tail, made of osier wands and covered with shirt fabric, fitted them to his shoulders, and took off by running downhill into the wind, hanging from the fabric and landing on his feet at the bottom of the hill. In 1896 he experimented with a small motor to flap the wings. Working with his brother Gustavus he made over 2,000 flights in various gliders, many from a special hill which he built near Berlin, before being killed in a crash. He also studied the science of bird flight and published the results, demonstrating the superiority of a curved over a flat wing.

Lilith /ˈlɪlɪθ/ a female demon of Jewish folklore, who tries to kill new-born children. In the Talmud she is the first wife of Adam, dispossessed by Eve. [f. Heb., = night-monster]

Lilliburlero /lɪlɪbəˈlɪərəʊ/ the title and part of the refrain of a song ridiculing the Irish, popular at the end of the 17th c. especially among soldiers and supporters of William III during the revolution of 1688. The tune (of unknown origin) first appeared in print in 1686, and was set to satirical verses, with the mock Irish word 'Lilliburlero' as a refrain, in the following year; it has remained a song of the Orange party, set to different words, as 'Protestant Boys'.

lilliputian /lɪlɪˈpjuːʃ(ə)n/ n. a diminutive person or thing.

—adj. diminutive. [f. *Lilliput*, place in Swift's 'Gulliver's Travels', inhabited by people 6 inches high]

Lilongwe /lɪˈlɒŋweɪ/ the capital of Malawi; pop. 102,924.

lilt n. a light pleasant rhythm; a song or tune with this. —v.t./i. to move or utter with a lilt. [orig. unkn.]

lily /ˈlɪlɪ/ n. a plant of the genus *Lilium*, growing from a bulb, with white, yellow, orange, or purple flowers on a tall slender stem; its flowers; a heraldic figure of a lily. —attrib. delicately white. —**lily-livered** adj. cowardly. **lily of the valley**, a spring plant (*Convallaria majalis*) with fragrant white bell-shaped flowers. [OE f. L *lilium*]

Lima /ˈliːmə/ the capital of Peru, founded by Pizarro in 1535; pop. 3,595,000.

limb[1] /lɪm/ n. 1. a projecting part of an animal body, used in movement or in grasping things. 2. a main branch of a tree. 3. an arm of a cross. —**out on a limb**, isolated, stranded, at a disadvantage. [OE]

limb[2] /lɪm/ n. (*Astron.*) a specified edge of the sun etc. [f. F or L *limbus* border]

limber[1] /ˈlɪmbə(r)/ adj. flexible; lithe, agile. —v.t./i. to make limber. —**limber up**, to exercise in preparation for athletic activity etc. [perh. f. foll., with ref. to movement of shafts]

limber[2] n. the detachable front part of a gun-carriage. —v.t. to attach a limber to (a gun). [app. rel. to L *limonarius* (*limo* shaft)]

limbo[1] /ˈlɪmbəʊ/ n. 1. (in medieval Christian theology) a region on the border of hell, the supposed abode of pre-Christian righteous persons and of unbaptized infants. 2. an intermediate state or condition (e.g. of a plan awaiting decision); a condition of being neglected and forgotten. [f. L phr. *in limbo* (as LIMB[2])]

limbo[2] /ˈlɪmbəʊ/ n. (*pl.* **-os**) a West Indian dance in which the dancer bends backwards to pass under a horizontal bar which is progressively lowered. [West Indian word]

lime[1] n. a white substance (calcium oxide) obtained by heating limestone and used for making mortar, as a fertilizer, etc. —v.t. to treat with lime. —**lime-kiln** n. a kiln for heating limestone. [OE]

lime[2] n. the round fruit of the tree *Citrus medica*, like a lemon but smaller and more acid. —**lime green**, the pale-green colour of the lime. [F f. Prov. or Sp. f. Arab. (as LEMON)]

lime[3] n. an ornamental tree of the genus *Tilia*, with heart-shaped leaves and fragrant yellow blossom (ill. TREES). [alt. of *line* = *lind* = LINDEN]

limelight n. an intense white light obtained by heating a cylinder of lime in an oxyhydrogen flame, formerly used to illuminate the stages of theatres. —**the limelight**, the full glare of publicity.

limerick /ˈlɪmərɪk/ n. a humorous (often bawdy) five-line stanza. The form was popularized by Edward Lear in the 19th c. [said to be f. chorus 'Will you come up to Limerick?' sung after extempore verses contributed by each member of a party, f. *Limerick* in Ireland]

limestone n. a rock composed mainly of calcium carbonate.

Limey /ˈlaɪmɪ/ n. (*US slang*) a British person (originally a sailor) or ship. [f. LIME[2], f. the former issue of lime-juice on British ships as a drink to prevent scurvy]

limit /ˈlɪmɪt/ n. 1. the point, line, or level beyond which something does not or may not extend or pass. 2. the greatest or smallest amount permitted. —v.t. to set or serve as a limit to; to restrict. —**be the limit**, (*slang*) to be intolerable. **within limits**, with some degree of freedom. [f. L *limes* boundary]

limitation /lɪmɪˈteɪʃ(ə)n/ n. 1. limiting, being limited. 2. a lack of ability. 3. a limiting rule or circumstance. [as prec.]

limited adj. 1. confined within limits. 2. not great in scope or talents. 3. (of a monarch etc.) subject to constitutional restrictions. —**limited edition**, the production of a limited number of copies. **limited (liability) company**, a company whose members are legally responsible only to a limited degree for the debts of a company. [f. LIMIT]

limn /lɪm/ v.t. to paint (a picture), to portray. [f. obs. *lumine* illuminate (MSS) f. OF f. L (as ILLUMINATE)]

limnology /lɪmˈnɒlədʒɪ/ n. the study of fresh waters and their inhabitants. —**limnological** /-ˈlɒdʒɪk(ə)l/ adj., **limnologist** n. [f. Gk *limnē* lake + -LOGY]

Limoges /lɪˈməʊʒ/ a city of west central France, famous in the 16th–17th c. for enamel work and later for porcelain.

limousine /lɪmʊˈziːn/ n. a motor car with a closed body

and a partition behind the driver; a luxurious motor car. [F, orig. = caped cloak worn in province of *Limousin*]

limp[1] *v.i.* **1.** to walk lamely. **2.** (of a damaged ship etc.) to proceed with difficulty. **3.** (of verse) to be defective. —*n.* a lame walk. [rel. to OE *lemphealt* lame (as HALT[2])]

limp[2] *adj.* **1.** not stiff or firm, easily bent. **2.** without will or energy. —**limply** *adv.*, **limpness** *n.* [orig. unkn.]

limpet /ˈlɪmpɪt/ *n.* a marine shellfish that sticks tightly to rocks. —**limpet mine**, a mine attached to a ship's hull and exploding after a set time. [OE (as LAMPREY)]

limpid /ˈlɪmpɪd/ *adj.* clear, transparent. —**limpidity** /-ˈpɪdɪtɪ/ *n.* [f. F or L *limpidus*]

Limpopo /lɪmˈpəʊpəʊ/ a river of SE Africa (1,770 km, 1,100 miles) flowing into the Indian Ocean in Mozambique. For much of its course it forms the northern boundary of the Transvaal with Botswana and Zimbabwe.

Linacre /ˈlɪnəkə(r)/, Thomas (1460?–1524), English physician and classical scholar who has been called the 'restorer of learning' in England. He wrote elementary and advanced textbooks on Latin grammar, and his students of Greek included Thomas More and probably Erasmus. Linacre's translations into Latin from Galen's Greek works on medicine and philosophy brought about a revival of studies in anatomy, botany, and clinical medicine in Britain. He founded medical lectureships in Oxford and Cambridge, and was instrumental in founding the College of Physicians in London, being its first president.

linchpin *n.* **1.** a pin passed through the axle-end to keep a wheel in position. **2.** a person or thing vital to an organization etc. [f. OE *lynis* + PIN]

Lincoln /ˈlɪŋkən/, Abraham (1809–65), 16th President of the USA 1860–5. Having established an early reputation as a lawyer in rural Illinois, Lincoln became a nationally known figure as a result of his unsuccessful campaign for election to the Senate in 1858. His election as Republican President two years later, on a platform held by the Southern States to be antipathetic to their interests, helped precipitate the American Civil War. As war leader Lincoln eventually managed to unite the Union cause behind the cause of emancipation, largely as a result of his diplomatic ability in handling both his political colleagues and the army, and easily won re-election in 1864. He was assassinated by a Southern fanatic in Ford's Theatre, Washington, in April 1865, shortly after the surrender of the main Confederate army had brought the war to an end.

Lincolnshire /ˈlɪŋkənʃɪə(r)/ an eastern county of England.

Lincoln's Inn /ˈlɪŋkənz/ one of the Inns of Court (see INN). Thomas de Lincoln, king's sergeant in the 14th c., may have been an early landlord.

Lincs. *abbr.* Lincolnshire.

linctus *n.* a medicine, especially a soothing syrupy cough-mixture. [L *lingere* lick)]

Lind, Jenny (Johanna), Swedish soprano, known as 'the Swedish nightingale', noted for the purity and agility of her voice. She sang in opera, oratorio, and concerts all over Europe and in the USA, creating a sensation wherever she appeared. She did much work for charitable causes in England and Sweden.

Lindbergh /ˈlɪndbɜːg/, Charles Augustus (1902–74), American aviator of Swedish descent who made the first solo transatlantic flight, taking 33½ hours, on 20/21 May 1927, from New York to Paris, in a single-engined monoplane *Spirit of St Louis*. A popular figure, almost a folk-hero, he moved to Europe with his wife to escape the publicity ensuing from the kidnapping and murder of his two-year-old son. In the early years of the Second World War he vigorously opposed American involvement.

linden /ˈlɪnd(ə)n/ *n.* = LIME[3]. [f. OE *lind*]

Lindisfarne /ˈlɪndɪsfɑːn/ a small island (since the 11th c. also called *Holy Island*) off the coast of Northumberland, site of a church and monastery founded by St Aidan (635), a missionary centre of the Celtic Church.

line[1] *n.* **1.** a long narrow mark traced on a surface; its use in art; a thing resembling such a traced mark, a band of colour, a furrow or wrinkle. **2.** a straight or curved continuous extent of length without breadth, the track of a moving point. **3.** a curve connecting all points having a specified common property. **4.** a straight line. **5.** a limit, a boundary; a mark limiting the area of play in sports; the starting-point in a race. **6.** a row of persons or things; a direction as indicated by them, a trend; (*US*) a queue. **7.** a piece of cord, rope, etc., serving a specified purpose. **8.** a wire or cable for a telephone or telegraph; a connection by this. **9.**

a contour, outline, or lineament; the shape to which a garment is designed. **10.** a course of procedure, conduct, thought, etc.; (in *pl.*) a plan, a draft, a manner of procedure. **11.** a row of printed or written words, a verse; (in *pl.*) a piece of poetry, the words of an actor's part, a specified amount of text etc. to be written out as a school punishment. **12.** a single track of a railway; one branch of a railway system; the whole system under one management. **13.** a regular succession of buses, ships, aircraft, etc., plying between certain places; a company conducting this. **14.** a connected series of persons following one another in time (esp. several generations of a family); lineage, stock. **15.** a direction, a course, a track. **16.** a department of activity, a province, a branch of business; a class of commercial goods. **17.** a connected series of military fieldworks; an arrangement of soldiers side by side, ships etc. drawn up in battle array. **18.** each of the very narrow horizontal sections forming a television picture. —*v.t.* **1.** to mark with lines. **2.** to position or stand at intervals along. —**the line**, the equator. **all along the line**, at every point. **bring** (*or* **come**) **into line**, to make conform, to conform. **drop a person a line**, to send him a short letter etc. **get a line on**, (*colloq.*) to learn something about. **in line for**, likely to receive. **in line with**, in accordance with. **lay** *or* **put it on the line**, to speak frankly. **line-drawing** *n.* one done with pen or pencil. **line of fire**, the path of a bullet etc. about to be shot. **line of vision**, the straight line along which an observer looks. **line-out** *n.* (in Rugby football) parallel lines of opposing forwards at right angles to the touch-line for the throwing in of the ball. **line printer**, a machine that prints the output from a computer a line at a time. **line up**, to arrange or be arranged in line(s). **line-up** *n.* a line of people for inspection; an arrangement of persons in a team etc. **out of line**, not in alignment; discordant. [OE & f. OF f. L *linea* (*linum* flax)]

line[2] *v.t.* **1.** to cover the inside surface of (a garment, box, etc.) with a layer of material. **2.** to serve as a lining for. **3.** to fill (a purse, stomach, etc.). [f. obs. *line* fine linen (used for linings), f. L *linum* flax]

lineage /ˈlɪnɪdʒ/ *n.* lineal descent, ancestry. [f. OF (as LINE[1])]

lineal /ˈlɪnɪəl/ *adj.* **1.** in the direct line of descent or ancestry. **2.** linear. —**lineally** *adv.* [as prec.]

lineament /ˈlɪnɪəmənt/ *n.* (usu. in *pl.*) a distinctive feature or characteristic, especially of the face. [f. L (as LINE[1])]

linear /ˈlɪnɪə(r)/ *adj.* **1.** of or in lines. **2.** long and narrow and of uniform breadth. —**linearity** /-ˈærɪtɪ/ *n.* [as prec.]

Linear A the earlier of two related forms of writing discovered at Knossos in Crete by Sir Arthur Evans between 1894 and 1901, found on fewer than 400 tablets and stone vases dating from *c.*1700 to 1450 BC and still largely unintelligible. —**Linear B,** the later form, occurring also on the mainland of Greece, found on thousands of tablets dating from *c.*1450 to 1200 BC, shown in 1952 by the British architect and scholar Michael Ventris to be a syllabary imperfectly adapted to the writing of Mycenaean Greek. The scripts are composed of linear signs derived from older hieroglyphic or pictographic script, and were used to record details of palace administration.

lineation /lɪnɪˈeɪʃ(ə)n/ *n.* marking with or an arrangement of lines. [as LINEAMENT]

linen /ˈlɪnɪn/ *n.* **1.** cloth woven from flax. **2.** (*collect.*) articles made (or originally made) of linen, e.g. sheets, shirts, undergarments —*adj.* made of linen. [OE (as LINE[2])]

liner[1] /ˈlaɪnə(r)/ *n.* a ship or aircraft etc. carrying passengers on a regular route. —**liner train**, a fast freight train with detachable containers on permanently coupled wagons. [f. LINE[1]]

liner[2] /ˈlaɪnə(r)/ *n.* a removable lining. [f. LINE[2]]

linesman *n.* (*pl.* **-men**) an umpire's or referee's assistant who decides whether a ball falls within the playing area or not.

ling[1] *n.* a long slender sea-fish (*Molva molva*). [prob. f. MDu.]

ling[2] *n.* a kind of heather, especially *Calluna vulgaris*. [f. ON]

-ling *suffix* forming nouns denoting a person or thing connected with (*hireling*) or having the property of being (*weakling*) or undergoing (*starveling*), or denoting a diminutive (*duckling*), often derog. (*lordling*). [OE]

linga /ˈlɪŋɡə/ *n.* (also **lingam**) a phallus, especially as the symbol of the Hindu god Siva. [Skr., = mark, symbol]

linger /ˈlɪŋɡə(r)/ *v.i.* **1.** to stay a long time, especially as if reluctant to leave; to dawdle. **2.** to remain alive although becoming weaker, to be slow in dying. [frequent of obs. *long* remain (as LONG[1])]

lingerie /ˈlæ̃ʒərɪ/ *n.* women's underwear and night-clothes. [F (*linge* linen)]

lingo /ˈlɪŋgəʊ/ *n.* (*pl.* **-os**) (*colloq.*) **1.** a foreign language. **2.** the vocabulary of a special subject or class of people. [prob. f. Port. *lingoa* f. L *lingua* tongue]

lingua franca /ˌlɪŋgwə ˈfræŋkə/ a language used by speakers whose native languages are different; a system for mutual understanding. [It., = Frankish tongue]

lingual /ˈlɪŋgw(ə)l/ *adj.* **1.** of or formed by the tongue. **2.** of speech or languages. —**lingually** *adv.* [f. L (*lingua* tongue, language)]

linguist /ˈlɪŋgwɪst/ *n.* a person skilled in languages or linguistics. [f. L *lingua* language]

linguistic /lɪŋˈgwɪstɪk/ *adj.* of language or linguistics. —**linguistically** *adv.* [as prec.]

linguistics /lɪŋˈgwɪstɪks/ *n.* the study of language or languages, especially as regards their nature and structure. Concern with language started early. By the 4th c. BC in India there was a flourishing tradition of grammatical analysis of language which must be older than its best-known exponent (Pāṇini, 4th c. BC), and work on the subject continued thereafter though it did not make any impact on the West until the 19th c. General discussion of a semi-philosophical nature about language started in Greece in the 5th-4th c. BC and grammatical analysis developed soon after, creating a new linguistic terminology and defining a number of categories (e.g. the parts of speech) used to analyse Greek. These were accepted with modifications in Rome and applied to Latin—thus marking the beginning of the Western grammatical tradition which continued in the Middle Ages when the grammar of Priscian was standard for a long period. During the 13th and 14th c. speculative grammar tried to establish parallels between grammatical and metaphysical categories; languages were deemed to diverge because of superficial differences only. The Renaissance saw a great expansion in the number of languages known and analysed and this increase in knowledge was encouraged by the various translations of the Bible prompted by the Reformation. The problem of the connection between linguistic and logical categories, between language and thought, was discussed at length in the 17th and 18th c. in France and elsewhere. The *Grammaire générale et raisonnée* of Port-Royal, which had immense importance, explicitly aimed at recognizing the underlying features common to all languages and showing their link with logical categories. The 19th c. shifted its interests to historical and comparative linguistics, aiming at identifying language families, reconstructing disappeared protolanguages, and tracing the history of languages (see INDO-EUROPEAN). It was argued that linguistic facts could be explained only in historical and not in logical terms and it was assumed that this period had seen the start of 'scientific' linguistics. Most of the concrete results are still valid but similar claims about 'scientificity' have been made more than once in the 20th c. where the emphasis has shifted from historical to descriptive and theoretical linguistics (concerned with spoken and not written language) and where we have seen the rise of structuralism and of generative and transformational grammar. [f. prec.]

liniment /ˈlɪnɪmənt/ *n.* an embrocation, usually made with an oil. [f. L (*linire* smear)]

lining /ˈlaɪnɪŋ/ *n.* a layer of material used to line a surface. [f. LINE[2]]

link *n* **1.** one loop or ring of a chain etc. **2.** a connecting part; a thing or person that unites or provides continuity, one in a series; the state or a means of connection. **3.** a cuff-link. —*v.t./i.* **1.** to make or be a connection between. **2.** to be joined (to a system, company, etc.). [f. ON]

linkage *n.* a system of links; linking; a link. [f. LINK]

linkman *n.* (*pl.* **-men**) a person providing continuity in a broadcast programme.

links *n.* (treated as *sing.* or *pl.*) a golf-course. [pl. of *link* rising ground (OE, perh. rel. to LEAN[1])]

Linnaean /lɪˈniːən/ *adj.* of Linnaeus or his system of classifying plants. [f. foll.]

Linnaeus /lɪˈniːəs/, Carolus (Latinized name of Carl Linné, 1707-78), Swedish naturalist, founder of modern systematic botany and zoology. In the 18th c. there were conflicting systems of classification. Interest in the variety of stamens in flowers led Linnaeus to devise a system of twenty-four classes of plants grouped on this basis, and he became the authority to whom an army of correspondents all over the world sent specimens. He described over 7,000 plants, giving them binomial Latin names—*genus* or group-name, and *species* identifying the plant, often describing its use, appearance, or geographical location. It was a practical classification and the use of Latin made it internationally acceptable; it forms the basis of modern plant nomenclature, although his classification was later superseded by that of Jussieu. His classification of animals was less satisfactory as he paid little attention to internal anatomy. He was an astute observer and his experiments in controlling insect pests with other insects led him to the idea of a 'balance in nature' where there is a continual 'war of all against all'.

linnet /ˈlɪnɪt/ *n.* a songbird, the common brown or grey finch (*Carduelis cannabina*). [f. OF *linette* (*lin* flax, f. its food)]

lino /ˈlaɪnəʊ/ *n.* (*pl.* **-os**) linoleum. [abbr.]

linocut /ˈlaɪnəʊkʌt/ *n.* a design cut in relief on a block of linoleum; a print made from this.

linoleum /lɪˈnəʊlɪəm/ *n.* a floor-covering of canvas backing thickly coated with a preparation of linseed oil and powdered cork etc. [f. L *linum* flax + *oleum* oil]

Linotype /ˈlaɪnəʊtaɪp/ *n.* [P] a composing-machine producing lines of words as single strips of metal, used especially for newspapers. [= *line o' type*]

linseed /ˈlɪnsiːd/ *n.* **1.** the seed of flax. **2.** an oil extracted from it and used in paint and varnish. [OE *line* flax (as LINE[2]) + SEED]

linsey-woolsey /ˌlɪnzɪˈwʊlzɪ/ *n.* a fabric of coarse wool woven on a cotton warp. [prob. f. *Lindsey* in Suffolk + WOOL]

lint *n.* **1.** linen with one side made fluffy by scraping, used for dressing wounds. **2.** fluff. [perh. f. OF *linette* linseed (*lin* flax)]

lintel /ˈlɪnt(ə)l/ *n.* a horizontal timber or stone across the top of a door or window (ill. HOUSES). [f. OF (as LIMIT)]

lion /ˈlaɪən/ *n.* **1.** a large powerful tawny African and South Asian carnivorous animal (*Felis leo*) of the cat family. **2.** a brave or celebrated person. **3.** the Lion, the sign or constellation Leo. **4. Lions**, the Rugby Union team representing Britain, so called from the symbol on their official tie. —**lion-heart** *n.* a courageous person. **lion-hearted** *adj.* courageous. **Lion of the North**, a name given to Gustavus Adolphus, king of Sweden, in recognition of his military exploits. **lion's share**, the largest or best portion. —**lioness** *n.fem.* [f. AF f. L *leo* f. Gk]

lionize *v.t.* to treat as a celebrity. [f. LION]

lip *n.* **1.** either of the fleshy parts forming the edges of the mouth-opening. **2.** the edge of a cup etc.; the edge of a vessel shaped for pouring from. **3.** (*slang*) impudent speech. —*v.t.* (**-pp-**) **1.** to touch with the lips; to apply the lips to. **2.** to touch lightly. —**bite one's lip**, to repress emotion, laughter, etc. **curl one's lip**, to express scorn. **lip-read** *v.t./i.* (esp. of a deaf person) to understand speech (of) entirely from observing the speaker's lip-movements. **lip-service** *n.* an insincere expression of support. **smack one's lips**, to part the lips noisily in relish or anticipation, especially of food —**lipped**, **-lipped** *adj.* [OE]

Lipari Islands /ˈlɪpərɪ/ a group of volcanic islands (the ancient Aeolian Islands) north of Sicily, in Italian possession.

lipid /ˈlɪpɪd/ *n.* any of a group of compounds that are esters of fatty acids or fatlike substances. [f. F f. Gk *lipos* fat]

Lippi[1] /ˈlɪpɪ/, Filippino (*c.*1457-1504), Italian painter, son of Fra Filippo Lippi (see foll.). Having trained with his father and probably with Botticelli he worked (*c.*1481-3) on scenes from the life of St Peter in the Brancacci Chapel, Florence, a project begun by Masolino and Masaccio. In 1488 he went to Rome to decorate the Carafa Chapel, and his style was greatly influenced by this Roman experience. It could be said that his work borders on the bizarre at times, anticipating mannerist developments. At his best in a painting such as *Vision of St Bernard* (*c.*1486) his sensitivity to Flemish colour influences is seen. Highly regarded in his own lifetime, Filippino's reputation suffered a decline until 20th-c. criticism redefined his *œuvre*.

Lippi[2] /ˈlɪpɪ/, Fra Filippo (*c.* 1406-69), Italian early Renaissance Florentine painter. He joined a Carmelite order but left it shortly after executing a fresco *The Relaxation of the Carmelite Rule* (*c.*1432). His love affair with a novice (by whom he had a son; see prec.), romantically embroidered by Vasari, has given rise to the picture of a worldly Renaissance artist, rebelling against the discipline of the Church, which inspired Browning. Until *c*.1440 Masaccio's influence is clearly detected in Filippo's work, after which his style became less monumental and more decorative. Characteristically he preferred subjects with the Madonna as the central feature, stressing the human aspect of the theme, and his style served as a major source for the 19th-c. Pre-Raphaelites.

Lippizaner /lɪpɪˈtsɑːnə(r)/ *n.* a horse of a fine white breed used especially in displays of dressage. [G, f. *Lippiza* in Yugoslavia, the home of the former Austrian Imperial Stud where such a strain of horses was orig. bred]

lipsalve *n.* an ointment for sore lips.

lipstick *n.* a small stick of cosmetic for colouring the lips.

liquefy /ˈlɪkwɪfaɪ/ *v.t./i.* to make or become liquid. —**liquefaction** /-ˈfækʃ(ə)n/ *n.* [f. F f. L *liquefacere* (as LIQUID)]

liqueur /lɪˈkjʊə(r)/ *n.* any of several strong sweet alcoholic spirits, variously flavoured. [F, = LIQUOR]

liquid /ˈlɪkwɪd/ *adj.* 1. having a consistency like that of water or oil, flowing freely but not gaseous; having the qualities of water in appearance. 2. (of sounds) clear and pure. 3. (of assets) easily converted into cash. —*n.* 1. a liquid substance. 2. the sound of *l* or *r*. [f. L (*liquere* be liquid)]

liquidate /ˈlɪkwɪdeɪt/ *v.t./i.* 1. to wind up the affairs of (a company or firm) by ascertaining liabilities and apportioning its assets. 2. to undergo liquidation. 3. to pay off (a debt). 4. to put an end to or get rid of (esp. by violent means). —**liquidator** *n.* [f. L (as prec.)]

liquidation /lɪkwɪˈdeɪʃ(ə)n/ *n.* the liquidating of a company etc. —**go into liquidation,** (of a company etc.) to be wound up and have the assets apportioned. [f. prec.]

liquidity /lɪˈkwɪdɪtɪ/ *n.* the state of being liquid or having liquid assets. [F or L (as LIQUID)]

liquidize /ˈlɪkwɪdaɪz/ *v.t.* to reduce to a liquid state. [f. LIQUID]

liquidizer *n.* a machine for making purées etc. [f. prec.]

liquor /ˈlɪkə(r)/ *n.* 1. alcoholic drink. 2. juice or other liquid (esp. produced in cooking). [f. OF f. L (as LIQUID)]

liquorice /ˈlɪkərɪs, -ɪʃ/ *n.* 1. a black substance used as a sweet and in medicine. 2. the plant (*Glycyrrhiza glabra*) from whose root it is obtained. [f. AF f. L f. Gk *glukurrhiza* (*glukus* sweet, *rhiza* root)]

lira /ˈlɪərə/ *n.* (*pl.* **-re** /-reɪ/, **-ras**) the currency unit in Italy and in Turkey. [It. f. Prov. f. L *libra* pound]

Lisbon /ˈlɪzbən/ the capital and chief port of Portugal, at the mouth of the river Tagus; pop. (est. 1981) 812,400.

lisle /laɪl/ *n.* a fine smooth cotton thread for stockings etc. [f. *Lille* in France]

lisp *n.* a speech defection in which /s/ is pronounced /θ/ and /z/ is pronounced /ð/. —*v.t./i.* to speak or say with a lisp. [OE (imit.)]

lissom /ˈlɪsəm/ *adj.* lithe, agile. —**lissomness** *n.* [as LITHE, -SOME]

list[1] *n.* 1. a number of connected items, names, etc., written or printed together as a record or to aid the memory. 2. (in *pl.*) palisades enclosing a tilt-yard; the scene of a contest. —*v.t.* 1. to make a list of, to enter in a list. 2. to include (a building) in a list of those considered to be of special architectural or historic interest, having official protection from demolition or from alteration or extension affecting its character. —**enter the lists,** to issue or accept a challenge. [OE, orig. = edging, strip]

list[2] *v.i.* (of a ship etc.) to lean over to one side. —*n.* a listing position, a tilt. [orig. unkn.]

listen /ˈlɪs(ə)n/ *v.i.* 1. to make an effort to hear something, to wait alertly for a sound. 2. to hear with attention as a person speaks; to pay attention. 3. to allow oneself to be persuaded by a suggestion or request. —**listen in,** to tap a communication made by telephone; to listen to a radio broadcast. [OE]

listener /ˈlɪsnə(r)/ *n.* one who listens; a person listening to a radio broadcast. [f. prec.]

Lister /ˈlɪstə(r)/, Joseph, 1st Baron (1827–1912), English surgeon, inventor of antiseptic techniques in surgery. In 1865 he became acquainted with Pasteur's theory that putrefaction is due to micro-organisms, and realized its significance in connection with sepsis in wounds, a major cause of deaths in patients who had undergone surgery; this was the first application of the theory to human disease. In the same year at Glasgow Royal Infirmary Lister first used carbolic acid dressings as a protective barrier against infection, and later used a carbolic spray in the operating theatre. After about 1883 aseptic rather than antiseptic techniques became popular, though Lister believed in the use of both.

listless *adj.* without energy or enthusiasm. —**listlessly** *adv.*, **listlessness** *n.* [f. obs. *list* inclination (as LUST) + -LESS]

Liszt /lɪst/, Franz (Ferenc) (1811–86), Hungarian composer and pianist. A child prodigy, he gave his first recital at the age of 9. Many of his piano works demand great technical skill, as well as expressing the lyrical side of his nature. His orchestral works are equally important and innovative in conception, particularly those inspired by literary sources such as the Faust and Dante Symphonies (1854–7, 1855–6), Liszt's affair with the Countess Marie d'Agoult produced three children, one of whom, Cosima, was to marry Wagner. In 1865 he took minor orders, becoming the Abbé Liszt, and the oratorios *The Legend of St Elizabeth* (1857–62) and *Christus* (1862–7) date from this period. Liszt's championing of Wagner, the forming of a 'New German' school of composers, and above all his own startling originality, were to have far-reaching consequences for the music of the 19th and 20th c.

lit past & p.p. of LIGHT[1] and LIGHT[2].

Li (Tai) Po /liː taɪ ˈpəʊ/ (701–62), major Chinese poet, a romantic Bohemian whose vain attempts to win official position alternated with long periods of wandering. Favourite themes include wine, friendship, and the beauties of nature.

litany /ˈlɪtənɪ/ *n.* a series of supplications to God recited by a priest etc. with set responses by the congregation; **the Litany,** that in the Book of Common Prayer. [f. OF f. L f. Gk (*litē* supplication)]

litchi /ˈliːtʃiː/ *n.* a sweetish pulpy fruit in a thin brown shell; the tree (orig. Chinese) bearing this (*Litchi chinensis*). [f. Chin.]

literacy /ˈlɪtərəsɪ/ *n.* the ability to read and write. [f. LITERATE]

literal /ˈlɪtər(ə)l/ *adj.* 1. taking words in their usual sense without metaphor or allegory. 2. exactly corresponding to the original words. 3. (of a person) tending to interpret things in a literal way, unimaginative. 4. so called without exaggeration. 5. of a letter or letters of the alphabet. —*n.* a misprint of a letter. —**literally** *adv.*, **literalness** *n.* [f. OF or L (as LETTER)]

literalism *n.* insistence on literal interpretation, adherence to the letter. —**literalist** *n.* [f. prec.]

literary /ˈlɪtərərɪ/ *adj.* 1. of, concerned with, or interested in literature or books or written composition. 2. (of a word or idiom) used chiefly by writers, not in ordinary speech. —**literariness** *n.* [f. L (as LETTER)]

literate /ˈlɪtərət/ *adj.* able to read and write. —*n.* a literate person. [f. L *litteratus* (as LETTER)]

literati /lɪtəˈrɑːtiː/ *n.pl.* men of letters, the learned class. [L (as prec.)]

literature /ˈlɪtərətʃə(r)/ *n.* 1. written works, especially those valued for their beauty of form and style. 2. the writings of a country, period, or particular subject. 3. a literary production. 4. (*colloq.*) printed matter, leaflets, etc. [f. L (as LITERATE)]

lithe /laɪð/ *adj.* flexible, supple [OE]

lithium /ˈlɪθɪəm/ *n.* a soft silver-white element of the alkali-metal group, symbol Li, atomic number 3. It is the lightest of these metals. First discovered in 1817, lithium and its compounds now have numerous commercial uses in alloys, lubricating greases, chemical reagents, etc. Lithium carbonate is used in the treatment of manic depression. [f. Gk *litheios* made of stone (*lithos* stone)]

litho /ˈlaɪθəʊ/ *n.* (*colloq.*) (*pl.* **-os**) the lithographic process. —*adj.* lithographic. —*v.t.* (*colloq.*) to lithograph. [abbr.]

lithograph /ˈlɪθəɡrɑːf/ *n.* a print produced by lithography. —*v.t.* to produce a lithographic print of. [f. foll.]

lithography /lɪˈθɒɡrəfɪ/ *n.* the process of obtaining prints from a stone, metal, or other flat surface so treated that what is to be printed can be inked but the remaining area rejects ink. —**lithographer** *n.*, **lithographic** /-ˈɡræfɪk/ *adj.*, **lithographically** *adv.* [f. G f. Gk *lithos* stone + -GRAPHY] This planographic printing technique was invented in 1798 by a Bavarian playwright, Aloys Senefelder, while experimenting with methods of duplicating his plays. He first drew images in greasy ink or crayon on a flat piece of local limestone. When the stone was mildly etched with acid, treated with gum arabic, and subsequently moistened with water, it remained uniformly damp in the non-greasy areas. Ink then applied over the whole surface was repelled by the damp areas but retained by the greasy images, from which a replica could be obtained by pressing a piece of paper on to the stone. Nowadays, in place of stones, thin metal printing plates (usually aluminium) carry the image. In the printing press, these are wrapped round a cylinder and damped and inked alternately by rollers. This rotary process considerably speeds the taking of multiple lithographic prints. In offset lithography, the inked image is transferred (or set off) from the printing plate on to an intermediate rubber-covered transfer cylinder before being printed on to the chosen substrate. Photo litho offset involves the photographic capture and deposition of the image on to a specially sensitized plate, which is then appropriately processed before use on the press. Half-tone screens, which break material up into suitably sized dots, are used when transferring images of varying tonal values from original to plate, via either a camera or a special scanning device.

Lithuania /lɪθjuːˈeɪnɪə/ an area between Latvia and Poland, a State of medieval Europe that became a province of the Russian empire in the 18th c. It was declared an independent republic in 1918, but in 1940 was incorporated in the USSR as a constituent republic, the Lithuanian SSR; capital Vilnius (Vilna).

Lithuanian /lɪθjuːˈeɪnɪən/ adj. of Lithuania or its people or language. —n. 1. a native or inhabitant of Lithuania. 2. the language of Lithuania, spoken by some 2,500,000 people, most closely related to Latvian, with which it constitutes the Baltic language group. [f. prec.]

litigant /ˈlɪtɪgənt/ n. a party to a lawsuit. —adj. engaged in a lawsuit. [as foll.]

litigate /ˈlɪtɪgeɪt/ v.t./i. to go to law; to contest (a point) at law. —**litigation** /-ˈgeɪʃ(ə)n/ n. [f. L litigare (lis lawsuit)]

litigious /lɪˈtɪdʒəs/ adj. fond of litigation, contentious. —**litigiousness** n. [f. OF or L (as prec.)]

litmus /ˈlɪtməs/ n. a blue colouring matter got from lichens that is turned red by acid and restored to blue by alkali. —**litmus paper**, paper stained with litmus and used as a test for acids or alkalis. [f. ONorw., = dye-moss]

litotes /laɪˈtəʊtiːz/ n. an ironic understatement, especially using a negative of its contrary (e.g. I shan't be sorry = I shall be glad). [L f. Gk (litos meagre)]

litre /ˈliːtə(r)/ n. a metric unit of capacity, equal to 1 cubic decilitre or about 1¾ pints. [F (litron obs. measure of capacity f. L f. Gk litra Sicilian monetary unit)]

Litt. D. abbr. Doctor of Letters. [f. L. Litterarum Doctor]

litter n. 1. refuse, especially paper, discarded on streets etc.; odds and ends lying about. 2. a vehicle containing a couch and carried on men's shoulders or by beasts of burden. 3. a kind of stretcher for the sick and wounded. 4. the young animals brought forth at a birth. 5. straw etc. as bedding for animals. 6. straw and dung, of a farmyard etc. —v.t. 1. to make (a place) untidy by discarding rubbish. 2. to give birth to (whelps etc., or absol.). 3. to provide (a horse etc.) with litter as bedding; to spread straw etc. on (a stable-floor etc.). [f. AF f. L lectaria (lectus bed)]

litterbug n. (also **litter-lout**) a person who carelessly leaves litter in a street etc.

little adj. (compar. LESS, LESSER, littler; superl. LEAST, littlest) 1. small in size, amount, degree, etc., not great or big; short in stature; of short distance or duration. 2. relatively unimportant; operating on a small scale. 3. young or younger; 4. smaller or smallest of the name. 5. trivial, paltry, mean. 6. not much; a certain though small amount of. —n. not much, only a small amount; a certain but no great amount; a short time or distance. —adv. (compar. LESS; superl. LEAST) 1. to a small extent only. 2. not at all. —**Little Bear**, Ursa Minor. **little by little**, gradually, by a small amount at a time. **the Little Corporal**, a nickname given to Napoleon by the soldiers in his army, with whom he was always very popular. **little end**, the smaller end of a connecting-rod, attached to a piston. **Little Englander**, (hist.) one desiring to restrict the dimensions of the British Empire and Britain's responsibilities. **Little Masters**, English mistranslation of the German word Kleinmeister or 'Masters in Little', which describes a group of 16th-c. Nürnberg engravers, all influenced by Dürer, who worked small-dimension metal plates with biblical, mythological, and genre scenes. **the little people**, the fairies. **Little Russian**, Ukrainian. **little theatre**, a small playhouse, especially one

used for experimental productions. **the little woman**, (colloq.) one's wife. [OE]

littoral /ˈlɪtər(ə)l/ adj. of or on the shore. —n. a region lying along the shore. [f. L (litus shore)]

Littré /ˈliːtreɪ/, Émile (1801–81), French philosopher and lexicographer, author of the Dictionnaire de la langue française (1863–77). He was a follower of Comte, after whose death he became the leading exponent of the positivist philosophy. He also edited and translated the works of Hippocrates (1839–61) and wrote an Histoire de la langue française (1862).

liturgy /ˈlɪtədʒɪ/ n. the fixed form of public worship used in churches; the Book of Common Prayer. —**liturgical** /lɪˈtɜːdʒɪk(ə)l/ adj., **liturgically** adv. [f. F or L f. Gk leitourgia public worship]

live[1] /lɪv/ v.t./i. 1. to have life, to be or remain alive. 2. to subsist or feed on; to depend for livelihood, subsistence, or position. 3. to have one's home. 4. to lead (one's life) or arrange one's habits in a specified way; to express in one's life. 5. to enjoy life to the full. 6. (of a thing) to survive or endure. —**live down**, to cause (past guilt or scandal etc.) to be forgotten by blameless conduct thereafter. **live it up**, (colloq.) to live gaily and extravagantly. **live off**, to derive support or sustenance from. **live together**, (esp. of a couple not married to each other) to share a home and have a sexual relationship. **live up to**, to live or behave in accordance with (principles etc.). [OE]

live[2] /laɪv/ attrib. adj. 1. that is alive, living. 2. actual, not pretended or toy. 3. burning or glowing. 4. (of a match, bomb, etc.) ready for use, not yet exploded or kindled. 5. (of a wire etc.) charged with or carrying electricity. 6. (also predic., of a performance, broadcast, etc.) transmitted during the occurrence or undertaken with an audience present. 7. of current or intense interest or importance; moving or imparting motion. —**live wire**, a highly energetic and forceful person. [f. ALIVE]

liveable /ˈlɪvəb(ə)l/ adj. 1. (of life) worth living. 2. (of a house, person, etc.) fit to live in or with. [f. prec.]

livelihood /ˈlaɪvlɪhʊd/ n. a means of living, sustenance. [OE (as LIFE, lād course)]

livelong /ˈlɪvlɒŋ/ adj. in its entire length. [as LIEF + LONG[1], assim. to LIVE[1]]

lively /ˈlaɪvlɪ/ adj. full of life, vigorous, energetic; cheerful; keen. —**liveliness** n. [OE (as LIFE)]

liven /ˈlaɪv(ə)n/ v.t./i. to make or become lively, to cheer. [f. LIFE]

liver[1] /ˈlɪvə(r)/ n. 1. a large glandular organ in the abdomen of vertebrates, secreting bile (ill. BODY 2; see below). 2. the flesh of some animals' liver as food. 3. dark reddish-brown. —**liver salts**, salts for curing dyspepsia or biliousness. **liver sausage**, sausage of cooked liver etc. [OE]
The liver's main function is the chemical processing of the products of digestion into substances which will be useful to the rest of the body. It makes many of the proteins of blood-plasma, converts glucose into glycogen (which it stores for reconversion into glucose when the body needs it), neutralizes harmful substances absorbed from the intestine, and stores certain minerals, such as iron, and vitamins. Its other major function is the secretion of bile, which is essential for the proper digestion and absorption of fats.
The liver was anciently supposed to be the seat of love and of violent passion generally, whence expressions such as lily-livered (= cowardly).

liver[2] /ˈlɪvə(r)/ n. a person who lives in a specified way. [f. LIVE[1]]

liveried /ˈlɪvərɪd/ adj. wearing livery. [f. LIVERY]

liverish /ˈlɪvərɪʃ/ adj. suffering from a disorder of the liver; peevish, glum. [f. LIVER[1]]

Liverpudlian /lɪvəˈpʌdlɪən/ n. a native of Liverpool. —adj. of Liverpool. [f. Liverpool in NW England]

liverwort /ˈlɪvəwɜːt/ n. a round flat bryophyte of the class Hepaticae, without stems or leaves and sometimes with a lobed body; a mosslike plant of the same group. [f. LIVER[1], f. the shape of some species]

livery /ˈlɪvərɪ/ n. 1. a distinctive uniform worn by a male servant or by a member of a City Company. 2. a distinctive guise or marking. 3. an allowance of fodder for horses. —**at livery**, (of a horse) kept for the owner for a fixed charge. **livery company**, any of the London City Companies that formerly had a distinctive costume. **livery stable**, a stable where horses are kept at livery or let out for hire. [f. AF liveré (livrer deliver)]

lives pl. of LIFE.

livestock /ˈlaɪvstɒk/ n. animals kept or dealt in for use or profit. [f. LIVE² + STOCK]

livid /ˈlɪvɪd/ adj. **1.** of a bluish leaden colour. **2.** (colloq.) very angry. [f. F or L (livēre be bluish)]

living /ˈlɪvɪŋ/ n. **1.** being alive. **2.** a means of earning or providing enough food etc. to sustain life. **3.** a position held by a clergyman, providing an income. —adj. **1.** having life; now alive. **2.** contemporary. **3.** (of a likeness) lifelike, exact. **4.** (of a language) still in vernacular use. —living-room n. a room for general use during the day. living wage, a wage on which one can live without privation. within living memory, within the memory of people still alive. [f. LIVE¹]

Livingstone /ˈlɪvɪŋstən/, David (1813–73), Scottish missionary and explorer. He first went to Bechuanaland as a missionary in 1841, travelling extensively in the interior, discovering Lake Ngami (1849) and the Zambesi River (1851), before undertaking a great journey from Cape Town to west central Africa (1852–6) on which he discovered Victoria Falls. Welcomed back to Britain in 1855 as a popular hero, Livingstone returned to Africa as consul at Quelimane (1858–64), and made further expeditions into the interior in the Zambesi region, before returning once again to Britain to attempt to expose the Portuguese slave trade. He returned to Africa for the last time in 1866 to lead an expedition into central Africa in search of the source of the Nile. His disappearance became a Victorian cause célèbre and he was eventually found in poor health by the explorer Stanley at Ujiji on the eastern shore of Lake Tanganyika in 1871. He died in Africa and his body was brought home and buried in Westminster Abbey.

Livy /ˈlɪvɪ/ (Titus Livius, 59 BC–AD 17) Roman historian, born at Padua. His history of Rome from its foundation to his own time contained 142 books of which 35 survive (including the earliest history of the war with Hannibal). Livy's genius lay in his power of vivid historical reconstruction as he sought to give Rome a history that in conception and style should be worthy of her imperial rise and greatness. Though falling below modern critical standards in use of sources, and liable to mislead through ignorance of military matters and Roman institutions, he reproduces tradition faithfully. His success was immediate and lasting, and the popularity of his work endured into the Middle Ages, the Renaissance, and beyond.

lizard /ˈlɪzəd/ n. a reptile of the suborder Lacertilia, having usually a long body and tail, four legs, and a rough or scaly hide. [f. OF f. L lacertus]

LJ abbr. (pl. **LJJ**) Lord Justice.

'll v. (colloq., usu. after pronouns) shall, will. [abbr.]

llama /ˈlɑːmə/ n. a South American ruminant (Lama glabra) kept as a beast of burden and for its soft woolly hair. [Sp., prob. f. Quechua]

Lloyd /lɔɪd/, Marie (1870–1922), real name Matilda Wood, the most famous English music-hall singer of all time, known for her saucy songs and extravagant costumes.

Lloyd George /lɔɪd ˈdʒɔːdʒ/, David, 1st Earl Lloyd George of Dwyfor (1863–1945), British Liberal statesman who early established a reputation as a radical orator. As Chancellor of the Exchequer (1908–15) under Asquith his social reforms included the introduction of old-age pensions and of national insurance, while his People's Budget (1909), proposing a tax on the value of land, was rejected by the Lords and led to a prolonged political crisis and reform of the House of Lords. He became dissatisfied with Asquith's leadership and overthrew him at the end of 1916. As Prime Minister, Lloyd George proved a good war leader and was re-elected with a large majority after the war. He successfully pressed for a moderate treaty at the Paris peace talks, but at home his administration was threatened by economic problems and trouble in Ireland. He was forced to resign in 1922 after the Conservatives on whom he had depended since his revolt against Asquith withdrew their support, and although he eventually returned to the Liberal Party as leader in 1926, he never held office again.

Lloyd's /lɔɪdz/ an association of underwriters in London (not, as is often supposed, an insurance firm) incorporated by statute in 1871. Its members are private syndicates, elected after close scrutiny of their finances and required to deposit a substantial sum as security against their underwriting activities. It is named after the 17th-c. coffee-house of Edward Lloyd (d. 1713), in which underwriters and merchants congregated. For the benefit of his customers Lloyd built up an unrivalled intelligence system and displayed lists of the latest ship movements. Out of this practice a newspaper, Lloyd's List, was started in 1734,

giving daily news of the movements etc. of shipping. Originally Lloyd's dealt only in marine insurance, but it now undertakes most other kinds, and its business in marine and aircraft insurance is international. (See also LUTINE.) Lloyd's Register of Shipping is a separate and independent society which surveys and classifies ships over a certain tonnage, publishing details of these each year on the basis of reports by its surveyors. In the 18th-c. the finest ships were classed as 'A1 at Lloyd's', indicating (by A) that the hull was in first-class condition and (by 1) that the same was true of the fittings; whence 'A1' has passed into the language as a standard of excellence.

lm abbr. lumen.

lo /ləʊ/ int. (archaic) look. —lo and behold, an introduction to the mentioning of a surprising fact. [OE, = int. of surprise, and f. obs. lo = loke (as LOOK)]

loach n. a small freshwater fish of the family Cobitidae. [f. OF loche]

load n. **1.** what is carried or to be carried; the debris carried along by a river. **2.** an amount usually or actually carried; this as a weight or measure of some substances. **3.** a weight of care, responsibility, etc. **4.** the amount of power carried by an electric circuit or supplied by a generating station. **5.** a material object or force acting as a weight etc. **6.** (in pl., colloq.) plenty. —v.t./i. **1.** to put a load on or aboard; to place (a load) aboard ship, on a vehicle, etc.; (of a ship, vehicle, or person) to take a load aboard. **2.** to burden, to strain. **3.** to supply or assail overwhelmingly. **4.** to put ammunition in (a gun), a film in (a camera), a cassette in (a tape-recorder), etc.; to put (a program or data etc.) in a computer. —get a load of, (slang) to take note of. **loaded question**, one put in such a way as to evoke a required answer. **load line**, a Plimsoll line. —loader n., -loading adj. (of a gun or machine). [OE, = way (as LEAD¹)]

loaded adj. (slang) **1.** rich. **2.** drunk. **3.** (US) drugged. [f. LOAD]

loadstone n. **1.** a magnetic oxide of iron. **2.** a piece of it used as a magnet. **3.** a thing that attracts. [= way stone, f. LOAD (in its orig. sense) + STONE]

loaf¹ n. (pl. **loaves**) **1.** a quantity of bread baked alone or as a separate or separable part of a batch, usually of a standard weight. **2.** minced or chopped meat made in the shape of a loaf and cooked. **3.** (slang) the head. [OE]

loaf² v.i. to spend time idly, to hang about. —loafer n. [perh. f. G landläufer vagabond]

loam n. a rich soil of clay, sand, and decayed vegetable matter. —loamy adj., loaminess n. [OE (rel. to LIME¹)]

loan n. **1.** a thing lent, especially a sum of money to be returned with or without interest. **2.** lending, being lent. —v.t. (D) to lend. —loan-word n. a word adopted by one language from another in a more or less modified form (e.g. morale, naïve). on loan, being lent. [f. ON]

loath /ləʊθ/ predic. adj. averse, disinclined. [OE]

loathe /ləʊð/ v.t. to regard with hatred and disgust. —loathing n. [OE (as prec.)]

loathsome /ˈləʊðsəm/ adj. arousing hatred and disgust; repulsive. [f. loath n. disgust (f. LOATHE) + -SOME]

loaves pl. of LOAF¹.

lob v.t./i. (-bb-) to send or strike (a ball) slowly in a high arc in cricket or tennis etc. —n. a lobbed ball; a slow underarm delivery in cricket. [prob. f. LDu.]

Lobachevski /lɒbəˈtʃefskɪ/ Nikolai Ivanovich (1792–1856), Russian mathematician who, at about the same time as Gauss in Germany and János Bolyai in Hungary, discovered non-Euclidean geometry. His work was entirely independent of theirs despite suggestions to the contrary in the song by the American singer Tom Lehrer that has immortalized his name.

lobar /ˈləʊbə(r)/ adj. of a lobe, especially of the lung. [f. LOBE]

lobate /ˈləʊbeɪt/ adj. having a lobe or lobes. [f. LOBE]

lobby n. **1.** an entrance-hall, a porch; an ante-room, a corridor. **2.** (in the House of Commons) a large hall open to the public used especially for interviews between MPs and others; (in full **division lobby**) each of two corridors to which members retire to vote. **3.** a body of lobbyists. —v.t./i. to seek to influence (an MP etc.) to support one's cause; to get (a bill etc.) through by interviews etc. in a lobby. [f. L lobia, lobium lodge]

lobbyist n. a person who lobbies an MP etc. [f. prec.]

lobe n. a rounded flattish part or projection, especially of an organ of the body; the lower soft pendulous part of the outer ear. [f. L f. Gk lobos lobe, pod]

lobelia /ləˈbiːliə/ n. a herbaceous plant of the genus *Lobelia* with brightly coloured flowers. [f. M de *Lobel*, Flemish botanist in England (d. 1616)]

lobotomy /ləˈbɒtəmi/ n. an incision into the white tissue of the frontal lobe of the brain to relieve some cases of mental disorder. [f. LOBE + -TOMY]

lobscouse /ˈlɒbskaʊs/ n. a sailor's dish of meat stewed with vegetables and ship's biscuit. [orig. unkn.]

lobster n. a large edible sea crustacean of the family Homaridae, with stalked eyes and heavy pincer-like claws, that turns from bluish-black to scarlet when boiled; its flesh as food. —**lobster-pot** n. a basket for trapping lobsters. [OE, corrupt. of L *locusta* crustacean, = LOCUST]

lobworm /ˈlɒbwɜːm/ n. a large earthworm used as a fishing-bait. [f. LOB in obs. sense 'pendulous object']

local /ˈləʊk(ə)l/ adj. 1. in regard to place. 2. belonging to or affecting a particular place or a small area; of one's own neighbourhood. 3. (of a train or bus etc.) of the neighbourhood, not long-distance; stopping at all points on a route. —n. 1. an inhabitant of a particular district. 2. a local train, bus, etc. 3. (colloq.) the local public house. —**local authority,** a body charged with the administration of local government. **local colour,** details characteristic of the place in which a story etc. is set, added to make it seem more real. **local government,** a system of administration of a county or district etc. by elected representatives of those living there. **Local Group,** the cluster of galaxies of which our Galaxy is a member. —**locally** adv. [f. OF f. L (*locus* place)]

locale /ləʊˈkɑːl/ n. the scene or locality of operations or events. [f. F *local* (as prec.)]

locality /ləʊˈkælɪtɪ/ n. 1. a thing's position; the site or scene of something, especially in relation to the surroundings. 2. a district. [f. F or L (as LOCAL)]

localize /ˈləʊkəlaɪz/ v.t. 1. to assign or confine to a particular place. 2. to invest with the characteristics of a particular place. 3. to decentralize. [f. LOCAL]

locate /ləˈkeɪt/ v.t. 1. to discover the place where something is. 2. to establish in a place; to state the locality of. [f. L *locare* (as LOCAL)]

location /ləˈkeɪʃ(ə)n/ n. 1. a particular place. 2. locating. —**on location,** (of filming) in a natural setting rather than in a studio. [as prec.]

locative /ˈlɒkətɪv/ n. (Gram.) the case expressing location. —adj. (Gram.) of or in the locative. [as LOCATE]

loc. cit. abbr. in the place cited. [f. L *loco citato*]

loch /lɒx, lɒk/ n. a Scottish lake or land-locked arm of the sea. [f. Gael.]

Loch Ness monster an immense aquatic creature alleged to live in the deep waters of Loch Ness in Highland, Scotland. Reported appearances date from the time of St Columba (6th c.), who, according to a chronicler, saw it about to attack a man in the water and commanded it to go away, whereupon it retreated. The construction of a motor road immediately beside the loch in 1933 unleashed a flood of alleged sightings.

loci pl. of LOCUS.

lock¹ n. 1. a mechanism for fastening a door, lid, etc., with a bolt that requires a key of a particular shape to work it. 2. a section of a canal or river confined within sluiced gates for moving boats from one level to another. 3. a mechanism for exploding the charge of a gun. 4. the turning of the front wheels of a vehicle; the maximum extent of this. 5. an interlocked or jammed state. 6. a wrestling-hold that keeps the opponent's arm etc. fixed. 7. (in full **lock forward**) a player in the second row of the scrum in Rugby football. —v.t./i. 1. to fasten with a lock. 2. to shut into or out of a place by locking. 3. to store away securely or inaccessibly. 4. to bring or come into a rigidly fixed position, to jam; —**lock-keeper** n. a person in charge of a lock on a canal or river. **lock-knit** adj. knitted with an interlocking stitch. **lock-out** n. an employer's procedure of refusing the entry of workers to their place of work until certain terms are agreed to. **lock-stitch** n. see separate entry. **lock, stock, and barrel,** the whole of a thing, completely. **lock-up** n. premises that can be locked up; the time or process of locking up; a house or room for the temporary detention of prisoners; (adj.) able to be locked up. [OE]

lock² n. a portion of hair that hangs together; (in pl.) the hair of the head. [OE]

Locke¹ /lɒk/, John (1632–1704), English philosopher, a founder of empiricism and political liberalism. In 1690 he published his *Two Treatises of Government*, designed to combat the theory of the 'divine right of kings' and to

justify the Revolution of 1688, finding the origin of the civil State in a contract: the authority of rulers has a human origin, and is limited. His views on the philosophy of politics were influential throughout the following century. Locke's most famous work, *An Essay concerning Human Understanding* (1690), is an attempt to demonstrate what can and cannot be known, in order to guide us to the proper use of our understanding and show us how we should live. Denying that any ideas are innate he argued instead for the central empiricist tenet that all knowledge is derived from sense-experience, and attempted a classification of the sources of various ideas. He concluded that we can know something of the world but not everything, and that we cannot know why things are as they are, that the same was true of morality, and our limited knowledge must be reinforced by faith; in his last major work *The Reasonableness of Christianity* (1695) Locke turned firmly to revelation.

Locke² /lɒk/, Joseph (1805–60), English railway designer who in a lifelong association with Thomas Brassey built lines in England, the west coast line to Scotland, and trunk lines in France. He is honoured on both sides of the Channel as one of the great railway pioneers.

locker n. a small lockable cupboard or compartment. [f. LOCK¹]

locket /ˈlɒkɪt/ n. a small ornamental case containing a portrait or lock of hair and usually hung from the neck. [f. OF dim. of *loc* latch (as LOCK¹)]

lockjaw n. a form of tetanus in which the jaws become rigidly closed.

locksmith n. a maker and mender of locks.

lock-stitch n. a secure sewing-machine stitch made by locking together two threads or stitches. The needle descends through the fabric, carrying the thread; when it rises the thread forms a loop on the under-side of the fabric, a second thread from a shuttle or bobbin is passed through this loop, and the interlocked threads are pulled tight when the fabric is advanced for the next stitch.

loco¹ /ˈləʊkəʊ/ n. (pl. -os) (colloq.) a locomotive engine. [abbr.]

loco² /ˈləʊkəʊ/ adj. (US slang) crazy. [Sp.]

locomotion /ləʊkəˈməʊʃ(ə)n/ n. 1. motion or the power of motion from place to place. 2. travel, a way (esp. artificial) of travelling. [f. L *locus* place + MOTION]

locomotive /ˈləʊkəməʊtɪv/ n. (in full **locomotive engine**) an engine for drawing trains. —adj. of, having, or effecting locomotion, not stationary. [as prec.]

locum tenens /ləʊkəm ˈtiːnenz/ (also (colloq.) **locum**) a deputy, especially one acting for a doctor or clergyman in his absence. [L, = (one) holding place]

locus /ˈləʊkəs/ n. (pl. **loci** /ˈləʊsaɪ/) the line or curve etc. made by all points satisfying certain conditions, or by the defined motion of a point or surface. [L, = place]

locus classicus /ləʊkəs ˈklæsɪkəs/ the best known or most authoritative passage on a subject. [L, = classic place]

locust /ˈləʊkəst/ n. 1. an African or Asian grasshopper of the family Acridiae, migrating in swarms and consuming all vegetation. 2. a person of devouring or destructive propensities. 3. any of various kinds of tree and their fruit, especially the false acacia (*Robinia pseudoacacia*). [f. OF f. L *locusta* lobster, locust]

locution /ləˈkjuːʃ(ə)n/ n. 1. a word, phrase, or idiom. 2. style of speech. [f. OF or L (*loqui* speak)]

lode n. a vein of metal ore. [var. of LOAD, orig. = leading, way]

lodestar n. 1. a star used as a guide in navigation, especially the pole-star. 2. a guiding principle; an object of pursuit.

lodge n. 1. a small house at the entrance to a park or the grounds of a large house, occupied by a gate-keeper or other employee. 2. a small house used in sporting seasons. 3. a porter's room at the entrance or gateway of a factory, college, etc. 4. the members or meeting-place (orig. a mason's hut or workshop on a building site) of a branch of the Freemasons or other society. 5. a beaver's or otter's lair. —v.t./i. 1. to provide with temporary accommodation. 2. to live as a lodger. 3. to deposit (money etc.) for security. 4. to submit (a complaint etc.) for attention. 5. to place (power etc.) in or with a person. 6. to stick or become embedded in; to cause to do this. [f. OF *loge* f. L *lobia* (as LOBBY)]

lodger n. a person receiving accommodation in another's house for payment. [f. prec]

lodging n. accommodation in hired rooms, a dwelling-

-place; (in *pl.*) a room or rooms rented for lodging in. [f. LODGE]

loess /ˈloʊɪs/ *n.* a layer of fine light-coloured soil, found in large areas of Asia, Europe, and America and very fertile when irrigated, thought to have been deposited by winds during the ice age. [f. G *löss* f. Swiss G *lösch* loose]

Lofoten and Vesteraalen Islands /loʊˈfəʊtən, ˈvestərəːlən/ a group of islands off the NW coast of Norway.

loft *n.* **1.** a space (with a floor) under the roof of a house; a similar space under the roof of a stable or barn, used for storing hay etc. **2.** a gallery in a church or hall. **3.** a pigeon-house. **4.** a backward slope on the face of a golf-club. **5.** a lofting stroke. —*v.t.* to send (a ball) in a high arc. [f. ON, = air, upper room (as LIFT)]

lofty *adj.* **1.** towering, of imposing height. **2.** haughty, keeping aloof. **3.** exalted, noble. —**loftily** *adv.*, **loftiness** *n.* [f. LOFT (as in *aloft*)]

log¹ *n.* **1.** an unhewn piece of a felled tree; any large rough piece of wood, especially one cut for firewood. **2.** a floating device used to ascertain a ship's speed. **3.** a log-book. —*v.t.* (**-gg-**) **1.** to enter in a ship's log-book. **2.** to enter (data etc.) in a regular record; to attain (a cumulative total thus recorded). **3.** to cut into logs. —**log-book** *n.* a book in which details of a voyage or journey or the registration of a vehicle are recorded. **log cabin**, a hut built of logs. **log in** (*or* **out**), to begin (or finish) operations at a terminal of a multi-access computer. **log-line** *n.* a line to which the float of a ship's log is attached. [orig. unkn.]

log² *n.* a logarithm. [abbr.]

logan /ˈloʊgən/ *n.* (in full **logan-stone**) a poised heavy stone rocking at a touch. [= *logging* (*log* to rock)]

loganberry /ˈloʊgənberɪ/ *n.* a dark-red fruit, a hybrid of the raspberry and an American blackberry. [f. J. H. *Logan*, American horticulturist (d.1928) + BERRY]

logarithm /ˈlɒgərɪð(ə)m/ *n.* any of a series of arithmetic exponents tabulated to simplify computation by making it possible to use addition and subtraction instead of multiplication and division (see NAPIER). —**logarithmic** /-ˈrɪðmɪk/ *adj.*, **logarithmically** *adv.* [f. Gk *logos* reckoning, ratio + *arithmos* number]

loggerhead /ˈlɒgəhed/ *n.* **at loggerheads**, disagreeing, disputing. [f. dial. *logger* block of wood + HEAD]

loggia /ˈloʊdʒə/ *n.* an open-sided gallery or arcade; an open-sided extension to a house. [It., = LODGE]

logic /ˈlɒdʒɪk/ *n.* **1.** the science of reasoning (see below); a particular system or method of reasoning; a chain of reasoning (regarded as sound or unsound); use of or ability in argument. **2.** (in computers) the principles or circuitry involved in carrying out processes, on electrical or other signals, analogous to the processes of reasoning, deduction, etc. **3.** necessity, the compulsive power of events etc. [f. OF f. L f. Gk (as LOGOS)]

Logic is the systematic study of the patterns of argument, and in particular of those patterns of argument that are valid, i.e. such that if the premisses are true then of necessity the conclusion is true. The chief instrument of advance has been the development of symbols which make it possible to abstract from particular premisses and conclusions and consider only the patterns. The process was begun by Aristotle, who gave rules for which syllogisms are valid. Since the 19th c. the formulation of such rules has drawn on the concepts and techniques of mathematics, using symbols to replace ordinary language; the greatest advance was made by Gottlob Frege (1848–1925) who devised a simple method of handling 'all' and 'some'. (Questions can be raised about how far the systems of Frege and Russell preserve what is ordinarily meant by the words they replace with symbols.) In the 20th c. there have come to be two branches. *Philosophical logic* is the study of certain expressions of ordinary language to see how they do work: the goal of seeing which inferences are valid may be forgotten. *Mathematical* or *formal logic*, see MATHEMATICAL.

logical /ˈlɒdʒɪk(ə)l/ *adj.* **1.** of or according to logic; correctly reasoned; defensible or explicable on the ground of consistency. **2.** using or capable of correct reasoning. —**logicality** /-ˈkælɪtɪ/ *n.*, **logically** *adv.* [f. L (as LOGIC)]

logical positivism the theories of the Vienna Circle (influentially expounded by A. J. Ayer in *Language, Truth, and Logic*, 1936) aimed at evolving formal methods, similar to those of the mathematical sciences, for the verification of empirical questions and therefore eliminating metaphysical and more speculative questions. A statement, they held, has meaning only if its truth or falsity can be tested empirically; logical and mathematical statements are tauto-

logous because they are valid only within their own system; moral and value judgements are subjective and therefore without universal application; metaphysical and religious speculation is logically ill-founded. —**logical positivist**, one who holds such theories.

logician /lɒˈdʒɪʃ(ə)n/ *n.* a user of or expert in logic. [f. LOGIC]

logistics /ləˈdʒɪstɪks/ *n.pl.* the art of supplying and organizing (orig. military) services and equipment etc. —**logistic** *adj.*, **logistically** *adv.* [f. F (*loger* lodge)]

logo /ˈloʊgəʊ, ˈlɒ-/ *n.* (*pl.* **-os**) (*colloq.*) a logotype. [abbr.]

Logos /ˈlɒgɒs/ *n.* the Word of God, or the Second Person of the Trinity, incarnate in Jesus Christ according to the fourth Gospel. [Gk, = word, reason (*legō* speak)]

logotype /ˈlɒgəʊtaɪp/ *n.* a non-heraldic design or symbol as the badge of an organization; a piece of type with this. [as prec. + TYPE]

logwood *n.* a West Indian tree (*Haematoxylon campechianum*); the wood of this used in dyeing.

-logy /-lədʒɪ/ *suffix* forming nouns denoting a subject of study (*biology*), or body of writings (*trilogy, martyrology*), or a character of speech or language (*tautology*). [f. F or L or Gk *-logia* (as LOGOS)]

Lohengrin /ˈloʊhɪŋgrɪn/ (*French & German legend*) son of Perceval. He was summoned from the temple of the Grail and borne in a swan-boat to Antwerp to defend Elsa of Brabant against Frederick of Telramund, who wished to marry her (against her will). He overcame Frederick and consented to marry Elsa on condition that she did not ask who he was, but Elsa broke this condition and he was carried away again in the swan-boat. This forms the subject of a music-drama by Wagner, produced in 1850. A similar tale is told of Helias, the legendary grandfather of Godfrey de Bouillon (leader of the 1st Crusade).

loin *n.* **1.** (in *pl.*) the side and back of the body between the ribs and hip-bones. **2.** (in *sing.*) a joint of meat that includes the loin vertebrae. [f. OF *loigne* f. L *lumbus*]

loincloth *n.* a cloth worn round the hips, especially as the sole garment.

Loire /ləˈwɑː(r)/ the longest river of France (1,015 km, 630 miles), flowing from the Massif Central north and west to the Atlantic Ocean at St Nazaire. Principal cities upon it are Orléans, Tours, and Nantes; the valley is particularly noted for the châteaux that lie along its course.

loiter *v.i.* to stand about idly, to linger; to move or proceed indolently with frequent pauses. —**loiterer** *n.* [f. MDu. *loteren* wag about]

Loki /ˈloʊkɪ/ (*Scand. myth.*) a spirit of evil and mischief who contrived the death of Balder.

Lola Montez /ˈloʊlə ˈmɒntɪz/ (1818–61), stage name of the actress and adventuress Marie Dolores Eliza Rosanna Gilbert, who, after making a considerable name for herself as a dancer, became the mistress of Ludwig I of Bavaria and all but ruled the country through him until banished as a result of foreign influence.

loll *v.t./i.* **1.** to recline, sit, or stand in a lazy attitude. **2.** to rest (one's head or limbs) lazily on something. **3.** to hang (one's tongue) out; (of the tongue) to hang out. [prob. imit.]

Lollard /ˈlɒləd/ *n.* any of the followers of John Wyclif or those who held opinions similar to his on the necessity for the Church to aid men to live a life of evangelical poverty and imitate Christ. The name itself was a term of contempt, derived from a Dutch word meaning 'mumbler'. Official attitudes to the Lollards varied considerably, but they were generally held to be heretics and often severely persecuted. Their ideas influenced the thought of John Huss, who in turn influenced Martin Luther. [f. Du. (*lollen* mumble)]

lollipop /ˈlɒlɪpɒp/ *n.* a large round usually flat boiled sweet on a small stick. —**lollipop lady** *or* **man**, (*colloq.*) an official using a circular sign on a stick to stop traffic for children to cross a road. [perh. f. dial. *lolly* tongue + POP¹]

lollop *v.i.* (*colloq.*) to move in ungainly bounds; to flop about. [prob. f. LOLL, assoc. with TROLLOP]

lolly *n.* **1.** (*colloq.*) a lollipop; an ice lolly. **2.** (*slang*) money. [abbr. of LOLLIPOP]

Lombard /ˈlɒmbəd/ *n.* a member of a Germanic people from the lower Elbe who invaded Italy in 568 and founded a kingdom (overthrown by Charlemagne in 774) in the valley of the Po. —*adj.* of the Lombards or Lombardy. —**Lombard Street**, a street in the City of London formerly occupied by Lombard bankers and still containing many of the chief London banks. [f. OF or MDu., ult. f. L *Longobardus* (*longus* long, *Bardi* name of people)]

Lombardy /'lɒmbədɪ/ a region of central northern Italy, lying mainly between the Alps and the River Po, which became part of the kingdom of Italy in 1859. Milan is its principal city.

Lomé /lɔː'meɪ/ the capital and chief port of Togo; pop. (est. 1980) 283,000.

London /'lʌnd(ə)n/ the capital of the United Kingdom, a port on the River Thames and a commercial, business, and cultural centre; pop. (1981) 6,696,000. Settled by the Romans as a port and trading centre (*Londinium*), London has flourished since the Middle Ages. After the plague of 1665 and the fire of 1666 much of it was rebuilt under the direction of Sir Christopher Wren. Air raids in the Second World War obliterated whole areas of streets and damaged most public buildings; post-war reconstruction has added tower blocks of geometrical aspect to the landscape. — **London clay**, a geological formation in the lower division of the Eocene in SE England. **London pride**, a pink-flowered saxifrage (*Saxifraga* × *urbium*). —**Londoner** *n.*

Londonderry /'lʌndənderɪ/ **1.** a county of Northern Ireland. **2.** its county town, reputedly founded by St Columba in 546. The town was named 'Derry' [f. Gael., = oak grove], a name still retained in the titles of certain organizations etc., until 1613 when it was given to the City of London as part of the area to be colonized, and was renamed Londonderry. In 1689 it was beseiged by James II for 105 days before being relieved.

lone *attrib. adj.* **1.** solitary, without companions. **2.** uninhabited, lonely. —**lone hand**, a hand played or a player playing against the rest at cards; a person or action without allies. **lone wolf**, a loner. [f. ALONE]

lonely *adj.* **1.** lacking friends or companions; despondent because of this. **2.** isolated, unfrequented, uninhabited. —**loneliness** *n.* [f. LONE]

loner /'ləʊnə(r)/ *n.* a person or animal preferring to act alone or not to associate with others. [f. LONE]

lonesome /'ləʊnsəm/ *adj.* lonely, causing loneliness. [f. LONE + -SOME]

long[1] *adj.* **1.** having great length in space or time. **2.** having a specified length or duration. **3.** seeming to be longer than it really is, tedious. **4.** lasting, reaching far into the past or future. **5.** far-reaching, acting at a distance; involving a great interval or distance. **6.** of elongated shape. **7.** (of a vowel sound or a syllable) having the greater of two recognized durations. **8.** (of stocks etc.) bought in large quantities in advance, with the expectation of a rise in price. —*n.* **1.** a long interval or period. **2.** a long syllable or vowel. —*adv.* for a long time; by a long time; throughout a specified duration; (in *compar.*) after an implied point of time. —**as** *or* **so long as**, provided that. **in the long run**, over a long period, eventually. **the long and the short of it**, all that need be said, the eventual outcome. **long-distance** *adj.* travelling or operating between distant places. **long division**, division of numbers with the details of the calculation written down. **long-drawn (-out)** *adj.* prolonged. **long face**, a dismal expression. **long-haired** *adj.* intellectual; hippie. **long-headed** *adj.* shrewd, far-seeing; sagacious. **long-house** *n.* a large communal village house in certain parts of Malaysia and Indonesia. **long in the tooth**, rather old. **long johns**, (*colloq.*) long underpants. **long jump**, an athletic contest of jumping as far as possible along the ground in one leap. **long leg**, the position of a fieldsman in cricket far behind the batsman on the leg side (ill. SPORTS). **long-life** *adj.* (of milk etc) treated to prolong the period of usability. **long-lived** *adj.* having a long life, durable. **long odds**, very uneven odds. **long off**, **long on**, the position of fieldsmen in cricket far behind the bowler and towards the off (or on) side. **long on**, (*colloq.*) well supplied with. **Long Parliament**, the Parliament which sat from Nov. 1640 to March 1653, was restored for a short time in 1659 and finally voted its own dissolution in 1660. It was summoned by Charles I and sat through the English Civil War and on into the interregnum which followed. **long-playing** *adj.* (of a gramophone record) playing for 15-30 minutes on each side. **long-range** *adj.* having a long range; relating to a long period of future time. **long ship**, (*hist.*) a warship with many rowers (ill. SAILING-SHIPS). Such ships were used by Scandinavian maritime peoples until the mid-18th c. **long shot**, a wild guess or venture; a bet at long odds (*not by a long shot*, by no means). **long-sighted** *adj.* able to see clearly only what is at a distance; having imagination or foresight. **long-standing** *adj.* that has long existed. **long-suffering** *adj.* bearing provocation patiently. **long suit**, many cards of one suit in a hand; one's strong

point. **long-term** *adj.* occurring in or relating to a long period of time. **long ton**, see TON. **long wave** a radio wave of frequency less than 300 kHz. **long-winded** *adj.* (of a speech or writing) tediously lengthy. **night of the long knives**, a treacherous massacre, as (according to legend) the Britons by Hengist in 472, or of Ernst Roehmand his associates by Hitler on 29-30 June 1934; a similar ruthless or decisive action. [OE]

long[2] *v.i.* to feel a strong desire; to wish ardently. [OF, = seem long to (as LONG[1])]

long. *abbr.* longitude.

longboat *n.* the largest boat carried by a sailing-ship.

longbow *n.* a large bow drawn by hand and shooting a long feathered arrow. —**longbowman** *n.* (*pl.* **-men**)

longeron /'lɒndʒərən/ *n.* (usu. in *pl.*) a longitudinal member of an aeroplane's fuselage. [F, = girder]

longevity /lɒn'dʒevɪtɪ/ *n.* long life. [f. L (*longaevus* aged)]

Longfellow /'lɒŋfeləʊ/, Henry Wadsworth (1807-82), American poet, who was professor of modern languages at Harvard (1836-54) having travelled extensively in Europe. His first wife died in Holland and his prose romance *Hyperion* (1839) is a product of his bereavement into which are woven philosophical discourses, poems, and legends. His *Ballads and other Poems* (1841) contains such well-known pieces as 'The Wreck of the Hesperus' and 'The Village Blacksmith'. Longfellow's popularity increased with subsequent volumes, including *Evangeline* (1849) set in Acadia (now Nova Scotia) with fine evocations of 'the forest primeval' and his best-known work, *The Song of Hiawatha* (1855), a narrative poem reproducing American Indian stories; its metre and novel subject-matter attracted many parodies and imitations.

longhand *n.* ordinary writing as distinct from typing, shorthand, etc.

longhorn *n.* one of a breed of cattle with long horns.

longing /'lɒŋɪŋ/ *n.* an intense desire. [f. LONG[2]]

Longinus /lɒn'dʒaɪnəs/ the name given to the author of a Greek literary treatise *On the Sublime* (probably of the 1st c. AD), a critical analysis of what constituted literary greatness, showing concern with the moral function of literature and impatience with pedantry. The period of its greatest influence extends from Boileau's French translation (1674) to the early 19th c.

Long Island an island of New York State, separated from the mainland of Connecticut by **Long Island Sound**, an arm of the Atlantic Ocean.

longitude /'lɒŋgɪtjuːd, 'lɒndʒ-/ *n.* **1.** the angular distance east or west from the meridian of Greenwich or other standard meridian to that of any place (see ill. NAVIGATION). **2.** (*Astron.*) a body's or point's angular distance especially along an ecliptic. [f. L *longitudo* (*longus* long)]

longitudinal /lɒŋgɪ'tjuːdɪn(ə)l, lɒndʒ-/ *adj.* **1.** of longitude. **2.** of or in length. **3.** lying longways. —**longitudinally** *adv.* [f. prec.]

long-shore *adj.* **1.** found on the shore. **2.** employed along the shore, especially near a port. —**long-shore drift**, the gradual movement of beach materials (such as sand and shingle) along a shore. [f. *along shore*]

longshoreman *n.* (*pl.* **-men**) a person employed in loading and unloading ships from the shore.

longways *adv.* (also **longwise**) lengthways.

loo *n.* (*colloq.*) a lavatory. [perh. f. WATERLOO, but there are a number of other possible derivations]

loofah /'luːfɑː/ *n.* the dried pod of a kind of gourd (*Luffa aegyptiaca*) used as a rough sponge while bathing. [f. Egyptian Arab.]

look /lʊk/ *v.t./i.* **1.** to use or direct one's eyes in order to see, search, or examine. **2.** to direct one's attention, to consider. **3.** to have a specified appearance, to seem. **4.** (of a thing) to face in a certain direction. **5.** to indicate (an emotion etc.) by one's looks. —*n.* **1.** the act of looking, a gaze or glance. **2.** an inspection or search. **3.** (in *sing.* or *pl.*) the appearance of the face, the expression, the personal aspect. **4.** (of a thing) appearance. —*int.* (also **look here!**) of protest or demanding attention. —**look after**, to attend to, to take charge of. **look-alike** *n.* a person or thing closely resembling another. **look down on** *or* **down one's nose at**, to regard with contempt or a feeling of superiority. **look for**, to expect; to try to find. **look forward to**, to await (an expected event) eagerly or with specified feelings. **look in**, to make a short visit or call. **look-in** *n.* a brief visit; a chance of participation or success. **look into**, to investigate. **look on**, to regard (*as*); to be a spectator. **look out**, to be vigilant or prepared; to search for and produce; to have an outlook *on* or *over*. **look over**, to inspect. **look-see** *n.* (*slang*) an inspection. **look sharp**, to make haste. **look to**, to consider; to be careful about; to rely on. **look up**, to seek information about in a reference book etc.; to improve in prospect; (*colloq.*) to go to visit. **look up to**, to respect or admire (a senior or superior person). **not like the look of**, to find alarming or suspicious. [OE]

looker *n.* **1.** a person of specified appearance. **2.** (*colloq.*) an attractive woman. —**looker-on** *n.* a spectator. [f. LOOK]

looking-glass *n.* a glass mirror.

look-out *n.* **1.** a careful watch. **2.** an observation-post. **3.** a person etc. stationed to keep watch. **4.** a prospect. **5.** a person's own concern.

loom[1] *n.* an apparatus for weaving cloth. The craft of weaving is an ancient one, and hand-operated looms are still in use as a craft or cottage industry. A horizontal loom is pictured on a pottery dish, dating from *c.*4400 BC, found at al-Badari in Egypt; the vertical loom dates from the time of the 18th Dynasty (*c.*1567-1320 BC). Similar devices were known in many other early civilizations. The power-loom was invented by Cartwright (1785), and modern looms are power-driven using either a flying shuttle, which is given sufficient impulse to carry it across the warp, or air or water jets to blow the weft thread across the warp. [OE, = tool]

loom[2] *v.i.* to appear dimly, to be seen in vague and often magnified or threatening form (*lit.* or *fig.*). [prob. f. LDu.]

loon *n.* **1.** a kind of diving bird with a wild cry, especially a grebe or large diver. **2.** (*slang*) a crazy person (cf. foll.). [alt. f. *loom* f. ON]

loony *n.* (*slang*) a lunatic. —*adj.* (*slang*) crazy. —**loony-bin** *n.* (*slang*) a mental home or mental hospital. [abbr.]

loop[1] *n.* **1.** the figure produced by a curve or doubled thread etc. that crosses itself. **2.** a thing, path, or pattern forming roughly this figure; a length of cord or wire etc. that crosses itself and is fastened at the crossing; a fastening shaped thus. **3.** a curved piece of metal serving as a handle etc. **4.** a contraceptive coil. **5.** a complete circuit for an electrical current. **6.** an endless strip of tape or film allowing continuous repetition. **7.** a sequence of computer operations repeated until some condition is satisfied. —*v.t./i.* **1.** to form (into) a loop or loops. **2.** to enclose with or as with a loop. **3.** to fasten or join with a loop or loops. —**loop-line** *n.* a railway or telegraph line that diverges from the main line and joins it again. **loop the loop**, to perform an aerobatic loop, with the aircraft turning upside down between climb and dive (ill. FLIGHT). [orig. unkn.]

loop[2] *n.* a loophole in a fort etc. [orig. unkn.]

looper *n.* a caterpillar (of a kind of moth) that progresses by arching itself into loops. [f. LOOP[1]]

loophole *n.* **1.** a means of evading a rule etc. without infringing the letter of it. **2.** a narrow vertical slit in the wall of a fort etc. for shooting or looking through or to admit light or air (ill. CASTLES). [f. LOOP[2] + HOLE]

loopy *adj.* (*slang*) crazy. [f. LOOP[1]]

loose *adj.* **1.** not or no longer held by bonds or a restraint. **2.** detached or detachable from its place, not held together or contained or fixed. **3.** slack, relaxed. **4.** inexact, indefinite, vague or incorrect. **5.** not compact or dense. **6.** morally lax. —*v.t.* **1.** to free, untie, or detach. **2.** to release. **3.** to discharge (a missile). **4.** to loosen, to relax. —**at a loose end**, without definite occupation. **loose box**, a stall in which a horse can move about. **loose cover**, a removable cover for an armchair etc. **loose-leaf** *adj.* (of a notebook etc.) with each leaf separately removable. **on the loose**, enjoying oneself freely. —**loosely** *adv.*, **looseness** *n.* [f. ON]

loosen /'luːs(ə)n/ *v.t./i.* to make or become loose or looser. —**loosen a person's tongue**, to make him talk freely. [f. prec.]

loot *n.* goods taken from an enemy or by theft. —*v.t./i.* to plunder, to take as loot; to steal from shops or houses left unprotected after a violent event. —**looter** *n.* [f. Hindi]

lop[1] *v.t.* (**-pp-**) to cut away the branches or twigs of; to cut off. [cf. obs. *lip* to prune]

lop[2] *v.i.* (**-pp-**) to hang limply. —**lop-eared** *adj.* having drooping ears. [rel. to LOB]

lope *v.i.* to run with a long bounding stride. —*n.* a long bounding stride. [f. ON (as LEAP)]

lopsided /lɒp'saɪdɪd/ *adj.* with one side lower etc., unbalanced. [f. LOP[2] + SIDE]

loquacious /lə'kweɪʃəs/ *adj.* talkative. —**loquaciously** *adv.*, **loquacity** /-'kwæsɪtɪ/ *n.* [f. L (*loqui* speak)]

Lorca /'lɔːkə/, Federico Garcia (1898-1936), Spanish poet

and dramatist. His volumes of verse include *Romancero gitano* (*Gypsy Ballads*, 1928), strongly influenced by the folk poetry of his native Andalusia. A reaction against the label of 'poet of the gypsies' took him to New York in 1929, a visit which resulted in his surrealist collection, *Poeta en Nueva York* published posthumously in (1940). On his return to Spain in 1930 he started a government-sponsored travelling theatre company which brought new and classic drama to peasant audiences; his own plays included the lyrical, intense, poetic tragedies *Bodas de sangre* (1933), *Yerma* (1934), *La Casa de Bernada Alba* (published posthumously in 1945), and several plays evoking the primitive passions of Spanish peasant life. Lorca was murdered by Nationalist partisans after the outbreak of the Spanish civil war.

lord *n.* **1.** a master or ruler; (*hist.*) a feudal superior, especially of a manor. **2.** a nobleman; **Lord**, the title of a marquis, earl, viscount, baron, or (before a Christian name) of the younger son of a duke or marquis, or in the titles of certain high officials. —*int.* expressing surprise or dismay etc. —*v.t.* (with *it*) to domineer. —**the Lord**, God or Christ. **the Lords**, the House of Lords. **Lord Chamberlain**, the head of management in the Royal Household. **Lord Chief Justice**, the president of the Queen's Bench Division. **Lord (High) Chancellor**, the highest officer of the Crown, presiding in the House of Lords etc. **Lord Lieutenant**, the chief executive authority and head of magistrates in each county; (*hist.*) the viceroy of Ireland. **Lord Mayor**, the title of the mayor in some large cities. **Lord President of the Council**, the Cabinet minister presiding at the Privy Council. **Lord Privy Seal**, a senior Cabinet minister without official duties. **Lord's day**, Sunday. **Lord's Prayer**, the prayer taught by Christ to his disciples (Matt. 6 : 9-13), beginning 'Our Father'. **Lords Spiritual**, the bishops in the House of Lords. **Lord's Supper**, the Eucharist. **Lords Temporal**, the members of the House of Lords who are not bishops. They consist of all hereditary peers and peeresses of England, Scotland, Great Britain, and the United Kingdom who have not disclaimed their peerages, life peers and peeresses, and those Lords of Appeal who are created life peers (Law Lords). **Our Lord**, Christ. [OE, orig. = bread-keeper (as LOAF[1], WARD)]

lordly *adj.* **1.** haughty, imperious. **2.** suitable for a lord. —**lordliness** *n.* [f. LORD]

Lord's Cricket Ground the premier cricket ground of the world, in London, home of the MCC. It is named after the cricketer Thomas Lord (1755-1832), and has been situated on its present site in St John's Wood since 1814.

lordship *n.* the title used in addressing or referring to a man with the rank of Lord. [f. LORD + -SHIP]

lore[1] *n.* the body of traditions and facts on a subject. [OE (as LEARN)]

lore[2] *n.* a straplike surface between the eye and upper mandible of birds or between the eye and nostril of snakes. [f. L *lorum* strap]

Lorelei /'lɔːrəlaɪ/ a rock or cliff on the Rhine with a remarkable echo, in German legend the home of a siren of the same name whose song lured boatmen to destruction.

Lorentz /'lɒrents/, Hendrik Antoon (1853-1928), Dutch physicist, who shared the 1902 Nobel Prize for physics with his pupil, Pieter Zeeman (1865-1943) for their work on electromagnetic theory. His name is applied to various concepts and phenomena which he described. —**Fitzgerald-Lorentz contraction**, the hypothesis (postulated independently by G. F. Fitzgerald) that there is a contraction or foreshortening of a moving body in a direction parallel to its line of motion, small except at speeds comparable to that of light. **Lorentz transformation**, the set of equations which in Einstein's special theory of relativity relate the space and time coordinates of one frame of reference to those of another.

Lorenz /'lɒrents/, Konrad (1903-), Austro-German zoologist, pioneer of a scientific study of behaviour emphasizing inherited instinct rather than Pavlovian reflex action. The major influences on Lorenz were studies of ornithology, especially of goose and jackdaw communities, From his observations on birds he generalized to supposed human and social behaviour patterns. He compared the ill-effects of the domestication of animals to human civilizing processes, and argued for the need to impose racial policies to prevent degeneration. These studies earned him a 1973 Nobel Prize for medicine and many academic honours.

Loreto /le'reɪtəʊ/ a town near Ancona in eastern central Italy to which pilgrims travel to see the 'Holy House', said to have been the home of the Virgin Mary in Nazareth and (according to legend) brought to Loreto by angels in 1295.

lorgnette /lɔːˈnjet/ *n.* a pair of eyeglasses or opera-glasses held to the eyes on a long handle. [F (*lorgner* squint)]

loris /ˈlɔːrɪs/ *n.* a small slender tailless nocturnal arboreal lemur, with very large dark eyes, especially the **slender loris** (*Loris gracilis*) of southern India etc. and the **slow loris** (*Bradicebus tardigradus*) of southern and SE Asia. [F, perh. f. obs. Du. *loeris* clown]

lorn *adj.* (*archaic*) desolate, forlorn. [OE, p.p. of obs. *leese* lose]

Lorraine /ləˈreɪn/ a medieval kingdom on the west bank of the Rhine, extending from the North Sea to Italy, and divided into two duchies, Upper and Lower Lorraine, in the 10th c. Upper Lorraine (south of the Ardennes), as a province of France, passed to the French Crown in 1766; part of Lorraine was acquired (with Alsace) by Germany in 1871 but was restored to France after the First World War. [f. L *Lotharingia*, f. *Lothair* name of king]

lorry *n.* a large strong motor vehicle for transporting goods etc. [orig. N. Engl., perh. f. name *Laurie*]

Los Angeles /lɒs ˈændʒɪliːz/ a city on the coast of California, the second largest in the USA; pop. (1980) 7,477,657. Its suburb, Hollywood, is the centre of the American cinema industry.

lose /luːz/ *v.t./i.* (*past* & *p.p.* **lost**) **1.** to be deprived of; to cease to have or maintain. **2.** to become unable to find; to fail to keep in sight or follow or grasp mentally. **3.** to let or have pass from one's control or reach. **4.** to get rid of. **5.** to fail to obtain or catch or perceive. **6.** to be defeated in (a contest, lawsuit, argument, etc.). **7.** to have to forfeit. **8.** to spend (time, efforts, etc.) to no purpose. **9.** to suffer loss or detriment; to be the worse off. **10.** to cause a person the loss of. **11.** (of a clock etc.) to become slow (by a specified time). **12.** (in *pass.*) to disappear, to perish, to die or be dead. —**be lost** *or* **lose oneself in,** to be engrossed in. **be lost on,** to be wasted on, not to be noticed or appreciated by. **be lost to,** to be no longer affected by or accessible to. **get lost,** (*slang*, usu. in *imper.*) to go away. **lose out,** (*colloq.*) to be unsuccessful, not to get a full chance or advantage. **losing battle,** (esp. *fig.*) a battle in which defeat seems certain. [OE, = perish]

loser /ˈluːzə(r)/ *n.* a person who loses, especially a contest or game; (*colloq.*) one who regularly fails. [f. LOSE]

loss *n.* **1.** losing, being lost. **2.** a thing or amount lost. **3.** detriment resulting from losing. —**at a loss,** (sold etc.) for less than was paid for it. **be at a loss,** to be puzzled or uncertain. **loss-leader** *n.* an article sold at a loss so as to attract customers. [prob. back-formation f. LOST]

lost *past* & *p.p.* of LOSE. —**lost-head nail,** one without a raised or projecting head (ill. CARPENTRY). **Lost Tribes,** the ten tribes of Israel taken away *c.*720 BC by Sargon II to captivity in Assyria (2 Kings 17: 6), from which they are believed never to have returned, while the tribes of Benjamin and Judah remained.

lot *n.* **1.** (*colloq.* often in *pl.*) a large number or amount; much. **2.** each of a set of objects used in making a chance selection; this method of deciding; a share or office resulting from it. **3.** a person's destiny or appointed task etc. **4.** a piece of land; (*US*) an area for a particular purpose. **5.** an article or set of articles for sale at an auction etc. **6.** a number or quantity of associated persons or things. —**bad lot,** a person of bad character. **cast** *or* **draw lots,** to decide with lots. **throw in one's lot with,** to decide to share the fortunes of. **the (whole) lot,** the total number or quantity. [OE]

loth var. of LOATH.

Lothario /ləˈθeərɪəʊ/ *n.* (*pl.* **-os**) a libertine. [character in Rowe's *Fair Penitent* (1703)]

Lothian /ˈləʊðɪən/ a local government region in SE central Scotland.

Loti /ˈləʊtɪ/, Pierre (pseudonym of Louis Marie Julien Viaud, 1850-1923), French novelist whose novels and travel books were written while he served as a naval officer. He first made his name with romances of sentimental adventure in exotic Oriental or tropical settings. His fame now rests on three novels: *Mon frère Yves* (1883), *Pêcheur d' Islande* (1886), and *Matelot* (1893), tales of the struggles of sailors who leave Brittany to fish in Iceland, and the heartbreak of those left behind.

lotion /ˈləʊʃ(ə)n/ *n.* a medicinal or cosmetic liquid preparation applied to the skin. [f. OF or L [(*lavare* wash)]

lottery /ˈlɒtərɪ/ *n.* **1.** a means of raising money by selling numbered tickets and giving prizes to the holders of numbers drawn at random. **2.** a thing whose outcome is governed by chance. [prob. f. Du. (as LOT)]

Lotto /ˈlɒtəʊ/ Lorenzo (*c.*1480-1556), Italian painter, born in Venice and trained in Giovanni Bellini's studio, probably with Giorgione and Titian. A restless man, he roamed a great deal, living in Venice and its environs, and incorporating in his art rich elements of the northern tradition and influences from Leonardo and from Dürer, who was in Venice in 1505-6. His sometimes dislocated images, highlighted in cold light, are unlike the contemplative warmth of his contemporary Giorgione, and place him as an active participant in the early mannerist tradition.

lotto /ˈlɒtəʊ/ *n.* a game of chance similar to bingo but with the numbers drawn instead of called. [It.]

lotus /ˈləʊtəs/ *n.* **1.** a legendary plant inducing luxurious languor when eaten. **2.** a kind of water-lily etc., especially as used symbolically in Hinduism and Buddhism. —**lotuseater** *n.* a person given to indolent enjoyment. **lotus position,** a cross-legged position of meditation with the feet resting on the thighs. [L f. Gk]

loud *adj.* **1.** strongly audible, producing much noise. **2.** (of colours etc.) gaudy, obtrusive. —*adv.* loudly. —**loud hailer,** an electronic device for amplifying the sound of the voice so that it can be heard at a distance. **out loud,** aloud, —**loudly** *adv.*, **loudness** *n.* [OE]

loudspeaker /laʊdˈspiːkə(r)/ *n.* an apparatus that converts electrical impulses into sound.

lough /lɒx, -x/ *n.* (*Ir.*) a lake, an arm of the sea. [f. Ir. (as LOCH)]

Louis[1] /ˈluːɪ/ the name of 18 kings of France:

Louis IX (1214-70), son of Louis VIII, reigned 1226-70, canonized as St Louis. Renowned for his honesty and pure character, Louis far exceeded the normal medieval moral standards of kingship, displaying such fairness (although not weakness) in his exercise of power as to be recognized in many ways as the arbiter of Europe. His reign was dominated by his two crusades to the Holy Land, neither of which proved successful: the first (1248-50) ended in disaster with his capture by the Egyptians, the second (1270) in his own death of plague at Carthage.

Louis XI (1423-83), son of Charles VII, reigned 1461-83. Frequently known as the 'Spider King' because of his frequent recourse to intrigue, Louis completed the work of his father in rebuilding France as a modern European power. His reign was dominated by his struggle with Charles the Rash, Duke of Burgundy, a struggle which ended with Charles's death in battle against the Swiss in 1477 and the French absorption of much of Burgundy's former territory along their border.

Louis XIV (1638-1715), son of Louis XIII, reigned 1643-1715. The reign of Louis XIV represented the high point of the Bourbon dynasty and of French power in Europe. Its magnificence earned him the name of the 'Sun King', but his brand of absolutism was to leave severe troubles for his less powerful successors, while his almost constant wars of expansion united Europe against him, and, despite the reforms of Colbert, gravely weakened France's financial position. The Treaty of Utrecht, which ended the War of the Spanish Succession, was symbolic of the ultimate failure of Louis's attempt at European hegemony, preventing as it did the union of the French and Spanish crowns.

Louis XVI (1754-93), grandson and successor of Louis XV, reigned 1774-92. A well-intentioned but weak monarch, Louis was unable to prevent political discontent in France leading to revolution. When the French Revolution broke out, the King persistently misinterpreted the situation and took refuge in a series of half-measures which proved disastrous to his cause. Eventually, with the revolution becoming progressively more extreme and with foreign invaders massing on the borders, the monarchy was abolished and Louis was executed.

Louis[2] /ˈluːɪ/, Joe (real name Joseph Louis Barrow, 1914-81), American boxer, known as the 'Brown Bomber', heavyweight champion of the world 1937-49.

Louisiana /luːiːzɪˈænə/ a State in the south-western USA, bordering on the Gulf of Mexico. The territory was claimed by France in 1682 and named in honour of Louis XIV. It was sold by the French republic to the USA in 1803, becoming the 18th State in 1812; capital, Baton Rouge. —**Louisiana purchase,** territory sold by France to the USA in 1803, comprising the western part of the Mississippi valley. The area had been explored by France, ceded to Spain in 1762, and returned to France in 1800.

Louis Philippe /ˈluːɪ fɪˈliːp/ (1773–1850), king of France 1830–48. As the Duc d'Orléans, Louis Philippe participated in the early, liberal phase of the French Revolution, but later went into exile abroad, building up a considerable fortune in England. Returning to France after the restoration of the Bourbons, he became the focus for liberal discontent, and after the overthrow of Charles X in 1830 was made king. His bourgeois-style regime was popular at first, and presided over a period of commercial growth, but it was gradually undermined by radical discontent and overthrown in a brief uprising in 1848, with Louis retiring once more to exile in England.

lounge /laʊndʒ/ v.i. to recline casually and comfortably; to loll; to stand or move about idly. —n. 1. a public room (e.g. in a hotel) for sitting in. 2. a waiting-room at an airport etc. with seats for waiting passengers. 3. a sitting-room in a house. 4. a spell of lounging. —**lounge-suit** n. a man's suit for ordinary wear. —**lounger** n. [perh. f. obs. *lungis* lout, laggard]

lour /laʊə(r)/ v.i. to frown, to look sullen or (of the sky etc.) dark and threatening. [orig. unkn.]

Lourdes /lʊəd/ a town in SW France where in 1858 a peasant girl, Bernadette Soubirous, claimed to have had visions of the Virgin Mary. At the same time a spring appeared, and miraculous healings were reported. It is now a major centre of pilgrimage.

louse /laʊs/ n. 1. (pl. lice) any of various insects of the orders Anoplura (sucking-lice) and Mallophaga (biting-lice), parasitic on mammals, birds, fish, or plants (ill. INSECTS); a parasitic insect (*Pediculus humanus*, order Anoplura) infesting human hair and skin and transmitting many diseases. 2. (slang, pl. louses) a contemptible person. —v.t. to remove lice from. —**louse up**, (slang) to spoil, to mess up. [OE]

lousy /ˈlaʊzɪ/ adj. 1. infected with lice. 2. (slang) disgusting, very bad. 3. (slang) swarming, well supplied. —**lousily** adv., **lousiness** n. [f. prec.]

lout n. a hulking or rough-mannered fellow. —**loutish** adj. [perh. f. archaic *lout* v. to bow, stoop]

Louvre /luːvr/ the national museum and art gallery of France, in Paris, housed in the former royal palace, on the site of an earlier fortress and arsenal, built by Francis I (d. 1547) and later extended. When the court moved to Versailles in 1678 its conversion into a museum was begun. It was Francis I who set the pattern for royal collecting and patronage which persisted until the Revolution, and the royal collections, greatly increased by Louis XIV, formed the nucleus of the national collection which is an epitome of French history and culture.

louvre /ˈluːvə(r)/ n. 1. any of a set of overlapping slats arranged to admit air and exclude light or rain. 2. a domed erection on a roof with side openings for ventilation etc. [f. OF *lov(i)er* skylight]

lovable /ˈlʌvəb(ə)l/ adj. inspiring love or affection. [f. LOVE]

lovage /ˈlʌvɪdʒ/ n. a herb (*Levisticum officinale*) used for flavouring. [f. OF *levesche* f. L *levisticum*]

love /lʌv/ n. 1. warm liking or affection for a person or thing. 2. sexual passion; sexual relations. 3. a beloved one, a sweetheart (often as a form of address); (colloq.) a person of whom one is fond. 4. affectionate greetings. 5. (often Love) a representation of Cupid. 6. (in games) no score, nil. —v.t./i. 1. to feel love for. 2. to like greatly, to delight in. 3. to be inclined, especially as a habit. —**for love**, because of affection; without receiving payment. **in love (with)**, feeling (esp. sexual) love (for). **love-affair** n. a romantic or sexual relationship between two people who are in love. **love-bird** n. a parakeet (esp. of the genus Agapornis) seeming to show great affection for its mate. **love-child** n. an illegitimate child. **love game**, a game in which the loser makes no score. **love-hate relationship**, an intense emotional response involving ambivalent feelings of love and hate towards the same object. **love-in-a-mist** n. a blue-flowered garden plant (*Nigella damascena*). **love-letter** n. a letter between sweethearts, expressing their love. **love-lies-bleeding** n. a garden plant (*Amaranthus caudatus*) with drooping spikes of purple-red bloom. **love-match** n. a marriage between two people who are in love with each other. **love-song** n. a song expressing love. **love-story** n. a story in which the theme is romantic love. **make love**, to have sexual intercourse; to pay amorous attentions to. **not for love or money**, not in any circumstances. [OE, rel. to LIEF]

Lovelace /ˈlʌvleɪs/, Richard (1618–57/8), English Cavalier poet. In 1642 he was committed to prison, where he

probably wrote the song 'To Althea from Prison'. He rejoined Charles I in 1645 and was again imprisoned in 1648; during this time he prepared his *Lucasta* which includes some of his best lyrics. Lovelace died in poverty, having spent his fortune in the Royalist cause.

loveless adj. unloving or unloved or both. [f. LOVE + -LESS]

Lovell /ˈlʌv(ə)l/, Sir (Alfred Charles) Bernard (1913–), English physicist and astronomer, a pioneer of radio astronomy, founder and director of Jodrell Bank observatory.

lovelorn adj. pining from unrequited love.

lovely adj. exquisitely beautiful; (colloq.) pleasing, delightful. —n. (colloq.) a pretty woman. —**loveliness** n. [OE (as LOVE)]

lover n. 1. a person (esp. a man) in love with another; a man with whom a woman is having sexual relations; (in pl.) a pair in love. 2. one who likes or enjoys something. [f. LOVE]

lovesick adj. languishing with love.

lovey-dovey /ˈlʌvɪdʌvɪ/ adj. (colloq.) fondly affectionate and sentimental. [f. LOVE]

loving /ˈlʌvɪŋ/ adj. feeling or showing love. —**loving-cup** n. a large drinking-vessel with two or more handles, passed from hand to hand at a banquet etc. so that each person may drink from its contents. —**lovingly** adv. [as LOVE]

low[1] /ləʊ/ adj. 1. not high or tall, not extending far upwards; coming below the normal or average level. 2. not elevated in position. 3. ranking below others in importance or quality. 4. of a small or less than normal amount, extent, intensity, etc.; (of opinion) unfavourable. 5. dejected, lacking vigour. 6. unfavourable. 7. ignoble, vulgar. 8. (of a sound or voice) deep not shrill, having slow vibrations; not loud. 9. (in compar.) situated on less high land or to the south; (of a geological period) earlier (called 'lower' because of the position of the corresponding rock formations); (of animals or plants etc.) of relatively simple structure, not highly developed. —n. 1. a low or the lowest level or number. 2. an area of low pressure. —adv. 1. in or to a low position (lit. or fig.). 2. in a low tone; (of a sound) at or to a low pitch. **Low Church**, the section of the Church of England which gives a relatively unimportant or 'low' place to the claims of the episcopate, priesthood, and sacraments, and approximates to Protestant Nonconformists in its beliefs. Originally used of the Latitudinarians, the term has been applied, since the time of the Oxford Movement, to Evangelicals. **low comedy**, that in which the subject and its treatment border on farce. **Low Countries**, the district now forming the Netherlands, Belgium, and Luxemburg. **low-down** adj. ignoble, dishonourable. **low-down** n. (slang) the relevant information (on). **low frequency**, (in radio) 30–300 kilohertz. **low-key** adj. restrained, lacking intensity. **low-level language**, a computer language close in form to a machine-readable code. **low-pitched** adj. (of a sound) low; (of a roof) having only a slight slope. **low pressure**, a low degree of activity or exertion; a condition of the atmosphere with the pressure below average. **low season**, the period of fewest visitors at a resort etc. **Low Sunday**, the Sunday after Easter. **low tide**, a tide of the lowest level; the time of this. **low water**, low tide; *in low water*, short of money. [f. ON (as LIE[1])]

low[2] /ləʊ/ n. the deep sound made by cows, a moo. —v.i. to make this sound. [OE]

lowbrow adj. (colloq.) not intellectual or cultured. —n. (colloq.) a lowbrow person.

Lowell[1] /ˈləʊəl/, Amy Lawrence (1874–1925), American poet. After producing her first volume of relatively conventional poetry she took up imagism and visited England in 1913 and 1914 where she met Pound (who adopted the expression 'Amy-gism') and other imagists. Her subsequent volumes show her increasing allegiance to the movement and her experiments in 'polyphonic prose', including *Men, Women and Ghosts* (1916; which contains 'Patterns'); her love of New England is expressed in 'Lilacs' and 'Purple Grackles' (in *What's O'Clock*, 1925).

Lowell[2] /ˈləʊəl/, James Russell (1819–91), American poet and critic. His works include volumes of verse, the satirical *Biglow Papers* (1848 and 1867; prose and verse), memorial odes after the Civil War, and various volumes of essays including *Among my Books* (1870) and *My Study Window* (1871).

Lowell[3] /ˈləʊəl/, Robert Traill Spence (1917–77), American poet, born in Boston of distinguished New England ancestry. In 1940 he married novelist Jean Stafford (he subsequently married writers Elizabeth Hardwick, 1949, and

Caroline Blackwood, 1973) and became a fanatical convert to Roman Catholicism. His first volume *Land of Unlikeness* (1944) betrays the conflict of Catholicism and his Boston ancestry. During the Second World War he was imprisoned as, in effect, a conscientious objector. Subsequent volumes include *Life Studies* (1959) and *For the Union Dead* (1964), and he reached the height of his public fame during his opposition to the Vietnam war and support of Senator McCarthy, as recorded in *Notebook 1967–1968* (1968). He suffered recurring bouts of manic disorder and alcoholism and his confessional volume of poems *The Dolphin* (1973) caused a scandal with its revelations of marital anguish. A legendary figure in his lifetime, he was an ironic intellectual whose ambiguous complex imagery satisfied the demands of contemporary criticism.

lower[1] /ˈləʊə(r)/ *adj.* **1.** less high in place or position. **2.** situated on lower ground or to the south. **3.** ranking below others. **4.** (of a geological or archaeological period) earlier (cf. UPPER). —*v.t.* **1.** to let or haul down. **2.** to make or become lower; to reduce in amount or quantity etc. **3.** to direct (one's gaze) downwards. —**lower case,** see CASE². **Lower Chamber** *or* **House,** the lower and usually elected body in a legislature, especially the House of Commons. [compar. of LOW¹]

lower[2] var. of LOUR.

lowermost *adj.* lowest. [f. LOWER¹ + -MOST]

lowland *n.* a low-lying country. —*adj.* of or in a lowland. —**lowlander** *n.*

lowly /ˈləʊlɪ/ *adj.* of humble rank or condition. —**lowliness** *n.* [f. LOW¹]

Lowry /ˈlaʊrɪ/, Lawrence Stephen (1887–1976), English artist. He spent most of his life in Salford, near Manchester, which became the characteristic industrial landscape of his pictures. Deliberately adopting a childlike manner of visualization, he painted small matchstick figures set against the iron and brick expanse of the town, to provide a wry perspective on life in the industrial North, combining penetration and compassion, revealing the alienation of the lonely and man's inconsequence against the juggernaut of industrialism.

loyal /ˈlɔɪəl/ *adj.* faithful; steadfast in allegiance, devoted to the legitimate sovereign etc. —**loyal toast,** a toast to the sovereign. —**loyally** *adv.*, **loyalty** *n.* [f. OF f. L *legalis*, = LEGAL]

loyalist *n.* one who remains loyal to the legitimate sovereign etc., especially in the face of rebellion or usurpation; **Loyalist,** (in Northern Ireland) one who favours retaining Ulster's link with Britain. —**loyalism** *n.* [f. prec.]

lozenge /ˈlɒzɪndʒ/ *n.* **1.** a small sweet or medicinal etc. tablet to be dissolved in the mouth. **2.** a rhombus, a diamond figure. **3.** a lozenge-shaped object. [f. OF]

LP *abbr.* long-playing (record).

L-plate /ˈelpleɪt/ *n.* a sign bearing the letter L, attached to the front and rear of a motor vehicle to indicate that it is being driven by a learner.

Lr *symbol* lawrencium.

LSD *abbr.* lysergic acid diethylamide, a powerful hallucinogenic drug.

£.s.d. /elesˈdiː/ *n.* pounds, shillings, and pence (in former British currency); money, riches. [f. L *librae, solidi, denarii*]

LT *abbr.* low tension.

Lt. *abbr.* **1.** Lieutenant. **2.** light.

Ltd. *abbr.* Limited.

Lu *symbol* lutetium.

Luanda /luːˈændə/ the capital of Angola; pop. (est. 1979) 475,300.

lubber *n.* a clumsy fellow, a lout. —**lubberly** *adj.* [perh. f. OF, = swindler]

lubricant /ˈluːbrɪkənt/ *n.* an oil or grease etc. used to reduce friction in machinery etc. [as foll.]

lubricate /ˈluːbrɪkeɪt/ *v.t.* to apply a lubricant to; to make slippery. —**lubrication** /-ˈkeɪʃ(ə)n/ *n.*, **lubricator** *n.* [f. L *lubricare (lubricus* slippery)]

lubricity /luːˈbrɪsɪtɪ/ *n.* **1.** slipperiness. **2.** skill in evasion. **3.** lewdness. [f. F or L (as prec.)]

Lucan /ˈluːk(ə)n/ (Marcus Annaeus Lucanus, 39–65) Roman poet of Spanish origin, nephew of the younger Seneca. At first an intimate of Nero, he was forced to commit suicide after joining a conspiracy against the emperor. His major work, a hexameter epic in ten books *The Civil War* (also known as the *Pharsalia*), deals with the civil war between Julius Caesar and Pompey; his republican and

Stoic ideals find expression in the depiction of Cato; a rhetorical and hyperbolical manner is the vehicle for the extravagant horrors of the subject-matter.

Lucas van Leyden /luːkəs væn ˈlaɪd(ə)n/ (1494–1533), Dutch painter of portraits and religious works who was also an outstanding graphic artist, influenced by Dürer. Early technical masterpieces include *Muhammad and the Monk*, an engraving of 1508 done when he was only 14 years old, and *Ecce Homo* (1510). Perspective was less important to him than the genre anecdote, as seen in his painting *Chess Players* (*c.*1508). He died at an early age, contemporary historians placing him at the forefront of 16th-c. Dutch art, although he was untouched by the Renaissance and did not exercise much influence over many artists, Rembrandt standing as an exception.

lucerne /luːˈsɜːn/ *n.* a cloverlike plant (*Medicago sativa*) used for fodder. [f. F f. Prov. = glow-worm, f. its shiny seeds]

lucid /ˈluːsɪd/ *adj.* **1.** expressed or expressing things clearly. **2.** sane. —**lucidity** /-ˈsɪdɪtɪ/ *n.*, **lucidly** *adv.* [f. F or It. or L *lucidus* bright (*lucēre* shine)]

Lucifer /ˈluːsɪfə(r)/ **1.** Satan, the Devil, whose fall from heaven Jerome and other early Christian writers thought was alluded to in Isaiah 14: 12 (where the word *Lucifer* (L, = light-bringer) is an epithet of the king of Babylon). **2.** (*poet.*) the planet Venus when it appears in the sky before sunrise, the morning star. [f. L (*lux* light, *ferre* bring)]

luck *n.* chance regarded as a bringer of good or bad fortune; the circumstances of life (beneficial or not) brought by this; good fortune, success due to chance. —**down on one's luck,** in a period of bad fortune. **hard luck,** worse fortune than one deserves. **push one's luck,** to take undue risks. **try one's luck,** to make a venture. **worse luck,** unfortunately. [f. LG]

luckless *adj.* **1.** invariably having bad luck. **2.** ending in failure. [f. LUCK + -LESS]

Lucknow /ˈlʌknaʊ/ the capital of Uttar Pradesh in India. The city was besieged twice by native insurgents during the Indian Mutiny in 1857.

lucky *adj.* having or resulting from good luck, especially as distinct from skill or design or merit; bringing good luck. —**lucky dip,** a tub etc. containing articles of different value into which one may dip at random on payment of a small sum. —**luckily** *adv.* [f. LUCK]

lucrative /ˈluːkrətɪv/ *adj.* profitable, producing much money. —**lucrativeness** *n.* [f. L (*lucrari* to gain, as foll.)]

lucre /ˈluːkə(r)/ *n.* (*derog.*) money, money-making as a motive for action. [f. F or L *lucrum* profit]

Lucretia /luːˈkriːʃjə/ (*Rom. legend*) wife of Tarquinius Collatinus. She was raped by a son of Tarquin the Proud and took her own life; this led to the expulsion of the Tarquins from Rome by a rebellion under Brutus.

Lucretius /luːˈkriːʃəs/ (Titus Lucretius Carus, *c.*94–*c.*55 BC) Roman didactic poet, of whose life little is known (the story that he committed suicide after being driven mad by a love-potion is probably apocryphal). His hexameter poem *On the Nature of Things* is an exposition of the atomist physics of the Epicureans; a thoroughgoing materialism is directed to the evangelical goal of giving men peace of mind by showing that their fear of the gods and of death is baseless; despite an apparently unpromising subject, the combination of philosophical zeal and poetic sublimity is unequalled in Latin.

Lucullan /loˈkʌlən, luː-/ *adj.* (esp. of a feast) very sumptuous or luxurious. [f. *Lucullus* (1st c. BC), Roman general, famous for his lavish banquets]

Lucy /ˈluːsɪ/, St (late 3rd c.), Sicilian virgin and martyr, much venerated in the early Church.

Luddite /ˈlʌdaɪt/ *n.* **1.** a member of the bands of English craftsmen who, when their jobs were threatened by the progressive introduction of machinery into their trades in the early 19th c., attempted to reverse the trend towards mechanization by wrecking the offending machines. Although the Luddites were never well organized, they were taken very seriously by the government of the day which was haunted by the spectre of a popular uprising. **2.** a person similarly seeking to obstruct progress. —*adj.* of Luddites. [perh. f. Ned *Lud*, an insane person said to have destroyed two stocking-frames *c.*1779]

ludicrous /ˈluːdɪkrəs/ *adj.* absurd, ridiculous, laughable. —**ludicrously** *adv.* [f. L (*ludicrum* stage-play, as foll.)]

ludo /ˈluːdəʊ/ *n.* a simple game played with dice and counters on a special board. [L, = I play]

Ludwig /ˈlʊdvɪg/ the name of three kings of Bavaria:

Ludwig I (1786–1868), reigned 1825–48. In the early years of his reign Ludwig pursued relatively moderate reform policies, but after the 1830 liberal disturbances across Europe he inclined more and more towards reactionary catholicism. His domination by the dancer Lola Montez led to increasing unrest against his rule, and after a series of radical protests in 1847–8 he was forced to abdicate in favour of his son Maximilian.

Ludwig II (1845–86), reigned 1864–86. Ludwig II sided with the losing Austrians in the Austro-Prussian War of 1866, but afterwards came increasingly under Prussian influence and eventually joined the new German Empire, having obtained special legislative concessions for his country. A patron of the arts, and a friend of Wagner, in the last years of his reign he became a recluse and concentrated on building a series of elaborate castles at ruinous expense to his kingdom. He was declared insane and deposed in 1886 and drowned himself in Lake Starnberg almost immediately afterwards.

luff *n*. the side of a fore-and-aft sail next to the mast or stay (ill. SAILING-SHIPS). —*v.t./i.* **1.** to bring a ship's head nearer the wind; to bring the head of (a ship) thus. **2.** to raise or lower (a crane's jib). [f. OF *lof* prob. f. LG]

Luftwaffe /ˈlʊftvɑːfə/ *n*. the German air force before and during the Second World War. [G, = air weapon]

lug *v.t./i.* (-gg-) to drag or carry with great effort; to pull hard. —*n.* **1.** a hard or rough pull. **2.** a projection on an object by which it may be carried, fixed in place, etc. **3.** (*colloq.*) an ear. [prob. f. Scand.]

luge /luːʒ/ *n*. a short raised toboggan for one person seated. —*v.i.* to ride on a luge. [Swiss F]

luggage /ˈlʌgɪdʒ/ *n*. suitcases, bags, etc., for containing a traveller's belongings. [f. prec.]

lugger *n*. a small ship with four-cornered sails. [f. foll.]

lugsail *n*. a four-cornered sail on a yard. [prob. f. LUG]

lugubrious /luːˈguːbrɪəs/ *adj*. doleful. —**lugubriously** *adv*. [f. L *lugēre* mourn]

lugworm *n*. a large marine worm (*Arenicola marina*) used as bait. [orig. unkn.]

Luini /luːˈiːnɪ/, Bernardino (*c.*1485–1532), Italian painter of the Milanese school, indebted to Leonardo da Vinci but lacking his richness and innovation. The many examples of his work in Lombardy have in common a naïvety and slightness which prevents him from being regarded as a great painter, although his sentimental style appealed to Victorian taste.

Luke /luːk/, St **1.** an Apostle, physician, possibly the son of a Greek freedman of Rome, closely associated with St Paul, and traditionally the author of the third Gospel and the Acts of the Apostles. Feast day, 18 Oct. **2.** the third Gospel. —**St Luke's summer,** a period of fine weather expected about 18 Oct.

lukewarm /ˈluːkwɔːm/ *adj*. **1.** moderately warm, tepid. **2.** not enthusiastic, indifferent. [f. dial. *luke* tepid + WARM]

lull *v.t./i.* **1.** to soothe or send to sleep. **2.** to calm (suspicions etc.), usually by deception. **3.** (of a storm or noise) to lessen, to become quiet. —*n.* an intermission in a storm etc.; a temporary period of inactivity or quiet. [imit. of sounds used in lulling a child]

lullaby /ˈlʌləbaɪ/ *n*. a soothing song to send a child to sleep. [as prec.]

Lully /ˈluːlɪ/, Jean-Baptiste (1632–87), composer who was born in Florence but lived in France from the age of 14, changing his name and his nationality in 1661. He entered the service of the young Louis XIV as a dancer and soon became one of the most powerful figures at court. He created and drummed into superb shape a small orchestra of string players known as the Petits Violons, and in 1672 bought the privilege to establish a Royal Academy of Music together with the right of veto on any work which involved singing throughout. Lully's own operas mark the beginning of the French operatic tradition; many were not only popular in his own lifetime—the inevitable result of his monopoly—but also continued to hold the stage in France for nearly a century after their composition. They marked his skill as an orchestrator and his sensitivity to French declamation. He died from gangrene as the result of striking his foot with the long staff he used for beating time on the floor.

lumbago /lʌmˈbeɪgəʊ/ *n*. a rheumatic muscular pain in the lower part of the back. [L (*lumbus* loin)]

lumbar /ˈlʌmbə(r)/ *adj*. of the loins. [f. L (as prec.)]

lumber *n*. **1.** disused and cumbersome articles; useless stuff. **2.** partly prepared timber. —*v.t./i.* **1.** to encumber. **2.** to fill up space inconveniently; to obstruct (a place). **3.** to move in a blundering noisy way. **4.** to cut and prepare forest timber. —**lumber-jacket** *n*. a jacket of the kind worn by lumberjacks. **lumber-room** *n*. a room in which disused articles are kept. [v. perh. imit.; n. perh. in part assoc. with obs. *lumber* pawnbroker's shop]

lumberjack *n*. one who fells and removes lumber (= timber).

lumen /ˈluːmen/ *n*. a unit of luminous flux, the flux per unit solid angle from a uniform source of one candela. [L, = light]

Lumière /ˈljuːmɪeə(r)/, Auguste (1862–1954) and Louis (1864–1948), French inventors and pioneers of cinema. Their Cinématographe, initially a camera and projector in one, was patented in 1895 and gave its first public performance later in the same year.

luminary /ˈluːmɪnərɪ/ *n*. **1.** a natural light-giving body, especially the sun or moon. **2.** a person as a source of intellectual or spiritual light. [f. OF or L (*lumen* light)]

luminescent /luːmɪˈnes(ə)nt/ *adj*. emitting light without heat. —**luminescence** *n*. [as prec.]

luminous /ˈluːmɪnəs/ *adj*. shedding light, phosphorescent and so visible in darkness. —**luminosity** /-ˈnɒsɪtɪ/ *n*. [f. OF or L (as LUMINARY)]

lump¹ *n*. **1.** a hard or compact mass of no particular or regular shape. **2.** a protuberance or swelling on a surface. **3.** (*slang*) a great quantity, a lot. **4.** a heavy, dull, or ungainly person. —*v.t.* to put or consider together; to treat as all alike. —**the lump,** casual workers especially in the building trade who are paid in lump sums. **in the lump,** generally, taking things as a whole. **lump in one's throat,** a feeling of discomfort there due to anxiety or emotion. **lump sugar,** sugar in small lumps or cubes. **lump sum,** a sum covering a number of items; money paid down all at once. [perh. f. Scand.]

lump² *v.t.* (*colloq.*) to put up with ungraciously. [imit.]

lumpish *adj*. **1.** heavy and clumsy. **2.** stupid, lethargic. [f. LUMP¹]

lumpy *adj*. full of or covered with lumps; (of water) choppy. —**lumpily** *adv.*, **lumpiness** *n*. [f. LUMP¹]

lunacy /ˈluːnəsɪ/ *n*. **1.** insanity. **2.** great folly. [f. LUNATIC]

lunar /ˈluːnə(r)/ *adj*. of, like, or concerned with the moon. —**lunar (excursion) module,** a module for making a journey from an orbiting spacecraft to the moon's surface and back. **lunar month,** the period of the moon's revolution, especially a lunation; (*pop.*) a period of four weeks. [f. L (*luna* moon)]

lunate /ˈluːneɪt/ *adj*. crescent-shaped. [as prec.]

lunatic /ˈluːnətɪk/ *adj*. insane; extremely reckless or foolish. —*n.* a lunatic person. —**lunatic asylum,** (*hist.*) a mental home or mental hospital. **lunatic fringe,** a fanatical or eccentric or visionary minority of a party etc. [f. OF f. L (as prec.), because formerly believed to be affected by changes of moon]

lunation /luːˈneɪʃ(ə)n/ *n*. the interval between new moons, about 29½ days. [f. L (as LUNAR)]

lunch *n*. **1.** the midday meal. **2.** a light refreshment at mid-morning. —*v.t./i.* **1.** to take lunch. **2.** to provide lunch for. [f. foll.]

luncheon /ˈlʌntʃ(ə)n/ *n*. (*formal*) the midday meal. —**luncheon meat,** tinned meat loaf of pork etc. **luncheon voucher,** a voucher given to an employee as part of his pay and exchangeable for food at certain restaurants and shops. [orig. unkn.]

lung *n*. either of the pair of air-breathing organs in man and most vertebrates. (ill. BODY 3). —**lung-fish** *n*. a freshwater bony fish of the order Dipnoi, with a sac-shaped air-breathing organ in addition to or in place of gills. Extant species occur in South America, Africa, and Australia. [OE, rel. to LIGHT²]

lunge *n*. **1.** a sudden forward movement of the body in thrusting, hitting, or kicking; a thrust. **2.** a long rope on which a horse is held and made to move in a circle round its trainer. —*v.t./i.* **1.** to deliver or make a lunge; to drive (a weapon etc.) violently in some direction. **2.** to exercise (a horse) on a lunge. [f. F *allonger* lengthen (as LONG¹)]

lupin /ˈluːpɪn/ *n*. a garden or fodder plant of the genus *Lupinus*, with long tapering spikes of flowers. [f. L]

lupine /ˈluːpaɪn/ *adj*. of or like wolves. [f. L *lupinus* (*lupus* wolf)]

lupus /'lu:pəs/ *n.* an ulcerous skin disease, especially tuberculosis of the skin. [L, = wolf]

lurch¹ *n.* a sudden lean or deviation to one side, a stagger. —*v.i.* to make a lurch, to stagger. [orig. Naut., f. *lee-lurch* alt. of *lee-latch* drifting to leeward]

lurch² *n.* **leave in the lurch**, to abandon (a friend or ally) to an awkward situation; to desert in difficulties. [f. F *lourche* game like backgammon, bad defeat in this]

lurcher *n.* a dog cross-bred between a collie or sheep-dog and a greyhound, often used by poachers for retrieving game. [f. obs. *lurch* var. of LURK]

lure /ljʊə(r)/ *v.t.* **1.** to entice. **2.** to recall with a lure. —*n.* **1.** a thing used to entice; the enticing quality of a pursuit etc. **2.** a falconer's apparatus for recalling a hawk. [f. F *luere*]

lurid /'ljʊərɪd/ *adj.* **1.** strong and glaring in colour. **2.** sensational, showy. **3.** horrifying. **4.** ghastly, wan. —**luridly** *adv.*, **luridness** *n.* [f. L (*luror* wan or yellow colour)]

lurk *v.i.* **1.** to linger furtively or unobtrusively. **2.** to lie hidden while waiting to attack. **3.** to be latent. [perh. f. LOUR]

Lusaka /lu:'sɑːkə/ the capital of Zambia; pop. (est. 1980) 641,000.

luscious /'lʌʃəs/ *adj.* **1.** richly sweet in taste or smell. **2.** (of style) over-rich. **3.** voluptuously attractive. —**lusciously** *adv.*, **lusciousness** *n.* [perh. f. obs. *licious* f. DELICIOUS]

lush *adj.* **1.** (of grass etc.) luxuriant and succulent. **2.** luxurious. —**lushly** *adv.*, **lushness** *n.* [perh. f. obs. *lash* soft f. OF (as LAX)]

Lusitania¹ /lu:sɪ'teɪnɪə/ an ancient province of Hispania, almost identical with modern Portugal.

Lusitania² /lu:sɪ'teɪnɪə/ a Cunard liner which was sunk by a German submarine in the Atlantic in May 1915 with the loss of over 1,000 lives. The anti-German feeling that this event generated in the USA was a factor in bringing that country into the First World War.

lust *n.* **1.** strong sexual desire. **2.** any passionate desire or enjoyment. **3.** sensuous appetite regarded as sinful. —*v.i.* to have a strong or excessive (esp. sexual) desire. —**lustful** *adj.*, **lustfully** *adv.* [OE]

lustre /'lʌstə(r)/ *n.* **1.** the soft brightness of a smooth or shining surface. **2.** glory, distinction. **3.** an iridescent metallic glaze on pottery and porcelain; pottery and porcelain with this. —**lustrous** *adj.* [F f. It. (L *lustrare* illuminate)]

lusty *adj.* healthy and strong; vigorous, lively. —**lustily** *adv.*, **lustiness** *n.* [f. LUST]

lute¹ /lu:t/ *n.* a plucked stringed instrument with frets and a round body, resembling a halved pear. In Europe it was one of the most important solo instruments from the 16th to the 18th c., and with the 20th-c. revival of interest in music of this period it has regained something of its former popularity. The lute was brought to Spain by the Moors at least as early as the 11th c., at that time having no frets and being plucked by a plectrum rather than the fingers. The word is also used to describe the many different plucked instruments of Asia and eastern Europe which have a bowl-shaped body: a form of 'long lute' (with neck longer than the body) was known in Mesopotamia in the 2nd millennium BC, while a short-necked instrument was played in Greece from *c.*800 BC. [f. F, ult. f. Arab.]

lute² /lu:t/ *n.* clay or cement for making joints airtight etc. —*v.t.* to treat with lute. [f. OF f. L *lutum* mud]

lutenist /'lu:tənɪst/ *n.* a lute-player. [f. L (as LUTE¹)]

lutetium /lu:'ti:ʃəm/ *n.* a metallic element, the heaviest and last of the lanthanide series, symbol Lu, atomic number 71, first discovered in 1907. It has few commercial uses at present. [F f. L *Lutetia* ancient name of Paris, native city of its discoverer (G. Urbain, d. 1938)]

Luther /'lu:θə(r)/, Martin (1483-1546), German Protestant theologian, founder of the German Reformation. One of the giants of history, his religious ideas brought political consequences which influenced European history for centuries. In 1505 he became an Augustinian friar, and later taught at the newly founded university of Wittenberg, latterly as professor of Scripture. His study of the Bible, the influence of Augustine and late medieval German mysticism, and his own experience of the religious life led him to see an analogy between the religion of his day and the Judaism St Paul had relinquished, and the Pauline doctrine of justification by faith became for Luther the touchstone of reform. Public controversy, sparked off by his 95 *Theses* (1517), led quickly to a break between Luther and the Church. Justification by faith alone implied for him the freedom of the Christian man to dispense with a priestly system mediating between men and God. Marriage of the clergy, restoration of the chalice to the laity, the translation of the Scriptures, all pointed to the equality of men before God, though, as Luther's opposition to the Peasants' Revolt (1524-6) revealed, this had no political consequences. Through his German Bible and hymns, Luther's influence on German religion and on the German language has been enormous.

Lutheran /'lu:θərən/ *adj.* of Martin Luther or the Lutheran Church. —*n.* a follower of Luther; a member of the Lutheran Church. —**Lutheran Church**, the Church accepting the Augsburg Confession of 1530, with justification by faith alone as its cardinal doctrine. —**Lutheranism** *n.* [f. prec.]

Lutine Bell /'lu:ti:n/ the bell of HMS *Lutine*, which sank in 1799. The ship was carrying a large amount of coin and bullion, and the loss fell on the underwriters, who were members of Lloyd's of London. When the bell was recovered during salvage operations it was taken to Lloyd's, where it now hangs. It is rung (and business is halted) whenever there is an important announcement to be made to the underwriters. [F, fem. of *lutin* spirit, imp]

Lutyens¹ /'lʌtjənz/, (Agnes) Elizabeth (1906-), English composer, daughter of Sir Edwin Lutyens. She was one of the first English composers to use the 12-note system. Her works include operas, orchestral and choral works, and chamber music; she has written nearly 200 scores for films and radio, and incidental music for plays.

Lutyens² /'lʌtjənz/, Sir Edwin Landseer (1869-1944), English architect who dominated design in the early 1900s. He established his reputation designing country houses, moving from a romantic red-brick style to Palladian-influenced formal designs. His immense output included the British Embassy, Washington (1926), and, most importantly, his work in designing the Indian capital, New Delhi (1915-30), where his mature public style is dramatically demonstrated.

lux /lʌks/ *n.* (*pl.* same) a unit of illumination, one lumen per square metre. [L, = light]

luxe /lʌks,lʊks/ *n.* luxury, cf. DE LUXE. [F f. L *luxus*]

Luxemburg /'lʌksəmbɜːg/ a country in western Europe, situated between Belgium, Germany, and France; pop. (1983) 365,500; official language, French; capital, Luxemburg, seat of the European Court of Justice and the Secretariat of the parliament of the EEC; pop. (1983) 78,900. The country is rich in iron ore and its economic prosperity is based chiefly on its large iron and steel industries. Becoming a Hapsburg possession in the 15th c., Luxemburg was Spanish until 1713 and then Austrian until annexed by France in 1795. As a result of the Treaty of Vienna in 1815 it became a grand duchy, though in 1839 it lost its western province to Belgium. Occupied by Germany during both World Wars, Luxemburg formed a customs union with Belgium in 1922 which was extended in 1948 into the Benelux Customs Union which included the Netherlands. —**Luxemburger** *n.*

Luxor /'lʌksə(r)/ a city of Egypt, site of the southern complex of monuments of ancient Thebes. [f. Arab, = castles]

luxuriant /lʌg'zjʊərɪənt/ *adj.* growing profusely; exuberant, florid. —**luxuriance** *n.* [f. *luxuriare* grow rank (as LUXURY)]

luxuriate /lʌg'zjʊərɪeɪt/ *v.i.* to revel or feel keen delight; to abandon oneself to enjoyment or ease. [as prec.]

luxurious /lʌg'zjʊərɪəs/ *adj.* **1.** supplied with luxuries, extremely comfortable. **2.** fond of luxury. —**luxuriously** *adv.*, **luxuriousness** *n.* [f. OF f. L (as foll.)]

luxury /'lʌkʃərɪ/ *n.* **1.** choice or costly surroundings, possessions, food, etc.; the habitual use or enjoyment of these. **2.** a thing desirable for comfort or enjoyment but not essential. **3.** (*attrib.*) comfortable and expensive. [f. OF f. L *luxuria* abundance)]

LV *abbr.* luncheon voucher.

lx *abbr.* lux.

LXX *abbr.* the Septuagint. [Latin numeral, = 70]

Lyceum /laɪ'sɪəm/ *n.* **1.** the garden at Athens where Aristotle taught. **2.** his followers, his philosophy. [L f. Gk (*Lukeios* epithet of Apollo, whose temple stood near by)]

lychee /'laɪtʃiː/ var. of LITCHI.

lychgate /'laɪtʃɡeɪt/ var. of LICHGATE.

Lycia /'lɪsɪə/ the ancient name for the region of SW Asia Minor between Caria and Pamphylia. —**Lycian** *adj. & n.*

Lycurgus /laɪ'kɜːɡəs/ the reputed founder of the constitution of ancient Sparta, probably of about the end of the 9th c. BC.

Lydgate /'lɪdgeɪt/, John (?1370–1449), English poet, a prolific writer of verse often in a Chaucerian vein. His longer works include the *Troy Book* (1412–20), telling the 'noble storye' of Troy, written at the request of Prince Henry (later Henry V), *The Siege of Thebes* (1420–2) and *The Fall of Princes* (1431–8). He enjoyed great popularity up to the 17th c. but later critics have found his work dull and prolix.

Lydia /'lɪdɪə/ the ancient name for the region of western Asia Minor south of Mysia and north of Caria. It was a powerful kingdom *c.*700–*c.*546 BC, and by the time of its last king (Croesus) had considerably extended its territory. Lydia was probably the first realm to use coined money. —**Lydian** *adj.* & *n.*

lye /laɪ/ *n.* water made alkaline with wood ashes; any alkaline solution for washing things. [OE]

Lyell /'laɪəl/, Sir Charles (1797–1875), Scottish geologist whose textbook *Principles of Geology* (1830–3) influenced a generation of geologists. He held that the earth's features were shaped over a long period of time by natural processes, and not during short periodic tremendous upheavals as proposed by the 'catastrophist' school of thought. In this he revived the theories of James Hutton, but his influence on geological opinion was much greater. His views cleared the way for Darwin's theory of evolution which Lyell, after some hesitation, accepted.

lying *partic.* of LIE[1], LIE[2].

Lyly /'lɪlɪ/, John (?1554–1606), English poet and dramatist. His most popular works in Elizabethan times were his prose romances *Euphues: The Anatomy of Wit* (1578) and *Euphues and his England* (1580), written in a characteristically elaborate style where ornament takes priority over sense; their peculiar style became known as 'Euphuism'. His plays, all written for performance by boy actors to courtly audiences, are now admired for their flexible use of dramatic prose and their grace and wit.

lymph /lɪmf/ *n.* the colourless fluid from the tissues or organs of the body, containing white blood-cells; this fluid used as a vaccine. [f. F or L *lympha* water]

lymphatic /lɪmˈfætɪk/ *adj.* **1.** of, secreting, or conveying lymph. **2.** (of a person) flabby, pale, sluggish. [orig. = frenzied, now assoc. w. LYMPH]

lynch /lɪntʃ/ *v.t.* (of a mob) to execute or punish violently without lawful trial. —**lynch law,** such a procedure by a self-constituted illegal court. [app. f. Capt. W. *Lynch*, judge in Virginia *c.*1780]

lynchet /'lɪntʃɪt/ *n.* a ridge or ledge formed by prehistoric ploughing on a slope. [f. OE *hlinc*; cf. LINKS]

lynx /lɪŋks/ *n.* a wild animal of the subgenus *Lynx* of the cat genus, with a short tail, spotted fur, and proverbially keen sight. —**lynx-eyed** *adj.* keen-sighted. [f. L f. Gk]

Lyra /'laɪrə/ a northern constellation, the Lyre, whose brightest star, Vega, dominates the heavens in summer and is the fifth brightest star visible.

lyre /laɪə(r)/ *n.* a plucked stringed instrument in which strings are fixed to a crossbar supported by two arms. It was one of the most important instruments of ancient Greece (Homer describes Achilles playing the lyre when the embassy from Agamemnon visited him in his tent) but is widespread now only in eastern Africa. —**lyre-bird** *n.* an Australian bird of the genus *Menura*, the male of which has a lyre-shaped tail display. [f. OF f. L f. Gk]

lyric /'lɪrɪk/ *adj.* **1.** (of poetry) expressing the writer's emotions, usually briefly and in stanzas or groups of lines; (of a poet) writing in this manner. **2.** of or for the lyre; meant to be sung; fit to be expressed in song; of the nature of song. —*n.* **1.** a lyric poem. **2.** (esp. in *pl.*) the words of a song. **3.** (in *pl.*) lyric verses. [f. F f. L f. Gk (as prec.)]

lyrical /'lɪrɪk(ə)l/ *adj.* **1.** resembling or using language appropriate to lyric poetry. **2.** (*colloq.*) highly enthusiastic. —**lyrically** *adv.* [as prec.]

lyricist /'lɪrɪsɪst/ *n.* a writer of lyrics [f. LYRIC]

Lysander /laɪˈsændə(r)/ (d. 395 BC) Spartan general and statesman, who was instrumental in the final defeat of Athens in the Peloponnesian War. He destroyed the Athenian navy at Aegospotami in 405 BC, and conducted the subsequent blockade of the Piraeus.

Lysenko /lɪˈseŋkəʊ/, Trofim Denisovich (1898–1976), Soviet biologist and geneticist, an adherent of Lamarck's theory of evolution by inheritance of acquired characteristics. Since Lysenko's ideas harmonized with Marxist ideology he was favoured by Stalin, and dominated Soviet genetics until 1948. Many false claims resulted during this unfortunate phase, notably that wheat grown in cold climates would 'vernalize' or become adapted genetically to resist low temperatures.

Lysippus /laɪˈsɪpəs/ (4th c. BC) Greek sculptor of Sicyon, official portraitist and favourite court sculptor of Alexander the Great. There are no works extant which are indisputably attributed to him but clear literary evidence survives, especially through Pliny, of his great influence on contemporaries and later artists. Although he also worked in marble, his bronze athletes, especially the Apoxyomenos (athlete cleaning himself, *c.*320–315 BC, of which a Roman copy exists) are his best-known works and support the tradition that he introduced a new scheme of proportions for the human body. He can be seen as the last great sculptor in the 4th-c. tradition, his innovations maturing in the works of Hellenistic sculptors.

-lysis /-lɪsɪs/ *suffix* forming nouns denoting disintegration or decomposition (*electrolysis*). [L f. Gk *lusis* loosening (*luō* loosen)]

-lyte /-laɪt/ *suffix* forming nouns denoting substances that can be decomposed (*electrolyte*). [L f. Gk *lutos* loosed (as prec.)]

Lytton /'lɪt(ə)n/, Edward George Earle, 1st Baron Lytton of Knebworth (1803–73), British novelist and politician, son of General Bulwer, added his mother's name of Lytton when he inherited her estate, Knebworth, in 1843. Educated at Cambridge, he embarked on a political career (first as Liberal, later as Tory MP), and financed his extravagant life-style by a prolific and versatile literary output which spanned the many changes in 19th-c. fiction from his first success *Pelham* (1828), which presents an archetypal wit and dandy as hero, to his immensely successful but now little-read historical romances, such as *The Last Days of Pompeii* (1834). Of his plays *Money* (1840) has been successfully revived.

M

M,m /em/ *n.* (*pl.* **Ms, M's**) **1.** the thirteenth letter of the alphabet. **2.** (as a Roman numeral) 1,000.

M *abbr.* **1.** mega-. **2.** motorway.

M. *abbr.* **1.** Master. **2.** *Monsieur.*

m *abbr.* **1.** metre(s). **2.** mile(s). **3.** million(s). **4.** milli-. **5.** minute(s). **6.** (also **m.**) masculine; married; male.

'm (*colloq.*) = *am* in *I'm.*

MA *abbr.* Master of Arts.

ma /mɑː/ *n.* (*colloq.*) mother. [abbr. of MAMMA].

ma'am /mæm, mɑːm, məm/ *n.* madam (used esp. in addressing a royal lady or an officer in the WRAC etc.). [abbr.]

Maat /mɑːt/ (*Egyptian myth.*) the goddess of truth, justice, and cosmic order, daughter of Ra. She was the feather (this as a hieroglyphic sign means 'true' or 'just') against which the heart of the deceased was weighed in the balance at the judgement of the dead. She is depicted as a young and beautiful woman, standing or seated, with a feather on her head.

Mabinogion /mæbɪˈnɔʊgɪən/ a collection of Welsh prose tales of the 11th-13th c., dealing with Celtic legends and mythology. [Welsh *Mabinogi* instruction for young bards]

Mabuse /məˈbjuːz/ (*c.*1478-1533/6), Flemish painter thus called because of his birthplace, Maubeuge (his real name was Jan Gossaert). Nothing is known of his early life and training, but soon after 1507 he entered the permanent service of Philip of Burgundy. He travelled in Italy where the art of the High Renaissance made a lasting impression on him and he became one of the first artists to disseminate the Italian style in the Netherlands. His works are largely nudes, studies of the Virgin and Child, and commissioned portraits.

mac *n.* (*colloq.*) a mackintosh. [abbr.]

macabre /məˈkɑːbr/ *adj.* grim, gruesome. [f. OF, perh. f. *Macabé* Maccabee, with ref. to play containing slaughter of the Maccabees]

macadam /məˈkædəm/ *n.* a material for road-making with successive layers of broken stone compacted; tar macadam (see TAR¹). [f. J. L. *McAdam*, Scottish engineer (d. 1836) who advocated this method]

macadamize /məˈkædəmaɪz/ *v.t.* to surface with macadam. [f. prec.]

macaque /məˈkɑːk/ *n.* a monkey of the genus *Macaca*, e.g. the rhesus monkey, of India and SE Asia. [F f. Port., = monkey]

macaroni /mækəˈrəʊnɪ/ *n.* **1.** pasta formed into tubes. **2.** (*pl.* **-ies**) an 18th-c. dandy. [f. It. f. Gk *makaria* barley food]

macaronic /mækəˈrɒnɪk/ *adj.* (of verse) of burlesque form containing Latin or other foreign words and vernacular words with Latin etc. terminations. [f. obs. It., joc. (as prec.)]

macaroon /mækəˈruːn/ *n.* a small cake or biscuit made with ground almonds or coconut. [f. F f. It. (as MACARONI)]

MacArthur /məˈkɑːθə(r)/, Douglas (1880-1964), American general who commanded US (later Allied) forces in the SW Pacific during the Second World War. He was in charge of the ceremony at which Japan surrendered, and administered that country during the Allied occupation that followed. In 1950-1 he was commander of military forces in Korea.

Macaulay¹ /məˈkɔːlɪ/, Dame (Emilie) Rose (1881-1958), English novelist, much acclaimed in the 1920s for her light satirical novels. Her witty scholarly accounts of her travels in the Mediterranean, written in later life, are also noteworthy.

Macaulay² /məˈkɔːlɪ/, Thomas Babington, 1st Baron (1800-59), English historian, essayist, and philanthropist. As a Civil Servant in India he established an English system of education there, and devised a new criminal code, before returning to Britain and devoting himself to literature and politics. Among his best-known works were the *Lays of Ancient Rome* (1842), but his greatest achievement was his detailed *History of England* (1849-61) from the accession of James II to the death of William III, written with compelling narrative force and lucidity (with a distinct Whig bias)

which did much to establish history as the discipline it is today.

macaw /məˈkɔː/ *adj.* an American parrot of the genus *Ara* etc., with bright colours and a long tail. [f. Port. *Macao*]

Macbeth /məkˈbeθ/ (*c.*1005-57), king of Scotland 1040-57, the subject of one of Shakespeare's tragedies. A far more effective ruler than the play suggests, Macbeth came to the throne after murdering Duncan I, but was himself killed 17 years later by Malcolm III.

Maccabees /ˈmækəbiːz/ *n.* **1.** a Jewish family which was mainly instrumental in freeing Judaea from the oppression of the Syrian king, Antiochus Epiphanes, and thus stemming the threatened destruction of Judaism by the advance of Hellenism. The revolt was begun in 168 BC by Mattathias, then an aged priest, and the struggle was carried on by his five sons, three of whom (Judas, Jonathan, and Simon) led the Jews in their struggle. **2.** four books of Jewish history and theology, of which the first two (whose hero is Judas Maccabaeus) are included in the Apocrypha. —**Maccabean** /-ˈbiːən/ *adj.* [f. L *Maccabaeus* f. Gk, epithet of Judas, perh. f. Heb. *maqāb* hammer]

McCarthy /məˈkɑːθɪ/, Mary (1912-), American novelist and critic. Her novels include *The Groves of Academe* (1952), which describes the political persecutions of McCarthyism (see foll.); *The Group* (1963), a study of the lives and careers of eight college girls; *Birds of America* (1971), deploring the effects of growing tourism; and *Cannibals and Missionaries* (1980), dealing with a hijacking in Holland. She has also published volumes of essays and criticism, short stories, and descriptive profiles of two Italian cities in *Venice Observed* (1956) and *The Stones of Florence* (1959). She was married to and divorced from the essayist and critic Edmund Wilson.

McCarthyism /məˈkɑːθɪɪz(ə)m/ *n.* anti-Communist persecution, verging on public hysteria, prevalent in the USA in the decade following the Second World War. Under the leadership of Senator J. R. McCarthy (d. 1957) this witch-hunt for people suspected of Communist beliefs, and their removal especially from Government departments, resulted in the ruin of many careers and a nationwide suspicion of Communism which is still apparent in the USA today.

McCoy /məˈkɔɪ/ *n.* **the real McCoy**, (*colloq.*) the real thing, the genuine article. [orig. unkn.]

Macdonald¹ /məkˈdɒn(ə)ld/, Flora (1722-90), a popular Jacobite heroine who aided Charles Edward Stuart's escape from Scotland, after his defeat at Culloden in 1746, by smuggling him over to the Isle of Skye in a small boat under the eyes of government forces.

MacDonald² /məkˈdɒn(ə)ld/, James Ramsay (1866-1937), British statesman. Leader of the Parliamentary Labour Party before the First World War, he resigned because of his pacifist views. Resuming leadership of the party in 1922, he led the short-lived Labour government of 1924 and was elected Prime Minister again in 1929, but without an overall majority. Faced with economic crisis, and weakened by splits in his own party, he formed a National Government with some Conservatives and Liberals, an act for which he was expelled from the Labour Party. MacDonald remained Prime Minister until succeeded by Baldwin in 1935.

mace¹ *n.* **1.** a staff of office, especially the symbol of the Speaker's authority in the House of Commons (ill. PARLIAMENT). **2.** (*hist.*) a heavy club usually having a metal head and spikes. [f. OF]

mace² *n.* the dried outer covering of the nutmeg as a spice. [f. OF f. L *macir* spicy bark]

macédoine /ˈmæsɪdwɑːn/ *n.* mixed fruit or vegetables, especially cut up small or in jelly. [F]

Macedon /ˈmæsɪd(ə)n/ ancient Macedonia.

Macedonia /mæsɪˈdəʊnɪə/ **1.** an ancient country (now a region of northern Greece and SE Yugoslavia) at the NE end of the Greek peninsula, including the coastal plain around Salonika and the mountain ranges behind. It was the seat of a kingdom which under Philip II and Alexander the Great became a world power. **2.** a constituent republic of Yugoslavia. —**Macedonian** *adj.* & *n.*

macerate /'mæsəreɪt/ *v.t./i.* **1.** to make or become soft by soaking. **2.** to waste away by fasting. —**maceration** /-'reɪʃ(ə)n/ *n.* [f. L *macerare*]

Mach /mɑːk/, Ernst (1838–1916), Austrian physicist and philosopher of science. His belief that all knowledge of the world comes from sensations, and that science should be solely concerned with observables, inspired the logical positivist philosophers of the Vienna Circle in the 1920s, and also scientists such as Einstein in the formulation of his theory of relativity, and the 'Copenhagen school' of quantum mechanics. In commemoration of his work on aerodynamics, his name has been preserved in the Mach number (see entry).

machete /mə'tʃetɪ, -'tʃeɪtɪ/ *n.* a broad heavy knife used in Central America and the West Indies. [Sp. (*macho* hammer, f. L)]

Machiavelli /mækɪə'velɪ/, Niccolo di Bernardo dei (1469–1527), Florentine statesman and political philosopher. After holding high office he was exiled by the Medicis on suspicion of conspiracy, but was subsequently restored to some degree of favour. He produced an important study of the art of war and a series of works on political philosophy, but his best-known work was *The Prince* (1513), a treatise on statecraft directed to the attainment of a united Italy by means that included cruelty and bad faith. Selected maxims from it were translated into French, and attacked by the French Huguenot Gentillet, and it was from an English translation of this treatise that the Elizabethans derived their knowledge of, and hostility to, Machiavelli.

machiavellian /mækɪə'velɪən/ *adj.* elaborately cunning; deceitful, perfidious. [f. prec.]

machicolation /məʃɪkə'leɪʃ(ə)n/ *n.* an opening between the corbels of a projecting parapet, through which missiles etc. could be hurled down on attackers; a structure with such openings (ill. CASTLES). [f. OF, ult. f. Prov. (*macar* crush, *col* neck)]

machinate /'mækɪneɪt, 'mæʃ-/ *v.i.* to lay plots, to intrigue. —**machination** /-'neɪʃ(ə)n/ *n.*, **machinator** *n.* [f. L *machinari* contrive (as foll.)]

machine /mə'ʃiːn/ *n.* **1.** an apparatus for applying mechanical power, having several parts each with a definite function. **2.** a bicycle, motor cycle, etc., an aircraft; a computer. **3.** the controlling system of an organization. **4.** a person who acts mechanically. —*v.t.* to make or operate on with a machine (esp. of sewing or printing). —**machine-readable** *adj.* in a form that a computer can process. **machine tool,** a mechanically operated tool for working on metal, wood, or plastics. [f. F f. L *machina* f. Gk (as MECHANIC)]

machine-gun *n.* a mounted automatic gun giving continuous fire (see below). —*v.t.* (**-nn-**) to shoot at with a machine-gun.
The first mechanically operated (hand-cranked) 'revolving battery gun' was the invention of a London lawyer, James Puckle, and was patented in 1718. It was actually produced, but its flintlock mechanism was unreliable. Other notable inventors include R. J. Gatling (1862), B. B. Hotchkiss (1877), I. N. Lewis, and J. M. Browning; the first satisfactory fully automatic weapon was that of H. S. Maxim (1884). The machine-gun dominated the battlefields in the First World War and continued in use in the Second.

machinery *n.* **1.** machines; a mechanism. **2.** an organized system; a means arranged. [f. prec.]

machinist *n.* **1.** one who operates a machine, especially a sewing-machine or a machine tool. **2.** one who makes machinery. [f. F & f. MACHINE]

machismo /mə'tʃɪzməʊ/ *n.* assertive manliness, masculine pride. [Sp. (as MACHO)]

Mach number /mɑːk, mæk/ the ratio of the speed of a body to the speed of sound in the surrounding medium. [f. E. MACH]

macho /'mætʃəʊ/ *adj.* manly, virile. —*n.* (*pl.* **-os**) **1.** a macho man. **2.** machismo. [Sp., = male, f. L *masculus*]

Machu Picchu /mætʃuː 'pɪtʃuː/ a fortified Inca town in Peru, which the invading Spaniards never found. Perhaps not an important fortress, it is dramatically perched on a steep-sided ridge. The town contains a palace, a temple to the sun, and extensive cultivation terraces. Discovered in 1911, it was named after the mountain that rises above it.

mack var. of MAC.

Mackenzie¹ /mə'kenzɪ/, Sir Alexander (1764–1820), Scot-

tish explorer of Canada. Mackenzie entered the service of the North West Fur Company in 1779, undertaking explorations all over NW Canada. He discovered the Mackenzie River in 1789 and in 1793 became the first white man to reach the Pacific Ocean by land along a northern route.

Mackenzie² /mə'kenzɪ/, Sir (Edward Montague) Compton (1883–1972), English novelist and author of essays, memoirs, and poems. One of his best-known works is the semi-autobiographical *Sinister Street* (1913–14), a novel about growing up. In later life his works were in a lighter vein and include the humorous novel *Whisky Galore* (1947, filmed 1949), a story (based on an actual event) of the foundering of a whisky-laden ship near the shore of an island and the subsequent abstraction of its cargo by the local population.

Mackenzie³ /mə'kenzɪ/, William Lyon (1795–1861), Canadian revolutionary. Unhappy with the pace of reform in the colony of Upper Canada, Mackenzie, a radical journalist, led a short-lived rebellion in 1837, unsuccessfully attempting to set up a new government in Toronto.

Mackenzie River the longest river of Canada, 1,700 km (1,060 miles) long, flowing NE from the Great Slave Lake to the Beaufort Sea, a section of the Arctic Ocean. It is named after Sir Alexander Mackenzie (see entry).

mackerel /'mækər(ə)l/ *n.* (*pl.* same) a sea-fish (*Scomber scombrus*) used as food. —**mackerel sky,** a sky dappled with rows of small white fleecy clouds (cirrocumulus). [f. AF]

McKinlay /mə'kɪnlɪ/, John (1819–72), Scottish-born explorer. Having emigrated to New South Wales in 1836, McKinlay was appointed by the South Australia government in 1861 to lead an expedition to search for the missing explorers Burke and Wills. Although he found only traces of part of the Burke and Wills party, he carried out valuable exploratory work in the interior and got his entire party back safely despite tremendous hardships. On another expedition into the interior in 1865, it was once again his skill as a leader which saved the group when faced with extraordinarily unfavourable climatic conditions.

mackintosh /'mækɪntɒʃ/ *n.* **1.** a waterproof coat or cloak. **2.** cloth waterproofed with rubber. [f. C. *Macintosh*, Scottish inventor of the material (d. 1843)]

MacNeice /mək'niːs/, (Frederick) Louis (1907–63), British poet, born in Belfast, educated in England, a contemporary of Auden (with whom he collaborated in *Letters from Iceland*, 1937) at Oxford, where he published his first volume of poems in 1929. MacNeice used many classic verse forms but his distinctive contribution was his deployment of assonance, internal rhythms, and ballad-like repetitions absorbed from the Irish background of his youth. He was an outstanding writer of documentaries and parable plays for radio, notably *The Dark Tower* (1947). Although overshadowed by Auden in the 1930s and 1940s, his reputation revived with the publication of his *Collected Poems* (1960).

macramé /mə'krɑːmɪ/ *n.* the art of knotting cord or string in patterns to make decorative articles; work so made. [f. Turk. *makrama* bedspread, f. Arab.]

macro- *in comb.* long, large, large-scale. [f. Gk (*makros* long)]

macrobiotic /mækrəʊbaɪ'ɒtɪk/ *adj.* of or following a Zen Buddhist dietary system (comprising pure vegetable foods, brown rice, etc.) intended to prolong life. [f. Gk (MACRO-, *biotos* life)]

macrocosm /'mækrəʊkɒz(ə)m/ *n.* the universe; any great whole. [f. F f. L (MACRO-, Gk *kosmos* world)]

macroeconomics /mækrəʊiːkə'nɒmɪks/ *n.* the study of the economy as a whole.

macromolecule /'mækrəʊmɒlɪkjuːl/ *n.* a molecule containing a very large number of atoms.

macron /'mækrɒn/ *n.* the written or printed mark (‾) over a long or stressed vowel. [Gk, neut. of *makros* long]

macroscopic /mækrəʊ'skɒpɪk/ *adj.* **1.** visible to the naked eye. **2.** regarded in terms of large units. —**macroscopically** *adv.* [f. MACRO- + -SCOPIC]

macula /'mækjʊlə/ *n.* (*pl.* **-lae** /-liː/) a dark spot; a spot, especially a permanent one, in the skin. —**maculation** /-'leɪʃ(ə)n/ *n.* [L]

mad *adj.* **1.** having a disordered mind, insane. **2.** extremely foolish. **3.** wildly enthusiastic or infatuated. **4.** frenzied. **5.** (*colloq.*) angry. **6.** wildly light-hearted. —**like mad,** (*colloq.*) with great energy or enthusiasm. —**madness** *n.* [OE]

Madagascar /mædə'gæskə(r)/ an island country in the Indian Ocean, off the east coast of Africa; pop. (approx.) 9,000,000; official languages, Malagasy and French; capital, Antananarivo. The island's geological history is puzzling, and many of its plants and animals are not found elsewhere. The people are of mixed Polynesian, Arab, and Black origin, and the economy is mainly agricultural. The fourth largest island in the world, Madagascar was heavily influenced by Arab settlers before the Portuguese discovery in 1500. The island, despite rival French and British attempts at domination, remained independent until finally colonized by the French in 1896. It regained its independence as the Malagasy Republic in 1960, changing its name back to Madagascar in 1975.

madam /'mædəm/ n. **1.** a polite or respectful formal address or mode of reference to a woman. **2.** (colloq.) a conceited or precocious young woman. **3.** a woman brothel-keeper. [f. OF (as foll.)]

Madame /'mædəm, mæ'dɑ:m/ n. (pl. **Mesdames** /mei'dɑ:m, -'dæm/) the title used of or to a French-speaking woman, corresponding to Mrs or madam. [F, = my lady]

madcap n. a wildly impulsive person. —adj. wildly impulsive.

madden v.t./i. to make or become mad; to irritate. [f. MAD]

madder n. **1.** a herbaceous plant (Rubia tinctoria) with yellowish flowers. **2.** the red dye obtained from its root; a synthetic substitute for this. [OE]

made past & p.p. of MAKE. —adj. (of a person) **1.** built or formed (well-made; loosely-made). **2.** successful. —**have it made**, (slang) to be sure of success. **made for**, ideally suited to. **made of**, consisting of. **made of money**, (colloq.) very rich.

Madeira[1] /mə'dɪərə/ the largest of a group of islands (**the Madeiras**) in the Atlantic Ocean off NW Africa which are in Portuguese possession but partially autonomous; pop. (1978) 265,600; capital, Funchal. [Port., = timber (f. L materia matter), from its thick woods]

Madeira[2] /mə'dɪərə/ n. a fortified white wine from Madeira. —**Madeira cake**, a rich cake containing no fruit. [f. prec.]

Mademoiselle /mædəmwə'zel/ n. (pl. **Mesdemoiselles** /meidm-/) **1.** the title used of or to an unmarried French-speaking woman, corresponding to Miss or madam. **2.** **mademoiselle**, a young Frenchwoman; a French governess. [F (ma my, demoiselle as DAMSEL]

madhouse n. **1.** (colloq.) a mental home or mental hospital. **2.** a scene of confused uproar.

Madhya Pradesh /'mɑ:dɪə prə'deʃ/ a State in central India, formed in 1956; capital, Bhopal.

madly adv. in a mad manner; (colloq.) passionately, extremely. [f. MAD]

madman n. (pl. **-men**) a man who is mad.

madonna /mə'dɒnə/ n. a picture or statue of the Virgin Mary. —**madonna lily**, a tall white lily (Lilium candidum) often depicted in pictures of the Annunciation. [It., = my lady]

Madras /mə'drɑ:s, -æs/ a seaport on the east coast of India, capital of Tamil Nadu; pop. 4,300,000.

Madrid /mə'drɪd/ the capital (since 1561) of Spain, situated on a high plateau almost exactly in the centre of the country; pop. (est. 1981) 3,267,500.

madrigal /'mædrɪg(ə)l/ n. **1.** a part-song for several voices (see below). **2.** a short amatory poem. The form was developed and perfected by Petrarch. [f. It. f. L matricalis mother (as MATRIX)]

The term was used in the 14th c. for a genre of Italian song for two or three voices, often comprising two or three stanzas, each of three lines. Today, however, the term is usually thought of in connection with 16th- and early 17th-c. song, a multi-voiced composition but with no fixed form, following the vagaries of the verse and frequently dwelling on particular descriptive or emotive words or phrases. The 20th c. has seen a considerable revival of madrigal singing in Britain and America.

madwoman n. (pl. **-women**) a woman who is mad.

Maecenas /mai'si:nəs/, Gaius (c.70–8 BC), a wealthy Roman of Etruscan origin who was a close friend and adviser of Augustus but shunned official position, and was renowned for his luxurious habits. Himself a writer, he was an important patron and friend of poets (an occupation for which his name is a byword), among whom were Virgil, Propertius, and Horace.

maelstrom /'meilstrɒm/ n. **1.** a great whirlpool. **2.** a confused state. [Du.]

maenad /'mi:næd/ n. a bacchante. [f. L f. Gk (mainomai rave)]

maestro /'maistrəʊ/ n. (pl. **-ri** /-ri:/) **1.** a great conductor, composer, or teacher of music. **2.** a masterly performer in any sphere. [It., = master]

Maeterlinck /'meitəlɪŋk/, Maurice (1862–1949), Belgian poet, dramatist, and essayist. He became a leading figure in the symbolist movement with his play La Princesse Maleine (1889) and is now chiefly remembered for his Pelléas et Mélisande (1892), the source of Debussy's opera of that name (1902), and for the fairy play L'Oiseau bleu (The Blue-bird, 1909). He drew on traditions of fairy-tale and romance, and the characteristic tone of much of his drama is doom-laden mystery and timeless melancholy. He was awarded the Nobel Prize for literature in 1911.

Mae West /mei 'west/ (slang) an inflatable life-jacket that gives the wearer a somewhat feminine figure. [professional name of Amer. film actress (d. 1980), with a plump figure]

Mafeking /'mæfɪkɪŋ/ a South African town in which a small British force under the command of Baden-Powell was besieged by the Boers for 215 days in 1899–1900. Although the town was of little strategic significance, its successful defence, at a time when the Boer War was going very badly for the British, excited great interest, while its relief was hailed almost with a national sense of jubilation.

Mafia /'mæfɪə/ n. **1.** a secret organization, opposed to legal authority and engaged in crime, that originated in Sicily in the 13th c. and later spread to North and South America, at first among Italian immigrants. Calling itself 'Cosa Nostra' [It., = our affair], it became an integral part of the sophisticated and ruthless organized crime that developed in the USA. **2.** **mafia,** a network of persons regarded as exerting hidden influence. [It. dial., = bragging]

Mafioso /mæfɪ'əʊsəʊ, mɑː-/ n. (pl. **-si** /-si:/) a member of the Mafia. [It. (as prec.)]

magazine /mægə'zi:n/ n. **1.** a periodical publication (now usually illustrated) containing contributions by various writers. **2.** a store for arms, ammunition, and provisions, for use in war; a store for explosives. **3.** a chamber for holding the supply of cartridges to be fed automatically to the breech of a gun; a similar device in a camera, slide-projector, etc. [f. F f. It. f. Arab., = store-house]

magdalen /'mægdəlɪn/ n. a reformed prostitute. [f. Mary Magdalen(e) (see MARY 2)]

Magdalenian /mægdə'li:nɪən/ adj. of the latest palaeolithic industry of Europe, named after the type-site at La Madelaine in the Dordogne region of France and dated to c.15,000–11,000 BC. It is characterized by a range of bone and horn tools, including elaborate bone harpoons; cave art reached a zenith during this period (see ALTAMIRA). —n. this industry.

Magdeburg hemispheres /'mægdɪbɜːg/ a pair of copper hemispheres joined to form a hollow globe from which the air could be extracted, after which they were practically inseparable, devised by a German physicist, Otto von Guericke (1602–86), to demonstrate the effect of air pressure. [name of town in E. Germany]

Magellan /mə'gelən/, Ferdinand (c.1480–1521), Portuguese explorer. On Portuguese service in the East Indies in 1511–12 he explored the Spice Islands, but in 1517 offered his services to Spain to undertake a voyage to the same islands by the western route. Leaving Spain with five vessels in 1519, Magellan reached South America and wintered at Port St Julien before rounding the continent through the strait which now bears his name. In 1521 he discovered the Philippines, but soon after was killed in a native war on Cebu. The survivors of this disaster escaped to the Moluccas and sailed back to Spain round Africa, with the one remaining vessel, thereby completing the first circumnavigation of the globe.

Magellanic clouds /mædʒɪ'lænɪk/ two diffuse luminous regions of the southern sky, now known to be galaxies of irregular shape, containing millions of stars, that are nearest to the Galaxy. [f. prec.]

magenta /mə'dʒentə/ n. a bluish-crimson colour; an aniline dye of this colour. —adj. of or coloured with magenta. [f. Magenta in N. Italy, town near which the Austrians were defeated by the French under Napoleon III in 1859, the year of the dye's discovery]

maggot /'mægət/ n. a larva, especially of the bluebottle or cheese-fly. —**maggoty** adj. [perh. alt. of maddock f. ON]

magi *pl.* of MAGUS.

magic /ˈmædʒɪk/ *n.* **1.** the supposed art of influencing the course of events by the occult control of nature or of spirits, witchcraft. **2.** conjuring tricks. **3.** an inexplicable or remarkable influence; an enchanting quality or phenomenon. —*adj.* of magic; producing surprising results. —*v.t.* (**-ck-**) to change or make by or as if by magic. —**magic carpet,** a mythical carpet able to transport the person on it to any place. **magic eye,** a photoelectric device for automatic control. **magic lantern,** a simple form of image-projector using slides. —**magical** *adj.*, **magically** *adv.* [f. OF f. L f. Gk (as MAGUS)]

magician /məˈdʒɪʃ(ə)n/ *n.* **1.** one skilled in magic. **2.** a conjuror. [as prec.]

magisterial /mædʒɪˈstɪərɪəl/ *adj.* **1.** imperious; having authority. **2.** of a magistrate. —**magisterially** *adv.* [f. L (as MASTER)]

magistracy /ˈmædʒɪstrəsɪ/ *n.* magisterial office; magistrates collectively. [f. foll.]

magistrate /ˈmædʒɪstreɪt/ *n.* a civil officer with authority to administer the law; a person conducting a court for minor cases and preliminary hearings. [f. L *magistratus* (as MAGISTERIAL)]

Maglemosian /mæɡləˈməʊzɪən/ *adj.* of the first mesolithic industries in northern Europe, named after the type-site at Maglemose in Denmark, and dated to *c.*8300–6500 BC. The people were fishers and fowlers, hunting game and gathering natural crops (hazel nuts were relished), but not cultivating crops deliberately nor domesticating animals (except for dogs of a wolfish type). —*n.* this industry.

magma *n.* (*pl.* **-as** or **magmata**) a fluid or semi-fluid material under the earth's crust, from which igneous rock is formed by cooling. [L f. Gk (*massō* knead)]

Magna Charta /ˈmæɡnə ˈkɑːtə/ the political charter which King John was forced to sign by his rebellious barons at Runnymede in 1215. The barons, discontented with John's high-handedness, were led by Archbishop Langton to frame a charter which effectively redefined the limits of royal power. Although the charter was often violated by medieval kings, it eventually came to be seen as the seminal document of English constitutional practice. Among its chief provisions were that no freeman should be imprisoned or banished except by the law of the land, and that supplies should not be exacted without the consent of the Common Council of the realm. [L, = great charter]

magnanimous /mæɡˈnænɪməs/ *adj.* noble and generous in feelings or conduct, not petty. —**magnanimity** /-nəˈnɪmɪtɪ/ *n.*, **magnanimously** *adv.* [f. L (*magnus* great, *animus* mind)]

magnate /ˈmæɡneɪt/ *n.* a wealthy and influential person, especially in business. [f. L *magnas* (*magnus* great)]

magnesia /mæɡˈniːʃə/ *n.* **1.** magnesium oxide. **2.** hydrated magnesium carbonate, used as an antacid and laxative. [f. *Magnesia* in Asia Minor]

magnesium /mæɡˈniːzɪəm/ *n.* a silver-white metallic element of the alkaline-earth metal group, symbol Mg, atomic number 12. It is a common element in the earth's crust and in the sea. Because of its low density magnesium is used to make strong light alloys in the aerospace industry and for certain consumer goods. It is also used in flash-bulbs and pyrotechnics, as it burns in air with a brilliant white flame. Magnesium compounds have various uses, including as important reagents in organic chemistry; magnesium hydroxide is a commonly used antacid and laxative. Magnesium is necessary to life, and in particular forms part of the chlorophyll molecule. [f. prec.]

magnet /ˈmæɡnɪt/ *n.* **1.** a piece of iron, steel, alloy, ore, etc., having the properties of attracting iron and of pointing approximately north and south when suspended (ill. MAGNETISM); a loadstone. **2.** a person or thing that attracts. [f. L f. Gk, = stone of Magnesia (as MAGNESIA)]

magnetic /mæɡˈnetɪk/ *adj.* **1.** having the properties of a magnet. **2.** produced or acting by magnetism; capable of acquiring the properties of or of being attracted by a magnet. **3.** strongly attractive. —**magnetic compass,** one using a magnetic needle. **magnetic field,** see FIELD. **magnetic needle,** an indicator made of magnetized steel, pointing north and south on the dial of a compass. **magnetic north,** the direction indicated by a magnetic needle, close to the geographical north but not identical with it. **magnetic pole,** the point near the north or south pole where a magnetic needle dips vertically. **magnetic storm,** a disturbance of the earth's magnetic field by charged

particles from the sun etc. **magnetic tape,** a plastic strip coated or impregnated with magnetic particles for the recording and reproduction of signals. —**magnetically** *adv.* [as prec.]

magnetism /ˈmæɡnɪtɪz(ə)m/ *n.* **1.** magnetic phenomena; the science of these; the natural agency producing them (see below, also FIELD and ill. pp. 500–1). **2.** great charm and attraction. [f. prec.].

The phenomenon of magnetism has been known since ancient times. It derived its name in antiquity from an iron ore found near Magnesia in Asia Minor, which had the power to attract iron and other pieces of ore, and also to induce a similar power of attraction in iron. The constant direction of a freely suspended magnetic needle (i.e. a magnetic compass) was first discovered in China and was apparently introduced to Europe in the 12th c. William Gilbert in *De Magnete* (1600) established that the Earth is a great magnet, and raised magnetism to the status of an exact experimental science; before this the mysterious attractive power of a magnet, which was able to pass through wood and stone, had placed magnetism firmly in the sphere of natural magic.

It was Ampère who first suggested that the powers of a magnet are due to the combined effect of tiny electric currents circulating in its atoms. In 1820 Oersted demonstrated that a wire carrying an electric current gave rise to a magnetic field, and in 1831 the converse of this effect, in which a moving magnet induces a current in a wire, was demonstrated by Faraday. It is now generally accepted that all magnetism, including that of the Earth, is due to circulating electric currents. In magnetic materials the magnetism is produced by electrons orbiting within the atoms. In most substances the magnetic effects of different electrons cancel each other out, but in some, such as iron, a net magnetic field can be induced. The magnetism of the Earth itself is thought to be caused by the circulation of molten iron and nickel in the core.

The earliest uses of magnets were as compasses, but nowadays magnetism and especially electromagnetic phenomena have many applications, being fundamental to the operation of electric generators and motors, loud-speakers, lifting magnets, transformers, etc.

magnetize /ˈmæɡnɪtaɪz/ *v.t.* **1.** to give magnetic properties to; to make into a magnet. **2.** to attract (*lit.* or *fig.*) as a magnet does. —**magnetization** /-ˈzeɪʃ(ə)n/ *n.* [f. MAGNET]

magneto /mæɡˈniːtəʊ/ *n.* (*pl.* **-os**) an electric generator using permanent magnets (esp. for ignition in an internal-combustion engine). [abbr. of *magneto-electric* (comb. form of MAGNET, ELECTRIC)]

Magnificat /mæɡˈnɪfɪkæt/ *n.* a canticle, the song of praise (so called from the first word of the Latin text) in Luke 1: 46–55 sung when the Virgin Mary was greeted by her cousin Elizabeth as the mother of the Lord. Some scholars have argued that Luke attributed it originally to Elizabeth and not to Mary. [L, = magnifies (i.e. extols)]

magnification /mæɡnɪfɪˈkeɪʃ(ə)n/ *n.* magnifying; the amount of this. [f. MAGNIFY]

magnificent /mæɡˈnɪfɪs(ə)nt/ *adj.* **1.** splendid in appearance etc.; sumptuously constructed or adorned; splendidly lavish. **2.** (*colloq.*) excellent. —**magnificence** *n.*, **magnificently** *adv.* [F or f. L *magnificus* (*magnus* great, *facere* make)]

magnify /ˈmæɡnɪfaɪ/ *v.t.* **1.** to make (a thing) appear larger than it is, as with a lens. **2.** to exaggerate; to intensify. **3.** (*archaic*) to extol. —**magnifying glass,** a lens used to magnify things (ill. LIGHT). —**magnifier** *n.* [f. OF or L *magnificare* (as prec.)]

magnitude /ˈmæɡnɪtjuːd/ *n.* **1.** largeness; size. **2.** importance. **3.** a measure of the relative brightness of stars and other celestial objects, based originally on a scale devised in the 2nd c. BC by Hipparchus (who classified the brightest stars as of the first magnitude, less bright as second, and so on in six classes), but now quantified by a mathematical formula involving the logarithm of the measured energy, and with the scale extended beyond the range of discrimination of unaided vision. —**absolute magnitude,** the magnitude that a star would seem to have if at a distance of 10 parsecs or 32.6 light-years. **apparent magnitude,** as seen from the earth. [f. L *magnitudo* (*magnus* great)]

magnolia /mæɡˈnəʊlɪə/ *n.* a tree of the genus *Magnolia*, with dark-green foliage and waxlike flowers. [f. P. *Magnol*, French botanist (d. 1715)]

magnum /ˈmæɡnəm/ *n.* a bottle containing two reputed quarts of wine or spirits. [L, neut. of *magnus* great]

Magnetism

Magnets

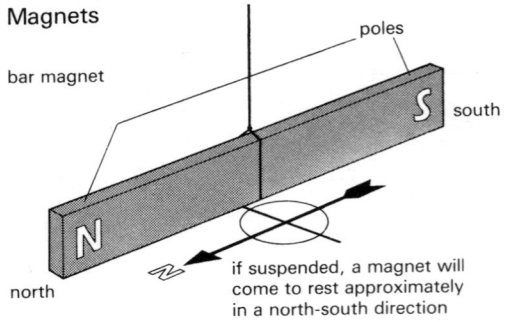

bar magnet

poles

south

north

if suspended, a magnet will come to rest approximately in a north-south direction

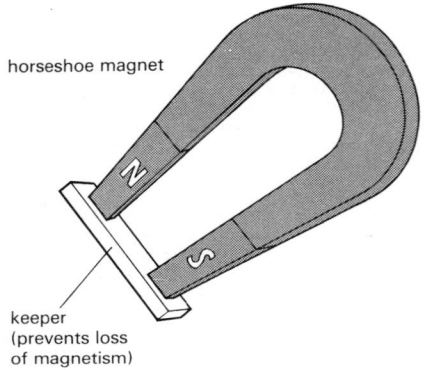

horseshoe magnet

keeper (prevents loss of magnetism)

Magnetic fields

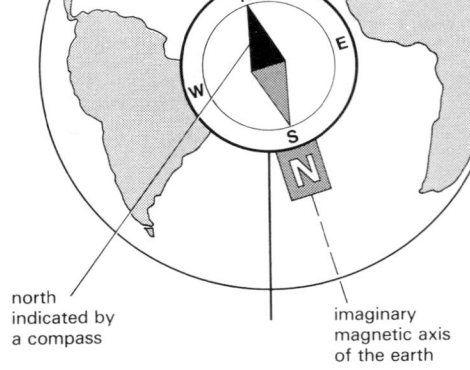

the earth

geographical north (earth's axis)

magnetic north

north indicated by a compass

imaginary magnetic axis of the earth

the earth has a magnetic field which behaves as if it contained a magnet slightly out of line with its axis

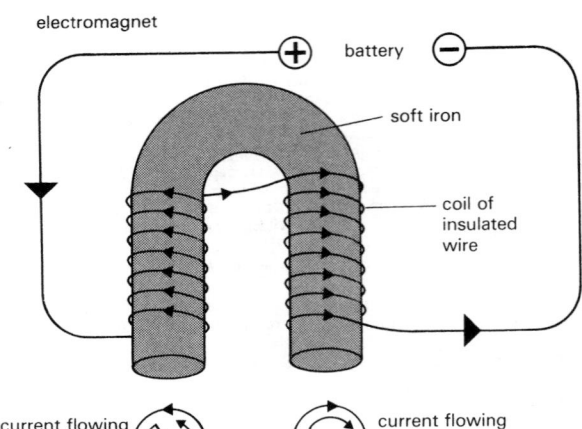

electromagnet

battery

soft iron

coil of insulated wire

current flowing anticlockwise, polarity north

current flowing clockwise, polarity south

a coil of insulated wire (a solenoid) carrying a direct steady current has a magnetic effect

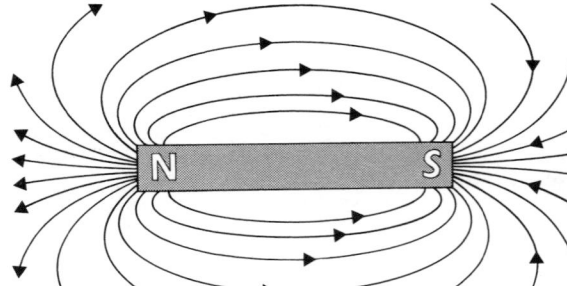

magnetic field

direction of flow is always N – S

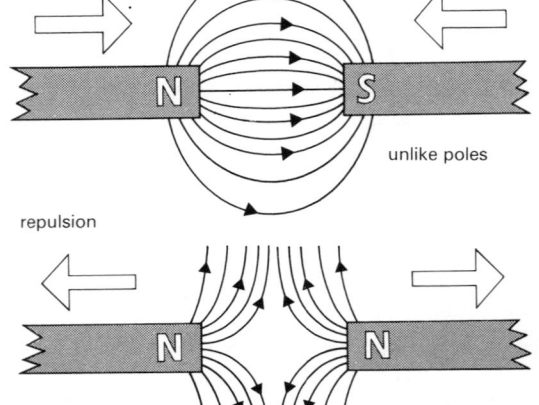

attraction

unlike poles

repulsion

like poles

Some uses of electromagnets

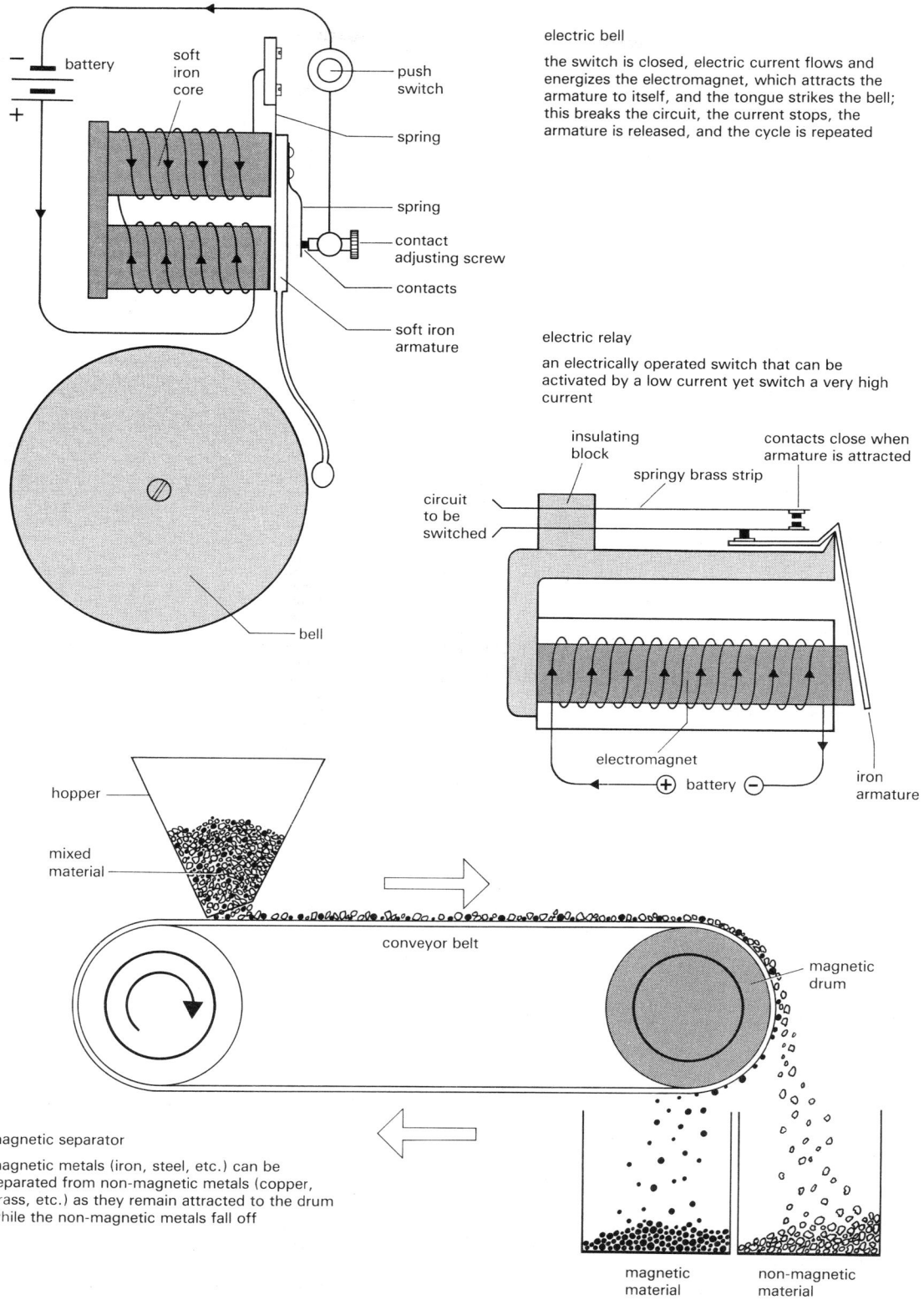

battery

soft iron core

push switch

spring

spring

contact adjusting screw

contacts

soft iron armature

bell

electric bell

the switch is closed, electric current flows and energizes the electromagnet, which attracts the armature to itself, and the tongue strikes the bell; this breaks the circuit, the current stops, the armature is released, and the cycle is repeated

electric relay

an electrically operated switch that can be activated by a low current yet switch a very high current

insulating block

contacts close when armature is attracted

springy brass strip

circuit to be switched

electromagnet

battery

iron armature

hopper

mixed material

conveyor belt

magnetic drum

magnetic separator

magnetic metals (iron, steel, etc.) can be separated from non-magnetic metals (copper, brass, etc.) as they remain attracted to the drum while the non-magnetic metals fall off

magnetic material

non-magnetic material

magnum opus /ˈmægnəm ˈɔʊpəs/ a great work of literature etc.; an author's greatest work. [L]

Magog see GOG AND MAGOG.

magpie /ˈmægpaɪ/ *n.* **1.** a kind of crow (*Pica pica*) with black-and-white plumage and a long tail, reputed to collect objects. **2.** a random collector. **2.** a chatterer. [f. *Mag* abbr. of woman's name *Margaret* + PIE²]

magus /ˈmeɪgəs/ *n.* (*pl.* **magi** /-dʒaɪ/) a poet of ancient Persia; a sorcerer. —**the Magi**, the 'wise men' from the East who brought offerings to the infant Christ (Matt. 2: 1-12). The gospel does not mention their number (the later tradition that there were three probably arose from the three gifts of gold, frankincense, and myrrh). The tradition that they were kings appears first in Tertullian (2nd c.); their names, Caspar, Melchior, and Balthasar, are first mentioned in the 6th c. In the Middle Ages they were venerated as saints, and what are claimed to be their relics lie in Cologne cathedral. [f. L f. Gk f. Pers.]

Magyar /ˈmægjɑː(r)/ *n.* **1.** a member of the people now predominant in Hungary. **2.** the Hungarian language. —*adj.* of this people or their language. [native name]

Mahabharata /mɑːhɑːˈbɑːrətə/ *n.* one of the two great Sanskrit epics of the Hindus (the other is the Ramayana) that evolved over centuries to reach its present form *c.* AD 400. Containing almost 100,000 stanzas, it is probably the longest single poem in the world. The main story describes the civil war waged between the five Pandava brothers and their hundred stepbrothers at Kuruksetra near modern Delhi, and there is much legendary, philosophical, and religious material; the numerous interpolated episodes include the Bhagavadgita. [Skr., = the great epic of the Bharata dynasty]

maharaja /mɑːhɑːˈrɑːdʒə/ *n.* (also **maharajah**) (*hist.*) the title of some Indian princes. [f. Hindi, = great rajah]

maharanee /mɑːhɑːˈrɑːniː/ *n.* (also **maharani**) (*hist.*) a maharaja's wife or widow. [f. Hindi, = great ranee]

Maharashtra /mɑːhɑːˈræʃtrə/ a State in Western India bordering on the Arabian Sea, formed in 1960 from the SE part of the former Bombay State; capital, Bombay. —**Maharashtrian** *adj.* & *n.*

maharishi /mɑːhɑːˈrɪʃɪ/ *n.* a great Hindu sage. [f. Hindi]

mahatma /məˈhætmə/ *n.* (in India etc.) **1.** a title of respect for a person regarded with reverence. **2.** a member of a class of persons supposed by some Buddhists to have preternatural powers. [f. Skr., = great soul]

Mahayana /mɑːhəˈjɑːnə/ *n.* the more general form of Buddhism (see HINAYANA). It survived in India until the Muslim era and also spread to Central Asia, China, Japan, Java, and Sumatra. The stress of the ancient schools (e.g. Theravada) on personal enlightenment is superseded by the ideal of the bodhisattva who postpones his own salvation for the love of others. [Skr., = great vehicle]

Mahdi /ˈmɑːdɪ/ *n.* (in Islam) a spiritual and temporal leader who will be sent by divine command to prepare human society for the end of earthly time through perfectly just government. Not part of orthodox doctrine, this concept was introduced into popular Islam through Sufi channels influenced by Christian doctrine. For Shiites, the title refers to the twelfth imam. The title has been claimed by various individuals who sought to establish popular movements of resistance; the most widely known of these was the Sudanese Muhammad Ahmad, who proclaimed himself Mahdi in 1881 in the Sudan and led his followers in resisting Egyptian rule in 1884-5. —**Mahdist** *n.* [f. Arab., = guided one (*hadā* guide)]

mah-jong /mɑːˈdʒɒŋ/ *n.* an old Chinese game resembling certain card-games, introduced into Europe and America in the early 1920s, played usually by four persons using 136 or 144 pieces called *tiles*. [f. Chin. dial. *ma-tsiang* sparrows]

Mahler /ˈmɑːlə(r)/, Gustav (1860-1911), Austrian composer, conductor, and pianist. His name is especially remembered in connection with the Viennese Opera, where he was Director 1897-1907, setting standards still scarcely surpassed; he was forced to leave by the anti-Semitic faction, despite his conversion to the Roman Catholic faith. Mahler was a master of the large-scale form, notably in his symphonies and orchestral songs. For many years his works were regarded with fanatical admiration by a handful of disciples and equally fanatical scorn by a larger number of musicians, but in the 1950s there was a fervent revival of interest. The unconventional form of the symphonies, complex and subtle polyphony, contrasts of irony, pathos, simplicity, and psychological insight, all appealed to later 20th-c. composers and audiences.

mahlstick /ˈmɑːlstɪk/ var. of MAULSTICK.

mahogany /məˈhɒgənɪ/ *n.* **1.** a reddish-brown wood, especially of a tropical American tree (*Swietenia majogani*), used for furniture. **2.** its colour. **3.** a tree yielding mahogany. [orig. unkn.]

mahout /məˈhaʊt/ *n.* (in India etc.) an elephant-driver. [f. Hindi f. Skr.]

Maia /ˈmaɪə/ **1.** (*Gk myth.*) the daughter of Atlas and mother of Hermes [Gk, = mother, nurse]. **2.** (*Rom. myth.*) a goddess associated (for unknown reasons) with Vulcan and also (by confusion with 1 above) with Mercury. She was worshipped on 1 May and 15 May; that month is named after her. [perh. f. L root *mag-* growth, increase]

maid *n.* **1.** a female servant. **2.** (*archaic*) a girl; a young woman. —**maid of all work**, a female servant doing general housework; a person doing many jobs. **maid of honour**, an unmarried lady attending a queen or princess; a kind of small custard tart; (*US*) a principal bridesmaid. [abbr. of foll.]

maiden /ˈmeɪd(ə)n/ *n.* **1.** a girl, a young unmarried woman. **2.** a maiden over. **3.** a maiden horse. —*adj.* **1.** unmarried. **2.** (of a female animal) unmated. **3.** (of a horse) that has never won a prize; (of a race) open only to such horses. **4.** (of a speech, voyage, etc.) first. —**maiden name**, a woman's surname before marriage. **maiden over**, an over in cricket in which no runs are scored. —**maidenhood** *n.*, **maidenly** *adj.* [OE]

maidenhair *n.* a fern of the genus *Adiantum* with fine hairlike stalks and delicate fronds.

maidenhead *n.* virginity; the hymen.

maidservant *n.* a female servant.

Maigret /ˈmeɪgreɪ/ a detective-superintendent in the crime stories of Georges Simenon.

mail¹ *n.* **1.** matter conveyed by post; this system of conveyance; letters, parcels, etc., sent, collected, or delivered at one place on one occasion. **2.** a vehicle carrying post. —*v.t.* to send by post. —**mail-bag** *n.* a large bag for carrying mail. **mailing list**, a list of persons to whom mail (esp. advertising matter) is to be posted. **mail order**, purchase of goods by post. [f. OF *male* wallet]

mail² *n.* armour composed of metal rings or plates (ill. ARMOUR). —**coat of mail**, a jacket or tunic covered with mail. [f. OF f. L *macula* spot, mesh]

Mailer /ˈmeɪlə(r)/, Norman (1923-), American novelist and essayist, whose naturalistic first novel *The Naked and the Dead* (1948) was based on his army experiences in the Pacific during the Second World War. Much of his work is of a more unorthodox genre, combining journalism, autobiography, political commentary, and fictional passages in a wide range of styles. His works include an ambitious novel, *Ancient Evenings* (1983), set in ancient Egypt.

maim *v.t.* to cripple, to disable, to mutilate. [f. OF *mahaignier*]

Maimonides /maɪˈmɒnɪdiːz/ Moses ben Maimon (1135-1204), Spanish-Jewish philosopher and Rabbinic scholar, known to Jewish writers as 'Rambam'. He wrote in Hebrew and Arabic, and was much influenced by Aristotelian philosophy; his work had great influence on medieval Christian thought.

main *adj.* **1.** principal, most important. **2.** greatest in size or extent; exerted to the full. —*n.* **1.** a principal channel, duct, etc., for water or sewage etc.; (usu in *pl.*) a principal cable for the supply of electricity. **2.** (*archaic*) the mainland; the high seas. —**have an eye to the main chance**, to consider one's own interests. **in the main**, for the most part. **main brace**, a brace attached to the main yard. **main line**, an important railway line linking large cities. **main-topmast** *n.* the mast above the maintop. **main yard**, the yard on which the mainsail is extended. [f. ON & OE]

Maine /meɪn/ a north-eastern State of the USA, on the Atlantic coast, visited by Cabot in 1498 and colonized from England in the 17th-18th c. It became the 23rd State of the USA in 1820; capital, Augusta.

mainframe *n.* **1.** the central processing unit of a computer. **2.** (often *attrib.*) a large computer as distinct from a microcomputer etc.

mainland /ˈmeɪnlənd/ *n.* a large continuous extent of land, excluding neighbouring islands etc.

mainly *adv.* for the most part, chiefly. [f. MAIN]

mainmast *n.* the principal mast of a ship (ill. SAILING-SHIPS).

mainsail /ˈmeɪnseɪl/, -s(ə)l/ *n.* (in a square-rigged vessel) the lowest sail on a mainmast (ill. SAILING-SHIPS); (in a fore-and-aft rigged vessel) a sail set on the after part of a mainmast.

mainspring *n.* **1.** the principal spring of a watch, clock, etc. **2.** a chief motivating force or initiative.

mainstay *n.* **1.** the chief support. **2.** the stay from the maintop to the foot of the foremast.

mainstream *n.* **1.** the principal current of a river etc. **2.** the prevailing trend of opinion, fashion, etc.

maintain /meɪnˈteɪn/ *v.t.* **1.** to cause to continue; to continue one's action in; to keep in existence. **2.** to take action to preserve (a machine, house, etc.) in good order. **3.** to support, to provide sustenance for; to provide means for. **4.** to assert as true. —**maintained school,** a school supported from public funds. [f. OF *maintenir* f. L *manu tenēre* hold in the hand]

maintenance /ˈmeɪntɪnəns/ *n.* **1.** maintaining, being maintained. **2.** keeping equipment etc. in repair. **3.** provision of the means to support life; an allowance of money for this. [as prec.]

Maintenon /ˈmæ̃tənɔ̃/, Françoise d'Aubigné, Marquise de (1635–1719), mistress and later second wife of the French king Louis XIV. Devoutly religious and already a middle-aged widow, Madame de Maintenon came to Louis' attention while looking after his children by his previous mistress, Madame de Montespan. After his own wife's death in 1683, Louis married de Maintenon morganatically, and in the last years of his reign she turned him increasingly towards piety.

maintop *n.* a platform above the head of the lower mainmast.

maisonette /meɪzəˈnet/ *n.* **1.** part of a house let or used separately (usually not all one one floor). **2.** a small house. [f. F, dim. of *maison* house]

maize *n.* **1.** a cereal plant (*Zea mays*) of North American origin. **2.** the grain of this. **3.** the yellow colour of its ripe cobs. [f. F or Sp., of Carib orig.]

majestic /məˈdʒestɪk/ *adj.* stately and dignified, imposing. —**majestically** *adv.* [f. foll.]

majesty /ˈmædʒɪstɪ/ *n.* **1.** impressive stateliness. **2.** sovereign power. —**Christ in Majesty,** a representation of Christ enthroned within an aureole. **His, Her, Your,** etc., **Majesty,** a title used in addressing or referring to a king or queen or a sovereign's wife or widow. [f. OF f. L *majestas* (as MAJOR)]

majolica /məˈjɒlɪkə, -ˈdʒɒl-/ *n.* Italian earthenware of the Renaissance period with coloured ornamentation on white enamel; a modern imitation of this. [f. It., f. former name of *Majorca*, ships of which brought Spanish wares to Italy]

major /ˈmeɪdʒə(r)/ *adj.* **1.** greater or relatively great in size or importance. **2.** of full legal age. **3.** (*Mus.*, of a scale) having intervals of a semitone above its third and seventh notes; (of an interval) normal or perfect (cf. MINOR); (of a key) based on a major scale. —*n.* **1.** an army officer next below lieutenant-colonel. **2.** an officer in charge of a section of band instruments. **3.** a person of full legal age. **4.** (*US*) a student's special course or subject. —*v.i.* (*US*) to specialize (in a subject). —**major-general** *n.* an army officer next below lieutenant-general. [f. L, compar. of *magnus* great]

Majorca /məˈjɔːkə/ the largest of the Balearic Islands; pop. (1970) 460,030; capital, Palma.

major-domo /meɪdʒəˈdəʊməʊ/ *n.* (*pl.* **-os**) the chief steward of a great household; a house-steward, a butler. [f. Sp. & It. f. L *major domus* highest official of household]

majority /məˈdʒɒrɪtɪ/ *n.* **1.** the greater number or part of a group etc. **2.** the number by which votes for the winning party etc. exceed those for the next or for all others combined; the party etc. receiving a majority of votes. **3.** full legal age (in Britain, since 1970 the age of 18 years, formerly 21 years). **4.** the rank of major. —**majority rule,** the principle that the greater number should exercise the greater power. [f. F f. L (as MAJOR)]

majuscule /ˈmædʒəskjuːl/ *adj.* (of lettering) large; written in large lettering. —*n.* large lettering; a large letter, whether capital or uncial. [F f. L *majuscula* (*littera* letter), dim. of MAJOR]

make *v.t./i* (*past & p.p.* MADE) **1.** to construct, create, or prepare from parts or other substances. **2.** to bring about, to cause to exist, to give rise to. **3.** to frame in the mind. **4.** to draw up as a legal document etc. **5.** to establish (a distinction, rule, or law). **6.** to gain or acquire. **7.** to secure the advancement or success of. **8.** to cause to be or become or seem. **9.** to cause or compel (to). **10.** to proceed, to act as if intending (to). **11.** to perform (an action etc.). **12.** to consider to be, to estimate as. **13.** to constitute, to amount to. **14.** to serve for, to be adequate as; to form or be reckoned as; to bring to (a chosen value etc.). **15.** to accomplish or achieve (a distance, speed, score, etc.); to achieve a place in (a team, prize-list, etc.); to arrive at, to come in sight of; (*slang*) to catch (a train etc.). —*n.* **1.** the way a thing is made. **2.** the origin of manufacture, a brand. —**make away with,** to get rid of; to kill; to squander. **make believe,** to pretend. **make-believe** *adj.* pretended; (*n.*) pretence. **make a day** *or* **night** etc. **of it,** to devote a whole day etc. to an activity or relaxation. **make do,** to manage with the limited or inadequate means available. **make for,** to conduce to; to proceed towards (a place); to attack. **make good,** to repay, repair, or compensate for; to achieve (a purpose), to be successful. **make the grade,** to succeed. **make it,** to achieve one's purpose, to be successful. **make much** (*or* **little**) **of,** to treat as important (or unimportant). **make nothing of,** to treat as trifling; to be unable to understand or use or deal with. **make off,** to depart hastily. **make off with,** to carry away, to steal. **make or break,** to cause the success or ruin of; to be crucial for. **make out,** to discern or understand; to fare or progress; to write out (a document etc.) or fill in (a form); to prove or try to prove to be; to pretend or claim. **make over,** to transfer possession of; to refashion or convert to a new purpose. **make time,** to contrive to find time to do something. **make up,** to put or get together; to prepare, to invent (a story etc.); to compensate (for); to complete (an amount originally deficient); to form or constitute; to apply cosmetics (to). **make (it) up** to be reconciled. **make-up** *n.* cosmetics; the way a thing is made or composed; character or temperament. **make up to,** to court, to curry favour with. **on the make,** (*slang*) intent on gain. [OE]

maker *n.* **1.** one who makes something. **2.** our **Maker,** God. [f. MAKE]

makeshift *n.* a temporary substitute or device. —*adj.* serving as this.

makeweight *n.* **1.** a small quantity added to make up the weight. **2.** a person or thing supplying a deficiency.

making *n.* **1.** (in *pl.*) earnings, profits. **2.** (in *pl.*) the essential qualities for becoming. —**be the making of,** to be the main factor in the success or favourable development of. **in the making,** in the course of being made or formed. [OE (as MAKE)]

mal- /mæl/ *prefix* bad (*malpractice*); badly (*maltreat*); faulty (*malfunction*); not (*maladroit*). [f. F *mal* badly f. L *male*]

Malabar /ˈmæləbɑː(r)/ a coastal district of SW India. —**Malabar Christians,** a group of Christians of SW India, tracing their origin to St Thomas, who according to their tradition landed in these parts.

Malabo /məˈlɑːbəʊ/ (formerly *Santa Isabel*) the capital of Equatorial Guinea; pop. (est. 1974) 25,000.

Malacca cane /məˈlækə/ a rich-brown cane from the stem of the palm-tree *Calamus rotang*, used for walking-sticks etc. [f. *Malacca* State and city of Malaysia]

Malachi /ˈmæləkaɪ/ the last book of the Old Testament in the English versions, belonging to a period before Ezra and Nehemiah. (Malachi is probably not a personal name.) [f. Heb., = my messenger]

malachite /ˈmæləkaɪt/ *n.* a green mineral used for ornament. [f. OF f. L f. Gk *molokhitis* (*molokhē* mallow)]

maladjusted /mælədˈʒʌstɪd/ *adj.* (of a person) not satisfactorily adjusted to his or her environment and conditions of life. —**maladjustment** *n.*

maladminister /mælədˈmɪnɪstə(r)/ *v.t.* to manage badly or improperly. —**maladministration** /-ˈstreɪʃ(ə)n/ *n.*

maladroit /mæləˈdrɔɪt, ˈmæ-/ *adj.* clumsy, bungling. —**maladroitly** *adv.*, **maladroitness** *n.* [F (as MAL-, ADROIT)]

malady /ˈmælədɪ/ *n.* a disease or ailment (*lit.* or *fig.*). [f. OF (*malade* sick)]

Malagasy /mæləˈgæsɪ/ *adj.* of Madagascar or its people or language. —*n.* **1.** a native or inhabitant of Madagascar. **2.** the official language of Madagascar, spoken by its 7 million inhabitants. It is a Malayo-Polynesian language, related to Malay, although the other languages of this group are spoken thousands of miles to the east. [orig. *Malegass*, f. MADAGASCAR]

malaise /mæˈleɪz/ *n.* bodily discomfort, especially without the development of a specific disease; an uneasy feeling. [F (as MAL-, EASE)]

malapropism /ˈmæləprɒpɪz(ə)m/ *n.* a ludicrous misuse of a word especially in mistake for one resembling it (e.g. *it will* *percussion the blow* for *cushion the blow*). [f. Mrs *Malaprop* (f. foll.) in Sheridan's *The Rivals*]

malapropos /ˌmæləprə'pəʊ/ *adv. & adj.* inopportunely said, done, or happening. [f. F *mal à propos* (*mal* ill, *à propos* to the purpose)]

malaria /mə'leərɪə/ *n.* a recurrent fever caused by a protozoan parasite of the genus *Plasmodium*, transmitted from infected persons by the bite of a female *Anopheles* mosquito after developing in the body of this insect. One type of malaria causes fever and sweating to occur every third day, another every fourth day, while malignant malaria causes a nearly continuous fever and is associated with dangerous complications and death. Anti-malarial drugs used in treating the disease are usually successful (the earliest known was quinine), and preventive drugs can be taken, but the best means of prevention is to attack the mosquitoes not only with insecticides but by draining the swamps and stagnant waters where they breed. Some mosquitoes have proved able to survive the insecticides used, however, and the disease is still a problem. —**malarial** *adj.* [f. It. *mala aria* bad air, the unwholesome condition of the atmosphere which results from the exhalations of marshy districts, to which the disease was formerly attributed]

malarkey /mə'lɑːkɪ/ *n.* (*slang*) humbug, nonsense. [orig. unkn.]

malathion /ˌmælə'θaɪən/ *n.* an insecticide containing phosphorous and relatively harmless to plants and animals. [f. chemical name]

Malawi /mə'lɑːwɪ/ a country of south central Africa, landlocked and almost totally dependent upon Mozambique for access to the sea; pop. (est. 1981) 6,370,000; official language, English; capital, Lilongwe. The Great Rift Valley runs through the country from north to south. Much of the eastern border is formed by Lake Malawi, the third largest lake in Africa, with a length of *c.*580 km (360 miles). Malawi is the former Nyasaland, a British protectorate from 1891 (following Livingstone's exploration), and from 1953 to 1963 a part of the Federation of Rhodesia and Nyasaland; it became an independent State within the Commonwealth under President Hastings Banda in 1964, and a republic in 1966. —**Malawian** *adj. & n.*

Malay /mə'leɪ/ *adj.* of a people predominating in Malaysia and Indonesia, or their language. —*n.* **1.** a member of this people. **2.** their language, which belongs to the Malayo-Polynesian language group and is spoken mainly in Malaysia, where it is the mother tongue of about half the population (6 million people). Meaning is shown by the order and grouping of words, not by inflexions. It is virtually the same language as Indonesian. From the 14th c. Malay was written in Arabic script but in the 19th c. the British constructed a Roman-based alphabet which is in general use today. —**Malayan** *adj.* [f. Malay *malāyu*]

Malayalam /ˌmælei'ɑːləm/ *n.* the Dravidian language of the Malabar district of southern India. [native name]

Malay Archipelago a very large group of islands, including Sumatra, Java, Borneo, the Philippines, and New Guinea, lying SE of Asia and north and NE of Australia.

Malayo-Polynesian *adj.* of a family of languages (also called *Austronesian*) extending from Madagascar in the west to the Pacific in the east. They are spoken by some 140 million people of whom all but one million speak a language of the Indonesian group, such as Indonesian, Tagalog, or Malagasy. The other groups are Micronesian, Melanesian, and Polynesian.

Malaysia /mə'leɪʒə/ a country in SE Asia, a federation composed of East Malaysia (the northern part of Borneo, including Sarawak and Sabah) and West Malaysia (the Malayan Peninsula south of Thailand), separated from each other by 650 km (400 miles) of the South China Sea; pop. (1980) 13,435,588; official language, Malay; capital, Kuala Lumpur. West Malaysia is the world's leading producer of rubber and leading exporter of tin, while East Malaysia, although considerably less developed, is an important exporter of oil. The area was opened up by the Portuguese and Dutch in the 16th and 17th c., but was under British influence from the early 19th c. It federated as an independent State of the Commonwealth in 1963 despite opposition from its neighbours Indonesia and the Philippines. —**Malaysian** *adj. & n.*

Malcolm /'mælkəm/ the name of four kings of Scotland: **Malcolm III** (*c.*1031–93), son of Duncan I, reigned 1058–93, killer of Macbeth. One of the monarchs most responsible for welding Scotland into an organized kingdom, Malcolm spent a large part of his reign involved in intermittent

border warfare with the new Norman regime in England, eventually being killed in battle near Alnwick. His wife Margaret (see entry) was later canonized.
Malcolm IV (1141–65), grandson of David I, reigned 1153–65, popularly known as 'the Maiden'. The reign of this youthful and sickly king witnessed a progressive loss of power to Henry II of England.

malcontent /'mælkəntent/ *n.* a discontented person. —*adj.* discontented. [F (as MAL-, CONTENT²)]

Maldives /'mɔːldaɪvz/ a country consisting of a chain of coral islands in the Indian Ocean SW of Sri Lanka; pop. (est. 1982) 160,200; official language, a form of Sinhalese; capital, Male. The islands were a British protectorate from 1887 until they became independent under the rule of a sultan in 1965 and then a republic in 1968, with a limited form of membership of the Commonwealth since 1982. —**Maldivian** /-'dɪvɪən/ *adj. & n.*

Male /'mɑːleɪ/ the capital of the Maldives; pop. (1982) 160,200.

male *adj.* **1.** of the sex that can beget offspring by performing the fertilizing function; (of plants or flowers) containing stamens but no pistil; of men or male animals or plants. **2.** (of parts of machinery etc.) designed to enter or fill a corresponding hollow part. —*n.* a male person or animal. [f. OF *ma(s)le* f. L *masculus*]

malediction /ˌmælɪ'dɪkʃ(ə)n/ *n.* a curse; the uttering of a curse. —**maledictory** *adj.* [f. L (*male* ill, *dicere* speak)]

malefactor /'mælɪfæktə(r)/ *n.* a criminal; an evil-doer. —**malefaction** /-'fækʃ(ə)n/ *n.* [f. L (*male* ill, *facere* do)]

malevolent /mə'levələnt/ *adj.* wishing ill to others. —**malevolence** *adj.* [f. OF or L (*male* ill, *volens* willing)]

malfeasance /mæl'fiːzəns/ *n.* misconduct, especially in an official capacity. [f. AF (MAL-, *faire* do)]

malformation /ˌmælfɔː'meɪʃ(ə)n/ *n.* faulty formation. —**malformed** /-'fɔːmd/ *adj.*

malfunction /mæl'fʌŋkʃ(ə)n/ *n.* a failure to function in the normal manner. —*v.i.* to function faultily.

Malherbe /mɑː'lerb/ François de (1555–1628), French poet, court poet from 1605 until his death. An architect of classicism in poetic form and grammar, he sternly criticized excess of emotion and ornamentation and the use of Latin and dialectal forms. His teaching was mainly oral or circulated in commentaries, and his own poems, painstakingly written and eloquent, were lacking in inspiration.

Mali /'mɑːlɪ/ an inland country in West Africa, south of Algeria; pop. (est. 1980) 6,900,000; official language, French; capital, Bamako. The north of the country is desert and most of the population, who depend on livestock for their living, are to be found pursuing a semi-nomadic existence in the south. Colonized by the French in the late 19th c. (and known as Soudan), Mali became a partner with Senegal in the Federation of Mali in 1959 and achieved full independence a year later. —**Malian** *adj. & n.*

malice /'mælɪs/ *n.* desire to harm or cause difficulty to others, ill-will; (*Law*) harmful intent. [f. OF f. L *malitia* (*malus* bad)]

malicious /mə'lɪʃəs/ *adj.* feeling, showing, or arising from malice. —**maliciously** *adv.*, **maliciousness** *n.* [f. prec.]

malign /mə'laɪn/ *adj.* **1.** harmful; (of a disease) malignant. **2.** malevolent. —*v.t.* to slander, to speak ill of. —**malignity** /-'lɪgnɪtɪ/ *n.* [f. OF or L *malignus* (*malus* bad)]

malignant /mə'lɪgnənt/ *adj.* **1.** (of a tumour) tending to spread and to recur after removal, cancerous. **2.** (of a disease) very virulent. **3.** feeling or showing intense ill-will. **4.** harmful. —**malignancy** *n.*, **malignantly** *adv.* [f. L *malignare* (as prec.)]

malinger /mə'lɪŋgə(r)/ *v.i.* to pretend to be ill to escape a duty. —**malingerer** *n.* [f. F *malingre* sickly]

Malinowski /ˌmælɪ'nɒfski/, Bronislaw Kaspar (1884–1942), Polish anthropologist, who initiated the technique of what came to be known as 'participant observation' —living for an extended period among the people he was studying (those of the Trobriand Islands, now part of Papua New Guinea), and participating in their activities, while gathering information.

mall /mæl, mɔːl/ *n.* a sheltered walk or promenade. [var. of MAUL, used of the hammer in the croquet-like game of pall-mall; applied to *The Mall* in London, orig. an alley where this game was played]

mallard /'mælɑːd/ *n.* (*pl.* same) a kind of wild duck (*Anas boscas*) of which the male has a green head. [f. OF (prob. as MALE)]

Mallarmé /ˌmɑːlɑː'meɪ/, Stéphane (1842–98), French poet, a leading symbolist and more recently a hero of structuralism. His best-known poems are 'Herodiade' (c.1871) and 'L'après-midi d'un faun' (1876). His pursuit of perfection led him to use elaborate symbols and metaphors, and to experiment with rhythm and syntax by transposing words and omitting grammatical elements. These tendencies culminated in 'Un coup de dès jamais n'abolira le hasard' (1897), which makes revolutionary use of typographical possibilities to suggest a musical score, and to render the 'prismatic subdivisions of the idea'.

malleable /ˈmælɪəb(ə)l/ adj. **1.** (of a metal etc.) that can be shaped by hammering. **2.** adaptable, pliable. —**malleability** /-ˈbɪlɪtɪ/ n. [f. OF f. L (malleare to hammer, as MALLET)]

mallet /ˈmælɪt/ n. **1.** a hammer, usually of wood (ill. CARPENTRY). **2.** a similarly shaped implement with a long handle, for striking the ball in croquet or polo. [f. OF maillet (mail hammer f. L malleus)]

mallow /ˈmæləʊ/ n. a flowering plant of the genus Malva, with purple, pink, or white flowers and hairy stems and leaves. [OE f. L malva]

malmsey /ˈmɑːmzɪ/ n. a sweet fortified wine made in Madeira, Cyprus, the Canary Islands, etc., from a kind of grape which came originally from the eastern Mediterranean. [f. MDu. or MLG f. Monemvasia in Greece]

malnutrition /mælnjuːˈtrɪʃ(ə)n/ n. insufficient nutrition; a condition where the diet omits some foods that are necessary for health.

malodorous /mælˈəʊdərəs/ adj. evil-smelling.

Malory /ˈmælərɪ/, Sir Thomas (d. 1471), English writer. Although his exact identity is uncertain, he is identified by his modern editor, Vinaver, as Sir Thomas Malory of Newbold Revel, Warwickshire, who after 1450 was charged with crimes of violence, theft, and rape. His major work, Le Morte D'Arthur (printed 1483), is a prose translation of a collection of the legends of King Arthur, skilfully selected from French and other sources. Malory wrote the work in prison and it was one of the earliest works to be printed by Caxton.

Malpighi /mælˈpiːgɪ/, Marcello (?1628-94), Italian microscopist. Seeking a mechanical interpretation of animal bodies he looked for and found visible structures underlying physiological functions. He saw the alveoli and capillaries in the lungs and demonstrated the pathway of blood from arteries to veins (confirming Harvey's theory of circulation); he saw the fibres and red cells of clotted blood, and investigated the structures of the kidney and skin. His interest in fine structure led him to embryology as the means by which the machine of the body was put together. He also studied the anatomy of the silkworm, discovered the breathing system of animals, and extended the search for structure into an examination of plant cells. A layer of developing cells in skin tissue (Malpighian layer) and a cluster of capillaries in the kidney are named after him.

Malplaquet /mælplæˈkeɪ/ a village in northern France, scene of a victory (1709) of allied British and Austrian troops over the French (see MARLBOROUGH).

malpractice /mælˈpræktɪs/ n. **1.** wrong-doing; an illegal action for one's own benefit while in a position of trust. **2.** the improper or negligent treatment of a patient by a physician.

malt /mɔːlt, mɒlt/ n. **1.** grain (usually barley) prepared by steeping, germination, and drying, for brewing etc. **2.** (colloq.) malt liquor; malt whisky. —v.t. to convert (grain) into malt. —**malted milk**, a drink made from dried milk and extract of malt. **malt whisky**, whisky made entirely of malted barley. [OE]

Malta /ˈmɔːltə, ˈmɒl-/ an island country in the central Mediterranean, a member State of the Commonwealth, lying about 100 km (60 miles) south of Sicily; pop. (1981) 341,000; official languages, Maltese and English; capital, Valletta. The island was held in turn by Phoenicians, Greeks, Carthaginians, and Arabs, and in 1090 was conquered by Roger of Normandy. Given to the Knights of St John by the Emperor Charles V in 1530, Malta successfully withstood a long siege by Turkish invaders and remained headquarters for the Order until captured by the French in 1798. It was annexed by Britain in 1814 and subsequently became an important naval base. During the Second World War the island was awarded the George Cross for its endurance under heavy air attack between 1940 and 1942. Independence was granted in 1964, but since that time, despite income from tourism, the economy has experienced

considerable difficulties because of the decline of the naval base.

Maltese /mɔːlˈtiːz, mɒl-/ adj. of Malta or its people or language. —n. **1.** a native or inhabitant of Malta. **2.** the Semitic language of Malta, much influenced by Italian. —**Maltese cross,** a cross with the arms broadening outwards, often indented at the ends (ill. VESTMENTS). [f. MALTA]

Malthus /ˈmælθəs/, Thomas Robert (1766-1834), English clergyman, a pioneer of the science of political economy. Malthus propounded the theory, very controversial at the time, that the rapidly growing population would soon increase beyond the capacity to feed it and that controls on population were therefore necessary to prevent catastrophe. —**Malthusian** /-ˈθjuːzɪən/ adj.

maltreat /mælˈtriːt/ v.t. to ill-treat. —**maltreatment** n.

malversation /mælvəˈseɪʃ(ə)n/ n. corrupt behaviour in a position of trust; corrupt administration of public money etc. [F (malverser f. L male badly, versari behave)]

Malvinas /mælˈviːnəs/ the name by which the Falkland Islands are known in Argentina.

mama var. of MAMMA.

mamba /ˈmæmbə/ n. a kind of venomous African snake of the genus Dendroaspis. [f. Zulu m'namba]

Mameluke /ˈmæmɪluːk/ n. a member of a body of Turkoman warriors who were originally brought to Egypt as slaves to act as a bodyguard for the caliphs and sultans, and themselves became powerful, ruling as sultans from 1250 until the Ottoman Turks conquered Egypt in 1517, and locally as governors under a Turkish viceroy. Napoleon defeated them in 1798, and the surviving Mamelukes were massacred by Muhammad Ali in 1811. —adj. of the Mamelukes. [f. F, ult. f. Arab., = slave]

mamma /məˈmɑː/ n. (archaic) mother. [imit. of child's ma, ma]

mammal /ˈmæm(ə)l/ n. a vertebrate of the class Mammalia, characterized by secretion of milk by the female to feed the young. Mammals evolved from reptiles about 200 million years ago but remained relatively small and inconspicuous until the dinosaurs died out at the end of the Cretaceous period, when they evolved rapidly and became the dominant land vertebrates. There are about 4,000 living species, of which nearly half are rodents and almost another quarter are bats. They are a very diverse group in terms of size, appearance, and behaviour (see ill., pp. 506-7). Mammals display a number of distinctive features which help to account for their success as a group. Along with birds they are warm-blooded, and so can remain active at night or in cold climates; a covering of hair and a layer of fat beneath the skin help to conserve their body heat. Mammals differ from reptiles in the position of their limbs, which are held more vertically beneath the body, making for more efficient locomotion, and in their teeth, which have evolved into a number of different types as an adaptation to particular diets. The mammalian brain is also relatively larger than that of other vertebrate groups, permitting more complex and adaptable behaviour. The three major subgroups of mammals are monotremes (egg-laying mammals, represented only by the platypus and echidnas), marsupials, and placental mammals, which include most of the familiar types: primates (including man), carnivores (such as dogs, cats, and bears), hoofed mammals, rodents, bats, whales, etc. —**mammalian** /məˈmeɪlɪən/ adj. & n. [f. L mammalis (mamma breast)]

mammary /ˈmæmərɪ/ adj. of the breasts. [as prec.]

Mammon /ˈmæmən/ n. wealth regarded as an idol or evil influence. 'Mammon' was the Aramaic word for 'riches' used in the Greek text of the New Testament in Matt. 6: 24 and Luke 16: 9-13, and retained in the Vulgate. It was taken by medieval writers as the name of the devil of covetousness, and this use was revived by Milton in Paradise Lost. [f. L f. Gk f. Aram.]

mammoth /ˈmæməθ/ n. a large extinct elephant of the genus Mammuthus, with a hairy coat and curved tusks. —adj. huge. [f. Russ.]

man n. (pl. **men**) **1.** a creature of the genus Homo (see entry), distinguished from other animals by superior mental development, power of articulate speech, and upright stance; (collect.) the human race, mankind. **2.** an adult human male. **3.** a person of a particular type or historical period. **4.** (in indefinite or general application, without specification of sex) a person. **5.** an individual person, especially in the role of assistant, opponent, or expert, or considered in terms of suitability. **6.** a husband. **7.** (usu. in

Mammals

Variations in body design, reflecting adaptation to different ways of life

leaping
(kangaroo)

powerfully developed hind limbs

arms lengthened
for swinging from
branches of trees

tree-climbing
(gibbon)

long neck can
reach tree-tops

feeding and
camouflage
(giraffe)

pattern on body
simulates dappled shadows

flying
(bat)

thumb

wings formed by
membranes stretched
between limbs

thumb

fingers

running
(deer)

hind limbs absorbed
into streamlined body

fore-limbs
become flippers

swimming
(dolphin)

hoof

long legs with weight
taken on the toes

living on land
and in the sea
(walrus)

burrowing
(mole)

fur can move easily
in all directions

ears and eyes
hidden in fur

fore-limbs
adapted for digging

blubber beneath skin
for insulation

flippers for swimming
also give support on land

Some unusual mammals

pangolin or scaly ant-eater

protected by an armour
of horny scales

kangaroo

young develop
and suckle
in pouch

duck-billed platypus

an egg-laying mammal

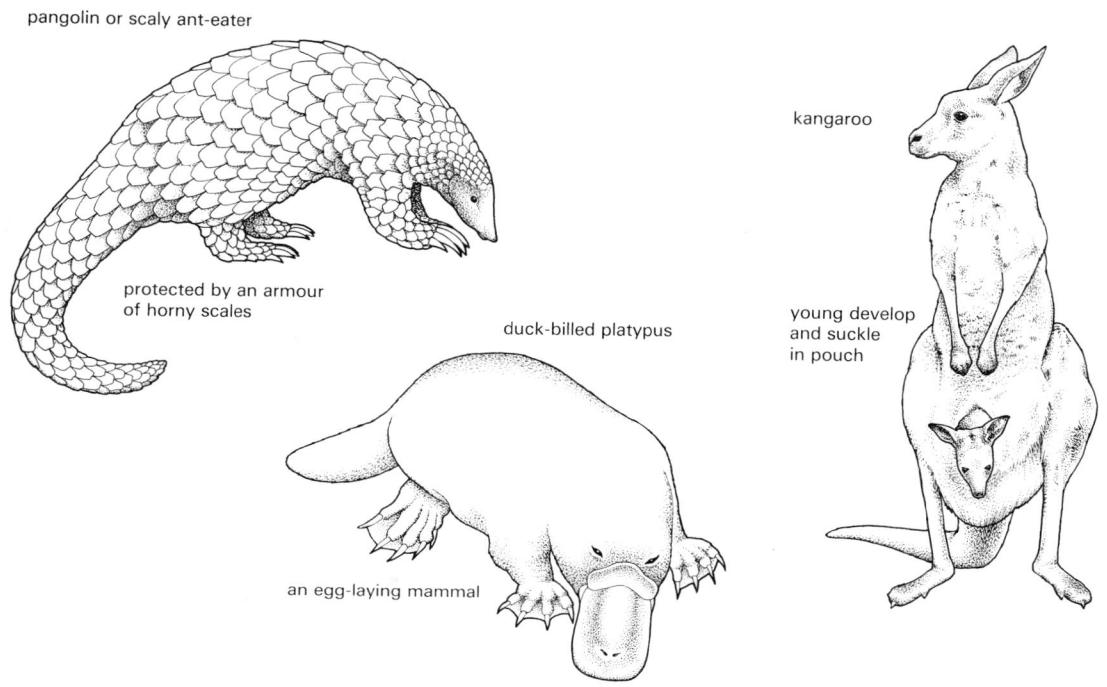

Foot formation and number of toes

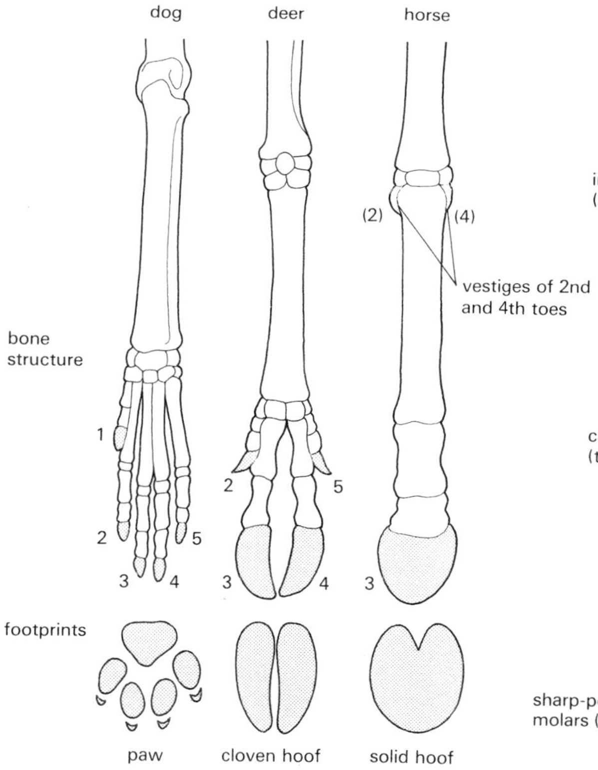

dog

deer

horse

(2)   (4)

vestiges of 2nd
and 4th toes

bone
structure

1

2   5

3   4

2   5

3   4

3

footprints

paw

cloven hoof

solid hoof

Teeth

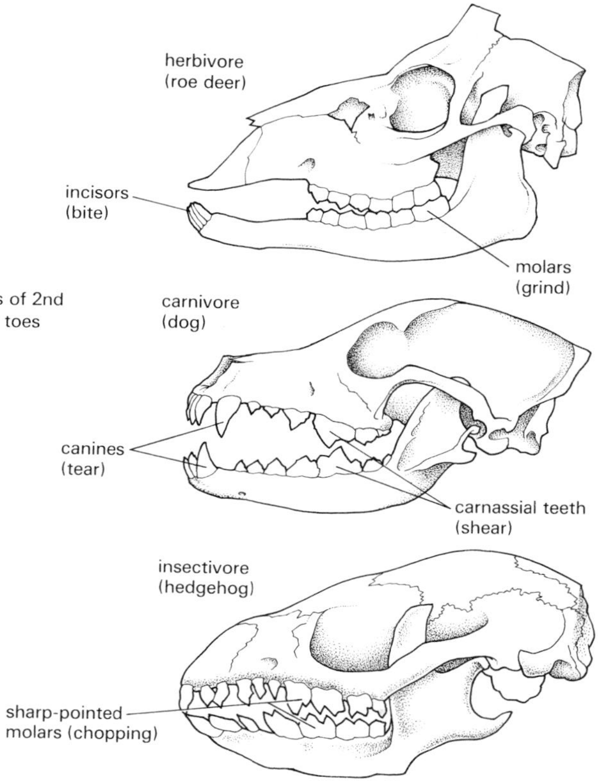

herbivore
(roe deer)

incisors
(bite)

molars
(grind)

carnivore
(dog)

canines
(tear)

carnassial teeth
(shear)

insectivore
(hedgehog)

sharp-pointed
molars (chopping)

pl.) an employee, a workman. **8.** (usu. in *pl.*) a member of the armed forces, especially of those not officers. **9.** (*colloq.*) as a form of address. **10.** one of a set of objects used in playing chess, draughts, etc. —*v.t.* (**-nn-**) to supply with a man or manpower for service or to operate something. —**as one man,** in unison. **be one's own man,** to be independent. **man about town,** a fashionable socializer. **man-at-arms** *n.* (*pl.* **men-at-arms**) (*archaic*) a soldier. **man-hour** *n.* the work done by one person in one hour. **man-hunt** *n.* an organized search for a person (especially a criminal). **Man in the Iron Mask,** see separate entry. **man in the street,** an ordinary average man. **man-made** *adj.* artificially made. **man-of-war** *n.* (*pl.* **men-of-war**) an armed ship of a country's navy. **man of the world,** see WORLD. **man-sized** *adj.* of the size of a man; adequate to a man, large. **man to man,** candidly. **to a man,** without exception. —**mannish** *adj.* [OE]

-man /-mən/ *suffix* (*pl.* **-men**) denoting a man concerned with (*clergyman*), or skilful with (*oarsman*), or describable as (*Welshman*). [= prec.]

manacle /ˈmænək(ə)l/ *n.* (usu. in *pl.*) **1.** a fetter for the hand, a handcuff. **2.** a restraint. —*v.t.* to fetter with manacles. [f. OF f. L *manicula* (*manus* hand)]

manage /ˈmænɪdʒ/ *v.t./i.* **1.** to organize or regulate; to be the manager of (a business etc.). **2.** to succeed in achieving, to contrive; to succeed with limited resources or means, to be able to cope (with). **3.** to secure the co-operation of (a person) by tact, flattery, etc. **4.** to have under effective control. **5.** to use or wield (a tool etc.) effectively. [f. It. *maneggiare* f. L *manus* hand]

manageable /ˈmænɪdʒəb(ə)l/ *adj.* that may be managed. [f. prec.]

management *n.* **1.** managing, being managed. **2.** the administration of business concerns or public undertakings; persons engaged in this. [f. MANAGE]

manager *n.* **1.** a person conducting a business, institution, etc.; a person controlling the activities of a person or team in sport, entertainment, etc. **2.** a person who manages money, household affairs, etc., in a specified way. —**manageress** /-ˈres/ *n.fem.*, **managerial** /mænəˈdʒɪərɪəl/ *adj.* [as prec.]

Managua /məˈnɑːgwə/ the capital of Nicaragua; pop. (est. 1978) 517,700. The city was almost completely destroyed by an earthquake in 1972.

Manama /məˈnɑːmə/ the capital of Bahrain; pop. (est. 1980) 150,000.

mañana /mənˈjɑːnə/ *n. & adv.* tomorrow (as a symbol of easy-going procrastination); the indefinite future. [Sp.]

Manasseh /məˈnæsɪ, -sə/ **1.** Hebrew patriarch, son of Joseph (Gen. 48: 19). **2.** the tribe of Israel traditionally descended from him.

Manasses see PRAYER OF MANASSES.

manatee /mænəˈtiː/ *n.* a large tropical aquatic mammal of the genus *Trichechus*, feeding on plants. [f. Sp. f. Carib.]

Manchu /mænˈtʃuː/ *n.* **1.** a member of a Tartar people who conquered China and founded the Ch'ing dynasty. **2.** their language, which belongs to the Tungusic group in the Altaic family of languages. At one time it was an official language of China, but it is now spoken only in parts of northern Manchuria. —*adj.* of this people or their language. [Manchu, = pure]

Manchuria /mænˈtʃʊərɪə/ a region forming the NE portion of China. In 1932 it was declared an independent State by Japan and renamed *Manchukuo*; it was restored to China in 1945.

Mancunian /mæŋˈkjuːnɪən/ *adj.* of Manchester. —*n.* a native or inhabitant of Manchester. [f. L *Mancunium* Roman settlement on the site of Manchester]

Mandaean /mænˈdiːən/ *n.* **1.** a member of a Gnostic sect of Mesopotamia (see SABIAN) regarding St John the Baptist as the Messiah. **2.** the Aramaic dialect in which their sacred books are written. —*adj.* of the Mandaeans or their language. [Mandaean, = having knowledge (tr. Gk *gnōstikoi*, see GNOSTIC)]

mandala /ˈmændələ/ *n.* a circular figure as a religious symbol of the universe. [f. Skr.]

mandamus /mænˈdeɪməs/ *n.* a judicial writ issued as a command to an inferior court, or ordering a person to perform a public or statutory duty. [L, = we command]

mandarin /ˈmændərɪn/ *n.* **1.** an influential person, especially a reactionary or secretive bureaucrat. **2.** (*hist.*) a Chinese official. **3. Mandarin,** the language formerly used by officials and educated persons in China; any of the

varieties of this spoken as a common language in China, especially the Northern variety. **4.** a small flat orange with a loose skin. [f. Port. f. Malay ult. f. Skr. *mantrin* counsellor]

mandatary /ˈmændətərɪ/ *n.* a holder or receiver of a mandate. [f. L (as foll.)]

mandate /ˈmændeɪt/ *n.* **1.** authority to act for another; the political authority supposed to be given by the electors to a government. **2.** a judicial or legal command from a superior. —/mænˈdeɪt/ *v.t.* **1.** to give authority to (a delegate). **2.** to commit (a territory) to a mandatary. [f. L *mandatum* (*mandare* command, entrust)]

mandatory /ˈmændətərɪ/ *adj.* compulsory; of or conveying a command. —**mandatorily** *adv.* [f. L (as prec.)]

Mandeville /ˈmændvɪl/, Sir John, the reputed author of a 14th-c. book of travels and travellers' tales which takes the reader to Turkey, Tartary, Persia, Egypt, and India. Written in French and much translated, it was actually compiled by an unknown hand from the works of several writers.

mandible /ˈmændɪb(ə)l/ *n.* a jaw, especially the lower jaw in mammals (ill. BODY 1) and fishes; the upper or lower part of a bird's beak (ill. BIRDS); either half of the crushing organ in the mouth-parts of an insect etc. (ill. INSECTS). [f. OF or L *mandibula* (*mandere* chew)]

mandolin /ˈmændəlɪn/ *n.* a plucked stringed instrument of the lute family with metal strings tuned in pairs and a characteristic tremolo when sustaining long notes. It is played chiefly in folk music. [F f. It.]

mandorla /mænˈdɔːlə/ *n.* = VESICA 2. [It., = almond]

mandragora /mænˈdrægərə/ *n.* the mandrake, especially as a narcotic (Shakespeare *Othello* III. iii. 330). [f. L F. Gk (as foll.)]

mandrake /ˈmændreɪk/ *n.* a plant of the genus *Mandragora*, with white or purple flowers and a large yellow fruit, having emetic and narcotic properties. Its root was formerly thought to resemble human form and to shriek when plucked. [prob. f. MDu., ult. f. Gk *mandragoras*, assoc. w. MAN, *drake* dragon]

mandrel /ˈmændr(ə)l/ *n.* **1.** a lathe-shaft to which work is fixed while being turned. **2.** a cylindrical rod round which metal or other material is forged or shaped. [orig. unkn.]

mandrill /ˈmændrɪl/ *n.* a kind of large baboon (*Mandrillus sphinx*) of West Africa, with highly coloured patches and callosities on its face and hindquarters. [prob. f. MAN + DRILL[4]]

mane *n.* **1.** the long hair on the neck of an animal, especially a horse (ill. HORSE) or lion. **2.** the long hair of a person. [OE]

manège /məˈneɪʒ/ *n.* **1.** a riding-school. **2.** horsemanship. **3.** the movements of a trained horse. [F f. It. (as MANAGE)]

Manes /ˈmeɪniːz/ (*c.*215-75) the Persian founder of Manichaeism (see entry).

Manet /mæˈneɪ/, Édouard (1832-83), French painter, sometimes called the 'father of modern art'. He was greatly admired by the young impressionists from whom, however, he stood somewhat aloof, seeking (with indifferent success) recognition from the official Salon. Manet was essentially a realist: his aim was 'to paint spontaneously what one sees', and the indignation which his paintings aroused can be explained by their challenge to the Old Masters through the introduction of contemporary reality into themes which had become hallowed and innocuous by the unreality conferred on them when they appeared in mythological and historical paintings. His abandonment of half-tones and shadings in favour of a bold use of pure colour added to the effect of frankness and lack of sentimentality. Among his works are some of the most familiar pictures in the world—*The Picnic* (*Déjeuner sur l'herbe*, 1863), created a scandal which led to the closing of the exhibition in which it appeared; *Olympia* (1865), also caused a scandal although Baudelaire and Zola came forward in his support; and *A Bar at the Folies-Bergère* (1882), his last great work. Afflicted by a wasting disease of the nervous system he resorted to small pictures of flowers when he no longer had strength for larger themes and canvases.

Manetho /mæˈneɪθəʊ/ (3rd c. BC) an Egyptian priest who in *c.*280 BC wrote a history of Egypt from mythical times to 323 BC. He arbitrarily divided the succession of rulers known to him into 31 dynasties, an arrangement which it is still convenient to use.

Manhattan /mænˈhæt(ə)n/ an island at the mouth of the Hudson River, which was the site of the original Dutch settlement of New Amsterdam, later the city of New York. It is now a borough containing the commercial and cultural centre of the city.

Manhattan Project the code name for an American project set up in 1942 to develop an atomic bomb.

manful *adj.* brave, resolute. —**manfully** *adv.* [f. MAN + -FUL]

manganese /ˈmæŋɡəniːz/ *n.* **1.** a hard grey metallic element, symbol Mn, atomic number 25, first isolated in 1774. The presence of manganese is essential to the process of steel manufacture, and special steels high in manganese are produced for heavy-duty work. The element is also required in small amounts by plants and many animals. **2.** an oxide of this, a black mineral used in glass-making etc. [f. F f. It., f. MAGNESIA]

mange /meɪndʒ/ *n.* a skin disease in hairy and woolly animals. [f. OF *mangeue* itch (*mangier* eat f. L *manducare* chew)]

mangel-wurzel /ˈmæŋɡ(ə)l wɜːz(ə)l/ *n.* a large beet used as cattle food. [G (*mangold* beet, *wurzel* root)]

manger /ˈmeɪndʒə(r)/ *n.* a long open box or trough for horses or cattle to eat from. [f. OF *mangeoire* f. L (as MANGE)]

mangle¹ /ˈmæŋɡ(ə)l/ *v.t.* **1.** to hack or mutilate by blows; to cut roughly so as to disfigure. **2.** to spoil (a text etc.) by gross blunders. [f. AF *ma(ha)ngler* (app. as MAIM)]

mangle² /ˈmæŋɡ(ə)l/ *n.* a machine of two or more cylinders for squeezing water from and pressing washed clothes etc. —*v.t.* to press (clothes) in a mangle. [f. Du., ult. f. Gk *magganon* pulley]

mango /ˈmæŋɡəʊ/ *n.* (*pl.* **-oes**) a tropical fruit with yellowish flesh; the tree (*Mangifera indica*) bearing this. [f. Port. f. Malay f. Tamil]

mangold /ˈmæŋɡ(ə)ld/ *n.* = MANGEL-WURZEL. [G, = beet]

mangrove /ˈmæŋɡrəʊv/ *n.* a tropical tree or shrub of the genus *Rhizophora*, growing in shore-mud with many tangled roots above ground. [orig. unkn.; assim. to GROVE]

mangy /ˈmeɪndʒɪ/ *adj.* **1.** having mange. **2.** squalid, shabby. [f. MANGE]

manhandle *v.t.* **1.** to move by human effort alone. **2.** to treat roughly.

manhole *n.* an opening (usually with a lid) through which a person can enter a sewer, conduit, etc., to inspect or repair it.

manhood *n.* **1.** the state of being a man. **2.** manliness, courage. **3.** the men of a country. [f. MAN + -HOOD]

mania /ˈmeɪnɪə/ *n.* **1.** violent madness. **2.** extreme enthusiasm. [f. L f. Gk, = madness (*mainomai* be mad)]

-mania /-meɪnɪə/ *suffix* forming nouns denoting a special type of mental disorder (*megalomania*), or enthusiasm or admiration. [as. prec.]

maniac /ˈmeɪnɪæk/ *n.* a person affected with mania. —*adj.* of or affected with mania. [as MANIA]

-maniac /-meɪnɪæk/ *suffix* forming nouns with the sense 'a person affected with -mania' and adjectives with the sense 'affected with -mania'. [as prec.]

maniacal /məˈnaɪək(ə)l/ *adj.* of or like a mania or a maniac. —**maniacally** *adv.* [as MANIA]

manic /ˈmænɪk/ *adj.* of or affected with mania. —**manic-depressive** *adj.* relating to a mental disorder with alternating periods of elation and depression; (*n.*) a person having such a disorder. [f. MANIA]

Manichaeism /ˈmænɪkiːɪz(ə)m/ *n.* a religious system with Christian, Gnostic, and pagan elements, founded in Persia in the 3rd c. by Manes (*c.*216-76) and spread widely in the Roman Empire and in Asia, surviving in Chinese Turkestan until the 13th c. The system was based on a supposed primeval conflict between light and darkness, teaching that matter is evil but within each person's brain is imprisoned a particle of the divine 'light' which can be released by the practice of religion, and that Christ, Buddha, the Prophets, and Manes had been sent to help in this task. Severe asceticism was practised within the sect, with the 'elect' living a more rigorous life than the 'hearers' who supported them. [f. MANES or *Manichaeus*]

manicure /ˈmænɪkjʊə(r)/ *n.* cosmetic treatment of the hands and finger-nails. —*v.t.* to apply such treatment to. —**manicurist** *n.* [F f. L *manus* hand, *cura* care]

manifest /ˈmænɪfest/ *adj.* clear and unmistakable. —*v.t./i.* **1.** to show clearly, to give signs of; to make or become apparent or visible. **2.** to be evidence of, to prove. **3.** to record in a manifest. —*n.* a list of cargo or passengers carried by a ship or aircraft etc. —**manifestation** /-ˈsteɪʃ(ə)n/ *n.*, **manifestly** *adv.* [f. OF or L *manifestus*]

manifesto /mænɪˈfestəʊ/ *n.* (*pl.* **-os**) a public declaration of policy, especially by a political party. [It. (as prec.)]

manifold /ˈmænɪfəʊld/ *adj.* **1.** many and various. **2.** having various forms, applications, component parts, etc. —*n.* **1.** a pipe or chamber (in a piece of a mechanism) with several openings. **2.** a manifold thing. [OE (as MANY, -FOLD)]

manikin /ˈmænɪkɪn/ *n.* a little man, a dwarf. [f. Du. dim. (as MAN)]

Manila /məˈnɪlə/ the capital and chief port of the Philippines; pop. (est.) approx. 8 million.

manila /məˈnɪlə/ *n.* (also **manilla**) **1.** the strong fibre of a Philippine tree (*Musa textilis*). **2.** a brown paper originally made from this, used esp. for envelopes. [f. prec.]

Man in the Iron Mask a mysterious prisoner in the Bastille and other prisons in 17th-c. France. According to Dumas' novel of the same name, the man was the twin brother of Louis XIV, his face concealed by a mask so as to prevent his recognition, and a threat to Louis' position on the throne. Various other theories as to the identity of the prisoner (who almost certainly did exist) have been advanced, but it is now considered most likely that he was an Italian agent, Count Matthioli, who had seriously annoyed the king.

manioc /ˈmænɪɒk/ *n.* cassava; flour made from this. [f. Tupi *mandioca*]

maniple /ˈmænɪp(ə)l/ *n.* **1.** a strip of material worn over the left arm by a priest celebrating the Eucharist. **2.** a subdivision of a legion in the army of ancient Rome. [OF, or f. L *manipulus* handful, troop (*manus* hand)]

manipulable /məˈnɪpʊləb(ə)l/ *adj.* that may be manipulated. [f. foll.]

manipulate /məˈnɪpjʊleɪt/ *v.t.* **1.** to handle, manage, or use (a thing) skilfully. **2.** to examine manually and treat (a part of the body) for a fracture etc. **3.** to arrange or influence cleverly or unfairly. —**manipulation** /-ˈleɪʃ(ə)n/ *n.*, **manipulator** *n.* [f. F. *manipuler* f. L *manipulus* (see MANIPLE)]

Manipur /mænɪˈpʊə(r)/ a State of India, east of Assam; capital, Imphal. —**Manipuri** *adj.* & *n.*

Manitoba /mænɪˈtəʊbə/ a province of central Canada (from 1870) with a coastline on Hudson Bay. The area was ceded to Canada by the Hudson's Bay Company in 1869; capital, Winnipeg.

mankind /mænˈkaɪnd/ *n.* **1.** human beings in general, the human species. **2.** /ˈmæn-/ men in general.

manly *adj.* having the qualities associated with a man (e.g. strength and courage); befitting a man. —**manliness** *n.* [f. MAN]

Mann, Thomas (1875-1955), German novelist and essayist who combined elegance and lucidity of style with acute analytical powers. He achieved literary fame with his first novel *Buddenbrooks* (1901), which describes the decline of a merchant family and has strongly autobiographical features. The role and character of the artist in relation to society is a constant theme in his works, and is linked with the problem of Nazism in *Dr Faustus* (1947), in which a composer epitomizes the degeneration of 20th-c. Germany, exposing Nietzsche and Wagner as its sponsors. Originally a man of somewhat conservative sympathies, he caused surprise by quickly lending his public support to the Weimar Republic. When Hitler came to power Mann was forced into exile, and became a US citizen in 1936. He was awarded the Nobel Prize for literature in 1929.

manna /ˈmænə/ *n.* **1.** a substance miraculously supplied as food to the Israelites in the wilderness (Exod. 16). **2.** something unexpected and delightful. [OE ult. f. Heb., prob. = Arab. *mann* exudation of tamarisk]

manned *adj.* (of a spacecraft etc.) having a human crew. [f. MAN]

mannequin /ˈmænɪkɪn/ *n.* **1.** a person, usually a woman, employed by a dress designer etc. to model clothes. **2.** a dummy for the display of clothes in a shop. [F, = MANIKIN]

manner /ˈmænə(r)/ *n.* **1.** the way a thing is done or happens. **2.** a person's bearing or way of behaving towards others, style of speaking, etc. **3.** (in *pl.*) modes of life, conditions of society. **4.** (in *pl.*) social behaviour; polite social behaviour. **5.** style in literature or art. **6.** kind, sort. —**all manner of,** every kind of. **comedy of manners,** a comedy with satirical portrayal of the manners of society. **in a manner of speaking,** in some sense, to some extent, so to speak. [f. AF f. L *manuarius* (*manus* hand)]

mannered *adj.* **1.** behaving in a specified way (*ill-, well-mannered*). **2.** full of mannerisms. [f. prec.]

mannerism /ˈmænərɪz(ə)m/ *n.* **1.** a distinctive gesture or feature of style; excessive use of these in art etc. **2.** a style of Italian art (see below). —**mannerist** *n.* [f. MANNER]

Although the terms *mannerist* and *mannered* are sometimes applied to any art that is excessively refined and affected, *mannerism* is usually reserved for a definable phase of Italian art from *c.*1530 to 1590, the period after the High Renaissance. The term derives from the Italian word *maniera*, which in the 16th c. had a particular currency as meaning anything (in art or behaviour) that was especially stylish or graceful. It was a quality sought and admired by painters; only in the 17th c. was the term applied negatively, as defining a highly artificial and overwrought (and therefore degenerate) style, and this prejudice was inherited and legitimized in the 19th c. by the first generation of professional art historians. Mannerist art is characterized by a sense of extreme elegance and grace and is often highly imaginative; in stylistic terms it relies on fine drawing and rich, acid, often artificial colour, with a strong sense of movement and contrast. In their use of perspective mannerist painters often sought a self-conscious virtuosity and deliberately played visual tricks. Pontormo, Vasari, and the later Michelangelo (particularly for his *Last Judgement* 1536-41) are among the typical exponents of the mannerist sensibility. The term is sometimes applied to architecture, notably to the buildings of Giulio Romano near Mantua (from 1526) and to Michelangelo's Laurentian Library at Florence (1524-34), where both deliberately infringed the rules of humanist architecture, and created un-classical combinations of classical elements.

mannerly *adj.* well-behaved, polite. [as prec.]

manœuvre /məˈnuːvə(r)/ *n.* **1.** a planned and controlled movement of a vehicle or body of troops etc.; (in *pl.*) large-scale exercises of troops or ships. **2.** a deceptive or elusive movement; a skilful plan. —*v.t./i.* **1.** to move (a thing, esp. a vehicle) carefully. **2.** to perform manœuvres; to cause (troops or ships) to do this. **3.** to guide skilfully or craftily. [f. F f. L *man(u)operari* work by hand (*manus* hand, *operari* to work)]

manometer /məˈnɒmɪtə(r)/ *n.* a pressure-gauge for gases and liquids. [f. F f. Gk *manos* thin + -METER]

manor /ˈmænə(r)/ *n.* **1.** a large landed estate or its house (also **manor-house**). **2.** (*hist.*) a territorial unit under the feudal control of a lord. **3.** (*slang*) an area for which a police unit is responsible. —**manorial** /məˈnɔːrɪəl/ *adj.* [f. AF f. L *manēre* remain]

manpower *n.* the number of persons available for work or military service.

manqué /ˈmɑ̃keɪ/ *adj.* (placed after a noun) that might have been but is not. [F (*manquer* lack)]

mansard /ˈmænsɑːd/ *n.* a roof with each face having two slopes, with the steeper one below (ill. HOUSES). The style was popularized by François Mansart (see foll.) but had been in existence earlier, e.g. in part of the roof of the Louvre dating from the mid-16th c. [f. foll.]

Mansart /mɑ̃ˈsɑːr/, François (1598-1666), French classical architect. His first major work was the rebuilding of part of the château of Blois, which incorporated the type of roof now named after him (see prec.). Other buildings include a number of town houses in Paris, the château of Maisons (1642-6), and the church of Val-de-Grâce (1645), but his uncompromising disposition and obstinate refusal to keep to any final plan for a building led to his being deprived of this and other commissions. His great-nephew by marriage, Jules Hardouin-Mansart (1646-1708), became architect to Louis XIV and from 1678 was in charge of building at Versailles.

manse *n.* an ecclesiastical residence, especially a Scottish Presbyterian minister's house. [f. L (as MANOR)]

manservant *n.* (*pl.* **menservants**) a male servant.

Mansfield /ˈmænsfiːld/, Katherine (Kathleen Mansfield Beauchamp, 1888-1923), New Zealand-born short-story writer. Her stories, influenced by Chekhov, are marked by intensity and poetic feeling and often pathos or irony.

mansion /ˈmænʃ(ə)n/ *n.* a large grand house. —**the Mansion House**, the official residence of the Lord Mayor in the City of London, built in 1737-53. [f. OF f. L (as MANOR)]

manslaughter *n.* the unlawful killing of a human being without intentional malice.

Mantegna /mænˈtenjə/, Andrea (1431-1506), Italian painter and engraver, noted especially for his frescoes, which include the *Triumph of Caesar*, bought by Charles I in 1627 and now at Hampton Court. His frescoes for the bridal chamber of the ruling family at Mantua, where he was court painter, show portraits of the family arrayed as narrative pictures round the walls in an illusionist style that makes their events seem to be happening in and outside the room, and a ceiling where the centre appears to be open to the sky. Mantegna had a considerable influence on Giovanni Bellini, who was his brother-in-law.

mantel /ˈmænt(ə)l/ *n.* **1.** a structure of wood or marble etc. above and around a fireplace (ill. HOUSES). **2.** a mantelpiece. [var. of MANTLE]

mantelpiece *n.* a shelf over a fireplace.

mantilla /mænˈtɪlə/ *n.* a lace scarf worn esp. by Spanish women over the hair and shoulders. [Sp. (as MANTLE)]

mantis /ˈmæntɪs/ *n.* (in full **praying mantis**) a predacious insect (*Mantis religiosa*) that holds its forelegs in a position suggesting hands folded in prayer (ill. INSECTS). [Gk, = prophet]

mantle *n.* **1.** a loose sleeveless cloak; a covering. **2.** a fragile tube fixed round a gas-jet to give an incandescent light. **3.** a bird's back, scapulars, and wing-coverts, especially when these are of a distinctive colour (ill. BIRDS). **4.** the region between the earth's crust and its core (ill. GEOLOGY). —*v.t.* to clothe in or as in a mantle; to conceal, to envelop. [f. OF f. L *mantellum*]

mantling /ˈmæntlɪŋ/ *n.* (in heraldry) an ornamental representation of drapery etc. behind and round a shield (ill. HERALDRY). [f. prec.]

mantra /ˈmæntrə/ *n.* **1.** a sacred syllable, word, or phrase (especially in Buddhism and Hinduism) believed to possess supernatural powers. A personal mantra is given by the guru at initiation and used as an object of meditation. **2.** a Vedic hymn. [Skr., = instrument of thought (*man* think)]

mantrap *n.* a trap for catching trespassers etc.

Manu /ˈmɑːnuː/ *n.* the archetypal first man of Hindu mythology, survivor of the great flood, and father of the human race, and legendary author of the most famous codes of Hindu religious law, the *Manusmriti* (*The Laws of Manu*) composed in Sanskrit and dating in its present form from the 1st c. BC. [Skr., = man (*man* think)]

manual /ˈmænjʊəl/ *adj.* of or done with the hands; worked by hand, not by automatic equipment. —*n.* **1.** a handbook; a reference book. **2.** an organ keyboard played with the hands not the feet. —**manually** *adv.* [f. OF f. L *manualis* (*manus* hand)]

manufacture /mænjʊˈfæktʃə(r)/ *v.t.* **1.** to produce (articles) by labour, especially by machinery on a large scale. **2.** to invent or fabricate (evidence or a story etc.). —*n.* the manufacturing of articles; a branch of such an industry. —**manufacturer** *n.* [F f. It. & L (*manu facere* make by hand)]

manure /məˈnjʊə(r)/ *n.* a fertilizer, especially dung. —*v.t.* to apply manure to (land). [f. AF (as MANŒUVRE)]

manuscript /ˈmænjʊskrɪpt/ *n.* **1.** a book or document written by hand. **2.** an author's copy, written by hand or typed (not printed). **3.** manuscript state. —*adj.* written by hand. [f. L (*manu scribere* write by hand)]

Manx /mæŋks/ *adj.* of the Isle of Man or its people or language. —*n.* the Celtic language of the Isle of Man, a dialect of Gaelic. There are no native speakers alive now but it is still in use for ceremonial purposes. —**the Manx**, the Manx people. **Manx cat**, a cat of a tailless variety. **Manxman** *n.* (*pl.* **-men**), **Manxwoman** *n.fem.* (*pl.* **-women**) [f. ON f. OIr. *Manu* Isle of Man]

many /ˈmenɪ/ *adj.* (*compar.* MORE, *superl.* MOST) great in number, numerous. —*n.pl.* many people or things. —**the many**, the multitude of people. **a good many**, a fair number. **a great many**, a large number. [OE]

Manzoni /mænˈtsəʊnɪ/, Alessandro (1785-1873), Italian novelist, dramatist, and poet, author of the greatest of Italian historical novels *I promessi sposi* (*The Betrothed*, 1825-42). The novel (which had immense patriotic appeal) is set in Lombardy in 1628-31, during the period of Spanish administration, and is remarkable for its powerful characterization of historical figures and ordinary people and for its coherent reconstruction of events.

Maoism /ˈmaʊɪz(ə)m/ *n.* the Communist doctrines of Mao Tse-tung. —**Maoist** *n.* [f. MAO Tse-tung]

Maori /ˈmaʊrɪ/ *n.* **1.** a member or the Polynesian language of the brown aboriginal people of New Zealand. Having arrived there first as part of a wave of migration from

Tahiti, probably in the 9th c., by 1200 they had established settlements in various parts of the islands. The Maoris now number about 280,000. **2.** their Polynesian language, spoken by about 100,000 persons in New Zealand. *—adj.* of the Maoris or their language. **—Maori Wars,** wars fought intermittently in 1845–8 and 1860–72 between Maoris and the colonial government of New Zealand over the enforced sale of Maori lands to Europeans (see WAITANGI). [native name]

Mao Tse-tung /maʊ tsiːˈtʊŋ/ (also **Mao Zedong,** 1893–1976) Chinese statesman. Leader of the Chinese Communist revolution, Mao was successful in organizing and uniting peasant forces, to whom he gave central importance, and eventually defeated both the occupying Japanese and rival Chinese nationalist forces to form, in 1949, the Chinese People's Republic of which he became President. He resigned as Head of State in 1959 but retained his position as chairman of the Communist Party.

map *n.* **1.** a representation (usually on a flat surface) of the earth's surface or a part of it; a similar representation of the sky (showing the positions of stars etc.) or of the moon etc. **2.** a diagram showing an arrangement or the components of a thing. *—v.t.* (**-pp-**) to represent on a map. **—map out,** to plan in detail. [f. L *mappa* napkin]

maple /ˈmeɪp(ə)l/ *n.* a kind of tree or shrub of the genus *Acer* grown for wood, ornament, shade, or sugar; its wood. **—maple-leaf** *n.* the emblem of Canada. **maple sugar,** a sugar obtained by evaporating the sap of some kinds of maple. **maple syrup,** a syrup made by evaporating maple sap or dissolving maple sugar. [f. OE]

Maputo /məˈpuːtəʊ/ the capital and chief port of Mozambique; pop. (1980) 755,300.

maquette /məˈket/ *n.* a preliminary model or sketch. [F f. It. (*macchia* spot)]

Maquis /ˈmækiː, ˈmɑː-/ *n.* a secret army of patriots in France during the German occupation in 1940–5; a member of this. [F, = brushwood, scrub (traditionally used as a refuge by fugitives)]

mar *v.t.* (**-rr-**) to spoil, to disfigure, to impair the perfection of. [OE]

Mar. *abbr.* March.

marabou /ˈmærəbuː/ *n.* a kind of stork (*Leptoptilus crumeniferus*); its down as a trimming etc. [F, f. Arab. = holy man (the stork being regarded as holy)]

maraca /məˈrækə/ *n.* a clublike gourd containing beans, beads, etc., held in the hand and shaken (usually in pairs) as a musical instrument (ill. MUSICAL INSTRUMENTS). [f. Port., prob. f. Tupi]

maraschino /mærəˈskiːnəʊ/ *n.* (*pl.* **-os**) a sweet liqueur made from cherries. **—maraschino cherry,** a cherry preserved in this. [It. (*marasca* small black cherry f. *amaro* bitter)]

Marat /ˈmærɑː/, Jean Paul (1743–93), French revolutionary. A doctor by training, Marat made a reputation for himself during the early days of the French Revolution as one of the most virulent critics of the moderate Girondins. His murder in his bath by a Royalist fanatic, Charlotte Corday, was used as a pretext by Robespierre and the Jacobins to purge their Girondin rivals.

marathon /ˈmærəθən/ *n.* a long-distance foot-race over roads, especially of 26 miles 385 yards (42.195 km) as a principal event of modern Olympic Games. It is named after Marathon in Greece, where the Athenians in 490 BC successfully defeated an invading Persian army; news of the victory was announced in Athens by an unnamed courier who ran all the way from the field of battle and fell dead on arrival. **2.** a feat of endurance; an undertaking of long duration.

maraud /məˈrɔːd/ *v.t./i.* to make a plundering raid (on); to go about pilfering. **—marauder** *n.* [f. F *marauder* (*maraud* rogue)]

marble *n.* **1.** a kind of limestone able to take a high polish, used in sculpture and architecture. **2.** this as a type of hardness or durability or smoothness (often *attrib.*). **3.** (in *pl.*) a collection of sculptures. **4.** a small ball of glass etc. as a toy; (in *pl.*) a game using these. *—v.t.* to stain or colour to look like variegated marble. [f. OF f. L *marmor* f. Gk]

Marble Arch an arch with three gateways erected in 1827 in front of Buckingham Palace, and moved in 1851 to its present site at the NE corner of Hyde Park.

marbled *adj.* **1.** looking like variegated marble. **2.** (of meat) streaked with fat. [f. MARBLE]

marcasite /ˈmɑːkəsaɪt/ *n.* crystalline iron sulphide; a piece of this as an ornament. [f. L f. Arab. f. Pers.]

March *n.* the third month of the year. **—mad as a March hare,** a proverb referring to the seemingly insane antics of male hares in the breeding season (March), when they are seen bucking on stiff legs, boxing each other standing on hind legs, etc. [f. OF f. L *Martius* (*mensis* month) of Mars]

march[1] *v.t./i.* **1.** to walk in a military manner with a regular and measured tread; to advance thus. **2.** to walk purposefully. **3.** (of events) to proceed steadily. **4.** to cause to march or walk. *—n.* **1.** the marching of troops; the uniform step of troops etc.; the distance covered by marching troops etc. **2.** a long toilsome walk. **3.** a procession as a protest or demonstration. **4.** a piece of music meant to accompany a march. **—marching orders,** a command to troops to depart for war etc.; a dismissal. **march past,** the marching of troops in line past a saluting-point at a review. **—marcher** *n.* [f. F *marcher* f. L *marcus* hammer]

march[2] *n.* (*hist.*) **1.** a boundary or frontier (often in *pl.*, esp. of the borderland between England and Scotland or Wales). **2.** a tract of land, often disputed, between two countries. *—v.i.* (of countries, estates, etc.) to have a common frontier, to border. [f. OF (as MARCH)]

marchioness /ˈmɑːʃənɪs, -ˈnes/ *n.* a marquis's wife or widow; a woman holding the rank of a marquis in her own right. [f. L (*marchio* captain of the marches, as prec.)]

Marconi /mɑːˈkəʊni/, Guglielmo (1874–1937), Italian electrical engineer, generally regarded as the father of radio. His achievement lay in appreciating the potential of earlier work by Heinrich Hertz on electric waves and of Oliver Lodge's coherer for their detection. Marconi demonstrated radio transmission over a distance of a mile at Bologna in 1895, and by 1901 he was able to transmit a signal across the Atlantic from Poldhu in Cornwall to St John's in Newfoundland. By 1912 he could produce a continuously oscillating wave, essential for transmission of sounds other than Morse code, and went on to develop short-wave transmission over long distances. Shipowners and navies were enthusiastic, and among the first customers were Lloyd's of London. In 1909 he was awarded the Nobel Prize for physics. Marconi had great business ability and set up companies (which flourished) to exploit his work.

Marco Polo /ˈmɑːkəʊ ˈpəʊləʊ/ (*c.*1254–*c.*1324), Venetian traveller. Between 1271 and 1275 he accompanied his father and uncle on a journey east from Acre into central Asia, eventually reaching China and the court of Kublai Khan. Polo entered the Mongol diplomatic service, travelling widely in the empire for a decade and a half before returning home (1292–5) via Sumatra, India, and Persia. Captured by the Genoese in 1298, he dictated the story of his travels to a fellow inmate during a year of imprisonment. His book was widely read in subsequent years, adding considerable impetus to the European quest to discover the riches of the East.

Marcus Aurelius see AURELIUS.

Mardi Gras /mɑːdɪ ˈɡrɑː/ Shrove Tuesday; the merrymaking then, at the end of a carnival. [F, = fat Tuesday]

mare[1] /meə(r)/ *n.* the female of a horse or related animal. **—mare's nest,** an illusory discovery. **mare's tail,** a slender perennial marsh plant (*Hippuris vulgaris*); (in *pl.*) long straight streaks of cirrus cloud. [OE]

mare[2] /ˈmɑːrɪ/ *n.* (*pl.* **maria** /ˈmɑːrɪə/) a large flat area on the moon, once thought to be a sea. [L, = sea]

Marengo /məˈreŋɡəʊ/ a village near Turin, scene of a decisive French victory of Napoleon's campaign in Italy in 1800. After military reverses had all but destroyed French power in Italy, Napoleon crossed the Alps to defeat and capture an Austrian army, returning Italy to French possession.

Margaret /ˈmɑːɡərɪt/, St (*c.*1046–93), Scottish queen, wife of Malcolm III. She exerted a strong influence over royal policy during her husband's reign, and was canonized for her reform of the Scottish Church.

margarine /mɑːdʒəˈriːn, mɑːɡ-/ *n.* a substance used like butter, made from animal or vegetable fats. The world's first substitute food, it was first developed in France in the mid-19th c. [F, ult. f. Gk *margaron* pearl]

marge *n.* (*colloq.*) margarine. [abbr.]

margin /ˈmɑːdʒɪn/ *n.* **1.** an edge or border of a surface. **2.** a plain space beside the main body of print etc. on a page. **3.** an extra amount (of time, money, etc.) over and above the necessary or minimum; a sum deposited with a stock-broker to cover the risk of loss on a transaction. **4.** a condition near the limit below or beyond which a thing ceases to be possible. —*v.t.* to furnish with a margin or with marginal notes. —**margin of error,** the difference allowed for miscalculation or mischance. [f. L *margo*]

marginal /ˈmɑːdʒɪn(ə)l/ *adj.* **1.** written in a margin. **2.** of or at an edge. **3.** (of a constituency) having an elected MP with only a small majority that may be lost at the next election. **4.** close to the limit, especially of no profit, barely adequate or provided for. —**marginal cost,** the cost of producing one extra item of output. —**marginally** *adv.* [f. L (as prec.)]

marginalia /mɑːdʒɪˈneɪlɪə/ *n.pl.* marginal notes. [L (as prec.)]

marguerite /mɑːgəˈriːt/ *n.* an ox-eye daisy or similar flower. [F, f. L *margarita* pearl f. Gk]

Mari /ˈmɑːrɪ/ an ancient city on the west bank of the Euphrates, in Syria. Its strategic position commanding major trade routes ensured rapid growth, and by *c.*2500 BC it was thriving, influenced by Sumerian culture. Its period of greatest importance and individuality was from the late 19th–mid 18th c. BC, when it was a kingdom with hegemony over the middle Euphrates valley. The vast palace of the last king, Zimrilim, famous in its day, has yielded an archive of 25,000 tablets, inscribed in cuneiform, which are the principal source for the history of northern Syria and Mesopotamia at that time. The city was sacked by Hammurabi of Babylon in 1759 BC.

maria *pl.* of MARE[2].

Mariana Islands /mærɪˈɑːnə/ (also **Marianas**) a group of islands in the NW Pacific, administered by the USA. The ocean trench (**Mariana Trench**) to the south-east of the islands is the greatest known ocean depth (11,033 m, 36,198 ft.).

Maria Theresa /məˈraɪə (-ˈriːə) təˈriːsə (-ˈreɪzə)/ (1717–80) Archduchess of Austria, queen of Hungary and Bohemia 1740–80. The daughter of the Emperor Charles VI, Maria Theresa married the future Emperor Francis I in 1736 and succeeded to the Hapsburg dominions in 1740 by virtue of the Pragmatic Sanction. Her accession was the occasion of the War of the Austrian Succession (1740–8) in which Silesia was lost to Frederick the Great of Prussia. She strengthened and reformed Austria-Hungary, but once again suffered at the hands of the Prussians in the Seven Years War (1756–63). After the death of Francis I in 1765 she ruled, until her death, in conjunction with her son, the Emperor Joseph II.

Marie Antoinette /ˈmɑːrɪ ãtwaˈnet/ (1755–93), queen of France. An Austrian princess, Marie Antoinette married the future Louis XVI of France in 1770, becoming queen four years later. Her lack of formal education minimized her ability to participate in State affairs, while her reckless spending severely strained royal finances and won her widespread unpopularity. Like her husband she was eventually imprisoned during the French Revolution, and was finally executed in October 1793.

marigold /ˈmærɪgəʊld/ *n.* any of various plants, especially of the genus *Calendula* or *Tagetes*, with golden or bright yellow flowers. [f. *Mary* (prob. the Virgin) + dial. *gold* marigold]

marijuana /mærɪˈhwɑːnə/ *n.* (also **marihuana**) the dried leaves and flowers and stems of common hemp, smoked as an intoxicant. [Amer. Sp.]

marimba /məˈrɪmbə/ *n.* **1.** a xylophone of Africa and Central America. **2.** a modern orchestral instrument evolved from this. [of Congolese orig.]

marina /məˈriːnə/ *n.* a place with moorings for pleasure-yachts etc. [It. & Sp. f. L (as MARINE)]

marinade /mærɪˈneɪd/ *n.* a mixture of wine, vinegar, oil, herbs, etc., for steeping meat or fish; meat or fish so steeped. —*v.t.* to steep in a marinade. [F f. Sp. (*marinar* pickle in brine, as MARINE)]

marinate /ˈmærɪneɪt/ *v.t.* to marinade. [f. It. or F (as prec.)]

marine /məˈriːn/ *adj.* **1.** of, found in, or produced by the sea. **2.** of shipping or naval matters. **3.** for use at sea. —*n.* **1.** a member of a corps trained to serve on land or sea. In Britain, the Corps of the Royal Marines, first formed in 1664, is part of the Royal Navy. **2.** a country's shipping, fleet, or navy. [f. OF f. L *marinus* (*mare* sea)]

Mariner /ˈmærɪnə(r)/ a series of US planetary probes (1962–77). Mariners 1 and 8 suffered launch failure, 2 and 5 made close-up observations of Venus, 3 failed to achieve its intended trajectory, 4, 6, 7, and 9 were successful probes

to Mars, 10 visited Venus and Mercury, 11 and 12 were renamed Voyager 1 and 2.

mariner /ˈmærɪnə(r)/ *n.* a seaman. [f. AF f. L *marinarius* (as MARINE)]

Marinetti /mærɪˈnetɪ/, Filippo Tommaso (1876–1944), Italian dramatist, poet, and novelist. He launched the futurist movement in his Manifesto, published in *Le Figaro* (1909), which exalted the machine age, glorified war, and demanded revolution and innovation in the arts. In his poems he abandoned syntax and grammar, and pioneered visual poetry; in the theatre he destroyed the barriers between stage and audience, staged unrelated actions simultaneously, and initiated the 'synthetic' play. He has profoundly influenced 20th-c. culture but his reputation has been compromised by his support for Fascism.

marionette /mærɪəˈnet/ *n.* a puppet worked by strings. [f. F (*Marion* dim. of *Marie* Mary)]

marital /ˈmærɪt(ə)l/ *adj.* of marriage; of or between a husband and wife. —**maritally** *adv.* [f. L (*maritus* husband)]

maritime /ˈmærɪtaɪm/ *adj.* **1.** situated or living or found near the sea. **2.** connected with the sea or seafaring. —**Maritime Provinces** (also **Maritimes**), the Canadian Provinces of New Brunswick, Nova Scotia, Prince Edward Island, and sometimes Newfoundland, with coastlines on the Gulf of St Lawrence or the Atlantic. [f. L *maritimus* (*mare* sea)]

Marius /ˈmærɪəs/, Gaius (*c.*157–86 BC), Roman general and politician. A 'new man' (i.e. not of the old aristocracy), his political power was based on popular and military support. Consul for the first time in 107 BC, he established his dominance by victories over Jugurtha and invading Germanic tribes, and reformed the Roman army. Subsequently in and out of power, he was expelled from Italy by Sulla, only to return and take Rome by force in 87 BC. He died in the following year.

marjoram /ˈmɑːdʒərəm/ *n.* an aromatic herb of the genus *Origanum* or *Majorana*, used in cookery. [f. OF f. L *majorana*]

Mark, St **1.** an Apostle, companion of St Peter and St Paul, traditional author of the second Gospel. Feast day, 25 April. **2.** the second Gospel (the earliest in date).

mark[1] *n.* **1.** a line or area that visibly breaks the uniformity of a surface, especially one that spoils its appearance. **2.** a written or printed symbol; this as an assessment of conduct or proficiency; a numerical unit awarded for merit in an examination etc. **3.** something that indicates the presence of a quality or feeling. **4.** a sign or symbol placed on a thing to identify it or indicate its origin. **5.** a cross etc. made in place of a signature by an illiterate person. **6.** a lasting effect or influence. **7.** a target or other object to be aimed at; a desired object. **8.** a line etc. serving to indicate a position; a standard; a runner's starting-point in a race. **9.** (followed by a numeral) a particular type or design of equipment etc. —*v.t.* **1.** to make a mark on. **2.** to distinguish with a mark; to characterize. **3.** to assign marks of merit to (a student's work etc.). **4.** to attach figures indicating prices to (goods). **5.** to notice, to watch carefully. **6.** to keep close to (an opposing player) in football etc. so as to hamper him if he receives the ball. —**make one's mark,** to attain distinction. **mark down,** to make a written note of; to mark at a lower price. **mark-down** *n.* a reduction in price. **mark off,** to separate, to mark the limits of. **mark out,** to mark the boundaries of; to trace (a course); to destine; to single out. **mark time,** to move the feet as in marching but without advancing; to occupy time routinely while awaiting events or an opportunity. **mark up,** to mark at a higher price. **mark-up** *n.* an amount the seller adds to the cost-price of an article to cover his profit margin etc. **off the mark,** having made a start; irrelevant. **on the mark,** ready to start; relevant. [OE]

mark[2] *n.* the currency unit of East and West Germany (Ostmark, Deutschmark) and of Finland. [G]

Mark Antony see ANTONY[2].

marked *adj.* clearly noticeable or evident. —**marked man,** one singled out, especially as an object of attack etc. —**markedly** /-ɪdlɪ/ *adv.* [f. MARK[1]]

marker *n.* **1.** a thing marking a position. **2.** a person or thing that marks. **3.** a scorer in a game etc. [f. MARK[1]]

market /ˈmɑːkɪt/ *n.* **1.** a gathering for the purchase and sale of provisions, livestock, etc.; a space or building used for this. **2.** a demand for a commodity or service; a place or group providing such a demand; the conditions as regards buying or selling; the opportunity for this. **3.** the rate of purchase and sale. —*v.t./i.* to sell; to offer for sale; to buy or sell goods in a market. —**in the market for,** wishing to buy. **market-day** n. a day on which markets are regularly held. **market garden,** a place where vegetables are grown for market. **market-place** n. an open space where a market is held in a town; the scene of actual dealings. **market price,** the price in current dealings. **market research,** study of consumers' needs and preferences. **market town,** a town where a market is held. **market value,** the value as a saleable thing. **on the market,** offered for sale. [f. Old Saxon f. L *mercatus* (*mercari* buy)]

marketable *adj.* able or fit to be sold. [f. prec.]

marking n. **1.** an indentification mark. **2.** the colouring of an animal's fur or feathers etc. [f. MARK¹]

Markova /maːˈkəʊvə/, Dame Alicia (1910-), real name Lillian Alicia Marks, English dancer. With the Ballet Rambert and Vic-Wells Ballet she danced the ballerina roles in the first English productions of the classics and created many roles in Ashton's early ballets such as *Façade* (1931). She formed groups with Dolin in 1935, 1945, and 1949, the last becoming the London Festival Ballet in 1950, with Markova prima ballerina until 1952.

marksman n. (*pl.* **-men**) a skilled shot, especially with a rifle. —**marksmanship** n.

marl n. a soil consisting of clay and lime, used as a fertilizer. —*v.t.* to apply marl to. —**marly** *adj.* [f. OF f. L *margila*]

Marlborough /ˈmɔːlbərə/, John Churchill, 1st Duke of (1650-1722), English soldier. After an eventful early military career, which saw him play a leading role in the suppression of the Monmouth rebellion and in the accession of William III, Marlborough was appointed commander of British and Austrian troops in the War of Spanish Succession and won a reputation as one of Britain's greatest military commanders as a result of a series of victories that drove the French armies of Louis XIV, most notably Blenheim (1704), Ramillies (1706), Oudenarde (1708), and Malplaquet (1709), which spelt the end of Louis' attempts to dominate Europe. Dismissed from all his posts by Queen Anne in 1711, largely as a result of personal antagonisms, he was restored by George I in 1714 but retired four years later after a stroke.

marlinspike /ˈmaːlɪnspaɪk/ n. a pointed tool used to separate strands of rope or wire. [f. *marline* line of two strands, f. Du.]

Marlowe /ˈmaːləʊ/, Christopher (1564-93), English dramatist and poet. Born in the same year as Shakespeare, he was the son of a Canterbury shoemaker and was educated at Cambridge University. As a dramatist he came to fame with *Tamburlaine the Great* (1587/8), which shows a new vitality and strength in the use of blank verse which he developed in his other major plays, including *Doctor Faustus* (c.1590), *Edward II* (1592), and *The Jew of Malta* (1592). His finest poem is the unfinished *Hero and Leander* (1598; completed by George Chapman). Marlowe had many admirers including Jonson, who praised his 'mighty line', and he profoundly influenced Shakespeare's early historical plays. Marlowe held and propagated atheist opinions, and probably became involved in political intrigues. He was killed in obscure circumstances after a brawl in a Deptford tavern.

marmalade /ˈmaːməleɪd/ n. a preserve of citrus fruit (usually oranges) made like jam. [f. F f. Port. *marmelada* (*marmelo* quince)]

Marmara /ˈmaːmərə/, Sea of a small inland sea in Turkey connected by the Bosporus to the Black Sea and by the Dardanelles to the Aegean.

marmoreal /maːˈmɔːrɪəl/ *adj.* of or like marble. [f. L (as MARBLE)]

marmoset /ˈmaːməzet/ n. a small monkey of the family Callithricidae, with a bushy tail. [f. OF *marmouset* grotesque image]

marmot /ˈmaːmət/ n. a burrowing rodent of the genus *Arctomys*, of the squirrel family. [f. F prob. f. Romansch *murmont* f. L, = mouse of the mountain]

marocain /ˈmærəkeɪn/ n. a kind of crêpe dress-fabric. [F, = Moroccan]

Maronite /ˈmærənaɪt/ n. a member of a Christian sect of Syrian origin, living chiefly in Lebanon. They claim to have been founded by St Maro, a friend of Chrysostom (d. 407), but it seems certain that their origin does not go back beyond the 7th c. Since 1181 they have been in communion with the Roman Catholic Church. [f. Sp *Maro*]

maroon¹ /məˈruːn/ *adj.* brownish-crimson. —n. **1.**

brownish-crimson colour. **2.** a kind of firework that explodes with a sound like a cannon, used as a warning signal. [f. F *marron* a chestnut [f. It. f. Gk]

maroon² /məˈruːn/ *v.t.* **1.** to put (a person) ashore in a desolate place and abandon him there. **2.** to make unable to leave a place safely. [orig. = fugitive slave living rough, f. F f. Sp. *cimarrón* wild (*cima* peak)]

marque /maːk/ n. a make of motor car, as opposed to a specific model. [F, = MARK¹]

marquee /maːˈkiː/ n. a large tent used for a party or exhibition etc. [f. MARQUISE, taken as pl.]

Marquesas Islands /maːˈkeɪsəs/ a group of islands in the Pacific, in French possession; pop. (1971) 5,593.

marquess var. of MARQUIS.

marquetry /ˈmaːkɪtrɪ/ n. inlaid work in wood, ivory, etc. [F (*marqueter* variegate f. MARQUE)]

Marquette /maːˈket/, Jacques (1637-75), French Jesuit missionary and explorer. He came to North America in 1666, and played a prominent part in the attempt to Christianize the North American Indians, especially during his mission among the Ottawa tribe. In 1673 he accompanied Louis Jolliet on a voyage down the Wisconsin and Mississippi Rivers as far as the mouth of the Arkansas and then back to Lake Michigan via the Illinois River.

marquis /ˈmaːkwɪs/ n. a nobleman ranking between a duke and (in the UK) an earl or (elsewhere) a count. [f. OF *marchis* (as MARCH²)]

marquise /maːˈkiːz/ n. (in foreign nobility) a marchioness. [F (as prec.)]

marram /ˈmærəm/ n. a shore grass that binds sand (*Ammophila arenaria*). [f. ON, = sea-haulm]

marriage /ˈmærɪdʒ/ n. **1.** the condition of a man and woman legally united for the purpose of living together and usually procreating lawful offspring. **2.** an act or ceremony etc. establishing this condition. **3.** a particular matrimonial union. —**marriage bureau,** an establishment arranging introductions between persons wishing to marry. **marriage certificate,** a certificate stating that a marriage ceremony has taken place. **marriage guidance,** the counselling of married couples who have problems in living together harmoniously. **marriage lines,** a marriage certificate. **marriage of convenience,** a marriage not made primarily for love. **marriage settlement,** an arrangement securing property to the wife. [f. OF (as MARRY)]

marriageable *adj.* old enough to marry; (of an age) fit for marriage. [f. prec.]

marron glacé /mærɒn ˈglæseɪ/ a chestnut preserved in sugar as a sweet. [F, = iced chestnut]

marrow /ˈmærəʊ/ n. **1.** a gourd (the fruit of *Cucurbita pepo*) with whitish flesh, cooked as a vegetable. **2.** the fatty substance in the cavities of bones. —**to the marrow,** right through. [OE]

marrowbone n. a bone containing edible marrow.

marrowfat n. a kind of large pea.

marry /ˈmærɪ/ *v.t./i.* **1.** to take, give, or join in marriage; to enter into a marriage. **2.** to unite intimately, to correlate as a pair. [f. OF *marier* f. L (*maritus* husband)]

Marryat /ˈmærɪət/, Captain Frederick (1792-1848), English novelist, who resigned his commission in the Navy in 1830 and wrote many novels. Successful among these were his sea-stories, *Peter Simple* (1834), *Mr Midshipman Easy* (1836), and *Masterman Ready* (1841). His works for children include the popular historical story *The Children of the New Forest* (1847).

Mars /maːz/ **1.** (*Rom. myth.*) next to Jupiter, the chief ancient Italian god. He is usually considered a war-god and equated with Ares, but has agricultural functions also. **2.** (*Astron.*) the fourth planet in order of distance from the sun, with an orbit lying between that of the earth and Jupiter, a rocky body 6,796 km in diameter. Its characteristic red colour, clearly visible to the naked eye, arises from the iron-rich minerals covering its surface. A tenuous atmosphere of carbon dioxide is dense enough to whip up periodic dust storms which can cover the entire planet, and causes erosion of surface features over long periods. Sinuous channels on the surface, resembling river beds on Earth, and extinct volcanoes hint at vigorous past geological activity, perhaps associated with flows of liquid water, of which none remains. The polar caps are of frozen carbon dioxide, but may contain some water ice. Investigations by space probes show no evidence for the 'canals' reported by the American astronomer Percival Lowell in the early 20th c., nor is there any evidence for life on the planet. There are two small satellites, Phobos and Deimos.

Marsala /maːˈsɑːlə/ n. a dark usually sweet fortified wine. [f. *Marsala* in Sicily]

Marseillaise /maːsəˈleɪz, -seɪˈjeɪz/ the French national anthem, composed by a young engineer officer, Rouget de Lisle, in 1792, on the declaration of war against Austria, and first sung in Paris by Marseilles patriots. [f. foll.]

Marseilles /maːˈseɪ, -ˈseɪlz/ a French seaport on the Mediterranean coast, on the site of an ancient Greek colony (*Massilia*); pop. 878,689.

marsh n. low-lying watery land. —**marsh gas**, methane. **marsh mallow**, a shrubby herb (*Althaea officinalis*). **marsh marigold**, a plant (*Caltha palustris*) with golden flowers, growing in moist meadows. —**marshy** adj. [OE]

marshal /ˈmaːʃ(ə)l/ n. **1.** a high-ranking officer of State or in the armed forces. **2.** an official arranging ceremonies, controlling the procedure at races, etc. —v.t. (**-ll-**) **1.** to arrange in due order. **2.** to conduct (a person) ceremoniously. —**marshalling yard**, a railway yard in which goods trains etc. are assembled. **Marshal of the RAF**, the highest rank in the RAF. [f. OF *mareschal* f. L]

Marshall /ˈmaːʃ(ə)l/, George Catlett (1880–1959), US Secretary of State 1947–9 who in 1947 initiated a plan to supply certain Western European countries with financial assistance (**Marshall Aid**) to further their recovery after the Second World War.

Marshall Islands /ˈmaːʃ(ə)l/ a group of islands in the NW Pacific, administered by the USA under trusteeship of the United Nations; pop. (1971) 23,166.

marshmallow n. a soft sweet made from sugar, albumen, gelatine, etc.

Marston Moor a moor about 11 km (7 miles) west of York, site of the largest battle (1644) of the English Civil War, in which the combined Royalist armies of Prince Rupert and the Duke of Newcastle were defeated by the English and Scottish Parliamentary armies. The defeat destroyed Royalist power in the north of England and fatally weakened Charles I's cause.

marsupial /maːˈsuːpɪəl/ n. a mammal of the order Marsupialia, which includes the kangaroo and opossum. The young, which are born in a very undeveloped state, are nourished and complete their development attached to the teats of the milk-secreting glands, on the mother's abdomen; the external pouch or *marsupium*, from which the order takes its name, is found in many species but is not a universal feature. Apart from the American opossums, present-day marsupials, of which there are under 200 species, are confined to Australasia. —adj. of marsupials. [f. L f. Gk *marsupion* pouch]

Marsyas /ˈmaːsɪəs/ (*Gk myth.*) a satyr who took to fluteplaying. He challenged Apollo to a musical contest and was flayed alive when he lost.

mart n. a trade centre; an auction-room, a market. [f. obs. Du., = MARKET]

Martello tower /maːˈteləʊ/ any of the small circular forts erected along the coasts of Britain during the Napoleonic Wars to repel expected French landings. They have massive walls and flat roofs on which guns were mounted. [f. Cape *Mortella* in Corsica where such a tower offered a stubborn resistance to the British in 1794]

marten /ˈmaːtɪn/ n. an animal of the genus *Martes*, like a weasel, with valuable fur. [f. MDu. f. OF]

Martha /ˈmaːθə/ sister of Lazarus and Mary and friend of Jesus Christ (Luke 10: 40). Her name is used allusively for one much concerned with domestic affairs; in Christian allegory she symbolizes the active life and her sister the contemplative life.

Martial /ˈmaːʃ(ə)l/ (Marcus Valerius Martialis, c.40–c.104) Roman epigrammatist, originally from Spain. His fifteen books of epigrams, in a variety of metres, reflect all facets of Roman life. He specialized in the witty surprise-ending, and is the chief ancient model for modern epigrammatists.

martial /ˈmaːʃ(ə)l/ adj. of or appropriate to warfare; warlike, brave, fond of fighting. —**martial arts**, fighting sports such as judo and karate. **martial law**, military government, by which ordinary law is suspended. [f. OF or L *martialis* of Mars, god of war]

Martian /ˈmaːʃ(ə)n/ adj. of the planet Mars. —n. a hypothetical inhabitant of Mars. [f. OF or L (as prec.)]

Martin, /ˈmaːtɪn/ St (d. 397), a patron saint of France. While serving in the Roman army he gave half his cloak to a beggar at Amiens and received a vision of Christ, after which he was baptized. He joined Hilary at Poitiers and founded the first monastery in Gaul. Becoming bishop of Tours c.372, he pioneered the evangelization of the rural areas. Feast day, 11 Nov. —**St Martin's summer,** a period of fine mild weather occurring about this date.

martin /ˈmaːtɪn/ n. a bird, especially the house-martin (see HOUSE) and sand-martin (see SAND), of the swallow family. [prob. f. prec.]

martinet /maːtɪˈnet/ n. a strict disciplinarian. [f. J. *Martinet*, 17th-c. French drill-master]

martingale /ˈmaːtɪŋgeɪl/ n. a strap, or set of straps, fastened at one end to the nose-band and at the other end to the girth, to prevent a horse from rearing etc. [F; orig. unkn.]

Martini[1] /maːˈtiːnɪ/ n. [P] vermouth; a cocktail made of gin and vermouth. [f. *Martini* & Rossi, firm selling vermouth]

Martini[2] /maːˈtiːnɪ/, Simone (c.1284–1344), Italian painter, whose work reflects a sense of sumptuous Byzantine colour combined with the strong outline and elegant gesture of the French Gothic manner. To him is attributed the first equestrian portrait in European art—the fresco of an Italian commander on the wall of the Palazzo Pubblico, Siena, opposite his earlier *Maestà* (1315). *The Annunciation* (1333) represents the epitome of Simone's lyrical and decorative contribution to the new Gothic taste. His fame spread, and he painted for the papal court at Avignon from c.1340.

Martinique /maːtɪˈniːk/ a French West Indian island, one of the Lesser Antilles; capital, Fort de France. Its former capital, St Pierre, was completely destroyed by an eruption of Mont Pelée in 1902.

Martinmas /ˈmaːtɪnməs/ n. St Martin's day, 11 Nov. It was formerly the usual time in England for hiring servants and for slaughtering cattle to be salted for the winter. [f. St MARTIN + MASS[2]]

martlet /ˈmaːtlɪt/ n. (in heraldry) an imaginary footless bird as a charge (ill. HERALDRY). [f. F, f. dim. of MARTIN]

martyr /ˈmaːtə(r)/ n. one who undergoes the death penalty for persistence in the Christian faith or obedience to the law of the Church, or undergoes death or suffering for any great cause. —v.t. **1.** to put to death as a martyr. **2.** to torment. —**martyr to,** a constant sufferer from (an ailment). [OE f. L f. Gk, orig. = witness]

martyrdom n. the sufferings and death of a martyr; torment. [f. prec.]

martyrology /maːtəˈrɒlədʒɪ/ n. a list or history of martyrs. —**martyrologist** n. [f. L f. Gk (as MARTYR -LOGY)]

Maruts /ˈmaːrʊts/ n.pl. (*Hinduism*) the sons of Rudra, hence also called the Rudras. In the Rig-Veda they are the storm gods, Indra's henchmen.

marvel /ˈmaːv(ə)l/ n. a wonderful thing; a wonderful example. —v.i. (**-ll-**) to feel surprise or wonder. [f. OF *merveille* f. L *mirabilia* (*mirari* wonder at)]

Marvell /ˈmaːv(ə)l/, Andrew (1621–78), English poet and politician. He was employed as tutor in the households of Lord Fairfax and Cromwell (who is honoured in several of his poems), and in 1657 became assistant to Milton who was a secretary to Cromwell's government. As an MP (1659–78) Marvell wrote pamphlets and verse satires that attacked Charles II and his ministers, particularly for corruption at court and in Parliament. In his lifetime he was almost unknown as a lyric poet, although famed as patriot, satirist, and foe to tyranny; today his oblique and enigmatic treatment of conventional poetic materials has intrigued the modern mind and set him high among the metaphysical poets.

marvellous /ˈmaːvələs/ adj. astonishing; excellent. —**marvellously** adv. [f. OF (as MARVEL)]

Marx /maːks/, Karl Heinrich (1818–83), German political philosopher and economist. Born of Jewish parents, he studied in Bonn and in Berlin, where he joined the radical followers of Hegel. His rebellious political outlook made a university career impossible and he turned to journalism, living variously in Paris and Brussels until in 1849 he was exiled to England, where his friend and collaborator Engels was already settled. Their pamphlet the *Communist Manifesto,* still the classic exposition of communism, had been published in 1848; it detailed a programme for socialist revolution to be led by workers of the more industrially advanced States, and appeared at a time when factory workers were suffering the worst results of the Industrial Revolution. In London Marx spent much of his time reading in the British Museum, enlarging the theory of this pamphlet into a series of books, the most important being the three-volume *Das Kapital*, of which the first volume appeared in 1867 and the remainder after his death. At no time did he concern himself greatly with the practical problems of how the socialist society should be run; his interest was in the revolution itself. He was also a leading figure in the founding of the First International. The prophet of communism, Marx became famous after his death as movements all over the world looked to his writings for the ultimate truth on matters of economics, politics, and philosophy, and the influence of his theories on the socialist movements of modern times has been greater than that of any other man.

Marxism /ˈmɑːksɪz(ə)m/ *n.* the political and economic theory of Karl Marx, especially that, as labour is basic to wealth, historical development, following scientific laws determined by dialectical materialism, must lead to the violent overthrow of the capitalist class and the taking over of the means of production by the proletariat. Events would then progress towards the ideal of a classless society, but the initial transition could not be effected without violent revolution. —**Marxist** *n.* [f. prec.]

Mary[1] /ˈmeərɪ/ (in the Bible) **1.** the Blessed Virgin Mary, mother of Jesus Christ, daughter of Joachim and Anne, betrothed to Joseph at the time of the Annunciation. **2.** Mary Magdalene (= of Magdala), a follower of Christ, commonly identified with the 'sinner' of Luke 7: 37. Feast day, 22 July.

Mary[2] /ˈmeərɪ/ the name of two queens of England:
Mary I (1516-58), daughter of Henry VIII, reigned 1553-8. Having regained the throne after the brief attempt to install Lady Jane Grey in her place, Mary attempted to reverse the country's turn towards Protestantism, which had begun to gain momentum during the short reign of her brother Edward VI. She married Philip II of Spain, and after putting down several revolts, began the series of religious persecutions which earned her the name of 'Bloody Mary'. Mary died childless, however, and the accession of her Protestant sister Elizabeth I guaranteed that England would not revert permanently to Catholicism.
Mary II (1662-94), daughter of James II, reigned 1689-94. Although her father James II was converted to Catholicism, Mary remained a Protestant, and was invited to replace him on the throne after his deposition in 1689. She insisted that her Dutch husband William of Orange be crowned along with her (see WILLIAM III) and afterwards left most of the business of the kingdom to him, although she frequently had to act as sole head of State because of her husband's absence on campaign on the Continent.

Mary Celeste /meərɪ sɪˈlɛst/ an American brig that set sail from New York for Genoa and was found in the North Atlantic in December 1872 in perfect condition but abandoned and without her boats. The fate of the crew was never discovered, and the abandonment of the ship remains one of the great mysteries of the sea.

Maryland /ˈmeərɪlænd/ a State on the Atlantic coast of the USA, colonized from England in the 17th c. and named after Queen Henrietta Maria, wife of Charles I. It was one of the original 13 States of the USA (1788); capital, Annapolis.

Mary, Queen of Scots (1542-87), daughter of James V, queen of Scotland 1542-67. Mary was sent to France as an infant, and married briefly to Francis II, but after his premature death returned to Scotland in 1561 to resume personal rule. A devout Catholic, she proved unequal to the task of controlling her Protestant lords led by her half-brother the Earl of Moray. Her position was made even more difficult by two disastrous marriages to Lord Darnley and the Earl of Bothwell, and after the defeat of her supporters she fled to eventual imprisonment in England in 1567. There she became the centre of several Catholic plots against Elizabeth I, and, after the discovery of one of these, was beheaded.

Mary Rose a heavily armed ship of 600 tons, built for Henry VIII and named in honour of his sister Mary Tudor. For some years from 1512 onwards the ship took part in Henry's wars with the French, always as the flagship of the Lord High Admiral, and when going out to engage the French fleet off Portsmouth in July 1545 she was swamped and quickly sank with the loss of nearly all her company. The hull was discovered by skin-divers in 1968, and raised in 1982.

marzipan /ˈmɑːzɪpæn/ *n.* a paste of ground almonds, sugar, etc. [G f. It.]

Masaccio /mæˈsætʃɪəʊ/, Tommaso Giovanni di Mone

(1401-28), Italian early Renaissance painter, who worked in Florence until a move to Rome in the last year of his short life. He is noted for two important innovations: the central-perspective system, which he learnt from Brunelleschi and used most notably in his fresco of the Trinity, and the use of light to define the construction of the body and its draperies and (in his later works) to unify a whole composition.

Masada /məˈsɑːdə/ a fortress on a steep rocky hill west of the Dead Sea, site of a palace and fortifications built by Herod the Great, but best known as the Jewish stronghold in the Zealots' revolt of AD 66-73. In AD 73 the defenders committed mass suicide rather than surrender to the Romans who had finally breached the citadel after a siege of nearly two years.

Masai /ˈmɑːsaɪ, məˈsaɪ/ *n.* (*pl.* same) **1.** a member of a pastoral people of mixed Hamitic stock, inhabiting some of the best grazing lands in Kenya and Tanzania, whose life and livelihood revolve round their cattle-herds. Their contempt for the agriculture practised by their neighbours is well known. The Masai are traditionally credited with fierce raiding of neighbouring tribes, undertaken to protect their herds and prove prowess, not for food. **2.** their Nilotic language. [Bantu]

mascara /mæˈskɑːrə/ *n.* a cosmetic for darkening the eyelashes etc. [It., = mask]

mascot /ˈmæskɒt/ *n.* a person or animal or thing supposed to bring luck. [f. F f. Prov. (*masco* witch)]

masculine /ˈmæskjʊlɪn/ *adj.* **1.** of men; having the qualities appropriate to a man. **2.** (*Gram.*) of the gender proper to men's names. **3.** (of a rhyme or line-ending) having a final stressed syllable. —*n.* (*Gram.*) the masculine gender; a masculine word. —**masculinity** /-ˈlɪnɪtɪ/ *n.* [f. OF f. L (as MALE)]

Masefield /ˈmeɪsfiːld/, John Edward (1878-1967), English poet. His fascination for the sea is reflected in his first published book *Salt-Water Ballads* (which contained 'I must go down to the sea again'; 1902). His works include the verse narratives, *The Daffodil Fields* (1913), *The Everlasting Mercy* (1911), *Reynard the Fox* (1919), several novels, and the classic children's story *The Midnight Folk* (1927). He was appointed Poet Laureate in 1930.

maser /ˈmeɪzə(r)/ *n.* a device for amplifying microwaves. [f. *m*icrowave *a*mplification by *s*timulated *e*mission of *r*adiation]

Maseru /mæsəˈruː/ the capital of Lesotho; pop. (1980) 60,000.

mash *n.* **1.** a soft or confused mixture; a mixture of boiled grain, bran, etc., used as animal food. **2.** (*colloq.*) mashed potatoes. **3.** a mixture of malt and hot water used in brewing. —*v.t.* **1.** to reduce (potatoes etc.) to a uniform mass by crushing; to crush to a pulp. **2.** to mix (malt) with hot water. [OE]

mask /mɑːsk/ *n.* **1.** a covering for all or part of the face, worn as a disguise, for protection, or (by a surgeon etc.) to prevent infection of the patient. **2.** a respirator used to filter inhaled air or to supply gas for inhalation. **3.** a likeness of a person's face, especially (as *death-mask*) one made by taking a mould from the face. **4.** a disguise or pretence. —*v.t.* to cover or disguise with a mask; to conceal or protect. —**masking tape**, adhesive tape used in painting to cover areas on which paint is not wanted. [f. F *masque* f. It. f. Arab., = buffoon]

masochism /ˈmæsəkɪz(ə)m/ *n.* **1.** a form of (esp. sexual) perversion in which the sufferer derives pleasure from his own pain or humiliation. **2.** (*colloq.*) enjoyment of what appears to be painful or tiresome. —**masochist** *n.*, **masochistic** /-ˈkɪstɪk/ *adj.* [f. L. von Sacher-*Masoch*, Austrian novelist (d. 1895)]

Mason /ˈmeɪs(ə)n/, Alfred Edward Woodley (1865-1948), English novelist, author of adventure stories (including *The Four Feathers*, 1902), historical novels (including *Musk and Amber*, 1942), detective novels featuring Inspector Hanaud of the Sûreté, and several plays.

mason /ˈmeɪs(ə)n/ *n.* **1.** one who builds with stone. **2.** Mason, a Freemason. [f. OF *masson*]

Mason-Dixon line /meɪs(ə)n ˈdɪks(ə)n/ (also **Mason and Dixon line**) the boundary line between Pennsylvania and Maryland as laid out in 1763-7 by the English surveyors Charles Mason and Jeremiah Dixon. The term was later applied to the entire southern boundary of Pennsylvania, and regarded as the border between North and South in the USA. In the years before the American Civil War it formed the northern boundary of the slave-owning States.

Masonic /mə'sɒnɪk/ *adj.* of Freemasons. [f. MASON]

masonry /'meɪs(ə)nrɪ/ *n.* **1.** a mason's work; stonework. **2.** **Masonry,** Freemasonry. [as prec.]

Masorete /'mæsəriːt/ *n.* any of the Jewish scholars who, between the 6th and 10th c. AD, established a recognized text of the Old Testament (the **Masoretic text**), providing marginal notes and commentaries in order to preserve this from accretion or alteration. They also introduced vowel points and accents to indicate how the words should be pronounced at a time when Hebrew was ceasing to be a spoken language. —**Masoretic** *adj.* [f. F & L f. Heb., perh. = bond (of the covenant)]

masque /mɑːsk/ *n.* an amateur dramatic and musical entertainment especially in the 16th–17th c., with scenery and elaborate costumes, originally in dumb show but later with metrical dialogue; a dramatic composition for this. The masque derived from a primitive folk ritual featuring the arrival of guests, usually in disguise, bearing gifts to a king or nobleman, who with his household then joined the visitors in a ceremonial dance. The presentation of the gifts soon became an excuse for flowery flattering speeches, while the wearing of outlandish or beautiful costumes and masks led to miming and dancing. The Civil War put an end to the masque, which was never revived. (Milton's *Comus*, though sometimes described as a masque, is strictly a pastoral drama.) [var. of MASK]

masquerade /mɑːskə'reɪd/ *n.* **1.** a false show, a pretence. **2.** a ball at which the guests wear masks. —*v.i.* to appear in disguise, to assume a false appearance. [f. Sp. (*mascara* mask)]

mass¹ /mæs/ *n.* **1.** a coherent body of matter of indefinite shape. **2.** a dense aggregation of objects. **3.** (in *sing.* or *pl.*) a large number or amount. **4.** an unbroken expanse of colour etc. **5.** the quantity of matter a body contains, measured in terms of resistance to acceleration by a force (i.e., its inertia; see below). —*v.t./i.* to gather into a mass; to assemble into one body. —*adj.* of or relating to large numbers of persons or things, large-scale. —**the mass,** the majority. **the masses,** the ordinary people. **in the mass,** in the aggregate. **mass media,** means of communication (e.g. newspapers or broadcasting) to large numbers of people. **mass meeting,** a large assembly of people. **mass production,** the production of large quantities of a standardized article by mechanical processes. **mass spectrograph,** a mass spectrometer in which the particles are detected photographically. **mass spectrometer,** an apparatus separating atoms and molecules according to mass by passage in ionic form through electric and magnetic fields, and detecting them photographically or electrically (originally applied specifically to apparatus with electrical detection). It has become an indispensable tool in nuclear physics, analytical chemistry, and (more recently) organic chemistry. [f. OF f. L *massa* f. Gk *maza* barley-cake]

The earliest scientific concept of mass was formulated in the Middle Ages as a refinement of the vernacular meaning of mass as an aggregation of matter of any kind or shape. In keeping with this older tradition Newton defined mass informally as quantity of matter; subsequently he found it necessary to introduce a more precise conception of mass, and based his new definition on 'inertia', a property possessed by all bodies in all circumstances, the innate resistance which is called into play while any body is being set in motion. For Newton all bodies with the same inertia have the same mass. He also demonstrated that all bodies with the same weight have the same inertia and, therefore, the same mass. The modern scientific concept of mass is an uneasy fusion of the various meanings given to it by Newton. It is regarded as one of the most obscure and abstract and also as one of the most important concepts of physics.

Einstein in his special theory of relativity showed that mass increases with velocity; further, he suggested that the total energy content of every body was measured by the equation $E = mc^2$ (where E is energy, m is mass, and c is the speed of light), and that mass can be converted into energy—a great deal of energy, since c^2 is a very large number. The equation suggests that the release of energy which accompanies even a small loss of mass is enormous. This has been borne out fully by nuclear science; the atomic bomb and nuclear energy depend upon this equation. Einstein's general theory of relativity also provides a rationale for the identity of inertial and gravitational mass, a phenomenon which in Newtonian physics was an unexplained coincidence.

mass² /mæs, mɑːs/ *n.* a celebration of the Eucharist, now especially in the Roman Catholic and High Church; the liturgy used in this; a musical setting for parts of it. [OE f. L *missa* (*mittere* dismiss), perh. from the concluding words *Ite, missa est*]

Massachusetts /mæsə'tʃuːsɪts/ a State in the northeastern USA, bordering on the Atlantic. The Pilgrim Fathers landed there in 1620 and founded a Puritan colony. It was one of the original 13 States of the USA (1788); capital, Boston.

massacre /'mæsəkə(r)/ *n.* **1.** a general slaughter (of persons, occasionally of animals). **2.** utter defeat or destruction. —*v.t.* to make a massacre of; to murder (a large number of people) cruelly or violently. [F]

massage /'mæsɑːʒ/ *n.* the rubbing, kneading, etc., of the muscles and joints of the body with the hands, to stimulate their action, cure strains, etc. —*v.t.* **1.** to treat (a part or person) thus. **2.** to manipulate the presentation of (figures, data, etc.) so as to give a more acceptable result. [F]

masseur /mæ'sɜː(r)/ *n.* one who provides massage professionally. —**masseuse** /-'sɜːz/ *n. fem.* [F (as prec.)]

massif /'mæsiːf, -'siːf/ *n.* mountain heights forming a compact group. [F (as MASSIVE)]

Massine /mæ'siːn/, Léonide Fedorovich (1895–1979), Russian-American dancer, choreographer, ballet master, and teacher. As dancer he was most successful in character roles, and as choreographer he was important for his contributions to the comedy genre and as the originator of the symphonic ballet. His many symphonic ballets include *Les Présages* (Tchaikovsky's Fifth, 1934) and *Seventh Symphony* (Beethoven, 1938).

Massinger /'mæsɪndʒə(r)/, Philip (1583–1640), English dramatist, who collaborated with John Fletcher, and became principal dramatist of the leading theatrical company, the King's Men. His writings include tragedies and tragicomedies, but his most enduring plays are his social comedies *A New Way to Pay Old Debts* (1625/6) and *The City Madam* (1632), which show a contempt for the arrogance of an effete aristocracy.

massive /'mæsɪv/ *adj.* **1.** large and heavy or solid. **2.** substantial, unusually large. —**massiveness** *n.* [f. F *massif* (as MASS¹)]

mast¹ /mɑːst/ *n.* **1.** a long upright post set up on a ship's keel to support the sails (ill. SAILING-SHIPS). **2.** a post or lattice-work upright to support a radio or television aerial. **3.** a flag-pole. —**before the mast,** as an ordinary sailor. —**masted** *adj.* [OE]

mast² /mɑːst/ *n.* the fruit of the beech, oak, etc., especially as food for pigs. [OE]

mastaba /'mæstəbə/ *n.* **1.** an ancient Egyptian tomb, rectangular in shape and with a flat roof, standing to a height of 5–6 metres, with an underground burial chamber and rooms above, in the superstructure, to store offerings etc. **2.** a bench of stone or other material attached to a house in Islamic countries. [f. Arab., = bench]

mastectomy /mæ'stektəmɪ/ *n.* surgical removal of a breast. [f. Gk *mastos* breast + -ECTOMY]

master /'mɑːstə(r)/ *n.* **1.** a person having control of people or things, especially an employer; the male head of a household or of a college etc.; the male owner of an animal or slave; (in full **master mariner**) the captain of a merchant ship. **2.** a male teacher or tutor, a schoolmaster. **3.** one who has or gets the upper hand. **4.** a skilled workman, or one in business on his own account. **5.** a holder of a master's degree from a university, originally giving the holder authority to teach in a university; a revered teacher in philosophy etc. **6.** a great artist; a picture by one. **7.** a chess player of proved ability at international level. **8.** a thing from which a series of copies (e.g. of a film or gramophone record) is made. **9.** **Master,** a title prefixed to the name of a boy not old enough to be called *Mr.* —*adj.* **1.** commanding, superior. **2.** main, principal. **3.** controlling others. —*v.t.* **1.** to overcome, to bring under control. **2.** to acquire knowledge or skill in. —**master-key** *n.* a key that opens several locks, each also having its own key. **Master of Ceremonies,** a person in charge of a ceremonial or social occasion, a person introducing the speakers at a banquet or the performers at a variety show. **Master of the Rolls,** the Court of Appeal judge in charge of the Public Record Office. **master-stroke** *n.* an outstandingly skilful act of policy etc. **master-switch** *n.* a switch controlling the electricity etc. supply to an entire system. [OE f. L *magister*]

masterful *adj.* **1.** imperious, domineering. **2.** masterly. —**masterfully** *adv.* [f. prec. + -FUL]

masterly *adj.* worthy of a master; very skilful. [f. MASTER]

mastermind *n.* **1.** a person with an outstanding intellect. **2.** a person directing an intricate operation. —*v.t.* to plan and direct (a scheme).

masterpiece *n.* an outstanding piece of artistry; one's best work. [prob. f. Du. or G (as MASTER, PIECE), orig. denoting the piece of work by which a craftsman gained from his guild the recognized rank of 'master']

mastery /ˈmɑːstərɪ/ *n.* **1.** complete control, supremacy. **2.** masterly skill or knowledge. [f. OF (as MASTER)]

masthead *n.* **1.** the highest part of a ship's mast (ill. SAILING-SHIPS). **2.** the title details of a newspaper at the head of its front or editorial page.

mastic /ˈmæstɪk/ *n.* **1.** a gum or resin exuded from certain trees (esp. *Pistacia lentiscus*). **2.** a type of cement. [f. OF f. L f. Gk (perh. as foll.)]

masticate /ˈmæstɪkeɪt/ *v.t.* to grind (food) with the teeth, to chew. —**mastication** /-ˈkeɪʃ(ə)n/ *n.*, **masticatory** *adj.* [f. L f. Gk *mastikhaō* gnash the teeth]

mastiff /ˈmæstɪf/ *n.* a large strong kind of dog. [ult. f. OF *mastin* f. L *mansuetus* tame]

mastodon /ˈmæstədɒn/ *n.* a large extinct animal of the genus *Mammut*, resembling the elephant. [f. Gk *mastos* breast + *odous* tooth, f. the nipple-shaped tubercles on its molars]

mastoid /ˈmæstɔɪd/ *adj.* shaped like a woman's breast. —*n.* the conical prominence on the temporal bone behind the ear (also **mastoid process**); (*colloq.*, usu. in *pl.*) inflammation of this. [f. F f. Gk (*mastos* breast)]

masturbate /ˈmæstəbeɪt/ *v.t./i.* to produce sexual orgasm or arousal (of) by stimulation of the genitals other than by sexual intercourse. —**masturbation** /-ˈbeɪʃ(ə)n/ *n.*, **masturbatory** *adj.* [f. L]

mat[1] *n.* **1.** a piece of coarse material as a floor-covering or for wiping shoes on, especially a doormat. **2.** a piece of cork, rubber, plastic, etc., to protect a surface from the heat or moisture of an object placed on it. **3.** a piece of resilient material for landing on in gymnastics or wrestling. —*v.t./i.* (**-tt-**) **1.** to make or become entangled in a thick mass. **2.** to cover or furnish with mats. —**on the mat**, (*slang*) being reprimanded. [OE, f. L *matta*]

mat[2] var. of MATT.

Matabele /mætəˈbiːlɪ/ *n.* (*pl.* same) a member of a people of Zulu stock living in Zimbabwe. [f. *Ndebele*, native name]

matador /ˈmætədɔː(r)/ *n.* a bullfighter whose task is to kill the bull. [Sp. (*matar* kill, f. Pers.)]

Mata Hari /mɑːtə ˈhɑːrɪ/ (real name Margaretha Geertruida Zelle, 1876–1917) Dutch courtesan and secret agent. She became a professional dancer in Paris in 1905 and probably worked for both French and German intelligence services before being executed by the French in 1917.

match[1] *n.* **1.** a contest or game of skill etc. in which persons or teams compete against each other. **2.** a competitor able to contend with another as an equal; a person equal to another in some quality. **3.** a person or thing exactly like or corresponding to another. **4.** a marriage. **5.** a person viewed in regard to eligibility for marriage. —*v.t./i.* **1.** to be equal; to correspond in some essential respect. **2.** to place in competition or conflict. **3.** to find a material etc. that matches (another). **4.** to find a person or thing suitable for another. —**match point**, the state of a game when one side needs only one more point to win the match; this point. [OE, f. companion (as MAKE)]

match[2] *n.* **1.** a short thin piece of wood etc. tipped with a composition that bursts into flame when rubbed on a rough or specially prepared surface. **2.** a fuse for firing a cannon etc. [f. OF *mesche*]

matchboard *n.* a board with a tongue cut along one edge and a groove along the other, so as to fit with similar boards. [f. MATCH[1] + BOARD]

matchbox *n.* a box for holding matches.

matchless *adj.* incomparable. [f. MATCH[2] + -LESS]

matchmaker *n.* a person fond of scheming to bring about marriages. —**matchmaking** *adj. & n.*

matchstick *n.* the stem of a match.

matchwood *n.* **1.** wood suitable for making matches. **2.** wood reduced to minute splinters.

mate[1] *n.* **1.** a companion, a fellow worker; (*colloq.*) a general form of address to an equal. **2.** one of a pair, especially of birds; (*colloq.*) a partner in marriage. **3.** a subordinate officer on a merchant ship. **4.** an assistant to a worker. —*in comb.* a fellow member or joint occupant of (*team-mate, room-mate*). —*v.t./i.* **1.** to bring or come together in marriage or for breeding. **2.** to put or come together as a pair or as corresponding. [f. MLG]

mate[2] *n.* a checkmate. —*v.t.* to checkmate. [f. F *mat(er)*; see CHECKMATE]

mater /ˈmeɪtə(r)/ *n.* (*archaic slang*) mother. [L]

material /məˈtɪərɪəl/ *n.* **1.** the substance or things from which something is or can be made; (in *pl.*) the things needed for an activity. **2.** a person or thing suitable for a specified purpose. **3.** cloth, fabric. **4.** information etc. to be used in writing a book etc. —*adj.* **1.** of matter; consisting of matter; of the physical (opp. spiritual) world. **2.** of bodily comfort etc. **3.** important, significant, relevant. [f. OF f. L (as MATTER)]

materialism *n.* **1.** the tendency to prefer material possessions and physical comfort to spiritual values. **2.** the theory that nothing exists but matter and its movements and modifications. —**materialist** *n.*, **materialistic** /-ˈlɪstɪk/ *adj.* [f. prec.]

materialize *v.t./i.* **1.** to become a fact, to happen. **2.** to appear, to become visible. **3.** to represent in or assume bodily form. —**materialization** /-ˈzeɪʃ(ə)n/ *n.* [f. MATERIAL]

materially *adv.* substantially, considerably. [as prec.]

maternal /məˈtɜːn(ə)l/ *adj.* **1.** of or like a mother, motherly. **2.** related through one's mother. **3.** of the mother in pregnancy and childbirth. —**maternally** *adv.* [f. OF or L *maternus* (*mater* mother)]

maternity /məˈtɜːnɪtɪ/ *n.* **1.** motherhood. **2.** motherliness. **3.** (*attrib.*) for women in pregnancy or childbirth. [f. F f. L (as prec.)]

matey /ˈmeɪtɪ/ *adj.* sociable, familiar and friendly. —*n.* (*colloq.*, as a form of address) mate. —**matily** *adv.*, **matiness** *n.* [f. MATE[1]]

mathematical /mæθɪˈmætɪk(ə)l/ *adj.* of or involving mathematics. —**mathematical logic**, the part of mathematics concerned with the study of formal languages, formal reasoning, the nature of mathematical proof, provability of mathematical statements, computability, and other aspects of the foundations of mathematics. Its roots lie in Boole's mid-19th-c. algebraic description of logic. Its growth was enormously stimulated by *Principia Mathematica* (1910–13) in which A. N. Whitehead and Bertrand Russell attempted to express all of mathematics in formal logical terms, and by Gödel's incompleteness theorem (1931) which, by showing that no such enterprise could ever succeed, has led to investigation of the boundary between what is possible in mathematics and what is not. —**mathematically** *adv.* [as MATHEMATICS]

mathematician /mæθɪməˈtɪʃ(ə)n/ *n.* one who is skilled in mathematics. [f. foll.]

mathematics /mæθɪˈmætɪks/ *n.pl.* (also treated as *sing.*) **1.** the body of knowledge and reasoning about numbers, spatial forms, logic, and relationships between them, and applications to measurement and prediction in science and other areas. The main parts of pure mathematics are algebra (including arithmetic), analysis, geometry (including topology), logic. Applied mathematics includes classical mechanics, continuum mechanics (hydrodynamics, elasticity, etc.), quantum mechanics, relativity theory, statistics, and many other newer areas of application to computing, economics, biological sciences, etc. **2.** (as *pl.*) the use of this in calculation etc. [f. F f. L f. Gk (*mathēma* science f. *manthanō* learn)]

maths /mæθs/ *n.* (*colloq.*) mathematics. [abbr.]

Matilda /məˈtɪldə/ (1102–67), queen of England for a few months in 1135, widowed wife of the Emperor Henry V (d.1125), and the only legitimate child of Henry I of England. (See STEPHEN.)

matinée /ˈmætɪneɪ/ *n.* an afternoon performance at a theatre or cinema. —**matinée coat**, a baby's short coat. [F, = what occupies a morning (as foll.)]

matins /ˈmætɪnz/ *n.pl.* the service of morning prayer, especially in the Church of England. [f. OF f. L (*matutinus* of morning)]

Matisse /mæˈtiːs/, Henri Emile Benoît (1869–1954), French painter who first studied law, which he abandoned after 1890. Matisse was influenced by the impressionists and by Gauguin and Cézanne, colour and simplified design playing an increasingly important role in his art. About 1904 he was experimenting with a free neo-impressionist technique, but by then he was associated with Derain and Vlaminck and was already regarded as a leader of the Fauve group, notorious for their crude compositions and arbitrary use of colour. His *Bonheur de vivre*, exhibited in 1906, heralded a new more personal style—a sense of rhythmic decorative pattern (with a clear debt to the aesthetics of art nouveau) imposed on a flat ground. The imagery of Arcadia, of nude figures frolicking in a Golden Age, was to become a lifelong obsession. He continued to develop throughout his life a style based on simple reductive line on a field of rich, saturated colour, and has exerted a powerful influence on 20th-c. art. Matisse also made prints and sculpture, and produced ballet designs for Diaghilev and Massine.

matriarch /'meɪtrɪɑːk/ *n.* a woman who is head of a family or tribe. —**matriarchal** /-'ɑːk(ə)l/ *adj.* [f. L *mater* mother, on false analogy of PATRIARCH]

matriarchy /'meɪtrɪɑːkɪ/ *n.* a social organization in which the mother is head of the family and descent is reckoned through the female line. [f. prec.]

matricide /'meɪtrɪsaɪd/ *n.* 1. the crime of killing one's own mother. 2. one who is guilty of this. —**matricidal** *adj.* [f. L (*mater* mother, -CIDE)]

matriculate /mə'trɪkjʊleɪt/ *v.t./i.* to admit (a student) to membership of a university; to be thus admitted. [f. L (*matricula* register, as MATRIX)]

matriculation /mətrɪkjʊ'leɪʃ(ə)n/ *n.* matriculating; an examination to qualify for this. [f. prec.]

matrilineal /mætrɪ'lɪnɪəl/ *adj.* of or based on kinship with the mother or the female line of ancestors. [f. L *mater* mother + LINEAL]

matrimony /'mætrɪmənɪ/ *n.* 1. the rite of marriage. 2. the state of being married. —**matrimonial** /-'məʊnɪəl/ *adj.*, **matrimonially** *adv.* [f. AF f. L *matrimonium* (as MATER)]

matrix /'meɪtrɪks/ *n.* (*pl.* **-ices** /-ɪsiːz/) 1. a mould in which a thing is cast or shaped. 2. a place in which a thing is developed. 3. a mass of rock enclosing gems etc. 4. a rectangular array of mathematical quantities treated as a single quantity. [L, = womb (as MATER)]

matron /'meɪtrən/ *n.* 1. a married woman, especially one who is middle-aged or elderly and dignified. 2. a woman managing the domestic arrangements of a school etc. 3. a woman in charge of nurses in a hospital (now usu. called *senior nursing officer*). —**matron of honour,** a married woman attending the bride at a wedding. —**matronly** *adj.* [f. OF f. L *matrona* (as MATER)]

matt *adj.* (of a colour etc.) dull, not lustrous. [f. F (as MATE²)]

matter *n.* 1. that which occupies space and possesses rest mass, including atoms, their major constituents, and substances made of atoms, but not light and other electromagnetic radiation (see below); physical substance in general, as distinct from mind and spirit. 2. a particular substance or material. 3. a discharge from the body, pus. 4. material for thought or expression; the content of a book, speech, etc. 5. a thing or things of a specified kind. 6. a situation or business being considered. 7. (with *of*) a quantity or extent of; a thing that depends on. —*v.i.* to be important. —**the matter,** the thing that is amiss, the trouble or difficulty. **as a matter of fact,** in reality (esp. to correct a falsehood or misunderstanding). **for that matter,** as far as that is concerned; and indeed also. **a matter of course,** a thing to be expected. **matter-of-fact** *adj.* strictly factual and not imaginative or emotional. **no matter,** it is of no importance. [f. AF f. L *materia*]

Until the 19th c., Western scientific thought regarded all bodies as forms of matter or as matter united to spirit. With the advent of Faraday's concept of electric and magnetic fields, and the discovery that light is a form of electromagnetic radiation, a new fundamental distinction gained prominence in physics, that between matter and field. Matter is distinguished from light, radio waves, X-rays, electric and magnetic fields, and gravitational fields. Most material bodies are composed of protons, neutrons, and electrons. Matter may be partly or wholly transformed into kinetic energy and electromagnetic radiation; such transformations account for nuclear energy and for nuclear explosions.

Matterhorn /'mætəhɔːn/ a spectacular Alpine peak on the Swiss–Italian border, rising to 4,477 m (14,688 ft.).

Matthew /'mæθjuː/, St 1. an Apostle, a tax-gatherer from Capernaum in Galilee, traditionally but erroneously supposed to be the author of the first Gospel. Feast day, 21 Sept. 2. the first Gospel, written after AD 70 and based largely on that of St Mark.

Matthew Paris (*c.*1199–1259) English chronicler, a Benedictine monk at St Albans. His *Chronica Majora*, a history of the world from the Creation to 1259, is a valuable source

for contemporary events, notable for its trenchant criticism of ecclesiastical abuses.

Matthews /'mæθjuːz/, Sir Stanley (1917-), English Association football player who played for England 54 times. His career in first-class football lasted until he was 50.

matting *n.* fabric for mats. [f. MAT¹]

mattock /'mætək/ *n.* an agricultural tool like a pickaxe with an adze and a chisel edge as the ends of its head. [OE]

mattress /'mætrɪs/ *n.* a pad of soft or firm or springy material enclosed in a fabric case, used on or as a bed. [f. OF *materas* f. It. f. Arab.]

maturate /'mætjʊreɪt/ *v.i.* (of a boil etc.) to come to maturation. [f. L (as MATURE)]

maturation /mætjʊ'reɪʃ(ə)n/ *n.* maturing, development; (of a boil etc.) the formation of purulent matter. [f. F or L (as foll.)]

mature /mə'tjʊə(r)/ *adj.* 1. with fully developed powers of body and mind, adult. 2. complete in natural development, ripe. 3. (of thought, intentions, etc.) duly careful and adequate. 4. (of a bill etc.) due for payment. —*v.t./i.* to make or become mature. —**maturely** *adv.*, **maturity** *n.* [f. L *maturus*]

matutinal /mætjuː'taɪn(ə)l/ *adj.* of or occurring in the morning; early. [f. L *matutinus* (as MATINS)]

maudlin /'mɔːdlɪn/ *adj.* weakly or tearfully sentimental, especially from drunkenness. [orig. = St Mary Magdalen, f. OF *Madeleine* f. L]

Maugham /mɔːm/, William Somerset (1874-1965), English novelist and dramatist. His first novel *Lisa of Lambeth* (1897) was followed by many others, including *Of Human Bondage* (1915), *Cakes and Ale* (1930), and *The Razor's Edge* (1944). Among his successful plays are *The Circle* (1921) and *East of Suez* (1922). Maugham's wide travels provided exotic settings for many of his stories; he made his home on the French Riviera in 1926. He was a cynical observer of human frailties, and although his novels remain popular, he states in his autobiography (*The Summing Up*, 1938) that he stood 'in the very front row of the second-raters', a judgement that most critics have endorsed.

maul /mɔːl/ *v.t.* 1. to treat roughly; to injure by rough handling or clawing. 2. to make damaging criticisms of. —*n.* 1. a loose scrum in Rugby football. 2. a brawl. 3. a heavy hammer. [f. OF f. L *malleus* hammer]

maulstick /'mɔːlstɪk/ *n.* a stick used to support the hand in painting. [f. Du. *maalstok* (*malen* to paint)]

Mau Mau /mau mau/ an African secret society, an underground anti-British terrorist movement functioning within the Kikuyu tribe in Kenya between 1953 and 1957, vehicle of native discontent with colonial rule. As the result of a well-organized counter-insurgency campaign the British were eventually able to subdue the terrorists, and went on to institute widespread political and social reforms, eventually leading to Kenyan independence in 1963.

maunder /'mɔːndə(r)/ *v.i.* 1. to talk in a dreamy or rambling manner. 2. to move or act listlessly or idly. [perh. f. obs. *maunder* beggar, to beg]

Maundy /'mɔːndɪ/ *n.* the ceremony of washing the feet of a number of poor people, performed by royal or other eminent persons, or by ecclesiastics, on the Thursday before Easter, and commonly followed by the distribution of clothing, food, or money. It was instituted in commemoration of Christ's washing the Apostles' feet at the Last Supper (John 13). In Britain (except in the RC Church) the distribution of Maundy money (see below) is all that remains of this ceremony. From the time of Henry IV the number of recipients has corresponded to the number of years in the sovereign's age, and the value in pence of the amount received by each now corresponds similarly. —**Maundy money,** specially minted silver coins distributed by the sovereign to the poor on Maundy Thursday. The first were issued in 1662. **Maundy Thursday,** the Thursday before Easter, celebrated in memory of the Last Supper. [f. OF *mandé* f. L, = commandment (as MANDATE), ref. to John 13: 34]

Maupassant /məʊpa'sɑ̃/, Guy de (1850-93), French short-story writer and novelist, a disciple of Flaubert and one of the naturalist writers of Zola's circle. He contributed 'Boule de Suif' to their *Les Soirées de Médan* (1880) and became an immediate celebrity. In his brief creative life he wrote about 300 short stories and six novels, portraying a wide range of society and embracing themes of war, mystery, hallucination, and horror, written in a simple direct narrative style. His best-known novels are *Une Vie* (1883),

Bel-Ami (1885), and *Pierre et Jean* (1888). He suffered from syphilis which resulted in a mental disorder, and spent the last 18 months of his life in an asylum.

Mauretania /mɒrɪˈteɪnɪə/ the ancient name for the land of the Moors (Latin *Mauri*) in North Africa, reaching from the Atlantic to Numidia, formed into two Roman provinces by the emperor Claudius. It is now part of Morocco and Algeria. —**Mauretanian** *adj. & n.*

Mauritania /mɒrɪˈteɪnɪə/ a country in West Africa with a coastline on the Atlantic Ocean; pop. (est. 1980) 1,634,000; official language, French; capital, Nouakchott. The country, which is mainly desert in the north but more fertile in the south, supports a largely pastoral economy. A French protectorate from 1902 and a colony from 1920, Mauritania achieved full independence in 1961. —**Mauritanian** *adj. & n.*

Mauritius /məˈrɪʃəs/ an island country in the Indian Ocean, about 850 km (550 miles) east of Madagascar; pop. (est. 1982) 949,686; official language, English; capital, Port Louis. Discovered by the Portuguese in the early 16th c., Mauritius was held by the Dutch (who named it in honour of Prince Maurice) from 1598 to 1710 and then by the French until 1810, when it was ceded to Britain; after 158 years as a Crown colony it became independent as a member of the Commonwealth in 1968. The economy is largely dependent on sugar, and overpopulation and severe unemployment cause continuing social problems. —**Mauritian** *adj. & n.*

Maurya /ˈmaʊrɪə/ **1.** a dynasty of ancient India (321–*c.*184 BC) founded by Chandragupta Maurya, who introduced a centralized government and script and developed a highway network which led to Mauryan control of most of the Indian subcontinent. **2.** a member of this dynasty. The oldest extant Indian art originated in this era, which was a period of lively contact between India, the Middle East, and the Mediterranean. —**Mauryan** *adj.*

mausoleum /mɔːsəˈliːəm/ *n.* a large magnificent tomb. The term was originally applied to the marble tomb at Halicarnassus in Caria (one of the Seven Wonders of the World) ordered for himself by Mausolus king of Caria (d. 353 BC) and erected by his queen Artemisia. It has been variously reconstructed but appears to have consisted of a colonnade (enclosing the sarcophagus) above which rose a pyramid-like structure; fragments of the sculptures which adorned it are in the British Museum.

mauve /məʊv/ *adj.* pale purple. —*n.* mauve colour or dye. [F, = mallow, f. L *malva*]

maverick /ˈmævərɪk/ *n.* **1.** an unorthodox or independent person. **2.** an unbranded calf or yearling. [f. S. A. *Maverick*, Texan who did not brand his cattle (*c.*1850)]

maw *n.* **1.** the stomach, especially of an animal. **2.** the jaws or throat of a voracious animal. [OE]

mawkish *adj.* sentimental in a feeble or sickly way. —**mawkishly** *adv.*, **mawkishness** *n.* [f. obs. *mawk* maggot]

max. *abbr.* maximum.

maxi- /ˈmæksɪ-/ *in comb.* very large or long (*maxi-coat*). [abbr. of MAXIMUM; cf. MINI-]

maxilla /mækˈsɪlə/ *n.* (*pl.* **-lae** /-liː/) **1.** the jaw, especially (in vertebrates) the upper one (ill. BODY 1). **2.** a masticatory mouth-part of insects and other arthropods (ill. INSECTS). —**maxillary** *n.* [L]

maxim /ˈmæksɪm/ *n.* the succinct expression of a general truth or rule of conduct. [f. F or L *maxima* (*propositio*) (as MAXIMUM)]

maximal /ˈmæksɪm(ə)l/ *adj.* being or related to a maximum. —**maximally** *adv.*

Maximilian /mæksɪˈmɪlɪən/, Ferdinand Maximilian Joseph (1832–67), emperor of Mexico. Brother of the Austro-Hungarian emperor Franz Joseph and Archduke of Austria, Maximilian was established as emperor of Mexico under French auspices in 1864. In 1866, however, Napoleon III was forced to withdraw his support as a result of American pressure, and Maximilian was confronted by a popular uprising led by Juárez. His forces proved unable to resist the rebels on their own and in 1867 he was captured and shot.

maximize /ˈmæksɪmaɪz/ *v.t.* to increase or enhance to the utmost. —**maximization** /-ˈzeɪʃ(ə)n/ *n.* [f. L (as foll.)]

maximum /ˈmæksɪməm/ *n.* (*pl.* **-ima**) the highest amount possible, attained, usual, etc. —*adj.* that is a maximum. [neut. of L *maximus* greatest]

Maxwell /ˈmækswel/, James Clerk (1831–79), Scottish physicist whose electromagnetic theory became the chief inspiration for modern theoretical physics. He became the first Cavendish professor of physics at Cambridge in 1871, where he designed the new laboratory named after Henry Cavendish, whose unpublished papers on electricity he edited. He contributed to thermodynamics, the kinetic theory of gases (he showed the importance of the statistical approach), colour vision (he demonstrated one of the earliest colour photographs in 1861), and to the theory of Saturn's rings, but his greatest achievement was to extend the ideas of Faraday and Kelvin into his field equations of electromagnetism; these not only unified electricity and magnetism, but also identified the electromagnetic nature of light and predicted the existence of other electromagnetic radiation, verified later experimentally by Hertz.

May *n.* the fifth month of the year. —**May Day,** 1 May especially as a festival (originally associated with spring fertility rites) celebrated with dancing, or (since 1889) as an international holiday in honour of workers. **May Queen** *or* **Queen of the May,** a girl chosen to be queen of the games on May Day. [f. OF f. L *Maius* (*mensis*) (month) of goddess Maia]

may[1] *n.* the hawthorn; its blossom [= prec.]

may[2] *v.aux.* (3 *sing. pres.* **may**; *past* MIGHT[1]) expressing possibility, permission, wish, uncertainty. [OE]

Maya /ˈmɑːjə/ *n.* (*pl.* same or **-s**) **1.** a member of an American Indian people of Yucatan and Central America who still maintain aspects of their ancient culture (see below). **2.** their language, which is still spoken in various forms by several million people. —*adj.* of the Maya or their language. —**Mayan** *adj. & n.* [Sp.]
The Maya civilization developed over an extensive area and reached its peak in the 4th–8th c., a period distinguished by a spectacular flowering of art and learning, contrasting with primitive agriculture in an area surrounded by primeval forests. Remains include stone temples built on pyramids and ornamented with sculptures; the distinctive art style of this period is highly ornamented and detailed. Among the most striking of the Maya achievements are a system of pictorial writing (still largely undeciphered) and a calendar system, more accurate than the Julian, that was still in use at the time of the Spanish conquest in the 16th c.

maya /ˈmɑːjə/ *n.* (*Hinduism*) illusion, magic, the supernatural power wielded by gods and demons; (in Hindu and Buddhist philosophy) the power by which the universe becomes manifest, the illusion or appearance of the phenomenal world. [f. Skr. (*ma* create)]

maybe /ˈmeɪbɪ/ *adv.* perhaps, possibly. [f. *it may be*]

mayday /ˈmeɪdeɪ/ *n.* an international radio distress-signal used by ships and aircraft. [repr. pronunc. of F *m'aider* help me]

Mayflower /ˈmeɪflaʊə(r)/ the ship in which, in 1620, the Pilgrim Fathers sailed from Plymouth to establish the first permanent colony in New England. It arrived at Cape Cod (Mass.) on 21 Nov., after a voyage of 66 days.

mayflower *n.* any of various flowers that bloom in May.

mayfly *n.* an insect of the order Ephemoptera, which lives briefly in spring (ill. INSECTS).

mayhem /ˈmeɪhem/ *n.* **1.** violent or damaging action. **2.** (*hist.*) the crime of injuring a person so as to render him wholly or partly defenceless. [f. AF & OF (as MAIM)]

mayn't /meɪnt/ (*colloq.*) may not.

mayonnaise /meɪəˈneɪz/ *n.* a dressing made of egg-yolks, oil, vinegar, etc.; a dish dressed with this. [F, perh. = of Port *Mahon* in Minorca]

mayor /meə(r)/ *n.* the head of the municipal corporation of a city or borough; the head of a district council with the status of a borough. —**mayoral** *adj.* [f. OF *maire* f. L (as MAJOR)]

mayoralty /ˈmeərəltɪ/ *n.* the office of mayor; the period of this. [as prec.]

mayoress /ˈmeərɪs/ *n.* a mayor's wife; a lady fulfilling the ceremonial duties of a mayor's wife; a woman mayor. [f. MAYOR]

maypole *n.* a pole decked with ribbons, for dancing round in celebrations on May Day. [f. MAY + POLE]

Mazarin /ˈmæzəræ̃/, Jules (1602–61), Sicilian-born French statesman. He became the Italian papal legate in Paris in 1634 and was made a cardinal in 1641. In 1642 he succeeded Richelieu as chief minister of France, which he governed during the minority of Louis XIV, imposing an administration which aroused such opposition as to provoke the civil wars of the Fronde, 1648–53.

mazarine /mæzəˈriːn/ n. & adj. rich deep blue. [perh. f. prec., or Duchesse de *Mazarin*, French noblewoman (d. 1699)]

Mazdaism /ˈmæzdaɪz(ə)m/ n. Zoroastrianism, worship of Ahura Mazda. [f. Avestan *mazda*, the good principle in ancient Persian theology]

maze n. **1.** a complicated network of paths, a labyrinth; a network of paths and hedges designed as a puzzle in which to try and find one's way. **2.** a state of bewilderment; a confused mass etc. [rel. to AMAZE]

mazurka /məˈzɜːkə/ n. a lively Polish dance in triple time; the music for this. [F or f. G f. Polish, = woman of province *Mazovia*]

MB abbr. Bachelor of Medicine. [f. L *Medicinae Baccalaureus*]

Mbabane /əmbɑːˈbɑːnɪ/ the capital of Swaziland; pop. (1976) 23,100.

MBE abbr. Member of the Order of the British Empire.

MC abbr. **1.** Master of Ceremonies. **2.** Military Cross.

MCC abbr. the Marylebone Cricket Club, founded in 1787, with its headquarters at Lord's Cricket Ground. It held the tacitly accepted power to maintain, and if necessary amend, the laws of cricket, until government of the game became the official responsibility of the newly created Cricket Council in 1969.

MD abbr. Doctor of Medicine. [f. L *Medicinae Doctor*]

Md symbol mendelevium.

me[1] /miː, mɪ/ pron. obj. case of I; (colloq.) = I. [OE, acc. & dat. of I[2]]

me[2] /miː/ n. (Mus.) the third note of the major scale in tonic sol-fa (see entry). [f. *mira* (see GAMUT)]

mead n. an alcoholic drink made from fermented honey and water. [OE]

meadow /ˈmedəʊ/ n. a piece of grassland, especially one used for hay; low well-watered ground, especially near a river. —**meadowy** adj. [OE]

meadowsweet n. a plant (*Filipendula ulmaria*) with masses of fragrant creamy-white flowers, often growing in profusion in damp meadows.

meagre /ˈmiːgə(r)/ adj. of poor quality and scanty in amount; (of a person) lean. [f. OF *maigre* f. L *macer*]

meal[1] n. **1.** an occasion when food is eaten. **2.** the food eaten on one occasion. —**make a meal of,** to treat (a task etc.) too laboriously or fussily. **meals-on-wheels** n. a public service whereby meals are delivered to old people, invalids, etc. **meal ticket,** a source of food or income. [OE]

meal[2] n. **1.** coarsely ground grain or pulse. **2.** (Sc.) oatmeal. **3.** (US) maize flour. [OE]

mealie /ˈmiːlɪ/ n. (in southern Africa) maize, a cob with the corn on it. [f. Afrik. f. Port. f. L *milium* millet]

mealtime n. the (usual) time of eating.

mealy adj. of, like, or containing meal; dry and powdery. —**mealy-mouthed** adj. trying excessively to avoid offending people. [f. MEAL[2]]

mean[1] v.t. (past & p.p. **meant** /ment/) **1.** to have as one's purpose or intention. **2.** to design or destine for a purpose. **3.** to intend to convey (a specified sense) or indicate or refer to (a thing). **4.** to signify; (of words) to have as an equivalent in the same or another language. **5.** to entail; to involve; to be likely or certain to result in. **6.** to be of specified importance to. —**mean it,** not to be joking or exaggerating. **mean well,** to have good intentions. [OE]

mean[2] adj. **1.** miserly, niggardly, not generous. **2.** poor in quality or capacity; poor in appearance, not imposing. **3.** malicious, ill-tempered; (US) vicious, nastily behaved. **4.** (US slang) skilful. —**no mean,** very good. —**meanly** adv., **meanness** n. [OE]

mean[3] n. **1.** a condition, quality, or course of action equally removed from two opposite extremes. **2.** the quotient of the sum of several quantities and their number. **3.** a term between the first and last of an arithmetical etc. progression, especially of three terms. —adj. (of a point or quantity) equally far from two extremes. —**in the mean time,** meanwhile. **mean sea level,** the level half-way between high and low water. [f. OF *meien, moien* f. L (as MEDIAN)]

meander /mɪˈændə(r)/ v.i. **1.** (of a stream) to wind about. **2.** to wander at random. —n. **1.** (in pl.) the sinuous windings of a river (ill. RIVERS). **2.** a circuitous journey. [L f. Gk *Maiandros*, winding river in Phrygia]

meaning n. what is meant, the significance. —adj. expressive, significant. —**meaningful** adj., **meaningfully** adv., **meaningless** adj., **meaninglessly** adv. [f. MEAN[1]]

means n.pl. **1.** (usu. treated as sing.) that by which a result is brought about. **2.** money resources, wealth. —**by all means,** certainly. **by no means,** not at all; far from it; certainly not. **means test,** an official inquiry to establish need before financial assistance is given. [as MEAN[3]]

meant past & p.p. of MEAN[1].

meantime adv. meanwhile. [f. MEAN[3] + TIME]

meanwhile adv. **1.** in the intervening period of time. **2.** at the same time. [f. MEAN[3] + WHILE]

meany n. (colloq.) a niggardly or small-minded person. [f. MEAN[2]]

measles /ˈmiːz(ə)lz/ n. an infectious virus disease marked by a red rash. [f. MLG *masele* or MDu. *masel* pustule]

measly /ˈmiːzlɪ/ adj. **1.** of or affected with measles. **2.** (slang) meagre; inferior, contemptible. [f. prec.]

measure /ˈmeʒə(r)/ n. **1.** the size or quantity of something, found by measuring. **2.** a unit, standard, or system used in measuring. **3.** a device used in measuring, especially a rod, tape, or vessel marked with standard units. **4.** degree or extent. **5.** (often in pl.) suitable action taken to achieve some end; a law or proposed law. **6.** that by which a thing is computed. **7.** a prescribed quantity or extent. **8.** a poetical rhythm, a metre; the metrical group of a dactyl or two disyllabic feet; (archaic) a dance. **9.** a stratum containing a mineral. —v.t./i. **1.** to find the extent or quantity of (a thing) by comparison with a fixed unit or with an object of known size; to ascertain the size and proportions of (a person etc.) for fitting clothing etc. **2.** to be of a specified size. **3.** to mark out (a given length) or deal out as a specified quantity. **4.** to estimate (a quality etc.) by comparing it with some standard. **5.** to bring into competition. —**beyond measure,** very great, very much. **for good measure,** in addition to what is necessary. **in some measure,** partly, to some extent. **made to measure,** made from measurements specially taken. **measure up (to),** to reach the necessary standard. [f. OF f. L *mensura (metiri* to measure)]

measured adj. **1.** rhythmical, regular in movement. **2.** (of language) carefully considered. [f. prec.]

measurement n. an act or the result of measuring; (in pl.) detailed dimensions. [f. MEASURE]

meat n. **1.** animal flesh as food (usually excluding fish and poultry). **2.** the essence or chief part. —**meat and drink,** a source of great pleasure to. **meat-safe** n. a ventilated cupboard for storing meat. [OE, = food]

meatball n. a small ball of minced meat.

meatus /mɪˈeɪtəs/ n. (pl. same or **-uses**) a channel or passage in the body; its opening. —**auditory meatus,** a channel of the ear. [L, = passage (*meare* flow, run)]

meaty adj. **1.** like meat. **2.** full of meat, fleshy. **3.** full of informative matter. —**meatiness** n. [f. MEAT]

Mecca /ˈmekə/ **1.** the holiest city of the Islamic faith, an oasis town located in the Hijaz region (on the Red Sea coast, in W. Arabia) of the Arabian peninsula, now in Saudi Arabia. A trading centre in pre-Islamic times, it was in Mecca that the Prophet Muhammad was born and brought up, and it was with local people here that he shared his first revelations. Expelled from the city for his 'disruptive' preaching, he returned to Mecca eight years later as the head of a non-tribally based religious community and made it his capital until his death two years later in AD 632. The centre of Islamic ritual (see KAABA, HADJ) and site of the Great Mosque, Mecca receives thousands of visitors each year at the time of the annual pilgrimage. **2.** a place one aspires to visit. —**Meccan** adj.

mechanic /mɪˈkænɪk/ n. a skilled worker, especially one who makes or uses or repairs machinery. [f. OF or L f. Gk (as MACHINE)]

mechanical /mɪˈkænɪk(ə)l/ adj. **1.** of machines or a mechanism. **2.** working or produced by machinery. **3.** (of a person or action) like a machine, acting or done without conscious thought; lacking originality; (of work) needing little or no thought. **4.** of or belonging to the science of mechanics. —**mechanically** adv. [f. prec.]

mechanics /mɪˈkænɪks/ n.pl. (usu. treated as sing.) **1.** the branch of applied mathematics dealing with motion and tendencies to motion. **2.** the science of machinery. **3.** (as pl.) the processes by which something is done or functions. [f. MECHANIC]

mechanism /ˈmekənɪz(ə)m/ n. **1.** the structure or parts of a machine or other set of mutually adapted parts. **2.** the mode of operation of a process or machine. [f. Gk (as MACHINE)]

mechanize /'mekənaɪz/ v.t. **1.** to introduce or use machines in; to equip with machines. **2.** to give a mechanical character to. —**mechanization** /-ˈzeɪʃ(ə)n/ n. [f. MECHANIC]

Med n. (colloq.) the Mediterranean Sea. [abbr.]

medal /'med(ə)l/ n. a piece of metal, usually in the form of a coin, struck or cast with an inscription and device to commemorate an event etc., or awarded as a distinction to a soldier, athlete, etc. [f. F f. It. ult. f. L metallum (as METAL)]

medallion /mɪˈdæljən/ n. **1.** a large medal. **2.** a thing so shaped, e.g. a decorative panel, a portrait. [f. F f. It. (as prec.)]

medallist /'medəlɪst/ n. a winner of a medal. [f. MEDAL]

Medawar /'medəwə(r)/, Sir Peter Brian (1915-), English immunologist, who in 1960 shared a Nobel Prize for his studies of the biology of tissue transplantation. His early work showed that rejection of grafts was the result of an immune mechanism; his subsequent discovery of 'acquired' tolerance of grafts encouraged the early attempts at human organ transplantation.

meddle v.i. **1.** to interfere in people's affairs. **2.** to tinker. —**meddler** n. [f. OF var. of mesler, ult. f. L miscēre mix]

meddlesome adj. fond of meddling. [f. prec. + -SOME]

Mede /miːd/ n. a member of an ancient Indo-European people whose homeland, Media, lay SW of the Caspian Sea. In the 7th-6th c. BC they were masters of an empire that included most of modern Iran and extended to Cappadocia and Syria; it passed into Persian control after the defeat of King Astyages by Cyrus in 549 BC.

Medea /mɪˈdiːə/ (Gk legend) a sorceress, daughter of Aeetes king of Colchis. She helped Jason to obtain the Golden Fleece, and married him, but was deserted in Corinth and avenged herself by killing their two children. [Gk, = cunning]

Media /'miːdɪə/ the country of the Medes.

media pl. of MEDIUM.

mediaeval var. of MEDIEVAL.

medial /'miːdɪ(ə)l/ adj. situated in the middle. —**medially** adv. [f. L (medius middle)]

median /'miːdɪən/ adj. medial. —n. **1.** the straight line drawn from any vertex of a triangle to the middle of the opposite side (ill. SHAPES). **2.** a medial number or point in a series. **3.** (in statistics) the value of a quantity such that exactly half of a given population have greater values of that quantity. [f. F or L (as prec.)]

mediate /'miːdɪeɪt/ v.t./i. **1.** to act as negotiator or peacemaker between the two sides in a dispute. **2.** to bring about (a result) thus. —/'miːdɪət/ adj. connected not directly but through some other person or thing. —**mediation** /-ˈeɪʃ(ə)n/ n., **mediator** n. [f. L mediare (as MEDIAL)]

medic /'medɪk/ n. (colloq.) a medical practitioner or student. [f. L medicus physician (medēri heal)]

medical /'medɪk(ə)l/ adj. of the science of medicine in general or as distinct from surgery. —n. (colloq.) a medical examination. —**medical certificate**, a certificate of fitness or unfitness to work etc. **medical examination**, an examination to determine a person's physical fitness. **medical officer**, a person in charge of the health services of a local authority or other organization. —**medically** adv. [f. F or L (as prec.)]

medicament /mɪˈdɪkəmənt/ n. a substance used in curative treatment. [f. F or L (as MEDICATE)]

medicate /'medɪkeɪt/ v.t. **1.** to treat medically. **2.** to impregnate with a medicinal substance. —**medication** /-ˈkeɪʃ(ə)n/ n., **medicative** adj. [f. L medicare (as MEDIC)]

Medici /'medɪtʃɪ/ an Italian family which dominated Florence in the 15th c., particularly during the lifetimes of Cosimo (1389-1464) and Lorenzo (frequently called 'the Magnificent') (1449-92). In the following century the family rose to become grand dukes of Tuscany, while two members of it reached the papacy (Leo X, d. 1521, and Clement VII, d. 1534) and two others were married to kings of France (Catherine to Henry II, Marie to Henry IV).

medicinal /mɪˈdɪsɪn(ə)l/ adj. of medicine; having healing properties. —**medicinally** adv. [f. OF f. L (as foll.)]

medicine /'medsɪn, -sɪn/ n. **1.** the art of restoring and preserving health, especially by means of remedial substances etc. as distinct from surgery (see below). **2.** a substance used in this, especially one taken internally. —**medicine-man** n. a witch-doctor. **take one's medicine**, to submit to rebuke or punishment etc. [f. OF f. L medicina (as MEDIC)]

Although medicine was practised in ancient Egypt and Mesopotamia, and was studied at Cnidos in Asia Minor in the 7th c. BC, it is the Greek physician Hippocrates (5th c. BC) who is regarded as the 'father of medicine', with his careful recording and comparison of actual clinical cases and discarding of ancient superstitions and theories. Greek physicians were famous, and Galen (2nd c. AD) dominated medical knowledge for nearly 1,500 years. The modern study of anatomy dates from the publication of Vesalius' account of human anatomy in 1543, while William Harvey's discovery of blood circulation was the major advance in physiology in the 17th c. The invention of the microscope made it possible for the Dutchman Anton van Leeuwenhoek to investigate the previously invisible world of microorganisms. In the 1860s Pasteur made his first investigations which led to the germ theory of disease. This and the discovery of anaesthetics and antiseptics brought about a transformation in medicine, while a host of scientific discoveries (including X-rays) accompanied and succeeded them. The growth of organic chemistry and the work of the German bacteriologist Paul Ehrlich made possible the science of chemotherapy, and antibiotics came into general use during the Second World War (see PENICILLIN). Many virus diseases can be prevented or controlled by inoculation (see JENNER). Improvements in general standards of living, hygiene, and nutrition have all but eliminated many diseases that were formerly common, but increased stress, and longevity itself, have brought their own problems.

medico /'medɪkəʊ/ n. (pl. -os) (colloq.) a medical practitioner or student. [It. f. L, = MEDIC]

medieval /medɪˈiːv(ə)l/ adj. of or imitating the Middle Ages. [f. L medius middle + aevum age]

Medina /meˈdiːnə/ an oasis in NW Arabia, approximately 320 km (200 miles) north of Mecca. Considered the second holiest city of Islam (after Mecca), it was the destination of the Prophet Muhammad's infant Muslim community when they left Mecca in AD 622. He had been invited to Yathrib —as the oasis town was then known—by its populace to assume the role of arbiter in an ongoing conflict between two tribal groups. In Yathrib/Medina the community grew and was consolidated around the home of the Prophet, which is considered the first mosque (masjid) in the history of Islam and the model for later structures meant for worship and communal gatherings. The community was based upon the city of Mecca capitulated to Muhammad in AD 630. Muhammad is buried in Medina (its name means 'the city'), and it is customary for the pilgrim to visit the Prophet's tomb following the series of ritual events constituting the formal pilgrimage (hadj) to Mecca.

mediocre /miːdɪˈəʊkə(r)/ adj. of middling quality; second-rate. [f. F or L mediocris (as MEDIAL)]

mediocrity /miːdɪˈɒkrɪtɪ/ n. **1.** mediocre quality. **2.** a mediocre person. [f. F f. L (as prec.)]

meditate /'medɪteɪt/ v.t./i. **1.** to think deeply and quietly; to do this in religious contemplation. **2.** to plan in one's mind. —**meditation** /-ˈteɪʃ(ə)n/ n., **meditator** n. [f. L meditari]

meditative /'medɪtətɪv/ adj. inclined to meditate; indicative of meditation. —**meditatively** adv. [f. prec.]

Mediterranean /medɪtəˈreɪnɪən/ adj. **1.** of or characteristic of the Mediterranean Sea or the countries in and round it. **2.** of or belonging to an extremely artificial sub-racial grouping of people who, as a population, are short (average height c.163 cm, 5 ft.) with dark skin, hair, and eyes, and dolichocephalic. —**Mediterranean Sea**, an almost land-locked sea between southern Europe and Africa, connected with the Atlantic Ocean by the Strait of Gibraltar and with the Red Sea by the Suez Canal. [f. L, = inland (medius middle, terra land)]

medium /'miːdɪəm/ n. (pl. -ia, in sense 6 -iums) **1.** a middle quality or degree of intensiveness etc. **2.** a substance or surroundings in which something exists, moves, or is transmitted; an environment. **3.** an agency or means by which something is done. **4.** (in pl., sometimes treated erron. as sing.) the mass media (see MASS[1]). **5.** the material or form used by an artist or composer etc. **6.** (pl. -iums) a person claiming to be able to communicate with the spirits of the dead etc. —adj. intermediate between two degrees or amounts; average, moderate. —**medium wave**, a radio wave of frequency between 300 kHz and 3 MHz. [L, neut. of medius middle]

mediumistic /miːdɪəˈmɪstɪk/ adj. of a spiritualist medium. [f. prec.]

medlar /'medlə(r)/ n. a fruit like a small apple, eaten when decayed; the trée bearing this (*Mespilus germanica*). [f. OF f. L f. Gk *mespilē*]

medley /ˈmedlɪ/ *n.* a varied mixture, a miscellany; a collection of musical items from various sources. [f. OF f. L (as MEDDLE)]

medulla /mɪˈdʌlə/ *n.* **1.** the marrow within a bone; the substance of the spinal cord. **2.** the hindmost section of the brain. **3.** the central part of some organs, e.g. that of the kidneys (ill. BODY 2). **4.** the soft internal tissue of plants. —**medullary** *adj.* [L]

Medusa /mɪˈdjuːsə/ (*Gk myth.*) one of the Gorgons, the only mortal one, slain by Perseus, who cut off her head.

medusa /mɪˈdjuːzə/ *n.* (*pl.* **-ae** or **-as**) a jellyfish. [f. prec., snake-haired Gorgon]

meek *adj.* quiet and obedient, making no protest. —**meekly** *adv.*, **meekness** *n.* [f. ON]

meerschaum /ˈmɪəʃəm/ *n.* a white substance resembling clay; a tobacco-pipe with the bowl made of this. [G, = sea-foam]

meet[1] *v.t./i.* (*past & p.p.* **met**) **1.** to come by accident or design into the company of, to come face to face (with). **2.** to go to a place to be present at the arrival of (a person, train, etc.). **3.** to come together or into contact (with). **4.** to make the acquaintance of, to be introduced (to). **5.** (of people or a group) to assemble. **6.** to deal with or answer (a demand, objection, etc.) effectively; to satisfy or conform with (a person's wishes). **7.** to pay (the cost, a bill at maturity). **8.** to experience or receive (one's death, fate, etc.). **9.** to oppose or be in opposition in a contest etc. —*n.* a meeting of persons and hounds for a hunt. —**meet the case**, to be adequate. **meet the eye** (*or* ear), to be visible (or audible) (*more in it than meets the eye*, hidden qualities or complications). **meet a person's eye**, to look into the eyes of a person looking at one. **meet a person half-way**, to respond to his advances, to make a compromise with him. **meet up with**, (*colloq.*) to happen to meet (a person). [OE]

meet[2] *adj.* (*archaic*) fitting, proper. [OE (rel. to METE)]

meeting *n.* **1.** coming together. **2.** an assembly of people, e.g. for discussion or (especially of Quakers) worship. **3.** a race-meeting. [f. MEET[1]]

mega- /megə-/ *in comb.* **1.** large. **2.** one million. [Gk (*megas* great)]

megadeath /ˈmegədeθ/ *n.* the death of one million people (especially as a unit in estimating casualties of war).

Megaera /mɪˈgɪərə/ (*Gk myth.*) one of the Furies. [Gk, perh. = she who bewitches]

megahertz /ˈmegəhɜːts/ *n.* a unit of frequency, equal to one million cycles per second.

megalith /ˈmegəlɪθ/ *n.* a large stone, especially one forming (part of) a prehistoric monument. —**megalithic** /-ˈlɪθɪk/ *adj.* [f. MEGA- + Gk *lithos* stone]

megalomania /megələˈmeɪnɪə/ *n.* a mental disorder involving an exaggerated idea of one's own importance; a passion for grandiose schemes etc. —**megalomaniac** *n.* [f. Gk *megas* great + MANIA]

megaphone /ˈmegəfəʊn/ *n.* a large funnel-shaped device for sending the sound of the voice to a distance. [f. MEGA- + Gk *phōnē* voice, sound]

megaton /ˈmegətʌn/ *n.* a unit of explosive force equal to one million tons of TNT.

megavolt /ˈmegəvəʊlt/ *n.* a unit of electromotive force equal to one million volts.

megawatt /ˈmegəwɒt/ *n.* a unit of electrical power equal to one million watts.

Meghalaya /megəˈleɪə/ a State of India, created in 1970 from parts of Assam; capital, Shillong.

megohm /ˈmegəʊm/ *n.* a unit of electrical resistance equal to one million ohms. [f. MEGA- + OHM]

meiosis /maɪˈəʊsɪs/ *n.* (*pl.* **-oses** /-siːz/) **1.** litotes. **2.** the process of division of cell nuclei forming gametes each containing half the normal number of chromosomes. [f. Gk (*meioō* make less)]

Meissen /ˈmaɪs(ə)n/ an East German town, near Dresden, where the earliest European porcelain factory was founded and still exists. —**Meissen china** etc., porcelain made there, often called Dresden china.

Meistersinger /ˈmaɪstəsɪŋə(r)/ *n.* (*pl.* same) a member of one of the guilds of German lyric poets and musicians. These guilds, usually of burghers and respected master craftsmen, began to be organized from 1311 and continued to flourish until the 17th c. Their technique was elaborate and they were subject to rigid regulations, depicted in Wagner's opera *Die Meistersinger von Nürnberg* (1868). They represented a middle- and lower-class continuation of the aristocratic minnesinger of preceding centuries. [G, = master singer]

Mekong /miːˈkɒŋ/ the major river of SE Asia, rising in Tibet and flowing south-east and south for 4,180 km (2,600 miles). For part of its course it forms the Burma/Laos and Thailand/Laos border before continuing south across Kampuchea and Vietnam to its extensive delta on the South China Sea.

melamine /ˈmeləmiːn/ *n.* a tough resilient kind of plastic. [f. *melam* (arbitrary) + AMINE]

melancholia /melənˈkəʊlɪə/ *n.* a mental disorder marked by depression and ill-founded fears. [L (as MELANCHOLY)]

melancholic /melənˈkɒlɪk/ *adj.* melancholy; liable to melancholy. [f. OF f. L f. Gk (as foll.)]

melancholy /ˈmelənkəlɪ/ *n.* pensive sadness; mental depression; a habitual or constitutional tendency to this. —*adj.* **1.** sad, gloomy. **2.** saddening, depressing. **3.** (of words etc.) expressing sadness. [f. OF f. L f. Gk (*melas* black, *kholē* bile)]

Melanchthon /məˈlæŋkθən/, Philipp (1497–1560), German Protestant reformer (real name Schwarzerd) who in 1521 succeeded Luther as leader of the Reformation movement in Germany. Professor of Greek at Wittenberg, he helped to systematize Luther's teachings and produced the first ordered exposition of Reformation doctrine. His attitude to Christianity was humanistic, and he cared for learning as such, writing textbooks that were used for several generations in upper schools and universities.

Melanesia /melɑˈniːʃə/ an island-group in the SW Pacific containing the Bismarck Archipelago, the Solomon Islands, Santa Cruz, Vanuatu, New Caledonia, Fiji, and the intervening islands. —**Melanesian** *adj.* & *n.* [f. Gk *melas* black (from the colour of the predominant native people), *nēsos* island]

mélange /meɪˈlɑːʒ/ *n.* a medley. [F (*mêler* mix)]

melanin /ˈmelənɪn/ *n.* a dark pigment in the hair, skin, etc. [f. Gk *melas* black]

Melba /ˈmelbə/, Dame Nellie (real name Helen Porter Mitchell, 1859–1931), Australian soprano singer, born near Melbourne, from which city she took her professional name.

Melba toast thin crisp toast. [f. prec.]

Melbourne[1] /ˈmelbən, -bɔːn/ the capital of Victoria and second-largest city in Australia; pop. (est. 1982) 2,836,800.

Melbourne[2] /ˈmelbən, -bɔːn/ William Lamb, 2nd Viscount (1779–1848), British statesman. During his early parliamentary career Melbourne was a supporter of the moderate policies of Canning. He became Home Secretary in Lord Grey's administration in 1830 and succeeded Grey as Prime Minister in 1834. Out of office briefly in 1834-5, Melbourne then went on to serve as Prime Minister until 1841, pursuing a moderate reform policy despite troubles with Chartist and anti-Corn Laws agitation.

Melchior /ˈmelkɪɔː(r)/ the traditional name of one of the Magi, represented as a king of Nubia.

Melchizedek /melˈtʃɪzɪdek/ king of Salem (which is doubtfully identified with Jerusalem) and priest of the most high God, to whom Abraham paid tithes (Gen. 14: 18). He is sometimes quoted as the type of self-originating power, with reference to Heb. 7: 3-4.

Meleager[1] /melɪˈeɪgə(r)/ (*Gk myth.*) a hero at whose birth the Fates declared that he would die when a brand then on the fire was consumed. His mother Althaea seized the brand and kept it, but threw it into the fire when he quarrelled with and killed her brothers in a hunting expedition, whereupon he died.

Meleager[2] /melɪˈeɪgə(r)/ (*c.*140-*c.*70 BC) Greek poet who lived at Tyre and on the island of Cos, author of many epigrams and of short poems on love and death.

mêlée /ˈmeleɪ/ *n.* **1.** a confused fight or struggle. **2.** a muddle. [F (as MEDLEY)]

mellifluous /meˈlɪfluəs/ *adj.* sweet-sounding. —**mellifluously** *adv.*, **mellifluousness** *n.* [f. OF or L (*mel* honey, *fluere* flow)]

mellow /ˈmeləʊ/ *adj.* **1.** (of fruit) sweet and rich in flavour from being fully ripe; (of wine) well-matured; (of soil) rich, loamy. **2.** made kindly and sympathetic by age or experience. **3.** genial, jovial. **4.** (of sound, colour, or light) soft and rich, free from harshness or sharp contrast. —*v.t./i.* to make or become mellow. —**mellowly** *adv.*, **mellowness** *n.* [perh. rel. to MEAL[2]]

melodeon /mɪˈləʊdɪən/ n. **1.** an American organ (see entry). **2.** an accordion on which the notes are produced by buttons. This type of instrument was first patented in 1829. [f. MELODY + HARMONIUM]

melodic /mɪˈlɒdɪk/ adj. of melody. [f. F f. L f. Gk (as MELODY)]

melodious /mɪˈləʊdɪəs/ adj. of or producing melody; sweet-sounding. —**melodiously** adv., **melodiousness** n. [f. OF (as MELODY)]

melodrama /ˈmelədrɑːmə/ n. **1.** a play with a sensational plot and crude appeal to the emotions; such plays as a genre (see below). **2.** behaviour or an occurrence suggestive of this. —**melodramatic** /-drəˈmætɪk/ adj., **melodramatically** adv. [f. F f. Gk melos music + F drame (as DRAMA)]

This type of play was popular all over Europe in the 19th c. The term derives from the use of incidental music in spoken dramas in Germany and from the French mélodrame, a dumb show accompanied by music; its application to Gothic tales of horror and mystery, vice, and virtue triumphant stems from the early works of Goethe and Schiller. The music gradually became less important and the setting less Gothic, and in England there were domestic melodramas, melodramas based on real-life or legendary crimes (as the anonymous Maria Marten in the 1830s), and dramatizations of popular novels (Mrs Henry Wood's East Lynne, 1861). Melodrama died out early in the 20th c.

melody /ˈmelədɪ/ n. **1.** sweet music. **2.** a musical arrangement of words, a song or tune. **3.** an arrangement of single notes in a musically expressive succession; the principal part in harmonized music. [f. OF f. L f. Gk melōidia (as prec., ODE)]

melon /ˈmelən/ n. the sweet fruit of various gourds; a gourd producing this, especially the musk-melon (see MUSK) and water-melon (see WATER). [f. OF f. L, abbr. of melopepo f. Gk, = apple-gourd]

Melpomene /melˈpɒmɪnɪ/ (Gk & Rom. myth.) the Muse of tragedy. [Gk, = singer]

melt v.t./i. (p.p. **melted**, or (as adj., of substances not easily melted) MOLTEN) **1.** to change from solid to liquid by heat. **2.** to become softened or dissolved easily. **3.** to make or become gentler through pity or love. **4.** to dwindle or fade away; to pass slowly into another form. **5.** (colloq.) to depart unobtrusively. —**melt down**, to melt (metal articles) in order to use the metal as a raw material; to become liquid and lose structure. **melting-point** n. the temperature at which a solid melts. **melting-pot** n. a container (e.g. a crucible) in which substances are melted; a place or situation where ideas etc. are being fused or reconstructed. **melt-water** n. water resulting from the melting of ice or snow, especially that of a glacier. [OE]

meltdown n. the melting of (and consequent damage to) a structure, e.g. the overheated core of a nuclear reactor.

Melville /ˈmelvɪl/, Herman (1819–91), American novelist and poet. In 1839 he took to the sea as a cabin boy, and a voyage (1841) on a whaler to the South Seas provided the basis for his masterpiece Moby-Dick (1851), a dramatic celebration of man's defiance of a demonic God whose agent is the symbolic white whale Moby-Dick; this brilliant work was noted by some critics but few readers. His successful fictional travel narrative Typee (1846) and its sequel Omoo (1847) were followed by others, all based on his experiences in the South Seas, but his novel Pierre (1852) was a critical failure. The Confidence-Man (1857) was his last novel and his great creative period perished from public neglect. In addition to his stringent sombre tales and the novella Billy Budd (1924, the basis of Benjamin Britten's opera) he was a powerful poet, a satirist, romantic allegorist, and analyst of national character. It was not until the 1920s that he was rediscovered by literary scholars.

member n. **1.** a person or thing belonging to a particular society or group. **2. Member,** (in full **Member of Parliament** or (US) **of Congress**) a person formally elected to take part in the proceedings of a parliament (in the UK the House of Commons; in the USA Congress). **3.** a part of a complex structure. **4.** a part or organ of the body. [f. OF f. L membrum limb]

membership n. **1.** being a member. **2.** the number of members; the body of members. [f. prec. + -SHIP]

membrane /ˈmembreɪn/ n. a pliable sheetlike tissue connecting or lining structures in an animal or vegetable body. —**membranous** /ˈmembreɪnəs/ adj. [f. L membrana (as MEMBER)]

memento /mɪˈmentəʊ/ n. (pl. **-oes**) an object serving as a reminder or souvenir. [L, imper. of meminisse remember]

Memnon /ˈmemnɒn/ (Gk legend) Ethiopian king who went to Troy to help Priam, his uncle, and was killed. The 'colossi of Memnon', statues (supposed to represent him) near Thebes in Egypt, whose stones, before the restoration of the statues, were said to sing at dawn, are inscribed with the name of Amenophis III.

memo /ˈmeməʊ/ n. (pl. **-os**) (colloq.) a memorandum. [abbr.]

memoir /ˈmemwɑː(r)/ n. **1.** a record of events, written from personal knowledge or special sources of information. **2.** (usu. in pl.) an autobiography; a biography. **3.** an essay on a learned subject specially studied by the writer. [f. F mémoire (as MEMORY)]

memorabilia /memərəˈbɪlɪə/ n.pl. noteworthy things. [L (as foll.)]

memorable /ˈmemərəb(ə)l/ adj. **1.** worth remembering. **2.** easily remembered. —**memorability** /-ˈbɪlɪtɪ/ n., **memorably** adv. [f. F or L memorabilis (memorare bring to mind)]

memorandum /meməˈrændəm/ n. (pl. **memoranda** or **-ums**) **1.** a note or record made for future use. **2.** an informal written message, especially in business etc. [L, = to be remembered (as prec.)]

memorial /mɪˈmɔːrɪəl/ n. an object, institution, or custom established in memory of a person or event. —adj. serving as a memorial. [f. OF or L (as MEMORY)]

memorize /ˈmeməraɪz/ v.t. to learn by heart. [f. foll.]

memory /ˈmemərɪ/ n. **1.** the faculty by which things are recalled to or kept in the mind; this in an individual. **2.** remembering; a person or thing remembered. **3.** posthumous repute. **4.** the length of time over which memory extends. **5.** the store for data in a computer. —**from memory,** without verification. **in memory of,** to keep alive the remembrance of. [f. OF f. L memoria (memor mindful)]

Memphis /ˈmemfɪs/ an ancient city of Egypt, about 15 km (nearly 10 miles) south of Cairo. It was the capital of Egypt from early dynastic times, and is said to have been founded by Menes, the first ruler of a united Egypt (c.3000 BC); it remained one of the principal cities even after the pharaohs of the 18th Dynasty made Thebes their capital (c.1550 BC). The monuments of Giza and Saqqara form part of its extensive necropolis.

memsahib /ˈmemsɑːɪb, -sɑːb/ n. (hist.) a European married woman as spoken of or to by Indians. [f. MA'AM + SAHIB]

men pl. of MAN.

menace /ˈmenɪs/ n. **1.** a threat. **2.** a dangerous or obnoxious person or thing. —v.t. to threaten. —**menacing** adj., **menacingly** adv. [f. AF f. L minaciae (minax threatening)]

ménage /meɪˈnɑːʒ/ n. a domestic establishment. —**ménage à trois** /ɑː trwɑː/ a household consisting of a husband, wife, and the lover of one of these. [f. OF f. L (as MANSION)]

menagerie /mɪˈnædʒərɪ/ n. a collection of wild animals in captivity for exhibition etc. [f. F (as prec.)]

Menai Strait /ˈmenaɪ/ the channel separating Anglesey from NW Wales.

Menander /məˈnændə(r)/ (342/1–293/89 BC) the leading writer of comedy in the Hellenistic period, of great influence and popularity in antiquity, but whose works survive only as fragments in papyrus finds. His plays, set in contemporary Greece, deal with domestic situations, with recurring features such as foundling children, kidnapped daughters, and scheming slaves; a love-interest is constant. His verse stays close to colloquial speech and his characters are lifelike; in antiquity he was praised for representing life.

Mencius /ˈmensɪəs/ (Latinization of Chinese Meng-tzu Meng the Master) **1.** Chinese philosopher of the 4th c. BC. **2.** one of the four great texts of Confucianism published in AD 1190, containing his teachings. The central doctrine is that human nature tends towards the good as water tends to flow downhill.

mend v.t./i. **1.** to make whole (something that is damaged), to repair. **2.** to regain health. **3.** to improve. —n. a place where a material etc. has been repaired. —**mend one's fences,** to make peace with a person. **on the mend,** improving in health or condition. [f. AF (as AMEND)]

mendacious /menˈdeɪʃəs/ adj. untruthful, lying. —**mendaciously** adv., **mendacity** /-ˈdæsɪtɪ/ n. [f. L mendax]

Mendel /ˈmend(ə)l/, Gregor Johann (1822–84), Moravian monk, the 'father of genetics'. From his experiments with peas he argued (1855–6) that hybrids of plants showing different characters produced second-generation offspring in which parental characters were inherited in precise ratios. Hybrids exhibit the dominant parental character and produce offspring in which the parental characters re-emerge unchanged. The importance of Mendel's work lies in the fact that he recognized that it is not the characters themselves which are inherited, but the predisposing factors underlying them. After the rediscovery of his ratios in 1900, Mendelism was often thought, wrongly, to be the antithesis of the Darwinian theory of natural selection; in fact, Mendel had demonstrated the primary source of variability in plants and animals, on which natural selection could then operate.

Mendeleev /mende'leɪef/, Dmitri Ivanovich (1834-1907), Russian chemist who developed the periodic table in which he classified chemical elements according to their atomic weights in groups with similar properties. This allowed him to systematize much of the existing chemical information, pinpoint elements with incorrectly assigned atomic weights, and also predict the existence of several new elements. His study of gases and liquids led him to the concept of critical temperature, independently of Thomas Andrews (1813-85). The artificial element mendelevium was named after him in 1955.

mendelevium /mend(ə)l'iːvɪəm/ n. an artificially made transuranic radioactive metallic element, symbol Md, atomic number 101, first obtained in 1955 by bombarding einsteinium with helium ions. [f. prec.]

Mendelian /men'diːlɪən/ adj. of Mendel's theory of heredity by genes. [f. MENDEL]

Mendelism /'mendəlɪz(ə)m/ n. that part of genetics concerned with the manner in which hereditary factors (genes) and the characteristics they control are inherited during the course of sexual reproduction. The main principles were first outlined by Mendel, although they have been modified by later discoveries. [f. MENDEL]

Mendelssohn /'mend(ə)ls(ə)n/, (Jakob Ludwig) Felix (1809-47), German composer, born of a Jewish banking family which adopted the Christian faith after moving to Berlin in 1811. He was a child prodigy; his 13 string symphonies, composed 1821-3, reveal a firm grasp of counterpoint and mastery of the classical style, and his overture to A Midsummer Night's Dream was composed at the age of 17. Pianist, organist, and conductor, he combined his musical accomplishments with wide literary knowledge and was a good painter; his love of landscape provides the inspiration for the descriptive Fingal's Cave (1830) and the Fourth (Italian) Symphony (1832). The poetic elegance of his work has caused it to be regarded as superficial because of its lack of impassioned features, and its popularity during his lifetime was followed (from the 1860s) by a severe reaction, but the pendulum has swung again and the craftsmanship, restraint, poetry, and melodic freshness of his compositions are now highly valued.

mendicant /'mendɪkənt/ adj. begging; (of a friar) living solely on alms. —n. a beggar; a mendicant friar. [f. L mendicare (mendicus beggar)]

Menelaus /menɪ'leɪəs/ (Gk legend) king of Sparta, brother of Agamemnon and husband of Helen who was stolen from him by Paris, an event which provoked the Trojan war. They were reunited after the fall of Troy.

menfolk n. **1.** men in general. **2.** the men in a family.

Meng-tzu /meŋ'tsuː/ see MENCIUS.

menhir /'menhɪə(r)/ n. a tall upright prehistoric monumental stone. [f. Breton men stone, hir long]

menial /'miːnɪəl/ adj. (of work) lowly, degrading. —n. a lowly domestic servant; a person who does humble tasks. —**menially** adv. [f. AF (meinie retinue)]

meninges /mɪ'nɪndʒiːz/ n.pl. the membranes enclosing the brain and spinal cord. [f. Gk mēnigx -iggos membrane]

meningitis /menɪn'dʒaɪtɪs/ n. inflammation of the meninges. [f. prec. + -ITIS]

meniscus /mɪ'nɪskəs/ n. (pl. -sci /-saɪ/) **1.** the curved upper surface of a liquid in a tube, usually concave upwards when the walls are wetted and convex when they are dry, because of the effects of surface tension. **2.** a lens that is convex on one side and concave on the other. [f. Gk, = crescent (mēnē moon)]

Mennonite /'menənaɪt/ n. a member of a Christian sect which arose in Friesland in the 16th c. maintaining principles similar to those of the Anabaptists, being opposed to infant baptism, the taking of oaths, military service, and the holding of civic offices. In the following centuries many emigrated, first to other European countries and to Russia, later to North and South America, in search of political freedom. [f. Menno Simons (1496-1561), their early leader]

menopause /'menəpɔːz/ n. the final cessation of the menses; the period of a woman's life (usually 40-50) when this occurs. —**menopausal** adj. [f. Gk mēn month + PAUSE]

menorah /mə'nɔːrə/ n. a holy seven-branched candelabrum used in the ancient Temple in Jerusalem; a candelabrum with any number of branches used in modern synagogues. [Heb., = candlestick]

menses /'mensiːz/ n.pl. the flow of blood etc. from the mucous lining of the human or primate womb, occurring in women at monthly intervals from puberty until middle age. [L, pl. of mensis month]

Menshevik /'menʃəvɪk/ n. a member of a minority faction of the Russian Socialist Party who opposed the Bolshevik policies of non-co-operation with other opponents of the Tsarist regime and violent revolutionary action by a small political élite. The Mensheviks, along with the other revolutionary groups, were completely defeated by the Bolsheviks in the power struggle following the successful overthrow of the Tsar in 1917. [f. Russ., = member of the minority; cf. BOLSHEVIK]

menstrual /'menstruəl/ adj. of menstruation. [f. L (menstruus monthly f. mensis month)]

menstruate /'menstrueɪt/ v.i. to discharge the menses. —**menstruation** /-'eɪʃ(ə)n/ n. [f. L. menstruare (as prec.)]

mensurable /'mensjʊrəb(ə)l/ adj. measurable; having fixed limits. [F or f. L (mensurare to measure)]

mensuration /mensjʊə'reɪʃ(ə)n/ n. measuring; the mathematical rules for finding lengths, areas, and volumes. [f. L (as prec.)]

menswear n. clothes for men.

-ment /-mənt/ suffix forming nouns expressing the result or means of a verbal action (fragment, ornament, treatment); also forming nouns from adjectives (merriment, oddment). [f. F f. L -mentum]

mental /'ment(ə)l/ adj. **1.** of the mind; done by the mind. **2.** caring for mental patients. **3.** (colloq.) affected with mental disorder. —**mental age**, the degree of a person's mental development expressed as the age at which the same degree is attained by the average child. **mental deficiency**, imperfect mental development leading to abnormally low intelligence. **mental patient**, a sufferer from mental illness. —**mentally** adv. [f. OF of L (mens mind)]

mentality /men'tælɪtɪ/ n. mental character or outlook; mental ability. [f. prec.]

menthol /'menθɒl/ n. a camphor-like substance obtained from oil of peppermint etc., used as a flavouring or to relieve local pain etc. [G, f. L mentha mint]

mentholated /'menθəleɪtɪd/ adj. treated with or containing menthol. [f. prec.]

mention /'menʃ(ə)n/ v.t. to refer to briefly or by name. —n. **1.** mentioning. **2.** a formal acknowledgement of merit. —**don't mention it**, a polite reply to thanks or an apology. **not to mention**, and also. [f. OF f. L]

mentor /'mentɔː(r)/ n. an experienced and trusted adviser. [F, f. Mentor adviser of young Telemachus, son of Odysseus]

menu /'menjuː/ n. **1.** a list of the dishes available in a restaurant etc. or to be served at a meal. **2.** a list of options, displayed on a screen, from which a user selects what he requires a computer to do. [F, = detailed list (as MINUTE²)]

MEP abbr. Member of the European Parliament.

Mephistopheles /mefɪ'stɒfɪliːz/ in the legend of Faust, the demon to whom Faust sold his soul. —**mephistophelean** /-stə'fiːlɪən/ adj.

mercantile /'mɜːkəntaɪl/ adj. of trade, commercial; trading. —**mercantile marine**, the merchant navy. [F f. It. (as MERCHANT)]

mercantilism /'mɜːkəntɪlɪz(ə)m/ n. an economic theory that money is the only form of wealth. [f. prec.]

Mercator /mɜː'keɪtə(r)/, Gerardus (Latinized name of Gerhard Kremer, 1512-94), Flemish geographer, inventor of a system of map-projection in which the globe is projected on to a cylinder and the meridians of longitude are at right angles to the parallels of latitude. His world map of 1659 shows a navigable north-west passage between Asia and America, and a large southern continent. This was immediately influential, whereas his more enduring projection was not adopted for many years.

mercenary /'mɜːsɪnərɪ/ adj. working merely for money or

other reward; hired. —*n.* a hired soldier in foreign service. —**mercenarily** *adv.* [f. L *mercenarius* (*merces* reward)]

mercer /ˈmɜːsə(r)/ *n.* a dealer in textile fabrics. [f. AF f. L *merx* goods]

mercerize /ˈmɜːsəraɪz/ *v.t.* to treat (cotton fabric or thread) with caustic alkali to give greater strength and lustre. [f. J. *Mercer*, alleged inventor of process (d. 1866)]

merchandise /ˈmɜːtʃəndaɪz/ *n.* the commodities of commerce; goods for sale. —*v.t./i.* to promote the sales of (goods etc.); to trade. [f. OF *marchandise* (as foll.)]

merchant /ˈmɜːtʃ(ə)nt/ *n.* **1.** a wholesale trader, especially with foreign countries. **2.** (*US & Sc.*) a retail trader. **3.** (*slang*) a person fond of an activity etc. —**merchant bank,** a bank whose main business is the providing of long-term credit and the financing of trading enterprises. **merchant navy,** shipping engaged in commerce. **merchant prince,** a wealthy merchant. **merchant ship,** a ship carrying merchandise. [f. OF *marchand* f. L *mercari* trade (as MERCER)]

merchantable *adj.* saleable. [f. prec.]

merchantman *n.* (*pl.* -**men**) a merchant ship.

Mercia /ˈmɜːʃə/ a kingdom that was founded in central England by the invading Angles in the 6th c. and became powerful under Offa in the second half of the 8th c. Its borders fluctuated considerably as a result of the endemic warfare of the period, and by the end of the 9th c. it had lost its separate identity. The name has been revived in 'West Mercia Authority', an area of police administration covering the counties of Hereford and Worcester, and Shropshire. —**Mercian** *adj. & n.* [L f. OE, = people of the marches (i.e. borders, with ref. to the border with Wales)]

merciful /ˈmɜːsɪfʊl/ *adj.* **1.** having, showing, or feeling mercy. **2.** giving relief from pain etc. —**mercifully** *adv.*, **mercifulness** *n.* [f. MERCY + -FUL]

merciless /ˈmɜːsɪlɪs/ *adj.* showing no mercy. —**mercilessly** *adv.*, **mercilessness** *n.* [f. MERCY + -LESS]

mercurial /mɜːˈkjʊərɪəl/ *adj.* **1.** (of a person) volatile, ready-witted. **2.** of or containing mercury. [f. OF or L (as foll.)]

Mercury /ˈmɜːkjʊrɪ/ **1.** (*Rom. myth.*) the god of eloquence, skill, trading, and thieving, the messenger of the gods, early identified with Hermes. **2.** (*Astron.*) the innermost planet of the solar system. Somewhat larger than the moon (its diameter is 4,878 km), it was discovered by the Mariner 10 space probe to have a heavily cratered surface. Early theories that its rotation period was the same as its orbital period, so that it always kept the same face turned towards the sun, are now known to be incorrect, but its 'day' of 58.65 days is precisely two-thirds the length of its 87.97-day 'year' because of the influence of tidal forces from the nearby sun, and daytime temperatures average 170 °C. There is no atmosphere, nor has the planet any satellites. [f. L *merx mercis* merchandise]

mercury /ˈmɜːkjʊrɪ/ *n.* a silvery-white heavy metallic element, symbol Hg, atomic number 80, liquid at room temperatures. Known to the ancient world, it has long been used in medicines and ointments, although recently its use has declined as its toxicity has become recognized. Its main use is now in batteries, switches, lamps, and other electrical equipment. It is also used in thermometers and barometers, and in alloys (amalgams) with other metals. It can occur in the uncombined state in nature, but its main source is the sulphide, cinnabar. Pollution of seas and lakes by mercury and its compounds has become a serious problem in recent years, although efforts are now being made to control it. —**mercuric** /-ˈkjʊərɪk/ *adj.*, **mercurous** *adj.* [f. prec. (Roman god)]

mercy /ˈmɜːsɪ/ *n.* **1.** refraining from inflicting punishment or pain on an offender or enemy etc. who is in one's power. **2.** a tendency to behave in this way. **3.** a merciful act; a thing to be thankful for. —**at the mercy of,** wholly in the power of; liable to danger or harm from. **mercy killing,** euthanasia. [f. OF f. L *merces* reward, later = pity, thanks]

mere[1] /mɪə(r)/ *attrib. adj.* that is solely or no more or better than what is specified. [f. AF f. L *merus* unmixed]

mere[2] /mɪə(r)/ *n. poetic* a lake. [OE]

Meredith /ˈmɛrədɪθ/, George (1828–1909), English novelist and poet. His finest volume of verse, *Modern Love* (1862), describes the disillusionment of married love; Meredith's first marriage, to Mary Ellen Nichols (daughter of T. L. Peacock), had not been happy, and she deserted him in 1857. During 1861–2 he lodged for a time with Swinburne

and Rossetti in Chelsea. His reputation rests on his novels which began with *The Ordeal of Richard Feverel* (1859); more successful were *Evan Harrington* (1861), largely autobiographical, the celebrated *The Egoist* (1879), and *Diana of the Crossways* (1885). He received much praise for his narrative skill and his intense psychological exploration, but the elliptic character of his prose has tended to obscure his genius.

merely *adv.* only, just. [f. MERE[1]]

meretricious /mɛrɪˈtrɪʃəs/ *adj.* showily attractive but cheap or insincere. —**meretriciously** *adv.*, **meretriciousness** *n.* [f. L (*meretrix* prostitute)]

merganser /mɜːˈɡænsə(r)/ *n.* a diving duck of the genus *Mergus* etc. [f. L *mergus* diver + *anser* goose)]

merge /mɜːdʒ/ *v.t./i.* **1.** to unite or combine into a whole. **2.** to pass slowly into something else; to blend or become blended. [f. L *mergere* dip]

merger /ˈmɜːdʒə(r)/ *n.* the combining of two commercial companies etc. into one. [f. AF (as prec.)]

meridian /məˈrɪdɪən/ *n.* **1.** a circle of constant longitude, passing through a given place and the terrestrial poles; a corresponding line on a map or the sky. **2.** prime, full splendour. [f. OF or L (*meridies* midday)]

meridional /məˈrɪdɪən(ə)l/ *adj.* **1.** of the south, especially of Europe, or its inhabitants. **2.** of a meridian. [f. OF f. L (as prec.)]

meringue /məˈræŋ/ *n.* a mixture of white of egg, sugar, etc., baked crisp. [F]

merino /məˈriːnəʊ/ *n.* (*pl.* -**os**) **1.** a variety of sheep with fine wool. **2.** a soft woollen yarn or fabric originally of merino wool. [Sp.]

merit /ˈmɛrɪt/ *n.* **1.** the quality of deserving to be praised, excellence. **2.** a feature or quality that deserves praise. —*v.t.* to deserve. —**Order of Merit,** an order, founded in 1902, for distinguished achievement. [f. L *meritum* (*merēri* deserve)]

meritocracy /mɛrɪˈtɒkrəsɪ/ *n.* government by persons selected for their merit. [as prec. + -CRACY]

meritorious /mɛrɪˈtɔːrɪəs/ *adj.* having merit, praiseworthy. —**meritoriously** *adv.*, **meritoriousness** *n.* [f. L (as MERIT)]

Merlin /ˈmɜːlɪn/ (in Arthurian legend) a magician who aided and supported King Arthur. Geoffrey of Monmouth (12th c.) identifies him with a boy (Ambrosius), without mortal sire, who, according to Nennius in his *Historia Britonum* (*c.*796), interpreted an omen for the British king Vortigern.

merlin /ˈmɜːlɪn/ *n.* a kind of small falcon (*Falco columbarius*). [f. AF]

merlon /ˈmɜːlən/ *n.* the solid part of an embattled parapet, between two embrasures (ill. CASTLES). [F, f. It. *merlone* (*merlo* battlement)]

mermaid /ˈmɜːmeɪd/ *n.* a legendary sea-creature with a woman's head and trunk and a fish's tail. The mermaid legend involves the concept of an ideal but fatal love, embodied in a hauntingly beautiful, mysterious, and unattainable feminine being; its persistence is not surprising. For centuries there were reports of sightings in many parts of the world until in the 18th c. scepticism set in. In Victorian times stuffed mermaids of regulation design, usually constructed by enterprising Japanese fishermen from the trunk of a monkey and the skin of a fish, were exhibited at fairs. Ancient Babylonian and Semitic mythologies include fish-deities (the male seems earlier than the female), and the Tritons were the mermen of Greek (or rather, pre-Greek) mythology, but all these are a long way from the beautiful mermaid who beguiles sailors to their destruction. If a real animal is sought as the basis of the tradition credit usually goes to the manatee and the dugong, because of the pectoral position of the breasts and the horizontally flattened tail, or (in colder latitudes) to one of the seal family, but to be mistaken for a human form these would have to be seen at a considerable distance. [f. MERE[2] in obs. sense 'sea' + MAID]

Merovingian /mɛrəˈvɪndʒɪən/ *n.* a member of the Frankish dynasty who created a kingdom in what is now France in the 5th c. and (after feuding had weakened royal authority) were overthrown in the mid-8th c., to be replaced by the Carolingians. —*adj.* of this dynasty. [f. F f. L *Meroveus* name of reputed founder]

merry *adj.* joyous, full of laughter or gaiety; (*colloq.*) slightly tipsy. —**make merry,** to be festive. **merry-go-round** *n.* a revolving machine with horses, cars, etc., for riding on at a fair etc., a revolving device in a playground, a cycle of bustling activities. **merry-making** *n.* festivity. —**merrily** *adv.*, **merriment** *n.* [OE (as MIRTH)]

Mersey /ˈmɜːzɪ/ an English river rising in the Peak district and flowing into the Irish Sea near Liverpool.

Merseyside /ˈmɜːzɪsaɪd/ a metropolitan county of NW England.

mesa /ˈmeɪsə/ *n.* (*US*) a high tableland with steep sides. [Sp., = table]

mésalliance /meɪˈzælɪɑ̃s/ *n.* marriage with a social inferior. [F., = MISALLIANCE]

mescal /ˈmeskæl/ *n.* the peyote cactus. —**mescal buttons**, its disc-shaped dried tops. [f. Sp. f. Nahuatl]

mescaline /ˈmeskəliːn/ *n.* a hallucinogenic alkaloid present in mescal buttons. [f. prec.]

Mesdames *pl.* of MADAME; also used as *pl.* of MRS.

Mesdemoiselles *pl.* of MADEMOISELLE.

mesembryanthemum /mɪzembrɪˈænθɪməm/ *n.* a plant of the genus *Mesembryanthemum*, with flowers that are open in the middle of the day. [f. Gk *mesēmbria* noon + *anthemon* flower]

mesh *n.* **1.** the open spaces between the threads or wires in a net, sieve, wire screen, etc. **2.** network fabric. **3.** (in *pl.*) a network; a trap or snare. —*v.t./i.* **1.** (of toothed wheels) to engage with another or others. **2.** to be harmonious. **3.** to catch in a net (*lit.* or *fig.*). —**in mesh**, (of the teeth of wheels) engaged. [f. MDu.]

mesmerize /ˈmezməraɪz/ *v.t.* to hypnotize (see HYPNO-SIS); to fascinate, to dominate the attention or will of. —**mesmeric** /-ˈmerɪk/ *adj.*, **mesmerism** *n.* [f. A. *Mesmer*, Austrian physician (d. 1815)]

meso- /mesə-/ *in comb.* middle, intermediate. [f. Gk *mesos* middle]

Meso-America the central region of America, from northern Mexico to Nicaragua, especially as a region of American-Indian cultures before the arrival of the Spaniards. —**Meso-American** *adj.* & *n.*

mesolithic /mesəˈlɪθɪk/ *adj.* of the transitional period between the palaeolithic and neolithic, especially in Europe, where it falls between the end of the last glacial period (mid-9th millennium BC) and the beginnings of agriculture (see NEOLITHIC). The period is characterized by the use of microliths and the first domestication of any animal (the dog). [f. MESO- + Gk *lithos* stone]

mesomorph /ˈmesəmɔːf/ *n.* a person with a compact muscular build of body (see ECTOMORPH). [f. MESO- + Gk *morphē* form]

meson /ˈmiːzɒn/ *n.* an unstable elementary particle intermediate in mass between a proton and an electron. [alt. of earlier *mesotron* (MESO-)]

mesopause /ˈmesəpɔːz/ *n.* the boundary between the mesosphere and the thermosphere, where the temperature stops decreasing with height and starts to increase (ill. WEATHER).

Mesopotamia /mesəpəˈteɪmɪə/ a region of SW Asia lying between the rivers Tigris and Euphrates. Its alluvial plains were the site of the ancient civilizations of Sumer, Babylon, and Assyria, and now lies within Iraq. —**Mesopotamian** *adj.* & *n.* [f. Gk *mesos* middle, *potamos* river]

mesosphere /ˈmesəsfɪə(r)/ *n.* the region of the earth's atmosphere from the top of the stratosphere to an altitude of about 80 km (ill. WEATHER).

Mesozoic /mesəˈzəʊɪk/ *adj.* of the geological era between the Palaeozoic and Cainozoic, comprising the Triassic, Jurassic, and Cretaceous periods, and lasting from about 248 to 65 million years ago. It was a time of abundant vegetation and saw the dominance of the reptiles, although by its close they were being rapidly replaced by the mammals. —*n.* this era. [f. Gk *mesos* middle + *zōion* animal]

mess *n.* **1.** a dirty or untidy state of things; an untidy collection of things; something spilt. **2.** a difficult or confused situation, trouble. **3.** a disagreeable substance or concoction; excreta. **4.** (*colloq.*) a person who looks untidy, dirty, or slovenly. **5.** a group of people who take meals together, especially in the armed services; the room where such meals are taken; a meal so taken. **6.** a portion of liquid or pulpy food. —*v.t./i.* **1.** to make untidy or dirty. **2.** to muddle or bungle (often with *up*). **3.** to potter or fool *about* or *around*; to tinker. **4.** to take one's meals with a military or other group. —**make a mess of**, to bungle. —**mess-jacket** *n.* a short close-fitting coat worn at mess. **mess-kit** *n.* a soldier's cooking and eating utensils. [f. OF f. L *missus* course at dinner (*mittere* send)]

message /ˈmesɪdʒ/ *n.* **1.** a spoken or written communication sent or transmitted from one person to another. **2.** an inspired or significant communication from a prophet, writer, preacher, etc. —**get the message**, (*colloq.*) to understand what is meant. [f. OF, ult. f. L *mittere* send]

messenger /ˈmesɪndʒə(r)/ *n.* one who carries a message. [as prec.]

Messiaen /ˈmesiɑ̃/, Olivier (1908–), French composer, organist, and teacher. His music, which is amongst the most influential and idiosyncratic of this century, is compounded from his deep Catholic faith, his celebration of human love, and his love of nature. In organ music he makes special use of acoustic reverberations and contrasts of timbres; his interest in Indian music influenced the massive *Turangalîla-symphonie* (1946-8). Birdsong is also a major feature (he has notated the songs of all French birds).

Messiah /mɪˈsaɪə/ *n.* **1.** the expected deliverer and ruler of the Jewish people, whose coming was prophesied in the Old Testament. **2.** Christ, regarded by Christians as this. **3.** a liberator of oppressed people. [f. OF, ult. f. Heb., = anointed]

Messianic /mesɪˈænɪk/ *adj.* of the Messiah; inspired by hope or belief in a Messiah. [f. F (as prec.)]

Messieurs *pl.* of MONSIEUR.

Messina /meˈsiːnə/ a city and harbour of NE Sicily, situated on the **Strait of Messina** which separates Sicily from Italy.

Messrs /ˈmesəz/ *n.* used as *pl.* of MR, especially as a prefix to the name of a firm or to a list of men's names. [abbr. of prec.]

messuage /ˈmeswɪdʒ/ *n.* (*Law*) a dwelling-house with outbuildings and land. [f. AF, perh. alt. of *mesnage* dwelling (as MÉNAGE)]

messy *adj.* **1.** untidy or dirty. **2.** causing or accompanied by a mess. **3.** difficult to deal with. —**messily** *adv.*, **messiness** *n.* [f. MESS]

met[1] *adj.* (*colloq.*) **1.** meteorological. **2.** metropolitan. —**the Met**, the Meteorological Office; the Metropolitan Opera House (New York). [abbr.]

met[2] *past & p.p.* of MEET[1].

meta- /metə/ *prefix* denoting a position or condition behind, after, beyond or transcending (*metacarpus*), or a change of position or condition (*metabolism*). [Gk (*meta* with, after)]

metabolism /mɪˈtæbəlɪz(ə)m/ *n.* the sum total of the organized chemical reactions taking place in a living cell, tissue, or organism in order to maintain life. It consists of *anabolism*, the building up of tissue etc. by the construction of the proteins, carbohydrates, and fats from which it is made, and *catabolism*, the chemical breakdown of complex substances and the consequent production of waste matter. —**metabolic** /metəˈbɒlɪk/ *adj.* [f. Gk *metabolē* change (META-, *ballō* throw)]

metabolize /mɪˈtæbəlaɪz/ *v.t.* to process (food) in metabolism. [f. prec.]

metacarpus /metəˈkɑːpəs/ *n.* (*pl.* **-pi** /-paɪ/) the part of the hand between the wrist and the fingers; the set of bones in this (ill. BODY 1). —**metacarpal** *adj.* [f. Gk (as META-, CARPUS)]

metal /ˈmet(ə)l/ *n.* **1.** any of a large class of elements which in general can take the form of opaque solids having a characteristic lustre (see below); an alloy of these. **2.** (in *pl.*) the rails of a railway-line; road-metal (see ROAD). —*adj.* made of metal. —*v.t.* (**-ll-**) **1.** to furnish or fit with metal. **2.** to make or mend (a road) with road-metal. [f. OF or L f. Gk *metallon* mine]

Metals have traditionally been defined as substances which exhibit some or all of the following properties: high density, malleability, ductility, fusibility, strength, hardness, opacity, a characteristic lustre, and an ability to conduct heat and electricity. Because no single combination of these properties applies to all metals but to no other substances, a strict definition of a metal in terms of such properties is not possible. This is partly because many new elements with varying properties have been discovered in recent centuries and classified among the metals. In the ancient world only seven metallic elements were known—gold, silver, copper, iron, lead, tin, and mercury. The modern theory of metals circumvents the problem of definition by describing as a metal any substance in which each atom 'loses' one or more orbiting electrons, which are then able to move freely throughout the metal. This so-called 'sea' of mobile electrons can be shown to account for most of the properties of metals listed above. By this definition about three-quarters of the 105 known elements are metals when uncombined, although many are too reactive to exist in a stable state in air.

metallic /mɪˈtælɪk/ *adj.* **1.** of metal; characteristic of metals. **2.** sounding like struck metal. —**metallically** *adv.* [f. F f. L f. Gk (as prec.)]

metalliferous /metəˈlɪfərəs/ *adj.* (of rocks etc.) containing metal. [f. L (as METAL, -FEROUS)]

metallize /ˈmetəlaɪz/ *v.t.* **1.** to render metallic. **2.** to coat with a thin layer of metal. —**metallization** /-ˈzeɪʃ(ə)n/ *n.* [f. METAL]

metallography /metəˈlɒɡrəfɪ/ *n.* the descriptive science of metals. [f. METAL + -GRAPHY]

metallurgy /mɪˈtælədʒɪ, ˈmetəlɜːdʒɪ/ *n.* **1.** the science of the properties of metals. **2.** the art of working metals, especially of extracting metals from ores. —**metallurgical** /metəˈlɜːdʒɪk(ə)l/ *adj.*, **metallurgist** *n.* [f. Gk (as METAL, -ourgia working)]

metamorphic /metəˈmɔːfɪk/ *adj.* **1.** of or characterized by metamorphism. **2.** (of rock) that has undergone structural, chemical, or mineralogical change by natural agencies, especially heat and pressure (cf. IGNEOUS, SEDIMENTARY), as in the transformation of limestone into marble. The term does not include alterations caused by weathering or consolidation of sediments. [f. META- + Gk *morphē* form]

metamorphism /metəˈmɔːfɪz(ə)m/ *n.* the process of metamorphic change in rock. [f. prec. + -ISM]

metamorphose /metəˈmɔːfəʊz/ *v.t.* to change into a new form; to change the nature of. [f. F (as foll.)]

metamorphosis /metəˈmɔːfəsɪs, -ˈfəʊsɪs/ *n.* (*pl.* -**oses** /-siːz/) a change of form, especially by magic or natural development (ill. INSECTS; a change of character, conditions, etc. [L f. Gk (as METAMORPHIC)]

metaphor /ˈmetəfə(r)/ *n.* an application of a name or descriptive term or phrase to an object or action where it is not literally applicable (e.g. *a glaring error*). —**metaphorical** /-ˈfɒrɪk(ə)l/ *adj.*, **metaphorically** *adv.* [f. F or L f. Gk (*metapherō* transfer)]

metaphysical /metəˈfɪzɪk(ə)l/ *adj.* **1.** of or involving metaphysics. **2.** based on abstract reasoning, over-subtle. —**metaphysical poets**, a classification of 17th-c. poets, addicted to fanciful conceits and far-fetched imagery, generally taken to include John Donne (regarded as the founder of the 'school'), George Herbert, Richard Crashaw, Henry Vaughan, Andrew Marvell, and Thomas Traherne. The term is misleading since none of these poets is seriously interested in metaphysics and, further, they have little in common. Their reputation dwindled after the Restoration with the new taste for clarity and the impatience with figurative language. Their dramatic revival was delayed until after the First World War; the revaluation of metaphysical poetry was a major feature of the rewriting of English literary history in the first half of the 20th c. [f. foll.]

metaphysics /metəˈfɪzɪks/ *n.pl.* (usu. treated as *sing.*) **1.** the branch of speculative inquiry that deals with such concepts as being, knowing, substance, cause, identity, time, space, etc. It discusses, for example, whether there are only minds and their states (*idealism*) or only physical things (*materialism*), or both mental properties and physical things, each distinct from the other. **2.** (*pop.*) abstract or subtle talk, mere theory. [f. OF ult. f. Gk *ta meta ta phusica*, the title applied, at least from the 1st c. AD, to the 13 books of Aristotle dealing with questions of ontology. The title doubtless originally referred to the position which these books occupied in the received arrangement of Aristotle's writings, being placed after (*meta*) the *Physics* (i.e. treatises on natural science), but it was from an early period used as a name for the branch of study treated in these books and hence came to be misinterpreted as meaning 'the science of things transcending what is physical or natural'.]

metastasis /meˈtæstəsɪs/ *n.* (*pl.* -**ases** /-əsiːz/) the transfer of disease etc. from one part of the body to another. [L f. Gk, = removal, change]

metatarsus /metəˈtɑːsəs/ *n.* (*pl.* -**si** /-saɪ/) the part of the foot between the ankle and the toes; the set of bones in this (ill. BODY 1). —**metatarsal** *adj.* [as META- + TARSUS]

mete /miːt/ *v.t.* to allot or deal (a punishment, reward, etc.). [OE (as MEET²)]

meteor /ˈmiːtɪə(r)/ *n.* a bright moving body formed by a small mass of matter from outer space rendered incandescent by friction with the air as it passes through the earth's atmosphere. [f. Gk (*meteōros* high in the air)]

meteoric /miːtɪˈɒrɪk/ *adj.* **1.** of meteors. **2.** like a meteor in

brilliance, sudden appearance, or transience. —**meteorically** *adv.* [f. prec.]

meteorite /ˈmiːtɪəraɪt/ *n.* a fallen meteor, a fragment of rock or metal from outer space, of sufficient size to survive a fiery passage through the atmosphere and reach the surface of the earth. Rarely more than a few pounds in weight, some have been of much greater mass, their impact leaving a crater, of which perhaps the most famous is Meteor Crater, Flagstaff, Arizona. [f. METEOR]

meteoroid /ˈmiːtɪərɔɪd/ *n.* a body moving through space, of the same nature as those which become visible as meteors. [as prec.]

meteorological /miːtɪərəˈlɒdʒɪk(ə)l/ *adj.* of meteorology. —**Meteorological Office**, a government department providing weather forecasts etc. [as foll.]

meteorology /miːtɪəˈrɒlədʒɪ/ *n.* the study of the phenomena of the atmosphere, especially for weather forecasting. —**meteorologist** *n.* [f. Gk (as METEOR, -LOGY)]

meter /ˈmiːtə(r)/ *n.* an instrument for recording the amount of a substance supplied or used, time spent, distance travelled, etc. —*v.t.* to measure by a meter. [f. METE]

-meter /-mɪtə(r)/ *suffix* forming names of automatic measuring instruments (*thermometer*, *voltmeter*) or of lines of verse with a specified number of measures (*pentameter*). [f. Gk *metron* measure]

methane /ˈmiːθeɪn/ *n.* an inflammable hydrocarbon gas of the paraffin series. [f. METHYL]

methinks /mɪˈθɪŋks/ *v.i.* (*impers.*) (*past* **methought** /mɪˈθɔːt/) (*archaic*) it seems to me. [OE (as ME¹, THINK)]

method /ˈmeθəd/ *n.* **1.** a procedure or way of doing something. **2.** orderliness; the orderly arrangement of ideas. **3.** a theory and practice of acting in which the actor seeks to achieve a true interpretation of his part by mentally identifying himself with the character he is playing. Based on the system evolved by Stanislavsky, it came into prominence in the USA in the 1930s and was most successful in the work of modern American playwrights such as Tennessee Williams. [f. F or L f. Gk *methodos* pursuit of knowledge (META-, *hodos* way)]

methodical /mɪˈθɒdɪk(ə)l/ *adj.* characterized by method or order. —**methodically** *adv.* [f. L f. Gk (as prec.)]

Methodist /ˈmeθədɪst/ *n.* a member of a Protestant denomination originating in an 18th-c. evangelistic movement which grew out of a religious society (nicknamed the 'Holy Club') established within the Church of England (from which it formally separated in 1791) by John and Charles Wesley at Oxford. Its theology is Arminian, and its ordained ministry usually presbyterian; its governing body is the Conference, composed of ministers and laymen. How the term 'Methodist' came to be applied to the Wesleys' followers is uncertain. —**Methodism** *n.* [f. METHOD]

Methodius /mɪˈθəʊdɪəs/, St (*c.*815-85), brother of St Cyril (see CYRIL²).

methodology /meθəˈdɒlədʒɪ/ *n.* **1.** the science of method. **2.** the body of methods used in an activity. [f. METHOD + -LOGY]

methought *past* of METHINKS.

meths *n.* (*colloq.*) methylated spirit. [abbr.]

Methuselah /mɪˈθjuːzələ/ a patriarch, grandfather of Noah, said (Gen. 5: 27) to have lived 969 years.

methyl /ˈmeθɪl, ˈmiːθaɪl/ *n.* the chemical radical present in methane etc. —**methyl alcohol**, a colourless volatile inflammable liquid. [G or F, ult. f. Gk *methu* wine + *hulē* wood]

methylated /ˈmeθɪleɪtɪd/ *adj.* mixed or impregnated with methyl alcohol. —**methylated spirit(s)**, alcohol so treated to make it unfit for drinking and so exempt from duty. [f. prec.]

meticulous /mɪˈtɪkjʊləs/ *adj.* giving great or excessive attention to details, very careful and precise. —**meticulously** *adv.*, **meticulousness** *n.* [f. L (*metus* fear)]

métier /ˈmeɪtjeɪ/ *n.* one's trade, profession, or field of activity; one's forte. [F (as MINISTRY)]

Metonic cycle /mɪˈtɒnɪk/ a period of 19 years (235 lunar months), after the lapse of which the new and full moons return to the same day of the year. It was the basis of the ancient Greek calendar and is still used for calculating movable feasts such as Easter. [f. Gk *Metōn*, Athenian astronomer (5th c. BC)]

metonymy /mɪˈtɒnɪmɪ/ *n.* substitution of the name of an attribute or adjunct for that of the thing meant (e.g. *crown* for *king*). [f. L f. Gk (META-, *onoma* name)]

metope /'metəʊp/ *n.* a square space between triglyphs in a Doric frieze (ill. TEMPLES). [f. L f. Gk (as META-, *opē* hole for beam-end)]

metre[1] /'miːtə(r)/ *n.* any form of poetic rhythm, determined by the character and number of feet; a metrical group. [OE, ult. f. Gk *metron* measure]

metre[2] /'miːtə(r)/ *n.* the base unit of length (symbol m), defined in 1983 as the length of the path travelled by light in a vacuum during a time interval of 1/299 792 458 of a second. When the metric system (see entry) was standardized careful measurements were made of the polar quadrant of the earth through Paris, and the metre was originally defined as one ten millionth part of this arc. To overcome the impracticality of the definition the French Academy of Sciences used a platinum bar whose length was equal to the theoretical length, and this (despite an imperfection in its calculation) was used for the next 90 years. In 1889 the International Metre was redefined as the distance between two lines engraved on an alloy bar, and this held until 1960 when the metre was defined in terms of the wavelength of the krypton-86 atom; it was redefined again in 1983. [f. F *mètre* (as prec.)]

metric /'metrɪk/ *adj.* **1.** of or based on the metre as a unit. **2.** metrical. —**metric system,** see separate entry. —**metrically** *adv.* [f. F *métrique* (as prec.)]

-metric *suffix* (also **-metrical**) forming adjectives from nouns in *-meter* or *-metry*. [f. F f. L (as foll.)]

metrical /'metrɪk(ə)l/ *adj.* **1.** of or composed in metre. **2.** of or involving measurement. —**metrically** *adv.* [f. L f. Gk (as METRE)]

metricate /'metrɪkeɪt/ *v.t./i.* to change or adapt to the metric system. —**metrication** /-'keɪʃ(ə)n/ *n.* [f. METRIC]

metric system a decimal measuring-system with the metre, litre, and gram as the units of length, capacity, and weight or mass. It is the culmination of a long endeavour to devise a system which is exact, convenient, based on reliable natural units, and employs a rational notation. The system, first proposed by Gabriel Mouton of Lyons in 1670, was based on two natural units—the second, which is a sexagesimal fraction of the day, and the metre, which was intended to be a decimal fraction of a meridional quadrant of the earth's surface. It was standardized in France under the Republican government in the 1790s and its use was made compulsory there in 1801; decimal measures based on the metre were introduced for areas and volumes. Napoleon's conquests facilitated the spread of the system to many European countries; it is still not adopted for general use in the USA. The most recent development of the metric system is the *Système International* (see SI).

metronome /'metrənəʊm/ *n.* an instrument that sounds a click at a selected interval, used to indicate tempo while practising music. [f. Gk *metron* measure + *nomos* law]

metropolis /mɪ'trɒpəlɪs/ *n.* the chief city of a county or region, a capital. [L f. Gk (*mētēr* mother, *polis* city)]

metropolitan /metrə'pɒlɪt(ə)n/ *adj.* **1.** of a metropolis. **2.** of or forming the mother country as distinct from colonies etc. —*n.* **1.** a bishop with authority over the bishops of a province. **2.** an inhabitant of a metropolis. —**metropolitan county,** each of the six conurbations (other than Greater London) established in England by the local government reorganization of 1974, with powers analogous to those of counties. **metropolitan district,** each of the areas into which a metropolitan county is divided.

Metropolitan Museum of Art an important museum of art and archaeology, in New York, founded in 1870. [f. L f. Gk (as prec.)]

-metry /-mɪtrɪ/ *suffix* forming names of procedures and systems involving measurement (*geometry*). [f. Gk *-metria* (as METRE)]

Metternich /'metənɪx/, Prince Clemens Wenzel Lothar Metternich-Winneburg (1773–1859), Austrian statesman. He was one of the organizers of the Congress of Vienna in 1814–15 which devised the settlement of Europe after the Napoleonic Wars, and thereafter he presided over the maintenance of order and stability in Europe, espousing a particularly reactionary brand of conservatism, until forced to resign by the Vienna mob during the revolutionary disturbances of 1848.

mettle *n.* quality or strength of character, courage. —**on one's mettle,** incited to do one's best. [var. of METAL]

mettlesome *adj.* spirited. [f. prec. + -SOME]

Meuse /mɜːz/ a river of NE France, Belgium, and the Netherlands, flowing into the North Sea.

mew[1] *n.* the characteristic cry of a cat. —*v.i.* to utter a mew. [imit.]

mew[2] *n.* a gull. [OE]

mews /mjuːz/ *n.pl.* (treated as *sing.*) a set of stables round an open yard or lane, now often converted into dwellings. [orig. sing. *mew* = cage for hawks while moulting, f. OF f. L *mutare* change; orig. of royal stables on site of hawks' cages at Charing Cross in London]

Mexico /'meksɪkəʊ/ a country in Central America with extensive coastlines on the Atlantic and Pacific Oceans, bordered by the USA to the north; pop. (1980) 67,383,000; official language, Spanish; capital, Mexico City, pop. (est.) 16,000,000. Agriculture is heavily dependent on irrigation. Mexico is now a major oil-producing country and recent industrialization, centred upon these oil resources, has revolutionized its economy, but the country has massive international debts. The Aztecs are said to have fulfilled an ancient prophecy when they saw an eagle perched on a cactus eating a snake; on this site they founded a city, and the symbol of the eagle, snake, and cactus is the national emblem of Mexico. The centre of Aztec and Mayan civilization, Mexico was conquered and colonized by the Spanish in the early 16th c., remaining under Spanish rule until independence was achieved in 1821; a republic was established three years later. Texas rebelled and broke away in 1836, while all the remaining territory north of the Rio Grande was lost to the USA in the Mexican War of 1846–8. Half a century of political instability, including a brief French occupation and imperial rule by Maximilian (1864–7) ended with the establishment of Diaz as president in the 1870s, but civil war broke out again in 1910–20, leading to partial reform of the political organization. Mexico is now a one-party State. Mexico City suffered a severe earthquake in 1985. —**Mexican** *adj.* & *n.* [f. *Mexitli*, Aztec war-god]

Meyerbeer /'maɪəbɪə(r)/, Giacomo (Jakob) (1791–1864), German-Jewish composer, who settled in Paris. His collaboration with the librettist Augustin Scribe resulted in the grand operas *Robert le Diable* (1831), *Les Huguenots* (1836), and *Le Prophète* (1849), which placed him firmly as the leading opera composer in France. He gave Wagner financial and other help in getting his early operas performed, and had some influence on his orchestration, but in later years Wagner attacked him in a pamphlet *Judaism in Music*. Revivals of Meyerbeer's operas have revealed virtues which were his alone.

mezzanine /'metsəniːn/ *n.* an extra storey between two others, usually between the ground and first floors. [F f. It. (*mezzano* middle, as MEDIAN)]

mezzo /'metsəʊ/ *adv.* (esp. *Mus.*) half, moderately. —**mezzo forte,** fairly loud. **mezzo piano,** fairly soft. **mezzo-soprano,** a voice between soprano and contralto, a singer with this voice. [It. f. L *medius* middle]

mezzotint /'metsəʊtɪnt/ *n.* **1.** a method of engraving using a uniformly roughened plate, on which the rough areas give shaded parts and the areas scraped smooth give light. This technique was much used in the 17th, 18th, and early 19th c. for the reproduction of paintings. It was invented by Ludwig von Siegen of Utrecht *c.*1640, and introduced to England by Prince Rupert (nephew of Charles I) who demonstrated it to Evelyn, who publicized it in his *Sculptura* (1662). **2.** a print produced by this. [f. It. (as prec. + TINT)]

mf *abbr.* mezzo forte.

Mg *symbol* magnesium.

mg *abbr.* milligram(s).

Mgr. *abbr.* Monsignor; Monseigneur.

MHz *abbr.* megahertz.

mi var. of ME[2].

miaow /mɪ'aʊ/ *n.* the cry of a cat, a mew. —*v.i.* to make this cry. [imit.]

miasma /mɪ'æzmə, maɪ-/ *n.* (*pl.* **-mata**) an infectious or noxious escape of air etc. [Gk, = defilement (*miainō* pollute)]

mica /'maɪkə/ *n.* a kind of mineral found as small glittering scales in granite etc. or in crystals separable into thin transparent plates. [L, = crumb]

Micah /'maɪkə/ **1.** a Hebrew minor prophet. **2.** a book of the Old Testament bearing his name, foretelling the destruction of Samaria and of Jerusalem.

Micawber /mɪ'kɔːbə(r)/ *n.* a person who is perpetually hoping that something good will turn up while making no positive effort. —**Micawberish** *adj.*, **Micawberism** *n.* [character in Dickens's novel *David Copperfield*, for whom the model was Dickens's father]

mice *pl.* of MOUSE.

Michael /ˈmaɪk(ə)l/, St, one of the archangels, usually represented slaying a dragon (see Rev. 12:7). Feast day, 29 Sept. (Michaelmas Day).

Michaelmas /ˈmɪkəlməs/ *n.* the feast of St Michael, 29 Sept. —**Michaelmas daisy**, an aster flowering in autumn. **Michaelmas term**, the university and law term beginning near Michaelmas. [f. St *Michael* + MASS²]

Michelangelo Buonarroti /maɪk(ə)lˈændʒələʊ bəʊnəˈrɒti/ (1475-1564), Italian sculptor, painter, architect, and poet. Essentially self-taught, he was apprenticed to Ghirlandaio and enjoyed the patronage of Lorenzo de Medici. In Rome (1496-1501) he carved the two statues which established his fame—the *Bacchus* and the *Pietà*; the latter is his only signed work, tragically expressive, beautiful, and harmonious. The years 1501-5 in Florence mark a great creative period epitomized by his marble *David*, which embodies civic virtue and Herculean heroism. In Rome again from 1505 his greatest works were executed under papal patronage. The decoration of the Sistine ceiling (1508-12) marks a peak in his *œuvre* and assured him a place as a leader in the High Renaissance. In 1536-41 he painted the *Last Judgement* on the east wall of the Sistine Chapel, its elongated forms predicting the mannerist movement. His architectural achievements included the directing, from 1546, of rebuilding at St Peter's and designing its great dome. His poetry, first published by his grandnephew in 1623, offers an insight into Michelangelo the man, as he explores his faith, art, and the notion of love.

He embodied the perfect multi-talented Renaissance man. An exponent of Neoplatonic ideals, he was fêted by popes, enjoying success and power in his own time, and he represented a new status of artist, no longer a mere craftsman as in medieval times. He was the epitome of 'the artist as genius', and his influence on later artists has been profound.

Michelozzo /miːkeˈlɒtsəʊ/ di Bartolommeo (1396-1472), Florentine architect and sculptor. He was in partnership with Ghiberti (from *c.*1420) and then Donatello (1423-38), and led a revival of interest in Roman architecture. He was the favourite architect of Cosimo de Medici for whom he built, amongst other works, the Medici Palace (1444-*c.*1459). One of the most important palace designs of the quattrocento, it constantly influenced later architecture in Florence.

Michelson /ˈmɪtʃ(ə)ls(ə)n/, Albert Abraham (1852-1931), American physicist who specialized in precision measurement in experimental physics, for which he became in 1907 the first American to be awarded a Nobel Prize. He performed a number of accurate determinations of the velocity of light, begun in 1878, but his crucial experiment, which demonstrated that the hypothetical 'ether' (postulated as the medium through which light and other electromagnetic waves travelled) did not exist, was first performed in 1881, and again in 1887 with the chemist Morley using improved apparatus. The Michelson-Morley result contradicted Newtonian physics and was eventually resolved in 1905 by Einstein's special theory of relativity. In 1920 Michelson used similar apparatus for determining the diameter of the star Betelgeuse.

Michigan /ˈmɪʃɪgən/ a State in the north-western USA, with its northern boundary formed by Lakes Huron and Superior. Explored by the French in the 17th c., it was ceded to Britain in 1763 and acquired by the USA in 1783, becoming the 26th State in 1837; capital, Lansing. **Lake Michigan**, one of the five Great Lakes of North America and the only one wholly within the USA. The cities of Chicago and Milwaukee are on its shores.

mickey *n.* (*slang*) **take the mickey (out of),** to tease or mock. [orig. unkn.]

Mickey Mouse a Disney cartoon character, who first appeared as Mortimer Mouse in 1927, becoming Mickey in 1928. For the next decade he remained one of the staple figures of Disney's growing reputation. Disney himself always spoke the sound-track for Mickey's voice.

mickle *adj.* much, great. —*n.* a large amount. (The proverb *many a mickle makes a muckle* is an error for *many a little* (or *pickle*) *makes a mickle.*) [f. ON]

micro- /maɪkrəʊ-/ *in comb.* **1.** small. **2.** one millionth of (*microgram, microsecond*). [f. Gk *mikros* small]

microbe /ˈmaɪkrəʊb/ *n.* a micro-organism, especially a bacterium causing disease or fermentation. —**microbial** /-ˈrəʊbɪ(ə)l/ *adj.*, **microbially** *adv.* [F f. Gk (as MICRO-, *bios* life)]

microbiology /maɪkrəʊbaɪˈɒlədʒɪ/ *n.* the study of micro-organisms.

microchip /ˈmaɪkrəʊtʃɪp/ *n.* a tiny piece of semiconductor carrying many electrical circuits.

microcircuit /ˈmaɪkrəʊsɜːkɪt/ *n.* an integrated circuit or other very small electrical circuit.

microclimate /ˈmaɪkrəʊklaɪmət/ *n.* the climate of a small area.

microcomputer /maɪkrəʊkəmˈpjuːtə(r)/ *n.* a small computer in which the central processor is a microprocessor.

microcosm /ˈmaɪkrəkɒz(ə)m/ *n.* **1.** a complex thing, especially man, viewed as an epitome of the universe. **2.** a miniature representation. —**microcosmic** /-ˈkɒzmɪk/ *adj.* [f. F or L f. Gk *mikros kosmos* little world]

microdot /ˈmaɪkrəʊdɒt/ *n.* a photograph of a document etc. reduced to the size of a dot.

microelectronics /maɪkrəʊiːlekˈtrɒnɪks/ *n.* the design, manufacture, and use of microcircuits.

microfiche /ˈmaɪkrəʊfiːʃ/ *n.* (*pl.* same) a small sheet of film bearing tiny photographs of pages of documents etc. [f. MICRO- + F *fiche* slip of paper]

microfilm /ˈmaɪkrəʊfɪlm/ *n.* a length of film bearing a microphotograph of a document etc. —*v.t.* to record on this.

microlight /ˈmaɪkrəʊlaɪt/ *n.* a kind of motorized hang-glider. [f. MICRO- + LIGHT²]

microlith /ˈmaɪkrəʊlɪθ/ *n.* a very small worked flint, usually mounted on a piece of bone, wood, or horn as part of a composite tool, characteristic especially of mesolithic industries in Europe. —**microlithic** *adj.* [f. MICRO- + Gk *lithos* stone]

micrometer /maɪˈkrɒmɪtə(r)/ *n.* an instrument for measuring small lengths or angles. [f. MICRO- + -METER]

micron /ˈmaɪkrɒn/ *n.* one millionth of a metre. [Gk, neut. of *mikros* small]

Micronesia /maɪkrəʊˈniːzɪə/ part of the western Pacific Ocean including the Mariana, Caroline, and Marshall Islands and Kiribati.

micro-organism /maɪkrəʊˈɔːgənɪz(ə)m/ *n.* an organism not visible to the naked eye, e.g. a bacterium or virus.

microphone /ˈmaɪkrəfəʊn/ *n.* an instrument for converting sound-waves into electrical energy which may be reconverted into sound elsewhere. [f. MICRO- + Gk *phōnē* sound]

microprocessor /ˈmaɪkrəʊprəʊsesə(r)/ *n.* a miniature computer, or a unit of this, consisting of one or more microchips.

microscope /ˈmaɪkrəskəʊp/ *n.* an instrument magnifying small objects by means of a lens or lenses so as to reveal details invisible to the naked eye (ill. LIGHT). So-called 'simple microscopes' of one lens (such as those used by Leeuwenhoek, or the modern magnifying glass) were used as early as the 15th c. for examining insects. The compound microscope, which first appeared at the beginning of the 17th c., consists of at least two lenses, mounted in a tube: an 'objective' lens, placed near the specimen, which produces an enlarged image of it, and an eyepiece lens which magnifies this image. Compound microscopes thus permit much greater magnification, but the early instruments also produced distortions of colour or shape in the image, and these problems were fully overcome only in the 19th c. The wave nature of light itself sets a limit to the power of the light microscope to discriminate between points which are closer together than the wavelength of light; beyond this limit an electron microscope (see entry) has to be employed. [f. MICRO- + -SCOPE]

microscopic /maɪkrəˈskɒpɪk/ *adj.* **1.** too small to be visible without a microscope. **2.** extremely small. **3.** of or by means of a microscope. —**microscopically** *adv.* [f. prec.]

microscopy /maɪˈkrɒskəpɪ/ *n.* use of the microscope. [f. MICROSCOPE]

microsurgery /ˈmaɪkrəʊsɜːdʒərɪ/ *n.* surgery using a microscope to see the tissue and instruments involved.

microwave /ˈmaɪkrəʊweɪv/ *n.* an electromagnetic wave having a wavelength of between about 30 cm and 1 mm. Microwaves have wavelengths which are shorter than those of normal radio-waves (whence their name) but longer than those of infra-red radiation. They are used in radar, in communications, and in microwave ovens where the moisture present in food selectively absorbs the microwaves, converts the energy into heat, and quickly cooks the food.

micturition /mɪktjʊəˈrɪʃ(ə)n/ *n.* urination. [f. L, = desire to urinate (*mingere* urinate)]

mid *adj.* **1.** in the middle of (usu. as comb.: *mid-air*; *mid-week*). **2.** that is in the middle, medium, half. **—mid-off, mid-on** *ns.* the positions of fieldsmen in cricket near the bowler on the off or on side (ill. SPORTS). **Mid West,** = Middle West. [OE]

Midas /ˈmaɪdəs/ (*Gk legend*) a king of Phrygia, of whom several stories are told, the most famous being the following. (1) He was given by Dionysus the power of turning everything he touched into gold. Unable to eat or drink, he prayed to be relieved of the gift and was instructed to wash in the river Pactolus, which since then has had golden sands. (2) He declared Pan a better flute-player than Apollo, who thereupon bestowed ass's ears upon him. Midas tried to hide them but his barber whispered the secret to some reeds, which repeat it whenever they rustle in the wind.

midday /ˈmɪddeɪ/ *n.* noon; the time near noon.

midden /ˈmɪd(ə)n/ *n.* a dunghill, a refuse-heap. [cf. Da. *mødding* (as MUCK, *dynge* heap)]

middle *attrib. adj.* **1.** at an equal distance from extremities. **2.** (of a member of a group) so placed as to have the same number of members on each side. **3.** intermediate in rank, quality, etc.; average. **—n. 1.** a middle point, position, or part. **2.** the waist. **—in the middle of,** during or half-way through (an activity or process). **middle age,** the middle part of normal life. **middle-aged** *adj.* of middle age. **Middle Ages,** the period in Europe after the Dark Ages (*c.*1000–1400) or in a wider sense *c.*600–1500. **middle C,** the C near the middle of the piano keyboard, the note between the treble and bass staves. **middle class,** the social class between the upper and lower, including professional and business people. **middle ear,** the cavity behind the ear-drum. **Middle East,** the region comprising the countries lying between the Near and Far East, especially Egypt, Iran, and the countries between them. **Middle Kingdom,** a period of ancient Egyptian history (see EGYPT). **middle name,** a given name between the first name and the surname; a person's most characteristic quality. **middle-of-the-road** *adj.* (of a person or action) moderate, avoiding extremes. **middle school,** a school for children from about 9 to 13. **middle-sized** *adj.* of medium size. **Middle West,** that part of the USA occupying the northern half of the Mississippi River basin, including the States of Ohio, Indiana, Illinois, Michigan, Wisconsin, Iowa, and Minnesota.

middleman *n.* (*pl.* **-men**) **1.** any of the traders who handle a commodity between its producer and its customer. **2.** an intermediary.

Middleton /ˈmɪd(ə)lt(ə)n/, Thomas (1580–1627), English dramatist, who wrote and collaborated on many masques and pageants for city ceremonies, and rollicking comedies of London life. His anti-Catholic anti-Spanish satire *A Game at Chesse* (1624) caused him and his players to be summoned before the Privy Council. He is remembered for his two tragedies, *The Changeling* (in collaboration with William Rowley, 1622) and *Women Beware Women* (1620/7).

middleweight *n.* the boxing-weight between welterweight and heavyweight (see BOXING-WEIGHT).

middling *adj.* moderately good; fairly well in health. **—adv.** fairly, moderately. [f. MID]

midfield *n.* the part of a football pitch away from the goals.

Midgard /ˈmɪdgɑːd/ (*Scand. myth.*) the region, encircled by the sea, in which men live, the earth. **—Midgard serpent,** a monstrous serpent, the offspring of Loki, thrown by Odin into the sea, where, with its tail in its mouth, it encircled the earth.

midge *n.* a gnatlike insect, specifically one of the family Chironomidae. [OE]

midget /ˈmɪdʒɪt/ *n.* an extremely small person or thing. **—adj.** extremely small. [f. prec.]

Mid Glamorgan /ɡləˈmɔːgən/ a county of South Wales.

midland /ˈmɪdlənd/ *adj.* of the middle part of a country. **—the Midlands,** the inland counties of central England.

midnight /ˈmɪdnaɪt/ *n.* 12 o'clock at night; the time near this; the middle of the night. **—midnight blue,** very dark blue. **midnight sun,** the sun visible at midnight during summer in polar regions.

Midrash /ˈmɪdræʃ/ *n.* (*pl.* **-im** /-ˈræʃiːm/) an ancient Jewish commentary on part of the Hebrew scriptures, attached to the Biblical text. The earliest Midrashim come from the 2nd c. AD, although much of their content is older. [f. Heb., = commentary (*darash* study)]

midriff /ˈmɪdrɪf/ *n.* the region of the front of the body just above the waist. [OE, = mid-belly]

midshipman /ˈmɪdʃɪpmən/ *n.* (*pl.* **-men**) a naval officer ranking next above cadet.

midst *n.* the middle part. **—in the midst of,** among; in the middle of. [earlier *middest* f. *in middes* (IN, MID)]

midsummer /mɪdˈsʌmə(r), ˈmɪ-/ *n.* the period of or near the summer solstice, about 21 June. **—Midsummer's Day,** 24 June.

midway *adv.* half-way between.

midwicket /mɪdˈwɪkɪt/ *n.* a position in cricket on the leg side opposite the middle of the pitch (ill. SPORTS).

midwife *n.* (*pl.* **midwives** /-vz/) a person trained to assist women in childbirth. **—midwifery** /-wɪfrɪ/ *n.* [f. obs. *mid* with + WIFE, in sense 'one who is with the mother']

midwinter /mɪdˈwɪntə(r)/ *n.* the period of or near the winter solstice, about 22 Dec.

mien /miːn/ *n.* a person's bearing or look. [f. obs. *demean* behave (as DEMEANOUR)]

Mies van der Rohe /miːz væn də ˈrəʊ/, Ludwig (1886–1969), German-American architect who succeeded Gropius as director of the Bauhaus (1930–3). His buildings, devoid of ornament, depend on subtlety of proportion and mechanical precision of finish. In the 1920s he produced pioneer projects for skyscrapers, and designed the German pavilion at the 1929 Barcelona exhibition, now regarded as the classic example of pure geometrical architecture. He also pioneered in furniture design, including the first tubular metal cantilevered chair (1927). In 1937 he emigrated to the USA. Among his most important works there is the high-rise Seagram Building, New York (1958).

might[1] /maɪt/ *v.aux.* used as *past tense* of MAY[1] esp. (1) in reported speech, (2) with a perfect infinitive expressing possibility based on a condition not fulfilled, or based on an obligation not fulfilled; also used (*loosely*) as = MAY[2]. **—might-have-been** *n.* an event etc. that might have happened but did not. [as MAY[1]]

might[2] /maɪt/ *n.* great strength or power. **—with might and main,** with all one's power. [OE (as MAY[1])]

mightn't /ˈmaɪt(ə)nt/ (*colloq.*) might not.

mighty /ˈmaɪtɪ/ *adj.* **1.** powerful, strong. **2.** massive, bulky; (*colloq.*) great, considerable. **—adv.** (*colloq.*) very. **—mightily** *adv.*, **mightiness** *n.* [as MIGHT[2]]

mignonette /mɪnjəˈnet/ *n.* an annual plant of the genus *Reseda* with small fragrant flowers. [f. F dim. of *mignon* small]

migraine /ˈmiːgreɪn/ *n.* a severe recurring form of headache, often with nausea and disturbance of the vision. [F, f. L f. Gk *hēmikrania* (as HEMI-, CRANIUM)]

migrant /ˈmaɪgrənt/ *adj.* that migrates. **—n.** a migrant person or animal, especially a bird. [as foll.]

migrate /maɪˈgreɪt/ *v.i.* **1.** to leave one place and settle in another. **2.** (of animals) to go periodically from one area to another, living in each place for part of a year. **—migration** *n.*, **migratory** /ˈmaɪgrətərɪ/ *adj.* [f. L *migrare*]

mihrab /ˈmiːrɑːb/ *n.* a niche or slab in a mosque, used to show the direction of Mecca. [f. Arab., = praying-place]

mikado /mɪˈkɑːdəʊ/ *n.* (*pl.* **-os**) the emperor of Japan. [Jap., = august door]

mike *n.* (*colloq.*) a microphone. [abbr.]

milady /mɪˈleɪdɪ/ *n.* an English noblewoman. [F, f. *my lady*]

milch /mɪltʃ/ *adj.* giving milk. **—milch cow,** a cow kept for milk; a source of regular or easy profit. [as MILK]

mild /maɪld/ *adj.* **1.** moderate in intensity, character, or effect, not severe or harsh or drastic; (of climate etc.) moderately warm. **2.** gentle in manner. **3.** not strongly flavoured, not sharp or bitter in taste. **—n.** mild ale. **—mild steel,** steel that is tough but not easily tempered. **—mildly** *adv.*, **mildness** *n.* [OE]

mildew /ˈmɪldjuː/ *n.* a growth of minute fungi forming on surfaces exposed to damp. **—v.t./i.** to taint or be tainted with mildew. **—mildewed** *adj.*, **mildewy** *adj.* [OE, = honey dew]

mile *n.* **1.** a unit of linear measure, equal to 1,760 yds. (1.609 km). It was originally the Roman lineal measure of 1,000 paces. Its length as a unit used in Britain etc. has varied considerably at different periods and in different localities, chiefly owing to the influence of the agricultural system of measures with which it was brought into relation (see FURLONG). The nautical mile, used in navigation, is a unit of 2,025 yds. (1.852 km). **2.** a great distance or amount. **3.** a race extending over a mile. [OE, ult. f. L *mille* thousand]

mileage n. 1. the number of miles travelled. 2. the advantage to be derived from something. [f. MILE]

miler /'maɪlə(r)/ n. a person or horse specializing in races of one mile. [f. MILE]

milestone n. 1. a stone set up beside a road to mark the distance in miles. 2. a significant event or stage in life or history.

milfoil /'mɪlfɔɪl/ n. a plant (*Achillea millefolium*) with small white flowers and finely divided leaves, yarrow. [f. OF f. L *millefolium* (*mille* thousand, *folium* leaf)]

Milhaud /'mi:jəʊ/, Darius (1892-1974), French composer and pianist, who travelled in Brazil before becoming a member of the Paris group of composers known as 'Les Six'. He composed the music to Cocteau's *Le Boeuf sur le toit* (1919), and his experience of Latin-American music bore fruit in the piano work *Saudades do Brasil* (1920-1), while a taste for jazz after a visit to the USA found expression in the ballet *La Création du monde* (1923).

milieu /'mi:ljə:/ n. (pl. **-ieux** /-jə:z/) an environment; a state of life; social surroundings. [F (*mi* mid, *lieu* place]

militant /'mɪlɪtənt/ adj. 1. prepared to take aggressive action in support of a cause. 2. engaged in warfare. —n. a militant person. —**Militant Tendency**, a movement dedicated to upholding Trotskyist principles within the Labour Party. —**militancy** n., **militantly** adv. [f. OF f. L (as MILITATE)]

militarism /'mɪlɪtərɪz(ə)m/ n. military spirit; an aggressive policy of reliance on military strength and means. —**militarist** n., **militaristic** /-'rɪstɪk/ adj. [f. F (as MILITARY)]

militarize /'mɪlɪtəraɪz/ v.t. 1. to make military or warlike. 2. to equip with military resources. 3. to imbue with militarism. —**militarization** /-'zeɪʃ(ə)n/ n. [f. foll.]

military /'mɪlɪtərɪ/ adj. of or for or done by soldiers or the armed forces. —**the military** (as *sing.* or *pl.*), the army (as distinct from the police or civilians). —**militarily** adv. [f. F or L *militaris* (*miles* soldier)]

militate /'mɪlɪteɪt/ v.i. (of facts or evidence) to tell or serve as a strong influence (*against*, rarely *in favour of*, a conclusion etc.). [f. L *militare* (as prec.)]

militia /mɪ'lɪʃə/ n. a military force, especially one raised from the civil population and supplementing the regular army in an emergency. [L, = military service (as MILITARY)]

milk n. 1. an opaque white fluid secreted by female mammals for the nourishment of their young; milk, especially of the cow, as a food. 2. a milklike liquid, e.g. in a coconut. —v.t. 1. to draw milk from (an animal). 2. to exploit or extract money etc. from (a person). —**milk and honey**, abundant means of prosperity. **milk and water**, a feeble or insipid or mawkish discourse or sentiment. **milk float**, a light low vehicle used in delivering milk. **milk run**, a routine expedition or mission. **milk shake**, a drink of milk and a flavouring mixed or shaken until frothy. **milk-tooth** n. any of the first temporary teeth in young mammals. [OE]

milkmaid n. a woman who milks or works in a dairy.

milkman /'mɪlkmən/ n. (pl. **-men**) a man who sells or delivers milk.

milksop n. a weak or timid man or youth.

milkweed n. any of various wild plants with a milky juice, especially sowthistle (*Sonchus oleraceus*).

milky adj. of, like, or containing milk; (of a liquid) cloudy, unclear. —**milkiness** n. [f. MILK]

Milky Way a faint band of light crossing the sky, clearly visible on dark moonless nights and discovered by Galileo to be made up of vast numbers of faint stars. It is the plane of our Galaxy in which most stars are located, and telescopic observations in the constellation of Sagittarius, looking towards the galactic centre, show 'clouds' of millions of stars, hosts of nebulae, and a great richness of other celestial phenomena.

Mill, John Stuart (1806-73), English philosopher and economist, strongly influenced by Bentham, who was a friend of his father. His chief concern was to oppose justification that depends on appeal to intuition, authority, custom, or revelation, and his most thorough-going defence of this view was in his *System of Logic* (1843), in which he argued that even knowledge of deductive inferences and mathematical truths was empirical. Mill is best known for his political and moral works. In *Utilitarianism* (1863) he developed Bentham's theory, refining it to deal with criticism, and considering explicitly the relation between utilitarianism and justice; his work has become the classic statement of the view. In *On Liberty* (1859) he argued for the importance of individuality, and claimed that self-

protection was the only proper reason for interfering with another's freedom. In other works he argued for representative democracy, criticized the contemporary treatment of married women, claimed that an end to economic growth was desirable as well as inevitable, and advocated the replacement of a divisive socio-economic class structure by a system of worker ownership.

mill n. 1. a building fitted with mechanical apparatus for grinding corn; such apparatus. 2. an apparatus for grinding any solid substance to a powder or pulp. 3. a building fitted with machinery for manufacturing-processes etc.; such machinery. —v.t./i. 1. to grind (corn) in a mill; to produce (flour) in a mill. 2. to produce regular markings on the edge of (a coin). 3. to cut or shape (metal) with a rotating tool. 4. (of people or animals) to move in an aimless manner. —**go** (*or* **put**) **through the mill**, to undergo (or cause to undergo) training or experience or suffering. **mill-pond** n. a pond formed by damming a stream to use the water in a mill. **mill-race** n. a current of water that works a mill-wheel. **mill-wheel** n. a wheel used to drive a water-mill. [OE ult. f. L *mola* millstone (*molere* grind)]

Millais /'mɪleɪ/, Sir John Everett (1829-96), English painter. A prodigious youthful talent saw him studying at the Royal Academy at the age of eleven. There he met Holman Hunt and, with Rossetti, formed the Pre-Raphaelite Brotherhood in 1848. His early work in that style (e.g. *Christ in the House of His Parents*, 1850) was totally uncompromising in its adherence to a pure vision of nature with vivid colouring, harsh outline, and unidealized figures, and brought the wrath of the critical establishment on his head until defended by Ruskin, whose former wife he married in 1855. However, with growing success he gradually slipped away from the moral and aesthetic rigour of the Pre-Raphaelites to become the archetypal mid-Victorian artist, producing beautifully painted portraits, landscapes, and sentimental genre pictures that cemented his fame (e.g. *Bubbles*, 1886).

millennium /mɪ'lenɪəm/ n. (pl. **-iums** or **-ia**) 1. a period of 1,000 years. 2. Christ's prophesied reign of 1,000 years on earth (Rev. 20). 3. a coming time of justice and happiness. —**millennial** adj. [f. L *mille* thousand + *annus* year]

millepede /'mɪlɪpi:d/ n. a many-legged arthropod of the class Diplopoda, having two pairs of legs to each segment. (Cf. CENTIPEDE.) [f. L, = wood-louse (*mille* thousand, *pes pedis* foot)]

Miller /'mɪlə(r)/, Arthur (1915-), American playwright. His tragedy *Death of a Salesman* (1949) was a powerful indictment of American values. *The Crucible* (1953) was based on the Salem witch trials of 1692. He was married to Marilyn Monroe from 1955 to 1961.

miller n. one who works or owns a mill, usually a corn-mill. —**miller's thumb**, a kind of small fish of the genus *Cottus*. [f. MILL]

millesimal /mɪ'lesɪm(ə)l/ adj. 1. thousandth. 2. consisting of thousandths. —n. a thousandth part. [f. L *millesimus* (*mille* thousand)]

millet /'mɪlɪt/ n. a cereal plant, especially *Panicum miliaceum*, with small nutritious seeds; these seeds. [f. F dim. f. L *milium*]

milli- /mɪlɪ-/ *in comb.* 1. thousand. 2. one thousandth. [f. L *mille* thousand]

milliard /'mɪljəd/ n. one thousand million. [F (*mille* thousand)]

millibar /'mɪlɪbɑ:(r)/ n. a unit of pressure equal to one thousandth of a bar. [f. MILLI- + BAR²]

milligram /'mɪlɪgræm/ n. a metric unit of mass, equal to 0.001 gram.

millilitre /'mɪlɪli:tə(r)/ n. a metric unit of capacity, equal to 0.001 litre.

millimetre /'mɪlɪmi:tə(r)/ n. a metric unit of length, equal to 0.001 metre or about 0.04 in.

milliner /'mɪlɪnə(r)/ n. a person who makes or sells women's hats. —**millinery** n. [f. *Milan* in Italy; orig. = vendor of goods from Milan]

million /'mɪljən/ adj. & n. (for plural usage, see HUNDRED). 1. one thousand thousand. 2. a million pounds or dollars. 3. (in *pl.*) very many. —**millionth** adj. n. [f. OF prob. f. It. (*mille* thousand)]

millionaire /mɪljə'neə(r)/ n. a person possessing a million pounds, dollars, etc.; a very rich person. [f. F (as prec.)]

millipede /'mɪlɪpi:d/ var. of MILLEPEDE.

millstone n. 1. either of two circular stones for grinding corn. 2. a heavy burden or responsibility.

millwright /'mɪlraɪt/ n. one who designs or erects mills.

milometer /maɪ'lɒmɪtə(r)/ n. an instrument for measuring the number of miles travelled by a vehicle. [f. MILE + -METER]

Milos /'maɪlɒs, 'miː-/ a Greek island in the Cyclades, where a Hellenistic marble statue of Aphrodite was found in 1820 (see VENUS OF MILO).

milt n. **1.** the reproductive gland or sperm of a male fish. **2.** the spleen of mammals. [OE]

Milton /'mɪlt(ə)n/, John (1608–74), English Puritan poet. A London scrivener's son, he attended St Paul's School and Christ's, Cambridge, dedicating himself, as a youth, to the stern chaste life he deemed needful for poetry, and writing three early masterpieces: the 'Nativity Ode', *Comus* (a masque), and 'Lycidas', an elegy for a drowned friend. He became politically active during the Civil War, publishing a renowned plea for a free press (*Areopagitica*, 1644), and, after his unhappy first marriage (1642), several pioneering tracts urging legalization of divorce. As Secretary of State for Foreign Tongues to Cromwell's government he produced propaganda defending Charles I's execution, and the unremitting work destroyed his sight. His three major poems, all completed after he had gone blind (1652), have biblical subjects: *Paradise Lost* (1667, revised 1674), an epic on the fall of man; *Paradise Regained*, on Christ's temptations, and (published with it in 1671) *Samson Agonistes*, in Greek tragic form.

mimbar /'mɪmbɑː(r)/ n. a pulpit in a mosque. [f. Arab.]

mime n. acting with gestures and without words; a performance involving this. —v.t./i. to perform in the form of a mime. [f. L f. Gk *mimos*]

mimeograph /'mɪmɪəgrɑːf/ n. an apparatus for making copies from stencils. —v.t. to reproduce by means of this. [f. Gk *mimeomai* imitate + -GRAPH]

mimetic /mɪ'metɪk/ adj. of or given to imitation or mimicry. [f. Gk *mimētikos* as prec.]

mimic /'mɪmɪk/ v.t. (-ck-) **1.** to copy the appearance or ways of (a person etc.) playfully or for entertainment. **2.** to copy minutely or servilely. **3.** (of a thing) to resemble closely. —n. a person skilled in imitation, especially for entertainment. —**mimicry** n. [f. L f. Gk (as MIME)]

mimosa /mɪ'məʊzə/ n. any of several usually tropical shrubs, especially those of the genus *Mimosa*, with small fragrant globular flower-heads. [app. f. L (as MIME), because the leaves imitate animals in their sensitivity]

Min. abbr. **1.** Minister. **2.** Ministry.

min. abbr. **1.** minute(s). **2.** minimum. **3.** minim.

mina /'maɪnə/ n. a talking bird (*Gracula religiosa*) of the starling family. [f. Hindi]

Minaean /mɪ'niːən/ n. **1.** a member of a Semitic-speaking people who established a kingdom in southern Arabia *c.*400 BC, absorbed into the Sabaean kingdom by the late 1st c. BC. **2.** their language. —adj. of the Sabaeans or their language. [f. L f. Arab.]

minaret /mɪnə'ret, 'mɪ-/ n. a slender turret connected with a mosque, from which a muezzin calls at the hours of prayer. [F or Sp. f. Turk. f. Arab.]

minatory /'mɪnətərɪ/ adj. threatening, menacing. [f. L (*minari* threaten)]

mince v.t./i. **1.** to cut into very small pieces, especially in a machine. **2.** to walk or speak in an affected way. —n. minced meat. —**mince pie,** a pie containing mincemeat. **not to mince matters** or **one's words,** to speak plainly. [f. OF f. L (as MINUTIAE)]

mincemeat n. a mixture of currants, sugar, spices, suet, etc. —**make mincemeat of,** to defeat or refute utterly.

mind /maɪnd/ n. **1.** the seat of consciousness, thought, volition, and feeling. **2.** intellectual powers as distinct from the will and emotions. **3.** remembrance. **4.** opinion; this as expressed. **5.** a way of thinking or feeling; a direction of thought or desires. **6.** the normal condition of the mental faculties. **7.** a person as embodying mental faculties. —v.t./i. **1.** to object to (usu. with neg. or interrog.); **2.** to remember and take care (about). **3.** to have charge of for a while. **4.** to apply oneself to; to concern oneself about. —**be in two minds,** to be undecided. **change one's mind,** to discard one's opinion etc. in favour of another. **do you mind?** (*iron.*) please stop that. **have a mind of one's own,** to be capable of an independent opinion. **have a (good) mind to,** to feel (much) inclined or tempted to. **have in mind,** to think of; to intend. **in one's mind's eye,** in one's imagination. **make up one's mind,** to decide, to resolve. **mind one's P's and Q's,** to be careful in speech

or conduct. **mind out,** to be careful; (in *imper.*) let me pass. **mind-reader** n. one who claims to be able to become aware of another's thoughts. **mind (you),** please take note. **never mind,** do not be troubled (about); I prefer not to answer; you may ignore. **on one's mind,** in one's thoughts; worrying one. [OE]

minded adj. **1.** inclined to think in a specified way or concern oneself with a specified thing. **2.** having a mind of a specified kind. **3.** inclined or disposed (to do something). [f. MIND]

minder n. one whose business it is to attend to something, especially a child or machinery. [f. MIND]

mindful adj. taking thought or care (of something). —**mindfully** adv., **mindfulness** n. [f. MIND + -FUL]

mindless adj. **1.** lacking intelligence, stupid. **2.** heedless (of). —**mindlessly** adv., **mindlessness** n. [f. MIND + -LESS]

mine[1] poss. pron. of or belonging to me; the thing(s) belonging to me. [OE (as ME[1])]

mine[2] n. **1.** an excavation in the earth for extracting metal, coal, salt, etc. **2.** an abundant source (*of* information etc.). **3.** a receptacle filled with explosive placed in or on the ground or in the water for destroying enemy personnel, material, or ships. —v.t./i. **1.** to obtain (metal, coal, etc.) from a mine; to dig in the earth etc. for ore etc. **2.** to lay explosive mines under or in. [f. OF]

minefield n. **1.** an area where explosive mines have been laid. **2.** a subject etc. presenting many unseen hazards.

minelayer n. a ship or aircraft for laying explosive mines.

miner n. one who works in a mine. [f. MINE[2]]

mineral /'mɪnər(ə)l/ n. **1.** a substance obtained by mining. **2.** a natural inorganic substance having a definite chemical composition and usually a characteristic crystalline structure. A rock may be made up of one type or several types of mineral. **3.** an artificial mineral water or similar drink. —adj. **1.** obtained by mining. **2.** inorganic, not animal or vegetable. —**mineral water,** water found in nature impregnated with a mineral substance; an artificial imitation of this; a non-alcoholic effervescent drink. [f. OF f. L (*minera* ore, f. OF)]

mineralogy /mɪnə'rælədʒɪ/ n. the science of minerals. —**mineralogical** /-rə'lɒdʒɪk(ə)l/ adj., **mineralogist** n. [f. prec. + -LOGY]

Minerva /mɪ'nɜːvə/ (*Rom. myth.*) goddess of handicrafts, widely worshipped and regularly identified with Athene, which led to her being regarded also as the goddess of war.

minestrone /mɪnɪ'strəʊnɪ/ n. an Italian soup containing vegetables and pasta or rice. [It.]

minesweeper n. a ship for clearing explosive mines from the sea.

mineworker n. a miner.

Ming the name of the Chinese dynasty founded in 1368 by Chu Yuan-chang after the collapse of Mongol authority in China, and ruling until succeeded by the Manchus in 1644 (see CH'ING). It was a period of expansion and exploration, with lasting contact established in the 16th c. between China and Europe, and a culturally productive period in which the arts flourished. The capital was established at Peking in 1421. —n. Chinese porcelain of this period.

mingle /'mɪŋg(ə)l/ v.t./i. to mix, to blend. —**mingle with,** to go about among. [f. obs. *meng* (OE, rel. to AMONG)]

mingy /'mɪndʒɪ/ adj. (*colloq.*) mean, stingy. —**mingily** adv. [prob. f. MEAN[2] + STINGY]

Mini /'mɪnɪ/ n. [P] a type of small car. [abbr.]

mini /'mɪnɪ/ n. (*colloq.*) a miniskirt. [abbr.]

mini- /mɪnɪ-/ in comb. miniature, small of its kind (*minicar*; *mini-budget*). [abbr.]

miniature /'mɪnɪtʃə(r)/ adj. **1.** much smaller than normal. **2.** represented on a small scale. —n. **1.** a small minutely finished portrait. **2.** miniature thing. —**in miniature,** on a small scale. [f. It. f. L *miniare* (*minium* red lead)]

miniaturist /'mɪnɪtʃərɪst/ n. a painter of miniatures. [f. prec.]

miniaturize /'mɪnɪtʃəraɪz/ v.t. **1.** to make miniature. **2.** to produce in a smaller version. [f. MINIATURE]

minibus /'mɪnɪbʌs/ n. a small bus for about twelve passengers.

minicab /'mɪnɪkæb/ n. a small car like a taxi, that can be booked but does not ply for hire.

minicomputer /mɪnɪkəm'pjuːtə(r)/ n. a computer that is smaller than a main-frame but larger than a microcomputer.

minim /'mɪnɪm/ n. **1.** (*Mus.*) a note half as long as a semibreve (ill. MUSICAL NOTATION). **2.** (*hist.*) one sixtieth of a fluid drachm, about 1 drop. [f. L (as MINIMUM)]

minimal /'mɪnɪm(ə)l/ *adj.* being or related to a minimum; very small or slight. —**minimally** *adv.* [as prec.]

minimize /'mɪnɪmaɪz/ *v.t.* **1.** to reduce to a minimum. **2.** to estimate at the smallest possible amount or degree; to estimate or represent at less than the true value or importance. —**minimization** /-'zeɪʃ(ə)n/ *n.* [as MINIM]

minimum /'mɪnɪməm/ *n.* (*pl.* **-ma**) the least amount possible, attained, usual, etc. [L, neut. of *minimus* least]

minion /'mɪnjən/ *n.* (*derog.*) a subordinate, an assistant. [orig. = favourite child etc., f. F *mignon* dainty]

miniskirt /'mɪnɪskɜːt/ *n.* a skirt ending well above the knees (ill. DRESS).

minister /'mɪnɪstə(r)/ *n.* **1.** a person at the head of a government department or a main branch of this. **2.** a clergyman, especially in the Presbyterian and Nonconformist Churches. **3.** a diplomatic agent, usually ranking below ambassador. **4.** a person employed in the execution of one's purpose, will, etc. —*v.t./i.* to render aid or service (to a person, cause, etc.). —**Minister of State,** a departmental senior minister between departmental head and junior minister. —**ministerial** /-'stɪərɪ(ə)l/ *adj.* [f. OF f. L *minister* servant]

ministration /mɪnɪ'streɪʃ(ə)n/ *n.* giving aid or service; ministering, especially in religious matters. —**ministrant** /'mɪnɪstrənt/ *adj.* & *n.* [f. OF or L (as prec.)]

ministry /'mɪnɪstrɪ/ *n.* **1.** a government department; the building occupied by it. **2.** the body of ministers of the government; a period of government under one Prime Minister. **3.** office as a minister in the Christian Church; period of this. **4.** ministering; ministration. —**the ministry,** the clerical profession. [f. L *ministerium* (as MINISTER)]

mink *n.* **1.** a small stoatlike animal of the family Mustelidae, especially *Mustela vison*. **2.** its fur. **3.** a coat made from this. [cf. Sw. *mänk*]

minnesinger /'mɪnɪsɪŋə(r)/ *n.* (*pl.* same) any of the aristocratic German poet-musicians of the 12th–14th c., the German equivalent of troubadours. [G (*minne* love, from the courtly love that was their chief theme)]

Minnesota /mɪnɪ'səʊtə/ a State in the north central USA on the Canadian border. Part of it was ceded to Britain by the French in 1763 and acquired by the USA in 1783, the remainder forming part of the Louisiana Purchase (1803). It became the 32nd State in 1858; capital, St Paul.

minnow /'mɪnəʊ/ *n.* a small freshwater fish (esp. *Phoxinus phoxinus*). [OE, prob. infl. by F *menu* (*poisson*) small fish (as MINUTE²)]

Minoan /mɪ'nəʊən/ *adj.* of the Bronze Age civilization of Crete *c.*3000–1100 BC (see below) or its people, culture, or language. —*n.* **1.** an inhabitant of Minoan Crete or other parts of the Minoan world. **2.** the language or scripts associated with the Minoan civilization. [f. MINOS]

This civilization, the earliest on European soil, was first revealed by the excavations of Sir Arthur Evans, who gave it its name, from 1900 onwards after Crete became independent of Turkish rule. It had reached its zenith by the beginning of the late Bronze Age, extending over the islands of the south Aegean while its wares were exported to Cyprus, Syria, and Egypt. Urban centres were constructed, dominated by palaces at Knossos, Mallia, Phaistos, and Zakro. Divided into two periods by an earthquake destruction *c.*1700 BC, the Minoan civilization, noted particularly for its Linear A script and distinctive palatial art and architecture, greatly influenced the Mycenaeans, whose presence in Crete is attested from the 16th c. BC and who succeeded the Minoans in control of the Aegean *c.*1400 BC; the precise dating of successive phases and of the collapse of Minoan civilization is highly controversial.

minor /'maɪnə(r)/ *adj.* **1.** lesser or relatively less in size or importance. **2.** under full legal age. **3.** (*Mus.*) (of a scale) having intervals of a semitone above its second and seventh notes; (of an interval) less by a semitone than a major interval; (of a key) based on a minor scale. —*n.* **1.** a person under full legal age. **2.** (*US*) a student's subsidiary subject or course. —*v.i.* (*US*) to undertake study (in a subject) as a subsidiary course. —**minor planets,** (also called *asteroids*) the small rocky bodies (less than a few kilometres across) orbiting the sun. Mostly found in a broad belt between the orbits of Mars and Jupiter, some are found closer to the sun, and may pass within a few million kilometres of Earth. Many satellites of the planets are thought to be captured asteroids. [L, = smaller, lesser]

Minorca /mɪ'nɔːkə/ the most easterly and second largest of the Balearic Islands; pop. (1970) 50,217. The capital and chief port, Mahon, was intermittently under British rule from 1708–82.

Minorite /'maɪnəraɪt/ *n.* a Franciscan friar, so called because the Franciscans regarded themselves as of humbler rank than members of other orders. [f. MINOR]

minority /maɪ'nɒrɪtɪ, mɪ-/ *n.* **1.** the smaller number or part of a group etc. **2.** the state of having fewer than half the votes. **3.** a small group of persons differing from others in race, religion, language, opinion on a topic, etc. **4.** the state or period of being under full legal age (see MAJORITY). [f. F or L (as prec.)]

Minos /'maɪnɒs/ a legendary king of Crete. The traditions concerning him preserve faint reminiscences of the might of the civilization now called Minoan. In Attic tradition his wife was Pasiphaë, and he was a cruel tyrant who every year exacted a tribute of Athenian youths and maidens to be devoured by the Minotaur. —**Palace of Minos,** a building (excavated and reconstructed by Sir Arthur Evans) identified with the largest Minoan palace of Knossos, which yielded local coins portraying the labyrinth as the city's symbol and a Linear B religious tablet which, when eventually deciphered, was found to refer to the 'lady of the labyrinth'.

Minotaur /'maɪnətɔː(r)/ (*Gk myth.*) the creature half-man, half-bull, offspring of Pasiphaë and a bull with which she fell in love, confined in Crete in a labyrinth made by Daedalus and eventually slain by Theseus. [f. Gk, = bull of Minos]

minster *n.* a large or important church; the church of a monastery. [OE (as MONASTERY)]

minstrel /'mɪnstr(ə)l/ *n.* **1.** a medieval singer or musician, who sang or recited (often his own) poetry; (in earlier use) an entertainer of any kind. **2.** (usu. in *pl.*) a member of a band of public entertainers, with blackened faces etc., performing songs and music ostensibly of Black origin. [f. OF *menestral* attendant f. L (as MINISTERIAL)]

minstrelsy /'mɪnstrəlsɪ/ *n.* a minstrel's art or poetry. [as prec.]

mint¹ *n.* **1.** an aromatic herb of the genus *Mentha*, used in cooking. **2.** peppermint; a small sweet flavoured with this. —**the Mint,** the Royal Mint (see ROYAL). —**minty** *adj.* [OE f. L *ment*(*h*)*a* f. Gk]

mint² *n.* **1.** a place where money is coined, usually under State authority. **2.** a vast sum or amount. —*v.t.* **1.** to make (a coin) by stamping metal. **2.** to coin (a word or phrase). —**in mint condition,** as new, unsoiled. [OE f. L *moneta* (as MONEY)]

minuet /mɪnjʊ'et/ *n.* a slow stately dance in triple measure; music for this, or in the same rhythm and style (often as a movement in a suite, sonata, or symphony). [f. F *menuet* (as MENU)]

minus /'maɪnəs/ *prep.* **1.** with the subtraction of (symbol −). **2.** below zero. **3.** (*colloq.*) deprived of. —*adj.* **1.** (of a number) less than zero, negative. **2.** having a negative electrical charge. **3.** (in evaluating) rather worse or lower than. —*n.* **1.** a minus sign. **2.** a disadvantage. **3.** a negative quantity. —**minus sign,** the symbol −. [L, neut. of MINOR]

minuscule /'mɪnəskjuːl/ *adj.* **1.** extremely small. **2.** lowercase. **3.** (of a kind of cursive script developed in the 7th c.) small. —*n.* **1.** a lower-case letter. **2.** a letter in minuscule script. [F, f. L *minusculus* (dim. of MINOR)]

minute¹ /'mɪnɪt/ *n.* **1.** a period of 60 seconds, a sixtieth part of an hour; the distance traversed in this. **2.** a very brief portion of time. **3.** a particular point of time. **4.** a sixtieth part of a degree of measurement of angles. **5.** (in *pl.*) a brief summary of the proceedings of an assembly, committee, etc. **6.** an official memorandum authorizing or recommending a course of action. **7.** a rough draft, a memorandum. —*v.t.* **1.** to record in minutes; to make a note of. **2.** to send a minute to (a person). —**in a minute,** very soon. **minute steak,** a thin slice of steak that can be cooked quickly. **up to the minute,** having the latest information; in the latest fashion. [f. OF f. L *minutus* (as foll.)]

minute² /maɪ'njuːt/ *adj.* **1.** very small. **2.** precise, detailed. —**minutely** *adv.*, **minuteness** *n.* [f. L *minutus* (*minuere* lessen)]

minutiae /maɪ'njuːʃiː, mɪ-/ *n.pl.* very small or unimportant details. [L (as prec.)]

minx /mɪŋks/ *n.* a pert or mischievous or sly girl. [orig. unkn.]

Miocene /'maɪəsiːn/ *adj.* of the fourth epoch of the Tertiary

Mirabeau /ˈmiːrəbəʊ/, Honoré Gabriel Riqueti, Comte de (1749–91), French revolutionary. A long-time opponent of the Bourbon regime, Mirabeau rose to prominence in the early days of the French Revolution when he rose to the leadership of the Third Estate in the Estates General, trying to find a moderate solution to the crisis by pressing for a form of constitutional monarchy. He died before the Revolution entered its extremist phase and was later accused, unfairly, of being a royal agent.

period, following the Oligocene and preceding the Pliocene, lasting from about 24.6 to 5.1 million years ago. It was a period of great earth movements during which the Alps and Himalayas were being formed. —*n.* this epoch. [f. Gk *meiōn* less + *kainos* new]

miracle /ˈmɪrək(ə)l/ *n.* **1.** a marvellous and welcome event that seems impossible to explain by means of the known laws of nature and is therefore attributed to a supernatural agency; a remarkable occurrence. **2.** a remarkable specimen. **3.** a miracle play (see MYSTERY PLAY). [f. OF f. L *miraculum* object of wonder (*mirari* wonder at)]

miraculous /mɪˈrækjʊləs/ *adj.* **1.** that is a miracle, supernatural. **2.** remarkable. —**miraculously** *adv.* [f. F or L (as prec.)]

mirage /mɪˈrɑːʒ/ *n.* **1.** an optical illusion caused by atmospheric conditions, especially the appearance of a sheet of water in the desert or on a hot road. **2.** an illusory thing. [F (*se mirer* be reflected)]

mire *n.* **1.** swampy ground, a bog. **2.** mud. —*v.t.* **1.** to plunge in mire. **2.** to involve in difficulties. **3.** to defile, to bespatter (*lit.* or *fig.*). —**in the mire**, in difficulties. —**miry** *adj.* [f. ON, rel. to MOSS]

Miró /mɪˈrəʊ/, Joan (1893–), Spanish painter, from *c.*1923 among the most prominent of the surrealists. Many of his pictures contain enlarged amoebic forms in rhythmically balanced composition.

mirror /ˈmɪrə(r)/ *n.* **1.** a polished surface (usu. of amalgam-coated glass) reflecting an image. **2.** what gives a faithful reflection or true description of a thing. —*v.t.* to reflect as in a mirror. —**mirror image**, a reflection or copy in which the left and right sides are reversed. [f. OF f. L *mirare* look at]

mirth *n.* merriment; laughter. —**mirthful** *adj.*, **mirthless** *adj.* [OE (as MERRY)]

mis- *prefix* **1.** to verbs and verbal derivatives, in the sense 'amiss', 'badly', 'wrongly', 'unfavourably' (*mislead*, *misshapen*, *mistrust*). **2.** to verbs, adjectives, and nouns, in the sense 'amiss', 'badly', 'wrongly', or negative (*misadventure*, *mischief*). [sense 1 OE; sense 2 f. OF *mes-* f. L (as MINUS)]

misadventure /mɪsədˈventʃə(r)/ *n.* **1.** a piece of bad luck. **2.** the killing of a person by a lawful act without negligence or any intention of hurt, for which there is no criminal responsibility.

misalliance /mɪsəˈlaɪəns/ *n.* an unsuitable alliance, especially a marriage with a social inferior.

misanthrope /ˈmɪsənθrəʊp, ˈmɪz-/ *n.* a hater of mankind; one who avoids human society. —**misanthropic** /-ˈθrɒpɪk/*adj.*, **misanthropically** /-ˈθrɒpɪkəlɪ/ *adv.* [F f. Gk (*misos* hatred, *anthrōpos* man)]

misanthropy /mɪˈsænθrəpɪ, mɪˈz-/ *n.* the condition or habits of a misanthrope. [f. prec.]

misapply /mɪsəˈplaɪ/ *v.t.* to apply (esp. funds) wrongly. —**misapplication** /-æplɪˈkeɪʃ(ə)n/ *n.*

misapprehend /mɪsæprɪˈhend/ *v.t.* to misunderstand. —**misapprehension** /-ʃ(ə)n/ *n.*

misappropriate /mɪsəˈprəʊprɪeɪt/ *v.t.* to take wrongly; to apply (another's money) wrongly to one's own use. —**misappropriation** /-ʃ(ə)n/ *n.*

misbegotten /mɪsbɪˈɡɒt(ə)n/ *adj.* **1.** contemptible, disreputable. **2.** bastard.

misbehave /mɪsbɪˈheɪv/ *v.i.* to behave improperly. —**misbehaviour** *n.*

miscalculate /mɪsˈkælkjʊleɪt/ *v.t./i.* to calculate wrongly. —**miscalculation** /-ˈleɪʃ(ə)n/ *n.*

miscall /mɪsˈkɔːl/ *v.t.* to misname.

miscarriage /mɪsˈkærɪdʒ, ˈmɪs-/ *n.* **1.** a spontaneous abortion; a delivery of the foetus in the 12th–28th week of pregnancy. **2.** the miscarrying of a plan etc. —**miscarriage of justice**, the failure of a legal procedure to achieve justice. [f. foll.]

miscarry /mɪsˈkærɪ/ *v.i.* **1.** (of a woman) to have a miscarriage. **2.** (of a scheme etc.) to go wrong, to fail. **3.** (of a letter etc.) to fail to reach its destination.

miscast /mɪsˈkɑːst/ *v.t.* (*past & p.p.* **miscast**) to allot an unsuitable part to (an actor).

miscegenation /mɪsɪdʒɪˈneɪʃ(ə)n/ *n.* interbreeding of races, especially of Whites with non-Whites. [f. L *miscēre* mix + *genus* race]

miscellaneous /mɪsəˈleɪnɪəs/ *adj.* **1.** of various kinds. **2.** of mixed composition or character. [f. L (*miscellus* mixed, as prec.)]

miscellany /mɪˈselənɪ/ *n.* **1.** a mixture, a medley. **2.** a book containing various literary compositions etc. [f. F (as prec.)]

mischance /mɪsˈtʃɑːns/ *n.* misfortune.

mischief /ˈmɪstʃɪf/ *n.* **1.** troublesome but not malicious conduct, especially of children; playful malice or archness. **2.** harm or injury, especially caused by a person. —**make mischief**, to create discord. [f. OF (MIS-, *chever* come to an end, as CHIEF)]

mischievous /ˈmɪstʃɪvəs/ *adj.* (of a person) disposed to mischief; (of conduct) playfully malicious, mildly troublesome; (of a thing) having harmful effects. —**mischievously** *adv.*, **mischievousness** *n.* [f. AF (as prec.)]

miscible /ˈmɪsɪb(ə)l/ *adj.* that can be mixed. —**miscibility** /-ˈbɪlɪtɪ/ *n.* [f. L (*miscēre* mix)]

misconceive /mɪskənˈsiːv/ *v.t./i.* to have a wrong idea or conception (of). —**misconception** /-ˈsepʃ(ə)n/ *n.*

misconduct /mɪsˈkɒndʌkt/ *n.* **1.** improper conduct, especially adultery. **2.** bad management.

misconstrue /mɪskənˈstruː/ *v.t.* to misinterpret. —**misconstruction** *n.*

miscopy /mɪsˈkɒpɪ/ *v.t.* to copy wrongly.

miscount /mɪsˈkaʊnt/ *v.t./i.* to make a wrong count; to count (things) wrongly. —*n.* a wrong count, especially of votes.

miscreant /ˈmɪskrɪənt/ *n.* a wrongdoer, a villain. [f. OF (MIS-, *creant* believer)]

misdeal /mɪsˈdiːl/ *v.t./i.* (*past & p.p.* **misdealt** /-ˈdelt/) to make a mistake in dealing (cards). —*n.* such a mistake; a misdealt hand.

misdeed /mɪsˈdiːd/ *n.* a wrong or improper act, a crime.

misdemeanour /mɪsdɪˈmiːnə(r)/ *n.* a misdeed; (*Law*) an indictable offence, formerly (in the UK) one less heinous than a felony.

misdirect /mɪsdɪˈrekt, -daɪ-/ *v.t.* to direct wrongly. —**misdirection** *n.*

misdoing /mɪsˈduːɪŋ/ *n.* a misdeed.

mise en scène /miːz ɑ̃ ˈseɪn/ *n.* **1.** the scenery and properties of an acted play. **2.** the surroundings of an event. [F, p.p. of *mettre* put f. L *mittere* miss- send, put]

miser /ˈmaɪzə(r)/ *n.* a person who hoards wealth, especially one who lives miserably. —**miserliness** *n.*, **miserly** *adj.* [L, = wretched]

miserable /ˈmɪzərəb(ə)l/ *adj.* **1.** full of misery, wretchedly unhappy or uncomfortable. **2.** wretchedly poor in quality etc., contemptible. **3.** causing wretchedness. —**miserably** *adv.* [f. F f. L, = pitiable (*miserari* pity)]

misericord /mɪˈzerɪkɔːd/ *n.* a projection under a hinged seat in a choir stall serving (when the seat is turned up) to support a person standing. [f. OF f. L *misericordia* compassion]

misery /ˈmɪzərɪ/ *n.* **1.** a condition or feeling of extreme unhappiness or discomfort. **2.** a cause of this. **3.** (*colloq.*) a constantly grumbling or doleful person. [f. OF or L *miseria* (as MISER)]

misfire /mɪsˈfaɪə(r)/ *v.i.* **1.** (of a gun, motor, engine, etc.) to fail to go off or start its action or function regularly. **2.** (of a plan etc.) to fail to have the intended effect. —*n.* such a failure.

misfit /ˈmɪsfɪt/ *n.* **1.** a person unsuited to his environment or work. **2.** a garment etc. that does not fit properly.

misfortune /mɪsˈfɔːtʃuːn/ *n.* bad luck; an instance of this.

misgive /mɪsˈɡɪv/ *v.t.* (*past* **-gave**, *p.p.* **-given**) (of a person's mind, heart, etc.) to fill (him or her) with misgivings.

misgiving *n.* a feeling of doubt, mistrust, or apprehension. [f. prec.]

misgovern /mɪsˈɡʌvən/ *v.t.* to govern badly. —**misgovernment** *n.*

misguided /mɪsˈɡaɪdɪd/ *adj.* mistaken in thought or action. —**misguidedly** *adv.*

mishandle /mɪsˈhænd(ə)l/ *v.t.* **1.** to deal with incorrectly or ineffectively. **2.** to handle (a person or thing) roughly or rudely.

mishap /'mɪshæp/ n. an unlucky accident.

mishear /mɪs'hɪə(r)/ v.t. (past & p.p. **-heard** /-hɜːd/) to hear incorrectly or imperfectly.

mishit /mɪs'hɪt/ v.t. (**-tt-**; past & p.p. **-hit**) to hit (a ball) faultily or badly. —/'mɪshɪt/ n. a faulty or bad hit.

mishmash /'mɪʃmæʃ/ n. a confused mixture. [redupl. of MASH]

Mishnah /'mɪʃnɑː/ n. an authoritative collection of exegetical material embodying the oral tradition of Jewish law. Written in Hebrew and traditionally attributed to Rabbi Judah ha-Nasi (c. AD 200), it forms the first part of the Talmud, with an influence on Judaism second only to that of the Scriptures. —**Mishnaic** /-'neɪɪk/ adj. [f. Heb., = (teaching by) repetition]

misinform /mɪsɪn'fɔːm/ v.t. to give wrong information to. —**misinformation** /-fə'meɪʃ(ə)n/ n.

misinterpret /mɪsɪn'tɜːprɪt/ v.t. to give a wrong interpretation to; to make a wrong inference from. —**misinterpretation** /-'teɪʃ(ə)n/ n.

misjudge /mɪs'dʒʌdʒ/ v.t./i. **1.** to have a wrong opinion of. **2.** to judge wrongly. —**misjudgement** n.

mislay /mɪs'leɪ/ v.t. (past & p.p. **-laid**) to put (a thing) in a place and be unable to remember where it is; to lose temporarily.

mislead /mɪs'liːd/ v.t. (past & p.p. **-led**) to lead astray, to cause to go wrong in conduct or belief.

mismanage /mɪs'mænɪdʒ/ v.t. to manage badly or wrongly. —**mismanagement** n.

mismatch /mɪs'mætʃ/ v.t. to match unsuitably or incorrectly. —/'mɪsmætʃ/ n. a bad match.

misname /mɪs'neɪm/ v.t. to name wrongly or unsuitably.

misnomer /mɪs'nəʊmə(r)/ n. a name or term used wrongly; the use of a wrong name. [f. AF (MIS-, nommer name f. L nominare)]

misogynist /mɪ'sɒdʒɪnɪst/ n. one who hates all women. —**misogyny** n. [f. Gk (misos hatred, gunē woman)]

misplace /mɪs'pleɪs/ v.t. **1.** to put in the wrong place. **2.** to bestow (affections or confidence) on the wrong object. **3.** to time (words or an action) badly. —**misplacement** n.

misprint /'mɪsprɪnt/ n. a mistake in printing. —/mɪs'prɪnt/ v.t. to print wrongly.

misprision /mɪs'prɪʒ(ə)n/ n. (Law) a wrong act or an omission. —**misprision of treason** or **of felony**, concealment of one's knowledge of a treasonable or felonious intent. [f. AF (MIS-, prendre take)]

mispronounce /mɪsprə'naʊns/ v.t. to pronounce (a word etc.) wrongly. —**mispronunciation** /-nʌnsɪ'eɪʃ(ə)n/ n.

misquote /mɪs'kwəʊt/ v.t. to quote inaccurately. —**misquotation** /-'teɪʃ(ə)n/ n.

misread /mɪs'riːd/ v.t. (past & p.p. **-read** /-'red/) to read or interpret wrongly.

misrepresent /mɪsreprɪ'zent/ v.t. to give a false account of, to represent wrongly. —**misrepresentation** /-'teɪʃ(ə)n/ n.

misrule /mɪs'ruːl/ n. **1.** bad government. **2.** disorder. —v.t. to govern badly.

miss[1] v.t./i. **1.** to fail to hit, reach, or catch (an object). **2.** to fail to catch (a train etc.) or see (an event) or meet (a person); to fail to keep (an appointment) or seize (an opportunity). **3.** to fail to hear or understand. **4.** to notice or regret the loss or absence of. **5.** to avoid. **6.** (of an engine) to misfire; to fail. —n. a failure to hit or attain what is aimed at. —**miss out**, to omit, to leave out. **miss out (on)**, (colloq.) to fail to get benefit or enjoyment (from). [OE]

miss[2] n. **1.** a girl or unmarried woman. **2. Miss**, the title of an unmarried woman or girl; the title of a beauty queen from a specified region etc. [abbr. of MISTRESS]

missal /'mɪs(ə)l/ n. (in the RC Church) the book containing the service of the Mass for the whole year. As a liturgical book, the missal appeared from about the 10th c., combining in one book the devotions that had previously appeared in several. [f. L (missa Mass)]

missel-thrush /'mɪs(ə)lθrʌʃ/ n. a large thrush (Turdus viscivorus) that feeds on mistletoe etc. berries. [f. OE mistel mistletoe]

misshapen /mɪs'ʃeɪpən/ adj. ill-shaped, deformed; distorted. [f. MIS- + shapen, old p.p. of SHAPE]

missile /'mɪsaɪl/ n. **1.** an object or weapon suitable for throwing at a target or for discharge from a machine. **2.** a weapon directed by remote control or automatically. [f. L missilis (mittere send)]

missing adj. **1.** not in its place, lost. **2.** (of a person) not yet traced or confirmed as alive but not known to be dead. **3.** not present. —**missing link**, a thing lacking to complete a series; a hypothetical creature called upon to bridge the gap between man and his evolutionary non-human ancestors. The rise of Darwinian evolutionary theory during mid- to late 19th-c. Victorian England questioned biblical authority on man's temporal and physical integrity. During this time it was becoming apparent that modern man may have been the result of evolutionary change from some as yet unidentified extinct species. This unknown predecessor was expected to exhibit both ape-like and human physical attributes, for it was popularly, though wrongly, thought that modern man somehow evolved from the extant higher primates, while professionally the belief was that man and the higher primates shared a common ancestor. The 'common ancestor or early human' searched for by the scientifically minded, and the hybrid ape-men demanded by popular thought, gave rise to the concept of a 'missing link'. This concept is now defunct for it is known that the evolution of the genus Homo (man) has occurred over at least 2 million years: a time that has seen the rise and decline of a series of tool-using hominids of which several evolved no further and have hence become extinct. It is now clear that there is no single 'missing link' to be found in our past but rather a complicated collection of often concurrently existing men or man-like creatures from whom we are derived. [f. MISS[1]]

mission /'mɪʃ(ə)n/ n. **1.** a body of persons sent to conduct negotiations or propagate a religious faith. **2.** a missionary post. **3.** a task to be performed; a journey for such a purpose; an operational sortie; the dispatch of an aircraft or spacecraft. **4.** a person's vocation. [F or f. L (as MISSILE)]

missionary adj. of religious etc. missions. —n. a person doing missionary work. [as prec.]

missis /'mɪsɪz/ n. (vulgar) as a form of address to a woman. —**the missis**, my or your wife. [corrupt. of MISTRESS; cf. MRS]

Mississippi /mɪsɪ'sɪpɪ/ **1.** the greatest river of North America, rising near the Canadian border in Minnesota and flowing south to a delta on the Gulf of Mexico. With its chief tributary, the Missouri, it is 5,970 km (3,710 miles) long; it provided a route for early explorers into North America. **2.** a State of the USA lying east of the lower Mississippi River. A French colony in the 18th c., it was ceded to Britain in 1763 and to the USA in 1783, becoming the 20th State in 1817; capital, Jackson.

missive /'mɪsɪv/ n. an official or long and serious letter. [f. L (as MISSILE)]

Missouri /mɪ'zʊərɪ/ **1.** one of the main tributaries of the Mississippi, rising in the Rocky Mountains in Montana and flowing into it from the west. **2.** a State of the USA lying west of the Mississippi River, acquired as part of the Louisiana Purchase (1803) and becoming the 24th State of the USA in 1821; capital, Jefferson City.

misspell /mɪs'spel/ v.t. (past & p.p. **-spelt, -spelled**) to spell wrongly.

misspend /mɪs'spend/ v.t. (past & p.p. **-spent**) to spend amiss or wastefully.

misstate /mɪs'steɪt/ v.t. to state wrongly. —**misstatement** n.

mist n. **1.** water vapour near the ground in droplets smaller than raindrops and obscuring the atmosphere. **2.** a condensed vapour obscuring windscreens etc. **3.** a dimness or blurring of sight caused by tears etc. —v.t./i. to cover or become covered with or as with mist. [OE]

mistake /mɪ'steɪk/ n. an incorrect idea or opinion; a thing incorrectly done or thought. —v.t./i. (past **mistook** /-'stʊk/, p.p. **mistaken**) **1.** to misunderstand the meaning or intention of. **2.** to choose or identify wrongly.

mistaken /mɪ'steɪkən/ adj. wrong in opinion; ill-judged. —**mistakenly** adv. [f. prec.]

mister n. **1.** a person without a title of nobility etc. **2.** (vulgar) as a form of address to a man. [var. of MASTER; cf. MR]

mistime /mɪs'taɪm/ v.t. to say or do (a thing) at the wrong time.

mistletoe /'mɪs(ə)ltəʊ/ n. a parasitic plant (Viscum album) growing on apple and other trees and bearing white berries. [OE misteltan (as MISSEL-THRUSH, tan twig)]

mistook past of MISTAKE.

mistral /'mɪstr(ə)l, -'trɑːl/ n. a cold north or north-west wind in southern France. [F f. Prov. f. L *magistralis* (as MAGISTRATE)]

mistreat /mɪsˈtriːt/ *v.t.* to treat badly. —**mistreatment** *n.*

mistress /ˈmɪstrɪs/ *n.* **1.** a woman in authority or with power; the female head of a household or of a college etc.; the female owner of an animal or slave. **2.** a female teacher or tutor, a schoolmistress. **3.** a woman having an illicit sexual relationship with a (usu. married) man. [f. OF *maistresse* (*maistre* master)]

mistrial /mɪsˈtraɪəl/ *n.* a trial vitiated by an error.

mistrust /mɪsˈtrʌst/ *v.t.* to feel no confidence in; to be suspicious of. —*n.* lack of confidence, suspicion. —**mistrustful** *adj.*, **mistrustfully** *adv.*

misty *adj.* **1.** of or covered with mist. **2.** of dim outline; (*fig.*) obscure, vague. —**mistily** *adv.*, **mistiness** *n.* [OE (as MIST)]

misunderstand /mɪsʌndəˈstænd/ *v.t.* (*past* & *p.p.* **-stood** /-ˈstʊd/) to understand in a wrong sense; (esp. in *p.p.*) to misinterpret the words or action of.

misunderstanding *n.* **1.** failure to understand correctly. **2.** a slight disagreement or quarrel.

misusage /mɪsˈjuːsɪdʒ/ *n.* **1.** a wrong or improper usage. **2.** ill-treatment.

misuse /mɪsˈjuːz/ *v.t.* **1.** to use wrongly, to apply to a wrong purpose. **2.** to ill-treat. —/mɪsˈjuːs/ *n.* wrong or improper use or application.

Mitanni /mɪˈtænɪ/ a political and geographic term of unknown derivation, first encountered in Egyptian inscriptions dating to Tuthmosis I (*c.*1520 BC) in reference to a Late Bronze Age hegemony of north Mesopotamian and Syrian States composed of a predominantly Hurrian-speaking populace and ruled by a succession of Indo-European kings. —*n.pl.* its people. —**Mitannian** *adj.* & *n.* [orig. unkn.]

Mitchell /ˈmɪtʃ(ə)l/, Reginald Joseph (1895–1937), English aeronautical engineer who designed many successful aircraft for the Schneider Trophy contest in the 1920s and a range of flying boats and amphibious aircraft. His last design was the Spitfire fighter aircraft much used in the Second World War.

mite *n.* **1.** a small arachnid of the order Acari, especially of a kind found in cheese etc. **2.** a modest contribution. **3.** a small object or child. [OE]

Mithras /ˈmɪθræs/ (*Pers. myth.*) a god of light, truth, and the plighted word, whose titles include 'Saviour from Death', 'Victorious', and 'Warrior'. These partly explain his attraction for the Roman world, its army, merchants, and those hoping for immortality, and made his worship the principal rival of Christianity in the first three centuries AD. But how, when, and where the god of Persian Zoroastrianism evolved into the Roman god, slayer of the mystic bull and worshipped with secret rites and initiations in a mystery-cult, is an unsolved problem. —**Mithraic** /-ˈreɪɪk/ *adj.*, **Mithraism** /ˈmɪθreɪɪz(ə)m/ *n.*

Mithridates /mɪθrɪˈdeɪtiːz/ king of Pontus 120–63 BC. His expansionist policies led to a war with Rome (88–85 BC), in which he occupied most of Asia Minor and much of Greece, until driven back by the Roman general Sulla. Two further wars followed; he was finally defeated by Lucullus and Pompey, and fled to the Crimea. In cunning, courage, and organizing ability Mithridates was Rome's stoutest oriental antagonist, but he failed in the arts of a strategist and could not keep the loyalty of his subordinates. His portraits show that he copied Alexander in personal appearance.

mitigate /ˈmɪtɪgeɪt/ *v.t.* to make milder or less intense or severe; (of circumstances) to excuse (wrongdoing) partially. —**mitigation** /-ˈgeɪʃ(ə)n/ *n.* [f. L *mitigare* (*mitis* mild)]

mitosis /maɪˈtəʊsɪs, mɪt-/ *n.* (*pl.* **-oses** /-siːz/) a process of division of cell nuclei in which two new nuclei each with the full number of chromosomes are formed. —**mitotic** /-ˈtɒtɪk/ *adj.* [f. Gk *mitos* thread]

mitre /ˈmaɪtə(r)/ *n.* **1.** a head-dress forming part of the insignia of a bishop in the Western Church, and worn also by abbots and other ecclesiastics as a mark of exceptional dignity. In its modern form it is a tall cap, deeply cleft at the top, the outline of the front and back having the shape of a pointed arch (ill. VESTMENTS). **2.** a joint of two pieces of wood or other material at an angle of 90°, such that the line of junction bisects this angle. —*v.t.* **1.** to bestow a mitre on. **2.** to join with a mitre. [f. OF f. L f. Gk *mitra* turban; sense 2 of *n.* and *v.* perh. a different wd]

mitt *n.* **1.** a mitten. **2.** a baseball-player's glove. **3.** (*slang*) a hand. [abbr. of foll.]

mitten /ˈmɪt(ə)n/ *n.* a kind of glove that leaves the fingers and thumb-tip bare, or that has no partitions between the fingers. [f. OF *mitaine* f. L *medietas* half (as MOIETY)]

Mitty, Walter, hero of a story (by James Thurber) who indulged in extravagant daydreams of his own triumphs.

mix *v.t./i.* **1.** to combine or put together (two or more substances or things) so that the constituents of each are diffused among those of the other(s). **2.** to prepare (a compound, cocktail, etc.) by mixing the ingredients. **3.** to be capable of being blended. **4.** to combine; (of things) to be compatible. **5.** (of a person) to be harmonious or sociable; to have dealings. —*n.* a mixture; the proportion of materials in this; a mixture prepared commercially from suitable ingredients for making something. —**be mixed up in** *or* **with**, to be involved in or with. **mix it**, (*colloq.*) to start fighting. **mix up**, to mix thoroughly, to confuse. **mix-up** *n.* a confusion; a misunderstanding. [back-formation f. foll.]

mixed /mɪkst/ *adj.* **1.** of diverse qualities or elements. **2.** (of a group of persons) containing persons from various races or social classes. **3.** for persons of both sexes. —**mixed bag**, a diverse assortment. **mixed blessing**, a thing having advantages but also disadvantages. **mixed doubles**, (in tennis) a doubles game with a man and woman as partners on each side. **mixed farming**, farming of both crops and livestock. **mixed feelings**, a mixture of pleasure and dismay. **mixed grill**, a dish of various grilled meats and vegetables. **mixed marriage**, a marriage between persons of different race or religion. **mixed metaphor**, a combination of inconsistent metaphors. **mixed-up** *adj.* (*colloq.*) mentally or emotionally confused, socially ill-adjusted. [f. earlier *mixt* f. OF f. L *mixtus*, p.p. of *miscēre* mix]

mixer *n.* **1.** a device for mixing or blending foods etc. **2.** a person who manages socially in a specified way. **3.** a drink to be mixed with another. [f. MIX]

Mixtec /ˈmɪkstek/ *n.* (*pl.* same or **-s**) a member or the language of a people of southern Mexico who were outstanding craftsmen in pottery and metallurgy. In the 15th c. they were conquered by the Aztecs. —*adj.* of the Mixtec or their language. [Sp.]

mixture /ˈmɪkstʃə(r)/ *n.* the process or result of mixing; a thing made by mixing; a combination of ingredients, qualities, characteristics, etc. —**the mixture as before**, the same treatment repeated. [f. F or L *mixtura* (as MIXED)]

mizen *n.* (also **mizen-sail**) the lowest fore-and-aft sail of a full-rigged ship's mizen-mast. —**mizen-mast** *n.* the mast next aft of the mainmast (ill. SAILING-SHIPS). [f. F *misaine* f. It. (as MEZZANINE)]

Mizoram /ˈmɪzɔːrəm/ a Union Territory of India, separated in 1972 from Assam; capital, Aizawl.

ml *abbr.* millilitre(s).

Mlle(s) *abbr.* Mademoiselle, Mesdemoiselles.

MM *abbr.* **1.** Messieurs. **2.** Military Medal.

mm *abbr.* millimetre(s).

Mme(s) *abbr.* Madame, Mesdames.

Mn *symbol* manganese.

mnemonic /nɪˈmɒnɪk/ *adj.* of or designed to aid the memory. —*n.* **1.** a mnemonic device. **2.** (in *pl.*) the art of or a system for improving the memory. —**mnemonically** *adv.* [f. Gk (*mnēmōn* mindful)]

Mnemosyne /niːˈmɒzɪnɪ/ (*Gk myth.*) mother of the Muses. [Gk, = memory]

MO *abbr.* **1.** Medical Officer. **2.** money order.

Mo *symbol* molybdenum.

mo /məʊ/ *n.* (*slang*) (*pl.* **mos**) a moment. [abbr.]

moa /ˈməʊə/ *n.* an extinct flightless New Zealand bird of the family Dinorthidae, resembling the ostrich. [Maori]

Moabite /ˈməʊəbaɪt/ *adj.* of Moab, an ancient region by the Dead Sea, or its people. —*n.* a member of a Semitic people traditionally descended from Lot, living in Moab. —**Moabite Stone**, a monument erected by Mesha, king of Moab, *c.*850 BC which describes the campaign between Moab and Israel (2 Kings 3), and furnishes an early example of an inscription in the Phoenician alphabet. It is now in the Louvre. [f. *Moab* name of region]

moan *n.* **1.** a long murmur expressing physical or mental suffering; the low plaintive sound of wind etc. **2.** a complaint, a grievance. —*v.t./i.* to make a moan or moans; to utter with moans. [OE]

moat *n.* a defensive ditch round a castle, town, etc., usually filled with water. —**moated** *adj.* [f. OF *mot(t)e* mound]

mob *n.* **1.** a disorderly crowd, a rabble. **2.** the common people. **3.** (*slang*) a gang; an associated group of persons.

—*v.t.* (**-bb-**) to crowd round in order to attack or admire. [abbr. of *mobile* obs. n. = L *mobile vulgus* excitable crowd]

mob-cap *n.* (*hist.*) a woman's large indoor cap covering all the hair. [f. obs. *mob* slut + CAP]

mobile /ˈməʊbaɪl/ *adj.* **1.** movable, not fixed; able to move or be moved easily. **2.** (of the face etc.) readily changing its expression. **3.** (of a shop etc.) accommodated in a vehicle so as to serve various places. **4.** (of a person) able to change social status. —*n.* a light decorative structure that may be hung so as to turn freely. —**mobile home,** a caravan. —**mobility** /məˈbɪlɪtɪ/ *n.* [f. F f. L *mobilis* (*movēre* move)]

mobilize /ˈməʊbɪlaɪz/ *v.t./i.* **1.** to assemble (troops etc.) for service; to prepare for war or other emergency. **2.** to assemble for a particular purpose. —**mobilization** /-ˈzeɪʃ(ə)n/ *n.* [as prec.]

Möbius strip /ˈməʊbɪəs/ a surface with only one side and one edge, formed by joining the ends of a rectangular strip after twisting one end through 180° (ill. SHAPES). [f. A. F. *Möbius*, German mathematician (d. 1868)]

mobster *n.* (*slang*) a gangster. [f. MOB]

moccasin /ˈmɒkəsɪn/ *n.* a soft heelless shoe as originally worn by North American Indians. [f. Amer. Ind.]

mocha /ˈmɒkə, ˈməʊ-/ *n.* a kind of coffee; flavouring made with this. [f. *Mocha*, port on Red Sea]

Mochica /məˈtʃiːkə/ *n.* (*pl.* same) a member or the language of a pre-Inca people living on the coast of Peru AD 100–800, with a highly developed agricultural system, depending on artificial irrigation, and no cities but concentrated ceremonial complexes where the ruling dynasty and administrators lived. [Sp., f. an Indian word; cf. *Moche*, site and valley on NW coast of Peru]

mock *v.t./i.* **1.** to make fun of by imitating, to mimic. **2.** to scoff or jeer; to defy contemptuously. —*attrib. adj.* sham, imitation (esp. without intent to deceive). —**mocking-bird** *n.* a bird (esp. the American songbird *Mimus polyglottus*) that mimics the notes of other birds. **mock orange,** a shrub (*Philadelphus coronarius*) with fragrant white flowers. **mock turtle soup,** a soup made from a calf's head etc., to resemble turtle soup. **mock-up** *n.* an experimental model or replica of a proposed structure etc. [f. OF *mo(c)quer*]

mockery /ˈmɒkərɪ/ *n.* **1.** derision; the subject or occasion of this. **2.** a counterfeit or absurdly inadequate representation. **3.** a ludicrously or insultingly futile action etc. [as prec.]

mod *n.* (*colloq.*) a modification. —*adj.* modern. —**mod cons,** modern conveniences. [abbr.]

modal /ˈməʊd(ə)l/ *adj.* **1.** of mode or form as opposed to substance. **2.** (*Gram.*) of the mood of a verb; (of a verb, e.g. *would*) used to express the mood of another verb. [f. L (as MODE)]

mode *n.* **1.** the way or manner in which a thing is done; a method of procedure. **2.** the prevailing fashion or custom. **3.** (*Mus.*) any of the scale systems or types of melody that make up the characteristic sound of the music of a country or tradition. [F & f. L *modus*]

model /ˈmɒd(ə)l/ *n.* **1.** a representation in three dimensions of an existing person or thing or of a proposed structure, especially on a smaller scale. **2.** a simplified description of a system for calculations etc. **3.** a figure in clay, wax, etc., to be reproduced in another material. **4.** a particular design or style of structure, especially of a motor vehicle. **5.** a person or thing regarded as excellent of its kind and proposed for imitation. **6.** a person employed to pose for an artist, or to display clothes etc. by wearing them. **7.** a garment etc. by a well-known designer; a copy of this. —*adj.* exemplary, ideally perfect. —*v.t./i.* (**-ll-**) **1.** to fashion or shape (a figure) in clay, wax, etc. **2.** to design or plan on or after the model of. **3.** to act or pose as an artist's or fashion model; to display (clothes) thus. —**the (New) Model,** the plan for the reorganization of the Parliamentary army, passed by the House of Commons in 1644–5. **Model Parliament,** that of Nov. 1295, summoned by Edward I to obtain financial aid for his wars and so called in the 19th c. because it was more representative than any previous parliament—but the pattern did not survive. [f. F f. It. *modello* f. L (as MODULUS)]

modem /ˈməʊdem/ *n.* a combined device for modulation and demodulation, e.g. between a computer and a telephone line. [portmanteau word]

moderate /ˈmɒdərət/ *adj.* **1.** medium in amount, intensity, or quality etc.; avoiding extremes. **2.** temperate in conduct or expression; not holding extremist views. **3.** fairly large or good, tolerably so. **4.** (of prices) fairly low. —*n.* one who

holds moderate views in politics etc. —/-eɪt/ *v.t./i.* to make or become moderate or less intense etc.; to act as a moderator of. —**moderately** *adv.*, **moderateness** *n.* [f. L (*moderare* reduce, control)]

moderation /mɒdəˈreɪʃ(ə)n/ *n.* **1.** moderating. **2.** moderateness. —**in moderation,** in moderate amounts or degree. [f. OF f. L (as prec.)]

moderator *n.* **1.** an arbitrator, a mediator. **2.** a presiding officer; a Presbyterian minister presiding over a church court or assembly. **3.** a substance used in nuclear reactors to retard neutrons. [f. L (as MODERATE)]

modern /ˈmɒd(ə)n/ *adj.* of present and recent times; in current fashion, not antiquated. —*n.* a person living in modern times. —**modern dance,** see BALLET. —**modern English,** English from the 16th c. onwards (see ENGLISH). —**modernity** /-ˈdɜːnɪtɪ/ *n.* [f. F or L (*modo* just now)]

modernism *n.* **1.** modern views or methods. **2.** a tendency in matters of religious belief to subordinate tradition to harmony with modern thought, especially a movement in the Roman Catholic Church in the late 19th c., officially condemned by Pope Pius X in 1907. **3.** a modern term or usage. —**modernist** *n.*, **modernistic** /-ˈnɪstɪk/ *adj.* [f. prec.]

modernize *v.t./i.* to make modern, to adapt to modern needs or habits; to adopt modern ways or views. —**modernization** /-ˈzeɪʃ(ə)n/ *n.*

modest /ˈmɒdɪst/ *adj.* **1.** having a humble or moderate estimate of one's own merits. **2.** diffident, not putting oneself forward. **3.** decorous in manner and conduct. **4.** (of a demand, statement, etc.) not excessive or exaggerated. **5.** unpretentious in appearance, amount, etc. —**modestly** *adv.*, **modesty** *n.* [f. F f. L, = keeping due measure]

modicum /ˈmɒdɪkəm/ *n.* a small quantity. [L, neut. of *modicus* moderate]

modification /mɒdɪfɪˈkeɪʃ(ə)n/ *n.* **1.** modifying, being modified. **2.** a change made. —**modificatory** *adj.* [F or f. L (as foll.)]

modify /ˈmɒdɪfaɪ/ *v.t.* **1.** to make less severe or decided, to tone down. **2.** to make partial changes in. **3.** (*Gram.*) to qualify the sense of (a word etc.). [f. OF f. L *modificare* (as MODE)]

Modigliani /mɒdiːˈljɑːnɪ/, Amedeo (1884–1920), Italian painter and sculptor who settled in Paris in 1906. He worked chiefly as a painter of female nudes, in which a somewhat mannered stylization of form was coupled with strong linear qualities and a knowing use of colour, often compared with the style of Botticelli. His friendship with the sculptor Brancusi (d. 1957) saw the production of some assured sculpture reliant on tribal art for its directness and visual power.

modish /ˈməʊdɪʃ/ *adj.* fashionable. —**modishly** *adv.*, **modishness** *n.* [f. MODE]

modiste /mɒˈdiːst/ *n.* a milliner, a dressmaker. [F (as MODE)]

modular /ˈmɒdjʊlə(r)/ *adj.* consisting of modules or moduli. [f. L MODULUS]

modulate /ˈmɒdjʊleɪt/ *v.t./i.* **1.** to regulate or adjust; to moderate. **2.** to adjust or vary the tone or pitch of (the speaking voice); to alter the amplitude or frequency of (a wave) by a wave of lower frequency to convey a signal; (*Mus.*) to pass from one key to another. —**modulation** /ˈleɪʃ(ə)n/ *n.* [f. L *modulari* (as foll.)]

module /ˈmɒdjuːl/ *n.* a standardized part or independent unit in construction (esp. of furniture), buildings, spacecraft, etc., or in an academic course. [F or f. L (as foll.)]

modulus /ˈmɒdjʊləs/ *n.* (*pl.* **-li** /-laɪ/) a constant factor or ratio. [L, = measure (as foll.)]

modus operandi /ˈməʊdəs ɒpəˈrændɪ/ the way a person goes about a task; the way a thing operates. [L, = mode of working]

modus vivendi /ˈməʊdəs vɪˈvendɪ/ a way of living or coping; an arrangement whereby those in dispute can carry on pending a settlement. [L, = mode of living]

mog *n.* (also **moggie**) (*slang*) a cat. [dial.]

Mogadishu /mɒɡəˈdɪʃuː/ the capital of Somalia; pop. (est. 1982) 600,000.

Mogul /ˈməʊɡ(ə)l/ *adj.* Mongolian; of the Moguls. —*n.* a Mongolian; a member of the Mongolian (Muslim) dynasty in India whose empire was consolidated, after the conquests of Tamerlane, by his descendant Babur (reigned *c.*1525–30) and greatly extended by Akbar. Gradually broken up by wars and revolts, and faced by European commercial expansion, the Mogul empire did not finally disappear until after the Indian Mutiny in 1857. —**the (Great** or **Grand) Mogul,** the Mogul emperor. [f. Pers. & Arab., as MONGOL]

mogul /ˈmoʊɡ(ə)l/ n. (colloq.) an important or influential person. [f. prec.]

mohair /ˈmoʊheə(r)/ n. the hair of the Angora goat; a yarn or fabric from this. [ult. f. Arab., = choice]

Mohammed var. of MUHAMMAD.

Mohawk /ˈmoʊhɔːk/ n. a member or the language of a tribe of North American Indians (see IROQUOIS). [native name]

Mohenjo-Daro /məhendʒoʊˈdɑːroʊ/ an ancient city of the Indus Valley civilization (see entry), in SE Pakistan.

Mohican /moʊˈhiːkən/ n. a member of a warlike tribe of North American Indians, of Algonquian stock, formerly occupying the western parts of Connecticut and Massachusetts.

moho /ˈmoʊhoʊ/ n. (pl. **-os**) (in full **Mohorovičić discontinuity** /məhendʒoʊˈroʊvɪtʃɪtʃ/) the boundary surface between the earth's crust and its mantle, where there is a change in the seismological properties of the rocks. It is believed to exist at a depth of about 10-12 km under the ocean beds and 40-50 km under the continents. [f. A. Mohorovičić, Yugoslav seismologist (d. 1936)]

Mohs /moʊz/, Friedrich (1773-1839), German mineralogist who developed a classification of minerals based on physical appearance rather than on chemical properties, but is now chiefly remembered for his classification of the hardness of minerals (Mohs' scale) described in 1812, and consisting of ten reference minerals of increasing hardness, from talc (hardness 1) to diamond (hardness 10). The reference minerals are talc 1, gypsum 2, calcite 3, fluorspar 4, apatite 5, orthoclase 6, quartz 7, topaz 8, corundum 9, diamond 10. Each can scratch the softer metals, and be scratched only by the harder metals, within this scale.

moiety /ˈmɔɪɪti/ n. (Law or literary) a half; either of the two parts of a thing. [f. OF f. L medietas (medius middle)]

moil v.i. to drudge. [f. OF moillier paddle in mud]

moire /mwɑː(r)/ n. (also **moire antique**) a watered fabric, usually silk. [F, f. MOHAIR]

moiré /ˈmwɑːreɪ/ adj. **1.** (of silk) watered. **2.** (of metal) having a clouded appearance like watered silk. [F (as prec.)]

Moissan /ˈmwɑːsɑ̃/, Ferdinand Frédéric Henri (1852-1907), French chemist and influential teacher of inorganic chemistry, who in 1886 succeeded in isolating the very reactive element fluorine, and who invented in 1892 an electric arc furnace that bears his name, in which he claimed to have synthesized diamonds. This is now in doubt, but the very high temperatures achieved in his furnace made it possible to reduce some uncommon metals from their ores. He was awarded the Nobel Prize for chemistry in 1906.

moist adj. slightly wet, damp; (of a season) rainy. —**moistness** n. [f. OF, perh. f. L mucidus (cf. MUCUS)]

moisten /ˈmɔɪs(ə)n/ v.t./i. to make or become moist. [f. prec.]

moisture /ˈmɔɪstʃə(r)/ n. liquid diffused in a small quantity as a vapour, within a solid, or condensed on a surface. [f. OF (as MOIST)]

moisturize v.t. to make less dry (esp. the skin by use of a cosmetic). —**moisturization** /-ˈzeɪʃ(ə)n/ n., **moisturizer** n. [f. prec.]

moke n. (slang) a donkey. [perf. f. a proper name]

moksha /ˈmɒkʃə/ n. (Hinduism & Jainism) liberation from the chain of births impelled by the law of karma; the bliss attained by this liberation (cf. NIRVANA). [Skr., = release (muc to release)]

molar /ˈmoʊlə(r)/ adj. (esp. of a mammal's back teeth) serving to grind. —n. a molar tooth (ill. BODY 1). [f. L molaris (mola millstone)]

molasses /məˈlæsɪz/ n. uncrystallized syrup drained from raw sugar; (US) treacle. [f. Port. f. L mellaceum must (mel honey)]

Moldavia /mɒlˈdeɪvɪə/ **1.** a Danubian principality from which, together with Wallachia, the kingdom of Romania was formed in 1859. **2.** the Moldavian SSR, a constituent republic of the USSR, formed from territory ceded by Romania in 1940; capital, Kishinev. —**Moldavian** adj. & n.

mole[1] n. **1.** a small burrowing mammal of the genus Talpa, with usually blackish velvety fur and very small eyes (ill. MAMMALS). **2.** a spy established deep within an organization and usually dormant for a long period while attaining a position of trust. [prob. f. MDu. or MLG]

mole[2] n. a small permanent dark spot on the human skin. [OE]

mole[3] n. a massive structure usually of stone, as a pier, breakwater, or causeway; an artificial harbour. [f. F f. L moles mass]

mole[4] n. the base unit of amount of substance (symbol mol; established in 1971 for international use), the amount of substance of a system which contains as many elementary entities as there are atoms in 0.012 kilogram of carbon 12. The elementary entities must be specified and may be atoms, molecules, ions, electrons, other particles, or specified groups of such particles. [f. G mol (molekül, as MOLECULE)]

molecular /məˈlekjʊlə(r)/ adj. of, relating to, or consisting of molecules. —**molecular weight,** the ratio between the mass of one molecule of a substance and one-twelfth of the mass of an atom of the isotope carbon 12. —**molecularity** /-ˈlærɪtɪ/ n. [f. foll.]

molecule /ˈmɒlɪkjuːl/ n. the smallest particle (usually a group of atoms) to which a substance can be reduced by subdivision without losing its chemical identity. [f. F, as MOLE[3]]

molehill n. a small mound thrown up by a mole in burrowing. —**make a mountain out of a molehill,** to over-react to a small difficulty.

molest /məˈlest/ v.t. to annoy or pester (a person) in a hostile or injurious way. —**molestation** /-ˈsteɪʃ(ə)n/ n. [f. OF or L molestare (molestus troublesome)]

Molière /ˈmɒlɪeə(r)/ the name assumed by Jean-Baptiste Poquelin (1622-73), French comic dramatist. He began his career as groom-upholsterer to the king, but soon turned to the stage, became an actor, and founded a dramatic company for which he composed comedies and farces. His real genius is first shown in Les Précieuses ridicules (1659), in which, abandoning imitations of Plautus and Terence, he introduced the ridicule of actual French society, with its various types of folly, oddity, pedantry, or vice, as the subject of French comedy. Among his most famous plays, showing a profound understanding of the incongruities of human nature, are Le Tartuffe (1664), Don Juan (1665), Le Misanthrope (1666), L'Avare (1669), Le Bourgeois Gentilhomme (1670), and Le Malade imaginaire (1673). He was the creator of French classical comedy, with a genius for reconciling the comic and the intellectual.

moline /məˈlaɪn/ adj. (in heraldry, of a cross) having each extremity broadened and curved back like the ends of an upper millstone's support (ill. HERALDRY). [prob. f. AF (molin MILL)]

moll n. (colloq.) **1.** a prostitute. **2.** a gangster's female companion. [pet-form of Mary]

mollify /ˈmɒlɪfaɪ/ v.t. to appease; to soothe the anger of. —**mollification** /-fɪˈkeɪʃ(ə)n/ n. [f. F or L mollificare (mollis soft)]

mollusc /ˈmɒləsk/ n. an animal of the phylum Mollusca, of soft-bodied usually hard-shelled animals including snails, oysters, mussels, etc. [f. L molluscus (mollis soft)]

mollycoddle /ˈmɒlɪkɒd(ə)l/ v.t. to coddle excessively, to pamper. —n. an effeminate man or boy, a milksop. [as MOLL + CODDLE]

Moloch /ˈmoʊlɒk/ a Canaanite god to whose image children were sacrificed as burnt offerings (Lev. 18: 21, 2 Kings 23: 10).

Molotov /ˈmɒlətɒf/, Vyacheslav Mikhailovich (1890-), Russian statesman, an early member of the Bolsheviks and one of the most important members of the Stalinist party. Prime Minister from 1930 to 1941, he took over responsibility for foreign affairs in 1939, negotiating the Nazi-Soviet Pact and remaining Foreign Secretary throughout the Second World War. He returned to the Foreign Ministry in 1953 after Stalin's death but quarrelled with Khruschev and was expelled from his party posts in 1956. —**Molotov cocktail,** a makeshift incendiary hand-grenade consisting of a breakable container with inflammable liquid and a means of ignition.

molten /ˈmoʊlt(ə)n/ adj. melted, especially made liquid by heat. [f. MELT]

Molucca Islands /məˈlʌkə/ (also **Moluccas**) a group of islands of Indonesia, SE of the Philippines, formerly called the Spice Islands; pop. (1971) 1,088,945; capital, Amboina.

moly /ˈmoʊlɪ/ n. (Gk legend) a magical plant with a white flower and black root, given by Hermes to Odysseus as a charm against the sorceries of Circe. [L, F. Gk mōlu]

molybdenum /məˈlɪbdɪnəm/ n. a hard silver-white

metallic element, symbol Mo, atomic number 42, first isolated in 1782. The pure metal is used where resistance to very high temperatures is required, but its main use is as a component in special steels and other alloys, where it imparts strength at high temperatures and resistance to corrosion. [f. L f. Gk, = plummet (*molubdos* lead)]

moment /ˈməʊmənt/ *n.* **1.** a very brief portion of time. **2.** an exact point of time. **3.** importance. **4.** the product of a force and the distance of its line of action from the centre of rotation. —**at the moment**, at this time, now. **in a moment**, very soon. **man** etc. **of the moment**, the one of importance at the time in question. **moment of truth**, a time of crisis or test. [f. OF f. L, = MOMENTUM]

momentary /ˈməʊməntərɪ/ *adj.* lasting only a moment. —**momentarily** *adj.* [f. L (as prec.)]

momentous /məˈmentəs/ *adj.* having great importance. [f. MOMENT]

momentum /məˈmentəm/ *n.* (*pl.* **-ta**) the quantity of motion of a moving body, the product of its mass and its velocity; impetus gained by movement (*lit.* or *fig.*). [L (*movimentum* f. *movēre* move)]

Mommsen /ˈmɒms(ə)n/, Theodor (1817-1903), German historian. His most celebrated works are his *History of Rome* (1854-6, 1885), and his treatises on Roman constitutional law (1871-88) and on criminal law (1899); he was also editor of the monumental *Corpus Inscriptionum Latinarum* (1863-) for the Berlin Academy. Mommsen took an active part in politics and was a keen critic of Bismarck. He was awarded the Nobel Prize for literature in 1902.

Mon. *abbr.* Monday.

Mona /ˈməʊnə/ an island between Ireland and Scotland, traditionally supposed to have been inhabited by the Druids, now thought to have been either the Isle of Man or Anglesey.

Monaco /ˈmɒnəkəʊ/ a principality in southern Europe on the Mediterranean coast, an enclave within French territory near the Italian frontier; pop. (1983) approx. 28,000; official language, French; capital, Monaco (pop. 1,443). Ruled by the Genoese from medieval times, and by the Grimaldi family from 1297, Monaco was under French occupation from 1793 to 1814 and then was a Sardinian protectorate until 1861. It became a constitutional monarchy in 1911, although the constitution was briefly suspended in 1959–62. The smallest sovereign State in the world apart from the Vatican, Monaco is almost entirely dependent on the tourist trade with over a million visitors a year, and maintains a customs union with France. —**Monacan** *adj.* & *n.*

monad /ˈmɒnæd/ *n.* **1.** the number one, unity; an arithmetical unit. **2.** any of the ultimate units of being (e.g. a soul, an atom, a person, God), especially in the philosophy of Leibniz. [f. F or L f. Gk *monas* unit (*monos* alone)]

Mona Lisa /ˌməʊnə ˈliːzə/ a painting (now in the Louvre) executed 1503-6 by Leonardo da Vinci and known also as La Gioconda, the sitter being the wife of Francesco di Bartolommeo del Giocondo di Zandi. Her enigmatic smile has become the most famous image in the world, whether inspiring reverence (e.g. Walter Pater's prose poem in his *Renaissance*) or ridicule (e.g. Marcel Duchamp's Dada gesture of adding a moustache).

monarch /ˈmɒnək/ *n.* a sovereign with the title of king, queen, emperor, empress, or the equivalent; a supreme ruler (*lit.* or *fig.*). —**monarchic** /məˈnɑːkɪk/ *adj.*, **monarchical** /məˈnɑːkɪk(ə)l/ *adj.* [f. F or L f Gk (*monos* alone, *arkhō* rule)]

monarchism /ˈmɒnəkɪz(ə)m/ *n.* the advocacy of or principles of monarchy. —**monarchist** *n.* [f. F (as foll.)]

monarchy /ˈmɒnəkɪ/ *n.* a form of government with a monarch at the head; a State governed in this way. [f. OF f. L f. Gk (as MONARCH)]

monastery /ˈmɒnəstərɪ/ *n.* the residence of a community of monks. [f. L f. Gk (*monazō* live alone, as MONO-)]

monastic /məˈnæstɪk/ *adj.* **1.** of or like monks, nuns, friars, etc. **2.** of monasteries. —**monastically** *adv.*, **monasticism** /məˈnæstɪsɪz(ə)m/ *n.* [f. F f. L f. Gk (as prec.)]

Monck /mʌŋk/, George (1608-70), English general, created 1st Duke of Albemarle. Although initially a royalist in the Civil War, he became a supporter of Cromwell and campaigned capably in Scotland, subduing that country by the end of 1651, and fought at sea in the Dutch war of 1652-4. Excluded from influence in the subsequent military government, however, he and his troops advanced on London, and Monck was instrumental in restoring the monarchy (1660).

Monday /ˈmʌndeɪ, -dɪ/ *n.* the day of the week following Sunday. —*adv.* (*colloq.*) on Monday. [OE, = day of the moon]

Mondrian /ˈmɒndrɪɑːn/, Piet (Pieter Cornelis Mondriaan, 1872-1944), Dutch painter. A founder of the periodical *De Stijl* in 1917, he became the main exponent of a new kind of geometrical abstract painting which he named neo-plasticism. The basic elements that he used were straight lines meeting at right angles, and a limited number of primary colours. He influenced the art and taste of the 1930s, including contemporary fashion in commercial and advertisement design.

Monégasque /mɒneɪˈgæsk/ *adj.* of Monaco or its people. —*n.* a Monégasque person. [F]

Monet /ˈmɒneɪ/, Claude Oscar (1840-1926), French painter, one of the founders of French impressionism (his *Impression: Sunrise*, 1873, gave the movement its name). In his youth he was introduced to landscape painting, and developed a firm predilection for painting out of doors. An early picture *Women in the Garden* (1867) shows his growing interest in light, and from *c.*1870 he restricted himself almost completely to landscape and to rendering harmonies of colour hue in varying conditions of light. Among the most celebrated are those of Rouen Cathedral, painted at different times of day in different lights, the views of the Gare St Lazare, and a series of water-lily pictures. He has been regarded as perhaps the most powerful exponent of that aspect of impressionism which is concerned with the representation of atmosphere and colour.

monetarism /ˈmʌnɪtərɪz(ə)m/ *n.* advocacy of the control of money as the chief method of stabilizing the economy. This economic theory is based on the belief that the supply of money is the crucial determinant of the level of demand, which argues that strict government control of the money supply is necessary to prevent high inflation, and is opposed to the Keynesian idea that the money supply is largely unimportant in determining demand. Britain, predominantly Keynesian in the 1960s, experienced a strong monetarist backlash in the late 1970s in the government's attempts at controlling inflation. —**monetarist** *n.* [f. foll.]

monetary /ˈmʌnɪtərɪ/ *adj.* of the currency in use; of or consisting of money. —**monetarily** *adv.* [f. F or L (as MONEY)]

money /ˈmʌnɪ/ *n.* **1.** the current medium of exchange in the form of coins and banknotes. **2.** (in *pl.* **moneys** or **monies**) sums of money. **3.** wealth, property viewed as convertible into money. **4.** a rich person or rich people. —**in the money**, having or winning plenty of money. **make money**, to acquire wealth. **money-bag** *n.* a bag for money; (in *pl.* treated as *sing.*, *colloq.*) a wealthy person. **money-box** *n.* a closed box for holding money dropped in through a slit. **money-changer** *n.* one whose business it is to change money, especially at an official rate. **money for jam,** (*slang*) a profit for little or no trouble. **money-grabber** *n.* one greedily intent on amassing money. **money-grabbing** *adj.* given to this practice; (*n.*) this practice. **money-lender** *n.* one whose business it is to lend money at interest. **money-making** *adj.* producing wealth; (*n.*) the acquisition of wealth. **money-market** *n.* the sphere of operation of dealers in short-dated loans, stocks, etc. **money of account,** a unit of money used in accounting but not current as a coin or note. **money order,** an order for the payment of a specified sum, issued by a bank or the Post Office. **money-spider** *n.* a small spider supposed to bring good luck in money or other matters to the person over whom it crawls. **money-spinner** *n.* a thing that brings in much profit. **money's-worth** *n.* good value for one's money. **put money into,** to make an investment in. [f. OF f. L *moneta* mint]

moneyed /ˈmʌnɪd/ *adj.* wealthy; consisting of money. [f. prec.]

monger /ˈmʌŋgə(r)/ *n.* (chiefly *in comb.*) **1.** a dealer or trader (*fishmonger*). **2.** (usu. *derog.*) a spreader (*scandalmonger*, *scaremonger*). [OE f. L *mango*]

Mongol /ˈmɒŋg(ə)l/ *adj.* **1.** of an Asian people now inhabiting Mongolia. **2.** having Mongoloid characteristics. —*n.* a Mongol person. [native name, perh. f. *mong* brave]

mongol /ˈmɒŋg(ə)l/ *adj.* suffering from Down's syndrome. —*n.* a mongol person. —**mongolism** *n.* [f. prec.]

Mongolia /mɒŋˈgəʊlɪə/ a large and sparsely populated country of eastern Asia, bordered by the USSR and China; pop. (1984) approx. 1,820,400; official language, Mongolian; capital, Ulan Bator. The economy is predominantly pastoral and the bulk of the international trade is with the Soviet

Union. The centre of the medieval Mongol empire, Mongolia subsequently became a Chinese province, achieving *de facto* independence in 1911. In 1924 it became a Communist State after the Soviet model, and has since gravitated towards the USSR.

Mongolian /mɒŋˈɡəʊlɪən/ *adj.* of Mongolia or its people or language. —*n.* 1. a native or inhabitant of Mongolia. 2. a member of a racial division of mankind (see below). 3. the language of Mongolia, spoken by some 1,500,000 people, chief among a number of related languages and dialects which together form the Mongolian group in the Altaic language family. [f. prec.]

Mongolians form one of the major racial divisions of mankind defined by Blumenbach. They occupy three distinct geographical areas: eastern Asia, SE Asia, and the Arctic region of North America, and are characterized by dark eyes, very dark coarse straight hair, pale ivory to dark skin, scant facial and body hair, and the epicanthic skin-fold.

Mongoloid /ˈmɒŋɡəlɔɪd/ *adj.* resembling the Mongolians in racial origin or in having a broad flat (yellowish) face. —*n.* a Mongoloid person. [f. MONGOL]

mongoose /ˈmɒŋɡuːs/ *n.* (*pl.* **-gooses**) a small carnivorous tropical mammal of the genus *Herpestes*, especially a species common in India, able to kill venomous snakes unharmed. [f. Marathi]

mongrel /ˈmʌŋɡr(ə)l/ *n.* 1. a dog of no definable breed. 2. an animal or plant resulting from the crossing of different breeds or types. —*adj.* of mixed origin, nature, or character. [rel. to MINGLE]

Monica /ˈmɒnɪkə/, St (*c.*331–87), mother of St Augustine of Hippo. Feast day, 24 Aug.

moniker /ˈmɒnɪkə(r)/ *n.* (*slang*) a name, a nickname. [orig. unkn.]

monism /ˈmɒnɪz(ə)m/ *n.* the theory that there is only a single ultimate principle or kind of being, not two or more (opp. DUALISM and PLURALISM); any of the theories that deny the duality of matter and mind. —**monist** *n.*, **monistic** /-ˈnɪstɪk/ *adj.* [f. Gk *monos* single]

monitor /ˈmɒnɪtə(r)/ *n.* 1. a pupil in a school with disciplinary or other duties. 2. a television receiver used in selecting or verifying the broadcast picture; a highly definitive screen used with a computer. 3. one who listens to and reports on foreign broadcasts etc. 4. a detector of radioactive contamination. —*v.t./i.* 1. to act as a monitor (of); to maintain regular surveillance (over). 2. to regulate the strength of (a recorded or transmitted signal). —**monitor lizard,** a lizard of the family Varanidae, found in tropical and subtropical regions. —**monitorial** /-ˈtɔːrɪəl/ *adj.*, **monitress** *n.fem.* [L (*monēre* warn)]

monitory /ˈmɒnɪtərɪ/ *adj.* giving or serving as a warning. [f. L *monitorius* (as prec.)]

monk /mʌŋk/ *n.* a member of a community of men living apart under religious vows. —**monkish** *adj.* [OE, ult. f. Gk *monakhos* solitary]

monkey /ˈmʌŋkɪ/ *n.* 1. a mammal of a group closely allied to and resembling man, especially a small long-tailed member of the order Primates. 2. a mischievous person, especially a child. 3. (*slang*) £500; (*US*) $500. —*v.i.* 1. to play mischievously. 2. to tamper or play mischief with tricks. —**monkey business,** (*slang*) mischief. **monkey-nut** *n.* a peanut. **monkey-puzzle** *n.* a prickly tree of the genus *Araucaria* with interlaced branches, the Chile pine. **monkey-tricks** *n.pl.* (*slang*) mischief. **monkey-wrench** *n.* a wrench with an adjustable jaw. [orig. unkn.]

Mon-Khmer /məʊnˈkmeə(r)/ *adj.* of a group of Indo-Chinese languages of which the most important are Mon (spoken in eastern Burma and western Thailand) and Khmer (=CAMBODIAN). Mon is now a relatively minor language but in the 13th c. it was extremely influential throughout Burma.

monkshood /ˈmʌŋkshʊd/ *n.* a poisonous plant (*Aconitum napellus*) with hood-shaped flowers.

Monmouth /ˈmʌnməθ/ James Scott, Duke of (1649–85), illegitimate son of Charles II. His repeated attempts to have himself legitimized as Charles's heir led to his being banished on several occasions, despite his military services to the regime. On the accession of James II, Monmouth raised an insurrection against him in the West Country but was defeated at Sedgemoor and subsequently beheaded.

mono /ˈmɒnəʊ/ *adj.* monophonic. —*n.* (*pl.* **-os**) a monophonic record, reproduction, etc. [abbr.]

mono- *in comb.* (before a vowel usu. **mon-**) one, alone, single. [Gk (*monos* alone)]

monochromatic /mɒnəkrəˈmætɪk/ *adj.* 1. (of light or other radiation) containing only one colour or wavelength. 2. executed in monochrome. —**monochromatically** *adv.*

monochrome /ˈmɒnəkrəʊm/ *n.* a picture done in one colour or different tints of this, or in black and white only. —*adj.* having or using only one colour. [f. Gk (MONO-, *khrōma* colour)]

monocle /ˈmɒnək(ə)l/ *n.* a single eyeglass. [F, orig. f. L *monoculus* one-eyed]

monocotyledon /mɒnəkɒtɪˈliːd(ə)n/ *n.* a flowering plant with a single cotyledon. —**monocotyledonous** *adj.*

monocular /məˈnɒkjʊlə(r)/ *adj.* with or for one eye. [f. L (as MONOCLE)]

monodrama /ˈmɒnədrɑːmə/ *n.* a dramatic piece for one performer.

monody /ˈmɒnədɪ/ *n.* 1. an ode sung by a single actor in a Greek play. 2. a poem in which a mourner bewails someone's death. —**monodist** *n.* [f. L f. Gk *monōidia* (as MONO-, ODE)]

monogamy /məˈnɒɡəmɪ/ *n.* the practice or state of being married to one person at a time. —**monogamist** *n.*, **monogamous** *adj.* [f. F f. L f. Gk (MONO-, *gamos* marriage)]

monogram /ˈmɒnəɡræm/ *n.* two or more letters, especially a person's initials, interwoven as a device. —**monogrammed** *adj.* [f. F f. L (as MONO-, -GRAM)]

monograph /ˈmɒnəɡrɑːf/ *n.* a separate treatise on a single subject or aspect of it. [f. MONO- + -GRAPH]

monolith /ˈmɒnəlɪθ/ *n.* 1. a single block of stone, especially shaped into a pillar etc. 2. a person or thing like a monolith in being massive, immovable, or solidly uniform. —**monolithic** /-ˈlɪθɪk/ *adj.* [f. F f. Gk (MONO-, *lithos* stone)]

monologue /ˈmɒnəlɒɡ/ *n.* 1. a scene in a drama where a person speaks alone; a dramatic composition for one performer. 2. a long speech by one person in a company. [F f. Gk *monologos* speaking alone]

monomania /mɒnəˈmeɪnɪə/ *n.* an obsession of the mind by one idea or interest. —**monomaniac** /-ɪæk/ *adj. & n.* [f. F (as MONO-, -MANIA)]

monophonic /mɒnəˈfɒnɪk/ *adj.* (of reproduction of sound) using only one channel of transmission. [f. MONO- + Gk *phōnē* sound]

Monophysite /məˈnɒfɪzaɪt/ *n.* an adherent of the doctrine that there was in the person of Christ only a single nature, part divine and part human, the human element being totally subordinate to the divine. Its followers became a distinct body after the Council of Chalcedon (451) had defined the orthodox doctrine that there were two natures in Christ, separate and unconfused. Despite attempts at reconciliation by the Byzantine emperors, who saw the unity of the empire threatened, the break became final in the 6th c., and the Coptic and several other Eastern Churches have remained Monophysite. [f. L f. Gk (*monos* one, *phusis* nature]

monoplane /ˈmɒnəpleɪn/ *n.* an aeroplane with one pair of wings.

monopolist /məˈnɒpəlɪst/ *n.* one who has or advocates a monopoly. —**monopolistic** /-ˈlɪstɪk/ *adj.* [f. MONOPOLY]

monopolize /məˈnɒpəlaɪz/ *v.t.* 1. to obtain exclusive possession or control of (a trade or commodity). 2. to dominate or prevent others from sharing in (a conversation etc.). —**monopolization** /-ˈzeɪʃ(ə)n/ *n.* [f. foll.]

monopoly /məˈnɒpəlɪ/ *n.* 1. exclusive possession of the trade in some commodity. 2. exclusive possession, control, or exercise (*of*, (*US*) *on*). 3. a thing of which one person or firm etc. has a monopoly. [f. L f. Gk (MONO-, *pōleō* sell)]

monorail /ˈmɒnəʊreɪl/ *n.* a railway in which the track consists of a single rail.

monosyllable /ˈmɒnəsɪləb(ə)l/ *n.* a word of one syllable. —**monosyllabic** /-ˈlæbɪk/ *adj.*

monotheism /ˈmɒnəθiːɪz(ə)m/ *n.* the doctrine that there is only one god. —**monotheist** *n.*, **monotheistic** /-ˈɪstɪk/ *adj.* [f. MONO- + Gk *theos* god]

Monothelite /məˈnɒθəlaɪt/ *n.* an adherent of the doctrine that there was in the person of Christ only one will. The theory (condemned as heresy in 681) was put forward as an attempt to reconcile the orthodox and Monophysite doctrines, but it led only to fresh controversy. [f. L f. Gk (*monos* one, *thelēma* will)]

monotone /ˈmɒnətəʊn/ *n.* 1. a sound or utterance continuing or repeated on one note without change of pitch. 2. sameness in style of writing. —*adj.* without change of pitch. [f. Gk (as MONO-, TONE)]

monotonous /mə'nɒtənəs/ *adj.* lacking in variety, wearisome through sameness. —**monotonously** *adv.*, **monotony** *n.* [f. prec.]

monotreme /'mɒnətri:m/ *n.* a mammal of the subclass Monotremata of primitive egg-laying Australasian animals with a single vent. [f. MONO- + Gk *trēma* hole]

Monotype /'mɒnətaɪp/ *n.* [P] a composing-machine that casts and sets up pieces of type singly.

monovalent /'mɒnəveɪlənt/ *adj.* univalent. [f. MONO- + -*valent* (VALENCE¹)]

monoxide /mə'nɒksaɪd/ *n.* an oxide containing one oxygen atom.

Monroe¹ /mən'rəʊ/, James (1758–1831), President of the USA (1817–25), and formulator of the **Monroe Doctrine,** that interference by any European State in the affairs of Spanish-American republics would be regarded as an act unfriendly to the USA, and that the American continents were no longer open to European colonial settlement.

Monroe² /mən'rəʊ/, Marilyn (Norma Jean Mortenson, later Baker, 1926–62), American film actress. In the 1940s she became a photographic model and a forces' pin-up, subsequently appearing in comedy films (e.g. *Gentlemen Prefer Blondes*, 1953) in which she was promoted as a sex symbol. Later she starred in more serious films, the last of which (*The Misfits*, 1961) was written for her by her third husband, Arthur Miller. Her private life was much publicized; after bouts of depression she died from an overdose of barbiturates.

Monrovia /mɒn'rəʊvɪə/ the capital of Liberia; pop. (est.) 300,000.

Mons /mɒnz/ a town in Belgium, site of the first British battle on the Continent in the First World War, in August 1914. The Germans were repulsed with heavy losses by accurate British rifle fire.

Monseigneur /mɒnsen'jɜ:(r)/ *n.* the title given to an eminent Frenchman, especially a prince, cardinal, archbishop, or bishop. [F (*mon* my, SEIGNEUR)]

Monsieur /mə'sjɜ:(r)/ *n.* (*pl.* **Messieurs** /me'sjɜ:(r)/) the title used of or to a French-speaking man, corresponding to Mr or sir. [F (*mon* my, *sieur* lord)]

Monsignor /mɒn'si:njə(r)/ *n.* the title of various Roman Catholic prelates. [It., after MONSEIGNEUR]

monsoon /mɒn'su:n/ *n.* a wind in southern Asia, especially in the Indian Ocean, blowing from the south-west in summer and from the north-east in winter; the rainy season accompanying the south-west monsoon. [f. obs. Du. f. Port. f. Arab., = fixed season]

monster *n.* **1.** an imaginary creature, usually large and frightening, compounded of incongruous elements. **2.** a misshapen animal or plant. **3.** an inhumanly cruel or wicked person. **4.** an animal or thing of huge size. —*adj.* huge. [f. OF f. L, = portent (*monēre* warn)]

monstrance /'mɒnstrəns/ *n.* (in the RC Church) a vessel in which the Host is exposed for veneration. [f. L *monstrantia* (*monstrare* show)]

monstrosity /mon'strɒsɪtɪ/ *n.* **1.** a misshapen animal or plant; an outrageous thing. **2.** monstrousness. [f. L (as foll.)]

monstrous /'mɒnstrəs/ *adj.* **1.** like a monster; huge. **2.** abnormally formed. **3.** outrageously wrong or absurd, atrocious. —**monstrously** *adv.* [f. OF or L (as MONSTER)]

montage /mɒn'tɑ:ʒ/ *n.* **1.** a composite picture or piece of music etc. made of heterogeneous juxtaposed items, a pastiche; production of this. **2.** (in cinematography) combination of images in quick succession to compress background information or provide atmosphere; a system of editing in which the narrative is modified or interrupted to include images that are not necessarily related to the dramatic development. The latter technique was used notably by Eisenstein. [F (*monter* to mount)]

Montagna /mɒn'tɑ:njə/, Bartolommeo Cincani (1450–1523), Italian painter. Probably trained in Venice, he settled in Vicenza and helped establish it as a centre of art. His *Madonna and Child* is a good example of his work, with its strong unaffected composition and muted tonality.

Montaigne /mɒn'teɪn/, Michel Eyquem de (1533–92), French writer, generally regarded as the inventor of the modern 'essay'. His famous *Essais* (1580–95), vividly translated into English by John Florio (d. 1625), became the subject of philosophical expansion in the 17th c. They reveal the author as a man of insatiable intellectual curiosity, kindly and sagacious, condemning pedantry and lying, but tolerant of an easy morality.

Montana /mɒn'tænə/ a State of the USA on the Canadian border east of the Rocky Mountains, forming part of the Louisiana Purchase in 1803. It became the 41st State of the USA in 1889; capital, Helena.

Montanist /'mɒntənɪst/ *n.* a member of a heretical Christian movement, founded in Phrygia in the 2nd c., which reacted against the growing secularism of the Church, desired a stricter adhesion to the principles of primitive Christianity, and prepared for the earthly kingdom of Christ. —**Montanism** *n.* [f. *Montanus* its founder]

Mont Blanc /mɔ̃ 'blɑ̃/ a peak in the Alps on the border of France and Italy, the highest mountain in Europe (4,180 m, 15,781 ft.).

montbretia /mɒn'bri:ʃə/ *n.* a hybrid plant of the iris family (genus *Crocosmia*) with bright orange-coloured flowers. [f. A. F. E. Coquebert de *Montbret*, French botanist (d. 1801)]

Montcalm /mɒn'kɑ:m/, Louis Joseph de Montcalm-Gozon, Marquis de (1712–59), French soldier, who defended Quebec against Wolfe and was mortally wounded in the battle which followed the scaling of the Heights of Abraham.

Monte Carlo /mɒntɪ 'kɑ:ləʊ/ one of the three communes of the principality of Monaco, famous as a gambling resort and as the terminus of a car rally; pop. 9,948.

Monte Cassino /mɒntɪ kə'si:nəʊ/ a hill midway between Rome and Naples, site of the principal monastery of the Benedictines, founded by St Benedict *c*.529. In 1944, during the Second World War, Allied forces advancing towards Rome were halted by German defensive positions to which Monte Cassino was the key; they succeeded in capturing the site only after four months of bitter fighting. The monastery, previously demolished and rebuilt several times, was almost totally destroyed, but has since been restored.

Montenegro /mɒntɪ'ni:grəʊ/ a constituent republic of Yugoslavia.

Montespan /mɔ̃tespã/, Françoise-Athénaïs de Rochechouart, Marquise de (1641–1707), mistress of Louis XIV. A great beauty with a notorious temper, de Montespan dominated the king for more than a decade (1667–79), giving him many illegitimate children. Very unpopular at court, she was the subject of repeated plots aimed at supplanting her with a more amenable woman.

Montessori /mɒntɪ'sɔ:rɪ/, Maria (1870–1952), Italian educationist. Her success with mentally retarded children led her, in 1907, to apply similar methods to younger children of normal intelligence. The Montessori system, which became world-wide in the 1910s and 1920s, emphasizes free but guided play with apparatus designed to encourage sense perception and mental interest, with less rigid discipline than was formerly common.

Monteverdi /mɒntɪ'veədɪ/, Claudio (1567–1643), Italian composer of sacred and secular music, whose place in the history of Renaissance music can be compared to Shakespeare's in literature. He transformed every genre in which he worked by imaginative use of existing styles rather than by revolutionary means. His madrigals cover a period of forty years, and he introduced instrumental accompaniments and chromatic modulations. His *Orfeo* (1607) is the earliest opera to enjoy widespread popularity, while the operas he composed for the newly opened public opera houses in Venice portray clearly defined characters rather than the customary symbolic figures. Above all, the melodic genius and fertility of his music and its harmonic adventurousness are what make it so attractive and 'contemporary' in the 20th c.

Montevideo /mɒntɪvɪ'deɪəʊ/ the capital and chief port of Uruguay, on the Río de la Plata; pop. (1981) 345,858.

Montezuma /mɒntɪ'zu:mə/ (1466–1520), the last ruler of the Aztec empire in Mexico. Defeated by the Spanish conquistadors under Cortés, Montezuma was imprisoned, but subsequently killed while trying to pacify some of his former subjects who had risen against his captors.

Montfort /'mɒntfət/, Simon de (1208–65), Earl of Leicester, leader of baronial opposition to Henry III. His campaign against royal encroachment on the privileges gained through Magna Carta, and his use of a parliament which included not only barons, knights, and ecclesiastics but two citizens from every borough in England, established him as one of the earliest exponents of limitations on the authority of the throne. After his defeat and capture of Henry at Lewes in 1264 he enjoyed a brief period as effective ruler of England, but was defeated and killed by reorganized royal forces under Henry's son (later Edward I) at Evesham in 1265.

Montgolfier /mɒnˈgɒlfɪeɪ, -ə(r)/, Joseph (1740-1810) and Jacques Étienne (1745-99), French paper-manufacturers and balloonists, the first to arouse scientific and popular interest in ballooning. They began experiments in 1782 and built a large globe of linen and paper, lit a fire on the ground, and let the hot air float up into the globe through its open base so as to lift it. With this they successfully lifted a sheep, goat, and duck on 19 Sept. 1782; manned ascents followed in 1783. Joseph was the only brother to fly, once, in the largest ever hot-air balloon *La Flesselle* (19 Jan. 1784).

Montgomery /mɒntˈgʌmərɪ, -ˈgɒm-/, Bernard Law, Viscount Montgomery of Alamein (1887-1976), British soldier, who rose to prominence with his appointment to command the Eighth Army in the Western Desert in mid-1942, where his victory at El Alamein proved the decisive battle in the campaign to secure Egypt (and the Suez Canal), and later commanded British forces in the invasion of German-occupied France in 1944. By no means the most brilliant of generals, Montgomery achieved results by concentrating on meticulous planning and attention to logistics, and did much to sustain the spirit of the British Army through an intensive public relations campaign.

month /mʌnθ/ n. 1. any of usually 12 periods of time into which the year is divided or any period between the same dates in successive such portions (see below). 2. a period of 28 days. —**month of Sundays,** a very long period. [OE (as MOON)]
    The primitive calendar month of ancient nations began on the day of a new moon or the day after, and thus coincided (except for fractions of a day) with the lunar month. Among many peoples, however, it was from a very early period found desirable that the calendar year should contain an integral number of the smaller periods used in ordinary reckoning, and the lunar months were superseded by a series of twelve periods each having a fixed number of days. In the Julian calendar the months in leap year had alternately 31 and 30 days while in other years February had only 29 instead of 30. This symmetrical arrangement was under Augustus broken up by the transference of one day from February to August, and one from September and November to October and December respectively, producing the system now in use.

monthly adj. produced or occurring once every month. —adv. every month. —n. a monthly periodical. [f. prec.]

Montmartre /mɔ̃ˈmɑːtr/ a district in Paris much frequented by artists at the beginning of the 19th c. when it was a village separated from Paris. Many of its buildings have artistic associations, e.g. the Moulin de la Galette painted by Renoir, the Bateau-Lavoir occupied successively by Renoir, van Dongen, and Picasso, and the various houses associated with Utrillo.

Montreal /mɒntrɪˈɔːl/ a port on the St Lawrence and the largest city in Canada; pop. (1981) 2,828,349.

Montrose /mɒnˈtrəʊz/, James Graham, Marquis of (1612-50). Although one of the leaders of early Scottish resistance to Charles I, Montrose supported the king when his country entered the English Civil War and, commanding a small army of Irish and Scottish irregulars, inflicted a dramatic series of defeats on the stronger Covenanter forces in the north in 1644-5 before being defeated at Philiphaugh while trying to bring his men south to aid the failing Royalist cause in England. After several years in exile, he returned to Scotland in an ill-fated bid to restore the new king Charles II.

Mont St Michel /mɔ̃ sæ miːˈʃel/ an islet off the coast of Normandy, a rocky peak crowned by a medieval Benedictine abbey-fortress.

Montserrat /mɒntsəˈræt/ one of the Leeward Islands in the West Indies, discovered by Columbus in 1493 and named after a monastery in Spain. It was colonized by Irish settlers in 1632 and is now a British dependency; pop. (1980) 12,073; official language, English; chief town, Plymouth.

monument /ˈmɒnjʊmənt/ n. 1. anything enduring (especially a structure or building) designed or serving to celebrate or commemorate a person or event etc. 2. a structure preserved because of its historical importance. —**the Monument,** a Doric column 60.6 m (202 ft.) high in the City of London, designed by Robert Hooke and Sir Christopher Wren (1671-7) to commemorate the Great Fire of 1666, which broke out in Pudding Lane near by. [f. F f. L (*monēre* remind)]

monumental /mɒnjʊˈment(ə)l/ adj. 1. of or serving as a monument. 2. (of a literary work) massive and of permanent

importance. 3. extremely great. —**monumental mason,** a maker of tombstones etc. —**monumentally** adv. [f. prec.]

moo n. the characteristic vocal sound of the cow, a low. —v.i. to make this sound. [imit.]

mooch v.t./i. (slang) 1. to loiter, to walk slowly. 2. to steal. [prob. f OF *muchier* skulk]

mood[1] n. 1. a state of mind or feeling. 2. (in pl.) fits of melancholy or bad temper. —**in the mood,** disposed or inclined. [OE]

mood[2] n. (Gram.) a form or forms of a verb serving to indicate whether it is to express a fact, command, wish, etc.; a group of such forms, a distinction of meaning expressed by this. [var. of MODE]

moody adj. gloomy, sullen, subject to moods. —**moodily** adv., **moodiness** n. [f. MOOD[1]]

moon n. 1. (also **Moon**) a satellite of Earth (see below), revolving round it monthly, illuminated by the sun and reflecting some light to Earth; this when visible. 2. (poet.) a month. 3. any rocky or icy body orbiting a planet as a satellite. 4. something regarded as unlikely to be attained. —v.i. to move or look dreamily or listlessly. —**moon-daisy** n. an ox-eye daisy. **over the moon,** (colloq.) in raptures; highly excited. [OE]
    The moon orbits Earth at a mean distance of some 400,000 km, and was familiar to our earliest ancestors as the source of night-time illumination. The bright and dark features which outline the face of 'the Man in the Moon' are seen through a telescope to be highland and lowland regions, the former heavily pockmarked by craters due to the impact of millions of meteorites when the solar system was still young. The moon has now been visited by the Apollo astronauts, and the samples of rock and dust which they collected are still being analysed to determine the nature and history of our airless companion.

moonbeam n. a ray of moonlight.

moonlight n. the light of the moon. —adj. lighted by the moon. —v.i. (colloq.) to have two paid occupations, especially one by day and one by night. —**moonlight flit,** a hurried removal by night to avoid paying rent.

moonlit adj. lighted by the moon.

moonshine n. 1. visionary talk or ideas. 2. illicitly distilled or smuggled alcoholic liquor.

moonstone n. a feldspar with a pearly appearance.

moonstruck adj. deranged in mind.

moony adj. 1. of or like the moon. 2. foolishly dreamy. —**moonily** adv. [f. MOON]

Moor /ˈmʊə(r)/ n. a member of a Muslim people of mixed Berber and Arab descent, inhabiting NW Africa. —**Moorish** adj. [f. OF f. L f. Gk *Mauros* inhabitant of Mauretania]

moor[1] /ˈmʊə(r)/ n. a stretch of open uncultivated land with low shrubs (e.g. heather); this used for preserving game for shooting. [OE]

moor[2] /ˈmʊə(r)/ v.t. to attach (a boat etc.) to a fixed object. [prob. f. MLG]

moorage n. a place or charge made for mooring. [f. MOOR[2]]

Moore[1] /ˈmʊə(r)/, Francis (1657-?1715), physician, astrologer, and schoolmaster, who in 1699 published an almanac containing weather predictions in order to promote the sale of his pills, and in 1700 some with astrological observations. There are now several almanacs called 'Old Moore', and predictions range far beyond the weather.

Moore[2] /ˈmʊə(r)/, George (1852-1933), Anglo-Irish novelist, who studied painting in Paris and there became influenced by the naturalist techniques of Zola and the Goncourts, evident in his novels *A Mummer's Wife* (1885), set in the Potteries, and *Esther Waters* (1894), which defied Victorian conventions by exploring the problems facing the servant classes. He became involved in the Irish literary revival and collaborated in the planning of the Irish National Theatre. His autobiographical *Confessions of a Young Man* (1888) shows Moore as the champion of aestheticism and French impressionist painting.

Moore[3] /ˈmʊə(r)/, Henry (1898-), English sculptor and draughtsman. One of the most important 20th-c. sculptors, his eminence is due to his pioneering and sustained exploration of the suggestive area lying between figuration and abstraction, such ambiguity giving sculpture an enriched potential for expressive communication, particularly in exploiting the human body/landscape analogy. His discovery of African and pre-Columbian art in the 1920s led him to reject modelling for direct carving in stone and wood, working the material sympathetically and allowing natural qualities of grain and texture to influence form. His development of pierced and, later, broken form allowed the fullest interaction between sculpture and environment (e.g. *Reclining Figure* 1938), and much of his work is seen at its best in the open air. His work as a war artist (1940-2) emphasized the human aspect of his art, as in his drawings of sleeping air-raid victims.

Moore[4] /mʊə(r)/, Sir John (1761-1809), British general during the Napoleonic Wars, developer of special light-infantry training within the British army. Moore led an expeditionary force into French-held Spain in 1800 and, confronted by a much larger French army under Marshal Soult, conducted a successful 250-mile retreat in mid-winter, then won a brilliant victory over his pursuers while covering the embarkation of his army at Corunna, being mortally wounded in the process.

moorhen *n.* a small water-hen (*Gallinula chloropus*).

mooring *n.* (usu. in *pl.*) **1.** permanent anchors and chains laid down for ships to be moored to. **2.** a place where a vessel is moored.

moorland *n.* an area of moor.

moose *n.* (*pl.* same) a North American animal (*Alces americana*) closely allied to or the same as the European elk. [f. N. Amer. Indian *moos*]

moot *adj.* debatable. —*v.t.* to raise (a question) for discussion. —*n.* (*hist.*) an assembly. [OE, rel. to MEET[1]]

mop *n.* **1.** a bundle of coarse yarn or cloth fastened at the end of a stick, for cleaning floors etc., a similarly shaped instrument for various purposes. **2.** a thick head of hair like a mop. —*v.t.* (**-pp-**) **1.** to wipe or clean (as) with a mop. **2.** to wipe tears, sweat, etc., from (the face etc.); to wipe (tears etc.) thus. —**mop up**, to wipe up (as) with a mop; (*slang*) to absorb; (*slang*) to dispatch or make an end of; to complete the military occupation of (a district etc.) by capturing or killing the troops left there; to capture or kill (stragglers). [perh. as MAP]

mope *v.i.* to be depressed and listless. —*n.* **1.** one who mopes. **2.** (in *pl.*) low spirits. —**mopy** *adj.* [orig. unkn.]

moped /ˈməʊped/ *n.* a motorized bicycle. [Sw. (*motor*, *pedal*er pedals)]

moppet /ˈmɒpɪt/ *n.* (as a term of endearment) a baby or small child. [f. obs. *moppe* baby, doll]

moquette /mɒˈket/ *n.* a material of wool on cotton with a looped pile, used for upholstery etc. [F, perh. f. obs. It. *mocaiardo* mohair]

moraine /mɒˈreɪn/ *n.* debris carried down and deposited by a glacier (ill. MOUNTAINS). —**morainic** *adj.* [F]

moral /ˈmɒr(ə)l/ *adj.* **1.** concerned with goodness or badness of character or disposition or with the principles of what is right and what is wrong. **2.** virtuous in general conduct. **3.** (of rights or duties etc.) founded on moral law. **4.** capable of moral action. —*n.* **1.** the moral lesson of a fable, story, event, etc. **2.** (in *pl.*) moral habits, e.g. sexual conduct. —**moral certainty**, a probability so great as to leave no reasonable doubt. **moral courage**, the courage to face disapproval rather than abandon the right course of action. **moral law**, the conditions to be fulfilled by any right course of action. **moral philosophy**, that concerned with ethics. **moral support**, that giving psychological rather than physical help. **moral victory**, a defeat that has some of the satisfactory elements of a victory. —**morally** *adv.* [f. L *moralis* (*mos* custom)]

morale /mɒˈrɑːl/ *n.* the mental attitude or bearing of a person or group, especially as regards confidence, discipline, etc. [respelling of F. *moral* (= prec.)]

moralist /ˈmɒrəlɪst/ *n.* one who practises or teaches morality; one who follows a natural system of ethics. —**moralistic** /-ˈlɪstɪk/ *adj.* [f. MORAL]

morality /mɒˈrælɪtɪ/ *n.* **1.** degree of conformity to moral principles. **2.** (esp. good) moral conduct. **3.** moralizing. **4.** the science of morals; a particular system of morals. —**morality play**, any of the medieval dramatic dramas, teaching a moral lesson, in which the main characters are personified human qualities. They belong mainly to the 15th c. Among the most celebrated English examples are *Everyman*; *Ane Satire of the Thrie Estaitis* by Sir David Lyndsay; *Magnificence* by Skelton; *King John* by John Bale; *Mankind*; *The Castle of Perseverance*. [f. OF or L (as MORAL)]

moralize /ˈmɒrəlaɪz/ *v.t./i.* **1.** to indulge in moral reflection or talk. **2.** to interpret morally. **3.** to make (more) moral. —**moralization** /-ˈzeɪʃ(ə)n/ *n.* [f. F or L (as MORAL)]

morass /məˈræs/ *n.* **1.** a marsh or bog. **2.** an entanglement or confusion. [f. Du. f. OF (as MARSH)]

moratorium /mɒrəˈtɔːrɪəm/ *n.* (*pl.* **-s**) **1.** a legal authorization to debtors to postpone payment; the period of this. **2.** a temporary prohibition or suspension on an activity. [f. L *moratorius* (*morari* to delay)]

Moravian /məˈreɪvɪən/ *adj.* **1.** of Moravia, a region of Czechoslovakia round the River Morava. **2.** of a Protestant sect holding Hussite doctrines and a simple unworldly form of Christianity with the Bible as the only source of faith, founded in Saxony in 1722 by emigrants from Moravia. —*n.* **1.** a native or inhabitant of Moravia. **2.** a member of the Moravian Church. [f. *Moravia*]

morbid /ˈmɔːbɪd/ *adj.* **1.** (of the mind, ideas, etc.) unwholesome, sickly. **2.** given to morbid feelings; (*colloq.*) melancholy. **3.** of the nature of or indicative of disease. —**morbidity** /-ˈbɪdɪtɪ/ *n.*, **morbidly** *adv.*, **morbidness** *n.* [f. L *morbidus* (*morbus* disease)]

mordant /ˈmɔːd(ə)nt/ *adj.* **1.** (of sarcasm etc.) caustic, biting, pungent. **2.** corrosive or cleansing. **3.** serving to fix colouring matter. —*n.* a mordant acid or substance. —**mordancy** *n.* [f. F f. L *mordēre* bite]

More /mɔː(r)/, Sir Thomas (1478-1535), Lord Chancellor of England 1529-32, a deeply religious, learned, and ascetic man, whose house in Chelsea was a centre of intellectual life. His most famous work, *Utopia*, describes an ideal community living (without private property) according to natural law and practising a natural religion, and contains satiric side-thrusts at contemporary abuses. From the time of the accession of Henry VIII (1509) More held a series of public offices, but the turning-point in his fortunes came when he opposed the king's divorce from Catherine of Aragon. He was forced to resign office and lived in retirement until 1534, when he refused to take the oath on the Act of Succession and was imprisoned. In 1535 he was accused of high treason on the ground of his opposition to the Act of Supremacy which confirmed Henry as supreme head of the Church of England, and was beheaded. It would, however, be a mistake to assume that he died in defence of papal power and authority. He was canonized in 1935. Feast day, 22 June.

more /mɔː(r)/ *adj.* **1.** greater in quantity or degree. **2.** additional, further. —*n.* a greater quantity or number. —*adv.* **1.** in a greater degree. **2.** again. **3.** moreover. **4.** forming the comparative of adjectives and adverbs (e.g. *more absurd*, *more easily*), especially those of more than one syllable. —**more or less**, in a greater or less degree, approximately. **what is more**, as an additional point, moreover. [OE]

moreish /ˈmɔːrɪʃ/ *adj.* (*colloq.*) pleasant to eat, causing a desire for more. [f. MORE]

morello /məˈreləʊ/ *n.* (pl. **-os**) a bitter kind of dark cherry. [f. It. = blackish, f. L (as MOOR)]

moreover /mɔːˈrəʊvə(r)/ *adv.* besides, in addition to that already said.

mores /ˈmɔːriːz/ *n.pl.* the customs or conventions regarded as characteristic of or essential to a community. [L, pl. of *mos* custom]

Morgan /ˈmɔːɡən/, Thomas Hunt (1866-1945), American zoologist, best known for showing the mechanism in the animal cell responsible for the genetics of inheritance. Morgan's studies with the rapidly reproducing fruit-fly Drosophila showed that the genetic information was carried by genes arranged along the length of the chromosomes. Though this work was not widely accepted initially, he was awarded a Nobel Prize in 1933.

morganatic /mɔːɡəˈnætɪk/ *adj.* (of a marriage) between a man of high rank and a woman of lower rank, the wife and children having no claim to the possessions or title of the father; (of a wife) so married. —**morganatically** *adv.* [f. F or G f. L, prob. f. Gmc, = morning gift, with ref. to husband's gift to wife on the morning after consummation (her sole claim on his possessions)]

Morgan le Fay /ˈmɔːɡən lə ˈfeɪ/ (in Arthurian legend) 'Morgan the Fairy', a magician, sister of King Arthur. (See FATA MORGANA.)

morgue /mɔːɡ/ *n.* **1.** a mortuary. **2.** (in journalism) the repository where miscellaneous material for reference is kept. [F, orig. = building in Paris where those found dead were exposed for identification]

moribund /ˈmɒrɪbʌnd/ *adj.* at the point of death (*lit.* or *fig.*). [f. L (*mori* die)]

Morland /ˈmɔːlənd/, George (1763-1804), English genre

painter. Although indebted to Dutch 17th-c. painters, such as Teniers, his pictures of taverns, cottages, and farmyards were local in inspiration (e.g. *Inside a Stable*, 1791, and *Outside the Ale-House Door*, 1792) and helped to create that fictitious rural England so popular in the 18th and 19th c. His art achieved wide popularity through the engravings of W. and J. Ward.

Morley /ˈmɔːlɪ/, Edward Williams (1838-1923), American chemist who specialized in accurate quantitative measurements such as those of the combining weights of hydrogen and oxygen, but who is best remembered for his collaboration with Michelson (see entry) in their experiment in 1887 to determine the speed of light.

Mormon /ˈmɔːmən/ n. an adherent of the Church of Jesus Christ of Latter-day Saints, founded at New York (1830) by Joseph Smith (1805-44), who claimed to have discovered, through divine revelation, the 'Book of Mormon', which he translated, relating the history of a group of Hebrews who migrated to America c.600 BC; this work is accepted by Mormons as Scripture along with the Bible. A further revelation led him to institute polygamy, a practice which brought the Mormons into conflict with the Federal Government and was abandoned in 1890. Smith was succeeded as leader by Brigham Young (1801-77), who moved the Mormon headquarters to Salt Lake City, Utah, in 1847. Mormon teaching is strongly adventist; the movement has no professional clergy, self-help is emphasized, and tithing and missionary work are demanded from its members.

morn n. (*poetic*) morning. [OE]

mornay /ˈmɔːneɪ/ n. a cheese-flavoured white sauce. [orig. unkn.]

morning n. the early part of the day, ending at noon or at the hour of the midday meal. —**morning after,** (*colloq.*) a time of hangover. **morning-after pill,** a contraceptive pill effective when taken some hours after intercourse. **morning coat,** a coat with the front cut away to form tails. **morning dress,** formal dress for a man of a morning coat and striped trousers. **morning glory,** a twining plant of the genus *Ipomoea* with trumpet-shaped flowers. **morning star,** a planet, especially Venus, seen in the east before sunrise. [as MORN]

Morocco /məˈrɒkəʊ/ a country in the NW corner of Africa, with coastlines on the Mediterranean Sea and Atlantic Ocean; pop. (1982) 20,419,555; official language, Arabic; capital, Rabat. The economy is sustained by a well-developed mining industry, the country being one of the leading exporters of phosphates, but agriculture remains the main occupation of its inhabitants. Conquered by the Arabs in the 7th c., Morocco was penetrated by the Portuguese in the 15th c. and later fell under French and Spanish influence, each country establishing protectorates in the early 20th c. It became a fully fledged independent State after the withdrawal of the colonial powers in 1956. —**Moroccan** adj. & n.

morocco /məˈrɒkəʊ/ n. (*pl.* -os) a fine flexible leather of goatskin tanned with sumac. [f. prec.]

moron /ˈmɔːrɒn/ n. 1. an adult with an intelligence equal to that of an average child of 8-12 years. 2. (*colloq.*) a very stupid person. —**moronic** /məˈrɒnɪk/ adj. [f. Gk, neut. of *mōros* foolish]

morose /məˈrəʊs/ adj. sullen, gloomy, and unsociable. —**morosely** adv., **moroseness** n. [f. L (*mos* manner)]

morpheme /ˈmɔːfiːm/ n. a morphological element considered in respect of its functions in a linguistic system; the smallest morphological unit of a language (*farmer* consists of two morphemes, *farm* and *-er*; *farmers* of three, *farm*, *-er*, *-s*). [f. F (after *phoneme*), f. Gk *morphē* form]

Morpheus /ˈmɔːfɪəs/ (*Rom. myth.*) son of Somnus (god of sleep) and sender of dreams of human forms.

morphia /ˈmɔːfɪə/ n. morphine. [as foll.]

morphine /ˈmɔːfiːn/ n. the narcotic constituent of opium, used to alleviate pain. [f. G f. L MORPHEUS]

morphology /mɔːˈfɒlədʒɪ/ n. the study of the forms of things, especially of plants and animals; the study of the forms of words, the system of forms in a language. —**morphological** /-əˈlɒdʒɪk(ə)l/ adj. [f. Gk *morphē* form + -LOGY]

Morris¹ /ˈmɒrɪs/, William (1834-96), English writer, artist, and designer. Distressed by the poverty of mass-produced design, he championed a return to an ideal of beauty through utility and simplicity. The establishment of his firm, Morris and Co., in 1861 allowed the realization of his essentially medieval aesthetic, recreating a hand industry

in a machine age, with craftsmen producing stained glass, wall-paper, tapestry, furniture, and fabrics for the home. The founding of the Kelmscott Press in 1890 influenced English book design. His reformist doctrines were of vital importance to the English Arts and Crafts movement (see entry). Ironically, despite a link with the socialist revival of the 1880s, Morris's greatest success was in the decoration of the homes of the wealthy.

Morris² /ˈmɒrɪs/, William Richard (1877-1963), see NUFFIELD.

morris dance /ˈmɒrɪs/ a vigorous (male) folk-dance of ancient date, characteristic of rural England. There are many styles, traditionally associated with different localities, and dress etc. varies: some use handkerchiefs and bells, others sticks. Such dances are referred to in the 14th c. but are probably much earlier, dating back to pre-Christian pagan rituals. By the end of the 19th c. they were dying out and were saved from almost certain extinction by the efforts of Cecil Sharp. [f. *morys* var. of MOORISH (dance)]

morrow /ˈmɒrəʊ/ n. (*poetic*) the following day. [as MORN]

Morse¹ /mɔːs/, Samuel Finley Breese (1791-1872), American painter, noted for his portraits, and a pioneer in the use of the electric telegraph. He conceived the idea for this device in 1832, had the first working model ready a few years later, and extended its range and capabilities in 1837 by means of electromagnetic relays, helped considerably by the physicist Joseph Henry (1797-1878). In England, however, he had been anticipated by Wheatstone. The US Congress gave financial support in 1843 for an experimental line from Washington, DC, to Baltimore, over which Morse sent the famous message 'What hath God wrought' on 24 May 1844, using his system of dots and dashes (the Morse code; see foll.).

Morse² n. (also **Morse code**) a signalling code in which letters are represented by various combinations of two signs, e.g. dot and dash, long and short flash (ill. ALPHABET). Invented by S. F. B. Morse (see prec.) it was adopted internationally in wireless or radiotelegraphy when this superseded wire telegraphy. —*adj.* of this code. —*v.t./i.* to signal by Morse code. [f. prec.]

morse n. the clasp, often jewelled or ornamented, of a cope. [f. OF f. L *morsus* bite, catch (*mordēre* bite)]

morsel /ˈmɔːs(ə)l/ n. a small piece or quantity; a mouthful; a fragment. [f. OF (*mors* a bite, as MORDANT)]

mortal /ˈmɔːt(ə)l/ adj. 1. subject to death. 2. causing death, fatal; (of a combat) fought to the death. 3. accompanying death. 4. (of an enemy) implacable. 5. (of a pain, fear, affront, etc.) intense, very serious. 6. (*colloq.*) whatsoever. 7. (*colloq.*) long and tedious. —n. a mortal being; a human being. —**mortal sin,** a sin that causes the death of the soul or is fatal to salvation. —**mortally** adv. [f. OF or L (*mors* death)]

mortality /mɔːˈtælɪtɪ/ n. 1. being subject to death. 2. loss of life on a large scale. 3. the number of deaths in a given period etc. —**mortality rate,** the death rate. [f. OF f. L (as prec.)]

mortar /ˈmɔːtə(r)/ n. 1. a mixture of lime or cement, sand, and water, for joining stones or bricks in building. 2. a short large-bore cannon for throwing shells at high angles. 3. a vessel in which ingredients are pounded with a pestle. —v.t. 1. to plaster or join with mortar. 2. to attack or bombard with mortars. —**mortar-board,** a board for holding mortar; an academic cap with a stiff square top. [f. AF f. L *mortarium*]

mortgage /ˈmɔːgɪdʒ/ n. conveyance of a property by a debtor to a creditor as security for a debt (especially one incurred by the purchase of the property), with the proviso that it shall be returned on payment of the debt within a certain period; the deed effecting this; a sum of money lent by this. —v.t. to convey (property) by a mortgage. [f. OF, = dead pledge (as GAGE¹)]

mortgagee /mɔːgɪˈdʒiː/ n. the creditor in a mortgage. [f. prec.]

mortgager /ˈmɔːgɪdʒə(r)/ n. (*Law* **mortgagor**) the debtor in a mortgage. [f. MORTGAGE]

mortician /mɔːˈtɪʃ(ə)n/ n. (*US*) an undertaker. [f. L *mors* death]

mortify /ˈmɔːtɪfaɪ/ v.t./i. 1. to humiliate greatly; to wound (feelings). 2. to subdue by discipline or self-denial. 3. (of flesh) to be affected by gangrene or necrosis. —**mortification** /-fɪˈkeɪʃ(ə)n/ n. [f. OF f. L *mortificare* kill (as prec.)]

mortise /ˈmɔːtɪs/ n. a hole in a framework to receive the end of another part, especially a tenon (ill. CARPENTRY).

—*v.t.* to join securely, especially by a mortise and tenon; to cut a mortise in. —**mortise lock**, a lock recessed in the edge of a door etc. [f. OF f. Arab., = fixed in]

Morton[1] /'mɔːt(ə)n/, 'Jelly Roll' (1885-1941), American jazz pianist, composer, and band-leader. He was one of the principal links between ragtime and jazz proper, and formed his own band, the Red Hot Peppers, to make some classic jazz recordings.

Morton[2] /'mɔːt(ə)n/, John (*c.*1420-1500), English statesman, who rose to become Henry VII's chief adviser, being appointed Archbishop of Canterbury in 1486 and Chancellor a year later. He is generally associated with the Crown's stringent taxation policies, which gained great unpopularity for the regime in general and Morton in particular. —**Morton's fork**, the argument he used in demanding gifts for the royal treasury: that if a man lived handsomely he was obviously rich, and if simply that economy must have made him so and he could afford a donation.

mortuary /'mɔːtjʊərɪ/ *n.* a building in which dead bodies may be kept for a time. —*adj.* of death or burial. [f. AF f. L (*mortuus* dead)]

Mosaic /məʊ'zeɪɪk/ *adj.* of Moses. [f. F (*Moses* f. Heb.)]

mosaic /məʊ'zeɪɪk/ *n.* **1.** a picture or pattern produced by juxtaposing small pieces of glass, stone, etc., of different colours; this form of art (see below). **2.** a thing consisting of divers elements in juxtaposition. [f. F, ult. f. Gk *mous(e)ion* (as MUSE)]

The first extensive use of mosaic was by the Romans, and a crucial technical advance was their invention of a durable and waterproof cement in which the fragments were fixed. Well-preserved examples survive from all parts of the Roman world, a testimony of their durability. The classical Roman mosaic tradition was continued in the Christian period, and survived longest and most splendidly in the Byzantine world, fine examples ranging from the Emperor Justinian's sequences at Ravenna (6th c.) to Hosios Loukas in mainland Greece (11th c.) and the mosaic cycles of Norman Sicily (12th c.) and St Mark's in Venice (13th c.), which deliberately sought to emulate the splendours of the Byzantine court. In the West, from the 13th c. the stylized mosaic technique was superseded by the new naturalistic possibilities of fresco painting. It is a seldom-used art form now, but examples of more modern mosaics include those by Watts and Stevens in St Paul's Cathedral (1863-92).

Moscow /'mɒskəʊ/ the capital of the USSR, on the central Russian plain; pop. (1984) 8,546,000. Moscow is first heard of in 1146; at that time it was a typical Russian village, built on the high right bank of the Moskva River. It soon became the centre of the increasingly powerful Muscovite princes, one of whom in 1380 succeeded in defeating the Tartar overlords of the Russians, and in the 16th c., when Ivan the Terrible proclaimed himself Tsar of all the Russias, Moscow became the capital of the new empire, its central position giving it supreme military and economic value. Though Peter the Great moved his capital to St Petersburg (now Leningrad) in 1712, Moscow remained the heart of Russia, and was the target for the main attacks by Napoleon in 1812 and Hitler in 1941. Three-quarters of the city was destroyed by fire during Napoleon's occupation, but by the mid-19th c. Moscow had become a large and growing industrial city, and after the revolution of 1917 was made the capital of the USSR. Its centre is the Kremlin.

Moseley /'məʊzlɪ/, Henry Gwyn Jeffreys (1887-1915), English physicist who, while working under Rutherford, discovered that there existed a relationship between the atomic numbers of elements and the wavelengths of their emitted X-rays. Thus he demonstrated experimentally the connection between nuclear charge and atomic number, that the element's chemical properties were determined by this number, and that there were only 92 naturally-occurring elements. His short life ended tragically when he was killed in the Gallipoli campaign in the First World War.

moselle /məʊ'zel/ *n.* a white wine produced in the valley of the Moselle and its tributaries in Germany.

Moses /'məʊzɪz/ Hebrew patriarch who, according to the Pentateuch, was born in Egypt and led the Jews away from their bondage there, across the desert. During the journey he was inspired by God on Mount Sinai to write down the Ten Commandments on tablets of stone (Exod. 20); he died in Moab, within sight of the Promised Land.

Moslem /'mɒzləm/ var. of MUSLIM.

Mosley /'məʊzlɪ/, Sir Oswald Ernald (1896-1980), English

Fascist leader. One of the brightest young politicians of his day, Mosley sat successively as a Conservative, Independent, and Labour MP before founding the British Union of Fascists in 1932, a political party which failed to find the mass support enjoyed by its European cousins. He was imprisoned for most of the Second World War and made an unsuccessful attempt to form a new right-wing party in Britain after its end.

mosque /mɒsk/ *n.* a Muslim place of worship. The earliest mosques grew out of the needs of the community and its rituals, and during the first century of the faith a dominant form of mosque architecture developed: a courtyard, forming a place for communal gathering; a covered area used for worship, on the side facing Mecca, frequently domed, with its mihrab or niche oriented towards the Kaaba and showing the direction of prayer; sometimes a space for princes (the *maqsura*); and a fountain for ablutions, obligatory before prayer. Representations of the human form are forbidden, and decoration is by geometric designs and Arabic calligraphy (e.g. of verses from the Koran). [f. F, ult. f. Arab. *masjid*]

mosquito /mɒs'kiːtəʊ/ *n.* (*pl.* -oes) a gnat especially of the genus *Culex* or *Anopheles*, of which the female punctures the skin of man and animals and sucks their blood. —**mosquito-net** a net to keep mosquitoes from a bed, room, etc. [Sp. & Port., dim. of *mosca* fly]

Moss, Stirling (1929-), English motor-racing driver who was especially successful in the 1950s, winning various Grand Prix and other competitions, though the drivers' world championship always eluded him.

moss *n.* any of a class of small cryptogams of the class Musci, growing in dense clusters in bogs or on the surface of the ground, trees, stones, etc. Such plants bear structures resembling roots, stems, and leaves but, unlike higher plants, have no specialized vascular (conducting) tissue. —**moss-rose** *n.* a variety of rose with a mosslike growth on the calyx and stalk. —**mossy** *adj.* [OE]

Mossad /məʊ'sɑːd/ the Israeli secret service. [Heb., = agency]

most /məʊst/ *adj.* greatest in quantity or degree; the majority of. —*n.* the greatest quantity or degree; the majority. —*adv.* **1.** in the highest degree. **2.** forming the superlative of adjectives and adverbs (as *most absurd, most easily*), especially those of more than one syllable. —**at (the) most,** as the greatest amount. **for the most part,** in the main; usually. **make the most of,** to use or enjoy to the best advantage. **Most Reverend,** see REVEREND. [OE]

-most *suffix* forming adjectives with a superlative sense from prepositions and other words indicating relative position (*foremost, inmost, topmost, uttermost*). [OE]

mostly *adv.* for the most part. [f. MOST]

mot /məʊ/ *n.* a witty saying. —**mot juste** /ʒuːst/ an exactly appropriate expression. [F, = word]

MOT *abbr.* (hist.) **1.** Ministry of Transport. **2.** (in full **MOT test**) (*colloq.*) a compulsory annual test of motor vehicles of more than a specified age.

mote *n.* a particle of dust. [OE]

motel /məʊ'tel/ *n.* a roadside hotel often consisting of a group of furnished cabins accommodating motorists and their vehicles. [portmanteau word f. MOTOR + HOTEL]

motet /məʊ'tet/ *n.* a short usually unaccompanied anthem in the Roman Catholic or Lutheran Church. [f. OF (as MOT)]

moth *n.* a lepidopterous mainly nocturnal insect resembling a butterfly (see entry); an insect of this kind (of the family Tineidae) breeding in cloth etc., on which its larvae feed. —**moth-eaten** *adj.* damaged or destroyed by moths, antiquated, time-worn. [OE]

mothball *n.* a small ball of naphthalene etc. placed in stored clothes to keep away moths. —**in mothballs**, stored out of use for a considerable time.

mother /'mʌðə(r)/ *n.* **1.** a female parent. **2.** a quality or condition etc. that gives rise to something else. **3.** the head of a female religious community. **4.** (*colloq.*) a title used to or of an elderly woman. —*v.t.* **1.** to give birth to; to be the origin of. **2.** to look after in a motherly way. —**Mother Carey's chickens**, stormy petrels. **mother country,** a country in relation to its colonies. **mother earth,** the earth as the mother of its inhabitants. **mother goddess,** see separate entry. **Mother Goose rhyme,** (*US*) a nursery rhyme. **Mothering Sunday,** the fourth Sunday in Lent, with the old custom of giving one's mother a gift. **mother-**

in-law *n.* (*pl.* **mothers-in-law**) a wife's or husband's mother. **mother-of-pearl** *n.* a smooth shining iridescent substance forming the inner layer of the oyster etc. shell. **Mother's Day,** Mothering Sunday. **mother tongue,** one's native language. —**motherhood** *n.* [OE]

mothercraft *n.* skill in looking after one's children as a mother.

mother goddess a mother-figure deity (also called the Great Mother), goddess of the entire complex of birth and growth, commonly a central figure of early nature-cults where maintenance of fertility was of prime importance in the religion. Such a figure is found in pantheons all over the world; Isis, Astarte, Cybele, and Demeter were traditional mother goddesses in the eastern Mediterranean. The term is often applied to prehistoric female figurines with exaggerated sexual parts, but though these are associated with fertility they do not necessarily represent a female deity.

motherland *n.* one's native land.

motherly *adj.* having or showing the good qualities of a mother. —**motherliness** *n.* [OE (as MOTHER)]

mothproof *adj.* (of clothes) treated so as to repel moths. —*v.t.* to treat (clothes) thus.

mothy /ˈmɒθɪ/ *adj.* infested with moths. [f. MOTH]

motif /məʊˈtiːf/ *n.* **1.** a distinctive feature or dominant idea in an artistic, literary, or musical composition. **2.** an ornament sewn separately on to a garment. **3.** an ornament on a vehicle identifying the maker etc. [F (as MOTIVE)]

motion /ˈməʊʃ(ə)n/ *n.* **1.** moving, change of position. **2.** manner of movement. **3.** change of posture; a particular movement; a gesture. **4.** a formal proposal that is to be discussed and voted on at a meeting; an application for an order from a judge. **5.** an evacuation of the bowels; (in *sing.* or *pl.*) faeces. —*v.t./i.* to direct by a gesture etc.; to make such a gesture. —**go through the motions,** to do a thing perfunctorily or superficially. **in motion,** not at rest, moving. **motion picture,** a film recording a story or events with movement as in real life. [f. OF f. L (as MOVE)]

motionless *adj.* not moving. —**motionlessly** *adv.* [f. prec. + -LESS]

motivate /ˈməʊtɪveɪt/ *v.t.* **1.** to supply a motive to, to be the motive of; to cause (a person) to act in a particular way. **2.** to stimulate the interest of (a person) in an activity. —**motivation** /-ˈveɪʃ(ə)n/ *n.* [f. foll.]

motive /ˈməʊtɪv/ *n.* **1.** what induces a person to act in a particular way. **2.** a motif. —*adj.* tending to initiate movement; concerned with movement. —**motive power,** moving or impelling power, especially the source of energy used to drive machinery. [f. OF f. L *motivus* (as MOVE)]

motley /ˈmɒtlɪ/ *adj.* **1.** diversified in colour. **2.** of varied character. —*n.* (*hist.*) a jester's particoloured dress. [perh. as MOTE]

moto-cross /ˈməʊtəʊkrɒs/ *n.* (also called *scrambling*) a form of motor-cycle racing held on a closed circuit consisting of a variety of cross-country terrain and natural obstacles. The sport was developed in southern England in the 1920s. [f. MOTOR + CROSS]

motor *n.* **1.** a machine (especially an internal-combustion engine) supplying the motive power for a vehicle etc. or for some other device with moving parts. **2.** a motor car (see separate entry). —*adj.* **1.** giving, imparting, or producing motion. **2.** driven by a motor. **3.** of or for motor vehicles. —*v.t./i.* to go or convey in a motor car. —**motor bicycle,** a motor cycle; a moped. **motor bike,** (*colloq.*) a motor cycle. **motor cycle,** see separate entry. **motor-cyclist** *n.* the rider of a motor cycle. **motor nerve,** a nerve carrying impulses from the brain or spinal cord to a muscle. **motor vehicle,** a vehicle driven by a motor (esp. an internal-combustion engine). [L, = mover (as MOVE)]

motorcade /ˈməʊtəkeɪd/ *n.* a procession or parade of motor cars. [f. prec., after *cavalcade*]

motor car a short-bodied motor-driven vehicle that can carry a driver and usually passengers. Attempts to devise mechanical propulsion began in the 18th c., and the first self-propelled road vehicle—which represented one of the most important advances in the history of transport—was a steam-driven carriage designed and built in France by Joseph Cugnot in 1769; other pioneers included Trevithick of Cornwall. In Britain development clashed with the interests of the promoters of the new railway lines, who used their considerable capital and influence to secure a law (1865) which effectively killed it, requiring every power-driven vehicle on the roads to have a man walking 100 yards in front with a red flag by day and a red lantern

by night; the provisions of this law were not abolished until 1896. On the Continent, however, progress was being made with the internal-combustion engine, which Daimler fitted to a cycle and Benz to a three-wheeled vehicle (1885) that carried two passengers. Early cars were very small two-seat carts, with no roofs, poor springs, and wooden- or wire-spoked wheels. Motorists had to cope with flint roads and discarded nails from horseshoes, and to carry spare tyres etc., for there were no garages to serve them; petrol was obtainable from chemists' shops.

The motor car became significant in its social effects when it began to be built in large numbers by low-cost mass-production methods (see Henry FORD). It is now ubiquitous in industrialized countries and both town and country are planned to accommodate it. Its future is threatened by the increasing cost and future scarcity of the highly specific types of oil fuel on which it relies; introduction of an electrically powered car awaits the design of a suitable battery.

motor cycle a two-wheeled motor-driven road vehicle, now without pedal propulsion. A cycle powered by a steam-engine was patented in France in 1868, and a charcoal-fired steam-powered motor cycle was built by S. H. Roper in the USA in 1869. The first practical machine was built in 1885 by Daimler, who fitted an internal-combustion engine into a wooden cycle frame, but it was some years before sustained efforts were made towards its improvement. From this was developed the motor car, but the motor cycle continued as a distinct vehicle, being lighter, cheaper, and more stable on rough ground. After the Second World War it lost sales to the scooter, developed in Italy, and the moped, mostly a French development, but the motor cycle proper was given a new lease of life when Japan entered the market with a large range of models and quickly became the world's largest supplier.

motorist *n.* the driver of a motor car. [f. MOTOR]

motorize *v.t./i.* **1.** to equip with motor transport. **2.** to equip (a device etc.) with a motor. —**motorization** /-ˈzeɪʃ(ə)n/ *n.* [f. MOTOR]

motorway *n.* a road designed for fast traffic.

motte /mɒt/ *n.* a mound forming the site of an ancient castle, camp, etc., found in Britain and parts of northern France, dating from the Norman period onwards (ill. CASTLES). [f. F (as MOAT)]

mottle *v.t.* (esp. in *p.p.*) to mark with spots or smears of colour. [back-formation f. MOTLEY]

motto /ˈmɒtəʊ/ *n.* (*pl.* **-oes**) **1.** a maxim adopted as a rule of conduct or as expressing the aims and ideals of a family, country, institution, etc. **2.** a sentence inscribed on an object. **3.** a maxim, verse, or riddle etc. inside a paper cracker. [It., as MOT]

mould[1] /məʊld/ *n.* **1.** a hollow container into which molten metal etc. is poured or soft material is pressed to harden in a required shape. **2.** a vessel used to give a shape to puddings etc.; a pudding etc. so shaped. **3.** form, shape. **4.** a pattern or shape used in making mouldings. —*v.t.* **1.** to bring into a particular shape or form. **2.** to influence or control the development of. [f. OF *modle* f. L (as MODULUS)]

mould[2] /məʊld/ *n.* a furry growth of fungi on things of animal or vegetable origin that lie for some time in moist warm air. [prob. f. p.p. of *moul* grow mouldy, f. ON]

mould[3] /məʊld/ *n.* loose earth; the upper soil of cultivated land, especially when rich in organic matter. [OE, rel. to MEAL]

moulder /ˈməʊldə(r)/ *v.i.* to decay to dust, to rot or decline. [perh. f. prec.]

moulding *n.* **1.** a moulded object, especially an ornamental strip of wood. **2.** an ornamental variety of outline in the cornices etc. of a building; a similar shape in woodwork etc. [f. MOULD[1]]

mouldy *adj.* **1.** covered with mould. **2.** out-of-date, stale. **3.** (*slang*) dull, miserable. —**mouldiness** *n.* [f. MOULD[2]]

Moulin Rouge /muːlæ ˈruːʒ/ a cabaret in Montmartre, Paris, a favourite resort of poets and artists around the turn of the century. Toulouse-Lautrec immortalized its dancers in his posters.

moult /məʊlt/ *v.t./i.* to shed feathers, hair, skin, etc., before a new growth; to shed (feathers etc.) thus. —*n.* the process of moulting. [earlier *moute* ult. f. L *mutare* change]

mound *n.* **1.** a mass of piled-up earth or stones. **2.** a small hill. **3.** a heap or pile. [orig. unkn.]

mount[1] *v.t./i.* **1.** to ascend; to go upwards; to rise to a higher level or rank etc. **2.** to get or put on (a horse etc.) in order to ride; to provide with a horse for riding. **3.** to increase in amount or intensity. **4.** to put into place on a support; to fix in position for use, display, or study. **5.** to arrange and carry out (a programme, campaign, etc.). **6.** to place on guard. **7.** to put (a play) on the stage. —*n.* **1.** a horse for riding. **2.** something on which a thing is mounted for support or display etc. [f. OF f. L (as foll.)]

mount² *n.* a mountain or hill (*archaic* exc. before a name, as in *Mount Everest*). [OE & f. OF f. L *mons*]

mountain /ˈmaʊntɪn/ *n.* **1.** a mass of land that rises to a great height, especially of over 1,000 ft. (See ill. p. 548.) **2.** a large heap or pile; a huge quantity. **3.** a large surplus stock. —**mountain ash**, a tree (*Sorbus aucuparia*) bearing scarlet berries, rowan. **mountain dew**, (*colloq.*) whisky, especially that illicitly distilled. **mountain goat**, a white goatlike animal (*Oreamnos montanus*) of the Rocky Mountains etc. **mountain lion**, the puma. [f. OF *montaigne* (as prec.)]

mountaineer /maʊntɪˈnɪə(r)/ *n.* one skilled in mountain-climbing. —*v.i.* to climb mountains as a recreation (see below). [f. prec.]

From time immemorial people living in mountainous countries have crossed mountain passes in order to get to one valley from another, and in Europe a thousand years ago a few established routes, such as that over the Great St Bernard pass, were in regular use by pilgrims and other travellers. In the 14th c. a few isolated climbs were made by inquiring naturalists to study flowers or rocks, and by the 16th c. some adventurous people were wandering among the Alps for pleasure. In the 18th c. a number of the higher Alpine peaks were climbed for the first time. It was the British who first organized mountaineering as a sport, and in the decade 1855–65 made many first ascents of peaks and crossings of high passes in the Alps before turning their attention to more distant ranges in South America, New Zealand, and Africa, and in the Himalayas. The introduction of artificial aids such as pitons and fixed ropes aroused much controversy. Attempts to conquer the world's highest mountain, Mount Everest, began in 1920 but were unsuccessful until the British expedition led by Sir John Hunt culminated in the ascent to the summit by Sir Edmund Hillary and Sherpa Tenzing Norgay in 1953.

mountainous /ˈmaʊntɪnəs/ *adj.* **1.** having many mountains. **2.** huge. [f. MOUNTAIN]

mountainside *n.* the sloping side of a mountain.

Mountbatten /maʊntˈbæt(ə)n/, Louis, 1st Earl Mountbatten of Burma (1900–79), British sailor, soldier, and statesman. A great-grandson of Queen Victoria, Mountbatten served in the Royal Navy before rising to become supreme Allied commander in SE Asia in 1943–5. The qualities of tact and diplomacy that he displayed in this difficult job stood him in good stead when as Viceroy and then Governor-General he oversaw the independence of India and Pakistan in 1947–8. He later went on to become First Sea Lord; he was murdered by the IRA in Ireland while in retirement.

mountebank /ˈmaʊntɪbæŋk/ *n.* **1.** a swindler, a charlatan. **2.** (*hist.*) an itinerant quack. [f. It., = mount on bench]

mounted *adj.* serving on horseback etc. [f. MOUNT¹]

Mountie /ˈmaʊntɪ/ *n.* (*colloq.*) a member of the Royal Canadian Mounted Police. [abbr.]

mourn /mɔːn/ *v.t./i.* to feel or show deep sorrow or regret for (a dead person, a lost or regretted thing); to grieve. [OE]

mourner *n.* one who mourns; one who attends a funeral. [f. prec.]

mournful *adj.* sorrowful, showing grief. —**mournfully** *adv.*, **mournfulness** *n.* [f. MOURN + -FUL]

mourning *n.* **1.** expression of sorrow at a death etc. **2.** black or dark clothes worn as a conventional sign of bereavement. [f. MOURN]

mouse *n.* (*pl.* **mice**) **1.** a small rodent, especially of the genus *Mus*; a species of this (*M. musculus*) infesting houses etc. **2.** a shy or timid person. **3.** a small hand-held device for controlling the position of the cursor on the visual display unit of a computer. —*v.i.* to hunt mice. —**mouser** *n.* [OE]

mousetrap *n.* **1.** a trap for catching mice. **2.** (*colloq.*) cheese of poor quality.

moussaka /muːˈsaːkə/ *n.* a Greek dish of minced meat, aubergines, eggs, etc. [Gk or Turk.]

mousse /muːs/ *n.* a dish of cold whipped cream or a similar substance flavoured with fruit, chocolate, or meat or fish purée. [F, = moss, froth]

moustache /məˈstaːʃ/ *n.* hair left to grow on a man's upper lip. [F, f. It. *mostaccio* f. Gk]

Mousterian /muːˈstɪərɪən/ *adj.* of the flint industries of the middle palaeolithic period, named after the type-site, the Moustier cave in the Dordogne region of France, and dated to *c.*70,000–30,000 BC. They are attributed to the Neanderthal peoples living in Europe and around the Mediterranean. —*n.* such an industry. [f. Le *Moustier*]

mousy /ˈmaʊsɪ/ *adj.* **1.** greyish-brown. **2.** shy, timid; quiet. [f. MOUSE]

mouth /maʊθ/ *n.* (*pl.* **-s** /maʊðz/) **1.** the external opening in the head, with a cavity behind it, through which food is taken in and from which the voice is emitted; this cavity. **2.** the opening of a bag, cave, cannon, trumpet, etc. **3.** the place where a river enters the sea. **4.** an individual as needing sustenance. —/maʊð/ *v.t./i.* **1.** to utter or speak with affectation, to declaim. **2.** to grimace; to move the lips silently. —**mouth-organ** *n.* a thin rectangular musical instrument played by blowing and sucking air through it (ill. MUSICAL NOTATION). **keep one's mouth shut**, (*slang*) to refrain from revealing a secret. **mouth-watering** *adj.* making one's mouth water, appetizing. **put words into a person's mouth**, to tell him what to say; to represent him as having said such words. **take the words out of a person's mouth**, to say what he was about to say. [OE]

mouthful *n.* **1.** an amount that fills the mouth. **2.** a small quantity of food etc. **3.** a lengthy word or phrase; something difficult to utter. [f. MOUTH + -FUL]

mouthpiece *n.* **1.** the part of a pipe, musical instrument, telephone, etc., placed between or near the lips. **2.** a person who speaks for another or others.

mouthwash *n.* a liquid for rinsing the mouth or gargling.

movable /ˈmuːvəb(ə)l/ *adj.* that can be moved; varying in date from year to year. [f. MOVE]

move /muːv/ *v.t./i.* **1.** to change or cause to change position, place, or posture. **2.** to be or cause to be in motion. **3.** to change one's place of residence or business. **4.** to live or be active in a specified group. **5.** to provoke a reaction or emotion in, to stimulate; to prompt or incline, to motivate. **6.** to cause (bowels) to empty; to be emptied thus. **7.** (of goods etc.) to be sold. **8.** to propose (a resolution) formally at a meeting. **9.** to initiate action. —*n.* **1.** the act or process of moving. **2.** a change of residence, business premises, etc. **3.** the moving of a piece in chess etc.; a player's turn to do this. **4.** a calculated action done to achieve some purpose. —**get a move on**, (*colloq.*) to hurry. **move house**, to change one's place of residence etc. **move in**, to take possession of a new residence etc. **move over** *or* **up**, to adjust one's position to make room for another. **on the move**, progressing, moving about. —**mover** *n.* [f. AF f. L *movēre*]

movement /ˈmuːvmənt/ *n.* **1.** moving, being moved. **2.** action, activity. **3.** the moving parts of a mechanism, especially of a clock or watch. **4.** a campaign to achieve some purpose; a group undertaking this. **5.** a trend. **6.** market activity in some commodity. **7.** any of the principal divisions in a long musical work. [f. OF f. L (as MOVE)]

movie /ˈmuːvɪ/ *n.* (*US slang*) a motion picture. [f. *moving* picture]

moving *adj.* emotionally affecting. —**movingly** *adv.* [f. MOVE]

mow /maʊ/ *v.t.* (*p.p.* **mowed** or **mown**) to cut (grass etc.) with a scythe or machine; to cut down the grass of (a lawn) or the produce of (a field) thus. —**mow down**, to kill or destroy randomly or in great numbers. [OE]

mower /ˈmaʊə(r)/ *n.* **1.** a mowing machine, especially a lawn-mower. **2.** a person who mows. [f. MOW]

Mozambique /məʊzæmˈbiːk/ a country on the east coast of Africa, bordered by the Republic of South Africa in the south and west; pop. (est. 1982) 12,000,000; official language, Portuguese; capital, Maputo. The country is largely agricultural, and in relation to its area the export trade is very small. Discovered by Vasco da Gama, Mozambique was colonized by the Portuguese in the early 16th c. and did not gain full independence as a republic until 1975. It has been troubled by the guerrilla activity rife in southern Africa for the past decade. —**Mozambican** *adj.* & *n.*

Mozart /ˈmɔːtsaːt/, Wolfgang Amadeus (1756–91), Austrian composer, born at Salzburg, typically Austrian in that in him a basically Teutonic nature was Italianized. A child prodigy as harpsichordist and composer, he was taken by his father on tours of western Europe and Italy, but most of his mature years were spent at Salzburg and, latterly, Vienna. His flow of unsurpassable Italianate

Mountains and Glaciers

A mountain valley during . . .

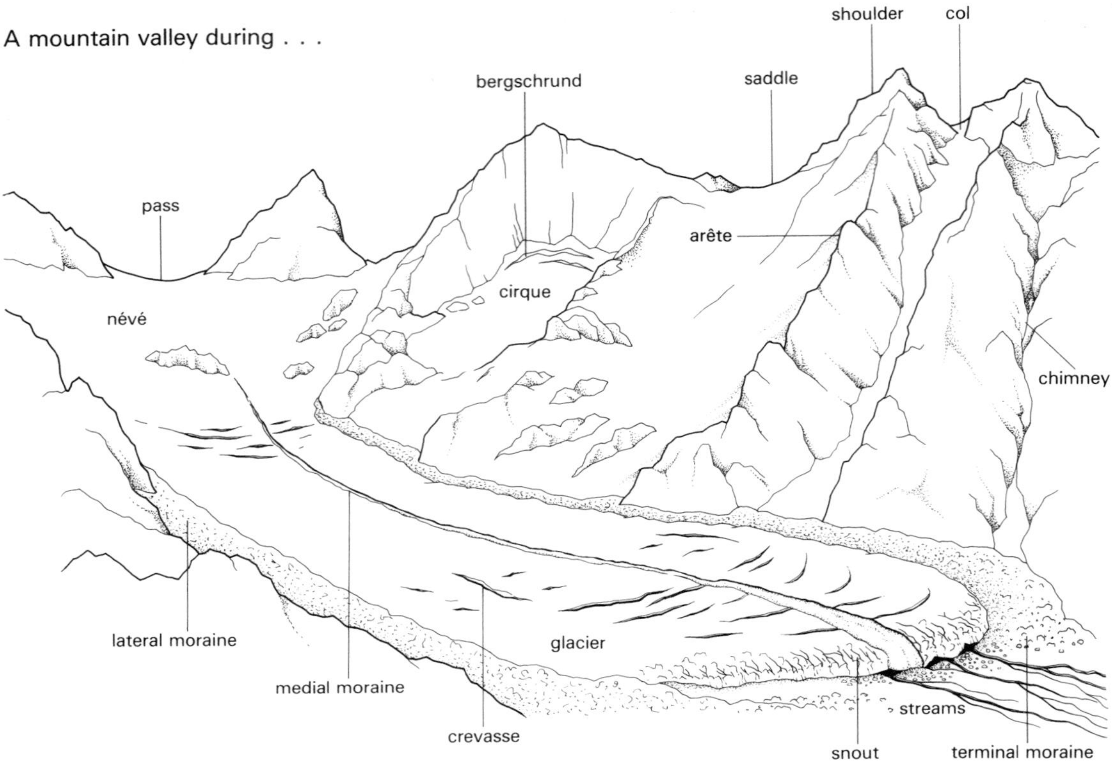

pass

bergschrund

shoulder

col

saddle

arête

cirque

névé

chimney

lateral moraine

medial moraine

glacier

crevasse

snout

streams

terminal moraine

. . . and after glaciation

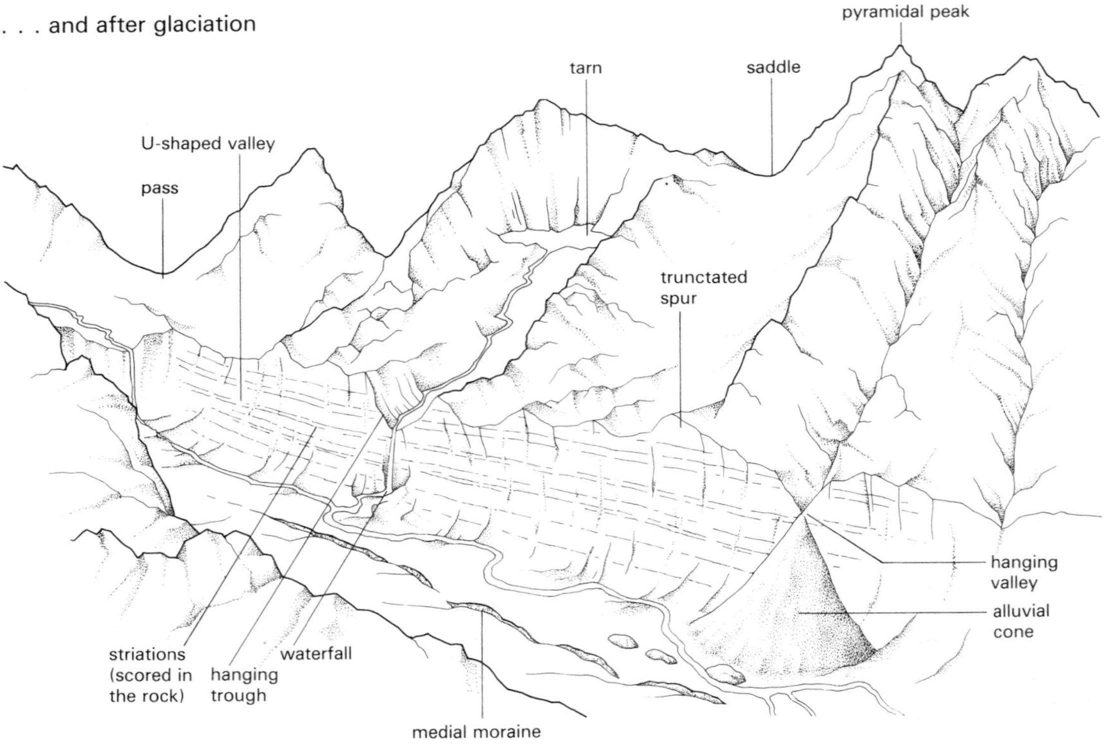

pyramidal peak

tarn

saddle

U-shaped valley

pass

trunctated
spur

hanging
valley

alluvial
cone

striations
(scored in
the rock)

hanging
trough

waterfall

medial moraine

melodic invention and seemingly effortless command of German technique are displayed in more than forty symphonies, nearly thirty piano concertos, and a vast quantity of orchestral and other instrumental music. This kind of symbiosis is still more obvious in his operas, in the greatest of which comedy is always liable to become serious, and even tragic in *Don Giovanni* (1787). In *The Magic Flute* (1791) extremes of profundity and buffoonery are juxtaposed with no sense of incongruity. The most straight-forwardly comic is probably *The Marriage of Figaro* (1786). Mozart's subtle creation of character in terms of music is comparable with Shakespeare's in terms of poetry.

MP *abbr.* Member of Parliament.

mp *abbr. mezzo piano.*

m.p.g. *abbr.* miles per gallon.

m.p.h. *abbr.* miles per hour.

Mr /ˈmɪstə(r)/ *n.* (*pl.* MESSRS) the title of a man without a higher title, or prefixed to a designation of an office etc. (*Mr Jones; Mr Speaker*). [abbr. of MISTER]

Mrs /ˈmɪsɪz/ *n.* (*pl.* same or **Mesdames**) the title of a married woman without a higher title. [abbr. of MISTRESS]

MS *abbr.* **1.** manuscript. **2.** multiple sclerosis.

Ms /mɪz/ *n.* the title of a woman without a higher title, whether or not married. [comb. of MRS, MISS]

M.Sc. *abbr.* Master of Science.

MSS /emˈesɪz/ *abbr.* manuscripts.

Mt *abbr.* Mount.

mu /mjuː/ *n.* the twelfth letter of the Greek alphabet, = m. [Gk]

much *adj.* existing in great quantity. —*n.* a great quantity. —*adv.* **1.** in a great degree. **2.** often; for a large part of one's time. **3.** approximately. —**as much**, that amount etc. **much of a muchness**, very alike, very nearly the same. **not much**, (*colloq.*) certainly not. **not much of a**, (*colloq.*) not a great or good example of. [f. *muchel* = MICKLE]

mucilage /ˈmjuːsɪlɪdʒ/ *n.* a viscous substance extracted from plants; an adhesive gum. [f. F f. L *mucilago* musty juice (as MUCUS)]

muck *n.* farmyard manure; (*colloq.*) dirt, filth; (*colloq.*) mess. —*v.t./i.* **1.** to manure. **2.** to make dirty. —**make a muck of**, (*slang*) to bungle. **muck about** *or* **around**, (*slang*) to potter or fool about; to interfere. **muck in**, (*colloq.*) to share tasks etc. equally. **muck out**, to remove the manure from. **muck-raking** *n.* (*colloq.*) searching out and revealing scandal. **muck sweat**, (*colloq.*) a profuse sweat. **muck up**, (*slang*) to bungle, to spoil. [prob. f. Scand.]

muckle *adj. & n.* = MICKLE.

mucky *adj.* covered with muck, dirty. [f. MUCK]

mucous /ˈmjuːkəs/ *adj.* of or covered with mucus. —**mucous membrane**, the skin lining the nose and other cavities of the body. —**mucosity** /-ˈkɒsɪtɪ/ *n.* [f. L *mucosus* (as foll.)]

mucus /ˈmjuːkəs/ *n.* the slimy substance secreted by the mucous membrane. [L]

mud *n.* **1.** wet soft earth. **2.** a liquid (commonly a suspension of clay and other substances in water) used as a lubricant and sealant etc. of the drill pipe in the drilling of an oil or gas well. —**mud-flat** *n.* a stretch of muddy land uncovered at low tide. **mud pack**, a cosmetic paste applied thickly to the face. **one's name is mud**, one is in disgrace. **sling** *or* **throw mud**, to speak slanderously. [prob. f. MLG]

muddle *v.t./i.* **1.** to bring into disorder. **2.** to confuse (a person) mentally. **3.** to confuse (one thing etc.) with another. **4.** to act in a confused way. —*n.* disorder, a muddled condition. —**muddle-headed** *adj.* confused, stupid. **muddle through**, to succeed despite one's inefficiency etc. —**muddler** *n.* [perh. f. MDu., = dabble in mud (as prec.)]

muddy *adj.* **1.** like mud. **2.** covered in or full of mud. **3.** confused, obscure. —*v.t.* to make muddy. —**muddiness** *n.* [f. MUD]

Mudéjar /muːˈðeɪhɑː(r)/ *n.* a Christianized Moor in medieval Spain. —*adj.* of a style of architecture originated by these (11th–16th c.). [Sp. f. Arab., = allowed to remain]

mudguard *n.* a curved strip or cover over the upper part of a wheel to protect a rider or another road-user from spray thrown up by the wheel.

muesli /ˈmjuːzlɪ/ *n.* a food of crushed cereals, dried fruit, nuts etc. [Swiss G]

muezzin /muːˈezɪn/ *n.* a Muslim crier who proclaims the hours of prayer, usually from a minaret. [f. Arab.]

muff¹ *n.* a tubular covering, especially of fur, in which the hands are put to keep them warm (ill. DRESS). [f. Du. *mof* f. L]

muff² *v.t.* to bungle; to miss (a catch, ball, etc.); to blunder in (a theatrical part etc.). [orig. unkn.]

muffin /ˈmʌfɪn/ *n.* a light flat round spongy cake eaten toasted and buttered. [orig. unkn.]

muffle *v.t.* **1.** to wrap or cover for warmth or protection, or to deaden sound. **2.** (usu. in *p.p.*) to deaden the sound of. [perh. f. OF *enmoufler* (*moufle* thick glove, as MUFF¹]

muffler *n.* **1.** a scarf or wrap worn for warmth. **2.** a thing used to deaden sound. [f. prec.]

mufti /ˈmʌftɪ/ *n.* plain clothes worn by one who normally wears uniform (esp. *in mufti*). [f. Arab., orig. = Muslim priest]

mug¹ *n.* **1.** a drinking-vessel, usually cylindrical, with a handle, and used without a saucer; its contents. **2.** (*slang*) the face or mouth. **3.** (*slang*) a gullible person, a simpleton. —*v.t.* (**-gg-**) to attack and rob, especially in a public place. —**a mug's game**, an unprofitable or senseless occupation. —**mugger** *n.* [prob. f. Scand.]

mug² *v.t./i.* (**-gg-**) (with *up*) to learn (a subject) by concentrated study. [orig. unkn.]

Mugabe /muːˈɡɑːbɪ/, Robert Gabriel (1924–), African statesman, first prime minister (1980) of Zimbabwe upon its independence.

muggins /ˈmʌɡɪnz/ *n.* (*pl.* **-ses** or same) (*colloq.*) a person who allows himself to be outwitted. [perh. f. surname *Muggins*]

muggy *adj.* (of the weather etc.) oppressively humid and warm. —**mugginess** *n.* [f. dial. *mug* mist, f. ON]

Muhammad /məˈhæmɪd/ (*c.*570–632) the founder of the Islamic faith and community. Born in Mecca to poor parents of noble lineage, as a young man he entered commerce, then through his marriage to the wealthy widow Khadīja gained some prominence in the business community as he assumed direction of his wife's commercial ventures. In 610 he received the first of a series of revelations (see KORAN) which shaped his message to the Muslim community and became the doctrinal and legislative basis of Islam. In the face of opposition from the merchants of Mecca—resistance based not only on the alien idea of a monotheistic doctrine in place of devotion to the traditional Arabian deities but also on social and economic concerns, for Muhammad's vision of social organization ran counter to that of a tribally based society—he and his small group of supporters were forced to flee north to Medina in 622. After consolidation of the community there, he led his followers into a series of battles which resulted in the capitulation of Mecca in 630. Muhammad died two years later, having successfully united tribal factions of the Hijāz into a force which would expand the frontiers of Islam. He was buried in Medina; a visit to his tomb is a traditional sequel to the requisite pilgrimage to Mecca. Muslims consider Muhammad to be 'seal of the Prophets', the final messenger sent by God to warn mankind against the consequences of rebelliousness against the divinely ordered way.

Muhammadan /məˈhæmɪd(ə)n/ *adj.* of Muhammad; Muslim. —*n.* a Muslim. [f. prec.]

mulatto /mjuːˈlætəʊ/ *n.* (*pl.* **-os**) a person of mixed White and Black parentage. [f. Sp. (as MULE¹)]

mulberry /ˈmʌlbərɪ/ *n.* **1.** a tree of the genus *Morus*, bearing purple or white edible berries and with leaves which are used to feed silkworms. **2.** its fruit. **3.** dull purplish-red. [earlier *murberie*, f. L *morum* mulberry + BERRY]

mulch *n.* a mixture of wet organic material spread to protect the roots of newly planted trees etc. —*v.t.* to treat with mulch. [prob. f. obs. *mulsh* soft]

mulct *v.t.* to extract money from by fine, taxation, or fraudulent means. [f. F f. L *mulctare* to fine]

mule¹ /mjuːl/ *n.* **1.** an animal that is the offspring of a mare and a male ass, or (*loosely*) of a she-ass and a stallion (*properly* HINNY), known for its stubbornness. **2.** a kind of spinning-machine invented in 1779 by Samuel Crompton (d. 1827) so called because it was a cross between Arkwright's 'water frame' and Hargreaves' spinning jenny. It was an improvement upon both, producing yarn of higher quality at greater speed. [f. OF f. L *mulus*]

mule² /mjuːl/ *n.* a backless slipper. [F]

muleteer /mjuːlɪˈtɪə(r)/ *n.* a mule-driver. [f. F *muletier* (as MULE¹)]

mulish *adj.* obstinate. [f. MULE¹]

mull¹ *v.t./i.* to think (over), to ponder. [perh. f. *mull* grind to powder, f. MDu.]

mull² *v.t.* to make (wine or beer) into a hot drink with sugar, spices, etc. [orig. unkn.]

mull³ *n.* (*Sc.*) a promontory. [cf. Gael. *maol*]

mullah /ˈmʌlə/ *n.* a Muslim learned in Islamic theology and sacred law. [f. Pers., Turk. & Urdu f. Arab.]

Müller¹ /ˈmylə(r)/, Johannes Peter (1801–58), German anatomist and biologist, a pioneer of comparative and microscopical methods in biology, regarded as one of the most distinguished scientists of 19th-c. Germany.

Müller² /ˈmylə(r)/, Paul Hermann (1899–1965), Swiss chemist, who synthesized DDT (1939) and discovered its insecticidal properties. He was awarded the 1948 Nobel Prize for medicine.

mullet¹ /ˈmʌlɪt/ *n.* a sea-fish of the families Mullidae or Mugilidae, valued for food. [f. OF f. L *mullus* f. Gk]

mullet² /ˈmʌlɪt/ *n.* (in heraldry) a star-shaped figure, usually with five points, given as a mark of cadency for a third son (ill. HERALDRY). [f. OF, = rowel]

mulligatawny /mʌlɪgəˈtɔːnɪ/ *n.* a highly seasoned soup, originally from India. [f. Tamil, = pepper-water]

mullion /ˈmʌljən/ *n.* a vertical bar dividing the lights in a window (ill. HOUSES). [prob. alt. f. *monial*, f. OF *moinel* (as MEAN³)]

multi- /mʌltɪ-/ *prefix* many. [L (*multus* much, many)]

multi-access /mʌltɪˈækses/ *adj.* (of a computer system) allowing access to the central processor from several terminals at the same time.

multicoloured /ˈmʌltɪkʌləd/ *adj.* of many colours.

multifarious /mʌltɪˈfeərɪəs/ *adj.* many and various; having a great variety. —**multifariously** *adv.* [f. L *multifarius*]

multiform /ˈmʌltɪfɔːm/ *adj.* having many forms, of many kinds.

multilateral /mʌltɪˈlætər(ə)l/ *adj.* **1.** (of an agreement, treaty, etc.) in which three or more parties participate. **2.** having many sides.

multilingual /mʌltɪˈlɪŋɡw(ə)l/ *adj.* in, using, or speaking many languages.

multimillionaire /mʌltɪmɪljəˈneə(r)/ *n.* a person possessing several million pounds, dollars, etc.

multinational /mʌltɪˈnæʃən(ə)l/ *adj.* operating in several countries. —*n.* a multinational company.

multiple /ˈmʌltɪp(ə)l/ *adj.* **1.** having several parts, elements, or components. **2.** many and various. —*n.* a quantity that contains another some number of times without a remainder. —**least** or **lowest common multiple,** the least quantity that is a multiple of two or more given quantities. **multiple-choice** *adj.* (of a question in an examination) accompanied by several possible answers from which the correct one is to be selected. **multiple sclerosis,** see SCLEROSIS. [F f. L *multiplus* (as foll.)]

multiplex /ˈmʌltɪpleks/ *adj.* of many elements, manifold. [L (MULTI-, -*plex* -fold)]

multiplicand /mʌltɪplɪˈkænd/ *n.* a quantity to be multiplied by another. [f. L, gerundive of *multiplicare* (as MULTIPLY)]

multiplication /mʌltɪplɪˈkeɪʃ(ə)n/ *n.* multiplying, especially the arithmetical process. —**multiplication sign,** ×, as in 2 × 3. **multiplication table,** a table of the products of pairs of factors, especially from 1 to 12. [f. OF or L (as MULTIPLY)]

multiplicity /mʌltɪˈplɪsɪtɪ/ *n.* a great variety or number. [f. L (as MULTIPLEX)]

multiplier /ˈmʌltɪplaɪə(r)/ *n.* the quantity by which a multiplicand is multiplied. [f. foll.]

multiply /ˈmʌltɪplaɪ/ *v.t./i.* **1.** to obtain from (a number) another that is a specified number of times its value. **2.** to increase in number, as by breeding. **3.** to produce a large number of (instances). **4.** to breed (animals); to propagate (plants). [f. OF f. L *multiplicare* (as MULTIPLEX)]

multi-purpose /mʌltɪˈpɜːpəs/ *adj.* serving many purposes.

multiracial /mʌltɪˈreɪʃ(ə)l/ *adj.* composed of or concerning people of various races.

multi-storey /ˈmʌltɪstɔːrɪ/ *adj.* having several storeys.

multitude /ˈmʌltɪtjuːd/ *n.* **1.** a crowd of people. **2.** a great number. —**the multitude,** the common people. [f. OF f. L *multitudo* (*multus* many)]

multitudinous /mʌltɪˈtjuːdɪnəs/ *adj.* very numerous; consisting of many individuals. [f. L (as prec.)]

mum¹ *adj.* (*colloq.*) silent. —**mum's the word,** say nothing. [imit. of closed lips]

mum² *v.i.* (-mm-) to act in a mime. [cf. prec., and MLG *mummen*]

mum³ *n.* (*colloq.*) = MUMMY². [abbr.]

mumble *v.t./i.* to speak or utter indistinctly. —*n.* an indistinct utterance. —**mumbler** *n.* [f. MUM¹; cf. LG *mummelen*]

mumbo-jumbo /mʌmbəʊˈdʒʌmbəʊ/ *n.* **1.** meaningless ritual. **2.** language or action intended to mystify or confuse. **3.** an object of senseless veneration. [f. *Mumbo Jumbo*, a supposed African idol]

mummer /ˈmʌmə(r)/ *n.* an actor in a traditional mime. —**mummers' play,** the best-known type of English folk-play, which appears to derive from the folk festivals of primitive agricultural communities. The central theme is the death and resurrection of one of the characters, an obvious re-enactment in human terms of the earth awakening from the death of winter. Texts show a remarkable similarity. The play is first mentioned towards the end of the 18th c. and flourished until the mid-19th c.; it can still be seen in a few English villages. [f. OF *momeur* (as MUM²)]

mummery /ˈmʌmərɪ/ *n.* **1.** a performance by mummers. **2.** a ridiculous (esp. religious) ceremonial. [f. OF *momerie* (as prec.)]

mummify /ˈmʌmɪfaɪ/ *v.t.* to preserve (a body) as a mummy. —**mummification** /-fɪˈkeɪʃ(ə)n/ *n.* [f. foll.]

mummy¹ *n.* (*colloq.*) mother. [imit. of child's pronunc.; cf. MAMMA]

mummy² /ˈmʌmɪ/ *n.* the body of a person or animal embalmed for burial, especially in ancient Egypt. The concept of mummification was based on the belief that the preservation of the body was necessary so that the soul and the ka might meet it again and live with it. The practice developed in the predynastic period with the change from simple desert burials, which had dehydrated and preserved the body naturally, to burial in coffins. Mummification procedures evolved, reaching a peak by the late New Kingdom. The essential steps were removing the viscera, dehydrating the body with natron, treating it with resin, bandaging, and decorating it. The ceremonial aspects were considered crucial, and the procedure could take 70 days. [f. F, ult. f. Pers. *mūm* wax]

mumps *n.* an infectious disease with swelling of the neck and face. [f. obs. *mump* grimace]

Munch /mʌŋk/, Edvard (1863–1944), Norwegian painter and engraver, one of the chief sources of German expressionism. His subjects had an intense emotionalism, and he explored the use of violent colour and linear distortion to express anxiety, fear, love, and hatred; among his most famous works is *The Cry* (1895).

munch *v.t./i.* to eat steadily with marked action of the jaws. [imit.]

Munchausen /mʌnˈtʃaʊz(ə)n/, Baron, hero of a book of fantastic travellers' tales (1785) written in English by a German, Rudolph Erich Raspe. The original Freiherr von Münchhausen is said to have lived in 1720–97, to have served in the Russian army against the Turks, and to have related extravagant tales of his prowess.

Munda /ˈmuːndə/ *n.* **1.** a member of an ancient people surviving in present times as primitive tribes living in NE India. **2.** the group of languages which includes their dialects. —*adj.* of the Mundas or their languages. [native name]

mundane /mʌnˈdeɪn/ *adj.* **1.** dull or routine. **2.** of this world, worldly. [f. OF f. L (*mundus* world)]

Munich /ˈmjuːnɪk/ a city in SW Germany, capital of Bavaria; pop. (1981) 1,294,000. —**Munich Pact** or **Agreement,** an agreement between Britain, France, Germany, and Italy, signed at Munich on 29 Sept. 1938, under which part of Czechoslovakia was ceded to Germany. It is remembered as an act of appeasement.

municipal /mjuːˈnɪsɪp(ə)l/ *adj.* of or concerning a municipality or its self-government. —**municipally** *adv.* [f. L (*municipium* self-governing town of Italy or a Roman province)]

municipality /mjuːnɪsɪˈpælɪtɪ/ *n.* **1.** a town or district having local self-government. **2.** the governing body of this. [f. F (as prec.)]

munificent /mjuːˈnɪfɪs(ə)nt/ *adj.* splendidly generous. —**munificence** *n.,* **munificently** *adv.* [f. L *munificus* (*munus* gift)]

muniment /ˈmjuːnɪmənt/ *n.* (usu. in *pl.*) a document kept as evidence of rights or privileges. [f. OF f. L *munimentum* title-deed, orig. = defence (as foll.)]

munition /mjuːˈnɪʃ(ə)n/ *n.pl.* military weapons, ammunition, equipment, and stores. [F f. L (*munire* fortify)]

muntjak /ˈmʌntjæk/ *n.* a small deer originally of SE Asia, of the genus *Muntiacus*, the male of which has small tusks and antlers. [f. native name]

mural /ˈmjʊər(ə)l/ *adj.* of or like a wall; on a wall. —*n.* a mural painting etc. [F f. L *muralis* (*murus* wall)]

Murat /ˈmjuːrɑː/, Joachim (*c.*1767-1815), French general, king of Naples 1808-14. One of the most flamboyant of Napoleon's marshals, Murat made his name as a cavalry commander, but like several of his colleagues was not always equal to the challenge of independent command. Having deserted Napoleon in 1814, he returned to his cause in 1815, but was defeated and eventually captured and executed.

murder *n.* **1.** the intentional and unlawful killing of one person by another. **2.** (*colloq.*) a highly troublesome or dangerous state of affairs. —*v.t.* **1.** to kill (a person) unlawfully with malice aforethought; to kill wickedly or inhumanly. **2.** (*colloq.*) to spoil by bad performance, mispronunciation, etc. **3.** (*colloq.*) to defeat utterly. —**cry blue murder,** (*slang*) to make an extravagant outcry. **get away with murder,** (*colloq.*) to do whatever one wishes. —**murderer** *n.*, **murderess** *n.fem.* [OE]

murderous /ˈmɜːdərəs/ *adj.* capable of, intent on, or involving murder or great harm. [f. prec.]

Murdoch /ˈmɜːdɒk/, Iris Jean (1919-), English novelist, born in Dublin of Anglo-Irish parents, and educated at Oxford where she subsequently lectured in philosophy. Her first novel *Under the Net* (1954) was followed by many other successful works portraying sophisticated sexual relationships. Her plots have an operatic quality combining comic, macabre, and bizarre incidents, showing an acute observation of 20th-c. middle-class life and a great ingenuity.

Murillo /mjʊəˈrɪləʊ/, Bartolomé Esteban (1618-82), Spanish painter. Born in Seville, his early work's dramatic chiaroscuro shows an indebtedness to Zurbarán. His mature subject-matter incorporated two basic themes: genre scenes of sentimentalized urchins and peasants and devotional pictures of delicate colour and ethereal form—his 'estilo vaporoso' (e.g. *Immaculate Conception*). In 1660 he became first director of the Seville Academy. His reputation and influence stood high throughout the 18th c. but fell sharply because of the mannered vapidity of his imitators.

murk *n.* darkness, poor visibility. [prob. f. Scand.]

murky *adj.* **1.** dark, gloomy; (of liquid etc.) thick and dirty. **2.** suspiciously obscure. —**murkily** *adv.*, **murkiness** *n.* [f. MURK]

murmur /ˈmɜːmə(r)/ *n.* **1.** a subdued continuous sound. **2.** softly spoken or nearly inarticulate speech. **3.** a subdued expression of discontent. —*v.t./i.* to make a murmur; to utter (words) softly; to complain in low tones. —**murmurous** *adj.* [f. OF or L]

murphy /ˈmɜːfi/ *n.* (*slang*) a potato. [Irish surname, from the potato being regarded as the staple food of Ireland]

Murphy's law a name humorously given to various expressions of the apparent perverseness of things (roughly, 'anything that can go wrong will go wrong'). [Irish surname; orig. of phrase uncertain]

murrain /ˈmʌrɪn/ *n.* an infectious disease in cattle. [f. AF *moryn*]

Murray[1] /ˈmʌri/ the principal river of Australia, rising in New South Wales and flowing 2,590 km (1,610 miles) westward to the Indian Ocean.

Murray[2] /ˈmʌri/, Sir James Augustus Henry (1837-1915), Scottish-born lexicographer, chief editor of the largest of all dictionaries, the *Oxford English Dictionary* (1884-1928; originally entitled *A New English Dictionary on Historical Principles*). The original plan of a four-volume work, to be completed in ten years (i.e. by 1889), was defeated by the complexities of the English language and its development over nine centuries, and nine years' editing produced only the first volume of a work that was to consist ultimately of twelve. In spite of the drain on its resources the University of Oxford recognized that the project was already a national asset: new instalments were eagerly awaited by scholars around the world, and the parts already issued were becoming the final authority on the English language. Murray did not live to see the Dictionary completed; he died after finishing a section of the letter T, two years short of his 80th birthday.

muscadine /ˈmʌskədiːn, -daɪn/ *n.* a musk-flavoured kind of grape. [perh. f. MUSCAT]

Muscat /ˈmʌskæt/ the capital of Oman; pop. (est. 1973) 15,000.

muscat /ˈmʌskət/ *n.* **1.** a muscadine. **2.** wine made from muscadines. [F f. Prov. (as MUSK)]

muscatel /mʌskəˈtel/ *n.* **1.** a muscadine. **2.** wine or a raisin made from this. [f. OF (as prec.)]

muscle /ˈmʌs(ə)l/ *n.* **1.** the contractile tissue that produces movement in an animal's body (see below); a structure composed of such tissue, especially a skeletal muscle of a vertebrate (ill. BODY 2). **2.** that part of the animal body which is composed of muscles, the chief constituent of flesh. **3.** power, strength. —*v.i.* (*slang*) to force one's way. —**muscle-bound** *adj.* with the muscles stiff and inelastic through excessive exercise or training. **muscle-man** *n.* a man with highly-developed muscles, especially as an intimidator. [F f. L *musculus*]
In all animals except the protozoa and most of the sponges certain cells function as muscle-cells. These cells are very small, but when grouped may form conspicuous columns, bands, or sheets of muscle. Muscular tissue makes movement and stance possible; it converts chemical into mechanical energy, and its chemical reactions produce most of the heat which keeps mammals' and birds' temperature above that of their surroundings. In vertebrates there are three main types of muscle tissue. Skeletal muscles are under voluntary control (at least in man); they are attached to bones by tendons and move the joints. Cardiac muscle, found only in the heart, is not under direct voluntary control; it is notable for its ability to contract spontaneously and rhythmically (see HEART). Smooth or visceral muscle, which is also controlled involuntarily, is found chiefly in the walls of hollow organs such as the stomach and intestines. Under the microscope voluntary muscle has a striped appearance, while involuntary or smooth muscle shows no stripes. In invertebrates distinctions between different types of muscle tissue are less clear.

Muscovite /ˈmʌskəvaɪt/ *adj.* of Moscow. —*n.* a citizen of Moscow. [as foll.]

Muscovy /ˈmʌskəvi/ **1.** a principality in west central Russia, founded by Daniel, son of Alexander Nevski, in the late 13th c. Muscovy gradually expanded, despite repeated Tartar depredations, uniting with the neighbouring principality of Vladimir to form the nucleus of the modern Russian State. **2.** (*archaic*) Russia. —**Muscovy duck,** a tropical American duck (*Cairina moschata*) with a slight smell of musk (and no connection with Russia). [f. obs. F, ult. f. Russ. *Moskva* Moscow]

muscular /ˈmʌskjʊlə(r)/ *adj.* **1.** of or affecting the muscles. **2.** having well-developed muscles. —**muscularity** /-ˈlærɪtɪ/ *n.* [as MUSCLE]

Muse /mjuːz/ *n.* **1.** (*Gk & Rom. myth.*) any of the goddesses who presided over the arts and sciences. They were the daughters of Zeus and Mnemosyne, traditionally nine in number (Calliope, Clio, Euterpe, Terpsichore, Erato, Melpomene, Thalia, Polyhymnia, and Urania), though their functions and names vary considerably in different sources. **2.** **muse,** a poet's inspiring genius. [f. OF or L f. Gk *mousa*]

muse /mjuːz/ *v.t./i.* to ponder, to meditate; to say meditatively. [f. OF perh. f. L *musus* muzzle]

musette /mjuːˈzet/ *n.* **1.** the bagpipe of 17th-18th-c. French society; a small simple instrument of 19th-c. France, resembling the oboe. **2.** a popular dance at the court of Louis XIV and XV, a rustic form of the gavotte. Its name derives from the music's bagpipe-like bass drone. [f. OF, dim. of *muse* bagpipe + -ETTE]

museum /mjuːˈzɪəm/ *n.* a building used for the exhibition and storage of objects illustrating antiquities, natural history, the arts, etc. —**museum piece,** a specimen of art, manufacture, etc., fit for a museum; an old-fashioned person or machine etc. [L f. Gk, = seat of the Muses]

mush[1] *n.* **1.** soft pulp. **2.** feeble sentimentality. **3.** (*US*) maize porridge. [app. var. of MASH]

mush[2] *v.i.* (*N. Amer.*) **1.** to travel across snow with a dog-sledge. **2.** (as a command to sledge-dogs) get moving. [prob. corrupt. f. F *marchons* let us advance (as MARCH[2])]

mushroom /ˈmʌʃrʊm/ *n.* an edible fungus, especially *Agaricus campestris*, with a stem and domed cap. —*v.i.* **1.** to spring up rapidly. **2.** to expand and flatten like a mushroom cap. **3.** to gather mushrooms. —**mushroom cloud,** a cloud of mushroom shape, especially from a nuclear explosion. [f. OF *mousseron* f. L]

Musical Notation and some Instruments

(see also **The Orchestra**)

Values of notes and rests

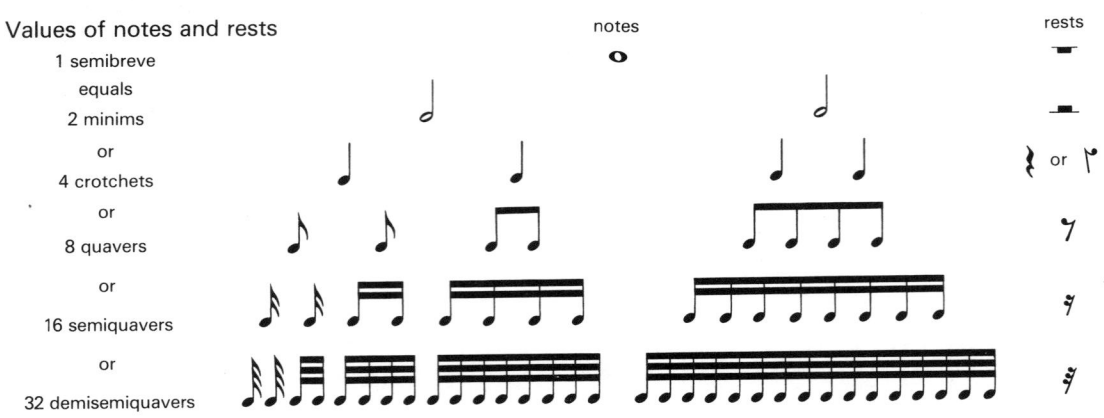

notes

rests

1 semibreve

equals

2 minims

or

4 crotchets

or

8 quavers

or

16 semiquavers

or

32 demisemiquavers

Some common symbols

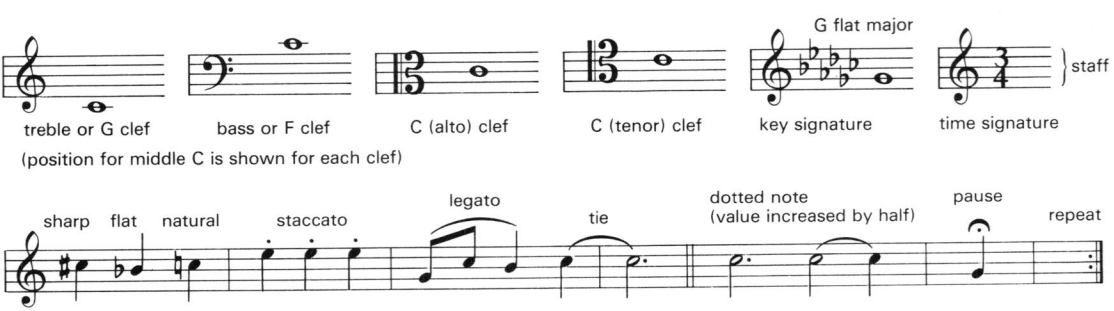

treble or G clef   bass or F clef   C (alto) clef   C (tenor) clef   key signature   time signature

G flat major

) staff

(position for middle C is shown for each clef)

sharp   flat   natural   staccato   legato   tie   dotted note (value increased by half)   pause   repeat

Some instruments from overseas

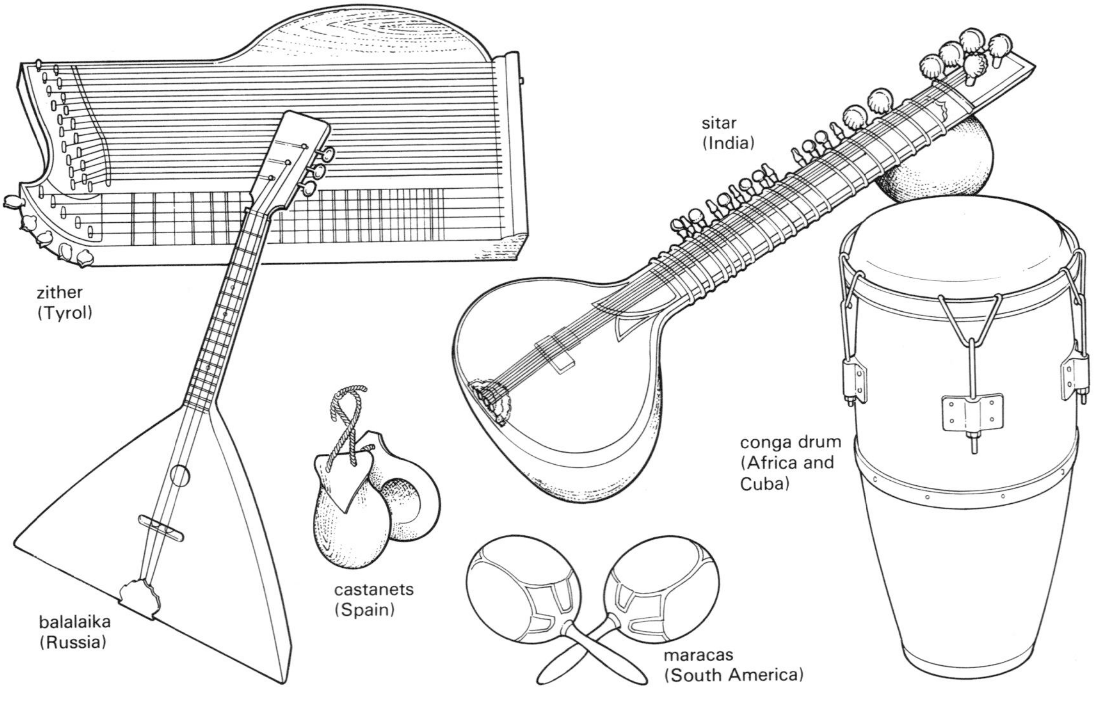

zither
(Tyrol)

balalaika
(Russia)

castanets
(Spain)

maracas
(South America)

sitar
(India)

conga drum
(Africa and
Cuba)

The piano

action of a modern grand piano

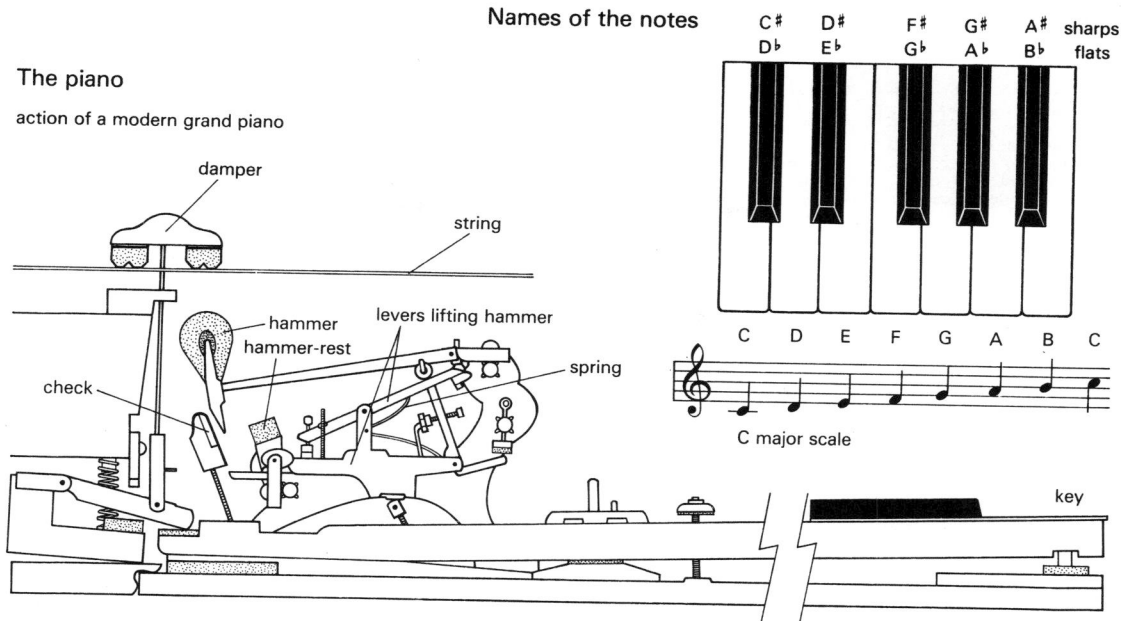

C# / Db   D# / Eb   F# / Gb   G# / Ab   A# / Bb   sharps flats

damper

string

hammer
hammer-rest

levers lifting hammer

check

spring

C D E F G A B C

C major scale

key

Some popular and band instruments

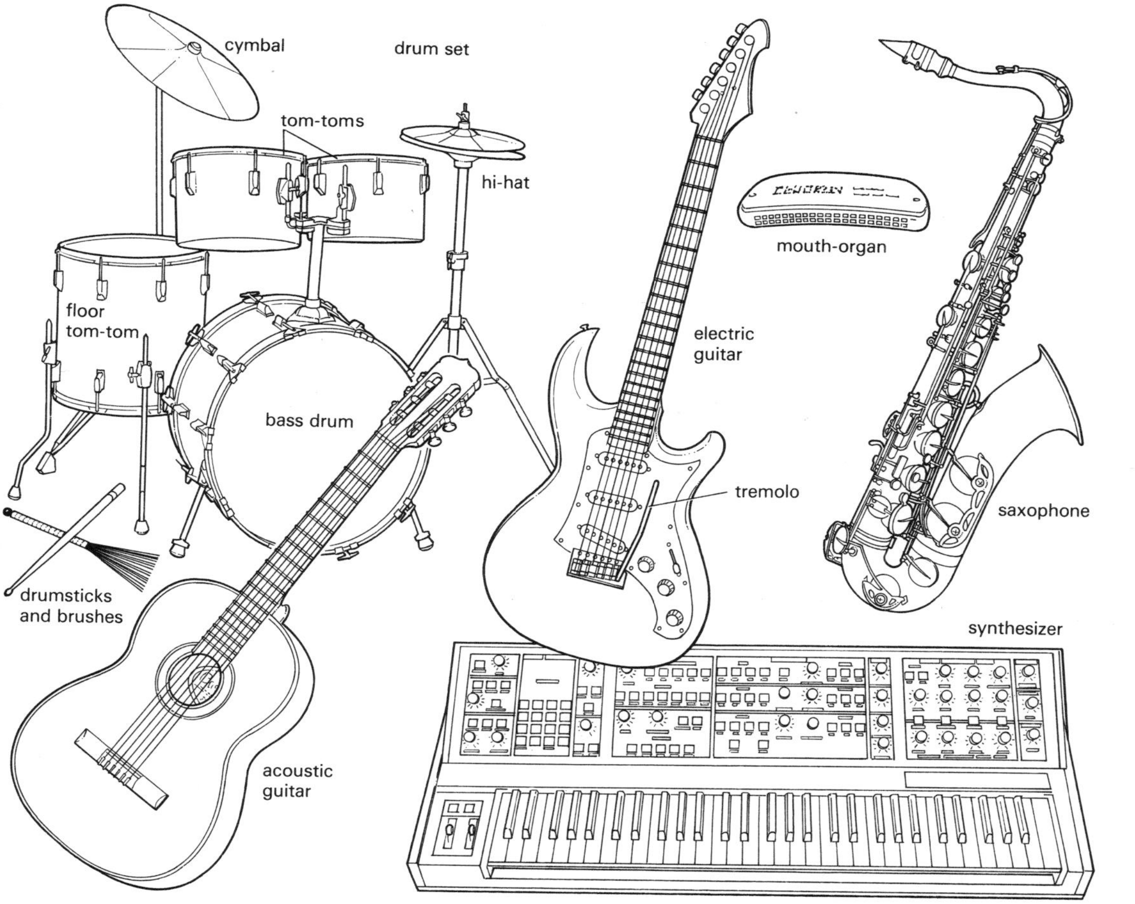

cymbal

drum set

tom-toms

hi-hat

floor
tom-tom

bass drum

electric
guitar

mouth-organ

tremolo

saxophone

drumsticks
and brushes

acoustic
guitar

synthesizer

mushy adj. **1.** like mush, soft. **2.** feebly sentimental. —**mushily** adv., **mushiness** n. [f. MUSH¹]

music /ˈmjuːzɪk/ n. **1.** the art of combining vocal and/or instrumental sounds in harmonious and expressive ways; the sounds so produced. **2.** a musical composition; a printed or written score of this. **3.** a pleasant natural sound. —**face the music,** to face one's critics etc., not to shirk the consequences. **music centre,** equipment combining a radio, record-player, and tape-recorder. **music-hall** n. see separate entry. **music-stool** n. a stool with adjustable height of the seat, for a pianist. **music to one's ears,** what one is pleased to hear. [f. OF f. L f. Gk, = of the Muses (as MUSE)]

musical /ˈmjuːzɪk(ə)l/ adj. **1.** of music. **2.** (of a sound etc.) melodious or harmonious. **3.** fond of or skilled in music. **4.** set to or accompanied by music. —n. a film or play etc. with music and song as the principal feature. —**musical box,** a box containing a mechanism (usually a revolving toothed cylinder striking a comblike metal plate) for playing a certain tune when set in motion. **musical chairs,** a party game in which players walk round chairs (one fewer than the number of players) until the music stops, when the player who finds no chair is eliminated and a chair is removed before the next round. —**musicality** /-ˈkælɪtɪ/ n., **musically** adv. [as prec.]

musical comedy an entertainment in which a story is told by a combination of spoken dialogue and songs. Originally the plot was very slight, but with the importation of more serious themes, particularly in the USA, the word 'comedy' was dropped and the genre became known simply as the 'musical'. Musical comedy dates from the end of the 19th c. and reached its peak in the USA in the work of such composers as Jerome Kern, Irving Berlin, Cole Porter, George Gershwin, and Richard Rodgers.

music-hall n. a type of entertainment, or a place for performing this, which flourished in Britain during the second half of the 19th and early 20th c. Originally a simple stage in a hall furnished with tables, chairs, and a bar, the whole presided over by a chairman, it developed into an elaborate two- or three-tier auditorium with a fully equipped stage behind a proscenium arch. The 'turns' on a normal evening's bill—sometimes as many as 25—ranged from acrobats and jugglers to comedians and singers. In its heyday music-hall was the entertainment most loved by working people, but it was killed by the advent of the cinema, radio, and above all television.

musician /mjuːˈzɪʃ(ə)n/ n. a person skilled in music, especially one practising it professionally. —**musicianship** n. [f. OF (as MUSIC)]

musicology /mjuːzɪˈkɒlədʒɪ/ n. the study of the history and forms of music as distinct from study to perform or compose it. —**musicologist** n. [f. F (as MUSIC, -LOGY)]

musique concrète /mjuːziːk kɔ̃ˈkret/ concrete music (see CONCRETE). [F]

musk n. **1.** a substance secreted by the male musk-deer, used as the basis of perfumes. **2.** a plant (esp. *Mimulus moschatus*) which has or used to have a musky smell. —**musk-deer** n. a small hornless ruminant of Central Asia, of the genus *Moschus*. **musk-duck** n. the Muscovy duck. **musk-melon** n. the common yellow melon (*Cucumis melo*). **musk-ox** n. a shaggy ruminant (*Ovibos moschatus*) with curved horns. **musk-rat** n. a large North American aquatic rodent (*Ondatra zibethica*) with a musky smell; its fur. **musk-rose** n. a rambling rose (*Rosa moschata* etc.) with a musky fragrance. [f. L f. Pers.]

musket /ˈmʌskɪt/ n. (hist.) an infantryman's (esp. smooth-bored) light gun. [f. F f. It. *moschetto* crossbow bolt]

musketeer /mʌskɪˈtɪə(r)/ n. a soldier armed with a musket. [f. prec.]

Muskogean /mʌskəˈɡɪən, -ˈkəʊɡɪən/ n. a family of American Indian languages in south-eastern North America. —adj. of this family. [f. *Muskogee* its speakers, perh. of Algonquian origin]

musky adj. smelling like musk. —**muskiness** n. [f. MUSK]

Muslim /ˈmʊslɪm, -z-/ n. a believer in Islam. —adj. of Muslims. [f. Arab., = one who submits (as ISLAM)]

muslin /ˈmʌzlɪn/ n. a fine delicately woven cotton fabric. [f. F f. It. (*Mussolo* Mosul in Iraq, where it was made)]

musquash /ˈmʌskwɒʃ/ n. **1.** the musk-rat. **2.** its fur. [Algonquian]

mussel /ˈmʌs(ə)l/ n. a bivalve mollusc, especially the edible kind (genus *Mytilus*). [OE (ult. as MUSCLE)]

Mussolini /mʊsəˈliːnɪ/, Benito (1883-1945), Italian dic-tator, founder and leader of the Italian Fascist Party. He began his political life as a Marxist, calling Marx his 'father and teacher' and 'the magnificent philosopher of working-class violence', and though he broke with Marxism because it was unpatriotic his ideology contained socialist elements right to the end. Mussolini gained power in 1922 and quickly organized his government along dictatorial lines. Although he achieved a certain degree of success with domestic reforms, his aggressive foreign policy led first to the conquest of Ethiopia in 1935-6 and then Italy's entry into the Second World War on Germany's side in 1940. He was captured and executed by Italian Communist par-tisans in April 1945, a few weeks before the end of the war.

Mussorgsky /məˈsɔːɡskɪ/, Modest (1839-81), Russian composer. He trained for the army but resigned his com-mission to study music in St Petersburg, where he later became a member of the group of composers known as 'The Five', or 'The Mighty Handful'. Most of his best-known works are vocal, his interest in speech rhythms combining with a natural lyricism in his songs. After his death many of his works were completed and altered by Rimsky-Korsakov and others, but recently there has been a tendency to return to Mussorgsky's original scoring, particularly in his monumental opera *Boris Godunov* (1868-74).

must¹ v.aux. (pres. & past **must**; no other parts used) expressing obligation, insistence, rightness or advisability, certainty or likelihood. —n. (colloq.) a thing that must be done, seen, etc. [OE]

must² n. grape-juice before the end of fermentation; new wine. [OE f. L *mustum*]

mustang /ˈmʌstæŋ/ n. a half-wild domestic horse of Mexico and California. [f. Sp. *mestengo* & *mostrenco*]

mustard /ˈmʌstəd/ n. **1.** a plant (*Brassica nigra*) with yellow flowers. **2.** a condiment made by grinding the seeds of this and making them into a paste with water or vinegar. **3.** a fodder plant (*Sinapis alba*) the seed-leaves of which form part of 'mustard and cress'. **4.** a brownish-yellow colour. —**mustard gas,** a colourless oily liquid or its vapour, a powerful irritant. **mustard plaster,** a plaster containing mustard, applied to the skin as a poultice. [f. OF f. L (as MUST²), the condiment being orig. prepared with must]

muster v.t./i. **1.** to assemble or cause to assemble (orig. of soldiers assembled to check numbers etc. or for inspection). **2.** to summon (courage, strength, etc.). —n. an assembly or gathering. —**pass muster,** to be accepted as adequate. [f. OF *mo(u)strer* f. L *monstrare* show]

mustn't /ˈmʌs(ə)nt/ (colloq.) must not.

musty adj. **1.** mouldy, stale. **2.** antiquated. —**mustily** adv., **mustiness** n. [perh. alt. f. *moisty* (MOIST)]

mutable /ˈmjuːtəb(ə)l/ adj. liable to change; fickle. —**mutability** /-ˈbɪlɪtɪ/ n. [f. L *mutabilis* (*mutare* change)]

mutant /ˈmjuːt(ə)nt/ adj. resulting from mutation. —n. a mutant form. [f. L (as MUTATION)]

mutate /mjuːˈteɪt/ v.t./i. to undergo mutation; to cause to do this. [f. foll.]

mutation /mjuːˈteɪʃ(ə)n/ n. **1.** a change, an alteration. **2.** a genetic change which when transmitted to an offspring gives rise to heritable variation. **3.** a mutant. **4.** umlaut. [f. L (*mutare* change)]

mutatis mutandis /muːˈtɑːtɪs muːˈtændɪs/ with due alter-ation of details in comparing cases). [L]

mute /mjuːt/ adj. **1.** silent, refraining from speech. **2.** not emitting articulate sound; (of a person or animal) dumb. **3.** (of a letter) not pronounced. **4.** not expressed in speech. —n. **1.** a dumb person. **2.** an actor whose part is in dumb show. **3.** a device to deaden the sound of a musical instrument. **4.** a mute consonant. —v.t. **1.** to deaden or soften the sound of (esp. a musical instrument). **2.** to tone down, to make less intense. —**mute swan,** the common white swan (*Cygnus olor*). —**mutely** adv., **muteness** n. [f. OF f. L *mutus*]

mutilate /ˈmjuːtɪleɪt/ v.t. **1.** to injure or disfigure by cutting off an important part. **2.** to render (a book etc.) imperfect by excision etc. —**mutilation** /-ˈleɪʃ(ə)n/ n., **mutilator** n. [f. L *mutilare* (*mutilus* maimed)]

mutineer /mjuːtɪˈnɪə(r)/ n. one who mutinies. [f. F (*mutin* rebellious f. *muete* movement f. L *movere* move)]

mutinous /ˈmjuːtɪnəs/ adj. rebellious, ready to mutiny. —**mutinously** adv. [f. obs. mutine rebellion (as prec.)]

mutiny /ˈmjuːtɪnɪ/ n. an open revolt against authority, especially by servicemen against officers. —v.i. to engage in a mutiny, to revolt. [as prec.]

mutt *n.* (*slang*) a stupid person. [abbr. of *mutton-head*]

mutter *v.t./i.* **1.** to speak or utter in a low unclear tone. **2.** to utter subdued grumbles. —*n.* muttering; muttered words. [as MUTE]

mutton *n.* the flesh of the sheep as food. —**mutton dressed as lamb,** a middle-aged or elderly woman dressed to look young. **mutton-head** *n.* (*colloq.*) a stupid person. —**muttony** *adj.* [f. OF f. L *multo* sheep]

mutual /ˈmjuːtjʊəl/ *adj.* **1.** (of feeling, action, etc.) felt or done by each to or towards the other. **2.** standing in (a specified) relation to each other. **3.** (*colloq.*) (**D**) common to two or more persons. —**mutuality** /-ˈælɪtɪ/ *n.*, **mutually** *adv.* [f. OF f. L *mutuus*]

mutualism /ˈmjuːtjʊəlɪz(ə)m/ *n.* mutually beneficial symbiosis. [f. prec.]

Muzak /ˈmjuːzæk/ *n.* [P] a system of music transmission for playing in shops, factories, etc.; recorded light music as a background. [cf. MUSIC]

muzzle *n.* **1.** the projecting part of an animal's head including the nose and mouth. **2.** the open end of a firearm. **3.** a contrivance of strap or wire etc. put over an animal's head to prevent it from biting or feeding. —*v.t.* **1.** to put a muzzle on. **2.** to impose silence on. [f. OF f. L *musum*]

muzzy *adj.* **1.** dazed, feeling stupefied. **2.** indistinct. —**muzzily** *adv.*, **muzziness** *n.* [orig. unkn.]

MW *abbr.* megawatt(s).

my /maɪ/ *poss. adj.* **1.** of or belonging to me. **2.** used in affectionate collocations and as an exclamation of surprise. [f. MINE¹]

myalgia /maɪˈældʒɪə/ *n.* pain in muscle(s). [f. Gk *mus* muscle + *algos* pain]

myall /ˈmaɪəl/ *n.* an Australian acacia with hard scented wood used for fences etc. [f. Aboriginal *maiāl*]

Mycenae /maɪˈsiːniː/ a city of ancient Greece, situated in the NE Peloponnese a few kilometres from the sea, dominating various land and sea routes, famous in Greek legend as the home of Agamemnon. Its greatest era was the period from *c.*1400 to 1200 BC, during which were constructed the massive walls of Cyclopaean masonry (including the 'Lion Gate', *c.*1250 BC) and the palace on the summit of the hill.

Mycenaean /maɪsɪˈniːən/ *adj.* of the culture developed in mainland Greece in the late Bronze Age, *c.*1580-1100 BC, illustrated by remains at Mycenae and other ancient cities of the Peloponnese (see below). —*n.* a Mycenaean person. [f. L *Mycenaeus*]
The Mycenaeans inherited control of the Aegean after the collapse of the Minoan civilization *c.*1400 BC. Their cities, such as those of Mycenae, Tiryns, and Pylos, were well populated and prosperous, with fortified citadels enclosing impressive palaces. Artefacts of ivory, gold, and inlaid bronze, of advanced technique and exquisite workmanship, are found in tombs that must have been those of royalty. The language they used was a form of Greek, and their actions were recorded in the script known as Linear B. Trade with other Mediterranean countries flourished, and Mycenaean products are found from southern Italy to Palestine and Syria. The end of Mycenaean power coincided with a period of general upheaval and migrations associated with the end of the Bronze Age in the Mediterranean.

mycology /maɪˈkɒlədʒɪ/ *n.* the study of fungi. —**mycologist** *n.* [f. Gk *mukēs* mushroom + -LOGY]

myna, mynah var. of MINA.

myopia /maɪˈəʊpɪə/ *n.* short-sightedness. —**myopic** /-ˈɒpɪk/ *adj.*, **myopically** /-ˈɒpɪkəlɪ/ *adv.* [f. Gk (*muō* shut, *ōps* eye)]

myriad /ˈmɪrɪəd/ *n.* (*literary*) **1.** (in *pl.*) an indefinitely great number. **2.** ten thousand. —*adj.* (*literary*) innumerable. [f. L f. Gk (*murioi* 10,000)]

myriapod /ˈmɪrɪəpɒd/ *n.* a small crawling arthropod with many legs, of the group Myriapoda comprising centipedes and millepedes. [as prec. + Gk *pous podos* foot]

myrmidon /ˈmɜːmɪd(ə)n/ *n.* a hired ruffian, a base servant. [f. *Myrmidons*, Thessalians who followed Achilles to Troy]

Myron /ˈmaɪrən/ (mid-5th c. BC) Greek sculptor. Only two certain copies of his work survive, the most important being the 'Discobolus' (discus-thrower) demonstrating his interest in symmetry and the drama of physical endeavour, a preoccupation of this phase of early classical sculpture.

myrrh /mɜː(r)/ *n.* a gum resin from trees of the genus *Commiphora*, used in perfumes, medicine, and incense. [OE f. L f. Gk *murra*]

myrtle /ˈmɜːt(ə)l/ *n.* an evergreen shrub of the genus *Myrtus*, with shiny leaves and fragrant white flowers. [f. L dim. (*myrta, myrtus* f. Gk)]

myself /maɪˈself/ *pron.* emphat. & refl. form of I, ME¹. [f. ME¹ + SELF]

Mysia /ˈmɪsɪə/ the ancient name for the region of NW Asia Minor south of the Hellespont and the Sea of Marmara. —**Mysian** *adj.* & *n.*

Mysore /maɪˈsɔː(r)/ see KARNATAKA.

mysterious /mɪˈstɪərɪəs/ *adj.* **1.** full of or wrapped in mystery. **2.** (of a person) enjoying mystery. —**mysteriously** *adv.* [f. F (as foll.)]

mystery /ˈmɪstərɪ/ *n.* **1.** an inexplicable or secret matter. **2.** secrecy, obscurity. **3.** the practice of making a secret of things. **4.** a fictional work dealing with a puzzling event, especially a crime. **5.** a religious truth that is beyond human powers to understand. **6.** (in *pl.*) secret cults in the ancient world, which generally included mystic ideas and involved initiation rites. **7.** a mystery play (see separate entry). —**mystery tour** *or* **trip,** a pleasure excursion to an unspecified destination. [f. OF or L f. Gk *mustērion* (as MYSTIC)]

mystery play any of the vernacular religious dramas of the Middle Ages. Some writers have drawn a distinction between 'mystery plays' (dealing with Gospel events only) and 'miracle plays' (based on stories of the saints), but this is not generally observed in English where originally 'miracle' was used for both kinds of play, though a parallel distinction between *mystère* and *miracle* exists in French. A further confusion arises because the plays were often acted by the trade guilds (these were also religious fraternities) which were called 'mysteries' from the old use of this term to mean 'occupation'. Early religious dramas were performed in churches, often on feast days (which were also public holidays), especially Corpus Christi, Christmas, Easter, and Whitsun. They became increasingly secular and were moved outdoors, performed on temporary stages or on wagons which were trundled along an established route, stopping at fixed points where the audience awaited them. Individual dramas merged into a cycle of plays, and the four great English collections are known by the names of the towns where they are said to have been performed—York, Chester, Coventry, and Wakefield (also called Towneley, from the owners of the manuscript).

mystic /ˈmɪstɪk/ *n.* one who seeks by contemplation and self-surrender to obtain union with or absorption into the Deity, or who believes in the spiritual apprehension of truths beyond the understanding. —*adj.* **1.** mysterious and awe-inspiring. **2.** spiritually allegorical or symbolic. **3.** occult, esoteric; of hidden meaning. [f. OF or L f. Gk (*mustēs* initiated person)]

mystical *adj.* **1.** of mystics or mysticism. **2.** having direct spiritual significance. —**mystically** *adv.* [as prec.]

mysticism /ˈmɪstɪsɪz(ə)m/ *n.* **1.** mystical quality. **2.** being a mystic. Mysticism is a widespread experience in Christianity and in many non-Christian religions, e.g. Buddhism, Taoism, Hinduism, and Islam. [f. MYSTIC]

mystify /ˈmɪstɪfaɪ/ *v.t.* to cause to feel puzzled. —**mystification** /-fɪˈkeɪʃ(ə)n/ *n.* [f. F (as MYSTIC or MYSTERY)]

mystique /mɪˈstiːk/ *n.* an atmosphere of mystery and veneration attending some activity or person; a skill or technique impressive to the layman. [F (as MYSTIC)]

myth /mɪθ/ *n.* **1.** a traditional narrative usually involving supernatural or imaginary persons etc. and embodying popular ideas on natural or social phenomena etc.; such narratives collectively. **2.** an imaginary person or thing. **3.** a widely held but false notion. **4.** an allegory. —**mythical** *adj.*, **mythically** *adv.* [f. L f. Gk *muthos*]

mythology /mɪˈθɒlədʒɪ/ *n.* **1.** a body of myths. **2.** the study of myths. —**mythological** /mɪθəˈlɒdʒɪk(ə)l/ *adj.*, **mythologically** *adv.*, **mythologist** *n.* [f. F or L f. Gk (as MYTH, -LOGY)]

myxomatosis /mɪksəməˈtəʊsɪs/ *n.* a virus disease in rabbits, with tumours in mucous tissue. [f. Gk *muxa* mucus]

N

N, n /en/ *n.* (*pl.* **Ns, N's**) **1.** the fourteenth letter of the alphabet. **2.** an indefinite number. —**to the nth degree,** to the utmost.

N *abbr.* **1.** (in chess) knight. **2.** newton(s).

N *symbol* nitrogen.

N. *abbr.* **1.** New. **2.** North, Northern.

n. *abbr.* **1.** name. **2.** neuter. **3.** note.

Na *symbol* sodium. [f. L *natrium*]

NAAFI /'næfi/ *abbr.* Navy, Army, and Air Force Institutes (a canteen for servicemen).

nab *v.t.* (**-bb-**) (*slang*) **1.** to catch (a wrongdoer) in the act; to arrest. **2.** to seize, to grab. [also *nap*, as in KIDNAP; orig. unkn.]

Nabataean /næbə'ti:ən/ *n.* **1.** a member of an ancient Arabian people (see below). **2.** their language, a form of Aramaic strongly influenced by Arabic. —*adj.* of the Nabataeans or their language. [f. L & Gk (*Nebatu* native name of country)]
  The Nabataeans seem originally to have been a nomadic Arab tribe. They formed an independent State 312-63 BC, prospering from control of the transit trade, conveying South Arabian goods to the Mediterranean, which converged at their capital Petra (now in Jordan). Their culture reflects Babylonian, Arab, Greek, and Roman influence in its speech, religion, art, and architecture. From AD 63 they became allies and vassals of Rome, and in AD 106 Trajan transformed their kingdom into the Roman province of Arabia. Nabataean prosperity declined after this with the rise of a rival trading metropolis, Palmyra, to the north.

Nabi /'na:bi/ *n.* a member of a group of late 19th-c. French Post-Impressionists. Paul Sérusier, a follower of Gauguin, and Maurice Denis stressed the rejection of naturalism for a pictorial reality that dealt with ideas and mystic perceptions. Paul Ranson, K.-X. Roussel, Pierre Bonnard, Édouard Vuillard, and Félix Vallotton were all members of the group, working variously in painting, book illustration, posters, and other media. The flat areas of emphatic colour that typify their work owe a stylistic debt to Gauguin and Japanese prints. [f. Heb. *nabi* prophet]

nabob /'neibɒb/ *n.* **1.** (*hist.*) a Muslim official or governor under the Mogul empire. **2.** (*archaic*) a wealthy luxury-loving person, especially one who has returned from India with a fortune. [f. Port. or Sp. f. Urdu (as NAWAB)]

Nabokov /nə'bɔːkɒf, 'næbək-/, Vladimir Vladimorovich (1899-1977), Russian novelist and poet. He left Russia for Germany in 1919, studied at Trinity College, Cambridge (1919-23), lived in Berlin (1923-37), in Paris (1937-40), and in 1940 moved to the USA where he became professor of poetry at Cornell University. The outstanding success of his novel *Lolita* (1955) enabled him to devote himself entirely to writing. From 1959 he lived in Montreux. He was a stylist with great narrative and descriptive skill combined with an unusual linguistic inventiveness in both Russian and English; his critical work *Lectures on English Literature* (1980) shows his admiration for Dickens, Stevenson, and Joyce.

nacre /'neikə(r)/ *n.* mother-of-pearl; the shellfish yielding this. —**nacreous** /-kriəs/ *adj.* [F]

nadir /'neidiə(r)/ *n.* **1.** the point of the heavens directly under the observer (opp. ZENITH; ill. NAVIGATION). **2.** the lowest point, the state or time of greatest depression etc. [f. OF f. Arab., = opposite (to zenith)]

naevus /'ni:vəs/ *n.* (*pl.* **-vi** /-vai/) a birthmark in the form of a sharply-defined red mark in the skin; a mole (MOLE²). [L]

nag¹ *v.t./i.* (**-gg-**) **1.** to find fault or scold persistently. **2.** (of pain etc.) to be persistent. —**nagger** *n.* [perh. f. Scand. or LG]

nag² *n.* (*colloq.*) a horse. [orig. unkn.]

Naga /'na:gə/ *n.* **1.** a member of a group of tribes living in or near the Naga Hills of Burma and in NE India. **2.** their language, a member of the Tibetan language group. [as foll.]

naga /'na:gə/ *n.* (*Hinduism*) a member of a race of semi-divine creatures, half-snake half-human. [Skr., = serpent]

Nagaland /'na:gəlænd/ a State in NE India; capital, Kohima.

Nagar Haveli see DADRA AND NAGAR HAVELI.

Nagasaki /nægə'sa:ki/ Japanese city, target of the second atomic bomb attack, on 9 Aug. 1945 (see HIROSHIMA); pop. (est. 1976) 447,235.

Nahuatl /na:'wa:t(ə)l/ *n.* **1.** a group of peoples in southern Mexico and Central America; a member of this group. **2.** their language, that of the Aztecs and Toltecs. —*adj.* of this group or their language. [Sp. f. Nahuatl]

Nahum /'neihəm/ **1.** a Hebrew minor prophet. **2.** a book of the Old Testament containing his prophecy of the fall of Nineveh (early 7th c. BC).

naiad /'naiæd/ *n.* a water-nymph. [f. L f. Gk]

nail *n.* **1.** the horny covering of the upper surface of the tip of a finger or toe. **2.** a small metal spike hammered in to hold things together or serve as a peg or ornament (ill. CARPENTRY). —*v.t.* **1.** to fasten with a nail or nails. **2.** to secure, catch, or arrest (a person, thing, attention, etc.). **3.** to identify precisely. —**nail down,** to bind to a promise etc.); to define precisely. **nail in a person's coffin,** a thing hastening a person's death. **nail-punch** *n.* a driving punch for nails (ill. CARPENTRY). **on the nail,** (esp. of payment) without delay. [OE]

nainsook /'neinsʊk/ *n.* a fine soft cotton fabric, originally from India. [f. Hindi]

Nairobi /nai'rəʊbi/ the capital of Kenya, situated at 1,680 m (*c.*5,500 ft.); pop. approx. 1,000,000.

naïve /na:'i:v/ *adj.* **1.** simple, unaffected, unconsciously artless. **2.** (of art etc.) straightforward in style, eschewing subtlety or conventional technique. —**naïvely** *adv.*, **naïveté** /-'i:vtei/ *n.*, **naïvety** /-'i:vti/ *n.* [F, fem. of *naïf* f. L *nativus* native]

naked /'neikid/ *adj.* **1.** unclothed, nude. **2.** without the usual covering or furnishings; unsheathed or unprotected. **3.** undisguised. **4.** (of the eye) unassisted by a telescope or microscope etc. —**nakedly** *adv.*, **nakedness** *n.* [OE]

namby-pamby /næmbi'pæmbi/ *adj.* insipid, feeble, un-manly. —*n.* a person of this kind. [f. *Ambrose* Philips, English pastoral writer (d. 1749)]

name *n.* **1.** the word by which an individual person, animal, place, or thing is spoken of or to. **2.** the word denoting an object of thought, especially one applicable to many individuals. **3.** a reputation. **4.** a person as known, famed, etc. **5.** a family, a clan.—*v.t.* **1.** to give a name to. **2.** to state the name of. **3.** to mention, to specify, to cite. **4.** to nominate or appoint. —**call a person names,** to address or speak of him abusively. **have to one's name,** to possess. **in the name of,** invoking; as representing. **in name only,** not in reality. **name-dropping** *n.* familiar mention of famous names as a form of boasting. **name-plate** *n.* a plate with a name inscribed on it, identifying the occupant etc. [OE, rel. to L *nomen*]

nameable *adj.* that may be named. [f. NAME]

nameless *adj.* **1.** having no name or no known name. **2.** left unnamed. **3.** unmentionable, loathsome. [f. NAME + -LESS]

namely *adv.* that is to say, in other words, specifically. [f. NAME]

namesake *n.* a person or thing with the same name as another. [prob. f. *for the name's sake*]

Namibia /nə'mibiə/ a country in SW Africa, between Angola and Cape Province; pop. (est. 1982) 1,039,400; official languages, Afrikaans and English; capital, Windhoek. Namibia is an arid country, with few perennial streams and with large tracts of desert along the coast and in the east. As South West Africa, from 1884 it was a German protectorate, but in 1919 was mandated to South Africa by the League of Nations. Despite increasing international insistence, after 1946, that this mandate has ended, South Africa has continued to administer the country, assimilating it to the South African political system. Since

1970 South Africa has accepted the principle of Namibian independence, but the terms of the constitution are still under discussion. —**Namibian** adj. & n. [f. Namib, desert on western coast of southern Africa]

nancy /ˈnænsɪ/ n. (slang) an effeminate or homosexual man or boy. [f. Nancy, pet-form of woman's name Ann]

Nandi /ˈnændɪ/ (Hinduism) the bull of Siva, which is his vehicle and symbolizes fertility. [Skr., = the happy one]

nankeen /nænˈkiːn/ n. 1. a yellow cotton cloth. 2. the colour of this. [f. Nankin(g) in China]

Nanking /nænˈkɪŋ/ a city of China on the Yangtze River, that has served at times as the capital; pop. (est. 1974) 2,400,000. [Chinese, = southern capital]

nanny n. 1. a child's nurse or minder. 2. (colloq.) grandma. —**nanny-goat** n. a female goat. [as NANCY]

nano- /nænəʊ-, neɪnəʊ-/ in comb. one thousand millionth. [f. L f. Gk nanos dwarf]

Nansen /ˈnæns(ə)n/, Fridtjof (1861-1930), Norwegian polar explorer and statesman. In 1888 he led the first expedition to cross the Greenland ice-fields. His most famous Arctic adventure, however, began in 1893 when he sailed his tiny vessel the Fram north of Siberia, intending to reach the North Pole by allowing the ship to become frozen in the ice and letting the current carry it towards Greenland. It drifted as far north as 84° 4′ and in 1895 Nansen and one companion left here and made for the Pole on foot, reaching a latitude of 86° 14′, the highest then achieved. In 1922 Nansen was awarded the Nobel Peace Prize for organizing relief work after the First World War among prisoners of war, refugees, and victims of the Russian famine.

Nantes /nãt/ a city of western France, on the River Loire. —**Edict of Nantes,** the edict of Henry IV of France (1598) granting toleration to Protestants, revoked by Louis XIV (1685).

naos /ˈneɪɒs/ n. (pl. **naoi**) the inner part of an ancient Greek temple (ill. TEMPLES). [Gk, = temple]

nap[1] n. a short period of light sleep, especially during the day. —v.i. (**-pp-**) to have a nap. —**catch a person napping,** to take him or her unawares; to find him or her remiss. [OE]

nap[2] n. a surface of cloth consisting of fibre-ends raised, cut even, and smoothed. [f. MDu. or MLG]

nap[3] n. 1. a card-game like whist, with bidding. 2. a racing tip claimed to be almost a certainty. —v.t. (**-pp-**) to name (a horse) as an almost certain winner. —**go nap,** to make the highest bid in nap; to risk everything. [abbr. of NAPOLEON]

napalm /ˈneɪpɑːm/ n. a thickening agent made from naphthalene and coconut oil; jellied petrol made from this, used in bombs. —v.t. to attack with napalm bombs. [f. naphthenic acid (in petroleum) + palmitic acid (in coconut oil)]

nape n. the back of the neck. [orig. unkn.]

Naphtali /ˈnæftəlɪ/ n. 1. Hebrew patriarch, son of Jacob and Bilhah (Gen. 30: 7-8). 2. the tribe of Israel traditionally descended from him.

naphtha /ˈnæfθə/ n. an inflammable oil distilled from coal etc. [L f. Gk]

naphthalene /ˈnæfθəliːn/ n. a white crystalline substance obtained in distilling coal-tar. [f. prec.]

Napier /ˈneɪpɪə(r)/, John (1550-1617), Scottish landowner, famous as the inventor (simultaneously with, but completely independently of, the German Joost Bürgi) of logarithms. His tables, modified and republished by Henry Briggs, had an immediate and lasting influence on mathematics. —**Napier's bones,** slips of bone etc. marked with digits and formerly used to facilitate the operations of multiplication and division, according to a method devised by Napier.

napkin n. 1. a piece of cloth or paper used at meals for wiping the lips and fingers or protecting the clothes. 2. a nappy. [f. nappe f. L mappa (as MAP)]

Naples /ˈneɪp(ə)lz/ a city and port on the west coast of Italy south of Rome; pop. (est. 1981) 1,210,503. It was formerly the capital of the Kingdom of Naples and Sicily (see SICILY).

Napoleon /nəˈpəʊlɪən/ the name of three rulers of France: **Napoleon I** (Napoleon Bonaparte, 1769-1821), emperor 1804-14. Having risen to power in the service of Revolutionary France, Napoleon became successively First Consul and Emperor, and, after a series of dramatic military victories, including Austerlitz (1805), Jena (1806), and Wagram (1809), established a French empire stretching from Spain to Poland. He also made his brother Joseph

(1768-1844) king of Naples 1806-8 and of Spain 1808-13, and his younger brother Louis (1778-1846) king of Holland 1806-10. British seapower, however, frustrated his plans to invade England, and resulted in the destruction of the French fleet at Trafalgar; then, after the disastrous failure of his attack on Russia in 1812, his conquests were gradually lost to a coalition of all his major opponents. Forced into exile in 1814, he returned briefly to power a year later, but after his defeat at Waterloo he was once again exiled, this time to the island of St Helena, where he died.
    Napoleon III (Charles Louis Napoléon Bonaparte, 1808-73), emperor 1852-70. A nephew of Napoleon I, Napoleon III came to power in a coup launched in the confused situation prevailing after the 1848 revolution. Modelling his regime very much upon that of his uncle, he embarked on an aggressive foreign policy, including intervention in Mexico, participation in the Crimean War, and war against Austria in Italy. At home, however, his position became uncertain, and after his defeat at Sedan in the Franco-Prussian War he abdicated and went into exile in England.

Napoleonic Wars /nəpəʊlɪˈɒnɪk/ a series of campaigns (1800-15) of French armies under Napoleon I against Austria, Russia, Great Britain, Portugal, Prussia, and other European powers.

nappy n. a piece of material wrapped round the lower part of a baby's body and between its legs to hold or absorb excreta. [abbr. of NAPKIN]

narcissism /nɑːˈsɪsɪz(ə)m/ n. abnormal self-love or self-admiration. —**narcissistic** /-ˈsɪstɪk/ adj. [f. foll.]

Narcissus /nɑːˈsɪsəs/ (Gk myth.) a beautiful youth who, falling in love with his own reflection in a spring, pined away and was changed into the flower that bears his name. (See also ECHO.)

narcissus /nɑːˈsɪsəs/ n. (pl. **-si** /-saɪ/) a flowering bulb of the genus Narcissus (which includes the daffodil), especially the white-flowered N. poeticus. [f. prec.]

narcosis /nɑːˈkəʊsɪs/ n. an insensible state; the induction of this. [f. Gk (narkoō benumb)]

narcotic /nɑːˈkɒtɪk/ adj. (of a substance) inducing sleep, drowsiness, or stupor, etc.; (of a drug) affecting the mind. —n. a narcotic substance, drug, or influence. [f. OF or L f. Gk (as prec.)]

nard n. spikenard; the plant (probably Nardostachys jatamansi) yielding this. [f. L f. Gk]

nark v.t. (slang) to annoy. —n. (slang) a police informer or spy. [f. Romany nāk nose]

Narragansett /nærəˈgænsət/ n. a member or the Algonquian language of an American Indian people originally living in New England. —adj. of this people or their language. [f. Algonquian, = people of the small point (of land)]

narrate /nəˈreɪt/ v.t./i. to tell (a story), to give an account of; to write or speak a narrative. —**narration** n., **narrator** n. [f. L narrare]

narrative /ˈnærətɪv/ n. a spoken or written account of connected events in order of happening. —adj. of or by narration. [f. F f. L (as prec.)]

narrow /ˈnærəʊ/ adj. 1. of small width in proportion to length, not broad. 2. with little scope or variety. 3. with little margin. 4. narrow-minded. —n. (usu. in pl.) the narrow part of a sound, strait, river, pass, or street. —v.t./i. to make or become narrower; to lessen, to contract. —**narrow boat,** a canal boat. **narrow-minded** adj. intolerant; rigid or restricted in one's views. **narrow seas,** the English Channel and the Irish Sea. —**narrowly** adv., **narrowness** n. [OE]

narwhal /ˈnɑːw(ə)l/ n. an Arctic mammal (Monodon monoceros) the male of which has a long tusk. [f. Du. f. Da.]

NASA /ˈnæsə/ (also **Nasa**) abbr. National Aeronautics and Space Administration, a body (set up in 1958) responsible for organizing research in extraterrestrial space conducted by the USA.

nasal /ˈneɪz(ə)l/ adj. 1. of the nose. 2. (of a letter or sound) pronounced with the nose passage open (e.g. m, n, ng). 3. (of a voice or speech) having many nasal sounds. —n. a nasal letter or sound. —**nasally** adv. [F or f. L (nasus nose)]

nasalize /ˈneɪzəlaɪz/ v.t./i. to speak nasally; to give a nasal sound to. [f. prec.]

nascent /ˈnæs(ə)nt, ˈneɪ-/ adj. in the process of birth, incipient, not mature. —**nascence** n., **nascency** n. [f. L nasci be born]

Naseby /ˈneɪzbɪ/ a village in Northamptonshire, scene of the last major battle (1645) of the main phase of the English Civil War, in which the last Royalist army in England, commanded by Prince Rupert and the King himself, was comprehensively defeated by the larger and better organized New Model Army under Fairfax and Oliver Cromwell. Following the destruction of his army Charles I's cause collapsed completely; the monarchy was never so powerful again.

Nash[1], John (1752-1835), English architect, designer of the terraces near Regent's Park, London, and also of Regent Street (the buildings have since been replaced) and other parts of London.

Nash[2] Ogden (1902-71), American writer of sophisticated doggerel verse, renowned for his puns, epigrams, wildly asymmetrical lines, and other verbal eccentricities, with witty observations on social and domestic life.

Nash[3], Paul (1889-1946), English painter, print-maker, and designer. His first mature paintings date from his experience as a war artist in the First World War, with scenes of devastation recorded in a modernist fashion. In the 1920s he became known as a designer, particularly in book illustration. In 1933 he founded 'Unit One'—a cross-section of avant-garde tendencies in British art. It was surrealism, however, that liberated his imagination in the 1930s, resulting in a number of enigmatic and haunting pictures based on dream-experience or provocative landscape motifs, e.g. *Pillar and Moon*. As a war artist in the Second World War he recorded the Battle of Britain in pictures—e.g. *Totes Meer*—that transmogrified the conflict into another reality.

Nash[4], Richard, 'Beau Nash' (1674-1762), English gambler and fashion-setter. An accomplished gamester, Nash established Bath as the centre of fashionable society and dictated fashion and etiquette in the early Georgian age.

Nashe /næʃ/, Thomas (1567-1601), English pamphleteer and dramatist, who made fervent attacks on Puritanism in satirical works such as the pamphlet *Pierce Pennilesse* (1592). His best-known work *The Unfortunate Traveller* (1594) is an exuberant medley of picaresque narrative and pseudo-historical fantasy. His dramatic works include *Summer's Last Will and Testament* (1600), and *The Isle of Dogs* (1897, with Ben Jonson) which attacked so many current abuses that he and others were imprisoned for seditious and slanderous language.

Nassau /ˈnæsɔː/ the capital of the Bahamas; pop. (1980) 135,437.

Nasser /ˈnɑːsə(r)/, Gamel Abdel (1918-70), Egyptian statesman. After leading a military coup to depose King Farouk in 1952, Nasser became President of the new Republic of Egypt in 1956 after an election at which voting was compulsory and he was the only candidate. His nationalization of the Suez Canal brought war with Britain, France, and Israel in 1956, while as effectively leader of the Arab world, seeking to advance the cause of Arab unity, he was largely responsible for the escalation of tension leading to the Arab-Israeli War of 1967. With massive Russian aid he launched a programme of domestic modernization, including the building of the high dam at Aswan.

nasturtium /nəˈstɜːʃ(ə)m/ *n.* a trailing garden plant of the genus *Tropaeolum*, with bright orange, yellow, or red flowers. [L, = a kind of cress]

nasty /ˈnɑːstɪ/ *adj.* **1.** unpleasant. **2.** unkind, malicious. **3.** difficult to deal with. —**nasty piece of work**, (*colloq.*) an unpleasant or undesirable person. —**nastily** *adv.*, **nastiness** *n.* [orig. unkn.]

Nat. *abbr.* **1.** National; Nationalist. **2.** Natural.

Natal /nəˈtæl/ the eastern coastal province of the Republic of South Africa; capital, Pietermaritzburg. It was first settled by a few British traders in 1823, then by Boers in 1838, when it became a Boer republic. Annexed by the British in 1845, it acquired internal self-government in 1893; from 1910 it was a province of the Union of South Africa. [named *Terra Natalis* (L, = land of the day of birth) by Vasco da Gama because he sighted the entrance to what is now Durban harbour on Christmas Day, 1497]

natal /ˈneɪt(ə)l/ *adj.* of or concerning birth. [f. L *natalis* (as foll.)]

nation /ˈneɪʃ(ə)n/ *n.* a community of people of mainly common descent, language, history, or political institutions and usually sharing one territory and government. —**nation-wide** *adj.* extending over the whole nation. [f. OF f. L *natio* (*nasci* be born)]

national /ˈnæʃ(ə)n(ə)l/ *adj.* of a nation; affecting or concerning a whole nation. —*n.* a citizen or subject of a specified country; one's fellow countryman. —**the National,** the Grand National. **national anthem,** a song of patriotism or loyalty adopted by a nation. **National Debt,** a debt

incurred by a central government and secured against the national income. The permanent national debt in Britain was first established as a result of borrowing to finance the wars against Louis XIV of France at the end of the 17th c., and has been managed by the Bank of England since 1750. **National Front,** an extreme right-wing British political party, formed in 1967 by a merger of the British National Party with the League of Empire Loyalists, holding extreme reactionary views on immigration etc. **national grid,** a network of high-voltage electric power-lines between major power-stations; a metric system of geographical co-ordinates used in maps of the British Isles (see ill. NAVIGATION). **National Guard,** (*US*) a reserve force partly maintained by individual States of the USA but available for federal use. **National Health Service,** a system of national medical service financed by taxation. **National Insurance,** a system of compulsory contribution from the employee and the employer to provide State assistance in sickness, unemployment, retirement, etc. **national park,** an area of countryside under State supervision to preserve its natural state for public enjoyment. **national service,** service by conscription in the armed services. **National Socialism,** the political creed of the National Socialist German Workers' Party, more commonly known as Nazism (see entry). —**nationally** *adv.* [F (as prec.)]

National Gallery a gallery in Trafalgar Square, London, holding one of the chief national collections of pictures. The collection began in 1824 when Parliament voted money for the purchase of 38 pictures from the J. J. Angerstein collection. The present building, built in 1833-7 at first shared with the Royal Academy, was opened in 1838.

nationalism *n.* **1.** patriotic feeling, principles, or efforts. **2.** a policy of national independence. —**nationalist** *n.* [f. NATIONAL]

nationality /næʃəˈnælɪtɪ/ *n.* **1.** the status of belonging to a particular nation. **2.** distinctive national quality, being national. **3.** an ethnic group forming part of one or more political nations. [f. NATIONAL]

nationalize /ˈnæʃ(ə)nəlaɪz/ *v.t.* to make national; to convert (an industry, institution, etc.) to public ownership. —**nationalization** /-ˈzeɪʃ(ə)n/ *n.* [as prec.]

National Trust a trust for the preservation of places of historic interest or natural beauty in England, Wales, and Northern Ireland, founded in 1893, incorporated in 1907, and supported by endowment and private subscription. *The National Trust for Scotland* is a Scottish institution (founded in 1931) with similar aims.

native /ˈneɪtɪv/ *adj.* **1.** inborn, innate, natural. **2.** of one's birth; belonging to one by right of birth. **3.** born in a particular place, indigenous; of the natives of a place. **4.** (of metal etc.) found in a pure or uncombined state. —*n.* **1.** one born in a particular place. **2.** a local inhabitant. **3.** a member of a non-European or less civilized indigenous people; (in South Africa) a Black. **4.** an indigenous animal or plant. [f. OF or L *nativus* (as NATION)]

nativity /nəˈtɪvɪtɪ/ *n.* birth; **the Nativity,** that of Christ; a festival celebrating this. [f. OF f. L (as prec.)]

NATO /ˈneɪtəʊ/ *abbr.* (also **Nato**) North Atlantic Treaty Organization, an association of European and North American States, formed in 1949 for the defence of Europe and the North Atlantic against the perceived threat of Soviet aggression. Under strong influence from its most powerful member, the USA, it now includes all the major non-neutral Western powers.

natter *v.i.* (*colloq.*) to chat, to chatter idly. —*n.* (*colloq.*) a chat, idle chatter. [orig. Sc., imit.]

natterjack /ˈnætədʒæk/ *n.* a kind of small toad (*Bufo calamita*), with a yellow stripe down its back, that runs instead of hopping. [perh. f. prec. (from its loud croak) + JACK]

natty *adj.* neat and trim, dapper. —**nattily** *adv.* [perh. rel. to NEAT]

Natufian /nɑːˈtuːfɪən/ *adj.* of a late mesolithic industry of Palestine, which provides evidence for the first settled villages and is characterized by the use of microliths and of bone for implements. It is named after the type-site, a cave at Wadi an-Natuf, 27 km (17 miles) north of Jerusalem. —*n.* this industry. [f. Wadi an-*Natuf*]

natural /ˈnætʃər(ə)l/ *adj.* **1.** of, existing in, or produced by nature. **2.** conforming to the ordinary course of nature, normal. **3.** suited to be such by nature. **4.** not affected in manner etc. **5.** not surprising, to be expected. **6.** (of a child) illegitimate. **7.** (*Mus.*, of a note) neither a sharp nor a flat. —*n.* **1.** a person or thing that seems naturally suited (for a role, purpose, etc.). **2.** (*Mus.*) a natural note; a sign denoting this (ill. MUSICAL NOTATION). **3.** pale fawn colour. —**natural gas,** gas found in the earth's crust, not manufactured. **natural history,** the study of animal and vegetable life. **natural law,** a correct statement of the invariable sequence between specified conditions and a specified phenomenon. **natural number,** any whole number greater than 0. **natural religion,** religion based on reason without accepting revelation (cf. DEISM). **natural science,** science dealing with natural or material phenomena. **natural selection,** see separate entry. **natural theology,** knowledge of God gained by reason and without the aid of revelation. —**naturalness** *n.* [f. OF f. L (as NATURE)]

naturalism /ˈnætʃər(ə)lɪz(ə)m/ *n.* **1.** realistic method or adherence to nature in literature and art (see below). **2.** action based on natural instincts. **3.** a theory of the world, and of man's relation to it, in which only the operation of natural (as opp. to supernatural or spiritual) laws and forces is assumed; the theory that moral concepts can be explained wholly in terms of concepts applicable to natural phenomena. —**naturalistic** /-ˈlɪstɪk/ *adj.* [f. prec.]

In its simplest usage naturalism means the representation of form as found in nature, with avoidance of stylized or conceptual forms; in this sense the art of classical Greece is naturalistic (in contrast to Egyptian art), and that of the Italian Renaissance is a revival of naturalism; a work of art is conceived as a mirror for natural beauty. As applied to a particular school of painting the term was first used of the 17th-c. followers of Caravaggio, with reference to their doctrine of copying nature faithfully whether it seems to us ugly or beautiful. It was later applied specifically to an artistic and literary movement of the 19th c., influenced by Darwin's evolutionary theories, Comte's scientific ideas applied to the study of society, and the historian Taine's deterministic approach. It is characterized by a refusal to idealize experience and by the persuasion that human life is strictly subject to natural laws. The new naturalism can be detected in minutely detailed and closely observed painting (its influence is apparent in the works of Van Gogh and the Barbizon painters), and in the rise of the naturalist novel, Zola's *Le Roman expérimental* (1880) being regarded as the manifesto of the movement. Among the dramatists influenced by naturalism are Henry Becque, Hauptmann, Strindberg, Ibsen, Chekhov, and Dreiser.

naturalist *n.* **1.** an expert in natural history. **2.** an adherent of naturalism. [f. F, & NATURAL]

naturalize *v.t.* **1.** to admit (an alien) to citizenship. **2.** to introduce and acclimatize (an animal or plant) into a country where it is not native. **3.** to adopt (a foreign word or custom). **4.** to cause to appear natural. —**naturalization** /-ˈzeɪʃ(ə)n/ *n.* [f. F (as NATURAL)]

naturally *adv.* **1.** in a natural manner. **2.** of course, as might be expected. [f. NATURAL]

natural selection the process favouring the survival of those organisms that are best adapted to their environment. The way that this operates can be seen in the survival and numerical predominance of darker-coloured moths in industrially polluted areas of Britain, where they are less visible against dark tree-trunks than are the lighter-coloured species, of which a considerable number are eaten by predators. (See EVOLUTION.)

nature /ˈneɪtʃə(r)/ *n.* **1.** the phenomena of the physical world as a whole, the physical power causing these; **Nature,** these personified. **2.** a thing's essential qualities; a person's or animal's innate character. **3.** a kind or class. **4.** vital force, functions, or needs. —**by nature,** innately. **by** *or* **in the nature of things,** inevitable, inevitably. **call of nature,** the need to urinate or defecate. **in a state of nature,** in an uncivilized or uncultivated state; totally naked. **nature trail,** a path through the countryside planned to show interesting natural objects. —**-natured** *adj.* (*good-natured*). [f. OF f. L *natura* (*nasci nat-* be born)]

naturist *n.* a nudist. —**naturism** *n.* [f. prec.]

naught /nɔːt/ *n.* (*archaic*) nothing, nought. —*predic. adj.* (*archaic*) worthless, useless. —**come to naught,** not to succeed; to come to nothing. **set at naught,** to despise. [OE (as NO, WIGHT)]

naughty /ˈnɔːtɪ/ *adj.* **1.** badly behaved, disobedient. **2.** mildly indecent. —**naughtily** *adv.*, **naughtiness** *n.* [f. prec.]

Nauru /naʊˈruː/ a small but relatively rich country that is an island in the SW Pacific, lying near the Equator; pop. (1977) 7,254; official language, English. Discovered by the British in 1798, it was annexed by Germany in 1888, and

became a British mandate after the First World War. Since 1968 it has been an independent republic with a limited form of membership of the Commonwealth. Its economy is heavily dependent upon the mining of phosphates, of which it has the world's richest deposits. —**Nauruan** *adj.* & *n.*

nausea /ˈnɔːzɪə/ *n.* **1.** inclination to vomit (orig. = seasickness). **2.** loathing. —**nauseous** *adj.* [L f. Gk (*naus* ship)]

nauseate /ˈnɔːzɪeɪt/ *v.t./i.* **1.** to affect with nausea, to disgust. **2.** to loathe. **3.** to feel nausea. [f. prec.]

nautch /nɔːtʃ/ *n.* a performance of Indian dancing girls. [f. Urdu f. Skr.]

nautical /ˈnɔːtɪk(ə)l/ *adj.* of sailors or navigation. —**nautical mile,** see MILE. —**nautically** *adv.* [f. F or L f. Gk *nautikos* (*nautēs* sailor)]

nautilus /ˈnɔːtɪləs/ *n.* (*pl.* **-luses, -li** /-laɪ/) a mollusc of the genus *Nautilus,* with a spiral shell divided into compartments. [L f. Gk, = sailor (as prec.)]

Navajo /ˈnævədʒəʊ/ *n.* (also **Navaho**) (*pl.* **-os**) a member or the language of an American Indian people in New Mexico and Arizona. —*adj.* of this people or their language. [Sp., = pueblo]

naval /ˈneɪv(ə)l/ *adj.* of the or a navy; of ships. [f. L (*navis* ship)]

Navarre /nəˈvɑː(r)/ a former Franco-Spanish kingdom in the Pyrenees area. Navarre achieved independence in the 10th c. under Sancho III, but during the Middle Ages fell at various times under French or Spanish domination. The southern part of the country was conquered by Ferdinand V in 1512 while the northern part passed to France in 1589 through inheritance by Henry IV.

nave[1] *n.* the body of a church (apart from the choir or chancel, aisles, and transepts) (ill. CHURCH). [F. L *navis* ship]

nave[2] *n.* the hub of a wheel. [OE]

navel /ˈneɪv(ə)l/ *n.* **1.** the hollow in the belly left by the detachment of the umbilical cord. **2.** the central point of anything. —**navel orange,** an orange with a navel-like formation on the top. [OE (as prec.)]

navigable /ˈnævɪgəb(ə)l/ *adj.* **1.** (of a river etc.) suitable for ships to sail in. **2.** (of a ship etc.) seaworthy. **3.** (of a balloon) steerable. —**navigability** /-ˈbɪlɪtɪ/ *n.*, **navigably** *adv.* [F or f. L (as foll.)]

navigate /ˈnævɪgeɪt/ *v.t./i.* **1.** to sail in or through (a sea or river etc.). **2.** to direct the course of (a ship, aircraft, or vehicle etc.). —**navigator** *n.* [f. L *navigare* (*navis* ship, *agere* drive)]

navigation /nævɪˈgeɪʃ(ə)n/ *n.* navigating; methods of determining a ship's or aircraft's position and course by geometry and astronomy or radio signals (see below and ill. pp. 560-1). —**navigation satellite,** an artificial satellite whose orbit is accurately known and made available, so that signals from it may be used for navigational purposes. [F, or f. L *navigatio* (as prec.)]

In ancient times navigation depended upon observation of landmarks and the positions of the stars. Navigational instruments included the compass, introduced in the 12th-13th c. (see COMPASS), the astrolabe, and the quadrant. The problem of determining longitude was not solved until the 18th c., with the development of an accurate marine chronometer and the sextant. The 20th c. has seen the introduction of radio signals, with the use of radar and of navigation satellites for both sea and air navigation. —**navigational** *adj.* [F or f. L (as prec.)]

navvy /ˈnævɪ/ *n.* a labourer employed in excavating for roads, railways, canals, etc. —*v.i.* to work as a navvy. [abbr. of *navigator*]

navy /ˈneɪvɪ/ *n.* **1.** a State's warships with their crews and organization (see below). **2.** the officers and men of the navy. **3.** (*poetic*) a fleet. —**navy (blue),** dark blue as of naval uniforms. [f. OF *navie* f. L (as NAVAL)]

Creation of the basis of a naval force is usually credited to Alfred the Great (9th c.), who sought to defend his land against the marauding Norsemen. In medieval times England's navy was generally provided by the Cinque Ports, but the Tudor monarchs Henry VIII and Elizabeth I began to establish a regular government-controlled force. Reforms and expansion in the 17th c. built the Royal Navy into the most powerful in the world, a position it retained until the Second World War.

nawab /nəˈwɑːb/ *n.* **1.** the title of a distinguished Muslim in Pakistan. **2.** (*hist.*) the title of a governor or nobleman in India. [f. Urdu f. Arab., = deputy; cf. NABOB]

Navigation and Surveying

Navigation

Celestial sphere

meridian and
azimuth circle
for point A

north celestial pole

zenith for
point A

winter
solstice

Earth

summer
solstice

ecliptic

equinox

celestial equator

nadir for
point A

south celestial pole

Points of the compass

N
N by E
NNE
NE by N
NE
NE by E
ENE
E by N
E
E by S
ESE
SE by E
SE
SE by S
SSE
S by E
S
S by W
SSW
SW by S
SW
SW by W
WSW
W by S
W
W by N
WNW
NW by W
NW
NW by N
NNW
N by W

0°
45°
90°
135°
180°
225°
270°
315°

modern compass roses are
usually marked in degrees only

Sextant

used to find
latitude at sea

star or sun

mirror A

half-silvered
mirror B

telescope

horizon

arc

index bar

60°
30°
0°

The index bar is swung until the chosen star is
reflected from mirror A on to the silvered half of mirror
B. The reflected image is lined up with the horizon
seen through the other half of the mirror. The altitude
of the star is indicated by the position of the index bar
on the arc.

Latitude and longitude

any point on the Earth's surface
can be defined by two references
(e.g. 51° 48' N, 2° 27' W)

lines of
latitude

North Pole

75°N
60°N
45°N — meridian
30°N
15°N

tropic of
Cancer
(23½° N)

west

75° 45° 30° 15° 0° 15° 30° 45° 75°
60°   60°

0° east
equator
15°S
30°S
45°S
60°S
75°S

tropic of
Capricorn
(23½° S)

lines of longitude

South Pole

Finding north and south by the stars

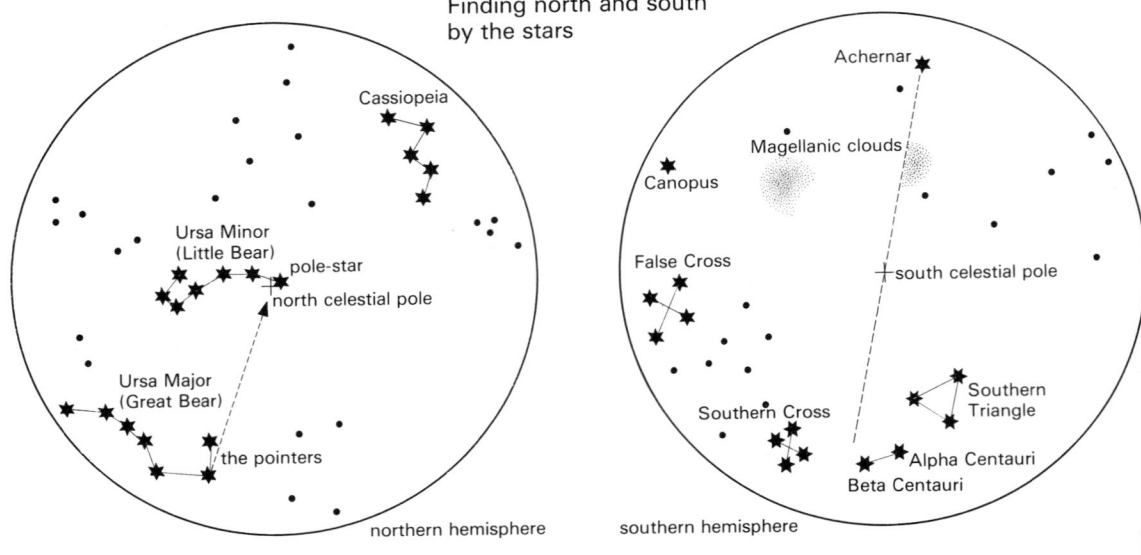

Cassiopeia

Ursa Minor
(Little Bear)

pole-star

north celestial pole

Ursa Major
(Great Bear)

the pointers

northern hemisphere

Achernar

Magellanic clouds

Canopus

False Cross

south celestial pole

Southern
Triangle

Southern Cross

Alpha Centauri

Beta Centauri

southern hemisphere

Inertial navigation system

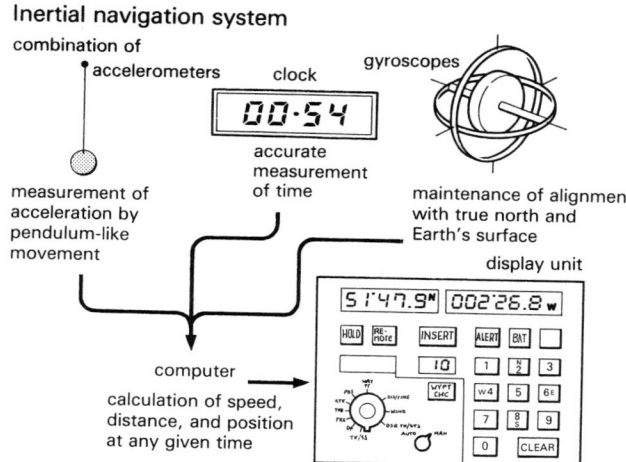

combination of

accelerometers · clock · gyroscopes

00·54

accurate measurement of time

measurement of acceleration by pendulum-like movement

maintenance of alignment with true north and Earth's surface

display unit

51°47.9″N 002°26.8″W

HOLD · REMOTE · INSERT · ALERT · BAT

computer →

calculation of speed, distance, and position at any given time

(used by nuclear submarines, which remain submerged for long periods, and by aircraft)

Hyperbolic navigation system

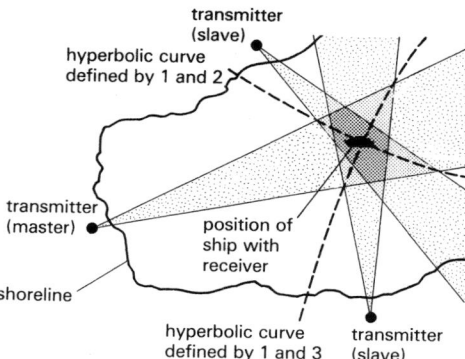

transmitter (slave)

hyperbolic curve defined by 1 and 2

transmitter (master)

position of ship with receiver

shoreline

hyperbolic curve defined by 1 and 3

transmitter (slave)

Radio waves received by a ship from two transmitters (1 and 2) define its position as somewhere on a hyperbolic curve. Use of another transmitter (3) in conjunction with one of these produces a second curve, and the intersection of these two curves gives the ship's actual position.

Surveying

Bearings

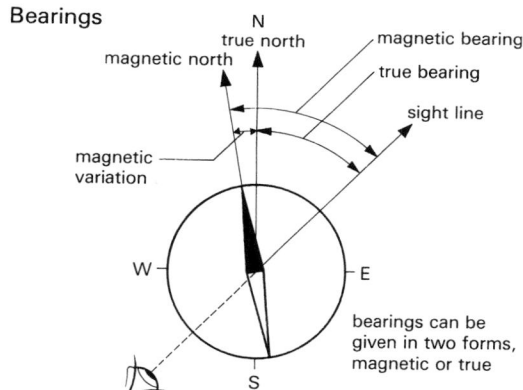

N true north

magnetic north

magnetic bearing

true bearing

sight line

magnetic variation

W — E

S

bearings can be given in two forms, magnetic or true

Triangulation

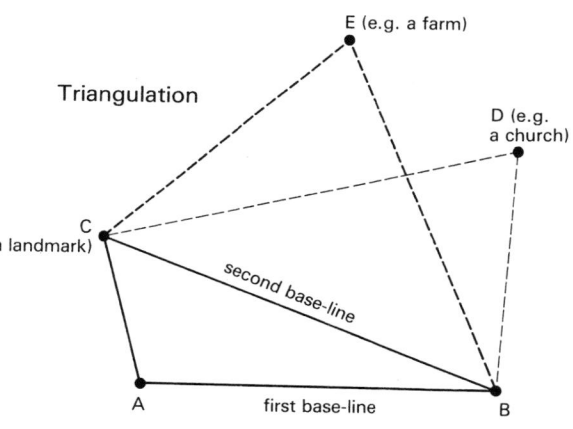

E (e.g. a farm)

D (e.g. a church)

C (a landmark)

second base-line

A   first base-line   B

Bearings are basic to surveying. The length of the base-line AB is measured; the angles CAB and CBA are measured; the length of the line CB can then be calculated and becomes the second base-line, from which further triangles can be built up and landmarks plotted.

The National Grid reference system

For the purposes of National Grid references the British Isles are divided into 100km squares identified by a pair of letters, e.g.

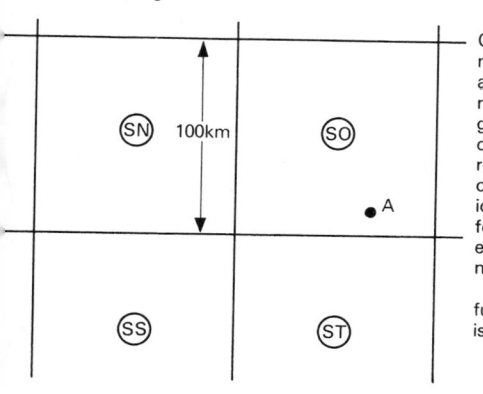

SN · 100km · SO

A

SS · ST

Ordnance Survey maps show grid lines at 1km intervals and a reference can be given to an accuracy of 100m. The reference is made up of the grid square identification, followed by an easting and a northing.

full reference for A is SO 689 120

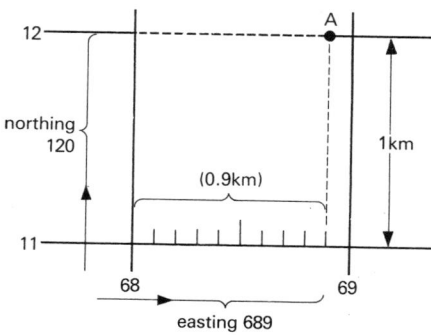

12

northing 120

northing

11

(0.9km)

1km

A

68   69

easting 689

nay *adv.* **1.** (*archaic*)no. **2.** or rather, and even, and more than that. —*n.* the word 'nay'. —**say nay**, to refuse, to contradict. [f. ON (*ne* not, as AYE²)]

Nazarene /ˌnæzəˈriːn, ˈnæ-/ *adj.* of Nazareth or the Nazarenes. —*n.* **1.** a person of Nazareth, especially Christ. **2.** (in Jewish or Muslim use) a Christian. **3.** a member of a group of German painters called the Brotherhood of St Luke, founded in 1809, who aspired to revive religious painting by a return to the art and working practices of medieval Germany and early Renaissance Italy. From 1810 they lived and worked in the disused monastery of San Isidoro, Rome; their style was marked by strong outlines and pure colour reminiscent of quattrocento art. The most important participants were Cornelius, Overbeck, Pforr, and Schadow. [f. L f. Gk (*Nazaret* Nazareth)]

Nazareth /ˈnæzərəθ/ a town of lower Galilee, now in Israel, first mentioned in the Gospels, where Mary and Joseph lived and Christ spent his youth.

Nazarite /ˈnæzəraɪt/ *n.* (more correctly **Nazirite**) any of the Israelites specially consecrated to the service of God who were under vows to abstain from wine, let their hair grow, and avoid the defilement of contact with a dead body. [f. L f. Heb. (*nazar* consecrate oneself)]

Nazi /ˈnɑːtsɪ/ *n.* a member of the German National Socialist (Workers') Party in Germany, led by Adolf Hitler (see foll.). —*adj.* of this party. [repr. pronunc. of *Nati* in G *Nationalsozialist*]

Nazism /ˈnɑːtsɪz(ə)m/ *n.* the political creed of the Nazis (see prec.). The National Socialist (Workers') Party was formed in Munich soon after the First World War to espouse a right-wing brand of nationalist authoritarianism. It was dominated from its early days by Hitler who forced his own ideas upon it, most notably anti-Semitism, a belief in the racial superiority of Aryan Germans, a determination to overthrow the Treaty of Versailles, and a pervasive ethos of leader-worship. The initial popularity of Nazism (as witnessed by an increase in party membership from 176,000 in 1929 to 2,000,000 in early 1933) was due to Hitler's charismatic appeal and to the dreadful conditions prevalent in Germany during the Depression. After his election as Chancellor in January 1933, Hitler built up a Nazi dictatorship in which the party effectively controlled the State at all levels. The Nazi Party collapsed at the end of the Second World War and was formally outlawed by the new West German constitution. [f. prec.]

NB *abbr.* note well. [f. L *nota bene*]

Nb *symbol* niobium.

NCO *abbr.* non-commissioned officer.

Nd *symbol* neodymium.

n.d. *abbr.* no date.

Ndjaména /əndʒəˈmeɪnə/ (formerly *Fort-Lamy*) the capital of Chad; pop. (est. 1979) 303,000.

NE *abbr.* North-East, North-Eastern.

Ne *symbol* neon.

Neanderthal man /nɪˈændətɑːl/ the first fossil hominid to be identified as such, and the best known, named after remains found in the Neanderthal valley in western Germany in 1856. *Homo* (*sapiens*) *neanderthalensis* is found throughout Europe and the Near East, and also the remainder of the Old World in variant forms, during the late Middle and Upper Pleistocene c.80,000–c.30,000 years ago. Within western Europe his remains are associated with the middle palaeolithic Mousterian stone-tool industries that disappeared with the arrival of Cro-Magnon man (fully modern man). Neanderthal man developed from *Homo erectus*, though the widespread distribution of intermediate forms hinders an attempt to resolve any single geographical locality as the origin of the development. The fate of the Neanderthal populations is equally hard to discern: they either became assimilated into the encroaching fully modern populations or died out in the time-honoured evolutionary manner. Neanderthal man was a fully erect biped of stocky build, with a long low skull, prominent brow ridges and occiputs, and a jutting face. The popular impression of him as a stooping brute is incorrect and derives from the original poor reconstruction of the first find from the Neanderthal valley; it has also been suggested that this individual suffered from a vitamin D deficiency (rickets) and/or syphilis.

neap *n.* (in full **neap tide**) the tide at times of the month when there is least difference between high and low water. [OE *nēpflōd* (cf. FLOOD); orig. unkn.]

Neapolitan /nɪəˈpɒlɪt(ə)n/ *adj.* of Naples. —*n.* a native of Naples. [f. L (*Neapolis* Naples, f. Gk)]

near *adv.* **1.** to, at, or within a short distance in space or time. **2.** closely, nearly. —*prep.* **1.** near to in space, time, condition, or semblance. **2.** (*in comb.*) resembling, intended as a substitute for (*near-silk*), that is almost (*near-hysterical*). —*adj.* **1.** with only a short distance or interval between. **2.** closely related. **3.** (of part of a vehicle, horse, or road) nearer to the side of the road when facing forward, usually left. **4.** with little margin. **5.** niggardly. —*v.t./i.* to draw near (to), to approach. —**near by**, not far off. **Near East**, the region comprising the countries of the eastern Mediterranean, sometimes also including those of the Balkan peninsula, SW Asia, or north Africa. **near miss**, something that misses its objective only narrowly; a narrowly avoided collision. **near-sighted** *adj.* short-sighted. **near thing**, a narrow escape. —**nearness** *n.* [f. ON, orig. = *nigher* (NIGH)]

nearby *adj.* close in position.

nearly *adv.* **1.** almost. **2.** closely. —**not nearly**, nothing like, far from. [f. NEAR]

neat *adj.* **1.** simple, clean, and orderly in appearance. **2.** done or doing things in a precise and skilful way. **3.** (of alcoholic drink) undiluted. —**neatly** *adv.*, **neatness** *n.* [f. F, = NET²]

neaten *v.t.* to make neat. [f. prec.]

neath *prep.* (*poetic*) beneath. [f. BENEATH]

Nebraska /nɪˈbræskə/ a State in the central USA, acquired as part of the Louisiana Purchase in 1803. It became the 37th State of the USA in 1867; capital, Lincoln.

Nebuchadnezzar /ˌnebjʊkədˈnezə(r)/ king of Babylon 605–562 BC, who rebuilt the city with massive fortification walls, a huge temple, and a ziggurat, and extended his rule over ancient Palestine and neighbouring countries. In 586 BC he captured and destroyed Jerusalem and deported its leaders.

nebula /ˈnebjʊlə/ *n.* (*pl.* **-ae** /-iː/) a cloud of gas or dust situated within the interstellar space of a galaxy (usually our own) and appearing as either a bright or a dark cloud according to whether or not there are stars present to make it luminous. Some distant galaxies were formerly known as spiral or extragalactic nebulae. The term was originally applied to any indistinct cloud-like patch revealed by a telescope. [L, = mist]

nebular /ˈnebjʊlə(r)/ *adj.* of a nebula or nebulae. —**nebular theory** *or* **hypothesis**, the theory that the solar and stellar systems were developed from nebulae. [f. prec.]

nebulous /ˈnebjʊləs/ *adj.* cloudlike, indistinct, having no definite form. [f. F or L (as NEBULA)]

necessary /ˈnesəsərɪ/ *adj.* **1.** indispensable, required in order to achieve something. **2.** inevitable, determined by natural laws or predestination and not by free will. —*n.* (usu. *pl.*) a thing without which life cannot be maintained or is unduly harsh. —**the necessary**, (*slang*) the money or action needed for a purpose. —**necessarily** *adv.* [f. OF f. L *necessarius* (*necesse* needful)]

necessitarianism /nɪˌsesɪˈteərɪənɪz(ə)m/ *n.* the denial of free will and the belief that all action is determined by causes. —**necessitarian** *adj. & n.* [f. NECESSITY]

necessitate /nɪˈsesɪteɪt/ *v.t.* to make necessary, to involve as a condition, accompaniment, or result. [f. L *necessitare* (as NECESSITY)]

necessitous /nɪˈsesɪtəs/ *adj.* needy. [f. F or f. foll.]

necessity /nɪˈsesɪtɪ/ *n.* **1.** constraint or compulsion regarded as a law governing all human action. **2.** the constraining power of circumstances. **3.** an imperative need. **4.** an indispensable thing. **5.** poverty, hardship. —**of necessity**, unavoidably. [f. OF f. L *necessitas* (as NECESSARY)]

Nechtansmere /ˈnektənzmɪə(r)/ the site (near Forfar in Tayside, Scotland) of a battle in 685 in which the Northumbrians were decisively defeated by the Picts. Their expansion northward was permanently thwarted, and they were forced to withdraw south of the Firth of Forth.

neck *n.* **1.** the narrow part of the body connecting the head with the shoulders. **2.** a narrow part, piece, or channel; the lower part of a capital, above the astragal terminating the shaft of a column (ill. TEMPLES). **3.** the part of a garment around the neck. **4.** the length of a horse's head and neck as a measure of its lead in a race. **5.** the flesh of an animal's neck as food. **6.** (*slang*) impudence. —*v.i.* (*slang*) to kiss and caress amorously. —**get it in the neck**, (*colloq.*) to suffer a heavy blow, to be severely reprimanded or punished. **neck and neck**, running level in a race. **risk** (*or* **save**) **one's**

neck, to risk (or save) one's own life. **up to one's neck,** (*colloq.*) very deeply involved; very busy. [OE]

neckband *n.* a strip of material round the neck of a garment.

neckerchief /ˈnekətʃɪf/ *n.* a square of cloth worn round the neck. [f. NECK + KERCHIEF]

necklace /ˈneklɪs/ *n.* an ornament of beads, precious stones, etc., worn round the neck.

necklet /ˈneklɪt/ *n.* an ornament or fur garment for the neck. [f. NECK + -LET]

neckline *n.* the outline of a garment-opening at the neck.

necktie *n.* a band of material tied round a shirt-collar.

necro- /nekrəʊ-/ *in comb.* corpse. [f. Gk (*nekros* corpse)]

necromancy /ˈnekrəʊmænsɪ/ *n.* dealings with the dead as a means of divination; magic. —**necromancer** *n.* [f. OF f. L f. Gk (NECRO-, *mantis* seer)]

necrophilia /nekrəʊˈfɪlɪə/ *n.* abnormal (esp. erotic) attraction to corpses. [NECRO- + Gk -*philia* loving]

necropolis /neˈkrɒpəlɪs/ *n.* a cemetery, especially an ancient one. [Gk (NECRO-, *polis* city)]

necrosis /neˈkrəʊsɪs/ *n.* (*pl.* **necroses** /-siːz/) the death of a piece of bone or tissue. —**necrotic** /-ˈkrɒtɪk/ *adj.* [f. Gk (*nekroō* kill)]

nectar /ˈnektə(r)/ *n.* **1.** a sweet fluid produced by plants and made into honey by bees. **2.** (*Gk & Rom. myth.*) the drink of the gods. **3.** any delicious drink. —**nectarous** *adj.* [f. L f. Gk]

nectarine /ˈnektərɪn, -iːn/ *n.* a kind of peach with a smooth downless skin. [f. prec.]

nectary /ˈnektərɪ/ *n.* a plant's nectar-secreting organ. [f. NECTAR]

NEDC *abbr.* (*colloq.* **Neddy**) National Economic Development Council.

neddy *n.* (*colloq.*) a donkey. [pet-form of man's name *Edward*]

née /neɪ/ *adj.* born (used in adding a married woman's maiden name after her surname: *Anne Hall, née Browne*). [F, fem. p.p. of *naître* be born]

need *n.* **1.** circumstances requiring some course of action. **2.** a requirement or want. **3.** a time of difficulty or crisis. **4.** destitution or poverty. —*v.t./i.* (in neg. interrog. *to* can be omitted, and 3 *sing. pres.* is **need**) **1.** to be in need of, to require. **2.** to be under a necessity or obligation. —**have need of,** to require. **need not have done,** did not need to do (but did). [OE]

needful *adj.* necessary. —**the needful,** (*slang*) money or action needed for a purpose. —**needfully** *adv.* [f. NEED + -FUL]

needle *n.* **1.** a long slender piece of polished steel pointed at one end and with an eye for thread at the other, used in sewing. **2.** a similar larger instrument of bone or plastic etc. without an eye, used in knitting or crocheting etc. **3.** a piece of metal etc. transmitting the vibrations from a revolving gramophone record, a stylus. **4.** the pointer of a compass or other instrument. **5.** the pointed end of a hypodermic syringe. **6.** the slender pointed leaf of a fir or pine. **7.** a sharp rock or peak. **8.** an obelisk. —*v.t.* (*colloq.*) to annoy or provoke. —**needle game** *or* **match,** a game or match closely contested or arousing exceptional personal feeling. **needle-point** *n.* embroidery on canvas; lace made with needles, not bobbins. [OE]

needlecord *n.* a finely ribbed corduroy fabric.

needless *adj.* unnecessary, uncalled for. —**needlessly** *adv.* [f. NEED + -LESS]

needlewoman *n.* (*pl.* **-women**) a seamstress; a woman or girl who sews.

needlework *n.* sewing or embroidery.

needn't (*colloq.*) need not.

needs *adv.* (*archaic*) of necessity (esp. in **must needs** or **needs must**). [as NEED]

needy *adj.* lacking the necessaries of life, extremely poor. —**neediness** *n.* [f. NEED]

ne'er /neə(r)/ *adv.* (*poetic*) never. [contr.]

ne'er-do-well *n.* a good-for-nothing person. —*adj.* good-for-nothing.

nefarious /nɪˈfeərɪəs/ *adj.* wicked. —**nefariously** *adv.* [f. L *nefarius* (*nefas* wrong)]

Nefertiti /nefəˈtiːtɪ/ the chief wife of Akhenaten, possibly co-ruler towards the end of his reign. She fully supported her husband's religious reforms and is invariably represented beside him, with their daughters, on reliefs from Tell el-Amarna. Best known from the painted limestone bust of her (now in West Berlin), she merited her name which means 'the beautiful (one) is come' (which did not, however, allude to her own beauty).

neg. *abbr.* negative.

negate /nɪˈgeɪt/ *v.t.* to nullify; to imply or involve the non-existence of. —**negation** *n.* [f. L *negare* deny]

negative /ˈnegətɪv/ *adj.* **1.** expressing or implying denial, prohibition, or refusal. **2.** not positive, lacking positive attributes; marked by an absence of qualities. **3.** (of a quantity in algebra) less than zero; to be subtracted from others or from zero. **4.** in the direction opposite that regarded as positive. **5.** of or containing or producing the kind of electrical charge carried by electrons. **6.** (of a photograph) having the lights and shades of the actual objects or scene reversed, or the colours replaced by complementary ones. —*n.* **1.** a negative statement or word. **2.** a developed photographic film etc. bearing a negative image from which positive pictures are obtained. —*v.t.* **1.** to veto; to refuse consent to. **2.** to serve to disprove. **3.** to contradict (a statement). **4.** to neutralize (an effect). —**in the negative,** with a refusal; with a negative statement or reply. —**negative sign,** the minus sign −. —**negatively** *adv.* [f. OF or L (as NEGATE)]

Negev /ˈnegev/ a triangular semi-desert region of southern Israel between Beersheba and the Gulf of Aqaba.

neglect /nɪˈglekt/ *v.t.* **1.** to pay too little or no attention to. **2.** to fail to take proper care of. **3.** to omit to do, to be remiss about. —*n.* neglecting, being neglected; disregard. —**neglectful** *adj.* [f. L *neglegere* (*neg-* not, *legere* choose, pick up)]

negligé /ˈneglɪʒeɪ/ *n.* a woman's light flimsy dressing-gown. [F, p.p. of *négliger* = prec.]

negligence /ˈneglɪdʒ(ə)ns/ *n.* lack of proper care or attention, carelessness. —**negligent** *adj.*, **negligently** *adv.* [f. OF or L (as NEGLECT)]

negligible /ˈneglɪdʒɪb(ə)l/ *adj.* too small or unimportant to be considered. [obs. F (as NEGLECT)]

negotiable /nɪˈgəʊʃəb(ə)l/ *adj.* **1.** that can be modified after discussion. **2.** (of a cheque etc.) that can be converted into cash or transferred to another person. [f. foll.]

negotiate /nɪˈgəʊʃɪeɪt/ *v.t./i.* **1.** to try to reach agreement by discussion; to arrange (an affair) or bring about (a result) thus. **2.** to get or give the money value for (a cheque or bonds etc.). **3.** to get over or through (an obstacle or difficulty). —**negotiation** /-ˈeɪʃ(ə)n/ *n.*, **negotiator** *n.* [f. L *negotiari* (*negotium* business)]

Negrillo /nɪˈgrɪləʊ/ *n.* (*pl.* **-os**) a member of a dwarf Negro people in central and southern Africa. [Sp., dim. of NEGRO]

Negrito /nɪˈgriːtəʊ/ *n.* (*pl.* **-os**) a member of a small Negroid people in the Malayo-Polynesian region (see PYGMY). [as prec.]

Negro /ˈniːgrəʊ/ *n.* a member of the black- or dark-skinned group of human populations that exist or originated in Africa south of the Sahara. Their physical attributes include woolly hair, thick lips, a broad short nose, projecting jaws, and legs that are long relative to the torso. —*adj.* of Negroes, black- or dark-skinned. —**Negress** *n.fem.* [Sp. & Port., f. L *niger* black]

Negroid /ˈniːgrɔɪd/ *adj.* of the group having physical characteristics resembling those of Negroes. —*n.* a Negroid person. [f. prec.]

Negus /ˈniːgəs/ *n.* (*hist.*) the title of the ruler of Ethiopia. [f. Amharic, = king]

negus /ˈniːgəs/ *n.* hot sweetened wine with water. [f. Col. F. *Negus* (d. 1732), its inventor]

Nehemiah /nɪəˈmaɪə/ **1.** a Jewish leader who (*c.*444 BC) supervised the rebuilding of the walls of Jerusalem and (*c.*432 BC) introduced moral and religious reforms. His work was continued by Ezra. **2.** a book of the Old Testament telling of this rebuilding and of the reforms.

Nehru /ˈneəruː/, Pandit Jawaharlal (1889-1964), Indian statesman. An early associate of Gandhi, Nehru was among the early leaders of the Indian National Congress, eventually playing a major part in the negotiations preceding independence. He then served as the first Prime Minister of independent India from 1947 until his death. Two years later his daughter, Mrs Indira Gandhi (see entry), became prime minister.

neigh /neɪ/ *n.* the cry of a horse. —*v.i.* to utter a neigh. [OE (imit.)]

neighbour /ˈneɪbə(r)/ *n.* **1.** a person who lives next door or near by. **2.** a person or thing near or next to another. **3.**

a fellow human being. **4.** (*attrib.*) neighbouring. —*v.t./i.* to adjoin, to border (on). [OE (as NIGH, BOOR)]

neighbourhood *n.* **1.** a district. **2.** the people of a district. **3.** nearness, vicinity. —**in the neighbourhood of,** approximately. [f. prec. + -HOOD]

neighbourly *adj.* like a good neighbour, friendly, helpful. —**neighbourliness** *n.* [as prec.]

neither /ˈnaɪðə(r), ˈniːðə(r)/ *adv.* not either, not on the one hand (introducing one of two negative statements, the other often introduced by *nor*). —*adj. & pron.* not either, not the one nor the other. —*conj.* (*archaic*) nor, not yet. [OE (as NO, WHETHER)]

nelly *n.* **not on your nelly,** (*slang*) certainly not. [perh. f. woman's name *Nelly*]

Nelson /ˈnels(ə)n/, Horatio, Viscount Nelson, Duke of Bronté (1758–1805), British admiral whose victories at sea during the early years of the Napoleonic Wars assured British naval supremacy and made him a national hero, though his affair with Emma, Lady Hamilton, caused great scandal. While still a captain he played a crucial part in the victory over the Spanish at Cape St Vincent in 1797; in the following year he destroyed the French fleet in the Mediterranean at Aboukir Bay, and in 1801 at Copenhagen disobeyed his superior's order to withdraw and won a total victory over the Danes. His final and most famous victory, over the combined fleets of France and Spain at Trafalgar in 1805, effectively ended Napoleon's challenge to British sea power and saved Britain from invasion, although Nelson himself was mortally wounded in the course of the battle.

nelson /ˈnels(ə)n/ *n.* a wrestling hold in which the arm is passed under the opponent's arm from behind and the hand applied to his neck. [app. f. name *Nelson*]

nematode /ˈnemətəʊd/ *n.* a slender unsegmented worm of the phylum Nematoda. [f. Gk *nēma* thread]

nem. con. *abbr.* with no one dissenting. [f. L *nemine contradicente*]

nemesia /nɪˈmiːʒə/ *n.* a South African plant of the genus *Nemesia*, cultivated for its variously coloured irregular flowers. [f. Gk *nemesion* name of a similar plant]

Nemesis /ˈnemɪsɪs/ (*Gk myth.*) a goddess, usually the personification of retribution or righteous indignation, especially that of the gods at human wrongdoing. It is puzzling, however, that she is also a deity of the type of Artemis, pursued amorously by Zeus and taking various non-human forms to evade him. [Gk, = retribution (*nēmeō* give what is due)]

nemesis /ˈnemɪsɪs/ *n.* inevitable retribution. [f. prec.]

Nennius /ˈneniəs/ (*c.*800) Welsh writer, the author or reviser of the *Historia Britonum*, a collection of notes from several sources on the history and geography of Britain. It is chiefly interesting for the account it purports to give of the historical Arthur.

neo- /niːəʊ-/ *in comb.* new, modern; a new form of. [Gk (*neos* new)]

neoclassic /niːəʊˈklæsɪk/ *adj.* neoclassical.

neoclassical /niːəʊˈklæsɪk(ə)l/ *adj.* of a revival of classical style or treatment in the arts.

neoclassicism /niːəʊˈklæsɪsɪz(ə)m/ *n.* neoclassical style etc. In art, the term refers to an aesthetic movement and artistic style which originated in Rome in the mid-18th c. and spread rapidly over Europe and North America, combining a reaction against the excesses of the late baroque and rococo with a new interest in the antique. It was stimulated by discoveries at Herculaneum and Pompeii, the publication of illustrations of archaeological and architectural remains, and the writings of the German art historian Winckelmann, who praised the calm simplicity and noble grandeur of antique art. In music, the term refers to a trend which developed in the 1920s when several composers, especially Stravinsky and Hindemith, wrote works in 17th- and 18th-c. forms and styles as a reaction against the elaborate orchestration of the late 19th-c. Romantics.

neodymium /niːəˈdɪmɪəm/ *n.* a metallic element of the lanthanide series, symbol Nd, atomic number 60, discovered in 1885. The metal is used in certain alloys; its compounds are used in ceramics and for colouring glass. [f. NEO- + *didymium* (f. Gk. *didumos* twin, from being closely associated with lanthanum) substance orig. regarded as an element]

Neo-Impressionism *n.* a movement in French painting. The term was coined by the critic Félix Fénéon in 1886 on seeing pointillist works by Seurat, Signac, and Pissarro at the last impressionist exhibition. The Neo-Impressionists saw themselves as refining and improving upon impressionist style by introducing greater compositional structure to painting and rationalizing impressionist colour technique. They adhered to classical principles of pictorial composition in pictures that are made up of small dots of pure unmixed colour in an attempt to give greater luminosity. —**Neo-Impressionist** *adj.* & *n.*

neolithic /niːəˈlɪθɪk/ *adj.* of the later part of the Stone Age, when ground or polished stone weapons and implements prevailed. —*n.* this period, which saw the introduction of agriculture and the domestication of animals, sometimes called the 'Neolithic Revolution', turning man from being dependent on nature to controlling it at least partially and indirectly. The change led to the establishment of settled communities, accumulation of food and wealth, and heavier growth of population. In the Old World, agriculture began in the Near East by the 8th millenium BC and had spread to northern Europe by the 4th millennium BC. [f. NEO- + Gk *lithos* stone]

neologism /niːˈɒlədʒɪz(ə)m/ *n.* **1.** a newly-coined word. **2.** the coining of words. [f. F (as NEO-, -LOGY)]

neon /ˈniːɒn/ *n.* a colourless odourless element of the noble gas group, symbol Ne, atomic number 10, discovered in 1898. Obtained by the distillation of liquid air, neon is mainly used in fluorescent lamps and advertising signs as it emits a reddish-orange glow when conducting electricity. It has no known chemical compounds. [Gk, neut. of *neos* new]

neophyte /ˈniːəʊfaɪt/ *n.* **1.** a new convert. **2.** a religious novice. **3.** a beginner. [f. L f. Gk (NEO-, *phuton* plant)]

neo-plasticism *n.* a movement or style in art originated by the Dutch painter Piet Mondrian, characterized by the use of primary colours and abstract forms.

Neoplatonism /niːəʊˈpleɪtənɪz(ə)m/ *n.* the revived Platonism—really a synthesis of elements from the philosophies of Plato, Pythagoras, Aristotle, and the Stoics, with overtones of Oriental mysticism—which was the dominant philosophy of the pagan world from the mid-3rd c. AD down to the closing of the pagan schools by Justinian in 529, and strongly influenced medieval and Renaissance thought. Its abiding shape was given to it by Plotinus, whose central doctrine postulates a hierarchy of being, at the summit of which is the transcendent One, immaterial and indescribable. The human soul aspires to knowledge of this One through ascetic virtue and sustained contemplation, and in doing so rises above the imperfection and multiplicity of the material world. —**Neoplatonist** *n.*

Neoptolemus /niːɒpˈtɒlɪməs/ (*Gk legend*) the son of Achilles. [Gk, = young warrior]

Nepal /nəˈpɔːl/ a country in southern Asia, bordered by China (Tibet) to the north and India to the south, dominated by the Himalayas including Mount Everest; pop. (est.) 16,000,000; official language, Nepali; capital, Kathmandu. A remote landlocked and mountainous country, Nepal has a very poor transportation and communications system and few regular contacts with the outside world. The country was conquered by the Gurkhas in the 18th c. and despite defeats by the British in the early 19th c. has maintained its independence, supplying contingents of soldiers to fight in British armies up to the present day. Gautama Buddha was born in Nepal. —**Nepalese** /-ˈliːz/ *adj.* & *n.*

Nepali /nəˈpɔːlɪ/ *n.* **1.** the official language of Nepal, spoken also in parts of NE India. It belongs to the Indic branch of the Indo-European family of languages. **2.** a Nepalese. —*adj.* of the Nepalese or their language. [f. prec.]

nephew /ˈnefjuː, -v-/ *n.* one's brother's or sister's son. [f. OF f. L *nepos*]

nephritic /neˈfrɪtɪk/ *adj.* of or in the kidneys. [f. L f. Gk (*nephros* kidney)]

nephritis /neˈfraɪtɪs/ *n.* inflammation of the kidneys. [L f. Gk (as prec.)]

ne plus ultra /neɪ plʊs ˈʊltrɑː/ **1.** the furthest attainable point. **2.** the acme, perfection. [L, = not further beyond (supposed inscription on Straits of Gibraltar)]

nepotism /ˈnepətɪz(ə)m/ *n.* favouritism shown to relatives in conferring offices (orig. by popes for their illegitimate sons, euphemistically called nephews). [f. F f. It. (*nepote* nephew)]

Neptune /ˈneptjuːn/ **1.** (*Rom. myth.*) the god of water (not of the sea, though his identification with Poseidon extended his cult in this aspect). **2.** (*Astron.*) the third largest of the planets, most distant of the giant planets of the solar system, orbiting the sun at a distance of almost four and a half thousand million km. It was discovered in 1846 by J. G. Galle, working at the Berlin Observatory and using the calculations of Le Verrier (similar predictions had been made by the English mathematician John Couch Adams). Little is known of this world (49,500 km in diameter) save that it possesses a dense cold atmosphere of hydrogen and helium, probably lying on top of a mantle of icy materials which surround a dense solid core. The surface temperature is probably less than 60° above absolute zero. There are two moons, Triton and Nereid. [orig. unkn.]

Neptunian /nepˈtjuːnɪən/ adj. **1.** (Geol.) produced by the action of water; maintaining that the action of water played a principal part in the formation of certain rocks (see foll.). **2.** of the planet Neptune. [f. prec.]

Neptunist /ˈneptjuːnɪst/ n. a person (esp. in the 18th c.) maintaining the Neptunian theory of the origin of certain rocks (opp. Plutonist or Vulcanist). [as prec.]

neptunium /nepˈtjuːnɪəm/ n. a transuranic radioactive metallic element, symbol Np, atomic number 93, first obtained in 1940 by irradiating uranium with neutrons and since discovered in trace amounts in nature. [f. NEPTUNE, planet next beyond Uranus (see URANIUM)]

Nereid /ˈnɪərɪɪd/ n. any of the sea-nymphs, daughters of Nereus. They include Thetis, mother of Achilles. [f. NEREUS]

nereid /ˈnɪərɪɪd/ n. a long sea-worm or centipede. [f. prec.]

Nereus /ˈnɪərɪəs/ (Gk myth.) an old sea-god who had the power, like Proteus, of assuming various forms.

Nero /ˈnɪərəʊ/ (Nero Claudius Caesar, 15-68) Roman emperor 54-68, the adopted successor of Claudius. His reign started promisingly, but after procuring the murder of his mother Agrippina in 59, he became increasingly capricious and repressive. Executions of leading Romans on charges of treason led to conspiracies against him and more executions; his unpopularity was increased by a fire which destroyed half of Rome in 64 and during which he was rumoured to have recited his own poem on the fall of Troy. A wave of uprisings in 68 led to his flight from Rome and to suicide. A lover of things Greek, he was an extravagant practitioner and patron of the arts.

Nerva /ˈnɜːvə/, Marcus Cocceius (30-98), Roman emperor 96-8. Appointed emperor by the Senate after the murder of Domitian, he returned to a liberal and constitutional form of rule after the autocracy of his predecessor.

nerve n. **1.** a fibre or bundle of fibres conveying impulses of sensation or of movement between the brain or spinal cord and other parts of the body; the material constituting these. **2.** courage, coolness in danger. **3.** (colloq.) impudent boldness. **4.** (pl.) nervousness; a condition of mental and physical stress. **5.** (Bot.) the rib of a leaf. —v.t. to give strength, courage, or vigour to; to brace (oneself) to face danger etc. —**bundle of nerves,** a very nervous person. **get on a person's nerves,** to irritate him. **lose one's nerve,** to become timid or irresolute. **nerve-cell** n. a cell transmitting impulses in nerve tissue. **nerve-centre** n. a group of closely-connected ganglion-cells; a centre of control. **nerve gas,** a poison gas that affects the nervous system. **nerve-racking** adj. greatly taxing the nerves. **strain every nerve,** to do one's utmost. [f. L nervus sinew]

nerveless adj. lacking vigour or spirit; incapable of effort. [f. prec. + -LESS]

Nervi /ˈnɜːvɪ/, Pier Luigi (1891-1979), Italian architectural engineer, regarded as one of Europe's most innovative designers of the 20th c. He is known for his mastery of new technology and materials, especially reinforced concrete, which he used with effect in his Giovanni Berta stadium in Florence (1929-32). His Exhibition Hall at Turin (1948-9) incorporated his theories on 'strength through form', with an enormous lightweight roof, similar to his earlier military hangar designs (from 1935). In 1952 he was appointed one of the architects to collaborate on the design of the UNESCO building in Paris. His major architectural projects of the 1950s include Naples Railway Station (1954) and the Pirelli skyscraper in Milan of 1958; his later works include San Francisco Cathedral.

nervous /ˈnɜːvəs/ adj. **1.** timid and anxious, easily agitated; fearful. **2.** of or affecting the nerves or nervous system; full of nerves. —**nervous breakdown,** loss of emotional and mental stability. —**nervously** adv., **nervousness** n. [f. L nervosus (as NERVE)]

nervous system the nerves and nerve-centres as a whole, allowing an animal to co-ordinate its response to its environ-

ment, and (in some) to initiate behaviour. —**autonomic nervous system,** (in man and other vertebrates) that controlling or influencing involuntary functions (e.g. heart-beat, digestive processes). **central nervous system,** the brain and spinal cord of vertebrates; an equivalent concentration of nerve cells in invertebrates. **peripheral nervous system,** (in vertebrates) that consisting of the cranial nerves (supplying the face and head), spinal nerves (distributed to the limb and trunk muscles and skin), and the autonomic nervous system.

nervure /ˈnɜːvjʊə(r)/ n. **1.** any of the tubes forming the framework of an insect's wing. **2.** the principal vein of a leaf. [F (nerf nerve)]

nervy adj. nervous, easily excited. [f. NERVE]

Nesbit /ˈnezbɪt/, Edith (1858-1924), English writer, best remembered for her humorous imaginative stories for children, such as The Treasure Seekers (1899) and The Would-begoods (1901). Other titles with a lasting appeal include The Phoenix and the Carpet (1904) and The Railway Children (1906). She and her first husband, Hubert Bland, were founder members of the Fabian Society.

nescient /ˈnesɪənt/ adj. not having knowledge (of). —**nescience** n. [f. L (nescire not know)]

ness n. a headland. [OE]

-ness /-nɪs/ suffix forming nouns from adjectives, expressing a state or condition (happiness) or an instance of this (a kindness). [OE]

nest n. **1.** a structure or place where a bird lays eggs and shelters its young; an animal's or insect's building-place or lair. **2.** a snug retreat or shelter. **3.** a brood or swarm. **4.** a group or set of similar objects, often of different sizes. —v.t./i. **1.** to have or build a nest. **2.** to take wild birds' nests or eggs. **3.** (of objects) to fit together or one inside another. —**nest-egg** n. a sum of money saved for the future. [OE]

nestle /ˈnes(ə)l/ v.t./i. **1.** to curl oneself up or press comfortably into a soft place. **2.** to lie half-hidden or sheltered or embedded. [OE (as NEST)]

nestling /ˈnestlɪŋ/ n. a bird too young to leave the nest. [f. NEST or NESTLE]

Nestor /ˈnestə(r)/ (Gk legend) a king of Pylos in the Peloponnese, who in old age led his subjects to the Trojan War, where his wisdom and eloquence were proverbial.

Nestorianism /nesˈtɔːrɪənɪz(ə)m/ n. the doctrine that there were two separate persons, one human and one divine, in the incarnate Christ, as opposed to the orthodox teaching that there was a single person, both God and man. The theory takes its name from Nestorius, patriarch of Constantinople from 428. What he actually taught, and how far it was heretical, is now disputed, but a violent controversy developed over the use of the term theotokos (= bearer of God) as an epithet of the Virgin Mary, and Nestorius was deposed and banished. His supporters in Syria and Persia gradually constituted themselves into a separate Nestorian Church, which became active in missionary work in India, Arabia, and China before suffering drastic losses in the Mongol invasions of Persia in the 14th c.

net[1] n. **1.** open-work material of thread, cord, or wire, etc. woven or jointed at intervals. **2.** a piece of this for a particular purpose, e.g. catching fish, covering or protecting something, or enclosing a goal-space. —v.t./i. (-tt-) **1.** to catch or procure (as) with a net. **2.** to cover or confine with nets. **3.** to put (a ball) into a net, especially of the goal. **4.** to make cord etc. into a net. [OE]

net[2] adj. **1.** remaining after necessary deductions. **2.** (of a price) off which a discount is not allowed. **3.** (of an effect, result, etc.) ultimate; excluding unimportant effects or those that cancel each other out. —v.t. (-tt-) to gain or yield (a sum) as net profit. —**net profit,** the actual profit after working expenses have been paid. **net weight,** that excluding the weight of wrappings etc. [F (as NEAT)]

netball n. a seven-a-side game in which a ball has to be thrown so as to fall through an elevated horizontal ring from which a net hangs. It was introduced into England from the USA in 1895 as the indoor version of basketball, and is played almost entirely by girls and women, and mainly in English-speaking countries.

nether /ˈneðə(r)/ adj. lower. —**nether regions** or **world,** hell, the underworld. —**nethermost** adj. [OE]

Netherlands /ˈneðələndz/ **1.** a country (often called Holland) in western Europe bordering on the North Sea, with Belgium on its southern frontier; pop. (est. 1984) 14,394,589; official language, Dutch; capital, Amsterdam;

seat of government, The Hague. **2.** (*hist.*) the area now occupied by Holland, Belgium, Luxemburg, and small parts of France and Germany. —**Netherlander** *n.* [f. Du. (as prec., LAND)]

The area was occupied by Celts and Frisians who came under Roman rule from the 1st c. BC until the 4th c. AD, and was then overrun by German tribes with the Franks establishing an ascendancy (5th–8th c.). During the Middle Ages it was divided between numerous principalities. Part of the Hapsburg empire in the 16th c., the northern (Dutch) part revolted against Spanish attempts to crush the Protestant faith and won independence in a series of wars lasting into the 17th c., becoming a Protestant republic; meanwhile the southern part passed to the Spanish Hapsburgs and then in 1713 to the Austrian Hapsburgs. Prior to wars with England and France the country enjoyed great prosperity and became a centre of art and scholarship as well as a leading maritime power, building up a vast commercial empire in the East Indies, South Africa, and Brazil, but in the 18th c. sharply declined as a European power. In 1814 north and south were united under a monarchy, but the south revolted in 1830 and became an independent kingdom, Belgium, in 1839; Luxemburg gained its independence in 1867. The Netherlands managed to maintain its neutrality in the First World War but was occupied by the Germans in the Second. The post-war period has seen the country turn away from its traditional dependence on agriculture to emerge as an industrial power.

netsuke /ˈnetsʊkeɪ/ *n.* a carved button-like ornament formerly worn with Japanese dress to hang articles from a girdle. [Jap.]

nett var. of NET².

netting *n.* netted fabric; a piece of this. [f. NET¹]

nettle *n.* a plant of the genus *Urtica* covered with stinging hairs; a plant resembling this. —*v.t.* to irritate or provoke. —**nettle-rash** *n.* a skin eruption like nettle-stings. [OE]

network *n.* **1.** an arrangement or pattern with intersecting lines and interstices; a complex system of railways etc. **2.** a chain of interconnected persons, operations, electrical conductors, etc.; a group of broadcasting stations connected for simultaneous broadcasts of the same programme. —*v.t.* to broadcast by this.

Neumann /ˈnɔɪmən/, John von (1903–57), Hungarian-born mathematician who migrated to the USA in 1930. His fundamental contributions ranged over the whole of mathematics, from the purest parts of logic and set theory to the most practical areas of application in economics, computer design, aerodynamics, meteorology, and astrophysics. His analysis (1927–32) of the mathematics of quantum mechanics supplied that infant theory with the necessary environment in which to grow and founded a vigorous new area of mathematical research (algebras of operators in Hilbert space). He founded the mathematical theory of games and, with Oskar Morgenstern, exhibited its applications to economics and policy-making. But perhaps his most influential contributions were his work at Los Alamos on the harnessing of nuclear energy both for military and for peacetime uses, and his work on the design and use of high-speed electronic computing machines, the immediate forerunners of the ubiquitous computers that have so enormously changed our world.

neural /ˈnjʊər(ə)l/ *adj.* of the nerves. —**neurally** *adv.* [f. Gk *neuron*]

neuralgia /njʊəˈrældʒə/ *n.* an intense intermittent pain in the nerves especially of the face and head. —**neuralgic** *adj.* [as prec. + Gk *algos* pain]

neurasthenia /njʊərəsˈθiːnɪə/ *n.* debility of the nerves causing fatigue etc. —**neurasthenic** *adj.* [as NEURAL + Gk *astheneia* weakness]

neuration /njʊəˈreɪʃ(ə)n/ *n.* the distribution of nervures. [as NEURAL]

neuritis /njʊəˈraɪtɪs/ *n.* inflammation of a nerve or the nerves. [as NEUR- + -ITIS]

neuro- /njʊərəʊ-/ *in comb.* nerve, nerves. [f. Gk *neuron* nerve]

neurology /njʊəˈrɒlədʒɪ/ *n.* the scientific study of nerve systems. —**neurological** /-ˈlɒdʒɪk(ə)l/ *adj.*, **neurologist** *n.* [as prec. + -LOGY]

neurone /ˈnjʊərəʊn/ *n.* (also **neuron** /-rɒn/) a nerve-cell and its appendages. [as NEURO-]

neuropterous /njʊəˈrɒptərəs/ *adj.* of the Neuroptera, an order of insects having four membranous transparent wings with a network of nervures. [f. NEURO- + Gk *pteruх* wing]

neurosis /njʊəˈrəʊsɪs/ *n.* (*pl.* **-oses** /-siːz/) a disorder of the nervous system producing depression or irrational behaviour. [as NEURO- + -OSIS]

neurotic /njʊəˈrɒtɪk/ *adj.* caused by or suffering from neurosis; (*colloq.*) abnormally anxious or obsessive. —*n.* a neurotic person. —**neurotically** *adv.* [f. prec.]

neuter /ˈnjuːtə(r)/ *adj.* **1.** (of a noun etc.) neither masculine nor feminine. **2.** (of plants) having neither pistils nor stamens. **3.** (of insects) sexually undeveloped, sterile. —*n.* **1.** a neuter word; the neuter gender. **2.** a sexually undeveloped female insect, especially a bee or ant. **3.** a castrated animal. —*v.t.* to castrate. [f. OF or L, = neither]

neutral /ˈnjuːtr(ə)l/ *adj.* **1.** not helping or supporting either of two opposing sides, impartial; belonging to a neutral State etc. **2.** having no positive or distinctive characteristics, indeterminate; (of colours) not strong or positive, grey or fawn. **3.** (of a gear) in which the engine is disconnected from the driven parts. **4.** (*Chem.*) neither acid nor alkaline. **5.** (*Electr.*) neither positive nor negative. **6.** (*Biol.*) sexually undeveloped, asexual. —*n.* **1.** a neutral State or person; a subject of a neutral State. **2.** a neutral gear. —**neutrality** /-ˈtrælɪtɪ/ *n.*, **neutrally** *adv.* [f. obs. F or f. L, = of neuter gender (as prec.)]

neutralize *v.t.* **1.** to make neutral, to make ineffective by an opposite force or effect. **2.** to exempt or exclude (a place) from the sphere of hostilities. —**neutralization** /-ˈzeɪʃ(ə)n/ *n.* [f. F f. L (as prec.)]

neutrino /njuːˈtriːnəʊ/ *n.* (*pl.* **-os**) an elementary particle with zero electric charge and probably zero mass. [It., dim. of *neutro* neutral (as NEUTER)]

neutron /ˈnjuːtrɒn/ *n.* an elementary particle of about the same mass as a proton but without electric charge, present in all atomic nuclei except the common isotope of hydrogen (see below). —**neutron bomb**, a nuclear bomb that kills by intense radiation but does little damage to buildings etc. **neutron star**, a hypothetical object of very small radius (typically 30 km), thought to form after a supernova explosion near the end of the life cycle of a massive star, when the original atomic material of the star has been compressed to such high densities that neutrons form from electrically charged particles. [f. NEUTRAL]

Intense research into the structure and properties of atomic nuclei led to the discovery of the neutron (the term was suggested by Rutherford) in 1932. Although neutrons have no resultant electric charge they behave like tiny magnets, which suggests that they have an internal electrical structure. Free neutrons are unstable, with a half-life of approximately 1,000 seconds. Because they are electrically neutral, a beam of neutrons can easily penetrate the nucleus of an atom, rendering it unstable and inducing radioactive fission. Neutrons are particularly important in nuclear reactors where a controlled flux of slow neutrons, produced in the reaction itself, also maintains that reaction.

Nevada /nɪˈvɑːdə/ a State of the western USA, bordering on the Pacific, acquired from Mexico in 1848. It became the 36th State in 1864; capital, Carson City.

névé /ˈneveɪ/ *n.* an expanse of granular snow not yet compressed into ice at the head of a glacier (ill. MOUNTAINS). [Swiss F, = glacier f. L *nix nivis* snow]

never /ˈnevə(r)/ *adv.* **1.** at no time, on no occasion, not ever. **2.** not at all. **3.** (*colloq.*) surely not. —**never-never** *n.* (*colloq.*) hire-purchase. **well I never**, an exclamation of surprise. [OE (*ne* not, as EVER)]

nevermore *adv.* at no future time.

nevertheless /nevəðəˈles/ *adv.* for all that, notwithstanding.

Nevis /ˈniːvɪs/ one of the Leeward Islands, forming part of the State of St Kitts and Nevis; pop. approx. 9,300; capital, Charlestown.

Nevsky /ˈnevskɪ/, Alexander (1220–63), Russian soldier prince, famous for his victories over the invading Swedes in 1240 on the River Neva (from which he got his name) and the Teutonic Knights two years later on the ice of Lake Peipus.

new /njuː/ *adj.* **1.** not existing before; of recent origin or arrival; made, invented, discovered, acquired, or experienced recently or now for the first time. **2.** in the original condition, not worn or used. **3.** renewed or reformed; now invigorated. **4.** changed or different from a previous one; additional to another or others already existing. **5.** unfamiliar or strange. **6.** later, modern; (*derog.*) newfangled; advanced in method or doctrine; (in place-names) discovered or founded later than and named after. —*adv.* newly, recently (*new-born, new-found, new-laid*). —**New**

Kingdom, a period of ancient Egyptian history (see EGYPT). **the new mathematics,** the system using set theory (see SET²) in elementary teaching. **New Model Army,** see MODEL. **new moon,** the moon when first seen as a crescent after conjunction with the sun; the time of such an appearance. **new potatoes,** the earliest potatoes of the new crop. **new star,** a nova. **New Style,** (of a date) reckoned by the reformed or Gregorian Calendar. **new town,** a town established as a completely new settlement with government sponsorship. **New World,** North and South America. **new year,** the year about to begin or just begun; the first few days of the year. **New Year's Day,** 1 Jan. **New Year's Eve,** 31 Dec. —**newness** n. [OE]

New Brunswick /'brʌnzwɪk/ a maritime province (from 1867) of south-east Canada, settled by the French and ceded to Britain in 1713; capital, Fredericton.

Newcomen /'nju:kʌmən/, Thomas (1663-1729), English metal-worker, inventor of the first practical steam-engine, which is named after him. The engine was a steam-operated pump; its design infringed the patent held by Thomas Savery, and was later greatly improved by James Watt.

newcomer n. a person recently arrived.

New Commonwealth those countries which have achieved self-government within the British Commonwealth since 1945, as opposed to the old Dominions.

New Deal the economic measures introduced by Franklin D. Roosevelt as President of the USA in 1933 to counteract the effects of the Great Depression which had gravely affected the American economy. The New Deal depended largely on a massive public works programme, complemented by the large-scale granting of loans, and succeeded in reducing unemployment by between 7 and 10 million.

newel /'nju:əl/ n. the supporting central pillar of a winding stair; a post supporting a stair-handrail at the top or bottom of a flight of stairs (ill. HOUSES). [f. OF no(u)el knob f. L (nodus knot)]

New England part of the USA comprising the States of Maine, New Hampshire, Vermont, Massachusetts, Rhode Island, and Connecticut. The name was given to it by the English explorer John Smith in 1614.

newfangled /nju:'fæŋg(ə)ld/ adj. objectionably new in method or style. [orig. = fond of novelty, f. NEW + -fangle (OE fang seize)]

New Forest an area of heath and woodland in south Hampshire, reserved as Crown property since 1079, originally (by William I) as a royal hunting area. William II was killed by an arrow when hunting there in 1100.

Newfoundland /'nju:fəndlənd, -'faʊ-/ a large island at the mouth of the St Lawrence River. It was discovered in 1497 by John Cabot, and founded as an English colony by Sir Humphrey Gilbert; in 1949 it was united with Labrador (as Newfoundland and Labrador) as a province of Canada; capital, St John's. —**Newfoundlander** n.

Newgate /'nju:geɪt/ a former London prison, originally the gatehouse of the main west gate to the city, first used as a prison in the early Middle Ages and rebuilt and enlarged with funds left to the city by Richard Whittington. Its unsanitary conditions became notorious in the 18th c. before the building was burnt down in the anti-Catholic riots of 1780. A new edifice was erected on the same spot soon after but was demolished in 1902 to make way for the Central Criminal Court. The Newgate Calendar (or Malefactors' Bloody Register) was published c.1774 and dealt with notorious crimes from 1700 to that date; later series were issued c.1826.

New Hampshire /'hæmpʃə(r)/ a State in the north-eastern USA, bordering on the Atlantic. It was settled from England in the 17th c. and was one of the original 13 States of the USA; capital, Concord.

New Jersey /'dʒɜːzɪ/ a State of the USA, bordering on the Atlantic, colonized by Dutch settlers and ceded to England in 1664. It was one of the original 13 States of the USA; capital, Trenton.

Newlands /'nju:ləndz/, John Alexander Reina (1837-98), English industrial chemist who proposed a periodic table shortly before Mendeleev, based on his 'law of octaves'. He observed that if elements were arranged in order of atomic weight, similar chemical properties appeared in every eighth element, a pattern he likened to the musical scale. The significance of his idea was not understood until Mendeleev's periodic table of chemical classification, based on his periodic law, had been accepted.

newly adv. recently, afresh, new-; —**newly-weds** n.pl. a recently married couple (or couples). [f. NEW]

Newman¹ /'nju:mən/, Barnett (1905-70), American painter, one of the originators (c.1948) of colour field painting, in which pictorial incident within the painting is replaced by an overall effect orientated to the canvas edge. The characteristic look of his paintings was of large rectangular bands of uniformly saturated pigment dividing the canvas into two or more coloured areas. A dramatic move away from the dynamic gestural painting of abstract expressionism, his art had a profound influence in the 1950s.

Newman² /'nju:mən/, John Henry (1801-91), a leader of the Oxford Movement, and later cardinal. He wrote twenty-four of the Tracts for the Times, initially defending Anglicanism, but from 1839 he came increasingly to doubt the Anglican claims, and in 1845 was received into the Roman Catholic Church. His works include Apologia pro vita sua (1864), written in answer to Charles Kingsley, and his poem The Dream of Gerontius (1865), depicting the soul's journey to God.

New Mexico /'meksɪkəʊ/ a State in the south-western USA, obtained from Mexico in 1848 and 1854. It became the 47th State of the USA in 1912; capital, Santa Fé.

news /nju:z/ n.pl. (usu. treated as sing.) information about recent events, especially when published or broadcast; a broadcast report of news; new or interesting information. —**news-stand** n. a stall for the sale of newspapers. **news-vendor** n. a newspaper-seller. [f. NEW]

newsagent n. a dealer in newspapers.

newscast n. a radio or television broadcast of news reports.

newscaster n. a person who reads a newscast. [f. prec.]

newsletter n. an informal printed report issued to members of a club or some other group.

New South Wales a State in SE Australia, first colonized from Britain in 1788 and federated with the other States of Australia in 1901; capital, Sydney.

newspaper n. a printed publication (usu. daily or weekly) containing news, advertisements, correspondence, etc.; the sheets of paper forming this. Daily publication of news dates back to ancient Rome where, in 59 BC, the practice began of writing public announcements about social and political matters (the Acta Diurna, = daily gazette) on a large whitened board in the city centre. For centuries news was circulated to important persons by letters. Handwritten news-sheets circulated reports of current events, and the invention of printing enabled more to be circulated at lower cost. The first regular public newspapers appeared in Europe in the mid-17th c., and the first English daily paper, the Daily Courant, in 1702; they were subject to various kinds of control. In England, government censorship was not ended until 1695, and reporting of Parliamentary debates was forbidden until 1772. The papers were often corrupt (bribes were used to control their comments on public figures) and prosecutions for libel were freely made by the royal family, government, and Church authorities who were the recipients of published criticism. A tax on newspapers, instituted in 1712, continued under various forms for nearly 150 years. During the 18th c., however, increasing revenue from advertisements encouraged editors to resist bribes, and reporting became more independent. During the 19th c. improvements in printing technology, and the setting up of international news agencies, together with the spread of literacy (which newspapers aided) all contributed to the general expansion of newspapers, and from the 1890s a more popular approach, offering amusing or sensational items of news, was introduced from America (see NORTHCLIFFE). In the 20th c. many newspapers have merged into large groups and a number of the less successful papers have ceased to be published. Introduction of computer technology is to transform established methods of production.

Newspeak /'nju:spi:k/ n. ambiguous euphemistic language used especially in political propaganda. [name of artificial official language in Orwell's Nineteen Eighty-Four]

newsprint n. the type of paper on which newspapers are printed.

newsreel n. a cinema film giving recent news. The regular issue of newsreels in the conventional sense—several short items grouped together—was begun in 1908. During the 1930s they appeared once or twice a week in Britain and America and lasted about 15 minutes, forming a familiar part of cinema programmes. Newsreels played an important role in the Second World War, but after the war the greater topicality of television caused them to be dropped.

newsworthy *adj.* topical, noteworthy as news.

newsy /'nju:zɪ/ *adj.* (*colloq.*) full of news.

newt /nju:t/ *n.* a small tailed amphibian especially of the genus *Triturus*, allied to the salamander (ill. AMPHIBIANS). [*a newt* f. *an ewt* (var. of EFT)]

New Testament the 27 books of the Bible recording the life and teaching of Christ and some of his earliest followers, written originally in Greek. At an early date the Church came to regard some of its own writings, especially those held to be of Apostolic origin, as of equal authority and inspiration to those received from Judaism. The canon of the New Testament, based on the four Gospels and the Epistles of St Paul, came into existence largely without definition. It was probably formally fixed at Rome in 382 when the Christian Old Testament (based on the Septuagint) was also defined.

Newton /'nju:t(ə)n/, Sir Isaac (1642–1726), English mathematician and physicist, the greatest single influence on theoretical physics until Einstein. His most productive period, which he called his *annus mirabilis* (1666–7), was when Cambridge University, where he had taken his bachelor's degree in 1665, was closed because of the plague. Retreating to his parents' home in Lincolnshire he laid the foundations of his future successes in mathematics, optics, dynamics (mechanics), and astronomy. He discovered the binomial theorem, and made contributions to algebra, geometry, and the theory of infinite series, all somewhat overshadowed by his most famous contribution to mathematics—the differential calculus (his 'method of fluxions') for finding rates of change of varying quantities, and his discovery of its relationship with what is now called integration (then 'quadrature'), the problem of finding the area of a figure circumscribed by curved boundaries. A bitter quarrel with the philosopher Leibniz ensued, as to which of them had discovered calculus first. His optical experiments, begun in 1666, led to his discovery that white light is made up of a mixture of coloured rays. In his major treatise, *Philosophiae Naturalis Principia Mathematica*, he gave a mathematical description of the laws of mechanics and gravitation, and applied this theory to explain planetary and lunar motion. For most purposes Newtonian mechanics has survived even the 20th-c. introduction of relativity theory and quantum mechanics (to both of which theories it stands as a first, but very good, approximation) as a mathematical description of terrestrial and cosmological phenomena. In 1699 Newton was appointed Master of the Mint, and was responsible for an urgently needed reform of the coinage. He entered Parliament as MP for Cambridge University in 1701, and in 1703 was elected President of the Royal Society, whose reputation he greatly increased over the following twenty-four years. Newton interested himself also in alchemy, astrology, and theology, and attempted a biblical chronology. He disliked criticism, and was involved in several bitter controversies with fellow scientists. The newton (see foll.) is named in his honour. He is buried in Westminster Abbey.

newton /'nju:t(ə)n/ *n.* a unit of force, the force that acting for 1 second on a mass of 1 kg gives it a velocity of 1 metre per second per second. [f. prec.]

Newtonian /nju:'təʊnɪən/ *adj.* of Sir Isaac Newton or his theory of the universe; (of mechanics) classical (see NEWTON); (of a telescope) with an oblique mirror to reflect the image to the side of the tube. [f. NEWTON]

New York 1. a State of the USA, bordering on the Atlantic, one of the original 13 States of the Union (1788); capital, Albany. 2. the richest and most populous city of the USA (pop. (1982) 7,068,096), and its greatest port, containing the financial centre Wall Street, industries of every kind, two universities, and an opera house, art galleries and museums that are world famous, and the headquarters of the United Nations. The Hudson River and Manhattan Island were discovered in 1609, and in 1629 Dutch colonists purchased Manhattan from the Indians for 24 dollars' worth of trinkets, establishing a settlement there which they called New Amsterdam. In 1664 the English naval officer who received the Dutch surrender renamed it in honour of the Duke of York (later James II), who was at that time Lord High Admiral of England. In 1789 George Washington took his oath as first President of the USA in New York. Because of the island's small area and the firm foundations afforded by its rock, Manhattan has been

built upwards, with skyscrapers that give its characteristic skyline.

New Zealand /'zi:lənd/ a country in the South Pacific, a member State of the Commonwealth, about 1,900 km (1,200 miles) east of Australia, consisting of two major islands (North and South Islands) separated by Cook Strait, and several smaller islands; pop. (est. 1983) 3,230,000; capital, Wellington. The discoverers and first colonists of the country were Polynesians (see MAORI). It was sighted by the Dutch navigator Tasman in 1642, and named after the Netherlands province of Zeeland. The islands were circumnavigated by Cook in 1769–70, and came under British sovereignty in 1840; colonization led to a series of wars with the native Maoris in the 1860s and 1870s. Full dominion status was granted in 1907, and independence in 1931. In recent years there has been a huge increase in Polynesian immigrants. The economy is heavily agricultural, with meat, wool, and dairy products forming the principal exports; there has been a boom in horticulture and an increase in small manufacturing industries. The country has reserves of coal and iron ore, and natural gas is also found. Tourism is an expanding industry. —**New Zealander** *n.*

next *adj.* 1. being, lying, or living nearest (*to*). 2. nearest in order or time, soonest come to. —*adv.* 1. in the next place or degree. 2. on the next occasion. —*n.* the next person or thing. —*prep.* next to. —**next-best** *adj.* second-best. **next door,** in the next room or house. **next of kin,** one's closest living relative. **next to,** almost. **the next world,** life after death. [OE, superl. of NIGH]

nexus /'neksəs/ *n.* a connected group or series. [L (*nectere* bind)]

Ney /neɪ/, Michel (1768–1815), French marshal, one of Napoleon's leading generals, known for his personal courage as 'the bravest of the brave'. He commanded the French cavalry at Waterloo, and after Napoleon's defeat and final overthrow was executed by the Bourbons despite attempts by Wellington and other allied leaders to intervene on his behalf.

NHS *abbr.* National Health Service.

NI *abbr.* 1. National Insurance. 2. Northern Ireland.

Ni *symbol* nickel.

niacin /'naɪəsɪn/ *n.* nicotinic acid. [f. *nicotinic acid*]

Niagara /naɪ'ægərə/ a river forming the US–Canada border between Lakes Erie and Ontario, famous for its spectacular waterfalls which are over 45 m (150 ft.) high. The falls are a major source of hydroelectric power.

Niamey /'njɑːmeɪ/ the capital of Niger; pop. (est.) 100,000.

nib *n.* 1. a pen-point. 2. (in *pl.*) crushed coffee- or cocoa-beans. 3. a small projection on a tile (ill. BUILDING TECHNIQUES). [prob. f. MDu. or MLG]

nibble *v.t./i.* 1. to take small quick or gentle bites at. 2. to eat in small amounts. 3. (with *at*) to show a cautious interest in (an offer etc.). —*n.* 1. an act of nibbling. 2. a very small amount of food. [prob. f. LDu.; cf. LG *nibbeln* gnaw]

Nibelung /'ni:bəlʊŋ/ (*Scand. myth.*) 1. a member of a Scandinavian race of dwarfs, owners of a hoard of gold and magic treasures, who were ruled by Nibelung, king of Nibelheim (land of mist). 2. (in the Nibelungenlied) any of the supporters of Siegfried, the subsequent possessor of the hoard; any of the Burgundians who stole it from him.

Nibelungenlied /'ni:bəlʊŋənli:d/ a 13th-c. Germanic poem, embodying a story found in the Edda, telling of the life and death of Siegfried, a prince of the Netherlands, and of its avenging by his wife Kriemhild, a Burgundian princess. There have been many adaptations of the story, including Wagner's epic music drama *Der Ring des Nibelungen* (1852–74). [f. prec. + G *lied* song]

nibs /nɪbz/ *n.* (*slang*) **his nibs,** a burlesque title of an important or self-important person. [f. earlier (cant) *nabs*]

Nicaragua /nɪkə'rægjʊə/ the largest country in Central America, with a coastline on both the Atlantic and the Pacific Ocean; pop. (1980) 2,700,000; official language, Spanish; capital, Managua. Columbus sighted the eastern coast in 1502, and the country was colonized by the Spaniards in the early 16th c. It broke away in 1821, and after brief membership of the Central American Federation became an independent republic in 1838. Since then its history has been scarred by border disputes and internal disturbances, the last witnessing the successful overthrow of the dictator Anastasio Somoza in 1979, followed by a continuing counter-revolutionary campaign against the new left-wing Sandinista regime. The country's economy, frequently disrupted by war, is overwhelmingly agricultural. —**Nicaraguan** adj. & n.

nice adj. **1.** pleasant, satisfactory, (of a person) kind, good-natured. **2.** (iron.) bad, difficult, awkward. **3.** needing precision and care; subtle. **4.** fastidious, delicately sensitive. —**nice and**, satisfactorily. —**nicely** adv., **niceness** n. [orig. = stupid, f. OF f. L nescius ignorant]

Nicene Creed /'naɪsiːn/ a formal statement of Christian belief, that appears in the Thirty-nine Articles, based on that adopted at the first Council of Nicaea (325). [f. L f. Gk (Nikaia Nicaea, town in Asia Minor)]

nicety /'naɪsɪtɪ/ n. **1.** precision. **2.** a subtle distinction or detail. —**to a nicety**, exactly. [f. OF (as NICE)]

niche /nɪtʃ, niːʃ/ n. **1.** a shallow recess, especially in a wall. **2.** a comfortable or suitable position in life or employment. [F (nicher make a nest f. L nidus nest)]

Nicholas¹ /'nɪkələs/ the name of two emperors of Russia: **Nicholas I** (1796–1855), brother of Alexander I, reigned 1825–55. A far harsher character than his predecessor Alexander, Nicholas pursued rigidly conservative policies, maintaining serfdom and building up a large secret police which proved more than a match for radical reformers. He was largely concerned with keeping the peace in Europe, but his expansionist policies in the Near East finally brought war with Britain and France in the Crimea. **Nicholas II** (1868–1918), son of Alexander III, reigned 1894–1917. Reactionary and ineffective, Nicholas proved incapable of coping with the dangerous political legacy left him by his father and tended to fall too easily under the sway of favourites such as Rasputin who, like the Tsar, failed to perceive the need for reform. After the disastrous war with Japan (1904–5) Russia was racked by unrest, but the programme of reforms initiated thereafter (including the creation of the Duma) did no more than paper over the cracks, and the Tsarist regime disintegrated altogether under the strain of fresh military disasters during the First World War. Nicholas was forced to abdicate after the Russian Revolution in 1917 and was murdered along with his family by the Bolsheviks a year later.

Nicholas² /'nɪk(ə)ləs/, St (4th c.), bishop of Myra in Lycia and patron saint of children, sailors, and Russia. Little is known of his life but he was the subject of many legends, and immensely popular in the West following the translation of his supposed remains to Bari in SE Italy (1087). The cult of Santa Claus (a corruption of his name) arose in North America from the Dutch custom of giving gifts to children on his feast-day (6 Dec.), a practice now usually transferred to Christmas.

nick n. **1.** a small cut or notch. **2.** (slang) prison; a police station. **3.** (slang) condition. —v.t. **1.** to make a nick or nicks in. **2.** (slang) to steal. **3.** (slang) to catch, to arrest. —**in the nick of time**, only just in time. [orig. unkn.]

nickel /'nɪk(ə)l/ n. **1.** a hard silver-white metallic element, symbol Ni, atomic number 28 (see below). **2.** (US) a five-cent piece. —**nickel silver**, an alloy of nickel, zinc, and copper. **nickel steel**, an alloy of nickel with steel. [abbr. of G kupfernickel, the one whence it was first obtained] Nickel, first isolated in 1751, is widely used in alloys (especially with iron, where it imparts strength and resistance to corrosion) and in coinage. The unalloyed metal is used to form a protective and decorative coat on other metals, and as a catalyst in the hydrogenation of oils to form fats, notably in the manufacture of margarine.

nickelodeon /nɪkə'ləʊdɪən/ n. (US colloq.) a juke-box. [f. prec. + MELODEON]

nicker n. (pl. same) (slang) £1 sterling. [orig. unkn.]

nickname n. a familiar or humorous name given to a person or thing instead of or as well as the real name. —v.t. to give a nickname to. [a nickname f. an eke-name (eke addition, NAME)]

Nicobar Islands see ANDAMAN AND NICOBAR ISLANDS.

Nicosia /nɪkə'siːə/ the capital of Cyprus; pop. (est. 1980) 161,000.

nicotine /'nɪkətiːn/ n. a poisonous alkaloid extracted as an oily liquid from tobacco. [F, f. generic name (nicotiana herba) of tobacco, f. J. Nicot, French diplomat who introduced tobacco into France 1560]

nicotinic acid /nɪkə'tɪnɪk/ a vitamin of the B group, formed by oxidation of nicotine and acting to prevent pellagra. [f. prec.]

nictitate /'nɪktɪteɪt/ v.i. to blink, to wink. —**nictitating membrane**, the third or inner eyelid of many animals (including birds and fishes). —**nictitation** /-'teɪʃ(ə)n/ n. [f. L (nictare blink)]

niece /niːs/ n. one's brother's or sister's daughter. [f. OF f. L neptis grand-daughter]

nielsbohrium /niːlz'bɔːrɪəm/ n. the Russian name for the element of atomic number 105, a short-lived artificially produced radioactive transuranic element (cf. HAHNIUM). [f. Niels BOHR]

Nietzsche /'niːtʃə/, Friedrich Wilhelm (1844–1900), German philosopher and writer of Polish descent, an admirer and sometime friend of Wagner. He was briefly a professor at Basle but spent most of his life writing in isolation, frustrated at lack of recognition; in 1889 his lack of mental balance developed into permanent insanity. Roused by Darwin he argued forcefully that since human life has no meaning bestowed upon it supernaturally it must create meaning; this theme appears in his novel Thus Spake Zarathustra (1883), where he speaks of the 'death of God'. The principal features of his doctrine are contempt for Christianity with its compassion for the weak, and exaltation of the 'will to dominate' and of the 'superman', unscrupulous and pitiless, superior to ordinary morality, who tramples on the feeble and will replace the Christian ideal. He divided mankind into a small dominant 'master-class' and a large dominated 'herd'—a thesis which became part of the Nazi culture after Nietzsche's death. His writings are often obscure and open to different interpretations.

niff n. (slang) a smell, a stink. —v.i. (slang) to smell, to stink. —**niffy** adj. [orig. dial.]

nifty adj. (slang) **1.** smart, stylish. **2.** excellent, clever. [orig. unkn.]

Niger¹ /'naɪdʒə(r)/ a river of West Africa, flowing in a curve from the NE frontier of Sierra Leone to the Gulf of Guinea, length 4,100 km (2,550 miles). [L, = black]

Niger² /niː'ʒeə(r)/ a landlocked country of West Africa, lying mainly in the Sahara, taking its name from the river that flows through the SW part of its territory, and bounded by Mali, Algeria, and Libya on its west and north, by Upper Volta, Nigeria, and Chad on its south and east; pop. (est. 1981) 5,466,000; official language, French; capital, Niamey. A French colony (part of French West Africa) from 1922, it became an autonomous republic within the French Community in 1958 and fully independent in 1960. Ground-nuts are a main export and the country's uranium deposits are being exploited.

Niger-Congo a group of languages, the largest in Africa, named after the rivers Niger and Congo. It includes the languages spoken by most of the indigenous peoples of western, central, and southern Africa: the important Bantu group, the Mande group (West Africa), the Voltaic group (Burkina), and the Kwa group (Nigeria) which includes Yoruba and Ibo.

Nigeria /naɪ'dʒɪərɪə/ a country on the west coast of Africa, a member State of the Commonwealth, bordered by the River Niger to the north; pop. (est.) 85,000,000; official language, English; capital, Lagos. The country was the site of highly developed kingdoms in the Middle Ages, and the coast was explored by the Portuguese in the 15th c. The area of the Niger delta came gradually under British influence in the 18th and 19th c., particularly during the period between the annexation of Lagos in 1861 and the unification of the protectorates of Southern and Northern Nigeria into a single colony in 1914. Independence came in 1960 and the State became a republic in 1963, but since that time it has been troubled by political instability, particularly a civil war with the breakaway eastern area of Biafra (1967–70). The discovery of oil in the 1960s and 1970s resulted in a dramatic expansion of the economy and a shift away from the traditional industries of farming, fishing, and forestry. Nigeria has emerged as one of the world's major exporters of oil, which now accounts for over 90 per cent of its export earnings and makes its economy vulnerable to changes in the world prices of oil. —**Nigerian** adj. & n.

niggard /'nɪgəd/ n. a stingy person. [prob. of Scand. orig.; cf. NIGGLE]

niggardly adj. stingy. —**niggardliness** n. [f. prec.]

nigger n. (offensive) a Black, a dark-skinned person. —**nigger in the woodpile**, a hidden cause of trouble or inconvenience. [f. F nègre f. Sp. (as NEGRO)]

niggle v.t./i. **1.** to fuss over details, to find fault in a petty way. **2.** to irritate, to nag. [app. of Scand. orig.]

niggling adj. petty, troublesome; nagging. [f. prec.]

nigh /naɪ/ adv., prep., & adj. (archaic & dial.) near. [OE]

night /naɪt/ *n.* **1.** the period of darkness between one day and the next, the time from sunset to sunrise. **2.** nightfall. **3.** the darkness of night. **4.** a night or evening appointed for some activity. —**make a night of it,** to spend most or all of the night enjoying oneself. **night-club** *n.* a club that is open at night and provides refreshment and entertainment. **night-dress** *n.* a woman's or girl's loose garment worn in bed. **night-gown** *n.* a night-dress or night-shirt. **night-life** *n.* the entertainment available at night in a town. **night-light** *n.* a short thick candle or dim bulb kept burning in a bedroom at night. **night-long** *adj. & adv.* throughout the night. **night safe,** a safe with an opening in the outer wall of a bank for the deposit of money etc. when the bank is closed. **night school,** a school providing evening classes for those working by day. **night-shirt** *n.* a man's or boy's long shirt for sleeping in. **night-time** *n.* the time of darkness. **night-watchman** *n.* a person employed to look after unoccupied premises at night; (in cricket) an inferior batsman sent in near the close of play to avoid the dismissal of a better one in adverse conditions. [OE]

nightcap *n.* **1.** a cap worn in bed. **2.** a hot or alcoholic drink taken at bedtime.

nightfall *n.* the end of daylight.

Nightingale /ˈnaɪtɪŋgeɪl/, Florence (1820-1910), British nurse and medical reformer who became famous during the Crimean War for her attempts to publicize and improve the state of the army's medical arrangements. She took a party of nurses to the unhealthy and dangerous army hospital at Scutari, where she became known as the 'Lady of the Lamp' for her nightly rounds, and devoted the rest of her life to attempts to improve public health and hospital care.

nightingale /ˈnaɪtɪŋgeɪl/ *n.* a small bird of the genus *Luscinia* of the thrush family, of which the male sings melodiously both by day and by night. [OE, = night-singer]

nightie *n.* (*colloq.*) a night-dress. [abbr.]

nightjar *n.* a nocturnal bird of the family Caprimulgidae with a harsh cry. [f. NIGHT + JAR[1]]

nightly *adj.* **1.** happening, done, or existing in the night. **2.** recurring every night. —*adv.* every night. [f. NIGHT]

nightmare *n.* **1.** a terrifying dream. **2.** (*colloq.*) a terrifying or very unpleasant experience or situation; a haunting fear. —**nightmarish** *adj.* [orig. = monster supposed to sit on and suffocate sleepers, f. NIGHT + obs. *mare* goblin]

nightshade *n.* a plant of the genus *Solanum* with poisonous berries. —**deadly nightshade,** belladonna.

nihilism /ˈnaɪɪlɪz(ə)m/ *n.* **1.** negative doctrines or total rejection of current beliefs in religion or morals, often involving a general sense of despair coupled with the belief that life is devoid of meaning. **2.** philosophical scepticism that denies all existence. **3.** the doctrine of a Russian extreme-revolutionary party in the 19th-20th c. finding nothing to approve of in the established order or social and political institutions. —**nihilist** *n.*, **nihilistic** /-ˈlɪstɪk/ *adj.* [f. L *nihil* nothing]

Nijinsky /nɪˈʒɪnskɪ/, Vaslav Fomich (1890-1950), Russian dancer and choreographer. As a dancer he had exceptional technical virtuosity and instinctive dramatic gifts. Diaghilev made him the star of his Paris seasons and later his touring ensemble, and he was idolized for his performances in the classics and Fokine's ballets, including *Spectre de la Rose* (1911). Diaghilev encouraged him to attempt choreography; the outcome was Debussy's *L'Après-midi d'un faune* (1912) and *Jeux*, and Stravinsky's *Le Sacre du printemps* (1913), which foreshadowed many developments of later avant-garde choreography. Nijinsky's career declined after his separation from Diaghilev, and was brought to a premature end by *dementia praecox*.

Nike /ˈnaɪkɪ/ (*Gk myth.*) the goddess of victory. [Gk, = victory]

nil *n.* nothing, no number or amount, especially as a score in games. [L, = *nihil* nothing]

Nile /naɪl/ a river which flows from east central Africa 6,695 km (4,160 miles) northwards through Egypt to the Mediterranean Sea. Seasonal flooding in Egypt has been controlled by the construction of a dam at Aswan which also provides hydroelectric power. —**Blue Nile,** the easterly of the Nile's two main branches, flowing from the Ethiopian Highlands to a confluence with the White Nile at Khartoum. **White Nile,** the westerly and longer branch.

Nilotic /naɪˈlɒtɪk/ *adj.* **1.** of the Nile or this region or its inhabitants. **2.** of a group of languages spoken in Egypt and the Sudan, and further south in Kenya and Tanzania. The

western group includes Luo (Kenya), Dinka (Sudan), and Lango (Uganda); the eastern group includes Masai (Kenya and Tanzania) and Turkana (Kenya).

nimble *adj.* quick and light in movement or action, agile; (of the mind) quick, clever. —**nimbleness** *n.*, **nimbly** *adv.* [OE, = quick to seize]

nimbo-stratus /nɪmbəʊˈstreɪtəs, -ˈstrɑː-/ *n.* a low dark-grey layer of cloud (ill. WEATHER). [f. foll. + STRATUS]

nimbus /ˈnɪmbəs/ *n.* (*pl.* **-bi** /-baɪ/, **-buses**) **1.** a halo, an aureole. **2.** a storm-cloud. [L]

Nimrod /ˈnɪmrɒd/ the great-grandson of Noah, traditional founder of the Babylonian dynasty, noted as a mighty hunter.

Nimrud /ˈnɪmrʊd/ the modern name of ancient Kalhu, (*Calah* of Genesis) situated on the eastern bank of the Tigris south of Nineveh. It was inaugurated as the Assyrian capital in 879 BC by Ashurnasirpal II (883-859 BC) which was later supplanted by Khorsabad with the accession of Sargon II (722-705 BC), and finally destroyed by the Medes in 612 BC. British excavations under Henry A. Layard and later Sir Max Mallowan uncovered palaces of the Assyrian kings with monumental sculptured reliefs, carved ivory furniture inlays, and metalwork.

nincompoop /ˈnɪnkəmpuːp/ *n.* a foolish person. [orig. unkn.]

nine *adj. & n.* **1.** one more than eight; the symbol for this (9, ix, IX). **2.** the size etc. denoted by nine. —**the Nine,** the Muses. **Nine Days' Queen,** Lady Jane Grey. **nine days' wonder,** a thing attracting interest for a short time. [OE]

ninefold *adj. & adv.* **1.** nine times as much or as many. **2.** consisting of nine parts. [f. NINE + -FOLD]

ninepins *n.pl.* a kind of skittles.

nineteen /naɪnˈtiːn/ *adj. & n.* **1.** one more than eighteen; the symbol for this (19, xix, XIX). **2.** the size etc. denoted by nineteen. —**nineteenth** *adj. & n.* [OE (as NINE, -TEEN)]

ninety *adj. & n.* **1.** nine times ten; the symbol for this (90, xc, XC). **2.** (in *pl.*) the numbers, years, or degrees of temperature from 90 to 99. —**ninetieth** *adj. & n.* [OE (as NINE)]

Nineveh /ˈnɪnɪvə/ the capital of Assyria from the reign of Sennacherib (704-681 BC) until its sack by a coalition of Babylonians and Medes in 612 BC, located east of the Tigris opposite Mosul. First excavated by the French and later by the British, Nineveh is noted for its monumental Neo-Assyrian palace, library, and statuary as well as for its crucial sequence of prehistoric pottery.

Ninian /ˈnɪnɪən/, St (*c.*360-*c.*432), Scottish missionary. According to Bede he founded a church at Whithorn in Wigtownshire and from there evangelized the 'southern Picts'.

ninny *n.* a foolish person. [perh. for *innocent*]

ninth /naɪnθ/ *adj.* next after the eighth. —*n.* each of nine equal parts into which a thing may be divided. —**ninthly** *adv.* [f. NINE]

Niobe /ˈnaɪəbɪ/ (*Gk myth.*) daughter of Tantalus, and mother of a large family. Apollo and Artemis, enraged because she boasted herself superior to their mother Leto, slew her children. Niobe herself was turned into a stone, and her tears into streams that trickled from it. The figure carved on a mountain east of Manisa in Turkey, formerly identified as that seen by Pausanias and others, is now thought to be a fertility goddess and of Hittite workmanship, and the identification has been transferred to a natural formation resembling a weeping woman, found near the town of Manisa.

niobium /naɪˈəʊbɪəm/ *n.* a rare metallic element, symbol Nb, atomic number 41, used in a number of alloys. First discovered in 1801, it is normally found in ores containing tantalum, which has similar chemical properties. [f. prec.]

nip[1] *v.t./i.* (**-pp-**) **1.** to pinch or squeeze sharply; to bite quickly with the front teeth. **2.** to pinch *off*. **3.** to pain or harm with biting cold. **4.** (*colloq.*) to go quickly or nimbly. —*n.* **1.** a sharp pinch, squeeze, or bite. **2.** biting coldness. —**nip in the bud,** to destroy at an early stage of development. [prob. f. L Du.]

nip[2] *n.* a small quantity of spirits. [abbr. of *nipperkin* small measure]

nipper *n.* **1.** a crustacean's claw. **2.** (in *pl.*) pincers or forceps for gripping things or cutting things off. **3.** (*colloq.*) a young child. [f. NIP[1]]

nipple *n.* **1.** a small projection in which the mammary ducts of either sex of mammals terminate and from which in females milk is secreted for the young. **2.** the teat of a feeding-bottle. **3.** a nipple-like protuberance. [perh. f. *neb* beak, tip]

Nipponese /nɪpɒˈniːz/ *adj. & n. (pl.* same) Japanese. [f. Jap. *Nippon* Japan]

nippy *adj. (colloq.)* **1.** nimble, quick. **2.** chilly, cold. [f. NIP¹]

nirvana /nɜːˈvɑːnə/ *n.* the final goal of Buddhism, a transcendent state in which there is neither suffering, desire, nor sense of self (*atman*), with release from the effects of karma. [f. Skr., = extinction (i.e. the extinction of illusion, since suffering, desire, and self are all illusions)]

Nissen hut /ˈnɪs(ə)n/ *n.* a tunnel-shaped hut of corrugated iron with a cement floor. [f. P. N. *Nissen*, British engineer (d. 1930)]

nit *n.* **1.** a louse or other parasite; its egg. **2.** *(slang)* a stupid person. —**nit-picking** *n. & adj. (colloq.)* fault-finding in a petty way. [OE]

nitrate¹ /ˈnaɪtreɪt/ *n.* **1.** a salt or ester of nitric acid. **2.** potassium or sodium nitrate used as a fertilizer. [F (as NITRE)]

nitrate² /naɪˈtreɪt/ *v.t.* to treat, combine, or impregnate with nitric acid. [f. foll.]

nitre /ˈnaɪtə(r)/ *n.* saltpetre. [f. OF f. L f. Gk *nitron*]

nitric /ˈnaɪtrɪk/ *adj.* of or containing nitrogen. —**nitric acid**, a pungent corrosive caustic liquid. [f. F (as prec.)]

nitride /ˈnaɪtraɪd/ *n.* a binary compound of nitrogen. [f. NITRE]

nitrify /ˈnaɪtrɪfaɪ/ *v.t.* to turn into a nitrite or nitrate. —**nitrification** /-frˈkeɪʃ(ə)n/ *n.* [f. F (as NITRE)]

nitrite /ˈnaɪtraɪt/ *n.* a salt or ester of nitrous acid. [f. NITRE]

nitro- /naɪtrəʊ-/ *in comb.* of or made with nitric acid, nitre, or nitrogen. —**nitro-glycerine** *n.* a yellowish oily highly explosive liquid made by adding glycerine to nitric and sulphuric acids. [Gk (as NITRE)]

nitrogen /ˈnaɪtrədʒ(ə)n/ *n.* a colourless odourless gaseous element, symbol N, atomic number 7, forming 78 per cent of the earth's atmosphere by volume. Pure nitrogen is obtained mainly by distillation of liquefied air. It is a comparatively unreactive element, and is used in situations where an inert atmosphere is needed. Liquid nitrogen is used as a coolant. Nitrogen is essential to life, being a major constituent of proteins and other biological molecules. It forms a range of compounds including nitric acid, ammonia, and nitrogenous fertilizers. —**nitrogenous** /-ˈtrɒdʒɪnəs/ *adj.* [f. F (as NITRO-, -GEN]

nitrogen cycle the cycle in which nitrogen is absorbed from and replaced in the atmosphere. Nitrogen exists in a free state in the air; it is converted to ammonia and thence into compounds mainly by the action of certain bacteria. These compounds are deposited in the soil, from which they are assimilated by plants which are eaten by animals, and returned to the atmosphere when these organic substances decay.

nitrous /ˈnaɪtrəs/ *adj.* of, like, or impregnated with nitre. —**nitrous acid**, a liquid resembling nitric acid but containing less oxygen. **nitrous oxide**, a colourless gas used as an anaesthetic, laughing-gas. [f. L (as NITRE)]

nitty-gritty *n. (slang)* the realities or basic facts of a matter. [orig. unkn.]

nitwit *n. (colloq.)* a stupid person. [perh. f. NIT + WIT]

nix *n. (slang)* nothing. [G, colloq. form of *nichts* nothing]

Nkruma /nˈkruːmə/, Kwame (1909–72), the first leader of Ghana after it achieved independence in 1957. Nkruma became one of the most influential African statesmen as a result of his flamboyant style of politics, but his corrupt dictatorial methods seriously damaged his country's economy and eventually led to his overthrow in 1966.

NNE *abbr.* north-north-east.

NNW *abbr.* north-north-west.

No *symbol* nobelium.

No. *abbr.* number. [f. L *numero* (*numerus* number)]

no /nəʊ/ *adj.* **1.** not any. **2.** not a, quite other than. **3.** hardly any. —*adv.* **1.** (as a negative answer to a question etc.) it is not so, I do not agree, I shall not, etc. **2.** (with *compar.*) by no amount, not at all. **3.** (after *or*) not. —*n. (pl.* **noes**) **1.** the word or answer 'no'. **2.** a denial or refusal; a negative vote. —**no-ball** *n.* an unlawfully delivered ball in cricket etc. **no-claim bonus,** a reduction of an insurance premium for a person who has not claimed payment under the insurance since a previous renewal. **no go,** it is hopeless or impossible. **no-go area,** one to which entry is forbidden or restricted. **no man's land,** the space between two opposing enemies;

an area not assigned to any owner. **no one,** no person, nobody. **no way,** *(colloq.)* it is impossible; not at all. [f. NONE, orig. before consonants]

Noah /ˈnəʊə/ a Hebrew patriarch represented as tenth in descent from Adam. According to the story in Genesis he made the ark which saved his family and specimens of every animal from the flood sent by God to destroy the world, and his sons Ham, Shem, and Japheth were regarded as ancestors of all the races of mankind (Gen. 5–10). The tradition of a great flood in very early times is found also in other countries (see DEUCALION and GILGAMESH).

nob¹ *n. (slang)* a person of wealth or high social standing. —**nobby** *adj.* [orig. unkn.]

nob² *n. (slang)* the head. [perh. var. of KNOB]

nobble *v.t. (slang)* **1.** to tamper with (a racehorse) to prevent its winning. **2.** to influence (a person) by underhand means; to get possession of dishonestly. **3.** to catch (a criminal). [prob. = dial. *knobble* beat (f. KNOB)]

nobelium /nəʊˈbiːlɪəm/ *n.* an artificially made transuranic radioactive metallic element, symbol No, atomic number 102, first obtained in 1958 by bombarding curium with carbon ions. [f. NOBEL (see foll.)]

Nobel Prize /nəʊbel/ any of the (orig. five) prizes awarded annually to the person or persons adjudged by Swedish learned societies to have done the most significant recent work in physics, chemistry, medicine, and literature, and to the person who is adjudged by the Norwegian parliament to have rendered the greatest service to the cause of peace. They were established by the will of Alfred Bernhard Nobel (1833–96), Swedish chemist, engineer, and inventor of dynamite and other high explosives, and are traditionally awarded on 10 Dec., the anniversary of his death. A Nobel Prize for economic sciences was added in 1969, financed by the Swedish National Bank.

nobility /nəʊˈbɪlɪtɪ/ *n.* nobleness of character, mind, birth, or rank. —**the nobility,** the aristocracy. [f. OF or L *nobilitas* (as foll.)]

noble /ˈnəʊb(ə)l/ *adj.* **1.** belonging to the aristocracy by birth or rank. **2.** of excellent character, free from pettiness or meanness, magnanimous. **3.** of imposing appearance, excellent. —*n.* a nobleman or noblewoman. —**noble gas,** any of the 6 chemically similar gaseous elements helium, neon, argon, krypton, xenon, and radon. They are very unreactive and were formerly believed never to combine with other elements, but a few compounds of krypton, xenon, and radon have now been prepared. **noble metal,** a metal (e.g. gold) that resists chemical attack. —**nobleness** *n.*, **nobly** *adv.* [f. OF f. L *nobilis*]

nobleman *n. (pl.* **-men**) a peer.

noblesse oblige /nəʊˈbles ɒˈbliːʒ/ privilege entails responsibility. [F]

noblewoman *n. (pl.* **-women**) a peeress.

nobody /ˈnəʊbədɪ/ *pron.* **1.** no person. **2.** a person of no importance.

nock *n.* a notch on a bow or arrow for the bowstring. [perh. = *hock* upper corner of sail, f. MDu.]

nocturnal /nɒkˈtɜːn(ə)l/ *adj.* **1.** of or in the night. **2.** done or active by night. —**nocturnally** *adv.* [f. L (*nocturnus* of night, f. *nox* night)]

nocturne /ˈnɒktɜːn/ *n.* **1.** a dreamy musical piece. **2.** a picture of a night scene. [F (as prec.)]

nod *v.t./i.* (**-dd-**) **1.** to incline the head slightly and briefly in greeting, assent, or command. **2.** to let the head droop in drowsiness; to be drowsy. **3.** to incline (the head); to signify (assent etc.) by a nod. **4.** (of flowers etc.) to bend downwards and sway. **5.** to make a mistake due to a momentary lack of alertness or attention. —*n.* a nodding of the head. —**nod off,** to fall asleep. [orig. unkn.]

noddle *n. (colloq.)* the head. [orig. unkn.]

Noddy a character in the writings of Enid Blyton, a toy figure of a boy whose head is so fixed that he has to nod when he speaks.

noddy *n.* **1.** a simpleton. **2.** a tropical sea-bird of the genus *Anous*, resembling the tern. [prob. f. obs. *noddy* foolish (as NOD)]

node *n.* **1.** a knob-like swelling. **2.** the point on the stem of a plant where a leaf or bud grows out. **3.** a point at which a curve crosses itself. **4.** the intersecting point of a planet's orbit and the ecliptic or of two great circles of the celestial sphere. —**nodal** *adj.* [f. L *nodus* knot]

nodule /ˈnɒdjuːl/ *n.* a small rounded lump; a small node. —**nodular** *adj.* [f. L *nodulus* dim. of *nodus* knot]

Noel /nəʊˈel/ n. (in carols etc.) Christmas. [F f. L (as NATAL)]

Noether /ˈnɜːtə(r)/, Emmy (1882–1935), German mathematician whose uncanny ability to distil the essentials from an algebraic situation and generalize to exactly the right level led her to simplify and greatly extend the work of her predecessors, particularly Hilbert and Dedekind, on rings and their ideals. Her colleagues were more aware than she was of her lack of status in what was then a man's world: Hilbert's argument to a meeting of the Göttingen faculty in 1915, that this was a university and not a bathing establishment, was unsuccessful, and her position there remained insecure and unsalaried until terminated by the anti-Semitic laws of 1933. Nevertheless, through her lectures, seminars, and conversations she exercised an enormous influence and inaugurated the modern period in algebraic geometry and abstract algebra.

nog[1] n. a small block or peg of wood. [orig. unkn.]

nog[2] n. **1.** strong beer. **2.** an egg-nog. [orig. unkn.]

noggin /ˈnɒgɪn/ n. **1.** a small mug. **2.** a small (usually ¼-pint) measure. **3.** (slang) the head. [orig. unkn.]

nogging n. brickwork in a wooden frame (ill. HOUSES). [f. NOG[1]]

Noh /nəʊ/ n. a form of traditional Japanese drama, evolved from Shinto rites and dating from the 14th to the 15th c. It flourished in the 17th–19th c. and has since been revived. The plays were short, and five made up a complete programme. The general tone was noble, the language honorific and sonorous, and the subject-matter taken mainly from Japan's classical literature. The players were all male, the chorus playing a passive narrative role and even chanting the lines of the principal characters while the latter executed certain dances. About two hundred Noh plays are extant; they are comparable in various respects with early Greek drama. [Jap.]

noise /nɔɪz/ n. **1.** a sound, especially a loud or unpleasant one; a series of loud sounds. **2.** irregular fluctuations accompanying a transmitted signal. **3.** (in pl.) utterances, especially conventional remarks. —v.t. to make public, to make generally known. [f. OF = outcry, f. L (as NAUSEA)]

noiseless adj. without a sound. —**noiselessly** adv. [f. prec. + -LESS]

noisome /ˈnɔɪsəm/ adj. (literary) noxious, disgusting, especially to the smell. [f. obs. noy (f. ANNOY)]

noisy /ˈnɔɪzɪ/ adj. full of, making, or attended with noise; given to making a noise. —**noisily** adv., **noisiness** n. [f. NOISE]

Nolan /ˈnəʊlən/, Sidney (1917–), Australian painter, internationally known for his paintings of events from Australian history around which legends have gathered, beginning with his Ned Kelly paintings (1946). His interpretations are often whimsical and at times humorous.

nomad /ˈnəʊmæd/ n. a member of a tribe roaming from place to place for pasture; a wanderer. —**nomadic** /-ˈmædɪk/ adj., **nomadism** n. [f. F f. L f.Gk (nemō to pasture)]

nombril /ˈnɒmbrɪl/ n. (in heraldry) the point half-way between the fess point and the base of a shield (ill. HERALDRY). [F, = navel]

nom de plume /nɒm də ˈpluːm/ n. (pl. noms pr. same) a writer's assumed name. [sham F, = pen-name]

nomen /ˈnəʊmen/ n. (in ancient Rome) the second or family name, e.g. Marcus Tullius Cicero. [L, = name]

nomenclature /nəʊˈmenklətʃə(r)/ n. a system of names or naming, terminology. [F f. L (as prec., calare call)]

nominal /ˈnɒmɪn(ə)l/ adj. **1.** of, as, or like a noun. **2.** of or in names. **3.** existing in name only, not real or actual. **4.** (of a sum of money etc.) virtually nothing, much below the actual value. —**nominal value**, face value. —**nominally** adv. [f. F or L (as NOMEN)]

nominalism /ˈnɒmɪnəlɪz(ə)m/ n. the theory that universals or general ideas (abstract concepts) are mere names (opp. REALISM). —**nominalist** n., **nominalistic** /-ˈlɪstɪk/ adj. [as prec.]

nominate /ˈnɒmɪneɪt/ v.t. to appoint to or propose for election to an office; to name or appoint (a date etc.). —**nominator** n. [f. L nominare (as NOMEN)]

nomination /nɒmɪˈneɪʃ(ə)n/ n. **1.** nominating, being nominated. **2.** the right of nominating. [f. OF or L (as prec.)]

nominative /ˈnɒmɪnətɪv/ n. (Gram.) the case expressing the subject of a verb. —adj. (Gram.) of or in the nominative. [f. OF or L (as NOMINATE)]

nominee /nɒmɪˈniː/ n. a person who is nominated [as NOMINATE]

non- prefix not; (with v. to form adj.) not doing (non-skid), not behaving in a specified way (non-stick), not to be treated in a specified way (non-iron). [f. OF f. L non not]

nonage /ˈnəʊnɪdʒ, ˈnɒn-/ n. being under full legal age, minority; immaturity. [f. AF (as NON-, AGE)]

nonagenarian /nəʊnədʒɪˈneərɪən, nɒn-/ n. a person from 90 to 99 years old. [f. L (nonageni ninety each)]

nonagon /ˈnɒnəgɒn/ n. a plane figure with nine sides and angles. [L (nonus ninth, Gk -gōnos angled)]

non-aligned adj. (of a State) not in alliance with any major bloc.

non-belligerent adj. taking no active or open part in a war. —n. a non-belligerent State.

nonce n. the time being, the present, esp. in **for the nonce**, for the occasion only. —**nonce-word** n. a word coined for one occasion. [f. obs. than anes the one (occasion), alt. by wrong division]

nonchalant /ˈnɒnʃələnt/ adj. not feeling or showing anxiety or excitement, calm and casual. —**nonchalance** n., **nonchalantly** adv. [F (NON-, chaloir be concerned)]

non-com. abbr. non-commissioned (officer).

non-combatant adj. not fighting (esp. in war, as being a civilian, army chaplain, etc.). —n. such a person.

non-commissioned adj. (esp. of an officer) of a grade below those with commissions.

non-committal adj. not committing oneself to a definite opinion, course of action, etc. —**non-committally** adv.

non compos mentis /nɒn ˈkɒmpɒs ˈmentɪs/ adj. not in one's right mind, insane. [L, = not in control of one's mind]

non-conductor n. a substance that does not conduct heat or electricity.

nonconformist /nɒnkənˈfɔːmɪst/ n. **1.** one who does not conform to the doctrine or discipline of an established Church; **Nonconformist**, a member of a (usu. Protestant) sect dissenting from the Anglican Church. **2.** one who does not conform to a prevailing principle.

nonconformity /nɒnkənˈfɔːmɪtɪ/ n. **1.** nonconformists or their principles etc. **2.** failure to conform. **3.** lack of correspondence between things.

non-contributory adj. not involving contributions.

non-co-operation n. failure or refusal to co-operate, especially as a protest.

nondescript /ˈnɒndɪskrɪpt/ adj. indeterminate, lacking distinctive characteristics. —n. a nondescript person or thing. [f. NON- + descript described (as DESCRIBE)]

none /nʌn/ pron. not any, no one; no person(s). —adj. not any (usu. with the reference supplied by an earlier or later noun). —adv. by no amount. —**none the less** nevertheless. [OE, = not one]

nonentity /nɒˈnentɪtɪ/ n. **1.** a person or thing of no importance. **2.** non-existence; a non-existent thing. [f. L (as NON-, ENTITY)]

nones /nəʊnz/ n.pl. the 7th day of March, May, July, Oct., the 5th of the other months, in the ancient Roman calendar. [f. OF f. L nonae (nonus ninth)]

nonesuch var. of NONSUCH.

non-event n. an event that turns out to be insignificant (usu. contrary to hopes or expectations).

non-existent adj. not existing.

non-ferrous adj. (of a metal) not iron or steel.

non-fiction n. a classification of literature that includes books in all subjects other than fiction.

non-intervention n. the principle or practice of not interfering in others' disputes.

non-moral adj. not concerned with morality.

non-nuclear adj. not involving nuclei or nuclear energy.

nonpareil /ˈnɒnpər(ə)l/ adj. unrivalled, unique. —n. such a person or thing. [F (NON-, pareil equal)]

non-party adj. independent of political parties.

nonplus /nɒnˈplʌs/ v.t. (-ss-) to perplex completely. [f. L non plus not more]

non-profit-making adj. (of an enterprise) not conducted primarily with a view to making profits.

non-proliferation n. limitation of the number especially of nuclear weapons.

nonsense /ˈnɒnsəns/ n. **1.** words put together in a way that does not make sense. **2.** absurd or foolish talk, ideas, or behaviour. —*int.* you are talking nonsense. —**nonsensical** /-'sensɪk(ə)l/ *adj.*, **nonsensically** *adv.* [f. NON- + SENSE]

non sequitur /nɒn 'sekwɪtə(r)/ *n.* a conclusion that does not logically follow from the premises. [L, = it does not follow]

non-skid *adj.* that does not, or is designed not to, skid.

non-smoker *n.* **1.** a person who does not smoke. **2.** a compartment in a train etc. where smoking is forbidden.

non-starter *n.* (*colloq.*) an idea or person not worth consideration.

non-stick *adj.* (of a saucepan etc.) to which food will not stick during cooking.

non-stop *adj.* **1.** (of a train etc.) not stopping at intermediate stations. **2.** not ceasing, done without pausing. —*adv.* without stopping.

nonsuch /'nʌnsʌtʃ/ *n.* **1.** an unrivalled person or thing, a paragon. **2.** a plant (*Medicago lupulina*) resembling lucerne with black pods. [f. NONE + SUCH]

non-U *adj.* (*colloq.*) not characteristic of upper-class speech or behaviour.

non-union *adj.* not belonging to or not made by members of a trade union.

non-voting *adj.* (of shares) not entitling the holder to a vote.

non-White *adj.* belonging to a race other than the White race. —*n.* a non-White person.

noodle *n.* **1.** a simpleton. **2.** (*slang*) the head. [orig. unkn.]

noodles /'nuːd(ə)lz/ *n.pl.* narrow strips of pasta used in soups etc. [f. G *nudel*]

nook /nʊk/ *n.* a secluded corner or recess. [orig. unkn.]

noon *n.* twelve o'clock in the day, midday. [OE, f. L *nona* (*hora*) ninth hour (as NONES)]

noonday *n.* midday.

noose *n.* a loop in a rope etc. with a running knot; a snare, a bond. —*v.t.* to catch with or enclose in a noose. [perh. f. OF *no(u)s* f. L *nodus* knot]

nor *conj.* and not; and not either. [contr. f. obs. *nother* (as NO[1], WHETHER)]

nor' *abbr.* north, esp. in compounds (*nor'ward, nor'wester*).

Nordic /'nɔːdɪk/ *adj.* **1.** of or belonging to an extremely artificial sub-racial grouping of people who, as a population, are tall, with fair colouring, and dolichocephalic. **2.** of Scandinavia, Finland, or Iceland. —*n.* a Nordic person. [f. F *nordique* (*nord* north)]

Norfolk /'nɔːfək/ a county of eastern England. —**Norfolk jacket,** a man's loose single-breasted belted jacket.

norm *n.* a standard, pattern, or type; a standard amount of work etc.; customary behaviour. [f. L *norma*, lit. = carpenter's square]

normal /'nɔːm(ə)l/ *adj.* **1.** conforming to what is standard or usual; typical. **2.** free from mental or emotional disorder. **3.** (of a line) at right angles, perpendicular. —*n.* **1.** the normal value of a temperature etc.; the usual state, level, etc. **2.** a line at right angles (ill. SHAPES). —**normalcy** *n.*, **normality** /-'mælɪtɪ/ *n.* [F or f. L *normalis* (as prec.)]

normalize *v.t./i.* to make or become normal; to cause to conform. —**normalization** /-'zeɪʃ(ə)n/ *n.* [f. prec.]

normally *adv.* **1.** in a normal manner. **2.** usually. [f. NORMAL]

Norman /'nɔːmən/ *n.* **1.** a native or inhabitant of Normandy, a descendant of a mixed Scandinavian and Frankish people established there in early medieval times. They were the dominant military power in western Europe in the 11th c., conquering England and setting up Norman kingdoms as far afield as Sicily, Greece, and the Holy Land. **2.** any of the kings of England from William I to Stephen. **3.** the style of architecture developed by the Normans and employed in England after the Conquest, with rounded arches and heavy pillars. —*adj.* of the Normans or their style of architecture. —**Norman Conquest,** see CONQUEST. **Norman French,** the form of medieval French spoken by the Normans; the later form of this in English legal use. [f. OF f. ON (as NORTH, MAN)]

Normandy /'nɔːməndɪ/ **1.** a region and former province of NW France with its coastline on the English Channel. It was given by Charles III of France to Rollo, first Duke of Normandy, in 912, and was contested between France and Britain throughout the Middle Ages until finally conquered by France in the mid-15th c. **2.** the name of the royal house including William I and II, Henry I, and Stephen, which ruled England from 1066 until 1154.

normative /'nɔːmətɪv/ *adj.* of or establishing a norm. [f. F f. L *norma* (as NORM)]

Norn *n.* (*Scand. myth.*) the personification of fate or destiny, usually in the form of a virgin goddess (Urd, Urdar, Verdandi, Skuld). [ON]

Norse *n.* **1.** the Norwegian language. **2.** the Scandinavian language group. —*adj.* of ancient Scandinavia, especially Norway. —**the Norse,** the Norwegians. **Old Norse,** the Germanic language of Norway and its colonies, or of Scandinavia, down to the 14th c. It is the ancestor of the Scandinavian languages and is most clearly preserved in the saga literature of Iceland. [f. Du. (*noord* north)]

Norseman /'nɔːsmən/ *n.* (*pl.* **-men**) a Viking.

north *n.* **1.** the point of the horizon corresponding to the compass point 90° anticlockwise from east; the direction in which this lies. **2.** (usu. **North**) the part of a country or town lying to the north. —*adj.* **1.** towards, at, near, or facing the north. **2.** (of wind) blowing from the north. —*adv.* towards, at, or near the north. —**North Atlantic Drift,** see GULF STREAM. **north country,** the northern part of England. **north-north-east** *n., adj., & adv.* midway between north and north-east. **north-north-west** *n., adj., & adv.* midway between north and north-west. **North Pole,** the northern end of the earth's axis of rotation. **North Star,** the pole-star (see POLARIS). [OE]

North America the northern half of the American land mass, connected to South America by the Isthmus of Panama, bordered by the Atlantic Ocean to the east and the Pacific Ocean to the west. (See AMERICA.) The southern part of the continent was colonized by the Spanish in the 16th c., while the eastern coast was opened up by the British and French in the 17th c., rivalry between the two ending in British victory during the Seven Years War. The American colonies won their independence in the American War of Independence (1775–83), while Canada was granted its own constitution in 1867. The 19th c. saw the gradual development of the western half of the continent, the emergence of Mexico as an independent State, and the growth of the United States as a world power. The USA has progressively dominated the continent, both economically and politically, Canada having a very small population relative to its size and Mexico sharing, albeit to a much lesser extent, the problems of its Central American neighbours to the south.

Northamptonshire /nɔː'θæmptənʃɪə(r)/ an east midland county of England.

Northants *abbr.* Northamptonshire.

North Carolina /kærə'laɪnə/ a State of the USA on the Atlantic coast, settled by the English and named after Charles I. It was one of the original 13 States of the USA (1788); capital, Raleigh.

Northcliffe /'nɔːθklɪf/, Alfred Charles William Harmsworth, Viscount (1865–1922), British newspaper proprietor. With his younger brother Harold (later Lord Rothermere), Northcliffe built up a large newspaper empire in the years preceding the First World War, including *The Times*, the *Daily Mail*, and the *Daily Mirror*. During the war he used his press empire to exercise a strong if at times erratic influence over British war policy and in 1918 was given control of overseas propaganda.

North Dakota /də'kəʊtə/ a State in the north central USA, bordering on Canada, acquired partly by the Louisiana Purchase in 1803 and partly from Britain by treaty in 1818. It became the 39th State of the USA in 1889; capital, Bismarck.

north-east *n.* **1.** the point midway between north and east; the direction in which this lies. **2.** (usu. **North-East**) the part of a country or town lying to the north-east. —*adj.* of, towards, or coming from the north-east. —*adv.* towards, at, or near the north-east. —**North-east passage,** a passage for vessels along the northern coasts of Europe and Asia, formerly thought of as a possible course by which to make voyages to the East. —**north-easterly** *adj. & adv.*, **north-eastern** *adj.*

northeaster /nɔː'θiːstə(r)/ *n.* a north-east wind. [f. prec.]

northerly /'nɔːðəlɪ/ *adj. & adv.* **1.** in a northern position or direction. **2.** (of wind) blowing from the north (approximately). [f. NORTH]

northern /'nɔːð(ə)n/ *adj.* of or in the north. —**Northern Cross,** CYGNUS. **northern lights,** the aurora borealis. —**northernmost** *adj.* [OE (as NORTH)]

northerner *n.* a native or inhabitant of the north. [f. NORTH]

Northern Ireland a unit of the UK comprising the six north-eastern counties of Ireland, established in 1920 when these withdrew from the newly constituted Irish Free State (see IRELAND); pop. (1981) 1,556,039. At first a self-governing province with its parliament meeting at Stormont Castle in Belfast, it was dominated by the Ulster Unionist party, opposed by an increasing Roman Catholic minority favouring union with the Irish Republic. Discrimination against the latter group in local government, employment, and housing led to violent conflicts and (from 1969) the presence of British army units to keep the peace. Continuing terrorist activities resulted in the suspension of the Stormont assembly and imposition of direct rule from Westminster. Attempts to organize an agreed and permanent system of government have so far met with failure.

Northern Territory a territory in central north Australia, the administration of which was taken over from South Australia by the Commonwealth of Australia in 1911; it became self-governing within the Commonwealth in 1978; capital, Darwin.

northing /'nɔːθɪŋ/ n. (Naut. etc.) 1. a distance travelled or measured northward. 2. a northerly direction. [f. NORTH]

Northman n. (pl. -men) a native of Scandinavia, especially of Norway.

North Sea that part of the Atlantic Ocean between the mainland of Europe and the east coast of Britain. Since 1960 it has become important for the exploitation of oil and gas deposits under the sea-bed.

Northumb. abbr. Northumberland.

Northumberland /nɔː'θʌmbələnd/ a county in the extreme north-east of England.

Northumbria /nɔː'θʌmbrɪə/ an ancient Anglo-Saxon kingdom extending from the Humber to the Forth. The name has been revived in 'Northumbria Authority', an area of police administration in NE England. —**Northumbrian** adj. & n.

northward /'nɔːθwəd/ adj. & (also **northwards** /-z/) adv. towards the north. —n. a northward direction or region. [f. NORTH + -WARD]

north-west n. 1. the point midway between north and west; the direction in which this lies. 2. (usu. **North-West**) the part of a country or town lying to the north-west. —adj. of, towards, or coming from the north-west. —adv. towards, at, or near the north-west. —**North-west passage**, a passage for vessels along the north coast of America, formerly thought of as a possible channel for navigation between the Atlantic and the Pacific, and sought by Sebastian Cabot and others. —**north-westerly** adj. & adv., **north-western** adj.

northwester /nɔː'θwestə(r)/ n. a north-west wind. [f. prec.]

Northwest Territories the part of Canada lying north of the 60th parallel, administered by the Hudson's Bay Company from 1670 and transferred by Britain to Canada in 1870.

Northwest Territory a region of the USA lying between the Mississippi and Ohio Rivers and the Great Lakes, acquired in 1783 after the War of American Independence.

North Yorkshire /'jɔːkʃɪə(r)/ a county of NE England.

Norway /'nɔːweɪ/ a country (its name means 'north way') occupying the northern and western part of the Scandinavian peninsula; pop. (est. 1983) 4,106,651; official language, Norwegian; capital, Oslo. An independent if often divided kingdom in Viking and early medieval times, Norway was united with Denmark and Sweden by the Union of Kolmar in 1397, and after the latter's departure in 1523, was reduced to little more than a Danish territory. Ceded to Sweden in 1814, it finally regained its independence in 1905, only to lose it for the period of the Nazi occupation of 1940-5. With a small population confined to a mountainous coastal strip, Norway is heavily dependent on foreign trade, although the opening up of the North Sea oil fields has recently benefited the economy greatly.

Norwegian /nɔː'wiːdʒ(ə)n/ adj. of Norway or its people or language. —n. 1. a native or inhabitant of Norway. 2. the official language of Norway, spoken by its 4 million inhabitants, which belongs to the Scandinavian language group. During the Middle Ages Danish gradually replaced Norwegian as the language of the upper classes in Norway, the peasants continuing to speak Norwegian, and there are still two separate forms of the modern language, Bokmål or Riksmål, the more widely used (also called Dano-Norwegian), a modified form of the Danish language used in Norway after its separation from Denmark (1814) following

four centuries of union, and Nynorsk (= new Norwegian, formerly called Landsmål), a literary form devised by the Norwegian philologist Ivar Aasen (d. 1896) from the country dialects most closely descended from Old Norse, and considered to be a purer form of the language than Bokmål. [f. L Norvegia Norway]

Nos. abbr. numbers. [cf. No.]

nose /nəʊz/ n. 1. the organ above the mouth on the face or head of a man or animal, used for smelling and breathing. 2. the sense of smell. 3. the ability to detect a particular thing. 4. an odour or perfume, e.g. of a wine. 5. the open end of a tube, pipe, etc.; the front end or projecting part of a thing, e.g. of a car or aircraft. 6. (slang) a police informer. —v.t./i. 1. to perceive a smell of; to discover by smell; to detect. 2. to thrust one's nose against or into. 3. to pry or search. 4. to make one's way cautiously forward. —**by a nose**, a very narrow margin. **keep one's nose clean**, to stay out of trouble. **pay through the nose**, to have to pay an exorbitant price. **put a person's nose out of joint**, to embarrass or disconcert him. **rub a person's nose in it**, to remind him humiliatingly of an error etc. **turn up one's nose**, to show disdain. **under one's nose**, right before one. **with one's nose in the air**, haughtily. [OE]

nosebag n. a bag containing fodder, hung on a horse's head.

noseband n. the lower band of a bridle passing over the horse's nose and attached to the cheek-straps (ill. HORSE).

nosebleed n. bleeding from the nose.

nose-cone n. the cone-shaped nose of a rocket etc.

nosedive n. a steep downward plunge by an aeroplane; a sudden plunge or drop. —v.i. to make a nosedive.

nosegay /'nəʊzgeɪ/ n. a small bunch of flowers. [f. NOSE + obs. gay ornament]

nosh v.t./i. (slang) to eat. —n. (slang) food, especially a snack. —**nosh up** n. (slang) a large meal. [Yiddish]

nostalgia /nɒ'stældʒɪə/ n. 1. sentimental yearning for the past. 2. homesickness. —**nostalgic** adj., **nostalgically** adv. [f. Gk nostos return home + algos pain]

Nostradamus /nɒstrə'deɪməs/ the Latinized name of Michel de Notredame (1503-66), Provençal astrologer whose extensive prophecies, decidedly apocalyptic in tone, were given extensive credence in the mid-16th c. at the French court, where he was for a time personal physician to Charles IX.

nostril /'nɒstrɪl/ n. either of the openings in the nose. [OE, = nose-hole]

nostrum /'nɒstrəm/ n. 1. a quack remedy, a patent medicine. 2. a pet scheme, especially for political or social reform. [L, = of our own make]

nosy /'nəʊzɪ/ adj. inquisitive, prying. —**Nosy Parker**, a busybody. —**nosily** adv., **nosiness** n. [f. NOSE]

not adv. expressing negation (also colloq. **-n't** as in don't, haven't); expressing denial or refusal, or used ellipt. for a negative phrase etc. —**not at all**, (in a polite reply to thanks) there is no need to thank me. [contr. of NOUGHT]

notable /'nəʊtəb(ə)l/ adj. worthy of notice, remarkable, eminent. —n. an eminent person. —**notability** /-'bɪlɪtɪ/ n., **notably** adv. [f. OF f. L notabilis (as NOTE)]

notary /'nəʊtərɪ/ n. (in full **notary public**) a person with the authority to draw up deeds and perform other legal formalities. —**notarial** /-'teərɪəl/ adj. [f. L, = secretary (as NOTE)]

notate /nəʊ'teɪt/ v.t. to write in notation. [back-formation f. foll.]

notation /nəʊ'teɪʃ(ə)n/ n. the representing of numbers, quantities, music sounds, etc., by symbols; any set of such symbols. [F or f. L (as NOTE)]

notch n. 1. a V-shaped cut or indentation. 2. a step in a graded system. —v.t. 1. to make a notch or notches in. 2. (often with up) to score (as) with notches. [f. AF]

note n. 1. a brief record of facts, topics, etc., written down to aid the memory. 2. a short or informal letter; a memorandum; a formal diplomatic communication. 3. a short comment on or explanation of a word or passage in a book etc. 4. a banknote. 5. a written promise of payment. 6. notice, attention; eminence. 7. a written sign representing the pitch and duration of a musical sound (ill. MUSICAL NOTATION); a single tone of definite pitch made by a musical instrument, a voice, etc.; a key of a piano etc. 8. a significant sound or feature of expression. 9. a characteristic, a distinguishing feature. —v.t. 1. to notice, to give attention to. 2. (often with down) to record as a thing to be remembered or observed. 3. (in p.p.) celebrated, well known for. —**hit**

or **strike the right note,** to speak or act in exactly the right manner. [f. OF f. L *nota* mark, *notare* to mark]

notebook *n.* a small book with blank pages in which to write memoranda.

notecase *n.* a wallet for holding bank-notes.

notelet /ˈnəʊtlɪt/ *n.* a small folded card or sheet for an informal letter.

notepaper *n.* paper for writing letters.

noteworthy *adj.* worthy of attention, remarkable.

nothing /ˈnʌθɪŋ/ *n.* **1.** no thing; not anything. **2.** a person or thing of no importance. **3.** non-existence, what does not exist. **4.** no amount, nought. —*adv.* not at all, in no way. —**for nothing,** at no cost, without payment; to no purpose. **have nothing on,** to be naked. **have nothing on (a person),** to possess no advantage over; to be much inferior to. **nothing doing,** (*colloq.*) no prospect of success or agreement. [OE (as NO¹, THING)]

nothingness *n.* **1.** non-existence. **2.** worthlessness, triviality. [f. prec.]

notice /ˈnəʊtɪs/ *n.* **1.** attention, observation; heed. **2.** news or information of what has happened or is about to happen; a warning. **3.** written or printed information or instructions displayed publicly. **4.** formal declaration of one's intention to end an agreement or leave employment at a specified time. **5.** an account or review in a newspaper or magazine. —*v.t.* **1.** to perceive, to become aware of. **2.** to remark upon. —**at short notice,** with little warning. **notice-board** *n.* a board for displaying notices. **take (no) notice,** to show (no) signs of interest. **take notice of,** to observe; to act upon. [f. OF f. L *notitia* being known (*notus* known)]

noticeable *adj.* **1.** noteworthy. **2.** perceptible. —**noticeably** *adv.* [f. prec.]

notifiable /ˈnəʊtɪfaɪəb(ə)l/ *adj.* (of a disease or pest etc.) that must be notified to a public authority [f. foll.]

notify /ˈnəʊtɪfaɪ/ *v.t.* **1.** to inform. **2.** to report; to make (a thing) known. —**notification** /-fɪˈkeɪʃ(ə)n/ *n.* [f. OF f. L *notificare* (as NOTICE)]

notion /ˈnəʊʃ(ə)n/ *n.* **1.** a concept or idea, a conception; a vague view or opinion. **2.** an understanding; an inclination; an intention. **3.** (in *pl.*, *US*) small items used in sewing, haberdashery. [f. L *notion* (as NOTICE)]

notional *adj.* hypothetical; imaginary. —**notionally** *adv.* [obs. F, or f. L (as prec.)]

notochord /ˈnəʊtəʊkɔːd/ *n.* a flexible longitudinal rod found at some stage of the life cycle of all chordates. In adult vertebrates its place is taken by the spinal column. [f. Gk *nōton* back + CHORD²]

notorious /nəʊˈtɔːrɪəs/ *adj.* well known, especially for an unfavourable reason. —**notoriety** /-təˈraɪɪtɪ/ *n.*, **notoriously** *adv.* [f. L (as NOTICE)]

Notre-Dame /nɒtrə ˈdɑːm/ the gothic cathedral church of Paris, dedicated to the Virgin Mary, on the Île de la Cité (an island in the Seine), begun in 1163 and effectively finished by 1250. It is especially noted for its innovatory flying buttresses, sculptured façade, and great rose windows with 13th-c. stained glass. [F, = our lady]

Nottinghamshire /ˈnɒtɪŋəmʃɪə(r)/ a midland county of England.

Notts. *abbr.* Nottinghamshire.

notwithstanding /nɒtwɪθˈstændɪŋ, -wɪð-/ *prep.* in spite of, without prevention by. —*adv.* nevertheless. [f. NOT + WITHSTAND]

Nouakchott /ˈnwækʃɒt/ the capital of Mauritania; pop. (1977) 135,000.

nougat /ˈnuːgɑː/ *n.* a sweet made from sugar or honey, nuts, and egg-white. [F f. Prov. (*noga* nut)]

nought /nɔːt/ *n.* **1.** the figure 0. **2.** (*poetic* or *archaic*) nothing. —**noughts and crosses,** a game in which two players seek to complete a row of three of either kind in a square array of usually nine spaces. [OE (*ne* not, AUGHT)]

noun /naʊn/ *n.* a word used as the name of a person, place, or thing. [f. AF f. L *nomen* name]

nourish /ˈnʌrɪʃ/ *v.t.* **1.** to sustain with food (*lit.* or *fig.*). **2.** to foster or cherish (a feeling etc.). [f. OF f. L (as NUTRIMENT)]

nourishing *adj.* containing much nourishment. [f. prec.]

nourishment *n.* **1.** sustenance, food. **2.** nourishing. [f. NOURISH]

nous /naʊs/ *n.* **1.** (*Philos.*) the mind or intellect. **2.** (*colloq.*) common sense. [Gk]

nouveau riche /nuːvəʊ ˈriːʃ/ (*pl.* **-x -s,** pr. same) one who has acquired wealth only recently, especially one who displays this ostentatiously. [F, = new rich]

Nov. *abbr.* November.

nova /ˈnəʊvə/ *n.* (*pl.* **-ae, -as**) a star showing a sudden large increase in brightness and then subsiding. The so-called 'new stars' of early astronomers, these are actually old stars which undergo a dramatic outburst, increasing in brightness by a factor of many thousands and returning to their original state over the space of a few months. They are classed as a type of cataclysmic variable, where material falling from a companion star to the surface of a white dwarf collects for several thousand years, increasing in density and temperature until it suddenly undergoes a runaway thermonuclear reaction, blasting much of the accumulated material back into space. Novae are often visible at peak brightness in small telescopes, and may sometimes become bright enough to be visible to the naked eye. [L, fem. of *novus* new]

Nova Scotia /nəʊvə ˈskəʊʃə/ a province of SE Canada, comprising a peninsula projecting into the Atlantic and the adjoining Cape Breton island. Settled by the French in the early 18th c. (see ACADIA) it changed hands several times between the French and English until ceded to Britain in 1713, becoming a province of Canada in 1867; capital, Halifax. —**Nova Scotian** *adj.* & *n.*

novel /ˈnɒv(ə)l/ *adj.* of a new kind, strange, hitherto unknown. —*n.* a fictitious prose story published as a complete book. [f. OF f. L *novellus* (as prec.)]

novelette /nɒvəˈlet/ *n.* a short novel. [f. prec. + -ETTE]

novelist /ˈnɒvəlɪst/ *n.* a writer of novels. [f. NOVEL]

novella /nəˈvelə/ *n.* a short novel or narrative story. [It. (as NOVEL)]

novelty /ˈnɒvəltɪ/ *n.* **1.** the quality of being novel. **2.** a novel thing or occurrence. **3.** a small unusual object. [f. OF (as NOVEL)]

November /nəʊˈvembə(r)/ *n.* the eleventh month of the year. [f. OF f. L (*novem* nine, because orig. the ninth month in the Roman calendar)]

novena /nəˈviːnə/ *n.* a Roman Catholic devotion consisting of special prayers or services on nine successive days. [L (*novem* nine)]

Noverre /nɒˈve(r)/, Jean-Georges (1727–1810), French dancer, choreographer, ballet master, and dance theorist, a great reformer who stressed the dramatic mission of the ballet.

novice /ˈnɒvɪs/ *n.* **1.** a probationary member of a religious order. **2.** a new convert. **3.** an inexperienced person, a beginner. [f. OF f. L *novicius* (as NOVA)]

noviciate /nəˈvɪʃɪət/ *n.* (also **novitiate**) **1.** the period of being a novice. **2.** a religious novice. **3.** novices' quarters. [f. F or L (as prec.)]

now *adv.* **1.** at the present or mentioned time. **2.** by this time. **3.** immediately. **4.** on this further occasion. **5.** in the present circumstances. **6.** (without reference to time, giving various tones to a sentence) surely, I insist, I wonder, etc. —*conj.* (also with *that*) as a consequence of the fact. —*n.* this time, the present. —**for now,** until a later time. **now and again** *or* **then,** from time to time, intermittently. [OE]

nowadays /ˈnaʊədeɪz/ *adv.* at the present time or age, in these times. —*n.* the present time. [f. NOW + A³ + DAY]

nowhere /ˈnəʊweə(r)/ *adv.* in or to no place. —*pron.* no place. —**get nowhere,** to make no progress. **nowhere near,** not nearly. [OE (as NO¹, WHERE)]

nowt *n.* (*colloq.* or *dial.*) nothing. [var. of NOUGHT]

noxious /ˈnɒkʃəs/ *adj.* harmful, unwholesome. [f. L *noxius* (*noxa* harm)]

nozzle *n.* the spout of a hose etc. for a jet to issue from. [dim. of NOSE]

Np *symbol* neptunium.

npn *abbr.* in which a p-type layer occurs between two n-type layers.

nr. *abbr.* near.

NS *abbr.* New Style. **2.** new series. **3.** Nova Scotia.

NSPCC *abbr.* National Society for the Prevention of Cruelty to Children (incorporated in 1884).

NSW *abbr.* New South Wales.

n't see NOT.

NT *abbr.* **1.** New Testament. **2.** (*Austral.*) Northern Territory.

n-type *adj.* (of a semiconductor device or a region in this) having negative carriers of electricity.

nu /nju:/ *n.* the thirteenth letter of the Greek alphabet, = n. [Gk]

nuance /'nju:ãs/ *n.* a subtle difference in or shade of meaning, feeling, colour, etc. [F (*nuer* to shade)]

nub *n.* **1.** (also **nubble**) a small lump, especially of coal. **2.** the central point or core of a matter or problem etc. —**nubbly** *adj.* [app. var. of *knub* knob]

Nubia /'nju:bɪə/ a region of southern Egypt and northern Sudan which includes the Nile valley between Aswan and Khartoum and the Nubian Desert to the east. Nubia fell under ancient Egyptian rule from the time of the Middle Kingdom, soon after 2,000 BC, and from about the 15th c. BC was ruled by an Egyptian viceroy. The country was Egyptianized, and trade (especially in gold) flourished. By the 8th c. BC, however, as Egypt's centralized control disintegrated, a Nubian kingdom emerged, and for a brief period extended its power over Egypt. Much of Nubia is now drowned by the waters of Lake Nasser, formed by the building of the two dams at Aswan. Nubians constitute an ethnic minority group in Egypt. —**Nubian** *adj.* & *n.*

nubile /'nju:baɪl/ *adj.* (of a woman) marriageable, sexually attractive. —**nubility** /-'bɪlɪtɪ/ *n.* [f. L (*nubere* become wife of)]

nuclear /'nju:klɪə(r)/ *adj.* **1.** of or constituting a nucleus. **2.** using nuclear energy. —**nuclear energy,** energy released or absorbed during reactions (nuclear fission or fusion) taking place in atomic nuclei. **nuclear family,** a father, mother, and their child or children. **nuclear fission,** see separate entry. **nuclear fuel,** a source of nuclear energy. **nuclear fusion,** see separate entry. **nuclear physics,** physics dealing with atomic nuclei and their reactions. **nuclear power,** power derived from nuclear energy; a country possessing nuclear weapons. **nuclear reactor,** see separate entry. **nuclear weapon,** a bomb or warhead deriving its destructive power from the rapid uncontrolled release of nuclear energy. **nuclear winter,** a conjectural period of changed climatic conditions following a nuclear war, characterized by extreme cold temperatures and other effects catastrophic to animal and vegetable life, caused by an atmospheric layer of smoke and dust particles blocking the sun's rays. [f. NUCLEUS]

nuclear fission the splitting of an atomic nucleus into smaller nuclei of roughly equal size, with consequent release of energy, discovered in 1938 by two German chemists, Otto Hahn and F. Strassmann. It can occur either spontaneously or after the impact of another particle. The principal elements capable of undergoing fission are plutonium, uranium, and thorium.

nuclear fusion the union of atomic nuclei to form heavier nuclei. For the lighter elements this process results in an enormous release of energy, but it can occur only at very high temperatures. The sun's energy arises mainly from the conversion of its hydrogen into helium by fusion. This is also the principle behind the hydrogen bomb, the necessary high temperatures being created by an initial atomic explosion. Research continues into harnessing fusion so that it can be used in power stations, the major obstacle being how to contain the reacting substances, whose temperatures can rise to millions of degrees Celsius.

nuclearize /'nju:klɪəraɪz/ *v.t.* to supply or equip (a nation) with nuclear weapons. —**nuclearization** /-'zeɪʃ(ə)n/ *n.* [f. NUCLEAR]

nuclear reactor an assembly of fissile and other materials (e.g. moderators) in which a controlled chain reaction can take place, the peaceful application of the chain reaction that was first used in the atomic bomb. The heat obtained when a reactor is in operation is continually carried away to where it can be used in a boiler to generate electrical power. Some reactors are involved in the production of radioactive material for medical and other purposes. The first atomic 'pile' or reactor was built by the physicist Enrico Fermi at the University of Chicago in 1942.

nucleate /'nju:klɪeɪt/ *v.t./i.* **1.** to form (into) a nucleus. **2.** (in *p.p.*) possessing a nucleus. [f. L (as NUCLEUS)]

nucleic acid /nju:'kli:ɪk/ either of two acids (DNA and RNA) present in all living cells. [f. NUCLEUS]

nucleon /'nju:klɪɒn/ *n.* a proton or neutron; a particle of which these are regarded as different states. [f. NUCLEUS]

nucleonic /nju:klɪ'ɒnɪk/ *adj.* of nucleons or nucleonics. —**nucleonics** *n.pl.* (usu. treated as *sing.*) the branch of science and technology concerned with atomic nuclei and nucleons, especially the practical use of nuclear phenomena. [f. NUCLEAR & f. prec., after *electronics*]

nucleoprotein /nju:klɪəʊ'prəʊti:n/ *n.* a compound of a protein with nucleic acid. [f. NUCLEUS + PROTEIN]

nucleosynthesis /nju:klɪəʊ'sɪnθɪsɪs/ *n.* the formation of atoms more complicated than the hydrogen atom by cosmic processes. [f. NUCLEUS + SYNTHESIS]

nucleus /'nju:klɪəs/ *n.* (*pl.* **nuclei** /-laɪ/) **1.** the central part or thing around which others collect; the central part of an atom (see below), of a seed, or of a plant or animal cell. **2.** a kernel, an initial part meant to receive additions. [L, = kernel (*nux* nut)]

Ernest Rutherford in 1911 and afterwards established that the positive charge and most of the mass of each atom is concentrated in a volume which is about 1/10,000 of the diameter of the atom as a whole. He called this dense core the atomic 'nucleus' in 1912; its diameter is approximately 10^{-13} cm. Subsequent research established that the nucleus consists of protons and neutrons only, bound together by very powerful forces which do not extend significantly beyond the nucleus itself. The nucleus can vibrate, rotate, and alter its shape, properties which can be recognized through energy changes and by means of various other phenomena.

nude /nju:d/ *adj.* naked, bare, unclothed. —*n.* a picture or sculpture etc. of a nude human figure; a nude person. —**in the nude,** in an unclothed state, naked. —**nudity** *n.* [f. L *nudus*]

nudge *v.t./i.* **1.** to prod gently with the elbow to attract attention. **2.** to push gradually. —*n.* such a prod or push. [orig. unkn.]

nudist /'nju:dɪst/ *n.* a person who advocates or practises going unclothed. —**nudism** *n.* [f. NUDE]

Nuer /'nu:ə(r)/ *n.* (*pl.* same) a member or the language of an African people living in south-eastern Sudan. —*adj.* of this people or their language. [native name]

Nuffield /'nʌfi:ld/, William Richard Morris, 1st Viscount (1877-1963), the most influential British motor manufacturer, a good engineer and a good business man. Working in Oxford, he started (like most early car-makers) by building bicycles. He made his first car in 1913 and afterwards introduced automobile mass-manufacture to Britain in his Oxford factory. In later life he devoted his considerable fortune to philanthropic purposes, and the University of Oxford in particular has benefited greatly, both in the provision of hospital buildings and in the endowment of chairs of medicine and surgery; his name is also preserved in Nuffield College which he endowed for the study of social sciences.

nugatory /'nju:gətərɪ/ *adj.* **1.** futile, trifling. **2.** inoperative, not valid. [f. L (*nugari* to trifle)]

nugget /'nʌgɪt/ *n.* **1.** a lump of gold etc. as found in the earth. **2.** something valuable. [f. dial. *nug* lump]

nuisance /'nju:s(ə)ns/ *n.* a source of trouble or annoyance; an annoying person, thing, or circumstance. [f. OF, = hurt (*nuire* to hurt)]

nuke /nju:k/ *n.* (*slang*, esp. *US*) a nuclear bomb, weapon, etc. [abbr. NUCLEAR]

Nuku'alofa /nu:ku:ə'lɔʊfə/ the capital of Tonga; pop. 21,000.

null *adj.* **1.** void, not valid. **2.** characterless, expressionless. **3.** non-existent. —**nullity** *n.* [f. F or L *nullus* none]

nullify /'nʌlɪfaɪ/ *v.t.* to neutralize, to invalidate. —**nullification** /-'keɪʃ(ə)n/ *n.* [f. NULL]

Numa Pompilius /'nju:mə pɒm'pɪlɪəs/ the legendary second king of Rome, successor to Romulus, revered by the ancient Romans as the founder of nearly all their religious institutions.

numb /nʌm/ *adj.* deprived of feeling or the power of motion. —*v.t.* to make numb; to stupefy, to paralyse. —**numbly** *adv.,* **numbness** *n.* [f. *nome* p.p. of obs. *nim* take (as NIMBLE)]

numbat /'nʌmbæt/ *n.* the banded anteater *Myrmecobius fasciatus,* a small rare marsupial native to SW Australia. [Aboriginal]

number *n.* **1.** a count, sum, or aggregate of persons, things, or abstract units (see below). **2.** an arithmetical value showing position in a series; a symbol or figure representing this. **3.** a person or thing having a place in a series; a single issue of a magazine; an item in a programme etc. **4.** numerical reckoning. **5.** a company, a collection, a group. **6.** (in *pl.*) numerical preponderance. **7.** (*Gram.*) the class of word-forms including all singular, all plural, or all dual etc. forms. **8. Numbers,** the fourth book of the Old Testament, relating the experiences of the Israelites under Moses during their wanderings in the desert. The English title is explained by its two records of a census; its Hebrew title means 'in the wilderness'. —*v.t.* **1.** to count. **2.** to assign a number or numbers to. **3.** to have or amount to a specified number. **4.** to include as a member of a class. **5.** (in *pass.*) to be restricted in number. —**by numbers,** following simple instructions identified by numbers. **have a person's number,** (*slang*) to understand him or his motives. **one's number is up,** (*colloq.*) one is doomed to die. **number one,** (*colloq.*) oneself; the most important. **number-plate** *n.* a plate on a vehicle giving the registration number. **without number,** innumerable. [f. AF f. L *numerus*]

Numbers are mathematical abstractions originally (and still mainly) used for counting and measurement. Natural numbers, also known as positive integers, are the numbers 1, 2, 3,... (sometimes 0 is also included) used in counting. Integers are natural numbers, 0, and their negatives -1, -2, -3,.... Rational numbers are the fractions p/q (where p and q are integers and q is not 0). Real numbers are the numbers used in measurement; they are limits of sequences of rational numbers; usually described by decimal expansions that go on for ever. Complex numbers are numbers of the form $a + bi$ in which a and b are real numbers and i is an imagined square root of -1. Note the hierarchy: all natural numbers are integers, all integers are rational numbers, all rational numbers are real numbers, all real numbers are complex numbers. Algebraic numbers are those (complex numbers) that are roots of polynomial equations with integer coefficients; transcendental numbers are the complex numbers that are not algebraic. Transfinite numbers are the cardinal and ordinal numbers assigned to infinite sets in Cantor's set theory.

numberless *adj.* innumerable. [f. prec. + -LESS]

numerable /ˈnjuːmərəb(ə)l/ *adj.* countable. [f. L (as NUMBER)]

numeral /ˈnjuːmər(ə)l/ *n.* a symbol denoting a number. —*adj.* of or denoting a number. [f. L (as NUMBER)]

numerate /ˈnjuːmərət/ *adj.* acquainted with the basic principles of mathematics and science. —**numeracy** *n.* [f. L *numerus* number, after *literate*]

numeration /njuːməˈreɪʃ(ə)n/ *n.* a method or process of numbering; calculation. [f. L (as NUMBER)]

numerator /ˈnjuːməreɪtə(r)/ *n.* the number above the line in a vulgar fraction showing how many of the parts indicated by the denominator are taken. [f. F or L (as NUMBER)]

numerical /njuːˈmerɪk(ə)l/ *adj.* of, in, or denoting a number or numbers. —**numerically** *adv.* [f. L (as NUMBER)]

numerology /njuːməˈrɒlədʒɪ/ *n.* the study of the occult significance of numbers. [f. L *numerus* number + -LOGY]

numerous /ˈnjuːmərəs/ *adj.* many; consisting of many. [f. L *numerosus* (as prec.)]

Numidia /njuːˈmɪdɪə/ an ancient kingdom (later a Roman province) in North Africa, east of Mauretania and west of Carthage, now part of Algeria. —**Numidian** *adj. & n.*

numinous /ˈnjuːmɪnəs/ *adj.* indicating the presence of a divinity; spiritual, awe-inspiring. [f. L (*numen* deity)]

numismatic /njuːmɪzˈmætɪk/ *adj.* of coins or coinage or medals. —**numismatist** /-ˈmɪzmətɪst/ *n.* [f. F f. L f. Gk *nomisma* current coin]

numismatics *n.pl.* (usu. treated as *sing.*) the study of coins or medals. [f. prec.]

numskull *n.* a stupid person. [f. NUMB + SKULL]

nun *n.* a member of a community of women living apart under religious vows. [OE & f. OF f. L *nonna*]

Nunc dimittis /nʌŋk ˈdɪmɪtɪs/ the canticle beginning thus (L, = 'Lord, now lettest thou thy servant depart'), the first words of the Song of Simeon (Luke 2: 29).

nuncio /ˈnʌnʃɪəʊ/ *n.* (*pl.* **-os**) an ambassador of the pope, accredited to a civil government. [It., f. L *nuntius* messenger]

nunnery *n.* a convent of nuns. [as NUN]

nuptial /ˈnʌpʃ(ə)l/ *adj.* of marriage or a wedding. —*n.* (usu. in *pl.*) a wedding. [F or f. L (*nuptiae* wedding)]

Nuremberg /ˈnjʊərəmbɜːɡ/ a city of Bavaria in West Germany, a leading cultural centre in the 15th and 16th c. Nazi party congresses were held here in the 1930s, as were the trials of war criminals at the end of the Second World War.

Nureyev /ˈnjʊərief, njʊˈreɪef/, Rudolf (1939-), Russian ballet-dancer, who defected to the West in 1961. A dancer of dazzling virtuosity and vigorous but controlled expressiveness, he has taken the leading roles of the classical and standard modern repertory and created others, particularly

in a noted partnership with Margot Fonteyn. He has also choreographed and staged a number of works.

nurse *n.* **1.** a person trained to assist doctors in caring for the sick or infirm. **2.** a woman employed to take charge of young children. —*v.t./i.* **1.** to work as a nurse; to attend to (a sick person). **2.** to feed or be fed at the breast. **3.** to hold or treat carefully. **4.** to foster, to promote the development of; to pay special attention to. —**nursing home,** a privately run hospital or home for invalids, old people, etc. [f. OF *norice* f. L (as NOURISH)]

nurseling *n.* (also **nursling**) an infant that is being suckled. [f. prec.]

nursemaid *n.* a young woman employed to take charge of a child or children.

nursery /ˈnɜːsərɪ/ *n.* **1.** a room or place equipped for young children; a day nursery. **2.** a place where plants are reared for sale. —**nursery rhyme,** a simple traditional song or story in rhyme for children. **nursery school,** a school for children below normal school age. **nursery slopes,** slopes suitable for beginners at skiing. [as NURSE]

nurseryman *n.* (*pl.* **-men**) an owner of or a worker in a plant nursery.

nurture /ˈnɜːtʃə(r)/ *n.* **1.** bringing up, fostering care. **2.** nourishment. —*v.t.* to bring up, to rear. [f. OF *nour(e)ture* (as NOURISH)]

Nut /nʊt/ (*Egyptian myth.*) the sky-goddess, thought to swallow the sun at night and give birth to it in the morning. She is usually depicted as a naked woman, with her body arched above the earth which she touches with her feet and hands.

nut *n.* **1.** a fruit consisting of a hard or tough shell round an edible kernel; this kernel. **2.** a pod containing hard seeds. **3.** a small usually hexagonal piece of metal with a hole through it screwed on the end of a bolt to secure it. **4.** (*slang*) the head. **5.** (*slang*) a crazy person. **6.** a small lump (of coal etc.). —*v.i.* (**-tt-**) to seek or gather nuts. —**do one's nut,** (*slang*) to be very angry. **nut-case** *n.* (*slang*) a crazy person. **nuts and bolts,** the practical details. **nut-tree** *n.* a tree bearing nuts, especially the hazel. [OE]

nutation /njuːˈteɪʃ(ə)n/ *n.* **1.** nodding. **2.** the oscillation of the earth's axis. [f. L (*nutare* nod)]

nutcracker *n.* (usu. in *pl.*) an instrument for cracking nuts. —**Nutcracker man,** a nickname for the fossil hominid *Australopithecus boisei*, especially the specimen discovered at Olduvai, Tanzania, in 1959. Similar remains, including the characteristic large premolar teeth, have also been found in South Africa.

nuthatch /ˈnʌthætʃ/ *n.* a small climbing bird (*Sitta europaea*) feeding on nuts, insects, etc.

nutmeg *n.* the hard aromatic seed of an East Indian tree (*Myristica fragrans*), ground or grated as a spice. [partial transl. of OF *nois mug(u)ede* musky nut]

nutria /ˈnjuːtrɪə/ *n.* the skin or fur of the coypu. [Sp., = otter]

nutrient /ˈnjuːtrɪənt/ *adj.* serving as or providing nourishment. —*n.* a nutrient substance. [f. L *nutrire* nourish]

nutriment /ˈnjuːtrɪmənt/ *n.* nourishing food (*lit.* or *fig.*). [f. L *nutrimentum* (as prec.)]

nutrition /njuːˈtrɪʃ(ə)n/ *n.* food, nourishment. —**nutritional** *adj.*, **nutritionally** *adv.* [F or f. L (as NUTRIENT)]

nutritious /njuːˈtrɪʃəs/ *adj.* efficient as food. —**nutritiously** *adv.*, **nutritiousness** *n.* [f. L (as NURSE)]

nutritive /ˈnjuːtrɪtɪv/ *adj.* of nutrition; nutritious. [f. F f. L (as NUTRIENT)]

nuts *adj.* (*slang*) crazy, mad. —**nuts about** or **on,** (*slang*) very fond of or enthusiastic about. [pl. of NUT]

nutshell *n.* the hard exterior covering of a nut. —**in a nutshell,** in a few words.

nutter *n.* (*slang*) a crazy person. [f. NUT]

nutty *adj.* **1.** full of nuts. **2.** tasting like nuts. **3.** (*slang*) crazy. —**nuttily** *adv.*, **nuttiness** *n.* [f. NUT]

nux vomica /nʌks ˈvɒmɪkə/ the seed of an East Indian tree (*Strychnos nux-vomica*), yielding strychnine. [L (*nux* nut, as VOMIT)]

nuzzle *v.t./i.* **1.** to press or rub gently with the nose. **2.** to nestle, to lie snug. [f. NOSE]

NW *abbr.* North-West, North-Western.

NY *abbr.* New York.

Nyerere /njeˈreərɪ/, Julius Kambarage (1922-), African statesman who became the first premier of Tanganyika following its independence in 1961 and President a year later. In 1964 he successfully negotiated a union with

Zanzibar and remained President of the new State of Tanzania until his retirement in 1985.

nylon /'naɪlɒn/ *n.* **1.** a strong light synthetic polymer that may be produced as filaments, bristles, or sheets and as moulded objects (see below). **2.** fabric made from nylon yarn. **3.** (in *pl.*) nylon stockings. [invented word, with *-on* suggested by *cotton* and *rayon*; there is no evidence to support the derivations frequently given for this word in popular sources]

Nylon was devised by the American chemist W. H. Carothers, of the du Pont chemical company; its production was announced in 1938. Unlike natural fibres it is resistant to destruction by bacteria, fungus, insects, or rodents, and is widely used for textile fabrics and in industry.

nymph /nɪmf/ *n.* **1.** a mythological semi-divine maiden of the sea, woods, etc. **2.** (*poetic*) a maiden. **3.** an immature insect which from the time of hatching has a general resemblance to the adult. [f. OF f. L f. Gk *numphē*]

nymphet /'nɪmfet, -'fet/ *n.* **1.** a young nymph. **2.** a nymph-like or sexually attractive girl. [f. prec.]

nympho /'nɪmfəʊ/ *n.* (*pl.* **-os**) (*colloq.*) a nymphomaniac. [abbr.]

nymphomania /nɪmfəʊ'meɪnɪə/ *n.* excessive sexual desire in women. —**nymphomaniac** *n.* [NYMPH + -MANIA]

nystagmus /nɪ'stægməs/ *n.* continual rapid oscillation of the eyeballs; an eye-disease characterized by this. [f. Gk *nustagmos* nodding (*nustazō* nod)]

NZ *abbr.* New Zealand.

O

O¹, o /əʊ/ n. (pl. **Os, O's**) the fifteenth letter of the alphabet; (as a numeral, in telephone numbers etc.) nought, zero.

O² /əʊ/ int. prefixed to a name in the vocative or expressing a wish, entreaty, etc. [natural excl.]

O symbol oxygen.

o' /ə/ prep. of, on (esp. in phrases, e.g. o'clock, will-o'-the-wisp). [abbr.]

oaf n. (pl. **oafs**) an awkward lout. —**oafish** adj. [f. ON (as ELF)]

oak n. a forest tree (Quercus robur or Q. petraea) with hard wood, acorns, and lobed leaves (ill. TREES); its wood; an allied or similar tree; (attrib.) of oak. —**oak-apple** or **oak-gall** n. = gall³. **Oak-apple Day,** 29 May, the day of Charles II's restoration in 1660, on which oak-apples or oak-leaves were worn in memory of the royal-oak incident (see ROYAL). **the Oaks,** an annual horse-race for 3-year-old fillies run at Epsom in Surrey, England, over the same course as the Derby and three days after it. It was first run in 1779, and is named after the 12th Earl of Derby's shooting-box, 'The Oaks'. —**oaken** adj. [OE]

oakum /ˈəʊkəm/ n. loose fibre obtained by picking old rope to pieces. [OE, = off-combings]

OAP abbr. old-age pension(er).

oar /ɔ:(r)/ n. **1.** a pole with a blade used to propel a boat by leverage against the water. **2.** a rower. —**put one's oar in,** to interfere. [OE]

oarsman n. (pl. **-men**) a rower. —**oarsmanship** n., **oarswoman** n.fem.

OAS abbr. Organization of American States, an association of American countries founded in 1948 to work for peace and prosperity in the region and to uphold the sovereignty of member nations. Its headquarters are in Washington, DC.

oasis /əʊˈeɪsɪs/ n. (pl. **oases** /-iːz/) **1.** a fertile spot in the desert, with a spring or well of water. **2.** a thing or circumstance offering relief in difficulty. [L f. Gk, app. of Egyptian orig.]

oast n. a kiln for drying hops. —**oast-house** n. a building containing this. [OE]

oat n. **1.** (in pl.) a hardy cereal (Avena sativa) grown as food; the grain yielded by this. **2.** an oat-plant or a variety of it. —**off one's oats,** (colloq.) lacking appetite for food. —**oaten** adj. [OE]

oatcake n. a thin unleavened cake made of oatmeal.

Oates /əʊts/, Titus (1649-1705), Protestant clergyman, fabricator of the Popish Plot, which he 'discovered' while serving as chaplain to the Protestant servants of the Catholic Duke of Norfolk. He was condemned and imprisoned for perjury, but subsequently released and granted a pension.

oath n. (pl. /əʊðz/) **1.** a solemn declaration or undertaking naming God or a revered object as witness. **2.** casual use of the name of God etc. in anger or emphasis; an obscenity. —**on** or **under oath,** having made a solemn oath. [OE]

oatmeal n. meal made from oats.

OAU abbr. Organization of African Unity, an association of African States founded in 1963 for mutual co-operation and the elimination of colonialism.

ob- prefix (usu. **oc-** before c, **of-** before f, **op-** before p) esp. in words from Latin, expressing exposure, meeting, facing, direction, compliance, opposition, resistance, hindrance, concealment, finality, completeness. [L (ob towards, against, in the way of)]

ob. abbr. he or she died. [f. L obiit]

Obadiah /əʊbəˈdaɪə/ **1.** a Hebrew minor prophet. **2.** the shortest book of the Old Testament, bearing his name.

obbligato /ɒblɪˈɡɑːtəʊ/ n. (pl. **-os**) (Mus.) a part or accompaniment forming an integral part of a composition. [It., = obligatory]

obdurate /ˈɒbdjʊərət/ adj. hardened, stubborn. —**obduracy** n. [f. L (OB-, durare harden f. durus hard)]

OBE abbr. Officer of the Order of the British Empire.

obedient /əʊˈbiːdɪənt/ adj. obeying, ready to obey; submiss-ive to another's will. —**obedience** n., **obediently** adv. [f. OF f. L (as OBEY)]

obeisance /əʊˈbeɪsəns/ n. a bow, curtsey, or other respectful gesture; homage. —**obeisant** adj. [f. OF (as OBEY)]

obelisk /ˈɒbəlɪsk/ n. a tapering usually four-sided stone pillar as a monument. [f. L f. Gk (dim. of foll.)]

obelus /ˈɒbələs/ n. (pl. **-li** /-laɪ/) a dagger-shaped mark of reference (†). [L f. Gk, = spit]

Oberammergau /əʊbəˈræməɡaʊ/ a village in the Bavarian Alps of SW Germany, site of the most famous of the few surviving Passion plays. It has been performed every tenth year (with few exceptions) from 1634 as a result of a vow made during an epidemic of plague, and remains entirely amateur, the villagers dividing the parts among themselves and being responsible also for the production, music, costumes, and scenery.

obese /əʊˈbiːs/ adj. very fat. —**obesity** n. [f. L, = having eaten oneself fat (OB-, edere eat)]

obey /əʊˈbeɪ/ v.t./i. **1.** to do what is commanded by. **2.** to be obedient. **3.** to be actuated by (a force or impulse). [f. OF f. L obedire (OB-, audire hear)]

obfuscate /ˈɒbfʌskeɪt/ v.t. **1.** to obscure or confuse (the mind, a topic, etc.). **2.** to stupefy, to bewilder. —**obfuscation** /-ˈkeɪʃ(ə)n/ n. [f. L (OB-, fuscus dark)]

obituary /əˈbɪtjʊərɪ/ n. a notice of a person's death especially in a newspaper, often with an account of the life of the deceased person. —adj. of or serving as an obituary. [f. L (obitus death)]

object /ˈɒbdʒɪkt/ n. **1.** a material thing that can be seen or touched. **2.** a person or thing to which an action or feeling is directed. **3.** a thing sought or aimed at. **4.** (Gram.) a noun or its equivalent governed by an active transitive verb or by a preposition. **5.** (Philos.) a thing external to the thinking mind or subject. —/əbˈdʒekt/ v.t./i. **1.** to express opposition; to feel or express dislike or reluctance. **2.** to adduce as contrary or damaging. —**no object,** not forming an important or restricting factor. **object-glass** n. the lens in a telescope etc. nearest to the object observed. **object-lesson** n. a striking practical example of some principle. —**objector** /əbˈdʒektə(r)/ n. [f. L (OB-, jacere throw)]

objectify /ɒbˈdʒektɪfaɪ/ v.t. **1.** to make objective. **2.** to embody. [f. prec.]

objection /əbˈdʒekʃ(ə)n/ n. **1.** a feeling of disapproval or opposition; a statement of this. **2.** a reason for objecting; a drawback in a plan etc. [f. OF or L (as OBJECT)]

objectionable adj. open to objection; unpleasant, offensive. —**objectionably** adv. [f. prec.]

objective /əbˈdʒektɪv/ adj. **1.** external to the mind, actually existing. **2.** dealing with outward things or exhibiting facts uncoloured by feelings or opinions. **3.** (Gram., of a case or word) constructed as or appropriate to the object. **4.** aimed at. —n. **1.** something sought or aimed at. **2.** (Gram.) the objective case. **3.** an object-glass. —**objectively** adv., objectivity /ɒbdʒekˈtɪvɪtɪ/ n. [f. L (as OBJECT)]

objet d'art /ɒbʒeɪ ˈdɑː(r)/ (pl. **objets d'art** pr. same) a small decorative object. [F, = object of art]

objurgate /ˈɒbdʒɜːɡeɪt/ v.t. (literary) to rebuke, to scold. —**objurgation** /-ˈɡeɪʃ(ə)n/ n. [f. L objurgare quarrel (OB-, jurgium strife)]

oblate /ˈɒbleɪt, əˈbleɪt/ adj. (of a spheroid) flattened at the poles. [f. OB- + -late (as in PROLATE)]

oblation /əˈbleɪʃ(ə)n/ n. a thing offered to a divine being. [f. OF or L (as OFFER)]

obligate /ˈɒblɪɡeɪt/ v.t. (usu. in p.p.) to oblige (a person legally or morally) to do a thing. [f. L (as OBLIGE)]

obligatory /əˈblɪɡətərɪ/ adj. required by law, contract, or custom etc., not optional. —**obligatorily** adv. [f. L (as foll.)]

obligation /ɒblɪˈɡeɪʃ(ə)n/ n. **1.** being obliged to do something; the compelling power of a law, contract, duty, etc. **2.** a duty, a task one must perform. **3.** indebtedness for a service or benefit. —**under (an) obligation,** owing gratitude. [f. OF f. L (as OBLIGE)]

oblige /əˈblaɪdʒ/ v.t./i. **1.** to compel by law, contract, custom etc., or necessity. **2.** to help or gratify by performing a small service. —**be obliged to a person**, to be indebted or grateful to him. **much obliged**, thank you. [f. OF f. L *obligare* (OB-, *ligare* bind)]

obliging *adj.* courteous and helpful, accommodating. —**obligingly** *adv.* [f. prec.]

oblique /ə'bli:k/ *adj.* **1.** declining from the vertical or horizontal, diverging from a straight line or course. **2.** not going straight to the point, roundabout, indirect. **3.** (*Gram.*, of a case) other than the nominative or vocative. —*n.* an oblique stroke (/). —**obliquely** *adv.*, **obliquity** /ə'blɪkwɪtɪ/ *n.* [f. F f. L *obliquus*]

obliterate /ə'blɪtəreɪt/ *v.t.* to blot out, to destroy and leave no clear traces of. —**obliteration** /-'reɪʃ(ə)n/ *n.*, **obliterator** *n.* [f. L *oblit(t)erare* erase (OB-, *litera* letter)]

oblivion /ə'blɪvɪən/ *n.* **1.** the state of being forgotten. **2.** the state of being oblivious. [f. OF f. L *oblivisci* forget)]

oblivious /ə'blɪvɪəs/ *adj.* unaware or unconscious (with *of* or *to*). [f. L (as prec.)]

oblong /'ɒblɒŋ/ *adj.* of a rectangular shape with adjacent sides unequal. —*n.* an oblong figure or object. [f. L, orig. = somewhat long]

obloquy /'ɒbləkwɪ/ *n.* **1.** abuse intended to damage a person's reputation. **2.** discredit brought by this. [f. L *obloquium* contradiction (OB-, *loqui* speak)]

obnoxious /əb'nɒkʃəs/ *adj.* offensive, objectionable, disliked. —**obnoxiously** *adv.* [f. L (OB-, *noxa* hard)]

oboe /'əʊbəʊ/ *n.* **1.** a double-reed wood-wind instrument of treble pitch, with a range of over two-and-a-half octaves, developed in France in the 17th c. (ill. ORCHESTRA). **2.** its player. **3.** an organ reed-stop of similar quality. —**oboist** /-'bəʊɪst/ *n.* [f. F *hautbois* (*haut* high, *bois* wood)]

obscene /əb'si:n/ *adj.* offensively indecent; (*Law*, of a publication) tending to deprave or corrupt; (*colloq.*) highly offensive. —**obscenely** *adv.*, **obscenity** /-'senɪtɪ/ *n.* [f. F or L *obsc(a)enus*, orig. = ill-omened]

obscure /əb'skjʊə(r)/ *adj.* **1.** not clearly expressed, not easily understood. **2.** dark, indistinct. **3.** hidden, unnoticed; (of a person) undistinguished, hardly known. —*v.t.* to make obscure or unintelligible; to conceal. —**obscurely** *adv.*, **obscurity** *n.* [f. OF f. L *obscurus*]

obsequies /'ɒbsɪkwɪz/ *n.pl.* funeral rites. [f. AF f. L *obsequiae*]

obsequious /əb'si:kwɪəs/ *adj.* excessively or sickeningly respectful. —**obsequiously** *adv.*, **obsequiousness** *n.* [f. L *obsequium* compliance)]

observance /əb'zɜ:vəns/ *n.* **1.** the keeping or performance of a law, duty, etc. **2.** a rite, a ceremonial act. [f. OF f. L *observantia* (as OBSERVE)]

observant *adj.* **1.** quick at noticing things. **2.** attentive in observance. —**observantly** *adv.* [F (as OBSERVE)]

observation /ɒbzə'veɪʃ(ə)n/ *n.* **1.** observing, being observed. **2.** a comment or remark. **3.** facts or data; the recording of these. —**observational** *adj.* [f. L (as OBSERVE)]

observatory /əb'zɜ:vətərɪ/ *n.* a building designed and equipped for scientific observation of the stars or weather etc. [f. L (as foll.)]

observe /əb'zɜ:v/ *v.t./i.* **1.** to see and notice; to watch carefully. **2.** to keep or pay attention to (rules etc.). **3.** to celebrate or perform (an occasion, rite, etc.). **4.** to note and record (facts or data). **5.** to remark. —**observable** *adj.* & *n.* [f. OF f. L *observare* (OB-, *servare* watch)]

observer *n.* one who observes; an interested spectator. [f. prec.]

obsess /əb'ses/ *v.t.* to occupy the thoughts of (a person) continually. [f. L *obsidere* besiege]

obsession /əb'seʃ(ə)n/ *n.* **1.** obsessing, being obsessed. **2.** a persistent idea dominating a person's thoughts. —**obsessional** *adj.* [as prec.]

obsessive /əb'sesɪv/ *adj.* of, causing, or showing obsession. —**obsessively** *adv.* [as OBSESS]

obsidian /əb'sɪdɪən/ *n.* a dark vitreous lava or volcanic rock that looks like a coarse glass. [f. L f. *Obsius*, name of finder of a similar stone, mentioned by Pliny]

obsolescent /ɒbsə'lesənt/ *adj.* becoming obsolete. —**obsolescence** *n.* [f. L *obsolescere* (OB-, *solēre* be accustomed)]

obsolete /'ɒbsəli:t/ *adj.* no longer used, antiquated. [as prec.]

obstacle /'ɒbstək(ə)l/ *n.* a thing obstructing progress. [f. OF f. L *obstare* stand in the way)]

obstetrician /ɒbstɪ'trɪʃ(ə)n/ *n.* a specialist in obstetrics. [f. foll.]

obstetrics /ɒb'stetrɪks/ *n.pl.* (usu. treated as *sing.*) the branch of medicine and surgery dealing with childbirth. —**obstetric** *adj.*, **obstetrical** *adj.* [f. L *obstetricius* (*obstetrix* midwife)]

obstinate /'ɒbstɪnət/ *n.* stubborn, intractable; firmly continuing in one's action or opinion and not yielding to persuasion. —**obstinacy** *n.*, **obstinately** *adv.* [f. L (*obstinare* persist)]

obstreperous /əb'strepərəs/ *adj.* noisy, unruly. —**obstreperously** *adv.* [f. L (*obstrepere* shout against)]

obstruct /əb'strʌkt/ *v.t.* **1.** to prevent or hinder passage along (a path etc.) by means of an object etc. placed in it. **2.** to prevent or hinder the movement, progress, or activities of. —**obstructor** *n.* [f. L (OB-, *struere* build)]

obstruction /əb'strʌkʃ(ə)n/ *n.* **1.** obstructing, being obstructive. **2.** a thing that obstructs, a blockage. [as prec.]

obstructive *adj.* causing or intended to cause obstruction. [f. OBSTRUCT]

obtain /əb'teɪn/ *v.t./i.* **1.** to get, to come into possession of (a thing) by effort or as a gift. **2.** to be established or in use as a rule or customary practice. —**obtainment** *n.* [f. OF f. L *obtinēre* (OB-, *tenēre* hold)]

obtainable *adj.* that may be obtained. [f. prec.]

obtrude /əb'tru:d/ *v.t./i.* to force (oneself or one's ideas) upon others; to be or become obtrusive. —**obtrusion** *n.* [f. L *obtrudere* (OB-, *trudere* thrust)]

obtrusive /əb'tru:sɪv/ *adj.* obtruding oneself; unpleasantly noticeable. —**obtrusively** *adv.* [as prec.]

obtuse /əb'tju:s/ *adj.* **1.** stupid, slow at understanding. **2.** of blunt shape, not sharp-edged or pointed. **3.** (of an angle) more than 90° but less than 180°. —**obtusely** *adv.*, **obtuseness** *n.* [f. L (OB-, *tundere* beat)]

obverse /'ɒbvɜ:s/ *n.* **1.** the side of a coin or medal etc. that bears the head or principal design; the front or proper or top side of a thing. **2.** the counterpart. [f. L *obvertere* turn towards]

obviate /'ɒbvɪeɪt/ *v.t.* to make unnecessary; to get round (a danger or hindrance etc.). [f. L *obviare* withstand (OB-, *via* way)]

obvious /'ɒbvɪəs/ *adj.* easily seen or recognized or understood. —**obviously** *adv.* [f. L (*ob viam* in the way)]

OC *abbr.* Officer Commanding.

OC- see OB-.

ocarina /ɒkə'ri:nə/ *n.* a small egg-shaped terracotta or metal wind instrument with holes for the fingers. Invented *c.*1860, it was used mainly as a toy and sometimes nicknamed 'sweet potato' (as in the once-popular song *Sweet Potato Piper*). [It. (*oca* goose, from its shape)]

OCAS *abbr.* Organization of Central American States, an association founded in 1951 (a new charter being negotiated in 1962) for economic and political co-operation. It is also known as the Organizacion de Estados Centro Americanos (ODECA).

O'Casey /əʊ'keɪsɪ/, Sean (1880–1964), Irish playwright, born in Dublin of poor Protestant parents. He spent 9 years from 1903 as a railway labourer and developed an enthusiasm for the theatre through amateur dramatics. His three tragicomedies, *The Shadow of a Gunman* (1923), *Juno and the Paycock* (1924), and *The Plough and the Stars* (1926), deal realistically with the dangers of Irish patriotism, with tenement life, self-deception, and survival. He settled in England permanently in 1926. *The Silver Tassie* (1928) introduced the symbolic expressionist techniques which he developed in later works.

Occam /'ɒkəm/ see WILLIAM OF OCCAM.

occasion /ə'keɪʒ(ə)n/ *n.* **1.** a special event or happening; a particular time marked by this. **2.** a reason, a need. **3.** a suitable juncture, an opportunity. **4.** an immediate but subordinate cause. **5.** (in *pl.*) affairs, business. —*v.t.* to cause (esp. incidentally). —**on occasion**, now and then, when the need arises. [f. OF or L (*occidere* go down)]

occasional *adj.* **1.** happening irregularly and infrequently. **2.** made, intended for, or acting on a special occasion. —**occasionally** *adv.* [f. prec.]

Occident /'ɒksɪdənt/ *n.* (*poetic* or *rhet.*) the West (especially Europe and America) as opposed to the Orient. [f. OF f. L, = sunset, west (as OCCASION)]

occidental /ɒksɪ'dent(ə)l/ *adj.* of the Occident, western. —*n.* a native or inhabitant of the Occident. [as prec.]

occiput /'ɒksɪpʌt/ *n.* the back of the head. —**occipital** /ɒk'sɪpɪt(ə)l/ *adj.* [f. L (OC-, *caput* head)]

occlude /ɒ'klu:d/ *v.t.* **1.** to obstruct, to stop up. **2.** to absorb and retain (gases). —**occluded front,** the atmospheric condition that occurs when a cold front overtakes a mass of warm air, and warm air is driven upwards, producing a long period of steady rain (ill. WEATHER). —**occlusion** n. [f. L occludere (OC-, claudere shut)]

occult[1] /ɒˈkʌlt/ adj. **1.** involving the supernatural, mystical, magical. **2.** esoteric, recondite. —**the occult,** occult phenomena generally. [f. L occulere to hide]

occult[2] /ɒˈkʌlt/ v.t. to conceal, to cut off from view by passing in front (usu. Astron. of a concealing body much greater in apparent size than the concealed body). —**occultation** /-ˈteɪʃ(ə)n/ n. [f. L occultare frequent. of occulere (see prec.)]

occupant /ˈɒkjʊpənt/ n. a person occupying a dwelling, office, or position. —**occupancy** n. [f. OF f. L (as OCCUPY)]

occupation /ɒkjʊˈpeɪʃ(ə)n/ n. **1.** an activity that keeps a person busy; one's employment. **2.** occupying, being occupied; taking or holding possession of a country or district by military force. [f. OF f. L (as OCCUPY)]

occupational adj. of or connected with one's occupation. —**occupational disease** or **hazard,** a disease or hazard to which a particular occupation renders one especially liable. **occupational therapy,** mental or physical activity to assist recovery from a disease or injury. [f. prec.]

occupier /ˈɒkjʊpaɪə(r)/ n. a person residing in a house etc. as its owner or tenant. [f. foll.]

occupy /ˈɒkjʊpaɪ/ v.t. **1.** to reside in, to be a tenant of. **2.** to take up or fill (a space or time or place). **3.** to hold (a position or office). **4.** to take military possession of; to place oneself in (a building etc.) forcibly or without authority. **5.** to keep (a person or his time) filled with activity. [f. OF f. L occupare seize]

occur /əˈkɜː(r)/ v.i. (**-rr-**) **1.** to come into being as an event or process. **2.** to be met with or found to exist in some place or condition. —**occur to,** to come into the mind of. [f. L occurrere present itself]

occurrence /əˈkʌrəns/ n. **1.** occurring. **2.** a thing that occurs, an event. [f. occurrent adj. f. F f. L (as prec.)]

ocean /ˈəʊʃ(ə)n/ n. **1.** the sea surrounding the continents of the earth, especially one of five named divisions of this (Atlantic, Pacific, Indian, Arctic, and Antarctic Oceans; ill. SEA). **2.** an immense expanse or quantity. —**ocean-going** adj. (of a ship) able to cross the ocean. —**oceanic** /əʊʃɪˈænɪk/ adj. [f. OF f. L f. Gk, = stream encircling the earth]

Oceania /əʊʃɪˈeɪnɪə/ the islands of the Pacific and adjacent seas. —**Oceanian** adj. & n. [f. F f. L (as OCEAN)]

oceanography /əʊʃəˈnɒgrəfɪ/ n. the study of oceans. —**oceanographer** n. [f. OCEAN + -GRAPHY]

Oceanus /əʊsɪˈeɪnəs/ (Gk myth.) the son of Uranus and Ge, and father of the ocean nymphs (Oceanids) and river gods. He is the personification of the river encircling the whole world.

ocellus /əˈseləs/ n. (pl. **ocelli** /-laɪ/) **1.** any of the simple (as opp. compound) eyes of insects etc. **2.** a facet of a compound eye. [L, dim. of oculus eye]

ocelot /ˈəʊsɪlɒt, ˈɒ-/ n. a leopard-like feline (Felis pardalis) of South and Central America. [F, abbr. by Buffon f. Nahuatl tlalocelotl jaguar of the field, and applied to a different animal]

och /ɒx/ int. (Sc. & Ir.) oh, ah. [Gael. & Ir.]

oche /ˈɒkɪ/ n. var. of HOCKEY[2].

ochre /ˈəʊkə(r)/ n. **1.** an earth used as a yellow or brown or red pigment. **2.** a pale brownish-yellow colour. —**ochrous** adj. [f. OF f. L f. Gk (ōkhros pale yellow)]

o'clock /əˈklɒk/ adv. = of the clock, used to specify an hour.

Oct. abbr. October.

oct-, octa- in comb. eight. [f. L or Gk (L octo, Gk oktō eight)]

octagon /ˈɒktəgən/ n. a plane figure with eight sides and angles. —**octagonal** /-ˈtægən(ə)l/ adj. [f. L f. Gk (OCTA-, -gōnos angled)]

octahedron /ɒktəˈhiːdrən/ n. (pl. **-s**) a solid figure contained by eight plane faces and usually by eight triangles (ill. SHAPES). —**octahedral** adj. [f. Gk (OCTA-, hedra base)]

octane /ˈɒkteɪn/ n. a hydrocarbon compound of the paraffin series occurring in petrol. —**high-octane** adj. (of fuel used in internal-combustion engines) not detonating rapidly during the power stroke. **octane number,** a number indicating the anti-knock properties of fuel. [f. OCT-]

octave /ˈɒktɪv/ n. **1.** (Mus.) a note seven diatonic degrees from a given note and having the same name; the interval

between a given note and its octave; the series of notes filling this. **2.** the seventh day after a religious festival; the period of eight days including the festival and its octave. **3.** an eight-line stanza. —**law of octaves,** that formulated (1863-6) by J. A. R. Newlands, who noted that the chemical elements, when arranged in order of their atomic weights, exhibited a recurring regularity of properties after each series of 8 elements, an anticipation of the periodic law. [f. OF f. L (octavus eighth)]

Octavian /ɒkˈteɪvɪən/ the name (Gaius Julius Caesar Octavianus) taken by Gaius Octavius on his recognition in 43 BC as the adopted son of Julius Caesar, and by which he was known until his assumption of the title Augustus in 27 BC.

octavo /ɒkˈteɪvəʊ/ n. (pl. **-os**) the size of a book or page given by folding a sheet of standard size three times to form eight leaves; a book or sheet of this size. [L (as OCTAVE)]

octet /ɒkˈtet/ n. (also **octette**) **1.** a musical composition for eight performers; these performers. **2.** any group of eight. **3.** the set of eight lines beginning a sonnet. [f. It. or G (OCT-, after duet, quartet)]

octo- in comb. eight. [as OCT-, OCTA-]

October /ɒkˈtəʊbə(r)/ n. the tenth month of the year. [OE f. L (octō eight, because orig. the eighth month in the Roman calendar)]

octogenarian /ɒktəʊdʒɪˈneərɪən/ n. a person from 80 to 89 years old. [f. L (octogeni 80 each)]

octopus /ˈɒktəpəs/ n. (pl. **-uses**) a sea-mollusc of the family Octopodidae, with eight suckered tentacles. [f. Gk (OCTO-, pous foot)]

ocular /ˈɒkjʊlə(r)/ adj. of or connected with the eyes or sight, visual. [f. F f. L (oculus eye)]

oculist /ˈɒkjʊlɪst/ n. a specialist in the treatment of eye diseases and defects. [as prec.]

odalisque /ˈəʊdəlɪsk/ n. (hist.) an Oriental female slave or concubine, especially in the Turkish sultan's seraglio. [F f. Turk. (oda chamber, lik function)]

odd adj. **1.** unusual, strange, eccentric. **2.** not regular, occasional; not normally noticed or considered; unconnected. **3.** (of numbers such as 3 and 5) not integrally divisible by two; bearing such a number. **4.** left over when the rest have been distributed or divided into pairs; detached from a set or series. **5.** (appended to a number, sum, weight, etc.) something more than; by which a round number, given sum, etc., is exceeded. —**odd man out,** a person or thing differing from all others of a group in some respect. —**oddly** adv., **oddness** n. [f. ON odda- in odda-mathr third man (oddi angle, triangle)]

oddball n. (colloq.) an eccentric person.

oddity /ˈɒdɪtɪ/ n. **1.** strangeness; a peculiar trait. **2.** a strange person, thing, or event. [f. ODD]

oddment n. an odd article, something left over; (in pl.) odds and ends. [f. ODD]

odds n.pl. (sometimes treated as sing.). **1.** the ratio between the amounts staked by the parties to a bet, based on the expected probability either way. **2.** the balance of advantage or probability. **3.** advantageous difference. —**at odds,** in conflict, at variance. **odds and ends,** remnants, stray articles. **odds-on** n. a state when success is expected to be more likely than failure. **over the odds,** above the generally agreed price etc. [app. pl. of ODD]

ode n. (in ancient literature) a poem intended or adapted to be sung; (in modern use) a rhymed (rarely unrhymed) lyric, often in the form of an address, generally dignified or exalted in subject, feeling, and style, but sometimes (in earlier use) simple and familiar (though less so than a song). [f. F f. L f. Gk ōidē song]

Odessa /əʊˈdesə/ a Ukrainian city and seaport on the NW coast of the Black Sea; pop. (1983) 1,113,000.

Odin /ˈəʊdɪn/ (Scand. myth.) the supreme god and creator, god of victory and the dead, represented as an old one-eyed man of great wisdom. Wednesday is named after him.

odious /ˈəʊdɪəs/ adj. hateful, repulsive. —**odiously** adv., **odiousness** n. [f. OF f. L (as foll.)]

odium /ˈəʊdɪəm/ n. widespread dislike or disapproval felt towards a person or action. [L, = hatred]

odometer /əʊˈdɒmɪtə(r)/ n. an instrument for measuring the distance travelled by a wheeled vehicle. [f. F (Gk hodos way, -METER)]

odoriferous /əʊdəˈrɪfərəs/ adj. diffusing a (usu. agreeable) odour. [f. L (odor smell, ferro carry)]

odour /ˈəʊdə(r)/ *n.* **1.** a smell. **2.** a savour, a trace. **3.** favour, repute. —**odorous** *adj.* [f. AF f. L *odor*]

Odysseus /əˈdɪsjəs/ (*Gk legend*) king of Ithaca, called Ulysses by the Romans, renowned for cunning. He survived the Trojan War but Poseidon kept him from home for ten years while his wife Penelope waited. (See ODYSSEY.)

Odyssey /ˈɒdɪsɪ/ a Greek hexameter epic poem in 24 books traditionally ascribed to Homer. It tells of the travels of the ever-resourceful Odysseus during his years of wandering after the sack of Troy, and of his eventual return home to Ithaca and his slaying of the evil suitors of his faithful wife Penelope. His adventures include amorous liaisons with Calypso and the witch Circe, hospitality at the court of the pleasure-loving Phaeacians, the evocation of the famous dead from the underworld, and encounters with a number of fabulous monsters, including the Cyclops Polyphemus and Scylla and Charybdis.

odyssey /ˈɒdɪsɪ/ *n.* a long adventurous journey. [f. prec.]

OECD *abbr.* Organization for Economic Co-operation and Development, an association of Western States founded in 1961 to assist the economy of member nations and to promote world trade. Its headquarters are in Paris.

OED *abbr.* Oxford English Dictionary.

oedema /iːˈdiːmə, ɪˈd-/ *n.* a swollen state of tissue in the body. —**oedematous** *adj.* [L f. Gk (*oideō* swell)]

Oedipus /ˈiːdɪpəs/ (*Gk legend*) son of Laius king of Thebes, and Jocasta. He unwittingly killed his father and married Jocasta, and when the facts were discovered went mad and put out his own eyes, while Jocasta hanged herself. [Gk = swollen foot, from the story that Laius ran a spike through the infant's feet before leaving it to die]

Oedipus complex the manifestation of a child's sexuality towards its parents, with attraction to the parent of the opposite sex (especially the mother) and jealousy of the other parent. —**Oedipal** *adj.* [f. prec.]

Oenone /iːˈnəʊnɪ/ (*Gk legend*) a nymph of Mount Ida and lover of Paris, who deserted her for Helen.

o'er /ˈɔːə(r)/ *prep.* & *adv.* (chiefly *poetic*) = OVER. [contr.]

Oersted /ˈɜːsted/, Hans Christian (1777–1851), Danish physicist, who in 1820 discovered that an electric current has a magnetic effect. He noticed the deflection of a compass needle placed near a wire carrying a current. The unit of magnetic field strength named after him (the *oersted*) is replaced in the SI system by the ampere per metre.

oesophagus /iːˈsɒfəgəs/ *n.* (*pl.* **-gi** /-dʒaɪ/) the canal from the mouth to the stomach, the gullet (ill. BODY 2). [f. Gk]

oestrogen /ˈiːstrədʒ(ə)n/ *n.* a sex hormone maintaining or developing female bodily characteristics. [f. Gk *oistros* frenzy + -GEN]

œuvre /ˈəvr/ *n.* **1.** a work of art, music, or literature. **2.** the corpus of work produced by an artist, composer, or writer, considered as a whole. [F, = work, f. L *opera*]

of /ɒv, emphat. ɒv/ *prep.* **1.** belonging to; originating from. **2.** concerning. **3.** composed or made from. **4.** with reference or regard to. **5.** for, involving, directed towards. **6.** so as to bring separation or relief from. **7.** during; regularly on a specified day or time. —**of itself**, by or in itself. [OE]

of- see OB-.

off *adv.* **1.** away, at, or to a distance. **2.** out of position; not on or touching or attached, loose, separate; gone; so as to be rid of; incorrect, insufficient. **3.** so as to break continuity or continuance; discontinued, stopped; not available on the menu etc. **4.** to the end, entirely, so as to be clear. **5.** situated as regards money, supplies, etc. **6.** off-stage. **7.** (of food etc.) beginning to decay. —*prep.* **1.** from, away or down or up from, not on. **2.** temporarily relieved of or abstaining from or not achieving. **3.** using as a source or means of support. **4.** leading from, not far from; at a short distance to sea from. —*adj.* far, further; (of a part of a vehicle, animal, or road) further from the side of a road when facing forward, usually the right; (in cricket) designating the half of the field (as divided lengthways through the pitch) to which the striker's feet are pointed. —*n.* **1.** the off side in cricket. **2.** the start of a race. —**a bit off**, (*slang*) rather annoying or unfair or unwell. **off and on**, intermittently, now and then. **off-beat** *adj.* eccentric, unconventional. **off chance,** a remote possibility. **off colour,** not in good health; (*US*) somewhat indecent. **off-day** *n.* a day when one is not at one's best. **off-key** *adj.* out of tune; not quite suitable or fitting. **off-licence** *n.* a shop selling alcoholic drink for consumption elsewhere; a licence for this. **off-line** *adj.* (of computer equipment or a computer process) not directly controlled by or connected to a central processor. **off-load**

v.t. to unload. **off-peak** *adj.* used or for use at times other than those of greatest demand. **off-putting** *adj.* (*colloq.*) disconcerting; repellent. **off-season** *n.* a time when business etc. is slack. **off-stage** *adj.* & *adv.* not on the stage and so not visible or audible to the audience. **off-white** *adj.* white with a grey or yellowish tinge. [var. of OF]

Offa /ˈɒfə/ (d. 796) king of Mercia 757–96. —**Offa's Dyke,** a series of earthworks running from near the mouth of the Wye to near the mouth of the Dee, built or repaired by Offa to mark the boundary established by his wars with the Welsh.

offal /ˈɒf(ə)l/ *n.* **1.** the edible parts of a carcass (especially the heart, liver, etc.) cut off as less valuable. **2.** refuse, scraps. [f. MDu. *afval* (as OFF, FALL)]

offcut *n.* a remnant of timber etc. after cutting.

Offenbach /ˈɒf(ə)nbɑːx/, Jacques (1819–80), German-born French composer, Jacques Eberst, who adopted the name of the German town in which his father lived. He began composing operettas in 1853, writing no fewer than ninety in the next quarter-century. His two-act opera *Orphée aux enfers* (Orpheus in the Underworld) was produced in 1858, and by the 1860s his fame as a witty and satirical composer was widespread. Later he turned away from the frivolous style, which was less to the taste of the Parisian public than it had been before the war of 1870–1, and composed *Les Contes d'Hoffmann* (Tales of Hoffmann), based on three stories by the German writer E. T. A. Hoffmann; it was not produced until after his death.

offence /əˈfens/ *n.* **1.** an illegal act, a transgression. **2.** wounding of the feelings; annoyance or resentment caused thus. **3.** an aggressive action. [f. F or OF f. L (as foll.)]

offend /əˈfend/ *v.t./i.* **1.** to cause offence to; to displease or anger. **2.** to do wrong. —**offender** *n.* [f. OF f. L *offendere*, orig. = strike against]

offensive /əˈfensɪv/ *adj.* **1.** causing offence, insulting. **2.** disgusting, repulsive. **3.** aggressive, attacking; (of a weapon) meant for attacking. —*n.* an aggressive attitude, action, or campaign. —**offensively** *adv.*, **offensiveness** *n.* [f. F or L (as OFFENCE)]

offer *v.t./i.* **1.** to present for acceptance or refusal or for consideration. **2.** to express readiness or show intention to do, pay, or give. **3.** to provide, to give opportunity for. **4.** to make available for sale. **5.** to present to sight or notice; to present itself, to occur. —*n.* **1.** an expression of readiness to do or give if desired, or to buy or sell (for a certain amount); the amount offered; a bid. **2.** a proposal, especially of marriage. —**on offer**, for sale at a certain (esp. reduced) price. [OE or f. OF f. L *offerre*]

offering *n.* a thing offered as a gift, contribution, sacrifice, etc. [f. prec.]

offertory /ˈɒfətərɪ/ *n.* **1.** the offering of bread and wine at the Eucharist. **2.** a collection of money at a religious service. [f. L (as OFFER)]

offhand *adj.* **1.** curt or casual in manner. **2.** without preparation in. —*adv.* in an offhand way. —**offhanded** /-ˈhændɪd/ *adj.*, **offhandedly** *adv.*

office /ˈɒfɪs/ *n.* **1.** a room or building used as a place of business, especially for clerical or administrative work; a room or department for a particular business. **2.** a position with duties attached to it; tenure of an official position. **3.** the quarters, staff, or collective authority of a government department. **4.** a duty, a task, a function. **5.** a piece of kindness, a service. **6.** an authorized form of religious worship. **7.** (in *pl.*) rooms in a house that are devoted to household work, storage, etc. [f. OF f. L *officium* (*opus* work, *facere* do)]

officer /ˈɒfɪsə(r)/ *n.* **1.** a person holding a position of authority or trust, especially one with a commission in the armed services or mercantile marine, or on a passenger ship. **2.** a policeman. **3.** a holder of a post in a society (e.g. the president or secretary). —*v.t.* (usu. in *p.p.*) to provide with officers. [f. AF f. L *officiarius* (as prec.)]

official /əˈfɪʃ(ə)l/ *adj.* **1.** of an office or its tenure. **2.** characteristic of officials and bureaucracy. **3.** properly authorized. —*n.* a person holding office or engaged in official duties. —**officialdom** *n.*, **officially** *adv.* [f. OF or L (as OFFICE)]

officiate /əˈfɪʃɪeɪt/ *v.i.* **1.** to act in an official capacity. **2.** to perform divine service. [f. L (as OFFICE)]

officious /əˈfɪʃəs/ *adj.* asserting one's authority, domineering; intrusively kind. —**officiously** *adv.* [f. L, = obliging (as OFFICE)]

offing *n.* the more distant part of the sea in view. —**in the**

offing, not far away; likely to appear or happen. [perh. f. OFF]

offish adj. (colloq.) inclined to be aloof. [f. OFF]

offprint n. a printed copy of an article etc. originally forming part of a larger publication.

offset n. **1.** a side-shoot from a plant serving for propagation. **2.** compensation, a consideration or amount diminishing or neutralizing the effect of a contrary one. **3.** a sloping ledge in a wall etc.; a bend in a pipe etc. to carry it past an obstacle. **4.** (in full **offset process**) a method of printing with the transfer of ink from a plate or stone to a rubber or other surface and thence to paper (see LITHOGRAPHY). —/also -'set/ v.t. (-tt-; p.p. **offset**) **1.** to counterbalance, to compensate. **2.** to print by the offset process.

offshoot n. **1.** a side-shoot or branch. **2.** a derivative.

offshore adj. **1.** at sea some distance from the shore. **2.** (of a wind) blowing from the land towards the sea.

offside /ɒf'saɪd/ adj. (of a player in a field game) in a position where he may not play the ball.

offspring n. (pl. same) a person's child or children or descendants; an animal's young or descendants. [OE (as OF from, SPRING)]

oft /ɒft/ adv. (archaic) often. [OE]

often /'ɒf(ə)n/ adv. **1.** frequently, many times. **2.** at short intervals. **3.** in many instances. —**every so often,** from time to time. [extended f. prec.]

ogee /'əʊdʒiː, -'dʒiː/ n. a sinuous line of a double continuous curve as in S; a moulding with such a section. —**ogee arch,** an arch with two ogee curves meeting at the apex (ill. CHURCH). [app. f. foll.]

ogham /'ɒɡəm/ n. **1.** an ancient British and Irish alphabet of 20 characters, probably invented in the 4th c. AD, formed by parallel strokes on either side of or across a continuous line. **2.** an inscription in this. **3.** any of the characters. [OIr. ogam, f. Ogma supposed inventor]

ogive /'əʊdʒaɪv, -'dʒaɪv/ n. **1.** the diagonal rib of a vault. **2.** a pointed arch. [f. F, ult. orig. unkn.]

ogle /'əʊɡ(ə)l/ v.t./i. to look amorously (at). —n. an amorous glance. [prob. f. LDu.]

ogre /'əʊɡə(r)/ n. **1.** a man-eating giant in folklore. **2.** a terrifying person. —**ogress** n.fem., **ogrish** adj. [f. F]

oh /əʊ/ int. expressing surprise, pain, entreaty, etc. [var. of O²]

O'Higgins /əʊ'hɪɡɪnz/, Bernado (c. 1778-1842), Chilean revolutionary leader, son of a Spanish officer of Irish origin. He put himself at the head of the independence movement in Chile and, with the help of San Martín, liberator of Argentina, led the army which triumphed over Spanish forces in 1817 and won independence for his country. For the next six years he was supreme director of Chile, but then fell from power and was obliged to live in exile in Peru for the remainder of his life.

Ohio /əʊ'haɪəʊ/ a State in the north-eastern USA, bordering on Lake Erie. Acquired by Britain from France in 1763 and by the USA in 1783, it became the 17th State of the USA in 1803; capital, Columbus.

Ohm /əʊm/, Georg Simon (1789-1854), German physicist who discovered the law, named after him, that the electric current flowing through a wire is directly proportional to the potential difference (voltage) and inversely proportional to the resistance. The ohm (see foll.) is named in his honour.

ohm /əʊm/ n. a unit of electrical resistance, transmitting a current of one ampere when subjected to a potential difference of one volt. [f. OHM]

OHMS abbr. On Her (or His) Majesty's Service.

oho /əʊ'həʊ/ int. expressing surprise or exultation. [f. O² + HO]

oil n. **1.** any of various liquid viscid unctuous, usually inflammable, chemically neutral substances lighter than and insoluble in water but soluble in alcohol and ether (see below). **2.** (US) petroleum. **3.** (often in pl.) oil-colour. **4.** an oil-painting. **5.** (colloq., usu. in pl.) oilskins. —v.t. **1.** to apply oil to; to lubricate, impregnate, or treat with oil. **2.** to supply oil to. —**oil-colour** n. (usu. in pl.) a paint made by mixing powdered pigment in oil. **oil-fired** adj. using oil as a fuel. **oil-paint** n. oil-colour. **oil-painting** n. the art of painting in oil-colours (Vasari attributes its invention to Jan van Eyck at the beginning of the 15th c.); a picture painted thus. **oil rig**, equipment for drilling an oil well. **oil-slick** n. a smooth patch of oil, especially on the sea. **oil well**, a well from which mineral oil is drawn. [f. AF f. L oleum olive oil]

Oils are classified thus: (i) non-volatile *fatty* or *fixed oils* of animal or vegetable origin, used as varnishes, lubricants, illuminants, soap constituents, etc., chemically identical with fats, (ii) *essential* or *volatile oils*, chiefly of vegetable origin, giving plants etc. their scent, used in medicine and perfumery, and (iii) *mineral oils*, consisting mainly of hydrocarbons, thought to be the remains of tiny living organisms deposited millions of years ago and now found trapped in underground reservoirs, detectable by seismic surveys and by drilling. The modern mineral oil industry dates from 1859, when a well was bored at Titusville in Pennsylvania. (This was not the first strike; oil had been found in Ohio in 1841 during drilling for salt.) Petroleum oils are the main source of energy in developed countries for heating and transport, and are used as the basis of a whole range of chemicals, particularly plastics.

oilcake n. compressed linseed from which oil has been expressed, used as cattle food or manure.

oilcloth n. a fabric, esp. canvas, water-proofed with oil.

oiled adj. (slang) drunk. [f. OIL]

oilfield n. a district yielding mineral oil.

oilskin n. cloth waterproofed with oil; a garment of this; (in pl.) a suit of this.

oily adj. **1.** of or like oil. **2.** covered or soaked with oil. **3.** unpleasantly smooth in manner; ingratiating. —**oiliness** n. [f. OIL]

ointment /'ɔɪntmənt/ n. a smooth greasy healing or beautifying preparation for the skin. [f. OF f. L (as UNGUENT)]

Oireachtas /'ɪərəxθæs/ n. the legislature of the Republic of Ireland, consisting of the President, Dáil, and Seanad. [Ir., = assembly]

Oisin /'əʊʃiːn/ see OSSIAN.

Ojibwa /əʊ'dʒɪbweɪ/ n. a member or the language of an Algonquian people of North American Indians inhabiting the lands round Lake Superior and (more recently) certain adjacent areas. —adj. of this people or their language. [native name, f. root meaning 'puckered', with ref. to their moccasins]

OK /əʊ'keɪ/ (also **okay**) adj. & adv. all right, satisfactory; (as int.) I agree. —n. approval, agreement to a plan etc. —v.t. to give one's approval or agreement to. [orig. US, app. from the initials of oll (or orl) korrect, joc. spelling of all correct, and first used in 1839; it was used as a slogan for a candidate from Old Kinderhook in the American election of 1840; other suggestions about its origin are without acceptable foundation]

okapi /ə'kɑːpɪ/ n. a brightly coloured partially striped ruminant of Central Africa (*Okapia johnstoni*), discovered in 1900, resembling the giraffe but with a shorter neck and striped body. [Central Afr. native name]

okay var. of OK.

Oklahoma /əʊklə'həʊmə/ a State of the USA lying west of Arkansas, acquired as part of the Louisiana Purchase in 1803. In 1834-89 it was declared Indian territory in which Europeans were forbidden to settle. It became the 46th State of the USA in 1907; capital, Oklahoma City.

okra /'əʊkrə, 'ɒk-/ n. a tall originally African plant (*Hibiscus esculentus*) with seed-pods used for food. [W. Afr. native name]

Olaf /'əʊlæf/ the name of two kings of Norway:

Olaf I Tryggvason (969-1000), reigned 995-1000. According to legend he was brought up in Russia, being converted to Christianity and carrying out extensive Viking raids before returning to Norway to be accepted as king. He jumped overboard and disappeared after his fleet was defeated by the combined forces of Denmark and Sweden at the battle of Svöld, but his exploits as a warrior and his popularity as sovereign made him a national legend.

Olaf II Haraldsson (c.995-1030), reigned 1016-30. Notable for his attempts to spread Christianity in his kingdom, Olaf was forced into exile by a rebellion in 1028 and killed in battle at Stiklestad while attempting to return. He was canonized in 1164 and became the patron saint of Norway.

old /əʊld/ adj. **1.** having lived or existed for a long time. **2.** made long ago; used, established, or known for a long time; shabby from age or wear. **3.** having the characteristics, experience, feebleness, etc. of age; skilled through long experience. **4.** not recent or modern; belonging chiefly to the past; former, original. **5.** of a specified age (ten years old). **6.** (colloq.) as a term of fondness or casual reference. —**the old,** old people. **of old,** of or in past times. **old age,** the later part of normal lifetime. **old-age pension,** a State

Oil

On-shore drilling rig

— derrick

For clarity machinery is shown on a much larger scale than the rock structure. Usually oil is found at a considerable depth below ground level.

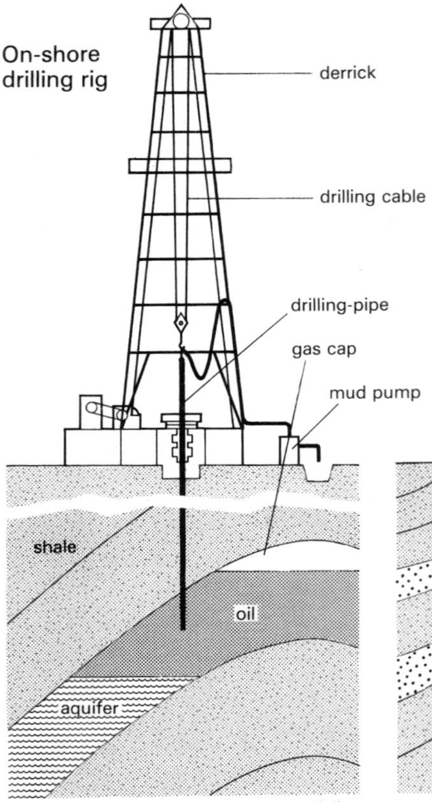

— drilling cable

— drilling-pipe

gas cap

mud pump

pumping unit

oil and some gas

gas

shale

oil

plunger

pump

aquifer

salt dome

sandstone

anticline

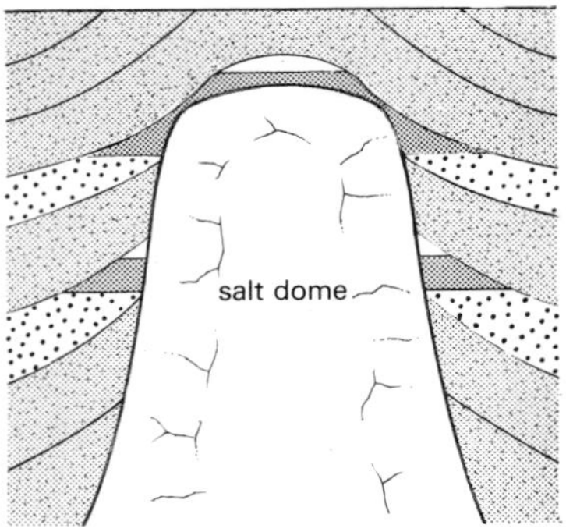

salt dome

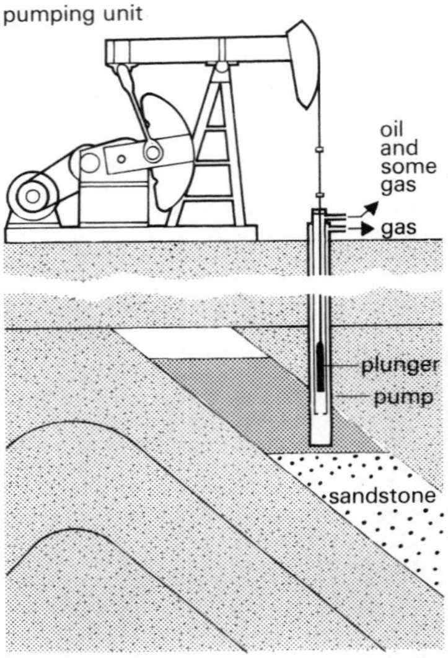

unconformity

Some types of oil-trap

Offshore drilling rig

flare stack

derrick

power-station

heliport

platform

sea

Supertanker

bridge and cabins

vents

pipes for loading and unloading oil

oil tanks

ballast tanks

bunker tanks

subdivisions separate different grades of oil and, by reducing the effect of liquid moving about, help to stabilize the vessel at sea

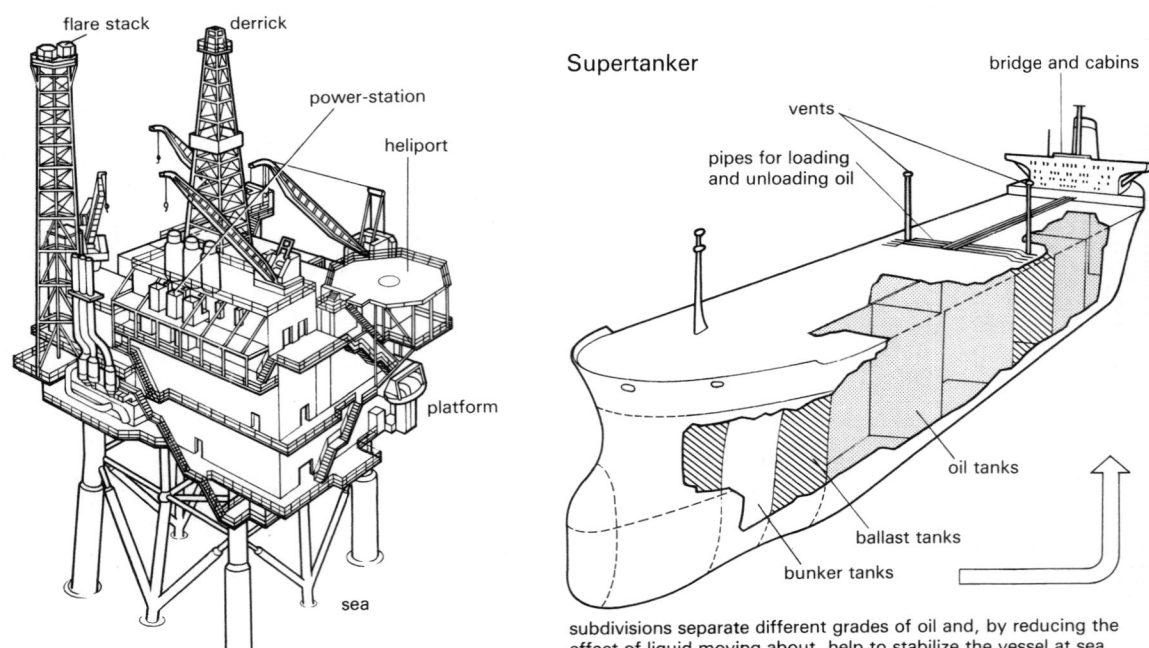

Treatment unit

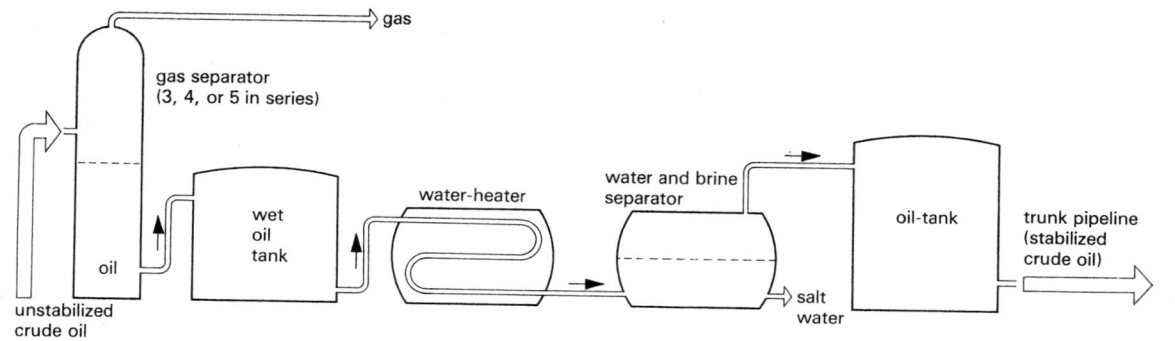

gas

gas separator
(3, 4, or 5 in series)

oil

unstabilized
crude oil

wet
oil
tank

water-heater

water and brine
separator

salt
water

oil-tank

trunk pipeline
(stabilized
crude oil)

Refinery

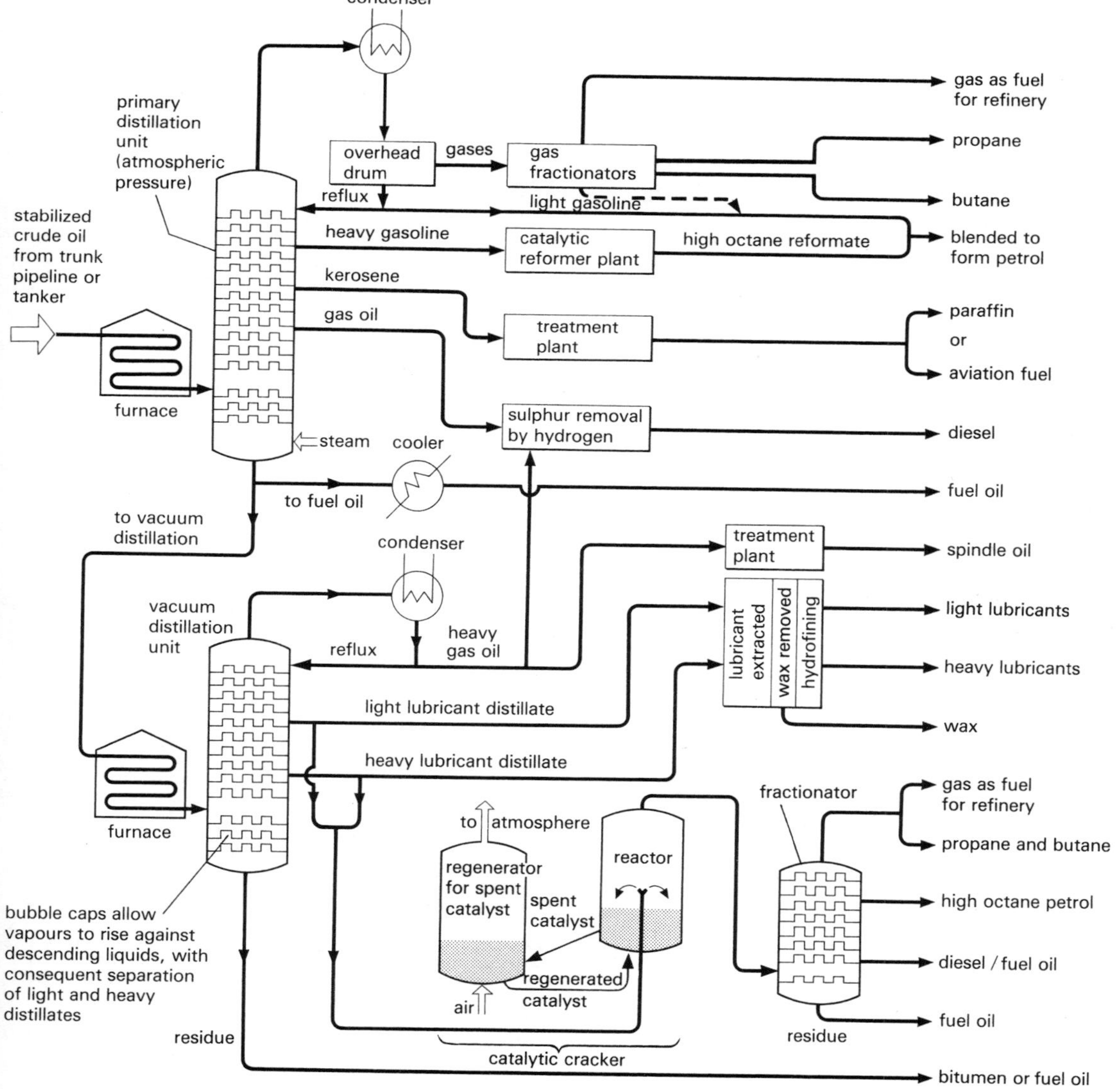

condenser

primary distillation unit (atmospheric pressure)

stabilized crude oil from trunk pipeline or tanker

furnace

overhead drum

gases

gas fractionators

gas as fuel for refinery

propane

butane

reflux

light gasoline

heavy gasoline

catalytic reformer plant

high octane reformate

blended to form petrol

kerosene

gas oil

treatment plant

paraffin
or
aviation fuel

steam

cooler

sulphur removal by hydrogen

diesel

to fuel oil

fuel oil

to vacuum distillation

condenser

treatment plant

spindle oil

vacuum distillation unit

reflux

heavy gas oil

lubricant extracted | wax removed | hydrofining

light lubricants

heavy lubricants

light lubricant distillate

heavy lubricant distillate

wax

furnace

to atmosphere

fractionator

gas as fuel for refinery

propane and butane

regenerator for spent catalyst

spent catalyst

reactor

high octane petrol

bubble caps allow vapours to rise against descending liquids, with consequent separation of light and heavy distillates

diesel / fuel oil

regenerated catalyst

air

fuel oil

residue

residue

catalytic cracker

bitumen or fuel oil

pension paid to people above a certain age, introduced in Britain by Lloyd George in 1908. **old-age pensioner**, a person receiving this. **old boy**, a former member of a school; (*colloq.*) an elderly man; (as a form of address) old man. **the old country**, one's mother country. **old-fashioned** *adj.* in or according to fashion or tastes no longer current, antiquated. **old girl**, a former member of a school; (*colloq.*) an elderly woman; (*colloq.*) as a fond form of address. **Old Glory**, (*US*) the Stars and Stripes. **old gold**, a dull brownish gold colour. **Old Guard**, the French Imperial Guard created by Napoleon I in 1804. **old guard**, the original or past or conservative members of a group. **old hat**, (*colloq.*) something tediously familiar. **Old Hickory**, (*US*) the nickname of Andrew Jackson (President of the USA 1829-37), from his toughness of character. **Old Kingdom**, a period of ancient Egyptian history (see EGYPT). **Old Lady of Threadneedle Street**, the nickname of the Bank of England. **old maid**, an elderly spinster; a prim and fussy person; a card game in which the object is to avoid the holding of an unpaired card. **old man**, (*colloq.*) one's father, husband, or employer etc.; (*colloq.*) as a fond form of address. **old man's beard**, a kind of clematis (*Clematis vitalba*) with grey fluffy hairs round the seeds. **old master**, a great painter of former times, especially of the 13th-17th c. in Europe, a painting by such a painter. **Old Nick**, the Devil. **Old Pals Act**, the doctrine that friends should always help one another. **Old Pretender**, see PRETENDER. **Old Style**, (of a date) reckoned by the Julian calendar. **old-time** *adj.* belonging to former times. **old-timer** *n.* a person with long experience or standing. **old wives' tale**, an old but foolish belief. **old woman**, (*colloq.*) a wife or mother; a fussy or timid man. **Old World**, Europe, Asia, and Africa, the part known by the ancients to exist. **old year**, the year just ended or about to end. —**oldness** *n.* [OE]

Old Bailey the Central Criminal Court, formerly standing in an ancient bailey of London city wall. The present court, trying offences committed in the City and the Greater London area, and certain other offences, was built in 1903-6 on the site of Newgate Prison.

Old Contemptibles the veterans of the British Expeditionary Force sent to France in 1914, so named because of a German reference to the contemptible little army facing them.

Old Dominion a name adopted by the colony of Virginia after it had been raised to the status of Dominion by Charles II for its prompt recognition of him after his restoration to the throne in 1660.

olden *adj.* (*archaic*) old; of old. [f. OLD]

oldie *n.* (*colloq.*) an old person or thing. [f. OLD]

Old Testament the first 39 books of the Bible, the Jewish scriptures containing an account of the creation, the origin of mankind, God's covenant with the Jews, and their early history. Most of the books were written in Hebrew, some in Aramaic. They were classified by the Jews into three groups: the Law (i.e. the Pentateuch), the Prophets (Joshua, Judges, 1 & 2 Samuel, 1 & 2 Kings, Isaiah, Jeremiah, Ezekiel, and the twelve Minor Prophets), and the 'Writings', comprising the remaining books; the canon of the Jewish scriptures was probably settled by about AD 100.

Olduvai Gorge /ˈɒlduvaɪ/ a gorge 48 km (30 miles) long and up to 90 metres (300 ft.) deep, in northern Tanzania, in which the exposed strata contain numerous fossils spanning the full range of the Pleistocene period. Most importantly, the Gorge has provided the longest sequence of hominid presence and activity yet discovered anywhere in the world, with fossils, stone-tool industries, and other evidence of hominid activities that date from *c.*2.1-1.7 million years ago for the oldest dated deposits to *c.*22,000 years ago for the most recent fossil-bearing deposits. The hominids found at individual sites within the Gorge include *Australopithecus boisei* (the *Zinjanthropus* fossils), *Homo habilis*, and *Homo erectus*.

Old Vic the popular name of a London theatre, opened in 1818 as the Royal Coburg and renamed the Royal Victoria Theatre in honour of Princess (later Queen) Victoria in 1833. Its standards declined and it suffered various vicissitudes until under the management of Lilian Baylis from 1912 it gained an enduring reputation for its Shakespearian productions.

oleaginous /əʊlɪˈædʒɪnəs/ *adj.* 1. having the properties of or producing oil. 2. oily (*lit.* or *fig.*). [f. F f. L (as OIL)]

oleander /əʊlɪˈændə(r)/ *n.* an evergreen flowering Mediterranean shrub (*Nerium oleander*). [L]

oleaster /əʊlɪˈæstə(r)/ *n.* a wild olive (*Olea oleaster*). [f. L (*olea* olive-tree)]

olefin /ˈəʊləfɪn/ *n.* a hydrocarbon of a type containing less than the maximum amount of hydrogen. [f. F *oléfiant* oil-forming]

O level ordinary level in the GCE examination. [abbr.]

olfactory /ɒlˈfæktərɪ/ *adj.* concerned with smelling. [f. L *olfacere* to smell]

oligarch /ˈɒlɪɡɑːk/ *n.* a member of an oligarchy. [f. Gk (*oligoi* few, *arkhō* rule)]

oligarchy /ˈɒlɪɡɑːkɪ/ *n.* a form of government in which power is in the hands of a small group of people; this group; a State governed in this way. —**oligarchic** /-ˈɡɑːkɪk/ *adj.*, **oligarchical** /-ˈɡɑː-/ *adj.* [f. F or L f. Gk (as prec.)]

Oligocene /ˈɒlɪɡəsiːn/ *adj.* of the third epoch of the Tertiary period, following the Eocene and preceding the Miocene, lasting from about 38 to 24.6 million years ago. It was a time of falling world temperatures. —*n.* this epoch. [f. Gk *oligos* small + *kainos* new]

olive /ˈɒlɪv/ *n.* 1. a small oval hard-stoned fruit, green when unripe and bluish-black when ripe. 2. the tree bearing it (*Olea europaea*); its wood. 3. leaves or a branch or wreath of olive as an emblem of peace. 4. the colour of an unripe olive. —*adj.* 1. of green colour like an unripe olive. 2. (of the complexion) yellowish-brown. —**olive-branch** *n.* something done or offered as the sign of a wish to make peace. **olive oil**, oil extracted from olives. [f. OF f. L *oliva* f. Gk]

Oliver /ˈɒlɪvə(r)/ see ROLAND.

Olivier /əˈlɪvɪeɪ/, Laurence Kerr, Baron (1907-), English actor and director, famous as a Shakespearian actor and producer and with a considerable career in the cinema since 1929. He was director of the National Theatre for ten years from 1963.

olivine /ˈɒlɪviːn/ *n.* a mineral, usually olive-green, composed of magnesium iron silicate. [f. L *oliva* olive]

Olmec /ˈɒlmek/ *n.* (*pl.* same) 1. a member of a prehistoric people inhabiting the coast of Veracruz and western Tabasco on the Gulf of Mexico *c.*1500-100 BC, who established what was probably the first developed civilization of Mesoamerica. They are noted for their sculptures, especially the massive stone-hewn heads with realistic features and round helmets, and small jade carvings featuring a jaguar. 2. a member of a native American people living in the highlands of Mexico or migrating to the Gulf coast during the 12th c. [f. Nahuatl, = people of the rubber(-tree) country]

Olympia /əˈlɪmpɪə/ the site (in the western Peloponnese) of the chief sanctuary of Zeus in ancient Greece, the venue of the pan-Hellenic Olympic Games, after which the site is named.

Olympiad /əˈlɪmpɪæd/ *n.* 1. a period of four years between Olympic games, used by the ancient Greeks in dating events. 2. a celebration of the modern Olympic games. 3. a regular international contest in chess etc. [f. F or L f. Gk (as OLYMPIC)]

Olympian /əˈlɪmpɪən/ *adj.* 1. of Olympus, celestial. 2. (of manner etc.) magnificent, condescending, superior. 3. Olympic. —*n.* 1. a dweller in Olympus, a Greek god. 2. a person of great attainments or superhuman calm. [f. Mt. *Olympus* in Thessaly (where Greek gods were thought to dwell) or f. foll.]

Olympic /əˈlɪmpɪk/ *adj.* of the Olympic Games. —*n.* (in *pl.*) the Olympic Games. [f. L f. Gk *Olumpikos* of Olympus or Olympia]

Olympic Games a festival of sport held at Olympia (traditionally from 776 BC, every fourth year) by the ancient Greeks, with athletic, musical, and literary competitions, in honour of Olympian Zeus, until abolished by the emperor Theodosius in AD 393, after Greece had lost its independence. A modern revival of this, an international athletic and sports meeting, has been held at various centres every four years since 1896 (except during the two World Wars). The initiative for this revival came from the French aristocrat Baron de Coubertin, troubled by the growing commercialism of 19th-c. sport, as an amateur championship for the world's sportsmen.

Olympus /əˈlɪmpəs/, **Mount** a lofty mountain in Greece at the east end of the range dividing Thessaly from Macedonia. In Greek mythology it was the home of the gods and the court of Zeus. [pre-Greek wd, = mountain]

OM *abbr.* (Member of the) Order of Merit.

om (esp. in Buddhism and Hinduism) a mystic syllable, considered the most sacred mantra. It appears at the beginning and end of most Sanskrit recitations, prayers, and texts. [Skr., a universal affirmation]

Oman /əʊˈmɑːn/ a country in SW Asia at the eastern corner of the Arabian Peninsula; pop. (est. 1982) 850,000; official language, Arabic; capital, Muscat. An independent sultanate, known as Muscat and Oman until 1970, Oman fell increasingly under British influence in the mid-19th c., becoming a protectorate in 1891, and despite the general British withdrawal from the area in the post-war years, the sultanate still retains links with the UK. The discovery of oil in 1964 revolutionized the Oman economy, bringing wealth out of all proportion to its size and small population. —**Omani** adj. & n.

Omar I /ˈəʊmɑː(r)/ (c.581-644) Muslim caliph, 634-44. An early opponent of Muhammad, Omar was converted to Islam in 617 and after becoming Caliph in 634 began an extensive series of conquests, adding Syria, Palestine, and Egypt to the Muslim empire before being assassinated by a Persian slave at Medina.

Omar Khayyám /ʊmɑː kaɪˈɑːm/ (d. 1123) Persian poet, mathematician, and astronomer. He is remembered for his *rubais* (quatrains) containing his meditations on the mysteries of existence, translated and adapted by Edward Fitzgerald in *The Rubaiyat of Omar Khayyám* (1859) into a cynical yet poetic sequence, sceptical of divine providence and concentrating on the pleasures of the fleeting moment. The felicitously phrased aphorisms are frequently quoted, particularly the counsel to drink and make merry while life lasts.

ombudsman /ˈɒmbʊdzmæn/ n. (pl. **-men**) an official appointed to investigate complaints by individuals against maladministration by public authorities. In the UK (where the first one took office in 1967) he or she is officially called the Parliamentary Commissioner for Administration. [Sw., = legal representative]

Omdurman /ˈɒmdɜːmən/ the capital of the Mahdist State of Sudan following the British recapture of Khartoum in 1885, scene of Kitchener's decisive victory over the Mahdi's successor, the Khalifa, in 1898, which marked the end of the Dervish uprising.

omega /ˈəʊmɪɡə/ n. **1.** the last letter of the Greek alphabet, = o. **2.** the last of a series; the final development. [Gk, ō mega = great O]

omelette /ˈɒmlɪt/ n. beaten eggs cooked in a frying pan and often served folded round a savoury or sweet filling. [F]

omen /ˈəʊmen/ n. an occurrence or thing regarded as a prophetic sign; prophetic significance. [L]

omicron /əˈmaɪkrɒn/ n. the fifteenth letter of the Greek alphabet, = o. [Gk, o micron = small O]

ominous /ˈɒmɪnəs/ adj. looking or seeming as if trouble is at hand, inauspicious. —**ominously** adv. [f. L (as OMEN)]

omission /əˈmɪʃ(ə)n/ n. **1.** omitting, being omitted. **2.** a thing omitted or not done. [f. OF or L (as foll.)]

omit /əˈmɪt/ v.t. (**-tt-**) **1.** to leave out, not to insert or include. **2.** to leave not done, to neglect or fail to do. [f. L omittere (OB-, mittere send)]

omni- in comb. all. [L (omnis all)]

omnibus /ˈɒmnɪbəs/ n. **1.** a bus. **2.** a volume containing several novels etc. previously published separately. —adj. serving several objects at once; comprising several items. [F f. L, = for everybody]

omnifarious /ɒmnɪˈfeərɪəs/ adj. of all sorts. [f. L (OMNI-; cf. MULTIFARIOUS)]

omnipotent /ɒmˈnɪpət(ə)nt/ adj. all-powerful. —**omnipotence** n., **omnipotently** adv. [f. OF f. L (as OMNI-, POTENT)]

omnipresent /ɒmnɪˈprez(ə)nt/ adj. ubiquitous. —**omnipresence** n. [f. L (as OMNI-, PRESENT)]

omniscient /ɒmˈnɪsɪənt/ adj. knowing everything or much. —**omniscience** n. [f. L (OMNI-, scire know)]

omnivorous /ɒmˈnɪvərəs/ adj. **1.** feeding on many kinds of food, especially on both plants and flesh. **2.** reading or observing etc. whatever comes one's way. [f. L (OMNI-, vorare devour)]

on prep. **1.** supported by, attached to, covering, enclosing; carried with. **2.** during; exactly at; contemporaneously with; immediately after or before; as a result of. **3.** having or so as to have membership of (a committee etc.). **4.** supported financially by. **5.** close to, just by; in the direction of, against, so as to threaten. **6.** touching, striking. **7.** having as a basis or motive; having as a standard, confirmation, or guarantee.

8. concerning; using, engaged with; so as to affect; to be paid by. **9.** added to. **10.** in a specified manner or state. —adv. **1.** so as to be supported by, attached to, or covering something. **2.** in an appropriate direction, towards something. **3.** further toward; in an advanced position or state. **4.** with continued movement or action. **5.** in operation or activity; being shown or performed. —adj. (in cricket) being in, from, or towards the part of the field on the striker's side and in front of his wicket. —n. the on side in cricket. —**be on,** (of an event) to be due to take place; (colloq.) to be willing to participate or approve; to accept a proposition or wager; to be practicable or acceptable. **be on at,** (colloq.) to nag or grumble at. **be on to,** to realize the significance or intentions of. **on and off,** intermittently, now and then. **on and on,** continually, at tedious length. **on-line** adj. (of computer equipment or a computer process) directly controlled by or connected to a central processor. **on time,** punctual, punctually. **on to,** to a position on. [OE]

onager /ˈɒnəɡə(r)/ n. a wild ass (esp. Equus onager). [f. L f. Gk (onos ass, agrios wild)]

onanism /ˈəʊnənɪz(ə)m/ n. masturbation. [f. F f. Onan (Gen. 38: 9)]

once /wʌns/ adv. **1.** on one occasion only. **2.** at some point or period in the past. **3.** ever, at all. **4.** multiplied by one; by one degree. —conj. as soon as. —n. one time or occasion. —**all at once,** without warning, suddenly; all together. **at once,** immediately; simultaneously. **(every) once in a while,** from time to time. **for once,** on this (or that) occasion, even if at no other. **once again** or **more,** another time. **once and for all,** in a final manner, esp. after much hesitation or uncertainty. **once or twice,** a few times. **once-over** n. (colloq.) a rapid preliminary inspection. **once upon a time,** at some vague time in the past. [orig. gen. of ONE]

oncology /ɒŋˈkɒlədʒɪ/ n. the study of tumours. [f. Gk ogkos mass + -LOGY]

oncoming adj. approaching from the front.

one /wʌn/ adj. **1.** single and integral in number. **2.** (with a noun implied) a single person or thing of a kind expressed or implied. **3.** particular but undefined, especially as contrasted with another. **4.** only such. **5.** forming a unity. **6.** identical, the same. —n. **1.** the lowest cardinal numeral, a thing numbered with it (l, i, I); unity, a unit. **2.** a single thing, person, or example (often referring to a noun previously expressed or implied). **3.** a drink. **4.** a story or joke. —pron. **1.** a person of a specified kind. **2.** any person, as representing people in general. **3.** (colloq.) I. —**all one,** a matter of indifference (to). **at one,** in agreement. **one another,** each the other (as a formula of reciprocity). **one-armed bandit,** (slang) a fruit machine with a long handle. **one day,** on an unspecified day; at some unspecified future date. **one-horse,** adj. using a single horse; (slang) small, poorly equipped. **one-man** adj. involving or operated by only one man. **one-off** adj. (colloq.) made as the only one, not repeated. **one or two,** (colloq.) a few. **one-sided** adj. unfair, partial. **one-time** adj. former. **one-track mind,** a mind preoccupied with one subject. **one-up** adj. (colloq.) having a particular advantage. **one-upmanship** n. (colloq.) the art of maintaining a psychological advantage. **one-way** adj. allowing movement, travel, etc., in one direction only. [OE]

Onega /əˈniːɡə/ the second largest European lake, in the USSR, on the Finnish border.

Oneida Community /əʊˈnaɪdə/ a radical religious community, founded in New York State in 1848. Originally embracing primitive Christian beliefs, communal economic practices, and polygamous marital practices, the Oneida Community proved a considerable economic success, and, although it gradually gave up its radical social and economic ideas, has continued to flourish since becoming a joint-stock company (1881), carrying on various industries, especially the manufacture of silver plate, as a commercial venture. [name of N. Amer. Indian tribe orig. inhabiting New York State]

O'Neill /əʊˈniːl/, Eugene Gladstone (1888-1953), American playwright. His first full-length play *Beyond the Horizon* (1920) won a Pulitzer Prize, and was followed by *Anna Christie* (1921) and many other plays, some of which powerfully and poetically criticized contemporary materialistic values. He adapted the theme of the Oresteia to the aftermath of the American Civil War in his trilogy *Mourning Becomes Electra* (1931). His most important later plays were *The Iceman Cometh* (1946), a tragedy about a collection of bar-room derelicts, and his masterpiece *Long Day's Journey into Night* (1956), a semi-autobiographical tragedy portraying mutually destructive inter-family relationships. O'Neill was awarded the Nobel Prize for literature in 1936.

oneness *n.* **1.** being one, singleness, uniqueness. **2.** agreement. **3.** sameness, changelessness. [f. ONE]

onerous /ˈɒnərəs, ˈəʊn-/ *adj.* burdensome. [f. OF f. L (*onus* burden)]

oneself /wʌnˈself/ *pron.* the reflexive and emphatic form of *one*.

ongoing *adj.* continuing, in progress.

onion /ˈʌnjən/ *n.* a vegetable (*Allium cepa*) with an edible bulb of pungent smell and flavour. —**oniony** *adj.* [f. AF f. L *unio*]

onlooker *n.* a spectator.

only /ˈəʊnlɪ/ *attrib. adj.* **1.** existing alone of its or their kind. **2.** best or alone worth knowing. —*adv.* **1.** without anything or anyone else, and that is all. **2.** no longer ago than; not until. **3.** with no better result than. —*conj.* except that, but then. —**if only**, I wish that. **only too**, extremely. [OE (as ONE)]

o.n.o. *abbr.* or near offer.

onomatopoeia /ɒnəmætəˈpiːə/ *n.* formation of a word from a sound resembling that associated with the thing named (e.g. *cuckoo, sizzle*). —**onomatopoeic** *adj.* [L f. Gk (*onoma* name, *poieō* make)]

onrush *n.* an onward rush.

onset *n.* **1.** an attack. **2.** a beginning.

onshore *adj.* **1.** on the shore. **2.** (of a wind) blowing from the sea towards the land.

onside *adj.* (of a player in a field game) not offside.

onslaught /ˈɒnslɔːt/ *n.* a fierce attack. [f. MDu. (as ON, *slag* blow)]

Ontario /ɒnˈteərɪəʊ/ a province of south-east Canada (from 1867), settled by the French and English in the 17th c. and ceded to Britain in 1763; capital, Toronto. —**Lake Ontario**, the smallest and most easterly of the Great Lakes, lying between the province and New York State.

ontology /ɒnˈtɒlədʒɪ/ *n.* the branch of metaphysics dealing with the nature of being. —**ontological** /-ˈlɒdʒɪk(ə)l/ *adj.* [f. Gk *ont-* being + -LOGY]

onus /ˈəʊnəs/ *n.* a burden, a duty, a responsibility. [L]

onward /ˈɒnwəd/ *adv.* (also **onwards**) further on; towards the front; with advancing motion. —*adj.* directed onwards. [f. ON + -WARD]

onyx /ˈɒnɪks/ *n.* a kind of chalcedony with coloured layers. [f. OF f. L f. Gk, orig. = finger-nail]

oodles /ˈuːd(ə)lz/ *n. pl.* (*colloq.*) a very great amount. [orig. US; etym. unkn.]

ooh /uː/ *int.* expressing surprise, delight, pain, etc. [natural exclam.]

oolite /ˈəʊəlaɪt/ *n.* a granular limestone. —**oolitic** /-ˈlɪtɪk/ *adj.* [f. F (Gk *ōon* egg, *lithos* stone)]

oops /ʊps, uːps/ *int.* on making an obvious mistake. [natural excl.]

ooze *v.t./i.* **1.** (of a fluid) to trickle or leak slowly out. **2.** to exude moisture. **3.** to exude or exhibit (a feeling) freely. —*n.* **1.** wet mud. **2.** a sluggish flow. —**oozy** *adj.* [f. OE *wos* juice, sap]

op *n.* (*colloq.*) an operation. [abbr.]

op- see OB-.

op. *abbr.* opus.

opacity /əʊˈpæsɪtɪ/ *n.* opaqueness. [f. F f. L (as OPAQUE)]

opal /ˈəʊp(ə)l/ *n.* a precious stone usually of a milky or bluish colour with iridescent reflections. [f. F or L, prob. ult. f. Skr. *upalas* precious stone]

opalescent /əʊpəˈles(ə)nt/ *adj.* iridescent. —**opalescence** *n.* [f. OPAL]

opaline /ˈəʊpəlaɪn/ *adj.* opal-like, opalescent. [f. OPAL]

opaque /əʊˈpeɪk/ *adj.* **1.** not transmitting light, impenetrable to sight. **2.** unclear, obscure. [f. L *opacus*]

op art (*colloq.*) optical art (see OPTICAL). [abbr.]

op. cit. *abbr.* in the work already quoted. [f. L *opere citato*]

OPEC /ˈəʊpek/ *abbr.* Organization of Petroleum-Exporting Countries, an association of the eleven major oil-producing countries, formed in 1960 to co-ordinate policies.

open /ˈəʊpən/ *adj.* **1.** not closed or locked or blocked up; not sealed; giving access. **2.** not covered or concealed or confined; not restricted. **3.** spread out, unfolded, expanded. **4.** with wide spaces between solid parts. **5.** undisguised, public, manifest. **6.** (of an exhibition, shop, etc.) admitting visitors or customers, ready for business. **7.** (of a competition

etc.) unrestricted as to who may compete. **8.** not yet settled or decided; (of an offer or vacancy) still available; (with *to*) willing or liable to receive. **9.** (of the bowels) not constipated. —*n.* **1.** *the* open air; *the* country. **2.** an open competition or championship. —*v.t./i.* **1.** to make or become open or more open. **2.** to begin or establish; to make a start. **3.** to declare ceremonially to be open to the public. —**open air**, outdoors. **open-and-shut** *adj.* (*colloq.*) perfectly straightforward. **open book**, one who is easily understood; not having secrets. **open day**, a day when the public may visit a place normally closed to them. **open-ended** *adj.* without limit or restriction. **open a person's eyes**, to make him realize something unexpected. **open-handed** *adj.* generous. **open-hearted** *adj.* frank and kindly. **open-heart surgery**, surgery with the heart exposed and blood made to bypass it. **open letter**, a letter of protest etc. addressed to a person by name but printed in a newspaper etc. **open-minded** *adj.* accessible to new ideas, unprejudiced; undecided. **open-plan** *adj.* with few interior walls. **open prison**, a prison with few physical restraints on prisoners. **open question**, a matter on which no final verdict has yet been made or on which none is possible. **open sandwich**, a slice of bread covered with a layer of meat or cheese etc. **open sea**, the expanse of sea away from the land. **open secret**, one known to so many people that it is no longer a secret. **open society**, one without a rigid structure and with freedom of belief. **open verdict**, one affirming the commission of a crime but not specifying a criminal or (in the case of violent death) a cause. —**openness** *n.* [OE (as UP)]

opencast *adj.* (of a mine or mining) with removal of surface layers and working from above, not from shafts.

opener *n.* **1.** a person or thing that opens something. **2.** a device for opening tins or bottles etc. [f. OPEN]

open-hearth process a process for making steel, in which scrap iron or steel, limestone, and molten or cold pig-iron are melted together using a shallow reverberatory furnace. First operated *c.*1860, the process was producing most of the world's steel until *c.*1955. Although slower than the Bessemer process it is under closer control and can melt scrap and cold iron, which the Bessemer process cannot. (See STEEL.)

opening *n.* **1.** a space or gap; a place where something opens. **2.** the beginning of something. **3.** an opportunity. —**opening-time** *n.* the time at which public houses may legally open for custom. [f. OPEN]

openly *adv.* without concealment, publicly; frankly. [f. OPEN]

Open University a university (founded in Britain in 1969) with no formal requirements for entry to its first-degree courses, and providing instruction by a combination of television, radio, and correspondence courses and by audio-visual centres.

opera[1] /ˈɒpərə/ *n.* a dramatic performance or composition of which music is an essential part; the branch of art concerned with this (see below). —**opera-glasses** *n.pl.* small binoculars for use at the opera or theatre. **opera-hat** *n.* a man's collapsible hat. **opera-house** *n.* a theatre for operas. [It. f. L, = labour, work]

Opera was born in Italy in the 16th c. Although there had previously been stage works involving music, the creation of a dramatic work to be sung throughout was a new concept, derived from theories of the nature of the music of the ancient Greeks and put into practice by a group of intellectuals based in Florence. The earliest operas involved the talents of the composers Jacopo Peri (*Dafne*, 1598, now lost, and *Euridice*, 1600, including some settings by his rival Caccini) and Giulio Caccini (*Euridice*, 1600–2, the first published opera), and the poet Ottavio Rinuccini; better known today are the operas of Claudio Monteverdi. The first public opera house, the Teatro San Cassiano, was opened in Venice in 1637, and since then opera has become celebrated, and among those with a puritan streak notorious, for the extravagance of its plots, the range of its emotional power, the huge sums of money needed to attract star singers (and the volatile temperament of its prima donnas), and the irresistible and inexhaustible attraction it holds for its lovers.

opera[2] *pl.* of OPUS.

operable /ˈɒpərəb(ə)l/ *adj.* **1.** that can be operated. **2.** suitable for treatment by a surgical operation. [f. L (as foll.)]

operate /ˈɒpəreɪt/ *v.t./i.* **1.** to be in action; to produce an effect. **2.** to control the functioning of. **3.** to perform a surgical operation. —**operating-theatre** *n.* a room for surgical operations. [f. L *operari* to work (as OPUS)]

operatic /ɒpəˈrætɪk/ *adj.* of or like an opera. —**operatically** *adv.* [f. OPERA[1]]

operation /ɒpəˈreɪʃ(ə)n/ *n.* **1.** operating, being operated; the way a thing works; validity, scope. **2.** a piece of work, something to be done. **3.** an act performed by a surgeon on any part of the body to remove or deal with a diseased, injured, or deformed part. **4.** a piece of military activity. **5.** a financial or other transaction. **6.** (*Math.*) the subjection of a number, quantity, or function to a process affecting its value or form, e.g. multiplication, differentiation. [f. OF f. L (as OPERATE)]

operational *adj.* **1.** of, engaged in, or used for operations. **2.** able or ready to function. —**operational research**, the application of scientific principles to business etc. management. —**operationally** *adv.* [f. prec.]

operative /ˈɒpərətɪv/ *adj.* **1.** in operation, having an effect; practical; having principal relevance. **2.** of or by surgery. —*n.* a worker, especially in a factory. —**operatively** *adv.* [f. L (as OPERATE)]

operator /ˈɒpəreɪtə(r)/ *n.* **1.** a person who operates a machine etc.; one who engages in business; (*colloq.*) a person acting in a specified way. **2.** one who makes connections of lines at a telephone exchange. **3.** (*Math.*) a symbol or function denoting an operation. [as OPERATE]

operculum /əˈpɜːkjʊləm/ *n.* (*pl.* **-ula**) a fish's gill-cover (ill. FISH); a similar structure in a plant; the valve closing the mouth of a shell. [L (*operire* to cover)]

operetta /ɒpəˈretə/ *n.* a one-act or short opera; a light opera. [It. (dim. of OPERA)]

ophidian /əˈfɪdɪən/ *n.* a member of the Ophidia or Serpentes, a suborder of reptiles including the snakes; a snake. —*adj.* of this order; snakelike. [f. Gk *ophis* snake]

Ophir /ˈəʊfə(r)/ (in the Old Testament) an unidentified region, perhaps in SE Arabia, famous for its fine gold and precious stones.

ophthalmia /ɒfˈθælmɪə/ *n.* inflammation of the eye, especially conjunctivitis. [L f. Gk (*ophthalmos* eye)]

ophthalmic /ɒfˈθælmɪk/ *adj.* **1.** of or for the eye. **2.** of, for, or affected with ophthalmia. —**ophthalmic optician**, an optician qualified to prescribe as well as dispense spectacles etc. [f. L (as prec.)]

ophthalmology /ɒfθælˈmɒlədʒɪ/ *n.* the study of the eye and its diseases. —**ophthalmologist** *n.* [f. Gk *ophthalmos* eye + -LOGY]

ophthalmoscope /ɒfˈθælməskəʊp/ *n.* an instrument for examining the eye. [as prec. + -SCOPE]

opiate /ˈəʊpɪət/ *adj.* **1.** containing opium. **2.** narcotic, soporific. —*n.* **1.** a drug containing opium and easing pain or inducing sleep. **2.** a soothing influence. [f. L (as OPIUM)]

Opie /ˈəʊpɪ/, John (1761–1807), English painter. A carpenter's son, he was promoted on his arrival in London (1781) as the 'Cornish wonder'—a self-taught genius—and was made a Royal Academician in 1787. His portraiture (e.g. *Mary Wollstonecraft*) brought him wealth and reputation, while his history painting, especially for Boydell's Shakespeare Gallery, was both popular and influential.

opine /əʊˈpaɪn/ *v.t.* to express or hold as one's opinion. [f. L *opinari* believe]

opinion /əˈpɪnjən/ *n.* **1.** a belief based on grounds short of proof, a view held as probable. **2.** what one thinks about something. **3.** a piece of professional advice. —**opinion poll**, an estimate of public opinion made by questioning a representative sample of people. [f. OF f. L *opinio* (as prec.)]

opinionated /əˈpɪnjəneɪtɪd/ *adj.* having strong opinions and holding them dogmatically. [f. prec.]

opium /ˈəʊpɪəm/ *n.* a drug made from the juice of the poppy *Papaver somniferum*, used especially as a narcotic or sedative. [L f. Gk *opion*]

Opium War the war between Britain and China (1839–42) and later (1856–60) Britain and France against China, following China's attempt to prohibit the (illegal) importation of opium from British India into China, and Chinese restrictions on foreign trade. Defeat of the Chinese resulted in the ceding of Hong Kong to Britain and the opening of five 'treaty ports' to traders.

opossum /əˈpɒsəm/ *n.* **1.** an American marsupial of the family Didelphidae. **2.** a similar Australian marsupial of the family Phalangeridae, living in trees. [f. Virginian Indian]

opp. *abbr.* opposite.

Oppenheimer /ˈɒpənhaɪmə(r)/, Julius Robert (1904–67), American theoretical physicist who, as director of the laboratory at Los Alamos in New Mexico, USA, led the team which designed and built the first atomic bomb during the Second World War. After the war he opposed development of the hydrogen bomb and—like a number of intellectuals of his day—fell foul of the Senate committee investigating alleged un-American activities. His security clearance was withdrawn in 1953 and his advisory activities stopped; with the passing of the McCarthy era his public standing was restored.

opponent /əˈpəʊnənt/ *n.* a person or group opposing another in a contest or war. [f. L *opponere* set against (OP-, *ponere* place)]

opportune /ˈɒpətjuːn/ *adj.* (of time) well-chosen, favourable; (of an action or event) well-timed. —**opportunely** *adv.* [f. OF f. L *opportunus* (OP-, *portus* harbour), orig. of wind driving ship towards harbour]

opportunism /ˈɒpətjuːnɪz(ə)m/ *n.* the grasping of opportunities, often in an unprincipled way. —**opportunist** *n.* [f. prec.]

opportunity /ɒpəˈtjuːnɪtɪ/ *n.* a time or set of circumstances suitable for a particular purpose. [f. OF f. L (as OPPORTUNE)]

oppose /əˈpəʊz/ *v.t.* **1.** to place in opposition or contrast. **2.** to set oneself against, to resist; to argue against. —**as opposed to**, in contrast with. [f. OF f. L (as OPPONENT)]

opposite /ˈɒpəzɪt/ *adj.* **1.** (often with *to*) having a position on the other or further side, facing or back to back. **2.** of a contrary kind, as different as possible. —*n.* an opposite thing, person, or term. —*adv.* in the opposite position. —*prep.* opposite to. —**opposite number**, a person holding the equivalent position in another group or organization. [as prec.]

opposition /ɒpəˈzɪʃ(ə)n/ *n.* **1.** resistance, being hostile or in conflict or disagreement. **2.** placing or being placed opposite, contrast; a diametrically opposite position, esp. of two heavenly bodies when their longitude differs by 180° (opp. *conjunction*). **3.** the people who oppose a proposal etc.; a group of opponents or rivals. —**the Opposition**, the chief parliamentary party opposed to that in office. [f. OF f. L (as OB-, POSITION)]

oppress /əˈpres/ *v.t.* **1.** to govern harshly, to treat with continual cruelty or injustice; to keep in subservience. **2.** to weigh down with cares or unhappiness. —**oppression** *n.*, **oppressor** *n.* [f. OF f. L (as OP-, PRESS)]

oppressive *adj.* **1.** oppressing. **2.** difficult to endure. **3.** (of weather) sultry and tiring. —**oppressively** *adv.*, **oppressiveness** *n.* [f. F f. L (as prec.)]

opprobrious /əˈprəʊbrɪəs/ *adj.* (of language) severely scornful, abusive. [f. L (as foll.)]

opprobrium /əˈprəʊbrɪəm/ *n.* great disgrace brought by shameful conduct. [L, f. *opprobrium* disgraceful act]

oppugn /əˈpjuːn/ *v.t.* to controvert, to call in question. [f. L *oppugnare* attack (OP-, *pugnare* fight)]

opt *v.i.* to make a choice, to decide (*for* an alternative). —**opt out (of)**, to choose not to participate (in). [f. F f. L *optare* choose, wish]

optative /ɒpˈteɪtɪv, ˈɒptə-/ *adj.* (*Gram.*, esp. of a mood in Greek) expressing a wish. [f. F f. L (as prec.)]

optic /ˈɒptɪk/ *adj.* of the eye or sight. [f. F or L f. Gk (*optos* seen)]

optical /ˈɒptɪk(ə)l/ *adj.* **1.** of sight, visual. **2.** aiding sight. **3.** of or according to optics. —**optical fibre**, thin glass fibre used in fibre optics. **optical illusion**, an involuntary mental misinterpretation of a thing seen, due to its deceptive appearance (e.g. a mirage). —**optically** *adv.* [f. prec.]

optical art a form of abstract art and visual decoration, developed in the 1960s, in which optical effects are used to provide illusions of movement in the patterns produced, or designs in which conflicting patterns emerge and overlap. Bridget Riley and Victor Vasarely are its most famous exponents.

optician /ɒpˈtɪʃ(ə)n/ *n.* a maker or seller of spectacles and other optical instruments; one trained to provide means to correct the defects of people's eyesight. [f. F f. L (as OPTIC)]

optics /ˈɒptɪks/ *n.pl.* (usu. treated as *sing.*) the science of light and vision (see ill. LIGHT). [f. OPTIC]

optimal /ˈɒptɪm(ə)l/ *adj.* the best or most favourable. [f. L *optimus* best]

optimism /ˈɒptɪmɪz(ə)m/ *n.* **1.** a hopeful view or disposition; a tendency to expect a favourable outcome. **2.** the belief that the actual world is the best possible. **3.** the belief that good must ultimately prevail over evil. —**optimist** *n.* [f. F f. L (as OPTIMUM)]

optimistic /ɒptɪˈmɪstɪk/ adj. showing optimism; hopeful. —**optimistically** adv. [f. F f. L optimum best]

optimize /ˈɒptɪmaɪz/ v.t. to make optimum, to make the most of. [f. L optimus best]

optimum /ˈɒptɪməm/ n. (pl. **-ima**) the best or most favourable conditions or amount etc. —adj. optimal. [L, neut. of optimus best]

option /ˈɒpʃ(ə)n/ n. **1.** a choice; a thing that is or may be chosen. **2.** the liberty of choosing. **3.** the right to buy or sell something at a certain price within a limited time. —**keep or leave one's options open**, to remain uncommitted. [F or L f. L (as OPT)]

optional adj. open to choice, not obligatory. —**optionally** adv. [f. prec.]

opulent /ˈɒpjʊlənt/ adj. **1.** wealthy. **2.** abundant, luxuriant. **3.** luxurious. —**opulence** n., **opulently** adv. [f. L (opes wealth)]

opus /ˈəʊpəs, ˈɒp-/ n. (pl. **opera** /ˈɒpərə/) a musical composition numbered as one of a composer's works. [L, = work]

or[1] conj. introducing an alternative or another name for the same thing or an afterthought. [OE]

or[2] n. & adj. (usu. placed after n.) (in heraldry) gold, yellow. [F f. L aurum]

oracle /ˈɒrək(ə)l/ n. **1.** (in classical antiquity) a place where deities were consulted through the medium of a priest etc. for advice or prophecy; the reply given. **2.** a person or thing regarded as a source of wisdom etc. **3.** **Oracle** [P], the teletext service provided by the IBA. —**oracular** /ɒˈrækjʊlə(r)/ adj. [f. OF f. L (orare speak)]

oral /ˈɔːr(ə)l/ adj. **1.** spoken, verbal, by word of mouth. **2.** done or taken by mouth. —n. (colloq.) a spoken examination. —**orally** adv. [f. L (os mouth)]

Orange[1] /ɒˈrɑ̃ʒ/ a town and principality on the Rhône, which in the 16th c. passed to the House of Nassau, later rulers of the Netherlands. —**House of Orange** /ˈɒrɪndʒ/, the Dutch royal house. **William of Orange,** William III. [f. L Arausio name of the town]

Orange[2] /ˈɒrɪndʒ/ adj. of the extreme Protestants in Ireland, especially in Ulster, in reference to the secret political Association of Orangemen formed in 1895 for the defence of Protestantism and maintenance of Protestant ascendancy in Ireland. It was probably named from the wearing of orange badges etc. as a symbol of adherence to William III, of the House of Orange, who defeated the Catholic James II at the battle of the Boyne in 1690.

orange /ˈɒrɪndʒ/ n. **1.** a round juicy citrus fruit with reddish-yellow peel; the tree bearing it (Citrus aurantium). **2.** reddish-yellow colour. —adj. orange-coloured. —**orange-blossom** n. the fragrant white flowers of the orange, traditionally worn by brides (the custom appears to have been introduced from France c.1820-30). [f. OF ult. f. Arab. nāranj f. Pers.]

orangeade /ɒrɪndʒˈeɪd/ n. a drink made from orange-juice or a synthetic substitute. [f. prec.]

Orange Free State /ˈɒrɪndʒ/ an inland province of the Republic of South Africa; capital, Bloemfontein. First settled by Boers trekking from Cape Colony (1836-8), it was annexed by Britain in 1848 but restored in 1854 to the Boers, who established the Orange Free State Republic. It was re-annexed by Britain in 1900, as the Orange River Colony, was given internal self-government in 1907, and became a province of the Union of South Africa in 1910, as the Orange Free State. [f. House of ORANGE[1]]

Orangeman n. (pl. **-men**) see ORANGE[2].

Orange River the longest river in South Africa, flowing westward for 1,859 km (1,155 miles) into the Atlantic across almost the whole breadth of the continent.

orangery /ˈɒrɪndʒərɪ/ n. a building or hot-house for orange-trees. [f ORANGE]

orang-utan /ɔːˈræŋuːˈtæn/ n. a large long-armed anthropoid ape (Pongo pygmaeus) of the East Indies. [Malay, = wild man]

oration /ɔːˈreɪʃ(ə)n/ n. a formal or ceremonial speech. [f. L oratio (orare speak, pray)]

orator /ˈɒrətə(r)/ n. a maker of a formal speech; a skilful speaker. [f. AF f. L (as prec.)]

oratorical /ɒrəˈtɒrɪk(ə)l/ adj. of or like oratory. [f. ORATORY]

oratorio /ɒrəˈtɔːrɪəʊ/ n. (pl. **-os**) **1.** a musical composition, usually on a sacred theme, for solo voices, chorus, and orchestra. The first oratorios proper were composed in the early 17th c. **2.** this as a musical form. [It. (as foll.), orig.

of musical services held at Oratory of St Philip Neri in Rome]

oratory[1] /ˈɒrətərɪ/ n. the art of or skill in public speaking. [f. L oratoria (ars art) of speaking (as ORATION)]

oratory[2] /ˈɒrətərɪ/ n. a small chapel, a place for private worship. [f. AF f. L oratorium (as ORATOR)]

orb n. **1.** a sphere, a globe. **2.** a globe surmounted by a cross as part of the royal regalia; a heavenly body. **3.** (poetic) the eye. [f. L orbis ring]

orbicular /ɔːˈbɪkjʊlə(r)/ adj. spherical, circular. [f. L (orbiculus dim. of orbis, as prec.)]

orbit /ˈɔːbɪt/ n. **1.** the curved (usually closed) course of a planet, comet, satellite, spacecraft, etc., the closed path followed by an object constrained by a tangential velocity to remain bound to a massive body (a planet or star) while not falling directly towards the centre of attraction. **2.** the path of an electron round an atomic nucleus. **3.** a range or sphere of action. —v.t./i. **1.** to move in an orbit (round). **2.** to put into orbit. —**orbiter** n. [f. L, = track of wheel or moon (orbis ring)]

orbital /ˈɔːbɪt(ə)l/ adj. **1.** of an orbit or orbits. **2.** (of a road) passing round the outside of a city. —n. a state or function representing the possible motion of an election round an atomic nucleus. —**orbitally** adv. [f. prec.]

Orcadian /ɔːˈkeɪdɪən/ n. a native or inhabitant of Orkney. —adj. of Orkney. [f. L Orcades Orkney Islands]

Orcagna /ɔːˈkɑːnjə/ the nickname (= archangel) of Andrea di Cione (active c.1308-68), Florentine painter, sculptor, and architect occupying a key position between Giotto and Fra Angelico. His painting represents a return to a hieratic brightly coloured style fusing Gothic and Byzantine elements, in opposition to Giotto's naturalism, and may have been a product of new devotional attitudes in the aftermath of the Black Death (1348). His sculpture follows Andrea Pisano in style (e.g. the tabernacle reliefs on Or San Michele, Florence, 1359). As an architect he worked on the cathedrals of Orvieto and Florence. He had two brothers: Nardo (fl. c.1343-66) and Jacopo di Cione (fl. 1365-98) who worked in a similar style.

orchard /ˈɔːtʃəd/ n. an enclosed piece of land planted with fruit-trees. [OE (L hortus garden, YARD[2])]

orchestra /ˈɔːkɪstrə/ n. **1.** a body of musicians playing together on stringed, wind, and percussion instruments according to an established scheme (see below and ill. pp. 592-3). **2.** the area in a theatre etc. assigned to them (called orchestra-pit when on a lower level). **3.** the semi-circular space in front of the stage of an ancient Greek theatre, where the chorus danced and sang (ill. THEATRE). —**orchestral** /ɔːˈkestr(ə)l/ adj. [L f. Gk (orkheomai to dance)]

In its modern definition the orchestra dates from the 18th c. when the forces required for orchestral music settled into four main categories with standard members: woodwind (flutes, clarinets, oboes, bassoons), brass (horns, trumpets, trombones, tubas), percussion (drums, with many optional extras), and strings (first and second violins, violas, cellos, double basses). The 19th c. saw a great increase in the number and variety of instruments in the orchestra, but in the 20th c. a return has frequently been made to smaller, chamber groups.

orchestrate /ˈɔːkɪstreɪt/ v.t. **1.** to compose, arrange, or score for an orchestral performance. **2.** to arrange or combine (various elements) harmoniously or for maximum effect. —**orchestration** /-ˈstreɪʃ(ə)n/ n. [f. prec.]

orchid /ˈɔːkɪd/ n. any plant of the family Orchidaceae, often with brilliant flowers. [f. L orchis f. Gk, orig. = testicle (from shape of tuber in some species)]

Orczy /ˈɔːkzɪ/, Baroness Emmusca (1865-1947), Hungarian-born British novelist whose best-known novel is The Scarlet Pimpernel (1905), telling of the adventures of an English nobleman smuggling aristocrats out of France during the French Revolution.

ordain /ɔːˈdeɪn/ v.t. **1.** to appoint ceremonially to perform religious duties in the Christian Church. **2.** to destine. **3.** to appoint or decree authoritatively. [f. AF f. L ordinare (ordo -inis as prec.)]

ordeal /ɔːˈdiːl/ n. **1.** a severe or testing trial or experience. **2.** (hist.) a method of determining guilt by making a suspect undergo physical harm, the safe endurance of which betokened innocence. [OE]

order n. **1.** a condition in which every part or unit is in its right place or in a normal or efficient state; the arrangement of things relative to one another; a proper or customary sequence. **2.** the prevalence of constitutional authority and obedience to the law. **3.** a system of rules or procedure. **4.** a command, an authoritative instruction; a direction to supply something, the thing (to be) supplied; a written instruction to pay money or giving authority to do something. **5.** a social class or rank. **6.** a monastic organization or institution; a Masonic or similar fraternity; a company to which distinguished persons are admitted as an honour or reward; the insignia of this. **7.** any of the ancient orders of architecture (see below). **8.** a group of plants or animals classified as similar in many ways, below a class and above a family. —*v.t.* **1.** to put in order, to arrange methodically. **2.** to command; to prescribe. **3.** to give an order for (goods etc.); to tell a waiter etc. to serve. —**holy orders,** the status of an ordained clergyman. **in order,** in correct sequence or position; according to rules etc.; in good condition. **in order to** or **that,** with the intention that; for the purpose of. **on order,** ordered but not yet received. **Order in Council,** a sovereign's order on an administrative matter given by the advice of the Privy Council. **order-paper** *n.* a written or printed order of a day's proceedings, especially in Parliament. **orders of architecture,** the styles of ancient architecture distinguished by the type of column used (ill. TEMPLES). The principal classical orders are the Doric, Ionic, Corinthian, Tuscan, and Composite, the first three being Greek in origin and the others Roman. The simplicity or elaborateness of each influenced the overall look of the building, and their differing proportional relations determined those of the whole edifice. **out of order,** not in order. **to order,** as specified by a customer. [f. OF *ordre* f. L *ordo*]

orderly /ˈɔːdəlɪ/ *adj.* **1.** well arranged, in good order; tidy. **2.** methodical. **3.** obedient to discipline, well-behaved. —*n.* **1.** a soldier in attendance on an officer to assist him or take messages etc. **2.** an attendant in a hospital. —**orderly officer,** the officer on duty on a particular day. **orderly room,** a room where business is conducted in a military barracks. —**orderliness** *n.* [f. prec.]

ordinal /ˈɔːdɪn(ə)l/ *adj.* (of a number) defining a thing's position in a series (e.g. *first, tenth, hundredth*). —*n.* an ordinal number. [f. L (as ORDER)]

ordinance /ˈɔːdɪnəns/ *n.* **1.** a decree. **2.** a religious rite. [f. OF f. L (as ORDAIN)]

ordinand /ˈɔːdɪnænd/ *n.* a candidate for ordination. [f. L (as ORDAIN)]

ordinary /ˈɔːdɪnərɪ/ *adj.* usual, customary, not exceptional. —*n.* **1.** a rule or book laying down the order of divine service. **2.** an ungeared bicycle of an early type, with a large front wheel and small rear wheel, so called for some years after the introduction of the 'safety' type (see BICYCLE). **3.** (in heraldry) a charge of the earliest, simplest, and commonest kind (esp. chief, pale, bend, fess, bar, chevron, cross, saltire). —**in the ordinary way,** in normal circumstances, usually. **ordinary level,** the lowest level in the GCE examination. **ordinary seaman,** a seaman of a lower rating than an able seaman. **out of the ordinary,** unusual. —**ordinarily** *adv.* [f. L *ordinarius* (as ORDER)]

ordinate /ˈɔːdɪnət/ *n.* (*Math.*) a coordinate measured usually vertically. [f. L (as ORDAIN)]

ordination /ɔːdɪˈneɪʃ(ə)n/ *n.* ordaining, conferring of holy orders. [f. OF or L (as ORDAIN)]

ordnance /ˈɔːdnəns/ *n.* artillery and military supplies; the government department dealing with these. —**Ordnance Survey,** the government survey of the UK producing accurate and detailed maps of the whole country. [var. of ORDINANCE]

Ordovician /ɔːdəˈvɪsɪən/ *adj.* of the second period of the Palaeozoic era, following the Cambrian and preceding the Silurian, lasting from about 505 to 438 million years ago. It saw both the diversification of many invertebrate groups and the appearance of the first vertebrates (jawless fish). —*n.* this period. [f. L *Ordovices* ancient British tribe in N. Wales]

ordure /ˈɔːdjʊə(r)/ *n.* dung. [f. OF (*ord* foul f. L *horridus*)]

ore /ɔː(r)/ *n.* solid rock or mineral from which metal or other valuable substances may be extracted. [OE]

oregano /ɒrɪˈɡɑːnəʊ/ *n.* dried wild marjoram as a seasoning. [Sp., = ORIGAN]

Oregon /ˈɒrɪɡən/ a State of the USA, on the Pacific coast, occupied jointly by British and Americans until 1846, when it was ceded to the USA. It became the 33rd State in 1859; capital, Salem. —**Oregon Trail,** the route from the Missouri across Oregon, some 3,000 km (2,000 miles) in

length followed by settlers moving west, especially in the 1840s.

Orestes /ɒˈrestiːz/ (*Gk legend*) son of Agamemnon and Clytemnestra. He killed his mother and her lover Aegisthus to avenge the murder of Agamemnon.

organ /ˈɔːɡən/ *n.* **1.** a musical instrument consisting of pipes that sound when air is forced through them, operated by keyboards and pedals (see below); a similar electronic instrument without pipes; a harmonium. **2.** a part of an animal or plant body serving a particular function. **3.** a medium of communication (e.g. a newspaper) representing a party or interest. —**organ-grinder** *n.* the player of a barrel-organ. **organ-loft** *n.* a gallery for an organ. [OE & f. OF f. L f. Gk *organon* tool]

The organ has been associated with the church for nearly a millennium, but its invention *c.*246 BC is attributed to Ktesibios, an engineer based in Alexandria. His instrument used water to pump the bellows and a row of reed pipes for making the sound. Roman interest in the organ was attested in 1931 when an instrument built in AD 228 was excavated at Aquincum in Hungary, but its importance in the West stems from a gift of one from Emperor Constantine V to Pepin, king of the Franks, in 757. In the mid-10th c. a huge organ belonging to Winchester Cathedral apparently required no fewer than 70 strong men to work the 26 bellows. Among celebrated organ builders are 'Father' Smith (*c.*1630-1708), who built instruments for the Banqueting House in Whitehall, Westminster Abbey, and Durham Cathedral, and Aristide Cavaillé-Coll (1811-98), who revolutionized the tonal design, incorporating a rich variety of orchestral stops.

organdie /ˈɔːɡəndɪ, -ˈɡændɪ/ *n.* fine translucent muslin, usually stiffened. [f. F]

organic /ɔːˈɡænɪk/ *adj.* **1.** of or affecting a bodily organ or organs. **2.** (of plants or animals) having organs or an organized physical structure. **3.** (of food etc.) produced without the use of artificial fertilizers or pesticides. **4.** organized or arranged as a system of related parts. **5.** (of a compound etc.) containing carbon in its molecules. **6.** inherent, structural. —**organic chemistry,** the chemistry of carbon compounds, which are present in all living matter and in substances derived from it. —**organically** *adv.* [f. F f. L f. Gk *organikos* (as ORGAN)]

organism /ˈɔːɡənɪz(ə)m/ *n.* **1.** an individual animal or plant. **2.** an organized body. [f. F (as ORGANIZE)]

organist /ˈɔːɡənɪst/ *n.* the player of an organ. [f. ORGAN]

organization /ɔːɡənaɪˈzeɪʃ(ə)n/ *n.* **1.** organizing, being organized. **2.** an organized body of people; an organized system. —**organizational** *adj.* [f. foll.]

organize /ˈɔːɡənaɪz/ *v.t.* **1.** to give an orderly structure to, to systematize. **2.** to initiate or make arrangements for; to enlist (a person or group) in this. **3.** to make organic, to make into living tissue. —**organizer** *n.* [f. OF f. L (as ORGAN)]

organza /ɔːˈɡænzə/ *n.* a thin stiff transparent dress-fabric of silk or synthetic fibre. [prob. f. *Lorganza* (US trade mark)]

orgasm /ˈɔːɡæz(ə)m/ *n.* the climax of sexual excitement. **orgasmic** /-ˈɡæzmɪk/ *adj.* [f. F f. Gk *orgaō* swell)]

orgy /ˈɔːdʒɪ/ *n.* **1.** a wild drunken or licentious party or revelry. **2.** excessive indulgence in an activity. **3.** (in ancient Greece and Rome) secret rites in the worship of various gods, especially Bacchus, with wild drinking etc. —**orgiastic** /-ˈæstɪk/ *adj.* [f. F f. L f. Gk *orgia* pl.]

oriel /ˈɔːrɪəl/ *n.* a polygonal recess with windows projecting from the wall of a house at an upper level (ill. HOUSES). [f. OF *oriol* gallery]

Orient /ˈɔːrɪənt/ *n.* the East, the countries east of the Mediterranean, especially East Asia. [f. OF f. L *oriens* rising, sunrise (*oriri* rise)]

orient /ˈɔːrɪənt/ *v.t.* **1.** to place or determine the position of with regard to the points of the compass. **2.** to site (a building etc.) so that it faces east. **3.** to face or turn (towards a specified direction); to bring into clearly understood relations, to direct. —**orient oneself,** to get one's bearings; to accustom oneself to a new situation etc. [= prec.]

oriental /ɔːrɪˈent(ə)l, ɒr-/ *adj.* of the Orient, of the eastern or East Asian world or its civilization. —*n.* a native or inhabitant of the Orient. [as ORIENT]

orientate /ˈɔːrɪənteɪt/ *v.t./i.* to orient. [f. foll.]

orientation /ɔːrɪənˈteɪʃ(ə)n/ *n.* **1.** orienting, being oriented. **2.** position relative to surroundings. [f. ORIENT]

orienteering /ɔːrɪənˈtɪərɪŋ/ *n.* the competitive sport of

The Orchestra (see also **Musical Notation and some Instruments**)

Typical layout of a modern orchestra

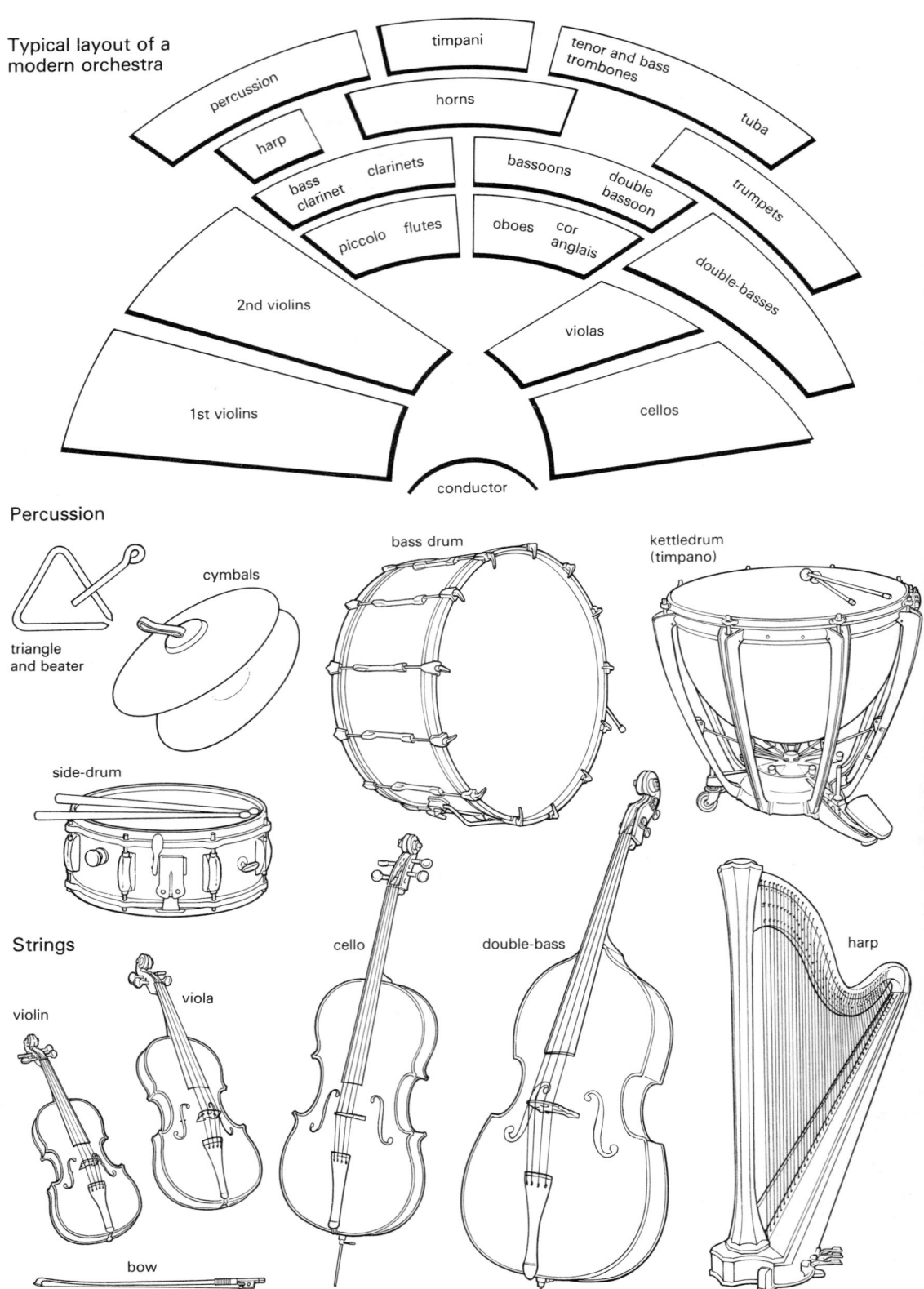

percussion

timpani

tenor and bass trombones

horns

tuba

harp

bass clarinet clarinets

bassoons double bassoon

trumpets

piccolo flutes

oboes cor anglais

double-basses

2nd violins

violas

1st violins

cellos

conductor

Percussion

triangle and beater

cymbals

bass drum

kettledrum (timpano)

side-drum

Strings

violin

viola

cello

double-bass

harp

bow

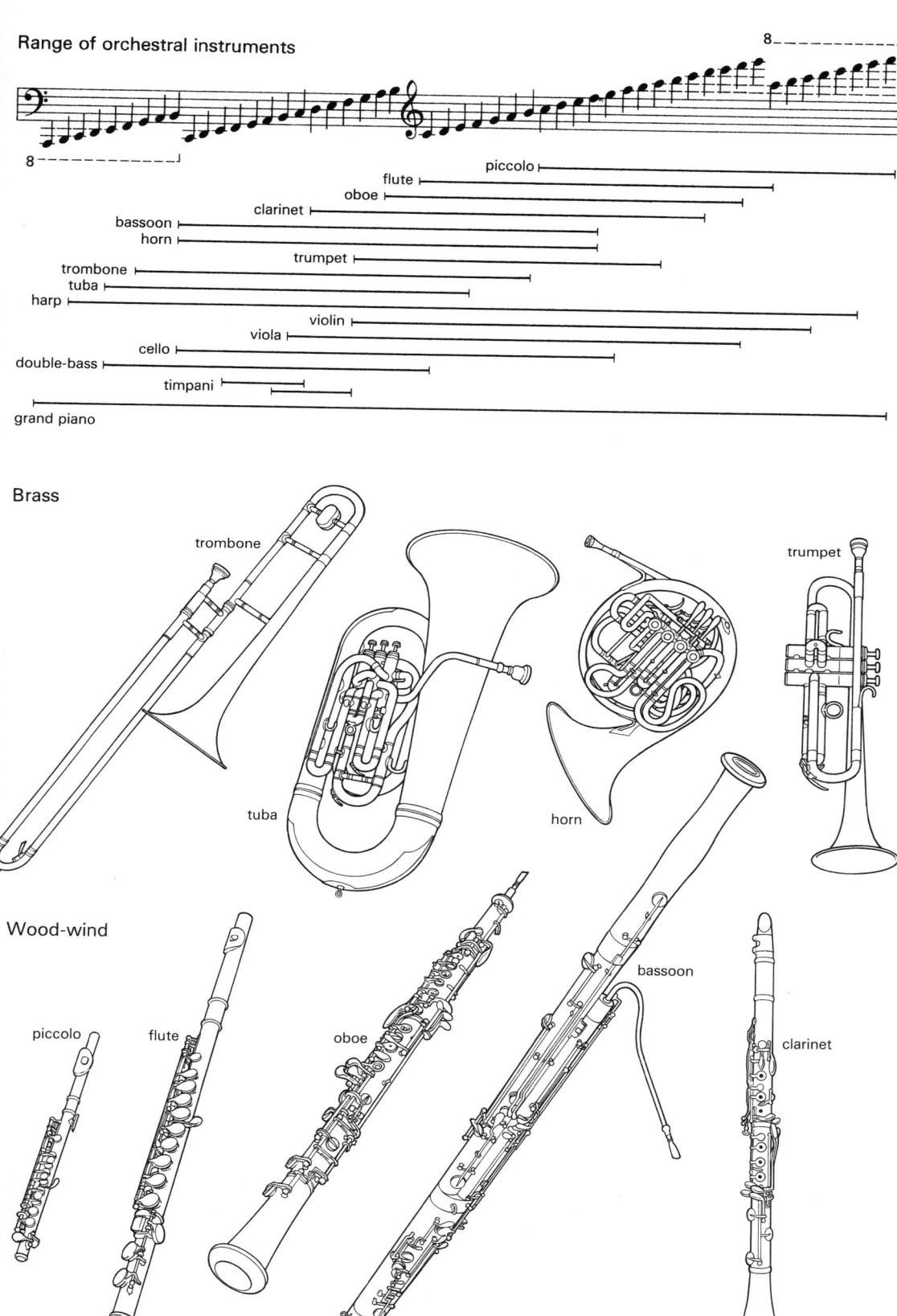

Range of orchestral instruments

piccolo
flute
oboe
clarinet
bassoon
horn
trumpet
trombone
tuba
harp
violin
viola
cello
double-bass
timpani
grand piano

Brass

trombone

tuba

horn

trumpet

Wood-wind

piccolo

flute

oboe

bassoon

clarinet

finding one's way on foot across rough country with map and compass. Although 'chart and compass' races were held in the sports meetings of British army units in the early 20th c., orienteering is generally recognized as being of Scandinavian origin, first introduced as a sport for young people in Sweden in 1918. [f. Sw. *orientering*]

orifice /ˈɒrɪfɪs/ *n.* an aperture, the mouth of a cavity, a vent. [F f. L *orificium* (*os* mouth)]

origami /ɒrɪˈgɑːmɪ/ *n.* the art of folding paper intricately into decorative shapes. [Jap.]

origan /ˈɒrɪgən/ *n.* (also **origanum** /-ˈgɑːnəm/) wild marjoram (*Origanum vulgare*). [f. L f. Gk]

Origen /ˈɒrɪdʒ(ə)n/ (*c.*185–*c.*254) Alexandrian biblical scholar and theologian. Of his numerous works the most famous was the *Hexapla*, an edition of the Old Testament with six or more parallel versions. He recognized literal, moral, and allegorical interpretations of Scripture, preferring the last. Many of his writings have perished and most of the others survive only in fragments or in Latin translations, partly because of later condemnations of his teaching and partly because of the exorbitant length and diffusiveness of his work.

origin /ˈɒrɪdʒɪn/ *n.* **1.** the point, source, or cause from which a thing begins its existence. **2.** parentage, ancestry. **3.** (*Math.*) a point from which coordinates are measured. [f. F or L *origo* (*oriri* rise)]

original /əˈrɪdʒɪn(ə)l/ *adj.* **1.** existing from the first, earliest; primitive; innate. **2.** that has served as a pattern, of which a copy or translation has been made. **3.** new in concept, not derived or imitative. **4.** thinking or acting for oneself, inventive, creative. —*n.* the first form of something, the thing from which another is copied or translated. —**original sin,** (in Christian theology) the innate depravity held to be common to all human beings in consequence of the Fall. Medieval theologians were particularly occupied with its nature and transmission, but from the 18th c. onwards the influence of rationalism and natural science has attenuated the dogma, which has been given up almost completely by Liberal Protestantism and Modernism. —**originality** /-ˈnælɪtɪ/ *n.*, **originally** *adv.* [f. OF or L (as prec.)]

originate /əˈrɪdʒɪneɪt/ *v.t./i.* **1.** to have its origin, to begin. **2.** to initiate or give origin to; to be the origin of. —**origination** /-ˈneɪʃ(ə)n/ *n.*, **originator** *n.* [f. L (as ORIGIN)]

Orinoco /ɒrɪˈnəʊkəʊ/ a river in the north of South America, 2,060 km (1,280 miles) long, flowing from the Guiana Highlands through Venezuela to the Atlantic Ocean.

oriole /ˈɔːrɪəʊl/ *n.* a bird of the genus *Oriolus*, especially (**golden oriole**) one with black and yellow plumage in the male. [f. OF f. L *aureolus* (*aureus* golden)]

Orion /əˈraɪən/ **1.** (*Gk legend*) a giant and hunter, said to have been changed into a constellation at his death. The association of his name with the constellation occurs in Homer, making it an unprecedentedly early star-myth. **2.** (*Astron.*) a conspicuous constellation containing many bright stars including **Orion's belt**, three stars in a short line.

Orissa /ɒˈrɪsə/ a State in eastern India; capital, Bhubaneswar.

Oriya /ɒˈriːə/ *adj.* **1.** of Odra, an ancient region of India corresponding to the State of Orissa. **2.** of Orissa (which takes its name from Odra). —*n.* **1.** a native of Odra. **2.** the Indo-European language of Odra/Orissa, which is descended from Sanskrit and closely related to Bengali, spoken by some 20 million people. [Hindi, f. *Odra*]

Orkney Islands /ˈɔːknɪ/ (also **Orkneys**) a group of islands off the NE tip of Scotland, colonized by the Vikings in the 9th c. and ruled by Norway and Denmark until they came into Scottish possession (together with Shetland) in 1472 as security against the unpaid dowry of Margaret of Denmark after her marriage to James III. They constitute an islands area (Orkney) of Scotland.

Orleans /ɔːˈliːənz/ a French city on the River Loire, scene of Joan of Arc's first victory over the English during the Hundred Years War.

Ormazd /ˈɔːmæzd/ see AHURA MAZDA.

ormolu /ˈɔːməluː/ *n.* **1.** gilded bronze. **2.** a gold-coloured alloy. **3.** articles made of or decorated with ormolu. [f. F *or moulu* powdered gold]

Ormuz /ˈɔːmʊz/ var. of HORMUZ.

ornament /ˈɔːnəmənt/ *n.* **1.** a decorative object or detail. **2.** decoration, adornment. **3.** a person or quality that brings honour or adds distinction. —/-ment/ *v.t.* to decorate; to be an ornament to. —**ornamental** /-ˈment(ə)l/ *adj.*, **orna-**

mentally *adv.*, **ornamentation** /-ˈteɪʃ(ə)n/ *n.* [f. AF f. L (*ornare* adorn)]

ornate /ɔːˈneɪt/ *adj.* elaborately ornamented; (of literary style) embellished with flowery language. [f. L (as prec.)]

ornithology /ɔːnɪˈθɒlədʒɪ/ *n.* the study of birds. —**ornithological** /-ˈlɒdʒɪk(ə)l/ *adj.*, **ornithologist** *n.* [f. Gk (*ornis* bird, -LOGY)]

orogenesis /ɒrəˈdʒenɪsɪs/ *n.* the process of formation of mountains. —**orogenetic** /-dʒɪˈnetɪk/ *adj.* [f. Gk *oros* mountain + GENESIS]

orogeny /ɒˈrɒdʒənɪ/ *n.* **1.** orogenesis. **2.** a geological period of mountain-building. —**orogenic** /ɔːrəˈdʒenɪk/ *adj.* [as prec.]

orotund /ˈɒrətʌnd/ *adj.* (of an utterance) dignified, imposing; pompous. [f. L *ore rotundo*, lit. 'with round mouth']

orphan /ˈɔːf(ə)n/ *n.* a child whose parents are dead. —*adj.* being an orphan; of or for orphans. —*v.t.* to make (a child) an orphan. [f. L f. Gk, = bereaved]

orphanage *n.* an institution where orphans are housed and cared for. [f. prec.]

Orpheus /ˈɔːfjəs/ either a real person, founder of Orphism, or purely mythical. He appears in ancient Greek literature and art as a singer who, with his lyre, sang and played so wonderfully that wild beasts were spellbound by his music. He visited the underworld and persuaded its lord to release his wife Euridice from the dead, but lost her because he failed to obey the condition that he must not look back at her until they had reached the world of the living.

Orphic /ˈɔːfɪk/ *adj.* of Orpheus or Orphism (sense 1). [f. L f. Gk (f. prec.)]

Orphism /ˈɔːfɪz(ə)m/ *n.* **1.** a mystic religion of ancient Greece, originating in the 7th or 6th c. BC and based in poems (now lost) attributed to Orpheus, emphasizing the mixture of good (or divine) and evil in human nature and the necessity that the individual should rid himself of the evil part by ritual and moral purification throughout a series of reincarnations. It sank to the level of a superstition in the 5th c., though the profound thoughts which underlay it were perceived by Pindar and Plato; its high ideas were mixed up with crude myths, and misused by base priests and charlatans. **2.** a short-lived art movement (*c.*1912) within cubism, pioneered by a group of French painters calling themselves *La Section d'Or* (Golden Section), which emphasized the lyrical use of colour in pure abstract designs rather than the austere intellectual cubism of Picasso, Braque, and Gris. [f. ORPHEUS]

orpiment /ˈɔːpɪmənt/ *n.* arsenic trisulphide as a mineral, formerly used as a yellow dye and artists' pigment. [f. OF f. L *auripigmentum* (*aurum* gold, *pigmentum* pigment)]

orrery /ˈɒrərɪ/ *n.* a clockwork model of the planetary system. [f. 4th Earl of *Orrery*, for whom one was made]

orris /ˈɒrɪs/ *n.* a kind of iris, especially *Iris florentina*. —**orris-root** *n.* a violet-scented iris root used in perfumery etc. [app. alt. of IRIS]

ortho- *in comb.* right, straight, correct. [f. Gk *orthos* straight]

orthoclase /ˈɔːθəkleɪz/ *n.* common felspar in crystals with two cleavages at right angles. [f. ORTHO- + Gk *klasis* breaking]

orthodontics /ɔːθəˈdɒntɪks/ *n.* correction of irregularities in the teeth and jaws. —**orthodontic** *adj.*, **orthodontist** *n.* [f. ORTHO- + Gk *odous* tooth]

orthodox /ˈɔːθədɒks/ *adj.* holding the usual or currently accepted views, especially on religion; generally approved, conventional. —**Orthodox Church,** the Eastern or Greek Church separated from the Western Church in the 9th c. over doctrinal differences and refusal to accept papal supremacy, recognizing the Patriarch of Constantinople as its head, and the national Churches of Russia, Romania, etc., in communion with it. —**orthodoxy** *n.* [f. L f. Gk (ORTHO-, *doxa* opinion)]

orthography /ɔːˈθɒgrəfɪ/ *n.* spelling (esp. with reference to its correctness). —**orthographic** /-ˈgræfɪk/ *adj.*, **orthographical** *adj.* [f. OF f. L f. Gk (as ORTHO-, -GRAPHY)]

orthopaedics /ɔːθəˈpiːdɪks/ *n.* the branch of surgery dealing with the correction of deformities of the bones or muscles, originally in children. —**orthopaedic** *adj.*, **orthopaedist** *n.* [f. F (ORTHO-, Gk *paideia* rearing of children)]

orthoptic /ɔːˈθɒptɪk/ *adj.* relating to the correct or normal use of the eyes. [f. ORTHO- + OPTIC]

orthoptics /ɔːˈθɒptɪks/ *n.* remedial treatment of the eye-muscles. —**orthoptist** *n.* [f. prec.]

ortolan /ˈɔːtələn/ *n.* a European bunting (*Emberiza hortulana*) eaten as a delicacy. [F f. Prov., = gardener, f. L *hortulanus*]

Orwell /ˈɔːwel/, George (pseudonym of Eric Arthur Blair, 1903–50), English novelist and essayist with socialist preoccupations, an acute observer of social deprivation and injustice. Born in Bengal, he served with the Indian Imperial Police in Burma (1922–7), and his experiences are reflected in his first novel *Burmese Days* (1934). He resigned to escape from imperialism and 'man's dominion over man', returning to Europe to live in poverty as described in *Down and Out in Paris and London* (1933). Subsequent works include *The Road to Wigan Pier* (1937), an impassioned documentary of unemployment and proletarian life. In the Spanish Civil War he fought on the side of the Republicans and returned, demoralized and with a throat injury that permanently impeded his speech, to criticize Communist beliefs in *Homage to Catalonia* (1939) and the satire *Animal Farm* (1945). *Nineteen Eighty-four* (1949) is a nightmare view of a future totalitarian State; Orwell wrote it in an isolated house on the island of Jura in the Hebrides, financially secure with the royalties from *Animal Farm* but knowing that his life was drawing to its close because of the tuberculosis from which he shortly died.

oryx /ˈɒrɪks/ *n.* a large straight-horned African antelope of the genus *Oryx*. [f. L f. Gk *orux* stonemason's pickaxe, f. its pointed horns]

OS *abbr.* **1.** old style. **2.** ordinary seaman. **3.** Ordnance Survey. **4.** outsize.

Os *symbol* osmium.

Osborne /ˈɒzbɔːn/, John James (1929–), English dramatist. His first play *Look back in Anger* (1956) startled contemporary taste with the vehemence of its tirades against middle-class values, and earned him the cachet 'angry young man'. Later plays include *The Entertainer* (1957) and *Luther* (1961).

Oscan /ˈɒskən/ *n.* an ancient Italic language allied to Latin, surviving only in inscriptions in an alphabet derived from Etruscan. —*adj.* of this language. [f. L *Oscus*]

Oscar /ˈɒskə(r)/ *n.* each of several gold statuettes awarded annually by the Academy of Motion Picture Arts and Sciences (Hollywood, USA) for excellence in film acting, directing, etc. Such 'Academy awards' have been made annually since 1928. [man's given name; the statuette is said to have reminded Margaret Herrick, then librarian of the Academy and later its Executive Director, of her Uncle Oscar (i.e. Oscar Pierce, American wheat and fruit grower)]

oscillate /ˈɒsɪleɪt/ *v.t./i.* **1.** to swing to and fro; to cause to do this. **2.** to vacillate, to vary between extremes. **3.** (of an electric current) to reverse its direction with high frequency. —**oscillation** /-ˈleɪʃ(ə)n/ *n.* [f. L *oscillare* swing]

oscillator *n.* an instrument for producing oscillations. [f. prec.]

oscillograph /əˈsɪləɡrɑːf/ *n.* a device for recording oscillations. [as OSCILLATE + -GRAPH]

oscilloscope /əˈsɪləskəʊp/ *n.* a device for displaying oscillations, especially on the screen of a cathode-ray tube. [as OSCILLATE + -SCOPE]

osier /ˈəʊzɪə(r), ˈəʊʒə(r)/ *n.* a willow (*Salix viminalis* etc.) used in basketwork; a shoot of this. [f. OF]

Osiris /əˈsaɪrɪs/ (*Egyptian myth.*) a divinity originally connected with fertility, known chiefly through the legend (made famous by Plutarch) of his death (at the hands of his brother Seth) and subsequent restoration to a new life as ruler of the after-life. In the Old Kingdom he was identified with the deceased pharaoh, but eventually all the dead could claim the title 'the Osiris'.

-osis /-əʊsɪs/ *suffix* forming nouns denoting a process or condition (*metamorphosis*), especially a pathological state (*neurosis*, *thrombosis*). [f. L or Gk]

Osler /ˈəʊzlə(r)/, Sir William (1849–1919), Canadian-born physician and classical scholar, professor of medicine at McGill, Pennsylvania, Johns Hopkins, and Oxford University, whose *Principles and Practice of Medicine* (1892) became the chosen clinical textbook for English-speaking medical students. At Johns Hopkins he instituted a model teaching unit in which clinical observation was combined with laboratory research, but, in spite of the often extravagant homage subsequently paid to Osler's memory, medical education in the USA and elsewhere has followed a different model in which medical teachers are rarely engaged in medical practice.

Oslo /ˈɒzləʊ/ the capital and chief port of Norway; pop. (1983) 448,747.

Osman /ˈɒzmən/ (1259–1326) Turkish conqueror, founder of the Ottoman or Osmanli dynasty. After succeeding his father as leader of the Seljuk Turks in 1288 Osman reigned as sultan, conquering NW Asia Minor, and assumed the title of Emir in 1299.

osmium /ˈɒzmɪəm/ *n.* a hard bluish-white metallic element, symbol Os, atomic number 76. It is thought to be the densest non-radioactive element, and was first isolated in 1804. Its main use is in alloys with platinum and related metals, where it contributes hardness; an alloy with iridium is used in fountain-pen nibs. Osmium tetroxide is commonly used for staining tissues in electron microscopy. [f. Gk *osmē* smell (from the pungent smell of its tetroxide)]

osmosis /ɒzˈməʊsɪs/ *n.* the tendency of a solvent to pass from a less concentrated into a more concentrated solution through a semipermeable membrane, permeable to the solvent but not to the solute. It occurs partly because of interactions between the solute molecules and the solvent, and partly because the presence of the solute reduces the number of molecules of solvent per unit area on one side of the partition. The process continues until the pressure of the more concentrated solution exceeds that of the less concentrated; this pressure difference is known as the osmotic pressure. Osmosis was first studied by Jean Nollet (1700–70). It is now recognized as a very important mechanism in plant and animal physiology, playing a vital role in the passage of water into and out of living cells. It also has applications in the desalination of water. —**osmotic** /-ˈmɒtɪk/ *adj.* [ult. f. Gk *ōsmos* thrust]

osprey /ˈɒsprɪ/ *n.* a large raptorial bird (*Pandion haliaetus*) preying on fish in inland waters. [f. OF ult. f. L *ossifraga* (*os* bone, *frangere* break)]

Ossa /ˈɒsə/ a lofty mountain in Thessaly, Greece, south of Olympus. (See PELION.)

osseous /ˈɒsɪəs/ *adj.* of bone; having bones, bony. [f. L *osseus* (*os* bone)]

Ossian /ˈɒʃɪən, ˈɒs-/ anglicized form of Oisín, a legendary Irish warrior and bard, whose name became well known internationally in 1760–3 when the Scottish poet James Macpherson published what was later discovered to be his own verse as an alleged translation of 3rd-c. Gaelic tales.

ossicle /ˈɒsɪk(ə)l/ *n.* a small bone or piece of hard substance in an animal structure. [f. L *ossiculum* (as prec.)]

ossify /ˈɒsɪfaɪ/ *v.t./i.* **1.** to turn into bone, to harden. **2.** to make or become rigid and unprogressive. —**ossification** /-fɪˈkeɪʃ(ə)n/ *n.* [f. F (as OSSEOUS)]

Ostade /ɒˈstɑːdə/, Adriaen van (1610–85), Dutch painter and engraver. Trained at Haarlem, possibly in Frans Hals's studio, his early work depicts lively scenes of peasants carousing or brawling in crowded taverns or barns, but he is known principally for his genre scenes. His brother and pupil, Isaak (1621–49), painted for only a decade but produced genre pictures—usually outdoor peasant scenes—that hint at a great talent cut short by his early death.

ostensible /ɒˈstensɪb(ə)l/ *adj.* pretended, professed, put forward to conceal what is real. —**ostensibly** *adv.* [F f. L (*ostendere* show)]

ostensive /ɒˈstensɪv/ *adj.* directly showing. —**ostensively** *adv.* [f. L (as prec.)]

ostentation /ɒstenˈteɪʃ(ə)n/ *n.* pretentious display of wealth etc., showing off. —**ostentatious** *adj.*, **ostentatiously** *adv.* [f. OF f. L (as OSTENSIBLE)]

osteo- /ˈɒstɪə(ʊ)-/ *in comb.* bone. [f. Gk *osteon* bone]

osteopath /ˈɒstɪəpæθ/ *n.* a practitioner of osteopathy. [f. foll.]

osteopathy /ɒstɪˈɒpəθɪ/ *n.* treatment of disease by manipulation of bones (especially the spine) and muscles (their deformity being the supposed cause of problems). The system was founded by an American doctor, A. T. Still, who, after failing to persuade various medical schools to accept his ideas, established a new school in Missouri in 1892 to put them into practice. [f. OSTEO- + Gk *patheia* suffering]

Ostia /ˈɒstɪə/ the ancient city and harbour of Latium, said to be the first colony founded by Rome. It was buried, and its ruins were preserved, by the gradual silting up of the River Tiber.

ostler /ˈɒslə(r)/ *n.* a person in charge of stabling horses at an inn. [f. AF *hosteler* (as HOSTEL)]

Ostmark /ˈɒstmɑːk/ *n.* the currency unit in the German Democratic Republic. [G, f. *Ost* east + MARK²]

Ostpolitik /ˈɒstpɒlɪtiːk/ *n.* the policy of a West European country with regard to the Communist countries of East Europe. [G (*ost* east, *politik* politics)]

ostracize /ˈɒstrəsaɪz/ *v.t.* **1.** (in ancient Athens) to banish (a dangerously powerful or unpopular citizen) by a voting-system in which the name of the person proposed for banishment was written on a potsherd. **2.** to exclude from society, favour, or common privileges. —**ostracism** *n.* [f. Gk *ostrakon* potsherd]

ostrich /ˈɒstrɪtʃ/ *n.* **1.** a large swift-running flightless African bird (*Struthio camelus*), that swallows hard substances to assist the working of its gizzard and is reputed to bury its head in the sand when pursued, believing that it cannot then be seen. **2.** a person who refuses to acknowledge an awkward truth. [f. OF f. L *avis* bird, *struthio* ostrich f. Gk]

Ostrogoth /ˈɒstrəɡɒθ/ *n.* a member of the eastern branch of the Goths, who conquered Italy in the 5th–6th c. —**Ostrogothic** /-ˈɡɒθɪk/ *adj.* [f. L, = eastern Goth]

Oswald /ˈɒzw(ə)ld/, St (d. 992), early English churchman. A Benedictine monk who rose first to become Bishop of Worcester and then Archbishop of York, St Oswald, along with St Dunstan, was responsible for the revival of the Church and of learning in 10th-c. England.

OT *abbr.* Old Testament.

other /ˈʌðə(r)/ *adj.* **1.** not the same as one or some already mentioned or implied; separate in identity, distinct in kind. **2.** alternative; additional; being the remaining one of a set of two or more. —*n.* or *pron.* another person or thing. —*adv.* otherwise. —**the other day** etc., a few days, nights, etc., ago. **other than,** different from. **other-worldly** *adj.* concerned or preoccupied with life after death or in some imagined world to the neglect of the present or real one. [OE]

otherwise *adv.* **1.** in a different way. **2.** in other respects. **3.** in different circumstances. **4.** or else. —*adj.* in a different state. [OE (as prec., WISE²)]

Othman /ˈɒθmən/ var. of OSMAN.

Otho /ˈəʊθəʊ/, Marcus Salvius (32–69), acclaimed Roman emperor on 15 Jan. 69 after he had procured the death of Galba in a conspiracy of the Praetorian Guard. The legions of the Rhine, however, had already chosen Vitellius and Otho committed suicide on 16 Apr. after they had defeated his own troops.

otiose /ˈəʊʃɪəʊs, -əʊt-/ *adj.* not required, serving no practical purpose. [f. L *otiosus* (*otium* leisure)]

Otomi /əʊtəˈmiː/ *n.* (*pl.* same) a member or the language of an Indian people inhabiting parts of central Mexico. [Sp. f. Nahuatl]

Ottawa /ˈɒtəwə/ the federal capital of Canada, on the Ottawa River (a tributary of the St Lawrence) and the Rideau Canal; pop. (1981) 303,114. Founded in 1827, the city received its present name in 1854 and was chosen as capital (of the United Provinces of Canada) by Queen Victoria in 1858.

otter /ˈɒtə(r)/ *n.* an aquatic fish-eating mammal of the genus *Lutra* etc. with webbed feet, thick brown fur, and a pointed tail somewhat flattened horizontally, feeding chiefly on fish; its fur. [OE]

Otto /ˈɒtəʊ/, Nikolaus August (1832–91), German engineer who has given his name to the four-stroke cycle on which most internal-combustion engines work. This consists of an induction stroke during which a mixture of fuel and air is drawn in; a compression stroke, at the end of which the mixture is ignited by a spark; an expansion stroke during which hot gases force the piston up; an exhaust stroke when the cylinder contents are ejected to the atmosphere. Otto's patent of 1876 was invalidated ten years later when it was found that Beau de Rochas had described the successful cycle earlier, so enabling other manufacturers to adopt it.

Otto I /ˈɒtəʊ/ 'the Great' (912–73), German ruler. Succeeding his father Henry I as king of the Germans in 936, Otto carried out a policy of eastward expansion from his Saxon homeland and defeated the invading Hungarians in 955. He was crowned Holy Roman Emperor in 962 and began to establish a strong imperial presence in Italy to rival that of the papacy.

Ottoman /ˈɒtəmən/ *adj.* of the dynasty of Osman or Othman I, his branch of the Turks, or the empire ruled by his descendants (see OTTOMAN EMPIRE). —*n.* an Ottoman person. [F f. Arab.]

ottoman /ˈɒtəmən/ *n.* **1.** a long cushioned seat without back or arms. **2.** a storage box with a padded top. [= prec.]

Ottoman empire the Turkish empire, established in northern Anatolia by Osman or Othman at the end of the 13th c. and expanded by his successors to include all of Asia Minor and much of SE Europe. Ottoman power received a severe check with the invasion of Tamerlane in

1401, but expansion resumed several decades later, resulting in the capture of Constantinople in 1453. The empire reached its zenith under Suleiman in the mid-16th c., dominating the eastern Mediterranean and threatening central Europe, but thereafter it began to decline. Still powerful in the 17th c., it had, by the 19th c., become the 'sick man of Europe', eventually collapsing in the early 20th c.

Otway /ˈɒtweɪ/, Thomas (1652–85), English playwright. After failing as an actor he wrote for the stage and achieved success with his second play *Don Carlos* (1676), a tragedy in rhymed verse. He had a burning passion for the actress Mrs Elizabeth Barry who acted in his two great blank verse tragedies, *The Orphan* (1680) and *Venice Preserved* (1682), probably the finest tragedies of the period. He also wrote several comedies and poems.

Ouagadougou /wɑɡəˈduːɡuː/ the capital of Burkina; pop. (est. 1980) 235,000.

oubliette /uːblɪˈet/ *n.* a secret dungeon with a trapdoor entrance. [F (*oublier* forget)]

ouch *int.* expressing sharp or sudden pain. [natural excl.]

Oudenarde /ˈuːdənɑːd/ a town in eastern Flanders in Belgium, scene of a victory (1708) of allied British and Austrian troops under Marlborough and Prince Eugene over the French.

ought¹ /ɔːt/ *v.aux.* (as present and past, the only form now in use; *neg.* **ought not**) expressing rightness or duty, advisability, or strong probability. [OE, past tense of OWE]

ought² /ɔːt/ *n.* (*colloq.*) the figure 0, nought. [f. *an ought* for *a nought*]

oughtn't /ˈɔːt(ə)nt/ (*colloq.*) = ought not.

Ouida /ˈwiːdə/ (pseudonym of Marie Louise de la Ramée 1839–1908) English novelist, who lived a lavish life mostly in Italy and wrote 45 novels, often set in a fashionable world far removed from reality. These include *Under Two Flags* (1867), *Folle-Farine* (1871), and *Two Little Wooden Shoes* (1874). She suffered frequent ridicule for her extravagantly portrayed heroes, miracles of strengh, courage, and beauty, but her faults were redeemed by her vigorous narrative.

Ouija /ˈwiːdʒə/ *n.* [P] (also **Ouija-board**) a board marked with the alphabet and other signs used with a movable pointer to obtain messages in spiritualistic seances. [f. F *oui* yes + G *ja* yes]

ounce¹ /aʊns/ *n.* **1.** a unit of weight equal to one sixteenth of a pound (about 28 grams). **2.** a very small quantity. [f. OF f. L *uncia* twelfth part of pound or foot]

ounce² /aʊns/ *n.* an Asian feline (*Panthera uncia*), the mountain panther or snow-leopard, smaller than the leopard but similarly marked. [f. OF *once* for earlier *lonce* (*l* mistaken for the definite article), ult. f. L LYNX]

our *poss. adj.* of or belonging to us; that we are concerned with or thinking of. —**Our Father,** the Lord's Prayer, beginning with these words (Matt. 6: 9–13). **Our Lady,** the Virgin Mary. [OE]

ours /ˈaʊəz/ *poss. pron.* of or belonging to us; the thing(s) belonging to us. [f. OUR]

ourself /aʊəˈself/ *pron.* corresponding to MYSELF when used by a sovereign etc.

ourselves /aʊəˈselvz/ *pron.* emphat. and refl. form of WE, US.

ousel var. of OUZEL.

oust /aʊst/ *v.t.* to eject, to drive out of office or power; to seize the place of. [f. AF f. L *obstare* oppose]

out *adv.* **1.** expressing movement or position away from a centre or beyond or regardless of stated or implied limits, or a state other than the right or usual one; away from or not in a place; not at home, not in one's office etc.; not in its normal or usual state. **2.** (so as to be) excluded. **3.** not in effective or favourable action; no longer in fashion or season or office; (in cricket etc.) having had one's innings ended; (of workers) on strike; (of a light or fire etc.) no longer burning; no longer visible. **4.** in or into the open; so as to be clear or perceptible; (of flowers) open, (of plants) in bloom; (of a secret) revealed; (of a book) published; (after a superlative) among known examples etc. **5.** to or at an end, completely. **6.** in error. **7.** unconscious. **8.** (of a jury) considering its verdict in private. **9.** with attentiveness (*watch out*). —*prep.* out of. —*n.* a way of escape. —*int.* get out! —*v.t.* **1.** to put out. **2.** (*colloq.*) to eject forcibly. **3.** (in boxing) to knock out. —**out and about,** active outdoors. **out and away,** by far. **out and out,** thoroughly, **out-and-out** *adj.* complete, thorough. **out for,** intent on, determined to get. **out of,** from within; from among; beyond the range of; because of; by the use of, (of an animal) having as its dam; so as to be without a supply of. **out of doors,** in or into the open air. **out to,** determined to. [OE]

out- *prefix* **1.** out of, away from, outward. **2.** external, separate. **3.** so as to surpass or exceed. [= OUT]

outage /'aʊtɪdʒ/ *n.* a period of non-operation of a power-supply etc. [f. OUT]

outback *n.* the remote inland districts of Australia.

outbid /aʊt'bɪd/ *v.t.* (-dd-) to bid higher than.

outboard *adj.* **1.** towards the outside of a ship, aircraft, or vehicle. **2.** (of a motor) attached externally to the stern of a boat; (of a boat) using such a motor.

outbreak *n.* a breaking out of anger, war, disease, fire, etc.

outbuilding *n.* an outhouse.

outburst *n.* a bursting out, especially of emotion in vehement words.

outcast *n.* a person cast out of his home or rejected by society. —*adj.* homeless, rejected.

outclass /aʊt'klɑːs/ *v.t.* to surpass in quality.

outcome *n.* the result or effect of an event etc.

outcrop *n.* **1.** part of an underlying stratum, vein, or rock that emerges on the surface of the ground etc.; such emergence. **2.** a breaking out, a noticeable manifestation.

outcry *n.* **1.** a loud cry. **2.** a strong protest.

outdated /aʊt'deɪtɪd/ *adj.* out of date, obsolete.

outdistance /aʊt'dɪstəns/ *v.t.* to get far ahead of.

outdo /aʊt'duː/ *v.t.* (3 *sing. pres.* **outdoes** /-'dʌz/; *past* **outdid**; *p.p.* **outdone**) to do better than, to surpass.

outdoor *adj.* of, done, or for use out of doors; fond of the open air.

outdoors /aʊt'dɔːz/ *n.* the open air. —*adv.* in or into the open air.

outer *adj.* further from the centre or the inside; external, exterior. —**outer space,** the universe beyond the earth's atmosphere. —**outermost** *adj.* [f. OUT]

outface /aʊt'feɪs/ *v.t.* to disconcert by staring or by a display of confidence.

outfall *n.* an outlet of a river, drain, etc.

outfield *n.* the outer part of a cricket or baseball pitch.

outfit *n.* **1.** a set of equipment or clothes. **2.** (*colloq.*) a group of persons, an organization.

outfitter *n.* a supplier of equipment, especially men's clothes.

outflank /aʊt'flæŋk/ *v.t.* to extend beyond or get round the flank of (an enemy); to outmanœuvre, outwit.

outflow *n.* an outward flow; what flows out.

outfox /aʊt'fɒks/ *v.t.* to outwit.

outgoing *adj.* **1.** going out; retiring from office. **2.** sociable and friendly. —*n.* (in *pl.*) expenditure.

outgrow /aʊt'grəʊ/ *v.t.* (*past* **outgrew**; *p.p.* **outgrown**) **1.** to grow faster or taller than. **2.** to grow too big for; to be too old or developed for.

outgrowth *n.* **1.** an offshoot. **2.** a natural development or product.

outhouse *n.* a small building belonging to but separate from the main house.

outing *n.* a pleasure-trip or excursion. [f. OUT *v.*]

outlandish /aʊt'lændɪʃ/ *adj.* looking or sounding very strange or foreign, bizarre. —**outlandishness** *n.* [OE (*ūtland* foreign country)]

outlast /aʊt'lɑːst/ *v.t.* to last longer than.

outlaw *n.* a fugitive from the law (originally one placed beyond the protection of the law). —*v.t.* **1.** to declare (a person) an outlaw. **2.** to make illegal, to proscribe.

outlay *n.* expenditure.

outlet *n.* **1.** a means of exit or escape. **2.** a means of expressing feelings. **3.** a market for goods.

outline *n.* **1.** a line or lines showing the shape or boundary of something. **2.** a summary; a statement of the chief facts. —*v.t.* to draw or describe in outline; to mark the outline of. —**in outline,** giving only an outline.

outlive /aʊt'lɪv/ *v.t.* to live longer than (a person) or beyond (a period); to live through (an experience).

outlook *n.* **1.** a view on which one looks out. **2.** a mental attitude. **3.** future prospects.

outlying *adj.* situated far from a centre, remote.

outmanœuvre /aʊtmə'nuːvə(r)/ *v.t.* to outdo in manœuvring.

outmatch /aʊt'mætʃ/ *v.t.* to be more than a match for.

outmoded /aʊt'məʊdɪd/ *adj.* out of fashion; obsolete.

outnumber /aʊt'nʌmbə(r)/ *v.t.* to exceed in number.

outpace /aʊt'peɪs/ *v.t.* to go faster than; to outdo in a contest.

out-patient *n.* a patient not residing in hospital during treatment.

outpost *n.* **1.** a detachment stationed at some distance from an army. **2.** a distant branch or settlement.

output *n.* **1.** the amount produced. **2.** the electrical power etc. delivered by an apparatus. **3.** the place where energy, information, etc., leaves a system. **4.** the results etc. supplied by a computer. —*v.t./i.* (*past & p.p.* **output** or **outputted**) (of a computer) to supply (results etc.).

outrage *n.* **1.** an extreme or shocking violation of others' rights, sentiments, etc.; a gross offence or indignity. **2.** fierce resentment. —*v.t.* to subject to an outrage, to commit an outrage against; to shock and anger. [f. OF (*outrer* exceed f. L *ultra* beyond)]

outrageous /aʊt'reɪdʒəs/ *adj.* greatly exceeding what is moderate or reasonable; grossly cruel, immoral, or offensive. —**outrageously** *adv.* [f. OF (as prec.)]

outrank /aʊt'ræŋk/ *v.t.* to be superior in rank to.

outré /'uːtreɪ/ *adj.* eccentric, violating decorum. [F, p.p. of *outrer* (as OUTRAGE)]

outrider *n.* a mounted attendant or motor-cyclist riding ahead of a procession etc.

outrigger *n.* **1.** a spar or framework projecting from or over a ship's side. **2.** a strip of wood fixed parallel to a canoe to stabilize it; a canoe with this. [perh. partly after obs. (Naut.) *outligger*]

outright /aʊt'raɪt/ *adv.* altogether, entirely, not gradually; without reservation, openly. —/'aʊtraɪt/ *adj.* complete, thorough.

outrun /aʊt'rʌn/ *v.t.* (-nn-; *past* **outran**; *p.p.* **outrun**) **1.** to run faster or further than. **2.** to go beyond (a point or limit).

outsell /aʊt'sel/ *v.t.* (*past & p.p.* **outsold** /-'səʊld/) to sell more than; to be sold in greater quantities than.

outset *n.* the beginning (usu. in **at** *or* **from the outset**).

outshine /aʊt'ʃaɪn/ *v.t.* (*past & p.p.* **outshone** /-'ʃɒn/) to shine brighter than; to surpass in excellence etc.

outside /aʊt'saɪd, 'aʊt-/ *n.* **1.** the outer side of a surface or part. **2.** the outer part(s). **3.** outward appearance; all that is without. **4.** a position on the outer side. —/'aʊtsaɪd/ *adj.* **1.** of, on, or coming from the outside; outer. **2.** not belonging to some circle or institution. **3.** nearer to the outside of a games field. **4.** the greatest existent or possible. —/aʊt'saɪd/ *adv.* on, at, or to the outside; in or into the open air. —/aʊt'saɪd/ *prep.* **1.** on the outer side of; not in; at or to the outer side of. **2.** other than. **3.** not included in. —**at the outside,** (of amounts) at the most. **outside broadcast,** one not made from a studio. **outside chance,** a remote possibility.

outsider *n.* **1.** a non-member of some circle, party, profession, etc. **2.** a competitor thought to have little chance.

outsize *adj.* unusually large. —*n.* an outsize garment etc. or person.

outskirts *n.pl.* the outer area of a town etc.

outsmart /aʊt'smɑːt/ *v.t.* to outwit, to be cleverer than.

outspan /aʊt'spæn/ *v.t.* (-nn-) (*S. Afr.*) to unyoke, to unharness. [f. Du. (as OUT, SPAN¹)]

outspoken /aʊt'spəʊkən/ *adj.* speaking or spoken without reserve, frank.

outspread /aʊt'spred/ *adj.* spread out. —*v.t.* to spread out.

outstanding /aʊt'stændɪŋ/ *adj.* **1.** conspicuous, especially from excellence. **2.** still to be dealt with. —**outstandingly** *adv.*.

outstay /aʊt'steɪ/ *v.t.* to stay longer than.

outstretched /aʊt'stretʃt/ *adj.* stretched out.

outstrip /aʊt'strɪp/ *v.t.* (-pp-) **1.** to go faster than. **2.** to surpass.

out-tray *n.* a tray for outgoing documents.

outvote /aʊt'vəʊt/ *v.t.* to defeat by a majority of votes.

outward /'aʊtwəd/ *adj.* **1.** situated on or directed towards the outside. **2.** going towards the outside. **3.** external, material, apparent. —*adv.* (also **outwards**) in an outward direction, towards the outside. **outward bound,** going away from home. [OE (as OUT, -WARD)]

outwardly *adv.* on the outside; in appearance.

outwardness *n.* external existence, objectivity.

outweigh /aʊtˈweɪ/ v.t. to exceed in weight, value, importance, or influence.

outwit /aʊtˈwɪt/ v.t. (-tt-) to be too clever for, to overcome by greater ingenuity.

outwork n. an advanced or detached part of a fortification.

outworn /aʊtˈwɔːn/ adj. worn out, obsolete, exhausted.

ouzel /ˈuːz(ə)l/ n. 1. a small bird (*Turdus torquatus*) of the thrush family (**ring ouzel**). 2. a diving bird of the genus *Cinclus* (**water ouzel**), a dipper. [OE, = blackbird]

ouzo /ˈuːzəʊ/ n. a Greek drink of aniseed-flavoured spirits. [modern Gk]

ova pl. of OVUM.

oval /ˈəʊv(ə)l/ adj. having a rounded symmetrical shape longer than it is broad, elliptical or ellipsoidal. —n. a thing of oval shape or outline. [f. L (as OVUM)]

ovary /ˈəʊvərɪ/ n. 1. either of two reproductive organs in which ova are produced in female animals (ill. BODY 2). 2. the lower part of the pistil in a plant, from which the fruit is formed (ill. FLOWERS). —**ovarian** /-ˈveərɪən/ adj. [f. OVUM]

ovate /ˈəʊveɪt/ adj. egg-shaped (as a solid or in outline), oval. [f. L (*ovum* egg)]

ovation /əˈveɪʃ(ə)n/ n. enthusiastic applause or reception. [f. L (*ovare* exult)]

oven /ˈʌv(ə)n/ n. an enclosed compartment for heating or cooking food etc. [OE]

ovenware n. dishes in which food can be cooked in an oven.

over /ˈəʊvə(r)/ adv. expressing movement or position or state above or beyond something stated or implied: 1. outward and downward from the brink or from an erect position. 2. so as to cover or touch a whole surface. 3. with movement from one side to the other or so that a different side is showing; upside down; across a street or other space; with transference or change from one hand, part, etc., to another. 4. with motion above something, so as to pass across. 5. from beginning to end, with repetition; thoroughly, with detailed consideration. 6. too, in excess, in addition, besides. 7. apart; until a later time. 8. at an end, settled. 9. (in a radio conversation) it is your turn to transmit. 10. (as an umpire's call in cricket) change ends for bowling etc. —prep. 1. in or to a position higher than. 2. out and down from; down from the edge of. 3. so as to clear; on or to the other side of. 4. so as to cover. 5. concerning. 6. while occupied with. 7. with or achieving superiority or preference to. 8. throughout the length or extent of; during. 9. beyond; more than. 10. transmitted by. 11. in comparison with. —n. a sequence of six (or eight) balls in cricket, bowled between two calls of 'over', play resulting from this. —adj. upper, outer, superior, extra (usu. as *prefix*; see OVER-). —**over and above**, besides. **over and over**, repeatedly. **over to you**, it is your turn to act. [OE]

overact /əʊvərˈækt/ v.t./i. to act with exaggeration.

overall adj. 1. from end to end. 2. total, inclusive of all. —/also -ˈɔːl/ adv. in all parts, taken as a whole. —n. a protective outer garment; (in pl.) protective outer trousers or suit.

overarm adj. & adv. with the arm brought forward and down from above shoulder level.

overawe /əʊvərˈɔː/ v.t. to overcome with awe.

overbalance /əʊvəˈbæləns/ v.t./i. to lose one's balance and fall; to cause to do this.

overbear /əʊvəˈbeə(r)/ v.t. (past -**bore**; p.p. -**borne**) 1. to bear down by weight or force. 2. to repress by power or authority.

overbearing adj. domineering, bullying.

overblown /əʊvəˈbləʊn/ adj. 1. pretentious. 2. (of a flower) too fully open, past its prime.

overboard adv. from within a ship into the water. —**go overboard**, (colloq.) to show extreme enthusiasm.

overbook /əʊvəˈbʊk/ v.t. to make too many bookings for (an aircraft flight, hotel, etc., or *absol.*).

Overbury /ˈəʊvəbərɪ/, Sir Thomas (1581–1613), English poet and courtier, remembered for his 'Characters', on the model of those of Theophrastus. He was sent to the Tower on the pretext of his refusal of a diplomatic post, where he was poisoned to death by the agents of Lady Essex whose marriage to his patron Robert Carr (afterwards Earl of Somerset) he had opposed. The subsequent prosecution of the conspirators was conducted by Francis Bacon. The whole business is a historical mystery.

overcast /əʊvəˈkɑːst/ adv. (of the sky) covered with cloud.

—v.t. (past & p.p. -**cast**) to stitch over (an edge) to prevent fraying.

overcharge /əʊvəˈtʃɑːdʒ/ v.t. 1. to charge too high a price to (a person) or for (a thing). 2. to put an excessive charge into; to overfill.

overcheck n. a check pattern superimposed on a pattern of smaller checks.

overcoat n. a warm outdoor coat.

overcome /əʊvəˈkʌm/ v.t./i. (past -**came**; p.p. -**come**) 1. to win a victory over, to succeed in subduing; to be victorious. 2. to make helpless, to deprive of proper self-control. 3. to find a way of dealing with (a problem etc.).

overcrowd /əʊvəˈkraʊd/ v.t. to crowd too many people into (a place or vehicle etc.).

overdevelop /əʊvədɪˈveləp/ v.t. to develop excessively.

overdo /əʊvəˈduː/ v.t. (3 sing. pres. -**does** /-ˈdʌz/; past -**did**; p.p. -**done** /-ˈdʌn/) 1. to do (a thing) excessively, to go too far in. 2. to cook too much. 3. to exhaust. —**overdo it**, to work too hard; to exaggerate; to carry an action too far.

overdose n. an excessive dose, especially of a drug.

overdraft n. overdrawing of a bank account; the amount by which an account is overdrawn.

overdraw /əʊvəˈdrɔː/ v.t. (past -**drew**; p.p. -**drawn**) to draw more from (a bank account) than the amount in credit; (in p.p.) having overdrawn one's account.

overdress /əʊvəˈdres/ v.t./i. to dress ostentatiously or with too much formality.

overdrive n. a mechanism in a vehicle providing a gear ratio higher than that of the usual gears.

overdue /əʊvəˈdjuː/ adj. past the due time for payment, arrival, etc.

overeat /əʊvərˈiːt/ v.i. (past -**ate**; p.p. -**eaten**) to eat too much.

over-emphasize /əʊvərˈemfəsaɪz/ v.t. to emphasize excessively. —**over-emphasis** n.

overestimate /əʊvərˈestɪmeɪt/ v.t. to form too high an estimate of. —/-ət/ n. too high an estimate.

over-expose /əʊvərɪkˈspəʊz/ v.t. to expose for too long. —**over-exposure** n.

overfeed /əʊvəˈfiːd/ v.t./i. (past & p.p. -**fed**) to feed too much.

overfish /əʊvəˈfɪʃ/ v.t. to fish (a river etc.) too much so that next season's supply is reduced.

overflow /əʊvəˈfləʊ/ v.t./i. 1. to flow over (a brim etc.); to flood (a surface or area). 2. (of a crowd etc.) to spread beyond the limits of (a room etc.). 3. (of a receptacle etc.) to be so full that the contents overflow; (of kindness, a harvest, etc.) to be very abundant. —/ˈəʊvə-/ n. 1. what overflows or is superfluous. 2. an outlet for excess liquid.

overfly /əʊvəˈflaɪ/ v.t. (past -**flew**; p.p. -**flown** /-ˈfləʊn/) to fly over or beyond (a place or territory).

overfull /əʊvəˈfʊl/ adj. filled too much, too full.

overgrown /əʊvəˈgrəʊn/ adj. 1. covered with plants, weeds, etc. 2. grown too big. —**overgrowth** n.

overhang /əʊvəˈhæŋ/ v.t./i. (past & p.p. -**hung**) to jut out (over). —/ˈəʊvə-/ n. overhanging; an overhanging part or amount.

overhaul /əʊvəˈhɔːl/ v.t. 1. to check over thoroughly and make any necessary repairs to. 2. to overtake. —/ˈəʊvə-/ n. a thorough check with repairs if necessary.

overhead /əʊvəˈhed/ adv. above one's head, in the sky. —/ˈəʊvə-/ adj. placed overhead. —/ˈəʊvə-/ n. (in pl.) the routine administrative and maintenance expenses of a business.

overhear /əʊvəˈhɪə(r)/ v.t. (past & p.p. -**heard** /-ˈhɜːd/) to hear unintentionally or without the speaker's knowledge.

overheat /əʊvəˈhiːt/ v.t./i. to make or become too hot.

overjoyed /əʊvəˈdʒɔɪd/ adj. filled with extreme joy.

overkill n. a surplus of capacity for destruction above what is needed to defeat or destroy an enemy.

overland /əʊvəˈlænd/ adv. by land. —/ˈəʊvə-/ adj. entirely or mainly by land.

Overlander /ˈəʊvəlændə(r)/ n. (*Austral. hist.*) one whose occupation was to drive large herds of livestock over a long distance or from one colony to another. [f. prec.]

overlap /əʊvəˈlæp/ v.t./i. (-pp-) 1. to extend beyond the edge of and partly cover. 2. to coincide partly. —/ˈəʊvə-/ n. overlapping; an overlapping part or amount.

overlay /əʊvəˈleɪ/ v.t. (past & p.p. -**laid**) 1. to lie on top of. 2. to cover the surface of with a coating etc. —/ˈəʊvə-/ n. a thing laid over another.

overleaf /ˌəʊvəˈliːf/ *adv.* on the other side of a leaf of a book.

overlie /ˌəʊvəˈlaɪ/ *v.t.* (*past* **-lay**; *p.p.* **-lain**; *partic.* **-lying**) to lie on top of; to smother thus.

overload /ˌəʊvəˈləʊd/ *v.t.* to put too great a load on or into. —/ˈəʊvə-/ *n.* a load that is too great.

overlook /ˌəʊvəˈlʊk/ *v.t.* **1.** to fail to observe or consider. **2.** to take no notice of, to allow (an offence) to go unpunished. **3.** to have a view of from above. **4.** to supervise.

overlord *n.* a supreme lord.

overly *adv.* (chiefly *Sc.* & *US*) excessively, too. [f. OVER]

overman /ˌəʊvəˈmæn/ *v.t.* (**-nn-**) to provide with too many people as staff or crew.

overmantel *n.* ornamental shelves etc. over a mantelpiece (ill. HOUSES).

overmuch /ˌəʊvəˈmʌtʃ/ *adv.* too much.

overnight /ˌəʊvəˈnaɪt/ *adv.* **1.** during the course of a night. **2.** on the preceding evening regarded from the next day. **3.** (*colloq.*) instantly. —/ˈəʊvə-/ *adj.* done or for use etc. during a night.

overpass /ˈəʊvəpɑːs/ *n.* a road that passes over another by means of a bridge.

overpay /ˌəʊvəˈpeɪ/ *v.t.* to pay too highly.

overplay /ˌəʊvəˈpleɪ/ *v.t.* to give too much importance to. —**overplay one's hand,** to act with overestimation of one's strength.

overpower /ˌəʊvəˈpaʊə(r)/ *v.t.* to overcome by greater strength or numbers.

overpowering *adj.* extreme, too intense.

overprint /ˌəʊvəˈprɪnt/ *v.t.* to print over (something already printed). —/ˈəʊvə-/ *n.* a thing overprinted.

overrate /ˌəʊvəˈreɪt/ *v.t.* to have too high an opinion of.

overreach /ˌəʊvəˈriːtʃ/ *v.t.* to outwit, to circumvent. —**overreach oneself,** to fail through being too ambitious.

over-react /ˌəʊvərɪˈækt/ *v.i.* to respond more strongly than is justified.

override /ˌəʊvəˈraɪd/ *v.t.* (*past* **-rode**; *p.p.* **-ridden**) **1.** to have or claim superior authority or precedence over; to set aside (an order etc.) thus. **2.** to intervene and cancel the operation of. **3.** to move so as to extend over or overlap.

overrider *n.* either of a pair of vertical attachments to the bumper of a car to prevent another bumper from becoming locked behind it.

overripe /ˌəʊvəˈraɪp/ *adj.* too ripe.

overrule /ˌəʊvəˈruːl/ *v.t.* to set aside (a decision etc.) by superior authority; to set aside a decision of (a person) thus.

overrun /ˌəʊvəˈrʌn/ *v.t.* (**-nn-**; *past* **-ran**; *p.p.* **-run**) **1.** to swarm or spread over. **2.** to conquer (a territory) by force of numbers. **3.** to exceed (a limit).

overseas *adj.* & *adv.* across or beyond the sea.

oversee /ˌəʊvəˈsiː/ *v.t.* (*past* **-saw**; *p.p.* **-seen**) to superintend.

overseer /ˈəʊvəsɪə(r)/ *n.* a superintendent.

overset /ˌəʊvəˈset/ *v.t.* (**-tt-**; *past* & *p.p.* **-set**) to overturn, to upset.

oversew /ˌəʊvəˈsəʊ/ *v.t.* (*p.p.* **-sewn** or **-sewed**) to sew together (two edges) with stitches lying over them.

overshadow /ˌəʊvəˈʃædəʊ/ *v.t.* **1.** to appear much more prominent or important than. **2.** to cast into the shade.

overshoe /ˈəʊvəʃuː/ *n.* an outer protective shoe worn over an ordinary shoe.

overshoot /ˌəʊvəˈʃuːt/ *v.t.* (*past* & *p.p.* **-shot**) to pass or send beyond (a target or limit).

overshot *adj.* (of a water-wheel) turned by water falling on it from above.

oversight /ˈəʊvəsaɪt/ *n.* **1.** failure to do or note something; an inadvertent mistake. **2.** supervision.

over-simplify /ˌəʊvəˈsɪmplɪfaɪ/ *v.t.* to distort or misrepresent by putting in too simple terms.

overskirt *n.* an outer skirt (ill. DRESS).

oversleep /ˌəʊvəˈsliːp/ *v.i.* (*past* & *p.p.* **-slept**) to sleep beyond an intended time of waking.

overspend /ˌəʊvəˈspend/ *v.i.* (*past* & *p.p.* **-spent**) to spend beyond one's means.

overspill *n.* **1.** what spills over or overflows. **2.** surplus population moving to a new area.

overstaff /ˌəʊvəˈstɑːf/ *v.t.* (esp. in *p.p.*) to provide with too many staff.

overstate /ˌəʊvəˈsteɪt/ *v.t.* to state too strongly, to exaggerate. —**overstatement** *n.*

overstay /ˌəʊvəˈsteɪ/ *v.t.* to stay longer than.

oversteer *v.i.* (of a vehicle) to have a tendency to turn more sharply than was intended. —*n.* this tendency.

overstep /ˌəʊvəˈstep/ *v.t.* (**-pp-**) to pass beyond (a limit).

overstock /ˌəʊvəˈstɒk/ *v.t.* to stock too many of; to stock with too many items.

overstrung /ˌəʊvəˈstrʌŋ/ *adj.* **1.** (of a person or the nerves) too highly strung. **2.** (of a piano) with strings arranged in sets crossing each other obliquely.

overstuffed /ˌəʊvəˈstʌft/ *adj.* (of cushions etc.) filled with much or too much stuffing.

over-subscribed /ˌəʊvəsəbˈskraɪbd/ *adj.* (esp. of shares for sale) not enough to meet the amount subscribed.

overt /ˈəʊvɜːt, ˈəʊ-/ *adj.* done openly, unconcealed. —**overtly** *adv.* [f. OF, p.p. of *ovrir* open f. L]

overtake /ˌəʊvəˈteɪk/ *v.t.* (*p.t.* **-took** /-tʊk/, *p.p.* **-taken**) **1.** to pass (a person or vehicle travelling in the same direction); to come abreast or level with. **2.** to exceed (a compared value or amount).

overtax /ˌəʊvəˈtæks/ *v.t.* **1.** to make excessive demands on. **2.** to tax too highly.

overthrow /ˌəʊvəˈθrəʊ/ *v.t.* (*past* **-threw** /-ˈθruː/; *p.p.* **-thrown**) **1.** to remove forcibly from power. **2.** to conquer. **3.** to knock down, to upset. —/ˈəʊvə-/ *n.* **1.** defeat, downfall. **2.** a fielder's throwing of a ball beyond an intended point.

overthrust *n.* a thrust of (esp. lower) strata on one side of a fault over those on the other side (ill. GEOLOGY).

overtime *n.* time worked in addition to one's regular hours; payment for this. —*adv.* as or during overtime.

overtone *n.* **1.** a subtle extra quality or implication. **2.** (*Mus.*) any of the tones above the lowest in a harmonic series.

overtrick *n.* a trick taken in excess of one's contract in the game of bridge.

overture /ˈəʊvətjʊə(r)/ *n.* **1.** an orchestral piece opening an opera etc.; a composition in this style. **2.** (often in *pl.*) a friendly approach showing willingness to begin negotiations; a formal proposal or offer. [f. OF f. L (as APERTURE)]

overturn /ˌəʊvəˈtɜːn/ *v.t./i.* **1.** to turn over or fall down; to cause to do this. **2.** to overthrow; to subvert.

over-use /ˌəʊvəˈjuːz/ *v.t.* to use excessively. —/-ˈjuːs/ *n.* excessive use.

overview *n.* a general survey.

overweening /ˌəʊvəˈwiːnɪŋ/ *adj.* arrogant, presumptuous. [f. OVER- + obs. *ween* think]

overweight /ˌəʊvəˈweɪt/ *adj.* more than the allowed or normal or desired weight. —/ˈəʊvə-/ *n.* excess weight.

overwhelm /ˌəʊvəˈwelm/ *v.t.* **1.** to overpower, especially with an emotion or burden. **2.** to overcome by force of numbers. **3.** to bury or drown beneath a huge mass.

overwind /ˌəʊvəˈwaɪnd/ *v.t.* (*past* & *p.p.* **-wound**) to wind (a watch etc.) beyond the proper stopping-point.

overwork /ˌəʊvəˈwɜːk/ *v.t./i.* to work or cause to work too hard; to weary or exhaust with too much work. —*n.* excessive work.

overwrought /ˌəʊvəˈrɔːt/ *adj.* suffering a nervous reaction from over-excitement.

ovi- /ˈəʊvɪ-/ *in comb.* egg, ovum. [f. L (as OVUM)]

Ovid /ˈɒvɪd/ (Publius Ovidius Naso, 43 BC–*c.*AD 17) the youngest and most productive of the great Roman poets who wrote under Augustus. His wit and fluency are most clearly seen in his elegiac poems on love: the *Amores* (Loves), three books of personal love-poems, the *Heroides* (Heroines), imaginary letters from legendary heroines to their absent lovers, the *Ars Amatoria* (Art of Love) and the *Remedia Amoris* (Remedies for Love), mock-didactic poems on the art of falling in and out of love. The *Metamorphoses* is a hexameter epic, a kaleidoscopic retelling of Greek and Roman myths arranged in roughly chronological order. Their irreverent attitudes offended Augustus, and in AD 8, possibly after a scandal involving the latter's daughter Julia, he was exiled to Tomis on the Black Sea, from where he continued to write elegiac poems describing his plight and unsuccessfully seeking pardon.

oviduct /ˈəʊvɪdʌkt/ *n.* a canal through which ova pass from the ovary, especially in oviparous animals. [f. OVI- + DUCT]

oviform /ˈəʊvɪfɔːm/ *adj.* egg-shaped. [f. OVI- + -FORM]

ovine /ˈəʊvaɪn/ *adj.* of or like sheep. [f. L (*ovis* sheep)]

oviparous /əʊˈvɪpərəs/ *adj.* producing young from eggs expelled from the body before being hatched (cf. VIVIPAROUS). [f. L (OVI-, -*parus* bearing)]

ovipositor /ˌəʊvɪˈpɒzɪtə(r)/ *n.* a pointed tubular organ by

which a female insect deposits eggs (ill. INSECTS). [f. OVI-
+ POSIT]

ovoid /'əʊvɔɪd/ adj. (of a solid) egg-shaped. [f. F (as OVUM)]

ovulate /'ɒvjʊleɪt/ v.i. to discharge an ovum or ova from
an ovary; to produce ova. —**ovulation** /-'leɪʃ(ə)n/ n. [as
foll.]

ovule /'əʊvjuːl/ n. 1. a germ-cell in a female plant (ill.
FLOWERS). 2. an unfertilized ovum. [F f. L (dim. of
foll.]

ovum /'əʊvəm/ (pl. **ova**) 1. a female germ-cell in animals,
from which by fertilization with male sperm the young is
developed. 2. an egg, especially of a mammal or fish or
insect. [L, = egg]

ow int. expressing sudden pain. [natural excl.]

owe /əʊ/ v.t. 1. to be under an obligation to pay or repay
(money etc. to a person); to be in debt. 2. to have a duty to
render. 3. to feel (gratitude etc. towards another) in return
for a service. 4. to be indebted for (a thing) to a cause or to
another's work etc. [OE]

Owen[1] /'əʊɪn/, Robert (1771-1858), British socialist and
philanthropist. A pioneer socialist thinker, Owen attempted
to put his ideas into action in the New Lanark cotton mills
and in a series of co-operative communities. Although these
ideas did not always work well in practice, they had an
important long-term effect on the development of
British socialist thought and on the practice of industrial
relations.

Owen[2] /'əʊɪn/, Wilfrid (1893-1918), English poet of the
First World War. He was invalided out of the army in 1917
and in hospital met Siegfried Sassoon who encouraged him
to speak out against the war; on returning to the trenches
he found his own voice as a poet. Only five of his poems
appeared in his lifetime and his reputation has grown
since Sassoon's edition of his poems in 1920 and Edmund
Blunden's in 1931; among the most famous are 'Strange
Meeting' and 'Anthem for Doomed Youth'. Owen adopted
technical experiments using assonantal rhyme to produce
bleak realism and indignation at the horrors of war and pity
for its victims—of whom he became one, killed in action in
the last hours of the war.

Owens /'əʊɪnz/, James Cleveland (Jesse) (1913-80),
American athlete of track and field events, who in 1935
equalled or broke six world records in 45 minutes, and in
1936 won four gold medals at the Olympic Games in Berlin,
equalling or breaking twelve Olympic records.

owing predic. adj. owed, not yet paid. —**owing to,** caused
by, because of. [f. OWE]

owl n. a nocturnal bird of prey of the order Strigiformes,
with a large head and eyes and a hooked beak. [OE]

owlet /'aʊlɪt/ n. a small or young owl. [earlier howlet, dim.
of OWL, assim. to HOWL]

owlish adj. like an owl; solemn and dull. —**owlishly** adv.
[f. OWL]

own /əʊn/ adj. belonging to oneself or itself. —v.t./i. 1. to
have as property, to possess. 2. to acknowledge paternity,
authorship, or possession of. 3. to admit as existent, valid,
true, etc. —**come into one's own,** to receive one's due, to
achieve recognition. **of one's own,** belonging to oneself
exclusively. **on one's own,** alone; independent, independently, without help. **own goal,** a goal scored by a member
of a team against his own side. **own to,** to confess to. **own
up (to),** to confess frankly. —**owned** adj. [OE]

owner n. a possessor. **owner-occupier,** one who owns
and occupies a house. —**ownership** n.

ox n. (pl. **oxen**) an animal of the kinds of large usually
horned cloven-footed ruminant kept for draught, milk, and
meat; a fully-grown bullock of the domesticated species
(Bos taurus) of this. —**ox-bow** n. a horseshoe bend in a
river; a lake formed from this when the river cuts across
the narrow end (ill. RIVERS). **ox-eye** n. any of several plants
(esp. Leucanthemum vulgare) with flowers like the eye of an
ox. [OE]

oxalic acid /ɒk'sælɪk/ a highly poisonous and sour acid
originally found in wood sorrel and other plants. [f. F f. L
f. Gk oxalis wood sorrel]

Oxbridge /'ɒksbrɪdʒ/ n. the universities of Oxford and
Cambridge, especially in contrast to newer universities.
—adj. characteristic of these. [f. Ox(FORD) + (CAM)BRIDGE]

oxen pl. of ox.

Oxfam abbr. Oxford Commitee for Famine Relief.

Oxford /'ɒksfəd/ a midland city on the River Thames, the
seat of a major English university organized as a federation
of colleges. A university (studium generale) was organized

there soon after 1167, perhaps as a result of a migration of
students from Paris. The first colleges were founded in the
13th c.—University (1249), Balliol (1263), and Merton
(1264)—and Oxford rose to equal status with the great
European medieval universities, numbering among its
scholars the philosopher and scientist Roger Bacon, and Sir
Thomas More; Erasmus lectured there. A centre of royalism
during the 17th c., Oxford declined during the 18th c. but
was revived in the 1800s, particularly as a result of a
renaissance in religious thought. The University includes
the Bodleian Library (see entry). The first women's college,
Lady Margaret Hall, was founded in 1878. In 1982-3 there
were 9,401 undergraduates in residence (5,972 men,
3,429 women) and 2,921 postgraduates (2,018 men, 903
women). —**Oxford blue,** dark blue. **Oxford English Dictionary,** see MURRAY[2].

Oxford Movement a movement (1833-45), centred at
Oxford and led by Keble, Newman, and Pusey, which
aimed at restoring traditional Catholic teaching within the
Church of England; its principles were set out in the Tracts
for the Times. The Movement emphasized ceremonial, set
up the first Anglican religious communities, and contributed to social work and scholarship. At first it met with
much hostility, but its concern for a higher standard of
worship has ultimately influenced most groups within the
Church of England and even many Nonconformists.

Oxfordshire /'ɒksfədʃɪə(r)/ a SE midland county of
England.

oxherd n. a cowherd.

oxhide n. the hide of an ox; leather from this.

oxidant /'ɒksɪdənt/ n. an oxidizing agent. [F, partic. of
oxider (as OXIDE)]

oxidation /ɒksɪ'deɪʃ(ə)n/ n. oxidizing, being oxidized. [F
(as foll.)]

oxide /'ɒksaɪd/ n. a binary compound of oxygen. [F (as
OXYGEN)]

oxidize /'ɒksɪdaɪz/ v.t./i. 1. to combine or cause to combine
with oxygen. 2. to make or become rusty. 3. to coat (metal)
with an oxide. —**oxidization** /-'zeɪʃ(ə)n/ n. [f. prec.]

Oxon. abbr. 1. Oxfordshire. 2. of Oxford University. [f. L
Oxoniensis (as foll.)]

Oxonian /ɒk'səʊnɪən/ adj. of Oxford or Oxford University. —n. 1. a member of Oxford University. 2. a citizen of
Oxford. [f. Oxonia Latinized form of Ox(en)ford]

oxtail n. the tail of an ox, much used for soup-making.

Oxus /'ɒksəs/ the former name of the Amu Darya (see
entry).

oxy-acetylene /ɒksɪə'setɪliːn/ adj. of or using a mixture
of oxygen and acetylene, especially in the cutting or welding
of metals. [f. foll. + ACETYLENE]

oxygen /'ɒksɪdʒ(ə)n/ n. an odourless tasteless gaseous element, symbol O, atomic number 8, which is essential to
living organisms (see below). —**oxygen mask,** a mask
placed over the nose and mouth to supply oxygen for
breathing. **oxygen tent,** a tentlike enclosure supplying a
patient with air having increased oxygen content. [f. F
oxygène acidifying principle (Gk oxus sharp, -GEN), because
it was at first held to be the essential principle in the
formation of acids]

Oxygen was discovered in 1774 by Joseph Priestley (see
entry). It forms about 20 per cent of the earth's atmosphere
by volume. Many rocks are formed chiefly of oxygen
compounds, and it is the most abundant element in the
earth's crust. It exists in two forms: atmospheric oxygen,
which consists of diatomic molecules, and ozone (see entry).
Oxygen is essential to plant and animal life. It is a constituent of most of the compounds found in living organisms,
and the processes of respiration and combustion involve its
ability to combine readily with other elements. Water is a
compound of hydrogen and oxygen. Industrially, pure
oxygen is obtained by distillation of liquefied air; it is
used in the steel-making and chemical industries, and in
medicine.

oxygenate /'ɒksɪdʒəneɪt/ v.t. to supply, treat, or mix with
oxygen, to oxidize. —**oxygenation** /-'neɪʃ(ə)n/ n. [f. F (as
prec.)]

oxymoron /ɒksɪ'mɔːrɒn/ n. a figure of speech with pointed
conjunction of apparent contradictions (e.g. cheerful pessimist). [f. Gk, = pointedly foolish (oxus sharp, mōros
foolish)]

oxytocin /ɒksɪ'təʊsɪn/ n. a pituitary hormone controlling
uterine contraction and the release of milk, used in synthetic

form to induce labour etc. [f. Gk *oxutokia* (as OXY-, *tokos* childbirth)]

oyez /əʊˈjes/ *int.* (also **oyes**) a cry uttered usually three times by a public crier or court officer to call for attention. [f. AF, imper. of *oïr* hear f. L *audire*]

oyster *n.* **1.** a bivalve mollusc of the genus *Ostrea* or family Ostreidae, used as a food and in some types producing a pearl. **2.** a symbol of all one desires. **3.** white with a grey tinge. —**oyster-catcher** *n.* a shore-bird of the genus *Haematopus*. [f. OF f. L *ostrea, ostreum* f. Gk]

oz. *abbr.* ounce(s).

ozone /ˈəʊzəʊn/ *n.* **1.** a form of oxygen with three atoms in the molecule, having a pungent smell. It can be formed by passing an electrical discharge through oxygen, and is present in the air after a thunderstorm. The greatest concentration of ozone is in the upper atmosphere, where it forms as a result of the interaction of oxygen and ultraviolet rays from the sun, forming a layer which by absorbing these rays protects the earth from excessive ultraviolet radiation. **2.** (*pop.*) invigorating air at the seaside etc. [f. G f. Gk (*ozō* smell)]

P

P, p /piː/ *n.* (**Ps, P's**) the sixteenth letter of the alphabet.
P *abbr.* pawn (in chess).
P *symbol* phosphorus.
p *abbr.* **1.** penny, pence. **2.** (*Mus.*) piano (= PIANO²).
p. *abbr.* page.
PA *abbr.* **1.** personal assistant. **2.** public address. **3.** Press Association.
Pa *symbol* protactinium. —*abbr.* pascal.
pa /pɑː/ *n.* (*colloq.*) father. [abbr. of PAPA]
p.a. *abbr.* per annum.
pace¹ *n.* **1.** a single step in walking or running; the space traversed in this. **2.** speed in walking or running. **3.** any of the various gaits of (esp. a trained) horse etc. —*v.t./i.* **1.** to walk with a slow or regular pace; to traverse by pacing. **2.** to set the pace for (a rider, runner, etc.). **3.** to measure (a distance) by pacing. **4.** (of a horse) to amble. —**keep pace**, to advance at an equal rate. **put a person through his paces**, to test his qualities in action etc. **set the pace**, to set the speed, especially by leading. [f. OF *pas* f. L *passus*]
pace² /ˈpeɪsɪ, ˈpɑːtʃeɪ/ *prep.* (in announcing a contrary opinion) with all due deference to (the person named). [L, abl. of *pax* peace]
pacemaker *n.* **1.** a runner etc. who sets the pace in a race. **2.** a structure or device for stimulating the heart muscle.
pachyderm /ˈpækɪdɜːm/ *n.* a thick-skinned mammal, especially an elephant or rhinoceros. —**pachydermatous** /-ˈdɜːmətəs/ *adj.* [f. F f. Gk (*pakhus* thick, *derma* skin)]
Pacific /pəˈsɪfɪk/ *adj.* of the Pacific Ocean. —*n.* the Pacific Ocean. —**Pacific Ocean**, the world's largest ocean, covering one third of the earth's surface (181,300,000 sq. km, 70 million sq. miles), separating Asia and Australia from North and South America and extending from Antarctica in the south to the Bering Strait (which links it to the Arctic Ocean) in the north. It was named by its first European navigator, Magellan, because he experienced calm weather there. [= foll.]
pacific /pəˈsɪfɪk/ *adj.* peaceful; making or loving peace. —**pacifically** *adv.* [f. F or L (*pax* peace)]
pacifist /ˈpæsɪfɪst/ *n.* one who rejects war and violence and believes that disputes should be settled by peaceful means. —**pacifism** *n.* [f. F (as prec.)]
pacify /ˈpæsɪfaɪ/ *v.t.* **1.** to calm and quieten, to appease. **2.** to establish peace in. —**pacification** /-fɪˈkeɪʃ(ə)n/ *n.*, **pacificatory** /pəˈsɪfɪkətərɪ/ *adj.* [f. OF or L (as PACIFIC)]
pack¹ *n.* **1.** a collection of things wrapped up or tied together for carrying. **2.** (usu. *derog.*) a lot or set. **3.** a set of playing-cards. **4.** a group of wild animals, hounds, etc.; an organized group of Cub Scouts or Brownies. **5.** a team's forwards in Rugby football. **6.** a medicinal or cosmetic substance applied to the skin. **7.** an area of pack-ice. **8.** a method of packing. —*v.t./i.* **1.** to put (things) together in a bundle, bag, etc. for transport, storing, or marketing, etc.; to fill with things thus; to fill a case etc. with one's belongings. **2.** to be able to be packed. **3.** to put closely together; to fill (a space) in this way; to fill (a theatre or meeting etc.) with persons. **4.** to cover or protect with something pressed tightly round or inside. **5.** to carry (a gun etc.); to be capable of delivering (a punch) with skill or force. **6.** (of animals) to form a pack. —**pack-drill** *n.* a military punishment of drill in full marching equipment (*no names no pack-drill*, discretion will prevent punishment).
pack-horse *n.* a horse for carrying packs. **pack-ice** *n.* large crowded floating pieces of ice in the sea. **pack it in**, (*slang*) to cease doing something. **pack off**, to send away.
pack-saddle *n.* a saddle adapted for supporting packs. **pack up**, to put one's things together in readiness for departure or ceasing work; (*slang*, of machinery etc.) to break down. **send packing**, (*colloq.*) to dismiss summarily. —**packer** *n.* [f. MDu. or MLG]
pack² *v.t.* to select (a jury etc.) so as to secure a decision biased in one's favour. [prob. f. obs. v. *pact* f. PACT]
package *n.* **1.** a bundle of things packed. **2.** a parcel, a box, etc., in which things are packed. **3.** a package deal. —*v.t.* to make up into or enclose in a package. —**package deal**,

a transaction or proposals offered or agreed to as a whole. **package holiday** *or* **tour** etc., one with all arrangements made at an inclusive price. [f. PACK¹]
packaging *n.* wrapping(s) or container(s) for goods. [f. prec.]
packet /ˈpækɪt/ *n.* **1.** a small package. **2.** (*colloq.*) a large sum of money won or lost. —**packet-boat** *n.* a mail-boat. [f. PACK¹]
packing *n.* material used to pack and protect fragile articles etc. —**packing-case** *n.* a wooden case or framework for packing goods. [f. PACK¹]
packthread *n.* stout thread for sewing or tying up packs.
pact *n.* an agreement, a treaty. [f. OF f. L *pactum* (*pacisci* agree)]
pad¹ *n.* **1.** a piece of soft stuff used to reduce friction or jarring, rub things, fill out hollows, hold or absorb liquid, etc. **2.** a number of sheets of blank paper fastened together at one edge. **3.** the fleshy underpart of an animal's foot. **4.** a guard for the leg and ankle in cricket etc. **5.** a flat surface for a helicopter take-off and landing or a rocket launching. **6.** (*slang*) a lodging. —*v.t.* (**-dd-**) **1.** to provide with a pad or padding; to stuff. **2.** to fill (a book etc.) with unnecessary material in order to lengthen it. —**padded cell**, a room with padded walls in a mental hospital. [prob. of Du. or LG orig.]
pad² *v.t./i.* (**-dd-**) **1.** to walk with a soft dull steady sound of steps. **2.** to travel (along) on foot. [f. LG *pad* path or *padden* tread]
padding *n.* **1.** material used to pad things. **2.** superfluous words in a book, sentence, etc.
paddle¹ *n.* **1.** a short broad-bladed oar used without a rowlock. **2.** a paddle-shaped instrument or part. **3.** a fin, a flipper. **4.** any of the boards fitted round the circumference of a paddle-wheel or mill-wheel. **5.** an act or spell of paddling. —*v.t./i.* to move on water or propel (a canoe) by means of paddles; to row gently. —**paddle-boat** *n.* a boat propelled by a paddle-wheel. **paddle-wheel** *n.* a wheel for propelling a ship, with boards round the circumference so as to press backward against the water as the wheel revolves. —**paddler**, *n.* [orig. unkn.]
paddle² *v.t./i.* to walk barefoot in shallow water; to dabble (the feet or hands) in shallow water. —*n.* an act or spell of paddling. [cf. LG *paddeln* tramp about]
paddock /ˈpædək/ *n.* **1.** a small field, especially for keeping horses in. **2.** a turf enclosure adjoining a racecourse where horses are assembled before a race; a similar enclosure at a motor-racing circuit. **3.** (*Austral.* & *NZ*) a field, a plot of land. [app. var. of dial. *parrock* (as PARK)]
Paddy *n.* (*colloq.*) a nickname for an Irishman. [pet-form of Irish *Padraig* Patrick]
paddy¹ *n.* (in full **paddy-field**) a field where rice is grown. **2.** rice before threshing or in the husk. [f. Malay]
paddy² *n.* (*colloq.*) a rage, a fit of temper. [as PADDY]
padlock *n.* a detachable lock hanging by a pivoted hook from the object it fastens. —*v.t.* to secure with a padlock. [f. LOCK¹; first element unkn.]
padre /ˈpɑːdrɪ/ *n.* (*colloq.*) a chaplain in an army etc. [It., Sp., & Port., = father]
paean /ˈpiːən/ *n.* a song of praise or triumph. [L f. Doric Gk *paian* hymn to Apollo]
paediatrics /piːdɪˈætrɪks/ *n.pl.* the branch of medicine dealing with children and their diseases. —**paediatric** *adj.*, **paediatrician** /piːdɪəˈtrɪʃ(ə)n/ *n.* [f. PAEDO- + Gk *iatros* physician]
paedo- /ˈpiːdə(ʊ)-/ *in comb.* child. [f. Gk *pais* boy, child]
paedophilia /piːdəˈfɪlɪə/ *n.* sexual love directed towards children. [f. prec. + -PHILIA]
paella /pɑːˈelə/ *n.* a Spanish dish of rice, saffron, chicken, seafood, etc., cooked and served in a large shallow pan. [Catalan, f. OF f. L *patella* pan]
pagan /ˈpeɪɡən/ *adj.* **1.** heathen; irreligious. **2.** holding the belief that deity exists in natural forces; nature-worshipping, especially in contrast to believing in Christian-

ity, Judaism, etc. —*n.* **1.** a pagan person. **2.** one with pagan beliefs. —**paganism** *n.* [f. L *paganus* (*pagus* village)]

Paganini /ˌpægəˈniːniː/, Niccolò (1782–1840), Italian violinist and composer, who lived an extraordinary life as a travelling violinist. He possessed a brilliant technical skill, a personal magnetism, and a mephistophelean appearance that mesmerized his audiences (particularly the female members) and led some critics to speak of diabolical powers. He did not confine his skills to playing the violin but took up the guitar during a love affair in the 1830s; he also commissioned Berlioz to write a viola concerto for him (which, however, he never played), and his own compositions for the violin bear witness to his prowess.

Page /peɪdʒ/, Sir Frederick Handley (1885–1962), English aircraft designer, founder of Handley Page Ltd. (1909), the first British aircraft manufacturing company. He was responsible for the design and construction of many famous aircraft including Handley Page bombers of the First World War, Hannibal airliners, Hampden and Halifax bombers of the Second World War, and many post-war aircraft. In 1919 he formed Handley Page Transport Ltd., operating London–Paris and London–Brussels–Switzerland flights until 1924. He was also famous for his design of the slotted aerofoil.

page¹ *n.* a leaf of a book etc.; one side of this; what is written or printed on this; an episode that might fill a page in a written history etc. —*v.t.* to paginate. [F f. L *pagina*]

page² *n.* a boy or man, usually in livery, employed to run errands, attend to a door, etc.; a boy employed as a personal attendant of a person of rank, a bride, etc. —*v.t.* to summon (as) by a page. [f. OF perh. ult. f. Gk *paidion* small boy]

pageant /ˈpædʒ(ə)nt/ *n.* a brilliant spectacle, especially an elaborate parade; a spectacular procession, or play performed in the open, illustrating historical events; a tableau etc. on a fixed stage or moving vehicle. [orig. unkn.]

pageantry *n.* a spectacular show or display; what serves to make a pageant. [f. prec.]

paginate /ˈpædʒɪneɪt/ *v.t.* to number the pages of (a book etc.). —**pagination** /-ˈneɪʃ(ə)n/ *n.* [f. F f. L (as PAGE¹)]

pagoda /pəˈɡəʊdə/ *n.* a Hindu or Buddhist temple or sacred building, especially a tower, in India and the Far East; an ornamental imitation of this. [f. Port., prob. ult. f. Pers.]

pah /pɑː/ *int.* expressing disgust or contempt. [natural excl.]

Pahlavi /ˈpɑːləvɪ/ *n.* the language of Persia under the Sassanian kings. It was closely related to Avestan and was written in a version of the Aramaic script. [f. Pers., = Parthian]

paid *past* & *p.p.* of PAY.

pail *n.* a bucket. —**pailful** *n.* [OE]

pain *n.* **1.** an unpleasant feeling caused by injury or disease of the body; mental suffering. **2.** (in *pl.*) careful effort. **3.** punishment; the threat of this. —*v.t.* to inflict pain on; (in *p.p.*) expressing pain. —**pain in the neck,** (*colloq.*) an annoying or tiresome person or thing. **pain-killer** *n.* a medicine for alleviating pain. [f. OF *peine* f. L *poena* punishment]

painful *adj.* **1.** causing pain; (of a part of the body) suffering pain. **2.** causing trouble or difficulty, laborious. —**painfully** *adv.*, **painfulness** *n.* [f. PAIN + -FUL]

painless *adj.* not causing pain. [f. PAIN + -LESS]

painstaking /ˈpeɪnzteɪkɪŋ/ *adj.* careful, industrious.

paint *n.* colouring-matter, especially in liquid form for applying to a surface; (in *pl.*) a collection of tubes or cakes of paint. —*v.t./i.* **1.** to coat or decorate with paint; to colour thus. **2.** to depict or portray with paint(s); to make pictures thus. **3.** to describe. **4.** to apply a liquid or cosmetic to (the skin or face); to apply (liquid etc.) thus. —**painted lady**, an orange-red butterfly (*Vanessa cardui*) with black and white spots. **paint the town red**, (*slang*) to enjoy oneself flamboyantly. [f. OF f. L *pingere*]

paintbox *n.* a box holding dry paints for use by an artist.

paintbrush *n.* a brush for applying paint.

painter¹ *n.* one who paints, especially as an artist or decorator. —**painterly** *adj.* [f. PAINT]

painter² *n.* a rope attached to the bow of a boat for tying it to a quay etc. [prob. f. OF *penteur* rope from mast-head]

painting *n.* a painted picture. [f. PAINT]

pair *n.* **1.** a set of two persons or things used together or regarded as a unit. **2.** an article consisting of two joined or corresponding parts. **3.** an engaged or married couple; a mated couple of animals. **4.** the other member of a pair. **5.**

two playing-cards of the same denomination. **6.** either or both of two MPs of opposing parties who are absent from a division by mutual arrangement. —*v.t./i.* **1.** to arrange or be arranged in couples. **2.** (of animals) to mate. **3.** to partner (a person) with a member of the opposite sex. **4.** to make a pair in Parliament. —**pair off**, to form into pairs. [f. OF f. L *paria* (as PAR)]

Paisley /ˈpeɪzlɪ/ *adj.* having a distinctive pattern of curved abstract figures. [f. *Paisley* in Scotland]

Pakistan /pɑːkɪˈstɑːn, pæk-/ a country in southern Asia, bordered by Afghanistan to the north and India to the east; pop. (1981) 83,780,000; official language, Urdu; capital, Islamabad. Part of the Indian subcontinent, Pakistan was created as a separate country, comprising the territory to the NE and NW of India in which the population was predominantly Muslim, following the British withdrawal in 1947. East Pakistan became the independent State of Bangladesh in 1972 after war between India and Pakistan in December 1971; Pakistan withdrew from the Commonwealth as a protest against the decision of Britain, Australia, and New Zealand to recognize Bangladesh. Pakistan's history since independence has been characterized by border disputes with India over Kashmir, the involvement of the army in politics, and recently by the threat to its northern frontier caused by the war in Afghanistan. The economy is predominantly agricultural, wheat, cotton, and rice being the principal crops. —**Pakistani** *adj.* & *n.* [f. Punjab, *Afghan* Frontier, *Kashmir*, *Baluchistan*, lands where Muslims predominated]

pal *n.* (*colloq.*) a friend, a mate. —*v.i.* (**-ll-**) (with *up*) (*colloq.*) to become friends. [f. Romany, ult. as BROTHER]

palace /ˈpælɪs/ *n.* **1.** an official residence of a sovereign, president, archbishop, or bishop. **2.** a splendid mansion, a spacious building. —**palace revolution**, the overthrow of a sovereign etc. without a civil war. [f. OF f. L *Palatium* house of Augustus at Rome]

Palace of Westminster see WESTMINSTER and ill. PARLIAMENT.

paladin /ˈpælədɪn/ *n.* **1.** any of the Twelve Peers of Charlemagne's court, of whom the Count Palatine was the chief. **2.** a knight errant, a champion. [f. F f. It. f. L (as PALATINE)]

palaeo- /ˈpælɪə(ʊ)-/ *in comb.* ancient, of ancient times. [f. Gk *palaios*]

Palaeocene /ˈpælɪəsiːn/ *adj.* of the first epoch of the Tertiary period, following the Cretaceous period and preceding the Eocene epoch, lasting from about 65 to 54.9 million years ago. The sudden diversification of the mammals is a notable feature of the epoch. —*n.* this epoch. [f. prec. + Gk *kainos* new]

palaeography /pælɪˈɒɡrəfɪ/ *n.* the study of ancient writing and documents. —**palaeographer** *n.*, **palaeographic** /-ˈɡræfɪk/ *adj.* [f. F (as PALAEO-, -GRAPHY)]

palaeolithic /pælɪəˈlɪθɪk, peɪ-/ *adj.* of the earlier part of the Stone Age, when primitive stone implements were used. —*n.* this period, which extends from the first appearance of artefacts, some 2.5 million years ago, to the end of the last ice age *c.*10,000 BC. It has been divided into the *lower palaeolithic*, with the earliest forms of man and the presence of hand-axe industries, ending *c.*80,000 BC, *middle palaeolithic* (or Mousterian), the era of Neanderthal man, ending *c.*33,000 BC, and *upper palaeolithic*, which saw the development of *Homo sapiens*. [f. PALAEO- + Gk *lithos* stone]

palaeontology /pælɪɒnˈtɒlədʒɪ/ *n.* the study of life in the geological past. —**palaeontologist** *n.* [f. PALAEO- + Gk *onta* beings (*eimi* be) + -LOGY]

Palaeozoic /pælɪəʊˈzəʊɪk/ *adj.* of the geological era between the Precambrian and the Mesozoic. The era comprises the Cambrian, Ordovician, Silurian, Devonian, Carboniferous, and Permian periods. It lasted from about 590 to 248 million years ago, beginning with the first appearance of fossils bearing hard shells and ending with the rise to dominance of the reptiles. —*n.* this era. [f. PALAEO- + Gk *zōē* life, *zōos* living]

palais /ˈpæleɪ/ *n.* a public hall for dancing. —**palais glide**, a type of ballroom dance in which large groups dance simultaneously. [F *palais* (*de danse*) public hall (for dancing), = PALACE]

palanquin /pælənˈkiːn/ *n.* (also **palankeen**) an eastern covered litter for one person. [f. Port.; cf. Hindi *palki*]

palatable /ˈpælətəb(ə)l/ *adj.* pleasant to the taste; agreeable to the mind. [f. PALATE]

palatal /ˈpælət(ə)l/ *adj.* of the palate; (of a sound) made by placing the tongue against the palate. —*n*. a palatal sound. —**palatally** *adv*. [F (as foll.)]

palate /ˈpælət/ *n*. **1.** the structure forming the upper part of the mouth cavity in vertebrates (ill. BODY 2). **2.** the sense of taste. **3.** mental taste, liking. [f. L *palatum*]

palatial /pəˈleɪʃ(ə)l/ *adj*. like a palace, spacious, splendid. —**palatially** *adv*. [f. L (as PALACE)]

palatinate /pəˈlætɪneɪt/ *n*. a territory under a Count Palatine. [f. foll.]

Palatine /ˈpælətaɪn/ *adj*. possessing royal privileges, having jurisdiction (within a territory) such as elsewhere belongs only to the sovereign. —**Count Palatine,** (in the later Roman Empire) a count (*comes*) attached to the imperial palace and having supreme judicial authority in certain causes; (under the German emperors) a count having supreme jurisdiction in his fief; (in English history) an **Earl Palatine,** the proprietor of a County Palatine, now applied to the earldom of Chester and duchy of Lancaster, dignities which are attached to the Crown. **County Palatine,** (in England) a county of which the earl formerly had royal privileges, with exclusive jurisdiction (now Cheshire and Lancashire, formerly also Durham, Pembroke, Ely, etc.). [f. F f. L (as PALACE)]

palaver /pəˈlɑːvə(r)/ *n*. **1.** fuss; profuse or idle talk. **2.** (*slang*) an affair, a business. **3.** (esp. *hist*.) a parley between African or other natives and traders etc. —*v.t./i*. to talk profusely; to wheedle. [f. Port. *palavra* word f. L (as PARABLE)]

pale[1] *adj*. **1.** (of a person or complexion) having little colour, lighter than normal. **2.** (of colour or light) faint, not bright or vivid; only faintly coloured. —*v.t./i*. **1.** to make or become pale. **2.** to become feeble in comparison. —**pale-face** *n*. a supposed North American Indian name for a white man. —**palely** *adv*., **paleness** *n*. [f. OF f. L *pallidus*]

pale[2] *n*. **1.** a stake used in a fence etc.; a boundary. **2.** (*hist*.) a district or territory within determined bounds or subject to a particular jurisdiction. **3.** (in heraldry) a vertical stripe in the middle of a field (ill. HERALDRY). —**beyond the pale,** outside the bounds of civilized behaviour etc. **the English Pale,** (*hist*.) the small area round Calais, the only part of France remaining in English hands after the Hundred Years War; (also **the Pale**) that part of Ireland, varying in extent at different times, over which England exercised jurisdiction. [f. OF f. L *palus* stake]

Palestine /ˈpælɪstaɪn/ a territory in SW Asia on the eastern coast of the Mediterranean Sea, which in biblical times comprised the kingdoms of Israel and Judah (see ISRAEL[1]). There have been many changes in the frontiers in the course of history. The land was controlled at various times by the Egyptian, Assyrian, Persian, and Roman empires before being conquered by the Arabs in AD 634. It remained in Muslim hands, except for a brief hiatus during the Crusades (1098–1197), until the First World War, being part of the Ottoman empire from 1516 to 1917, when Turkish and German forces were defeated by the British at Megiddo. The name 'Palestine' was revived as an official political title for the land west of the Jordan mandated to Britain in 1920. Jewish immigration, encouraged by the Balfour Declaration of 1917, became quite heavy, and Palestine ceased to exist as a political entity in 1948 when the State of Israel was established. The name continues to be used, however, to describe a geographical entity, particularly in the context of Arab aims for the resettlement of people who left the area when the State of Israel was established, or in subsequent struggles. —**Palestinian** *adj*. & *n*. [f. Gk *Palaistinē* (used in early Christian writing), L (*Syria*) *Palaestina* (name of Roman province), f. *Philistia* land of the Philistines]

Palestine Liberation Organization a politico-military body formed in 1964 to unite various Palestinian Arab groups. From 1967 it was dominated by the Al Fatah group led by Yasser Arafat, and was soon active in guerrilla activities against Israel. The activities of radical factions of the movement caused trouble with the host country Jordan, and following a brief civil war in 1970, it moved to Lebanon and Syria. In 1974 the organization was recognized by the Arab nations as the representative of all Palestinians and in 1976 was invited to take part in a UN debate. The Israeli invasion of Lebanon in 1982 disorganized its military power and caused serious strains within its political superstructure. It regrouped in Libya.

Palestrina /pæleˈstriːnə/, Giovanni Pierluigi da (1525/6–1594), Italian composer, who took his name from his birthplace, a small hill town near Rome. He composed several madrigals but is known for his sacred music, and

his flowing style came to represent the lost purity of Roman Catholic music for worship in the years after instruments were admitted into church services.

palette /ˈpælət/ *n*. an artist's thin wooden slab etc. used for laying and mixing colours on. —**palette-knife** *n*. a thin steel blade with a handle for mixing colours or applying paint; a kitchen knife with a long blunt round-ended flexible blade. [F, dim. of *pale* shovel f. L]

palfrey /ˈpɔːlfrɪ/ *n*. (*archaic*) a horse for ordinary riding, especially for ladies. [f. OF f. L *paraveredus* (Gk *para* beside, extra, L *veredus* light horse)]

Pali /ˈpɑːlɪ/ *n*. an Indic language, closely related to Sanskrit, in which the sacred texts of Theravada Buddhism are written. It was spoken in northern India in the 5th–2nd c. BC. As the language of a large part of the Buddhist scriptures it was brought to Sri Lanka and Burma, and, though not spoken there, became the vehicle of a large literature of commentaries and chronicles. [f. Skr. *pālī-bhāsā* (*pālī* canon, *bhāsā* language)]

palimpsest /ˈpælɪmpsest/ *n*. a writing-material or manuscript on which the original writing has been effaced to make room for other writing; a monumental brass turned and re-engraved on the reverse side. [f. L f. Gk (*palin* again, *psaō* rub smooth)]

palindrome /ˈpælɪndrəʊm/ *n*. a word or verse etc. that reads the same backwards as forwards (e.g. *rotator, nurses run*). —**palindromic** /-ˈdrɒmɪk/ *adj*. [f. L *palindromos* (*palin* back again, *drom-* run)]

paling /ˈpeɪlɪŋ/ *n*. **1.** a fence of pales. **2.** a pale. [f. PALE[2]]

palisade /pælɪˈseɪd/ *n*. **1.** a fence of pales or of iron railings. **2.** a strong pointed wooden stake. —*v.t*. to enclose or furnish with a palisade. [f. F f. Prov. f. L *palus* stake]

Palissy /ˈpælɪsɪ/, Bernard (*c*.1510–90), French master potter, who enjoyed court patronage and became famous for his richly coloured ware ornamented in relief with snakes, lizards, frogs, fish, foliage, etc., cast from the life, for which he was given the title 'inventor of the king's rustic pottery'. Wares of this type continued to be produced regionally in France for some two centuries after his death.

pall[1] /pɔːl/ *n*. **1.** a cloth spread over a coffin, hearse, or tomb. **2.** a woollen shoulder-band with front and back pendants, worn by the pope and some metropolitans and archbishops. **3.** something forming a dark heavy covering. [OE f. L *pallium* cloak]

pall[2] /pɔːl/ *v.t./i*. to become uninteresting; to satiate, to cloy. —**pall on,** to cease to interest or attract. [f. APPAL]

Palladian /pəˈleɪdɪən/ *adj*. in the neoclassical style of Palladio. The term is applied to a phase of English architecture from *c*.1715, when a revival of interest in the ideas and designs of Palladio and his English follower, Inigo Jones, led to a reaction against the baroque. —**Palladianism** *n*. [f. foll.]

Palladio /pəˈlɑːdɪəʊ/, Andrea (1508–80), Italian architect, born in Padua, who was one of the most important architect/theorists of 16th-c. Italy. He went to Rome in 1540–1 and published a guide to the antiquities of that city, and this interest in classical harmony of proportion permeates all his own works. Among his architectural designs were villas for use as summer residences, their façades often having the appearance of an antique temple. His palace designs often show classical influence and he executed much distinctive work on Venetian churches. He published a philosophical and visual analysis of his work, *I Quattro Libri dell'Architettura* (1570), which was very influential and was the main source of inspiration for the English Palladian movement.

palladium /pəˈleɪdɪəm/ *n*. a rare hard white metallic element, symbol Pd, atomic number 46, chemically related to platinum. First isolated in 1803, palladium is important as a catalyst, and the metal and its alloys are used in electrical contacts, precision instruments, and jewellery. [f. *Pallas* (f. foll.) an asteroid discovered just previously]

Pallas /ˈpæləs/ (*Gk myth*.) one of the names (of unknown meaning) of Athene.

pallbearer *n*. a person helping to carry the coffin at a funeral.

pallet[1] /ˈpælɪt/ *n*. a straw mattress; a mean or makeshift bed. [f. AF f. L *palea* straw]

pallet[2] /ˈpælɪt/ *n*. a portable platform for transporting and storing goods. [f. F, = PALETTE]

palliasse /ˈpælɪæs/ *n*. a straw mattress. [f. F *paillasse* f. It. f. L (as PALLET[1])]

palliate /ˈpælɪeɪt/ *v.t*. **1.** to alleviate (a disease) without

curing. **2.** to excuse, to extenuate. —**palliative** adj. &
n., **palliation** /-ˈeɪʃ(ə)n/ n. [f. L palliare to cloak (as
PALL[1])]

pallid /ˈpælɪd/ adj. pale, especially from illness. [f. L (as
PALE[1])]

pallium /ˈpælɪəm/ n. (pl. **-a**) **1.** a man's large rectangular
cloak as worn by the ancient Greeks. **2.** the pall worn by
the pope etc. **3.** the mantle of a mollusc. [L, = cloak]

pall-mall /ˈpælˈmæl, pelˈmel/ n. a 16th- and 17th-c. game
in which a boxwood ball was driven with a mallet through
an iron ring suspended at the end of a long alley. The street
Pall Mall in London was on the site of a pall-mall alley,
whence its name. [F. It. palla ball, maglio mallet]

pallor /ˈpælə(r)/ n. pallidness, paleness. [L (pallēre be pale)]

pally /ˈpælɪ/ (colloq.) friendly. —**palliness** n. [f. PAL]

palm[1] /pɑːm/ n. **1.** a chiefly tropical tree of the family
Palmae, with no branches and a mass of large leaves at the
top. **2.** a leaf of this as the symbol of victory. **3.** supreme
excellence; the prize for this. —**palm-oil** n. the oil from
various palms. **Palm Sunday**, the Sunday before Easter,
on which Christ's entry into Jerusalem is celebrated by
processions in which branches of palms are carried. [OE f.
L palma (as foll.)]

palm[2] /pɑːm/ n. the inner surface of the hand between the
wrist and the fingers; the part of a glove that covers this.
—v.t. to conceal in the hand. —**palm off**, to impose or
thrust fraudulently on a person; to put (a person) off with.
—**palmar** /ˈpɑːmə(r)/ adj. [f. OF f. L palma]

palmate /ˈpælmeɪt/ adj. shaped like the palm of the hand,
having lobes etc. like spread fingers (of leaves, ill. PLANTS).
—**palmately** adv. [f. L (as prec.)]

Palmerston /ˈpɑːməst(ə)n/, Henry John Temple, 3rd Viscount (1784–1865), British statesman. Foreign Secretary
between 1830 and 1841, and again from 1846 to 1851,
Palmerston actively pursued liberal policies in all spheres
of British influence, supporting Belgian independence,
sustaining Turkey against Russian expansionism, and declaring the Opium War against China. As Prime Minister
(1855–8 and 1859–65) Palmerston was the dominant political figure of the mid-19th c., overseeing the successful
conclusion of the Crimean War, the suppression of the
Indian Mutiny, and the maintenance of neutrality during
the American Civil War.

palmetto /pælˈmetəʊ/ n. (pl. **-os**) a palm-tree, especially of
small size. [f. Sp. palmito (as PALM[1])]

palmistry /ˈpɑːmɪstrɪ/ n. the pseudo-science of divination
by the lines and swellings of the hand. It can be traced back
to ancient China and flourished in classical Greece and
medieval Christendom. The parts of the hand were held to
correspond to various parts of the body, traits of personality,
and to the heavenly bodies. There was a close link between
palmistry and astrology, both claiming the ability to predict
the future; one practitioner is said to have foretold the
election of Pope Leo X by reading his palm. Palmistry
enjoyed a considerable vogue in Renaissance Europe, often
associated with physiognomy and other forms of divination;
English writers in this field drew heavily on the Continental
tradition. Simple cheap guides brought the basic rules to a
vast audience. Palmistry was always a controversial subject:
while practitioners claimed support from Scripture, other
contemporaries denounced it as diabolic, and it was condemned by papal bulls in 1586 and 1631. After a long
decline it enjoyed a certain revival in the 19th c., linked to
the renewed interest in physiognomy. —**palmist** n. [f.
PALM[2]]

palmy /ˈpɑːmɪ/ adj. **1.** of, like, or abounding in palms. **2.**
full of success, flourishing. [f. PALM[1]]

Palmyra /pælˈmaɪrə/ the Greek name for the Semitic
Tadmor (= city of palms), an oasis settlement in the Syrian
desert, known from the 1st c. BC first as an independent
State and then, after AD 18, as a Roman dependency which
flourished between the 1st–3rd c. AD, supplanting Petra as
the leading caravan city on the east–west trade route. Built
mainly during the 1st c. AD on the model of a Roman city,
Palmyra briefly regained its independence in the 260s as
the capital of the dynasts Oeleanthus, Vaballath, and Queen
Zenobia who dominated Syria-Palestine as far as Egypt
before being defeated by Aurelian who destroyed Palmyra
in 273.

palomino /pæləˈmiːnəʊ/ n. (pl. **-os**) a golden or cream-
coloured horse with a light-coloured mane and tail. [f. Sp.,
= young pigeon]

palp n. a segmented organ at or near the mouth of certain

insects and crustaceans, used for feeling and tasting things.
[f. L (palpare touch gently)]

palpable /ˈpælpəb(ə)l/ adj. that can be touched or felt;
readily perceived by the senses or mind. —**palpability**
/-ˈbɪlɪtɪ/ n., **palpably** adv. [as PALP]

palpate /pælˈpeɪt/ v.t. to examine (esp. medically) by
touch. —**palpation** /-ˈpeɪʃ(ə)n/ n. [as PALP]

palpitate /ˈpælpɪteɪt/ v.i. to pulsate, to throb; to tremble
(with pleasure, fear, etc.). [f. L palpitare frequent. of palpare
touch gently]

palpitation /pælpɪˈteɪʃ(ə)n/ n. throbbing, trembling; increased activity of the heart due to exertion, agitation, or
disease. [f. prec.]

palsy /ˈpɔːlzɪ/ n. paralysis, especially with involuntary
tremors; a cause or state of powerlessness. —v.t. to affect
with palsy. [f. OF f. L (as PARALYSIS)]

paltry /ˈpɔːltrɪ/ adj. worthless, contemptible, trivial.
—**paltriness** n. [f. dial. palt rubbish]

palynology /pælɪˈnɒlədʒɪ/ n. the study of pollen in connection with plant geography, the dating of fossils, allergies,
etc. —**palynological** /-əˈlɒdʒɪk(ə)l/ adj. [f. Gk palunō
sprinkle + -LOGY]

Pamirs /pəˈmɪəz/ a mountain system of central Asia, partly
in the USSR and partly in Afghanistan.

pampas /ˈpæmpəs/ n.pl. the large treeless plains in South
America. —**pampas-grass** n. a large ornamental grass
(Cortaderia selloana) originally from South America. [Sp.
f. Quechua]

pamper v.t. to over-indulge (a person, taste, etc.); to spoil
(a person) with luxury. [f. obs. pamp cram]

pamphlet /ˈpæmflɪt/ n. a small usually unbound booklet
or leaflet containing information or a treatise. [f. Pamphilet
pet-name of Pamphilus 12th-c. amatory poem]

pamphleteer /pæmflɪˈtɪə(r)/ n. a writer of (esp. political)
pamphlets. [f. prec.]

Pamphylia /pæmˈfɪlɪə/ the ancient name for the southern
coastal region of Asia Minor, between Lycia and Cilicia.
—**Pamphylian** adj. & n.

Pan (Gk myth.) a god of flocks and herds, native to Arcadia,
thought of as loving mountains, caves, and lonely places,
and as musical (his instrument being the pan-pipe), capable
of causing 'panic' terror like that of a frightened and
stampeding herd. He is represented with the horns, ears,
and legs of a goat on a man's body. [Gk, prob. = the feeder
(i.e. herdsman); the ancients regularly associated his name
with Gk pas or pan = all, interpreting this as implying a
'universal' god, but this has nothing to do with his native
worship or any normal developments of it]

pan[1] n. **1.** a metal, earthenware, or plastic vessel used for
cooking and other domestic purposes; a panlike vessel in
which substances are heated etc. **2.** the bowl of a pair of
scales; the bowl of a lavatory. **3.** the part of the lock that
held the priming in obsolete types of gun. **4.** a hollow in
the ground. —v.t. (**-nn-**) to criticize severely. —**pan out**,
(of gravel) to yield gold; (of an action etc.) to turn out (well
etc.); to be successful. —**panful** n. [OE]

pan[2] v.t./i. (**-nn-**) to swing (a cine-camera) horizontally to
give a panoramic effect or follow a moving object; (of a
camera) to be moved thus. —n. a panning movement. [f.
PANORAMA]

pan- in comb. all, relating to the whole of a continent, racial
group, religion, etc. (pan-American). [Gk (pan neut. of pas
all)]

panacea /pænəˈsɪə/ n. a universal remedy. [L f. Gk (PAN-,
akos remedy)]

panache /pəˈnæʃ/ n. an assertively or flamboyantly confident style or manner. [F, = plume]

Panama /pænəˈmɑː/ a country in Central America, situated
on the isthmus which connects North and South America;
pop. (est. 1980) 1,940,000; official language, Spanish; capital, Panama City. Colonized by Spain in the early 16th c.,
Panama was freed from imperial control in 1821 and briefly
joined the Federation of Grand Colombia before becoming
a Colombian province. It gained full independence in 1903,
although the construction of the Panama Canal and the
leasing of the zone around it to the USA until 1977 split
the country in two. The economy is largely agricultural,
although shipping registration and newly discovered copper
deposits also provide important sources of income. —
Panamanian /-ˈmeɪnɪən/ adj. & n.

panama /ˈpænəmɑː/ n. a hat of strawlike material made
from the leaves of a pine-tree. [f. prec.]

Panama Canal a canal about 81 km (51 miles) long, across the isthmus of Panama, connecting the Atlantic and Pacific Oceans. It was begun by Ferdinand de Lesseps in 1882, abandoned through bankruptcy in 1889, and built by the USA in 1904-14 in territory (the *Panama Canal Zone*) that was ceded in perpetuity from the Republic of Panama; by a treaty of 1977 this reverted to Panamanian jurisdiction.

Panama City the capital of Panama; pop. (1980) 386,400.

panatella /pænə'telə/ *n.* a long thin cigar. [f. Sp., = long thin biscuit]

pancake *n.* **1.** a thin flat batter-cake usually fried in a pan. **2.** a flat cake (e.g. of make-up). —**Pancake Day,** Shrove Tuesday (on which pancakes are traditionally eaten). **pancake landing,** a heavy landing of an aircraft descending too steeply in a level horizontal position.

panchromatic /pænkrə'mætɪk/ *adj.* (of film etc.) sensitive to all visible colours of the spectrum.

pancreas /'pæŋkrɪəs/ *n.* a gland near the stomach discharging a digestive secretion into the duodenum and insulin into the blood (ill. BODY 2). —**pancreatic** /-'ætɪk/ *adj.* [f. Gk (*pan*, *kreas* flesh)]

panda /'pændə/ *n.* **1.** (also **giant panda**) a large black-and-white bearlike mammal (*Ailuropoda melanoleuca*), native to limited mountainous forested areas in China. First described by the French missionary Armand David (d. 1900) in 1869, it was known as the particoloured bear until its zoological relationship to the red panda (see sense 2) was established in 1901. **2.** an Indian racoon-like animal (*Ailurus fulgens*) with reddish-brown fur and a long bushy ring-marked tail. —**panda car,** a police patrol car (originally white with black stripes on the doors). [Nepali name]

pandemic /pæn'demɪk/ *adj.* (of a disease) prevalent over a whole region or the world. [f. Gk (PAN-, *dēmos* people)]

pandemonium /pændɪ'məʊnɪəm/ *n.* uproar, utter confusion; a scene of this. [name of capital of hell in Milton, f. PAN- + DEMON]

pander *v.i.* (with *to*) to gratify or indulge a person or weakness etc. —*n.* **1.** a go-between in illicit love-affairs; a procurer. **2.** one who panders. [f. *Pandarus*, name of Cressida's uncle in the medieval legend of Troilus and Cressida, who acted as go-between for the lovers]

Pandora /pæn'dɔːrə/ (*Gk myth.*) in Hesiod's tale, Zeus punished mankind in general by creating woman to their confusion. The first woman was called Pandora, because she had 'all gifts' from the gods (she is probably, in reality, an earth-goddess, the All-giver). Prometheus' simple brother, Epimetheus (= After-thinker) married her despite his brother's warnings, and she let out all the evils from the store-jar where they were kept; hope alone remained to assuage the lot of mankind. The tale is a piece of satire against women (compare the part played by Eve in the Hebrew myth). —**Pandora's box,** a thing that once activated will generate many unmanageable problems.

P. & O. *abbr.* Peninsular and Oriental Steamship Company.

p. & p. *abbr.* postage and packing.

pane *n.* a single sheet of glass in a window or door (ill. HOUSES). [f. OF *pan* f. L *pannus* piece of cloth]

panegyric /pænɪ'dʒɪrɪk/ *n.* a laudatory discourse, a eulogy. —**panegyrical** *adj.* [f. F f. L f. Gk (PAN-, *agora* assembly)]

panel /'pæn(ə)l/ *n.* **1.** a distinct usually rectangular section of a surface (e.g. of a wall, door (ill. HOUSES), vehicle). **2.** a strip of material as part of a garment. **3.** a team in a broadcast or public quiz programme etc.; a body of experts assembled for discussion or consultation. **4.** a list of jurors, a jury. —*v.t.* (-ll-) to cover or decorate with panels. —**panel game,** a quiz etc. played by a panel. **panel-saw** *n.* a saw with small teeth for cutting thin wood for panels (ill. CARPENTRY). [f. OF, = piece of cloth (as PANE)]

panelling *n.* panelled work; wood for making panels. [f. prec.]

panellist *n.* a member of a panel. [f. PANEL]

pang *n.* a sudden sharp pain or painful emotion. [var. of earlier *pronge*, cf. MLG *prange* pinching]

Pangaea /pæn'dʒɪə/ *n.* a vast continental area or supercontinent comprising all the continental crust of the earth which is postulated to have existed in late Palaeozoic or Mesozoic times before breaking up into Gondwanaland and Laurasia. [f. PAN- + Gk *gaia* land, earth]

pangolin /pæŋ'gəʊlɪn/ *n.* the scaly ant-eater, a large mammal of the genus *Manis* (ill. MAMMALS). [f. Malay, = roller (because it rolls itself up)]

panic /'pænɪk/ *n.* a sudden uncontrollable fear or alarm; infectious fright. —*adj.* of, connected with, or resulting from panic. —*v.t./i.* (-ck-) to affect or be affected with panic. —**panic-stricken** *or* **-struck** *adj.* affected with panic. —**panicky** *adj.* [f. F f. Gk (see PAN)]

panicle /'pænɪk(ə)l/ *n.* a loose branching cluster of flowers (ill. PLANTS). [f. L *paniculum*, dim. of *panus* thread]

panjandrum /pæn'dʒændrəm/ *n.* a mock title of an exalted personage. [invented by S. Foote in nonsense verse (1755)]

Pankhurst /'pæŋkhɜːst/, Mrs Emmeline (1858-1928), British suffragette leader. A convinced feminist, she founded the Women's Social and Political Union in 1903 and was more responsible than anyone else for keeping the suffragette cause in the public eye and eventually winning the vote for women, although her militant activities frequently resulted in terms of imprisonment.

pannier /'pænɪə/ *n.* **1.** a basket, especially one of a pair carried by a beast of burden or on a bicycle, motor cycle, etc. **2.** (*hist.*) a part of a skirt looped up round the hips (ill. DRESS); a frame supporting this. [f. OF f. L *panarium* bread-basket (*panis* bread)]

panoply /'pænəplɪ/ *n.* **1.** a complete suit of armour. **2.** a complete or splendid array. [f. F f. Gk (PAN-, *hopla* arms)]

panorama /pænə'rɑːmə/ *n.* **1.** a view of a wide area; a picture or photograph of this. **2.** a view of a constantly changing scene or series of events etc. —**panoramic** /-'ræmɪk/ *adj.* [f. PAN- + Gk *horama* view (*horaō* see)]

pan-pipe *n.* (in *sing.* or *pl.*) a musical instrument formed from three or more tubes of different lengths joined in a row (or in some areas of a block of wood with tubes drilled down into it) with mouthpieces in line, and sounded by blowing across the top. It is known to have been used in neolithic times, though probably not in the West until about the 6th c. BC. Our name for it derives from the legend in which the god Pan was frustrated in his pursuit of the nymph Syrinx by her transformation into a reed which Pan cut into pieces and then, relenting, kissed, his breath causing the broken reed to sound. [f. PAN + PIPE]

pansy /'pænzɪ/ *n.* **1.** a garden plant (hybrids of *Viola tricolor*) with flowers of various rich colours. **2.** (*colloq.*) an effeminate man; a male homosexual. [f. F *pensée* thought, pansy (*penser* think f. L *pensare* frequent. of *pendere* weigh)]

pant *v.t./i.* to breathe with short quick breaths; to utter breathlessly; to yearn; (of the heart etc.) to throb violently. —*n.* a panting breath; a throb. [f. OF *pantaisier* ult. f. Gk (as FANTASY)]

Pantaloon /pæntə'luːn/ *n.* a Venetian character in Italian comedy represented as a foolish old man wearing pantaloons, spectacles, and slippers. [f. It., perh. f. *San Pantalone*, favourite Venetian saint in former times]

pantaloons /pæntə'luːnz/ *n.pl.* (esp. *US*) trousers. [f. F f. prec.]

pantechnicon /pæn'teknɪkən/ *n.* a large van for transporting furniture. [short for *pantechnicon van* (*pantechnicon* furniture warehouse, orig. a bazaar, as PAN-, TECHNIQUE)]

pantheism /'pænθɪɪz(ə)m/ *n.* the belief that God is everything and everything God. —**pantheist** *n.*, **pantheistic** /-'ɪstɪk/ *adj.* [f. PAN- + Gk *theos* god]

pantheon /'pænθɪən/ *n.* **1.** a temple dedicated to all the gods, especially (**Pantheon**) the circular one still standing in Rome, erected in the early 2nd c. AD probably on the site of an earlier one built by Agrippa. **2.** the deities of a people collectively. **3. Pantheon,** a building in which the illustrious dead are buried or have memorials, especially (Panthéon) the former church of St Geneviève in Paris (which in some respects resembles the Pantheon in Rome). [f. L f. Gk (PAN-, *theios* divine)]

panther /'pænθə(r)/ *n.* a leopard (see entry). [f. OF f. L f. Gk]

panties /'pæntɪz/ *n.pl.* (*colloq.*) short-legged or legless knickers worn by women and girls. [dim. of PANTS]

pantihose /'pæntɪhəʊz/ *n.* women's tights. [f. prec. + HOSE]

pantile /'pæntaɪl/ *n.* a curved roof-tile (ill. BUILDING TECHNIQUES). [f. PAN¹ + TILE]

panto /'pæntəʊ/ *n.* (*colloq.*) a pantomime. [abbr.]

pantograph /'pæntəgrɑːf/ *n.* **1.** an instrument with jointed rods for enlarging or reducing a plan etc. **2.** a jointed framework conveying current to an electric vehicle from overhead wires. [f. *panto-* all (as PAN-) + -GRAPH]

pantomime /'pæntəmaɪm/ *n.* **1** a dramatic entertainment usually produced about Christmas and based on a fairy-tale (see below). **2.** gestures and facial expression used to convey meaning. —**pantomimic** /-'mɪmɪk/ *adj.* [F or f. L f. Gk (*panto-* as PAN- + MIME)]

In ancient Rome the Latin *pantomimus* denoted a player who represented in dumb show the different characters in a short scene based on classical history or mythology. In England it became the name by which the harlequinade (see entry) was known. By the 20th c. the form of this had changed. The entertainment (still known as pantomime), primarily for children and associated with Christmas, is now based on the dramatization of a fairy-tale or nursery story, and includes (as well as the traditional transformation scene) songs and topical jokes, buffoonery and slapstick, and standard characters such as a pantomime 'dame' played by a man, a principal boy played by a woman, and a pantomime animal (e.g. a horse, cat, goose) played by actors dressed in a comic costume, with some regional variations. Although less popular than formerly, pantomimes remain a feature of the English Christmas season.

pantry /ˈpæntrɪ/ n. **1.** a room or cupboard in which crockery, cutlery, table-linen, etc. are kept. **2.** a larder. [f. OF (*panetier* baker. L *panis* bread)]

pants n.pl. **1.** (*colloq.*) underpants, panties. **2.** (*US*) trousers. [abbr. of PANTALOONS]

Paolo Veronese see VERONESE.

pap[1] n. **1.** soft or semi-liquid food for infants or invalids. **2.** undemanding reading matter. [prob. f. MLG or MDu. f. L *pappare* eat]

pap[2] n. (*archaic* or *dial.*) a nipple of the breast. [f. Scand., imit. of sucking]

papa /pəˈpɑː/ n. (*archaic*; esp. as child's word) father. [F f. L f. Gk *pap(p)as*]

papacy /ˈpeɪpəsɪ/ n. **1.** the pope's office or tenure. **2.** the papal system. [f. L *papatia* (*papa* pope)]

papal /ˈpeɪp(ə)l/ adj. of the pope or his office. —**papally** adv. [f. OF f. L (as prec.)]

Papal States the territory held by the Church in central Italy, based originally on the 8th-c. Donation of Pepin, which promised Frankish conquests of former Lombard lands to the pope. The Church's holdings were greatly extended by Innocent III in the early 13th c. and re-conquered by Julius II 300 years later. At their greatest extent the Papal States included Romagna, Ferrara, Ravenna, and much of Tuscany. The States were incorporated in Italy in 1860, as was Rome itself ten years later.

papaw /pəˈpɔː, ˈpɔːpɔː/ n. **1.** an oblong orange fruit with a thick fleshy rind, and numerous black seeds embedded in its pulp, used as food. **2.** the palmlike tropical American tree (*Carica papaya*) bearing this. **3.** (*US*) a North American tree (*Asimina triloba*) bearing purple flowers and an oblong edible fruit. [earlier *papay(a)* f. Sp. & Port. f. Carib]

paper /ˈpeɪpə(r)/ n. **1.** a substance in thin sheets made from pulp of wood or other fibrous material, used for writing or drawing or printing on, as a wrapping material, etc. (see below). **2.** a document; documents attesting identity or credentials; the documents belonging to a person or relating to a matter. **3.** a newspaper. **4.** wallpaper. **5.** a piece of paper, especially as a wrapper etc. **6.** a set of questions to be answered at one session in an examination; the written answers to these. **7.** an essay or dissertation, especially one read to a learned society. —adj. made of or flimsy like paper; existing only in theory. —v.t. to decorate (a wall etc.) with paper. —**on paper,** in writing; in theory; to judge from written or printed evidence. **paper-boy, paper-girl** n. one who delivers or sells newspapers. **paper-clip** n. a clip of bent wire or of plastic for holding a few sheets of paper together. **paper-knife** n. a blunt knife for opening letters etc. **paper money,** money in the form of banknotes. **paper tiger,** a threatening but ineffectual person or thing. [f. AF f. L, = PAPYRUS]
The essence of paper-making is the compact interlacing of natural fibres. It originated in China over 2,000 years ago, when the fibres used were bamboo, rags, and old fishing-nets. In the 8th c. the Arabs learnt the process from Chinese prisoners captured in war; they used mostly flax as fibre. Knowledge of it spread to Baghdad by the 8th c. (the time of Haroun al-Raschid of *Arabian Nights* fame), and thence to Egypt and Morocco. The Moors brought it to Spain in the 12th c. and it spread northwards in Europe, reaching England (where paper had been used since the early 14th c.) in the 15th c. Rags were the main source of fibre until the 19th c., when wood fibres came into use and are now the main constituent, though rags, straw, esparto grass, and waste paper are important ingredients for mixing with wood fibres. The fibres are pulped, and this pulp is washed, bleached, and dried before passing to a paper mill, where it is dissolved in water and beaten to a uniform consistency, often with additives such as size, dye, or filler. A thin stream is made to flow on to a wire mesh belt which allows water to drain away, leaving a felt of sufficient strength to pass between heated rollers which compress and dry the paper. Special papers are coated with, for example, white clay to give an especially smooth surface for fine printing of illustrations.

paperback adj. bound in stiff paper, not boards. —n. a paperback book.

paperweight n. a small heavy object for keeping loose papers in place.

paperwork n. routine clerical or administrative work.

papery adj. like paper in thinness or texture. [f. PAPER]

Paphlagonia /pæflæˈɡəʊnɪə/ the ancient name for the region of northern Asia Minor lying along the Black Sea between Bithynia and Pontus. —**Paphlagonian** adj. & n.

papier mâché /ˌpæpjeɪˈmæʃeɪ/ moulded paper pulp used for boxes, trays, etc. [F, = chewed paper]

papilla /pəˈpɪlə/ n. (*pl.* **-lae** /-liː/) a small nipple-like protuberance in or on the body. [L, = nipple]

papillary /pəˈpɪlərɪ/ adj. papilla-shaped. [f. prec.]

papillon /ˈpæpɪljɒ̃/ n. a dog of a toy breed related to the spaniel, having a white coat with a few darker patches and erect ears resembling the shape of a butterfly's wings. [F, = butterfly]

papist /ˈpeɪpɪst/ n. an advocate of papal supremacy; (usu. derog.) a Roman Catholic. [f. F f. L *papa* pope]

papoose /pəˈpuːs/ n. a North American Indian baby. [Algonquin]

paprika /ˈpæprɪkə/ n. a ripe red pepper; the red condiment made from it. [Magyar]

Papua New Guinea /ˈpæpʊə, ˈɡɪnɪ/ a country in the Pacific off the NE coast of Australia; pop. (est. 1983) 3,160,000; official language, English; capital, Port Moresby. Papua was discovered in 1526-7 by a Portuguese navigator, who gave it its name (a Malayan word, = woolly-haired). Papua New Guinea was formed from the administrative union, in 1949, of Papua (SE New Guinea with adjacent islands), an Australian Territory since 1906, and the Trust Territory of New Guinea (NE Guinea), an Australian trusteeship since 1921. In 1975 the combined territories became an independent State within the Commonwealth. It is a country of 700 different languages. **Papua New Guinean** adj. & n.

papyrology /pæpɪˈrɒlədʒɪ/ n. the study of ancient papyri. —**papyrologist** n. [f. foll. + -LOGY]

papyrus /pəˈpaɪrəs/ n. (*pl.* **-ri** /-riː/) **1.** an aquatic plant (*Cyperus papyrus*) of the sedge family. **2.** an ancient writing material made from the stem of this (see below); a manuscript written on it. [f. L f. Gk]
Sheets of papyrus were a major export of ancient Egypt. Production and marketing of this as a writing-material was a royal monopoly, and the secret of its preparation was jealously guarded. Pliny the Elder describes the process of cutting tissue-thin strips of the stem of the plant and laying them across each other, but his account is defective. After the introduction of papermaking, the production of papyrus in Egypt rapidly declined and then ceased altogether, and the papyrus plant itself disappeared from the country until recently re-introduced.

par n. **1.** an average or normal amount, degree, condition, etc. **2.** equality, an equal status or footing. **3.** (in golf) the number of strokes a scratch player should normally require for a hole or course. **4.** the face value of stocks and shares etc. **5.** (in full **par of exchange**) the recognized value of one country's currency in terms of another's. [L, = equal]

para /ˈpærə/ n. (*colloq.*) a paratrooper. [abbr.]

para-[1] /ˈpærə-/ prefix **1.** beside (*parabola, paramilitary*). **2.** beyond (*paradox, paranormal*). [f. Gk]

para-[2] /ˈpærə-/ in comb. to protect, to ward off (*parachute, parasol*). [F f. It. (*parare* defend)]

para. abbr. paragraph.

parable /ˈpærəb(ə)l/ n. a narrative of imagined events used to illustrate a moral or spiritual lesson; an allegory. [f. OF f. L *parabola* comparison (as foll.)]

parabola /pəˈræbələ/ n. an open plane curve formed by the intersection of a cone with a plane parallel to its slanting side (ill. SHAPES). [f. Gk *parabolē* placing side by side]

parabolic /pærəˈbɒlɪk/ adj. **1.** of or expressed in a parable. **2.** of or like a parabola. —**parabolically** adv. [f. L f. Gk (as prec.)]

Paracelsus /pærəˈselsəs/ (real name Theophrastus

Phillipus Aureolus Bombastus von Hohenheim, *c.*1493-1541), Swiss physician, of an iconoclastic and violent temper, who developed a totally new approach to medicine and philosophy. He lectured in German rather than the accepted Latin, and condemned all current academic medical teaching not based on observation and experience. He introduced chemical remedies to replace traditional herbal ones and turned alchemy away from its limited aims of discovering the philosopher's stone and the elixir of life and gave it a wider perspective. Paracelsus had a new concept of disease: he saw illness as coming from a specific external cause rather than being caused by an imbalance of the humours in the body. This modernity was countered by his overall occultist perspective in which the cosmos and man were interconnected by spiritual forces, and the powers of the stars could send down the seeds of disease. His study of a disease of miners was one of the first accounts of an occupational disease. His influence was greatest in the hundred years after his death, when most of his writings were published.

paracetamol /pærə'si:təmɒl, -set-/ *n.* a compound forming a white powder, used to relieve pain and reduce fever; a tablet of this. [f. its chemical name]

parachute /'pærəʃu:t/ *n.* an umbrella-shaped apparatus of silk, nylon, etc. allowing a person or heavy object to descend safely from a height, especially from an aircraft (see below and ill. FLIGHT); (*attrib.*) (to be) dropped by parachute. —*v.t./i.* to descend or convey by parachute. —**parachutist** *n.* [F (as PARA-², CHUTE)]
The principle of the parachute had, like many principles, been noted by Leonardo da Vinci. The first man to demonstrate it in action was L. S. Lenormand of France in 1783, jumping from a high tower. A few years later French balloonists made successful descents, and in the 19th c. hot-air balloons were used by parachutists who jumped for public entertainment. In the 20th c. parachuting has become a sophisticated sport.

Paraclete /'pærəkli:t/ *n.* the Holy Spirit as an advocate or counsellor. [f. OF f. L f. Gk, = called in aid (PARA-¹, *kaleō* call)]

parade /pə'reɪd/ *n.* **1.** a muster of troops for inspection. **2.** a public procession. **3.** an ostentatious display. **4.** a public square or promenade. **5.** a parade-ground. —*v.t./i.* **1.** to assemble for a parade. **2.** to march through (streets etc.) in procession, to march ceremonially. **3.** to display ostentatiously. —**parade-ground** *n.* a place for the muster of troops. [F, = show, f. It. & Sp. f. L *parare* prepare]

paradigm /'pærədaɪm/ *n.* an example or pattern, especially of the inflexions of a noun, verb, etc. —**paradigmatic** /-dɪg'mætɪk/ *adj.* [f. L f. Gk (PARA-¹, *deiknumi* show)]

paradise /'pærədaɪs/ *n.* **1.** the abode of God and of the righteous after death, heaven. **2.** a region or state of supreme bliss. **3.** (in Gen. 2, 3) the garden of Eden. —**paradisiac** /-'daɪsɪæk/ *adj.*, **paradisiacal** /-dɪ'saɪək(ə)l/ *adj.*, **paradisal** *adj.* [f. OF ult. f. Avestan *pairidaēza* park]

paradox /'pærədɒks/ *n.* **1.** a seemingly absurd though perhaps actually well-founded statement. **2.** a self-contradictory or essentially absurd statement. **3.** a person or thing conflicting with a preconceived notion of what is reasonable or possible. **4.** paradoxical nature. —**paradoxical** /-'dɒksɪk(ə)l/ *adj.*, **paradoxically** *adj.* [f. L f. Gk (PARA-¹, *doxa* opinion)]

paraffin /'pærəfɪn/ *n.* **1.** an inflammable waxy or oily substance obtained by distillation from petroleum and shale and used especially as a fuel. **2.** a hydrocarbon of the methane series, containing the maximum amount of hydrogen. —**liquid paraffin**, a tasteless mild laxative. **paraffin wax**, paraffin in a solid form. [G, f. L *parum* little + *affinis* related]

paragon /'pærəgən/ *n.* a model of excellence, a supremely excellent person or thing; a model (*of* virtue etc.). [obs. F f. It. *paragone* touchstone f. Gk]

paragraph /'pærəgrɑ:f/ *n.* one or more sentences on a single theme, forming a distinct section of a piece of writing and beginning on a new (usually indented) line. —*v.t.* to arrange in paragraphs. —**paragraphic** /-'græfɪk/ *adj.* [f. F or L f. Gk *paragraphos* short stroke marking break in sense (PARA-¹, *graphō* write)]

Paraguay /'pærəgwaɪ/ an inland country in South America, situated between Argentina, Bolivia, and Brazil; pop. (1982) 3,026,165; official language, Spanish; capital, Asunción. Once part of the Spanish viceroyalties of Peru and La Plata, Paraguay achieved its independence in 1811, but

was devastated, losing over half of its population, in the megalomaniac dictator Solano Lopez's war against Brazil, Argentina, and Uruguay in 1865-70. It gained land to the west as a result of the Chaco War with Bolivia in 1932-5, but the country has remained backward and agricultural with a low standard of living and an uncertain political system. —**Paraguayan** *adj.* & *n.*

parakeet /'pærəki:t/ *n.* any of various small usually long-tailed species of parrot. [f. OF, perh. ult. f. dim. of *Pierre* Peter]

parallax /'pærəlæks/ *n.* the apparent difference in position or direction of an object caused by a change of the point of observation; the angular amount of this. —**parallactic** /-'læktɪk/ *adj.* [f. F f. Gk *parallaxis* change, alternation]

parallel /'pærəlel/ *adj.* **1.** (of lines or planes) continuously equidistant; (of a line or plane) having this relation. **2.** analogous, having features that correspond. —*n.* **1.** a person or thing that is analogous to another. **2.** a comparison. **3.** (in full **parallel of latitude**) each of the imaginary parallel circles of constant latitude on the earth's surface; a corresponding line on a map. **3.** two parallel lines (‖) as a reference mark. —*v.t.* (*p.t.* **paralleled**) **1.** to be parallel to, to correspond to. **2.** to represent as similar, to compare. **3.** to adduce a parallel instance to. —**in parallel**, (of an electric circuit) arranged so as to join at common points at each end. **parallel bars**, a pair of parallel rails on posts for gymnastics. [f. F f. L f. Gk, = alongside each other (PARA-¹, *allēlos* one another)]

parallelepiped /pærəle'lepɪped, -ə'paɪped/ *n.* a solid body of which each face is a parallelogram. [f. Gk (as prec., *epipedon* plane surface, EPI-, *pedon* ground)]

parallelism *n.* being parallel; correspondence. [f. PARALLEL]

parallelogram /pærə'leləgræm/ *n.* a four-sided plane rectilinear figure with the opposite sides parallel (ill. SHAPES). [f. F f. L f. Gk (as PARALLEL, *grammē* line)]

paralyse /'pærəlaɪz/ *v.t.* **1.** to affect with paralysis. **2.** to render powerless; to bring to a standstill. [f. F (as foll.)]

paralysis /pə'rælɪsɪs/ *n.* **1.** impairment or loss of the power of movement, caused by disease or injury to nerves. **2.** a state of powerlessness; inability to move or operate normally. [L f. Gk (PARA-¹, *luō* loosen)]

paralytic /pærə'lɪtɪk/ *adj.* **1.** affected by paralysis. **2.** (*slang*) very drunk. —*n.* a person affected by paralysis. [f. OF f. L f. Gk (as prec.)]

Paramaribo /pærə'mærɪbəʊ/ the capital of Surinam; pop. (1980) 67,700.

paramedical /pærə'medɪk(ə)l/ *adj.* (of services etc.) supplementing and supporting medical work.

parameter /pə'ræmɪtə(r)/ *n.* **1.** a quantity that is constant in the case considered but which varies in different cases. **2.** a variable quantity or quality that restricts or gives a particular form to the thing it characterizes. [f. Gk *para* beside + *metron* measure]

paramilitary /pærə'mɪlɪtərɪ/ *adj.* organized like a military force but not part of the armed services. —*n.* a member of a paramilitary organization.

paramount /'pærəmaʊnt/ *adj.* supreme; in supreme authority. [f. AF (OF *par* by, *amont* above; see AMOUNT)]

paramour /'pærəmʊə(r)/ *n.* (*archaic*) a married person's illicit lover. [f. OF *par amour* by love]

parang /'pɑ:ræŋ/ *n.* a heavy Malayan sheath-knife. [Malay]

paranoia /pærə'nɔɪə/ *n.* **1.** a mental disorder with delusions of grandeur, persecution, etc. **2.** an abnormal tendency to suspect and mistrust others. [f. Gk (PARA-¹, *noos* mind)]

paranoiac /pærə'nɔɪæk/ *adj.* (also **paranoic** /pærə'nəʊɪk/) paranoid. —*n.* a paranoid person. [f. prec.]

paranoid /'pærənɔɪd/ *adj.* affected by paranoia. —*n.* a paranoid person. [f. PARANOIA]

paranormal /pærə'nɔːm(ə)l/ *adj.* (of phenomena or powers) presumed to operate according to natural laws beyond or outside those considered normal or known.

parapet /'pærəpɪt/ *n.* a low wall at the edge of a roof, balcony, etc., or along the sides of a bridge etc.; a defence of earth or stone to conceal and protect troops. [F or f. It., = breast-high wall (PARA-², *petto* breast)]

paraphernalia /pærəfə'neɪlɪə/ *n.pl.* miscellaneous belongings, accessories, etc. [L f. Gk, = personal articles which a woman could keep after marriage, as opp. to her dowry which went to her husband (PARA-¹, *phernē* dowry)]

paraphrase /'pærəfreɪz/ *n.* expression of the meaning of a passage in other words. —*v.t.* to express the meaning of (a passage) in other words. [F or f. L f. Gk (PARA-, *phrazō* tell)]

paraplegia /ˌpærəˈpliːdʒə/ *n.* paralysis of the legs and part or the whole of the trunk. [f. Gk (PARA-¹, *plēssō* strike)]

paraplegic /ˌpærəˈpliːdʒɪk/ *adj.* of paraplegia. —*n.* one who suffers from paraplegia. [f. prec.]

parapsychology /ˌpærəsaɪˈkɒlədʒɪ/ *n.* the study of mental phenomena outside the sphere of ordinary psychology (hypnosis, telepathy, etc.).

paraquat /ˈpærəkwɒt/ *n.* an extremely poisonous quick-acting herbicide that becomes inactive on contact with the soil. [f. PARA-¹ + QUATERNARY (with ref. to its chemical composition)]

parasite /ˈpærəsaɪt/ *n.* **1.** an animal or plant living in or on another and drawing nutriment directly from it. **2.** a person who lives off or exploits another or others. —**parasitic** /-ˈsɪtɪk/ *adj.*, **parasitically** /-ˈsɪtɪkəlɪ/ *adv.*, **parasitism** *n.* [f. L f. Gk, = one who eats at another's table (PARA-¹, *sitos* food)]

parasol /ˈpærəsɒl/ *n.* a light umbrella used to give shade from the sun. [F f. It. (PARA-², *sole* sun)]

paratrooper /ˈpærətruːpə(r)/ *n.* a member of the para-troops. [f. foll.]

paratroops /ˈpærətruːps/ *n.pl.* parachute troops. [f. PARA-CHUTE + TROOPS]

paratyphoid /ˌpærəˈtaɪfɔɪd/ *n.* a fever resembling typhoid but caused by a different bacterium.

parboil /ˈpɑːbɔɪl/ *v.t.* **1.** to boil (food) until it is partly cooked. **2.** to subject (a person) to great heat. [f. OF f. L *perbullire* (*per-* thoroughly, confused with PART)]

parcel /ˈpɑːs(ə)l/ *n.* **1.** a thing or things wrapped as a single package for carrying or for sending by post. **2.** a piece of land. **3.** the quantity dealt with in one commercial transaction. —*v.t.* (**-ll-**) **1.** to wrap up as a parcel. **2.** to divide (*out*) into portions. [f. OF dim. of L *particula* (as PARTICLE)]

parch *v.t./i.* **1.** to make or become hot and dry. **2.** to roast (peas, corn, etc.) slightly. [orig. unkn.]

parchment /ˈpɑːtʃmənt/ *n.* **1.** a heavy paper-like material made from animal skins. **2.** a manuscript written on this. **3.** a high-grade paper made to resemble parchment. [f. OF f. L *pergamina* f. PERGAMUM which from the 2nd c. BC was noted for the production of parchment]

pardon /ˈpɑːd(ə)n/ *n.* **1.** forgiveness. **2.** remission of the legal consequences of a crime or conviction. **3.** courteous forbearance. —*v.t.* **1.** to forgive. **2.** to make courteous allowances for, to excuse. —**I beg your pardon,** (*colloq.*) **pardon (me),** a formula of apology or disagreement, or a request to repeat something said. [f. OF f. L *perdonare* concede]

pardonable *adj.* that may be pardoned, easily excused. —**pardonably** *adv.* [f. prec.]

pare *v.t.* **1.** to trim or shave by cutting away the surface or edge. **2.** to diminish little by little. [f. OF f. L *parare* prepare]

paregoric /ˌpærɪˈɡɒrɪk/ *n.* a camphorated tincture of opium used as an analgesic; an anodyne. —*adj.* soothing. [f. L f. Gk (PARA-¹, *-agoros* speaking f. *agora* assembly)]

parent /ˈpeərənt/ *n.* **1.** one who has begotten or borne offspring, a father or mother. **2.** a forefather. **3.** a person who has adopted a child. **4.** an animal or plant from which others are derived. **5.** a source from which other things are derived. —*v.t./i.* to be a parent (of). —**parent-teacher association,** an organization consisting of, and promoting good relations between, teachers and the parents of their pupils. —**parental** /pəˈrent(ə)l/ *adj.*, **parentally** *adv.*, **parenthood** *n.* [f. OF f. L (*parere* bring forth)]

parentage *n.* lineage, descent from parents. [as prec.]

parenthesis /pəˈrenθəsɪs/ *n.* (*pl.* **-eses** /-əsiːz/) **1.** a word, clause, or sentence inserted as an explanation or after-thought into a passage which is grammatically complete without it, and usually marked off by brackets, dashes, or commas. **2.** (in *pl.*) a pair of round brackets () used for this. —**in parenthesis,** as a parenthesis; as an aside or digression. [L f. Gk (*parentithēmi* put in beside (as PARA-¹, EN-, *tithēmi* place)]

parenthesize /pəˈrenθəsaɪz/ *v.t.* to insert as a parenthesis; to put (words) between parentheses. [f. prec.]

parenthetic /ˌpærənˈθetɪk/ *adj.* of or inserted as a paren-thesis. —**parenthetical** *adj.*, **parenthetically** *adv.* [f. PARENTHESIS]

par excellence /pɑːr eksəˈlɑ̃s/ *adv.* above all others that may be so called. [F, = by virtue of special excellence]

parfait /ˈpɑːfeɪ/ *n.* **1.** a rich iced pudding of whipped cream, eggs, etc. **2.** layers of ice-cream, fruit, etc., served in a tall glass. [F, = PERFECT]

parget /ˈpɑːdʒɪt/ *v.t.* to plaster (a wall etc.) especially with an ornamental pattern (ill. HOUSES); to roughcast. —*n.* plaster; roughcast. [f. OF *pargeter* (*par* all over, *jeter* throw)]

pariah /pəˈraɪə/ *n.* **1.** a member of a low or no caste. **2.** a social outcast. [f. Tamil]

Parian /ˈpeərɪən/ *adj.* of the Greek island of Paros in the Aegean Sea, famous since the 6th c. BC for its fine-textured white marble, much used by sculptors.

parietal /pəˈraɪət(ə)l/ *adj.* of the wall of the body or any of its cavities. —**parietal bone,** either of a pair of bones form-ing part of the skull (ill. BODY 1). [f. F or L (*paries* wall)]

paring /ˈpeərɪŋ/ *n.* a strip or piece cut off. [f. PARE]

Paris¹ /ˈpærɪs/ the capital of France and its political, com-mercial, and cultural centre, situated on the River Seine; pop. (est. 1982) 2,188,918. It developed as a Roman town (*Lutetia*) and became firmly established as a capital after 987, when Hugo Capet became king of France.

Paris² /ˈpærɪs/ (*Gk legend*) son of Priam and Hecuba, he was known also as Alexander. Appointed by the gods to adjudge the prize of beauty among the three goddesses Hera, Athene, and Aphrodite, he awarded it to Aphrodite, who promised him the fairest woman in the world — Helen, wife of Menelaus king of Sparta. He abducted Helen, thus bringing about the Trojan War in which he was killed. The 'Judgement of Paris' is a favourite theme in art from the mid-7th c. BC onwards. Its story is essentially a folk-tale of choice (between kingship, warlike prowess, and love, offered by the goddesses respectively) comparable to the Hebrew story of Solomon's choice (between wisdom, long life, riches, and destruction of enemies) told in 1 Kings 3: 5 ff.

Paris³ /ˈpærɪs/, Matthew (d. 1259), English historian, a monk at the Benedictine monastery of St Albans where he became chief chronicler. From 1235 to 1259 he continued the compilation of the *Chronica Maiora*, his greatest work, which he expanded to include accounts of events in foreign countries as well as England, from the Creation to 1259. It surpasses any other English chronicle for the vigour and brightness of its narrative.

parish /ˈpærɪʃ/ *n.* **1.** an area having its own church and clergyman. **2.** a district constituted for the purposes of local government (see below). **3.** the inhabitants of a parish. —**parish clerk,** an official performing various duties con-cerned with a church. **parish council,** the administrative body in a civil parish. **parish register,** a book recording christenings, marriages, and burials, at a parish church. [f. OF f. L *parochia* f. Gk, = sojourning (PARA-¹, *oikeō* dwell)]
From the 17th c. parishes and churchwardens were en-trusted with local administration, chiefly relating to Poor Law and highways. Urban parishes were abolished as a unit of local government in 1933, but rural parishes have continued even after the local government reorganization of 1974; their responsibilities now include recreational facilities, allotments, cemeteries, etc.

parishioner /pəˈrɪʃənə(r)/ *n.* an inhabitant of a parish. [f. obs. *parishen* in same sense (as prec.)]

Parisian /pəˈrɪzɪən/ *adj.* of the city of Paris. —*n.* a native or inhabitant of Paris. [f. PARIS¹]

parity /ˈpærɪtɪ/ *n.* **1.** equality, equal status or pay etc. **2.** the equivalence of one currency in another; being at par. [f. F or L *paritas* (as PAR)]

Park, Mungo (1771–1806), Scottish explorer. A surgeon in the mercantile marine, Park undertook a series of explo-rations in West Africa in 1795–6, sailing up the River Gambia, crossing Senegal and navigating the River Niger before being captured by a local Arab chief. He escaped from captivity four months later and returned to Britain after a year and a half in the interior. Bored with his medical practice in Scotland, Park returned to the Niger in 1805 but was drowned during a fight with Africans a year later.

park *n.* **1.** a large public garden in a town, for recreation. **2.** a large enclosed piece of ground, usually with woodland and pasture, attached to a country house etc. **3.** a large tract of land in its natural state for public enjoyment. **4.** an area for motor cars etc. to be left in. **5.** (*US*) a sports ground. —*v.t.* **1.** to place and leave (a vehicle, or *absol.*) temporarily. **2.** (*colloq.*) to deposit temporarily. —**park oneself,** (*colloq.*) to sit down. **parking-lot** *n.* (*US*) an outdoor area for

Parliament

Plan of the Palace of Westminster (principal floor)

N

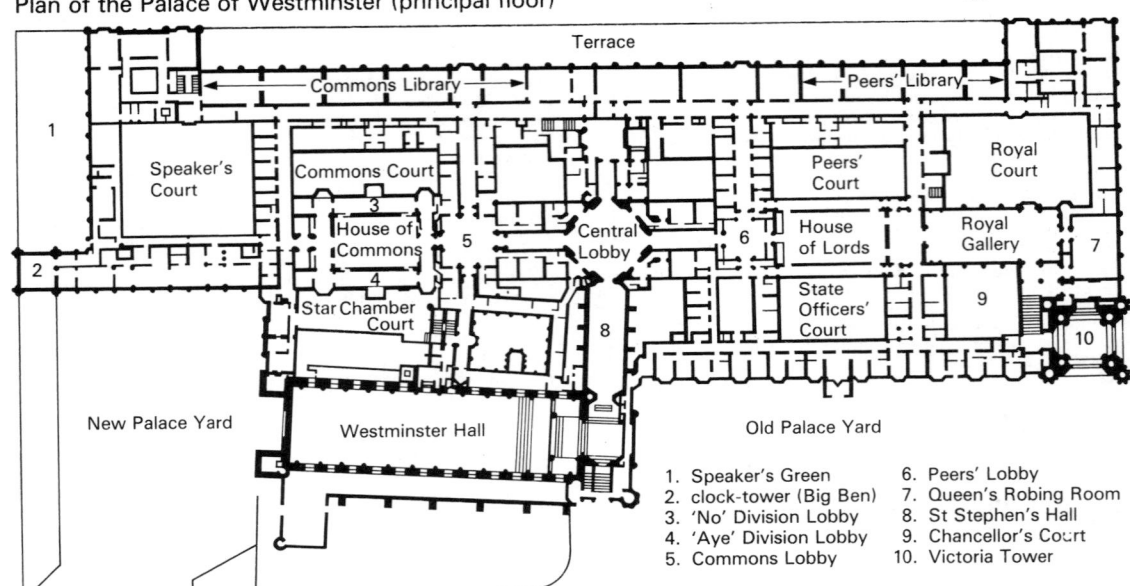

Terrace

Commons Library — Peers' Library

1 — Speaker's Court — Commons Court — Peers' Court — Royal Court

House of Commons — Central Lobby — House of Lords — Royal Gallery — 7

2 — House of Commons — 5 — 6 — House of Lords

Star Chamber Court — State Officers' Court — 9 — 10

8

New Palace Yard — Westminster Hall — Old Palace Yard

1. Speaker's Green
2. clock-tower (Big Ben)
3. 'No' Division Lobby
4. 'Aye' Division Lobby
5. Commons Lobby
6. Peers' Lobby
7. Queen's Robing Room
8. St Stephen's Hall
9. Chancellor's Court
10. Victoria Tower

House of Commons

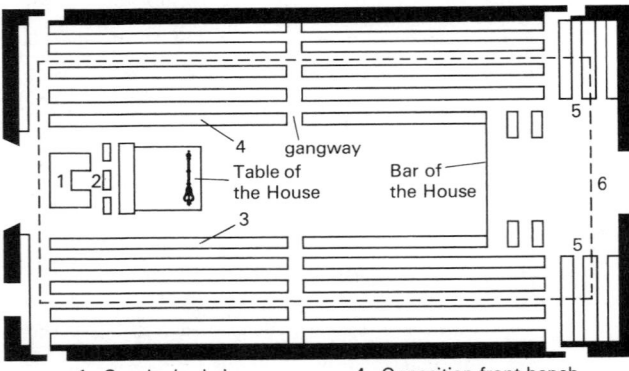

4 gangway
Table of the House
Bar of the House
1 2
3
5
6
5

1. Speaker's chair
2. clerks' chairs
3. Government front bench
4. Opposition front bench
5. cross-benches
6. public gallery above

House of Lords

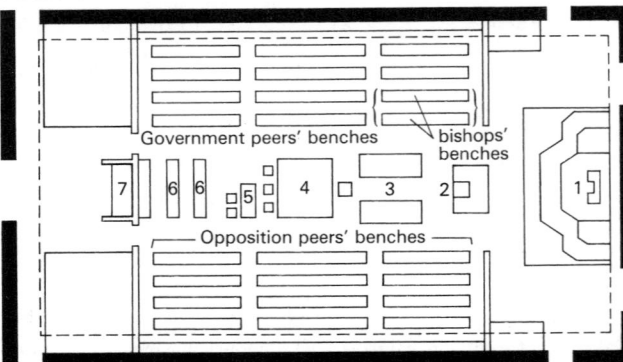

Government peers' benches — bishops' benches
7 6 6 5 4 3 2 1
Opposition peers' benches

1. throne
2. Woolsack on which the Lord Chancellor sits and the mace rests
3. Woolsacks on which judges sit at the opening of Parliament
4. Table of the House
5. Hansard reporters' table
6. cross-benches where Independent peers sit
7. Bar of the House

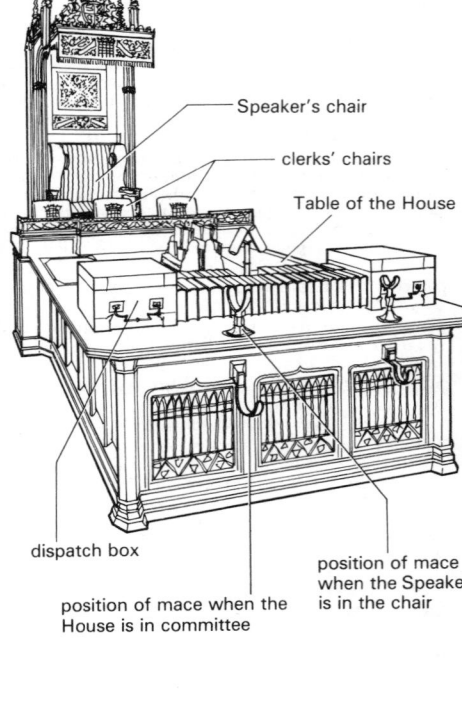

Speaker's chair

clerks' chairs

Table of the House

dispatch box

position of mace when the House is in committee

position of mace when the Speaker is in the chair

the mace, symbolic of the power and privileges of the House of Commons (nearly 2 metres in length and weighing over 7 kg) parking vehicles. **parking-meter** *n.* a coin-operated meter which receives the fees for vehicles parked in a street and indicates the time available. **parking-ticket** *n.* a notice of a fine etc. imposed for parking a vehicle illegally. [f. OF *parc*]

parka /ˈpɑːkə/ *n.* a skin jacket with a hood, worn by Eskimos; a similar windproof fabric garment worn by mountaineers etc. [Aleutian]

Parker[1], Charlie (Christopher) (1920-55), American jazz saxophonist. In New York he played with some of the great names of jazz, including Thelonious Monk and Dizzy Gillespie, and became one of the key figures of the 'bebop' movement, making some classic recordings with Miles Davis in 1945.

Parker[2], Dorothy Rothschild (1893-1967), American humorous writer and drama critic, noted for her viperish wit.

Parkinson's disease /ˈpɑːkɪns(ə)nz/ (also **Parkinsonism**) a progressive disease of the nervous system with tremor, muscular rigidity, and emaciation. [f. J. *Parkinson*, English surgeon, who described it in 1817 under the names 'shaking palsy' and 'paralysis agitans']

Parkinson's law /ˈpɑːkɪns(ə)nz/ the notion that 'work expands so as to fill the time available for its completion'. [f. C. N. *Parkinson*, English writer (1909-)]

parkland *n.* open grassland with clumps of trees etc.

parky *adj.* (*slang*) chilly. [orig. unkn.]

parlance *n.* way of speaking, phraseology. [OF (*parler* speak, ult. f. L *parabola*, as PARABLE)]

parley /ˈpɑːlɪ/ *n.* a conference for debating points in dispute, especially a discussion of the terms for an armistice etc. —*v.i.* to hold a parley. [perh. f. OF *parlee*, fem. p.p. of *parler* (as prec.)]

parliament /ˈpɑːləmənt/ *n.* the legislative assembly of a country; **Parliament**, that of the UK (see below and ill. p. 610). —**Houses of Parliament**, the House of Commons and House of Lords. [f. OF *parlement* speaking (as PARLANCE)]

The British Parliament now consists of a council forming, with the Sovereign, the supreme legislature of the United Kingdom, consisting of the House of Lords (Spiritual and Temporal) and the House of Commons (elected representatives of towns etc.). It emerged in medieval times as the assembly of the king and his Lords, meeting irregularly, summoned and dismissed by the king, to discuss judicial and other matters of general importance, especially finances. To these assemblies, since the establishment of the idea that taxation required consent, from the 13th c. knights and burgesses who represented their shires and boroughs were occasionally summoned. The practice developed of the 'Commons' assembly meeting separately from the 'Lords', but it remained for a long time in the shadow of the latter, not gaining its own meeting chamber until the 16th c. and not having free speech, regular meetings, and control over taxation established as rights until the Glorious Revolution in the late 17th c. After the passing of the first Reform Act (1832) the traditional influence of the landed aristocracy began to decline, and the Parliament Act of 1911 reduced the power of the House of Lords to simple delay of legislation. A further Act in 1949 reduced the period of delay and ended it completely for financial legislation; the House of Commons is now unequivocally the more powerful and important body. The building in which Parliament meets was designed by Sir Charles Barry and erected after the destruction by fire of the Palace of Westminster, its meeting-place, in 1834.

parliamentarian /pɑːləmənˈtɛərɪən/ *n.* a skilled debater in parliament. [f. prec.]

parliamentary /pɑːləˈmentərɪ/ *adj.* 1. of parliament; enacted or established by a parliament. 2. (of language) admissible in parliament, (*colloq.*) polite. [f. PARLIAMENT]

parlour /ˈpɑːlə(r)/ *n.* 1. a sitting-room in a private house. 2. a room in a hotel, convent, etc., for private conversation. 3. a shop providing specified goods or services. —**parlour game**, an indoor game, especially a word-game. [f. AF (as PARLANCE)]

parlous /ˈpɑːləs/ *adj.* (*archaic*) perilous, hard to deal with. —*adv.* (*archaic*) extremely. [= PERILOUS]

Parma /ˈpɑːmə/ a city and province (formerly a duchy) of north Italy.

Parmenides /pɑːˈmenɪdiːz/ (early 5th c. BC) Greek philosopher from Elea in southern Italy. By a vigorous analysis, set out in a hexameter poem, of the term 'to be' he deduced

that what is must be one, eternal, perfect, and indivisible, and that the plurality of objects in the common-sense world have no real being and cannot be the object of true knowledge.

Parmesan /pɑːmɪˈzæn, (*attrib.*) ˈpɑː-/ *n.* a kind of hard cheese made originally at Parma and used especially in a grated form. [F f. It. *parmegiano* (*Parma* in Italy)]

Parmigianino /pɑːmɪdʒaˈniːnəʊ/, Girolano Francesco Maria Mazzola (1503-40), Italian painter from Lombardy, sometimes called Parmigiano. A follower of Correggio, his etiolated and graceful figure style ranks as one of the highest points of refinement of mannerism. His work includes religious and mythological paintings and frescoes, portraiture, and some of the earliest known Italian etchings.

Parnassus /pɑːˈnæsəs/ a mountain of central Greece, which rises above Delphi. In antiquity it was a sacred mountain, associated with Apollo and the Muses and hence a symbol of poetry. —**Parnassian** *adj.*

Parnell /pɑːˈnel/, Charles Stewart (1846-91), Irish Nationalist leader. Elected to Parliament in 1875, Parnell became leader of the supporters of Home Rule for Ireland, and, through his mastery of parliamentary tactics, was successful in gaining great public exposure for Irish grievances. His political influence increased greatly after the 1885 elections, which left the Irish Nationalists the balance of power, and he supported Gladstone following the latter's acceptance of Home Rule. In 1890, however, involvement in a divorce case ruined Parnell's career and he died in obscurity a year later.

parochial /pəˈrəʊkɪəl/ *adj.* 1. of a parish. 2. (of affairs, views, etc.) merely local, confined to a narrow area. —**parochialism** *n.*, **parochially** *adv.* [f. AF f. L (as PARISH)]

parody /ˈpærədɪ/ *n.* 1. a humorous exaggerated imitation of an author, literary work, style, etc. 2. a grotesque imitation, a travesty. —*v.t.* to compose a parody of, to mimic humorously. —**parodist** *n.* [f. L or Gk *parōidia* burlesque poem (PARA-[1], *ōidē* song)]

parole /pəˈrəʊl/ *n.* 1. release of a prisoner (temporarily for a special purpose, or completely) before expiry of the sentence, on promise of good behaviour; such a promise. 2. a person's word of honour. —*v.t.* to release on parole. [F, = word, f. L *parabola* (as PARABLE)]

parotid /pəˈrɒtɪd/ *adj.* situated near the ear. —*n.* the parotid gland. —**parotid gland**, the salivary gland in front of the ear. [f. F or L f. Gk *parōtis* (PARA-[1], *ous* ear)]

paroxysm /ˈpærəksɪz(ə)m/ *n.* a sudden attack or outburst of rage, laughter, etc.; a spasm. —**paroxysmal** /-ˈsɪzm(ə)l/ *adj.* [f. F f. L f. Gk (*paroxunō* exasperate)]

parquet /ˈpɑːkeɪ, -kɪ/ *n.* flooring of wooden blocks arranged in a pattern. —*v.t.* to floor (a room) thus. —**parquetry** /-kɪtrɪ/ *n.* [F, = small compartment (as PARK)]

Parr /pɑː(r)/, Catherine (1512-48), sixth wife of Henry VIII. Having married the king in 1543 she nursed him through his last years, successfully avoiding the worst effects of his erratic bouts of temper.

parr /pɑː(r)/ *n.* a young salmon. [orig. unkn.]

parricide /ˈpærɪsaɪd/ *n.* 1. the crime of killing one's own parent or other near relative. 2. one who is guilty of this. —**parricidal** *adj.* [F, or f. L (assoc. with *pater* father, *parens* parent, -CIDE)]

parrot /ˈpærət/ *n.* 1. a mainly tropical bird with a short hooked bill of the order Psittaciformes, of which many species have vivid plumage and some can imitate words. 2. a person who mechanically repeats another's words or imitates his actions. —*v.t.* to repeat mechanically. [prob. f. dial. F (dim. of *Pierre* Peter)]

Parry /ˈpærɪ/, Sir (Charles) Hubert (Hastings) (1848-1918), director of the Royal College of Music from 1894 until his death, and Professor of Music at Oxford University 1900-8. His literary interests informed his vocal music to inspire such fine works as the cantata *Blest Pair of Sirens* (1887) and the six motets called *Songs of Farewell*, written in 1916 during the First World War. His setting of William Blake's *Jerusalem* (1916) has achieved the status of a national song.

parry /ˈpærɪ/ *v.t.* 1. to ward off (a weapon or blow) by using one's own weapon etc. to block the thrust. 2. to evade (an awkward question) by an adroit reply. —*n.* parrying. [prob. f. F *parer* f. It. *parare* ward off]

parse /pɑːz/ *v.t.* to describe (a word in context) grammatically, stating its inflexion, relation to the sentence, etc.; to resolve (a sentence) into its component parts and describe them grammatically. [perh. f. obs. *pars* parts of speech f. OF (as PART)]

parsec /ˈpɑːsek/ n. a unit of distance used in astronomy, about 3.26 light-years, the distance at which a star would have a parallax of one second of an arc, i.e. at which the mean radius of the earth's orbit subtends this angle. [f. PARALLAX + SECOND²]

Parsee /pɑːˈsiː/ n. **1.** an adherent of Zoroastrianism in India, a descendant of the Persians who fled to India from Muslim persecution in the 7th–8th c. **2.** Pahlavi. [f. Pers. *Parsi* Persian]

parsimony /ˈpɑːsɪmənɪ/ n. carefulness in the use of money or resources; meanness, stinginess. —**parsimonious** /-ˈməʊnɪəs/ adj., **parsimoniously** adv. [f. L (*parcere* spare)]

parsley /ˈpɑːslɪ/ n. a herb (*Petroselinum crispum*) used for seasoning and garnishing dishes. [f. OF f. L f. Gk *petroselinon* (*petra* rock, *selinon* parsley)]

parsnip /ˈpɑːsnɪp/ n. a plant (*Pastinaca sativa*) with a pale yellow tapering root used as a culinary vegetable; its root. [f. OF f. L *pastinaca*, assim. to *nep* turnip]

parson /ˈpɑːs(ə)n/ n. a rector; a vicar or any beneficed clergyman; (colloq.) any (esp. Protestant) clergyman. —**parson's nose**, the rump of a (cooked) fowl. [f. OF f. L, = PERSON]

parsonage n. the house provided for a parson. [f. prec.]

part n. **1.** some but not all of a thing or number of things. **2.** an integral member or component. **3.** a division of a book, broadcast serial, etc., especially as much as is issued etc. at one time. **4.** each of several equal portions of a whole. **5.** a portion allotted, a share; a person's share in an action, his duty. **6.** a character assigned to an actor on the stage; the words spoken by an actor on the stage; a copy of these. **7.** (Mus.) a melody or other constituent of harmony assigned to a particular voice or instrument. **8.** a side in an agreement or dispute. **9.** (in pl.) a region, a district. **10.** (in pl.) abilities. —v.t./i. **1.** to divide or separate into parts; to cause to do this. **2.** to separate (the hair of the head on either side of a parting) with a comb. **3.** to quit one another's company. **4.** (colloq.) to part with one's money, to pay. —adv. in part, partly. —**for my part**, so far as I am concerned. **in part**, partly. **on the part of**, proceeding from, done etc. by. **part and parcel**, an essential part of. **part-exchange** n. a transaction in which an article is given as part of the payment for a more expensive one. **part of speech**, each of the grammatical classes of words (in English usually noun, adjective, pronoun, verb, adverb, preposition, conjunction, interjection). **part-song** n. a song for several voice-parts, often unaccompanied. **part time**, less than full time. **part-time** adj. occupying or using only part of the available working time. **part-timer** n. one employed in part-time work. **part with**, to give up possession of, to hand over. **take in good part**, not to be offended by. **take part**, to assist or have a share (in). **take the part of**, to support, to back up. [f. OF f. L *pars*]

partake /pɑːˈteɪk/ v.i. (past **partook** /-ˈtʊk/, p.p. **partaken**) **1.** to participate. **2.** to take a share, especially of food or drink. —**partaker** n. [back-formation f. *partaker* = part-taker]

parterre /pɑːˈteə(r)/ n. **1.** a level space in a garden occupied by flower-beds. **2.** the pit of a theatre. [F, = *par terre* on the ground]

parthenogenesis /pɑːθɪnəʊˈdʒenəsɪs/ n. reproduction from gametes without fertilization. —**parthenogenetic** /-dʒɪˈnetɪk/ adj. [f. Gk *parthenos* virgin + GENESIS]

Parthenon /ˈpɑːθɪnən/ the temple of Athene Parthenos (= the maiden), built on the Acropolis at Athens in 447–432 BC by Pericles to honour the city's patron goddess and to commemorate the recent Greek victory over the Persians. Designed by the architects Ictinus and Callicrates with sculptures by Phidias, including a colossal gold and ivory statue of Athene (known from descriptive accounts) and the 'Elgin marbles' now in the British Museum, the Parthenon was partly financed by tribute from the league of Greek States led by Athens, and housed the treasuries of Athens and the league.

Parthian /ˈpɑːθɪən/ adj. of the ancient Asian kingdom of Parthia or its people, whose homeland lay SE of the Caspian Sea. From c.250 BC–c.AD 230 they ruled an empire stretching from the Euphrates to the Indus, with Ecbatana as its capital. Their culture contained a mixture of Greek and Iranian elements. The Parthians were superb horsemen, original and competent in warfare. —n. a native of Parthia. —**Parthian shot**, a telling remark reserved for the moment of departure, so called from the trick used by Parthians of shooting arrows while in real or pretended flight.

partial /ˈpɑːʃ(ə)l/ adj. **1.** not complete, forming only a part. **2.** biased, unfair. —**partial eclipse**, an eclipse in which only part of the luminary is covered or darkened. **partial to**, having a liking for. —**partially** adv. [f. OF f. L (as PART)]

partiality /pɑːʃɪˈælɪtɪ/ n. **1.** bias, favouritism. **2.** a strong liking. [f. OF f. L (as prec.)]

participant /pɑːˈtɪsɪpənt/ n. a participator. [as foll.]

participate /pɑːˈtɪsɪpeɪt/ v.i. to have a share, to take part. —**participation** /-ˈpeɪʃ(ə)n/ n., **participator** n. [f. L (*particeps* taking part f. *pars* part + *-cip-* f. *capere* take)]

participle /ˈpɑːtɪsɪp(ə)l/ n. a word formed from a verb (e.g. *going, gone, being, been*) and used in compound verb-forms (e.g. *is being, has been*) or as an adjective (*going concern, painted wall*). —**participial** /-ˈsɪpɪəl/ adj. [f. OF f. L *participium* (as prec.)]

particle /ˈpɑːtɪk(ə)l/ n. **1.** a minute portion of matter. **2.** the least possible amount. **3.** a minor part of speech, especially a short indeclinable one; a common prefix or suffix such as *un-*, *-ship*. [f. L *particula* (as PART)]

particoloured /ˈpɑːtɪkʌləd/ adj. partly in one colour and partly in another. [f. OF *parti* divided (as PARTY) + COLOURED]

particular /pəˈtɪkjʊlə(r)/ adj. **1.** relating to one person or thing as distinct from others, individual. **2.** more than usual, special. **3.** scrupulously exact, fastidious; detailed. —n. **1.** a detail, an item. **2.** (in pl.) information, a detailed account. —**in particular**, especially; specifically. [f. OF f. L (as PARTICLE)]

particularity /pətɪkjʊˈlærɪtɪ/ n. **1.** the quality of being individual or particular. **2.** fullness or minuteness of detail in description. [f. prec.]

particularize /pəˈtɪkjʊləraɪz/ v.t. to name specially or one by one; to specify (items). —**particularization** /-ˈzeɪʃ(ə)n/ n. [f. F (as PARTICULAR)]

particularly adv. especially, very. [f. PARTICULAR]

parting n. **1.** leave-taking; departure. **2.** the dividing line where hair is combed in different directions. **3.** division, separating. [f. PART]

partisan /pɑːtɪˈzæn, ˈpɑː-/ n. **1.** a strong (often uncritical) supporter of a party, cause, etc. **2.** a guerrilla. —**partisanship** n. [F f. It. dial. *partigiano* (as PART)]

partition /pɑːˈtɪʃ(ə)n/ n. **1.** division into parts. **2.** a part formed thus. **3.** a structure separating two such parts, a thin wall. —v.t. **1.** to divide into parts; to share out thus. **2.** to divide, to separate (part of a room etc.) by means of a partition. [f. OF f. L (*partiri* divide, as PART)]

partitive /ˈpɑːtɪtɪv/ adj. (Gram., of a word, form, etc.) denoting a part of a group or quantity. —n. a partitive word (e.g. *some, any*) or form. —**partitively** adv. [f. F or L (as prec.)]

partly adv. with respect to a part, in some degree. [f. PART]

partner /ˈpɑːtnə(r)/ n. **1.** one who shares or takes part with another or others, especially in a business firm with shared risks and profits. **2.** either of two people dancing together or playing tennis or cards etc. on the same side and scoring jointly. **3.** a husband or wife. —v.t. to be a partner of; to associate as partners. —**partnership** n. [alt. of *parcener* joint heir]

partridge /ˈpɑːtrɪdʒ/ n. a game-bird of the genus *Perdix* etc., especially the brown and grey varieties. [f. OF f. L f. Gk *perdix*]

parturient /pɑːˈtjʊərɪənt/ adj. about to give birth. [f. L *parturire* to be in labour (*parere* bring forth)]

parturition /pɑːtjʊəˈrɪʃ(ə)n/ n. the act of bringing forth young, childbirth. [as prec.]

party¹ n. **1.** a social gathering, usually of invited guests. **2.** a body of persons working or travelling together. **3.** a group of people united in a cause, opinion, etc., especially a political group organized on a national basis. **4.** a person or persons forming one side in an agreement or dispute. **5.** an accessory (*to* an action etc.) **6.** (colloq.) a person. —**party line**, the policy adopted by a political party; a telephone line shared by two or more subscribers. **party-wall** n. a wall common to the two buildings or rooms that it divides. [f. OF *partie* (as PARTITION)]

party² adj. (in heraldry) divided into parts of different tinctures (ill. HERALDRY). [as prec.]

Parvati /ˈpɑːvətɪ/ (Hinduism) a benevolent goddess, wife of Siva, mother of Ganesha and Skanda. She is often identified with Uma, Sati, Devi, and Sakti, and in her malevolent aspect with Durga and Kali. [Skr., = daughter of the mountain]

pas /pɑː/ *n.* (*pl.* same) a step in dancing. —**pas de deux** /dəˈdɜː/, a dance for two persons. [F, = step]

Pascal[1] /ˈpæˈskɑːl/ *n.* a computer language used esp. in training. [f. foll.]

Pascal[2] /pæsˈkɑːl/, Blaise (1623–62), French mathematician, physicist, and religious philosopher. A mathematical child prodigy, before the age of 16 he had proved one of the most important theorems in the projective geometry of conics, and at 19 constructed an arithmetic calculating machine to assist his father in his accounting. It was the first mechanical calculator to be offered for sale, of which seven still exist. From barometric experiments he concluded that air has weight; he confirmed the view that the vacuum could exist; while from his hydrostatic experiments he derived 'Pascal's principle' that the pressure of a fluid at rest is transmitted equally in all directions. He founded the theory of probabilities in 1654 when corresponding with Fermat, and also developed a forerunner of integral calculus. After a spiritual experience in 1654 he entered a Jansenist convent, where he wrote two classics of French devotional thought, his *Lettres Provinciales* (1656–7), directed against the casuistry of the Jesuits, and his posthumously published *Pensées* (1670), directed principally against free-thinkers. The pascal (see foll.) and a computer language (see prec.) are named in his honour.

pascal /ˈpæsk(ə)l/ *n.* a unit of pressure, one newton per square metre. [f. prec.]

paschal /ˈpæsk(ə)l, ˈpɑː-/ *adj.* 1. of the Jewish Passover. 2. of Easter. —**paschal lamb**, a lamb sacrificed at Passover; (*fig.*) Christ. [f. OF f. L (*pascha* Passover f. Gk f. Aram.)]

pasha /ˈpɑːʃə/ *n.* (*hist.*) the title (placed after the name) of a Turkish officer of high rank. [f. Turk.]

Pashto /ˈpʌʃtəʊ/ *n.* the Iranian language of the Pathans, the official language of Afghanistan, spoken by some 10 million people there and another 6 million in NW Pakistan. It is an Indo-Iranian language and, like Persian, is written in a form of the Arabic script. —*adj.* of or in this language. [Pashto]

Pasiphaë /pəˈsɪfəɪ/ (*Gk legend*) wife of Minos and mother of the Minotaur.

pass[1] /pɑːs/ *v.t./i.* (*p.p.* **passed** /pɑːst/ or as *adj.* PAST) 1. to go or move onward or past something, to proceed; to leave (a thing) on one side or behind, to disregard. 2. to go from one person or place etc. to another, to be transferred. 3. to surpass, to be too great for. 4. to cause to move across, over, or past; (in football etc.) to send (the ball, or *absol.*) to a player of one's own side. 5. to discharge from the body as or with excreta. 6. to change from one state or condition etc. into another; to cease or come to an end; (of time) to go by. 7. to happen, to be done or said. 8. to occupy (time). 9. to circulate or cause to circulate; to be accepted or currently known in a certain way. 10. to be tolerated, to go uncensured. 11. to examine and declare satisfactory; to approve (a law etc.), especially by vote. 12. to achieve the required standard in performing (a test); to be accepted as satisfactory. 13. to go beyond. 14. to utter; to pronounce as a decision. 15. (in cards etc.) to refuse one's turn, e.g. in bidding. —*n.* 1. passing, especially of a test or at cards; a status of degree etc. without honours. 2. a permit to go into or out of a place or to be absent from one's quarters. 3. (in football etc.) transference of the ball to a player of one's own side. 4. a movement made with the hand(s) or with something held. 5. a critical state of affairs. —**bring to pass**, to cause to happen. **come to pass**, to happen, to occur. **in passing**, by the way, in the course of speech. **make a pass at**, (*colloq.*) to try to attract sexually. **pass away**, (*euphem.*) to die. **pass for**, to be accepted as. **pass off**, to cease gradually; (of an event) to take place and be completed (in a specified way); to offer or dispose of (a thing) under false pretences; to evade or dismiss (an awkward remark etc.) lightly. **pass out**, to become unconscious; to complete one's military training. **pass over**, to omit, ignore, or disregard; to take the claims (of a person) to promotion etc. **pass up**, (*colloq.*) to refuse or neglect (an opportunity etc.). [f. OF *passer* f. L *passus* (as PACE[1])]

pass[2] /pɑːs/ *n.* a narrow route through mountains (ill. MOUNTAINS). [var. of PACE[1]]

passable /ˈpɑːsəb(ə)l/ *adj.* 1. (barely) satisfactory, adequate. 2. that can be passed. —**passably** *adv.* [f. PASS[1]]

passage /ˈpæsɪdʒ/ *n.* 1. passing; transition from one state

to another; a journey by sea or air. 2. (also **passageway**) a narrow way for passing along, especially with walls on either side. 3. a tubelike structure through which air or secretions etc. pass in the body. 4. the liberty or right to pass through; the right of conveyance as a passenger by sea or air. 5. a short section of a book etc. or of a piece of music. 6. (in *pl.*) an interchange of words etc. —**passage of arms**, a fight; a dispute. [f. OF (as PASS[1])]

passbook *n.* a book issued by a bank or building society to an account-holder, recording the sums deposited and withdrawn.

passant /ˈpæs(ə)nt/ *adj.* (in heraldry, of an animal) walking and looking to the dexter side, with three paws on the ground and the right fore-paw raised (ill. HERALDRY). [f. OF f. *passer* pass]

Passchendaele /ˈpæʃ(ə)ndeɪl/ a Belgian village marking the furthest point of the British advance during the Ypres offensive of 1917. Eight weeks of heavy rain had made conditions for the exhausted armies almost impossible. Here (as on the Somme) there was heavy loss of life, tolerated only in the fervent patriotism of the time.

passé /ˈpæseɪ/ *adj.* 1. behind the times. 2. past the prime. [F, p.p. of *passer* (as PASS[1])]

passenger /ˈpæsɪndʒə(r)/ *n.* 1. a traveller in or on a public or private conveyance (other than the driver, pilot, crew, etc.). 2. (*colloq.*) a member of a team, crew, etc. who does no effective work. [f. OF *passager* (as PASSAGE)]

passer-by *n.* one who goes past especially by chance. [f. PASS[1]]

passerine /ˈpæsəraɪn/ *adj.* of the order Passeriformes, the perching birds, whose feet are adapted for gripping branches and stems. —*n.* a passerine bird. [f. L *passer* sparrow]

passim /ˈpæsɪm/ *adv.* throughout or at many points in a book or article etc. [L (*passus* spread out)]

passion /ˈpæʃ(ə)n/ *n.* 1. strong emotion. 2. an outburst of anger. 3. sexual love. 4. great enthusiasm. 5. **Passion**, the sufferings of Christ on the Cross; a narrative of this from the Gospels; a musical setting of this narrative. —**passion-flower** *n.* a plant of the genus *Passiflora* with a flower thought to resemble the crown of thorns and other things associated with the Passion of Christ. **passion-fruit** *n.* the edible fruit of some species of passion-flower. **passion-play** *n.* a medieval religious drama in the vernacular dealing with the events of Christ's Passion from the Last Supper to the Crucifixion. The establishment of the feast of Corpus Christi in 1313 gave a great impetus to the enactment of passion-plays throughout Europe, but most of them died out during the 15th c. The best-known of the few that survive is that given at Oberammergau (see entry). **Passion Sunday**, the fifth Sunday in Lent. [f. OF f. L (*pati* suffer)]

passionate /ˈpæʃənət/ *adj.* 1. full of passion; showing or moved by strong emotion. 2. (of emotion) intense. —**passionately** *adv.* [f. L (as prec.)]

passive /ˈpæsɪv/ *adj.* 1. suffering an action, acted upon. 2. not resisting, submissive. 3. (of substances) not active, inert. 4. (*Gram.*) indicating that the subject undergoes the action of the verb (e.g. in *he was seen*). —**passive resistance**, resistance by non-violent refusal to co-operate. **passive voice**, (*Gram.*) that comprising the passive forms of verbs. —**passively** *adv.*, **passiveness** *n.*, **passivity** /-ˈsɪvɪtɪ/ *n.* [f. OF or L (as PASSION)]

passkey *n.* 1. a private key to a door or gate etc. 2. a master-key.

Passover *n.* 1. (Heb. *Pesach*) the Jewish festival celebrated each spring, held from 14 to 21 Nisan and commemorating the liberation of the Israelites from slavery in Egypt (see EXODUS). It may have been originally an agricultural feast. 2. the Paschal lamb. [f. *pass over*, with reference to the exemption of the Israelites from the death of the first-born which afflicted the Egyptians (Exod. 12)]

passport /ˈpɑːspɔːt/ *n.* 1. an official document issued by a government certifying the holder's identity and citizenship, and entitling him to travel under its protection to and from a foreign country. 2. a thing that secures admission to or attainment of something. [f. F (as PASS[1], PORT[1])]

password *n.* a selected word or phrase known only to one's own side, enabling sentries to distinguish friend from enemy.

past /pɑːst/ *adj.* 1. belonging to the time before the present; (of time) gone by. 2. (*Gram.*) expressing a past action or state. —*n.* 1. (esp. **the past**) past time; past events. 2. a person's past life or career, esp. one that is discreditable.

3. the past tense. —*prep.* **1.** beyond in time or place. **2.** beyond the range, limits, powers, or stage of. —*adv.* so as to pass by. —**not put it past,** (*colloq.*) to believe it possible of (a person). **past it,** (*slang*) incompetent or unusable through age. **past master,** an expert; a former master of a Freemason's lodge etc. [f. PASS[1]]

pasta /ˈpæstə/ *n.* dried paste made with flour and produced in various shapes (e.g. lasagne, macaroni); a cooked dish made with this. [It. (as foll.)]

paste /peɪst/ *n.* **1.** any moist fairly stiff mixture, especially of a powder and liquid. **2.** a dough of flour with fat, water, etc. **3.** a liquid adhesive for paper etc. **4.** an easily spread preparation of ground meat, fish, etc. **5.** a hard vitreous composition used in making imitation gems. —*v.t.* **1.** to fasten or coat with paste. **2.** (*slang*) to beat, thrash, bomb, etc. heavily. —**paste-up** *n.* a document prepared for copying etc. by pasting sections on a backing. [f. OF f. L *pasta* lozenge f. Gk *pastē* (*pastos* sprinkled)]

pasteboard *n.* a kind of thin board made of layers of paper or wood fibres pasted together.

pastel /ˈpæst(ə)l/ *n.* **1.** a crayon made of dried paste compounded of pigments with gum solution. **2.** a drawing made with this. **3.** a light delicate shade of colour. [F or f. It. (as PASTE)]

pastern /ˈpæstɜːn/ *n.* the part of a horse's foot between fetlock and hoof (ill. HORSE). [f. OF *pasturon* (*pasture* cord used to tether, f. L, ult. as PASTOR)]

Pasternak /ˈpæstənæk/, Boris Leonidovich (1890–1960), Russian poet and novelist. Born into a cultured Jewish family he studied music, which he abandoned for poetry, and philosophy; his third volume of poems *My Sister, Life* (1922) established his reputation. In the 1930s his position became increasingly difficult and he began his 'long silent duel' with Stalin; after 1933 none of his works could be published in Russia. During this time he made important translations of Goethe's *Faust*, of many of Shakespeare's plays, and of other English writers. His greatest work, *Doctor Zhivago* (1957) was internationally successful but has never been published in the USSR; the work witnessed the experience of the Russian intelligentsia before, during, and after the Revolution and the heroine, Lara, was based on Olga Ivinskaya (Pasternak's companion of his later years) who was subsequently imprisoned. Pasternak was awarded the Nobel Prize for literature in 1958, but declined it after a vehement political campaign against him.

Pasteur /pæsˈtɜː(r)/, Louis (1822–95), French chemist and bacteriologist. His early work laid the basis for a new approach to chemical structures and composition, but he became a French hero and is popularly remembered for his 'germ theory': Pasteur argued that each fermentation process could be traced to a specific living micro-organism. By sterilization or 'pasteurization' a product, such as milk or wine, could be preserved; from this he developed an interest in diseases. Although not as original as once suggested, Pasteur worked on problems of immediate economic and industrial application. He isolated bacilli attacking silkworms and found methods both of detecting diseased stock and of preventing the disease from spreading; this saved the silk industry of France and other countries. He then turned to the fatal cattle disease of anthrax and the problem of chicken cholera; in both areas he was able to isolate the bacillus responsible and cultivate attenuated forms which he then used to inoculate healthy animals. His last triumph was to make a successful vaccine against rabies.

pasteurize /ˈpɑːstʃəraɪz/ *v.t.* to subject (milk etc.) to a process of partial sterilization by heating. —**pasteurization** /-ˈzeɪʃ(ə)n/ *n.* [f. prec.]

pastiche /pæsˈtiːʃ/ *n.* **1.** a picture or musical or literary composition made up of selections from various sources. **2.** a literary or other work composed in the style of a well-known author. [F, f. It. *pasticcio* f. L *pasta* paste]

pastille /ˈpæstɪl, -stiːl/ *n.* **1.** a small medicinal or flavoured lozenge. **2.** a small roll of aromatic paste burnt as a fumigator etc. [F f. L, = little loaf, lozenge (*panis* loaf)]

pastime /ˈpɑːstaɪm/ *n.* something done to pass time pleasantly, a recreation. [f. PASS[1] + TIME]

pastor /ˈpɑːstə(r)/ *n.* a minister in charge of a church or congregation; a person exercising spiritual guidance. [f. OF f. L, = shepherd (*pascere* feed)]

pastoral /ˈpɑːstər(ə)l/ *adj.* **1.** of or portraying shepherds or country life. **2.** (of land) used for pasture. **3.** of a pastor; concerned with Christian spiritual guidance. —*n.* **1.** a pastoral poem, play, picture, etc. **2.** a letter from a pastor

(esp. a bishop) to the clergy or people. —**pastorally** *adv.* [f. L (as prec.)]

pastoralist /ˈpɑːstərəlɪst/ *n.* (*Austral.*) a sheep- or cattle-farmer. [f. prec.]

pastorate /ˈpɑːstərət/ *n.* **1.** a pastor's office or tenure. **2.** a body of pastors. [f. PASTOR]

pastrami /pæˈstrɑːmɪ/ *n.* seasoned smoked beef. [Yiddish]

pastry /ˈpeɪstrɪ/ *n.* **1.** a dough made of flour, fat, and water, used for covering pies or holding filling. **2.** food made with this. **3.** a cake made wholly or partly of pastry. —**pastry-cook** *n.* a cook who makes pastry, especially for public sale. [f. PASTE]

pasturage /ˈpɑːstʃərɪdʒ/ *n.* **1.** pasture-land. **2.** pasturing. [as foll.]

pasture /ˈpɑːstʃə(r)/ *n.* **1.** land covered with grass etc. suitable for grazing animals; a piece of such land. **2.** grass etc. on this. —*v.t./i.* to put (animals) to graze in a pasture; (of animals) to graze. [f. OF f. L *pastura* (as PASTOR)]

pasty[1] /ˈpæstɪ/ *n.* pastry with a sweet or savoury filling baked without a dish. [f. OF *pasté(e)* f. L *pasta* paste]

pasty[2] /ˈpeɪstɪ/ *adj.* **1.** of, like, or covered in paste. **2.** unhealthily pale. —**pastily** *adv.*, **pastiness** *n.* [f. PASTE]

pat *v.t.* (**-tt-**) to strike gently with the hand or a flat surface; to flatten or mould thus. —*n.* **1.** a light stroke or tap; the sound made by this. **2.** a small mass of butter or other soft substance. —*adj.* **1.** apposite, opportune. **2.** known thoroughly and ready for any occasion. —*adv.* in a pat manner, appositely. —**have off pat,** to know or have memorized perfectly. **pat on the back,** a congratulatory acknowledgement. [prob. imit.]

Pat. *abbr.* Patent.

Patagonia /pætəˈɡəʊnɪə/ the southernmost region of South America, chiefly a dry barren plateau in southern Argentina and Chile between the Andes and the Atlantic. —**Patagonian** *adj. & n.* [f. obs. *Patagon* member of a tribe of South American Indians alleged by 17th–18th c. travellers to be the tallest known people]

patch *n.* **1.** a piece of material or metal etc. put on to mend a hole or as a reinforcement. **2.** a piece of plaster or a pad put over a wound; a shield worn to protect an injured eye. **3.** a distinguishable area on a surface; an isolated area or period of time. **4.** a piece of ground; this covered by specified plants; (*colloq.*) an area assigned to a particular policeman etc. **5.** a scrap, a remnant. —*v.t.* **1.** to put a patch or patches on; (of a material) to serve as a patch to. **2.** to piece together (*lit.* or *fig.*). —**not a patch on,** (*colloq.*) greatly inferior to. **patch-pocket** *n.* one made of a piece of cloth sewn on a garment. **patch up,** to repair with patches; to settle (a quarrel etc.) esp. hastily or temporarily; to put together hastily. [perh. f. *pieche,* = PIECE]

patchouli /ˈpætʃʊlɪ/ *n.* a fragrant plant of the genus *Pogostemon,* grown in the Far East, the leaves of which yield an essential oil; perfume made from this. [native name in Madras]

patchwork *n.* **1.** needlework in which assorted small pieces of cloth are joined edge to edge, often in a pattern. **2.** a thing made of assorted pieces.

patchy *adj.* **1.** uneven in quality. **2.** having or existing in patches. —**patchily** *adv.*, **patchiness** *n.* [f. PATCH]

pate *n.* (*archaic* or *colloq.*) the head, often as the seat of the intellect. [orig. unkn.]

pâté /ˈpæteɪ/ *n.* **1.** a paste of meat etc. **2.** a pie, a patty. —**pâté de foie gras,** /də fwɑː grɑː/ a paste of fatted goose liver. [F (as PASTY)]

patella /pəˈtelə/ *n.* (*pl.* **-lae** /-liː/) the kneecap (ill. BODY 1). —**patellar** *adj.* [L, = small pan (as foll.)]

paten /ˈpæt(ə)n/ *n.* a shallow dish used for the bread at the Eucharist (ill. VESTMENTS). [f. OF or L *patina*]

patent /ˈpeɪt(ə)nt, ˈpæ-/ *n.* **1.** an official document (orig. **letters patent**) conferring a right or title etc., especially the sole right to make, use, or sell some invention; the right granted by this. **2.** an invention or process so protected. —*adj.* **1.** conferred or protected by a patent; (of a food, medicine, etc.) proprietary. **2.** obvious, plain. **3.** (*colloq.*) ingenious, well-contrived. —*v.t.* to obtain a patent for (an invention). —**patent leather,** leather with a glossy varnished surface. **Patent Office,** the government office from which patents are issued. **patent theatre,** one established by royal patent, (in London) the theatres of Covent Garden and Drury Lane, whose patents were granted by Charles II in 1662. —**patently** *adv.* [f. OF or L (*patēre* lie open)]

Patents for inventions seem to have been introduced in

Italy in the 15th c. and spread to other European States. In England, Elizabeth I and James I granted monopolies to favourites by means of *literae patentes* ('letters patent'), open letters addressed to all to whom they might come, relating not only to new inventions etc. but also to known commodities. General dissatisfaction with this system led to the passing of the Statute of Monopolies (1623), which declared such grants void but allowed future patents to confer exclusive rights on an inventor for a period of 14 years. The granting of patents in the UK is now regulated by statute, and patents are issued by and under the seal of the Patent Office.

patentee /peɪtən'tiː/ *n.* one who takes out or holds a patent; a person for the time being entitled to the benefit of a patent. [f. prec.]

Pater /'peɪtə(r)/, Walter Horatio (1839-94), English essayist and critic, greatly influenced by the Pre-Raphaelites. Among his friends were Swinburne and Rossetti. He came to fame with *Studies in the History of the Renaissance* (1873) which included his essays on the then neglected Botticelli, and on Leonardo da Vinci with its celebrated evocation of the Mona Lisa. Though attacked by some as unscholarly and morbid the work had a profound influence on under-graduates of the time and on the aesthetic movement. His other major works include *Marius the Epicurean* (1885), a fictional biography set in the Rome of Marcus Aurelius, which develops his ideas on 'art for art's sake', and *Appreciations: with an Essay on Style* (1889) which established his position as a critic and a master of English prose.

pater /'peɪtə(r)/ *n.* (*archaic, slang*) father. [L]

paternal /pə'tɜːn(ə)l/ *adj.* 1. of or like a father. 2. related through the father. 3. (of a government etc.) limiting freedom and responsibility by well-meant regulations. —**paternally** *adv.* [f. L *paternalis* (*pater* father)]

paternalism *n.* the policy of governing in a paternal way. —**paternalistic** /-'lɪstɪk/ *adj.* [f. prec.]

paternity /pə'tɜːnɪtɪ/ *n.* 1. fatherhood. 2. one's paternal origin. 3. authorship, source. [f. OF or L (as PATERNAL)]

paternoster /pætə'nɒstə(r)/ *n.* the Lord's Prayer, especially in Latin. [OE f. L, = our father]

path /pɑːθ/ *n.* (*pl.* /pɑːðz/) 1. a way or track laid down for walking or made by walking. 2. a line along which a person or thing moves. 3. a course of action. [OE]

Pathan /pə'tɑːn/ *n.* a member of a people inhabiting NW Pakistan and SE Afghanistan. —*adj.* of this people. [Hindi]

pathetic /pə'θetɪk/ *adj.* arousing pity or sadness; arousing contempt; miserably inadequate. —**pathetic fallacy**, crediting inanimate things with human emotions. —**pathetically** *adv.* [f. F f. L f. Gk (as PATHOS)]

pathfinder *n.* an explorer. [OE]

pathogen /'pæθədʒ(ə)n/ *n.* an agent causing disease. —**pathogenic** /-'dʒenɪk/ *adj.* [f. Gk *pathos* suffering (as PATHOS) + -GEN]

pathological /pæθə'lɒdʒɪk(ə)l/ *adj.* 1. of pathology. 2. of or caused by a physical or mental disorder. —**pathologically** *adv.* [f. foll.]

pathology /pə'θɒlədʒɪ/ *n.* 1. the science of bodily diseases. 2. abnormal changes in body tissue, caused by disease. —**pathologist** *n.* [f. F (as PATHOGEN + -LOGY)]

pathos /'peɪθɒs/ *n.* a quality in speech, writing, events, etc., that arouses pity or sadness. [f. Gk, = suffering (*paskhō* suffer)]

pathway *n.* a footway or track, especially one made by walking.

patience /'peɪʃ(ə)ns/ *n.* 1. calm endurance of hardship, annoyance, inconvenience, delay, etc. 2. perseverance. 3. a card-game (usually for one player) in which cards are brought into a specified arrangement. [f. OF f. L (as foll.)]

patient /'peɪʃ(ə)nt/ *adj.* having or showing patience. —*n.* a person receiving (or registered to receive) medical or dental treatment. —**patiently** *adv.* [f. OF f. L (*pati* suffer)]

patina /'pætɪnə/ *n.* 1. an incrustation, usually green, on the surface of old bronze; a similar alteration on other surfaces. 2. the gloss produced by age on woodwork. [It. f. L (as PATEN)]

patio /'pætɪəʊ/ *n.* (*pl.* -os) 1. a paved, usually roofless area adjoining a house. 2. an inner court open to the sky in a Spanish or Spanish-American house. [Sp.]

patisserie /pə'tiːsərɪ/ *n.* a pastry-cook's shop or wares. [f. F f. L *pasticium* pastry (as PASTE)]

Patmos /'pætmɒs/ a Greek island in the Aegean Sea, where,

according to legend, St John lived in exile and saw the visions of the Apocalypse.

Patna /'pætnə/ the capital city of Bihar; pop. approx. 500,000. —**Patna rice,** long-grained rice, originally that of Patna, now also grown elsewhere, especially in the USA.

patois /'pætwɑː/ *n.* (*pl.* same /-ɑːz/) 1. the dialect of the common people of a region, differing fundamentally from the literary language. 2. jargon. [F, = rough speech]

patriarch /'peɪtrɪɑːk/ *n.* 1. the male head of a family or tribe. 2. (in the Orthodox and RC Churches) a bishop of high rank. 3. a venerable old man. —**the Patriarchs,** the men named in Genesis as the ancestors of mankind or of the tribes of Israel. —**patriarchal** /-'ɑːk(ə)l/ *adj.* [f. OF f. L f. Gk (*patria* family, *-arkhēs* -ruler)]

patriarchate /'peɪtrɪɑːkət/ *n.* the office, see, or residence of an ecclesiastical patriarch. [f. L (as prec.)]

patriarchy /'peɪtrɪɑːkɪ/ *n.* a patriarchal system of society, government, etc. [f. L f. Gk (as PATRIARCH)]

patrician /pə'trɪʃ(ə)n/ *n.* an ancient Roman noble. —*adj.* 1. noble, aristocratic. 2. of the ancient Roman nobility. [f. OF f. L, = having a noble father (*pater* father)]

patricide /'pætrɪsaɪd/ *n.* 1. the crime of killing one's own father. 2. one who is guilty of this. —**patricidal** *adj.* [f. L, alt. of *parricida* (as PARRICIDE)]

Patrick /'pætrɪk/, St (5th c.), apostle and patron saint of Ireland. His *Confessions* (spiritual autobiography) are the chief source for the events of his life; early accounts by others are confused and full of the miraculous. Of Romano-British parentage, he was captured at the age of 16 by raiders and carried off to Ireland as a slave; there he experienced a religious conversion. Escaping after six years, probably to Gaul, he was ordained and returned to Ireland *c.*432. The details of his mission are uncertain but he travelled about the country, did much to convert the pagan west, organized the scattered Christian communities which he found in the north, and founded the archiepiscopal see of Armagh *c.*444. Favourite legends include his expulsion of snakes from Ireland. Feast day, 17 March.

patrilineal /pætrɪ'lɪnɪəl/ *adj.* of or based on kinship with the father or the male line of ancestors. [f. L *pater* father + LINEAL]

patrimony /'pætrɪmənɪ/ *n.* property inherited from one's father or ancestors; a heritage (*lit.* or *fig.*). —**patrimonial** /-'məʊnɪəl/ *adj.* [f. OF f. L (as PATER)]

patriot /'pætrɪət, 'peɪ-/ *n.* one who is devoted to and ready to defend his country. —**patriotic** /-'ɒtɪk/ *adj.*, **patriotically** /-'ɒtɪklɪ/ *adv.*, **patriotism** *n.* [f. F f. L f. Gk (*patrios* of one's father)]

patristic /pə'trɪstɪk/ *adj.* of the early Christian writers (the Church Fathers) or their work. [f. G f. L (as PATER)]

patrol /pə'trəʊl/ *v.t./i.* (-ll-) to walk or travel round (an area, or *absol.*) in order to protect or supervise it; to act as a patrol. —*n.* 1. patrolling. 2. a person or persons or vehicle(s) assigned or sent out to patrol. 2. a unit of usually six in a Scout troop or Guide company. [f. F *patrouiller* paddle in mud]

patrolman *n.* (*pl.* -men) (*US*) a policeman of the lowest rank.

patron /'peɪtrən/ *n.* 1. one who gives financial or other support to a person, activity, or cause. 2. a customer of a shop, restaurant, etc. —**patron saint,** a saint regarded as protecting a person or place etc. —**patroness** *n. fem.* [f. OF f. L *patronus* protector of clients (as PATER)]

patronage /'pætrənɪdʒ/ *n.* 1. a patron's or customer's support. 2. the right of bestowing or recommending for an appointment. 3. patronizing airs. [f. OF (as prec.)]

patronize /'pætrənaɪz/ *v.t.* 1. to act as a patron towards, to support. 2. to treat condescendingly. —**patronizing** *adj.*, **patronizingly** *adv.* [f. obs. F or L (as PATRON)]

patronymic /pætrə'nɪmɪk/ *n.* a name derived from that of a father or male ancestor. [f. L f. Gk (*pater* father, *onoma* name)]

patten /'pæt(ə)n/ *n.* a shoe with the sole set on an iron ring etc. to raise the wearer's foot above the level of surface mud etc. [f. OF *patin* (*patte* paw)]

patter[1] *v.i.* 1. to make a rapid succession of taps, as rain on a window-pane. 2. to run with short quick steps. —*n.* a series of taps or short light steps. [f. PAT]

patter[2] *n.* rapid and often glib or deceptive speech, e.g. that used by a salesman or conjuror. —*v.t./i.* to repeat (prayers etc.) in a rapid mechanical way; to talk glibly. [f. *pater* = PATERNOSTER]

pattern /'pætən/ n. **1.** a decorative design as executed on a carpet, wallpaper, cloth, etc. **2.** a model, design, or instructions from which a thing is to be made. **3.** an excellent example or model. **4.** a regular form or order. **5.** a sample of cloth etc. —v.t. **1.** to model (a thing *after* or *on* a design etc.). **2.** to decorate with a pattern. [f. PATRON]

patty n. **1.** a small pie or pasty. **2.** (*US*) a small flat cake of minced meat etc. [f. F *pâté* (as PASTY¹)]

paucity /'pɔːsɪtɪ/ n. smallness of quantity or supply. [f. OF or L *paucitas* (*paucus* few)]

Paul, St (1st c. AD), a Jew (also called Saul) of Tarsus, with the status of a Roman citizen. He was brought up as a Pharisee and at first opposed the followers of Christ, assisting at the martyrdom of St Stephen. On a mission to Damascus he was converted to Christianity after a vision, and became the 'Apostle of the Gentiles' and the first great Christian missionary and theologian. His missionary journeys are described in the Acts of the Apostles, and the letters to the Churches written by or attributed to him form part of the New Testament. He was martyred at Rome *c.*AD 64. Feast day, 29 June.

pauldron /'pɔːldrən/ n. (*hist.*) a piece of armour covering the shoulder (ill. ARMOUR). [f. OF (cf. F *épaule* shoulder)]

Pauli /'paʊlɪ/, Wolfgang (1900–58), Austrian-born physicist, best remembered for his 'exclusion principle', postulated in 1925, according to which at most two electrons could occupy each energy level or orbital around the atomic nucleus, but only if they had opposite spin. This made it easier to understand the structure of the atom and the chemical properties of the elements. The principle was later extended to a whole class of subatomic particles, the fermions, which includes the electron. In 1931 he proposed the existence of a new subatomic particle, the neutrino, later discovered by Fermi. He was awarded the 1945 Nobel Prize for physics.

Pauline /'pɔːlaɪn/ adj. of St Paul. [f. PAUL]

Pauling /'pɔːlɪŋ/, Linus Carl (1901–), American chemist, particularly renowned for his study of molecular structure and chemical bonding, especially of living tissue such as the complex protein molecule, for which he received the 1954 Nobel Prize for chemistry. After the Second World War he became increasingly involved with the peace movement and attempts to ban nuclear weapons, for which he was awarded the Nobel Peace Prize in 1962 and thus (like Madame Curie) achieved the rare distinction of receiving two Nobel Prizes.

Paul Jones /pɔːl 'dʒəʊnz/ a ballroom dance during which the dancers change partners after circling in concentric rings of men and women. [f. name of John *Paul Jones* (d. 1792), Scottish-born naval officer noted for his victories for the Americas during the War of Independence]

Paul Pry /'praɪ/ an inquisitive person. [character in US song (1820)]

paunch /pɔːntʃ/ n. **1.** the stomach or belly. **2.** a protruding abdomen. —v.t. to disembowel (an animal). —**paunchy** adj. [f. AF f. L *pantex* bowels]

pauper /'pɔːpə(r)/ n. a very poor person; (*hist.*) a recipient of poor-law relief. —**pauperism** n. [L, = poor]

pauperize /'pɔːpəraɪz/ v.t. to make into a pauper; to impoverish greatly. [f. prec.]

Pausanias /pɔːˈseɪnɪæs/ (2nd c.) Greek traveller and geographer. His *Description of Greece* (in ten books) is a guide to the topography and antiquities of Greece, and is still an invaluable source of information.

pause /pɔːz/ n. **1.** a temporary stop in action, sound, speech, etc. **2.** (*Mus.*) a character placed over a note or rest indicating that it is to be lengthened at the performer's discretion (ill. MUSICAL NOTATION). —v.i. to make a pause. —**give pause to,** to cause to hesitate. [f. OF or L *pausa* f. Gk (*pauō* stop)]

pavan /pəˈvæn/ n. (also **pavane**) a stately dance in slow duple time; the music for this. [f. F f. Sp. (*pavon* peacock)]

pave v.t. to cover (a street, floor, etc.) with a durable surfaceᴄ. —**pave the way,** to make preparations. [f. OF *paver* (as foll.)]

pavement n. a paved surface or path, especially (for pedestrians) at the side of a road. [f. OF f. L *pavimentum* (*pavire* ram)]

pavilion /pəˈvɪljən/ n. **1.** a light building in a park etc. used as a shelter. **2.** a building on a sports ground for players and spectators. **3.** an ornamental building for public entertainment. **4.** a large tent. [f. OF f. L *papilio*, orig. = butterfly]

paving /'peɪvɪŋ/ n. a paved surface; the material for this. [f. PAVE]

Pavlov /'pævlɒf/, Ivan Petrovich (1849–1936), Russian physiologist who was awarded a Nobel Prize in 1904 for his work on digestion, but is best known for his later studies on the conditioned reflex. He showed by experiment with dogs how the secretion of saliva can be stimulated not only by food but also by the sound of a bell which has been paired repeatedly with the presentation of food, and comes to elicit salivation when presented alone. Pavlov then applied his findings to show the importance of such reflexes in human and animal behaviour. His experiments form the basis for much current research in the field of conditioning.

Pavlova /'pævləvə, -'ləʊvə/, Anna Pavlovna (1881–1931), Russian dancer. By 1906 she had danced all the traditional ballerina roles and in 1907 she created Fokine's *Dying Swan*, her most famous solo dance. In 1908 she began to tour abroad, making her New York and London débuts in 1910, settling in England where she assembled her own company, and embarking on numerous tours which made her a pioneer of classical ballet all over the world. She had a unique lightness, grace, poetry, and spirituality, and became a household name; her aesthetic principles were strictly conservative.

pavlova /pæv'ləʊvə/ n. a meringue cake served with cream and fruit. [f. prec.]

paw n. **1.** the foot of an animal having claws or nails. **2.** (*colloq.*) a person's hand. —v.t./i. **1.** to strike with a paw. **2.** to scrape (the ground) with a hoof. **3.** (*colloq.*) to touch awkwardly or rudely with the hand(s). [f. OF *poue*]

pawky adj. (*Sc. & dial.*) drily humorous. —**pawkily** adv., **pawkiness** n. [f. Sc. & N. Engl. dial. *pawk* trick]

pawl n. **1.** a lever with a catch for the teeth of a wheel or bar. **2.** (*Naut.*) a short bar to prevent a capstan etc. from recoiling. [perh. f. LG & Du. *pal*]

pawn¹ n. **1.** a chess-man of the smallest size and value. **2.** an unimportant person subservient to others' plans. [f. AF *poun* f. L *pedo* foot-soldier]

pawn² v.t. **1.** to deposit (a thing) with a pawnbroker as security for money borrowed. **2.** to pledge in the hope of receiving something in return. —n. the state of being pawned. [f. OF *pan*, *pand*, etc. pledge]

pawnbroker n. one who lends money at interest on the security of personal property deposited. —**pawnbroking** n. the business of a pawnbroker. Such a practice existed in China more than 2,000 years ago, but in Europe it dates from the Middle Ages. It was introduced into England by the Lombards in the 13th c.; the symbol of the three golden balls derives from the Medici coat of arms.

pawnshop n. a pawnbroker's place of business.

pawpaw var. of PAPAW.

Paxton /'pækst(ə)n/, Sir Joseph (1801–65), one of the great Victorians. He became head gardener to the Duke of Devonshire at Chatsworth when only 23, and designed a series of greenhouses, using iron and glass, predecessors of the Crystal Palace for which he is chiefly remembered. He also designed parks and conventional country houses.

pay v.t./i. (*past & p.p.* **paid**) **1.** to hand over (money) in return for goods or services or in discharge of a debt; to give (a person) what is owed; to hand over the amount of (wages, a debt, ransom, etc.). **2.** to bear the cost of something. **3.** to be profitable, beneficial, or worth while (to). **4.** to bestow, render, or express. **5.** to suffer (a penalty etc.) **6.** to let out (a rope) by slackening it. —n. payment; wages. —**in the pay of,** employed by. **pay-as-you-earn,** a method of collecting income tax by deducting it at source from wages etc. **pay for,** to suffer or be punished because of. **pay in,** to pay into a bank account etc. **paying guest,** one who pays for his board and lodging. **pay its way,** to make enough profit to cover expenses. **pay off,** to pay in full and be free from (a debt) or discharge (an employee); (*colloq.*) to yield good results. **pay-off** n. (*slang*) payment; reward or retribution; a climax, especially of a joke or story. **pay one's way,** not get into debt. **pay out,** to punish or be revenged on. **pay-packet** n. a packet containing an employee's wages. **pay phone,** a telephone with a coin-box for prepayment of calls. **pay up,** to pay in full; to pay what is demanded. —**payer** n. [f. OF f. L *pacare* appease (*pax* peace)]

payable adj. that must or may be paid. [f. PAY]

PAYE abbr. pay-as-you-earn.

payee /peɪ'iː/ n. a person to whom money is (to be) paid. [f. PAY]

payload *n.* the part of an aircraft's load from which revenue is derived; the total weight of bombs or instruments carried by an aircraft or rocket etc.; goods etc. carried on a road vehicle.

paymaster *n.* an official who pays troops, workers, etc. —**Paymaster General,** the minister at the head of the department of the Treasury through which payments are made.

payment *n.* **1.** paying. **2.** an amount paid. **3.** reward, recompense.

payola /peɪˈəʊlə/ *n.* a bribe or bribery offered in return for illicit or unfair help in promoting a commercial product. [f. PAY + -ola after *Pianola* etc.]

payroll *n.* a list of employees receiving regular pay.

Pb *symbol* lead. [f. L *plumbum*]

PC *abbr.* **1.** police constable. **2.** Privy Counsellor.

p.c. *abbr.* **1.** per cent. **2.** postcard.

Pd *symbol* palladium.

pd. *abbr.* paid.

PE *abbr.* physical education.

pea *n.* **1.** a hardy climbing plant (*Pisum sativum*) whose seeds grow in pods and are used for food. **2.** its seed. **3.** any of various similar plants. —**pea-green** *adj.* & *n.* bright green. **pea-shooter** *n.* a toy tube from which dried peas are shot by blowing. **pea-souper** *n.* (*colloq.*) a thick yellow fog. [f. PEASE taken as pl.]

peace /piːs/ *n.* **1.** quiet, tranquillity; mental calm. **2.** freedom from or cessation of war. **3.** a treaty ending a war. **4.** freedom from civil disorder. —**at peace,** in a state of peace, not in strife. **hold one's peace,** to keep quiet. **keep the peace,** to prevent or refrain from strife. **make one's peace,** to bring oneself back into friendly relations (*with*). **peace offering,** something offered to show that one is willing to make peace. **peace-pipe** a tobacco-pipe as a token of peace among North American Indians. **peace-time** *n.* a period when a country is not at war. [f. AF f. L *pax*]

peaceable /ˈpiːsəb(ə)l/ *adj.* **1.** desiring to be at peace with others, not quarrelsome. **2.** peaceful. —**peaceably** *adv.* [f. OF f. L *placabilis* pleasing (as PLEASE)]

peaceful *adj.* characterized by or concerned with peace; not violating or infringing peace. —**peacefully** *adv.*, **peacefulness** *n.* [f. PEACE + -FUL]

peacemaker *n.* one who brings about peace.

peach *n.* **1.** a round juicy fruit with a downy yellowish or reddish skin. **2.** the tree (*Prunus persica*) bearing it. **3.** its yellowish-pink colour. **4.** (*slang*) a person or thing of superlative merit; an attractive young woman. —**peach Melba,** a dish of ice-cream and peaches with a raspberry sauce. —**peachy** *adj.* [f. OF *peche* f. L *persicum* (*malum*) peach (lit. 'Persian apple')]

Peacock /ˈpiːkɒk/, Thomas Love (1785–1866), English novelist and poet. His satirical romances, which include *Headlong Hall* (1816), *Nightmare Abbey* (1818), *Crotchet Castle* (1831), and *Gryll Grange* (1860–1), survey the contemporary cultural scene from a radical viewpoint, often in convivial argument between strange characters (some based on real people, including his friend Shelley) at dinner in a country house; the plots are slender and are diversified by clever songs. Peacock's sceptical attitude to the fashionable cult of the arts is apparent in his critical work *The Four Ages of Poetry* (1820), to which Shelley replied in *A Defence of Poetry* (1821).

peacock *n.* the male peafowl, a bird with brilliant plumage and a tail that can be spread upright like a fan. —**peacock blue,** the lustrous blue of the peacock's neck. **peacock butterfly,** a butterfly (*Inachis io*) with conspicuous 'eyes' on its wings (ill. INSECTS). [*pea* (OE f. L *pavo* peacock) + COCK[1]]

peafowl *n.* a kind of pheasant of the genus *Pavo*, a peacock or peahen. [as prec. + FOWL]

peahen *n.* the female of the peafowl. [as PEACOCK + HEN]

pea-jacket /ˈpiːdʒækɪt/ *n.* a sailor's short double-breasted overcoat of coarse woollen cloth. [prob. f. Du. *pijjakker*]

peak[1] *n.* **1.** a pointed top, especially of a mountain. **2.** any shape, edge, or part that tapers to form a point. **3.** the projecting part (usually at the front) of the brim of a cap. **4.** the highest point of achievement, intensity, etc. **5.** (*attrib.*) maximum, most busy or intense etc. —*v.i.* to reach the highest value, quality, etc. —**Peak District,** an area in Derbyshire where there are many peaks. [f. dial. *picked* pointed (as PICK)]

peak[2] *v.i.* **1.** to waste away. **2.** (in *p.p.*) pinched, drawn. [orig. unkn.]

peaky *adj.* sickly, peaked. —**peakiness** *n.* [f. PEAK[2]]

peal *n.* **1.** the loud ringing of a bell or bells, especially a series of changes on a set of bells. **2.** a set of bells with different notes. **3.** a loud outburst of sound, especially of thunder or laughter. —*v.t./i.* to sound or cause to sound in a peal. [f. APPEAL]

peanut *n.* **1.** a plant (*Arachis hypogaea*) bearing pods that ripen underground, containing seeds used as food and yielding oil. **2.** its seed. **3.** (in *pl.*, *slang*) a paltry or trivial thing or amount, especially of money. —**peanut butter,** a paste of ground roasted peanuts.

pear /peə(r)/ *n.* **1.** a rounded fleshy fruit tapering towards the stalk. **2.** the tree bearing it (*Pyrus communis*). [OE, ult. f. L *pirum*]

pearl /pɜːl/ *n.* **1.** a smooth lustrous mass, usually white or bluish-grey, formed within the shell of certain oysters and used as a gem; an imitation of this. **2.** a thing like a pearl in form. **3.** a precious thing, the finest example. —*adj.* like a pearl in form or colour. —*v.t./i.* **1.** to fish for pearls. **2.** to reduce (barley etc.) to small rounded grains. **3.** to form pearl-like drops. **4.** to sprinkle with pearly drops. —**pearl barley,** barley rubbed into small rounded grains. **pearl button,** a button of real or imitation mother-of-pearl. **pearl-diver,** *n.* one who dives for oysters containing pearls. [f. OF *perle* prob. ult. f. L *perna* leg (applied to a kind of bivalve)]

Pearl Harbor a harbour on the island of Oahu, one of the Hawaiian islands, site of a major American naval base, where a surprise attack on 7 Dec. 1941, delivered (without a declaration of war) by Japanese carrier-borne aircraft, inflicted heavy damage and brought the USA into the Second World War. [tr. Hawaiian *Wai Momi*, lit. = pearl waters]

pearly *adj.* like or adorned with pearls. —*n.* (in *pl.*) costermongers' clothes decorated with pearl buttons. —**Pearly Gates,** the gates of heaven. **pearly king** (*or* **queen**), a leading London costermonger (or his wife) wearing pearlies.

peasant /ˈpez(ə)nt/ *n.* (in some rural or agricultural countries) a worker on the land, a farm labourer; a small farmer. —**peasantry** *n.* [f. AF *paisant* (*païs* country f. L *pagus* village)]

Peasants' Revolt an uprising in England (1381) when widespread unrest, caused by poor economic conditions and repressive legislation, culminated in revolt among the peasant and artisan classes, particularly in Kent and Essex. The rebels marched on London, occupying the city and executing unpopular ministers, but after the death of their leader, Wat Tyler, they were persuaded to disperse after the young king Richard II had granted some of their demands. Afterwards the government went back on its promises and rapidly re-established control.

pease /piːz/ *n.* (*archaic*) peas. —**pease-pudding** *n.* a pudding of boiled peas, eggs, etc. [OE *pise* pea f. L *pisum*]

peat *n.* vegetable matter decomposed in water and partly carbonized, used for fuel, in horticulture, etc.; a cut piece of this. —**peaty** *adj.* [perh. rel. to PIECE]

peatbog *n.* a bog composed of peat.

pebble *n.* a small stone worn and rounded by the action of water. —**pebble-dash** *n.* mortar with pebbles in it as a coating for a wall. —**pebbly** *adj.* [OE]

pecan /ˈpiːkən, pɪˈkæn/ *n.* the pinkish-brown smooth nut of a hickory (*Carya illinoensis*) of the Mississippi region; this tree. [f. Algonquian]

peccadillo /pekəˈdɪləʊ/ *n.* (*pl.* **-oes**) a trivial offence. [f. Sp. (dim. of *pecado* sin f. L *peccare* to sin)]

peccary /ˈpekərɪ/ *n.* a wild pig of the genus *Tayassu* of tropical America. [f. Carib]

peck[1] *v.t./i.* **1.** to strike, nip, or pick up with the beak; to make (a hole) with the beak. **2.** to kiss hastily or perfunctorily. **3.** (*colloq.*) to eat in a nibbling or listless fashion. **4.** to carp *at*. **5.** to mark with short strokes. —*n.* **1.** a stroke, nip, or mark made by a beak. **2.** a hasty or perfunctory kiss. —**pecking order,** a social hierarchy, originally as observed among domestic fowls, where aggressive behaviour towards those of inferior status took the form of pecking. [prob. f. MLG]

peck[2] *n.* **1.** a measure of capacity for dry goods, = 2 gallons or 8 quarts. **2.** a lot. [f. AF]

pecker *n.* (*in comb.*) a bird that pecks. —**keep your pecker up,** (*slang*) stay cheerful. [f. PECK[1]]

peckish *adj.* (*colloq.*) hungry. [f. PECK[1]]

pectin /ˈpektɪn/ *n.* a soluble gelatinous carbohydrate found in ripe fruits etc. and used as a setting agent in jams and jellies. [f. Gk *pēktos* congealed]

pectoral /ˈpektər(ə)l/ *adj.* of or for the breast or chest; worn on the breast. —*n.* a pectoral fin or muscle. [f. OF f. L (*pectus* breast)]

peculate /ˈpekjʊleɪt/ *v.t./i.* to embezzle (money). —**peculation** /-ˈleɪʃ(ə)n/ *n.*, **peculator** *n.* [f. L (rel. to foll.)]

peculiar /pɪˈkjuːlɪə(r)/ *adj.* **1.** strange, eccentric. **2.** belonging exclusively *to*; belonging to the individual. **3.** particular, special. —**peculiarly** *adv.* [f. L (*peculium* private property, as PECUNIARY)]

peculiarity /pɪkjuːlɪˈærɪtɪ/ *n.* **1.** being peculiar. **2.** a characteristic. **3.** an oddity, an eccentricity. [f. prec.]

pecuniary /pɪˈkjuːnɪərɪ/ *adj.* of or consisting of money. [f. L (*pecunia* money f. *pecu* cattle, because in early Rome wealth consisted in cattle and sheep)]

pedagogue /ˈpedəɡɒɡ/ *n.* (*archaic*) a schoolmaster; (*derog.*) one who teaches in a pedantic way. [f. L f. Gk *paidagōgos* (*pais* boy, *agōgos* guide)]

pedagogy /ˈpedəɡɒɡɪ/ *n.* the science of teaching. —**pedagogic** /-ˈɡɒɡɪk/ *adj.*, **pedagogical** /-ˈɡɒɡɪk(ə)l/ *adj.* [f. F f. Gk (as prec.)]

pedal /ˈped(ə)l/ *n.* a lever or key operated by the foot, especially in a bicycle or motor vehicle or some musical instruments (e.g. the organ and the harp). —*v.t./i.* (**-ll-**) **1.** to move or operate by means of pedals. **2.** to ride a bicycle. —/also ˈpiː-/ *adj.* of the foot or feet. [f. L or f. F f. It. f. L (*pes* foot)]

pedalo /ˈpedələʊ/ *n.* (*pl.* **-os**) a small pedal-operated pleasure-boat. [f. prec.]

pedant /ˈped(ə)nt/ *n.* one who lays excessive emphasis on detailed points of learning or procedure. —**pedantic** /pɪˈdæntɪk/ *adj.*, **pedantically** /pɪˈdæntɪkəlɪ/ *adv.*, **pedantry** *n.* [f. F f. It., app. as PEDAGOGUE]

peddle *v.t.* to sell (goods) as a pedlar; to carry about and offer for sale (*lit.* & *fig.*). [f. PEDLAR]

pederast /ˈpedəræst/ *n.* one who commits pederasty. [as foll.]

pederasty *n.* a homosexual act with a boy. [f. Gk (*pais* boy, *erastēs* lover)]

pedestal /ˈpedɪst(ə)l/ *n.* **1.** a base supporting a column, pillar, or statue etc. **2.** each of the two supporting columns of a knee-hole desk etc. —**put on a pedestal,** to admire or respect greatly. [f. F *piédestal* f. It. (*piede* foot, as STALL[1])]

pedestrian /pɪˈdestrɪən/ *n.* a person who is walking, especially in a street. —*adj.* **1.** prosaic, dull. **2.** of walking; going or performed on foot. **3.** for walkers. —**pedestrian crossing,** a part of a road where crossing pedestrians have priority over the traffic. —**pedestrianism** *n.* [f. F or L *pedester* (*pes* foot)]

pedicure /ˈpedɪkjʊə(r)/ *n.* **1.** care or treatment of the feet and toe-nails. **2.** a person who practises this professionally. [f. F (L *pes* foot, *curare* care for)]

pedigree /ˈpedɪɡriː/ *n.* **1.** a genealogical table. **2.** ancestral line (especially a distinguished one) of a person or animal. **3.** derivation. **4.** (*attrib.*) having a recorded line of descent, especially one showing pure breeding. [f. earlier *pedegru* f. AF & OF, = crane's foot, mark denoting succession in pedigrees]

pediment /ˈpedɪmənt/ *n.* a triangular part crowning the front of a building, especially over a portico (ill. TEMPLES). [earlier *periment*, perh. corrupt. of PYRAMID]

pedlar /ˈpedlə(r)/ *n.* **1.** a travelling vendor of small articles that are usually carried in a pack. **2.** a seller of illegal drugs. **3.** a retailer *of* gossip etc. [alt. of obs. *pedder* (*ped* pannier)]

pedology /pɪˈdɒlədʒɪ/ *n.* the science of natural soils. —**pedological** /-dəˈlɒdʒɪk(ə)l/ *adj.*, **pedologist** *n.* [f. Russ. f. Gk *pedon* ground + -LOGY]

pedometer /pɪˈdɒmɪtə(r)/ *n.* an instrument for estimating the distance travelled on foot by recording the number of steps taken. [f. F (as PEDESTRIAN, -METER)]

peduncle /pɪˈdʌŋk(ə)l/ *n.* the stalk of a flower, fruit, or cluster, especially the main stalk bearing a solitary flower or subordinate stalks. —**peduncular** /pɪˈdʌŋkjʊlə(r)/ *adj.* [f. L *pes* foot]

pee *v.i.* (*colloq.*) to urinate. —*n.* (*colloq.*) **1.** urination. **2.** urine. [f. *piss*]

peek *v.i.* to peep, to glance. —*n.* a peep, a glance. [orig. unkn.]

Peel, Sir Robert (1788-1850), British statesman. Peel proved an outstanding Home Secretary (1822-7 and 1828-30), establishing the Metropolitan Police and carrying through a wide-ranging series of legal and penal reforms. As leader of the Conservatives, his Tamworth Manifesto (1834) established his belief in reform where necessary, and although his first term as Prime Minister lasted only a few months (1834-5), his second term (1841-6) proved a model of good government. His repeal of the Corn Laws in 1846, however, split the Conservative Party and forced his resignation. In the last years of his career, he and his remaining followers generally supported the Whig policies of free trade. Peel himself died in 1850 after a riding accident.

peel *n.* the outer skin of certain fruits and vegetables; the outer coating of prawns etc. —*v.t./i.* **1.** to remove the peel from; to take *off* (peel etc.); to be able to be peeled. **2.** to come *off* in strips or layers; to lose skin or bark etc. thus. **3.** (*slang*) to strip off one's clothes before exercise. —**peel off,** to veer away from a formation of which one formed part. —**peeler** *n.* [f. earlier *pill*, perh. f. L *pilare* remove hair from (*pilus* hair)]

peeling *n.* a piece peeled off, especially the skin of a fruit or vegetable. [f. PEEL]

Peelite /ˈpiːlaɪt/ *n.* a Conservative supporting Peel, especially with reference to the repeal of the Corn Laws (1846). [f. PEEL]

peep[1] *v.i.* **1.** to look quickly or surreptitiously; to look through a narrow opening or from a concealed place. **2.** to come briefly or partially into view; to emerge slightly. —*n.* **1.** a brief or surreptitious look. **2.** the first appearance (of dawn, day, etc.). —**peep-hole** a small hole to peep through. **Peeping Tom,** a furtive voyeur (from the name of a Coventry tailor said to have peeped at Lady Godiva when she rode naked through Coventry). **peep-of-day boys,** a Protestant organization in Ireland (1784-95) searching opponents' houses at daybreak for arms. **peep-toe(d)** *adj.* (of shoes) with a small opening at the tip of the toe. [rel. to PEEK, PEER[1]]

peep[2] *n.* a weak high chirping sound like that made by young birds. —*v.i.* to make this sound. [imit.]

peep-show *n.* a device, usually in the form of a box, with a small eyepiece, inside which are arranged the receding elements of a perspective view. Originally a scientific toy for the educated rich, in the latter part of the 17th c. it became a public entertainment, a fairground sideshow, and a children's plaything. Peep-shows have vanished from contemporary life, though some of the children's peep-shows have been preserved.

peer[1] *v.i.* **1.** to look searchingly or with difficulty. **2.** (*archaic*) to appear, to come into view. [var. of earlier *pire* f. LG; perh. partly f. APPEAR]

peer[2] *n.* **1.** one who is equal to another in rank, standing, merit, etc.; a member of the same age-group or social set. **2.** a member of one of the degrees (duke, marquis, earl, viscount, baron) of nobility in the United Kingdom (see below); a noble of any country. —**peer group,** a person's associates who are of the same age or social status as himself. [f. AF f. L *par* equal]

Of the British peers, earls and barons were the earliest to appear; dukes were created from 1337, marquises from the end of the 14th c., and viscounts from 1440. The main privilege of peers nowadays is to sit and vote in the House of Lords; they are debarred from election to the House of Commons.

peerage *n.* **1.** peers, the nobility. **2.** the rank of peer or peeress. **3.** a book containing a list of peers. [f. PEER[2]]

peeress /ˈpɪərɪs/ *n.* a female holder of a peerage; a peer's wife. [f. PEER[2]]

peerless *adj.* unrivalled, superb. [f. PEER[2] + -LESS]

peeve *v.t./i.* (*slang*) **1.** to irritate, to annoy. **2.** to grumble. —*n.* (*slang*) **1.** a cause of annoyance. **2.** a mood of vexation. [back-formation f. PEEVISH]

peeved /piːvd/ *adj.* (*slang*) annoyed, vexed. [f. foll.]

peevish /ˈpiːvɪʃ/ *adj.* irritable, querulous. —**peevishly** *adv.*, **peevishness** *n.* [earlier = silly, mad, spiteful; orig. unkn.]

peewit /ˈpiːwɪt/ *n.* a kind of plover (*Vanellus vanellus*) named from its cry. [imit.]

peg *n.* **1.** a pin or bolt of wood, metal, etc., for holding things together, hanging things on, holding a tent-rope taut, marking a position, or as a stopper. **2.** a clothes-peg. **3.** any of a series of pins or screws for adjusting the tension in a string of a violin etc. **4.** an occasion or opportunity, a pretext. **5.** a drink or measure of spirits. —*v.t./i.* (**-gg-**) **1.** to fix or mark with a peg or pegs. **2.** to maintain (prices or wages) at a certain level. —**off the peg,** (of clothes) ready-made. **peg away,** to work diligently, to be persistent. **peg-board** *n.* a board with holes and pegs for displaying or hanging things on. **peg-leg** *n.* an artificial leg; a person with this. **peg out,** to mark out the boundaries of; (*slang*) to die. **square peg in a round hole,** a person not suited to his surroundings, position, etc. **take a person down a peg (or two),** to humble or humiliate him or her. [prob. f. LDu.]

Pegasus /ˈpeɡəsəs/ **1.** (*Gk myth.*) a winged horse sprung from the blood of Medusa when Perseus cut off her head. He became the favourite of the Muses, and carried the thunderbolt of Zeus. His legend probably goes back to pre-Greek Asia Minor. In ancient sources he has no connection with poets beyond the fact that he created the spring Hippocrene; in Roman times he became a symbol of immortality. **2.** (*Astron.*) a northern constellation, figured as a winged horse, containing three stars of moderate brightness forming with one star of Andromeda a large square (the 'square of Pegasus').

PEI *abbr.* Prince Edward Island.

Peirce /ˈpɪəs/, Charles Sandars (1839-1914), American philosopher, one of the founders of American pragmatism. He held that the aim of philosophical inquiry was to secure stability in beliefs, and that the fixation of beliefs should be based on the method of science. On his conception of scientific method, a theory is to be assessed according to its practical consequences; accordingly connections between beliefs and the actions that result from them were crucial to his view of philosophy. His theory of meaning is suggestive of the verification demanded by the logical positivists, but unlike some other pragmatists he insisted on the difference between true and merely useful beliefs. He also worked extensively in formal logic, arriving independently at some of the conclusions first reached by Frege.

pejorative /pɪˈdʒɒrətɪv, ˈpiːdʒə-/ *adj.* derogatory, disparaging. —*n.* a pejorative word. —**pejoratively** *adv.* [f. F f. L *pejorare* (*pejor* worse)]

peke /piːk/ *n.* (*colloq.*) a Pekingese dog. [abbr.]

Peking /piːˈkɪŋ/ (now transliterated as *Beijing*) the capital of China; pop. (1982) 9,230,687. The city developed from Kublai Khan's capital built in the late 13th c. and was the capital of China, except for brief periods, from 1421. At its centre lies the 'Forbidden City', a walled area containing a number of buildings including the imperial palaces of the emperors of China (1421-1911), entry to which was forbidden to all except the imperial family and servants. [Chinese, = northern capital]

Pekingese /piːkɪˈniːz/ *n.* (*pl.* same) **1.** a native or inhabitant of Peking. **2.** a dog of a short-legged snub-nosed breed with long silky hair, originally brought to Europe from the Summer Palace at Peking in 1860. [f. prec.]

Peking man a fossil hominid (*Homo erectus pekinensis*) first described from remains found in 1926 in caves near the village of Choukoutien near Peking and at that time assigned to a new species (*Sinanthropus pekinensis*). All the fossils found before the Second World War, except for two teeth, were lost during the war (casts of the originals survive), but the excavations that were resumed in 1949 have since produced large quantities of cranial fossils and abundant evidence of the activities of these hominids, including the use of controlled fire and the manufacture and use of stone tools. The cave deposits in which the fossils were found have been dated to c.500,000 years ago for the oldest and c.230,000 years ago for more recent levels (the middle Pleistocene period).

pekoe /ˈpiːkəʊ/ *n.* a superior kind of black tea. [f. Chin. dial. *pek-ho* white down (leaves being picked young with down on them)]

Pelagius /pəˈleɪdʒɪəs/ (died *c.*420) the Latinized name of a British (or perhaps Irish) lay monk and theologian who denied the doctrine of original sin and maintained that the human will is capable of good without the help of divine grace. He went to Rome *c.*400; his doctrines were opposed by St Augustine of Hippo and condemned as heresy.— **Pelagian** *adj.* & *n.*, **Pelagianism** *n.*

pelargonium /pelɑːˈɡəʊnɪəm/ *n.* a plant of the genus *Pelargonium*, with showy flowers. [f. Gk *pelargos* stork; cf. GERANIUM]

Pelasgian /pɪˈlæzɡɪən/ *n.* a member of an ancient people inhabiting the coasts and islands of the eastern Mediterranean, especially the Aegean Sea, before the arrival of Greek-speaking peoples in the Bronze Age. —*adj.* of the Pelasgians. [f. Gk *Pelasgoi*]

pelf *n.* (usu. *derog.* or *joc.*) money, wealth. [rel. to OF *pelfre* spoils (as PILFER)]

pelican /ˈpelɪkən/ *n.* a large water-bird of the genus *Pelicanus*, with a pouch in the bill for storing fish. —**pelican crossing,** a pedestrian crossing with traffic lights operated by pedestrians. [OE & f. OF f. L f. Gk (*pelekus* axe, with ref. to its bill)]

Pelion /ˈpiːlɪən/ a wooded mountain near the coast of SE Thessaly, Greece, the home of the centaurs in Greek mythology. The giants were said to have piled Olympus on Ossa and Ossa on Pelion in their attempt to reach heaven and destroy the gods.

pelisse /peˈliːs/ *n.* **1.** a woman's cloaklike garment with armholes or sleeves, reaching to the ankles. **2.** a fur-lined mantle or cloak, especially as part of a hussar's uniform. [F f. L *pellicia* fur garment (*pellis* skin)]

pellagra /pɪˈlæɡrə, -ˈleɪɡrə/ *n.* a deficiency disease with cracking of the skin, often ending in insanity. [It. (*pelle* skin)]

pellet /ˈpelɪt/ *n.* **1.** a small rounded closely packed mass of a soft substance. **2.** a slug of small shot. [f. OF f. L *pila* ball]

pellicle /ˈpelɪk(ə)l/ *n.* a thin skin; a membrane; a thin layer. [f. F f. L *pellicula* dim. of *pellis* skin]

pell-mell /pelˈmel/ *adv.* & *adj.* in a hurrying disorderly manner; headlong. [f. F f. OF *pesle-mesle* redupl. of *mesle* (*mesler* mix)]

pellucid /pɪˈljuːsɪd, -ˈluː-/ *adj.* **1.** transparent, not distorting images or diffusing the light. **2.** clear in style, expression, or thought. [f. L (as PER-, LUCID)]

pelmet /ˈpelmɪt/ *n.* a valance or pendent border, especially over a window or door to conceal curtain rods. [prob. f. F *palmette* palm-leaf ornament (as PALM¹)]

Peloponnese /ˈpeləpəniːs/ the mountainous southern peninsula of Greece, connected to the mainland by the Isthmus of Corinth.

Peloponnesian War /peləpəˈniːʃ(ə)n/ the war of 431-404 BC fought against Athens by Sparta and her allies, hostile to the Athenian empire. It ended in the total defeat of Athens and the transfer, for a brief period, of the leadership of Greece to Sparta.

Pelops /ˈpiːlɒps/ (*Gk myth.*) son of Tantalus, brother of Niobe, and father of Atreus. (See TANTALUS.)

pelota /pɪˈləʊtə/ *n.* a Basque or Spanish game played in a walled court with a ball and a basket-like structure fitted over the hand. It was originally played with the bare hand, a glove, or a short bat; the basket-glove (*chistera*) was adopted in about 1860. [Sp., = ball, f. L *pila*]

pelt¹ *v.t./i.* **1.** to attack or strike repeatedly with missiles. **2.** (of rain etc.) to beat down fast. **3.** to run fast. —*n.* pelting. —**at full pelt,** as fast as possible. [orig. unkn.]

pelt² *n.* an animal skin, especially with the hair or fur still on it. [f. OF, ult. f. L *pellis* skin]

pelvis /ˈpelvɪs/ *n.* the basin-shaped cavity formed by the bones of the haunch with the sacrum and other vertebrae (ill. BODY 1). —**pelvic** *adj.* [L, = basin]

pemmican /ˈpemɪkən/ *n.* a North American Indian cake of dried and pounded meat mixed with melted fat; beef so treated and flavoured with currants etc. for Arctic and other travellers. [f. Cree *pimecan* (*pime* fat)]

pen¹ *n.* **1.** an instrument for writing in ink (orig. a sharpened quill, now usu. a device with a metal nib). **2.** writing, especially as a profession. —*v.t.* (**-nn-**) to write (a letter etc.). —**pen-friend** *n.* a friend acquired and known mainly or only from correspondence. **pen-name** *n.* a literary pseudonym. **pen-pushing** *n.* (*colloq.*) clerical work. [f. OF f. L *penna* feather]

pen² *n.* a small enclosure for cows, sheep, poultry, etc. —*v.t.* (**-nn-**) to enclose, to shut in or as if in a pen. [OE *penn* (orig. unkn.)]

pen³ *n.* a female swan. [orig. unkn.]

penal /ˈpiːn(ə)l/ *adj.* of or involving punishment, especially by law; (of an offence) punishable. —**penally** *adv.* [f. OF or L (*poena* punishment)]

penalize /ˈpiːnəlaɪz/ *v.t.* **1.** to inflict a penalty on. **2.** to place at a comparative disadvantage. **3.** to make or declare (an action) penal. [f. prec.]

penalty /'penəltı/ *n.* **1.** a punishment for breaking a law, rule, or contract; a fine or loss etc. incurred by this. **2.** a disadvantage imposed by an action or circumstances. **3.** a disadvantage to which a player or team in a sport must submit for breach of a rule. —**penalty area,** the area in front of the goal on a football field in which a foul by the defenders involves the award of a penalty kick. [f. F f. L *penalitas* (as PENAL)]

penance /'penəns/ *n.* **1.** an act of self-mortification as an expression of repentance. **2.** (in the RC and Orthodox Churches) a sacrament involving confession, absolution, and an act of repentance imposed by a priest. —**do penance,** to perform such an act. [f. OF f. L *poenitentia* (as PENITENT)]

Penang /pɪ'næŋ/ a State of Malaysia; capital, Georgetown.

Penates /pɪ'nɑːtiːz/ *n.pl.* gods of the store-cupboard, worshipped in close conjunction with Vesta and the Lares by households in ancient Rome. [L (*penus* store of food)]

pence *pl.* of PENNY.

penchant /'pɑ̃ʃɑ̃/ *n.* an inclination or liking. [F (*pencher* incline)]

pencil /'pens(ə)l/ *n.* **1.** an instrument for drawing or writing, especially of graphite, chalk, etc., enclosed in a cylinder of wood or a metal etc. case with a tapering end. **2.** something used or shaped like this. —*v.t.* (**-ll-**) to write, draw, or mark with a pencil. [f. OF f. L *penicillum* paintbrush (ult. as PENIS)]

pendant /'pend(ə)nt/ *n.* a hanging ornament, especially one attached to a necklace, bracelet, etc. [f. OF f. L *pendēre* hang]

pendent /'pend(ə)nt/ *adj.* **1.** hanging, overhanging. **2.** undecided, pending. —**pendency** *n.* [var. of prec.]

pendentive /pen'dentıv/ *n.* a spherical triangle formed by the intersection of a dome with two adjacent arches springing from supporting columns. [F (as PENDANT)]

Penderecki /pendə'retskı/, Krzysztof (1933–), Polish composer. His music frequently uses unorthodox means for effect, including sounds drawn from extra-musical sources and note-clusters, and his best-known works have religious themes. In 1960 he composed a *Threnody to the Victims of Hiroshima.*

pending *adj.* **1.** waiting to be decided or settled. **2.** about to come into existence. —*prep.* **1.** until. **2.** during. [after F *pendant* (as PENDANT)]

pendulous /'pendjʊləs/ *adj.* hanging down, hanging so as to swing freely. [f. L (*pendēre* hang)]

pendulum /'pendjʊləm/ *n.* **1.** a body suspended so that it can swing freely or oscillate. **2.** an instrument consisting of a rod with a weight or 'bob' at the end, so suspended as to swing to and fro by the action of gravity and used for various mechanical etc. purposes, especially as an essential part of a clock, serving (by the evenness of its vibrations) to regulate and control the movement of the works so as to maintain a constant rate of going and enable it to keep regular time. The principle of the pendulum was discovered by Galileo in the 16th c. (See ill. TIME.) [as prec.]

Penelope /pɪ'neləpı/ (*Gk legend*) wife of Odysseus. When her husband did not return after the fall of Troy she was pressed to marry one of her numerous suitors, but put them off for a while by saying that she would marry only when she had finished the piece of weaving on which she was engaged, and every night unravelling the work she had done during the day.

peneplain /'peniplein/ *n.* a region that has become almost a plain as a result of erosion. [f. L *paene* almost + PLAIN]

penetrable /'penıtrəb(ə)l/ *adj.* that can be penetrated. —**penetrability** /-'bılıtı/ *n.* [as foll.]

penetrate /'penıtreıt/ *v.t./i.* **1.** to make a way into or through. **2.** to enter and permeate. **3.** to see into or through (darkness etc.). **4.** to explore or comprehend mentally. **5.** to be absorbed by the mind. —**penetration** /-'treıʃ(ə)n/ *n.* [f. L *penetrare* (*penitus* inmost)]

penetrating *adj.* **1.** having or showing great insight. **2.** (of a voice or sound) easily heard through or above other sounds, carrying. —**penetratingly** *adv.* [f. prec.]

penguin /'peŋgwın/ *n.* a flightless sea-bird of the family Spheniscidae of the southern hemisphere, with the wings developed into flippers for swimming under water. [orig. = great auk; etym. unkn.]

penicillin /penı'sılın/ *n.* an antibiotic of the group produced naturally on moulds. It was the first antibiotic to be

used therapeutically, during the Second World War. (See FLOREY.) [f. *Penicillium* genus of moulds f. L (as PENCIL)]

peninsular /pɪ'nınsjʊlə/ *n.* a piece of land almost surrounded by water or projecting far into the sea. —**peninsular** *adj.* [f. L *paeninsula* (*paene* almost, *insula* island)]

Peninsular War the campaign waged on the Spanish peninsula between the French and the British, the latter assisted by Spanish and Portuguese allies, from 1808 to 1814 during the Napoleonic Wars. Although an early British expedition (commanded in the later stages by Sir John Moore) was forced to evacuate the peninsula in 1809 after its Spanish allies had been defeated, a second expedition, led by Wellington, finally drove the French back over the Pyrenees in early 1814 after a long and bloody campaign in which the advantage swung from one side to the other several times.

penis /'piːnıs/ *n.* the sexual and (in mammals) urinatory organ of a male animal (ill. BODY 2). [L, orig. = tail]

penitent /'penıt(ə)nt/ *adj.* repentant. —*n.* a repentant sinner; a person doing penance under the direction of a confessor. —**penitence** *n.,* **penitently** *adv.* [f. OF f. L (*paenitēre* repent)]

penitential /penı'tenʃ(ə)l/ *adj.* of penitence or penance. [as prec.]

penitentiary /penı'tenʃərı/ *n.* (*US*) a prison for offenders convicted of serious crimes. —*adj.* **1.** of penance. **2.** of reformatory treatment. [f. L (as PENITENCE)]

penknife *n.* a small folding knife, especially for carrying in the pocket.

penmanship *n.* **1.** skill or style in writing or handwriting. **2.** the process of literary composition.

Penn, William (1644–1718), Quaker and founder of Pennsylvania, eldest son of Admiral Sir William Penn who captured Jamaica from the Dutch (1655). Sent down from Oxford University in 1661 for refusing to conform with the restored Anglicanism, he was imprisoned in the Tower for writing in defence of Quaker practices. Acquitted in 1670, he became increasingly interested in the foundation of a colony in America which would ensure freedom of conscience for Quakers and others; this he achieved when in 1682 Charles II granted him a charter to a large tract of land in North America, for which he drew up a constitution permitting all forms of worship compatible with monotheism and religious liberty.

pennant /'penənt/ *n.* a tapering flag, especially that flown at the mast-head of a vessel in commission; a pennon. [blend of PENDANT and PENNON]

penniless /'penılıs/ *adj.* having no money; poor, destitute. [f. PENNY + -LESS]

Pennines /'penaınz/ *n.pl.* (also **Pennine Chain**) a range of hills in northern England extending northwards from the Peak District in Derbyshire to the Scottish border, described as the 'Backbone of England'.

pennon /'penən/ *n.* **1.** a long narrow flag, triangular or swallow-tailed. **2.** a long pointed streamer of a ship. [f. OF f. L *penna* feather]

Pennsylvania /pensıl'veınıə/ a State of the north-eastern USA, founded by William Penn and named after Admiral Sir William Penn, his father. It was one of the original 13 States of the USA (1787); capital, Harrisburg.

penny *n.* (*pl.* **pennies** for separate coins, **pence** for a sum of money) **1.** a British bronze coin work $\frac{1}{100}$ of a pound, or formerly a coin worth $\frac{1}{12}$ of a shilling (see below); the monetary unit represented by this. **2.** (*US colloq.*) a cent. —**in for a penny, in for a pound,** a thing once begun should be concluded at all costs. **in penny numbers,** in small quantities at a time. **pennies from heaven,** unexpected benefits. **penny black,** the first adhesive postage stamp (1840), printed in black. **the penny drops,** understanding dawns (from the use of a coin to operate slot-machines etc.). **penny farthing,** a former type of bicycle with a large front wheel and a small rear one (see ORDINARY and BICYCLE). **penny-pinching** *adj.* niggardly; (*n.*) niggardliness. **penny post,** post for the conveyance of letters at a standard charge of one penny each instead of at varying rates according to distance, especially that established in the UK in 1840 at the instigation of Sir Rowland Hill, who invented (amongst other things) an adhesive stamp. **penny whistle,** one with six holes for the different notes. **penny wise (and pound foolish),** careful or thrifty in small matters (but wasteful in large ones). **a pretty penny,** a large sum of money. **two a penny,** commonly found and of little value. [OE] The coining of silver pennies for general circulation in

Britain ceased with the reign of Charles II; a small number have since been regularly coined as Maundy money. Copper pennies began to be coined in 1797, and the term 'copper' for 'penny' has remained in use long after this ceased to be the material used.

pennyweight *n.* a unit of weight equal to 24 grains, $\frac{1}{20}$ ounce troy.

pennyroyal /penɪˈrɔɪəl/ *n.* a creeping species of mint (*Pulegium vulgare*). [f. AF *puliol real* royal thyme]

pennywort *n.* a plant with rounded leaves, **wall pennywort** (*Umbilicus rupestris*) or **marsh pennywort** (*Hydrocotyle vulgaris*).

pennyworth *n.* as much as can be bought for a penny.

penology /piːˈnɒlədʒɪ/ *n.* the study of punishment and prison management. —**penological** /-ˈlɒdʒɪk(ə)l/ *adj.*, **penologist** *n.* [f. L *poena* penalty + -LOGY]

pension[1] /ˈpenʃ(ə)n/ *n.* a periodic payment made by the State to a person above a specified age or to a widowed or disabled person, or by an employer to a retired employee. —*v.t.* to grant a pension to. —**pension off,** to dismiss with a pension; to cease to employ (a person) or use (a thing). [f. OF f. L, = payment (*pendere* pay)]

pension[2] /ˈpɑ̃sɪ̃/ *n.* a continental boarding-house. [F, = prec.]

pensionable *adj.* entitled or entitling one to a pension. [f. PENSION[1]]

pensionary *adj.* of a pension. —*n.* a recipient of a pension. [f. L (as PENSION[1])]

pensioner *n.* a recipient of a retirement or other pension. [f. PENSION[1]]

pensive /ˈpensɪv/ *adj.* deep in thought. —**pensively** *adv.*, **pensiveness** *n.* [f. OF (*penser* think f. L *pensare*)]

penstock /ˈpenstɒk/ *n.* a sluice, a flood-gate (ill. ELECTRICAL POWER). [f. PEN[2] in sense 'mill-dam' + STOCK]

pent *adj.* shut in a confined space. [p.p. of *pend* var. of PEN[2]]

penta- *in comb.* five. [Gk (*pente* five)]

pentacle /ˈpentək(ə)l/ *n.* a figure used as a symbol, especially in magic, e.g. a pentagram. [f. L *pentaculum* (as PENTA-)]

Pentagon the headquarters of the US Department of Defense, near Washington, DC. Built in 1941-3 in the form of five concentric pentagons, it covers 13.8 hectares (34 acres) and is one of the world's largest office buildings. The name is used allusively for the US military leadership. [= foll.]

pentagon /ˈpentəgən/ *n.* a plane figure with five sides and angles (ill. SHAPES). —**pentagonal** /-ˈtægən(ə)l/ *adj.* [f. F or L f. Gk (PENTA-, -*gōnos* -angled)]

pentagram /ˈpentəgræm/ *n.* a five-pointed star (ill. SHAPES). [f. Gk (as PENTA-, -GRAM)]

pentameter /penˈtæmɪtə(r)/ *n.* a line of five metrical feet. [L f. Gk (as PENTA-, -METER)]

Pentateuch /ˈpentətjuːk/ *n.* the first five books of the Old Testament, traditionally ascribed to Moses but now held by scholars to have been compiled from documents dating from 9th to 5th c. BC incorporating material from oral traditions of varying dates. [f. L f. Gk *pente* five, *teuchos* implement, book]

pentathlon /penˈtæθlən/ *n.* an athletic contest in which each competitor takes part in the five different events which it comprises. It was a feature of the Olympic Games in ancient Greece. The modern men's pentathlon consists of fencing, shooting, swimming, riding, and cross-country running; the women's pentathlon consists of sprinting, hurdling, long jump, high jump, and putting the shot. [f. Gk *pente* five, *athlon* contest]

pentatonic /pentəˈtɒnɪk/ *adj.* of a five-note musical scale. [f. PENTA- + TONE]

Pentecost /ˈpentɪkɒst/ *n.* 1. the Jewish harvest festival on the fiftieth day after the second day of Passover. 2. Whit Sunday. —**pentecostal** /-ˈkɒst(ə)l/ *adj.* [OE & OF f. L f. Gk, = fiftieth day]

Pentecostal Churches a religious movement that began in the early 20th c. among believers who seek the same experience and gifts as those recorded in Acts 2:1-4 at Pentecost. Emphasis is on the corporate element in worship (often involving great spontaneity) and speaking in 'tongues' (often generally unintelligible utterances, arising from the intensity of emotion and religious experience), with prophecy, healing, and exorcism. Manifestations of this nature, occurring in revivalist meetings at Los Angeles in 1906, were the first to attract world-wide attention.

Penthesilea /penθesɪˈliːə/ (*Gk legend*) queen of the Amazons, who came to the help of Troy after the death of Hector and was slain by Achilles.

penthouse /ˈpenthaʊs/ *n.* 1. a separate apartment or flat etc. on the roof of a tall building. 2. a sloping roof, especially as a subsidiary structure attached to the wall of a main building. [f. OF *apentis* f. L *appendicium* (as APPEND)]

penult /pɪˈnʌlt, ˈpiː-/ *adj.* & *n.* (esp. of a syllable) penultimate. [abbr. of foll.]

penultimate /pɪˈnʌltɪmət/ *adj.* & *n.* last but one. [f. L *paenultimus* (*paene* almost, as ULTIMATE)]

penumbra /pɪˈnʌmbrə/ *n.* (*pl.* -**ae** /-iː/ or -**as**) a partly shaded region round the shadow of an opaque body (ill. LIGHT), especially of the moon or earth in eclipse; partial shadow. —**penumbral** *adj.* [f. L *paene* almost + UMBRA]

penurious /pɪˈnjʊərɪəs/ *adj.* 1. poverty-stricken. 2. scanty. 3. grudging, stingy. [f. L (as foll.)]

penury /ˈpenjʊrɪ/ *n.* 1. extreme poverty. 2. lack, scarcity. [f. L *penuria*]

peony /ˈpiːənɪ/ *n.* a garden plant of the genus *Paeonia* with large round red, pink, or white flowers. [OE f. L f. Gk (*Paean* physician of the gods)]

people /ˈpiːp(ə)l/ *n.* 1. human beings in general. 2. the persons belonging to a place or forming a group or social class; the subjects or citizens of a State. 3. ordinary persons, those not having high rank or office etc. 4. a person's parents or other relatives. —*v.t.* to fill with people, to populate. [f. AF f. L *populus*]

pep *n.* (*slang*) vigour, spirit. —*v.t.* (-**pp**-) (*slang*) to fill with vigour, to enliven. —**pep pill,** a pill containing a stimulant drug. **pep talk,** a talk urging the listener to greater effort or courage. —**peppy** *adj.* [abbr. of foll.]

pepper *n.* 1. a pungent aromatic condiment obtained from the dried berries of certain plants, especially *Piper nigrum*. 2. a capsicum plant grown as a vegetable; its fruit. —*v.t.* 1. to sprinkle with or as with pepper. 2. to pelt with missiles. —**pepper-and-salt** *adj.* (of cloth) woven so as to show small dots of dark and light colour intermingled. **pepper-mill** *n.* a mill for grinding peppercorns by hand. **pepper-pot** *n.* a small container with a perforated lid for sprinkling pepper. [OE f. L *piper* f. Gk f. Skr.]

peppercorn *n.* a dried pepper-berry. —**peppercorn rent,** a nominal or very low rent.

peppermint *n.* 1. a kind of mint (*Mentha × piperita*) grown for its strong fragrant oil. 2. a lozenge or sweet flavoured with this. 3. the oil itself.

peppery *adj.* 1. of, like, or abounding in pepper; hot and spicy. 2 (of persons) irascible; (of remarks etc.) pungent. [f. PEPPER]

pepsin /ˈpepsɪn/ *n.* an enzyme contained in gastric juice. [G, f. Gk *pepsis* digestion (as foll.)]

peptic /ˈpeptɪk/ *adj.* digestive. —**peptic ulcer,** an ulcer in the stomach or duodenum. —**peptically** *adv.* [f. Gk (*peptos* cooked)]

peptide /ˈpeptaɪd/ *n.* a compound consisting of a chain of amino acids, chemically linked. Some are important as hormones, others as antibiotics. Polypeptides are the constituents of proteins. [f. G (as prec.)]

Pepys /piːps/, Samuel (1633-1703), English diarist. He became secretary of the Admiralty in 1672 but was deprived of his post in 1679 and committed to the Tower for his alleged complicity in the Popish Plot, being reappointed in 1684. Pepys is remembered for his *Diary* which remains an important document of contemporary life and manners, seen through the author's own experiences as Admiralty official and observer of court life, written with engaging sincerity and humanity. The *Diary* remained in cipher until 1825 when it was deciphered by John Smith.

per *prep.* 1. for each. 2. through, by, by means of. —**as per,** in accordance with. **as per usual,** (*colloq.*) as usual. [L, = through]

per- *prefix.* 1. through or all over (*pervade*). 2. completely, very (*perturb*). 3. to destruction (*perdition*); to the bad (*pervert*). [f. L (as prec.)]

peradventure /pərədˈventʃə(r)/ (*archaic* or *joc.*) *adv.* perhaps; by chance. —*n.* uncertainty, chance, conjecture; doubt. [f. OF, = by chance (as PER, ADVENTURE)]

perambulate /pəˈræmbjʊleɪt/ *v.t./i.* to walk through, over, or about (a place); to walk about or from place to place. —**perambulation** /-ˈleɪʃ(ə)n/ *n.* [f. L (PER-, *ambulare* walk)]

perambulator /pəˈræmbjʊleɪtə(r)/ *n.* a pram. [f. prec.]

per annum /pɜːr ˈænəm/ *adv.* for each year. [L]

percale /pə'keɪl/ n. a closely-woven cotton fabric. [F]

per caput /pɜː 'kæpʊt/ adv. & adj. (also **per capita** /pɜː 'kæpɪtə/) for each person. [L, = by head(s)]

perceive /pə'siːv/ v.t. to become aware of with the mind or through one of the senses; to see or notice. [f. OF f. L *percipere* orig. = seize (PER-, *capere* take)]

per cent /pə'sent/ adv. in every hundred. —n. a percentage; one part in every hundred. [f. PER + *cent* f. L *centum* hundred]

percentage /pə'sentɪdʒ/ n. a rate or proportion per cent; a proportion. [f. prec.]

perceptible /pə'septɪb(ə)l/ adj. that can be perceived. —**perceptibility** /-'bɪlɪti/ n., **perceptibly** adv. [OF or f. L (as PERCEIVE)]

perception /pə'sepʃ(ə)n/ n. perceiving; the ability to perceive. [f. L (as PERCEIVE)]

perceptive /pə'septɪv/ adj. **1.** of perception. **2.** having or showing insight and sensitive understanding. —**perceptively** adv., **perceptiveness** n., **perceptivity** /-'tɪvɪti/ n. [f. L (as PERCEIVE)]

perceptual /pə'septjʊəl/ adj. of or involving perception. [as prec.]

perch[1] n. **1.** a branch or bar etc. serving as a bird's resting-place. **2.** an elevated position. **3.** a former measure of length (esp. for land) equal to 5½ yards (see GUNTER). —v.t./i. to rest or place on or as if on a perch. —**percher** n. [f. OF f. L *pertica* pole]

perch[2] n. (pl. same) a spiny-finned freshwater food-fish of the genus *Perca*. [f. OF f. L *perca* f. Gk]

perchance /pə'tʃɑːns/ adv. (archaic) **1.** by chance. **2.** possibly, maybe. [f. AF *par chance* (*par* by, CHANCE)]

percipient /pə'sɪpɪənt/ adj. perceiving, perceptive. —**percipience** n. [f. L (as PERCEIVE)]

percolate /'pɜːkəleɪt/ v.t./i. **1.** to filter or cause to filter, especially through small holes. **2.** to permeate. **3.** to prepare (coffee) in a percolator. —**percolation** /-'leɪʃ(ə)n/ n. [f. L *percolare* (PER-, *colum* strainer)]

percolator /'pɜːkəleɪtə(r)/ n. a pot for making and serving coffee, in which boiling water is made to rise up a central tube and down through a perforated drum of ground coffee. [f. prec.]

percussion /pə'kʌʃ(ə)n/ n. **1.** the forcible striking of one object against another. **2.** the group of percussion instruments in an orchestra (see below). **3.** a gentle tapping of the body in medical diagnosis. —**percussion cap**, a small metal or paper device containing explosive powder and exploded by the fall of a hammer, used as a detonator or in a toy pistol. **percussion instrument**, a musical instrument played by striking a resonating surface with a stick, the hand, a clapper, etc. —**percussive** adj. [F or f. L (*percutere* strike)]

In an orchestra the standard percussion instruments are the drums and cymbals, but there is a long list of possible extras which includes the glockenspiel, xylophone, triangle, gongs and bells of various kinds, castanets, rattles, and tambourine, not to mention thunder and wind machines and such 'instruments' as a typewriter or a gun. Percussion instruments fall into two categories: those tunable to a definite pitch, and those of indefinite pitch, used for their quality of sound rather than to provide any specific note or notes.

Percy /'pɜːsɪ/, Sir Henry, 'Hotspur' (1364-1403), English soldier. Son of the First Earl of Northumberland, he was one of the most eminent English soldiers of the day and was eventually killed at the battle of Shrewsbury during his father's revolt against Henry IV.

perdition /pə'dɪʃ(ə)n/ n. damnation; eternal death. [f. OF or L (*perdere* destroy)]

peregrine /'perɪɡrɪn/ n. a kind of falcon (*Falco peregrinus*) used for hawking. [f. L *peregrinus* foreign (*peregre* abroad)]

peremptory /pə'remptərɪ, 'perɪm-/ adj. imperious, insisting on obedience. —**peremptorily** adv., **peremptoriness** n. [f. AF f. L (*perimere* destroy, put an end to)]

perennial /pə'renɪəl/ adj. lasting through the year; lasting long or for ever; (of a plant) living for several years. —n. a perennial plant. —**perennially** adv. [f. L *perennis* (PER-, *annus* year)]

perfect /'pɜːfɪkt/ adj. **1.** complete and with all necessary qualities; faultless, not deficient. **2.** exact, precise. **3.** (colloq.) excellent, most satisfactory. **4.** entire, unqualified. **5.** (Gram., of a tense) denoting a completed event or action viewed in relation to the present (e.g. *he has gone*). —n. (Gram.) the perfect tense. —/pə'fekt/ v.t. to make perfect

or complete. —**perfect interval**, (Mus.) an interval between the tonic and the fourth or fifth or octave in a major or minor scale. —**perfectly** adv. [f. OF f. L (*perficere* complete)]

perfectible /pə'fektɪb(ə)l/ adj. that can be perfected. —**perfectibility** /-'bɪlɪti/ n. [f. prec.]

perfection /pə'fekʃ(ə)n/ n. **1.** making or being perfect; faultlessness. **2.** a perfect person or thing. —**to perfection**, perfectly. [f. OF f. L (as PERFECT)]

perfectionist n. one who is satisfied with nothing less than what he thinks is perfect. —**perfectionism** n. [f. prec.]

perfidy /'pɜːfɪdɪ/ n. a breach of faith, treachery. —**perfidious** /pə'fɪdɪəs/ adj., **perfidiously** adv. [f. L *perfidia* (*perfidus* treacherous)]

perfoliate /pə'fəʊlɪət/ adj. having the stalk apparently passing through the leaf (ill. PLANTS).

perforate /'pɜːfəreɪt/ v.t. to make a hole or holes through, to pierce; to make a row of small holes in (paper etc.) so that part may be torn off easily. —**perforation** /-'reɪʃ(ə)n/ n. [f. L *perforare* (PER-, *forare* bore through)]

perforce /pə'fɔːs/ adv. unavoidably, necessarily. [f. OF *par force* (*par* by, FORCE)]

perform /pə'fɔːm/ v.t./i. **1.** to carry into effect, to be the agent of, to do. **2.** to go through (some process), to execute (a function, piece of music, etc.). **3.** to act in a play etc., to play an instrument or sing etc. before an audience. **4.** to function. —**performing arts**, those (such as drama) that require public performance. —**performer** n. [f. AF f. OF *parfournir* (as PER-, FURNISH)]

performance /pə'fɔːməns/ n. **1.** the process or manner of performing. **2.** a notable or (colloq.) a ridiculous action. **3.** the performing of or in a play etc. [f. prec.]

perfume /'pɜːfjuːm/ n. **1.** a sweet smell. **2.** a fragrant liquid for giving a pleasant smell, especially to the body. —v.t. to give a sweet smell to; to apply perfume to. [f. F *parfumer* f. obs. It. (as PER-, FUME); orig. of smoke from burning substance]

perfumery /pə'fjuːmərɪ/ n. perfumes; the making of selling of these. [f. prec.]

perfunctory /pə'fʌŋktərɪ/ adj. done superficially or without much care or interest, as a duty or routine; (of a person) acting thus. —**perfunctorily** adv., **perfunctoriness** n. [f. L (PER-, *fungi* perform)]

Pergamum /'pɜːɡəməm/ (now Bergama in Turkey) the dynastic capital of the Attalid kings (3rd-2nd c. BC), situated on a rocky hill near the western coast of Asia Minor, one of the greatest and most beautiful of the Hellenistic cities. With its palace, famous school of sculpture, library second only to that of Alexandria, and kings who were philosophers at least in their spare time, Pergamum was a cultural even more than a political and commercial centre. —**Pergamene** /-miːn/ adj. & n.

pergola /'pɜːɡələ/ n. an arbour or covered walk formed of growing plants trained over trellis-work. [It. f. L *pergula* projecting roof]

perhaps /pə'hæps, præps/ adv. it may be, possibly. [f. PER + HAP]

peri /'pɪərɪ/ (Persian myth.) a fairy, a good (orig. evil) genius; a beautiful or graceful being. [f. Pers.]

peri- /perɪ-/ prefix round, about. [f. Gk]

perianth /'perɪænθ/ n. the outer part of a flower. [f. F (PERI-, Gk *anthos* flower)]

pericardium /perɪ'kɑːdɪəm/ n. (pl. -ia) the membranous sac enclosing the heart. [f. Gk (PERI-, *kardia* heart)]

pericarp /'perɪkɑːp/ n. a vessel containing the seed, with the pulp if present, formed from the wall of the ripened ovary (ill. FLOWERS). [f. F (PERI-, Gk *karpos* fruit, shell)]

Pericles /'perɪkliːz/ (c.495-429 BC) Athenian statesman and general. The most influential politician in mid-5th c. Athens, he promoted an imperialist policy and masterminded Athenian strategy in the Peloponnesian War. He was building commissioner for the Parthenon and other buildings, a great orator, and a friend of leading philosophers, writers, and artists, including Anaxagoras, Sophocles, and Phidias. His name is inseparably attached to the greatest age of Athens.

perigee /'perɪdʒiː/ n. the point in the orbit of the moon, a planet, or an artificial satellite when it is nearest to the earth. [f. F f. Gk (PERI-, *gē* earth)]

Périgord /perɪ'ɡɔːr/ a district (a former province) in SW France.

perihelion /perɪˈhiːlɪən/ n. (pl. -ia) the point of closest approach to the sun by an orbiting planet or satellite. Such a position can generally be calculated by the laws of classical mechanics, but the systematic change in the perihelion position of Mercury could be explained only by Einstein's general theory of relativity, for which it constituted an important test. [f. PERI- + Gk *hēlios* sun]

peril /ˈperɪl/ n. serious danger. —**perilous** adj., **perilously** adv. [f. OF f. L *peric(u)lum*]

perimeter /pəˈrɪmɪtə(r)/ n. 1. the circumference or outline of a closed figure; the length of this. 2. the outer boundary of an enclosed area. [f. F or L f. Gk (PERI-, *metron* measure)]

perineum /perɪˈniːəm/ n. the region of the body between the anus and the scrotum or vulva. —**perineal** adj. [f. L f. Gk *perinaion*]

period /ˈpɪərɪəd/ n. 1. a length or portion of time; a distinct portion of history, life, etc.; a time forming part of a geological era. 2. the interval between recurrences of an astronomical or other phenomenon. 3. the time allocated for a lesson in school. 4. an occurrence of menstruation; the time of this. 5. a complete sentence, especially one consisting of several clauses. 6. a full stop in punctuation. —adj. belonging to or characteristic of some past period. [f. OF f. L f. Gk *periodos* (PERI-, *hodos* way)]

periodic /pɪərɪˈɒdɪk/ adj. appearing or occurring at intervals. —**periodic table**, a tabular arrangement of the elements in order of atomic numbers, which also brings together those whose atoms have a similar pattern of orbiting electrons. Chemically related elements consequently tend to appear in the same column or row of the table. The earliest form of the table was devised by Mendeleev. [as prec.]

periodical /pɪərɪˈɒdɪk(ə)l/ adj. periodic. —n. a magazine etc. published at regular intervals. —**periodically** adv. [f. prec.]

periodicity /pɪərɪəˈdɪsɪtɪ/ n. being periodic; the tendency to recur at intervals. [f. PERIODIC]

periodontal /perɪəˈdɒnt(ə)l/ adj. of the tissues surrounding the teeth. [f. PERI- + Gk *odous odontos* tooth]

peripatetic /perɪpəˈtetɪk/ adj. going from place to place, itinerant; **Peripatetic**, Aristotelian (so called from Aristotle's custom of walking in the Lyceum while teaching). —n. a traveller, an itinerant; **Peripatetic**, an Aristotelian. [f. OF or L f. Gk (PERI-, *pateō* walk)]

peripheral /pəˈrɪfər(ə)l/ adj. 1. of minor but not central importance. 2. of a periphery. —n. (in a computer system) any input, output, or storage device that can be controlled by the central processing unit. [f. foll.]

periphery /pəˈrɪfərɪ/ n. the boundary of a surface, area, or subject etc.; the region just outside or inside this. [f. L f. Gk, = circumference (PERI-, *pherō* bear)]

periphrasis /pəˈrɪfrəsɪs/ n. (pl. -ases /-əsiːz/) a roundabout phrase or way of speaking, a circumlocution. —**periphrastic** /perɪˈfræstɪk/ adj. [L f. Gk (PERI-, *phrazō* declare)]

periscope /ˈperɪskəʊp/ n. an apparatus with a tube and mirrors by which an observer in a submerged submarine, a trench, the rear of a crowd, etc., can see things otherwise out of sight. —**periscopic** /-ˈskɒpɪk/ adj. [f. PERI- + -SCOPE]

perish /ˈperɪʃ/ v.t./i. 1. to be destroyed, to suffer death or ruin. 2. to lose or cause (a fabric etc.) to lose its normal qualities, to rot. 3. to distress or wither by cold or exposure; to suffer thus. [f. OF f. L *perire*]

perishable adj. liable to perish, subject to speedy decay. —n. (usu. in pl.) perishable goods (esp. foods). [f. prec.]

perisher n. (slang) an annoying person, especially a child. [f. PERISH]

perishing adj. 1. (colloq.) intensely cold. 2. (colloq.) confounded. [as prec.]

peristyle /ˈperɪstaɪl/ n. a row of columns surrounding a temple, court, cloister, etc.; the space surrounded by these (ill. TEMPLES). [f. F f. L f. Gk (PERI-, *stulon* pillar)]

peritoneum /perɪtəˈnɪəm/ n. (pl. -ums) the membrane lining the cavity of the abdomen. —**peritoneal** adj. [L f. Gk *-tonos* stretched)]

peritonitis /perɪtəˈnaɪtɪs/ n. inflammation of the peritoneum. [f. prec. + -ITIS]

periwig /ˈperɪwɪg/ n. (esp. hist.) a wig (ill. DRESS). [alt. of PERUKE]

periwinkle[1] /ˈperɪwɪŋk(ə)l/ n. an evergreen trailing plant of the genus *Vinca*, with blue or white flowers. [f. AF *pervenke* f. L *pervinca*, assim. to foll.]

periwinkle[2] /ˈperɪwɪŋk(ə)l/ n. a winkle. [orig. unkn.]

perjure /ˈpɜːdʒə(r)/ v.refl. to cause *oneself* to be guilty of perjury; (in *p.p.*) guilty of or involving perjury. [f. OF f. L *perjurare* (PER-, *jurare* swear)]

perjury /ˈpɜːdʒərɪ/ n. wilful utterance of a false statement while on oath. —**perjurious** /-ˈdʒʊərɪəs/ adj. [f. AF f. L *perjurium* (as prec.)]

perk[1] v.t./i. (colloq., usu. with *up*) 1. to regain or cause to regain courage, confidence, or liveliness. 2. to smarten. 3. to raise (the head etc.) briskly. [perh. f. var. of PERCH[1]]

perk[2] n. (colloq.) a perquisite. [abbr.]

Perkin /ˈpɜːkɪn/, Sir William Henry (1838-1907), English chemist who prepared the first synthetic dyestuff, mauve, made from aniline. The discovery was made almost by accident, at the age of 18, when he was trying to synthesize the important drug quinine.

perky adj. lively and cheerful. —**perkily** adv., **perkiness** n. [f. PERK[1]]

perm[1] n. (colloq.) a permanent wave. —v.t. (colloq.) to give a permanent wave to. [abbr.]

perm[2] n. (colloq.) a permutation. —v.t. (colloq.) to make a permutation of. [abbr.]

permafrost /ˈpɜːməfrɒst/ n. permanently frozen subsoil, especially in polar regions. [f. PERMANENT + FROST]

permanency /ˈpɜːmənənsɪ/ n. a permanent thing or arrangement. [f. foll.]

permanent /ˈpɜːmənənt/ adj. lasting or intended to last or function indefinitely. —**permanent wave**, a long-lasting artificial wave in the hair. **permanent way**, the finished road-bed of a railway. —**permanence** n., **permanently** adv. [f. OF or L (PER-, *manēre* remain)]

permeable /ˈpɜːmɪəb(ə)l/ adj. admitting the passage of liquid etc. —**permeability** /-ˈbɪlɪtɪ/ n. [f. foll.]

permeate /ˈpɜːmɪeɪt/ v.t./i. to pass, flow, or spread into every part of; to diffuse itself. —**permeation** /-ˈeɪʃ(ə)n/ n. [f. L *permeare* (PER-, *meare* pass)]

Permian /ˈpɜːmɪən/ adj. of the final period of the Palaeozoic era, following the Carboniferous and preceding the Triassic, lasting from about 286 to 248 million years ago. The climate was hot and dry in many parts of the world during this period, which also saw the extinction of many marine animals, including trilobites, and the proliferation of reptiles. —n. this period. [f. *Perm* in Russia]

permissible /pəˈmɪsɪb(ə)l/ adj. that can be permitted. —**permissibility** /-ˈbɪlɪtɪ/ n., **permissibly** adv. [f. F or L (as PERMIT)]

permission /pəˈmɪʃ(ə)n/ n. consent or authorization to do something. [f. OF or L (as PERMIT)]

permissive /pəˈmɪsɪv/ adj. 1. tolerant, allowing much freedom especially in social conduct and sexual matters. 2. giving permission. —**permissively** adv., **permissiveness** n. [f. OF or L (as foll.)]

permit /pəˈmɪt/ v.t./i. (-tt-) 1. to give permission or consent to; to authorize, to allow. 2. to give an opportunity; to make possible; to admit *of* (alteration, delay, etc.). —/ˈpɜːmɪt/ n. a written order giving permission to act, especially for entry into a place; permission. [f. L *permittere* (PER-, *mittere* let go, send)]

permittivity /pɜːmɪˈtɪvɪtɪ/ n. a quantity measuring a substance's ability to store energy in an electric field. [f. prec.]

permutation /pɜːmjuːˈteɪʃ(ə)n/ n. 1. variation of the order of a set of things. 2. any one such arrangement. 3. a combination or selection of a specified number of items from a larger group (especially of matches in a football pool). [f. OF or L (PER-, *mutare* change)]

pernicious /pəˈnɪʃəs/ adj. having a very harmful effect. —**pernicious anaemia**, a severe (formerly often fatal) form of anaemia. [f. L (*pernicies* ruin)]

pernickety /pəˈnɪkɪtɪ/ adj. (colloq.) fastidious; over-precise. [orig. Sc.; etym. unkn.]

Peron /peəˈrɒn/, Juan Domingo (1895-1974), Argentinian statesman. A career army officer, Peron was a member of the military junta which seized power in Argentina in 1943. He was elected President in 1946 and re-elected in 1951, deriving much of his own popularity from the charismatic appeal of his wife Eva. Following her death in 1952, his popularity declined sharply, particularly after he came into conflict with the Catholic Church, and in 1955 he was forced into exile. Following a resurgence by the Peronist party in the early 1970s, Peron returned to power in October 1973, only to die less than a year later. His second wife succeeded him as leader but was overthrown by the army in March 1976. —**Peronist** adj. & n.

peroration /perə'reɪʃ(ə)n/ *n.* a lengthy speech; the concluding part of a speech. [f. L (PER-, *orare* speak)]

peroxide /pə'rɒksaɪd/ *n.* a compound of oxygen with another element containing the maximum proportion of oxygen; (in full **hydrogen peroxide**) a colourless liquid used in a water solution, especially to bleach the hair. —*v.t.* to bleach (hair) with peroxide. [f. PER- + OXIDE]

perpendicular /pɜːpən'dɪkjʊlə(r)/ *adj.* **1.** at right angles to a given line, plane, or surface. **2.** upright, at right angles to the horizontal. **3.** (of a cliff etc.) having a vertical face; very steep. **4. Perpendicular,** of the style of English Gothic architecture (14th–15th c.) characterized by vertical tracery in large windows with regular horizontal divisions resulting in rows of panels (ill. CHURCH). —*n.* a perpendicular line; a perpendicular position or direction. —**perpendicularity** /-'lærɪtɪ/ *n.*, **perpendicularly** *adv.* [f. L (*perpendiculum* plumb-line)]

perpetrate /'pɜːpɪtreɪt/ *v.t.* to commit or perform (a blunder, crime, hoax, thing regarded as outrageous). —**perpetration** /-'treɪʃ(ə)n/ *n.*, **perpetrator** *n.* [f. L (PER-, *patrare* effect)]

perpetual /pə'petjʊəl/ *adj.* lasting for ever or indefinitely; unceasing; continuous; (*colloq.*) frequent, much repeated. —**perpetual motion,** the motion of a hypothetical machine running for ever unless subject to external forces or wear. —**perpetually** *adv.* [f. OF f. L (*perpetuus* f. *perpes* continuous)]

perpetuate /pə'petjʊeɪt/ *v.t.* to make perpetual, to cause to be always remembered. —**perpetuation** /-'eɪʃ(ə)n/ *n.*, **perpetuator** *n.* [f. L (as prec.)]

perpetuity /pɜːpɪ'tjuːɪtɪ/ *n.* **1.** the state or quality of being perpetual. **2.** a perpetual possession, or position, or annuity. —**in perpetuity,** for ever. [f. OF f. L (as PERPETUAL)]

perplex /pə'pleks/ *v.t.* **1.** to bewilder, to puzzle greatly. **2.** to complicate or confuse (a matter). [f. OF or L *perplexus* involved (PER-, *plectere* plait)]

perplexedly /pə'pleksɪdlɪ/ *adv.* in a perplexed manner. [f. prec.]

perplexity /pə'pleksɪtɪ/ *n.* **1.** perplexing, being perplexed. **2.** a thing that perplexes. [as PERPLEX]

per pro. *abbr.* by proxy, through an agent. [f. L *per procurationem*]

perquisite /'pɜːkwɪzɪt/ *n.* a profit, allowance, or privilege etc. given or looked upon as one's right in addition to wages or salary etc. [f. L *perquirere* search diligently for (PER-, *quaerere* seek)]

Perrault /'perəʊ/, Charles (1628-1703), French poet and critic, a member of the *Académie française* from 1671. He is remembered for his fairy tales, translated into English as 'Mother Goose Tales' by Robert Samber in 1729, containing among others, 'Sleeping Beauty', 'Little Red Riding Hood', 'Puss in Boots', and 'Cinderella'.

Perry /'perɪ/, Frederick John (1909-), English lawn tennis and table tennis player, a brilliant match player who won a number of titles. His record of winning the men's singles championship at Wimbledon in three successive years (1934-6) was unequalled until the success of Bjorn Borg (1976-80).

perry /'perɪ/ *n.* a drink made from fermented pear-juice. [f. OF *peré* f. L *pirum* pear]

per se /pɜː 'seɪ/ by or in itself, intrinsically. [L]

persecute /'pɜːsɪkjuːt/ *v.t.* to subject to constant hostility and ill-treatment, especially because of religious or political beliefs; to harass. —**persecution** /-'kjuːʃ(ə)n/ *n.*, **persecutor** *n.* [f. OF f. L (*persequi* pursue)]

Persephone /pə'sefənɪ/ (*Gk myth.*) a pre-Greek goddess later identified with the virgin daughter (Kore) of the corn-goddess Demeter, with whom she was often worshipped. She was carried off by Pluto and made queen of the underworld. Demeter, vainly seeking her, refused to let the earth bring forth its fruits until her daughter was restored to her, but Persephone had eaten some pomegranate-seeds in the other world and so could not return entirely but was obliged to spend some part of every year underground. Her story symbolizes the life and growth of corn.

Persepolis /pə'sepɒlɪs/ an ancient Persian city, ceremonial capital of the Achaemenids, founded by Darius I and almost completed by his successors, Xerxes and Artaxerxes, before its destruction and looting by Alexander the Great in 330 BC. Impressive remains of functional and ceremonial buildings adorned by sculptured friezes and cuneiform inscriptions in Old Persian were rediscovered in the 16th c. and first excavated in the 1930s.

Perseus /'pɜːsjəs/ **1.** (*Gk myth.*) son of Zeus and Danae. He cut off the head of the gorgon Medusa and gave it to Athene, rescued and married Andromeda, and became king of Tiryns in Greece. **2.** (*Astron.*) a northern constellation between Cassiopeia and Taurus, including part of the Milky Way.

persevere /pɜːsɪ'vɪə(r)/ *v.i.* to continue steadfastly, especially in something that is difficult or tedious. —**perseverance** *n.*, **persevering** *adj.* & *n.* [f. OF f. L *perseverare* (PER-, *severus* strict)]

Persia /'pɜːʃə/ the ancient and now the alternative name of Iran. It was the site of an ancient kingdom that in the 6th c. BC formed an empire by Cyrus' conquests of Media, Lydia, and Babylonia; at its greatest the empire included all western Asia, Egypt, and parts of eastern Europe, until overthrown by Alexander the Great (331 BC). (See IRAN).

Persian /'pɜːʃ(ə)n/ *n.* **1.** a native or inhabitant of (esp. ancient) Persia. **2.** the language of Persia (see FARSI). —*adj.* of Persia or its people or language. **Persian cat,** a cat of a breed with long silky hair. **Persian lamb,** the silky tightly-curled fur of karacul lambs. [f. prec.]

Persian Gulf an arm of the Arabian Sea, to which it is connected by the Strait of Hormuz and the Gulf of Oman, separating the Arabian peninsula from mainland Asia.

persiflage /'pɜːsɪflɑːʒ/ *n.* banter. [F (PER-, *siffler* whistle)]

persimmon /pə'sɪmən/ *n.* an American or East Asian tree of the genus *Diospyros*; its edible orange plumlike fruit. [corrupt. of Algonquian word]

persist /pə'sɪst/ *v.i.* **1.** to continue firmly or obstinately. **2.** to continue in existence, to survive. —**persistence** *n.*, **persistency** *n.*, **persistent** *adj.*, **persistently** *adv.* [f. L *persistere* (PER-, *sistere* stand)]

person /'pɜːs(ə)n/ *n.* **1.** an individual human being. **2.** the living body of a human being. **3.** (*Gram.*) each of the three classes of personal pronouns, verb-forms, etc., denoting respectively the person etc. speaking (**first person**), spoken to (**second person**), or spoken of (**third person**). **4.** God as Father, Son, or Holy Ghost. —**in person,** physically present. [f. OF f. L *persona* (as foll.)]

persona /pɜː'səʊnə/ *n.* (*pl.* -ae /-iː/) an aspect of one's personality as perceived by others. [L, orig. = actor's mask]

personable *adj.* pleasing in appearance or behaviour. [f. PERSON]

personage /'pɜːsənɪdʒ/ *n.* a person, especially an important one. [as prec.]

persona grata /pɜː'səʊnə 'grɑːtə/ a person acceptable to certain others, especially a diplomat acceptable to a foreign government. —**persona non grata,** one who is not acceptable. [L]

personal /'pɜːsənəl/ *adj.* **1.** of one's own or a particular person's own. **2.** done or made etc. in person. **3.** directed to or concerning an individual; of one's own or another's private life; referring (esp. in a hostile way) to an individual's private life or concerns. **4.** of the body. **5.** of or existing as a person; (*Gram.*) of or denoting one of the three persons. —**personal column,** a column of private advertisements or messages in a newspaper. **personal property,** all property except land and those interests in land that pass to one's heirs. [as PERSON]

personality /pɜːsə'nælɪtɪ/ *n.* **1.** the distinctive character or qualities of a person. **2.** personal existence or identity, being a person. **3.** a famous person, a celebrity. **4.** (in *pl.*) personal remarks. [as prec.]

personalize /'pɜːsənəlaɪz/ *v.t.* **1.** to make personal, especially by marking with the owner's name etc. **2.** to personify. [f. prec.]

personally *adv.* **1.** in person. **2.** for one's own part. [f. PERSONAL]

personate /'pɜːsəneɪt/ *v.t.* **1.** to play the part of (a character in a drama etc.). **2.** to impersonate for fraudulent purposes. —**personation** /-'neɪʃ(ə)n/ *n.*, **personator** *n.* [f. L *personare* (as PERSON)]

personify /pə'sɒnɪfaɪ/ *v.t.* **1.** to represent (a thing or abstraction) as having a personal nature. **2.** to symbolize (a quality) by a figure in human form. **3.** (esp. in *p.p.*) to embody in one's own person or exemplify (a quality). —**personification** /-fɪ'keɪʃ(ə)n/ *n.* [f. F (as PERSON)]

personnel /pɜːsə'nel/ *n.* the body of employees, the staff (in a public undertaking, armed forces, an office, etc.). —**personnel department,** the department of a firm etc. dealing with the appointment and welfare of employees. [F, = personal]

perspective /pə'spektɪv/ *n.* **1.** the art of drawing solid

objects on a plane surface so as to give the right impression of their relative positions, size, etc. (see below); a picture so drawn. **2.** the apparent relation between visible objects as to position, distance, etc. **3.** a mental view of the relative importance of things. **4.** a view or prospect (*lit.* or *fig.*). —*adj.* of or in perspective. —**in perspective,** drawn or viewed according to the rules of perspective; correctly regarded as to relative importance. [f. L (*ars*) *perspectiva* (*perspicere* look through, examine)]
   Brunelleschi (early 15th c.) is generally acknowledged to have been the originator of the first demonstration of scientific perspective. Shortly afterwards his fellow architect Alberti devised a perspective construction for the special use of painters, described in his treatise *On Painting* (1436).

Perspex /ˈpɜːspeks/ *n.* [P] a tough light transparent plastic. [as prec.]

perspicacious /pɜːspɪˈkeɪʃəs/ *adj.* having or showing great insight. —**perspicaciously** *adv.*, **perspicacity** /-ˈkæsɪtɪ/ *n.* [f. L *perspicax* (as PERSPECTIVE)]

perspicuous /pəˈspɪkjʊəs/ *adj.* **1.** easily understood, clearly expressed. **2.** expressing things clearly. —**perspicuity** /pɜːspɪˈkjuːɪtɪ/ *n.*, **perspicuously** *adv.*, **perspicuousness** *n.* [f. L orig. = transparent (as PERSPECTIVE)]

perspiration /pɜːspɪˈreɪʃ(ə)n/ *n.* sweat, sweating. [F (as foll.)]

perspire /pəˈspaɪə(r)/ *v.t./i* to sweat. [f. F f. L (PER-, *spirare* breathe)]

persuade /pəˈsweɪd/ *v.t.* to cause (a person) to do or believe something, especially by reasoning, to induce. —**persuadable** *adj.*, **persuasible** *adj.* [f. L (PER-, *suadēre* induce)]

persuasion /pəˈsweɪʒ(ə)n/ *n.* **1.** persuading. **2.** persuasiveness. **3.** a belief or conviction; a sect holding a particular religious belief. [f. L (as prec.)]

persuasive /pəˈsweɪsɪv/ *adj.* able or tending to persuade. —**persuasively** *adv.*, **persuasiveness** *n.* [f. F or L (as PERSUADE)]

pert *adj.* **1.** cheeky. **2.** jaunty, lively. —**pertly** *adv.*, **pertness** *n.* [f. OF *apert* f. L *apertus* open, & f. OF *aspert* f. L *expertus* (as EXPERT)]

pertain /pəˈteɪn/ *v.i.* **1.** to be relevant or appropriate. **2.** to belong as a part, appendage, or accessory. [f. OF f. L *pertinēre* belong]

Perth the capital of the State of Western Australia, on the estuary of the River Swan; pop. (est. 1981) 918,000 (including the port of Fremantle).

pertinacious /pɜːtɪˈneɪʃəs/ *adj.* holding firmly to an opinion or course of action; persistent, determined. —**pertinaciously** *adv.*, **pertinacity** /-ˈnæsɪtɪ/ *n.* [f. L *pertinax* (as PER-, TENACIOUS)]

pertinent /ˈpɜːtɪnənt/ *adj.* relevant to the matter in hand; to the point. —**pertinence** *n.*, **pertinency** *n.*, **pertinently** *adv.* [f. OF or L (as PERTAIN)]

perturb /pəˈtɜːb/ *v.t.* to disturb greatly, to make anxious or uneasy. —**perturbation** /pɜːtɜːˈbeɪʃ(ə)n/ *n.* [f. OF f. L *perturbare* (PER-, *turbare* disturb)]

Peru /pəˈruː/ a country in South America on the Pacific coast, traversed throughout its length by the Andes; pop. (1972) 14,121,564; official languages, Spanish and Quechua; capital, Lima. Agriculture is important, and cattle, sheep, llamas, and alpacas are bred in the mountain districts. Fish-meal is exported, and mineral exports include lead, zinc, copper, iron ore, and silver. The centre of the Inca empire, Peru was conquered by the Spanish conquistador Pizarro in 1532 and remained under Spanish control for nearly three centuries until liberated by Bolivar and San Martin in 1820–4; a democratic republic was then established. It lost territory in the south to Chile in the War of the Pacific (1879–83) and had border disputes with Colombia and Ecuador to the north in the 1930s and 1940s. Although beset by communication difficulties due to the mountainous terrain, Peru's mining industry has given it one of the most stable of South American economies. —**Peruvian** *adj.* & *n.*

peruke /pəˈruːk/ *n.* (esp. *hist.*) a wig. [f. F f. It.]

peruse /pəˈruːz/ *v.t.* to read or study (a document etc.) thoroughly or carefully. —**perusal** *n.* [prob. as PER- + USE]

pervade /pəˈveɪd/ *v.t.* to spread or be present throughout, to permeate. —**pervasion** *n.* [f. L *pervadere* (PER-, *vadere* go)]

pervasive /pəˈveɪsɪv/ *adj.* pervading. —**pervasiveness** *n.* [as prec.]

perverse /pəˈvɜːs/ *adj.* deliberately or stubbornly doing something different from what is reasonable or required; having this tendency, intractable. —**perversely** *adv.*, **perverseness** *n.*, **perversity** *n.* [f. OF f. L (as PERVERT)]

perversion /pəˈvɜːʃ(ə)n/ *n.* **1.** perverting, being perverted. **2.** preference for a form of sexual activity that is considered abnormal or unacceptable. [f. L (as foll.)]

pervert /pəˈvɜːt/ *v.t.* **1.** to turn (a thing) from its proper use or nature; to misapply (words etc.). **2.** to lead astray from right behaviour or beliefs. **3.** (in *p.p.*) showing perversion. —/ˈpɜːvɜːt/ *n.* a perverted person; one showing perversion of sexual instincts. [f. OF or L *pervertere* (PER-, *vertere* turn)]

pervious /ˈpɜːvɪəs/ *adj.* **1.** permeable, allowing passage. **2.** accessible (*to* reason etc.). [f. L *pervius* (PER-, *via* way)]

peseta /pəˈseɪtə/ *n.* the currency unit of Spain. [Sp., dim. of *pesa* weight]

Peshitta /pəˈʃiːtə/ *n.* the official ancient Syriac version of the Bible in Syriac-speaking Christian lands from the early 5th c. [f. Syriac, = simple, plain]

pesky /ˈpeskɪ/ *adj.* (*US colloq.*) troublesome, annoying. [perh. f. PEST]

peso /ˈpeɪsəʊ/ *n.* (*pl.* **-os**) the currency unit of Chile, several Latin-American countries, and the Philippines. [Sp., = weight, f. L *pensum* (as POISE)]

pessary /ˈpesərɪ/ *n.* a device worn in the vagina to prevent uterine displacement or as a contraceptive; a vaginal suppository. [f. L f. Gk *pessos* oval stone]

pessimism /ˈpesɪmɪz(ə)m/ *n.* **1.** a gloomy view or disposition; a tendency to expect an unfavourable outcome. **2.** the belief that the actual world is the worst possible, or that all things tend to be evil. —**pessimist** *n.* [f. L *pessimus* worst]

pessimistic /pesɪˈmɪstɪk/ *adj.* showing pessimism; gloomy. —**pessimistically** *adv.* [f. prec.]

pest *n.* **1.** a troublesome or annoying person or thing. **2.** an insect or animal that is destructive to plants, food, etc. [f. F or L *pestis* plague]

pester *v.t.* to trouble or annoy, especially with frequent or persistent requests. [prob. f. F *empestrer* encumber; infl. by prec.]

pesticide /ˈpestɪsaɪd/ *a* substance for destroying harmful insects etc. [f. PEST + -CIDE]

pestiferous /peˈstɪfərəs/ *adj.* troublesome, harmful. [f. L (as PEST, *ferre* bear)]

pestilence /ˈpestɪləns/ *n.* a fatal epidemic disease, especially bubonic plague. [f. OF f. L (as foll.)]

pestilent /ˈpestɪlənt/ *adj.* **1.** destructive to life, deadly; harmful. **2.** (*colloq.*) troublesome, annoying. [f. L (*pestis* plague)]

pestilential /pestɪˈlenʃ(ə)l/ *adj.* of a pestilence, pestilent. [f. L (as prec.)]

pestle /ˈpes(ə)l/ *n.* a club-shaped instrument for pounding substances in a mortar. [f. OF f. L *pistillum* (*pinsere* pound)]

pestology /peˈstɒlədʒɪ/ *n.* the scientific study of harmful insects and of the methods of dealing with them. [f. PEST + -LOGY]

pet[1] *n.* **1.** a domesticated animal treated with affection and kept for pleasure or companionship. **2.** a darling, a favourite. —*adj.* **1.** of, for, or in the nature of a pet. **2.** favourite, particular. **3.** expressing fondness or familiarity. —*v.t.* (**-tt-**) **1.** to fondle (esp. erotically). **2.** to treat with affection. [orig. unkn.]

pet[2] *n.* offence at being slighted, ill-humour. [orig. unkn.]

peta- /petə-/ *in comb.* denoting a factor of 10^{15}. [perh. f. PENTA-]

petal /ˈpet(ə)l/ *n.* each division of the corolla of a flower. —**petalled** *adj.* [f. L f. Gk *petalon* leaf]

petard /peˈtɑːd/ *n.* (*hist.*) a small bomb used to blast down a door etc. —**hoist with his own petard,** injured by his own devices against others. [f. F (*péter* break wind)]

Peter /ˈpiːtə(r)/, St (died *c*.AD 67), an Apostle, originally called Simon, prominent among the disciples, a man of action, ardent and impetuous. The tradition connecting him with Rome is early; in Roman Catholic belief he was the founder and first bishop of the Church there. He was martyred, probably in Rome; in popular belief he is represented as the keeper of the door of heaven, whence his attribute of a set of keys. Feast day, 29 June. —**Epistle of St Peter,** either of the two epistles in the New Testament ascribed to St Peter. **Peter's Pence,** (*hist.*) in England, an annual tribute of a penny from every householder having land of a certain value, paid to the papal see at Rome from Anglo-Saxon times (c.787) until discontinued by statute in 1534 after Henry VIII's break with Rome. [f. Gk (*petros* stone)]

Peter I /'piːtə(r)/ 'the Great' (1672–1725), emperor of Russia 1682–1725. After a troubled minority during which he was denied effective power by his half-sister Sofia, Peter finally established his authority in 1689–94 and began a policy of expansion to the south and north-west. He reformed his armed forces along Western lines and engaged in a long war with Charles XII of Sweden, a war from which Russia, after severe initial setbacks, finally emerged victorious. On the domestic front, Peter's reign was characterized by a systematic attempt to reform Russian government and administration similarly, and although he faced considerable internal opposition, and was engaged in almost constant warfare along his borders, he succeeded in transforming Russia into a modern European power which would henceforth play a significant part in international affairs in central Europe.

peter /'piːtə(r)/ *v.i.* **peter out,** to diminish gradually and come to an end. [orig. unkn.]

Peterloo /piːtə'luː/ an event of 16 Aug. 1819, an attack by Manchester Yeomanry against a large but peaceable crowd. Sent to arrest the speaker at a rally of supporters of political reform in St Peter's Field, Manchester, the local yeomanry lost their heads and charged the crowd. In the resulting fracas, named Peterloo in ironical reference to the Battle of Waterloo, 11 civilians were killed and more than 500 injured.

Peter Pan the hero of J. M. Barrie's play of the same name (1904), a boy who never grew up.

petersham /'piːtəʃəm/ *n.* a thick ribbed silk ribbon. [f. Lord *Petersham*, English army officer (d. 1851)]

Peter the Hermit (c.1050–1115) French monk, one of the most eloquent preachers of the First Crusade, who set out for the Holy Land in 1096 with an enthusiastic band of peasants, most of whom were massacred by the Turks. After his death he became the hero of many legends.

petiole /'petɪəʊl/ *n.* a slender stalk joining a leaf to a stem. [f. F f. L *petiolus* little foot, stalk]

Petipa /pe'tiːpə/, Marius (1818–1910), French dancer, choreographer, and ballet master, who became principal dancer in St Petersburg in 1847 and first ballet master in 1862. He choreographed about 50 ballets for the Imperial Theatres in St Petersburg and Moscow, collaborating closely with Tchaikovsky on the *Nutcracker*, and was responsible for leading the Tsarist ballet to its magnificent climax. His noble classicism and consciousness of form were once considered old-fashioned, but were vindicated by Diaghilev's production of *The Sleeping Princess* in 1921; his *œuvre* is now considered one of the greatest achievements in the history of ballet.

petit bourgeois /pəti: 'bʊəʒwɑː/ a member of the lower middle classes. [F]

petite /pə'tiːt/ *adj.* (of a woman) small and dainty in build. [F, fem. of *petit* small]

petit four /pəti: 'fʊə(r)/ (*pl.* **petits fours** *pr.* same) a very small fancy cake. [F, = little oven]

petition /pə'tɪʃ(ə)n/ *n.* **1.** asking, supplication. **2.** a formal written request, especially one signed by many people, appealing to an authority for a right or benefit etc. **3.** an application to a court for a writ, order, etc. —*v.t./i.* **1.** to make or address a petition to. **2.** to ask earnestly or humbly. —**petitioner** *n.* [f. OF f. L (*petere* seek)]

petit mal /pəti: 'mɑːl/ mild form of epilepsy without loss of consciousness. [F, = small sickness]

petit point /pəti: 'pwæ̃/ embroidery on canvas using small stitches. [F]

Petra /'petrə/ an ancient city in southern Jordan, that was the capital of the Nabataeans by 312 BC. After AD 105 it ceased to be the administrative centre but remained the religious metropolis of Arabia. Petra lies in a hollow surrounded by mountains; the only access is by narrow gorges. The ruins of the city itself, though extensive, are not impressive, but the rock-hewn temples and tombs in the surrounding hills are magnificent ('a rose-red city, half as old as Time'); the site was rediscovered in 1812 by the Swiss traveller Burckhardt.

Petrarch /'petrɑːk/ Francesco Petrarca, (1304–74) Italian poet, who has been called the father of modern poetry. His verse, especially his love-poems to the idealized woman he calls Laura, made him a national celebrity; he was crowned poet laureate in Rome in 1341. He was also important as a leader, with his friend Boccaccio, in the rediscovery of classical antiquity, rejecting medieval scholasticism and insisting on the continuity between pagan and Christian culture.

petrel /'petr(ə)l/ *n.* a kind of sea-bird, of the family Procellariidae or Hydrobatidae, that flies far from land. [orig. unkn.]

Petrie /'piːtrɪ/, Sir William Matthew Flinders (1853–1942), English Egyptologist who introduced scientific field archaeology to Egypt and laid the foundations of all modern studies of ancient Egypt with his technique of 'artefact analysis' and his system of 'sequence dating'—comparative dating on typological grounds—which he devised and presented in the publications of his excavations in Egypt and Palestine.

petrify /'petrɪfaɪ/ *v.t./i.* **1.** to paralyse with fear, astonishment, etc. **2.** to turn or be turned into stone. —**petrification** /-fɪ'keɪʃ(ə)n/ *n.* [f. F f. L *petrificare* (*petra* rock f. Gk)]

petrochemical /petrəʊ'kemɪk(ə)l/ *n.* a substance industrially obtained from petroleum or natural gas. [f. PETROLEUM + CHEMICAL]

petrodollar /'petrəʊdɒlə(r)/ *n.* a dollar held by a petroleum-exporting country. [f. PETROLEUM + DOLLAR]

petrography /pɪ'trɒɡrəfɪ/ *n.* the scientific description of the composition and formation of rocks. —**petrographic** /petrə'ɡræfɪk/ *adj.* [f. Gk *petra* rock + -GRAPHY]

petrol /'petr(ə)l/ *n.* refined petroleum used as fuel in motor vehicles, aircraft, etc. —**petrol station,** a filling station. [f. F f. L (as foll.)]

petroleum /pɪ'trəʊlɪəm/ *n.* a hydrocarbon oil found in the upper strata of the earth, refined for use as a fuel etc. —**petroleum jelly,** a translucent solid mixture of hydrocarbons obtained from petroleum and used as a lubricant etc. [L (*petra* rock f. Gk, *oleum* oil)]

petrology /pɪ'trɒlədʒɪ/ *n.* the study of the origin, structure, etc., of rocks. —**petrological** /-'lɒdʒɪk(ə)l/ *adj.* [f. Gk *petra* rock + -LOGY]

Petronius Arbiter /pɪ'trəʊnɪəs/ (1st c. AD) Roman writer, author of the *Satyricon*, a satirical novel of which only fragments survive. Its most complete episode tells of the tastelessly extravagant banquet of the *nouveau-riche* Trimalchio. The author is probably identical with the Petronius who was 'arbiter elegentiae' (= master of taste) at Nero's court, who committed suicide in AD 66.

petticoat /'petɪkəʊt/ *n.* **1.** a woman's or girl's dress-length undergarment hanging from the waist or shoulders. **2.** (*attrib.*) feminine, of or by women. [f. *petty coat*]

pettifogging /'petɪfɒɡɪŋ/ *adj.* **1.** quibbling or wrangling about unimportant details. **2.** practising legal chicanery. [*pettifogger* inferior legal practitioner (PETTY, *fogger* underhand dealer)]

pettish *adj.* peevish, petulant, irritable. —**pettishly** *adv.*, **pettishness** *n.* [f. PET²]

petty *adj.* **1.** unimportant, trivial. **2.** small-minded. **3.** minor; inferior; on a small scale. —**petty cash,** money kept for small cash items of expenditure. **petty officer,** a naval NCO. **petty sessions,** a meeting of two or more magistrates for the summary trial of certain offences. —**pettily** *adv.*, **pettiness** *n.* [f. OF *petit* small]

petulant /'petjʊlənt/ *adj.* peevishly impatient or irritable. —**petulance** *n.*, **petulantly** *adv.* [f. F f. L (*petere* seek)]

petunia /pɪ'tjuːnɪə/ *n.* a plant of the genus *Petunia* with funnel-shaped flowers of vivid purple, red, white, etc. [f. F f. Guarani, = tobacco]

pew *n.* **1.** a long backed bench or enclosed compartment in a church. **2.** (*colloq.*) a seat. [f. OF *puye* balcony f. L (as PODIUM)]

pewter /'pjuːtə(r)/ *n.* **1.** a grey alloy of tin with lead or other metal. **2.** articles made of this. [f. OF *peutre*]

peyote /peɪ'əʊtɪ/ *n.* **1.** a Mexican cactus of the genus *Lophophora*. **2.** a hallucinogenic drug prepared from it. [Amer. Sp., f. Nahuatl]

pfennig /'pfenɪɡ/ *n.* a small German coin worth ¹⁄₁₀₀ of a mark. [G (as PENNY)]

PG *abbr.* paying guest.

pH /piː'eɪtʃ/ *n.* a measure of the acidity or alkaline level of a solution. [G (*potenz* power, *H* (symbol for hydrogen) dissolved hydrogen ions)]

Phaedra /'fiːdrə/ (*Gk legend*) wife of Theseus. She conceived a passion for her stepson Hippolytus, who rejected her, whereupon she hanged herself, leaving behind a letter which accused him. Theseus would not believe his son's protestations of innocence and banished him.

Phaethon /ˈfeɪəθən/ (*Gk myth.*) son of Helios the sun-god. He asked to drive his father's solar chariot for a day, but could not control the immortal horses and the chariot plunged too near the earth until Zeus, to save the earth from destruction, killed Phaethon with a thunderbolt.

phaeton /ˈfeɪtən/ *n.* a light four-wheeled open carriage, usually drawn by a pair of horses. [f. prec.]

phagocyte /ˈfæɡəsaɪt/ *n.* a leucocyte etc. capable of absorbing foreign matter (esp. bacteria) in the body. [f. Gk phag-eat + -CYTE]

phalanger /fəˈlændʒə(r)/ *n.* (in Australia & New Zealand) a tree-dwelling marsupial of the family Phalangeridae, with webbed hind feet. [f. Gk *phalaggion* spider's web, f. its webbed toes]

phalanx /ˈfælæŋks/ *n.* (*pl.* **phalanxes**) **1.** (in ancient Greece) a line of battle, especially a body of infantry drawn up in close order. **2.** a set of persons etc. forming a compact mass or banded together for a common purpose. **3.** (*pl.* **phalanges**) a bone of the finger or toe (ill. BODY 1). [L f. Gk]

phallus /ˈfæləs/ *n.* (*pl.* **-uses**) an image of the penis (usu. in erection) as a symbol of generative power. —**phallic** *adj.* [L f. Gk]

phantasm /ˈfæntæz(ə)m/ *n.* an illusion, a phantom. —**phantasmal** /-ˈtæzm(ə)l/ *adj.* [f. OF f. L f. Gk (*phantazō* make visible)]

phantasmagoria /fæntæzməˈɡɔːrɪə/ *n.* a shifting scene of real or imagined figures. —**phantasmagoric** /-ˈɡɒrɪk/ *adj.* [prob. f. F *fantasmagorie* (as prec., with fanciful ending)]

phantom /ˈfæntəm/ *n.* **1.** a ghost, an apparition. **2.** something without substance or reality, a mental illusion. —*adj.* merely apparent, illusory. [f. OF *fantosme* f. Gk (as PHANTASM)]

Pharaoh /ˈfeərəʊ/ *n.* the title of the ruler of ancient Egypt. [f. L f. Gk f. Heb. f. Egyptian, = great house]

Pharisee /ˈfærɪsiː/ *n.* **1.** a member of an ancient Jewish sect (see below). **2.** a self-righteous person, a hypocrite. —**Pharisaic** /-ˈseɪɪk/ *adj.* [OE, ult. f. Aram., f. Heb. *parush* separated]

The Pharisees are mentioned only by Josephus and in the New Testament, where they are held to have pretensions to superior sanctity. Unlike the Sadducees, who tried to apply Mosaic law strictly, the Pharisees allowed some interpretation, and although in the Gospels they are represented as the chief opponents of Christ they seem to have been less hostile than the Sadducees to the nascent Church, with whom they shared belief in the resurrection.

pharmaceutical /fɑːməˈsjuːtɪk(ə)l/ *adj.* of or engaged in pharmacy; of the use or sale of medicinal drugs. [f. L f. Gk (*pharmakeutēs* druggist f. *pharmakon* drug)]

pharmaceutics *n.pl.* (usu. treated as *sing.*) pharmacy (PHARMACY sense 1). [f. prec.]

pharmacist /ˈfɑːməsɪst/ *n.* a person engaged in pharmacy. [f. PHARMACY]

pharmacology /fɑːməˈkɒlədʒɪ/ *n.* the science of the action of drugs on the body. —**pharmacological** /-ˈlɒdʒɪk(ə)l/ *adj.*, **pharmacologist** *n.* [f. Gk *pharmakon* drug + -LOGY]

pharmacopoeia /fɑːməkəˈpiːə/ *n.* **1.** a book (especially one published officially) containing a list of drugs with directions for their use. **2.** a stock of drugs. [f. Gk (*pharmakopoios* drug-maker, as prec. + -poios* making)]

pharmacy /ˈfɑːməsɪ/ *n.* **1.** the preparation and dispensing of drugs. **2.** a pharmacist's shop; a dispensary. [f. OF f. L f. Gk (*pharmakeus* druggist, as PHARMACEUTICAL)]

Pharos /ˈfeərɒs/ a lighthouse, one of the earliest known, erected by Ptolemy II *c.*280 BC on the island of Pharos, off the coast of Alexandria. Often considered one of the Seven Wonders of the World, it is said to have been over 130 m (440 ft.) high and to have been visible from 67 km (42 miles) away. It was finally destroyed in 1375.

pharyngitis /færɪnˈdʒaɪtɪs/ *n.* inflammation of the pharynx. [f. PHARYNX + -ITIS]

pharynx /ˈfærɪŋks/ *n.* the cavity behind the mouth and nose (ill. BODY 2). —**pharyngeal** /-ɪnˈdʒiːəl/ *adj.* [f. Gk *pharugx*]

phase /feɪz/ *n.* **1.** a stage of change or development. **2.** an aspect of the moon or a planet, according to the amount of illumination. **3.** a stage in a periodically recurring sequence of changes, e.g. of alternating current or light-vibrations. —*v.t.* to carry out (a programme etc.) in phases or stages. —**phase in** *or* **out**, to bring gradually into (or out of) use. [f. F f. Gk *phasis* appearance]

Ph.D. *abbr.* Doctor of Philosophy. [f. L *philosophiae doctor*]

pheasant /ˈfez(ə)nt/ *n.* a long-tailed game-bird with bright plumage, especially *Phasianus colchicus*, originally Asian but long naturalized in Europe. [f. AF f. Gk *phasianus* (*Phasis* river in Asia Minor)]

phenol /ˈfiːnɒl/ *n.* a hydroxyl derivative of aromatic hydrocarbons. [f. F (*phène* benzene)]

phenomenal /fɪˈnɒmɪn(ə)l/ *adj.* of the nature of a phenomenon; extraordinary, remarkable. —**phenomenally** *adv.* [f. PHENOMENON.]

phenomenalism /fɪˈnɒmɪnəlɪz(ə)m/ *n.* the theory that phenomena are the only objects of knowledge, that statements which appear to speak about physical objects are in fact speaking only about sense-experience. —**phenomenalist** *n.*, **phenomenalistic** /-ˈlɪstɪk/ *adj.* [f. prec.]

phenomenology /fɪnɒmɪˈnɒlədʒɪ/ *n.* **1.** the philosophical movement that concentrates on the study of consciousness and its immediate objects (see HUSSERL). **2.** the science of phenomena as distinct from that of being (*ontology*). [f. foll. + -LOGY]

phenomenon /fɪˈnɒmɪnən/ *n.* (*pl.* **-ena**) **1.** a fact or occurrence that appears or is perceived, especially a thing the cause of which is in question. **2.** a remarkable person or thing. [f. L f. Gk (*phainomai* appear)]

pheromone /ˈferəməʊn/ *n.* a substance secreted and released by an animal for detection and response by another of the same (or a closely related) species. [f. Gk *pherō* convey + HORMONE]

phew /fjuː/ *int.* expressing relief, weariness, surprise, etc. [imit. of puffing]

phi /faɪ/ *n.* the twenty-first letter of the Greek alphabet, = ph. [Gk]

phial /ˈfaɪəl/ *n.* a small glass bottle, especially for liquid medicine. [f. OF f. L f. Gk (as VIAL)]

Phi Beta Kappa /faɪ biːtə ˈkæpə/ the oldest American college fraternity, an honorary society to which distinguished undergraduate (and occasionally graduate) scholars may be elected, named from the initial letters of its Greek motto, = 'philosophy the guide to life'.

Phidias /ˈfɪdɪæs, ˈfaɪ-/ (5th c. BC) Athenian sculptor. His two greatest works, both executed in gold and ivory, were colossal statues of Zeus at Olympia and of Athene Parthenos for the Parthenon in Athens. He was appointed in 447 BC by the statesman Pericles to plan and supervise public building on the Acropolis and transformed Pericles' ideal of the grandeur of Athens into a reality, but both fell foul of political envy and Phidias was sent to trial in 432 BC accused of misappropriating gold and ivory. His career seems to have terminated then but he remains the most innovative highly individual artist of his time, and his sculptures can be seen as epitomizing the pinnacle of achievement in Greek art.

Phidippides /faɪˈdɪpɪdiːz/ the Athenian herald who was sent to Sparta to ask for aid when the Persians were known to have landed at Marathon in 490 BC. He is said to have covered the 250 km (150 miles) in two days on foot.

phil- see PHILO-.

Philadelphia /fɪləˈdelfɪə/ the chief city of Pennsylvania, founded by William Penn and other Quakers; pop. (1982) 1,665,382. [f. Gk, = brotherly love]

philander /fɪˈlændə(r)/ *v.i.* (of a man) to flirt. —**philanderer** *n.* [f. Gk *philandros* fond of men, taken as name of lover]

philanthropy /fɪˈlænθrəpɪ/ *n.* concern for the welfare of mankind, especially as shown by acts of benevolence. —**philanthropic** /-ˈθrɒpɪk/ *adj.*, **philanthropically** /-ˈθrɒpɪkəlɪ/ *adv.*, **philanthropist** *n.* [f. L f. Gk (PHIL-, *anthrōpos* human being)]

philately /fɪˈlætəlɪ/ *n.* the collecting and study of postage-stamps. —**philatelic** /-ˈtelɪk/ *adj.*, **philatelist** *n.* [f. F f. Gk PHIL-, *ateleia* exemption from payment (*a-* not, *telos* tax). When a letter was 'carriage-free' or carriage prepaid by the sender, it was formerly stamped with the word *free*; the fact is now indicated by its bearing a postage stamp or a frank]

-phile /-faɪl/ *suffix* (also **-phil**) forming nouns and adjectives in the sense 'one who is fond of' (*bibliophile*). [f. Gk *philos* loving]

Philemon[1] /fɪˈliːmən/ (*Gk myth.*) a good old countryman who lived with his wife Baucis in Phrygia, and offered hospitality to Zeus and Hermes who had come to earth, without revealing their identities, to test men's piety. Philemon and Baucis were subsequently saved from a flood which covered the district.

Philemon[2] /fɪˈlimən/ **Epistle to Philemon,** a book of the New Testament, an epistle of St Paul to a well-to-do Christian living probably at Colossae in Phrygia.

philharmonic /fɪlɑːˈmɒnɪk/ adj. (in the names of orchestras and music societies) fond of music. [f. F f. It. (as PHIL-, HARMONIC)]

Philip[1] /ˈfɪlɪp/, St **1.** an Apostle, commemorated with St James the Less on 1 May. **2.** 'the Evangelist', one of seven deacons appointed to superintend the secular business of the Church at Jerusalem (Acts 6: 5-6).

Philip[2] /ˈfɪlɪp/ the name of five kings of Macedonia:
Philip II (c.382-336 BC), reigned 359-336 BC, father of Alexander the Great. He unified Macedonia and fostered its economic growth, and introduced the phalanx formation in the army. His victory over Athens and Thebes at the battle of Chaeronea in 338 BC established his hegemony over Greece. He was assassinated as he was about to lead an expedition against Persia.
Philip V (238-179 BC), reigned 221-179 BC. A brilliant soldier, his aggressive policies led to a series of confrontations with the Romans, who forced a peace settlement on him after defeating him at Cynoscephalae in Thessaly in 197 BC.

Philip[3] /ˈfɪlɪp/ (Fr. Philippe) the name of several kings of France:
Philip II 'Philip Augustus' (1165-1223), son of Louis VII, reigned 1180-1223. His reign was marked by the most dramatic expansion of Capetian influence for several centuries. Having first come to terms with his own nobility, Philip proceeded to attack the English Plantagenet empire in France, getting the better, by a mixture of force and diplomacy, of Henry II, Richard I, and John, and occupying Normandy, Anjou, and Poitou. At the end of his reign, as a result of the Albigensian Crusade, Philip also succeeded in adding fresh territories in the south to his kingdom.
Philip IV 'the Fair' (1268-1314), son of Philip III, reigned 1285-1314. Philip IV continued the Capetian policy of extending French dominions, engaging in wars of expansion with England and Flanders. His reign, however, was dominated by his struggle with the papacy, during which he was excommunicated by Boniface VIII before establishing French domination over the Holy See, and by his persecution of the Knights Templar, for financial reasons, which ended with the dissolution of the order, the execution of its leaders, and the seizure of its property by the Crown.
Philip VI of Valois (1293-1350), cousin of Charles IV, reigned 1328-50. The founder of the Valois dynasty, Philip came to the throne under the Salic Law when the posthumous child of his cousin Charles IV, to whom he had been declared regent, proved to be a girl. His claim was disputed by the English king Edward III, who could trace a claim through the female line, and war between the two countries, which was to develop into the Hundred Years War, ensued. Philip got much the worse of the early engagements of the war, losing the battle of Crécy in 1346 with heavy casualties to his army.

Philip[4] /ˈfɪlɪp/ (Sp. Felipe) the name of several kings of Spain:
Philip I (1478-1506), son of Maximilian I of Austria, reigned 1504-6. Philip became Duke of Burgundy in 1482 and married Juana of Castile, daughter of Ferdinand and Isabella, ten years later. After Isabella's death in 1504 he ruled Castile jointly with his wife, but did not actually return to Spain until 1506. He died three months later, possibly poisoned, but he had established the Hapsburgs as the ruling dynasty in his new country.
Philip II (1527-98), reigned 1556-98. The son of Charles V, who abdicated in his favour in 1556, Philip married four times, his second wife (1554) being Mary I of England. His reign was entirely dominated by an anti-Protestant crusade which exhausted the Spanish economy and led to the country's rapid decline in the 17th c. Philip failed to suppress the revolt in the Netherlands (1567-79) and although he conquered Portugal in 1580-1, his war against England (1587-9) also proved a failure, an attempted Spanish invasion being thwarted by the defeat of the Armada in 1588.
Philip V (1683-1746), grandson of Louis XIV, reigned 1700-24, 1724-46. First Bourbon king of Spain, Philip's selection as successor to Charles II led to the War of the Spanish Succession (1701-14). Formally recognized as king by the Treaty of Utrecht, Philip abdicated in favour of his son Louis in 1724 but returned to the throne following Louis' death eight months later.

Philippi /fɪˈlɪpaɪ/ an ancient city in eastern Macedonia, the scene in 42 BC of the two battles in which Antony and Octavian defeated Brutus and Cassius.

Philippians /fɪˈlɪpɪənz/ **Epistle to the Philippians,** a book of the New Testament, an epistle of St Paul to the Church at Philippi in Macedonia.

philippic /fɪˈlɪpɪk/ n. a bitter invective. [f. L f. Gk (Philippos Philip); orig. applied to the orations of Demosthenes against Philip II of Macedon]

Philippines /ˈfɪlɪpiːnz/ a country in SE Asia consisting of a chain of over 7,000 islands of the Malay Archipelago, the chief of which are Luzon in the north and Mindanao in the south, all separated from the Asian mainland by the South China Sea; pop. (est. 1980) 48,098,460; official languages Pilipino and English; capital, Manila. The Portuguese navigator Magellan visited the islands in 1521 and was killed there. Conquered by Spain in 1565, and named 'Filipinas' after the king's son, the islands were ceded to the USA following the Spanish-American War in 1898. Occupied by the Japanese between 1941 and 1944, the Philippines achieved full independence as a republic in 1946; it has continued to maintain close links with the USA. Most of the area remains backward and agricultural, with the exception of the major population centre on Luzon.

Philistine /ˈfɪlɪstaɪn/ n. a member of an ancient non-Semitic people who settled in the coastal region of Canaan (see below). —adj. of the Philistines. [ult. f. Heb.]
The Philistines ('Peleset' of Egyptian inscriptions from the time of Rameses III, c.1190 BC), from whom the country of Palestine took its name, were one of the Sea Peoples who, according to the Bible, came from Caphtor/Crete and settled the southern coastal plain of Canaan in the 12th c. BC. Governed by a league of five city-states (Gaza, Ashkelon, Ashdod, Gath, and Ekron), they gained control of the land and sea routes and acquired a monopoly of metal technology. After repeated conflicts with the Israelites they were defeated by David c.1000 BC and subsequently declined into obscurity after losing control of the sea trade to the Phoenicians.

philistine /ˈfɪlɪstaɪn/ n. one who is hostile or indifferent to culture, or whose interests are material or commonplace. —adj. having such characteristics. —**philistinism** /-ɪnɪz(ə)m/ n. [= prec.]

Philo /ˈfaɪləʊ/ (c.20 BC-c. AD 50), Jewish philosopher of Alexandria, author of numerous works (written in Greek). His most influential achievement was his development of the allegorical interpretation of Scripture, which enabled him to discover much of Greek philosophy in the Old Testament.

philo- /-fɪlə(ʊ)-/ in comb. (**phil-** before a vowel or h) liking, fond of. [f. Gk (phileō to love)]

philology /fɪˈlɒlədʒɪ/ n. **1.** the study (esp. historical and comparative) of language(s). **2.** (US) the study of literature. **3.** (archaic) love of learning and literature. —**philologian** /-ˈləʊdʒɪən/ n., **philological** /-ˈlɒdʒɪk(ə)l/ adj., **philologist** n. [f. F, ult. f. Gk, = love of learning]

Philomel /fɪləˈmel/, **Philomela** /-ˈmelə/ (Gk myth.) the daughter of a legendary king of Athens. She was turned into a swallow and her sister Procne into a nightingale (or, in Latin versions, into a nightingale and Procne into a swallow).

philosopher /fɪˈlɒsəfə(r)/ n. **1.** one engaged or learned in philosophy or a branch of it. **2.** one who lives by philosophy or acts philosophically. —**philosopher's stone** an object sought by alchemists as a means of turning other metals into gold or silver. [f. AF f. L f. Gk (as PHILOSOPHY)]

philosophical /fɪləˈsɒfɪk(ə)l/ adj. (also **philosophic**) **1.** of or according to philosophy. **2.** skilled in or devoted to philosophy. **3.** calmly reasonable; bearing unavoidable misfortune unemotionally. —**philosophically** adv. [f. L (as PHILOSOPHY)]

philosophize /fɪˈlɒsəfaɪz/ v.i. to reason like a philosopher; to speculate, to theorize; to moralize. [app. f. F philosopher (as foll.)]

philosophy /fɪˈlɒsəfɪ/ n. **1.** the use of reason and argument in the search for truth and the knowledge of reality, especially of the causes and nature of things, and of the principles governing existence, perception, human behaviour, and the material universe. **2.** a particular system or set of beliefs preached by this. **3.** a system of conduct in life. **4.** a philosophical attitude to misfortune etc. **5.** advanced learning in general. [f. OF, ult. f. Gk, = love of wisdom]

philtre /'fɪltə(r)/ n. a drink supposed to be able to excite sexual love. [f. F f. L f. Gk *philtron* (*phileō* love)]

phlebitis /flɪ'baɪtɪs/ n. inflammation of the walls of a vein. —**phlebitic** /-'bɪtɪk/ adj. [f. Gk *phleps* vein + -ITIS]

phlegm /flem/ n. **1.** a thick viscous substance secreted by the mucous membranes of the respiratory passages, discharged by coughing. **2.** (*archaic*) this substance regarded as a humour (see HUMOUR n. 4). **3.** calmness; sluggishness. [f. OF f. L f. Gk, = inflammation]

phlegmatic /fleg'mætɪk/ adj. calm, not easily agitated; sluggish. —**phlegmatically** adv. [f. prec.]

phloem /'fləʊem/ n. the soft tissue of stems (opp. XYLEM) that carries the food materials made by photosynthesis to all parts of the plant. [f. Gk *phloos* bark]

phlogiston /flɒ'dʒɪst(ə)n/ n. a substance formerly supposed to cause combustion. [f. Gk (*phlogizō* set on fire, f. *phlox* flame)]

phlox /flɒks/ n. a plant of the genus *Phlox*, with clusters of reddish or purple or white flowers. [L f. Gk name of a plant (lit. 'flame')]

Phnom Penh /nɒm 'pen/ the capital of Kampuchea; pop. (est. 1981) 500,000.

-phobe /-fəʊb/ suffix forming nouns and adjectives in the sense '(a person) disliking or fearing' (*Anglophobe*). [F f. L f. Gk (*phobos* fear)]

phobia /'fəʊbɪə/ n. a persistent abnormal fear or dislike of something. [as foll.]

-phobia /-fəʊbɪə/ suffix forming abstract nouns corresponding to adjectives in -*phobe* (*xenophobia*). —**-phobic** adj. [L f. Gk (*phobos* fear)]

Phoebe, Phoebus /'fi:bɪ, 'fi:bəs/ (*Gk myth.*) Artemis and Apollo as goddess of the moon and god of the sun; the moon and sun personified. [f. Gk, = bright, radiant]

Phoenician /fɪ'nɪʃ(ə)n/ adj. of Phoenicia, the ancient name for the area occupied by the Phoenicians (see below), or its people or colonies. —n. a Phoenician person. The Phoenicians were a Semitic-speaking people of unknown origin but culturally descended from the Canaanites of the 2nd millennium BC, who occupied the coastal plain of modern Lebanon and Syria in the early 1st millennium BC and derived their prosperity from trade and manufacturing industries in textiles, glass, metalware, carved ivory, wood, and jewellery. Their trading contacts extended throughout Asia, and reached westwards as far as Africa (where they founded Carthage), Spain, and possibly Britain. The Phoenicians continued to thrive under Assyrian and then Persian suzerainty until 332 BC when the capital, Tyre, was sacked and the country incorporated in the Greek world by Alexander the Great. The Phoenician alphabet was borrowed by the Greeks and thence passed down into Western cultural tradition. [f. F f. L f. Gk]

phoenix /'fi:nɪks/ n. a mythical bird of the Arabian desert, the only one of its kind, said to live for five or six centuries and then burn itself on a funeral pyre, rising from its ashes with renewed youth to live through another cycle. [OE, ult. f. Gk *phoinix* Phoenician, purple, phoenix]

phone /fəʊn/ n. (*colloq.*) a telephone. —v.t./i. (*colloq.*) to telephone. —**phone-in** n. a broadcast programme in which listeners participate by telephoning the studio. [abbr.]

phoneme /'fəʊni:m/ n. a unit of significant sound in a specified language (e.g. the sound of *c* in *cat*, which differs from the *b* in *bat* and distinguishes the two words). —**phonemic** /-'ni:mɪk/ adj., **phonemics** n.pl. (also as sing.) [f. F f. Gk, = sound, speech (as foll.)]

phonetic /fə'netɪk/ adj. of or representing vocal sounds; (of a spelling) corresponding to the pronunciation. —**phonetically** adv. [f. Gk (*phōneō* speak)]

phonetician /fəʊnɪ'tɪʃ(ə)n/ n. an expert in phonetics. [f. foll.]

phonetics /fə'netɪks/ n.pl. phonetic phenomena; (as sing.) the study of these. —**phonetician** /-ɪ'tɪʃ(ə)n/ n. [f. PHONETIC]

phoney /'fəʊnɪ/ adj. (*slang*) sham, counterfeit, fictitious. —n. (*slang*) a phoney person or thing. [orig. unkn.]

phonic /'fəʊnɪk, 'fɒ-/ adj. of sound; of vocal sound. —**phonically** adv. [f. Gk *phōnē* voice, sound]

phono- /fəʊnə(ʊ)-/ in comb. sound. [f. Gk *phōnē* (as prec.)]

phonograph /'fəʊnəgrɑːf/ n. an early form of gramophone; (*US*) a gramophone. [f. PHONO- + -GRAPH]

phonology /fə'nɒlədʒɪ/ n. the study of the sounds in a language. —**phonological** /-'lɒdʒɪk(ə)l/ adj. [f. PHONO- + -LOGY]

phosphate /'fɒsfeɪt/ n. a salt or ester of phosphoric acid;

an artificial fertilizer composed of or containing this. [F (as PHOSPHORUS)]

phosphor /'fɒsfə(r)/ n. a synthetic fluorescent or phosphorescent substance. [G f. L, = PHOSPHORUS]

phosphoresce /fɒsfə'res/ v.i. to show phosphorescence. [f. foll.]

phosphorescence /fɒsfə'res(ə)ns/ n. radiation similar to fluorescence but detectable after the excitation ceases; emission of light without combustion or perceptible heat. —**phosphorescent** adj. [f. PHOSPHORUS]

phosphorus /'fɒsfərəs/ n. a non-metallic element, symbol P, atomic number 15, existing in a number of allotropic forms which can be grouped together in three major categories: white phosphorus, red phosphorus, and black phosphorus. Of these, white phosphorus is the most reactive. Usually yellowish because of impurities, it is waxy, poisonous, and luminous in the dark. It was first isolated in the 17th c.; its discovery led to attempts to obtain instant flame, and eventually to the invention of matches. Phosphorus is essential to life, and a major use of phosphorus compounds is as fertilizers. Other uses are as insecticides and poison gases. —**phosphoric** /-'fɒrɪk/ adj., **phosphorous** adj. [L, = morning star, f. Gk (*phōs* light, -*phoros* bringing)]

Photius /'fəʊtɪəs/ (*c.*820-?897) Byzantine scholar and patriarch of Constantinople. His most important work is the *Library* (*Bibliotheca*), a critical account of 280 earlier prose works and an invaluable source of information about many works now lost.

photo n. (*pl.* -**os**) a photograph. —**photo finish,** a close finish of a race with the winner determined by scrutiny of a photograph; any close-run thing. [abbr.]

photo- /fəʊtə(ʊ)-/ in comb. **1.** light. **2.** photography. [f. Gk *phōs* light, or as prec.]

photocopier /'fəʊtəʊkɒpɪə(r)/ n. a machine for photocopying documents etc.

photocopy /'fəʊtəʊkɒpɪ/ n. a copy of a document etc. made on a machine employing a light-sensitive process. —v.t. to make a photocopy of.

photoelectric /fəʊtəʊɪ'lektrɪk/ adj. with or using the emission of electrons from substances exposed to light. —**photoelectric cell,** a device using this effect to generate current. —**photoelectricity** /-'trɪsɪtɪ/ n.

photofit /'fəʊtəʊfɪt/ n. a composite picture made from photographs of separate features assembled from descriptions put together to form a likeness, especially of a person sought by the police.

photogenic /fəʊtəʊ'dʒenɪk, -dʒi:nɪk/ adj. **1.** apt to be a good subject for photography, coming out well in photographs. **2.** producing, or emitting light. —**photogenically** adv. [f. PHOTO- + Gk -*genēs* born]

photograph /'fəʊtəgrɑːf/ n. a picture formed by the chemical action of light or other radiation on a sensitive film (see PHOTOGRAPHY). —v.t. **1.** to take a photograph of. **2.** to come out in a specified way when photographed. [f. PHOTO- + -GRAPH]

photographer /fə'tɒgrəfə(r)/ n. one who takes photographs. [f. prec.]

photographic /fəʊtə'græfɪk/ adj. **1.** of or produced by photography. **2.** (of the memory) recalling in detail from a single sight. —**photographically** adv. [f. PHOTOGRAPH]

photography /fə'tɒgrəfɪ/ n. the taking and processing of photographs (see below). [f. PHOTO- + -GRAPHY]
The world's first photograph was taken in 1826 by a Frenchman, J. N. Niepce, who (by an exposure lasting several hours) produced a picture of barn-roofs, the view from his window, on a pewter plate, using a substance that hardened under the influence of light. The next landmark in photographic history was the daguerrotype (see entry), first shown to the public in 1838-9—a single and unique image with fine detail in the definition. This was followed by the invention of a negative process, devised by an English amateur scientist, W. H. Fox Talbot, by which an unlimited number of prints could be produced; subsequent developments consisted mainly of improvements of his work. The introduction in 1856 of flexible film instead of a glass plate made it possible for cameras to be not only smaller and lighter but simpler and cheaper (see CAMERA). Colour photography developed from the experiments of Clerk Maxwell in 1861.
Photography has become important in science and industry, in aerial reconnaissance, and in medicine. Interest in it as an art form is as old as the process itself. Photographic

societies were soon formed and techniques were explored at first with the idea of giving to the medium the manipulative latitude of painting, then (by *c.*1890) for their own sake. New freedoms in the other arts, and especially in painting, were paralleled in photography as surrealists experimented with dark-room tricks, and Max Ernst and others produced photomontages, until realism again became popular in the 1930s. An immense range of photographic materials, equipment, and skills now makes photography as versatile a medium as painting.

photogravure /ˌfəʊtəgrəˈvjʊə(r)/ *n.* a picture produced from a photographic negative transferred to a metal plate and etched in. [F (PHOTO-, *gravure* etching)]

photolithography /ˌfəʊtəʊlɪˈθɒgrəfɪ/ *n.* lithography with the plates made by photography.

photometer /fəʊˈtɒmɪtə(r)/ *n.* an instrument for measuring light. —**photometric** /ˌfəʊtəˈmetrɪk/ *adj.*, **photometry** *n.* [f. PHOTO- + -METER]

photon /ˈfəʊtɒn/ *n.* a quantum of electromagnetic radiation energy, proportional to the frequency. [f. Gk *phōs* light, after *electron*]

photorealism /ˌfəʊtəʊˈrɪəlɪz(ə)m/ *n.* detailed and un-idealized representation in art, characteristically of the banal, vulgar, or sordid aspects of life.

photosensitive /ˌfəʊtəʊˈsensɪtɪv/ *adj.* reacting chemically etc. to light.

photosphere /ˈfəʊtəsfɪə(r)/ *n.* the luminous envelope of the sun or a star from which its light and heat radiate. The temperature of the photosphere is quoted as the 'surface temperature' of the sun or star.

Photostat /ˈfəʊtəʊstæt/ *n.* [P] a photographic copy of a document etc. made by the Photostat process. —*v.t.* (-**tt**-) to make a Photostat of. [f. PHOTO- + -*stat* (as in *thermostat* etc.)]

photosynthesis /ˌfəʊtəʊˈsɪnθɪsɪs/ *n.* the process by which carbon dioxide is converted into organic matter in the presence of the chlorophyll of plants under the influence of light, which in all plants except some bacteria involves the production of oxygen from water.

phrase /freɪz/ *n.* **1.** a group of words forming a conceptual unit and usually without a predicate, grammatically equivalent to a noun, adjective, or adverb. **2.** an idiomatic or short pithy expression; a mode of expression. **3.** (*Mus.*) a group of notes forming a distinct unit within a longer melody. —*v.t.* **1.** to express in words. **2.** to divide (music) into phrases, especially in performance. —**phrase-book** *n.* a book for travellers, listing phrases and their foreign equivalents. —**phrasal** *adj.* [f. L *phrasis* f. Gk (*phrazō* declare)]

phraseology /ˌfreɪzɪˈɒlədʒɪ/ *n.* choice or arrangement of words; mode of expression. —**phraseological** /-ˈlɒdʒɪk(ə)l/ *adj.* [as prec. + -LOGY]

phrenology /frɪˈnɒlədʒɪ/ *n.* the study of the external form of the cranium as a supposed indication of a person's character and mental faculties. —**phrenological** /ˌfrenəˈlɒdʒɪk(ə)l/ *adj.*, **phrenologist** *n.* [f. Gk *phrēn* mind + -LOGY]

Phrygia /ˈfrɪdʒɪə/ the ancient name for an area of the central plateau and western Asia Minor, south of Bithynia. Its inhabitants were immigrants from Thrace, who established a kingdom centred at Gordion, west of present-day Ankara, that reached the peak of its power in the 8th c. BC under Midas and was overthrown by the Cimmerians *c.*680 BC. After its absorption by the powerful kingdom of Lydia in the 6th c. BC Phrygia was never independent again. —**Phrygian** *adj.* & *n.*

phthisis /ˈθaɪsɪs/ *n.* a progressive wasting disease, now especially pulmonary tuberculosis. [L f. Gk (*phthīnō* decay)]

phut /fʌt/ *n.* a dull sound of impact, the collapse of an inflated object, etc. —**go phut**, to explode or collapse with this sound; (*colloq.*) to collapse; to come to nothing. [f. Hindi, = to burst]

phylactery /fɪˈlæktərɪ/ *n.* **1.** a small leather box containing Hebrew texts, worn by Jews at morning weekday prayer to remind them to keep their law. **2.** an amulet or charm. [f. L f. Gk, = amulet (*phulassō* guard)]

phylum /ˈfaɪləm/ *n.* (*pl.* **phyla**) a major division of the animal or plant kingdom. [f. Gk *phulon* race]

physic /ˈfɪzɪk/ *n.* (*archaic*) **1.** the art of healing, medicine (excluding surgery). **2.** a medicine. [f. OF f. L f. Gk (*phusis* nature)]

physical /ˈfɪzɪk(ə)l/ *adj.* **1.** of matter, material (opp. moral, spiritual, or imaginary). **2.** of the body. **3.** of nature,

according to its laws. **4.** of physics. —**physical chemistry,** the branch of chemistry in which physics is applied to the study of substances and their reactions. **physical geography,** that dealing with natural features. **physical jerks,** (*colloq.*) physical exercises. **physical science,** the study of inanimate natural objects. —**physically** *adv.* [f. L f. Gk (as prec.)]

physician /fɪˈzɪʃ(ə)n/ *n.* a doctor, especially a specialist in medical diagnosis and treatment. [f. OF (as PHYSIC)]

physicist /ˈfɪzɪsɪst/ *n.* an expert in physics. [f. foll.]

physics /ˈfɪzɪks/ *n.pl.* (usu. treated as *sing.*) the science dealing with the properties and interactions of matter and energy (see below); (as *pl.*) these properties. [as PHYSIC]

The subject-matter of physics has undergone marked changes throughout the centuries. For Aristotle it included the study of all natural phenomena, but excluded quantitative subjects such as mechanics, music, and optics which were regarded as dealing with artefacts. By the 17th c. astronomy, mechanics, and optics were being treated mathematically, but a qualitative experimental physics remained, dealing especially with so-called 'imponderable fluids' such as heat, electricity, and magnetism. During the 18th c. physics concentrated increasingly on the more fundamental and general properties of matter, other phenomena being dealt with under the disciplines of chemistry, biology, etc. Mathematics was applied to all branches of physics during the 19th c. and by 1900 the structure of 'classical physics', describing the properties of matter on the macroscopic scale and at relatively low velocities, was largely complete. Since that time, however, the theories of modern physics, and in particular relativity, quantum theory, and the physics of atomic and subatomic particles, have transformed our overall understanding of the universe.

physiognomy /ˌfɪzɪˈɒnəmɪ/ *n.* **1.** the features of the face; a type of face. **2.** the art of judging character from facial or bodily features. **3.** the external features of a country etc. —**physiognomist** *n.* [f. OF f. L f. Gk (as PHYSIC, GNOMON)]

physiography /ˌfɪzɪˈɒgrəfɪ/ *n.* **1.** the description of nature or natural phenomena, or of a class of objects. **2.** physical geography. —**physiographer** *n.* [f. F (as PHYSIC, -GRAPHY)]

physiology /ˌfɪzɪˈɒlədʒɪ/ *n.* the science of the functions and phenomena of living organisms and their parts; these functions. —**physiological** /-ˈlɒdʒɪk(ə)l/ *adj.*, **physiologist** *n.* [f. F or L f. Gk (as PHYSIC, -LOGY)]

physiotherapy /ˌfɪzɪəʊˈθerəpɪ/ *n.* the treatment of disease or injury by massage, exercises, heat, etc., not by drugs. —**physiotherapist** *n.* [as PHYSIC + THERAPY]

physique /fɪˈziːk/ *n.* bodily structure and development. [F (as PHYSIC)]

pi /paɪ/ *n.* **1.** the sixteenth letter of the Greek alphabet, = p. **2.** (π) the symbol of the ratio of the circumference of a circle to the diameter (approx. 3.14159). [Gk]

Piaget /ˈpjæʒeɪ/, Jean (1897-1980), Swiss psychologist whose work has provided the single biggest impact on the study of the development of thought processes. His central thesis is that children initially lack intellectual and logical abilities, which they acquire through experience and inter-action with the world around them, proceeding through a series of fixed stages of cognitive development, each being a prerequisite for the next.

pia mater /ˌpaɪə ˈmeɪtə(r)/ the delicate inner membrane enveloping the brain and spinal cord. [L, = tender mother]

pianissimo /ˌpiːæˈnɪsɪməʊ/ *adv.* (*Mus.*) very softly. —*n.* (*Mus.*) a passage to be played very softly. [It., superl. of PIANO²]

pianist /ˈpɪənɪst/ *n.* a player of the piano. [f. F (as foll.)]

piano¹ /pɪˈænəʊ/ *n.* (*pl.* -**os**) a musical instrument with metal strings struck by hammers worked by levers from a keyboard (vibration being stopped by dampers when keys are released), and with pedals regulating the quality of the tone. (See PIANOFORTE and ill. MUSICAL NOTATION). —**piano-accordion** *n.* an accordion with the melody played on a small piano-like keyboard. [It., abbr. of PIANOFORTE]

piano² /pɪˈɑːnəʊ/ *adv.* (*Mus.*) softly. —*n.* (*Mus.*) a passage to be played softly. [It. f. L *planus* flat, (of sound) soft]

pianoforte /ˌpiːænəˈfɔːtɪ/ *n.* (*formal* or *archaic*) a piano. The pianoforte (commonly called 'piano') was developed in Italy in the early 18th c. and so called because it was designed to produce both soft (*piano*) and loud (*forte*) notes. It superseded the clavichord and harpsichord, having a louder tone than the former and a greater expressive range than the latter. Two instruments survive by Bartolomeo Cristofori, who has some claim to be the inventor of the piano, dating from 1720 and 1726 respectively. Today the most common forms are the grand piano (ranging in size from 'baby grand' to 'concert grand') and the upright, with strings running perpendicularly rather than horizontally, but the earliest models were of harpsichord shape; in the mid-18th c. the square piano was the principal domestic instrument.

Pianola /pɪəˈnəʊlə/ n. [P] a kind of automatic mechanical piano. [dim. of PIANO[1]]

pibroch /ˈpiːbrɒk/ n. a series of variations for the bagpipe. They are generally of martial character but include dirges. [f. Gael., = art of piping]

pica /ˈpaɪkə/ n. 1. a unit of type-size (⅙ inch). 2. a size of letters in typewriting (ten per inch). [f. L, = 15th-c. book of rules about church feasts (perh. as PIE[2])]

picador /ˈpɪkədɔː(r)/ n. a mounted man with a lance in a bullfight. [Sp. (picar prick)]

Picardy /ˈpɪkədɪ/ a former province of northern France between Normandy and Flanders, the scene of heavy fighting in the First World War.

picaresque /pɪkəˈresk/ adj. (of a style of fiction) dealing with the adventures of rogues. [F f. Sp. (picaro rogue)]

Picasso /pɪˈkæsəʊ/, Pablo (1881–1973), Spanish painter. Widely considered to be the most inventive of all 20th-c. painters, his achievement includes major contributions to painting, sculpture, and graphics. His earliest work (1901–4) is known as his Blue Period—pictures of society's outsiders painted predominantly in blue, and redolent of fin-de-siècle melancholia. This gave way, with his permanent settling in Paris (1904), to the less sentimental treatment of circus performers in the Rose Period of 1905–6. From 1907 to 1914 he worked with Georges Braque in the monumental enterprise of cubism which challenged for the first time since the Renaissance the whole function of painting, replacing mimesis with a new self-sufficient pictorial order distinct from everyday visual habits. The 1920s and 1930s saw the protean development of a heavy neo-classical figurative style, designs for Diaghilev's Ballets Russes, pictures using quasi-surrealist imagery, engraved work (particularly, the Minotaur series), and the development of sculpture; 1937 saw the completion of Guernica—his response to the destruction of the Basque capital by Fascist bombs—possibly his greatest and most distinctive single picture. In his later years a certain playfulness imbued his work, but the seemingly inexhaustible imaginative creativity that typified his art never faltered.

picayune /pɪkəˈjuːn/ n. (US) 1. a small coin. 2. (colloq.) an insignificant person or thing. —adj. (US colloq.) mean, contemptible; petty. [f. F picaillon Piedmontese coin]

piccalilli /pɪkəˈlɪlɪ/ n. a pickle of chopped vegetables, mustard, and spices. [perh. f. PICKLE + CHILLI]

piccaninny /pɪkəˈnɪnɪ/ n. a small Black or Australian Aboriginal child. [W. Ind. Negro f. Sp. pequeño little]

piccolo /ˈpɪkələʊ/ n. (pl. -os) a small flute, sounding an octave higher than the ordinary (ill. ORCHESTRA). [It., = small]

pick v.t./i. 1. to select (esp. carefully or thoughtfully). 2. to detach (a flower, fruit, etc.) from the plant bearing it. 3. to make a hole in or break the surface of with the fingers or a sharp instrument; to make (a hole) thus. 4. to open (a lock) with a pointed instrument, especially to force entry. 5. to probe or dig at to remove unwanted matter. 6. to eat (food) desultorily or in small bits. 7. to clear (a bone or carcass) of its flesh. —n. 1. picking, selection; the right to select. 2. the best or most wanted part. 3. a pickaxe. 4. an instrument for picking; a plectrum. —**pick and choose**, to select fastidiously. **pick at**, to find fault with; to eat desultorily. **pick a person's brains**, to extract ideas or information from him for one's own use. **pick holes in**, to find fault with. **pick-me-up**, n. a tonic (lit. or fig.) to restore health or revive the spirits. **pick off**, to pluck off; to select and shoot (a target or succession of targets) with care. **pick on**, to find fault with; to nag at; to select. **pick out**, to take from a large number; to identify or recognize; to distinguish from the surrounding objects; to play (a tune) by ear on a piano etc. **pick over**, to look over item by item; to choose the best from. **pick a person's pocket**, to steal its contents from him. **pick a quarrel**, to provoke or seize an opportunity for one. **pick to pieces**, to criticize harshly. **pick up**, to take hold of and lift; to learn routinely; to stop for and take with one; to take (cargo etc.) on board; (of the police) to catch and take into custody; to acquire by chance or casually; to encounter and get to know (a person); to manage to receive (a broadcast signal etc.); to improve, to recover health, (of an engine) to recover speed. **pick-up** n. picking-up; a person met casually; the part of a

record-player carrying the stylus; a small open motor truck. —**picker** n. [orig. unkn.]

pick-a-back /ˈpɪkəbæk/ var. of PIGGY-BACK.

pickaxe /ˈpɪkæks/ n. a heavy iron tool with a point at one end and a wooden handle at right angles to it, for breaking up hard ground etc. [f. OF picois, rel. to PIKE]

picket /ˈpɪkɪt/ n. 1. one or more persons stationed by strikers outside a place of work to dissuade others from entering. 2. a small body of troops acting as a patrol, a party of sentries. 3. a pointed stake driven into the ground. —v.t./i. 1. to place or act as a picket outside (a place of work). 2. to post as a military picket. 3. to tether (an animal). 4. to secure (a place) with stakes. [f. F piquet pointed stake (piquer prick)]

pickings n.pl. 1. casual profits or perquisites. 2. gains from pilfering. 3. the remaining scraps, gleanings. [f. PICK]

pickle n. 1. a food, especially a vegetable, preserved in brine, vinegar, or a similar liquor; pickled used. 2. (colloq.) a plight. —v.t. 1. to preserve in or treat with pickle. 2. (in p.p., slang) drunk. [f. MDu. or MLG pekel]

pickpocket n. one who steals from people's pockets.

Pickwickian /pɪkˈwɪkɪən/ adj. (of words or their sense) not in accordance with the usual meaning, conveniently interpreted so as to avoid offence etc. [f. Pickwick, character in Dickens's Pickwick Papers (1836–7)]

picky adj. (colloq.) excessively fastidious. [f. PICK]

picnic /ˈpɪknɪk/ n. 1. a pleasure outing including an informal outdoor meal; the meal itself. 2. (colloq.) something readily or easily accomplished. —v.i. (-ck-) to take part in a picnic. —**picnicker** n. [f. F pique-nique, orig. unkn.]

pico- /ˈpaɪkəʊ-, pɪ-/ in comb. denoting a factor of 10⁻¹² one billionth (picometre). [f. Sp. pico beak, peak, little bit]

picot /ˈpiːkəʊ/ n. a small loop of twisted thread in an edging to lace etc. [F, dim. of pic peak, point]

picric acid /ˈpɪkrɪk/ a yellow bitter substance used in dyeing and explosives. [f. Gk pikros bitter]

Pict n. a member of an ancient people, of disputed origin and ethnological affinities, who formerly inhabited parts of northern Britain. In Roman writings (c.AD 300) the term Picti is applied to the hostile tribes occupying the area north of the Antonine Wall. According to chroniclers the Pictish kingdom was united with the Scottish under Kenneth MacAlpine in 843, and the name of the Picts as a distinct people gradually disappeared. —**Pictish** adj. [f. L Picti, perh. = painted people, or perh. assim. to native name]

pictograph /ˈpɪktəɡrɑːf/ n. (also **pictogram**) 1. a pictorial symbol used as a form of writing. 2. a pictorial representation of statistics. —**pictographic** /-ˈɡræfɪk/ adj. [f. L pingere paint + -GRAPH, -GRAM]

pictorial /pɪkˈtɔːrɪəl/ adj. of or expressed in a picture or pictures; illustrated. —n. a periodical with pictures as the main feature. —**pictorially** adv. [f. L pictorius (pictor painter)]

picture /ˈpɪktʃə(r)/ n. 1. a likeness or representation of a subject produced by painting, drawing, or photography; a portrait. 2. a beautiful object or person. 3. a scene, a total visual or mental impression produced. 4. an image on a television screen. 5. a cinema film; (in pl.) a performance at a cinema. —v.t. 1. to form a mental picture of, to imagine. 2. to represent in a picture. 3. to describe graphically. —**in the picture**, fully informed; noticed. **picture postcard**, a postcard with a picture on one side. **picture window**, a large window facing an attractive view. [f. L (pingere paint)]

picturesque /pɪktʃəˈresk/ adj. 1. striking and pleasant to look at. 2. (of language) graphic, expressive. —**picturesquely** adv., **picturesqueness** n. [f. F pittoresque f. It. (as PICTORIAL)]

piddle v.i. 1. to work or act in a trifling way. 2. (colloq.) to urinate. [sense 1 perh. f. PEDDLE; sense 2 prob. f. PISS + PUDDLE]

piddling adj. (colloq.) trifling, trivial. [f. prec.]

pidgin /ˈpɪdʒɪn/ n. a simplified form of a language, used for communication between persons of different nationality etc. —**pidgin English**, a jargon, chiefly of English words, used originally between Chinese and Europeans. [corrupt. of business]

pi-dog var. of PYE-DOG.

pie[1] n. 1. a dish of meat, fish, or fruit, etc. enclosed in or covered with pastry or other crust and baked. 2. a confused mass of printers' type; chaos. —**easy as pie**, very easy. **pie chart**, a diagram representing various quantities as sectors of a circle. **pie in the sky**, a delusive prospect of future happiness, especially as a reward in heaven for virtue or suffering on earth. [perh. = foll.]

pie² *n.* a magpie. [f. OF f. L *pica*]

piebald /'paɪbɔːld/ *adj.* (of a horse etc.) with irregular patches of white and black or other dark colour. —*n.* a piebald animal. [f. PIE² + BALD]

piece /piːs/ *n.* **1.** any of the distinct portions of which a thing is composed or into which it is divided or broken; a detached portion. **2.** a single example or specimen, an item. **3.** a distinct section or area (of land etc.). **4.** any of the things of which a set is composed. **5.** a definite quantity in which a thing is made up for sale etc. **6.** a fixed unit of work. **7.** a (usu. short) literary, dramatic, or musical composition. **8.** a coin. **9.** a man in board-games, especially a chess-man (usu. other than a pawn). **10.** a firearm; an artillery weapon. **11.** (*derog.*) a person, especially a woman. —*v.t.* to form into a whole, to join the pieces of. —**go to pieces**, to lose self-control; to collapse. **in one piece**, not broken, unharmed. **of a piece**, uniform, consistent. **piece-goods** *n.pl.* textile fabrics woven in standard lengths. **pieces of eight**, (*hist.*) Spanish dollars. **piece-work** *n.* work paid at a rate per piece. **say one's piece**, to give one's opinion; to make a prepared statement. **take to pieces**, to separate the parts of; to be divisible thus. [f. AF, prob. f. Celtic]

pièce de résistance /pɪes də reˈzɪstãs/ the most important or remarkable item; the main dish at a meal. [F]

piecemeal /'piːsmiːl/ *adv.* piece by piece or part at a time. —*adj.* done etc. piecemeal. [f. PIECE + MEAL]

pied /paɪd/ *adj.* particoloured. [f. PIE²]

pied-à-terre /pjeɪdɑːˈteə(r)/ *n.* (*pl.* **pieds-à-terre** *pr.* same) a place kept available as temporary quarters when needed. [F, lit. 'foot to earth']

Piedmont /'piːdmɒnt/ a district of NW Italy, united with Italy in 1859.

pie-dog var. of PYE-DOG.

Pied Piper /paɪd ˈpaɪpə(r)/ the hero of *The Pied Piper of Hamelin*, a poem by Robert Browning (1842), based on an old legend. He rid the town of Hamelin in Brunswick of rats by luring them away with his music, and when refused the promised payment he lured away all the children. The event was long regarded as historical and supposed to have occurred in 1284; the piper's name was Bunting. [= PIED]

pier /pɪə(r)/ *n.* **1.** a structure running out into the sea and serving as a promenade, or landing-stage, or breakwater. **2.** a support of an arch or of a span of a bridge (ill. BRIDGES); a pillar (ill. CHURCH). **3.** the solid masonry between windows etc. —**pier-glass** *n.* a large mirror of a kind originally placed between windows. [f. L *pera*]

pierce /pɪəs/ *v.t./i.* **1.** to penetrate (*lit.* & *fig.*). **2.** to prick with or like a sharp instrument; to make (a hole) thus. **3.** to force one's way through or into. [f. OF ult. f. L *pertundere* bore through (PER-, *tundere* thrust)]

piercing *adj.* **1.** (of pain or cold etc.) intense, penetrating sharply. **2.** (of a look or sound) sharp or shrill, fierce. [f. prec.]

Piero della Francesca /pɪerəʊ delə frænˈtʃeskə/ (1416-92), Italian painter, for a long time forgotten but regarded in 20th-c. criticism as one of the greatest quattrocento painters. The world of his artistic imagination has clarity, dignity, and order, and the outlines of his figures tend towards the grace and regularity of curves in geometry. His interest in perspective and mathematical relationships is witnessed in an assured naturalism, with protagonists placed firmly in credible landscapes and inhabiting real space. He was capable of investing his art with hieratic solemnity and power by using the severity of frontal or profile poses and formal presentation of the figure (e.g. *The Resurrection*, c.1463).

Pierrot /'pɪərəʊ/ a stock character in the French and English theatres (*fem.* **Pierrette**), with whitened face and loose white costume. Originally a robust country bumpkin, he was transformed by the French player Deburau in the 1820s into an ever-hopeful always disappointed lover, a concept which became well known in London. The character was ousted from the harlequinade by the English clown, but regained much of his old vigour when the pierrot troupes, or concert parties, were formed towards the end of the 19th c. [F, dim. of *Pierre* Peter]

pietà /pɪeɪˈtɑː/ *n.* a picture or sculpture of the Virgin Mary holding the dead body of Christ on her lap. [It. f. L (as PIETY)]

pietism /'paɪətɪz(ə)m/ *n.* **1.** pious sentiment; exaggeration

or affectation of this. **2. Pietism**, a movement originated at Frankfurt c.1670 by P. J. Spener for the revitalizing of orthodox Lutheranism, with devotional circles for prayer, Bible study, etc. Pietism influenced similar movements elsewhere including that of John Wesley. [f. G (as foll.)]

piety /'paɪətɪ/ *n.* piousness; an act etc. showing this. [f. OF f. L (as PIOUS)]

piezoelectricity /paɪiːzəʊɪlekˈtrɪsɪtɪ, piːzəʊ-/ *n.* the phenomenon, exhibited especially by certain crystals such as quartz, in which a substance becomes electrically polarized when subjected to pressure. Piezoelectricity was first discovered by Pierre Curie and his brother in 1880. The converse effect, in which a voltage applied to such a material causes a mechanical deformation, also occurs. These effects are of great practical importance because piezoelectric substances are able to convert mechanical signals (such as sound waves) into electrical signals, and vice versa. They are therefore widely used in microphones, gramophone pick-ups, earphones, etc. They can also be made to resonate very accurately at a fixed frequency, and as such form the basis of accurate time-keeping devices such as quartz clocks. —**piezoelectric** *adj.* [f. Gk *piezō* press + ELECTRIC]

piffle *n.* (*slang*) nonsense, worthless talk. —*v.i.* (*slang*) to talk or act feebly or frivolously. [imit.]

piffling *adj.* (*slang*) trivial, worthless. [f. prec.]

pig *n.* **1.** a wild or domesticated animal of the family Suidae with a broad snout, stout bristly body, and short legs. **2.** pork. **3.** (*colloq.*) a greedy, dirty, or unpleasant person. **4.** (*slang, derog.*) a policeman. **5.** an oblong mass of metal (especially iron or lead) from a smelting-furnace. —*v.t./i.* to live or behave like a pig (esp. *pig it*). —**pig in a poke**, a thing acquired or offered without previous sight or knowledge of it. **pig-iron** *n.* crude iron from a smelting-furnace (see IRON). [f. OE]

pigeon-hole *n.* **1.** a small recess for a pigeon to rest in. **2.** each of a set of small compartments in a cabinet or on a wall for papers, letters, etc. —*v.t.* **1.** to put in a pigeon-hole. **2.** to put aside for future consideration or indefinitely. **3.** to classify mentally.

piggery *n.* a place where pigs are bred; a pigsty. [f. PIG]

piggish *adj.* like a pig, greedy or dirty. [f. PIG]

piggy *n.* a little pig. —**piggy bank**, a money-box in the form of a hollow pig. [f. PIG]

piggy-back *n.* a ride on the shoulders and back of another. —*adv.* by means of a piggy-back. [for earlier *pick-a-back;* orig. unkn.]

pigheaded *adj.* obstinate, stubborn.

piglet /'pɪglɪt/ *n.* a young pig. [f. PIG + -LET]

pigment /'pɪgmənt/ *n.* colouring-matter. —*v.t.* to colour (skin or other tissue) with natural pigment. —**pigmentation** /-ˈteɪʃ(ə)n/ *n.* [f. L *pigmentum* (*pingere* paint)]

pigskin *n.* a pig's skin; leather made from this.

pigsty *n.* **1.** a partly-covered pen for pigs. **2.** a very dirty or untidy place.

pigswill *n.* the swill of a kitchen or brewery fed to pigs.

pigtail *n.* a plait of hair hanging from the back of the head.

pike *n.* **1.** (*pl.* same) a large voracious freshwater fish with a long narrow snout. **2.** a peaked top of a hill. **3.** (*hist.*) an infantry weapon consisting of a long wooden shaft with a pointed metal head. [OE, = point]

piked /paɪkt/ *adj.* (in diving and gymnastics) with the legs straight and forming an angle with the body at the hips (ill. SPORTS). [orig. unkn.]

pikelet /'paɪklɪt/ *n.* a crumpet. [f. Welsh (*bara*) *pyglyd* pitchy (bread)]

pikestaff *n.* the wooden shaft of a pike. —**plain as a pikestaff**, quite plain or obvious.

pilaff /'pɪlæf/ *n.* an oriental dish of rice with meat, spices, etc. [f. Turk.]

pilaster /pɪˈlæstə(r)/ *n.* a rectangular column, especially one fastened into a wall (ill. HOUSES). [f. F f. It. f. L (*pila* pillar)]

Pilate /'paɪlət/, Pontius (1st c. AD), the governor of Judaea AD 26-36 who presided at the trial of Jesus Christ.

pilau /pɪˈlaʊ/ var of PILAFF.

pilchard /'pɪltʃəd/ *n.* a small sea-fish (*Sardinia pilchardus*) related to the herring. [orig. unkn.]

pile¹ *n.* **1.** a number of things lying one upon another. **2.** (*colloq.*) a large quantity, especially of money. **3.** a grand or lofty building. **4.** (in full **funeral pile**) a heap of wood etc.

on which a corpse is burnt. **5.** a series of plates of dissimilar metals laid alternately to produce an electric current. **6.** (in full **atomic pile**) a nuclear reactor. —*v.t./i.* **1.** to heap, stack, or load. **2.** to crowd. —**pile it on,** (*colloq.*) to exaggerate. **pile up,** to accumulate, to cause (a vehicle or aircraft) to crash. **pile-up** *n.* a collision of several motor vehicles. [f. OF f. L *pila* pillar]

pile[2] *n.* **1.** a pointed stake or post. **2.** a heavy beam of metal, concrete, or timber driven vertically into the ground as a foundation or support for a building or bridge. —**pile-driver** *n.* a machine for driving piles into the ground. **pile-dwelling** *n.* a lake-dwelling (see LAKE[1]). [OE f. L *pilum* javelin]

pile[3] *n.* the soft surface of a fabric with a tangible depth formed by cut or uncut loops. [prob. f. AF f. L *pilus* hair]

pile[4] *n.* (usu. in *pl.*) a haemorrhoid. [prob. f. L *pila* ball]

pilfer *v.t./i.* to steal, especially in small quantities. —**pilferer** *n.* [f. AF *pelfrer* pillage]

pilgrim /ˈpɪlgrɪm/ *n.* one who journeys to a sacred or revered place as an act of religious devotion. —**Pilgrim Fathers,** the pioneers of British colonization of North America, a group of 100 (or according to some reports 102) persons who sailed in the *Mayflower* and founded a settlement at New Plymouth, Mass., in 1620. The expedition was initiated by a group of English Puritans fleeing religious persecution. [f. Prov. F. L, = PEREGRINE]

pilgrimage *n.* a pilgrim's journey. [f. prec.]

Pilipino /pɪlɪˈpiːnəʊ/ *n.* the national language of the Republic of the Philippines, based on Tagalog. [f. FILIPINO]

pill *n.* **1.** a small ball or flat piece of medicinal substance for swallowing whole. **2.** something that has to be endured, a humiliation. —**the pill,** (*colloq.*) the contraceptive pill. [f. MDu. or MLG (prob. as PILULE)]

pillage /ˈpɪlɪdʒ/ *n.* plundering, especially in war. —*v.t.* to plunder. —**pillager** *n.* [f. OF (*piller* plunder)]

pillar /ˈpɪlə(r)/ *n.* **1.** a slender vertical structure of stone etc. used as a support or ornament. **2.** an upright mass of air, water, rock, etc. **3.** a person regarded as a main supporter of a cause or principle. —**from pillar to post,** rapidly from one place or situation to another. **pillar-box** *n.* a hollow pillar in which letters may be posted. Such structures were introduced by the novelist Anthony Trollope during his time in the Post Office. **Pillars of Hercules,** see HERCULES. [f. AF *piler* ult. f. L *pila* pillar]

pillbox *n.* **1.** a shallow circular box for holding pills. **2.** a small concrete shelter for a gun emplacement.

pillion /ˈpɪljən/ *n.* a seat for a passenger behind a motorcyclist etc. —**ride pillion,** to ride on this as a passenger. [f. Gaelic, = small cushion, f. L *pellis* skin]

pillory /ˈpɪlərɪ/ *n.* a wooden framework with holes for the head and hands, into which offenders were formerly locked for exposure to public ridicule. —*v.t.* **1.** to put in a pillory. **2.** to expose to ridicule. [f. OF]

pillow /ˈpɪləʊ/ *n.* **1.** a cushion used as a support for the head, especially in a bed. **2.** a pillow-shaped block or support. —*v.t.* to rest or prop up on a pillow. [OE, ult. f. L *pulvinus* cushion]

pillowcase *n.* (also **pillowslip**) a washable cover of cotton etc. for a pillow.

pilot /ˈpaɪlət/ *n.* **1.** a person who operates the controls of an aircraft. **2.** a person qualified to take charge of ships entering or leaving a harbour or travelling through certain waters. **3.** a guide. —*v.t.* **1.** to act as the pilot of. **2.** to guide. —*adj.* experimental, testing (on a small scale) how a scheme etc. will work. —**pilot-light** a small gas-burner kept alight and lighting a larger burner when this is turned on; an electric indicator light or control light. **pilot officer,** the lowest commissioned rank in the RAF. [f. F f. L ult. f. Gk *pēdon* oar]

Pilsener /ˈpɪlznə(r), -s-/ *n.* a pale-coloured lager beer with a strong hop flavour, of the type brewed at Pilsen (Plzeň) in Czechoslovakia.

Piltdown man /ˈpɪltdaʊn/ a fraudulent fossil (*Eoanthropus dawsoni*) composed of a human cranium and an ape jaw that was presented to the scientific community in 1912 as a genuine hominid of great antiquity. The fossil was allegedly discovered in a gravel-pit on Piltdown Common near Lewes, East Sussex, in association with early Pleistocene fossil fauna in addition to stone and bone artefacts of 'pre-Acheulian' type. Although suspicions concerning its genuineness were voiced the fraud was not proved until 1953, when J. S. Weiner and K. P. Oakley demonstrated beyond any doubt, by fluorine dating and other tests, that

Piltdown man was a hoax. The problems of human evolution, although still complex and much disputed, were made less difficult with the removal of *Eoanthropus dawsoni* from the competition. Perpetration of the hoax has been variously credited to the skull's 'discoverer' (Charles Dawson), his friends Samuel Woodhead (county analyst for Sussex) and Teilhard du Chardin, and Sir Arthur Conan Doyle.

pilule /ˈpɪljuːl/ *n.* a small pill. [F f. L *pilula* dim. of *pila* ball]

pimento /pɪˈmentəʊ/ *n.* (*pl.* **-os** 1.) a West Indian tree (*Pimenta officinalis*) the ground berry of which produces allspice. **2.** this spice. **3.** a sweet pepper. [f. Sp. f. L (as PIGMENT)]

pimp *n.* one who solicits clients for a prostitute or brothel. —*v.i.* to act as a pimp. [orig. unkn.]

pimpernel /ˈpɪmpənel/ *n.* an annual plant (*Anagallis arvensis*) with small scarlet, blue, or white flowers that close in cloudy or rainy weather. [f. OF, ult. f. L *piper* pepper]

pimple *n.* a small hard inflamed spot on the skin; a similar slight swelling on a surface. —**pimply** *adj.* [OE, = break out in pustules]

pin *n.* **1.** a thin usually cylindrical piece of metal with a sharp point and round broadened head for fastening together papers, fabrics, etc. or (with an ornamental head) as a decoration. **2.** a larger similar object of wood or metal for various purposes. **3.** the projecting part of a dovetail joint (ill. CARPENTRY). **4.** (in golf) a stick with a flag on it marking the position of a hole. **5.** (in *pl.*, *colloq.*) the legs. —*v.t.* (**-nn-**) **1.** to fasten with a pin or pins. **2.** to fix the responsibility for (a deed *on* a person). **3.** to seize and hold fast (against a wall etc.). **4.** to transfix with a pin, lance, etc. —**pin-ball** *n.* a game in which small metal balls are shot across a sloping board and strike against pins. **pin down,** to make (a person) declare his intentions etc. clearly; to restrict the actions of (an enemy etc.); to specify (a thing) precisely. **pin one's faith** *or* **hopes on,** to rely absolutely on. **pin-money,** a small sum of money, originally that allowed to a woman or earned by her for private expenses. **pins and needles,** a tingling sensation in a limb recovering from numbness. **pin-stripe** *n.* a very narrow stripe in cloth. **pin-table** *n.* a table used in pin-ball. **pin-tuck** *n.* a very narrow ornamental tuck. **pin-up** *n.* a picture of an attractive or famous person, pinned up on a wall etc.; such a person. **pin-wheel** *n.* a small Catherine wheel. [OE f. L *pinna* point etc.]

pinafore /ˈpɪnəfɔː(r)/ *n.* a full-length apron. —**pinafore dress,** a dress without a collar and sleeves, worn over a blouse or jumper. [f. PIN + AFORE]

pince-nez /ˈpæ̃sneɪ/ *n.* (*pl.* same) a pair of eyeglasses with a spring that clips on the nose. [F, = pinch-nose]

pincers /ˈpɪnsəz/ *n.pl.* **1.** (also **pair of pincers**) a gripping-tool of two pivoted limbs forming jaws. **2.** a similar organ of crustaceans etc. —**pincer movement,** a military movement in which forces converge from each side on an enemy position. [f. AF (OF *pincier* pinch)]

pinch *v.t./i.* **1.** to squeeze tightly between two surfaces, especially between finger and thumb. **2.** (of cold, hunger, etc.) to affect painfully; to cause to shrivel. **3.** to stint, to be niggardly. **4.** (*slang*) to steal. **5.** (*slang*) to arrest. —*n.* **1.** pinching, squeezing. **2.** the stress of circumstances. **3.** as much as can be taken up with the tips of the finger and thumb. —**at a pinch,** in an emergency, if necessary. **pinch off** *or* **out,** to shorten or remove (buds etc.) by pinching. [f. OF *pincier* ult. f. L *pungere* prick]

pinchbeck *n.* a goldlike alloy of copper and zinc used in cheap jewellery etc. —*adj.* counterfeit, sham. [f. C. Pinchbeck, English watchmaker (d. 1732)]

pincushion *n.* a small cushion or pad into which pins are stuck to keep them ready for use.

Pindar /ˈpɪndə(r)/ (518–438 BC) Greek lyric poet. Of his various works there survive four books of odes in honour of victories won, chiefly by Greek rulers and aristocrats, in athletic contests. They are usually in the form of choral hymns, written in a grand style; the celebration of victory is seen as a religious occasion. —**Pindaric** /-ˈdærɪk/ *adj.*

pine[1] *n.* an evergreen coniferous tree of the genus *Pinus* with needle-shaped leaves growing in clusters (ill. TREES); its wood. —**pine-cone** *n.* the seed-head of the pine. [OE & f. OF f. L *pinus*]

pine[2] *v.i.* **1.** to waste away through grief or yearning. **2.** to feel an intense longing. [OE]

pineal /ˈpɪnɪəl/ *adj.* shaped like a pine-cone. —**pineal body** *or* **gland,** a conical gland in the brain, of unknown function (ill. BODY 4). [f. F f. L *pinea* pine-cone]

pineapple /ˈpaɪnæp(ə)l/ n. **1.** a large juicy tropical fruit with a yellow flesh and tough segmented skin. **2.** the plant (*Ananas comosus*) bearing this. [f. PINE¹ + APPLE (f. the resemblance of the fruit to a pine-cone)]

Pinero /pɪˈnɪərəʊ/, Sir Arthur Wing (1855–1934), English dramatist, who began as an actor and encouraged by Sir Henry Irving became a prolific author of many successful farces, such as *The Magistrate* (1885), and several more serious plays, including *The Profligate* (1889) and the enduringly popular *The Second Mrs Tanqueray* (1893). In his later years his reputation became eclipsed by the rising popularity of the new theatre of Shaw and Ibsen.

ping n. an abrupt single ringing sound. —v.t./i. to make or cause to make this sound. —**pinger** n. [imit.]

ping-pong n. table tennis. [imit., f. sound of bat striking ball]

pinion¹ /ˈpɪnjən/ n. a small cog-wheel engaging with a larger one; a cogged spindle engaging with a wheel. [f. F *pignon* f. L (as PINEAL)]

pinion² /ˈpɪnjən/ n. **1.** the outer segment of a bird's wing. **2.** (*poetic*) a wing. **3.** a flight-feather. —v.t. **1.** to clip the wings of (a bird) to prevent it from flying. **2.** to restrain (a person) by holding or binding his arms; to bind (arms) thus. [f. OF, ult. f. L *pinna* feather]

pink¹ n. **1.** pale red colour. **2.** pink clothes or material. **3.** a garden plant of the genus *Dianthus* with fragrant flowers. **4.** the best or most perfect condition. —adj. **1.** of pale red colour. **2.** (*slang*) mildly communist. —**in the pink,** (*slang*) in very good health. **pink gin,** gin flavoured with angostura bitters. —**pinkness** n. [perh. f. obs. *pink-eyed* small-eyed]

pink² v.t. **1.** to pierce slightly. **2.** to cut a scalloped or zigzag edge on. —**pinking shears,** a dressmaker's serrated scissors for cutting a zigzag edge. [perh. f. L Du.; cf. LF *pinken* strike, peck]

pink³ v.i. (of a vehicle engine) to emit high-pitched explosive sounds when running faultily. [imit.]

Pinkerton /ˈpɪŋkət(ə)n/, Allan (1819–84), American detective. An immigrant from Scotland, Pinkerton established the first American private detective agency in Chicago in 1850 and became a national figure after solving a series of express robberies. In the early years of the American Civil War he served as the secret service chief of the Union general McClellan and was later prominent as a strike-breaker, particularly in the eastern coal industry.

pinnace /ˈpɪnɪs/ n. a warship's or other ship's small boat. [f. F]

pinnacle /ˈpɪnək(ə)l/ n. **1.** a small ornamental turret crowning a buttress, roof, etc. **2.** a natural peak. **3.** the highest point (of fame, success, etc.). [f. OF f. L *pinnaculum* (*pinna* wing, point)]

pinnate /ˈpɪnɪt/ adj. (of a compound leaf) with leaflets on each side of the leaf-stalk. —**pinnately** adv. [f. L *pinnatus* feathered]

pinny n. (*colloq.*) a pinafore. [abbr.]

pin-point n. **1.** the point of a pin. **2.** something very small or sharp. —v.t. to locate or designate with high precision. —adj. **1.** seeming as small or sharp as the point of a pin. **2.** performed with or exhibiting high precision.

pinprick n. a trifling irritation.

pint /paɪnt/ n. **1.** a measure of capacity of liquids etc., ⅛ of a gallon (in Britain 4546 cc, in the USA 3785 cc). **2.** this quantity of liquid, especially milk or beer. —**pint-sized** adj. (*colloq.*) diminutive. [f. OF]

pinta /ˈpaɪntə/ n. (*colloq.*) a pint of milk etc. [corrupt. (orig. in advertising slogan) of *pint of*]

pintail n. a duck or grouse with a pointed tail.

Pinter /ˈpɪntə(r)/, Harold (1930–), English playwright. His plays are marked by humorous misunderstandings and often also by a sense of brooding menace, as in *The Caretaker* (1960) and *The Homecoming* (1965).

pintle /ˈpɪnt(ə)l/ n. a bolt or pin, especially one on which some other part turns. [OE, = penis]

pioneer /paɪəˈnɪə(r)/ n. an original explorer or settler or investigator of a subject etc.; an initiator of an enterprise. —v.t./i. to be a pioneer; to originate (a course of action etc. followed later by others). [f. F *pionnier* foot-soldier (as PEON)]

pious /ˈpaɪəs/ adj. **1.** devout in religion. **2.** ostentatiously virtuous. **3.** dutiful. —**piously** adv., **piousness** n. [f. L *pius*]

pip¹ n. a seed of an apple, orange, grape, etc. [abbr. of PIPPIN]

pip² n. **1.** each spot on playing-cards, dice, or dominoes. **2.**

a star (up to three according to rank) on the shoulder of an army officer's uniform. [earlier *peep* (orig. unkn.)]

pip³ v.t. (-**pp**-) **1.** (*colloq.*) to hit with a shot. **2.** (also **pip at the post**) to forestall; to defeat narrowly or at the last moment. [f. prec. or PIP¹]

pip⁴ n. a short high-pitched sound, especially one produced electronically e.g. as a time-signal. [imit.]

pip⁵ n. **1.** a disease of poultry, hawks, etc. **2.** (*slang*) a fit of disgust, depression, or bad temper. [f. MDu. or MLG, perh. ult. f. L *pituita* slime]

pipe n. **1.** a tube of metal, plastic, etc., especially for conveying water, gas, etc. **2.** a narrow tube with a bowl at one end containing tobacco for smoking; the quantity of tobacco held by this. **3.** a wind-instrument of a single tube; each tube by which the sound is produced in an organ; (in *pl.*) bagpipes. **4.** a tubular organ, vessel, etc., in an animal body. **5.** a boatswain's whistle; the sounding of this. **6.** a cask for wine, especially as a measure (usu. = 105 gal.). —v.t./i. **1.** to convey (oil, water, gas, etc.) by pipes. **2.** to transmit (recorded music etc.) by wire or cable for hearing elsewhere. **3.** to play on a pipe or pipes. **4.** to utter in a shrill voice. **5.** to lead or guide (a person etc.) by the sound of a pipe; to summon by sounding a whistle. **6.** to decorate or trim with piping. **7.** to furnish with pipes. —**pipe-cleaner** n. a piece of flexible tuft-covered wire to clean inside a tobacco-pipe. **pipe down,** (*colloq.*) to be quiet or less insistent. **pipe-dream** n. an unattainable or fanciful hope or scheme, as indulged in when smoking a pipe (orig. of opium). **pipe up,** to begin to sing, play a tune, etc.; to interject a remark. [OE, ult. f. L *pipare* chirp]

pipeclay n. a fine white clay for tobacco-pipes or for whitening leather etc.

pipeline n. **1.** a series of pipes conveying oil etc. to a distance. **2.** a channel of supply or information. —**in the pipeline,** being considered, prepared, etc.

pip emma /pɪp ˈemə/ (*colloq.*) p.m. [former signallers' names for letters *P.M.*]

Piper /ˈpaɪpə(r)/, John (1903–), English painter and decorative designer. His early paintings were abstract, but in the 1930s he turned to a Romantic naturalism. During the Second World War he was one of the artists commissioned to record the effects of the war upon Britain. He is best known for his water-colours and aquatints of buildings (e.g. Windsor Castle, 1941–2), stage designs at Glyndebourne and elsewhere, and stained glass for Llandaff and Coventry Cathedrals.

piper n. one who plays on a pipe, especially the bagpipes. [f. PIPE]

pipette /pɪˈpet/ n. a slender tube for transferring or measuring small quantities of liquids. [F dim. (as PIPE)]

piping /ˈpaɪpɪŋ/ n. **1.** a length of pipe; a system of pipes. **2.** a pipelike fold enclosing a cord as a decoration for the edges or seams of upholstery etc. **3.** ornamental cordlike lines of icing on a cake. —adj. **piping hot,** (of food or water) very hot.

pipistrelle /pɪpɪˈstrel/ n. a small bat of the genus *Pipistrellus*. [f. F f. It. f. L *vespertilio* bat (*vesper* evening)]

pipit /ˈpɪpɪt/ n. a small bird of the family Motacillidae, resembling a lark. [prob. imit.]

pippin /ˈpɪpɪn/ n. an apple grown from seed; any of various red and yellow dessert apples. [f. OF *pepin*]

pip-squeak n. (*slang*) a small or unimportant but self-assertive fellow.

piquant /ˈpiːkənt/ adj. **1.** pleasantly sharp in its taste or smell, appetizing. **2.** pleasantly stimulating or exciting to the mind. —**piquancy** n., **piquantly** adv. [F (*piquer* prick)]

pique /piːk/ v.t. **1.** to wound the pride or self-respect of. **2.** to irritate to arouse (curiosity or interest). —n. a feeling of resentment or hurt pride. [f. F (as prec.)]

piquet /pɪˈket/ n. a card-game for two players with a pack of 32 cards (omitting the low cards two to six). [F]

Piraeus /paɪˈriːəs/ the chief port of Athens in ancient and modern times, 8 km (5 miles) SW of the city.

Pirandello /pɪrænˈdeləʊ/, Luigi (1867–1936), Italian dramatist and novelist, born in Sicily, who challenged the conventions of naturalism and greatly influenced European drama. Of his ten plays the best-known include *Six Characters in Search of an Author* (1921) and *Henry IV* (1922), in which he anticipated the theatre of Brecht while probing the conflict between reality and appearance, self and persona, actor and character, face and mask. Among his novels are *The Outcast* (1901), dealing with woman's desire for independence within patriarchal Sicily, *The Late Mattia*

Pascal (1904), and *The Old and the Young* (1909). He was awarded the Nobel Prize for literature in 1934.

Piranesi /pɪrəˈneɪsɪ/, Giovanni Battista (1720–78), Italian engraver. An enthusiastic devotee of Roman architecture, in his prints he relied on atypical viewpoints and dramatic chiaroscuro to aggrandize its power and scale. His *Prisons* (1745–61) extended this imagery into the realms of fantasy, producing a nightmare vision of claustrophobic space and endless dimensions that prefigured later Romantic concerns.

piranha /pɪˈrɑːnə, -njə/ n. a voracious South American freshwater fish of the genus *Serrasalmus*. [Port. f. Tupi]

pirate /ˈpaɪərət/ n. 1. a seafaring robber attacking other ships etc.; a ship used by a pirate. 2. one who infringes another's copyright or business rights or who broadcasts without authorization. —v.t. 1. to plunder. 2. to reproduce (a book etc.) or trade (goods) without due authorization. —**piracy** n., **piratical** /paɪˈrætɪk(ə)l/ adj. [f. L f. Gk (*peiraō* attempt, assault)]

pirouette /pɪruːˈet/ n. a ballet-dancer's spin on one foot or the point of the toe. —v.i. to perform a pirouette. [F, = spinning-top]

Pisa /ˈpiːzə/ a city in northern Italy, noted for its 'Leaning Tower', the campanile of its cathedral. Built at the end of the 12th c., the circular tower in eight storeys is 55 m (181 ft.) high and leans about 5 m (17 ft.) from the perpendicular, part of this inclination dating from its construction.

Pisano[1] /pɪˈsɑːnəʊ/, Andrea (c.1290–1348) and Nino (died c.1368), Italian sculptors, unrelated to Nicola and Giovanni Pisano. Andrea is first mentioned in 1329, when he received the commission to make a pair of bronze doors for the baptistery at Florence. His son Nino was one of the earliest to specialize in free-standing life-size figures.

Pisano[2] /pɪˈsɑːnəʊ/, Nicola (active c.1258–78) and Giovanni, his son (active c.1265–1314), Italian sculptors. The father can be seen as one of the greatest medieval sculptors, and he explored the revival of interest in classical form within a Gothic framework. He executed the carvings on the pulpit in Pisa Baptistery (c.1260), and reliefs on the pulpit of Siena Cathedral (1265–8); he worked with Giovanni on his last great project, a large fountain in Perugia which was finished in 1278. Giovanni's works show a further refinement of the Gothic ideal, and he is seen as the precursor of the sculptural renaissance which followed. His works include the façade of Siena Cathedral (from 1284), reliefs for the pulpit in S. Andrea at Pistoia (completed in 1301), and what appears to have been his last commission, a monument to Margaret of Luxemburg (1313), in which she is shown not as dead or sleeping but as rising from the grave; since no sculptor hitherto had depicted the flight of the soul in this way, Giovanni's innovation was a dramatic one.

piscatorial /pɪskəˈtɔːrɪəl/ adj. of fishermen or fishing. [f. L (*piscator* fisherman)]

Pisces /ˈpaɪsiːz/ n. a constellation and the twelfth sign of the zodiac, the Fishes, which the sun enters about 20 Feb. —**Piscean** adj. & n. [L, = fishes]

piscina /pɪˈsiːnə/ n. 1. a perforated stone basin near the altar in a church for carrying away water used in rinsing the chalice etc. (ill. VESTMENTS). 2. a fish-pond. [L (as prec.)]

Pisidia /paɪˈsɪdɪə/ the ancient name for the region of Asia Minor between Pamphylia and Phrygia. —**Pisidian** adj. & n.

Pisistratus /paɪˈsɪstrətəs/ (6th c. BC) ruler of Athens. He seized power in 561 BC and after twice being expelled ruled continuously from 546 until his death in 527 BC. A benevolent tyrant who also succeeded in placating the nobles, he promoted the financial prosperity and cultural pre-eminence of Athens.

piss v.t./i. (*vulgar*) 1. to urinate. 2. (in *p.p.*) drunk. —n. (*vulgar*) urine; urination. [f. OF *pisser* (imit.)]

Pissarro /pɪˈsɑːrəʊ/, Camille (1830–1903), French painter and graphic artist. Born in the West Indies, he moved to France in the 1850s and studied in Paris with Monet. At first heavily influenced by Corot, he later developed a *plein-air* style that contributed to the formation of impressionism in the 1870s. Always open to new developments, he made use of Seurat's pointillist theories in the 1880s as well as supporting Cézanne and Gauguin in their search for a valid Post-Impressionist style.

pistachio /pɪˈstæʃɪəʊ/ n. (pl. **-os**) a nut with a greenish edible kernel; the tree (*Pistacia vera*) bearing this. [f. It. & Sp., ult. f. Pers. *pistah*]

piste /piːst/ n. a ski-track of compacted snow. [F, = racetrack]

pistil n. the female organ of a flower, comprising the ovary, style, and stigma. —**pistillate** adj. [f. F or L (as PESTLE)]

pistol /ˈpɪst(ə)l/ n. a small gun. —v.t. (**-ll-**) to shoot with a pistol. —**pistol-grip** n. a handle shaped like the butt of a pistol. **pistol-whip** v.t. to beat with a pistol. [f. F f. G f. Czech]

piston /ˈpɪst(ə)n/ n. 1. a sliding cylinder fitting closely in a tube and moving up and down in it, used in steam and internal-combustion engines to impart motion, or in a pump to receive motion. 2. a sliding valve in a trumpet etc. —**piston-rod** n. the rod by which a piston impacts motion. [F f. It. (as PESTLE)]

pit n. 1. a large hole in the ground, especially one made in digging for a mineral etc. or for industrial purposes. 2. a coal-mine. 3. a covered hole as a trap for animals. 4. a hollow on a surface. 5. a part of the auditorium of a theatre on the floor of the house; the sunken part before the stage, accommodating the orchestra. 6. a sunken area in a workshop floor for access to the underside of motor vehicles. 7. an area of the side of the track at a racecourse, where racing cars are serviced etc. during a race. —v.t. 1. to match or set in competition. 2. (esp. in *p.p.*) to make pits or scars in. 3. to put into a pit. —**pit-head** n. the top of the shaft of a coal-mine; the area surrounding this. **pit of the stomach**, the depression below the breastbone. [OE f. L *puteus* well]

pita /ˈpiːtə/ n. (also **pitta**) a flat bread originating in Greece and the Middle East. [modern Gk, = cake]

pit-a-pat /ˈpɪtəpæt/ n. a sound as of quick light steps or quick tapping. —adv. with this sound. [imit.]

Pitcairn Islands /pɪtˈkeən, ˈpɪt-/ a British dependency comprising a group of islands in the South Pacific, NE of New Zealand; pop. (1982) about 54. Pitcairn Island, the chief of the group, was discovered in 1767 by a British naval officer and named after the sailor who first sighted it. It remained uninhabited until settled in 1790 by mutineers from HMS *Bounty*; some of their descendants still dwell there.

pitch[1] v.t./i. 1. to erect and fix (a tent or camp); to fix in a definite position. 2. to throw or fling. 3. to cause (a bowled ball in cricket) to strike the ground at a particular point; (of a ball) to strike the ground thus. 4. to express in a particular style or at a particular level. 5. to fall heavily; (of a ship or aircraft) to plunge alternately backwards and forwards in a lengthwise direction (ill. FLIGHT). 6. (*Mus.*) to set at a particular pitch. 7. (*slang*) to tell (a tale, a yarn). —n. 1. the act or process of pitching. 2. an area marked out for play in outdoor games; (in cricket) the area between or near the wickets. 3. (*Mus.*) the relative sound of a note, governed by the rate of vibration of a string etc.; the degree of highness or lowness of tone. 4. the place at which a street vendor etc. is stationed. 5. an approach taken in advertising or sales-talk. 6. the intensity of a quality etc. 7. the distance between successive ridges of a screw, teeth of a cog, etc.; the steepness of a slope. —**absolute pitch**, ability to recognize or reproduce the pitch of a note (also **perfect pitch**); a fixed standard of pitch. **pitched battle**, a battle fought between armies in prepared positions and formations; a fierce argument. **pitched roof**, one that slopes. **pitch in**, (*colloq.*) to set to work vigorously. **pitch into**, (*colloq.*) to attack forcefully. [perh. rel. to OE *picung* stigmata]

pitch[2] n. a dark resinous substance from the distillation of tar or turpentine, used for caulking the seams of ships etc. —v.t. to coat with pitch. —**pitch-black** or **pitch-dark** adj. dark with no light at all. **pitch-pine** n. a pine-tree (*Pinus rigida*) yielding much resin. —**pitchy** adj. [OE f. L *pix*]

pitchblende /ˈpɪtʃblend/ n. uranium oxide found in pitch-like masses and yielding radium. [f. G (as prec., BLENDE)]

pitcher[1] n. a large jug with a handle or two ears and usually a lip, for holding liquids. —**pitcher-plant** n. a plant, especially of the genus *Sarracenia*, with pitcher-shaped leaves holding a secretion in which insects become trapped. [f. OF (as BEAKER)]

pitcher[2] n. the player who delivers the ball in baseball. [f. PITCH[1]]

pitchfork n. a long-handled fork with two prongs, used for pitching hay. —v.t. 1. to throw (as) with a pitchfork. 2. to thrust (a person) forcibly into a position, office, etc.

piteous /ˈpɪtɪəs/ adj. deserving or arousing pity. —**piteously** adv. [f. AF (as PITY)]

pitfall *n.* **1.** an unsuspected danger or difficulty. **2.** a covered hole as a trap for animals.

pith *n.* **1.** the spongy tissue in plant stems and branches or lining the rind of an orange etc. **2.** the essential part. **3.** physical strength, vigour. [OE]

Pithecanthropus /pɪθɪˈkænθrəpəs/ *n.* (also called Java man) a genus of hominids first defined on the basis of human fossils found in Java in 1891 within deposits of Middle Pleistocene age, dating from *c.*1,000,000–500,000 years ago. It has now been subsumed under the genus *Homo erectus.* [f. Gk *pithēkos* ape, *anthrōpos* man]

pithy *adj.* **1.** terse, condensed, and forcible. **2.** of or like pith. **—pithiness** *n.* [f. PITH]

pitiable /ˈpɪtɪəb(ə)l/ *adj.* deserving or arousing pity or contempt. **—pitiably** *adv.* [f. OF (as PITY)]

pitiful /ˈpɪtɪfʊl/ *adj.* **1.** causing pity. **2.** contemptible. **—pitifully** *adv.* [f. PITY + -FUL]

pitiless /ˈpɪtɪlɪs/ *adj.* showing no pity. **—pitilessly** *adv.* [f. PITY + -LESS]

piton /ˈpiːtɒn/ *n.* a spike or peg with a hole through which a rope can be passed, driven into rock or crack as a support in rock-climbing. [F, = eye-bolt]

Pitot /ˈpiːtəʊ/, Henri (1695–1771), French scientist whose name is used to designate devices based upon his inventions. **—pitot tube,** a right-angled tube open at both ends, used in anemometers and for determining the velocity of fluids; a similar device used for measuring the velocity of aircraft.

Pitt¹, William, 'the Elder', Earl of Chatham (1708–78), British statesman, a brilliant parliamentary orator who made his reputation as an opposition spokesman in the 1740s and, despite earning the King's disfavour, became Prime Minister in 1756 after early military failures in the Seven Years War. As war leader Pitt proved a brilliant success, concentrating on a maritime strategy to defeat France and masterminding the conquest of French possessions overseas, particularly in Canada and India. Forced to resign in 1761, he suffered increasingly from ill health, and although he returned to office in 1766 he never again exercised effective political control.

Pitt², William, 'the Younger' (1759–1806), British statesman, son of Pitt the Elder. He became Prime Minister in 1783, at 24 the youngest ever to hold this office, and in the ensuing ten years of peace restored the authority of Parliament, with himself in undisputed ascendancy, introduced financial reforms, reduced the enormous National Debt which he had inherited, and reformed the administration of India. With Britain's entry into war against France (1793) in the wake of the French Revolution, Pitt became almost entirely occupied as a war leader, proving as successful as his father, and after the Irish uprising in 1798 secured the Union of Great Britain and Ireland (1800). Although he resigned a year later over the issue of Catholic emancipation (which George III refused to accept) he returned to office in 1804 after hostilities with France had been resumed, and died in office early in 1806, his health undermined by the strain of organizing the war.

pittance /ˈpɪt(ə)ns/ *n.* a very small allowance or remuneration. [f. OF f. L (as PITY)]

pitter-patter /ˈpɪtəpætə(r)/ *n.* & *adv.* pit-a-pat. [imit.]

Pitti /ˈpɪtɪ/ an art gallery and museum in Florence, housed in the Pitti Palace which was begun in 1440 but not completed until after 1549. It contains about 500 masterpieces from the Medici collections, a profusion of art treasures including Gobelin tapestries, and a rich collection of plate, goldsmiths' work, ivories, enamels, etc.

Pitt-Rivers, Augustus Henry Lane Fox (1827–1900), English lieutenant-general, archaeologist, anthropologist, founder of the ethnological museum in Oxford which bears his name. From his studies of weaponry he realized that something analogous to the biological evolution of species could be traced in artefacts, and did pioneering work in establishing typological sequences of objects from different cultures. On retiring in 1882 he began a series of large-scale excavations of the prehistoric, Roman, and Saxon sites on his Wiltshire estate, organized and recorded with meticulous care. His approach greatly advanced the technique of archaeology both because of his thoroughness, in contrast to the sampling or object-seeking common in his day, and through his emphasis on the importance of commonplace objects as distinct from rarities; he is rightly regarded as the father of modern excavation.

pituitary /pɪˈtjuːɪtərɪ/ *n.* the pituitary gland. **—pituitary**

gland *or* **body,** a pea-sized endocrine gland at the base of the brain (ill. BODY 4) with an important influence on growth and bodily functions, especially through its effect on other glands. Its anterior lobe secretes various hormones including one which stimulates body growth, others regulating the activity of the gonads and the adrenal and thyroid glands, and another which stimulates the growth of the mammary glands and causes them to secrete milk. Its posterior lobe, consisting mainly of nervous tissue, releases two hormones, oxytocin and an antidiuretic hormone which acts on the kidney and may also act on the smooth muscle-tissue of the blood-vessels and affect blood pressure. [f. L (*pituita* slime, phlegm, referring to the fact that the gland was once thought to secrete nasal mucus)]

pity /ˈpɪtɪ/ *n.* **1.** a feeling of sorrow for another's suffering. **2.** a cause for regret. **—***v.t.* to feel pity (often with contempt) for. **—take pity on,** to feel or act compassionately towards. [f. OF *pité* f. L (as PIETY)]

pivot /ˈpɪvət/ *n.* **1.** a short pin or shaft on which something turns or oscillates. **2.** a person or point that is crucial. **—***v.t./i.* **1.** to turn (as) on a pivot. **2.** to provide with a pivot. **3.** to depend crucially, to hinge. **—pivotal** *adj.* [F]

pixie /ˈpɪksɪ/ *n.* (*also* **pixy**) a supernatural being akin to a fairy. **—pixie hood,** a hood with a pointed crown. [orig. unkn.]

Pizarro /pɪˈzɑːrəʊ/, Francisco (*c.*1478–1541), Spanish conquistador. After service in the Italian wars and under Balboa during the discovery of the Pacific, Pizarro set out from Panama in 1531 with less than 200 men to conquer the Inca empire in Peru. Crossing the mountains, he defeated the Incas and executed their emperor Atahualpa (1533), setting up an Inca puppet monarchy at Cuzco and building his own capital at Lima. Pizarro was then faced by a serious native revolt which was put down in 1537 only after the return of his rival Amalgro from Chile. This was followed by a power struggle between Pizarro and Amalgro which ended in 1538 with the latter's capture and execution. Amalgro's supporters, however, conspired against the ageing Pizarro and assassinated him in his house in Lima.

pizza /ˈpiːtsə/ *n.* an Italian dish of a layer of dough baked with a savoury topping. [It., = pie]

pizzicato /pɪtsɪˈkɑːtəʊ/ *adv.* (*Mus.*) with a string of the violin etc. plucked instead of played with the bow. **—***n.* (*pl.* **-os**) a note or passage to be played in this way. [It.]

pl. *abbr.* plural.

placable /ˈplækəb(ə)l/ *adj.* easily appeased, forgiving. **—placability** /-ˈbɪlɪtɪ/ *n.* [f. OF or L (*placare* appease)]

placard /ˈplækɑːd/ *n.* a large notice for public display. **—***v.t.* **1.** to put placards on (a wall etc.). **2.** to advertise by placards. **3.** to display as a placard. [f. OF (*plaquier* to plaster f. MDu.)]

placate /pləˈkeɪt/ *v.t.* to conciliate, to pacify. **—placatory** *adj.* [f. L *placare*]

place *n.* **1.** a particular part of space or of an area on a surface. **2.** a particular town, district, building, etc. **3.** (in names) a short street; a square or the buildings round it; a country mansion. **4.** a passage or part in a book etc.; the point one has reached in reading. **5.** a proper space for a thing; position in a series. **6.** rank, position in a community, etc.; a duty appropriate to this. **7.** a position of employment. **8.** a space, seat, or accommodation for a person; one's home or dwelling. **9.** (in racing) a position among placed competitors, especially other than the winner. **10.** a step in the progression of an argument or statement etc. **11.** the position of a figure in a series as indicating its value in decimal or other notation. **—***v.t.* **1.** to put into a particular or proper place, state, rank, order, etc.; to find a place for. **2.** to locate; to identify in relation to circumstances etc. **3.** to put or give (goods, an order for these) into the hands of a firm etc.; to invest (money). **—be placed,** to be among the first three in a race. **give place to,** to make room for; to yield precedence to; to be succeeded by. **go places,** (*colloq.*) to be successful. **in place,** in the right place; suitable. **in place of,** in exchange for, instead of. **in places,** at some places but not others. **out of place,** in the wrong place; unsuitable. **place-kick** *n.* a kick in football with the ball placed on the ground. **place-mat** *n.* a table-mat for a person's place at table. **place-setting** *n.* a set of cutlery or dishes for one person at table. **put a person in his place,** to snub a presumptious person. **take place,** to occur. **take the place of,** to be substituted for. **—placement** *n.* [f. OF f. L *platea* broad way f. Gk]

placebo /pləˈsiːbəʊ/ *n.* (*pl.* **-os**) a medicine intended to cure by reassuring the patient rather than by its physiological effect; a dummy pill etc. used in a controlled trial. [L, = I shall be acceptable (*placēre* please), first word of Ps. 114: 9 in Vulgate]

placenta /pləˈsentə/ *n.* (*pl.* **-ae** /-iː/ or **-as**) **1.** a flattened circular spongy vascular structure that develops in the uterus of pregnant mammals (other than marsupials and monotremes) by interlocking of foetal and maternal tissue, through which the developing foetus is supplied with nutriment and rid of waste products, and to which it is attached by the umbilical cord. **2.** (in plants) the part of the carpel to which ovules are attached. —**placental** *adj.* [L f. Gk, = flat cake]

placer /ˈpleɪsə(r), ˈplæ-/ *n.* a deposit of sand or gravel etc. containing valuable minerals in particles. [Amer. Sp.]

placid /ˈplæsɪd/ *adj.* calm and peaceful; not easily made anxious or upset. —**placidity** /pləˈsɪdɪtɪ/ *n.*, **placidly** *adv.* [f. F or L *placidus* (*placēre* please)]

placket /ˈplækɪt/ *n.* an opening or slit in a woman's skirt, for fastenings or access to a pocket. [var. of PLACARD]

plagiarize /ˈpleɪdʒəraɪz/ *v.t.* to pass off (another's ideas, writings, or inventions) as one's own. —**plagiarism** *n.*, **plagiarist** *n.* [f. L *plagiarius* kidnapper]

plague /pleɪg/ *n.* **1.** a deadly contagious disease transmitted to man by rats' fleas, especially bubonic plague (see below). **2.** an infestation of a pest. **3.** a great trouble or affliction; (*colloq.*) a nuisance. —*v.t.* **1.** to afflict with plague. **2.** (*colloq.*) to pester, to annoy. [f. L *plaga* stroke]

Epidemics of plague broke out in Europe in the Middle Ages. The first killed millions in the mid-14th c. (see BLACK DEATH), and the disease re-emerged periodically for several centuries thereafter, the last serious outbreak in Britain killing almost 100,000 inhabitants of London in 1665-6.

plaice *n.* (*pl.* same) a kind of edible marine flat-fish (*Pleuronectes platessa*). [f. OF f. L *platessa*]

plaid /plæd/ *n.* a long piece of twilled woollen cloth with a chequered or tartan pattern, the outer article of Highland costume; the cloth used for this. —*adj.* made of or having a plaidlike pattern. [Gaelic]

Plaid Cymru /plaɪd ˈkʌmrɪ/ the Welsh nationalist party, founded in 1925 and dedicated to seeking autonomy for Wales. [Welsh, = party of Wales]

plain *adj.* **1.** clear and unmistakable, easily perceived or understood. **2.** not elaborate or intricate; not luxurious; (of food) not rich or highly seasoned. **3.** straightforward, candid. **4.** undistinguished in appearance, not beautiful or good-looking. **5.** homely in manner, without affectation. —*n.* **1.** a large level tract of country. **2.** the ordinary stitch in knitting, producing a smooth surface towards the knitter. —*adv.* plainly, simply. —**plain chocolate,** chocolate made without milk. **plain clothes,** civilian clothes as distinct from uniform or official dress. **plain flour,** flour that does not contain a raising agent. **plain sailing,** a simple situation or course of action. **plain-spoken** *adj.* frank. —**plainly** *adv.*, **plainness** *n.* [f. OF f. L *planus*]

Plains of Abraham a plateau in eastern Canada above Quebec City, scene of the decisive battle for North America in 1759. The British army under General Wolfe surprised the French defenders by scaling the heights above the city under cover of darkness, and the city fell. The battle led to British control over Canada, but both Wolfe and the French commander Montcalm died of their wounds.

plainsong *n.* (also **plainchant**) traditional church music in medieval modes and in free rhythm depending on accentuation of the words, sung in unison, with a single line of vocal melody to words taken from the liturgy. The chant of the Roman Church is generally known as 'Gregorian', after Pope Gregory the Great (d. 604), but it is likely that the role he played had more to do with organizing and standardizing the various schools of chant then in use than with composing, a role taken up with enthusiasm in the 8th c. by Pepin, king of the Franks, and especially by Charlemagne.

plaint *n.* **1.** (*Law*) an accusation, a charge. **2.** (*poetic*) a lamentation, a complaint. [f. OF f. L (*plangere* lament)]

plaintiff /ˈpleɪntɪf/ *n.* the party who brings a suit into a lawcourt. [f. OF, = foll.]

plaintive /ˈpleɪntɪv/ *adj.* mournful-sounding. —**plaintively** *adv.* [f. OF (as PLAINT)]

plait /plæt/ *n.* an interlacing of three or more strands of hair or ribbon or straw etc.; material thus interlaced. —*v.t.* to form into a plait. [f. OF f. L *plicare* fold]

plan *n.* **1.** a method or procedure, thought out in advance, by which a thing is to be done. **2.** a map of a town or

district. **3.** a drawing showing the relative position and size of the parts of a building or structure. **4.** a scheme of arrangement. —*v.t./i.* (**-nn-**) **1.** to arrange or work out the details of (a procedure, enterprise, etc.) beforehand; to make plans. **2.** to make a plan of or design for. **3.** (in *p.p.*) done in accordance with a plan. —**plan on,** (*colloq.*) to aim at or envisage. —**planner** *n.* [F f. It. *pianta* plan of building (as PLANT)]

planchette /plænˈʃet/ *n.* a small board supported on castors and a pencil, said to trace letters etc. at spiritualist seances without conscious direction when one or more persons rest their fingers lightly on the board. [F dim. (as PLANK)]

Planck /plæŋk/, Max Karl Ernst Ludwig (1858-1947), German theoretical physicist, the originator of the quantum theory which, with Einstein's general theory of relativity, forms the foundation of 20th-c. physics. During the 1880s he published fundamental papers on thermodynamics before taking up the problem of black-body radiation. The characteristic radiation spectra produced by such, in theory, perfect absorbers of radiant energy had foxed classical physicists. In 1900 he announced his 'radiation law', according to which this electromagnetic radiation was not emitted as a continuous flow but was made up of discrete units or 'quanta' of energy, and mathematical investigation showed that the size of these units involved a fundamental physical constant (Planck's constant). The quantum concept could now be invoked to explain atomic structure. Einstein applied it to the photoelectric effect, and Bohr to his model of the atom. For his achievement Planck received the 1918 Nobel Prize for physics. In his personal life he suffered a series of cruel misfortunes, including the execution of his son, Erwin, by the Nazis in 1944 for his part in the July plot to assassinate Hitler.

plane[1] *n.* **1.** a surface such that a straight line joining any two points in it lies wholly in it; a level surface. **2.** a level of attainment or knowledge etc. **3.** an aeroplane; a main aerofoil. —*adj.* level as or lying in a plane. [f. L *planus* (as PLAIN)]

plane[2] *n.* a tool for smoothing the surface of wood by paring shavings from it (ill. CARPENTRY). —*v.t.* to pare or make smooth with a plane. [f. OF f. L (as prec.)]

plane[3] *n.* a tall spreading broad-leaved tree of the genus *Platanus*. [f. OF f. L *platanus* f. Gk]

planet /ˈplænɪt/ *n.* any of the heavenly bodies in orbit round the sun (see below). —**planetary** *adj.* [f. OF f. L f. Gk, lit. = wanderer (*planaomai* wander), orig. distinguished from fixed stars by apparently having a motion of its own, and including the sun and moon]

Planets fall into two main classes, depending on whether they have extensive gaseous atmospheres or are predominantly rocky bodies. The former comprises Jupiter, Saturn, Uranus, and Neptune, all with dense atmospheres of hydrogen-rich gases subject to violent winds and eddies. These giant planets have their own retinues of satellites (some as large as the other planets) and are associated with concentric rings of orbiting small pàrticles. Of the rocky planets, only Earth and Venus have substantial atmospheres, and only Earth has significant amounts of surface water. None but Earth is known to support life.

planetarium /plænɪˈteərɪəm/ *n.* (*pl.* **-ums**) a device for projecting an image of the night sky as seen at various times and places; a building containing this. [as prec.]

plangent /ˈplændʒənt/ *adj.* **1.** loud and reverberating. **2.** loud and plaintive. —**plangency** *n.* [f. L (as PLAINT)]

plank *n.* **1.** a long flat piece of timber. **2.** an item of a political or other programme. —*v.t.* **1.** to furnish or cover with planks. **2.** (*colloq.*) to put down roughly or violently; to pay (money) on the spot. —**walk the plank,** (*hist.*) to be made to walk blindfold into the sea along a plank laid over the side of a ship. [f. OF f. L *planca*]

planking *n.* planks collectively; a structure or surface of planks. [f. PLANK]

plankton /ˈplæŋktən/ *n.* the forms of organic life (chiefly microscopic) that drift or float in the sea or fresh water. —**planktonic** /-ˈtɒnɪk/ *adj.* [G f. Gk, = wandering]

plano- /ˈpleɪnəʊ-/ *in comb.* level, flat; having one surface plane. [f. L *planus* flat]

planographic /pleɪnəˈgræfɪk/ *adj.* printing from a flat surface. [f. prec. + -GRAPHIC]

plant /plɑːnt/ *n.* **1.** an organism that obtains its food by photosynthesis or by absorption, and that has neither power of locomotion nor special organs of sensation or digestion; a small organism of this kind as distinguished from a tree or shrub. **2.** the machinery and implements etc. used in

Plants

Some divisions of the plant kingdom

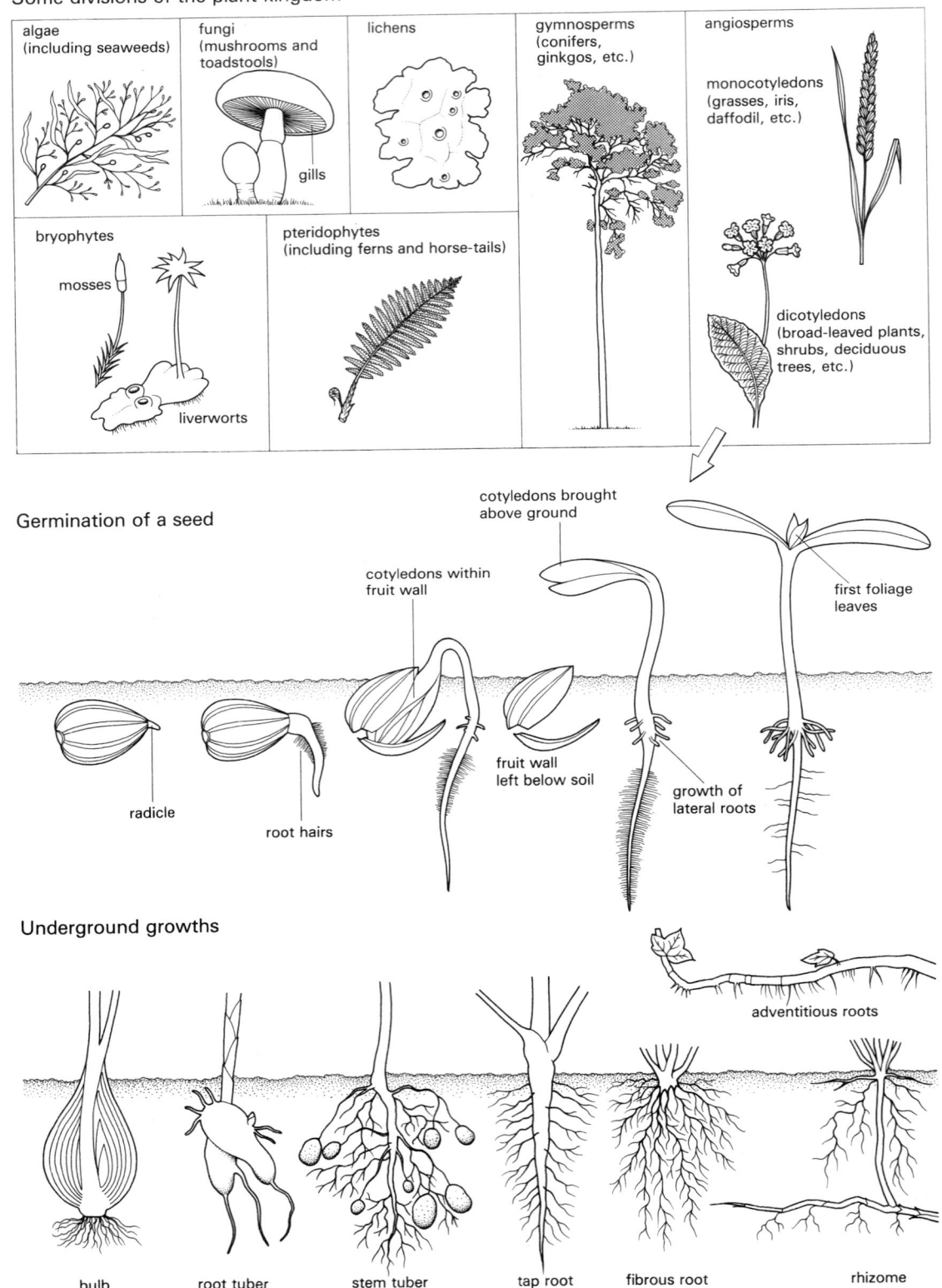

algae
(including seaweeds)

fungi
(mushrooms and
toadstools)

gills

lichens

gymnosperms
(conifers,
ginkgos, etc.)

angiosperms

monocotyledons
(grasses, iris,
daffodil, etc.)

bryophytes

mosses

liverworts

pteridophytes
(including ferns and horse-tails)

dicotyledons
(broad-leaved plants,
shrubs, deciduous
trees, etc.)

Germination of a seed

cotyledons brought
above ground

cotyledons within
fruit wall

first foliage
leaves

radicle

root hairs

fruit wall
left below soil

growth of
lateral roots

Underground growths

adventitious roots

bulb

root tuber

stem tuber

tap root

fibrous root

rhizome

Leaves

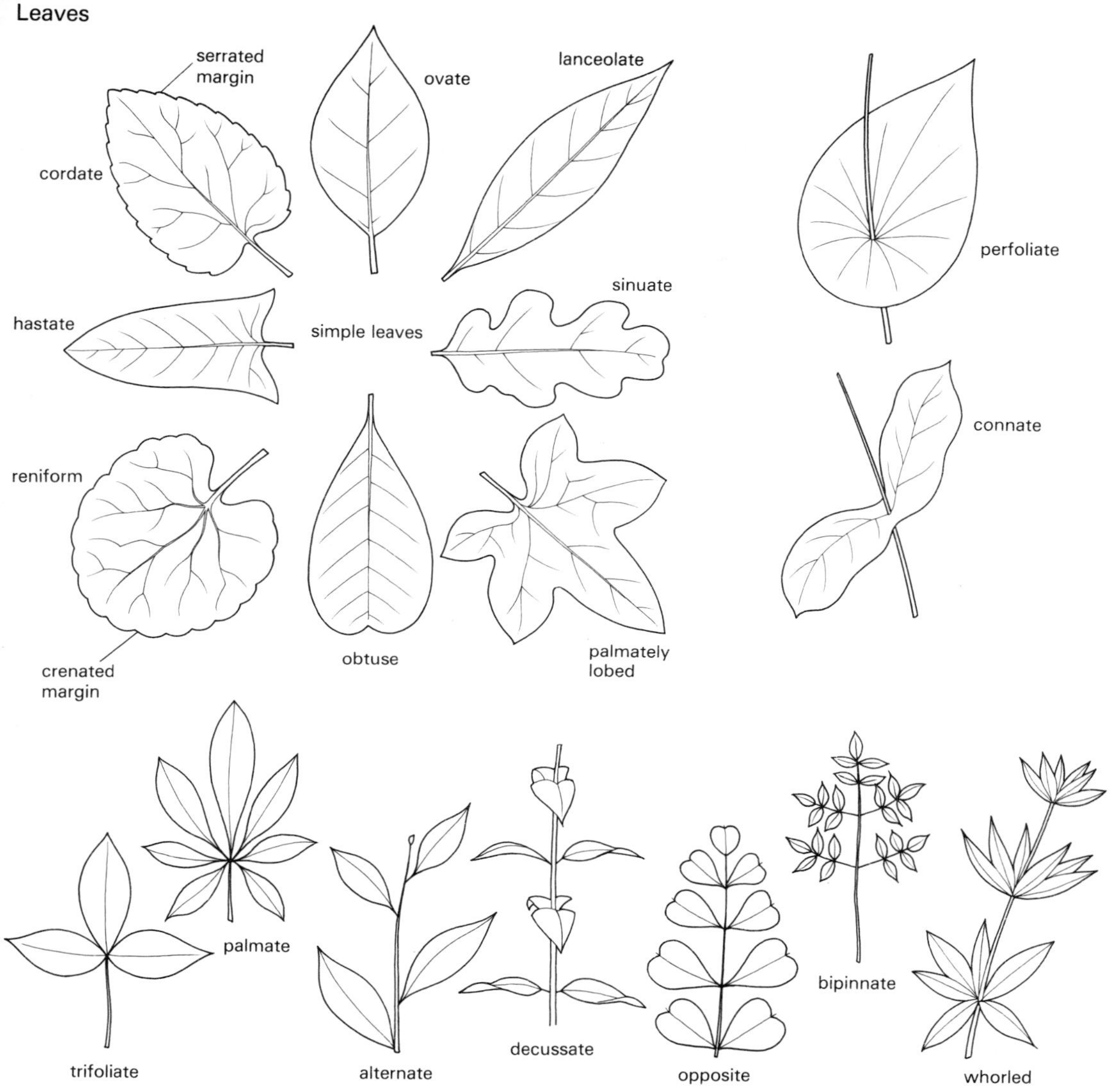

serrated margin

ovate

lanceolate

cordate

perfoliate

hastate

simple leaves

sinuate

connate

reniform

crenated margin

obtuse

palmately lobed

trifoliate

palmate

alternate

decussate

opposite

bipinnate

whorled

Inflorescences

racemes

racemose inflorescences

simple

compound

spike

panicle

corymb

cymes

umbels

bracteole

bract

simple

compound

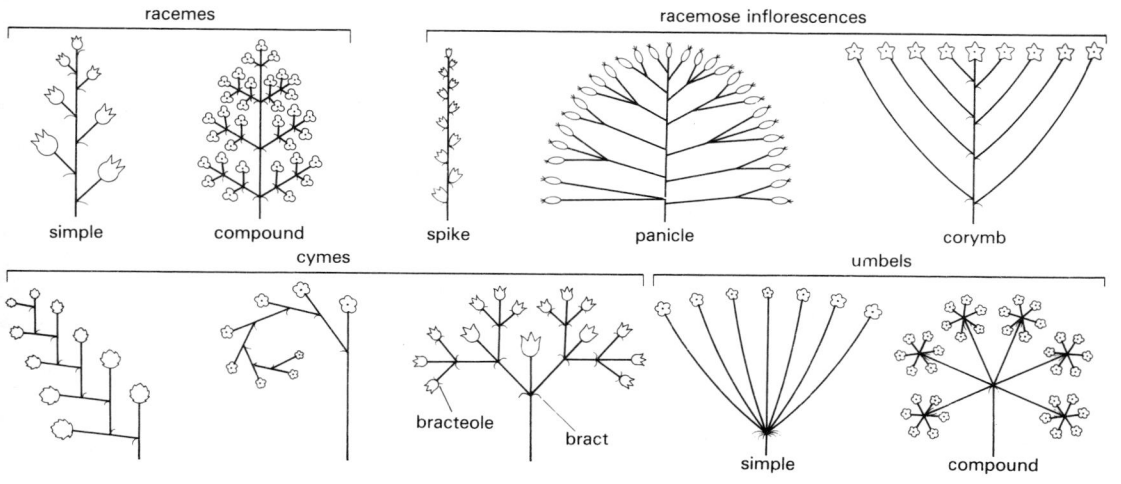

industrial processes; a factory and its equipment. **3.** (*slang*) a thing deliberately placed for discovery by others; a hoax or trap. —*v.t.* **1.** to place in the ground or soil for growing; to put plants or seeds into (the ground or soil). **2.** to put or fix firmly in position. **3.** to station (a person), especially as a look-out or spy. **4.** to cause (an idea etc.) to be established in the mind. **5.** to deliver (a blow or thrust) with deliberate aim. **6.** (*slang*) to conceal, especially with a view to misleading a later discoverer. **7.** to settle or establish (a colony, community, etc.). —**plant kingdom**, the taxonomic group that contains the plants. The term originally included fungi and bacteria as well as green plants, but nowadays these two groups, along with single-celled organisms, are frequently assigned to separate kingdoms and the term 'plant kingdom' restricted to the multicellular green plants, of which the main groups are multicellular algae, mosses, ferns, gymnosperms, and angiosperms (flowering plants). [f. OE & F f. L *planta* sprout, cutting]

Plantagenet /plæn'tædʒənɪt/ originally the nickname of Geoffrey, Count of Anjou, father of Henry II of England, derived from the sprig of broom (L *planta* plant, *genista* broom) worn as a distinctive mark. It was adopted as a surname (*c.*1460) by Richard, Duke of York, and applied to the royal house which came to the English throne in 1154 (Henry II). In the 15th c. it was divided into two branches, the house of Lancaster and the house of York, which came to an end with the death of Richard III (1485).

plantain[1] /'plæntɪn/ *n.* a herb of the genus *Plantago* with broad flat leaves spread close to the ground and seeds used for food for cage-birds. [f. OF f. L *plantago* (*planta* sole of foot)]

plantain[2] /'plæntɪn/ *n.* a tropical banana-like fruit; the treelike plant (*Musca paradisiaca*) bearing this. [f. Sp. *pla(n)tano* plane-tree (as PLANE[3])]

plantation /plɑː'teɪʃ(ə)n/ *n.* **1.** an extensive collection or area of cultivated trees or plants. **2.** an estate for the cultivation of cotton, tobacco, rubber, etc. **3.** (*hist.*) colonization; a settlement in a new or conquered country, a colony. —**Plantation of Ireland**, the government-sponsored settlement of British families in Ireland, on confiscated land, in the 16th–17th c. [f. OF or L (as PLANT)]

planter *n.* **1.** the owner or manager of a plantation. **2.** a container for house plants. [f. PLANT]

plaque /plɑːk, plæk/ *n.* **1.** a flat tablet or plate of metal or porcelain etc. fixed on a wall as an ornament or memorial. **2.** film on teeth, where bacteria can proliferate. [F f. Du. *plak* (as PLACARD)]

plasma /'plæzmə/ *n.* **1.** the colourless coagulable part of blood, lymph, or milk, in which corpuscles or fat-globules float. **2.** a gas in which there are positive ions and free negative electrons, usually in approximately equal numbers throughout and therefore electrically neutral; any analogous collection of charged particles in which one or both kinds are mobile, as the conduction electrons in a metal or the ions in a salt solution. (See below.) [L, = mould, f. Gk (*plassō* to shape)]

Plasmas include the following: the hot ionized gases found in the sun, other stars, and artificial fusion reactions; the material of glowing electrical discharges; the gaseous interior of working fluorescent lamps; metals (in which some of the electrons can move freely: see METAL); and molten salts. Salts in the solid state are not included, although they consist of ionized particles, because the particles are not free to move and so cannot conduct electricity. In a narrower sense, however, the term *plasma* frequently refers specifically to the hot ionized gases found in the sun and in fusion reactions. Such plasmas behave differently from ordinary un-ionized gases, notably in being affected by magnetic fields. For this reason they are sometimes regarded as constituting a fourth state of matter alongside solids, liquids, and gases; more than 99 per cent of matter in the universe is estimated to be in this state. The study of plasmas is very important for developing controlled fusion reactions (see NUCLEAR FUSION). Fusion can take place only at extremely high temperatures, which would immediately vaporize any container in which the hydrogen fuel was kept. However, because hydrogen is a plasma at these temperatures, its response to a magnetic field can be utilized to keep it from touching the walls of its container; this property removes one obstacle to the practicability of controlled fusion.

plasmid /'plæzmɪd/ *n.* any genetic structure in a cell that can replicate independently of the chromosomes. [as prec.]

Plassey /'plæsɪ/ a village north-west of Calcutta in former Bengal, scene of a British victory in 1757, when a very small British army under Robert Clive defeated a much larger native force under the Nawab of Bengal partly because Clive had previously bribed some of the Indian generals. The victory established British supremacy in Bengal.

plaster /'plɑːstə(r)/ *n.* **1.** a soft mixture of lime, sand, and water, for spreading on walls etc. to form a smooth surface and harden by drying. **2.** a medicinal or protective substance spread on fabric and applied to the body. **3.** sticking-plaster. **4.** plaster of Paris. —*v.t.* **1.** to cover (a wall etc.) with plaster or a similar substance. **2.** to coat or daub, to cover thickly. **3.** to stick or fix (a thing) like plaster on a surface; to make (hair) smooth with a fixative etc. **4.** (*slang*) to bomb or shell heavily. **5.** (in *p.p.*, *slang*) drunk. —**plaster of Paris**, a fine white plaster of gypsum for making moulds or casts. —**plasterer** *n.* [OE & OF f. L f. Gk *emplastron*]

plasterboard *n.* board with a core of plaster used for partitions, walls, etc.

plastic /'plæstɪk/ *n.* a synthetic polymeric organic substance that can be given any permanent shape (see below); a material formed from such a substance together with fillers, colouring agents, etc. —*adj.* **1.** made of plastic. **2.** capable of being moulded; pliant, supple. **3.** giving form to clay or wax etc. —**plastic arts**, the arts concerned with modelling or with the representation of solid objects. **plastic bomb**, one containing putty-like explosive. **plastic surgeon**, a specialist in plastic surgery. **plastic surgery**, the repair or replacement of injured or defective tissue. —**plasticity** /plæ'stɪsɪtɪ/ *n.* [f. F or L f. Gk (as PLASMA)]

Plastics are artificial substances consisting of long chain-like organic molecules (polymers) intertwined with one another. The first plastics, such as celluloid (developed in 1869) used chemically modified forms of cellulose or other natural polymers. In the 20th c., however, polymers made artificially from small molecules became available, leading to the great diversity of plastics available today. The structure of plastics allows them to be softened during manufacture, and thus they can be moulded into many different forms. Other advantages of plastics include toughness, insulating ability, resistance to chemical and biological attack (although this leads to environmental problems), and ability to be given any desired colour. Among the major successes of the plastics industry are celluloid (which became a household name), bakelite (the first heat-proof plastic), and nylon (see entries).

Plasticine /'plæstɪsiːn/ *n.* [P] a plastic substance used for modelling. [f. prec.]

plasticize /'plæstɪsaɪz/ *v.t./i.* to make or become plastic. —**plasticizer** *n.* [f. prec.]

plastron /'plæstrən/ *n.* (*hist.*) **1.** a steel breastplate (ill. ARMOUR). **2.** an ornamental front on a woman's bodice. [F, f. It. *piastra* f. L *emplastrum* plaster]

Plate /pleɪt/, River, an estuary on the eastern side of South America between Uruguay and Argentina. The chief rivers flowing into it are the Paraná and the Uruguay, and the cities of Buenos Aires and Montevideo stand on its shores. Its name refers to the export of silver (Sp. *plata*) in the Spanish colonial period. In 1939 it was the scene of a naval battle between British and German warships.

plate *n.* **1.** a shallow usually circular vessel from which food is eaten or served; the contents of this. **2.** a similar vessel used for the collection of money in churches etc. **3.** (*collect.*) utensils of silver, gold, or other metal; objects of plated metal. **4.** a piece of metal with a name or inscription for affixing to something. **5.** an illustration on special paper in a book. **6.** a thin sheet of metal, glass, etc., coated with a sensitive film for use in photography etc. **7.** a flat thin usually rigid sheet of metal etc. **8.** each of a number of nearly rigid pieces of the earth's crust which each cover a large area, some of them including whole continents, and which together constitute the surface of the earth (ill. GEOLOGY). They lie on top of a more plastic region on which they move slowly relative to one another, the boundaries between adjacent plates being associated with well-defined belts of seismic, volcanic, and tectonic activity. **9.** a smooth piece of metal etc. for engraving; an impression from this. **10.** a silver or gold cup as a prize for a horse-race etc.; such a race. **11.** a thin piece of plastic material, moulded to the shape of the gums etc., to which artificial teeth are attached; (*colloq.*) a denture. —*v.t.* **1.** to cover (another metal) with a thin coat especially of silver, gold, or tin. **2.** to cover with plates of metal. —**on a plate**, (*colloq.*) available with little trouble to the recipient. **on one's plate**, for one to deal with or consider. **plate armour**, armour consisting of metal plates (ill. ARMOUR). **plate glass,** see GLASS. **plate tectonics,** a theory of the earth's surface based on the concepts of moving plates (see sense 8 above) and spreading of the sea floor. This theory, which since the 1960s has revolutionized the geological sciences, provides explanations for the phenomenon of continental drift and the distribution of earthquakes, mid-ocean ridges, deep-sea trenches, and mountain chains. [f. OF f. L *plata* plate armour]

plateau /ˈplætəʊ/ n. (pl. **-eaux** /-əʊz/) 1. an area of fairly level high ground. 2. a state of little variation after an increase. [F f. OF *platel* (*plat* flat)]

plateful n. 1. as much as a plate will hold. 2. (colloq.) a great deal (of work etc.). [f. PLATE + -FUL]

platelayer n. a person employed in fixing and repairing railway rails.

platelet /ˈpleɪtlɪt/ n. a small colourless disc found in the blood and involved in clotting. [f. PLATE + -LET]

platen /ˈplæt(ə)n/ n. a plate in a printing-press by which the paper is pressed against the type; the roller in a typewriter against which the paper rests as it is struck by the letters. [f. OF *platine* flat piece (as PLATEAU)]

plateresque /plætəˈresk/ adj. richly ornamented in a style suggesting silverware. [f. Sp. (*platero* silversmith f. *plata* silver)]

platform n. 1. a raised level surface, especially one from which a speaker addresses an audience. 2. a raised area along the side of a line at a railway station, where passengers board or alight from trains. 3. the floor area at the entrance to a bus. 4. a thick sole of a shoe. 5. the declared policy of a political party. [f. F, = ground-plan (as PLATEAU, FORM)]

Plath /plæθ/, Sylvia (1932–63), American poet and novelist, married in 1956 to the English poet Ted Hughes. In 1960 she published her first volume of poetry *The Colossus*. Her only novel *The Bell Jar* (1963) gives a witty and disturbing account of her nervous breakdown and ECT treatment. Her best-known collection, *Ariel* (1965), published posthumously after her suicide, established her reputation with its courageous and controlled treatment of extreme and painful states of mind.

platinum /ˈplætɪnəm/ n. a rare white heavy metallic element, symbol Pt, atomic number 78 (see below). —**platinum blonde,** a woman with silvery-blonde hair; this colour. [f. earlier *platina* f. Sp., dim. of *plata* silver]
Platinum occurs uncombined in nature, usually alloyed with other metals. It has a high melting-point and is resistant to chemical attack. The pure metal and its alloys have many uses, in jewellery, electrical contacts, and laboratory equipment, and it is an important industrial catalyst.

platitude /ˈplætɪtjuːd/ n. a commonplace remark, especially one solemnly delivered. —**platitudinous** /-ˈtjuːdɪnəs/ adj. [F (*plat* flat), after *certitude* etc.]

Plato /ˈpleɪtəʊ/ (429–347 BC), Greek philosopher, of aristocratic birth, a disciple of Socrates. His philosophy is presented in the form of dialogues, of high literary merit, with Socrates as the principal speaker. His most famous work, the *Republic*, presents a long inquiry into the best form of life for people and States. Plato's main political principle, that government is a science and requires expert knowledge, led him to the strongest condemnation of democracy. Seeking to discover the real nature of knowledge he developed the doctrine of 'ideas' or 'forms'—abstracts, perfect entities outside the physical world, and of which the material things that we see and handle are ephemeral and imperfect copies. His hypothesis has among its consequences that the soul is immortal; this is elaborately argued in the *Phaedo*. Plato's thought profoundly influenced Christian theology and Western philosophy. He was buried in the grounds of the Academy which he founded in Athens and which he served for 40 years.

Platonic /pləˈtɒnɪk/ adj. 1. of Plato or his philosophy. 2. platonic, confined to words or theory, not leading to action, harmless; (of love or friendship) purely spiritual, not sexual. [f. L f. Gk (*Platōn* Plato)]

Platonism /ˈpleɪtənɪz(ə)m/ n. 1. the doctrines of Plato or his followers. 2. any of various revivals of these doctrines or related ideas, especially Neoplatonism (3rd–5th c. AD), and Cambridge Platonism (17th c.) centred on Cambridge. 3. (in the philosophy of mathematics) the theory that arithmetical statements are about numbers, entities that exist apart from physical collections of things, and over and above the symbols that represent them. —**Platonist** n. [f. PLATO]

platoon /pləˈtuːn/ n. 1. a subdivision of a military company.

2. a group of persons acting together. [f. F *peloton* small ball (as PELLET)]

platter n. a flat dish or plate, especially for food. [AF *plater* (as PLATE)]

platypus /ˈplætɪpəs/ n. an Australian egg-laying aquatic and burrowing mammal (*Ornithorhynchus anatinus*) with a ducklike beak and flat tail (ill. MAMMALS). When the first complete platypus skin was brought to the British Museum in 1798 it was believed to be a hoax (that was the age of such hoaxes), but four years later a complete carcass arrived and its authenticity was attested. [f. Gk (*platus* broad, flat, *pous* foot)]

plaudit /ˈplɔːdɪt/ n. (usu. in pl.) a round of applause; an emphatic expression of approval. [f. L *plaudite*, imper. of *plaudere* clap (said by Roman actors at end of play)]

plausible /ˈplɔːzɪb(ə)l/ adj. (of a statement etc.) seeming reasonable or probable; (of a person) persuasive but deceptive. —**plausibility** /-ˈbɪlɪtɪ/ n., **plausibly** adv. [f. L (as prec.)]

Plautus /ˈplɔːtəs/, Titus Maccius (c.250–184 BC), Roman comic playwright. His plays, of which 21 survive, are based on models from Greek but with the addition of much specifically Roman material. Fantasy and imagination are more important than realism in the development of the plots; the characters, including stock types such as cunning slaves, boastful soldiers, courtesans, and long-lost daughters, are often larger than life, and the language is correspondingly exuberant.

play v.t./i. 1. to occupy oneself in a game or other recreational activity; to act light-heartedly or flippantly. 2. to take part in (a game). 3. to compete against in a game. 4. to occupy (a specified position) in a team for a game; to assign (a player) to a position. 5. to move (a piece) or put (a card) on the table or strike (a ball etc.) in a game. 6. to perform (on a musical instrument); to perform (a piece of music etc.); to cause (a record or record-player etc.) to produce sound. 7. to act in a drama etc.; to act the part of; to perform (a drama or role) on stage. 8. to move about lightly or irregularly; to allow (light or water etc.) to fall on something; (of a fountain or hosepipe) to discharge water. 9. to allow (a fish) to exhaust itself pulling against the line. —n. 1. playing; recreation, amusement, especially as the spontaneous activity of children. 2. the playing of a game; the action or manner of this. 3. a literary work written for performance on the stage; a similar work for broadcasting. 4. activity, operation. 5. free movement; space or scope for this. 6. a brisk, light, or fitful movement. 7. gambling. —**in** (or **out of**) **play,** (of the ball etc. in a game) in (or not in) position for continued play according to the rules. **make a play for,** (slang) to seek to acquire. **make play with,** to use effectively or ostentatiously. **play about** or **around,** to behave irresponsibly. **play along,** to pretend to co-operate. **play at,** to perform or engage in halfheartedly. **play back,** to play (sounds recently recorded). **play-back** n. the playing back of sound. **play by ear,** to perform (music) without having seen a score; to proceed step by step going by one's instinct or by results. **play down,** to minimize the importance of. **played out,** exhausted of energy or usefulness. **play fast and loose,** to act unreliably. **play for time,** to seek to gain time by delaying. **play the game,** to observe the rules, to behave honourably. **play havoc** or **hell with,** (colloq.) to produce great disorder in. **play into a person's hands,** to act so as unwittingly to give him an advantage. **play the market,** to speculate in stocks etc. **play off,** to oppose (a person *against* another) especially for one's own advantage; to play an extra match to decide a draw or tie. **play-off** n. a match so played. **play on,** to take advantage of (a person's feelings etc.). **play on words,** to pun; a pun. **play-pen** n. a portable enclosure for a young child to play in. **play safe** or **for safety,** to avoid risks. **play up,** to behave mischievously; to annoy thus; to put all one's energy into a game. **play up to,** to flatter so as to win favour etc. **play with fire,** to take foolish risks. [OE]

playbill n. a poster announcing a theatre programme.

playboy n. a pleasure-seeking usually wealthy man.

player n. 1. a person taking part in a game. 2. a performer on a musical instrument. 3. an actor. 4. a record-player. [f. PLAY]

Playfair /ˈpleɪfeə(r)/, John (1748–1819), Scottish mathematician and geologist, a friend of James Hutton. He is chiefly remembered for his *Illustrations of the Huttonian Theory of the Earth* (1802), which presented Hutton's views—and some of his own—in a concise and readable form, enabling them to reach a far wider audience than Hutton's own writings.

playfellow *n.* a playmate.

playful *adj.* **1.** full of fun. **2.** in a mood for play, not serious; done in fun. —**playfully** *adv.*, **playfulness** *n.* [f. PLAY + -FUL]

playgoer *n.* one who goes to the theatre.

playground *n.* an outdoor area for children to play on.

playgroup *n.* a group of pre-school children who play regularly together under supervision.

playhouse *n.* a theatre.

playing-card *n.* a small oblong card with rounded corners used in games; one of a set of usually 52 divided into four suits. The origin of playing-cards is uncertain. They were not known to Graeco-Roman antiquity, and though it has been argued that they reached Europe from the Far East, European and Asian cards are so different that there may be no need to assume a common origin. They have been in use in Europe since the 14th c. and in the East for at least as long. From the 14th c. the various suit systems were becoming established in different parts of Europe. The standard pack now contains 52 cards divided into 4 suits of 13 cards each. Each suit has an ace, nine cards numbered 2 to 10, and three picture or 'court cards' (Jack or Knave, Queen, and King); the English pack also includes a Joker. Aces were a Victorian invention (early packs had numbered these cards 1; as ace in most card-games they count the highest). The ornamental ace of spades in English packs dates from the 18th c. when a duty was levied on the cards and this one was selected to bear the government stamp (forging it was an offence punishable by hanging); this duty was not entirely removed until 1960. The signs of the four suits reached England from France in about the 15th c.; since then no major change has been made in the composition of the pack, and figures on the court cards are still clad in the costume of Henry VII's reign. The double head was introduced in the 19th c., for convenience, so that cards laid on the table looked the same way up to players on each side.

playing-field *n.* a field used for outdoor games.

playmate *n.* a child's companion in play.

plaything *n.* a toy or other thing to play with.

playtime *n.* time for play or recreation.

playwright *n.* a dramatist.

PLC *abbr.* Public Limited Company.

plea *n.* **1.** an appeal, an entreaty. **2.** (*Law*) a formal statement by or on behalf of a defendant. **3.** a pleading argument, an excuse. [f. AF f. L *placitum* decree (as PLEASE)]

pleach *v.t.* to entwine or interlace (esp. branches to form a hedge). [f. OF f. L *plectere* plait]

plead *v.t./i.* **1.** to address a lawcourt as an advocate; to put forward (a case) in a lawcourt. **2.** to declare oneself to be (guilty or not guilty) to a charge; to allege formally as a plea. **3.** to offer as an excuse. **4.** to make an appeal or entreaty. —**plead with**, to entreat earnestly. [f. AF (as PLEA)]

pleasant /ˈplez(ə)nt/ *adj.* pleasing to the mind, feelings, or senses. —**pleasantly** *adv.*, **pleasantness** *n.* [f. OF (as PLEASE)]

pleasantry *n.* **1.** jocularity. **2.** humorous speech; a joking or polite remark. [f. F (as prec.)]

please /pliːz/ *v.t./i.* **1.** to give pleasure (to); to make satisfied or glad. **2.** to think fit; to have the desire; to be the wish of. **3.** (short for *may it please you*) used in polite requests. —**if you please**, if you are willing, esp. (*iron.*) to indicate unreasonableness. **please oneself**, to do as one likes. [f. OF *plaisir* f. L *placēre*]

pleasurable /ˈpleʒərəb(ə)l/ *adj.* causing pleasure. —**pleasurably** *adv.* [f. foll.]

pleasure /ˈpleʒə(r)/ *n.* **1.** a feeling of satisfaction or joy, enjoyment. **2.** a source of pleasure or gratification. **3.** one's will or desire. **4.** (*attrib.*) done or used for pleasure. [OF (as PLEASE)]

pleat *n.* a fold or crease, especially a flattened fold in cloth doubled upon itself. —*v.t.* to make a pleat or pleats in. [var. of PLAIT]

pleb *n.* (*slang*) a person of the lower classes. [abbr. of foll.]

plebeian /plɪˈbiːən/ *n.* a commoner, especially in ancient Rome. —*adj.* of low birth, of the common people; uncultured; coarse, ignoble. [f. L *plebs* common people)]

plebiscite /ˈplebɪsɪt/ *n.* a direct vote of all the electors of a

State on an important public question. [f. F f. L (as prec., *scitum* decree)]

plectrum *n.* (*pl.* **-tra**) a small thin piece of horn or metal etc. for plucking the strings of a guitar etc. [L f. Gk (*plēssō* strike)]

pledge *n.* **1.** a thing given as security for the fulfilment of a contract, payment of a debt, etc., and liable to forfeiture in case of failure; a thing put in pawn. **2.** a thing given as a token of favour etc. or of something to come. **3.** a solemn promise. **4.** the drinking of a health, a toast. —*v.t.* **1.** to deposit as security, to pawn. **2.** to promise solemnly by pledge of (one's honour, word, etc.); to bind by a solemn promise. **3.** to drink to the health of. [OF (rel. to PLIGHT²)]

Pleiades /ˈplaɪədiːz/ *n.pl.* the 'Seven Sisters', the best-known galactic cluster in the sky, found in the constellation Taurus, a beautiful association of some half-dozen stars visible to the naked eye (more if the observer's eyesight is good) but actually containing over two hundred members. [L f. Gk]

plein air /plen ˈeə(r)/ (in painting) representing effects of atmosphere and light that are not observable in a studio. —**plein-airism** *n.* [F, = open air, orig. of French impressionists *c.*1870]

Pleistocene /ˈplaɪstəsiːn/ *adj.* of the first of the two epochs forming the Quaternary period. The Pleistocene epoch followed the Pliocene and preceded the Holocene (Recent); it lasted from about 2,000,000 to 10,000 years ago, is notable for a succession of ice ages, and also saw the evolution of modern man. Towards the end of the epoch many animal species became extinct. —*n.* this epoch. [f. Gk *pleistos* most + *kainos* new]

plenary /ˈpliːnəri/ *adj.* **1.** entire, unqualified. **2.** (of an assembly) to be attended by all members. [f. L (*plenus* full)]

plenipotentiary /plenɪpəˈtenʃəri/ *n.* a person (especially a diplomat) invested with full power of independent action. —*adj.* having this power. [f. L (as prec., *potentia* power)]

plenitude /ˈplenɪtjuːd/ *n.* fullness, completeness; abundance. [f. OF f. L (as PLENARY)]

plenteous /ˈplentɪəs/ *adj.* (*literary*) plentiful. [f. OF (as PLENTY)]

plentiful /ˈplentɪfʊl/ *adj.* existing in ample quantity. —**plentifully** *adv.* [f. foll. + -FUL]

plenty *n.* quite enough, as much as one could need or desire. —*adv.* (*colloq.*) quite, fully. [f. OF f. L *plenitas* (as PLENARY)]

pleonasm /ˈpliːənæz(ə)m/ *n.* the use of extra words not needed to give the sense (e.g. *hear with one's ears*). —**pleonastic** /-ˈnæstɪk/ *adj.* [f. L f. Gk (*pleonazō* be superfluous)]

plesiosaurus /pliːsɪəˈsɔːrəs/ *n.* an extinct marine reptile with a long neck, short tail, and four large paddles. [f. Gk *plēsios* near + *sauros* lizard]

plethora /ˈpleθərə/ *n.* an over-abundance. [L f. Gk *plēthōrē* (*plēthō* be full)]

pleura /ˈplʊərə/ *n.* (*pl.* **-ae** /-iː/) the membrane enveloping the lungs. [L f. Gk, = rib]

pleurisy /ˈplʊərɪsɪ/ *n.* inflammation of the pleura. —**pleuritic** /-ˈrɪtɪk/ *adj.* [f. OF f. L f. Gk *pleuritis* (as prec.)]

plexus /ˈpleksəs/ *n.* the network of nerves or vessels in an animal body. [L (*plectere* plait)]

pliable /ˈplaɪəb(ə)l/ *adj.* **1.** bending easily, flexible. **2.** easily influenced; compliant. —**pliability** /-ˈbɪlɪtɪ/ *n.*, **pliably** *adv.* [F (*plier* bend f. L *plicare*)]

pliant /ˈplaɪənt/ *adj.* pliable. —**pliancy** *n.*, **pliantly** *adv.* [f. OF (as prec.)]

pliers /ˈplaɪəz/ *n.pl.* pincers with parallel flat surfaces for holding small objects, bending wire, etc. [f. dial. *ply* bend (as PLY¹)]

plight¹ /plaɪt/ *n.* a condition or state, especially an unfortunate one. [AF *plit* (as PLAIT)]

plight² /plaɪt/ *v.t.* (*archaic*) to pledge. [f. OE, = danger; cf. PLEDGE]

plimsoll /ˈplɪms(ə)l/ *n.* a rubber-soled canvas sports shoe. [as foll.]

Plimsoll line /ˈplɪms(ə)l/ (also **Plimsoll mark**) a marking on a ship's side showing the limit of legal submersion in summer or under various conditions. It is named after Samuel Plimsoll, the English politician (d. 1898) whose agitation in the 1870s put an end to the practice of sending to sea overloaded and heavily insured old ships from which the owners made a profit if they sank.

plinth *n.* the lower square member of the base of a column;

a base supporting a vase or statue etc. [f. F or L f. Gk, = tile]

Pliny[1] /'plını/ 'the Elder' (Gaius Plinius Secundus, 23/4–79), Roman statesman, a scholar who combined a busy life in public affairs with prodigious activity in reading and writing. His *Natural History* is a vast encyclopaedia of the natural and human worlds, widely read in later ages. His scientific curiosity led to his death from suffocation while observing the eruption of Vesuvius in AD 79.

Pliny[2] /'plını/ 'the Younger' (Gaius Plinius Caecilius Secundus, *c*.61–*c*.112), nephew of Pliny the Elder, Roman senator and writer who led a busy public life under a succession of emperors. Nine books of literary letters, carefully edited for publication, deal with a wide variety of public and private affairs; a tenth book contains his correspondence, as governor of Bithynia, with Trajan, and includes one of the earliest pagan accounts of the Christians.

Pliocene /'plaɪəsiːn/ *adj.* of the final epoch of the Tertiary period, following the Miocene and preceding the Pleistocene, lasting from about 5.1 to 2 million years ago. It was a time when world temperatures were falling and many species of mammals that had flourished earlier in the Tertiary were becoming extinct. —*n.* this epoch. [f. Gk *pleiōn* more + *kainos* new]

PLO *abbr.* Palestine Liberation Organization.

plod *v.i.* (-dd-) **1.** to walk doggedly or laboriously, to trudge. **2.** to work slowly and steadily. —*n.* a spell of plodding. —**plodder** *n.* [prob. imit.]

plonk[1] *n.* a heavy thud. —*v.t.* to set down hurriedly or clumsily; to put firmly. [imit.]

plonk[2] *n.* (*slang*) cheap or inferior wine. [perh. f. prec. or F *vin blanc* white wine]

plop *n.* a sound as of an object dropping into water without a splash. —*v.t./i.* (-pp-) to fall or cause to fall with a plop. —*adv.* with a plop. [imit.]

plosive /'pləʊsɪv/ *adj.* (of a consonant, e.g. p, d, k) pronounced with a sudden release of the breath. —*n.* a consonant of this kind. [f. EXPLOSIVE]

plot *n.* **1.** a defined and usually small piece of ground. **2.** the interrelationship of main events in a play, novel, film, etc. **3.** a conspiracy, a secret plan. —*v.t.* (-tt-) **1.** to make a plan or map of. **2.** to mark on a chart or diagram; to make (a curve etc.) by marking out a number of points. **3.** to plan or contrive (a crime etc.); to plan secretly. —**plotter** *n.* [OE & f. OF *complot* secret plan]

Plotinus /plə'taɪnəs/ (*c*.205–70) Greek philosopher, the founder and leading exponent of Neoplatonism. Born in Upper Egypt, he accompanied the emperor Gordian (d. 243) on a military expedition to Persia to acquaint himself with Eastern thought, and finally settled in Rome in 244, where he set up a school of philosophy. His writings were published after his death by his pupil Porphyry. (See NEOPLATONISM.)

plough /plaʊ/ *n.* **1.** an implement for cutting furrows in soil and turning it up (see below). **2.** an implement resembling this (e.g. a snow-plough). **3. the Plough,** a constellation also known as the Great Bear. —*v.t.* **1.** to turn up (earth, or *absol.*) or cast out (roots etc.) with a plough; to cut (a furrow). **2.** to make one's way or advance laboriously (through snow, a book, etc.). **3.** to advance with irresistible penetration and damage. **4.** (*slang*) to fail in (an examination); to declare that (a candidate) has failed. —**plough back,** to turn (growing grass etc.) into the soil to enrich it; to reinvest (profits) in the business producing them. [OE f. ON]

One of the earliest agricultural tools, the plough is used to loosen and aerate the soil, to bury stubble and weeds, and to expose fresh soil to weathering so that it can be harrowed into a good seed-bed. The essential parts of a plough are a coulter (a vertical knife which cuts a thin vertical slice), a share, which cuts a horizontal slice below the earth to be turned by the mould-board or breast, thus exposing a furrow which is subsequently filled by the next slice of turned earth. The first ploughs were made of wood; later, metal reinforcement was introduced, and finally all-metal ploughs came into use in the 18th c. An important development was the use of chilled cast iron, which resists abrasion, for the ploughshare. Disc ploughs consist of a row of concave discs which break up the surface layer in hard dry soils and leave enough stubble to bind the surface soil and so prevent erosion by wind. Animal traction was used from 2000 BC onwards and is still widespread in developing countries. Steam-engines were developed during the 19th c. in England to haul ploughs of up to 8-furrow

capacity by means of winches and cables, but were replaced in the 20th c. by tractors. Most modern ploughs are mounted on the rear of a tractor and the depth of the furrow is controlled hydraulically.

ploughman *n.* (*pl.* **-men**) a man who guides a plough. —**ploughman's lunch,** a meal of bread and cheese etc.

ploughshare *n.* the cutting-blade of a plough.

plover /'plʌvə(r)/ *n.* a medium-sized wading bird of the family Charadriidae, e.g. the peewit. [AF, ult. f. L *pluvia* rain]

ploy *n.* (*colloq.*) a cunning manœuvre used to gain an advantage. [orig. Sc.; etym. unkn.]

PLR *abbr.* Public Lending Right.

pluck *v.t./i.* **1.** to pick or pull out or away. **2.** to strip (a bird) of feathers. **3.** to pull at, to twitch. **4.** to sound (the string of a musical instrument) with the finger or a plectrum. **5.** to plunder, to swindle. —*n.* **1.** courage, spirit. **2.** plucking, a twitch. **3.** an animal's heart and liver and lungs as food. —**pluck up courage,** to summon up one's courage. [OE]

plucky *adj.* brave, spirited. —**pluckily** *adv.*, **pluckiness** *n.* [f. prec.]

plug *n.* **1.** a piece of solid material fitting tightly into a hole, used to fill a gap or cavity or act as a wedge or stopper. **2.** a device of metal pins in an insulated casing fitting into holes in a socket for making an electrical connection; (*colloq.*) the socket. **3.** a sparking-plug. **4.** (*colloq.*) favourable publicity for a commercial product etc. **5.** (*colloq.*) the release-mechanism of a water-closet flushing-apparatus. **6.** a cake or stick of tobacco; a piece of this for chewing. —*v.t./i.* (-gg-) **1.** to put a plug into; to stop with a plug. **2.** (*slang*) to shoot or strike (a person etc.). **3.** (*colloq.*) to mention favourably; to seek to popularize (a song, product, policy, etc.) by constant recommendation. **4.** (*colloq.*) to work steadily. —**plug in,** to connect electrically by inserting a plug into a socket. **plug-in** *adj.* able to be connected thus. [f. MDu. & MLG *plugge*]

plum *n.* **1.** a roundish fleshy fruit with sweet pulp and a flattish pointed stone; the tree (*Prunus domestica*) bearing it; the dried fruit used in cooking. **2.** a thing that is highly prized or the best of its kind. —**plum pudding,** a boiled pudding containing raisins etc. [OE, ult. f. L *prunum*]

plumage /'pluːmɪdʒ/ *n.* a bird's feathers. [f. OF (as PLUME)]

plumb[1] /plʌm/ *n.* a ball of lead, especially attached to the end of a line for finding the depth of water or testing whether a wall etc. is vertical. —*adj.* vertical. —*adv.* **1.** exactly; vertically. **2.** (*US slang*) quite, utterly. —*v.t.* **1.** to measure or test with a plumb-line. **2.** to reach or experience (depths of feeling etc.). **3.** to get to the bottom of (a matter). —**out of plumb,** not vertical. **plumb-line** *n.* a line with a plumb attached. [f. L *plumbum* lead]

plumb[2] /plʌm/ *v.t./i.* **1.** to work as a plumber. **2.** to provide with a plumbing system; to fit (a thing) as part of this. [back-formation f. PLUMBER]

plumbago /plʌm'beɪɡəʊ/ *n.* **1.** graphite. **2.** a herbaceous plant of the genus *Plumbago* with spikes of tubular white, blue, or purplish flowers. [L (as PLUMB[1])]

plumber /'plʌmə(r)/ *n.* a person who fits and repairs the domestic apparatus of a water-supply. [as PLUMB[2]]

plumbing /'plʌmɪŋ/ *n.* **1.** the system or apparatus of a water-supply. **2.** the work of a plumber. **3.** (*colloq.*) lavatory installations. [f. prec.]

plume /pluːm/ *n.* a feather, especially a large one used for ornament; an ornament of feathers etc. attached to a helmet or hat or worn in the hair; something resembling this. —*v.t.* **1.** to furnish with a plume or plumes. **2.** to pride (oneself). **3.** (of a bird) to preen (itself or its feathers). [f. OF f. L *pluma*]

plummet /'plʌmɪt/ *n.* **1.** a plumb; a plumb-line; a sounding-lead. **2.** a weight attached to a fishing-line to keep a float upright. —*v.i.* to fall or plunge rapidly. [f. OF *plommet* (as PLUMB[1])]

plummy *adj.* **1.** of plums; full of plums. **2.** (*colloq.*) good, desirable. **3.** (of a voice) sounding affectedly rich in tone. [f. PLUM]

plump[1] *adj.* having a full rounded shape, fleshy. —*v.t./i.* to make or become plump; to fatten. —**plumpness** *n.* [f. MDu. or MLG, = blunt, shapeless]

plump[2] *v.t./i.* to drop or plunge with an abrupt descent. —*n.* an abrupt or heavy fall. —*adv.* **plump for,** to choose; to decide on. [f. MLG or MDu. (imit.)]

plumy /'pluːmɪ/ *adj.* **1.** plumelike, feathery. **2.** adorned with plumes. [f. PLUME]

plunder *v.t.* to rob (a place or person) forcibly of goods, especially (as) in war; to rob systematically; to steal or embezzle. —*n.* the violent or dishonest acquisition of property; the property so acquired; (*slang*) profit, gain. —**plunderer** *n.* [f. LG *plündern*]

plunge /plʌnj/ *v.t./i.* **1.** to thrust or go suddenly or violently into something; to jump or dive into water; to immerse completely. **2.** to enter or cause to enter a condition, course, or set of circumstances. **3.** to descend suddenly; to move with a rush. **4.** (*slang*) to gamble heavily; to run deeply into debt. —*n.* a plunging action or movement, a dive. —**take the plunge**, to take a bold decisive step. [f. OF, ult. f. L *plumbum* lead]

plunger *n.* **1.** a part of a mechanism that works with a plunging or thrusting movement. **2.** a rubber cup on a handle for the removal of blockages from pipes by a plunging action. **3.** (*slang*) a reckless gambler. [f. prec.]

pluperfect /pluːˈpɜːfɪkt/ *adj.* (*Gram.*, of a tense) denoting action completed prior to some past point of time (e.g. *he had said*). —*n.* (*Gram.*) the pluperfect tense. [f. L *plus quam perfectum* more than perfect]

plural /ˈpluər(ə)l/ *adj.* **1.** more than one in number. **2.** (*Gram.*, of a word or form) denoting more than one. —*n.* (*Gram.*) a plural word or form; the plural number. [f. OF f. L (*plus* more)]

pluralism /ˈpluərəlɪz(ə)m/ *n.* **1.** the theory that there is more than one ultimate principle or kind of being (cf. MONISM); (in moral philosophy) the theory that there is more than one value and that they cannot be reduced one to another. **2.** a form of society in which members of minority groups maintain independent traditions. **3.** the holding of more than one office at a time. —**pluralist** *n.*, **pluralistic** /-ˈlɪstɪk/ *adj.* [f. prec.]

plurality /pluəˈrælɪtɪ/ *n.* **1.** the state of being plural. **2.** pluralism, a benefice or office held with another. **3.** (*US*) a majority that is not absolute. [as PLURAL]

plus *prep.* **1.** with addition of (symbol +). **2.** (of a temperature) above zero. **3.** (*colloq.*) with, having gained; possessing. —*adj.* **1.** additional, extra. **2.** (after a number) at least, rather better than. **3.** (*Math.*) positive. **4.** having positive electrical charge. —*n.* the symbol +. **2.** an additional quantity; a positive quantity. **3.** an advantage. [L, = more]

plus-fours /plʌsˈfɔːz/ *n.pl.* long wide knickerbockers (ill. DRESS). [so named because, to produce the overhang, four inches are added to ordinary knickerbockers]

plush *n.* a cloth of silk or cotton etc. with a long soft nap. —*adj.* **1.** made of plush. **2.** plushy. [f. F *peluche* f. It., ult. f. L *pilus* hair]

plushy *adj.* luxurious. —**plushiness** *n.* [f. prec.]

Plutarch /ˈpluːtɑːk/ (Lucius Mestrius Plutarchus, *c.*46–*c.*120) Greek Platonist philosopher and biographer, for the latter part of his life a priest at Delphi. He was a prolific writer, producing a varied collection of rhetorical, antiquarian, religious, and philosophical works, including short treatises on themes of popular moral philosophy, derivative in content, with his warm and sympathetic personality never far beneath the surface. His most influential work was the *Lives* of great men, tantalizing and treacherous to the historian but winning the affection of many generations by his vivid and memorable narrative, a mine of information about the ancient world. Montaigne, Shakespeare, Dryden, and Rousseau are among his debtors.

Pluto /ˈpluːtəʊ/ **1.** (*Gk myth.*) see HADES. **2.** (*Astron.*) the ninth planet of the solar system, discovered in 1930 by Clyde Tombaugh, following analysis of perturbations in the orbit of Neptune which were attributed to the gravitational influence of a then unknown planet. Although these calculations predicted a position close to where Pluto was discovered, it is now believed that Pluto is too small a body (diameter about 2,500 km) to have produced the measured perturbations, so that its discovery may have been serendipitous. Its orbit lies well out of the ecliptic plane in which the other planets lie, and is furthermore highly eccentric, so that its closest approach to the sun brings it within the orbit of Neptune. It was discovered in 1978 to have one satellite, Charon. [f. Gk, = rich]

plutocracy /pluːˈtɒkrəsɪ/ *n.* **1.** government by the wealthy; a State so governed. **2.** a wealthy élite. [f. Gk (*ploutos* wealth, -CRACY)]

plutocrat /ˈpluːtəkræt/ *n.* **1.** a member of a plutocracy. **2.** a wealthy man. —**plutocratic** /-ˈkrætɪk/ *adj.* [f. prec.]

plutonic /pluːˈtɒnɪk/ *adj.* **1.** (of igneous rocks) formed by crystallization of molten material at a great depth underground. **2.** attributing most geological phenomena to the action of internal heat (opp. *Neptunian*). [f. L *Pluto* god of the underworld, f. Gk]

Plutonist /ˈpluːtənɪst/ *n.* a person (esp. in the 18th c.) maintaining the plutonic theory (see prec., sense 2; opp. *Neptunist*). [f. prec.]

plutonium /pluːˈtəʊnɪəm/ *n.* a fissile transuranic radioactive metallic element, symbol Pu, atomic number 94, first obtained in 1940 by bombarding uranium with deuterons, and since found in trace amounts in nature. There are several isotopes. Plutonium was discovered in the course of the development of the atomic bomb, and the weapon exploded at Nagasaki in 1945 was a plutonium bomb. The use of plutonium as a nuclear fuel is economically important because it can be manufactured in nuclear reactors from the commonest but non-fissile isotope of uranium, 'uranium-238'. [f. PLUTO, planet next beyond Neptune (see NEPTUNIUM)]

pluvial /ˈpluːvɪəl/ *adj.* **1.** of rain, rainy. **2.** (*Geol.*) caused by rain; of periods of relatively high average rainfall in low and intermediate latitudes during the geological past (especially in the Pleistocene epoch) which alternated with interpluvial periods in a cycle which may be correlated with or related to the better-known cycle of glacial and interglacial periods in higher latitudes. —*n.* a period of prolonged rainfall, especially in the Pleistocene epoch. [f. L (*pluvia* rain)]

ply¹ /plaɪ/ *n.* **1.** a thickness or layer of cloth or wood etc. **2.** a strand of rope or yarn etc. [f. F *pli* (as PLIABLE)]

ply² /plaɪ/ *v.t./i.* **1.** to use or wield (a tool or weapon). **2.** to work steadily (at). **3.** to supply continuously with food or drink etc.; to approach repeatedly with questions etc. **4.** (of a vehicle etc.) to travel regularly to and fro between; to work (a route) thus. **5.** (of a taxi-driver etc.) to attend regularly for custom. [f. APPLY]

Plymouth Brethren /ˈplɪməθ/ a Christian denomination with no formal creed and no official order of ministers, named after its first centre, established in 1830 by J. N. Darby at Plymouth in Devon. Its teaching combines elements of Calvinism and Pietism, and emphasis is often placed on an expected millennium. Of austere outlook, members renounce many secular occupations, allowing only those compatible with New Testament standards. Controversies within the movement led in 1849 to a division between the 'Open Brethren' and the 'Exclusive Brethren'.

Plymouth Rock /ˈplɪməθ/ a granite boulder at Plymouth, Mass., on which the Pilgrim Fathers are supposed to have stepped from the *Mayflower*.

plywood /ˈplaɪwʊd/ *n.* a strong thin board made by gluing layers with the direction of the grain alternating through 90°. [f. PLY¹ + WOOD]

PM *abbr.* **1.** Prime Minister. **2.** post-mortem.

Pm *symbol* promethium.

p.m. *abbr.* after noon. [f. L *post meridiem*]

pneumatic /njuːˈmætɪk/ *adj.* **1.** filled with wind or air. **2.** working by means of compressed air. —**pneumatic drill,** a machine for breaking up the hard surface of a road etc., driven by compressed air. **pneumatic tyre,** a tyre inflated with air. The first pneumatic tyres, with an air-filled inner tube, were invented in 1845 by a Scottish engineer, R. W. Thomson, but proved expensive to make and awkward to fit; the idea lapsed until 1888 when J. B. Dunlop (see entry) made some for his son's tricycle, and they were soon in wide use. —**pneumatically** *adv.* [f. F or L f. Gk (*pneuma* wind)]

pneumonia /njuːˈməʊnɪə/ *n.* inflammation of one or both lungs. [L f. Gk (*pneumōn* lung)]

pnp *abbr.* in which an n-type layer occurs between two p-type layers.

PO *abbr.* **1.** Post Office. **2.** postal order. **3.** Petty Officer. **4.** Pilot Officer.

Po /pəʊ/ Italy's longest river, flowing eastward for nearly 670 km (416 miles) from the Alps to the Adriatic Sea.

Po *symbol* polonium.

po /pəʊ/ *n.* (*pl.* **pos**) (*colloq.*) a chamber-pot. —**po-faced** *adj.* (*colloq.*) solemn-faced, humourless. [F pronunc. of POT]

poach¹ /pəʊtʃ/ *v.t./i.* **1.** to catch (game or fish, or *absol.*) illegally. **2.** to trespass or encroach (on the property or idea etc. of another). [perh. f. F *pocher* (as foll.)]

poach² /pəʊtʃ/ *v.t./i.* **1.** to cook (an egg) without the shell in boiling water or in a poacher. **2.** to cook by simmering in a small amount of liquid. [f. OF *pochier* (*poche* bag; cf. POKE²)]

poacher¹ *n.* one who poaches (see POACH¹). [f. POACH¹]

poacher² *n.* a pan with one or more cup-shaped containers in which eggs (without the shells) are placed for cooking over boiling water. [f. POACH²]

Pocahontas /pəʊkəˈhɒntəs/ the daughter of Powhattan, an American Indian chief in Virginia. According to the story of an English colonist, Captain John Smith, she rescued him from death at the hands of her father who had captured him. She was seized as a hostage in 1612, and married a colonist, John Rolfe. In 1616 she was taken to England, where she died.

pock *n.* an eruptive spot on the skin, especially in small-pox. —**pock-marked** *adj.* bearing the scars left by such spots. [OE]

pocket /ˈpɒkɪt/ *n.* **1.** a small bag sewn into or on clothing, for carrying small articles. **2.** a pouchlike compartment in a suitcase, car door, etc. **3.** money resources. **4.** an isolated group or area. **5.** a cavity in the earth filled with gold or other ore. **6.** a pouch at the corner or on the side of a billiard-table into which balls are driven. **7.** an air pocket. —*adj.* **1.** of suitable size or shape for carrying in a pocket. **2.** smaller than the usual size. —*v.t.* **1.** to put into one's pocket. **2.** to appropriate (esp. dishonestly). **3.** to confine as in a pocket. **4.** to submit to (an injury or affront). **5.** to conceal or suppress (feelings). **6.** to drive (a billiard ball) into a pocket. —**in a person's pocket,** close to or intimate with him, under his control. **in pocket,** having gained in a transaction. **out of pocket,** having lost. **pocket-book** *n.* a notebook; a booklike case for papers or money carried in the pocket. **pocket borough,** see BOROUGH. **pocket-knife** *n.* a knife with a folding blade or blades, for carrying in the pocket. **pocket-money** *n.* money for minor expenses, especially that allowed to children. [f. AF dim. (as POKE¹)]

pocketful *n.* (*pl.* **-fuls**) as much as a pocket will hold. [f. prec. + -FUL]

pod *n.* a long seed-vessel, especially of the pea or bean. —*v.t./i.* (**-dd-**) **1.** to bear or form pods. **2.** to remove (seeds etc.) from pods. [f. dial. *podware, podder* field crops]

podgy /ˈpɒdʒɪ/ *adj.* short and fat; plump, fleshy. —**podgily** *adv.*, **podginess** *n.* [f. *podge* short fat person]

podium /ˈpəʊdɪəm/ *n.* (*pl.* **-ia**) **1.** a continuous projecting base or pedestal round a room or house etc. **2.** a rostrum. [L f. Gk *podion* (dim. of *pous* foot)]

Poe /pəʊ/, Edgar Allan (1809-49), American short-story writer, poet, and critic. His first collection *Tales of the Grotesque and Arabesque* (1839/40) contains his famous gothic romance 'The Fall of the House of Usher'. His poem 'The Raven' (1845) brought him fame but not fortune, and his family suffered continuing poverty and ill health, while Poe struggled with alcohol addiction. His posthumous reputation and influence has been great: Freudian critics have been intrigued by the macabre and pathological ele-ments in his works, ranging from necrophilia in his poem 'Annabel Lee' (1849) to the sadism of 'The Pit and the Pendulum' (1843). His other stories include the first detec-tive story, 'The Murders in the Rue Morgue' (1841). Of his critical writings the most influential was 'The Philosophy of Composition' (1846); 'The Poetic Principle' (1850) preaches a form of 'art for art's sake'.

poem /ˈpəʊɪm/ *n.* **1.** a metrical composition, especially one concerned with feeling or imaginative description; an elevated composition in verse or prose. **2.** something with poetic qualities. [f. F or L f. Gk *poēma* (*poieō* make)]

poesy /ˈpəʊɪsɪ/ *n.* (*archaic*) poetry. [f. OF f. L f. Gk *poēsis* (as prec.)]

poet /ˈpəʊɪt/ *n.* a writer of poems; one possessing high powers of imagination or expression etc. —**Poet Laureate,** see LAUREATE. —**poetess** *n.fem.* [f. OF f. L f. Gk *poētēs* (as POEM)]

poetaster /pəʊɪˈtæstə(r)/ *n.* a paltry or inferior poet. [as prec. + L *-aster* derog. suffix]

poetic /pəʊˈetɪk/ *adj.* of or like poetry or poets. —**poetic justice,** well-deserved punishment or reward. **poetic licence,** a writer's or artist's exaggeration or disregard of rules, for effect. —**poetically** *adv.* [f. F f. L f. Gk (as POET)]

poetical /pəʊˈetɪk(ə)l/ *adj.* poetic; written in verse. —**poeti-cally** *adv.* [as prec.]

poetry /ˈpəʊɪtrɪ/ *n.* **1.** the art or work of a poet. **2.** poems collectively. **3.** a quality that pleases the mind as poetry does. [f. L *poetria* (as POET)]

pogo /ˈpəʊgəʊ/ *n.* (*pl.* **-os**) (also **pogo stick**) a stiltlike toy with a spring, used for jumping about on. [orig. unkn.]

pogrom /ˈpɒgrəm/ *n.* an organized massacre (originally of Jews in Russia 1905-6). [Russ., = devastation]

poignant /ˈpɔɪnjənt/ *adj.* **1.** painfully sharp to the senses or feelings, deeply moving. **2.** sharp or pungent in taste or smell; pleasantly piquant. **3.** arousing sympathy. —**poignancy** *n.*, **poignantly** *adv.* [f. OF f. L (as POINT)]

Poincaré /ˈpwæːkɑːreɪ/, Jules-Henri (1854-1912), French mathematician and philosopher of science who made far-reaching contributions to pure and applied mathematics. He worked extensively on differential equations which allowed him to transform celestial mechanics (the branch of astronomy concerned with the movement of celestial bodies under the influence of gravitational forces), and was one of the pioneers of algebraic topology. By 1900 he was proposing a relativistic philosophy, suggesting that a consequence of this was the absolute velocity of light which nothing could exceed. His brother Raymond was President of France during the First World War.

poinsettia /pɔɪnˈsetɪə/ *n.* a plant (*Euphorbia pulcherrima*) with large scarlet bracts surrounding small yellowish flowers. [f. J. R. *Poinsett,* American ambassador to Mexico (d. 1851)]

point *n.* **1.** the sharp or tapered end of something; the tip or extremity. **2.** (in geometry) that which has position but no magnitude (e.g. the intersection of two lines). **3.** a dot; this used as a punctuation-mark; a dot or small stroke used in Semitic languages to indicate vowels or distinguish consonants; a decimal point. **4.** a particular place or spot; an exact moment; a stage or degree of progress or increase; the level of temperature at which a change occurs. **5.** each of the 32 directions marked on the compass; a corresponding direction towards the horizon. **6.** a unit of measurement or value or scoring. **7.** a separate item or detail. **8.** a distinctive or significant feature; the essential thing; the thing intended or under discussion; the salient feature of a story, joke, remark, etc. **9.** effectiveness, purpose, value. **10.** (usu. in *pl.*) a tapering movable rail by which a train may pass from one line to another. **11.** an electrical socket, a power point. **12.** (usu. in *pl.*) an electrical contact device in the distributor of an internal-combustion engine. **13.** (in cricket) a fields-man on the off side near the batsman; his position (ill. SPORTS). —*v.t./i.* **1.** to direct or aim; to be directed or aimed; to direct attention, to indicate. **2.** to provide with a point or points. **3.** to give force to (words or actions). **4.** to fill the joints of (brickwork etc.) with smoothed mortar or cement. —**at** or **on the point of,** on the verge of. **beside the point,** irrelevant, irrelevantly. **in point of,** as a matter of (fact etc.). **make a point of,** to indicate the necessity of; to call particular attention to (an action). **point-duty** *n.* (of a policeman etc.) being stationed at a particular point to control traffic. **point of no return,** the point in a journey or enterprise at which it becomes essential or more practical to continue to the end. **point of view,** a position from which a thing is viewed; a way of considering a matter. **point out,** to indicate, to draw attention to. **points of sailing,** the headings of a sailing vessel in relation to the wind (ill. SAILING-SHIPS). **point-to-point** *n.* a horse-race over a course defined only by certain landmarks. **point up,** to emphasize. **to the point,** relevant, relevantly. **up to a point,** to some extent but not completely. [f. F f. L *punctum, puncta* (*pungere* prick)]

point-blank *adj.* **1.** (of a shot) aimed or fired at a range very close to the target; (of range) very close. **2.** (of a remark etc.) blunt, direct. —*adv.* **1.** at point-blank range. **2.** bluntly, directly.

pointed *adj.* **1.** sharpened or tapering to a point. **2.** (of a remark or manner etc.) clearly aimed at a particular person or thing; emphasized. —**pointedly** *adv.* [f. POINT]

pointer *n.* **1.** a thing that points, e.g. the index hand of a gauge etc.; a rod for pointing to the features on a chart etc. **2.** (*colloq.*) a hint. **3.** a dog of a breed that on scenting game stands rigid looking towards it. **4.** (in *pl.*) two stars (Dubhe and Merak) in the constellation the Great Bear, a straight line through which points nearly to the pole-star; the two stars in the Southern Cross which are nearly in a line with the south pole of the heavens. (See ill. NAVIGATION.) [f. POINT]

pointillism /ˈpwæntɪlɪz(ə)m/ *n.* a technique of impression-ist painting, developed by Seurat to give painting greater luminosity, in which pigment is applied in small spots of various pure colours which are blended by the spectator's eye. Under the general title of 'divisionism' the style was influential in France, Holland, and Italy in the 1890s and early 1900s. —**pointillist** *n.* [f. F (*pointiller* mark with dots, as POINT)]

pointing *n.* the cement filling the joints of brickwork; the facing produced by this. [f. POINT]

pointless *adj.* without point or force; lacking purpose or meaning. —**pointlessly** *adv.* [f. POINT + -LESS]

Poirot /ˈpwarəʊ/, Hercule. A Belgian private detective in the crime stories of Agatha Christie. Short and bald, with luxuriant moustaches, he constantly advocates orderliness and the use of observation and reasoning.

poise /pɔɪz/ *v.t./i.* **1.** to balance or be balanced. **2.** to hold suspended or supported. **3.** to carry (one's head etc.) in a specified way. —*n.* **1.** balance, the way something is poised. **2.** a dignified and self-assured manner. [f. OF f. L *pensare* (*pendere* weigh)]

poison /ˈpɔɪz(ə)n/ *n.* **1.** a substance that when introduced into or absorbed by a living organism causes death or injury, especially one that kills by rapid action even in a small quantity. **2.** a harmful influence. —*v.t.* **1.** to administer poison to; to kill, injure, or infect with poison; (esp. in *p.p.*) to smear (a weapon) with poison. **2.** to corrupt or pervert (a person or the mind). **3.** to spoil or destroy (a person's pleasure etc.). —**poison ivy,** a North American climbing plant (*Rhus toxicodendron*) secreting an irritant oil from the leaves. **poison pen,** an anonymous writer of libellous or scurrilous letters; the practice of writing these. —**poisoner** *n.*, **poisonous** *adj.* [f. OF (as POTION)]

poke[1] *v.t./i.* **1.** to thrust with the end of a finger or a stick etc. **2.** to stir (a fire) with a poker. **3.** to produce (a hole etc.) by poking. **4.** to thrust or be thrust forward, to protrude. **5.** to pry or search. **6.** to potter. —*n.* the act of poking; a thrust or nudge. —**poke fun at,** to ridicule. **poke one's nose into,** to pry or intrude into. [f. MDu. & MLG *poken*]

poke[2] *n.* a bag, a sack (*dial.* exc. in *a pig in a poke*). [f. OF (cf. POUCH)]

poker[1] *n.* a stiff metal rod with a handle, for stirring a fire. [f. POKE[1]]

poker[2] *n.* a card-game in which players bet on the value of their hands. —**poker-face** *n.* an impassive countenance appropriate to a poker-player; a person with this. [cf. G *pochen* to brag]

poky /ˈpəʊkɪ/ *adj.* (of a room etc.) small and cramped. —**pokiness** *n.* [f. POKE[1]]

Poland /ˈpəʊlənd/ a country in eastern Europe with a coastline on the Baltic Sea, bordered by East Germany, Czechoslovakia, and the USSR; pop. (1982) 36,400,000; official language, Polish; capital, Warsaw. First united in the 11th c., Poland emerged from a period of internal division to become the dominant East European power in the 16th c. Thereafter it suffered severely from the rise of Russian, Swedish, Prussian, and Austrian power, losing territory and eventually its independent identity in three partitions between 1772 and 1795; the country did not regain full independence until (as a republic) after the First World War. Its invasion by German forces in 1939 precipitated the Second World War, and since 1945 it has been dominated, albeit to a fluctuating extent, by the USSR. The country has deposits of copper and iron, and some of the largest coalfields in the world. Despite rapid advances in urbanization and industrialization, however, Poland is still affected by severe economic problems, while the rise of the independent trade union movement, Solidarity (see entry), has led to fresh socio-political tensions within the country.

polar /ˈpəʊlə(r)/ *adj.* **1.** of or near either pole of the earth or the celestial sphere. **2.** having electric or magnetic polarity. **3.** directly opposite in character. —**polar bear,** a large white bear (*Thalarctos maritimus*) living in Arctic regions. **polar circles,** the parallels at 23° 27′ from the poles. [f. F (as POLE[2])]

Polaris /pəˈlɑːrɪs/ alpha Ursae Minoris, the North star or pole-star, located within one degree of the celestial pole, the focal point about which the heavens wheel during the course of a night (ill. NAVIGATION). The 49th brightest star in the sky, it is actually a double star, the bright component being a cepheid variable. [as POLAR]

polariscope /pəˈlærɪskəʊp/ *n.* an instrument for showing the polarization of light or for viewing objects in polarized light. [f. POLAR + -SCOPE]

polarity /pəˈlærɪtɪ/ *n.* **1.** the tendency of a magnet etc. to point with its extremities to the earth's magnetic poles, or of a body to lie with its axis in a particular direction. **2.** the possession of two poles having contrary qualities. **3.** the electrical condition of a body as positive or negative. [f. POLAR]

polarize /ˈpəʊləraɪz/ *v.t./i.* **1.** to restrict the vibrations of (light-waves etc.) so that they have different amplitudes in different planes. **2.** to give electric or magnetic polarity

to. **3.** to set or become set at opposite extremes of opinion. —**polarization** /-ˈzeɪʃ(ə)n/ *n.* [f. POLAR]

Polaroid /ˈpəʊlərɔɪd/ *n.* [P] a material in thin sheets polarizing light passing through it; a camera able to develop a negative and produce a print within a short time of exposure.

polder /ˈpəʊldə(r)/ *n.* a piece of low-lying land reclaimed from the sea or a river, especially in the Netherlands. [f. MDu.]

Pole *n.* a native or inhabitant of Poland. [G f. Polish]

pole[1] *n.* **1.** a long slender rounded piece of wood or metal, especially one used as part of a supporting structure or in propelling a barge etc. **2.** (as a measure) a perch (PERCH[1] sense 3). —**pole-jump** or **pole-vault** *n.* a vault over a high bar with the help of a pole held in the hands (SPORTS). **up the pole,** (*slang*) in a difficulty; crazy. [OE f. L *palus* stake]

pole[2] *n.* **1.** either of the ends of the earth's axis of rotation; either of two points in the celestial sphere about which the stars appear to revolve; the North Pole or South Pole. **2.** each of the two opposite points on the surface of a magnet at which the magnetic forces are concentrated. **3.** each of the two terminals (positive and negative) of an electric cell or battery etc. **4.** each of two opposed principles. —**be poles apart,** to differ greatly. **pole-star.** see POLARIS. [f. L f. Gk *polos* axis]

pole-axe *n.* **1.** a battleaxe with a long handle. **2.** a butcher's axe with a hammer at the back. —*v.t.* to slaughter or strike with a pole-axe. [f. MDu. or MLG (as POLL, AXE)]

polecat /ˈpəʊlkæt/ *n.* **1.** a small dark-brown mammal of the weasel family, especially *Mustela putorius*. **2.** (*US*) a skunk. [f. CAT; first element unkn.]

polemic /pəˈlemɪk/ *n.* a verbal attack; a controversial discussion. —*adj.* (also **polemical**) controversial, involving dispute. —**polemically** *adv.* [f. L f. Gk (*polemos* war)]

polemics /pəˈlemɪks/ *n.pl.* the art or practice of controversial discussion. [f. prec.]

poleyn /pəʊˈleɪn/ *n.* (*hist.*) a piece of armour covering the knee (ill. ARMOUR). [f. OF; orig. unkn.]

police /pəˈliːs/ *n.* **1.** a civil force responsible for maintaining public order (see below); (as *pl.*) its members. **2.** a force with a similar function of enforcing the regulations of an organization etc. —*v.t.* **1.** to maintain order in (a place) by means of police; to provide with police. **2.** to keep order in, to control. —**police state,** a totalitarian State regulated by means of a national police force controlling citizens' activities. **police station,** an office of a local police force. [F f. L (as foll.)]

Police forces are organized along different lines in various parts of the world. Compared with many countries (where the role of the military was not always sharply distinguished from that of the police) Britain was rather tardy in establishing a regular force, the first being that organized in London in 1829 by Sir Robert Peel. From medieval times a petty or parish constable was appointed to preserve the peace in his area and to execute the orders of Justices of the Peace; in towns, the 'watch' patrolled and guarded the streets with varying degrees of diligence. In London in the 18th c. some justices organized bodies of constables, of which the Bow Street Runners were one. The modern British police force is not a national one; a number of forces exist for defined areas, maintained by local police authorities, the Home Office being responsible for the Metropolitan Police.

policeman *n.* (*pl.* **-men**) a man who is a member of a police force. —**policewoman** *n.fem.* (*pl.* **-women**)

policy[1] /ˈpɒlɪsɪ/ *n.* **1.** a course of action adopted by a government or party or person. **2.** prudent conduct, sagacity. [f. OF f. L f. Gk (as POLITY)]

policy[2] /ˈpɒlɪsɪ/ *n.* a contract of insurance; a document containing this. [f. F, = bill of lading, ult. f. Gk *apodeixis* evidence]

polio /ˈpəʊlɪəʊ/ *n.* (*colloq.*) poliomyelitis. [abbr.]

poliomyelitis /ˌpəʊlɪəʊmaɪˈlaɪtɪs/ *n.* an infectious viral disease which may cause temporary or permanent localized paralysis as a result of the infection and death of nerve cells in the spinal cord or brain stem. [f. Gk *polios* grey + *muelos* marrow]

Polish /ˈpəʊlɪʃ/ *adj.* of Poland or the Poles or their language. —*n.* the official language of Poland, which belongs to the Slavonic language group and is spoken by its 36 million inhabitants and by some 2,500,000 people in the USA. [f. POLE]

polish /ˈpɒlɪʃ/ *v.t./i.* **1.** to make or become smooth and glossy by rubbing. **2.** (esp. in *p.p.*) to refine or improve, to add finishing touches to. —*n.* **1.** a substance used for polishing things. **2.** smoothness or glossiness produced by friction. **3.** refinement, elegance. —**polish off**, to finish off quickly. —**polisher** *n.* [f. OF f. L *polire*]

Politbureau /'pɒlɪtbjʊərəʊ/ *n.* the highest policy-making committee of the USSR or of some other Communist countries. [f. Russ., = political bureau]

polite /pə'laɪt/ *adj.* **1.** having good manners, socially correct. **2.** cultivated, cultured; refined, elegant. —**politely** *adv.*, **politeness** *n.* [f. L *politus* (as POLISH)]

politic /'pɒlɪtɪk/ *adj.* (of an action) judicious, expedient; (of a person) prudent, sagacious. —*v.i.* (**-ck-**) to engage in politics. [f. OF f. L f. Gk (*politēs* citizen)]

political /pə'lɪtɪk(ə)l/ *adj.* **1.** of or engaged in politics. **2.** of or affecting the State or its government; of public affairs. **3.** relating to a person's or organization's status or influence. —**political asylum**, see ASYLUM. **political economy**, the study of the economic problems of government. **political geography**, that dealing with the boundaries and possessions of States. **political prisoner**, a person imprisoned for a political offence. **political science**, the study of the factors involved in politics; the scientific analysis of political activity and behaviour. —**politically** *adv.* [f. L (as prec.)]

politician /pɒlɪ'tɪʃ(ə)n/ *n.* one who is engaged in politics, especially as a profession; one who is skilled in political affairs. [as POLITIC]

politicize /pə'lɪtɪsaɪz/ *v.t./i.* **1.** to engage in or talk politics. **2.** to give a political character to. —**politicization** /-'zeɪʃ(ə)n/ *n.* [as POLITIC]

politics /'pɒlɪtɪks/ *n.pl.* **1.** (also treated as *sing.*) the science and art of government; political affairs or life. **2.** political principles or practice. [f. POLITIC]

polity /'pɒlɪtɪ/ *n.* **1.** the form or process of civil government. **2.** an organized society, a State. [f. L f. Gk *politeia* (*politēs* citizen f. *polis* city)]

polka /'pɒlkə/ *n.* a lively dance originating in Bohemia; music for this. —*v.i.* to dance the polka. —**polka dot**, a round dot as one of many forming a regular pattern on a textile fabric etc. [F & G f. Czech, = half-step]

poll /pəʊl/ *n.* **1.** voting at an election; the result of voting; the number of persons voting or of votes recorded. **2.** an opinion poll (see OPINION). **3.** the head; the crown or top of the head. —*v.t./i.* **1.** to vote at an election. **2.** (of a candidate) to receive as votes. **3.** to cut off the horns of (cattle) or the top of (a tree etc.). —**poll-tax** *n.* a tax levied on every person. [perh. f. LDu.]

pollack /'pɒlæk/ *n.* a marine food-fish (*Pollachius pollachius*) related to the cod. [f. earlier *podlock*; orig. unkn.]

Pollaiuolo /pɒ'laɪwələʊ/, Antonio (1432–98) and Piero di Benci (1441–96), Florentine brothers who worked as painters, sculptors, and designers. Antonio assisted Ghiberti with the Florence Baptistery doors (1452) and produced the monuments in St Peter's to Popes Sixtus IV and Innocent VIII. His innovatory anatomical studies seem to have determined the composition and choice of subject in his paintings (e.g. *Battle of the Naked Men* and the *Hercules* panels). Piero was primarily a painter, producing chastely decorative figures when working independently but collaborating with his brother in the *Martyrdom of St Sebastian* (1475) and other works.

pollard /'pɒləd/ *n.* **1.** an animal that has cast or lost its horns; an ox, sheep, or goat of a hornless breed. **2.** a tree polled so as to produce a close rounded head of young branches. —*v.t.* to make (a tree) into a pollard. [f. POLL]

pollen /'pɒlən/ *n.* a fine powdery substance discharged from a flower's anther, containing the fertilizing element. —**pollen analysis**, palynology. **pollen count**, an index of the amount of pollen in the air, published as a warning to those allergic to it. [L, = fine flour]

pollinate /'pɒlɪneɪt/ *v.t.* to sprinkle the stigma of (a flower) with pollen. —**pollination** /-'neɪʃ(ə)n/ *n.*, **pollinator** *n.* [as prec.]

pollock var. of POLLACK.

pollster /'pəʊlstə(r)/ *n.* a person who organizes an opinion poll. [f. POLL]

pollute /pə'luːt/ *v.t.* **1.** to make foul or impure. **2.** to corrupt. —**pollutant** *adj. & n.*, **pollution** *n.* [f. L *polluere*]

Pollux /'pɒləks/ **1.** (*Gk myth.*) one of the Dioscuri (see entry). **2.** (*Astron.*) a bright star in the constellation Gemini.

polo /'pəʊləʊ/ *n.* a four-a-side game resembling hockey, played on horseback with a long-handled mallet (polo-stick). It is of eastern origin, first described in Persia in

about 600 BC. Having spread over Asia to China and Japan, by the 19th c. it survived only in a few mountain areas in the NW and NE frontiers of India, where it was discovered by visiting British officers who adopted it with enthusiasm. —**polo neck**, a high round turned-over collar on a jumper etc. [Kashmir dialect, = ball]

polonaise /pɒlə'neɪz/ *n.* a slow processional dance of Polish origin; music for this. [F, = Polish (as foll.)]

polonium /pə'ləʊnɪəm/ *n.* a rare radioactive metallic element, symbol Po, atomic number 84, occurring naturally as a product of radioactive decay of uranium. Discovered in 1898 by Marie Curie, occurring in minute amounts in pitchblende, it can now also be created artificially in nuclear reactors. It has some use as an energy source in satellites. [f. L *Polonia* Poland (discoverer's native country)]

polony /pə'ləʊnɪ/ *n.* a sausage of partly cooked pork etc. [app. for *Bologna* sausage]

poltergeist /'pɒltəgaɪst/ *n.* a mischievous ghost or spirit manifesting itself by making a noisy disturbance. [G (*poltern* create disturbance, *geist* ghost)]

poltroon /pɒl'truːn/ *n.* (*archaic*) a spiritless coward. —**poltroonery** *n.* [f. F f. It. (*poltro* sluggard)]

poly /'pɒlɪ/ *n.* (*pl.* **polys**) (*colloq.*) a polytechnic. [abbr.]

poly- /pɒlɪ-/ *prefix* **1.** many (*polygamy*). **2.** polymerized (*polyester*). [f. Gk (*polus* much)]

polyandry /'pɒlɪændrɪ/ *n.* polygamy in which one woman has more than one husband. —**polyandrous** /-'ændrəs/ *adj.* [f. Gk (as POLY-, *anēr* man, husband)]

polyanthus /pɒlɪ'ænθəs/ *n.* a cultivated primrose produced from hybridized primulas. [f. POLY- + Gk *anthos* flower]

Polybius /pə'lɪbɪəs/ (*c.*200–after 118 BC) Greek historian of Rome. After an early political career in Greece, he was deported to Rome. His 40 books of *Histories* (partially extant) chronicled the rise of Rome to world-supremacy from 220 to 146 BC; by ancient standards he is an accurate and honest historian.

Polycarp /'pɒlɪkɑːp/, St (traditionally *c.*69–*c.*155 but possibly later), bishop of Smyrna in Asia Minor, where he seems to have been the leading Christian figure in the mid-2nd c. He was arrested during a pagan festival, refused to recant his faith, and was burnt to death.

polychromatic /pɒlɪkrə'mætɪk/ *adj.* **1.** many-coloured. **2.** (of radiation) consisting of more than one wavelength. —**polychromatically** *adv.*

polychrome /'pɒlɪkrəʊm/ *adj.* in many colours. —*n.* a polychrome work of art. [F f. Gk (as POLY-, *khrōma* colour)]

Polyclitus /pɒlɪ'klaɪtəs/ (5th c. BC) Greek sculptor, who concentrated largely on nude male statues, although his best-known work in contemporary times was a colossal Hera, which was also depicted on coins. Two copies of his works survive, both idealized athletes, 'Doryphoros' (the spear-bearer) and 'Diadumenos' (youth fastening a band round his head). Polyclitus was known for his sensitivity in depicting the varying ages of his models, ideal or human, from young boyhood to maturity.

polyester /pɒlɪ'estə(r)/ *n.* a synthetic resin or fibre.

polyethylene /pɒlɪ'eθɪliːn/ *n.* polythene.

polygamy /pə'lɪgəmɪ/ *n.* the practice of having more than one wife or (less usually) husband at once. —**polygamist** *n.*, **polygamous** *adj.* [f. F f. Gk (as POLY-, *gamos* marriage)]

polyglot /'pɒlɪglɒt/ *adj.* knowing or using or written in several languages. —*n.* a polyglot person. [f. F f. Gk (as POLY-, *glōtta* tongue)]

polygon /'pɒlɪgɒn/ *n.* a figure with many (usually five or more) sides and angles. —**polygonal** /pə'lɪgən(ə)l/ *adj.* [f. L f. Gk (as POLY-, *-gōnos* angled)]

polygraph /'pɒlɪgrɑːf/ *n.* a machine for reading physiological characteristics (e.g. the pulse-rate), and made to serve as a lie-detector. [f. Gk (as POLY-, -GRAPH)]

polygyny /pə'lɪdʒɪnɪ/ *n.* polygamy in which one man has more than one wife. —**polygynous** *adj.* [f. POLY- + Gk *gunē* woman, wife]

polyhedron /pɒlɪ'hiːdrən/ *n.* (*pl.* **-dra**) a solid figure with many (usually seven or more) faces. —**polyhedral** *adj.* [f. Gk (as POLY-, *hedra* base)]

Polyhymnia /pɒlɪ'hɪmnɪə/ (*Gk & Rom. myth.*) the Muse of the mimic art. [Gk, = she of the many hymns]

polymath /'pɒlɪmæθ/ *n.* a person with wide knowledge of many subjects. [f. Gk (as POLY-, *manthanō* learn)]

polymer /'pɒlɪmə(r)/ *n.* a compound whose molecule is formed from many repeated units of one or more compounds. —**polymeric** /-'merɪk/ adj. [G f. Gk *polumeros* having many parts]

polymerize /'pɒlɪməraɪz/ v.t./i. to combine or become combined into a polymer. —**polymerization** /-'zeɪʃ(ə)n/ n. [f. prec.]

polymorphic /pɒlɪ'mɔːfɪk/ adj. (also **polymorphous** /-əs/) varying in individuals, passing through successive variations. [f. Gk (as POLY-, *morphē* form)]

Polynesia /pɒlɪ'niːzjə/ the islands of the central and western Pacific or (more usually) the easternmost of the three great groups of these islands, including New Zealand, Hawaii, and Samoa. —**Polynesian** adj. & n. [f. POLY- + Gk *nēsos* island]

polynomial /pɒlɪ'nəʊmɪəl/ adj. (of an algebraic expression) consisting of three or more terms. —n. a polynomial expression. [f. POLY-, after BINOMIAL]

polyp /'pɒlɪp/ n. **1.** a simple organism with a tube-shaped body, e.g. an individual coelenterate. **2.** a small growth of mucous membrane. [f. F (as POLYPUS)]

polypeptide /pɒlɪ'peptaɪd/ n. a peptide formed by combination of many amino acids.

Polyphemus /pɒlɪ'fiːməs/ (*Gk legend*) the Cyclops from whom Odysseus and some of his companions escaped by putting out his one eye while he slept.

polyphonic /pɒlɪ'fɒnɪk/ adj. **1.** having many voices. **2.** contrapuntal. **3.** (of a letter or symbol) representing more than one sound. —**polyphony** /pə'lɪfənɪ/ n. [f. Gk (as POLY-, *phōnē* voice, sound)]

polyploid /'pɒlɪplɔɪd/ adj. having more than two haploid sets of chromosomes. —n. a polyploid cell or organism. [G (as POLY-, after HAPLOID)]

polystyrene /pɒlɪ'staɪriːn/ n. a kind of plastic, a polymer of styrene.

polysyllabic /pɒlɪsɪ'læbɪk/ adj. **1.** having many syllables. **2.** characterized by polysyllables.

polysyllable /'pɒlɪsɪləb(ə)l/ n. a polysyllabic word.

polytechnic /pɒlɪ'teknɪk/ adj. giving instruction in many (including vocational) subjects at an advanced level. —n. a polytechnic institution, especially a college. The original Polytechnic Institution (in Regent Street, London) was founded in 1838 by George Cayley (see entry) and others. [f. F f. Gk (as POLY-, *tekhnē* art)]

polytheism /'pɒlɪθiːɪz(ə)m/ n. the belief in or worship of more than one god. —**polytheist** n., **polytheistic** /-'ɪstɪk/ adj. [f. F f. Gk (as POLY-, *theos* god)]

polythene /'pɒlɪθiːn/ n. a tough light plastic. [f. POLYETHYLENE]

polyunsaturated /pɒlɪʌn'sætʃəreɪtɪd/ adj. of those kinds of fat or oil that are not associated with the formation of cholesterol in the blood.

polyurethane /pɒlɪ'jʊərɪθeɪn/ n. a synthetic resin or plastic used especially as foam, as an electrical insulator, and in varnish. [f. POLY- + UREA + ETHANE]

polyvinyl chloride /pɒlɪ'vaɪnɪl/ a vinyl plastic used as an insulation or as a fabric.

pom n. **1.** a Pomeranian. **2.** (*Austral. & NZ slang*) a pommy. [abbr.]

pomace /'pʌmɪs/ n. the mass of crushed apples in cider-making. [f. L, = cider (*pomum* apple)]

pomade /pə'mɑːd/ n. a scented ointment for the hair and the skin of the head. [f. F f. It. (as prec.)]

pomander /pə'mændə(r)/ n. a ball of mixed aromatic substances; a round container for this. [f. OF f. L, = apple of ambergris]

pomegranate /'pɒmɪɡrænɪt/ n. a tropical fruit with a tough rind and reddish pulp enclosing many seeds; the tree (*Punica granatum*) bearing it. [f. OF f. L, lit. = many-seeded apple]

pomelo /'pɒmɪləʊ/ n. (*pl.* -os) a shaddock or grapefruit. [orig. unkn.]

Pomeranian /pɒmə'reɪnɪən/ n. a small dog of a breed with long silky hair. [f. *Pomerania* region in Germany and Poland]

pomfret-cake /'pʌmfrɪt, 'pɒ-/ n. a small round flat liquorice sweet. [f. Pontefract (earlier *Pomfret*) in West Yorkshire.]

pommel /'pʌm(ə)l/ n. **1.** a knob, especially at the end of a sword-hilt. **2.** the upward projecting front of a saddle (ill. HORSE). **3.** either of pair of handgrips fitted to a vaulting-horse. —v.t. (-ll-) to pummel. [f. OF *pomel* dim. f. L *pomum* apple]

pommy n. (also **pommie**) (*Austral. & NZ slang*) a British person, especially a recent immigrant. [orig. unkn.]

pomp n. **1.** a stately and splendid display. **2.** specious glory. [f. OF f. L f. Gk, = procession]

Pompadour /'pɒmpəduə(r)/, Marquise de. Jeanne Antoinette Poisson le Normant (1721-64), favourite of Louis XV. Pompadour became the king's confidante from 1745 until her death nineteen years later. Although her relationship with the king was platonic, certainly after the first few years, she maintained her hold over him by procuring him young mistresses and became very unpopular with the king's critics, particularly among the nobility who did not approve of her humble origins.

Pompeii /pɒm'peɪɪ/ an ancient town SE of Naples. Its sudden end in the Vesuvius eruption of AD 79, described by the Younger Pliny (and in which his uncle, the Elder Pliny, perished), struck the imagination of the ancient world as well as the modern. The site, forgotten in the Middle Ages, was rediscovered in 1748, since when excavation and restoration has proceeded intermittently. The remains, buried and preserved beneath 4-6 metres of volcanic ash, include not only buildings and mosaics but wall-paintings, furniture, graffiti, and personal possessions of the inhabitants, providing an unusually vivid insight into Roman life, art, and architecture of the period.

Pompey /'pɒmpɪ/ 'the Great' (Gnaeus Pompeius, 106-48 BC), Roman general and politician. His greatest achievements were the suppression of the Mediterranean pirates (66 BC), and the defeat of Mithridates in the east (63 BC). Disagreement with Caesar ended in civil war and defeat for Pompey at the battle of Pharsalus, after which he fled to Egypt where he was murdered.

pom-pom[1] /'pɒmpɒm/ n. an automatic quick-firing gun. [imit.]

pom-pom[2] var. of POMPON.

pompon /'pɒmpɒn/ n. **1.** a decorative tuft or ball on a hat or shoe etc. **2.** a dahlia etc. with small tightly clustered petals. [F]

pompous /'pɒmpəs/ adj. ostentatiously or affectedly grand or solemn; (of language) pretentious, unduly grand. —**pomposity** /-'pɒsɪtɪ/ n., **pompously** adv. [f. OF f. L (as POMP)]

ponce n. **1.** a man who lives off a prostitute's earnings. **2.** (*slang*) an effeminate or homosexual man. —v.i. **1.** to act as a ponce. **2.** (*slang*) to move in an effeminate way; to potter. [perh. f. POUNCE]

Ponce de Leon /'pɒnθeɪ də 'leɪɒn/, Juan (c.1460-1521), Spanish explorer who accompanied Columbus on his second voyage to the New World in 1493 and in 1510 became Governor of Puerto Rico. He discovered Florida in 1513, but was wounded in a skirmish with natives on a return voyage in 1521 and later died of his injuries in Cuba.

poncho /'pɒntʃəʊ/ n. (*pl.* -os) a blanket-like piece of cloth with a slit in the middle for the head, worn as a cloak; a garment shaped like this. [S. Amer. Sp.]

pond n. a small area of still water. [var. of POUND³]

ponder v.t./i. **1.** to think over, to consider. **2.** to muse, to be deep in thought. [f. OF f. L *ponderare* weigh]

ponderable adj. having appreciable weight or significance. [f. L (as prec.)]

ponderous /'pɒndərəs/ adj. **1.** heavy, unwieldy. **2.** (of a style) dull, tedious. —**ponderously** adv. [f. L (*pondus* weight)]

Pondicherry /pɒndɪ'tʃerɪ/ a Union Territory in SE India, formed from several former French territories incorporated in India in 1954; capital, Pondicherry.

pondweed n. an aquatic herb especially of the genus *Potamogeton*, growing in still water.

pong n. (*slang*) a stink. —v.i. (*slang*) to stink. [orig. unkn.]

poniard /'pɒnjəd/ n. (*hist.*) a dagger. [f. F f. L *pugnale* (*pugnus* fist)]

Pontefract-cake /'pɒntɪfrækt/ n. a small round flat cake of liquorice, made at Pontefract in West Yorkshire.

pontiff n. a bishop, a chief priest; the pope. [f. F f. L *pontifex*]

pontifical /pɒn'tɪfɪk(ə)l/ adj. **1.** of or befitting a pontiff. **2.** pompously dogmatic. —**pontifically** adv. [f. F or L (as PONTIFF)]

pontificate /pɒn'tɪfɪkeɪt/ v.i. **1.** to speak in a pontifical way. **2.** to play the pontiff. — /pɒn'tɪfɪkət/ n. the office of bishop or pope; the period of this. [f. L (as PONTIFF)]

pontoon[1] /pɒn'tuːn/ n. a card-game in which players try to acquire cards with a face-value totalling 21 and no more. [prob. corrupt. of *vingt-un* vingt-et-un]

pontoon² /pɒnˈtuːn/ n. **1.** a flat-bottomed boat used as a ferry-boat or to carry lifting-gear etc. **2.** each of several boats etc. used to support a temporary bridge (**pontoon bridge**). [f. F f. L *ponto* (*pons* bridge)]

Pontormo /pɒnˈtɔːməʊ/, Jacopo da (1494-1557), Florentine painter. Although a pupil of Andrea del Sarto, his admiration for Michelangelo saw the development of strong mannerist tendencies in his work—in particular, dynamic composition, anatomical exaggeration, and abrupt contrasts (e.g. *Joseph in Egypt*, 1518-19). His portrait style is less exuberant and, with his drawings, justly admired.

Pontus /ˈpɒntəs/ the ancient name for the region in northern Asia Minor north of Cappadocia, stretching along the Black Sea coast.

pony /ˈpəʊnɪ/ n. a horse of any small breed. —**pony-tail** n. hair drawn back, tied, and hanging down behind the head.
pony-trekking n. travelling across country on ponies for pleasure. [perh. f. F *poulenet* dim. of *poulain* foal]

Pony Express a system of mail delivery in the USA in 1860-1, over a distance of 2,900 km (1,800 miles), between St Joseph in Missouri and Sacramento in California, by continuous relays of horse-riders. William Cody ('Buffalo Bill') was one of its riders.

poodle n. a dog of a breed with thick curling hair often elaborately clipped and shaved. [f. G *pudel*(*hund*), as PUDDLE]

poof /puːf/ n. (*slang*) an effeminate or homosexual man. [cf. PUFF]

pooh /puː/ int. expressing contempt or impatience. [imit.]

Pooh-Bah /puːˈbɑː/ n. a holder of many offices at once. [character in W. S. Gilbert's *The Mikado* (1885)]

pooh-pooh /puːˈpuː/ v.t. to express contempt for, to ridicule. [redupl. of POOH]

pool¹ n. **1.** a small body of still water, usually of natural formation. **2.** a small shallow body of any liquid. **3.** a deep place in a river. **4.** a swimming-pool. [OE]

pool² n. **1.** a common fund, e.g. of the profits of separate firms or of players' stakes in gambling. **2.** a common supply of persons, vehicles, commodities, etc., for sharing by a group of people; a group of persons sharing duties etc. **3.** an arrangement between competing parties to fix prices and share business. **4.** (*US*) a game played on a billiard-table with usually 16 balls. —v.t. to put into a common fund; to share in common. —**the pools**, football pools, especially as conducted on a weekly basis. [f. F *poule*, orig. = hen]

poop n. **1.** the stern of a ship. **2.** the aftermost and highest deck (ill. SAILING-SHIPS). [f. OF f. L *puppis*]

poor /pʊə(r)/ adj. **1.** having little money or means. **2.** deficient in a specified quality or possession. **3.** scanty, inadequate; less good than is usual or expected. **4.** deserving pity or sympathy, unfortunate. **5.** spiritless, despicable. **6.** humble, insignificant. —**Poor Clares**, see CLARE. **poor man's**, an inferior or cheaper substitute for. **poor white**, (*US derog.*) a member of a socially inferior group of white people. —**poorness** n. [f. OF *povre* f. L *pauper*]

poorhouse n. (*hist.*) the workhouse.

Poor Law (*hist.*) law relating to the support of the poor in England. In Elizabethan times it placed the responsibility for the relief of the poor on the parish, and levied a compulsory rate for the provision of funds. In the 17th-18th c. there was an inefficient system of workhouses and outdoor relief. Successive legislation resulted in a gradual improvement of the system in the 19th c., and in the 20th c. it was finally supplanted by schemes of social security.

poorly adv. in a poor manner, badly. —*predic. adj.* unwell. [f. POOR]

pop¹ n. **1.** a sudden sharp explosive sound, as of a cork when drawn. **2.** an effervescing drink. —v.t./i. **1.** to make or cause to make a pop. **2.** to go, move, or put abruptly. **3.** (*slang*) to pawn. —adv. with the sound of a pop. —**pop-eyed** adj. with eyes bulging or wide open. **pop off**, (*slang*) to die. **pop the question**, (*colloq.*) to propose marriage. **pop-shop** n. (*slang*) a pawnbroker's shop. **pop-up** adj. involving parts that pop up automatically. [imit.]

pop² adj. (*colloq.*) **1.** in a popular modern style. **2.** performing popular music. —n. (*colloq.*) pop music or records. —**pop art**, art that uses themes drawn from popular culture. The term is applied specifically to the works of a group of artists who, largely in the mid-1950s and 1960s, were interested in the subject-matter and techniques of commercial culture and mass production, and were opposed to contemporary

aesthetic standards. Artists such as Warhol in America and Hockney in Britain produced works including images of media stars, modern transport, and industrial machinery and products. **pop music,** modern popular music (e.g. rock music) appealing particularly to younger people. [abbr. POPULAR]

pop³ n. (*colloq.*) father; any older man. [f. PAPA]

popcorn n. maize which when heated bursts open to form fluffy balls.

Pope /pəʊp/, Alexander (1688-1744), English poet, crippled by a childhood spinal affliction, and largely self-educated, who showed his precocious metrical skill and biting wit in his 'Pastorals' (1709) and his *Essay on Criticism* (1711) which made him known to Addison's literary circle. Later he associated with Swift, Gay, and others. *The Rape of the Lock* (1712) is perhaps his finest achievement, showing his masterful use of the mock heroic. His translation of the *Iliad* (1715-20) into heroic couplets, though not an accurate version of the original, is one of the great poems of the age and, supplemented in 1725-6 by a translation of the *Odyssey*, helped to finance the comfortable house in Twickenham where he spent the remainder of his life.

pope¹ n. **1.** the Bishop of Rome as head of the Roman Catholic Church. **2.** the head of the Coptic Church. [OE f. L *papa* f. Gk, = father]

pope² n. a parish priest of the Orthodox Church in Russia etc. [f. Russ. *pop* (as prec.)]

Pope Joan according to a legend widely believed in the Middle Ages, a woman in male disguise who (c.1100) became a distinguished scholar and then pope, reigned for more than two years, and died after giving birth to a child during a procession. The legend is rejected by all serious scholars as an invention.

popery /ˈpəʊpərɪ/ n. (*derog.*) the papal system; the Roman Catholic religion. [f. POPE¹]

popgun n. a child's toy gun firing a cork etc. by the action of compressed air.

popinjay /ˈpɒpɪndʒeɪ/ n. a fop; a conceited person. [f. OF *papingay* f. Sp. f. Arab.]

popish /ˈpəʊpɪʃ/ adj. (*derog.*) of popery. —**Popish Plot,** a fictitious Jesuit plot to kill Charles II of England, massacre Protestants, and put the Catholic Duke of York on the throne, concocted by a Protestant clergyman, Titus Oates, in 1678. The 'discovery' of the plot led to a major panic and the execution of about 35 Catholics, most notably the Primate of Ireland. [f. POPE¹]

poplar /ˈpɒplə(r)/ n. a tall slender tree of the genus *Populus*, with a straight trunk and often tremulous leaves. [f. AF *popler* (*pople* f. L *populus*)]

poplin /ˈpɒplɪn/ n. a plain-woven fabric usually of cotton. [f. obs. F *papeline* perh. f. It. (as PAPAL)]

poppadam /ˈpɒpədəm/ n. a thin crisp biscuit made with lentil-flour. [f. Tamil]

popper n. (*colloq.*) a press-stud. [f. POP¹]

poppet /ˈpɒpɪt/ n. (*colloq.*) (esp. as a term of endearment) a small or dainty person. [ult. f. L *pu(p)pa* doll]

popping-crease n. (in cricket) the line in front of and parallel to the wicket within which a batsman stands (ill. SPORTS). [f. POP¹]

poppy n. a plant of the genus *Papaver* with showy (esp. scarlet) flowers and milky juice. —**Poppy Day,** Remembrance Sunday, when artificial poppies are worn (see FLANDERS POPPY). [OE f. L *papaver*]

poppycock n. (*slang*) nonsense. [OE f. Du. dial. *pappekak*]

populace /ˈpɒpjʊləs/ n. the common people. [F f. It. *popolaccio* (*popolo* people)]

popular /ˈpɒpjʊlə(r)/ adj. **1.** liked or admired by many people. **2.** of, for, or prevalent among the general public. —**popular music,** music that appeals to general taste, not highbrow or classical. —**popularity** /-ˈlærɪtɪ/ n., **popularly** adv. [f. AF or L (*populus* people)]

Popular Front 1. an international political alliance of Communist, radical, and socialist elements formed in 1935 and gaining power in France (1936-8), Spain (1936), and Chile (1938-42). In Europe it was largely ineffective after 1938. **2.** (also **popular front**) a similar party or coalition representing left-wing elements.

popularize v.t. **1.** to make generally liked. **2.** to present (a subject) in a readily understandable form. —**popularization** /-ˈzeɪʃ(ə)n/ n., **popularizer** n. [f. prec.]

populate /ˈpɒpjʊleɪt/ v.t. **1.** to inhabit, to form the population of. **2.** to supply with inhabitants. [f. L *populare* (as PEOPLE)]

population /pɒpjʊ'leɪʃ(ə)n/ *n.* **1.** the inhabitants of a place or country etc.; the total number of these. **2.** the extent to which a place is populated. —**population explosion,** a sudden large increase of population. [f. L (as PEOPLE)]

populist /'pɒpjʊlɪst/ *n.* an adherent of a political party claiming to the interests of ordinary people. [f. L *populus* people]

populous /'pɒpjʊləs/ *adj.* thickly inhabited. [f. L *populosus* (as PEOPLE)]

porcelain /'pɔ:slɪn/ *n.* fine earthenware with a translucent body and a transparent glaze; articles made of this. [F f. It. *porcellana* cowrie shell, china ware resembling this polished substance, f. *porcella* dim. of *porca* sow (perh. from resemblance of shells to a sow's vulva)]

porch *n.* a covered approach to the entrance of a building. [f. OF f. L *porticus*]

porcine /'pɔ:saɪn/ *adj.* of or like a pig. [f. F or L (as PORK)]

porcupine /'pɔ:kjʊpaɪn/ *n.* a rodent of the family Hystricidae with a body and tail covered with erectile spines. [f. OF *porcespin* (as PORK, SPINE)]

pore[1] *n.* a minute opening in the surface of a skin or leaf etc. through which fluids may pass. [f. OF f. L f. Gk *poros*]

pore[2] *v.i.* (with *over*) to be absorbed in studying (a book etc.); to meditate or think intently about. [perh. rel. to PEER[1]]

pork *n.* the flesh (esp. unsalted) of a pig used as food. —**pork pie,** a raised pie of minced pork etc., eaten cold. **pork-pie hat,** a hat with a flat rimmed crown and the brim turned up all round. [OF *porc* f. L *porcus* pig]

porker *n.* a pig raised for pork. [f. PORK]

porky *adj.* **1.** of or like pork. **2.** (*colloq.*) fleshy. —**porkiness** *n.* [f. PORK]

porn *n.* (*colloq.*) pornography. [abbr.]

pornography /pɔ:'nɒgrəfɪ/ *n.* the explicit representation of sexual activity visually or descriptively to stimulate erotic rather than aesthetic feelings; pictures or literature etc. containing this. —**pornographer** *n.,* **pornographic** /-'græfɪk/ *adj.* [f. Gk *pornē* prostitute, -GRAPHY]

porous /'pɔ:rəs/ *adj.* **1.** containing pores. **2.** able to be permeated by fluid or air. —**porosity** /-'rɒsɪtɪ/ *n.* [f. OF f. L (as PORE[1])]

Porphyry /'pɔ:fɪrɪ/ (*c.*232-303) Neoplatonist philosopher and opponent of Christianity, pupil of Plotinus whose works he edited after the latter's death.

porphyry /'pɔ:fɪrɪ/ *n.* a hard rock composed of crystals of red or white feldspar in a red matrix. —**porphyritic** /-'rɪtɪk/ *adj.* [f. L *porphyreum* ult. f. Gk *porphura* purple dye]

porpoise /'pɔ:pəs/ *n.* a sea mammal of the genus *Phocaena* related to the whale, with a blunt rounded snout. [f. OF f. L *porcus* pig + *piscis* fish]

porridge /'pɒrɪdʒ/ *n.* a food made by boiling oatmeal or other meal or cereal in water or milk. [alt. f. POTTAGE]

porringer /'pɒrɪndʒə(r)/ *n.* (*archaic*) a small soup-basin, especially for a child. [alt. f. earlier *pottinger* f. OF *potager* (as POTTAGE)]

Porsche /pɔ:ʃ/, Ferdinand (1875-1952), Austrian designer of cars, of which the best known is the original German Volkswagen (= people's car), planned as a small economical vehicle (and with Adolf Hitler's backing), though Porsche's real passion was for high-performance sports and racing cars.

Porsen(n)a /'pɔ:sɪnə/, Lars. According to legend (probably based on a confusion of the historical facts) an Etruscan chieftain, who was summoned by the exiled Tarquin the Proud (6th c. BC) and vainly laid siege to Rome.

port[1] *n.* a harbour; a town or place possessing a harbour; a place where customs officers are stationed to supervise the entry of goods into a country. —**port of call,** a place where a ship or person stops during a journey. [OE f. L *portus*]

port[2] *n.* a strong sweet usually dark-red fortified win. [f. *Oporto* in Portugal, whence shipped]

port[3] *n.* the left-hand side (when facing forward) of a ship or aircraft. —*v.t.* to turn (the helm) to port. —**port tack,** a tack with the wind on the port side. [prob. orig. the side turned towards port (PORT[1])]

port[4] *n.* **1.** an opening in a ship's side for entrance or loading etc. **2.** a porthole. [OF f. L *porta* gate]

port[5] *v.t.* to carry (a rifle) diagonally across and close to the body. [f. F f. L *portare* carry]

portable /'pɔ:təb(ə)l/ *adj.* easily movable, convenient for

carrying. —*n.* a portable form of typewriter, television set, etc. —**portability** /-'bɪlɪtɪ/ *n.* [f. OF or L (as prec.)]

portage /'pɔ:tɪdʒ/ *n.* the carrying of boats or goods between two navigable waters; a place at which this is necessary; the charge for it. —*v.t.* to convey (a boat or goods) over a portage. [f. OF (as PORT[5])]

portal /'pɔ:t(ə)l/ *n.* a gate or doorway etc., especially an elaborate one. —**portal frame bridge,** a type of bridge with a solid rectangular framed structure (ill. BRIDGES). **portal vein,** a vein conveying blood to the liver or some other organ except the heart. [f. OF f. L *portale* (as PORT[4])]

Port-au-Prince /pɔ:təʊ'prɪns/ the capital of Haiti; pop. (est. 1978) 745,800.

portcullis /pɔ:t'kʌlɪs/ *n.* a strong heavy grating sliding up and down in vertical grooves, lowered to block a gateway in a fortress etc. (ill. CASTLES). [f. OF, = sliding door]

portend /pɔ:'tend/ *v.t.* to foreshadow, as an omen, to give warning of. [f. L *portendere* (as PRO-, TEND[1])]

portent /'pɔ:tent/ *n.* **1.** an omen; a significant sign of something to come. **2.** a prodigy, a marvellous thing. [f. L *portentum* (as prec.)]

portentous /pɔ:'tentəs/ *adj.* **1.** being or like a portent. **2.** pompously solemn. [f. prec.]

Porter[1] /'pɔ:tə(r)/, Cole (1891-1964), American composer. He was as set on following a musical career as his parents were against it, and was a skilful enough song composer to make a success of it and live independently of them. His main successes came during and after the 1930s, with a long series of Broadway musicals including *Gay Divorce* (1932), *Anything Goes* (1934), and *Kiss me, Kate* (1948). He wrote his own song lyrics, such as the witty and original 'Begin the Beguine'.

Porter[2] /'pɔ:tə(r)/, Peter (Neville Frederick) (1929-), Australian poet, who settled in England in 1951 where he has worked from copywriter to full-time critic, broadcaster, and writer. His early collections (*Once Bitten, Twice Bitten*, 1961; *Poems, Ancient and Modern*, 1964; *The Last of England*, 1970) provide a sharply satiric portrait of London in the 1960s. His work became increasingly meditative, complex, and allusive, with a wide range of reference from Italian baroque to classical mythology and German romanticism, which add both richness and obscurity. Later volumes (*The Cost of Seriousness*, 1978; *English Subtitles*, 1981) introduce a new sombre exploration of the poet's conflicting responsibilities to his art and to others.

porter[1] *n.* **1.** a person employed to carry luggage etc. **2.** a dark beer brewed from charred or browned malt. [f. OF f. L *portator* (as PORT[5])]

porter[2] *n.* a doorman or gate-keeper, especially of a large building. [AF f. L *portarius* (as PORT[4])]

porterage *n.* the hire of porters. [f. PORTER[1]]

porterhouse steak a thick choice steak of beef. [said to derive its name from a porter-house, i.e. one selling porter (= dark beer; PORTER[1]), in New York]

portfolio /pɔ:t'fəʊlɪəʊ/ *n.* (*pl.* -os) **1.** a case for loose drawings, sheets of paper, etc. **2.** a list of investments held by a person or company etc. **3.** the office of a minister of State. —**Minister without portfolio,** a minister not in charge of any department of State. [f. It. *portafogli* (*portare* carry, *foglio* sheet of paper)]

porthole *n.* an aperture, usually glazed, in a ship's or aircraft's side for the admission of light and air to a ship or light to an aircraft. [f. PORT[4] + HOLE]

portico /'pɔ:tɪkəʊ/ *n.* (*pl.* -oes) a colonnade, a roof supported by columns at regular intervals, usually attached as a porch to a building. [It. f. L, = PORCH]

portion /'pɔ:ʃ(ə)n/ *n.* **1.** a part or share. **2.** the amount of food allotted to one person. **3.** a dowry. **4.** one's destiny or lot. —*v.t./i.* **1.** to divide into portions; to distribute. **2.** to give a dowry to. [f. OF f. L *portio*]

Portland cement /'pɔ:tlənd/ cement manufactured from chalk and clay. It was patented in 1824 by Joseph Aspdin, a bricklayer of Leeds, who fancied that it bore some resemblance to the limestone of Portland Island in Dorset.

Portland stone a valuable building limestone. [cf. prec.]

Portland vase a Roman vase dating from *c.*1st c. AD, of dark-blue transparent glass with an engraved figured decoration in white opaque glass. Acquired in the 18th c. by the Duchess of Portland from the Barberini Palace in Rome, it is now in the British Museum, where it was damaged by a madman in 1845.

portly *adj.* corpulent and dignified. —**portliness** *n.* [f. OF *port* deportment (as PORT[5])]

portmanteau /pɔːtˈmæntəʊ/ *n.* (*pl.* **-eaus**) a trunk for clothes etc., opening into two equal parts. —**portmanteau word,** a factitious word blending the sounds and combining the meanings of two others. (e.g. CHORTLE). [f. F (as PORT⁵, MANTLE)]

Port-of-Spain the capital of Trinidad and Tobago; pop. (1980) approx. 55,800.

Porto Novo /pɔːtəʊ ˈnəʊvəʊ/ the capital of Benin; pop. (est. 1980) 123,000.

portrait /ˈpɔːtrɪt/ *n.* **1.** a likeness of a person or animal made by drawing, painting, or photography. **2.** a description in words. —**portraitist** *n.* [F (as PORTRAY)]

portraiture /ˈpɔːtrɪtʃə(r)/ *n.* **1.** portraying. **2.** a portrait. **3.** a description in words. [as foll.]

portray /pɔːˈtreɪ/ *v.t.* **1.** to make a picture of. **2.** to describe in words. —**portrayal** *n.* [f. OF *portraire*]

Port Said /saɪd/ a seaport of Egypt, at the north end of the Suez Canal.

Portsmouth /ˈpɔːtsməθ/ a city and port in Hampshire, the chief naval station of Britain.

Portugal /ˈpɔːtjʊg(ə)l/ a country occupying the western part of the Iberian peninsula in SW Europe, bordering on the Atlantic Ocean; pop. (est. 1979) 9,862,700; official language, Portuguese; capital, Lisbon. In Roman times the province of Lusitania, the country's history was linked with that of the rest of the peninsula (see SPAIN) until it became an independent kingdom under Alfonso I in the 12th c. Dynastic disputes with the Spanish kingdoms to the east resulted in the formation of Portugal's long-standing alliance with England in the 14th c., and in the following two hundred years it emerged as one of the leading European colonial powers. Independence was lost to Philip II of Spain in 1580 and not regained until 1688, by which time Portugal had been relegated to a position of secondary importance in European affairs, a state of events exacerbated by domestic political instability which has continued through much of the 20th c. A republic since 1911, after the expulsion of the monarchy, the country remains poor by European standards, its economy still largely based on agriculture. Portugal became a member of the EEC on 1 Jan. 1986.

Portuguese /pɔːtjʊˈgiːz/ *adj.* of Portugal or its people or language. —*n.* (*pl.* same) **1.** a native or inhabitant of Portugal. **2.** the official language of Portugal and its territories and of Brazil, where it was taken by 15th-c. explorers. It is a Romance language, most closely related to (but clearly distinct from) Spanish, with 10 million speakers in Portugal and 55 million in Brazil. —**Portuguese man-of-war,** a tropical or subtropical hydrozoan of the genus *Physalia*, with a sail-shaped crest and a poisonous sting. [f. Port. f. L *portugalensis*]

pose /pəʊz/ *v.t./i.* **1.** to put into or assume a desired position for a portrait or photograph etc. **2.** to take a particular attitude for effect or to impress others. **3.** (with *as*) to pretend to be. **4.** to present (a question or problem). —*n.* **1.** an attitude in which a person etc. is posed. **2.** an affectation, a pretence. [f. F f. L *pausare* pause; confused in part with L *ponere* place]

Poseidon /pəˈsaɪd(ə)n/ (*Gk myth.*) the god of earthquakes and water, and secondarily of the sea, brother of Zeus. In cult he is prominent as the sea-god, displacing Nereus (who is probably a more ancient god) from the position which it would seem that he once held. The Romans identified Neptune with him.

poser *n.* a puzzling question or problem. [f. POSE]

poseur /pəʊˈzɜː(r)/ *n.* a person who poses for effect or behaves affectedly. [F (as POSE)]

posh *adj.* (*slang*) high-class, smart. —*v.t.* (*slang*) to smarten. [perh. f. slang *posh* money, a dandy. The suggestion that this word is derived from the initials of 'port out, starboard home', referring to the more expensive side for accommodation in ships formerly travelling between England and India, is often put forward but lacks foundation]

posit /ˈpɒzɪt/ *v.t.* to assume as a fact, to postulate. [f. L (as foll.)]

position /pəˈzɪʃ(ə)n/ *n.* **1.** the place occupied by a person or thing. **2.** the proper place. **3.** being advantageously placed. **4.** the way in which a thing or its parts are placed or arranged. **5.** a mental attitude; a way of looking at a question. **6.** a situation in relation to others. **7.** rank or status; high social standing. **8.** paid (official or domestic) employment. **9.** a place where troops are posted for strategic purposes. **10.** a configuration of chess-men etc during a game. —*v.t.*

to place in a position. —**positional** *adj.* [f. OF or L (*ponere* place)]

positive /ˈpɒzɪtɪv/ *adj.* **1.** formally or explicitly stated. **2.** definite, unquestionable. **3.** (of a person) convinced, confident or over-confident in an opinion. **4.** absolute, not relative. **5.** (*colloq.*) downright, out-and-out. **6.** constructive. **7.** marked by the presence and not absence of qualities. **8.** dealing only with matters of fact, practical. **9.** tending in the direction naturally or arbitrarily taken as that of increase or progress. **10.** (of a quantity in algebra) greater than zero. **11.** of, containing, or producing the kind of electrical charge produced by rubbing glass with silk. **12.** (of a photograph) showing the lights and shades or colours as in the original image cast on a film etc. **13.** (*Gram.*, of an adjective or adverb) in the primary form expressing a simple quality without comparison. —*n.* a positive adjective, photograph, quantity, etc. —**positive vetting,** an intensive inquiry into the background and character of a candidate for a senior post in the civil service etc. —**positively** *adv.*, **positiveness** *n.* [f. OF or L (as prec.)]

positivism /ˈpɒzɪtɪvɪz(ə)m/ *n.* **1.** the theory (held by Bacon and Hume amongst others, including Comte) that every rationally justifiable assertion can be scientifically verified or is capable of logical or mathematical proof, and that philosophy can do no more than attest to the logical and exact use of language through which such observation or verification can be expressed. **2.** logical positivism (see LOGICAL). **3.** the theory that laws are to be understood as social rules, valid because they are enacted by the 'sovereign' or derive logically from existing decisions, and that ideal or moral considerations (e.g. that a rule is unjust) should not limit the scope or operation of the law. —**positivist** *n.*, **positivistic** /-ˈvɪstɪk/ *adj.* [f. F (as prec.)]

positron /ˈpɒzɪtrɒn/ *n.* an elementary particle with the mass of an electron and a charge the same as an electron's but positive. [f. POSITIVE]

posse /ˈpɒsɪ/ *n.* a body (of constables); a strong force or company. [L, = to be able]

possess /pəˈzes/ *v.t.* **1.** to hold as belonging to oneself, to have or own. **2.** to have (a faculty or quality etc.). **3.** to occupy or dominate the mind of. —**like one possessed,** with great energy. —**possessor** *n.* [f. OF f. L *possidere*]

possession /pəˈzeʃ(ə)n/ *n.* **1.** possessing, being possessed. **2.** a thing possessed. **3.** occupancy. **4.** (in *pl.*) property, wealth. **5.** a subject territory. —**take possession of,** to become the owner or possessor of. [f. OF or L (as prec.)]

possessive /pəˈzesɪv/ *adj.* **1.** showing a desire to possess or to retain what one possesses. **2.** (*Gram.*, of a word or form) indicating possession (e.g. *Anne's, my, mine*). —*n.* (*Gram.*) a possessive case or word. —**possessively** *adv.*, **possessiveness** *n.* [f. L (as POSSESS)]

possibility /pɒsɪˈbɪlɪtɪ/ *n.* **1.** the fact or condition of being possible. **2.** something that may exist or happen. **3.** capability of being used or of producing good results. [as foll.]

possible /ˈpɒsɪb(ə)l/ *adj.* capable of existing, happening, being done, etc. —*n.* **1.** a possible candidate, member of a team, etc. **2.** the highest possible score, especially in shooting. [f. OF or L (as POSSE)]

possibly /ˈpɒsɪblɪ/ *adv.* **1.** in accordance with possibility. **2.** perhaps, for all one knows to the contrary. [f. prec.]

possum /ˈpɒsəm/ *n.* **1.** (*colloq.*) an opossum. **2.** (*Austral. & NZ*) a member of a large family of arboreal phalangers, some of which have a prehensile tail. —**play possum,** (*colloq.*) to pretend to be unconscious or unaware of something (from the opossum's habit of seeming to feign death if attacked). [abbr. OPOSSUM]

post¹ /pəʊst/ *n.* **1.** a long stout piece of timber or metal set upright in the ground etc. to support something, mark a position or boundary, etc. **2.** the pole marking the start or finish of a race. —*v.t.* (also with *up*) **1.** to attach (a paper etc.) in a prominent place. **2.** to announce or advertise by a placard or in a published list. [OE f. L *postis*]

post² /pəʊst/ *n.* **1.** the official conveying of parcels, letters, etc. (see below). **2.** the letters etc. conveyed; a single collection or delivery of these. **3.** a place where letters etc. are dealt with. —*v.t.* **1.** to put (a letter etc.) into the post. **2.** (esp. in *p.p.*) to supply (a person) with information. **3.** to enter (an item) in a ledger; to complete (a ledger) thus. —**post-bag** *n.* a mail-bag. **post-box** *n.* a box into which letters are inserted for dispatch or are delivered. **post-code** *n.* a group of letters and numerals in a postal address to assist sorting. **post-free** *adj.* & *adv.* carried by post without charge to the recipient. **post-haste** *adv.* with great speed. **post-office,** a building or room where postal business is

carried on. **Post Office,** the public department or corporation responsible for postal services. **post-paid** adj. on which postage has been paid. [f. F f. It. *posta* f. L (as POSITION)]
In medieval England messengers transported government documents around the country. From the beginning of the 16th c. the term 'post' was applied to men with horses stationed or appointed in places at suitable distances along the routes, the duty of each being to ride with, or forward with all speed to the next stage, the king's 'packet' or mail, and subsequently the letters of other persons also, as well as to furnish horses for use in this. The term corresponds to the *equites dispositi* (L, = posted horsemen) of classical and later times. The corresponding terms in French and Italian are used by Marco Polo of the stations, 25 miles apart on the great roads, at which the messengers of the Emperor of China changed horses, and at each of which 300–400 horses are said to have been kept for their service. In 18th-c. England stage-coaches carried the mail, succeeded in the mid-19th c. by the railways. In 1840 the 'penny post' was introduced, and similar developments in other countries led to the establishment of a 'Postal Union' in 1874 which stimulated the development of international mail services. The first regular airmail service (London–Paris) was introduced in 1919.

post³ /pəʊst/ n. **1.** a situation of paid employment. **2.** the appointed place of a soldier etc. on watch; a place of duty. **3.** a place (especially a frontier fort) manned by soldiers; the soldiers there. **4.** a trading station. —v.t. **1.** to place (a soldier etc.) at his post. **2.** to appoint to a post or command. **—last post,** a military bugle-call at the time of retiring for the night or at a funeral. [f. F f. It. *posto* (as prec.)]

post- /pəʊst-/ prefix after, behind. [f. L *post* adv. & prep.]

postage /'pəʊstɪdʒ/ n. the amount charged for sending a letter etc. by post. **—postage stamp,** an official adhesive stamp for sticking on a letter etc. indicating the amount of postage paid (see STAMP). [f. POST²]

postal /'pəʊst(ə)l/ adj. of or by post. **—postal code,** a post-code. **postal order,** a kind of money order issued by the Post Office. **—postally** adv. [F (as POST²)]

postcard n. a card for sending by post without an envelope.

postdate /pəʊst'deɪt/ v.t. **1.** to follow in time. **2.** to give a date later than the true date to.

poster /'pəʊstə(r)/ n. **1.** a placard in a public place. **2.** a large printed picture. [f. POST¹]

poste restante /pəʊst re'stɑ̃t/ a department in a post office where letters are kept until called for. [F, = letters remaining]

posterior /pɒ'stɪərɪə(r)/ adj. **1.** later, coming after in a series or in order of time. **2.** situated behind or at the back. —n. the buttocks. [L, compar. of *posterus* following (as POST-)]

posterity /pɒ'sterɪtɪ/ n. **1.** future generations. **2.** a person's descendants. [f. OF f. L (as prec.)]

postern /'pɒstɜːn/ n. a small entrance at the back or side of a fortress etc. [f. OF f. L *posterula* dim. f. *posterus* (see POSTERIOR)]

postgraduate /pəʊst'grædjʊət/ adj. (of studies) carried on after taking a first degree; (of a student) engaged in such studies. —n. a postgraduate student.

posthumous /'pɒstjʊməs/ adj. **1.** occurring after death. **2.** published after the author's death. **3.** born after the father's death. **—posthumously** adv. [f. L *postumus* last (as POSTERIOR), assoc. with *humus* ground]

postilion /pə'stɪljən/ n. a rider on the near horse drawing a coach etc. where there is no coachman. [f. F f. It., = post-boy (as POST²)]

Post-Impressionism n. the theory or practice of the Post-Impressionist school in art, an extension of impressionism. **—Post-Impressionist** n. a member of a movement in French painting in the late 19th and early 20th c. who sought to reveal the subject's structural form without strict fidelity to its natural appearance. The term was unknown to those French painters to whom it is applied (in their day labelled as impressionists, neo-impressionists, or symbolists) being invented by Roger Fry in 1910. In seeking an acceptable title for the 1910 autumn exhibition of modern French painting at the Grafton Gallery in London, Fry settled on what he called this 'somewhat negative title', naming the exhibition 'Manet and the Post-Impressionists' from the fact that they came, chronologically, after impressionism. The term is most readily applied to the three luminaries of that exhibition—Gauguin, Van Gogh, and Cézanne—but it should not be forgotten that Seurat, Denis, Sérusier, and even Matisse were also included.

postman n. (pl. **-men**) one who delivers or collects letters etc.

postmark n. an official mark on a letter etc. cancelling the stamp and giving the place and date. —v.t. to stamp with a postmark.

postmaster n. the official in charge of a post office. **—postmistress** n.fem.

post-mortem /pəʊst'mɔːtəm/ n. **1.** an examination made after death, especially to determine its cause. **2.** (colloq.) a discussion after the conclusion of a game, election, etc. —adv. & adj. after death. [L]

post-natal /pəʊst'neɪt(ə)l/ adj. of or concerning the period after childbirth.

postpone /pəʊst'pəʊn/ v.t. to cause or arrange to take place at a later time. **—postponement** n. [f. L *postponere* (POST-, *ponere* place)]

postprandial /pəʊst'prændɪəl/ adj. (usu. joc.) after lunch or dinner. [f. POST- + L *prandium* dinner]

postscript /'pəʊstskrɪpt/ n. an additional paragraph, especially at the end of a letter after the signature. [f. L (POST-, *scribere* write)]

postulant /'pɒstjʊlənt/ n. a candidate, especially for admission to a religious order. [F or f. L (as foll.)]

postulate /'pɒstjʊleɪt/ v.t. to assume or require to be true, especially as a basis for reasoning; to claim; to take for granted. — /'pɒstjʊlət/ n. a thing postulated. **—postulation** /-'leɪʃ(ə)n/ n. [f. L *postulare* demand]

posture /'pɒstʃə(r)/ n. **1.** an attitude of the body or mind; the relative position of parts, especially of the body. **2.** a condition or state (of affairs etc.). —v.t./i. **1.** to assume a posture, especially for effect. **2.** to dispose the limbs of (a person) in a particular way. **—postural** adj., **posturer** n. [F f. It. f. L (as POSITION)]

post-war /pəʊst'wɔː(r)/ attrib. 'pəʊst- adj. occurring or existing after a war.

posy /'pəʊzɪ/ n. a small bunch of flowers. [contr. of POESY]

pot¹ n. **1.** a rounded vessel of earthenware, metal, or glass, for holding liquids or solids or for cooking in. **2.** a chamber-pot, teapot, etc. **3.** the contents of a pot. **4.** the total amount bet in a game etc.; (colloq.) a large sum. **5.** (slang) a prize in an athletic contest, especially a silver cup. **6.** (slang) a pot-belly. —v.t./i. (**-tt-**) **1.** to plant in a pot. **2.** to sit (a child) on a chamber-pot. **3.** to send (a ball) into the pocket in billiards etc. **4.** to shoot, to hit or kill (an animal) by a pot-shot. **5.** to seize or secure. **6.** to abridge or epitomize. **7.** (esp. in p.p.) to preserve (food) in a sealed pot etc. **—go to pot,** (colloq.) to deteriorate, to be ruined. **pot-belly** n. a protruding belly; a person with this. **pot-boiler** n. a piece of art, writing, etc., done merely to earn money. **pot-herb** n. a herb used in cooking. **pot-hole** n. a deep hole in rock; a rough hole worn in a road surface. **pot-holing** n. exploring pot-holes in rock. **pot-hook** n. a hook over a fireplace for hanging or lifting a pot; a curved stroke in handwriting. **pot-hunter** n. a sportsman who shoots at random; a person who takes part in a contest merely for the sake of the prize. **pot luck,** whatever is available for a meal etc. **pot plant,** a plant grown in a flower-pot. **pot-roast** n. a piece of meat cooked slowly in a covered dish; (v.t.) to cook thus. **pot-shot** n. a random shot; a casual attempt. **potting-shed** n. a shed in which plants are grown in pots for planting out later. [OE]

pot² n. (slang) marijuana. [prob. f. Mex. Sp. *potiguaya*]

potable /'pəʊtəb(ə)l/ adj. drinkable. [F or f. L (*potare* drink)]

potage /pɒ'tɑːʒ/ n. thick soup. [F, = POTTAGE]

potash /'pɒtæʃ/ n. any of various salts of potassium, especially potassium carbonate. [f. Du. (as POT¹, ASH¹)]

potassium /pə'tæsɪəm/ n. a soft silver-white metallic element, symbol K, atomic number 19, first isolated by Sir Humphry Davy in 1807. It is essential to life. The metal itself is very reactive and has few uses, but its compounds are widely used in the manufacture of fertilizers, soaps, glass, etc. [f. prec.]

potation /pəʊ'teɪʃ(ə)n/ n. drinking; a drink. [f. OF or L (as POTABLE)]

potato /pə'teɪtəʊ/ n. (pl. **-oes**) a plant (*Solanum tuberosum*) with starchy tubers used as food; its tuber. Now one of the main food crops of the world, the potato was introduced into Europe c.1570 by the Spaniards who had encountered it in their explorations of South America. [f. Sp. *patata* f. S.Amer. Indian name]

poteen /pɒˈtiːn/ n. (in Ireland) whisky from an illicit still. [f. Ir. *poitín* dim. (as POT¹)]

Potemkin /pəˈtemkɪn/, Grigori Alexandrovich (1739–91), Russian soldier and statesman. The chief favourite of Catherine the Great from 1771, he was responsible for considerable Russian expansion towards the south.

potent¹ /ˈpəʊt(ə)nt/ adj. **1.** powerful, strong; (of a reason) forceful, cogent. **2.** (of a man) not sexually impotent. —**potency** n. [f. L *potens* (*posse* be able)]

potent² /ˈpəʊt(ə)nt/ adj. (in heraldry) with a crutch-head shape; formed by a series of such shapes. —n. **1.** (in heraldry) a fur formed thus. [f. OF *potence* crutch f. L *potentia* power (as prec.)]

potentate /ˈpəʊtənteɪt/ n. a monarch or ruler with great power. [f. OF or L (as prec.)]

potential /pəˈtenʃ(ə)l/ adj. capable of coming into being or of being developed or used etc. —n. **1.** ability or capacity available for use or development; usable resources. **2.** a quantity determining the energy of a mass in a gravitational field, of a charge in an electric field, etc. —**potentiality** /-ʃɪˈælɪtɪ/ n., **potentially** adv. [f. OF or L (*potentia* power, as POTENT)]

pother /ˈpɒðə(r)/ n. (literary) a commotion, fuss. [orig. unkn.]

potion /ˈpəʊʃ(ə)n/ n. a liquid for drinking as a medicine or drug. [f. OF f. L (*potus* having drunk)]

Potiphar /ˈpɒtɪfɑː(r)/ an Egyptian officer whose wife tried to seduce Joseph and then falsely accused him of attempting to rape her (Gen. 39).

Potomac /pəˈtəʊmæk/ a river of the USA flowing into Chesapeake Bay and forming part of the northern boundary of Virginia.

pot-pourri /pəʊˈpʊrɪ/ n. **1.** a scented mixture of dried petals and spices. **2.** a musical or literary medley. [F, = rotten pot]

potsherd /ˈpɒtʃɜːd/ n. a broken piece of earthenware (esp. in archaeology).

pottage n. (archaic) a soup, a stew. [f. OF *potage* (as POT¹)]

Potter, (Helen) Beatrix (1866–1943), English writer for children. *The Tale of Peter Rabbit* (1901) was the first in a series of animal stories, charmingly illustrated in water-colour by the author, which remain popular to this day.

potter¹ v.i. to work on trivial tasks in a leisurely relaxed way. —**potterer** n. [frequent. of dial. *pote* push]

potter² n. a maker of earthenware vessels. —**potter's wheel**, a horizontal revolving disc to carry clay during moulding. The wheel probably came into use during the 4th millennium BC. At first it was turned by hand (the 'slow wheel'), later by a foot-operated wheel. Known in Mesopotamia by c.3500 BC, over a period of centuries it spread to Egypt and other parts of the Near East and to India, reaching Crete and China by about 2000 BC, Europe at varying dates, and southern Britain in the mid-1st c. BC. It was unknown in America until the arrival of European conquerors and settlers. [OE (as POT¹)]

pottery n. **1.** vessels etc. made of baked clay (see below). **2.** a potter's work or workshop. —**the Potteries**, a district in north Staffordshire, seat of the English pottery industry. [f. OF (as prec.)]
The shaping and baking of clay vessels is among the oldest and most widely practised of all the crafts: earthenware pottery dating from about 9,000 years ago has been found on the Anatolian plateau of Turkey. At first it was shaped entirely by hand, and many centuries passed before the introduction of the potter's wheel (see prec.). The brilliant achievements of the Chinese and their neighbours, especially in the field of glazed stoneware and porcelain, were almost unknown in Europe until the opening up of the direct sea-route in the 16th c., though these wares were not without influence on the Islamic pottery of the Near East. In medieval times pottery was little used at table but by the 18th c. there was an immense demand for table and ornamental wares of all kinds, and new factories appeared in many countries. In Britain, where the Industrial Revolution was beginning, the rise of Staffordshire as the pottery centre saw technical and practical innovations which culminated, during the life of Josiah Wedgwood, in the change from craft to industry.

potty¹ adj. (slang) **1.** crazy, foolish. **2.** insignificant, trivial. [orig. unkn.]

potty² n. (colloq.) a chamber-pot, especially for a child. [f. POT¹]

pouch n. **1.** a small bag or detachable outside pocket. **2.** a baglike formation. —v.t. **1.** to put into a pouch; to pocket. **2.** to make (part of a dress etc.) hang like a pouch. [f. OF (cf. POKE²)]

pouffe /puːf/ n. a padded stool without legs, large enough to be used as a seat. [F]

Poulenc /ˈpuːlæk/, Francis (1899–1963), French composer, a member of the group dubbed 'Les Six'. In his lightness of touch, wit, and adoption of the idioms of popular music (music-hall, jazz, café music, etc.) he was a true disciple of Satie and Cocteau, but his works are also characterized by a lyricism and an almost romantic charm, at its most attractive in his many songs and in such instrumental works as the sonatas for flute (1957), oboe (1962), and clarinet (1962). His works for the theatre include the ballet *Les Biches* (1923) and the large-scale religious opera *Dialogues des Carmélites* (1957) based on events of the French Revolution.

poult /pəʊlt/ n. a young domestic fowl, turkey, or game-bird. [contr. of PULLET]

poulterer /ˈpəʊltərə(r)/ n. a dealer in poultry and usually game. [f. earlier *poulter* f. OF *pouletier* (as PULLET)]

poultice /ˈpəʊltɪs/ n. a soft heated mass of bread or kaolin etc. applied to a sore part of the body. —v.t. to apply a poultice to. [orig. *pultes* pl. f. L *puls* pottage, pap]

poultry /ˈpəʊltrɪ/ n. domestic fowls, ducks, geese, turkeys, etc., especially as a source of food. [f. OF (as POULTERER)]

pounce v.i. **1.** to spring or swoop down in a sudden attack. **2.** to seize *on* (an opportunity, mistake, etc.) eagerly. —n. a pouncing movement. [perh. as PUNCH¹]

Pound /paʊnd/, Ezra Weston Loomis (1885–1972), American poet and critic, who left for Europe in 1908 and in London became a leader of the imagist movement. To this period belong *Ripostes* (1912), 'Homage to Sextus Propertius', and *Hugh Selwyn Mauberley* (1920). Gradually he moved away from imagism, using a wide range of reference including Chinese, Old English, Provençal, Greek, and Latin towards the multi-cultural world of the *Cantos* (1917–70) on which his reputation rests. He settled in Italy in 1925 where his preoccupation with economics led to anti-Semitism and support for Mussolini; he made anti-democratic broadcasts on Italian radio during the Second World War and in 1945 was charged with treason but adjudged insane and committed to a mental institution until 1958. The tragedies of his later years obscured his reputation, but he is widely accepted as a master of verse form and as the regenerator of the poetic idiom of his day.

pound¹ n. **1.** a unit of weight, equal to 16 oz. avoirdupois (454 g), 12 oz. troy (373 g). **2.** (pl. **pounds** or **pound**) the currency unit of the UK (in full **pound sterling**); the currency unit of some other countries. —**pound note**, a banknote for one pound. **pound of flesh**, any legal but morally offensive demand (with allusion to Shylock's demand for a pound of Antonio's flesh, pledged as security for a loan, in Shakespeare's *Merchant of Venice*). [OE f. L *pondo* Roman pound weight]

pound² v.t./i. **1.** to crush or beat with heavy repeated strokes. **2.** to deliver heavy blows or gunfire etc. **3.** to make one's way heavily. **4.** (of the heart) to beat heavily. [OE]

pound³ n. an enclosure where stray animals or officially removed vehicles are kept until claimed. [f. OE (cf. POND)]

poundage n. a commission or fee of so much per pound in money or weight. [f. POUND¹]

pounder n. a thing that weighs a pound or (**-pounder**) so many pounds; a gun carrying a shell of such weight.

pour /pɔː(r)/ v.t./i. **1.** to flow or cause to flow especially downwards in a stream or shower; to serve by pouring. **2.** to rain heavily. **3.** to come or go in profusion or rapid succession. **4.** to discharge or send freely. **5.** to utter at length or in a rush. —**pourer** n. [orig. unkn.]

Poussin /ˈpuːsæ̃/, Nicolas (1594–1665), French painter. Although considered the chief representative of French classicism in art, his work could almost be seen as part of the development of painting in Italy from where he took all his inspiration and where he chose to live for thirty-nine of the last forty-one years of his life. At first influenced by Italian mannerist and baroque painting, his study of the antique and the paintings of Raphael and Titian led him to a cogent and lucid style suffused with a rich and vibrant colour sense. His subject-matter ranged over biblical scenes (*The Entombment*), classical mythology (*Arcadia*), and, particularly towards the end of his life, historical landscapes.

pout v.t./i. to push forward one's lips as a sign of displeasure or sulking; to protrude (the lips); (of the lips) to be pushed forward thus. —*n.* a pouting expression. [orig. unkn.]

pouter *n.* a kind of pigeon that can inflate its crop greatly. [f. POUT]

poverty /'pɒvətɪ/ *n.* **1.** being poor, great lack of money or resources. **2.** scarcity, lack. **3.** inferiority, poorness. —**poverty line,** the minimum income level needed to secure the necessities of life. **poverty-stricken** *adj.* greatly affected by poverty. **poverty trap,** a situation in which an increase of income incurs loss of State benefits so that the recipient is no better off than before. [f. OF f. L *paupertas* (as PAUPER)]

POW *abbr.* prisoner of war.

powder *n.* **1.** a mass of fine dry particles. **2.** a medicine or cosmetic in this form. **3.** gunpowder. —*v.t.* **1.** to apply a powder to. **2.** to reduce to a fine powder. —**powder blue,** pale blue. **powder-puff** *n.* a soft pad for applying powder to the skin. **powder-room** *n.* a ladies' lavatory in a public building. —**powdery** *adj.,* **powderiness** *n.* [f. OF *poudre* f. L *pulvis*]

Powell /paʊ(ə)l/, Anthony Dymoke (1905–), English novelist, whose initial reputation as a satirist and comedian rests on five pre-war books beginning with *Afternoon Men* (1931). After the war he embarked on his ambitious sequence of 12 novels (*A Dance to the Music of Time*) beginning with *A Question of Upbringing* (1951) and ending with *Hearing Secret Harmonies* (1975); the whole is seen through the detached eyes of narrator Nicholas Jenkins, whose generation grew up in the shadow of the First World War to find their lives dislocated by the Second, and gives a rich and broad panorama, part humorous, part melancholy, of English life.

power *n.* **1.** the ability to do something; a particular faculty of the body or mind. **2.** vigour, energy. **3.** an active property or function. **4.** (*colloq.*) a large amount. **5.** control, influence; ascendancy. **6.** authorization. **7.** an influential person or organization etc.; a State having international influence. **8.** a deity. **9.** capacity for exerting mechanical force. **10.** mechanical or electrical energy as opposed to hand labour; (*attrib.*) operated by this. **11.** the electricity supply. **12.** the product obtained by multiplying a number by a given number of factors equal to it. **13.** the magnifying capacity of a lens. —*v.t.* to supply with mechanical or electrical energy. —**power-point** *n.* a socket in a wall etc. for connecting an electrical device to the mains. **power-station** *n.* a building where electrical power is generated for distribution (ill. ELECTRICAL POWER). **the powers that be,** those in authority. [AF *poer* f. L (as POTENT)]

powerful *adj.* having great power or influence. —**powerfully** *adv.,* **powerfulness** *n.* [f. prec. + -FUL]

powerhouse *n.* **1.** a power-station. **2.** a person etc. of great energy.

powerless *adj.* without power; wholly unable. —**powerlessly** *adv.,* **powerlessness** *n.* [f. POWER + -LESS]

powwow /'paʊwaʊ/ *n.* a conference or meeting for discussion (originally among North American Indians). —*v.i.* to hold a powwow. [f. Algonquian, = magician]

Powys /'pəʊɪs, 'paʊ-/ an inland county of Wales.

pox *n.* a virus disease with pocks; (*colloq.*) syphilis. [alt. spelling of *pocks* pl. of POCK]

pp. *abbr.* pages.

p.p. *abbr. per pro.*

pp *abbr.* pianissimo.

p.p.m. *abbr.* parts per million.

PPS *abbr.* **1.** Parliamentary Private Secretary. **2.** additional postscript (*postpostscript*).

PR *abbr.* **1.** proportional representation. **2.** public relations.

Pr *symbol* praseodymium.

practicable /'præktɪkəb(ə)l/ *adj.* that can be done or used; possible in practice. —**practicability** /-'bɪlɪtɪ/ *n.* [f. F (as foll.)]

practical /'præktɪk(ə)l/ *adj.* **1.** involving activity as distinct from study or theory. **2.** suited to use or action. **3.** (of a person) inclined to action; able to do or make functional things well. **4.** virtual. —*n.* a practical examination or lesson. —**practical joke,** a humorous trick played on a person. —**practicality** /-'kælɪtɪ/ *n.* [f. obs. F or L f. Gk (*prattō* do)]

practically *adv.* **1.** virtually, almost. **2.** in a practical way. [f. prec.]

practice /'præktɪs/ *n.* **1.** a habitual action, a custom. **2.** repeated exercise to improve a skill; a spell of this. **3.** action as opposed to theory. **4.** the professional work of a doctor,

---

lawyer, etc.; this as a business; the patients or clients regularly consulting these. —**out of practice,** temporarily lacking a former skill etc. [f. foll.]

practise /'præktɪs/ *v.t./i.* **1.** to do habitually; to carry out in action. **2.** to do repeatedly as an exercise to improve a skill. **3.** to pursue (a profession, religion, etc.; also *absol.*). **4.** (in *p.p.*) experienced, expert. [f. OF or L f. Gk (as PRACTICAL)]

practitioner /præk'tɪʃənə(r)/ *n.* a person practising a profession, especially medicine. [f. prec.]

Prado /'prɑːdəʊ/ the Spanish national art gallery, in Madrid. Established in 1818 by Ferdinand VII and Isabella of Braganza, it houses the greatest collection in the world of Spanish masters—Velazquez, el Greco, Zurbarán, Ribera, Murillo, Goya—as well as important examples of Flemish and Venetian art collected as a result of political ties with these countries in the reign of Charles V, Philip II, and Philip IV. Work produced after 1850 is deemed ineligible for inclusion.

praenomen /priː'nəʊmen/ *n.* an ancient Roman's first or personal name (e.g. *Marcus* Tullius Cicero). [L (*prae* before, *nomen* name)]

praetor /'priːtə(r)/ *n.* a magistrate in ancient Rome, ranking below a consul and performing some of his duties. [f. F or L, perh. f. *prae* before, *ire* go]

praetorian /prɪ'tɔːrɪən/ *adj.* of a praetor. —**Praetorian Guard,** (in ancient Rome) soldiers who formed the bodyguard of a general or of the emperor. [f. L (as prec.)]

pragmatic /præg'mætɪk/ *adj.* **1.** dealing with matters from a practical point of view. **2.** treating the facts of history with reference to their practical lessons. —**pragmatically** *adv.* [f. L f. Gk (*pragma* deed)]

Pragmatic Sanction a document drafted by the Emperor Charles VI after the birth of his daughter Maria Theresa in 1717 to allow her to succeed to all his territories should he die without a son. The Sanction was accepted by the Diets of Austria, Hungary, and the Austrian Netherlands in 1720–3, but the campaign to have it recognized by the rest of Europe dominated the international diplomatic scene for two decades afterwards, and, on Charles's death in 1740, led to the War of the Austrian Succession.

pragmatism /'prægmətɪz(ə)m/ *n.* **1.** the matter-of-fact treatment of things. **2.** a philosophy that evaluates assertions solely by their practical consequences and bearing on human interests (see William JAMES). —**pragmatist** *n.* [f. Gk *pragma* (as prec.)]

Prague /prɑːg/ the capital of Czechoslovakia, situated on the River Vltava; pop. (1980) 1,182,900. It first achieved prominence in the 13th c., when the kings of Bohemia established it as their capital. Its university, founded in 1348 by the future emperor Charles IV, is among the oldest in Europe.

prairie /'preərɪ/ *n.* a large treeless area of grassland, especially in North America. —**prairie-dog** *n.* a North American rodent of the genus *Cynomys* with a bark like a dog's. **prairie oyster,** a raw egg seasoned and swallowed whole. [f. OF, ult. f. L *pratum* meadow]

praise /preɪz/ *v.t.* **1.** to express warm approval or admiration of. **2.** to glorify (God) in words. —*n.* praising; approval expressed in words. [f. OF *preisier* f. L *pretiare* (*pretium* price)]

praiseworthy *adj.* worthy of praise.

praline /'prɑːliːn/ *n.* a sweet made by browning nuts in boiling sugar. [F, f. Marshal de Plessis-*Pralin* (d. 1675), whose cook invented it]

pram *n.* a four-wheeled carriage for a baby, pushed by a person walking. The invention dates from the mid-19th c. [abbr. of PERAMBULATOR]

prance /prɑːns/ *v.i.* **1.** to walk or behave in an elated or arrogant manner. **2.** (of a horse) to raise the forelegs and spring from the hind legs. —*n.* prancing; a prancing movement. [orig. unkn.]

Prandtl /'prænt(ə)l/, Ludwig (1875–1953), German physicist with a world-wide reputation for his studies on both aerodynamics and hydrodynamics. His work established the existence of a boundary layer (see BOUNDARY) and he made important studies on streamlining. Design of efficient shape, weight, and mass of aircraft and ships owes much to his work.

prang *v.t.* (*slang*) **1.** to crash (an aircraft or vehicle); to damage by impact. **2.** to bomb (a target) successfully. —*n.* (*slang*) a crash; damage by impact. [imit.]

prank *n.* a practical joke, a piece of mischief. [orig. unkn.]

prankster *n.* a person fond of playing pranks. [f. prec.]

praseodymium /ˌpreɪsɪəˈdɪmɪəm/ *n.* a metallic element of the lanthanide series, symbol Pr, atomic number 59, discovered in 1885. The metal is a component of certain alloys and its compounds are used for colouring glass and ceramics. [f. G f. Gk *prasios* leek-green (from its green salts), as NEODYMIUM]

prat *n.* (*slang*) **1.** a fool. **2.** the buttocks. [orig. unkn.]

prate *v.i.* to chatter, to talk too much; to talk foolishly or irrelevantly. —*n.* prating, idle talk. [f. MDu. or MLG, prob. imit.]

prattle *v.i.* to chatter or say in a childish way. —*n.* childish chatter; inconsequential talk. [as prec.]

prawn *n.* an edible shellfish of the genus *Palaemon, Penaeus*, etc., like a large shrimp. [orig. unkn.]

Praxiteles /prækˈsɪtəliːz/ (mid-4th c. BC) Athenian sculptor. He and Phidias were the greatest Greek sculptors of their age. The *Hermes* (Olympia) is considered a fine example (or copy) of work that justifies his renown, with its physical repose qualified by submerged undercurrents of latent energy—a subtlety that is lost in the copies of his *Sauroctonus* (Apollo slaying a lizard) and Cnidian *Aphrodite* (the first important female nude).

pray *v.t./i.* **1.** to say prayers. **2.** to make a devout supplication; to entreat; to ask earnestly (for). **3.** (*archaic*, before an imperative) = please. —**praying mantis**, see MANTIS. [f. OF *preier* f. L *precari*]

prayer[1] /ˈpreə(r)/ *n.* **1.** a solemn request or thanksgiving to God or to an object of worship; a formula used in praying. **2.** the act of praying; a religious service consisting largely of prayers. **3.** an entreaty to a person. —**prayer-book** *n.* a book of set prayers. **prayer-mat** *n.* a small rug on which Muslims kneel to pray. **Prayer of Manasses** /məˈnæsiːz/, a book of the Apocrypha consisting of a penitential prayer put into the mouth of Manasseh, king of Judah (2 Kings 21: 1-18). **prayer-wheel** *n.* a revolving cylindrical box inscribed with or containing prayers, used especially by the Buddhists of Tibet. [f. OF f. L (as PRECARIOUS)]

prayer[2] /ˈpreɪə(r)/ *n.* one who prays. [f. PRAY]

pre- *prefix* before (in time, place, order, degree, or importance). [f. L *prae* before]

preach *v.t./i.* **1.** to deliver a sermon or religious address; to deliver (a sermon); to make (the Gospel) known by preaching. **2.** to give moral advice in an obtrusive way. **3.** to advocate or urge people to (a quality or practice etc.). —**preacher** *n.* [f. OF f. L *praedicare* proclaim]

preamble /priːˈæmb(ə)l/ *n.* a preliminary statement; the introductory part of a statute or document etc. [f. OF f. L (as PRE-, AMBLE)]

pre-arrange /priːəˈreɪndʒ/ *v.t.* to arrange beforehand. —**pre-arrangement** *n.*

prebend /ˈprebənd/ *n.* the stipend of a canon or member of a chapter; the portion of land or tithe from which this is drawn. —**prebendal** *adj.* [f. OF f. L *praebenda* pension (*praebēre* grant)]

prebendary /ˈprebəndərɪ/ *n.* a holder of a prebend; an honorary canon. [f. L (as prec.)]

Precambrian /priːˈkæmbrɪən/ *adj.* of the geological era preceding the Cambrian period and Palaeozoic era. The Precambrian era includes the whole of the earth's history from its origin about 4,600 million years ago to the beginning of the Cambrian about 590 million years ago. Fossils of animals with hard skeletons are absent from Precambrian rocks, and the era was once considered to be devoid of organic life, but it is now known that a variety of organisms did exist during that time (see ill. GEOLOGY). The oldest known Precambrian rocks on earth are about 3,800 million years old. —*n.* this era.

precarious /prɪˈkeərɪəs/ *adj.* uncertain, dependent on chance; insecure. —**precariously** *adv.*, **precariousness** *n.* [f. L, = obtained by entreaty (*prex* prayer)]

pre-cast /priːˈkɑːst/ *adj.* (of concrete) cast in blocks before use.

precaution /prɪˈkɔːʃ(ə)n/ *n.* an action taken beforehand to avoid a risk or ensure a good result. —**precautionary** *adj.* [f. F f. L (as PRE-, CAUTION)]

precede /prɪˈsiːd/ *v.t.* to come, go, or place before in time, order, importance, etc. [f. OF f. L *praecedere* (*prae* before, *cedere* go)]

precedence /ˈpresɪdəns/ *n.* priority in time or order etc.; the right of preceding others. [f. foll.]

precedent /ˈpresɪdənt/ *n.* a previous case taken as an example for subsequent cases or as a justification. —*adj.* preceding in time or order etc. [f. OF (as PRECEDE)]

precentor /prɪˈsentə(r)/ *n.* one who leads the singing or (in a synagogue) the prayers of a congregation. [f. F or L *praecentor* (*prae* before, *canere* sing)]

precept /ˈpriːsept/ *n.* **1.** a command, a rule of conduct. **2.** a writ, a warrant. [f. L *praeceptum* f. *praecipere* warn, instruct]

preceptor /prɪˈseptə(r)/ *n.* a teacher, an instructor. —**preceptorial** /-ˈtɔːrɪəl/ *adj.*, **preceptress** *n.fem.* [as prec.]

precession /prɪˈseʃ(ə)n/ *n.* the slow movement of the axis of a spinning body round another axis (e.g. that of a spinning-top, initially vertical but describing a cone round its original position as the top slows down). —**precession of the equinoxes**, the apparent slow retrograde motion of the equinoctial points along the ecliptic; the resulting earlier occurrence of the equinoxes in each successive sidereal year. As the Earth rotates about its axis it responds to the gravitational attraction of the sun upon its equatorial bulge, so that its axis of rotation describes a circle in the sky. The celestial equator moves backward along the sun's apparent path (the ecliptic), and the points where these two great circles intersect, which define the sun's position at the equinoxes, therefore travel through the constellations of the zodiac once in a period of about 26,000 years. The equinoctial position of the sun at the time of Hipparchus (*c.*125 BC) was a point in the constellation of Aries; the corresponding position, although now in Pisces, is still known as the First Point of Aries. [f. L (as PRECEDE)]

pre-Christian /priːˈkrɪstjən/ *adj.* before Christianity.

precinct /ˈpriːsɪŋkt/ *n.* **1.** an enclosed area, especially round a place of worship. **2.** (in full **pedestrian precinct**) an area in a town where traffic is prohibited. **3.** (in *pl.*) environs. **4.** (*US*) a subdivision of a county, city, or ward for election and police purposes. [f. L (*praecingere* encircle)]

preciosity /ˌpreʃɪˈɒsɪtɪ/ *n.* over-refinement, especially in choice of words. [f. OF f. L (as foll.)]

precious /ˈpreʃəs/ *adj.* **1.** of great value or worth. **2.** beloved; much prized. **3.** affectedly refined. **4.** (*colloq.*, often *iron.*) considerable. —*adv.* (*colloq.*) extremely, very. —**precious metals**, gold, silver, and platinum. **precious stone**, a piece of mineral having great value, especially as used in jewellery. —**preciously** *adv.*, **preciousness** *n.* [f. OF f. L *pretiosus* (*pretium* price)]

precipice /ˈpresɪpɪs/ *n.* a vertical or steep face of a rock, cliff, mountain, etc. [f. F f. L (as PRECIPITATE)]

precipitance /prɪˈsɪpɪt(ə)ns/ *n.* (also **precipitancy**) rash haste. [f. obs. F (as foll.)]

precipitate /prɪˈsɪpɪteɪt/ *v.t.* **1.** to cause to happen suddenly or soon; to make occur prematurely. **2.** to send rapidly into a certain state or condition. **3.** to throw down headlong. **4.** to cause (a substance) to be deposited in solid form from a solution. **5.** to condense (a vapour) into drops which fall as rain etc. —/-tət/ *adj.* headlong, violently hurried; (of a person or act) hasty, rash, inconsiderate. —/-tət/ *n.* a substance precipitated from a solution; moisture condensed from vapour and falling as rain etc. —**precipitately** *adv.* [f. L *praecipitare* (*praeceps* headlong)]

precipitation /prɪˌsɪpɪˈteɪʃ(ə)n/ *n.* **1.** precipitating, being precipitated. **2.** rash haste. **3.** rain or snow etc. falling to the ground; the quantity of this. [f. F or L (as prec.)]

precipitous /prɪˈsɪpɪtəs/ *adj.* of or like a precipice, dangerously steep; precipitate. —**precipitously** *adv.* [f. obs. F f. L (as PRECIPITATE)]

précis /ˈpreɪsiː/ *n.* (*pl.* same /-iːz/) a summary, an abstract. —*v.t.* to make a précis of. [F, = foll.]

precise /prɪˈsaɪs/ *adj.* **1.** accurately expressed. **2.** exact, definite. **3.** scrupulous in being exact. [f. F f. L (*praecidere* cut short)]

precisely *adv.* **1.** in a precise manner, exactly. **2.** in exact terms. **3.** (as a reply) quite so, as you say. [f. prec.]

precision /prɪˈsɪʒ(ə)n/ *n.* **1.** accuracy. **2.** (*attrib.*) characterized by or adapted for precision. [f. F or L (as PRECISE)]

preclude /prɪˈkluːd/ *v.t.* to exclude the possibility of, to prevent. [f. L *praecludere* (*prae* before, *claudere* shut)]

precocious /prɪˈkəʊʃəs/ *adj.* (of a person) having developed certain abilities or characteristics earlier than is usual; (of abilities etc.) showing such development. —**precocity** /prɪˈkɒsɪtɪ/ *n.*, **precociously** *adv.* [f. L *praecox* prematurely ripe]

precognition /ˌpriːkɒɡˈnɪʃ(ə)n/ *n.* (supposed) foreknowledge, especially of a supernatural kind.

Pre-Columbian /ˌprɪkəˈlʌmbɪən/ *adj.* of the period before the discovery of America by Columbus.

preconceive /priːkənˈsiːv/ *v.t.* to form (an idea or opinion etc.) beforehand.

preconception /priːkənˈsepʃ(ə)n/ *n.* a preconceived idea; a prejudice.

pre-condition /priːkənˈdɪʃ(ə)n/ *n.* a condition that must be fulfilled before something else can happen.

precursor /p.ːˈkɜːsə(r)/ *n.* **1.** a forerunner, a harbinger. **2.** a thing that precedes a later and more developed form. [f. L (*praecurrere* run before)]

predacious /prɪˈdeɪʃəs/ *adj.* (of an animal) predatory. [f. L *praeda* plunder]

pre-date /priːˈdeɪt/ *v.t.* to antedate.

predator /ˈpredətə(r)/ *n.* a predatory animal. [f. L (*praedari* seize as plunder)]

predatory *adj.* **1.** (of an animal) preying naturally upon others. **2.** plundering or exploiting others. [as prec.]

predecease /priːdɪˈsiːs/ *v.t.* to die earlier than (another person).

predecessor /ˈpriːdɪsesə(r)/ *n.* **1.** a former holder of an office or position with respect to a later holder. **2.** an ancestor. **3.** a thing to which something else has succeeded. [f. OF f. L (as PRE-, DECEASE)]

predella /prɪˈdelə/ *n.* **1.** an altar-step; a painting on the vertical face of this. **2.** a raised shelf at the back of an altar (ill. VESTMENTS); a painting or sculpture on this. [It., = stool]

predestination /prɪdestɪˈneɪʃ(ə)n/ *n.* God's foreordaining of all that happens, or that certain souls are destined for salvation and eternal life and others are not. [f. L *praedestinare* (*prae* before, *destinare* destine)]

predestine /priːˈdestɪn/ *v.t.* to determine beforehand; to ordain by divine will or as if by fate. [as prec.]

predetermine /priːdɪˈtɜːmɪn/ *v.t.* to decide beforehand, to predestine. —**predetermination** /-ˈneɪʃ(ə)n/ *n.*

predicable /ˈpredɪkəb(ə)l/ *adj.* that may be predicated or affirmed. [as PREDICATE]

predicament /prɪˈdɪkəmənt/ *n.* a difficult or unpleasant situation. [as PREDICATE]

predicate /ˈpredɪkeɪt/ *v.t.* to assert or affirm as true or existent. —/-kət/ *n.* **1.** (in logic) what is predicated (e.g. *mortal* in *all men are mortal*). **2.** (*Gram.*) what is said about the subject of a sentence etc. (e.g. *went home* in *John went home*). —**predication** /-ˈkeɪʃ(ə)n/ *n.* [f. L *praedicare* proclaim]

predicative /prɪˈdɪkətɪv/ *adj.* forming part or all of the predicate (e.g. *old* in *the dog is old* but not in *the old dog*). —**predicatively** *adv.* [as prec.]

predict /prɪˈdɪkt/ *v.t.* to foretell, to prophesy. —**predictor** *n.* [f. L *praedicere* (*prae* before, *dicere* say)]

predictable *adj.* that can be predicted or is to be expected. —**predictability** /-ˈbɪlɪtɪ/ *n.*, **predictably** *adv.* [f. prec.]

prediction /prɪˈdɪkʃ(ə)n/ *n.* **1.** predicting, being predicted. **2.** a thing predicted. [f. PREDICT]

predilection /priːdɪˈlekʃ(ə)n/ *n.* a preference or special liking. [f. F f. L *praediligere* prefer]

predispose /priːdɪˈspəʊz/ *v.t.* **1.** to influence favourably in advance. **2.** to render liable or inclined. —**predisposition** /-pəˈzɪʃ(ə)n/ *n.*

predominant /prɪˈdɒmɪnənt/ *adj.* predominating; being the strongest or main element. —**predominance** *n.*, **predominantly** *adv.* [as foll.]

predominate /prɪˈdɒmɪneɪt/ *v.i.* **1.** to have or exert control, to be superior. **2.** to be the stronger or main element. [f. L (*prae* before, *dominari* dominate)]

pre-dynastic /priːdaɪˈnæstɪk/ *adj.* of the period before dynasties, especially in ancient Egypt.

pre-eminent /priːˈemɪnənt/ *adj.* excelling others, outstanding. —**pre-eminence** *n.*, **pre-eminently** *adv.*

pre-empt /priːˈempt/ *v.t.* to obtain by pre-emption; to appropriate beforehand; to forestall. [back-formation f. foll.]

pre-emption /priːˈempʃ(ə)n/ *n.* the purchase or taking of a thing by one person or party before an opportunity is offered to others. [f. L (*prae* before, *emere* buy)]

pre-emptive /priːˈemptɪv/ *adj.* pre-empting; (of a military action) intended to prevent an attack by disabling the enemy. [as prec.]

preen *v.t.* (of a bird) to tidy (the feathers) with the beak;

(of a person) to smarten (oneself or one's clothes etc.). —**preen oneself,** to congratulate oneself, to show self-satisfaction. [var. of obs. *prune* v., assoc. with dial. *preen* pierce]

pre-exist /priːɪgˈzɪst/ *v.t./i.* to exist beforehand or prior to. —**pre-existence** *n.*

prefab /ˈpriːfæb/ *n.* (*colloq.*) a prefabricated building. [abbr.]

prefabricate /priːˈfæbrɪkeɪt/ *v.t.* to manufacture in sections that are ready for assembly on a site. —**prefabrication** /-ˈkeɪʃ(ə)n/ *n.*

preface /ˈprefəs/ *n.* **1.** an introduction to a book, stating its subject, scope, etc. **2.** the preliminary part of a speech. —*v.t.* **1.** to provide or introduce with a preface. **2.** to lead up to (an event). [f. OF f. L (*prae* before, *fari* speak)]

prefatory /ˈprefətərɪ/ *adj.* of or serving as a preface, introductory. [as prec.]

prefect /ˈpriːfekt/ *n.* **1.** the chief administrative officer of certain departments in France, Japan, etc. **2.** a senior pupil in a school etc. authorized to maintain discipline. [f. OF f. L (*praeficere* set in authority)]

prefecture /ˈpriːfektjʊə(r)/ *n.* a district under the government of a prefect; a prefect's office or tenure. [f. F or L (as prec.)]

prefer /prɪˈfɜː(r)/ *v.t.* (**-rr-**) **1.** to choose as more desirable, to like better. **2.** to submit (information, an accusation, etc.) for consideration. **3.** to promote (a person to an office). [f. OF f. L *praeferre* (*prae* before, *ferre* bear)]

preferable /ˈprefərəb(ə)l/ *adj.* to be preferred; more desirable. —**preferably** *adv.* [f. prec.]

preference /ˈprefərəns/ *n.* **1.** preferring, being preferred. **2.** a thing preferred. **3.** the favouring of one person etc. before others. **4.** a prior right. —**in preference to,** as a thing preferred over (another). **preference shares** or **stock,** shares or stock on which a dividend is paid before profits are distributed to holders of ordinary shares etc. [f. F f. L (as PREFER)]

preferential /prefəˈrenʃ(ə)l/ *adj.* of or involving preference; giving or receiving favour. —**preferentially** *adv.* [as prec.]

preferment /prɪˈfɜːmənt/ *n.* promotion to an office. [f. PREFER]

prefigure /priːˈfɪgə(r)/ *v.t.* to represent or imagine beforehand.

prefix /ˈpriːfɪks/ *n.* **1.** a verbal element placed at the beginning of a word to qualify the meaning (e.g. *ex-, non-*). **2.** a title placed before a name (e.g. *Mr*). —*v.t.* **1.** to put as an introduction. **2.** to join as a prefix (to a word).

preform /priːˈfɔːm/ *v.t.* to form beforehand.

pregnant /ˈpregnənt/ *adj.* **1.** (of a woman or female animal) having a child or young developing in the womb. **2.** full of meaning, significant or suggestive. **3.** (with *with*) full of. **4.** fruitful in results. —**pregnancy** *n.* [f. F or L, prob. F. *prae* before, (*g*)*nasci* be born]

prehensile /prɪˈhensaɪl/ *adj.* (of a tail or limb) capable of grasping things. [f. F f. L (*prehendere* seize)]

prehistoric /priːhɪˈstɒrɪk/ *adj.* **1.** of the period before written records (see below). **2.** (*derog.*) antiquated, long out of date. —**prehistorically** *adv.*, **prehistory** /-ˈhɪstərɪ/ *n.* [f. F (as PRE-, HISTORIC)]

The prehistoric era is conventionally divided into a Stone Age, Bronze Age, and Iron Age, on the basis of the material used for weapons and tools. The system was devised by Christian Thomsen (1788–1865) as a means of classifying the collections in the National Museum of Denmark, of which he was curator. It was later elaborated and refined, and confirmed (at least for European areas) by stratification of finds, but is neither a guide to absolute dates nor an essential evolutionary sequence: not all its stages are represented in all parts of the world, and there is often a considerable time-lag between the first appearance of metal artefacts and a fully developed metal-working technology in an area. Until its invention, however, there was no framework into which archaeological discoveries could be fitted, and it remains a convenient terminology.

pre-ignition /priːɪgˈnɪʃ(ə)n/ *n.* the premature firing of an explosive mixture in an internal combustion engine.

prejudge /priːˈdʒʌdʒ/ *v.t.* to pass judgement on (a person) before a trial or proper enquiry; to form a premature judgement on.

prejudice /ˈpredʒʊdɪs/ *n.* **1.** a preconceived opinion, like, or dislike. **2.** injury to someone's rights etc. —*v.t.* **1.** (esp. in *p.p.*) to cause to have a prejudice. **2.** to injure (a person's right etc.). —**without prejudice,** without detriment to an existing right or claim. [f. OF f. L (*prae* before, *judicium* judgement)]

prejudicial /predʒʊ'dɪʃ(ə)l/ adj. causing prejudice; detrimental (to rights, interests, etc.). —**prejudicially** adv.

prelacy /'preləsɪ/ n. **1.** church government by prelates. **2.** prelates collectively. **3.** the office or rank of prelate. [f. AF f. L (as foll.)]

prelate /'prelət/ n. a high ecclesiastical dignitary, e.g. a bishop. —**prelatical** /prɪ'lætɪk(ə)l/ adj. [f. OF f. L *praelatus* (as PREFER)]

prelim /prɪ'lɪm/ n. **1.** (colloq.) a preliminary examination. **2.** (in pl.; also /'pri:lɪmz/) the front matter of a book, the pages preceding the text. [abbr.]

preliminary /prɪ'lɪmɪnərɪ/ adj. introductory, preparatory. —n. (usu. in pl.) a preliminary action or arrangement. —adv. preparatory. —**preliminarily** adv. [f. F (as PRE-, L *limen* threshold)]

prelude /'prelju:d/ n. **1.** an action, event, or situation that precedes another and leads up to it. **2.** the introductory part of a poem etc. **3.** (Mus.) the introductory movement or first part of a suite; a short piece of music of a similar type. —v.t./i. to serve as a prelude to; to introduce with a prelude. [f. F or L *praeludium* (prae before, *ludere* play)]

pre-marital /pri:'mærɪt(ə)l/ adj. of the time before marriage; occurring before marriage.

premature /'premətjʊə(r)/ adj. occurring or done before the usual or proper time, too early; hasty; (of a baby) born 3–12 weeks before the expected time. —**prematurely** adv., **prematureness** n., **prematurity** /-'tjʊərɪtɪ/ n. [f. L, = very early (prae early, *maturus* mature)]

premedication /pri:medɪ'keɪʃ(ə)n/ n. (also (colloq.) pre-med) medication in preparation for an operation etc.

premeditate /pri:'medɪteɪt/ v.t. (esp. in p.p.) to plan beforehand. —**premeditation** /-'teɪʃ(ə)n/ n.

pre-menstrual /pri:'menstrʊəl/ adj. of the time immediately before each menstruation.

premier /'premɪə(r)/ adj. first in importance, order, or time. —n. **1.** (orig. short for *premier minister*; see PRIME MINISTER) a Prime Minister. **2.** the head of the government of a province of Canada or State of Australia. —**premiership** n. [f. OF, = first, f. L (as PRIMARY)]

première /'premɪeə(r)/ n. the first performance or showing of a play or film. —v.t. to give a première to. [F, fem. of *premier* adj. (as prec.)]

premise /'premɪs/ n. **1.** a premiss. **2.** (in pl.) a house or building with its grounds and appurtenances. **3.** (Law) the houses, lands, or tenements previously specified in a document etc. —**on the premises**, in the house etc. concerned. [f. OF f. L *praemissa* (*praemittere* send in front)]

premiss /'premɪs/ n. a statement from which another is inferred. [var. of prec.]

premium /'pri:mɪəm/ n. **1.** an amount to be paid for a contract of insurance. **2.** a sum added to interest, wages, etc. **3.** a reward or prize. —**at a premium**, above the usual or nominal price, highly valued. **Premium (Savings) Bond,** a British government security without interest but with chances of cash prizes, issued since 1956. **put a premium on,** to provide or act as an incentive to; to attach special value to. [f. L *praemium* reward]

premolar /pri:'məʊlə(r)/ n. a tooth nearer the front of the mouth than the molars (ill. BODY I). —adj. of these teeth.

premonition /pri:mə'nɪʃ(ə)n, pre-/ n. a forewarning, a presentiment. —**premonitory** /prɪ'mɒnɪtərɪ/ adj. [f. F or L (*praemonēre* warn)]

pre-natal /pri:'neɪt(ə)l/ adj. of the period before being born or before childbirth.

preoccupation /pri:ɒkjʊ'peɪʃ(ə)n/ n. **1.** the state of being preoccupied. **2.** a thing that engrosses one's mind.

preoccupy /pri:'ɒkjʊpaɪ/ v.t. **1.** (of a thought etc.) to dominate or engross the mind of so as to exclude other thoughts; (in p.p.) inattentive because of this. **2.** to appropriate beforehand.

pre-ordain /pri:ɔ:'deɪn/ v.t. to decree or determine beforehand.

prep n. school work that a pupil is required to do outside lessons; a school period when this is done. —**prep school,** a preparatory school. [abbr.]

preparation /prepə'reɪʃ(ə)n/ n. **1.** preparing, being prepared. **2.** a specially prepared substance. **3.** = prep. **4.** (usu. in pl.) a thing done to make ready. [f. OF f. L (as PREPARE)]

preparatory /prɪ'pærətərɪ/ adj. serving to prepare, introductory. —adv. in a preparatory way. —**preparatory**

school, a school preparing pupils for a higher school or (US) for a college or university. [f. L (as foll.)]

prepare /prɪ'peə(r)/ v.t. **1.** to make or get ready. **2.** to make (food or other substances) ready for use; to assemble (a meal etc.) for eating. —**be prepared to,** to be disposed or willing to. [f. F or L *praeparare* (prae before, *parare* make ready)]

prepay /pri:'peɪ/ v.t. to pay (a charge) beforehand; to pay the postage on (a letter or parcel etc.) beforehand, e.g. by buying and affixing a stamp. —**prepayment** n.

preponderate /prɪ'pɒndəreɪt/ v.i. to be greater in influence, quantity, or number; to weigh more; to predominate. —**preponderance** n., **preponderant** adj., **preponderantly** adv. [f. L *praeponderare* (prae before, *pondus* weight)]

preposition /prepə'zɪʃ(ə)n/ n. a word governing (and usually preceding) a noun or pronoun and expressing the relation to another word or element (e.g. the man *on* the platform, came *after* dinner, went *by* train). —**prepositional** adj. [f. L (*praeponere* place in front)]

prepossess /pri:pə'zes/ v.t. **1.** (usu. in pass., of an idea etc.) to take possession of (a person). **2.** to prejudice (usu. favourably and at first sight). —**prepossession** n.

prepossessing adj. attractive, making a good impression on others. [f. prec.]

preposterous /prɪ'pɒstərəs/ adj. utterly absurd, outrageous; contrary to nature, reason, or common sense. —**preposterously** adv. [f. L, lit. = back to front (prae before, *posterus* coming after)]

prepuce /'pri:pju:s/ n. the foreskin; a similar structure at the tip of the clitoris. [f. L *praeputium*]

Pre-Raphaelite /pri:'ræfɪəlaɪt/ n. an artist or writer who aimed at producing work in the spirit that prevailed before the time of Raphael. The Pre-Raphaelite Brotherhood was founded in 1848 by seven young English artists and writers, the major figures being Holman Hunt, Millais, and Rossetti. Abhorring the slickness and sentimentality of much Victorian painting they sought to purify art by a return to the truth and seriousness of the early Renaissance, adopting a minutely detailed method of study from nature and painting in bright colours over a wet white ground. Much criticized for their espousal of 'ugliness', they were defended by Ruskin. The movement began to dissipate in the early 1850s: Millais eloped with Ruskin's wife and became a successful Royal Academician, Rossetti retreated into the world of medieval romance, Hunt went to Palestine to paint biblical scenes, but the style they had created was continued by a number of inferior imitators.

prerequisite /pri:'rekwɪzɪt/ adj. required as a precondition. —n. a prerequisite thing.

prerogative /prɪ'rɒgətɪv/ n. a right or privilege exclusive to an individual or class. [f. OF or L *praerogativa*, orig. = tribe voting first (*praerogare* ask first)]

presage /'presɪdʒ/ n. **1.** an omen, a portent. **2.** a presentiment. —/ also prɪ'seɪdʒ/ v.t. **1.** to portend, to be an advance sign of. **2.** to predict, to have a presentiment of. [f. F f. L *praesagium* (prae before, *sagire* perceive keenly)]

presbyter /'prezbɪtə(r)/ n. (in the Episcopal Church) a minister of the second order, a priest; (in the Presbyterian Church) an elder. [L f. Gk, = elder]

Presbyterian /prezbɪ'tɪərɪən/ adj. (of a Church) governed by elders all of equal rank, especially the national Church of Scotland. —n. a member of the Presbyterian Church; an adherent of the Presbyterian system. —**Presbyterianism** n. [f. L *presbyterium* (as foll.)]

presbytery /'prezbɪtərɪ/ n. **1.** a body of presbyters, especially the court next above the kirk-session. **2.** the eastern part of a chancel. **3.** the house of a Roman Catholic priest. [f. OF f. L f. Gk (as PRESBYTER)]

preschool /'pri:sku:l/ adj. of the time before a child is old enough to attend school.

prescient /'presɪənt/ adj. having foreknowledge or foresight. —**prescience** n. [f. L *praescire* (prae before, *scire* know)]

prescribe /prɪ'skraɪb/ v.t. **1.** to lay down as a course or rule to be followed. **2.** to advise the use of (a medicine etc.). [f. L *praescribere* direct in writing]

prescript /'pri:skrɪpt/ n. an ordinance, a law, a command. [f. L *praescriptum* (as prec.)]

prescription /prɪ'skrɪpʃ(ə)n/ n. **1.** prescribing. **2.** a doctor's (usually written) instruction for the composition and use of a medicine; a medicine thus prescribed. [f. OF f. L (as PRESCRIBE)]

prescriptive /prɪ'skrɪptɪv/ adj. **1.** prescribing; laying down rules. **2.** based on prescription; prescribed by custom. [as PRESCRIBE]

presence /ˈprezəns/ *n.* **1.** being present in a place; the place where a person is. **2.** a person's appearance or bearing, especially when imposing. **3.** a person or thing that is present. —**presence of mind**, calmness and self-command in a sudden difficulty etc. [f. OF f. L (as foll.)]

present[1] /ˈprez(ə)nt/ *adj.* **1.** being in the place in question. **2.** now existing, occurring, or being such. **3.** now being considered etc. **4.** (*Gram.*) expressing an action etc. now going on or habitually performed. —*n.* **1.** the time now passing. **2.** (*Gram.*) the present tense. —**at present**, now. **by these presents**, (*Law*) by this document. **for the present**, just now, as far as the present is concerned. **present-day** *adj.* of this time, modern. [f. OF f. L (*praeesse* be at hand)]

present[2] /ˈprez(ə)nt/ *n.* a thing given. [as prec.]

present[3] /prɪˈzent/ *v.t.* **1.** to introduce (a person) to another or others. **2.** to give as a gift or award; to offer for acceptance, attention, consideration, etc. **3.** to show, to reveal (a quality etc.). **4.** to level or aim (a weapon). —**present arms**, to hold a rifle etc. vertically in front of the body as a salute. —**presenter** *n.* [f. OF f. L *praesentare* (as PRESENT[1])]

presentable /prɪˈzentəb(ə)l/ *adj.* of good appearance, fit to be presented. —**presentability** /-ˈbɪlɪtɪ/ *n.*, **presentably** *adv.* [f. prec.]

presentation /prezənˈteɪʃ(ə)n/ *n.* **1.** presenting, being presented. **2.** a thing presented. [as PRESENT[3]]

presentiment /prɪˈzentɪmənt/ *n.* a vague expectation, a foreboding (esp. of evil). [f. obs. F (as PRE-, SENTIMENT)]

presently *adv.* **1.** soon, after a short time. **2.** (esp. *US & Sc.*) at the present time, now. [f. PRESENT[1]]

preservative /prɪˈzɜːvətɪv/ *n.* a substance for preserving perishable foodstuffs etc. —*adj.* tending to preserve. [as foll.]

preserve /prɪˈzɜːv/ *v.t.* **1.** to keep safe; to keep in an unchanged condition; to retain (a quality or condition). **2.** to keep from decay; to treat (food etc.) so as to prevent decomposition or fermentation. **3.** to protect (game, or a river etc.) for private use. —*n.* **1.** (also in *pl.*) preserved fruit, jam. **2.** a place where game etc. is preserved. **3.** a sphere regarded by a person as being for him alone. —**preservation** /prezəˈveɪʃ(ə)n/ *n.*, **preserver** *n.* [f. OF f. L *praeservare* (*prae* before, *servare* keep)]

preside /prɪˈzaɪd/ *v.i.* to be chairman or president; to have the position of authority or control. [f. F f. L *praesidēre* (*prae* before, *sedēre* sit)]

presidency /ˈprezɪdənsɪ/ *n.* the office of president; the period of this. [f. F. L (as prec.)]

president /ˈprezɪdənt/ *n.* **1.** the head of a republican State. **2.** a person who is head of a society or council etc.; the head of some colleges; (*US*) the head of a university or company etc.; the person in charge of a meeting. —**presidential** /-ˈdenʃ(ə)l/ *adj.* [f. OF f. L (as PRESIDE)]

presidium /prɪˈsɪdɪəm/ *n.* a standing committee in a Communist organization, especially that of the Supreme Soviet in the Soviet Union which functions as the ultimate legislative authority when the Soviet itself is not sitting. [f. Russ. f. L *praesidium* garrison (as PRESIDE)]

Presley /ˈprezlɪ/, Elvis Aaron (1935–77), American singer, the dominant personality of early rock and roll from the mid-1950s, noted for the vigour and frank sexuality of his style.

press[1] *v.t./i.* **1.** to apply steady force to (a thing in contact). **2.** to compress or squeeze (a thing) so as to flatten, shape, or smooth it or extract juice etc.; to make by pressing; to squeeze out (juice etc.); to iron (clothes etc.). **3.** to be urgent, to require immediate action. **4.** to throng closely; to push one's way; to hasten. **5.** to exert pressure on (an enemy etc.); to oppress. **6.** to urge or entreat; to make an insistent demand (upon). **7.** to force the acceptance of; to insist upon. **8.** (in golf) to strike the ball imperfectly by trying too hard for a long hit. —*n.* **1.** pressing. **2.** a device or machinery for compressing, flattening, or shaping something, or for extracting juice. **3.** a printing-press; a printing or publishing firm. **4.** newspapers and periodicals generally; journalists and photographers etc. involved in these; publicity in newspapers etc. **5.** crowding; a throng of people. **6.** haste; the pressure of affairs. **7.** a large usually shelved cupboard for clothes, books, etc. —**be pressed for**, to have barely enough (time etc.). **go** or **send to press**, to go or send to be printed. **press agent**, a person employed to attend to advertising and press publicity. **press conference**, an interview given to a body of journalists. **press-gallery** *n.* a gallery for reporters especially in a legislative assembly. **press-stud** *n.* a small fastening device engaged by pressing the two parts together. **press-up** *n.* (usu. in *pl.*) an exercise in which a person lying prone presses down on the hands to straighten the arms so that head, shoulders, and trunk are raised. [f. OF f. L *pressare* frequent. of *premere* press]

press[2] *v.t.* (*hist.*) to force to serve in the army or navy. —**press-gang** *n.* (*hist.*) a body of men employed to force men to serve in the army or navy; a group using coercive methods; (*v.t.*) to force into service. **press into service**, to bring into use as a makeshift. [alt. of obs. *prest* f. OF, = loan, advance pay, f. L *praestare* furnish]

pressing *adj.* urgent; urging strongly. —*n.* a thing made by pressing, especially a gramophone record; a series of such made at one time. [f. PRESS[1]]

pressure /ˈpreʃə(r)/ *n.* **1.** the exertion of continuous force on or against a body by another in contact with it; the force so exerted; the amount of this (expressed by the force on a unit area), especially that of the atmosphere. **2.** urgency. **3.** an affliction or difficulty. **4.** a constraining influence. —*v.t.* to apply pressure to; to coerce, to persuade. —**pressure group**, a group seeking to influence a policy by concerted action and propaganda. [f. L (as PRESS[1])]

pressure-cooker *n.* a sealed pan for cooking food in a short time under steam pressure. The earliest vessel of this kind was described by its French inventor, Denis Papin, in 1681, and called by him 'Papin's Digester'; the diarist John Evelyn describes a supper prepared in it.

pressurize *v.t.* **1.** to raise to a high pressure; (esp. in *p.p.*) to maintain normal atmospheric pressure in (an aircraft cabin etc.) at high altitude. **2.** coerce. —**pressurized water reactor**, a nuclear reactor in which the coolant is water at high pressure (ill. ELECTRICAL POWER). —**pressurization** *n.* [f. prec.]

Prester John (i.e. 'Presbyter' John) a legendary medieval Christian king of Asia, said to have defeated the Muslims and to be destined to bring help to the Holy Land. The legend spread in Europe in the mid-12th c. He was later identified with a real king of Ethiopia; another theory identifies him with a Chinese prince who defeated the sultan of Persia in 1141. The legend may contain a nucleus of historical fact.

prestidigitator /prestɪˈdɪdʒɪteɪtə(r)/ *n.* a conjuror. — **prestidigitation** /-ˈteɪʃ(ə)n/ *n.* [f. F (as PRESTO, DIGIT)]

prestige /preˈstiːʒ/ *n.* influence or good reputation derived from past achievements, associations, etc. —*adj.* having or conferring prestige. [F, = illusion, glamour (as foll.)]

prestigious /preˈstɪdʒəs/ *adj.* having or showing prestige. [orig. = deceptive, f. L (*praestigiae* juggler's tricks)]

presto /ˈprestəʊ/ *adv.* (*Mus.*) in quick tempo. —*n.* (*pl.* **-os**) (*Mus.*) a movement to be played this way. [It. f. L *praestus* (*praesto* ready)]

Prestonpans /prestənˈpænz/ a village just east of Edinburgh, near which the first major engagement of the Jacobite Rebellion of 1745 took place. A small Hanoverian army under Sir John Cope was routed by the Highlanders at the equally small Jacobite army, leaving the way clear for the Young Pretender's subsequent invasion of England.

pre-stressed /priːˈstrest/ *adj.* (of concrete) strengthened by means of stretched wires within it (see CONCRETE).

presumably /prɪˈzjuːməblɪ/ *adv.* it is or may be reasonably presumed. [f. foll.]

presume /prɪˈzjuːm/ *v.t./i.* **1.** to suppose to be true, to take for granted. **2.** to take the liberty, to be impudent enough, to venture; to be presumptuous. —**presume on** or **upon**, to take advantage of or make unscrupulous use of (a person's good nature etc.). [f. OF f. L *praesumere* anticipate]

presumption /prɪˈzʌmpʃ(ə)n/ *n.* **1.** presumptuous behaviour. **2.** presuming a thing to be true; a thing that is, or may be, presumed to be true; a ground for presuming something. [as prec.]

presumptive /prɪˈzʌmptɪv/ *adj.* giving grounds for presumption. —**presumptively** *adv.* [as PRESUME]

presumptuous /prɪˈzʌmptjʊəs/ *adj.* behaving with impudent boldness; acting without due authority. —**presumptuously** *adv.*, **presumptuousness** *n.* [as PRESUME]

presuppose /priːsəˈpəʊz/ *v.t.* **1.** to assume beforehand. **2.** to imply the existence of. —**presupposition** /-sʌpəˈzɪʃ(ə)n/ *n.* [f. OF (as PRE-, SUPPOSE)]

pre-tax /priːˈtæks/ *adj.* (of income) before the deduction of taxes.

pretence /prɪˈtens/ *n.* **1.** pretending, make-believe. **2.** a claim, e.g. to merit or knowledge. **3.** false profession of purpose, a pretext. **4.** ostentation, show. —**in pretence,** (in heraldry) borne on an inescutcheon to indicate pretension or claim. [f. AF (as foll.)]

pretend /prɪ'tend/ v.t./i. **1.** to claim or assert falsely so as to deceive. **2.** to imagine to oneself in play. **3.** (in p.p.) falsely claimed to be such. —**pretend to,** to lay claim to (a right or title); to profess to have. —**pretendedly** adv. [f. F or L praetendere (prae before, tendere stretch)]

pretender n. **1.** one who pretends. **2.** one who claims a throne or title. —**Old Pretender, Young Pretender,** the son and grandson of James II, claimants to the British throne. [f. prec.]

pretension /prɪ'tenʃ(ə)n/ n. **1.** the assertion of a claim; a justifiable claim. **2.** pretentiousness. [f. L (as PRETEND)]

pretentious /prɪ'tenʃəs/ adj. making an excessive claim to great merit or importance; ostentatious. —**pretentiously** adv., **pretentiousness** n. [f. F (as prec.)]

preterite /'pretərɪt/ adj. (Gram.) expressing a past action or state. —n. (Gram.) the preterite tense of a verb. [f. OF or L (praeterire pass)]

preternatural /pri:tə'nætʃr(ə)l/ adj. outside the ordinary course of nature, unusual. —**preternaturally** adv. [f. L (praeter naturam beyond nature)]

pretext /'pri:tekst/ n. an ostensible reason, an excuse offered. [f. L praetextus outward display (prae before, texere weave)]

Pretoria /prɪ'tɔ:rɪə/ the capital of Transvaal and administrative capital of the Republic of South Africa; pop. (1980) approx. 528,000. [f. A. W. J. Pretorius (1799-1853), S.Afr. Boer leader, one of the founders of Transvaal]

pretty /'prɪtɪ/ adj. **1.** attractive in a delicate way. **2.** fine or good of its kind. **3.** (iron.) considerable. —adv. fairly, moderately. —**pretty much,** or **nearly** or **well,** almost, very nearly. **pretty-pretty** adj. with the prettiness overdone. —**prettily** adv., **prettiness** n. [OE]

prevail /prɪ'veɪl/ v.i. **1.** to be victorious, to gain the mastery. **2.** to be more usual or prominent; to exist or occur in general use or experience. —**prevail on** or **upon,** to persuade. [f. L praevalere (prae before, valēre have power)]

prevalent /'prevələnt/ adj. generally existing or occurring, predominant. —**prevalence** n., **prevalently** adv. [as prec.]

prevaricate /prɪ'værɪkeɪt/ v.i. to speak or act evasively or misleadingly; to quibble, to equivocate. —**prevarication** /-'keɪʃ(ə)n/ n., **prevaricator** n. [f. L, orig. = walk crookedly]

prevent /prɪ'vent/ v.t. to keep from happening or doing something; to hinder, to make impossible. —**prevention** n. [orig. = anticipate, f. L praevenire come before]

preventable adj. that may be prevented. [f. prec.]

preventative /prɪ'ventətɪv/ adj. & n. preventive. [as foll.]

preventive /prɪ'ventɪv/ adj. serving to prevent, especially preventing a disease. —n. a preventive agent, measure, drug, etc. —**preventive detention,** the imprisonment of a person thought likely to commit a crime. [f. PREVENT]

preview /'pri:vju:/ n. a showing of a film or play etc. before it is seen by the general public. —v.t. to view or show in advance of public presentation.

previous /'pri:vɪəs/ adj. **1.** coming before in time or order; prior. **2.** done or acting hastily. —**previous to,** before. —**previously** adv. [f. L praevius (prae before, via way)]

Prévost /pre'vəʊ/, Antoine-François, l'Abbé ('Prévost d'Exiles') (1696-1763), French novelist, successively Jesuit novice, professional soldier, and Benedictine priest. Unfitted for the cloister he fled in 1728 and took refuge in Holland and England. He is remembered for his novel Manon Lescaut (1731), the story of a mutually destructive passion between a noble man and a demi-mondaine, which inspired operas by Massenet and Puccini. He wrote many novels and translations of Richardson's major novels which introduced his countrymen to English life and literature.

pre-war /pri:'wɔ:(r), attrib. 'pri:-/ adj. occurring or existing before a war.

prey /preɪ/ n. **1.** an animal that is hunted or killed by another for food. **2.** a person or thing that falls victim to an enemy, disease, fear, etc. —v.i. **prey on** or **upon,** to seek or take as prey; (of a disease or emotion etc.) to exert a harmful influence on. —**beast** or **bird of prey,** one that kills and devours other animals. [f. OF f. L praeda plunder]

Priam /'praɪæm/ (Gk legend) king of Troy at the time of its destruction by the Greeks under Agamemnon. He was slain by Neoptolemus, son of Achilles.

Priapus /'praɪəpəs/ (Gk myth.) a god of fertility, whose

symbol was the phallus. He was originally worshipped in the Hellespont area and his cult spread to Greece after Alexander's conquest, and thence to Italy. By this time the Greeks had outgrown the more crudely naturalistic worship and Priapus seems to have been found broadly funny. He was adopted as a god of gardens, where his statue (a misshapen little man with enormous genitals) was a sort of combined scarecrow and guardian deity.

price n. **1.** the amount of money for which a thing is bought or sold. **2.** what must be given or done etc. to obtain or achieve something. **3.** the odds in betting. —v.t. to fix or find the price of (a thing for sale); to estimate the value of. —**at a price,** at a high cost. **price-fixing** n. the maintaining of prices at a certain level by agreement between competing sellers. **price on a person's head,** a reward for his capture or death. **price-tag** n. a label on an item showing its price, the cost of an undertaking etc. **what price . . . ?** (colloq.) what is the chance of . . . ?; the vaunted . . . has failed. [f. OF pris f. L pretium]

priceless adj. **1.** invaluable. **2.** (colloq.) very amusing or absurd. [f. PRICE + -LESS]

pricey adj. (compar. **pricier;** superl. **priciest**) (colloq.) expensive. [f. PRICE]

prick v.t./i. **1.** to pierce slightly, to make a small hole in. **2.** to mark with pricks or dots. **3.** to trouble mentally. **4.** to feel a pricking sensation. —n. **1.** a small hole or mark made by pricking. **2.** a pain caused (as) by pricking. **3.** (vulgar) the penis; (derog.) a man. —**prick out,** to plant out (seedlings) in small holes pricked in soil. **prick up one's ears,** (of a dog) to make the ears erect when on the alert; (of a person) to become suddenly attentive. —**pricker** n. [OE]

prickle n. **1.** a small thorn. **2.** the hard-pointed spine of a hedgehog etc. **3.** a prickling sensation. —v.t./i. to affect or be affected with a sensation as of pricking. [OE]

prickly adj. **1.** having prickles. **2.** (of a person) irritable. **3.** tingling. —**prickly heat,** inflammation of the skin near the sweat glands with an eruption of vesicles and a prickly sensation, common in hot countries. **prickly pear,** a cactus of the genus Opuntia with a pear-shaped edible fruit; this fruit. —**prickliness** n. [f. prec.]

pride n. **1.** a feeling of elation or satisfaction at one's achievements, qualities, or possessions etc. **2.** an object of this feeling. **3.** unduly high opinion of one's own importance or merits etc. **4.** a proper sense of what befits one's position, self-respect. **5.** the best condition, the prime. **6.** a group or company (of lions etc.). —v.refl. (with on or upon) to be proud of. —**pride of place,** the most important or prominent position. **take pride in,** to be proud of. [OE (as PROUD)]

Pride's Purge the exclusion or arrest of about 140 Members of Parliament by soldiers under the command of Colonel Pride when, in December 1648, the army, seeking a trial of the captive Charles I, decided to remove those Members likely to vote against it. Following the purge, the remaining Members, known as the Rump Parliament, voted for the trial which resulted in Charles being executed.

prie-dieu /pri:'djɜ:/ n. a desk at which one kneels for prayer. [F, = pray God]

priest /pri:st/ n. an ordained minister of the Roman Catholic or Orthodox Church, or of the Anglican Church (above a deacon and below a bishop); an official minister of a non-Christian religion. —v.t. to make (a deacon) into a priest. —**priesthood** n. [OE (ult. as PRESBYTER)]

priestess /'pri:stɪs/ n. a female priest of a non-Christian religion. [f. prec.]

Priestley[1] /'pri:stlɪ/, John Boynton (1894-1984), English novelist, playwright, and critic. His good-humoured optimistic novels include The Good Companions (1929). Some of his plays, such as Time and the Conways (1937), are influenced by the time theories of J. W. Dunne. Priestley was a popular broadcaster, known for his forthright down-to-earth comments. His prodigious literary output earned him a fortune and popular esteem, but critical acclaim was more sparing.

Priestley[2] /'pri:stlɪ/, Joseph (1733-1804), English chemist, natural philosopher, and theologian, author of about 150 books, mostly theological or educational. He was introduced to the study of electricity (electrostatics) by Franklin, but his most important work was done in 'pneumatic' chemistry (the study of gases), in which, by means of improved techniques, he managed to isolate a number of gases, including ammonia, sulphur dioxide, and nitrous oxide and nitrogen dioxide, but his most significant discovery was of 'dephlogisticated air' in 1774, which he reported to

Lavoisier who gave it the modern name of oxygen. He demonstrated the importance of oxygen to animal life, and that plants require sunlight and yield this gas. In his theology he espoused what eventually became known as Unitarianism. His support of the French Revolution provoked so much hostility that he left Birmingham in 1794 and settled in America.

priestly *adj.* of, like, or befitting a priest. —**priestliness** *n.* [f. PRIEST]

prig *n.* a self-righteously correct or moralistic person. —**priggery** *n.*, **priggish** *adj.* [orig. unkn.]

prim *adj.* (of a person or manner) stiffly formal and precise, demure; disliking what is rough or improper, prudish. —**primly** *adv.*, **primness** *n.* [prob. f. OF *prin* fine, delicate (as PRIME¹)]

prima ballerina /ˈpriːmə/ a ballerina of the highest rank; the leading ballerina of a ballet company. [It., = first female dancer]

primacy /ˈpraɪməsɪ/ *n.* **1.** pre-eminence. **2.** the office of primate. [as PRIMATE]

prima donna /priːmə ˈdɒnə/ **1.** the chief female singer in an opera. **2.** a temperamentally self-important person. [It., = first lady]

prima facie /praɪmə ˈfeɪʃiː/ at first sight; (of evidence) based on the first impression. [L]

primal /ˈpraɪm(ə)l/ *adj.* **1.** primitive, primeval. **2.** chief, fundamental. —**primally** *adv.* [f. L (as PRIME¹)]

primary /ˈpraɪmərɪ/ *adj.* **1.** earliest in time or order; first in a series, not derived. **2.** of the first importance, chief. —*n.* a thing that is primary; a primary feather etc.; (*US*) a primary election. —**primary battery,** a battery producing electricity by an irreversible chemical action. **primary colours,** see COLOUR. **primary education,** the first stage of education in which the rudiments of knowledge are taught. **primary election,** (*US*) an election to appoint party conference delegates or to select candidates for a principal election. **primary feather,** any of the large flight-feathers of a bird's wing (ill. BIRDS). **primary school,** a school where primary education is given. —**primarily** *adv.* [f. L *primarius* (as PRIME¹)]

primate /ˈpraɪmət, -eɪt/ *n.* **1.** an archbishop. **2.** a member of the order Primates, the highest order of mammals, including man, apes, monkeys, tarsiers, and lemurs. —**Primate of England,** the Archbishop of York. **Primate of all England,** the Archbishop of Canterbury. [f. OF f. L, = of first rank (*primus* first)]

prime¹ *adj.* **1.** chief, most important. **2.** first-rate, excellent. **3.** primary, fundamental. —*n.* **1.** the state of highest perfection; the best part. **2.** a beginning. **3.** the second canonical hour of prayer. **4.** a prime number. —**prime minister,** see separate entry. **prime number,** a natural number other than 1 that can be divided exactly only by itself and unity. **prime time,** the time at which a television etc. audience is expected to be largest. [f. OF f. L *primus* first]

prime² *v.t.* **1.** to prepare (a thing) for use or action; to prepare (a gun) for firing or (an explosive) for detonation. **2.** to pour (liquid) into a pump to make it start working. **3.** to prepare (wood etc.) for painting by applying a substance that prevents the paint from being absorbed. **4.** to equip (a person) with information. **5.** to ply (a person) with food or drink in preparation for something. [orig. unkn.]

prime minister the chief minister of a government. In Britain the term was originally merely descriptive and unofficial. In the early 18th c. (perhaps from its prior application to the sole minister of a despotic ruler) it was regarded as odious; it was applied opprobriously to Sir Robert Walpole and disowned by him, as later by Lord North. It was little used in the later part of the 18th c., 'premier' (also 'first minister') being often substituted, but by the middle of the 19th c. it had become usual and began to creep into official use from 1878. In 1905 it was fully recognized and the precedence of the Prime Minister defined by King Edward VII.

primer¹ *n.* a substance used to prime wood etc. [f. PRIME²]

primer² *n.* **1.** an elementary school-book for teaching children to read. **2.** a small book introducing a subject. [f. AF f. L (as PRIMARY)]

primeval /praɪˈmiːv(ə)l/ *adj.* of the first age of the world; ancient, primitive. —**primevally** *adv.* [f. L (*primus* first, *aevum* age)]

primitive /ˈprɪmɪtɪv/ *adj.* **1.** ancient, at an early stage of civilization. **2.** undeveloped, crude, simple. —*n.* an untutored painter with a direct naïve style; a picture by

such a painter. —**primitively** *adv.*, **primitiveness** *n.* [f. OF or L *primitivus* first of its kind (as PRIME¹)]

primogeniture /praɪməʊˈdʒɛnɪtʃə(r)/ *n.* **1.** the fact of being the first-born child. **2.** the right of succession or inheritance belonging to the eldest son. [f. L (*primo* first, *genitura* begetting)]

primordial /praɪˈmɔːdɪ(ə)l/ *adj.* existing at or from the beginning, primeval. —**primordially** *adv.* [f. L (as PRIME¹, *ordiri* begin)]

primp *v.t.* to make (the hair etc.) tidy; to smarten. [dial. var. of PRIM]

primrose /ˈprɪmrəʊz/ *n.* **1.** a plant (*Primula vulgaris*) bearing a pale yellow flower in spring; its flower. **2.** the colour of this flower. —**Primrose Day,** the anniversary of the death of Disraeli (19 Apr. 1881). **Primrose League,** a political association, formed in memory of Disraeli (whose favourite flower was supposedly the primrose) in 1883, to promote and sustain conservative principles in Britain. It is still in existence today. **primrose path,** the unjustified pursuit of ease or pleasure (with ref. to Shakespeare *Hamlet* I. iii. 50). [f. OF f. L, = first rose]

primula /ˈprɪmjʊlə/ *n.* a herbaceous perennial of the genus *Primula* with flowers of various colours. [L, dim. of *primus* first]

Primus /ˈpraɪməs/ *n.* [P] a brand of portable stove burning vaporized paraffin for cooking etc. [L, = first]

prince *n.* **1.** a male member of a royal family who is not a reigning king; (in Britain) a son or grandson of the sovereign. **2.** a ruler, especially of a small State. **3.** a nobleman of some countries. **4.** a person who is outstanding of his kind. —**prince consort,** the husband of a reigning queen who is himself a prince. The title was conferred on Prince Albert, husband of Queen Victoria, to avoid the word 'king' as Albert was not regnant. **Prince Regent,** a prince acting as regent, especially the future George IV who was regent 1811–20. [f. OF f. L *princeps* chieftain]

Prince Charming a fairy-tale hero. The name is a partial translation of the French *Roi Charmant*, the name of the hero of the Comtesse d'Aulnoy's *L'Oiseau Bleu* (*The Blue Bird*, 1697). In English it first appears as that of the hero of Planché's *King Charming* or *Prince Charming*, and was later adopted for the hero of various fairy-tale pantomimes.

Prince Edward Island the smallest province of Canada (from 1873), an island in the Gulf of St Lawrence, captured by the British from the French settlers in 1758; capital, Charlottetown.

Prince Imperial Napoléon Eugène Louis Jean Joseph (1856–79), son of Napoleon III. Trained as a soldier in Britain after his father's overthrow, he was allowed, at his own request, to join the British forces in the Zulu War and was killed in a skirmish in Zululand.

princeling /ˈprɪnslɪŋ/ *n.* a young or petty prince. [f. prec. + -LING]

princely *adj.* **1.** of or worthy of a prince. **2.** sumptuous, splendid, generous. [f. PRINCE]

Prince of Wales a title, formerly adopted by various Welsh rulers, usually conferred (since 1301; see EDWARD II) on the heir apparent to the English (later the British) throne.

Princes in the Tower the young sons of Edward IV, supposedly murdered in the Tower of London. Edward, Prince of Wales, and Richard, Duke of York, were housed in the royal apartments of the Tower of London following the death of their father and the seizure of the throne by Richard III. They disappeared soon after their arrival there in 1483, and although many theories as to their fate are subsequently advanced, it is generally assumed that they were murdered, either by their uncle Richard III or by Henry Tudor (later Henry VII).

princess /prɪnˈses, *attrib.* ˈprɪn-/ *n.* **1.** the wife of a prince. **2.** a female member of a royal family who is not a reigning queen; (in Britain) a daughter or granddaughter of the sovereign. —**princess royal,** a title that may be conferred on the sovereign's eldest daughter. [as PRINCE]

principal /ˈprɪnsɪp(ə)l/ *adj.* (usu. *attrib.*) first in rank or importance, chief; main, leading. —*n.* **1.** the person with highest authority in an organization etc.; the head of some schools, colleges, and universities. **2.** a person who takes a leading part in an activity or in a play etc. **3.** a capital sum as distinct from interest or income. **4.** a person for whom another is agent. **5.** a civil servant of the grade below Secretaries. —**principal boy,** the leading male part in a pantomime, usually played by a woman. **principal parts,**

the parts of a verb from which all the other parts can be deduced. —**principally** *adv.* [as PRINCE]

principality /prɪnsɪˈpælɪtɪ/ *n.* a State ruled by a prince. —**the Principality,** Wales. [as prec.]

principle /ˈprɪnsɪp(ə)l/ *n.* **1.** a fundamental truth or a general law or doctrine that is used as a basis of reasoning or action. **2.** a personal code of right conduct; (in *pl.*) such rules of conduct. **3.** a general law in physics. **4.** a law of nature forming the basis for the construction or working of a machine. **5.** (*Chem.*) a constituent of a substance, especially one giving rise to some quality etc. **6.** a fundamental source, a primary element. —**in principle,** as regards fundamentals but not necessarily in detail. **on principle,** from a settled moral motive. [f. OF f. L *principium* source]

prink *v.t.* **1.** to make (oneself) smart. **2.** (of a bird) to preen. **3.** to walk daintily. [cf. *prank* in similar sense, rel. to Du. *pronk* finery]

print *n.* **1.** an indentation or mark left on a surface by the pressure of a thing in contact. **2.** printed lettering or writing; words in printed form. **3.** a picture or design printed from a block or plate. **4.** a photograph produced from a negative. **5.** a printed cotton fabric. —*v.t.* **1.** to produce (a book, picture, etc., or *absol.*) by applying inked types, blocks, or plates to paper etc. (see PRINTING); to express or publish in print. **2.** to impress or stamp (a surface, or a mark or design in or on a surface). **3.** to write (words, letters, or *absol.*) without joining, in imitation of typography. **4.** to produce (a photograph) from a negative. **5.** to mark (a textile fabric) with a coloured design. **6.** to impress (an idea or scene etc. on the mind or memory). **7.** to make (a printed circuit or component). —**in** *or* **out of print,** (of a book etc.) available (or no longer available) from a publisher. **printed circuit,** an electric circuit with lines of conducting material printed on a flat insulating sheet (instead of using wires). [f. OF f. L *premere* (as PRESS)]

printer *n.* **1.** one whose job or business is the printing of books, newspapers, etc. **2.** a device that prints. —**Printers' Bible,** one said to have had *Printers* for *Princes* in Ps. 119: 161, reading 'Printers have persecuted me without a cause'. [f. prec.]

printing *n.* **1.** the production of printed books etc. (see below). **2.** a single impression of a book. **3.** printed letters or writing imitating them. —**printing-press** *n.* a machine for printing from types or plates etc. [f. PRINT]

Printing involves transferring any number of times an image, or group of images, from an original master to a receptive substrate such as paper, board, or cloth. It is most commonly achieved by inking a suitable form of the master image (i.e. printers' type, a rubber stamp, or litho plate) and transferring the ink to the substrate by flat or rolling pressure. The process originated in China in about the 8th c. and spread to Europe in the 15th c. A major advance was Johann Gutenberg's invention of movable type by which each letter is cast separately, allowing words and spaces to be formed into lines and pages, which in turn form relief master images for inking and impressing on to paper. This method has been largely superseded by photographic image-forming techniques and faster rotary printing. Film is now the most universal master-image material, through which the printing-surface is selectively sensitized and etched, ready for the modern rotary printing-press. Multicolour images are formed by superimposing one printed colour upon another in register. A growing method of printing is that whereby master images are held by computer in digital form, and then output on to a suitable substrate by plotting, xerographic, ink-jet, or laser techniques.

printout *n.* computer output in printed form.

prior /ˈpraɪə(r)/ *adj.* earlier; coming before in time, order, or importance. —*n.* a superior of a religious house or order; (in an abbey) the deputy of the abbot. —**prior to,** before. —**prioress** *n.fem.* [f. OF or L, = former (*prae* before)]

priority /praɪˈɒrɪtɪ/ *n.* **1.** being earlier or more important; precedence in rank etc.; the right to be first. **2.** an interest having a prior claim to attention. [as prec.]

priory /ˈpraɪərɪ/ *n.* a monastery governed by a prior; a nunnery governed by a prioress. [f. AF (as PRIOR)]

Priscian /ˈprɪʃən/ (Priscianus, 6th c.) Byzantine grammarian. His Latin *Grammatical Institutions* was one of the standard grammatical works in the Middle Ages.

prise /praɪz/ *v.t.* to force open or out by leverage. [OF, = levering instrument (as PRIZE[2])]

prism /ˈprɪz(ə)m/ *n.* **1.** a solid figure whose two ends are equal parallel rectilinear figures, and whose sides are parallelograms. **2.** a transparent body of this form, usually

triangular, with refracting surfaces at an acute angle with each other. —**prism binoculars,** binoculars in which triangular prisms are used to shorten the instrument. [f. L f. Gk *prisma* thing sawn (*prizō* saw)]

prismatic /prɪzˈmætɪk/ *adj.* of or like a prism; (of colours) formed or distributed (as if) by a transparent prism. —**prismatically** *adv.* [f. F f. Gk (as prec.)]

prison /ˈprɪz(ə)n/ *n.* **1.** a place where people are confined after being convicted (or in certain cases accused) of crimes (see below). **2.** any place of custody or confinement. **3.** imprisonment, confinement. —**prison-camp** *n.* a camp serving as a prison for prisoners of war etc. [f. OF f. L *prensio* (*prehendere* seize)]

There have been prisons at all periods of history. Originally imprisonment was not a mode of punishment but a means of holding offenders awaiting trial or execution; it was used also as a means of extorting payment of money, and even by the 19th c. a high proportion of prisoners were debtors. The modern idea of prison grew from the 'house of correction', a place which, in the 16th c., was used for housing beggars and vagrants who threatened the peace of the community, and for setting them to work. By the mid-16th c. such places, modelled on and named after the Bridewell organized in London, were established in every county under the local justices (a similar movement sprang up on the Continent); their original functions were superseded by that of imprisoning petty offenders. Bad insanitary surroundings, oppression, cruelty, and lack of supervision made prison conditions notorious and towards the end of the 18th c. John Howard began a vigorous crusade for reform; this was only one aspect of a European movement. In 1878 the government assumed control of all prisons. Thinking about prisons was affected then and thereafter by the development of penological theory, particularly stressing the individualism of punishment and criticizing imprisonment as not suitable in all cases.

prisoner /ˈprɪz(ə)nə(r)/ *n.* **1.** a person kept in prison. **2.** (also **prisoner at the bar**) a person in custody on a criminal charge and on trial. **3.** a captive. **4.** a person or thing held in confinement or in another's grasp etc. —**prisoner of conscience,** a person in prison for an act of conscientious protest etc. **prisoner of war,** one who has been captured in a war. **prisoners' base,** a game played by two groups of children who each occupy a distinct base or home. It was played as a street game in France in the Middle Ages. In England it was prohibited in the avenues of the Palace of Westminster during sessions of Parliament in the reign of Edward III because it interfered with the passage of members. **take prisoner,** to seize and hold as a prisoner. [f. AF (as prec.)]

prissy *adj.* prim. —**prissily** *adv.*, **prissiness** *n.* [perh. f. PRIM + SISSY]

pristine /ˈprɪstiːn, -aɪn/ *adj.* **1.** in the original condition, unspoilt. **2.** (**D**) spotless, fresh as if new. **3.** ancient, primitive. [f. L *pristinus* former]

privacy /ˈprɪvəsɪ, ˈpraɪ-/ *n.* being alone or undisturbed; the right to this; freedom from intrusion or public attention. [f. foll.]

private /ˈpraɪvɪt/ *adj.* **1.** belonging to an individual, one's own, personal. **2.** confidential, not to be disclosed to others. **3.** kept from public knowledge or observation; (of a place) secluded. **4.** not open to the public. **5.** (of a person) not holding a public office or official position. **6.** (of medical treatment) conducted outside the State system, at the patient's expense. —*n.* **1.** a private soldier. **2.** (in *pl.*) the genitals. —**in private,** privately, not in public. **private bill,** a parliamentary bill affecting an individual or corporation only. **private company,** one with restricted membership and no issue of shares. **private detective,** one engaged privately, outside the official police force. **private enterprise,** a business or businesses privately owned and free of direct State control. **private eye,** (*colloq.*) a private detective. **private hotel,** one not obliged to take all comers. **private means,** income from investments etc., apart from earned income. **private member,** an MP not holding a government appointment. **private parts,** the genitals. **private school,** a school supported wholly by pupils' fees and by endowments. **private sector,** the part of the economy free of direct State control. **private soldier,** an ordinary soldier, not an officer. —**privately** *adv.* [f. L *privatus* (*privare* deprive)]

privateer /praɪvəˈtɪə(r)/ *n.* **1.** an armed vessel owned and officered by private persons holding a commission from the government and authorized to use it against a hostile nation, especially in the capture of merchant shipping. **2.** its commander. —**privateering** *n.* [f. prec.]

privation /praɪˈveɪʃ(ə)n/ *n.* a lack of the comforts or necessaries of life. [as PRIVATE]

privative /ˈprɪvətɪv/ *adj.* consisting in or showing loss or absence; (*Gram.*) indicating lack or absence. [f. F or L (as prec.)]

privatize /ˈpraɪvətaɪz/ *v.t.* to assign to private enterprise, to denationalize. —**privatization** /-ˈzeɪʃ(ə)n/ *n.* [f. PRIVATE]

privet /ˈprɪvɪt/ *n.* a bushy evergreen shrub of the genus *Ligustrum*, with smooth dark-green leaves, used for hedges. [orig. unkn.]

privilege /ˈprɪvɪlɪdʒ/ *n.* a special right, advantage, or immunity belonging or granted to a person, group, or office; a special benefit or honour. —*v.t.* to invest with a privilege. [f. OF f. L, = law affecting an individual (*privus* private, *lex legis* law)]

privileged *adj.* having a privilege or privileges. [f. prec.]

privy /ˈprɪvɪ/ *adj.* hidden, secluded, secret. —*n.* (*archaic* or *US*) a lavatory. —**privy purse,** an allowance from public revenue for the sovereign's private expenses. **privy seal,** a State seal formerly attached to documents that were afterwards to pass the Great Seal, or to ones of lesser importance not requiring the Great Seal. **Lord Privy Seal,** a senior Cabinet minister without official duties (formerly keeper of the privy seal). **privy to,** sharing in the secret of (a person's plans etc.). —**privily** *adv.* [f. OF *privé* f. L, = PRIVATE]

Privy Council a sovereign's or governor-general's private counsellors (see below); (in the USA) an advisory council consisting of the heads of executive departments. —**Privy Counsellor,** a member of the Privy Council of the UK.

In Britain, the Privy Council originated in the *Curia Regis* (king's council) of the Norman kings. This took two forms: a large council of the realm (which grew into the parliament), and a select body of officials who met regularly to carry on everyday government, becoming known in the 14th c. as the Privy (= private) Council, with political, judicial, and administrative functions. In the 18th c. the importance of the Cabinet increased and the Privy Council's functions became chiefly formal, except in certain judicial capacities. It now consists of about 300 members, chosen by the sovereign (usually as a personal honour) and includes those who hold or have held high political, legal, or ecclesiastical office in the UK or Commonwealth. It is summoned as a body only to sign the proclamation of the accession of a new sovereign, and when the sovereign announces an intention to marry.

prize[1] *n.* **1.** something that can be won in a competition or lottery etc. **2.** an award given as a symbol of victory or superiority. **3.** something striven for or worth striving for. —*adj.* **1.** to which a prize is awarded. **2.** excellent of its kind. —*v.t.* to value highly. —**prize-fighter** *n.* a professional boxer; (*hist.*) one who fought to the finish (in bare fists) for a prize or stake, before the introduction of Queensberry Rules. [var. of PRICE]

prize[2] *n.* a ship or property captured in naval warfare. [f. OF *prise* f. L *prehendere* seize]

prize[3] var. of PRISE.

PRO *abbr.* public relations officer.

pro[1] /prəʊ/ *n.* (*pl.* **pros**) (*colloq.*) a professional. [abbr.]

pro[2] /prəʊ/ *adj.* & *prep.* (of an argument or reason) for, in favour (of). —*n.* (*pl.* **pros**) a reason for or in favour (esp. in **pros and cons**). [L, = for, on behalf of]

pro-[1] *prefix* **1.** as a substitute or deputy for, substituted for. **2.** favouring, siding with. **3.** forwards (*produce*). **4.** forwards and downwards (*prostrate*). **5.** onwards (*proceed*). **6.** in front of (*protect*). [f. L (as prec.)]

pro-[2] *prefix* before (in time, place, or order). [f. Gk *pro* before]

probability /prɒbəˈbɪlɪtɪ/ *n.* **1.** being probable; likelihood. **2.** something that is probable, the most probable event. **3.** the extent to which an event is likely to occur, measured by the ratio of favourable cases to all possible cases. —**in all probability,** most probably. [f. F or L (as foll.)]

probable /ˈprɒbəb(ə)l/ *adj.* that may be expected to happen or prove true; likely. —*n.* a probable candidate, member of a team, etc. —**probably** *adv.* [f. OF or L (as PROVE)]

probate /ˈprəʊbeɪt/ *n.* **1.** the official proving of a will. **2.** a verified copy of a will with a certificate as handed to the executors. [f. L]

probation /prəˈbeɪʃ(ə)n/ *n.* **1.** the testing of the character or abilities of a person, especially of a candidate for employ-

ment or membership. **2.** a system whereby certain offenders are supervised by an official as an alternative to imprisonment. —**on probation,** undergoing probation before full admission to employment or membership, or as a criminal offender. **probation officer,** an official supervising offenders on probation. —**probationary** *adj.* [as PROVE]

probationer *n.* a person undergoing a probationary period of testing, e.g. a hospital nurse at an early stage of training. [f. prec.]

probative /ˈprəʊbətɪv/ *adj.* affording proof. [as PROVE]

probe *n.* **1.** a device for exploring an otherwise inaccessible place or object etc.; a blunt-ended surgical instrument for exploring a wound. **2.** an unmanned exploratory spacecraft transmitting information about its environment. **3.** a penetrating investigation. —*v.t.* **1.** to explore with a probe. **2.** to penetrate (a thing) with a sharp instrument. **3.** to examine or enquire into closely. [f. L *proba* (as PROVE)]

probity /ˈprəʊbɪtɪ/ *n.* uprightness, honesty. [f. F or L (*probus* good)]

problem /ˈprɒbləm/ *n.* **1.** a doubtful or difficult matter requiring solution. **2.** something hard to understand, accomplish, or deal with. **3.** an exercise in mathematics or chess etc. [f. OF or L f. Gk. *problēma* (PRO-[2], *ballō* throw)]

problematic /prɒbləˈmætɪk/ *adj.* (also **problematical**) **1.** hard to understand, accomplish, or deal with. **2.** doubtful, questionable. —**problematically** *adv.* [f. F or L f. Gk (as prec.)]

proboscis /prəˈbɒsɪs/ *n.* (*pl.* **-ises**) **1.** an elephant's trunk; the long flexible snout of the tapir etc. **2.** an elongated part of the mouth of some insects, used for sucking things. [L f. Gk (PRO-[2], *boskō* feed)]

procedure /prəˈsiːdjə(r), -dʒə(r)/ *n.* **1.** a mode of conducting business or a legal action. **2.** a series of actions conducted in a certain order or manner. —**procedural** *adj.* [f. F (as foll.)]

proceed /prəˈsiːd/ *v.i.* **1.** to go forward or onward; to make one's way. **2.** to continue in an activity; (of an action) to be carried on or continued. **3.** to adopt a course of action. **4.** to go on to say. **5.** to start a lawsuit (against a person). **6.** to come forth, to originate. [f. OF f. L (PRO-[1], *cedere* go)]

proceeding *n.* **1.** an action, a piece of conduct. **2.** (in *pl.*) a legal action. **3.** (in *pl.*) a published report of discussions or a conference. [f. prec.]

proceeds /ˈprəʊsiːdz/ *n.pl.* money produced by a sale or performance etc. [pl. of obs. *proceed* n. f. PROCEED]

process[1] /ˈprəʊses/ *n.* **1.** a series of actions or proceedings used in making, manufacturing, or achieving something. **2.** progress, course. **3.** a natural or involuntary operation or series of changes. **4.** a lawsuit; a summons or writ. **5.** a natural appendage or outgrowth on an organism. —*v.t.* to put through a manufacturing or other process; to treat, especially so as to prevent decay. [as PROCEED]

process[2] /prəˈses/ *v.i.* (*colloq.*) to walk in procession. [back-formation f. foll.]

procession /prəˈseʃ(ə)n/ *n.* a number of persons or vehicles etc. going along in orderly succession, especially as a ceremony or demonstration or festivity; the action of this. [as PROCEED]

processional *adj.* of processions; used, carried, or sung in processions. —*n.* a processional hymn. [f. L (as prec.)]

processor /ˈprəʊsesə(r)/ *n.* a machine that processes things. —**central processor,** the part of a computer that controls and co-ordinates the activities of the other units and performs the actions specified in the program. [f. PROCESS[1]]

proclaim /prəˈkleɪm/ *v.t.* **1.** to announce publicly or officially, to declare; to declare (a person) to be (a king, traitor, etc.). **2.** to reveal as being. [f. L *proclamare* cry out (PRO-[1], *clamare* cry)]

proclamation /prɒkləˈmeɪʃ(ə)n/ *n.* **1.** proclaiming. **2.** a thing proclaimed. [f. prec.]

proclivity /prəˈklɪvɪtɪ/ *n.* a tendency or natural inclination. [f. L (*proclivis* inclined f. PRO-[1], *clivus* slope)]

Procne /ˈprɒknɪ/ (*Gk myth.*) sister of Philomel (see entry).

procrastinate /prəˈkræstɪneɪt/ *v.i.* to defer action; to be dilatory. —**procrastination** /-ˈneɪʃ(ə)n/ *n.*, **procrastinator** *n.* [f. L (PRO-[1], *crastinus* of tomorrow)]

procreate /ˈprəʊkrɪeɪt/ *v.t.* to bring (offspring) into existence by the natural process of reproduction. —**procreation** /-ˈeɪʃ(ə)n/ *n.* (as PRO-[1], CREATE)]

Procrustean /prəˈkrʌstɪən/ *adj.* seeking to enforce uniformity by violent methods. [f. foll.]

Procrustes /prɒˈkrʌstiːz/ (*Gk legend*) a robber who forced travellers to lie on a bed and made them fit it by stretching their limbs or cutting bits off. Theseus killed him in like manner. [Gk, = the stretcher]

proctor /ˈprɒktə(r)/ *n.* each of two university officers at Oxford and Cambridge, appointed annually and having mainly disciplinary functions. —**Queen's** *or* **King's Proctor,** an official who has the right to intervene in probate, divorce, and nullity cases when collusion or suppression of facts is alleged. —**proctorial** /-ˈtɔːrɪəl/ *adj.,* **proctorship** *n.* [syncopation of PROCURATOR]

procuration /prɒkjʊəˈreɪʃ(ə)n/ *n.* 1. procuring. 2. the function or an authorized action of an attorney. [as PROCURE]

procurator /ˈprɒkjʊəreɪtə(r)/ *n.* an agent or proxy, especially with power of attorney. —**procurator fiscal,** an officer of a sheriff's court in Scotland, acting as public prosecutor of a district and with other duties similar to those of a coroner. **procurator general,** the head of the Treasury law department. [as foll.]

procure /prəˈkjʊə(r)/ *v.t./i.* 1. to obtain by care or effort, to acquire. 2. to bring about. 3. to act as a procurer or procuress (of). —**procurement** *n.* [f. OF f. L (PRO-¹, *curare* look after)]

procurer *n.* one who obtains women for prostitution. —**procuress** *n.fem.* [f. OF f. L, = PROCURATOR]

prod *v.t./i.* (**-dd-**) 1. to poke. 2. to urge or stimulate to action. —*n.* 1. a poke. 2. a stimulus to action. 3. a pointed instrument for prodding things. [perh. imit.]

prodigal /ˈprɒdɪg(ə)l/ *adj.* 1. recklessly wasteful or extravagant. 2. lavish. —*n.* a prodigal person. —**prodigal son,** a repentant wastrel, a returned wanderer (Luke 15 : 11-32). —**prodigality** /-ˈgælɪtɪ/ *n.,* **prodigally** *adv.* [f. L *prodigus* lavish]

prodigious /prəˈdɪdʒəs/ *adj.* 1. marvellous. 2. enormous. 3. abnormal. —**prodigiously** *adv.* [f. L (as foll.)]

prodigy /ˈprɒdɪdʒɪ/ *n.* 1. a person with exceptional qualities or abilities, especially a precocious child. 2. a marvellous thing; a wonderful example of something. [f. L *prodigium* portent]

produce /prəˈdjuːs/ *v.t.* 1. to bring forward for consideration, inspection, or use. 2. to bring (a play or performance etc.) before the public; to be the producer of. 3. to manufacture (goods) from raw materials etc. 4. to bear or yield (offspring, fruit, a harvest, etc.); to bring into existence; to cause or bring about (a reaction etc.). 5. to extend or continue (a line). —/ˈprɒdjuːs/ *n.* what is produced, especially agricultural and natural products generally; the amount of this. [f. L *producere* (PRO-¹, *ducere* lead)]

producer /prəˈdjuːsə(r)/ *n.* 1. one who produces articles or agricultural products etc. (opp. *consumer*). 2. a person who directs the acting of a play. 3. a person in charge of the expenditure, schedule, and quality of a film or a broadcast programme. [f. prec.]

product /ˈprɒdʌkt/ *n.* 1. a thing or substance produced by a natural process or by manufacture. 2. a result. 3. a quantity obtained by multiplying. [as PRODUCE]

productive /prəˈdʌktɪv/ *adj.* 1. of or engaged in the production of goods; producing commodities of exchangeable value. 2. producing much. 3. (with *of*) producing, giving rise to. —**productively** *adv.,* **productiveness** *n.* [f. F or L (as PRODUCE)]

production /prəˈdʌkʃ(ə)n/ *n.* 1. producing; being produced or manufactured, especially in large quantities. 2. the total yield. 3. a thing produced, especially a literary or artistic work, a play or film, etc. [f. OF f. L (as prec.)]

productivity /prɒdʌkˈtɪvɪtɪ/ *n.* capacity to produce; effectiveness of productive effort, especially in industry. [f. prec.]

proem /ˈprəʊem/ *n.* an introductory discourse. [f. OF or L f. Gk *prooimion* (PRO-², *oimē* song)]

Prof. *abbr.* Professor.

profane /prəˈfeɪn/ *adj.* 1. not sacred, secular. 2. irreverent, blasphemous. —*v.t.* to treat (a sacred thing) with irreverence or disregard; to violate or pollute (what is entitled to respect). —**profanation** /-ˈneɪʃ(ə)n/ *n.,* **profanely** *adv.* [f. OF f. L, = before (i.e. outside) the temple]

profanity /prəˈfænɪtɪ/ *n.* a profane act or profane language, blasphemy. [f. prec.]

profess /prəˈfes/ *v.t.* 1. to claim openly to have (a quality or feeling); to pretend, to allege. 2. to declare. 3. to affirm one's faith in or allegiance to. [f. L *profitēri* declare publicly (PRO-¹, *fatēri* confess)]

professed /prəˈfest/ *adj.* 1. avowed, openly acknowledged

by oneself. 2. pretended, alleged. 3. having taken the vows of a religious order. —**professedly** *adv.* [f. prec.]

profession /prəˈfeʃ(ə)n/ *n.* 1. an occupation, especially in some branch of advanced learning or science. 2. the body of persons engaged in this. 3. a declaration, an avowal. [f. OF f. L (as PROFESS)]

professional *adj.* 1. of, belonging to, or connected with a profession. 2. having or showing the skill of a professional. 3. engaged in a specified activity as one's main paid occupation (often as distinct from *amateur*). —*n.* a professional person. —**professionalism** *n.,* **professionally** *adv.* [f. prec.]

professor /prəˈfesə(r)/ *n.* 1. a university teacher of the highest (in the USA, of high) rank. 2. one who makes a profession (of a religion etc.). —**professorial** /-ˈsɔːrɪəl/ *adj.,* **professorship** *n.* [f. OF or L (as PROFESS)]

proffer *v.t.* to offer. [f. AF (as PRO-¹, OFFER)]

proficient /prəˈfɪʃənt/ *adj.* able to do something correctly or competently through training or practice, skilled. —**proficiency** *n.,* **proficiently** *adv.* [f. L *proficere* make progress]

profile /ˈprəʊfaɪl/ *n.* 1. an outline (especially of a human face) as seen from one side; a representation of this. 2. a short biographical or character sketch. 3. a vertical cross-section of a structure or of layers of soil etc. —*v.t.* to represent in profile. —**keep a low profile,** to remain inconspicuous. [f. obs. It. *profilare* draw in outline]

profit /ˈprɒfɪt/ *n.* 1. an advantage or benefit obtained from doing something. 2. money gained in a business transaction; the excess of returns over outlay. —*v.t./i.* 1. to be beneficial (to). 2. to obtain an advantage or benefit. —**profit-sharing** *n.* the practice of allowing the employees of a company to share directly in its profits. [f. OF f. L *profectus* (as PROFICIENT)]

profitable *adj.* bringing profit or benefits. —**profitability** /-ˈbɪlɪtɪ/ *n.,* **profitably** *adv.* [f. prec.]

profiteer /prɒfɪˈtɪə(r)/ *v.t./i.* to make or seek excessive profits out of others' needs, especially in times of scarcity. —*n.* a person who profiteers. [f. PROFIT]

profiterole /prəˈfɪtərəʊl/ *n.* a small hollow cake of choux pastry with sweet or savoury filling. [F. dim. of *profit* (as PROFIT)]

profligate /ˈprɒflɪgət/ *adj.* 1. licentious, dissolute. 2. recklessly wasteful or extravagant. —*n.* a profligate person. —**profligacy** *n.* [f. L *profligare* overthrow, ruin)]

pro forma /prəʊ ˈfɔːmə/ 1. for form's sake. 2. (in full **pro forma invoice**) an invoice sent to a purchaser in advance of the goods for the completion of business formalities. [L]

profound /prəˈfaʊnd/ *adj.* 1. having or showing great knowledge or insight into a subject. 2. requiring much study or thought. 3. deep, intense; far-reaching. —**profoundly** *adv.,* **profundity** /-ˈfʌndɪtɪ/ *n.* [f. OF f. L *profundus* deep]

profuse /prəˈfjuːs/ *adj.* 1. lavish, extravagant. 2. plentiful. —**profusely** *adv.,* **profuseness** *n.,* **profusion** /-ˈfjuːʒ(ə)n/ *n.* [f. L *profusus* (PRO-¹, *fundere* pour)]

progenitor /prəˈdʒenɪtə(r)/ *n.* an ancestor; a predecessor, an original. [f. OF f. L (PRO-¹, *gignere* beget)]

progeny /ˈprɒdʒənɪ/ *n.* 1. offspring. 2. an outcome. [f. OF f. L *progenies* (as prec.)]

progesterone /prəʊˈdʒestərəʊn/ *n.* a sex hormone causing uterine changes in the latter part of the menstrual cycle and maintaining pregnancy. [f. G (as PRO-², GESTATION, STEROID)]

prognosis /prɒgˈnəʊsɪs/ *n.* (*pl.* **-oses** /-iːz/) a forecast or advance indication, especially of the course of a disease. [L f. Gk (PRO-², *gignōskō* know)]

prognostic /prɒgˈnɒstɪk/ *n.* an advance indication or omen; a prediction. —*adj.* foretelling, predictive. [f. OF f. L f. Gk (as prec.)]

prognosticate /prɒgˈnɒstɪkeɪt/ *v.t.* to foretell or foresee; (of a thing) to betoken. —**prognostication** /-ˈkeɪʃ(ə)n/ *n.,* **prognosticator** *n.* [f. L (as PROGNOSIS)]

programmable *adj.* that may be programmed. [f. foll.]

programme /ˈprəʊgræm/ *n.* (*US* & in computing **program**) *n.* 1. a plan of intended procedure. 2. a descriptive list or notice of a series of events; these events. 3. a broadcast performance or entertainment. 4. **program,** a series of instructions to control the operation of a computer. —*v.t.* (**-mm-**) 1. to make a programme of. 2. **program,** to express (a problem) or instruct (a computer etc.) by means of a program. —**programmatic** /-ˈmætɪk/ *adj.,* **programmer** *n.* [f. L f. Gk (*prographō* write publicly)]

progress /ˈprəʊgres/ n. **1.** forward or onward movement. **2.** an advance or development, especially to a better state. **3.** (archaic) a State journey, especially by a royal person. — /prəˈgres/ v.t./i. **1.** to move forward or onward. **2.** to advance or develop, especially to a better state. **3.** to deal with at successive stages. —**in progress,** taking place, in the course of occurrence. [f. L progressus (progredi go forward)]

progression /prəˈgreʃ(ə)n/ n. **1.** progressing. **2.** a succession or series. [f. OF or L (as prec.)]

progressive /prəˈgresɪv/ adj. **1.** making continuous forward movement. **2.** proceeding steadily or in regular degrees. **3.** favouring political or social reform; advancing in social conditions, efficiency, etc. **4.** (of a disease etc.) continuously increasing in severity or extent. **5.** (of a card-game, dance, etc.) with a periodic change of partners. **6.** (of taxation) at rates increasing with the sum taxed. **7.** (Gram., of a tense) expressing an action in progress. —n. an advocate of a progressive policy. —**progressively** adv., **progressiveness** n. [f. F or L (as PROGRESS)]

prohibit /prəˈhɪbɪt/ v.t. to forbid or prevent. —**prohibited degrees,** see DEGREE. —**prohibitor** n., **prohibitory** adj. [f. L prohibēre]

prohibition /prəʊhɪˈbɪʃ(ə)n, prəʊɪ-/ n. **1.** forbidding, being forbidden. **2.** an edict or order that forbids something. **3.** the forbidding by law of the manufacture and sale of intoxicants, especially (**Prohibition**) that established in the USA in 1919, after a long campaign, by the 18th Amendment to the Constitution, and repealed in 1933 by the 21st Amendment. [f. OF or L (as prec.)]

prohibitionist n. an advocate of legal prohibition. [f. prec.]

prohibitive /prəˈhɪbɪtɪv/ adj. prohibiting; (of prices, costs, taxes, etc.) extremely high. —**prohibitively** adv. [f. F or L (as PROHIBIT)]

project /ˈprɒdʒekt/ n. **1.** a plan or scheme; a planned undertaking. **2.** a task set as an educational exercise, requiring students to do their own research and present the results. —/prəˈdʒekt/ v.t./i. **1.** to plan or contrive (a scheme etc.). **2.** to cause (a light, shadow, or image) to fall on a surface. **3.** to send or throw outward or forward. **4.** to extend outwards from a surface. **5.** to imagine (a thing or person or oneself) as having another's feelings, being in another situation or in the future, etc.; to attribute (one's own feelings) to another person or thing, esp. unconsciously. **6.** to extrapolate (results to a future time etc.). **7.** to make a projection (of the earth or sky etc.). [f. L projicere throw forward (PRO-¹, jacere throw)]

projectile /prəˈdʒektaɪl/ n. an object to be hurled or projected forcibly, especially from a gun. —adj. of or serving as a projectile. [as prec.]

projection /prəˈdʒekʃ(ə)n/ n. **1.** projecting, being projected. **2.** a thing that projects from a surface. **3.** a representation on a plane surface of (any part of) the surface of the earth or of a celestial sphere. **4.** a mental image viewed as objective reality. [as PROJECT]

projectionist n. a person who operates a projector. [f. prec.]

projector /prəˈdʒektə(r)/ n. an apparatus for projecting the image of a film etc. on a screen. [f. PROJECT]

Prokofiev /prəˈkɒfief/, Sergei (1891–1953), Russian composer. His gifts as a composer revealed themselves early, together with a talent for iconoclasm which brought him both fame and a certain notoriety. The wit and vigour of his opera *The Love for Three Oranges* (1921), and the *Lieutenant Kijé* suite (1934), stand in contrast to the opera *War and Peace* (begun 1941), the later symphonies including the deeply pessimistic Sixth (1945–7), and the romantic and widely popular ballet music for *Romeo and Juliet* (1935–6). *Peter and the Wolf* (1936) is perhaps his best-known work, an enduring, touching, and instructive young persons' guide to the orchestra.

prolapse /ˈprəʊlæps/ n. (also **prolapsus**) the slipping forward or downward of a part or organ, especially of the womb or rectum. —/prəˈlæps/ v.i. to undergo a prolapse. [f. L (PRO-¹, labi slip)]

prolate /ˈprəʊleɪt/ adj. (of a spheroid) lengthened along the polar diameter. [f. L, = brought forward, prolonged]

prolegomena /prəʊlɪˈgɒmɪnə/ n.pl. a preliminary discourse or matter prefixed to a book etc. [L f. Gk, neut. pass. partic. of prolegō say beforehand]

proletarian /prəʊlɪˈteərɪən/ adj. of the proletariat. —n. a member of the proletariat. [f. L, = one who served the State not with property but with offspring (proles)]

proletariat /prəʊlɪˈteərɪət/ n. the working class (contrasted with the bourgeoisie). [f. F (as prec.)]

proliferate /prəˈlɪfəreɪt/ v.t./i. **1.** to reproduce itself or grow by the multiplication of elementary parts; to produce (cells) thus. **2.** to increase rapidly in numbers etc. —**proliferation** /-ˈreɪʃ(ə)n/ n. [f. F f. L proles offspring, ferre bear]

prolific /prəˈlɪfɪk/ adj. producing much offspring or output; abundantly productive. —**prolifically** adv. [f. L (as prec.)]

prolix /ˈprəʊlɪks/ adj. lengthy, tediously wordy. —**prolixity** /prəˈlɪksɪtɪ/ n. [f. OF or L prolixus long, extended]

prologue /ˈprəʊlɒg/ n. **1.** an introduction to a poem or play etc. **2.** an act or event serving as an introduction. [f. OF f. L f. Gk (as PRO-², logos speech)]

prolong /prəˈlɒŋ/ v.t. to extend in duration or spatial length. —**prolongation** /prəʊlɒŋˈgeɪʃ(ə)n/ n. [f. OF & L prolongare (PRO-¹, longus long)]

prom n. (colloq.) **1.** a promenade. **2.** a promenade concert. [abbr.]

promenade /prɒməˈnɑːd/ n. **1.** a public place for walking, especially a paved area along the sea front in a seaside town. **2.** a leisurely walk, especially for pleasure. —v.t./i. **1.** to take a leisurely walk (through). **2.** to lead (a person) about a place, especially for display. —**promenade concert,** a concert with an area for a part of the audience to stand and move about. The most famous series of such concerts is the annual BBC Promenade Concerts ('the Proms'), instituted by Sir Henry Wood, and held (since the Second World War) in the Albert Hall. **promenade deck,** the upper deck on a passenger ship. [F (se promener walk)]

Prometheus /prəˈmiːθɪəs/ (Gk myth.) a demigod, one of the Titans, who was worshipped by craftsmen. The two principal tales told of him are (i) that when Zeus hid fire away from man Prometheus stole it by trickery and brought it to earth again, (ii) to punish him Zeus chained him to a rock where an eagle fed each day on his liver which (since he was immortal) grew again each night; he was rescued by Hercules.

promethium /prəˈmiːθɪəm/ n. a radioactive metallic element of the lanthanide series, symbol Pm, atomic number 61. Not found in nature, it was first synthesized in a nuclear reactor in the 1940s. Its radiation has been used to power miniature batteries. [f. prec.]

prominence /ˈprɒmɪnəns/ n. **1.** being prominent. **2.** a prominent thing. [obs. F f. L (as foll.)]

prominent adj. **1.** jutting out, projecting. **2.** conspicuous. **3.** distinguished, well-known. —**prominently** adv. [f. L prominēre project (cf. EMINENT)]

promiscuous /prəˈmɪskjʊəs/ adj. **1.** having casual sexual relations with many people. **2.** casual, indiscriminate. **3.** of mixed and indiscriminate composition or kinds. —**promiscuity** /prɒmɪˈskjuːɪtɪ/ n., **promiscuously** adv. [f. L promiscuus (PRO-¹, miscēre mix)]

promise /ˈprɒmɪs/ n. **1.** an assurance as to what one will or will not do, or of help or giving something. **2.** an indication of something that may be expected to come or occur. **3.** an indication of future achievement or good result. —v.t./i. **1.** to make a promise, to give an assurance; to give (a person) a promise of (a thing); (colloq.) to assure. **2.** to seem likely. —**promised land,** Canaan, promised by God to Abraham and his descendants (Gen. 17: 8); any place of expected happiness. [f. L promissum (promittere send forth, promise)]

promising adj. likely to turn out well or produce good results. —**promisingly** adv. [f. prec.]

promissory /ˈprɒmɪsərɪ/ adj. conveying or implying a promise. —**promissory note,** a signed document containing a written promise to pay a stated sum. [as PROMISE]

promontory /ˈprɒməntərɪ/ n. a point of high land jutting out into the sea etc., a headland. [f. L promunturium (perh. f. PRO-¹, mons mountain)]

promote /prəˈməʊt/ v.t. **1.** to raise (a person) to a higher rank or office. **2.** to help forward or encourage (an enterprise or result). **3.** to publicize (a product) in order to sell it. **4.** to initiate (a project). **5.** to take the necessary steps for the passing of (a private bill in Parliament). —**promotion** n., **promotional** adj. [f. L promovēre (as PRO-¹, movēre move)]

promoter n. one who promotes an enterprise financially, especially the formation of a joint-stock company or the holding of a sporting event etc. [f. prec.]

prompt adj. **1.** acting or done without delay or at once. **2.** punctual. —adv. punctually. —v.t. **1.** to incite or urge (a person) to action. **2.** to inspire or give rise to (a feeling or action). **3.** to help (an actor etc., or absol.) by supplying the words that come next; to assist (a hesitant person) with a suggestion etc. —*n.* a thing said to help the memory, especially of an actor. —**prompt side,** the side of a stage (usually to the actors' left) where the prompter is placed. —**promptitude** *n.*, **promptly** *adv.*, **promptness** *n.* [f. OF or L (*promere* produce)]

prompter *n.* a person (placed out of sight of the audience) who prompts the actors on a stage. [f. prec.]

promulgate /ˈprɒməlgeɪt/ *v.t.* to make known to the public, to disseminate; to proclaim (a decree or news). —**promulgation** /-ˈgeɪ(ə)n/ *n.*, **promulgator** *n.* [f. L *promulgare* (PRO-¹, *mulgēre* milk, cause to come forth)]

prone *adj.* **1.** lying face downwards (opp. *supine*); lying flat, prostrate. **2.** disposed (*to*), liable or likely (*to*). —**proneness** *n.* [f. L *pronus* (*pro* forwards)]

prong *n.* each of the two or more projecting pointed parts at the end of a fork etc. [perh. rel. to MLG *prange* pinching instrument]

pronged *adj.* having a specified number or kind of prongs. [f. prec.]

pronominal /prəˈnɒmɪn(ə)l/ *adj.* of or of the nature of a pronoun. [f. L (as foll.)]

pronoun /ˈprəʊnaʊn/ *n.* **1.** a word used instead of a noun to designate (without naming) a person or thing. **2.** a pronominal adjective. [f. PRO-¹ + NOUN, after L *pronomen*]

pronounce /prəˈnaʊns/ *v.t./i.* **1.** to utter (a word or speech-sound) distinctly or correctly or in a specified way. **2.** to utter or declare formally. **3.** to declare as one's opinion; to pass judgement. [f. OF f. L *pronuntiare* (PRO-¹, *nuntiare* announce)]

pronounceable *adj.* (of a word etc.) that may be pronounced. [f. prec.]

pronounced *adj.* noticeable, strongly marked. [f. PRONOUNCE]

pronouncement *n.* a formal statement, a declaration. [as prec.]

pronto /ˈprɒntəʊ/ *adv.* (*slang*) promptly, quickly. [Sp. f. L, = prompt]

pronunciation /prənʌnsɪˈeɪʃ(ə)n/ *n.* the way in which a word is pronounced; a person's way of pronouncing words. [f. OF or L (as PRONUNCIATE)]

proof *n.* **1.** a fact or thing that shows or helps to show that something is true or exists. **2.** a demonstration of the truth of something. **3.** the process of testing whether something is true, good, or valid. **4.** a standard of strength for distilled alcoholic liquors. **5.** a trial impression of printed matter, produced for correction. **6.** a trial print of a photograph. —*adj.* impervious to penetration, damage, or undesired action. —*v.t.* **1.** to make a proof of (printed matter). **2.** to make (a thing) proof, against something; to make (a fabric etc.) waterproof. — **-proof** *in comb.* in the sense 'impervious', 'resistant', forming adjectives (*bullet-proof*; *waterproof*) and verbs (*soundproof*). —**proof-read** *v.t.* to read and correct (printed proofs). **proof-reader** *n.* a person who does this. **proof spirit,** a mixture of alcohol and water having a standard strength. [f. OF f. L *proba* (as PROVE)]

prop¹ *n.* **1.** a rigid support, especially not a structural part of the thing supported. **2.** a person etc. depended on for help or support. —*v.t.* (**-pp-**) to support (as) with a prop (often with *up*). [prob. f. MDu.]

prop² *n.* (*colloq.*) an aircraft propeller. [abbr.]

prop³ *n.* (*colloq.*) a stage property in a theatre. [abbr.]

propaganda /prɒpəˈgændə/ *n.* publicity intended to spread ideas or information; (usu. *derog.*) the ideas etc. thus propagated. —**propagandist** *n.* [It. f. L *congregatio de propaganda fide,* title of RC committee in charge of foreign missions (as foll.)]

propagate /ˈprɒpəgeɪt/ *v.t./i.* **1.** to breed or reproduce from parent stock. **2.** to disseminate (news or ideas etc.). **3.** to transmit (a vibration, earthquake, etc.). **4.** to be propagated. —**propagation** /-ˈgeɪʃ(ə)n/ *n.*, **propagator** *n.* [f. L *propagare* multiply plants from layers (PRO-¹, *pangere* fix, layer)]

propane /ˈprəʊpeɪn/ *n.* a hydrocarbon of the paraffin series. [f. *propionic acid* (PRO-², Gk *piōn* fat)]

propel /prəˈpel/ *v.t.* (**-ll-**) to drive or push forward, to give onward motion to. —**propellent** *adj.* [f. L *propellere* (PRO-¹, *pellere* drive)]

propellant *n.* a propelling agent. [f. prec.]

propeller *n.* (in full **screw-propeller**) a device with blades on a revolving shaft for propelling a ship or aircraft to which it is fitted. [f. PROPEL]

propensity /prəˈpensɪtɪ/ *n.* an inclination or tendency. [f. L *propensus* inclined]

proper /ˈprɒpə(r)/ *adj.* **1.** suitable, appropriate. **2.** correct, according to rules. **3.** respectable, in conformity with social standards or conventions. **4.** real or genuine; rightly so called; (usu. placed after the noun) strictly so called. **5.** belonging or relating exclusively or distinctively (*to*). **6.** (*colloq.*) thorough, complete. —**proper fraction,** a fraction less than unity, with the numerator less than the denominator. **proper name** *or* **noun,** the name of an individual person, place, or thing. —**properly** *adv.* [f. OF f. L *proprius* one's own]

propertied /ˈprɒpətɪd/ *adj.* having property, especially of real estate. [f. foll.]

Propertius /prəˈpɜːʃəs/, Sextus (*c.*50–after 16 BC), Roman poet from Assisi. His four books of elegies are largely concerned with the joys and sufferings of his love-affair with Cynthia, though the later poems also deal with mythological and historical themes. He is noted for the intensity of his love-poems and for the energetic wit and occasional obscurity of his style.

property /ˈprɒpətɪ/ *n.* **1.** a thing or things owned. **2.** real estate, a person's land or house etc. **3.** a movable object used on a theatre stage or in a film etc. [f. OF f. L *proprietas* (as PROPER)]

prophecy /ˈprɒfɪsɪ/ *n.* **1.** the power of prophesying. **2.** a prophetic utterance. **3.** the foretelling of future events. [as PROPHET]

prophesy /ˈprɒfɪsaɪ/ *v.t./i.* to speak as a prophet; to foretell future events; to foretell. [f. OF *profecier* (as foll.)]

prophet /ˈprɒfɪt/ *n.* **1.** an inspired teacher, a person regarded as revealing or interpreting divine will. **2.** any of the prophetical writers in the Old Testament; **the Prophets,** their writings. **3.** one who foretells events. **4.** a spokesman or advocate of a principle etc. —**major prophets,** Isaiah, Jeremiah, Ezekiel, Daniel. **minor prophets,** Hosea to Malachi, whose surviving writings are not lengthy. **the Prophet,** Muhammad. —**prophetess** *n.fem.* [f. OF f. L f. Gk, orig. = spokesman (PRO-², *phēmi* speak)]

prophetic /prəˈfetɪk/ *adj.* (also **prophetical**) **1.** of a prophet. **2.** predicting or containing a prediction of (an event etc.). —**prophetically** *adv.* [f. F or L f. Gk (as prec.)]

prophylactic /prɒfɪˈlæktɪk/ *adj.* tending to prevent a disease or other misfortune. —*n.* a prophylactic medicine or course of action. —**prophylactically** *adv.* [f. F f. Gk (PRO-², *phulassō* guard)]

prophylaxis /prɒfɪˈlæksɪs/ *n.* preventive treatment against a disease etc. [f. PRO-² + Gk *phulaxis* guarding]

propinquity /prəˈpɪŋkwɪtɪ/ *n.* **1.** nearness in place. **2.** close kinship. [f. OF or L (*propinquus* near)]

propitiate /prəˈpɪʃɪeɪt/ *v.t.* to win the favour or forgiveness of, to placate. —**propitiation** /-ˈeɪʃ(ə)n/ *n.* [f. L *propitiare* (as PROPITIOUS)]

propitiatory /prəˈpɪʃətərɪ/ *adj.* serving or intended to propitiate. [as prec.]

propitious /prəˈpɪʃəs/ *adj.* favourable, giving a good omen or a suitable opportunity. —**propitiously** *adv.* [f. OF or L *propitius*]

proponent /prəˈpəʊnənt/ *n.* a person who puts forward a proposal; a person who supports a cause etc. [f. L *proponere* (as PROPOUND)]

proportion /prəˈpɔːʃ(ə)n/ *n.* **1.** a fraction or comparative share of a whole. **2.** a ratio. **3.** the correct relation in size, amount, or degree between one thing and another or between a thing's parts. **4.** (in *pl.*) dimensions, size. —*v.t.* to give correct proportions to; to make (one thing) proportionate to another. —**proportionment** *n.* [f. OF or L (as PRO-¹, PORTION)]

proportional *adj.* in correct proportion; corresponding in size, amount, or degree. —**proportional representation,** an electoral system in which each party is allocated a number of seats in proportion to the number of votes for its candidates. —**proportionally** *adv.* [f. L (as prec.)]

proportionate /prəˈpɔːʃənət/ *adj.* in due proportion. —**proportionately** *adv.* [f. prec.]

proposal /prəˈpəʊz(ə)l/ *n.* **1.** the proposing of something. **2.** a course of action etc. proposed. **3.** an offer of marriage. [f. foll.]

propose /prəˈpəʊz/ *v.t./i.* **1.** to put forward for consideration. **2.** to have and declare as one's plan or intention; to make a proposal. **3.** to make an offer of marriage. **4.** to offer (a person or a person's health) as the subject for the drinking of a toast. **5.** to nominate (a person) as a member of a society etc. [f. OF f. L (as PROPOUND)]

proposition /prɒpə'zıʃ(ə)n/ *n.* **1.** a proposal, a scheme proposed. **2.** a statement, an assertion. **3.** (*colloq.*) a thing to be considered, dealt with, or undertaken. **4.** a formal statement of a theorem or problem, often including a demonstration. —*v.t.* (*colloq.*) to put a proposal to; to suggest extramarital sexual intercourse to. [f. OF or L (as foll.)]

propound /prə'paʊnd/ *v.t.* to put forward for consideration. —**propounder** *n.* [f. L *proponere*, lit. = place in front]

proprietary /prə'praıətərı/ *adj.* **1.** of a proprietor. **2.** holding property. **3.** held in private ownership. **4.** manufactured and sold by one particular firm, usually under a patent. [f. L *proprietarius* (as PROPERTY)]

proprietor /prə'praıətə(r)/ *n.* the holder of a property; the owner of a business. —**proprietorial** /-'tɔ:rıəl/ *adj.*, **proprietress** *n.fem.* [f. prec.]

propriety /prə'praıtı/ *n.* **1.** being proper or suitable. **2.** correctness of behaviour or morals. **3.** (in *pl.*) the details of correct conduct. [f. OF, = PROPERTY]

propulsion /prə'pʌlʃ(ə)n/ *n.* driving or pushing forward. —**propulsive** *adj.* [f. obs. *propulse* v. f. L *propulsare* frequent. of *propellere* propel]

propulsor /prə'pʌlsə(r)/ *n.* a ducted propeller which can be swivelled to give forward, upward, or downward flight to an airship (ill. FLIGHT). [as prec.]

pro rata /prəʊ 'rɑ:tə/ proportional; in proportion. [L, = according to the rate]

prorogue /prə'rəʊg/ *v.t./i.* to discontinue the meetings of (a parliament etc.) without dissolving it; (of a parliament etc.) to be prorogued. —**prorogation** /prəʊrə'geıʃ(ə)n/ *n.* [f. OF f. L *prorogare* prolong (PRO-¹, *rogare* ask)]

prosaic /prə'zeıık/ *adj.* **1.** like prose, lacking in poetic beauty. **2.** unromantic, commonplace, dull. —**prosaically** *adv.* [f. F or L (as PROSE)]

proscenium /prəʊ'si:nıəm/ *n.* (*pl.* **-s**) the part of a theatre stage in front of a drop or curtain, especially with the enclosing arch (ill. THEATRE). [L f. Gk (as PRO-², SCENE)]

proscribe /prə'skraıb/ *v.t.* **1.** to forbid by law. **2.** to denounce as dangerous etc. **3.** to put (a person) outside the protection of the law; to banish, to exile. —**proscription** /-'skrıpʃ(ə)n/ *n.*, **proscriptive** /-'skrıptıv/ *adj.* [f. L *proscribere* (PRO-¹, *scribere* write)]

prose /prəʊz/ *n.* **1.** written or spoken language not in verse form. **2.** dull or matter-of-fact quality. —*v.i.* to talk tediously. —**prose poem,** an elevated prose composition. [f. OF f. L *prosa* (*oratio*) straightforward discourse (*prorsus* direct)]

prosecute /'prɒsıkju:t/ *v.t.* **1.** to institute legal proceedings against (a person, or *absol.*) or with reference to (a crime or claim etc.). **2.** to carry on or be occupied with. [f. L *prosequi* (PRO-¹, *sequi* follow)]

prosecution /prɒsı'kju:ʃ(ə)n/ *n.* **1.** the institution and carrying on of legal proceedings. **2.** the prosecuting party. **3.** prosecuting, being prosecuted. [f. OF or L (as prec.)]

prosecutor /'prɒsıkju:tə(r)/ *n.* one who prosecutes, especially in a criminal court. [f. PROSECUTE]

proselyte /'prɒsılaıt/ *n.* **1.** a person converted from one opinion or belief etc. to another. **2.** a Gentile convert to the Jewish faith. [f. L f. Gk (*proserkhomai* come to a place)]

proselytism /'prɒsılıtız(ə)m/ *n.* **1.** being a proselyte. **2.** the practice of proselytizing. [f. prec.]

proselytize /'prɒsılıtaız/ *v.t.* to seek to make a proselyte of (a person, or *absol.*). [f. PROSELYTE]

Proserpine /'prɒsə:pıni/ the Roman name for Persephone.

prosody /'prɒsədı/ *n.* the science of versification; the study of speech-rhythms. —**prosodic** /prə'sɒdık/ *adj.*, **prosodically** /prə'sɒdıkəlı/ *adv.*, **prosodist** *n.* [f. L f. Gk (*pros* to, as ODE)]

prospect /'prɒspekt/ *n.* **1.** what one is to expect; a chance (of success etc.). **2.** an extensive view of a landscape etc.; a mental scene or view of matters. **3.** (*colloq.*) a possible or likely customer etc. —/prə'spekt/ *v.t./i.* to explore or search (for gold etc.); to look out *for.* —**prospector** /prə'spektə(r)/ *n.* [f. L, = PROSPECTUS]

prospective /prə'spektıv/ *adj.* expected to be or occur; future, possible. [f. obs. F or L (as prec.)]

prospectus /prə'spektəs/ *n.* a printed document describing the chief features of a school or business etc. [L, = prospect (*prospicere* look forward)]

prosper /'prɒspə(r)/ *v.i.* to be successful, to thrive. [f. obs. F or L *prosperare* (as PROSPEROUS)]

prosperity /prɒ'sperıtı/ *n.* prosperous state or condition, wealth. [f. foll.]

prosperous /'prɒspərəs/ *adj.* **1.** financially successful, thriving. **2.** auspicious. —**prosperously** *adv.* [f. obs. F f. L *prosperus*]

prostate /'prɒsteıt/ *n.* (in full **prostate gland**) the large gland round the neck of the bladder, accessory to the male genital organs (ill. BODY 2). —**prostatic** /-'tætık/ *adj.* [F f. Gk *prostatēs* one who stands before]

prosthesis /'prɒsθısıs/ *n.* (*pl.* **-theses** /-i:z/) **1.** the making up of bodily deficiencies, e.g. by an artificial limb. **2.** a part supplied for this. —**prosthetic** /-'θetık/ *adj.* [L f. Gk, = placing in addition]

prostitute /'prɒstıtju:t/ *n.* a woman who engages in sexual intercourse for payment; a man who engages in homosexual acts for payment. —*v.t.* to make a prostitute of (esp. *oneself*); to sell or make use of (one's honour or abilities etc.) unworthily. —**prostitution** /-'tju:ʃ(ə)n/ *n.* [f. L *prostituere* offer for sale (PRO-¹, *statuere* set up)]

prostrate /'prɒstreıt/ *adj.* **1.** lying with one's face to the ground, especially in submission or humility. **2.** lying in a horizontal position. **3.** overcome, overthrown. **4.** physically exhausted. —/prɒ'streıt/ *v.t.* **1.** to throw (oneself) down prostrate. **2.** to overcome, to make submissive. **3.** (of fatigue etc.) to reduce to extreme physical weakness. —**prostration** /prɒ'streıʃ(ə)n/ *n.* [f. L *prosternere* (PRO-¹, *sternere* lay flat)]

prosy /'prəʊzı/ *adj.* prosaic, dull. —**prosily** *adv.*, **prosiness** *n.* [f. PROSE]

protactinium /prəʊtæk'tınıəm/ *n.* a naturally-occurring radioactive metallic element, symbol Pa, atomic number 91, first discovered in 1913. It is so named because one of its isotopes decays to form actinium. [G (as PROTO- + ACTINIUM)]

protagonist /prəʊ'tægənıst/ *n.* **1.** the chief person in a drama or the plot of a story; the principal performer. **2.** (**D**) a champion or advocate of a course or method etc. [f. Gk (PROTO-, *agonistēs* actor)]

protean /'prəʊtıən, -'ti:ən/ *adj.* variable, versatile; taking many forms. [f. PROTEUS]

protect /prə'tekt/ *v.t.* **1.** to keep from harm or injury. **2.** to guard (a home industry) against competition by import duties on foreign goods. [f. L *protegere* (PRO-¹, *tegere* cover)]

protection /prə'tekʃ(ə)n/ *n.* **1.** protecting, being protected. **2.** a person or thing that protects. **3.** the system of protecting home industries. **4.** immunity from molestation obtained by payment under threat of violence; money so paid. [f. OF or L (as prec.)]

protectionism *n.* the principle or practice of economic protection. —**protectionist** *n.* [f. prec.]

protective *adj.* protecting; giving or intended for protection. —**protective custody,** the detention of a person actually or allegedly for his own protection. —**protectively** *adv.* [f. PROTECT]

protector *n.* **1.** a person or thing that protects. **2.** a regent in charge of a kingdom during the minority or absence of a sovereign. **3. Protector,** the title taken by Oliver Cromwell during his government of Britain in 1653-8, and passed on to his son (see foll.). —**protectorship** *n.*, **protectress** *n.fem.* [f. OF f. L (as PROTECT)]

protectorate /prə'tektərət/ *n.* **1.** the office of protector of a kingdom or State, especially that under the Cromwells in 1653-9 (see below). **2.** protectorship of a weak or under-developed State by a stronger one; a State thus protected. [f. prec.]

Oliver Cromwell was appointed Lord Protector in December 1653 at the behest of the army and retained the position until his death in September 1658. Although the Protectorate achieved considerable success in foreign wars, it depended almost entirely on its leader's personality at home and was continually threatened by the unstable relationship between the Protector, Parliament, and the army. After the elder Cromwell's death his son Richard proved incapable of holding the regime together, and its subsequent collapse led to the restoration of Charles II.

protégé /'prɒteʒeı/ *n.* a person to whom another is protector or patron. —**protégée** *n.fem.* [F (as PROTECT)]

protein /'prəʊti:n/ *n.* any of a class of large molecules which form an essential part of all living things. They have many different functions. Some form strong fibres and hold the skeleton together, others are enzymes (see ENZYME), others again are antibodies which prevent disease. Proteins are made from about twenty amino acids which are arranged in different orders in long chains. One or a small number of such chains make one protein molecule, which may be of fibrous or globular shape depending on the type and order of the amino acids present. The information needed for the synthesis of particular proteins comes from the DNA in a cell's nucleus. [f. F & G f. Gk *prōteios* primary]

pro tem /prəʊ ˈtem/ (*colloq.*) pro tempore. [abbr.]

pro tempore /prəʊ ˈtempərɪ/ for the time being. [L]

protest /prəˈtest/ *v.t./i.* **1.** to express disapproval or dissent; (*US*) to object to (a decision etc.). **2.** to declare solemnly or firmly, especially in reply to an accusation etc. **3.** to write or obtain a protest in regard to (a bill). —/ˈprəʊtest/ *n.* **1.** a formal statement or action of disapproval or dissent. **2.** a written declaration that a bill has been presented and payment or acceptance refused. —**under protest**, unwillingly and after making protests. —**protestor** /prəˈtestə(r)/ *n.* [f. OF f. L *protestari* (PRO-¹, *testari* assert on oath)]

Protestant /ˈprɒtɪst(ə)nt/ *n.* **1.** a member or adherent of any of the Christian bodies that separated from the Roman communion in the Reformation (16th c.), or their offshoots. **2.** (*hist.*, in *pl.*) those German princes and free cities who made a declaration (*Protestatio*) of dissent from the decision of the Diet of Spires (1529) which reaffirmed the edict of the Diet of Worms against the Reformation. —**Protestantism** *n.* [f. L (as prec.)]
In the 16th c., the name 'Protestant' was generally taken in Germany by the Lutherans, while the Swiss and French called themselves 'Reformed'. In England the use has varied with time and circumstances. In the 17th c., 'Protestant' was generally accepted and used by members of the Established Church, and was even so applied to the exclusion of Presbyterians, Quakers, and Separatists; it was primarily opposed to 'papist'. Later, it was opposed to 'Roman Catholic' or to 'Catholic', and was viewed with disfavour by those who laid stress on the claim of the Anglican Church to be equally Catholic with the Roman.

protestation /prɒteˈsteɪʃ(ə)n/ *n.* a solemn affirmation; a protest. [as PROTEST]

Proteus /ˈprəʊtjəs/ (*Gk myth.*) a minor sea-god with the power of assuming different shapes.

Protista /prəˈtɪstə/ *n.pl.* a kingdom of organisms (bacteria, protozoa, etc.) not distinguished as animals or plants. [f. Gk (*prōtos* first)]

proto- /ˈprəʊtə(ʊ)-/ *in comb.* first. [f. Gk (*prōtos* first)]

protocol /ˈprəʊtəkɒl/ *n.* **1.** official formality and etiquette; observance of this. **2.** the original draft of a diplomatic document, especially of the agreed terms of a treaty. —*v.t./i.* (-ll-) to draw up a protocol or protocols; to record in a protocol. [f. OF f. L f. Gk, = flyleaf (PROTO-, *kolla* glue)]

proton /ˈprəʊtɒn/ *n.* a positively charged elementary particle found in the nuclei of all atoms. The charge on the proton is equal and opposite to the charge on the electron, although the mass of the proton is 1,836 times greater. The atom of each chemical element has a characteristic number of protons in the nucleus; the common isotope of hydrogen has a nucleus consisting of a single proton. Protons are approximately 10^{-13} cm in diameter, although their size is not sharply defined. The atomic number of each atom is the number of protons it contains and this, together with an equal number of electrons, determines the chemical properties of the corresponding element. Protons, or positively charged ions, are partly responsible for heat radiation, for the conduction of electricity in electrolytes and in hot gases, and also for the gamma radiation from excited nuclei. High-velocity protons are used in particle accelerators to probe the structure of atomic nuclei. Protons were identified by W. Wien in 1898 and J. J. Thomson in 1910; they were named 'protons' by Rutherford in 1920. [f. Gk *prōtos* first, reflecting their character as primitive constituents of all atomic nuclei; also perhaps suggested by the name of William *Prout* (d. 1850), English chemist and physician, who suggested that hydrogen was a constituent of all the elements]

protoplasm /ˈprəʊtəplæz(ə)m/ *n.* the contents of a living cell. In the 19th c. protoplasm was thought of as a complex but essentially homogeneous form of matter having the basic properties of life such as irritability and metabolism. With the realization, especially after the invention of the electron microscope, that there is a complex structural organization within cells, the concept of protoplasm as a special substance has lost much of its significance.

—protoplasmic /-ˈplæzmɪk/ *adj.* [f. Gk (as PROTO-, PLASMA)]

protoplast /ˈprəʊtəplæst/ *n.* (*Biol.*) the contents of a cell after the cell wall has been removed. [f. F or L f. Gk (PROTO-, *plastos* moulded; cf. PLASMA)]

prototype /ˈprəʊtətaɪp/ *n.* an original thing or person in relation to a copy or imitation or developed form; a trial model, a preliminary version (e.g. of an aeroplane). [F or f. L f. Gk (as PROTO-, TYPE)]

protozoon /prəʊtəˈzəʊən/ *n.* (*pl.* **-zoa**) an animal of the subkingdom or phylum Protozoa, usually unicellular and microscopic. First observed by Leeuwenhoek in the 17th c., protozoa are ubiquitous in aquatic and damp habitats and there are numerous parasitic species, among them the trypanosomes which cause sleeping sickness, and the malaria parasite. Protozoa display a great variety of form; important groups include the flagellates, amoebas, and ciliates, and some bear shells, the residue of which forms a significant proportion of some limestone rocks. —**protozoan** *adj. & n.* [as PROTO- + Gk *zōion* animal]

protract /prəˈtrækt/ *v.t.* to prolong in duration. —**protraction** *n.* [f. L *protrahere* (PRO-¹, *trahere* draw)]

protractor *n.* an instrument for measuring angles, usually a semicircle marked off in degrees. [f. prec.]

protrude /prəˈtruːd/ *v.t./i.* to project or cause to project from a surface; to thrust forward. —**protrusion** *n.*, **protrusive** /-ˈtruːsɪv/ *adj.* [f. L *protrudere* (PRO-¹, *trudere* thrust)]

protuberant /prəˈtjuːbərənt/ *adj.* bulging out, prominent. —**protuberance** *n.* [f. L (PRO-¹, *tuber* bump)]

proud *adj.* **1.** feeling or showing justifiable pride; marked by or causing such feeling. **2.** feeling oneself greatly honoured. **3.** full of self-respect and indignation. **4.** having an unduly high opinion of one's own qualities or merits. **5.** (of a thing) imposing, splendid. **6.** slightly projecting; (of flesh) overgrown round a healing wound. —**do a person proud**, to treat him with great generosity or honour. —**proudly** *adv.* [OE f. OF *prud* valiant]

Proudhon /pruːˈdɔ̃/, Pierre Joseph (1809–65), French social reformer, largely self-educated, whose writings argue that property is theft and that for a just society orderly anarchy should replace government.

Proust /pruːst/, Marcel (1871–1922), French novelist, essayist, and critic. In the 1890s he moved in the most fashionable Paris circles. Severe asthma precluded any regular profession; his neurotic disposition, aggravated by efforts to conceal his homosexuality, made him a virtual recluse in his later years. He published a collection of essays, poems, and stories, *Les Plaisirs et les jours* (1896), translations of Ruskin whose artistic ideas influenced his own; he was also influenced by the philosophy of Bergson. Proust explored his own literary aesthetic in *Contre Sainte-Beuve* (1954) where he defines the artist's task as the releasing of creative energies of past experience from the unconscious, an aesthetic which found its most developed literary expression in his novel *À la recherche du temps perdu* (1913–27) which occupied him from *c.*1907 until his death.

provable /ˈpruːvəb(ə)l/ *adj.* that may be proved. —**provability** /-ˈbɪlɪtɪ/ *n.* [f. foll.]

prove /pruːv/ *v.t./i.* **1.** to give or be proof of. **2.** to be found to be, to emerge as. **3.** to establish the validity of (a will). **4.** to rise or cause (dough) to rise. **5.** (*archaic*) to test the qualities of. —**not proven**, (*Sc. Law*) the evidence is insufficient to establish guilt or innocence. **prove oneself**, to demonstrate one's abilities etc. [f. OF f. L *probare* test, demonstrate (*probus* good)]

provenance /ˈprɒvənəns/ *n.* origin, place of origin. [F, f. L *provenire* come forth (PRO-¹, *venire* come)]

Provençal /prɒvɑ̃ˈsaːl/ *adj.* of Provence or its people or language. —*n.* **1.** a native or inhabitant of Provence. **2.** its dialect of French; a Romance language of this region, closely related to French, Italian, and Catalan. In the 12th–14th c. it was the language of the troubadours and cultured speakers of southern France, but the subsequent spread of the northern dialects of French led to its gradual decline despite attempts to revive it. [as foll.]

Provence /prɒˈvɑ̃s/ a district and former province of SE France east of the lower Rhône, which contains Marseilles and the French Riviera. [f. L *provincia* province, as L colloq. name for southern Gaul, which was the first Roman province to be established outside Italy]

provender /ˈprɒvɪndə(r)/ *n.* fodder; (*colloq.*) food for humans. [f. OF f. L *praebenda* (as PREBEND)]

proverb /ˈprɒvɜːb/ *n.* **1.** a short pithy saying in general use, stating a truth or giving advice. **2.** a person or thing that is widely known as exemplifying something. **3. Proverbs,** a didactic poetical book of the Old Testament containing maxims ascribed to Solomon and others. [f. OF or L *proverbium* (PRO-[1], *verbum* word)]

proverbial /prəˈvɜːbɪəl/ *adj.* **1.** of or expressed in proverbs. **2.** well-known, notorious. —**proverbially** *adv.* [f. L (as prec.)]

provide /prəˈvaɪd/ *v.t./i.* **1.** to cause (a person) to have possession or use of something; to supply. **2.** to supply the necessities of life. **3.** to make due preparation (for or against a contingency). **4.** to stipulate, to give as a condition. —**provided** *or* **providing (that),** on the condition or understanding that. [f. L *providēre* foresee (PRO-[1], *vidēre* see]

providence /ˈprɒvɪd(ə)ns/ *n.* **1.** being provident; foresight, timely care. **2.** the beneficent care of God or nature. **3. Providence,** God in this aspect. [f. OF or L (as prec.)]

provident /ˈprɒvɪd(ə)nt/ *adj.* having or showing wise foresight for future needs or events; thrifty. —**Provident Society,** a Friendly Society. [as PROVIDE]

providential /prɒvɪˈdenʃ(ə)l/ *adj.* **1.** of or by divine foresight or intervention. **2.** opportune, lucky. —**providentially** *adv.* [f. PROVIDENCE]

provider /prəˈvaɪdə(r)/ *n.* one who provides; the breadwinner of a family etc. [f. PROVIDE]

province /ˈprɒvɪns/ *n.* **1.** each of the principal administrative divisions of certain countries. **2.** a district consisting of a group of adjacent dioceses, under the charge of an archbishop. **3.** a sphere of responsibility or concern or of knowledge; a branch of learning. **4.** (in Roman history) a territory under Roman rule, outside Italy. —**the Province,** (in recent use) Northern Ireland. **the provinces,** the whole of a country outside its capital city. [f. OF f. L *provincia*]

provincial /prəˈvɪnʃ(ə)l/ *adj.* **1.** of a province or provinces. **2.** having restricted views or the interests or manners etc. attributed to inhabitants of the provinces. —*n.* an inhabitant of a province or the provinces. —**provincialism** *n.* [as prec.]

provision /prəˈvɪʒ(ə)n/ *n.* **1.** providing; preparation for a future contingency. **2.** a provided amount of something; (in *pl.*) a supply of food and drink. **3.** a formally stated condition or stipulation. —*v.t.* to supply with provisions. [f. OF f. L (as PROVIDE)]

provisional /prəˈvɪʒən(ə)l/ *adj.* arranged or agreed upon temporarily but possibly to be altered later. —**Provisional** *n.* a member of the Provisional wing of the IRA. The name is taken from the 'Provisional Government of the Republic of Ireland' which was declared in 1916. —**provisionally** *adv.* [f. prec.]

proviso /prəˈvaɪzəʊ/ *n.* (*pl.* **-os**) a stipulation, a clause giving a stipulation in a document. [f. F or L (as PROVIDE)]

provisory /prəˈvaɪzərɪ/ *adj.* **1.** conditional. **2.** making provision. [f. F or L (as PROVIDE)]

provocation /prɒvəˈkeɪʃ(ə)n/ *n.* **1.** provoking, being provoked. **2.** something that provokes anger or retaliation. [f. OF or L (as PROVOKE)]

provocative /prəˈvɒkətɪv/ *adj.* **1.** tending or intended to arouse anger, interest, or sexual desire. **2.** deliberately annoying. —**provocatively** *adv.* [f. obs. F f. L (as foll.)]

provoke /prəˈvəʊk/ *v.t.* **1.** to rouse or incite (a person) to a feeling or action. **2.** to annoy or irritate. **3.** to cause or give rise to (a feeling or reaction etc.). **4.** to tempt, to allure. [f. OF f. L *provocare* (PRO-[1], *vocare* summon)]

provost /ˈprɒvəst/ *n.* **1.** the head of some colleges. **2.** the head of a Scottish municipal corporation or burgh. **3.** (in full **provost marshal** /prəˈvɒʊ/) the head of the military police in a camp or on active service. [OE & f. OF f. L *propositus* for *praepositus* placed in charge)]

prow /praʊ/ *n.* the projecting front part of a ship or boat. [f. F, ult. f. Gk *prōira*]

prowess /ˈpraʊɪs/ *n.* great ability or daring. [f. OF (as PROUD)]

prowl /praʊl/ *v.t./i.* to go about stealthily in search of prey or to catch others unawares; to traverse (a place) thus; to pace or wander restlessly. —*n.* prowling. —**prowler** *n.* [orig. unkn.]

prox. *abbr.* proximo.

proximate /ˈprɒksɪmət/ *adj.* **1.** nearest, next before or after (in time or order, in causation etc.). **2.** approximate. [f. L (*proximus* nearest)]

proximity /prɒkˈsɪmɪtɪ/ *n.* **1.** nearness in space or time. **2.** neighbourhood. [f. F or L (as prec.)]

proximo /ˈprɒksɪməʊ/ *adj.* (in commerce) of the next month. [L, = in the next (*mense* month)]

proxy /ˈprɒksɪ/ *n.* **1.** a person authorized to act for another; the agency of such a person. **2.** a document authorizing a person to vote on behalf of another; a vote so given. [f. obs. *procuracy* f. L (as PROCURATION)]

prude /pruːd/ *n.* a person of extreme or exaggerated propriety in conduct or speech, one who is easily shocked by sexual matters. —**prudery** *n.*, **prudish** *adj.*, **prudishly** *adv.*, **prudishness** *n.* [F, f. *prudefemme* fem. of *prud'homme* good man and true (as PROUD)]

prudent /ˈpruːd(ə)nt/ *adj.* showing care and foresight, avoiding rashness. —**prudence** *n.*, **prudently** *adv.* [f. OF or L (as PROVIDENT)]

prudential /pruːˈdenʃ(ə)l/ *adj.* of, involving, or characterized by prudence. —**prudentially** *adv.* [f. prec.]

prune[1] *v.t.* **1.** to trim by cutting away dead or overgrown branches or shoots, especially to promote growth. **2.** to remove or reduce (what is regarded as superfluous or excessive); to remove items thus from. [f. OF *pr(o)ignier*]

prune[2] *n.* a dried plum. [f. OF f. L *prunum* plum]

prurient /ˈprʊərɪənt/ *adj.* given to or arising from the indulgence of lewd thoughts. —**prurience** *n.*, **pruriently** *adv.* [f. L *prurire* itch]

Prussia /ˈprʌʃə/ a former German kingdom, originally centred in NE Europe along the south coast of the Baltic. Prussia rose to prominence in the 17th c. when the Electors of Brandenburg became the pre-eminent German military power under Frederick the Great in the mid-18th c. Its territory was expanded southwards and westwards by conquest and treaty and in 1866-70 served as the nucleus for the new German empire created by Bismarck under the king of Prussia. Most of the original Prussian territories are now in Poland or the Soviet Union.

Prussian /ˈprʌʃ(ə)n/ *adj.* of Prussia. —*n.* a native of Prussia. —**Prussian blue,** a deep blue pigment. [f. prec.]

prussic /ˈprʌsɪk/ *adj.* of or obtained from Prussian blue. —**prussic acid,** a highly poisonous aqueous solution of hydrogen cyanide. [f. F (as prec.)]

pry /praɪ/ *v.i.* to inquire impertinently (into a person's affairs etc.); to look or peer inquisitively and often furtively. [orig. unkn.]

PS *abbr.* postscript.

psalm /sɑːm/ *n.* a sacred song, especially one of those in the Book of Psalms. —**(Book of) Psalms,** a book of the Old Testament containing psalms, used in both Jewish and Christian worship. The popular belief that David was the author of the whole Psalter can no longer be sustained, but many of the psalms date from the early years of the monarchy in Israel. [OE f. L f. Gk *psalmos* song sung to the harp (*psallō* pluck the strings)]

psalmist *n.* an author of psalms. [f. L (as prec.)]

psalmody /ˈsɑːmədɪ, ˈsælmədɪ/ *n.* the practice or art of singing psalms etc., especially in public worship. [f. L f. Gk (as PSALM, *ōidē* singing)]

Psalter /ˈsɔːltə(r), ˈsɒ-/ *n.* **1.** the Book of Psalms. **2. psalter,** a copy or version of this. [f. L f. Gk *psaltērion* stringed instrument (as PSALM)]

psaltery /ˈsɔːltərɪ, ˈsɒ-/ *n.* an ancient and medieval instrument like a dulcimer but played by plucking the strings. [f. OF f. L (as prec.)]

psephology /pseˈfɒlədʒɪ, se-/ *n.* the study of trends in elections and voting. —**psephologist** *n.* [f. Gk *psēphos* pebble used in voting + -LOGY]

pseudo- /sjuːdəʊ-/ *in comb.* false, apparent, supposed but not real. [Gk (*pseudēs* false)]

pseudonym /ˈsjuːdənɪm/ *n.* a fictitious name, especially one assumed by an author. —**pseudonymity** /-ˈnɪmɪtɪ/ *n.*, **pseudonymous** /-ˈdɒnɪməs/ *adj.* [f. F f. Gk (PSEUDO-, *onoma* name)]

pseudopodium /sjuːdəˈpəʊdɪəm/ *n.* (*pl.* **-ia**) a temporary footlike protrusion of cell tissue, used for movement, feeding, etc., by some protozoa and other animals. [f. PSEUDO- + Gk *podion* dim. of *pous podos* foot]

psi /psaɪ/ *n.* the twenty-third letter of the Greek alphabet, = ps. [Gk]

psoriasis /sɔːˈraɪəsɪs/ *n.* a skin disease with red scaly patches. [f. Gk (*psōriaō* have itch)]

psst *int.* to attract the attention surreptitiously. [imit.]

PSV *abbr.* public service vehicle.

Psyche /ˈsaɪkɪ/ (*Gk myth.*) the soul personified as female, or sometimes represented as a butterfly. She is associated with Eros, either in quiet harmony or being tormented by him as the seat of passions. The allegory of Psyche's love for Cupid is told in the 'Golden Ass' of Apuleius.

psyche /ˈsaɪkɪ/ n. the human soul or spirit; the human mind. [L f. Gk]

psychedelic /saɪkɪˈdelɪk/ adj. **1.** hallucinatory, expanding the mind's awareness. **2.** having intensely vivid colours or sounds etc. [as prec. + Gk dēlos clear]

psychiatric /saɪkɪˈætrɪk/ adj. (also **psychiatrical**) of or concerning psychiatry. —**psychiatrically** adv. [f. foll.]

psychiatry /saɪˈkaɪətrɪ/ n. the study and treatment of mental disease. —**psychiatrist** n. [PSYCHO- + Gk iatreia healing]

psychic /ˈsaɪkɪk/ adj. psychical, able to exercise psychical or occult powers. —n. **1.** a person susceptible to psychical influence, a medium. **2.** (in pl.) the study of psychical phenomena. —**psychically** adv. [f. Gk (as PSYCHE)]

psychical /ˈsaɪkɪk(ə)l/ adj. of the soul or mind, of phenomena and conditions apparently outside the domain of physical law. —**psychically** adv. [as prec.]

psycho- /saɪkəʊ-/ in comb. mind, soul. [f. Gk (as PSYCHE)]

psychoanalyse /saɪkəʊˈænəlaɪz/ v.t. to treat by psychoanalysis. —**psychoanalyst** n. [f. foll.]

psychoanalysis /saɪkəʊəˈnælɪsɪs/ n. **1.** a therapeutic method originated by Freud for treating disorders of the personality or behaviour by bringing into a patient's consciousness his unconscious conflicts and fantasies (attributed chiefly to the development of the sexual instinct), e.g. through the free association of ideas, and the analysis and interpretation of dreams, helping the patient to understand his condition. **2.** a theory of personality and psychical life derived from this, based on concepts of the ego, id, and super-ego, the conscious, pre-conscious, and unconscious levels of the mind, and the repression of the sexual instinct. —**psychoanalytic** /-ænəˈlɪtɪk/ adj., **psychoanalytical** /-ænəˈlɪtɪk(ə)l/ adj.

psychological /saɪkəˈlɒdʒɪk(ə)l/ adj. of the mind; of psychology. —**psychological moment,** the psychologically appropriate moment; (colloq.) the most appropriate time. **psychological warfare,** warfare achieving its aims by weakening the enemy's morale. [f. foll.]

psychology /saɪˈkɒlədʒɪ/ n. **1.** the science of the human mind; a treatise on or system of this. **2.** (colloq.) mental characteristics. —**psychologist** n. [as PSYCHO- + -LOGY]

psychometry /saɪˈkɒmɪtrɪ/ n. **1.** divination of facts concerning an object (e.g. its source, ownership) from contact with it. **2.** measurement of mental abilities. —**psychometric** /-kəˈmetrɪk/ adj. [f. PSYCHO- + -METRY]

psychoneurosis /saɪkəʊnjʊəˈrəʊsɪs/ n. a neurosis, especially with indirect expression of emotional feelings. —**psychoneurotic** /-ˈrɒtɪk/ adj.

psychopath /ˈsaɪkəpæθ/ n. a person suffering from chronic mental disorder especially with aggressive antisocial behaviour; a mentally or emotionally unstable person. —**psychopathic** /-ˈpæθɪk/ adj., **psychopathy** /-ˈkɒpəθɪ/ n. [f. PSYCHO- + Gk -pathēs sufferer]

psychopathology /saɪkəʊpəˈθɒlədʒɪ/ n. the science of mental disorders.

psychosis /saɪˈkəʊsɪs/ n. (pl. **-oses** /-iːz/) a severe mental derangement involving the whole personality. [f. Gk, = principle of life (as PSYCHE)]

psychosomatic /saɪkəʊsəˈmætɪk/ adj. of the mind and the body; (of a disease etc.) caused or aggravated by mental stress. —**psychosomatically** adv.

psychosurgery /saɪkəʊˈsɜːdʒərɪ/ n. brain surgery as a means of treating mental disorder.

psychotherapy /saɪkəʊˈθerəpɪ/ n. treatment of mental disorders by psychological means. —**psychotherapeutic** /-ˈpjuːtɪk/ adj., **psychotherapist** n.

psychotic /saɪˈkɒtɪk/ adj. of or suffering from psychosis. —n. a psychotic person. [as PSYCHOSIS]

PT abbr. physical training.

Pt symbol platinum.

pt. abbr. **1.** part. **2.** pint. **3.** point. **4.** port.

PTA abbr. parent-teacher association.

Ptah /tɑː/ (Egyptian myth.) an ancient deity of Memphis, originally a god of artisans (the Greeks called him Hephaestus) and creator of the universe. He acquired a solar character and became one of the chief deities of Egypt.

ptarmigan /ˈtɑːmɪgən/ n. a bird of the grouse family (Lagopus mutus). [f. Gaelic]

Pte abbr. Private (soldier).

pteridophyte /ˈterɪdəfaɪt/ n. a fern or similar plant. [f. Gk pteris fern + phuton plant]

pterodactyl /terəˈdæktɪl/ n. an extinct winged reptile. [f. Gk pteron wing + daktulos finger]

PTO abbr. please turn over.

Ptolemaic /tɒlɪˈmeɪɪk/ adj. **1.** of or according to the theory of Ptolemy (see PTOLEMY²) that the earth is the stationary centre round which the sun and stars revolve. **2.** of the Ptolemies (rulers of Egypt). [f. PTOLEMY¹,²]

Ptolemy¹ /ˈtɒləmɪ/ the name of all the Macedonian kings of Egypt, a dynasty founded by Ptolemy, the close friend and general of Alexander the Great, who took charge of Egypt after his master's death and declared himself king in 304 BC. The dynasty ended with the death of Cleopatra in 30 BC. Under the Ptolemies their capital, Alexandria, became a leading commercial and cultural centre of the Greek world.

Ptolemy² /ˈtɒləmɪ/ (2nd c.) Greek astronomer and geographer, who worked in Alexandria. His major work, known by its Arabic title the Almagest, was a complete textbook of astronomy based on the geocentric system of Hipparchus. His teachings had enormous influence on medieval thought, the geocentric view of the cosmos being adopted as Church doctrine until the late Renaissance. Besides placing the Earth at the centre of the universe and explaining the motions of the planets by combining individual circular motions, the Almagest included detailed tables of lunar and solar motion with eclipse predictions, and a star catalogue giving the positions and magnitudes (graded from 1 to 6) of 1022 stars. Ptolemy's Geography, giving lists of places with their longitudes and latitudes, was also a standard work for centuries, despite its inaccuracies.

ptomaine /ˈtəʊmeɪn/ n. any of various amines (some toxic) in putrefying animal and vegetable matter. [f. F f. It. f. Gk ptōma corpse]

p-type adj. (of a semiconductor device or a region in this) having positive carriers of electricity.

Pu symbol plutonium.

pub n. (colloq.) a public house. —**pub crawl,** a series of visits to several pubs with drinking at each. [abbr.]

puberty /ˈpjuːbətɪ/ n. the stage at which a person becomes capable of procreation through the natural development of the reproductive organs. —**pubertal** adj. [f. F or L (puber adult)]

pubes /ˈpjuːbiːz/ n. the lower part of the abdomen. [L]

pubescence /pjuːˈbes(ə)ns/ n. **1.** arrival at puberty. **2.** soft down on a plant or animal. —**pubescent** adj. [F or f. L (pubescere reach puberty)]

pubic /ˈpjuːbɪk/ adj. of the pubes or pubis. [f. PUBES]

pubis /ˈpjuːbɪs/ n. (pl. **pubes** /-iːz/) the bone forming the front of each half of the pelvis. [f. L os pubis bone of the pubes]

public /ˈpʌblɪk/ adj. **1.** of, concerning, or for the use of the people as a whole. **2.** representing the people; done by or for the people. **3.** open to general observation or knowledge, openly done or existing. **4.** of or engaged in the people's affairs or service. —n. the community in general; members of it; a section of the community. —**in public,** openly, for all to see or know. **public-address system,** a system of loud-speakers etc. for a speaker at a large gathering. **public company,** one with shares available to all buyers. **public house,** a place licensed for and mainly concerned with selling alcoholic drink for consumption on the premises. **Public Lending Right,** the right of authors to payment when their books are lent by public libraries. **public relations,** the promotion of good relations between a business etc. and the public. **public school,** see separate entry. **public servant,** a State official. **public-spirited** adj. ready to do things for the benefit of people in general. **public transport,** buses, trains, etc., available to the public and having fixed routes. **public utility,** an organization supplying gas or electricity or water, etc., and regarded as a public service. **public works,** building operations undertaken by the State. —**publicly** adv. [f. OF or L publicus (populus people, infl. by pubes adult population)]

publican /ˈpʌblɪkən/ n. **1.** the keeper of a public house. **2.** (Rom. hist. & in the New Testament) a tax-collector. [f. OF f. L, = tax-collector]

publication /pʌblɪˈkeɪʃ(ə)n/ n. **1.** the issuing of a book or periodical etc. to the public. **2.** a book etc. so issued. **3.** making publicly known. [f. OF f. L (as PUBLISH)]

publicist /ˈpʌblɪsɪst/ n. **1.** a writer on or a person skilled in current public affairs. **2.** an expert in publicity. [f. F f. L (jus) publicum public (law)]

publicity /pʌbˈlɪsɪtɪ/ n. **1.** public attention; the means of attracting it, the business of advertising. **2.** being open to general observation; notoriety. [f. F (as PUBLIC)]

publicize /'pʌblɪsaɪz/ v.t. to make publicly known, especially by advertisement. [f. PUBLIC]

public school 1. an endowed secondary school (usually a boarding-school) for fee-paying pupils (see below). **2.** (in Scotland, USA, etc.) a school managed by public authorities.
  In England, public schools had their origin in the grammar schools of the Tudor period or earlier, endowed for the use or benefit of the public and carried on under some kind of public management or control; they were contrasted with 'private schools' which were carried on at the risk and for the profit of their proprietors, and with education at home under a tutor. In the 19th c. there was a surge of expansion, as well-to-do members of the middle class sought for their sons the education that they had not had themselves, and of reform, under the influence of headmasters such as Butler of Shrewsbury and Arnold of Rugby, who set new standards of work and behaviour. Among the foremost are Winchester (founded in 1382), Eton (1440), Shrewsbury (1552), Westminster (1560), Rugby (1567), Harrow (1571), and Charterhouse (1611).

publish /'pʌblɪʃ/ v.t. **1.** to issue copies of (a book, or periodical, newspaper, etc., or absol.) for sale to the public (see below). **2.** to make generally known, to announce formally. [f. OF f. L *publicare* (as PUBLISH)]
  The trade in books is now shared by the publisher (who takes the commercial risks on a book's production, and the responsibility for marketing it to booksellers and the public), the printer (who prints the book to a publisher's order), and the bookseller (who offers it to the buying public). Before the invention of printing, texts were 'published' by being read aloud to an audience. In the early days of printing the printer was also publisher and bookseller, but during the 15th-16th c. these functions began to separate and developed into separate trades. Technological developments in the printing industry in the 19th c. dramatically increased output and reduced prices. In the 20th c. the introduction of paperbacks, pioneered in the Penguin series in 1935, tapped a wider market by offering books at an unprecedentedly low price, and after the Second World War social and economic changes, and the spread of university education, resulted in an increased demand for books of all kinds. The advent of computers is likely to change many aspects of publishing in a technological revolution as important as the invention of printing.

publisher n. a person or firm that issues and distributes copies of a book, periodical, newspaper, etc. [f. prec.]

Puccini /pʊ'tʃiːnɪ/, Giacomo (1858–1924), Italian composer. He decided to devote his musical gifts to opera after seeing Verdi's *Aida* in 1876, but his first major success did not come until 1893 when *Manon Lescaut* was produced at Turin. His most famous operas followed soon after: *La Bohème* in 1896, *Tosca* in 1900, *Madama Butterfly* in 1904, and *La Fanciulla del West* in 1910. These works, among the most popular in the repertory, are saved from cloying sentimentality by Puccini's sense of the dramatic, his great melodic gift, and the skill and effectiveness of his handling of the orchestra.

puce adj. & n. brownish-purple. [F, = flea, flea-colour, f. L *pulex*]

Puck 1. a merry mischievous sprite or goblin believed, especially in the 16th and 17th c., to haunt the English countryside. He was also called Robin Goodfellow or Hobgoblin. **2.** (in earlier superstition) an evil demon. [OE, = mischievous demon]

puck n. a rubber disc used in ice hockey. [orig. unkn.]

pucker v.t./i. to gather or cause to gather into wrinkles, folds, or bulges, intentionally or as a fault. —n. such a wrinkle or bulge. [prob. frequent. (as POKE², POCKET)]

pud /pʊd/ n. (colloq.) pudding. [abbr.]

pudding /'pʊdɪŋ/ n. **1.** any sweet food made with sugar, eggs, etc.; a dessert. **2.** food of various kinds containing or enclosed in a mixture of flour (or a similar substance) and other ingredients and cooked by baking, boiling, or steaming. **3.** a kind of sausage. **4.** a dumpy slow-witted person. —**puddingy** adj. [f. OF *boudin* black pudding, ult. f. L *botellus* sausage]

puddle n. **1.** a small pool especially of rain on a road etc. **2.** clay made into a watertight coating. —v.t. **1.** to make muddy. **2.** to knead (clay and sand) with water into a muddy mixture. **3.** to stir (molten iron) to produce wrought iron by expelling the carbon. —**puddly** adj. [dim. of OE *pudd* ditch]

pudenda /pjuː'dendə/ n.pl. the genitals, especially of a woman. [L, = things to be ashamed of]

Pudovkin /pʊ'dɒfkɪn/, Vsevolod Ilarionovich (1893–1953), Russian film director whose works were consistently successful in the USSR. His three major films *Mother* (1926), *The End of St. Petersburg* (1927), and *The Heir to Ghenghis Khan* (1928) have a warmth that contrasts with the contemporaneous work of Eisenstein. His editing aimed at supporting the narrative by linking images in a meaningful way, the montage drawing the audience along a smooth narrative line.

Pueblo /'pwebləʊ/ n. (pl. -os) a member of certain Indian peoples occupying a pueblo settlement. Their prehistoric period is known as the Anasazi culture. [f. foll.]

pueblo /'pwebləʊ/ n. (pl. -os) a type of settlement in the southwestern USA and Latin America, especially of Indians, with multistorey adobe dwellings occupied by a number of families. [Sp., = people, village, f. L *populus*]

puerile /'pjʊəraɪl/ adj. suitable only for children, silly and immature. —**puerility** /-'rɪlɪtɪ/ n. [f. F or L (*puer* boy)]

puerperal /pjuː'ɜːpər(ə)l/ adj. of or due to childbirth. —**puerperal fever**, a fever following childbirth and caused by uterine infection. [f. L *puerperus* (*puer* child, -*parus* bearing)]

Puerto Rico /pwɜːtəʊ 'riːkəʊ/ an island of the Greater Antilles in the West Indies; pop. (1980) 3,187,570; official language, Spanish; capital, San Juan. Discovered in 1493 by Christopher Columbus, the island was one of the earliest Spanish settlements in the New World. It was ceded to the USA in 1898 after the Spanish-American war, and was established as a Commonwealth with full powers of local government in 1952. In recent decades there has been considerable progress in industrialization and welfare. —**Puerto Rican** adj. & n.

puff n. **1.** a short quick blowing of breath or wind etc.; its sound; a small quantity of smoke or vapour etc. emitted at a puff. **2.** the act of smoking a pipe etc. **3.** a powder-puff. **4.** a cake of light pastry. **5.** a piece of extravagant praise as a review or advertisement etc. —v.t./i. **1.** to emit a puff or puffs; to emit (smoke etc.) in puffs; to smoke (a pipe etc.) in puffs. **2.** to come (out or up) in puffs. **3.** to blow (dust etc.) away with a puff. **4.** to breathe hard, to pant; to put out of breath. **5.** to make or become inflated; to swell. **6.** to advertise (goods etc.) with extravagant praise. —**puff-adder** n. a large venomous African viper (esp. *Bitis arietans*) that inflates the upper part of its body when excited. **puff-ball** n. a fungus of the genus *Lycoperdon* with a ball-shaped sporecase. **puff pastry**, light flaky pastry. **puff** or **puffed sleeve**, a short sleeve that is very full at the shoulder. **puff up**, (esp. in p.p.) to elate, to make proud. [prob. imit.]

puffin /'pʌfɪn/ n. a North Atlantic auk (*Fratercula arctica*) with a short striped bill. [orig. unkn.]

puffy adj. **1.** puffed out, swollen. **2.** short-winded. —**puffily** adv., **puffiness** n. [f. PUFF]

pug n. a dog of a dwarf breed with a broad flat nose and wrinkled face. —**pug-nosed** adj. having a short flattish nose. [perh. f. L Du.]

pugilist /'pjuːdʒɪlɪst/ n. a professional boxer. —**pugilism** n., **pugilistic** /-'lɪstɪk/ adj. [f. L *pugil*]

Pugin /'pjuːdʒɪn/, Augustus Welby Northmore (1812–52), English architect, theorist, and designer. His chief importance lies in his proselytizing zeal as apologist for the Gothic revival in England. Converted to Roman Catholicism in 1835, he championed the Gothic case in *Contrasts* (1836), where medieval Christian society and architecture were favourably compared with the inadequacies of their contemporary equivalents. Other works, e.g. *Principles* (1841) and *Apology* (1843), continued this theoretical assault. His practical schemes, however, although accurate in revivalist detail, appear flimsy overall, indicating perhaps that for all his functionalist justification of Gothic architecture his inspiration was visual rather than structural.

pugnacious /pʌg'neɪʃəs/ adj. disposed to fight, aggressive. —**pugnaciously** adv., **pugnacity** /-'næsɪtɪ/ n. [f. L *pugnax* (*pugnare* fight)]

puisne /'pjuːnɪ/ n. a judge of a superior court who is inferior in rank to a chief justice. [F (*puis* after (f. L *postea*), né born f. L *natus*)]

puissance /'pwiːsɑːns/ n. (in show-jumping) a test of a horse's ability to jump high obstacles. [as foll.]

puissant /'pjuːɪs(ə)nt, 'pwiː-/ adj. (literary) having great power or influence, mighty. [f. OF f. L *posse* be able (cf. POTENT)]

puke *v.t./i.* to vomit. —*n.* vomit. [prob. imit.]

pukka /ˈpʌkə/ *adj.* (*colloq.*) genuine; of good quality. [f. Hindi, = cooked]

pulchritude /ˈpʌlkrɪtjuːd/ *n.* (*literary*) beauty. —**pulchritudinous** /-ˈtjuːdɪnəs/ *adj.* [f. L (*pulcher* beautiful)]

pule *v.i.* to whimper, to cry querulously or weakly. [prob. imit.]

Pulitzer /ˈpʊlɪtsə(r)/, Joseph (1847–1911), American newspaper-owner and editor, of Hungarian origin, one of the founders of American sensational journalism. His object was the remedy of abuses and the reform of social and economic inequalities by the exposure of striking instances and by the vigorous expression of democratic opinion. The success of this appeal to the emotions found many imitators among journalists not actuated by the same creditable motives. —**Pulitzer Prize** /ˈpjuː-/, any of a group of money prizes established under his will and offered annually to American citizens for work in music, journalism, American history and biography, poetry, drama, and fiction.

pull /pʊl/ *v.t./i.* **1.** to exert force on (a thing) so as to move it towards oneself or towards the origin of the force; to cause to move thus; to exert such a force. **2.** to remove (a cork or tooth) by pulling. **3.** to damage (a muscle etc.) by abnormal strain. **4.** to move (a boat) by pulling on its oars; (of a boat etc.) to be caused to move, especially in a specified direction. **5.** to proceed with effort. **6.** to bring out (a weapon) for use. **7.** to restrain the speed of (a horse). **8.** to attract (customers). **9.** to draw (liquor) from a barrel etc. **10.** (in cricket) to strike (a ball) to the leg side; (in golf) to strike (a ball) widely to the left. **11.** to print (a proof etc.). —*n.* **1.** the act of pulling; the force thus exerted. **2.** a means of exerting influence, an advantage. **3.** a deep draught of liquor. **4.** a prolonged effort, e.g. in going up a hill. **5.** a handle etc. for applying pull. **6.** a printer's proof. **7.** a pulling stroke in cricket or golf. — **pull apart** *or* **to pieces**, to separate the parts of forcibly; to criticize severely. **pull back,** to retreat or cause to retreat. **pull down,** to demolish; to humiliate. **pull a fast one,** (*slang*) to gain an advantage by unfair or deceitful means. **pull in,** to earn or acquire; (of a train etc.) to enter a station; (of a vehicle) to move to the side of or off a road; (*colloq.*) to arrest. **pull-in** *n.* a place for a vehicle to pull in off the road. **pull a person's leg,** to deceive him playfully. **pull off,** to remove by pulling; to succeed in achieving or winning. **pull oneself together,** to recover control of oneself. **pull out,** to depart; to withdraw from an undertaking; (of a train etc.) to leave a station; (of a vehicle) to move from the side of a road, or into position to overtake another. **pull one's punches,** to avoid using one's full force. **pull rank,** to take unfair advantage of seniority. **pull round** *or* **through,** to recover from an illness. **pull strings,** to exert (esp. clandestine) influence. **pull up,** to stop or cause to stop moving; to reprimand; to pull out of the ground; to check oneself. **pull one's weight,** to do one's fair share of work. [OE]

pullet /ˈpʊlɪt/ *n.* a young domestic fowl, especially a hen that has begun to lay but not yet moulted. [f. OF dim. of *poule* f. L *pullus*]

pulley /ˈpʊlɪ/ *n.* **1.** a grooved wheel for a cord etc. to pass over, set in a block and used for changing the direction of a force. **2.** a wheel or drum fixed on a shaft and turned by a belt, used especially to increase speed or power. [f. OF *polie* prob. ult. f. Gk (as POLE²)]

Pullman /ˈpʊlmən/ *n.* **1.** a type of railway carriage with luxurious furnishings and without compartments; a luxurious motor coach. **2.** a sleeping-car. [f. G. M. *Pullman*, American designer (d. 1897)]

pullover *n.* a knitted garment (with no fastenings) for the upper part of the body, put on over the head.

pullulate /ˈpʌljʊleɪt/ *v.i.* **1.** to sprout; to develop. **2.** to abound *with.* —**pullulation** /-ˈleɪʃ(ə)n/ *n.* [f. L *pullulare* sprout (as PULLET)]

pulmonary /ˈpʌlmənərɪ/ *adj.* **1.** of, in, or affecting the lungs. **2.** affected with or subject to lung-disease. [f. L (*pulmo* lung)]

pulp *n.* **1.** the fleshy part of a fruit, animal body, etc. **2.** a soft shapeless mass, especially that of rags or wood etc., from which paper is made. **3.** (*attrib.*, of a magazine etc.) of a kind originally printed on rough paper made from wood pulp, often with sensational or poor-quality writing. —*v.t./i.* to reduce to or become pulp. —**pulpy** *adj.*, **pulpiness** *n.* [f. L *pulpa*]

pulpit /ˈpʊlpɪt/ *n.* a raised enclosed platform in a church etc. from which a preacher delivers a sermon (ill. VESTMENTS). [f. L *pulpitum*]

pulsar /ˈpʌlsɑː(r)/ *n.* a cosmic source from which light or

radio waves are emitted in short bursts with great regularity. When discovered in 1968, this regularity was at first attributed to signals from intelligent beings, but is now believed to be due to the interaction of the magnetic field of a rapidly rotating neutron star with circumstellar material, accelerating electrons which radiate energy in a beam; as this beam sweeps past the observer up to hundreds of times a second, the characteristic 'pulsations' in signal strength are noted. [f. *pulsating* star]

pulsate /pʌlˈseɪt, ˈpʌl-/ *v.i.* to expand and contract rhythmically, to throb; to vibrate, to quiver. —**pulsation** /-ˈseɪʃ(ə)n/ *n.*, **pulsator** /-ˈseɪtə(r)/ *n.*, **pulsatory** /ˈpʌlsətərɪ/ *adj.* [f. L *pulsare* (as foll.)]

pulse¹ *n.* **1.** the rhythmical throbbing of the arteries as blood is propelled along them; each successive beat of the arteries or heart; the rate of this beat. **2.** a single vibration of sound or light or electric current etc., especially as a signal. **3.** a throb or thrill of life or emotion; a latent feeling. —*v.i.* to pulsate. [f. L *pulsus* (*pellere* drive, beat)]

pulse² *n.* **1.** (as *sing.* or *pl.*) the edible seeds of leguminous plants, e.g. peas, beans, lentils. **2.** any kind of these. [f. OF f. L *puls* meal porridge]

pulverize /ˈpʌlvəraɪz/ *v.t./i.* **1.** to reduce or crumble to powder or dust; to demolish. **2.** to defeat utterly. —**pulverization** /-ˈzeɪʃ(ə)n/ *n.* [f. L (*pulvis* dust)]

puma /ˈpjuːmə/ *n.* a large tawny American feline (*Felis concolor*). [Sp., f. Quechua]

pumice /ˈpʌmɪs/ *n.* (also **pumice-stone**) a light porous lava used for removing stains from the skin etc. or as a powder for polishing; a piece of this. [f. OF f. L *pumex*]

pummel /ˈpʌm(ə)l/ *v.t.* (**-ll-**) to strike repeatedly, especially with the fist. [alt. f. POMMEL]

pump¹ *n.* a machine or device of various kinds for raising or moving liquids or gases; a machine for raising water for domestic use. —*v.t./i.* **1.** to raise, move, or inflate by using a pump; to use a pump; to empty by using a pump. **2.** to pour or cause to pour forth as if by pumping. **3.** to move vigorously up and down like a pump-handle. **4.** to question (a person) persistently to obtain information. [orig. naut.; prob. imit.]

pump² *n.* **1.** a plimsoll. **2.** a light shoe for dancing etc. **3.** (*US*) a court shoe. [orig. unkn.]

pumpernickel /ˈpʌmpənɪk(ə)l, ˈpʊ-/ *n.* German wholemeal rye bread. [G, orig. = lout, stinker (*pumpe(r)n* break wind, *Nickel* Nicholas)]

pumpkin *n.* **1.** the large round orange-coloured fruit of a trailing vine, *Cucurbita pepo*, used as a vegetable and (in the USA) a filling for pies. **2.** this vine. [f. earlier *pompon*, ult. f. Gk *pepōn* large melon]

pun *n.* humorous use of a word to suggest different meanings, or of words of the same sound with a different meaning (e.g. 'the sole has no feet and therefore no sole, poor soul'). —*v.i.* (**-nn-**) to make a pun or puns. [perh. f. obs. *pundigrion*]

Punch a grotesque hook-nosed hump-backed buffoon, the English variant of a stock character derived from Italian popular comedy (*Pulcinella*; in France *Polichinelle*; in England *Punchinello* or *Punch*). The name is now preserved chiefly as the title of an English humorous weekly periodical (founded in 1841) and in 'Punch and Judy'. —**as pleased** *or* **proud as Punch,** showing great pleasure or pride. **Punch and Judy,** an English puppet-show of uncertain origin, probably introduced into England from the Continent in the 17th c. (Pepys saw a show in 1662). It is presented on the miniature stage of a tall collapsible booth traditionally covered with striped canvas, and was once a familiar sight in large cities and can still be seen in seaside towns. In the standard version of the play Punch, with his humped back and hooked nose, is on the manipulator's right hand, remaining on stage all the time, while the left hand provides a series of characters—baby, wife (Judy), priest, doctor, policeman, hangman—for him to nag, beat, and finally kill. His live dog, Toby, sits on the ledge of the booth. [abbr. *Punchinello*, perh. dim. of It. *pollecena* young turkey-cock (with hooked beak which the nose of Punch's mask resembles); the name of Punch's wife (Judy) is of later date]

punch¹ *v.t.* **1.** to strike with the fist. **2.** to pierce a hole in (metal, paper, a ticket, etc.) as or with a punch; to pierce (a hole) thus. —*n.* **1.** a blow with the fist; the ability to deliver this. **2.** (*slang*) vigour, effective force. **3.** an instrument or machine for cutting holes or impressing a design in leather, metal, paper, etc. —**punch-ball** *n.* an inflated ball held on a stand etc. and punched as a form of exercise. **punch-drunk** *adj.* stupefied through having been severely punched (*lit.* or *fig.*). **punch-line** *n.* the words giving the point of a joke or story. **punch-up** *n.* a fist-fight, a brawl. [var. of *pounce* emboss]

punch² *n.* a drink usually of wine or spirits mixed with hot or cold water, spice, etc. —**punch-bowl** *n.* a bowl in which punch is mixed; a round deep hollow in a hill. [orig. unkn.]

punch³ *n.* (in full **Suffolk punch**) a short-legged thickset draught horse. [prob. as PUNCH]

punched card a card perforated according to a specified code, used in recording and analysing data. Such cards (introduced by the American engineer Hollerith) were first used in the US census of 1890, and thereafter found widespread use in business and later for scientific and technical purposes. Early computers were often fed with information from punched cards of the Hollerith type.

punchy *adj.* having vigour, forceful. [f. PUNCH¹]

punctilio /pʌŋkˈtɪlɪəʊ/ *n.* (*pl.* **-os**) 1. a delicate point of ceremony or honour; the etiquette of such points. 2. petty formality. [f. It. & Sp. dim. (as POINT)]

punctilious /pʌŋkˈtɪlɪəs/ *adj.* attentive to formality or etiquette; precise in behaviour. —**punctiliously** *adv.*, **punctiliousness** *n.* [f. F (as prec.)]

punctual /ˈpʌŋktjʊəl/ *adj.* observant of the appointed time; neither early nor late. —**punctuality** /-ˈælɪtɪ/ *n.*, **punctually** *adv.* [f. L (as POINT)]

punctuate /ˈpʌŋktjʊeɪt/ *v.t.* 1. to insert punctuation marks in. 2. to interrupt at intervals. 3. to emphasize, to accentuate. [f. L *punctuare* (as prec.)]

punctuation /pʌŋktjʊˈeɪʃ(ə)n/ *n.* punctuating; the system used for this. —**punctuation mark,** any of the marks (e.g. full stop and comma) used in writing to separate sentences and phrases etc. and clarify meaning. Before the invention of printing, texts were 'published' by being read aloud to an audience from manuscript, and punctuation marks, consisting of simple 'points' or stops, were used to indicate to the reader the pauses which mark off the sense units (phrases, clauses, and sentences) in the spoken language. Since these pauses frequently correlate with a rise or fall in voice pitch, punctuation marks, particularly in liturgical manuscripts, also seem to have been used to indicate changes of intonation, i.e. as a primitive form of musical notation. When printing made the written language directly available to the literate without the intervention of the reader's voice, new punctuation marks were introduced (e.g. brackets, question marks, exclamation and quotation marks) to provide visual clarification of the text. [as prec.]

puncture /ˈpʌŋktʃə(r)/ *n.* a prick or pricking, especially an accidental piercing of a pneumatic tyre; a hole thus made. —*v.t./i.* to make a puncture in; to undergo a puncture; to prick or pierce. [f. L *punctura* (*pungere* prick)]

pundit /ˈpʌndɪt/ *n.* 1. a learned Hindu. 2. a learned expert or teacher. —**punditry** *n.* [f. Hind. f. Skr., = learned]

pungent /ˈpʌndʒ(ə)nt/ *adj.* 1. having a sharp or strong taste or smell. 2. (of remarks) penetrating, biting, caustic. 3. mentally stimulating. —**pungency** *n.*, **pungently** *adv.* [as PUNCTURE]

Punic Wars /ˈpjuːnɪk/ three wars between Rome and Carthage, which led to the unquestioned dominance of Rome in the western Mediterranean, a position of power which was not endangered for centuries afterwards. In the first (264–241 BC) Rome secured Sicily from Carthage and established herself as a naval power; in the second (218–201 BC) the defeat of Hannibal (largely through the generalship of Fabius Cunctator and Scipio) put an end to Carthage's position as a Mediterranean power; the third (149–146 BC) ended in the total destruction of the city of Carthage. [f. L *Punicus* Carthaginian]

punish /ˈpʌnɪʃ/ *v.t.* 1. to cause (an offender) to suffer for an offence; to inflict a penalty for (an offence). 2. (*colloq.*) to inflict severe blows on (an opponent). 3. to tax severely, to subject to severe treatment. [f. OF f. L *punire* (*poena* penalty)]

punishable *adj.* liable to be punished, especially by law. [f. prec.]

punishment *n.* 1. punishing, being punished. 2. that which an offender is made to suffer for his offence. 3. severe treatment or suffering. [f. PUNISH]

punitive /ˈpjuːnɪtɪv/ *adj.* inflicting or intended to inflict punishment. [f. F or L (as PUNISH)]

Punjab /pʌnˈdʒɑːb, ˈpʌn-/ a State of India, formerly a north-western province of British India; capital, Chandigarh. —**Punjabi** *adj.* & *n.*

punk *n.* (*colloq.*) 1. a worthless person or thing. 2. punk rock; a devotee of this or of the bizarre dress, hair-style, etc., associated with it. —**punk rock,** a type of pop music using aggressive and outrageous effects. [orig. unkn.]

punnet /ˈpʌnɪt/ *n.* a small basket or container for fruit etc. [perh. dim. of dial. *pun* pound (POUND¹)]

punster *n.* a habitual maker of puns. [f. PUN]

punt¹ *n.* a flat-bottomed shallow boat propelled by a long pole thrust against the bottom of a river etc. Formerly used for transporting goods and cattle, such boats are now used for pleasure and sometimes for racing. —*v.t./i.* to propel (a punt) with a pole in this way; to travel or convey in a punt. —**punter¹** *n.* [f. MLG or MDu. f. L *ponto* Gaulish transport vessel]

punt² *v.t.* to kick (a football) after it has dropped from the hands and before it reaches the ground. —*n.* such a kick. —**punter²** *n.* [prob. f. dial. *punt* push forcibly]

punt³ *v.i.* 1. (in some card-games) to lay a stake against the bank. 2. (*colloq.*) to bet on a horse etc.; to speculate in shares etc. [f. F *ponter* (*ponte* player against bank f. Sp., as POINT)]

punter³ *n.* 1. one who punts (PUNT³). 2. (*colloq.*) the victim of a swindler or confidence trickster; a customer or client etc., a spectator. [f. PUNT³]

puny /ˈpjuːnɪ/ *adj.* undersized, weak, feeble. —**puniness** *n.* [phonetic spelling of PUISNE]

pup *n.* a young dog; a young wolf, rat, seal, etc. —*v.t.* (**-pp-**) (of a bitch etc.) to bring forth (young, or *absol.*). —**in pup,** (of a bitch) pregnant. **sell a person a pup,** to swindle him or her, especially by selling a thing on its prospective value. [f. PUPPY]

pupa /ˈpjuːpə/ *n.* (*pl.* **-ae**) an insect in its passive phase of development between larva and imago (ill. INSECTS). —**pupal** *adj.* [L, = doll]

pupate /pjuːˈpeɪt/ *v.t.* to become a pupa. —**pupation** /-ˈpeɪʃ(ə)n/ *n.* [f. prec.]

pupil /ˈpjuːpɪl/ *n.* 1. one who is taught by another; a schoolchild; a disciple. 2. the circular opening in the centre of the iris of the eye (ill. BODY 2). [f. OF f. L *pupillus*, *pupilla*, dim. of *pupus* boy, *pupa* girl]

puppet /ˈpʌpɪt/ *n.* 1. an inanimate figure representing a human being or an animal etc., ranging in size from a few inches to larger than life, moved by various means as an entertainment (see below). 2. a person whose acts are controlled by another. —**puppet state,** a country that is apparently independent but actually under the control of another power. —**puppetry** *n.* [var. of POPPET]

Puppetry as a form of theatre is probably as old as the theatre itself. There are hand or glove puppets, rod puppets, marionettes or string puppets, and the flat puppets of the shadow-show. Famous hand puppets include the English Punch, the French Guignol, and the Italian Pulcinella, but the true home of puppetry is the Far East and Eastern Europe, where its uses range from elementary education to cabaret shows.

puppy *n.* 1. a young dog. 2. a vain empty-headed young man. —**puppy-fat** *n.* temporary fatness of a child or adolescent. [perh. f. OF *po(u)pee* doll (as PUPPET)]

Purana /pʊˈrɑːnə/ *n.* any of a class of Sanskrit sacred poems of Hindu mythology, of varying date and origin. The most ancient dates from the 8th c. [f. Skr., = ancient (legend), f. *purā* formerly]

purblind /ˈpɜːblaɪnd/ *adj.* 1. partly blind, dim-sighted. 2. stupid, dim-witted. [orig. *pur(e)* (= utterly) *blind*]

Purcell /ˈpɜːs(ə)l/, Henry (1659–95), the first English opera composer. His *Dido and Aeneas* (1689) moved away from the tradition of the masque, breaking new dramatic ground and accommodating a wide emotional range. His versatility enabled him to feel equally at home in the composition of religious, occasional, and purely instrumental music. The aptness of Purcell's treatment of the English language in his vocal music has inspired and influenced British song composers of the 20th c.

purchase /ˈpɜːtʃəs/ *v.t.* 1. to buy. 2. to obtain or achieve with a specified cost or sacrifice. —*n.* 1. buying. 2. a thing bought. 3. an annual rent or return from land. 4. a firm hold on a thing to move it or prevent it slipping, leverage. —**purchaser** *n.* [f. AF (as PRO-¹, CHASE¹)]

purdah /ˈpɜːdə/ *n.* a system of screening Muslim or Hindu women from strangers by means of a veil or curtain. [f. Urdu & Pers., = veil, curtain]

pure *adj.* 1. not mixed with any other substance; free from impurities; of unmixed origin. 2. morally or sexually undefiled; chaste. 3. mere, nothing but. 4. (of sound) not discordant, perfectly in tune. 5. dealing with theory only, not with practical applications. —**pureness** n. [f. OF f. L *purus*]

purée /ˈpjʊəreɪ/ n. a pulp of vegetables or fruit etc. reduced to a smooth cream. [F]

purely adv. in a pure manner; merely; solely, exclusively; entirely. [f. PURE]

purgative /ˈpɜːgətɪv/ adj. **1.** serving to purify. **2.** strongly laxative. —n. a purgative thing; a laxative. [f. OF or L (as PURGE)]

purgatory /ˈpɜːgətərɪ/ n. **1.** the condition or a place of spiritual cleansing, especially in the RC and Orthodox Church) of souls departing this life in the grace of God but having to expiate venial sins etc. **2.** a place or state of temporary suffering or expiation. —**purgatorial** /-ˈtɔːrɪəl/ adj. [f. AF f. L (as foll.)]

purge v.t. **1.** to make physically or spiritually clean; to remove by a cleansing process. **2.** to rid of persons regarded as undesirable. **3.** to empty (the bowels); to empty the bowels of (a person). **4.** (*Law*) to atone for or wipe out (an offence, esp. contempt of court). —n. **1.** the act or process of purging. **2.** a purgative. [f. OF f. L *purgare* (as PURE)]

purify /ˈpjʊərɪfaɪ/ v.t. to cleanse or make pure; to make ceremonially clean; to clear of extraneous elements. —**purification** /-fɪˈkeɪʃ(ə)n/ n., **purificatory** adj., **purifier** n. [f. OF f. L (as PURE)]

purist /ˈpjʊərɪst/ n. **1.** a stickler for or affecter of scrupulous purity, especially in language. **2. Purist**, an adherent of Purism, an early 20th-c. movement in painting arising out of a rejection of cubism and characterized by a return to the representation of recognizable objects, with emphasis on purity of geometric form. The movement was founded by Le Corbusier and Amédée Ozenfant, launched theoretically in their book *After Cubism* (1918); their pictures, chiefly still-lifes of machine-made objects, are painted in cool muted tones and have the impersonality of the engineer's blueprint. —**purism** n., **puristic** /-ˈrɪstɪk/ adj. [f. F (as PURE)]

Puritan /ˈpjʊərɪt(ə)n/ n. **1.** a member of the more extreme English Protestants who, dissatisfied with the Elizabethan settlement, sought a further purification of the Church from supposedly unscriptural forms. At first they attacked church ornaments, vestments, organs, etc.; from 1570 the more extreme attacked the institution of episcopacy itself. Puritans were one of the main targets of Archbishop Laud. The Civil War of 1642 and after led to the temporary triumph of Puritanism but also to its proliferation into sects, and the term 'Puritan' ceased to be applicable. **2. puritan**, a person practising or affecting extreme strictness in religion or morals. —adj. **1.** of the Puritans. **2. puritan**, scrupulous in religion or morals. —**puritanical** /-ˈtænɪk(ə)l/ adj., **puritanism** n. [f. L *puritas* purity (*purus* pure)]

purity /ˈpjʊərɪtɪ/ n. pureness, cleanness; freedom from physical or moral pollution. [f. OF (as PURE)]

purl[1] n. **1.** a knitting-stitch with the needle put into the stitch in an opposite to the normal direction, producing a ridge towards the knitter. **2.** a chain of minute loops, a picot. —v.t. to make (a stitch, or *absol.*) purl. [f. Sc. *pirl* twist]

purl[2] v.i. (of a brook etc.) to flow with a swirling motion and babbling sound. [prob. imit.]

purler n. (*colloq.*) a headlong fall. [f. *purl* overturn (prob. as PURL[1])]

purlieu /ˈpɜːljuː/ n. **1.** one's bounds or limits or usual haunts. **2.** (*hist.*) a tract on the border of a forest. **3.** (in *pl.*) outskirts, an outlying region. [prob. alt. of AF *purale(e)* perambulation to settle boundaries]

purlin /ˈpɜːlɪn/ n. a horizontal beam along a roof (ill. HOUSES). [f. L *perlio*]

purloin /pɜːˈlɔɪn/ v.t. to steal, to pilfer. [f. AF (as PRO-, *loign* far f. L *longe*)]

purple n. **1.** a colour between red and blue. **2.** (in full **Tyrian purple**) a crimson colour obtained from some molluscs. **3.** a purple robe, especially as the dress of an emperor etc. **4.** the scarlet official dress of a cardinal. —adj. of a purple or Tyrian purple colour. —v.t./i. to make or become purple. —**born in the purple**, born to a reigning family; belonging to the most privileged class. [tr. L *porphyrogenitus*, orig. used of one born of the imperial family at Constantinople and (it is said) in a chamber called the *Porphyra*] **purple passage** or **patch**, an over-ornate passage in a literary composition. —**purplish** adj. [OE f. L *purpura* f. Gk *porphura* (shellfish yielding) purple]

purport /pəˈpɔːt/ v.t. **1.** to profess, to be intended to seem.

2. (of a document or speech) to have as its meaning, to state. —/ˈpɜːpɔːt/ n. an ostensible meaning; the sense or tenor of a document or statement. —**purportedly** adv. [f. AF f. L *proportare* (PRO-[1], *portare* carry)]

purpose /ˈpɜːpəs/ n. **1.** an intended result, something for which effort is being made. **2.** intention to act, determination. —v.t. to have as one's purpose, to intend. —**on purpose**, intentionally. **purpose-built** or **purpose-made** etc. adj. built etc. for a specific purpose. **to little** or **no purpose**, with little or no result or effect. **to the purpose**, relevant, useful. [f. AF f. L, =PROPOSE]

purposeful adj. having or indicating a (conscious) purpose; intentional; acting or done with determination. —**purposefully** adv., **purposefulness** n. [f. prec. + -FUL]

purposely adv. on purpose. [f. PURPOSE]

purposive /ˈpɜːpəsɪv/ adj. having, serving, or done with a purpose; purposeful. [as prec.]

purpure /ˈpɜːpjʊə(r)/ adj. & n. (in heraldry) purple. [as PURPLE]

purr /pɜː(r)/ v.i. (of a cat etc.) to make a low vibratory sound expressing pleasure; (of machinery etc.) to make a similar sound. —n. such a sound. [imit.]

purse n. **1.** a small pouch of leather etc. for carrying money on the person. **2.** (*US*) a handbag. **3.** money, funds. **4.** a sum given as a present or prize for a contest. —v.t. to pucker or contract (the lips or brow) in wrinkles; to become wrinkled. —**hold the purse-strings**, to have control of expenditure. [OE f. L *bursa* f. Gk, = leather]

purser n. an officer on a ship who keeps the accounts, especially the head steward in a passenger vessel. [f. prec.]

pursuance /pəˈsjuːəns/ n. carrying out or observance (of a plan, rules, etc.). [as foll.]

pursuant /pəˈsjuːənt/ adj. (with *to*) in accordance with. [f. OF (as foll.)]

pursue /pəˈsjuː/ v.t./i. **1.** to follow with intent to overtake, capture, or do harm to. **2.** to continue, to proceed along or with (a route, course of action, topic, etc.). **3.** to engage in (a study or other activity). **4.** to seek to attain. **5.** (of misfortune etc.) to assail persistently. —**pursuer** n. [f. AF f. L (as PRO-[1] or PER-, SUE)]

pursuit /pəˈsjuːt/ n. **1.** pursuing. **2.** an occupation or activity pursued. [f. OF (as PRO-[1] or PER-, SUIT)]

pursuivant /ˈpɜːsɪv(ə)nt/ n. an officer of the College of Arms below a herald. [f. OF (as PURSUE)]

purulent /ˈpjʊərʊlənt/ adj. of, containing, or discharging pus. —**purulence** n. [F or f. L (as PUS)]

purvey /pəˈveɪ/ v.t. to provide or supply (articles of food) as one's business. —**purveyor** n. [f. AF f. L *providere* provide]

purview /ˈpɜːvjuː/ n. **1.** the scope or range of a document or scheme etc. **2.** the range of physical or mental vision. [as prec.]

pus /pʌs/ n. yellowish viscous matter produced from inflamed or infected tissue. [L *pus puris*]

Pusey /ˈpjuːzɪ/, Edward Bouverie (1800–82), leader of the Oxford Movement after the withdrawal of J. H. Newman (1841). He was Professor of Hebrew at Oxford from 1828.

push /pʊʃ/ v.t./i. **1.** to exert force on (a thing) so as to move it away from oneself or from the origin of the force; to cause to move thus; to exert such a force. **2.** to thrust outwards; to cause to project. **3.** to move forward or extend by effort. **4.** to make a vigorous effort in order to succeed to surpass others. **5.** to urge or impel; to put a strain on the abilities or tolerance of. **6.** to promote the use or sale or adoption of (e.g. by advertising); to sell (a drug) illegally. —n. **1.** the act of pushing; the force thus exerted. **2.** a vigorous effort; a military attack in force. **3.** enterprise, determination to succeed; use of influence to advance a person. **4.** the pressure of affairs, a crisis. —**be pushed for**, (*colloq.*) to have very little of. **push around**, to bully. **push-bike** n. (*colloq.*) a pedal cycle. **push-button** n. a button to be pushed especially to operate an electrical device; (adj.) operated thus. **push-chair** n. a folding chair on wheels, in which a child can be pushed along. **push for**, to demand. **push one's luck**, see LUCK. **push off**, to push with an oar etc. against the bank etc. in order to get a boat out into a stream; (*slang*) to go away. **push-over** n. (*colloq.*) something easily done; a person who is easily convinced or charmed. **push-start** n. the starting of a motor vehicle by pushing it to turn the engine; (v.t.) to start (a vehicle) thus. **push through**, to get completed or accepted quickly. —**pusher** n. [f. OF *pousser* f. L *pulsare* (as PULSATE)]

pushful *adj.* self-assertive, determined to succeed. —**pushfully** *adv.*, **pushfulness** *n.* [f. PUSH + -FUL]

pushing *adj.* **1.** (of a person) pushful. **2.** (*colloq.*) having nearly reached (a specified age). [f. PUSH]

Pushkin /ˈpʊʃkɪn/, Alexander Sergeevich (1799–1837), the first national poet of Russia, born in Moscow and educated in St Petersburg, but was expelled from the Lyceum in 1820 for writing revolutionary epigrams. He was also expelled from the Civil Service for atheistic writings, and his subsequent seclusion at his mother's estate prevented him from partaking in the unsuccessful revolt of 1825. One of the most influential Russian writers, he wrote prolifically in many genres, including lyric and narrative verse and an epic poem *The Bronze Horseman* (1833). His great verse novel *Eugene Onegin* (1823–31) formed the basis of Tchaikovsky's opera (1879), and his blank-verse historical drama *Boris Godunov* (1825) that of Mussorgsky's opera (1874). He was fatally wounded in a duel with his wife's admirer, Baron Georges D'Anthès.

Pushtu /ˈpʌʃtuː/ *n.* & *adj.* Pashto. [f. Pers.]

pushy *adj.* (*colloq.*) pushful. [f. PUSH]

pusillanimous /pjuːsɪˈlænɪməs/ *adj.* lacking courage, timid. —**pusillanimity** /-ˈnɪmɪtɪ/ *n.*, **pusillanimously** *adv.* [f. L (*pusillus* small, *animus* mind)]

puss /pʊs/ *n.* **1.** a cat (esp. as a form of address). **2.** (*colloq.*) a playful or coquettish girl. [prob. f. MLG or Du.]

pussy /ˈpʊsɪ/ *n.* **1.** (also **pussy-cat**) a cat. **2.** (*vulgar*) the vulva. —**pussy willow**, a willow with furry catkins. [f. PUSS]

pussyfoot *v.i.* (*colloq.*) **1.** to move stealthily. **2.** to shirk dealing with or referring directly to a problem etc.

pustulate /ˈpʌstjʊleɪt/ *v.t./i.* to form into pustules. [f. L *pustulare* (as foll.)]

pustule /ˈpʌstjuːl/ *n.* a pimple or blister, especially one containing pus. —**pustular** *adj.* [f. OF or L *pustula*]

put /pʊt/ *v.t./i.* (**-tt-**; past & *p.p.* **put**) **1.** to move to or cause to be in a specified place or position. **2.** to bring into a specified condition or state. **3.** to impose as a tax etc. **4.** to submit for consideration or attention. **5.** to express or state. **6.** to estimate. **7.** to place as an investment; to stake (money) in a bet. **8.** to lay (blame). **9.** (of a ship) to proceed. **10.** to hurl (the shot or weight) as an athletic exercise. —*n.* a throw of a shot or weight. —**put across**, to succeed in communicating (an idea etc.); to cause to seem acceptable. **put away**, (*colloq.*) to put into prison or into a mental home; (*colloq.*) to consume as food or drink. **put back**, to restore to a former place; to move back the hands of (a clock or watch). **put by**, to save for future use. **put down**, to suppress by force or authority; to snub; to have (an animal) destroyed; to record or enter in writing; to enter (a person's name) as one who will subscribe; to reckon or consider; to attribute. **put-down** *n.* a snub. **put in**, to make (an appearance); to enter (a claim etc.); to spend (time) in working etc. **put in for**, to apply for. **put it across**, (*slang*) to trick or get the better of. **put it to a person**, to challenge him to deny. **put off**, to postpone; to postpone an engagement with (a person); to make excuses and try to avoid; to dissuade or repel; to put (an electrical device or light etc.) out. **put on**, to stage (a play etc.); to cause (an electrical device or light etc.) to function; to advance the hands of (a clock or watch); to feign (an emotion); to increase one's weight by (so much). **put oneself in a person's place**, to imagine oneself in his or her situation etc. **put out**, to disconcert, to annoy, to inconvenience; to cause (a fire or light etc.) to cease to burn or function. **put over**, to put across. **put through**, to carry out or complete; to connect by telephone. **put under**, to make unconscious. **put up**, to build, to erect; to raise (a price etc.), to provide with or receive accommodation; to engage in (a fight, struggle, etc.) as a form of resistance; to present (a proposal); to present oneself as a candidate; to provide (money as a backer); to offer for sale or competition; to concoct. **put-up** *adj.* fraudulently concocted. **put upon**, (*colloq.*) unfairly burdened or deceived. **put a person up to**, to instigate him in. **put up with**, to tolerate, to submit to. [f. OE]

putative /ˈpjuːtətɪv/ *adj.* reputed, supposed. [f. OF or L (*putare* think)]

putlog /ˈpʌtlɒg/ *n.* each of the short horizontal timbers projecting from a wall, on which scaffold floor-boards rest. [orig. unkn.]

putrefy /ˈpjuːtrɪfaɪ/ *v.i.* to rot, to decay; to fester or suppurate. —**putrefaction** /-ˈfækʃ(ə)n/ *n.* [f. L *putrefacere* (*puter* rotten, *facere* make)]

putrescent /pjuːˈtres(ə)nt/ *adj.* decaying, rotting; of or accompanying this process. —**putrescence** *n.* [f. L *putrescere* (as foll.)]

putrid /ˈpjuːtrɪd/ *adj.* **1.** decomposed, rotten. **2.** foul, noxious. **3.** (*slang*) of poor quality; very unpleasant. —**putridity** /-ˈtrɪdɪtɪ/ *n.* [f. L (*putrēre* rot)]

putsch /pʊtʃ/ *n.* an attempt at a political revolution. [Swiss G, = thrust]

putt /pʌt/ *v.t./i.* to strike (a golf-ball) gently to get it into or nearer to a hole on a putting-green. —*n.* such a stroke. —**putting-green** *n.* (in golf) the smooth area of grass round a hole. [var. of PUT]

puttee /ˈpʌtɪ/ *n.* a long strip of cloth wound spirally round the leg from the ankle to the knee for protection and support. [f. Hindi, = bandage]

putter /ˈpʌtə(r)/ *n.* a golf-club used in putting. [f. PUTT]

putty /ˈpʌtɪ/ *n.* a soft hard-setting paste of chalk powder and linseed oil for fixing glass in a frame, filling up holes in woodwork, etc. —*v.t.* to fix or fill with putty. [f. F *potée* (as POT)]

puzzle *n.* **1.** a difficult or confusing problem. **2.** a problem or toy designed to test knowledge or ingenuity. —*v.t./i.* to confound or disconcert mentally; to require much thought to comprehend. —**puzzle about** or **over**, to be confused about; to ponder about. **puzzle out**, to solve or understand by hard thought. —**puzzlement** *n.* [orig. unkn.]

puzzler *n.* a difficult question or problem. [f. prec.]

PVC *abbr.* polyvinyl chloride.

PW *abbr.* Policewoman.

PWR *abbr.* pressurized water reactor.

pyaemia /paɪˈiːmɪə/ *n.* blood-poisoning with formation of abscesses in the viscera. [f. Gk *puon* pus + *haima* blood]

pye-dog /ˈpaɪdɒg/ *n.* a vagrant mongrel of the East. [f. Hindi *pahi* outsider + DOG]

Pygmalion[1] /pɪgˈmeɪlɪən/ (*Gk legend*) a legendary king of Cyprus who (according to Ovid) fashioned an ivory statue of a beautiful woman and loved it so deeply that at his prayer Aphrodite gave it life. The woman (at some point named Galatea) bore him a daughter, Paphos.

Pygmalion[2] /pɪgˈmeɪlɪən/ legendary king of Tyre, brother of Elissa (Dido), whose husband he killed in the hope of obtaining his fortune.

pygmy /ˈpɪgmɪ/ *n.* **1.** a member of a population whose average male height is not greater than 150 cm (4 ft. 11 in.), e.g. the Bambuti of tropical central Africa (the term 'Negrito' is used of similar populations of SE Asia). **2.** a very small person or thing. **3.** an insignificant person or thing. —*adj.* **1.** of pygmies. **2.** very small. [f. L f. Gk (*pugmē* length from elbow to knuckles)]

pyjamas /pɪˈdʒɑːməz/ *n.pl.* a suit of loose trousers and jacket for sleeping in; a similar garment for beach or evening wear by women. [f. Urdu, = leg-clothing]

pylon /ˈpaɪlən/ *n.* **1.** a tall lattice-work structure used as a support for overhead electricity cables or as a boundary. **2.** a structure marking a path for aircraft. **3.** a structure supporting the engine of an aircraft. **4.** a gateway or gate-tower, especially the monumental gateway to an Egyptian temple, usually formed by two truncated pyramidal towers connected by a lower architectural member containing the gate. [f. Gk *pulōn* (*pulē* gate)]

Pyongyang /pjʌŋˈjɑːŋ/ the capital of North Korea; pop. (1982) approx. 1,500,000.

pyorrhoea /paɪəˈrɪə/ *n.* discharge of pus, especially in disease of the tooth-sockets. [f. Gk *puon* pus + *rhoia* flux]

pyracantha /paɪərəˈkænθə/ *n.* an evergreen thorny shrub of the genus *Pyracantha* with white flowers and scarlet or orange berries. [L f. Gk]

pyramid /ˈpɪrəmɪd/ *n.* **1.** a monumental structure, especially in ancient Egypt, usually with a square base and with four equal triangular sides meeting at an apex (see below). **2.** a solid of this shape with a base of three or more sides. **3.** a thing or pile of things shaped like this. —**pyramid selling**, a system of selling goods in which agency rights are sold to an increasing number of distributors at successively lower levels. —**pyramidal** /-ˈræmɪd(ə)l/ *adj.* [f. L f. Gk *puramis*]

The pyramid is the characteristic tomb built for Egyptian kings from the 3rd Dynasty (*c.*2649 BC) until *c.*1640 BC. There are two principal types: the step pyramid (e.g. that of Djoser at Saqqara), consisting of several stepped levels rising to a flat top, and the true pyramid, which developed from this and was introduced in the 4th Dynasty (*c.*2575 BC, e.g. at Giza). The pyramid was the focal point of a vast funerary complex, including a temple at its side, linked by a causeway to a lower temple near the cultivated land and flood-waters of the river. The internal structure of most true pyramids consists of a series of stepped buttresses surrounding the central core; these were packed with rubble and finished with casing blocks. Inclined ramps were used in the building process, but the exact procedure, and the mathematical calculations involved, remain (like the reason for the choice of the pyramidal shape) unknown. The hallmark of Egypt, the pyramids are imposing in their austere simplicity; those at Giza were one of the Seven Wonders of the World.

Monuments of similar shape are associated with the civilizations of Mesoamerica and South America *c.*1200 BC– AD 750. They were built by the Aztecs and Mayas as centres of worship, usually as one component in a complex of courtyards, platforms, and temples.

Pyramus /ˈpɪrəməs/ (*Rom. legend*) a Babylonian youth, lover of Thisbe. Their story is almost unknown except from Ovid. Forbidden to marry by their parents, who were neighbours, the lovers conversed through a chink in the wall and agreed to meet at a tomb outside the city. There, Thisbe was frightened away by a lioness coming from its kill, and Pyramus, seeing her bloodstained cloak and supposing her dead, stabbed himself. Thisbe, finding his body when she returned, threw herself upon his sword. Their blood stained a mulberry-tree, whose fruit has ever since been black when ripe, in sign of mourning for them.

pyre /ˈpaɪə(r)/ *n.* a heap of combustible material, especially a funeral pile for burning a corpse. [f. L f. Gk *pura* (as PYRO-)]

Pyrenees /pɪrəˈniːz/ a range of mountains rising to over 3,380 m (11,000 ft.), separating France from the Iberian Peninsula. —**Pyrenean** /-ˈniːən/ *adj.*

pyrethrum /paɪˈriːθrəm/ *n.* **1.** a chrysanthemum with finely divided leaves (esp. *Chrysanthemum coccineum* and *C. cinerariifolium*). **2.** an insecticide made from its dried flowers. [L f. Gk, = feverfew]

pyretic /paɪˈretɪk, pɪ-/ *adj.* of or producing fever. [f. Gk *puretos* fever]

Pyrex /ˈpaɪreks/ *n.* [P] a hard heat-resistant glass. [invented word]

pyrexia /paɪˈreksɪə/ *n.* fever. [f. Gk *purexis* (*puressō* be feverish, as PYRO-)]

pyrites /paɪˈraɪtiːz/ *n.* a mineral that is a sulphide of iron

(*iron pyrites*) or of copper and iron (*copper pyrites*). [L f. Gk (as PYRO-)]

pyro- /paɪrəʊ-/ *in comb.* fire. [f. Gk (*pur* fire)]

pyromania /paɪrəʊˈmeɪnɪə/ *n.* an uncontrollable impulse to start fires. —**pyromaniac** *n. & adj.* [f. PYRO- + -MANIA]

pyrotechnics /paɪrəʊˈtekniks/ *n.pl.* **1.** the art of making fireworks. **2.** a display of fireworks. **3.** any loud or brilliant display. —**pyrotechnic** *adj.* [f. PYRO- + Gk *tekhnē* art]

Pyrrha /ˈpɪrə/ (*Gk myth.*) wife of Deucalion (see entry).

pyrrhic /ˈpɪrɪk/ *adj.* (of a victory) won at too great a cost. [f. *Pyrrhus* king of Epirus, who defeated the Romans thus in 279 BC]

Pythagoras /paɪˈθægərəs/ (late 6th c. BC) Greek philosopher, founder of a religious, political, and scientific society at Croton in southern Italy. No writings by him survive, his achievements were early confused with those of his followers, and his life is obscured by legend. The Pythagoreans held that the soul is condemned to a cycle of re-incarnation, from which it may escape by attaining a state of purity. Pythagoras is said to have discovered the numerical ratios determining the principal intervals of the musical scale, whence he was led to interpret the world as a whole through numbers, the systematic study of which he thus originated. He is the probable discoverer (though not in its Euclidean form) of the geometrical theorem named after him—that the square on the hypotenuse of a right-angled triangle is equal to the sum of the squares on the other two sides. In astronomy, his analysis of the courses of the sun, moon, and stars into circular motions was not set aside until the 17th c. (see KEPLER). —**Pythagorean** /-ˈriːən/ *adj. & n.*

Pythia /ˈpɪθɪə/ the priestess of Apollo at Delphi in ancient Greece, who delivered the oracles. [as foll.]

Pythian /ˈpɪθɪən/ *adj.* of Delphi or Apollo's oracle and priestess there. —*n.* Apollo or his priestess at Delphi. —**Pythian games,** those celebrated by the ancient Greeks every four years at Delphi. [f. L f. Gk *Puthios* (*Puthō* older name of Delphi)]

python /ˈpaɪθ(ə)n/ *n.* a large snake (esp. of the genus *Python*) that kills its prey by compressing and asphyxiating it. [L f. Gk *Puthōn* huge serpent or monster slain near Delphi (cf. prec.) by Apollo in myth]

pyx /pɪks/ *n.* **1.** a vessel in which bread consecrated for the Eucharist is kept (ill. VESTMENTS). **2.** a box in which specimen coins are deposited at the Royal Mint. —**trial of the pyx,** an annual test of specimen coins at the Royal Mint by a group of members (called a *jury*) of the Goldsmith's Company. [f. L f. Gk *puxis* (*puxos* box)]

Q

Q, q /kjuː/ *n.* (*pl.* **Qs, Q's**) the seventeenth letter of the alphabet, derived from a Phoenician letter representing a guttural *k* sound. The letter, followed by *v*, was used in Latin to represent the double sound *kw*-, and *qu*- is used in English to represent this sound in many native English words as well as in those derived from Latin, even when these have now the pronunciation *k*- (as in words derived through French).

Q. *abbr.* **1.** Queen('s). **2.** question.

Qatar /ˈkætɑː(r), ˈgæ-/ a sheikdom on a peninsula on the west coast of the Persian Gulf; pop. (est. 1982) 250,000; official language Arabic; capital, Doha. The country became a British protectorate in 1916, and until 1971 (when it became a sovereign independent State) was in special treaty relations with Britain. Oil is the chief source of revenue. —**Qatari** *adj.* & *n.*

QC *abbr.* Queen's Counsel.

QED *abbr.* which was the thing to be proved. [initials of L *quod erat demonstrandum*]

Qld. *abbr.* Queensland.

qr. *abbr.* quarter(s).

qt. *abbr.* quart(s).

q.t. *abbr.* (*slang*) quiet (*on the q.t.*).

qua /kweɪ/ *conj.* in the capacity of. [L, = in the manner in which]

quack¹ *n.* the harsh cry of a duck. —*v.i.* **1.** to utter a quack. **2.** to talk loudly. [imit.]

quack² *n.* a person who falsely claims to have medical skill or to provide remedies which will cure disease, a charlatan. —*adj.* **1.** being a quack. **2.** characteristic of or used by a quack. —**quackery** *n.* [abbr. of Du. *quacksalver*, f. *quacken* boast, *salf* salve, ointment]

quad¹ /kwɒd/ *n.* (*colloq.*) **1.** a quadruplet. **2.** a quadrangle. **3.** quadraphony. —*adj.* quadraphonic. [abbr.]

quad² /kwɒd/ *n.* a small metal block used by printers in spacing. [abbr. of *quadrat*, f. L *quadratus* made square]

Quadragesima /kwɒdrəˈdʒesɪmə/ *n.* the first Sunday in Lent. [f. L, = fortieth (day), Lent having 40 days]

quadrangle /ˈkwɒdræŋg(ə)l/ *n.* **1.** a four-cornered figure, especially a square or rectangle. **2.** a four-sided court bordered by large buildings, especially in colleges. —**quadrangular** /-ˈræŋgjʊlə(r)/ *adj.* [f. OF f. L (as QUADRI-, ANGLE)]

quadrant /ˈkwɒdrənt/ *n.* **1.** a quarter of a circle's circumference; a quarter of a circle as cut by two diameters at right angles (ill. SHAPES); a quarter of a sphere as cut by two planes intersecting at right angles at the centre. **2.** a thing shaped like a quarter-circle, especially a graduated strip of metal etc.; an instrument including this for taking angular measurements. [f. L *quadrans* quarter (*quattuor* four)]

quadraphonic /kwɒdrəˈfɒnɪk/ *adj.* (of sound-reproduction) using four transmission channels. —**quadraphonically** *adv.*, **quadraphony** /-ˈrɒfənɪ/ *n.* [f. QUADRI- + (STEREO)PHONIC]

quadrat /ˈkwɒdræt/ *n.* a small area marked out for study of the plants and animals it contains. [f. L *quadratus* made square]

quadrate /ˈkwɒdreɪt/ *adj.* square, rectangular. [as prec.]

quadratic equation /kwɒdˈrætɪk/ an equation involving the square and no higher power of an unknown quantity or variable. [f. F or L (as QUADRAT)]

quadrennial /kwɒdˈrenɪəl/ *adj.* **1.** lasting for four years. **2.** recurring every four years. —**quadrennially** *adv.* [as foll.]

quadrennium /kwɒdˈrenɪəm/ *n.* (*pl.* **-s**) a period of four years. [f. L *quadriennium* (QUADRI-, *annus* year)]

quadri- /ˈkwɒdrɪ/ *in comb.* four. [L (*quattuor* four)]

quadrilateral /kwɒdrɪˈlætər(ə)l/ *adj.* having four sides. —*n.* a quadrilateral figure (ill. SHAPES). [f. L (QUADRI-, *latus* side)]

quadrille¹ /kwəˈdrɪl/ *n.* a square dance usually containing five figures; music for this. [F f. Sp. *cuadrilla* squadron (*cuadra* square)]

quadrille² /kwəˈdrɪl/ *n.* a card-game fashionable in the 18th c., played by four persons with 40 cards (i.e. an ordinary pack without the 8s, 9s, and 10s). [F, perh. f. Sp. (*cuarto* fourth)]

quadrillion /kwəˈdrɪljən/ *n.* (for *pl.* usage see HUNDRED) **1.** a million raised to the fourth power (1 followed by 24 ciphers). **2.** (*Amer.*) a thousand raised to the fifth power (1 followed by 15 ciphers). [QUADRI-, + MILLION]

quadriplegia /kwɒdrɪˈpliːdʒɪə/ *n.* paralysis of all four limbs. —**quadriplegic** *adj.* and *n.* [f. QUADRI- + Gk *plēgē* blow]

quadrivium /kwɒdˈrɪvɪəm/ *n.* a medieval university course comprising arithmetic, geometry, astronomy, and music. [L, = place where four roads meet (QUADRI-, *via* road)]

quadroon /kwəˈdruːn/ *n.* the offspring of a White and a mulatto, a person of one-quarter Negro blood. [f. Sp. *cuarterón* (*cuarto* fourth)]

quadruped /ˈkwɒdrʊped/ *n.* a four-footed animal, especially a mammal. [f. F or L (QUADRI-, *pes* foot)]

quadruple /ˈkwɒdrʊp(ə)l/ *adj.* **1.** fourfold; having four parts; being four times as many or as much. **2.** (of time in music) having four beats in a bar. —*n.* a fourfold number or amount. —*v.t./i.* to multiply by four. —**Quadruple Alliance**, an alliance of four powers, (1) that formed in 1718 when Austria joined Britain, the Dutch Republic, and France against Spain (who had seized Sicily and Sardinia); (2) that of 1813 (renewed in 1815) when Britain, Russia, Austria, and Prussia united to defeat Napoleon and to maintain the international order established in Europe by the Peace of Paris at the end of the Napoleonic Wars; (3) that of 1834 between Britain, France, Spain, and Portugal to expel pretenders from the last two named countries. —**quadruply** *adv.* [f. F f. L *quadruplus* (as QUADRI-)]

quadruplet /ˈkwɒdrʊplɪt, -ˈruːp-/ *n.* each of four children born at one birth. [f. prec., after *triplet*]

quadruplicate /kwɒˈdruːplɪkət/ *adj.* **1.** fourfold. **2.** of which four copies are made. —/-eɪt/ *v.t.* **1.** to multiply by four. **2.** to make four copies of. —**in quadruplicate**, in four copies. [f. L (*quadruplex* fourfold)]

quaestor /ˈkwiːstə(r)/ *n.* a magistrate in ancient Rome who acted as the State treasurer, paymaster, etc. [f. L (*quaerere* seek)]

quaff /kwɒf, kwɑːf/ *v.t./i.* (*literary*) to drain (a cup etc.) in copious draughts; to drink deeply. [perh. imit.]

quagmire /ˈkwægmaɪə(r), ˈkwɒg-/ *n.* a quaking bog, a marsh, a slough. [f. *quag* marsh, or dial. *quag* to shake + MIRE]

Quai d'Orsay /keɪ dɔːˈseɪ/ a riverside street on the left bank of the Seine in Paris. The name is often used to denote the French ministry of foreign affairs, which has its headquarters there.

quail¹ *n.* (*pl.* same or **-s**) a bird of the genus *Coturnix* related to the partridge. [f. OF f. L *coacula* (prob. imit.)]

quail² *v.i.* to flinch, to show fear. [orig. unkn.]

quaint *adj.* piquantly or attractively unfamiliar or old-fashioned, daintily odd. —**quaintly** *adv.*, **quaintness** *n.* [orig. = cunning, f. OF f. L *cognitus* (*cognoscere* ascertain)]

quake *v.i.* to shake or tremble from unsteadiness; (of a person) to shake with fear etc. —*n.* (*colloq.*) an earthquake. [OE]

Quaker /ˈkweɪkə(r)/ *n.* a member of the Society of Friends (see entry). —**Quakerism** *n.* [f. prec.; the reason for the name is disputed]

qualification /kwɒlɪfɪˈkeɪʃ(ə)n/ *n.* **1.** qualifying. **2.** an accomplishment fitting a person for a position or purpose. **3.** a thing that modifies or limits a meaning etc. —**qualificatory** *adj.* [F or f. L (as foll.)]

qualify /ˈkwɒlɪfaɪ/ *v.t./i.* **1.** to make competent or fit for a position or purpose; to make legally entitled. **2.** (of a person) to satisfy the conditions or requirements. **3.** to modify or make (a statement etc.) less absolute. **4.** to moderate, to mitigate, to make less extreme. **5.** to attribute a quality to, to describe as. —**qualifier** *n.* [f. F. f. L *qualificare* (*qualis* such as, of what kind)]

qualitative /'kwɒlɪtətɪv/ *adj.* concerned with or depending on quality. [f. L (as foll.)]

quality /'kwɒlɪtɪ/ *n.* **1.** degree or level of excellence. **2.** general excellence. **3.** an attribute or faculty. **4.** (of a voice or sound) timbre. **5.** (*archaic*) high social standing. [f. OF f. L (as QUALIFY)]

qualm /kwɑːm/ *n.* **1.** a misgiving, an uneasy doubt, a scruple of conscience. **2.** a momentary faint or sick feeling. [orig. unkn.]

quandary /'kwɒndərɪ/ *n.* a perplexed state, a practical dilemma. [orig. unkn.]

quango /'kwæŋgəʊ/ *n.* (*pl.* **-os**) a semi-public body with financial support from and senior appointments made by the government. The term came into use *c.* 1973 (its full form is found in 1967) in the USA. [abbr. of *qua*si-*a*utonomous *n*on-*g*overnmental *o*rganization]

quanta *pl.* of QUANTUM.

quantifiable /'kwɒntɪfaɪəb(ə)l/ *adj.* that may be quantified. [f. foll.]

quantify /'kwɒntɪfaɪ/ *v.t.* to express as a quantity; to determine the quantity of. —**quantification** /-fɪ'keɪʃ(ə)n/ *n.* [f. L *quantificare* (*quantus* how much)]

quantitative /'kwɒntɪtətɪv/ *adj.* concerned with quantity; measured or measurable by quantity. [f. L (as foll.)]

quantity /'kwɒntɪtɪ/ *n.* **1.** ability to be measured through having size, weight, amount, or number. **2.** an amount or number of things; a specified or considerable amount or number. **3.** length or shortness of vowel sounds or syllables. **4.** a thing having quantity. —**quantity surveyor,** a person who measures and prices the work of builders. [f. OF f. L (as QUANTIFY)]

quantum /'kwɒntəm/ *n.* (*pl.* **quanta**) **1.** a minimum amount of a physical quantity (such as energy or momentum) which can exist in a given situation and by multiples of which changes in the quantity occur (see below). **2.** a required, desired, or allowed amount. —**quantum mechanics,** a mathematical form of quantum theory dealing with the motion and interaction of (esp. subatomic) particles and incorporating the concept that these particles can also be regarded as waves. **quantum theory,** the body of theory based on the existence of quanta of energy. [L, neut. of *quantus* how much]

The development of quantum theory in the 20th c. has, along with the theory of relativity, revolutionized our understanding of the physical world. The first step occurred in 1900 when Max Planck accounted for certain puzzling characteristics of the electromagnetic radiation given off by hot bodies by postulating that energy could be emitted only in discrete 'lumps' rather than as a continuum—a radical break with traditional views. In 1905 Einstein took this idea further by suggesting that light itself, along with other electromagnetic radiation, could be regarded as consisting of discrete particles or quanta of energy. (These particles are now called *photons*.) In 1913 Niels Bohr proposed a model of the atom that incorporated quantum theory: electrons are postulated to circle round a central nucleus, but are restricted to particular orbits which correspond to possessing discrete amounts of energy. In 1924 L. de Broglie conjectured that, just as light waves possess some of the attributes of particles, perhaps particles such as electrons also had the properties of waves. This idea was taken up and over the rest of the decade was developed by Schrödinger, Heisenberg, and others into a more sophisticated theory of atomic structure called quantum mechanics, in which the fixed orbits of Bohr's model are replaced by more diffuse 'orbitals', reflecting the dual nature of the electron as behaving both like a wave and like a particle. This 'wave-particle duality' appeared paradoxical to many, as did the so-called 'uncertainty principle' enunciated by Heisenberg in 1927, which set a definite theoretical limit to the accuracy with which properties of a particle, such as position and momentum, can be measured simultaneously. Philosophical debate has continued about whether the uncertainty principle means that there is after all some 'spontaneity' in the physical world, in the sense that not every event is completely determined by previous events. In 1928 quantum mechanics was further refined by P. A. M. Dirac, who incorporated into it the principles of relativity. Since then the ideas of quantum mechanics have been extended to include nuclear physics and the properties of electromagnetic fields. Quantum theory also explains certain properties of solids such as superconductivity, and overall continues to be an extremely successful and accurate account of the fundamental structure of the physical world.

quarantine /'kwɒrəntiːn/ *n.* isolation imposed on a ship, persons, or animals to prevent infection or contagion; the period of this. —*v.t.* to put into quarantine. [f. It., = forty days (*quaranta* forty)]

quark /kwɑːk, kwɔːk/ *n.* any of a group of (originally three) hypothetical components of elementary particles. Quarks are held to carry a charge one third or two thirds that of the proton. Many predictions of this theory have been corroborated by experiments but free quarks have yet to be observed. In a sense, quark theory recapitulates at a deeper level efforts earlier this century to explain all atomic properties in terms of electrons, protons, and neutrons. [coined by M. Gell-Mann, 1964, from phrase 'Three quarks for Muster Mark!' in James Joyce's *Finnegans Wake* (1939)]

quarrel /'kwɒr(ə)l/ *n.* **1.** a violent disagreement; a break in friendly relations. **2.** a cause for complaint. —*v.i.* (**-ll-**) **1.** to engage in a quarrel; to break off friendly relations. **2.** to find fault. [f. OF f. L *querel(l)a* complaint (*queri* complain)]

quarrelsome *adj.* given to quarrelling. —**quarrel-someness** *n.* [f. prec. + -SOME]

quarry[1] /'kwɒrɪ/ *n.* a place from which stone is extracted for building etc. —*v.t./i.* to extract (stone) from a quarry. —**quarry tile,** an unglazed floor-tile. [f. L f. OF *quarriere* f. L *quadrum* square]

quarry[2] /'kwɒrɪ/ *n.* an intended prey or victim being hunted; something sought or pursued. [f. OF *cuiree*, ult. f. L *cor* heart; orig. = parts of deer given to hounds]

quart /kwɔːt/ *n.* a liquid measure equal to one quarter of a gallon. [f. OF f. L (*quartus* fourth)]

quarter /'kwɔːtə(r)/ *n.* **1.** each of four equal parts into which a thing is divided. **2.** a period of three months, especially one ending on a quarter-day. **3.** a point of time 15 minutes before or after any hour. **4.** 25 US or Canadian cents; a coin for this. **5.** a division of a town, especially as occupied by a particular class. **6.** a point of the compass; the region at this; a direction; a district; a person or group regarded as a possible source of supply. **7.** (in *pl.*) lodgings; an abode, a station of troops. **8.** one fourth of a lunar month; the moon's position between the first two (**first quarter**) and the last two (**last quarter**) of these. **9.** each of the four parts into which a carcass is divided. **10.** (in *pl.*) the hind legs and adjoining parts of a quadruped; the hindquarters. **11.** exemption from being put to death, on condition of surrender; a grain-measure of 8 bushels, one quarter of a hundredweight. —*v.t.* **1.** to divide into quarters; (*hist.*) to divide (the body of an executed person) thus. **2.** to put (troops etc.) into quarters; to provide with lodgings. **3.** to place (coats of arms) on four parts of a shield's surface. —**cry quarter,** to ask for mercy. **quarter-day** *n.* any of the four days beginning an official quarter of the year for fiscal purposes (in England 25 March, 24 June, 29 Sept., 25 Dec.; in Scotland 2 Feb., 15 May, 1 August, 11 Nov.). **quarter-final** *n.* a match or round preceding a semi-final. **quarter-light** *n.* a small vertically opening window in a motor vehicle. **quarter sessions,** (*hist.*) a court with limited criminal and civil jurisdiction, usually held quarterly. [f. AF f. L *quartarius* (as prec.)]

quarterdeck *n.* the part of a ship's upper deck near the stern, usually reserved for officers.

quartering *n.* (often in *pl.*) coats of arms arranged on one shield to denote alliances of families (ill. HERALDRY). [f. QUARTER]

quarterly *adv.* **1.** once in each quarter of a year. **2.** (in heraldry) in the four, or in two diagonally opposite, quarters of a shield. —*adj.* **1.** done, published, or due quarterly. **2.** (in heraldry, of a shield) quartered. —*n.* a quarterly publication. [as prec.]

quartermaster *n.* **1.** a regimental officer in charge of quartering, rations, etc. **2.** a naval petty officer in charge of steering, signals, etc.

quarterstaff *n.* a stout pole, six to eight feet long, formerly used by peasantry as a weapon.

quartet /kwɔː'tet/ *n.* (also **quartette**) **1.** a musical composition for four performers; these performers. **2.** any group of four. [f. F f. It. (*quarto* fourth, f. L *quartus* four)]

quarto /'kwɔːtəʊ/ *n.* (*pl.* **-os**) the size of a book or page given by twice folding a sheet of standard size to form four leaves; a book or sheet of this size. [f. L (*in*) *quarto* (in) fourth (of sheet)]

quartz /kwɔːts/ *n.* silica in various forms. —**quartz clock** or **watch,** one operated by electric vibrations of a quartz crystal. **quartz lamp,** a quartz tube with mercury vapour as the light-source. [f. G f. Slavonic]

quasar /ˈkweɪsɑː(r)/ n. any of a class of point-like sources of light visible in large telescopes, often associated with intense radio emission. Their spectra show large red-shifts, suggesting great remoteness and high velocities of recession. If they are indeed at such distances, they must be emitting exceptionally large amounts of energy, the nature of which is not fully understood. [f. *quasi* + stell*ar*]

quasi- /ˈkweɪzaɪ/ *prefix* seeming(ly), not real(ly); almost. [f. L *quasi* as if]

Quasimodo[1] /kweɪsɪˈmɑʊdəʊ/ the deformed bell-ringer of Notre Dame in Victor Hugo's *Notre Dame de Paris* (1831).

Quasimodo[2] /kwɑːzɪˈmɑʊdəʊ/, Salvatore (1901-68), Italian poet, who was awarded the Nobel Prize for literature in 1959. His early work was influenced by the symbolist movement; his later work is more extrovert and concerned with social issues. Some of his best poetry is inspired by his Sicilian background, for which he felt a nostalgic tenderness.

quassia /ˈkwɒʃə/ n. **1.** a South American tree (*Quassia amara*); its wood, bark, or root. **2.** a bitter tonic from these. [f. G. *Quassi*, 18th-c. Surinam Negro, who discovered its medicinal properties]

quaternary /kwəˈtɜːnərɪ/ adj. **1.** having four parts. **2. Quaternary**, of the second period of the Cainozoic era, comprising the Pleistocene and Holocene (Recent) epochs and extending from about 2 million years ago to the present. —**Quaternary** n. this period. [f. L (*quaterni* four each)]

quatrain /ˈkwɒtreɪn/ n. a four-line stanza. [F (*quatre* four)]

quatrefoil /ˈkætrəfɔɪl/ n. **1.** a four-cusped figure (ill. CHURCH). **2.** a four-lobed leaf or flower. [f. AF (*quatre* four, *foil* leaf)]

quattrocento /kwɑːtrəʊˈtʃentəʊ/ n. Italian art of the 15th c. [It., = 1400, used of years 14—]

quaver /ˈkweɪvə(r)/ v.t./i. **1.** to tremble, to vibrate. **2.** to say or speak in a trembling voice; to sing with trembling. —n. **1.** a quavering sound; quavering speech. **2.** a trill. **3.** (*Mus.*) a note half as long as a crotchet (ill. MUSICAL NOTATION). —**quavery** adj. [frequent. of obs. *quave* (imit.)]

quay /kiː/ n. an artificial landing-place for loading and unloading ships. [f. OF *kay*]

queasy /ˈkwiːzɪ/ adj. **1.** feeling slight nausea; having an easily upset digestion. **2.** (of food) causing nausea. **3.** (of a conscience or person) over-scrupulous. —**queasily** adv., **queasiness** n. [perh. rel. to OF *coisier* hurt]

Quebec /kwɪˈbek/ **1.** a province of eastern Canada (from 1867), settled by the French and ceded to the British in 1763. Its culture remains predominantly French. **2.** its capital city, on the St Lawrence river, captured from the French by a British force in 1759 (see PLAINS OF ABRAHAM).

Quechua /ˈketʃwə/ n. **1.** (*pl.* same) a member of an Indian people of Peru and neighbouring parts of Bolivia, Chile, Colombia, and Ecuador. **2.** the language (actually a group of related languages) spoken by this people. It is one of the two official languages of Peru (the other being Spanish). —**Quechuan** adj. & n. [Sp. f. Quechua, = plunderer, despoiler]

queen n. **1.** a female sovereign (esp. hereditary) ruler of an independent State. **2.** a king's wife. **3.** a woman, country, or thing regarded as pre-eminent in a specified field, area, or class. **4.** a perfect fertile female of the bee, ant, etc. **5.** the most powerful piece in chess. **6.** a court-card with a picture of a queen. **7.** (*slang*) a male homosexual. —v.t. to convert (a pawn in chess) to a queen when it reaches the opponent's end of the board; (of a pawn) to be thus converted. —**Queen-Anne** adj. in the style of English design characteristic of the early 18th c. **queen consort**, a king's wife. **queen it**, to act the queen. **queen mother**, a king's widow who is the mother of a sovereign. **queen-post** n. either of the two upright posts between the tie-beam and the main rafters (ill. BUILDING TECHNIQUES). —**queenly** adj., **queenliness** n. [OE]

Queensberry Rules /ˈkwiːnzbərɪ/ the standard rules of boxing, drafted in 1867 under the name and patronage of the Marquess of Queensberry. They formed the basis of modern glove-fighting as distinct from earlier bare-knuckle contests. The rules called for the wearing of gloves, and rounds of 3 minutes' duration interspersed with a minute's rest, and prohibited wrestling.

Queensland /ˈkwiːnzlənd/ a State comprising the north-eastern part of Australia. Originally established in 1824 as a penal settlement, it was constituted a separate colony in 1859, having previously formed part of New South Wales,

and was federated with the other States of Australia in 1901; capital, Brisbane. —**Queenslander** n.

queer adj. **1.** strange, odd, eccentric. **2.** suspect, of questionable character. **3.** slightly ill, faint. **4.** (*slang*, esp. of a man) homosexual. —n. (*slang*) a homosexual (esp. male) person. —v.t. (*slang*) to spoil, to put out of order. —**in Queer Street**, (*slang*) in debt or trouble or disrepute. **queer the pitch for**, to spoil the chances of (a person) beforehand. —**queerly** adv., **queerness** n. [perh. f. G *quer* oblique]

quell v.t. to suppress; to reduce to submission. [OE, = kill]

quench v.t. **1.** to satisfy (one's thirst) by drinking. **2.** to extinguish (a fire or light). **3.** to cool, especially with water. **4.** to stifle or suppress (a desire etc.). [OE]

Quercia /ˈkwɜːʃə/, Jacopo della (1374-1438), Italian sculptor, a native of Siena. His achievement has been overshadowed by his contemporaries, Ghiberti and Donatello, with whom he worked on the Siena Baptistry reliefs (1417-31). His biblical reliefs for the portal of S. Petronio, Bologna (1425) are reckoned to constitute his masterpiece and reveal the pungency and vigour of his mature style.

quern /kwɜːn/ n. **1.** a simple apparatus for grinding corn, consisting of two hard stones, the upper of which is rubbed to and fro, or rotated, on the lower one. **2.** a small hand-mill for pepper etc. [OE]

querulous /ˈkwerʊləs/ adj. complaining peevishly. —**querulously** adv., **querulousness** n. [f. L (*queri* complain)]

query /ˈkwɪərɪ/ n. **1.** a question. **2.** a question mark or the word *query* spoken or written as a mark of interrogation. —v.t. **1.** to ask or inquire. **2.** to call in question, to dispute the accuracy of. [anglicized form of L *quaere* (imper. of *quaerere* ask)]

quest n. **1.** seeking, a search. **2.** a thing sought. —v.i. to seek or search for something. —**in quest of**, seeking. [f. OF f. L *quaerere* seek]

question /ˈkwestʃ(ə)n/ n. **1.** a sentence so worded or expressed as to seek information. **2.** a doubt or dispute about a matter; the raising of such doubt etc. **3.** the matters to be discussed or decided. **4.** a problem for solution. **5.** a thing depending on the conditions *of*. —v.t. **1.** to ask questions of; to subject to examination. **2.** to call in question; to throw doubt on. —**beyond (all) question**, certainly. **call in question**, to express doubts about, to dispute. **in question**, being mentioned or discussed. **out of the question**, impracticable, not worth considering. **question mark**, the punctuation mark (?) indicating a question. **question-master** n. the person who puts the questions to people taking part in a quiz game or similar entertainment. **question time**, a period in Parliament when MPs may question ministers. —**questioner** n. [as prec.]

questionable adj. of doubtful truth, validity, or advisability; suspect. —**questionably** adv. [f. prec.]

questionnaire /kwestʃəˈneə(r)/ n. a formulated series of questions put to a number of people, especially as part of a survey. [F (as QUEST)]

Quetzalcóatl /ketsəlkəʊˈɑːt(ə)l/ the Plumed Serpent of the Toltec and Aztec civilizations, traditionally known as the god of the morning and evening star, later as the patron of priests, inventor of books and of the calendar, and as the symbol of death and resurrection. His worship involved human sacrifice. Legend said that he would return in another age, and when Montezuma, last king of the Aztecs, received news of the landing of Cortés and his men in 1519, his first thought was that Quetzalcóatl had indeed returned.

queue /kjuː/ n. **1.** a line or sequence of persons or vehicles etc. awaiting their turn. **2.** a pigtail. —v.i. (often with *up*) to stand in or join a queue. [F f. L *cauda* tail]

quibble n. **1.** a petty objection, a trivial point of criticism. **2.** a play on words, a pun. **3.** an equivocation, an evasion; an argument depending on the ambiguity of a word or phrase. —v.i. to use quibbles. —**quibbler** n. [dim. of obs. *quib* prob. f. L *quibus* dat. and abl. pl. of *qui* who (used in legal documents)]

quiche /kiːʃ/ n. an open tart, usually with a savoury filling. [F]

quick adj. **1.** taking only a short time to do something or to traverse a distance or to be done or obtained etc. **2.** able to notice or learn or think quickly; alert. **3.** (of temper) easily roused. **4.** (*archaic*) living, alive. —adv. quickly, at a rapid rate; in a fairly short time. —n. **1.** the sensitive flesh below the nails or skin or a sore. **2.** the seat of feeling or emotion. —**quick-freeze** v.t. to freeze (food) rapidly for storing, so that it keeps its natural qualities. **quick-witted**

adj. alert; quick to understand a situation; quick at making jokes. —**quickly** *adv.* **quickness** *n.* [OE, orig. = alive]

quicken *v.t./i.* **1.** to make or become quicker, to accelerate. **2.** to make or become livelier, to stimulate. **3.** (of a woman or foetus) to reach the stage of pregnancy when the foetus makes movements that can be felt by the mother. [f. prec.]

quickie *n.* (*colloq.*) a thing made or done quickly. [f. QUICK]

quicklime *n.* unslaked lime.

quicksand *n.* an area of loose wet sand into which heavy objects readily sink.

quickset *adj.* formed of live plants set to grow in a hedge. —*n.* a hedge formed thus.

quicksilver *n.* **1.** mercury. **2.** a mercurial temperament.

quickstep *n.* a ballroom dance with quick steps; the music for this.

quid[1] *n.* (*pl.* same) (*slang*) one pound sterling. —**quids in,** able to profit. [prob. f. *quid* nature of a thing, f. L what, something]

quid[2] *n.* a lump of tobacco for chewing. [dial. var. of CUD]

quiddity /ˈkwɪdɪtɪ/ *n.* **1.** the essence of a thing. **2.** a quibble, a captious subtlety. [f. L *quidditas* (*quid* what)]

quid pro quo /kwɪd prəʊ ˈkwəʊ/ a thing given as compensation. [L, = something for something]

quiescent /kwɪˈesənt/ *adj.* inactive, dormant. —**quiescence** *n.* [as foll.]

quiet /ˈkwaɪət/ *adj.* **1.** with little or no sound or motion. **2.** of gentle or peaceful disposition. **3.** unobtrusive, not showy. **4.** not overt, private, disguised. **5.** undisturbed, uninterrupted; free or far from vigorous action; informal. **6.** enjoyed in quiet; not anxious or remorseful. —*n.* an undisturbed state, tranquillity; repose; stillness, silence. —*v.t./i.* to make or become quiet or calm. —**be quiet,** (*colloq.*) to cease talking etc. **keep quiet,** to say nothing. **on the quiet,** unobtrusively, secretly. —**quietly** *adv.,* **quietness** *n.* [f. OF f. L (*quiescere* become calm)]

quieten *v.t./i.* to make or become quiet. [f. prec.]

quietism /ˈkwaɪətɪz(ə)m/ *n.* a passive contemplative attitude to life, as a form of religious mysticism. —**quietist** *n.* & *adj.* [f. It. (as QUIET)]

quietude /ˈkwaɪɪtjuːd/ *n.* quietness. [f. QUIET]

quietus /kwaɪˈiːtəs/ *n.* release from life, final riddance. [f. L *quietus* (*est* he is) quit, used in receipts]

quiff *n.* a lock of hair plastered down or brushed up on the forehead. [orig. unkn.]

quill *n.* **1.** a large feather of a bird's wing or tail; a pen made from this. **2.** the hollow stem of a feather (ill. BIRDS); a plectrum or other device made from this. **3.** one of a porcupine's spines. [prob. f. MLG]

quilt *n.* a coverlet, especially of quilted material. —*v.t.* to line (a coverlet or garment) with padding held between two layers of cloth etc. by cross-lines of stitching. [f. OF *coilte* f. L *culcita* cushion]

quin *n.* (*colloq.*) a quintuplet. [abbr.]

quince *n.* an acid pear-shaped fruit used in jams etc.; the tree (*Cydonia oblonga*) bearing it. [orig. pl. of obs. *quoyn* f. OF f. L *cotoneum, cydoneum* (*Cydonia* in Crete)]

quincentenary /kwɪnsenˈtiːnərɪ/ *n.* a 500th anniversary; a celebration of this. —*adj.* of a quincentenary. [f. L *quinque* five + CENTENARY]

quincunx /ˈkwɪnkʌŋks/ *n.* **1.** the centre and four corner points of a square or rectangle. **2.** five trees etc. so placed. [L, = five-twelfths (*quinque* five, *uncia* twelfth part; see OUNCE[1])]

Quine /kwaɪn/, Willard Van Orman (1908–), American philosopher and logician, who developed and revised the work on the foundations of mathematics begun by Frege and Russell. Many of his broader philosophical concerns can be seen as reactions against Carnap, by whom he was greatly influenced. He has argued against the sentence-by-sentence analysis of language, claiming that theories were to be treated as wholes, to which adjustment was to be made on pragmatic grounds. He has been sceptical about the significance of the concepts of meaning and necessity, and raised again traditional questions of existence, claiming that what we take to exist depends upon our choice of language, and that that choice should be made to provide the simplest expression of physics.

quinine /ˈkwɪniːn/ *n.* a bitter drug obtained from the bark of the cinchona tree, used to reduce fever and as a tonic. [f. *quina* cinchona bark (Sp. f. Quechua *kina* bark)]

Quinquagesima /kwɪŋkwəˈdʒesɪmə/ *n.* the Sunday before Lent (50 days before Easter). [L (*quinquagesimus* fiftieth; cf. QUADRIGESIMA)]

quinquennial /kwɪŋˈkwenɪəl/ *adj.* lasting or recurring every five years. —**quinquenially** *adv.* [f. L *quinquennis* (as foll.)]

quinquennium /kwɪŋˈkwenɪəm/ *n.* (*pl.* **-iums**) a period of five years. [L (*quinque* five, *annus* year)]

quinquereme /ˈkwɪŋkwɪriːm/ *n.* an ancient galley (see entry), probably with five men at each oar. [f. L (*quinque* five, *remus* oar)]

quinsy /ˈkwɪnzɪ/ *n.* inflammation of the throat, especially with an abscess on the tonsil(s). [f. OF f. L *quinancia* f. Gk]

quintessence /kwɪnˈtes(ə)ns/ *n.* **1.** the purest and most perfect form or manifestation or embodiment of a quality etc. **2.** a highly refined extract. —**quintessential** /-tɪˈsenʃ(ə)l/ *adj.,* **quintessentially** *adv.* [f. F f. L *quinta essentia* fifth essence (underlying the four elements)]

quintet /kwɪnˈtet/ *n.* **1.** a musical composition for five performers; these performers. **2.** any group of five. [f. F f. It. (*quinto* fifth, f. L)]

Quintilian /kwɪnˈtɪlɪən/ (Marcus Fabius Quintilianus, *c.*30–*c.*96) Roman rhetorician. A famous teacher, whose chief work is his *Education of an Orator,* a comprehensive treatment of the art of rhetoric and of the training of the orator, inspired by a humanist educational ideal of combined technical and moral proficiency. The work was highly influential in the Middle Ages and Renaissance.

quintuple /ˈkwɪntjʊp(ə)l/ *adj.* fivefold; having five parts; being five times as many or as much. —*n.* a fivefold number or amount. —*v.t./i.* to multiply by five. [f. F f. L *quintus* fifth]

quintuplet /ˈkwɪntjʊplɪt, -ˈtjuː-/ *n.* each of five children born at one birth. [f. prec., after *triplet* etc.]

quintuplicate /kwɪnˈtjuːplɪkət/ *adj.* **1.** fivefold. **2.** of which five copies are made. [as QUINTUPLE, after QUADRUPLICATE]

quip *n.* a clever saying, an epigram. —*v.i.* (**-pp-**) to make quips. [perh. f. L *quippe* forsooth]

quire *n.* **1.** 25 (formerly 24) sheets of writing paper. **2.** each of the folded sheets that are sewn together in bookbinding. —**in quires,** unbound. [f. OF f. L *quaterni* (as QUATERNARY)]

quirk *n.* **1.** a peculiarity of behaviour. **2.** a trick of fate. **3.** a flourish in writing. —**quirky** *adj.* [orig. unkn.]

quisling /ˈkwɪzlɪŋ/ *n.* a traitor, especially one who collaborates with an enemy occupying his country. [f. V. *Quisling* Norwegian collaborator (d. 1945)]

quit *v.t.* (**-tt-**) **1.** to give up or abandon. **2.** to cease. **3.** to leave or depart (from). —*predic. adj.* rid. [earlier = release, f. OF f. L *quittus, quietus* (as QUIET)]

quitch *n.* a weed with long creeping roots, couch-grass (*Elymus repens*). [OE]

quite *adv.* **1.** completely, entirely, wholly. **2.** really, actually. **3.** somewhat, to some extent. —**quite a few,** a fair number. **quite (so),** I grant the truth of that. **quite something,** remarkable. [var. of *quit* adj. (QUIT)]

Quito /ˈkiːtəʊ/ the capital of Ecuador, situated at 2,850 m (9,350 ft.) at the foot of the Pichincha volcano; pop. (est. 1981) 800,000.

quits *predic. adj.* on even terms by retaliation or repayment. —**call it** or **cry quits,** to acknowledge that things are now even, to agree to stop quarrelling etc. [perh. abbr. of L *quittus* (as QUIT)]

quittance /ˈkwɪt(ə)ns/ *n.* (*archaic*) **1.** release from an obligation. **2.** an acknowledgement of payment. [f. OF (as QUIT)]

quitter *n.* a deserter, a shirker. [f. QUIT]

quiver[1] /ˈkwɪvə(r)/ *v.i.* to tremble or vibrate with a slight rapid motion. —*n.* a quivering motion or sound. [f. obs. *quiver* nimble]

quiver[2] /ˈkwɪvə(r)/ *n.* a case for holding arrows. [f. OF *quivre* f. WG]

qui vive /kiː ˈviːv/ **on the qui vive,** on the alert. [F, = (long) live who? (as sentry's challenge)]

Quixote /ˈkwɪksəʊt/, Don. The hero of a romance (1605–15) by Cervantes, written to ridicule books of chivalry.

quixotic /kwɪkˈsɒtɪk/ *adj.* chivalrous and unselfish to an extravagant or impractical extent. —**quixotically** *adv.,* **quixotry** /ˈkwɪksətrɪ/ *n.* [f. prec.]

quiz *n.* (*pl.* **quizzes**) a series of questions testing people's knowledge, especially as a form of entertainment. —*v.t.* (**-zz-**) **1.** to interrogate. **2.** (*archaic*) to stare at curiously or critically. **3.** (*archaic*) to make fun of. [orig. unkn.]

quizzical /ˈkwɪzɪk(ə)l/ *adj.* **1.** expressing or done with mild or amused perplexity. **2.** strange, comical. —**quizzically** *adv.* [f. QUIZ]

Qumran /kʊmˈrɑːn/ a region on the western shore of the Dead Sea, now in Israel, site of caves in which the Dead Sea scrolls (see entry) were found and of the settlement of an ancient Jewish community to whom these manuscripts belonged.

quod *n.* (*slang*) prison. [orig. unkn.]

quoin /kɔɪn/ *n.* **1.** an outside corner of a building. **2.** a corner-stone (ill. BUILDING TECHNIQUES). **3.** an inside corner of a room. **4.** a wedge used for various purposes. [var. of COIN]

quoit /kɔɪt/ *n.* **1.** a ring thrown at a mark or to encircle a peg. **2.** (in *pl.*) a game using these. It was a well-known game from at least the reign of Edward III, when it was included among the many sports and pastimes that were forbidden because they diverted servants, apprentices, and labourers from recreations of a more warlike character (e.g. archery) at a time of recurring wars against the French. Such edicts were conspicuously unsuccessful. [orig. unkn.]

quondam /ˈkwɒndæm/ *adj.* that once was, sometime, former. [L, = formerly]

quorum /ˈkwɔːrəm/ *n.* the number of members that must be present to constitute a valid meeting. —**quorate** *adj.* [L, = of which people]

quota /ˈkwəʊtə/ *n.* **1.** the share to be contributed to or received from a total by one of the parties concerned. **2.** the total number or amount required or permitted. [f. L *quota* (*pars*) how great (a part) (*quot* how many)]

quotable /ˈkwəʊtəb(ə)l/ *adj.* worth quoting. [f. foll.]

quotation /kwəʊˈteɪʃ(ə)n/ *n.* **1.** quoting. **2.** a passage or price quoted. —**quotation-marks** *n.pl.* inverted commas (' ' or " ") used at the beginning and end of quoted passages or words. [f. L (as foll.)]

quote *v.t./i.* **1.** to cite or appeal to (an author or book) in confirmation of some view. **2.** to repeat or copy out a passage from; to repeat or copy out (a passage). **3.** to enclose (words) in quotation marks. **4.** to state the price of (usu. *at a* figure). —*n.* (*colloq.*) **1.** a passage or price quoted. **2.** (usu. in *pl.*) a quotation-mark. [f. L *quotare* mark with numbers (as QUOTA)]

quoth /kwəʊθ/ *v.t.* (*archaic*) (only with *I* or *he* or *she* placed after) said. [OE]

quotidian /kwəˈtɪdɪən/ *adj.* **1.** daily; (of a fever) recurring every day. **2.** everyday, commonplace. [f. OF f. L (*quotidie* daily)]

quotient /ˈkwəʊʃənt/ *n.* the result of a division sum. [f. L *quotiens* how many times]

q.v. *abbr.* which see (in references). [f. L *quod vide*]

qy. *abbr.* query.

R

R, r /ɑ:(r)/ *n.* (*pl.* **Rs, R's**) the eighteenth letter of the alphabet. —**the three Rs,** reading, (w)riting, (a)rithmetic.
R *abbr.* (in chess) rook.
Ⓡ *symbol* registered as a trademark.
R. *abbr.* **1.** *Regina.* **2.** *Rex.* **3.** River.
r. *abbr.* right.
RA *abbr.* **1.** Royal Academician; Royal Academy. **2.** Royal Artillery.
Ra /rɑ:/ (*Egyptian myth.*) the sun-god (or initially the sun itself), a notable deity to whom other gods could be assimilated. He is often portrayed with a falcon's head bearing the solar disc. He appears travelling in his ship with other gods, crossing the sky by day and journeying through the underworld of the dead at night. From earliest times he was associated with the king.
Ra *symbol* radium.
Rabat /rə'bɑ:t/ the capital of Morocco; pop. 518,616.
rabbet /'ræbɪt/ *n.* & *v.t.* = REBATE². [f. OF *rab(b)at* recess (as REBATE¹)]
rabbi /'ræbaɪ/ *n.* a Jewish religious leader; a Jewish scholar or teacher, especially of the law. —**rabbinical** /-'bɪnɪk(ə)l/ *adj.* [ult. f. Heb., = my master]
rabbit /'ræbɪt/ *n.* **1.** a herbivorous mammal (*Oryctolagus cuniculus*), native to western Europe, allied to the hare but with shorter legs and smaller ears, brownish-grey in the natural state, also black, white, or pied in domestication. **2.** (*US*) a hare. **3.** (*colloq.*) a poor performer at a game. —*v.i.* **1.** to hunt rabbits. **2.** (*slang*) to talk lengthily or in a rambling way. —**rabbit punch,** a short chop with the edge of the hand to an opponent's nape, such as is used for breaking a rabbit's neck. —**rabbity** *adj.* [perh. f. OF]
rabble *n.* a disorderly crowd, a mob; a contemptible or inferior set of people; the lower or disorderly classes of the populace. [orig. unkn.]
Rabelais /'ræbəleɪ/, François (*c.*1494-1553), French humanist, satirist, and physician, who became successively a monk, priest, bishop's secretary, and Bachelor of Medicine. He travelled in France and Italy, acquiring a widespread reputation for his erudition and medical skill, and enjoyed ecclesiastical and royal patronage. He is remembered for his five great books: *Pantagruel* (1532/3), *Gargantua* (1534), *Tiers Livre* (1546), *Quart Livre* (1548-52), and *Cinquième Livre* (1562-4) which is of doubtful authenticity. Linked together by a narrative thread the whole provides a vivid panorama of contemporary society through which the author reveals his own humanism, his hatred of asceticism, and his contempt for scholasticism. His command of the vernacular, sustained by an encyclopaedic vocabulary, extends beyond French to a dozen contemporary languages. The work was officially condemned for its insulting reference to theologians, and Rabelais is often censured for his lapses into obscenity and coarse wit, but his work gained wide popularity and remains a unique expression of Renaissance energy and plenitude.
rabid /'ræbɪd/ *adj.* **1.** furious, raging. **2.** fanatical. **3.** of or affected with rabies. —**rabidity** /rə'bɪdɪtɪ/ *n.*, **rabidly** *adv.* [f. L (*rabere* rave)]
rabies /'reɪbi:z, -ɪz/ *n.* a contagious virus disease of dogs and other warm-blooded animals, which produces paralysis or a vicious excitability and in man causes a fatal encephalitis with convulsions and with throat spasm on swallowing. [L (as prec.)]
race¹ *n.* **1.** a contest of speed in reaching a certain point or in doing or achieving something; (in *pl.*) a series of these for horses or dogs at a fixed time on a regular course. **2.** a strong fast current of water. **3.** a channel for the balls in a ball-bearing. —*v.t./i.* **1.** to compete in a race; to have a race with; to cause to race. **2.** to move or cause to move or operate at full or excessive speed. **3.** to take part in horse-racing. —**race-meeting** *n.* a series of horse-races at one venue at fixed times. **race-track** *n.* a course for racing horses, vehicles, etc. —**racer** *n.* [orig. = running, f. ON]
race² *n.* **1.** each of the major divisions of mankind with distinct inherited physical characteristics; the fact or concept of division into races. The term is often used imprecisely; even among anthropologists there is no generally accepted classification or terminology. (See below.) **2.** a group of persons, animals, or plants connected by common descent; a genus, species, breed, or variety of animals or plants. —**the human race,** mankind. **race relations,** relations between members of different races in the same country or community. **race riot,** an outbreak of violence due to racial antagonism. [F f. It. *razza*]
  The term has been applied to various national or cultural as well as physical groupings (including 'human race' for the entire species of mankind). For centuries geographical races were identified by the most observable physical differences, especially the colour of the skin, hair, and eyes. The reason for human variation has been a subject of interest and speculation since antiquity. Christian tradition of the unity of mankind, descended from a common ancestor, became scientific orthodoxy in medieval Europe, with national genealogies traced to a descendant of Noah, but from the time of Paracelsus onwards a diversity of human origins was argued. In the 19th c. a combination of European overseas migration and the heightening of national consciousness strengthened interest in the differences between human groups, generally with the underlying assumption that the 'races' were once separate and that subsequent obscuring of pure racial types had occurred. In the early 20th c. Franz Boas put forward the theory that racial typing on a purely physical basis was arbitrary and argued the cultural origin of mental differences. His approach became dominant, though the Nazis burned his book. Human variation continues to be studied but the notion of 'race' as a rigid classification or genetic system has largely been abandoned.
racecourse *n.* a ground for horse-racing.
racegoer *n.* one who frequents horse-races.
racehorse *n.* a horse bred or kept for racing.
raceme /rə'si:m/ *n.* a flower-cluster with flowers attached by short stalks at intervals along a stem (ill. PLANTS). [f. L *racemus* grape-bunch]
racemose /'ræsɪməʊs/ *adj.* **1.** in the form of a raceme (ill. PLANTS). **2.** (of a gland etc.) clustered. [as RACEME]
rachel /rə'ʃel/ *n.* a light tannish colour of face-powder. [f. *Rachel*, stage-name of Elisa Félix (1820-58), French actress]
Rachmaninov /ræk'mænɪnɒf/, Sergei Vasilyevich (1873-1943), Russian composer. He was a celebrated pianist and his works for the instrument overshadow in fame, if not in importance, his songs, choral works including *The Bells* (1913), and three symphonies. From 1897 he held a conducting post with a private opera company in Moscow (the then unknown Chaliapin was among its members), but in 1917 left Russia for America; until 1933 his music was banned in his native country after he signed a letter attacking the Soviet regime.
racial /'reɪʃ(ə)l/ *adj.* of or characteristic of a race; concerning or caused by race. —**racially** *adv.* [f. RACE²]
racialism *n.* **1.** belief in the superiority of a particular race. **2.** antagonism towards a particular race. —**racialist** *n.* & *adj.* [f. prec.]
Racine /ræ'si:n/, Jean (1639-99), French dramatist, one of the greatest figures of the French classical period. He was admitted to the *Académie* in 1673 and became historiographer to Louis XIV in 1677. His tragedies derive from various sources; from Greek and Roman literature (*Andromaque* 1667, *Iphigénie* 1674, *Phèdre* 1677), from Roman history (*Britannicus* 1669, *Bérénice* 1670, and *Mithridate* 1673), from contemporary Turkish history (*Bajazet* 1672), and from the Bible (*Esther* 1689, *Athalie* 1691); his one comedy *Les Plaideurs* (1668) was drawn from Aristophanes. Central to the majority of his tragedies is a perception of the blind folly of human passion.
racism /'reɪsɪz(ə)m/ *n.* **1.** racialism. **2.** the theory that human abilities etc. are determined by race. —**racist** *n.* & *adj.* [f. RACE²]

rack[1] *n*. **1.** a framework, usually with bars or pegs etc., for holding things or hanging things on. **2.** a cogged or toothed bar or rail engaging with a wheel or pinion etc. **3.** (*hist*.) an instrument of torture, a frame with a roller at each end to which the victim's wrists and ankles were tied so that his joints were stretched when the rollers were turned. —*v.t*. **1.** (of a disease or pain) to inflict suffering on. **2.** (*hist*.) to torture (a person) on a rack. **3.** to place on or in a rack. **4.** to shake violently; to injure by straining. —**on the rack**, in pain or distress. **rack one's brains**, to try hard to remember or think of something. **rack-railway** *n*. a mountain railway with a cogged rail in which a pinion on the locomotive engages. **rack-rent** *n*. an exorbitant rent. [f. Du or MLG]

rack[2] *n*. destruction (esp. in *rack and ruin*). [var. of WRACK]

racket[1] /ˈrækɪt/ *n*. **1.** a bat having a round or oval frame strung with catgut or nylon etc., used in ball-games such as tennis and rackets. **2.** (in *pl*.) a ball-game for two or four persons, played with rackets in a plain four-walled court. Each player strikes the ball in turn and tries to keep it rebounding from the end wall of the court. The game in its modern form developed in England in the 19th c., but its origins may be traced to medieval handball. It was played in open courts in the backyards of inns and taverns; the rackets court in the Fleet debtors' prison in London is depicted by Rowlandson and described by Dickens. Indoor courts were built at the Prince's Club, London, in 1853, a development which speeded up the game and (because it was now more expensive to play) altered its social character. The extension of the game to other parts of the world was due largely to the influence of the British Army and the Royal Navy. [f. F, ult. f. Arab., = palm of the hand]

racket[2] /ˈrækɪt/ *n*. **1.** a din, a noisy fuss. **2.** a business or other scheme in which dishonest means are used. **3.** (*slang*) a line of business; a dodge. —*v.i*. to move about noisily; to engage in wild social activities. —**stand the racket**, (*colloq*.) to bear the costs or consequences. [perh. imit.]

racketeer /rækɪˈtɪə(r)/ *n*. one who operates a dishonest scheme. —**racketeering** *n*. [f. prec.]

rackety *adj*. noisy, rowdy. [f. RACKET[2]]

raconteur /rækɒnˈtɜ:(r)/ *n*. a teller of anecdotes. —**raconteuse** /-ˈtɜ:z/ *n.fem*. [F (*raconter* relate)]

racoon /rəˈku:n/ *n*. a North American mammal (*Procyon lotor*) with a bushy tail, sharp snout, and greyish-brown fur. [Algonquian dial.]

racy /ˈreɪsɪ/ *adj*. **1.** lively and vigorous in style. **2.** (*US*) risqué. **3.** of a distinctive quality; retaining traces of its origin. —**racily** *adv*., **raciness** *n*. [f. RACE[2]]

rad *abbr*. **1.** radian(s). **2.** radical.

radar /ˈreɪda:(r)/ *n*. **1.** a system for detecting the presence of objects at a distance, or ascertaining their position and motion, by transmitting short radio waves and detecting or measuring their return after they are reflected; a similar system in which the return signal consists of radio waves that a suitably equipped target automatically transmits when it receives the outgoing waves. (See below.) **2.** an apparatus or installation used for this system. —**radar trap**, an arrangement using radar to detect vehicles etc. travelling faster than the speed limit. [f. *radio detection and ranging*]

The principle of radar was established when Heinrich Hertz showed (in 1886) that radio waves could be reflected from solid objects, but use of this remained chiefly theoretical until 1922 when Marconi suggested that radio echoes could be used for the detection of ships in bad visibility, and the idea was tested experimentally in the USA. Radar systems were developed in Britain, France, Germany, and the USA in the 1930s, and used by both sides in the Second World War. They are now widely employed in sea and air navigation.

raddle *n*. red ochre. —*v.t*. to colour with raddle, or with much rouge crudely used. [var. of RUDDLE]

raddled *adj*. worn out. [f. prec.]

Radha /ˈra:da:/ *n*. (*Hinduism*) wife of a cowherd, she was the favourite mistress of the god Krishna, and an incarnation of Lakshmi. In devotional religion she represents the longing of the human soul for God. [f. Skr., = prosperity]

radial /ˈreɪdɪəl/ *adj*. **1.** of or arranged like rays or radii; having spokes or lines radiating from a centre. **2.** acting or moving along lines that diverge from a centre. **3.** (of a tyre; also **radial-ply**) having fabric layers with cords lying radial to the hub of the wheel (not crossing each other). —*n*. a radial-ply tyre. —**radially** *adv*. [f. L (as RADIUS)]

radian /ˈreɪdɪən/ *n*. a unit of plane angle; the angle at the

centre of a circle formed by the radii of an arc with a length equal to the radius. [f. RADIUS]

radiant /ˈreɪdɪənt/ *adj*. **1.** emitting rays of light. **2.** looking very bright and happy; (of beauty) splendid, dazzling. **3.** (of light) issuing in rays. —*n*. a point or object from which light or heat radiates. —**radiant heat**, heat transmitted by radiation. —**radiance** *n*., **radiancy** *n*., **radiantly** *adv*. [f. L *radiare* (as RADIUS)]

radiate /ˈreɪdɪeɪt/ *v.t./i*. **1.** to emit rays of light, heat or other radiation; to emit from a centre; (of light or heat) to issue in rays. **2.** to diverge or spread from a central point; to cause to do this. **3.** to exude or show (a feeling etc.) clearly. —/ˈreɪdɪət/ *adj*. having the parts radially arranged. [as prec.]

radiation /reɪdɪˈeɪʃ(ə)n/ *n*. **1.** radiating, being radiated. **2.** the emission of energy as electromagnetic waves or as moving particles. **3.** energy thus transmitted. —**radiation sickness**, sickness caused by exposure to excessive amounts of radioactivity. [as RADIATE]

radiator /ˈreɪdɪeɪtə(r)/ *n*. **1.** an apparatus for heating a room etc. by the radiation of heat, especially a metal structure through which steam or hot water circulates, or one heated electrically. **2.** an engine-cooling apparatus in a motor vehicle or aeroplane, with a large surface for cooling circulating water. [f. prec.]

radical /ˈrædɪk(ə)l/ *adj*. **1.** fundamental, far-reaching, thorough. **2.** advocating radical reforms; holding extreme views, revolutionary. **3.** forming the basis, primary. **4.** of the root of a number or quantity. **5.** of the roots of words. —*n*. **1.** a person holding radical views or belonging to a radical party. **2.** a group of atoms forming part of a compound and remaining unaltered during its ordinary chemical changes. **3.** the root of a word. **4.** a mathematical quantity forming or expressed as the root of another. —**radicalism** *n*., **radically** *adv*. [f. L (*radix* root)]

radicle /ˈrædɪk(ə)l/ *n*. the part of a plant embryo that develops into the primary root (ill. PLANTS); a rootlet. [f. L *radicula* dim. of *radix* root]

radii *pl*. of RADIUS.

radio /ˈreɪdɪəʊ/ *n*. (*pl*. -os) **1.** the transmission and reception of messages etc. by electromagnetic waves of radio-frequency, without a connecting wire, pioneered by Marconi (see entry). **2.** an apparatus for transmitting or receiving signals by radio. **3.** sound broadcasting; a station engaged in this. —*adj*. **1.** of, using, or sent by radio; equipped with radio. **2.** of or concerned with stars or other celestial bodies from which radio waves are received or reflected. —*v.t./i*. to send (a message) by radio; to communicate (with) or broadcast by radio. —**radio astronomy**, see separate entry. **radio star**, a small celestial object emitting strong radio waves. **radio telescope**, see separate entry. [short for *radio-telegraphy* etc.]

radio- /reɪdɪəʊ-/ *in comb*. of or connected with rays, radiation, radioactivity, or radio. [f. RADIUS]

radioactive /reɪdɪəʊˈæktɪv/ *adj*. of or exhibiting radioactivity.

radioactivity /reɪdɪəʊækˈtɪvɪtɪ/ *n*. the property of spontaneous disintegration of atomic nuclei, usually with emission of penetrating radiation or particles. Radioactivity was discovered in 1896 by Becquerel, who found that uranium salt crystals affected a photographic emulsion. Studies by Rutherford and others from 1898 onwards showed that there are three main types of radiation emitted by radioactive substances: alpha rays, which are identical with nuclei of the element helium; beta rays, which are fast-moving electrons; and gamma radiation, which is electromagnetic radiation of very high energy. Naturally occurring radioactive minerals such as uranium and thorium are believed to be largely responsible for the heating of the earth's core and for volcanic heat; they are also responsible for a large proportion of the background radiation experienced at the surface of the earth. Other contributions come from the radioactivity released in nuclear explosions and in the waste products of nuclear reactors. Although man has evolved in an environment which has always had background radiation, severe damage can be caused to living tissue by dosages which are significantly in excess of this background.

radio astronomy the branch of astronomy which monitors radio emission from celestial objects. Long-wavelength radiation originates in such objects as pulsars and supernovae remnants, and radio galaxies and quasars, where poorly understood processes involving large amounts of energy operate. The discovery in 1965 that a uniform background of radiation existed throughout the universe at microwave wavelengths is now believed to be a direct observation of the remnant of radiation from the 'big bang' associated with the formation of the universe. (See RADIO TELESCOPE.)

radio-carbon *n.* a radioactive isotope of carbon, especially carbon 14 which has been used since the late 1940s in a technique of assigning absolute dates to ancient organic material. All living things absorb carbon, either from the carbon dioxide in the atmosphere or by eating plants etc. that contain it. Once they are dead, the proportion of carbon 14 in their remains falls at a steady rate, and by measuring the concentration of this isotope the approximate date of death of the specimen can be calculated. The figure for the half-life of carbon 14 is usually given as 5568 ± 30 years (that is, after 5568 years one half of the C14 will have been lost, after another 5568 years one half of the remainder will have gone, and so on); this figure is subject to correction. The amount of carbon 14 in the atmosphere, however, has not remained constant throughout all time, and carbon 14 dates have been calibrated against dates based on dendrochronology in efforts to produce a secure chronological framework.

radio-controlled *adj.* controlled from a distance by radio.

radio-frequency *n.* frequency of radio waves, between about 10 kilohertz and 0.1 terahertz.

radiogram /ˈreɪdɪəʊɡræm/ *n.* **1.** a combined radio and gramophone. **2.** a telegram sent by radio. **3.** a picture obtained by X-rays etc. [f. RADIO- + -GRAM]

radiograph /ˈreɪdɪəɡrɑːf/ *n.* **1.** a picture obtained by X-rays etc. **2.** an instrument for recording the intensity of radiation. —*v.t.* to obtain a picture by X-rays etc. —**radiographer** /-ˈɒɡrəfə(r)/ *n.*, **radiography** /-ˈɒɡrəfɪ/ *n.* [f. RADIO- + -GRAPH]

radio-isotope *n.* a radioactive isotope.

radiolarian /reɪdɪəˈleərɪən/ *n.* a protozoan of the order Radiolaria, with a silicious skeleton and radiating pseudopodia. [f. L *radiolus* dim. of RADIUS]

radiology /reɪdɪˈɒlədʒɪ/ *n.* the study of X-rays and other high-energy radiation, especially for use in medicine. —**radiologist** *n.* [f. RADIO- + -LOGY]

radiometry /reɪdɪˈɒmətrɪ/ *n.* measurement of radioactivity or ionizing radiation. —**radiometric** /-əˈmetrɪk/ *adj.* [f. RADIO- + -METRY]

radioscopy /reɪdɪˈɒskəpɪ/ *n.* the examination by X-rays etc. of objects opaque to light. [f. RADIO- + -SCOPY]

radio-telegraphy *n.* telegraphy using radio.

radio-telephony *n.* telephony using radio.

radio telescope an instrument used to detect radio emissions from the sky, whether from natural celestial objects or from artificial satellites. Most familiar as a large dish antennae, like the fully steerable reflector at Jodrell Bank, they may also be constructed as linear arrays of aerials, or as grids of sensitive detectors distributed over large areas of the countryside. Radio signals from outside the Earth's atmosphere were first detected in 1932 by an American radio engineer, Karl Jansky. A few years later Grote Reber, an Illinois engineer, built an apparatus with a parabolic reflector to detect and focus radio waves; the development of radio astronomy had begun.

radio-therapy *n.* the treatment of disease by radiation, especially X-rays.

radish /ˈrædɪʃ/ *n.* a plant (*Raphanus sativus*) with a crisp pungent root eaten raw; this root. [OE f. L *radix* root]

radium /ˈreɪdɪəm/ *n.* a radioactive element, the heaviest member of the alkaline-earth metal group, symbol Ra, atomic number 88, discovered in pitchblende in 1898 by Pierre and Marie Curie. Because of its radioactive properties it was formerly used extensively in the treatment of tumours and in luminous materials, but it has now been largely replaced by other substances for these purposes. [f. L *radius* ray]

radius /ˈreɪdɪəs/ *n.* (*pl.* **radii** /-ɪaɪ/) **1.** a straight line from the centre to the circumference of a circle or sphere (ill. SHAPES); the length of this; distance from a centre. **2.** any of a set of lines diverging from a point like the radii of a circle. **3.** the thicker and shorter bone in the forearm on the same side as the thumb (ill. BODY 1); the corresponding bone in an animal's foreleg or bird's wing. [L, = spoke, ray]

radix /ˈreɪdɪks/ *n.* (*pl.* **-ices** /-siːz/) a number or symbol used as the basis of a numeration scale. [L, = root]

radon /ˈreɪdɒn/ *n.* a radioactive gaseous element, the heaviest of the noble gases, symbol Rn, atomic number 86.

It is produced naturally by the disintegration of radium. [f. RADIUM, after *argon* etc.]

Raeburn /ˈreɪbɜːn/, Sir Henry (1756-1823), Scottish portrait painter. After moving to London (1784) and travelling in Italy he returned to Edinburgh in 1787 and established a successful portrait practice there, portraying the local intelligentsia and Highland chieftains in a broad and distinctive *bravura* style. His rising fame was marked by several honours, and he is often considered to be the Scottish equivalent of Sir Joshua Reynolds.

RAF *abbr.* Royal Air Force.

raffia /ˈræfɪə/ *n.* a fibre from the leaves of a kind of palm-tree, used for tying up plants and making mats and baskets etc.; this tree (*Raphia ruffia*). [Malagasy]

raffish *adj.* disreputable, rakish; tawdry. —**raffishness** *n.* [f. *raff* rubbish]

raffle *n.* a sale of articles by lottery, especially for charity. —*v.t.* to sell by a raffle. [orig. = dice-game, f. OF *raf(f)le*]

Raffles[1] /ˈræf(ə)lz/, A. J., a debonair cricket-loving gentleman burglar in novels (1899 onwards) by E. W. Hornung.

Raffles[2] /ˈræf(ə)lz/, Sir Thomas Stamford Bingley (1781-1826), English colonial administrator, founder of Singapore. Although forced to retire early from the East India Company by ill health, Raffles was responsible for one of the Company's most momentous decisions, persuading it to purchase the undeveloped Singapore Island and then undertaking much of the preliminary work for turning it into an important international port and centre of commerce.

raft /rɑːft/ *n.* a flat floating structure of wood or fastened logs etc., used in water for transport or as an emergency boat. [f. ON, rel. to foll.]

rafter /ˈrɑːftə(r)/ *n.* any of the sloping beams forming the framework of a roof (ill. HOUSES). [OE]

rag[1] *n.* **1.** a torn, frayed or worn piece of woven material. **2.** (in *pl.*) old or torn or worn clothes. **3.** (*collect.*) rags used as a material for making paper, stuffing, etc. **4.** (*derog.*) a newspaper. —**in rags**, much torn. **rag-and-bone man,** *n.* an itinerant dealer in old clothes, furniture, etc. **rag-bag** *n.* a bag for old rags; a miscellaneous collection. **rags to riches**, poverty to affluence. **rag trade,** (*colloq.*) the clothing business. [prob. back-formation f. RAGGED]

rag[2] *n.* **1.** a programme of stunts, parades, and entertainment, staged by students to collect money for charity. **2.** (*colloq.*) a prank. **3.** (*slang*) a rowdy celebration; a noisy disorderly scene. —*v.t./i.* (**-gg-**) (*slang*) **1.** to tease, to play rough jokes on. **2.** to engage in rough play, to be noisy and riotous. [orig. unkn.]

rag[3] *n.* a piece of ragtime. [perh. f. RAGGED]

ragamuffin /ˈræɡəmʌfɪn/ *n.* a person in ragged dirty clothes. [f. RAG[1] with fanciful ending]

rage *n.* **1.** fierce or violent anger; a fit of this. **2.** the violent operation of a natural force. —*v.i.* **1.** to be fiercely angry; to speak furiously or madly. **2.** (of a wind or battle etc.) to be violent, to be at its height. —**be all the rage**, to be temporarily very popular or fashionable. [f. OF f. L, = RABIES]

ragged /ˈræɡɪd/ *adj.* **1.** torn, frayed. **2.** wearing ragged clothes. **3.** having a broken jagged outline or surface. **4.** faulty, lacking finish or smoothness or uniformity. —**run a person ragged**, to exhaust or debilitate him or her. —**raggedly** *adv.*, **raggedness** *n.* [f. ON, = tufted]

raglan /ˈræɡlən/ *n.* (usu. *attrib.*) a garment, especially an overcoat, with sleeves that continue to the neck and are joined to the body of the garment by sloping seams. —**raglan sleeve**, a sleeve of this kind. [f. Lord *Raglan*, British commander in Crimea (d. 1855)]

Ragnarök /ˈræɡnərøk/ *n.* (*Scand. myth.*) the great battle between the gods and the powers of evil, the Scandinavian equivalent of the *Götterdämmerung*, the twilight of the gods (see TWILIGHT). [tr. Icel. *ragna rök* (*rökr* twilight) altered from the original *ragna rök* (= the history or judgement of the gods)]

ragout /ˈræɡuː/ *n.* a highly-seasoned stew of meat and vegetables. [f. F (*ragoûter* revive taste of)]

ragtag (and bobtail) riff-raff, disreputable people. [f. RAG[1]]

ragtime *n.* music with a syncopated melodic line and regularly-accented accompaniment. It evolved among American Black musicians in the 1890s, and was the immediate precursor of jazz. [prob. f. RAG[3] + TIME]

ragwort /ˈræɡwɜːt/ *n.* a wild plant of the genus *Senecio* with yellow flowers and ragged leaves.

raid *n.* **1.** a sudden attack and withdrawal made by a military party or by ships or aircraft. **2.** an attack made in order to steal or do harm. **3.** a surprise visit by police etc. to arrest suspected persons or to seize illicit goods. —*v.t./i.* to make a raid (on). —**raider** *n.* [Sc. form of ROAD]

rail¹ *n.* **1.** a level or sloping bar or series of bars used to hang things on, as the top of banisters, as part of a fence, as a protection against contact or falling over etc. **2.** a horizontal piece (cf. STILE²) in the frame of a panelled door etc. (ill. HOUSES). **3.** a steel bar or continuous line of bars laid on the ground usually as one of two forming a railway track. **3.** railways as a means of transport. —*v.t.* **1.** to furnish with a rail. **2.** to enclose with rails. —**off the rails,** disorganized, out of order or control; crazy. [f. OF *reille* f. L *regula* rule]

rail² *v.i.* to complain or protest fiercely or abusively. [f. F *railler*]

rail³ *n.* a small wading bird of the family Rallidae. [f. OF *raille* (perh. imit.)]

railcar *n.* a self-propelled railway coach.

railhead *n.* **1.** the furthest point reached by a railway under construction. **2.** the point on a railway at which the road transport of goods begins or ends.

railing *n.* a fence or barrier made of rails. [f. RAIL¹]

raillery /'reɪlərɪ/ *n.* good-humoured ridicule. [f. F *raillerie* (as RAIL²)]

railman *n.* (*pl.* **-men**) a railway-man.

railroad *n.* (*US*) a railway. —*v.t.* to rush or force into hasty action.

railway *n.* **1.** a track or set of tracks of steel rails for the passage of trains conveying passengers and goods (see below). **2.** a system of transport using these; the organization and personnel required for its working. **3.** a track on which wheeled equipment is run.

When a workable steam locomotive was first evolved the idea of a well-laid track of wooden or iron rails on which a 'train' of wagons could be drawn by a horse with less effort than on a rough-surfaced road was already familiar. Such tracks had long been used at collieries, and it was on one of these that Richard Trevithick's steam locomotive ran in 1804. After the success of George Stephenson's definitive *Rocket* in 1830, railways were proposed for many parts of the country. Development was rapid, though opposed by private landowners (who demanded vast payments for a route over their land), and by canal companies (who feared loss of business), but urged by manufacturers and traders who wanted this new form of quick and reliable transport. Railways played a large part in the growing industrial power of Britain in the 19th c., and until the 1860s were an exclusively British industry. By 1920 Britain had 36,800 km (23,000 miles) of track, but after that the railways ceased to grow and road transport began to expand; in recent decades many of the less used lines have been abandoned. Steam locomotives have largely given way to diesel-electric, in which an engine-driven generator supplies power to a number of electric motors driving several axles, and speeds of up to 200 kilometres an hour (125 m.p.h.) are used on main lines. Many busy routes are now electrified, using either insulated overhead wires or an insulated third rail to supply electricity to the motors of the train. Such a system will allow nuclear power to supply the system even when fossil fuels are scarce.

railwayman *n.* (*pl.* **-men**) a railway employee.

raiment /'reɪmənt/ *n.* (*archaic*) clothing. [f. obs. *arrayment* (as ARRAY)]

rain *n.* **1.** condensed moisture of the atmosphere falling in drops; a fall of these; (in *pl.*) falls of rain, the season of these. **2.** falling liquid or solid particles or objects (*lit.* or *fig.*); a rainlike descent of these. —*v.t./i.* **1.** to fall or send down as or like rain; to send down rain. **2.** to supply in large quantities. —**it rains** *or* **is raining,** rain falls or is falling. **rain forest,** luxuriant tropical forest with heavy rainfall. **rain off,** (esp. in *pass.*) to cause to be cancelled because of rain. **rain-shadow** *n.* a region in the lee of mountains where rainfall is low because it is sheltered from the prevailing winds. **rain-water** *n.* water that has fallen as rain, not obtained from wells etc. [OE]

rainbow /'reɪnbəʊ/ *n.* an arch of colours formed in the sky by the refraction and dispersion of the sun's rays in falling rain or in spray or mist. —*adj.* many-coloured. —**rainbow trout,** a large trout (*Salmo gairdnerii*) originally of the Pacific coast of North America. [OE (as RAIN, BOW¹)]

raincoat *n.* a waterproof or water-resistant coat.

raindrop *n.* a single drop of rain.

rainfall *n.* a fall of rain; the quantity of rain falling within a given area in a given time.

rainy *adj.* (of the weather, a day, region, etc.) in or on which rain is falling or much rain usually falls. —**rainy day,** a time of special need in the future. [OE (as RAIN)]

raise /reɪz/ *v.t.* **1.** to put or take into a higher position; to cause to rise or stand up or be vertical. **2.** to construct or build up. **3.** to levy, to collect, to manage to obtain. **3.** to cause to be heard or considered. **4.** to set going or bring into being; to breed (animals) or grow (crops). **5.** to bring up, to educate. **6.** to increase the amount, value, or strength of. **7.** to promote to a higher rank. **8.** to multiply (a quantity to a power). **9.** to cause (bread) to rise. **10.** (in a card-game) to bet more than (another player). **11.** to abandon or force an enemy to abandon (a siege etc.). **12.** to remove (a barrier). **13.** to cause (a ghost etc.) to appear. **14.** (*colloq.*) to find (a person etc. who is wanted). —*n.* an increase in a stake or bid; (*US*) an increase in salary. —**raise from the dead,** to restore to life. **raise a laugh,** to cause others to laugh. **raise one's eyebrows,** to look supercilious or shocked. **raise the wind,** to procure money for a purpose. [f. ON]

raisin /'reɪz(ə)n/ *n.* a partially dried grape. [f. OF f. L *racemus* grape-bunch]

raison d'être /reɪzɔ̃ 'detr/ the purpose or reason that accounts for or justifies or originally caused a thing's existence. [F]

raj /rɑːdʒ/ *n.* British sovereignty in India. [Hindi, = reign]

raja /'rɑːdʒə/ *n.* (also **rajah**) (*hist.*) an Indian king or prince; a noble or petty dignitary. [f. Hindi f. Skr. *rājan* king]

Rajasthan /rɑːdʒə'stɑːn/ a State in NW India; capital, Jaipur. —**Rajasthani** *adj.* & *n.*

rake¹ *n.* an implement of a pole with a toothed cross-bar at the end for drawing together hay etc. or smoothing loose soil or gravel; an implement like this, e.g. to draw in money at a gaming-table. —*v.t./i.* **1.** to collect or gather (as) with a rake; to make tidy or smooth with a rake; to use a rake. **2.** to search thoroughly, to ransack. **3.** to direct gunfire along (a line) from end to end; to direct one's eyes or a camera thus. **4.** to scratch or scrape. —**rake in,** (*colloq.*) to amass (profits etc.). **rake-off** *n.* (*colloq.*) a commission or share, especially in a disreputable deal. **rake up,** to revive (unwelcome memories etc.). [OE]

rake² *n.* a dissipated or immoral man of fashion. [f. *rakehell* (as RAKE¹, HELL)]

rake³ *v.t./i.* to set or be set at a sloping angle; (of a mast or funnel) to incline from the perpendicular towards the stern. —*n.* a raking position or build; the amount by which a thing rakes. [prob. rel. to G *ragen* project]

rakish /'reɪkɪʃ/ *adj.* like a rake (RAKE²); dashing, jaunty. —**rakishly** *adv.*, **rakishness** *n.* [f. RAKE²]

Raleigh /'rɔːlɪ, 'rɔː-, 'ræ-/, Sir Walter (*c.*1552–1618), explorer and courtier, a favourite of Elizabeth I who conferred a knighthood upon him. He organized several voyages of exploration and colonization to North America, including the first unsuccessful attempt to settle Virginia (now North Carolina); from his expeditions he brought back the potato and the tobacco plant. Raleigh was imprisoned in 1603 by the new king James I on a flimsy charge of conspiracy; while in the Tower of London he wrote his *History of the World*. Released to undertake an expedition in search of the fabled land of El Dorado, he became involved in military action with the Spanish, and on his return empty-handed was executed on the original charge of conspiracy.

rallentando /rælən'tændəʊ/ *adv.* (*Mus.*) with a gradual decrease of speed. —*n.* (*pl.* **-os**) (*Mus.*) a passage to be played this way. [It.]

rally¹ /'rælɪ/ *v.t./i.* **1.** to bring or come together as support or for united effort. **2.** to bring or come together again after a rout or dispersion. **3.** to rouse or revive (courage etc.); to recover after an illness; (of share-prices etc.) to increase after a fall. —*n.* **1.** rallying, being rallied. **2.** a mass meeting of supporters or persons having a common interest. **3.** a competition for motor vehicles, usually over public roads. **4.** a series of strokes in tennis etc. before a point is decided. [f. F *rallier* (as RE-, ALLY)]

rally² *v.t.* to subject to good-humoured ridicule. [f. F *railler* (as RAIL²)]

RAM *abbr.* random-access memory (see RANDOM).

ram *n.* **1.** an uncastrated male sheep. **2. the Ram,** the constellation or sign of the zodiac Aries. **3.** a battering-ram. **4.** the falling weight of a pile-driving machine. **5.** a hydraulic water-raising or lifting machine. —*v.t.* (**-mm-**) **1.** to force or squeeze into place by pressure; to beat or drive (*down* or *in* etc.) by heavy blows. **2.** to strike and push heavily, to crash against. —**ram-jet** *n.* a simple form of jet engine in which the air used for combustion is compressed solely by the forward motion of the engine. —**rammer** *n.* [OE]

Rama /'rɑːmə/ the hero of the Indian epic the Ramayana. He is the Hindu model of the ideal man, the seventh incarnation of Vishnu. [f. Skr., = black, dark]

Ramadan /ræmə'dɑːn/ *n.* the ninth month of the lunar calendar of Islam, which Muslims are obligated to spend in fasting and ritual prayer. This is one of the five 'Pillars of the Faith' or basic ritual duties. The fast (which entails abstinence from food, water, tobacco, and sexual intercourse) takes place from dawn to sundown every day of the month, and Muslims are enjoined to perform devotions (prayer, reading of the Koran) in addition to the usual five daily ritual sequences of prayer. Emphasis is on Allah's forgiveness and the atonement of sins. Those fasting are expected to live in especial simplicity during the month and to provide more than usual for the needy members of the community. [f. Arab. (*ramada* be hot); reason for name uncertain]

Raman /'rɑːmən/, Sir Chandrasekhara Venkata (1888-1970), Indian physicist, discoverer of the Raman effect, that there is a change in the wavelength of light scattered within a substance (e.g. a liquid). His discovery, for which he was awarded the 1930 Nobel Prize for physics, was important for the study of molecular structure.

Ramayana /rɑː'maɪənə/ *n.* a Sanskrit epic of India, composed *c.*300 BC. It describes how Rama, aided by his brother and the monkey Hanuman, rescued his wife Sita from the clutches of Ravana, the ten-headed demon king of Lanka (according to some, modern Sri Lanka). [Skr., = exploits of Rama]

Rambert /'rɑːmbe(r)/, Dame Marie (1888-1982), real name Cyvia Rambam, then Miriam Ramberg, Polish-British dancer, teacher and ballet director. She opened a ballet school in London in 1920, the company being originally called Marie Rambert Dancers, then Ballet Club from 1930 and Ballet Rambert from 1935. One of the pioneers of modern British ballet, she discovered many young choreographers and dancers.

ramble *v.i.* **1.** to walk for pleasure, with or without a definite route. **2.** to talk or write disconnectedly. —*n.* a walk taken for pleasure. [prob. f. MDu. *rammelen* (of an animal) wander about in sexual excitement, frequent. of *rammen* copulate with (rel. to RAM)]

rambler *n.* **1.** one who rambles. **2.** a vigorously growing and straggling climbing rose. [f. prec.]

rambling *adj.* that rambles; (of a house, street, etc.) irregularly arranged; (of a plant) straggling, climbing. [f. RAMBLE]

Rameau /rɑː'məʊ/, Jean-Philippe (1683-1764), French composer, best remembered for his stage works. His first opera was composed in 1733, when he was 50, but the 25 or so such works which followed mark him as a worthy successor to Lully and an important predecessor to Gluck.

ramekin /'ræmɪkɪn/ *n.* a small dish for baking and serving an individual portion of food; food served in this. [f. F *ramequin*]

Rameses /'ræmsiːz/ the name of 11 Egyptian pharaohs: **Rameses II** 'the Great' (1290-1224 BC, 19th Dynasty), famed for his numerous self-aggrandizing monuments which are a testimony to Egypt's wealth at the time. For practical reasons, early in his reign he established a new capital in the eastern part of the Nile delta. His major foreign campaign was his offensive against the Hittites, leading his troops in person; the campaign ended indecisively but a treaty followed. Having outlived much of his family Rameses was succeeded by his thirteenth son, Merneptah.
Rameses III (1194-1163 BC, 20th Dynasty), the last great imperial pharaoh. He fought decisive battles against the Libyans and the Sea Peoples who attempted invasions, thus salvaging Egypt's integrity until the Persian period. After his death the power of Egypt declined steadily.

ramify /'ræmɪfaɪ/ *v.t./i.* **1.** to form branches or subdivisions or offshoots, to branch out. **2.** (usu. in *pass.*) to cause to branch out; to arrange in a branching manner. —**ramification** /-fɪ'keɪʃ(ə)n/ *n.* [f. F f. L *ramificare* (*ramus* branch)]

Ramillies /'ræmɪliz/ a village in Belgium, scene of a battle in 1706 (see MARLBOROUGH).

Ramón y Cajal /rəməʊn iː kə'hɑːl/, Santiago (1852-1934),

Spanish histologist who was awarded a Nobel Prize in 1906 (jointly with Golgi) for establishing that the neurone or nerve cell is the fundamental unit of the nervous system.

ramp[1] *n.* **1.** a slope joining two levels of ground or floor etc. **2.** movable stairs for entering or leaving an aircraft. —*v.t./i.* **1.** to furnish or build with a ramp. **2.** to take a threatening posture. **3.** to rampage. [f. F *rampe* (OF *ramper* creep)]

ramp[2] *n.* (*slang*) a swindle, a racket, especially one involving exorbitant prices. —*v.t./i.* (*slang*), to engage in a ramp; to subject (a person etc.) to a ramp. [orig. unkn.]

rampage /ræm'peɪdʒ/ *v.i.* to rush wildly or violently about; to rage, to storm. —/'ræmpeɪdʒ/ *n.* wild or violent behaviour. —**on the rampage**, rampaging. —**rampageous** /ræm'peɪdʒəs/ *adj.* [perh. f. RAMP[1]]

rampant /'ræmpənt/ *adj.* **1.** (in heraldry, esp. of a lion) standing on the left hind foot with forefeet raised, right higher than left, facing dexter (ill. HERALDRY). **2.** unrestrained, flourishing excessively. **3.** violent or extravagant in action or opinion. —**rampancy** *n.* [f. OF (as RAMP[1])]

rampart /'ræmpɑːt/ *n.* **1.** a defensive wall with a broad top and usually a stone parapet; a walkway on this. **2.** a defence, a protection. [f. F (*remparer* fortify)]

ramrod /'ræmrɒd/ *n.* **1.** a rod for ramming down the charge of a muzzle-loaded firearm. **2.** a thing that is very straight or rigid.

Ramsay[1] /'ræmzɪ/, Allan (1713-84), Scottish portrait painter. The grace and sensitivity of his style, particularly in his portraits of women (e.g. his wife, Margaret Lindsay, 1755) was much sought after and he was a serious rival to Reynolds in the 1750s. However, in the 1760s he increasingly delegated work to his studio assistants to leave him free to pursue the literary and archaeological interests that dominated his last years.

Ramsay[2] /'ræmzɪ/, Sir William (1852-1916), Scottish chemist, discoverer of the rare gases of the atmosphere, for which he was awarded the 1904 Nobel Prize for chemistry. This work was initiated after a discussion with Lord Rayleigh (see entry) in 1892 about why nitrogen prepared in the laboratory should be slightly less dense than when isolated from the air, a phenomenon already observed by Cavendish in 1785; Ramsay decided that atmospheric nitrogen must be contaminated by a heavier gas. Between 1894 and 1903 he discovered the existence of five chemically inert gases: argon, helium and, with the help of the chemist Morris William Travers (1872-1961), neon, krypton, and xenon, and determined their atomic weights and places in the periodic table. In 1910 with Soddy and Sir Robert Whytlaw-Gray (1877-1958) he identified the last member of the rare (or noble) gases, radon, the product of radioactive decay.

ramshackle /'ræmʃæk(ə)l/ *adj.* tumbledown, rickety. [f. p.p. of obs. *ransackle* (as RANSACK)]

ran *past* of RUN.

ranch /rɑːntʃ/ *n.* **1.** a cattle-breeding establishment especially in the USA and Canada. **2.** a farm where certain other animals are bred. —*v.i.* to farm on a ranch. —**rancher** *n.* [f. Sp. *rancho* persons eating together]

rancid /'rænsɪd/ *adj.* smelling or tasting like rank stale fat. —**rancidity** /-'sɪdɪtɪ/ *n.* [f. L *rancidus*]

rancour /'ræŋkə(r)/ *n.* inveterate bitterness, malignant hate. —**rancorous** *adj.*, **rancorously** *adv.* [f. OF f. L (as prec.)]

rand /rænd, rɑːnt/ *n.* the currency unit of South African countries. [f. the *Rand*, gold-field near Johannesburg]

R & D *abbr.* research and development.

random /'rændəm/ *adj.* made or done etc. without method or conscious choice. —**at random**, without aim or purpose or principle. **random access**, (in computers, usu. *attrib.*) a memory or file all parts of which are directly accessible so that it need not be processed sequentially. —**randomly** *adv.* [f. OF *randon* great speed (*randir* gallop)]

randy *adj.* lustful, eager for sexual gratification; —**randily** *adv.*, **randiness** *n.* [perh. f. obs. Du. *randen* rant]

ranee /'rɑːnɪ/ *n.* a raja's wife or widow. [f. Hindi f. Skr. *rājnī* fem. of *rājan* king]

rang *past* of RING[2].

range /reɪndʒ/ *n.* **1.** the area over which a thing is found or has effect or relevance, scope. **2.** the region between limits of variation; such limits. **3.** the distance attainable or to be covered by a gun or missile etc.; the distance that can be covered by a vehicle or aircraft without refuelling; the distance between a camera and the subject to be photographed. **4.** a row or series, especially of mountains. **5.** an open or enclosed area with targets for shooting. **6.** a fireplace with ovens and hotplates for cooking. **7.** a large open area for grazing or hunting. —*v.t./i.* **1.** to place in a row or rows or in a specified arrangement. **2.** to rove or wander. **3.** to reach; to lie; to spread out; to be found over a specified area; to vary between limits. **4.** to traverse in all directions. —**range-finder** *n.* an instrument to determine the distance of an object for shooting or photography. [f. OF, = row (as RANK[1])]

ranger /ˈreɪndʒə(r)/ *n.* **1.** a keeper of a royal or national park or forest. **2.** a member of a body of mounted troops. **3. Ranger,** a senior Guide. [f. prec.]

Rangoon /ræŋˈguːn/ the capital and a seaport of Burma, on the Rangoon river, one of the mouths of the Irrawaddy; pop. 2,458,712.

rangy /ˈreɪndʒɪ/ *adj.* tall and lanky. [f. RANGE]

rani var. of RANEE.

rank[1] *n.* **1.** a place in a scale of quality or value etc.; a position or grade. **2.** high social position. **3.** a line of people or things. **4.** a place where taxis stand to await hire. —*v.t./i.* **1.** to have a specified rank or place. **2.** to assign a rank to, to classify. **3.** to arrange in a rank. —**close ranks,** to maintain solidarity. **rank and file,** ordinary undistinguished people. **the ranks,** common soldiers. [f. OF, as RING[1]]

rank[2] *adj.* **1.** too luxuriant, coarse; choked with or apt to produce weeds or excessive foliage. **2.** foul-smelling; loathsome, corrupt. **3.** flagrant, unmistakably bad, complete. —**rankly** *adv.,* **rankness** *n.* [OE]

rankle *v.i.* (of envy or disappointment etc. or their cause) to cause persistent annoyance or resentment. [f. OF, = festering sore, f. L *dra(cu)nculus* dim. of *draco* serpent]

ransack /ˈrænsæk/ *v.t.* **1.** to pillage or plunder. **2.** to search thoroughly. [f. ON (*rann* house, *-saka* seek)]

ransom /ˈrænsəm/ *n.* a sum of money or other payment demanded or paid for the release of a prisoner; liberation of a prisoner in return for this. —*v.t.* **1.** to buy the freedom or restoration of, to redeem. **2.** to hold to ransom. **3.** to release for a ransom. —**hold to ransom,** to hold (a captive) and demand a ransom for his release; to demand concessions from (a person etc.) by threatening some damaging action. [f. OF f. L, = redemption (as REDEEM)]

rant *v.t./i.* to use bombastic language; to declaim, to recite theatrically; to preach noisily. —*n.* a piece of ranting. [f. Du.]

ranunculus /rəˈnʌŋkjʊləs/ *n.* (*pl.* **-uses**) a plant of the genus *Ranunculus,* including the buttercup. [L, orig. dim. of *rana* frog]

rap[1] *n.* **1.** a quick sharp blow. **2.** a knock, a sharp tapping sound. **3.** (*slang*) blame, punishment. —*v.t./i.* (**-pp-**) **1.** to strike quickly and sharply. **2.** to knock, to make the sound of a rap. **3.** to criticize adversely. —**rap out,** to utter abruptly; to express by raps. [prob. imit.]

rap[2] *n.* a small amount, the least bit. [orig. = counterfeit halfpenny, abbr. of Ir. *ropaire*]

rapacious /rəˈpeɪʃəs/ *adj.* grasping, extortionate; predatory. —**rapaciously** *adv.,* **rapacity** /rəˈpæsɪtɪ/ *n.* [f. L *rapax* (*rapere* snatch)]

rape[1] *n.* **1.** the act or crime of having sexual intercourse with a person (usually a woman) without freely given consent. **2.** violent assault or interference. —*v.t.* to commit rape on. [f. AF f. L (as prec.)]

rape[2] *n.* a plant (*Brassica napus*) grown as fodder and for its seed from which oil is made. [f. L *rapum, rapa* turnip]

rape[3] *n.* the refuse of grapes that is left after wine-making. [f. F f. L *raspa*]

Raphael[1] /ˈræfeɪ(ə)l/ one of the seven archangels enumerated in the Book of Enoch. He is said to have 'healed' the earth when it was defiled by the sins of the fallen angels. [f. Heb., = God has healed]

Raphael[2] /ˈræfeɪəl/, Raffaello Sanzio (1483–1520), Italian painter whose refined elegant style epitomizes the humanistic spirit of the High Renaissance, influenced by Perugino, Leonardo da Vinci, and Michelangelo. By the age of 25 his reputation was sufficiently established for him to be entrusted with frescoes for one of the papal rooms in the Vatican, and in 1514 he was appointed as chief architect of St Peter's. Raphael's numerous versions of the Virgin and Child show a serenity of expression and sense of deep inner integrity; in Rome (probably in 1512) he painted his greatest altarpiece, the *Sistine Madonna,* where Mother and Child appear among the clouds, still triumphantly and splendidly

human but transcending the earthly conditions in which he had earlier represented them. His influence was widely spread: he became 'the divine painter', the model of all academies, and through a long tradition his forms and motifs have been used with a steady diminution of their values. In much 20th-c. criticism his naturalism and religious feeling have been at a discount, but his place is secure: in the technical ability to render rounded forms on a two-dimensional surface he remains an unrivalled executant, and he used his great formal sensibility to create memorable symbols of the traditional doctrines of the Christian Church. As well as his frescoes and oil paintings Raphael produced designs for tapestries, mosaics, and architectural projects, including a survey of ancient Rome. His important achievements as an architect, undertaken in later life, should not be underrated, and the elegant classicism of a building such as the Villa Madama has been no less influential on future generations than his painting. Raphael died in Rome in 1520, aged only 37 and at the height of his powers.

rapid /ˈræpɪd/ *adj.* **1.** quick, swift; acting or completed in a short time. **2.** (of a slope) descending steeply. —*n.* (usu. in *pl.*) a steep descent in a river-bed with a swift current. —**rapidity** /rəˈpɪdɪtɪ/ *n.,* **rapidly** *adv.* [f. L *rapidus* (*rapere* seize)]

rapier /ˈreɪpɪə(r)/ *n.* a light slender double-edged sword used for thrusting. [prob. f. Du. or LG, f. F *rapière* (orig. unkn.)]

rapine /ˈræpaɪn/ *n.* plundering. [f. OF or L *rapina* (*rapere* seize)]

rapist /ˈreɪpɪst/ *n.* one who commits rape. [f. RAPE[1]]

rapport /ræˈpɔː(r)/ *n.* an understanding relationship or communication between people. [F (*rapporter,* as RE-, AP-, *porter* f. L *portare* carry)]

rapprochement /ræˈprɒʃmɑ̃/ *n.* resumption of harmonious relations, especially between States. [F (as RE-, APPROACH)]

rapscallion /ræpˈskælɪən/ *n.* a rascal. [earlier *rascallion,* perh. f. RASCAL]

rapt *adj.* fully intent or absorbed, enraptured; carried away with emotion or lofty thought. [f. L *raptus* p.p. of *rapere* seize]

raptorial /ræpˈtɔːrɪəl/ *adj.* predatory. —*n.* a predatory animal or bird. [f. L *raptor* ravisher, plunderer (as prec.)]

rapture /ˈræptʃə(r)/ *n.* ecstatic delight; (in *pl.*) great pleasure or enthusiasm, the expression of this. —**rapturous** *adj.,* **rapturously** *adv.* [obs. F, or f. L *raptura* as RAPT)]

rare[1] *adj.* **1.** seldom done or found or occurring, very uncommon, unusual. **2.** exceptionally good. **3.** of less than usual density. —**rare earth,** see separate entry. —**rareness** *n.* [f. L *rarus*]

rare[2] *adj.* (of meat) underdone. [OE]

rarebit /ˈreəbɪt/ *n.* a Welsh rarebit (see WELSH). [alt. of (*Welsh*) *rabbit*]

rare earth any of a class of 17 chemically similar metallic elements or their oxides, including scandium, yttrium, and the lanthanides (the term is sometimes applied to the lanthanides alone). These elements are not in fact 'rare' compared with many better-known metals, but they tend to occur together in nature and are difficult to separate from one another. It took over a century for all the elements to be identified after the oxide of the first, yttrium, was isolated in 1794. Nowadays mixtures of rare earths, as well as purified individual elements, have a wide variety of specialized uses, notably as industrial catalysts and in alloys.

rarefy /ˈreərɪfaɪ/ *v.t./i.* **1.** to make or become less solid or dense. **2.** to refine. **3.** to make (an idea etc.) subtle. —**rarefaction** /-ˈfækʃ(ə)n/ *n.* [f. OF or L *rarefacere* (*rarus* rare, *facere* make)]

rarely *adv.* seldom, not often; exceptionally. [f. prec.]

raring /ˈreərɪŋ/ *adj.* (*colloq.*) enthusiastic, eager (*to go* etc.). [partic. of *rare,* dial. var. of REAR[2]]

rarity /ˈreərɪtɪ/ *n.* **1.** rareness. **2.** an uncommon thing. [f. F or L (as RARE[1])]

rascal /ˈrɑːsk(ə)l/ *n.* a dishonest or mischievous person. —**rascally** *adj.* [f. OF *rascaille* rabble]

rash[1] *adj.* acting or done without due consideration of the possible consequences or risks. —**rashly** *adv.,* **rashness** *n.* [f. OE, = MDu. *rasch*]

rash[2] *n.* **1.** an eruption of spots or patches on the skin. **2.** a sudden widespread onset. [cf. OF *ra(s)che* eruptive sores]

rasher *n.* a thin slice of bacon or ham. [orig. unkn.]

rasp /rɑːsp/ *n.* **1.** a coarse kind of file having separate teeth. **2.** a grating sound. —*v.t./i.* **1.** to scrape with a rasp; to scrape roughly. **2.** to make a grating sound; to say gratingly. **3.** to grate upon (a person or his feelings). [f. OF *raspe*, *rasper*]

raspberry /ˈrɑːzbərɪ/ *n.* **1.** an edible sweet usually red conical berry; the plant (*Rubus idaeus*) bearing this. **2.** (*slang*) a sound expressing derision or dislike. —**raspberry-cane** *n.* a raspberry plant. [f. obs. *raspis* (orig. unkn.) + BERRY]

Rasputin /ræsˈpuːtɪn/, Grigori Efimovich (1871–1916), Russian religious fanatic who came to exert great influence over Tsar Nicholas II and his family during the First World War by claiming miraculous powers to heal the heir to the throne, who suffered from haemophilia. A libertine and mystic, Rasputin was responsible in a large measure for the Tsar's failure to respond to the rising tide of discontent which eventually resulted in the Russian Revolution. He was murdered by a group of nobles.

Rasta /ˈræstə/ *n.* a Rastafarian. [abbr.]

Rastafarian /ræstəˈfeərɪən/ *adj.* of the Rastafari sect, of Jamaican origin, which believes that Blacks are the chosen people, that the late Emperor Haile Selassie of Ethiopia was God Incarnate, and that he will secure their repatriation to their homeland in Africa. —*n.* a member of this sect. [f. the title and name *Ras Tafari* (Amharic, *ras* chief) by which Haile Selassie was known from 1916 until his accession in 1930]

rat *n.* **1.** a rodent of the genus *Rattus* like a large mouse; a similar rodent. **2.** (*colloq.*) an unpleasant or treacherous person. —*v.i.* (**-tt-**) **1.** to hunt or kill rats. **2.** to act as an informer. —**rat on,** to desert or betray (a person). **rat race,** a fiercely competitive struggle, especially to maintain one's position in work or life. **smell a rat,** to begin to suspect treachery etc. [OE & OF]

ratafia /rætəˈfiːə/ *n.* **1.** a liqueur flavoured with almonds or fruit-kernels. **2.** a kind of small almond biscuit. [F, prob. rel. to *tafia* kind of rum]

ratatouille /rɑːtaˈtuːi/ *n.* a Provençal dish of vegetables (chiefly aubergines, tomatoes, onions, and peppers) stewed in oil. [F dial.]

ratchet /ˈrætʃɪt/ *n.* **1.** a set of teeth on the edge of a bar or wheel with a catch allowing motion in one direction only. **2.** (in full **ratchet-wheel**) a wheel with a rim so toothed. [f. F *rochet* lance-head]

rate[1] *n.* **1.** a stated numerical proportion between two sets of things (the second usually expressed as unity), especially as a measure of amount or degree or as the basis of calculating an amount or value. **2.** a fixed or appropriate charge, cost, or value; a measure of this. **3.** rapidity of movement or change. **4.** class, rank. **5.** an assessment by a local authority levied on the value of buildings and land owned or leased; (in *pl.*) the amount payable. Liability to rates originated in the Poor Relief Act of 1801. —*v.t./i.* **1.** to estimate or assign the worth or value of. **2.** to consider, to regard as; to rank or be regarded in a specified way. **3.** to subject to the payment of a local rate; to value for the assessment of rates. **4.** (*US*) to be worthy of, to deserve. —**at any rate,** in any case, whatever happens. **at this rate,** if this example is typical. [f. OF f. L *rata* (*rēri* reckon)]

rate[2] *v.t./i.* to scold angrily. [orig. unkn.]

rateable /ˈreɪtəb(ə)l/ *adj.* liable to rates. —**rateable value,** the value at which a house etc. is assessed for rates. [f. RATE[1]]

ratepayer *n.* a person liable to pay rates.

rath /rɑːθ/ *n.* (in Ireland & SW Wales) a small circular hill-fort. [Ir.]

rather /ˈrɑːðə(r)/ *adv.* **1.** by preference, more willingly. **2.** more truly; as the more likely alternative. **3.** more precisely. **4.** slightly, to some extent. **5.** (*colloq.*, in an answer) most certainly. —**had rather,** would rather. [f. OE, = earlier]

ratify /ˈrætɪfaɪ/ *v.t.* to confirm or accept (an agreement made in one's name) by formal consent, signature, etc. —**ratification** /-fɪˈkeɪʃ(ə)n/ *n.* [f. OF f. L *ratificare* (as RATE[1], *facere* make)]

rating[1] /ˈreɪtɪŋ/ *n.* **1.** a place in a rank or class. **2.** the estimated standing of a person as regards credit etc. **3.** a non-commissioned sailor. **4.** the amount fixed as a local rate. **5.** the relative popularity of a broadcast programme as determined by the estimated size of the audience. [f. RATE[1]]

rating[2] /ˈreɪtɪŋ/ *n.* an angry reprimand. [f. RATE[2]]

ratio /ˈreɪʃɪəʊ/ *n.* (*pl.* **-os**) the quantitative relation between two similar magnitudes determined by the number of times one contains the other. [L (as RATE[1])]

ratiocinate /rætɪˈɒsɪneɪt/ *v.i.* to reason, especially using syllogisms. —**ratiocination** /-ˈneɪʃ(ə)n/ *n.* [f. L (as prec.)]

ration /ˈræʃ(ə)n/ *n.* an allowance or portion of food or clothing etc., especially an official allowance in time of shortage; (usu. in *pl.*) a fixed daily allowance of food in the armed forces etc. —*v.t.* to limit (persons or provisions) to a fixed ration; to share (food etc.) in fixed quantities. [F, f. It. or Sp. f. L *ratio* reckoning, ratio]

rational /ˈræʃən(ə)l/ *adj.* **1.** of or based on reason; sane, sensible. **2.** endowed with reason. **3.** rejecting what is unreasonable or cannot be tested by reason in religion or custom. **4.** (of a quantity or ratio) expressible as a ratio of integers. —**rationality** /-ˈnælɪtɪ/ *n.*, **rationally** *adv.* [f. L (as prec.)]

rationale /ræʃəˈnɑːl/ *n.* a fundamental reason; a logical basis. [neut. of L *rationalis* (as RATION)]

rationalism /ˈræʃ(ə)nəlɪz(ə)m/ *n.* **1.** the practice of explaining the supernatural in religion in a way that is consonant with reason, or of treating reason as the ultimate authority in religion as elsewhere. **2.** the theory that reason is the foundation of certainty in knowledge (opp. EMPIRICISM, SENSATIONALISM). —**rationalist** *n.*, **rationalistic** /-ˈlɪstɪk/ *adj.* [f. RATIONAL]

rationalize *v.t.* **1.** to offer a reasoned but specious explanation of (behaviour or an attitude). **2.** to make logical and consistent. **3.** to make (an industry) more efficient by reorganizing it to reduce or eliminate waste. **4.** to explain by rationalism. —**rationalization** /-ˈzeɪʃ(ə)n/ *n.* [as prec.]

ratline /ˈrætlɪn/ *n.* (also **ratlin**) any of the small lines fastened across a sailing-ship's shrouds like ladder-rungs. [orig. unkn.]

rattan /rəˈtæn/ *n.* **1.** a palm of the genus *Calamus* etc. with long thin many-jointed pliable stems. **2.** a piece of rattan stem used as a cane etc. [f. Malay]

rat-tat /rætˈtæt/ *n.* a rapping sound, especially of a knocker. [imit.]

Rattigan /ˈrætɪgən/, Sir Terence Marvyn (1911–77), English dramatist. His first West End success, the comedy *French Without Tears* (1936), was followed by many other works, including *The Winslow Boy* (1946), *The Browning Version* (1948), and *Ross* (1960), which was based on the life of T. E. Lawrence. In the 1950s and 1960s there was a reaction against the middle-class middle-brow nature of his plays, but later they were again in favour and are still performed.

rattle *v.t./i.* **1.** to make or cause to make a rapid succession of short sharp hard sounds; to cause such sounds by shaking something. **2.** to move or travel with a rattling noise. **3.** (usu. with *off*) to say or recite rapidly; (usu. with *on*) to talk in a lively thoughtless way. **4.** (*slang*) to disconcert, to alarm. —*n.* **1.** a rattling sound. **2.** a device or toy etc. for making a rattling sound. [prob. f. MDu. or LG (imit.)]

rattlesnake *n.* a poisonous American snake of the genus *Crotalus* with a rattling structure of horny rings in its tail.

rattletrap *n.* a rickety old vehicle etc.

rattling *adj.* brisk, vigorous. —*adv.* remarkably. [f. RATTLE]

ratty *adj.* **1.** relating to or infested with rats. **2.** (*slang*) irritable, angry. [f. RAT]

raucous /ˈrɔːkəs/ *adj.* harsh-sounding, loud and hoarse. —**raucously** *adv.*, **raucousness** *n.* [f. L *raucus*]

raunchy /ˈrɔːntʃɪ/ *adj.* coarse, earthy; boisterous. [orig. unkn.]

ravage /ˈrævɪdʒ/ *v.t./i.* to devastate, to plunder, to make havoc (in). —*n.* **1.** devastation; **2.** (usu. in *pl.*) destructive effect. [f. F, alt. of *ravine* rush of water (as RAVINE)]

rave *v.i.* **1.** to talk wildly or furiously (as) in delirium. **2.** to speak with rapturous admiration. —*n.* **1.** (*colloq.*) a highly enthusiastic review (of a film or play etc.). **2.** (*slang*) an infatuation. —**rave-up** *n.* (*slang*) a lively party. **raving beauty,** an excitingly beautiful person. **raving mad,** completely mad. [prob. f. OF *raver*]

Ravel /ræˈvel/, Maurice (1875–1937), French composer. The best-known of Debussy's contemporaries, he was equally influenced by the Oriental music brought to Paris in the 1889 World Exhibition and by impressionism, but combined his love of apt descriptive sonorities with a cool classicism and a recognition of Liszt's legacy of brilliance and vigour. His works span all genres: opera, ballet, orchestral music, and song. Among his later works were the two great piano concertos (both 1931); the first is for left hand only, composed for Paul Wittgenstein who lost his right arm in the First World War.

ravel /'rævəl/ v.t./i. (**-ll-**) **1.** to entangle or become entangled. **2.** to confuse or complicate (a question or problem). **3.** to fray out; **4.** to disentangle, to unravel; to distinguish the separate threads or subdivisions of. —n. a tangle, a knot; a complication. [perh. f. Du. *ravelen*]

raven[1] /'reɪv(ə)n/ n. a large crow (*Corvus corax*) with glossy blue-black feathers and a hoarse cry. —adj. (usu. of hair) glossy black. [OE]

raven[2] /'ræv(ə)n/ v.t./i. **1.** to plunder, to seek prey or booty. **2.** to devour voraciously. [f. OF *raviner* ravage f. L (as RAPINE)]

Ravenna /rə'venə/ a city near the Adriatic coast in NE central Italy. An important centre in Roman times, Ravenna became the capital of the Ostrogothic kingdom of Italy in the 5th c. and afterwards served as capital of the Byzantine Empire of Italy. The richest mosaics of the early Christian period are found there. It became an independent republic in the 13th c. and then a papal possession in 1509, remaining in papal hands until 1859.

ravenous /'rævənəs/ adj. very hungry; voracious; rapacious. —**ravenously** adv. [f. OF (as prec.)]

ravine /rə'vi:n/ n. a deep narrow gorge. [F f. L, = RAPINE]

ravioli /rævi'əʊli/ n. small pasta cases containing meat etc. [It.]

ravish /'rævɪʃ/ v.t. **1.** to commit rape on. **2.** to enrapture, to fill with delight. —**ravishment** n. [f. OF f. L *rapere* seize]

raw adj. **1.** uncooked. **2.** in its natural state, not yet or not fully processed or manufactured. **3.** inexperienced; untrained. **4.** stripped of skin and having the underlying flesh exposed; sensitive to the touch from being so exposed. **5.** (of atmosphere or a day etc.) damp and chilly. **6.** crude in artistic quality, lacking finish. **7.** (of an edge of cloth) not a selvage and not hemmed. —**in the raw**, in its natural state without mitigation; naked. **raw-boned** adj. gaunt. **raw deal**, see DEAL[1]. **raw material**, that from which a process of manufacture makes articles. **touch a person on the raw**, to wound his feelings on a point where he is sensitive. —**rawness** n. [OE]

rawhide n. untanned leather; a rope or whip of this.

Rawlplug /'rɔ:lplʌg/ n. [P] a thin cylindrical plug for holding a screw or nail in masonry. [f. J. J. & W. R. *Rawl*ings, English electrical engineers + PLUG]

Rawls /rɔːlz/, John (1921–), American philosopher, author of *A Theory of Justice* (1972) which presents a systematic moral theory in opposition to utilitarianism. The central claim of the book is that a system is just if and only if it accords with the principles which would be agreed upon by rational people making a kind of social contract. Rawls argues for principles which give weight to basic liberties and improvement for the worst off, in preference to any form of utilitarianism.

Ray /reɪ/, John (1627-1705), English naturalist who developed early systematic classifications of plants and animals. His principal interest was botany, and his major work, the *Historia Plantarum*, appeared in three volumes between 1686 and 1704. Ray toured Europe in search of specimens. He was the first to classify flowering plants into monocotyledons and dicotyledons, and he established the species as a basic taxonomic unit.

ray[1] n. **1.** a single line or narrow beam of light or other radiation. **2.** a straight line in which radiation is propagated to a given point; (in pl.) radiation of a specified type. **3.** a remnant or beginning of an enlightening or cheering influence. **4.** any of a set of radiating lines, parts, or things. **5.** the marginal part of a composite flower (e.g. a daisy). [f. OF *rai* f. L, = RADIUS]

ray[2] n. a large sea-fish of the order *Hypotremata*, related to the shark and used as food. [f. OF f. L *raia*]

ray[3] n. (Mus.) the second note of the major scale in tonic sol-fa (see entry). [f. *resonare* (see GAMUT)]

Rayleigh /'reɪli/, John William Strutt, 3rd Baron (1842-1919), English physicist who made significant contributions to several branches of the science. In 1877-8 he published a major work on acoustics, *The Theory of Sound*. He studied the scattering of light by small particles, thereby explaining why the sky is blue. In 1879-84 he was director of the Cavendish Laboratory at Cambridge, succeeding James Clerk Maxwell. His researches included the establishment of electrical units of resistance, current, and electromotive force. A brilliant and successful experimentalist, he worked

with Sir William Ramsay from 1894, and their accurate measurement of the constituent gases of the atmosphere led to the discovery of argon and other inert gases. In 1904 Rayleigh was awarded the Nobel Prize for physics and Ramsay that for chemistry.

rayon /'reɪɒn/ n. an artificial textile fibre or fabric made from cellulose. [f. RAY[1]]

raze v.t. to destroy completely, to tear down (usu. *to the ground*). [f. OF, = shave close, ult. f. L *radere* scrape]

razor /'reɪzə(r)/ n. an instrument with a sharp blade used in cutting hair especially from the skin. —**razor-bill** n. an auk (*Alca torda*) with a sharp-edged bill. **razor-blade** n. a blade used in a razor, especially a flat piece of metal with two sharp edges used in a safety razor. **razor-edge** n. a keen edge; a sharp mountain ridge; a critical situation; a sharp line of division. [f. OF (as prec.)]

razzle n. (slang) a spree, a lively outing. [f. foll.]

razzle-dazzle /'ræz(ə)ldæz(ə)l/ n. (slang) **1.** excitement, bustle, a spree. **2.** (slang) noisy advertising. [redupl. of DAZZLE]

razzmatazz /ræzmə'tæz/ n. (colloq.) **1.** excitement, bustle. **2.** noisy advertising. **3.** insincere actions, humbug. [prob. alt. f. prec.]

Rb symbol rubidium.

RC abbr. Roman Catholic.

Rd. abbr. road.

Re symbol rhenium.

re[1] /riː/ prep. in the matter of (as the first word in a heading, especially of a legal document); (colloq.) about, concerning. [L, abl. of *res* thing]

re[2] /reɪ/ var. of RAY[3].

're abbr. are.

re-[1] prefix (sometimes **red-** before vowels: *redolent*) in verbs and verbal derivatives denoting: in return, mutually (*react*, *resemble*), opposition (*repel*, *resist*), behind or after (*relic*, *remain*), retirement or secrecy (*recluse*, *reticence*), off, away, down (*recede*, *relegate*, *repress*), frequentative or intensive force (*redouble*, *refine*, *resplendent*), negative force (*recant*, *reveal*). [f. L]

re-[2] prefix attachable to almost any verb or its derivative in senses (1) once more, afresh, anew; (2) back, with return to a previous state. A hyphen is normally used when the word begins in *e-* (*re-enact*) or to distinguish the compound from a more familiar one-word form (*re-form* = form again). [as prec.]

reach v.t./i. **1.** to stretch out or extend. **2.** to stretch out the hand etc. in order to touch or grasp or take something; to make a reaching motion or effort (lit. or fig.). **3.** to get as far as, to arrive at, to attain. **4.** to make contact by hand etc. or by telephone etc. **5.** to sail with the wind abeam or abaft the beam. —n. **1.** an act of reaching. **2.** the extent to which a hand etc. can be reached out, an influence exerted, or a mental power used. **3.** a continuous extent, especially the part of a river that can be looked along at once between two bends, or part of a canal between locks. **4.** (in sailing) the distance traversed in reaching (**broad reach**, with the wind aft the beam but not so far aft that the vessel is running. **close reach**, with the wind forward of the beam but not so far forward that the vessel is close-hauled; ill. SAILING-SHIPS). —**reach-me-down** adj. (colloq.) ready-made. [OE]

reachable adj. that may be reached.

react /riː'ækt/ v.i. **1.** to respond *to* a stimulus, to undergo a change or show behaviour that is due to some influence. **2.** to be actuated by repulsion *against*, to tend in a reverse or backward direction.

reaction /riː'ækʃ(ə)n/ n. **1.** reacting; a responsive feeling. **2.** an occurrence of a condition after its opposite. **3.** tendency to oppose change or to return to a former system, especially in politics. **4.** the interaction of substances undergoing chemical change. [f. prec.]

reactionary /riː'ækʃənərɪ/ adj. showing reaction; opposed to progress or reform. —n. a reactionary person. [f. prec.]

reactivate /riː'æktɪveɪt/ v.t. to restore to a state of activity. —**reactivation** /-'veɪʃ(ə)n/ n.

reactive /riː'æktɪv/ adj. showing reaction. —**reactivity** /-'tɪvɪtɪ/ n. [f. REACT]

reactor /riː'æktə(r)/ n. a nuclear reactor (see entry). [f. REACT]

read /riːd/ v.t./i. (past & p.p. **read** /red/) **1.** to reproduce mentally or vocally the words of (an author, book, letter, etc.) while following their symbols with the eyes or fingers.

2. to be able to understand the meaning of (written or printed words or symbols). **3.** to interpret mentally, to find implications; to declare the interpretation of. **4.** (of a measuring instrument) to show (a figure etc.). **5.** to have a specified wording. **6.** to study or discover by reading; to study (a subject at university); to carry out a course of study. **7.** (of a computer) to copy or transfer (data). —*n.* a spell of reading. —**read between the lines,** to look for and find a hidden or implicit meaning. **read-only memory,** (in computers) a memory whose contents can usually be read at high speed but cannot be changed by program instructions. **read up,** to make a special study of (a subject). **take as read,** to dispense with actual reading or discussion of. **well read,** (of a person) having knowledge of a subject or good general acquaintance with literature through reading. [OE]

readable *adj.* able to be read; interesting to read. [f. READ]

readdress /riːəˈdres/ *v.t.* to alter the address on (a letter).

Reade /riːd/, Charles (1814-84), English dramatist and novelist who wrote several propagandist novels on social reform, successful stage works, and is chiefly remembered for his historical romance *The Cloister and the Hearth* (1861), set in the 15th c. and relating the adventures of Gerard, whose son became the future Erasmus.

reader *n.* **1.** one who reads. **2.** a book containing passages for practice in reading by students learning a language. **3.** a device to produce an image that can be read from a microfilm etc. **4.** a university lecturer of a higher grade. **5.** a publisher's employee who reports on submitted manuscripts; a printer's proof-corrector. [f. READ]

readership *n.* the readers of a newspaper etc. [f. prec.]

readily /ˈredɪlɪ/ *adv.* **1.** without showing reluctance, willingly. **2.** without difficulty. [f. READY]

readiness *n.* **1.** a ready or prepared state. **2.** willingness. **3.** facility, quickness in argument or action. [f. READY]

reading *n.* **1.** the act of one who reads. **2.** an entertainment at which a thing is read. **3.** matter to be read; its specified quality. **4.** literary knowledge. **5.** a figure etc. given by a measuring instrument. **6.** an interpretation. **7.** each of the three occasions on which a Bill must be presented to a legislature for acceptance. —**reading-room** *n.* a room in a club, library, etc., for those wishing to read. [f. READ]

readjust /riːəˈdʒʌst/ *v.t./i.* to adjust (a thing) again; to adapt oneself again. —**readjustment** *n.*

ready /ˈredɪ/ *adj.* **1.** with preparations complete; in a fit state for immediate use or action. **2.** willing; about or inclined to do something. **3.** easily available; within reach. **4.** prompt, quick, facile. —*adv.* beforehand, so as to be ready when the time comes. —*n.* (*slang*) ready money. —*v.t.* to make ready, to prepare. —**at the ready,** ready for action. **ready-made** *adj.* (esp. of clothes) made for immediate wear, not to measure. **ready money,** actual coin or notes; payment on the spot. **ready reckoner,** a book or table of the results of arithmetical computations of the kind commonly wanted in business etc. [OE]

Reagan /ˈreɪgən/, Ronald Wilson (1911-) 40th President of the USA, 1981- . A film actor before entering politics, he was governor of California 1966-74.

reagent /riːˈeɪdʒ(ə)nt/ *n.* a substance used to cause a chemical reaction, especially to detect another substance.

real[1] /ˈrɪəl/ *adj.* **1.** existing as a thing or occurring in fact, not imaginary. **2.** genuine, rightly so called; not artificial or imitation. **3.** (*Law*) consisting of immovable property such as land or houses. **4.** (of income or value etc.) appraised by purchasing power. —*adv.* (*Sc. & US colloq.*) really, very. —**real money,** coin, cash. **real tennis,** see TENNIS. **real time,** the actual time of a process analysed by a computer. [AF & f. L *realis* (*res* thing)]

real[2] /reɪˈɑːl/ *n.* (*hist.*) a silver coin in Spanish-speaking countries. [Sp. (as ROYAL)]

realgar /rɪˈælgə(r)/ *n.* a mineral consisting of arsenic sulphide, used as a pigment and in fireworks. [f. L f. Arab., = dust of the cave]

realign /riːəˈlaɪn/ *v.t./i.* **1.** to align again. **2.** to regroup in politics etc. —**realignment** *n.*

realism /ˈrɪəlɪz(ə)m/ *n.* (usu. opp. IDEALISM) **1.** the practice of regarding things in their true nature, and dealing with them as they are; practical views and policy. **2.** fidelity of representation, truth to nature, insistence upon details; the showing of life as it is without glossing over what is ugly or painful. **3.** the medieval theory that universals or general ideas have objective existence (cf. NOMINALISM, CONCEPTUALISM). **4.** belief that matter as an object of perception has real existence (in the 20th c. the term has been applied to philosophical theories reacting against 19th-c. idealism

which, while they agree in affirming that external objects exist independently of the mind, differ in their accounts of appearance, perception, and illusion); the theory that the world has a reality that transcends the mind's analytical capacity, and hence that propositions are to be assessed in terms of their truth in reality rather than in terms of their verifiability. —**realist** *n.* [f. REAL[1]]

realistic /rɪəˈlɪstɪk/ *adj.* **1.** regarding things as they are, following a policy of realism. **2.** based on facts rather than ideals. **3.** (of wages or prices) high enough to pay the worker or seller adequately. —**realistically** *adv.* [f. prec.]

reality /rɪˈælɪtɪ/ *n.* **1.** what is real or existent or underlies appearances. **2.** real existence, being real. **3.** resemblance to an original. [f. L or F (as REAL[1])]

realize /ˈriːəlaɪz/ *v.t.* **1.** to be fully aware of; to present or conceive as real; to understand clearly. **2.** (usu. in *pass.*) to convert (a hope or plan) into a fact. **3.** to convert (securities or profit) into money by selling. **4.** to acquire (a profit); to be sold for (a specified price). —**realization** /-ˈzeɪʃ(ə)n/ *n.* [f. REAL[1]]

really /ˈriːəlɪ/ *adv.* **1.** in reality, in fact. **2.** indeed, I assure you. **3.** as an expression of interest, surprise, or mild protest. [f. REAL[1]]

realm /relm/ *n.* **1.** a kingdom. **2.** a field of activity or interest. [f. OF f. L, = REGIMEN]

realty /ˈrɪəltɪ/ *n.* real estate. [f. REAL[1]]

ream[1] *n.* **1.** twenty quires of paper (about 500 sheets). **2.** (usu. in *pl.*) a large quantity of writing. [f. OF ult. f. Arab., = bundle]

ream[2] *v.t.* to enlarge or give a smooth finish to (a hole drilled in metal etc.) by a borer. —**reamer** *n.* [orig. unkn.]

reap *v.t.* **1.** to cut or gather (a crop, esp. grain) as harvest; to harvest the crop of (a field etc.). **2.** to receive as the consequence of one's own or another's actions. [OE]

reaper *n.* **1.** a person who reaps. **2.** a machine for reaping crops. A crude corn-reaping machine was in use in Roman Gaul in the 1st c. AD, but the first machines of any efficiency date from the early 19th c. **3.** death personified. [f. REAP]

reappear /riːəˈpɪə(r)/ *v.i.* to appear again. —**reappearance** *n.*

reappraise /riːəˈpreɪz/ *v.t.* to appraise again, to reconsider. —**reappraisal** *n.*

rear[1] *n.* **1.** the back part, the space behind, position at the back of something. **2.** (*colloq.*) the buttocks. —*adj.* at the back, in the rear. —**bring up the rear,** to come last. **Rear Admiral,** see ADMIRAL. **rear-lamp** or **rear-light** *n.* a light, usually red, on the back of a vehicle. [prob. f. REARWARD or REARGUARD (cf. VAN[2])]

rear[2] *v.t./i.* **1.** to bring up and educate (children); to breed and care for (animals); to cultivate (crops). **2.** (of a horse etc.) to raise itself on its hind legs. **3.** to set upright, to build; to hold upwards. **4.** to extend to a great height. [OE]

rearguard *n.* a body of troops detached to protect the rear of the main force; especially in retreats. —**rearguard action,** an engagement between the rearguard and the enemy (*lit.* or *fig.*). [f. OF *rereguarde* (as RETRO-, GUARD)]

rearm /riːˈɑːm/ *v.t./i.* to arm again, especially with improved weapons. —**rearmament** *n.*

rearmost *adj.* furthest back. [f. REAR[1]]

rearrange /riːəˈreɪndʒ/ *v.t.* to arrange in a different way. —**rearrangement** *n.*

rearward /ˈrɪəwəd/ *n.* the rear (esp. in prepositional phrases: *to the rearward of, in the rearward*). —*adj.* to the rear. —*adv.* (also **rearwards**) towards the rear. [f. AF *rerewarde* (as REARGUARD)]

reason /ˈriːz(ə)n/ *n.* **1.** a motive, cause, or justification; a fact adduced or serving as this. **2.** the intellectual faculty by which conclusions are drawn from premisses. **3.** sanity. **4.** good sense, sensible conduct; what is right or practical or practicable; moderation. —*v.t./i.* **1.** to form or try to reach conclusions by connected thought, to state as a step in this. **2.** to try to persuade a person by giving reasons. —**by reason of,** owing to. **in** or **within reason,** within the bounds of moderation. **with reason,** not unjustifiably. [f. OF f. L, = RATIO]

reasonable *adj.* **1.** having or based on sound judgement or moderation; sensible, not expecting too much. **2.** not excessive, not expensive or extortionate. **3.** ready to listen to reason. —**reasonableness** *n.*, **reasonably** *adv.* [as prec.]

reassemble /riːəˈsemb(ə)l/ *v.t./i.* to assemble again.

reassure /riːəˈʃʊə(r)/ *v.t.* to restore confidence to, to dispel the apprehensions of. —**reassurance** *n.*

Réaumur /reɪəʊˈmjʊə(r)/, René Antoine Ferchault de (1683–1757), French entomologist, one of the greatest naturalists of his age, who was put in charge of compiling a list of France's arts, industries, and professions. As a consequence, he suggested improvements in several manufacturing processes, including the making of porcelain, mirrors, tinplate, iron, and steel, but he is chiefly remembered for his thermometer scale, now obsolete. The traditional Réaumur scale has eighty divisions between 0° (the melting-point of ice) and 80° (the boiling-point of water), but the original alcohol thermometer had only one fixed point, that of melting ice, and its divisions were marked volumetrically rather than lineally.

reave v.t. (past & p.p. **reft**) (archaic) to deprive forcibly; to take by force or carry off. [OE]

rebarbative /rɪˈbɑːbətɪv/ adj. (literary) repellent, unattractive. [f. F (barbe beard)]

rebate[1] /ˈriːbeɪt/ n. a deduction from a sum to be paid, a discount; a partial refund. [f. OF rebattre (as RE-[1], ABATE)]

rebate[2] /ˈriːbeɪt/ n. a step-shaped channel etc. cut along the edge or face of wood etc., usually to receive the edge or tongue of another piece (ill. CARPENTRY). —v.t. to join or fix with a rebate; to make a rebate in. [as RABBET, after prec.]

rebec /ˈriːbek/ n. a medieval usually three-stringed instrument played with a bow. [f. F f. OF f. Arab.]

rebel /ˈreb(ə)l/ n. 1. a person who fights against, resists, or refuses allegiance to the established government; a person or thing that resists authority or control. 2. (attrib.) rebellious; of rebels; in rebellion. —/rɪˈbel/ v.i. (-ll-) 1. to act as a rebel. 2. to feel or display repugnance (against a custom etc.). [f. OF f. L rebellare (RE-[1], bellum war)]

rebellion /rɪˈbeljən/ n. open resistance to authority, especially organized armed resistance to the established government. [f. OF f. L (as prec.)]

rebellious /rɪˈbeljəs/ adj. 1. in rebellion. 2. disposed to rebel, defying lawful authority. 3. (of a thing) unmanageable, refractory. —**rebelliously** adv., **rebelliousness** n. [f. prec.]

rebirth /riːˈbɜːθ/ n. 1. a new incarnation; a return to life or activity, a revival. 2. spiritual enlightenment.

rebound /rɪˈbaʊnd/ v.i. 1. to spring back after impact. 2. (of an action) to have an adverse effect upon the originator. —/ˈriːbaʊnd/ n. 1. an act of rebounding, a recoil. 2. reaction after disappointment or other emotion. [f. OF (as RE-[1], BOUND[1])]

rebuff /rɪˈbʌf/ n. an unkind or contemptuous rejection; snub. —v.t. to give a rebuff to. [f. F f. It. (as RE-[1], buffo puff)]

rebuild /riːˈbɪld/ v.t. (past & p.p. **rebuilt**) to build again after destruction or demolition.

rebuke /rɪˈbjuːk/ v.t. to reprove sharply or severely. —n. a sharp or severe reproof. [f. AF rebuker (RE-[1] + OF buchier beat)]

rebus /ˈriːbəs/ n. a representation of a word (especially a name) by pictures etc. suggesting its syllables. [f. F f. L rebus, abl. pl. of res thing]

rebut /rɪˈbʌt/ v.t. (-tt-) 1. to refute or disprove (evidence or an accusation). 2. to force or turn back. —**rebutment** n. **rebuttal** n. [f. AF (as RE-[2], BUTT[1])]

recalcitrant /rɪˈkælsɪtrənt/ adj. obstinately disobedient, resisting authority or discipline. —**recalcitrance** n. [f. L recalcitrare kick out (calx heel)]

recall /rɪˈkɔːl/ v.t. 1. to summon to return. 2. to bring back to the attention or memory etc. 3. to recollect, to remember. 4. to revoke or annul (an action or decision). —n. 1. a summons to come back. 2. the act of remembering; ability to remember. 3. the possiblity of revoking or annulling.

recant /rɪˈkænt/ v.t./i. to withdraw and renounce (a former belief or statement etc.) as erroneous or heretical; to disavow a former opinion, especially with a public confession of error. —**recantation** /riːkænˈteɪʃ(ə)n/ n. [f. L recantare (RE-[1], cantare sing)]

recap /ˈriːkæp/ v.t. (colloq.) (-pp-) to recapitulate. —n. (colloq.) recapitulation. [abbr.]

recapitulate /riːkəˈpɪtjʊleɪt/ v.t./i. to state again briefly; to repeat the main points of. [f. L recapitulare (RE-[2], capitulum chapter)]

recapitulation /riːkəpɪtjʊˈleɪʃ(ə)n/ n. 1. recapitulating. 2. (Mus.) the part of a movement in which the themes from the exposition are restated. [f. OF or L (as prec.)]

recapture /riːˈkæptʃə(r)/ v.t. 1. to capture again (a person or thing that has escaped or been lost to an enemy). 2. to re-experience (a past emotion etc.). —n. recapturing.

recast /riːˈkɑːst/ v.t. (past & p.p. **recast**) to put into a new form, to improve the arrangement of. —n. 1. recasting. 2. a recast form.

recce /ˈreki/ n. (slang) a reconnaissance. —v.t./i. (slang) to reconnoitre. [abbr.]

recede /rɪˈsiːd/ v.i. 1. to go or shrink back or further off; to be left at an increasing distance by the observer's motion. 2. to slope backwards. 3. to decline in force or value etc. [f. L recedere (RE-[1], cedere go)]

receipt /rɪˈsiːt/ n. 1. receiving, being received. 2. a written acknowledgement that something has been received or that money has been paid. 3. (archaic) a recipe. —v.t. to put a written receipt on (a bill). [f. AF receite (as foll.)]

receive /rɪˈsiːv/ v.t. 1. to acquire, accept, or take in (something offered, sent, or given). 2. to have conferred or inflicted upon one; to experience; to be treated with. 3. to take the force, weight, or impact of. 4. to consent to hear (a confession or an oath) or consider (a petition). 5. to accept (stolen goods knowingly; also absol.). 6. to serve as a receptacle for; to be able to hold or accommodate. 7. to allow to enter as a member or guest; to greet or welcome in a specified manner. 8. to be marked (lit. or fig.) more or less permanently with (an impression etc.). 9. to convert (broadcast signals) into sound or a picture. 10. (esp. in p.p.) to give credit to, to accept as authoritative or true. —**be at** or **on the receiving end,** (colloq.) to bear the brunt of something unpleasant. **received pronunciation,** the form of English speech used (with local variations) by the majority of educated English-speaking people. [f. OF f. L recipere recover (RE-[2], capere take)]

receiver n. 1. a person or thing that receives something. 2. an official who administers property under a receiving-order. 3. a person who accepts stolen goods while knowing them to be stolen. 4. the part of a telephone that receives incoming sound and is held to the ear. 5. a radio or television receiving apparatus. [f. prec.]

receiving-order n. a lawcourt's order to an official (the receiver) to take charge of the property of a bankrupt or insane person or of property that is the subject of litigation. [f. RECEIVE]

recent /ˈriːs(ə)nt/ adj. 1. not long past, that happened or began to exist or existed shortly before the present. 2. **Recent,** (Geol.) Holocene. —**Recent** n. (Geol.) the Holocene epoch. —**recency** n., **recently** adv. [f. F or L recens recentis]

receptacle /rɪˈseptək(ə)l/ n. a container, something for holding or containing what is put into it. [as foll.]

reception /rɪˈsepʃ(ə)n/ n. 1. receiving, being received. 2. the way in which a person or thing is received. 3. a social occasion for receiving guests, especially after a wedding. 4. the place where guests or clients are registered or welcomed on arrival at a hotel or office etc. 5. the receiving of broadcast signals; the quality of this. —**reception room,** a room available or suitable for receiving company or visitors. [f. OF or L (as RECEIVE)]

receptionist n. a person employed to receive guests or clients etc. [f. prec.]

receptive /rɪˈseptɪv/ adj. able or quick to receive knowledge, impressions, ideas, etc. —**receptiveness** n., **receptivity** /riːsepˈtɪvɪti/ n. [f. F or L (as RECEIVE)]

receptor /rɪˈseptə(r)/ n. an organ able to respond to light, heat, a drug, etc., and transmit a signal to a sensory nerve. [f. OF or L (as prec.)]

recess /rɪˈses/ n. 1. a part or space set back from the line of a wall etc.; a small hollow place inside something; a remote or secret place. 2. temporary cessation from business (esp. of Parliament); a time of this. —v.t./i. 1. to make a recess in or of (a wall etc.). 2. (US) to take a recess, to adjourn. [f. L recessus (as RECEDE)]

recession /rɪˈseʃ(ə)n/ n. 1. a temporary decline in economic activity or prosperity. 2. receding or withdrawal from a place or point. [as prec.]

recessional /rɪˈseʃən(ə)l/ adj. sung while the clergy and choir withdraw after a service. —n. a recessional hymn. [f. prec.]

recessive /rɪˈsesɪv/ adj. 1. tending to recede. 2. (of an inherited characteristic) remaining latent when a dominant characteristic is present. —**recessively** adv. [f. RECESS]

Rechabite /ˈrekəbaɪt/ n. 1. a member of a Jewish family, descended from Jonadab son of Rechab, who refused to drink wine or live in houses (Jer. 35: 2–19). 2. a total abstainer; a member of the Independent Order of Rechabites, a benefit society founded in 1835. [f. *Rechab*]

recharge /riːˈtʃɑːdʒ/ *v.t.* to charge (a battery or gun) again. —**recharge one's batteries,** to have a period of rest and recovery.

rechargeable /riːˈtʃɑːdʒəb(ə)l/ *adj.* that may be recharged. [f. prec.]

recherché /rəˈʃeəʃeɪ/ *adj.* devised or selected with care or difficulty; far-fetched. [F (RE-¹, *chercher* seek)]

rechristen /riːˈkrɪs(ə)n/ *v.t.* to christen again; to give a new name to.

recidivist /rɪˈsɪdɪvɪst/ *n.* one who relapses into crime. —**recidivism** *n.* [f. F f. L *recidivus* falling back (RE-², *cadere* fall)]

recipe /ˈresɪpɪ/ *n.* 1. a statement of the ingredients and procedure for preparing a dish etc. in cookery. 2. a procedure to be followed in order to achieve something. [L, imper. of *recipere* receive (RE-², *capere* take)]

recipient /rɪˈsɪpɪənt/ *n.* a person who receives something. [f. F f. It. or L (as prec.)]

reciprocal /rɪˈsɪprək(ə)l/ *adj.* 1. given or received in return. 2. mutual; (*Gram.*) (of a pronoun) expressing mutual relation (e.g. *each other*). 3. corresponding but the other way round. —*n.* a mathematical expression or function so related to another that their product is unity. —**reciprocally** *adv.* [f. L *reciprocus*, orig. = moving backwards and forwards (*re*- back, *pro* forward)]

reciprocate /rɪˈsɪprəkeɪt/ *v.t./i.* 1. to give and receive mutually; to make a return for something done, given or felt. 2. (of a machine part) to go with alternate backward and forward motion. —**reciprocation** /-ˈkeɪʃ(ə)n/ *n.* [f. L *reciprocare* (as prec.)]

reciprocity /resɪˈprɒsɪtɪ/ *n.* 1. the condition of being reciprocal. 2. a mutual action. 3. give-and-take, especially the interchange of privileges. [f. F (as RECIPROCAL)]

recital /rɪˈsaɪt(ə)l/ *n.* 1. reciting. 2. a long account of a series of facts or events. 3. a musical entertainment given by one performer or group; a similar entertainment of any kind (e.g. by a dancer). [f. RECITE]

recitation /resɪˈteɪʃ(ə)n/ *n.* 1. reciting. 2. a thing recited. [f. F or L (as RECITE)]

recitative /resɪtəˈtiːv/ *n.* musical declamation of the kind usual in the narrative and dialogue parts of opera and oratorio. [f. It. *recitativo* (as foll.)]

recite /rɪˈsaɪt/ *v.t./i.* 1. to repeat aloud or declaim (a poem or passage) from memory; to give a recitation. 2. to state (facts) in order. [f. OF or L *recitare* (RE-², CITE)]

reckless /ˈreklɪs/ *adj.* regardless of consequences or danger etc. —**recklessly** *adv.*, **recklessness** *n.* [OE (*reck* concern oneself)]

reckon /ˈrekən/ *v.t./i.* 1. to count up; to compute by calculation. 2. to include in a total or as a member of a particular class. 3. to have as one's opinion; to consider or regard; to feel confident. —**day of reckoning,** the time when something must be atoned for or avenged. **reckon on,** to rely or count or base plans on. **reckon with,** to take into account; to settle accounts with (a person). [OE]

reckoner *n.* an aid to reckoning, a ready reckoner (see READY). [f. prec.]

reclaim /rɪˈkleɪm/ *v.t.* 1. to seek the return of (one's property); to take action so as to recover possession of. 2. to bring (flooded or waste land) under cultivation. 3. to win back or away from vice, error, or waste condition. —**reclamation** /rekləˈmeɪʃ(ə)n/ *n.* [f. OF f. L *reclamare* cry out against (RE-², *clamare* shout)]

recline /rɪˈklaɪn/ *v.t./i.* to assume or be in a horizontal or leaning position, to put in this position. [f. OF or L *reclinare* (RE-², *clinare* bend)]

recluse /rɪˈkluːs/ *n.* a person given to or living in seclusion or isolation. [f. OF f. L *recludere* shut away (RE-¹, *claudere* shut)]

recognition /rekəgˈnɪʃ(ə)n/ *n.* recognizing, being recognized. [f. L (as RECOGNIZE)]

recognizable /ˈrekəgnaɪzəb(ə)l/ *adj.* that can be identified or detected. —**recognizably** *adv.* [f. RECOGNIZE]

recognizance /rɪˈkɒgnɪz(ə)ns/ *n.* a bond by which a person undertakes before a court or magistrate to observe some condition, e.g. to appear when summoned; a sum pledged as surety for such an observance. [f. OF (as RE-¹, COGNIZANCE)]

recognize /ˈrekəgnaɪz/ *v.t.* 1. to identify as known before. 2. to realize or discover the nature of. 3. to realize or admit (a fact). 4. to acknowledge the existence, validity, character, or claims of. 5. to show appreciation of, to reward. [f. OF f. L *recognoscere* (RE-², *cognoscere* learn)]

recoil /rɪˈkɔɪl/ *v.i.* 1. to move suddenly or spring back, or shrink mentally, in horror, disgust, or fear. 2. to rebound after impact. 3. to have an adverse reactive effect upon the originator. 4. (of a gun) to be driven backwards by a discharge. —/also ˈriːkɔɪl/ *n.* the act or sensation of recoiling. [f. OF *reculer* f. L *culus* buttocks]

recollect /rekəˈlekt/ *v.t.* to remember; to succeed in remembering, to call to mind. [f. L *recolligere* (RE-², *colligere* collect)]

recollection /rekəˈlekʃ(ə)n/ *n.* 1. recollecting. 2. a thing recollected. 3. a person's memory; the time over which it extends. [F or f. L (as prec.)]

recommence /riːkəˈmens/ *v.t./i.* to begin again. —**recommencement** *n.*

recommend /rekəˈmend/ *v.t.* 1. to suggest as fit for employment or favour or trial. 2. to advise (a course of action etc.). 3. (of qualities or conduct etc.) to make acceptable or desirable. 4. to commend or entrust (to a person or his care). —**recommendation** /-ˈdeɪʃ(ə)n/ *n.* [f. L *recommendare* (RE-¹, *commendare* commend)]

recompense /ˈrekəmpens/ *v.t.* 1. to make amends to (a person) or for (a loss etc.). 2. to requite, reward, or punish (a person or action). —*n.* a reward, a requital; retribution. [f. OF f. L *recompensare* (RE-¹, *compensare* compensate)]

reconcilable /ˈrekənsaɪləb(ə)l/ *adj.* that may be reconciled. [f. foll.]

reconcile /ˈrekənsaɪl/ *v.t.* 1. to make friendly again after an estrangement or quarrel. 2. to induce to accept or be submissive to (an unwelcome fact or situation). 3. to harmonize (facts), to show the compatibility of. —**reconciliation** /-sɪlɪˈeɪʃ(ə)n/ *n.* [f. OF or L *reconciliare* (RE-², *conciliare* conciliate)]

recondite /ˈrekəndaɪt/ *adj.* (of a subject or knowledge) abstruse, out of the way, little known; (of an author or style) dealing in recondite knowledge or allusion, obscure. [f. L *reconditus* (RE-¹, *condere* hide)]

recondition /riːkənˈdɪʃ(ə)n/ *v.t.* to overhaul, to renovate to make usable again.

reconnaissance /rɪˈkɒnɪs(ə)ns/ *n.* a survey of a region, especially a military examination to locate an enemy or ascertain strategic features; a preliminary survey. [F (as foll.)]

reconnoitre /rekəˈnɔɪtə(r)/ *v.t./i.* to make a reconnaissance (of). [f. obs. F f. L, = RECOGNIZE]

reconquer /riːˈkɒŋkə(r)/ *v.t.* to conquer again. —**reconquest** /riːˈkɒŋkwest/ *n.*

reconsider /riːkənˈsɪdə(r)/ *v.t.* to consider again, especially for a possible change of decision. —**reconsideration** /-ˈreɪʃ(ə)n/ *n.*

reconstitute /riːˈkɒnstɪtjuːt/ *v.t.* 1. to reconstruct, to reorganize. 2. to restore the previous constitution of (dried food etc.) by adding water. —**reconstitution** /-ˈtjuːʃ(ə)n/ *n.*

reconstruct /riːkənˈstrʌkt/ *v.t.* 1. to construct or build again. 2. to piece together (past events) into an intelligible whole, by imagination or by re-enacting them. 3. to reorganize. —**reconstruction** *n.*

recopy /riːˈkɒpɪ/ *v.t.* to make a fresh copy of.

record /rɪˈkɔːd/ *v.t.* 1. to set down for remembrance or reference, to put in writing or other permanent form. 2. to convert (sound or visual scenes, esp. television pictures) to a permanent form for later reproduction. 3. (of a measuring instrument) to register. —/ˈrekɔːd/ *n.* 1. the state of being recorded or preserved in writing etc. 2. a piece of recorded evidence or information; an account of a fact preserved in a permanent form; a document or monument preserving it. 3. an official report of public or legal proceedings. 4. the known facts about a person's past; a list and the details of previous offences. 5. a disc (formerly a cylinder) from which recorded sound can be reproduced. 6. an object serving as a memorial, portrait, etc. 7. (often *attrib.*) the best performance or most remarkable event of its kind on record. —**for the record,** so that facts may be recorded officially. **go on record,** to state an opinion openly so that it is published. **have a record,** to have been convicted on a previous occasion. **off the record,** unofficially, confidentially. **on record,** officially recorded, publicly known. **recorded delivery,** a Post Office service whereby safe delivery is recorded by the signature of the recipient. **record-player** *n.* a gramophone (see entry). [f. OF f. L *recordari* remember (RE², *cor* heart)]

recorder /rɪˈkɔːdə(r)/ n. **1.** a keeper of records. **2.** a barrister or solicitor appointed to act for a period as a part-time judge of a Crown Court; (*hist.*) a judge in certain courts. **3.** an apparatus for recording things, especially a tape-recorder. **4.** a vertical instrument like a flute, one of a family with various ranges, of which the earliest surviving example comes from the 14th c. [f. prec.]

recording /rɪˈkɔːdɪŋ/ n. **1.** a process by which audio or video signals are recorded for later reproduction. **2.** the material or programme thus recorded. [f. RECORD]

recordist /rɪˈkɔːdɪst/ n. a person who records sound. [as prec.]

recount /rɪˈkaʊnt/ v.t. to narrate, to tell in detail. [f. AF *reconter* (as RE-², COUNT)]

re-count /riːˈkaʊnt/ v.t. to count again. —/ˈriːkaʊnt/ n. re-counting, especially of election votes.

recoup /rɪˈkuːp/ v.t. **1.** to recover or regain (a loss). **2.** to compensate or reimburse for loss. —**recoup oneself**, to recover a loss. —**recoupment** n. [f. F (RE-¹, *couper* cut)]

recourse /rɪˈkɔːs/ n. **1.** resorting to a possible source of help. **2.** person or thing forming such a source. —**have recourse to**, to adopt as an adviser or helper or as an expedient. [f. OF f. L (as RE-², COURSE)]

recover /rɪˈkʌvə(r)/ v.t./i. **1.** to regain possession, use, or control of. **2.** to come back to health or consciousness or to a normal state or position. **3.** to obtain or secure by legal process. **4.** to retrieve or make up for (a loss or setback etc.). —**recover oneself**, to regain calmness or consciousness or control of one's limbs. [f. AF *recoverer* f. L (as RECUPERATE)]

recoverable adj. that may be recovered. [f. prec.]

recovery n. the act or process of recovering or being recovered. [f. AF *recoverie* (as RECOVER)]

recreant /ˈrekrɪənt/ adj. (*literary*) craven, cowardly. —n. a coward. [f. OF (*recroire* yield in trial by combat, f. L (*se*) *recredere*)]

re-create /riːkrɪˈeɪt/ v.t. to create again.

recreation /rekrɪˈeɪʃ(ə)n/ n. the process or a means of refreshing or entertaining oneself after work by some pleasurable activity. —**recreational** adj. [f. OF f. L (as RE-², CREATION)]

recriminate /rɪˈkrɪmɪneɪt/ v.i. to make mutual or counter accusations. —**recrimination** /-ˈneɪʃ(ə)n/ n., **recriminatory** adj. [f. L *recriminare* accuse (RE-¹, *crimen* accusation)]

recross /riːˈkrɒs/ v.t./i. to cross again, to go back across.

recrudesce /riːkruːˈdes, rek-/ v.i. (of a disease or sore or discontent etc.) to break out again. —**recrudescence** n., **recrudescent** adj. [f. L *recrudescere* (RE-², *crudus* raw)]

recruit /rɪˈkruːt/ n. a serviceman newly enlisted and not yet fully trained; a new member of a society etc.; a beginner. —v.t./i. **1.** to enlist (a person) as a recruit; to enlist recruits for (an army etc.); to get or seek recruits. **2.** to replenish or reinvigorate (numbers or strength etc.). —**recruitment** n. [f. obs. F dial. *recrute* f. L *recrescere* grow again]

rectal /ˈrekt(ə)l/ adj. of or by means of the rectum. [f. RECTUM]

rectangle /ˈrektæŋɡ(ə)l/ n. a four-sided plane rectilinear figure with four right angles, especially one with adjacent sides unequal. —**rectangular** /-ˈtæŋɡʊlə(r)/ adj. [F or f. L *rectangulum* (*rectus* straight, *angulus* angle)]

rectifiable /ˈrektɪfaɪəb(ə)l/ adj. that may be rectified. [f. foll.]

rectify /ˈrektɪfaɪ/ v.t. **1.** to put right, to correct. **2.** to purify or refine, especially by repeated distillation. **3.** to convert (alternating current) to direct current. —**rectification** /-fɪˈkeɪʃ(ə)n/ n., **rectifier** n. [f. OF f. L *rectificare* (*rectus*) straight, right, *facere* make)]

rectilinear /rektɪˈlɪnɪə(r)/ adj. **1.** bounded or characterized by straight lines. **2.** in or forming a straight line. [f. L *rectilineus* (*rectus* straight, *linea* line)]

rectitude /ˈrektɪtjuːd/ n. moral goodness; correctness of behaviour or procedure. [f. OF or L *rectitudo* (as RECTIFY)]

recto /ˈrektəʊ/ n. (*pl.* -os) the right-hand page of an open book; the front of a leaf of a manuscript etc. (opp. *verso*). [f. L *recto* (*folio*) on the right leaf]

rector /ˈrektə(r)/ n. **1.** an incumbent of a Church of England parish where all the tithes formerly passed to the incumbent; the head priest of a Roman Catholic church. **2.** the head of a university, college, or religious institution. —**rectorship** n. [f. OF or L, = ruler (*regere* rule)]

rectory n. the house provided for a rector. [f. AF or L (as prec.)]

rectrix /ˈrektrɪks/ n. (*pl.* **rectrices** /-ɪsiːz/) any of a bird's strong tail-feathers, directing its flight (ill. BIRDS). [L, fem. of RECTOR]

rectum /ˈrektəm/ n. (*pl.* **-ums**) the final section of the large intestine, terminating at the anus (ill. BODY 2). [f. L, = straight (intestine)]

recumbent /rɪˈkʌmbənt/ adj. lying down, reclining. [f. L *recumbere* (RE-², *cumbere* lie)]

recuperate /rɪˈkjuːpəreɪt, -ˈkuː-/ v.t./i. to recover from illness, exhaustion, or loss etc.; to regain (health or losses etc.). —**recuperation** /-ˈreɪʃ(ə)n/ n. **recuperative** adj. [f. L *recuperare*]

recur /rɪˈkɜː(r)/ v.i. (**-rr-**) **1.** to occur again, to be repeated. **2.** to go back in thought or speech. —**recurring decimal**, a decimal fraction in which the same figures are repeated indefinitely. [f. L *recurrere* run back (RE-², *currere* run)]

recurrent /rɪˈkʌrənt/ adj. recurring, happening repeatedly. —**recurrence** n. [as prec.]

recusant /ˈrekjʊz(ə)nt/ n. **1.** one who refuses submission to authority or compliance with a regulation. **2.** (*hist.*) one (esp. a Roman Catholic, *Popish recusant*) who refused to attend the services of the Church of England. From *c.*1570 to 1791 this was punishable by a fine, and involved many civil disabilities. —**recusancy** n. [f. L *recusare* refuse]

recycle /riːˈsaɪk(ə)l/ v.t. to return (a material) to a previous stage of a cyclic process; to convert (waste) into a form in which it can be reused.

red adj. **1.** of the colour of blood or a colour approaching this (ranging to pink or orange); flushed in the face with shame, anger, etc.; (of the eyes) sore, bloodshot; (of the hair) reddish-brown, tawny. **2.** having to do with bloodshed, burning, violence, or revolution. **3. Red**, Russian, Soviet; socialist, communist. —n. **1.** red colour or pigment. **2.** red clothes or material. **3.** a socialist or communist. —**in the red**, in debt. **red admiral**, see ADMIRAL. **red-blooded** adj. virile, vigorous. **red card**, such a card shown by the referee at a football match to a player whom he is sending off the field. **red carpet**, privileged treatment of an important visitor. **red cent**, (*US*) the smallest (orig. copper) coin. **Red Crescent**, the equivalent of the Red Cross in Muslim countries. **Red Cross**, see separate entry. **red flag**, a symbol of danger or of revolution. **The Red Flag**, a socialist song by James Connell (1889), secretary to the Workmen's Legal Friendly Society. **red giant**, see separate entry. **Red Guard**, any of various radical groups and their members, especially (i) an organized detachment of workers during the Russian Bolshevik revolution of 1917, (ii) a youth movement during the Cultural Revolution in China, 1966–76. **red-handed** adj. in the act of committing a crime or doing wrong etc. **red hat**, a cardinal's hat, the symbol of his office. **red herring**, an irrelevant distraction. **red-hot** adj. heated to redness; highly exciting or excited; angry; (of news) fresh, completely new. **red-hot poker**, a garden plant of the genus *Kniphofia* with spikes of red or yellow flowers. **Red Indian**, a North American Indian, with reddish skin. **red lead**, a pigment made from red oxide of lead. **red-letter day**, one that is pleasantly noteworthy or memorable (originally a festival marked in red on a calendar). **red light**, a signal to stop on a road or railway; a warning. **red-light district**, one containing many brothels. **red pepper**, cayenne pepper; the ripe fruit of a capsicum plant. **red rag**, a thing that excites a person's rage. **red rose**, the emblem of Lancashire or Lancastrians. **red-shift** n. the displacement of spectral lines towards longer wavelengths (the red end of the spectrum) in radiation from distant galaxies etc., interpreted as a Doppler shift arising from a velocity of recession. **red squirrel**, a squirrel of the native English species (*Sciurus leucouros*) with reddish fur. **red tape**, excessive use of or adherence to formalities especially in public business. —**reddish** adj., **redly** adv., **redness** n. [OE]

red- see RE-¹.

redbreast n. a robin.

redbrick adj. (of English universities) founded in the 19th c. or early 20th c., as distinct from Oxford and Cambridge (*Oxbridge*).

redcap n. a member of the military police.

redcoat n. (*hist.*) a British soldier.

Red Cross an organization set up, at the instigation of the Swiss philanthropist Henri Dunant (d.1910), according to the Geneva Convention of 1864 for the treatment of the sick and wounded in war and those suffering by large-scale natural disasters. The international organization (which operates through national societies) has twice won the

Nobel Peace Prize (1917, 1944). Its headquarters are at Geneva in Switzerland, and its emblem, a red cross on a white ground, is the Swiss flag with its colours reversed. Its national branches include the British Red Cross Society (incorporated in 1908), which undertakes first-aid and welfare work as well as participating in relief work abroad. Muslim countries have adopted a red crescent as their emblem.

redcurrant *n.* a small round red edible berry; the shrub (*Ribes sylvestre*) bearing it.

redden /ˈred(ə)n/ *v.t./i.* to make or become red. [f. RED]

redecorate /riːˈdekəreɪt/ *v.t.* to decorate freshly. —**redecoration** /-ˈreɪʃ(ə)n/ *n.*

redeem /rɪˈdiːm/ *v.t.* 1. to buy back, recover by expenditure of effort or by a stipulated payment. 2. to make a single payment to cancel (a regular charge or obligation). 3. to convert (tokens or bonds) into goods or cash. 4. to save, rescue, or reclaim; to deliver from damnation or from the consequences of sin. 5. to make amends for, to serve as a compensating factor; to save from a defect or from blame. 6. to purchase the freedom of (a person); to save (a person's life) by a ransom. 7. to fulfil (a promise). [f. OF or L *redimere* (RE-², *emere* buy)]

redeemable *adj.* that may be redeemed. [f. prec.]

redeemer *n.* one who redeems. —**the Redeemer,** Christ, who redeemed mankind. [f. REDEEM]

redemption /rɪˈdempʃ(ə)n/ *n.* 1. redeeming, being redeemed. 2. a thing that redeems. [as REDEEM]

redeploy /riːdɪˈplɔɪ/ *v.t.* to send (troops or workers etc.) to a new place or task. —**redeployment** *n.*

redevelop /riːdɪˈveləp/ *v.t.* to develop (esp. land) afresh. —**redevelopment** *n.*

red giant an extended star of high luminosity and low surface temperature, generally understood to be in a late stage of evolution when no further hydrogen remains in the central regions to undergo nuclear fusion, but reactions involving hydrogen may continue in a spherical shell. The radius may exceed 150 million km, so that the entire orbit of Earth about the sun could be fitted inside the star's envelope. Temperatures may be as low as 3,000 °C, but the enormous emitting area renders such a star many times more luminous than the sun. Typical examples are Betelgeuse in Orion and Aldebaran in Taurus.

rediffusion /riːdɪˈfjuːʒ(ə)n/ *n.* the relaying of broadcast programmes, especially by wire from a central receiver.

redirect /riːdɪˈrekt/ *v.t.* to direct or send to another place, to readdress. —**redirection** *n.*

rediscover /riːdɪˈskʌvə(r)/ *v.t.* to discover again (what has been lost).

Redmond /ˈredmənd/, John Edward (1856–1916), Irish statesman who led the Parnellites after Parnell's death. During his leadership the Irish obtained control of local government, and the statutory establishment of an Irish parliament. His aim was to establish a free Ireland within the British Empire, but his moderate approach lost the confidence of his country which passed into the control of extreme nationalists under de Valera.

redo /riːˈduː/ *v.t.* (*past* redid; *p.p.* redone /-ˈdʌn/) 1. to do again. 2. to redecorate.

redolent /ˈredələnt/ *adj.* strongly smelling or suggestive or reminiscent *of*; fragrant. —**redolence** *n.* [f. L *redolēre* (RE-¹, *olēre* smell)]

redouble /riːˈdʌb(ə)l/ *v.t./i.* 1. to make or grow greater or more intense or numerous. 2. to double again a bid in bridge already doubled by an opponent. —*n.* redoubling of a bid in bridge.

redoubt /rɪˈdaʊt/ *n.* an outwork or fieldwork without flanking defences. [f. F f. It. f. L *reductus* refuge (as REDUCE)]

redoubtable /rɪˈdaʊtəb(ə)l/ *adj.* formidable, especially as an opponent. [f. OF (*redouter* fear)]

redound /rɪˈdaʊnd/ *v.i.* to come back as an advantage or disadvantage, to accrue. [f. OF f. L *redundare* overflow (RE-¹, *unda* wave)]

redpoll *n.* 1. a bird with a red forehead (esp. *Carduelis flammea*) similar to a linnet. 2. an animal of a red breed of polled cattle.

redress /rɪˈdres/ *v.t.* to set right; to rectify (a wrong or grievance etc.). —*n.* reparation, amends for a wrong done; redressing of a grievance etc. —**redress the balance,** to restore equality. [f. OF (as RE-², DRESS)]

Red Sea a long narrow land-locked sea separating Africa from the Arabian Peninsula, connected to the Arabian Sea by the Gulf of Aden and to the Mediterranean Sea by the Suez Canal.

redshank *n.* a large kind of sandpiper (*Tringa totanus*).

redskin *n.* a Red Indian.

redstart *n.* a small red-tailed songbird of the genus *Phoenicurus*. [RED + OE *steort* tail]

reduce /rɪˈdjuːs/ *v.t./i.* 1. to make or become smaller or less. 2. to bring by force or necessity to some state or action. 3. to convert to another (esp. simpler) form; to convert (a fraction) to the form with the lowest terms; to bring, simplify, or adapt by classification or analysis to its components etc. 4. to subdue, to bring back to obedience. 5. to make lower in status or rank. 6. to slim. 7. to weaken; to impoverish. 8. to convert (an oxide etc.) to a metal; to remove oxygen from or add hydrogen or electrons to. 9. to restore (a broken or dislocated part) to its original or proper position; to remedy (a dislocation) thus. —**reducer** *n.* [f. L *reducere* (RE-², *ducere* bring)]

reducible *adj.* that may be reduced. [f. prec.]

reductio ad absurdum /rɪdʌktɪəʊ æd əbˈsɜːdəm/ *n.* proof of falsity by showing the absurd logical consequence; the carrying of a principle to unpractical lengths. [L, = reduction to the absurd]

reduction /rɪˈdʌkʃ(ə)n/ *n.* 1. reducing, being reduced; an instance of this. 2. the amount by which something is reduced, especially in price. 3. a reduced copy of a picture or version of a musical score etc. [f. OF or L (as REDUCE)]

reductive /rɪˈdʌktɪv/ *adj.* causing reduction. [as prec.]

redundant /rɪˈdʌnd(ə)nt/ *adj.* 1. superfluous; that can be omitted without loss of significance. 2. (of a worker) no longer needed for any available job and therefore liable to dismissal. —**redundancy** *n.* [f. L (as REDOUND)]

reduplicate /rɪˈdjuːplɪkeɪt/ *v.t.* to make double, to repeat; to repeat (a word or syllable) exactly or with a slight change (e.g. *hurly-burly, see-saw*). —**reduplication** /-ˈkeɪʃ(ə)n/ *n.*, **reduplicative** /-kətɪv/ *adj.* [f. L *reduplicare* (RE-², *duplicare* duplicate)]

redwing *n.* a thrush (*Turdus iliacus*) with red flanks.

redwood *n.* a very large North American tree (*Sequoia sempervirens*) yielding reddish wood.

re-echo /riːˈekəʊ/ *v.t./i.* to echo repeatedly, to resound.

reed *n.* 1. a water or marsh plant of the genus *Phragmites* with a firm stem; a tall straight stalk of this. 2. the vibrating part of some wind instruments. 3. (usu. in *pl.*) such an instrument. —**reed-stop** *n.* a reeded organ-stop. [OE]

reeded *adj.* with a vibrating reed. [f. REED]

reedy *adj.* 1. full of reeds. 2. like a reed in slenderness or (of grass) thickness. 3. like a reed instrument in tone. —**reediness** *n.* [f. REED]

reef¹ *n.* 1. a ridge of rock or sand etc. at or near the surface of the sea etc. 2. a lode of ore; the bedrock surrounding this. [f. MDu. or MLG f. ON (as foll.)]

reef² *n.* each of several strips along the top or bottom of a sail that can be taken in or rolled up to reduce the sail's surface in high wind. —*v.t.* to take in the reef(s) of (a sail). —**reef-knot** *n.* a double knot made symmetrically. [f. Du. f. ON, = RIB]

reefer *n.* 1. a marijuana cigarette. 2. a thick double-breasted jacket. [f. prec.]

reek *v.i.* to smell strongly or unpleasantly; to have unpleasant or suspicious associations. —*n.* 1. a foul or stale smell. 2. (esp. *Sc.*) smoke, vapour, a visible exhalation. [OE]

reel *n.* 1. a cylindrical device on which thread, silk, yarn, paper, film, wire, etc., are wound; a quantity of thread etc. wound on a reel; a device for winding and unwinding a line as required, especially in fishing. 2. a revolving part in various machines. 3. a lively folk-dance or Scottish dance; the music for this. —*v.t./i.* 1. to wind (thread, a fishing-line, etc.) on or off reel. 2. to draw (a fish etc.) in by using a reel. 3. to stand, walk, or run unsteadily; to be shaken physically or mentally; to rock from side to side, to swing violently. 4. to dance a reel. —**reel off,** to say or recite very rapidly and without apparent effort. [OE]

re-elect /riːɪˈlekt/ *v.t.* to elect again. —**re-election** *n.*

re-enter /riːˈentə(r)/ *v.t./i.* to enter again. —**re-entry** *n.*

re-entrant /riːˈentrənt/ *adj.* (of an angle) pointing inwards, reflex.

re-establish /riːɪˈstæblɪʃ/ *v.t.* to establish again. —**re-establishment** *n.*

reeve¹ *n.* (*hist.*) the chief magistrate of a town or district. [OE]

reeve² *v.t.* (*past* rove) (*Naut.*) to thread (a rope or rod etc.)

through a ring or other aperture; to fasten (a rope or block etc.) thus. [prob. f. Du. *reven* (as REEF²)]

reeve³ *n.* a female ruff. [orig. unkn.]

re-examine /riːɪgˈzæmɪn/ *v.t.* to examine again. —**re-examination** /-ˈneɪʃ(ə)n/ *n.*

ref *n.* (*colloq.*) a referee in sports. [abbr.]

reface /riːˈfeɪs/ *v.t.* to put a new facing on (a building).

refectory /rɪˈfektərɪ, ˈrefɪk-/ *n.* a room for communal meals, especially in a monastery or college. —**refectory table,** a long narrow table. [f. L *refectorium* (*reficere* refresh)]

refer /rɪˈfɜː(r)/ *v.t./i.* (**-rr-**) **1.** to ascribe; to consider as belonging to a specified date, place or class. **2.** to send on or direct (a person, a question for discussion) to an authority or source of information; to make an appeal or have recourse thus. **3.** to make an allusion; to direct attention by words; to interpret (a statement) as being directed, (of a statement) to have relation or be directed (to what is specified). —**referred pain,** pain felt in a part of the body other than its true source. —**referral** *n.* [f. OF f. L *referre* carry back (RE-², *ferre* carry)]

referable /rɪˈfɜːrəb(ə)l, ˈrefər-/ *adj.* that may be referred. [f. prec.]

referee /refəˈriː/ *n.* **1.** a person to whom a dispute is or may be referred for decision. **2.** an umpire, especially in football or boxing. **3.** a person willing to testify to the character of an applicant for employment etc. —*v.t./i.* to act as a referee (for). [f. REFER]

reference /ˈrefərəns/ *n.* **1.** the referring of a matter for decision, settlement, or consideration to some authority. **2.** the scope given to such an authority. **3.** relation, respect, or correspondence *to.* **4.** allusion. **5.** a direction to a book etc. (or a passage in it) where information may be found; a book or passage so cited. **6.** the act of looking up a passage etc. or of referring to a person etc. for information. **7.** a written testimonial supporting an applicant for employment etc.; a person giving this. —**in** *or* **with reference to,** regarding, as regards, about. **reference book,** a book for occasional consultation, providing information for reference but not designed to be read straight through. **reference library** *or* **room,** one providing books that may be consulted but not taken away. —**referential** /-ˈrenʃ(ə)l/ *adj.* [as prec.]

referendum /refəˈrendəm/ *n.* (*pl.* **-ums**) the referring of a political question to the electorate for a direct decision by a general vote. [L, gerund of *referre* refer]

refill /riːˈfɪl/ *v.t.* to fill again. —/ˈriːfɪl/ *n.* a new filling; the material for this.

refine /rɪˈfaɪn/ *v.t./i.* **1.** to free from impurities or defects. **2.** to make or become more polished or elegant or cultured. [f. RE-¹, + FINE¹, & F *raffiner*]

refined *adj.* characterized by polish, elegance, or subtlety. [f. prec.]

refinement *n.* **1.** refining, being refined. **2.** fineness of feeling or taste; polish or elegance in behaviour or manners. **3.** an added development or improvement. **4.** a piece of subtle reasoning, a fine distinction. [f. REFINE]

refiner *n.* one who refines, especially one whose business is to refine crude oil or sugar or metal etc. [as prec.]

refinery *n.* a place where oil etc. is refined. [f. REFINE]

refit /riːˈfɪt/ *v.t./i.* (**-tt-**) to make or become fit again (especially of a ship undergoing renewal and repairs). —/ˈriːfɪt/ *n.* refitting. —**refitment** *n.*

reflate /riːˈfleɪt/ *v.t.* to cause the reflation of (a currency or economy etc.). [f. RE-², after *deflate, inflate*]

reflation /riːˈfleɪʃ(ə)n/ *n.* the inflation of a financial system to restore the previous condition after deflation. —**reflationary** *adj.* [f. RE-², after *deflation, inflation*]

reflect /rɪˈflekt/ *v.t./i.* **1.** (of a surface or body) to throw back (heat, light, or sound). **2.** (of a mirror etc.) to show an image of; to reproduce to the eye or mind; to correspond in appearance or effect to. **3.** (of an action or result etc.) to show or bring (credit etc.) on the person or method responsible; (*absol.*) to bring discredit on the person etc. responsible. **4.** to think deeply, to consider; to remind oneself of past events. [f. OF or L *reflectere* (RE-², *flectere* bend)]

reflection /rɪˈflekʃ(ə)n/ *n.* (also **reflexion**) **1.** reflecting, being reflected. **2.** reflected light or heat etc; a reflected image (ill. LIGHT). **3.** discredit; a thing bringing this. **4.** reconsideration. **5.** deep thought; an idea or statement produced by this. [as prec.]

reflective *adj.* **1.** (of a surface etc.) giving back a reflection or image. **2.** (of mental faculties) concerned in reflection or thought; (of a person or mood etc.) thoughtful, given to meditation. [f. REFLECT]

reflector *n.* **1.** a piece of glass or metal etc. for reflecting light in a required direction, e.g. a red one on the back of a motor vehicle. **2.** a mirror producing images; a telescope equipped with this. [as prec.]

reflex /ˈriːfleks/ *adj.* **1.** (of an action) independent of the will, as an automatic response to nerve-stimulation (e.g. a sneeze). **2.** (of an angle) exceeding 180°. —*n.* **1.** a reflex action. **2.** a secondary manifestation, a corresponding result. **3.** reflected light; a reflected image. —**reflex camera,** a camera in which the image is reflected by a mirror to allow focusing up to the moment of exposure. [f. L *reflexus* (as REFLECT)]

reflexive /rɪˈfleksɪv/ *adj.* (*Gram.*) (of a word or form) implying the subject's action on himself or itself. —*n.* a reflexive word or form, especially a pronoun (e.g. *myself*). [as prec.]

refloat /riːˈfləʊt/ *v.t.* to set (a stranded ship) afloat again.

reflux /ˈriːflʌks/ *n.* backward flow; (*Chem.*) a method of boiling in which vapour is liquefied and returned to the boiler.

reform /rɪˈfɔːm/ *v.t./i.* to make or become better by the removal of faults or errors; to abolish or cure (an abuse or malpractice). —*n.* the removal of faults or abuses, especially of a moral or political or social kind; an improvement made or suggested. —**Reform Acts,** measures of electoral reform undertaken in Britain in the 19th c. The first Reform Bill (1832) disenfranchised various rotten boroughs, redistributed their seats among the counties and newly grown towns, and widened the electorate by about 50 per cent to include most of the upper middle class. The second (1867) carried out a further redistribution of seats and doubled the electorate (to two million) by lowering the property qualification. The third (1884) extended the franchise approved for the towns by the second to cover the entire country, increasing the electorate to about five million. **Reformed Church,** any of the Protestant Churches which have accepted the principles of the Reformation, especially of those following Calvinist rather than Lutheran doctrines (see PROTESTANT). **Reform Jew,** an adherent of Reform Judaism. **Reform Judaism,** a liberalizing movement, initiated in Germany by the philosopher Moses Mendelssohn (1729-86), to accommodate the Jewish faith to European intellectual enlightenment. —**reformer** *n.* [f. OF or L *reformare* (RE-², *formare* form)]

re-form /riːˈfɔːm/ *v.t./i.* to form again.

reformation /refəˈmeɪʃ(ə)n/ *n.* reforming, being reformed, especially a radical change for the better in public affairs. —**the Reformation,** the movement that led to the division of Western Christendom in the 16th c. Pressure for the reform of medieval Christendom came from many quarters: unease at the political power of the Italian papacy, distress at the externality of much medieval religion, a sense of the gulf between contemporary theology and religious life and that found in the New Testament and Patristic period, made increasingly evident by the access provided by the humanists, especially Erasmus, to the original text of the New Testament and the Fathers. Reluctance by the papacy to allow a reforming council meant that Luther's protest against indulgences led to schism. A parallel movement in Switzerland, led by Zwingli, effected a still more complete break with medieval religion, and the Reformation, influenced in the second generation especially by Calvin, spread to most European countries. All Protestants rejected the authority of the papacy, both religious and political, and found authority in the original text of the Scriptures, made available to all in vernacular translation. The authority of the clergy and the sacramental system was weakened in varying degrees, and the way opened for religious individualism. [as REFORM]

reformative /rɪˈfɔːmətɪv/ *adj.* tending or intended to produce reform. [f. OF or L (as REFORM)]

reformatory /rɪˈfɔːmətərɪ/ *adj.* reformative. —*n.* (*US & hist.*) an institution to which young offenders are sent to be reformed. [f. REFORMATION]

refract /rɪˈfrækt/ *v.t.* (of water, air, glass, etc.) to deflect (a ray of light etc.) at a certain angle when it enters obliquely from another medium of different density (ill. LIGHT). —**refraction** *n.*, **refractive** *adj.* [f. L *refringere* (RE-¹, *frangere* break)]

refractor *n.* a refracting medium or lens; a telescope using a lens to produce an image. [f. prec.]

refractory /rɪ'fræktərɪ/ *adj.* **1.** resisting control or discipline, stubborn. **2.** (of a disease or wound etc.) not yielding to treatment. **3.** (of a substance) resistant to heat; hard to fuse or work. [f. L *refractarius* (as REFRACT)]

refrain[1] /rɪ'freɪn/ *v.i.* to abstain or keep oneself (*from* a thing or action). [f. OF f. L *refrenare* (RE-[2], *frenum* bridle)]

refrain[2] /rɪ'freɪn/ *n.* a recurring phrase or lines especially at the end of stanzas; the music accompanying this. [f. OF ult. f. L (as REFRACT)]

refrangible /rɪ'frændʒɪb(ə)l/ *adj.* that can be refracted. [as REFRACT]

refresh /rɪ'freʃ/ *v.t.* to give fresh spirit or vigour to; to stimulate (one's memory). [f. OF (as RE-[2], FRESH)]

refresher *n.* **1.** an extra fee to counsel in a prolonged lawsuit. **2.** (*colloq.*) a drink. —**refresher course,** a course reviewing previous studies, or giving instruction in modern methods etc. [f. prec.]

refreshment *n.* **1.** refreshing, being refreshed. **2.** a thing that refreshes, especially food and drink, (usu. in *pl.*) this when not regarded as constituting a meal. [as REFRESH]

refrigerant /rɪ'frɪdʒərənt/ *n.* a substance used for refrigeration. —*adj.* refrigerating. [f. foll.]

refrigerate /rɪ'frɪdʒəreɪt/ *v.t./i.* to make or become cool or cold; to subject (food etc.) to cold in order to freeze or preserve it. —**refrigeration** /-'reɪʃ(ə)n/ *n.* [f. L *refrigerare* (RE-[2], *frigus* cold)]

refrigerator *n.* a cabinet or room in which food etc. is refrigerated. A refrigerator contains a chamber that is kept cooler than its surroundings by making use of the cooling effect produced when a liquid is made to evaporate. The liquid (now usually a fluorine compound) is pumped through a valve that causes it to expand and become a vapour; this vapour is made to condense back to a liquid outside the refrigerator, where it gives up the heat it acquired from the interior when it became a vapour. [f. prec.]

Ice-cooled pits or cellars were known in ancient Mesopotamia, Greece, and Rome, and the principle continued in use up to the 19th c.; ice was collected in winter from frozen rivers, and lasted into the summer without melting, while food stored in it stayed fresh for several months. In the mid-19th c. ice was used to cool the air in railway wagons for transporting meat in the USA, and by the 1880s refrigerating machines had been developed for use in ships, transporting meat successfully on sea journeys of two or three months. A cooling apparatus had long been used in the brewing industry, and it was from this that the first mechanically operated domestic refrigerator was developed *c.*1880, powered by a small steam pump. Electric refrigeration was a development of the 1920s.

reft see REAVE.

refuel /riː'fjuːəl/ *v.t./i.* (-ll-) to replenish the fuel supply (of).

refuge /'refjuːdʒ/ *n.* shelter from pursuit or danger or trouble; a person or place etc. offering this. [f. OF f. L *refugium* (RE-[1], *fugere* flee)]

refugee /refjʊ'dʒiː/ *n.* a person taking refuge, especially in a foreign country from war or persecution or natural disaster. [f. F *réfugié* (as prec.)]

refulgent /rɪ'fʌldʒ(ə)nt/ *adj.* shining, gloriously bright. —**refulgence** *n.* [f. L (RE-[1], *fulgēre* shine)]

refund /riː'fʌnd/ *v.t./i.* to pay back (money or expenses); to reimburse (a person); to make repayment. —/'riːfʌnd/ *n.* refunding, repayment. [orig. = pour back, f. OF or L *refundere* (RE-[2], *fundere* pour)]

refurbish /riː'fɜːbɪʃ/ *v.t.* to brighten up, to redecorate.

refusal /rɪ'fjuːz(ə)l/ *n.* **1.** refusing, being refused. **2.** the right or privilege of deciding to accept or refuse a thing before it is offered to others. [f. foll.]

refuse[1] /rɪ'fjuːz/ *v.t./i.* **1.** to say or show that one is unwilling to accept, give, or do (what is requested); to indicate unwillingness; not to grant a request made by (a person). **2.** (of a horse) to be unwilling to jump (a fence etc.). [f. OF prob. f. L *recusare* refuse after *refutare* refute]

refuse[2] /'refjuːs/ *n.* what is rejected as worthless, waste. [perh. f. OF (as prec.)]

refutable /rɪ'fjuːtəb(ə)l/ *adj.* that may be refuted. [f. foll.]

refute /rɪ'fjuːt/ *v.t.* to prove the falsity or error of (a statement etc. or a person advancing it); to rebut by

argument. —**refutation** /refjuː'teɪʃ(ə)n/ *n.* [f. L *refutare*; cf. CONFUTE]

regain /rɪ'geɪn/ *v.t.* **1.** to obtain possession, use, or control of after loss. **2.** to reach (a place) again.

regal /'riːg(ə)l/ *adj.* of or by a king or kings; fit for a king, magnificent. —**regality** /rɪ'gælɪtɪ/ *n.*, **regally** *adv.* [f. OF or L *regalis* (*rex* king)]

regale /rɪ'geɪl/ *v.t.* to entertain lavishly with feasting or talk etc.; (of beauty, flowers, etc.) to give delight to. [f. F *régaler* (OF *gale* pleasure)]

regalia /rɪ'geɪljə/ *n.pl.* the insignia of royalty used at coronations; the insignia of an order or civic dignity. [L (as REGAL)]

regard /rɪ'gɑːd/ *v.t.* **1.** to gaze steadily at (usu. in a specified way). **2.** to give heed to, to take into account. **3.** to look upon or contemplate mentally in a specified way, to consider to be. —*n.* **1.** a steady gaze. **2.** heed, consideration. **3.** respectful or kindly feeling. **4.** reference, a point attended to. **5.** (in *pl.*) an expression of friendliness in a letter etc., compliments. —**as regards,** about, concerning, in respect of. **in** or **with regard to,** regarding, in respect of. [f. F *regarder* (as RE-[1], GUARD)]

regardant /rɪ'gɑːdənt/ *adj.* (in heraldry) looking backwards (ill. HERALDRY). [f. AF & OF (as REGARD)]

regardful *adj.* mindful *of.* [f. REGARD + -FUL]

regarding *prep.* about, concerning, with reference to. [f. REGARD]

regardless *adj.* without regard or consideration (*of*). —*adv.* without paying attention. [f. REGARD + -LESS]

regatta /rɪ'gætə/ *n.* a meeting for boat or yacht races. [It. (Venetian dialect)]

regency /'riːdʒ(ə)nsɪ/ *n.* the office of a regent; a commission acting as regent; a regent's or regency commission's period of office. —**the Regency,** the period of 1810–20 in Britain when George, Prince of Wales, acted as regent, or 1715–23 in France with Philip, Duke of Orleans, as regent. [f. L (as REGENT)]

regenerate /rɪ'dʒenəreɪt/ *v.t./i.* **1.** to generate again; to form afresh. **2.** to give new life or vigour to. **3.** to reform spiritually or morally. —/rɪ'dʒenərət/ *adj.* spiritually born again, reformed. —**regeneration** /-'reɪʃ(ə)n/ *n.*, **regenerative** *adj.* [f. L *regenerare* (as RE-[2], GENERATE)]

regent /'riːdʒ(ə)nt/ *n.* a person appointed to administer a State during the minority, absence, or incapacity of a monarch. —*adj.* (placed after a noun) acting as regent. [f. OF or L *regere* rule]

reggae /'regeɪ/ *n.* a kind of music, of Jamaican origin, characterized by a strongly accentuated subsidiary beat and often a prominent bass. [orig. unkn.; perh. rel. to Jamaican English *rege-rege* quarrel, row]

regicide /'redʒɪsaɪd/ *n.* **1.** the killing of a king. **2.** the persons guilty of or involved in this. —**the Regicides,** those involved in trying and executing Charles I of England or Louis XVI of France. —**regicidal** /-'saɪd(ə)l/ *adj.* [f. L *rex regis* king + -CIDE]

regime /reɪ'ʒiːm/ *n.* a method or system of government; the prevailing order or system of things. [f. F (as foll.)]

regimen /'redʒɪmen/ *n.* a prescribed course of exercise, way of life, and especially diet. [L (*regere* rule)]

regiment /'redʒɪmənt/ *n.* **1.** a permanent unit of the army usually commanded by a colonel and divided into several companies, troops, or batteries and often into two or more battalions. **2.** an operational unit of artillery etc. **3.** a large array or number of things. —/also -ment/ *v.t.* to organize rigidly into groups or according to a system; to form into regiment(s). —**regimentation** /-'teɪʃ(ə)n/ *n.* [f. OF f. L (as prec.)]

regimental /redʒɪ'ment(ə)l/ *adj.* of a regiment. —*n.* (in *pl.*) military uniform, especially of a particular regiment. —**regimentally** *adv.* [f. prec.]

Regina /rɪ'dʒaɪnə/ *n.* the reigning queen (in the titles of lawsuits, e.g. *Regina* v. *Jones,* the Crown versus Jones). [L, = queen]

region /'riːdʒ(ə)n/ *n.* **1.** a continuous part of a surface, space, or body, with or without definite boundaries or with certain characteristics. **2.** an administrative division of a country, especially in Scotland. **3.** the sphere or realm of a subject etc. —**in the region of,** approximately. —**regional** *adj.*, **regionally** *adv.* [f. OF f. L *regio* direction, district (*regere* direct)]

register /'redʒɪst(ə)r/ *n.* **1.** an official list of names, items, attendances, etc.; the book or other document(s) in which this is kept. **2.** a mechanical device for indicating or recording speed, force, numbers, etc., automatically. **3.** an adjustable plate for widening or narrowing an opening and regulating draught, especially in a fire-grate. **4.** the compass of a voice or instrument; a part of the voice-compass. **5.** a set of organ-pipes; a sliding device controlling this. **6.** exact correspondence of position in printing etc. —*v.t./i.* **1.** to enter or cause to be entered in a register. **2.** to set down formally in writing; to present for consideration. **3.** to entrust (a letter etc.) to a post office for transmission by registered post. **4.** (of an instrument) to indicate or record automatically. **5.** to notice and remember. **6.** to express (an emotion) facially or by a gesture. **7.** to make an impression on a person's mind. —**registered post**, a procedure with special precautions for safety and for compensation in case of loss. **register office**, a place where records of births, marriages, and deaths are made and where civil marriages are performed. [f. OF or L (*regesta* things recorded, RE-², *gerere* carry)]

registrar /redʒɪˈstrɑː(r)/ *n.* **1.** a person charged with keeping a register; the senior administrative officer in a university etc. **2.** a doctor undergoing hospital training as a specialist. [f. L (as prec.)]

registration /redʒɪˈstreɪʃ(ə)n/ *n.* registering, being registered. —**registration mark** *or* **number**, a combination of letters and figures uniquely identifying a motor vehicle. [f. obs. F or L (as REGISTER)]

registry /ˈredʒɪstrɪ/ *n.* a place or office where registers are kept. —**registry office**, a register office. [f. L *registerium* (as REGISTER)]

Regius professor /ˈriːdʒɪəs/ the holder of a chair founded by a sovereign (especially one at Oxford or Cambridge instituted by Henry VIII) or filled by Crown appointment. [L, = royal (*rex regis* king)]

regnant /ˈregnənt/ *adj.* reigning. [f. L *regnare* reign]

regress /rɪˈgres/ *v.i.* **1.** to move backwards. **2.** to go back to an earlier or more primitive state. —/ˈriːgres/ *n.* regressing; relapse, backward tendency. —**regression** *n.*, **regressive** *adj.* [f. L *regredi* (RE-², *gradi* to step)]

regret /rɪˈgret/ *v.t.* (**-tt-**) to feel or express sorrow, repentance, or distress over (an action or loss etc.); to say with sorrow or remorse. —*n.* a feeling of sorrow or repentance etc. over an action or loss etc. —**give** *or* **send** etc. **one's regrets**, to decline an invitation. [f. OF *regreter* bewail, perh. rel. to GREET²]

regretful *adj.* feeling or showing regret. —**regretfully** *adv.* [f. prec. + -FUL]

regrettable *adj.* (of events or conduct) undesirable, unwelcome, deserving censure. —**regrettably** *adv.* [f. REGRET]

regroup /riːˈgruːp/ *v.t./i.* to form into new groups.

regular /ˈregjʊlə(r)/ *adj.* **1.** conforming to a rule or principle or to a standard of procedure; consistent; symmetrical. **2.** acting, done, or recurring uniformly or calculably in time or manner; habitual, constant, orderly. **3.** conforming to a standard of etiquette or procedure. **4.** properly constituted or qualified; devoted exclusively or primarily to its nominal function. **5.** (*Gram.*, of a noun, verb, etc.) following the normal type of inflexion. **6.** (*colloq.*) thorough, indubitable. **7.** bound by a religious rule; belonging to a religious or monastic order. —*n.* **1.** a regular soldier. **2.** (*colloq.*) a regular customer, visitor, etc. **3.** a member of the regular clergy. —**regularity** /-ˈlærɪtɪ/ *n.* **regularly** *adv.* [f. OF & L (*regula* rule)]

regularize /ˈregjʊləraɪz/ *v.t.* to make regular. [f. prec.]

regulate /ˈregjʊleɪt/ *v.t.* **1.** to control or direct by rule(s); to subject to restrictions. **2.** to adapt to requirements; to alter the speed of (a machine or clock) so that it will work accurately. —**regulator** *n.* [f. L *regulare* (as prec.)]

regulation /regjʊˈleɪʃ(ə)n/ *n.* **1.** regulating, being regulated. **2.** a prescribed rule. —*adj.* in accordance with regulations, of the correct type etc.; usual. —**the Queen's Regulations**, those applying to the armed forces. [f. prec.]

regurgitate /rɪˈgɜːdʒɪteɪt/ *v.t./i.* **1.** to bring (swallowed food) up again to the mouth. **2.** to cast or pour out again; to gush back. —**regurgitation** /-ˈteɪʃ(ə)n/ *n.* [f. L *regurgitare* (RE-², *gurges* whirlpool)]

rehabilitate /riːhəˈbɪlɪteɪt/ *v.t.* **1.** to restore to effectiveness or normal life by training, especially after imprisonment or illness. **2.** to restore to privileges, reputation, or proper condition. —**rehabilitation** /-ˈteɪʃ(ə)n/ *n.*

rehash /riːˈhæʃ/ *v.t.* to put (old material) into a new form without significant change or improvement. —/ˈriːhæʃ/ *n.* rehashing; material rehashed.

rehearsal /rɪˈhɜːs(ə)l/ *n.* rehearsing; a trial performance or practice. [f. foll.]

rehearse /rɪˈhɜːs/ *v.t./i.* **1.** to practise before performing in public. **2.** to train by rehearsal. **3.** to recite, to say over; to give a list of, to enumerate. [f. AF & OF, perh. as RE-², *hercer* harrow]

re-heat /riːˈhiːt/ *v.t.* to heat again. —**reheater** *n.*

Rehoboam /riːhəˈbəʊəm/ (10th c. BC) son of Solomon. He succeeded his father as king of Israel, but the northern tribes broke away from his rule and set up a new kingdom under Jeroboam, after which Rehoboam continued as the first king of Judah (1 Kings 11-14).

rehoboam /riːhəˈbəʊəm/ *n.* a large winebottle, twice the size of a jeroboam. [f. prec.]

rehouse /riːˈhaʊz/ *v.t.* to provide with new accommodation.

Reich /raɪx, -k/ *n.* the German State or commonwealth, especially during the period 1871-1945. —**Third Reich,** the regime under the rule of Hitler and the Nazi party, 1933-45. The German expression was coined with allusion to the former Holy Roman Empire (962-1806) and the Hohenzollern empire (1871-1918). Apart from *Third Reich,* such collocations with an ordinal do not constitute recognized English historical terminology. [G, = kingdom, realm, State]

Reichstag /ˈraɪxstɑːx, -g/ *n.* the supreme legislature of the former German Empire and of the Republic; the building in Berlin in which this met, burnt down on the Nazi accession to power (1933).

reign /reɪn/ *n.* sovereignty, rule; the period during which a sovereign reigns. —*v.i.* **1.** to be king or queen. **2.** to prevail. —**Reign of Terror,** see TERROR. [f. OF f. L *regnum* kingdom (*rex* king)]

reimburse /riːɪmˈbɜːs/ *v.t.* to repay (a person who has expended money, a person's expenses). —**reimbursement** *n.* [f. RE-² + obs. *imburse* f. L (as IM-¹, PURSE)]

Reims /riːmz/ an ancient cathedral city of northern France.

rein /reɪn/ *n.* (in *sing.* or *pl.*) **1.** a long narrow strap with each end attached to a bit, used to guide or check a horse etc. in riding or driving (ill. HORSE); a similar device to restrain a child etc. **2.** a means of control. —*v.t.* **1.** to check or control with reins; to pull or hold (as) with reins. **2.** to restrain, to control. —**give free rein to,** to allow free scope to. **keep a tight rein on,** to allow little freedom to. [f. OF f. L *retinēre* (see RETAIN)]

reincarnation /riːɪnkɑːˈneɪʃ(ə)n/ *n.* the rebirth of a soul in a new body. —**reincarnate** /-ˈkɑːnɪt/ *adj.*

reindeer /ˈreɪndɪə(r)/ *n.* (*pl.* usu. same) a subarctic deer (*Rangifer tarandus*) with large antlers. [f. ON]

reinforce /riːɪnˈfɔːs/ *v.t.* to strengthen or support, especially by additional men or material or by an increase of numbers, quantity, size, etc. —**reinforced concrete,** see CONCRETE. [f. F *renforcer* (as RE-¹, ENFORCE)]

reinforcement *n.* **1.** reinforcing, being reinforced. **2.** a thing that reinforces; (in *pl.*) additional personnel, ships, etc. sent to reinforce armed forces etc. [f. prec.]

Reinhardt /ˈraɪnhɑːt/, Max (1873-1943), real name Goldmann, Austrian director and impresario, who dominated the stage in Berlin during the first two decades of the 20th c., mainly as owner of the Deutsches Theater. His integrated productions established the director's pre-eminence, especially in works of symbolism and impressionism. No stage was too big for him, two of his most remarkable productions being Sophocles' *Oedipus the King* (1910) and Vollmöller's *The Miracle* (1911).

reinstate /riːɪnˈsteɪt/ *v.t.* to restore to or replace in a lost position or privileges etc. —**reinstatement** *n.* [f. RE-² + *instate* establish in office (IN-¹, STATE)]

reinsure /riːɪnˈʃʊə(r)/ *v.t./i.* to insure again (esp. of an insurer securing himself by transferring risk to another insurer). —**reinsurance** *n.*

reissue /riːˈɪsjuː/ *v.t.* to issue (a thing) again. —*n.* a thing reissued.

reiterate /riːˈɪtəreɪt/ *v.t.* to say or do again or repeatedly. —**reiteration** /-ˈreɪʃ(ə)n/ *n.*, **reiterative** /-ˈɪtərətɪv/ *adj.*

Reith /riːθ/, John Charles Walsham, 1st Baron Reith (1889-1971), first General Manager and later first Director-General (1927-38) of the BBC. An uncompromising idealist, closely associated with the development of radio broadcasting in Britain, Reith later served in various Cabinet posts during the Second World War.

reject /rɪˈdʒekt/ *v.t.* **1.** to refuse to accept or believe in. **2.** to put aside or send back as not to be used or done or complied with etc. —/ˈriːdʒekt/ *n.* a person or thing rejected. —**rejection** /rɪˈdʒekʃ(ə)n/ *n.*, **rejector** *n.* [f. L *rejicere* (RE-², *jacere* throw)]

rejig /riːˈdʒɪg/ *v.t.* (**-gg-**) to re-equip (a factory etc.) for a new kind of work; (*colloq.*) to rearrange.

rejoice /rɪˈdʒɔɪs/ *v.t./i.* **1.** to feel or show great joy; to take delight. **2.** to cause joy to. —**rejoicing** *n.* [f. OF *rejoir* (as RE-¹, JOY)]

rejoin¹ /riːˈdʒɔɪn/ *v.t./i.* to join together again, to reunite.

rejoin² /rɪˈdʒɔɪn/ *v.t./i.* to say in answer, to retort; to reply to a charge or pleading in a lawsuit. [f. OF *rejoindre* (as RE-², JOIN)]

rejoinder /rɪˈdʒɔɪndə(r)/ *n.* what is said in reply or rejoined, a retort. [as prec.]

rejuvenate /rɪˈdʒuːvəneɪt/ *v.t.* to make (as if) young again. —**rejuvenation** /-ˈneɪʃ(ə)n/ *n.*, **rejuvenator** *n.* [f. RE-² + L *juvenis* young]

relapse /rɪˈlæps/ *v.i.* to fall back into a previous condition, or into a worse state after improvement. —*n.* relapsing, especially after partial recovery from illness. [f. L (RE-², *labi* slip)]

relate /rɪˈleɪt/ *v.t./i.* **1.** to narrate, to tell in detail. **2.** to bring into relation. **3.** to have reference. **4.** to bring oneself into a sympathetic or successful relationship (to a person or thing). [f. L (as REFER)]

related *adj.* connected, especially by blood or marriage; having a common descent or origin. [f. prec.]

relation /rɪˈleɪʃ(ə)n/ *n.* **1.** the way in which one person or thing is related to another; a similarity, correspondence, or contrast between people or things or events. **2.** (in *pl.*) dealings with others; sexual intercourse. **3.** a person who is a relative. **4.** being related. **5.** narration, a narrative. —**in relation to,** as regards. —**relationship** *n.* [f. OF or L (as REFER)]

relative /ˈrelətɪv/ *adj.* **1.** considered in relation to something else. **2.** proportionate; comparative. **3.** corresponding in some way, related to each other; having reference or relation *to*. **4.** (*Gram.*, of a word) referring to an expressed or implied antecedent and attaching a subordinate clause to it; (of a clause) attached to an antecedent by a relative word. —*n.* **1.** a person who is related to another by parentage, descent, or marriage. **2.** a species related to another by a common origin. **3.** (*Gram.*) a relative word, especially a pronoun. —**relatively** *adv.*, **relativeness** *n.* [f. OF or L (as REFER)]

relativity /reləˈtɪvɪtɪ/ *n.* **1.** being relative. **2.** a theory based on the principle that all motion is relative and that light travels with a constant maximum speed in a vacuum (also **special relativity**), a theory extending this to gravitation and accelerated motion (**general relativity**; see GRAVITATION). [f. prec.]

The special theory of relativity is largely the outcome of experimental and theoretical efforts late last century to produce a coherent theory of electromagnetism. The chief architect of the theory was Einstein, whose investigations led him to reject the idea of a stationary 'ether' pervading space, and the notions of absolute space and time as a common framework of reference for all bodies in the universe. Special relativity places great importance on distinguishing systematically between the viewpoint or framework of the observer and that of the object or process being observed. Fundamental principles of the theory, well confirmed by experiment, are that the measured velocity of every beam of light is the same for all observers, whatever their mutual velocities, and that the mathematical form of those laws of physics which apply to moving objects or systems is independent of the motion of the framework of the observer, provided the latter motion is uniform. Although mathematically the theory is surprisingly uncomplicated its results are far-reaching, changing the basis of physics and undermining intuitive common-sense notions. Among its consequences are the following: nothing can go faster than the speed of light in a vacuum; the mass of a body increases and its length (in the direction of motion) shortens as its speed increases; the time interval between two events occurring in a moving body appears (to a stationary observer) to increase; and mass and energy are equivalent and interconvertible. All of these are well attested by experiment. Their explanation, however, quite eludes modern physics and they tend to be regarded as a basic datum of nature.

relax /rɪˈlæks/ *v.t./i.* **1.** to make or become less stiff, rigid, or tense. **2.** to make or become less formal or strict. **3.** to reduce or abate (one's attention or efforts etc.). **4.** to cease

work or effort; to indulge in recreation. —**relaxation** /-ˈseɪʃ(ə)n/ *n.* [f. L *relaxare* (RE-², *laxus* lax)]

relay /ˈriːleɪ/ *n.* **1.** a fresh set of people or animals taking the place of others who have completed a spell of work. **2.** a fresh supply of material to be used or worked on. **3.** a relay race. **4.** a device activating an electric circuit; a device that receives and transmits a telegraph message or broadcast etc. **5.** a relayed message or transmission. —also ri:ˈleɪ/ *v.t.* to receive (a message, broadcast etc.) and transmit to others. —**relay race,** a race between teams of which each member in turn covers part of the distance. [f. OF *relai* (as RE-¹, L *laxare*; cf. RELAX)]

re-lay /riːˈleɪ/ *v.t.* (*past & p.p.* **re-laid**) to lay again.

release /rɪˈliːs/ *v.t.* **1.** to set free (*lit.* or *fig.*); to unfasten. **2.** to remove or allow to move from a fixed position; to allow to fall or fly etc. **3.** to make (information or a recording etc.) public; to issue (a film etc.) for general exhibition. —*n.* **1.** releasing, being released. **2.** a handle or catch etc. that unfastens a device or machine-part. **3.** a document etc. made available for publication; a film or record etc. that is released; the releasing of a document or film etc. thus. [f. OF *relesser* f. L *relaxare* relax]

relegate /ˈrelɪgeɪt/ *v.t.* to consign or dismiss to an inferior position; to transfer (a sports team) to a lower division of a league etc.; to banish. —**relegation** /-ˈgeɪʃ(ə)n/ *n.* [f. L *relegare* (RE-¹, *legare* send)]

relent /rɪˈlent/ *v.i.* to relax one's severity, to abandon a harsh intention, to yield to compassion. [f. RE-² + L *lentare* bend]

relentless *adj.* unrelenting. —**relentlessly** *adv.*, **relentlessness** *n.* [f. prec. + -LESS]

relevant /ˈrelɪv(ə)nt/ *adj.* related to the matter in hand. —**relevance** *n.* [f. L *relevare* (as RELIEVE)]

reliable /rɪˈlaɪəb(ə)l/ *adj.* that may be relied on. —**reliability** /-ˈbɪlɪtɪ/ *n.*, **reliably** *adv.* [f. RELY]

reliance /rɪˈlaɪəns/ *n.* relying; trust, confidence. [f. RELY]

relic /ˈrelɪk/ *n.* **1.** something that survives from an earlier age; a surviving custom or belief etc. from a past age; an object that is interesting because of its age or associations. **2.** a part of a holy person's body or belongings kept after his or her death as an object of reverence. **3.** (in *pl.*) residue, surviving scraps; the dead body or remains of a person. [f. OF f. L *reliquiae* (as RELINQUISH)]

relict /ˈrelɪkt/ *n.* **1.** a person's widow. **2.** a geological or other object surviving in a primitive form. [f. L *relinquere* (see RELINQUISH)]

relief /rɪˈliːf/ *n.* **1.** alleviation of or deliverance from pain, distress, anxiety, etc. **2.** a feature etc. that breaks up monotony or relaxes tension. **3.** assistance given to persons in special danger, need, or difficulty. **4.** the replacing of a person or persons on duty by another or others; the person(s) thus taking over. **5.** a thing supplementing another in some service. **6.** a method of moulding, carving, or stamping in which the design stands out from the surface; a piece of sculpture etc. in relief; representation of relief given by the arrangement of line, colour, or shading. **7.** deliverance of a besieged place, especially by raising the siege. **8.** redress of a hardship or grievance. —**relief map,** a map showing hills and valleys by shading or colouring etc. rather than by contour lines alone. **relief road,** a road by which traffic can avoid a congested area. [f. AF & F f. It. (as foll.)]

relieve /rɪˈliːv/ *v.t.* **1.** to give relief, bring or be a relief to. **2.** to mitigate the tedium or monotony of. **3.** to release (a person) from duty by taking his place or providing a substitute. —**relieve one's feelings,** to use strong language or vigorous behaviour when annoyed. **relieve oneself,** to urinate or defecate. **relieve a person of,** to take (a burden or responsibility etc.) from him. [f. OF *relever* f. L *relevare* lift (RE-², *levis* light)]

relievo /rɪˈliːvəʊ/ *n.* (*pl.* **-os**) relief in sculpture etc. [f. It. (as RELIEF)]

religion /rɪˈlɪdʒ(ə)n/ *n.* **1.** belief in a superhuman controlling power, especially in a personal God or gods entitled to obedience and worship; the expression of this in worship. **2.** a particular system of faith. **3.** a thing that one is devoted to. **4.** life under monastic vows. [f. AF f. L *religio* obligation, bond, reverence]

religious /rɪˈlɪdʒəs/ *adj.* **1.** believing firmly in a religion and paying attention to its practices. **2.** of or concerned with religion. **3.** of or belonging to a monastic order. **4.** scrupulous, conscientious. —*n.* (*pl.* same) a person bound by monastic vows. —**religiously** adv. [f. AF f. L religiosus (as prec.)]

relinquish /rɪˈlɪŋkwɪʃ/ v.t. **1.** to give up or cease from (a habit, plan, or belief etc.). **2.** to resign or surrender (a right or possession). **3.** to relax one's hold of. —**relinquishment** n. [f. OF f. L relinquere leave behind (RE-¹, linquere leave)]

reliquary /ˈrelɪkwərɪ/ n. a receptacle for relics. [f. F reliquaire (as RELIC)]

relish /ˈrelɪʃ/ n. **1.** great liking or enjoyment. **2.** appetizing flavour, attractive quality. **3.** a thing eaten with plainer food to add flavour. **4.** a distinctive taste or tinge of. —v.t. to get pleasure from, to enjoy greatly. [f. OF, = remainder (as RELEASE)]

relive /riːˈlɪv/ v.t. to live (an experience etc.) over again, especially in the imagination.

reload /riːˈləʊd/ v.t./i. to load again.

relocate /riːləʊˈkeɪt/ v.t./i. to locate in or move to a new place. —**relocation** /-ˈkeɪʃ(ə)n/ n.

reluctant /rɪˈlʌkt(ə)nt/ adj. unwilling, with consent grudgingly given. —**reluctance** n., **reluctantly** adv. [f. L reluctari (RE-¹, luctari struggle)]

rely /rɪˈlaɪ/ v.i. (with on or upon) to trust confidently, to depend on for help. [orig. = rally, be vassal of, f. OF relier bind together f. L religare (RE-², ligare bind)]

remain /rɪˈmeɪn/ v.i. **1.** to be left after other parts have been removed, used, or dealt with. **2.** to be in the same place or condition during further time; to continue to be. [f. OF f. L remanēre (RE-¹, manēre stay)]

remainder /rɪˈmeɪndə(r)/ n. **1.** the remaining persons, things, or part. **2.** the number left after subtraction or division. **3.** the copies of a book left unsold when demand has almost ceased. —v.t. to dispose of (the remainder of the copies of a book) at a reduced price. [f. AF (as prec.)]

remains n.pl. **1.** what remains after other parts have been removed or used etc. **2.** relics of antiquity, especially of buildings. **3.** a dead body. [f. OF (as REMAIN)]

remand /rɪˈmɑːnd/ v.t. to send back (a prisoner) into custody while further evidence is sought. —n. remanding, being remanded. —**on remand,** held in custody after being remanded. **remand centre** or **home,** an institution to which young offenders may be sent. [f. L remandare (RE-², mandare commit)]

remanent /ˈremənənt/ adj. remaining, residual. —**remanent magnetism,** magnetization remaining after the source of excitation has been removed. [f. L (as REMAIN)]

remark /rɪˈmɑːk/ v.t./i. **1.** to say by way of comment. **2.** to take notice of, to regard with attention. —n. **1.** a written or spoken comment, anything said. **2.** noticing. [f. F remarquer (as RE-¹, MARK¹)]

remarkable adj. worth notice, exceptional, unusual. —**remarkably** adv. [f. F (as prec.)]

remarry /riːˈmærɪ/ v.t./i. to marry again. —**remarriage** n.

Rembrandt /ˈrembrɒnt/ (full name Rembrandt Harmensz van Rijn, 1606–69), the greatest of Dutch painters. The son of a miller, he worked at first in Leyden but from 1632 established himself in Amsterdam. His initial success owed much to highly-finished society portraits, strongly lit in the manner of Caravaggio, and some financial independence came with his marriage to the well-to-do Saskia in 1634. By 1642, when she died, his style was evolving as his art became ever more searching and profound. The great Night Watch (1642) transformed the traditional Dutch portrait convention into a haunting mystery. Though his wordly affairs now decayed (he was bankrupted in 1656), yet his imaginative power became ever richer. The emotional resonance of his later work, his ability to paint human flesh as if lit from within by the spirit, in the surrounding darkness, surpasses at its finest the power of any painter in history. The great series of over 60 self-portraits is an unique autobiography in paint, but he found his subjects in genre, religion, and landscape, and in drawing and etching he is a supreme master. His work is represented in almost all the major art galleries of the Western world.

remediable /rɪˈmiːdɪəb(ə)l/ adj. that may be remedied. [f. REMEDY]

remedial /rɪˈmiːdɪəl/ adj. providing a remedy for a disease or deficiency; (of teaching) for slow or backward children. —**remedially** adv. [f. L (as foll.)]

remedy /ˈremɪdɪ/ n. **1.** something that cures or relieves a disease or that puts right a matter. **2.** redress, legal or other

reparation. —v.t. to be a remedy for; to put right. [f. AF f. L remedium (RE-¹, medēri heal)]

remember /rɪˈmembə(r)/ v.t. **1.** to keep in one's mind, not to forget. **2.** to recall (knowledge or an experience etc.) to one's mind; to be able to do this. **3.** to think of (a person), especially in making a gift etc. **4.** to convey greetings from. [f. OF f. L rememorari (RE-², memor mindful)]

remembrance /rɪˈmembrəns/ **1.** remembering, being remembered; memory. **2.** a memento; a memorial. **3.** (in pl.) greetings conveyed through a third person. —**Remembrance Sunday,** the Sunday nearest 11 Nov., when those who were killed in the First and Second World Wars are commemorated. [f. OF (as prec.)]

remind /rɪˈmaɪnd/ v.t. to cause (a person) to remember or think of. [f. RE-² + MIND]

reminder n. a thing that reminds or is a momento. [f. prec.]

reminisce /remɪˈnɪs/ v.i. to indulge in reminiscences. [back-formation f. foll.]

reminiscence /remɪˈnɪs(ə)ns/ n. **1.** remembering of things past. **2.** (in pl.) an account of facts and incidents remembered, especially in literary form. **3.** a thing that is reminiscent of something else. [f. L reminisci remember)]

reminiscent adj. **1.** inclined to reminisce. **2.** reminding or suggestive of. —**reminiscently** adv. [as prec.]

remiss /rɪˈmɪs/ adj. careless of one's duty, lax, negligent. [f. L remissus (as REMIT)]

remission /rɪˈmɪʃ(ə)n/ n. **1.** shortening of a prison sentence on account of good behaviour; the remitting of a debt or penalty etc. **2.** diminution of force or intensity especially of a disease or pain. **3.** God's pardon or forgiveness of sins. [f. OF or L (as foll.)]

remit /rɪˈmɪt/ v.t./i. (-tt-) **1.** to cancel (a debt etc.); to refrain from inflicting (a punishment). **2.** to make or become less intense; to cease. **3.** to send (money etc.) in payment. **4.** to refer (a matter for decision etc.) to some authority. **5.** to postpone. **6.** (of God) to pardon or forgive (sins). —/also ˈriːmɪt/ n. **1.** an item remitted for consideration. **2.** the terms of reference of a committee etc. [f. L remittere (RE-², mittere send)]

remittance /rɪˈmɪtəns/ n. the sending of money to a person; the money sent. [f. prec.]

remittent adj. that abates at intervals. [as REMIT]

remnant /ˈremnənt/ n. **1.** a small remaining quantity, part, or number of people or things; a surviving trace. **2.** a piece of cloth etc. left when the greater part has been used or sold. [f. OF remenant (as REMAIN)]

remodel /riːˈmɒd(ə)l/ v.t. to model again or differently; to reconstruct or reorganize.

remonstrance /rɪˈmɒnstrəns/ n. **1.** (hist.) a formal statement of public grievances. **2.** remonstrating, a protest. **3. Remonstrance,** a document drawn up in 1610 by the Arminians of the Dutch Reformed Church, presenting the differences between their doctrines and those of the strict Calvinists. —**Grand Remonstrance,** that presented by the House of Commons to the Crown in 1641. —**Remonstrant** n. [as foll.]

remonstrate /ˈremənstreɪt/ v.t./i. to make a protest (with a person). [f. L remonstrare (RE-¹, monstrare show)]

remorse /rɪˈmɔːs/ n. deep regret for a wrong committed; compunction. [f. OF f. L (remordēre vex, RE-¹, mordēre bite)]

remorseful adj. filled with remorse. —**remorsefully** adv. [f. prec. + -FUL]

remorseless adj. relentless, without compassion. —**remorselessly** adv. [f. REMORSE + -LESS]

remote /rɪˈməʊt/ adj. **1.** far apart; far away in place or time. **2.** far from civilization etc.; secluded. **3.** not closely related. **4.** slight. **5.** aloof, not friendly. —**remote control,** control of apparatus etc. from a distance, usually by means of an electrically operated device, radio, etc. —**remotely** adv., **remoteness** n. [f. L remotus (as REMOVE)]

remould /riːˈməʊld/ v.t. to mould again, to refashion; to reconstruct the tread of (a tyre). —/ˈriːməʊld/ n. a remoulded tyre.

removable /rɪˈmuːvəb(ə)l/ adj. that may be removed. [f. REMOVE]

removal /rɪˈmuːv(ə)l/ n. removing, being removed; transfer of furniture etc. to a different house. [f. foll.]

remove /rɪˈmuːv/ v.t./i. **1.** to take off or away from the place occupied; to convey to another place. **2.** to get rid of. **3.** to dismiss from office. **4.** to take off (clothing). **5.** (in p.p.) distant, remote. —n. **1.** distance, degree of remoteness.

2. a stage in gradation. **3.** a form or division in some schools. —**cousin once, twice, etc., removed,** see COUSIN. —**remover** n. [f. OF f. L (as RE-¹, MOVE)]

remunerate /rɪ'mju:nəreɪt/ v.t. to pay or reward (a person) for a service rendered; to pay for or reward (work etc.). —**remuneration** /-'reɪʃ(ə)n/ n., **remunerative** adj. [f. L remunerari (RE-¹, munus gift)]

Remus /'ri:məs/ (Rom. legend) the twin brother of Romulus (see entry).

Renaissance /rɪ'neɪs(ə)ns, -sãs/ n. **1.** the revival of art and learning under the influence of classical models which began in Italy in the late Middle Ages and reached its peak at the end of the 15th c. before spreading northwards into the rest of Europe; the period of this; the style of art and architecture developed by it. **2.** renaissance, any similar revival. [F, = rebirth (as RENASCENT)]

renal /'ri:n(ə)l/ adj. of the kidneys. [f. F f. L (renes kidneys)]

rename /ri:'neɪm/ v.t. to give a fresh name to.

Renan /rə'nã/, Ernest (1823-92), French historian and philologist,. He was educated for the priesthood but his scepticism of the divine inspiration of the Bible and the fundamental doctrines of orthodox religion found him unable to take his vows. His controversial Vie de Jésus (1863) rejects the supernatural element in Jesus' life. Through the persuasive force of his reasoning and his erudition he became a major representative of 19th-c. French thought. His belief that the future of the world lay in the progress of science found expression in L'Avenir de la science (1890).

renascent /rɪ'næs(ə)nt/ adj. springing up anew, being reborn. —**renascence** n. [f. L (RE-², nasci be born)]

rend v.t./i. (past & p.p. rent) (archaic) to tear or wrench forcibly. [OE]

render v.t. **1.** to cause to be or become. **2.** to give or pay (money, a service, etc.) especially in return or as a thing due; to give (assistance). **3.** to present, to send in. **4.** to represent or portray; to act (a role); to perform (music). **5.** to translate. **6.** to melt down (fat). **7.** to cover (stone or brick) with a first coat of plaster. [f. AF rendre f. L reddere (RE-¹, dare give)]

rendezvous /'rɒndeɪvu:/ n. (pl. same /-u:z/) an agreed or regular meeting-place; a meeting by agreement. —v.i. (3 sing. pres. -vouses /-vu:z/, past -voused /-vu:d/, partic. -vousing /-vu:ɪŋ/) to meet at a rendezvous. [f. F rendez-vous present yourselves]

rendition /ren'dɪʃ(ə)n/ n. the rendering or interpretation of a dramatic role, musical piece, etc. [obs. F (as RENDER)]

renegade /'renɪgeɪd/ n. one who deserts his or her party or principles. [f. Sp. renegado f. L (as foll.)]

renege /rɪ'ni:g, -'neɪg/ v.t./i. **1.** to deny, to renounce. **2.** (US, in cards) to revoke. —**renege on,** to fail to keep (a promise etc.); to disappoint (a person). [f. L renegare (RE-¹, negare deny)]

renew /rɪ'nju:/ v.t. **1.** to restore to its original state; to revive, to regenerate. **2.** to replace with a fresh supply etc. **3.** to repeat, to re-establish; to make, get, or give again; to arrange for a continuation or continued validity of (a licence, subscription, lease, etc.). —**renewal** n.

reniform /'ri:nɪfɔ:m/ adj. kidney-shaped (ill. PLANTS). [f. L ren kidney + FORM]

rennet /'renɪt/ n. curdled milk found in the stomach of an unweaned calf, or a preparation of a bovine stomach-membrane or of a plant, used in curdling milk for cheese or junket. [prob. rel. to RUN]

Rennie /'renɪ/, John (1761-1821), Scottish civil engineer, much of whose work is still to be seen. He built some distinguished bridges, including three in London, the Waterloo, Southwark, and New London bridges, of which Southwark remains, and many docks including some in London, Hull, Malta, and Bermuda, while his great breakwater at Plymouth (1811-48) is an enduring monument.

Renoir¹ /rə'nwɑ:(r), 'ren-/, Jean (1894-), French film director, second son of Pierre Auguste Renoir. His fame is based chiefly on the deeply moving films that he made in France in the 1930s, including La Grande Illusion (1937) and his masterpiece La Reigle du Jeu (1939). All his works are notable for their humanity, grace, and style.

Renoir² /rə'nwɑ:(r), 'ren-/, Pierre Auguste (1841-1919), French impressionist painter, a close friend of Monet and Sisley. He introduced the so-called 'rainbow palette' restricted to pure tones at maximum intensity with no use of black, and a more throrough use of divisionism and the subordination of outline. The human figure played a larger part in his painting than in that of his colleagues, and he

delighted in the intrinsic charm of lovely women, children, flowers, and beautiful scenes; nowhere in his landscape is there a suggestion of sadness or melancholy. His later subjects are mostly female nudes of a fine fleshiness and sensuality. Among his best-known works are Les grandes baigneuses (1885-7), Les grandes laveuses (1912), and Le jugement de Paris (c.1914).

renounce /rɪ'naʊns/ v.t. **1.** to give up (a claim or right etc.) formally. **2.** to repudiate, to refuse to recognize any longer; to decline further association or disclaim a relationship with. [f. OF renoncer f. L renuntiare (RE-¹, nuntiare announce)]

renovate /'renəveɪt/ v.t. to restore to a good condition, to repair. —**renovation** /-'veɪʃ(ə)n/ n., **renovator** n. [f. L renovare (RE-², novus new)]

renown /rɪ'naʊn/ n. fame, high distinction. [f. AF & OF (renomer make famous (as RE-², NOMINATE)]

renowned adj. famous, celebrated. [f. prec.]

rent¹ n. a tenant's periodical payment to an owner or landlord for the use of land or premises; payment for the use of equipment etc. —v.t. **1.** to pay rent for occupation or use of. **2.** to let or hire for rent; to be let at a specified rent. [f. OF rente (as RENDER)]

rent² n. a large tear in a garment etc.; an opening in clouds etc. [as REND]

rent³ past & p.p. of REND.

rentable /'rentəb(ə)l/ adj. that may be rented. [f. RENT¹]

rental /'rent(ə)l/ n. **1.** the amount paid or received as rent. **2.** renting. [f. AF or L (as RENT¹)]

rentier /'rɑ̃tɪeɪ/ n. a person living on income from property or investments. [F (rente dividend)]

renumber /ri:'nʌmbə(r)/ v.t. to change the numbering of.

renunciation /rɪnʌnsɪ'eɪʃ(ə)n/ n. renouncing; the giving up of things. [as RENOUNCE]

reopen /ri:'əʊpən/ v.t./i. to open again.

reorder /ri:'ɔ:də(r)/ v.t. **1.** to order again. **2.** to put into a new order.

reorganize /ri:'ɔ:gənaɪz/ v.t. to organize again in a different way. —**reorganization** /-'zeɪʃ(ə)n/ n.

rep¹ n. a textile fabric with a corded surface, used in curtains and upholstery. [f. F reps]

rep² n. (colloq.) a representative, especially a commercial traveller. [abbr.]

rep³ n. (colloq.) a repertory theatre or company. [abbr.]

repaint /ri:'peɪnt/ v.t. to paint again or differently. —/'ri:peɪnt/ n. **1.** repainting. **2.** a repainted thing.

repair¹ /rɪ'peə(r)/ v.t. **1.** to restore to a good condition after damage or wear. **2.** to set right or make amends for (a loss or wrong etc.). —n. **1.** restoring to a sound condition; the act or result of doing this. **2.** condition as regards being repaired. —**repairer** n. [f. OF reparer f. L reparare (RE-², parare make ready)]

repair² /rɪ'peə(r)/ v.i. to go, resort, or have recourse to. [f. OF f. L repatriare (as REPATRIATE)]

reparable /'repərəb(ə)l/ adj. (of a loss etc.) that can be made good. [F f. L (as REPAIR²)]

reparation /repə'reɪʃ(ə)n/ n. making amends; compensation. [f. OF f. L (as REPAIR²)]

repartee /repɑ:'ti:/ n. a witty retort; the making of witty retorts. [f. F repartie (repartir reply promptly)]

repast /rɪ'pɑ:st/ n. a meal; the food and drink for a meal. [f. OF f. L repascere (past)]

repatriate /ri:'pætrɪeɪt/ v.t./i. to restore (a person) to his native land; to return thus. —/-ət/ n. a repatriated person. —**repatriation** /-'eɪʃ(ə)n/ n. [f. L repatriare (RE-², patria native land)]

repay /ri:'peɪ/ v.t./i. **1.** to pay back (money) ; to pay back money to (a person). **2.** to give in return or recompense; to make recompense for (a service etc.); to requite (an action). —**repayment** n.

repayable adj. that can or must be repaid. [f. prec.]

repeal /rɪ'pi:l/ v.t. to annul or revoke (a law etc.). —n. repealing. [f. AF & OF (as RE-², APPEAL)]

repeat /rɪ'pi:t/ v.t./i. **1.** to say, do, or provide again. **2.** to say, recite, or report (something heard or learnt). **3.** to recur, to appear again or repeatedly. **4.** (of food) to be tasted intermittently for some time after being swallowed. —n. **1.** repeating. **2.** a thing repeated; a repeated broadcast programme; (Mus.) a passage intended to be repeated, a mark indicating this (ill. MUSICAL NOTATION); each occurrence of a pattern repeated in wallpaper etc. —**repeat itself,** to recur in the same form. **repeat oneself,** to say or do the same thing over again. [f. OF f. L repetere (RE-², petere seek)]

repeatable *adj.* that may be repeated; suitable for being repeated. [f. prec.]

repeatedly *adv.* many times over. [f. REPEAT]

repeater *n.* a person or thing that repeats, especially a firearm that fires several shots without reloading, or a watch etc. that strikes the last quarter etc. again when required; a device that repeats a signal. [as prec.]

repel /rɪ'pel/ *v.t.* (-ll-) **1.** to drive back, to ward off; to refuse admission, approach, or acceptance to. **2.** to be impenetrable by. **3.** to be repulsive or distasteful to. [f. L *repellere* (RE-¹, *pellere* drive)]

repellent *adj.* that repels. —*n.* a substance that repels something (esp. insects). [f. prec.]

repent /rɪ'pent/ *v.t./i.* to feel deep sorrow or regret about (one's wrongdoing or omission etc.). —**repentance** *n.*, **repentant** *adj.* [f. OF *repentir* (as RE-¹, PENITENT)]

repercussion /ri:pə'kʌʃ(ə)n/ *n.* **1.** an indirect effect or reaction of an event or act. **2.** a recoil after impact. **3.** an echo. [f. OF or L (as RE-¹, PERCUSSION)]

repertoire /'repətwɑː(r)/ *n.* a stock of pieces etc. that a performer or company knows or is prepared to give; a stock of regularly performed pieces, regularly used techniques, etc. [f. F f. L (as foll.)]

repertory /'repətərɪ/ *n.* **1.** a repertoire. **2.** theatrical performance of various plays for short periods by one company. **3.** a store or collection, especially of information or instances etc. [f. L *repertorium* (*reperire* find)]

repetition /repɪ'tɪʃ(ə)n/ *n.* **1.** repeating, being repeated. **2.** a thing repeated; a copy. —**repetitious** *adj.*, **repetitive** /rɪ'petɪtɪv/ *adj.*, **repetitively** *adv.* [f. F or L (as REPEAT)]

repine /rɪ'paɪn/ *v.i.* to fret, to be discontented. [f. RE-¹ + PINE², after *repent*]

replace /rɪ'pleɪs/ *v.t.* **1.** to put back in place. **2.** to take the place of. **3.** to find or provide a substitute for.

replaceable *adj.* that may be replaced. [f. prec.]

replacement *n.* **1.** replacing, being replaced. **2.** a person or thing that takes the place of another. [f. REPLACE]

replant /ri:'plɑ:nt/ *v.t.* to plant again or differently.

replantation /ri:plɑ:n'teɪʃ(ə)n/ *n.* **1.** replanting. **2.** permanent reattachment to the body of a part which has been removed or severed. [f. prec.]

replay /ri:'pleɪ/ *v.t.* to play (a match, recording, etc.) over again. —/'ri:pleɪ/ *n.* the replaying (of a match, a recording of an incident in a game, etc.).

replenish /rɪ'plenɪʃ/ *v.t.* to fill up again (*with*); to renew (a supply etc.). —**replenishment** *n.* [f. OF *replenir* (RE-², *plein* full f. L *plenus*)]

replete /rɪ'pli:t/ *adj.* filled or well supplied; full, gorged, sated. —**repletion** *n.* [f. OF or L *replēre* (RE-¹, *plēre* fill)]

replica /'replɪkə/ *n.* an exact copy, especially a duplicate made by an original artist of his picture etc.; a model, especially on a smaller scale. [It. (*replicare*, as REPLY)]

reply /rɪ'plaɪ/ *v.t./i.* to make an answer; to say in answer. —*n.* **1.** replying. **2.** what is replied, an answer. [f. OF f. L *replicare*, lit. = fold again (RE-², *plicare* fold)]

report /rɪ'pɔːt/ *v.t./i.* **1.** to bring back or give an account of; to state as a fact or news; to narrate, describe, or repeat, especially as an eye-witness or hearer etc.; to describe (an event etc.) for publication or broadcasting; to make an official or formal statement about. **2.** to make a formal accusation about (an offence or offender). **3.** to present oneself as having returned or arrived. **4.** to be responsible to a specified person as one's superior or supervisor. —*n.* **1.** a spoken or written account of something seen, done, or studied. **2.** a description for publication or broadcasting. **3.** a periodical statement on a pupil's work, conduct, etc. **4.** rumour, a piece of gossip. **5.** the sound of an explosion or firing of a gun. —**reported speech,** a speaker's words as given in a report of them, with person and tense etc. adapted. [f. OF f. L *reportare* (RE-², *portare* carry)]

reporter *n.* a person employed to gather and report news for a newspaper or broadcast. [f. prec.]

repose¹ /rɪ'pəʊz/ *n.* **1.** cessation of activity, excitement, or toil; sleep. **2.** a peaceful or quiescent state, tranquillity. —*v.t./i.* to rest, to lie; to be supported. [f. OF f. L *repausare* (RE-¹, *pausare* pause)]

repose² /rɪ'pəʊz/ *v.t.* to place (trust etc.) *in.* [f. RE-¹ + POSE²]

reposeful *adj.* inducing or exhibiting repose. —**reposefully** *adv.* [f. REPOSE¹ + -FUL]

repository /rɪ'pɒzɪtərɪ/ *n.* a place where things are stored, especially a warehouse or museum; a receptacle; a recipient of secrets etc. [f. obs. F or L (as REPOSE²)]

repossess /ri:pə'zes/ *v.t.* to regain possession of (esp.

goods on which hire-purchase payments are in arrears). —**repossession** *n.*

repp var. of REP¹.

reprehend /reprɪ'hend/ *v.t.* to rebuke, to blame. [f. L *reprehendere* (RE-¹, *prehendere* seize)]

reprehensible /reprɪ'hensɪb(ə)l/ *adj.* deserving rebuke. —**reprehensibly** *adv.* [f. prec.]

represent /reprɪ'zent/ *v.t.* **1.** to be an example or embodiment of. **2.** to symbolize. **3.** to present a likeness or description of to the mind or senses. **4.** to describe or depict, *as,* to declare *to be*; to declare. **5.** to show or play the part of in a picture or stage play etc. **6.** to be a deputy, agent, or spokesman for; to be the elected representative of (the people of an area) in a legislative assembly. [f. OF or L *repraesentare* (RE-², *praesentare* present)]

representation /reprɪzen'teɪʃ(ə)n/ *n.* **1.** representing, being represented. **2.** a thing that represents something. **3.** (esp. in *pl.*) a statement made by way of an allegation or to convey an opinion. —**representational** *adj.* [as prec.]

representative /reprɪ'zentətɪv/ *adj.* **1.** typical of a group or class. **2.** containing examples of all or many types. **3.** consisting of elected deputies or representatives; based on the representation of a nation etc. by such deputies. **4.** serving as a portrayal or symbol *of.* —*n.* **1.** a sample, or specimen, or typical embodiment. **2.** an agent of a person, or firm, or society; a firm's travelling salesman. **3.** a delegate, a person chosen to represent another or others, or to take part in a legislative assembly on their behalf. —**House of Representatives,** see CONGRESS. [f. OF or L (as REPRESENT)]

repress /rɪ'pres/ *v.t.* to keep down, to suppress; to keep (emotions etc.) from finding an outlet; (in *p.p.*) suffering from repression of the emotions. —**repression** *n.*, **repressive** *adj.*, **repressively** *adv.* [f. L *reprimere* (RE-¹, *premere* press)]

reprieve /rɪ'priːv/ *v.t.* **1.** to postpone or remit the execution of (a condemned person). **2.** to give a respite to. —*n.* **1.** reprieving, being reprieved; remission or commutation of a capital sentence; a warrant for this. **2.** a respite. [f. AF *repris* (*reprendre* take back)]

reprimand /'reprɪmɑːnd/ *n.* a formal or offical rebuke. —*v.t.* to administer a reprimand to. [f. F f. Sp. f. L *reprimenda* (as REPRESS)]

reprint /ri:'prɪnt/ *v.t.* to print again. —/'ri:prɪnt/ *n.* the reprinting of a book etc.; a book etc. reprinted.

reprisal /rɪ'praɪz(ə)l/ *n.* an act of retaliation. [f. AF (as REPREHEND)]

reprise /rɪ'priːz/ *n.* a repeated passage in music; a repeated song etc. in a musical programme. [F (as REPRIEVE)]

reproach /rɪ'prəʊtʃ/ *v.t.* to express disapproval to (a person) for a fault or offence. —*n.* **1.** reproaching; an instance of this. **2.** a thing that brings disgrace or discredit. **3.** disgraced or discredited state. —**beyond reproach,** deserving no blame, perfect. [f. OF *reprocher* f. L (RE-¹, *prope* near)]

reproachful *adj.* inclined to or expressing reproach. —**reproachfully** *adv.* [f. prec. + -FUL]

reprobate /'reprəbeɪt/ *n.* an unprincipled or immoral person. [f. L (as REPROVE)]

reprobation /reprə'beɪʃ(ə)n/ *n.* strong condemnation. [as prec.]

reproduce /ri:prə'djuːs/ *v.t./i.* **1.** to produce a copy or representation of. **2.** to cause to be seen or heard etc. again or to occur again. **3.** to produce further members of the same species by natural means; to produce offspring of.

reproducible *adj.* that may be reproduced. [f. prec.]

reproduction /ri:prə'dʌkʃ(ə)n/ *n.* **1.** reproducing, being reproduced. **2.** a copy of a painting etc. **3.** (*attrib.,* of furniture etc.) made in imitation of an earlier style. [f. REPRODUCE]

reproductive /ri:prə'dʌktɪv/ *adj.* of or concerning reproduction. [as prec.]

reprography /rɪ'prɒgrəfɪ/ *n.* the science and practice of copying documents by photography, xerography, etc. —**reprographic** /ri:prə'græfɪk/ *adj.* [f. REPRODUCE + -GRAPHY]

reproof /rɪ'pruːf/ *n.* an expression of condemnation for a fault or offence. [f. OF *reprove* (as foll.)]

reprove /rɪ'pruːv/ *v.t.* to give a reproof to (a person) or for (conduct etc.). [f. OF *reprover* f. L *reprobare* disapprove]

reptile /'reptaɪl/ *n.* a vertebrate animal of the class Reptilia, which includes snakes, lizards, crocodiles, turtles, and tortoises. Reptiles, which first appeared in the Carboniferous period, probably evolved from amphibians, but they differ from them in several important respects. They breathe air all their lives, they are protected from desiccation by a scaly skin, and their eggs have shells, so that they can be laid on land without drying up; the young when hatched resemble their parents and do not undergo metamorphosis. Present-day reptiles are cold-blooded; there are about 6,000 living species, but there were formerly many more, especially in the Mesozoic era (284–265 million years ago), when dinosaurs dominated the earth. The closest living relatives of the now extinct dinosaurs are the crocodiles and the birds, which descended from one group of bipedal dinosaurs. [f. L *reptilis* (*repere* crawl)]

reptilian /rep'tɪliən/ *adj.* 1. of reptiles. 2. (of animals) creeping. —*n.* a reptile. [f. prec.]

republic /rɪ'pʌblɪk/ *n.* a State in which supreme power is held by the people or its elected representatives or by an elected or nominated president, not by a monarch etc. [f. F f. L *respublica* (*res* concern, *publicus* public)]

republican *adj.* 1. of or constituted as a republic; characteristic of republics. 2. advocating or supporting republican government. —*n.* 1. a person advocating or supporting republican government. 2. **Republican,** a member of the Republican Party. —**republicanism** *n.* [f. prec.]

Republican Party one of the two chief political parties in the USA (the other being the Democratic Party). It was formed in 1854 to resist the extension of slave territory; Abraham Lincoln was the first of its leaders to become President. It is now chiefly identified with business interests and favours restrictions on central power.

repudiate /rɪ'pju:dɪeɪt/ *v.t.* to reject or disown utterly; to deny; to refuse to recognize or obey (an authority or treaty) or discharge (an obligation or debt). —**repudiation** /-'eɪʃ(ə)n/ *n.*, **repudiator** *n.* [f. L *repudiare* (*repudium* divorce)]

repugnant /rɪ'pʌɡnənt/ *adj.* 1. strongly distasteful or objectionable. 2. (of ideas etc.) inconsistent, incompatible. —**repugnance** *n.* [f. F or L (*repugnare* fight against)]

repulse /rɪ'pʌls/ *v.t.* 1. to drive back (an attack or attacking enemy) by force of arms. 2. to rebuff. 3. to refuse (a request or offer, or its maker). —*n.* 1. repulsing, being repulsed. 2. a rebuff. [f. L (as REPEL)]

repulsion /rɪ'pʌlʃ(ə)n/ *n.* 1. repelling, being repelled. 2. a feeling of strong distaste, revulsion. [as REPEL]

repulsive /rɪ'pʌlsɪv/ *adj.* 1. arousing strong distaste, loathsome. 2. causing repulsion. —**repulsively** *adv.*, **repulsiveness** *n.* [f. F *répulsif* or REPULSE]

reputable /'repjʊtəb(ə)l/ *adj.* of good repute, respected. —**reputably** *adv.* [obs. F or f. L (as REPUTE)]

reputation /repjʊ'teɪʃ(ə)n/ *n.* 1. what is generally said or believed about a person or thing. 2. the state of being well thought of. [f. L (as foll.)]

repute /rɪ'pju:t/ *n.* reputation. —*v.t.* (in *pass.*) to be generally considered. [f. OF f. L *reputare* (RE-¹, *putare* think)]

reputed /rɪ'pju:tɪd/ *adj.* said or thought to be but possibly not. —**reputed pint** etc., a bottle of wine or spirits etc. sold as a pint etc. but not guaranteed as an imperial measure. —**reputedly** *adv.* [f. prec.]

request /rɪ'kwest/ *n.* 1. asking for something. 2. a thing asked for. 3. the state of being sought after, demand. —*v.t.* to make a request for (a thing) or of (a person); to seek permission. —**by** or **on request,** in response to an expressed wish. **request stop,** a place where a bus etc. stops only on a passenger's (or intended passenger's) request. [f. OF f. L *requaerere* (as REQUIRE)]

requiem /'rekwɪem/ *n.* a form of Mass for the repose of souls of the dead; the music for this. [f. L (accusative of *requies* repose)]

require /rɪ'kwaɪə(r)/ *v.t.* 1. to be unable to do without, to depend on for success, fulfilment, growth, etc. 2. to lay down as imperative; to order or oblige. 3. to wish to have. [f. OF f. L *requirere* (RE-¹, *quaerere* seek)]

requirement *n.* a thing required; a need. [f. prec.]

requisite /'rekwɪzɪt/ *adj.* required by circumstances, necessary to success. —*n.* a thing needed for some purpose. [f. L *requisitus* (as prec.)]

requisition /rekwɪ'zɪʃ(ə)n/ *n.* 1. an official order laying claim to the use of property or materials; a formal written demand that some duty should be performed. 2. being called or put into service. —*v.t.* to demand use or supply of, especially by a formal requisition. [f. F or L (as REQUIRE)]

requite /rɪ'kwaɪt/ *v.t.* to make a return for (a service) to avenge (a wrong or injury etc.); to make a return to (a person); to repay with good or evil. —**requital** *n.* [f. RE-¹ + *quite* var. of QUIT]

reredos /'rɪədɒs/ *n.* an ornamental screen covering the wall above the back of an altar (ill. VESTMENTS). [f. OF *areredos* (*arere* behind, *dos* back; cf. ARREAR)]

re-route /ri:'ru:t/ *v.t.* to send or carry by a different route.

rerun /ri:'rʌn/ *v.t.* (**-nn-**) to run again. —/'ri:rʌn/ *n.* an act of rerunning; a repeat of a film etc.

resale /ri:'seɪl/ *n.* sale to another person of something one has bought.

rescind /rɪ'sɪnd/ *v.t.* to abrogate, to revoke, to cancel. —**rescission** /-ʒ(ə)n/ *n.* [f. L *rescindere* (RE-¹, *scindere* cut)]

rescript /'ri:skrɪpt/ *n.* 1. a Roman emperor's or pope's written reply to an appeal for a decision; any papal decision. 2. an official edict or announcement. [f. L *rescriptum* (*rescribere* write back)]

rescue /'reskju:/ *v.t.* to save or bring away from capture, danger, harm, etc. —*n.* rescuing, being rescued. —**rescuer** *n.* [f. OF *rescoure* (RE-¹, L *executere* shake out)]

research /rɪ'sɜ:tʃ, (D) 'ri:-/ *n.* systematic investigation and study in order to establish facts and reach new conclusions. —*v.t./i.* to do research (into). —**researcher** *n.* [f. obs. F (as RE-¹, SEARCH)]

resell /ri:'sel/ *v.t.* (*past* & *p.p.* **resold** /-'səʊld/) to sell (what one has bought) to another person.

resemble /rɪ'zemb(ə)l/ *v.t.* to be like (another person or thing). —**resemblance** *n.* [f. OF *resembler* f. L (RE-¹, *similis* like)]

resent /rɪ'zent/ *v.t.* to feel indignation at or retain bitter feelings about (an action or injury etc.); to feel offended by (a person). [f. obs. F *resentir* (RE-¹, L *sentire* feel)]

resentful *adj.* feeling resentment. —**resentfully** *adv.* [f. prec. + -FUL]

resentment *n.* indignant or bitter feelings. [f. F or It. (as RESENT)]

reservation /rezə'veɪʃ(ə)n/ *n.* 1. reserving, being reserved. 2. a reserved seat or hotel accommodation etc.; a record of this. 3. a limitation on one's agreement or acceptance of an idea etc. 4. a strip of land between the carriageways of a road. 5. a tract of land set apart by a government for some special purpose or for the exclusive use of certain persons, e.g. American or Canadian Indians, African Blacks, Australian Aborigines. [as foll.]

reserve /rɪ'zɜ:v/ *v.t.* 1. to put aside or keep back for a later occasion or special use. 2. to order to be specially retained or allocated for a particular person at a particular time. 3. to retain (a right etc.). 4. to postpone delivery of (a judgement). —*n.* 1. a thing reserved for future use; an extra amount or stock kept available for use when needed. 2. a limitation or exception attached to something. 3. self-restraint, reticence; coolness of manner. 4. a company's profit added to the capital. 5. (in *sing.* or *pl.*) troops withheld from action to reinforce or protect others; forces outside the regular ones but available in an emergency. 6. a member of a military reserve. 7. an extra player chosen in case a substitute should be needed in a team. 8. a place reserved for special use, especially as a habitat. —**in reserve,** unused and available if needed. **reserve price,** the lowest acceptable price stipulated for an item sold at an auction. [f. OF f. L *reservare* (RE-¹, *servare* keep)]

reserved *adj.* reticent, uncommunicative; tending not to reveal emotions or opinions. [f. prec.]

reservist *n.* a member of a military reserve. [f. RESERVE]

reservoir /'rezəvwɑ:(r)/ *n.* 1. a large natural or artificial lake as the source of an area's water supply. 2. a container for a supply of fuel or other liquid. 3. a supply of information etc. [f. F (as RESERVE)]

reshuffle /ri:'ʃʌf(ə)l/ *v.t.* to shuffle (cards) again; to interchange the posts or responsibilities of (a group of people). —*n.* reshuffling.

reside /rɪ'zaɪd/ *v.i.* 1. to have one's home or dwell permanently (in a specified place). 2. (of power, right, or quality etc.) to be vested or present (in a specified person etc.). [prob. back-formation f. RESIDENT]

residence /'rezɪd(ə)ns/ *n.* 1. residing. 2. a place where one resides. 3. a house, especially of considerable pretension. —**in residence,** dwelling at a specified place especially for the performance of duties or work. [as foll.]

resident /'rezɪd(ə)nt/ *n.* a permanent inhabitant, not a visitor; (in a hotel) a person staying overnight. —*adj.* having quarters on the spot; residing; in residence; located. [f. OF or L *residēre* (RE-¹, *sedēre* sit)]

residential /rezɪ'denʃ(ə)l/ *adj.* 1. suitable for or occupied by private houses. 2. used as a residence. 3. based on or connected with residence. —**residentially** *adv.* [f. RESIDENCE]

residual /rɪˈzɪdjʊəl/ *adj.* left as a residue or residuum. —*n.* a residual quantity. —**residually** *adv.* [f. RESIDUE]

residuary /rɪˈzɪdjʊərɪ/ *adj.* 1. of the residue of an estate. 2. residual. [f. RESIDUUM]

residue /ˈrezɪdju:/ *n.* 1. the remainder, what is left or remains over. 2. what remains of an estate after the payment of charges, debts, and bequests. [f. OF f. L, = foll.]

residuum /rɪˈzɪdjʊəm/ *n.* (*pl.* -ua) what remains, especially a substance left after combustion or evaporation. [L (*residuus* remaining, as RESIDENT)]

resign /rɪˈzaɪn/ *v.t./i.* to give up or surrender (one's job, property, claim, etc.); to give up one's job. —**resign oneself to,** to come to accept or tolerate; to regard as inevitable. [f. OF f. L *resignare* unseal, cancel (RE-¹, *signare* sign, seal)]

resignation /rezɪgˈneɪʃ(ə)n/ *n.* 1. resigning, especially of a job. 2. a letter etc. conveying that one wishes to resign. 3. a resigned attitude or expression. [as prec.]

resigned /rɪˈzaɪnd/ *adj.* having resigned oneself; content to endure, showing patient acceptance of an unwelcome task or situation. —**resignedly** /-nɪdlɪ/ *adv.* [f. RESIGN]

resilient /rɪˈzɪlɪənt/ *adj.* 1. springing back to its original form after compression etc. 2. (of a person) readily recovering from shock or depression etc. —**resilience** *n.,* **resiliently** *adv.* [f. L *resilire* spring back (RE-², *salire* jump)]

resin /ˈrezɪn/ *n.* 1. a sticky substance secreted by many plants and trees, used in making varnish etc. 2. a similar synthetic substance, especially an organic compound made by polymerization and used as a plastic or in plastics. —*v.t.* to rub or treat with resin. —**resinous** *adj.* [f. L *resina*]

resist /rɪˈzɪst/ *v.t./i.* 1. to be undamaged or unaffected by; to stop the course of. 2. to refrain from accepting or yielding to (a pleasure or temptation etc.). 3. to oppose, to strive against, to try to impede; to refuse to comply (with). [f. OF or L *resistere* stop (RE-¹, stand)]

resistance /rɪˈzɪstəns/ *n.* 1. resisting, refusal to comply; the power to resist; ability to resist harsh or bad conditions. 2. an influence that hinders or stops something. 3. the property of failing to conduct electricity or heat etc.; the measure of this; a resistor. 4. (also **Resistance**) a secret organization resisting the authorities, especially in a conquered or enemy-occupied country. —**line of least resistance,** the easiest method or course. —**resistant** *adj.* [f. F f. L (as prec.)]

resistivity /rezɪsˈtɪvɪtɪ/ *n.* the power of a specified material to resist the passage of an electric current. [f. RESIST]

resistor /rɪˈzɪstə(r)/ *n.* a device having resistance to the passage of an electric current. [as prec.]

resit /ri:ˈsɪt/ *v.t.* (-**tt**-) to take (an examination) again, usually after failing.

resoluble /rɪˈzɒljʊb(ə)l/ *adj.* that can be resolved; analysable. [f. F or L (as RESOLVE)]

resolute /ˈrezəlu:t, -lju:t/ *adj.* showing great determination, not vacillating or shrinking. —**resolutely** *adv.,* **resoluteness** *n.* [as RESOLVE]

resolution /rezəˈlu:ʃ(ə)n, -ˈlju:-/ *n.* 1. the quality of being resolute, great determination. 2. a thing resolved on, an intention. 3. a formal expression of opinion agreed on by a committee or assembly. 4. the solving of a doubt, problem, or question. 5. separation into constituent parts; conversion into another form; causing musical discord to pass into concord; the smallest interval measurable by a scientific instrument. [as foll.]

resolve /rɪˈzɒlv/ *v.t./i.* 1. to decide firmly; to cause to do this. 2. (of an assembly or meeting) to pass a resolution. 3. to separate into constituent parts; to analyse mentally. 4. to solve or settle (a doubt, argument, etc.). 5. (*Mus.*) to convert (discord) or be converted into concord. —*n.* 1. a firm decision or intention. 2. determination. —**resolving power,** the ability of a lens etc. to distinguish very small or very close objects. [f. L *resolvere* (RE-¹, *solvere* solve)]

resolved *adj.* resolute, determined. [f. prec.]

resonant /ˈrezənənt/ *adj.* resounding, echoing. —**resonance** *n.* [f. F or L *resonare* (RE-¹, *sonare* sound)]

resonate /ˈrezəneɪt/ *v.i.* to produce or show resonance, to resound. [f. L (as prec.)]

resonator /ˈrezəneɪtə(r)/ *n.* 1. an instrument responding to a single note and used for detecting it in combinations. 2. an appliance for giving resonance to sounds or other vibrations. [f. prec.]

resort /rɪˈzɔ:t/ *n.* 1. a place frequented especially for holidays

or for a specified purpose. 2. a thing to which recourse is had, an expedient; recourse. 3. frequenting, or being frequented. —*v.i.* 1. to turn for aid or as an expedient. 2. to go in large numbers or as a frequent or customary practice. —**in the last resort,** when all else has failed, as a final attempt. [f. OF (RE-², *sortir* go out)]

resound /rɪˈzaʊnd/ *v.t./i.* 1. (of a place) to be filled with sound, to echo; to re-echo (a sound). 2. (of a voice, instrument, sound, etc.) to produce echoes; to go on sounding; to fill a place with sound. 3. (of a reputation etc.) to be much talked of, to produce a sensation.

resounding *adj.* 1. that resounds. 2. notable, decisive. —**resoundingly** *adv.* [f. prec.]

resource /rɪˈsɔ:s, -ˈzɔ:s/ *n.* 1. something to which one can turn for help or support or to achieve one's purpose. 2. (usu. in *pl.*) available assets, a stock that can be drawn on; (in *pl.*) a country's sources of wealth or means for defence. 3. ingenuity; quick wit. [f. F (RE-¹, L *surgere* rise)]

resourceful *adj.* good at devising expedients. —**resourcefully** *adv.,* **resourcefulness** *n.* [f. prec. + -FUL]

respect /rɪˈspekt/ *n.* 1. admiration felt or shown towards a person or thing that has good qualities or achievements; politeness arising from this. 2. heed, consideration for something. 3. an aspect or detail. 4. reference, relation. 5. (in *pl.*) polite greetings. —*v.t.* 1. to feel or show respect for. 2. to avoid interfering with or harming; to refrain from offending. —**in respect of,** as concerns, with reference to. **pay one's respects,** to make a polite visit. **pay one's last respects,** to show respect for a dead person, especially by attending the funeral. [f. OF or L *respectus* (*respicere* look back at)]

respectable /rɪˈspektəb(ə)l/ *adj.* 1. deserving respect. 2. of moderately good social standing; honest and decent; proper in appearance or behaviour. 3. of a moderately good standard or size etc.; not bringing disgrace or embarrassment. —**respectability** /-ˈbɪlɪtɪ/ *n.,* **respectably** *adv.* [f. prec.]

respecter *n.* one who respects. —**be no respecter of persons,** to treat everyone in the same way without being influenced by their importance etc. [f. RESPECT]

respectful *adj.* showing respect. —**respectfully** *adv.,* **respectfulness** *n.* [as prec. + -FUL]

respecting *prep.* in respect of, concerning. [f. RESPECT]

respective *adj.* concerning or appropriate to each of several individually; comparative. [f. F or L (as RESPECT)]

respectively *adv.* for each separately or in turn, and in the order mentioned. [f. prec.]

Respighi /reˈspi:gɪ/, Ottorino (1879–1936), Italian composer, string-player, and pianist. His highly popular suites *Fountains of Rome* (1914–16) and *Pines of Rome* (1923–4) reveal his gifts for bright evocative orchestration, which can be seen also in his arrangements of other composers' music. In his operas he reacted against the 'realism' of Puccini, but some of his most tender and exquisite work is to be found in his shorter vocal pieces.

respiration /respəˈreɪʃ(ə)n/ *n.* 1. breathing. 2. a plant's absorption of oxygen and emission of carbon dioxide. 3. the biochemical processes within living cells by which carbon compounds are broken down to obtain energy, usually involving as a final step the combining of carbon with atmospheric oxygen to form carbon dioxide. 4. a single inspiration and expiration, a breath. [F or f. L (as RESPIRE)]

respirator /ˈrespəreɪtə(r)/ *n.* 1. an apparatus worn over the mouth and nose to warm, filter, or purify inhaled air or to prevent inhalation of a poison, gas, etc. 2. an apparatus for maintaining artificial respiration (see IRON LUNG). [as RESPIRE]

respiratory /ˈrespəreɪtərɪ, rɪˈspaɪərət-/ *adj.* of respiration. [as foll.]

respire /rɪˈspaɪə(r)/ *v.t./i.* to breathe; (of plants) to perform the process of respiration. [f. OF or L *respirare* (RE-², *spirare* breathe)]

respite /ˈrespaɪt, -ɪt/ *n.* 1. an interval of rest or relief. 2. a delay permitted before an obligation must be discharged or a penalty suffered. —*v.t.* to grant or bring respite to. [f. OF *respit* f. L, = RESPECT]

resplendent /rɪˈsplendənt/ *adj.* brilliant with colour or decorations. —**resplendence** *n.,* **resplendency** *n.,* **resplendently** *adv.* [f. L *resplendēre* (RE-¹, *splendēre* glitter)]

respond /rɪˈspɒnd/ *v.i.* 1. to make an answer; to act or behave in an answering or corresponding manner. 2. to show sensitiveness to a stimulus or action etc., by behaviour or change. [f. L *respondēre* (RE-¹, *spondēre* pledge)]

respondent *n.* a defendant, especially in an appeal or divorce case. —*adj.* in the position of a defendant. [as prec.]

response /rɪ'spɒns/ *n.* **1.** an answer given in word or act. **2.** a feeling, movement, or change etc. caused by a stimulus or influence. **3.** any part of the liturgy said or sung in answer to a priest etc. [f. OF or L *responsum* (as RESPOND)]

responsiblity /rɪspɒnsɪ'bɪlɪti/ *n.* **1.** being responsible. **2.** something for which one is responsible. **3.** responsible quality. [f. foll.]

responsible /rɪ'spɒnsɪb(ə)l/ *adj.* **1.** legally or morally obliged to take care of something or to carry out a duty, liable to be blamed for loss or favour etc.; having to account for one's actions *to* a specified person. **2.** capable of rational conduct. **3.** evidently trustworthy, of good credit or repute. **4.** being the primary cause. **5.** involving important duties. —**responsibly** *adv.* [obs. F, f. L (as RESPOND)]

responsive /rɪ'spɒnsɪv/ *adj.* **1.** responding readily to a stimulus; responding warmly and favourably. **2.** answering; by way of answer. —**responsively** *adv.*, **responsiveness** *n.* [f. F or L (as RESPOND)]

respray /ri:'spreɪ/ *v.t.* to spray again, especially to change the colour of paint on a vehicle. —/'ri:spreɪ/ *n.* the act or process of respraying.

rest[1] *v.t./i.* **1.** to cease from work, exertion, or action etc.; to be still or asleep, especially in order to regain one's vigour; to cause or allow to do this. **2.** to place or be placed for support. **3.** to rely. **4.** (of a look etc.) to alight, to be directed. **5.** (of a subject) to be left without further investigation or discussion. **6.** to lie buried. **7.** (in *p.p.*) refreshed or invigorated by resting. —*n.* **1.** inactivity or sleep as a way of regaining vigour; a period of this. **2.** a support for holding or steadying something. **3.** (*Mus.*) an interval of silence between notes; a sign indicating this (ill. MUSICAL NOTATION). —**at rest**, not moving; no longer anxious; (of the dead) free from trouble or anxiety. **be resting**, (of an actor) to be out of work. **rest mass**, the mass of a body when at rest. **rest one's case**, to conclude presentation of it. **rest-cure** *n.* a prolonged period of rest (usually in bed) as medical treatment. **rest on one's oars**, to relax one's efforts. **rest-room** *n.* a lavatory and other facilities for employees or customers. [OE]

rest[2] *n.* **the rest**, the remaining part(s) or individuals, the others; the remaining quantity etc. —*v.i.* to remain in a specified state. —**rest with**, to be left in the hands or charge of. [f. OF *reste* (*rester* remain behind, f. L *restare*, RE-[1], *stare* stand)]

restaurant /'restərɒnt/ *n.* a place where meals can be bought and eaten. —**restaurant car**, a dining car. [F (*restaure* restore)]

restaurateur /restərə'tɜ:(r)/ *n.* a restaurant-keeper. [as prec.]

restful *adj.* inducing rest or a feeling of rest. —**restfully** *adv.*, **restfulness** *n.* [f. REST[1] + -FUL]

restitution /restɪ'tju:ʃ(ə)n/ *n.* **1.** restoration of a thing to its proper owner or to its original state. **2.** reparation for injury or damage. [f. OF or L *restituere* restore (RE-[2], *statuere* establish)]

restive /'restɪv/ *adj.* restless, resisting control because made impatient by delay or restraint. —**restively** *adv.*, **restiveness** *n.* [f. OF (as REST[2])]

restless *adj.* **1.** unable to rest or to be still; constantly in motion or fidgeting. **2.** without rest or sleep. —**restlessly** *adv.*, **restlessness** *n.* [f. REST[1] + -LESS]

restock /ri:'stɒk/ *v.t./i.* to stock again, to replenish one's stock.

restoration /restə'reɪʃ(ə)n/ *n.* **1.** restoring, being restored. **2.** a model, drawing, or reconstruction representing the supposed original form of an extinct animal, ruined building, etc. —**the Restoration,** the restoration of the Stuart monarchy in Britain with the return of Charles II to the throne in 1660. After the death of Oliver Cromwell in 1658, his son Richard proved incapable of maintaining the Protectorate, and, with no other viable form of government possible, a faction led by General Monck organized the King's return from exile. [as RESTORE]

restorative /rɪ'stɒrətɪv/ *adj.* that tends to restore health or strength. —*n.* a restorative food or medicine etc. [as foll.]

restore /rɪ'stɔ:(r)/ *v.t.* **1.** to bring back to its original state, e.g. by rebuilding or repairing. **2.** to bring back to good health or vigour. **3.** to put back in its former position; to reinstate; to give back to its original owner. **4.** to make a representation of the supposed orignal form of (an extinct animal, a ruin, etc.). —**restorer** *n.* [f. OF f. L *restaurare*]

restrain /rɪ'streɪn/ *v.t.* to hold back from movement or action; to keep under control or within bounds. [f. OF f. L *restringere* (RE-[1], *stringere* tie)]

restraint /rɪ'streɪnt/ *n.* **1.** restraining, being restrained. **2.** an agency or influence that restrains. **3.** self-control; avoidance of excess or exaggeration; reserve of manner. **4.** confinement, especially because of insanity. [as prec.]

restrict /rɪ'strɪkt/ *v.t.* to put a limit on, to subject to limitations. —**restriction** *n.* [f. L *restringere* (as RESTRAIN)]

restrictive /rɪ'strɪktɪv/ *adj.* restricting. —**restrictive practice,** an agreement or practice that limits efficiency or output in industry. [f. OF or L (as prec.)]

restructure /ri:'strʌktʃə(r)/ *v.t.* to give a new structure to; to rebuild, to rearrange.

result /rɪ'zʌlt/ *n.* **1.** that which is produced by an activity or operation, an effect, a consequence; a satisfactory outcome. **2.** a quantity or formula etc. obtained by calculation. **3.** a statement of the score, marks, or name of the winner in a sporting event, competition, or examination; (in *pl.*) a list of these. —*v.i.* **1.** to occur as a result. **2.** to have a specified result. [f. L *resultare* spring back (RE-[2], *saltare* frequent. of *salire* jump)]

resultant /rɪ'zʌltənt/ *adj.* occurring as a result, especially as the total outcome of more or less opposed forces. —*n.* a force etc. equivalent to two or more acting in different directions at the same point. [as prec.]

resume /rɪ'zju:m/ *v.t./i.* **1.** to begin again or go on after interruption, to begin to speak, work, or use again. **2.** to get or take again or back. [f. OF or L *resumere* (RE-[2], *sumere* take up)]

résumé /'rezju:meɪ/ *n.* a summary. [F (as prec.)]

resumption /rɪ'zʌmpʃ(ə)n/ *n.* resuming. —**resumptive** *adj.* [as RESUME]

resurface /ri:'sɜ:fɪs/ *v.t./i.* **1.** to put a new surface on. **2.** to return to the surface.

resurgent /rɪ'sɜ:dʒ(ə)nt/ *adj.* rising or arising again after defeat, destruction, or disappearance. —**resurgence** *n.* [f. L (RE-[2], *surgere* rise)]

resurrect /rezə'rekt/ *v.t.* **1.** to revive the practice or memory of. **2.** to take from the grave, to exhume. **3.** to dig up. [back-formation f. foll.]

resurrection /rezə'rekʃ(ə)n/ *n.* **1.** rising from the dead, especially (**Resurrection**) that of Christ. **2.** revival after disuse, inactivity, or decay. [f. OF f. L (as RESURGENT)]

resuscitate /rɪ'sʌsɪteɪt/ *v.t./i.* **1.** to revive from unconsciousness or apparent death. **2.** to revive (an old custom or institution etc.); to return or restore to vogue, vigour, or vividness. —**resuscitation** /-'teɪʃ(ə)n/ *n.* [f. L *resuscitare* (RE-[2], *suscitare* rouse)]

retable /rɪ'teɪb(ə)l/ *n.* a shelf, or frame enclosing decorative panels, above the back of an altar. [f. F f. L *retrotabulum* rear table (as RETRO-, TABLE)]

retail /'ri:teɪl/ *n.* the selling of things in small quantities to the general public and usually not for resale. —*adj.* of retail. —*adv.* by retail. —*v.t./i.* **1.** to sell or be sold by retail. **2.** /also rɪ:'teɪl/ to recount, to relate details of. —**retailer** *n.* [f. OF *retaille* piece cut off (as RE-[1], TAIL[2])]

retain /rɪ'teɪn/ *v.t.* **1.** to keep possession of, not to lose; to continue to have, practise, or recognize. **2.** to keep in one's memory. **3.** to keep in place, to hold fixed. **4.** to secure the services of (a person, especially a barrister) with a preliminary payment. [f. AF f. L *retinēre* (RE-[1], *tenēre* hold)]

retainer *n.* **1.** a person or thing that retains. **2.** a fee for retaining a barrister etc. **3.** (*hist.*) a dependant or follower of a person of rank. —**old retainer,** (*joc.*) a faithful old servant. [f. prec.]

retake /ri:'teɪk/ *v.t.* (*past* **retook**; *p.p.* **retaken**) to take again; to recapture.

retaliate /rɪ'tælɪeɪt/ *v.t./i.* to repay (an injury or insult etc.) in kind; to make a counter-attack. —**retaliation** /-'eɪʃ(ə)n/ *n.*, **retaliatory** /-ljətəri/ *adj.* [f. L *retaliare* (RE-[1], *talis* such)]

retard /rɪ'tɑ:d/ *v.t.* to make slow or late, to delay the progress or accomplishment of. —**retardation** /ri:tɑ:'deɪʃ(ə)n/ *n.* [f. F f. L *retardare* (RE-[1], *tardus* slow)]

retarded *adj.* backward in mental or physical development. [f. prec.]

retch *v.i.* to make a motion as in vomiting, esp. involuntarily and without effect. [OE, = spit (imit.)]

retell /ri:'tel/ *v.t.* (*past & p.p.* **retold** /-'təʊld/) to tell (a story etc.) again.

retention /rɪ'tenʃ(ə)n/ *n.* retaining, being retained. [f. OF or L (as RETAIN)]

retentive /rɪˈtentɪv/ adj. tending to retain; (of the memory) not forgetful. —**retentiveness** n. [as prec.]

rethink /riːˈθɪŋk/ v.t. (past & p.p. **rethought** /-ˈθɔːt/) to consider afresh, especially with a view to making changes. —/ˈriːθɪŋk/ n. rethinking, a reassessment.

reticence /ˈretɪsəns/ n. avoidance of expressing all one knows or feels or more than is necessary; disposition to silence, taciturnity. —**reticent** adj., **reticently** adv. [f. L reticentia (RE-¹, tacēre be silent)]

reticle /ˈretɪk(ə)l/ n. a network of fine threads or lines in the focal plane of an optical instrument to help accurate observation. [f. L reticulum dim. of rete net]

reticulate /rɪˈtɪkjʊleɪt/ v.t./i. to divide or be divided in fact or appearance into a network. —/rɪˈtɪkjʊlət/ adj. reticulated. [f. L (as RETICULE)]

reticulation /rɪtɪkjʊˈleɪʃ(ə)n/ n. (usu. in pl.) a netlike marking or arrangement. [as prec.]

reticule /ˈretɪkjuːl/ n. **1.** a reticle. **2.** a woman's bag of woven or other material, carried or worn to serve the purpose of a pocket (ill. DRESS). [f. F f. L (as foll.)]

reticulum /rɪˈtɪkjʊləm/ n. (pl. **-la**) **1.** a ruminant's second stomach. **2.** a netlike structure, a fine network in cytoplasm etc., a reticulated membrane etc. [L, dim. of rete net]

retina /ˈretɪnə/ n. (pl. **-as**) the layer at the back of the eyeball sensitive to light (ill. BODY 4). —**retinal** adj. [f. L (rete net)]

retinue /ˈretɪnjuː/ n. a body of attendants accompanying an important person. [f. OF (as RETAIN)]

retire /rɪˈtaɪə(r)/ v.t./i. **1.** to give up one's regular work because of advancing age; to cause (an employee) to do this. **2.** to withdraw; to go away; to retreat. **3.** to seek seclusion or shelter; to go to bed. **4.** (of a batsman at cricket) to terminate voluntarily or be compelled to suspend one's innings. —**retire into oneself,** to become uncommunicative or unsociable. —**retirement** n. [f. F retirer (RE-², tirer draw)]

retired adj. **1.** who has retired. **2.** withdrawn from society or observation, secluded. [f. prec.]

retiring adj. shy, avoiding society, fond of seclusion. [f. RETIRE]

retort¹ /rɪˈtɔːt/ n. an incisive, witty, or angry reply. —v.t./i. **1.** to say by way of retort; to make a retort. **2.** to repay (an insult or attack) in kind. [f. L retorquēre (RE-², torquēre twist)]

retort² /rɪˈtɔːt/ n. **1.** a vessel (usually of glass) with a long downward-bent neck, used in distilling liquids. **2.** a vessel for heating mercury for purification, coal to generate gas, or iron and carbon to make steel. [f. F f. L (as prec.)]

retouch /riːˈtʌtʃ/ v.t. to improve (a picture or photograph etc.) by fresh touches or alterations. [f. F retoucher (as RE-², TOUCH)]

retrace /rɪˈtreɪs/ v.t. to go back over; to trace back to the source or beginning; to recall the course of in memory. [f. F (as RE-², TRACE¹)]

retraceable adj. that may be retraced. [f. prec.]

retract /rɪˈtrækt/ v.t./i. **1.** to draw or be drawn back or in. **2.** to withdraw (a statement or opinion etc.); to refuse to keep (an agreement). —**retraction** n., **retractor** n. [f. OF or L retractare (RE-², tractare frequent. of trahere draw)]

retractable adj. that may be retracted. [f. prec.]

retractile /rɪˈtræktaɪl/ adj. (esp. of a bodily part) retractable. [f. RETRACT]

retread /riːˈtred/ v.t. to put a fresh tread on (a tyre). —/ˈriːtred/ n. a retreaded tyre.

retreat /rɪˈtriːt/ v.i. **1.** to withdraw after defeat or when faced with danger or difficulty; to go away to a place of shelter. **2.** to recede. —n. **1.** retreating; the military signal for this; a military bugle-call at sunset. **2.** withdrawal into privacy or security; a place of shelter or seclusion. **3.** a period of withdrawal from worldly activities for prayer and meditation. —**beat a retreat,** to retreat, to abandon an undertaking. [f. OF f. L retrahere (RE-², trahere draw)]

retrench /rɪˈtrentʃ/ v.t./i. to reduce the amount of (expense or its cause); to reduce one's expenditure or operations. —**retrenchment** n. [f. obs. F retrencher cut back] (as RE-¹, TRENCH)]

retrial /riːˈtraɪəl/ n. the retrying of a lawsuit. [f. RETRY]

retribution /retrɪˈbjuːʃ(ə)n/ n. a deserved punishment, requital, usually for evil done. —**retributive** /rɪˈtrɪbjʊtɪv/ adj. [f. L (RE-¹, tribuere assign)]

retrievable /rɪˈtriːvəb(ə)l/ adj. that may be retrieved. [f. foll.]

retrieve /rɪˈtriːv/ v.t. **1.** to regain possession of; to recover

by investigation or effort of memory. **2.** to find again (stored information etc.). **3.** (of a dog) to find and bring in (killed or wounded game etc.). **4.** to rescue, to restore to a flourishing state. **5.** to repair or set right (a loss or error etc.). —n. possiblity of recovery. —**retrieval** n. [f. OF (RE-², trover find)]

retriever n. a dog of a breed used for retrieving game. [f. prec.]

retro- /retrəʊ-/ prefix. **1.** backwards; back again; in return. **2.** behind. [f. L retro backwards]

retroactive /retrəʊˈæktɪv/ adj. having a retrospective effect. —**retroactively** adv.

retrograde /ˈretrəɡreɪd/ adj. **1.** directed backwards. **2.** reverting, especially to an inferior state; declining. **3.** reversed. —v.i. to move backwards, to recede; to decline, to revert. [f. L retrogradus (retrogradi move backwards)]

retrogress /retrəˈɡres/ v.i. to move backwards, to deteriorate. —**retrogression** /-eʃ(ə)n/ n., **retrogressive** adj. [f. RETRO-, after PROGRESS]

retro-rocket /ˈretrəʊrɒkɪt/ n. an auxiliary rocket for slowing down a spacecraft etc.

retrospect /ˈretrəspekt/ n. a survey of or reference to past time or events etc. —**in retrospect,** when one looks back on a past event or situation. [f. RETRO-, after PROSPECT]

retrospection /retrəˈspekʃ(ə)n/ n. looking back, especially on the past. [as prec.]

retrospective /retrəˈspektɪv/ adj. **1.** looking back on or dealing with the past. **2.** (of a statute etc.) applying to the past as well as the future. —**retrospectively** adv. [f. RETROSPECT]

retroussé /rəˈtruːseɪ/ adj. (of the nose) turned up at the tip. [F, p.p. of retrousser tuck up (as RE-², TRUSS)]

retroverted /ˈretrəvɜːtɪd/ adj. (esp. of the womb) turned backwards. [f. L (RETRO-, vertere turn)]

retry /riːˈtraɪ/ v.t. to try (a defendant or lawsuit) again.

retsina /retˈsiːnə/ n. a resin-flavoured Greek wine. [modern Gk]

return /rɪˈtɜːn/ v.t./i. **1.** to come or go back. **2.** to bring, give, put, or send back; to pay back or reciprocate, to give in response; to yield (a profit). **3.** to say in reply, to retort. **4.** to send (a ball) back in cricket or tennis etc. **5.** to state or describe officially, especially in answer to a writ or formal demand. **6.** (of a constituency) to elect as an MP etc. —n. **1.** coming or going back. **2.** bringing, giving, putting, or sending back; paying back. **3.** a thing given etc. back. **4.** a return ticket. **5.** (in sing. or pl.) the proceeds or profit of an undertaking; the coming in of these. **6.** a formal report compiled or submitted by order. —**by return (of post),** by the next available post in the return direction. **in return,** as an exchange or reciprocal action. **many happy returns (of the day),** a birthday or festival 'greeting. **return crease,** (in cricket) each of two lines joining the popping-crease and bowling-crease and extending beyond the latter (ill. SPORTS). In his delivery stride the bowler's back foot must land within the return crease. **returning officer,** an official conducting an election in a constituency and announcing the name of the person elected. **return ticket,** a ticket for the journey to a place and back to the starting point. [f. OF retorner (as RE-², TURN)]

retype /riːˈtaɪp/ v.t. to type again.

Reuben /ˈruːbən/ **1.** a Hebrew patriarch, eldest son of Jacob and Leah (Gen. 29: 32). **2.** the tribe of Israel traditionally descended from him.

reunion /riːˈjuːnjən/ n. **1.** reuniting, being reunited. **2.** a social gathering of people who were formerly associated. [f. F (as RE-², UNION)]

reunite /riːjuːˈnaɪt/ v.t./i. to unite again after separation.

Reuter /ˈrɔɪtə(r)/, Paul Julius, Baron von (1816-99), pioneer in the use of the telegraph for international news. In 1851 he established in London the headquarters of a press service (Reuters) which still operates throughout the world.

reuse /riːˈjuːz/ v.t. to use again. —/-ˈjuːs/ n. using or being used again.

rev n. (colloq.) a revolution (of an engine). —v.t./i. (**-vv-**) (colloq.) **1.** (of an engine) to cause the crankshaft to rotate. **2.** to rev up. —**rev up,** to cause (an engine) to run quickly, to increase the speed of its revolution. [abbr.]

Rev. abbr. Reverend.

revalue /riːˈvæljuː/ v.t. to reassess the value of; to give a new (higher) value to a currency etc. —**revaluation** /-ˈeɪʃ(ə)n/ n.

revamp /riːˈvæmp/ v.t. to renovate, to give a new appearance to.

Revd abbr. Reverend.

reveal /rɪˈviːl/ v.t. to make known (a secret etc.); to uncover and allow to be seen. —n. the internal side surface of an opening or recess, especially of the aperture of a door or window. [f. OF or L revelare (RE-¹, velum veil]

reveille /rɪˈvælɪ/ n. a military waking-signal. [f. F réveillez imper. of réveiller wake up]

revel /ˈrev(ə)l/ v.i. (-ll-) 1. to make merry, to be riotously festive. 2. to take keen delight. —n. (in sing. or pl.) revelling, merry-making; an instance of this. —**reveller** n. [f. OF reveler riot f. L, = REBEL]

revelation /revəˈleɪʃ(ə)n/ n. 1. the revealing of a fact. 2. the disclosing of knowledge, or knowledge disclosed, to man by a divine or supernatural agency; **the Revelation (of St John the Divine)**, the last book of the New Testament (see APOCALYPSE). 3. something revealed, a startling disclosure. [as REVEAL]

revelry /ˈrevəlrɪ/ n. revelling, revels. [f. REVEL]

revenge /rɪˈvendʒ/ n. 1. punishment or injury inflicted in return for what one has suffered; desire to inflict this; the act of retaliation. 2. opportunity to defeat in a return game an opponent who won an earlier game etc. —v.t. to avenge. —**be revenged** or **revenge oneself**, to obtain revenge. [f. OF f. L revindicare (as RE-¹, VINDICATE)]

revengeful adj. eager for revenge. —**revengefully** adv. [f. prec. + -FUL]

revenue /ˈrevənjuː, -vɪn-/ n. 1. income, especially of a large amount, from any source; (in pl.) items constituting this. 2. a State's annual income from which public expenses are met; the department of the Civil Service collecting this. [f. OF (revenir come back]

reverberate /rɪˈvɜːbəreɪt/ v.t./i. (of sound, light, or heat) to be returned or reflected; to return (a sound etc.) thus. —**reverberant** adj., **reverberation** /-ˈreɪʃ(ə)n/ n., **reverberative** adj. [f. L reverberare (RE-², verberare lash f. verbera scourge)]

Revere /rɪˈvɪə(r)/, Paul (1735–1818), American patriot, famous for his midnight ride from Charlestown to Lexington in April 1775 to warn fellow American revolutionaries of the approach of British troops from Boston.

revere /rɪˈvɪə(r)/ v.t. to feel deep respect or religious veneration for. [f. F or L reverēri (RE-¹, verēri fear)]

reverence /ˈrevərəns/ n. 1. revering, being revered. 2. a feeling of awe and respect or veneration. —v.t. to regard or treat with reverence. —**His, Your,** etc. **Reverence,** (archaic or joc.) a title used in addressing or referring to a clergyman. [f. OF f. L (as prec.)]

reverend /ˈrevərənd/ adj. deserving reverence. —**the Reverend,** the title of a clergyman (**Very Reverend,** of a dean; **Right Reverend,** of a bishop; **Most Reverend,** of an archbishop). **Reverend Mother,** the Mother Superior of a convent. [f. OF or L reverendus (as REVERE)]

reverent /ˈrevərənt/ adj. feeling or showing reverence. —**reverently** adv. [f. L reverens (as REVERE)]

reverential /revəˈrenʃ(ə)l/ adj. of the nature of, due to, or characterized by reverence. —**reverentially** adv. [as REVERENCE]

reverie /ˈrevərɪ/ n. a fit of abstracted musing, a day-dream; being engaged in this. [f. OF, = rejoicing, revelry (rever be delirious]

revers /rɪˈvɪə(r)/ n. (pl. same /-ɪəz/) a turned-back edge of a garment revealing the under-surface; the material on this surface. [F (as REVERSE)]

reversal /rɪˈvɜːs(ə)l/ n. reversing, being reversed. [f. foll]

reverse /rɪˈvɜːs/ v.t./i. 1. to turn the other way round or up or inside out. 2. to change to the opposite character or effect. 3. to travel or cause to travel backwards; to make (an engine etc.) work in the contrary direction. 4. to revoke or annul (a decree, act, etc.). —adj. 1. facing or moving in the opposite direction. 2. opposite in character or order. 3. upside down. —n. 1. the opposite; the opposite of the usual manner. 2. a piece of misfortune; a defeat in battle. 3. reverse gear or motion. 4. the reverse side; the back of a coin etc. bearing a secondary design; the verso of a leaf. —**reverse arms,** to hold rifles butt upwards. **reverse the charges,** to make the recipient of a telephone call responsible for payment. **reverse gear,** one used to make a vehicle etc. travel backwards. **the reverse of,** far from, not at all. **reversing light,** a white light at the rear of a vehicle, operated when a vehicle travels backwards.

—**reversely** adv. [f. OF f. L reversare (RE-², versare frequent. of vertere turn)]

reversible adj. that may be reversed. [f. REVERSE]

reversion /rɪˈvɜːʃ(ə)n/ n. 1. the legal right (esp. of an original owner or his or her heirs) to possess or succeed to property on the death of the present possessor. 2. return to a previous state, esp. (Biol.) to an earlier type. [as prec.]

revert /rɪˈvɜːt/ v.i. 1. to return to a former state, practice, subject, etc. 2. (of property, an office, etc.) to return by reversion. [as REVERSE]

revetment /rɪˈvetmənt/ n. a facing of masonry on a rampart or wall; a retaining wall. [f. revêtir f. L, as RE-², VEST)]

review /rɪˈvjuː/ n. 1. a general survey or assessment of a subject or thing; a survey of past events. 2. re-examination, reconsideration. 3. a display and formal inspection of troops etc. 4. a published report assessing the merits of a book or play etc.; a periodical publication with critical articles on current events, the arts, etc. —v.t. 1. to look back on. 2. to re-examine, to reconsider. 3. to hold a review of (troops etc.). 4. to write a review of (a book or play etc.). —**reviewer** n. [f. obs. F (revoir see again (RE-², voir see)]

revile /rɪˈvaɪl/ v.t. to criticize abusively. —**revilement** n. [f. OF reviler (as RE-¹, VILE)]

revise /rɪˈvaɪz/ v.t. 1. to re-examine and alter or correct. 2. to go over (work learnt or done) in preparation for an examination. —n. a printer's proof-sheet embodying corrections made in an earlier proof. —**Revised Version,** the revision made in 1870–84 of the Authorized Version of the Bible. **Revised Standard Version,** the revision made in 1946–57 of the American Standard Version (the latter was based on the English RV and published in 1901). [f. F or L revisere (RE-², visere intensive of vidēre see)]

revision /rɪˈvɪʒ(ə)n/ n. 1. revising, being revised. 2. a revised edition or form. [f. L (as prec.)]

revisit /riːˈvɪzɪt/ v.t. to pay another visit to (a place).

revisory /rɪˈvaɪzərɪ/ adj. of revision. [f. REVISE]

revival /rɪˈvaɪv(ə)l/ n. 1. reviving, being revived. 2. something brought back into use or fashion; a new production of an old play etc. 3. a reawakening of religious fervour; a campaign to promote this. [f. REVIVE]

revivalist n. one who promotes a religious revival. —**revivalism** n. [f. prec.]

revive /rɪˈvaɪv/ v.t./i. 1. to come or bring back to consciousness, life, or strength. 2. to come or bring back to existence, use, notice, etc. —**reviver** n. [f. OF or L revivere (RE-², vivere live)]

revivify /riːˈvɪvɪfaɪ/ v.t. to restore to life or strength or activity. —**revivification** /-fɪˈkeɪʃ(ə)n/ n. [f. F or L revivificare (as RE-², VIVIFY)]

revocable /ˈrevəkəb(ə)l/ adj. that may be revoked. [OF or f. L (as foll.)]

revoke /rɪˈvəʊk/ v.t./i. 1. to withdraw or cancel (a decree or promise etc.). 2. to fail to follow suit in a card-game when able to do so. —n. revoking in a card-game. [f. OF or L revocare (RE-², vocare call)]

revolt /rɪˈvəʊlt/ v.t./i. 1. to rise in rebellion; to be in a mood of protest or defiance. 2. to affect with strong disgust. 3. to feel or turn away in strong disgust. —n. 1. an act or state of rebelling or defying authority. 2. a sense of strong disgust. [f. F, ult. as REVOLVE]

revolting adj. disgusting. [f. prec.]

revolution /revəˈluːʃ(ə)n/ n. 1. the forcible overthrow of a government or social order, in favour of a new system; (in English history) the Glorious Revolution of 1688 (see GLORIOUS); (in American history) the overthrow of British supremacy (see AMERICAN REVOLUTION); (in French history) the French Revolution (see separate entry); (in Russian history) a series of revolutionary movements in Russia in 1917, beginning with a revolt of workers, peasants, and soldiers in March (February Old Style, whence 'February Revolution') and the formation of a provisional government, and culminating in the Bolshevik Revolution in November (October Old Style, whence 'October Revolution') which led to the establishment of the USSR. 2. any fundamental change or reversal of conditions or ideas. 3. revolving; a single completion of an orbit or rotation; the time taken for this; cyclic recurrence. [f. OF or L (as REVOLVE)]

revolutionary adj. 1. involving great change. 2. of or causing political revolution; **Revolutionary,** of the American or other specific revolution. —n. an instigator or supporter of political revolution. [f. prec.]

revolutionize v.t. to introduce fundamental change to. [f. REVOLUTION]

revolve /rɪˈvɒlv/ v.t./i. **1.** to turn or cause to turn round, especially on an axis. **2.** to move in orbit. **3.** to ponder (a problem etc.) in one's mind. —**revolving door,** a door with several radial partitions turning round a central axis. [f. L *revolvere* (RE-², *volvere* roll)]

revolver /rɪˈvɒlvə(r)/ n. a pistol with revolving chambers enabling several shots to be fired without reloading. The Colt revolver was patented in 1835. [f. prec.]

revue /rɪˈvjuː/ n. **1.** a theatrical entertainment consisting of a number of short items—songs, dances, sketches, monologues—which are normally unrelated. The players reappear in various items throughout the programme, and the material is usually topical. In France revues were seen in the 1820s, but it was not until the end of the 19th c. that they spread to England and America. The genre declined largely because satirical programmes on television were able to achieve a topicality impossible in the theatre. **2.** an elaborate musical show consisting of numerous unrelated scenes. [F, = review]

revulsion /rɪˈvʌlʃ(ə)n/ n. **1.** a feeling of strong disgust. **2.** a sudden violent change of feeling. [F or f. L (RE-², *vellere* pluck)]

reward /rɪˈwɔːd/ n. **1.** something given or received in return for what was done, or for a service or merit. **2.** a sum of money offered for the detection of a criminal, recovery of lost property, etc. —v.t. to give a reward to (a person) or for (a service etc.). [f. AF, = REGARD]

rewarding adj. (of an activity etc.) well worth doing. [f. prec.]

rewind /riːˈwaɪnd/ v.t. (*past* & *p.p.* **rewound**) to wind (a film or tape etc.) back to the beginning.

rewire /riːˈwaɪə(r)/ v.t. to renew the wiring of (a house etc.).

reword /riːˈwɜːd/ v.t. to change the wording of.

rewrite /riːˈraɪt/ v.t. (*past* **rewrote**; *p.p.* **rewritten**) to write again or differently. —/ˈriːraɪt/ n. a thing rewritten.

Rex n. the reigning king (in use as REGINA). [L, = king]

Reykjavik /ˈreɪkjəvɪk/ the capital of Iceland; pop. (1983) 87,106.

Reynolds /ˈren(ə)ldz/, Sir Joshua (1723–92), English painter and first President of the Royal Academy. He spent three years in Italy (1749–52) studying antique, Renaissance, and Baroque art, and laying the foundations for the philosophy of art that he would develop practically in his portraits and theoretically in the *Discourses* delivered at the Royal Academy between 1769 and 1790—the lofty calling of the artist and the intellectual nobility of painting. These concerns are evident in his formal portraits where the dignity of history painting adds an extra dimension of solemnity to the sitter (e.g. *Mrs Siddons as the Tragic Muse*). As President of the Royal Academy and a member of London's intellectual circle he did a great deal to advance the whole profession of painting in England.

Rf *symbol* rutherfordium.

Rh *symbol* rhodium.

r.h. *abbr.* right hand.

Rhadamanthus /rædəˈmænθəs/ (*Gk myth.*) son of Zeus and Europa, and brother of Minos. He did not die but went to Elysium where he is represented as a ruler and judge of the dead, renowned for his justice.

rhapsodize /ˈræpsədaɪz/ v.i. to utter or write rhapsodies. [f. foll.]

rhapsody /ˈræpsədɪ/ n. **1.** an ecstatic spoken or written statement. **2.** a romantic musical composition in an irregular form. —**rhapsodic** /-ˈsɒdɪk/ adj., **rhapsodical** /-ˈsɒdɪk(ə)l/ adj. [f. Gk *rhapsōidos* (*rhaptō* stitch, *ōdē* song)]

Rhea /ˈriːə/ (*Gk myth.*) one of the Titans, wife of Cronus and mother of Zeus, Demeter, Poseidon, and Hades.

Rheims var. of REIMS.

Rhenish /ˈriːnɪʃ, ˈren-/ adj. (*archaic*) of the Rhine or neighbouring regions. [f. AF f. L (*Rhenus* Rhine)]

rhenium /ˈriːnɪəm/ n. a rare hard heavy metallic element, symbol Re, atomic number 75, is not found uncombined in nature. The metal and its alloys have a number of specialized uses. [f. L *Rhenus* Rhine]

rhesus /ˈriːsəs/ n. a small Indian monkey (*Macaca mulatta*). —**rhesus factor,** an antigen occurring in the red blood cells of most persons and some animals (first described by Landsteiner in 1940). **rhesus negative,** not having this factor. **rhesus positive,** having this factor. [f. *Rhesus* mythical king of Thrace (the use of the name is arbitrary)]

rhetoric /ˈretərɪk/ n. **1.** the art of speaking or writing impressively. **2.** language used for its impressive sound (often with an implication of insincerity, exaggeration, etc.). [f. OF f. L f. Gk (*rhētōr* orator)]

rhetorical /rɪˈtɒrɪk(ə)l/ adj. expressed with a view to impressive effect; the nature of rhetoric. —**rhetorical question,** a question asked not for information but to produce an effect (e.g. *who cares?*). —**rhetorically** adv. [f. L f. Gk (as prec.)]

rheumatic /ruːˈmætɪk/ adj. of, caused by, or suffering from rheumatism. —n. (in *pl.*, *colloq.*) rheumatism. —**rheumatic fever,** a serious form of rheumatism with fever, especially in children. —**rheumatically** adv., **rheumaticky** adj. [f. OF or L f. Gk (*rheuma* watery secretion)]

rheumatism /ˈruːmətɪz(ə)m/ n. any of several diseases causing pain in the joints, muscles, or fibrous tissue, especially rheumatoid arthritis. [as prec.]

rheumatoid /ˈruːmətɔɪd/ adj. having the character of rheumatism. —**rheumatoid arthritis,** a chronic progressive disease causing inflammation and stiffening of the joints. [f. prec.]

rheumatology /ruːməˈtɒlədʒɪ/ n. the study of rheumatic diseases. —**rheumatologist** n. [f. RHEUMATISM + -LOGY]

Rhine /raɪn/ a river of Western Europe flowing from the Swiss Alps to the North Sea in the Netherlands. Most of its course (1,320 km, 820 miles) lies within West Germany and it forms part of an important inland waterway network.

Rhineland /ˈraɪnlænd/ the region of West Germany through which the Rhine flows, especially the part to the west of the river. The area was demilitarized as part of the Versailles Treaty in 1919 but was reoccupied by Hitler in 1936.

rhinestone /ˈraɪnstəʊn/ n. an imitation diamond. [f. RHINE + STONE]

rhino /ˈraɪnəʊ/ n. (*pl.* same or **-os**) (*colloq.*) a rhinoceros. [abbr.]

rhizome /ˈraɪzəʊm/ n. a rootlike stem growing along or under the ground and emitting both roots and shoots (ill. PLANTS). [f. Gk *rhizōma* (*rhizoō* take root)]

rho /rəʊ/ n. the seventeenth letter of the Greek alphabet, = rh. [Gk]

Rhode Island /rəʊd/ a State in the north-eastern USA, on the Atlantic coast, settled from England in the 17th c. It was one of the original 13 States of the USA; capital, Providence.

Rhodes¹ /rəʊdz/ the largest of the Dodecanese Islands in the SE Aegean, off the Turkish coast, acquired by Italy from Turkey in 1912 and returned to Greece in 1947; pop. (1971) 66,606.

Rhodes² /rəʊdz/, Cecil John (1853–1902), South African statesman. Born in Britain, Rhodes went to South Africa for reasons of health and made a huge fortune in diamond mining. A convinced imperialist, he was instrumental in extending British territory in South Africa and in the development of Rhodesia, and served as Premier of the Cape Colony from 1890 until forced to resign in 1896 as a result of implication in the Jameson Raid. Much of his fortune was used to set up the system of Rhodes Scholarships to allow students from the Empire, the United States, and Germany to study at Oxford University.

Rhodesia /rəʊˈdiːʃə/ **1.** the former name of a large area of southern Africa south of Zaïre, divided into Northern Rhodesia and Southern Rhodesia. The region was developed by Sir Cecil Rhodes and the British South Africa Company, which administered it until Southern Rhodesia became a self-governing British colony in 1923 and Northern Rhodesia a British protectorate in 1924. From 1953 to 1963 Northern and Southern Rhodesia were united with Nyasaland (now Malawi) to form the Federation of Rhodesia and Nyasaland. **2.** the name adopted by Southern Rhodesia when Northern Rhodesia left the Federation in 1963 to become the independent republic of Zambia. For its subsequent history see ZIMBABWE. —**Rhodesian** adj. & n.

rhodium /ˈrəʊdɪəm/ n. a hard white metallic element, symbol Rh, atomic number 45, usually found associated with platinum. It is chiefly used in alloys with platinum, where it increases hardness, but the pure metal is used in electroplating for decorative purposes and to form reflecting surfaces. [f. Gk *rhodon* rose (from colour of solution of its salts)]

rhododendron /rəʊdəˈdendrən/ n. an evergreen shrub of the genus *Rhododendron*, with large clusters of trumpet-shaped flowers. [L, = oleander, f. Gk (*rhodon* rose, *dendron* tree)]

rhomboid /'rɒmbɔɪd/ *adj.* like a rhombus. —*n.* a quadrilateral of which only the opposite sides and angles are equal. —**rhomboidal** *adj.* [f. F or L f. Gk (as foll.)]

rhombus /'rɒmbəs/ *n.* (*pl.* **-uses**) an oblique equilateral parallelogram, such as the diamond on playing-cards (ill. SHAPES). [L f. Gk *rhombos*]

Rhône /rəʊn/ a river rising in the Swiss Alps and flowing west and south 812 km (505 miles) through France to the Mediterranean Sea. The cities of Geneva, Lyons, and Avignon lie along its course.

rhubarb /'ru:bɑ:b/ *n.* **1.** a garden plant of the genus *Rheum* with fleshy leaf-stalks used like fruit; these stalks. **2.** the root of a Chinese plant of the genus *Rheum;* a purgative made from this. The earliest use of rhubarb was medicinal; the dried rootstock, principally of Chinese species imported via Russia and the Levant, was employed as a purgative. Culinary use of the leaf-stalks (the plants now used are of hybrid origin) dates only from the mid-18th c., and it did not become popular until the introduction of forced rhubarb in the early 19th c. [f. OF f. L *rhabarbarum* foreign rha (*rha* f. Gk, perh. f. *Rha* ancient name of river Volga)]

rhumb /rʌm/ *n.* **1.** any of the 32 points of the compass. **2.** the angle between the directions of any two successive compass-points. **3.** a rhumb-line. —**rhumb-line** *n.* a line cutting all meridians at the same angle; the line followed by a ship sailing according to a fixed compass-bearing. [f. F prob. f. Du. *ruim* room, assoc. with L *rhombus*]

rhyme /raɪm/ *n.* **1.** identity of sound between the endings of words or of verse-lines. **2.** (in *sing.* or *pl.*) a verse having rhymes. **3.** the use of rhyme. **4.** a word providing a rhyme to another. —*v.t./i.* **1.** to form a rhyme; to have rhymes. **2.** to write rhymes; to put or make (a story etc.) into rhyme. **3.** to treat (a word) as rhyming with another. —**rhyming slang,** slang which replaces words by words or phrases that rhyme with them (e.g. *stairs* by *apples and pears*). **without rhyme or reason,** lacking discernible sense or logic. [f. OF *rime* f. L f. Gk (as RHYTHM)]

rhymester /'raɪmstə(r)/ *n.* a writer of (esp. simple) rhymes. [f. prec.]

rhythm /'rɪð(ə)m/ *n.* **1.** the pattern produced by various relations of emphasis and duration of notes in music or by long and short or accented and unaccented syllables; the aspect of composition concerned with this. **2.** a movement with a regular succession of strong and weak elements. **3.** a regularly recurring sequence of events. —**rhythm and blues,** popular music with blues themes and a strong rhythm. **rhythm method,** contraception by avoiding sexual intercourse near the time of ovulation (which recurs regularly). —**rhythmic** *adj.*, **rhythmical** *adj.*, **rhythmically** *adv.* [f. F or L f. Gk *rhuthmos* (cf. *rheō* flow)]

rhyton /'raɪt(ə)n/ *n.* an ancient Greek form of drinking-cup, shaped like an animal's head and with a hole at the bottom through which the wine ran. [f. Gk (*rheō* flow)]

Rialto /rɪ'æltəʊ/ an island and district of Venice, containing the old mercantile quarter. The Rialto Bridge, completed in 1591, crosses the Grand Canal in a single span between Rialto and San Marco islands.

rib *n.* **1.** each of the bones articulated in pairs to the spine and curving round to protect the thoracic cavity and its organs (ill. BODY¹). **2.** a joint of meat from this part of an animal. **3.** a ridge or long raised piece often of stronger or thicker material across a surface or through a structure, serving to support or strengthen; any of the hinged rods forming the framework of an umbrella. **4.** a combination of plain and purl stitches in knitting, producing a ribbed somewhat elastic fabric. —*v.t.* (**-bb-**) **1.** to provide with ribs. **2.** to knit as rib. **3.** (*colloq.*) to tease. —**rib-cage** *n.* the framework of ribs round the thoracic cavity. [OE]

ribald /'rɪbəld/ *adj.* (of language or its user) coarsely or disrespectfully humorous. [orig. = low-born retainer, f. OF *ribault* (*riber* pursue licentious pleasures)]

ribaldry /'rɪbəldrɪ/ *n.* ribald talk. [f. prec.]

riband /'rɪbənd/ *n.* a ribbon. [f. OF *riban*]

ribbed /rɪbd/ *adj.* **1.** having ribs or riblike markings. **2.** knitted in rib. [f. RIB]

ribbon /'rɪbən/ *n.* **1.** a narrow strip or band of silk or other ornamental material, used for decoration or for tying something; material in this form. **2.** a ribbon of a special colour or pattern worn to indicate some honour or membership of a sports team etc. **3.** a long narrow strip of anything, e.g. inked material used in a typewriter. **4.** (in *pl.*) ragged strips. —**ribbon development,** the building of houses in a narrow strip along a road outwards from a town or village. [var. of RIBAND]

Ribera /rɪ'beərə/, José (Jusepe) de (1591–1652), Spanish painter and etcher. In 1616 he settled in Naples (at that time a Spanish possession) where because of his small stature he gained the sobriquet Il Spagnoletto (the little Spaniard). His early paintings, chiefly of religious subjects and scenes of everyday life, show dramatic chiaroscuro effects, and his *penchant* for martyrdoms and the realistic depiction of torture prompted Byron's line 'Il Spagnoletto tainted his brush with all the blood of all the Sainted'; his later paintings show a softer style and have a spiritual quality.

ribonucleic acid /raɪbəʊnju:'kli:ɪk/ a nucleic acid yielding ribose on hydrolysis (see RNA). [f. *ribose* a sugar + NUCLEIC]

rice *n.* a kind of grass (*Oryza sativa*) grown in marshes, especially in Asia, producing seeds that are used as food; these seeds. —**rice-paper** *n.* paper made from the pith of an oriental tree (*Tetrapanax papyriferum*) and used for painting and in cookery. [f. OF *ris* f. It. f. L f. Gk *oruza*]

rich *adj.* **1.** having much wealth. **2.** having a large supply of something; having great natural resources; (of soil) full of nutrients, fertile. **3.** splendid, made of costly materials, elaborate. **4.** producing or produced abundantly. **5.** (of food or diet) containing a large proportion of fat, oil, eggs, spice, etc. **6.** (of a mixture in an internal-combustion engine) containing a high proportion of fuel. **7.** (of colour, sound, or smell) pleasantly deep or strong. **8.** (of an incident or assertion etc.) highly amusing or ludicrous. —**richness** *n.* [OE & f. OF *riche*]

Richard /'rɪtʃəd/ the name of three kings of England:

Richard I (1157–99), son of Henry II, reigned 1189–99. Richard's military exploits won him the nickname 'Coeur de Lion' (Lionheart) and made him a medieval legend, but he was absent from his kingdom too frequently to govern effectively. In his youth he twice rebelled against his father and soon after succeeding him he left to take part in the Third Crusade. He defeated Saladin at Arsuf, but failed to capture Jerusalem, and was captured on his way home by Duke Leopold of Austria. Held captive at the behest of the Emperor Henry VI, Richard was released in 1194 only after the payment of a huge ransom. After staying in England for little more than a matter of weeks he embarked on a campaign against Philip II Augustus of France, eventually dying from wounds received at the siege of the castle of Châlus.

Richard II (1367–1400), son of the Black Prince, reigned 1377–99. Though Richard behaved bravely when still a minor during the Peasants' Revolt, he proved a weak king, heavily dependent on favourites and on his uncle John of Gaunt. In 1386–8 noble opponents of his administration, known as the Lords Appellant, successfully removed many of the King's confidants. Ten years later Richard exacted revenge, executing or banishing most of his former opponents, but when he confiscated John of Gaunt's estate after the latter's death, the dispossessed heir returned from exile to overthrow Richard and reign in his place as Henry IV. Richard died in prison in Pontefract Castle, apparently of starvation.

Richard III (1452–85), brother of Edward IV, reigned 1483–5. He succeeded his brother after the latter's heir Edward V had been declared (on dubious grounds) to be illegitimate. Historical opinion on the popular picture of Richard as a bloodthirsty usurper is still divided; what is certain is that, after suppressing several plots in the early months of his reign, he ruled with some success for a brief period before being defeated and killed at Bosworth in 1485 by Henry Tudor, who then took the throne as Henry VII.

Richards /'rɪtʃədz/, Sir Gordon (1904–), English jockey, who between 1925 and 1953 was champion jockey 26 times.

Richardson /'rɪtʃəds(ə)n/, Samuel (1689–1761), English novelist, of humble background, who became a prosperous printer. A request by two booksellers for a series of model letters on the problems and concerns of everyday life resulted in his first novel *Pamela* (1740–1) which, in spite of his rival Fielding's stinging parodies, was a successful and pioneering novel in epistolary form. This technique was further developed in his masterpiece, *Clarissa Harlowe* (1747–8), about a heroine of rare beauty and virtue, and in his final novel, *Sir Charles Grandison* (1754), an attempted portrayal of the ideal Christian gentleman. In these works he explored, with psychological intensity, moral issues in a detailed social context, and greatly influenced the development of future fiction.

Richelieu /ˈriːʃljɜː/ Armand Jean du Plessis, (1585-1642), French Cardinal and statesman. Chief minister of Louis XIII from 1624 until his death in 1642, Richelieu completely dominated French government, establishing a strong central government at home, and pursuing an aggressive foreign policy, particularly against Spain, which made France indisputably the strongest nation in Europe.

riches /ˈrɪtʃɪz/ n.pl. a great quantity of money, property, valuable possessions, natural resources, etc. [as RICH]

richly adv. 1. in a rich way. 2. fully, thoroughly. [f. RICH]

Richter /ˈrɪktə(r), ˈrɪx-/, Johann Friedrich, see JEAN PAUL.

Richter scale /ˈrɪktə(r), ˈrɪx-/ a scale for stating the strength of an earthquake. [f. C. F. Richter, American seismologist (1900-85)]

rick¹ n. a stack of hay etc. [OE]

rick² v.t. to sprain or strain slightly. —n. a slight sprain or strain. [f. MLG wricken]

rickets /ˈrɪkɪts/ n. (as sing. or pl.) a children's deficiency disease with softening of the bones. —**rickettsial** /rɪˈketsɪəl/ adj. [orig. unkn.]

rickety /ˈrɪkɪtɪ/ adj. 1. shaky, weak-jointed, insecure. 2. suffering from rickets. —**ricketiness** n. [f. prec.]

rickrack var. of RICRAC.

rickshaw /ˈrɪkʃɔː/ n. (also **ricksha**) a light two-wheeled hooded vehicle drawn by one or more persons. [abbr. of jinricksha(w) f. Jap. (jin person, riki power, sha vehicle)]

ricochet /ˈrɪkəʃeɪ, -ʃet/ v.i. (past **ricocheted** /-eɪd/; partic. **ricocheting** /-eɪɪŋ/) to rebound from a surface as a missile does when it strikes with a glancing blow. —n. a rebound of this kind; a hit made after it. [F; orig. unkn.]

ricrac /ˈrɪkræk/ n. a zigzag braided trimming for garments. [redupl. of RACK¹]

rid v.t. (-dd-; past & p.p. rid) to free from something unpleasant or unwanted. —**get rid of**, to cause to go away; (colloq.) to succeed in selling. [orig. = clear (land etc.), f. ON]

riddance /ˈrɪd(ə)ns/ n. ridding. —**good riddance,** welcome deliverance from an unwanted person or thing. [f. RID]

riddel /ˈrɪd(ə)l/ n. an altar-curtain (ill. VESTMENTS). [f. OF (cf. F. rideau)]

ridden p.p. of RIDE.

riddle¹ n. 1. a question or statement testing ingenuity in finding its answer or meaning. 2. a puzzling fact, thing, or person. —v.i. to speak in or propound riddles. [OE, rel. to READ]

riddle² v.t. 1. to pierce with many holes. 2. (in p.p.) thoroughly permeated (with faults etc.). 3. to pass through a riddle. —n. a coarse sieve for gravel or cinders etc. [OE]

ride v.t./i. (past rode; p.p. ridden /ˈrɪd(ə)n/) 1. to sit on and control or be carried by (a horse etc.). 2. to travel on horseback, a bicycle, train, or other conveyance; to travel thus over or through. 3. to be carried on or conveyed by, to be supported on; to float or seem to float. 4. to yield to (a blow) so as to reduce its impact. 5. to give a ride to. —n. 1. a spell of riding; a journey on a horse etc. or in a vehicle. 2. a track for riding on, especially through woods. 3. a roundabout or other device on which people ride at a fairground etc. 4. the quality of sensations felt when riding. —**let a thing ride**, to leave it undisturbed. **ride down**, to overtake or trample on horseback. **ride out**, to come safely through (a storm etc., or a danger or difficulty). **ride up**, (of a garment) to work upwards when worn. **riding-light** n. a light shown by a ship at anchor. **take for a ride**, (slang) to hoax or deceive. [OE]

rider n. 1. one who rides a horse or bicycle etc. 2. an additional clause amending or supplementing a document, a corollary; a recommendation etc. added to a verdict; (Math.) a problem arising as a corollary of a theorem etc. [f. RIDE]

riderless adj. without a rider. [f. prec. + -LESS]

ridge /rɪdʒ/ n. 1. the line of junction of two surfaces sloping upwards towards each other; a long narrow hill-top, a mountain range, a watershed; any narrow elevation across a surface. 2. an elongated region of high barometric pressure. 3. a raised strip of arable land, usually one of a set separated by furrows. —**ridge-piece** n. a beam along the ridge of a roof (ill. CHURCH). **ridge-pole** n. a horizontal pole of a long tent. —**ridgy** adj. [OE]

ridgeway /ˈrɪdʒweɪ/ n. a road along a ridge, sometimes dating back to medieval or perhaps even prehistoric times.

ridicule /ˈrɪdɪkjuːl/ n. making or being made an object of

derision. —v.t. to make fun of, to subject to ridicule. [F or f. L ridiculum (ridēre laugh)]

ridiculous /rɪˈdɪkjʊləs/ adj. 1. deserving to be laughed at, especially in a malicious or scornful way. 2. not worth serious consideration, preposterous. —**ridiculously** adv. [as prec. or f. L ridiculosus]

riding /ˈraɪdɪŋ/ n. a former administrative division of Yorkshire (East, North, and West Riding). [OE f. ON, = third part]

Ridley /ˈrɪdlɪ/, Nicholas (c.1500-55), English Protestant martyr. One of Archbishop Cranmer's chaplains, he rose to become successively Bishop of Rochester and of London and one of the leaders of the Protestant Reformation in the reign of Edward VI. He opposed the Catholic policies of Edward's sister and successor Mary I and was imprisoned and eventually burnt for heresy at Oxford.

Riemann /ˈriːmən/, (Georg Friedrich) Bernhard (1826-66), German mathematician whose achievements were characterized by their outstandingly imaginative character. Riemann surfaces are the modifications of the complex number plane required for a proper understanding of algebraic and other many-valued functions; Riemannian geometry is the study of intrinsic properties of curved space, now fundamental to the relativistic description of our universe. His name is attached to several other concepts and theorems in mathematics, of which the most famous is an assertion about the complex numbers which are roots of a certain transcendental equation. This assertion, known as the Riemann hypothesis, has many deep implications, particularly about the distribution of prime numbers, but after more than 100 years it remains one of the greatest of the unsolved problems of mathematics.

Riesling /ˈriːslɪŋ/ n. a kind of dry white wine made from a European variety of grape; this grape. [G]

rife predic. adj. 1. of common occurrence, widespread. 2. well provided, full. [OE prob. f. ON, = acceptable]

riffle v.t./i. to turn (pages) in quick succession; to leaf quickly (through a book); to thumb (a block of paper or pack of cards etc.), releasing the edges in (rapid) sucession. [perh. var. of RUFFLE]

riff-raff /ˈrɪfræf/ n. a rabble, disreputable or undesirable persons. [f. rif et raf]

rifle /ˈraɪf(ə)l/ n. 1. a gun with a long rifled barrel, especially one fired from shoulder level. 2. (in pl.) riflemen. —v.t. 1. to search and rob. 2. to make spiral grooves in (a gun or its barrel or bore) to make the bullet spin and so travel more accurately when fired. [f. OF rifler scratch, plunder, f. ODu.]

rifleman n. (pl. -men) a soldier armed with a rifle.

rifling /ˈraɪflɪŋ/ n. the arrangement of grooves in a rifle. [f. RIFLE]

rift n. 1. a crack or split in an object. 2. a cleft in the earth or a rock. 3. a disagreement, a breach in friendly relations. —**rift-valley** n. a steep-sided valley formed by subsidence of the earth's crust (ill. GEOLOGY). [Scand., rel. to RIVEN]

rig¹ v.t. (-gg-) 1. to provide (a ship) with spars and ropes etc. 2. (often with out or up) to provide with clothes or other equipment. 3. to set up hastily or as a makeshift. 4. to assemble and adjust the parts of (an aircraft). —n. 1. the arrangement of a ship's masts and sails etc. 2. equipment for a special purpose, e.g. a radio transmitter. 3. an oil-rig. —**rig-out** n. (colloq.) an outfit of clothes. [perh. Scand. (cf. Norw. rigga bind)]

rig² v.t. (-gg-) to manage or conduct fraudulently. —**rig the market**, to cause an artificial rise or fall in prices. [orig. unkn.]

Rigel /ˈraɪg(ə)l/ the seventh brightest star in the sky, found in the constellation Orion. Its name is derived from an Arabic phrase meaning 'left leg of the Great One'. Blue in colour, it is a supergiant star nearly sixty thousand times as luminous as our sun.

rigging n. a ship's spars and ropes etc. used to support masts and set or work the sails (ill. SAILING-SHIPS). [f. RIG¹]

right /raɪt/ adj. 1. (of conduct etc.) morally good, in accordance with justice, equity, or duty. 2. proper, correct, true; preferable, most suitable; (of a side of a fabric) meant for show or use. 3. in a good or normal condition; sane; well-advised, not mistaken. 4. on or towards the right-hand side. 5. politically to the right (see sense 4 below). 6. (archaic or colloq.) real, properly so called. —n. 1. what is just; a fair claim or treatment. 2. being entitled to a privilege or immunity; a thing one is entitled to. 3. the right-hand part, region, or direction; the right hand; a blow with this; (in marching) the right foot. **4.** (often **Right**) the right wing of a political party or other group; conservatives collectively. —*v.t.* **1.** to restore to a proper, correct, or vertical position. **2.** to set right, to make amends or take vengeance for; to vindicate, to justify; to rehabilitate. **3.** to correct. —*adv.* **1.** straight. **2.** (*colloq.*) immediately. **3.** all the way, completely. **4.** exactly, quite. **5.** on or to the right-hand side. **6.** rightly. **7.** all right; what you say is correct; I agree. **8.** (*archaic*) very, to the full. —**by right(s)**, if right were done. **in one's own right**, through one's own position or effort etc. **in the right**, having justice or truth on one's side. **on the right side of**, in the favour of (a person); somewhat less than (a stated age). **put** *or* **set to rights**, to arrange in proper order. **right and left**, on all sides. **right angle**, an angle of 90°, made by lines meeting with equal angles on either side (**at right angles**, placed to form a right angle). **right ascension**, the celestial co-ordinate corresponding to longitude, measured eastwards on the celestial sphere from the point known as the First Point of Aries, where the ecliptic intersects the celestial equator. **right bank**, the bank of a river on the right as one faces downstream. **right hand**, the hand that in most people is used more than the left, on the side opposite the left hand; a right-hand man. **right-hand** *adj.* of, on, or towards this side of a person or the corresponding side of a thing. **right-handed** *adj.* using the right hand by preference as more serviceable; made by or for the right hand; turning to the right. **right-hander** *n.* a right-handed person or blow. **right-hand man**, an indispensable or chief assistant. **Right Honourable**, the title of earls, viscounts, barons, Privy Counsellors, and certain others. **right-minded** *adj.* having proper or honest principles. **right of way**, the right to pass over another's ground; a path that is subject to such a right; the right to proceed while another vehicle etc. must wait. **right-oh!** (*colloq.*) an expression of agreement to what is suggested. **Right Reverend**, see REVEREND. **rights issue**, an issue of shares offered by a company at a special price to its existing shareholders. **rights of man**, = human rights (see HUMAN). The phrase is associated with the declaration of the rights of man and of the citizen adopted by the French National Assembly in 1789 and serving as a preface to the French Constitution of 1791. Other declarations to the same effect include the American Declaration of Independence. **right wing**, the right-hand side of a football team etc. on the field; a player in this position; the supporters of more conservative or traditional policies than others in their group. **right-winger** *n.* a person on the right wing. — **rightly** *adv.*, **rightness** *n.* [OE]

righteous /'raɪtʃəs/ *adj.* doing what is morally right; making a show of this; morally justifiable. —**righteously** *adv.*, **righteousness** *n.* [OE (as prec. + -WISE), after *bounteous* etc.]

rightful *adj.* in accordance with what is just, proper, or legal; (of property etc.) to which one is entitled. —**rightfully** *adv.* [OE (as RIGHT, -FUL)]

rightism *n.* political conservatism. —**rightist** *n.* [f. RIGHT]

rightward /'raɪtwəd/ *adv.* (also **rightwards**) towards the right. —*adj.* going towards or facing the right. [f. RIGHT + -WARD]

rigid /'rɪdʒɪd/ *adj.* **1.** not flexible, that cannot be bent. **2.** inflexible, strict. —**rigidity** /-'dʒɪdɪtɪ/ *n.*, **rigidly** *adv.* [f. F or L *rigidus* (as RIGOR)]

rigmarole /'rɪgmərəʊl/ *n.* **1.** a rambling statement; meaningless talk. **2.** a lengthy procedure. [alt. f. obs. *ragman roll* = catalogue]

rigor /'raɪɡɔː(r), 'rɪɡə(r)/ *n.* a sudden chill with shivering. —**rigor mortis**, stiffening of the body after death. [f. L (*rigēre* be stiff)]

rigour /'rɪɡə(r)/ *n.* **1.** severity, strictness. **2.** (in *pl.*) harshness of weather or conditions. **3.** logical exactitude. —**rigorous** *adj.*, **rigorously** *adv.* [f. OF F L, = prec.]

Rig-Veda /rɪg'veɪdə, -'viː-/ *n.* a collection of hymns in Old Sanskrit used in the Vedic religion by the priest in charge of invoking the gods at the ritual sacrifice. Composed in the 2nd millenium BC, this is the oldest and most important of the four Vedas. [f. Skr. (*ric* praise, *vēda* knowledge)]

Rijksmuseum /'raɪksmʉzeɪəm/ the national gallery of Holland, in Amsterdam. Established in the late 19th c. and developed from the collection of the House of Orange, it now contains the most representative collection of Dutch art in the world.

rile *v.t. colloq.* to anger, to irritate. [var. of *roil* make turbid, perh. f. OF, = mix mortar, f. L *regulare*]

Riley /'raɪlɪ/, Bridget Louise (1931-), English painter, whose work belongs to the category known as op art. Her earlier works are in black and white (e.g. *Movement in Squares*, 1961; *Fall*, 1963), and through graded greys she advanced to colour compositions which arrived at similar effects.

rill *n.* a small stream. [cf. LG *ril(le)*]

rim *n.* a raised edge or border; the outer edge of a wheel, on which a tyre is fitted. [OE]

Rimbaud /'ræmbəʊ/, Arthur (1854-91), French poet of precocious genius, who at the age of 17 had written his most famous poem 'Le bateau ivre'. In the same year he began a passionate relationship with the poet Paul Verlaine and the pair led a dissolute life in Brussels and London until they quarrelled violently. He undertook a programme of 'disorientation of the senses' in an attempt to become a visionary, and his prose poems *Une Saison en enfer* (1873) and *Les Illuminations* (1886) explored the possibilities of this. By the age of 19 his poetic career was ·over and he succumbed to a vagabond life in Europe and in NE Africa, but he had become one of the most revolutionary figures in 19th-c. literature, whose verse was fiercely independent of religious, political, and literary orthodoxy.

rime *n.* frost; (*poetic*) hoar-frost. —*v.t.* to cover with rime. [OE]

rimmed *adj.* edged, bordered. [f. RIM]

Rimmon /'rɪmən/ a deity worshipped in ancient Damascus (2 Kings 5: 18). —**bow down in the house of Rimmon**, to compromise one's convictions.

Rimsky-Korsakov /rɪmskɪ 'kɔːsəkɒf/, Nikolai Andreievich (1844-1908), Russian composer. Born of an aristocratic family he attended the Corps of Naval Cadets in St Petersburg, at the same time pursuing his interest in music which, though he lacked formal·training, was keen enough to lead him to compose a much acclaimed First Symphony in 1861-5. He was appointed professor of composition at the St Petersburg Conservatory in 1871 and followed his early success with such works as the symphonic suite *Sheherazade* (1888). In 1905 his involvement with revolutionary students led to temporary suspension from the Conservatory; his attitude to autocracy found expression in his opera *The Golden Cockerel* (1909), after Pushkin's poem. He was a fine orchestrator, but today his versions of such works as Mussorgsky's *Khovanshchina* and *Boris Godunov* find less favour than do the originals.

rind /raɪnd/ *n.* a tough outer layer or skin on fruit, vegetables, cheese, bacon, etc. [OE]

rinderpest /'rɪndəpest/ *n.* a disease of ruminants (esp. cattle). [G (*rinder* cattle, as PEST)]

ring[1] *n.* **1.** a circlet, usually of precious metal, worn on a finger. **2.** a circular band of any material; (in *pl.*) a pair of metal or wooden rings 236 mm in diameter suspended 500 mm apart and 2,500 mm (approx. 8 ft.) above the ground, used in gymnastics competitions in which swinging and balancing movements are performed. **3.** a line or band round, or the rim of, a cylindrical or circular object. **4.** a mark or part etc. having the form of a circular band. **5.** a circular or other enclosure for a circus, boxing, betting at races, the showing of cattle, etc. **6.** persons or things arranged in a circle; such an arrangement; a combination of traders, politicians, spies, etc., acting together for the control of operations. **7.** a circular or spiral course. —*v.t.* **1.** to enclose with a ring, to encircle, to put a ring on (a bird etc.) to identify it. **3.** to cut a ring in the bark of (a tree), especially to retard its growth and improve fruit-production. —**the ring**, bookmakers. **make** *or* **run rings round**, to do things much better than (another person). **ring-dove** *n.* a large species of pigeon (*Columba palumbus*). **ring-finger** *n.* the third finger especially of the left hand, on which a wedding ring is usually worn. **ring main** *or* **circuit**, an electrical circuit serving many sockets in a continuous ring. **ring road**, a bypass encircling a town. [OE]

ring[2] *v.t./i.* (*past* **rang**; *p.p.* **rung**) **1.** to give out a clear resonant sound of or like that of a bell when struck. **2.** to make (a bell) ring; to sound (a peal etc.) on bells; to sound a bell as a summons; to signal by ringing. **3.** to make a telephone call (to). **4.** to resound. **5.** (of the ears) to be filled with a sensation of ringing. **6.** (*colloq.*) to alter and sell (a stolen vehicle). —*n.* **1.** a ringing sound or tone. **2.** the act of ringing a bell; the sound caused by this. **3.** a specified feeling conveyed by an utterance. **4.** (*colloq.*) a telephone call. **5.** a set of (church) bells. —**ring a bell**, (*colloq.*) to begin to revive a memory. **ring down** (or **up**) **the curtain**, to cause it to be lowered (or raised). **ring off**, to end a telephone call. **ring up,** to call by telephone; to record (an amount) on a cash register. [OE]

ringer *n.* **1.** a person who rings bells. **2.** (*US*) a racehorse etc. fraudulently substituted for another. **3.** a person's double. [f. RING²]

ringleader *n.* a leading instigator in crime, mischief etc.

ringlet /'rɪŋlɪt/ *n.* a long tubular curl of hair. —**ringleted** *adj.* [f. RING¹ + -LET]

ringmaster *n.* a person directing a circus performance.

ringside *n.* the area immediately beside a boxing or circus ring. —*adj.* (of a seat etc.) close to the scene of action.

ringworm *n.* a contagious fungus skin-disease forming circular patches, especially on a child's scalp.

rink *n.* **1.** an area of natural or artificial ice for skating or a game of curling etc.; a floor for roller-skating; a building containing either of these. **2.** a strip of bowling green. **3.** a team in bowls or curling. [perh. f. OF *renc*, = RANK¹]

rinse *v.t.* to wash out with clean water; to wash lightly; to put (clothes etc.) through clean water to remove soap etc.; to remove (impurities) by rinsing. —*n.* **1.** rinsing. **2.** a solution washed through hair to tint or condition it. [f. OF *rincer*]

Rio de Janeiro /riːəʊ də dʒəˈnɪərəʊ/ the chief port, second largest city, and former capital of Brazil; pop. (1980) 5,094,396.

Rio de la Plata /riːəʊ də lɑː ˈplɑːtə/ the River Plate.

Rio Grande /riːəʊ ˈgrænd/ a river of North America which rises in Colorado and flows 3,030 km (1,880 miles) SE to the Gulf of Mexico. It forms the USA–Mexico frontier from El Paso to the sea.

riot /'raɪət/ *n.* **1.** a wild disturbance by a crowd of people. **2.** loud revelry; a lavish display or enjoyment. **3.** (*colloq.*) a very amusing thing or person. —*v.i.* to make or take part in a riot. —**read the Riot Act,** to insist that noise or insubordination etc. must cease. **Riot Act,** an Act passed in 1715 by the Whig government in the wake of anti-Hanoverian rioting, which made it a felony for an assembly of more than twelve people to refuse to disperse after being ordered to do so by lawful authority. It was repealed in 1967. **riot helmet, riot shield,** a helmet or shield for use by police or soldiers dealing with riots. **run riot,** to behave in an unruly way; (of plants) to grow or spread uncontrolled. —**rioter** *n.* [f. OF *riote, rioter*]

riotous /'raɪətəs/ *adj.* **1.** disorderly, unruly. **2.** boisterous, unrestrained. —**riotously** *adv.* [f. RIOT]

RIP *abbr.* may he, she or they rest in peace. [f. L *requiesca(n)t in pace*]

rip¹ *v.t./i.* (**-pp-**) **1.** to tear or cut (a thing) quickly or forcibly away or apart; to make (a hole etc.) thus; to make a long tear or cut in. **2.** to come violently apart, to split. **3.** to rush along. —*n.* **1.** a long tear or cut. **2.** an act of ripping. **3.** a stretch of rough water. —**let rip,** (*colloq.*) to refrain from holding back the speed of or from interfering with (a person or thing); to speak violently. **rip-cord** *n.* a cord for releasing a parachute from its pack. **rip off,** (*slang*) to defraud; to steal. **rip-off** *n.* (*slang*) a fraud; a theft. **rip-roaring** *adj.* wildly noisy. **rip-saw** *n.* a saw for sawing wood along the grain. —**ripper** *n.* [orig. unkn.]

rip² *n.* **1.** a dissolute person. **2.** a worthless horse. [perh. var. of *rep* = REPROBATE]

riparian /raɪˈpeərɪən/ *adj.* of or on a river-bank. [f. L *riparius* (*ripa* bank)]

ripe *adj.* **1.** (of grain or fruit etc.) ready to be gathered and used; (of cheese or wine etc.) matured and ready to be eaten or drunk. **2.** mature, fully developed; (of a person's age) advanced. **3.** ready, in a fit state. —**ripely** *adv.*, **ripeness** *n.* [OE]

ripen *v.t./i.* to make or become ripe. [f. RIPE]

riposte /rɪˈpɒst/ *n.* **1.** a quick counterstroke; a retort. **2.** a quick return thrust in fencing. —*v.i.* to deliver a riposte. [f. F f. It. (as RESPONSE)]

ripple *n.* **1.** a ruffling of the surface of water, a small wave or series of waves. **2.** a gentle lively sound that rises and falls. **3.** a wavy appearance in hair etc. —*v.t./i.* **1.** to form or flow in ripples; to cause to do this. **2.** to show or sound like ripples. —**ripply** *adj.* [orig. unkn.]

Rip van Winkle /'wɪŋk(ə)l/ the good-for-nothing hero of a story (1820) by Washington Irving. He fell asleep in the Catskill Mountains and awoke after 20 years to find the world completely changed.

rise /raɪz/ *v.i.* (*past* **rose** /rəʊz/; *p.p.* **risen** /'rɪz(ə)n/) **1.** to come or go up; to grow, project, swell, or incline upwards; to become higher; to reach a higher position, level, intensity, or amount; to come to the surface; to become or be visible above the surroundings or horizon; (of bread or cake etc.) to swell by the action of yeast etc.; (of fish) to come to the surface to feed; (of a person's spirits) to become more cheerful. **2.** to get up from lying, sitting, or kneeling, or from a bed; (of a meeting etc.) to cease to sit for business, to recover a standing or vertical position, to become erect; to leave the ground; to come to life again. **3.** to cease to be quiet or submissive, to rebel; (of the wind) to begin to blow, to strengthen. **4.** (of a river etc.) to have its origin, to begin or begin to flow. —*n.* **1.** the act, manner, or amount of rising. **2.** an upward slope, a small hill. **3.** social advancement, upward progress; an increase in power, rank, price, amount, height, wages, etc. **4.** a movement of fish to the surface. **5.** origin. —**get a rise out of,** to cause to display temper or characteristic behaviour. **give rise to,** to cause. **rise to,** to develop powers equal to dealing with (an occasion). [OE]

riser *n.* the vertical piece between the treads of a staircase (ill. HOUSES). [f. RISE]

risible /'rɪzɪb(ə)l/ *adj.* **1.** laughable, ludicrous. **2.** inclined to laugh. [f. L *risibilis* (*ridēre* laugh)]

rising /'raɪzɪŋ/ *adj.* **1.** advancing to maturity or high standing. **2.** approaching a specified age). **3.** (of ground) sloping upwards. —*n.* a revolt. [f. RISE]

risk *n.* **1.** the possibility of meeting danger or suffering harm or loss; exposure to this. **2.** a person or thing causing risk or regarded in relation to risk. —*v.t.* to expose to risk; to accept the risk of; to venture on. —**at risk,** exposed to danger. **run a** or **the risk,** to expose oneself to danger or loss etc. [f. F *risque, risquer* f. It.]

risky *adj.* **1.** full of risk. **2.** risqué. —**riskily** *adv.*, **riskiness** *n.* [f. RISK]

Risorgimento /rɪsɔːdʒɪˈmentəʊ/ *n.* a movement in the mid-19th c. to unite and liberate Italy, associated with the names of Cavour, Mazzini, and Garibaldi. [It., = resurrection]

risotto /rɪˈzɒtəʊ/ *n.* (*pl.* **-os**) an Italian dish of rice containing chopped meat or cheese and vegetables. [It.]

risqué /'rɪskeɪ/ *adj.* (of a story etc.) slightly indecent. [F (as RISK)]

rissole /'rɪsəʊl/ *n.* a ball or cake of minced meat mixed with potato or breadcrumbs etc. and usually fried. [F, ult. f. L *russeolus* reddish]

ritardando /riːtɑːˈdændəʊ/ *adv.* & *n.* (*pl.* **-os**) rallentando. [It.]

rite *n.* a religious or other solemn ceremony; an action required or usual in this; the body of usage characteristic of a Church. [f. OF or L *ritus*]

ritual /'rɪtjʊəl/ *n.* **1.** the series of actions used in a religious or other rite; a particular form of this. **2.** a procedure regularly followed. —*adj.* of or done as a ritual. —**ritually** *adv.* [f. L (as prec.)]

ritualism *n.* regular or excessive practice of ritual. —**ritualist** *n.*, **ritualistic** /-'lɪstɪk/ *adj.*, **ritualistically** /-'lɪstɪkəlɪ/ *adv.* [f. prec.]

ritzy /'rɪtsɪ/ *adj.* (*colloq.*) high-class, luxurious, ostentatiously smart. [f. *Ritz*, name of luxurious hotels, f. C. *Ritz* (d.1918) Swiss hotel-owner]

rival /'raɪv(ə)l/ *n.* **1.** a person or thing competing with another. **2.** a person or thing that equals another in quality. —*attrib. adj.* being a rival or rivals. —*v.t.* (**-ll-**) to be a rival of or comparable to; to seem or claim to be as good as. —**rivalry** *n.* [f. L (*rivus* stream); orig. = one using the same stream]

riven /'rɪv(ə)n/ *adj.* split, torn violently. [*p.p.* of archaic *rive* f. ON]

river /'rɪvə(r)/ *n.* **1.** a copious natural stream of water flowing in a channel to the sea etc. (see ill. p. 711). **2.** a copious flow. —**sell down the river,** (*colloq.*) to defraud or betray. [f. AF *river(e)* river (bank) f. L (as RIPARIAN)]

riverside *n.* the ground along a river-bank.

rivet /'rɪvɪt/ *n.* a nail or bolt for holding metal plates etc. together, its headless end being beaten out or pressed down when in place. —*v.t.* **1.** to join or fasten with a rivet or rivets. **2.** to beat out or press down the end of (a nail or bolt). **3.** to fix, to make immovable; to direct (the eyes or attention etc.) intently; to engross (a person or his attention). —**riveter** *n.* [f. OF (*river* clench)]

Riviera /rɪvɪˈeərə/ that part of the Mediterranean coastal region of southern France and northern Italy extending

Rivers and their Landscape

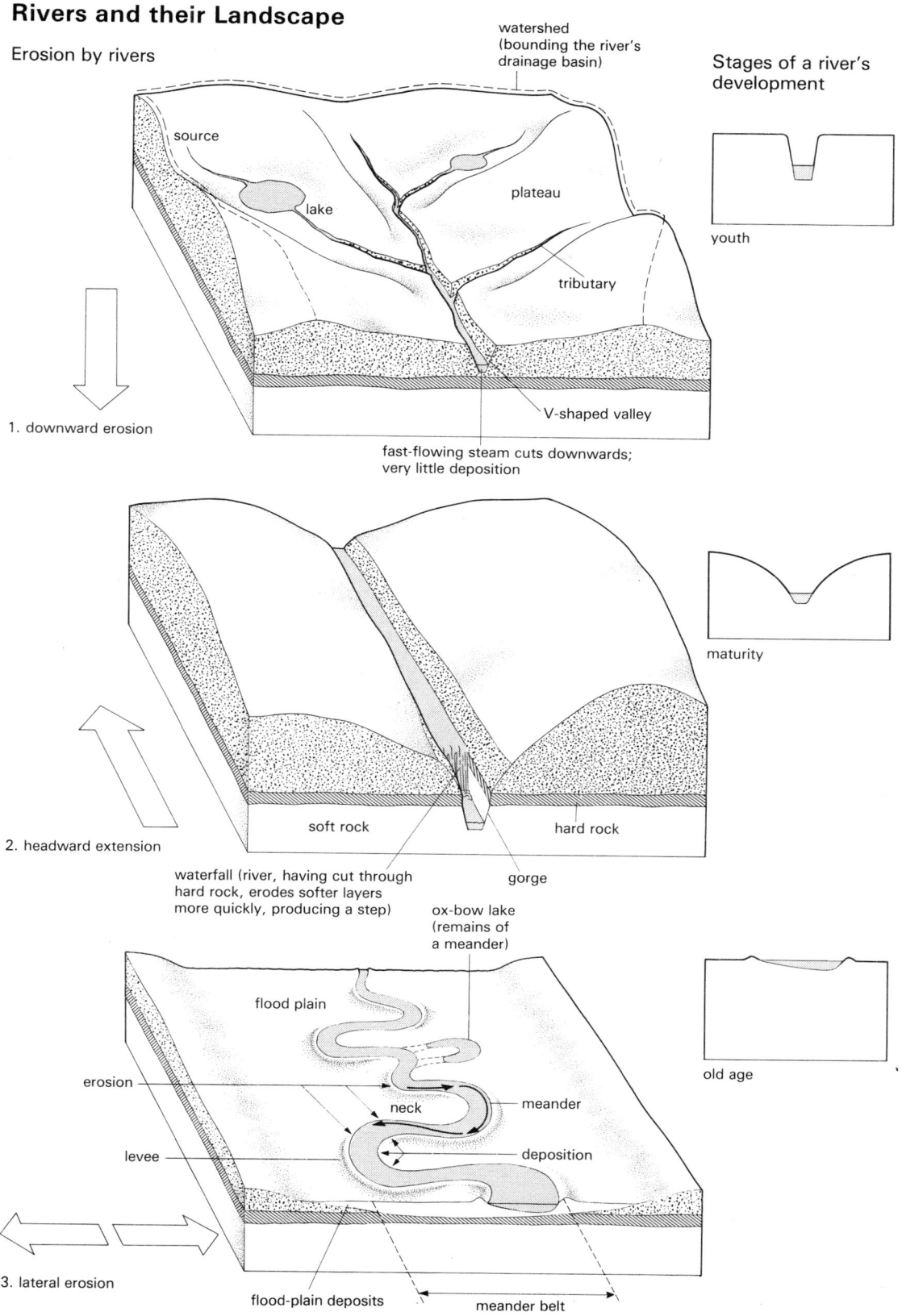

Erosion by rivers

Stages of a river's development

watershed (bounding the river's drainage basin)

source

lake

plateau

tributary

V-shaped valley

1. downward erosion

fast-flowing steam cuts downwards; very little deposition

youth

soft rock

hard rock

2. headward extension

waterfall (river, having cut through hard rock, erodes softer layers more quickly, producing a step)

gorge

maturity

ox-bow lake (remains of a meander)

flood plain

erosion

neck

meander

levee

deposition

old age

3. lateral erosion

flood-plain deposits

meander belt

from Nice to La Spezia, famous for its scenic beauty, fertility, and mild climate, and with many fashionable resorts; a region resembling this. [It., = sea-shore].

rivulet /ˈrɪvjʊlɪt/ *n.* a small stream. [alt. f. obs. *riveret* (F, dim. of RIVER)]

Riyadh /riːˈɑːd/ the capital of Saudi Arabia; pop. (est. 1980) 1,044,000.

RM *abbr.* Royal Marines.

RN *abbr.* Royal Navy.

Rn *symbol* radon.

RNA *abbr.* ribonucleic acid, a substance similar to DNA, found in all cells and having several functions, one of which is to act as a 'messenger', carrying instructions from DNA for controlling the synthesis of proteins (see DNA). In some viruses it is RNA (not DNA) that carries the genetic information.

roach *n.* a small freshwater fish (esp. *Rutilus rutilus*) of the carp family. [f. OF *roc(h)e*]

road *n.* **1.** a way by which people, animals, or vehicles may pass between places, especially one with a prepared surface. **2.** a way of getting to or achieving something. **3.** one's way or route. **4.** (usu. in *pl.*) also **roadstead**) a piece of water near a shore in which ships can ride at anchor. —**one for the road**, (*colloq.*) a final drink before departure. **on the road**, travelling, especially as a commercial traveller, itinerant performer, or vagrant. **road-block** *n.* a barricade set up by police etc. on a road to enable them to stop and search traffic. **road-hog** *n.* a reckless or inconsiderate motorist or cyclist. **road-holding** *n.* the stability of a moving vehicle. **road show**, a theatrical performance by a company on tour. **road test**, a test of a vehicle by use on the road. **road train**, (*Austral.*) a very large lorry hauling two or three trailers. **road-works** *n.pl.* construction or repair of roads. [OE (as RIDE)]

roadie /ˈrəʊdɪ/ *n.* (*colloq.*) an assistant of a touring band, responsible for equipment. [f. ROAD]

roadside *n.* the border of a road.

roadstead *n.* see ROAD 4.

roadster *n.* an open car without rear seats. [f. ROAD]

roadway *n.* a road; the part of a road intended for vehicles.

roadworthy *adj.* (of a vehicle) fit for use on a road. —**roadworthiness** *n.*

roam *v.t./i.* to wander (through). —*n.* a wander. [orig. unkn.]

roan *adj.* (of an animal) with a coat of which the prevailing colour is thickly interspersed with another, esp. bay, sorrel, or chestnut mixed with white or grey. —*n.* a roan animal, esp. a horse. [OE]

roar *n.* **1.** a long loud deep sound like that made by a lion. **2.** loud laughter. —*v.t./i.* **1.** to utter a roar; to express in this way. **2.** to function with the sound of a roar; to travel in a vehicle at high speed with the engine roaring. —**roarer** *n.* [OE (imit.)]

roaring *adj.* **1.** noisy. **2.** briskly active. —*adv.* **roaring drunk**, very or noisily drunk. —**roaring forties**, stormy ocean tracts between latitudes 40° and 50° S. [f. ROAR]

roast *v.t./i.* **1.** to cook (food, esp. meat) by exposure to heat or in an oven. **2.** to heat (coffee-beans) before grinding. **3.** to expose to fire or great heat. **4.** (*US*) to censure. **5.** to undergo roasting. —*attrib. adj.* (of meat, a potato, chestnut, etc.) roasted. —*n.* **1.** roast meat; a joint of meat for roasting. **2.** the operation of roasting. [f. OF *rostir*]

roaster *n.* **1.** a fowl etc. suitable for roasting. **2.** an apparatus that will roast meat etc. [f. prec.]

roasting *adj.* very hot. [f. ROAST]

rob *v.t.* (**-bb-**) to steal from, to deprive unlawfully. **2.** to deprive of what is due or normal. —**robber** *n.*, **robbery** *n.* [f. OF *rob(b)er*]

Robbia /ˈrɒbɪə/, della. The name of a family of Florentine sculptors and ceramists of whom Luca (1400-82) is the most famous. His Singing Gallery for Florence Cathedral (1431-8) reinterpreted in marble relief antique motifs of singing and dancing youths with a delightful tenderness and sympathy, and it is this quality in his work that characterizes his output, particularly his half-length Madonna and Child in glazed white terracotta on blue ground. His nephew Andrea (1435-1525) carried on the family business; the roundels of infants on the Foundling Hospital in Florence (1463-6) have been attributed to him.

Robbins /ˈrɒbɪnz/, Jerome (1918-), American choreographer and director, originally a dancer. His adaptation

of his first ballet *Fancy Free* (1944) as the musical *On the Town* led to a long series of successful musicals including *The King and I* (1951), *West Side Story* (1957), *Funny Girl* (1964), and *Fiddler on the Roof* (1964). Though much of his work draws on jazz and modern dance he has also created a number of ballets with music by classical composers.

robe *n.* **1.** a long loose garment. **2.** (often in *pl.*) a long outer garment worn as an indication of the wearer's rank or office etc. **3.** a dressing-gown. —*v.t./i.* to put on robes; to clothe in a robe; to dress. [f. OF (as ROB, orig. sense 'booty')]

Robert /ˈrɒbət/ the name of three kings of Scotland:
Robert I 'the Bruce' (1274-1329), reigned 1306-29. One of several competitors for the Scottish throne, Bruce eventually took up the leadership of the struggle against the English after the death of Sir William Wallace. Initially he suffered a series of defeats at the hands of Edward I and various Scottish rivals, but after several years as a fugitive he returned to lead a successful campaign against Edward II, culminating in his great victory at Bannockburn. He then went on to re-establish Scotland as a kingdom in its own right and to force the Plantagenets, at least temporarily, to give up their claim to overlordship.
Robert II 'the Steward' (1316-90), grandson of Robert the Bruce, reigned 1371-90. The first of the Stuart line, he succeeded his uncle David II at an advanced age and proved incapable of strong government. By the time of Robert's death the lawlessness of the Scottish nobility, which was to dominate the country's affairs for more than a century, had already become a serious problem.
Robert III (*c.*1337-1406), illegitimate son of Robert II, reigned 1390-1406, he changed his name from John to Robert on coming to the throne. Like his father, Robert III was senescent by the time he became king and proved unable to check the spread of noble lawlessness, in which his own brother Alexander, 'the Wolf of Badenoch', was a prime culprit. He described himself on his death-bed as 'the worst of kings and most miserable of men'.

Roberts /ˈrɒbəts/, Frederick Sleigh, 1st Earl Roberts of Kandahar (1832-1914), British military leader, whose career spanned the great age of British imperialism. He won a Victoria Cross during the Indian Mutiny and in 1880 commanded the British army which ended the Second Afghan War with a victory at Kandahar. In 1899 he was appointed Commander-in-Chief in South Africa and planned the successful march on the Boer capital of Pretoria.

Robeson /ˈrəʊbs(ə)n/, Paul Bustill (1898-1976), American Black actor and singer. His singing of 'Ole Man River' in the London production of *Show Boat* (1928) first revealed his superb bass voice, and he gave many recitals of Negro spirituals. He did much to further the interests of Blacks but his visit to Russia in 1963 as an avowed Communist aroused much controversy.

Robespierre /ˈrəʊbzpjeə(r)/, Maximilien François Marie Isidore de (1758-94), French revolutionary. A lawyer of some distinction, Robespierre entered politics in the early days of the French Revolution, and, although initially a moderate, drifted gradually towards the extreme left. Allying himself with the radical Jacobins, he purged the more moderate Girondins and instituted the Terror to rid himself of political opponents. As the pace of executions quickened, many of Robespierre's Revolutionary colleagues began to fear that he had gone mad and eventually they rose against him, sending him to the guillotine in July 1794.

Robey /ˈrəʊbɪ/, Sir George (1869-1954), the name adopted by George Edward Wade, British music-hall comedian, who became known as 'the Prime Minister of mirth'.

robin /ˈrɒbɪn/ *n.* a small brown red-breasted European bird (*Erithacus rubecula*); (*US*) a red-breasted thrush (*Turdus migratorius*); a bird of similar appearance etc. to either of these. [f. OF, pet-form of man's name *Robert*]

Robin Goodfellow /rɒbɪn ˈɡʊdfeləʊ/ see PUCK.

Robin Hood /ˈrɒbɪn hʊd/ a semi-legendary English medieval outlaw, reputed to have robbed the rich and helped the poor. Although generally associated with Sherwood Forest in Nottinghamshire in the legends which sprang up around him, it seems likely that the real Robin Hood operated further north, in Yorkshire, most probably in the early decades of the 13th c.

Robinson Crusoe /ˈkruːsəʊ/ the hero of a novel (1719) by Defoe, based on an adventure of Alexander Selkirk who lived alone on the uninhabited Pacific Island of Juan Fernandez for five years (1704-9).

robot /ˈrəʊbɒt/ *n.* **1.** a machine designed to function in place of a living agent (see ROBOTICS). **2.** an apparently human automaton; a machine like person. **3.** (*S.Afr.*) an automatic traffic-signal. [Czech, f. *robota* forced labour; used by K. Čapek in his play *R.U.R.* (Rossum's Universal Robots), 1920]

robotic /rə'botɪk/ *adj.* of robots; resembling a robot. —**robotics** *n.pl.* the design, construction, operation, and application of robots; the study of robots. The term originated in the science fiction stories of Isaac Asimov, American scientist and writer, but is now used of automatic processes in industry. The discipline is concerned with building robots, programmable devices consisting of fixed or mobile mechanical manipulators and sensory organs, which are linked to a computer. Simple robots are widely used in production engineering, especially where a variety of goods is to be produced with minimum changeover time. Such robots have very little (if any) sensory capability and follow a fixed but reprogrammable sequence of instructions. Important goals of robotics research in artifical intelligence are (i) to program robots off line using a high-level computing language, especially including a degree of automatic planning and recovery from errors, and (ii) to provide the robot with sensors—typically a television camera—and to use sensory perception to guide it in a flexible manner. Goals of robotic research in mechanical and production engineering are to improve dynamic prformance and to design robot systems able to handle the assembly of complex objects. [f. prec.]

Rob Roy (Robert MacGregor, 1671-1734), Scottish highland bandit, popularized in Sir Walter Scott's novel of the same name, who was heavily involved in blackmail and cattle theft in the area north of Loch Lomond. He proclaimed his support for the Old Pretender in 1715, but failed to commit his men to battle.

Robson /'robs(ə)n/, Dame Flora (1902-85), English actress, an outstanding player of parts demanding controlled nervous tension.

robust /rəʊ'bʌst/ *adj.* strong, vigorous. —**robustly** *adv.*, **robustness** *n.* [f. F or L *robustus* (*robur* strength)]

roc /rɒk/ *n.* a gigantic bird of Eastern legend. [f. Sp. f. Arab.]

roche moutonnée /rɒʃ muː'tɒneɪ/ a small mass of rock shaped by glacial action, with one side smooth and gently sloping and the other rough, steep, and irregular. [F, = fleecy rock]

Rochester /'rɒtʃɪstə(r)/, John Wilmot, 2nd Earl of (1647-80), English poet, one of the 'court wits' surrounding Charles II. According to Samuel Johnson he 'blazed out his youth and health in lavish voluptuousness'; at the end of his short life he had moved towards religious conversion. His poems (often erotic and sometimes pornographic) combine a brilliant wit with an emotional complexity, and with his social and literary verse satires he was one of the first Augustans. These works include his tough self-dramatization 'The Maimed Debauchee', the grimly funny 'Upon Nothing', and the *Satyr against Mankind* (1675).

rochet /'rɒtʃɪt/ *n.* a surplice-like vestment used chiefly by bishops and abbots. [f. OF]

rock¹ *n.* **1.** the hard part of the earth's crust underlying the soil; the hard compact material of which rock consists. **2.** a large detached stone. **3.** a mass of rock projecting and forming a hill, cliff, etc., or standing up into or out of water from the bottom. **4.** a hard sweet made in a cylindrical stick, usually flavoured with peppermint. —**on the rocks**, (*colloq.*) short of money, (of a drink) served neat with ice. **rock-bottom** *adj.* & *n.* (*colloq.* of prices etc.) the very lowest. **rock-bound** *adj.* (of a coast) rocky, very rugged. **rock-cake** *n.* a small fruit cake with a rugged surface. **rock-crystal** *n.* transparent colourless quartz usually in hexagonal prisms. **rock-garden** *n.* a rockery; a garden in which rockeries are the chief feature. **rock-plant** *n.* a plant growing on or among rocks. **rock salmon**, dogfish as sold for food. **rock-salt** *n.* common salt as a solid mineral. [f. OF *ro(c)que, roche*]

rock² *v.t./i.* **1.** to move or be moved gently to and fro while supported on something. **2.** to sway or shake violently. **3.** to disturb greatly by shock. —*n.* **1.** a rocking motion. **2.** a kind of modern popular music, usually with a strong beat; rock 'n' roll. —**rocking-chair** *n.* a chair mounted on rockers or springs so that it can be rocked by the sitter. **rocking-horse** *n.* a wooden horse mounted on rockers or springs so that it can be rocked by a child sitting on it. **rock 'n' roll**, a kind of popular music with a strong beat, containing elements of blues. [OE]

Rockefeller /'rɒkəfelə(r)/, John Davison (1839-1937),

American industrialist. One of the first to recognize the industrial possibilities of oil, Rockefeller established the Standard Oil Company and by the end of the 1870s exercised a virtual monopoly over oil refining and transportation in the USA. Early in the 20th c. he handed over his business interests to his son and devoted his immense private fortune to various philanthropic projects.

rocker *n.* **1.** a device for rocking or being rocked. **2.** each of the curved bars on which a rocking-chair etc. is mounted. —**off one's rocker**, (*slang*) crazy. [f. ROCK²]

rockery /'rɒkərɪ/ *n.* an artificial mound or bank containing large stones and planted with rock-plants. [f. ROCK¹]

rocket /'rɒkɪt/ *n.* **1.** a firework or similar device (e.g. as a signal) that rises into the air when ignited and then explodes. **2.** a projectile operating by the reaction of a continuous jet of gases released in the combustion of a propellant within it (see below); a device propelled by this, especially a bomb or spacecraft. **3.** (*slang*) a reprimand. —*v.t./i.* **1.** to move rapidly upwards or away. **2.** to bombard with rockets. [f. F *roquette* f. It. (*rocca* distaff)]

   The use of rockets (probably of the fireworks type) as a weapon of war dates from the 13th c. in both China and Europe. They were developed and used in warfare over the centuries, but by the mid-19th c. could not compete with improved artillery. In 1926 the work of the American physicist R. H. Goddard resulted in the launching of the first rocket to use liquid fuel, an important development in the history of rocketry. The Germans devoted considerable effort towards rocket research and experimentation in the 1930s, and used both guided and ballistic missiles (the V1 and V2) during the Second World War, after which von Braun and others of the German research team were recruited by the Americans to assist in the development of rockets which eventually launched vehicles into space.

rocketry *n.* the science or practice of rocket propulsion. [f. prec.]

rocky¹ *adj.* of or like a rock; abounding in rocks. [f. ROCK¹]

rocky² *adj.* (*colloq.*) unsteady, tottering. —**rockily** *adv.*, **rockiness** *n.* [f. ROCK²]

Rocky Mountains (also **Rockies**) the great mountain system of western North America extending from the US–Mexico border to the Yukon Territory of Canada. Several peaks rise to over 4,300 m (14,000 ft.).

rococo /rə'kəʊkəʊ/ *adj.* of an ornate style of art, music, and literature in Europe in the 18th c. —*n.* this style. [F, joc. alt. of *rocaille* fancy shell- and rock-work for fountains and grottoes, f. *roc* rock]

rod *n.* **1.** a slender straight round stick or metal bar. **2.** a cane or birch for use in flogging people. **3.** a fishing rod; an angler with the right to use this on a specified stretch of water. **4.** (as a measure) a perch (PERCH¹; see GUNTER). —**make a rod for one's own back**, to cause future trouble or effort for oneself. [OE]

rode *past* of RIDE.

rodent /'rəʊd(ə)nt/ *n.* an animal with strong incisors for gnawing things and no canine teeth (e.g. a rat, squirrel, beaver). —*adj.* gnawing; (of an ulcer) spreading slowly. —**rodent officer**, an official rat-catcher. [f. L *rodere* gnaw]

rodeo /rəʊ'deɪəʊ/ *n.* (*pl.* **-os**) **1.** an exhibition of cowboys' skill in handling animals. Rodeo was born in the southern States of the USA after the Civil War, when Texan cowboys, driving their cattle to the north and west in search of new markets, had to find their own amusements. They did so with riding and roping contests, which presently became public entertainments. **2.** a round-up of cattle on a ranch for branding etc. [Sp. (*rodear* go round)]

Rodgers /'rɒdʒəz/, Richard (1902-79), American songwriter. He collaborated with Lorenz Hart on musical shows such as *The Girl Friend* (1926). After Hart's death in 1943, Oscar Hammerstein II became his lyric-writer and together they produced such triumphs as *Oklahoma!* (1943), *Carousel* (1945), *South Pacific* (1949), *The King and I* (1951), and *The Sound of Music* (1959).

Rodin /'rəʊdæ̃/, Auguste (1840-1917), the most celebrated sculptor of the French Romantic school, primarily a modeller rather than a carver in spite of being deeply influenced by Michelangelo. His sketchy unfinished figures are reminiscent of contemporary impressionist paintings. Rodin began as a mason, but visited Italy in 1875, and first became known with a life-sized nude called *Bronze Age* (1877). Like that of his most famous work, the huge *Gate of Hell* (1880, unfinished), the title is virtually meaningless (the latter derives from Ghiberti's *Door of Paradise*); it is actually a collection of nude figures, including one re-used as *The*

Thinker (1904). His works exist in many replicas; there are large collections in Paris (Musée Rodin), London, and Philadelphia.

rodomontade /rɒdəmɒnˈteɪd/ *n.* boastful talk. [F, f. obs. It. (*Rodomonte* boastful character in Ariosto's *Orlando Furioso*)]

roe[1] /rəʊ/ *n.* a mass of eggs in a female fish's ovary (**hard roe**); a male fish's milt (**soft roe**). [f. MLG or MDu.]

roe[2] /rəʊ/ *n.* (*pl.* **roes** or **roe**) (also **roe-deer**) a small kind of deer (*Capreolus capreolus*). [OE]

roebuck *n.* a male roe-deer.

roentgen /ˈrʌntjən/ *n.* a former unit of ionizing radiation. [f. W. C. RÖNTGEN]

rogation /rəˈɡeɪʃ(ə)n/ *n.* (usu. in *pl.*) the litany of the saints chanted on the three Rogation days before Ascension Day. —**Rogation days**, certain days prescribed in the Western Church for prayer and fasting, on which intercession is made especially for the harvest. The Major Rogation (25 Apr.) is a Christianized version of pagan ritual processions through the cornfields to pray for the preservation of the crops from mildew. The Minor Rogations are kept on the three days before Ascension Day, and originated in 5th-c. Gaul to protect the land against earthquakes and other perils; these days (only) are prescribed in the Book of Common Prayer. In England the traditional ceremony of beating the parish bounds is associated with this observance. **Rogation Sunday**, the Sunday before Ascension Day. [f. L (*rogare* ask)]

roger /ˈrɒdʒə(r)/ *int.* (in telegraphy etc.) your message has been received and understood; (*slang*) I agree. [man's name *Roger*, used in signalling code for letter *R*]

rogue /rəʊɡ/ *n.* **1.** a dishonest or unprincipled person. **2.** a mischievous person, especially a child. **3.** a wild animal driven away or living apart from the herd and of savage temper. **4.** an inferior or defective specimen among many acceptable ones. —**rogue's gallery**, a collection of photographs of known criminals etc. —**roguery** *n.*, **roguish** *adj.*, **roguishly** *adv.*, **roguishness** *n.* [orig. unkn.]

roister *v.i.* to revel noisily, to be uproarious. [f. F *rustre* ruffian, f. L (as RUSTIC)]

Roland /ˈrəʊlənd/ the most famous of Charlemagne's paladins, hero of the *Chanson de Roland* (12th c.) and other (esp. French and Italian) medieval romances. He is said to have become a friend of Oliver, another paladin, after contending with him in single combat in which neither won. Roland was killed in a rearguard action at Roncesvalles (see entry). —**a Roland for an Oliver**, an equal exchange.

role /rəʊl/ *n.* **1.** an actor's part. **2.** a person's or thing's function. [f. F, = foll.]

roll /rəʊl/ *n.* **1.** a cylinder formed by turning a flexible material over and over on itself without folding; a thing of similar form. **2.** a small individual portion of bread separately baked. **3.** an official list or register. **4.** a rolling motion or gait; a spell of rolling. **5.** a continuous rhythmic sound of thunder or a drum. **6.** a complete revolution of an aircraft about its longitudinal axis (ill. FLIGHT). —*v.t./i.* **1.** to move, send, or go in some direction by turning on an axis. **2.** (of a vehicle) to advance or convey on wheels; (of a person) to be so conveyed. **3.** to turn over and over into a cylindrical or spherical shape; to make thus. **4.** to flatten by passing under or between rollers. **5.** to walk with a swaying gait; (of a ship or vehicle) to sway to and fro sideways; (of an aircraft) to turn (partially or completely) on its horizontal axis (ill. FLIGHT). **6.** to undulate; to show an undulating surface or motion; to go, propel, or carry with such a motion. **7.** to sound with a vibration or trill. —**be rolling in**, to have a large supply of. **Master of the Rolls**, one of the judges of the Court of Appeal, and Keeper of the Records at the Public Record Office. **roll by** *or* **on**, (of time) to pass steadily. **roll-call** *n.* the calling of a list of names to establish presence. **rolled gold**, a thin coating of gold applied to a base metal. **rolled into one**, combined in one person etc. **roll-film** *n.* a length of photographic film backed with opaque paper and rolled on a spool. **roll one's eyes**, to show the whites in various directions. **roll in**, to arrive in great numbers. **rolling-mill** *n.* a machine or factory for rolling metal into shape. **rolling-pin** *n.* a roller for pastry. **rolling-stock** *n.* stock of railway (or (*US*) road) vehicles. **rolling stone**, a person unwilling to settle for long in one place. **roll of honour**, a list of those honoured, especially the dead in a war. **roll-on** *n.* a light elastic corset; (*adj.*) (of a ship) on to which motor vehicles can be driven; (of a cosmetic) applied from a container with a rotating ball in its neck. **roll-top desk**, a desk with a

flexible cover sliding in curved grooves. **roll up**, to make into or form a roll; (*colloq.*) to arrive in a vehicle or on the scene. **strike off the rolls**, to debar from practising as a solicitor. [f. OF f. L *rotulus* (*rota* wheel)]

Rolland /rɒˈlɑ̃/, Romain (1866-1944), French writer and critic of art and music, who published an *Histoire de l'opéra* (1895) and achieved success with a lyrically written life of Beethoven (1903) and similar studies on Michelangelo (1908) and Tolstoy (1911). His stage works include three dramas of the Revolution; his best-known work *Jean-Christophe* (1906-12) is a *roman-fleuve* about a German composer. Rolland's pamphlet *Au-dessus de la mêlée* (1915) was an appeal to both sides to agitate for peace in place of fanatical patriotism; it aroused resentment in many quarters. He was awarded the Nobel Prize for literature in 1915.

roller /ˈrəʊlə(r)/ *n.* **1.** a hard cylinder for smoothing, spreading, or crushing things etc. **2.** a small cylinder on which the hair is rolled for setting. **3.** a long swelling wave. —**roller-coaster** *n.* a switchback at a fair etc. **roller-skate** *n.* see SKATE[1]. Although a primitive form of roller-skate was known in the Netherlands from the 18th c., the first practical four-wheel skate was patented in the USA in 1863. Its original purpose was to enable ice-skaters to practise when there was no natural ice, but roller-skating quickly developed as an independent sport. **roller towel**, a towel with the ends joined, hung on a roller. [f. ROLL]

rollicking /ˈrɒlɪkɪŋ/ *adj.* jovial and boisterous. [f. *rollick* (perh. f. ROMP + FROLIC)]

rollmops /ˈrəʊlmɒps/ *n.* (sometimes erroneously treated as *pl.*) a rolled fillet of herring, flavoured with sliced onions, spices, etc., and pickled in brine. [G]

Rolls /rəʊlz/, Charles Stewart (1877-1910), English motoring and aviation pioneer, one of the founder members of the Royal Automobile Club and the Royal Aero Club. In 1906 he and Royce (see entry) formed the company Rolls-Royce Ltd. with Royce as chief engineer and Rolls himself as demonstrator-salesman. He was the first Englishman to fly across the English Channel, and made the first double crossing in 1910 shortly before he was killed in an air crash, the first English victim of aviation.

roly-poly /rəʊlɪˈpəʊlɪ/ *n.* a pudding made of a sheet of suet pastry covered with jam etc., formed into a roll, and boiled or baked. —*adj.* (usu. of a child) podgy, plump. [prob. formed on ROLL]

ROM *abbr.* read-only memory (see READ).

rom. *abbr.* roman (type).

Roman /ˈrəʊmən/ *adj.* **1.** of ancient or modern Rome or the Roman republic or Empire. **2.** of the Roman Catholic Church. **3.** (of the nose) having a prominent upper part or bridge like those seen in portraits of ancient Romans. **4.** **roman**, of the plain upright lettering or type used in ordinary print (opp. *Gothic* or *black letter*, and *italic*). **5.** (of the alphabet) based on the ancient Roman system with letters A–Z. —*n.* **1.** a native or inhabitant of ancient or modern Rome, a citizen of the Roman republic or Empire; **(Epistle to the) Romans**, a book of the New Testament, an epistle of St Paul to the Church at Rome. **2.** a Roman Catholic. **3.** **roman**, roman type. —**Roman candle**, a tubular firework discharging a shower of sparks with coloured balls of flame. **Roman Catholic**, of the Roman Catholic Church (see separate entry); a member of this Church. **Roman Catholicism**, the beliefs and practice of this Church. **Roman Empire**, see separate entry. **Roman numerals**, Roman letters representing numbers (I = 1, V = 5, X = 10, L = 50, C = 100, D = 500, M = 1,000). [f. OF f. L *Romanus* (*Roma* Rome)]

Roman Catholic Church that part of the Christian Church which acknowledges the pope as its head, especially that which has developed since the Reformation. It has an elaborately organized hierarchy of bishops and priests, basing its claims on the power entrusted by Christ to his Apostles, particularly to St Peter, whose successors the popes are traditionally regarded as being. In doctrine, it is characterized by strict adherence to tradition combined with acceptance of the living voice of the Church and belief in its infallibility. The classic definition of its position was made in response to the Reformation at the Council of Trent (1545-63). During the Enlightenment the Church increasingly saw itself as an embattled defender of ancient truth, something that culminated in the proclamation of Papal Infallibility in 1870. The 20th c. has seen a great change as the Church has become more open to the world, a change given effect in the decrees of the 2nd Vatican Council (1962-5).

Romance /rəˈmæns/ *adj.* of the group of European languages descended from Latin. —*n.* this group, of which the main languages are French, Spanish, Portuguese, Italian, and Romanian. With the spread of the Roman Empire, Latin was introduced as the language of administration; with its decline the languages of separate areas began to develop in different ways, and the Latin from which they developed seems to have been not the classical Latin of Rome but the informal Latin of the soldiers. [f. OF f. L (as ROMANIC)]

romance /rəˈmæns/ *n.* **1.** an episode or story centred on highly imaginative and emotive scenes of love or heroism etc., originally a long verse narrative written in a Romance language; such stories as a genre; the atmosphere characterizing them; a mental tendency to be influenced by it, sympathetic imaginativeness. **2.** a love affair viewed as resembling a tale of romance; a love-story. **3.** a picturesque exaggeration or falsehood; an instance of this. —*v.i.* to exaggerate or distort the truth in an imaginative way. [f. prec.]

Roman Empire the period of ancient Roman history from 27 BC, when Octavian took power as what was effectively a constitutional monarch with the title of Augustus, until the barbarian invasions of the 4th-5th c. (which followed the death of Constantine) ended with the deposition of the last Roman emperor, Romulus Augustulus, in 476. At its greatest extent Roman rule or influence extended from Armenia and Mesopotamia in the east to the Iberian peninsula in the west, and from the Rhine and Danube in the north to Egypt and provinces on the Mediterranean coast of North Africa. The empire was divided by Theodosius (AD 395) into the Western or Latin and Eastern or Greek Empire, of which the Eastern lasted until 1453 and the Western, after lapsing in 476, was revived in 800 by Charlemagne and continued to exist as the Holy Roman Empire until 1806.

Romanesque /rəʊməˈnesk/ *n.* a style of art and architecture prevalent in Europe *c.*1050-1200, with massive vaulting and round arches. Although disseminated throughout Europe, the style reached its fullest development in central and northern France; the English version is usually termed Norman. —*adj.* of this style. [F (as ROMANCE)]

roman-fleuve /rəʊmɑ̃ˈflɜːv/ *n.* (*pl.* **-ns- -es**, pr. same) a sequence of self-contained novels [F, = river novel]

Romania /ruːˈmeɪnɪə/ a country in SE Europe with the USSR on its northern frontier and a coastline on the Black Sea; pop. (1982) 22,480,000; official language, Romanian; capital, Bucharest. In Roman times Romania formed the imperial province of Dacia, and in the Middle Ages the principalities of Walachia and Moldavia, each of which was swallowed up by the Ottoman empire in the 15th-16th c. The two principalities were unified in 1859 and gained independence in 1878, and although conquered in 1916 by the Central Powers, Romania emerged from the peace settlement with fresh territorial gains in Bessarabia and Transylvania. The present boundaries are a result of the Second World War (its oilfields were of vital importance to Germany, which it supported), after which Romania became a Communist State under Soviet influence. In the last twenty years the country has tended towards more independent policies and has benefited from a progressive industrialization of its economy.

Romanian /ruːˈmeɪnɪən/ *adj.* of Romania or its people or language. —*n.* **1.** a native of Romania. **2.** the official language of Romania, the only Romance language spoken in eastern Europe, which developed from the Latin introduced by Trajan when he invaded the area in the 2nd c. AD and has subsequently been heavily influenced by Slavonic languages. It is spoken by 8 million people in Romania itself, and a variety of it is spoken in the Soviet Union where it is known as Moldavian. [f. prec.]

Romanic /rəˈmænɪk/ *n.* Romance. —*adj.* **1.** of Romance; Romance-speaking. **2.** descended from the ancient Romans; inheriting their civilization etc. [f. L *Romanicus* (as ROMAN)]

romanize /ˈrəʊmənaɪz/ *v.t.* **1.** to make Roman or Roman Catholic in character. **2.** to put into the Roman alphabet or roman type. —**romanization** /-ˈzeɪʃ(ə)n/ *n.* [f. ROMAN]

Romano- /rəmeɪnəʊ-/ *in comb.* Roman. [f. ROMAN]

Romanov /ˈrəʊmənɒf/ the name of a dynasty that ruled in Russia from the accession of Michael Romanov in 1613 until the overthrow of the last tsar, Nicholas II, in 1917.

Romansh /rəˈmænʃ/ *n.* any of various Romance dialects of eastern Switzerland. —*adj.* of any of these dialects. [f. L *romanice* adv., as ROMANCE]

romantic /rəˈmæntɪk/ *adj.* **1.** of, characterized by, or suggestive of romance; (of a person) enjoying romance and situations etc. characterized by this. **2.** (freq. **Romantic**; of music, literature, painting, or the composers etc. involved) imaginative, charged with feeling and emotion and not conforming to classical conventions (see below). **3.** (of an idea etc.) characterized by fantasy, unpractical. —*n.* **1.** a romantic person. **2.** (freq. **Romantic**) a composer etc. in the Romantic style. —**romantically** *adv.* [f. *romaunt* tale of chivalry, f. OF (as ROMANCE)]

The Romantic movement originated in the 18th c. It was a reaction to the Enlightenment, with its rejection of authoritarianism, and recognized the claims of passion and emotion and the sense of mystery in life; the critical was replaced by the creative spirit, and wit by humour, pathos, and gentle melancholy. In music, the period embraces much of the 19th c., with Weber, Schubert, Schumann, Liszt, and Wagner (some critics would include Beethoven). In literature, the movement is usually dated from the publication of *Lyrical Ballads* (1898) by Wordsworth and Coleridge; other writers include Byron, Shelley, Keats, and Scott. In Germany the Romantic writers included Goethe, Schiller, and the philosophical criticism of A. W. Schlegel, and in France, where the tone of Romanticism was shaped by Rousseau's *Julie* (1761), they included Chateaubriand and Victor Hugo. A state of mind rather than a style, it included, in painting, such stylistically diverse artists as Blake, Turner, Delacroix, and Goya. In its implications for the idea of an artist as an isolated misunderstood genius the Romantic movement has not yet ended.

romanticism /rəˈmæntɪsɪz(ə)m/ *n.* **1.** a tendency towards romance or romantic views. **2.** (freq. **Romanticism**) the distinctive qualities or spirt of the Romantic movement in music, literature, and painting. —**romanticist** *n.* [f. prec.]

romanticize *v.t./i.* **1.** to make romantic. **2.** to indulge in romantic ideas etc. [f. ROMANTIC]

Romany /ˈrəʊmənɪ/ *adj.* of the gypsies or their language. —*n.* **1.** a gypsy. **2.** the distinctive language of gypsies, which shares common features with Sanskrit and the later Indian languages (indicating an origin in the Indian subcontinent), with regional variations reflecting the incorporation of loan-words and other local linguistic features absorbed in their travels. [f. Romany *Rom* man]

Romberg /ˈrɒmbɜːɡ/ Sigmund (1887-1951), Hungarian-born composer who settled in New York in 1913. He wrote a succession of popular operettas, including *Maytime* (1917), *The Student Prince* (1924), *The Desert Song* (1926), and *New Moon* (1928).

Rome the capital of Italy, situated on the River Tiber about 25 km (16 miles) inland; pop. (1981) 2,830,569. The name is used allusively of the ancient Roman republic (see below) and Empire, and (as the see of the pope) of the Roman Catholic Church. The ancient city, traditionally founded by Romulus in 753 BC, was ruled by kings until the expulsion of Tarquin the Proud in 510 BC. An aristocratic republic was established, and its history in the next 250 years was marked by internal class-struggle and external conflict with the surrounding peoples. By the mid-2nd c. BC Rome had subdued the whole of Italy; her power brought her into conflict with Carthaginian interests in the western Mediterranean and with the Hellenistic world in the east. Success in the Punic Wars gave Rome her first overseas possessions, and the Macedonian wars eventually left her dominant over Greece and much of Asia Minor. From about 135 BC provincial unrest, and dissatisfaction at home with the Senate's control of government, brought a series of ambitious military leaders to the fore in open rivalry, each able to count on the support of a devoted soldiery, until civil wars culminated in the defeat of Pompey by Julius Caesar. Cæsar's brief dictatorship established the principle of personal autocracy, and after his assassination by republican conspirators another round of civil war ended with Octavian's assumption of authority as a kind of constitutional monarch. (See ROMAN EMPIRE.) During the Middle Ages Rome emerged as the seat of the papacy and the spiritual capital of western Christianity, and became a centre of the Renaissance. It remained under papal control until 1871 when it was made the capital of a unified Italy.

Romeo /ˈrəʊmɪəʊ/ *n.* a romantic lover. [hero of Shakespeare's romantic tragedy *Romeo and Juliet*]

romer /ˈrəʊmə(r)/ *n.* a small piece of plastic or card marked with scales along two edges meeting at a right angle, or (if transparent) bearing a grid, used for measuring grid references on a map. [f. C. *Romer* (d.1951), British barrister, its inventor]

Rommel /ˈrɒm(ə)l/, Erwin (1891–1944), German general, best known for his victories as commander of the Afrika Korps in the Second World War. The Italian army had been all but defeated in its attempt to secure Egypt and the Suez Canal when Rommel assumed command in 1941. The Arabs saw him as a liberator, and his audacious attacks earned him his enemies' respect and the nickname the 'Desert Fox'. He drove the Allied forces east to 96 km (60 miles) from Alexandria, only to be defeated there at El Alamein (1942) and forced to withdraw, handicapped by the difficulty of maintaining his supply lines for so great a distance from friendly territory when the Allies held superiority in the air; in 1943 he was withdrawn from Africa to assume command of the Channel coastline. A professional soldier, he saw the inevitability of Germany's defeat. The discovery of his involvement with the conspirators who unsuccessfully attempted to assassinate Hitler in 1944, and who would have had Rommel succeed him as head of State, led to his enforced suicide.

Romney /ˈrɒmnɪ/, George (1734–1802), English portrait painter. He left his north country practice for London in 1762 and worked there for most of his professional life. In his day he was almost as popular as Reynolds and Gainsborough, and the elegance of his pictures with their lucid presentation and delicate colour was a distinctive contribution to 18th-c. portraiture.

romp *v.i.* **1.** to play about roughly and energetically. **2.** to succeed easily. —*n.* a spell of romping. [perh. var. of RAMP¹]

rompers *n.pl.* a young child's play-garment, usually covering the trunk only. [f. prec.]

Romulus /ˈrɒmjʊləs/ (*Rom. legend*) the founder of Rome, one of the twin sons of Mars by the Vestal Virgin Rhea Silvia, exposed at birth with his brother Remus and found and suckled by a she-wolf. He was worshipped after his death as Quirinus.

Roncesvalles /ˈrɒnsəvæl/ (also **Roncevaux** /-vəʊ/) a mountain pass in the Pyrenees, scene of the defeat of the rearguard of Charlemagne's army by native tribesmen in 778 and of the heroic death of one of his nobles, Roland, an event much celebrated in medieval literature.

rondeau /ˈrɒndəʊ/ *n.* a short poem with only two rhymes throughout and the opening words used twice as a refrain. [F (as foll.)]

rondel /ˈrɒnd(ə)l/ *n.* a rondeau, esp. of a special form. [f. OF (as ROUND); cf. ROUNDEL]

rondo /ˈrɒndəʊ/ *n.* (*pl.* **-os**) a piece of music with a leading theme which recurs several times. [It. f. F, = RONDEAU]

Röntgen /ˈrʌntjən/, Wilhelm Conrad von (1845–1923), German physicist, the discoverer of X-rays, for which he was awarded the first Nobel Prize for physics in 1901. Röntgen was trained as a mechanical engineer before taking up an academic career in physics, and he was a skilful experimenter. He worked on a variety of topics but the two pieces of research for which he is famous were outside his normal scope. In 1888 he demonstrated the existence of a magnetic field caused by the motion of electrostatic charges, predicted by Maxwell's electromagnetic theory and important for future electrical theory; then in 1895 he observed by chance that a fluorescent screen began to glow brightly as soon as a current was passed through a Crookes' vacuum tube some distance away. He investigated the properties of this invisible radiation, which he called X-rays because of their unknown origin, and startled the world with the photograph of the bones of his wife's hand, taken on 22 Dec. 1895. The roentgen (see entry) was named in his honour.

rood *n.* **1.** a crucifix, especially one raised on the middle of a rood-screen. **2.** a quarter-acre. —**rood-loft** *n.* a gallery above a rood-screen. **rood-screen** *n.* a carved wooden or stone screen separating the nave from the chancel in a church (ill. VESTMENTS), found in England and on the Continent especially in the 14th-mid-16th c. [OE]

roof *n.* the upper covering of a building; the top of a covered vehicle; the overhead rock in a cave or mine etc. —*v.t.* to cover with a roof; to be the roof of. —**hit** *or* **raise the roof**, (*colloq.*) to become very angry. **roof-garden** *n.* a garden on the flat roof of a building. **roof of the mouth**, the palate. **roof-rack** *n.* a framework to carry luggage etc. on the roof of a car. **roof-top** *n.* the outer surface of a roof. **roof-tree** *n.* the ridge-piece of a roof. [OE]

roofing *n.* material used for a roof. [f. ROOF]

rook¹ /rʊk/ *n.* a black bird (*Corvus frugilegus*) of the crow family, nesting in colonies. —*v.t.* **1.** to win money from at cards etc., especially by swindling. **2.** to charge (a customer) extortionately. [OE]

rook² /rʊk/ *n.* a chess piece with a battlement-shaped top. [f. OF f. Arab. (orig. sense uncertain)]

rookery /ˈrʊkərɪ/ *n.* **1.** a colony of rooks, penguins, or seals. **2.** (*archaic*) a crowded cluster of mean houses or tenements. [f. ROOK¹]

rookie /ˈrʊkɪ/ *n.* (*slang*) a recruit. [corruption of *recruit*]

room /ruːm, rʊm/ *n.* **1.** space that is or could be occupied by something. **2.** a part of a house enclosed by walls or partitions; the people in this; (in *pl.*) apartments, lodgings. **3.** opportunity, scope. —*v.i.* (*US*) to have a room or rooms, to lodge. —**rooming-house** *n.* a lodging-house. **room-mate** *n.* a person sharing a room. **room service**, provision of food etc. in a hotel bedroom. [OE]

roomy /ˈruːmɪ/ *adj.* having much room, spacious. —**roominess** *n.* [f. ROOM]

Roosevelt¹ /ˈrəʊzəvelt/, Franklin Delano (1882–1945), 32nd President of the USA 1932–45. His New Deal (see entry) successfully lifted the USA out of the Great Depression, and after the American entry into the Second World War he played a vital part in the co-ordination of the Allied war effort. In 1940 he became the first President to be elected for a third term in office, and four years later he was once again successful at the polls, but died of a cerebral haemorrhage several months later.

Roosevelt² /ˈrəʊzəvelt/, Theodore (1858–1919), 26th President of the USA 1901–8. After a varied early career in politics, Roosevelt won national fame for his service in the Spanish-American War. Elected Vice-President in 1900, he succeeded McKinley following the latter's assassination in 1901 and won re-election in 1904. At home he was notable for his anti-trust activities; while abroad, he successfully engineered the American bid to build the Panama Canal and won a Nobel Peace Prize for bringing the Russo-Japanese War to an end. He retired temporarily from politics in 1908 and was unsuccessful in his attempt to regain the Presidency in 1912 at the head of his own 'Bull Moose' party. The 'teddy-bear' is named after him, with allusion to his bear-hunting activities.

roost *n.* a bird's perching or resting place, especially a place where fowls sleep. —*v.i.* (of a bird or person) to settle for sleep; to be perched or lodged for the night. —**come home to roost**, to recoil upon the originator. [OE]

rooster *n.* (*US*) a domestic cock. [f. prec.]

root¹ *n.* **1.** the part of a plant that attaches it to the earth and conveys water and nourishment from the soil; (in *pl.*) fibres or branches of this (ill. PLANTS). **2.** a small plant with a root for transplanting. **3.** a plant with an edible root, such as a root. **4.** the embedded part of a hair, tooth, etc. **5.** (in *pl.*) what causes close emotional attachment to a place etc. **6.** a source or origin; a basis; a means of continuance. **7.** a number that when multiplied by itself a given number of times yields a given number, especially a square root (see SQUARE); the value of a quantity such that a given equation is satisfied. **8.** an ultimate element of a language from which words have been made by addition or modification. —*v.t./i.* **1.** to take root; to cause to do this. **2.** (esp. in *p.p.*) to fix or establish firmly. **3.** to drag or dig up by the roots. —**root and branch**, thoroughly, radically. **root out**, to find and get rid of. **root-stock** *n.* a rhizome; a plant into which a graft is inserted; a source from which offshoots have arisen. **take root**, to begin to draw nourishment from the soil; to become established. [OE]

root² *v.t./i.* **1.** to dig or turn up (the ground etc.) with the snout or beak in search of food. **2.** to rummage; to find or extract by rummaging —**root for**, (*US slang*) to encourage by applause or support. [OE]

rope *n.* **1.** stout cord made by twisting together strands of fibre or wire etc.; a piece of this. **2.** a quantity of similar things strung together. —*v.t.* **1.** to fasten, secure, or catch with a rope. **2.** to enclose with rope. **3.** to connect with rope. —**the rope**, a halter for hanging a person. **know** (*or* **learn**) **the ropes**, to know (or learn) the procedure for doing something. **rope in**, to persuade to take part. **rope-ladder** *n.* a ladder made of two long ropes connected by rungs. **rope-walk** *n.* a long piece of ground where ropes are made. **rope-walker** *n.* a performer on a tightrope. [OE]

ropy /ˈrəʊpɪ/ *adj.* **1.** like a rope; forming viscous or gelatinous threads. **2.** (*colloq.*) poor in quality. [f. ROPE]

Roquefort /ˈrɒkfɔː(r)/ *n.* [P] blue cheese originally made at Roquefort, a town in southern France, usually from ewes' milk and ripened in limestone caves, with a strong characteristic flavour.

rorqual /ˈrɔːkw(ə)l/ *n.* a whale of the genus *Balaenoptera*, with a dorsal fin. [F f. Norw. f. OIcel. *reythr* the specific name + *hvalr* whale]

Rorschach test /ˈrɔːʃɑːk/ a type of personality test in which a standard set of ink blots of different shapes and colours is presented one at a time to a subject who is asked to describe what they suggest or resemble. [f. Hermann *Rorschach* (d. 1922), Swiss psychiatrist, who first devised such a test]

Rosa /ˈrəʊzə/, Salvator (1615-73), Italian painter and etcher, born in Naples but active chiefly in Rome. His wide artistic abilities—including music and poetry—coupled with his colourful and dramatic life made him the epitome of the Romantic artist for the 18th and 19th c. His reputation now rests on his invention of a type of landscape, often peopled with bandits and containing scenes of violence, whose form and atmosphere blend together to create an overall feeling of sublime terror. These landscapes were, with those of Claude and Poussin, one of the determinants of 18th-c. taste and had a profound influence on Romantic art in England.

rosaceous /rəʊˈzeɪʃəs/ *adj.* of the Rosaceae, the large family of plants of which the rose is the type. [f. L (as ROSE[1])]

rosary /ˈrəʊzərɪ/ *n.* 1. (in the RC Church) a form of devotion in which five or fifteen decades of Aves are repeated, each decade preceded by the Paternoster and followed by the Gloria; a book containing this; a string of 55 or 165 beads for keeping count of these prayers. According to a tradition current since the 15th c., the devotion was founded by St Dominic, but in fact it seems to have developed gradually. 2. a similar form of bead-string used in other religions. [f. L *rosarium* rose-garden (*rosa* rose)]

Roscius /ˈrɒskɪəs/ (Quintus Roscius Gallus, d. 62 BC) the most famous Roman actor of his day, whose talents brought him wealth and the friendship of the great (including Cicero). His name became synonymous with all that was best in acting. Shakespeare referred to him in *Hamlet*, and many outstanding actors were nicknamed with reference to him (*the African, Scottish* etc. *Roscius*).

rose[1] /rəʊz/ *n.* 1. a prickly bush or shrub of the genus *Rosa*, bearing ornamental usually fragrant flowers; its flower; a flowering plant resembling this. 2. deep pink colour. 3. a representation of the flower; a design based on it. 4. the sprinkling-nozzle of a hose or watering-can. —*adj.* deep pink. —**rose-bay** *n.* a willow-herb (*Epilobium angustifolium*). **rose-bud** *n.* the bud of a rose. **rose-water** *n.* a fragrant liquid perfumed with roses. **rose-window** *n.* a circular window with a roselike pattern of tracery. **see things through rose-coloured spectacles,** to take an unduly cheerful view of things. **Wars of the Roses,** see separate entry. [f. OE f. L *rosa*]

rose[2] *p.p.* of RISE.

rosé /ˈrəʊzeɪ/ *n.* a light pink wine, coloured by only brief contact with the grape-skins. [F, = pink]

roseate /ˈrəʊzɪət/ *adj.* 1. deep pink. 2. unduly cheerful. [f. L *roseus* (as ROSE[1])]

rosemary /ˈrəʊzmərɪ/ *n.* an evergreen fragrant shrub (*Rosmarinus officinalis*) with leaves used as a culinary herb, in perfume, etc., and regarded as an emblem of remembrance. [f. OF or MDu. or L *ros marinus* dew of the sea]

rosery /ˈrəʊzərɪ/ *n.* a rose-garden. [f. ROSE[1]]

Rosetta stone /rəʊˈzetə/ an inscribed stone found near Rosetta on the western mouth of the Nile by one of Napoleon's officers in 1799. Its text, a decree commemorating the accession of Ptolemy V (reigned 205-180 BC) is written in two languages and three scripts: hieroglyphic and demotic Egyptian, and Greek. The decipherment of the Egyptian parts of the inscription by J.-F. Champollion in 1822 led to the interpretation of all the other early records of Egyptian civilization. The stone is now in the British Museum.

rosette /rəˈzet/ *n.* a roselike object, symbol, or arrangement of parts; a rose-shaped ornament of ribbons etc., especially as a supporter's badge, or as an award or a symbol of an award in a competition; a rose-shaped carving. [F dim. (as ROSE[1])]

rosewood *n.* any of several fragrant close-grained woods used in making furniture.

Rosicrucian /rəʊzɪˈkruːʃ(ə)n/ *n.* 1. a member of certain secret societies who venerated the emblems of the Rose and the Cross as twin symbols of Christ's Resurrection and

Redemption. Early in the 17th c. two anonymous writings were published in Germany relating the fabulous story of one Christian Rosenkreutz, who having learnt the wisdom of the Arabs founded a secret society devoted to the study of the hidden things of nature. The books were meant to be satirical but were taken seriously, and a number of societies with alchemistic tendencies sprang up under this title. 2. a member of various present-day societies that claim to continue the Rosicrucian tradition. —*adj.* of the Rosicrucians. [f. L *rosa crucis* (or *crux*, lit. rose cross) as Latinization of Rosenkreutz]

rosin /ˈrɒzɪn/ *n.* resin, esp. in a solid form. —*v.t.* to rub (esp. the bow of a violin etc.) with rosin. [alt. f. RESIN]

Rosinante /rɒsɪˈnæntɪ/ the name of Don Quixote's horse.

Ross[1], Sir James Clark (1800-62), English polar explorer. A nephew of Sir John Ross, he served his apprenticeship as a polar explorer in the 1820s under both Parry and his uncle. In 1831 he discovered the north magnetic pole and in 1838 undertook a magnetic survey of the United Kingdom. Between 1839 and 1843 Ross commanded the *Erebus* and the *Terror* on an expedition to the Antarctic (where Ross Sea, Ross Barrier, and Ross Island all now bear his name), for which he was knighted.

Ross[2], Sir John (1777-1856), Scottish polar explorer. After serving with distinction in the Napoleonic Wars, Ross led an expedition to Baffin Bay in 1818 and another in search of the North-west Passage between 1829 and 1833, during which he surveyed King William Land, Boothia Peninsula, and the Gulf of Boothia (the last two named in honour of the expedition's patron, Sir Felix Booth (d. 1850), head of a firm of distillers).

Rossellini /rɒseˈliːnɪ/, Roberto (1906-   ), Italian film director, noted for his 'neo-realist' style. Among his most successful films are those on the theme of the Italian resistance movement during the German occupation —*Open City* (1945), which incorporated documentary material filmed during the Second World War, and *General Della Rovere* (1959).

Rossetti[1] /rəˈzetɪ/, Christina Georgina (1830-94), English poet, sister of D. G. Rossetti (see foll.). She was deeply influenced by the Oxford Movement and her devotion to the Anglican faith is reflected in the religious poetry which constitutes the greater part of her prolific output. Marked by recurrent themes of melancholy, frustrated love and premature resignation, and great technical virtuosity, her work includes poems of fantasy, love lyrics, and poems for the young. Her first published work *Goblin Market and other Poems* (1862) shows a literary expression of Pre-Raphaelite ideals.

Rossetti[2] /rəˈzetɪ/, Dante Gabriel (Gabriel Charles Dante Rossetti, 1828-82), English poet and painter, son of a cultured Italian patriot. A founder-member of the Pre-Raphaelite brotherhood (1848), he contributed something of the mystic religiosity of quattrocento painting to the movement. Some of his poems appeared in the Pre-Raphaelite journal *The Germ* in 1850, including 'The Blessed Damozel' which was the subject of a later painting. *Poems* (1870) were attacked for its impurity and obscenity, but some readers have enjoyed the erotic and emotional power of his poetry.

Rossini /rɒˈsiːnɪ/, Gioachino Antonio (1792-1868), Italian composer, a precociously musical child who by the age of 31 was a successful enough opera composer for Stendhal (admittedly a partial witness) to declare 'The glory of the man is limited only by the limits of civilization'. Almost all of his works were written in the first half of his life. His combination of deft sophisticated humour and brilliant orchestral writing was to find its finest expression in *The Barber of Seville* (1816). Ranking equally with this work, however, is the grand opera *William Tell* (1829), a powerful recounting of the William Tell legend. A fine cook, Rossini also left to posterity a recipe for fillet steaks with artichoke hearts, *foie gras*, truffles, and Madeira sauce—tournedos Rossini.

Rostand /rɒˈstɑ̃/, Edmond (1868-1918), French playwright, who won sudden fame with his poetic drama *Cyrano de Bergerac* (1897) which remains his most popular and successful work, reviving in romantic guise the 17th-c. soldier and duellist of the title.

roster /ˈrɒstə(r)/ *n.* a list or plan showing turns of duty etc. —*v.t.* to put on a roster. [f. Du., orig. = grid-iron, with ref. to parallel lines]

rostrum /ˈrɒstrəm/ *n.* (*pl.* **-tra**) a platform for public speaking or for an orchestral conductor. [L, = beak (orig.

rostra in Roman forum adorned with beaks of captured galleys)]

rosy /ˈrəʊzɪ/ *adj.* **1.** rose-coloured, deep pink. **2.** promising, cheerful, helpful. —**rosily** *adv.*, **rosiness** *n.* [f. ROSE¹]

rot *v.t./i.* (**-tt-**) **1.** (of animal or vegetable matter) to lose its original form from chemical action caused by bacteria or fungi etc. **2.** to perish or become weak through lack of use or activity. **3.** to cause to rot. —*n.* **1.** rotting; rottenness. **2.** (*slang*) nonsense, an absurd statement or argument. **3.** a series of failures; a rapid decline. —*int.* expressing incredulity or ridicule. —**rot-gut** *n.* (*slang*) inferior or harmful liquor. [OE]

rota /ˈrəʊtə/ *n.* a list of persons acting, or duties to be done, in rotation; a roster. [L, = wheel]

Rotarian /rəʊˈteərɪən/ *n.* a member of Rotary. —*adj.* of Rotary. [f. foll.]

Rotary /ˈrəʊtərɪ/ *n.* (in full **Rotary International**) a worldwide society for business and professional men having as its aim the promotion of unselfish service and international goodwill. Its name derives from the fact that the first local group, formed at Chicago in 1905, met at each member's premises in rotation. —**Rotary Club**, a local branch of Rotary. [f. foll.]

rotary /ˈrəʊtərɪ/ *adj.* acting by rotation. [f. L *rotarius* (as ROTA)]

rotate /rəʊˈteɪt/ *v.t./i.* **1.** to move round an axis or centre, to revolve or cause to revolve. **2.** to arrange or deal with in rotation. —**rotator** *n.* [f. L *rotare* (as ROTA)]

rotation /rəʊˈteɪʃ(ə)n/ *n.* **1.** rotating, being rotated. **2.** recurrence; a recurrent series or period; a regular succession of various members of a group. **3.** the practice of growing a different crop each year on a plot of land in a regular order, to avoid exhausting the soil. —**rotational** *adj.* [as prec.]

rotatory /ˈrəʊtətərɪ/ *adj.* rotating; of rotation. [f. ROTATE]

rote *n.* **by rote**, by memory without thought of the meaning; by a fixed procedure. [orig. unkn.]

Rothschild /ˈrɒθstʃaɪld/ the name of a famous Jewish banking-house, first established in Frankfurt at the end of the 18th c. and eventually spreading its operations all over western Europe.

rotisserie /rəˈtɪsərɪ/ *n.* a cooking-device for roasting food on a revolving spit. [f. F (as ROAST)]

rotor /ˈrəʊtə(r)/ *n.* **1.** a rotary part of a machine. **2.** a horizontally-rotating vane of a helicopter (ill. FLIGHT). [irreg. for ROTATOR]

rotten /ˈrɒt(ə)n/ *adj.* **1.** rotting, rotted; falling to pieces or liable to break or tear from age or use. **2.** morally or politically corrupt; effete. **3.** contemptible, worthless. **4.** (*colloq.*) unpleasant. —**rotten borough**, see BOROUGH. —**rottenly** *adv.*, **rottenness** *n.* [f. ON (as ROT)]

rotter *n.* (*slang*) an objectionable or contemptible person. [f. ROT]

Rotterdam /ˈrɒtədæm/ a city and the principal port of the Netherlands, on the River Meuse; pop. 558,832.

rotund /rəʊˈtʌnd/ *adj.* **1.** (of a person) rounded, plump. **2.** (of speech or literary style etc.) sonorous, grandiloquent. —**rotundity** *n.* [f. L *rotundus* (as ROTATE)]

rotunda /rəʊˈtʌndə/ *n.* a circular building or hall, especially one with a dome. [f. It. *rotonda* (as prec.)]

rouble /ˈruːb(ə)l/ *n.* the currency unit of the USSR. [F. f. Russ.]

roué /ˈruːeɪ/ *n.* a dissolute person, esp. an elderly one. [F (*rouer* break on wheel, = one deserving this)]

rouge /ruːʒ/ *n.* a red cosmetic used to colour the cheeks. —*v.t.* to colour with rouge. [F, = red, f. L *rubeus*]

rough /rʌf/ *adj.* **1.** having an uneven or irregular surface, not smooth or level. **2.** not gentle or restrained or careful; violent, boisterous, harsh; severe, unpleasant, demanding. **3.** lacking finish or delicacy; not perfected or detailed; approximate. —*adv.* in a rough manner. —*n.* **1.** hardship. **2.** a hooligan, a ruffian. **3.** something rough, rough ground etc. **4.** an unfinished or natural state; a rough drawing or design etc. —*v.t.* **1.** to make rough. **2.** to shape, plan, or sketch *out* roughly. —**rough-and-ready** *adj.* rough or crude but effective; not elaborate or over-particular. **rough-and-tumble** *adj.* disorderly, irregular; (*n.*) a disorderly fight. **rough deal**, see DEAL¹. **rough diamond**, an uncut diamond; a person of good nature but rough manners. **rough-dry** *v.t.* to dry (clothes) without ironing. **rough house**, (*slang*) a disturbance, violent behaviour. **rough it**, to do without basic comforts. **rough justice**, treatment that is approximately fair. **rough-rider** *n.* one who rides unbroken

horses. **rough shooting**, shooting (as a sport) without the help of beaters. **rough up**, (*slang*) to attack (a person) violently. —**roughly** *adv.*, **roughness** *n.* [OE]

roughage /ˈrʌfɪdʒ/ *n.* indigestible fibrous material in plants which are used as food (e.g. bran, green vegetables, and certain fruits) that stimulates the action of the intestines. [f. prec.]

roughcast *n.* a plaster of lime and gravel, used on outside walls. —*v.t.* to coat with this.

roughen /ˈrʌf(ə)n/ *v.t./i.* to make or become rough. [f. ROUGH]

roughneck *n.* **1.** (*colloq.*) a driller on an oil rig. **2.** (*US slang*) a rough person.

roughshod *adj.* (of a horse) having shoes with nail-heads projecting to prevent slipping. —**ride roughshod over**, to treat inconsiderately or arrogantly.

roulette /ruːˈlet/ *n.* a gambling game played with a revolving compartmented wheel in which a ball rolls randomly. Its origins are obscure but probably French; it was only in the late 18th or early 19th c. that it became a fashionable attraction in the casinos of Europe. [F f. L (dim. of *rota* wheel)]

round *adj.* **1.** having a curved shape or outline; shaped like a circle, sphere, or cylinder. **2.** done with a circular motion. **3.** full, complete; candid. —*n.* **1.** a round object; a rung of a ladder; a slice of bread cut across the loaf; a sandwich made from whole slices of bread. **2.** a revolving motion; a circular or recurring course or series; a route on which things are to be delivered or inspected. **3.** a single provision of drinks etc. to each member of a group. **4.** one spell of play in a game etc.; one stage in a competition or struggle; one section of a boxing-match. **5.** the playing of all the holes in a golf-course once. **6.** a single shot or volley of shots from one or more firearms; ammunition for this. **7.** a solid form of sculpture etc. **8.** a musical composition for two or more voices in which each sings the same melody but starts at a different time. —*adv.* **1.** with a circular motion; in a circle or curve; with return to the starting-point or an earlier state; into consciousness after unconsciousness; so as to change to an opposite position (*lit.* or *fig.*). **2.** to, at, or affecting all or many points of a circumference or area or members of a company etc.; in every direction from a centre or within a radius. **3.** by a circuitous route; to a person's house etc. **4.** measuring (a specified distance) in girth. —*prep.* **1.** so as to encircle or enclose. **2.** with successive visits to; to all points of interest in. **3.** having as an axis or central point; coming close from various sides but not into contact (*lit.* or *fig.*). **4.** so as to pass in a curved course; having thus passed; in a position thus reached. —*v.t./i.* **1.** to give or take a round shape. **2.** (with *up* or *down*) to make (a number etc.) round by omitting units or fractions. **3.** to travel round (a cape, corner, etc.). —**go the rounds**, to go from person to person. **in the round**, with all features shown or considered; (of a sculpture) with all sides shown, not in relief; (of a theatre) with the audience all round the stage. **round about**, all round, on all sides (of); approximately. **round and round**, several times round. **round dance**, a dance with a circular movement or in which the dancers form a ring. **round figure**, *or* **number**, a figure or number without odd units or fractions. **round off**, to bring to a complete state. **round on**, to make an unexpected retort to or retaliation against. **round robin**, a petition with signatures in a circle to conceal the order of signing. **round shoulders**, shoulders bent forward so that the back is rounded. **Round Table**, that at which King Arthur and his knights sat so that none might have precedence. **round-table conference**, one with discussion by members round a table. **round trip**, a trip to one or more places and back again. **round up**, to gather or bring together. **round-up** *n.* a rounding up; a summary. [f. OF f. L (as ROTUND)]

roundabout *n.* **1.** a road junction with traffic passing in one direction round a central island. **2.** a merry-go-round or other revolving structure at a funfair. —*adj.* circuitous.

roundel /ˈraʊnd(ə)l/ *n.* **1.** a small disc, a medallion. **2.** a circular identifying mark. **3.** a rondeau. [f. OF *rondel(le)* (as ROUND)]

roundelay /ˈraʊndɪleɪ/ *n.* a short simple song with a refrain. [f. F *rondelet* (as RONDEL)]

rounders /ˈraʊndəz/ *n.* an outdoor game played with a bat and ball between teams of 9 players, having features in common with baseball (its original name). [f. ROUND]

Roundhead *n.* a member of the party (also known as *Parliamentarians*) opposing the king (Charles I) in the English Civil War, so called because of the style in which the Puritans, who were an important element in the forces, wore their hair.

roundly *adv.* **1.** thoroughly, severely. **2.** in a rounded shape. [f. ROUND]

roundsman *n.* (*pl.* **-men**) a tradesman's employee delivering goods on a regular round.

roundworm *n.* a worm with a rounded body, especially one of the genus *Ascaris*.

rouse /raʊz/ *v.t./i.* **1.** to wake; to cause to wake. **2.** to make active or excited. [orig. unkn.]

rousing *adj.* vigorous, stirring. [f. prec.]

Rousseau[1] /ˈruːsəʊ/, Henri Julien (1844-1910), French painter known as 'Le Douanier' from his job as a Parisian toll-inspector. He began painting in 1885 in a naïve style that was to appeal to Apollinaire's circle (including Jarry and Picasso) in its often dreamlike intensity and simplicity of vision. The unique stylization and authority of his pictures—e.g. *Sleeping Gypsy* (1897) and *Tropical Storm with Tiger* (1891)—have caused him to be considered a modern master and the doyen of all naïve painters.

Rousseau[2] /ˈruːsəʊ/, Jean-Jacques (1712-78), philosopher and novelist, born in Geneva. Lacking in stability of character he led an unsettled life, sometimes aided by benefactors (including Hume) whose kindness he ill repaid, sometimes occupying humble situations, as footman or music-master, living for twenty-five years with a kitchen-maid and (she claimed) depositing their five babies at the Foundling Hospital. He came into notice by the works in which he expounded his revolt against the existing social order. Believing in the original goodness of human nature he considered that the rise of property and human pride (*amour propre*) had corrupted the 'noble savage'. His most important work, the *Social Contract* (1762) expounded the theory that society is founded on a contract: the people sacrifice their natural rights to the general will in return for protection, and the head of the State is their mandatary not their master. These views had an effect on the American Declaration of Independence and were wildly acclaimed during the French Revolution, when his body was brought to Paris and reburied with pomp in the Panthéon.

Rousseau[3] /ˈruːsəʊ/, Théodore (1812-67), French landscape painter. His fruitless attempts to get his pictures accepted in the French Academy—an opponent of his *plein-air* aesthetic and bold handling—earned him the nickname of 'Le Grand Refusé', but the more liberal circumstances following the 1848 revolution saw the beginning of public recognition. In that year he settled at Barbizon in Fontainebleau Forest and worked in the company of others of the Barbizon school. His style ranged between luminous realism and deeply felt responses to the melancholy of nature.

roustabout /ˈraʊstəbaʊt/ *n.* **1.** a labourer on an oil rig. **2.** an unskilled or casual labourer. [f. dial. *roust* rout out + ABOUT]

rout[1] *n.* a disorderly retreat of defeated troops; utter defeat. —*v.t.* to put to flight, to defeat utterly. [f. AF *rute*]

rout[2] var. of ROOT[2].

route /ruːt/ *n.* the way taken in getting from a starting-point to a destination. —*v.t.* (*partic.* **routeing**) to send by a particular route. —**route march**, a training-march for troops. [f. OF, = road, ult. f. L *rumpere* break]

router /ˈraʊtə(r)/ *n.* a type of two-handled plane for cutting grooves etc. (ill. CARPENTRY). [f. ROUT[2]]

routine /ruːˈtiːn/ *n.* **1.** a regular course of procedure; the unvarying performance of certain acts. **2.** a set sequence of movements in a dance or other performance. **3.** a sequence of instructions to a computer. —*adj.* performed as a routine. —**routinely** *adv.* [F (as prec.)]

roux /ruː/ *n.* (*pl.* same) a mixture of fat and flour used as a basis for making a sauce etc. [F, = browned]

rove[1] *v.i.* to wander. —**rove-beetle** *n.* a long-bodied beetle of the family Staphylinidae. **roving commission,** authority to travel as may be necessary in conducting an inquiry or other work. **roving eye,** a tendency to flirt. [orig. archery term, = shoot at casual mark with range not determined, perh. f. dial. *rave* stray, prob. of Scand. orig.]

rove[2] past of REEVE[2].

rover[1] /ˈrəʊvə(r)/ *n.* a roving person, a wanderer. [f. ROVE[1]]

rover[2] /ˈrəʊvə(r)/ *n.* a pirate. [f. MLG or MDu. (*roven* rob)]

row[1] /rəʊ/ *n.* **1.** a number of persons or things in a more or less straight line. **2.** a line of seats across a theatre etc. **3.** a street with houses along one or each side. —**in a row,** (*colloq.*) in succession. [OE]

row[2] /rəʊ/ *v.t./i.* to propel (a boat) with oars; to convey (a passenger) in a boat thus. Rowing dates back to ancient times when it provided motive power for warships. The earliest literary reference to rowing as a sport occurs in Virgil's *Aeneid*, at the funeral games arranged by Aeneas in honour of his father. —*n.* a spell of rowing. —**rowing-boat** *or* **row-boat** *n.* a boat propelled by oars. [OE]

row[3] /raʊ/ *n.* (*colloq.*) **1.** a loud noise or commotion. **2.** a fierce quarrel or dispute. —*v.i.* (*colloq.*) to make or engage in a row. [orig. unkn.]

rowan /ˈrəʊən, ˈraʊ-/ *n.* the mountain ash (*Sorbus aucuparia*) its scarlet berry. [f. Scand.]

rowdy /ˈraʊdɪ/ *adj.* noisy and disorderly. —*n.* a rowdy person. —**rowdily** *adv.*, **rowdiness** *n.*, **rowdyism** *n.* [orig. unkn.]

Rowe /rəʊ/, Nicholas (1674-1718), English dramatist, who abandoned the legal profession for the theatre. His best-known tragedies were *The Fair Penitent* (1703) and *Jane Shore* (1714), both of which provided Mrs Siddons with celebrated roles, and *Tamerlane* (1701). They are marked by pathos and female suffering, and their strong moral tone is in sharp contrast to the licentiousness of the drama of the preceding 50 years.

rowel /ˈraʊəl/ *n.* a spiked revolving disc at the end of a spur. [f. OF *roel(e)* f. L (as ROULETTE)]

Rowlandson /ˈraʊlənds(ə)n/, Thomas (1756-1827), English draughtsman and print-maker. He trained at the Royal Academy in the 1770s and set up in London as a portrait painter in 1777, but he is remembered today as one of the finest and most acute commentators on contemporary English mores, satirizing the manners, morals, and occupations of English society, e.g. in *Vauxhall Gardens* (1784) and his illustrations to William Combe's *Tours of Dr Syntax* (1812-20). His style was essentially illustrative, a combination of graceful outline and delicate colour-washes.

rowlock /ˈrɒlək/ *n.* a device for holding an oar in place and serving as a fulcrum. [alt. of earlier *oarlock* (OAR, LOCK[1])]

royal /ˈrɔɪəl/ *adj.* **1.** of, suited to, or worthy of a king or queen. **2.** in the service or under the patronage of royalty; belonging to a king or queen or their family. **3.** splendid; on a great scale, of exceptional size etc. —*n.* **1.** (*colloq.*) a member of a royal family. **2.** a royal mast or sail (that above the topgallant; ill. SAILING-SHIPS). —**royal blue,** deep vivid blue. **Royal Commission,** a commission of inquiry appointed by the Crown at the request of the government. **Royal Family,** the family to which the sovereign belongs. **royal flush,** see FLUSH[3]. **royal icing,** hard icing for cakes, made with icing sugar and egg-white. **royal jelly,** a substance secreted by worker-bees and fed by them to future queen bees. **royal oak,** a sprig of oak worn on 29 May to commemorate the restoration of Charles II (1660) who hid in an oak-tree after the battle of Worcester (1651). **royal warrant,** a warrant authorizing a tradesman to supply goods to a specified royal person. —**royally** *adv.* [f. OF *roïal* f. L, = REGAL]

Royal Academy of Arts (London) an institution established with the sanction of George III in 1768. Its original purpose was to cultivate and improve the arts of painting, sculpture, and architecture; this implied raising the artist's social and economic status by demonstrating the seriousness of his calling—a task that Reynolds, its first President, emphasized in his annual lectures. Like most 18th-c. academies its schools instructed students in drawing from life and the antique, and an annual open exhibition selected by its own jury was established as a show-case for artistic talent. Its premises were successively in Pall Mall, Somerset Palace (1780), and with the National Gallery in Trafalgar Square from 1837, moving to Burlington House, Piccadilly, in 1867. Although it became increasingly unrepresentative of modernist tendencies (and often at odds with new talent), it is now seen as the repository of mainstream art in England and its annual summer exhibition (May-August) is something of a social event. The Royal Scottish Academy received its royal charter in 1838 as a regional focus for Scottish art but has never matched its English counterpart in prestige.

Royal Air Force the British air force, formed in 1918 by amalgamation of the Royal Flying Corps (1912) and the Royal Naval Air Service (1914).

Royal British Legion a national association of ex-members of the British armed forces, founded in 1921.

Royal Canadian Mounted Police the Canadian police force, founded in 1873 as the North West Mounted Police.

Royal Institution a society founded in London in 1799 for the dissemination of scientific knowledge.

royalist /'rɔɪəlɪst/ n. a monarchist, a supporter of a monarchy or the royal side in a civil war etc.; **Royalist**, a supporter of the Stuarts in the English Civil War. [f. prec.]

Royal Marines a British armed service founded in 1644 for service on land and at sea.

Royal Mint the establishment (since 1850, the only one) responsible for the manufacture of British coins. Set up in 1810 in a building near the Tower of London, it moved in 1968 to Llantrisant in South Wales. It also mints coins on behalf of certain foreign and Commonwealth governments, as well as medals, decorations, and seals. Since 1869 the office of Master Worker and Warden of the Mint has been nominally held by the Chancellor of the Exchequer, who has control of the establishment.

Royal Navy the British navy, whose origin dates from the fleet of warships created by King Alfred to defend the southern coast of England against Viking invaders in the 9th c. (see NAVY).

Royal Society the oldest and most prestigious scientific society in Britain, formed to promote scientific discussion especially in the physical sciences. Such societies had stormy beginnings in the 16th-c. Italy, for scientific discoveries, such as those of Galileo, contradicted the accepted ideas of the time and were frowned on by the Church. The Royal Society, which received its charter from Charles II in 1662, had originated privately among the followers of Francis Bacon, and numbered among its members such famous scientists as Boyle, Wren, and Newton, who was its president from 1703 to 1727. Its *Philosophical Transactions*, founded in 1665 and still published, is the earliest scientific journal.

royalty n. 1. being royal. 2. a royal person or persons. 3. the sum paid to a patentee for the use of a patent or to an author etc. for each copy of his book etc. sold or for each public performance of his work. 4. a royal right (now especially over minerals) granted by a sovereign to an individual or a corporation. [f. OF (as ROYAL)]

Royce /rɔɪs/, Sir Frederick Henry (1863–1933), English engine designer who founded the company of Rolls-Royce Ltd. with C. S. Rolls in 1906, after having started his own successful electrical manufacturing business in 1884 and designing and building his own car and engine in 1903. He became famous as the designer of the Rolls-Royce Silver Ghost motor car (produced 1906–25). His first aircraft engine was the Eagle, used extensively in the First World War, and subsequent designs included the Merlin, used in Spitfires and Hurricanes of the Second World War. A genius as an engineer, he was noted for his extraordinary modesty and remarkable memory. The symbol 'RR' on the front of Rolls-Royce motor cars was originally in maroon, but was changed to black because this often clashed with the colour scheme ordered by buyers. The decision to make the change had been taken shortly before Royce died but the fact that it was implemented after his death gave rise to the legend that the change was made in mourning.

r.p.m. abbr. revolutions per minute.

RSFSR abbr. Russian Soviet Federative Socialist Republic.

RSM abbr. Regimental Sergeant-Major.

RSPCA abbr. Royal Society for the Prevention of Cruelty to Animals (founded in 1824).

RSV abbr. Revised Standard Version (of the Bible).

RSVP abbr. (in an invitation etc.) please reply. [f. F *répondez s'il vous plaît*]

rt. abbr. right.

Rt. Hon. abbr. Right Honourable.

Rt. Revd abbr. Right Reverend.

Ru symbol ruthenium.

rub v.t./i. (-bb-) 1. to press one's hand or an object etc. against (a surface) and slide it to and fro; to apply thus. 2. to clean or polish by rubbing; to make or become dry, smooth, or sore etc. in this way; to remove by rubbing. 3. to move or slide (objects) against each other. —n. 1. the act or process of rubbing. 2. an impediment or difficulty. —**rub along**, (colloq.) to manage to get on without undue difficulty. **rub down**, to dry, smooth, or clean by rubbing. **rub it in**, to emphasize or repeat an embarrassing fact etc. **rub off on**, to be transferred to by contact (lit. or fig.). **rub shoulders with**, to associate with. **rub up**, to polish; to brush up (a subject etc.). **rub up the wrong way**, to irritate or repel. [perh. f. LG]

rubato /ruːˈbɑːtəʊ/ n. (pl. **-os**) (Mus.) a temporary relaxation of strict tempo. [It., = robbed]

rubber[1] n. 1. a tough elastic substance made from the latex of tropical plants or synthetically. 2. a piece of this or some other substance for erasing pencil or ink marks. 3. a device for rubbing things. 4 (slang) a condom. 5. (in pl., US) galoshes. —**rubber band**, a loop of rubber to hold papers etc. together. **rubber plant**, a plant yielding rubber, especially *Ficus elastica* grown as a house-plant. **rubber stamp**, a device for inking and imprinting on a surface; one who mechanically agrees to others' actions; an indication of such agreement. **rubber-stamp** v.t. to approve (an action) automatically without proper consideration. —**rubbery** adj. [f. RUB]

rubber[2] n. a match of usually three successive games between the same sides or persons at bridge etc. or cricket. [orig. unkn.]

rubberneck n. (US colloq.) an inquisitive person; a gaping sightseer. —v.i. (US colloq.) to behave as a rubberneck.

rubbing n. a reproduction or impression made of a memorial brass or other relief design by placing paper over it and rubbing with pigment.

rubbish n. 1. waste or worthless matter. 2. absurd ideas or suggestions, nonsense (often as an exclamation of contempt). —**rubbishy** adj. [f. AF *rubbous*]

rubble n. waste or rough fragments of stone or brick etc. —**rubbly** adj. [perh. f. OF *robe* spoils]

Rubbra /'rʌbrə/, Edmund (1901–86), English composer and pianist. Recognition came with the performance of his first symphony (1935–7). His prolific output includes ten symphonies, a piano concerto, a viola concerto, choral works, songs, and chamber music; among these is a large amount of religious music. His symphonies have a musical substance and spiritual grandeur which have still not been fully appreciated.

rubella /ruˈbelə/ n. German measles. [f. L *rubellus* reddish]

Rubens /'ruːbɪnz/, Sir Peter Paul (1577–1640), Flemish painter, the supreme master of northern baroque. He trained in Antwerp, but in Italy (1600–8) studied profoundly the work of Italian old masters, especially Titian. Based in Antwerp from 1609, his output from a superbly organized workshop was prodigious—in fresh departures in portraiture, in landscape, in religious subjects no less than historical or mythological scenes. His appetite for the female nude was robustly large, and he defined an enduringly valid type of feminine beauty (of his wives Isabella Brant, and secondly Hélène Fourment). In person sophisticated, handsome, of a learned but deftly worldly intelligence, he served also as a diplomat in Spain and in England: a prince amongst painters. The ease and vitality, the copious but sinuous rush of his strokes, are inexhaustibly influential, while his work is to be found amongst almost all the major galleries of the world.

Rubicon /'ruːbɪkɒn/ a stream in NE Italy marking the ancient boundary between Italy and Cisalpine Gaul. By taking his army across it (i.e. outside his own province) in 49 BC Julius Caesar committed himself to war against the Senate and Pompey. —**cross the Rubicon**, to take a decisive step that commits one to an enterprise.

rubicund /'ruːbɪkʌnd/ adj. (of a person or complexion) ruddy, high-coloured. [f. F or L *rubicundus* (*rubēre* be red)]

rubidium /ruˈbɪdɪəm/ n. a soft silvery metallic element of the alkali-metal group, symbol Rb, atomic number 37. First discovered spectroscopically by R. W. Bunsen and G. R. Kirchhoff in 1861, it has few commercial uses. [f. L *rubidus* reddish (with ref. to its spectrum lines)]

rubric /'ruːbrɪk/ n. 1. a direction for the conduct of divine service inserted in a liturgical book. 2. explanatory words. 3. a heading or passage in red or special lettering. [f. OF or L *rubrica* red ochre]

ruby /'ruːbɪ/ n. 1. a rare precious stone with a colour varying from deep crimson to pale rose. 2. a deep red colour. —adj. deep red. —**ruby wedding**, the 40th anniversary of a wedding. [f. OF *rubi* f. L (*rubeus* red)]

ruche /ruːʃ/ n. a frill or gathering of lace etc. [F, f. L *rusca* tree-bark]

ruck[1] n. 1. the main body of competitors not likely to overtake the leaders. 2. the undistinguished crowd of persons or things. 3. (in Rugby football) a loose scrum with the ball on the ground. [orig. = stack of fuel; app. Scand.]

ruck[2] v.t./i. to crease or wrinkle. [f. ON]

rucksack /'rʌksæk, 'rʊk-/ n. a bag slung by straps from

both shoulders and resting on the back. [G (*rucken* back, SACK[1])]

ruction /ˈrʌkʃ(ə)n/ *n.* (esp. in *pl.*, *colloq.*) protests and noisy argument, a row; a disturbance. [orig. unkn.]

rudder *n.* a flat piece hinged vertically to the stern of a vessel (ill. SAILING-SHIPS) or the rear of an aircraft (ill. FLIGHT) for steering. [OE]

ruddy *adj.* **1.** (of a person or complexion) freshly or healthily red. **2.** reddish. **3.** (*colloq.*) bloody, damnable. —**ruddily** *adv.*, **ruddiness** *n.* [OE]

rude *adj.* **1.** impolite, showing no respect or consideration; coarse. **2.** roughly made or done; primitive, uneducated. **3.** abrupt, sudden. **4.** vigorous, hearty. —**rudely** *adv.*, **rudeness** *n.* [f. OF f. L *rudis* unwrought]

rudiment /ˈruːdɪmənt/ *n.* **1.** (in *pl.*) the elements or first principles of knowledge or some subject. **2.** (in *pl.*) the imperfect beginnings of something undeveloped. **3.** a part or organ imperfectly developed because it is vestigial or has no function (e.g. the breast in males). —**rudimentary** /-ˈmentəri/ *adj.* [F or f. L (as prec.)]

Rudra /ˈrʊdrə/ **1.** (in the Rig-Veda) a minor god, associated with the storm, father of the Maruts. A destructive force, his arrows brought disease and disaster. **2.** one of the names of Siva, who may have evolved from the earlier deity. [f. Skr. = howler (*rud* howl, roar)]

rue[1] *v.t.* (*partic.* **ruing**) to repent of, to regret; to wish undone or non-existent. [OE]

rue[2] *n.* an evergreen shrub (*Ruta graveolens*) with bitter leaves. [f. OF f. L *ruta* f. Gk]

rueful /ˈruːf(ə)l/ *adj.* expressing good-humoured regret. —**ruefully** *adv.* [f. RUE[1] + -FUL]

ruff[1] *n.* **1.** a projecting starched frill worn round the neck especially in the 16th c. (ill. DRESS). **2.** a projecting or conspicuously coloured ring of feathers or hair round a bird's or animal's neck. **3.** a bird of the sandpiper family (*Philomachus pugnax*). **4.** a kind of pigeon. [perh. = ROUGH]

ruff[2] *v.t./i.* to trump at cards. —*n.* trumping. [orig. name of card-game f. OF *ro(u)ffle*]

ruffian /ˈrʌfɪən/ *n.* a violent lawless person. —**ruffianism** *n.*, **ruffianly** *adj.* [f. F f. It. *ruffiano*]

ruffle *v.t./i.* **1.** to disturb the smoothness or evenness of. **2.** to upset the calmness or even temper of (a person). **3.** to undergo ruffling. —*n.* a frill of lace etc. worn especially round the wrist or neck. [orig. unkn.]

rufous /ˈruːfəs/ *adj.* (esp. of animals) reddish-brown. [f. L *rufus*]

rug *n.* **1.** a thick floor-mat. **2.** a piece of thick material used as a blanket or coverlet. —**pull the rug from under,** to deprive of support, to weaken, to unsettle. [prob. f. Scand.]

Rugby /ˈrʌgbɪ/ *n.* (in full **Rugby football**) a form of football played with an oval ball which may be carried as well as kicked. It is named after Rugby School in Warwickshire where it was developed, though the exact date when the distinctive practice originated (in 1823 or later) of running while carrying the ball is in dispute. The oval ball owes its shape to the inflated pig's bladder which was used in ball-games for many centuries before being given (by the 16th c.) a leather outer cover. —**Rugby League,** a partly professional form of the game with teams of 13. It dates from 1895 when a group of northern clubs, exasperated by repeated refusals of the ruling body to allow them to compensate players for money lost by taking time off from work to play football, decided to break away from the Rugby Union. **Rugby Union,** an amateur form with teams of 15.

rugged /ˈrʌgɪd/ *adj.* **1.** having a rough uneven surface or outline; (of the features) irregular and strongly marked. **2.** (of manner etc.) rough but kindly and sincere. **3.** harsh-sounding. **4.** sturdy. —**ruggedly** *adv.*, **ruggedness** *n.* [prob. f. Scand.]

rugger /ˈrʌgə(r)/ *n.* (*colloq.*) Rugby football. [f. RUGBY]

Ruhr /rʊə(r)/ a tributary of the Rhine in West Germany, which has given its name to this region of coal-mining and heavy industry.

ruin /ˈruːɪn/ *n.* **1.** severe damage or destruction; a destroyed or wrecked state. **2.** complete loss of fortune, resources, or prospects. **3.** (in *sing.* or *pl.*) the remains of something that has suffered ruin. **4.** a cause of ruin. —*v.t.* to bring into a state of ruin; to damage so severely that it is in ruins; (in *p.p.*) reduced to ruins. —**ruination** /-ˈneɪʃ(ə)n/ *n.* [f. OF f. L *ruina* (*ruere* fall)]

ruinous /ˈruːɪnəs/ *adj.* **1.** bringing or likely to bring ruin, disastrous. **2.** in ruins, dilapidated. —**ruinously** *adv.* [f. L *ruinosus* (as RUIN)]

Ruisdael /ˈrɔɪsdɑːl/, Jacob Isaacksz van (1628/9–82), the most important Dutch landscape painter of the 17th c. Born in Haarlem, he painted the surrounding landscape from the mid-1640s until his move to Amsterdam in 1657, where he spent the rest of his life. His subdued palette suited his typical subject-matter of low horizons, dominant cloud-scapes, and wind-blown silvery atmosphere. His painting demonstrates the possibilities of investing landscape with an emotional quality that ranges from the subtlest inti-mations of mood to a sense of tragedy and transcendence (e.g. *Jewish Cemetery*, 1660s). Hobbema was his most famous pupil. His influence continued as far as the 18th and 19th c. affecting, among others, Gainsborough, Con-stable, and the Barbizon school.

rule *n.* **1.** a statement of what can, must, or should be done in a certain set of circumstances or in playing a game; the customary or normal state of things or course of action. **2.** government, exercise of authority, control. **3.** a graduated straight often jointed measuring device used by carpenters etc. **4.** a thin line or dash in printing. **5.** the code of discipline of a religious order. **6.** (*Law*) an order made by a judge or court with reference to a particular case only. —*v.t./i.* **1.** to have authoritative control over, to govern. **2.** to keep under control; to exercise a decisive influence over. **3.** to give a decision as judge or other authority. **4.** to mark parallel lines across (paper); to make (a straight line) with a ruler etc. —**as a rule,** usually, more often than not. **rule of thumb,** a rule based on experience or practice, not on theory. **rule out,** to exclude, to pronounce irrelevant or ineligible. **rule the roost,** to be in control, to dominate. [f. OF f. L *regula*]

ruler *n.* **1.** a person who rules by authority, especially over a country etc. **2.** a straight strip of wood or metal etc. used for measuring or for drawing straight lines. [f. RULE]

ruling *n.* an authoritative pronouncement. [f. RULE]

rum[1] *n.* a spirit distilled from sugar-cane or molasses. [perh. abbr. of 17th-c. forms *rumbullion*, *rumbustion*]

rum[2] *adj.* (*colloq.*) strange, odd. [16th-c. slang, orig. = excellent]

rumba /ˈrʌmbə/ *n.* a ballroom dance of Cuban origin, danced on the spot with a pronounced movement of the hips; the music for this. [Amer. Sp.]

rumble[1] *v.i.* to make a continuous deep sound as of distant thunder; (of a person or vehicle) to go along making such a sound. —*n.* a rumbling sound. [prob. f. MDu. *rommelen* (imit.)]

rumble[2] *v.t.* (*slang*) to see through (a deception), to detect the true character of. [orig. unkn.]

rumbustious /rʌmˈbʌstʃəs/ *adj.* (*colloq.*) boisterous, up-roarious. [prob. var. of *robustious* robust]

ruminant /ˈruːmɪnənt/ *n.* an animal that chews the cud. —*adj.* **1.** belonging to the ruminants. **2.** meditative. [as foll.]

ruminate /ˈruːmɪneɪt/ *v.i.* **1.** to chew the cud. **2.** to ponder, to meditate. —**rumination** /-ˈneɪʃ(ə)n/ *n.*, **ruminative** *adj.* [f. L *ruminari* (*rumen* throat)]

rummage /ˈrʌmɪdʒ/ *v.t./i.* **1.** to search by turning things over or disarranging them. **2.** to discover thus. —*n.* a search of this kind. —**rummage sale,** a jumble sale. [orig. = arranging of casks in hold, f. OF *arrumage* (*arrumer* stow)]

rummy *n.* a card-game played usually with two packs, each player seeking to dispose of his cards by forming sequences or sets. [20th c.; orig. unkn.]

rumour /ˈruːmə(r)/ *n.* information spread by word of mouth, of doubtful accuracy. —*v.t.* (usu. in *pass.*) to spread as a rumour. [f. OF f. L *rumor* noise]

rump *n.* **1.** the tail-end or buttocks of an animal, person, or bird. **2.** a cut of meat from an animal's hindquarters. **3.** an unimportant remnant. —**Rump Parliament,** that part of the Long Parliament which continued to sit after Pride's Purge in 1648. Dissolved by Cromwell in 1653, the Rump was briefly reconvened in 1659 but voted its own dissolution early in 1660. —**rump steak,** a steak cut from a rump of beef. [prob. f. Scand.]

rumple *v.t./i.* to make or become crumpled; to make (something smooth) untidy. [f. MDu. (*rompe* wrinkle)]

rumpus /ˈrʌmpəs/ *n.* (*colloq.*) an uproar; an angry dispute. [prob. fanciful]

run *v.t./i.* (**-nn-**; *past* **ran**; *p.p.* **run**) **1.** to move with quick steps, never having both or all feet on the ground at once; (in cricket) to traverse the pitch to score a run. **2.** to flee. **3.** to go or travel hurriedly or swiftly; (of a ship) to go straight and fast; (of salmon) to go up river in large numbers from the sea. **4.** to compete in a race or contest; to seek election. **5.** to advance (as) by rolling or on wheels, or smoothly or easily. **6.** to be in action or operation; to be current or valid. **7.** (of a bus, train, etc.) to travel from point to point; to convey (a person) in a vehicle; to smuggle (guns etc.). **8.** to extend; to have a course, order, or tendency. **9.** to flow or cause to flow; to fill (a bath etc.) thus; to exude liquid; to be wet. **10.** to spread rapidly or beyond the intended limit. **11.** to make one's way through or over (a course, race, distance, etc.); to perform (an errand). **12.** to own and use (a vehicle etc.); to operate (a business). **13.** to cause to run, go, extend, or function. **14.** (of a newspaper) to print as an item. **15.** to sew (fabric) with running stitches. —*n.* **1.** an act or spell of running. **2.** a short excursion; a distance travelled. **3.** a general tendency of development; a regular route. **4.** a continuous or long stretch, spell, or course; a high general demand; a quantity produced in one period of operation. **5.** the general or average type or class. **6.** a point scored in cricket or baseball. **7.** permission to make unrestricted use of something. **8.** an animal's regular track; an enclosure where domestic animals can range; a track for some purpose. **9.** a large number of salmon going up river from the sea. **10.** a ladder in a stocking etc. —**on the run,** fleeing from pursuit or capture. **run across,** to happen to meet or find. **run away,** to leave secretly or hastily. **run away with,** to elope with; to win (a prize etc.) easily; to accept (an idea) too hastily; to require (much money) in expense. **run down,** to knock down with a moving vehicle or ship; to reduce the numbers of; (of a clock) to stop because not rewound; to discover after searching; to disparage; (in *pass.*) to be weak or exhausted from overwork or undernourishment. **run-down** *n.* a reduction in numbers; a detailed analysis; (*adj.*) decayed after being prosperous. **run dry,** to cease to flow. **run for it,** to seek safety by fleeing. **run for one's money,** some return for outlay or effort. **run in,** to run (a new engine or vehicle) carefully in the early stages; (*colloq.*) to arrest. **run into,** to collide with; to encounter; to reach as many as. **run off,** to run away; to produce (copies etc.) on a machine; to decide (a race) after a tie or heats; to flow or cause to flow away; to write or recite fluently. **run-of-the-mill** *adj.* ordinary, undistinguished. **run out,** to come to an end, to become used up; to exhaust one's stock; to jut out; to put down the wicket of (a batsman who is running). **run out on,** (*colloq.*) to desert (a person). **run over,** to overflow; to study or repeat quickly; (of a vehicle or driver) to pass over, to knock down or crush. **run through,** to examine or rehearse briefly; to deal successively with. **run to,** to have the money or ability for; to reach (an amount or number; to show a tendency to (fat etc.). **run up,** to accumulate (a debt etc.) quickly; to build hurriedly; to make quickly by sewing; to add up (a column of figures); to raise (a flag). **run-up** *n.* the period preceeding an important event. **run up against,** to meet with (a difficulty). [OE]

runaway *n.* a fugitive. —*adj.* **1.** fugitive. **2.** (of a victory) won easily.

rune /ruːn/ *n.* **1.** any letter of the earliest Germanic alphabet, used especially by the Scandinavians and Anglo-Saxons from *c.* 3rd c. and formed by modifying Roman or Greek characters to suit carving. **2.** a letter of a similar alphabet of 8th-c. Mongolian Turks. **3.** a similar mark of mysterious or magical significance. **4.** a Finnish poem; a division of this. —**runic** *adj.* [f. ON, = magic signs]

rung[1] *n.* **1.** a cross-piece of a ladder (*lit.* or *fig.*). **2.** a short stick fixed as a cross bar in a chair etc. [OE]

rung[2] *p.p.* of RING[2].

runnel /ˈrʌn(ə)l/ *n.* **1.** a brook. **2.** a gutter. [OE (as RUN)]

runner *n.* **1.** one who or that which runs; a person or animal that runs in a race. **2.** a messenger. **3.** a creeping plant-stem that can take root. **4.** a rod, groove, or roller for a thing to move on; each of the long strips on which a sledge etc. slides. **5.** a long narrow strip of carpet, or of ornamental cloth for a table etc. —**runner bean,** a kind of climbing bean (*Phaseolus multiflorus*). **runner-up** *n.* a person or team finishing second in a competition. [f. RUN]

running *n.* the action of runners in a race etc.; the way a race proceeds. —*adj.* **1.** performed while running. **2.** continuous. **3.** consecutive. —**in** (*or* **out of**) **the running,** with a good (or no) chance of succeeding. **make the running,** to set the pace (*lit.* or *fig.*). **running commentary,** a spoken description of events as they occur. **running knot,** a knot that slips along a rope etc. so that the size of the loop is changed. **running repairs,** minor repairs and replacements. **running-stitch** *n.* a line of evenly-spaced

stitches made by a straight thread passing in and out of the material. [f. RUN]

runny *adj.* **1.** tending to flow or exude fluid. **2.** semi-liquid; excessively fluid. [f. RUN]

Runnymede /ˈrʌnimiːd/ a meadow at Egham on the south bank of the Thames near Windsor, famous for its association with Magna Carta which was signed by King John in the meadow or on the island near by.

runt *n.* an undersized person or animal; the smallest of a litter. [orig. unkn.]

runway *n.* a specially prepared surface for the taking off and landing of aircraft.

Runyon /ˈrʌnjən/, (Alfred) Damon (1884–1946), American journalist and sports writer, famous also for his short stories about New York City's Broadway and underworld characters, written in a highly individual style with much use of colourful slang idiom. His stories were the inspiration for the musical comedy *Guys and Dolls* (1950).

rupee /ruːˈpiː/ *n.* the currency unit of India, Pakistan, etc. [f. Hind. f. Skr., = wrought silver]

Rupert /ˈruːpət/, Prince (1619–82), a Royalist general of the English Civil War, son of the Elector Palatine and nephew of Charles I. Rupert was one of the most innovative and accomplished soldiers of his day, with a particular reputation as a dashing leader of cavalry. After being victorious in a series of engagements in the early years of the war, he was defeated by superior Parliamentarian forces at Marston Moor (1644) and Naseby (1645) and finally dismissed by the King for surrendering Bristol. Banished by Parliament, he led a series of expeditions against English shipping from the Low Countries before returning to Britain with Charles II to become one of the admirals in the Restoration Navy. Rupert was an active dilettante of science and the arts, an amateur etcher, and introduced mezzotint engraving to England. —**Prince Rupert's drops,** pear-shaped drops of glass with a long tail, made by dropping melted glass into water, and remarkable for the property, due to internal strain, of disintegrating explosively into powder when the tail is broken off or the surface scratched. **Prince Rupert's metal,** a gold-coloured alloy of about three parts copper and one part zinc.

rupture /ˈrʌptʃə(r)/ *n.* **1.** breaking, breach. **2.** a breach of harmonious relations, disagreement and parting. **3.** an abdominal hernia. —*v.t./i.* **1.** to burst or break (tissue etc.); to become burst or broken. **2.** to sever (a connection). **3.** to affect with or suffer a hernia. [f. OF or f. L (*rumpere* break)]

rural /ˈrʊər(ə)l/ *adj.* in, of, or suggesting the countryside. —**rural dean,** see DEAN[1]. **rural district,** (*hist.*) a group of country parishes governed by an elected council. [f. OF or L (*rus* the country)]

Rurik /ˈrʊərɪk/ the name of a dynasty that ruled in Russia from the 9th c. until 1598, reputedly founded by a Varangian chief who settled in Novgorod in 862. The Ruriks established themselves as rulers of the principality of Moscow and gradually extended their dominions into the surrounding territory.

Ruritania /rʊərɪˈteɪnɪə/ an imaginary Central-European kingdom used as a fictional background for court romances with chivalry and intrigue in a modern setting, as in the novels of Sir Anthony Hope (Hawkins) *The Prisoner of Zenda* (1894) and *Rupert of Hentzau* (1898). —**Ruritanian** *adj.* & *n.* [as RURAL, after *Lusitania*]

ruse /ruːz/ *n.* a stratagem, a trick. [f. OF (*ruser* drive back)]

rush[1] *v.t./i.* **1.** to go, move, or pass precipitately or with great speed. **2.** to impel or carry along rapidly. **3.** to act hastily; to force into hasty action. **4.** to attack or capture with a sudden assault. —*n.* **1.** rushing; an instance of this. **2.** a period of great activity. **3.** a sudden migration of large numbers. **4.** a sudden great demand for goods etc. **5.** (in *pl.*, *colloq.*) the first print or showing of a film after shooting, before it is cut and edited. —**rush one's fences,** to act with undue haste. **rush-hour** *n.* the time each morning and evening when traffic or business is heaviest. [F. AF *russher* = OF *ruser* (as prec.)]

rush[2] *n.* a marsh plant of the genus *Juncus* with slender pith-filled stems, used for making chair-seats or baskets etc.; a stem of this. —**rush candle,** a candle made by dipping the pith of a rush in tallow. —**rushy** *adj.* [OE]

rusk *n.* a slice of bread rebaked as a light biscuit, especially for feeding infants. [f. Sp. or Port. *rosca* twist, roll of bread]

Ruskin /ˈrʌskɪn/, John (1819–1900), English art and social critic. His voluminous writings profoundly influenced 19th-c. opinion and the development of the Labour movement. He was a champion of the painter Turner, who was then a controversial figure, and of Gothic architecture, which he saw as a religious expression of the piety of the Middle Ages: *The Stones of Venice* (1851–3), in its attacks on 'the pestilent art of the Renaissance', led on to his later attacks on capitalism in his lectures on 'The Political Economy of Art' (1857), and on utilitarianism in *Unto This Last* (1860). His *Fors Clavigera* (1871–8) or 'Letters to the Workmen and Labourers of Great Britain' was an attempt to spread his notions of social justice, coupled with aesthetic improvement; his religious and philanthropic instincts also expressed themselves in the founding of the Guild of St George in 1871, a major contribution to the Arts and Crafts movement, and in other public causes. His unfinished autobiography *Praeterita* (1885–9) was written in his final years of mental infirmity and semi-isolation.

Russell[1] /ˈrʌs(ə)l/, Bertrand Arthur William (1873–1970), 3rd Earl (though he rejected the title), British philosopher, mathematician, and reformer, important especially for his work on mathematical logic, which had great influence on symbolic logic and on set theory in mathematics. In *Principia Mathematica* (1910–13), written with A. N. Whitehead, he followed Frege in seeking to provide a secure foundation for mathematics by showing how its axioms could be deduced from those of logic. Although his philosophical views underwent continual development and revision, he remained constant in his admiration of physics and his belief that science provides the best understanding of all that exists. Kept from a traditional academic career by his radical views, he became widely known to the general public through campaigns and writings in favour of progressive views in politics, morals, education, and religion. He campaigned for women's suffrage, opposed the First World War, ran a progressive school, and demonstrated in favour of nuclear disarmament. He was awarded the Nobel Prize for literature in 1950, and retained his lucidity and wit to the end of his long life.

Russell[2] /ˈrʌs(ə)l/, George William (1867–1935), Irish poet who wrote under the pseudonym 'AE'. He met W. B. Yeats in 1886 and became interested in theosophy and mysticism, evident in his volume of verse, *Homeward; Songs by the Way* (1894). After the performance of *Deirdre* (1902) he became an established figure in the Irish literary revival. His interests extended to public affairs and he successfully edited *The Irish Homestead* (1905–23) and *The Irish Statesman* (1923–30).

Russell[3] /ˈrʌs(ə)l/, John, 1st Earl Russell (1792–1878), British Whig statesman who introduced the Reform Bill of 1832 into Parliament. He was Prime Minister 1846–52 and 1865–6.

russet /ˈrʌsɪt/ adj. reddish-brown —n. 1. russet colour. 2. an apple with a rough skin of this colour. [f. AF, ult. f. L *russus* red]

Russia /ˈrʌʃə/ a country in northern Asia and eastern Europe. The modern State originated from the expansion of Muscovy under the Rurik and Romanov dynasties, westwards towards Poland and Hungary, southwards to the Black Sea, and eastwards to the Pacific Ocean. Russia played an increasing role in Europe from the time of Peter the Great in the early 18th c. and pursued imperial ambitions in the east in the second half of the 19th c. Social and economic problems, exacerbated by the First World War, led to the overthrow of the Tsar in 1917 and the establishment of a Communist government. (See UNION OF SOVIET SOCIALIST REPUBLICS.)

Russian /ˈrʌʃ(ə)n/ adj. of Russia or its people or language. —n. 1. a native or inhabitant of Russia. 2. the official language of the USSR, the most important of the Slavonic languages, spoken in the USSR as a first language by about 142 million people and by another 42 million as a second language. It is written in the Cyrillic alphabet. —**Russian roulette**, the firing of a revolver held to one's head after spinning the cylinder with one chamber loaded. **Russian salad,** a salad of mixed diced vegetables coated with mayonnaise. [f. prec.]

Russian Soviet Federative Socialist Republic the largest and most important of the constituent republics of the USSR. It occupies more than three-quarters of the total area of the Union, contains more than half its population, and consists of twelve autonomous republics and numerous provinces; capital, Moscow.

Russo- /ˈrʌsəʊ-/ *in comb.* Russian. —**Russo-Japanese War,** a war of 1904–5, caused by conflict of Russian and Japanese interests in Manchuria and Korea. Russia suffered a series of defeats, and by the peace settlement Japan gained the ascendancy in that region.

rust n. 1. a reddish or yellowish-brown corrosive coating formed on iron or steel by oxidation. 2. reddish-brown. 3. a plant-disease with rust-coloured spots. 4. an impaired state due to disuse or inactivity. —v.t./i. 1. to make or become rusty. 2. to lose quality or efficiency by disuse or inactivity. [OE, rel. to RED]

rustic /ˈrʌstɪk/ adj. 1. having the appearance or qualities ascribed to country people or peasants, simple and unsophisticated, rough and unrefined. 2. made of untrimmed branches or rough timber. —n. a countryman, a peasant. —**rustically** adv., **rusticity** /-ˈtɪsɪtɪ/ n. [f. L *rusticus* (*rus* the country)]

rusticate /ˈrʌstɪkeɪt/ v.t./i. 1. to send down temporarily from a university as a punishment. 2. to retire to or live in the country. 3. to mark (masonry) with sunk joints or a roughened surface (ill. BUILDING TECHNIQUES). —**rustication** /-ˈkeɪʃ(ə)n/ n. [f. L *rusticare* live in the country (as prec.)]

rustle /ˈrʌs(ə)l/ v.t./i. 1. to make or cause to make a gentle sound as of dry leaves blown in a breeze. 2. to steal (cattle or horses). —n. a rustling sound. —**rustle up**, (*colloq.*) to produce when needed. —**rustler** n. [imit.]

rustless adj. not liable to rust. [f. RUST + -LESS]

rusty adj. 1. rusted, affected by rust. 2. stiff with age or disuse; (of knowledge etc.) faded or impaired by neglect. 3. rust-coloured; (of black clothes) discoloured by age. —**rustily** adv. **rustiness** n. [OE (as RUST)]

rut[1] n. 1. a deep track made by the passage of wheels. 2. a fixed pattern of behaviour difficult to change; a habitual usually dull course of life. [prob. f. OF (as ROUTE)]

rut[2] n. the periodic sexual excitement of male deer etc. —v.i. (**-tt-**) to be affected with rut. [f. OF f. L *rugitus* (*rugire* roar)]

Ruth /ruːθ/ a book of the Old Testament telling the story of Ruth, a Moabite woman, who married her husband's kinsman Boaz. King David (and therefore Christ, Matt. 1: 5) are descended from them.

ruthenium /ruːˈθiːnɪəm/ n. a rare hard white metallic element, symbol Ru, atomic number 44, chemically related to platinum. First isolated in the pure state in the 1840s, the metal is used in powdered form as a catalyst, and in alloys to increase the hardness of platinum and palladium. [f. L *Ruthenia* Russia (from its discovery in ores from the Urals)]

Rutherford /ˈrʌðəfəd/, Sir Ernest, 1st Baron Rutherford of Nelson (1871–1937), British physicist, born in New Zealand, successively professor at Montreal, Manchester, and Cambridge, widely regarded as the founder of nuclear physics, his researches having led to major discoveries concerning the nature of the atom. An experimental genius with a strategic approach to research, Rutherford had an unrivalled capacity for isolating a problem until there were only a small number of possible explanations, and then devising a series of simple experiments until all but one possibility has been eliminated. While studying radioactivity he established the nature of alpha and beta particles, and (with Soddy) proposed the laws of radioactive decay. From further experiments he concluded that the positive charge in an atom, and virtually all its mass, is concentrated in a central nucleus with negatively charged electrons in orbit round it; in essence his view is still held today. In 1919, after spending the war years developing means of detecting German submarines, Rutherford announced the first artificial transmutation of matter—an experiment which caught the public imagination: he bombarded nitrogen gas with alpha particles produced by natural radioactive substances, and found that the disruption of the nuclei had changed the nitrogen atoms into oxygen. For his considerable services to science he received many honours, including the Nobel Prize for chemistry in 1908, a knighthood in 1914, and a peerage in 1931. The artifical element rutherfordium is named in his honour.

rutherfordium /rʌðəˈfɔːdɪəm/ n. the American name for the element of atomic number 104, a short-lived artificially produced radioactive transuranic element (cf. KURCHATOVIUM). [f. prec.]

ruthless /ˈruːθlɪs/ adj. having no pity or compassion. —**ruthlessly** adv., **ruthlessness** n. [f. *ruth* pity, f. RUE[1]]

rutted /ˈrʌtɪd/ *adj.* marked with ruts. [f. RUT¹]

RV *abbr.* Revised Version (of the Bible).

Rwanda /ruːˈændə/ a country of central Africa east of Zaïre; pop. (est. 1981) 5,100,000; official languages, Rwanda (a Bantu language) and French; capital, Kigali. The area was claimed by Germany from 1890, and after the First World War it became part of a Belgian trust territory, gaining independence as a republic in 1962. —**Rwandan** *adj. & n.*

Ryder Cup /ˈraɪdə(r)/ a golf tournament played between teams of men professionals of the USA and of Great Britain and Ireland (and, since 1979, other European players), held every second year in September, alternately in the USA and Great Britain, from 1927; the trophy for this, donated by Samuel Ryder, a British seed-merchant.

rye /raɪ/ *n.* **1.** a cereal plant (*Secale cereale*); the grain of this, used for bread and fodder. **2.** (in full **rye whisky**) whisky distilled from rye. [OE]

rye-grass /ˈraɪgrɑːs/ *n.* a fodder grass of the genus *Lolium*. [alt. of earlier *ray-grass*]

S

S, s /es/ n. (pl. **Ss, S's** /ˈesɪz/) **1.** the nineteenth letter of the alphabet. **2.** an S-shaped thing.

S abbr. siemens.

S symbol sulphur.

S. abbr. **1.** Saint. **2.** south, southern.

s. abbr. **1.** second(s). **2.** shilling(s) [f. L solidus, orig = gold coin of the Roman Empire]. **3.** singular. **4.** son.

's abbr. has, is, us.

SA abbr. **1.** Salvation Army. **2.** South Africa. **3.** South Australia.

Sabaean /səˈbiːən/ n. a member of a Semitic-speaking people who by the 3rd c. AD had established an elaborate system of government and succeeded in uniting southern Arabia into a single State, overthrown by the Abyssinians in AD 525. —adj. of the Sabaeans. [f. L f. Gk, ult. f. Heb. Sheba people of Yemen (see SHEBA)]

Sabah /ˈsɑːbɑː/ a State of Malaysia, comprising North Borneo and some offshore islands. A British protectorate from 1888, it gained independence and joined Malaysia in 1963; capital, Kota Kinabalu.

Sabbatarian /sæbəˈteərɪən/ n. a person who observes the sabbath strictly. —**Sabbatarianism** n. [f. L (as foll.)]

sabbath /ˈsæbəθ/ n. **1.** a religious rest-day appointed for Jews on the last day of the week (Saturday). **2.** Sunday as a Christian day of abstinence from work and play. [OE, ult. f. Heb., = rest]

sabbatical /səˈbætɪk(ə)l/ adj. **1.** of the sabbath. **2.** (of leave) granted at intervals to a university professor etc. for study or travel etc. —n. a period of sabbatical leave. [f. L f. Gk (as prec.)]

Sabellian[1] /səˈbelɪən/ adj. of the Sabellians or their language or dialects. —n. a member of a group of tribes in ancient Italy (including Sabines, Samnites, Campanians, etc.), or their language or dialects. [f. L Sabellus]

Sabellian[2] /səˈbelɪən/ adj. of the Sabellians. —n. a holder of the doctrine of Sabellius (3rd c.), African heretic, that the Father, Son, and Holy Spirit are merely aspects of one divine Person. [f. Sabellius]

Sabian /ˈseɪbɪən/ n. **1.** an adherent of a religious sect mentioned in the Koran and by later Arabian writers. In the Koran, the Sabians are classed with Muslims, Jews, and Christians as believers in the true God. On account of the toleration extended to them by Muslims the name of Sabians was, some centuries after Muhammad, assumed not only by a half-Christian Gnostic sect, the Mandaeans (whose religion was perhaps akin to that of true Sabians), but also by certain actual polytheists. **2.** a member of a group of Syrian pagan star-worshippers. [f. Arab., prob. as Heb. saba host]

Sabin /ˈseɪbɪn/, Albert Bruce (1906–), Russian-born American microbiologist who in 1955 developed an orally administered vaccine, named after him, against polio-myelitis.

Sabine /ˈsæbaɪn/ adj. of the Sabines. —n. a member of a people of ancient Italy of the area NE of Rome, renowned in antiquity for their frugal and hardy character and their superstitious practices, finally conquered by Rome in 290 BC. The (unhistorical) legend of the Rape of the Sabine Women (said to have been carried off by the Romans at a spectacle to which the Sabines had been invited) reflects the early intermingling of Romans and Sabines; some Roman religious institutions were said to have a Sabine origin.

sable /ˈseɪb(ə)l/ n. **1.** a small dark-furred arctic mammal (Martes zibellina or M. americana); its fur or skin. **2.** (in heraldry) the colour black. —adj. black, gloomy. [f. OF, ult. f. Slav.]

sabot /ˈsæbəʊ/ n. a heavy wooden or wooden-soled shoe. [F]

sabotage /ˈsæbətɑːʒ/ n. malicious or wanton damage or destruction, especially for an industrial or political purpose. —v.t. to commit sabotage on; to destroy or render useless, to spoil. [F, f. saboter make a noise with sabots,

perform or execute badly, destroy (tools, machinery, etc.) wilfully]

saboteur /sæbəˈtɜː(r)/ n. one who commits sabotage. [F]

sabre /ˈseɪbə(r)/ n. **1.** a cavalry sword with a curved blade. **2.** a light fencing-sword with a tapering blade. —**sabre-rattling** n. a display or threats of military force. [F, earlier sable, ult. f. Polish or Magyar]

sac /sæk/ n. a membranous bag in an animal or vegetable organism. [F or f. L (as SACK¹)]

saccharin /ˈsækərɪn/ n. a very sweet substance used as a substitute for sugar. [G f. L saccharum sugar]

saccharine /ˈsækəriːn/ adj. intensely sweet, cloying. [as prec.]

sacerdotal /sækəˈdəʊt(ə)l/ adj. of priests or priestly office. [f. OF or L (sacerdos priest)]

sachet /ˈsæʃeɪ/ n. a small bag or packet containing a small portion of a substance or filled with a perfumed substance for laying among clothes etc. [F, dim. of sac f. L saccus f. Gk]

Sachs /sæks/, Hans (1494–1576), German writer, by trade a shoemaker of Nuremberg, prolific author of verse and some 200 plays. He became renowned in the Guild of Meistersinger, writing many songs using their elaborate technique, and celebrated Luther in a poem and the Protestant cause in prose dialogues. Despised in the 17th c., he was restored to fame by Goethe in his poem Hans Sachsens poetische Sendung (1776), and Wagner raised him to legendary status in Die Meistersinger von Nürnberg (1868).

sack[1] n. **1.** a large strong bag for storing or conveying goods. **2.** the quantity contained in a sack. **3.** a woman's loose-fitting dress. **4.** (slang) a bed. —v.t. **1.** to put into a sack or sacks. **2.** (colloq.) to dismiss from a job etc. —**the sack**, (colloq.) dismissal from a job etc. **hit the sack,** (slang) to go to bed. —**sackful** n. [OE f. L saccus f. Gk]

sack[2] v.t. to plunder and destroy (a captured town etc.). —n. the sacking of a town etc. [f. F sac (in phr. mettre à sac), f. It. sacco (as prec.)]

sack[3] n. (hist.) a white wine formerly imported from Spain and the Canary Islands. [orig. wyne seck, f. F vin sec dry wine]

sackbut /ˈsækbʌt/ n. an early form of trombone. [f. F saqueboute hook for pulling man off horse]

sackcloth n. **1.** a coarse fabric of flax or hemp. **2.** mourning or penitential garb (esp. in sackcloth and ashes).

sacking n. material for making sacks, sackcloth. [f. SACK¹]

Sackville-West /sækvɪlˈwest/, Hon. Victoria (Mary) (1892–1962), English novelist and poet. Her poem The Land (1927) is a fine evocation of the English countryside. She is said to be portrayed in her friend Virginia Woolf's novel Orlando (1928).

sacral /ˈseɪkr(ə)l/ adj. **1.** of the sacrum. **2.** of or for sacred rites. [f. SACRUM or f. L sacrum sacred rite (as foll.)]

sacrament /ˈsækrəmənt/ n. **1.** a religious ceremony or act regarded as an outward and visible sign of inward and spiritual grace. The term is applied by the Eastern, Pre-Reformation Western, and Roman Catholic Churches to the seven rites of baptism, confirmation, the Eucharist, penance, extreme unction, ordination, and matrimony; it is restricted by most Protestants to baptism and the Eucharist. **2.** (in full **Blessed** or **Holy Sacrament**) the Eucharist. **3.** a sacred thing, influence, etc. —**sacramental** /-ˈment(ə)l/ adj. [f. OF f. L (sacrare hallow, f. sacer holy)]

sacred /ˈseɪkrɪd/ adj. **1.** associated with or dedicated to God or a god; regarded with reverence because of this. **2.** connected with religion, not secular. **3.** dedicated to some person or purpose. **4.** safeguarded or required by religion or tradition, inviolable. —**sacred cow**, the cow as an object of veneration amongst Hindus; an idea or institution unreasonably held to be above criticism. **Sacred Heart,** the heart of Jesus (or of Mary) as an object of devotion. [p.p. of obs. sacre consecrate f. OF sacrer f. L sacrare (as prec.)]

sacrifice /ˈsækrɪfaɪs/ n. **1.** the giving up of a valued thing for the sake of something else that is more important, worthy, or urgent. **2.** the slaughter of a victim or presenting of a gift to win the favour of a deity. **3.** the thing thus given up or offered. **4.** (in games) a loss deliberately incurred to avoid greater loss or obtain a compensating advantage. —*v.t./i.* **1.** to give up or offer as a sacrifice. **2.** to devote *to*. —**sacrificial** /-'fɪʃ(ə)l/ *adj.* [f. OF f. L (as prec.)]

sacrilege /'sækrɪlɪdʒ/ *n.* disrespect or damage to something regarded as sacred. —**sacrilegious** /-'lɪdʒəs/ *adj.* [f. OF f. L (*sacrilegus* stealer of sacred things, f. *sacer* sacred + *legere* take possession of)]

sacristan /'sækrɪstən/ *n.* the person in charge of the sacristy and church contents. [f. L (as SACRED)]

sacristy /'sækrɪstɪ/ *n.* the repository for a church's vestments, vessels, etc. [f. F or It. or L *sacristia* (as prec.)]

sacro- /seɪkrəʊ-/ *in comb.* of the sacrum and. [f. SACRUM]

sacrosanct /'sækrəʊsæŋkt/ *adj.* reverenced or respected and therefore not to be violated or damaged. —**sacrosanctity** /-'sæŋkt-/ *n.* [f. L (as SACRED, SAINT)]

sacrum /'seɪkrəm/ *n.* the composite triangular bone forming the back of the pelvis. [f. L *os sacrum* sacred bone (from sacrificial use)]

sad *adj.* **1.** showing or causing sorrow, unhappy. **2.** regrettable; deplorably bad. **3.** (of cake or pastry) dense from not having risen. —**sadly** *adv.*, **sadness** *n.* [OE]

sadden *v.t./i.* to make or become sad. [f. prec.]

saddle *n.* **1.** a seat of leather etc., usually raised at the front and rear, fastened on a horse etc. for riding (ill. HORSE). **2.** the seat for the rider of a bicycle etc. **3.** a joint of meat consisting of the two loins. **4.** a ridge rising to a summit at each end (ill. MOUNTAINS). —*v.t.* **1.** to put a saddle on (a horse etc.). **2.** to burden (a person) with a task etc.; to put (a burden etc.) on a person. —**saddle-bag** *n.* one of a pair of bags laid across the back of a horse etc.; a bag attached behind the saddle of a bicycle etc. —**in the saddle**, on horseback; in office or control. [OE]

saddleback *n.* **1.** a saddlebacked hill or roof. **2.** a black pig with a white stripe across its back.

saddlebacked *adj.* with a concave upper outline.

saddler *n.* a maker of or dealer in saddles etc. [f. SADDLE]

saddlery *n.* a saddler's trade or goods. [as prec.]

Sadducee /'sædjʊsiː/ *n.* a member of a Jewish sect at the time of Christ emphasizing traditional law and denying the resurrection of the dead. [OE ult. f. Heb., prob. = descendant of Zadok (2 Sam. 8: 17)]

Sade /sɑːd/, Donatien-Alphonse-François, Comte (known as Marquis) de (1740–1814), French novelist and pornographer. His career as a cavalry officer was destroyed by the criminal debauchery of his life. During his prolonged periods of imprisonment for sexual offences he wrote his licentious novels *Justine ou les Malheurs de la vertu* (1791), *La philosophie dans le boudoir* (1795), and *Nouvelle Justine* (1797). Their obsession with the minutiae of sexual pathology and their hedonistic nihilism have persuaded recent critics that they anticipate Nietzsche and Freud. The word 'sadism' owes its origin to his name, referring to the sexual perversions to which he was prone.

sadhu /'sɑːduː/ *n.* a Hindu or Jain ascetic and religious mendicant. [Skr., = holy man]

sadism /'seɪdɪz(ə)m/ *n.* enjoyment of cruelty to others; a sexual perversion characterized by this. —**sadist** *n.*, **sadistic** /sə'dɪstɪk/ *adj.*, **sadistically** *adv.* [f. F f. SADE]

Sadler's Wells Theatre a London theatre so called because in 1683 Thomas Sadler discovered a medicinal spring in his garden and established a pleasure-garden which became known as Sadler's Wells. A wooden music room built there in 1685 became a theatre in 1753, whose stone-built successor remained in use until 1906. In 1927 Lilian Baylis took over the derelict building, erecting a new theatre which opened in 1931. At first drama, ballet, and opera productions alternated between Sadler's Wells and the Old Vic, but from 1934 Sadler's Wells became the home only of opera and ballet. In 1946 the ballet company moved to Covent Garden, but opera remained until 1968, when the company moved to the Coliseum as the English National Opera. The theatre has since housed visiting companies.

s.a.e. *abbr.* stamped addressed envelope.

safari /sə'fɑːrɪ/ *n.* an overland expedition, especially in Africa. —**safari park**, an area where wild animals are kept in the open for viewing from vehicles. [Swahili, f. Arab. *safara* travel]

safe *adj.* **1.** free from risk or danger; not dangerous. **2.** providing security or protection. —*n.* **1.** a strong lockable

cupboard or cabinet for valuables. **2.** a ventilated cabinet for storing food. —**on the safe side**, having a margin of security against risks. **safe conduct**, the right to pass through a district on a particular occasion without risk of arrest or harm; a document granting this. **safe deposit**, a building containing safes and strong-rooms that are let separately. **safe period**, the time during and near a menstrual period when sexual intercourse is least likely to result in conception. —**safely** *adv.*, **safeness** *n.* [f. AF *saf* f. L *salvus* uninjured]

safeguard *n.* a stipulation, circumstance, etc., that tends to prevent something undesirable. —*v.t.* to protect by a stipulation or precaution.

safety *n.* being safe, freedom from risk or danger. —**safety-belt** *n.* a strap securing a person safely, especially a seat-belt. **safety-catch** *n.* a device for locking a gun-trigger or preventing the accidental or dangerous operation of machinery. **safety curtain**, a fireproof curtain in a theatre to divide the auditorium from the stage in case of fire etc. **safety lamp**, a miner's lamp so protected as not to ignite firedamp. **safety match**, a match that ignites only on a specially prepared surface. **safety net**, a net placed to catch an acrobat etc. in case of a fall from a height. **safety-pin** *n.* see separate entry. **safety razor**, one with a guard to prevent the blade cutting the skin. Its invention dates from the mid-19th c. **safety valve**, a valve that opens automatically to relieve excessive pressure in a boiler etc.; a means of harmlessly releasing excitement, anger, etc. [f. OF f. L (as SAFE)]

safety-pin *n.* a pin with a point that is bent back to the head and can be held in a guard so that the user may not be pricked nor the pin come out unintentionally. Fasteners made on the same principle, consisting of a single length of metal wire coiled on itself at its middle point so as to form a spring, are known from the Bronze Age (13th c.) and seem to have been a European invention. The modern type (with a clasp) was re-invented and patented in the USA by Walter Ireland Hunt in 1849.

saffron /'sæfrən/ *n.* the orange-coloured stigmas of a crocus (*Crocus sativus*) used for colouring and flavouring; the colour of this. —*adj.* saffron-coloured. [f. OF f. Arab.]

sag *v.i.* (**-gg-**) **1.** to hang or subside loosely and unevenly; to sink or curve downwards in the middle under weight or pressure. **2.** (of prices) to fall. —*n.* the state or amount of sagging. [f. MLG or Du., = subside]

saga /'sɑːgə/ *n.* a long story of heroic achievement, especially of medieval tale of Scandinavian heroes; a series of connected books telling the story of a family etc. [ON, = narrative (rel. to SAW²)]

sagacious /sə'geɪʃəs/ *adj.* having or showing insight or good judgement. —**sagaciously** *adv.*, **sagacity** /-'gæsɪtɪ/ *n.* [f. L *sagax*]

sage¹ *n.* a kitchen herb (*Salvia officinalis*) with greyish-green leaves. —**sage-brush** *n.* the growth of plants (esp. of the genus *Artemisia*) in some sterile alkaline regions of the USA. [f. OF f. L *salvia* healing plant (as SAFE)]

sage² *adj.* profoundly wise, having wisdom gained from experience. —*n.* a profoundly wise man. —**sagely** *adv.* [f. OF f. L *sapere* be wise]

saggar /'sægə(r)/ *n.* a case of baked fireproof clay enclosing pottery while it is baked. [prob. contr. of SAFEGUARD]

Sagittarius /sædʒɪ'teərɪəs/ the ninth sign of the zodiac, the Archer. —**Sagittarian** *adj.* & *n.* [L, = archer]

sago /'seɪgəʊ/ *n.* (*pl.* **-os**) **1.** a starch used in puddings etc. **2.** a palm (esp. of the genus *Metroxylon*) with a pith yielding this. [f. Malay]

Sahara /sə'hɑːrə/ a great desert of North Africa, the largest in the world, covering an area of about 9,065,000 sq. km (3,500,000 square miles) from the Atlantic to the Red Sea. In recent years it has been increasing its southerly extent. [f. Arab., = desert]

Sahel /sə'hel/ the belt of dry savannah south of the Sahara in West Africa, comprising parts of Senegal, Mauritania, Mali, Niger, and Chad. —**Sahelian** /sə'hiːlɪən/ *adj.*

sahib /sɑːb, 'sɑːɪb/ *n.* (*hist.*) a form of address to European men in India. [Urdu f. Arab., = lord]

said *past* & *p.p.* of SAY.

sail *n.* **1.** a piece of canvas or other material extended on rigging to catch the wind and propel a vessel (ill. SAILING-SHIPS); a ship's sails collectively. **2.** a voyage or excursion in a sailing-vessel. **3.** a ship, especially as discerned from its sails. **4.** the wind-catching apparatus on a windmill. —*v.t./i.* **1.** to travel on water by the use of sails or engine-power. **2.** to navigate (the sea, a ship, etc.); to set (a toy boat) afloat. **3.** to start on a voyage. **4.** to glide or move smoothly or in a stately manner. —**sail close to the wind,** to sail as nearly against the wind as possible; to come close to indecency or dishonesty. **sailing-boat** *or* **-ship** *n.* one moved by sails (see ill. pp. 728-9). **sail into,** to attack with blows or words. **under sail,** with the sails set. [OE]

sailboard *n.* a kind of surfboard with a sail, a windsurfer.

sailboarding *n.* the sport of riding on a sailboard, windsurfing. —**sailboarder** *n.*

sailcloth *n.* **1.** canvas for sails. **2.** a canvas-like dress material.

sailor *n.* **1.** a seaman or mariner, especially one below the rank of officer. **2.** a person considered as liable or not liable to sea-sickness (*bad* or *good sailor*). [var. of *sailer*, f. SAIL]

sailplane *n.* a glider designed for soaring.

sainfoin /ˈsænfɔɪn/ *n.* a pink-flowered fodder plant (*Onobrychis sativa*). [f. obs. F *saintfoin*, orig. = lucerne, f. L *sanctum foenum* holy hay]

saint /seɪnt, or often before a name sənt/ (abbr. **St** or **S.**, in *pl.* **Sts** or **SS**) *n.* **1.** a holy person, one declared (in the Roman Catholic or Orthodox Church) worthy of veneration, whose intercession may be publicly sought (see below, and under names of individual saints). **2.** the title of such a person or of one receiving veneration, or used in the name of a church not named after a saint (e.g. St Saviour's, St Cross). **3.** each of the souls of the dead in paradise. **4.** a member of the Christian Church or (in certain religious bodies) of one's own branch of it. **5.** a very good, patient, or unselfish person. —*v.t.* to canonize; to call or regard as a saint; (in *p.p.*) sacred, worthy of sainthood. —**sainthood** *n.* [f. OF f. L *sanctus* holy (*sancire* consecrate)]

The original ideal of the saint (in sense 1) in Christianity was the martyr. The cessation of persecution in the 4th c. led to the transformation of this ideal: the monk tended to take the place of the martyr. A saint in this sense is one who is close to God and can therefore intercede with God on behalf of other Christians, and one through whom divine power is therefore manifest. A cult of the saints, focused on their physical remains, has early attestation (e.g. Polycarp, 2nd c.), and developed rapidly from the 4th c. onwards. Procedures for the approval of such veneration (called canonization) were gradually formalized, being eventually vested in the papacy in the West and episcopal synods in the East: miracles and a life of heroic sanctity are the criteria for canonization. At the Reformation the cult of the saints was attacked as blurring the unique status of Christ and as the occasion of deplorable religious commercialization. The persecution of Christians in some countries in the 20th c. has to an extent restored the primitive ideal of the saint as martyr.

Sainte-Beuve /sɛtˈbœv/, Charles-Augustin (1804-69), French critic, who studied medicine before turning to literature. His modest creative output included volumes of verse, a novel *Volupté* (1834), and love poems addressed to Victor Hugo's wife Adèle with whom he fell in love. *Port-Royal* (1840-59) is a remarkable study of Jansenism, and *Causeries du lundi* (1851-62) a collection of weekly critical and biographical essays. He is one of the founders of modern criticism and these works illustrate the range of his reading and the breadth of his views. His approach to criticism was objective and re-creative rather than dogmatic, believing that formative influences on the authors' characters were considered before reaching any conclusions.

St Helena /hɪˈliːnə/ a solitary island in the South Atlantic, a British dependency, famous as the place of Napoleon's exile (1815-21) and death; pop. (1982) 5,499; official language, English; capital, Jamestown. The island was discovered by the Portuguese in 1502 on 21 May, feast day of St Helena, mother of Constantine.

St James's Palace the old Tudor palace of the monarchs of England in London, built by Henry VIII on the site of an earlier leper hospital dedicated to St James the Less. The palace was the chief royal residence in London from 1697 (when Whitehall was burnt down) until Queen Victoria made Buckingham Palace the monarch's London residence. —**Court of St James's,** the official title of the British court, to which ambassadors from foreign countries are accredited.

St John Ambulance an organization providing first aid, nursing, ambulance, and welfare services. (See KNIGHTS HOSPITALLERS.)

St Kitts and Nevis /ˈniːvɪs/ a State in association with Britain (who has responsibility for defence and foreign affairs) consisting of two adjoining islands (St Kitts and Nevis) of the Leeward Islands in the West Indies; pop. (St Kitts) 35,000, (Nevis) 9,300; official language, English; capital, Basseterre (on St Kitts). St Kitts was discovered in 1493 by Columbus. He named it after his patron saint, St Christopher, but the name was shortened by settlers from England who arrived in 1623 and established the first successful English colony in the West Indies. Nevis, which consists almost entirely of a mountain, gained its name from the resemblance of the clouds around its peak to snow (Sp. *las nieves* the snows). A union between St Kitts, Nevis, and Anguilla was created in 1967, but Anguilla seceded within three months.

St Lawrence /ˈlɒrəns/ a river of North America flowing from Lake Ontario to the Atlantic Ocean. The St Lawrence Seaway, which includes a number of artificial sections to bypass rapids, was inaugurated by Canada and the USA in 1959 and enables large vessels to navigate the entire length of the river.

St Leger /ˈledʒə(r)/ an annual horse-race for 3-year-old colts and fillies, held in September at Doncaster, S.Yorks, instituted by Lieutenant-General St Leger in 1776.

St Lucia /ˈluːʃə/ an island of the West Indies, one of the Windward Islands; pop. (est. 1982) 124,000; official language, English; capital, Castries. Possession of the island was long disputed with France, and it did not pass finally into British hands until the early 19th c. Since 1979 it has been an independent State within the Commonwealth. —**St Lucian** *adj. & n.*

saintly *adj.* very holy or virtuous. —**saintliness** *n.* [f. prec.]

St Mark's Cathedral the church in Venice, its cathedral church since 1807, built in the 9th c. to house the relics of St Mark brought from Alexandria, and rebuilt in the 11th c. It is lavishly decorated with mosaics (11th-13th c.) and sculptures.

St Paul's Cathedral a cathedral on Ludgate Hill, London, built between 1675 and 1711 by Sir Christopher Wren to replace a medieval cathedral largely destroyed in the Great Fire.

St Peter's Basilica the Roman Catholic basilica in the Vatican City, Rome, the largest church in Christendom. The present 16th-c. building replaced a much older basilican structure, erected by Constantine on the supposed site of St Peter's crucifixion. A succession of architects (Bramante, Raphael, Peruzzi, Sangallo) in turn made drastic changes in the design; the dome closely follows a design of Michelangelo. The building was consecrated in 1626.

St Petersburg /ˈpiːtəzbɜːg/ see LENINGRAD.

Saint-Saëns /sæˈsɑ̃/, Camille (1835-1921), French composer, pianist, and organist. Born in Paris, he became an important figure in musical life there. He devoted much time and energy to the composition of opera (notably *Samson et Dalila*, 1877) and oratorio, but is best known today for his Third Symphony (with organ, 1886), the symphonic poem *Danse macabre* (1874), and the light, witty *Carnaval des animaux* (1886).

Saint-Simon[1] /sæsiˈmɔ̃/, Claude-Henri de Rouvroy, Comte de (1760-1825), French social scientist. An aristocrat (his father was a cousin of the Duc de Saint-Simon), reduced to poverty by profligacy, Saint-Simon devoted the last twenty years of his life to writing, promulgating a new theory of social organization in reaction to the chaos engendered by the French Revolution, arguing that society ought to be organized in an industrial order, controlled by leaders of industry and given spiritual direction to scientists. Such works as *L'Industrie* (1816), *Du système industriel* (1821), and *Nouveau Christianisme* (1825) were of great influence on later French social thinkers, earning Saint-Simon a reputation as the founder of French socialism.

Saint-Simon[2] /sæ siˈmɔ̃/, Louis de Rouvroy, Duc de (1675-1855), French writer. His *Mémoires* describe people and events of the latter years of Louis XIV's reign in graphic detail, although they are not the work of a critical and accurate historian.

St Sophia /səˈfiːə, -ˈfaɪə/ a church at Constantinople (now Istanbul), dedicated to the 'Holy Wisdom' (i.e. the Person of Christ), built by order of Justinian (532-7) and inaugurated in 537. The key monument of Byzantine architecture, its chief feature is the enormous dome, supported by piers, arches, and pendentives and pierced by 40 windows, which crowns the basilica. In 1453, on the day of the Turkish invasion, orders were given for its conversion into a mosque;

Sailing-ships . . .

Full-rigged ship

(The names of the upper masts and sails
given on the foremast and mainmast
are similar for all three masts.)

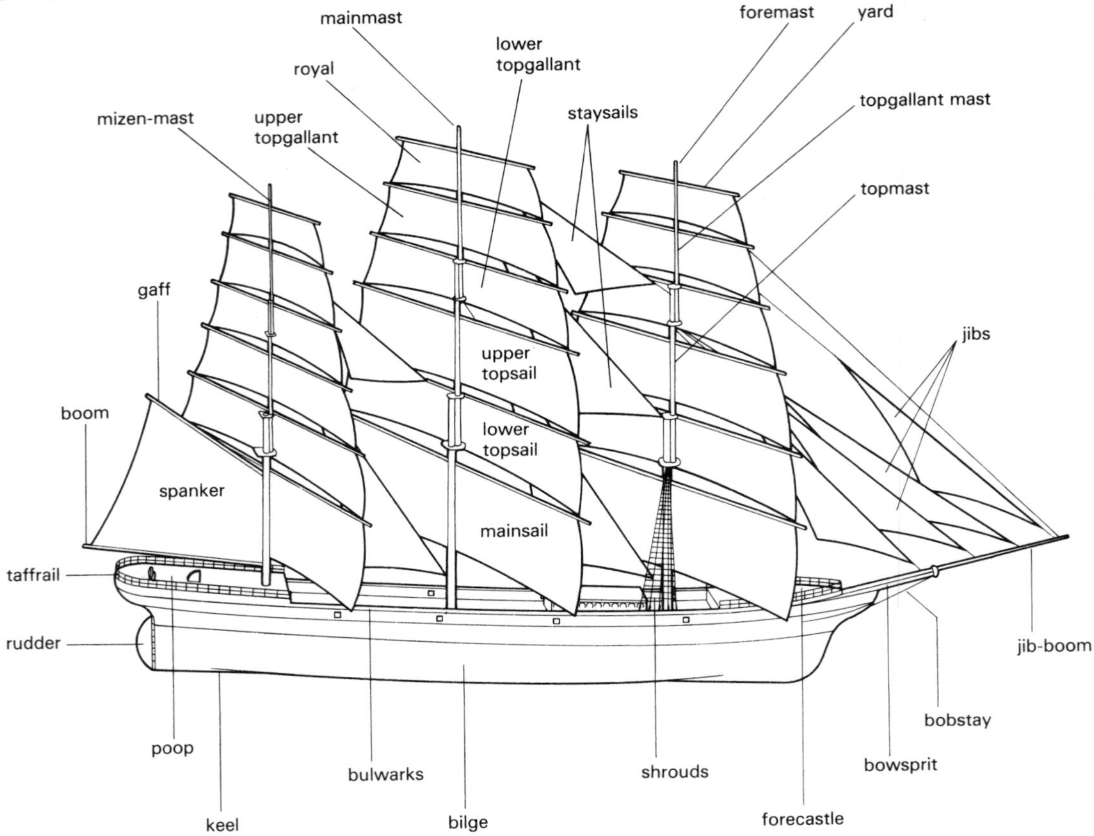

mainmast

royal

lower
topgallant

foremast   yard

staysails

topgallant mast

mizen-mast

upper
topgallant

topmast

gaff

jibs

boom

upper
topsail

lower
topsail

spanker

mainsail

taffrail

rudder

jib-boom

poop

bobstay

bulwarks

shrouds

bowsprit

keel

bilge

forecastle

Types of sailing-vessel

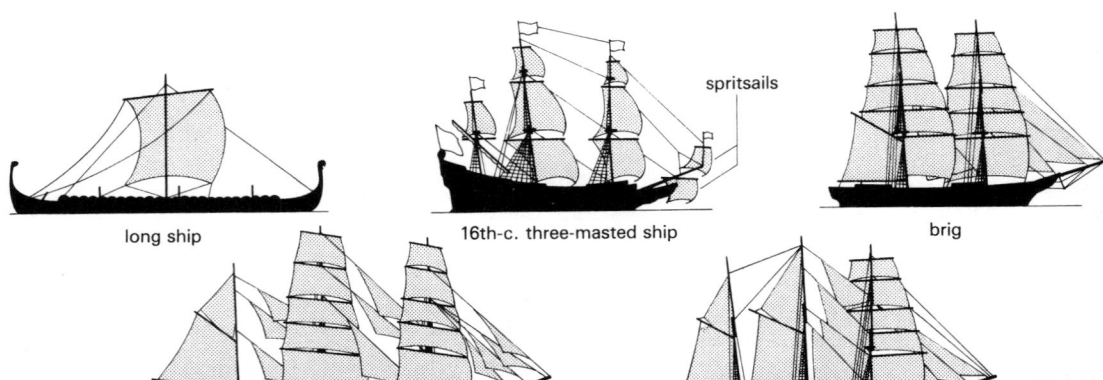

long ship

spritsails

16th-c. three-masted ship

brig

barque

barquentine

. . . and Boats

Parts of a sail

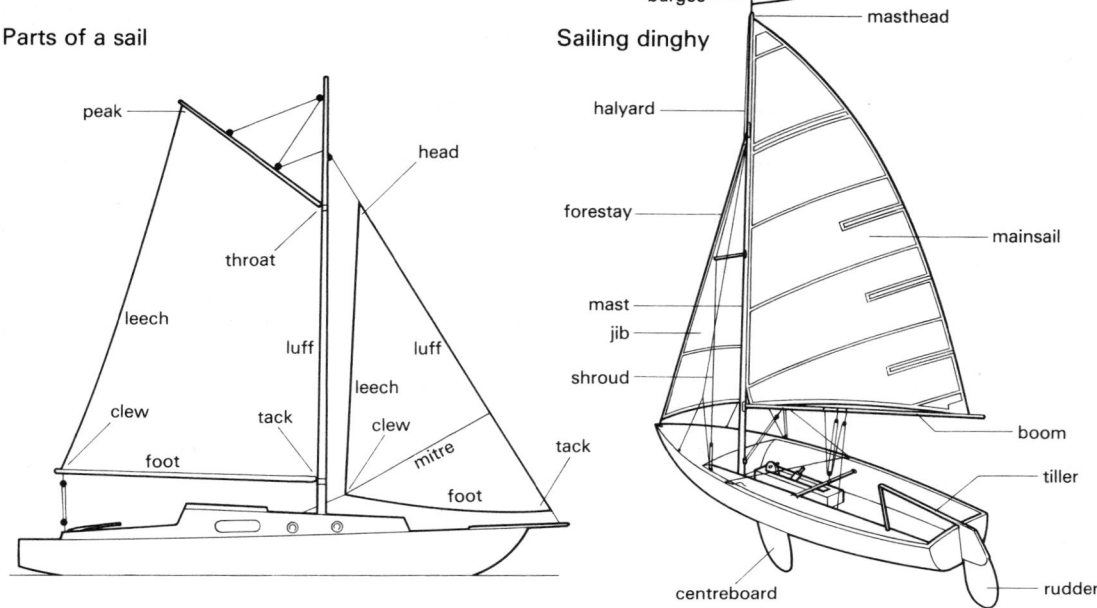

peak
head
throat
leech
luff
luff
leech
clew
tack
clew
mitre
foot
tack
foot

Sailing dinghy

burgee
masthead
halyard
forestay
mainsail
mast
jib
shroud
boom
tiller
centreboard
rudder

Bearings

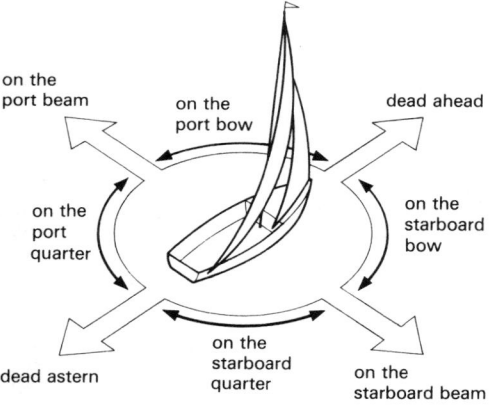

on the port beam
on the port bow
dead ahead
on the port quarter
on the starboard bow
on the starboard quarter
on the starboard beam
dead astern

Points of sailing

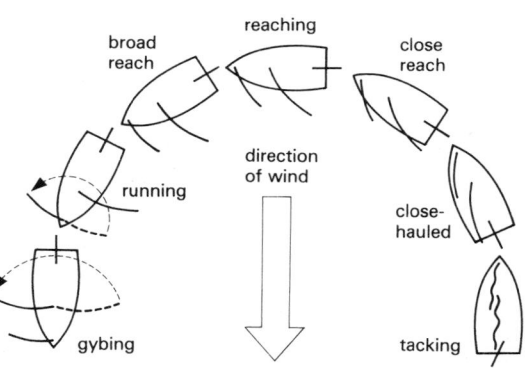

broad reach
reaching
close reach
running
direction of wind
close-hauled
gybing
tacking

Types of sailing-vessel

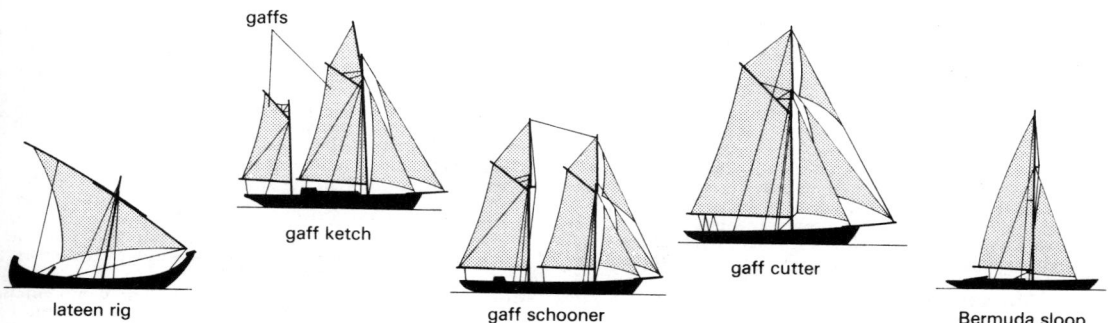

gaffs

lateen rig
gaff ketch
gaff schooner
gaff cutter
Bermuda sloop

the mosaics which adorned its interior were covered and partly destroyed, and minarets were added. It was used as a mosque until 1935, when Atatürk converted it into a museum.

St Stephens /ˈstiːvənz/ the House of Commons, so called from the ancient chapel of St Stephen, Westminster, in which the House used to sit (1537–1834).

St Trinian's /ˈtrɪnɪənz/ the name of a girls' school invented by the cartoonist Ronald Searle (1920–) in 1941, whose pupils are characterized by hoydenish behaviour, ungainly appearance, and unattractive school uniform. (Searle's daughters attended St Trinnean's school in Edinburgh.)

St Vincent /ˈvɪns(ə)nt/ an island State in the Windward Islands in the West Indies, consisting of the island of St Vincent and some of the Grenadines; pop. (est. 1982) 127,883; official language, English; capital, Kingstown. The French, Dutch, and British all made attempts at settlements in the 18th c., and it finally fell to British possession early in the 19th c. The State obtained full independence with a limited form of membership of the Commonwealth in 1979. It is the world's chief producer of arrowroot.

sake[1] *n.* **for the sake of, for (a person's) sake,** out of consideration for, in the interest of; in order to please, honour, get, or keep. **for heaven's** *or* **God's** etc. **sake,** an exclamation of dismay, annoyance, or supplication. [OE, = contention, charge]

sake[2] /ˈsɑːkɪ/ *n.* a Japanese fermented liquor made from rice. [Jap.]

Sakti /ˈʃɒktɪ/ (*Hinduism*) the power of the male god, usually Siva, personified as a goddess; the goddess as supreme deity (Devi). [f. Skr., = power, energy]

salaam /səˈlɑːm/ *n.* **1.** an oriental salutation 'Peace'; an Indian obeisance with or without this, a bow with the right palm on the forehead. **2.** (in *pl.*) respectful compliments. —*v.t./i.* to make a salaam (to). [f. Arab.]

salacious /səˈleɪʃəs/ *adj.* indecently erotic, lewd. —**salaciously** *adv.*, **salaciousness** *n.*, **salacity** /-ˈlæsɪtɪ/ *n.* [f. L *salax* (*salire* leap)]

salad /ˈsæləd/ *n.* a mixture of raw or cold vegetables, herbs, etc., usually seasoned with oil, vinegar, etc., and often eaten with or including cold meat, cheese, etc.; a vegetable or herb suitable for eating raw. —**salad days,** one's period of youthful inexperience. **salad-dressing** *n.* a mixture of oil, vinegar, etc., used with a salad. [f. OF f. Prov., ult. f. L *sal* salt]

Saladin /ˈsælədɪn/ (1137–93), sultan of Egypt, who successfully invaded the Holy Land and reconquered Jerusalem from the Crusaders before fighting off the Third Crusade, the leaders of which included Richard I. Saladin won a reputation not only for military skill but for honesty and chivalry, and was generally a match for his European opponents.

salamander /ˈsæləˌmændə(r)/ *n.* **1.** (in mythology) a lizard-like animal living in fire. **2.** a kind of tailed amphibian of the family Salamandridae. [f. OF f. L f. Gk]

salami /səˈlɑːmɪ/ *n.* a highly seasoned sausage, originally from Italy. [It., ult. f. L *sal* salt]

Salamis /ˈsæləmɪs/ an island in the Saronic Gulf in Greece. In the straits between it and the western coast of Attica the Greek fleet crushingly defeated the Persian fleet of Xerxes in 480 BC.

sal ammoniac /sæl əˈməʊnɪæk/ ammonium chloride, a hard white crystalline salt, said to have been made from camels' dung near the temple of Jupiter Ammon. [f. L (*sal* salt, *ammoniacus* of Jupiter Ammon)]

salary /ˈsælərɪ/ *n.* a fixed regular payment, usually calculated on an annual basis and paid monthly, made by an employer to an employee. —*v.t.* (esp. in *p.p.*) to pay a salary to. [f. AF f. L *salarium* orig. soldier's salt-money (*sal* salt)]

sale *n.* **1.** selling, being sold. **2.** an instance of this; the amount sold. **3.** an event at which goods are sold, especially by public auction or for charity. **4.** disposal of a shop's stock at reduced prices, e.g. at the end of a season. **5.** (in *pl.*) the department of a firm concerned with selling its products. —**for** *or* **on sale,** offered for purchase. **sale of work,** a sale for charity etc. of goods provided by supporters. **sale or return,** an arrangement by which a retailer can return to a wholesaler without payment any goods left unsold. **saleroom** *n.* a room in which auctions are held. **sales talk,** persuasive talk to promote the sale of goods or the acceptance of an idea etc. [OE f. ON (as SELL)]

saleable *adj.* fit for sale; likely to find a purchaser. —**saleability** /-ˈbɪlɪtɪ/ *n.* [f. prec.]

Salesian /səˈliːʒ(ə)n/ *adj.* of a Roman Catholic educational religious order named after St Francis de Sales (d. 1622), French bishop of Geneva. —*n.* a member of this order. [f. *Sales*]

salesman *n.* (*pl.* **-men**) a man employed to sell goods in a shop etc. or as a middleman between producer and retailer.

salesmanship *n.* skill in selling. [f. prec. + -SHIP]

salesperson *n.* a salesman or saleswoman.

saleswoman *n.* (*pl.* **-women**) a woman employed to sell goods.

Salic law /ˈsælɪk/ **1.** a Frankish law-book extant in Merovingian and Carolingian times. **2.** a law excluding females from dynastic succession, especially an alleged fundamental law of French monarchy (based on a quotation, not referring to such succession, from the law-book). In the 14th c. Edward III's claim to the French throne, based on descent from his mother, a Capetian princess, was denied by the French on the authority of this law and brought on the Hundred Years War. [f. F or L (*Salii* name of Frankish tribe)]

salicylic acid /sælɪˈsɪlɪk/ a benzene derivative used as an antiseptic and pain-killing substance. [f. F *salicyle* f. L *salix* willow]

salient /ˈseɪlɪənt/ *adj.* prominent, conspicuous; standing or pointing outwards. —*n.* a salient angle; a bulge in the line of a military attack or defence. [f. L *salire* leap]

saline /ˈseɪlaɪn/ *adj.* of salt or salts; containing or tasting of salt(s). —*n.* **1.** a saline substance, especially a medicine. **2.** a salt lake, spring, etc. —**salinity** /səˈlɪnɪtɪ/ *n.* [f. L *salinus* (*sal* salt)]

saliva /səˈlaɪvə/ *n.* the colourless liquid produced by glands in the mouth, assisting in chewing and digestion. —**salivary** *adj.* [L]

salivate /ˈsælɪveɪt/ *v.i.* to secrete or discharge saliva, especially in excess. —**salivation** /-ˈveɪʃ(ə)n/ *n.* [f. L *salivare* (as prec.)]

Salk vaccine /sælk/ the first vaccine developed against poliomyelitis, named after J. E. Salk (1914–), US virologist, who developed the vaccine in 1954.

sallow[1] /ˈsæləʊ/ *adj.* (esp. of the complexion) of sickly yellow or pale brown. —*v.t./i.* to make or become sallow. —**sallowness** *n.* [OE, = dusky]

sallow[2] /ˈsæləʊ/ *n.* a low-growing willow; a shoot or the wood of this. [OE]

Sallust /ˈsæləst/ (Gaius Sallustius Crispus, 86–35 BC) Roman historian, who retired to write after an unsuccessful political career. He is a moralizing historian, with a pessimistic view of the political and moral decline of Rome, a process which he dates from the fall of Carthage.

sally /ˈsælɪ/ *n.* **1.** a rush from a besieged place upon the besiegers, a sortie. **2.** an excursion. **3.** a lively or witty remark. —*v.i.* to make a sally. —**sally forth** *or* **out,** to go on a journey or walk etc. **sally-port** *n.* an opening in a fortification from which to make a sally (ill. CASTLES). [f. F *saillie* f. L (as SALIENT)]

Sally Lunn /sælɪ ˈlʌn/ a kind of sweet light teacake served hot. [perh. f. name of girl hawking them at Bath *c.*1800]

salmagundi /sælməˈgʌndɪ/ *n.* **1.** a dish of chopped meat, anchovies, eggs, onions, etc., and seasoning. **2.** a miscellaneous collection. [f. F *salmigondis*, orig. unkn.]

salmi /ˈsælmɪ/ *n.* a ragout or casserole, especially of game-birds. [F, abbr. f. as prec.]

salmon /ˈsæmən/ *n.* (*pl.* usu. same) **1.** a large fish of the genus *Salmo* etc. with orange-pink flesh, highly valued for food and sport. **2.** the colour of its flesh. —*adj.* orange-pink. —**salmon-trout** *n.* a sea trout. [f. AF f. L *salmo*]

salmonella /sælməˈnelə/ *n.* a bacterium of the genus *Salmonella*, especially of a species causing food poisoning. [f. D. E. *Salmon*, American veterinary surgeon (d. 1914)]

Salome /səˈləʊmɪ/ the name given by Josephus to the daughter of Herodias, who is mentioned but not named in the Gospels. She danced before Herod Antipas, and St John the Baptist was beheaded at her request.

Salon /ˈsælɔ̃/ the name given to the exhibitions of the French Royal Academy of Painting and Sculpture founded in the 17th c. by Colbert and Lebrun. The name derived from the fact that exhibitions were held in the Salon d'Apollon in the Louvre. Even after its reorganization in 1881 it retained its traditional hostility to new and creative artists. [= foll.]

salon /ˈsælɒn/ *n.* **1.** the reception-room of a large continental house. **2.** a meeting there of eminent people. **3.** a room or establishment where a hairdresser or couturier etc. receives clients. [F f. It. *salone* (*sala* hall)]

Salonica /sə'lɒnɪkə/ (Gk *Thessaloniki*, the ancient Thessalonica) a seaport in NE Greece, the capital of Macedonia. It was the scene of a campaign in the First World War by the French and British in support of Serbia, during which they occupied Salonica (Oct. 1915).

saloon /sə'lu:n/ *n.* **1.** a large public room for a specified purpose. **2.** a public room on a ship. **3.** (*US*) a place where alcoholic drinks may be bought and drunk. **4.** a saloon car. —**saloon-bar** *n.* a first-class bar in a public house. **saloon car,** a motor car with a closed body for driver and passengers. [f. F *salon* (as prec.)]

salsify /'sælsɪfɪ/ *n.* a plant (*Tragopogon porrifolius*) with a long fleshy root cooked as a vegetable. [f. F f. It. *salsefica,* orig. unkn.]

SALT /sɒlt/ *abbr.* Strategic Arms Limitation Talks, involving especially the USA and the Soviet Union, aimed at the limitation or reduction of nuclear armaments. (The last element is also understood as *Treaty.*)

salt /sɔ:lt, sɒlt/ *n.* **1.** (also **common salt**) sodium chloride, a substance found in sea-water and obtained in crystalline forms by mining or by evaporation of sea-water etc., and used especially to season or preserve food. **2.** a chemical compound of basic and acid radicals, the acid with the whole or part of its hydrogen replaced by a metal or metal-like radical. **3.** (often in *pl.*) a substance resembling common salt in taste, form, etc.; (in *pl.*) such a substance used as a laxative. **4.** piquancy, pungency, wit. **5.** a salt-cellar. **6.** (also **old salt**) an experienced sailor. —*adj.* containing or tasting of salt; cured, preserved, or seasoned with salt. —*v.t.* **1.** to cure, preserve, or season with salt or brine. **2.** to sprinkle with salt. **3.** (*slang*) to make (a mine) appear rich by fraudulently inserting precious metal into it before it is viewed (also *fig.*); to make fraudulent entries in (accounts etc.). —**salt away** *or* **down,** (*colloq.*) to save or put aside for the future. **salt-cellar** *n.* a container for salt at table. **salt-lick** *n.* a place where animals lick earth impregnated with salt. **salt-mine** *n.* a mine yielding rock-salt; a place of unremitting toil. **the salt of the earth,** the finest people, those who keep society wholesome. **salt-pan** *n.* a hollow near the sea where salt is got by evaporation. **take with a grain** *or* **pinch of salt,** to regard sceptically. **worth one's salt,** deserving one's position, competent. [OE]

salting /'sɔ:ltɪŋ, 'sɒ-/ *n.* a marsh overflowed by the sea. [f. SALT]

saltire /'sæltaɪə(r)/ *n.* an X-shaped cross (ill. VESTMENTS); this dividing a shield etc. into four sections (ill. HERALDRY). [f. OF *sau(l)toir* stirrup-cord, stile, f. L (*saltare* leap)]

saltpetre /sɒlt'pi:tə(r)/ *n.* potassium nitrate, a white crystalline salty substance used as a constituent of gunpowder, in preserving meat, and medicinally. [f. OF f. L *salpetra,* prob. = salt of the rock]

salty /'sɔ:ltɪ, 'sɒ-/ *adj.* **1.** containing or tasting of salt. **2.** piquant, pungent. —**saltiness** *n.* [f. SALT]

salubrious /sə'lu:brɪəs/ *adj.* health-giving, healthy. —**salubrity** *n.* [f. L *salubris* (*salus* health)]

saluki /sə'lu:kɪ/ *n.* a tall slender silky-coated dog. [f. Arab.]

salutary /'sæljʊtərɪ/ *adj.* producing good effects. —**salutarily** *adv.* [f. F or L *salutaris* (*salus* health)]

salutation /sælju:'teɪʃ(ə)n/ *n.* a sign or expression of greeting or respect; the use of these. —**salutatory** /sə'lju:tətərɪ/ *adj.* [as foll.]

salute /sə'lu:t, -'lju:t/ *n.* **1.** a gesture of respect or courteous recognition. **2.** a prescribed military movement of the hand or the firing of a gun or guns etc. as a formal or ceremonial sign of respect. —*v.t.* **1.** to greet with a polite gesture. **2.** to perform a military salute; to greet with this. **3.** to express respect for, to commend. [f. OF or L *salutare* (*salus* health)]

Salvador /'sælvədɔ:(r)/ see EL SALVADOR. —**Salvadorean** /-'dɔ:rɪən/ *adj.* & *n.*

salvage /'sælvɪdʒ/ *n.* **1.** the rescue of property from loss at sea or from fire etc.; payment made or due for this; property so saved. **2.** the saving and utilization of waste materials; materials salvaged. —*v.t.* **1.** to save from a wreck etc. **2.** to make salvage of. [F f. L *salvagium* (*salvare* save)]

salvation /sæl'veɪʃ(ə)n/ *n.* **1.** the saving of the soul from sin and its consequences; the state of being saved. **2.** preservation from loss or calamity; a thing that preserves from these. —**salvationist** *n.* [f. OF f. L (*salvare* save)]

Salvation Army an international organization for evangelistic and social work, founded in 1865 by William Booth. It is organized on a military basis, headed by a General,

and exacts unquestioning obedience from its members, who wear a distinctive uniform on public occasions. Public worship consists of open-air meetings marked by brass bands and banners. The Army is active in all kinds of social work, including the care of criminals and drunkards, soup kitchens, workers' hostels, and night shelters. Its headquarters are in London.

salve[1] *n.* **1.** a healing ointment. **2.** a thing that soothes or consoles. —*v.t.* to soothe. [OE]

salve[2] *v.t.* to save from a wreck or fire etc. —**salvor** *n.* [back-formation f. SALVAGE]

salver /'sælvə(r)/ *n.* a tray, usually metal, on which letters or refreshments etc. are handed. [f. F f. Sp. *salva* assaying of food (as SAVE)]

salvia /'sælvɪə/ *n.* a garden plant of the genus *Salvia,* especially a species with red flowers (*S. splendens*). [L, = SAGE[1]]

salvo /'sælvəʊ/ *n.* (*pl.* **-oes**) **1.** a simultaneous discharge of guns or bombs. **2.** a round of applause. [f. F f. It. *salva* salutation (as SAVE)]

sal volatile /sæl və'lætɪlɪ/ a solution of ammonium carbonate, used as a restorative in fainting etc. [L, = volatile salt]

Salyut /sæl'ju:t, 'sæ-/ any of a series of Soviet manned space stations, of which the first was launched into Earth orbit in 1971.

Samaria /sə'meərɪə/ **1.** the ancient capital of the northern kingdom of the Hebrews (see ISRAEL[1] 2). In 721 BC it was captured by the Assyrians and resettled with pagans from other parts of their empire (2 Kings 17, 18). **2.** the region surrounding this, west of the Jordan, bounded by Galilee and Judaea.

Samaritan[1] /sə'mærɪt(ə)n/ *n.* **1.** a native of Samaria (see below). **2.** the Aramaic dialect formerly spoken there. **3.** an adherent of the Samaritan religious system, accepting only the Pentateuch. **4.** (also **good Samaritan**) a person who readily gives help to one in distress who has no claim upon him (with ref. to Luke 10: 30 ff.). —*adj.* of Samaria or the Samaritans. [f. L f. Gk (*Samareia* Samaria)]

According to Jewish tradition, the Samaritans were descendants of the pagan settlers established by the Assyrians in 721 BC; the hostility of the Jews to them was proverbial. A few still survive, living near Nablus (now in Israel), and bear a striking resemblance to the Assyrians depicted on ancient monuments.

Samaritan[2] *n.* a member of an organization (**the Samaritans**), founded in 1953 by the Revd. Chad Varah, to enable help, compassion, and friendship to be given (especially through the telephone service) to the suicidal and despairing. [f. prec., sense 4]

samarium /sə'meərɪəm/ *n.* a metallic element of the lanthanide series, symbol Sm, atomic number 62, first discovered in 1879. The pure metal is used as a catalyst and its compounds are used in computer hardware, some types of electrode, special glasses, etc. [f. *samarskite* mineral in which its spectrum was first observed, f. *Samarski* 19th-c. Russian official]

Samarkand /sæmɑ:'kænd/ a city in central Asia. Destroyed by Alexander the Great in 329 BC, Samarkand later rose to fame as the centre of the silk trade, becoming the subject of much legend in the West. It was destroyed again by Genghis Khan in 1221 but later became the capital of Tamerlane's empire. By 1700 it was almost deserted, but in 1868 it was taken by Russia and in 1924 was incorporated into the Uzbek Soviet Socialist Republic, briefly becoming its capital.

Sama-Veda /sɑ:mə'veɪdə, -'vi:-/ *n.* one of the four Vedas, a collection of liturgical chants in Old Sanskrit used in the Vedic religion by the priest in charge of chanting aloud at the sacrifice. Its material is drawn largely from the Rig-Veda. [f. Skr. (*sāma* = chant, *vēda* = knowledge)]

samba /'sæmbə/ *n.* a ballroom dance of Brazilian origin; the music for this. —*v.i.* to dance the samba. [Port., of Afr. orig.]

Sam Browne /braʊn/ (in full **Sam Browne belt**) a belt with a supporting strap that passes over the right shoulder, worn by commissioned officers of the British Army and also by members of various police forces etc. [f. Sir *Samuel James Browne* (d. 1901), British general, its inventor]

same *adj.* **1.** being of one kind, not different; unchanged, unvarying. **2.** just mentioned. —*pron.* (**the same**) the same person or thing; the person or thing just mentioned. —*adv.* (**the same**) in the same way, similarly. —**all** *or* **just the same,** nevertheless. **be all** *or* **just the same,** to make no difference (to a person). **same here,** (*colloq.*) the same applies to me, I agree. —**sameness** *n.* [f. ON]

Samian /'seɪmɪən/ *adj.* of Samos, an island in the Aegean Sea, or its people. —*n.* **1.** a native of Samos. **2.** (in full **Samian pottery** *or* **ware**) a kind of glossy red pottery made in Gaul in the 1st–4th c. and common on archaeological sites of this period. It is also called *terra sigillata*; 'Samian' is a misnomer, deriving from a supposed but non-existent connection with Samos. [f. L f. Gk *Samios* of Samos]

samizdat /'sæmɪzdæt/ *n.* a system of clandestine publication of banned literature in the USSR. [Russ., = self-publishing (i.e. illegal)]

Samnite /'sæmnaɪt/ *n.* **1.** a member of a people of ancient Italy often at war with republican Rome. **2.** their language. —*adj.* of the Samnites or their language. [f. L, rel. to *Sabinus* Sabine]

Samoa /sə'məʊə/ a group of Polynesian Islands of which the eastern part is a US territory. —**Western Samoa,** see separate entry. —**Samoan** *adj.* & *n.*

Samos /'seɪmɒs/ a Greek island in the Aegean.

samovar /'sæməvɑː(r)/ *n.* a Russian tea-urn. [Russ., = self-boiler]

Samoyed /'sæmɔjed/ *n.* **1.** a member of a people of northern Siberia. **2.** their language. **3.** a dog of a white Arctic breed. —**Samoyedic** /-'jedɪk/ *adj.* [f. Russ. *samoed*]

sampan /'sæmpæn/ *n.* a small boat used on the rivers and coasts of China, Japan, and neighbouring islands, rowed with a scull (or two sculls) from the stern and usually having a sail of matting and an awning. [f. Chin. *san ban* (*san* three, *ban* board)]

samphire /'sæmfaɪə(r)/ *n.* a coastal plant (*Crithmum maritimum*) used in pickles. [f. F (*herbe de*) *Saint Pierre*, = St Peter's herb]

sample /'sɑːmp(ə)l/ *n.* a small separated part or quantity intended to show what the whole is like; a specimen; an illustrative or typical example. —*v.t.* to take or give a sample of; to try the qualities of; to get representative experience of. [f. AF *assample*, = EXAMPLE]

sampler *n.* a piece of embroidery worked in various stitches as a specimen of proficiency. [f. OF *essamplaire* (as EXEMPLAR)]

Samson /'sæms(ə)n/ (prob. 11th c. BC) an Israelite leader famous for his strength (Judges 13–16). He confided to a woman, Delilah, that his strength lay in his hair, and she betrayed him to the Philistines. They cut off his hair while he slept and captured and blinded him, but when his hair grew again his strength returned and he pulled down the pillars of a house, destroying himself and a large concourse of Philistines.

Samuel /'sæmjʊ(ə)l/ **1.** a Hebrew prophet who rallied the Israelites after their defeat by the Philistines and became their ruler. **2.** either of two books of the Old Testament covering the history of Israel from Samuel's birth to the end of the reign of David.

samurai /'sæmʊraɪ/ *n.* (*pl.* same) **1.** a Japanese army officer. **2.** (*hist.*) a member of the feudal warrior class of Japan which was bound by the code of bushido, emphasizing qualities of loyalty, bravery, and endurance. The samurai dominated Japanese society until the demise of the feudal order in the 19th c. [Jap.]

Sana'a /'sɑːnə/ the capital of the Yemen Arab Republic; pop. 277,817.

sanatorium /sænə'tɔːrɪəm/ *n.* (*pl.* **-ums**) **1.** an establishment for treating chronic diseases (e.g. tuberculosis) or convalescents. **2.** accommodation for sick persons in a school etc. [f. L (*sanare* heal)]

Sancho Panza /sæŋkəʊ 'pænzə/ the squire of Don Quixote (see entry), who accompanies the latter on his adventures. He is an ignorant and credulous peasant but has a store of proverbial wisdom, and is thus a foil to his master.

sanctify /'sæŋktɪfaɪ/ *v.t.* **1.** to make holy or sacred. **2.** to justify. —**sanctification** /-fɪ'keɪʃ(ə)n/ *n.* [f. OF f. L (*sanctus* holy)]

sanctimonious /sæŋktɪ'məʊnɪəs/ *adj.* making a show of righteousness or piety. —**sanctimoniously** *adv.*, **sanctimoniousness** *n.* [f. L *sanctimonia* sanctity (as SAINT)]

sanction /'sæŋkʃ(ə)n/ *n.* **1.** permission or approval for an action or behaviour etc. **2.** confirmation or ratification of a law etc. **3.** a penalty for disobeying a law or a reward for obeying it; (esp. in *pl.*) action taken by a country etc. to penalize and coerce a country or organization that is considered to have violated a law, code of practice, or basic human rights. —*v.t.* **1.** to give sanction or approval to, to

authorize. **2.** to ratify. **3.** to attach a penalty or reward to (a law). [F f. L (*sancire* make holy)]

sanctity /'sæŋktɪtɪ/ *n.* holiness, sacredness. [f. OF or L *sanctitas* (as SAINT)]

sanctuary /'sæŋktjʊərɪ/ *n.* **1.** a sacred place. **2.** the holiest part of a temple; the part of the chancel containing the altar. **3.** a place where birds or wild animals etc. are protected and encouraged to breed. **4.** (esp. *hist.*) a sacred place where a fugitive from the law, or a debtor, was secured by medieval Church law against arrest or violence; a place in which similar immunity was established by custom or law. **5.** a place of refuge. [f. AF f. L (as SAINT)]

sanctum /'sæŋktəm/ *n.* **1.** a holy place. **2.** a person's private room or study. [L (as SAINT)]

Sanctus /'sæŋktəs/ *n.* the hymn (from Isa. 6: 3) beginning 'Sanctus, sanctus, sanctus' or 'Holy, holy, holy', forming the conclusion of the Eucharistic preface; the music for this. —**Sanctus bell,** a bell in the turret at the junction of nave and chancel, or a handbell, rung at the sanctus or at the elevation of the host. [L, = holy]

Sand /sɑ̃/, George (pseudonym of Amandine-Aurore Lucille Dupin, Baronne Dudevant, 1804–76), French novelist, who left her husband to lead an independent literary life in Paris. She wrote romantic novels portraying women's struggles against conventional morals, including *Indiana* (1832) and *Lélia* (1833), and idyllic works of rustic life such as *La mare au diable* (1846) and *François le champi* (1850). *Elle et lui* (1859) is a fictionalized account of her affair with Alfred de Musset; *Un hiver à Majorque* (1841) describes an unhappy episode during her passionate liaison with Chopin.

sand *n.* the loose granular substance resulting from the wearing down of siliceous and other rocks and found on the sea-shore, river-beds, deserts, etc.; (in *pl.*) grains of sand, an expanse of sand, a sandbank. —*v.t.* **1.** to smooth or polish with sandpaper. **2.** to sprinkle, cover, or treat with sand. —**sand-blast** *n.* a jet of sand driven by compressed air or steam for cleaning a glass or stone etc. surface; (*v.t.*) to treat with this. **sand-castle** *n.* a structure of sand made by or for a child on the sea-shore. **sand-dune** *or* **-hill** *n.* a dune. **sand-glass** *n.* a wasp-waisted reversible glass with two bulbs containing enough sand to take a definite time in passing from the upper to the lower bulb (ill. TIME). **sand-martin** *n.* a bird (*Riparia riparia*) nesting in sandy banks. **sand-pit** *n.* a pit etc. containing sand for children to play in. **sand-wasp** *n.* a wasp of the family Sphecidae that makes its nest in sand (ill. INSECTS). **sand-yacht** *n.* a yachtlike vehicle on wheels for use on sand. [OE]

sandal¹ /sænd(ə)l/ *n.* a shoe with an open-work upper or no upper, usually fastened with straps. [f. L f. Gk *sandalion*]

sandal² /'sænd(ə)l/ *n.* (in full **sandal-wood**) a scented wood; a tree with this, especially one of the genus *Santalum*. [f. L ult. f. Skr.]

sandbag *n.* a bag filled with sand, used to protect a wall or building (e.g. in war) to make temporary defences, or as a ruffian's weapon. —*v.t.* (**-gg-**) **1.** to protect with sandbags. **2.** to hit with a sandbag.

sandbank *n.* a deposit of sand forming a shallow place in a sea or river.

sander *n.* a device for sanding things (ill. CARPENTRY). [f. SAND]

Sandhurst (in full 'The Royal Military Academy, Sandhurst') a training college, now at Camberley, Surrey, for officers for the British Army. It was formed in 1946 from an amalgamation of the Royal Military College at Sandhurst in Berkshire (founded 1799) and the Royal Military Academy at Woolwich, London (founded 1741).

sandman *n.* an imaginary person causing sleepiness in children, the personification of tiredness causing children's eyes to smart towards bedtime.

sand-painting *n.* an American Indian ceremonial art form, using coloured sands, also called *dry painting*; an example of this. Although sand-painting had largely died out by the early 20th c., it continues to be an important ritual among the Navajos (where it is associated with healing practices) and the Pueblos. The designs are executed with traditional gestures; the gods are represented in conventionalized form; the colours used are traditional, and the greater part of the design follows patterns handed down from memory, each sand-painting being destroyed after the ceremony.

sandpaper *n.* paper with a coating of sand or other abrasive for smoothing or polishing things. —*v.t.* to smooth or polish with sandpaper.

sandpiper *n.* a bird of the family Scolopacidae inhabiting wet sandy places.

Sandringham House /ˈsændrɪŋəm/ a holiday residence of the Royal Family, NE of King's Lynn in Norfolk. The estate was acquired in 1861 by Edward VII, then Prince of Wales.

sandstone *n.* a sedimentary rock of compressed sand.

sandstorm *n.* a storm with clouds of sand raised by the wind.

sandwich /ˈsænwɪdʒ/ *n.* **1.** two or more slices of bread with a filling between. **2.** a cake of two or more layers with jam or cream etc. between. —*v.t.* to put (a thing, statement, etc.) between two others of a different kind. —**sandwich-board** *n.* each of the two advertisement boards carried by a sandwich-man. **sandwich course**, a course of training with alternate periods of practical and theoretical work. **sandwich-man** *n.* a man walking in the street with advertisement boards hung one before and one behind him. [f. 4th Earl of *Sandwich* (d. 1792), said to have eaten only slices of bread and meat while gaming for 24 hours]

sandy *adj.* **1.** having much sand. **2.** sand-coloured. **3.** (of hair) yellowish-red; (of a person) having hair of this colour. —**sandiness** *n.* [f. SAND]

sane *adj.* **1.** having a sound mind, not mad. **2.** showing good judgement, sensible and practical. —**sanely** *adv.* [f. L *sanus* healthy]

San Francisco /frænˈsɪskəʊ/ a city and seaport on the coast of California, with a magnificent land-locked harbour entered by a channel called the Golden Gate; pop. (1983) 3,250,630.

sang past of SING.

sang-froid /sɑ̃ˈfrwɑː/ *n.* calmness in danger or difficulty. [F, = cold blood]

sangha /ˈsɑːŋə/ *n.* the Buddhist monastic order, including monks, nuns, and novices. [f. Skr., = community (*sam* together, *lan* come in contact)]

sangria /sænˈgriːə/ *n.* a Spanish drink of red wine with lemonade etc. [Sp., = bleeding]

sanguinary /ˈsæŋgwɪnərɪ/ *adj.* accompanied by or delighting in bloodshed; bloody, bloodthirsty. [f. L (*sanguis* blood)]

sanguine /ˈsæŋgwɪn/ *adj.* **1.** optimistic. **2.** (of the complexion) bright and florid. [f. OF f. L *sanguineus* (as prec.)]

Sanhedrin /ˈsænɪdrɪn/ *n.* the supreme Jewish council and highest court of justice at Jerusalem in New Testament times. It pronounced sentence of death on Christ. [f. Heb. f. Gk *sunedrion* (*sun* with, *hedra* seat)]

sanitarium /sænɪˈteərɪəm/ *n.* (*US*) a sanatorium. [as foll.]

sanitary /ˈsænɪtərɪ/ *adj.* **1.** of or assisting hygiene, hygienic. **2.** of sanitation. —**sanitary towel**, an absorbent pad used during menstruation. [f. F f. L *sanitas* (as SANITY)]

sanitation /sænɪˈteɪʃ(ə)n/ *n.* sanitary conditions, the maintenance or improvement of these; the disposal of sewage and refuse etc. [irreg. f. prec.]

sanitize /ˈsænɪtaɪz/ *v.t.* to make sanitary. [f. SANITARY]

sanity /ˈsænɪtɪ/ *n.* being sane. [f. L *sanitas* (as SANE)]

San José /sæn ˈxəʊseɪ, ˈhəʊ-/ the capital of Costa Rica; pop. (est. 1981) 843,800.

San Juan /sæn ˈxwɑːn, ˈhwɑːn/ the capital and chief port of Puerto Rico; pop. 808,919.

sank past of SINK.

San Marino /sæn məˈriːnəʊ/ a small republic near the Adriatic near Rimini, Italy, with a capital of the same name; pop. (1982) 22,053; official language, Italian. It is perhaps Europe's oldest State, claiming to have been independent almost continuously since its foundation in the 4th c.

San Martín /sæn mɑːˈtiːn/, José de (1778–1850), South American soldier and statesman. Having assisted in the liberation of Argentina from Spanish rule (1812–13) he went on to liberate Chile (1817–18) and Peru (1820–1), and was appointed Protector of Peru in 1821. He resigned a year later, having refused to oppose the ambitions of the other great liberator Bolivar, who, because of San Martin's retiring ways, has always received a disproportionate share of the credit for liberating South America.

San Salvador /sæn ˈsælvədɔː(r)/ the capital of El Salvador; pop. (est. 1980) 425,119.

sansculottes /sɑ̃kjuːˈlɒt/ *n.* (in the French Revolution) a republican of the poorer classes in Paris; an extreme republican or revolutionary. [F, lit. = without knee-breeches; usu. explained as one wearing trousers instead of the knee-breeches of the aristocracy]

sanserif /sænˈserɪf/ *adj.* without serifs. —*n.* a form of typeface without serifs. [app. f. F *sans* without, SERIF]

Sanskrit /ˈsænskrɪt/ *n.* the ancient language of Hindus in India, belonging to a branch of the Indo-European family of languages. It flourished in India as the language of learning for more than three millenniums, well into the 19th c., but has been gradually eclipsed by English and the modern Indian languages (e.g. Hindi, Bengali, Gujarati) to which, as a spoken language, it gave rise, and is now used only for religious purposes. It is written in the Devanagari script. —*adj.* of or in Sanskrit. —**Sanskritic** /-ˈkrɪtɪk/ *adj.* [f. Skr., = composed (*sam* together, *kr* make)]

Sansovino /sænsəˈviːnəʊ/, Jacopo Tatti (1486–1570), Italian sculptor and architect, city architect of Venice from 1529, where his buildings include St Mark's Library, the Loggia of the Campanile, and the Palazzo Corner, all of which show the influence of his early training in Rome and the development of antique architectural style for contemporary use. His sculpture includes reliefs for the Campanile Loggia and the sacristy doors of St Mark's, and the colossal *Mars* and *Neptune* for the staircase of the Ducal Palace.

Santa Claus /sæntə ˈklɔːz/ a person said to fill children's stockings with presents on the night before Christmas (see FATHER CHRISTMAS). [f. Du. dial., = St Nicholas]

Santayana /sæntəˈjɑːnə/, George (1863–1952), American philosopher and man of letters, born in Spain. For twenty-three years he was a professor at Harvard, but American culture held no appeal for him and he left for Europe in 1912, settling eventually in Rome. His outstanding early work is *The Life of Reason* (1905–6). Rejecting German idealism and the transcendental claims of religion, he held that the human mind is an effect of physical growth and organization, and matter is the only reality, yet our ideas and aesthetic appreciation, although of bodily origin, stand on a higher and non-material plane. Analysing religious and other institutions, he distinguished the ideal element from its material embodiment; thus the wisdom embodied in the ritual and dogmas of religion is truth not about existence but about the ideals on which mental strength and serenity are founded. With *Scepticism and Animal Faith* (1923) he modified this philosophy, holding that belief in the external world rests on an act of 'animal faith'; this concept he modified and supplemented in *The Realms of Being* (1927–40). Santayana is noted for the formal elegance of his prose style. He did not confine himself to philosophy but wrote also poems, a great deal of literary criticism, and a successful novel *The Last Puritan* (1935), in which he gave fictional form to his philosophy.

Santiago /sæntɪˈɑːgəʊ/ the capital of Chile; pop. approx. 4,000,000.

Santo Domingo /sæntəʊ dəˈmɪŋgəʊ/ the capital of the Dominican Republic, founded in 1496 by a brother of Christopher Columbus. It is the oldest city in the New World; pop. (1981) 1,550,739.

São Tomé and Principe /sɑːuː tɒˈmeɪ, ˈprɪnsɪpɪ/ a country consisting of two islands in the Gulf of Guinea, formerly an overseas province of Portugal; pop. (est. 1980) 113,000; official language, Portuguese; capital, São Tomé. The islands became independent in 1975. Cacao is the main product.

sap[1] *n.* **1.** the vital juice circulating in plants, carrying nutriment to all parts. **2.** vigour, vitality. **3.** sapwood. **4.** (*slang*) a foolish person. —*v.t.* (**-pp-**) **1.** to drain or dry (wood) of sap. **2.** to exhaust the vigour of, to weaken. [OE]

sap[2] *n.* **1.** a tunnel or trench to conceal assailants' approach to a fortified place. **2.** the insidious undermining of belief etc. —*v.t./i.* (**-pp-**) **1.** to dig saps; to undermine (a wall etc.). **2.** to destroy insidiously, to weaken. [f. F or It. *zappa* spade, spadework, prob. of Arab. orig.]

sapid /ˈsæpɪd/ *adj.* **1.** savoury, palatable. **2.** (of writings etc.) not insipid or vapid. —**sapidity** /səˈpɪdɪtɪ/ *n.* [f. L *sapidus* (*sapere* have flavour)]

sapient /ˈseɪpɪənt/ *adj.* (*literary*) wise, pretending to be wise. —**sapience** *n.* [f. OF or L *sapiens* (*sapere* be wise)]

Sapir /ˈsæpɪə(r)/, Edward (1884–1939), American linguistics scholar and anthropologist who, like Bloomfield, had an important role in the creation of American linguistic structuralism. He was immensely learned in a number of subjects and left important works on American-Indian languages and linguistic theory (e.g. his book *Language*, 1921). His approach is characterized by constant awareness of the links between language and culture, language and psychology, etc.

sapling *n.* a young tree. [f. SAP¹]

sapper *n.* **1.** one who digs saps. **2.** a soldier of the Royal Engineers (esp. as the official term for a private). [f. SAP²]

Sapphic /ˈsæfɪk/ *adj.* of Sappho or her poetry, esp. (of a stanza or verse) in four-line form with a short fourth line. [f. F f. L f. Gk, = of SAPPHO]

sapphire /ˈsæfaɪə(r)/ *n.* **1.** a transparent blue precious stone. **2.** its bright blue colour. —*adj.* of sapphire blue. [f. OF f. L f. Gk, = lapis lazuli]

Sappho /ˈsæfəʊ/ (early 7th c. BC) Greek lyric poetess from the island of Lesbos. The fragments of her poems, written in her local dialect, are chiefly on personal subjects; many concern young girls in her circle, and her affection and love for them.

sappy *adj.* **1.** full of sap. **2.** young and vigorous. [f. SAP¹]

saprophyte /ˈsæprəfaɪt/ *n.* a vegetable organism living on dead organic matter. —**saprophytic** /-ˈfɪtɪk/ *adj.* [f. Gk *sapros* putrid + *phuō* grow]

sapwood *n.* the soft outer layers of recently formed wood between the heartwood and the bark (ill. TREES).

Saqqara /səˈkɑːrə/ a cemetery of the necropolis at Memphis, with monuments dating from the early dynastic period (3rd millennium BC) to the Graeco-Roman age, including the step pyramid of King Djoser (*c.*2700 BC), the earliest type of pyramid and the first known building entirely of stone.

saraband /ˈsærəbænd/ *n.* a slow Spanish dance; the music for this. [f. F f. Sp. & It. *zarabanda*]

Saracen /ˈsærəs(ə)n/ *n.* an Arab or Muslim of the time of the Crusades. [f. OF, perh. ult. f. Arab., = eastern]

Sarah /ˈseərə/ the wife of Abraham and mother of Isaac (Gen. 17: 15 ff.).

Sarajevo /særəˈjeɪvəʊ/ a city in Yugoslavia, formerly capital of the Balkan province of Bosnia, where the Archduke Franz Ferdinand (heir to the Austrian throne) and his wife were assassinated on 28 June 1914. The event triggered off the First World War. The city was a centre of Slav opposition to Austrian rule, and connections between Bosnian nationalists and Serbian agents were used by the Austrians as a pretext for war with Serbia. Each side was supported by its European allies, so that within a few weeks most of the Continent was at war.

Saratoga /særəˈtəʊgə/ a city in New York State near which two battles were fought (1777) in the War of American Independence. The Americans were victorious in both, and in the second battle the British forces, under General Burgoyne, were decisively defeated. The defeat encouraged French support of the Americans and destroyed the best British opportunity to end the rebellion.

Sarawak /səˈrɑːwɒk/ a State of Malaysia on the NW coast of Borneo; capital, Kuching.

sarcasm /ˈsɑːkæz(ə)m/ *n.* an ironical remark or comment; the use of such remarks. [f. F or L f. Gk (*sarkazō* speak bitterly; orig. = tear flesh, f. *sarx* flesh)]

sarcastic /sɑːˈkæstɪk/ *adj.* using or showing sarcasm. —**sarcastically** *adv.* [as prec.]

sarcoma /sɑːˈkəʊmə/ *n.* (*pl.* **-mata**) a malignant tumour of connective tissue. [f. Gk (*sarkoō* become fleshy f. *sarx* flesh)]

sarcophagus /sɑːˈkɒfəgəs/ *n.* (*pl.* **-gi** /-gaɪ/) a stone coffin. [L f. Gk, = flesh-consuming (*sarx* flesh, *-phagos* eating)]

Sardanapalus /sɑːdəˈnæpələs/ (d. 626 BC) the last king of Assyria, notorious for his luxury and effeminacy.

sardine /sɑːˈdiːn/ *n.* a young pilchard or similar small fish, often tinned tightly packed in oil. —**like sardines,** crowded close together. [f. OF f. L *sardina,* perh. f. Gk *Sardō* Sardinia]

Sardinia /sɑːˈdɪnɪə/ a large island in the Mediterranean west of Italy, which became part of the kingdom of Italy in 1861; capital, Cagliari. —**Sardinian** *adj. & n.*

Sardis /ˈsɑːdɪs/ an ancient city that was the capital of Lydia.

sardonic /sɑːˈdɒnɪk/ *adj.* humorous in a grim or sarcastic way; full of bitter mockery; cynical. —**sardonically** *adv.* [f. F f. L f. Gk *Sardonios* (= Sardinian), substituted for Homeric *sardanios* (epithet of bitter or scornful laughter) because of belief that eating a Sardinian plant could result in convulsive laughter ending in death]

sardonyx /ˈsɑːdənɪks/ *n.* an onyx in which white layers alternate with yellow or orange ones. [f. L f. Gk (*sardios* a precious stone, as ONYX)]

sargasso /sɑːˈgæsəʊ/ *n.* (*pl.* **-os**) a seaweed of the genus

Sargassum, with berry-like air-vessels, found floating in island-like masses. [f. Port.; orig. unkn.]

Sargasso Sea /sɑːˈgæsəʊ/ a region of the western Atlantic Ocean around latitude 35 °N, so called because of the prevalence in it of floating sargasso seaweed. It is the breeding-place of eels from the rivers of Europe and eastern North America.

sarge *n.* (*slang*) a sergeant. [abbr.]

Sargent /ˈsɑːdʒ(ə)nt/, John Singer (1856-1925), American portrait painter. Born in Florence, he travelled and studied widely in Europe as a youth. In the 1870s he painted some impressionist landscapes, but it was in portraiture that he developed the loaded brush and bravura handling typical of his style. A painterly painter—he had profited from studying Manet, Hals, and Velazquez—his virtuoso technique was much in demand in Parisian circles, but the scandal over the supposed eroticism of *Madame Gautreau* (1884) made him move to London, where he dominated society portraiture for over twenty years. In about 1910 he produced a small number of water-colour landscapes and later worked as a war artist.

Sargon /ˈsɑːgɒn/ (2334-2279 BC) the semi-legendary founder of the ancient kingdom of Akkad.

Sargon II /ˈsɑːgɒn/ (d. 705 BC) king of Assyria 722-705 BC, who adopted the name of Sargon of Akkad (see prec.) and is famous for his conquest of a number of cities in Syria and Palestine.

sari /ˈsɑːrɪ/ *n.* a length of material draped around the body, worn as the main garment by Hindu women. [f. Hindi]

Sarmatia /sɑːˈmeɪʃə/ the name in ancient times of a region north of the Black Sea inhabited by ancestors of the Slavs, used occasionally by English poets to signify Poland. —**Sarmatian** *adj. & n.*

sarong /səˈrɒŋ/ *n.* a Malay and Javanese garment worn by both sexes, consisting of a long strip of cloth tucked round the waist or under the armpits. [Malay, lit. = sheath]

sarsaparilla /sɑːsəpəˈrɪlə/ *n.* a tropical American smilax especially *Smilax ornata*; its dried roots; a tonic made from these. [f. Sp. *zarzaparilla* (*zarza* bramble)]

sarsen /ˈsɑːs(ə)n/ *n.* a sandstone etc. boulder, a relict carried by ice in the glacial period. [prob. var. of SARACEN]

sarsenet /ˈsɑːsnɪt/ *n.* a soft silk fabric used especially as a lining. [f. AF *sarzinett* (perh. *sarzin* Saracen)]

sartorial /sɑːˈtɔːrɪ(ə)l/ *adj.* of clothes or tailoring. —**sartorially** *adv.* [f. L *sartor* tailor]

Sartre /sɑːtr/, Jean-Paul (1905-80), French philosopher, novelist, dramatist, and critic, a nephew of Albert Schweitzer. During the Second World War he was a prisoner of war and an active member of the Resistance. In his philosophy and literature, which established him as the leading figure in the existentialist movement, he set out to show that the human situation is characterized by lack of a permanent nature, essence, or divinely bestowed destiny, and as a result possesses a terrifying freedom of choice. His later philosophy, cast in a Marxist mould, explores the social setting of human relationships conditioned by material scarcity. His works include the treatise *Being and Nothingness* (1943), the novels *Nausea* (1938) and the trilogy *Les Chemins de la liberté* (*Roads to Freedom*, 1945-9), and the plays *Les Mouches* (*The Flies*, 1943) and *Huis clos* (*No Exit*, 1944). In 1964 he was offered but refused the Nobel Prize for literature. The novelist Simone de Beauvoir was friend and lover to him throughout most of his life.

Sarum /ˈseərəm/ the ecclesiastical name of Salisbury, Wilts., and its diocese. —**Old Sarum,** a hill 3 km (2 miles) from Salisbury on which a Norman castle and town were built, now deserted. **Sarum use,** the form of liturgy used in the diocese of Salisbury from the 11th c. to the Reformation. [L, perh. f. misreading of abbreviated form of L *Sarisburia* Salisbury]

sash¹ *n.* a long strip or loop of cloth etc. worn over one shoulder or round the waist as part of a uniform or insignia, or (by a woman or child) round the waist for ornament. [f. Arab., = muslin, turban]

sash² *n.* a frame holding the glass in a sash-window (ill. HOUSES). —**sash cord,** a strong cord attaching sash-weights to a sash. **sash-weight** *n.* a weight attached to each end of a sash to balance it at any height. **sash-window** *n.* a window usually made to slide up and down in grooves. [f. *sashes,* corrupt. of CHASSIS]

Saskatchewan /səˈskætʃɪwən/ **1.** a province of central Canada (from 1905), settled by the Hudson's Bay Company;

capital, Regina. **2.** a river of Canada, flowing from the Rocky Mountains to Lake Winnipeg.

sassafras /ˈsæsəfræs/ *n.* **1.** a small tree of the genus *Sassafras*, especially a North American species yielding bark that is used medicinally and in perfumes. **2.** this bark. [f. Sp. or Port.; orig. unkn.]

Sassanian /səˈseɪnɪən/ *adj. & n.* = foll. [as foll.]

Sassanid /ˈsæsənɪd/ *n.* a member (esp. a king) of the dynasty ruling the Persian empire (224-636) until driven from Mesopotamia by the Arabs. —*adj.* of the Sassanids. [f. *Sasan*, grandfather of the first Sassanid, Artaxerxes I]

Sassenach /ˈsæsənæx, -æk/ *n.* (*Sc. & Ir.*, usu. *derog.*) an Englishman. [f. Gael. or Ir. f. L (as SAXON)]

Sassoon /səˈsuːn/, Siegfried Louvain (1886-1967), English poet and prose writer, remembered for his starkly realistic poems written in the trenches during the First World War. In hospital, recovering from shell-shock, he met and inspired the poet Wilfred Owen. After the war his poetry became increasingly religious and he became a successful prose writer with *Memoirs of a Fox-Hunting Man* (1928), *Memoirs of an Infantry Officer* (1930), *Sherston's Progress* (1936), three volumes of autobiography, and an important biography of George Meredith (1948). His later works reflect his attachment to the countryside.

sat *past & p.p.* of SIT.

Sat. *abbr.* Saturday.

Satan /ˈseɪt(ə)n/ *n.* the Devil. [OE, ult. f. Heb. = adversary]

satanic /səˈtænɪk/ *adj.* of or like Satan; devilish, evil. —**satanically** *adv.* [f. prec.]

Satanism /ˈseɪtənɪz(ə)m/ *n.* **1.** the worship of Satan, with a travesty of Christian forms. **2.** the pursuit of evil. —**Satanist** *n.* [f. SATAN]

satchel /ˈsætʃ(ə)l/ *n.* a small bag usually with a shoulder-strap, especially for carrying school-books. [f. OF f. L *saccellus* (as SACK¹)]

sate *v.t.* to satiate. [prob. f. dial. *sade* (as SAD)]

sateen /sæˈtiːn/ *n.* a glossy cotton fabric woven like satin. [f. *satin* after *velveteen*]

satellite /ˈsætəlaɪt/ *n.* **1.** a heavenly body revolving round a planet. **2.** an artificial body placed in orbit round the Earth or other planet for purposes of observation, research, navigation or communications. The first artificial satellite (Sputnik I) was launched by the USSR on 4 Oct. 1957, but the idea had been put forward much earlier, e.g. in Jules Verne's *Begum's Fortune* (tr. 1880). **3.** a follower, a hanger-on; a member of a retinue. **4.** a small country etc. controlled by or dependent on another and following its lead. [F or f. L *satelles* guard]

Sati /ˈsɒtiː/ (*Hinduism*) wife of Siva, reborn as Parvati. According to some accounts, she died by throwing herself into the sacred fire, hence the custom of suttee. [f. Skr., = virtuous woman, chaste wife]

satiable /ˈseɪʃəb(ə)l/ *adj.* that may be satiated. [f. foll.]

satiate /ˈseɪʃɪeɪt/ *v.t.* to gratify fully, to surfeit. —**satiation** /-ˈeɪʃ(ə)n/ *n.* [f. L *satiare* (*satis* enough)]

Satie /ˈsɑːtiː/, Erik (1866-1925), French composer. He formed the centre of an irreverent avant-garde artistic set, associated not only with the composers of the group known as Les Six but also with Cocteau, Dadaism, and surrealism. He was fond of giving facetious titles to his short irresistibly naïve works: the *Trois Pièces en forme de poire* (1903), for example, is in fact a set of six pieces. One of his few large-scale works is the symphonic drama *Socrate* (1919) to a libretto based on Plato and scored for four sopranos and orchestra.

satiety /səˈtaɪətɪ/ *n.* the state or feeling of being satiated. [as SATIATE]

satin /ˈsætɪn/ *n.* a silky fabric so woven that it has a glossy surface on one side. —*adj.* smooth as satin. —*v.t.* to give a glossy surface to (paper). —**satiny** *adj.* [f. OF f. Arab., = of Tseutung in China]

satinwood *n.* a kind of choice glossy timber of any of various trees.

satire /ˈsætaɪə(r)/ *n.* **1.** the use of ridicule, irony, or sarcasm to expose folly or vice etc. **2.** a work or composition using satire. —**satirical** /səˈtɪrɪk(ə)l/ *adj.*, **satirically** *adv.* [F or f. L, orig. = medley)]

satirist /ˈsætɪrɪst/ *n.* a writer or performer of satires. [f. prec.]

satirize /ˈsætɪraɪz/ *v.t.* to attack with satire; to describe satirically. [f. F (as SATIRE)]

satisfaction /sætɪsˈfækʃ(ə)n/ *n.* **1.** satisfying, being satis-

fied. **2.** a thing that satisfies a desire or gratifies a feeling. **3.** a thing that settles an obligation or debt, or compensates for an injury or loss. [as SATISFY]

satisfactory /sætɪsˈfæktərɪ/ *adj.* satisfying expectations or needs; adequate. —**satisfactorily** *adv.*, **satisfactoriness** *n.* [f. F or L (as foll.)]

satisfy /ˈsætɪsfaɪ/ *v.t./i.* **1.** to give (a person) what he wants, demands, or needs; to make pleased or contented; to be adequate. **2.** to deal adequately with (an obligation, debt, etc.); to pay (a creditor). **3.** to put an end to (a demand or craving etc.) by giving what is required. **4.** to provide with sufficient information or proof; to convince. [f. OF f. L *satisfacere* (*satis* enough, *facere* make)]

satrap /ˈsætræp/ *n.* a provincial governor in the ancient Persian empire. [f. OF or L f. Gk f. OPers., = country-protector]

satsuma /sætˈsuːmə/ *n.* a kind of mandarin orange originally grown in Japan. [f. *Satsuma*, province of Japan]

saturate /ˈsætʃəreɪt, -tjʊr-/ *v.t.* **1.** to make thoroughly wet, to soak. **2.** to cause to absorb or accept as much as possible. [f. L *saturare* (*satur* full)]

saturation /sætʃəˈreɪʃ(ə)n, -tjʊr-/ *n.* the act or result of being saturated. —**saturation point**, the point beyond which no more can be absorbed or accepted. [f. prec.]

Saturday /ˈsætədeɪ, -dɪ/ *n.* the day of the week following Friday. —*adv.* (*colloq.*) on Saturday. [OE, = day of Saturn]

Saturn /ˈsætɜːn/ *n.* **1.** (*Rom. myth.*) an ancient god whose festival was 17 Dec., often interpreted (but not with certainty) as a god of agriculture, and also identified with the Greek Cronus (see entry). In historical times his festival was the merriest of the year, when slaves were allowed temporary liberty to do as they liked and presents were exchanged. By about the 4th c. AD much of this had been transferred to what was then New Year's Day, and so became one of the elements in the traditional celebrations of Christmas. **2.** (*Astron.*) a ringed planet of the solar system, sixth in distance from the sun, with a mean orbital radius of 1,427 million km. The planet has a radius of 60,000 km, but the rings, extending out to a distance twice as great, make this planet a glorious sight in any moderate to large telescope. Galileo recognized from his observations that the planet departed from sphericity, but could not provide the explanation. We now know that several thousand individual rings, composed of small icy particles, occupy a wide band of orbits, broken here and there by the so-called 'gaps', which are not true gaps in the particle distribution, but only regions of smaller particle density. The planet itself has a dense hydrogen-rich atmosphere, similar to that of Jupiter, but with more vigorous atmospheric circulation. There are at least fifteen moons, ranging in radius from the 2,560 km of Titan, which itself has a dense atmosphere of methane, to the few kilometres radius of the small moons which travel close to the outermost thin ring, 'shepherding' it into place.

Saturnalia /sætəˈneɪlɪə/ *n.* **1.** the ancient Roman festival of Saturn, observed as a time of unrestrained merry-making (see prec.). **2. saturnalia,** a scene or time of wild revelry or tumult. [f. prec.]

saturnine /ˈsætənaɪn/ *adj.* of gloomy forbidding temperament or appearance. [f. OF f. L (as prec.)]

satyr /ˈsætə(r)/ *n.* **1.** (*Gk myth.*) any of a class of woodland spirits, bestial in their desires and behaviour, in Hellenistic art and poetry, associated with Dionysus. In Greek art of the pre-Roman period they are represented with the tail and ears of a horse. Roman sculptors assimilated the satyr in some degree to the faun of their native mythology, giving it the ears, tail, and legs of a goat, with budding horns. **2.** a grossly lustful man. [f. OF or L f. Gk]

sauce /sɔːs/ *n.* **1.** a liquid or soft preparation served with food to add flavour or richness. **2.** impudence. —*v.t.* (*colloq.*) to be impudent to (a person). [f. OF ult. f. L *salsus* salted]

saucepan *n.* a metal cooking-vessel, usually round and with a long handle at the side, for use on top of a cooker etc.

saucer /ˈsɔːsə(r)/ *n.* **1.** a small shallow dish, especially for standing a cup on. **2.** a thing of this shape. [f. OF (as SAUCE)]

saucy /ˈsɔːsɪ/ *adj.* **1.** impudent. **2.** (*colloq.*) stylish, smart-looking. —**saucily** *adv.*, **sauciness** *n.* [f. SAUCE]

Saudi /ˈsaʊdɪ/ *n.* **1.** a native or inhabitant of Saudi Arabia. **2.** a member of the dynasty founded by Saud. —*adj.* of the Saudis or Saudi Arabia. [f. A. Ibn-*Saud* (d. 1953), Arab. king]

Saudi Arabia /saʊdɪ əˈreɪbɪə/ a country in SW Asia occupying most of the Arabian peninsula; pop. (est. 1976) 9,160,000; official language, Arabic; capital, Riyadh. The birthplace of Islam, Saudi Arabia emerged from the Arab revolt against the Turks during the First World War to become an independent kingdom in 1932. Since the Second World War the economy has been revolutionized by the exploitation of the area's oil resources, the export of oil now accounting for 85% of the government's revenue and making Saudi Arabia the largest oil producer in the Middle East. Ruled along traditional Islamic lines, the country has exercised a conservative influence over Middle Eastern politics, although the position of the ruling house of Saud was severely threatened by the brief seizure of the Great Mosque in Mecca by Islamic fanatics in 1979. —**Saudi Arabian** adj. & n.

sauerkraut /ˈsaʊəkraʊt/ n. a German dish of chopped pickled cabbage. [G (*saur* sour, *kraut* vegetable)]

Saul /sɔːl/ 1. the first king of Israel (11th c. BC). 2. (also **Saul of Tarsus**) the original name of St Paul.

sauna /ˈsɔːnə/ n. a Finnish-style steam-bath; a building or room for this. [Finnish]

saunter /ˈsɔːntə(r)/ v.i. to walk in a leisurely way. —n. a leisurely walk or walking-pace. [orig. unkn.]

saurian /ˈsɔːrɪən/ n. an animal of the lizard family. —adj. of or like a lizard. [f. Gk *saura* lizard]

sausage /ˈsɒsɪdʒ/ n. 1. minced meat seasoned and enclosed in a cylindrical case of thin membrane; a length of this. 2. a sausage-shaped object. —**not a sausage,** (slang) nothing at all. **sausage roll,** sausage meat baked in a cylindrical pastry-case. [f. OF *saussiche* f. L *salsicia* (as SAUCE)]

Saussure /sɒˈsjʊə(r), səʊ-/, Ferdinand de (1857–1913), Swiss linguistics scholar often treated as the founder of modern linguistics. The contrast he established between a synchronic and a diachronic approach to language and the priority he gave to the former also allowed him to treat language as a system in which each element is defined in terms of the other elements (see STRUCTURALISM). In his lifetime he published works of fundamental importance for Indo-European studies, but his theoretical work, *Cours de linguistique générale,* appeared posthumously (1916) and was put together from lecture-notes.

sauté /ˈsəʊteɪ/ adj. quickly and lightly fried in a little fat. —n. food cooked thus. —v.t. (past & p.p. **sautéd**) to cook thus. [F (*sauter* jump)]

Sauternes /səʊˈtɜːn/ n. a sweet white French wine. [f. *Sauternes* district of SW France]

Sauveterrian /səʊvˈterɪən/ adj. of an early mesolithic industry of France and western Europe, named after the type-site at Sauveterre-la-Lémance, France. —n. this industry.

savage /ˈsævɪdʒ/ adj. 1. in a primitive or uncivilized state. 2. wild and fierce. 3. cruel and hostile. 4. (colloq.) very angry. —n. 1. a member of a savage tribe. 2. a brutal or barbarous person. —v.t. 1. (of an animal) to attack savagely, to maul. 2. (of a critic etc.) to attack fiercely. —**savagely** adv., **savageness** n. [f. OF *sauvage* f. L *silvaticus* (*silva* forest)]

savagery /ˈsævɪdʒrɪ/ n. savage behaviour or state. [f. prec.]

savannah /səˈvænə/ n. a grassy plain in a tropical or subtropical region, with few or no trees. [f. Sp. *zavana,* perh. of Carib. orig.]

savant /ˈsæv(ə)nt/ n. a learned person. [F (*savoir* know)]

save v.t./i. 1. to rescue, to keep from danger, harm, or capture. 2. to keep for future use or enjoyment; to put aside (money) for future use. 3. to make unnecessary (for); to avoid wasting. 4. to effect the spiritual salvation of. 5. to avoid losing (a match or game etc.); (in football etc.) to prevent an opponent from scoring. —n. (in football etc.) the act of preventing an opponent from scoring. —prep. except, but. —conj. (archaic) unless, except. —**save-as-you-earn** n. a method of saving by regular deduction from earnings. —**saver** n. [f. AF *sa(u)ver* f. L *salvare* (*salvus* safe)]

saveloy /ˈsævəlɔɪ/ n. a highly seasoned dried sausage. [corrupt. of F *cervelas* f. It. (*cervello* brain)]

Savery /ˈseɪvərɪ/, Thomas ('Captain') (c.1650–1715), English inventor of a partially successful engine for raising water 'by the Impellent Force of Fire', patented in 1698. It was described as being suitable for raising water from mines, supplying towns with water, and operating mills. Its use of high-pressure steam made it very dangerous, but the patent covered the type of engine developed by Thomas

Newcomen, who was therefore obliged to join Savery in its exploitation.

saving /ˈseɪvɪŋ/ n. 1. the act of rescuing or keeping from danger etc. 2. (usu. in pl.) money put aside for future use. —adj. 1. that saves or redeems. 2. that makes economical use of (labour etc.). 3. (of a clause etc.) stipulating an exception or reservation. —prep. 1. except; with the exception of. 2. without offence to. —**savings bank,** a bank paying interest on small deposits. **savings certificate,** an interest-bearing document issued by the government for savers. [f. SAVE]

saviour /ˈseɪvjə(r)/ n. a person who saves others from harm or danger. —**our** or **the Saviour,** Christ. [f. OF f. L *salvator* (as SAVE)]

savoir faire /sævwɑː ˈfeə(r)/ knowledge of how to behave in any situation that may arise, tact. [F, = know how to do]

Savonarola /sævənəˈrəʊlə/, Girolamo (1452–98), Italian preacher and reformer. A Dominican monk and severe ascetic, in 1482 he moved to Florence, where he attracted great attention as a preacher by his passionate denunciations of the immorality of the people of Florence and of the clergy, and by his apocalyptic prophecies. He became virtual ruler of Florence in 1494–5, but his severity made him many enemies, and in 1495 the Pope forbade him to preach and summoned him to Rome. His refusal to comply with these orders led to his excommunication in 1497; he was hanged as a schismatic and heretic.

savory /ˈseɪvərɪ/ n. an aromatic herb of the genus *Satureia,* used in cookery. [perh. OE f. L *satureia*]

savour /ˈseɪvə(r)/ n. 1. a characteristic taste or smell (lit. or fig.). 2. the power to arouse enjoyment. —v.t./i. 1. to taste or smell (a thing) with enjoyment or deliberation (lit. or fig.). 2. to have a certain taste or smell. 3. to give a specified impression. [f. OF f. L *sapor* (*sapere* taste)]

savoury /ˈseɪvərɪ/ adj. 1. having an appetizing taste or smell. 2. having a salt or piquant and not a sweet taste. —n. a savoury dish, especially at the end of a meal or as an appetizer. —**savouriness** n. [as prec.]

Savoy /səˈvɔɪ/ a region in SE France bordering on NW Italy, ruled by the counts of Savoy from the 11th c. although frequently invaded and fought over by neighbouring States. In 1720 Savoy was formed with Sardinia and Piedmont into the Kingdom of Sardinia. In the mid-19th c. Sardinia served as the nucleus for the formation of a unified Italy, but at the time of unification (1860) Savoy itself was ceded to France.

savoy /səˈvɔɪ/ n. a cabbage with wrinkled leaves. [f. prec.]

savvy /ˈsævɪ/ v.t./i. (slang) to know. —n. (slang) knowingness, understanding. —adj. (US) knowing, wise. [orig. Negro & Pidgin f. Sp. *sabe* (*saber* you know]

saw[1] n. a tool with a toothed metal blade or edge for cutting wood, metal, stone, etc., by a to-and-fro or rotary motion (ill. CARPENTRY). —v.t./i. (p.p. **sawn** or **sawed**) 1. to cut (wood etc.) with a saw; to make (boards etc.) with a saw. 2. to move to and fro, or to divide (the air etc.) with the motion as of a saw or a person sawing. —**saw off,** to remove or reduce by sawing. **saw-tooth** or **-toothed** adj. shaped like the teeth of a saw, serrated. [OE]

saw[2] n. an old saying, a maxim. [OE (rel. to SAY)]

saw[3] past of SEE[1].

sawdust n. powdery fragments of wood produced in sawing.

sawfish n. a large sea-fish of the family Pristidae, having a blade-like snout with jagged edges that it uses as a weapon.

sawmill n. a mill for the mechanical sawing of wood.

sawn p.p. of SAW[1].

sawyer n. a workman who saws timber. [f. SAW[1]]

sax n. (colloq.) a saxophone. [abbr.]

saxe /sæks/ n. (also **saxe blue**) light blue with a greyish tinge. [F = Saxony]

Saxe-Coburg-Gotha /sækskəʊbɜːgˈɡəʊθə/ the name of the British royal house from the accession of Edward VII (1901), whose father Prince Albert, consort of Queen Victoria, was a prince of the German duchy of Saxe-Coburg and Gotha. In 1917, with anti-German feeling running high during the First World War, George V changed the family name to Windsor.

saxhorn /ˈsækshɔːn/ n. a brass wind instrument of the trumpet family made in several sizes, usually held with its mouth upwards. It was evolved by the Belgian instrument-maker A. Sax (d. 1894) and patented by him in 1846. [f. *Sax* + HORN]

saxifrage /'sæksɪfrɪdʒ/ n. a rock plant of the genus *Saxifraga* with tufted foliage. [f. OF or L *saxifraga* (*saxum* rock, *frangere* break)]

Saxon /'sæks(ə)n/ n. **1.** a member of a north German tribe, originally inhabitants of the area round the mouth of the Elbe, one branch of which, along with the Angles and the Jutes, conquered and colonized much of southern Britain in the 5th and 6th centuries. **2.** (also **Old Saxon**) the language of this tribe. **3.** Anglo-Saxon. **4.** a native of modern Saxony. **5.** the Germanic (as opposed to Latin or Romance) elements of English. —*adj.* of the Saxons or their language. [f. F f. L *Saxo*]

Saxony /'sæksənɪ/ a former province of east central Germany on the upper reaches of the Elbe, earlier part of the larger Kingdom of Saxony. —**Lower Saxony,** a *Land* ('State') of West Germany; capital, Hanover.

saxophone /'sæksəfəʊn/ n. a keyed brass wind instrument with a reed (ill. MUSICAL NOTATION), invented *c.*1840 by A. Sax (see SAXHORN) and patented in 1846. —**saxophonist** /-'sɒfənɪst/ n. [f. *Sax* + -PHONE]

say v.t./i. (*past* & *p.p.* **said** /sed/; 3 *sing. pres.* **says** /sez/) **1.** to utter or recite in a speaking voice. **2.** to state; to have a specified wording. **3.** to put into words; to convey information; to indicate or show. **4.** to give as an argument or excuse. **5.** to give as an opinion or decision. **6.** to suppose as a possibility; to select as an example etc.; to take a specified amount etc.) as being near enough. —*n.* **1.** what one wishes to say; an opportunity of saying this. **2.** a share in a discussion or decision; the power of final decision. —**go without saying,** to be obvious. **I'll say,** (*colloq.*) yes indeed. **I say,** an exclamation drawing attention, opening a conversation, or expressing surprise. **say-so** n. the power of decision; mere assertion. **says you,** (*slang*) I disagree. **that is to say,** in other words. [OE]

SAYE abbr. save-as-you-earn.

Sayers /'seɪəz/, Dorothy Leigh (1893-1957), English writer whose detective fiction, introducing the hero amateur detective Lord Peter Wimsey, is among the classics of the genre. In this she reached her peak with *Murder Must Advertise* (1933) and *The Nine Tailors* (1934). Her religious plays showed her as a formidable theological polemicist. She left unfinished a translation of Dante's *Divine Comedy* (1949-55).

saying n. a frequent or proverbial remark. [f. SAY]

Sb symbol antimony. [f. L *stibium*]

Sc symbol scandium.

sc. abbr. scilicet.

scab n. **1.** a crust formed over a sore in healing. **2.** a kind of skin-disease or plant-disease with scabs or scablike roughness. **3.** (*derog.*) a blackleg in a strike. —*v.i.* (**-bb-**) **1.** to form a scab; to heal over thus. **2.** (*derog.*) act as a blackleg. —**scabby** adj. [rel. to SHABBY]

scabbard /'skæbəd/ n. the sheath of a sword etc. [f. AF]

scabies /'skeɪbiːz/ n. a contagious skin-disease causing itching [L *scabere* scratch]

scabious /'skeɪbɪəs/ n. a wild or garden flower of the genus *Scabiosa* (or allied genera). [f. L *scabiosa* (*herba*) plant curing itch (as prec.)]

scabrous /'skeɪbrəs/ adj. **1.** (of the skin etc.) rough and scaly. **2.** indecent. [F or L (*scaber* rough)]

scaffold /'skæf(ə)ld/ n. **1.** a platform on which criminals are executed. **2.** scaffolding. [f. OF; cf. CATAFALQUE]

scaffolding n. **1.** a temporary structure of poles or tubes and planks providing platforms for building work; the materials for this. **2.** any temporary framework. [f. prec.]

scalar /'skeɪlə(r)/ adj. (*Math.*) having magnitude but not direction. —*n.* a scalar quantity. [f. L (as SCALE¹)]

scald¹ /skɔːld, skɒld/ v.t. **1.** to injure or pain with hot liquid or vapour. **2.** to heat (esp. milk or cream) to near boiling-point. **3.** to cleanse (a vessel) with boiling water. —*n.* an injury to the skin by scalding. [f. AF f. L *excaldare* (*calidus* hot)]

scald² var. of SKALD.

scale¹ n. **1.** a set of marks at fixed distances on a line for use in measuring etc.; a rule determining the intervals between these; a piece of metal etc. on which they are marked. **2.** relative dimensions or extent; the ratio of reduction or enlargement in a map, drawing, etc. **3.** a series of degrees; a ladder-like arrangement, a graded system. **4.** (*Mus.*) a set of sounds belonging to a key, arranged in order

of pitch. In Western music the 12 notes of the chromatic scale which make up the octave have been organized as three seven-note scale types, the major and the harmonic and melodic minor, since the 17th c., superseding the modes of earlier music. —*v.t.* **1.** to climb (a wall, precipice, etc.) with a ladder or by clambering. **2.** to represent in dimensions different from but proportional to the actual ones. —**in scale,** in proportion. **on a large** (*or* **small**) **scale,** to a large (or small) extent. **scale down** (*or* **up**), to make smaller (or larger) in proportion; to reduce (or increase) in size. **to scale,** with uniform reduction or enlargement. [f. L *scala* ladder]

scale² n. **1.** any of the small thin horny overlapping plates protecting the skin of many fishes (ill. FISH) and reptiles. **2.** a thin plate or flake resembling this. **3.** an incrustation inside a boiler or kettle etc. in which hard water is regularly used; tartar on teeth. —*v.t./i.* **1.** to remove scale(s) from. **2.** to form or drop off in scales. —**scaly** adj. [f. OF *escale* (cf. foll.)]

scale³ n. **1.** the pan of a weighing-balance. **2.** (in *pl.*) a weighing instrument; **the Scales,** the constellation or sign of the zodiac Libra. —*v.t.* to be found to weigh (a specified amount). —**pair of scales,** a simple balance. **tip** *or* **turn the scale(s),** to outweigh the opposite scale; to be the decisive factor. [f. ON, = bowl]

scalene /'skeɪliːn/ adj. (of a triangle etc.) having unequal sides. [f. L f. Gk *skalēnos* unequal]

Scaliger /'skælɪdʒə(r)/, Julius Caesar (1484-1558), Italian classical scholar and physician. Besides polemical works directed against Erasmus (1531) he wrote a long Latin treatise on poetics, scientific commentaries on botanical works, and a philosophical treatise, all showing encyclopaedic knowledge and acute observation marred by arrogance and vanity. His son Joseph Justus Scaliger (1540-1609), the greatest scholar of the Renaissance, has been described as 'the founder of historical criticism'. His edition of Manilius (1579) and his *De Emendatione Temporum* revolutionized understanding of ancient chronology by recognizing the historical material relating to the Jews, Persians, Babylonians, and Egyptians.

scallion /'skæljən/ n. a shallot; a long-necked bulbless onion. [f. AF f. L, = onion of *Ascalon* in Palestine]

scallop /'skɒləp/ n. **1.** a shellfish of the genus *Pecten*, with two fan-shaped ridged shells. **2.** one shell of this used as a container in which food is cooked and served. **3.** each of a series of ornamental semi-circular curves edging a fabric etc. —*v.t.* **1.** to cook in a scallop. **2.** to ornament (material etc.) with scallops. **3.** (usu. in *p.p.*) to bake (slices of potato) overlapping in a scallop-like arrangement. [f. OF, = ESCALOPE]

scalloping n. a scallop-edging. [f. prec.]

scallywag /'skælɪwæg/ n. a rascal. [orig. US slang; etym. unkn.]

scalp n. the skin and hair of the top of the head; this formerly cut off as a trophy by an American Indian. —*v.t.* **1.** to remove the scalp of. **2.** to criticize savagely. **3.** (*US colloq.*) to resell at a high or quick profit. [prob. f. Scand.]

scalpel /'skælp(ə)l/ n. a small surgical knife. [F or f. L dim. of *scalprum* chisel (*scalpere* scratch, carve)]

scamp n. a rascal. —*v.t.* to do (work etc.) perfunctorily or inadequately. [f. *scamp* rob on highway, prob. f. MDu. = decamp]

scamper v.i. to move or run hastily or impulsively, to run about playfully. —*n.* an act of scampering. [prob. as prec.]

scampi /'skæmpɪ/ n.pl. large prawns; these as food. [It.]

scan v.t./i. (**-nn-**) **1.** to look at all parts of (a thing) successively. **2.** to look over quickly or cursorily. **3.** to traverse with a controlled electronic or radar beam. **4.** to resolve (a picture) into its elements of light and shade for television transmission. **5.** to test the metre of (a line etc. of verse) by examining the nature and number of its feet and syllables; (of a line etc.) to be metrically correct. —*n.* an act or process of scanning. —**scanner** n. [f. L *scandere*, orig. = climb]

scandal /'skænd(ə)l/ n. **1.** a general feeling of (esp. moral) outrage or indignation; a thing causing this. **2.** malicious gossip about people's faults and wrongdoing. [f. OF f. L f. Gk, = stumbling-block]

scandalize /'skændəlaɪz/ v.t. to offend the moral feelings or sense of propriety of. [as prec.]

scandalmonger /'skændəlmʌŋgə(r)/ n. a person who disseminates scandal.

scandalous /'skændələs/ adj. containing or arousing

scandal, outrageous, shocking. —**scandalously** adv. [f. SCANDAL]

Scandinavia /ˌskændɪˈneɪvɪə/ a geographical unit consisting of Norway and Sweden with the addition of Denmark. Finland is sometimes included on geological and economic grounds; Iceland and the Faeroe Islands are often included on an ethnic and linguistic basis. [f. L]

Scandinavian adj. of Scandinavia or its people or languages. —n. **1.** a native of Scandinavia. **2.** the North Germanic branch of the Indo-European family of languages, including Danish, Norwegian, Swedish, and Icelandic, all descended from Old Norse. [f. prec.]

scandium /ˈskændɪəm/ n. a metallic element, symbol Sc, atomic number 21, included among the rare-earth metals. It was first discovered in 1879, after its existence had been predicted by Mendeleev on the basis of his periodic table. The metal and its compounds have at present few commercial uses. [f. L *Scandia* Scandinavia (source of minerals containing it)]

scansion /ˈskænʃ(ə)n/ n. metrical scanning. [f. L (as SCAN)]

scant adj. scanty, insufficient. —v.t. (archaic) to skimp, to stint. [f. ON (*skammr* short)]

scantling n. **1.** a timber beam of small cross-section. **2.** the size to which stone or timber is to be cut. **3.** a set of standard dimensions for parts of a structure, especially in shipbuilding. [f. obs. *scantlon* f. OF, = sample]

scanty adj. **1.** of small amount or extent. **2.** barely sufficient. —**scantily** adv., **scantiness** n. [as SCANT]

scapegoat /ˈskeɪpɡəʊt/ n. **1.** a goat allowed to escape when the Jewish chief priest had symbolically laid the sins of the people upon it (Lev. 16). **2.** a person who is made to bear blame or punishment that should rightly fall on others. [f. archaic *scape* escape + GOAT]

scapegrace /ˈskeɪpɡreɪs/ n. a wild and foolish or rash person, especially a child or young person who constantly gets into trouble. [as prec. + GRACE, = one who escapes the grace of God]

scapula /ˈskæpjʊlə/ n. (pl. **-lae** /-liː/) the shoulder-blade (ill. BODY 1). [L]

scapular /ˈskæpjʊlə(r)/ adj. of the scapula. —n. **1.** a monastic short cloak. **2.** a scapular feather (ill. BIRDS). [as prec.]

scar[1] n. **1.** a mark left by damage, especially on the skin by a healed wound or on a plant by the loss of a leaf etc. **2.** the lasting effect of grief etc. —v.t./i. (**-rr-**) to mark with a scar; to form a scar or scars. [f. OF f. L f. Gk *eskhara* scab]

scar[2] n. a precipitous craggy part of a mountain-side or cliff. [f. ON, = reef]

scarab /ˈskærəb/ n. **1.** a beetle of the family Scarabaeidae. **2.** the sacred dung-beetle of ancient Egypt. **3.** a carving of a beetle, engraved with symbols on the flat side and used in ancient Egypt as a charm. [f. L *scarabaeus* f. Gk]

scarce /skeəs/ adj. **1.** (usu. predic.) not plentiful, insufficient for demand or need. **2.** seldom found, rare. —adv. (literary) scarcely. —**make oneself scarce,** to go away; to keep out of the way. [f. AF ult. f. L *excerpere* (as EXCERPT)]

scarcely adv. **1.** almost not; not quite; only just. **2.** not; surely not; probably not. [f. prec.]

scarcity /ˈskeəsɪtɪ/ n. being scarce; a shortage. [f. SCARCE]

scare v.t./i. to strike or be struck with sudden fear, to startle and frighten; to drive (away, off, etc.) by fright; (in p.p.) frightened. —n. a sudden outbreak of fear; alarm caused by a rumour. [f. ON *skirra* frighten]

scarecrow n. **1.** a figure of a man dressed in old clothes and set up in a field to scare birds away from crops. **2.** a badly dressed or grotesque person.

scaremonger n. a person who raises unnecessary or excessive alarm. —**scaremongering** n.

scarf[1] n. (pl. **scarves** /skɑːvz/) **1.** a long narrow strip of material worn for warmth or ornament round the neck. **2.** a square piece of material worn round the neck or over a woman's hair. [prob. f. OF *escarpe* sash]

scarf[2] n. a joint made by thinning the ends of two pieces of timber etc. so that they overlap without an increase of thickness and fastening them with bolts etc. —v.t. to join with a scarf. [rel. to F *écarver*]

scarify[1] /ˈskeərɪfaɪ, ˈskæ-/ v.t. **1.** to loosen the surface of (soil etc.). **2.** to make slight incisions in (skin etc.); to cut off skin from. **3.** to criticize etc. mercilessly. —**scarification** /-fɪˈkeɪʃ(ə)n/ n. [f. F f. L f. Gk (*skariphos* stylus)]

scarify[2] /ˈskeərɪfaɪ/ v.t. (colloq.) to scare, to terrify. [f. SCARE]

scarlatina /ˌskɑːləˈtiːnə/ n. scarlet fever. [It. (as SCARLET)]

Scarlatti /skɑːˈlætɪ/, Alessandro (1660–1725), Italian composer, an important and prolific composer of operas. Over 70 survive, and in them can be found the elements which carried Italian opera through the baroque period and into the classical, together with a fine sense of the dramatic in music. His son Domenico (1685–1757) is best known today for over 500 keyboard sonatas, lively invigorating pieces in one movement.

scarlet /ˈskɑːlɪt/ adj. of brilliant red colour. —n. **1.** scarlet colour or pigment. **2.** scarlet clothes or material. —**scarlet fever,** an infectious fever with a scarlet rash. **scarlet runner,** a kind of bean; the scarlet-flowered climbing plant (*Phaseolus multiflorus*) bearing this. [f. OF *escarlate*]

Scarlet Pimpernel the name assumed by the hero of a series of novels by Baroness Orczy. He was a dashing but elusive English nobleman who rescued potential victims of the French Reign of Terror and smuggled them out of France.

scarp n. a steep slope, especially the inner side of a ditch in a fortification. —v.t. to make steep or perpendicular. [f. It. *scarpa*]

scarper v.i. (slang) to escape, to run away. [prob. f. It. *scappare* escape, infl. by rhyming slang *Scapa Flow* go]

scary /ˈskeərɪ/ adj. (colloq.) frightening. [f. SCARE]

scat[1] v.i. (**-tt-**) (colloq.) to depart quickly. —int. (colloq.) depart quickly. [perh. abbr. of SCATTER]

scat[2] n. wordless jazz singing using the voice as an instrument. —v.i. to sing in this style. [prob. imit.]

scathe /skeɪð/ v.t. (archaic) to harm or injure. —n. (archaic) harm, injury. [f. ON; cf. OE *sceatha* malefactor, injury]

scathing /ˈskeɪðɪŋ/ adj. (of a look, criticism, etc.) harsh, severe. [f. prec.]

scatology /skæˈtɒlədʒɪ/ n. preoccupation with obscene literature or with excrement. —**scatological** /ˌskætəˈlɒdʒɪk(ə)l/ adj. [f. Gk *skōr* dung + -LOGY]

scatter v.t./i. **1.** to throw or put here and there; to cover thus. **2.** to go or send in different directions. **3.** to deflect or diffuse (light or particles etc.). **4.** (in p.p.) not situated together, wide apart. —n. **1.** scattering. **2.** a small amount scattered. **3.** the extent of distribution, especially of shot. —**scatter-brain** n. a scatter-brained person. **scatter-brained** adj. lacking concentration; disorganized; flighty. [prob. var. of SHATTER]

scatty adj. (slang) scatter-brained, crazy. —**scattily** adv., **scattiness** n. [f. *scatter-brained*]

scaup n. a diving duck of the genus *Aythya*, frequenting northern coasts. [f. *scaup*, Sc. var. of *scalp* mussel-bed, which it frequents]

scaur var. of SCAR[2].

scavenge /ˈskævɪndʒ/ v.t./i. **1.** to be or act as a scavenger (of). **2.** to remove dirt, waste, or impurities etc. from. [back-formation f. foll.]

scavenger /ˈskævɪndʒə(r)/ n. **1.** a person who searches among or collects things unwanted by others. **2.** an animal or bird that feeds on carrion. [orig. = inspector of imports, f. AF (rel. to SHOW)]

Sc.D. abbr. Doctor of Science. [f. L *scientiae doctor*]

scenario /sɪˈnɑːrɪəʊ/ n. (pl. **-os**) **1.** the script or synopsis of a film, play, etc. **2.** an imagined sequence of future events. [It. (as SCENE)]

scene /siːn/ n. **1.** the place in which an event or series of events takes or took place. **2.** a portion of a play during which the action is continuous; a subdivision of an act; a similar portion of a film, book, etc. **3.** an incident thought of as resembling this. **4.** a dramatic outburst of temper or emotion; a stormy interview. **5.** a landscape or view as seen by a spectator. **6.** stage scenery. **7.** (slang) an area or subject of activity or interest; a way of life. —**behind the scenes,** behind stage, out of sight of the audience; not known to the public, working secretly. **come on the scene,** to arrive. **set the scene,** to describe the location of events etc. **scene-shifter** n. a person engaged in changing the scenery in a theatre. [f. L f. Gk *skēnē* tent, stage]

scenery /ˈsiːnərɪ/ n. **1.** structures used on a theatre stage to represent features in the scene of the action. Stage scenery is a comparatively recent innovation, Greek plays being acted against a stage wall. Modern scenery originated with the masque, which used a decorative proscenium arch behind which sets of side scenes framed the back scene on either side. **2.** the general appearance of a landscape; its picturesque features. [earlier *scenary* f. It. SCENARIO]

scenic /ˈsiːnɪk/ adj. **1.** having fine natural scenery. **2.** of scenery. **3.** of or on the stage. —**scenic railway,** a miniature railway running through artificial picturesque scenery as an amusement at a fair. —**scenically** adv. [as SCENE]

scent /sent/ n. **1.** a characteristic odour, especially a pleasant one. **2.** liquid perfume. **3.** the smell or trail left by an animal; a line of investigation or pursuit. **4.** the power of detecting or distinguishing smells or discovering the presence of something. —v.t. **1.** to discern by sense of smell. **2.** to sniff out. **3.** to begin to suspect the presence or existence of. **4.** to make fragrant, to apply perfume to. —**off the scent**, misled by false information etc. —**scented** adj. [f. OF sentir perceive, smell, f. L sentire feel, sense]

sceptic /'skeptɪk/ n. **1.** a sceptical person; one who doubts the truth of religious doctrines. **2.** a philosopher who questions the possibility of knowledge. —**scepticism** /-sɪz(ə)m/ n. [f. F or L f. Gk (skeptomai consider)]

sceptical /'skeptɪk(ə)l/ adj. inclined to disbelieve things; doubting or questioning the truth of claims or statements etc. —**sceptically** adv. [as prec.]

sceptre /'septə(r)/ n. a staff borne as a symbol of sovereignty. [f. OF f. L f. Gk skēptron (skēptō lean on)]

schadenfreude /'ʃɑːdənfrɔɪdə/ n. malicious enjoyment of others' misfortunes. [G (schade harm, freude joy)]

schedule /'ʃedjuːl/ n. **1.** a timetable or programme of planned events or work etc. **2.** a table of details or items, especially as an appendix to a document. —v.t. **1.** to make a schedule of; to include in a schedule; to appoint a time for. **2.** to include (an ancient monument) in a list of those considered to be of national importance and so to be preserved. —**on schedule**, to time, not late. **scheduled flight**, one operated on a regular timetable. [f. OF f. L schedula slip of paper, dim. of scheda f. Gk skhédē papyrus-leaf]

Scheherazade /ʃəherə'zɑːd/ the female narrator of the Arabian Nights.

schematic /skɪ'mætɪk/ adj. in the form of a diagram or chart. —n. a schematic diagram. —**schematically** adv. [as SCHEME]

schematize /'skiːmətaɪz/ v.t. to put into schematic form; to formulate in regular order. —**schematization** /-'zeɪʃ(ə)n/ n. [f. Gk, = assume a form (or as foll.)]

scheme /skiːm/ n. **1.** a plan of work or action. **2.** an orderly planned arrangement. **3.** a secret or underhand plan. —v.t./i. to make plans; to plan, especially in secret or in an underhand way. —**schemer** n. [f. L f. Gk skhēma form, figure]

scherzo /'skeətsəʊ/ n. (pl. -os) a vigorous often playful movement in a symphony or sonata etc.; a lively vigorous musical composition. [It., = jest]

Schiller /'ʃɪlə(r)/, Johann Christoph Friedrich von (1759–1805), German dramatist and poet. His early play Die Räuber (The Robbers, 1781) established him as the leading figure of this period of German literature; Kabale und Liebe (Intrigue and Love, 1784), on which Verdi based his opera Luisa Miller, attacked contemporary society. His historical plays include Wallenstein (1799), his greatest success, Mary Stuart (1800), and Die Jungfrau von Orleans (The Maid of Orleans, 1801); his last completed play was Wilhelm Tell (1804). These plays are concerned with the problem of freedom and responsibility either political, personal, or moral. Among his best-known poems are 'Die Künstler' ('The Artists'), on the humanizing influence of art, 'Das Ideal und das Leben' ('The Ideal and Life'), and 'An die Freude' ('Ode to Joy'), which Beethoven set to music in his 9th Symphony. His many essays on aesthetics include Über naive und sentimentalische Dichtung (On Naïve and Reflective Poetry, 1795–6), in which he contrasts his own 'modern' reflective style with Goethe's more 'antique' unselfconscious genius.

schism /'sɪz(ə)m, 'skɪ-/ n. division into opposing groups because of a difference in belief or opinion, especially in a religious body. —**schismatic** /-'mætɪk/ adj., **schismatically** adv. [f. OF f. L f. Gk skhisma cleft (skhizō split)]

schist /ʃɪst/ n. a layered crystalline rock. [f. F f. L f. Gk skhistos split (as prec.)]

schizo /'skɪtsəʊ/ n. (pl. -os) (colloq.) a schizophrenic. [abbr.]

schizoid /'skɪtsɔɪd/ adj. of or resembling schizophrenia or a schizophrenic. —n. a schizoid person. [f. foll.]

schizophrenia /skɪtsə'friːnɪə/ n. a mental disease marked by disconnection between thought, feelings, and actions, often with delusions and withdrawal from social relationships. —**schizophrenic** /-'frenɪk/ adj. & n. [f. Gk skhizō split + phrēn mind]

Schleswig /'ʃlesvɪk/ a former duchy of the Danish Crown, acquired by conquest by Prussia in 1864 and incorporated into the province of Schleswig-Holstein. The northern part of this territory was returned to Denmark in 1920 after a plebiscite held in accordance with the Treaty of Versailles. —**Schleswig-Holstein** /'hɒlstaɪn/, a province of the Federal Republic of Germany.

Schliemann /'ʃliːmən/, Heinrich (1822–90), German archaeologist. During the early part of his life he was very successfully engaged in commerce, and did not begin archaeological work until he was nearly 50. Convinced that if the city of Troy had existed remains of it must surely survive, he ignored the open derision of scholars and in 1871 began excavating, at his own expense, the mound of Hissarlik on the NE Aegean coast of Turkey. The remains of nine consecutive cities faced him, and (there being at that time no accepted method of scientifically excavating a complex site) he incorrectly identified the second oldest as Homer's Troy, and romantically called a hoard of jewellery (which he smuggled out of Turkey and had photographed adorning his wife) 'Priam's Treasure'. He subsequently excavated at Mycenae, where he believed he had discovered Agamemnon's tomb, and at other sites of mainland Greece. Schliemann is recognized as the discoverer of the Mycenaean civilization and the bringer of a new romance and excitement to archaeology.

schmaltz /ʃmɔːlts/ n. sugary sentimentalism, especially in music or literature. [Yiddish f. G, = dripping]

schnapps /ʃnæps/ n. a kind of strong gin. [G, = dram of liquor, f. LG & Du. snaps mouthful (as SNAP)]

Schneider /'ʃnaɪdə(r)/, Jacques (1879–1928), French flying enthusiast, who donated a trophy, the Jacques Schneider Maritime Cup, which he presented in 1913 to the winner of an international competition for seaplanes comprising an air race and seaworthiness trials. It was contested annually (with certain exceptions) until won outright by Great Britain in 1931.

schnitzel /'ʃnɪts(ə)l/ n. a veal cutlet. [G]

Schoenberg /'ʃənbɜːg/, Arnold (1874–1951), one of the most influential figures in the history of music. Born in Vienna, he worked as a professor of music there and in Berlin until 1933 when, after having his music branded (together with that of his pupils Berg and Webern) 'degenerate art' by Hitler, he emigrated to the USA. His dedication to the development of the musical language inherited from the late 19th c. led in 1908 to a break with tonal writing and the concept of atonality and, later, serialism. Such early works as the symphonic poem for string sextet Verklärte Nacht (1899) reveal the chromatic idiom being stretched to its limits; his first atonal works, the Five Orchestral Pieces, the monodrama Erwartung (both 1909), and the song-cycle Pierrot lunaire (1912), are expressionist and intense in their exploration of fundamental human emotion and violence; with the serial works Schoenberg returned to classical formal moulds and a quieter manner. One of the last works written by him before leaving Germany was Moses und Aron (1930–2), an opera reflecting his concern with religion at that time (he returned to the Jewish faith of his upbringing in 1933); it was left unfinished with its central problem unresolved at his death.

scholar /'skɒlə(r)/ n. **1.** a person with great learning in a particular subject; one who is skilled in academic work. **2.** a person who learns. **3.** a person who holds a scholarship. —**scholarly** adj. [f. OF f. L scholaris (as SCHOOL¹)]

scholarship n. **1.** an award of money towards education, usually gained by means of a competitive examination. **2.** learning or knowledge in a particular subject. **3.** the methods and achievements characteristic of scholars and academic work. [f. prec. + -SHIP]

scholastic /skɒ'læstɪk/ adj. of schools or education, academic. —**scholastically** adv. [f. L f. Gk (as SCHOOL¹)]

scholasticism /skə'læstɪsɪz(ə)m/ n. the educational tradition of the medieval 'schools' (i.e. universities), especially a method of philosophical and theological speculation which aimed at a better understanding of the revealed truths of Christianity by defining, systematizing, and reasoning. Its theoretical foundations were laid by St Augustine and Boethius, and among its most famous figures were St Anselm and Abelard (who perfected the technique). Of decisive importance was the introduction of the works of Aristotle into Western Europe, and the crowning achievement of scholastic theology was the work of Aquinas, whose Summa Theologica drew the line between faith and reason with the utmost clarity. From this time scholasticism declined, undermined by the writings of William of Occam, but it never wholly lost its vitality, and interest in it revived at the end of the 19th c. [f. prec.]

school[1] /sku:l/ *n*. **1.** an institution for educating children or giving instruction. **2.** (*US*) a university; a department of this. **3.** the buildings or pupils of such an institution; the time during which teaching is done. **4.** the process of being educated in a school; circumstances or an occupation serving to educate or discipline. **5.** a branch of study at a university. **6.** a group of thinkers, artists, etc., sharing the same principles, methods, characteristics, or inspirations. **7.** a group of card-players or gamblers. **8.** a medieval lecture-room. —*v.t.* **1.** to educate; to send to school. **2.** to discipline; to train or accustom. —**school-leaver** *n*. a person who has just left school. **school year,** the period when schools are in session, reckoned from the autumn term. [f. OE, ult. f. L *schola* school f. Gk *skholē* leisure, disputation, philosophy, lecture-place]

school[2] /sku:l/ *n*. a shoal of fish, whales, etc. [f. MLG or MDu., = OE *scolu* troop]

schoolchild *n*. (*pl*. **-children**) (also **schoolboy, schoolgirl**) a child who attends school.

schoolhouse *n*. the building of a school, especially that of a village.

schooling *n*. education, especially in a school.

schoolman *n*. (*pl*. **-men**) **1.** a teacher in a medieval European university. **2.** a theologian seeking to deal with religious doctrines by the rules of Aristotelian logic.

schoolmaster *n*. a male teacher in a school. —**schoolmistress** *n.fem.*

schoolroom *n*. a room used for lessons in a school or private house.

schoolteacher *n*. a teacher in a school.

schooner /ˈsku:nə(r)/ *n*. **1.** a fore-and-aft-rigged ship with more than one mast (ill. SAILING-SHIPS). **2.** a large glass of sherry etc. [orig. unkn.]

Schopenhauer /ˈʃəʊpənhaʊə(r), ˈʃɒp-/, Arthur (1788-1860), German author of a pessimistic philosophy which is an adaptation of Kant's and is embodied in his principal work *The World as Will and Idea* (1818). According to Schopenhauer the will, of which we have direct intuition, is the only reality and the means by which all other things are understood; what is real is one vast will, appearing in the whole natural world, animate and inanimate alike. This 'cosmic will' is a malignant thing, which inveigles us into reproducing and perpetuating life. Asceticism and chastity are the duty of man, with a view to terminating the evil. As a stage towards this goal he found a transient place of rest in the realms of poetry, art, and above all music. His theory of the predominance of the will anticipated that of Freud and later psychologists; in his ethical doctrines he was influenced by Buddhism. In private life he made no attempt to put into practice the asceticism which he extolled, but he bequeathed what material wealth he had to the relief of suffering.

schottische /ʃɒˈti:ʃ/ *n*. a kind of slow polka; the music for this. [f. G *der schottische tanz* the Scottish dance]

Schrödinger /ˈʃrədɪŋə(r)/, Erwin (1887-1961), Austrian theoretical physicist who in the 1920s developed wave mechanics, a mathematical theory which describes the structure and properties of atoms and the particles they contain. He shared the 1933 Nobel Prize for physics with Dirac, and (an ardent anti-Nazi) moved to Oxford. He spent the Second World War in Dublin, and wrote a book *What is Life?* which was the inspiration of many physicists who became molecular biologists.

Schubert /ˈʃu:bɜ:t/, Franz (1797-1828), Austrian composer. During his short life he produced over 600 songs, 9 symphonies, 15 string quartets, and 21 piano sonatas, as well as operas, church music, and a host of single-movement pieces for piano, chamber ensemble, etc. Schubert can be considered equally the most approachable and lovable of composers for his gift for exquisite miniatures and a master of sustained thought on a larger scale, particularly in the works of his last years. He has been criticized both for setting inferior verse and for missing the deeper implications of more serious poets, but to look for a refined literary sensibility in such a composer is to miss the essence of his genius. His response to poetry was immediate and overpowering in its intensity, allowing no time for meditation or qualification; as Richard Capell wrote in his study of the songs (1928), 'Schubert . . . knew nothing but the rapture and poignancy of first sensations, the loss of which is the beginning of wisdom'.

Schumann /ˈʃu:mən/, Robert Alexander (1810-56), German composer, who studied law before embarking on a musical career. He had ambitions to become a concert pianist but damaged his hand with a device intended to aid finger control; in 1840 he married Clara Wieck, the daughter of his piano teacher and herself a celebrated pianist. In 1854 Schumann attempted suicide by drowning, and his last two years were passed in a private asylum near Bonn. His most productive years were those following his marriage to Clara: in 1840 he composed the bulk of his many songs; 1841 saw the start of his symphonic writing, and in 1842 he produced much chamber music. His symphonies, Piano Concerto (1845), and chamber works have much to recommend them, but he was at his best on a smaller scale, as in the loosely linked miniatures for piano of *Papillons* (1829-31), *Carnaval* (1834-5), and *Waldscenen* (1848-9) and especially in the songs, where he reveals his sensitivity to the romanticism of contemporary poets.

Schütz /ʃu:ts/, Heinrich (1585-1672), German composer and organist, one of the greatest of Bach's predecessors. A visit to Italy in 1609-13 for a period of study provided an important influence, seen for example in the settings of *Psalmens Davids* (1619), and he composed what is thought to have been the first opera by a German (*Dafne*, now lost). His three settings of the Passion story represent a turning towards a simple meditative style, eschewing instrumental accompaniment and relying on voices alone for his depiction of Christ's suffering and crucifixion.

schwa /ʃwa:, ʃva:/ *n*. an indeterminate vowel sound (as in anoth*er*); the symbol (ə) representing this. [G f. Heb., app. = emptiness]

Schweitzer /ˈʃwaɪtsə(r), ˈʃvaɪ-/, Albert (1875-1965), theologian, musician, and physician, born in Alsace-Lorraine (then part of Germany), who devoted the early part of his life to learning and music and the remainder to the service of others. His book *The Quest of the Historical Jesus* (1906) ended an epoch of attempts to unearth an authentic portrait of Jesus from the Gospels by historical-critical research, showing that many such portraits were conditioned by 19th-c. ideals, and argued that Jesus was a more alien figure who had believed that the end of the world was imminent. Schweitzer was an accomplished organist and interpreter of Bach, on whom he wrote a monograph (1908). In 1913 he abandoned his academic career to become a doctor and missionary at Lambaréné in French Equatorial Africa (now Gabon). After being interned in France during the First World War he returned to restore his hospital and continue the work which embodied his ethical principle of 'reverence for life'. The greatest humanitarian of our time, Schweitzer was awarded the Nobel Peace Prize in 1952.

sciatic /saɪˈætɪk/ *adj*. **1.** of the hip; affecting the hip or sciatic nerve. **2.** suffering from or liable to sciatica. —**sciatic nerve,** the large nerve from the pelvis to the thigh. [f. F f. L f. Gk *iskhiadikos* (*iskhion* hip-joint)]

sciatica /saɪˈætɪkə/ *n*. neuralgia affecting the sciatic nerve. [L (as prec.)]

science /ˈsaɪəns/ *n*. **1.** the branch of knowledge involving systematized observation and experiment, especially one dealing with substances, or animal and vegetable life, and natural laws. **2.** systematic and formulated knowledge; the pursuit or principles of this. **3.** an organized body of knowledge on a subject. **4.** skilful technique. [f. OF f. L *scientia* knowledge (*scire* know)]

science fiction a class of prose narrative which assumes an imaginary technological or scientific advance, portrays space travel or life on other planets, or depends upon a spectacular change in the human environment. Although examples exist from the time of Lucian (2nd c. AD), it was not until the end of the 19th c. that the form emerged as we know it today. The works of Jules Verne are notable examples, but the first successful English author was H. G. Wells, using themes of invasion from outer space (*The War of the Worlds*, 1898), biological change or catastrophe (*The Food of the Gods*, 1904), time travel (*The Time Machine*, 1895), and air warfare (*The War in the Air*, 1908). Since the Second World War scientific developments and their possible consequences have been reflected in fictional forms often carrying apocalyptic undertones; the destruction of the world as a result of its own technological achievements is a favourite theme. The literary quality of the genre is extremely variable, ranging from violent strip cartoons in pulp magazines, through respectable 'domestic' novels, to more challenging intellectual ventures and philosophical inquiry into the nature of man and his behaviour. The impact of its tradition on films and television has been enormous, with products ranging from children's programmes to cinema epics.

scientific /saɪənˈtɪfɪk/ *adj.* **1.** of science; used or engaged in science. **2.** following the systematic methods of science. **3.** having, using, or requiring trained skill. —**scientifically** *adv.* [f. F or L (as SCIENCE)]

scientist /ˈsaɪəntɪst/ *n.* a student of or expert in one or more of the natural or physical sciences. [f. SCIENCE or prec.]

Scientology /saɪənˈtɒlədʒɪ/ *n.* a religious system based on the study of knowledge and seeking to develop the highest potentialities of its members, founded in 1951 by American science-fiction writer L. Ron Hubbard (1911–86). —**Scientologist** *n.* [f. L *scientia* (as SCIENCE)]

sci-fi /ˈsaɪfaɪ/ *n.* (*colloq.*) science fiction. [abbr.]

scilicet /ˈsaɪlɪset/ *adv.* that is to say (introducing a word to be supplied or an explanation of an ambiguous word). [L]

Scilly Islands /ˈsɪlɪ/ (also **Scillies**) a group of about 40 small islands off the western extremity of Cornwall; pop. 1,850; capital, Hugh Town (on St Mary's).

scimitar /ˈsɪmɪtə(r)/ *n.* a curved oriental sword. [f. F or It.]

scintilla /sɪnˈtɪlə/ *n.* a sign or trace. [L, = spark]

scintillate /ˈsɪntɪleɪt/ *v.i.* **1.** to sparkle; to give off sparks. **2.** to talk or act with brilliance. —**scintillation** /-ˈleɪʃ(ə)n/ *n.* [f. L *scintillare* (as prec.)]

sciolism /ˈsaɪəlɪz(ə)m/ *n.* superficial knowledge; a display of this. —**sciolist** *n.*, **sciolistic** /-ˈlɪstɪk/ *adj.* [f. L *sciolus* smatterer, dim. of *scius* knowing]

scion /ˈsaɪən/ *n.* **1.** a shoot of a plant, especially one cut for grafting. **2.** a descendant; a young member of a family. [f. OF, = shoot, twig]

Scipio[1] /ˈskɪpɪəʊ/ (Publius Cornelius Scipio Africanus Major, 236–184/3 BC) Roman general and politician. His tactical reforms of the army and offensive strategy were successful in concluding the second Punic War, firstly by the defeat of the Carthaginians in Spain in 206 BC, and then by the defeat of Hannibal in Africa in 202 BC (after which he was given the name Africanus); his victories pointed the way to Roman hegemony in the Mediterranean. His son was the adoptive father of Scipio[2].

Scipio[2] /ˈskɪpɪəʊ/ (Publius Cornelius Scipio Aemilianus Africanus, 185/4–129 BC), Roman general and politician. He achieved distinction in the third Punic War, and blockaded and destroyed Carthage in 146 BC. His successful campaign in Spain (133 BC) ended organized resistance in that country. Returning to Rome in triumph, he provoked a major political storm by initiating moves against the reforms introduced by his brother-in-law Tiberius Gracchus. Scipio's sudden death at the height of the crisis gave rise to the rumour that he had been murdered.

scissors /ˈsɪzəz/ *n. pl.* (also **pair of scissors**) a cutting instrument made of two blades so pivoted that their cutting edges close on what is to be cut. Scissors with overlapping blades and with a C-shaped spring at the handle end (like tongs) probably date from the Bronze Age; they were used in Europe until the end of the Middle Ages, and the design survived still later for some specific purposes (e.g. sheep-shearing). Scissors pivoted between handle and blade were used in Roman Europe and the Far East 2,000 years ago. In Europe they came into domestic use in the 16th c.; large-scale production dates from 1761 when Robert Hinchcliffe of Sheffield began to use cast steel in their manufacture. [f. OF f. L *cisorium* cutting instrument (as CHISEL), rel. to *scindere* cut]

sclerosis /sklɪəˈrəʊsɪs/ *n.* abnormal hardening of body tissue. —**disseminated** *or* **multiple sclerosis**, sclerosis spreading to all or many parts of the body. —**sclerotic** /-ˈrɒtɪk/ *adj.* [f. L f. Gk (*sklēroō* harden)]

scoff[1] *v.i.* to speak derisively; to jeer. —*n.* a scoffing remark, a jeer. —**scoffer** *n.* [perh. f. Scand.]

scoff[2] *v.t./i.* (*slang*) to eat greedily. —*n.* (*slang*) food, a meal. [f. Afrik. *schoff* quarter of a day]

scold /skəʊld/ *v.t./i.* to rebuke (esp. a child). —*n.* a nagging woman. [prob. f. ON (as SKALD)]

scolding *n.* a lengthy rebuke (esp. to a child). [f. SCOLD]

scollop var. of SCALLOP.

sconce[1] *n.* a wall-bracket holding a candlestick or light-fitting. [f. OF f. L *absconsa* covered light (as ABSCOND)]

sconce[2] *n.* a small fort or earthwork. [f. Du. *schans* brushwood]

Scone /skuːn/ a village in Tayside, the ancient Scottish capital where their kings were crowned. —**stone of Scone,** see CORONATION STONE.

scone /skɒn, skəʊn/ *n.* a small soft cake of flour, oatmeal,

or barley-meal baked quickly and eaten buttered. [perh. f. MDu. or LG, = fine (bread)]

scoop *n.* **1.** a deep shovel-like tool for taking up and moving grain, sugar, coal, etc. **2.** a ladle; a device with a small round bowl and a handle, for serving portions of ice-cream etc. **3.** the quantity taken with a scoop. **4.** a scooping movement. **5.** a large profit made quickly or by anticipating one's competitors. **6.** an exclusive item in a newspaper etc. —*v.t.* **1.** to lift or hollow with or as with a scoop. **2.** to secure (a large profit etc.) by sudden action or luck. **3.** to forestall (a rival newspaper etc.) with a news scoop. [f. MDu. or MLG, = bucket etc. (rel. to SHAPE)]

scoot *v.i.* (*colloq.*) to run or dart; to go away hastily. [for earlier *scout* (orig. unkn.)]

scooter *n.* **1.** a child's toy vehicle consisting of a footboard with a wheel at front and back and a long steering-handle, propelled by thrusting one foot against the ground while the other rests on the footboard. **2.** (also **motor scooter**) a kind of lightweight motor cycle with a protective shield extending from below the handles to where the rider's feet rest. —**scooterist** *n.* [f. prec.]

scope *n.* **1.** the reach or sphere of observation or action; the extent to which it is possible or permissible to range or develop etc. **2.** opportunity, outlet. [f. It. f. Gk, = target]

-scope *suffix* forming nouns denoting a thing looked at or through (*telescope*) or an instrument for observing or showing (*oscilloscope*). [f. Gk *skopeō* look at]

scorbutic /skɔːˈbjuːtɪk/ *adj.* of, like, or affected with scurvy. [f. L *scorbutus* scurvy]

scorch *v.t./i.* **1.** to burn or discolour the surface of with dry heat; to become burnt or discoloured thus. **2.** (*slang*) to go at a very high speed. —*n.* a mark made by scorching. —**scorched earth policy**, the policy of burning one's crops etc. and removing or destroying anything that might be useful to an occupying enemy. [perh. rel. to *skorkle* in same sense]

scorcher *n.* (*colloq.*) a very hot day. [f. prec.]

score *n.* **1.** the number of points or goals etc. made by a player or side in a game, or gained in a competition etc.; a list or total of these, a reckoning. **2.** (for plural usage see HUNDRED) a set of twenty; (in *pl.*) very many. **3.** a copy of a musical composition with the parts on a series of staves. **4.** the music for a musical comedy, film, etc. **5.** a reason or motive; a topic. **6.** (*colloq.*) a remark or act by which a person scores off another. **7.** a line or mark cut into a surface. **8.** a record of money owing. —*v.t./i.* **1.** to gain (a point or points) in a game etc.; to make a score; to achieve (a success, victory, etc.). **2.** to keep a record of the score; to record in a score. **3.** to have an advantage; to be successful, to have good luck; to make a clever retort that puts an opponent at a disadvantage. **4.** to cut a line or mark(s) into. **5.** to write out as a musical score; to arrange (a piece of music) for specified instruments. —**know the score,** to be aware of essential facts. **on that score,** so far as that matter is concerned. **pay off old scores,** to get one's revenge. **score-board** *or* **-book, -card, -sheet** *n.* a board etc. on which a score is entered or displayed. **score off,** (*colloq.*) to humiliate; to defeat in argument or repartee. **score out,** to delete. —**scorer** *n.* [f. ON = notch, tally, twenty (as SHEAR)]

scoria /ˈskɔːrɪə/ *n.* (*pl.* **-ae** /-iː/) slag, a clinker-like mass of lava. —**scoriaceous** /-ˈeɪʃəs/ *adj.* [L f. Gk, = refuse (*skōr* dung)]

scorn *n.* **1.** strong contempt. **2.** an object of this. —*v.t.* **1.** to feel or show strong contempt for. **2.** to reject as unworthy, to refuse scornfully. [f. OF; cf. OS *skern* mockery]

scornful *adj.* feeling or showing scorn. —**scornfully** *adv.*, **scornfulness** *n.* [f. SCORN + -FUL]

Scorpio /ˈskɔːpɪəʊ/ a constellation and the eighth sign of the zodiac, the Scorpion, which the sun enters about 23 Oct. It is noteworthy for its brightest member, the red giant star Antares, and its X-ray source Sco X-1 which is the brightest object in the X-ray sky. —**Scorpian** *adj. & n.* [L f. Gk, = scorpion]

scorpion /ˈskɔːpɪən/ *n.* **1.** a lobster-like arachnid of the order Scorpionida, with a jointed stinging tail. **2.** the Scorpion, the constellation or sign of the zodiac Scorpio. [f. OF f. L (as prec.)]

Scot *n.* **1.** a native of Scotland. **2.** (*hist.*) a member of a Gaelic tribe that migrated from Ireland to Scotland about the 6th c. [OE f. L *Scottus*]

Scotch /skɒtʃ/ *adj.* of Scotland or Scottish people or their form of English. —n. **1.** the form of English used (especially in the Lowlands) in Scotland. **2.** Scotch whisky. —**Scotch broth,** soup made from beef or mutton with vegetables, pearl barley, etc. **Scotch cap,** a man's wide beret, like that worn as part of Highland dress. **Scotch egg,** a hard-boiled egg enclosed in sausage-meat. **Scotch fir** *or* **pine,** a type of pine-tree (*Pinus sylvestris*). **Scotch mist,** thick mist and drizzle. **Scotch terrier,** a small rough-haired short-legged kind of terrier. **Scotch whisky,** whisky distilled in Scotland. **Scotch woodcock,** scrambled eggs on toast, garnished with anchovies. [contr. of SCOTTISH]

In recent years the word *Scotch* has been falling into disuse in England as well as in Scotland, out of deference to the Scotsman's supposed dislike of it; except for certain fixed collocations, such as those listed above, *Scottish* (less frequently *Scots*) is now the usual adjective, and *Scots* (pl.) designates the inhabitants of Scotland.

scotch /ˈskɒtʃ/ v.t. **1.** to put an end to decisively; to frustrate (a plan etc.). **2.** (*archaic*) to wound without killing. —n. a line on the ground for hopscotch. [orig. unkn.]

scot-free adj. unharmed, unpunished. [f. obs. *scot* tax, f. ON *skot* + FREE]

Scotland /ˈskɒtlənd/ the northern part of Great Britain and of the United Kingdom; pop. (1981) 5,130,735; capital, Edinburgh. Early inhabitants were the Picts, and Celtic peoples arrived from the Continent during the Bronze and early Iron Age. The limit of Roman subjugation of Britain was marked by Hadrian's Wall except for a period of about 40 years at the more northerly line of the Antonine Wall. An independent country in the Middle Ages, after the unification of various small Dark Age kingdoms between the 9th and 11th c. Scotland successfully resisted English attempts at domination but was amalgamated with her southern neighbour as a result of the union of the crowns in 1603 and of the parliaments in 1707. The northern part of the country is lightly populated, but the south and south-west benefited from the Industrial Revolution in the 18th and 19th c., although they have suffered badly from the effects of economic recession in the 20th c. while the discovery of North Sea oil has led to a boom on the east coast.

Scotland Yard 1. the headquarters of the Metropolitan Police, situated from 1829 to 1890 in Great Scotland Yard, a short street off Whitehall in London, from then until 1967 in New Scotland Yard on the Thames Embankment, and from 1967 in New Scotland Yard, Broadway, Westminster. **2.** the detective department of the Metropolitan Police force.

Scots adj. & n. Scottish (see note at SCOTCH). [orig. *Scottis,* northern var. of SCOTTISH]

Scotsman n. (*pl.* **-men**) a native of Scotland. —**Scotswoman** n.fem. (*pl.* **-women**)

Scott[1], Sir George Gilbert (1811–78), English architect. The most prolific Gothic revivalist, he built or 'improved' over 400 churches, 39 cathedrals, 25 university buildings, and fulfilled many private commissions. In 1858 he confronted Palmerston over the design for the new Foreign Office, the so-called 'Battle of Styles', and was compelled to adopt a classical solution; but his Albert Memorial (1872) reflects more accurately his preferred aesthetic. Although many of his alterations to religious buildings have been criticized for their excess, there is no doubt as to his qualities as an architect. His grandson, Sir Giles Scott (1880–1960), also worked as a revivalist architect and is best known for Liverpool Cathedral (begun in 1903), the last Gothic building to be built in England.

Scott[2], Sir Peter Markham (1909–), English naturalist, son of the Antarctic explorer Robert Falcon Scott. He is best known for his activities in wildlife conservation and for his paintings of birds; in 1946 he founded the Wildfowl Trust, based at Slimbridge in Gloucestershire.

Scott[3], Robert Falcon (1868–1912), English polar explorer. Entering the Royal Navy in 1881, Scott commanded the National Antarctic Expedition of 1900–4, surveying the interior of the continent, charting the Ross Sea, and discovering King Edward VII Land. On a second expedition (1910–12) Scott and four companions (Wilson, Oates, Bowers, and Evans) made a journey to the South Pole by sled, arriving there in January 1912 to discover that the Norwegian explorer Amundsen had beaten them to their goal by a month. On the journey back to base Scott and his companions were hampered by bad weather and illness, the last three finally dying of starvation and exposure in March. Their bodies and diaries were discovered by a search party

eight months later. Scott, a national hero, was posthumously knighted.

Scott[4], Sir Walter (1771–1832), Scottish novelist and poet, nicknamed 'the Wizard of the North'. Deeply influenced by the old and romantic poetry of France and Italy, and by the modern German poets, he developed an interest in the old Border tales and ballads which he collected (with imitations) in *The Minstrelsy of the Scottish Border* (1802). Among his original works were the romantic poem *The Lay of the Last Minstrel* (1805), *The Lady of the Lake* (1810), and *Rokeby* (1813). As a poet he was eclipsed by Byron, and found expression for his wide erudition, humour, and sympathies in the historical novel. Of these the Scottish Waverley novels were his masterpieces: *Waverley* (1814), *The Antiquary* (1816), *Old Mortality* (1816), and *The Heart of Midlothian* (1818). In 1826 the firm of booksellers, James Ballantyne & Co., in which Scott was a partner, became involved in bankruptcy, and he henceforth worked strenuously and prolifically to pay off his creditors. His influence as a novelist was incalculable: he established the form of the historical novel which was imitated throughout the 19th c., as was his treatment of rural themes; he influenced the development of the short story. His other works include plays, historical, literary, and antiquarian works, and editions of Swift and Dryden.

Scottie /ˈskɒtɪ/ n. (*colloq.*) **1.** a Scotsman. **2.** a Scotch terrier. [f. SCOT]

Scottish /ˈskɒtɪʃ/ adj. of Scotland or its inhabitants. —**Scottish National Party,** a political party formed in 1934 by an amalgamation of the National Party of Scotland and the Scottish Party, which seeks autonomous government for Scotland. **Scottish Nationalist,** a member of this party. [f. SCOT]

scoundrel /ˈskaʊndr(ə)l/ n. an unscrupulous person, a villain. —**scoundrelly** adj. [orig. unkn.]

scour[1] v.t. **1.** to clean or brighten by rubbing; to rub away (rust or a stain etc.). **2.** to clear (a channel or pipe etc.) by the force of water flowing over or through it. **3.** to purge drastically. —n. **1.** scouring. **2.** the action of water on a channel etc. [f. MDu. & MLG f. L *excurare* clean off (EX-[1], *curare* clean)]

scour[2] v.t./i. to search rapidly or thoroughly. [orig. unkn.]

scourer n. an abrasive pad or powder for scouring things. [f. SCOUR[1]]

scourge /skɜːdʒ/ n. **1.** a person or thing regarded as a bringer of vengeance or punishment. **2.** a whip for flogging people. —v.t. **1.** to chastise, to afflict greatly. **2.** to whip. [f. OF f. L *corrigia* whip]

scouse /skaʊs/ adj. (*slang*) of Liverpool. —n. (*slang*) **1.** a native of Liverpool. **2.** Liverpool dialect. [f. LOBSCOUSE]

scout[1] n. **1.** a person, especially a soldier, sent out to get information about an enemy etc. **2.** an act of seeking information. **3.** a talent-scout. **4. Scout,** a member of the Scout Association. **5.** a college servant at Oxford. **6.** (*colloq.*) a fellow, a person. —v.i. to act as a scout. —**scout about** *or* **around,** to search. [f. OF *escoute(r)* f. L *auscultare* listen]

scout[2] v.t. to reject (an idea etc.) with scorn. [f. Scand.; cf. ON *skúta* taunt]

Scout Association an organization (originally called the Boy Scouts) founded in 1908 by Lord Baden-Powell for helping boys to develop character by training them in open-air activities.

Scouter n. an adult leader in the Scout Association. [f. SCOUT[1]]

scow /skaʊ/ n. a flat-bottomed boat. [f. Du., = ferry-boat]

scowl n. a sullen or bad-tempered look on a person's face. —v.i. to make a scowl. [prob. f. Scand.; cf. Da. *skule* look down or sidelong]

Scrabble n. [P] a game in which players use small square blocks displaying individual letters to form words on a special board. [f. foll.]

scrabble v.i. **1.** to make a scratching movement or sound with the hands or feet. **2.** to grope busily; to struggle to find or obtain something. —n. scrabbling. [f. MDu., frequent. of *schrabben* scrape]

scrag n. **1.** (also **scrag-end**) the bony part of an animal's carcass as food; neck of mutton; the less meaty end of this. **2.** a skinny person or animal. —v.t. (**-gg-**) to seize roughly by the neck; to handle roughly, to beat up. [perh. alt. f. dial. *crag* neck]

scraggy adj. thin and bony. —**scraggily** adv., **scragginess** n. [f. SCRAG]

scram v.i. (-mm-) (slang, esp. in imper.) to go away. [perh. f. foll.]

scramble v.t./i. **1.** to move as best one can over rough ground or by clambering; to move hastily and awkwardly. **2.** to struggle eagerly to do or obtain something. **3.** (of aircraft or their crew) to hurry and take off quickly in an emergency. **4.** to mix together indiscriminately; to cook (egg) by mixing its contents and heating the mixture in a pan until it thickens. **5.** to make (a telephone conversation etc.) unintelligible except to a person with a special receiver by altering the frequencies on which it is transmitted. —n. **1.** a climb or walk over rough ground. **2.** an eager struggle to do or obtain something. **3.** a motor-cycle race over rough ground (see MOTO-CROSS). —**scrambled egg,** (colloq.) gold braid on an officer's cap. [imit.]

scrambler n. a device for scrambling telephone conversations. [f. prec.]

scrap[1] n. **1.** a small detached piece, a fragment. **2.** rubbish, waste material; discarded metal suitable for reprocessing. **3.** (with neg.) the smallest piece or amount. **4.** (in pl.) odds and ends, bits of uneaten food. —v.t. (-pp-) to discard as useless. —**scrap-book** n. a book in which newspaper cuttings or similar souvenirs are mounted. **scrap-merchant** n. a dealer in scrap. **scrap-yard** n. a place where scrap is collected. [f. ON, rel. to SCRAPE]

scrap[2] n. (colloq.) a fight or rough quarrel. —v.i. (-pp-) to have a scrap. [perh. f. foll.]

scrape v.t./i. **1.** to make (a thing) level, clean, or smooth by causing a hard edge to move across the surface; to apply (a hard edge) thus; to remove by scraping. **2.** to scratch or damage by scraping. **3.** to dig (a hollow etc.) by scraping. **4.** to draw or move with a sound (as) of scraping; to produce such a sound. **5.** to pass along or through something with difficulty, with or without touching it. **6.** to obtain or amass with effort or by parsimony. **7.** to be very economical. **8.** to draw back the foot in making a clumsy bow. —n. **1.** a scraping movement or sound. **2.** a scraped place or mark. **3.** a thinly applied layer of butter etc. on bread. **4.** an awkward situation resulting from an escapade. —**scrape acquaintance,** to contrive to become acquainted. **scrape the barrel,** to be driven to using one's last and inferior resources because the better ones are finished. **scrape through** etc., to get through a difficult situation or pass an examination by only a very narrow margin. [f. ON or MDu.]

scraper n. a device used for scraping things. [f. prec.]

scraping n. (esp. in pl.) a fragment produced by scraping. [f. SCRAPE]

scrappy adj. consisting of scraps or disconnected elements. —**scrappily** adv., **scrappiness** n. [f. SCRAP[1]]

scratch /skrætʃ/ v.t. **1.** to make a shallow mark or wound on (a surface) with something sharp. **2.** to make or form by scratching. **3.** to scrape with the finger-nail(s) in order to relieve itching. **4.** to make a thin scraping sound. **5.** to obtain with difficulty. **6.** (with off, out, or through) to delete by drawing a line through; to withdraw from a race, competition, or (US) election. —n. **1.** a mark, wound, or sound made by scratching; (colloq.) a trifling wound. **2.** a spell of scratching oneself. **3.** a line from which competitors start in a race, especially those receiving no handicap. —adj. **1.** collected by chance or from whatever is available. **2.** with no handicap given. —**from scratch,** from the beginning; without help or advantage. **scratch one's head,** to be perplexed. **scratch the surface,** to deal with a matter only superficially. **up to scratch,** up to the required standard. [prob. f. earlier scrat & cratch; orig. unkn.]

scratchy adj. **1.** tending to make scratches or a scratching noise. **2.** tending to cause itchiness. **3.** (of a drawing etc.) done in scratches or carelessly. —**scratchily** adv., **scratchiness** n. [f. prec.]

scrawl v.t./i. **1.** to write in a hurried untidy way. **2.** to cross out thus. —n. hurried writing; a scrawled note. [perh. f. obs. scrawl sprawl]

scrawny adj. lean, scraggy. [var. of dial. scranny]

scream v.t./i. **1.** to emit a piercing cry of pain, terror, annoyance, or excitement. **2.** to speak or sing (words etc.) in such a tone. **3.** to make or move with a shrill sound like a scream. **4.** to laugh uncontrollably. **5.** to be blatantly obvious. —n. **1.** a screaming cry or sound. **2.** (colloq.) an irresistibly funny occurrence or person. [OE]

scree n. (in sing. or pl.) a mass of small loose stones, sliding when trodden on; a mountain slope covered with these. [f. ON, = landslip]

screech n. a harsh high-pitched scream. —v.t./i. to utter with or make a screech. —**screech-owl** n. an owl that screeches instead of hooting, especially a barn-owl. [var. of earlier scritch (imit.)]

screed n. **1.** a tiresomely long letter or other document. **2.** a level strip of material formed or placed on a floor, road, etc., as a guide for the accurate finishing of it. **3.** a levelled layer of material forming part of a floor etc. —v.t. to level by means of a screed; to apply (material) as a screed. [prob. var. of SHRED]

screen n. **1.** an upright structure used to conceal, protect, or divide something. **2.** anything serving a similar purpose; an expression or measure etc. adopted for concealment; the protection given by this. **3.** a blank surface on which a film, televised picture, radar image, etc., is projected; the cinema industry. **4.** a sight-screen; a windscreen. **5.** a large sieve or riddle. **6.** a frame with fine wire netting to keep out flies, mosquitoes, etc. **7.** a system for showing the presence or absence of a disease, quality, etc. **8.** (Printing) a transparent finely-ruled plate or film used in half-tone reproduction. —v.t. **1.** to shelter, conceal, or protect. **2.** to protect from discovery or deserved blame by diverting suspicion. **3.** to show (images or a film etc.) on a screen. **4.** to prevent from causing electrical interference. **5.** to sieve. **6.** to test for the presence or absence of a disease, quality (esp. reliability or loyalty), etc. —**screen-printing** n. a process like stencilling with ink forced through a prepared sheet of fine material. [f. OF escren f. OHG skrank barrier]

screenplay n. the script of a film.

screw /skruː/ n. **1.** a cylinder or cone with a spiral ridge round the outside (**male screw**) or the inside (**female screw**); a metal male screw with a slotted head and a sharp point for fastening things (esp. of wood) together (see below and ill. CARPENTRY). **2.** a wooden or metal screw used to exert pressure; (in sing. or pl.) an instrument of torture operating thus. **3.** a propeller or other device acting like a screw. **4.** one turn of a screw. **5.** a small twisted-up paper of tobacco etc. **6.** (in billiards etc.) an oblique curling motion of the ball. **7.** (slang) a prison warder. **8.** (slang) the amount of one's salary or wages. **9.** (vulgar) sexual intercourse; a partner in this. —v.t./i. **1.** to fasten or tighten with a screw or screws. **2.** to turn (a screw); to twist or turn round like a screw. **3.** (of a ball etc.) to swerve. **4.** to put the screws on, to oppress; to extort (consent, money, etc.). **5.** to contort or contract (one's face etc.). **6.** (vulgar) to have sexual intercourse (with). —**have a screw loose,** (colloq.) to be slightly crazy. **put the screws on,** to exert pressure (on), to intimidate or extort money. **screw-cap** or **-top** n. a cap or top that screws on to a bottle etc. **screw up,** to contort or contract (one's eyes, face, etc.); to summon up (one's courage); (slang) to bungle or mismanage. [f. OF escroue female screw, nut, f. L scrofa female pig used for breeding]

The principle of the screw was used by the ancient Greeks in a water-raising device (see ARCHIMEDEAN SCREW), and from the 1st c. AD for exerting pressure in wine- and olive-presses. As fasteners, metal screws and nuts appear in the 16th c., turned with a box-wrench; some of those found in 16th-c. armour may have been turned with a pronged device. The metal screw for fixing various materials to wood is described by a German mining-engineer of the mid-16th c., but may have been in use for some time. The screwdriver as a hand-tool appears from c.1800.

screwball n. (US slang) a crazy or eccentric person.

screwdriver n. a tool with a shaped tip fitting into the slot of a screw to turn it. (See SCREW and ill. CARPENTRY.)

screwed adj. (slang) drunk. [f. SCREW]

screwy adj. (slang) crazy, eccentric; absurd. [f. SCREW]

Scriabin var. of SKRYABIN.

scribble v.t./i. **1.** to write carelessly or hurriedly. **2.** to make meaningless marks. —n. something scribbled; hurried or careless writing; scribbled meaningless marks. —**scribbler** n. [f. L scribillare dim. of L scribere write]

scribe n. **1.** an ancient or medieval copyist of manuscripts. **2.** a professional Jewish religious scholar in New Testament times. **3.** a pointed instrument for making marks on wood etc. —v.t. to mark with a scribe. —**scribal** adj. [f. L scriba (scribere write)]

scrim n. an open-weave fabric for lining or upholstery etc. [orig. unkn.]

scrimmage /ˈskrɪmɪdʒ/ n. a confused struggle; a skirmish. —v.i. to engage in a scrimmage. [var. of SKIRMISH]

scrimp v.t./i. to skimp. [perh. rel. to SHRIMP]

scrimshank /ˈskrɪmʃæŋk/ v.i. (slang) to shirk work, to malinger. [orig. unkn.]

scrip n. **1.** a provisional certificate of money subscribed entitling the holder to dividends; (collect.) such certificates. **2.** an extra share or shares issued instead of a dividend. [abbr. of subscription receipt]

script n. **1.** handwriting, written characters. **2.** type imitating handwriting. **3.** an alphabet or system of writing. **4.** the text of a play, film, broadcast talk, etc. **5.** an examinee's written answer. —v.t. to write the script for (a film etc.). —**script-writer** n. a writer for broadcasting or films etc. [f. OF f. L scriptum (scribere write)]

scripture /ˈskrɪptʃə(r)/ n. **1.** sacred writings. **2.** **Scripture** or **the Scriptures**, the sacred writings of the Christians (the Old and New Testaments) or the Jews (the Old Testament). (See TESTAMENT.) —**scriptural** adj. [f. L (as prec.)]

scrivener /ˈskrɪvənə(r)/ n. (hist.) a drafter of documents, a copyist, a notary. [f. OF escrivein f. L (as SCRIBE)]

scrofula /ˈskrɒfjʊlə/ n. a disease with glandular swellings, probably a form of tuberculosis. —**scrofulous** adj. [L dim. of scrofulae (pl.) scrofulous swelling f. scrofa (see SCREW)]

scroll /skrəʊl/ n. **1.** a roll of parchment or paper, especially with writing; a book of the ancient roll form. **2.** an ornamental design imitating a roll of parchment. —v.t. to move (the display on a VDU screen) up or down as new material appears. [orig. scrowle alt. f. rowle roll]

scrolled /skrəʊld/ adj. having a scroll ornament. [f. prec.]

Scrooge /skruːdʒ/, Ebenezer. A miserly curmudgeon in Charles Dickens's novel A Christmas Carol (1843). —n. a miser.

scrotum /ˈskrəʊtəm/ n. (pl. **scrota**) the pouch of skin containing the testicles (ill. BODY 2). —**scrotal** adj. [L]

scrounge v.t./i. (slang) to cadge; to collect by foraging. —**scrounger** n. [var. of dial. scrunge steal]

scrub[1] v.t./i. (-**bb-**) **1.** to rub hard so as to clean or brighten, especially with a hard brush; to use a brush thus. **2.** to remove impurities from (gas) in a scrubber. **3.** (slang) to scrap or cancel (a plan, order, etc.) —n. scrubbing, being scrubbed. —**scrub up**, (of a surgeon etc.) to clean the hands and arms by scrubbing before an operation. [prob. f. MLG or MDu.]

scrub[2] n. **1.** brushwood or stunted forest growth; land covered with this. **2.** a stunted or insignificant person etc. —**scrubby** adj. [var. of SHRUB]

scrubber[1] n. **1.** an apparatus for cleaning gases. **2.** (slang) an immoral or sluttish woman. [f. SCRUB[1]]

scrubber[2] n. (Austral.) an inferior animal, especially a bullock, living in scrub country. [f. SCRUB[2]]

scruff n. the back of the neck. [alt. of scuff, perh. f. ON, = soft hair]

scruffy adj. (colloq.) shabby and untidy. —**scruffily** adv., **scruffiness** n. [f. scruff var. of SCURF]

scrum n. a scrummage. —**scrum-half** n. the half-back who puts the ball into the scrum. [abbr.]

scrummage /ˈskrʌmɪdʒ/ n. (in Rugby football) the grouping of all forwards on each side to push against those of the other and seek possession of the ball thrown on the ground between them. [as SCRIMMAGE]

scrump v.t./i. (dial. or slang) to steal (apples), especially from orchards. [f. dial. scrump small apple]

scrumptious /ˈskrʌmpʃəs/ adj. (colloq.) delicious, delightful. [orig. unkn.]

scrumpy n. (colloq., orig. dial.) rough cider. [as SCRUMP]

scrunch n. a crunch. —v.t. to crunch. [var. of CRUNCH]

scruple /ˈskruːp(ə)l/ n. **1.** due regard to the morality or propriety of an action etc.; doubt or hesitation caused by this. **2.** (hist.) a unit of weight of 20 grains. —v.i. to feel or be influenced by scruples; (esp. with neg.) to be reluctant because of scruples. [f. F or L scrupulus (scrupus rough pebble)]

scrupulous /ˈskruːpjʊləs/ adj. **1.** careful to avoid doing wrong. **2.** conscientious or thorough even in small matters; painstakingly careful and thorough. —**scrupulosity** /-ˈlɒsɪtɪ/ n., **scrupulously** adv., **scrupulousness** n. [as prec.]

scrutineer /skruːtɪˈnɪə(r)/ n. a person who scrutinizes ballot-papers. [f. SCRUTINY]

scrutinize /ˈskruːtɪnaɪz/ v.t. to subject to scrutiny. [f. foll.]

scrutiny /ˈskruːtɪnɪ/ n. a careful look or examination; an official examination of ballot-papers to check their validity or the accuracy of counting. [f. L scrutinium (scrutari search)]

scuba /ˈskuːbə/ n. self-contained underwater breathing apparatus, designed to enable a swimmer to breathe while under the water. [acronym]

scud v.i. (-**dd-**) **1.** to run or fly straight and fast, to skim along. **2.** (Naut.) to run before the wind. —n. **1.** a spell of scudding; a scudding motion. **2.** vapoury driving clouds; a driving shower. [perh. alt. of SCUT]

scuff v.t./i. **1.** to walk with dragging feet, to shuffle. **2.** to graze or brush against; to mark or wear out (shoes etc.) thus. —n. a mark of scuffing. [imit.]

scuffle n. a confused struggle or fight at close quarters. —v.i. to engage in a scuffle. [prob. f. Scand. (cf. SHOVE)]

scull n. **1.** each of a pair of small oars used by a single rower. **2.** an oar that rests on the stern of a boat, used with a screwlike motion. **3.** (in pl.) a sculling race. —v.t. to propel (a boat, or absol.) with sculls. [orig. unkn.]

sculler n. **1.** a user of a scull or sculls. **2.** a boat for sculling. [f. SCULL]

scullery /ˈskʌlərɪ/ n. a back kitchen; a room in which dishes etc. are washed. [f. OF esculerie (escuele dish f. L scutella salver dim. of scutra wooden platter)]

scullion /ˈskʌljən/ n. (archaic) a cook's boy, one who washes dishes. [orig. unkn.]

sculpt v.t./i. (colloq.) to sculpture. [abbr.]

sculptor /ˈskʌlptə(r)/ n. one who sculptures. —**sculptress** n. fem. [L (as foll.)]

sculpture /ˈskʌlptʃə(r)/ n. **1.** the art of forming representations in the round or in relief by chiselling stone, carving wood, modelling clay, casting metal, etc. **2.** a work of sculpture. —v.t./i. to represent in or adorn with sculpture; to practise sculpture. —**sculptural** adj., **sculpturally** adv. [f. L sculptura (sculpere carve)]

scum n. **1.** a layer of dirt, froth, or impurities etc. that rises to the top of a liquid. **2.** a worthless part; a worthless person or persons. —v.t./i. (-**mm-**) to remove the scum from; to form a scum (on). —**scummy** adj. [f. MLG or MDu.]

scuncheon /ˈskʌntʃ(ə)n/ n. the inside face of a door-jamb, window-frame, etc. [f. OF escoinson (as EX-, COIN)]

scupper n. a hole in a ship's side to carry off water from the deck. —v.t. (slang) **1.** to sink (a ship) deliberately. **2.** to defeat or ruin (a plan etc.). **3.** to kill. [perh. f. AF deriv. of OF escopir spit, orig. imit.]

scurf n. flakes of dead skin, especially on the scalp. —**scurfy** adj. [OE, prob. rel. to sceorfian cut to shreds]

scurrilous /ˈskʌrɪləs/ adj. **1.** abusive and insulting. **2.** coarsely humorous. —**scurrility** /-ˈrɪlɪtɪ/ n., **scurrilously** adv. [f. L scurrilis (scurra buffoon)]

scurry /ˈskʌrɪ/ v.i. to run or move hurriedly, especially with short quick steps; to scamper. —n. **1.** an act or sound of scurrying; a rush. **2.** a flurry of rain or snow. [abbr. of hurry-scurry redupl. of HURRY]

scurvy /ˈskɜːvɪ/ n. a deficiency disease caused by lack of vitamin C in the diet. —adj. paltry, dishonourable, contemptible. —**scurvily** adv., **scurviness** n. [f. SCURF; the n. infl. by F scorbut (cf. SCORBUTIC)]

scut n. a short tail, especially of a rabbit, hare, or deer. [orig. unkn.]

scutter v.i. (colloq.) to scurry. —n. (colloq.) a scurry. [perh. alt. of SCUTTLE[3]]

scuttle[1] n. **1.** a receptacle for carrying and holding a small supply of coal. **2.** the part of a motor-car body between the windscreen and bonnet. [f. ON or OHG f. L scutella dish]

scuttle[2] n. a hole with a lid in a ship's deck or side. —v.t. to let water into (a ship), especially to sink it. [perh. f. obs. F f. Sp. escotilla hatchway (escota cutting out cloth)]

scuttle[3] v.i. to scurry, to flee from danger or difficulty. —n. **1.** a scuttling run. **2.** a precipitate flight or departure. [cf. dial. scuddle (as SCUD)]

Scylla /ˈsɪlə/ (Gk myth.) a female sea-monster who devoured men from ships when they tried to navigate the narrow channel between her cave and the whirlpool Charybdis. Later legend substituted a dangerous rock for the monster and located it on the Italian side of the Strait of Messina.

scythe /saɪð/ n. a mowing and reaping instrument with a long curved blade swung over the ground. —v.t. to cut with a scythe. [OE]

Scythia /ˈsɪθɪə/ the name given by the ancient Greeks to a country on the north shore of the Black Sea. Its inhabitants were an Indo-European people of Central Asian origin, skilful horsemen and craftsmen, known for their distinctive 'animal style' art. They were eventually absorbed by the Goths and other immigrants during the 3rd and 2nd c. BC. **—Scythian** adj. & n.

SDLP abbr. Social Democratic and Labour Party, a political party in Northern Ireland, founded in 1970.

SDP abbr. Social Democratic Party (see entry).

SE abbr. south-east, south-eastern.

Se symbol selenium.

sea n. **1.** the expanse of salt water that covers most of the earth's surface and surrounds the continents; any part of this as opposed to land or fresh water. (See ill. pp. 746-7) **2.** a named tract of salt water partly or wholly enclosed by land; a large freshwater inland lake. **3.** the waves of the sea; their motion or state. **4.** a vast quantity or expanse. — (attrib.) living or used in, on, or near the sea (often prefixed to the name of a marine animal, plant, etc., having a superficial resemblance to what it is named after). **—at sea**, in a ship on the sea; perplexed, confused. **by sea**, in a ship or ships. **go to sea**, to become a sailor. **on the sea**, in a ship at sea; situated on the coast. **sea anchor**, a bag to retard the drifting of a ship. **sea anemone**, a large polyp of the order Actiniaria, with petal-like tentacles. **sea-bird** n. a bird frequenting the sea or land near the sea. **sea-borne** adj. conveyed by the sea. **sea change**, a notable or unexpected transformation. **sea-cow** n. a sirenian; a walrus; a hippopotamus. **sea-dog** n. an old sailor, especially an Elizabethan captain. **Sea Dyak**, see IBAN. **sea-girt** adj. surrounded by the sea. **sea-green** adj. & n. bluish green. **sea-horse** n. a small fish of the genus Hippocampus with a head suggestive of a horse's at right angles to its body, and a tail that can be wrapped round a support; a mythical creature with a horse's head and a fish's tail. **sea-kale** n. a herb (Crambe maritima) with young shoots used as a vegetable. **sea-legs** n. pl. the ability to walk on the deck of a rolling ship. **sea-level** n. the mean level of the sea's surface, used in reckoning the height of hills etc. and as a barometric standard. **sea-lion** n. a large eared seal especially of the genus Zalophus or Otaria. **Sea Lord**, a naval member of the Admiralty Board. **sea mile**, a nautical mile (see MILE). **Sea Peoples** or **Peoples of the Sea**, groups of invaders who encroached on the Levant and Egypt by land and by sea in the late 13th c. Their identity is still being debated. In the Levant they are associated with destruction; the Egyptians were successful in driving them away. Some, including the Philistines, settled in Palestine. **—sea-room** n. space for a ship to turn etc. at sea. **sea-salt** n. salt produced by evaporating sea-water. **Sea Scout**, a member of the maritime branch of the Scout Association. **sea-shell**, the shell of a salt-water mollusc. **sea-shore** n. land close to the sea. **sea-urchin** n. a small sea-animal of the order Echinoidea with a prickly shell. **sea-way** n. a ship's progress; a place where a ship lies in open water; an inland waterway open to seagoing ships. [OE]

seaboard n. the seashore or line of a coast; a coastal region.

seafarer n. a sailor, a traveller by sea.

seafaring adj. & n. travelling by sea, especially as one's regular occupation.

seafood n. edible marine fish or shellfish.

seagoing adj. **1.** (of ships) fit for crossing the sea. **2.** (of a person) seafaring.

seagull n. a gull (GULL¹).

seal¹ n. **1.** a piece of wax, lead, paper, etc., with a stamped design, attached to a document as a guarantee of authenticity or to a receptacle, room, envelope, etc., as a sign that (while the seal is unbroken) the contents have not been tampered with since it was affixed. **2.** an engraved piece of metal etc. for stamping such a design. **3.** a substance or device to close an aperture etc. **4.** an act, gesture, or event regarded as a confirmation or guarantee. **5.** a decorative adhesive stamp. —v.t. **1.** to stamp or fasten with a seal; to fix a seal to; to certify as correct with a seal or stamp. **2.** to close securely or hermetically. **3.** to confine securely. **4.** to settle or decide. **—sealing-wax** n. a mixture of shellac and rosin softened by heating and used for seals. **seal off**, to prevent entry to and exit from (an area). **seals of office**, those held during tenure of office, especially by a Lord Chancellor or Secretary of State. **set one's seal to**, to authorize or confirm. [f. AF f. L sigillum dim. of signum sign]

seal² n. **1.** a fish-eating amphibious sea mammal of the family Phocidae, with flippers. **2.** sealskin. —v.i. to hunt seals. [OE]

sealant n. material for sealing things, especially to make them airtight or watertight. [f. SEAL¹]

sealer n. a ship or person engaged in hunting seals. [f. SEAL²]

sealskin n. the skin or prepared fur of a seal; a garment made from this.

Sealyham /'siːliəm/ n. a wire-haired short-legged terrier. [f. Sealyham in Dyfed, Wales]

seam n. **1.** the line where two edges join, especially of cloth or leather etc. or boards. **2.** a fissure between parallel edges. **3.** a wrinkle. **4.** a stratum of coal etc. —v.t. **1.** to join by a seam. **2.** (esp. in p.p.) to mark or score with a seam, fissure, or scar. **—seam bowler**, a bowler in cricket who makes the ball spin by bouncing it off its seam. [OE]

seaman n. (pl. **-men**) one whose occupation is on the sea; a sailor, especially below the rank of officer.

seamanship n. skill in managing a ship or boat. [f. prec. + -SHIP]

seamstress /'semstrɪs/ n. a woman who sews, especially as a job. [OE (as SEAM)]

seamy adj. marked with or showing seams. **—seamy side**, the disreputable or unattractive side. [f. SEAM]

Seanad /'ʃænəð/ n. the upper house of parliament in the Republic of Ireland, composed of 60 members, of whom 11 are nominated by the Taoiseach and 49 are elected by institutions etc. [Ir., = senate]

seance /'seɪɑ̃s/ n. a meeting for the exhibition or investigation of spiritualistic phenomena. [f. F, = a sitting]

seaplane n. an aircraft that can land on and take off from water using floats instead of an undercarriage. It differs from a flying boat in that its hull does not support it in the water.

seaport n. a port on the coast.

sear v.t. **1.** to scorch, to cauterize. **2.** to make (the conscience or feelings etc.) callous. [OE]

search /sɜːtʃ/ v.t./i. **1.** to look through or go over thoroughly in order to find something. **2.** to examine the clothes and body of (a person) to see if anything is concealed there. **3.** to examine thoroughly (lit. or fig.). —n. an act of searching; an investigation. **—in search of**, trying to find. **search me**, (colloq.) I do not know. **search out**, to look for, to seek out. **search-party** n. a group of people organized to look for a lost person or thing. **search-warrant** n. an official authority to enter and search a building. **—searcher** n. [f. AF f. L circare go round (as CIRCUS)]

searchlight n. an electric lamp with a powerful concentrated beam that can be turned in any direction; the light or beam from this.

seascape n. a picture or view of the sea. [f. SEA, after landscape]

seasick adj. suffering from sickness or nausea from the motion of a ship etc. **—seasickness** n.

seaside n. the sea-coast, especially as a holiday resort.

season /'siːz(ə)n/ n. **1.** each of the divisions of the year (spring, summer, autumn, winter) associated with a type of weather and a stage of vegetation. **2.** a proper or suitable time; the time when something is plentiful, active, or in vogue; the high season. **3.** the time of year regularly devoted to an activity, or to social life generally. **4.** an indefinite period. **5.** (colloq.) a season ticket. —v.t./i. **1.** to flavour or make palatable with salt, herbs, etc.; to enhance with wit etc.; to temper or moderate. **2.** to make or become suitable or in a desired condition, especially by exposure to air or weather. **—in season**, (of food) available in good condition and plentifully; (of an animal) on heat. **season-ticket** n. a ticket entitling the holder to any number of journeys, admittances, etc., in a given period. [f. OF saison f. L satio sowing]

seasonable adj. **1.** suitable or usual to the season. **2.** opportune; meeting the needs of the occasion. **—seasonably** adv. [f. prec.]

seasonal adj. of, depending on, or varying with the season. **—seasonally** adv. [f. SEASON]

seasoning n. flavouring added to food. [as prec.]

seat n. **1.** a thing made or used for sitting on; a place for one person in a theatre, vehicle, etc. **2.** occupation of a seat; the right to this, e.g. as a member of a board or of the House of Commons. **3.** the buttocks; the part of the trousers etc. covering them. **4.** the part of a chair etc. on which the sitter's weight directly rests; the part of a machine that supports or guides another part. **5.** a site or location. **6.** a country mansion, especially with large grounds. **7.** a person's manner of sitting on a horse etc. —v.t. **1.** to cause to sit. **2.** to provide sitting accommodation for. **3.** (in p.p.)

The Sea

Oceans

71% of the earth's surface is covered by water

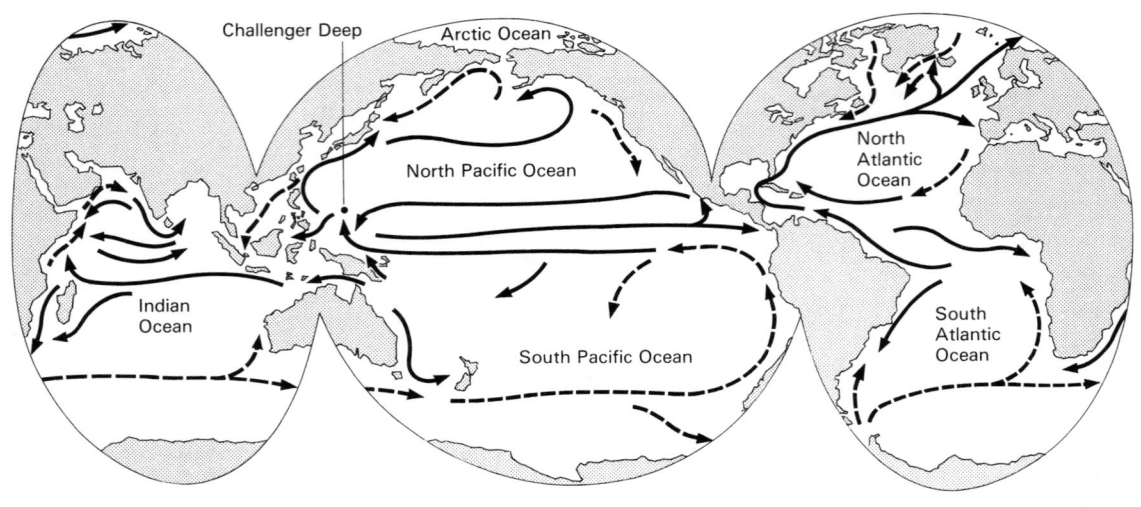

Challenger Deep

Arctic Ocean

North Pacific Ocean

North Atlantic Ocean

Indian Ocean

South Pacific Ocean

South Atlantic Ocean

→ warm ocean currents

----→ cold ocean currents

Some currents vary in direction seasonally or from year to year

Ocean depths

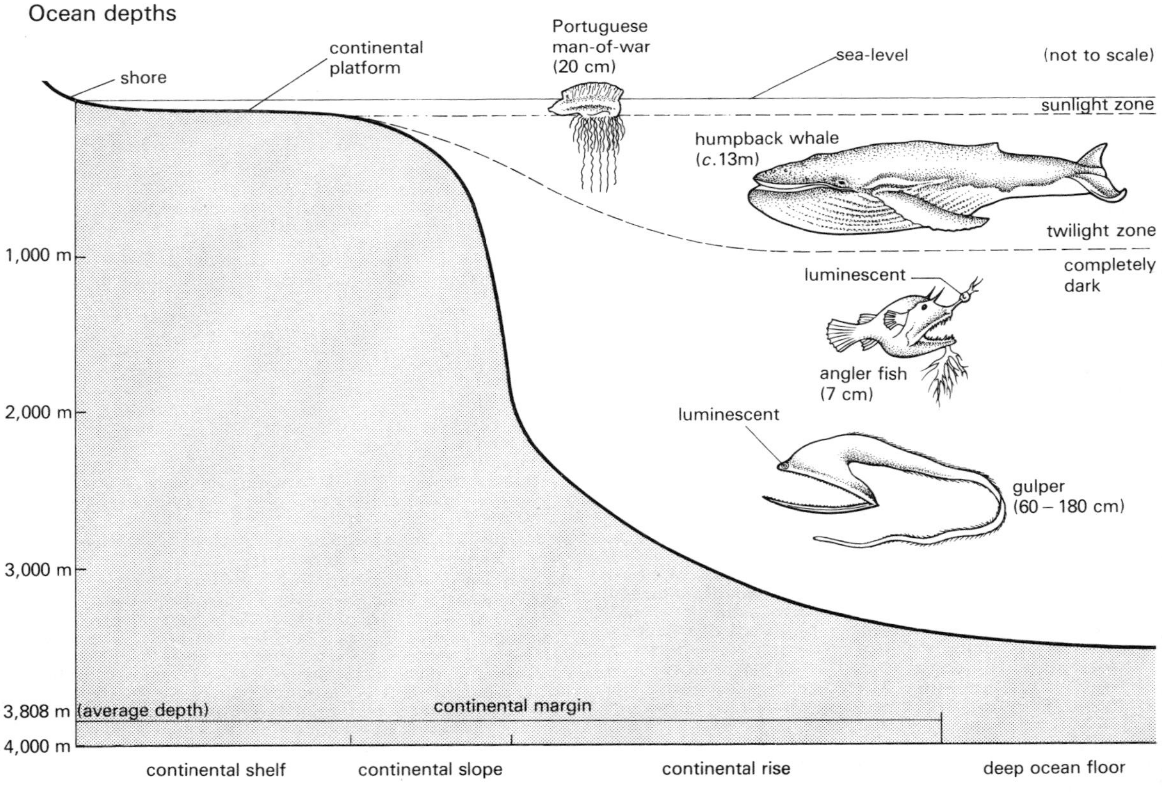

continental platform

Portuguese man-of-war (20 cm)

shore

sea-level

(not to scale)

sunlight zone

humpback whale (c.13m)

twilight zone

1,000 m

completely dark

luminescent

angler fish (7 cm)

2,000 m

luminescent

gulper (60 – 180 cm)

3,000 m

3,808 m (average depth)   continental margin

4,000 m

continental shelf   continental slope   continental rise   deep ocean floor

The earth's surface area

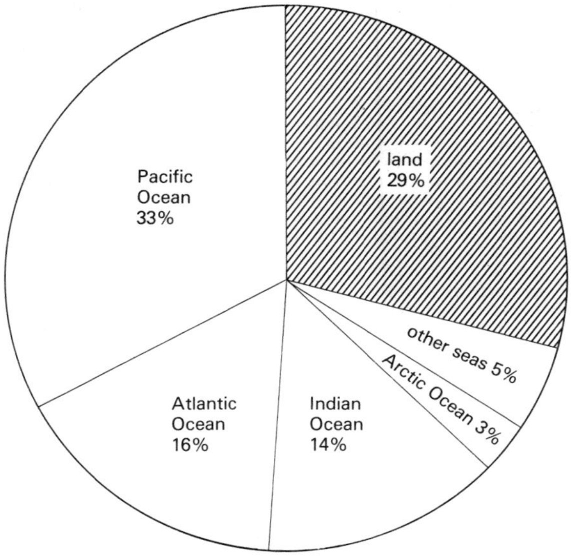

Pacific Ocean 33%

land 29%

other seas 5%

Arctic Ocean 3%

Atlantic Ocean 16%

Indian Ocean 14%

Food-chain (simplified)

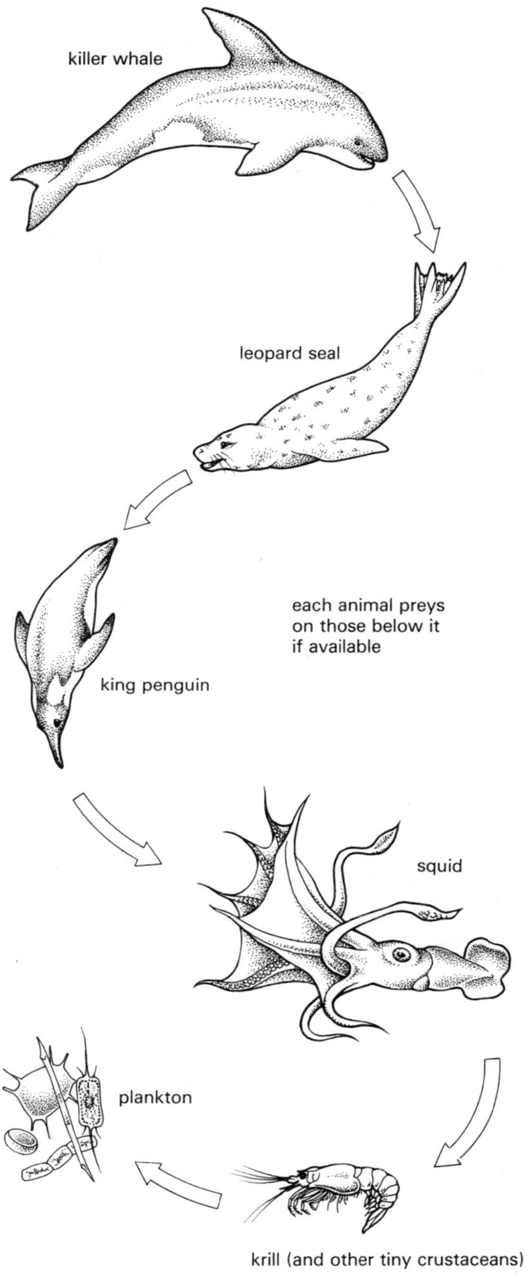

killer whale

leopard seal

each animal preys on those below it if available

king penguin

squid

plankton

krill (and other tiny crustaceans)

Depths attained by man

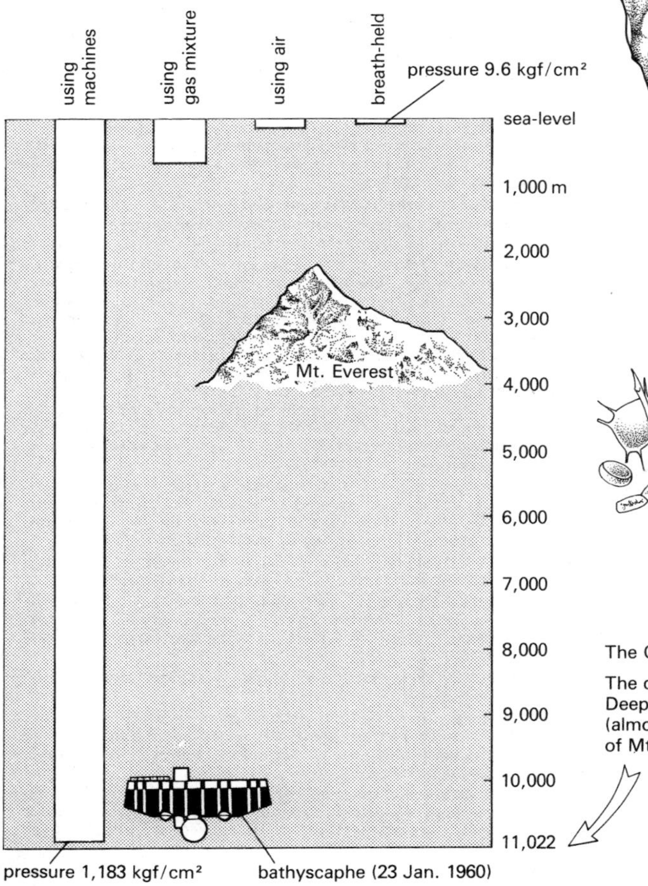

using machines

using gas mixture

using air

breath-held

pressure 9.6 kgf/cm²

sea-level

1,000 m

2,000

3,000

Mt. Everest

4,000

5,000

6,000

7,000

8,000

9,000

10,000

11,022

pressure 1,183 kgf/cm²   bathyscaphe (23 Jan. 1960)

The Challenger Deep

The deepest part of the ocean is in the Challenger Deep, part of the Mariana Trench, 11,022 metres (almost 7 miles). This depth is greater than the height of Mt. Everest.

sitting. **4.** to put or fit in position. **—be seated,** to sit down. **by the seat of one's pants,** by instinct rather than knowledge or logic. **seat-belt** *n.* a belt securing a person in the seat of a car or aircraft. **take a seat,** to sit down. **take one's seat,** to sit down, especially in one's appointed place; to assume one's official position, to be formally admitted to Parliament or to Congress. [f. ON (as SIT)]

-seater *in comb.* having a specified number of seats. [f. SEAT]

seating *n.* seats collectively, sitting accommodation. [f. SEAT]

seaward /ˈsiːwəd/ *adv.* (also **seawards**) towards the sea. *—adj.* going or facing towards the sea. *—n.* such a direction or position. [f. SEA + -WARD]

seaweed *n.* any alga growing in the sea or in rocks on the shore.

seaworthy *adj.* fit to put to sea.

sebaceous /sɪˈbeɪʃəs/ *adj.* fatty, secreting or conveying oily matter. [f. L (*sebum* tallow)]

Sebastian /sɪˈbæstɪən/, St (late 3rd c.), Roman martyr. According to legend he was sentenced by Diocletian to be shot by archers but recovered, confronted the Emperor, and was clubbed to death. Feast day, 20 Jan.

Sebastopol /sɪˈbæstəp(ə)l/ a Russian fortress and naval base in the Crimea, the focal point of military operations during the Crimean War. It eventually fell to Anglo-French forces in September 1855 after a year-long siege.

sec *adj.* (of wine) dry. [F f. L *siccus* dry]

Sec. *abbr.* Secretary.

sec. *abbr.* second(s).

secant /ˈsiːkənt/ *n.* a straight line that cuts a curve, especially a circle, at two points; the radius of a circle produced through one end of an arc to meet the tangent to the other end; the ratio of this to the radius. **—secant of an angle,** the ratio of the length of the hypotenuse to the length of the side adjacent to that angle in a right-angled triangle. [f. F f. L *secare* cut]

secateurs /sekəˈtɜːz/ *n.* pruning-clippers used with one hand. [f. F f. L *secare* cut]

secede /sɪˈsiːd/ *v.i.* to withdraw formally from an organization, e.g. a political federation. [f. L *secedere* (*se-* aside, *cedere* go)]

secession /sɪˈseʃ(ə)n/ *n.* seceding. **—secessionist** *n.* [f. F or L (as prec.)]

seclude /sɪˈkluːd/ *v.t.* to keep (a person) apart from others; to keep (a place) screened or sheltered from view. [f. L *secludere* (*se-* aside, *claudere* shut)]

seclusion /sɪˈkluːʒ(ə)n/ *n.* **1.** secluding, being secluded; privacy. **2.** a secluded place. [as prec.]

second¹ /ˈsekənd/ *adj.* **1.** next after first. **2.** another besides one or the first, additional. **3.** of subordinate importance or position etc., inferior. **4.** (*Mus.*) performing a lower or subordinate part. **5.** metaphorical, such as to be comparable to. *—n.* **1.** the person or thing that is second; the second day of a month. **2.** another person or thing besides the previously mentioned or principal one. **3.** second-class honours in a university degree. **4.** an assistant to a combatant in a duel, boxing match, etc. **5.** (in *pl.*) a second helping of food; a second course of a meal. *—v.t.* **1.** to back up, to assist. **2.** to support, (a resolution etc. or its proposer) formally so as to show that the proposer is not isolated or as a means of bringing it to a vote. **—second-best** *adj.* & *n.* next after the best; inferior in quality (*come off second-best,* to fail to win). **second chamber,** the upper house of a parliament. **second class,** the second-best group or category or accommodation etc.; the class of mail that does not have priority in delivery. **second-class** *adj.* & *adv.* of or by the second or inferior class. **second fiddle,** a subordinate position or role. **second-guess** *v.t./i.* (*US*) to anticipate the action of; to predict; to criticize by hindsight. **second-hand** *adj.* having had a previous owner, not new; (of a shop etc.) supplying such goods; (*adv.*) from a second-ary source (*at second hand,* indirectly). **second lieutenant,** an army officer next below lieutenant. **second nature,** an acquired tendency that has become instinctive. **second officer,** an assistant mate on a merchant ship. **second person,** see PERSON. **second-rate** *adj.* in the second class, inferior. **second sight,** the supposed power of perceiving future events. **second teeth,** adults' permanent teeth. **second thoughts,** a new opinion or resolution reached after further consideration. **second wind,** recovery of regular breathing during continued exertion after breath-lessness; renewed capacity for effort after tiredness. **Second

World War, see WORLD WAR. **—seconder** *n.* [f. OF f. L *secundus* (*sequi* follow)]

second² /sɪˈkɒnd/ *v.t* to transfer (an officer or official) temporarily to another appointment or department. **—secondment** *n.* [= prec.]

second³ /ˈsekənd/ *n.* **1.** the base unit of time (symbol s; established in 1967 for international use), the duration of 9,192,631,770 periods of the radiation of a certain transition of the caesium-133 atom. Originally the second was defined as the fraction 1/86,400 of the mean solar day, exact definition of which was left to astronomers, but this was shown to be insufficiently accurate on account of irregularities in the rotation of the Earth. **2.** one sixtieth part of an angle. **3.** (*colloq.*) a very short time. [f. OF f. L *secunda* (*minuta*) secondary minute, i.e. minute of a minute)]

secondary /ˈsekəndərɪ/ *adj.* **1.** coming after or next below what is primary; derived from, depending on, or supplementing what is primary; of lesser importance or rank etc. than the first. **2.** (of education, a school etc.) for those who have received primary education but have not yet proceeded to a university or occupation. *—n.* a thing that is secondary; a secondary feather (ill. BIRDS). **—secondary colours,** see COLOUR. **secondary feather,** any of those growing from the second joint of a bird's wing. **secondary picketing,** furtherance of an industrial dispute by picketing the premises of a firm not directly involved in it. **—secondarily** *adv.* [f. L (as SECOND¹)]

secondly *adv.* in the second place, furthermore. [f. SECOND¹]

secrecy /ˈsiːkrəsɪ/ *n.* keeping things secret; being kept secret. **—sworn to secrecy,** having promised to keep a secret. [f. foll.]

secret /ˈsiːkrɪt/ *adj.* **1.** kept or meant to be kept from the knowledge or view of others or of all but a few; to be known only by specified people. **2.** acting or operating secretly. **3.** fond of secrecy. *—n.* **1.** a thing kept or meant to be kept secret. **2.** a mystery, a thing for which an explanation is unknown or not widely known. **3.** a valid but not generally known method for achieving something. **—in secret,** in a secret manner. **secret agent,** a spy acting for a country. **secret ballot,** one in which individual voters' choices are not made public. **secret police,** a police force operating in secret for political ends. **secret service,** a government department concerned with espionage. **secret society,** one whose members are sworn to secrecy about it. **—secretly** *adv.* [f. OF f. L *secretus* f. *secernere* separate, set apart (*se-* aside, *cernere* sift)]

secretaire /sekrɪˈteə(r)/ *n.* an escritoire. [F (as SECRETARY)]

secretariat /sekrəˈteərɪət/ *n.* an administrative office or department; its members or premises. [f. F f. L (as foll.)]

secretary /ˈsekrətərɪ/ *n.* **1.** a person employed to assist with correspondence, keep records, make appointments, etc. **2.** an official appointed by a society etc. to conduct its correspondence, keep its records, etc. **3.** the principal assistant of a government minister, ambassador, etc. **—secretary-bird** *n.* a long-legged African bird (*Sagittarius serpentarius*) with a crest likened to quill pens placed behind a writer's ear. **Secretary-General** *n.* the principal administrator of an organization. **Secretary of State,** the head of a major government department; (*US*) the Foreign Secretary. **—secretarial** /-ˈteərɪəl/ *adj.*, **secretaryship** *n.* [f. L *secretarius* (as SECRET)]

secrete /sɪˈkriːt/ *v.t.* **1.** to put into a place of concealment. **2.** to separate (a substance) in a gland etc. from blood or sap for a function in the organism or for excretion. **—secretor** *n.* [f. SECRET or as back-formation f. foll.]

secretion /sɪˈkriːʃ(ə)n/ *n.* **1.** secreting, being secreted. **2.** a secreted substance. [f. F or L *secretio* (as SECRET)]

secretive /ˈsiːkrətɪv/ *adj.* making a secret of things unnecessarily, uncommunicative. **—secretively** *adv.*, **secretiveness** *n.* [back-formation f. *secretiveness* after F *secrétiveté* (as SECRET)]

secretory /sɪˈkriːtərɪ/ *adj.* of physiological secretion. [f. SECRETE]

sect *n.* a group of people with religious or other beliefs that differ from those more generally accepted; the followers of a particular philosophy or school of thought. [f. OF or L *secta* (*sequi* follow)]

sectarian /sekˈteərɪən/ *adj.* of or concerning a sect; bigoted or narrow-minded in following one's sect. *—n.* a member of a sect. **—sectarianism** *n.* [f. L *sectarius* adherent (as prec.)]

section /ˈsekʃ(ə)n/ *n.* **1.** a part cut off; one of the parts into which a thing is divided or divisible or out of which a structure can be fitted together; a subdivision of a book, statute, group of people, etc.; (*US*) an area of land, a district of a town; a subdivision of an army platoon. **2.** separation by cutting. **3.** the cutting of a solid by a plane; the resulting figure or area of this. —*v.t.* to arrange in or divide into sections. —**section-mark** *n.* a sign (§) used to indicate the start of a section of a book etc. [F or f. L (*secare* cut)]

sectional *adj.* **1.** of a section; **2.** made in sections. **3.** local rather than general; partisan. —**sectionally** *adv.* [f. prec.]

sector /'sektə(r)/ *n.* **1.** a distinct part or branch of an enterprise, of society or the economy, etc. **2.** the plane figure enclosed between two radii of a circle, ellipse, etc., and the arc cut off by them (ill. SHAPES). **3.** any of the parts into which a battle area is divided for control of operations. [L, orig. = cutter (as SECTION)]

secular /'sekjʊlə(r)/ *adj.* **1.** concerned with the affairs of this world, not spiritual or sacred. **2.** not ecclesiastical or monastic. **3.** occurring once in an age or century. —**secularity** /-'lærɪtɪ/ *n.* [f. F or L *saecularis* (*saeculum* an age)]

secularism *n.* the belief that morality or education should not be based on religion. —**secularist** *n.* [f. prec.]

secure /sɪ'kjʊə(r)/ *adj.* **1.** safe, especially against attack. **2.** certain not to slip or fail; reliable. —*v.t.* **1.** to make secure; to fasten or close securely. **2.** to succeed in obtaining. **3.** to guarantee, to make safe against loss. —**securely** *adv.* [f. L *securus*, orig. = free from worry (*se-* aside, *cura* care)]

security /sɪ'kjʊərɪtɪ/ *n.* **1.** the state or feeling of being secure; a thing that gives this. **2.** the safety of a State, organization, etc., against espionage, theft, or other danger; an organization for ensuring this. **3.** a thing deposited or pledged as a guarantee of the fulfilment of an undertaking or payment of a loan, to be forfeited in case of failure. **4.** (often in *pl.*) a document as evidence of a loan; a certificate of stock, a bond, etc. —**security risk,** a person whose presence may threaten security. [f. OF or L (as prec.)]

Security Council a principal council of the UN consisting of 15 members, of which five (China, France, UK, USA, USSR) are permanent and the rest are elected for two-year terms, charged with the duty of maintaining security and peace between nations.

Sedan /sɪ'dæn/ a town on the River Meuse in NE France, site of the decisive battle (1870) in the Franco-Prussian war of 1870-1, in which the Prussian army succeeded in surrounding a smaller French army under Napoleon III and forcing it to surrender, opening the way for a Prussian advance on Paris and marking the end of the Second Empire.

sedan /sɪ'dæn/ *n.* **1.** (also **sedan-chair**) an enclosed chair as a vehicle for one person (17th-18th c.), mounted on two horizontal poles and carried by two men. **2.** (*US*) an enclosed motor car for four or more persons. [perh. f. It. dial., ult. f. L *sella* saddle (*sedēre* sit)]

sedate[1] /sɪ'deɪt/ *adj.* tranquil and dignified, not lively. —**sedately** *adv.*, **sedateness** *n.* [f. L *sedare* make calm (*sedēre* sit)]

sedate[2] /sɪ'deɪt/ *v.t.* to treat with sedatives. —**sedation** /-'deɪʃ(ə)n/ *n.* [back-formation f. *sedation* f. F or L (as prec.)]

sedative /'sedətɪv/ *adj.* tending to calm or soothe. —*n.* a sedative medicine or influence. [f. OF or L (as SEDATE)]

sedentary /'sedəntərɪ/ *adj.* sitting; (of work etc.) characterized by much sitting and little physical exercise; (of a person) having or inclined to work etc. of this kind. [f. F or L (*sedēre* sit)]

sedge *n.* a waterside or marsh plant of the genus *Carex*, resembling coarse grass. —**sedgy** *adj.* [OE]

Sedgemoor /'sedʒmʊə(r)/ a plain in Somerset, scene of a battle (1685) in which Monmouth, who had landed on the Dorset coast as champion of the Protestant party, was defeated by James II's troops. Monmouth himself was captured, and was executed soon afterwards.

sediment /'sedɪmənt/ *n.* **1.** very fine particles of solid matter suspended in a liquid or settling to the bottom of it. **2.** solid matter (e.g. sand, gravel) carried by water or wind and deposited on the surface of the land. —**sedimentation** /-'teɪʃ(ə)n/ *n.* [f. F or L (as prec.)]

sedimentary /sedɪ'mentərɪ/ *adj.* **1.** of or like sediment. **2.** (of rock) formed from sediment (cf. IGNEOUS, METAMORPHIC). Such rocks are characteristically laid down in strata which are initially horizontal or nearly so. It is through the study of sequences of sedimentary rocks and the fossils associated with them that the geological time-scale was established. By volume, sedimentary rocks constitute only 5 % of the known crust of the earth, igneous rocks contributing the other 95 %. [f. prec.]

sedition /sɪ'dɪʃ(ə)n/ *n.* conduct or speech inciting people to rebellion. —**seditious** *adj.* [f. OF or L *seditio* (*se-* aside, *ire* go)]

seduce /sɪ'dju:s/ *v.t.* to tempt into (esp. extramarital) sexual intercourse; to persuade (esp. into wrongdoing) by offering temptations. —**seducer** *n.*, **seductress** /-'dʌktrɪs/ *n.fem.* [f. L (*se-* aside, *ducere* lead)]

seduction /sɪ'dʌkʃ(ə)n/ *n.* **1.** seducing, being seduced. **2.** a tempting or attractive thing or quality. [f. F or L (as prec.)]

seductive /sɪ'dʌktɪv/ *adj.* tending to seduce, alluring, enticing. —**seductively** *adv.*, **seductiveness** *n.* [f. prec.]

sedulous /'sedjʊləs/ *adj.* diligent and persevering. —**sedulity** /sɪ'dju:lɪtɪ/ *n.*, **sedulously** *adv.*, **sedulousness** *n.* [f. L *sedulus* zealous]

sedum /'si:dəm/ *n.* a fleshy-leaved plant of the genus *Sedum*, with pink, white, or yellow flowers. [L, = houseleek]

see[1] *v.t./i.* (*past* **saw**; *p.p.* **seen**) **1.** to perceive with the eyes; to have or use the power of doing this. **2.** to perceive with the mind, to understand; to ascertain; to consider, to take time to do this; to foresee; to find attractive qualities (in a person etc.). **3.** to watch, to be a spectator of. **4.** to look at for information; to learn (a fact) from a newspaper or other visual source. **5.** to meet; to be near and recognize. **6.** to grant or obtain an interview (with); to visit in order to consult. **7.** to interpret, to have an opinion of. **8.** to supervise, to ensure. **9.** to experience; to have presented to one's attention. **10.** to call up a mental picture of, to imagine. **11.** to escort or conduct. **12.** (in gambling, esp. poker) to equal (a bet); to equal the bet of (a player). —**see about,** to attend to. **see after,** to take care of. **see the back of,** to be rid of (an unwanted person or thing). **see into,** to investigate. **see the light,** to realize one's mistakes etc.; to undergo a religious conversion. **see off,** to accompany to a place of departure; to ensure the departure of (a person). **see out,** to accompany out of a building etc.; to finish (a project etc.) completely; to wait until the end of (a period). **see over,** to inspect, to tour and examine. **see red,** to become suddenly enraged. **see stars,** to see lights before one's eyes as a result of a blow on the head. **see through,** not to be deceived by, to detect the nature of. **see a person through,** to support him during a difficult time. **see a thing through,** to finish it completely. **see-through** *adj.* (esp. of clothing) transparent, diaphanous. **see to,** to attend to; to organize; to put right. [OE]

see[2] *n.* the area under the authority of a bishop or archbishop; his office or jurisdiction. [f. AF f. L *sedes* seat]

seed *n.* **1.** the unit of reproduction of a plant, a fertilized ovule capable of developing into another such plant; (*collect.*) seeds in any quantity, especially as collected for sowing. **2.** semen, milt. **3.** something from which a tendency or feeling etc. can develop. **4.** offspring, descendants. **5.** (in tennis etc.) a seeded player. —*v.t./i.* **1.** to plant seeds (in); to sprinkle (as) with seed. **2.** to produce or drop seed. **3.** to remove seeds from (fruit etc.). **4.** to place crystal etc. in (a cloud) to produce rain. **5.** to name (a strong player) as not to be matched against another named in this way in the early rounds of a knock-out tournament, so as to increase the interest of later rounds; to arrange (the order of play) thus. —**go** *or* **run to seed,** to cease flowering as the seed develops; to become degenerate or unkempt etc. **seed-bed** *n.* a bed of fine soil in which to sow seeds; a place of development. **seed-pearl** *n.* a very small pearl. **seed-potato** *n.* a potato kept for seed. [OE (as SOW[1])]

seedling *n.* a young plant, especially one raised from seed and not from a cutting etc. [f. SEED + -LING]

seedsman *n.* (*pl.* **-men**) a dealer in seeds.

seedy *adj.* **1.** full of seed; going to seed. **2.** shabby-looking. **3.** (*colloq.*) unwell. —**seedily** *adv.*, **seediness** *n.* [f. SEED]

seeing *n.* use of the eyes. —*conj.* (also **seeing that**) considering that, inasmuch as, because. [f. SEE]

seek *v.t./i.* (*past & p.p.* **sought** /sɔ:t/) **1.** to make a search or inquiry (for); to try or want to find, obtain, or reach or do. **2.** (*archaic*) to aim at, to attempt. —**seek out,** to seek specially, to single out for companionship etc. [OE]

seem *v.i.* to have the air, appearance, or feeling of being; to give a certain impression as to an action or state. —**it seems,** it appears to be true or the fact. [f. ON, = honour]

seeming *adj.* apparent but perhaps not real. [f. SEEM]

seemly *adj.* conforming to accepted standards of good taste; proper; suitable. —**seemliness** *n.* [as SEEM]

seen *p.p.* of SEE[1].

seep *v.i.* to ooze slowly out of or through; to percolate slowly. [perh. dial. form of OE, = soak]

seepage *n.* seeping; the quantity that seeps out. [f. SEEP]

seer *n.* 1. one who sees. 2. a person who sees visions, a prophet. [f. SEE[1]]

seersucker /ˈsɪəsʌkə(r)/ *n.* a striped material of linen or cotton etc. woven with a puckered surface. [f. Pers., lit. = milk and sugar]

see-saw *n.* 1. a device for children, with a long plank balanced on a central support and a child sitting at each end moving up and down alternately; a game played on this. 2. an up-and-down or to-and-fro motion. 3. a contest in which the advantage repeatedly changes from one side to the other. —*v.i.* 1. to play on a see-saw; to move up and down as on a see-saw. 2. to vacillate in policy etc. —*adj. & adv.* with an up-and-down or backward-and-forward motion. [redupl. of SAW[1]]

seethe /siːð/ *v.i.* 1. to bubble or surge as in boiling. 2. to be very agitated (esp. with anger) or excited. [OE]

segment /ˈsɛgmənt/ *n.* a part cut off or separable or marked off as though separable from the other parts of a thing; part of a circle or sphere etc. cut off by a line or plane intersecting it (ill. SHAPES). —/also -ˈment/ *v.t./i.* to divide into segments. —**segmental** /-ˈment(ə)l/ *adj.*, **segmentation** /-ˈteɪʃ(ə)n/ *n.* [f. L *segmentum* (*secare* cut)]

Segovia /seˈɡəʊvɪə/, Andrés (1893–), Spanish guitarist and composer. More than any other person he is responsible for the revival of interest in the guitar as a 'classical' instrument, elevating it to use as a major concert instrument rather than for a small room only.

segregate /ˈsɛgrɪgeɪt/ *v.t./i.* to put or come apart from the rest, to isolate; to separate (esp. a racial group) from the rest of the community. —**segregation** /-ˈgeɪʃ(ə)n/ *n.* [f. L *segregare* (*se-* apart, *grex* flock)]

segregationist /sɛgrɪˈgeɪʃənɪst/ *n.* a person who is in favour of racial segregation. [f. prec.]

seigneur /seɪˈnjɜː(r)/ *n.* a feudal lord. —**seigneurial** *adj.* [f. OF f. L, = SENIOR]

Seine /seɪn/ a river of northern France flowing 761 km (473 miles) from Burgundy to the English Channel near Le Havre. The cities of Paris and Rouen lie along its course.

seine /seɪn/ *n.* a fishing-net for encircling fish, with floats at the top and weights at the bottom edge. —*v.t./i.* to fish or catch with a seine. [f. OF & OE, ult. f. Gk *sagēnē*]

seise see SEIZE 5.

seismic /ˈsaɪzmɪk/ *adj.* of earthquakes; of earth vibrations produced artificially by explosions. —**seismic survey,** a survey of an area that is being explored for oil and gas, employing seismic methods. —**seismically** *adv.* [f. Gk *seismos* earthquake (*seiō* shake)]

seismogram /ˈsaɪzməgræm/ *n.* the record given by a seismograph. [as prec. + -GRAM]

seismograph /ˈsaɪzməgrɑːf/ *n.* an instrument for detecting, recording, and measuring the force and direction etc. of earthquakes. The first such instrument was devised by the Italian scientist, Luigi Palmieri, in the 1850s. [as SEISMIC + -GRAPH]

seismography /saɪzˈmɒgrəfɪ/ *n.* the study or recording of natural or artificially produced seismic phenomena. —**seismographer** *n.*, **seismographic** /-məˈgræfɪk/ *adj.* [as SEISMIC + -GRAPHY]

seismology /saɪzˈmɒlədʒɪ/ *n.* seismography. —**seismological** /-ˈlɒdʒɪk(ə)l/ *adj.*, **seismologist** *n.* [as SEISMIC + -LOGY]

seize /siːz/ *v.t./i.* 1. to take hold of (a thing) forcibly, suddenly, or eagerly. 2. to take possession of forcibly or by legal power. 3. to affect suddenly. 4. to grasp with the mind quickly or clearly. 5. (*Law* also **seise** /siːz/) to put in possession of. 6. (*Naut.*) to fasten by binding with turns of yarn etc. **seize on** *or* **upon,** to seize eagerly. **seize up,** (of a mechanism) to become stuck or jammed from undue heat or friction. [f. OF]

seizure /ˈsiːʒə(r)/ *n.* 1. seizing, being seized. 2. a sudden attack of apoplexy etc., a stroke. [f. prec.]

sejant /ˈsiːdʒ(ə)nt/ *adj.* (in heraldry, of an animal) sitting upright on its haunches (ill. HERALDRY). [f. OF, = sitting f. L *sedēre* sit]

Sekhmet /ˈsɛkmɛt/ (*Egyptian myth.*) a ferocious lioness-goddess, counterpart of the gentle cat-goddess Bastet, and wife of Ptah at Memphis. Her messengers were fearful creatures who could inflict disease and other scourges upon mankind.

seldom /ˈsɛldəm/ *adv.* rarely, not often. [OE]

select /sɪˈlɛkt/ *v.t.* to pick out as the best or most suitable. —*adj.* 1. chosen for excellence or fitness. 2. (of a society etc.) exclusive, cautious in admitting members. —**select committee,** a small parliamentary committee appointed to conduct a special inquiry. [f. L *seligere* (*se-* apart, *legere* pick)]

selection /sɪˈlɛkʃ(ə)n/ *n.* 1. selecting, being selected. 2. the selected person(s) or thing(s). 3. a collection of things from which a choice may be made. 4. the process by which some animals or plants thrive more than others, as a factor in evolution. [f. L *selectio* (as prec.)]

selective *adj.* 1. chosen or choosing carefully. 2. able to select. —**selectively** *adv.*, **selectivity** /-ˈtɪvɪtɪ/ *n.* [f. SELECT]

selector *n.* 1. a person who selects; a member of a committee selecting a national sports team. 2. a device in machinery making the required selection of gear etc. [as prec.]

Selene /sɪˈliːnɪ/ (*Gk myth.*) the goddess of the moon, identified with Artemis, perhaps because both had been identified with Hecate. She has few myths (for the best known see ENDYMION) and little cult in Greece; it is the moon itself rather than the goddess that played a role in Greek magic, folklore, and poetry. [Gk, = moon]

selenium /sɪˈliːnɪəm/ *n.* a semi-metallic element, symbol Se, atomic number 34, chemically related to sulphur. It occurs in a number of red, black, and grey allotropic forms. Selenium (which is a semiconductor) has various applications in electronics. It is used in rectifiers and photoelectric cells, and for colouring glass and ceramics. [f. Gk *selēnē* moon]

Seleucid /sɪˈluːsɪd/ *adj.* of the dynasty founded by Seleucus Nicator, one of the generals of Alexander the Great, ruling over Syria and a great part of western Asia 312–65 BC. Its capital was at Antioch. —*n.* a member of this dynasty. [f. *Seleucus*]

self *n.* (*pl.* **selves** /sɛlvz/) 1. a person's or thing's own individuality or essence. 2. a person or thing as the object of introspection or reflexive action. 3. one's own interests or pleasure; concentration on these. 4. (in commerce, or *colloq.*) myself, yourself, herself, etc. —*adj.* of the same colour as the rest or throughout. [OE]

self- *prefix* expressing a reflexive action in the senses 'of or by oneself or itself', 'on, in, for, or relating to oneself or itself'. [f. prec.]

self-abnegation *n.* self-sacrifice.

self-abuse *n.* masturbation.

self-addressed *adj.* addressed to oneself.

self-appointed *adj.* appointed by himself or herself, especially in an officious or self-righteous way, and not necessarily recognized by others.

self-assertive /sɛlfəˈsɜːtɪv/ *adj.* asserting oneself, one's rights, etc., confidently. —**self-assertion** *n.*

self-assured /sɛlfəˈʃʊəd/ *adj.* self-confident. —**self-assurance** *n.*

self-catering *adj.* catering for oneself, providing one's own meals, especially while on holiday.

self-centred /sɛlfˈsɛntəd/ *adj.* preoccupied with oneself or one's own affairs.

self-confessed *adj.* openly confessing oneself to be.

self-confident *adj.* having confidence in one's own abilities. —**self-confidence** *n.*

self-conscious *adj.* embarrassed or unnatural in manner from knowing that one is observed by others. —**self-consciousness** *n.*

self-contained *adj.* 1. complete in itself; (of accommodation) having all the necessary facilities and not sharing these. 2. (of a person) independent, able to do without the company of others; not communicating freely.

self-control *n.* ability to control one's behaviour and not act emotionally. —**self-controlled** *adj.*

self-deception *n.* deceiving oneself, especially about one's feelings etc.

self-defeating *adj.* (of a course of action etc.) frustrating the purpose it was intended to serve.

self-defence *n.* defence of oneself or of one's rights or good reputation etc.

self-denial *n.* deliberately going without the pleasures etc. that one would like to have.

self-determination *n.* 1. determination of one's own

fate or course of action, free will. **2.** a nation's determination of its own form of government or its allegiance.

self-discipline *n.* discipline and training of oneself.

self-drive *adj.* (of a hired vehicle) driven by the hirer.

self-educated *adj.* educated by oneself, with little or no help from schools etc.

self-effacing *adj.* keeping oneself in the background. —**self-effacement** *n.*

self-employed *adj.* working independently and not for an employer.

self-esteem *n.* good opinion of oneself.

self-evident *adj.* evident without proof, explanation, or further evidence.

self-explanatory *adj.* that needs no (further) explanation.

self-fertilizing *adj.* (of a plant) fertilizing itself by its own pollen, not from others. —**self-fertilization** *n.*

self-fulfilment *n.* fulfilment of one's own hopes and ambitions etc.

self-governing *adj.* governing itself. —**self-government** *n.*

self-help *n.* use of one's own abilities or resources to achieve success, without dependence on others.

self-important *adj.* having a high opinion of one's own importance, pompous. —**self-importance** *n.*

self-imposed *adj.* (of a task etc.) imposed by oneself on oneself.

self-induced *adj.* induced by oneself or itself.

self-indulgent *adj.* greatly indulging one's own desires for comfort and pleasure. —**self-indulgence** *n.*

self-inflicted *adj.* inflicted by oneself on oneself.

self-interest *n.* one's personal interest or advantage. —**self-interested** *adj.*

selfish *adj.* acting or done according to one's own interests and needs without regard for those of others; keeping good things for oneself and not sharing. —**selfishly** *adv.*, **selfishness** *n.* [f. SELF]

selfless *adj.* disregarding oneself or one's own interests, unselfish. —**selflessly** *adv.*, **selflessness** *n.* [f. SELF + -LESS]

self-loading *adj.* (of a firearm) reloading itself after firing, automatic.

self-locking *adj.* locking automatically when closed.

self-made *adj.* having risen from poverty or obscurity and achieved success by one's own efforts.

self-opinionated *adj.* stubbornly adhering to one's own opinions.

self-pity *n.* pity for oneself.

self-portrait *n.* a portrait of himself by an artist; an account of himself by a writer.

self-possessed *adj.* feeling or remaining calm and dignified, especially in difficulty. —**self-possession** *n.*

self-preservation *n.* protection of oneself from death, harm, or injury etc.; the instinct to ensure one's own survival.

self-propelled *adj.* propelled by itself or its own motor etc., not drawn or pushed. —**self-propulsion** *n.*

self-raising *adj.* (of flour) containing a raising agent and for use without additional baking-powder.

self-recording *adj.* (of a scientific instrument) recording measurements or changes etc. automatically.

self-regard *n.* regard for oneself.

self-reliant *adj.* reliant on or confident in one's own abilities and resources. —**self-reliance** *n.*

self-reproach *n.* reproach or blame directed by oneself at oneself.

self-respect *n.* respect for oneself, the feeling that one is behaving with honour, dignity, etc. —**self-respecting** *adj.*

self-restrained *adj.* able to restrain one's own emotions. —**self-restraint** *n.*

self-righteous *adj.* conceitedly aware of or asserting one's own righteousness. —**self-righteously** *adv.*

self-sacrifice *n.* sacrifice of one's own interests and wishes so that others may benefit. —**self-sacrificing** *adj.*

selfsame *adj.* the very same, identical.

self-satisfied *adj.* pleased or unduly satisfied with oneself or one's own achievements, conceited. —**self-satisfaction** *n.*

self-sealing *adj.* sealing automatically; (of a tyre etc.) having the means of automatically sealing small punctures.

self-seeking *adj.* & *n.* seeking to promote one's own interests rather than those of others.

self-service *n.* (often *attrib.*) the system in a shop or restaurant etc. by which customers serve themselves and pay for what they have taken.

self-sown *adj.* grown from seed that has dropped naturally from the plant.

self-starter *n.* an electric device for starting an internal-combustion engine.

self-styled *adj.* using a title or name etc. that one has given oneself, especially without authorization or right.

self-sufficient *adj.* able to supply one's own needs without outside help. —**self-sufficiency** *n.*

self-supporting *adj.* that supports oneself or itself without help; self-sufficient.

self-taught *adj.* having taught oneself without formal help from a teacher etc.

self-willed *adj.* obstinately determined to follow one's own wishes, intentions, etc.; stubborn. —**self-will** *n.*

self-winding *adj.* (of a watch or clock) having a mechanism that winds it automatically.

Seljuk /ˈseltʃʊk/ *n.* a member of the Turkish dynasty which ruled Asia Minor in the 11th–13th c., successfully invading the Byzantine Empire and defending the Holy Land against the Crusaders. —*adj.* of the Seljuks. [f. Turk. name of reputed ancestor]

Selkirk /ˈselkɜːk/, Alexander (1676–1721), Scottish sailor. While on a privateering expedition, Selkirk quarrelled with his captain and was put ashore, at his own request, on one of the uninhabited Juan Fernandez islands in the South Pacific, where he remained from 1704 to 1709 before being rescued. His experiences later formed the basis of Defoe's novel *Robinson Crusoe.*

sell *v.t./i.* (*past & p.p.* **sold** /səʊld/) **1.** to make over or dispose of in exchange for money. **2.** to keep a stock of (goods) for sale. **3.** (of goods) to find purchasers; to have a specified price. **4.** to betray or offer dishonourably for money or other reward. **5.** to promote sales of; to inspire with a desire to buy, acquire, or agree to. —*n.* (*colloq.*) **1.** the manner of selling. **2.** a deception, a disappointment. —**be sold on,** to be enthusiastic about. **selling-point** *n.* an advantage recommending a thing. **sell off,** to sell the remainder of (goods) at reduced prices. **sell out,** to sell (all one's stock, shares, etc., or *absol.*); to betray; to be treacherous or disloyal to. **sell-out** *n.* the selling of all tickets for a show etc., a commercial success; a betrayal. **sell short,** to disparage; to underestimate. **sell up,** to sell one's business, house, etc. [OE]

sellable *adj.* that may be sold, able to find purchasers. [f. SELL]

seller *n.* one who sells. —**seller's market,** a situation in which a commodity is scarce and therefore expensive. [f. SELL]

Sellotape /ˈseləʊteɪp/ *n.* [P] an adhesive usually transparent cellulose or plastic tape. Such tape was developed in the USA (where it was called Scotch tape) in 1928. —**sellotape** *v.t.* to fix or seal with tape of this kind. [f. CELL(ULOSE) + TAPE]

selvage /ˈselvɪdʒ/ *n.* **1.** an edge of cloth so woven that it does not unravel. **2.** a tape-like border along the edge of cloth, intended to be removed or hidden. [f. SELF + EDGE]

selves *pl.* of SELF.

semantic /sɪˈmæntɪk/ *adj.* of meaning in language; of connotation. —**semantically** *adv.* [f. F f. Gk (*sēmainō* signify)]

semantics *n.pl.* (usu. treated as *sing.*) **1.** the branch of philology concerned with meaning. **2.** meaning, connotation. **3.** interpretation of symbols (e.g. road signs) other than words. [f. prec.]

semaphore /ˈseməfɔː(r)/ *n.* **1.** a system of signalling by holding the arms or two flags in certain positions to indicate letters of the alphabet (ill. ALPHABETS). **2.** a signalling apparatus consisting of a post with movable arm(s) etc. used on railways etc. —*v.t./i.* to signal or send by semaphore. [f. F f. Gk *sēma* sign, *pherō* bear]

semblance /ˈsembləns/ *n.* **1.** an outward appearance (either real or pretended), a show. **2.** a resemblance or likeness. [f. OF f. L (as SIMULATE)]

Semele /ˈsemɪlɪ/ (*Gk myth.*) the mother, by Zeus, of Dionysus. She entreated Zeus to come to her in his full majesty and the fire of his thunderbolts killed her but made her child immortal.

semen /'si:men/ n. the whitish reproductive fluid produced by male animals, containing spermatozoa. [L, = seed]

semester /sɪ'mestə(r)/ n. a half-year course or term in (esp. German and US) universities. [G f. L *semestris* six-monthly (*sex* six, *mensis* month)]

semi /'semɪ/ n. (*colloq.*) a semi-detached house. [abbr.]

semi- *prefix* 1. half, partly. 2. occurring or appearing twice in a specified period (*semi-annual*). [F or L, = half (corresp. to Gk HEMI-)]

semibreve /'semɪbri:v/ n. (*Mus.*) the longest note in common use (ill. MUSICAL NOTATION).

semicircle /'semɪsɜ:k(ə)l/ n. half of a circle or of its circumference (ill. SHAPES).

semicircular /semɪ'sɜ:kjulə(r)/ adj. arranged in or shaped like a semicircle. —**semicircular canal**, each of three fluid-filled channels in the ear giving information to the brain to help to maintain balance (ill. BODY 4).

semicolon /semɪ'kəulən/ n. a punctuation mark (;) used where there is a more distinct break than that indicated by a comma but less than that indicated by a full stop.

semiconductor /semɪkən'dʌktə(r)/ n. a substance that has an electrical conductivity intermediate between insulators and metals. Modern electronics now relies principally upon devices made of semiconductors such as silicon and germanium, and increasing miniaturization of such devices has been achieved. The significance of semiconductors lies not only in their overall degree of conductivity but also in the fact that, in comparison with metals, their conductivity is liable to be much more sensitive to factors such as heat, light, applied voltage, and traces of impurities. This sensitivity means that the performance of transistors and other semiconductor devices can be very precisely controlled—control which is a prerequisite of creating electronic circuits that are able to process complicated information, as in a computer. Semiconductors are seldom used in the pure state but are normally mixed with traces of special impurities which increase conductivity and also help to determine its character. —**semiconducting** adj.

semi-detached adj. (of a house) joined to another on one side only.

semifinal /semɪ'faɪn(ə)l/ n. the match or round preceding the final. —**semifinalist** n.

seminal /'semɪn(ə)l/ adj. 1. of seed or semen; of reproduction. 2. (of ideas etc.) providing a basis for future development. —**seminal fluid**, semen. [f. OF or L (as SEMEN)]

seminar /'semɪnɑ:(r)/ n. 1. a small class at a university etc. for discussion and research. 2. a short intensive course of study. [G (as foll.)]

seminary /'semɪnərɪ/ n. a training-college for priests or rabbis etc. —**seminarist** n. [f. L, = seed-plot (*semen* seed)]

semiology /si:mɪ'ɒlədʒɪ/ n. the branch of linguistics concerned with signs and symbols. —**semiotic** adj. [f. Gk *sēmeion* sign (*sēma* mark) + -LOGY]

semi-permeable adj. (of a membrane etc.) allowing small molecules to pass through but not large ones; permeable to molecules of water but not to those of any dissolved substance.

semiprecious /semɪ'preʃəs/ adj. (of a gem) less valuable than the stones called precious.

semiquaver /'semɪkweɪvə(r)/ n. (*Mus.*) a note equal to half a quaver (ill. MUSICAL NOTATION).

Semiramis /sɪ'mɪrəmɪs/ (*Gk legend*) the daughter of a Syrian goddess. Exposed at birth, she was tended by doves until found by shepherds. Her second husband was Ninus, king of Assyria, after whose death she ruled for many years, renowned in war and (allegedly) as a builder of Babylon; at death she was changed into a dove. The historical figure behind this legend is almost certainly Sammuramat, wife of the Assyrian king Shamshi-Adad V, and herself regent 810-805 BC during the minority of her son.

semi-rigid adj. (of an airship) having a flexible gas-container to which is attached a stiffened keel or framework.

semi-skilled adj. (of work or a worker) having or needing some training but less than for a skilled worker.

Semite /'si:maɪt/ n. a member of any of the races supposedly descended from Shem, son of Noah (Gen. 10: 21 ff.), including the Jews, Phoenicians, Arabs, and Assyrians. —adj. of the Semites. [f. L f. Gk *Sēm* Shem]

Semitic /sɪ'mɪtɪk/ adj. 1. of the family of languages that includes Hebrew, Arabic, and Aramaic, and certain ancient languages such as Phoenician, Assyrian, and Babylonian.

They are closely related both in structure and in vocabulary. Almost all Semitic words are derived from verbs consisting of three consonants. 2. of Semites; of the Jews. [f. prec.]

semitone /'semɪtəun/ n. half a tone in the musical scale.

semi-trailer /semɪ'treɪlə(r)/ n. a trailer having wheels at the back and supported at the front by a towing vehicle.

semitropical /semɪ'trɒpɪk(ə)l/ adj. subtropical.

semivowel /'semɪvauəl/ n. a sound intermediate between a vowel and a consonant (e.g. *w*, *y*); a letter representing this.

Semmelweiss /'semǝlvaɪs/, Ignaz Philipp (1818-65), Austro-Hungarian obstetrician who discovered the infectious septic character of puerperal fever, a major cause of maternal mortality. He demonstrated that the infection was transmitted by the hands of doctors who examined patients after carrying out work in the dissecting room, and advocated rigorous cleanliness and the use of antiseptics. His results were spectacular, but though the younger medical men accepted his discoveries the weight of authority was against him; Virchow and others rejected his views, and his involvement in the 1848 revolution hindered his career. Disheartened and depressed by the years of opposition, he died in a mental hospital.

semolina /semə'li:nə/ n. the hard grains left after the milling of flour, used in milk puddings etc.; a pudding made of this. [f. It. *semolino* (*semola* bran)]

sempstress var. of SEAMSTRESS.

SEN abbr. State Enrolled Nurse.

sen. abbr. 1. Senator. 2. Senior.

senate /'senət/ n. 1. the State council of the ancient Roman republic and empire, composed (after the early period) of ex-magistrates and having a variety of administrative, legislative, and judicial functions. 2. the upper and smaller branch of the legislative assembly in the USA (see CONGRESS), France, States of the USA, etc. 3. the governing (academic) body of certain universities or (*US*) colleges. [f. OF f. L *senatus* (*senex* old man)]

senator /'senətə(r)/ n. a member of a senate. —**senatorial** /-'tɔ:rɪəl/ adj. [as prec.]

send v.t./i. (*past & p.p.* sent) 1. to order, cause, or enable to go to a certain destination; to have (a thing) conveyed. 2. to send a message or letter. 3. (of God, Providence, etc.) to grant, bestow, or inflict. 4. to cause to move or go. 5. to cause to become. 6. (*slang*) to affect emotionally, to put into ecstasy. —**send away for**, to order (goods etc.) by post from a dealer. **send down**, to rusticate or expel from a university; to put in prison. **send for**, to order (a person) to come to one's presence; to order (a thing) to be brought or delivered from elsewhere. **send off**, to dispatch (a letter etc.); to attend the departure of (a person) as a sign of respect etc.; (of a referee) to order (a player) to leave the field and take no further part in the game. **send-off** n. a demonstration of goodwill etc. at the departure of a person, the start of a project, etc. **send on**, to transmit to a further destination or in advance of one's own arrival. **send up**, to cause to go up; to transmit to higher authority; (*colloq.*) to satirize, to ridicule by comic imitation. **send-up** n. (*colloq.*) a satire or parody. **send word**, to send information. —**sender** n. [OE]

Seneca /'senɪkə/, Lucius Annaeus (4 BC/AD 1–AD 65), Roman writer and statesman, tutor and later political adviser and minister to Nero, until he fell from favour in AD 62. He was forced to commit suicide on a charge of conspiracy. Most of his prose works, including ethical treatises, letters, and a work on natural philosophy, expound Stoic philosophical ideas in a brilliant style, full of point and wit. His nine tragedies, on themes from Greek mythology, display a penchant for rhetoric and melodramatic horror.

Senegal /senɪ'gɔ:l/ a country on the west coast of Africa, with the River Senegal as its northern boundary and the Gambia forming a narrow strip within its territory; pop. (est. 1980) 5,661,000; official language, French; capital, Dakar. Part of the Mali empire in the 14th and 15th c., the area was colonized by the French in the second half of the 19th c. Senegal became part of French West Africa in 1895, a member of the French community in 1958, and part of the Federation of Mali in 1959 before becoming an independent republic in 1960. The economy is largely based on groundnuts, although the capital, Dakar, is industrialized. —**Senegalese** /-'li:z/ adj. & n.

Senegambia /senɪ'gæmbɪə/ a confederation of Senegal and Gambia, formed in 1982, with certain joint institutions and the integration of defence and security, each country remaining a sovereign and independent State.

senescent /sɪˈnes(ə)nt/ adj. growing old. —**senescence** n. [f. L senescere (senex old)]

seneschal /ˈsenɪʃ(ə)l/ n. the steward of a medieval great house. [f. OF f. L seniscalus]

senile /ˈsiːnaɪl/ adj. of or characteristic of old age; having the symptoms and weaknesses of old age. —**senility** /sɪˈnɪlɪtɪ/ n. [f. F or L senilis (as prec.)]

senior /ˈsiːnɪə(r)/ adj. 1. older or oldest in age; (placed after a name) older than another of the same name. 2. higher in rank or authority. 3. for older children. —n. 1. a senior person; one's senior in age or rank etc. 2. a member of a senior school. —**senior citizen**, an elderly person, especially an old-age pensioner. **senior nursing officer**, a person in charge of nurses in a hospital. **senior school**, a school for older children (especially those over 11). **senior service**, the Royal Navy. [L, compar. of senex old]

seniority /siːnɪˈɒrɪtɪ/ n. the state of being senior. [f. prec.]

senna /ˈsenə/ n. cassia; a laxative prepared from this. [f. f. Arab.]

Sennacherib /sɪˈnækərɪb/ king of Assyria 704–681 BC, who rebuilt the city of Nineveh, making it his capital. He was obliged to devote much of his reign to suppressing revolts in various parts of his empire, including Babylon which he sacked in 689 BC. In 701 BC he put down a Jewish rebellion, exacting tribute from Hezekiah and laying siege to Jerusalem but sparing it from destruction, according to 2 Kings 19: 35, after an epidemic of illness amongst his forces.

señor /senˈjɔː(r)/ n. (pl. **señores** /-rez/) a title used of or to a Spanish-speaking man. [Sp. f. L, = SENIOR]

señora /senˈjɔːrə/ n. a title used of or to a Spanish-speaking married woman. [fem., as prec.]

señorita /senjɔˈriːtə/ n. a title used of or to a Spanish-speaking unmarried woman. [as prec.]

sensation /senˈseɪʃ(ə)n/ n. 1. an awareness or feeling produced by stimulation of a sense-organ or of the mind, emotions, etc. 2. ability to feel such stimulation. 3. a condition of eager interest, excitement, or admiration aroused in a community or group of people; a person or thing arousing this. [f. L sensatio f. sensus sense]

sensational adj. 1. arousing eager interest, excitement, or admiration in a community or group of people. 2. (colloq.) extraordinary. —**sensationally** adv. [f. prec.]

sensationalism n. 1. pursuit of the sensational; use of subject-matter, words, or style etc. in order to produce excessive emotional excitement in people. 2. the theory that ideas are derived solely from sensation (opp. RATIONAL-ISM) —**sensationalist** n. [f. prec.]

sense n. 1. any of the special powers (usually reckoned as sight, hearing, smell, taste, touch) by which a living thing becomes aware of external objects and of changes in the condition of its own body. 2. ability to perceive, feel, or be conscious of a thing; awareness or recognition of something. 3. practical wisdom or judgement; conformity to this; common sense. 4. the meaning of a word etc.; possession of a meaning or of reasonableness. 5. the prevailing opinion. 6. (in pl.) a person's sanity or normal state of mind. —v.t. 1. to perceive by one or more of the senses. 2. to become aware of by receiving a mental impression; to realize. 3. (of a machine etc.) to detect. —**come to one's senses**, to regain consciousness; to be sensible after acting foolishly. **in a** or **one sense**, if the statement is understood in a particular way. **make sense**, to be intelligible or practicable. **make sense of**, to show or find the meaning of. **sense-datum** n. whatever is the immediate object of any of the senses, usually (but not always) with the implication that it is not a material object. **sense-organ** n. a bodily organ conveying external stimuli to the sensory system. [f. L sensus (sentire feel)]

senseless adj. 1. unconscious. 2. not showing good sense, wildly foolish; without meaning or purpose. —**senselessness** n. [f. prec. + -LESS]

sensibility /sensɪˈbɪlɪtɪ/ n. 1. the capacity to feel physically or emotionally. 2. exceptional or excessive sensitiveness; delicacy of feeling, susceptibility. 3. (in pl.) a tendency to feel offended etc. [f. L (as foll.)]

sensible /ˈsensɪb(ə)l/ adj. 1. having or showing good sense. 2. aware. 3. perceptible by the senses; great enough to be perceived. 4. (of clothing etc.) practical and functional rather than fashionable. —**sensibly** adv. [f. OF or L sensibilis (as SENSE)]

sensitive /ˈsensɪtɪv/ adj. 1. affected by stimuli or mental

impressions; receiving impressions quickly and easily. 2. alert and considerate about the feelings of others. 3. easily hurt or offended. 4. (of an instrument etc.) readily responsive to or recording slight changes; (of photographic materials etc.) prepared so as to respond to the action of light. 5. (of a topic) requiring tactful treatment so as to avoid embarrassment, ensure security, etc. —**sensitive plant**, a mimosa (Mimosa pudica) or other plant that droops or closes when touched; a sensitive person. —**sensitively** adv. [f. OF or L (as SENSE)]

sensitivity /sensɪˈtɪvɪtɪ/ n. the quality or degree of being sensitive. [f. prec.]

sensitize /ˈsensɪtaɪz/ v.t. to make sensitive. —**sensitization** /-ˈzeɪʃ(ə)n/ n. [f. SENSITIVE]

sensor /ˈsensə(r)/ n. a device to detect, record, or measure a physical property. [f. foll.]

sensory /ˈsensərɪ/ adj. of sensation or the senses; receiving or transmitting sensation. [f. L sensorium seat of feeling (as SENSE)]

sensual /ˈsensjʊəl/ adj. 1. physical, gratifying to the body. 2. indulging oneself with physical pleasures; showing that one does this. —**sensualism** n., **sensuality** /-ˈælɪtɪ/ n., **sensually** adv. [f. L (as SENSE)]

sensuous /ˈsensjʊəs/ adj. of, affecting, or appealing to the senses, esp. aesthetically. —**sensuously** adv. [as SENSE]

sent past & p.p. of SEND.

sentence /ˈsentəns/ n. 1. a set of words (or occasionally one word) that is complete in itself as an expression of thought, containing or implying a subject and a predicate and expressing a statement, question, exclamation, or command. 2. the decision of a lawcourt, especially the punishment allotted to a person convicted in a criminal trial; the declaration of this. —v.t. to pass sentence upon (a convicted person); to condemn to a specified punishment. —**sentential** /-ˈtenʃ(ə)l/ adj. (in Gram. sense). [f. OF f. L sententia opinion]

sententious /senˈtenʃəs/ adj. affectedly or pompously formal or moralizing; aphoristic. —**sententiously** adv., **sententiousness** n. [f. L (as prec.)]

sentient /ˈsenʃənt/ adj. perceiving or capable of perceiving things by means of the senses. —**sentience** n., **sentiency** n. [f. L sentire feel]

sentiment /ˈsentɪmənt/ n. 1. a mental attitude produced by one's feeling about something; a verbal expression of this; an opinion. 2. emotion as opposed to reason; sentimentality. [f. OF f. L (as prec.)]

sentimental /sentɪˈment(ə)l/ adj. 1. of or characterized by romantic or nostalgic feeling. 2. showing or affected by emotion rather than reason. —**sentimental value**, the value of a thing to a particular person because of its associations. —**sentimentalism** n., **sentimentalist** n., **sentimentality** /-ˈtælɪtɪ/ n., **sentimentally** adv. [f. prec.]

sentimentalize /sentɪˈmentəlaɪz/ v.t. to show sentimentality. [f. prec.]

sentinel /ˈsentɪn(ə)l/ n. a look-out, a sentry. [f. F f. It.; orig. unkn.]

sentry /ˈsentrɪ/ n. a soldier etc. stationed to keep guard. —**sentry-box** n. a wooden cabin large enough to shelter a standing sentry. **sentry-go** n. the duty of pacing up and down as a sentry. [perh. f. obs. centrinel, var. of prec.]

Senussi /seˈnuːsɪ/ n. a Muslim religious fraternity founded in 1837 by Sidi Mohammad ibn Ali es-Senussi; a member of this fraternity. [name of founder]

Seoul /səʊl/ the capital of the Republic of Korea; pop. (1980) 8,367,000.

sepal /ˈsep(ə)l/ n. a division or leaf of the calyx (ill. FLOWERS). [f. F (coined 1790), perh. as SEPARATE + PETAL]

separable /ˈsepərəb(ə)l/ adj. that may be separated. —**separability** /-ˈbɪlɪtɪ/ n. **separably** adv. [f. F or L (as foll.)]

separate /ˈsepərət/ adj. not joined or united with others; forming a unit that is or may be regarded as apart or by itself, distinct, individual. —n. (in pl.) separate articles of dress suitable for wearing together in various combinations. —/-eɪt/ v.t./i. 1. to make separate, to divide, to keep apart; to prevent the union or contact of; to be between. 2. to become separate; to go different ways; to withdraw oneself from a union; to cease to live together as a married couple. 3. to divide into sorts or sizes etc.; to extract (an item or set of items etc.) thus. —**separately** adv. [f. L separare (se- apart, parare make ready)]

separation /sepəˈreɪʃ(ə)n/ n. 1. separating, being separate. 2. (in full **judicial** or **legal separation**) an arrangement by which a husband and wife remain married but live apart. [f. OF f. L (as prec.)]

separatism /ˈsepərətɪz(ə)m/ n. a policy of separation, especially for political or ecclesiastical independence. —**separatist** n. [f. SEPARATE]

separative /ˈsepərətɪv/ adj. tending to cause separation. [as prec.]

separator /ˈsepəreɪtə(r)/ n. a machine for separating things, e.g. cream from milk. [f. SEPARATE]

Sephardi /seˈfɑːdɪ/ n. (pl. -**im**) a Jew of Spanish or Portuguese descent (cf. ASHKENAZI). —**Sephardic** adj. [Heb., f. name of country (Sepharad) mentioned in Obad. 20 and held in late Jewish tradition to be Spain]

sepia /ˈsiːpɪə/ n. a dark reddish-brown colour or paint. [L f. Gk, = cuttlefish]

sepoy /ˈsiːpɔɪ/ n. (hist.) a native Indian soldier under British or other European discipline. [f. Urdu & Pers. sipāhī soldier]

sepsis /ˈsepsɪs/ n. a septic condition. [Gk as SEPTIC]

sept n. a clan, especially in Ireland. [prob. alt. of SECT]

Sept. abbr. September.

September /sepˈtembə(r)/ n. the ninth month of the year. [f. L (septem seven, because orig. the seventh month in the Roman calendar)]

septennial /sepˈtenɪəl/ adj. lasting or recurring every seven years. —**septennially** adv. [f. L septennium (septem seven, annus year)]

septet /sepˈtet/ n. 1. a musical composition for seven performers; these performers. 2. any group of seven. [f. G f. L septem seven]

septic /ˈseptɪk/ adj. infected with harmful micro-organisms that cause pus to form. —**septic tank,** a tank into which sewage is conveyed and in which it remains until the activity of bacteria makes it liquid enough to drain away. —**septically** adv. [f. L f. Gk sēptikos (sēpō make rotten)]

septicaemia /septɪˈsiːmɪə/ n. blood-poisoning. —**septicaemic** adj. [as prec. + Gk haima blood]

Septimius Severus /sepˈtɪmɪəs sɪˈvɪərəs/, Lucius (145/6–211), Roman emperor 193–211. After an unsuccessful invasion of Britain he died at York. He was active in reforms of the imperial administration and of the army, which he recognized as the real basis of imperial power.

septuagenarian /septjʊədʒɪˈneərɪən/ adj. from 70 to 79 years old. —n. a septuagenarian person. [f. L (septuageni seventy each)]

Septuagesima /septjʊəˈdʒesɪmə/ n. the Sunday before Sexagesima. [L, = seventieth (day) (as foll.), with ref. to period of 70 days from Septuagesima to Saturday after Easter]

Septuagint /ˈseptjʊədʒɪnt/ n. a Greek version of the Old Testament, including the Apocrypha, made for the use of Jewish communities in Egypt whose native language was Greek. It derives its name from the tradition that it was the work of about 70 translators who were said to have worked in separate cells, each translating the whole, and whose versions were found to be identical, thereby showing the work to be divinely inspired. Internal evidence shows that the work was divided between a number of translators and spread over the 3rd–2nd c. BC. The early Christian Church, whose language was Greek, used the Septuagint as its Bible, and it is still the standard version of the Old Testament in the Greek Church. [f. L septuaginta seventy]

septum /ˈseptəm/ n. (pl. **septa**) a partition such as that between the nostrils or the chambers of a poppy-fruit or a shell. [f. L (saepire fence off)]

septuple /ˈseptjʊp(ə)l/ adj. sevenfold; having seven parts; being seven times as many or as much. —n. a sevenfold number or amount. [f. L septuplus (septem seven)]

sepulchral /sɪˈpʌlkr(ə)l/ adj. 1. of a sepulchre or interment. 2. gloomy, funereal. [f. F or L (as foll.)]

sepulchre /ˈsepəlkə(r)/ n. a tomb, especially one cut in rock or built of stone or brick. —v.t. to place in a sepulchre; to serve as a sepulchre for. [f. OF f. L sepulc(h)rum (sepelire bury)]

sepulture /ˈsepəltʃə(r)/ n. burying, placing in a grave. [f. OF f. L sepultura (as prec.)]

sequel /ˈsiːkw(ə)l/ n. 1. what follows or arises out of an earlier event. 2. a novel or film etc. that continues the story of an earlier one. [f. OF or L sequela (sequi follow)]

sequence /ˈsiːkwəns/ n. 1. a succession; the order of succession. 2. a set of things belonging next to one another, an unbroken series. 3. a section of a cinema film, dealing with one scene or topic [f. L sequentia (as prec.)]

sequential /sɪˈkwenʃ(ə)l/ adj. forming a sequence or consequence. —**sequentially** adv. [f. prec.]

sequester /sɪˈkwestə(r)/ v.t. 1. to seclude, to isolate. 2. to sequestrate. [f. OF or L sequestrare (sequester person with whom a contested thing is deposited)]

sequestrate /sɪˈkwestreɪt, ˈsiː-/ v.t. to confiscate; to take temporary possession of (a debtor's estate etc.). —**sequestration** /siːkweˈstreɪʃ(ə)n/ n., **sequestrator** n. [f. L (as prec.)]

sequin /ˈsiːkwɪn/ n. a circular spangle on a dress etc. —**sequinned** adj. [F f. It. zecchino gold coin]

sequoia /sɪˈkwɔɪə/ n. a Californian coniferous tree of the genus Sequoia, growing to a great height. [f. Sequoiah, name of a Cherokee]

serac /seˈræk/ n. each of the castellated masses into which a glacier is divided at steep points by the crossing of crevasses. [f. Swiss F sérac, originally the name of a compact white cheese]

seraglio /seˈrɑːlɪəʊ/ n. (pl. -**os**) 1. a harem. 2. (hist.) a Turkish palace. [f. It. f. Turk. f. Pers. sarāy palace]

seraph /ˈserəf/ n. (pl. **seraphim** or **seraphs**) an angelic being of the highest order of the celestial hierarchy. —**seraphic** /səˈræfɪk/ adj., **seraphically** adv. [back-formation f. seraphim (ult. f. Heb.)]

Serapis /səˈreɪpɪs/ (Egyptian myth.) a god whose cult arose at Memphis in the temple where the deceased Apis bulls were entombed. Ptolemy I sought to make this an imperial cult, a combination of the Apis with Osiris, to unite Greeks and Egyptians in a common worship.

Serb n. a Serbian. —adj. Serbian. [f. Serbo-Croatian Srb]

Serbia /ˈsɜːbɪə/ a constituent republic of Yugoslavia, formed from a former Balkan kingdom with its capital at Belgrade. It was conquered by the Turks in the 14th c., but with the decline of Ottoman power in the 19th c., the Serbs successfully pressed for independence, finally winning nationhood in 1878. Subsequent Serbian ambitions to found a South Slav nation State brought the country into rivalry with the Austro-Hungarian empire and eventually contributed to the outbreak of the First World War. Despite early successes against the Austrians, Serbia was occupied by the Central Powers and never regained its pre-war identity, being absorbed into the new State of Yugoslavia after the end of hostilities. —**Serbian** adj. & n.

Serbo-Croat /sɜːbəʊˈkrəʊæt/ n. the language of the Serbs and Croats, generally considered to be one language (the differences between Serbian and Croatian are cultural rather than linguistic). Serbian is spoken by 10 million Serbs in Yugoslavia who belong to the Eastern Orthodox religion and so use the Cyrillic alphabet; Croat is spoken by the 5 million Croats who live in the same country and are Roman Catholic and use the Roman alphabet. Both belong to the Slavonic group of languages. —adj. of Serbo-Croat. —**Serbo-Croatian** adj. & n. [f. SERB + CROAT]

serenade /serəˈneɪd/ n. 1. a piece of music sung or played by a lover to his lady, or suitable for this. 2. an orchestral suite for a small ensemble. —v.t. to sing or play a serenade to. [f. F or It. serenata (as SERENE)]

serendipity /serənˈdɪpɪtɪ/ n. the faculty of making happy discoveries by accident. —**serendipitous** adj. [coined by Horace Walpole (1754) f. The Three Princes of Serendip (Sri Lanka), a fairy-tale]

serene /sɪˈriːn/ adj. 1. (of the sky, air, etc.) clear and calm; (of the sea) unruffled. 2. tranquil, calm and unperturbed. —**His, Her, Your Serene Highness,** titles used of or to members of some European royal families. —**serenely** adv., **serenity** /-ˈrenɪtɪ/ n. [f. L serenus]

serf n. 1. a labourer who could not be removed (except by manumission) from his lord's land on which he worked, and was transferred with it when it passed to another owner. Though free, he was restricted in his movements and in the disposal of his property, and was inferior in status to a free tenant. Serfdom in England lasted until the 14th or 15th c., but was not abolished in eastern Europe until the 19th c. 2. an oppressed labourer, a drudge. —**serfdom** n. [OF f. L servus slave]

serge n. a durable twilled worsted etc. fabric used for making clothes. [OF f. L serica (lana) (as SILK)]

sergeant /ˈsɑːdʒ(ə)nt/ n. 1. a non-commissioned Army or RAF officer next below warrant officer. 2. a police officer below inspector. —(**regimental**) **sergeant-major** n. a warrant officer assisting the adjutant of a regiment or battalion. [f. OF f. L serviens servant (as SERVE)]

Sergius /ˈsɜːdʒɪəs/, St (1314–92), Russian monastic reformer and mystic, who founded the monastery of the Holy Trinity near Moscow, and thereby re-established monasticism, which had been lost in Russia through the Tartar invasion. His influence was great: he stopped four civil wars between Russian princes, and inspired the resistance which saved Russia from the Tartars in 1380. Altogether, Sergius founded forty monasteries. He is regarded as the greatest of Russian Saints. Feast day, 25 Sept.

serial /ˈsɪərɪəl/ n. a story published or broadcast etc. in regular instalments. —adj. **1.** of, in or forming a series. **2.** (of a story etc.) in the form of a serial. **3.** (of music) using serial composition (see separate entry). —**serial number,** a number identifying an item in a series. —**serialism** n., **serially** adv. [f. SERIES]

serial composition a technique used in composing music whereby the twelve notes of the chromatic scale are arranged in a fixed order and form the basic core of a piece, generating melodies and harmonies and, strictly speaking, subject to change only in specific ways, such as by inversion or retrograde motion. Serialism was designed to combat the potential anarchy of atonality, which overthrew the traditional harmonic thinking associated with scale and key, and the first fully serial movements appeared in 1923 in works by Schoenberg. For some composers, notably Boulez and Stockhausen, serialism remains an important concept, but in general composers have looked elsewhere for means of musical integration.

serialize /ˈsɪərɪəlaɪz/ v.t. to publish or produce in instalments. —**serialization** /-ˈzeɪʃ(ə)n/ n. [f. SERIAL]

series /ˈsɪəriːz, -ɪz/ n. (pl. same) **1.** a number of things of the same kind, or related to each other in a similar way, occurring, arranged, or produced in order. **2.** a set of geological strata with a common characteristic. **3.** a set of stamps or coins etc. issued at one time or in one reign. **4.** an arrangement of the twelve notes of the chromatic scale as the basis for serial composition (see entry). —**in series,** in an ordered succession; (of a set of electrical circuits) arranged so that the same current passes through each circuit. [L, = row, chain (serere join)]

serif /ˈserɪf/ n. a slight projection finishing off the stroke of a printed letter (as in T, contrasted with sanserif T). [perh. f. Du. schreef line]

serio-comic /sɪərɪəʊˈkɒmɪk/ adj. combining the serious and the comic. —**serio-comically** adv. [f. foll. + COMIC]

serious /ˈsɪərɪəs/ adj. **1.** solemn and thoughtful, not smiling. **2.** sincere, in earnest, not casual or lighthearted. **3.** important, demanding thought. **4.** causing great concern, not slight. —**seriously** adv., **seriousness** n. [f. OF or L seriosus]

serjeant /ˈsɑːdʒ(ə)nt/ n. (also **serjeant-at-law**) (hist.) a barrister of the highest rank. —**serjeant-at-arms** n. an official of a court, city, or parliament, with ceremonial duties; an officer of each House of Parliament with the duty of enforcing the commands of the house, arresting offenders, etc. [var. of SERGEANT]

sermon /ˈsɜːmən/ n. **1.** a spoken or written discourse on religion or morals etc., especially one delivered by a clergyman during a religious service. **2.** a long moralizing talk. [f. AF f. L sermo discourse]

sermonize v.t./i. to deliver a moral lecture (to). [f. prec.]

serous /ˈsɪərəs/ adj. **1.** of or like serum, watery. **2.** (of a gland etc.) having a serous secretion. —**serosity** /-ˈrɒsɪtɪ/ n. [f. F or L (as SERUM)]

serpent /ˈsɜːpənt/ n. **1.** a snake, especially of a large kind. **2.** a sly or treacherous person. **3.** an old type of wind instrument, about 20 cm (8 inches) long and roughly S-shaped (whence its name), made of wood or sometimes of metal and giving a powerful deep note. First introduced towards the end of the 16th c. in France, where it was used in church, it became a popular military-band instrument and was used in English church bands until the mid-19th c. [f. OF f. L serpens (serpere creep)]

serpentine /ˈsɜːpəntaɪn/ adj. of or like a serpent, twisting and turning; cunning, treacherous. —n. a soft usually dark green rock, sometimes mottled. [as prec.]

serrated /seˈreɪtɪd/ adj. with a toothed edge like a saw. —**serration** n. [f. L serrare (serra saw)]

serried /ˈserɪd/ adj. (of ranks of soldiers) close together. [f. serry press close f. F serrer to close]

serum /ˈsɪərəm/ n. (pl. **sera** or **serums**) **1.** the thin amber-coloured fluid that remains from blood when the rest has clotted; this taken from an immunized animal and used for

inoculation. **2.** any watery fluid from animal tissue (e.g. in a blister). [L, = whey]

servant /ˈsɜːv(ə)nt/ n. **1.** a person employed to do domestic work in a household or as a personal attendant. **2.** an employee considered as performing services for his employer. **3.** a devoted follower, a person willing to serve another. [f. OF (as foll.)]

serve v.t./i. **1.** to perform services for; to be a servant to; to work for. **2.** to be employed or performing a spell of duty; to be a member of the armed forces. **3.** to be useful to or serviceable for; to do what is required; to provide a facility for. **4.** to go through a due period of (office, apprenticeship, a prison sentence, etc.). **5.** to set out or present (food) for those about to eat it; to act as a waiter; to attend to (a customer in a shop). **6.** (of a quantity of food) to be enough for. **7.** to treat or act towards (a person) in a specified way. **8.** to assist (the officiating priest) in a religious service. **9.** to make legal delivery of (a writ etc.). **10.** (in tennis etc.) to set the ball in play. **11.** (of an animal) to copulate with (a female). —n. a service in tennis etc.; a person's turn for this. —**serve a person right,** to be his deserved punishment or misfortune. **serve up,** to offer for acceptance. —**server** n. [f. OF servir f. L (servus slave)]

servery /ˈsɜːvərɪ/ n. **1.** a room from which meals are served and in which utensils are kept. **2.** a serving-hatch. [f. prec.]

Servian[1] /ˈsɜːvɪən/ adj. & n. former var. of SERBIAN.

Servian[2] /ˈsɜːvɪən/ adj. of Servius Tullius, the semi-legendary sixth king of ancient Rome (6th c. BC). —**Servian Wall,** the wall said to have been built by him round Rome. [f. Servius]

service /ˈsɜːvɪs/ n. **1.** the doing of work for another or for a community etc.; the work done; assistance or benefit given to someone; readiness to perform this. **2.** a provision or system of supplying some public need, e.g. transport or (in pl.) a supply of water, gas, electricity, etc. being a servant; employment or position as a servant. **3.** employment in a public organization or Crown department; such an organization or department; a branch of the armed forces; (attrib.) of the kind issued to the armed forces. **5.** a ceremony of worship; a form of liturgy for this. **6.** maintenance and repair of a vehicle, machine, appliance, etc., at intervals. **7.** assistance or advice given to customers after the sale of goods. **8.** the serving of food etc.; an extra charge nominally made for this. **9.** a set of dishes, plates, etc., required for serving a meal. **10.** the act or manner of serving in tennis etc.; a game in which one serves. —v.t. **1.** to maintain or repair (machinery etc.). **2.** to provide with service(s), to repair (a car or machine etc.). —**at a person's service,** ready to serve him. **in service,** employed as a servant; in use. **of service,** useful, helpful. **on active service,** serving in the armed forces in wartime. **see service,** to have experience of serving, especially in the armed forces; (of a thing) to be much used. **service area,** an area beside a major road for the supply of petrol, refreshments, etc.; an area served by a broadcasting station. **service-box** n. the marked area of a squash court within which a validly served ball must land (ill. SPORTS). **service charge,** an additional charge for service. **service-court** n. (in tennis etc.) the marked area within which a validly served ball must fall. **service flat,** a flat in which domestic service and sometimes meals are provided by the management. **service industry,** one providing services not goods. **service line,** (in tennis) the line bounding a service-court (ill. SPORTS). **service road,** a road serving houses lying back from a main road. **service station,** a place beside a road selling petrol and oil etc. to motorists. [f. OF or L servitium (as SERVE)]

serviceable adj. useful or usable, able to render service; durable, suited for use rather than ornament. —**serviceability** /-ˈbɪlɪtɪ/ n., **serviceably** adv. [f. prec.]

serviceman n. (pl. **-men**) **1.** a man in the armed forces. **2.** a man providing service or maintenance.

servicewoman n. (pl. **-women**) a woman in the armed forces.

serviette /sɜːvɪˈet/ n. a table-napkin. [f. OF (as SERVE)]

servile /ˈsɜːvaɪl/ adj. **1.** of or like a slave; suitable for a servant, menial. **2.** excessively submissive, lacking independence. —**servilely** adv., **servility** /-ˈvɪlɪtɪ/ n. [f. L servilis (as SERVE)]

serving n. a quantity of food for one person. —**serving-hatch** n. an aperture through which food is served. [f. SERVE]

servitor /ˈsɜːvɪtə(r)/ n. (archaic) a servant, an attendant. [f. OF or L (as SERVE)]

servitude /'sɜːvɪtjuːd/ *n.* slavery, subjection. [f. OF f. L (as SERVE)]

servo /'sɜːvəʊ/ *n.* (*pl.* **-os**) a servo-motor or -mechanism. [abbr.]

servo- /sɜːvəʊ-/ *in comb.* a means of powered automatic control of a larger system (*servo-assisted*, *-mechanism*, *-motor*). [f. F f. L *servus* slave]

sesame /'sesəmɪ/ *n.* an annual East Indian plant (*Sesamum indicum*) with oil-yielding seeds; its seeds. **—open sesame**, a magic formula used in an Arabian-Nights tale to cause a door to open; a magical or mysterious means of access to what is usually inaccessible. [f. L f. Gk, of Oriental origin]

Sesotho /se'suːtuː/ *n.* a Bantu language spoken by members of the Sotho people, one of the official languages of Lesotho. [Bantu, = language of the Sotho]

sesqui- /'seskwɪ/ *prefix* denoting one and a half (*sesquicentenary*). [L]

sessile /'sesaɪl/ *adj.* **1.** (of a flower or leaf or an eye etc.) attached directly by the base without a stalk or peduncle. **2.** fixed in one position, immobile. [f. L *sessilis* (*sedēre* sit)]

session /'seʃ(ə)n/ *n.* **1.** an assembly for deliberative or judicial business; a single meeting for such a purpose; a period during which such meetings are regularly held. **2.** an academic year; (*US*) a university term. **3.** a period devoted to an activity. **—in session**, assembled for business, not on vacation. **—sessional** *adj.* [f. OF or L *sessio* (as prec.)]

sestet /ses'tet/ *n.* **1.** the set of six lines ending a sonnet. **2.** a sextet. [f. It. (*sesto* f. L *sextus* sixth)]

set[1] *v.t./i.* (**-tt-**; *past & p.p.* **set**) **1.** to put or place; to cause to stand in position. **2.** to put in contact with, to apply (one thing) to another. **3.** to fix ready or in position; to adjust the hands of (a clock or watch); to adjust (an alarm-clock) to sound at the required time; to adjust the mechanism of (a trap etc.); to lay (a table) for a meal. **4.** to fix, decide, or appoint. **5.** to arrange and protect (a broken bone, limb, etc.) into the right relative position so that it will heal after fracture or dislocation; to arrange (the hair) while damp so that it will dry in the required style; to insert (a jewel) in a ring, framework, etc.; to decorate or provide (a surface etc.) with jewels, ornaments, etc. **6.** to put into a specified state, to cause to be or to do or begin doing. **7.** to represent (a story etc.) as happening at a certain time or place. **8.** to present or assign as work to be done. **9.** to exhibit as a type or model; to initiate (a fashion etc.); to establish (a record). **10.** to make or become hard, firm, or established. **11.** to provide a tune for (words). **12.** to arrange (type) or type for (a book etc.). **13.** to cause (a hen) to sit on eggs; to place (eggs) for a hen to sit on. **14.** (of the sun, moon, etc.) to be brought towards or below the horizon by the earth's movement. **15.** (of a tide or current etc.) to have a specified motion or direction. **16.** (in certain dances) to face another dancer and make certain steps. **17.** (*vulgar* or *dial.*) to sit. **—set about**, to begin (a task); to attack with blows or words. **set back**, to place further back in space or time; to impede the progress of; to cause a change for the worse; to cost (a person) a specified sum. **set-back** *n.* impeding of progress; a change for the worse. **set foot in** or **on**, to enter or arrive at (a place etc.). **set forth**, to set out. **set in**, to begin and become established. **set off**, to begin a journey; to cause to begin; to ignite (a firework etc.) or cause to explode; to serve as an adornment or foil to, to enhance; to use as a compensating item. **set on** or **upon**, to attack violently; to cause or urge to attack. **set out**, to begin a journey; to have a specified aim or intention; to arrange or exhibit; to declare, to make known. **set sail**, to hoist sail; to begin a voyage. **set to**, to begin doing something vigorously, to begin fighting, arguing, or eating; to begin making (a loud sound); to cause; to supply adequately; to restore or enhance the health of; to establish (a record). **set-up** *n.* an arrangement or organization; the structure of this. **set up house**, to establish a household. [OE]

set[2] *n.* **1.** a number of things or persons that are grouped together as similar or forming a unit; a section of society whose members consort together or have similar interests etc. **2.** a collection of implements, vessels, etc., needed for a specified purpose. **3.** a radio or television receiver. **4.** (in tennis etc.) a group of games forming a unit or part of a match. **5.** the way something sets or is set, placed, or arranged; the process or style of setting hair. **6.** the scenery in use for a play or film; the stage where this is performed. **7.** (also **sett**) a badger's burrow; a granite paving-block; a slip, shoot, bulb, or tuber for planting. **—dead set**, a determined attack or initiative. **set theory**,

the branch of mathematics which deals with sets (i.e. things grouped together as forming a unit) without regard to the nature of their individual constituents. It was originated by Cantor (and, less explicitly, Dedekind) in the years 1873–1900 and now exists both as a sophisticated subject, closely related to mathematical logic, which is extensively studied for its sake, and as an excellent language in which other parts of mathematics may be easily and precisely expressed. [sense 1 f. OF *sette* f. L (as SECT); senses 2–3 f. SET[1]]

set[3] *adj.* **1.** prescribed or determined in advance; unchanging, unmoving; (of a phrase or speech etc.) having an invariable or predetermined wording, not extempore. **2.** prepared for action. **—set on** or **upon**, determined to get or achieve etc. **set piece**, a formal or elaborate arrangement especially in art or literature; fireworks arranged on scaffolding etc. **set square**, a draughtsman's right-angled triangular plate for drawing lines in a certain relation to each other, usually at 90°, 45°, or 30°. [p.p. of SET[1]]

Seth /seθ/ (*Egyptian myth.*) the personification of evil, who appears in the myth of Osiris as the wicked brother who murders Osiris and wounds Osiris's son Horus. He was probably the beneficent deity of the people of Upper Egypt before he became absorbed into the Osiris myth. Seth is represented with the head of a beast with a long pointed snout.

sett *n.* var. of SET[2] sense 7.

settee /se'tiː/ *n.* a long seat, with a back and usually arms, for more than one person. [perh. fanciful var. of SETTLE[2]]

setter *n.* a dog of a long-haired breed trained to stand rigid when it scents game. [f. SET[1]]

setting *n.* **1.** the position, place, or manner etc. in which something is set. **2.** music for the words of a song etc. **3.** a set of cutlery or crockery for one person at table. [f. SET[1]]

settle[1] *v.t./i.* **1.** to place (a thing etc.) so that it stays in position. **2.** to establish or be established more or less permanently; to make one's home; to occupy as settlers. **3.** to sink or come to rest; to cause to do this; to become compact in this way. **4.** to make or become calm or orderly; to stop being restless. **5.** to arrange as desired; to end or arrange conclusively; to deal with; to pay (a debt etc., or *absol.*). **6.** to bestow by legal process. **7.** (in *p.p.*) not soon changing. **—settle down**, to become settled after disturbance or movement etc.; to adopt a regular or secure style of life; to apply oneself (to work etc.). **settle up**, to pay what is owing. **settle with**, to pay all or part of the amount due to (a creditor); to get revenge on. [OE (as foll.)]

settle[2] *n.* a wooden seat for two or more people, with a high back and arms and often with a box below the seat. [OE, = place to sit]

settlement *n.* **1.** settling, being settled. **2.** a place occupied by settlers. **3.** a political or financial etc. agreement; an arrangement ending a dispute; the terms on which property is settled on a person by legal process; a deed stating these; the amount of property given. **—Act of Settlement**, the statute of 1701 that established the Hanoverian succession to the British throne. It vested the Crown in Sophia of Hanover (granddaughter of James I of England) and her heirs; her son became George 1. [f. SETTLE[1]]

settler *n.* one who goes to live permanently in a previously unoccupied land, a colonist. [as prec.]

Seurat /sɜː'rɑː/, Georges (1859–91), French painter, the founder of Neo-impressionism. He became interested in scientific theories of colour vision and colour combination, and set himself to systematize the 'additive' method of juxtaposing colours to be combined through the seeing eye, a technique which had been to some extent anticipated by the impressionists and by Corot (see POINTILLISM). Among his major paintings was *Un Dimanche d'été à la Grande-Jatte*.

seven /'sev(ə)n/ *adj. & n.* **1.** one more than six; the symbol for this (7, vii, VII). **2.** the size etc. denoted by seven. **—seven deadly sins**, see DEADLY. **seven-league boots**, (in the fairy story of Hop-o'-my-Thumb) boots enabling the wearer to go seven leagues at each stride. **seven seas**, all the seas of the world; the Arctic, Antarctic, North and South Atlantic, North and South Pacific, and Indian Oceans. **Seven Sisters**, the Pleiades. [OE]

sevenfold *adj. & adv.* seven times as much or as many; consisting of seven parts. [f. prec. + -FOLD]

Seven Sages a traditional list (found in Plato) of seven wise Greeks of the 6th c. BC, to each of whom a moral saying is attributed. The seven are: Bias, Chilon, Cleobulus, Periander, Pittacus, Solon, Thales.

Seven Sleepers in early Christian legend, seven noble Christian youths of Ephesus who fell asleep in a cave while fleeing from the Decian persecution and awoke 187 years later. The legend was translated from the Syriac by Gregory of Tours (6th c.), and is also given by other authors; it occurs in the Koran.

seventeen /sevən'tiːn/ *adj. & n.* **1.** one more than sixteen; the symbol for this (17, xvii, XVII). **2.** the size etc. denoted by seventeen. —**seventeenth** *adj. & n.* [OE (as SEVEN, -TEEN)]

seventh *adj.* next after the sixth. —*n.* each of seven equal parts of a thing. —**Seventh-day Adventist,** a member of a sect of Adventists who originally expected the second coming of Christ in 1844 and still preach that his return is imminent. They are strict Protestants and are notable for observing Saturday as the Sabbath. **seventh heaven,** a state of intense joy; the highest of seven heavens in Muslim and some Jewish systems. —**seventhly** *adv.* [f. SEVEN]

seventy /'sevəntɪ/ *adj. & n.* **1.** seven times ten; the symbol for this (70, lxx, LXX). **2.** (in *pl.*) the numbers, years, or degrees of temperature from 70 to 79. —**seventieth** *adj. & n.* [OE (as SEVEN)]

Seven Wonders of the World the seven most spectacular man-made structures of the ancient world. The earliest extant list of these dates from the 2nd c.; traditionally they comprise (1) the pyramids of Egypt, especially those at Giza; (2) the Hanging Gardens of Babylon (see HANGING); (3) the Mausoleum of Halicarnassus; (4) the temple of Diana (Artemis) at Ephesus in Asia Minor, rebuilt in 356 BC, measuring 90 × 45 m (300 × 150 ft.) and with 127 columns; (5) the Colossus of Rhodes; (6) the huge ivory and gold statue of Zeus at Olympia in the Peloponnese, made by Phidias *c.*430 BC; (7) the Pharos of Alexandria (or in some lists, the walls of Babylon).

Seven Years War a war (1756–63) which ranged Britain, Prussia, and Hanover against Austria, France, Russia, Saxony, Sweden, and Spain. Its main issues were the struggle between Britain and France for supremacy overseas, and that between Prussia and Austria for the domination of Germany. After some early setbacks, the British made substantial gains over France abroad, capturing (under Wolfe) French Canada and (under Clive) undermining French influence in India. On the Continent, the war was most notable for the brilliant campaigns of Frederick the Great of Prussia against converging enemy armies. The war was ended by the Treaties of Paris and Hubertusburg in 1763, leaving Britain the supreme European naval and colonial power and Prussia in an appreciably stronger position than before in central Europe.

sever /'sevə(r)/ *v.t./i.* **1.** to divide, break, or make separate, especially by cutting. **2.** to terminate the employment contract of (a person). [f. AF f. L (as SEPARATE)]

several /'sevr(ə)l/ *adj. & pron.* **1.** a few, more than two but not many. **2.** separate, respective. —**severally** *adv.* [as prec.]

severance /'sevərəns/ *n.* severing, being severed; a severed state. —**severance pay,** the amount paid to an employee on the termination of his contract. [f. SEVER]

severe /sɪ'vɪə(r)/ *adj.* **1.** strict; without sympathy; imposing harsh treatment. **2.** intense, forceful. **3.** making great demands on endurance, energy, ability, etc. **4.** plain and without decoration. —**severely** *adv.*, **severity** /sɪ'verɪtɪ/ *n.* [f. F or L *severus*]

Severn /'sevɜːn/ the longest river of Britain, rising on Mount Plynlimon in eastern Wales and flowing about 300 km (220 miles) to the Bristol Channel.

Seville orange /'sevɪl/ a bitter orange used for marmalade. [f. *Seville* in Spain]

Sèvres /sevr/ *n.* porcelain made at Sèvres, south-west of Paris. The factory founded in 1738 in the Château de Vincennes, east of Paris, moved to Sèvres in 1756 and three years later was purchased by Louis XV to save it from closure; thereafter it became a subsidized royal venture, and its pieces display an opulence matching court life. In 1793 the French Republic took over the factory; it created a sophisticated style at the beginning of the 19th c., but the great designs faded and the factory took to producing copies of 18th-c. wares.

sew /saʊ/ *v.t./i.* (*p.p.* **sewn** or **sewed**) to fasten by passing thread again and again through material, using a threaded needle or an awl etc. or a sewing-machine; to make or attach by sewing; to use a needle and thread or a sewing-machine thus. —**sew up,** to join or enclose by sewing; (*colloq.*, esp. in *p.p.*) to arrange or finish dealing with (a project etc.). [OE]

sewage /'sjuːɪdʒ, 'suː-/ *n.* liquid waste matter drained away from houses, towns, factories, etc., for disposal. —**sewage farm,** a farm on which a town's sewage is treated and used for manure. **sewage works,** a place where sewage is purified so that it can safely be discharged into a river etc. [f. foll.]

sewer /'sjuːə(r), 'suː-/ *n.* a public drain for carrying away sewage and drainage water (see below). —*v.t.* to provide or drain with sewers. [f. AF, orig. = channel to carry off overflow from a fish-pond, ult. f. L *aqua* water (rel. to EWER)]

Sewers were known in the ancient world: the earliest that survives is at Mohenjodaro in the Indus valley (*c.*2500 BC) and there were elaborate domestic arrangements at the Palace of Minos in Crete (*c.*2000 BC). Many Roman cities had underground sewers, but after the decline of Roman power these were allowed to deteriorate. In medieval Europe there was no proper drainage system and the water-supply was inadequate and insanitary; disease was rife. When the Industrial Revolution swelled the numbers of people living in towns it became essential to devise a system of waste-disposal. The first underground sewers were constructed at Hamburg in Germany in 1843.

sewerage /'sjuːərɪdʒ, 'suː-/ *n.* a system of sewers; drainage by sewers. [f. prec.]

sewing-machine *n.* a machine for sewing or stitching things. The earliest patents for mechanical sewing were taken out in England by Charles Weisenthal in 1755 and Thomas Saint in 1790. The first chain-stitch machine was invented in 1829 by Barthélemy Thimonnier, a French tailor, but when (some years later) a number of these were put into operation to make French army uniforms they were smashed by rioting tailors alarmed at this threat to their livelihood. Independent efforts in the USA led to the design and patenting of machines producing a lock-stitch, and though the style and powering of modern machines varies the basic principle remains the same. The success of Isaac Singer (1811–75) was due not only to the worth of his machine but to the astuteness of his lawyer, who fought his patent-battles and pioneered selling by hire-purchase. Gandhi, who learned to use a sewing-machine while in prison, declared that it was one of the few useful things ever invented, and exempted it from his ban on the import of Western machinery.

sewn *p.p.* of SEW.

sex *n.* **1.** either of the two main divisions (male and female) into which living things are placed on the basis of their reproductive functions; the fact of belonging to one of these. **2.** sexual instincts, desires, etc., or their manifestation. **3.** (*colloq.*) sexual intercourse. —*adj.* of sex; arising from the difference or consciousness of sex. —*v.t.* **1.** to determine the sex of (a young animal etc.). **2.** (in *p.p.*) having sexual characteristics or instincts etc. —**sex appeal,** sexual attractiveness. **sex life,** a person's sexual activities. **sex-starved** *adj.* lacking sexual gratification. **sex symbol,** a person who is for many the epitome of sexual attraction and glamour. —**sexer** *n.* [f. OF or L *sexus*]

sexagenarian /seksədʒɪ'neərɪən/ *adj.* from 60 to 69 years old. —*n.* a sexagenarian person. [f. L (*sexageni* sixty each)]

Sexagesima /seksə'dʒesɪmə/ *n.* the Sunday before Quinquagesima. [L, = sixtieth (day), prob. named loosely as preceding Quinquagesima]

sexagesimal *adj.* of sixtieths or sixty; reckoning or reckoned by sixtieths. [f. L *sexagesimus* sixtieth]

sexism *n.* **1.** prejudice or discrimination against people (esp. women) because of their sex. **2.** the assumption that a person's abilities and social functions are predetermined because of his or her sex. —**sexist** *adj. & n.* [f. SEX]

sexless *adj.* **1.** lacking sex, neuter. **2.** not involving sexual feelings or attraction. —**sexlessly** *adv.* [f. SEX + -LESS]

sexology /sek'splədʒɪ/ *n.* the study of human sexual life or relationships. —**sexological** /-'lɒdʒɪk(ə)l/ *adj.*, **sexologist** *n.* [f. SEX + -LOGY]

sextant /'sekst(ə)nt/ *n.* an instrument with a graduated arc of 60° used in navigation and surveying for measuring the angular distance of objects by means of mirrors (ill. NAVIGATION). The instrument was first described by Robert Hooke in 1667 and was re-invented independently by John Hadley in England (1731) and Thomas Godfrey in America. [f. L *sextans* sixth part (*sexus* sixth), because early sextants all contained 60° i.e. one sixth of a circle]

sextet /sek'stet/ *n.* **1.** a musical composition for six performers; these performers. **2.** any group of six. [alt. of SESTET]

sexton /'sekst(ə)n/ n. a person who looks after a church and churchyard, often acting as bell-ringer and grave-digger. [f. AF f. L (as SACRISTAN)]

sextuple /'sekstjʊp(ə)l/ adj. sixfold, having six parts; being six times as many or as much. —n. a sixfold number or amount. [f. L sextuplus (sex six)]

sextuplet /'sekstju:plɪt/ n. each of six children born at one birth. [f. prec. after triplet etc.]

sexual /'seksjʊəl, 'sekʃ-/ adj. **1.** of sex or the sexes or the relationship or feelings etc. between them. **2.** (of reproduction) occurring by fusion of male and female gametes. —**sexual intercourse**, copulation (esp. of a man and a woman); insertion of the penis into the vagina, usually followed by the ejaculation of semen. —**sexuality** /-'ælɪti/ n. **sexually** adv. [f. L sexualis (as SEX)]

sexy adj. sexually attractive or stimulating. —**sexily** adv. **sexiness** n. [f. SEX]

Seychelles /seɪ'ʃelz/ a country in the Indian Ocean, a member State of the Commonwealth, consisting of a group of about 90 islands about 1,000 km (600 miles) NE of Madagascar; pop. (est. 1983) 64,410; official languages, English and French; capital, Victoria. The islands are said to have been named the 'Isles of Gold' by visiting Arab seafarers, perhaps in the 9th c. The Portuguese, who arrived there in the 16th c., called them the 'Seven Sisters', by which name they were known until the French annexed and settled them in the mid-18th c. They formed an excellent hide-out for pirates until these were hunted down by the British and French. The Seychelles were captured by Britain during the Napoleonic Wars and administered from Mauritius before becoming a separate colony in 1903 and finally an independent republic in 1976. Noted for their beauty, the islands attract a considerable tourist trade; the economy is also supported by exports of copra and cinnamon. —**Seychellois** /-ʃel'wɑ:/ adj. & n.

Seymour /'si:mɔ:(r)/, Jane (c.1509-37), third wife of Henry VIII, and mother of Edward VI. Jane Seymour finally provided the king with the male heir he wanted, and, although she died little over a year after her wedding, probably made the ageing king happier than any of his other wives. After her demise Henry donned mourning and ordered that she be buried beside him.

sez (slang) says.

SF abbr. science fiction.

sf abbr. sforzando.

sforzando /sfɔ:t'sændəʊ/ adj. & adv. (Mus.) with sudden emphasis. [It. (sforzare use force)]

sh int. hush.

shabby adj. **1.** worn and faded; not kept in good condition; (of a person) poorly dressed. **2.** contemptible, dishonourable. —**shabbily** adj., **shabbiness** n. [f. shab scab f. OE]

shack n. a roughly built hut or shed. —**shack up,** (slang) to cohabit. [perh. f. Mexican jacal wooden hut]

shackle n. **1.** a metal loop or link, closed by a bolt, to connect chains etc. **2.** a fetter enclosing an ankle or wrist. **3.** a restraint, an impediment. —v.t. **1.** to put shackles on. **2.** to impede, to restrict. [OE]

Shackleton /'ʃæk(ə)lt(ə)n/, Sir Ernest Henry (1874-1922), Irish-born polar explorer. A junior officer on Scott's first polar expedition of 1900-4, Shackleton commanded an expedition of his own in 1909, getting within 155 km (97 miles) of the South Pole (the farthest south anyone had reached at that time). On a second expedition to the Antarctic (1914-16) his ship the Endurance was crushed in the ice. Extracting his crew with great difficulty, Shackleton set out with five others from Elephant Island in an open boat on an epic 1300 km (800-mile) voyage to South Georgia to get help. On a final expedition to the Antarctic in 1920-2 he died on South Georgia.

shad n. (pl. **shads** or **shad**) a large edible fish of the genus Alosa. [f. OE]

shade n. **1.** comparative darkness (and usually coolness) caused by shelter from direct light and heat; a place or area sheltered from the sun. **2.** the darker part of a picture etc. **3.** a colour, especially with regard to its depth or as distinguished from one nearly like it. **4.** a slight amount or difference. **5.** a translucent cover for a lamp etc.; a screen excluding or moderating light; (US) a window-blind; (US, in pl.) sun-glasses. **6.** a ghost; (in pl.) reminders of some person or thing. —v.t./i. **1.** to screen from light. **2.** to cover, moderate, or exclude the light of. **3.** to darken (parts of a

drawing etc.), especially with parallel lines to represent shadow etc. **4.** to change or pass gradually into another colour or variety. —**in the shade,** in comparative obscurity. [OE]

shadoof /ʃæ'du:f/ n. a pole with a bucket at one end and a counterweight at the other, used for drawing water from a river etc., especially in Egypt. [f. Egyptian Arab.]

shadow /'ʃædəʊ/ n. **1.** shade; a patch of shade; a dark figure projected by a body intercepting rays of light. **2.** one's inseparable attendant or companion; a person secretly following another; **3.** a very slight trace. **4.** a weak or insubstantial thing, a remnant. **5.** the shaded part of a picture. **6.** gloom, sadness. —v.t. **1.** to cast a shadow over. **2.** to follow and watch secretly. —**shadow-boxing** n. boxing against an imaginary opponent as a form of training. **Shadow Cabinet, Chancellor,** etc., members of the opposition party serving as spokesmen for affairs for which Cabinet ministers have responsibility. —**shadower** n. [OE (as SHADE)]

shadow-show n. a form of puppetry in which flat jointed figures pass between a strong light and a translucent screen, while the audience, in front of the screen, sees only their shadows. It originated in the Far East, spread to Turkey and Greece, and as les Ombres Chinoises was popular in Paris for about 100 years. In the streets of London shadow-shows, known as the galanty show, were given until the end of the 19th c., usually in Punch and Judy booths. The shadow-show survives in its traditional form in Java and Bali.

shadowy adj. like a shadow; full of shadows; vague, indistinct. [f. SHADOW]

shady /'ʃeɪdɪ/ adj. **1.** giving shade. **2.** situated in the shade. **3.** disreputable, of doubtful honesty. —**shadily** adv., **shadiness** n. [f. SHADE]

shaft /ʃɑ:ft/ n. **1.** an arrow, spear, or similar device; its long slender stem. **2.** a remark intended to hurt or stimulate. **3.** a ray (of light); a bolt (of lightning). **4.** a stem or stalk; the central stem of a feather (ill. BIRDS); the stem or long handle of a tool, implement, etc.; a long narrow part supporting, connecting, or driving a part or parts of greater thickness etc.; a column, especially between the base and the capital (ill. CHURCH and TEMPLES). **5.** a long narrow vertical or sloping passage or opening giving access to a mine, or as an outlet for air or smoke; a vertical passage for movement of a lift etc. **6.** each of a pair of poles between which a horse is harnessed to a vehicle. **7.** (US slang) harsh or unjust treatment. —v.t. to treat harshly or unjustly. —**shaft grave,** a type of grave found in Late Bronze Age Greece and Crete in which the burial chamber is approached by a vertical shaft sometimes lined with stones and roofed over with beams, as seen in the more elaborate examples of the famous six at Mycenae. [f. OE]

Shaftesbury /'ʃɑ:ftsbəri/, Anthony Ashley Cooper, 7th Earl (1801-85), British philanthropist and social reformer. Shaftesbury was one of the dominating figures of the 19th-c. movement towards social reform, inspiring much of the legislation designed to improve the lot of the large working class created by Britain's Industrial Revolution.

shag n. **1.** a rough growth or mass of hair or fibre. **2.** a strong coarse kind of tobacco. **3.** a cormorant, especially the crested cormorant (Phalacrocorax aristotelis). [OE]

shaggy adj. **1.** having long rough hair or fibre. **2.** (of hair etc.) rough, thick, and untidy. —**shaggy-dog story,** a long inconsequential narrative or joke. —**shaggily** adv., **shagginess** n. [f. SHAG]

shagreen /ʃæ'gri:n/ n. a kind of untanned leather with a granulated surface; shark-skin (rough with natural papillae) used for rasping and polishing things. [var. of CHAGRIN sense 'rough skin']

shah /ʃɑ:/ n. the former ruler of Iran. [f. Pers., = king]

shake v.t./i. (past **shook** /ʃʊk/; p.p. **shaken**) **1.** to move violently or quickly up and down or to and fro; to tremble or vibrate, to cause to do this. **2.** to agitate or shock; (colloq.) to upset the composure of. **3.** to weaken or impair; to make less convincing or firm or courageous. **4.** (of a voice etc.) to make tremulous or rapidly alternating sounds, to trill. **5.** to make a threatening gesture with (one's fist, stick, etc.). **6.** (colloq.) to shake hands. —n. **1.** shaking, being shaken; a jerk or shock. **2.** a milk shake. **3.** (Mus.) a trill. **4.** (colloq.) a moment. —**the shakes,** a fit of trembling. **no great shakes,** (colloq.) not very good or significant. **shake down,** to settle or cause to fall by shaking; to settle down, to become established. **shake hands,** to clasp hands (with another person), especially when meeting or parting, in reconciliation or congratulation, or as a sign of a bargain. **shake one's head,** to move one's head from side to side in refusal, denial, disapproval, or concern. **shake off,** to get rid of (an unwanted thing, bad habit, illness, undesirable companion, worry, etc.). **shake out,** to empty by shaking; to spread or open (a sail, flag, etc.) by shaking. **shake up,** to mix (ingredients) by shaking; to restore to shape by shaking; to disturb or make uncomfortable; to rouse from lethargy, apathy, conventionality, etc. **shake-up** n. an upheaval, a reorganization. [OE]

shaker n. **1.** a person or thing that shakes. **2.** a container for shaking together the ingredients of cocktails etc. **3. Shaker,** a member of an American religious sect (named from their religious dances) with a simple life in celibate mixed communities. [f. SHAKE]

Shakespeare /ˈʃeɪkspɪə(r)/, William (1564–1616), English dramatist, born in Stratford-upon-Avon, the son of a merchant, and probably educated at the local grammar school. His wife Anne Hathaway (see entry) remained in Stratford while he pursued a successful career in London as actor, poet, and dramatist, initially under the patronage of the Earl of Southampton, to whom his *Sonnets* (1609) may have been dedicated. Little is known of his life but his plays, many of which were not printed in his lifetime, have subsequently made him the world's most famous dramatist. These include early comedies such as *Love's Labour's Lost*, which sparkle with verbal ingenuity; the more mature and complex comedies such as *Twelfth Night* and *As You Like It*; several highly theatrical historical plays, including *Henry IV Parts 1 and 2* which introduced perhaps his best-known comic character, Falstaff; the Roman plays, which include *Julius Caesar*; the so-called 'problem plays', enigmatic comedies which include *All's Well that Ends Well* and *Measure for Measure*; his great tragedies, *Hamlet*, *Othello*, *King Lear*, *Macbeth*, and *Antony and Cleopatra*; and the group of autumnal romantic tragicomedies with which he ended his career, his last work being *The Tempest*, in which, like Prospero, he bids his imagined world farewell. —**Shakespearian** /-ˈpɪərɪən/ adj.

shako /ˈʃækəʊ/ n. (pl. **-os**) a cylindrical peaked military hat with an upright plume or tuft. [f. F f. Magyar, = peaked (cap)]

shaky adj. **1.** unsteady, apt to shake, trembling. **2.** unsound, infirm; unreliable, wavering. —**shakily** adv., **shakiness** n. [f. SHAKE]

shale n. a soft rock that splits easily, resembling slate. —**shaly** adj. [prob. f. G, rel. to SCALE²]

shall /ʃ(ə)l/, emphat. ʃæl/ v. aux. (3 sing. **shall,** archaic 2 sing. (with *thou*) **shalt;** *past* SHOULD) expressing (1) (in the first person) a future action or state, (2) (in other persons) a strong assertion, promise, or command. —**shall I?** do you want me to? [OE]

shallot /ʃəˈlɒt/ n. an onion-like plant (*Allium ascalonicum*) with cloves like those of garlic. [f. F (as SCALLION)]

shallow /ˈʃæləʊ/ adj. **1.** of little depth. **2.** not thinking deeply; not thought out. **3.** not capable of deep feelings. —n. (often in *pl.*) a shallow place. —v.t./i. to make or become shallow. —**shallowly** adv., **shallowness** n. [rel. to SHOAL]

shalom /ʃəˈləʊm/ n. & int. a Jewish salutation at a meeting or parting. [f. Heb., = peace]

shalt see SHALL.

shalwar /ˈʃʌlvɑ(r)/ n. loose trousers worn by both sexes in some South Asian countries. [f. Pers.]

sham v.t./i. (**-mm-**) to pretend; to pretend to be. —n. a pretence; a thing or feeling that is not genuine; a person pretending to be something that he or she is not. —adj. pretended, not genuine. —**shammer** n. [perh. dial. var. of SHAME]

shaman /ˈʃæmən/ n. (in primitive religions) a person regarded as having direct access to, and influence in, the spiritual world which is usually manifested during a trance and empowers him or her to guide souls, cure illnesses, etc. The general pattern of beliefs, rituals, techniques, etc., associated with a shaman is found almost universally in primitive cultures at the food-gathering stage of development. —**shamanism** n. [f. G & Russ. f. Tungusian]

shamateur /ˈʃæmətə(r)/ n. a sports player classed as an amateur though often profiting like a professional. —**shamateurism** n. [f. SHAM + AMATEUR]

shamble v.i. to walk or run with a shuffling, awkward, or lazy gait. —n. a shambling gait. [perh. f. *shamble legs* with ref. to straddling trestles (as foll.)]

shambles /ˈʃæmb(ə)lz/ n. pl. (usu. treated as *sing.*) (*colloq.*) **1.** a butcher's slaughter-house. **2.** a scene or condition of

great bloodshed or disorder. [pl. of *shamble* stall, OE f. L *scamellum* dim. of *scamnum* bench]

shambolic /ʃæmˈbɒlɪk/ adj. (*colloq.*) chaotic, disorganized. [f. prec., after SYMBOLIC]

shame n. **1.** a feeling of distress or humiliation caused by consciousness of one's guilt or folly etc.; capacity for experiencing this feeling. **2.** a state of disgrace or discredit. **3.** a person or thing that brings disgrace etc.; a thing that is wrong or regrettable, a pity. —v.t. to bring shame on, to make ashamed; to put to shame; to force by shame. —**for shame!** a reproof to a person for not showing shame. —**put to shame,** to disgrace or humiliate by revealing superior qualities etc. [OE]

shamefaced adj. **1.** showing shame. **2.** bashful, shy.

shameful adj. causing shame, disgraceful. —**shamefully** adv. [f. SHAME + -FUL]

shameless adj. having or showing no feeling of shame; impudent. —**shamelessly** adv. [f. SHAME + -LESS]

shammy n. a chamois-leather. [corrupt pronunc. of CHAMOIS]

shampoo /ʃæmˈpuː/ n. **1.** a liquid or cream used to lather and wash the hair. **2.** a liquid or chemical for washing a car or carpet etc. **3.** the act or process of shampooing. —v.t. to wash with shampoo. [f. Hind. imper. of *chāmpnā* to press]

shamrock /ˈʃæmrɒk/ n. a trefoil (esp. *Trifolium minus*) used as the national emblem of Ireland. [f. Ir., dim. of *seamar* clover]

shandy /ˈʃændɪ/ n. beer mixed with lemonade or ginger-beer. [f. earlier *shandygaff* (orig. unkn.)]

Shang /ʃæŋ/ the name of a dynasty which ruled China during part of the 2nd millennium BC, probably 16th–11th c. BC. The discovery of inscriptions on bone oracles confirmed literary references to the existence of the Shang dynasty, which witnessed the invention of Chinese ideographic script and the discovery and development of bronze casting. [Chinese]

shanghai /ʃæŋˈhaɪ/ v.t. **1.** (*hist.*) to force (a person) aboard a ship to serve as a sailor, usually after stupefying him by drugs etc. **2.** to transfer forcibly; to abduct; to compel. [f. *Shanghai* seaport in China]

Shangri La /ʃæŋrɪ ˈlɑː/ a Tibetan utopia in James Hilton's novel *Lost Horizon* (1933); an earthly paradise, a place of retreat from the worries of modern civilization. [f. Tibetan *la* mountain pass]

shank n. **1.** the leg; the lower part of the leg; a shin-bone. **2.** a shaft or stem; the long narrow part of an implement etc. —**Shank's mare** or **pony,** one's own legs as a means of conveyance. [OE, rel. to MHG *schenkel* thigh]

Shannon /ˈʃænən/ the chief river of Ireland, flowing 390 km (240 miles) to its estuary on the Atlantic.

shan't /ʃɑːnt/ (*colloq.*) = shall not.

shantung /ʃænˈtʌŋ/ n. a soft undressed Chinese silk, usually undyed; fabric resembling this. [f. *Shantung*, Chinese province]

shanty¹ /ˈʃæntɪ/ n. a shack. —**shanty town,** a town consisting of shanties. [orig. N. Amer.; etym. unkn.]

shanty² /ˈʃæntɪ/ n. a song traditionally sung by sailors while hauling ropes etc. [prob. F *chantez*, imper. of *chanter* sing]

shape n. **1.** an external form or appearance, the total effect produced by a thing's outlines. **2.** a specific form or guise in which something appears. **3.** a kind, sort, or way. **4.** a definite or proper arrangement; condition, good condition. **5.** a person or thing as seen, especially as indistinctly seen or imagined. **6.** a mould or pattern; a jelly etc. shaped in a mould; a piece of material, paper, etc., made or cut in a particular form. —v.t./i. **1.** to give a certain shape or form to. **2.** to adapt or modify (one's ideas etc.); to frame mentally, to imagine. **3.** to assume or develop into a certain shape or condition; to give signs of future development. —**shape up,** to take a (specified form); to show promise; to make good progress. —**shaper** n. [OE, = creation]

shapeless adj. lacking proper shape or shapeliness. —**shapelessly** adv., **shapelessness** n. [f. SHAPE + -LESS]

shapely adj. well formed or proportioned; of an elegant or pleasing shape or appearance. —**shapeliness** n. [f. SHAPE]

shard n. var of SHERD. [OE, = crack]

share¹ n. **1.** a part given to an individual out of a larger amount which is being divided or of a commitment to or achievement; the part one is entitled to have or obliged to give or do. **2.** each of the equal parts forming a business company's capital and entitling the holder to a proportion of the profits. —v.t./i. **1.** to give portions of (a thing) to two

Shapes and Forms in Mathematics . . .

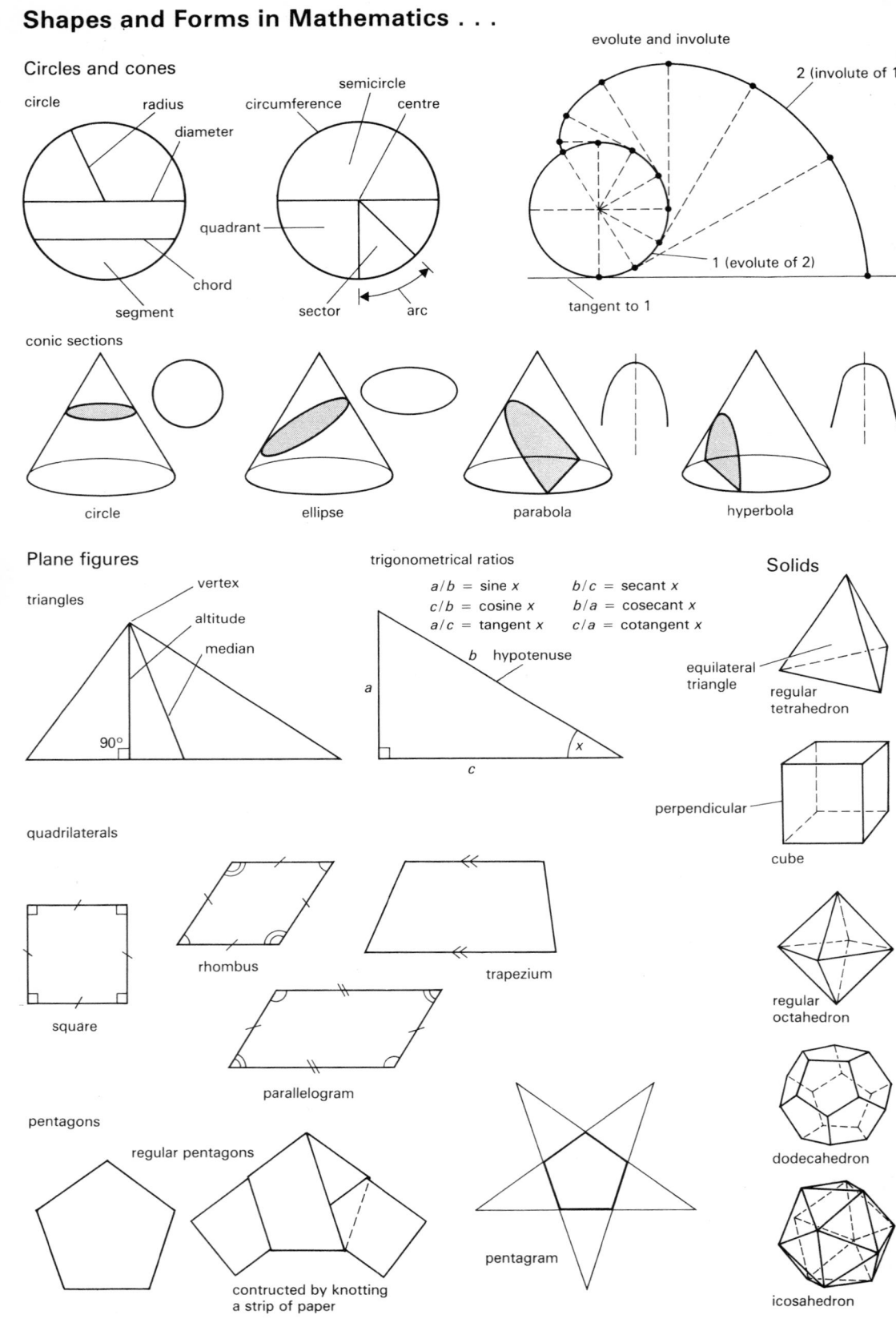

Circles and cones

evolute and involute

circle
radius
diameter
circumference
semicircle
centre
quadrant
chord
segment
sector
arc

2 (involute of 1)
1 (evolute of 2)
tangent to 1

conic sections

circle
ellipse
parabola
hyperbola

Plane figures

triangles

vertex
altitude
median
90°

trigonometrical ratios

a/b = sine x b/c = secant x
c/b = cosine x b/a = cosecant x
a/c = tangent x c/a = cotangent x

b hypotenuse
a
c
x

Solids

equilateral
triangle
regular
tetrahedron

perpendicular
cube

quadrilaterals

square
rhombus
trapezium
parallelogram

regular
octahedron

pentagons

regular pentagons
pentagram
contructed by knotting
a strip of paper

dodecahedron

icosahedron

. . . and in Everyday Life

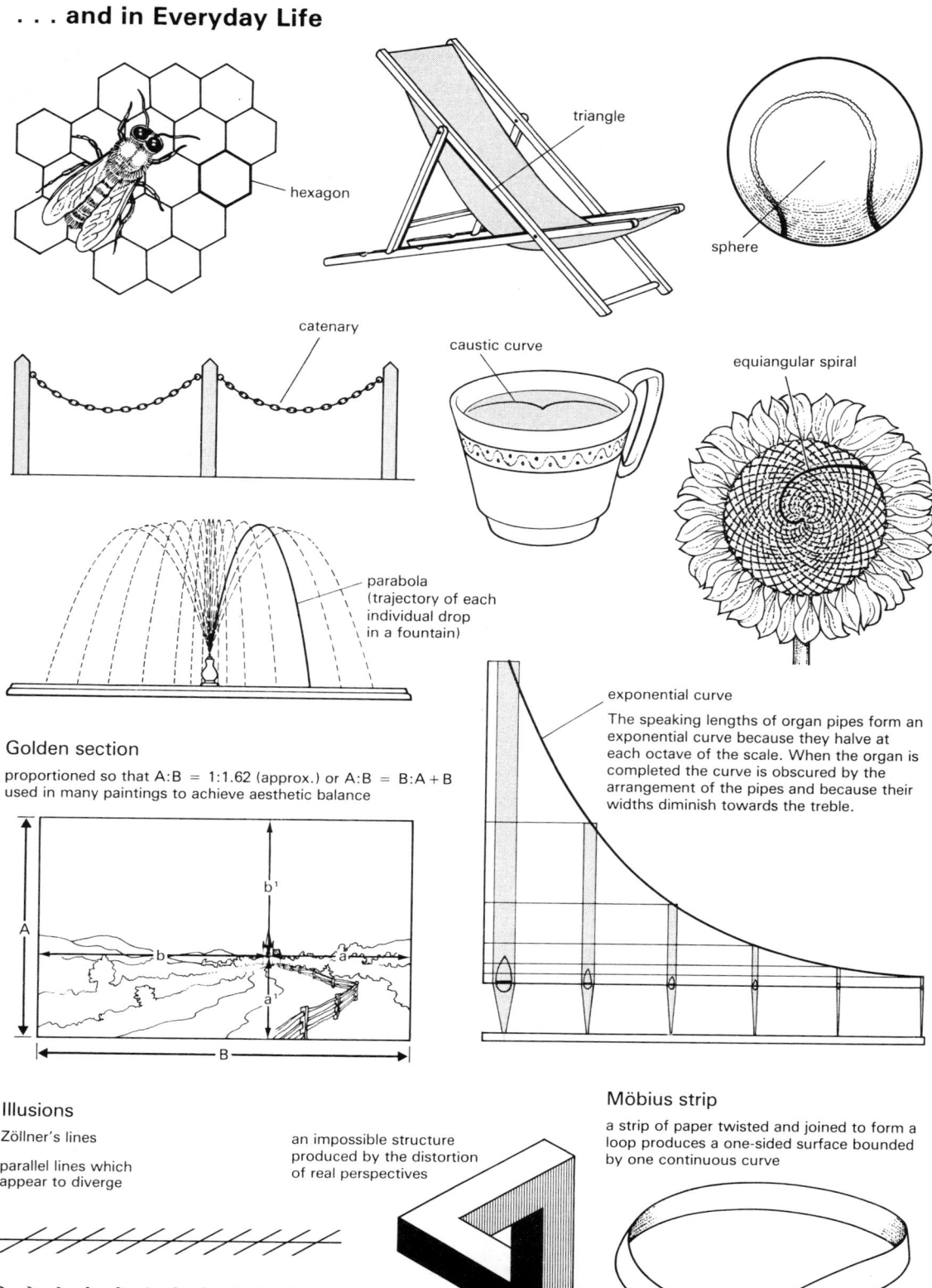

hexagon

triangle

sphere

catenary

caustic curve

equiangular spiral

parabola
(trajectory of each
individual drop
in a fountain)

exponential curve

The speaking lengths of organ pipes form an
exponential curve because they halve at
each octave of the scale. When the organ is
completed the curve is obscured by the
arrangement of the pipes and because their
widths diminish towards the treble.

Golden section

proportioned so that A:B = 1:1.62 (approx.) or A:B = B:A + B
used in many paintings to achieve aesthetic balance

Illusions

Zöllner's lines

parallel lines which
appear to diverge

an impossible structure
produced by the distortion
of real perspectives

Möbius strip

a strip of paper twisted and joined to form a
loop produces a one-sided surface bounded
by one continuous curve

or more people; to give away part of. **2.** to have a share of; to use, possess, endure, or benefit from (a thing) jointly with others. —**go shares**, to share. **share-cropper** *n.* a tenant farmer who pays part of his crop as rent to the owner. **share-cropping** *n.* this process. **share-out** *n.* a division and distribution, especially of profits or proceeds. —**sharer** *n.* [OE, rel. to SHEAR]

share² *n.* a ploughshare. [OE (as SHEAR)]

shareholder *n.* an owner of shares in a company.

shariah /ʃæˈriːə/ *n.* the sacred law of Islam, including the teachings of the Koran and the traditional sayings of Muhammad, prescribing religious and other duties. [f. Arab.]

shark *n.* **1.** a large voracious sea-fish of the order Selachii. **2.** a rapacious person; a swindler. [orig. unkn.]

sharkskin *n.* **1.** the skin of a shark. **2.** a wool, silk, or rayon fabric with a smooth slightly lustrous finish.

Sharp, Cecil (James) (1859-1924), English collector of folk-songs and folk-dances, whose enthusiasm inspired others to emulate him. He founded the English Folk Dance Society in 1911.

sharp *adj.* **1.** having an edge or point able to cut or pierce; tapering to a point or edge; abrupt, not gradual; steep, angular. **2.** well-defined, clean-cut, distinct. **3.** intense, forceful; loud and shrill; irritable, speaking harshly and angrily; (of tastes or smells) producing a smarting sensation. **4.** quick to see, hear, or notice things, intelligent. **5.** quick to take advantage; artful, unscrupulous, dishonest. **6.** vigorous, brisk. **7.** (*Mus.*, of a note) above the correct or normal pitch; a semitone higher than the corresponding note or key of natural pitch. —*adv.* **1.** punctually. **2.** suddenly. **3.** at a sharp angle. **4.** (*Mus.*) above the correct pitch. —*n.* **1.** (*Mus.*) a note that is a semitone higher than the corresponding one of natural pitch; the sign indicating this (ill. MUSICAL NOTATION). **2.** (*colloq.*) a swindler, a cheat. —**sharp end,** (*colloq.*) the bow of a ship; the place where decisions are made and correct action is taken. **sharp-eyed** *adj.* quick at noticing things. —**sharp practice,** dishonest or barely honest dealings. —**sharply** *adv.*, **sharpness** *n.* [OE]

sharpen *v.t./i.* to make or become sharp. —**sharpener** *n.* [f. prec.]

sharper *n.* a swindler, especially at cards. [f. SHARP]

sharpish *adj.* (*colloq.*) fairly sharp. —*adv.* (*colloq.*) fairly sharply, quite quickly. [f. SHARP]

sharpshooter *n.* a skilled marksman.

Shasta daisy /ˈʃæstə/ a kind of daisy (*Chrysanthemum × superbum*), a hybrid developed by Luther Burbank (d. 1926), with tall stems and large white flowers. [f. *Shasta* in California]

Shatt al-Arab a river of SE Iraq, formed by the confluence of the Tigris and Euphrates Rivers, flowing about 195 km (120 miles) SE to the Persian Gulf.

shatter *v.t./i.* **1.** to break or become broken violently into small pieces. **2.** to destroy utterly. **3.** to disturb or upset the calmness of. [rel. to SCATTER]

shave *v.t./i.* (*p.p.* **shaved** or (esp. as *adj.*) **shaven** /ˈʃeɪv(ə)n/) **1.** to cut (growing hair) from the chin etc. with a razor; to remove hair from the chin etc. (of). **2.** to cut thin slices from the surface of (wood etc.) to shape it. **3.** to graze gently in passing. **4.** to reduce or remove. —*n.* **1.** shaving, being shaved. **2.** (esp. **close shave**) a narrow miss or escape. **3.** a tool for shaving wood etc. [OE]

shaver *n.* **1.** a thing that shaves, especially an electric razor. **2.** (*colloq.*) a young lad. [f. SHAVE]

Shavian /ˈʃeɪvɪən/ *adj.* of or characteristic of the writer G. B. Shaw. —*n.* an admirer of Shaw. [f. *Shavius*, Latinized form of SHAW]

shaving *n.* (esp. in *pl.*) a thin strip shaved from the surface of wood etc. [f. SHAVE]

Shaw /ʃɔː/, George Bernard (1856-1950), Irish playwright who moved to London in 1876 and began his literary career as a critic and unsuccessful novelist. An active member of the Fabian Society, he was already well known as a socialist and public speaker when his first play was performed in 1892. After a slow start, Shaw was soon recognized as one of the wittiest, most provocative, and prolific writers of the age, whose intellectual comedies (e.g. *Man and Superman*, 1903; *Major Barbara*, 1907; *Pygmalion*, 1913; *Heartbreak House*, 1919) attacked conventional morality and thought with epigram, paradox, and a great fertility of theatrical invention. Shaw also wrote many prose works, including the lengthy Prefaces to his plays, and generously supported many progressive causes, including feminism. He was

awarded the Nobel Prize for literature in 1925. Abstemious, vegetarian, and indefatigable, he continued to work until the very end of his long life.

shawl *n.* a large piece of fabric, usually rectangular and often folded into a triangle, worn over the shoulders or head or wrapped round a baby. —*v.t.* (esp. in *p.p.*) to put a shawl on (a person). [f. Urdu f. Pers., prob. f. *Shaliat* in India]

shawm *n.* an obsolete musical instrument of the oboe type. [f. OF, ult. f. Gk *kalamos* reed]

she /ʃiː/ *pron.* (*obj.* HER; *poss.* HER, HERS; *pl.* THEY) the woman, girl, or female animal (or thing regarded as female, e.g. a ship) previously named or in question. —*n.* a female animal. —*adj.* (usu. with hyphen) female (*she-ass*). [OE]

sheaf *n.* (*pl.* **sheaves**) **1.** a bundle of stalks of corn etc. tied together after reaping. **2.** a bundle of arrows, papers, etc., laid lengthways together. —*v.t.* to make into sheaves. [OE (as SHOVE)]

shear *v.t./i.* (*past* **sheared**; *p.p.* **shorn** or **sheared**). **1.** to cut or trim with scissors, shears, etc.; to remove or take off by cutting; to clip wool off (a sheep etc.). **2.** to strip bare, to deprive. **3.** to break or distort by shear; to be broken or distorted by shear. —*n.* **1.** a type of distortion or fracture produced by pressure, in which each successive layer (e.g. of a mass of rock) slides over the next; transformation of a geometrical figure or solid in which one line or plane remains fixed and those parallel to it move sideways. **2.** (in *pl.*; also **pair of shears**) a clipping or cutting instrument working like scissors but much larger and usually operated with both hands. [OE]

sheath /ʃiːθ/ *n.* (*pl.* /ʃiːðz/) **1.** a covering into which a blade is thrust when not in use; a protective covering. **2.** a sheath-like covering in various animal and vegetable structures; the tubular fold of skin into which the penis of a horse, bull, dog, etc., is retracted. **3.** a condom. **4.** a woman's close-fitting dress. —**sheath-knife** *n.* a dagger-like knife carried in a sheath. [OE]

sheathe /ʃiːð/ *v.t.* to put into a sheath; to encase or protect with a sheath. [f. prec.]

sheave *v.t.* to make into sheaves. [f. SHEAF]

sheaves *pl.* of SHEAF.

Sheba /ˈʃiːbə/ the Biblical name of Saba, an ancient country in SW Arabia, famous for its trade in gold and spices. The Queen of Sheba visited King Solomon in Jerusalem. The Hebrew word is the name of the people (Sabaeans), but was erroneously assumed by Greek and Roman writers to be a place-name.

shebeen /ʃɪˈbiːn/ *n.* (*Ir.*) an unlicensed house selling alcoholic liquor. [f. Anglo-Ir. (*séibe* mugful)]

shed¹ *n.* a one-storied building for storing things or as a shelter for livestock etc., or for use as a workshop. [app. var. of SHADE]

shed² *v.t.* (**-dd-**; *past & p.p.* **shed**) **1.** to lose (a thing) by a natural falling off. **2.** to take off (clothes etc.). **3.** to reduce (an electrical power load) by disconnection etc. **4.** to allow to pour forth. **5.** to send forth, to diffuse, to radiate. —**shed light on,** to help to explain. [OE]

sheela-na-gig /ˈʃiːlənəgɪg/ *n.* a medieval carved stone female figure, sometimes found on churches or castles in Britain and Ireland, shown nude, in frontal aspect, and with the hands indicating the genitalia. [f. Ir., = Juno of the breasts]

sheen *n.* gloss, lustre. —**sheeny** *adj.* [f. obs. *sheen* beautiful f. OE; sense assim. to SHINE]

sheep *n.* (*pl.* **sheep**) **1.** a grass-eating animal of the genus *Ovis* with a thick woolly coat, esp. kept in flocks for its wool or meat. **2.** a bashful, timid, or silly person. **3.** (usu. in *pl.*) a member of a minister's congregation. —**separate the sheep from the goats,** to separate the good from the wicked (cf. Matt. 25: 33). **sheep-dip** *n.* a preparation for cleansing sheep of vermin etc.; a place where sheep are dipped in this. **sheep-dog** *n.* a dog trained to guard and herd sheep; a dog of a breed suitable for this. **sheep-fold** *n.* an enclosure for sheep. [OE]

sheepish *adj.* bashful; embarrassed through shame. —**sheepishly** *adv.*, **sheepishness** *n.* [f. per.]

sheepshank *n.* a knot used to shorten a rope temporarily.

sheepskin *n.* **1.** a garment or rug of sheep's skin with the wool on. **2.** leather of sheep's skin used in bookbinding etc.

sheer¹ *adj.* **1.** mere, pure, not mixed or qualified. **2.** (of a cliff or ascent etc.) with little or no slope, perpendicular. **3.** (of a textile) very thin, diaphanous. —*adv.* perpendicularly, directly. [prob. f. dial. *shire* clear, f. OE]

sheer[2] *v.i.* to swerve or change course. —**sheer off,** to go away, to leave a person or topic that one dislikes or fears. [perh. f. MLG, = SHEAR]

sheer-legs *n.* (also **sheers**) a hoisting-apparatus of two (or more) poles attached to or near the top and separated at the bottom, used for fitting masts to ships or putting in engines etc. [var. of SHEAR]

sheet[1] *n.* **1.** a large rectangular piece of cotton or other fabric, used esp. in pairs as inner bedclothes. **2.** a thin broad usually flat piece of material (e.g. paper or glass). **3.** a wide expanse of water, ice, flame, falling rain, etc. **4.** a newspaper. —*v.t./i.* **1.** to provide or cover with sheets. **2.** to form into sheets. **3.** (of rain etc.) to fall in sheets. —**sheet lightning,** lightning that looks like a sheet of light across the sky. **sheet metal,** metal formed into thin sheets by rolling, hammering, etc. **sheet music,** music published in separate sheets. [OE]

sheet[2] *n.* a rope or chain attached to the lower corner of a sail for securing or controlling it. —**sheet anchor,** a second anchor for use in emergencies; a person or thing depended on for security or stability. [OE (rel. to prec.)]

sheeting *n.* material for making sheets. [f. SHEET[1]]

sheikh /ʃeɪk, ʃiːk/ *n.* a chief, the head of an Arab tribe, family, or village; a Muslim leader. —**sheikhdom** *n.* [ult. f. Arab., = old man]

sheila /ˈʃiːlə/ *n.* (*Austral. & NZ slang*) a young woman, a girl. [orig. *shaler* (etym. unkn.)]

shekel /ˈʃek(ə)l/ *n.* **1.** the currency unit of Israel. **2.** an ancient Jewish etc. weight and silver coin. **3.** (in *pl.*, *colloq.*) money, riches. [f. Heb. (*shākal* weigh)]

sheldrake /ˈʃeldreɪk/ *n.* (*pl.* **shelduck**) a bright-plumaged wild duck of the genus *Tadorna*. [prob. f. dial. *sheld* pied + DRAKE]

shelduck *n.* **1.** a female sheldrake. **2.** (as *pl.*) see prec. [as prec. + DUCK]

shelf *n.* (*pl.* **shelves**) **1.** a horizontal board or slab etc. projecting from a wall or forming one tier of a bookcase or cupboard. **2.** something resembling this; a ledge, a horizontal steplike projection in a cliff face etc.; a reef or sandbank. —**on the shelf,** (esp. of a person) no longer active or of use; (of a woman) past the age when she might expect to get married. **shelf-life** *n.* the time for which a stored thing remains usable. **shelf-mark** *n.* a mark on a book to show its place in a library. [f. MLG, rel. to OE *scylfe* partition, *scylf* crag]

shell *n.* **1.** the hard outer covering of a nut-kernel, egg, seed, or fruit, or of an animal such as a crab, snail, or tortoise. **2.** a structure that forms a firm framework or covering. **3.** the walls or framework of an unfinished or gutted building or ship etc. **4.** an explosive projectile for firing from a large gun etc.; the hollow case containing explosives for a cartridge, firework, etc. **5.** a light rowing-boat for racing. **6.** a group of electrons in an atom, with almost equal energy. —*v.t.* **1.** to take out of a shell, to remove the shell or pod from. **2.** to fire shells at. —**come out of one's shell,** to become more communicative and less shy. **shell-keep** *n.* a form of Norman keep built on a mound (usually the site of an earlier fortress; ill. CASTLES). **shell out,** (*slang*) to pay out (money). **shell-shock** *n.* a nervous breakdown resulting from prolonged exposure to battle conditions. —**shell-less** *adj.*, **shelly** *adj.* [OE]

shellac /ʃəˈlæk/ *n.* a resinous substance used for making varnish etc. —*v.t.* (**-ck-**) to varnish with shellac. [f. SHELL + LAC]

shelled *adj.* **1.** having a shell. **2.** deprived of its shell. [f. SHELL]

Shelley[1] /ˈʃelɪ/, Mary Wollstonecraft (1797–1851), English novelist, daughter of W. Godwin and Mary Wollstonecraft. She eloped with P. B. Shelley in 1814 and married him in 1816. She is chiefly remembered as the author of *Frankenstein, or the Modern Prometheus* (1818). Her other works include the novels *The Last Man* (1826) and *Lodore* (1835), short stories (some with science fiction elements, others Gothic or historical), biographies, and an edition of her husband's poems (1830).

Shelley[2] /ˈʃelɪ/, Percy Bysshe (1792–1822), English poet. His pamphlet *The Necessity of Atheism* (1811; with T. J. Hogg) caused his expulsion from Oxford. This period of political activism, during which he married Harriet Westbrook (1811), is reflected in his ideological poem *Queen Mab* (1813). His marriage collapsed in 1814 and he eloped abroad with Mary Godwin and her step-sister 'Claire' Clairmont, marrying Mary in 1816 after Harriet had

drowned herself. From 1818 he settled permanently in Italy where, in spite of his increasingly troubled domestic situation, he composed his greatest works, including *Prometheus Unbound* (1820), a lyrical drama on his aspirations and contradictions as a poet and radical, *The Mask of Anarchy* (1819), a poem of political protest, 'Ode to the West Wind' (1819), *The Cenci* (1819), a verse tragedy, his famous prose work *The Defence of Poetry* (1821), vindicating the role of poetry in a progressive industrial society, and *Adonais* (1821), an elegy on the death of Keats. Shelley was drowned in a boating accident. Spectacular lyric powers, and his intellectual courage and originality, have earned him a high place among the Romantic poets.

shellfish *n.* (*pl.* same) a water animal with a shell, especially an edible mollusc or a crustacean.

Shelta /ˈʃeltə/ *n.* a cryptic jargon used by Irish gypsies and pipers, Irish and Welsh travelling tinkers, etc. It is composed partly of Irish or Gaelic words, mostly disguised by inversion or by arbitrary alteration of initial consonants. [orig. unkn.]

shelter *n.* **1.** something that serves as a shield or barrier against attack, danger, heat, wind, etc.; a structure providing this. **2.** refuge, a shielded condition. —*v.t./i.* **1.** to provide with shelter. **2.** to protect from blame, trouble, or competition. **3.** to find or take shelter. —**sheltered housing** etc., that provided for people who are old or handicapped, with special facilities or services. [perh. as SHIELD]

shelve *v.t./i.* **1.** to arrange on a shelf or shelves. **2.** to fit with shelves. **3.** to defer consideration of (a plan etc.); to remove (a person) from active work etc. **4.** (of ground) to slope away. [f. SHELF]

shelves *pl.* of SHELF.

shelving *n.* shelves collectively; material for shelves. [f. SHELVE]

Shem a son of Noah (Gen. 10: 21), traditional ancestor of the Semites.

Shema /ʃeˈmɑː/ *n.* a Hebrew text forming an important part of Jewish evening and morning prayer and used as a Jewish confession of faith, beginning 'Hear, O Israel, the Lord our God is one Lord'. [Heb., = hear]

shemozzle /ʃɪˈmɒz(ə)l/ *n.* (*slang*) a rumpus, a brawl; a muddle. [f. Yiddish after Heb., = of no luck]

shenanigan /ʃɪˈnænɪɡən/ *n.* (*colloq.*) nonsense; trickery; high-spirited behaviour. [orig. unkn.]

Sheol /ˈʃiːɒl/ *n.* (in the Old Testament) the underworld, the abode of the dead. [f. Heb.]

shepherd /ˈʃepəd/ *n.* **1.** a man who tends a flock of sheep at pasture. **2.** a spiritual leader, a priest. —*v.t.* **1.** to tend (sheep). **2.** to lead spiritually. **3.** to marshal, conduct, or drive (a crowd etc.) like sheep. —**shepherd's pie,** cottage pie. —**shepherdess** *n.fem.* [OE (as SHEEP, HERD)]

Sheraton /ˈʃerət(ə)n/ *n.* a style of furniture introduced in England *c.*1790, with delicate and graceful forms. [f. T. *Sheraton*, English furniture-maker (d. 1806)]

sherbet /ˈʃɜːbət/ *n.* **1.** an oriental drink of sweetened diluted fruit-juice. **2.** a fizzy flavoured drink; the powder for this. [f. Turk. or Pers. f. Arab., = drink (as SYRUP)]

sherd *n.* a potsherd. [var. of SHARD]

Sheridan /ˈʃerɪd(ə)n/, Richard Brinsley (1751–1816), Anglo-Irish dramatist, son of an actor-manager. After eloping to France with the beautiful singer Eliza Linley whom he married in 1773, he established his reputation with *The Rivals* (1775) which included the famous Mrs Malaprop among its characters, and continued his success with his masterpiece *The School for Scandal* (1777), both comedies of manners, skilfully constructed with great wit and elegance and continuously popular. He became principal director of Drury Lane Theatre in 1776 and sole proprietor in 1779. Already politically ambitious, Sheridan became the friend and supporter of Charles James Fox; he entered Parliament in 1780, where he became a celebrated orator, held senior government posts, and won the friendship of the Prince Regent. Meanwhile financial problems associated with Drury Lane became crushing; he died in poverty, but was given a magnificent funeral in Westminster Abbey.

sheriff /ˈʃerɪf/ *n.* **1.** (also **High Sheriff**) the chief executive officer of the Crown in a county, nominally charged with keeping the peace, administering justice through the courts, executing writs by deputy, presiding over elections, etc. **2.** an honorary officer elected annually in some towns. **3.** (*Sc.*; also **sheriff-depute**) the chief judge of a county or district.

4. (*US*) the chief law-enforcement officer of a county. [OE (as SHIRE, REEVE¹)]

Sherlock /ˈʃɜːlɒk/ *n.* a person who investigates mysteries or shows great perceptiveness; a private detective. [f. *Sherlock* HOLMES]

Sherman /ˈʃɜːmən/, William Tecumseh (1820–91), one of the great generals of the American Civil War. In March 1864 he succeeded Grant as chief commander in the west, and crushed the Confederate forces in his march through Georgia. Ordering his troops to live off the land, by deliberate and disciplined destruction he not only wiped out the South's sources of supply but sought to break the spirit of civilians as well as soldiers. In 1869 he became commander of the US army, a post he filled until his retirement in 1884.

Sherpa /ˈʃɜːpə/ *n.* a member of a Himalayan people living on the borders of Nepal and Tibet. [native name]

Sherrington /ˈʃerɪŋt(ə)n/, Sir Charles Scott (1857–1952), English physiologist whose researches opened up a new chapter in the understanding of the central nervous system. For his study of the neuron he shared the 1932 Nobel Prize for medicine.

sherry *n.* a white usually fortified wine originally from southern Spain; a glass of this. [f. *Xeres* (now Jerez de la Frontera) in Spain]

Shetland /ˈʃetlənd/ *adj.* of the Shetland Islands. —**Shetland Islands,** (also **Shetlands**) a group of about 100 Scottish islands NNE of the Orkneys, which have become important bases for the exploitation of oil and gas in the North Sea. They constitute an islands area (Shetland) of Scotland. (See also ORKNEY.) **Shetland pony,** a small hardy rough-coated pony. **Shetland wool,** fine loosely-twisted wool from Shetland sheep. —**Shetlander** *n.*

shew (*archaic*) var. of SHOW.

Shiah /ˈʃiːə/ *n.* the group of the Shiites. [f. Arab., = party (of Ali, Muhammad's cousin and son-in-law)]

shibboleth /ˈʃɪbəleθ/ *n.* an old-fashioned doctrine or formula of a party or sect; a catchword; a word, custom, or principle etc. regarded as revealing a person's orthodoxy etc. [f. Heb., = ear of corn, from the story in Judg. 12: 6 where it was a kind of password distinguishing those who could pronounce it from those who could not]

shield *n.* **1.** a piece of defensive armour carried in the hand or on the arm to protect the body against missiles or thrusts (ill. ARMOUR). **2.** an object, structure, or layer of material that protects something; a person giving protection; a shieldlike part in an animal or plant. **3.** a mass of ancient rock under a land area, a flat or gently convex platform usually forming the nucleus of a continent. The largest example is the Canadian shield, which occupies over two-fifths of the land area of Canada; it is drained by rivers flowing into Hudson Bay. **4.** a representation of a shield as a heraldic device displaying a coat of arms. **5.** a trophy in the form of a shield. —*v.t.* to protect or screen; to protect from discovery. [OE, prob. rel. to SCALE²]

shift *v.t./i.* **1.** to change or move from one position to another. **2.** to change form or character. **3.** to pass (responsibility etc.) on to someone else. **4.** (*slang*) to move quickly; to consume (food or drink). **5.** (*US*) to change gear in a motor vehicle. —*n.* **1.** a change of place, position, form, or character. **2.** a set of workers who start work as another set finishes; the period for which they work. **3.** a scheme for achieving something, an expedient. **4.** a trick, a piece of evasion. **5.** a woman's straight-cut dress. **6.** a change of position of typewriter type-bars to type capitals etc. **7.** a displacement of the lines of the spectrum. **8.** (*US*) a gear-change in a motor vehicle. —**make shift,** to manage in less than ideal circumstances. **shift for oneself,** to depend on one's own efforts. **shift one's ground,** to take a new position in an argument etc. —**shifter** *n.* [OE, = arrange, divide]

shiftless *adj.* lazy and inefficient; lacking resourcefulness. —**shiftlessly** *adv.,* **shiftlessness** *n.* [f. SHIFT]

shifty *adj.* evasive, deceitful, untrustworthy. —**shiftily** *adv.,* **shiftiness** *n.* [f. SHIFT]

Shiite /ˈʃiːaɪt/ *n.* a member of the Shia, one of the two major groups in Islam (opp. *Sunnite.*) centred chiefly in Iran. (See SUNNITE.) The Shiites followed a succession of imams, whom they believed to possess a Divine Light giving them special wisdom—indeed, infallibility—in matters of the faith and community of believers. There exist several subgroups, depending on which imam they believe to be the final one, regarded as forced to go into hiding through

the repressive political rule of the majority community and expected to return and to triumph over injustice. [as SHIAH]

shillelagh /ʃɪˈleɪlə, -lɪ/ *n.* an Irish cudgel. [f. *Shillelagh* in Co. Wicklow, Ireland]

shilling *n.* a former British currency unit and coin worth one-twentieth of a pound (i.e. 5p); a monetary unit in East African countries. [OE]

shilly-shally /ˈʃɪlɪʃælɪ/ *v.i.* to vacillate, to hesitate or be undecided. [redupl. of *shall I?* (SHALL)]

shim *n.* a thin wedge used in machinery etc. to make parts fit. —*v.t.* (**-mm-**) to fit or fill up thus. [orig. unkn.]

shimmer *v.i.* to shine with a tremulous or faint diffused light. —*n.* such a light. [OE (cf. SHINE)]

shin *n.* **1.** the front of the leg below the knee. **2.** (in full **shin of beef**) an ox's (esp. fore-)shank as a cut of meat. —*v.t./i.* (**-nn-**) to climb by clinging with arms and legs. —**shin-bone** *n.* the inner and usually larger of the two bones from knee to ankle. [OE]

shindig /ˈʃɪndɪɡ/ *n.* (also **shindy**) (*colloq.*) **1.** a festive gathering, especially a boisterous one. **2.** a din, a brawl. [perh. alt. of SHINTY]

shine *v.t./i.* (*past & p.p.* **shone** /ʃɒn/) **1.** to emit or reflect light, to be bright, to glow. **2.** (of the sun, a star, etc.) to be clearly visible. **3.** to be brilliant, to excel. **4.** to cause to shine (in a certain direction etc.). **5.** (*p.p.* **shined**) to polish so as to produce a shine. —*n.* brightness, a lustre, a polish; light, sunshine. —**take a shine to,** (*colloq.*) to take a liking to. [OE]

shiner /ˈʃaɪnə(r)/ *n.* (*colloq.*) a black eye. [f. SHINE]

shingle¹ /ˈʃɪŋɡ(ə)l/ *n.* (in *sing.* or *pl.*) pebbles in a mass, as on a sea-shore. —**shingly** *adj.* [orig. unkn.]

shingle² /ˈʃɪŋɡ(ə)l/ *n.* **1.** a rectangular piece of wood used as a roof-tile. **2.** shingled hair; shingling the hair. —*v.t.* **1.** to roof with shingles. **2.** to cut (a woman's hair) short so that it tapers from the back of the head to the nape of the neck so that all ends are exposed like roof-shingles. [app. f. L *scindula*]

shingles /ˈʃɪŋɡ(ə)lz/ *n.pl.* (usu. treated as *sing.*) an acute painful viral inflammation of nerve ganglia, with a skin eruption often forming a girdle around the middle of the body. [f. L *cingulus* girdle (*cingere* gird)]

Shinto /ˈʃɪntəʊ/ *n.* (also **Shintoism**) a Japanese religion revering ancestors and nature-spirits and embodying the beliefs and attitudes that are in accordance with this. The name was applied to the indigenous polytheistic religion of Japan of the 6th c. AD to distinguish it from Buddhism. Its oral traditions are recorded in the *Kojiki* (Records of Ancient Matters) and *Nihon Shoki* (Chronicles of Japan), both written *c.*712–20. Central to the religion is the belief in sacred power (*kami*) in both animate and inanimate things; in its mythology the sun-goddess was the ancestress of the imperial household. Shinto became closely associated with the State, a position that it held until after the Second World War, when it was disestablished and the Emperor Hirohito disavowed his claim to divine descent. —**Shintoist** *n.* [Jap. f. Chin., = way of the gods]

shinty /ˈʃɪntɪ/ *n.* **1.** a game like hockey, brought to Scotland by the invading Irish Gaels and sharing its history with hurling (see entry) until the mid-14th c. **2.** the stick or ball used in this. [earlier *shinny*, app. f. cry (*shin ye*) used in the game]

shiny /ˈʃaɪnɪ/ *adj.* having a shine; (of clothes) with the nap worn off. —**shinily** *adv.,* **shininess** *n.* [f. SHINE]

ship *n.* **1.** a large seagoing vessel (see below and ill. pp. 728–9). **2.** (*colloq.*) a spacecraft; (*US*) an aircraft. —*v.t./i.* (**-pp-**) **1.** to put, send, or take on board a ship for conveyance to a destination. **2.** to transport. **3.** to fix (a mast, rudder, etc.) in its place on a ship. **4.** to embark; (of a sailor) to take service on a ship. **5.** to take (oars) from the rowlocks and lay them inside the boat. **6.** to have (water, a sea) come into a boat etc. over the gunwale. —**ship burial,** burial in a ship under a mound. The practice is found in Scandinavia and parts of the British Isles in the pagan Anglo-Saxon and Viking periods (6th–11th c. AD). **ship-canal** *n.* a canal constructed to admit large ships. **ship's boat,** a small boat carried on a ship. **ship of the line,** (*hist.*) a ship with powerful enough armament to lie in the line of battle. **take ship,** to go on board a ship for a journey. **when one's ship comes home** *or* **in,** when one's fortune is made. [OE]

Ships is the generic name for sea-going vessels (as opposed to *boats*), originally personified as masculine but by the 16th c. almost universally expressed as feminine. Their origin is lost in the mists of antiquity, beginning when man discovered that wood and bundles of reeds would float and thought of using a river or the sea to convey himself and his goods, probably on a roughly-constructed raft. The need to acquire additional buoyancy and stowage-space was met first by the use of a hollowed-out tree trunk, then by development of stem and stern pieces fixed to a keel, and with ribs to support the two sides. Among the most ancient vessels known are a dug-out canoe found at Pese in Holland, dating from the 8th millennium BC, and the oared funeral ship, buried beside his tomb, of the Egyptian pharaoh Cheops (4th millennium BC). Early ships were propelled by sail, sometimes supplemented by oars. They were built of wood, but iron was introduced and then steel, which is now universal, though ships have also been made of concrete, glass-reinforced plastics, and light alloy. Steamships were evolved in the 19th c. using reciprocating steam-engines and later steam turbines; these in turn have been replaced by turbo-charged diesel engines or gas turbines. Modern ships are worked with small crews through extensive use of automatic control systems. The price of fuel oil and problems of its supply have led to renewed interest in the use of sail.

-ship *suffix* forming nouns denoting quality or condition (*friendship, hardship*), status, office, or honour (*authorship, lordship*), tenure of an office (*chairmanship*), skill in a certain capacity (*workmanship*), the collective individuals of a group (*membership*). [OE]

shipboard *n.* esp. in **on shipboard,** on board a ship.

shipbuilder *n.* a person engaged in the business of building ships. —**shipbuilding** *n.*

shipload *n.* the quantity of cargo or passengers that a ship can carry.

shipmate *n.* a person belonging to or sailing on the same ship as another.

shipment *n.* the placing of goods on a ship; the amount shipped. [f. SHIP]

shipowner *n.* a person owning or having shares in a ship or ships.

shipper *n.* one who ships goods, especially in import or export. [f. SHIP]

shipping *n.* ships collectively; transport of goods by ship. [f. SHIP]

shipshape *adv. & predic. adj.* in good order, neat and tidy.

shipwreck *n.* **1.** destruction of a ship at sea by storm or by striking rocks etc. **2.** the remains of a ship destroyed thus. **3.** the ruin of plans etc. —*v.t.* to cause to suffer a shipwreck.

shipwright *n.* **1.** a shipbuilder. **2.** a ship's carpenter.

shipyard a place where ships are built.

shire *n.* **1.** a county (see below). **2.** (*Austral.*) a rural area with its own elected council. —**shire-horse** *n.* a draught-horse of a heavy powerful breed, with long white hair covering the lower part of the legs. **shire-moot** *n.* the judicial assembly of the shire in Old English times. **the shires,** the band of English counties with names (formerly) ending in -*shire*, extending NE from Hampshire and Devon; the midland counties of England, comprising mainly Leicestershire and Northamptonshire. [OE, rel. to OHG, = care, official charge; orig. unkn.]

In pre-Norman times a shire was an administrative district made up of a number of smaller districts ('hundreds' or 'wapentakes'). Under Norman rule this division was retained but the term *shire* was replaced by French *counté* (= county). Until the local government reorganization of 1974 'shire' and 'county' were generally synonymous, indicating the major rural area of local government, but since that date the term 'shire county' has been applied to the non-metropolitan counties (see METROPOLITAN COUNTY).

shirk *v.t.* to avoid (a duty or work etc., or *absol.*) from laziness, cowardice, etc. —**shirker** *n.* [perh. f. G *schurke* scoundrel]

shirr *v.t.* to gather (fabric), especially with elastic or parallel threads run through it. [orig. unkn.]

shirt *n.* a loose sleeved garment of cotton or silk etc. for the upper part of the body. —**keep one's shirt on,** (*slang*) to keep one's temper. **put one's shirt on,** (*slang*) to bet all one's money on (a horse etc.). **shirt dress** a woman's dress with a bodice like a shirt. [OE]

shirting *n.* material for shirts. [f. SHIRT]

shirtwaister *n.* a shirt dress.

shirty *adj.* (*slang*) angry, annoyed. —**shirtily** *adv.,* **shirtiness** *n.* [f. SHIRT]

shish kebab /ʃiʃ kɪ'bæb/ pieces of meat and vegetable grilled on skewers. [f. Turk. (*shish* skewer, *kebab* roast meat)]

shit *v.t./i.* (**-tt-**; *past & p.p.* **shit**) (*vulgar*) to defecate; to get rid of as excrement. —*n.* (*vulgar*) **1.** faeces. **2.** an act of defecating. **3.** nonsense. **4.** a despicable person. —*int.* (*vulgar*) expressing anger or annoyance. [OE]

Shiva /'ʃiːvə/ var. of SIVA.

shiver[1] /'ʃɪvə(r)/ *v.i.* to tremble slightly, especially with cold or fear. —*n.* a shivering movement. —**the shivers,** an attack of shivering; a feeling or fear or horror. —**shivery** *adj.* [perh. f. obs. *chavele* chatter (as JOWL)]

shiver[2] /'ʃɪvə(r)/ *n.* (usu. in *pl.*) a small fragment, a splinter. —*v.t./i.* to break into shivers. [rel. to OHG *scivaro* splinter]

shoal[1] *n.* a multitude, a great number, especially of fish swimming together. —*v.i.* (of fish) to form a shoal or shoals. [prob. f. MDu., = SCHOOL²]

shoal[2] *n.* **1.** a shallow place in the sea; a submerged sandbank, especially one that shows at low water. **2.** (usu. in *pl.*) hidden danger. —*v.i.* to become shallow. [OE, rel. to SHALLOW]

shock[1] *n.* **1.** the effect of a violent impact or shake; a violent shake or tremor of the earth's crust in an earthquake. **2.** a sudden violent effect upon the mind or emotions; an acute state of prostration caused by physical injury or pain or by mental shock; an electric shock. **3.** great disturbance of or injury to an organization, stability, etc. —*v.t./i.* **1.** to affect with an electrical or mental shock. **2.** to appear horrifying or outrageous to. —**shock absorber,** a device on a vehicle etc. for absorbing vibration and shock. **shock therapy** *or* **treatment,** psychiatric treatment by means of a shock induced artificially by electricity or drugs. **shock troops,** troops specially trained for violent assaults. **shock wave,** an air-wave caused by an explosion or by a body moving faster than sound. [f. F *choc, choquer*]

shock[2] *n.* a group of corn-sheaves propped up together in a field. —*v.t.* to arrange (corn) in shocks. [= MDu. & MLG *schok*]

shock[3] *n.* an unkempt or shaggy mass of hair. [cf. obs. *shock(-dog)* shaggy-haired poodle]

shocker *n.* (*colloq.*) a person or thing that shocks; a very bad specimen of something; a sordid or sensational novel, film, etc. [f. SHOCK]

shocking *adj.* causing shock; scandalous; (*colloq.*) very bad. —**shockingly** *adv.* [f. SHOCK]

shod *past & p.p.* of SHOE.

shoddy *n.* fibre made from old cloth shredded; cloth made partly from this. —*adj.* of poor quality or workmanship. —**shoddily** *adv.,* **shoddiness** *n.* [orig. unkn.]

shoe /ʃuː/ *n.* **1.** an outer foot-covering of leather etc., especially one not reaching above the ankle. **2.** a thing like a shoe in shape or use. **3.** a metal rim nailed to a horse's hoof. **4.** a brake-shoe (see BRAKE¹). —*v.t.* (*past & p.p.* **shod**; *partic.* **shoeing**) **1.** to fit (a horse etc.) with a shoe or shoes. **2.** (in *p.p.*) having shoes etc. of a specified kind. —**in a person's shoes,** in his position or predicament. **shoe-lace** *n.* a cord for lacing a shoe. **shoe-string** *n.* a shoe-lace; (*colloq.*) a small or inadequate amount of money (especially as capital). **shoe-tree** *n.* a shaped block for keeping a shoe in shape. [OE]

shoehorn *n.* a curved piece of horn or metal etc. for easing the heel into a shoe.

shoemaker *n.* a person whose business is making and repairing boots and shoes. —**shoemaking** *n.*

shoeshine *n.* (*US*) the polishing of shoes.

shogun /'ʃəʊɡʊn/ *n.* the hereditary commander of the army in feudal Japan. Because of the military power concentrated in his hands, and the consequent weakness of the nominal head of State (Mikado or Emperor), the shogun was generally the real ruler of the country until feudalism was abolished in 1867. —**shogunate** *n.* [Jap., = general, f. Chinese *jiang jung*]

shone *past & p.p.* of SHINE.

shoo *int.* a sound used to frighten animals away. —*v.t./i.* to utter such a sound; to drive away thus. [imit.]

shook *past* of SHAKE.

shoot *v.t./i.* (*past & p.p.* **shot**) **1.** to cause (a weapon, or *absol.*) to discharge a missile; to kill or wound with a missile from a weapon. **2.** to hunt with a gun for sport. **3.** to come, go, or send swiftly or violently. **4.** to pass swiftly over (rapids etc.) or under (a bridge). **5.** (in football etc.) to take a shot at goal; to score (a goal). **6.** to photograph; to film. **7.** (of a plant) to put forth buds; (of a bud) to appear. **8.** (as *int.*, *US*) say what you have to say. —*n.* **1.** a young branch or sucker; the new growth of a plant. **2.** an expedition or party for shooting game; land in which game is shot. **3.** a chute. —**be** or **get shot of**, to be rid of. **shoot down**, to kill (a person) cold-bloodedly by shooting; to cause (an aircraft or its pilot) to fall to the ground by shooting; to argue effectively against (a proposal etc.). **shooting-brake** *n.* an estate car. **shooting-gallery** *n.* a place for shooting at targets with rifles etc. **shooting star**, a small meteor moving rapidly. **shooting-stick** *n.* a walking-stick with a handle folding out to form a small seat. **shoot one's mouth off**, (*slang*) to talk freely or indiscreetly. **shoot up**, to rise or grow rapidly; to destroy or terrorize by shooting. **the whole shoot**, (*slang*) everything. —**shooter** *n.* [OE]

shop *n.* **1.** a building or room where goods or services are on sale to the public. **2.** a place where manufacturing or repairing is done. **3.** one's work or profession as a subject of conversation (*to talk shop*). **4.** (*slang*) an institution, an establishment, a place of business etc. —*v.t./i.* (**-pp-**) **1.** to go to shops to make purchases etc. **2.** (*slang*) to inform against, especially to the police. —**all over the shop**, (*slang*) in great disorder, scattered everywhere. **shop around**, to look for the best bargain. **shop-assistant**, an employee in a retail shop. **shop-floor** *n.* the production area in a factory etc.; workers as distinct from management. **shop-soiled** *adj.* soiled or faded by having been on display in a shop. **shop-steward** *n.* an official of a trade union elected by fellow-workers as their spokesman. [f. AF & OF *eschoppe* booth, f. MLG]

shopkeeper *n.* the owner or manager of a shop.

shoplifter *n.* a person who steals goods from a shop after entering as a customer. —**shoplifting** *n.*

shopper *n.* **1.** a person who shops. **2.** a shopping-bag. [f. SHOP]

shopping *n.* **1.** buying goods from shops. **2.** the goods bought. —**shopping-bag** *n.* a bag for holding shopping. **shopping centre**, an area or complex of buildings where shops are concentrated. **shopping-trolley** *n.* a trolley with a large shopping-bag mounted on it. [f. SHOP]

shopwalker *n.* a supervisor in a large shop.

shore[1] *n.* the land that adjoins the sea or a large body of water. —**on shore**, ashore. [f. MDu. or MLG, perh. rel. to SHEAR]

shore[2] *n.* a prop, a beam set obliquely against a wall or ship etc. as a support. —*v.t.* to prop or support with shores. [f. MDu. or MLG = prop (orig. unkn.)]

shoreline *n.* the line of a shore.

shorn *p.p.* of SHEAR.

short *adj.* **1.** measuring little from end to end in space or time; soon traversed or finished. **2.** of small stature, not tall. **3.** not lasting, not reaching far into the past or future. **4.** not far-reaching, acting near at hand; insufficient, having an insufficient supply; (seemingly) less than the stated or usual amount etc. **5.** concise, brief; curt; (of temper) easily lost. **6.** (of an alcoholic drink) small and concentrated, made with spirits. **7.** (of a vowel sound or a syllable) relatively brief or light (cf. LONG[1] 7). **8.** (of pastry) rich and crumbly through containing much fat. **9.** (of a sale in stocks etc.) effected with borrowed stock in expectation of acquiring stock later at a lower price. **10.** (of a fielding position in cricket) close to the batsman. —*adv.* **1.** abruptly, suddenly. **2.** before the natural or expected time or place. **3.** in a short manner. —*n.* **1.** a short thing, especially a short syllable or vowel; a short film. **2.** (*colloq.*) a short circuit. **3.** (*colloq.*) a short drink. —*v.t./i.* (*colloq.*) to short-circuit. —**be caught** or **taken short**, to be put at a disadvantage; (*colloq.*) to have a sudden need to go to the lavatory. **come** or **fall short of**, to fail to reach or amount to. **for short**, as a short name. **in short**, briefly. **short-change** *v.t.* to rob or cheat, especially by giving insufficient change. **short circuit**, a connection (usually a fault) in an electrical circuit in which current flows through small resistance. **short-circuit** *v.t./i.* to cause a short circuit in; to have a short circuit; to shorten or avoid by taking a short cut. **short cut**, a shorter way or method than that usually followed. **short division**, division of numbers without writing down details of the calculation. **short for**, serving as an abbreviation of. **short-handed** *adj.* undermanned, with insufficient help. **short line**, a line across the width of a squash court (ill. SPORTS). **short list**, a list of selected candidates from which the final choice will

be made. **short-list** *v.t.* to put on a short list. **short-lived** *adj.* having a short life, ephemeral. **short of**, not having enough of; less than; distant from; without going so far as. **short on**, (*colloq.*) deficient in. **Short Parliament**, the first of two Parliaments summoned by Charles I in 1640. Owing to its insistence on seeking a general redress of grievances against the King before granting him the money he required, Charles dismissed it after only three weeks. **short-range** *adj.* having a short range; relating to a short period of future time. **short shrift**, curt attention or treatment. **short sight**, the ability to see clearly only what is comparatively near. **short-sighted** *adj.* having short sight; lacking imagination or foresight. **short-term** *adj.* occurring in or relating to a short period of time. **short-wave**, a radio wave of frequency greater than 3 MHz. **short-winded** *adj.* easily becoming breathless. —**shortness** *n.* [OE]

shortage *n.* a deficiency; the amount of this. [f. prec.]

shortbread *n.* a rich crumbly biscuit made with flour, butter, and sugar.

shortcake *n.* **1.** shortbread. **2.** a cake of short pastry, usually served with fruit.

shortcoming *n.* failure to reach a required standard, a deficiency.

shorten *v.t./i.* to make or become short or shorter. [f. SHORT]

shortening *n.* fat used for making short pastry. [f. prec.]

shortfall *n.* a deficit.

shorthand *n.* **1.** a method of rapid writing used in dictation etc. (see below). **2.** an abbreviated or symbolic mode of expression.

The use of shortened handwriting dates at least from ancient Roman times: Cicero's secretary devised a system for recording his speeches. Modern shorthand in England can be traced back to 1588 when Dr Timothy Bright published a system; it was difficult to learn, for nearly every word had its own special sign. Other systems were produced, based on the alphabet (Samuel Pepys kept his diaries in shorthand), but were gradually superseded by phonetic systems of which the best was that of Samuel Taylor (1786). Its brevity and simplicity attracted the attention of Sir Isaac Pitman (1813-97), who presently began anew on his own lines and issued his *Stenographic Sound-Hand* in 1873. His system is still widely used, though others are in common use; in the USA the system devised in 1888 by J. R. Gregg (1867-1948) is the most popular. Shorthand writing has become less essential in many contexts with the technological development of recordings of various kinds.

shorthorn *n.* one of a breed of cattle with short horns.

shortly *adv.* **1.** soon, not long, in a short time. **2.** in a few words. **3.** curtly. [f. SHORT]

shorts *n.pl.* **1.** trousers that do not reach to the knee. **2.** (*US*) underpants. [f. SHORT]

shorty *n.* (also **shortie**) (*colloq.*) a person or garment shorter than average. [f. SHORT]

Shostakovich /ʃɒstəˈkɒvɪtʃ/, Dmitri (1906-75), Russian composer. Born in St Petersburg, he lived there through the October Revolution and the forming of the Soviet State. His life was marked by conflict between his desire to serve the people of his country and the volatile response of the authorities to his music. His first brush with the authorities concerned an opera, *The Lady Macbeth of the Mtsensk District*, which had been praised on its first performance in 1934 but was criticized in *Pravda* two years later in an article entitled 'Chaos instead of Music'. A previous opera, *The Nose* (1930), had found favour for its biting mockery of bureaucracy, but in *The Lady Macbeth* Shostakovich had portrayed the life of a Soviet woman in music of uncompromising modernity. In subsequent works he successfully attempted a less formidable style, but another attack, this time on the Ninth Symphony (1945, written to celebrate the end of the war), caused a further retreat which was to end only with Stalin's death in 1953. From then on Shostakovich produced many works in which he expressed his most personal feelings, often despairing, including the last six symphonies and, in his last year, the Viola Sonata.

shot[1] *n.* **1.** the discharge of a gun etc.; the sound of this; an attempt to hit something by shooting or throwing etc. **2.** a stroke or kick in a ball-game. **3.** an attempt to do something. **4.** a possessor of a specified skill in shooting. **5.** a single missile for a gun etc., especially a non-explosive projectile; a small lead pellet of which several are used for a single charge; (as *pl.*) these collectively. **6.** the heavy metal ball used in shot-put. **7.** a photograph; the scene photographed;

a film sequence taken by one camera. **8.** the launch of a space-rocket. **9.** the injection of a drug etc. **10.** (*colloq.*) a dram of spirits. —**like a shot,** very quickly; without hesitation, willingly. **shot in the arm,** a stimulus or encouragement. **shot in the dark,** a mere guess. **shot-put** or **putting the shot,** an athletic contest of throwing a heavy metal ball. [OE (as SHOOT)]

shot² *past & p.p.* of SHOOT. —*adj.* **1.** that has been shot. **2.** (of fabric) woven or dyed so as to show different colours at different angles. —**shot through,** permeated, suffused.

shotgun *n.* a gun for firing small shot at short range. —**shotgun wedding,** one that is enforced, especially because of the bride's pregnancy.

should /ʃəd, *emphat.* ʃʊd/ *v.aux.* (*3 sing.* **should**) past tense of SHALL, used esp. in reported speech or to express obligation, condition, likelihood, or a tentative suggestion. [f. SHALL]

shoulder /ˈʃəʊldə(r)/ *n.* **1.** the part of the body to which the arm, wing, or foreleg is attached; either lateral projection below or behind the neck. **2.** the part of a garment covering the shoulder. **3.** an animal's upper foreleg as a joint of meat. **4.** (in *pl.*) the body regarded as bearing a burden, blame, etc. **5.** a part or projection resembling a human shoulder; a strip of land adjoining a metalled road-surface. —*v.t./i.* **1.** to push with one's shoulder; to make one's way thus. **2.** to take a burden on one's shoulders; to assume the responsibility or blame for. —**put one's shoulder to the wheel,** to make a strong effort. **shoulder arms,** to move a rifle to a position with the barrel against the shoulder and the butt in the hand. **shoulder-blade** *n.* either large flat bone of the upper back. **shoulder-strap** *n.* a strap passing over the shoulder to support something; a strap from the shoulder to the collar of a garment, especially with indication of military rank. **shoulder to shoulder,** side by side; with a united effort. **straight from the shoulder,** (of a blow) well delivered; (of criticism etc.) frank, direct. [OE]

shouldn't /ˈʃʊd(ə)nt/ (*colloq.*) = should not.

shout *n.* **1.** a loud utterance or vocal sound calling attention or expressing joy, excitement, disapproval, etc. **2.** (*Austral. & NZ colloq.*) one's turn to buy a round of drinks. —*v.t./i.* **1.** to emit a shout; to speak, say, or call loudly. **2.** (*Austral. & NZ colloq.*) to buy drinks etc. for. —**shout down,** to reduce to silence by shouting. [perh. rel. to SHOOT]

shove /ʃʌv/ *v.t./i.* to push vigorously; (*colloq.*) to put casually. —*n.* an act of shoving. —**shove-halfpenny** *n.* a game in which coins etc. are pushed along a marked board. **shove off,** to start from the shore in a boat; (*colloq.*) to depart. [OE]

shovel /ˈʃʌv(ə)l/ *n.* an implement shaped like a spade with the side edges turned up, used for scooping up earth, snow, coal, etc.; a machine or part of a machine with a similar function. —*v.t.* (**-ll-**) **1.** to move with or as with a shovel. **2.** to scoop or thrust roughly. —**shovel hat,** a broad-brimmed hat. —**shovelful** *n.* [OE (rel. to SHOVE)]

shovelboard *n.* a game played especially on a ship's deck by pushing discs over a marked surface.

shoveller /ˈʃʌvələ(r)/ *n.* a duck (*Anas clypeata*) with a shovel-like beak. [f. SHOVEL]

show /ʃəʊ/ *v.t./i.* **1.** to allow or cause to be seen; to offer for inspection or viewing; to exhibit in a show. **2.** to demonstrate, to point out, to prove; to cause to understand. **3.** to conduct. **4.** to give (specified treatment to a person or thing). **5.** to be visible or noticeable. —*n.* **1.** showing, being shown. **2.** a display; a public exhibition for competition, entertainment, or advertisement etc.; a pageant; (*colloq.*) any public entertainment or performance. **3.** (*slang*) a concern or undertaking; a business. **4.** an outward appearance; the impression produced; ostentation, mere display. **5.** a discharge of blood from the vagina in menstruation or at the start of childbirth. —**show business,** the entertainment industry. **show-case** *n.* a glazed case for displaying exhibits. **show-down** *n.* a final test or battle etc.; a disclosure of achievements or possibilities. **show one's hand,** to reveal one's intentions. **show house,** one house in an estate etc. furnished and prepared for inspection. **show-jumping** *n.* competitive jumping on horseback. **show off,** to display to advantage; to act in a flamboyant way in order to impress. **show-off** *n.* a person who shows off. **show of hands,** the raising of hands to vote for or against a proposal etc. **show-piece** *n.* an excellent specimen suitable for display. **show-place** *n.* an attractive or much visited place. **show trial,** a judicial trial regarded as intended mainly to impress public opinion. **show up,** to make or be visible or conspicu-

ous; to expose or humiliate; (*colloq.*) to appear or arrive. [OE]

shower /ˈʃaʊə(r)/ *n.* **1.** a brief fall of rain or snow etc., or of bullets, stones, dust, etc.; a sudden copious arrival of gifts or honours etc. **2.** (in full **shower-bath**) a bath in which water is sprayed from above; a room or device for this. **3.** (*slang*) a contemptible or unpleasant person or group. **4.** (*US*) a party for giving gifts, especially to a prospective bride. —*v.t./i.* **1.** to descend in a shower. **2.** to discharge (water or missiles etc.) in a shower; to bestow (gifts etc.) lavishly. **3.** to use a shower-bath. [OE]

showery /ˈʃaʊərɪ/ *adj.* (of weather) with many showers. [f. prec.]

showing /ˈʃəʊɪŋ/ *n.* a display or performance; the quality or appearance of a performance or achievement etc.; the evidence or putting of a case. [f. SHOW]

showman *n.* (*pl.* **-men**) **1.** a proprietor or organizer of public entertainment. **2.** a person skilled in showmanship.

showmanship *n.* capacity for exhibiting one's goods or capabilities to the best advantage.

shown *p.p.* of SHOW.

showroom *n.* a room where goods are displayed or kept for inspection.

showy /ˈʃəʊɪ/ *adj.* making a good or conspicuous display; gaudy. —**showily** *adv.*, **showiness** *n.* [f. SHOW]

shrank *past* of SHRINK.

shrapnel /ˈʃræpn(ə)l/ *n.* **1.** fragments of exploded bombs or shells. **2.** an artillery shell containing metal pieces which it scatters on explosion. [f. Gen. H. *Shrapnel*, who invented this shell *c.*1806]

shred *n.* **1.** a piece torn, scraped, or broken off; a scrap or fragment. **2.** the least amount. —*v.t.* (**-dd-**) to tear or cut into shreds. —**shredder** *n.* [OE]

shrew /ʃruː/ *n.* **1.** a small mouselike animal of the family Soricidae, with a long snout. **2.** a bad-tempered or scolding woman. [OE]

shrewd /ʃruːd/ *adj.* showing astute powers of judgement, clever and judicious. —**shrewdly** *adv.*, **shrewdness** *n.* [perh. f. prec. in sense 'evil person']

shrewish *adj.* scolding, bad-tempered. [f. SHREW]

shriek /ʃriːk/ *n.* a shrill scream or sound. —*v.t./i.* to make a shriek; to say in shrill tones. [imit.]

shrift *n.* (*archaic*) confession and absolution. —**short shrift,** see SHORT. [OE (as SHRIVE)]

shrike *n.* a bird of the family Laniidae, with a strong hooked and toothed bill. [perh. rel. to OE *scric* thrush (imit.)]

shrill *adj.* piercing and high-pitched in sound. —*v.t./i.* to sound or utter shrilly. —**shrilly** *adv.*, **shrillness** *n.* [rel. to LG *schrell* sharp in tone]

shrimp *n.* **1.** a small edible crustacean especially of the genus *Crangon*, pink when boiled. **2.** (*colloq.*) a very small person. —*v.i.* to go in search of shrimps. [prob. rel. to SCRIMP]

shrine *n.* **1.** a place for special worship or devotion. **2.** a tomb or casket containing sacred relics. **3.** a place hallowed by some memory or association etc. [OE f. L *scrinium* book-case]

shrink *v.t./i.* (*past* **shrank**; *p.p.* **shrunk** or (esp. as *adj.*) **shrunken**) **1.** to make or become smaller, especially by the action of moisture, heat, or cold; **2.** to draw back so as to avoid something; to withdraw; to be averse (from an action). —*n.* **1.** the act of shrinking. **2.** (*slang*, short for *head-shrinker*) a psychiatrist. —**shrink-wrap** *v.t.* to enclose (an article) in material that shrinks tightly round it. [OE]

shrinkage *n.* **1.** the process or amount of shrinking. **2.** (in commerce) loss by theft or wastage etc.

shrive *v.t.* (*past* **shrove**; *p.p.* **shriven** /ˈʃrɪv(ə)n/) (*archaic*) to hear the confession of and give absolution; to submit (oneself) for this. [OE, = impose as penance f. L *scribere* write]

shrivel /ˈʃrɪv(ə)l/ *v.t./i.* (**-ll-**) to contract into a wrinkled or curled-up state. [perh. f. ON; cf. Sw. dial. *skryvla* to wrinkle]

Shropshire /ˈʃrɒpʃɪə(r)/ a west midland county of England.

shroud *n.* **1.** a winding-sheet. **2.** something that conceals. **3.** (in *pl.*) the ropes supporting a ship's mast. —*v.t.* **1.** to clothe (a corpse) for burial. **2.** to cover and conceal or disguise. [OE (rel. to SHRED)]

shrove *past* of SHRIVE. —**Shrove Tuesday,** the day before Ash Wednesday, on which it was customary to be shriven. [f. SHRIVE]

Shrovetide *n.* Shrove Tuesday and the two preceding days. [f. prec. + TIDE]

shrub *n.* a woody plant smaller than a tree and usually with separate stems from or near the root. —**shrubby** *adj.* [f. OE, = shrubbery (rel. to SCRUB²)]

shrubbery *n.* an area planted with shrubs. [f. prec.]

shrug *v.t./i.* (**-gg-**) to raise (one's shoulders) slightly and momentarily to express indifference, helplessness, doubt, etc. —*n.* a shrugging movement. —**shrug off,** to dismiss as unimportant. [orig. unkn.]

shrunk *p.p.* of SHRINK.

shrunken see SHRINK.

shudder *n.* a sudden or convulsive shivering or quivering; a vibrating motion. —*v.i.* **1.** to experience a shudder; to feel strong repugnance or fear etc. **2.** to vibrate strongly. [f. MDu. or MLG]

shuffle *v.t./i.* **1.** to walk without lifting the feet clear of the ground; to move (one's feet) thus. **2.** to slide (cards) over one another so as to change their order; to rearrange, to jumble. **3.** to keep shifting one's position; to prevaricate, to be evasive. —*n.* **1.** a shuffling movement or walk; a shuffling dance. **2.** shuffling of cards etc. **3.** a general rearrangement. —**shuffle off,** to remove or get rid of. —**shuffler** *n.* [f. LG, = walk clumsily]

shun *v.t.* (**-nn-**) to avoid, to keep away from; to abstain from. [OE]

shunt *v.t./i.* **1.** to move (a train etc.) to another track; (of a train) to be shunted. **2.** to move or put aside; to redirect. —*n.* **1.** shunting, being shunted. **2.** a conductor joining two points of an electrical circuit for the diversion of current. **3.** (in surgery) an alternative path for the circulation of blood. **4.** (*slang*) a collision of vehicles, especially nose-to-tail. —**shunter** *n.* [perh. f. SHUN]

shush *int.* hush! —*v.t./i.* to call for silence (from); to be silent. [imit.]

shut *v.t./i.* (**-tt-**; *past & p.p.* **shut**) **1.** to move (a door, window, lid, etc.) into position to block an opening; (of a door etc.) to move or admit of being moved thus; to shut the door or lid etc. of (a room, box, eye, etc.). **2.** to bring (a book, telescope, etc.) into a folded-up or contracted state. **3.** to catch or pinch (a finger, dress, etc.) by shutting something on it. **4.** to bar access to (a place). —**be shut of,** (*slang*) to be rid of. **shut down,** to cease working or business, either at the end of a day or permanently; to cause to do this. **shut-down** *n.* this process. **shut-eye** *n.* (*slang*) sleep. **shut off,** to stop the flow of (water, gas, etc.); to separate from society etc. **shut up,** to shut securely or permanently; to imprison; to put away in a box etc.; (*colloq.,* esp. in *imper.*) to stop talking. **shut up shop,** to cease business or work at the end of the day or permanently. [OE]

Shute /ʃuːt/, Nevil (Nevil Shute Norway, 1899-1960), English novelist, by profession an aeronautical engineer. After the Second World War he settled in Australia, which provides the setting for a number of his novels, including *A Town Like Alice* (1950). In all his works, which are peopled by wholly credible characters, he excelled at showing how ordinary people act in extraordinary situations. *On the Beach* (1957), set in Australia and brilliantly effective in its understatement, portrays a community facing the gradual destruction of mankind in the aftermath of a nuclear war.

shutter *n.* **1.** a movable hinged cover for a window. **2.** a device that opens and closes the lens aperture of a camera to allow light to fall on the film. —*v.t.* to provide with shutters. —**put up the shutters,** to cease business at the end of the day or permanently. [f. SHUT]

shuttle *n.* **1.** a holder carrying the weft-thread to and fro between the threads of the warp in weaving. **2.** a moving holder carrying the lower thread in a sewing-machine. **3.** a vehicle used in a shuttle service; a space-shuttle. **4.** a shuttlecock. —*v.t./i.* to move, travel, or send to and fro. —**shuttle diplomacy,** negotiations conducted by a mediator who travels to several countries at brief intervals. **shuttle service,** a transport system operating to and fro over a relatively short distance. [OE, = a dart (as SHOOT)]

shuttlecock *n.* a small rounded piece of cork etc. with a ring of feathers attached, or of other material made in this shape, struck to and fro with a battledore in the old game of battledore and shuttlecock, and with a racket in badminton. [f. prec. + COCK, prob. f. flying motion]

shy¹ /ʃaɪ/ *adj.* **1.** timid and lacking self-confidence in the presence of others; avoiding company; reserved; (of behav-

iour) showing shyness. **2.** (of an animal) timid and avoiding observation. **3.** (as *suffix*) showing fear or distaste of (*work-shy*). —*v.i.* to jump or move suddenly in alarm. —*n.* an act of shying. —**shy of,** wary of. [OE]

shy² /ʃaɪ/ *v.t.* (*colloq.*) to fling or throw. —*n.* (*colloq.*) a throw. [orig. unkn.]

Shylock /ˈʃaɪlɒk/ a hard-hearted Jewish usurer in Shakespeare's *Merchant of Venice.*

shyster /ˈʃaɪstə(r)/ *n.* (*colloq.*) a person who acts unscrupulously or unprofessionally. [orig. unkn.]

SI *abbr.* International System of Units (tr. F *Système international d'unités*), a system of physical units (together with a set of prefixes indicating multiplication or division by a power of ten) based on the metre, kilogram, second, ampere, kelvin, candela, and mole as independent basic units, with each of the derived units defined in terms of these without any multiplying factor. It was instituted in 1957.

Si *symbol* silicon.

si /siː/ *n.* (*Mus.*) te. [perh. f. initials of *Sancte Iohannes* (see GAMUT)]

sial /ˈsaɪəl/ *n.* the discontinuous upper layer of the earth's crust represented by the continental masses, which are composed of relatively light rocks rich in silica and alumina and may be regarded as floating on a lower crustal layer of sima; the material of which these masses are composed. [f. SILICON + ALUMINA]

Siam /saɪˈæm/ the name until 1939 of Thailand.

Siamese /saɪəˈmiːz/ *adj.* of Siam or its people or language. —*n.* **1.** a native or the language (also called Thai; see entry) of Siam. **2.** a Siamese cat. —**Siamese cat,** a cat of a breed with short pale fur and dark markings. **Siamese twins,** identical twins that are physically conjoined at birth. The condition ranges from those joined only by the umbilical blood-vessels to those in whom the conjoined heads or trunks are inseparable. The name refers to two Siamese men (1811-74) joined by a fleshy band in the region of the waist; despite this conjunction they each married, and fathered several children. [f. SIAM]

sib *n.* a sibling. [OE]

Sibelius /sɪˈbeɪliəs/, Jean (1865-1957), Finnish composer. In 1885 he went to Helsinki, where he studied first law then music. He went on to further studies in Berlin and Vienna but maintained a deep feeling for his native country, revealed in his choice of the epic *Kalevala* as inspiration for many of his greatest works (the symphonic poem *Kullervo*, 1892; the four *Lemminkäinen* works which include *The Swan of Tuonela*, 1893; and *Pohjola's Daughter*, 1906). His seven symphonies move towards a cool but heartfelt purity of style and form the most substantial feature of his *œuvre*, but should not be allowed to detract from his songs (over 100), many of which set Swedish texts. The picture of him as an ascetic bleak figure is not supported by the facts of his far from austere life, nor is his music the 'cold, forbidding' art which some writers have portrayed.

Siberia /saɪˈbɪərɪə/ a region of the USSR in northern Asia, forming the larger part of the RSFSR. It has long been used as a place of exile for offenders. —**Siberian** *adj.*

sibilant /ˈsɪbɪlənt/ *adj.* sounded with a hiss; hissing. —*n.* a sibilant letter or sound. —**sibilance** *n.,* **sibilancy** *n.* [f. L *sibilare* hiss]

sibling *n.* each of two or more children having one or both parents in common. [f. SIB]

sibyl /ˈsɪbɪl/ *n.* any of the women who in ancient times acted as the reputed mouthpiece of a god, uttering prophecies and oracles, the most famous of whom was the sibyl of Cumae in south Italy who guided Aeneas through the underworld. [f. OF or L f. Gk *Sibulla*]

sibylline /ˈsɪbɪlaɪn/ *adj.* issuing from a sibyl; oracular, mysteriously prophetic. —**Sibylline books,** a collection of prophecies in Greek hexameter verses, ascribed to the sibyls, belonging to the State of ancient Rome and consulted by its magistrats for guidance in times of national calamity. They were destroyed in 83 BC in the burning of the Capitol and a new collection, from various sources, replaced them; these were later recopied (with many Jewish and Christian interpolations). The last known consultation of the books was in 363. [f. L (as prec.)]

sic /sɪk/ *adv.* thus used, spelt, etc. (used in brackets to confirm or call attention to the form of quoted words). [L, = thus]

Sicilian Vespers the massacre of the French inhabitants of Sicily in 1282, after a riot which began near Palermo while the vesper-bell was ringing. The ensuing war resulted in the unpopular Angevin dynasty being replaced by the Spanish House of Aragon.

Sicily /ˈsɪsɪlɪ/ a large triangular island in the Mediterranean Sea, separated from the 'toe' of Italy by the Strait of Messina; pop. approx. 5,000,000; capital, Palermo. Settled successively by Phoenicians, Greeks, and Carthaginians, it became a Roman province in 241 BC after the first Punic War. After various struggles Sicily and southern Italy became a Norman kingdom towards the end of the 11th c. It was conquered by Charles of Anjou in 1266, but the unpopularity of the Angevin regime led to the uprising known as the Sicilian Vespers (see entry) and the establishment in Sicily of the Spanish House of Aragon in its place; southern Italy remained under Angevin rule until reunited with Sicily in 1442. In 1816 the two areas were officially merged when the Spanish Bourbon Ferdinand styled himself King of the Two Sicilies. The island was liberated by Garibaldi in 1860 and finally incorporated into the new State of Italy. The Sicilian economy is predominantly agricultural and the island remains relatively backward in comparison with the Italian mainland. — **Sicilian** adj. & n.

sick adj. **1.** physically or mentally unwell, feeling the effects of a disease. **2.** vomiting, tending to vomit. **3.** of or for those who are sick (*sick-bed, -leave, -pay, -room*, etc.). **4.** greatly distressed or disgusted. **5.** (of humour) finding amusement in misfortune or in morbid subjects. —v.t. (colloq.) to vomit (esp. with *up*). —**be sick**, to vomit. **sick-bay** n. a room or rooms for sick people in an institution or on a ship etc. **sick of**, tired of, bored with through having already had too much of. [OE]

sicken v.t./i. to make or become sick or disgusted etc. —**sicken for**, to be in the first stages of (an illness). [f. SICK]

sickle n. **1.** an implement with a curved blade and a short handle, used for reaping or lopping etc. **2.** something shaped like this. —**sickle cell**, a sickle-shaped red blood-corpuscle, especially as found in a severe hereditary form of anaemia. [OE, f. L *sicula* (*secare* cut)]

sickly adj. **1.** liable to be ill, of weak health. **2.** unhealthy-looking, faint, pale. **3.** causing ill-health. **4.** inducing or connected with nausea; mawkish, weakly sentimental. —**sickliness** n. [f. SICK]

sickness n. **1.** being ill, disease. **2.** a specified disease. **3.** vomiting. [f. SICK]

Siddons /ˈsɪd(ə)nz/, Sarah (1755–1831), née Kemble, English actress. Her first London appearance, in 1775, was a failure, but after her second, in 1782, she was acclaimed as an incomparable tragic actress with beauty, tenderness, and nobility. She retained her pre-eminence until her retirement in 1812.

side n. **1.** any of the surfaces bounding an object, especially the vertical inner or outer surface or one of those distinguished from the top and bottom or front and back or ends. **2.** (*Math.*) each of the lines bounding a triangle, rectangle, etc.; each of the two quantities stated to be equal in an equation. **3.** either surface of a thing regarded as having only two; the amount of writing filling one side of a sheet of paper. **4.** the right or left part of a person's or animal's body; the corresponding half of a carcass. **5.** a direction; the part of an object or place etc. that faces a specified direction or is on an observer's right or left. **6.** the region to the right or left of (or nearer or further than) a real or imaginary dividing line; the part or area near the edge or away from the centre. **7.** a partial aspect of a thing; an aspect differing from or opposed to other aspects. **8.** each of two sets of opponents at war or competing in some way; the cause represented by these. **9.** the line of descent through one parent. **10.** (in billiards etc.) the spinning motion given to a ball by striking it on one side. **11.** (*slang*) assumption of superiority, swagger. —in comb. **1.** situated at or directed to or from a side (*side-door, -table; side-glance*). **2.** secondary, minor, incidental (*side-effect, -issue, -road, -street*). —v.i. to take part or be on the same side. —**-sided** adj. having a specified number or type of sides. —**by the side of**, close to; compared with. **on one side**, not in the main or central position; aside. **on the side**, as a sideline. **on the — side**, somewhat. **side by side**, standing close together, especially for mutual encouragement. **side-car** n. a passenger car attachable to the side of a motor cycle. **side-drum** n. a small double-headed drum (ill. MUSICAL NOTATION). **side-saddle** n. a saddle enabling a rider to have both feet on the same side of a horse; (*adv.*) sitting thus on a horse. **side-show** n. a small show at a fair

or exhibition; a minor or subsidiary activity or affair. **side-slip** n. a skid, a movement sideways; (*v.i.*) to move sideways. **side-splitting** adj. causing hearty laughter. **side-step** n. a step sideways; (*v.t.*) to avoid by stepping sideways; to evade (an issue etc.). **side-swipe** n. a glancing blow along the side; an indirect or incidental criticism etc.; (*v.t.*) to hit with a side-swipe. **side-track** v.t. to divert (a person) from the main course or issue. **side-whiskers** n.pl. those growing on the cheek. **side wind**, a wind coming from one side. [OE]

sideboard n. a table or flat-topped chest with drawers and cupboards for china etc.

sideburns n.pl. short side-whiskers. [f. Amer. General *Burnside* (d. 1881), who sported a moustache, whiskers, and clean-shaven chin]

sidekick n. (*US colloq.*) a close associate; a subordinate member of a pair or group.

sidelight n. **1.** light from the side. **2.** a piece of incidental information about a subject etc. **3.** each of a pair of small lights at the front of a vehicle. **4.** a light at the side of a moving ship.

sideline n. **1.** work etc. carried on in addition to one's main activity. **2.** (in *pl.*) the lines bounding the sides of a football pitch etc.; the space just outside these. **3.** a place for spectators as distinct from participants.

sidelong adj. directed to the side, oblique. —adv. to the side.

sidereal /saɪˈdɪərɪəl/ adj. of or determined by means of the stars. —**sidereal day**, the time between successive passages of any given star over a meridian. [f. L *sidereus* (*sidus* star)]

sidesman n. (*pl.* **-men**) an assistant churchwarden who takes the collection etc.

sidewalk n. (*US*) a pavement at the side of a road.

sideways adj. & adv. **1.** with the side foremost. **2.** to or from one side.

siding /ˈsaɪdɪŋ/ n. a short railway track to the side of a railway line, used for shunting.

sidle /ˈsaɪd(ə)l/ v.i. to walk obliquely; to move timidly or furtively. [back-formation f. *sideling* sidelong]

Sidney /ˈsɪdnɪ/, Sir Philip (1554–86), English soldier and poet. Generally considered to represent the apotheosis of the Elizabethan courtier, Sidney was one of the leading poets of the age, his most famous work being *Arcadia* (1580). He died of wounds received in the Low Countries while fighting the Spanish.

Sidon /ˈsaɪd(ə)n/ a city and seaport of the Phoenicians, now in Lebanon.

siege /siːdʒ/ n. the surrounding and blockading of a fortified place; the surrounding by the police etc. of a house occupied by a gunman etc. —**lay siege to**, to conduct a siege of. **raise a siege**, to end it. [f. OF *sege* seat]

Siegfried /ˈsiːɡfriːd/ the hero of the first part of the Nibelungenlied, who forged the Nothung sword, slew Fafner, the dragon guarding the stolen Rhine gold, and helped Gunther to win Brunhild. He was treacherously slain by Hagen, a Burgundian retainer, who was eventually slain with Siegfried's sword.

Siemens /ˈsiːmənz/, Ernst Werner von (1816–92), German electrical engineer, who developed electroplating and an electric generator using an electromagnet rather than a permanent magnetic field. He set up a factory in Berlin which manufactured telegraph systems and electric cables and pioneered electrical traction. His brother Karl Wilhelm (Charles William, 1823–83), was sent to England at the age of 20 and remained there all his life. He developed the open-hearth steel furnace, which was widely used, and designed the cable-laying steamship *Faraday* and one of the first electric railways in the UK, built at Portrush in Northern Ireland. A third brother Friedrich (1826–1904) worked both with Werner in Germany and with Charles in England; he applied the principles of the open-hearth furnace to glassmaking.

siemens /ˈsiːmənz/ n. the unit of electrical conductance, the reciprocal of the ohm. [f. E. W. von *Siemens* (see prec.)]

sienna /sɪˈenə/ n. a kind of clay used as a pigment; its colour of reddish-brown (**burnt sienna**) or yellowish-brown (**raw sienna**). [f. *Siena* in Italy]

sierra /sɪˈerə/ n. a long jagged mountain-chain in Spain or Spanish America. [Sp., f. L *serra* saw]

Sierra Leone /sɪerə lɪˈəʊn/ a country on the coast of West Africa, a member State of the Commonwealth; pop. (1974) 3,123,000; official language, English; capital, Freetown. An area of British influence from the late 18th c., the district around Freetown on the coast became a colony in 1807 but the large inland territory was not declared a protectorate until 1896. Sierra Leone achieved independence in 1961 and is now a one-party State. Its economy, though largely agricultural, benefits from iron mining and diamond exports. —**Sierra Leonian** adj. & n.

siesta /sɪˈestə/ n. an afternoon nap or rest, especially in hot countries. [Sp., f. L *sexta* (*hora*) sixth hour]

sieve /sɪv/ n. a utensil with a network or perforated bottom through which liquids or fine particles can pass while solid or coarser matter is retained, or used for reducing a soft mixture pressed through it to a uniform pulp. —v.t. to put through a sieve. [OE]

sift v.t./i. 1. to separate with or cause to pass through a sieve. 2. to sprinkle (flour etc.) from a sieve or perforated container. 3. to subject (information etc.) to close scrutiny or analysis. 4. (of snow etc.) to fall as if from a sieve. —**sifter** n. [OE (as prec.)]

sigh /saɪ/ n. a long deep audible breath expressing sadness, weariness, longing, relief, etc.; an act of making this; a sound resembling it. —v.t./i. 1. to make a sigh; to express with sighs. 2. to yearn *for* a person or thing desired or lost. [OE]

sight /saɪt/ n. 1. the faculty of perception through the response of the brain to the action of light on the eye. 2. seeing, being seen. 3. the range of vision; the region open to vision. 4. the way of regarding something, opinion. 5. a thing seen or visible or worth seeing; (in *pl.*) the noteworthy or attractive features of a town etc. 6. a person or thing regarded as unsightly or ridiculous-looking. 7. a precise aim with a gun or observation with an optical instrument; a device for assisting this. 8. (*colloq.*) a great quantity. —v.t. 1. to get a sight of, to observe the presence of. 2. to aim (a gun etc.) by using the sights. —**at first sight**, on the first glimpse or impression. **at** *or* **on sight**, as soon as a person or thing is seen. **catch sight of**, to begin to see or be aware of. **in sight**, visible, imminent. **set one's sights on**, to be determined to acquire or achieve etc. **a sight for sore eyes**, a person or thing one is delighted to see. **sight-read** v.t. to read (music) at sight, without preliminary practice or study of the score. **sight-screen** n. (in cricket) a large white screen placed near the boundary in line with the wicket to help the batsman see the ball. **sight unseen**, without previous inspection. [OE (as SEE¹)]

sighted adj. having sight, not blind. [f. prec.]

sightless adj. blind. [f. SIGHT + -LESS]

sightly adj. attractive to look at. —**sightliness** n. [f. SIGHT]

sightseer n. a person visiting the sights of a place. —**sightseeing** n.

sigma /ˈsɪgmə/ n. the eighteenth letter of the Greek alphabet, = s. [L f. Gk]

sign /saɪn/ n. 1. a thing perceived that suggests the existence of a fact, quality, or condition, either past, present, or future. 2. a mark or device with a special meaning, a symbol. 3. a motion or gesture used instead of words to convey information, a demand, etc. 4. each of the twelve divisions of the zodiac. 5. a publicly displayed symbol or device giving information; a signboard. —v.t./i. 1. to write one's name on (a document) to show its authenticity or one's agreement or acceptance; to write (one's name) thus. 2. to engage or be engaged by signing a contract. 3. to indicate or communicate by a gesture. —**sign away**, to relinquish a right to by signing. **sign-language** n. a series of signs used by deaf or dumb people for communication. **sign off**, to end work or a contract etc.; to indicate the end of a broadcast etc. **sign on**, to sign a contract of employment etc.; to register oneself (e.g. as available for employment); to indicate the start of a broadcast etc. [f. OF f. L *signum* mark, token]

Signac /siːˈnjæk/, Paul (1863–1935), French Neo-Impressionist painter, an ardent disciple of the views and methods of Seurat, though his own work had a liveliness and spontaneity not altogether in keeping with these. In 1899 he published a manifesto in defence of the movement, *D'Eugène Delacroix aux néoimpressionisme*.

signal /ˈsɪgn(ə)l/ n. 1. a sign (especially a pre-arranged one) conveying information or giving an instruction; a message made up of such signs. 2. a device on a railway giving instructions or warnings to train-drivers etc. 3. an event which causes immediate activity. 4. transmitted electrical impulses or radio waves; a sequence of these. —v.t./i. (**-ll-**) to make a signal or signals (to); to transmit or announce by a signal; to direct by a signal. —adj. remarkably good or bad, noteworthy. —**signal-box** n. a building from which

railway signals are controlled. —**signaller** n. [f. OF f. L *signalis* (as prec.)]

signalize v.t. to make noteworthy or remarkable. [f. prec.]

signally adv. remarkably, notably. [f. SIGNAL]

signalman n. (*pl.* **-men**) a person responsible for displaying or operating signals.

signatory /ˈsɪgnətərɪ/ adj. that has signed an agreement, especially a treaty. —n. a signatory party, especially a State. [as foll.]

signature /ˈsɪgnətʃə(r)/ n. 1. a person's name or initials used in signing. 2. the act of signing. 3. (*Mus.*) a sign put after the clef to indicate the key or time (ill. MUSICAL NOTATION). 4. a section of a book made from one sheet folded and cut; a letter or figure indicating a sequence of these. —**signature tune**, a tune used, especially in broadcasting, to announce a particular programme or performer etc. [f. L *signatura* (*signare* to mark, as SIGN)]

signboard n. a board with a name or symbol etc. displayed outside a shop or hotel etc.

signet /ˈsɪgnɪt/ n. a small seal used with or instead of a person's signature. —**signet ring**, a finger-ring with a signet set in it. [f. OF or L (as SIGN)]

significance /sɪgˈnɪfɪkəns/ n. 1. signifying. 2. what is meant. 3. importance. —**significancy** n. [OF or f. L (as SIGNIFY)]

significant /sɪgˈnɪfɪkənt/ adj. 1. having or conveying a meaning, especially an important or noteworthy one. 2. important. —**significant figure**, (*Math.*) a digit conveying information about a number containing it, and not a zero used simply to fill a vacant place at the beginning or end. —**significantly** adv. [f. L (as foll.)]

signify /ˈsɪgnɪfaɪ/ v.t./i. 1. to be a sign, symbol, or indication of. 2. to mean, to have as a meaning. 3. to make known. 4. to be of importance. —**signification** /-fɪˈkeɪʃ(ə)n/ n. [f. OF f. L *significare* (as SIGN, *facere* make)]

signor /ˈsiːnjɔː(r)/ n. (*pl.* **signori** /-ˈnjɔːrɪ/) the title used of or to an Italian man. [It. f. L, = SENIOR]

signora /siːnˈjɔːrə/ n. the title used of or to an Italian married woman. [fem. of prec.]

signorina /siːnjəˈriːnə/ n. the title used of or to an Italian unmarried woman. [as prec.]

signpost n. a post bearing a sign, especially one indicating direction. —v.t. to provide with a post or posts of this kind.

Sikh /siːk, sɪk/ n. an adherent of Sikhism. There are over 10 million Sikhs, most of whom live in Punjab. —**Sikh Wars**, wars between the Sikhs and the British in 1845 and 1848–9, culminating in the British annexation of the Punjab. [Hindi, = disciple, f. Skr.]

Sikhism /ˈsiːkɪz(ə)m, ˈsɪ-/ n. a monotheistic religion founded in the Punjab in the 15th c. by Guru Nanak. It combines elements of Hinduism and Islam, accepting the Hindu concepts of karma and reincarnation but rejecting the caste system, and has one sacred scripture, the Adi Granth. The tenth and last of the series of gurus, Gobind Singh, prescribed the distinctive outward forms (the so-called five Ks)—long hair (to be covered by a turban) and uncut beard (*kesh*), comb (*kangha*), short sword (*kirpan*), steel bangle (*kara*), and short trousers for horse-riding (*kaccha*). Originating as a religion, Sikkhism became a militant political movement within the Punjab. [f. prec.]

Sikkim /ˈsɪkɪm/ a State of India (since 1975) in the eastern Himalayas, previously an Indian protectorate; capital, Gangtok. —**Sikkimese** /-ˈmiːz/ adj. & n.

Sikorsky /sɪˈkɔːskɪ/, Igor Ivan (1889–1972), Russian-born aircraft designer who studied aeronautics in Paris before returning to Russia to build the world's first large four-engined aircraft, the Grand, in 1913. After experimenting unsuccessfully with helicopters he emigrated to New York (1919), where he established the Sikorski Aero Engineering Co. (1923) and produced many famous amphibious aircraft and flying boats. In the 1930s he again turned his attention to helicopters and personally flew the prototype of the world's first mass-produced helicopter in 1939; his name is closely associated with their subsequent development.

silage /ˈsaɪlɪdʒ/ n. 1. storage in a silo. 2. green fodder so stored. [alt. f. ENSILAGE after SILO]

silence /ˈsaɪləns/ n. 1. absence of sound. 2. avoidance of or abstinence from speech or making a noise. 3. avoidance of mentioning a thing or of betraying a secret etc. —v.t. to make silent by coercion or superior argument; to stop the sound of. —**in silence**, without speech or other sound. [f. OF or L *silentium* (as SILENT)]

silencer *n.* a device for reducing the noise made by a gun or a vehicle's exhaust etc. [f. prec.]

silent /ˈsaɪlənt/ *adj.* not speaking; not making or accompanied by a sound; saying little. —**silent majority**, people of moderate opinions who rarely make themselves heard. —**silently** *adv.* [f. L *silēre* be silent]

Silenus /saɪˈliːnəs/ (*Gk myth.*) one of the sileni (see foll.) with many weaknesses but also with intellectual talents, who was entrusted with the education of Dionysus. He is depicted either as dignified, inspired, and musical, or as an old drunkard. Portraits of Socrates and idealized heads of Silenus show great similarity.

silenus /saɪˈliːnəs/ *n.* (*pl.* **-i**) (*Gk myth.*) any of a class of woodland spirits, usually shown in art as old and with horse-ears, similar to the satyrs. [L f. Gk]

Silesia /saɪˈliːzjə/ a region of central Europe (now largely in SW Poland), an ancient district and duchy, partitioned at various times between the States of Prussia, Austria-Hungary, Poland, and Czechoslovakia. —**Silesian** *adj.* & *n.*

silhouette /sɪluːˈet/ *n.* **1.** a picture of a person in profile or of a thing in outline only, either dark against a light background or vice versa, or cut out in pages (see below). **2.** an appearance of a person or thing against the light so that only the outline is distinguishable. —*v.t.* to represent or (usu. in *pass.*) show in silhouette. [f. Étienne de *Silhouette*, Fr. author and politician (d. 1767), amateur maker of paper cut-outs]

The method of silhouette painting is seen in Egyptian and Greek art, but its main vogue was from the mid-18th c. to mid-19th c., when such portraiture was popularized by neoclassical taste until the introduction of photography relegated it to a position of curiosity value.

silica /ˈsɪlɪkə/ *n.* a mineral (silicon dioxide) occurring as quartz and as the main constituent of sandstone and other rocks. —**siliceous** /sɪˈlɪʃəs/ *adj.* [f. L *silex* flint]

silicate /ˈsɪlɪkeɪt/ *n.* a compound of a metal or metals, silicon and oxygen. [f. prec.]

silicon /ˈsɪlɪkən/ *n.* a non-metallic element, symbol Si, atomic number 14, the most abundant element in the earth's crust after oxygen (see below). —**silicon chip**, a microchip made of silicon. **Silicon Valley**, the Santa Clara valley SE of San Francisco, where many leading US microelectronic firms are situated. [as SILICA, replacing earlier *silicium*]

Silicon was first isolated and described as an element by Berzelius in 1823. It does not occur uncombined in nature, but most rocks of the earth's crust consist primarily of silica or silicates. Pure silicon, which can exist in a dark grey crystalline form or as an amorphous powder, is used in some alloys and (as a semiconductor) as the basis of many microelectronic devices, where it has largely replaced the chemically similar element germanium (which was used for the first transistors). Silicon compounds have for centuries been widely used: glass, pottery, and bricks are largely composed of silicate minerals.

silicone /ˈsɪlɪkəʊn/ *n.* one of many polymeric organic compounds of silicon with high resistance to cold, heat, water, and the passage of electricity, used in polishes, paints, lubricants, etc. [f. prec.]

silicosis /sɪlɪˈkəʊsɪs/ *n.* a lung disease caused by inhaling dust containing silica. [as SILICA]

silk *n.* **1.** the fine soft strong fibre produced by a silkworm in making its cocoon; thread or cloth made from or resembling this; (in *pl.*) clothing made from silk. **2.** a similar fibre produced by spiders or some insects. **3.** (*colloq.*) a King's or Queen's Counsel, as having the right to wear a silk gown. **4.** fine soft strands like threads of silk. **5.** (*attrib.*) made of silk. —**silk hat**, a tall cylindrical hat covered with silk plush. **silk-screen printing**, screen-printing. **take silk**, to become a King's or Queen's Counsel. [OE f. L *sericum* (*seres* f. Gk *Seres* the Chinese or neighbouring peoples)]

silken *adj.* of or resembling silk; soft, smooth, or lustrous. [as prec.]

silkworm *n.* a caterpillar of a kind of moth, which feeds on mulberry leaves and spins its cocoon of silk.

silky *adj.* **1.** soft and smooth like silk. **2.** suave. —**silkily** *adv.*, **silkiness** *n.* [f. SILK]

sill *n.* **1.** a slab of wood or stone etc. at the base of a window or doorway etc. (ill. HOUSES). **2.** a sheet of igneous rock intruded between other rocks. [OE]

sillabub var. of SYLLABUB.

silly *adj.* **1.** lacking good sense, foolish, unwise. **2.** weak-minded. **3.** (of a fielding position in cricket) very close to

the batsman. —*n.* (*colloq.*) a foolish person. —**silly-billy** *n.* (*colloq.*) a foolish person. —**silliness** *n.* [OE, = happy]

silo /ˈsaɪləʊ/ *n.* (*pl.* **silos**) **1.** a pit or airtight structure in which green crops are stored for fodder. **2.** a tower or pit for the storage of cement or grain etc. **3.** an underground place where a guided missile is kept ready for firing. [Sp. f. L f. Gk *siros* pit for corn]

Siloam /saɪˈləʊəm/ a spring and pool of water near ancient Jerusalem, where the man born blind was bidden to wash (John 9: 7).

silt *n.* sediment deposited by water in a channel or harbour etc. —*v.t./i.* to block or be blocked with silt. —**siltation** /-ˈteɪʃ(ə)n/ *n.* [perh. rel. to Da. *sylt* salt-marsh (as SALT)]

Silurian /saɪˈljʊərɪən/ *adj.* of the third period of the Palaeozoic era, following the Ordovician and preceding the Devonian, lasting from about 438 to 408 million years ago. The first land plants and the first true fish (with jaws) appeared during this period. —*n.* the Silurian period. [f. L *Silures* ancient British tribe in SE Wales]

silvan /ˈsɪlv(ə)n/ *adj.* of the woods; having woods, rural. [f. F or L (*silva* wood)]

silver *n.* **1.** a white lustrous precious metallic element, symbol Ag, atomic number 47 (see below). **2.** coins or articles made of or looking like silver. **3.** the colour of silver. **4.** a silver medal. —*adj.* of or coloured like silver. —*v.t./i.* **1.** to coat or plate with silver. **2.** to give a silvery appearance to. **3.** to provide (a mirror-glass) with a backing of tin amalgam etc. **4.** (of hair) to turn grey or white. —**silver birch**, the common birch (*Betula pendula*) with a silver-coloured bark. **silver-fish** *n.* a silver-coloured fish; a silvery bristletail (*Lepisma saccharina*) found in books and damp places. **silver jubilee**, a 25th anniversary. **Silver Latin**, see LATIN. **silver lining**, a consolation or hopeful feature in misfortune. **silver medal**, a medal of silver awarded as second prize. **silver paper**, tin foil. **silver plate**, articles plated with silver. **silver-plated** *adj.* plated with silver. **silver sand**, fine pure sand used in gardening. **silver wedding**, the 25th anniversary of a wedding. [OE]

Silver is found in the uncombined state in nature as well as in a number of ores. It has been used for jewellery and other ornaments since ancient times and it is also used in coins, cutlery, the coatings of mirrors, and dental amalgams; a further use is in printed circuits, as silver is a very good electrical conductor. The metal is generally resistant to corrosion but tarnishes in air through a reaction with small quantities of hydrogen sulphide gas. Silver salts are used in photographic films as they decompose when exposed to light, depositing metallic silver.

silver-point *n.* the process (now largely obsolete) of drawing with a silver-pointed instrument on paper coated with a special ground of powdered bone or zinc white. Fragments of metal deposited on the paper produce a very delicate fine line that does not smudge and cannot be erased. It was widely used in the 15th and 16th c. in Italy, the Netherlands, and Germany. Points of other metals, such as lead, were also used.

silverside *n.* the upper (and usually best) side of a round of beef.

silversmith *n.* one who makes articles in silver.

silverware *n.* articles made of or plated with silver.

silvery *adj.* **1.** like silver in colour or appearance. **2.** having a clear gentle ringing sound. [f. SILVER]

silviculture /ˈsɪlvɪkʌltʃə(r)/ *n.* cultivation of forest trees. [F (as SILVAN, CULTURE)]

sima /ˈsaɪmə/ *n.* the continuous basal layer of the earth's crust, composed of relatively heavy basic rocks rich in silica and magnesia, that underlies the sial of the continental masses and forms the crust under the oceans; the material of which it is composed. The lower limit of the sima is generally taken to be the Mohorovičić discontinuity. [f. SILICON + MAGNESIUM]

Simenon /ˈsiːmənɔ̃/, Georges (1903–), Belgian-French novelist, a prolific writer, who produced some 300 works between 1920 and 1973. His popularity rests on the series of detective novels featuring Commissaire Maigret, introduced in 1931, who sets out to discover, with great insight and sensitivity to local atmosphere, the human motives behind the crime.

Simeon /ˈsɪmɪən/ **1.** Hebrew patriarch, son of Jacob and Leah (Gen. 29: 33). **2.** the tribe of Israel traditionally descended from him.

Simeon Stylites /sɪmɪən staɪˈlaɪtiːz/, St (c.390–459) a hermit in northern Syria, the first ascetic to live on top of a pillar (Gk. *stulos*). The pillar eventually reached 40 cubits (*c*.20 m) in height. This novel form of austerity attracted many pilgrims and imitators in the East.

simian /ˈsɪmɪən/ *adj.* resembling an ape or monkey. —*n.* an ape or monkey. [f. L *simia* monkey]

similar /ˈsɪmɪlə(r)/ *adj.* **1.** like, alike; having a resemblance but not quite the same. **2.** of the same kind, nature, shape, or amount. —**similarity** /-ˈlærɪtɪ/ *n.*, **similarly** *adv.* [f. F or L (*similis* like)]

simile /ˈsɪmɪlɪ/ *n.* a figure of speech in which one thing is compared to another; the use of such a comparison. [L, neut. of *similis* like]

similitude /sɪˈmɪlɪtjuːd/ *n.* **1.** similarity, outward appearance. **2.** comparison; expression of comparison. [f. OF or L (as prec.)]

simmer *v.t./i.* **1.** to keep or be kept bubbling or boiling gently. **2.** to be in a state of anger or laughter which is only just suppressed. —*n.* a simmering condition. —**simmer down**, to become less agitated. [alt. f. earlier *simper* (perh. imit.)]

Simnel /ˈsɪmn(ə)l/, Lambert (*c*.1475–1525), son of an Irish baker, trained by Yorkists to impersonate the Earl of Warwick in an attempt to overthrow Henry VII. He was crowned in Dublin in 1487 as Edward VI but captured in the Yorkist uprising when the rebels were defeated at Stoke-on-Trent. As there was no real danger of his being taken to be the real Warwick (who was imprisoned in the Tower), he was not executed, but was given a menial post in the royal household.

simnel /ˈsɪmn(ə)l/ *n.* a rich cake, especially for Mothering Sunday or Easter, covered with marzipan and decorated. [f. OF, ult. f. L *simila* fine flour]

Simon /ˈsaɪmən/, St (1st c. AD), one of the twelve Apostles, who may have been a member of the Zealots. According to one tradition he preached and was martyred in Persia along with St Jude. Feast day (with St Jude), 28 Oct.

Simonides /saɪˈmɒnɪdiːz/ (*c*.556–468 BC) Greek lyric and elegiac poet, admired for his sweet and harmonious style. He wrote for the ruling men in Athens, Thessaly, and Syracuse, and composed verse inscriptions for the fallen of Marathon and for the Spartans who died at Thermopylae.

simony /ˈsaɪmənɪ/ *n.* the buying or selling of ecclesiastical offices. [f. OF f. L (*Simon* Magus (Acts 8: 18), with allusion to his offer of money to the Apostles to purchase the power of giving the Holy Ghost by the laying on of hands)]

simoom /sɪˈmuːm/ *n.* a hot dry dust-laden desert wind. [f. Arab. (*samma* to poison)]

simper *v.t./i.* to smile in a silly or affected way; to express by or with simpering. —*n.* such a smile. [cf. Da. & Norw. *semper* delicate]

simple *adj.* **1.** easily understood or done, presenting no difficulty. **2.** not complicated or elaborate; without luxury or sophistication. **3.** not compound, consisting of or involving only one element or operation etc. **4.** absolute, unqualified; straightforward; **5.** foolish, ignorant; gullible; feeble-minded. —**simple fracture**, a fracture of the bone only. **simple interest**, see INTEREST. **simple-minded** *adj.* unsophisticated, without cunning; feeble-minded. **simple time**, (*Mus.*) that with a binary subdivision of the unit (e.g. into two, four, eight). [f. OF f. L *simplus*]

simpleton /ˈsɪmp(ə)lt(ə)n/ *n.* a stupid or gullible person. [f. prec., after surnames from place-names in -*ton* (town)]

simplicity /sɪmˈplɪsɪtɪ/ *n.* the fact or quality of being simple. [f. L *simplex* (as SIMPLE)]

simplify /ˈsɪmplɪfaɪ/ *v.t.* to make simple or less difficult. —**simplification** /-fɪˈkeɪʃ(ə)n/ *n.* [f. F f. L *simplificare* make simple]

simplistic /sɪmˈplɪstɪk/ *adj.* excessively or affectedly simple or simplified. —**simplistically** *adv.* [f. SIMPLE]

Simplon /ˈsæplɔ̃/ a pass in the Alps in southern Switzerland reaching an altitude of 2,028 m (6,591 ft.). The nearby railway tunnel connecting Switzerland and Italy is the longest main-line railway tunnel in the world (19 km, 12 miles).

simply *adv.* **1.** in a simple manner. **2.** absolutely, without doubt. **3.** merely. [f. SIMPLE]

Simpson /ˈsɪmps(ə)n/, Sir James Young (1811–71), Scottish surgeon and obstetrician who discovered the usefulness of chloroform as an anaesthetic by experimentation on himself and his colleagues shortly after the first use of ether. He was active in the debate over which of the two was the best agent to use in surgery, and made a famous attack on Lister and antisepsis. Simpson was also a distinguished

antiquarian and historian, publishing monographs on archaeology and the history of medicine.

simulate /ˈsɪmjʊleɪt/ *v.t.* **1.** to pretend to be, have, or feel. **2.** to imitate or counterfeit; to imitate the conditions of (a situation etc.), e.g. for training. —**simulation** /-ˈleɪʃ(ə)n/ *n.*, **simulator** *n.* [f. L *simulare* (*similis* like)]

simultaneous /sɪmǝlˈteɪnɪəs/ *adj.* occurring or operating at the same time. —**simultaneity** /-tǝˈneɪɪtɪ/ *n.*, **simultaneously** *adv.* [f. L (*simul* at the same time)]

sin[1] *n.* **1.** the breaking of a religious or moral law, especially by a conscious act; an act that does this. **2.** a serious fault or offence. **3.** an act that is contrary to common sense. —*v.i.* (**-nn-**) to commit a sin. [OE]

sin[2] /saɪn/ *abbr.* sine.

Sinai /ˈsaɪnaɪ, -nɪaɪ/ a peninsula, mostly desert, at the north end of the Red Sea, now part of Egypt. In the south is Mount Sinai where according to Exod. 19-34 the Ten Commandments and the Tables of the Law were given to Moses.

since *prep.* after (a specified past event or time); between (a past event or time) and now. —*conj.* **1.** during or in the time after. **2.** for the reason that, because. —*adv.* **1.** from that time or event until now. **2.** ago. [OE, = after that]

sincere /sɪnˈsɪə(r)/ *adj.* free from pretence or deceit. —**sincerity** /sɪnˈserɪtɪ/ *n.* [f. L *sincerus* clean, pure]

sincerely *adv.* in a sincere manner. —**yours sincerely**, a formula for ending a letter. [f. prec.]

Sindbad /ˈsɪndbæd/ (also **Sinbad the Sailor**) hero of one of the tales in the *Arabian Nights*, who relates his fantastic adventures in a number of voyages.

sindonology /sɪndəˈnɒlədʒɪ/ *n.* study of the Holy Shroud of Turin, in which the body of Christ was reputedly wrapped. [f. OF or L f. Gk *sindōn* linen fabric, shroud + -LOGY]

sine /saɪn/ *n.* the ratio of the side of the opposite acute angle (in a right-angled triangle) to the hypotenuse. [f. L *sinus* curve, fold of toga, tr. Arab. *jayb* bosom, sine]

sinecure /ˈsaɪnɪkjʊə(r)/ *n.* a position that requires little or no work but yields profit or honour. [f. L *sine cura* without care]

sine die /saɪnɪ ˈdaɪiː, sɪneɪ ˈdiːeɪ/ *adv.* (of business adjourned indefinitely) with no appointed date. [L, = without a day]

sine qua non /sɪneɪ kwɑː ˈnəʊn, saɪnɪ kweɪ ˈnɒn/ an indispensable condition or qualification. [L, = without which not]

sinew /ˈsɪnjuː/ *n.* **1.** tough fibrous tissue joining a muscle to a bone; a piece of this. **2.** (in *pl.*) muscles, bodily strength. **3.** a thing that strengthens or sustains. [OE]

sinewy *adj.* having strong sinews. [f. prec.]

sinful *adj.* committing or involving sin; wicked. —**sinfully** *adv.*, **sinfulness** *n.* [f. SIN + -FUL]

sing *v.t./i.* (*past* **sang**; *p.p.* **sung**) **1.** to utter musical sounds with the voice, especially with a set tune; to utter or produce by singing. **2.** (of the wind, a kettle, etc.) to make a humming, buzzing, or ringing sound; (of the ears) to be affected with a ringing or buzzing sound. **3.** (*slang*) to act as an informer. —**sing-along** *n.* a song or recording to which one can sing in accompaniment; a sing-song to the accompaniment of a leader or tune. **sing out**, to shout. **sing the praises of**, to praise enthusiastically or continually. —**singer** *n.* [OE]

Singapore /sɪŋɡəˈpɔː(r)/ a country in SE Asia, a member State of the Commonwealth, consisting of the island of Singapore and about 54 smaller islands, lying just north of the equator off the southern tip of the Malay Peninsula to which it is linked by a causeway carrying a road and railway; pop. (1980) 2,413,945; official languages, Malay, Chinese, Tamil, and English. Sir Stamford Raffles established a trading post under the East India Company in 1819, and it was incorporated with Penang and Malacca to form the Straits Settlements in 1826; these became a Crown Colony in the following year. Singapore rapidly grew, by virtue of its large protected harbour, to become the most important commercial centre and naval base in SE Asia. It fell to the Japanese in 1942, and after liberation became first a British Crown Colony in 1946 and then a self-governing State in 1959. Federated with Malaysia in 1963, it regained full independence two years later and remains a world trade and financial centre; it also has an important oil-refining industry. —**Singaporean** /-ˈpɔːrɪən/ *adj.* & *n.*

singe /sɪndʒ/ *v.t./i.* (*partic.* **singeing**) to burn superficially or lightly; to burn off the tips or ends of. —*n.* **1.** a superficial burn. **2.** an act of singeing. [OE]

Singhalese var. of SINHALESE.

single /ˈsɪŋg(ə)l/ *adj.* **1.** one only, not double or multiple; united, undivided; designed for or used or done by one person etc. **2.** one by itself; regarded separately; not married. **3.** (of a ticket) valid for the outward journey only, not a return. **4.** (with neg. or interrog.) even one. **5.** (of a flower) having only one set of petals. —*n.* **1.** a thing that is single, a single item in a series. **2.** a single ticket. **3.** a pop record with one piece of music on each side. **4.** a hit for one run in cricket. **5.** (usu. in *pl.*) a game with one player on each side. —*v.t.* (with *out*) to choose for special attention etc.; to distinguish from others. —**single-breasted** *adj.* (of a coat etc.) having only one set of buttons and overlapping little across the breast. **single combat**, a duel. **single file**, a file of persons in one line. **single-handed** *adv.* without help from another; (*adj.*) done single-handed. **single-minded** *adj.* having or intent on only one purpose. —**singly** *adv.* [f. OF f. L *singulus* (rel. to SIMPLE)]

singlet /ˈsɪŋglɪt/ *n.* a man's sleeveless garment worn under or instead of a shirt. [f. prec., after *doublet*]

singleton /ˈsɪŋgəlt(ə)n/ *n.* a single person or thing, especially a player's only card of a suit. [f. SINGLE, after *simpleton*]

Sing Sing a New York State Prison, built in 1825–8 at Ossining village on the Hudson River and formerly notorious for its severe discipline. It is now called Ossining Correctional Facility.

singsong *adj.* uttered with a monotonous rhythm or cadence. —*n.* **1.** a singsong manner. **2.** an informal gathering for singing in chorus.

singular /ˈsɪŋgjʊlə(r)/ *adj.* **1.** unique; much beyond the average; extraordinary; eccentric, strange. **2.** (*Gram.* of a word or form) denoting one person or thing. —*n.* (*Gram.*) a singular word or form, the singular number. —**singularity** /-ˈlærɪtɪ/ *n.*, **singularly** *adv.* [f. OF f. L *singularis* (as SINGLE)]

Sinhala /ˈsɪnhələ/ *adj. & n.* = foll. [Sinh.]

Sinhalese /sɪnhəˈliːz/ *adj.* of the Sinhalese or their language. —*n.* (*pl.* same) **1.** a member of an Aryan people deriving from northern India and forming the majority of the population in Sri Lanka. **2.** their language, spoken by 9 million people in Sri Lanka. It is descended from Sanskrit and was brought by settlers from northern India in the 5th c. BC; its alphabet resembles that of the Dravidian languages of southern India. [f. Skr. *Sinhalam* Sri Lanka]

sinister /ˈsɪnɪstə(r)/ *adj.* **1.** suggestive of evil, looking malignant or villainous; wicked, criminal; of evil omen. **2.** (in heraldry) of or on the left-hand side (the observer's right) of a shield etc. (ill. HERALDRY). [f. OF or L, = left]

sink *v.t./i.* (*past* **sank**; *p.p.* **sunk** or (as *adj.*) **SUNKEN**) **1.** to fall slowly downwards; to come gradually to a lower level or pitch; to disappear below the horizon; to go or penetrate below the surface, especially of a liquid; (of a ship) to go to the bottom of the sea etc. **2.** to pass into a less active condition; to lose value or strength etc. gradually. **3.** to cause or allow to sink; to overlook or forget (one's differences etc.) to cause the failure or discomfiture of. **4.** to dig (a well); to bore (a shaft). **5.** to engrave (a die). **6.** to invest (money). **7.** to cause (a ball) to enter a pocket in billiards, a hole in golf, etc. —*n.* **1.** a fixed basin with a drainage pipe and usually with a water-supply. **2.** a place where foul liquid collects; a place of rampant vice etc. —**sink in**, to penetrate; to become understood. **sinking feeling**, a feeling of hunger or fear. **sinking fund**, a fund for the gradual repayment of a debt. **sunk fence**, a fence formed by or built along the bottom of a ditch. [OE]

sinker *n.* a weight used to sink a fishing-line or sounding-line. [f. SINK]

sinner *n.* one who sins. [f. SIN]

Sinn Fein /ʃɪn ˈfeɪn/ an Irish movement founded in 1905 by Arthur Griffith (1872–1922), Irish journalist and politician, originally aiming at the independence of Ireland and a revival of Irish culture and language and now dedicated to the political unification of Northern Ireland and the Republic of Ireland. Sinn Fein became increasingly republican with the failure of the Home Rule movement. After the failure of the Easter rising it began to win Irish seats in Parliament, its members refusing to go to Westminster and setting up their own Parliament in Ireland in 1919. The republican section of the party supported De Valera in his rejection of the Anglo-Irish Treaty, most of it joining his Fianna Fáil party on its formation in 1926. The remainder of the party began to function as the political wing of the

IRA, and in 1969 split like the IRA into Official and Provisional wings. [f. Ir., = we ourselves]

Sino- /saɪnəʊ-/ *in comb.* Chinese (and) (*Sino-American*; *Sinophobia*). [f. Gk *Sinai* the Chinese]

Sino-Japanese Wars wars fought between China and Japan. The first, in 1894–5, caused by rivalry over Korea, was ended by Treaty of Shimonoseki in Japan's favour. Poor Chinese performance in the war was a factor in the eventual overthrow of the Manchus in 1912. The second was in 1937–45; Japanese expansionism led to trouble in Manchuria in 1931 and to the establishment of a Japanese puppet State (Manchukuo) a year later. Hostilities began in earnest in 1937, but after two years of dramatic Japanese successes degenerated into stalemate. The Japanese position was gradually eroded by Communist guerrilla successes and finally collapsed at the end of the Second World War.

sinology /sɪˈnɒlədʒɪ, saɪ-/ *n.* the study of the Chinese language and history etc. —**sinologist** *n.* [f. SINO- + -LOGY]

Sino-Tibetan /saɪnəʊtɪˈbet(ə)n/ *adj.* of a language group which includes Chinese, Burmese, Tibetan, Nepalese, and Thai. They are tonal languages, but the exact relationships between them are far from clear. —*n.* this group of languages.

sinter *n.* a solid coalesced by heating. —*v.t./i.* to form into a sinter. [G, = CINDER]

sinuate /ˈsɪnjuːət/ *adj.* wavy-edged, with distinct inward and outward bends along the edge (ill. PLANTS). [f. L, p.p. of *sinuare* to bend]

sinuous /ˈsɪnjʊəs/ *adj.* with many curves, undulating, meandering. —**sinuosity** /-ˈɒsɪtɪ/ *n.*, **sinuously** *adv.* [f. F or L (as foll.)]

sinus /ˈsaɪnəs/ *n.* a cavity of bone or tissue, especially in the skull communicating with the nostrils (ill. BODY 2). [L, = bosom, recess]

sinusitis /saɪnəˈsaɪtɪs/ *n.* inflammation of the sinus. [f. prec. + -ITIS]

Sion var. of ZION.

Sioux /suː/ *n.* (*pl.* same) a member or the language of a group of North American Indian tribes. —*adj.* of the Sioux or their language. —**Siouan** /ˈsuːən/ *adj.* [F, f. native name]

sip *v.t./i.* (**-pp-**) to drink in repeated small mouthfuls or spoonfuls. —*n.* a small mouthful of liquid; an act of taking this. [perh. modification of SUP]

siphon /ˈsaɪf(ə)n/ *n.* **1.** a pipe or tube shaped like an inverted V or U with unequal legs, to convey liquid from a container to a lower level of atmospheric pressure. **2.** a bottle from which aerated water is forced out by the pressure of a gas. **3.** the sucking-tube of some insects or small animals. —*v.t./i.* to conduct or flow (as) through a siphon. [F or f. L f. Gk *siphōn* pipe]

sir /sɜː(r)/ *n.* **1.** a polite or respectful form of address or reference to a man. **2. Sir**, the title prefixed to the Christian name of a knight or baronet. [reduced form of SIRE]

sire *n.* **1.** the male parent of an animal, especially a stallion kept for breeding. **2.** (*archaic*) a form of address to a king. **3.** (*archaic*) a father or male ancestor. —*v.t.* (esp. of a stallion) to beget. [f. OF f. L *senior* (see SENIOR)]

siren /ˈsaɪrən/ *n.* **1.** (*Gk myth.*) any of the creatures (two or three in number) who had the power of luring seafarers to destruction by their song. When definite locations began to be attached to Homeric geography the sirens were associated with the coast of Italy, and were worshipped in Naples, Sorrentum, and Sicily. Their appearance is not described by Homer, but in art they are represented as half women and half birds, though in early examples male bearded sirens preponderate. The rapacious monsters of the archaic period are ennobled in classical art to mournful beautiful beings; in Hellenistic art and literature they are representative of music. **2.** a dangerously fascinating woman, a temptress; (*attrib.*) irresistibly tempting. **3.** a device for making a loud prolonged signal or warning sound; the sound made. [f. OF f. L f. Gk]

sirenian /saɪˈriːnɪən/ *adj.* of the order Sirenia of large aquatic plant-eating mammals that includes the dugong and the manatee. —*n.* a member of this order. [as prec.]

Sirius /ˈsɪrɪəs/ the Dog Star, alpha Canis Majoris, the brightest of the fixed stars, an unmistakable jewel in the winter sky of the northern hemisphere, apparently following on the heels of the hunter Orion. It was important to the ancient Egyptians as its heliacal rising coincided with the season of flooding of the Nile. It has a dim companion, Sirius B or the Pup, which is a white dwarf. The pronounced twinkling of Sirius, familiar to observers in northern latitudes, arises from atmospheric refraction and is not a property of the star itself.

sirloin /'sɜːlɔɪn/ *n.* **1.** the upper and choicer part of a loin of beef. **2.** (*US*) a rump steak. [f. OF (as SUR-², LOIN)]

sirocco /sɪ'rɒkəʊ/ *n.* (*pl.* **-os**) a hot moist wind in southern Europe. [F f. It. ult. f. Arab., = east wind]

sis *n.* (*colloq.*) sister. [abbr.]

sisal /'saɪs(ə)l/ *n.* fibre from the leaves of an agave. [f. *Sisal*, port of Yucatan]

siskin /'sɪskɪn/ *n.* a small songbird (*Spinus spinus*). [f. MDu.]

Sisley /'sɪslɪ/, Alfred (1839-99), French-born painter, of English parentage. His development towards impressionism from his early Corot-influenced landscapes was gradual and greatly indebted to Monet. He is chiefly remembered for his paintings of the Seine in the 1870s, with their concentration on reflecting surfaces, tonal mastery, and careful orchestration of fluid brush-work.

sissy *n.* an effeminate or cowardly person. *—adj.* characteristic of a sissy. [f. SIS]

sister *n.* **1.** a woman or girl in relation to the other sons and daughters of her parents. **2.** a close woman friend or associate; a female fellow member of the same church, trade union, or other association, or of the human race. **3.** a member of a sisterhood, especially a nun. **4.** a female hospital nurse in authority over others; (*colloq.*) any female nurse. **5.** (*attrib.*) of the same type, design, origin, etc. **—sister-in-law** *n.* (*pl.* **sisters-in-law**) the sister of one's husband or wife; one's brother's wife. **—sisterly** *adj.* [f. ON]

sisterhood *n.* **1.** the relationship (as) of sisters. **2.** a society of women bound by monastic views or devoting themselves to religious or charitable work. [f. prec. + -HOOD]

Sistine /'sɪstiːn/ *adj.* of any of the popes called Sixtus, especially Sixtus IV (pope 1471-84). **—Sistine chapel**, a chapel in the Vatican, built by Sixtus IV, containing Michelangelo's painted ceiling and his fresco of the Last Judgement. [f. It. *Sistino* (*Sisto* Sixtus)]

Sisyphean /sɪsɪ'fiːən/ *adj.* as of Sisyphus; endlessly laborious. [f. foll.]

Sisyphus /'sɪsɪfəs/ (*Gk myth.*) the son of Aeolus, condemned for his misdeeds to Hades where his eternal task was to roll a large stone to the top of a hill from which it always rolled down again.

sit *v.t./i.* (**-tt-**; *past & p.p.* **sat**) **1.** to take or be in a position in which the body is supported more or less upright by the buttocks resting on the ground or a raised seat etc. **2.** to cause to sit, to place in a sitting position. **3.** (of a bird) to perch; (of an animal) to rest with the hind legs bent and the body close to the ground. **4.** (of a bird) to remain on the nest to hatch eggs. **5.** to be engaged in an occupation in which the sitting position is usual; to pose for a portrait; to be a Member of Parliament *for* a constituency; to be a candidate *for* an examination etc.; to undergo (an examination). **6.** (of a parliament or court etc.) to be in session. **7.** to be in a more or less permanent position or condition. **8.** (of clothes etc.) to fit or hang in a certain way. **9.** to keep or have one's seat on (a horse etc.). **—be sitting pretty**, to be comfortably or advantageously placed. **sit at a person's feet**, to be his or her pupil. **sit back**, to relax one's efforts. **sit down**, to sit after standing; to cause to sit; to suffer tamely (under humiliation etc.). **sit-down** *adj.* (of a meal) eaten sitting. **sit-down strike**, a strike in which workers refuse to leave their place of work. **sit in**, to occupy a place as a protest. **sit-in** *n.* such a protest. **sit in judgement**, to assume the right of judging others; to be censorious. **sit in on**, to be present as a guest or observer at (a meeting). **sit on**, to be a member of (a committee etc.); to hold a session or inquiry concerning; (*colloq.*) to delay action about; (*slang*) to repress, rebuke, or snub. **sit on the fence**, to remain neutral or undecided. **sit out**, to take no part in (a dance etc.); to stay until the end of (an ordeal etc.). **sit tight**, (*colloq.*) to remain firmly in one's place; not to yield. **sit up**, to rise from a lying to a sitting position; to sit firmly upright; not to go to bed (until later than the usual time); (*colloq.*) to have one's interest or attention suddenly aroused. **sit-upon** *n.* (*colloq.*) the buttocks. [f. OE]

Sita /'siːtɑː/ (in the Ramayana) the wife of Rama, the Hindu model of the ideal woman, an incarnation of Lakshmi [f. Skr., = furrow]

sitar /sɪ'tɑː(r)/ *n.* an Indian long-necked lute, of Persian origin, one of the most important of Indian music and now well known also in the West (ill. MUSICAL NOTATION). The name derives from the Persian *sehtar*, 'three-stringed', and originally there were three melody strings (from four to seven are now common), together with a dozen or more 'sympathetic strings' (made of metal and providing a special background resonance) and two or three drone strings. The strings are plucked with a plectrum. [f. Hindi f. Pers.]

sitcom /'sɪtkɒm/ *n.* (*colloq.*) a situation comedy. [abbr.]

site *n.* **1.** the ground on which a town or building stood, stands, or is to stand. **2.** the place where some activity or event takes place or took place. *—v.t.* to locate; to provide with a site. [f. AF or L *situs* local position]

sitter *n.* **1.** one who sits, especially for a portrait. **2.** a baby-sitter. **3.** (*slang*) an easy catch or shot; something easy to do. [f. SIT]

sitting *n.* **1.** the time during which a person or assembly etc. sits continuously. **2.** a clutch of eggs. *—adj.* **1.** having sat down. **2.** (of an animal or bird) not running or flying. **—sitting duck** *or* **target**, a person or thing that is a helpless victim of attack. **sitting-room** *n.* a room for sitting in; space enough to accommodate seated persons. **sitting tenant,** one already occupying a house etc. [f. SIT]

situate /'sɪtjuːeɪt/ *v.t.* **1.** to place or put in a specified position, situation, etc.; (in *p.p.*) in specified circumstances. **2.** to establish or indicate the place of; to put in a context. *—/-ət/ adj.* (*archaic* or *Law*) situated. [f. L *situare* f. *situs* site]

situation /sɪtjuː'eɪʃ(ə)n/ *n.* **1.** a place (with its surroundings) that is occupied by something. **2.** a set of circumstances; a state of affairs; a condition. **3.** an employee's position or job. **—situation comedy**, a comedy (especially a serial) in which the humour derives largely from the particular conjunction of characters and circumstances. **—situational** *adj.* [f. F or L (as prec.)]

Sitwell /'sɪtwel/, Dame Edith (Louisa) (1887-1964), English poet and critic. Light-hearted and experimental, her early verse, like that of her brothers Osbert (1892-1969) and Sacheverell (1897-), marked a revolt against the prevailing Georgian style of the day; *Façade*, a group of her poems in notated rhythm declaimed to music by Sir William Walton, was performed in 1923. Her later verse is graver and more profound.

Siva /'siːvə, 'ʃiːvə/ (*Hinduism*) one of the major gods, perhaps a later development of the Vedic god Rudra. He is worshipped in many aspects: as fierce destroyer, naked ascetic, lord of the cosmic dance, lord of beasts and, most commonly, in the form of the phallus (linga). In his beneficent aspect, he lives in the Himalayas with his wife Parvati and their two sons, Ganesa and Skanda. His mount is the bull Nandi. Typically, Siva is depicted with a third eye in the middle of his forehead, wearing a crescent moon in his matted hair and a necklace of skulls at his throat, entwined with live snakes, and carrying a trident. [f. Skr., = auspicious]

six *adj. & n.* **1.** one more than five; the symbol for this (6, vi, VI). **2.** the size etc. denoted by six. **—at sixes and sevens**, in confusion or disagreement. **hit** *or* **knock for six**, (*colloq.*) to surprise utterly or overwhelm. **six-gun** *or* **-shooter** *n.* (*US*) a revolver with six chambers. [OE]

sixfold *adj. & adv.* six times as much or as many; consisting of six parts. [f. SIX + -FOLD]

sixpence *n.* the sum of 6p; (*formerly*) the sum of 6d., a silver coin worth this.

sixpenny *adj.* costing or worth sixpence.

sixteen /sɪks'tiːn/ *adj. & n.* **1.** one more than fifteen; the symbol for this (16, xvi, XVI). **2.** the size etc. denoted by sixteen. **—sixteenth** *adj. & n.* [OE (as SIX, -TEEN)]

sixth *adj.* next after the fifth. *—n.* each of six equal parts of a thing. **—sixth form**, a form in a secondary school for pupils over 16. **sixth-form college**, a college with special courses for such pupils. **sixth sense**, a supposed faculty giving intuitive or extra-sensory knowledge. **—sixthly** *adv.* [f. SIX]

sixty /'sɪkstɪ/ *adj. & n.* **1.** six times ten; the symbol for this (60, lx, LX). **2.** (in *pl.*) the numbers, years, or degrees of temperature from 60 to 69. **—sixtieth** *adj. & n.* [OE (as SIX)]

size¹ *n.* **1.** the extent of a thing; dimensions, magnitude. **2.** each of the series of standard measurements in which things of the same kind are made, grouped, sold, etc. *—v.t.* to group or sort according to size. **—size up**, to estimate the size of; (*colloq.*) to form a judgement of. **that is the size of it**, (*colloq.*) that is the truth of the matter. **—-sized** *adj.* of a specific size (*large-sized*). [f. OF (as ASSIZE)]

size[2] *n.* a gelatinous solution used in glazing paper, stiffening textiles, etc. —*v.t.* to treat with size. [perh. = prec.]

sizeable *adj.* fairly large. [f. SIZE[1]]

sizzle *v.i.* **1.** to make a spluttering or hissing noise as of frying. **2.** (*colloq.*) to be in a state of great heat or excitement etc. —*n.* a sizzling sound. [imit.]

SJ *abbr.* Society of Jesus.

sjambok /ˈʃæmbɒk/ *n.* (in South Africa) a rhinoceros-hide whip. [Afrik. f. Malay f. Urdu]

skald /skɔːld, skɒld/ *n.* an ancient-Scandinavian poet. [f. ON]

Skara Brae /skɑːrə ˈbreɪ/ a late neolithic (3rd millennium BC) settlement on the main island (Mainland) of Orkney, consisting of stone-built rooms with slab-shelves, chests, and hearths.

skate[1] *n.* each of a pair of blades, or (**roller-skate**) metal frames with four small wheels, fitted to the soles of boots or shoes so that the wearer can glide over ice or a hard surface. —*v.t./i.* to move on skates, to perform (a specified figure) on skates. —**get one's skates on,** (*slang*) to make haste. **skate on thin ice,** to behave rashly, to risk danger etc. **skate over,** to make only a passing reference (or no reference) to. —**skater** *n.* [f. Du. *schaats* f. OF *eschasse* stilt]

skate[2] *n.* (*pl.* **skate**) a fish that is a kind of ray (especially *Raja batis*). [f. ON]

skate[3] *n.* (*slang*) (also **cheap skate**) a contemptible or dishonest person. [orig. unkn.]

skateboard *n.* a short narrow board on roller-skate wheels for riding on while standing. —**skateboarder** *n.*, **skateboarding** *n.*

skedaddle /skɪˈdæd(ə)l/ *colloq.* *v.i.* to depart hurriedly. —*n.* a hurried departure. [orig. unkn.]

skein /skeɪn/ *n.* **1.** a loosely coiled bundle of yarn or thread. **2.** a flock of wild geese etc. in flight. [f. OF *escaigne*; orig. unkn.]

skeleton /ˈskelɪt(ə)n/ *n.* **1.** the hard framework of bones of an animal body (ill. BODY 1); the shell or other hard structure covering or supporting an invertebrate animal. **2.** any supporting framework or structure. **3.** a very thin person or animal. **4.** the remaining part of something after its life or usefulness is gone. **5.** an outline sketch, an epitome. **6.** (*attrib.*) having only the essential or minimum number of persons or parts etc. —**skeleton in the cupboard,** a discreditable or embarrassing fact kept secret. **skeleton key,** a key fitting many locks. —**skeletal** *adj.* [Gk, neut. of *skeletos* dried-up]

Skelton /ˈskelt(ə)n/, John (?1460–1529), English poet, who was created 'poet-laureate' by Oxford, Cambridge, and Louvain Universities and became tutor to the future Henry VIII. His principal works include *The Bowge of Courte*, a satire on the court of Henry VII, *Collyn Cloute*, *Speke Parrot*, and a morality play *Magnyfycence*. His satires contained attacks on Cardinal Wolsey, setting forth the evil consequences of his dominating position, and as a result Skelton was obliged to take sanctuary at Westminster, where he died. His favourite metre was designated 'a headlong voluble breathless doggerel', short lines with two or three stresses and quick recurring rhymes, now known as 'skeltonic'.

skep *n.* **1.** a wooden or wicker basket, the quantity contained in this. **2.** a straw or wicker beehive. [f. ON]

skerry *n.* a reef, a rocky island. [Orkney dial. f. ON, rel. to SCAR]

sketch *n.* **1.** a rough drawing or painting. **2.** a brief account of something. **3.** a short usually humorous play. **4.** a short descriptive piece of writing. **5.** a musical composition of a single movement. —*v.t./i.* to make a sketch or sketches (of). —**sketch-book** *n.* sheets of drawing-paper made up in the form of a book. **sketch in,** to indicate briefly or in outline. **sketch-map** *n.* a roughly drawn map with few details. —**sketcher** *n.* [f. Du. f. It. ult. f. Gk *skhedios* extempore]

sketchy *adj.* like a sketch, rough and not detailed; unsubstantial or imperfect, especially through haste. —**sketchily** *adv.*, **sketchiness** *n.* [f. prec.]

skew *adj.* set askew, slanting, oblique; distorted. —*n.* a skewed position, a slant. —*v.t./i.* **1.** to make skew; to distort. **2.** to move obliquely. —**on the skew,** askew. **skew-whiff** *adj.* (*colloq.*) askew. [f. OF as ESCHEW]

skewbald /ˈskjuːbɔːld/ *adj.* (of an animal) with irregular patches of white and another colour. —*n.* a skewbald animal, especially a horse. [f. obs. *skued* (orig. unkn.), after PIEBALD]

skewer *n.* a long pin designed for holding meat compactly

together while it is cooking. —*v.t.* to fasten together or pierce (as) with a skewer. [var. of dial. *skiver* (orig. unkn.)]

ski /skiː/ *n.* (*pl.* **skis**) each of a pair of long narrow pieces of wood fastened under the feet for travelling over snow (see below and ill. SPORTS); a similar device under a vehicle. —*v.i.* (*past & p.p.* **ski'd** or **skied** /skiːd/; *partic.* **skiing**) to travel on skis. —**ski-jump** *n.* a steep slope levelling off before a sharp drop to allow a skier to leap through the air. **ski-lift** *n.* a device for carrying skiers up a slope, usually on seats hung from an overhead cable. **ski-run** *n.* a slope suitable for skiing. —**skier** *n.* [Norw., f. ON *skíth* billet, snow-shoe]

The oldest skis that have been found, preserved in bogs in Sweden and Finland, date from the 3rd millennium BC, and a rock-carving in northern Norway of two men on skis from *c.*2000 BC; there are references to skis in Norse mythology. The Vikings used skis in the 10th–11th c., and ski troops were used in Scandinavia, Poland, and Russia in the 15th–16th c. The type of ski evolved in these countries, however, was unsuited to steep Alpine mountains, and skiing was virtually unknown in central Europe until it was introduced by Scandinavian and British visitors as a sport and recreation in the mid-19th and 20th c. Competitive skiing falls into two categories: Nordic (cross-country racing and jumping) and Alpine (downhill or straight racing, and slalom and giant slalom racing between series of set gates).

ski-bob *n.* a machine like a bicycle with skis instead of wheels, used in the sport (**ski-bobbing**) of downhill racing over snow, which began in Austria in the early 20th c.

skid *v.t./i.* (**-dd-**) (of a vehicle etc.) to slide (esp. sideways or obliquely) on a slippery road etc.; to cause (a vehicle) to skid. —*n.* **1.** an act of skidding. **2.** a piece of wood etc. serving as a support or fender etc. **3.** a braking device, especially a wooden or metal shoe on a wheel. **4.** a runner on an aircraft for use when landing. —**on the skids,** (*colloq.*) about to be discarded or defeated. **put the skids under,** to hasten the downfall or failure of. **skid-pan** *n.* a slippery surface prepared for vehicle-drivers to practise control of skidding. **skid row,** (*US*) a district frequented by vagrants. [orig. unkn.]

skiff *n.* a light rowing or sailing boat. [f. F *esquif* (as SHIP)]

skilful *adj.* having or showing skill. —**skilfully** *adv.* [f. SKILL + -FUL]

skill *n.* the ability to do something well. [f. ON, = distinction. (*skilja* distinguish)]

skilled *adj.* **1.** skilful. **2.** (of a worker) highly trained or experienced; (of work) requiring skill or special training. [f. SKILL]

skillet /ˈskɪlɪt/ *n.* **1.** a small metal cooking-pot with a long handle and usually legs. **2.** (*US*) a frying-pan. [perh. f. OF *escuelete* dim. of *escuele* platter f. pop. L *scutella*]

skim *v.t./i.* (**-mm-**) **1.** to take floating matter or cream etc. from the surface of a liquid; to clear (a liquid) thus. **2.** to pass over (a surface) almost touching it or touching it lightly; to glide along. **3.** to read or look at cursorily. —**skim milk,** milk from which the cream has been skimmed. —**skimmer** *n.* [back-formation f. foll.]

skimmer *n.* **1.** a ladle etc. for skimming liquids. **2.** a long-winged marine bird of the genus *Rynchops* that feeds by skimming over water with its knifelike lower mandible immersed. [f. OF f. *escume* scum]

skimp *v.t./i.* to supply or use a meagre amount or rather less than what is needed (of); to be parsimonious. [orig. unkn. (cf. SCRIMP)]

skimpy *adj.* meagre, not ample; scanty. —**skimpily** *adv.*, **skimpiness** *n.* [as prec.]

skin *n.* **1.** the flexible continuous covering of the human or animal body (see below and ill. BODY 4). **2.** a skin (with or without hair) removed from an animal; material made from this; a container for water or wine, made from an animal's whole skin. **3.** the colour or complexion of a person's skin. **4.** outer layer or covering; a film like a skin on the surface of a liquid. **5.** a ship's planking or plating. —*v.t./i.* (**-nn-**) **1.** to strip or scrape the skin from. **2.** to cover or become covered (as) with skin. **3.** (*slang*) to fleece, to swindle. —**be (all) skin and bone,** to be very thin. **by the skin of one's teeth,** by a very narrow margin. **get under a person's skin,** (*colloq.*) to interest or annoy him intensely. **have a thick (or thin) skin,** to be insensitive (or sensitive) to criticism etc. **no skin off one's nose,** (*colloq.*) of no consequence to one. **save one's skin,** to avoid death or harm etc. **skin-deep** *adj.* superficial, not deep or lasting. **skin-diver** *n.* one who swims underwater without a diving-

skinflint   776   slack

suit, usually with an aqualung and flippers. **skin-diving** n. such swimming. **skin-flick** n. (*slang*) a pornographic film. **skin-graft** n. a surgical transplanting of skin; the skin thus transferred. **skin-tight** adj. very close-fitting. [OE f. ON; cf. OHG *scinden* flay]

Skin protects the rest of the body from external injury, excessive heat or cold, fluid loss, and infection, and acts as a sense-organ, providing the body with information about the environment through special nerve-endings (temperature, touch, pressure, and pain receptors). Heat and water are lost through the skin, which thus plays an important part in controlling the temperature of the body and in maintaining the balance of body fluid. The skin's outer layer, the epidermis, itself consists of four layers, of which the innermost consists of continuously dividing cells; the other three are continually renewed as these are pushed outwards and become progressively impregnated with keratin. The outermost layer contains dead cells whose cytoplasm has been entirely replaced by keratin, and which are gradually sloughed off. The inner layer or true skin, the dermis, is a thick layer of living tissue within which are blood capillaries and lymph vessels, sensory nerve-endings, sweat glands and their ducts, sebaceous glands, and smooth muscle fibres.

skinflint n. a miserly person.

skinful n. (*colloq.*) enough alcoholic liquor to make one drunk. [f. SKIN + -FUL]

skinhead n. a youth with hair shaved off or cut very short, especially one of a group adopting this style.

Skinner /'skɪnə(r)/, Burrhus Frederic (1904-), American psychologist, ardent promoter of the view that the proper study of psychology should be to predict, and hence be able to control, behaviour. His experiments on animals demonstrated that arbitrary responses could be obtained provided that certain outcomes ('reinforcements') were made contingent upon them: rewards increased the frequency of response, punishments decreased it. He applied similar techniques in both clinical and educational practice, devising (in the 1930s) one of the first teaching machines, and was involved in the development of programmed learning. Skinner also attempted to account for the nature and development of language as being a response to conditioning.

skinny adj. thin or emaciated. —**skinniness** n. [f. SKIN]

skint adj. (*slang*) having no money. [= *skinned* (SKIN)]

skip[1] v.t./i. (**-pp-**) **1.** to move along lightly, especially by taking two steps with each foot in turn. **2.** to jump lightly from the ground; to jump using a skipping-rope. **3.** to pass quickly from one subject or point to another. **4.** to omit in reading or dealing with; (*colloq.*) not to participate in. **5.** (*colloq.*) to leave hurriedly. —n. a skipping movement or action. —**skip bail**, to jump bail. **skip it!** (*slang*) abandon the topic etc. **skipping-rope** n. a length of rope (usually with two handles) revolved over the head and under the feet while jumping as a game or exercise. [prob. f. Scand.]

skip[2] n. **1.** a large container for refuse etc. **2.** a cage or bucket etc. in which men or materials are raised or lowered in mines etc. [var. of SKEP]

skipper n. the captain of a ship, especially of a small trading or fishing vessel; the captain of an aircraft; the captain of a side in games. —v.t. to act as captain of. [f. MDu. or MLG *schipper* (as SHIP)]

skirl n. the shrill sound characteristic of bagpipes. —v.i. to make a skirl. [prob. Scand. (imit.)]

skirmish n. a minor fight especially between small or outlying parts of armies or fleets; a short argument or contest of wit etc. —v.i. to engage in a skirmish. [f. OF *eskirmir*]

skirt n. **1.** a woman's outer garment hanging from the waist; the part of a coat etc. that hangs below the waist. **2.** the hanging part round the base of a hovercraft. **3.** an edge, a border, an extreme part; skirt of beef (see below). —v.t./i. **1.** to go or lie along or round the edge of. **2.** to avoid dealing with (an issue etc.). —**skirting-board** n. a narrow board etc. along the bottom of a room-wall. **skirt of beef**, the diaphragm etc. as food; meat from the lower flank. [f. ON, = SHIRT]

skit n. a light usually short piece of satire or burlesque. [rel. to *skit* move lightly (perh. as SHOOT)]

skittish /'skɪtɪʃ/ adj. lively, playful; (of a horse etc.) nervous, inclined to shy. —**skittishly** adv., **skittishness** n. [perh. as prec.]

skittle n. **1.** (in *pl.*) a game played with usually nine wooden

pins set up at the end of an alley to be bowled down usually with a wooden ball or disc; a game played with similar pins set up on a board to be knocked down by a swinging suspended ball. **2.** a pin used in these games. —v.t. (with *out*) to get (batsmen in cricket) out in rapid succession. [orig. also *kittle-pins*; orig. unkn.]

skive v.t./i. (*slang*) to evade (a duty). —**skive off**, to depart evasively. —**skiver** n. [orig. = split (leather), f. ON]

skivvy /'skɪvɪ/ n. (*colloq.*, *derog.*) a female domestic servant. [orig. unkn.]

Skryabin /skrɪ'ɑːbɪn/, Alexander (1872-1915), Russian composer, born in Moscow where he studied at the Conservatory before embarking on a career as a concert pianist. Much of his music is influenced by the mystic theories he encountered in Brussels in 1908, especially the best known of his works, the symphonic poem *Prometheus*, or *The Poem of Fire* (1909-10), which is scored for orchestra, piano, optional choir, and 'keyboard of light' (projecting colours on to a screen) and is based on the chord he called 'mystic'.

skua /'skuːə/ n. a large predatory sea-bird of the genus *Stercorarius* etc. [f. Faeroese & ON]

skulduggery /skʌl'dʌgərɪ/ n. trickery; unscrupulous behaviour. [orig. Sc. = unchastity; etym. unkn.]

skulk v.i. to loiter, move, or conceal oneself stealthily, especially in cowardice, evasion of duty, or because intending mischief. [f. Scand.; cf. Norw. *skulka* lurk]

skull n. **1.** the bony case of the brain of a vertebrate. **2.** the bony framework of the head (ill. BODY 1); a representation of this. **3.** the head as the site of the intelligence. —**skull and cross-bones**, a representation of a skull with two thigh-bones crossed below it as an emblem of piracy or death. **skull-cap** n. a small close-fitting peakless cap. [orig. unkn.]

skunk n. **1.** a black white-striped bushy-tailed American animal of the genus *Mephitis* etc., about the size of a cat and able to emit a powerful stench from liquid secreted by its anal glands when attacked; its fur. **2.** a contemptible person. [f. Amer. Ind.]

sky /skaɪ/ n. (in *sing.* or *pl.*) the region of the clouds, atmosphere, and outer space seen from the earth. —v.t. to hit (a cricket ball) high into the air. —**sky-blue** adj. & n. bright clear blue. **sky-diving** n. parachuting in which the parachute is opened only at the last safe moment. **sky-high** adv. & adj. reaching the sky; very high. **sky-rocket** n. a rocket exploding high in the air; (v.i.) to rise very steeply or rapidly. **sky-writing** n. legible smoke-trails emitted by an aeroplane. **to the skies**, without reserve. [orig. = cloud(s), f. ON]

Skye /skaɪ/ the largest of the Inner Hebrides in NW Scotland. Much of the island is mountainous, especially the rugged Cuillin Hills. —n. (in full **Skye terrier**) a short-legged long-haired Scotch terrier.

skyjack v.t. (*slang*) to hijack (an aircraft). [f. SKY + HIJACK]

Skylab /'skaɪlæb/ a space laboratory (*Skylab 1*) launched into Earth orbit by the USA in 1973, where experiments were conducted in conditions of zero gravity. It was manned until 1974 and disintegrated in the atmosphere in 1979 after its orbit had become unstable, some parts crashing to earth in the desert of Western Australia.

skylark n. a lark (*Alauda arvensis*) that soars while singing. —v.i. to play tricks and practical jokes.

skylight n. a window in a roof.

skyline n. the outline of hills, buildings, etc., defined against the sky.

skyscraper n. a very tall building with many storeys, especially the type of office building that dominates Manhattan Island, New York, and the centres of other large American cities. Skyscrapers were first built because of the high cost of land in congested urban areas, and subsequently also for their prestige value even when they were not economical. They were made possible technically by the development of the steel-frame construction and the invention of the electric lift. Leroy S. Buffington, a Minneapolis architect, designed the first skyscraper in 1880, but the first one actually erected was the Home Insurance Building in Chicago, a 10-storey structure completed in 1885.

skyward /'skaɪwəd/ adv. (also **skywards**) & adj. towards the sky. [f. SKY + -WARD]

slab n. a flat thick usually square or rectangular piece of solid matter. [orig. unkn.]

slack[1] adj. **1.** lacking firmness or tautness. **2.** lacking energy or activity; sluggish; negligent. **3.** (of the tide etc.) neither ebbing nor flowing. —n. **1.** a slack period, slack part of a rope, etc.; (colloq.) a spell of inactivity. 2. (in pl.) informal trousers. —v.t./i. 1. to slacken. 2. (colloq.) to take a rest; to be lazy. —slack off, to loosen, to lose or cause to lose vigour. slack up, to reduce speed. —slackly adv., slackness n. [OE]

slack[2] n. coal-dust. [prob. f. LDu.]

slacken v.t./i. to make or become slack. [f. SLACK]

slacker n. a shirker, an indolent person. [f. SLACK]

slag n. solid non-metallic waste matter left when metal has been separated from ore by smelting. —v.i. (-gg-) to form slag. —slag-heap n. a hill of refuse from a mine etc. —slaggy adj. [f. MLG]

slain p.p. of SLAY.

slake v.t. 1. to assuage or satisfy (one's thirst, revenge, etc.). 2. to disintegrate (lime) by combination with water. [OE as SLACK]

slalom /'slɑːləm/ n. a ski-race down a zigzag course with artificial obstacles; an obstacle race in canoes. [Norw., = sloping track]

slam[1] v.t./i. (-mm-) 1. to shut forcefully with a loud bang; to put, knock, or move with a similar sound or violently. 2. (slang) to criticize severely; to hit, to beat; to gain an easy victory over. —n. the sound or action of slamming. [prob. f. Scand.]

slam[2] n. the gaining of every trick at cards. —grand slam, the winning of 13 tricks in bridge; the winning of all of a group of championships in a sport. [perh. f. obs. slampant trickery]

slander /'slɑːndə(r)/ n. a false statement maliciously uttered that is damaging to a person's reputation; the uttering of this. —v.t. to utter a slander about. —slanderous adj., slanderously adv. [f. AF & OF f. L (as SCANDAL)]

slang n. words and phrases, or particular meanings of these, that are found only in very informal language or in that of restricted groups of people (see below). —v.t./i. to use abusive language (to). —slanging-match n. a prolonged exchange of insults. —slangy adj. [orig. unkn.]
  Some words originally regarded as slang (e.g. clever, fun, frisky, mob, which were disliked by Dr Johnson and others in the 18th c.) have now passed into standard non-colloquial usage; others (e.g. quid = £1) have remained in the category of slang. Slang is used sometimes for fun, to be concise or picturesque, or to express feelings and attitudes (e.g. of hostility, ridicule, or affection) better than dignified words would do; it can make light of a serious or tragic situation, or refer to it by paraphrase; it can shock or attract attention; in particular, it can identify its users as members of a special group. Writers such as Dryden and Swift (17th–18th c.) thought that slang words and phrases were allowed too easy an entrance to the English language and proposed an Academy on the French model which they hoped might 'regulate' grammar and vocabulary. The proposal, however, came to nothing.

slant /slɑːnt/ v.t./i. 1. to slope, to lie or go at an angle from the vertical or horizontal; to cause to do this. 2. to present (information etc.) from a particular point of view or unfairly. —n. 1. a slope, an oblique position. 2. the way information etc. is presented; an attitude or bias. —adj. sloping, oblique. —on a or the slant, aslant. [var. of dial. slent, f. ON sletta dash]

slantwise adv. aslant. [f. prec. + -WISE]

slap v.t./i. (-pp-) 1. to strike with the palm of the hand or a flat object, or so as to make a similar noise. 2. to lay forcefully. 3. to put hastily or carelessly. —n. a blow with the palm of the hand or a flat object; a slapping sound. —adv. with a slap; directly, suddenly; exactly. —slap and tickle, (colloq.) lively (esp. amorous) amusement. slap-bang adv. violently, noisily, headlong. slap down, (colloq.) to snub; to reprimand. slap-happy adj. (colloq.) cheerfully casual or flippant. slap in the face, a rebuff or insult. slap on the back, congratulations. slap-up adj. lavish, first-class. [f. LG (imit.)]

slapdash adj. hasty and careless. —adv. in a slapdash manner.

slapstick n. boisterous knockabout comedy.

slash v.t./i. 1. to make a sweeping stroke or strokes with a sword, knife, whip, etc.; to strike or cut thus. 2. to make an ornamental slit in (a garment), especially so as to show underlying fabric. 3. to reduce (prices etc.) drastically. 4. (in partic.) vigorously incisive or effective. 5. to censure vigorously. —n. a slashing cut or stroke. [perh. f. OF, = break in pieces]

slat n. a thin narrow piece of wood or plastic etc., especially used in an overlapping series as in a fence or Venetian blind. [f. OF esclat splinter]

slate n. 1. a kind of metamorphic rock easily split into flat smooth plates. 2. a piece of such a plate used as a roofing-material (ill. BUILDING TECHNIQUES) or for writing on. 3. the dull blue or grey colour of slate. —v.t. 1. to cover with slates. 2. (colloq.) to criticize severely. 3. (US) to make arrangements for (an event etc.). 4. (US) to nominate for office etc. —clean slate, no discreditable history. clean the slate, to remove obligations, grievances, etc. —slaty adj. [f. OF esclate fem. of esclat (see prec.)]

slattern /'slætəːn/ n. a slovenly woman. —slatternliness n., slatternly adj. [rel. to dial. slatter spill, slop]

slaughter /'slɔːtə(r)/ n. 1. the killing of animals for food etc. 2. the ruthless killing of many persons or animals. —v.t. 1. to kill (animals) for food etc. 2. to kill ruthlessly in great numbers. 3. (colloq.) to defeat utterly. —slaughterer n. [f. ON (as SLAY)]

slaughterhouse n. a place for the slaughter of animals as food.

Slav /slɑːv/ n. a member of a group of peoples in central and eastern Europe, including the Russians, Poles, Czechs, Bulgarians, Serbo-Croats, etc., speaking languages of the Slavonic group. —adj. of the Slavs. [f. L Sclavus]

slave n. 1. a person who is owned by another and has to serve him. 2. a drudge, a person working very hard. 3. a helpless victim of some dominating influence. 4. a part of a machine directly controlled by another. —v.i. to work very hard. —slave-driver n. an overseer of slaves at work; a hard taskmaster. slave labour, forced labour. slave-trade n. the procuring, transporting, and selling of slaves, especially African Blacks. [f. OF esclave f. L (as prec.), the Slavonic peoples in parts of Central Europe having been reduced to bondage by conquest]

slaver[1] /'sleɪvə(r)/ n. a ship or person engaged in the slave-trade. [f. prec.]

slaver[2] /'slævə(r)/ n. 1. saliva running from the mouth. 2. flattery; drivel. —v.i. to let saliva run from the mouth, to dribble. [prob. f. LDu.; cf. SLOBBER]

slavery /'sleɪvərɪ/ n. 1. the condition or work of a slave. 2. very hard work, drudgery. 3. the custom of having slaves (see below). [f. SLAVE]
  A widespread institution in ancient times, slavery had died out in England by the 12th c. The transportation of slaves from Africa to the Americas by European traders began on a large scale in the 16th and 17th c., and although slavery became illegal in Britain in 1772, it remained an important feature of the economy of the Empire until the 19th c., the slave trade being abolished in 1807 and slavery itself throughout the Empire in 1833. In the American South slavery was an essential part of the cotton-based economy, and the abolition campaign waged during the first half of the 19th c. eventually led to the American Civil War and to final emancipation. In some parts of the world chattel slavery, the ownership of one person by another, continues to exist.

slavish /'sleɪvɪʃ/ adj. 1. of or like slaves; excessively submissive. 2. showing no independence or originality. —slavishly adv., slavishness n. [f. SLAVE]

Slavonic /sləˈvɒnɪk/ adj. 1. of the group of languages including Russian and Polish and Czech. 2. of the Slavs. —n. the Slavonic group of languages, a main division of the Indo-European family, including Russian, Czech, Serbo-Croat, Bulgarian, and Polish. The common Slavonic language from which they are all descended probably broke away from the main Indo-European family before Christian times. They have many characteristics in common: nouns and adjectives are highly inflected (Russian and Polish have as many as seven cases), verbs have few tenses but preserve an ancient distinction (called aspect) between actions thought of as finished or limited in time and those regarded as continuous, and final syllables are varied to show subtle changes of meaning. The two principal alphabets used are the Cyrillic and the Latin. —Church or Old (Church) Slavonic, the earliest written Slavonic language, surviving as a liturgical language in the Orthodox Church. It was a South Slavonic dialect from the region of Macedonia, used in the 9th c. by St Cyril and his brother St Methodius for their missionary purposes in the Slav countries of Moravia and Pannonia. Throughout the Middle Ages it was the language of culture for the Orthodox peoples of eastern Europe, playing a role similar to that of Latin in the West. Two different alphabets were used, Glagolitic and Cyrillic. [f. L S(c)lavonia country of the Slavs]

slay v.t. (past **slew** /sluː/; p.p. **slain**) to kill. [OE]

sleazy adj. squalid, tawdry; slatternly. —**sleazily** adv., **sleaziness** n. [orig. unkn.]

sled n. (US) a sledge. —v.t./i. (-**dd**-) (US) to sledge. [f. MLG (rel. to SLEDGE)]

sledge n. a vehicle on runners instead of wheels for conveying loads or passengers, especially over snow. —v.t./i. to travel or convey by sledge. [f. MDu. sleedse, rel. to prec.]

sledge-hammer n. **1.** a large heavy hammer. **2.** (attrib.) heavy and powerful. [OE slecg (as SLAY) + HAMMER]

sleek adj. **1.** (of hair or skin etc.) smooth and glossy. **2.** looking well-fed and comfortable. **3.** ingratiating. —v.t. to make sleek. —**sleekly** adv., **sleekness** n. [var. of SLICK]

sleep n. **1.** the naturally recurring condition of rest in animals, in which the eyes are closed, postural muscles relaxed, and consciousness suspended (see below); a sleep-like state. **2.** a spell of sleeping. **3.** the inert condition of hibernating animals. —v.t./i. **1.** to be in a state of sleep; to fall asleep. **2.** to stay for a night's sleep. **3.** to have sexual intercourse in bed together or with. **4.** to spend (time) in sleeping. **5.** to provide sleeping accommodation for. **6.** to be inactive or dead. —**go to sleep**, to enter the state of sleep; (of a limb etc.) to become numbed. **last sleep**, death. **put to sleep**, to anaesthetize; to kill (an animal) painlessly. **sleep around**, (colloq.) to be sexually promiscuous. **sleep in**, to remain asleep later than usual. **sleeping-bag** n. a lined or padded bag to sleep in, especially when camping etc. **sleeping-car** or **-carriage** n. a railway coach with beds or berths. **sleeping partner**, one not sharing in the actual work of a firm. **sleeping-pill** n. a pill to induce sleep. **sleeping sickness**, see separate entry. **sleep off**, to get rid of (a headache etc.) by sleeping. **sleep on it**, to refrain from deciding (a question etc.) until the next day. **sleep-walker** n. a person who walks about while asleep. **sleep-walking** n. this condition. [OE]

The capacity for sleep is very general. Most animals have it, and many insects show a marked difference between their daytime and night-time levels of activity. The pattern of sleep in mammals is usually related to their general habits and the importance of their different senses, with those dependent principally on vision for finding food etc. active by day and sleeping at night, but some (e.g. lions, horses, and sheep) show no clear-cut rhythm and may sleep at any time. Sleep varies not only in duration but in depth. The physiology of sleep has been studied by analysing the electrical activity of the human brain: the relatively fast electrical rhythm of the waking brain disappears during sleep and is replaced by slow waves and occasional bursts of fast activity. There is evidence that electrical activity of the brain changes when a sleeper dreams, and this is associated with rapid movements of the eyes. There is no general agreement, however, about why sleep is a feature of life.

sleeper n. **1.** one who sleeps. **2.** each of the beams on which railway rails run. **3.** a sleeping-car; a berth in this. **4.** a ring or stud worn in a pierced ear to keep the hole from closing. [f. SLEEP]

sleeping sickness any of several similar diseases caused by trypanosomes transmitted by the bite of the tsetse fly and characterized by changes in the central nervous system leading to apathy, coma, and death. Such diseases are prevalent in tropical Africa. The characteristic feature of the areas where they occur is a dense shade cast by thickly growing shrubs and small trees, such as may be found on the banks of watercourses and water-holes; there the fly flourishes, and one of the principal control methods is to eliminate such vegetation, especially around villages, fords, and other places where people congregate.

sleepless adj. **1.** lacking sleep; unable to sleep. **2.** continually active. —**sleeplessly** adv., **sleeplessness** n. [f. SLEEP + -LESS]

sleepy adj. **1.** ready for sleep, about to fall asleep. **2.** lacking activity or bustle. —**sleepy sickness**, an often fatal disease (encephalitis lethargica) widespread between 1916 and 1928, characterized in many of those who survived it by extreme somnolence due to physiological brain damage. —**sleepily** adv., **sleepiness** n. [f. SLEEP]

sleet n. snow and rain together; hail or snow melting as it falls. —v.i. to fall as sleet. —**it sleets** or **is sleeting**, sleet is falling. —**sleety** adj. [rel. to MLG sloten hail]

sleeve n. **1.** the part of a garment that encloses the arm or a part of it. **2.** the cover of a gramophone record. **3.** a tube enclosing a rod or smaller tube. **4.** a wind-sock. —**up one's sleeve**, concealed but ready for use. —**sleeved** adj. [OE]

sleeveless adj. without sleeves. [f. prec. + -LESS]

sleigh /sleɪ/ n. a sledge, especially one for riding on. —v.i. to travel on a sleigh. [f. Du. slee (as SLED)]

sleight /slaɪt/ n. (archaic) dexterity, cunning. —**sleight-of-hand** n. a display of dexterity; conjuring. [f. ON (as SLY)]

slender adj. **1.** of small girth or breadth; slim and graceful. **2.** relatively small in amount etc.; scanty. —**slenderness** n. [orig. unkn.]

slept past & p.p. of SLEEP.

sleuth /sluːθ/ n. a detective. —**sleuth-hound** n. a bloodhound; a detective. [orig. sleuth-hound, f. ON slóth track (cf. SLOT) + HOUND]

slew¹ /sluː/ v.t./i. to turn or swing forcibly or with effort to a new position. —n. such a turn. [orig. unkn.]

slew² past of SLAY.

slice n. **1.** a thin broad or wedge-shaped piece cut from something. **2.** a share or portion. **3.** an implement with a broad flat blade for lifting or serving fish etc. or for scraping or chipping things. **4.** (in golf) a slicing stroke. —v.t./i. **1.** to cut into slices; to cut from a larger piece. **2.** to cut cleanly or easily with or like a knife. **3.** (in golf) to strike (a ball) badly so that it deviates from the direction intended, going to the right of a right-handed player. —**sliced bread**, bread that is sliced and wrapped before being sold. —**slicer** n. [f. OF esclice splinter (cf. SPLIT)]

slick adj. **1.** skilful or efficient, especially in a superficial or pretentious way or with some trickery. **2.** smooth in manner or speech. **3.** shrewd, wily. **4.** smooth and slippery. —n. a slippery place or patch; a thick patch of oil floating on the sea. —v.t. to make sleek. —**slickness** n. [prob. f. OE, = polish; cf. SLEEK]

slide v.t./i. (past & p.p. **slid**) **1.** to move or cause to move along a smooth surface with constant friction on the same part of the thing moving. **2.** to move or go smoothly or quietly. **3.** to pass gradually or imperceptibly into a condition or habit. **4.** to glide more or less erect over ice or other smooth surface without using skates. —n. **1.** an act of sliding. **2.** a smooth surface for sliding on; an inclined plane down which goods etc. are slid or for children to play on. **3.** a sliding part of a machine or instrument. **4.** a thing slid into place; a mounted picture or transparency for showing by means of a projector; a small glass plate holding an object for examination under a microscope. **5.** a hair-slide. —**let things slide**, to fail to give them proper attention or control; to allow deterioration. **slide over**, to skate over (a delicate subject etc.). **slide-rule** n. a ruler with a sliding central strip, graduated logarithmically for use in making rapid calculations. **sliding scale**, a scale of fees, taxes, wages, etc., that varies as a whole according to changes in some standard. —**slider** n. [OE]

slight /slaɪt/ adj. **1.** not much, not great, not thorough; inconsiderable. **2.** slender and frail-looking, not heavily built. —v.t. to treat or speak of (a person etc.) with disrespect or as not worth attention. —n. an act of slighting. —**slightly** adv., **slightness** n. [f. ON, = level, smooth]

slim adj. **1.** of small girth or thickness, not heavily built. **2.** relatively small. —v.t./i. (-**mm**-) **1.** to make oneself slimmer by dieting, exercise, etc. **2.** to reduce (a work-force etc.) in size. —**slimly** adv., **slimmer** n., **slimness** n. [Du. or LG, = MLG slim(m) slanting]

slime n. an unpleasant slippery thick liquid substance. [OE, rel. to L limus mud, Gk limnē marsh]

slimline adj. of slender design.

slimy /ˈslaɪmɪ/ adj. **1.** like slime; covered with or full of slime. **2.** disgustingly obsequious, meek, or dishonest. —**slimily** adv., **sliminess** n. [f. SLIME]

sling¹ n. **1.** a belt, strap, or chain(s) etc. looped round an object to lift it or support it as it hangs. **2.** a bandage etc. looped round the neck to support an injured arm. **3.** a looped strap used to throw a stone or other missile. —v.t. (past & p.p. **slung**) **1.** to suspend or lift with a sling; to arrange so as to be held or moved from above. **2.** to hurl with a sling; (colloq.) to throw. —**sling-back** n. a shoe held in place by a strap above and behind the heel. **sling one's hook**, (slang) to make off. [prob. f. ON & LDu.]

sling² n. (US) a sweetened drink of gin or other spirits and water. [orig. unkn.]

slink v.i. (past & p.p. **slunk**) to move in a stealthy, guilty, or shamefaced manner. [OE, = crawl]

slinky adj. **1.** moving in a slinking manner; stealthy. **2.**

smooth and sinuous; (of clothes) close-fitting and sinuous. —**slinkily** adv., **slinkiness** n. [f. SLINK]

slip[1] v.t./i. (-**pp**-) **1.** to slide unintentionally or momentarily; to lose one's footing or one's balance thus. **2.** to go or put with a smooth movement or stealthily. **3.** to escape restraint or capture by being slippery or not grasped firmly. **4.** to make one's way quietly or unobserved. **5.** to make a careless or casual error; to fall below one's normal standard. **6.** to release from restraint or connection. **7.** (in knitting) to move (a stitch) to the other needle without looping the yarn through it. **8.** to escape from; to evade. —n. **1.** an act of slipping. **2.** an accidental or slight error. **3.** a loose covering or garment; a petticoat. **4.** a reduction in the movement or speed of a pulley or propeller etc. **5.** (in sing. or pl.) a slipway. **6.** (in cricket) a fieldsman close behind the wicket (ill. SPORTS); (in sing. or pl.) this part of the ground. —**give a person the slip,** to escape from or evade him. **let slip,** to release accidentally or deliberately; to miss (an opportunity); to utter inadvertently. **slip-case** or **-cover** n. a fitted cover for a book or furniture etc. **slip-knot** n. a knot that can be undone at a pull, a running knot. **slip of the pen** (or **tongue**), a small mistake in which something is written (or said) unintentionally. **slip-on** adj. (of shoes or clothes) that can be easily slipped on or off. **slipped disc,** a disc between the vertebrae that has become displaced and causes lumbar pain. **slip-road** n. a road for entering or leaving a motorway etc. **slip-stream** n. a current of air or water driven back by a propeller or moving vehicle. **slip up,** (colloq.) to make a mistake. **slip-up** n. (colloq.) a mistake, a blunder. [prob. f. MLG]

slip[2] n. **1.** a small piece of paper, especially for writing on. **2.** a cutting taken from a plant for grafting or planting. —**slip of a girl** etc., a small slim girl etc. [prob. f. MDu. or MLG]

slip[3] n. finely ground clay mixed with water for coating or decorating earthenware. [OE, = slime]

slipper n. a light loose shoe for indoor wear. [f. SLIP[1]]

slippery adj. **1.** difficult to grasp because of smoothness or wetness etc. **2.** (of a surface) on which slipping is likely. **3.** (of a person) unreliable, unscrupulous. —**slipperiness** n. [prob. made by Coverdale (1535) after Luther's schlipfferig; partly f. dial. slipper adj., f. OE]

slippy adj. (colloq.) slippery. —**look slippy,** to make haste. [f. SLIP[1]]

slipshod adj. **1.** slovenly, careless. **2.** having shoes that are down at heel.

slipway n. a sloping structure used for building ships or as a landing-stage.

slit n. a straight narrow incision or opening. —v.t. (-**tt**-; past & p.p. **slit**) to make a slit in; to cut into strips. [f. OE]

slither /ˈslɪðə(r)/ v.i. to slip or slide unsteadily. —n. an act of slithering. —**slithery** adj. [OE (frequent. of SLIDE)]

sliver /ˈslɪvə(r)/ n. a thin strip or piece of wood etc. —v.t./i. to break off as a sliver; to break or form into slivers. [rel. to dial. slive cleave]

Sloane /sləʊn/, Sir Hans (1660–1753), English physician and naturalist. He purchased the manor of Chelsea and endowed the Chelsea Physic Garden. His collections (including a large number of books and manuscripts) were purchased by the nation and placed in Montague House (afterwards the British Museum); the geological and zoological specimens formed the basis of the Natural History Museum in South Kensington, opened in 1881.

slob n. (colloq.) a large and coarse or stupid person. [f. Ir. slab mud]

slobber v.t./i. **1.** to slaver or dribble. **2.** to show excessive sentiment over a person etc. —n. slaver. —**slobbery** adj. [= Du. slobberen (imit.)]

sloe /sləʊ/ n. the blackthorn (Prunus spinosa); its small bluish-black fruit. [OE]

slog v.t./i. (-**gg**-) **1.** to hit hard. **2.** to work or walk doggedly. —n. **1.** a hard hit. **2.** hard steady work; a spell of this. —**slogger** n. [orig. unkn.; cf. SLUG[2]]

slogan /ˈsləʊgən/ n. a short catchy phrase used in advertising etc.; a party cry, a watchword. [f. Gael., = war-cry]

sloop n. a small one-masted fore-and-aft-rigged vessel (ill. SAILING-SHIPS). [f. Du. sloep]

slop v.t./i. (-**pp**-) **1.** to spill (liquid); to be spilt; to splash liquid on. **2.** to behave effusively. **3.** to plod clumsily through mud or puddles etc.; to move in a slovenly way. —n. **1.** slopped liquid. **2.** weak sentimentality. **3.** (in pl.) household liquid refuse; the contents of chamber-pots; dregs from teacups etc. **4.** (in sing. or pl.) unappetizing

liquid food. —**slop-basin** n. a basin for the dregs of cups at table. **slop out,** (in prison) to carry slops out from cells. **slop-pail** n. a pail for removing bedroom or kitchen slops. [earlier = slush, rel. to OE slyppe slimy substance]

slope n. **1.** a position, direction, or state at an angle from the horizontal or vertical; a state in which one end or side is at a higher level than the other; the difference in level between two ends or sides of a thing. **2.** a piece of rising or falling ground; a place for skiing on the side of a mountain —v.t./i. **1.** to have or take a slope. **2.** to cause to do this. —**slope arms,** to place a rifle in a sloping position against the shoulder. **slope off,** (slang) to go away. [f. aslope crosswise]

sloppy adj. **1.** having a liquid consistency and splashing easily; excessively liquid. **2.** unsystematic, careless. **3.** untidy and ill-fitting; loose-fitting. **4.** weakly sentimental. —**sloppily** adv., **sloppiness** n. [f. SLOP]

slosh v.t./i. **1.** to splash; to move with a splashing sound. **2.** to hit heavily. **3.** to pour (liquid) clumsily (on). —n. **1.** slush. **2.** an act or sound of splashing. **3.** (slang) a heavy blow. [var. of SLUSH]

sloshed adj. (slang) drunk. [f. SLOSH]

slot n. **1.** a slit or other narrow aperture in a machine etc. for something (especially a coin) to be inserted. **2.** a groove, channel, or slit into which something fits or in which something works. **3.** an allotted place in an arrangement or scheme. —v.t./i. (-**tt**-) **1.** to put into or be placed in a slot. **2.** to make a slot or slots in. —**slot-machine** n. a machine worked by the insertion of a coin, especially delivering small purchased articles or providing amusement. [orig. = hollow of the breast, f. OF esclot; orig. unkn.]

sloth /sləʊθ/ n. **1.** laziness, indolence. **2.** a South and Central American slow-moving arboreal mammal of the genera Choloepus and Bradypus. [f. SLOW]

slothful adj. lazy. —**slothfully** adv. [f. SLOTH + -FUL]

slouch v.i. to stand, move, or sit in a drooping ungainly fashion. —n. **1.** a slouching posture or movement. **2.** the downward bend of a hat-brim. **3.** (slang) a lazy, incompetent, or slovenly worker etc. —**slouch hat,** a hat with a wide flexible brim. —**sloucher** n. [orig. unkn.]

slough[1] /slaʊ/ n. a swamp, a miry place. —**Slough of Despond,** (in Bunyan's Pilgrim's Progress) a deep miry place between the City of Destruction and the wicket gate at the beginning of Christian's journey; a state of hopeless depression. [OE]

slough[2] /slʌf/ n. a snake's cast skin; dead tissue that drops away. —v.t./i. to cast or drop as slough. [perh. rel. to LG slu(we) husk]

Slovak /ˈsləʊvæk/ n. a native or the language of Slovakia (formerly part of Hungary, now the Slovak Socialist Republic, a part of Czechoslovakia). —adj. of the Slovaks. [f. Slovak etc. Slovák]

sloven /ˈslʌv(ə)n/ n. a slovenly person. [perh. f. Flemish sloef dirty]

Slovenia /sləˈviːnɪə/ a constituent republic of Yugoslavia. —**Slovenian** adj. & n.

slovenly /ˈslʌvənlɪ/ adj. careless and untidy, unmethodical. —adv. in a slovenly manner. —**slovenliness** n. [f. SLOVEN]

slow /sləʊ/ adj. **1.** not quick or fast; acting, moving, or done without haste or rapidity. **2.** tending to cause slowness. **3.** (of a clock etc.) showing a time earlier than the correct one. **4.** dull-witted, stupid; not understanding readily. **5.** lacking liveliness, slack or sluggish. **6.** (of a fire or oven) giving low heat. **7.** (of photographic film) not very sensitive to light, needing a long exposure; (of a lens) having only a small aperture. **8.** lacking the inclination. —adv. slowly (used when slow gives the essential point, as in go slow). —v.t./i. (with down or up) to reduce the speed of; to go more slowly. —**slow-down** n. the action of slowing down. **slow motion,** a speed of cinema film in which movements appear much slower than in real life; a simulation of this. —**slowly** adv., **slowness** n. [OE]

slowcoach n. a person who is slow in his actions, understanding, or work etc.

slow-worm n. a small European legless lizard (Anguis fragilis). [OE, first element of uncertain origin but not f. SLOW]

sludge n. **1.** thick greasy mud; muddy or slushy sediment. **2.** sewage. —**sludgy** adj. [cf. SLUSH]

slug[1] *n.* **1.** a small gastropod especially of the families Limacidae and Arionidae, like a snail but without a shell. **2.** a piece of metal; a bullet of irregular shape; a missile for an airgun. **3.** (*US*) a tot of liquor. [f. earlier *slugg(e)* sluggard, prob. f. Scand.]

slug[2] *v.t./i.* (*US*) (**-gg-**) to hit hard. —*n.* (*US*) a hard hit. [orig. unkn.; cf. SLOG]

sluggard /'slʌɡəd/ *n.* a lazy person. [f. *slug* be slothful (as SLUG[1])]

sluggish *adj.* inert, slow-moving. —**sluggishly** *adv.*, **sluggishness** *n.* [f. SLUG[1]]

sluice /sluːs/ *n.* **1.** (also **sluice-gate**) a sliding gate or other contrivance for regulating the flow or level of water. **2.** the water regulated by this. **3.** (also **sluice-way**) an artificial channel for carrying off water. **4.** a place for rinsing things. —*v.t./i.* **1.** to let out (water) by means of a sluice; (of water) to rush out freely (as) from a sluice. **2.** to flood, scour, or rinse with a flow of water. [f. OF *escluse* f. L (as EXCLUDE)]

slum *n.* a dirty overcrowded district inhabited by poor people. —*v.i.* (**-mm-**) **1.** to live in slumlike conditions. **2.** to visit a slum for curiosity or for charitable purposes. —**slummy** *adj.* [19th-c. slang]

slumber *v.t./i.* to sleep (*lit.* or *fig.*). —*n.* sleep (*lit.* or *fig.*). —**slumberer** *n.*, **slumberous** *adj.*, **slumbrous** *adj.* [f. OE]

slump *n.* a sudden severe or prolonged fall in prices and values and in demand for goods etc. —*v.i.* **1.** to undergo a slump. **2.** to sit or fall down limply. [orig. = sink in bog (imit.)]

slung *past* & *p.p.* of SLING[1].

slunk *past* & *p.p.* of SLINK.

slur *v.t./i.* (**-rr-**) **1.** to sound or write (words, musical notes, etc.) so that they run into one another. **2.** to put a slur upon (a person or character). **3.** to pass lightly or deceptively (over a fact etc.). —*n.* **1.** an imputation; discredit. **2.** an act of slurring. **3.** (*Mus.*) a curved line joining notes to be slurred. [orig. unkn.]

slurp *v.t.* (*colloq.*) to eat or drink with a noisy sucking sound. —*n.* (*colloq.*) this sound. [f. Du.]

slurry /'slʌrɪ/ *n.* thin mud; a suspension of fine solid material in water or other liquid; thin liquid cement. [rel. to dial. *slur* thin mud]

slush *n.* **1.** thawing snow; watery mud. **2.** silly sentimental talk or writing. —**slush fund,** money used to bribe officials etc., e.g. by illicit commission. —**slushy** *adj.* [orig. unkn.; cf. SLUDGE]

slut *n.* a slovenly woman. —**sluttish** *adj.* [orig. unkn.]

sly /slaɪ/ *adj.* **1.** done or doing things in an unpleasantly cunning and secret way. **2.** mischievous and knowing. —**on the sly,** secretly. —**slyly** *adv.*, **slyness** *n.* [f. ON, orig. = able to strike (as SLAY)]

Sm *symbol* samarium.

smack[1] *n.* **1.** a sharp slap or blow; a hard hit. **2.** a sharp sound as of a surface struck by a flat object; a loud kiss. —*v.t.* to slap; to move with a smack. —*adv.* (*colloq.*) with a smack; suddenly, directly, violently. —**smack in the eye,** a rebuff. [f. MDu. (imit.)]

smack[2] *v.t./i.* to have a slight flavour or trace of something. —*n.* a slight flavour or trace. [OE]

smack[3] *n.* a boat with a single mast, used for sailing or fishing. [f. Du.]

smacker *n.* (*slang*) **1.** a loud kiss, a sounding blow. **2.** £1; (*US*) $1. [f. SMACK[1]]

small /smɔːl/ *adj.* **1.** not large or big. **2.** not great in importance, amount, power, etc.; not much, insignificant. **3.** consisting of small particles. **4.** doing things on a small scale. **5.** socially undistinguished, poor or humble. **6.** mean, ungenerous; paltry. —*n.* **1.** the slenderest part of something (esp. *small of the back*). **2.** (in *pl.*, *colloq.*) small articles of laundry, especially underwear. —*adv.* into small pieces. —**feel** *or* **look small,** to be humiliated or ashamed. **small arms,** portable firearms. **small beer,** an insignificant thing. **small change,** coins, especially low denominations as opposed to notes. **small fry,** see FRY[2]. **small hours, the** period soon after midnight. **small-minded** *adj.* narrow or selfish in outlook. **small-scale** *adj.* made or occurring on a small scale. **small talk,** social conversation on unimportant matters. **small-time** *adj.* unimportant, petty. —**smallness** *n.* [OE]

smallholder *n.* an owner or user of a smallholding.

smallholding *n.* a piece of agricultural land smaller than a farm.

smallpox /'smɔːlpɒks/ *n.* an acute contagious virus disease with fever and pustules usually leaving permanent scars, the main devastating disease of the 17th and 18th c. Because it seldom attacked the same person more than once, it had been the practice in the East deliberately to infect healthy people with a mild form of the disease in order to confer upon them immunity from a more dangerous form, and this was introduced into England by the traveller and letter-writer Lady Mary Wortley Montagu (1689-1762). In 1796 Edward Jenner observed that the mild disease cowpox gave immunity from smallpox, and established the practice of vaccination; its systematic application resulted in the world-wide eradication of smallpox by 1979.

smarm *v.t.* (*colloq.*) **1.** to smooth, to slick. **2.** to flatter fulsomely. [orig. dial.; etym. unkn.]

smarmy *adj.* (*colloq.*) ingratiating. —**smarminess** *n.* [f. SMARM]

smart *adj.* **1.** clever, ingenious; quick-witted. **2.** neat and elegant; fashionable. **3.** forceful; brisk. —*v.i.* to feel acute pain or distress. —*n.* a stinging sensation or mental feeling. —**look smart,** to make haste. **smart alec,** a know-all. —**smartly** *adv.*, **smartness** *n.* [OE]

smarten *v.t./i.* (usu. with *up*) to make or become smart. [f. SMART]

smash *v.t./i.* **1.** to break or become broken suddenly and noisily into pieces. **2.** to destroy, defeat, or overthrow suddenly and completely; to suffer such destruction etc. **3.** to strike or move with great force; to strike (a ball) forcefully downwards in tennis etc. —*n.* **1.** an act or sound of smashing; a collision; a disaster, financial ruin. **2.** (also **smash hit**) a very successful play or song etc. —*adv.* with a smash. —**smash-and-grab** *adj.* (of a robbery) in which a thief smashes a window and seizes goods. [imit.]

smasher *n.* (*colloq.*) a very pleasing or beautiful person or thing. [f. SMASH]

smashing *adj.* (*colloq.*) excellent, wonderful; beautiful. [f. SMASH]

smattering /'smætərɪŋ/ *n.* a slight knowledge of something. [f. *smatter* talk ignorantly; orig. unkn.]

smear *v.t.* **1.** to daub or stain with a greasy or sticky substance. **2.** to smudge. **3.** to discredit or defame; to seek to do this. —*n.* **1.** the action or result of smearing. **2.** material smeared on a microscope slide etc. for examination; a specimen of this. **3.** discrediting, defaming; an attempt at this. —**smeary** *adj.* [OE]

smell *n.* **1.** the faculty of perception through the response of the brain to the action of odour on the nose. **2.** the quality in substances that affects this sense. **3.** an unpleasant odour. **4.** an act of inhaling to ascertain a smell. —*v.t./i.* (*past* & *p.p.* **smelt** *or* **smelled**) **1.** to perceive, detect, or examine by smell; to have or use the sense of smell. **2.** to give off a smell; to seem by smell to be; to be redolent *of* something specified. —**smelling-salts** *n.pl.* sharp-smelling solid substances sniffed to relieve faintness etc. **smell out,** to seek or discover by smelling or investigation. [prob. f. OE]

smelly *adj.* having a strong or unpleasant smell. —**smelliness** *n.* [f. SMELL]

smelt[1] *v.t.* to extract metal from (ore) by melting; to extract (metal) thus. [f. MDu. or MLG, rel. to MELT]

smelt[2] *n.* a small edible green and silver fish of the genus *Osmerus* etc. [OE]

smelt[3] *past* & *p.p.* of SMELL.

Smersh the popular name for the Russian counter-espionage organization, originating during the Second World War, which is responsible for maintaining security within the Soviet armed and intelligence services. [Russ. abbr. of *smert' shpionam*, lit. 'death to spies']

Smetana /'smetənə/, Bedřich (1824-84), Bohemian composer regarded as the founder of Czech music. His dedication to Czech nationalism is apparent in his operas (notably *The Bartered Bride*, 1866, and *Dalibor*, 1868) and in the cycle of symphonic poems *My Country* (1874-9). He also contributed to the cause through his work as conductor of the Provisional Theatre in Prague. Smetana died in an asylum after 10 years of suffering from the onset of syphilis, which had left him completely deaf in 1881, and was buried as a national hero.

smidgen /'smɪdʒ(ə)n/ *n.* (*colloq.*) a small bit or amount. [perh. f. synonymous *smitch*]

smilax /'smaɪlæks/ *n.* **1.** a climbing plant, often with a prickly stem, of the genus *Smilax*, some tropical species of which yield sarsaparilla from tuberous root-stocks. **2.** a South African climbing asparagus (*Asparagus asparagoides*) much used in decoration. [L f. Gk, = bindweed]

smile *v.t./i.* to make or have a facial expression indicating pleasure or amusement, with the lips stretched and turning upwards at their ends; to express by smiling; to give (a smile) of a specified kind. —*n.* an act of smiling; a smiling expression or aspect. —**smile on** *or* **at**, to look encouragingly on; (of a circumstance etc.) to favour. —**smiler** *n.* [perh. f. Scand. (rel. to SMIRK)]

Smiley /ˈsmaɪlɪ/, George. A quiet scholarly senior officer in the British intelligence bureaucracy in novels by John le Carré.

smirch *v.t.* to besmirch. —*n.* **1.** a smear or stain. **2.** discredit. [orig. unkn.]

smirk *n.* a silly or self-satisfied smile. —*v.i.* to give a smirk. [OE (*smerian* laugh at)]

smite *v.t./i.* (*past* **smote**; *p.p.* **smitten** /ˈsmɪt(ə)n/) **1.** (*archaic*) to hit hard; to chastise, to defeat. **2.** to have a sudden effect on. **3.** (*esp.* in *p.p.*) to strike with a disease, desire, emotion, or fascination. [OE *smitan* smear]

Smith[1], Adam (1723–90), Scottish philosopher and economist, founder of modern political economy, whose work marks a highly significant turning-point in the breakdown of mercantilist orthodoxy and the spread of *laissez-faire* ideas. A notable participant in the Scottish Enlightenment of the 18th c., with a considerable reputation as a philosopher, Smith retired from academic life to produce his seminal *Inquiry into the Nature and Causes of the Wealth of Nations* (1776), establishing theories of labour, distribution, wages, prices, and money, and putting forward a theory of the natural liberty of trade and commerce which was to prove highly influential in terms not only of economic but also of political theory in the following century. It appeared on the actual date of the Declaration of Independence of the American rebels, and contained the prophecy 'They will be one of the foremost nations of the world'.

Smith[2], Ian Douglas (1919–), Rhodesian statesman. Smith became Prime Minister of the White minority government of Rhodesia in 1964, and, after Britain refused to give the country its independence under his administration, unilaterally declared independence in 1965. He was forced to resign in 1979 to make way for majority Black rule. After the transformation of the country into the independent State of Zimbabwe he remained active in politics, leading the party that represented the interests of those Whites who chose to remain.

Smith[3], Joseph (1805–44), founder of the Mormon sect.

Smith[4], Stevie (Florence Margaret) (1902–71), English poet. She wrote three novels, including *Novel on Yellow Paper* (1936), but is more widely recognized for her witty, caustic, and enigmatic verse, often illustrated by her own comic drawings, in volumes which include *A Good Time was Had By All* (1937) and *Not Waving But Drowning* (1957). Her *Collected Poems* (1975) appeared posthumously.

Smith[5], Sydney (1771–1845), English churchman, essayist, and wit, author of the *Letters of Peter Plymley* (1807), in defence of Catholic emancipation.

Smith[6], William (1769–1839), English land-surveyor and self-taught geologist, one of the founders of stratigraphical geology, long known as the father of English geology. Working initially in the area around Bath, he discovered that rock strata could be distinguished on the basis of their characteristic assemblages of fossils, and that the identity of strata exposed in different places could thereby be established. Smith later travelled extensively in Britain, accumulating data which enabled him to produce the first geological map of the whole of England and Wales. Many of the names he devised for particular strata are still in use.

smith *n.* **1.** a worker in metal. **2.** a blacksmith. **3.** one who creates something (*song-smith*). [OE]

smithereens /smɪðəˈriːnz/ *n.pl.* small fragments. [f. dial. *smithers* (orig. unkn.)]

Smithfield /ˈsmɪθfiːld/ originally, an open area outside the NW walls of the City of London, a market for cattle and horses, which later became the central meat-market. In the 16th c. it was the scene of the burning of heretics.

Smithsonian Institution /smɪθˈsəʊnɪən/ the oldest US foundation for scientific research, established by Congress in 1838 and opened in 1846 in Washington, DC. It originated in a £100,000 bequest in the will of James Smithson (1765–1829), English chemist and mineralogist, for 'an

establishment for the increase and diffusion of knowledge among men'.

smithy /ˈsmɪðɪ/ *n.* a blacksmith's workshop, a forge. [f. SMITH]

smitten *p.p.* of SMITE.

smock *n.* **1.** a loose overall. **2.** (also **smock-frock**) a loose shirtlike garment often ornamented with smocking. —*v.t.* to decorate with smocking. [OE]

smocking *n.* ornamentation on cloth made by gathering it tightly with stitches into a honeycomb pattern. [f. SMOCK]

smog *n.* fog intensified by smoke. —**smoggy** *adj.* [portmanteau word]

smoke *n.* **1.** the visible vapour given off by a burning substance. **2.** an act or period of smoking tobacco. **3.** (*colloq.*) a cigarette or cigar. —*v.t./i.* **1.** to emit smoke or other visible vapour. **2.** to inhale and exhale the smoke of a cigarette, cigar, or pipe; to do this habitually; to use (a cigarette etc.) thus. **3.** to darken or preserve by the action of smoke. —**go up in smoke**, to come to nothing. **smoke-bomb** *n.* a bomb that emits dense smoke on exploding. **smoke out**, to drive out by means of smoke; to drive out of hiding or secrecy etc. —**smoke-stack** *n.* a chimney or funnel for discharging the smoke of a locomotive or steamer. [OE]

smokeless *adj.* having or producing little or no smoke. [f. SMOKE + -LESS]

smoker *n.* **1.** a person who smokes tobacco habitually. **2.** a part of a railway coach in which smoking is allowed. [f. SMOKE]

smokescreen *n.* **1.** a cloud of smoke concealing military or other operations. **2.** a device or ruse for disguising activities.

smoky *adj.* **1.** producing or emitting much smoke. **2.** covered or filled with smoke; obscured (as) with smoke. **3.** suggestive of or having the greyish colour of smoke. —**smokily** *adv.*, **smokiness** *n.* [f. SMOKE]

Smollett /ˈsmɒlɪt/, Tobias George (1721–71), Scottish novelist, who became a surgeon's mate in the Navy and was present at the abortive attack on Cartagena which is described in his first novel *Roderick Random* (1748). His other novels were *Peregrine Pickle* (1751), *Count Fathom* (1753), *Sir Launcelot Greaves* (1760–1), the story of an 18th-c. Don Quixote, and his most famous work *Humphrey Clinker* (1771) in epistolary form. These works are often described as picaresque and are characterized by fast-moving narrative, humorous caricature, and incident which sometimes distorts Smollett's professed moral purpose. He also edited periodicals, produced political pamphlets (often controversial), poems, plays, and a *Complete History of England* (1757–8), and translations of Voltaire, Cervantes, and Le Sage.

smolt /sməʊlt/ *n.* a young salmon at the stage between parr and grilse, when it is covered with silvery scales and migrates to the sea for the first time. [orig. Sc. & N. Engl.; orig. unkn.]

smooch *v.i.* (*colloq.*) to kiss and caress; to dance slowly and closely to a lazy romantic melody. —*n.* a spell of smooching; music for this. [imit.]

smooth /smuːð/ *adj.* **1.** having an even surface; without roughness, projections, or indentations; not hairy; (of water) without waves. **2.** having an even texture, without lumps. **3.** not harsh in sound or taste; moving evenly without jolts or bumping; progressing without hindrance. **4.** pleasantly polite but perhaps insincere. —*v.t./i.* **1.** to make or become smooth. **2.** to remove problems or dangers from. —*adv.* smoothly. —*n.* a smoothing touch or stroke. —**smoothly** *adv.*, **smoothness** *n.* [OE]

smorgasbord /ˈsmɔːɡəsbɔːd/ *n.* Swedish hors d'œuvres typically consisting of open sandwiches with an assortment of delicacies; a buffet meal with a variety of dishes. [Sw. (*smörgås* (slice of) bread and butter, *bord* table]

smote *past* of SMITE.

smother /ˈsmʌðə(r)/ *v.t./i.* **1.** to suffocate or stifle; to be suffocated. **2.** to cover thickly; to overwhelm (with gifts, kindness, etc.). **3.** to put out or keep down (a fire) by heaping ashes etc. on it. **4.** to repress or conceal. —*n.* a cloud of smoke or dust etc.; obscurity caused by this. [f. OE *smorian* suffocate]

smoulder /ˈsməʊldə(r)/ *v.i.* **1.** to burn slowly without flame or in a suppressed way. **2.** to burn inwardly with concealed anger or jealousy etc. **3.** (of feelings) to exist in a suppressed state. [rel. to LG *smöln*]

smudge *n.* a blurred or smeared mark. —*v.t./i.* **1.** to make a smudge on or of. **2.** to become smeared or blurred. —**smudgy** adj. [orig. unkn.]

smug adj. self-satisfied, complacent; consciously respectable. —**smugly** adv., **smugness** n. [f. LG smuk pretty]

smuggle v.t. to import or export (goods) illegally, especially without paying customs duties; to convey secretly. —**smuggler** n. [f. LG]

smut n. **1.** a small flake of soot; a small black mark made (as) by this. **2.** obscene talk, pictures, or stories. **3.** a cereal-disease turning parts of the plant to black powder. —v.t./i. (-**tt**-) **1.** to mark with smuts. **2.** to infect with or contract smut disease. —**smutty** adj., **smuttiness** n. [rel. to LG smutt (cf. SMUDGE)]

Smuts, Jan Christiaan (1870–1950), South African soldier, statesman, and philosopher. A lawyer by training, Smuts played an important part in the Boer War, leading a Boer guerrilla group in the Cape area, but afterwards supported Botha's policy of Anglo-Boer co-operation and was one of the founders of the Union of South Africa. During the First World War he became that country's foremost soldier, leading Imperial troops against the Germans in East Africa in 1916 and acting as South African representative in the British War Cabinet in 1917–18, during which time he played a crucial role in the formation of the Royal Air Force. After the war he held a series of high posts in the South African government, including that of Prime Minister in 1919–24 and 1939–48. During the Second World War he commanded the South African troops. As a statesman Smuts was respected internationally; he helped to found the League of Nations, drafted the preamble to the UN charter, and put forward the idea that the British Empire should evolve into a commonwealth of equal nations. In South Africa itself, however, he failed to grasp the strength of Afrikaner nationalism, and his support of Britain aroused resentment.

Sn symbol tin. [f. L stannum tin]

snack n. a small, casual, or hurried meal. —**snack bar,** a place where snacks are served. [orig. = a snap or bite, f. MDu. (snacken v., var. of snappen snap]

snaffle n. a simple bridle-bit without a curb (ill. HORSE). —v.t. **1.** to put a snaffle on. **2.** (slang) to take, to steal. [prob. f. LDu.; cf. MLG snavel beak, mouth]

snag n. **1.** an unexpected or hidden difficulty. **2.** a jagged projection. **3.** a tear in fabric caused by a snag. —v.t./i. (-**gg**-) to catch, tear, or be caught on a snag. —**snaggy** adj. [prob. f. Scand.; cf. Norw. dial. snag(e) sharp point]

snail n. a slow-moving gastropod mollusc, especially of the family Helicidae, with a spiral shell. —**snail's pace,** very slow movement. [OE]

snake n. **1.** a long limbless reptile of the suborder Ophidia. **2.** (also **snake in the grass**) a treacherous person; a secret enemy. —v.i. to move or twist etc. like a snake. —**snake-charmer** n. a person appearing to make snakes move to music etc. **snakes and ladders,** a game with counters moved, according to the throw of the dice, along a board with sudden advances up 'ladders' or returns down 'snakes' depicted on the board. [OE]

snaky /'sneɪkɪ/ adj. **1.** infested with snakes; (of the hair of the Furies) composed of snakes. **2.** snakelike in appearance or movements or in cunning, treachery, etc. —**snakily** adv. [f. prec.]

snap v.t./i. (-**pp**-) **1.** to make or cause to make a sharp cracking sound; to open or close thus. **2.** to break suddenly or with a cracking sound. **3.** to speak or say with sudden irritation. **4.** to make a sudden audible bite. **5.** to move quickly. **6.** to take a snapshot of. —n. **1.** an act or sound of snapping. **2.** a catch that fastens with a snap. **3.** a crisp brittle cake or biscuit. **4.** a snapshot. **5.** (also **cold snap**) a sudden brief spell of cold weather. **6.** a card-game in which players call 'Snap' when two similar cards are exposed (also as int. at the unexpected similarity of two things). **7.** vigour, liveliness. —adv. with a snapping sound. —adj. sudden; done or arranged etc. quickly or at short notice. —**snap fastener,** a press-stud. **snap one's fingers at,** to defy; to regard with contempt. **snap out of,** (slang) to throw off (a mood etc.) by a sudden effort. **snap up,** to pick up or buy hastily or eagerly. [prob. f. MDu. or MLG (imit.)]

snapdragon n. a plant of the genus Antirrhinum with a bag-shaped flower like a dragon's mouth.

snapper n. any of several food-fish, especially of the family Lutianidae. [f. SNAP]

snappish adj. inclined to snap; irritable, petulant. —**snappishly** adv. [f. SNAP]

snappy adj. (colloq.) **1.** brisk, full of zest. **2.** neat and elegant. —**make it snappy,** (colloq.) to be quick. —**snappily** adv. [f. SNAP]

snapshot n. a photograph taken informally or casually.

snare n. **1.** a trap, especially with a noose, for catching birds or animals. **2.** a thing that tempts or exposes one to danger or failure etc. **3.** (often in pl.) an arrangement of twisted gut or wire etc. stretched across the lower head of a side-drum to produce a rattling sound; (also **snare-drum**) a drum fitted with snares. —v.t. to catch in a snare; to ensnare. [OE f. ON]

snarl[1] v.t./i. **1.** to growl angrily with bared teeth. **2.** to speak irritably or cynically. —n. an act or sound of snarling. [f. earlier snar, f. LG]

snarl[2] v.t./i. (often with up) to tangle; to become entangled; to confuse and hamper the movement of (traffic etc.). —n. a tangle. —**snarl-up** n. a confusion or jam of traffic etc. [f. SNARE]

snatch v.t./i. to seize quickly, eagerly, or unexpectedly; to take quickly or when a chance occurs. —n. **1.** an act of snatching. **2.** a fragment of song or talk etc. **3.** a short spell of activity etc. [perh. rel. to SNACK]

snazzy /'snæzɪ/ adj. (slang) smart, stylish; excellent. —**snazzily** adv., **snazziness** n. [orig. unkn.]

sneak v.t./i. **1.** to go or convey furtively. **2.** (slang) to steal unobserved. **3.** (slang) to tell tales, especially at school. —n. a cowardly underhand person; (slang) a tell-tale, especially at school. —adj. acting or done without warning; secret. —**sneak-thief** n. a petty thief; a person who steals from open rooms etc. —**sneaky** adj. [perh. rel. to obs. snike creep]

sneakers n.pl. soft-soled shoes. [f. SNEAK]

sneaking adj. (of a feeling or suspicion etc.) persistent but not openly acknowledged. [f. SNEAK]

sneer n. a scornful smile or remark. —v.t./i. to show scorn by a sneer; to utter thus. [perh. f. LDu.]

sneeze n. a sudden involuntary expulsion of air from the nose and mouth caused by irritation in the nostrils. —v.i. to make a sneeze. —**not to be sneezed at,** (colloq.) not contemptible, worth having. [earlier snese, nese, fnese, f. ON]

snick v.t. **1.** to make a small notch or incision in. **2.** (in cricket) to hit (the ball) with a light glancing stroke. —n. such a notch or stroke. [suggested by snickersnee large knife]

snicker v.i. to snigger. —n. a snigger. [imit.]

snide adj. (colloq.) **1.** sneering, slyly derogatory. **2.** counterfeit. **3.** (US) mean, underhand. [19th c. slang]

sniff v.t./i. to draw up air audibly through the nose; to smell thus. —n. an act or sound of sniffing. —**sniff at,** to try the smell of; to show contempt for or disapproval of. [imit.]

sniffle v.i. to sniff repeatedly or slightly. —n. an act of sniffling; (in pl.) a cold in the head causing sniffling. [imit.; cf. SNIVEL]

sniffy adj. (colloq.) disdainful. —**sniffily** adv., **sniffiness** n. [f. SNIFF]

snifter n. (slang) a small drink of alcoholic liquor. [f. dial. snift sniff]

snigger n. a sly giggle. —v.i. to utter a snigger. [var. of SNICKER]

snip v.t./i. (-**pp**-) to cut with scissors or shears, especially in small quick strokes. —n. **1.** an act of snipping. **2.** a piece snipped off. **3.** (slang) something cheaply acquired or easily done. [f. LG or Du. (imit.)]

snipe n. (pl. **snipes** or (collect.) **snipe**) a wading bird of the genus Gallinago with a long straight bill. —v.i. **1.** to fire shots from a hiding-place, usually at long range. **2.** to make a sly critical remark attacking a person or thing. —**sniper** n. [prob. f. Scand.]

snippet /'snɪpɪt/ n. **1.** a small piece cut off. **2.** (usu. in pl.) a scrap or fragment of information or knowledge etc.; a short extract from a book etc. [f. SNIP]

snitch v.t. (slang) to steal. [orig. = fillip on the nose; etym. unkn.]

snivel /'snɪv(ə)l/ v.i. (-**ll**-) **1.** to cry or complain in a miserable whining way; to weep with sniffling. **2.** to run at the nose. —n. **1.** an act of snivelling. **2.** running mucus. —**sniveller** n. [f. OE (snofl mucus); cf. SNUFFLE]

snob n. a person who has an exaggerated respect for social position or wealth, or attainments or tastes, and despises those he considers inferior. —**snobbery** n., **snobbish** adj.,

snobbishly *adv.*, **snobbishness** *n.* [orig. = cobbler; etym. unkn.]

snoek /snuːk/ *n.* (in S. Afr.) a barracouta. [Afrik., f. Du. = pike; prob. rel. to SNACK]

snog *v.i.* (**-gg-**) (*slang*) to engage in kissing and caressing. —*n.* (*slang*) a spell of snogging. [orig. unkn.]

snood *n.* a loose baglike ornamental net in which a woman's hair is held at the back. [OE *snōd*; orig. unkn.]

snook /snuːk/ *n.* (*colloq.*) a contemptuous gesture with the thumb to the nose and the fingers spread. —**cock a snook at**, to make this gesture at; to show cheeky contempt for. [orig. unkn.]

snooker /ˈsnuːkə(r)/ *n.* **1.** a form of pool played with 15 red and 6 other coloured balls on a billiard table. **2.** a position in this game where a direct shot would lose points. —*v.t.* to subject to a snooker; (*slang*, esp. in *pass.*) to thwart, to defeat. [19th c.; orig. unkn.]

snoop *v.i.* to pry inquisitively. —*n.* an act of snooping. —**snooper** *n.*, **snoopy** *adj.* [f. Du., = eat on the sly]

snoot *n.* (*slang*) the nose. [var. of SNOUT]

snooty *adj.* (*colloq.*) supercilious, haughty, snobbish. —**snootily** *adv.* [orig. unkn.]

snooze *n.* a short sleep, especially in the daytime. —*v.i.* to take a snooze. [orig. unkn.]

snore *n.* a snorting or grunting sound in breathing during sleep. —*v.i.* to make such sounds. —**snorer** *n.* [prob. imit.]

Snorkel /ˈsnɔːk(ə)l/ *n.* [P] a piece of apparatus consisting of a platform which may be elevated and extended, used in fighting fires in tall buildings.

snorkel *n.* **1.** a breathing-tube for supplying air to an underwater swimmer. **2.** a device by which a submerged submarine can take in and expel air. —*v.i.* (**-ll-**) to swim with a snorkel. [f. G *schnorchel*]

Snorri Sturluson /ˈsnɔːrɪ ˈstɜːləs(ə)n/ (1178–1241), Icelandic historian, the most important figure in Old Icelandic literature, author of the prose *Edda* and the *Heimskringla*, a history of the kings of Norway, through which works he popularized Norse myth and Old Norse poetry. He was involved in the chief political intrigues of his time and King Hákon of Norway ordered his assassination.

snort *n.* **1.** an explosive sound made by the sudden forcing of breath through the nose, especially expressing indignation or incredulity; a similar sound made by an engine etc. **2.** (*colloq.*) a small drink of liquor. —*v.t./i.* to make a snort; to express or utter with a snort. [prob. imit.]

snorter *n.* (*slang*) something notably vigorous or difficult etc. [f. SNORT]

snot *n.* (*slang*) **1.** nasal mucus. **2.** a contemptible person. [prob. f. MDu. or MLG; rel. to SNOUT]

snotty *adj.* (*slang*) **1.** running or foul with nasal mucus. **2.** contemptible, bad-tempered. **3.** supercilious. —**snottily** *adv.*, **snottiness** *n.* [f. SNOT]

snout *n.* the projecting nose (and mouth) of an animal; (*derog.*) the human nose; the pointed front of a thing. [f. MDu. or MLG]

Snow /snəʊ/, Charles Percy (1905–80), English novelist, scientist, and administrator. His sequence of novels *Strangers and Brothers* deals with moral dilemmas and power-struggles in the academic world, and includes *The Masters* (1951) and *The Affair* (1960). He was created a life peer in 1964.

snow /snəʊ/ *n.* **1.** frozen atmospheric vapour falling to earth in light white flakes; a fall of this; a layer of it on the ground. **2.** a thing resembling snow in whiteness or texture etc.; (*slang*) cocaine. —*v.i.* to fall as or like snow; to come in large numbers or quantities. —**it snows** *or* **is snowing**, snow falls or is falling. **snow-berry** *n.* a garden shrub (*Symphoricarpos rivularis*) with white berries. **snow-blind** *adj.* temporarily blinded by the glare from snow. **snow-bound** *adj.* prevented by snow from going out or travelling. **snow-capped** *adj.* (of a mountain) covered at the top with snow. **snow-drift** *n.* a bank of snow heaped by the wind. **snowed in** *or* **up**, snow-bound. **snowed under**, covered (as) with snow; overwhelmed with a quantity of letters, work, etc. **snow goose**, the arctic white goose (*Anser caerulescens*). **snow-line** *n.* the level above which snow never melts entirely. **snow-plough** *n.* a device for clearing a road or railway of snow; a skiing movement turning the points of the skis inwards so as to stop (ill. SPORTS). **snow-shoe** *n.* a flat device like a racket attached to the foot for walking on snow without sinking in. **snow-white** *adj.* pure white. [OE]

snowball *n.* snow pressed together into a ball for throwing in play. —*v.t./i.* **1.** to throw or pelt with snowballs. **2.** to

increase rapidly. —**snowball-tree** *n.* a variety of guelder rose (*Viburnum opulus* var. *roseum*).

Snowdon /ˈsnəʊd(ə)n/ the highest mountain of Wales (1,085 m, 3,560 ft.).

snowdrop *n.* a spring-flowering plant (*Galanthus nivalis*) with white drooping flowers.

snowfall *n.* the amount of fallen snow.

snowflake *n.* each of the small collections of crystals in which snow falls.

snowman *n.* (*pl.* **-men**) a figure made of compressed snow roughly in the shape of a man.

snowmobile /ˈsnəʊməbiːl/ *n.* a motor vehicle, especially with runners or Caterpillar tracks, for travel over snow.

snowstorm *n.* a heavy fall of snow, especially with a high wind.

snowy *adj.* **1.** with snow falling; with much snow. **2.** covered with snow. **3.** as white as snow. —**snowy owl**, a large white owl (*Nyctea nyctea*). [f. SNOW]

SNP *abbr.* Scottish National Party.

Snr. *abbr.* Senior.

snub[1] *v.t.* (**-bb-**) to rebuff or humiliate with sharp words or a marked lack of cordiality. —*n.* an act of snubbing. [f. ON, = chide]

snub[2] *adj.* (of the nose) short and stumpy. **snub-nosed** *adj.* [f. prec. in sense 'check growth of']

snuff[1] *n.* the charred part of a candle-wick. —*v.t./i.* to remove the snuff from (a candle). —**snuff it**, (*slang*) to die. **snuff out**, to extinguish (a candle) by snuffing; to kill or put an end to (hopes etc.); (*slang*) to die. [orig. unkn.]

snuff[2] *n.* **1.** powdered tobacco or medicine taken by sniffing it up the nostrils. **2.** a sniff. —*v.t./i.* **1.** to take snuff. **2.** to sniff. —**snuff-box** *n.* a small box for holding snuff. **snuff-coloured** *adj.* dark yellowish-brown. [f. MDu., = snuffle]

snuffer *n.* a device for snuffing or extinguishing a candle. [f. SNUFF[1]]

snuffle *v.t./i.* **1.** to sniff in a noisy way; to breathe noisily (as) through a partly blocked nose. **2.** to speak or say with snuffles. —*n.* a snuffling sound. [prob. f. LG & Du. (as SNUFF[2]); cf. SNIVEL]

snug *adj.* cosy, sheltered and comfortable; (of a garment) close-fitting. —*n.* a small bar in a public house, with comfortable seating for a few people. —**snugly** *adv.* [orig. Naut.; prob. f. LDu.]

snuggery *n.* a snug place, especially a person's private room. [f. SNUG]

snuggle *v.t./i.* to settle or draw into a warm comfortable position. [f. SNUG]

so[1] /səʊ/ *adv.* & *conj.* **1.** in this or that way; in the manner, position, or state described or implied; to that or to such an extent. **2.** to a great or notable degree. **3.** (with verbs of saying or thinking etc.) thus, this, that. **4.** consequently, therefore; indeed; in actual fact. **5.** also. —**and so on** *or* **forth**, and others of the same kind; and in other similar ways. **or so**, approximately. **so as to**, in order to, in such a way as to. **so be it**, an expression of acceptance of or resignation to an event etc. **so-called** *adj.* called or named thus (but perhaps wrongly or inaccurately). **so long**, (*colloq.*) goodbye. **so many** (*or* **much**), a definite number (or amount); nothing but. **so much for**, that is all that need be said or done about. **so-so** *adj.* & *adv.* only moderately good or well. **so that**, in order that. **so to say** *or* **speak**, an expression of reserve or apology for an exaggeration or neologism etc. **so what?** that is irrelevant or of no importance. [OE]

soak *v.t./i.* **1.** to place or lie in a liquid so as to become thoroughly wet. **2.** (of liquid) to penetrate gradually; (of rain) to drench. **3.** to absorb (lit. or fig.). **4.** (*slang*) to extort money from. —*n.* **1.** the act or process of soaking. **2.** (*colloq.*) a hard drinker. —**soak-away** *n.* an arrangement for the disposal of water by percolation through the soil. **soak oneself in**, to absorb (a liquid or knowledge etc.). **soak through**, (of moisture) to penetrate, to make thoroughly wet. [OE (as SUCK)]

so-and-so /ˈsəʊənsəʊ/ *n.* (*pl.* **so-and-so's**) **1.** a particular person or thing not needing to be specified. **2.** (*colloq.*, to avoid use of a vulgar word) an unpleasant or objectionable person. [f. SO[1]]

Soane /səʊn/, Sir John (1753–1837), English architect. His highly individualistic manipulation of the classical canon makes him something of a Romantic classicist. From 1788 he was architect of the Bank of England and there developed his characteristic style of simple masses defined by flat surfaces and articulated with incised lines. By 1810 his style had become more severe, avoiding unnecessary ornament and adopting structural necessity as the basis of design. His picture collection, amassed as a result of his professional success, is housed in his self-designed home, the Sir John Soane Museum, London.

soap *n.* a cleansing substance made of fat or oil combined with an alkali, yielding lather when rubbed in water. —*v.t.* to apply soap to; to rub with soap. —**soap-box** *n.* a makeshift stand for a street orator. **soap-flakes** *n.pl.* flakes of soap prepared for washing clothes etc. **soap opera,** a sentimental domestic broadcast serial. **soap powder,** a powder, especially with additives, for washing clothes etc. [OE]

soapstone *n.* steatite.

soapsuds *n.pl.* suds.

soapy *adj.* **1.** of or like soap. **2.** containing or smeared with soap. **3.** unctuous, flattering. —**soapily** *adv.,* **soapiness** *n.* [f. SOAP]

soar *v.i.* **1.** to rise high in flight. **2.** to reach a high level or standard. [f. OF *essorer,* ult. f. L *aura* breeze]

sob *v.t./i.* (**-bb-**) to draw the breath in convulsive gasps usually with weeping; to utter with sobs. —*n.* the act or sound of sobbing. —**sob-story** *n.* (*colloq.*) a narrative meant to evoke sympathy. **sob-stuff** *n.* (*colloq.*) pathos, sentimental writing or behaviour. [prob. imit.]

sober /ˈsəʊbə(r)/ *adj.* **1.** not intoxicated; not given to heavy drinking. **2.** serious, sedate, not frivolous. **3.** moderate, well-balanced. **4.** (of colour etc.) quiet and inconspicuous. —*v.t./i.* to make or become sober. —**soberly** *adv.,* **sobriety** /səˈbraɪətɪ/ *n.* [f. OF f. L]

sobriquet /ˈsəʊbrɪkeɪ/ *n.* a nickname. [F, orig. = tap under chin]

Soc. *abbr.* **1.** Socialist. **2.** Society.

soccer /ˈsɒkə(r)/ *n.* (*colloq.*) Association football. [abbr. of *Association*]

sociable /ˈsəʊʃəb(ə)l/ *adj.* fond of company; characterized by friendly companionship. —**sociability** /-ˈbɪlɪtɪ/ *n.,* **sociably** *adv.* [F, or f. L (*sociare* unite, as foll.)]

social /ˈsəʊʃ(ə)l/ *adj.* **1.** of society or its organization; concerned with the mutual relationships of people or classes living in association. **2.** living in organized communities, not solitary. **3.** sociable. **4.** of or designed for companionship and sociability. —*n.* a social gathering, especially one organized by a club etc. —**social climber,** a person seeking to gain a higher rank in society. **social contract,** an agreement to co-operate for social benefits, especially involving submission to restrictions on individual liberty. **Social Democrat,** a member of a socialistic political party aiming at gradual advance towards socialism; (in the UK) a member of the Social Democratic Party (see separate entry). **social science,** the study of human society and social relationships. **social security,** State assistance to those lacking adequate means or welfare. **social services,** the welfare services provided by the State, including education, health, housing, pensions, etc. **social work,** organized work to alleviate social problems. **social worker,** a person engaged in this. —**socially** *adv.* [F of f. L (*socius* companion)]

Social Democratic Party a UK political party with moderate socialist aims, founded in 1981 by a group of former Labour MPs.

socialism /ˈsəʊʃ(ə)lɪz(ə)m/ *n.* a political and economic theory of social organization which advocates that the community as a whole should own and control the means of production, distribution, and exchange (see below); a policy or practice based on this theory. —**socialist** *n.,* **socialistic** /-ˈlɪstɪk/ *adj.* [f. F (as prec.)]

In its earliest forms, socialism tended to be little more than a romantic vision held by a minority of social reformers, many of them well-to-do philanthropists. It was revolutionized as a political ideal by Karl Marx in the mid-19th c., becoming a mass movement aimed at the transformation of society, but both the methods by which this transformation was to be achieved and the manner in which the new society was to be run have remained the subject of considerable disagreement and have produced a wide variety of socialist parties, ranging from moderate reformers to ultra-left-wing Communists dedicated to upheaval by violent revolution.

socialite /ˈsəʊʃ(ə)laɪt/ *n.* a person prominent in fashionable society. [f. SOCIAL]

socialize /ˈsəʊʃ(ə)laɪz/ *v.t./i.* **1.** to behave sociably; to

make social. **2.** to organize in a socialistic manner. —**socialization** *n.* [f. SOCIAL]

society /səˈsaɪətɪ/ *n.* **1.** an organized and interdependent community; the system of living in this. **2.** people of the higher social classes. **3.** company, companionship. **4.** an association of persons sharing a common aim or interest etc. —**Society of Jesus,** the Jesuits (see entry). [f. F f. L (as SOCIAL)]

Society Islands a group of islands in French Polynesia, including Tahiti. They were named by Captain Cook in honour of the Royal Society.

Society of Friends a body of Christians, also called Quakers, founded by George Fox. They were organized as a distinctive group in 1668, and began to engage in missionary work; in 1682 William Penn founded Pennsylvania on a Quaker basis. Until the Toleration Act of 1689 they were much persecuted, refusing to meet in secret, laying stress on outward observances in speech and in plainness of dress, and cutting themselves off from cultural life, which they regarded as frivolous. Their main activities were trade and philanthropic pursuits, for which they became famous. Central to their belief is the doctrine of the 'Inner Light', or sense of Christ's direct working in the soul; this has led them to reject the sacraments, the ministry, and all set forms of worship. Their meetings begin in silence until some member feels stirred to speak. They have a strong commitment to pacifism. Refusal of military service and of oaths has often brought members into conflict with the authorities, but their devotion to social and educational work (and, more recently, to international relief) has earned them general respect.

socio- /ˈsəʊsɪəʊ-, -ʃɪəʊ-/ *in comb.* of society or sociology (and). [f. L *socius* companion]

sociobiology /ˌsəʊʃɪəʊbaɪˈɒlədʒɪ/ *n.* the study of the biological (esp. ecological and evolutionary) bases of human and animal social behaviour. [f. SOCIO- + BIOLOGY]

sociology /ˌsəʊsɪˈɒlədʒɪ/ *n.* the study of society and social problems. —**sociological** /-sɪəˈlɒdʒɪk(ə)l/ *adj.* **sociologist** *n.* [f. F, as SOCIO- + -LOGY)]

sock¹ *n.* **1.** a short stocking, usually not reaching the knee. **2.** a loose insole. —**pull one's socks up,** (*colloq.*) to make an effort to improve. **put a sock in it,** (*slang*) to be quiet. [OE f. L *soccus* actor's shoe]

sock² *v.t.* (*slang*) to hit (a person) hard —*n.* (*slang*) a hard blow. —**sock it to,** to attack or address (a person) vigorously. [orig. unkn.]

socket /ˈsɒkɪt/ *n.* a natural or artificial hollow for something to fit into or stand firm or revolve in, especially a device receiving a plug or light-bulb etc. in, to make a electrical connection. [f. AF, dim. of OF *soc* ploughshare]

Socrates /ˈsɒkrətiːz/ (469–399 BC) Athenian philosopher. His interests lay not in the natural-philosophical speculation of earlier thinkers but in the question of how men should conduct their lives, an inquiry pursued through the method of cross-questioning those he met. Self-denying in his own life, he was the centre of a circle of devoted friends who included the great and the rich. Although he wrote nothing himself, he was immensely influential, particularly on Plato, in whose *Dialogues* he is the principal interlocutor. He was condemned to death by an Athenian jury on charges of introducing strange gods and corrupting the young.

Socratic /səˈkrætɪk/ *adj.* of Socrates or his philosophy. —**Socratic irony,** see IRONY. **Socratic method,** dialectic, procedure by question and answer. [f. prec.]

sod¹ *n.* turf, a piece of turf; the surface of the ground. —**under the sod,** in the grave. [f. MDu. or MLG; orig. unkn.]

sod² *n.* (*vulgar*) an unpleasant or despicable person; a fellow. —*v.t.* (**-dd-**) (*vulgar*) to damn. [abbr. of SODOMITE]

soda /ˈsəʊdə/ *n.* **1.** a compound of sodium in common use, especially sodium carbonate (**washing-soda**), bicarbonate (**baking-soda**), or hydroxide (**caustic soda**). **2.** (also **soda-water**) water made effervescent with carbon dioxide and used as a drink alone or with spirits etc. —**soda-bread** *n.* bread leavened with baking-soda. **soda-fountain** *n.* a device supplying soda-water; a shop equipped with this. [L, perh. f. *sodanum* glasswort]

sodden /ˈsɒd(ə)n/ *adj.* **1.** saturated with liquid, soaked through. **2.** rendered stupid or dull etc. with drunkenness. [p.p. of SEETHE]

Soddy /ˈsɒdɪ/, Frederick (1877–1956), English physicist who was awarded the 1921 Nobel Prize for chemistry for his work with Rutherford in Canada on radioactive decay, and especially for his theory of isotopes (the word was coined by him in 1913). He also assisted Ramsey in London in the discovery of helium. He wrote on economics, and later concentrated on creating an awareness of the social relevance of science.

sodium /ˈsəʊdɪəm/ n. a soft silver-white metallic element of the alkali metal group, symbol Na, atomic number 11, first isolated by Sir Humphry Davy in 1807. Sodium, which is essential to all living things, occurs commonly in the earth's crust, notably as rock salt (sodium chloride). Although very reactive, the liquid metal is used as a coolant in some types of nuclear reactor. Sodium compounds have many industrial uses. —**sodium bicarbonate,** a white crystalline compound used in baking-powder. **sodium carbonate,** = washing-soda. **sodium chloride,** common salt. **sodium hydroxide,** a compound of sodium with hydroxyl. **sodium lamp,** a lamp giving a yellow light from an electrical discharge in sodium vapour. [f. SODA]

Sodom /ˈsɒdəm/ a town of ancient Palestine, probably south of the Dead Sea, destroyed by fire from heaven (according to Genesis 19: 24), along with Gomorrah, for the wickedness of its inhabitants.

sodomite /ˈsɒdəmaɪt/ n. a person practising sodomy. [f. OF f. L f. Gk (as foll.)]

sodomy /ˈsɒdəmɪ/ n. an anal or other copulation-like act, especially between males or between a person and an animal. [f. L f. SODOM]

Sodor /ˈsəʊdə(r)/ a medieval diocese comprising the Hebrides and the Isle of Man, originally the 'southern isles' (Norse *Sudhr-eyjar*) of the kingdom of Norway. The Hebrides were separated in 1334, but *Sodor and Man* has been the official name for the Anglican diocese of the Isle of Man since 1684.

soever /səʊˈevə(r)/ adv. (literary) of any possible kind or extent.

sofa /ˈsəʊfə/ n. a long upholstered seat with a back and raised ends or arms. [F, ult. f. Arab.]

soffit n. an under-surface of an arch or lintel etc. [f. F or It. (as SUFFIX)]

Sofia /ˈsəʊfɪə, səˈfiːə/ the capital of Bulgaria; pop. (1980) 1,056,945.

soft adj. 1. not hard or firm, yielding to pressure; malleable, plastic, easily cut. 2. (of cloth etc.) smooth or fine in texture, not rough or stiff. 3. (of air etc.) mild, balmy. 4. (of water) free from mineral salts that prevent soap from lathering. 5. (of light or colour etc.) not brilliant or glaring; (of sound) not loud or strident. 6. (of a consonant) sibilant (as *c* in *ice*, *g* in *age*). 7. (of an outline etc.) not sharply defined. 8. (of an action or manner etc.) gentle, conciliatory; complimentary, amorous; (of the heart or feelings etc.) compassionate, sympathetic. 9. (of character etc.) feeble, effeminate, silly, sentimental. 10. (slang) (of a job etc.) easy. 11. (of drugs) not likely to cause addiction. 12. (of currency, prices, etc.) likely to depreciate. 13. (of pornography) not highly obscene. —adv. softly. —**be soft on,** (colloq.) to be lenient towards; to be infatuated with. **soft-boiled** adj. (of an egg) boiled so as to leave the yolk still soft. **soft drink,** a non-alcoholic drink. **soft fruit,** small stoneless fruits such as strawberries and currants. **soft furnishings,** curtains and rugs etc. **soft-hearted** adj. compassionate. **soft landing,** one made with little or no damage. **soft option,** the easier alternative. **soft palate,** the back part of the palate, which is not bony. **soft pedal,** the pedal on a piano making the tone softer. **soft-pedal** v.t./i. to refrain from emphasizing. **soft roe,** see ROE¹. **soft sell,** restrained salesmanship. **soft-soap** v.t. (colloq.) to persuade (a person) with flattery. **soft-spoken** adj. speaking with a soft voice. **soft spot,** a feeling of affection for a person or thing. **soft touch,** (slang) a person readily parting with money when asked. —**softly** adv., **softness** n. [OE *sōfte* agreeable]

softball n. a modified form of baseball using a softer and larger ball, originally devised (c.1887) as an indoor game.

soften /ˈsɒf(ə)n/ v.t./i. to make or become soft or softer. —**soften up,** to make weaker by a preliminary attack; to make more persuasible by preliminary approaches etc. —**softener** n. [f. SOFT]

softie /ˈsɒftɪ/ n. (colloq.) a person who is physically weak or not hardy, or who is soft-hearted. [f. SOFT]

software n. the programs and procedures required for computer operation, as opposed to the physical components of the system (*hardware*); other interchangeable material for performing functions.

softwood n. the wood of a coniferous tree.

soggy adj. 1. sodden. 2. moist and heavy in texture. —**soggily** adv., **sogginess** n. [f. dial. *sog* a swamp]

soh /səʊ/ n. (Mus.) the fifth note of the major scale in tonic sol-fa (see entry). [f. *solve* (see GAMUT)]

soigné /swaːˈnjeɪ/ adj. (fem. **soignée**) carefully finished or arranged; well-groomed and sophisticated. [p.p. of F *soigner* take care of]

soil¹ n. 1. the upper layer of earth in which plants grow. 2. the ground belonging to a nation, territory. [f. AF, perh. f. L *solium* seat]

soil² v.t./i. 1. to make or become dirty. 2. to defile, to bring discredit to. —n. 1. a dirty mark; defilement. 2. filth; refuse matter. —**soil-pipe** n. the discharge-pipe of a water-closet. [f. OF *suill(i)er* ult. f. L *sus* pig]

soirée /ˈswaːreɪ/ n. an evening party, especially for conversation or music. [F (*soir* evening)]

sojourn /ˈsɒdʒɜːn/ n. a temporary stay. —v.i. to make a sojourn. [f. OF *so(r)jorn(er)* f. L SUB-, *diurnum* day]

sol¹ n. a liquid solution or suspension of a colloid. [abbr. of SOLUTION]

sol² n. var. of SOH.

sola /ˈsəʊlə/ n. a pithy-stemmed East Indian swamp plant (*Aeschynomene aspera*). —**sola topi,** a sun-helmet made from its pith. [f. Urdu or Bengali]

solace /ˈsɒləs/ n. comfort in distress or disappointment or in tedium. —v.t. to give solace to. [f. OF f. L *solatium* (*solari* console)]

solan /ˈsəʊlən/ n. a large gooselike gannet (*Sula bassana*). [prob. f. ON, = gannet-duck]

solar /ˈsəʊlə(r)/ adj. of or reckoned by the sun. —n. 1. a solarium. 2. the upper chamber in a medieval house (ill. CASTLES). —**solar battery** or **cell,** a device converting solar radiation into electricity. **solar day,** the interval between meridian transits of the sun. **solar plexus,** the complex of radiating nerves at the pit of the stomach. **solar system,** see separate entry. **solar year,** see YEAR. [L *solaris* (*sol* sun)]

solarium /səˈleərɪəm/ n. (pl. **-ia**) a place for the enjoyment or medical use of sunshine. [L (as prec.)]

solar system the collection of nine planets and their moons in orbit round the sun, together with smaller bodies in the form of asteroids, meteors, and comets. Most of these objects lie within or close to the plane of the ecliptic, suggesting that the solar system originated in the collapse to a disc of a primordial gaseous nebula which fragmented to produce a large massive star at the centre of a group of orbiting inert bodies. It remains a mystery why the planets, with mass much less than that of the sun, should contain most of the angular momentum of the system.

sold past & p.p. of SELL.

solder /ˈsəʊldə(r), ˈsɒ-/ n. a fusible alloy used to join less fusible metals or wires etc. —v.t. to join with solder. —**soldering-iron** n. a tool to melt and apply solder (ill. HEAT). [f. OF *soudure* (*souder* f. L *solidare* fasten, as SOLID)]

soldier /ˈsəʊldʒə(r)/ n. 1. a member of an army; (also **common soldier**) a private or NCO in an army. 2. a military commander of specified ability. —v.i. to serve as a soldier. —**soldier of fortune,** an adventurous person ready to serve any State or person, a mercenary. **soldier on,** (colloq.) to persevere doggedly. —**soldierly** adj. [f. OF (*sou(l)de* soldier's pay, f. L, as SOLID)]

soldiery n. soldiers, especially of a specified character. [f. prec.]

sole¹ n. 1. the under-surface of the foot; the part of a shoe or sock etc. below the foot, especially the part other than the heel. 2. the lower surface or base of a plough, golf-club head, etc. —v.t. to provide (a shoe etc.) with a sole. [OE f. L *solea* sandal]

sole² n. a flat-fish of the genus *Solea* used as food. [f. OF f. L (as prec., from its shape)]

sole³ adj. one and only, single, exclusive. —**solely** adv. [f. OF f. L *solus* alone]

solecism /ˈsɒlɪsɪz(ə)m/ n. an offence against grammar, idiom, or etiquette. —**solecistic** /-ˈsɪstɪk/ adj. [f. F or L f. Gk (*soloikos* speaking incorrectly)]

solemn /ˈsɒləm/ adj. 1. not smiling or cheerful. 2. dignified and impressive. 3. formal, accompanied by ceremony. —**solemnly** adv., **solemnness** n. [f. OF f. L *sollemnis* customary (*sollus* entire)]

solemnity /səˈlemnɪtɪ/ n. 1. being solemn. 2. a solemn rite. [as prec.]

solemnize /ˈsɒləmnaɪz/ v.t. 1. to perform (a ceremony,

especially of marriage) with formal rites. **2.** to make solemn. —**solemnization** /-ˈzeɪʃ(ə)n/ n. [as SOLEMN]

Solemn League and Covenant an agreement of 1643 between the Parliamentarians and the Scots during the English Civil War. The Scots were to send 21,000 men to assist the English rebels, who would pay them, and in return a presbyterian system was to be established in England and Ireland. Scottish support was crucial; the arrival of their troops transferred the centre of operations from London to York, and after the battle of Marston Moor the loyal North passed under Scottish control. The conversion of the Church of England to Presbyterianism, however, was prevented by the action of Cromwell's army which in 1647 expelled the principal Presbyterian leaders from Parliament.

solenoid /ˈsəʊlənɔɪd/ n. a cylindrical coil of wire acting as a magnet when carrying an electric current. [f. F f. Gk *sōlēn* tube]

Solent /ˈsəʊlənt/ the west part of the channel between the Isle of Wight and the mainland of England.

sol-fa /ˈsɒlfɑː/ n. see TONIC SOL-FA. [f. *sol* var. of SOH + FA]

soli see SOLO.

solicit /səˈlɪsɪt/ v.t./i. **1.** to ask repeatedly or earnestly for; to seek to obtain. **2.** to make an immoral sexual offer; to accost and offer one's services as a prostitute. —**solicitation** /-ˈteɪʃ(ə)n/ n. [f. OF f. L *sollicitare* agitate (*sollicitus* anxious f. *sollus* entire + *citus* set in motion)]

solicitor n. a member of the legal profession competent to advise clients and instruct barristers but not appearing as an advocate except in certain lower courts. —**Solicitor-General** n. a law officer below the Attorney-General or Lord Advocate. [as prec.]

solicitous /səˈlɪsɪtəs/ adj. anxious and concerned, especially about a person's welfare or comfort. —**solicitously** adv. [f. L *sollicitus* (see SOLICIT)]

solicitude /səˈlɪsɪtjuːd/ n. solicitous concern. [as SOLICIT]

solid /ˈsɒlɪd/ adj. **1.** firm and stable in shape, not liquid or fluid. **2.** of solid material throughout, not hollow; of the same substance throughout. **3.** of strong material, construction, or build, not flimsy or slender etc. **4.** having three dimensions; concerned with solids. **5.** sound and reliable; sound but without special flair etc.; financially sound. **6.** (colloq.) (of time) uninterrupted. **7.** (colloq.) unanimous, undivided. —n. **1.** a solid substance or body. **2.** (in pl.) solid food. —**solid state**, see separate entry. —**solidly** adv. [f. OF or L *solidus* (rel. to *salvus* safe, *sollus* entire)]

Solidarity an independent trade-union movement in Poland, registered in Sept. 1980 and officially banned in Oct. 1982. [= foll., tr. Polish *Solidarność*]

solidarity /sɒlɪˈdærɪtɪ/ n. unity or agreement of feeling or action, especially among individuals with a common interest; mutual dependence. [f. F (as prec.)]

solidify /səˈlɪdɪfaɪ/ v.t./i. to make or become solid. —**solidification** /-fɪˈkeɪʃ(ə)n/ n. [f. F (as SOLID)]

solidity /səˈlɪdɪtɪ/ n. the state of being solid, firmness. [f. SOLID]

solid state a state of matter in which the constituent atoms or molecules occupy fixed positions with respect to each other and cannot move freely (see below). **solid-state** adj. of or relating to the solid state; using the electronic properties of solids, especially semiconductors, to replace those of valves.

The solid state is one of the fundamental states in which matter can exist, along with the liquid, gas, and plasma states. The atoms in a solid differ from those in a liquid and in a gas in that they are bound together at definite sites in the solid. When such an atom is displaced a little from its equilibrium position restoring forces are called into play which resist the displacement. This explains why solids oppose deforming forces and also why solid bodies do not easily penetrate each other. Solids may be roughly classified into crystalline and amorphous. In crystalline solids, such as ice, the atoms are arranged in an orderly and repeating manner. In amorphous solids, such as amorphous sulphur, this order is absent over distances large compared with inter-atomic distances, but there may still be some short-range crystalline structure.

soliloquize /səˈlɪləkwaɪz/ v.i. to utter a soliloquy. [f. foll.]

soliloquy /səˈlɪləkwɪ/ n. a speech in which a person expresses his thoughts aloud without addressing any specific person, especially in a play; a period of this. [f. L *solus* alone, *loqui* speak)]

solipsism /ˈsɒlɪpsɪz(ə)m/ n. the view that the self is all that

exists or can be known. —**solipsist** n. [f. L *solus* alone + *ipse* self]

solitaire /sɒlɪˈteə(r)/ n. **1.** a jewel set by itself; a piece of jewellery containing this. **2.** a game played on a special board by one person with marbles etc. removed one at a time after another has been jumped over each. **3.** (US) the card-game of patience, which is played by one person. [F f. L (= foll.)]

solitary /ˈsɒlɪtərɪ/ adj. **1.** alone, without companions; living alone, not gregarious. **2.** single, sole. **3.** (of a place) unfrequented, lonely. —n. **1.** a recluse. **2.** (slang) solitary confinement. —**solitary confinement**, isolation in a separate cell as a punishment. —**solitarily** adv., **solitariness** n. [f. L (*solus* alone)]

solitude /ˈsɒlɪtjuːd/ n. **1.** being solitary. **2.** a solitary place. [f. OF or L (as prec.)]

solmization /sɒlmɪˈzeɪʃ(ə)n/ n. the system of associating each note of the musical scale with a particular syllable (e.g. *do, re, mi,* etc., or *doh, ray, me,* etc.; see TONIC SOL-FA). [f. F (*sol* var. of SOH, *mi* var. of ME²)]

solo /ˈsəʊləʊ/ n. (pl. **-os**) **1.** (pl. also **-li** /-liː/) a musical composition or passage for a single voice or instrument, with or without accompaniment. **2.** a performance by one person; a pilot's flight in an aircraft without an instructor or companion. **3.** (in full **solo whist**) a card-game like whist in which one player may oppose the others. —adj. & adv. performed as a solo; unaccompanied, alone. [It. f. L (as SOLE³)]

soloist /ˈsəʊləʊɪst/ n. a performer of a solo, especially in music. [f. SOLO]

Solomon /ˈsɒləmən/ king of Israel c.970–930 BC, son of David, famed for his wisdom and magnificence. His grandiose schemes, including the building of the Temple with which his name is associated, and the fortifying of strategic cities, led to a system of levies and enforced labour, and the resulting discontent culminated in the secession of the northern tribes (see ISRAEL¹). —**Judgement of Solomon,** his proposal to cut in two the baby claimed by two women (1 Kings 3: 16–28), which he then gave to the woman who showed concern for its life. **Solomon's seal,** a herbaceous plant (*Polygonatum multiflorum*) with broad leaves and drooping greenish-white flowers on arching stems; a magic symbol formed by two interlaced triangles forming a six-pointed star. **Song of Solomon,** (also called the *Song of Songs* or *Canticles*) an anthology of love poems ascribed to Solomon but dating from a much later period. From an early date Jewish and Christian writers interpreted the book allegorically, in the Talmud as God's dealings with the congregation of Israel and in Christian exegesis as God's relations with the Church or the individual soul. **Wisdom of Solomon,** a book of the Apocrypha containing a meditation on wisdom which has given it its name. The ascription to Solomon is now believed to be a literary device; it probably dates from about 1st c. BC–1st c. AD.

Solomon Islands /ˈsɒləmən/ a country consisting of a group of islands in the South Pacific, SE of the Bismarck Archipelago; pop. (est. 1982) 244,000; official language, English; capital, Honiara. Discovered by the Spanish in 1658, the islands were divided between Britain and Germany in the late 19th c.; the southern islands became a British protectorate in 1893 while the north remained German until mandated to Australia in 1920. The scene of heavy fighting in 1942–3, the Solomons achieved self-government in 1976 and full independence as a member State of the Commonwealth two years later, with the exception of the northern part of the chain which is now part of Papua New Guinea. Copra and timber are the main exports.

Solon /ˈsəʊlɒn/ (early 6th c. BC) Athenian statesman and poet, one of the traditional Seven Sages. His economic reforms included the abolition of serfdom and of slavery for debt; his constitutional reforms, by which he divided the citizens into four classes based on wealth with a corresponding division of political responsibility, laid the foundations of the future democracy. His poetry is largely concerned with his political interests.

solstice /ˈsɒlstɪs/ n. each of two occasions during the year when the sun is at its highest or lowest point above the celestial equator (and appears to pause before returning) and the number of hours of daylight greatest (at the **summer solstice,** about 21 June) or smallest (**winter solstice,** about 22 Dec.). Since these events mark the turn of the seasons, they have been celebrated since prehistoric times by traditional festivities, and it is no coincidence that

soluble

787

songster

the feast of Christmas occurs so close to the winter solstice. [f. OF f. L (*sol* sun, *sistere* stand still)]

soluble /ˈsɒljuːb(ə)l/ *adj.* that can be dissolved (especially in water) or solved. —**solubility** /-ˈbɪlɪtɪ/ *n.*, **solubly** *adv.* [f. OF f. L (as SOLVE)]

solute /ˈsɒljuːt/ *n.* a dissolved substance. [as SOLVE]

solution /səˈluːʃ(ə)n, -ˈljuː-/ *n.* **1.** solving or the means of solving a problem or difficulty. **2.** the conversion of a solid or gas into a liquid by mixture with a liquid; the state resulting from this. **3.** dissolving, being dissolved. [f. OF f. L (as foll.)]

Solutrean /səˈluːtrɪən/ *adj.* of an upper palaeolithic industry of central and SW France and parts of Iberia, following the Aurignacian and preceding the Magdalenian, dated to *c.*19,000–18,000 BC. It is named after the type-site of Solutré in eastern France. —*n.* this industry. [f. *Solutré*]

solvable *adj.* that may be solved. [f. foll.]

Solvay process /ˈsɒlveɪ/ a manufacturing process for obtaining sodium carbonate (= washing-soda) from limestone, ammonia, and brine. [f. E. *Solvay* (d. 1922), Belgian chemist, who developed the process]

solve *v.t.* to find the answer to (a problem or puzzle); to find an action or course that removes or effectively deals with (a problem or difficulty). —**solver** *n.* [f. L *solvere* unfasten, release]

solvent /ˈsɒlvənt/ *adj.* **1.** able to dissolve or form a solution with something. **2.** having enough money to meet one's liabilities. —*n.* a solvent liquid etc. —**solvency** *n.* [as prec.]

Solzhenitsyn /sɒlʒəˈnɪtsɪn/, Alexander (1918–), Russian novelist, whose criticism of Stalin in 1945 led to his imprisonment for eight years, three of which were spent in a labour camp. After his release, his novel *One Day in the Life of Ivan Denisovich* (1962), describing life in such a camp, received international acclaim and was widely sold in the USSR, where it coincided with the de-Stalinization campaign begun in 1956. In 1963, however, he was again in conflict with the authorities and thereafter had difficulty in getting his books published in the Soviet Union. He was awarded the Nobel Prize for literature in 1970. The publication abroad of the first part of *The Gulag Archipelago* (1973–5) resulted in his deportation to West Germany in 1974, since when he has lived in the USA.

Som. *abbr.* Somerset.

soma /ˈsəʊmə/ *n.* the intoxicating juice of a plant, used in Vedic ritual and religion. [f. Skr. *sōma*]

Somali /səˈmɑːlɪ/ *n.* **1.** a member of a Hamitic Muslim people of Somalia. **2.** their language, which belongs to the Cushitic branch of the Hamito-Semitic family of languages and is the official language of Somalia. —*adj.* of the Somalis or their language. [native name]

Somalia /səˈmɑːlɪə/ a country in NE Africa, with a coastline on the Indian Ocean; pop. (est. 1983) 5,000,000; official language, Somali; capital, Mogadishu. The economy is largely agricultural, dependent upon nomadic stock-raising and (in the southern part of the country) some irrigated plantation-farming. Livestock, skins, and hides form the main export; the second largest export is the banana crop, most of which is imported by Italy. The area of the Horn of Africa was divided between British and Italian spheres of influence in the late 19th c., and the modern Somali Republic (which became an independent member of the United Nations in 1960) is a result of the unification of the former British Somaliland and Italian Somalia. Since independence, Somalia has been involved in border disputes with Kenya and Ethiopia, the latter leading to an intermittent war over the Ogaden Desert.

somatic /səˈmætɪk/ *adj.* of the body, not of the mind. —**somatically** *adv.* [f. Gk (*sōma* body)]

sombre /ˈsɒmbə(r)/ *adj.* dark, gloomy, dismal. —**sombrely** *adv.* [F f. L SUB-, *umbra* shade]

sombrero /sɒmˈbreərəʊ/ *n.* (*pl.* -**os**) a broad-brimmed hat worn especially in Latin American countries. [Sp. (*sombra* shade, as prec.)]

some /səm, *emphat.* sʌm/ *adj.* **1.** an unspecified amount or number of. **2.** that is unknown or unnamed. **3.** approximately. **4.** a considerable amount or number of; at least a small amount of. **5.** such to a certain extent; (*slang*) notably such. —*pron.* some people or things; some number or amount. —*adv.* (*colloq.*) to some extent. [OE]

-some /-səm/ *suffix* forming (1) adjectives in the senses 'adapted to, productive of' (*cuddlesome, fearsome*), 'characterized by being' (*fulsome*), 'apt to' (*tiresome, meddlesome*);

(2) nouns from numerals in the sense 'a group of' (*foursome*). [OE]

somebody *n.* & *pron.* **1.** some person. **2.** a person of importance.

somehow *adv.* **1.** in some unspecified or unexplained manner. **2.** for some reason or other.

someone *n.* & *pron.* somebody.

someplace *adv.* (*US*) somewhere.

somersault /ˈsʌməsɔːlt/ *n.* an acrobatic movement in which the body rolls head over heels either on the ground or in the air; a similar overturning movement. —*v.i.* to perform a somersault. [f. OF f. L *supra* above, *saltus* leap]

Somerset /ˈsʌməset/ a county of SW England.

something *n.* & *pron.* **1.** some unspecified or unknown thing. **2.** a known or understood but unexpressed quantity or quality or extent. **3.** an important or notable person or thing. —**see something of,** to meet (a person) occasionally or for a short time.

sometime *adv.* **1.** at some time. **2.** formerly. —*adj.* former.

sometimes *adv.* at some times.

somewhat *adv.* to some extent.

somewhere *adv.* in or to some place.

Somme /sɒm/ a river of NE France, running into the English Channel, the scene of heavy fighting in the First World War, especially in July–Nov. 1916.

somnambulism /sɒmˈnæmbjuːlɪz(ə)m/ *n.* sleep-walking. —**somnambulant** *adj.*, **somnambulist** *n.* [f. L *somnus* sleep + *ambulare* walk]

somnolent /ˈsɒmnələnt/ *adj.* sleepy, asleep; inducing drowsiness. —**somnolence** *n.* [f. OF or L (*somnus* sleep)]

son /sʌn/ *n.* **1.** a male child in relation to his parent(s). **2.** a male descendant, a male member of a family etc. **3.** a person regarded as inheriting an occupation or quality etc. **4.** a form of address to a boy. —**son-in-law** *n.* (*pl.* **sons-in-law**) a daughter's husband. **the Son of God** *or* **of Man,** Christ. [OE]

sonar /ˈsəʊnɑː(r)/ *n.* a system of detecting objects under water by reflected or emitted sound; the apparatus for this. The 'hydrophone' (a kind of underwater microphone) was used in the 1890s to detect sounds such as the operation of engines or propellers, but by 1918 a system of transmitting a pulse of sound and using its rebounding echo to detect a stationary submerged craft had been developed. It became known as 'asdic' (see entry) and later as 'sonar' (from the initials of the US development), and was widely used in the Second World War. Such apparatus also has civil applications, as in the location of shoals of fish. [f. *sound navigation and ranging*]

sonata /s(ə)ˈnɑːtə/ *n.* a composition for one instrument or two, normally with three or four movements contrasted in rhythm and speed but related in key (see below). —**sonata form,** a type of composition in which two themes ('subjects') are successively set forth, developed, and restated. [It., f. *sonare* sound (i.e. a piece to be played rather than sung)]
    The classical sonata has clear formal implications of a four-movement work, each movement of a standard type and in a particular order, and is scored for one or two solo instruments, such as piano, piano and violin; earlier uses of the term, however, have a common factor only in their use of instruments rather than voices. In the Romantic period the sonata lost its pre-eminence in favour of shorter pieces which depended on extra-musical rather than formal considerations for their integrity.

son et lumière /sɒn eɪ luːˈmjeə(r)/ an entertainment by night at a historic building etc. with recorded sound and lighting effects to give a dramatic narrative of its history. [F, = sound and light]

song *n.* **1.** singing, vocal music. **2.** a piece of music for singing, a short poem etc. set to music or meant to be sung; a musical composition suggestive of a song. —**for a song,** very cheaply. **song and dance,** an outcry, a commotion. **Song of Songs,** (i.e. greatest song; cf. *holy of holies*) the Song of Solomon. **Song of the Three (Holy Children),** a book of the Apocrypha, telling of the three Hebrew exiles thrown into the fiery furnace by Nebuchadnezzar. **song thrush,** a common thrush (*Turdus philomelos*) noted for its singing. [f. OE *sang* (as SING)]

songbird *n.* a bird with a melodious cry.

Song of Solomon see SOLOMON.

songster *n.* a singer, a songbird. —**songstress** *n. fem.* [OE, as SONG]

sonic /'sɒnɪk/ adj. of or involving sound or sound-waves. —**sonic bang** or **boom**, the noise made when an aircraft passes the speed of sound. **sonic barrier,** the sound barrier (see SOUND¹). [f. L. *sonus* sound]

sonnet /'sɒnɪt/ n. a poem of 14 lines with lengths and rhymes in accordance with one of several schemes, in English usually having 10 syllables per line. [F or f. It. *sonetto* dim. of *suono* sound]

sonny /'sʌnɪ/ n. (*colloq.*) a familiar form of address to a young boy. [f. SON]

sonorous /'sɒnərəs, sə'nɔːrəs/ adj. resonant, having a loud, full, or deep sound; (of speech etc.) sounding imposing. —**sonority** /sə'nɒrɪtɪ/ n., **sonorously** adv. [f. L (*sonor* sound)]

soon adv. **1.** after no long interval of time. **2.** relatively early, quickly. **3.** (after *as* or in compar.) readily, willingly. —**as** or **so soon as,** at the moment that; not later than, as early as. **sooner or later,** at some future time, eventually. [OE]

soot /sʊt/ n. a black powdery substance rising in smoke and deposited by it on surfaces. —v.t. to cover with soot. [OE]

sooth n. (*archaic*) truth. [OE *sōth* (orig. adj., = true)]

soothe /suːð/ v.t. to calm (a person or feelings etc.); to soften or mitigate (a pain etc.). —**soothing** adj. [OE, = verify (as prec.)]

soothsayer /'suːθseɪə(r)/ n. one who foretells the future, a diviner. [f. SOOTH + *sayer* (SAY)]

sooty /'sʊtɪ/ adj. **1.** covered with soot. **2.** like soot; black or brownish-black. [f. SOOT]

sop n. **1.** a piece of bread etc. dipped in liquid before being eaten or cooked. **2.** a concession made in order to pacify or bribe a troublesome person. **3.** a milksop. —v.t./i. (**-pp-**) **1.** to dip in liquid. **2.** to soak up (liquid) with something absorbent. [OE (rel. to SUP)]

sophism /'sɒfɪz(ə)m/ n. a false argument, especially one intended to deceive. [f. OF f. L f. Gk *sophisma* clever device (*sophizomai* become wise f. *sophos* wise)]

Sophist /'sɒfɪst/ n. a member of the last generations of Greek philosophers before Plato, of the period *c*.450 BC to *c*.400 BC. Their name (= 'expert') was originally a descriptive term, not a term of abuse. They were in business offering the equivalent of university education: for a hefty fee they would teach, in particular, rhetoric—how to argue a case in a lawcourt or an assembly. But they were also thinkers with argued views. Perhaps most important was the contrast they emphasized between *phusis*, what exists by nature, and *nomos*, what exists only by human convention. This led not only to moral relativism (what is right here depends entirely on what this society thinks right) but to amoralism (morality is a matter merely of conventions, which the intelligent and strong man will disregard). Such views, together with the thought that they taught how to make the worse case appear the better, made the word become an uncomplimentary one. [f. L f. Gk *sophistēs* (*sophizomai*; see prec.)]

sophist /'sɒfɪst/ n. a captious or fallacious reasoner, a quibbler (see prec.). —**sophistic** /-'fɪstɪk/ adj. [= prec.]

sophisticate /sə'fɪstɪkeɪt/ v.t. (esp. in *p.p.*) **1.** to make (a person etc.) worldly-wise, cultured, or refined. **2.** to make (equipment or techniques etc.) highly developed or complex. —/-kət/ adj. sophisticated. —/-kət/ n. a sophisticated person. —**sophistication** /-'keɪʃ(ə)n/ n. [f. L, = tamper with (as SOPHIST)]

sophistry /'sɒfɪstrɪ/ n. the use of sophisms; a sophism. [f. SOPHIST]

Sophocles /'sɒfəkliːz/ (*c*.496–406 BC) Greek dramatist. The second of the three great tragedians (the others were Aeschylus and Euripides), he took an active part in the political and religious life of contemporary Athens. His introduction of a third actor allowed the greater complexity of plot and fuller depiction of character for which his seven surviving plays are notable (*Antigone, Electra, Oedipus Tyrannus, Oedipus at Colonus, Philoctetes, Trachiniae*), as well as for their examination of the relationship between man and the divine order of the world.

sophomore /'sɒfəmɔː(r)/ n. (*US*) a second-year student at a university or high school. [app. f. *sophom* obs. var. of SOPHISM]

soporific /sɒpə'rɪfɪk/ adj. tending to produce sleep. —n. a soporific drug or influence. —**soporifically** adv. [f. L *sopor* sleep, *facere* make]

sopping adj. drenched. [f. SOP]

soppy adj. **1.** very wet. **2.** (*colloq.*) mawkishly sentimental; silly. —**soppily** adv., **soppiness** n. [f. SOP]

soprano /sə'prɑːnəʊ/ n. (*pl.* **-os**) **1.** the highest female or boy's singing-voice. **2.** a singer with such a voice; the part written for it. **3.** an instrument of the higher or highest pitch in its family. [It. (*sopra* above f. L *supra*)]

sorbet /'sɔːbət/ n. a water-ice; a sherbet. [F f. It., ult. f. Arab. (as SHERBET)]

Sorbonne /sɔː'bɒn/ originally a theological college founded in Paris by Robert de Sorbon, chaplain to Louis IX, *c*.1257; later, the faculty of theology in the University of Paris, suppressed in 1792; now, the seat of the faculties of science and letters of the University of Paris.

sorcerer /'sɔːsərə(r)/ n. a magician, a wizard. —**sorceress** n. *fem.*, **sorcery** n. [f. OF *sorcier* f. L *sors* lot]

sordid adj. **1.** dirty, squalid. **2.** ignoble, not honourable; mercenary. —**sordidly** adv., **sordidness** n. [f. F or L *sordidus* (*sordēre* be dirty)]

sore adj. **1.** causing or feeling pain from injury or disease. **2.** causing or feeling mental distress or annoyance. **3.** (*archaic*) serious, severe. —n. **1.** a sore place on the body. **2.** a source of distress or annoyance. —adv. (*archaic*) sorely. —**soreness** n. [OE]

sorely adv. very much; severely. [f. SORE]

sorghum /'sɔːgəm/ n. a tropical cereal grass of the genus *Sorghum*. [f. It. *sorgo*]

Soroptimist /sə'rɒptɪmɪst/ n. a member of the Soroptimist Club, an international club for professional and business women, founded in California in 1921 with the aim of providing service to the community. [app. f. L *soror* sister + OPTIMIST]

sorority /sə'rɒrɪtɪ/ n. **1.** a devotional sisterhood. **2.** (*US*) a women's society in a university or college. [f. L (*soror* sister)]

sorrel¹ /'sɒr(ə)l/ n. a sour-leaved herb (*Rumex acetosa*). [f. OF (as SOUR)]

sorrel² /'sɒr(ə)l/ adj. of a light reddish-brown colour. —n. **1.** this colour. **2.** a sorrel animal, especially a horse. [f. OF *sorel* (*sor* yellowish)]

sorrow /'sɒrəʊ/ n. **1.** mental distress caused by loss or disappointment etc. **2.** a thing causing sorrow. —v.i. to feel sorrow, to grieve. [OE]

sorrowful adj. feeling or showing sorrow; distressing. —**sorrowfully** adv. [f. prec. + -FUL]

sorry /'sɒrɪ/ adj. **1.** (*predic.*) feeling regret, regret, or sympathy. **2.** an expression of apology. **3.** (*attrib.*) wretched; paltry. —**sorry for oneself,** (*colloq.*) dejected. [OE (as SORE)]

sort n. **1.** a particular kind or variety. **2.** (*colloq.*) a person with regard to his (specified) character. —v.t. to arrange according to sort, size, destination, etc. —**of a sort** or **of sorts,** not fully deserving the name given. **out of sorts,** slightly unwell; in low spirits. **sort of,** (*colloq.*) as it were, to some extent. **sort out,** to separate into sorts; to select (things of one or more sorts) from a miscellaneous group; to disentangle; to put into order; to solve; (*slang*) to deal with or punish. —**sorter** n. [f. OF f. L *sors* lot, condition]

sortie /'sɔːtiː/ n. **1.** a sally, especially from a besieged garrison. **2.** an operational flight by a military aircraft. [F. (*sortir* go out)]

SOS /esəʊ'es/ n. (*pl.* **SOSs**) the international code-signal of extreme distress; an urgent appeal for help etc. [letters chosen as easily recognized in Morse code]

sostenuto /sɒstə'nuːtəʊ/ adv. (*Mus.*) in a sustained manner. —n. (*pl.* **-os**) a passage to be played in this way. [It. (as SUSTAIN)]

sot n. a habitual drunkard. —**sottish** adj. [OE & f. OF, = foolish]

Sothic /'səʊθɪk/ adj. of the dog-star. —**Sothic year,** the ancient Egyptian year of 365¼ days, fixed by the heliacal rising of the dog-star. **Sothic cycle,** a cycle (first fixed in AD 139) of 1460 Sothic years, after which the 365-day calendar year gives the same date for this rising. [f. Gk *Sōthis* f. Egyptian name of dog-star]

Sotho /'suːtuː/ n. **1.** a subdivision of the Bantu people which includes tribes living chiefly in Botswana, Lesotho, and the Transvaal. **2.** their Bantu languages. —adj. of this people or their languages. [native name]

sotto voce /sɒtəʊ 'vəʊtʃɪ/ in an undertone. [It., = under the voice]

sou /suː/ n. **1.** a former French coin of low value. **2.** (*colloq.*) a very small amount of money. —**not a sou,** no money at all. [F f. OF f. L *solidus* Roman gold coin]

soubrette /suːˈbret/ n. a pert maidservant etc. in comedy; an actress taking this part. [F f. Prov. (*soubret* coy)]

soubriquet var. of SOBRIQUET.

soufflé /ˈsuːfleɪ/ n. a light spongy dish usually made with stiffly beaten egg-whites. [F, = blown]

sough /sʌf, saʊ/ n. a moaning or whispering sound as of the wind in trees. —v.i. to make this sound. [f. OE, = resound]

sought past & p.p. of SEEK.

souk /suːk/ n. a market-place in Muslim countries. [f. Arab.]

soul /səʊl/ n. **1.** the spiritual or immaterial element in a person, often regarded as immortal. **2.** the moral, emotional, or intellectual nature of a person or animal. **3.** a personification or pattern. **4.** an individual; a person regarded with familiarity or pity etc. **5.** a person regarded as the animating or essential part. **6.** emotional or intellectual energy or intensity, especially as revealed in a work of art. **7.** the emotional or spiritual quality of Black American life and culture; soul music. —**soul-destroying** adj. deadeningly monotonous or depressing. **soul mate**, a person ideally suited to another. **soul music**, a kind of jazz played in a strong emotional style. **soul-searching** adj. examining one's own emotions or motives. **upon my soul**, an exclamation of surprise. [OE]

soulful adj. having, expressing, or evoking deep feeling. —**soulfully** adv. [f. SOUL + -FUL]

soulless adj. **1.** lacking sensitivity or noble qualities. **2.** undistinguished, uninteresting. [f. SOUL + -LESS]

sound[1] n. **1.** waves of pressure that travel through the air or other elastic medium (such as water) and are detectable at certain frequencies by the ear (see below and ill. pp. 790-1). **2.** the sensation produced by these; a particular kind of it. **3.** a sound made in speech. **4.** sound reproduced in a film etc. **5.** the mental impression produced by a statement or description etc. —v.t./i. **1.** to emit or cause to emit sound. **2.** to utter, to pronounce. **3.** to convey an impression when heard. **4.** to give an audible signal for (an alarm etc.). **5.** to test (the lungs etc.) by noting the sound produced. —**sound barrier,** the high resistance of the air to objects moving at speeds near that of sound. **sound effects**, sounds other than speech or music produced artificially for use in a play or film etc. **sounding-board** n. a canopy projecting sound towards an audience; a means of disseminating opinions etc. **sound off,** (colloq.) to talk loudly, to express one's opinions forcefully. **sound-wave** n. a wave of condensation and rarefaction, by which sound is transmitted in the air etc. —**sounder** n. [f. AF f. L *sonus*]

Sound consists of longitudinal waves of pressure (see WAVE) passing through solids, liquids, or gases; it cannot travel through a vacuum. The speed of sound tends to be independent of its frequency and to be a constant for any particular medium: for example, the speed of sound in air is about 344 metres (1,128 ft.) per second. In general, sound travels faster through solids than through liquids, and faster through liquids than through gases, although density and temperature are also important. The human ear responds to frequencies of sound that are between about 20 Hz and 20,000 Hz. Frequency is perceived as pitch: if one sound has twice the frequency of another, it is perceived (in musical terms) as being an octave above it. Most musical tones, however, are complex in form, including many higher frequencies or 'harmonics' as well as the fundamental frequency. Frequencies below and above the range of human hearing are called infrasonic and ultrasonic respectively. Some animals, such as dogs, bats, and dolphins, can hear frequencies in the ultrasonic range. Although the properties of sound waves do not suddenly change above 20,000 Hz, sound of very high frequency can be formed into a powerful beam, and ultrasound has a number of practical applications: it is used to form emulsions between immiscible liquids, as an alternative to X-rays in medical diagnosis, as a means of underwater detection, and for many other purposes.

sound[2] adj. **1.** healthy, not diseased or injured or rotten. **2.** (of an opinion or policy etc.) correct, orthodox, well-founded. **3.** financially secure; **4.** undisturbed. **5.** thorough. —adv. soundly. —**soundly** adv., **soundness** n. [f. OE]

sound[3] v.t. **1.** to test the depth or quality of the bottom of (the sea or a river etc.). **2.** (also with *out*) to inquire into the opinions or feelings of. —**sounder** n. [f. OF *sonder* f. L *sub* under, *unda* wave]

sound[4] n. a strait (of water). [OE, = swimming]

sounding n. **1.** measurement of the depth of water. **2.** (in pl.) the region near enough to the shore to allow sounding. [f. SOUND[3]]

soundproof adj. impervious to sound. —v.t. to make soundproof.

soundtrack n. a strip on cinema film or videotape for recording sound; the sound itself.

soup /suːp/ n. a liquid food made by stewing bones, vegetables, etc. —v.t. (usu. with *up*) (colloq.) **1.** to increase the power of (an engine etc.). **2.** to enliven. —**in the soup,** (slang) in difficulties or trouble. **soup-kitchen** n. an establishment supplying free soup etc. to the poor or in times of distress. **soup-plate** n. a large deep plate for soup. —**soupy** adj. [f. F *soupe* f. L (cf. SUP)]

soupçon /ˈsuːpsɔ̃/ n. a very small quantity, a trace or tinge. [F f. L, = SUSPICION]

sour adj. **1.** tasting or smelling sharp like unripe fruit; not fresh, tasting or smelling sharp or unpleasant from fermentation or staleness. **2.** (of soil) excessively acid; deficient in lime. **3.** bad-tempered, disagreeable in manner.—n. an acid drink, especially of whisky with lemon-juice or lime-juice. —v.t./i. to make or become sour. —**go** or **turn sour**, to turn out badly; to lose one's keenness. **sour grapes**, said when a person disparages what he desires but cannot attain. (From the fable of the fox who wanted some grapes but found that they were out of reach and so pretended that they were sour and undesirable anyway.) —**sourly** adv., **sourness** n. [OE]

source /sɔːs/ n. **1.** the place from which a thing comes or is obtained. **2.** a person or book etc. providing information. **3.** the starting-point of a river or stream. —**at source,** at the point of origin or issue. [f. OF *sors, sourse* f. *sourdre* rise f. L *surgere*)]

sourpuss n. (slang) a bad-tempered person.

Sousa /ˈsuːzə/, John Philip (1854-1932), American composer and conductor. He became director of the US Marine Band (1880) and then formed his own band in 1892. His works include over 100 marches, for example *The Stars and Stripes, King Cotton*, and *Hands Across the Sea*. The sousaphone (a helical form of bass tuba) was named in his honour on its invention in 1898.

souse /saʊs/ v.t./i. **1.** to steep in pickle. **2.** to plunge or soak in liquid; to drench; to throw (liquid) over a thing. **3.** (in p.p., slang) drunk. —n. **1.** pickle made with salt. **2.** (US) food in pickle. **3.** a plunge or soaking. [f. OF *sous* pickle f. OHG *sulza* brine (as SALT)]

soutane /suːˈtɑːn/ n. the cassock of a Roman Catholic priest. [F f. It. *sottana* (*sotto* under)]

south n. **1.** the point of the horizon opposite north; the compass point corresponding to this; the direction in which this lies. **2.** (usu. **South**) the part of a country or town lying to the south. —adj. **1.** towards, at, near, or facing the south. **2.** (of wind) blowing from the south. —adv. towards, at, or near the south. —**South Pole**, the southern end of the earth's axis of rotation. **south-south-east** n., adj., & adv. midway between south and south-east. **south-south-west** n., adj., & adv. midway between south and south-west. [OE]

South Africa a country occupying the southernmost part of the continent of Africa; pop. (est. 1980) 29,290,000; official languages, English and Afrikaans; administrative capital, Pretoria; seat of legislature, Cape Town. Settled by the Dutch in the 17th c., the Cape area later came under British occupation, setting in motion a series of conflicting political and economic developments leading to inland expansion, the subjugation of the native population, and finally war between the British and the Boer (Dutch) settlers at the end of the 19th c. The defeated Boer republics of the Transvaal and the Orange Free State were annexed as British Crown Colonies in 1902, but joined with the colonies of Natal and the Cape to form the self-governing Union of South Africa in 1910. After supporting Britain in both World Wars, in 1960-1 South Africa became a republic and left the Commonwealth. The dominant economic power in the southern half of the continent as a result of her well-developed agricultural and economic base and gold and diamond resources, South Africa has pursued a policy of White minority rule (apartheid) which keeps her in conflict with her Black African neighbours and complicates her international position. —**South African** adj. & n.

South America the southern half of the American land mass, connected to North America by the Isthmus of Panama, bordered by the Atlantic Ocean to the east and the Pacific Ocean to the west. (See AMERICA.) Colonized largely by the Spanish in the 16th c. (although the British,

Sound

Sound-waves

compressed
layers of air

amplitude

wavelength

tuning-fork prongs
vibrate layers of air
producing sound-waves

Distinguishing characteristics . . .

pitch (frequency)

mew   high frequency

'hum'   low frequency

Speech and hearing

nasal
cavity

cochlea (where mechanical
vibrations are converted
into electrical signals
which pass to the brain)

auditory nerve

ear-drum

tongue, lips, and teeth
(shaping sounds into words)

vocal
cords

air from lungs

Telephone

ear-piece

diaphragm

electrical impulses activate
the electromagnet and
vibrate the diaphragm
to produce sound-waves

electromagnet

diaphragm

electromagnet

mouthpiece

sound-waves vibrate the diaphragm,
inducing an electric current in
the coil and converting the
waves into electrical impulses

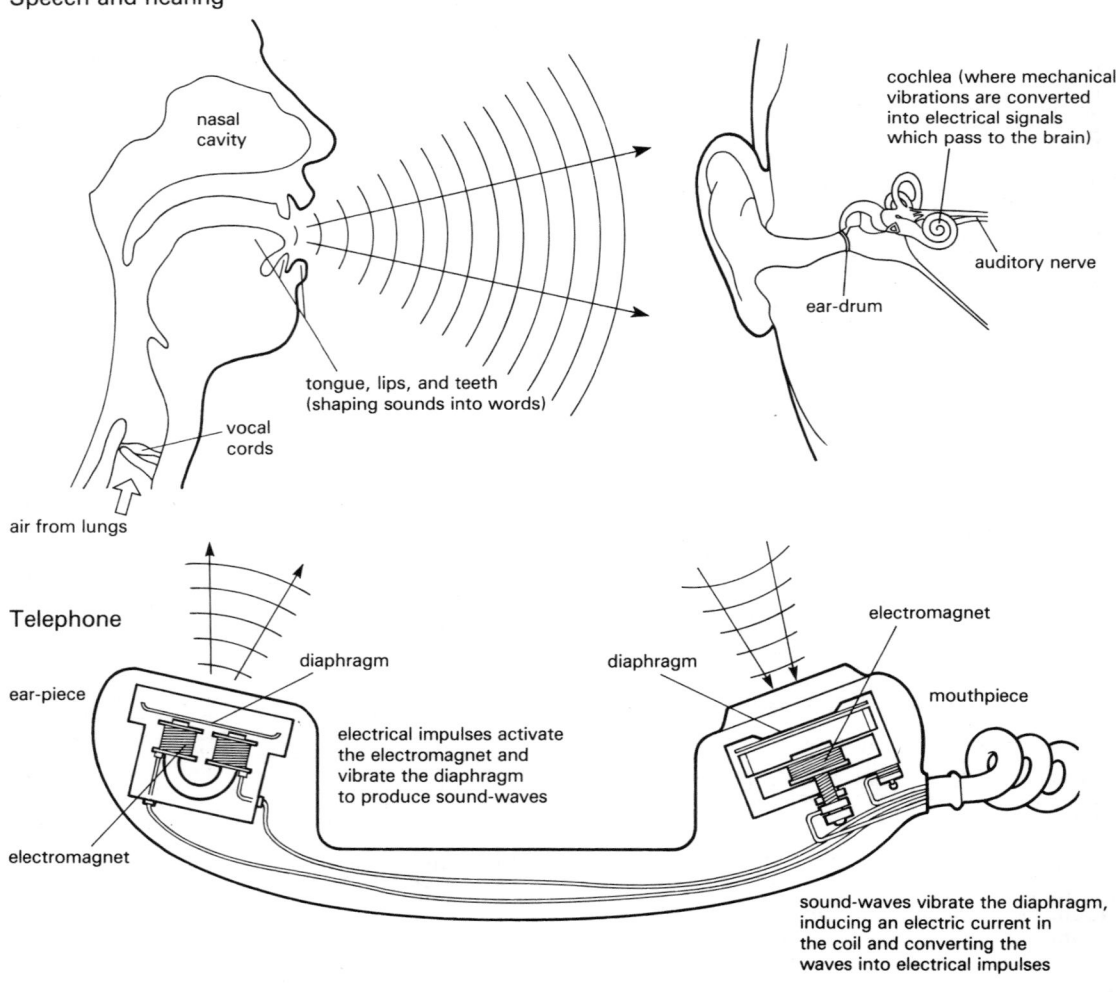

. . . of sound

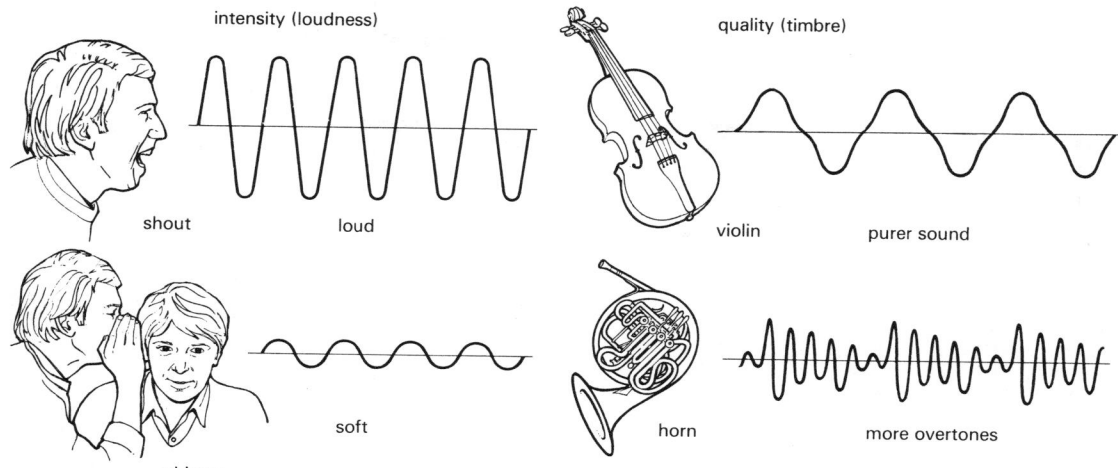

intensity (loudness)

shout — loud

whisper — soft

quality (timbre)

violin — purer sound

horn — more overtones

Acoustics and echoes

acoustic remedies for echo problems in the Royal Albert Hall

suspended fibreglass saucers to absorb echoes

20-metre reflector over orchestra

echo-sounding: depths can be calculated by timing the echo

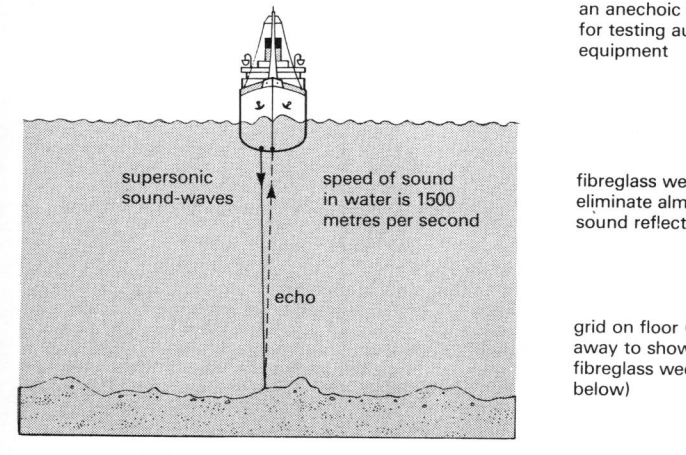

supersonic sound-waves

speed of sound in water is 1500 metres per second

echo

an anechoic chamber for testing audio equipment

fibreglass wedges eliminate almost all sound reflection

grid on floor (cut away to show fibreglass wedges below)

Dutch, and Portuguese were particularly active in the north-east), much of the continent remained part of Spain's overseas empire until liberated under the leadership of Bolivar and San Martín in the 1820s. Both culturally and ethnically the continent is now a mixture of native Indian and imported Hispanic influences, modified slightly by North European and North American penetration in the 19th and 20th centuries. Although many South American countries are still hampered by economic underdevelopment and political instability, a minority have emerged as world industrial powers in their own right.

South Australia a State comprising the central southern part of Australia. In 1836 it was constituted as a hybrid of a Crown colony and chartered colony, to which no convicts were to be sent. After financial collapse it lost its semi-independent status and became a regular Crown colony in 1841. It was federated with the other States of Australia in 1901; capital, Adelaide.

South Carolina /kærə'laɪnə/ a State of the USA on the Atlantic coast, settled by the Spanish and English (16th-17th c.) and named after Charles I. It was one of the original 13 States of the USA (1788); capital, Columbia.

South China Sea see CHINA SEA.

South Dakota /də'kəʊtə/ a State in the north central USA, acquired partly by the Louisiana Purchase in 1803. It became the 40th State of the USA in 1889; capital, Pierre.

south-east n. **1.** the point midway between south and east; the direction in which this lies. **2.** (usu. **South-East**) the part of a country or town lying to the south-east. —adj. of, towards, or coming from the south-east. —adv. towards, at, or near the south-east. —**south-easterly** adj. & adv., **south-eastern** adj.

southeaster n. a south-east wind.

southerly /'sʌðəlɪ/ adj. & adv. **1.** in a southern position or direction. **2.** (of wind) blowing from the south (approximately). [f. SOUTH]

southern /'sʌðən/ adj. of or in the south. —**southern lights**, the aurora australis. **Southern States**, those in the south (esp. south-east) of the USA. [OE (as SOUTH)]

Southern Cross a constellation in the southern sky, also known as Crux Australis, the smallest of the constellations officially recognized by the International Astronomical Union. It contains some noteworthy objects, such as Acrux, the 14th brightest star in the sky, and the beautiful galactic cluster of kappa Crucis (the Jewel Box).

southerner n. a native or inhabitant of the south. [as SOUTHERN.]

Southern Ocean the body of water surrounding the continent of Antarctica.

Southey /'sʌðɪ/, Robert (1774-1843), English poet and prose writer. His early revolutionary ideas, which he shared with his friends Coleridge and Wordsworth, later moderated and he became a leading contributor to the Tory *Quarterly Review*. His voluminous works include the long poems *Thalaba* (1801), *Madoc* (1805), and *Roderick* (1814), and the historical work *The Life of Nelson* (1813), but he is better remembered for his shorter poems, such as the ballad 'The Inchcape Rock' and 'The Battle of Blenheim'. In his verse he introduced metrical innovations; he was appointed Poet Laureate in 1813.

South Glamorgan a county of South Wales.

southing /'saʊθɪŋ/ n. (Naut. etc.) **1.** a distance travelled or measured southward. **2.** a southerly direction. [f. SOUTH]

southpaw adj. (colloq.) left-handed. —n. (colloq.) a left-handed person, especially a boxer.

South Sea (hist.) the Pacific Ocean. —**South Sea bubble**, the fever of speculation in stock of the South Sea Company (1720). The Company had been formed in 1711 to trade with Spanish America. In 1720 it assumed responsibility for the National Debt in return for a guaranteed profit, but the speculative boom in this and in ever more implausible projects was quickly followed by the Company's collapse and a general financial catastrophe; there were matching disasters in Paris and Amsterdam. The subsequent inquiry revealed corruption among the King's ministers. The situation was saved by Sir Robert Walpole, who transferred the South Sea stock to the Bank of England and the East India Company. A statute was passed severely restricting joint-stock companies for the future.

southward /'saʊθwəd/ adj. & (also **southwards**) adv. towards the south. —n. a southward direction or region. [f. SOUTH + -WARD]

south-west n. **1.** the point midway between south and west; the direction in which this lies. **2.** (usu. **South-West**) the part of a country or town lying to the south-west. —adj. of, towards, or coming from the south-west. —adv. towards, at, or near the south-west. —**south-westerly** adj. & adv., **south-western** adj.

southwester n. a south-west wind.

South Yorkshire a metropolitan county of northern England.

sou'wester /saʊ'westə(r)/ n. **1.** a waterproof hat with a broad flap at the back. **2.** a south-west wind. [f. SOUTHWESTER]

souvenir /su:və'nɪə(r)/ n. a thing kept as a reminder of a place, person, or event. [F f. L subvenire occur to the mind (SUB-, venire come)]

sovereign /'sɒvrɪn/ n. **1.** a supreme ruler, especially a monarch. **2.** a British gold coin (now rarely used) nominally worth £1. —adj. **1.** supreme; unmitigated. **2.** possessing sovereign power; independent; royal. **3.** very good or effective. —**sovereignty** n. [f. OF so(u)verain ult. f. L super over]

soviet /'səʊvɪət, 'sɒv-/ n. an elected council in a district of the USSR. [f. Russ. sovet council]

Soviet /'səʊvɪət, 'sɒ-/ adj. Russian; of the USSR. —n. (also in pl.) the Russian nation since 1922. —**Supreme Soviet**, the governing council of the USSR or of any of its constituent republics. As the highest legislative authority in the Soviet Union the Supreme Soviet is responsible for electing the Presidium, the supreme authority when the Soviet is not sitting. It is composed of two equal chambers: the Soviet of Union, composed of one delegate for every 300,000 citizens, and the Soviet of Nationalities, elected on a regional basis in the component republics and areas. [= prec.]

Soviet Union the Union of Soviet Socialist Republics.

sow[1] /səʊ/ v.t. (past **sowed**; p.p. **sown** or **sowed**) **1.** to put (seed) on or in the earth for the purpose of growth; to plant (land) with seed. **2.** to implant or spread (feelings or ideas). —**sower** n. [OE]

sow[2] /saʊ/ n. an adult female pig. [OE]

soy n. **1.** a sauce made from pickled soya beans. **2.** (also **soy bean**) a soya bean. [Jap. f. Chin. shi-you (shi salted beans, you oil)]

soya /'sɔɪə/ n. a leguminous plant (Soja hispida) yielding edible flour and oil. —**soya bean**, the seed of this plant. [f. Du. f. Malay (as prec.)]

sozzled /'sɒz(ə)ld/ adj. (slang) very drunk. [f. dial. sozzle mix sloppily (imit.)]

spa /spɑ:/ n. a curative mineral spring; a place with this. [f. Spa in Belgium, celebrated since medieval times for the curative properties of its mineral springs]

space n. **1.** the continuous expanse in which things exist and move; a portion of this; the amount of this taken by a particular thing or available for a particular purpose. **2.** the interval between points or objects; an empty area. **3.** an interval of time. **4.** the area of paper used in writing or printing something. **5.** outer space. **6.** a large area. —attrib. of or used for travel etc. in outer space. —v.t. to set or arrange at intervals; to put spaces between. —**space age**, the era of space travel. **space shuttle**, a spacecraft travelling repeatedly e.g. between earth and a space station (see SPACECRAFT). **space station**, an artificial satellite as a base for operations in outer space. **space-time**, the fusion of the concepts of space and time as a four-dimensional continuum. [f. OF espace f. L spatium]

spacecraft n. a vehicle for travelling in outer space. The first spacecraft to be launched into orbit was the Russian Sputnik I, launched on 4 Oct. 1957, the fortieth anniversary of the start of the Russian Revolution. The first manned spacecraft took the Russian pilot Yuri Gagarin into orbit on 12 Apr. 1961, and on 21 July 1969 two US astronauts landed on the moon. The first reusable spacecraft was the American space shuttle which made its first mission in 1981. (See ill. pp. 794-5.)

spaceman n. (pl. **-men**) a space traveller.

spaceship n. a spacecraft.

spacesuit n. a sealed pressurized suit allowing the wearer to survive in outer space.

spacious /'speɪʃəs/ adj. providing much space, roomy. —**spaciousness** n. [f. OF or L (as SPACE)]

spade[1] n. a digging-tool with a sharp-edged broad usually metal blade; a similar tool for various purposes. —**call a spade a spade**, to speak plainly or bluntly. —**spadeful** n. [OE]

spade[2] *n.* a playing-card of the suit (**spades**) marked with black figures shaped like an inverted heart with a short stem. [f. It. *spada* sword f. L f. Gk; assoc. with shape of prec.]

spadework *n.* hard preparatory work.

spadix /'speɪdɪks/ *n.* a spike of flowers closely arranged round a fleshy axis and usually enclosed in a spathe. [L f. Gk, = palm-branch]

spaghetti /spə'getɪ/ *n.* pasta made in solid strings, between macaroni and vermicelli in thickness. [It., pl. of dim. of *spago* string]

Spain a country in SW Europe, occupying the greater part of the Iberian peninsula; pop. (1981) 37,682,355; official language, Spanish; capital, Madrid. Conquered successively by the Carthaginians, Romans, Visigoths and Arabs, Spain was reunited by the marriage of Ferdinand of Aragon and Isabella of Castile at the end of the 15th c. and emerged under the Hapsburg kings of the 16th c. to become the dominant European power. Thereafter it declined, suffering as a result of the War of the Spanish Succession and the Napoleonic War, and losing most of its overseas empire in the early 19th c. Endemic political instability finally resulted in the Spanish Civil War (1936-9) and the establishment of a Fascist dictatorship under Franco. Franco's death in 1975 was followed by the re-establishment of a constitutional monarchy and a pronounced liberalization of the State, but the country's political problems have yet to be finally resolved. Despite some industrialization and a massive development of the tourist trade, Spain remains predominantly agricultural and, in European terms, economically underdeveloped. It became a member of the EEC on 1 Jan. 1986.

Spam *n.* [P] a tinned meat made mainly from ham. [arbitrary formation or f. *spiced ham*]

span[1] *n.* **1.** the full extent from end to end or across; the maximum lateral extent of an aeroplane or its wing. **2.** each part of a bridge between the supports (ill. BRIDGES). **3.** the maximum distance between the tips of the thumb and little finger, especially as a measure = 9 in. **4.** length in time from beginning to end. —*v.t.* (**-nn-**) to extend from side to side or end to end of; to bridge (a river etc.). [OE]

span[2] see SPICK.

spandrel /'spændr(ə)l/ *n.* the space between the curve of an arch and the surrounding rectangular moulding or framework (ill. CHURCH) or between the curves of adjoining arches and the moulding above. [perh. f. AF (*espaundre* expand)]

spangle *n.* a small piece of glittering material, especially one of many as an ornament of a dress etc. —*v.t.* (esp. in *p.p.*) to cover (as) with spangles. [f. *spang* f. MDu. & OHG, ON *spöng* brooch]

Spaniard /'spænjəd/ *n.* a native of Spain. [f. OF (*Espaigne* Spain)]

spaniel /'spænj(ə)l/ *n.* a dog of a breed with a long silky coat and drooping ears. [f. OF, = Spanish dog (as prec.)]

Spanish /'spænɪʃ/ *adj.* of Spain or its people or language. —*n.* the Spanish language (see below). —**the Spanish,** the people of Spain. **Spanish fly,** a dried insect (*Lytta vesicatoria*) used in medicine and as an aphrodisiac. **Spanish Main,** (*hist.*) the NE coast of South America and the adjoining part of the Caribbean Sea. [f. SPAIN]

Spanish is the most widely spoken of the Romance languages, with many Arabic words dating from the time when the Moors dominated Spain (8th-15th c.); there are in all about 225 million speakers. It is the official language of Spain and of every South American republic except Brazil and Guyana, and is widely spoken in the Southern States of the USA. In sound it is very like Italian, with a strong 'r' sound and with many masculine words ending in -o and feminine words in -a; the ñ sound /-nj-/ is characteristic. A variety of Spanish known as Ladino is spoken in Turkey and Israel by descendants of Jews expelled from Spain in 1492.

Spanish-American War the war between Spain and the USA in the Caribbean and the Philippines in 1898. American public opinion having been aroused by Spanish atrocities in Cuba and the destruction of the US warship *Maine* in Santiago harbour, the United States declared war and destroyed the Spanish fleets in both the Pacific and the West Indies before successfully invading Cuba, Puerto Rico, and the Philippines, all of which Spain gave up by the Treaty of Paris, signed at the end of the year.

Spanish Succession, War of the (1701-14), a European war, provoked by the death of the Spanish king Charles II without issue, marking the end of Louis XIV's attempts to establish French dominance over Europe. The Grand Alliance of Britain, Holland, and the Holy Roman Emperor, largely through the victories of Marlborough, threw back the French invasion of the Low Countries, and, although the Treaty of Utrecht (1713-14) confirmed the accession of a Bourbon king in Spain, it prevented Spain and France being united under one crown.

spank *v.t./i.* **1.** to slap on the buttocks. **2.** (of a horse etc.) to move briskly. —*n.* a slap given in spanking. [perh. imit.]

spanker *n.* a fore-and-aft sail on the after side of the mizen-mast (ill. SAILING-SHIPS). [f. SPANK]

spanking *n.* the process of spanking or being spanked. —*adj.* (*colloq.*) brisk, lively; excellent. —*adv.* (*colloq.*) briskly; excellently. [f. SPANK]

spanner *n.* a tool for turning a nut on a bolt etc. —**spanner in the works,** an upsetting element or influence. [G (*spannen* draw tight)]

spar[1] *n.* **1.** a stout pole as used for a ship's mast etc. **2.** the main longitudinal beam of an aeroplane wing. [f. OF *esparre* or ON *sperra*]

spar[2] *v.i.* (**-rr-**) **1.** to make the motions of attack and defence with closed fists; to use the hands (as) in boxing. **2.** to engage in argument etc. —*n.* a sparring motion; a boxing-match. —**sparring-partner** *n.* a boxer employed to practise with another in training; a person with whom one enjoys arguing. [OE, orig. unkn.; cf. ON *sperrask* kick out]

spar[3] *n.* an easily split crystalline mineral. [MLG, rel. to OE *spæren* of plaster, *spærstān* gypsum]

spare *v.t.* **1.** to refrain from hurting, harming, or destroying; to be merciful towards. **2.** to use with great restraint; to refrain from using. **3.** to part with, to be able to afford to give; to do without; to allow to have (a thing etc.), especially that one does not need). —*adj.* **1.** additional to what is usually needed or used; reserved for occasional or emergency use. **2.** (of a person etc.) thin; lean. **3.** small in quantity; frugal. —*n.* a spare part. —**go spare,** (*slang*) to become very angry. **not spare oneself,** to exert one's utmost efforts. **spare part,** a duplicate to replace a lost or damaged part. **spare-rib** *n.* a cut of pork from the lower ribs. **spare time,** leisure. **spare tyre,** (*colloq.*) a circle of fatness round or above the waist. —**sparely** *adv.*, **spareness** *n.* [OE]

sparing /'speərɪŋ/ *adj.* economical, not generous or wasteful; restrained. —**sparingly** *adv.* [f. SPARE]

Spark, Muriel (1918-), British author, of Scottish-Jewish descent. She became a Roman Catholic in 1954. Her novels include *Memento Mori* (1959), a comic and macabre study of old age; *The Ballad of Peckham Rye* (1960), a bizarre tale of the underworld; *The Prime of Miss Jean Brodie* (1961), a disturbing portrait of an Edinburgh schoolmistress and her favoured pupils; and *Loitering with Intent* (1981), on the problems of biography and autobiography. Her novels, with the exception of *The Mandelbaum Gate* (1965), are short, elegant, eccentric, and sophisticated, with touches of the bizarre and the perverse, and her use of narrative omniscience is highly distinctive.

spark *n.* **1.** a fiery particle, e.g. one thrown off by a burning substance or caused by friction. **2.** a flash of light produced by an electrical discharge; such a discharge serving to fire an explosive mixture in an internal-combustion engine. **3.** a flash of wit etc. **4.** a minute amount of a quality etc. **5.** a lively person. —*v.t./i.* **1.** to emit a spark or sparks. **2.** (also with *off*) to stir into activity, to initiate. —**spark-plug** or **sparking-plug** *n.* a device for making a spark in an internal combustion engine. [OE; orig. unkn.]

sparkle *v.i.* **1.** to shine brightly with flashes of light. **2.** to show brilliant wit or liveliness. **3.** (of wine) to effervesce. —*n.* sparkling light or brightness. [f. SPARK]

sparkler *n.* **1.** a sparking firework. **2.** (in *pl.*, *slang*) diamonds. [f. prec.]

sparrow /'spærəʊ/ *n.* a small brownish-grey bird of the genus *Passer*. —**sparrow-hawk** *n.* a small hawk (*Accipiter nisus*). [OE]

sparse *adj.* thinly scattered, not dense; infrequent. —**sparsely** *adv.*, **sparseness** *n.*, **sparsity** *n.* [f. L *sparsus* (*spargere* scatter)]

Sparta /'spɑːtə/ a city in the southern Peloponnese in Greece. After enslaving the surrounding populations as helots, in the 5th c. BC Sparta became the chief rival of Athens, whom she defeated in the Peloponnesian War. The ancient Spartans were renowned for the military

Space

Some significant steps in space exploration

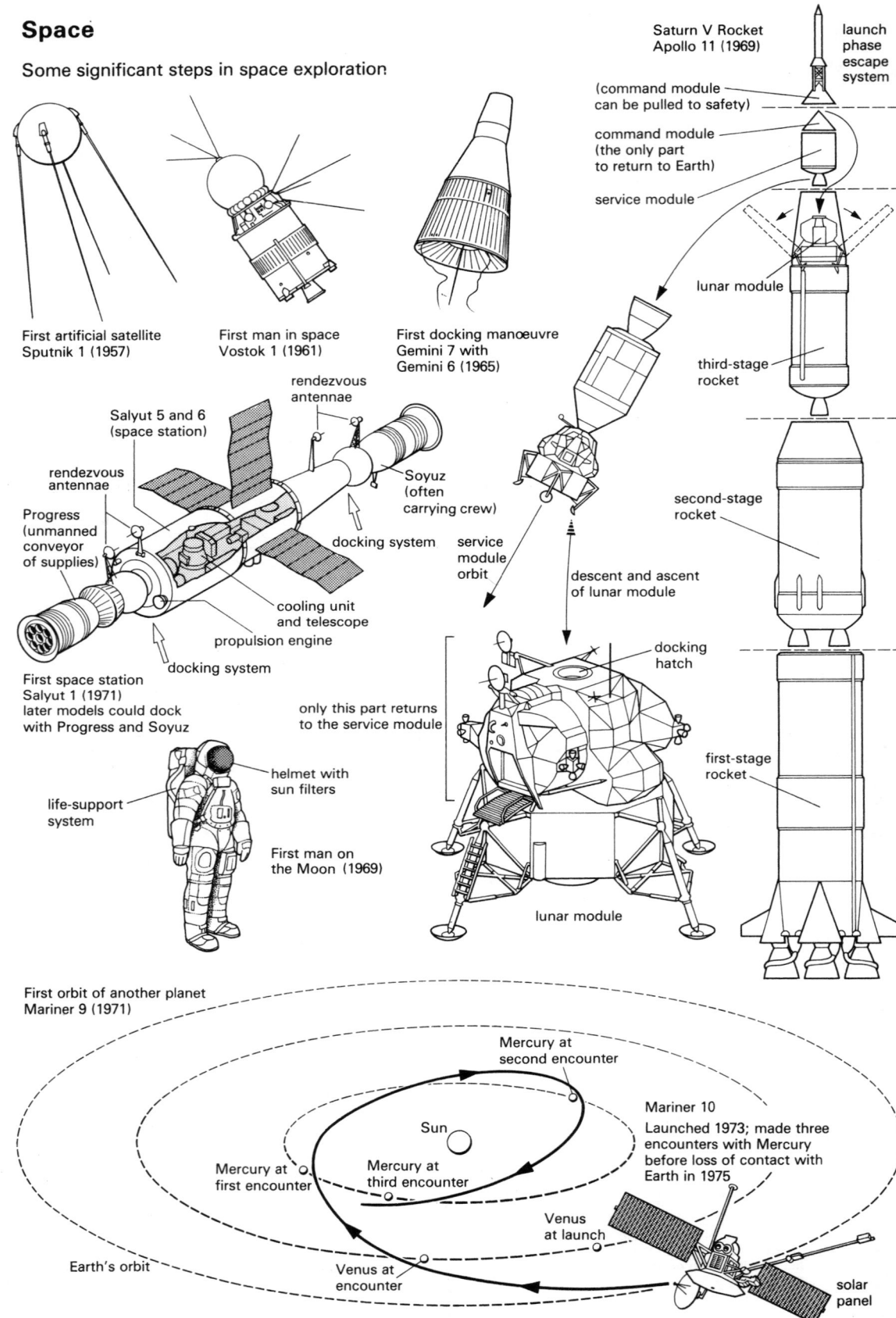

First artificial satellite
Sputnik 1 (1957)

First man in space
Vostok 1 (1961)

First docking manoeuvre
Gemini 7 with
Gemini 6 (1965)

Saturn V Rocket
Apollo 11 (1969)

launch
phase
escape
system

(command module
can be pulled to safety)

command module
(the only part
to return to Earth)

service module

lunar module

third-stage
rocket

second-stage
rocket

first-stage
rocket

rendezvous
antennae

Salyut 5 and 6
(space station)

rendezvous
antennae

Soyuz
(often
carrying crew)

docking system

Progress
(unmanned
conveyor
of supplies)

cooling unit
and telescope

propulsion engine

docking system

service
module
orbit

descent and ascent
of lunar module

First space station
Salyut 1 (1971)
later models could dock
with Progress and Soyuz

only this part returns
to the service module

docking
hatch

helmet with
sun filters

life-support
system

First man on
the Moon (1969)

lunar module

First orbit of another planet
Mariner 9 (1971)

Mercury at
second encounter

Sun

Mariner 10
Launched 1973; made three
encounters with Mercury
before loss of contact with
Earth in 1975

Mercury at
first encounter

Mercury at
third encounter

Venus
at launch

Earth's orbit

Venus at
encounter

solar
panel

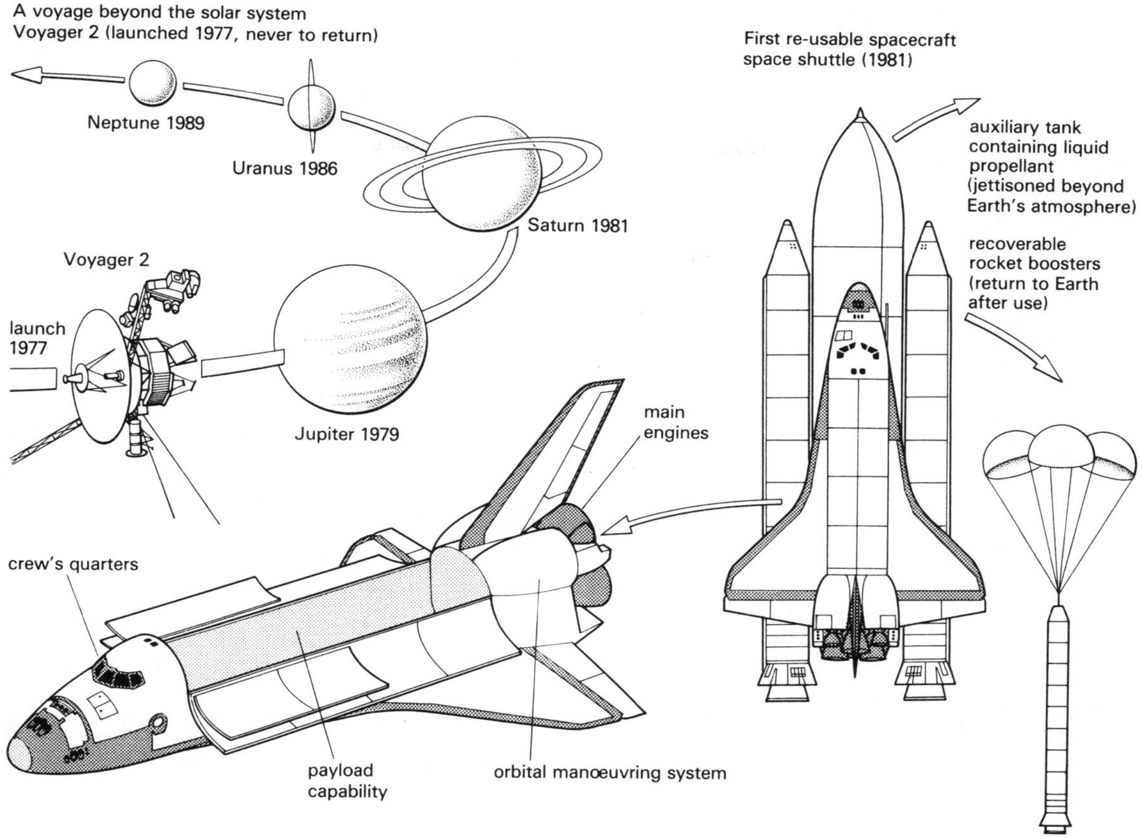

A voyage beyond the solar system
Voyager 2 (launched 1977, never to return)

Neptune 1989

Uranus 1986

Saturn 1981

Voyager 2

launch
1977

Jupiter 1979

First re-usable spacecraft
space shuttle (1981)

auxiliary tank
containing liquid
propellant
(jettisoned beyond
Earth's atmosphere)

recoverable
rocket boosters
(return to Earth
after use)

main
engines

crew's quarters

payload
capability

orbital manoeuvring system

Communications satellites

retransmitting to all parts of the globe

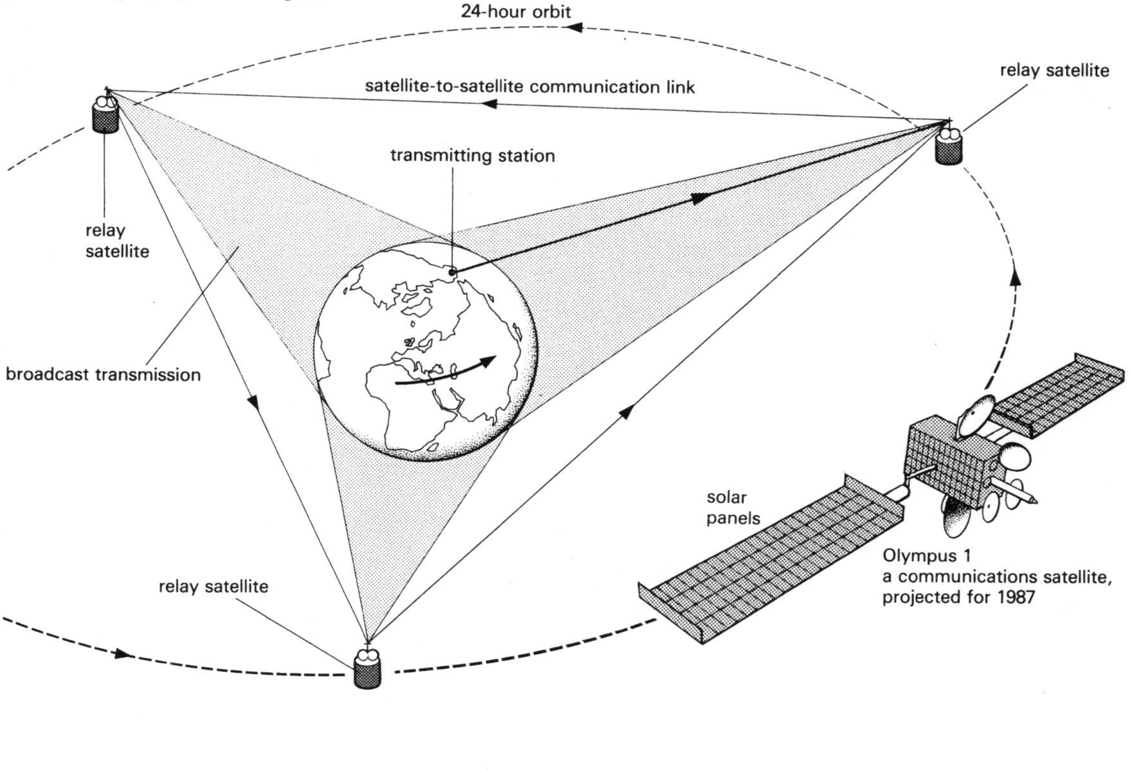

24-hour orbit

relay satellite

satellite-to-satellite communication link

transmitting station

relay
satellite

broadcast transmission

relay satellite

solar
panels

Olympus 1
a communications satellite,
projected for 1987

organization of their State and for their rigorous discipline, courage, and austerity.

Spartacus /ˈspɑːtəkəs/ (1st c. BC) Thracian gladiator who led a revolt against Rome in 73 BC. He defeated the Romans in a number of engagements in Italy; his army increased to a total of 90,000. He was eventually defeated by Crassus in 71 BC.

Spartan /ˈspɑːtən/ adj. **1.** of Sparta or its inhabitants. **2.** (of conditions) simple and sometimes harsh, without comfort or luxuries (with allusion to the hardy and austere life of Spartans). —n. **1.** a native of Sparta. **2.** an austere person. [f. prec.]

spasm /ˈspæz(ə)m/ n. **1.** a sudden involuntary muscular contraction. **2.** a sudden convulsive movement or emotion etc.; a brief spell of activity. [f. OF or L f. Gk (spaō pull)]

spasmodic /spæzˈmɒdɪk/ adj. of or occurring in spasms, intermittent. —**spasmodically** adv. [f. Gk spasmōdēs (as prec.)]

spastic /ˈspæstɪk/ adj. suffering from cerebral palsy with spasm of the muscles. —n. a spastic person. —**spastically** adv. [f. L f. Gk (as SPASM)]

spat[1] n. (usu. in pl.) a short gaiter covering the instep and reaching a little above the ankle (ill. DRESS). [abbr. of spatterdash (SPATTER)]

spat[2] n. the spawn of a shellfish, especially of the oyster. [AF; orig. unkn.]

spat[3] n. (US colloq.) a petty or brief quarrel. [prob. imit.]

spat[4] past & p.p. of SPIT[1].

spate n. **1.** a sudden flood. **2.** a large or excessive amount. —**in spate**, (of a river) flowing strongly at an abnormally high level. [orig. Sc. & N. Engl.; orig. unkn.]

spathe /speɪð/ n. a large bract or bracts enveloping a spadix or a flower-cluster. [f. L f. Gk, = broad blade]

spatial /ˈspeɪʃ(ə)l/ adj. of space. —**spatially** adv. [f. L spatium space]

spatter v.t./i. to splash or scatter in small drops. —n. a splash or splashes; the sound of spattering. [cf. Du. & LG spatten spout]

spatula /ˈspætjʊlə/ n. **1.** a tool like a knife with a broad blunt flexible blade, used especially by artists and in cookery. **2.** a strip of stiff material used by a doctor for pressing down the tongue etc. [L, f. dim. of spatha spathe]

spavin /ˈspævɪn/ n. a disease of a horse's hock with a hard bony swelling. —**spavined** adj. [f. OF espavin]

spawn v.t./i. **1.** (of fish, frogs, molluscs, etc.) to deposit spawn; to produce (spawn); to be produced as spawn or young. **2.** (derog.) to produce as offspring. **3.** to produce or generate in large numbers. —n. **1.** the eggs of fish, frogs, etc. (ill. AMPHIBIANS). **2.** (derog.) human or other offspring. **3.** the white fibrous matter from which fungi grow. [f. AF espaundre (as EXPAND)]

spay v.t. to remove the ovaries of (a female animal). [f. AF, = cut with sword (as ÉPÉE)]

speak v.t./i. (past **spoke**; p.p. **spoken**) **1.** to utter words in an ordinary voice (not singing). **2.** to hold a conversation; to make a speech; **3.** to utter or pronounce (words); to use (a specified language) in speaking; to make known in words. **4.** to convey an idea, to be evidence of something. —**generally** (or **strictly** etc.) **speaking**, in the general (or strict etc.) sense of the words. **not** (or **nothing**) **to speak of**, not (or nothing) worth mentioning. **on speaking terms**, sufficiently friendly or acquainted to hold a conversation. **speak for**, to act as a spokesman for; to speak in defence of; to bespeak. **speak for itself**, to be sufficient evidence. **speak out** or **up**, to speak loudly or freely; to give one's opinion etc. without hesitation or fear. **speak volumes (for)**, to be very significant (in terms of). [OE]

speakeasy n. (US slang) a place where alcoholic liquor is sold illicitly.

speaker n. **1.** one who speaks, especially in public; a person of a specified skill in speech-making; one who speaks a specified language. **2.** a loudspeaker. **3. Speaker**, the presiding officer of a legislative assembly (see below). [f. SPEAK]
The Speaker of the House of Commons is a member of that House, chosen to act as its representative (to 'speak' for it, whence his title) and to preside over its debates. The first person formally mentioned as holding the office was Sir Thomas de Hungerford in 1376-7. Originally a royal nominee, the Speaker has been elected since the late 17th c., and although no longer holding ministerial office or taking part in debate he remains chairman of the House with the casting vote and the power to censure, suspend,

or expel members. On appointment he is ceremonially dragged to his chair, the simulated reluctance being due to the fact that nine of his predecessors were beheaded. In the House of Lords the Speaker (who does not hold disciplinary powers) is now the Lord Chancellor or one acting as his deputy or substitute.

spear n. a thrusting or hurling weapon consisting of a stout staff with a pointed tip of metal etc. (ill. ARMOUR). —v.t. to pierce or strike (as) with a spear. [OE]

spearhead n. **1.** the pointed tip of a spear. **2.** a person or group leading an attack or challenge etc. —v.t. to act as the spearhead of (an attack etc.).

spearmint n. a common garden mint (Mentha spicata) used in cookery and to flavour chewing-gum.

spec n. (colloq.) a speculation. —**on spec**, as a speculation. [abbr.]

special /ˈspeʃ(ə)l/ adj. **1.** of a particular or peculiar kind, not general; for a particular purpose. **2.** exceptional in amount or degree etc. —n. a special constable, edition of a newspaper, dish on a menu, etc. —**Special Branch**, a section of the CID which deals with police matters involving political security. **special constable**, one assisting the police in routine duties or in emergencies. **special correspondent**, one appointed by a newspaper to report on a special event or facts. **special delivery**, a delivery of mail separately from the regular delivery. **special edition**, an edition of a newspaper including later news than the ordinary edition. **special licence**, a licence allowing a marriage to take place within a short time without banns. **special pleading**, (Law) pleading with particular reference to the circumstances of a case, as opposed to general pleading; (pop.) persuasive but unfair reasoning. —**specially** adv. [f. OF (= especial) or L specialis (as SPECIES)]

specialist n. one who specializes in a particular branch of a profession, especially medicine. [f. prec.]

speciality /speʃɪˈælɪtɪ/ n. **1.** a special feature. **2.** a special thing or activity; a special product; a subject in which one specializes. [as SPECIAL]

specialize /ˈspeʃəlaɪz/ v.t./i. **1.** to be or become a specialist. **2.** to make or become individual; to adapt for a particular purpose. —**specialization** /-ˈzeɪʃ(ə)n/ n. [f. F (as SPECIAL)]

specialty /ˈspeʃəltɪ/ n. a speciality. [f. OF (as SPECIAL)]

specie /ˈspiːʃiː, -ʃɪ/ n. coin as opposed to paper money. [L, abl. of foll.]

species /ˈspiːʃiːz, -ʃɪz/ n. (pl. same) **1.** a class of things having some common characteristics. **2.** a group of animals or plants within a genus. **3.** a kind or sort. [L, orig. = appearance (specere look)]

specific /spɪˈsɪfɪk/ adj. **1.** particular, clearly distinguished from others. **2.** exact, giving full details. **3.** peculiar, relating to a particular thing; (of a medicine etc.) having a distinct effect in curing a certain disease. —n. a specific detail or aspect; a specific medicine. —**specific gravity**, the ratio between the weight of a substance and that of the same volume of a substance used as a standard (usually water or air). —**specifically** adv., **specificity** /-ˈfɪsɪtɪ/ n. [f. L (as prec. + facere make)]

specification /spesɪfɪˈkeɪʃ(ə)n/ n. (usu. in pl.) a detail of the design and materials etc. (to be) used in a machine or project etc. [f. L (as foll.)]

specify /ˈspesɪfaɪ/ v.t. to name expressly, to mention definitely; to include in specifications. [f. OF or L (as SPECIFIC)]

specimen /ˈspesɪmɪn/ n. an individual or part taken as an example of a class or whole, especially when used for investigation; (colloq., usu. derog.) a person of a specified sort. [L. (specere look)]

specious /ˈspiːʃəs/ adj. apparently good or sound but not really so; superficially plausible. —**speciously** adv. [f. L speciosus attractive (as SPECIES)]

speck n. a small spot or stain; a particle. —v.t. (esp. in p.p.) to mark with specks. [OE]

speckle n. a speck, especially one of many markings on the skin etc. —v.t. (esp. in p.p.) to mark with speckles. [f. MDu.]

specs n.pl. (colloq.) spectacles. [abbr.]

spectacle /ˈspektək(ə)l/ n. **1.** an object of sight, especially of public attention; a striking, impressive, or ridiculous sight. **2.** a public show. **3.** (in pl.) a pair of lenses to correct or assist defective sight, set in a frame to rest on the nose and ears (see below). —**spectacled** adj. [f. OF f. L spectaculum (spectare look)]
Spectacles seem to have been invented in Europe and in China at about the same time (c.1300). In Europe they

797

originated in Italy, and for centuries were the mark of the learned man, since most people were unable to read and defective eyesight was not a great handicap. An early design shows a type of pince-nez; side-pieces came later. A portrait of St Jerome by Ghirlandaio (15th c.) shows the saint at a desk from which spectacles dangle, and he became the patron saint of the spectacle-maker's guild. With the increase of books and the spread of literacy the spectacle trade grew rapidly in the 16th c. The early rims were of horn or leather; metal ones date from c.1600. Bifocals worn on the nose are known from c.1760, when a pair was made for the American statesman Benjamin Franklin. During the 19th c. only the elderly and scholarly made use of spectacles, but with the spread of education and general health care spectacles have become common.

spectacular /spek'tækjʊlə(r)/ adj. striking, impressive, amazing. —n. a spectacular performance; a lavishly produced film etc. —**spectacularly** adv.

spectator /spek'teɪtə(r)/ n. one who watches a show, game, or incident etc. —**spectator sport**, a sport which attracts many spectators. [f. F or L (as SPECTACLE)]

spectra pl. of SPECTRUM.

spectral /'spektr(ə)l/ adj. 1. of a spectre or spectres; ghost-like. 2. of the spectrum or spectra. —**spectrally** adv. [f. foll.]

spectre /'spektə(r)/ n. 1. a ghost. 2. a haunting presentiment. [F or f. L, = SPECTRUM]

spectrograph /'spektrəgrɑːf/ n. an apparatus for photographing or otherwise reproducing spectra. —**mass spectrograph**, see MASS¹. —**spectrographic** /-'græfɪk/ adj. [f. SPECTRUM + -GRAPH]

spectrometer /spek'trɒmɪtə(r)/ n. a spectroscope that can be used for measuring observed spectra. —**mass spectrometer**, see MASS¹. [f. G or F (as SPECTRUM + -METER)]

spectroscope /'spektrəskəʊp/ n. an instrument for producing and examining spectra. —**spectroscopic** /-'skɒpɪk/ adj., **spectroscopically** /-'skɒpɪkəlɪ/ adv. [f. G or F (as foll. + -SCOPE)]

spectroscopy /spek'trɒskəpɪ/ n. the examination and investigation of spectra (see SPECTRUM). The technique was initiated by the German scientists Kirchhoff and Bunsen after the former's discovery in 1859 that each pure substance has its own characteristic spectrum. It led to the discovery of the elements caesium and rubidium, and has been used in the study of the structures of atoms and molecules and in the investigation of celestial bodies. [f. prec.]

spectrum /'spektrəm/ n. (pl. -tra) 1. the range of colours as seen in a rainbow or when white light is passed through a prism or a diffraction grating (see ill. LIGHT). The parts are arranged according to wavelength, ranging continuously from red (the longest wavelength) to violet (the shortest). It was Sir Isaac Newton who first analysed light in this way. 2. the whole range of other radiation or of sound in which the parts are arranged according to wavelength. 3. such a range characteristic of a body or substance when emitting or absorbing radiation. 4. a similar range of component parts of anything, arranged by degree, quality, etc. [L, = image, apparition (specere look)]

speculate /'spekjʊleɪt/ v.i. 1. to form or put forward opinions by conjecture, without definite knowledge. 2. to engage in risky financial transactions. —**speculation** /-'leɪʃ(ə)n/ n., **speculator** n. [f. L speculari spy out (specere look)]

speculative /'spekjʊlətɪv/ adj. involving speculation. —**speculatively** adv., **speculativeness** n. [f. prec.]

sped past & p.p. of SPEED.

speech n. 1. the act, faculty, or manner of speaking. 2. words spoken; a spoken communication to an audience. 3. the language of a nation or group etc. —**speech-day** n. an annual celebration at school when speeches are made. **speech therapy**, treatment to improve defective speech. [OE (as SPEAK)]

speechify /'spiːtʃɪfaɪ/ v.i. (colloq.) to make a speech or speeches. [f. prec.]

speechless adj. silent, temporarily unable to speak through emotion or surprise etc. —**speechlessly** adv., **speechlessness** n. [f. SPEECH + -LESS]

speed n. 1. rapidity of movement or operation; quick motion. 2. the rate of motion or action. 3. the gear appropriate to a range of speeds on a bicycle etc. 4. the relative sensitivity of a photographic film to light; the light-gathering power of a lens. 5. (archaic) success, prosperity. —v.t./i. (past & p.p. sped) 1. to go or send quickly. 2. (of a

motorist etc.; past & p.p. **speeded**) to travel at an illegal or dangerous speed. 3. (archaic) to be or make prosperous or successful. —**at full speed**, as fast as one can go or work. **at speed**, moving quickly. **speed limit**, the maximum permitted speed of a vehicle on a road etc. **speed up**, to move or work faster; to cause to do this. **speed-up**. [OE]

speedboat n. a motor boat designed for high speed.

speedo /'spiːdəʊ/ n. (pl. -os) (colloq.) a speedometer.

speedometer /spiː'dɒmɪtə(r)/ n. a device indicating the speed of a vehicle. [f. SPEED + -METER]

speedway n. 1. motor-cycle racing; an arena for this. 2. (US) a road or track for fast traffic.

speedwell n. a small plant of the genus Veronica with usually bright-blue flowers. [f. SPEED + WELL¹]

speedy adj. 1. moving quickly, rapid. 2. done or coming etc. without delay. —**speedily** adv., **speediness** n. [f. SPEED]

Speke /spiːk/, John Hanning (1827-64), English explorer who accompanied (Sir) Richard Burton on expeditions to trace the source of the Nile. After they had discovered Lake Tanganyika Speke went on alone and reached a great lake which he correctly identified as the 'source reservoir' of the Nile, and named it in honour of Queen Victoria. His claim to have found the Nile source was disputed, and on the day when he was to have debated the subject publicly with Richard Burton he was killed by his own gun in a shooting accident.

speleology /spelɪ'ɒlədʒɪ, spiː-/ n. the study of caves. —**speleological** /-'lɒdʒɪk(ə)l/ adj., **speleologist** n. [f. F f. L f. Gk spēlaion cave + -LOGY)]

spell¹ n. 1. words supposed to have magic power; the effect of these. 2. the fascination exercised by a person or activity etc. [OE]

spell² v.t./i. (past & p.p. **spelt** or **spelled**) 1. to write or name in their correct sequence the letters of (a word). 2. (of letters) to make up (a word). 3. (of circumstances etc.) to have as a consequence, to involve. —**spell out**, to make out (words etc.) laboriously or slowly; to spell aloud; to explain in detail. —**speller** n. [f. OF espel(l)er, rel. to prec.]

spell³ n. a period of time or work; a period of some activity; a period of a certain type of weather. —v.t. to relieve (a person) in work etc. by taking one's turn. [var. of dial. spele take place of f. OE spelian; orig. unkn.]

spellbound adj. held as if by a spell, fascinated.

spelling n. 1. the way a word is spelt. 2. ability to spell. [f. SPELL²]

spelt¹ n. a kind of wheat (Triticum spelta) giving very fine flour. [OE]

spelt² see SPELL².

Spencer /'spensə(r)/, Herbert (1820-1903), English philosopher, the leading English exponent of agnosticism in the 19th c. He worked for some years as a railway engineer and later as a sub-editor of The Economist, advocating a policy of laissez-faire. Spencer greeted Darwin's work with enthusiasm, coined the phrase 'survival of the fittest' (1864), and sought to trace an evolutionary principle in all branches of knowledge. In 1860 he published his Programme of a System of Synthetic Philosophy, to the elaboration of which he devoted the remainder of his life. Essentially an individualist, in his moral and political philosophy he deprecated State intervention and championed individual rights.

spend v.t./i. (past & p.p. **spent**) 1. to pay out (money) in buying something. 2. to use up, to consume (material or energy etc.). 3. to pass or occupy (time etc.). 4. (in p.p.) having lost its original force or strength. —**spend a penny**, (colloq.) to urinate or defecate. —**spender** n. [OE f. L (as EXPEND)]

Spender /'spendə(r)/, Sir Stephen (1909-), English poet and critic, a contemporary at Oxford of Auden, MacNeice, and Day Lewis, whose left-wing political convictions he shared. A period spent in Germany sharpened his political consciousness. During the Spanish Civil War he actively supported the Republicans, a period reflected in The Still Centre (1939). His Poems (1933) contained both personal and political poems including the notorious 'The Pylons' which gave the nickname of 'Pylon Poets' to himself and his friends; his critical work The Destructive Element (1935) argues the importance of 'politico-moral' subjects in literature. A gradual shift in his political allegiance is seen in his poetry and critical works, and in his autobiography World Within World (1951) he gives an account of his association with the Communist Party. His interest in the public and social duty of the writer has tended to obscure the essentially tender and private nature of much of his poetry.

spendthrift *n.* an extravagant person.

Spenser /'spensə(r)/, Edmund (*c.*1552–99), English poet. He dedicated his first major poem, *The Shepheardes Calendar* (1579) in twelve eclogues (one for each month of the year), to Sir Philip Sidney, nephew of his patron the Earl of Leicester. His greatest work is the allegorical romance, *The Faerie Queene* (1590, 1596). The general scheme is expounded in his introductory letter to Sir Walter Raleigh: by the Faerie Queene the poet celebrates Glory in the abstract and Queen Elizabeth in particular, and twelve knights were to represent the different virtues but only 6 of the 12 books were ever written. The poem is written in the stanza invented by Spenser (in which a ninth line of 12 syllables is added to 8 lines of 10 syllables); its chief beauties lie in the particular episodes with which the allegory is varied, and in the imaginative and musical descriptions such as in the Cave of Mammon. Spenser has been a major influence on many succeeding poets including Milton and Keats. He died in poverty but was buried in honour at Westminster Abbey. —**Spenserian** /-'sɪərɪən/ *adj.*

sperm *n.* (*pl.* **sperms** or **sperm**) semen; a spermatozoon. —**sperm whale,** a large whale (*Physeter catodon*) yielding spermaceti. —**spermatic** /-'mætɪk/ *adj.* [f. L f. Gk *sperma* seed]

spermaceti /spɜ:mə'setɪ/ *n.* a white waxy substance used for ointments etc. [f. L *sperma* sperm, *ceti* of whale, it being regarded as whale-spawn]

spermatozoon /spɜ:mətə'zəʊən/ *n.* (*pl.* **-zoa**) each of the male fertilizing elements in semen. [as SPERM + Gk *zōion* living creature]

spermicide /'spɜ:mɪsaɪd/ *n.* a substance killing spermatozoa. —**spermicidal** *adj.* [f. SPERM + -CIDE]

spew *v.t./i.* **1.** to vomit. **2.** to gush out; to cause to do this. [OE (imit.)]

sphagnum /'sfægnəm/ *n.* (*pl.* **-na**) a moss of the genus *Sphagnum* growing in bogs and peat. [f. Gk *sphagnos* a moss]

sphenoid /'sfi:nɔɪd/ *adj.* wedge-shaped. —**sphenoid bone,** a compound bone between the temporal bone and the eye (ill. BODY 1). [f. Gk (*sphēn* wedge)]

sphere /sfɪə(r)/ *n.* **1.** a solid figure with every point on its surface equidistant from the centre (ill. SHAPES); the surface of this. **2.** a globe, a ball. **3.** a field of action, influence, or existence; one's place in society. **4.** each of the revolving shells in which the heavenly bodies were formerly thought to be set. [f. OF f. L f. Gk *sphaira* ball]

spherical /'sferɪk(ə)l/ *adj.* **1.** shaped like a sphere. **2.** of spheres. **3.** (of a triangle etc.) bounded by the arcs of the great circles of a sphere. —**spherically** *adv.,* **sphericity** /-'rɪsɪtɪ/ *n.* [f. L f. Gk (as prec.)]

spheroid /'sfɪərɔɪd/ *n.* a spherelike but not perfectly spherical body. —**spheroidal** /-'rɔɪd(ə)l/ *adj.* [f. L f. Gk (as SPHERE)]

sphincter /'sfɪŋktə(r)/ *n.* a ring of muscle closing and opening an orifice. [L f. Gk (*sphiggō* bind tight)]

sphinx /sfɪŋks/ *n.* **1.** a mythological monster with a human head and the body of a lion. Originating in Egypt, it became known early to Syrians, Phoenicians, and Mycenaean Greeks. In Greek literature it is a female being. One tale associates it with Thebes, where it propounded a riddle about the three ages of man and devoured whoever failed to solve this until Oedipus was successful and the sphinx committed suicide (or was killed by him). In classical art the sphinx is humanized with a beautiful serious face, and becomes the wise, enigmatic, and musical messenger of divine justice. **2.** (in Egypt) a figure with a couchant lion's body and a man's or animal's head. The colossal figure of a sphinx at Giza is part of the complex of funerary monuments of the pharaoh Chephren (4th Dynasty, 3rd millennium BC). It is carved from the natural rock and completed with masonry; the beard and nose have disappeared because the monument served as a target for a Mameluke sultan. It is believed to be an effigy of Chephren, but it came to be identified with a god whom the Greeks called Harmachis (= Horus in the horizon), and received its own cult; the Arabs called it *Abu Hol* (= father of terror). **3.** an enigmatic or inscrutable person. [L f. Gk, app. f. *sphiggō* draw tight]

spice *n.* **1.** an aromatic or pungent vegetable substance used to flavour food; spices collectively. **2.** an interesting or piquant quality. **3.** a trace. —*v.t.* **1.** to flavour with spice. **2.** to enhance (with wit etc.). [f. OF *espice* f. L, = SPECIES]

Spice Islands the Molucca Islands.

spick and span /spɪk ənd 'spæn/ clean and tidy; new-looking. [f. earlier *spick and span new,* extension of obs. *span new* (ON, f. *spann* chip)]

spicy /'spaɪsɪ/ *adj.* **1.** of or flavoured with spice. **2.** piquant; slightly scandalous or improper. —**spicily** *adv.,* **spiciness** *n.* [f. SPICE]

spider /'spaɪdə(r)/ *n.* **1.** an eight-legged arthropod of the order Araneida, many species of which spin webs, especially to capture insects as food. **2.** a thing resembling a spider. —**spider-crab** *n.* a crab of the superfamily Oxyrhyncha, with long thin legs. **spider-man** *n.* a man working at a great height on a building. **spider monkey,** a monkey of the genus *Ateles* with long limbs and a long prehensile tail. [OE (as SPIN)]

spidery *adj.* of or like a spider; very thin or long. [f. prec.]

spiel /spiːl/ *n.* (*slang*) a speech or story, especially a glib or long one. —*v.t./i.* (*slang*) to speak lengthily or glibly. [G, = game]

spigot /'spɪgət/ *n.* a small peg or plug; a device for controlling the flow of liquor from a cask etc. [perh. f. Prov. *espigou(n)* f. L (as foll.)]

spike[1] *n.* **1.** a sharp projecting point; a pointed piece of metal, e.g. one of a set forming the top of an iron fence or worn on the bottom of a running-shoe to prevent slipping. **2.** (in *pl.*) running-shoes fitted with spikes. **3.** a large nail. **4.** a pointed metal rod standing upright on a base and used e.g. to hold unused matter in a newspaper office. —*v.t.* **1.** to put spikes on or into; to fix on a spike. **2.** (*colloq.*) to add alcohol to (a drink). **3.** (*hist.*) to plug the vent of (a gun) with a spike. —**spike a person's guns,** to spoil his plans. [perh. f. MLG or MDu., rel. to SPOKE[1]]

spike[2] *n.* a cluster of sessile flowers arranged closely on a long common axis; a separate sprig of any plant in which flowers form a spikelike cluster; an ear of corn. [f. L *spica* ear of corn]

spikenard /'spaɪknɑːd/ *n.* **1.** a tall sweet-smelling plant (*Nardostachys jatamansi*). **2.** an aromatic ointment formerly made from this. [f. L (as SPIKE[2], NARD)]

spiky *adj.* **1.** like a spike; having a spike or spikes. **2.** (*colloq.*) dogmatic; bad-tempered. —**spikily** *adv.,* **spikiness** *n.* [f. SPIKE[1]]

spill[1] *v.t./i.* (*past & p.p.* **spilt** or **spilled**) **1.** to cause or allow (a liquid or powder etc.) to run over the edge of its container. **2.** to become spilt. **3.** to shed (others' blood). **4.** to throw accidentally from a saddle or vehicle. **5.** (*slang*) to disclose (information etc.). —*n.* **1.** spilling, being spilt. **2.** being thrown from a saddle etc.; a tumble, a fall. —**spill the beans,** see BEAN. [OE, = kill]

spill[2] *n.* a thin strip of wood or paper used for transferring flame, e.g. for lighting a fire or pipe. [rel. to *spile* wooden peg, f. MDu. or MLG]

spillage *n.* **1.** the action of spilling. **2.** the amount spilt. [f. SPILL[1]]

spillikin /'spɪlɪkɪn/ *n.* a splinter of wood etc.; (in *pl.*) a game in which a heap of these is removed by taking one at a time without disturbing the others. [f. SPILL[2]]

spillway *n.* a passage for surplus water from a dam (ill. ELECTRICAL POWER).

spin *v.t./i.* (**-nn-**; *past & p.p.* **spun**) **1.** to turn or cause to turn rapidly on its own axis. **2.** to draw out and twist (raw cotton or wool etc.) into threads; to make (yarn) thus. **3.** (of a spider or silkworm) to make (a web or cocoon) by emitting a viscous thread. **4.** (of a person's head etc.) to be in a whirl through dizziness or astonishment; to toss (a coin). **5.** to spin-dry. **6.** to tell or compose (a story etc.). —*n.* **1.** a spinning movement. **2.** a short drive in a motor vehicle. **3.** a rotating dive of an aircraft (ill. FLIGHT). **4.** the intrinsic angular momentum of an elementary particle. —**spin bowler,** (in cricket) a bowler who imparts spin to a ball. **spin-drier** *n.* a machine for drying clothes by spinning them in a rotating drum so that moisture is squeezed out by centrifugal force. **spin-dry** *v.t.* to dry thus. **spin-off** *n.* an incidental or secondary result or benefit, especially in technology. **spin out,** to prolong (a speech or discussion etc.). **spun silk,** a cheap material of short-fibred and waste silk, often mixed with cotton. [OE]

spina bifida /'spaɪnə 'bɪfɪdə/ a congenital defect of the spine in which certain bones are not properly developed and allow the meninges or spinal cord to protrude. [L, = cleft spine]

spinach /'spɪnɪdʒ/ *n.* a vegetable (*Spinacia oleracea*) with succulent leaves cooked as food. [prob. f. MDu. f. OF, ult. f. Pers.]

spinal /'spaɪn(ə)l/ adj. of the spine. —**spinal column**, the spine. **spinal cord**, the cylindrical nervous structure within the spine. [f. L (as SPINE)]

spindle n. **1.** a slender rod or bar, often with tapered ends, to twist and wind thread. **2.** a pin or axis that revolves or on which a thing revolves. —**spindle-shanks** n. a person with long thin legs. **spindle-tree** n. a tree of the genus *Euonymus*, especially *E. europaeus* with a hard wood used for spindles. [OE (as SPIN)]

spindly adj. long or tall or thin. [f. prec.]

spindrift /'spɪndrɪft/ n. spray blown along the surface of the sea. [Sc. var. of *spoondrift* (*spoon* run before the wind + DRIFT)]

spine n. **1.** the column of small bones (vertebrae) extending from the skull down the centre of the back (ill. BODY **1**). **2.** a sharp needle-like outgrowth of an animal or plant. **3.** the part of a book's cover or jacket that encloses its page-fastening. **4.** a sharp ridge or projection. —**spine-chiller** n. a spine-chilling book or film etc. **spine-chilling** adj. frighteningly thrilling or exciting. [f. OF *espine* or L *spina* thorn]

spineless adj. **1.** lacking a backbone. **2.** lacking resoluteness or strength of character, feeble. —**spinelessness** n. [f. SPINE + -LESS]

spinet /spɪ'net/ n. (*hist.*) a small early keyboard instrument of the harpsichord family. [f. F f. It. *spinetta* (as SPINE)]

spinnaker /'spɪnəkə(r)/ n. a large triangular sail carried opposite the mainsail of a racing-yacht running before the wind. [f. *Sphinx*, name of first yacht to use it]

spinner n. **1.** a person or thing that spins, especially a manufacturer engaged in cotton-spinning. **2.** a spin bowler. **3.** (in fishing) a revolving bait as a lure. [f. SPIN]

spinneret /'spɪnəret/ n. **1.** the spinning-organ of a spider etc. **2.** a device for forming synthetic fibre. [f. prec.]

spinney /'spɪnɪ/ n. a small wood, a thicket. [f. OF f. L *spinetum* (as SPINE)]

spinning-jenny n. a machine for spinning fibres with more than one spindle at a time (see HARGREAVES).

spinning-top n. = TOP².

spinning-wheel n. a household device for spinning yarn or thread, with a spindle driven by a wheel operated originally by hand, later by a crank or treadle. The device is thought to have been introduced into Europe from India in the early 14th c.

Spinoza /spɪ'nəʊzə/, Baruch (Benedict) de (1632–77), Dutch rationalist philosopher of Jewish descent. Expelled from the Amsterdam synagogue in 1656 for his unorthodox views, he made his living by grinding and polishing lenses. Rejecting the Cartesian dualism of spirit and matter he saw only one infinite substance, of which finite existences are modes or limitations: God is all and all is God. For him, God was the immanent cause of the universe, not a ruler outside it; among his conclusions are determinism and a denial of personal immortality. Spinoza's *Ethics*, published posthumously, founded morality on the 'intellectual love of God', which becomes possible after the complete victory over the passions; virtue is its own reward. His political doctrine involved a 'social contract' in which man surrenders part of his natural rights to the State in order to obtain security. Spinoza's influence was at its height in the 19th c., especially in Germany.

spinster n. an unmarried woman; an (elderly) woman thought unlikely to marry. [orig. = woman who spins, f. SPIN]

spiny /'spaɪnɪ/ adj. having (many) spines. —**spininess** n. [f. SPINE]

spiracle /'spaɪərək(ə)l/ n. an external respiratory orifice in insects (ill. INSECTS); the blow-hole of a whale etc. [f. L *spirare* breathe)]

spiraea /spaɪ'riːə/ n. a garden plant of the genus *Spiraea*, related to meadowsweet. [L f. Gk (*speira* coil)]

spiral /'spaɪər(ə)l/ adj. coiled in a plane or as round a cylinder or cone; having this shape. —n. **1.** a spiral curve; a thing of spiral form. **2.** a continuous increase or decrease in two or more quantities alternately or in succession, because of their dependence on each other. —v.i. (**-ll-**) to move in a spiral course. —**spiral staircase**, a staircase rising round a central axis (ill. HOUSES). —**spirally** adv. [F or f. L (*spira* coil f. Gk)]

spirant /'spaɪərənt/ adj. uttered with a continuous expulsion of the breath. —n. a spirant consonant. [f. L *spirare* breathe]

spire n. a tapering structure like a tall cone or pyramid rising above a tower (ill. CHURCH); any tapering body. [OE]

spirit /'spɪrɪt/ n. **1.** a person's animating principle or intelligence. **2.** a person's soul. **3.** a person from an intellectual or moral viewpoint. **4.** a disembodied person or incorporeal being. **5.** a person's mental or moral nature. **6.** an attitude or mood. **7.** courage, self-assertion, vivacity. **8.** (in *pl.*) a state of mind. **9.** a tendency prevailing at a particular time etc. **10.** a principle or purpose underlying the form of a law etc. **11.** a volatile liquid produced by distillation; purified alcohol; (usu. in *pl.*) a strong distilled alcoholic liquor, e.g. whisky or gin. —v.t. to convey rapidly or mysteriously. —**in spirit**, inwardly. **spirit gum**, a quick-drying gum for attaching false hair. **spirit lamp**, a lamp burning methylated or other volatile spirit instead of oil. **spirit-level** n. a device consisting of a sealed glass tube nearly filled with liquid and containing an air-bubble, used to test levelness by the position of this bubble. Such devices were used on telescopes in the 17th c., but did not become a carpenter's and builder's tool until the mid-19th c. [f. AF f. L *spiritus* breath (as SPIRANT)]

spirited adj. **1.** full of spirit, lively, courageous. **2.** having a specified spirit or disposition (*poor-spirited*). —**spiritedly** adv. [f. prec.]

spiritless adj. lacking vigour or courage. [f. SPIRIT + -LESS]

spiritual /'spɪrɪtjʊəl/ adj. of or concerned with the spirit, not physical or worldly; of the Church or religion. —n. a religious song especially of American Blacks. —**spirituality** /-'ælɪtɪ/ n., **spiritually** adv. [f. OF f. L (as SPIRIT)]

spiritualism /'spɪrɪtjʊəlɪz(ə)m/ n. the belief that the spirits of the dead communicate with the living, especially through mediums (see below). —**spiritualist** n., **spiritualistic** /-'lɪstɪk/ adj. [f. prec.]
Belief that spirits of the dead can and do communicate with the living is very ancient and is an element in most primitive and some higher religions. Saul clandestinely consulted the woman of Endor (1 Sam. 28) in order to speak with the dead prophet Samuel, but the Jewish prophets disapproved of the practice and this repugnance was maintained by Christianity. In 1848 three sisters, Fox by name, living in New York State, heard strange rappings in their home and devised a simple code which, they asserted, was answered by rappings in such a way as to prove that they were made by an intelligent being. The news caused a sensation, and from this the modern spiritualistic movement had its origin. Hitherto most Christians had believed that spirits were evil and invoked only to do harm; now it was proclaimed that they dwelt in lands far better than this world, and were continually progressing. The impulse to make psychic communication the basis of a new religion comes from the natural longing (particularly evident after the two World Wars) to know what happens to people after death. In England the Society for Psychical Research was founded in 1882 for objective investigation not only of communication with the dead but of visions, telepathy, hauntings, etc. Although mediums appear to have access (in varying degrees) to knowledge beyond the ordinary, how it comes to them is still a mystery; it may proceed from some deep activity of the human mind, and any postulated type of 'communication' remains a hypothesis formulated to explain such knowledge.

spirituous /'spɪrɪtjʊəs/ adj. alcoholic, distilled and not only fermented. [f. SPIRIT]

spit¹ v.t./i. (**-tt-**; *past & p.p.* **spat** or **spit**) **1.** to eject from the mouth; to eject saliva from the mouth; to do this as a gesture of contempt. **2.** to utter (oaths or threats etc.) vehemently. **3.** to make a noise as of spitting. **4.** (of a fire or gun etc.) to throw out with an explosion. **5.** (of rain) to fall lightly. —n. **1.** spittle. **2.** spitting. —**the (dead or very) spit**, a spitting image. **spit and polish**, a soldier's cleaning and polishing work. **spit it out**, (*colloq.*) to speak candidly or louder. **spitting image**, an exact counterpart or likeness. [OE, orig. imit.]

spit² n. **1.** a rod on which meat is fixed for roasting over a fire etc. **2.** a long narrow strip of land projecting into the sea. —v.t. (**-tt-**) to pierce (as) with a spit. [OE]

spit³ n. a spade's depth of earth. [f. OE *spittan* dig with spade, prob. rel. to SPIT²]

spite n. malicious desire to hurt, annoy, or frustrate another person. —v.t. to hurt or annoy etc. through spite. —**in spite of**, not being prevented by, regardless of. [f. OF (as DESPITE)]

spiteful adj. full of spite; showing or caused by spite. —**spitefully** adv., **spitefulness** n. [f. SPITE + -FUL]

spitfire n. a person of fiery temper.

Spitsbergen /ˈspɪtsbɜːgən/ an archipelago in the Arctic Ocean, north of Norway, under Norwegian sovereignty.

spittle /ˈspit(ə)l/ n. saliva, especially as ejected from the mouth. [f. SPIT¹]

spittoon /spɪˈtuːn/ n. a vessel for spitting into. [f. SPIT¹]

spiv n. a man, especially a flashily-dressed one, living from shady dealings rather than regular work. —**spivish** adj. [perh. f. dial. spiff, spiffy smartly dressed]

splash v.t./i. 1. to cause (liquid) to fly about in drops; to wet with such drops; (of liquid) to be splashed. 2. to move or fall with splashing. 3. to decorate with scattered patches of colour etc. 4. to display (news) prominently. 5. to spend (money) freely and ostentatiously. —n. 1. the act or sound of splashing. 2. a quantity of liquid splashed; a mark etc. made by splashing. 3. a patch of colour or light. 4. a striking or ostentatious display. 5. (colloq.) a small quantity of soda-water etc. (in a drink). —**make a splash**, to attract much attention. **splash-down** n. the alighting of a spacecraft on the sea. **splash out**, (colloq.) to spend money freely. —**splashy** adj. [alt. f. plash (prob. imit.)]

splashback n. a panel behind a sink etc. to protect a wall from splashes.

splatter v.t./i. to splash noisily; to spatter. —n. a noisy splashing sound. [imit.]

splay v.t./i. to spread apart; (of an opening) to have the sides diverging; to make (an opening) have divergent sides. —n. a surface at an oblique angle to another (ill. CHURCH). —adj. splayed. [f. DISPLAY]

spleen n. 1. an abdominal organ maintaining the proper condition of the blood. 2. moroseness, irritability. [f. OF esplen f. L f. Gk splēn]

spleenwort /ˈspliːnwət/ n. a fern of the genus Asplenium, formerly used as a remedy for disorders of the spleen.

splendid /ˈsplendɪd/ adj. 1. magnificent, displaying splendour. 2. (colloq.) excellent. —**splendidly** adv. [f. F or L (splendēre shine)]

splendiferous /splenˈdɪfərəs/ adj. (colloq.) splendid. [f. foll. + L ferre bear]

splendour /ˈsplendə(r)/ n. brilliance, magnificent display or appearance; grandeur. [f. AF or L (as SPLENDID)]

splenetic /splɪˈnetɪk/ adj. bad-tempered, peevish. —**splenetically** adv. [f. L (as SPLEEN)]

splenic /ˈspliːnɪk, ˈsple-/ adj. of or in the spleen. [f. F or L f. Gk (as SPLEEN)]

splice v.t. 1. to join pieces of (ropes) by interweaving strands. 2. to join (pieces of wood or tape etc.) in an overlapping position. 3. (colloq., esp. in pass.) to join in marriage. —n. a junction made by splicing. —**splice the main brace**, (Naut.) to serve a free drink of spirits. [prob. f. MDu. splissen; orig. unkn.]

splint n. 1. a strip of wood etc. bound to a limb, especially to keep a broken bone in the right position while it heals. 2. a tumour or bony excrescence on the inside of a horse's leg. 3. (also **splint-bone**) either of two small bones in a horse's foreleg lying behind and close to the cannon-bone (ill. HORSE); the human fibula. —v.t. to secure with a splint. [f. MDu. or MLG, = metal plate or pin (rel. to foll.)]

splinter n. a small sharp piece broken off wood or glass etc. —v.t./i. to break or become broken into splinters. —**splinter group**, a small (esp. political) group that has broken away from a larger one. —**splintery** adj. [f. MDu., rel. to prec.]

split v.t./i. (-tt-; past & p.p. **split**) 1. to break or become broken into parts, especially lengthwise or with the grain or the plane of cleavage. 2. to divide into parts; to divide and share. 3. to remove or be removed by breaking or dividing. 4. to divide or become divided into disagreeing or hostile parties. 5. to cause fission of (an atom). 6. (slang) to betray secrets, to inform (on a person). —n. 1. an act or the result of splitting. 2. a disagreement or schism. 3. a dish made of bananas etc. split open, with ice-cream etc. 4. (in pl.) the feat of sitting down or leaping with the legs widely spread out at right angles to the body. 5. a half bottle of mineral water; a half glass of liquor. —**be splitting**, (of the head) to feel acute pain from a headache. **split hairs**, see HAIR. **split infinitive**, one with an adverb etc. inserted between to and the verb. **split-level** adj. built or having components at more than one level. **split pea**, a pea dried and split for cooking. **split personality**, a change of personality as in schizophrenia. **split pin**, a pin or bolt etc. held in place by the splaying of its split end. **split second**, a very brief moment. **split one's sides**, to laugh heartily. **splitting headache**, a very severe headache. **split up**, to

separate; (of a married couple etc.) to cease living together. [orig. Naut., f. MDu.]

splodge var. of SPLOTCH.

splosh v.t./i. (colloq.) to splash. —n. (colloq.) a splash. [imit.]

splotch n. a daub, blot, or smear. —v.t. to daub, to blot, to smear. [perh. f. SPOT + obs. plotch blotch]

splurge n. an ostentatious display or effort. —v.i. to make a splurge. [prob. imit.]

splutter v.t./i. 1. to make a rapid series of spitting sounds. 2. to speak or utter rapidly or incoherently. —n. a spluttering sound. [f. SPUTTER by assoc. with splash]

Spode /spəʊd/ n. a kind of fine pottery or porcelain named after the English potter Josiah Spode (1754-1827), its original maker.

spoil v.t./i. (past & p.p. **spoilt** or **spoiled**) 1. to make or become useless or unsatisfactory. 2. to diminish a person's enjoyment of. 3. to harm the character of (a person) by indulgence. 4. (of food etc.) to go bad. —n. (in sing. or pl.) 1. plunder, stolen goods, especially those taken by a victor. 2. profits; advantages accruing from success or an official position. —**be spoiling for**, to seek eagerly or aggressively. **spoil-sport** n. one who spoils other's enjoyment. **spoils system**, (US) the practice of giving public offices to adherents of the successful party. [f. OF f. L spoliare (spolium plunder)]

spoiler n. a device on an aircraft to retard it by interrupting the air-flow (ill. FLIGHT); a similar device on a vehicle to prevent it from being lifted off the ground at speed. [f. SPOIL]

spoke¹ n. 1. each of the bars or rods running from the hub to the rim of a wheel. 2. a rung of a ladder. —v.t. 1. to provide with spokes. 2. to obstruct (a wheel etc.) by thrusting a spoke in. —**put a spoke in a person's wheel**, to hinder or thwart his purpose. [OE (of SPIKE¹)]

spoke² past of SPEAK.

spoken p.p. of SPEAK. —adj. speaking in a specified way (soft-, well-spoken). [as SPEAK]

spokeshave /ˈspəʊkʃeɪv/ n. a tool for planing curved surfaces.

spokesman /ˈspəʊksmən/ n. (pl. **-men**) one who speaks on behalf of a group. —**spokeswoman** n.fem. [f. SPOKE² after craftsman etc.]

spoliation /spəʊlɪˈeɪʃ(ə)n/ n. plundering, pillage. [f. L (as SPOIL)]

spondee /ˈspɒndiː/ n. a metrical foot with two long or stressed syllables. —**spondaic** /-ˈdeɪɪk/ adj. [f. OF or L f. Gk (spondē libation, as being characteristic of music accompanying libations)]

sponge /spʌndʒ/ n. 1. a water animal of the phylum Porifera, with a porous body-wall and a tough elastic skeleton. 2. this skeleton, or a piece of a substance of similar texture, used for washing, cleaning, or padding things. 3. a thing of spongelike absorbency or consistency. 4. a sponge-cake. 5. the act of sponging; a wash with a sponge. —v.t./i. 1. to wipe or wash with a sponge. 2. to live parasitically on others, to scrounge. —**sponge-bag** n. a waterproof bag for toilet articles. **sponge-cake** (or **-pudding**) n. a light cake (or pudding) of spongelike consistency. **sponge rubber**, rubber made porous like a sponge. **throw in** or **up the sponge**, to abandon a contest, to admit defeat. [OE f. L f. Gk spoggia]

spongeable /ˈspʌndʒəb(ə)l/ adj. that may be sponged. [f. prec.]

sponger /ˈspʌndʒə(r)/ n. a person who habitually sponges on others. [f. SPONGE]

spongy /ˈspʌndʒɪ/ adj. like sponge in texture or absorbency, soft and springy. —**spongily** adv., **sponginess** n. [f. SPONGE]

sponson /ˈspɒns(ə)n/ n. 1. a projection from the side of a warship or tank to enable a gun to be trained forward and aft. 2. an air-filled structure fitted along the gunwale of a canoe to make it more stable and buoyant. 3. a short winglike projection from the hull of a seaplane, to stabilize it on water. [orig. unkn.]

sponsor /ˈspɒnsə(r)/ n. 1. a person who makes himself responsible for another, presents a candidate for baptism, introduces legislation, or contributes to a charity in return for a specified activity by another. 2. an advertiser who pays for a sporting event or a broadcast which includes an advertisement of his goods. —v.t. to be a sponsor for. —**sponsorial** /spɒnˈsɔːrɪəl/ adj., **sponsorship** n. [L (spondēre promise solemnly)]

spontaneous /spɒnˈteɪnɪəs/ *adj.* acting, done, or occurring without external cause or incitement; resulting from natural impulse; (of a style or manner) gracefully natural and unconstrained. —**spontaneous combustion,** ignition of a substance by chemical changes within it, not by flame etc. from an external source. **spontaneity** /spɒntəˈniːɪtɪ/ *n.*, **spontaneously** *adv.* [f. L (*sponte* of one's own accord)]

spoof *n.* (*colloq.*) a parody; a hoax, a swindle. —*v.t.* (*colloq.*) to parody; to hoax, to swindle. [invented by A. Roberts, English comedian (d. 1933)]

spook *n.* (*colloq.*) a ghost. [Du.; orig. unkn.]

spooky *adj.* (*colloq.*) ghostly, eerie. —**spookiness** *n.* [f. SPOOK]

spool *n.* a reel on which something is wound, e.g. yarn or magnetic tape; the revolving cylinder of an angler's reel. —*v.t.* to wind on a spool. [f. OF *espole* or MLG or MDu.; orig. unkn.]

spoon *n.* **1.** a utensil with an oval or round bowl and a handle, for conveying food (especially liquid) to the mouth or for stirring or measuring things. **2.** a spoon-shaped thing. **3.** (in full **spoon-bait**) a revolving spoon-shaped metal fish-lure. —*v.t./i.* **1.** to take or lift with a spoon. **2.** to hit (a ball) feebly upwards. **3.** (*colloq.*) to behave in an amorous way. —**spoon-feed** *v.t.* to feed (a baby etc.) with a spoon; to give such extensive help etc. to (a person) that they need make no effort for himself. —**spoonful** *n.* [OE, = chip of wood]

spoonbill *n.* a wading-bird of the family Plataleidae with a broad flat tip of the bill.

spoonerism /ˈspuːnərɪz(ə)m/ *n.* a transposition, usually accidental, of the initial letter etc. of two or more words. [f. W. A. *Spooner*, English scholar (d. 1930), reputed to have made such errors in speaking]

spoor *n.* an animal's track or scent. [Afrik. f. MDu.]

sporadic /spəˈrædɪk/ *adj.* occurring only here and there or occasionally. —**sporadically** *adv.* [f. L f. Gk (*sporas* scattered)]

spore *n.* each of the minute structures that are the reproductive cell of cryptogamous plants; a resistant form of bacterium etc. [f. Gk *spora* sowing, seed]

sporran /ˈspɒrən/ *n.* a pouch worn in front of a kilt. [f. Gael. f. L (as PURSE)]

sport *n.* **1.** an athletic (especially outdoor) activity (see ill. pp. 802-3); any game or pastime; an outdoor pastime such as hunting or fishing. **2.** such activities or pastimes collectively; the world of sport; (in *pl.*) a meeting for competing in sports, especially athletics. **3.** amusement, diversion, fun. **4.** (*colloq.*) a good fellow, a sportsmanlike person. **5.** an animal or plant differing from the normal type. —*v.t./i.* **1.** to play, to amuse oneself. **2.** to wear or display ostentatiously. —**in sport,** jestingly. **make sport of,** to ridicule. **sports car,** a low-built fast car. **sports coat** or **jacket,** a man's jacket for informal wear. [f. DISPORT]

sporting *adj.* **1.** interested or concerned in sport. **2.** sportsmanlike. —**a sporting chance,** some possibility of success. [f. SPORT]

sportive *adj.* playful. —**sportively** *adv.* [f. SPORT]

sportsman *n.* (*pl.* **-men**) **1.** a person fond of sport. **2.** a person who behaves fairly and generously. —**sportsman-like** *adj.,* **sportsmanship** *n.,* **sportswoman** *n.fem.*

sporty *adj.* (*colloq.*) **1.** fond of sport. **2.** rakish, showy. —**sportily** *adv.,* **sportiness** *n.* [f. SPORT]

spot *n.* **1.** a small roundish area or mark differing in colour or texture etc. from the surface it is on; a blemish or stain; a pimple. **2.** a particular place, a definite locality. **3.** (*colloq.*) one's (regular) position in an organization or programme etc. **4.** a small quantity of something; a drop (of liquid). **5.** a spotlight. —*v.t./i.* (**-tt-**) **1.** to mark with a spot or spots; to become marked thus. **2.** to make spots, to rain slightly. **3.** (*colloq.*) to pick out, to recognize, to catch sight of; to watch for and take note of (trains, talent, etc.). **4.** (in *p.p.*) marked or decorated with spots. —**in a** (**tight** etc.) **spot,** (*colloq.*) in difficulty. **on the spot,** at the scene of an action or event; (*colloq.*) in a position such that a response or action is required. **spot cash,** money paid immediately on a sale. **spot check,** a sudden or random check. **spot-on** *adj.* (*colloq.*) precise, on target. **spotted dick,** a suet pudding containing currants. **spot welding,** welding between points of metal surfaces in contact. —**spotter** *n.* [perh. f. MDu. or LG, = small piece]

spotless *adj.* free from stain or blemish, perfectly clean. [f. SPOT + -LESS]

spotlight *n.* **1.** a beam of light directed on a small area; a lamp projecting this. **2.** full attention or publicity. —*v.t.* **1.** to direct a spotlight on. **2.** to make conspicuous, to draw attention to.

spotty *adj.* **1.** marked with spots. **2.** patchy, irregular. —**spottily** *adv.,* **spottiness** *n.* [f. SPOT]

spouse /spaʊs/ *n.* a husband or wife. [f. OF f. L *sponsus, sponsa* p.p. of *spondēre* betroth]

spout *n.* **1.** a projecting tube or lip through which liquid etc. is poured or issues from a teapot, jug, roof-gutter, fountain, etc. **2.** a jet or column of liquid etc. —*v.t./i.* **1.** to discharge or issue forcefully or in a jet. **2.** to utter in a declamatory manner. —**up the spout,** (*slang*) useless, ruined; in trouble; pawned. [f. MDu. (imit.)]

sprain *v.t.* to injure (a joint or its muscles or ligaments) by wrenching it violently. —*n.* such an injury [orig. unkn.]

sprang *past* of SPRING.

sprat *n.* a small sea-fish (*Sprattus sprattus*). [OE]

sprawl *v.t./i.* **1.** to sit, lie, or fall with the limbs flung out or in an ungainly way; to spread (one's limbs) thus. **2.** to be of an irregular or straggling form. —*n.* a sprawling position, movement, or mass. [OE]

spray[1] *n.* **1.** water or other liquid flying in very small drops. **2.** a liquid preparation to be applied in this way with an atomizer etc.; a device for such an application. —*v.t.* to send out (a liquid) in very small drops; to sprinkle thus; to sprinkle (plants etc.) thus with insecticides. —**spray-gun** *n.* a gunlike device for spraying paint etc. —**sprayer** *n.* [perh. rel. to MDu. *spra(e)yen* sprinkle]

spray[2] *n.* **1.** a single shoot or branch with its leaves, twigs, and flowers. **2.** a bunch of cut flowers etc. arranged decoratively. **3.** an ornament in similar form. [orig. unkn.]

spread /spred/ *v.t./i.* (*past & p.p.* **spread**) **1.** to open out, to extend the surface of, to unroll or unfold; to cause to cover a larger surface, to display thus. **2.** to have a wide or specified extent; to become longer or wider. **3.** to cover the surface of, to apply as a layer; to be able to be spread. **4.** to make or become widely known or felt. **5.** to distribute or become distributed over an area or period. —*n.* **1.** spreading, being spread. **2.** a thing's extent, expanse, or breadth. **3.** expansion; increased bodily girth. **4.** the range of prices, rates, etc. **5.** (*colloq.*) a lavish meal. **6.** a sweet or savoury paste for spreading on bread etc. **7.** a bedspread. **8.** printed matter spread across more than one column. —**spread eagle,** a figure of an eagle with the legs and wings extended, as an emblem. **spread-eagle** *v.t.* to place (a person) in a position with the arms and legs spread out; to defeat utterly. **spread oneself,** to be lavish or discursive. [OE]

spree *n.* a lively outing, especially where one spends money freely; a bout of fun or drinking etc. [orig unkn.]

sprig *n.* **1.** a small branch, a shoot. **2.** an ornament resembling this, especially on fabric. **3.** (usu. *derog.*) a young man. —*v.t.* (**-gg-**) to ornament (fabric etc.) with sprigs. [f. or rel. to LG *sprick*]

sprightly /ˈspraɪtlɪ/ *adj.* lively, full of energy; brisk. —**sprightliness** *n.* [f. SPRITE]

spring *v.t./i.* (*past* **sprang**; *p.p.* **sprung**) **1.** to jump, to move rapidly or suddenly, especially in a single movement. **2.** to originate or arise (from ancestors or a source etc.). **3.** to produce, develop, or operate suddenly or unexpectedly. **4.** to rouse (game) from an earth or covert; to contrive the escape of (a prisoner etc.). **5.** (of wood etc.) to become warped or split. **6.** (usu. in *p.p.*) to provide with springs. —*n.* **1.** the act of springing, a jump. **2.** elasticity. **3.** a device (usually of bent or coiled metal) that reverts to its original position after being compressed, tightened, or stretched, used especially to drive clockwork or (in groups) to make a seat etc. more comfortable. **4.** the season in which vegetation begins to appear, from March to May in the northern hemisphere. **5.** a place where water or oil comes up naturally from the ground; a basin or flow so formed. **6.** a motive or origin of an action or custom etc. —**spring balance,** one that measures weight by the tension of a spring. **spring chicken,** a young fowl for eating; a youthful person. **spring-clean** *n.* a thorough cleaning of a house, especially in spring; (*v.t.*) to clean thus. **spring onion,** a young onion eaten raw. **spring roll,** a Chinese snack consisting of a pancake filled with vegetables and fried in the shape of a roll. **spring tide,** a tide of maximum height. **spring up,** to come into being, to appear. **sprung rhythm,** a poetic rhythm approximating to speech, each foot having one stressed syllable followed by a varying number of unstressed. The term was invented by G. M. Hopkins to describe his own idiosyncratic poetic metre. [OE]

Sports and Games

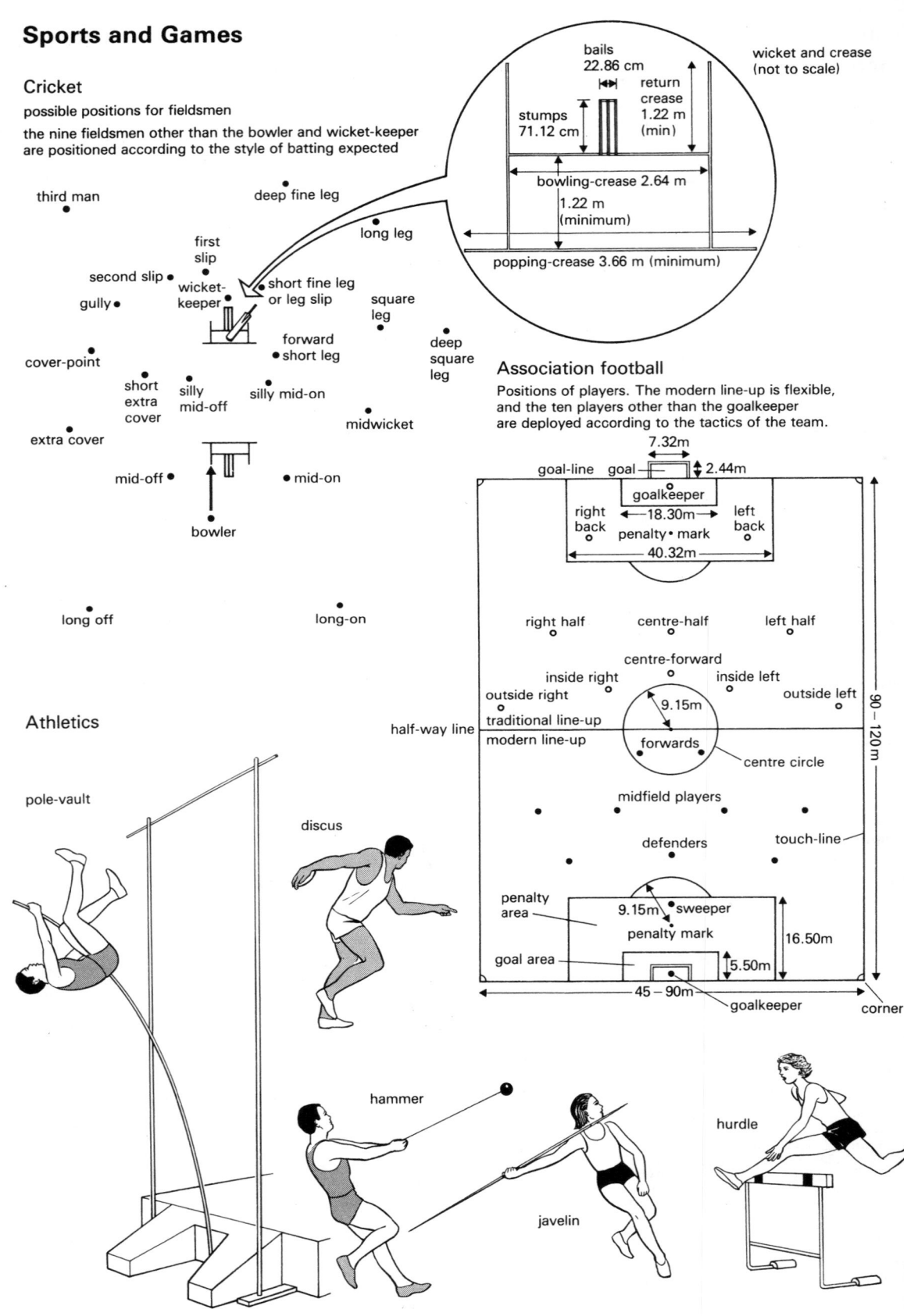

Cricket

possible positions for fieldsmen

the nine fieldsmen other than the bowler and wicket-keeper are positioned according to the style of batting expected

third man

deep fine leg

first slip

long leg

second slip

wicket-keeper

short fine leg or leg slip

gully

square leg

cover-point

deep square leg

short extra cover

silly mid-off

silly mid-on

forward short leg

extra cover

midwicket

mid-off

mid-on

bowler

long off

long-on

bails 22.86 cm

return crease 1.22 m (min)

wicket and crease (not to scale)

stumps 71.12 cm

bowling-crease 2.64 m

1.22 m (minimum)

popping-crease 3.66 m (minimum)

Association football

Positions of players. The modern line-up is flexible, and the ten players other than the goalkeeper are deployed according to the tactics of the team.

7.32m

goal-line   goal   2.44m

goalkeeper

right back   18.30m   left back

penalty • mark

40.32m

right half   centre-half   left half

centre-forward

inside right   inside left

outside right   9.15m   outside left

half-way line   traditional line-up

modern line-up

forwards

centre circle

midfield players

defenders   touch-line

penalty area   9.15m   • sweeper

penalty mark

goal area   16.50m

5.50m

45 – 90m   goalkeeper   corner

90 – 120m

Athletics

pole-vault

discus

hammer

javelin

hurdle

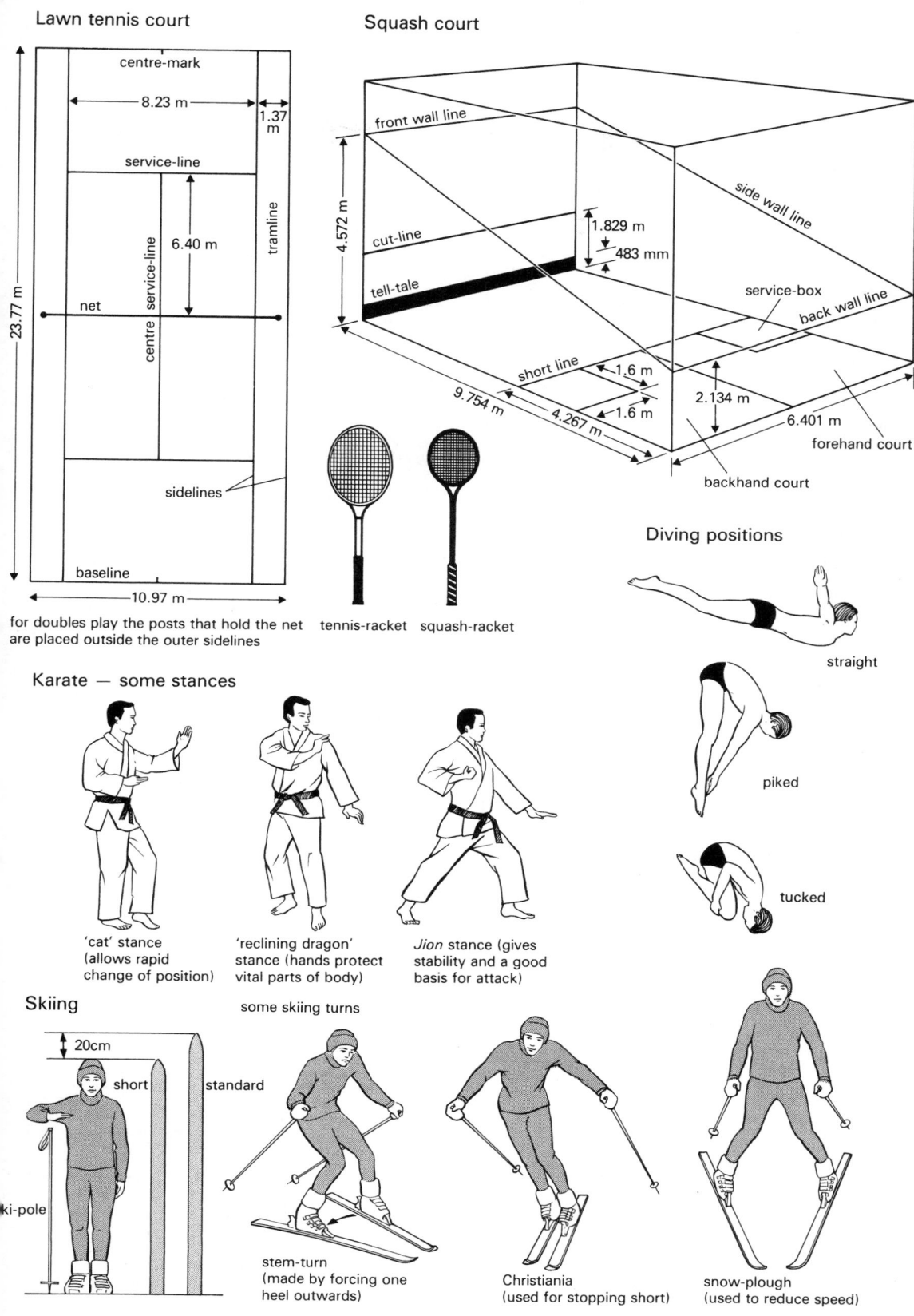

Lawn tennis court

centre-mark

8.23 m

1.37 m

service-line

6.40 m

tramline

23.77 m

centre service-line

net

centre service-line

sidelines

baseline

10.97 m

for doubles play the posts that hold the net are placed outside the outer sidelines

tennis-racket   squash-racket

Squash court

front wall line

4.572 m

cut-line

tell-tale

1.829 m

483 mm

side wall line

service-box

back wall line

short line

1.6 m

1.6 m

2.134 m

9.754 m

4.267 m

6.401 m

forehand court

backhand court

Diving positions

straight

piked

tucked

Karate — some stances

'cat' stance (allows rapid change of position)

'reclining dragon' stance (hands protect vital parts of body)

Jion stance (gives stability and a good basis for attack)

Skiing

20cm

short   standard

ski-pole

some skiing turns

stem-turn (made by forcing one heel outwards)

Christiania (used for stopping short)

snow-plough (used to reduce speed)

springboard *n.* a springy board giving an impetus in leaping or diving etc.; a source of impetus.

springbok /ˈsprɪŋbɒk/ *n.* **1.** a South African gazelle (*Antidorcas marsupialis*) with the habit of springing in play or when alarmed. **2. Springboks,** a South African national sporting team or touring party. [Afrik., f. Du. *springen* spring, *bok* antelope]

springer *n.* **1.** a small spaniel of a breed used to spring game. **2.** the part of an arch where the curve begins; the lowest stone of this (ill. BUILDING TECHNIQUES). [f. SPRING]

springtail *n.* a wingless insect of the order Collembola, leaping by means of a springlike caudal part.

springtime *n.* the season of spring.

springy *adj.* elastic, springing back quickly when squeezed or stretched. —**springily** *adv.*, **springiness** *n.* [f. SPRING]

sprinkle *v.t.* **1.** to scatter in small drops or particles. **2.** to scatter small drops etc. on (a surface). **3.** to distribute in small amounts. —*n.* sprinkling; a light shower. [perh. f. MDu. *sprenkelen*]

sprinkler *n.* a device for sprinkling water. [f. prec.]

sprinkling *n.* a small thinly distributed number or amount. [as prec.]

sprint *v.t./i.* to run at full speed, especially over a short distance. —*n.* such a run; a similar spell of maximum effort in swimming, cycling, etc. —**sprinter** *n.* [f. ON & Icel. *spretta;* orig. unkn.]

sprit *n.* a small diagonal spar from a mast to the upper outer corner of a sail. [OE *sprēot* pole; rel. to SPROUT]

sprite *n.* an elf, fairy, or goblin. [f. *sprit,* var. of SPIRIT]

spritely /ˈspraɪtlɪ/ *adj.* (*US*) = SPRIGHTLY.

spritsail /ˈsprɪts(ə)l/ *n.* a sail extended by a sprit; a sail extended by a yard set under the bowsprit (ill. SAILING-SHIPS).

sprocket /ˈsprɒkɪt/ *n.* each of the several teeth on a wheel engaging with the links of a chain. [orig. unkn.]

sprout *v.t./i.* to begin to grow or appear, to put forth shoots; to produce thus. —*n.* **1.** shoot of a plant. **2.** a Brussels sprout (see BRUSSELS). [OE]

spruce[1] /spruːs/ *adj.* neat in dress and appearance, smart. —*v.t./i.* to make or become spruce. —**sprucely** *adv.*, **spruceness** *n.* [perh. f. foll. in sense 'Prussian']

spruce[2] /spruːs/ *n.* a conifer of the genus *Picea* with dense conical foliage (ill. TREES); its wood. [alt. f. obs. *Pruce* Prussia]

sprung *p.p.* of SPRING.

spry /spraɪ/ *adj.* (*compar.* **spryer**; *superl.* **spryest**) lively, nimble. —**spryly** *adv.*, **spryness** *n.* [orig. unkn.]

spud *n.* **1.** a small narrow spade for weeding. **2.** (*slang*) a potato. —*v.t.* (**-dd-**) to dig with a spud. [orig. unkn.]

spume *n.* froth, foam. —*v.i.* to foam. —**spumy** *adj.* [f. OF or L *spuma*]

spun *p.p.* of SPIN.

spunk *n.* **1.** touchwood. **2.** (*colloq.*) mettle, spirit. **3.** (*slang*) semen. —**spunky** *adj.* [orig. unkn.]

spur *n.* **1.** a device with a small spike or spiked wheel attached to a rider's heel for urging a horse forward. **2.** a stimulus, an incentive. **3.** a spur-shaped thing, especially the hard projection on a cock's leg; a projection from a mountain or mountain range; a branch road or railway. —*v.t./i.* (**-rr-**) **1.** to prick (a horse) with a spur. **2.** to incite or stimulate; to urge on. **3.** (esp. in *p.p.*) to provide with spurs. —**on the spur of the moment** on a momentary impulse. [OE]

spurge *n.* a plant of the genus *Euphorbia*, with an acrid milky juice. [f. OF *espurge* (*espurgier* f. L, as EXPURGATE)]

spurious /ˈspjʊərɪəs/ *adj.* not genuine, not what it purports to be. —**spuriously** *adv.* [f. L *spurius,* orig. = illegitimate]

spurn *v.t.* to reject with disdain, to treat with contempt; to repel with one's foot. [OE, as SPUR]

spurt *v.t./i.* **1.** to gush, to send out (liquid) suddenly. **2.** to increase speed suddenly. —*n.* **1.** a sudden gush. **2.** a sudden increase in speed; a short burst of activity. [orig. unkn.]

sputnik /ˈspʊtnɪk, ˈspʌ-/ *n.* a Russian artificial satellite orbiting the Earth. The first such satellite was launched on 4 Oct. 1957. [Russ., = travelling companion]

sputter *v.t./i.* to splutter, to make a series of quick explosive sounds. —*n.* a sputtering sound. [f. Du. *sputteren* (imit.)]

sputum /ˈspjuːtəm/ *n.* (*pl.* **sputa**) saliva; expectorated matter, especially as used to diagnose disease. [L, p.p. of *spuere* spit]

spy /spaɪ/ *n.* a person secretly collecting and reporting information on the activities or movements of an enemy or competitor etc.; a person keeping a secret watch on others. —*v.t./i.* **1.** to discern, especially by careful observation. **2.** to act as a spy; to keep watch secretly. **3.** to pry. [f. OF *espier* espy]

spyglass *n.* a small telescope.

spyhole *n.* a peep-hole.

sq. *abbr.* square.

squab /skwɒb/ *n.* **1.** a short fat person. **2.** a young (unfledged) pigeon or other bird. **3.** a stuffed seat or cushion, especially as part (usually the back) of a seat in a motor car. —*adj.* short and fat, squat. [orig. unkn.; cf. obs. *quab* shapeless thing]

squabble /ˈskwɒb(ə)l/ *n.* a petty or noisy quarrel. —*v.i.* to engage in a squabble. [prob. imit.]

squad /skwɒd/ *n.* a small group of people sharing a task etc., especially a small number of soldiers. [f. F *escouade* f. It. *squadra* (as SQUARE)]

squadron /ˈskwɒdrən/ *n.* an organized body of persons etc., especially a cavalry division of two troops; a detachment of warships employed on a particular service; a unit of the RAF with 10 to 18 aircraft. —**squadron leader,** an officer commanding an RAF squadron, next below wing commander. [f. It. *squadrone* (as prec.)]

squalid /ˈskwɒlɪd/ *adj.* **1.** dirty and unpleasant, especially because of neglect or poverty. **2.** morally degrading. —**squalidly** *adv.* [f. L (*squalēre* be rough or dirty)]

squall /skwɔːl/ *n.* **1.** a sudden or violent wind-storm, especially with rain or snow or sleet. **2.** a discordant cry, a scream (especially of a baby). —*v.t./i.* to utter (with) a squall; to scream. —**squally** *adj.* [prob. f. SQUEAL, assoc. with *bawl*]

squalor /ˈskwɒlə(r)/ *n.* a squalid state. [L (as SQUALID)]

squander /ˈskwɒndə(r)/ *v.t.* to spend wastefully. [orig. unkn.]

square *n.* **1.** a rectangle with four equal sides (ill. SHAPES). **2.** an object or arrangement of (approximately) this shape. **3.** an open usually four-sided area surrounded by buildings. **4.** (in astrology) the aspect of two planets 90° apart, regarded as having an unfavourable influence. **5.** the product obtained when a number is multiplied by itself. **6.** an L- or T-shaped instrument for obtaining or testing right angles. **7.** (*slang*) a conventional or old-fashioned person. —*adj.* **1.** having the shape of a square. **2.** having or in the form of a right angle; at right angles, 90° apart; angular, not round. **3.** of or using units that express the measure of an area; (of a unit of measure) equal to the area of a square having each side one specified unit in length. **4.** level, parallel. **5.** properly arranged, settled; (also **all square**) not in debt, with no money owed; (of scores etc.) balanced, equal. **6.** fair and honest. **7.** direct, uncompromising. **8.** (*slang*) conventional, or old-fashioned. —*adv.* squarely; directly; fairly, honestly. —*v.t./i.* **1.** to make right-angled. **2.** to mark with squares. **3.** to multiply (a number) by itself. **4.** to place evenly or squarely. **5.** to make or be consistent. **6.** to settle or pay (a bill etc.); (*colloq.*) to pay or bribe (a person); to make the scores of (a match etc.) equal. —**back to square one,** (*colloq.*) back to the starting-point with no progress made. **on the square,** (*colloq.*) honest, honestly; fair, fairly. **out of square,** not at right angles. **square-bashing** *n.* (*slang*) military drill on a barrack-square. **square the circle,** to construct a square equal in area to a given circle; to do what is impossible. **square dance,** a dance with usually four couples facing inwards from four sides. **square deal,** a fair bargain or treatment. **square leg,** (in cricket) the position of the fieldsman at some distance on the batsman's leg-side and nearly opposite the stumps (ill. SPORTS). **square meal,** a substantial and satisfying meal. **square-rigged** *adj.* with the principal sails at right angles to the length of the ship. **square root,** a number that multiplied by itself gives a specified number. **square up,** to settle an account etc. **square up to,** to move towards (a person) in a fighting attitude; to face and tackle (a difficulty) resolutely. —**squarely** *adv.*, **squareness** *n.* [f. OF *esquar(r)e* ult. f. L *quadra* square.]

squash[1] /skwɒʃ/ *v.t./i.* **1.** to crush, to squeeze or become squeezed flat or into pulp. **2.** to pack tightly, to crowd, to squeeze into a small space. **3.** to suppress. **4.** to silence (a person) with a crushing reply, etc. —*n.* **1.** a crowd of people squashed together; a crowded state. **2.** a sound (as) of something being squashed. **3.** a drink made of crushed fruit. **4.** squash rackets (see separate entry). —**squashy** *adj.* [alt. f. QUASH]

squash² /skwɒʃ/ *n.* a trailing annual plant of the genus *Cucurbita;* a gourd of this. [f. Narraganset]

squash rackets a game played with rackets and a small soft ball in a closed court (ill. SPORTS). It is derived from the game of rackets (see entry), and originated at Harrow School in England, the word *squash* being derived from the softer hollow 'squashy' ball used.

squat /skwɒt/ *v.t./i.* (-**tt**-) **1.** to sit on one's heels, or on the ground with the knees drawn up, or in a hunched position. **2.** to put into a squatting position. **3.** (*colloq.*) to sit down. **4.** to act as a squatter. —*adj.* **1.** short and thick, dumpy. **2.** squatting. —*n.* **1.** a squatting posture. **2.** a place occupied by squatters. **3.** being a squatter. [f. OF *esquatir* flatten]

squatter /ˈskwɒtə(r)/ *n.* **1.** a person who takes unauthorized possession of unoccupied premises etc. **2.** an Australian sheep-farmer. [f. SQUAT]

squaw *n.* a North American Indian woman or wife. [f. Narraganset]

squawk *n.* **1.** a loud harsh cry especially of a bird. **2.** a complaint. —*v.i.* to utter a squawk. [imit.]

squeak *n.* **1.** a short high-pitched cry or sound. **2.** (also **narrow squeak**) a narrow escape; a success barely attained. —*v.t./i.* **1.** to make a squeak. **2.** to utter shrilly. **3.** (with *through* or *by* etc.; *colloq.*) to pass or succeed narrowly. **4.** (*slang*) to turn informer. —**squeaker** *n.* [imit., of *squeal*, *shriek*]

squeaky *adj.* making a squeaking sound. —**squeakily** *adv.*, **squeakiness** *n.* [f. prec.]

squeal *n.* a prolonged shrill sound or cry. —*v.t./i.* **1.** to make a squeal. **2.** to utter with a squeal. **3.** (*slang*) to turn informer. **4.** (*slang*) to protest vociferously. [imit.]

squeamish /ˈskwiːmɪʃ/ *adj.* **1.** easily nauseated, disgusted, or shocked. **2.** over-scrupulous about principles. —**squeamishly** *adv.*, **squeamishness** *n.* [f. AF *escoymos*; orig. unkn.]

squeegee /skwiːˈdʒiː/ *n.* an instrument with a rubber edge or roller on a long handle, used to remove liquid from surfaces. —*v.t.* to treat with a squeegee. [f. *squeege*, strengthened form of foll.]

squeeze *v.t./i.* **1.** to exert pressure on from opposite or all sides. **2.** to treat this so as to extract moisture or juice; to extract (juice) by squeezing; to reduce the size of or alter the shape of by squeezing. **3.** to force into or through; to force one's way; to crowd. **4.** to produce by pressure or effort. **5.** to obtain by compulsion or strong urging; to extort money from; to harass thus. —*n.* **1.** squeezing, being squeezed. **2.** an affectionate clasp or hug. **3.** a small amount of liquid produced by squeezing. **4.** a crowd or crush; the pressure of this. **5.** hardship or difficulty caused by a shortage of money or time etc. **6.** restrictions on borrowing and investment during a financial crisis. [earlier *squise*, intensive of obs. *queise* (orig. unkn.)]

squelch *v.t./i.* **1.** to make a sucking sound as of treading in thick mud; to move with a squelching sound. **2.** to disconcert, to silence. —*n.* an act or sound of squelching. [imit.]

squib *n.* a small firework burning with a hissing sound and usually with a final explosion. —**damp squib**, an unsuccessful attempt to impress etc. [perh. imit.]

squid *n.* a ten-armed marine cephalopod especially of the genus *Loligo*. [orig. unkn.]

squiffy /ˈskwɪfɪ/ *adj.* (*slang*) slightly drunk. [orig. unkn.]

squiggle *n.* a short curling line, especially in handwriting. —**squiggly** *adj.* [imit.]

squill *n.* **1.** a plant of the genus *Scilla*, growing from a bulb, resembling a bluebell. **2.** a crustacean of the genus *Squilla*. [f. L f. Gk *skilla*]

squinch *n.* a straight or arched structure across the interior angle of a square tower to carry a dome etc. [var. of obs. *scunch* abbr. of SCUNCHEON]

squint *v.i.* **1.** to have the eyes turned in different directions; to have a squint. **2.** to look obliquely or with half-shut eyes or through a narrow opening. —*n.* **1.** the abnormality of an eye which does not turn to match the other's direction. **2.** a stealthy or sidelong glance; (*colloq.*) a glance, a look. **3.** a narrow opening in a church wall giving a view of the altar. —*adj.* (*colloq.*) askew. [f. *asquint* adv. (cf. Du. *schuinte* slant)]

squire *n.* **1.** a country gentleman, especially the chief landowner in a country district. **2.** a woman's escort or gallant. **3.** (*hist.*) a knight's attendant. **4.** (*joc.*, as a form of address to a man) sir. —*v.t.* (of a man) to attend or escort (a woman). [f. OF, = ESQUIRE]

squirearchy /ˈskwaɪərɑːkɪ/ *n.* landowners collectively, especially as having political or social influence. [f. prec., after *hierarchy* etc.]

squirm *v.i.* **1.** to wriggle, to writhe. **2.** to show or feel embarrassment or discomfiture. —*n.* a squirming movement. [imit.]

squirrel /ˈskwɪr(ə)l/ *n.* a bushy-tailed usually arboreal rodent of the family Sciuridae; its fur. —*v.t.* (-**ll**-) (with *away*) to hoard. [f. AF ult. f. Gk *skiouros* (*skia* shade, *oura* tail)]

squirt *v.t./i.* to eject (liquid etc.) in a jet; to be ejected thus. —*n.* **1.** a jet of water etc. **2.** a device for ejecting this. **3.** (*colloq.*) an insignificant self-assertive person. [imit.]

squish *n.* a slight squelching sound. —*v.i.* to move with a squish. —**squishy** *adj.* [imit.]

Sr *symbol* strontium.

Sr. *abbr.* **1.** Senior. **2.** Señor.

sr *abbr.* steradian.

Sri Lanka /srɪ ˈlæŋkə/ (formerly Ceylon) an island off the SE coast of India; pop. (1981) 14,800,001; official language, Sinhalese; capital, Colombo. The economy is largely dependent on exports of tea, rubber, and coconuts. A centre of Buddhist culture from the 3rd c. BC, the island was ruled by a strong native dynasty from the 12th c. but was successively dominated by the Portuguese, Dutch, and British from the 16th c. and finally annexed by the last in 1815. A Commonwealth State from 1948, the country became an independent republic in 1972, taking the name of Sri Lanka (= resplendent island). Its political stability has been continually threatened by trouble between the Sinhalese and Tamil parts of the population. —**Sri Lankan** *adj.* & *n.*

SRN *abbr.* State Registered Nurse.

SS *abbr.* **1.** Saints. **2.** steamship. **3.** (*hist.*) the Nazi special police force (G *Schutz-Staffel*).

SSE *abbr.* south-south-east.

SSR *abbr.* Soviet Socialist Republic.

SSW *abbr.* south-south-west.

St *abbr.* Saint.

St. *abbr.* Street.

st. *abbr.* stone.

stability /stəˈbɪlɪtɪ/ *n.* being stable. [as STABLE¹]

stabilize /ˈsteɪbɪlaɪz/ *v.t./i.* to make or become stable. —**stabilization** /-ˈzeɪʃ(ə)n/ *n.* [f. STABLE¹]

stabilizer *n.* a device to keep a ship, aircraft, or child's bicycle steady. [f. prec.]

stab *v.t./i.* (-**bb**-) **1.** to pierce or wound with a pointed tool or weapon; to aim a blow with such a weapon. **2.** to cause a sensation like being stabbed. **3.** to hurt or distress (a person or feelings etc.). —*n.* **1.** an act or the result of stabbing; a wound or harm. **2.** (*colloq.*) an attempt. —**stab in the back**, a treacherous or slanderous attack. [orig. unkn.]

stable¹ /ˈsteɪb(ə)l/ *adj.* firmly fixed or established, not easily moved or changed or destroyed or decomposed; resolute, constant. [f. AF f. L *stabilis* (*stare* stand)]

stable² /ˈsteɪb(ə)l/ *n.* **1.** a building in which horses are kept. **2.** a place where racehorses are kept and trained; the racehorses of a particular stable. **3.** persons or products etc. having a common origin or affiliation; such an origin or affiliation. —*v.t.* to put or keep (a horse) in a stable. —**stable-companion** or **-mate** *n.* a horse of the same stable; a member of the same organization. —**stably** *adv.* [f. OF f. L *stabulum* n. (*stare* stand)]

stabling /ˈsteɪblɪŋ/ *n.* accommodation for horses. [f. prec.]

staccato /stəˈkɑːtəʊ/ *adj.* & *adv.* (esp. *Mus.*) in a sharp disconnected manner, not running on smoothly. [It., p.p. of *staccare* (as DETACH)]

stack *n.* **1.** a pile or heap, especially in an orderly arrangement. **2.** a haystack. **3.** (*colloq.*) a large quantity. **4.** a chimney-stack (ill. HOUSES); a tall factory chimney; a chimney or funnel for smoke on a steamer etc.; a tall steel structure from which unwanted gas produced in association with oil is burnt off. **5.** a stacked group of aircraft. **6.** a library's store of books to which readers do not usually have direct access. **7.** a high detached rock, especially off the coast of Scotland (ill. COASTS). —*v.t.* **1.** to pile in a stack or stacks. **2.** to arrange (cards) secretly for cheating; to manipulate (circumstances etc.) to one's advantage. **3.** to cause (aircraft) to fly round the same point at different levels while waiting to land. [f. ON *stakkr* haystack]

stadium /ˈsteɪdɪəm/ *n.* an enclosed athletic or sports ground with tiers of seats for spectators. [L f. Gk *stadion*]

staff *n.* **1.** a stick or pole used as a weapon, support, or measuring-stick, or as a symbol of office. **2.** a body of officers assisting a commanding officer and concerned with an army, regiment, or fleet etc. as a whole. **3.** a group of persons by whom a business is carried on; those responsible to a manager or other person in authority. **4.** persons in authority within an organization (as distinct from pupils etc.); those engaged in administrative as distinct from manual work. **5.** (*pl.* also **staves**) (*Mus.*) the set of usually five parallel lines to indicate the pitch of notes by position (ill. MUSICAL NOTATION). —*v.t.* to provide (an institution etc.) with a staff. —**staff college**, a college where officers are trained for staff duties. **staff nurse**, a nurse ranking just below a sister. **staff officer**, a member of a military staff. [OE]

Staffordshire /ˈstæfədʃɪə(r)/ a county of central England. **Staffs.** *abbr.* Staffordshire.

stag *n.* **1.** a male deer. **2.** a person who seeks to buy new shares and sell at once for profit. —**stag-beetle** *n.* a beetle of the family Lucanidae with branched mandibles like antlers (ill. INSECTS). **stag-party** *n.* a party for men only. [perh. orig. = male animal in its prime (cf. ON *staggr* male bird)]

stage *n.* **1.** a point or period in the course of a development or process. **2.** a platform, especially a raised one on which plays etc. are performed before an audience (ill. THEATRE). **3.** the acting or theatrical profession; dramatic art or literature. **4.** a scene of action. **5.** a regular stopping-place on a route; the distance between two of these. **6.** a section of a space-rocket with a separate means of propulsion. —*v.t.* **1.** to present (a play etc.) on the stage. **2.** to organize and carry out. —**stage direction**, an instruction in a play about an actor's movement, the sounds to be heard, etc. **stage fright**, nervousness on facing an audience, especially for the first time. **stage-hand** *n.* a person handling scenery etc. in a theatre. **stage-manage** *v.t.* to be the stage-manager of; to arrange and control for effect. **stage-manager** *n.* the person responsible for lighting and mechanical arrangements etc. on a stage. **stage-struck** *adj.* strongly wishing to be an actor or actress. **stage whisper**, an aside, a loud whisper meant to be heard by others than the person addressed. [f. OF *estage* ult. f. L *stare* stand]

stage-coach *n.* a large horse-drawn closed coach that formerly ran regularly by stages between two places. Such coaches were used in England from the mid-17th c. and reached their heyday in the early 19th c. as roads improved; in the USA they were often the only method available for long-distance travel. By the mid-19th c. their use was lapsing as they were superseded by the newly developed railways.

stagecraft *n.* skill or experience in writing or staging plays.

stager *n.* (esp. **old stager**) an experienced person. [f. STAGE]

stagflation /stægˈfleɪʃ(ə)n/ *n.* a state of inflation without a corresponding increase of demand and employment. [f. STAGNATION + INFLATION]

stagger *v.t./i.* **1.** to walk or move unsteadily; to cause to do this. **2.** (of news etc.) to shock or confuse (a person). **3.** to arrange (events or hours of work etc.) so that they do not coincide. **4.** to arrange (objects) so that they are not in line. —*n.* a staggering movement; (in *pl.*) a disease, especially of horses and cattle, causing staggering. [f. ON (*staka* push, *staggr*)]

staggering *adj.* astonishing, bewildering. [f. prec.]

staghound *n.* a large hound used in hunting deer.

staging /ˈsteɪdʒɪŋ/ *n.* **1.** the presentation of a play etc. **2.** a platform or support, especially a temporary one; shelves for plants in a greenhouse. —**staging post**, a regular stopping-place, especially on an air route. [f. STAGE]

stagnant /ˈstægnənt/ *adj.* **1.** (of water etc.) motionless, not flowing, still and stale. **2.** showing no activity. —**stagnancy** *n.* [as foll.]

stagnate /stægˈneɪt/ *v.i.* to be or become stagnant. —**stagnation** *n.* [f. L *stagnare* (*stagnum* pool)]

stagy /ˈsteɪdʒɪ/ *adj.* theatrical in style or manner. [f. STAGE]

staid *adj.* of quiet and sober character or demeanour, sedate. [= *stayed*, p.p. of STAY¹]

stain *v.t.* **1.** to discolour or be discoloured by the action of a liquid sinking in. **2.** to spoil or damage (a reputation or character etc.). **3.** to colour (wood or glass etc.) with a substance that penetrates the material; to treat (a microscopic specimen) with a colouring agent. —*n.* **1.** an act or the result of staining. **2.** a blot or blemish. **3.** damage to a reputation etc. **4.** a substance used in staining. —**stained glass**, pieces of glass, either dyed or superficially coloured, set in a framework (usually of lead) to form decorative or

pictorial designs. The art began in the service of the Christian Church and is of Byzantine origin, but its highest achievements are seen in the west and north of Europe. [f. earlier *distain* f. OF *desteindre* (as DIS-, TINGE)]

stainless *adj.* **1.** without stains. **2.** not liable to stain. —**stainless steel**, steel containing much chromium, that does not rust or tarnish under oxidizing conditions because it is protected by the film of oxide which forms on its surface. [f. STAIN + -LESS]

stair *n.* each of a set of fixed indoor steps; (in *pl.*) a set of these (ill. HOUSES). —**stair-rod** *n.* a rod for securing a carpet in the angle between two steps. [OE]

staircase *n.* a flight of stairs and the supporting structure (ill. HOUSES); the part of a building containing this.

stairway *n.* a flight of stairs; the way up this.

stake *n.* **1.** a stout stick pointed at one end for driving into the ground as a support or marker etc.; (*hist.*) a post to which a person was tied to be burnt alive; their death as a punishment. **2.** the money etc. wagered on an event. **3.** an interest or concern, especially financial. **4.** (in *pl.*) the money offered as the prize in a horse-race; the race itself. —*v.t.* **1.** to secure or support with stakes. **2.** to mark (an area) with stakes. **3.** to establish (a claim). **4.** to wager (money etc. *on* an event). **5.** (*US colloq.*) to give financial or other support to. —**at stake**, wagered, risked, to be won or lost. **stake out**, to place under surveillance. [OE]

stakeholder *n.* a third party with whom money etc. wagered is deposited.

Stakhanovite /stəˈkɑːnəvaɪt/ *n.* one who is exceptionally hard-working and productive. The term was first applied to a worker in the USSR during the 1930s and 1940s whose productivity exceeded the norms and who thus earned special privileges and rewards. —**Stakhanovism** *n.* [f. A. G. *Stakhanov*, Russian coal-miner (d. 1977), who in 1935 produced a phenomenal amount of coal by a combination of new methods and great energy, an achievement publicized by the Soviet authorities in their campaign to increase industrial output]

stalactite /ˈstæləktaɪt/ *n.* an icicle-like deposit of calcium carbonate hanging from the roof of a cave etc. [f. Gk *stalaktos* dripping (*stalassō* drip)]

stalagmite /ˈstæləgmaɪt/ *n.* a deposit like a stalactite rising like a spike from the floor of a cave etc. [f. Gk *stalagma* a dripping (as prec.)]

stale *adj.* **1.** not fresh; musty, insipid, or otherwise the worse for age or use; trite or unoriginal. **2.** (of an athlete or musician etc.) having his ability impaired by excessive exertion or practice. —*v.t./i.* to make or become stale. —**stalely** *adv.*, **staleness** *n.* [perh. f. AF *estaler* come to a standstill]

stalemate *n.* **1.** the state of a chess-game counting as a draw, in which one player cannot move without going into check. **2.** a deadlock in proceedings. —*v.t.* **1.** to bring (a player) to a stalemate. **2.** to bring a deadlock. [f. obs. *stale* in same sense (prob. f. AF *estale* position) + MATE²]

Stalin /ˈstɑːlɪn/ the name adopted by Joseph Vissarionovich Dzhugashvili (1879–1953), Russian dictator. An early member of the Bolshevik Party, he was imprisoned in 1913 and released only after the start of the Russian Revolution, when he rose rapidly to become one of Lenin's right-hand men. After Lenin's death, Stalin won a long struggle with Trotsky for the leadership and went on to become sole dictator. His large-scale purges gravely weakened Russia and the country only just survived Hitler's attack in 1941, but under Stalin's leadership it eventually went on to win the titanic struggle on the Eastern Front. Stalin stayed in power until his death, following his policy of removing anyone whose power might threaten his own. He was later denounced by Khruschev.

Stalingrad /ˈstɑːlɪŋgræd/ a city of the USSR (since 1961 called Volgograd) on the River Volga, at which in a long and bitterly fought battle in 1942–3, during the Second World War, the German advance into Russia was turned back. The city was called Tsaritsyn until 1925, and Stalingrad from then until 1961. [f. prec.]

stalk¹ /stɔːk/ *n.* a stem, especially the main stem of a herbaceous plant or the slender stem supporting a leaf or flower or fruit etc.; a similar support of an organ etc. in animals. [prob. dim. of *stale* rung of ladder (OE)]

stalk² /stɔːk/ *v.t./i.* **1.** to pursue or approach (a wild animal or an enemy etc.) stealthily. **2.** to stride, to walk in a stately or imposing manner. —*n.* **1.** a stalking of game. **2.** an imposing gait. —**stalking-horse** *n.* a horse behind which a hunter hides; a pretext concealing one's real intentions or actions. —**stalker** n. [f. OE prob. rel. to STEAL]

stall[1] /stɔːl/ n. **1.** a stable or cowhouse; a compartment for one animal in this. **2.** a trader's booth in a market etc. **3.** a fixed seat in a choir or chancel, more or less enclosed at the back and sides. **4.** (usu. in pl.) each of the seats on the ground floor of a theatre (ill. THEATRE). **5.** a compartment for one person in a shower-bath, one horse at the start of a race, etc. **6.** the stalling of an engine or aircraft; the condition resulting from this. —v.t./i. **1.** (of a motor vehicle or its engine) to stop because of inadequate fuel-supply or overloading of the engine etc.; (of an aircraft) to get out of control because its speed is insufficient. **2.** to cause (an engine etc.) to stall. **3.** to put or keep (cattle etc.) in a stall or stalls. [OE]

stall[2] /stɔːl/ v.t./i. to play for time when being questioned etc.; to delay or obstruct (a person). [f. stall pickpocket's confederate, orig. = decoy, f. AF estale (as STALEMATE)]

stallion /ˈstæljən/ n. an uncastrated male horse. [OF estalon (as STALL[1])]

stalwart /ˈstɔːlwət/ adj. **1.** strongly built, sturdy. **2.** courageous; strong and faithful; resolute. —n. a stalwart person, especially a loyal uncompromising partisan. [OE, = place-worthy]

Stamboul /stæmˈbuːl/ an obsolete name for Istanbul.

stamen /ˈsteimən/ n. the male fertilizing organ of a flowering plant (ill. FLOWERS). [L, lit. = warp-thread]

stamina /ˈstæminə/ n. ability to endure prolonged physical or mental strain. [L, pl. of prec.]

stammer v.t./i. to speak with halting articulation, especially with pauses or rapid repetitions of the same syllable; to utter (words) thus. —n. an act or the habit of stammering. —**stammerer** n. [OE]

stamp v.t./i. **1.** to bring down (one's foot) heavily on the ground etc.; to crush or flatten thus; to walk with heavy steps. **2.** to impress (a pattern or mark etc.) on a surface; to impress (a surface) with a pattern or mark etc. **3.** to affix a postage or other stamp to. **4.** to assign a specific character to; to mark out. —n. **1.** an instrument for stamping things. **2.** a mark or design made by this. **3.** (in full **postage stamp**) a small adhesive piece of paper showing the amount paid, affixed to letters etc. to be posted (see below); a piece of paper impressed with an official mark as evidence of payment of a tax or fee, for affixing to a licence or deed etc.; a similar decorative piece sold in aid of a charity. **4.** a mark impressed on or a label etc. fixed to a commodity as evidence of its quality etc. **5.** an act or sound of stamping of the foot. **6.** a characteristic mark or quality. —**stamp-collector**, n. one who collects postage stamps as a hobby. **stamp-duty** n. a duty imposed on certain kinds of legal document. **stamping-ground** n. a favourite place of resort or action. **stamp on**, to impress on (the memory etc.); to suppress. **stamp out**, to produce by cutting out with a die etc.; to put an end to, to destroy. [= OHG stampfōn to pound (rel. to STEP)]
The world's first postage stamps were the penny black and twopence blue, issued by Great Britain in May 1840 and showing the head of Queen Victoria in profile. The system of their use was introduced on the initiative of Sir Rowland Hill (1795-1879).
The name stamp was originally applied to the marks stamped or impressed by the Post Office on letters, to state whether they were 'prepaid', 'unpaid', 'free', etc. When adhesive labels were introduced in 1840 and took the place of these marks they appear to have been called 'postage stamps' from the first, though the official name was 'postage label', and the marks which continued to be impressed by the Post Office to show the place and date of postage, and to obliterate the 'label' so that it could not be reused, became called 'postmarks'.

stampede /stæmˈpiːd/ n. a sudden hurried rush of cattle or people etc., especially in fright; an uncontrolled or unreasoning action by a large number of people. —v.t./i. to take part in a stampede; to cause to do this. [f. Sp. estampida (rel. to prec.)]

stance /stɑːns, stæns/ n. **1.** an attitude or position of the body. **2.** a standpoint, an attitude. [F f. It., = STANZA]

stanch /stɑːntʃ/ v.t. to stop the flow of (blood) etc.); to stop the flow from (a wound). [f. OF estanchier]

stanchion /ˈstɑːnʃ(ə)n/ n. an upright post or support; a device for confining cattle in a stall etc. [f. AF (as STANCE)]

stand v.t./i. (past & p.p. **stood** /stʊd/) **1.** to have, take, or maintain an upright position, especially on the feet or a base. **2.** to be situated. **3.** to place, to set upright. **4.** to be

of a specified height. **5.** to remain firm or valid, or in a specified condition. **6.** to move to and remain in a specified position; to take a specified attitude (lit. or fig.); (of ships) to hold a specified course. **7.** to maintain a position; to avoid falling, moving, or being moved; to remain stationary or unused. **8.** to undergo; to endure or tolerate. **9.** to provide at one's own expense. **10.** to act as. —n. **1.** a standing or stationary condition. **2.** a position taken up, an attitude adopted (lit. or fig.). **3.** resistance to attack or compulsion. **4.** a rack or pedestal etc. on which something may be placed. **5.** a table, booth, or other (often temporary) structure on which things are exhibited or sold. **6.** a standing-place for vehicles. **7.** a raised structure for persons to sit or stand on, e.g. at a sports ground. **8.** (US) a witness-box. **9.** a halt made by a touring-company etc. to give a performance or performances. **10.** (in cricket) a prolonged stay at the wicket by two batsmen. **11.** a group of growing trees etc. —**as it stands**, in its present condition; in the present circumstances. **stand by**, to stand ready for action; to stand near; to look without interfering; to uphold or support (a person); to adhere to (a promise etc.). **stand-by** n. (pl. -bys) a person or thing ready if needed in an emergency etc.; (esp. attrib.) a system of allocating spare seats on an aircraft to passengers who have not booked in advance. **stand corrected**, to accept that one was wrong. **stand down**, to withdraw from a position or candidacy. **stand for**, to represent; to be a candidate for (esp. public office); (colloq.) to tolerate. **stand one's ground**, not to yield. **stand in**, to deputize. **stand-in** n. a deputy or substitute, especially for a principal film actor or actress while the cameras and lighting for a scene are set. **stand off**, to move or keep away; to dispense temporarily with the services of (an employee). **stand-off half**, a half-back in Rugby football who forms a link between the scrum-half and the three-quarters. **stand-offish** adj. cold or distant in manner. **stand on**, to insist on, to observe scrupulously. **stand on one's own (two) feet**, to be self-reliant or independent. **stand out**, to be prominent or outstanding; to persist in resistance or support. **stand to**, to stand ready for action; to abide by; to be likely or certain to. **stand to reason**, to be obvious or logical. **stand up**, to come to or remain in or place in a standing position; to be valid; (colloq.) to fail to keep an appointment with. **stand-up** adj. (of a meal) eaten standing; (of a fight) violent and thorough; (of a collar) upright, not turned down. **stand up for**, to defend or support, to side with. **stand up to**, to face (an opponent) courageously; to be resistant to the harmful effects of (use or wear etc.). **take one's stand**, to base an argument or reliance (on). [OE]

standard /ˈstændəd/ n. **1.** an object, quality, or specification serving as an example or principle to which others should conform or by which others are judged. **2.** a required or specified level of excellence etc. **3.** the average quality; the ordinary design or procedure etc. without added or novel features. **4.** a distinctive flag. **5.** an upright support or pipe. **6.** a treelike shrub with (or grafted on) an upright stem. — adj. **1.** serving or used as a standard. **2.** having a recognized and permanent value, authoritative. **3.** of normal or prescribed quality or size etc.; (of language) conforming to established educated usage. —**standard-bearer** n. a person who carries a distinctive flag; a prominent leader in a cause. **standard lamp**, a domestic lamp on a tall upright with a base. **standard of living**, the degree of material comfort enjoyed by a person or group. **standard time**, that established in a country or region by law or custom and based on the longitude. [f. AF (as EXTEND), in some senses infl. by prec.]

standardize v.t. to cause to conform to a standard. —**standardization** /-ˈzeiʃ(ə)n/ n. [f. prec.]

standee /stænˈdiː/ n. (colloq.) one who stands, especially when all seats are occupied. [f. STAND]

standing n. **1.** status; esteem, high repute. **2.** past duration. —adj. **1.** that stands, upright; (of corn) not yet harvested. **2.** (of a jump or start) performed from rest without a run-up. **3.** permanent, remaining effective or valid. **4.** (of water) not flowing. —**standing joke**, an object of permanent ridicule. **standing order**, an instruction to a banker to make regular payments, or to a newsagent etc. for the regular supply of a periodical etc. **standing orders**, the rules governing procedure in Parliament or a council etc. **standing room**, space to stand in. [f. STAND]

standpipe n. a vertical pipe for fluid to rise in, e.g. to provide a water supply outside or at a distance from buildings.

standpoint n. a point of view.

standstill n. a stoppage, inability to proceed.

Stanhope /ˈstænəp/, Lady Hester Lucy (1776–1839), niece of William Pitt the Younger, for whom she kept house from 1803 until his death in 1806, gaining a reputation as a brilliant political hostess. Becoming disillusioned with life in England she set out for the Middle East in 1810, and four years later established herself for the rest of her life at a ruined convent on Mount Lebanon, where she lived with a semi-oriental retinue which she ruled despotically. For several years her high rank and imperious character enabled her to meddle effectively in Middle Eastern politics, but later her debts accumulated, her eccentricity increased, and she sought to replace her waning political prestige by an undefined spiritual authority based on claims to be an inspired prophetess and mistress of occult sciences. She became a legendary figure in her lifetime and was visited by many distinguished European travellers.

Stanislaus /ˈstænɪslɔːs/, St (1030–79), the patron saint of Poland, who became bishop of Cracow in 1072. He came into conflict with King Boleslav II who (according to tradition) slew Stanislaus, while the latter was offering Mass, with his own hand. Feast day, 7 May.

Stanislavsky /stænɪsˈlæfskɪ/, Konstantin Sergeivich (Konstantin Alexeyev, 1863–1938), Russian director, actor, and teacher of acting. In 1898 he helped to found the Moscow Art Theatre, which opened a new epoch in Russian theatre. He trained his actors in a new way of acting, basing his methods on the psychological development of character and the drawing out of latent powers of self-expression. A whole system of actor training was built up on his theories, particularly in the USA where his system was elaborated into the 'method' (see entry). Among his greatest achievements were his productions of the plays of Chekhov and Gorky.

stank *past* of STINK.

Stanley /ˈstænlɪ/, Sir Henry Morton (1841–1904), explorer of central Africa. Born in Wales as John Rowlands, after a hard and unhappy youth he sailed to America as a cabin boy and changed his name to that of an American merchant who befriended him. He became a successful newspaper correspondent and in 1869 was dispatched to find the Scottish missionary-explorer, David Livingstone (see entry), in Central Africa. After Livingstone's death Stanley continued his exploration work in Africa and in 1874–7 traced the course of the Congo and crossed the continent. Supported by Belgium, he helped to organize and develop the Congo region, and laid the foundations for the establishment of the Congo Free State. In 1887 he led an expedition to rescue Emin Pasha during the Mahdist advance on the Sudan. A popular figure with the public, he was accorded many honours and his books on his travels had an immense sale. From 1895 until 1900 he was a Member of Parliament.

Stannaries /ˈstænərɪz/ *n.pl.* the tin-mining district of Cornwall and Devon. —**Stannary court,** a lawcourt for the regulation of tin-mines in the Stannaries. [f. L (*stannum* tin)]

stanza /ˈstænzə/ *n.* a group of lines (usually four or more rhymed) as a repeated metrical unit. [It., orig. = standing-place, f. L *stare* stand]

staphylococcus /stæfɪləˈkɒkəs/ *n.* (*pl.* **-cocci** /-iː/) a form of pus-producing bacterium. —**staphylococcal** *adj.* [f. Gk *staphulē* bunch of grapes + *kokkos* berry]

staple[1] /ˈsteɪp(ə)l/ *n.* **1.** a U-shaped metal bar or piece of wire with pointed ends, driven into wood etc. to hold something in place. **2.** a piece of metal or wire driven into sheets of paper etc. and clenched to fasten them together. —*v.t.* to fasten or furnish with a staple.—**stapler** *n.* [OE, = OHG *staffal* foundation, ON *stöpull* pillar]

staple[2] /ˈsteɪp(ə)l/ *adj.* principal, standard; important as a product or export. —*n.* **1.** an important (usually principal) article of commerce in a district or country. **2.** a chief element or material. **3.** the fibre of cotton or wool etc. as determining its quality. [f. OF *estaple* market f. MLG or MDu. (as prec.)]

star *n.* **1.** a celestial body appearing as a luminous point in the night sky (see below); a large self-luminous gaseous ball such as the sun; a celestial body regarded as influencing a person's fortunes etc. **2.** a thing resembling a star in shape or appearance; a figure or object with radiating points, e.g. as a decoration or mark of rank, or showing a category of excellence. **3.** a famous or brilliant person, especially an actor, actress, or other performer; a principal performer in a play or film etc. —*v.t./i.* (**-rr-**) **1.** to mark or adorn (as) with a star or stars. **2.** to present or perform as a star actor etc. —**star-dust** *n.* a multitude of stars looking like dust.

star-gazer *n.* (*colloq.*) an astronomer or astrologer. **Star of David,** a six-pointed star made of two interlaced equilateral triangles, used as the symbol of Judaism and of the State of Israel. **star-studded** *adj.* covered with stars; including many famous actors etc. **star turn,** the main item in an entertainment etc. [OE]

Stars are now known to be gaseous spheres, primarily of hydrogen and helium, in equilibrium between the force of self-gravity, which exerts a compressional force, and the pressure of radiation produced deep within the interior as a result of thermonuclear fusion reactions of the sort occurring in hydrogen bombs. Apart from the sun, the star nearest to Earth is Proxima Centauri, at a distance of some four light-years. Most are much further away than this, so that they appear hardly to change their relative positions in the sky. Some six thousand stars are visible to the naked eye; the actual number existing is vastly greater, more than a hundred thousand million in our own Galaxy, while billions of galaxies are known.

starboard /ˈstɑːbəd/ *n.* the right-hand side of a ship or aircraft looking forward. —*v.t.* to turn (the helm) to starboard. —**starboard tack,** a tack with the wind on the starboard side. [OE (as STEER[1], BOARD)]

starch *n.* **1.** a white carbohydrate that is an important element in human food, found in cereals, potatoes, and all other plants except fungi. **2.** a preparation of this for stiffening linen etc. **3.** stiffness of manner, formality. —*v.t.* to stiffen (as) with starch. [cf. OHG *sterken* stiffen (as STARK)]

Star Chamber an apartment in the royal palace at Westminster (said to have had gilt stars on the ceiling) where, in the 14th–15th c., the Privy Council in its judicial capacity tried civil and criminal cases, especially those affecting Crown interests. Under the Tudors and early Stuarts the court (**Court of Star Chamber**) became an instrument of tyranny, notorious for its arbitrary and oppressive judgements. It was abolished by Parliament in 1641.

starchy *adj.* **1.** of or like starch; containing much starch. **2.** stiff and formal in manner. —**starchily** *adv.*, **starchiness** *n.* [f. STARCH]

stardom *n.* the position or fame of a star actor etc. [f. STAR]

stare *v.t./i.* to look fixedly with the eyes wide open, especially with curiosity, surprise, or horror; to reduce (a person) to a specified condition by staring. —*n.* a staring gaze. —**stare a person in the face,** to be clearly evident or imminent. [OE]

starfish *n.* a star-shaped sea creature of the class Asteroidea.

stark *adj.* **1.** desolate, bare; cheerless. **2.** sharply evident. **3.** downright, complete. **4.** completely naked. **5.** (*archaic*) stiff, rigid. —*adv.* completely, wholly. —**starkly** *adv.*, **starkness** *n.* [OE]

starlet /ˈstɑːlɪt/ *n.* a young film actress likely to become a star. [f. STAR + -LET]

starlight *n.* light from the stars.

starling /ˈstɑːlɪŋ/ *n.* a noisy bird (*Sturnus vulgaris*) with glossy blackish speckled feathers, that forms large flocks. [OE]

starlit *adj.* lighted by stars; with stars visible.

starry *adj.* full of or bright with stars. —**starry-eyed** *adj.* (*colloq.*) bright-eyed, romantic but unpractical. [f. STAR]

Stars and Stripes the popular name of the flag of the USA. Originally it contained 13 alternating red and white stripes and 13 stars, representing the 13 States of the Union. Today it retains the 13 stripes, but has 50 stars, Hawaii having brought the number of States to 50 in 1959.

Star-spangled Banner a song composed by Francis Scott Key, inspired by the heroic defence of Fort McHenry in Baltimore harbour against the British in 1812, officially adopted as the US national anthem in 1931.

start *v.t./i.* **1.** to set in motion or action; to begin or cause to begin operating. **2.** to cause or enable to begin; to establish or found; to conceive (a baby). **3.** to begin a journey etc. **4.** to make a sudden movement from pain or surprise etc. **5.** to spring suddenly. **6.** to rouse (game etc.) from a lair. **7.** (of timber etc.) to become loose or displaced; to cause (timber) to do this. —*n.* **1.** the beginning; the place where a race is begun. **2.** an advantage granted in beginning a race; an advantageous initial position in life or business etc. **3.** a sudden movement of pain or surprise etc. —**for a start,** as a thing to start with. **starting-block** *n.* a shaped block against which a runner braces his feet at the start of a race. **starting-price** *n.* the final odds before the start of a horse-race etc. **start off,** to begin; to start to move. **start out,** to begin; to begin a journey. **start up,** to rise suddenly; to come or bring into existence or action. [cf. OHG *sturzen* overthrow, rush]

starter n. **1.** a device for starting the engine of a motor vehicle etc. **2.** a person giving the signal for the start of a race. **3.** a horse or competitor starting in a race. **4.** the first course of a meal. [f. START]

startle v.t. to give a shock or surprise to. [OE (as START)]

starve v.t./i. **1.** to die of hunger or suffer acutely from lack of food, to cause to do this; (*colloq.*) to feel very hungry or very cold. **2.** to be deprived or short of something needed or wanted; to cause to be in this position. **3.** to compel by starving. —**starvation** /-ˈveɪʃ(ə)n/ n. [OE, = die]

starveling /ˈstɑːvlɪŋ/ n. a starving person or animal. [f. prec.]

stash v.t. (*slang*) to conceal, to stow. —n. (*slang*) **1.** a hiding-place. **2.** a thing hidden. [orig. unkn.]

stasis /ˈsteɪsɪs, ˈstæ-/ n. (*pl.* **stases** /-iːz/) a stoppage of flow or circulation. [Gk, = standing]

state n. **1.** the quality of a person's or thing's characteristics or circumstances. **2.** (*colloq.*) an excited or agitated condition of mind. **3.** (often State) an organized community under one government or forming part of a federal republic; civil government. **4.** pomp. —adj. of or concerned with the State or its ceremonial occasions. —v.t. **1.** to express in speech or writing. **2.** to fix or specify. **3.** (*Mus.*) to play (a theme etc.), especially for the first time. —**in** or **into a fixed state,** in or into an excited or anxious or untidy condition. **lie in state,** to be laid in a public place of honour before burial. **State Department,** the department of foreign affairs in the government of the USA. **State Enrolled Nurse,** a nurse enrolled on a State register and having a qualification lower than that of a State Registered Nurse. **state of play,** the position in which a matter or business stands at a particular time. **State of the Union message,** a yearly address delivered by the President of the USA to Congress, giving the Administration's view of the state of the nation and its plans for legislation. **State Registered Nurse,** a nurse enrolled on a State register and more highly qualified than a State Enrolled Nurse. **the States,** the USA. [f. ESTATE and f. L *status* standing]

statehood n. the condition of being a State. [f. STATE + -HOOD]

stateless adj. having no nationality or citizenship. [f. STATE + -LESS]

stately adj. dignified, imposing. —**stately home,** a large grand house, especially one of historical interest. —**stateliness** n. [f. STATE]

statement /ˈsteɪtmənt/ n. **1.** stating, being stated. **2.** expression in words; a thing stated. **3.** a formal account of facts, especially of transactions in a bank account or of the amount due to a tradesman. [f. STATE]

stateroom n. **1.** a state apartment. **2.** a private compartment in a passenger ship.

statesman n. (*pl.* -**men**) a person skilled in affairs of State; a sagacious far-sighted politician. —**statesmanlike** adj., **statesmanship** n., **stateswoman** n.fem.

static /ˈstætɪk/ adj. **1.** stationary; not movable; not acting, not changing. **2.** concerned with bodies at rest or forces in equilibrium; of force acting by weight without motion (opp. *dynamic*). —n. **1.** static electricity. **2.** atmospherics. —**static electricity,** electricity present in a body and not flowing as current. —**statically** adv. [f. Gk *statikos* (sta- stand)]

statics n.pl. (usu. treated as *sing.*) **1.** the science of static bodies or forces. **2.** static. [f. prec.]

station /ˈsteɪʃ(ə)n/ n. **1.** a place or building etc. where a person or thing stands or is placed or where a particular activity, especially a public service, is based or organized. **2.** a regular stopping-place on a railway line; the buildings at this. **3.** an establishment engaged in broadcasting. **4.** a military or naval base; the inhabitants of this. **5.** position in life, rank or status. **6.** (*Austral.*) a large sheep-farm or cattle-farm. —v.t. to assign a station to; to put in position. —**station manager** or -**master** n. the official in charge of a railway station. **Stations of the Cross,** see separate entry. **station-wagon** n. (*US*) an estate car. [f. OF f. L *statio* (*stare* stand)]

stationary /ˈsteɪʃənərɪ/ adj. not moving; not intended to be moved; not changing in amount or quantity. [f. L (as prec.)]

stationer /ˈsteɪʃənə(r)/ n. a dealer in stationery. [as prec. in L sense 'shopkeeper' as opp. pedlar]

stationery /ˈsteɪʃənərɪ/ n. writing materials, office supplies,

etc. —**Stationery Office,** the government publishing-house in the UK. [f. prec.]

Stations of the Cross a series of 14 pictures or carvings, representing events in Christ's passion, before which devotions are performed in some Churches. The custom probably arose out of the practice, attested from an early date, of pilgrims at Jerusalem following the traditional route from Pilate's house to Calvary.

statistic /stəˈtɪstɪk/ n. a statistical fact or item. [f. G (as STATE)]

statistical /stəˈtɪstɪk(ə)l/ adj. of or concerned with statistics. —**statistically** adv. [f. prec.]

statistics /stəˈtɪstɪks/ n.pl. **1.** numerical data systematically collected. **2.** (usu. treated as *sing.*) the art of organizing numerical data so as to exhibit what is significant, especially the norm and deviations from it. —**statistical inference,** the science of drawing reliable conclusions from apparently random collections of numerical data, and of estimating the probability of the truth of those conclusions. —**statistician** /ˌstætɪˈstɪʃ(ə)n/ n. [f. STATISTIC]

Statius /ˈsteɪʃəs/, Publius Papinius (*c.*AD 45–96), Roman poet who flourished at the court of Domitian. His works include the *Silvae* (lit. = 'bits of raw material'), which are a miscellany of poems addressed to friends, and the *Thebais*, an epic written in a colourful and rhetorical style. His works were much admired in the Middle Ages. Statius was regarded by Dante as a Christian, and was a favourite of Chaucer's.

statuary /ˈstætjʊərɪ/ adj. of or for statues. —n. **1.** statues; the making of these. **2.** a maker of statues. [f. L (as foll.)]

statue /ˈstætjuː, -tʃuː/ n. a sculptured, moulded, or cast figure of a person or animal etc., usually of life size or larger. —**Statue of Liberty,** see LIBERTY. [f. OF f. L *statua* (*stare* stand)]

statuesque /ˌstætjʊˈesk, ˌstætʃ-/ adj. like a statue in size, dignity, or stillness. —**statuesquely** adv., **statuesqueness** n. [f. prec.]

statuette /ˌstætjʊˈet, ˌstætʃ-/ n. a small statue. [f. STATUE + -ETTE]

stature /ˈstætjə(r), -tʃə(r)/ n. **1.** the natural height of the body. **2.** greatness gained by ability or achievement. [f. OF f. L *statura* (as STATUE)]

status /ˈsteɪtəs/ n. **1.** a person's position or rank in relation to others; a person's or thing's legal position. **2.** high rank or prestige. —**status quo,** the state of affairs as it is or as it was before a recent change. **status symbol,** a possession or activity etc. regarded as evidence of a person's high status. [L, = standing (as STATION)]

statute /ˈstætjuːt/ n. **1.** a law passed by a legislative body. **2.** a rule of an institution. —**statute-book** n. the statute law; a book or books containing this. **statute law,** a statute; statutes collectively. **statute mile,** 1760 yds., about 1.6 km. [f. OF f. L (*statuere* set up, as prec.)]

statutory /ˈstætjʊtərɪ/ adj. enacted or required by statute. —**statutorily** adv. [f. prec.]

staunch /stɔːntʃ/ adj. **1.** firm in attitude, opinion, or loyalty. **2.** (of a ship or joint etc.) watertight, airtight. —**staunchly** adv. [f. OF *estanche*]

stave n. **1.** each of the curved pieces of wood forming the sides of a cask or pail etc. **2.** (*Mus.*) a staff. **3.** a stanza, a verse. —v.t. (*past & p.p.* **stove** or **staved**) to break a hole in; to knock out of shape. —**stave in,** to crush by forcing inwards. **stave off,** to avert or defer (danger or misfortune etc.). [var. of STAFF]

staves see STAFF.

stay[1] v.t./i. **1.** to continue to be in the same place or condition, not to depart or change. **2.** to dwell temporarily, especially as a guest or visitor. **3.** to stop or pause in movement, action, or speech; to cause to do this. **4.** to postpone (judgement etc.). **5.** to assuage (hunger etc.) especially for a short time. **6.** to show endurance. —n. **1.** an action or period of staying. **2.** suspension or postponement of the execution of a sentence etc. —**stay-at-home** adj. remaining habitually at home; (n.) a person who does this. **stay the course,** to endure a struggle etc. to the end. **stay in,** to remain indoors. **staying-power** n. endurance. **stay the night,** to remain until the next day. **stay put,** (*colloq.*) to remain where it is placed or where one is. [f. AF *estai-* f. L *stare* stand]

stay[2] n. **1.** a prop or support. **2.** a rope etc. supporting a mast or flagstaff etc. **3.** a tie-piece in an aircraft. **4.** (in *pl.*) a corset. [OE]

stayer n. a person or animal with great endurance. [f. STAY[1]]

staysail /'steɪseɪl, -s(ə)l/ n. a sail extended on a stay (ill. SAILING-SHIPS).

STD abbr. subscriber trunk dialling.

stead /sted/ n. **in a person's** or **thing's stead,** instead of him or her or it; as a substitute. **stand in good stead,** to be advantageous or serviceable to (a person). [OE (as STAND)]

steadfast /'stedfɑːst/ adj. firm and not changing or yielding. —**steadfastly** adv., **steadfastness** n. [OE (as prec. + FAST¹)]

steady /'stedɪ/ adj. **1.** firmly in position, not tottering or rocking or swaying. **2.** done, operating, or happening in a uniform and regular manner. **3.** constant in mind or conduct. **4.** serious and dependable in character. —v.t./i. to make or become steady. —adv. steadily. —n. (colloq.) a regular boy-friend or girl-friend. —**go steady with,** (colloq.) to have as a regular boy-friend or girl-friend. **steady on!** be careful! —**steadily** adv., **steadiness** n. [f. STEAD]

steady state an unvarying condition, especially in a physical process. The term is used specifically of a cosmological theory put forward by Sir James Jeans c.1920, again (revised) by Hermann Bondi and Thomas Gold in 1948, and further developed by Fred Hoyle, postulating that the universe maintains a constant average density, with more matter continuously created to fill the void left by galaxies that are known to be receding from one another. The theory has now largely been abandoned in favour of the 'big bang' theory, and an evolving universe, as a result of two major discoveries: (i) that the most distant quasars are very different in nature from nearby galaxies, and (ii) the discovery of the microwave radiation background, by use of radio telescopes, appears to provide direct evidence for very hot radiation in an early stage of the universe, immediately following the big bang.

steak /steɪk/ n. **1.** a thick slice of meat (especially beef) or fish, cut for grilling or frying. **2.** beef from the front of the animal, cut for stewing or braising. —**steak-house,** n. a restaurant specializing in beef-steaks. [f. ON, rel. to stikna be roasted]

steal v.t./i. (past **stole;** p.p. **stolen**) **1.** to take (another's property) illegally or without permission, esp. secretly. **2.** to obtain surreptitiously or by surprise; to gain insidiously or artfully etc. **3.** to move or come silently or gradually. —n. (US colloq.) **1.** stealing, theft. **2.** an (unexpectedly) easy task or good bargain. —**steal a march on,** to gain an advantage over by acting surreptitiously or anticipating. **steal a person's thunder,** see THUNDER. **steal the show,** to outshine the other performers unexpectedly. [OE]

stealth /stelθ/ n. secrecy, secret or surreptitious behaviour. [as prec.]

stealthy /'stelθɪ/ adj. acting or done by stealth. —**stealthily** adv., **stealthiness** n. [f. prec.]

steam n. **1.** the invisible gas into which water is changed by boiling, used as motive power. **2.** the visible vapour that forms when steam condenses in the air. **3.** (colloq.) energy, power. —v.t./i. **1.** to give out steam. **2.** to cook or treat by steam. **3.** to move by the power of steam; (colloq.) to work or move vigorously or rapidly. —**steam-hammer,** a forging-hammer worked by steam. **steam iron,** an electric iron emitting steam from its flat surface. **steam radio,** (colloq.) radio broadcasting regarded as antiquated by comparison with television. **steam train,** a train pulled by a steam-engine. **steam up,** to cover or become covered with condensed steam. **be** or **get steamed up,** to be or become excited or agitated. [OE]

steamboat n. a steam-driven boat, especially a paddle-wheel craft used widely on rivers in the 19th c. Such boats were constructed experimentally in the 1780s (John Fitch launched his invention on the Delaware River in 1787), but the most successful pioneer was Robert Fulton (see entry). In the USA the most famous steamboats were those on the Mississippi, noted for their ornate fittings and for the risk of fire and other hazards to which they were prone. The classic account of them is Mark Twain's Life on the Mississippi (1883), telling of his experiences as a river-boat pilot. (See also STEAMSHIP.)

steam-engine n. a locomotive or stationary engine in which the successive expansion and rapid condensation of steam forces a piston (or pistons) to move up and down in a cylinder (or cylinders) to produce motive power, which is transmitted to a crank by means of a connecting-rod. The power of steam had been demonstrated by Hero of Alexandria in AD 100, and condensed steam was made to drive a piston in experiments in the 18th c. The steam-engine proper, the first successful form of heat-engine, was developed and successively improved in the 18th c. by Newcomen, Watt, and others, after an early form had been invented by Captain Savery, and has changed little in its essentials since c.1820. It had reached its highest development by c.1900, when it was by far the most important heat-engine in existence: large stationary steam-engines provided the power for factories and blast furnaces, while smaller engines drove locomotives and tractors. It made possible the Industrial Revolution, being used first for pumping water from mines, later for driving machinery in mills, then for railway locomotives and for steamships. It has now been largely replaced by the steam turbine and the internal-combustion engine, but may again become popular because it can use coal rather than oil as a fuel.

steamer n. **1.** a steamship. **2.** a container for steaming food etc. [f. STEAM]

steamroller n. **1.** a heavy slow-moving locomotive with a roller, used in road-making. **2.** a crushing power or force. —v.t. to crush or move along (as) with a steamroller.

steamship n. a steam-driven ship. (See also SHIP and STEAMBOAT.) From the early 19th c. steam-engines were used to power ships. At first they were used as auxiliary engines on what were essentially sailing-ships, but in 1832 HMS Rhadamanthus crossed the Atlantic entirely under steam power, stopping at intervals to desalt the boilers, and in 1838 the Sirius crossed under continuous steam power, burning the cabin furniture, spare yards, and one mast en route in order to keep up steam in the boiler. Several steamship lines were established to exploit the profitable Atlantic route. The disadvantage of steamships for long journeys was that they were obliged to carry large amounts of fuel, and sailing-ships for carrying cargo survived into the 20th c.

steamy adj. **1.** of, like, or full of steam. **2.** (colloq.) erotic. —**steamily** adv., **steaminess** n. [f. STEAM]

steatite /'stiːətaɪt/ n. a kind of usually grey talc with a greasy feel. [f. L f. Gk (stear tallow)]

steed n. (literary) a horse. [OE stēda stallion, rel. to STUD²]

steel n. **1.** a malleable alloy of iron and carbon capable of being tempered to many different degrees of hardness (see below). **2.** a steel rod for sharpening knives. **3.** (literary; not in pl.) a sword. **4.** great strength or firmness. —adj. of or like steel. —v.t. to harden or make resolute. —**steel band,** a band of musicians who play music (chiefly calypso-style) on steel drums. **steel wool,** fine shavings of steel massed together for use as an abrasive. [OE]

In antiquity (c.1200 BC) steel surfaces were produced on iron weapons and tools by heating them over red-hot charcoal so that carbon was absorbed from the coals. By c.200 BC steel production had started in India, where iron fragments and wood chips were sealed into clay containers and heated until the iron had absorbed carbon—a process that later lapsed until it reappeared in 1740, when the 'crucible' method was developed in Sheffield. The basis of modern steelmaking is the removal of a large proportion of the non-ferrous elements from molten pig-iron by making them combine with oxygen. This can be done by any of several processes, including the Bessemer process, the open-hearth process, and (from c.1900) the electric-arc furnace, in which heat is provided by an electric arc. The most popular modern process, superseding the open-hearth, uses oxygen instead of air to reduce the carbon content without introducing impurities. The chief uses of steel are for structural purposes (e.g. girders), reinforcement for concrete, railways, ships, motor vehicles, machine tools, fastenings, and food containers.

Steele /stiːl/, Sir Richard (1672-1729), British essayist and dramatist, born in Dublin in the same year as Addison, with whom he was educated. He wrote several not very successful comedies, including The Funeral (1701) which broke away from Restoration drama in its true portrayal of virtue and vice. Today he is remembered for his essays in The Tatler (1709-11) which he founded, and The Spectator (1711-12) which he conducted with Addison; these had an important influence on the manners, morals, and literature of the time. He edited several other periodicals and in 1713 was elected MP, but his pamphlet The Crisis (1714) in favour of the Hanoverian succession led to his expulsion from the House. On the accession of George I he was appointed supervisor of Drury Lane Theatre and to other official posts; he was knighted in 1715.

steely adj. of or like steel; inflexibly severe. —**steeliness** n. [f. STEEL]

steelyard *n.* a weighing-apparatus with a graduated arm along which a weight slides.

steep[1] *adj.* **1.** sloping sharply, hard to climb. **2.** (of a rise or fall) rapid; **3.** (*colloq.*) exorbitant, unreasonable; exaggerated, incredible. —*n.* a steep slope, a precipice. —**steeply** *adv.*, **steepness** *n.* [OE, rel. to STOOP[1]]

steep[2] *v.t.* to soak or bathe in a liquid. —*n.* **1.** the action of steeping. **2.** a liquid for steeping things in. —**steep in,** to pervade or imbue with; to make deeply acquainted with (a subject etc.). [rel. to STOUP]

steepen *v.t./i.* to make or become steep. [f. STEEP[1]]

steeple *n.* a tall tower, especially one surmounted by a spire, above the roof of a church. (ill. CHURCH). [OE (as STEEP[1])]

steeplechase *n.* **1.** a horse-race across a tract of country or on a racecourse with hedges, ditches, etc., to jump (see below). **2.** a cross-country foot-race. —**steeplechasing** *n.* the sport of riding in steeplechases. —**steeplechaser** *n.* Steeplechasing is believed to have begun in Ireland in the 18th c., with matches between two horses across country, using steeples as landmarks, over a distance of four or five miles. The new sport soon spread to England, but it was not until 1830 that annual steeplechase fixtures began.

steeplejack *n.* a person who climbs steeples, tall chimneys, etc., to repair them.

steer[1] *v.t./i.* **1.** to direct the course of; to guide (a vehicle or boat etc.) by means of its mechanism. **2.** to be able to be steered. —**steer clear of,** to take care to avoid. **steering-column** *n.* the column on which a steering-wheel is mounted. **steering committee,** a committee deciding the order of business, the general course of operations, etc. **steering-wheel** *n.* the wheel by which a vehicle, vessel, etc., is steered. —**steerer** *n.* [OE]

steer[2] *n.* a young male ox, especially a bullock. [OE]

steerage *n.* **1.** steering. **2.** (*obs.*) the part of a ship assigned to passengers travelling at the cheapest rate. [f. STEER[1]]

steersman *n.* (*pl.* **-men**) one who steers a ship.

stein /staɪn/ *n.* a large earthenware mug, especially for beer. [G, = stone]

Steinbeck /ˈstaɪnbek/, John (Ernst) (1902–68), American novelist. His best work deals sympathetically and realistically with the poor and oppressed, especially the migrant agricultural workers of California, as in *The Grapes of Wrath* (1939).

Steinway /ˈstaɪnweɪ/, Henry Engelhard (1797–1871), German piano-builder. His name is used to designate a piano manufactured by him or by the firm which he founded in New York in 1853.

stela /ˈstiːlə/ *n.* (also **stele** /-iː/; *pl.* **stelae** /-iː/) an ancient upright slab or pillar, usually inscribed and sculptured, especially as a gravestone. [L f. Gk *stēlē* standing block]

stellar /ˈstelə(r)/ *adj.* of a star or stars. [f. L (*stella* star)]

stem[1] *n.* **1.** the main central part (usually above the ground) of a tree, shrub, or plant; a slender part supporting a fruit, flower, or leaf. **2.** any stem-shaped part, e.g. the slender part of a wineglass between bowl and foot. **3.** the root or main part of a noun or verb etc., to which case-endings etc. are added. **4.** the curved upright timber or metal piece at the fore end of a ship; a ship's bows. —*v.i.* (**-mm-**) **1.** (with *from*) to originate. **2.** to make headway against (the tide etc.). [OE]

stem[2] *v.t./i.* (**-mm-**) **1.** to restrain the flow of (*lit.* or *fig.*), to dam. **2.** (in skiing) to retard oneself by forcing the heel outwards. —*n.* (in skiing) the act of stemming. —**stem-turn** *n.* a turn made by stemming with one ski (ill. SPORTS). [f. ON; cf. STAMMER]

Sten *n.* (also **Sten gun**) a type of lightweight sub-machine-gun. [f. initials of designers R. V. Shepherd & H. J. Turpin + *En*field, Greater London (as in BREN)]

stench *n.* a foul smell. [OE *stenc* (any) smell (cf. STINK)]

stencil /ˈstens(ə)l/ *n.* a thin sheet in which a pattern is cut, used to produce a corresponding pattern on the surface beneath it by applying ink or paint etc.; a pattern so produced. —*v.t.* (**-ll-**) to produce (a pattern) with a stencil; to mark (a surface) thus. [orig. = ornament, f. OF *estanceler* cover with stars f. L *scintilla* spark]

Stendhal /ˈstɑːdɑːl/ (pseudonym of Henri Beyle, 1783–1842), French novelist who served under Napoleon in Italy, Germany, and Russia, and later held consular posts in Italy. His two recognized masterpieces are *Le Rouge et le Noir* (1830) and *La Chartreuse de Parme* (1839); each is remarkable for its political dimension, for the variety of experience portrayed, for the energy and passion of the principal characters, and for his penetrating psychological analysis. As well as novels he wrote studies of music, musicians, and Italian painting, travel books, three volumes of autobiography, and much journalism. His study *De l'amour* (1822) considers the passion both psychologically and in relation to historical and social questions, and with *Racine et Shakespeare* (1823, 1825) he linked himself with the Romantics in the Classic-Romantic controversy.

Steno /ˈstiːnəʊ/, Nicolaus (1638–86), Danish-born anatomist, geologist, and physician (Danish name Niels Steensen), who worked and studied in a number of European cities. He is remembered for proposing several ideas which are now part of modern geological thought: that fossils are the petrified remains of living organisms, that many rocks arise from consolidation of sediments, and that such rocks occur in layers in the order in which they were laid down, thereby constituting a record of the geological history of the earth. Steno later turned from science to religion, and ended his days as a bishop.

stenography /steˈnɒɡrəfɪ/ *n.* the writing of shorthand. —**stenographer** *n.* [f. Gk *stenos* narrow + -GRAPHY]

stentorian /stenˈtɔːrɪən/ *adj.* (of a voice etc.) loud and powerful. [f. Gk *Stentōr*, herald in Trojan War]

step *n.* **1.** a complete action of moving and placing one leg in walking or running; the distance covered by this; a unit of movement in dancing. **2.** a measure taken, especially one of several in a course of action. **3.** a surface on which the foot is placed in ascending or descending, a stair or tread; (in *pl.*) a step-ladder. **4.** a short distance. **5.** a mark or sound made by a foot in walking etc.; a manner of stepping. **6.** a stage in a scale of promotion or precedence etc. —*v.t./i.* (**-pp-**) **1.** to lift and set down the foot or alternate feet as in walking. **2.** to go a short distance or progress (as) by stepping. **3.** to measure (a distance) by stepping. —**break step,** to get out of step. **in step,** putting the foot to the ground at the same time as others, especially in marching; conforming to the actions etc. of others. **keep step,** to remain in step. **mind** or **watch one's step,** to take care. **out of step,** not in step, **step by step,** gradually, cautiously. **step down,** to resign. **step in,** to enter; to intervene. **step-ladder** *n.* a short self-supporting ladder with flat steps. **step on it,** (*slang*) to go or act faster. **step out,** to take long brisk steps; to go out to enjoy oneself socially. **stepping-stone** *n.* a raised stone (usually one of a series) as a means of crossing a stream etc.; a means of progress towards achieving something. **step up,** to come up or forward; to increase the rate or volume of. [OE]

step- *prefix* denoting a relationship like the one specified but resulting from a parent's remarriage. [OE (rel. to OHG, = bereave)]

stepbrother *n.* a male child of one's step-parent's previous marriage.

stepchild *n.* a spouse's child by a previous marriage.

stepdaughter *n.* a female stepchild.

stepfather *n.* a male step-parent.

stephanotis /stefəˈnəʊtɪs/ *n.* a fragrant tropical climbing plant of the genus *Stephanotis*. [f. Gk, = fit for a wreath (*stephanos*)]

Stephen[1] /ˈstiːv(ə)n/ (c.1097–1154), grandson of William I, king of England 1135–54. Stephen seized the throne of England from Matilda, the only legitimate child of Henry I, a few months after the latter's death in 1135. More popular with the English nobility than his rival, he forced her to flee the kingdom, but failed to restore royal authority in a time of great domestic unrest and was eventually obliged to recognize Matilda's son, the future Henry II, as heir to the throne.

Stephen[2] /ˈstiːv(ə)n/, St (d c.35), the first Christian martyr. One of the original seven deacons in Jerusalem appointed by the Apostles, he incurred the hostility of the Jews and was charged with blasphemy before the Sanhedrin and stoned; Saul (the future St Paul) was present at his execution. Feast day (in the Western Church) 26 Dec., in the Eastern Church) 27 Dec.

Stephen[3] /ˈstiːv(ə)n/, St (c.997–1038), the first king and patron saint of Hungary, who on his accession to the throne in 997 set out to christianize his country. Feast day, 2 Sept., but in Hungary 20 Aug., the day of the translation of his relics, is kept as his principal festival.

Stephenson /ˈstiːv(ə)ns(ə)n/, George (1781–1848), English engineer, generally regarded as the father of railways. Stephenson started as a colliery engineman and so had early acquaintance with steam power, which he proceeded to apply to haulage of coal wagons by cable. His first locomotive, the *Blucher*, was built in 1814. He became engineer to a company laying a railway track between Stockton and Darlington, and, having persuaded them to use steam-power instead of horse-drawn wagons, in 1825 drove the first train upon it, with a locomotive of his own design, at a speed of 19km an hour. His son Robert (1803-59) assisted him in the building of engines and of the Liverpool-Manchester railway for which they built the famous locomotive *Rocket* (1829), the prototype for all future steam locomotives. George invented a miners' safety lamp at about the same time as Sir Humphry Davy, while Robert became famous as both a locomotive builder and a bridge designer, notably the box-girder Britannia tubular bridge over the Menai Strait in Wales and other major bridges at Conway, Berwick, Newcastle, in Egypt, and at Montreal.

stepmother *n.* a female step-parent.

step-parent *n.* a mother's or father's later spouse.

steppe /step/ *n.* a level treeless plain. [f. Russ.]

stepsister *n.* a female child of one's step-parent's previous marriage.

stepson *n.* a male stepchild.

steradian /stə'reɪdɪən/ *n.* the unit of solid angle, equal to the angle at the centre of a sphere subtended by part of the surface whose area is equal to the square of the radius. [as STEREO- + RADIAN]

stereo /'sterɪəʊ, 'stɪər-/ *n.* (*pl.* -**os**) **1.** a stereophonic record-player etc. **2.** stereophony. **3.** a stereoscope. **4.** a stereotype. —*adj.* **1.** stereophonic. **2.** stereoscopic. [abbr.]

stereo- /sterɪəʊ-, stɪərɪəʊ-/ *in comb.* having three dimensions. [f. Gk *stereos* solid]

stereochemistry /sterɪəʊ'kemɪstrɪ, 'stɪər-/ *n.* the branch of chemistry dealing with the composition of matter as affected by the relations of atoms in space. [f. STEREO- + CHEMISTRY]

stereophonic /sterɪə'fɒnɪk, stɪər-/ *adj.* (of sound-reproduction) using two or more channels of transmission and reproduction so that the sound may seem to reach the listener from more than one direction and thus seems more realistic. —**stereophonically** *adv.*, **stereophony** /-'ɒfənɪ/ *n.* [f. STEREO- + PHONIC]

stereoscope /'sterɪəskəʊp, 'stɪər-/ *n.* a device by which two slightly different photographs etc. are viewed together, giving the impression of depth and solidity. —**stereoscopic** /-'skɒpɪk/ *adj.*, **stereoscopically** /-'skɒpɪkəlɪ/ *adv.* [f. STEREO- + -SCOPE]

stereotype /'sterɪətaɪp, 'stɪər-/ *n.* **1.** an unduly fixed mental impression; a conventional idea or opinion or character etc. **2.** a printing-plate cast from a mould of composed type. —*v.t.* **1.** (usu. in *p.p.*) to formalize, to make typical or conventional. **2.** to print from a stereotype; to make a stereotype of. [f. F (as STEREO-, TYPE)]

sterile /'steraɪl/ *adj.* **1.** not able to produce seed or offspring, barren. **2.** free from living micro-organisms. **3.** without result, unproductive. —**sterility** /-'rɪlɪtɪ/ *n.* [f. F or L *sterilis*]

sterilize /'sterɪlaɪz/ *v.t.* **1.** to make sterile or free from living micro-organisms. **2.** to deprive of the power of reproduction, especially by removal or obstruction of reproductive organs. —**sterilization** /-'zeɪʃ(ə)n/ *n.* [f. prec.]

sterling /'stɜːlɪŋ/ *adj.* **1.** of or in British money. **2.** (of coin or precious metal) genuine, of standard value or purity. **3.** (of a person or qualities etc.) of solid worth, genuine, reliable. —*n.* British money. —**sterling silver,** silver of 92.5% purity. [prob. f. OE, = coin with a star (*steorra*), some of the early Norman pennies having on them a small star]

stern[1] *adj.* strict and severe, not lenient or cheerful or kindly. —**sternly** *adv.*, **sternness** *n.* [OE]

stern[2] *n.* the rear part of a ship or boat; any rear part. —**stern-post** *n.* the central upright timber etc. of the stern, usually bearing the rudder. [prob. f. ON, = steering (as STEER[1])]

Sterne /stɜːn/, Laurence (1713-1768), British novelist, born in Ireland, who became a clergyman and prebendary of York cathedral (1741). He was fêted by London society after the publication of the first two volumes of his greatest novel *Tristram Shandy* (1759-67) in which he parodies the developing conventions of the still new 'novel' form and its problems in presenting reality, space, and time; in this Sterne excels as an innovator of the highest virtuosity, and in his use of the stream-of-consciousness technique he acknowledges his debt to Locke. He had been suffering from tuberculosis and in 1762 left for France in the hope of recuperation. His travels in France and Italy provided material for *A Sentimental Journey through France and Italy* (1767).

sternum *n.* (*pl.* **sternums** or **sterna**) the breastbone (ill. BODY 1). —**sternal** *adj.* [f. Gk *sternon* chest]

steroid /'stɪərɔɪd, 'ste-/ *n.* any of a large group of fat-soluble organic compounds whose molecules all have a basic structure that consists of four fused rings of carbon atoms. Examples of steroids include vitamin D, sex hormones, and sterols such as cholesterol. [f. foll.]

sterol /'stɪərɒl, 'ste-/ *n.* a complex solid alcohol important in vitamin synthesis. [f. CHOLESTEROL etc.]

stertorous /'stɜːtərəs/ *adj.* (of breathing etc.) laboured and noisy. —**stertorously** *adv.* [f. L *stertere* snore]

stethoscope /'steθəskəʊp/ *n.* an instrument used for listening to sounds within the body, e.g. those of the heart and lungs. The French physician R. T. H. Laennec in 1816 introduced a perforated wooden cylinder which concentrated the sounds of air flowing in and out of the lungs, and described the sounds which it revealed. The modern form, with two earpieces connected to the chest-piece by flexible tubes, developed later in the 19th c. —**stethoscopic** /-'skɒpɪk/ *adj.* [f. F f. Gk *stēthos* breast + -SCOPE]

stetson /'stets(ə)n/ *n.* a slouch hat with a very wide brim and a high crown. [f. J. B. *Stetson*, American hat-maker (d. 1906)]

stet *v. imper.* (placed beside a deleted word on a proof-sheet etc.) let it stand as printed or written. [L, 3 sing. pres. subjunctive of *stare* stand]

stevedore /'stiːvədɔː(r)/ *n.* a man employed in loading and unloading ships. [f. Sp. (*estivar* stow a cargo f. L *stipare* pack tight)]

Stevenson /'stiːv(ə)ns(ə)n/, Robert Louis (1850-94), British novelist, born in Edinburgh, where he studied law. He suffered from a chronic bronchial condition and spent much of his life abroad, in France, the USA, and the South Seas, finally settling in Samoa. He published a number of essays, short stories, and travel pieces; his poems include *A Child's Garden of Verses* (1885). His first full length fictional work, the adventure story *Treasure Island* (1883), brought him fame which continued with *The Strange Case of Dr. Jekyll and Mr. Hyde* (1886), *Kidnapped* (1886), its sequel *Catriona* (1893), and *The Master of Ballantrae* (1889); his masterpiece *Weir of Hermiston* (1896) is unfinished. In these works critics have detected beneath a lightness of touch a dark sense of apprehension, but his critical reputation has been obscured by his vivid personality and adventurous life.

stew *v.t./i.* **1.** to cook or be cooked by long simmering in a closed vessel with a liquid. **2.** (*colloq.*) to swelter. —*n.* **1.** a dish of stewed meat etc. **2.** (*colloq.*) an agitated or angry state. —**stew in one's own juice,** to be obliged to suffer the consequences of one's own actions without help or intervention from others. [f. OF *estuver* prob. ult. f. Gk *tuphos* steam]

steward /'stjuːəd/ *n.* **1.** a person employed to manage another's property, especially a great house or estate. **2.** a person responsible for supplies of food etc. for a college or club etc. **3.** a passengers' attendant on a ship, aircraft, or train. **4.** an official in charge of a race-meeting or show etc. —*v.t./i.* to act as a steward (of). —**Lord High Steward of England,** a high officer of State presiding at coronations. [OE f. *stig* house, *weard* ward]

stewardess *n.* a female steward, especially on a ship or aircraft. [f. prec.]

stewardship *n.* **1.** the position or work of a steward. **2.** the organized pledging of specific amounts of money etc. to be given regularly to the Church. [f. STEWARD + -SHIP]

Stewart var. of STUART[1].

stewed *adj.* **1.** cooked by stewing. **2.** (of tea) bitter or strong from infusing for too long. **3.** (*slang*) drunk. [f. STEW]

stick[1] *n.* **1.** a short slender branch or piece of wood, especially one trimmed for use as a support or weapon, or as firewood. **2.** a thin rod of wood etc. for a particular purpose; a thing resembling this in shape; the implement used to propel the ball in hockey or polo etc.; a gear-lever; a conductor's baton; a more or less cylindrical piece of a substance, e.g. celery or dynamite; (*colloq.*) an item of furniture etc. **3.** punishment, especially by beating; adverse criticism. **4.** (*colloq.*) a person, especially one who is dull or unsociable. —**stick insect,** an insect of the family Phasmidae, with a slender sticklike body resembling the twigs of the trees in which it lives (ill. INSECTS). [OE]

stick[2] *v.t./i.* (*past & p.p.* **stuck**) **1.** to insert or thrust (a thing or its point) into something; to stab. **2.** to fix on or upon a pointed object; (*colloq.*) to put. **3.** to fix or be fixed (as) by glue or solution etc.; (*colloq.*) to remain in the same place; (*colloq.* of an accusation etc.) to be convincing or regarded as valid. **4.** to lose or deprive of the power of motion or action through friction, jamming, or some other impediment or difficulty. **5.** (*slang*) to endure, to tolerate. **6.** (*colloq.*) to impose a difficult or unpleasant task upon. **7.** to provide (a plant) with a stick as a support. —**be stuck for,** (*colloq.*) to be at a loss for or in need of. **be stuck on,** (*slang*) to be captivated by. **be stuck with,** (*colloq.*) to be unable to get rid of. **get stuck in** or **into,** (*slang*) to begin in earnest. **stick around,** (*slang*) to linger, to remain at the same place. **stick at,** (*colloq.*) to persevere with. **stick at nothing,** to allow nothing, especially no scruples, to deter one. **stick by** or **with,** to stay close or faithful to. **stickingplaster** *n.* an adhesive plaster for wounds etc. **stick-in-the-mud** *n.* (*colloq.*) an unprogressive or old-fashioned person. **stick in one's throat,** to be against one's principles. **stick it out,** (*colloq.*) to endure something unpleasant. **stick one's neck out,** to expose oneself to danger etc. by acting boldly. **stick out,** to protrude or cause to protrude. **stick out for,** to persist in demanding. **stick to,** to remain fixed on or to, to remain faithful to, to keep to (a subject etc.). **stick together,** (*colloq.*) to remain united or mutually loyal. **stick up,** to protrude or cause to protrude; to be or make erect; to fasten to an upright surface; (*slang*) to rob or threaten with a gun. **stick-up** *n.* (*slang*) a robbery with a gun. **stick up for,** to support or defend (a person or cause). [OE]

sticker *n.* **1.** an adhesive label. **2.** a persistent person. [f. prec.]

stickleback /ˈstɪk(ə)lbæk/ *n.* a small spiny-backed fish of the family Gasterosteidae. [OE, = thorn-back]

stickler *n.* a person who insists on something. [f. obs. *stickle* be umpire]

stickpin *n.* (*US*) a tie-pin.

sticky *adj.* **1.** sticking or tending to stick to what is touched. **2.** (of weather) humid. **3.** (*colloq.*) making or likely to make objections. **4.** (*slang*) very unpleasant or difficult. —**sticky wicket,** (*colloq.*) a pitch that is drying after rain and is difficult for batsmen; difficult circumstances. —**stickily** *adv.*, **stickiness** *n.* [f. STICK²]

stiction /ˈstɪkʃ(ə)n/ *n.* static friction, the friction which tends to prevent surfaces at rest from being set in motion. [f. *static* + *friction*]

stiff *adj.* **1.** not flexible; not moving or changing its shape easily. **2.** not fluid, thick and hard to stir. **3.** difficult to move or deal with; (of a breeze) blowing strongly; (of a price or penalty) high, severe; (of a drink or dose) strong. **4.** formal in manner, not pleasantly sociable or friendly. **5.** (*colloq.*) to an extreme degree. —*n.* (*slang*) **1.** a corpse. **2.** a foolish or useless person. —**stiff-necked** *adj.* obstinate; haughty. **stiff upper lip,** fortitude in enduring grief etc. **stiff with,** (*slang*) abundantly provided with. —**stiffly** *adv.*, **stiffness** *n.* [OE]

stiffen *v.t./i.* to make or become stiff. —**stiffener** *n.* [f. STIFF]

stifle¹ /ˈstaɪf(ə)l/ *v.t./i.* **1.** to suffocate; to be or feel unable to breathe for lack of air. **2.** to restrain, to suppress. —**stifling** *adj.* [perh. f. OF *estouffer*]

stifle² /ˈstaɪf(ə)l/ *n.* the joint of a dog's or horse's etc. leg between hip and hock (ill. HORSE). [orig. unkn.]

stigma /ˈstɪgmə/ *n.* (*pl.* **-as**) **1.** a mark or sign of disgrace or discredit. **2.** the part of a pistil that receives the pollen in pollination (ill. FLOWERS). **3.** (in *pl.* **stigmata** /ˈstɪgmətə/) marks corresponding to those left on Christ's body by the nails and spear at his Crucifixion. Such marks are attributed to divine favour; they are first recorded as occurring on the person of St Francis of Assisi. [L f. Gk, = mark made by pointed instrument]

stigmatize /ˈstɪgmətaɪz/ *v.t.* to brand as unworthy or disgraceful. —**stigmatization** /-ˈzeɪʃ(ə)n/ *n.* [f. F or L f. Gk (as prec.)]

Stijl /staɪl/ *n.* a 20th-c. Dutch art movement which took its name from the Dutch periodical *De Stijl* (1917-32) founded by Theo van Doesburg and Piet Mondrian, devoted to the principles of neoplasticism. Its adherents sought an interdisciplinary application of their ideas and theory to painting, sculpture, architecture, and even poetry: form was reduced to the geometric simplicity of horizontals and verticals, and colour (which was used not as decoration but as an ancillary to special definition) was restricted to primary colours and black, white, and grey. Architects in the group included J. J. P. Oud (1890-1963), and Gerrit Rietveld (1888-1965). In the 1920s and 1930s De Stijl was influential in a European context, particularly on the Bauhaus and the constructivist movements and on Parisian purism. [Du., = the style]

stile¹ *n.* an arrangement of steps allowing people but not animals to climb over a fence or wall. [OE]

stile² *n.* a vertical piece (cf. RAIL¹) in the frame of a panelled door, wainscot, etc. (ill. HOUSES). [prob. f. Du. *stijl* pillar, door-post]

stiletto /stɪˈletəʊ/ *n.* (*pl.* **-os**) **1.** a short dagger. **2.** a pointed instrument for making eyelets etc. —**stiletto heel,** a high tapering heel of a shoe. [It., dim. of *stilo* dagger (as STYLUS)]

still¹ *adj.* **1.** without or almost without motion or sound. **2.** (of drinks) not effervescing. —*n.* **1.** silence and calm. **2.** an ordinary static photograph (as opposed to a motion picture), especially a single shot from a cinema film. —*adv.* **1.** without moving. **2.** even until or at a particular time. **3.** nevertheless, all the same. **4.** even, yet, increasingly. —*v.t./i.* to make or become still, to quieten. —**still birth,** a birth in which the child is born dead. **still life** (*pl.* **still lifes**), a painting of inanimate objects, e.g. fruits. —**stillness** *n.* [OE]

still² *n.* an apparatus for distilling spirituous liquors etc. —**still-room** *n.* a room for distilling, a housekeeper's store-room in a large house. [f. *still* v. f. DISTIL]

stillborn *adj.* **1.** born dead. **2.** (of an idea or plan etc.) not developing.

stilt *n.* **1.** each of a pair of poles with supports for the feet enabling the user to walk at a distance above the ground. **2.** each of a set of piles or posts supporting a building etc. [f. LG]

stilted *adj.* **1.** (of literary style etc.) stiff and unnaturally formal. **2.** standing on stilts. —**stiltedly** *adv.* [f. STILT]

Stilton /ˈstɪltən/ *n.* a rich blue-veined cheese originally made at various places in Leicestershire and formerly sold to travellers at a coaching inn at Stilton (now in Cambridgeshire) on the Great North Road from London.

stimulant /ˈstɪmjʊlənt/ *adj.* that stimulates, especially that increases bodily or mental activity. —*n.* a stimulant substance or influence. [f. L (as foll.)]

stimulate /ˈstɪmjʊleɪt/ *v.t.* **1.** to make more vigorous or active. **2.** to apply a stimulus to. —**stimulation** /-ˈleɪʃ(ə)n/ *n.*, **stimulative** *adj.*, **stimulator** *n.* [f. L *stimulare* (as foll.)]

stimulus /ˈstɪmjʊləs/ *n.* (*pl.* **-li** /-laɪ/) a stimulating thing or effect; something that produces a reaction in an organ or tissue. [L, = goad]

sting *n.* **1.** a sharp-pointed part or organ of an insect etc., used for wounding and often injecting poison. **2.** a stiff sharp-pointed hair on certain plants, causing inflammation if touched. **3.** the infliction of a wound by a sting; the wound so inflicted. **4.** any sharp bodily or mental pain; a wounding quality or effect. **5.** (*slang*) a swindle. —*v.t./i.* (*past & p.p.* **stung**) **1.** to wound or affect with a sting; to, be able to do this. **2.** to cause to feel sharp bodily or mental pain. **3.** to stimulate sharply as if by a sting. **4.** (*slang*) to swindle, especially by overcharging; to extort money from. —**stinging-nettle** *n.* a nettle that stings (opp. *dead-nettle*), a plant of the genus *Urtica*. **sting in the tail,** an unexpected pain or difficulty at the end. **sting-ray** *n.* a broad flat-fish, especially of the family Dasyatidae, with a stinging tail. [OE]

stinger *n.* a thing that stings, especially a sharp painful blow. [f. STING]

stingy /ˈstɪndʒɪ/ *adj.* spending, giving, or given grudgingly or in small amounts. —**stingily** *adv.*, **stinginess** *n.* [perh. f. dial. *stinge* sting]

stink *v.t./i.* (*past* **stank** or **stunk**; *p.p.* **stunk**) **1.** to give off an offensive smell. **2.** (*colloq.*) to be or seem very unpleasant, unsavoury, or dishonest. —*n.* **1.** an offensive smell. **2.** (*colloq.*) an offensive complaint or fuss. —**stink-bomb** *n.* a device emitting a stink when exploded. **stink out,** to drive out by a stink; to fill (a place) with a stink. [OE]

stinker *n.* **1.** a person or thing that stinks. **2.** (*slang*) a very objectionable person or thing; a difficult task; a letter etc. conveying strong disapproval. [f. STINK]

stinking *adj.* that stinks; (*slang*) very objectionable. —*adv.* (*slang*) extremely and usually objectionably. [f. STINK]

stint *v.t.* to restrict to a small allowance (of); to be niggardly with. —*n.* **1.** a limitation of supply or effort. **2.** a fixed or allotted amount of work. **3.** a small sandpiper of the genus *Calidris*. [OE, = to blunt]

stipend /ˈstaɪpend/ *n.* a salary, especially of a clergyman. [f. OF or L *stipendium* (*stips* wages, *pendere* to pay)]

stipendiary /staɪˈpendjərɪ, stɪ-/ *adj.* receiving a stipend.

—*n.* a person receiving a stipend. —**stipendiary magistrate,** a paid professional magistrate. [f. L (as prec.)]

stipple *v.t./i.* **1.** to paint, draw, or engrave with small dots (not with lines or strokes). **2.** to roughen the surface of (paint or cement etc.). —*n.* stippling; this effect. [f. Du. *stippelen* frequent. of *stippen* to prick (*stip* point)]

stipulate /ˈstɪpjʊleɪt/ *v.t./i.* to demand or specify as part of a bargain or agreement. —**stipulate for,** to mention or insist upon as essential. —**stipulation** /-ˈleɪʃ(ə)n/ *n.* [f. L *stipulari*]

stir[1] *v.t./i.* (**-rr-**) **1.** to move a spoon etc. round and round in (a liquid etc.) so as to mix the ingredients. **2.** to move or cause to move slightly; to be or begin to be in motion; to rise after sleeping. **3.** to arouse, inspire, or excite (emotions etc., or a person as regards these). —*n.* **1.** the act or process of stirring. **2.** a commotion or disturbance; excitement, a sensation. —**stir one's stumps,** (*colloq.*) to begin to move; to hurry. **stir up,** to mix thoroughly by stirring; to stimulate. [OE]

stir[2] *n.* (*slang*) prison. [orig. unkn.]

Stirling[1] /ˈstɜːlɪŋ/, James (1692–1770), Scottish mathematician. The formula named after him, giving the approximate value of the factorial of a large number, was first worked out by Abraham de Moivre (d. 1754).

Stirling[2] /ˈstɜːlɪŋ/, Robert (1796–1878), minister of the Presbyterian Church of Scotland, co-inventor with his brother James in 1816–17 of a type of external-combustion engine known as the Stirling engine. This engine achieved a modest success in the 1890s but development lapsed until 1938, and has not achieved commercial success despite post-war efforts.

stirrup /ˈstɪrəp/ *n.* a metal or leather support for a horse-rider's foot, hanging from the saddle (ill. HORSE). —**stirrup-cup** *n.* a drink offered to a person about to depart, originally on horseback. **stirrup-leather** *n.* a strap attaching a stirrup to a saddle. **stirrup-pump** *n.* a hand-operated water-pump with a stump-shaped foot-rest, used to extinguish small fires. [OE (*stigan* climb + ROPE)]

stitch *n.* **1.** a single pass of a threaded needle in and out of fabric in sewing or tissue in surgery; a thread etc. between two needle-holes. **2.** a single complete movement of a needle or hook in knitting or crochet; the loop of thread made thus. **3.** a particular method of arranging the thread(s). **4.** the least bit of clothing. **5.** an acute pain in the side induced by running etc. —*v.t./i.* to sew, to make stitches (in). —**in stitches,** (*colloq.*) laughing uncontrollably. **stitch in time,** a timely remedy. **stitch up,** to join or mend by sewing. [OE]

stoa /ˈstəʊə/ *n.* (in ancient Greek architecture) a portico or roofed colonnade (ill. TEMPLES). [Gk]

stoat *n.* an ermine, especially when the fur is brown. [orig. unkn.]

stock *n.* **1.** a store of goods etc. ready for sale or distribution etc.; a supply of things available for use. **2.** livestock. **3.** the capital of a business company; a portion of this held by an investor (differing from *shares* in that it is not issued in fixed amounts). **4.** one's reputation or popularity. **5.** money lent to a government at fixed interest. **6.** a line of ancestry. **7.** liquid made by stewing bones, vegetables, etc., as a basis for soup, sauce, etc. **8.** a base, support, or handle for an implement or machine etc.; the butt of a rifle etc. **9.** a plant into which a graft is inserted; the main trunk of a tree etc. **10.** a fragrant-flowered cruciferous plant of the genus *Matthiola*. **11.** (in *pl.*) supports for a ship during building. **12.** (in *pl.*, *hist.*) a timber frame with holes for the legs of a seated person, used like the pillory. **13.** a cravat worn e.g. as part of riding-kit; a piece of black or purple fabric worn over the shirt front by a clergyman, hanging from a clerical collar. —*adj.* **1.** kept in stock and readily available. **2.** commonly used, conventional; hackneyed. —*v.t./i.* **1.** to have (goods) in stock. **2.** to provide with goods, equipment, or livestock. **3.** to fit (a gun etc.) with a stock. —**in** (*or* **out of**) **stock,** available (or not available) immediately for sale etc. **on the stocks,** in construction or preparation. **stock-car** *n.* a specially strengthened car for use in racing in which deliberate bumping is allowed. **stock exchange,** see separate entry. **stock-in-trade** *n.* all the requisites of a trade or profession. **stock-market** *n.* a stock exchange; the transactions on this. **stock-pot** *n.* a pot for making soup stock. **stock-room** *n.* a room for storing goods. **stock-still** *adj.* motionless. **stock-taking** *n.* making the inventory of the stock in a shop etc.; a review of one's position and resources. **stock up,** to provide with or get stocks or supplies. **stock up with,** to gather a stock of. **take stock,**

to make an inventory of one's stock; to make a review or estimate of a situation etc. [OE (ON *stokkr* trunk)]

stockade /stɒˈkeɪd/ *n.* a line or enclosure of upright stakes. —*v.t.* to fortify with a stockade. [f. obs. F f. Sp. *estacada* (rel. to STAKE)]

stockbreeder *n.* a farmer who raises livestock.

stockbroker *n.* a person who buys and sells stocks and shares (from stockjobbers) on behalf of customers. —**stockbroking** *n.*

stock exchange a place where stocks and shares are publicly bought and sold. —**the Stock Exchange,** an association of dealers in stocks, conducting business according to fixed rules; the building occupied by these. An association was not formed in London until late in the 18th c., although dealings had previously taken place among bankers, brokers, and financial houses. Members of the new association met regularly at a coffee-house known as 'Jonathan's', and early in the 19th c. acquired a building of their own. The New York Stock Exchange had even humbler beginnings, for it started (at the end of the 18th c.) as a street market under a spreading tree in Lower Wall Street. The organization of the Stock Exchange in Britain differs from that of similar exchanges elsewhere. In Britain there is a rigid division of membership between the jobbers or dealers and those who act as brokers; in most other stock-markets all members carry on both functions.

Stockhausen /ˈstɒkhaʊz(ə)n/, Karlheinz (1928–), German composer. In 1952 he went to Paris for a year to study with Messiaen and Milhaud and work at the electronic music studios of Radio France. On his return to Cologne he joined the staff of West German Radio, becoming director in 1963. His experience with electronic music bore fruit in such works as the *Gesang der Jünglinge* (1955–6), which combines electrical sounds with the voice of a boy soprano altered by echo-effects, filters, etc. Another important early interest was in the serial works of Webern, and in *Gruppen* (1955–7) and *Momente* (1961–72), for example, he takes serialism to its limits, allowing it to govern every possible aspect of performance. In other works of the 1960s he concentrated on different timbres, frequently leaving the realization of details to the performers.

stockholder *n.* an owner of stocks or shares.

Stockholm /ˈstɒkhəʊm/ the capital of Sweden since 1634 and a major port; pop. (1980) 647,214.

stockinet /stɒkɪˈnet/ *n.* (also **stockinette**) fine stretchable machine-knitted fabric used for underwear etc. [prob. f. *stocking-net*]

stocking *n.* **1.** a close-fitting covering for the foot and all or part of the leg, usually knitted or woven of wool or nylon etc. **2.** a differently-coloured lower part of the leg of a horse etc. —**in one's stocking** *or* **stockinged feet,** wearing stockings but no shoes. **stocking mask,** a nylon stocking worn over the head as a criminal's disguise. **stocking-stitch** *n.* alternate rows of plain and purl in knitting, giving a plain smooth surface on one side. [f. STOCK in dial. sense 'stocking']

stockist *n.* one who stocks (certain) goods for sale. [f. STOCK]

stockjobber *n.* a member of the Stock Exchange who buys and sells stocks and shares so as to profit by fluctuations in their prices, dealing with stockbrokers but not with the general public.

stockman *n.* (*pl.* **-men**) (*Austral.*) a man in charge of livestock.

stockpile *n.* an accumulated stock of goods etc. held in reserve. —*v.t.* to accumulate a stockpile of.

stockrider *n.* (*Austral.*) a herdsman on an unfenced station.

stocky *adj.* short and strongly built. —**stockily** *adv.*, **stockiness** *n.* [f. STOCK]

stockyard *n.* an enclosure for sorting or temporary keeping of cattle.

stodge /stɒdʒ/ *n.* (*colloq.*) **1.** food of a thick heavy kind. **2.** an unimaginative person or work. —*v.t./i.* (*colloq.*) **1.** to stuff (oneself) with food etc. **2.** to trudge through mud etc.; to work laboriously. [imit., after *stuff* and *podge*]

stodgy /ˈstɒdʒɪ/ *adj.* **1.** (of food) heavy and thick, indigestible. **2.** dull and uninteresting. —**stodgily** *adv.*, **stodginess** *n.* [f. prec.]

Stoic /ˈstəʊɪk/ *n.* a member of the Greek philosophical school named after the *Stoa Poikilē* (painted colonnade) in Athens in which its founder Zeno (early 3rd c. BC) used to lecture. They taught that virtue, the highest good, is based on knowledge, and that only the wise man is truly virtuous; the wise man lives in harmony with the divine Reason (also identified with Fate and Providence) that governs nature, and is indifferent to the vicissitudes of fortune and to pleasure and pain (and hence 'stoic' in the popular sense). Stoicism was particularly influential among the Roman upper classes, numbering Seneca and Marcus Aurelius among its followers. —**Stoicism** /-sɪz(ə)m/ *n*. [f. L f. Gk]

stoic /'stəʊɪk/ *n*. a stoical person. —*adj*. stoical. —**stoicism** *n*. [= prec.]

stoical /'stəʊɪk(ə)l *adj*. having or showing great self-control in adversity. —**stoically** *adv*. [f. STOIC]

stoke *v.t./i*. (often with *up*) **1**. to tend and put fuel on (a fire or furnace etc.). **2**. (*colloq*.) to consume food steadily and in large quantities. [back-formation f. STOKER]

stokehold *n*. a compartment in which a steamer's fires are tended.

stokehole *n*. a space for stokers in front of a furnace.

Stoker /'stəʊkə(r)/, Abraham ('Bram') (1847–1912), Irish novelist, for several years business manager of the actor Sir Henry Irving. He is remembered as the author of the vampire story *Dracula* (see entry).

stoker /'stəʊkə(r)/ *n*. **1**. a person who stokes a furnace etc., especially on a ship. **2**. a mechanical device for doing this. [Du., f. *stoken* stoke f. MDu. *stoken* push (rel. to STICK[2])]

STOL *abbr*. short take-off and landing.

stole[1] *n*. **1**. a woman's long garment like a scarf, worn over the shoulders. **2**. a strip of silk etc. worn similarly as a vestment by a priest (ill. VESTMENTS). [OE f. L f. Gk *stolē* equipment]

stole[2] *past* of STEAL.

stolen *p.p.* of STEAL.

stolid /'stɒlɪd/ *adj*. not feeling or showing emotion or animation; not easily excited or moved. —**stolidity** /-'lɪdɪtɪ/ *n*., **stolidly** *adv*. [f. obs. F or L *stolidus*]

stomach /'stʌmək/ *n*. **1**. the internal organ in which the first part of digestion occurs (ill. BODY 2); one of the several digestive organs of an animal. **2**. the lower front of the body. **3**. an appetite or inclination. —*v.t.* to endure, to put up with. —**stomach-ache** *n*. a pain in the belly, especially in the bowels. **stomach-pump** *n*. a syringe for emptying the stomach or forcing liquid into it. **stomach upset**, a temporary slight digestive disorder. [f. OF f. L f. Gk, orig. = gullet (*stoma* mouth)]

stomacher /'stʌmək(r)/ *n*. (*hist.*) a pointed front-piece of a woman's dress, often jewelled or embroidered. [prob. f. OF *estomachier* (as prec.)]

stomp *n*. a lively jazz dance with heavy stamping. —*v.t./i.* to tread heavily (on); to dance a stomp. [US dial. var of STAMP]

stone *n*. **1**. the solid non-metallic mineral matter of which rock is made. **2**. a small piece of this; a piece of stone of a definite shape or for a particular purpose. **3**. a thing resembling a stone in hardness or form, e.g. a hard morbid concretion in the body or a hard case of the kernel in some fruits. **4**. a precious stone. **5**. (*pl.* same) the weight of 14 lb. —*adj*. made of stone. —*v.t.* **1**. to pelt with stones. **2**. to remove the stones from (fruit). **3**. (in *p.p.*, *slang*) very drunk; incapacitated or stimulated by drugs. —**cast** *or* **throw stones**, to make aspersions on the character etc. **leave no stone unturned**, to try every possible means. **Stone Age**, see separate entry. **stone-cold** *adj*. completely cold. **stone-dead** *adj*. completely dead. **stone-deaf** *adj*. completely deaf. **stone-fly** *n*. an insect of the order Plecoptera, with aquatic larvae found under stones, used as bait (ill. INSECTS). **stone-fruit** *n*. a fruit with flesh or pulp enclosing a stone. **a stone's throw**, a short distance. [OE]

Stone Age the first stage in the three-era classification of prehistoric periods (see PREHISTORY) when weapons and tools were made out of stone or of organic materials such as bone, wood, or horn. It is subdivided into the palaeolithic (formerly called the Old Stone Age), mesolithic (Middle Stone Age), and neolithic (New Stone Age).

stonechat *n*. a small black and white bird (*Saxicola torquata*) with an alarm-note like the knocking of pebbles.

stonecrop *n*. a creeping rock-plant of the genus *Sedum*, especially *S. acre*.

Stonehenge /stəʊn'hendʒ/ a unique megalithic monument on Salisbury Plain in Wiltshire, England. Its alleged connection with the Druids dates from the 17th c., when people's ideas about what constituted 'the past' were very vague. In the 12th c. it was believed to be a monument over King Arthur's grave; other theories have attributed it to

the Phoenicians, Romans, Vikings, and visitors from other worlds (see also DRUID); modern theory inclines to the view that it was a temple. Scientific study and excavation have identified three main constructional phases between *c*.3000 BC and *c*.1500 BC, i.e. it was completed in the Bronze Age. The circular bank and ditch, double circle of 'bluestones' (spotted dolerite), and circle of sarsen stones (some with stone lintels), are concentric, and the main axis is aligned on the midsummer sunrise—an orientation that was probably for ritual rather than scientific purposes.

stonemason *n*. a dresser of or builder in stone.

stonewall *v.i.* **1**. to obstruct discussion etc. with non-committal answers. **2**. (in cricket) to bat without attempting to score runs.

stoneware *n*. pottery made from very siliceous clay or from clay and flint.

stonework *n*. work built of stone, masonry.

stony /'stəʊnɪ/ *adj*. **1**. full of stones. **2**. like stone in texture, hard. **3**. unfeeling, uncompromising, unresponsive. **4**. (*slang*) = stony-broke. —**stony-broke** *adj*. (*slang*) = broke. —**stonily** *adv.*, **stoniness** *n*. [f. STONE]

stood *past* & *p.p.* of STAND.

stooge *n*. (*colloq.*) **1**. a comedian's assistant, used as a target for jokes. **2**. a subordinate who does routine work. **3**. a person who's actions are entirely controlled by another. —*v.i.* (*colloq.*) **1**. to act as a stooge. **2**. to move or wander aimlessly. [orig. unkn.; perh. f. STUDENT (students having frequently been employed as stage assistants)]

stool *n*. **1**. a movable seat without a back or arms, usually for one person; a footstool. **2**. (usu. in *pl.*) faeces. **3**. a root or stump of a tree or plant from which shoots spring. —**stool-pigeon** *n*. a pigeon as a decoy; a police informer. [OE]

stool-ball *n*. an old game resembling cricket, still played in Sussex etc. especially by women and girls. Forms of it were played in Elizabethan times, when it was a hand-game, not using bats, and the 'stool' or wicket may have been an ordinary stool.

stoop[1] *n*. **1**. to bend (one's shoulders or body) forwards and downwards; to carry one's head and shoulders thus. **2**. to condescend; to lower oneself morally. —*n*. a stooping posture. [OE, prob. rel. to STEEP[1]]

stoop[2] *n*. (*US*) a porch or small veranda or the steps in front of a house. [f. Du. *stoep* (rel. to STEP)]

stop *v.t./i.* (**-pp-**) **1**. to put an end to the movement, progress, or operation etc. of; to cause to halt or pause. **2**. to refrain from continuing, to cease motion or working. **3**. (*slang*) to receive (a blow etc.) on one's body. **4**. to remain, to stay for a short time. **5**. to close by plugging or obstructing; to put a filling in (a tooth). **6**. to keep back, to refuse to give or allow; to instruct a bank to withhold payment on (a cheque). **7**. to obtain the desired pitch in a musical instrument by pressing (a string) or blocking (a hole). —*n*. **1**. stopping, being stopped; a pause or check. **2**. a place where a bus or train etc. regularly stops. **3**. a sign to show a pause in written matter, especially a full stop. **4**. a device for stopping motion at a particular point. **5**. (*Mus.*) a change of pitch effected by stopping a string; (in an organ) a row of pipes of one character; a knob etc. operating these. **6**. (in optics and photography) a diaphragm; the effective diameter of a lens; a device reducing this. **7**. a plosive sound. —**pull out all the stops**, to make an extreme effort. **stop at nothing**, to be ruthless or unscrupulous. **stop-go** *n*. the alternate suppression and stimulation of progress. **stop off** *or* **over**, to break one's journey. **stopping train**, a train stopping at many intermediate stations. **stop-press** *n*. late news inserted in a newspaper after printing has begun. **stop-watch** *n*. a watch with a mechanism for instantly starting and stopping it, used in timing races etc. [OE]

stopcock *n*. an externally operated valve to regulate the flow in a pipe etc.

Stopes /stəʊps/, Marie Charlotte Carmichael (1880–1958), advocate of birth control, born in Scotland. She studied botany and specialized in fossil plants, establishing a considerable academic reputation, but after the failure in 1916 of her first marriage devoted herself to sex education and family planning, founding the first birth-control clinic in London in 1921.

stopgap *n*. a temporary substitute.

stopoff *n*. (also **stopover**) a break in one's journey.

stoppage *n*. the condition of being blocked or stopped. [f. STOP]

Stoppard /'stɒpɑːd/, Tom (1937–), Czech-born English

playwright, author of *Rosencrantz and Guildenstern are Dead* (1966) and other comedies. His plays are noted for their bizarre conjunctions and verbal dexterity.

stopper *n.* a plug for closing a bottle etc. —*v.t.* to close with a stopper. —**put a stopper on,** to cause to cease. [f. STOP]

stopping *n.* a filling for a tooth. [f. STOP]

storage /'stɔːrɪdʒ/ *n.* **1.** the storing of goods etc. **2.** a method of storing the space available for this. **3.** the cost of storing. **4.** the storing of data. —**storage battery** *or* **cell,** a battery or cell for storing electricity. **storage heater,** an electric heater accumulating heat outside peak hours for later release. [f. foll.]

store *n.* **1.** a quantity of something or (also in *pl.*) articles accumulated so as to be available for use. **2.** a large shop selling goods of many kinds; (*US*) a shop. **3.** a storehouse, a warehouse where things are stored. **4.** a device in a computer for storing data. —*v.t.* **1.** to accumulate for future use. **2.** to put (furniture etc.) into a warehouse for temporary keeping. **3.** to stock with something useful. **4.** (in computers) to enter or retain (data) for future retrieval. —**in store,** being stored; kept available for use; destined to happen, imminent. **set store by,** to consider important, to value greatly. **store-cattle** *n.* cattle kept for breeding or for future fattening. **store-room** *n.* a room used for storing things. [f. OF *estore, estorer* f. L *instaurare* renew]

storehouse *n.* a place where things are stored.

storekeeper *n.* **1.** a person in charge of a store or stores. **2.** (*US*) a shopkeeper.

storey /'stɔːrɪ/ *n.* **1.** each of the parts into which a building is divided horizontally; the whole of the rooms etc. having a continuous floor. **2.** a thing forming a horizontal division. —**storeyed** *adj.* [f. L *historia* history (perh. orig. a tier of painted windows)]

storied /'stɔːrɪd/ *adj.* celebrated in or associated with stories or legends. [f. STORY]

stork *n.* a tall usually white wading bird of the family Ciconiidae, with long legs and a long straight bill, sometimes nesting on buildings and humorously pretended to be the bringer of babies. [OE]

storm *n.* **1.** a violent disturbance of the atmosphere with thunder, strong wind, heavy rain or snow, or hail. **2.** a violent disturbance or commotion in human affairs; a violent dispute etc. **3.** a violent shower of missiles or blows; a violent outbreak of applause, abuse, etc. **4.** a direct military assault upon (and the capture of) a defended place. —*v.t./i.* **1.** (of wind or rain) to rage, to be violent. **2.** to move or behave violently or very angrily. **3.** to attract or capture by storm. —**storm-centre** *n.* the centre of a storm or cyclone; a subject etc. upon which agitation is concentrated. **storm-cloud** *n.* a heavy rain-cloud; something threatening. **storm-door** *n.* an additional outer door. **storm in a teacup,** great excitement over a trivial matter. **storm petrel,** a small black and white petrel (*Hydrobates pelagicus*) of the North Atlantic, said to be active before storms. **storm-trooper** *n.* a member of storm-troops. **storm-troops** *n.pl.* shock-troops; the Nazi political militia. **take by storm,** to capture by storm; to captivate quickly. [OE]

Stormont /'stɔːmənt/ a suburb of the east side of Belfast, the seat of the parliament of Northern Ireland (suspended since the imposition of direct rule from London in 1972).

stormy *adj.* **1.** full of storms; affected by storms. **2.** (of wind etc.) violent as in a storm. **3.** full of violent anger or outbursts. —**stormy petrel,** the storm petrel (see STORM); a person whose arrival seems to foreshadow or attract trouble. —**stormily** *adv.*, **storminess** *n.* [f. STORM]

story *n.* **1.** an account of an incident or of a series of incidents, either true or invented. **2.** the past course of a person's or institution's life. **3.** a report of an item of news; material suitable for this. **4.** (also **story-line**) the plot of a novel or play etc. **5.** (*colloq.*) a fib. [f. AF *estorie* f. L (as HISTORY)]

stoup /stuːp/ *n.* **1.** a basin for holy water, especially in the wall of a church. **2.** (*archaic*) a flagon, a beaker. [f. ON (rel. to STEEP²)]

stout *adj.* **1.** (of a person) solidly built and rather fat. **2.** of considerable thickness or strength. **3.** brave and resolute. —*n.* a strong dark beer brewed with roasted malt or barley. —**stoutly** *adv.*, **stoutness** *n.* [f. AF (e)*stout*]

stove¹ *n.* **1.** an apparatus containing an oven or ovens. **2.** a closed apparatus used for heating rooms etc. **3.** a hothouse with artificial heat. —**stove-enamel** *n.* a heat-proof enamel produced by treating enamelled objects in a stove. **stove-**

enamelled *adj.* [orig. = sweating-room, f. MDu. (perh. rel. to STEW)]

stove² see STAVE.

stow /stəʊ/ *v.t.* **1.** to place in a receptacle for storage. **2.** (*slang*, esp. in *imper.*) to cease from. —**stow away,** to put away in storage or in reserve; to conceal oneself as a stowaway. [f. BESTOW]

stowage *n.* stowing, being stowed; the space available for this; the charge for it. [f. STOW]

stowaway *n.* a person who hides on board a ship or aircraft etc. so as to travel without charge or unseen.

Stowe /stəʊ/, Mrs Harriet Beecher (1811–96), American novelist who won fame with her anti-slavery novel *Uncle Tom's Cabin* (1852) which stirred up great public feeling in its powerful and melodramatic descriptions of the sufferings of slaves. The novel's success brought her to England where she was rapturously received and honoured by Queen Victoria, though she later alienated British opinion by her *Lady Byron Vindicated* (1870) which charged Byron with incestuous relations with his half-sister.

strabismus /strə'bɪzməs/ *n.* squinting; a squint. [f. Gk (*strabizō* squint)]

Strabo /'streɪbəʊ/ (64/3 BC–after AD 21) Greek historian and geographer. His historical writing is lost; his *Geography*, probably written for the use of public figures, deals with theoretical and philosophical matters (he himself was a Stoic) before presenting a detailed physical and historical geography of the ancient world.

Strachey /'streɪtʃɪ/, (Giles) Lytton (1880–1932), English biographer, a prominent member of the Bloomsbury Group. He achieved recognition with *Eminent Victorians* (1918) which attacked the Victorian establishment through satirical biographies of Cardinal Manning, Florence Nightingale, Dr Thomas Arnold, General Gordon, and others. He influenced the development of biography with his irreverent biography of Queen Victoria (1921), and *Elizabeth and Essex* (1928) reveals his debt to Freud.

straddle *v.t./i.* **1.** to sit or stand (across) with the legs wide apart; to part (one's legs) widely. **2.** to drop shots or bombs short of and beyond (a specified point). —*n.* the act of straddling. [f. *striddlings* astride (as STRIDE)]

Stradivarius /strædɪ'veərɪəs/ *n.* a violin or other stringed instrument made by Antonio Stradivari (?1644–1737), the greatest of a family of violin-makers of Cremona in northern Italy, or his followers. Antonio Stradivari trained in the workshop of Nicolò Amati and produced over 1,100 instruments, of which perhaps 400 are known still to exist. Among the many famous Stradivarius violins are those nicknamed the 'Betts' (1704), now in the Library of Congress, and the 'Messie' (Messiah, named by the French violinist Alard on being shown 'what one waits for always but which never appears'; 1716), now in the Ashmolean Museum, Oxford. Stradivari's finest instruments are those dating from *c.*1700 onwards. [Latinized f. *Stradivari*]

strafe /strɑːf, streɪf/ *v.t.* to harass with gunfire or bombs. —*n.* an act of strafing. [adaptation of G 1914 catchword *Gott strafe* (God punish) *England*]

straggle *v.i.* **1.** to lack or lose compactness, to grow or spread in an irregular or untidy way. **2.** to go or wander separately, not in a group; to drop behind others. —*n.* a straggling group. —**straggler** *n.*, **straggly** *adj.* [perh. f. dial. *strake* go (rel. to STRETCH)]

straight /streɪt/ *adj.* **1.** extending or moving uniformly in the same direction, without a curve or bend etc. **2.** direct. **3.** in unbroken succession. **4.** level, tidy; in the proper order, place, or condition. **5.** honest; candid; not evasive. **6.** not modified or elaborate, without additions; (of a drink) undiluted. **7.** conventional, respectable; heterosexual. —*n.* **1.** the straight part of something, especially the concluding stretch of a racecourse. **2.** a straight condition. **3.** a sequence of five cards in poker. **4.** (*slang*) a heterosexual person. —*adv.* in a straight line; direct; in the right direction, correctly. —**go straight,** to live an honest life after being a criminal. **on the straight,** not on the bias. **straight away,** immediately. **straight eye,** the ability to draw or cut etc. in a straight line or to detect deviation from the straight. **straight face,** an expression concealing or not showing one's amusement etc. **straight fight,** a contest between two candidates only. **straight-man** *n.* the member of a comic act who makes remarks for the comedian to joke about. **straight off,** (*colloq.*) immediately; without hesitation. —**straightly** *adv.*, **straightness** *n.* [*p.p.* of STRETCH]

straighten /'streɪt(ə)n/ *v.t./i.* to make or become straight. —**straighten up,** to stand erect after bending. [f. prec.]

straightforward /streɪt'fɔ:wəd/ *adj.* **1.** honest, frank. **2.** (of a task etc.) uncomplicated. —**straightforwardly** *adv.*, **straightforwardness** *n.*

strain[1] *v.t./i.* **1.** to stretch tightly, to make or become taut or tense. **2.** to injure or weaken by excessive stretching or by over-exertion. **3.** to make an intensive effort; to use in this. **4.** to apply (a rule or meaning etc.) beyond its true application. **5.** to hold in a tight embrace. **6.** to pass (liquid) through a sieve or similar device in order to separate solids from the liquid in which they are dispersed; to filter out (solids) thus. —*n.* **1.** straining, being strained; the force exerted in straining. **2.** an injury caused by straining a muscle etc. **3.** a severe demand on mental or physical strength or on resources; distress caused by this. **4.** a passage from a piece of music or poetry. **5.** a tone or tendency in speech or writing. [f. OF *estreindre* f. L *stringere* draw tight]

strain[2] *n.* **1.** a line of descent of animals, plants, or micro-organisms; a variety or breed of these. **2.** a slight or inherited tendency as part of character. [OE, = progeny]

strained *adj.* **1.** (of behaviour or manner) produced by effort, not arising from genuine feeling. **2.** (of a relationship) characterized by unpleasant tension. [f. STRAIN[1]]

strainer *n.* a device for straining liquids. [f. STRAIN[1]]

strait *n.* **1.** (in *sing.* or *pl.*) a narrow channel of water connecting two large bodies of water. **2.** (usu. in *pl.*) a difficult state of affairs. —*adj.* (*archaic*) narrow, limited, strict. —**strait-laced** *adj.* very prim and proper, puritanical. [f. OF *estreit* tight f. L (as STRICT)]

straiten /'streɪt(ə)n/ *v.t.* to restrict; (in *p.p.*) of or characterized by poverty. [f. prec.]

strait-jacket *n.* **1.** a strong garment put on a violent person to confine his arms. **2.** restrictive measures. —*v.t.* **1.** to restrain with a strait-jacket. **2.** to restrict severely.

strake *n.* a continuous line of planking or plates from stem to stern of a ship. [rel. to OE *streccan* stretch]

stramonium /strə'məʊnɪəm/ *n.* a drug used to treat asthma; the plant yielding it (*Datura stramonium*). [perh. f. Tartar *turman* horse-medicine]

strand[1] *v.t./i.* **1.** to run or cause to run aground. **2.** (in *p.p.*) in difficulties, especially without money or means of transport. —*n.* a shore. [OE]

strand[2] *n.* **1.** each of the threads or wires twisted round each other to make a rope or cable etc. **2.** a single thread or strip of fibre; a lock of hair. **3.** an element or strain in any composite whole. [orig. unkn.]

strange /streɪndʒ/ *adj.* **1.** unusual, surprising; eccentric. **2.** unfamiliar, not one's own, alien. **3.** unaccustomed; not at one's ease. —**strangely** *adv.*, **strangeness** *n.* [f. OF *estrange* f. L (as EXTRANEOUS)]

stranger /'streɪndʒə(r)/ *n.* a person in a place or company that he does not know or belong to or where he is unknown; a person one does not know. —**a** (*or* **no**) **stranger to,** unaccustomed (or accustomed) to. [f. OF *estrangier* f. L (as prec.)]

strangle *v.t.* **1.** to squeeze the windpipe or neck of, especially so as to kill. **2.** to restrict or prevent the proper growth, operation, or utterance of. —**strangler** *n.* [f. OF f. L *strangulare* f. Gk (*straggalē* halter)]

stranglehold *n.* **1.** a strangling or deadly grip. **2.** firm or exclusive control.

strangulate /'stræŋɡjʊleɪt/ *v.t.* to compress (a vein or intestine etc.) so that nothing can pass through. [f. L (as STRANGLE)]

strangulation /stræŋɡjʊ'leɪʃ(ə)n/ *n.* **1.** strangling. **2.** strangulating. [as prec.]

strap *n.* **1.** a strip of leather or other flexible material often with a buckle, for holding things together or in place. **2.** a shoulder-strap. **3.** a loop for grasping to steady oneself in a moving vehicle. —*v.t.* (**-pp-**) **1.** to secure with a strap or straps. **2.** to beat with a strap. —**strapped for,** (*slang*) short of (cash etc.). [dial. form of STROP]

strapping *adj.* tall and healthy-looking. —*n.* **1.** straps; material for these. **2.** sticking-plaster etc. used for binding wounds or injuries. [f. STRAP]

strata *pl.* of STRATUM.

stratagem /'strætədʒəm/ *n.* a cunning plan or scheme; trickery. [f. F f. L f. Gk *stratēgēma* (*stratēgos* a general)]

strategic /strə'ti:dʒɪk/ *adj.* **1.** of strategy. **2.** giving an advantage. **3.** (of materials) essential in war. **4.** (of bombing) designed to disorganize or demoralize the enemy. —**strategic weapons,** missiles etc. that can reach the enemy's home territory (opp. *tactical weapons* which are for use at close quarters or in battle). —**strategically** *adv.* [f. F f. Gk (as prec.)]

strategy /'strætɪdʒɪ/ *n.* **1.** the art of war, especially the planning of the movements of troops into favourable positions etc. **2.** a plan of action or policy in business or politics etc. —**strategist** *n.* [f. F f. Gk, = generalship (as STRATAGEM)]

strath *n.* (*Sc.*) a broad valley. [f. Gael *srath*]

Strathclyde /stræθ'klaɪd/ a local government region in western Scotland.

strathspey /stræθ'speɪ/ *n.* a slow Scottish dance; music for this. [f. *Strathspey* valley of the river Spey]

stratify /'strætɪfaɪ/ *v.t.* (esp. in *p.p.*) to arrange in strata or grades etc. —**stratification** /-fɪ'keɪʃ(ə)n/ *n.* [f. F (as STRATUM)]

stratigraphy /strə'tɪɡrəfɪ/ *n.* the order and relative positions of strata; the study of these. —**stratigraphic** /-'ɡræfɪk/ *adj.*, **stratigraphically** /-'ɡræfɪkəlɪ/ *adv.* [f. STRATUM + -GRAPHY]

stratocumulus /strætəʊ'kju:mjʊləs/ *n.* dark masses of low cloud, frequently merging to cover the whole sky (ill. WEATHER). [f. STRATUS + CUMULUS]

stratopause /'strætəʊpɔ:z/ *n.* the interface between the stratosphere and the ionosphere. [f. STRATOSPHERE + PAUSE]

stratosphere /'strætəsfɪə(r)/ *n.* the layer of the atmosphere lying above the troposphere, in which the temperature does not decrease with increasing height (ill. WEATHER). —**stratospheric** /-'sferɪk/ *adj.* [f. foll. + SPHERE]

stratum /'stra:təm, 'streɪ-/ *n.* (*pl.* **strata**) **1.** each of a series of layers, especially of rocks in the earth's crust. **2.** a social level or class. [L, = something spread or laid down]

stratus /'stra:təs, 'streɪ-/ *n.* (*pl.* **-ti** /-ti:/) a continuous horizontal sheet of cloud (ill. WEATHER). [as prec.]

Strauss[1] /straʊs/, Johann (II) (1825–99), Austrian composer, who was born and died in Vienna. He was the son of a composer of dance music, particularly waltzes, also named Johann (I) (1804–49), and became known himself as 'the waltz king' after such successes as *The Blue Danube* (1867) and *Tales from the Vienna Woods* (1868). In 1874 he composed the ever popular operetta *Die Fledermaus* (*The Bat*, 1874), a triumph which was followed in 1885 with *Der Zigeunerbaron* (*The Gipsy Baron*), equally masterly in its combination of comic opera and operetta. He was a friend and admirer of Wagner, who, like Brahms and other composers including Schoenberg, were what we should now call 'fans' of Strauss, recognizing a supreme master of a genre who composed with style, elegance, taste, and wit.

Strauss[2] /straʊs/, Richard (1864–1949), German composer. His early works include a series of symphonic poems which remain among the staple fare of orchestras; *Don Juan* (1888–9) established him as the natural successor to Wagner, whose widow took a great interest in his career. He married the soprano Pauline de Ahna in 1894, and wrote many songs for her, appearing as her accompanist. In 1905 he produced the opera *Salome*, based on Oscar Wilde's play, and followed it in 1909 with *Elektra*: the two works both shocked and fascinated the musical public with music perfectly matched to the studies of emotional extremes and psychological abnormality. His subsequent operas were quite different in intention and effect, including the deliciously Viennese *Der Rosenkavalier* (1911), the combination of mythology and comedy of *Ariadne auf Naxos* (1912), and *Capriccio* (1942), which turns over, but does not resolve, the perennial question of whether the music should be master of the words or vice versa in opera.

Stravinsky /strə'vɪnskɪ/, Igor (1882–1971), Russian-born composer. In 1910 he began his travels with Diaghilev's ballet company, composing for it the ballets *The Firebird* (1909–10), *Petrushka* (1910–11), and, of course, *The Rite of Spring* (1911–13), which shocked Paris with its angular rhythms and liberal use of dissonance. He was prevented from returning to his native land by the 1917 revolution, but many works of this period have their roots in Russian folk-song, notably another ballet *Les Noces* (1914–23). He was fascinated also by the idioms of Western music and derived inspiration for his own neo-classical works from the baroque and classical periods. Stravinsky had moved from Paris to Los Angeles on the outbreak of the Second World War, and in the 1950s turned to serialism in such works as the cantatas *Canticum sacrum* (1955) and *Threni* (1957–8). In his final years he wrote short bare works, many of them religious in feeling and form. The overriding feature of his music is rhythm, and the sense of theatre and of the dance is never wholly absent even from his most austere works.

straw *n.* **1.** dry cut stalks of grain used as material for bedding, packing, fodder, etc. **2.** a single stalk or piece of straw. **3.** a thin hollow tube for sucking drink through. **4.** an insignificant thing. **5.** the pale yellow colour of straw. —**clutch at straws**, to try a hopeless expedient in desperation. **straw in the wind**, a slight hint of future developments. **straw poll** *or* **vote**, an unofficial ballot as a test of opinion. [OE (rel. to STREW)]

strawberry /ˈstrɔːbərɪ/ *n.* a pulpy red fruit having the surface studded with yellow seeds; the plant of the genus *Fragaria* bearing this. —**strawberry-mark** *n.* a reddish birthmark. [OE (as prec. + BERRY); reason for name unknown]

stray *v.i.* **1.** to leave one's group or proper place with no settled destination or purpose; to roam. **2.** to deviate from a direct course or from a subject. —*n.* a person or domestic animal that has strayed; a stray thing. —*adj.* **1.** that has strayed, lost. **2.** isolated, found or occurring occasionally or unexpectedly. **3.** unwanted, unintentional. [f. AF *estrayer* (as ASTRAY)]

streak *n.* **1.** a long thin usually irregular line or band, especially distinguished by its colour. **2.** a flash of lightning. **3.** a strain or element in a character. **4.** a spell or series. —*v.t./i.* **1.** to mark with streaks. **2.** to move very rapidly; (*colloq.*) to run naked through a public place. —**streaker** *n.* [f. prec.]

streaky *adj.* full of streaks; (of bacon) with alternate streaks of fat and lean. —**streakily** *adv.*, **streakiness** *n.* [f. prec.]

stream *n.* **1.** a body of water flowing in its bed, a brook or river. **2.** a flow of fluid or of a mass of things or people. **3.** the current or direction of something flowing or moving. **4.** (in some schools) a section into which children with the same level of ability are placed. —*v.t./i.* **1.** to flow or move as a stream. **2.** to emit a stream of; to run with liquid. **3.** to float or wave at full length. **4.** to arrange (schoolchildren) in streams. —**on stream**, in active operation or production. **stream of consciousness**, the continuous flow of a person's thoughts and reactions to events; a literary style depicting this, as in James Joyce's novel *Ulysses*. [OE]

streamer *n.* **1.** a long narrow flag. **2.** a long narrow ribbon or strip of paper attached at one or both ends. **3.** a banner headline. [f. prec.]

streamline *v.t.* **1.** to give a smooth even shape to (a vehicle, boat, etc.) so as to offer the least possible resistance to motion through air or water. **2.** to make more efficient by simplifying, removing superfluities, etc.

street *n.* a public road in a city, town, or village; this with the houses or buildings on each side; the persons who live or work in a particular street. —**on the streets**, working as a prostitute. **streets ahead (of)**, (*colloq.*) much superior (to). **street-walker** *n.* a prostitute seeking customers in the street. **up one's street**, (*colloq.*) within one's range of interest or knowledge, to one's liking. [OE f. L *strata* (*via*) paved (way)]

streetcar *n.* (*US*) a tram.

strength *n.* **1.** the quality, extent, or manner of being strong. **2.** what makes one strong. **3.** the number of persons present or available; the full complement. —**from strength to strength**, with ever-increasing success. **in strength**, in large numbers. **on the strength of**, relying on, on the basis of. [OE (as STRONG)]

strengthen /ˈstreŋθ(ə)n/ *v.t./i.* to make or become stronger. —**strengthener** *n.* [f. prec.]

strenuous /ˈstrenjʊəs/ *adj.* making or requiring great exertions, energetic. —**strenuously** *adv.*, **strenuousness** *n.* [f. L *strenuus*]

streptococcus /streptəˈkɒkəs/ *n.* (*pl.* -**cocci** /-aɪ/) a bacterium causing serious infections. —**streptococcal** *adj.* [f. Gk *streptos* twisted + *kokkos* berry]

streptomycin /streptəˈmaɪsɪn/ *n.* an antibiotic effective against some disease-producing bacteria. [f. Gk *streptos* (as prec.) + *mukēs* fungus]

stress *n.* **1.** pressure, tension; the measure of this. **2.** a demand on physical or mental strength; distress caused by this. **3.** emphasis; the extra force used on a syllable or on word(s) in speaking, or on a note or notes in music. —*v.t.* **1.** to lay stress on. **2.** to subject to stress. —**lay stress on**, to indicate as important. [f. DISTRESS or partly f. OF *estresse* narrowness, f. L (as STRICT)]

stressful *adj.* causing stress. —**stressfully** *adv.* [f. prec. + -FUL]

stretch *v.t./i.* **1.** to pull out tightly or into a greater length, extent, or size; to be able to be stretched without breaking; to tend to become stretched. **2.** to place or lie at full length or spread out; to extend one's limbs and tighten the muscles after being relaxed. **3.** to be continuous from a point or between points; to have a specified length or extension. **4.** to make great demands on the abilities of; to strain to the utmost or beyond a reasonable limit; to exaggerate (the truth). —*n.* **1.** stretching, being stretched; the ability to be stretched. **2.** a continuous expanse or tract; a continuous period of time. **3.** (*slang*) a period of imprisonment. **4.** (*US*) the straight part of a race-track. —*adj.* able to be stretched, elastic. —**stretch one's legs**, to exercise oneself by walking. **stretch out**, to extend (a hand or foot etc.); to last for a longer period; to prolong. **stretch a point**, to agree to something not normally allowed. [OE]

stretcher *n.* **1.** a framework of two poles with canvas etc. between for carrying a sick or injured person in a lying position. **2.** any of various devices for stretching things. **3.** a brick etc. placed lengthwise in the face of a wall (ill. BUILDING TECHNIQUES). [f. prec.]

stretchy *adj.* (*colloq.*) able or tending to stretch. —**stretchiness** *n.* [f. STRETCH]

strew /struː/ *v.t.* (*p.p.* **strewn** or **strewed**) to scatter or spread about over a surface; to cover or partly cover with scattered things. [OE]

stria /ˈstraɪə/ *n.* (*pl.* **striae** /-iː/) a slight furrow or ridge on a surface. [L]

striated /straɪˈeɪtɪd/ *adj.* marked with striae. —**striation** *n.* [f. STRIA]

stricken see STRIKE.

strict *adj.* **1.** precisely limited or defined, without exception or deviation. **2.** requiring or giving complete obedience or exact performance. —**strictly speaking**, if one uses words in their strict sense. —**strictly** *adv.*, **strictness** *n.* [f. L *strictus* (*stringere* draw tight)]

stricture /ˈstrɪktʃə(r)/ *n.* **1.** (usu. in *pl.*) a critical or censorious remark. **2.** abnormal constriction of a tubelike part of the body. [as prec.]

stride *v.t./i.* (*past* **strode**; *p.p.* **stridden** /ˈstrɪd(ə)n/) **1.** to walk with long steps. **2.** to cross with one step. **3.** to bestride. —*n.* **1.** a single long step; the length of this; gait as determined by the length of the stride. **2.** (usu. in *pl.*) progress. —**get into one's stride**, to settle into an efficient rate of work. **take in one's stride**, to manage without difficulty. [OE, rel. to MLG *striden* straddle]

strident /ˈstraɪdənt/ *adj.* loud and harsh. —**stridency** *n.*, **stridently** *adv.* [f. L *stridere* creak]

strife *n.* quarrelling, a state of conflict; a struggle between opposed persons or things. [f. OF *estrif* (as STRIVE)]

strike *v.t./i.* (*past & p.p.* **struck**) **1.** to subject to an impact; to bring or come into sudden hard contact (with); to inflict (a blow), to knock or propel with a blow or stroke. **2.** to attack suddenly; (of a disease) to afflict. **3.** (of lightning) to descend upon and blast. **4.** to produce (sparks or a sound etc.) by striking something; to produce (a musical note) by pressing a key; to make (a coin or medal) by stamping metal etc.; to ignite (a match) by friction. **5.** (of a clock) to indicate (time) by a sound; (of time) to be indicated thus. **6.** to bring suddenly into a specified state as if at one stroke. **7.** to reach (gold or mineral oil etc.) by digging or drilling. **8.** to agree on (a bargain). **9.** to put oneself theatrically into (an attitude). **10.** to occur to the mind of; to produce a mental impression on. **11.** to penetrate; to cause to penetrate; to fill with sudden fear etc. **12.** to insert (a plant cutting) in the soil to take root; (of a cutting) to take root. **13.** to cease work in protest about a grievance. **14.** to lower or take down (a flag or tent etc.). **15.** to take a specified direction. **16.** to arrive at (an average or balance) by balancing or equalizing the items. —*n.* **1.** an act or instance of striking. **2.** employees' concerted refusal to work unless a grievance is remedied; a similar concerted abstention from activity by persons attempting to obtain a concession or register a grievance. The first strike on record took place in Egypt in the mid-12th c. BC, in the reign of Rameses III, when tomb workers at Thebes downed tools because their rations had not arrived; it caused considerable alarm. **3.** a sudden find or success. **4.** an attack, especially from the air. —**be struck on**, (*slang*) to be infatuated with. **on strike**, taking part in an industrial strike. **strike-breaker** *n.* a person working or brought in in place of a striker. **strike home**, to deal an effective blow, to have an intended effect. **strike off**, to remove with a stroke; to delete (a name etc.) from a list. **strike out**, to hit out; to act vigorously; to delete (an item or name etc.). **strike pay**, an allowance paid by a trade union to members on strike. **strike up**, to start (an acquaintance, conversation, etc.) rapidly or casually; to begin playing (a tune etc.). [OE, = go, stroke]

striker *n.* **1.** a person or thing that strikes. **2.** an employee who is on strike. **3.** (in football) a player whose main function is to try to score goals. [f. prec.]

striking *adj.* sure to be noticed; attractive and impressive. —**strikingly** *adv.* [f. STRIKE]

Strindberg /'strɪndbɜːg/, (Johan) August (1849–1912), Swedish dramatist and novelist. The bitterness and misogyny of his starkly naturalistic earlier plays, notably *The Father* (1887), reflect his unhappy marriage and increasing paranoia. A more tranquil later period following a mental breakdown evoked expressionistic 'dream plays' as well as notable historical dramas.

Strine *n.* a comic transliteration of Australian speech; Australian English, especially of the uneducated type. [alleged pronunc. of 'Australian' in such speech]

string *n.* **1.** narrow cord, twine; a piece of this or a similar material used for tying or holding things together, for pulling, or interwoven in a frame to form the head of a racket. **2.** a piece of catgut, cord, or wire stretched and caused to vibrate so as to produce notes in a musical instrument; (in *pl.*) the stringed instruments played with a bow in an orchestra etc.; (*attrib.*) relating to or consisting of these. **3.** (in *pl.*) an awkward stipulation or complication. **4.** a set of things strung together; a series of people or events; a group of racehorses trained at one stable. **5.** a strip of tough fibre connecting two halves of a bean-pod etc. —*v.t./i.* (*past & p.p.* **strung**) **1.** to fit or fasten with string(s). **2.** to thread (beads etc.) on a string. **3.** to arrange in or as a string. **4.** to trim the tough fibre from (beans). **5.** (esp. in *p.p.*) to make (the nerves or resolution etc.) tense and ready for action. —**on a string,** under one's control or influence. **string along,** (*colloq.*) to deceive. **string along with,** (*colloq.*) to accompany. **string-course** *n.* a raised horizontal band of bricks etc. on a building. **string up,** to hang up on strings etc.; to kill by hanging. **string vest,** a vest of a material with large mesh. [OE]

stringed *adj.* (of musical instruments) having strings. [f. prec.]

stringent /'strɪndʒ(ə)nt/ *adj.* (of rules etc.) strict, severe, leaving no loophole for discretion. —**stringency** *n.*, **stringently** *adv.* [as STRICT]

stringer /'strɪŋə(r)/ *n.* **1.** a longitudinal structural member in a framework especially of a ship or aircraft. **2.** a newspaper correspondent not on the regular staff. [f. STRING]

stringy /'strɪŋɪ/ *adj.* like a string, fibrous. —**stringiness** *n.* [f. STRING]

strip[1] *v.t./i.* (**-pp-**) **1.** to remove the clothes or covering from; to undress oneself. **2.** to deprive of property or titles. **3.** to leave bare of accessories or fittings. **4.** to remove the old paint from. **5.** to damage the thread of (a screw) or the teeth of (a gear). —*n.* **1.** an act of stripping, especially of undressing in a strip-tease. **2.** (*colloq.*) the clothes worn by the members of a sports team. —**strip club,** a club where strip-tease is performed. **strip down,** to remove the accessory fittings of or take apart (a machine etc.). **strip-tease** *n.* an entertainment in which a woman (or occasionally a man) gradually undresses before an audience. [f. OE, = despoil]

strip[2] *n.* a long narrow piece or area. —**strip cartoon,** a comic strip. **strip light,** a tubular fluorescent lamp. **tear a person off a strip,** (*slang*) to rebuke him or her. [f. or rel. to MLG *strippe* strap, prob. rel. to foll.]

stripe *n.* **1.** a long narrow band or strip differing in colour or texture from the surface on either side of it. **2.** a chevron etc. denoting military rank. **3.** (*archaic,* usu. in *pl.*) a blow with a scourge or lash. [perh. back-formation f. foll.]

striped /straɪpt/ *adj.* marked with stripes. [orig. unkn.]

stripling *n.* a youth not fully grown. [prob. f. STRIP[2]]

stripper *n.* **1.** a person or thing that strips something. **2.** a device or solvent for removing paint etc. **3.** a strip-tease performer. [f. STRIP[1]]

stripy /'straɪpɪ/ *adj.* striped. [f. STRIPE]

strive *v.i.* (*past* **strove;** *p.p.* **striven** /'strɪv(ə)n/) **1.** to make great efforts. **2.** to carry on a conflict. [f. OF *estriver*]

strobe *n.* (*colloq.*) a stroboscope. [abbr.]

stroboscope /'strəʊbəskəʊp/ *n.* a lamp made to flash intermittently; a device using this to determine speeds of rotation etc. —**stroboscopic** /-'skɒpɪk/ *adj.* [f. Gk *strobos* whirling + -SCOPE]

strode *past* of STRIDE.

stroganoff /'strɒgənɒf/ *n.* (in full **beef stroganoff**) a dish of strips of beef cooked in a sauce containing sour cream. [f. Count Paul *Stroganov*, 19th-c. Russian diplomat]

stroke *n.* **1.** an act of striking. **2.** a sudden disabling attack, especially of apoplexy. **3.** an action or movement, especially as one of a series or in a game etc.; the slightest such action; a highly effective effort, action, or occurrence of a specified kind. **4.** the sound made by a striking clock. **5.** a movement in one direction of a pen or paintbrush etc.; a detail contributing to a general effect. **6.** a mode or action of moving an oar in rowing; a mode of moving the limbs in swimming. **7.** (in full **stroke oar**) the oarsman nearest the stern, who sets the time of the stroke. **8.** an act or spell of stroking. —*v.t.* **1.** to pass the hand gently along the surface of (hair or fur etc.). **2.** to act as stroke of (a boat or crew). —**at a stroke,** by a single action. **on the stroke (of),** punctually (at). [rel. to STRIKE]

stroll /strəʊl/ *v.i.* to walk in a leisurely way. —*n.* a short leisurely walk. —**strolling players,** actors etc. going from place to place performing. [prob. f. G (*strolch* vagabond)]

Stromboli /'strɒmbəlɪ/ an active volcano forming one of the Lipari Islands off the east coast of Italy, noted for its perpetual state of mild activity.

strong *adj.* **1.** having the power of resistance to being broken, damaged, disturbed, overcome, etc. **2.** capable of exerting great force or of doing much; physically powerful; powerful through numbers, resources, or quality; powerful in effect; (of an argument etc.) convincing. **3.** concentrated, having a large proportion of a flavouring or colouring element, or of a substance in water or other solvent; (of a drink) containing much alcohol. **4.** (placed after a noun) having a specified number of members. —*adv.* strongly, vigorously. —**strong-arm** *adj.* using force. **strong-box** *n.* a strongly made small chest for valuables. **strong language,** forceful language, swearing. **strong-minded** *adj.* having a determined mind. **strong point,** a fortified position; a thing at which one excels. **strong-room** *n.* a strongly built room for the storage and protection of valuables. **strong suit,** a suit at cards in which one can take tricks; a thing at which one excels. **strong verb,** a verb forming inflexions by vowel-change within the stem rather than by the addition of a suffix. —**strongly** *adv.* [OE]

stronghold *n.* **1.** a fortified place; a secure refuge. **2.** a centre of support for a cause etc.

strontium /'strɒntɪəm/ *n.* a soft silver-white metallic element of the alkaline-earth metal series, symbol Sr, atomic number 38, first detected in 1787 and isolated by Sir Humphry Davy in 1808. The metal has few uses, but strontium salts are used in fireworks and flares because they give a brilliant red light. The radioactive isotope strontium 90 is a particularly dangerous component of nuclear fallout as it can become concentrated in bones and teeth. [f. *Strontian* town in Scotland where the carbonate was discovered]

strop *n.* a device, especially a strip of leather, for sharpening razors. —*v.t.* (**-pp-**) to sharpen on or with a strop. [f. MDu. or MLG; cf. L *stroppus*]

stroppy /'strɒpɪ/ *adj.* (*slang*) bad-tempered, awkward to deal with. [orig. unkn.]

strove *past* of STRIVE.

struck *past & p.p.* of STRIKE.

structural /'strʌktʃər(ə)l/ *adj.* **1.** of a structure or framework. **2.** used in the construction of buildings etc. —**structural linguistics,** the study of a language viewed as a system made up of interrelated elements without regard to their historical development. —**structurally** *adv.* [f. STRUCTURE]

structuralism /'strʌktʃərəlɪz(ə)m/ *n.* **1.** (*Psychol.*) a method of investigating the structure of consciousness through the introspective analysis of simple forms of sensation, thought, images, etc. **2.** any theory or method in which a discipline or field of study is envisaged as comprising elements interrelated in systems and structures at various levels, being regarded as more significant than the elements considered in isolation. **3.** any of the theories of linguistics in which language is considered as a system or structure comprising elements at various phonological, grammatical, and semantic levels, especially after the work of F. de Saussure. —**structuralist** *n.* [f. prec.]

structure /'strʌktʃə(r)/ *n.* **1.** the way in which a thing is constructed or organized. **2.** a supporting framework or the essential parts of a thing. **3.** a constructed thing, a complex whole; a building. —*v.t.* to give a structure to, to organize. [f. OF or L *structura* (*struere* build)]

strudel /ˈstruːd(ə)l/ n. a confection of thin pastry filled especially with apple. [G]

struggle v.i. **1.** to throw one's limbs or body about in a vigorous effort to get free. **2.** to make a vigorous or determined effort under difficulties; to make one's way or a living etc. with difficulty. **3.** (with *with* or *against*) to try to overcome (an opponent) or deal with (a problem). —n. an act or period of struggling, a vigorous effort; a hard contest. [perh. imit.]

strum v.t./i. (**-mm-**) to play unskilfully or monotonously on (a stringed or keyboard instrument). —n. the act or sound of strumming. [imit.; cf. THRUM²]

strumpet /ˈstrʌmpɪt/ n. (archaic) a prostitute. [orig. unkn.]

strung past & p.p. of STRING.

strut n. **1.** a bar forming part of a framework and designed to strengthen and brace it. **2.** a strutting gait. —v.t./i. (**-tt-**) to walk in a stiff pompous way. **3.** to brace with struts. [OE, ? = be rigid]

'struth /struːθ/ int. (colloq.) an exclamation of surprise. [*God's truth*]

Struwwelpeter /ˈstruːəlpiːtə(r)/ a character in a children's book of the same name by Heinrich Hoffmann (1809-94), with long thick unkempt hair.

strychnine /ˈstrɪkniːn/ n. a highly poisonous alkaloid used in small doses as a stimulant. [f. L f. Gk *strukhnos* nightshade]

Stuart¹ /ˈstjuːət/ the name of the royal house of Scotland from the accession (1371) of Robert II, one of the hereditary stewards of Scotland, and of Britain from the accession of James VI of Scotland to the English throne as James I (1603) to the death of Queen Anne (1714).
  Charles Edward Stuart (1720-88), 'the Young Pretender', elder son of James Stuart (see below). A far more dashing and romantic figure than his father, on whose behalf he led the Jacobite uprising of 1745-6, Charles was not really able enough to face the task of overthrowing a reasonably well established Hanoverian regime. He made little impact on events after his flight from Scotland in the aftermath of Culloden and eventually succumbed to alcoholism, dying in obscurity in Rome.
  James Stuart (1688-1766), 'the Old Pretender', only son of James II of Britain, Jacobite claimant to the throne following his father's death. He spent his entire life in exile, failing to restore his fortunes as much because of the weakness of his political position as because of his lack of charisma and decisiveness. Arriving in Scotland too late to alter the outcome of the 1715 uprising, he left the leadership of a second major attempt in 1745 to his son Charles.

Stuart² /ˈstjuːət/, John McDouall (1815-66), Scottish emigrant to Australia who crossed the continent in 1861-2, at his sixth attempt, from south to north and back again. He was a man of indomitable courage and tenacity, who in all his journeys never lost a man of his expeditions, though his own health was destroyed as a result of the hardships he had suffered.

stub n. **1.** a short stump; a remnant of a pencil or cigarette etc. after use. **2.** the counterfoil of a cheque or receipt etc. —v.t. (**-bb-**) to strike (one's toe) against a hard object; (usu. with *out*) to extinguish (a cigarette etc.) by pressing the lighted end against something. [OE]

stubble n. **1.** the lower ends of the stalks of cereal plants left sticking up from the ground after the harvest is cut. **2.** a short stiff growth of hair or beard, especially that growing after shaving. —**stubbly** adj. [f. AF f. L, var. of *stipula* straw]

stubborn /ˈstʌbən/ adj. obstinate, not docile; not easy to control or deal with. —**stubbornly** adv., **stubbornness** n. [orig. unkn.]

Stubbs¹ George (1724-1806), English animal painter and engraver. Largely self-taught, he worked as a portrait painter in Leeds and studied anatomy at York. In 1759 he moved to London and there published his *Anatomy of the Horse* (1766), illustrated with his own engravings, which established his reputation. He was widely admired as a painter of horses, not only for his anatomical and observational knowledge but also for his ability to convey their spirit and dignity. His imaginative compositions, especially the horse and lion confrontations, show his proto-romantic nature, while the neo-classical purity of his line is evident in his mare and foals series.

Stubbs² William (1825-1901), English historian, Regius Professor of Modern History at Oxford (1866-1901), Bishop of Chester (1884) and of Oxford (1888). He showed his supreme professional skill, acquired from the German academic method, in his great *Constitutional History of England* (1874-8) which, together with his *Select Charters and other Illustrations of English Constitutional History to 1307* (1870), imposed a pattern and a method on the teaching of English history in British universities which lasted until the middle of the 20th c.

stubby adj. short and thick. —**stubbiness** n. [f. STUB]

stucco /ˈstʌkəʊ/ n. (pl. **-oes**) plaster or cement for coating walls or for moulding to form architectural decorations. —v.t. to coat with stucco. [It.]

stuck past & p.p. of STICK².

stuck-up adj. conceited, snobbish.

stud¹ n. **1.** a short large-headed nail, a rivet; a small knob projecting from a surface, especially for ornament. **2.** a device like a button on a shank, used e.g. to fasten a detachable shirt-collar. —v.t. (**-dd-**) to set (as) with stud. [OE]

stud² n. **1.** a number of horses kept for breeding etc.; the place where these are kept. **2.** a stallion. —**at stud,** (of a stallion) available for breeding on payment of a fee. **stud-book** n. a book containing pedigrees of horses. **stud-farm** n. a farm where horses are bred. **stud poker,** poker with betting after the dealing of successive cards face up. [OE]

studding n. the woodwork of a lath-and-plaster wall (ill. HOUSES). [f. STUD¹]

studding-sail /ˈstʌns(ə)l/ n. an extra sail set at the side of a square sail in light winds. [perh. f. MLG or MDu. *stotinge* a thrusting]

student /ˈstjuːdənt/ n. a person who is studying, especially at a university or other place of higher education; (attrib.) studying in order to become. [f. L *studēre* (as STUDY)]

studio /ˈstjuːdɪəʊ/ n. (pl. **-os**) **1.** the workroom of a painter, sculptor, photographer, etc. **2.** a room or premises where cinema films are made. **3.** a room from which radio or television programmes are regularly broadcast or in which recordings are made. —**studio couch,** a divan-like couch that can be converted into a bed. [It. f. L (as STUDY)]

studious /ˈstjuːdɪəs/ adj. **1.** assiduous in study or reading. **2.** painstaking; careful and deliberate. —**studiously** adv., **studiousness** n. [f. L *studiosus* (as foll.)]

study /ˈstʌdɪ/ n. **1.** giving one's attention to acquiring information or knowledge, especially from books. **2.** the object of this; a thing worth studying. **3.** a work presenting the result of investigations into a particular subject; a preliminary drawing; a written or other portrayal of an aspect of behaviour or character etc. **4.** a musical composition designed to develop a player's skill. **5.** a room used by a person for reading, writing, etc. —v.t./i. **1.** to make a study of; to examine attentively; to apply oneself to study. **2.** to give care and consideration to. **3.** (in p.p.) deliberate, carefully and intentionally contrived. [f. OF f. L *studium* zeal, study]

stuff n. **1.** the material that a thing is made of or that may be used for some purpose. **2.** a substance, things, or belongings of an indeterminate kind or quality or not needing to be specified; a particular knowledge or activity. **3.** (slang) valueless matter, trash. **4.** woollen fabric (as distinct from silk, cotton, or linen). —v.t./i. **1.** to pack or cram; to fill tightly; to stop up. **2.** to fill the empty skin of (an animal or bird etc.) with material to restore its original shape, e.g. for exhibition in a museum; to fill with padding; to fill (a fowl or rolled meat etc.) with minced seasoning etc. before cooking. **3.** to fill (a person or oneself) with food; to eat greedily. **4.** to push hastily or clumsily. **5.** (slang) to dispose of as unwanted. —**get stuffed!** (slang) go away; stop annoying me. **stuff and nonsense,** an exclamation of incredulity or ridicule. **stuffed shirt,** (colloq.) a pompous person. [f. OF *estoffe* (*estoffer* equip f. Gk *stuphō* draw together)]

stuffing n. **1.** padding used to stuff cushions etc. **2.** a savoury mixture used to stuff fowl etc. [f. STUFF]

stuffy adj. **1.** (of a room etc.) lacking ventilation or fresh air. **2.** (of the nose) blocked with secretions so that breathing is difficult. **3.** (colloq.) prim and pompous, old-fashioned or narrow-minded. **4.** (colloq.) showing annoyance. —**stuffily** adv., **stuffiness** n. [f. STUFF]

stultify /ˈstʌltɪfaɪ/ v.t. to make ineffective or useless, to impair. —**stultification** /-fɪˈkeɪʃ(ə)n/ n. [f. L *stultificare* (*stultus* foolish, *facere* make)]

stum n. unfermented grape-juice, must. —v.t. (**-mm-**) **1.** to prevent from fermenting, or from continuing to ferment, by using sulphur etc. **2.** to renew the fermentation of (wine) by adding stum. [f. Du. *stom* f. *stom* (adj.) dumb]

stumble *v.i.* **1.** to lurch forward or have a partial fall from catching or striking or misplacing the foot; to walk with repeated stumbling. **2.** to make a mistake or repeated mistakes in speaking or in playing music. —*n.* an act of stumbling. —**stumble across** *or* **on,** to discover accidentally. **stumbling-block** *n.* an obstacle or circumstance etc. causing difficulty or hesitation. [rel. to STAMMER]

stump *n.* **1.** the projecting remnant of a tree remaining in the ground after the rest has fallen or been cut down; a corresponding remnant of a broken tooth, amputated limb, or of something worn down. **2.** each of the three uprights of a wicket in cricket (ill. SPORTS). —*v.t./i.* **1.** to walk stiffly or noisily. **2.** to put (a batsman in cricket) out by touching the stumps with the ball while he is outside his crease. **3.** (*colloq.*) to be too difficult for, to baffle. —**stump up,** (*slang*) to pay or produce (money required); to pay what is owed. [f. MDu. or OHG]

stumpy *adj.* short and thick. —**stumpiness** *n.* [f. STUMP]

stun *v.t.* (**-nn-**) **1.** to knock senseless. **2.** to daze or shock by the impact of strong emotion. [f. OF, = ASTONISH]

stung *past* & *p.p.* of STING.

stunk see STINK.

stunner *n.* (*colloq.*) a stunning person or thing. [f. STUN]

stunning *adj.* (*colloq.*) extremely good or attractive. —**stunningly** *adv.* [f. STUN]

stunt[1] *v.t.* to retard the growth or development of. [*stunt* foolish, ON *stuttr* short]

stunt[2] *n.* (*colloq.*) something unusual or difficult done as a performance or to attract attention. —*v.i.* (*colloq.*) to perform stunts. —**stunt man,** a man employed to take an actor's place in performing dangerous stunts. [orig. unkn.]

stupa /ˈstjuːpə/ *n.* a round usually domed Buddhist monument, usually containing a sacred relic. [f. Skr., = heap, pile]

stupefy /ˈstjuːpɪfaɪ/ *v.t.* **1.** to dull the wits or senses of. **2.** to stun with astonishment. —**stupefaction** /-ˈfækʃ(ə)n/ *n.* [f. F f. L *stupefacere* f. *stupēre* be amazed, *facere* make]

stupendous /stjuːˈpendəs/ *adj.* amazing or prodigious, especially by its size or degree. —**stupendously** *adv.* [f. L (as prec.)]

stupid /ˈstjuːpɪd/ *adj.* **1.** not intelligent or clever, slow at learning or understanding things; typical of stupid persons. **2.** uninteresting, boring. **3.** in a state of stupor. —**stupidity** /-ˈpɪdɪtɪ/ *n.*, **stupidly** *adv.* [f. F or L (as prec.)]

stupor /ˈstjuːpə(r)n/ *n.* a dazed or torpid or helplessly amazed state. [L (as STUPEFY)]

sturdy /ˈstɜːdɪ/ *adj.* strongly built, hardy, vigorous.—**sturdily** *adv.*, **sturdiness** *n.* [orig. = recklessly violent, f. OF *est(o)urdi* dazed]

sturgeon /ˈstɜːdʒ(ə)n/ *n.* a large edible fish of the genus *Acipenser* etc. yielding caviare. [f. AF]

Sturt /stɜːt/, Charles (1795–1869), English explorer of Australia. Secretary to the Governor of New South Wales in 1827, he led several expeditions into the interior, discovering the Darling River and becoming surveyor-general for South Australia in 1833. He went blind during his third expedition in 1846 and returned to England, where he was Colonial Secretary in 1849–51.

stutter *v.t./i.* to stammer, especially by involuntarily repeating the first consonants of words; to utter (words) thus. —*n.* an act or habit of stuttering. —**stutterer** *n.* [frequent. of dial. *stut*]

sty[1] /staɪ/ *n.* a pigsty. [OE, prob. = *stig* hall]

sty[2] /staɪ/ *n.* an inflamed swelling on the edge of an eyelid. [shortened f. dial. *styany* = *styan* eye f. OE *stigend* sty, lit. riser + EYE, shortened as though = *sty on eye*]

Stygian /ˈstɪdʒɪən/ *adj.* of or like the Styx or Hades; gloomy, murky. [f. L f. Gk *Stugios* Styx]

style /staɪl/ *n.* **1.** a kind or sort, especially in regard to appearance and form. **2.** the manner of writing, speaking, or doing something; the distinctive manner of a person, school, or period. **3.** the correct way of designating a person or thing. **4.** elegance, distinction. **5.** shape; pattern; fashion (in dress etc.). **6.** a pointed implement for scratching or engraving things. **7.** a narrow extension of a plant's ovary, supporting the stigma (ill. FLOWERS). —*v.t./i.* **1.** to design or make etc. in a particular (especially a fashionable) style. **2.** to designate in a specified way. [f. OF f. L (as STYLUS)]

stylish *adj.* in fashionable style; elegant. —**stylishly** *adv.*, **stylishness** *n.* [f. STYLE]

stylist *n.* **1.** a person concerned with style, especially a writer having or aiming at a good literary style, or a designer of fashionable styles. **2.** a hairdresser who styles hair. [f. STYLE]

stylistic /staɪˈlɪstɪk/ *adj.* of literary or artistic style. —*n.* (in *pl.*) the study of literary style. —**stylistically** *adv.* [f. prec.]

stylite /ˈstaɪlaɪt/ *n.* any of the ascetics who lived on a platform on top of a pillar, especially in Syria in the 5th c. [f. Gk (*stulos* pillar)]

stylized /ˈstaɪlaɪzd/ *adj.* (of a work of art etc.) made to conform to a conventional style. [f. STYLE]

stylus *n.* (*pl.* **styluses**) **1.** a needle-like point for producing or following a groove in a gramophone record. **2.** a pointed writing-implement. [erron. spelling of L *stilus*]

stymie /ˈstaɪmɪ/ *n.* **1.** the situation in golf when an opponent's ball is between one's own ball and the hole. **2.** a difficult situation that blocks or thwarts one's activities. —*v.t.* **1.** to subject to a stymie. **2.** to block or thwart the activities of. [orig. unkn.]

styptic /ˈstɪptɪk/ *adj.* checking the flow of blood by causing blood-vessels to contract. [f. L f. Gk *stuphō* contract]

styrene /ˈstaɪriːn/ *n.* a liquid hydrocarbon easily polymerized and used in making plastics. [f. Gk *sturax* a resin]

Styx /stɪks/ (*Gk myth.*) one of the nine rivers of the underworld, over which Charon ferried the souls of the dead.

suasion /ˈsweɪʒ(ə)n/ *n.* persuasion. —**moral suasion,** a strong recommendation appealing to the moral sense. [f. OF or L (*suadēre* urge)]

suave /swɑːv/ *adj.* smooth-mannered. —**suavely** *adv.*, **suavity** *n.* [F or f. L *suavis* agreeable]

sub *n.* (*colloq.*) **1.** a submarine. **2.** a subscription. **3.** a substitute. **4.** a sub-editor. —*v.t./i.* (**-bb-**) (*colloq.*) **1.** to substitute. **2.** to sub-edit. [abbr.]

sub- *prefix* (in some Latin-derived words **suc-** before *c*, **suf-** before *f*, **sug-** before *g*, **sup-** before *p*, **sur-** before *r*, **sus-** before *s*) denoting **1.** under, at, to, or from a lower position (*subordinate*, *submerge*, *subtract*). **2.** secondary or inferior position (*subclass*, *sub lieutenant*, *subtotal*). **3.** nearly, more or less (*subarctic*). [f. L *sub* under]

subaltern /ˈsʌbəltən/ *n.* an officer of the rank next below a captain. [L (as SUB-, ALTERNATE)]

subaqua /sʌbˈækwə/ *adj.* (of a sport etc.) taking place underwater. [f. L *sub aqua* under the water]

subaquatic /sʌbəˈkwætɪk/ *adj.* underwater.

subaqueous /sʌbˈeɪkwɪəs/ *adj.* subaquatic.

subarctic /sʌbˈɑːktɪk/ *adj.* of or like the regions somewhat south of the Arctic Circle.

subatomic /sʌbəˈtɒmɪk/ *adj.* occurring in an atom; smaller than an atom.

subcommittee /ˈsʌbkəmɪtɪ/ *n.* a committee formed for a special purpose from some members of the main committee.

subconscious /sʌbˈkɒnʃəs/ *n.* the part of the mind that is considered to be not fully conscious but able to influence actions etc. —*adj.* of the subconscious. —**subconsciously** *adv.*

subcontinent /sʌbˈkɒntɪnənt/ *n.* a land-mass of great extent not classed as a continent.

subcontract /sʌbˈkɒntrækt/ *n.* an arrangement by which one who has contracted to do work arranges for it to be done by others. —/sʌbkənˈtrækt/ *v.t./i.* to make a subcontract (for). —**subcontractor** /-ˈtræktə(r)/ *n.*

subculture /ˈsʌbkʌltʃə(r)/ *n.* a social group or its culture within a larger culture.

subcutaneous /sʌbkjuːˈteɪnɪəs/ *adj.* under the skin.

subdivide /sʌbdɪˈvaɪd/ *v.t./i.* to divide again after the first division.

subdivision /ˈsʌbdɪvɪʒ(ə)n/ *n.* **1.** sub-dividing. **2.** a subordinate division.

subdue /səbˈdjuː/ *v.t.* **1.** to overcome, to bring under control. **2.** (esp. in *p.p.*) to make softer, gentler, or less intense. [f. OF *souduire* seduce f. L *subducere* withdraw, used with sense of L *subdere* conquer]

sub-edit *v.t.* to act as sub-editor of.

sub-editor *n.* **1.** an assistant editor. **2.** one who prepares material for printing in a newspaper or book etc. —**sub-editorial** /-ˈtɔːrɪ(ə)l/ *adj.*

subfusc /sʌbˈfʌsk/ *n.* the dull-coloured clothing worn in some universities on formal occasions. [f. L (SUB-, *fuscus* dark brown)]

subheading /ˈsʌbhedɪŋ/ *n.* a subordinate heading.

subhuman /sʌbˈhjuːmən/ adj. less than human; not fully human.

subject[1] /ˈsʌbdʒɪkt/ n. **1.** the person or thing being discussed, described, represented, or studied. **2.** a person under a particular political rule; any member of a State except the supreme ruler; a person owing obedience to another. **3.** a circumstance, person, or thing that gives occasion for a specified feeling or action. **4.** a branch of study. **5.** (logic & Gram.) the term about which something is predicated in a proposition; the word(s) in a sentence that name who or what does the action or undergoes what is stated in the verb. **6.** (Philos.) the conscious self as opposed to all that is external to the mind; the substance as opposed to the attributes of something. **7.** a principal theme in a piece of music. **8.** (esp. in medicine) a person with a specified (usually undesirable) bodily or mental tendency. —adj. not politically independent, owing obedience to another State etc. —adv. (with to) provided that (a specified condition is fulfilled). —**subject to,** owing obedience to; liable to. [f. OF f. L subjicere place beneath (SUB-, jacere throw)]

subject[2] /səbˈdʒekt/ v.t. **1.** (with to) to cause to undergo or experience. **2.** to bring (a country etc.) under one's control. —**subjection** n. [as prec.]

subjective /səbˈdʒektɪv/ adj. **1.** of or due to the consciousness or thinking or the percipient subject as opposed to real or external things, not objective; imaginary. **2.** giving prominence to or depending on personal opinions or idiosyncrasy. **3.** (Gram.) of the subject. —**subjectively** adv., **subjectivity** /-ˈtɪvɪtɪ/ n. [f. L (as SUBJECT[1])]

subjoin /səbˈdʒɔɪn/ v.t. to add (an anecdote or illustration etc.) at the end.

sub judice /sʌb ˈdʒuːdɪsɪ/ under judicial consideration, not yet decided (and in the UK therefore not to be commented on). [L, = under a judge]

subjugate /ˈsʌbdʒʊgeɪt/ v.t. to conquer, to bring into subjection or bondage. —**subjugation** /-ˈgeɪʃ(ə)n/ n., **subjugator** n. [f. L subjugare (SUB-, jugum yoke)]

subjunctive /səbˈdʒʌŋktɪv/ adj. (Gram., of a word) expressing a wish, supposition, or possibility (e.g. if I were you; suffice it to say). —n. a subjunctive mood or form. [f. F or L (as SUBJOIN)]

subkingdom /ˈsʌbkɪŋdəm/ n. a taxonomic category below a kingdom.

sublease /ˈsʌbliːs/ n. a lease granted to a subtenant. —/sʌbˈliːs/ v.t. to lease by a sublease.

sublet /sʌbˈlet/ v.t. (**-tt-**); past & p.p. **sublet**) to let to a subtenant.

sublimate /ˈsʌblɪmeɪt/ v.t. **1.** to divert the energy of (a primitive impulse etc.) into a culturally higher activity. **2.** to sublime (a substance); to refine, to purify. —/ˈsʌblɪmət/ n. a sublimed substance. —**sublimation** /-ˈmeɪʃ(ə)n/ n. [f. L sublimare (as foll.)]

sublime /səˈblaɪm/ adj. **1.** of the highest or most exalted sort, awe-inspiring. **2.** characteristic of one who has no fear of the consequences. —v.t./i. to convert (a substance) from a solid into a vapour by heat (and usually allow to solidify again); (of a substance) to undergo this process; to purify or make sublime. —**sublimely** adv., **sublimity** /-ˈlɪmɪtɪ/ n. [f. L sublimis]

subliminal /sʌbˈlɪmɪn(ə)l/ adj. below the threshold of consciousness; too faint or rapid to be consciously perceived. —**subliminally** adv. [f. SUB- + L limen threshold]

sublunar /sʌbˈluːnə(r)/ adj. (also **sublunary**) existing or situated beneath the moon or between its orbit and that of Earth; subject to the moon's influence.

sub-machine-gun n. a lightweight machine-gun held in the hand.

submarine /sʌbməˈriːn, ˈsʌb-/ n. a ship, especially an armed warship, equipped to operate below the surface of the sea (see below). —adj. existing or occurring or done below the surface of the sea.

Ancient Greek and Roman writers mention attempts to build submersible craft of various kinds, but the first authenticated vessel to be built seems to have been that of Cornelius Drebbel, a Dutch inventor (working for James I) who in the 1620s successfully manœuvred his craft 4–5 metres below the surface of the River Thames. In the following century a number of types were patented and the principle of buoyancy tanks devised. The submarine's use in naval warfare dates from the American Revolution, when a one-man craft, the Turtle, devised by the American inventor David Bushnell, attempted an underwater attack on a British warship. Robert Fulton experimented with submarines, but although initially backed by Napoleon his designs were not successful enough to attract serious attention. By the early 20th c. the invention of the internal-combustion engine, the electric motor, and new designs of torpedo enabled real progress to be made with the design of an effective war vessel, and submarines played a significant part in both World Wars, especially the Second. The greatest development in submarine construction came after the war, when the first nuclear-powered submarine, the Nautilus, was built. Since a nuclear reactor functions without the use of oxygen from the air, it enables the submarine to proceed submerged at or near her maximum speed for an indefinite period. The inertial navigation system (see ill. NAVIGATION) enables a vessel to fix its position without surfacing at intervals to take navigational observations of heavenly bodies. Speeds greatly in excess of anything previously attained have been made possible by streamlining of the hull and adoption of a 'teardrop' design. The arming of nuclear-powered submarines with ballistic missiles capable of being fired while the vessel is submerged is one of the great engineering feats of this century, with significant implications for international attack.

submerge /səbˈmɜːdʒ/ v.t./i. **1.** to place below the surface of water or other liquid; to flood. **2.** (of a submarine) to dive, to go below the surface. —**submergence** n., **submersion** n. [f. L submergere (SUB-, mergere dip)]

submersible /səbˈmɜːsɪb(ə)l/ adj. capable of submerging. —n. a submersible vessel. [f. submerse v. = prec.]

submicroscopic /sʌbmaɪkrəˈskɒpɪk/ adj. too small to be seen by an ordinary microscope.

submission /səbˈmɪʃ(ə)n/ n. **1.** submitting, being submitted. **2.** a thing submitted; a theory etc. submitted by counsel to a judge or jury. [f. OF or L (as SUBMIT)]

submissive /səbˈmɪsɪv/ adj. submitting to power or authority; meek, willing to obey. —**submissively** adv., **submissiveness** n. [f. prec.]

submit /səbˈmɪt/ v.t./i. (**-tt-**) **1.** to surrender (oneself) to the control or authority of another; to cease to resist or oppose. **2.** to present for consideration or decision. **3.** to subject (a person or thing) to a process or treatment. [f. L submittere (SUB-, mittere send)]

subnormal /sʌbˈnɔːm(ə)l/ adj. **1.** less than normal. **2.** below the normal standard of intelligence. —**subnormality** /-ˈmælɪtɪ/ n.

suborder /ˈsʌbɔːdə(r)/ n. a taxonomic category between order and family.

subordinary /səˈbɔːdɪnərɪ/ n. (in heraldry) a charge that is common but less so than ordinaries (ill. HERALDRY).

subordinate /səˈbɔːdɪnət/ adj. **1.** of lesser importance or rank. **2.** working under the control or authority of another. —n. a person in a subordinate position. —/-eɪt/ v.t. to make or treat as subordinate. —**subordinate clause,** a clause serving as a noun, adjective, or adverb within a sentence. —**subordination** /-ˈneɪʃ(ə)n/ n. [f. L (SUB-, ordinare ordain)]

suborn /səˈbɔːn/ v.t. to induce (especially by bribery) to commit perjury or some other crime. —**subornation** /-ˈneɪʃ(ə)n/ n. [f. L subornare incite secretly (SUB-, ornare equip)]

sub-plot n. a subordinate plot in a play.

subpoena /səbˈpiːnə/ n. a writ commanding a person's attendance in a law-court. —v.t. (past & p.p. **subpoenaed** /-nəd/) to serve a subpoena on. [f. L sub poena under penalty]

sub rosa /sʌb ˈrəʊzə/ in confidence or secretly. [L, = under the rose, as emblem of secrecy]

subscribe /səbˈskraɪb/ v.t./i. **1.** to contribute (a sum of money); to pay regularly for membership of an organization, receipt of a publication, etc. **2.** to sign (one's name) at the foot of a document; to sign (a document) thus. **3.** (with to) to express one's agreement with (an opinion or resolution). [f. L subscribere (SUB-, scribere write)]

subscriber n. **1.** one who subscribes. **2.** a person paying a regular sum for the hire of a telephone. —**subscriber trunk dialling,** the making of trunk calls by a subscriber without the assistance of an operator. [f. prec.]

subscript /ˈsʌbskrɪpt/ adj. written or printed below. —n. a subscript number or symbol. [f. L (as SUBSCRIBE)]

subscription /səbˈskrɪpʃ(ə)n/ n. **1.** subscribing. **2.** money subscribed; a fee for membership of an organization etc. —**subscription concert,** a concert (usually one of a series) paid for mainly by those who subscribe in advance. [as SUBSCRIBE]

subsection /ˈsʌbsekʃ(ə)n/ n. a division of a section.

subsequent /ˈsʌbsɪkwənt/ adj. following a specified or

implied event. —**subsequent to,** later than, after. —**subsequently** adv. [f. OF or L subsequi (SUB-, sequi follow)]

subservient /səbˈsɜːvɪənt/ adj. **1.** subordinate. **2.** servile, obsequious. **3.** of use in a minor role. —**subservience** n., **subserviently** adv. [f. L subservire (SUB-, servire serve)]

subside /səbˈsaɪd/ v.i. **1.** to sink or settle to a lower level or to the bottom. **2.** (of ground) to cave in, to sink. **3.** to become less active or intense or prominent. **4.** (of a person) to sink into a chair etc. —**subsidence** /səbˈsaɪdəns, ˈsʌbsɪdəns/ n. [f. L subsidere (SUB-, sidere settle, rel. to sedēre sit)]

subsidiary /səbˈsɪdɪərɪ/ adj. **1.** of secondary (not primary) importance. **2.** (of a company) controlled by another. —n. a subsidiary company, thing, or person. [f. L (as SUBSIDY)]

subsidize /ˈsʌbsɪdaɪz/ v.t. to provide with a subsidy; to reduce the cost of with a subsidy. [f. foll.]

subsidy /ˈsʌbsɪdɪ/ n. money contributed by the State or a public body etc. to keep prices at a desired level or to assist in meeting expenses etc. [f. AF f. L subsidium assistance]

subsist /səbˈsɪst/ v.i. to exist, to continue to exist, to get sustenance or a livelihood. [f. L subsistere stand firm (SUB-, sistere set, stand)]

subsistence /səbˈsɪst(ə)ns/ n. subsisting; a means of this. —**subsistence farming,** farming in which almost all the crops are consumed by the farmer's household. **subsistence level** or **wage,** merely enough to provide the bare necessities of life. [as prec.]

subsoil /ˈsʌbsɔɪl/ n. the soil immediately below the surface soil.

subsonic /sʌbˈsɒnɪk/ adj. relating to speeds less than that of sound. —**subsonically** adv.

subspecies /ˈsʌbspiːʃiːz/ n. a taxonomic category below a species, usually a more or less permanent variety geographically isolated.

substance /ˈsʌbst(ə)ns/ n. **1.** a particular kind of matter having more or less uniform properties. **2.** the essence of what is spoken or written. **3.** reality, solidity. **4.** wealth and possessions. **5.** content as distinct from form. —**in substance,** in the main points. [f. OF f. L, = essence (SUB-, stare stand)]

substandard /sʌbˈstændəd/ adj. below the usual or required standard.

substantial /səbˈstænʃ(ə)l/ adj. **1.** of real importance or value; considerable in amount. **2.** of solid structure. **3.** having substance, actually existing. **4.** well-to-do. **5.** essential, virtual. —**substantially** adv. [as SUBSTANCE]

substantiate /səbˈstænʃɪeɪt/ v.t. to support with evidence, to prove the truth of. —**substantiation** /-ˈeɪʃ(ə)n/ n. [f. L substantiare give substance to (as prec.)]

substantive /ˈsʌbstəntɪv, səbˈstæntɪv/ adj. **1.** having independent existence, not subordinate. **2.** actual, real, permanent. —/ˈsʌb-/ n. a noun. —**substantival** /-ˈtaɪv(ə)l/ adj. [as SUBSTANCE)]

substation /ˈsʌbsteɪʃ(ə)n/ n. a subordinate station; a station at which electrical current is switched, transformed, or converted, intermediate between a generating station and a low-tension distribution network.

substitute /ˈsʌbstɪtjuːt/ n. a person or thing acting or serving in place of another. —v.t. to put, use, or serve as a substitute. —adj. acting as a substitute. —**substitution** /-ˈtjuːʃ(ə)n/ n. [f. L substituere (SUB-, statuere set up)]

substratum /ˈsʌbstrɑːtəm, -streɪ-/ n. (pl. -**ta**) an underlying layer or substance. [p.p. of L substernere (SUB-, sternere strew)]

subsume /səbˈsjuːm/ v.t. to include (an instance etc.) under a particular rule or class. —**subsumption** /-ˈsʌmp(ə)n/ n. [f. L subsumere (SUB-, sumere take)]

subtenant /ˈsʌbtenənt/ n. a person renting a room or house etc. from one who is a tenant of it. —**subtenancy** n.

subtend /səbˈtend/ v.t. (of a line or arc) to form (an angle) at a point where lines drawn from each end of it meet; (of an angle or chord) to have bounding lines or points that meet or coincide with those of (a line or arc). [f. L subtendere (SUB-, tendere stretch)]

subterfuge /ˈsʌbtəfjuːdʒ/ n. a piece of trickery or deceit etc. used to escape blame or defeat etc.; the use of this. [F, or f. L subterfugere escape secretly (subter beneath, fugere flee)]

subterranean /sʌbtəˈreɪnɪən/ adj. underground. [f. L (SUB-, terra earth)]

subtitle /ˈsʌbtaɪt(ə)l/ n. **1.** a subordinate or additional title of a book etc. **2.** a caption of a cinema film, especially translating foreign dialogue. —v.t. to provide with a subtitle or subtitles.

subtle /ˈsʌt(ə)l/ adj. **1.** slight and difficult to detect or describe. **2.** making or able to make fine distinctions. **3.** ingenious, crafty. —**subtlety** n., **subtly** adv. [f. OF f. L subtilis]

subtopia /sʌbˈtəʊpɪə/ n. unsightly suburbs, especially those disfiguring a rural area. [f. SUB(URB) + (U)TOPIA]

subtotal /ˈsʌbtəʊt(ə)l/ n. the total of part of a group of figures to be added.

subtract /səbˈtrækt/ v.t. to deduct, to remove (a part, quantity, or number) from a greater one. —**subtraction** n. [f. L (SUB-, trahere draw)]

subtropical /sʌbˈtrɒpɪk(ə)l/ adj. **1.** bordering on the tropics. **2.** characteristic of subtropical regions.

suburb /ˈsʌbɜːb/ n. an outlying district of a city. [f. OF or L suburbium (SUB-, urbs city)]

suburban /səˈbɜːbən/ adj. of or characteristic of suburbs; having only limited interests and narrow-minded views. —**suburbanite** n. [f. L (as prec.)]

Suburbia /səˈbɜːbɪə/ n. (usu. derog.) the suburbs and their inhabitants. [f. SUBURB]

subvention /səbˈvenʃ(ə)n/ n. a subsidy. [f. OF f. L (subvenire come to a person's aid f. SUB-, venire come)]

subversive /səbˈvɜːsɪv/ adj. attempting subversion. —n. a subversive person. [f. L (as foll.)]

subvert /səbˈvɜːt/ v.t. to weaken or overthrow the authority of (a government etc.); to attempt to do this. —**subversion** n. [f. OF or L subvertere overturn (SUB-, vertere turn)]

subway /ˈsʌbweɪ/ n. **1.** an underground passage, especially for pedestrians. **2.** (US) an underground railway.

suc- prefix see SUB-.

succeed /səkˈsiːd/ v.t./i. **1.** to be successful. **2.** to come next in time or order, to follow. **3.** to come by inheritance or due order (to an office or title). [f. OF or L succedere (SUC-, cedere go)]

success /səkˈses/ n. **1.** a favourable outcome, the accomplishment of what was aimed at; the attainment of wealth, fame, or position. **2.** a thing or person that turns out well. [f. L successus (as prec.)]

successful adj. having success, prosperous. —**successfully** adv. [f. prec. + -FUL]

succession /səkˈseʃ(ə)n/ n. **1.** following in order; a series of people or things one after another. **2.** succeeding to the throne or to an office or inheritance; the right of doing this; a series of persons having such a right. —**in succession,** one after another. **in succession to,** as the successor of. [as SUCCEED]

successive /səkˈsesɪv/ adj. following in succession; in an unbroken series. —**successively** adv. [f. L (as SUCCEED)]

successor /səkˈsesə(r)/ n. a person or thing that succeeds another. [as SUCCEED]

succinct /səkˈsɪŋkt/ adj. concise, expressed briefly and clearly. —**succinctly** adv., **succinctness** n. [f. L succingere tuck up (SUC-, cingere gird)]

succour /ˈsʌkə(r)/ n. (literary) help given in time of need. —v.t. (literary) to give succour to. [f. OF f. L succurrere (SUC-, currere run)]

succulent /ˈsʌkjʊlənt/ adj. **1.** juicy (lit. or fig.). **2.** (of a plant) having thick fleshy leaves or stems. —n. a succulent plant. —**succulence** n. [f. L (succus juice)]

succumb /səˈkʌm/ v.i. to give way to something overpowering; to die. [f. OF f. L succumbere (SUC-, cumbere lie)]

such adj. **1.** of the kind or degree indicated or suggested. **2.** of the same kind. **3.** so great or extreme. —pron. such a person or persons or thing(s). —**as such,** as being what has been specified; in itself. **such-and-such** adj. (a person or thing) of a particular kind but not needing to be specified. **such as,** for example. [OE]

suchlike adj. of the same kind. —pron. (usu. pl.) things of this kind.

suck v.t./i. **1.** to draw (liquid) into the mouth by using the lip muscles; to draw liquid from (a thing) thus. **2.** to squeeze and extract the flavour from (a sweet etc.) in the mouth by using the tongue. **3.** to use a sucking action or make a sucking sound. **4.** to draw in; to obtain. —n. an act or period of sucking. —**suck dry,** to exhaust the contents of by sucking. **suck in** or **up,** to absorb; to engulf, to draw into itself. **suck up to,** (slang) to toady to. [OE]

sucker n. **1.** a shoot springing from a plant's root or its stem below ground. **2.** an organ in animals or a part of an apparatus for adhering by suction to surfaces. **3.** (*slang*) a gullible or easily deceived person. [f. SUCK]

sucking-pig *n.* a pig that is not yet weaned, especially one suitable for roasting whole.

suckle *v.t.* **1.** to feed (young) from the breast or udder. **2.** (of young) to take milk thus. [prob. back-formation f. foll.]

suckling *n.* an unweaned child or animal. [f. SUCK]

Sucre /ˈsuːkreɪ/ the legal capital and seat of the judiciary of Bolivia; pop. (1976) 63,000.

sucrose /ˈsjuːkrəʊz, ˈsuː-/ *n.* sugar obtained from sugar-cane, sugar-beet, etc. [f. F *sucre* sugar]

suction /ˈsʌkʃ(ə)n/ *n.* **1.** sucking. **2.** production of a partial vacuum causing adhesion of surfaces or enabling external atmospheric pressure to force a liquid etc. into the vacant space. [f. L *suctio* (*sugere* suck)]

Sudan /suːˈdɑːn, sʊ-/ a country in NE Africa south of Egypt, with a coastline on the Red Sea; pop. 19,500,000; official language, Arabic; capital, Khartoum. The NE area was part of ancient Nubia. Under Arab rule from the 13th c., the country was conquered by Egypt in 1820-2. The Sudan was separated from its northern neighbour by the Mahdist revolt of 1881-98, and administered after the reconquest of 1898 as an Anglo-Egyptian condominium. It became an independent republic in 1956, but suffered as a result of north-south tension within the country until the early 1970s. Cotton, grown in the irrigated areas of the south, forms the country's most important export. —**Sudanese** /suːdəˈniːz/ *adj. & n.* [f. Arab., = country of the Blacks]

sudden /ˈsʌd(ə)n/ *adj.* done or occurring etc. abruptly or unexpectedly. —**all of a sudden,** suddenly. **sudden death,** (*colloq.*) a decision (especially in a drawn contest) by the result of a single event. —**suddenly** *adv.*, **suddenness** *n.* [f. AF f. L (*subitus* sudden)]

Sudetenland /sʊˈdeɪt(ə)nlænd/ an area of Bohemia adjacent to the German border, allocated to the new State of Czechoslovakia after the First World War despite the presence of three million German-speaking inhabitants. The Sudetenland became the first object of German expansionist policies after the Nazis came to power, and, after war was threatened, was ceded to Germany as a result of the Munich Agreement of September 1938. In 1945 the area was returned to Czechoslovakia, and the German inhabitants were expelled and replaced by Czechs.

sudorific /sjuːdəˈrɪfɪk, suː-/ *adj.* causing sweating. —*n.* a sudorific drug. [f. L *sudor* sweat, *facere* make]

Sudra /ˈsuːdrə/ *n.* a member of the lowest of the four great Hindu castes (the labourer class), whose function is to serve the other three varnas; this class. [f. Skr.]

suds /sʌdz/ *n.pl.* froth of soap and water. —**sudsy** *adj.* [cf. MDu. & MLG *sudde* marsh]

sue /sjuː, suː/ *v.t./i.* **1.** to begin a lawsuit against (a person). **2.** to make an application. [f. AF, ult. f. L *sequi* follow]

suede /sweɪd/ *n.* **1.** kid or other skin with the flesh side rubbed to a nap. **2.** a cloth imitating this. [f. F (*gants de*) *Suède* (gloves of) Sweden]

suedette /sweɪˈdet/ *n.* a material designed to imitate the texture of suede, especially a type of cotton or rayon fabric with a suede-like nap. [f. SUEDE + -ETTE]

suet /ˈsjuːɪt, ˈsuː-/ *n.* the hard fat of the kidneys and loins of oxen or sheep etc. —**suety** *adj.* [f. OF f. L *sebum* tallow]

Suetonius /suːɪˈtəʊnɪəs/ (Gaius Suetonius Tranquillus, born *c.*69) Roman scholar and biographer. His surviving works include biographies of the first twelve Caesars, from Julius Caesar to Domitian, which detail the good and bad qualities and deeds of their subjects in a schematic but objective manner, and which provided a model for biography in the Middle Ages and Renaissance.

Suez /ˈsuːɪz/ an isthmus connecting Egypt to the Sinai peninsula, site of the **Suez Canal,** a shipping canal 171 km (106 miles) long connecting the Mediterranean (at Port Said) with the Red Sea, constructed in 1859-69 by Ferdinand de Lesseps. The Canal, now important for Egypt's economy as providing the shortest route for international sea traffic travelling between Europe and Asia, came under British control after Britain acquired majority shares in it, at Disraeli's instigation, in 1875, and after 1888 Britain acted as guarantor of its neutral status. It was nationalized by Egypt in 1956 and an Anglo-French attempt at intervention was called off after international protest.

suf- *prefix* see SUB-.

suffer *v.t./i.* **1.** to experience the effects of (something unpleasant); to feel pain or grief; to be subjected to damage.

2. to undergo (a change). **3.** to tolerate; (*archaic*) to permit. —**sufferer** *n.*, **suffering** *n.* [f. AF f. L *sufferre* (SUF-, *ferre* bear)]

sufferable *adj.* bearable. [f. prec.]

sufferance *n.* tacit consent, abstention from an objection. —**on sufferance,** tolerated but not supported. [as SUFFER]

suffice /səˈfaɪs/ *v.t./i.* to be enough or adequate; to meet the needs of (a person etc.). —**suffice it to say,** I will content myself with saying. [f. OF f. L *sufficere* (SUF-, *facere* make)]

sufficiency /səˈfɪʃ(ə)nsɪ/ *n.* a sufficient amount. [f. L (as foll.)]

sufficient /səˈfɪʃ(ə)nt/ *adj.* enough. —**sufficiently** *adv.* [f. OF or L (as SUFFICE)]

suffix /ˈsʌfɪks/ *n.* a letter or letters added at the end of a word to form a derivative. —*v.t.* to append, especially as a suffix. [f. L (as SUF-, FIX)]

suffocate /ˈsʌfəkeɪt/ *v.t./i.* **1.** to impede or stop the breathing of (a person etc.); to choke or kill thus. **2.** to be or feel suffocated. —**suffocation** /-ˈkeɪʃ(ə)n/ *n.* [f. L *suffocare* (SUF-, *fauces* throat)]

Suffolk /ˈsʌfək/ a county of eastern England.

suffragan /ˈsʌfrəgən/ *n.* **1.** a bishop appointed to assist a diocesan bishop. **2.** a bishop in relation to his archbishop. [f. AF f. L (as foll.); orig. of bishop summoned to vote in synod]

suffrage /ˈsʌfrɪdʒ/ *n.* **1.** the right of voting in political elections. **2.** a short prayer or petition. [f. L *suffragium*]

suffragette /sʌfrəˈdʒet/ *n.* (*hist.*) a woman who agitated, especially with violence, for women's suffrage. Under the leadership of the Pankhursts the Women's Suffrage Movement became an important political force in Britain in the early 20th c., eventually winning (in 1918) the vote for women over 30. Ten years later British women were given full equality with men in voting rights. [f. prec. + -ETTE]

suffuse /səˈfjuːz/ *v.t.* (of a colour or moisture etc.) to spread throughout or over. —**suffusion** *n.* [f. L *suffundere* (SUF-, *fundere* pour)]

Sufi /ˈsuːfɪ/ *n.* a Muslim ascetic mystic; a member of any of several orders of Islamic mystics (see below). —**Sufic** *adj.*, **Sufism** *n.* [f. Arab. *suf* wool (which was used for clothing by religious persons from pre-Islamic times)]

Sufism is the esoteric dimension of the Islamic faith, the inner way or spiritual path to mystical union with God. Its followers may be ascetics who isolate themselves from society, more usually they are members of a Sufi order. The many orders have each been founded by a devout individual, and the movement (which seems to have begun in the late 7th c., perhaps in response to the increasing worldliness of the expanding Muslim community) reached its peak in the 13th c. The devotional practices of various orders differ widely (see DERVISH). The Sufi have been responsible for world-wide missionary activity, and their mystical ideas spread through Persian and Arab poetry. In the 19th-20th c. Sufic orders have often taken on overtly political roles; the Sanusiyya of Libya led resistance to the Italian colonial occupation and founded the independent State after the Second World War.

sug- *prefix* see SUB-.

sugar /ˈʃʊgə(r)/ *n.* **1.** a sweet crystalline substance from sugar-cane, sugar-beet, and other plants, used in cookery, confectionery, etc. (see below). **2.** a soluble usually sweet crystalline carbohydrate, e.g. glucose. **3.** (*US colloq.*, as a term of address) darling. —*v.t.* to sweeten or coat with sugar. —**sugar-beet** *n.* a beet from whose roots sugar is made. **sugar-cane** *n.* a perennial tropical grass (*Saccharum officinarum*) with very tall stems from which sugar is made. **sugar-daddy** *n.* (*slang*) an elderly man who lavishes gifts on a young woman. **sugar-loaf** *n.* a conical moulded mass of sugar. **sugar soap,** an alkaline compound for cleaning or removing paint. [f. OF, ult. f. Arab. *sukkar*]

Cane-sugar was known in India in prehistoric times. In Europe it was known from the Roman period but only as a rare spice obtained from the East; the Venetian merchants later became prominent in this trade. In 1493 the plant was taken to the West Indies by Christopher Columbus, and has since been introduced into every tropical country. Sugar-beet (which will grow in colder climates) was long used as a vegetable and cattle-food. In 1747 the German chemist Andreas Marggraf found a way of extracting from it sugar in crystalline form, and its development as the basis of a successful industry dates from the period of the

Napoleonic Wars, when the British blockade prevented the importing of cane-sugar from the West Indies.

sugary *n.* **1.** containing or resembling sugar. **2.** attractively or excessively sweet or pleasant. —**sugariness** *n.* [f. prec.]

suggest /sə'dʒest/ *v.t.* **1.** to put forward for consideration or as a possibility; to propose tentatively. **2.** to cause (an idea) to present itself; to bring (an idea) into the mind. —**suggest itself,** to come into the mind. [f. L *suggerere* (SUG-, *gerere* bring)]

suggestible /sə'dʒestɪb(ə)l/ *adj.* **1.** easily influenced by suggestions. **2.** that may be suggested. —**suggestibility** /-'bɪlɪtɪ/ *n.* [f. prec.]

suggestion /sə'dʒestʃ(ə)n/ *n.* **1.** suggesting. **2.** a thing suggested. **3.** the insinuation of a belief or impulse into the mind. **4.** a hint or slight trace. [f. OF f. L (as SUGGEST)]

suggestive /sə'dʒestɪv/ *adj.* **1.** conveying a suggestion. **2.** tending to convey an indecent or improper meaning etc. —**suggestively** *adv.*, **suggestiveness** *n.* [f. SUGGEST]

suicidal /'su:ɪsaɪd(ə)l, 'sju:-, -'saɪ-/ *adj.* **1.** of or tending to suicide; (of a person) liable to commit suicide. **2.** extremely foolhardy, destructive to one's own interests etc. —**suicidally** *adv.* [f. foll.]

suicide /'su:ɪsaɪd, sju:-/ *n.* **1.** the intentional killing of oneself; an instance of this; a person who does this. **2.** an action destructive to one's own interests or reputation etc. [f. L *sui* of oneself + -CIDE]

sui generis /sjʊaɪ 'dʒenərɪs, su:i:/ of its own kind, unique. [L]

suit /su:t, sju:t/ *n.* **1.** a set of clothes for wearing together, especially of the same cloth and consisting of a jacket and trousers or skirt. **2.** clothing for a particular purpose. **3.** a set of pyjamas, armour, etc. **4.** any of the four sets (spades, hearts, diamonds, clubs) into which a pack of cards is divided. **5.** a lawsuit. **6.** (*archaic*) suing; the seeking of a woman's hand in marriage. —*v.t.* **1.** to satisfy, to meet the demands or needs of. **2.** to be convenient or right for. **3.** to give a pleasing appearance or effect upon. **4.** (of a climate, food, etc.) to improve or not impair the health of, to agree with. **5.** to adapt, to make suitable. —**suit oneself,** to do as one chooses; to find something that satisfies one. [f. AF *suite*; as SUE]

suitable *adj.* right or appropriate for the purpose or occasion etc. —**suitability** /-'bɪlɪtɪ/ *n.*, **suitably** *adv.* [f. prec.]

suitcase *n.* a rectangular case for carrying clothes etc., usually with a handle and a hinged lid.

suite /swi:t/ *n.* **1.** a set of rooms or furniture. **2.** a set of attendants, a retinue. **3.** (*Mus.*) a set of instrumental pieces. During the 17th-18th c. the suite was one of the most important forms of instrumental music. It was superseded in importance by the sonata and the symphony, and the title was given to works of a lighter type and assemblages of movements from opera or ballet scores; 20th-c. neo-classical composers (e.g. Stravinsky) have revived the term. [F (as SUIT)]

suitor /'su:tə(r), 'sju:-/ *n.* **1.** a man wooing a woman. **2.** a plaintiff or petitioner. [f. AF f. L *secutor* (*sequi* follow)]

Sulawesi /sʊlə'weɪsɪ/ a large island of Indonesia, east of Borneo, formerly called Celebes; pop. (1971) 8,535,164.

Suleiman I /'sʊlɪmɑ:n, -leɪ-/ 'the Magnificent', (?1495-1566), sultan of Turkey 1520-66, under whom the Ottoman empire reached its peak in military power and in cultural achievements.

sulfa var. of SULPHA.

sulk *v.i.* to be sulky. —*n.* (usu. in *pl.*) a sulky fit. [perh. back-formation f. foll.]

sulky *adj.* sullen and unsociable from resentment or bad temper. —*n.* a light two-wheeled one-horse vehicle for a single person, especially as used in trotting-races (see TROTTING), so called because it admits only one person. —**sulkily** *adv.*, **sulkiness** *n.* [perh. f. obs. *sulke* hard to dispose of]

Sulla /'sʌlə/ (Lucius Cornelius Sulla Felix, *c.*138-78 BC) Roman general and politician. In 88 BC he marched on Rome and ousted the supporters of Marius. After concluding the war in the east by a peace with Mithridates, Sulla invaded Italy in 88 BC and instituted ruthless proscriptions of his enemies. Elected dictator, he pushed through constitutional reforms in favour of the Senate, but resigned in 79 BC and returned to private status. Sulla never aimed at permanent tyranny, but he set the precedent for the use of military force against the State—and for its success.

sullen /'sʌlən/ *adj.* passively resentful, stubbornly ill-humoured, unresponsive. —**sullenly** *adv.*, **sullenness** *n.* [alt. f. earlier *solein* (as SOLE³)]

Sullivan /'sʌlɪv(ə)n/, Sir Arthur (1842-1900), English composer. He first collaborated with the librettist W. S. Gilbert in 1871, and they produced a string of highly popular light operas, many of them for Richard D'Oyly Carte's company at the Savoy theatre. Among the best known are *Trial by Jury* (1875), *HMS Pinafore* (1878), *The Pirates of Penzance* (1879), *Patience* (1881), *The Mikado* (1885), *Ruddigore* (1887), and *The Gondoliers* (1889). He also composed the hymn 'Onward, Christian Soldiers' (1871) and the song *The Lost Chord* (1877).

sully /'sʌlɪ/ *v.t.* to stain or blemish; to diminish the purity or splendour of (a reputation etc.). [perh. f. F *souiller* (as SOIL²)]

sulpha /'sʌlfə/ *adj.* sulphonamide. [abbr.]

sulphate /'sʌlfeɪt/ *n.* a salt of sulphuric acid. [f. F f. L *sulphur*]

sulphide /'sʌlfaɪd/ *n.* a binary compound of sulphur. [f. SULPHUR]

sulphite /'sʌlfaɪt/ *n.* a salt of sulphurous acid. [as SULPHATE]

sulphonamide /sʌl'fɒnəmaɪd/ *n.* a type of antibiotic drug. [f. G *sulfon* (as SULPHUR) + AMIDE]

sulphur /'sʌlfə(r)/ *n.* **1.** a pale-yellow non-metallic element, symbol S, atomic number 16 (see below). **2.** a pale slightly greenish yellow colour. **3.** a yellow butterfly of the family Pieridae. [f. AF f. L]

Sulphur, formerly also called brimstone, can occur uncombined in nature and has been known since ancient times. It was recognized as an element in 1777. Elemental sulphur, which can exist in a number of allotropic forms, burns with a blue flame and a suffocating smell, and is used in making gunpowder, matches, and as an antiseptic and fungicide. The most important compound of sulphur, produced in huge amounts, is sulphuric acid, much of which is in turn converted into other compounds. Sulphur compounds of one kind or another play a role in most manufacturing processes, and the element is also essential to living organisms.

sulphureous /sʌl'fjʊərɪəs/ *adj.* of or like sulphur. [f. L, = sulphur]

sulphuric /sʌl'fjʊərɪk/ *adj.* containing sulphur in a higher valency. —**sulphuric acid,** a dense oily highly acid and corrosive fluid. [f. F (as SULPHUR)]

sulphurous /'sʌlfərəs/ *adj.* **1.** of or like sulphur. **2.** containing sulphur in a lower valency. —**sulphurous acid,** an unstable weak acid used as a reducing and bleaching agent. [f. SULPHUR]

sultan /'sʌlt(ə)n/ *n.* **1.** a Muslim sovereign. **2.** (also **sweet sultan**) a sweet-scented plant (*Centaurea moschata* or *C. suaveolens*). [F or f. L f. Arab. = power, ruler]

sultana /sʌl'tɑ:nə/ *n.* **1.** a kind of seedless raisin. **2.** a sultan's wife, mother, concubine, or daughter. [It. (as prec.)]

sultanate /'sʌlt(ə)nət/ *n.* the position of or territory ruled by a sultan. [f. SULTAN]

sultry /'sʌltrɪ/ *adj.* **1.** (of weather etc.) hot and humid. **2.** of dark mysterious beauty; passionate, sensual. —**sultrily** *adv.*, **sultriness** *n.* [f. obs. *sulter* v.; rel. to SWELTER]

sum *n.* **1.** a total resulting from the addition of items. **2.** a particular amount of money. **3.** a problem in arithmetic; the working out of this. **4.** the whole amount. **5.** the substance, a summary (of facts etc.). —*v.t.* (-mm-) to find the sum of. —**in sum,** briefly, in summary. **sum up,** to find or give the total of; to express briefly, to summarize; to form or express a judgement or opinion of; (esp. of a judge) to recapitulate the evidence or argument. [f. OF f. L *summa* (*summus* highest)]

sumac /'ʃu:mæk/ *n.* a shrub of the genus *Rhus* yielding leaves that are dried and ground for use in tanning and dyeing; these leaves. [f. OF or L f. Arab.]

Sumatra /sʊ'mɑ:trə/ a large island of Indonesia, separated from the Malay Peninsula by the Strait of Malacca; pop. (1971) 20,812,682.

Sumer /'su:mə(r)/ the name used in antiquity from the 3rd millennium BC for southern Mesopotamia, the region inhabited by Sumerian-speaking people and later known as Babylonia.

Sumerian /su:'mɪərɪən/ *adj.* of a non-Semitic language, people, and civilization native to Sumer in the 4th millennium BC and possibly earlier. —*n.* a member of this people. The Sumerians were a hybrid stock, speaking an agglutinative language related structurally to Turkish, Hungarian, Finnish, and several Caucasian dialects. As the first historically attested civilization they are credited with the invention of cuneiform writing, the sexagesimal system of mathematics, and the socio-political institution of the city-state with bureaucracies, legal codes, division of labour, and a money economy. Their art, literature, and theology had a profound cultural and religious influence on the rest of Mesopotamia and beyond, which continued long after the Sumerian demise *c.* 2000 BC, as the prototype of Akkadian, Hurrian, Canaanite, Hittite, and eventually, biblical literature. [f. prec.]

summarize /ˈsʌməraɪz/ *v.t.* to make or be a summary of. [f. foll.]

summary /ˈsʌmərɪ/ *n.* a statement giving the main points of something. —*adj.* **1.** brief, giving the main points only. **2.** done or given without delay, details, or formalities. —**summarily** *adv.* [f. L (as SUM)]

summation /sʌˈmeɪʃ(ə)n/ *n.* **1.** the finding of a total. **2.** summarizing. [f. SUM]

summer *n.* **1.** the warmest season of the year, from June to August in the northern hemisphere. **2.** the mature stage of life etc. —*adj.* characteristic of or suitable for summer. —**summer-house** *n.* a light building in a garden or park, providing shade in summer. **Summer Palace,** a palace (now in ruins) of the Chinese emperors near Peking. **summer pudding,** a dish made by pressing soft fruits into a bowl lined and covered with bread or sponge-cake. **summer school,** a series of lectures etc. in summer, especially at a university. **summer-time** *n.* the season or weather of summer. **summer time,** the time shown by clocks advanced in summer to give long light evenings during the summer months. —**summery** *adj.* [OE]

summit /ˈsʌmɪt/ *n.* **1.** the highest point, the top. **2.** the highest level of achievement or status. **3.** (in full **summit meeting**) a discussion between heads of governments. [f. OF *somet* (*som* top f. L, as SUM)]

summon /ˈsʌmən/ *v.t.* **1.** to demand the presence of, to call together. **2.** to command (a person) to appear in a lawcourt. **3.** to call upon (a person etc.) to do something. **4.** to gather (one's strength, courage, or energy etc.) in order to do something. [f. OF *summonēre* (SUB-, *monēre* warn)]

summons /ˈsʌmənz/ *n.* an authoritative call to attend or do something, especially to appear before a judge or magistrate. —*v.t.* to serve with a summons. [as prec.]

sumo /ˈsuːməʊ/ *n.* (*pl.* **-os**) **1.** a kind of Japanese wrestling in which a person is considered defeated if he touches the ground except with his feet, or fails to keep within a marked area. **2.** a person who takes part in this. [Jap.]

sump *n.* **1.** a casing holding lubricating oil in an internal-combustion engine. **2.** a pit, well, or low area into which waste or superfluous liquid drains. [orig. = marsh, rel. to SWAMP]

sumptuary /ˈsʌmptjʊərɪ/ *adj.* regulating expenditure. [f. L (*sumptus* cost f. *sumere* take)]

sumptuous /ˈsʌmptjʊəs/ *adj.* splendid and costly-looking. —**sumptuously** *adv.*, **sumptuousness** *n.* [f. OF f. L (as prec.)]

sun *n.* **1.** (also **Sun**) the star that Earth travels round and receives warmth and light from (see below). **2.** such warmth or light or both. **3.** any fixed star with or without planets. **4.** (*poet.*) a day or year. —*v.t./i.* (**-nn-**) to expose (oneself etc.) to the sun. —**a place in the sun,** a favourable situation or condition. **sun-glasses** *n.pl.* spectacles with tinted lenses to protect the eyes from sunlight or glare. **sun-god** *n.* the sun worshipped as a deity. **Sun King,** Louis XIV of France, so called from the magnificence of his reign. **sun-lamp** *n.* a lamp giving ultraviolet rays for therapy or an artificial sun-tan. **sun lounge,** a room designed to receive much sunlight. **sun-roof** *n.* a roof with a sliding section in a saloon car. **sun-tan** *n.* tanning of the skin by exposure to the sun. **sun-tanned** *adj.* tanned by the sun. **sun-trap** *n.* a sunny place, especially one sheltered from the wind. **sun-up** *n.* (*US*) sunrise. **under the sun,** anywhere in the world. [OE]
  The central body of the solar system, the sun is a luminous body which provides the light and energy which sustains living creatures on Earth. It is a star of the type known to astronomers as a G2 subdwarf, a sphere of hydrogen and helium 1.4 million km in diameter which obtains its energy from nuclear fusion reactions deep within its interior. Temperatures at the centre must be high enough to sustain these reactions, say twenty million degrees or so; but the surface temperature is a little under 6000 °C. The visible surface is marked by occasional sunspots, local regions where temperatures are 2000° cooler than the rest of the surface, which appear to arise from local intense magnetic

fields. Above this region, known as the photosphere, are the chromosphere and corona, regions of much higher temperature. The apparent path of the sun across the sky (which is merely a reflection of the Earth's orbit about the sun) determines the terrestrial seasons.

Sun. *abbr.* Sunday.

sunbathe *v.i.* to expose one's body to the sun.

sunbeam *n.* a ray of sun.

sunburn *n.* tanning or inflammation of the skin caused by exposure to the sun. —**sunburnt** *adj.*

sundae /ˈsʌndeɪ/ *n.* a confection of ice-cream with fruit, syrup, etc. [perh. f. foll., either because the dish orig. included left-over ice-cream sold cheaply on Monday, or because it was at first sold only on Sunday, having been devised (according to some accounts) to circumvent Sunday legislation. The spelling is sometimes said to have been altered from *Sunday* out of deference to religious people's feelings]

Sunday /ˈsʌndeɪ/ *n.* **1.** the day of the week following Saturday, the Christian day of rest and worship (see below). **2.** a newspaper published on Sundays. —*adv.* (*colloq.*) on Sunday. —**Sunday best,** one's best clothes (kept for use on Sundays). **Sunday painter,** an amateur painter, one who paints solely for pleasure. **Sunday school,** a school held on Sundays for children, now only for religious instruction. Although there were earlier examples of schools for poor children on Sundays, the movement owes its success to Robert Raikes (1735-1811), a native of Gloucester, who in 1780 started a school in his own parish which became widely imitated. [OE, = day of the sun]
  The old pagan 'day of the sun' was given a Christian interpretation and referred to Christ, the 'sun of righteousness' (Mal. 4: 2), being called the 'day of the Lord'. Already in New Testament times Sunday began to replace (for Christians) the Jewish sabbath, chiefly in commemoration of the Resurrection. Its observance as a day of rest, consecrated especially to the service of God, began to be regulated by both ecclesiastical and civil legislation from the 4th c. In the 19th c. Sunday was still a day mainly devoted to duties of piety, but the increasing secularization of life in the 20th c. has considerably reduced its religious observance, though requirement to work on that day is regarded as unsocial.

sunder *v.t.* to break or tear apart, to sever. [OE; cf. ASUNDER]

sundial *n.* an instrument showing the time by the shadow of a rod or plate cast by the sun on a scaled dial (ill. TIME). It is probably the most ancient time-measuring instrument. Sundials in which the edge of the gnomon is parallel to the earth's axis (so that it points to the north celestial pole) can show solar time to an accuracy of a minute or two; for centuries they were used as a check on the accuracy of the clocks and watches which eventually superseded them, until telegraphic and radio time-signals became available.

sundown *n.* sunset.

sundry /ˈsʌndrɪ/ *adj.* various, several. —*n.* (in *pl.*) oddments, accessories, items not needed to be specified. —**all and sundry,** everyone. [OE, rel. to SUNDER]

sunfish *n.* a large globular fish, especially the ocean fish *Mola mola.*

sunflower *n.* a tall garden-plant of the genus *Helianthus* with large golden-rayed flowers.

Sung /sʊŋ/ *n.* the name of the dynasty which ruled in China 960-1279.

sung *p.p.* of SING.

sunk *past* & *p.p.* of SINK.

sunken *adj.* lying below the level of a surrounding area; (of cheeks etc.) shrunken, hollow. [p.p. of SINK]

sunless *adj.* without sunshine. [f. SUN + -LESS]

sunlight *n.* light from the sun.

sunlit *adj.* illuminated by sunlight.

Sunna /ˈsʌnə/ *n.* the traditional portion of Islamic law, based on Muhammad's words or acts but not written by him. [Arab., = form, way, rule]

Sunnite /ˈsʌnaɪt/ *n.* a member of one of the two major groups in Islam (opp. SHIITE), comprising the main community in most Muslim countries other than Iran. The split occurred early in the history of Islam over the question of allegiance to the nascent Ummayyad dynasty (supported by the Sunnis) versus the family of Ali, son-in-law of the Prophet Muhammad and fourth caliph. After his assassination and that of his son Husayn at the Battle of Kerbala (in present-day Iraq) in 680, one group of Muslims broke away from the main body, declaring their allegiance to the martyred sons, and calling themselves the Shia (= party). What became known as the Sunni Muslims continued to follow the reigning caliph. From the basic split in attitudes to leadership of the community have followed other differences in community organization and legal practice, but doctrinally Sunni and Shiite Muslims adhere to the same body of tenets. [f. SUNNA]

sunny *adj.* **1.** bright with or as sunlight; exposed to or warm with the sun. **2.** happy, cheerful. —**sunnily** *adv.*, **sunniness** *n.* [f. SUN]

sunrise *n.* the sun's rising; the moment of this; the eastern sky with the colours of the sunrise.

sunset *n.* the sun's setting; the moment of this; the western sky with the colours of the sunset.

sunshade *n.* a parasol or awning, giving shade from the sun.

sunshine *n.* **1.** the light of the sun; the area illuminated by it. **2.** fair weather. **3.** cheerfulness, bright influence.

sunspot *n.* a dark patch on the sun's surface.

sunstroke *n.* illness caused by excessive exposure to sun.

sunwise *adv.* in the direction of the sun's course (and hence lucky); opp. *widdershins*).

Sun Yat-sen /suːn jætˈsen/ (1866–1925), Chinese statesman, generally considered to be the 'Father of the Revolution'. Sun Yat-sen spent the period 1895–1911 in exile after an unsuccessful attempt to overthrow the Manchus, but returned to play a crucial part in the successful revolution and to organize the Kuomintang (1911–12). In the chaotic period that followed he was briefly provisional president of the Chinese Republic and a decade later president of the Southern Chinese Republic before dying of cancer.

sup *v.t./i.* (**-pp-**) **1.** to drink by sips or spoonfuls. **2.** to take supper. **3.** (*colloq.*) to drink (beer etc.). —*n.* a mouthful of liquid; (*colloq.*) a drink of beer etc. [OE; in second sense of v. f. OF (as SOUP)]

sup- *prefix* see SUB-.

super /ˈsuːpə(r), ˈsjuː-/ *adj.* (*slang*) excellent, superb. —*n.* (*colloq.*) **1.** a supernumerary. **2.** a superintendent. [abbr.]

super- /suːpə(r)-, sjuː-/ *prefix* above or beyond or over (*superstructure*, *supernormal*); to a great or extreme degree (*superabundant*, *supertanker*); higher in status (*superintendent*). [f. L *super* over]

superabundant /suːpərəˈbʌnd(ə)nt, sjuː-/ *adj.* very abundant, more than enough. —**superabundance** *n.*

superannuate /suːpərˈænjʊeɪt, sjuː-/ *v.t.* **1.** to discharge (an employee) into retirement with a pension. **2.** to discard as too old for use. [f. L (SUPER-, *annus* year)]

superannuation /suːpərænjʊˈeɪʃ(ə)n, sjuː-/ *n.* **1.** superannuating. **2.** a pension granted to an employee on retirement; payment(s) contributed towards this during his or her employment. [f. prec.]

superb /suːˈpɜːb, sjuː-/ *adj.* of the most impressive or splendid kind, excellent. —**superbly** *adv.* [F for L *superbus* proud]

supercargo *n.* (*pl.* **-oes**) a person in a merchant ship managing the sales etc. of cargo. [f. Sp. *sobrecargo* (*sobre* over, CARGO)]

supercharge *v.t.* **1.** to charge to extreme or excess (with energy etc.). **2.** to use a supercharger on.

supercharger *n.* a device forcing extra air or fuel into an internal-combustion engine so as to increase its power.

superciliary /suːpəˈsɪlɪərɪ, sjuː-/ *adj.* of the eyebrow; over the eye. [f. L *supercilium* eyebrow (SUPER-, *cilium* eyelid)]

supercilious /suːpəˈsɪlɪəs, sjuː-/ *adj.* with an air of superiority, haughty and scornful. —**superciliously** *adv.*, **superciliousness** *n.* [f. L (as prec.)]

superconductivity /suːpəkɒndʌkˈtɪvɪtɪ, sjuː-/ *n.* absence of electrical resistance in some substances at temperatures near absolute zero. Discovered in 1911 by H. Kamerlingh Onnes, superconductivity can now be explained in terms of quantum theory. Knowledge of the phenomenon has made possible the construction of large electromagnets which are able to operate without expending large quantities of electrical energy. —**superconductive** /-kənˈdʌktɪv/ *adj.*

supercool *v.t.* to cool (a liquid) below its freezing-point without its becoming solid or crystalline.

super-ego /suːpərˈiːɡəʊ, -ˈeɡəʊ/ *n.* a person's ideals for himself, acting like a conscience in directing his behaviour.

supererogation /suːpərerəˈɡeɪʃ(ə)n, sjuː-/ *n.* the doing of more than duty requires. [f. L *supererogare* pay out in

addition, orig. public money after formal request for permission (SUPER-, *rogare* ask)]

superfamily *n.* a taxonomic category between family and order.

superficial /suːpəˈfɪʃ(ə)l, sjuː-/ *adj.* **1.** of or on the surface only. **2.** without depth of knowledge or feeling etc. **3.** (of measure) square. —**superficiality** /-ʃɪˈælɪtɪ/ *n.*, **superficially** *adv.* [f. L (*superficies* surface f. SUPER-, *facies* face)]

superfine *adj.* extremely fine or refined.

superfluity /suːpəˈfluːɪtɪ, sjuː-/ *n.* **1.** a superfluous amount or thing. **2.** being superfluous. [f. OF f. L (as foll.)]

superfluous /suːˈpɜːfluəs, sjuː-/ *adj.* more than is needed or required; not needed. —**superfluously** *adv.*, **superfluousness** *n.* [f. L (SUPER-, *fluere* flow)]

supergrass *n.* (*slang*) one who informs against a large number of persons.

superheat *v.t.* to heat (liquid) above its boiling-point without allowing it to vaporize; to heat (vapour) above its boiling-point. —**superheater** *n.*

superhighway *n.* (*US*) a broad main road for fast traffic.

superhuman /suːpəˈhjuːmən, sjuː-/ *adj.* **1.** exceeding the normal human capacity or power. **2.** higher than humanity, divine.

superimpose /suːpərɪmˈpəʊz, sjuː-/ *v.t.* to lay or place (a thing) on top of something else. —**superimposition** /-pəˈzɪʃ(ə)n/ *n.*

superintend /suːpərɪnˈtend, sjuː-/ *v.t./i.* to supervise. —**superintendence** *n.* [f. L *superintendere* (SUPER-, INTEND)]

superintendent *n.* **1.** one who superintends. **2.** the director of an institution etc. **3.** a police officer above the rank of inspector. [f. prec.]

superior /suːˈpɪərɪə(r), sjuː-/ *adj.* **1.** higher in position or rank; (of figures etc.) written or printed above the line. **2.** better or greater in some way; of high or higher quality. **3.** showing that one feels oneself to be better or wiser etc. than others; conceited, supercilious. **4.** (with *to*) not influenced by; not yielding or resorting to. —*n.* **1.** a person or thing of higher rank, ability, or quality. **2.** the head of a monastery or other religious community. —**superiority** /-ˈɒrɪtɪ/ *n.* [f. OF f. L, compar. of *superus* situated above (*super* above)]

Superior, Lake one of the five Great Lakes of North America.

superlative /suːˈpɜːlətɪv, sjuː-/ *adj.* of the highest degree or quality, excellent. —*n.* (*Gram.*) the superlative degree; a superlative form. —**superlative adjective** (*or* **adverb**), an adjective (or adverb) in the superlative degree. **superlative degree**, the form expressing the highest or a very high degree of a quality (e.g. *bravest*, *most quickly*). —**superlatively** *adv.*, **superlativeness** *n.* [f. OF f. L (*superlatus* carried above f. SUPER-, p.p. of *ferre* bear)]

superman *n.* (*pl.* **-men**) **1.** the ideal superior man of the future, held by Nietzsche to be able to be evolved from the normal human type. **2.** a man of superhuman powers or achievement. [f. SUPER- + MAN, formed by G. B. Shaw after Nietzsche's G. *übermensch*]

supermarket *n.* a large self-service store usually selling food and some household goods.

supernatural /suːpəˈnætʃər(ə)l, sjuː-/ *adj.* of or manifesting phenomena not explicable by natural or physical laws. —**supernaturally** *adv.*

supernova /suːpəˈnəʊvə, sjuː-/ *n.* (*pl.* **-ae** *or* **-as**) a star that suddenly increases very greatly in brightness because of an explosion disrupting its structure and ejecting debris at speeds of up to a tenth that of light and temperatures of hundreds of thousands of degrees. Within the resulting shell of material may be left a pulsar or a black hole. Though frequently observed by astronomers in other galaxies, only three have been recorded in our own Galaxy: by Chinese astronomers in 1054, by Tycho Brahe in 1572, and by Kepler in 1604.

supernumerary /suːpəˈnjuːmərərɪ, sjuː-/ *adj.* in excess of the normal number, extra. —*n.* a supernumerary person or thing. [f. L *super numerum* beyond the number)]

superphosphate /suːpəˈfɒsfeɪt, sjuː-/ *n.* a fertilizer made from phosphate rock.

superpose /suːpəˈpəʊz, sjuː-/ *v.t.* to place (a geometrical figure) upon another so that their outlines coincide. —**superposition** /-pəˈzɪʃ(ə)n/ *n.*

superpower *n.* a nation or State having a dominant position in world politics, one with the power to act decisively in pursuit of interests affecting the whole world; the USA and USSR.

superscribe /ˈsuːpəskraɪb, ˈsjuː-/ v.t. to write (an inscription) at the top of or outside a document etc. [f. L *superscribere* (SUPER-, *scribere* write)]

superscript /ˈsuːpəskrɪpt, ˈsjuː-/ adj. written or printed just above and to the right of a word, figure, or symbol. —n. a superscript figure or symbol. [as prec.]

superscription /suːpəˈskrɪpʃ(ə)n, sjuː-/ n. superscribed words. [as SUPERSCRIBE]

supersede /suːpəˈsiːd, sjuː-/ v.t. to take the place of; to put or use another in place of. —**supercession** /-ˈseʃ(ə)n/ n. [f. OF f. L *supersedēre* be superior to (SUPER-, *sedēre* sit)]

supersonic /suːpəˈsɒnɪk, sjuː-/ adj. of or having a speed greater than that of sound. —**supersonically** adv.

superstar n. a great star in entertainment etc.

superstition /suːpəˈstɪʃ(ə)n, sjuː-/ n. **1.** belief in the existence or power of the supernatural; irrational fear of the unknown or mysterious; misdirected reverence. **2.** a religion, or practice, or opinion based on such tendencies. **3.** a widely held but wrong idea. —**superstitious** adj., **superstitiously** adv., **superstitiousness** n. [f. OF or L *superstitio* f. *superstare* (SUPER-, *stare* stand)]

superstore n. a large supermarket, especially one with a sales area of at least 2,500 sq. metres.

superstructure n. a structure built on top of something else; a building as distinct from its foundations.

supertanker n. a very large tanker.

supervene /suːpəˈviːn, sjuː-/ v.i. to occur as an interruption in or change from some state or process. —**supervention** n. [f. L *supervenire* (SUPER-, *venire* come)]

supervise /ˈsuːpəvaɪz, ˈsjuː-/ v.t. to direct and inspect (work, workers, or the operation of an organization). —**supervision** /-ˈvɪʒ(ə)n/ n., **supervisor** n., **supervisory** adj. [f. L *supervidēre* (SUPER-, *vidēre* see)]

supine /ˈsuːpaɪn, ˈsjuː-/ adj. **1.** lying face upwards. **2.** inactive, indolent. —n. a Latin verbal noun used only in the accusative and ablative cases. —**supinely** adv. [f. L *supinus* (*super* above)]

supper n. a light evening meal, the last meal of the day. [f. OF *soper*, *super* (as SUP)]

supplant /səˈplɑːnt/ v.t. to oust and take the place of. —**supplanter** n. [f. OF or L *supplantare* trip up (SUP-, *planta* sole)]

supple adj. bending easily, flexible, not stiff. —**supplely** adv., **suppleness** n. [f. OF f. L *supplex* submissive (as SUPPLICATE)]

supplement /ˈsʌplɪmənt/ n. **1.** a thing added as an extra or to make up for a deficiency. **2.** a part added to a book etc. to give further information or to treat a particular subject; a set of special pages issued with a newspaper. —/also -ˈment/ v.t. to provide or be a supplement to. —**supplemental** /-ˈment(ə)l/ adj., **supplementary** /-ˈmentərɪ/ adj., **supplementation** /-ˈteɪʃ(ə)n/ n. [f. L (as SUPPLY)]

suppliant /ˈsʌplɪənt/ n. a humble petitioner. —adj. supplicating [f. F (*supplier* f. L, as foll.)]

supplicate /ˈsʌplɪkeɪt/ v.t./i. to petition humbly. —**supplication** /-ˈkeɪʃ(ə)n/ n., **supplicatory** adj. [f. L *supplicare* (SUP-, *plicare* bend)]

supply /səˈplaɪ/ v.t. **1.** to give or provide with (something needed or useful); to make available for use. **2.** to make up for (a deficiency or need). —n. **1.** provision of what is needed. **2.** a stock or store, an amount of something provided or obtainable. **3.** (in *pl.*) the collected necessaries for an army, expedition, etc. **4.** a person, especially a schoolteacher or clergyman, acting as a temporary substitute for another. —**on supply,** (of a schoolteacher etc.) acting as a supply. **supply and demand,** the quantities available and required, as factors regulating the price of commodities. —**supplier** n. [f. OF f. L *supplēre* (SUP-, *plēre* fill)]

support /səˈpɔːt/ v.t. **1.** to keep from falling or sinking; to hold in position; to bear all or part of the weight of. **2.** to give strength to; to enable to last or continue; to supply with necessaries. **3.** to assist by one's approval or presence or by subscription to funds; to speak in favour of (a resolution etc.); to be actively interested in (a particular sport or team). **4.** to take a secondary part to (another performer). **5.** to bring facts to confirm (a statement etc.); to corroborate. **6.** to endure, to tolerate. —n. **1.** supporting, being supported. **2.** a person or thing that supports. —**in support of,** so as to support. **supporting film,** a less important film in a cinema programme. [f. OF f. L *supportare* (SUP-, *portare* carry)]

supporter n. **1.** a person or thing that supports; a person supporting a team or sport. **2.** (in heraldry) a representation of a living creature holding up or standing beside an escutcheon, usually as one of a pair on either side (ill. HERALDRY). [f. prec.]

supportive /səˈpɔːtɪv/ adj. providing support or encouragement. [f. SUPPORT]

suppose /səˈpəʊz/ v.t. **1.** to accept as true or probable, to be inclined to think. **2.** to take as a possiblity or hypothesis for the purpose of arguments; (in *imper.*) as a formula of proposal. **3.** (of a theory or result etc.) to require as a condition; to presuppose. **4.** (in *p.p.*) generally accepted as being so. —**be supposed to,** to be expected or required to; (*colloq.*, with *neg.*) ought not to, not to be allowed to. [f. OF (as SUP-, POSE)]

supposedly /səˈpəʊzɪdlɪ/ adv. as is generally supposed. [f. prec.]

supposition /sʌpəˈzɪʃ(ə)n/ n. **1.** a thing supposed. **2.** supposing. [f. SUPPOSE]

supposititious /sʌpəˈzɪʃəs/ adj. hypothetical. —**supposititiously** adv., **supposititiousness** n. [f. prec.]

supposititious /sʌpɒzɪˈtɪʃəs/ adj. substituted for the real person or thing, spurious. —**supposititiously** adv., **supposititiousness** n. [f. L *supponere* substitute (SUP-, *ponere* place)]

suppository /səˈpɒzɪtərɪ/ n. a medical preparation for insertion into the rectum or vagina, where it is left to melt. [f. L (as prec.)]

suppress /səˈpres/ v.t. **1.** to put an end to the activity or existence of, especially by force or authority. **2.** to prevent from being seen, heard, or known. **3.** to eliminate (electrical interference etc.) partially; to equip (a device) to reduce such interference as it produces. —**suppression** n., **suppressor** n. [f. L *supprimere* (SUP-, *premere* press)]

suppressible adj. that may be suppressed. [f. prec]

suppurate /ˈsʌpjʊreɪt/ v.i. to form pus, to fester. —**suppuration** /-ˈreɪʃ(ə)n/ n. [f. L *suppurare* (SUP-, *pus puris* pus)]

supra /ˈsuːprə/ adv. above or further back in the book etc. [L, = above]

supra- /ˈsuːprə-/ prefix above. [as prec.]

supranational /suːprəˈnæʃən(ə)l/ adj. transcending national limits.

supremacy /suːˈpreməsɪ, sjuː-/ n. being supreme; the highest authority. —**Act of Supremacy,** any Act of Parliament laying down the position of the sovereign as supreme head on earth of the Church of England (and excluding the authority of the pope) or supreme governor of England in spiritual and temporal matters, especially that of 1534. [f. foll.]

supreme /suːˈpriːm/ adj. **1.** highest in rank or authority. **2.** highest in importance, intensity, or quality; most outstanding; (of a penalty or sacrifice) involving death. —**Supreme Being,** God. **Supreme Court,** the highest judicial court in a State etc. [f. L *supremus*, superl. of *superus* (as SUPERIOR)]

supremo /suːˈpriːməʊ, sjuː-/ n. (*pl.* **-os**) a supreme leader or ruler. [Sp., = prec.]

sur-[1] prefix see SUB-.

sur-[2] prefix = SUPER- (*surcharge, surface, surrealism*). [OF]

surcease /sɜːˈsiːs/ n. (*archaic*) cessation. —v.i. (*archaic*) to cease. [f. OF *sursis* (*surseoir* refrain f. L, as SUPERSEDE)]

surcharge /ˈsɜːtʃɑːdʒ/ n. **1.** an additional charge or payment. **2.** a mark printed on a postage stamp, especially one changing its value. **3.** an additional or excessive load. —/also -ˈtʃɑːdʒ/ v.t. **1.** to exact a surcharge from; to exact (a sum) as a surcharge. **2.** to mark (a postage stamp) with a surcharge. **3.** to overload. [f. OF (as SUR-[2], CHARGE)]

surcoat /ˈsɜːkəʊt/ n. (*hist.*) a rich outer garment, especially (13th–14th c.) a loose garment worn over armour (ill. ARMOUR). [f. OF *surcot* (SUR-[2], COAT)]

surd adj. **1.** (of a number) irrational. **2.** (of a sound) uttered with breath and not voice (e.g. *f, k, p, s, t*). —n. **1.** a surd number, especially the root of an integer. **2.** a surd sound. [f. L *surdus* deaf]

sure /ʃʊə(r), ʃɔː(r)/ adj. **1.** having or seeming to have adequate reasons for one's belief; free from doubts; having satisfactory knowledge or trust. **2.** certain to do something or to happen. **3.** reliable, secure, unfailing. **4.** undoubtedly true or truthful. —adv. (*colloq.*) certainly. —**be sure to,** to take care to, not to fail to. **for sure,** (*colloq.*) without doubt. **make sure,** to make or become certain, to ensure. **sure enough,** (*colloq.*) in fact, certainly. **sure-fire** adj. (*colloq.*) certain to succeed. **sure-footed** adj. never stumbling or making a mistake. **to be sure,** it is undeniable or admitted. —**sureness** *n.* [f. OF *sur* f. L, = SECURE]

surely /ˈʃʊəlɪ, ˈʃɔː-/ *adv.* **1.** in a sure manner; with certainty; securely. **2.** used for emphasis, or (in questions) as an appeal to likelihood or reason. **3.** (as an answer) certainly, yes. [f. SURE]

surety /ˈʃʊərətɪ/ *n.* **1.** a person who makes himself responsible for another's performance of an undertaking or payment of a debt. **2.** (*archaic*) certainty. [f. OF f. L *securitas* security]

surf *n.* the foam of the sea breaking on the shore or on reefs. —*v.i.* to go surf-riding (see below). —**surf-riding** *n.* the sport of being carried over the surf to the shore on a board etc. —**surfer** *n.* [f. earlier *suff*; orig. unkn.]

Surfing or surf-riding originated in primitive societies living in coastal areas facing the open sea. It was a pastime for the peoples of the South Sea Islands before European mariners made their historic voyages, and was observed by Captain Cook in Tahiti in 1777. Body surfing (without a board) was practised by the early Hawaiians.

surface /ˈsɜːfɪs/ *n.* **1.** the outside of a thing; any of the limits terminating a solid. **2.** the top of a liquid or of soil etc. **3.** the outward aspect, what is perceived on a casual view or consideration. **4.** (*Geom.*) that which has length and breadth but no thickness. —(*attrib.*) *adj.* of the surface; superficial. —*v.t./i.* **1.** to give a (special) surface to (a road, paper, etc.). **2.** to rise to the surface; to become visible or known; (*colloq.*) to become conscious. **3.** to bring (a submarine) to the surface. —**surface mail,** mail carried overland and by sea. **surface tension,** tension of the surface of a liquid, tending to minimize its surface area. [F (as SUR-², FACE)]

surfboard *n.* a long narrow board used in surf-riding.

surfeit /ˈsɜːfɪt/ *n.* an excess, especially in eating or drinking; the resulting satiety. —*v.t./i.* to over-feed; to be or cause to be wearied through excess. [f. OF; cf. L *superficiens* excessive (SUPER-, *facere* do)]

surge *v.i.* **1.** to move to and fro (as) in waves. **2.** to move suddenly and powerfully; to increase in volume or intensity. —*n.* **1.** a powerful wave. **2.** a surging motion; an impetuous onset. [f. OF f. L *surgere* rise]

surgeon /ˈsɜːdʒ(ə)n/ *n.* a person skilled in surgery; a naval or military medical officer. [f. AF (OF *sirurgie* f. L *chirurgia* f. Gk, lit. = handiwork)]

surgery /ˈsɜːdʒərɪ/ *n.* **1.** the treatment of bodily injuries, disorders, and disease by cutting or manipulation of the affected parts (see below). **2.** the place where or time when a doctor or dentist etc. gives advice and treatment, or an MP or lawyer etc. is available for consultation. [f. OF (as prec.)]

The beginnings of surgery can be traced back to prehistoric times, when sharpened flints were used for opening abscesses, scarifying the skin, and for the serious operation of trepanning the skull. In the Middle Ages the practice of surgery became separated from that of medicine, largely because at different periods the Church forbade the practice of surgery by its clerics, who included not only those in monasteries (which played a great part in caring for the sick) but most educated doctors. Consequently surgery was left to barber-surgeons and other lowly practitioners, and for centuries the status of the surgeon was markedly inferior to that of the physician. In 1745 the Company of Surgeons was formed, becoming the Royal College of Surgeons in 1800. Advances in surgery in the 19th c. were made possible by overcoming two great problems—pain (see ANAESTHETIC), and infection (see ANTISEPTIC); an operation was no longer a desperate procedure undertaken only as a last resort. In the 20th c. the technical efficiency of the surgeon has been supplemented by a number of discoveries and techniques, including X-rays, safer anaesthetics, prompt replacement of blood and fluid loss, and effective antibiotics, while the present high level of surgical skill is partly due to the high degree of specialization which is one of the most striking features of modern medicine. Recent advances include open-heart surgery, cryosurgery, microsurgery, and the use of tomography.

surgical /ˈsɜːdʒɪk(ə)l/ *adj.* of or by surgeons or surgery; (of an appliance) used for surgery or in conditions suitable for surgery. —**surgical spirit,** methylated spirits used for cleansing etc. —**surgically** *adv.* [f. earlier *chirurgical* (*chirurgy* f. OF, as SURGEON)]

Surinam /sʊərɪˈnæm/ a country on the NE coast of South America; pop. (est. 1980) 390,000; official language, Dutch; capital, Paramaribo. The climate is subtropical and the population is largely concentrated on the coast. Surinam

has large timber resources, but the economy is chiefly dependent on bauxite, which makes up over three-quarters of its exports. Settled by the English in 1650, the country was ceded to the Dutch in 1667 but twice returned to British control before finally reverting to the Netherlands in 1815. Known until 1948 as Dutch Guiana, it attained a measure of autonomy in 1950 and 1954 followed by full independence in 1975. —**Surinamer** *n.*, **Surinamese** /-ˈmiːz/ *adj.* & *n.*

surly /ˈsɜːlɪ/ *adj.* bad-tempered and unfriendly. —**surlily** *adv.*, **surliness** *n.* [alt. of obs. *sirly* haughty f. SIR]

surmise /səˈmaɪz/ *n.* a conjecture. —*v.t./i.* to conjecture. [f. AF & OF p.p. of *surmettre* accuse f. L *supermittere* (SUPER-, *mittere* send)]

surmount /səˈmaʊnt/ *v.t.* **1.** to overcome (a difficulty); to get over (an obstacle). **2.** (in *p.p.*) capped or crowned by a specified thing. [f. OF (SUR-², *monter* mount)]

surmountable *adj.* that may be surmounted. [f. prec.]

surname /ˈsɜːneɪm/ *n.* the name common to all members of a family, a person's hereditary name. —*v.t.* to give a surname to. [alt. of *surnoun* f. AF (as SUR-², NOUN name)]

surpass /səˈpɑːs/ *v.t.* to do or be greater or better than, to excel; (in *partic.*) excelling or exceeding others. —**surpassingly** *adv.* [f. F (as SUR-², PASS¹)]

surplice /ˈsɜːplɪs/ *n.* a loose white linen vestment worn by clergy and choristers (ill. VESTMENTS). [f. AF f. L *superpellicium* (SUPER-, *pellicia* PELISSE)]

surplus /ˈsɜːpləs/ *n.* an amount left over when requirements have been met; the excess of revenue over expenditure. —*adj.* exceeding what is needed or used. [f. AF f. L (as SUR-², PLUS)]

surprise /səˈpraɪz/ *n.* **1.** the emotion aroused by something sudden or unexpected. **2.** an event or thing arousing such emotion. **3.** the catching of a person etc. unprepared. **4.** (*attrib.*) made or done etc. unexpectedly, without warning. —*v.t.* **1.** to affect with surprise, to turn out contrary to the expectations of; to shock, to scandalize. **2.** to capture or attack by surprise; to come upon (a person) off his guard. **3.** to startle into action by surprise. **4.** to discover (a secret etc.) by unexpected action. —**by surprise,** unexpectedly. —**surprising** *adj.*, **surprisingly** *adv.* [OF, p.p. of *surprendre* (SUR-², L *praehendere* seize)]

surrealism /səˈrɪəlɪz(ə)m/ *n.* a 20th-c. movement in art and literature purporting to express the unconscious mind by depicting the phenomena of dreams etc. (see below). —**surrealist** *adj.* & *n.*, **surrealistic** /-ˈlɪstɪk/ *adj.*, **surrealistically** /-ˈlɪstɪkəlɪ/ *adv.* [f. F (as SUR-², REALISM)]

This influential European movement, which began in literature with André Breton's manifesto of 1924, belongs to the 1920s and 1930s, but its elements are found also in later decades. It grew out of symbolism and Dada, and its participants (influenced by the ideas of Freud) sought to push beyond the accepted conventions of reality by representing in poetry and art the irrational imagery of dreams and the unconscious mind. This the poets achieved by 'automatic' writing, setting down words unfettered by the conscious mind, while in the visual arts surrealism hovered between a fluid abstracting style analogous to this (as in the works of Masson, Breton, Arp, Miro, and Cocteau) and a more photographic style which relied on deliberately ambiguous combinations of recognizable forms, with Magritte and Dali creating a disorientating realist imagery often based on dreams, hallucination, and paranoia. The surrealists readily experimented with new media: Ernst developed Dadaist collage and invented frottage (a rubbing process), while Man Ray and others experimented with photography and photo-montage. In 1928 the collaboration of Dali and Buñuel on *Un Chien andalou* initiated a phase of surrealist film-making.

surrender /səˈrendə(r)/ *v.t./i.* **1.** to hand over, to give into another's power or control, especially on demand or under compulsion. **2.** to give oneself up; to accept an enemy's demand for submission. **3.** to give up one's rights under (an insurance policy) in return for a small sum received immediately. —*n.* surrendering. —**surrender oneself to,** to give way to (an emotion). **surrender to one's bail,** to appear duly in a lawcourt after release on bail. [f. AF (as SUR-², RENDER)]

surreptitious /sʌrəpˈtɪʃəs/ *adj.* acting or done by stealth. —**surreptitiously** *adv.* [f. L *surripere* seize secretly. (SUR-¹, *rapere* seize)]

Surrey /ˈsʌrɪ/ a county of SE England.

surrogate /ˈsʌrəgət/ *n.* a deputy, especially of a bishop; a substitute. —**surrogacy** *n.* [f. L, p.p. of *surrogare* elect as substitute (SUR-[1], *rogare* ask)]

surround /sə'raʊnd/ *v.t.* to come to be all round; to enclose on all sides; to encircle with enemy forces. —*n.* a border or edging, especially between walls and carpet; a floor-covering for this. —**surrounded by** *or* **with,** having on all sides. [orig. = overflow, f. AF f. L *superundare* (SUPER-, *unda* wave)]

surroundings *n.pl.* the things or conditions around and liable to affect a person or thing. [f. prec.]

surtax /'sɜːtæks/ *n.* an additional tax, especially on incomes over a certain amount. —*v.t.* to impose a surtax on. [f. F (as SUR-[2], TAX)]

Surtees /'sɜːtiːz/, Robert Smith (1805-64), English journalist and novelist, who built up a reputation as a sporting journalist with his comic sketches of Mr Jorrocks, the sporting Cockney grocer, collected in *Jorrocks's Jaunts and Jollities* (1838). His second great character, Mr Soapy Sponge, appears in *Mr Sponge's Sporting Tour* (1853), and the celebrated Mr Facey Romford in his last novel *Mr Facey Romford's Hounds* (1865). These works deal convincingly with the characteristic aspects of English fox-hunting society and the illustrations by Leech, Alken, and Phiz have contributed to their success.

surveillance /sɜː'veɪləns/ *n.* close observation, especially of a suspected person. [F, f. *surveiller* keep watch on (SUR-[2], L *vigilare* keep watch)]

survey /sə'veɪ/ *v.t.* **1.** to look at and take a general view of. **2.** to make or present a survey of. **3.** to examine the condition of (a building etc.). **4.** to measure and map out the size, shape, position, elevation, etc. of (an area). See ill. pp. 560-1. —/'sɜːveɪ/ *n.* **1.** the act of surveying. **2.** a general examination of a situation or subject; an account of this. **3.** the surveying of land etc.; a map or plan produced by this. [f. AF f. L *supervidēre* (SUPER-, *vidēre* see)]

surveyor /sə'veɪə(r)/ *n.* one who surveys land or buildings professionally. [f. prec.]

survival /sə'vaɪv(ə)l/ *n.* **1.** surviving. **2.** something that has survived from earlier times. [f. foll.]

survive /sə'vaɪv/ *v.t./i.* **1.** to continue to live or exist. **2.** to live or exist longer than. **3.** to come alive through or continue to exist in spite of (a damage or accident etc.). —**survivor** *n.* [f. AF *survivre* f. L *supervivere* (SUPER-, *vivere* live)]

Surya /'suərɪə/ (*Hinduism*) one of several solar deities in the Vedic religion. He became the sun-god of later Hindu mythology. [f. Skr., = sun]

sus *n.* (*slang*) **1.** suspicion. **2.** a suspect. —*v.t.* (**-ss-**) (*slang*, often with *out*) to investigate, to reconnoitre. [abbr.]

sus- *prefix* see SUB-.

Susa /'suːsə/ an ancient city of SW Iran, the capital of Elam and later of Persia in Achaemenid times.

Susanna /suː'zænə/ a book of the Apocrypha telling of the false accusation of adultery brought against Susanna, a woman of Babylon, by the two elders, her condemnation, and her final deliverance by the sagacity of Daniel.

susceptibility /səseptɪ'bɪlɪtɪ/ *n.* **1.** being susceptible. **2.** (in *pl.*) a person's sensitive feelings. [f. foll.]

susceptible /sə'septɪb(ə)l/ *adj.* **1.** impressionable; falling in love easily. **2.** (*predic.*, with *to*) liable to be affected by, sensitive to; (with *of*) able to undergo, admitting. —**susceptibly** *adv.* [f. L *suscipere* take up (SUS-, *capere* take)]

susceptive /sə'septɪv/ *adj.* susceptible. [as prec.]

suspect /sə'spekt/ *v.t.* **1.** to have an impression of the existence or presence of; to have a partial or unconfirmed belief. **2.** to have suspicions or doubts about, to mistrust. —/'sʌspekt/ *n.* a suspected person. —/'sʌspekt/ *adj.* subject to suspicion or distrust. [f. L *suspicere* (SUS-, *specere* look)]

suspend /sə'spend/ *v.t.* **1.** to hang up; (in *p.p.*, of solid particles etc. in a fluid) sustained somewhere between top and bottom, kept from falling or sinking. **2.** to keep inoperative or undecided for a time, to postpone. **3.** to put a temporary stop to; to deprive temporarily of a position or right. —**suspended sentence,** a sentence of imprisonment that is not enforced, on condition of good behaviour. [f. OF or L *suspendere* (SUS-, *pendere* hang)]

suspender *n.* **1.** an attachment to hold up a stocking or sock by its top. **2.** (in *pl.*, *US*) a pair of braces. —**suspender belt,** a woman's undergarment with suspenders. [f. prec.]

suspense /sə'spens/ *n.* a state of anxious uncertainty or expectation. [f. AF f. L (as SUSPEND)]

suspension /sə'spenʃ(ə)n/ *n.* **1.** suspending, being sus-

pended. **2.** the means by which a vehicle is supported on its axles. **3.** a substance consisting of particles suspended in a fluid. —**suspension bridge,** a bridge with a roadway suspended from cables supported by towers (ill. BRIDGES). [F or f. L (as SUSPEND)]

suspicion /sə'spɪʃ(ə)n/ *n.* **1.** the feeling of one who suspects; a partial or unconfirmed belief. **2.** suspecting, being suspected. **3.** a slight trace. —**above suspicion,** too obviously good etc. to be suspected. **under suspicion,** suspected. [f. AF f. L (as SUSPECT)]

suspicious /sə'spɪʃəs/ *adj.* **1.** prone to or feeling suspicion. **2.** indicating or justifying suspicion. —**suspiciously** *adv.* [as prec.]

suss var. of SUS.

sustain /sə'steɪn/ *v.t.* **1.** to bear the weight of, to support, especially for a long period. **2.** to endure without giving way. **3.** to undergo, to suffer (a defeat or injury etc.). **4.** to confirm or uphold the validity of. **5.** to keep (a sound or effort etc.) going continuously. [f. AF f. L *sustinēre* (SUS-, *tenēre* hold)]

sustenance /'sʌstɪnəns/ *n.* **1.** the process of sustaining life by food. **2.** the food itself, nourishment. [as prec.]

Sutherland /'sʌðələnd/, Graham (1903-80), English painter. During the Second World War he was an official war artist, producing poignant pictures of ruined and shattered buildings. Among his portraits are those of Somerset Maugham and the controversial portrait of Sir Winston Churchill (destroyed by Churchill's family). Religious works include the *Crucifixion* for St Matthew's, Northampton (1944) and the tapestry, a figure of Christ in Glory, for the rebuilt Coventry Cathedral (1954-7).

sutler *n.* (*hist.*) a camp-follower selling food etc. [f. obs. Du. *soeteler* (*soetelen* perform mean duties)]

suttee /sʌ'tiː/ *n.* the former act or custom of a Hindu widow sacrificing herself on her husband's funeral pyre; a Hindu widow doing this. [Hindi & Urdu, f. Skr. = faithful wife]

Sutton Hoo an estate in Suffolk, site of a group of barrows, one of which was found (1939) to cover the remains of a Saxon ship burial (or perhaps a cenotaph; no body was discovered) of the 7th c. AD. The timbers had decayed and only their impression was left in the soil, with the iron bolts still in place, and in the centre was a magnificent collection of grave goods, including exotic jewellery, an iron standard, decorated shield, bronze helmet, and Merovingian gold coins.

suture /'suːtʃə(r)/ *n.* **1.** surgical stitching of a wound; a stitch or thread etc. used in this. **2.** a seamlike line of junction of two bones at their edges, especially in the skull (ill. BODY 1); a similar junction or parts in a plant or animal body. —*v.t.* to stitch (a wound). [F, or f. L *sutura* (*suere* sew)]

suzerain /'suːzəreɪn/ *n.* **1.** a feudal overlord. **2.** a sovereign or State having some control over another State that is internally autonomous. —**suzerainty** *n.* [F, app. f. *sus* above]

svelte /svelt/ *adj.* slender and graceful. [F, f. It. *svelto*]

SW *abbr.* south-west, south-western.

swab /swɒb/ *n.* **1.** a mop or other absorbent device for cleansing, drying, or absorbing things. **2.** an absorbent pad used in surgery. **3.** a specimen of a secretion taken for examination. —*v.t.* (**-bb-**) to clean with a swab; to take up (moisture) with a swab. [f. Du. *zwabber* f. Gmc = splash, sway]

Swabia /'sweɪbɪə/ a former German duchy (Ger. *Schwaben*). The region is now divided between Germany, Switzerland, and France. —**Swabian** *adj.* & *n.*

swaddle /'swɒd(ə)l/ *v.t.* to swathe in wraps, clothes, or warm garments. —**swaddling-clothes** *n.pl.* the narrow bandages formerly wrapped round a new-born child to restrain its movements. [f. SWATHE]

swag *n.* **1.** loot. **2.** a carved ornamental festoon of fruit, flowers, etc., hung by its ends. **3.** (*Austral.*) a bundle of personal belongings carried by a tramp etc. [f. *swag* sway, prob. f. Scand.]

swage *n.* **1.** a die or stamp for shaping wrought iron. **2.** a tool for bending metal etc. —*v.t.* to shape with a swage. [f. F *s(o)uage* decorative groove; orig. unkn.]

swagger *v.i.* to walk or behave with arrogance or self-importance. —*n.* a swaggering gait or behaviour; smartness. —*adj.* **1.** (*colloq.*) smart, fashionable. **2.** (of a coat) cut with a loose flare from the shoulders. —**swagger-stick** *n.* a short cane carried by a military officer. [app. f. SWAG]

Swahili /swɑː'hiːlɪ/ *n.* **1.** a Bantu people of Zanzibar and the adjacent coasts. **2.** their language, a Bantu language of the Niger-Congo group with a vocabulary heavily influenced by Arabic. It is the most important language in East Africa, spoken also in the central and southern regions and expanding rapidly to the west and north, and while it is the first language of only about a million people it is used as a common language by about 20 million who speak different mother tongues. It is the official language of Kenya and Tanzania. [f. Arab., pl. of *sāhil* coast]

swain *n.* **1.** (*archaic*) a country youth. **2.** (*poetic*) a young lover or suitor. [f. ON *sveinn* lad = OE *swān* swine-herd]

swallow[1] /'swɒləʊ/ *v.t./i.* **1.** to cause or allow (food etc.) to pass down one's throat; to perform the muscular movement (as) of swallowing something. **2.** to accept (a statement) with ready credulity; to accept (an insult) meekly. **3.** to repress (a sound or emotion etc.). **4.** to take in so as to engulf or absorb. —*n.* **1.** the act of swallowing. **2.** the amount swallowed in one movement. [OE]

swallow[2] /'swɒləʊ/ *n.* a migratory swift-flying bird of the genus *Hirundo* etc. with a forked tail. —**swallow-dive** *n.* a dive with the arms outspread until close to the water. —**swallow-tail** *n.* a deeply forked tail; a butterfly or humming-bird with a forked tail. [OE]

swam *past* of SWIM.

swami /'swɑːmɪ/ *n.* a Hindu religious teacher. [f. Hindi, = master]

Swammerdam /'swɑːmədæm/, Jan (1637–80), one of a number of Dutch investigators into what is now called biology. Qualified in medicine, he preferred to commit himself to research, and worked extensively on insects, describing their anatomy and life histories and classifying them into four groups. A pioneer in the use of lenses, he was the first to observe red blood cells; other work included an elegant demonstration of the fact that muscles do not change in volume during motion.

swamp /swɒmp/ *n.* a piece of wet spongy ground. —*v.t.* to overwhelm, flood, or soak with water; to overwhelm or make invisible etc. with an excess or large amount of something. —**swampy** *adj.* [prob. f. Gmc, = sponge, fungus]

Swan /swɒn/, Sir Joseph Wilson (1828–1914), English physicist and chemist, a pioneer of electric lighting. In 1860 he devised an electric light-bulb consisting of a carbon filament inside a glass bulb, and for nearly twenty years worked to perfect it. He formed a partnership in 1883 with the American inventor, Edison, to manufacture the bulbs. Swan also devised a dry photographic plate and (in 1878) bromide paper for the printing of negatives.

swan /swɒn/ *n.* a large web-footed swimming bird usually of the genus *Cygnus*, with a long gracefully-curved neck, especially *C. olor*, with pure white plumage in the adult, black legs and feet, and a red bill with a black knob. —*v.i.* (-**nn**-) (*slang*) to go in a leisurely majestic way, like a swan. —**Swan of Avon**, Shakespeare. **swan-song** *n.* a person's final composition or performance etc. (from the old belief that a swan sang sweetly when about to die). **swan-upping** *n.* the annual taking up and marking (by the appropriate authorities) of swans on the Thames. [OE]

swank *n.* (*colloq.*) **1.** boastful behaviour, ostentation. **2.** a person who swanks. —*v.i.* (*colloq.*) to behave with swank. —**swanky** *adj.*, **swankily** *adv.*, **swankiness** *n.* [orig. Midland dial.]

swannery /'swɒnərɪ/ *n.* a place where swans are kept. [f. SWAN]

swansdown /'swɒnzdaʊn/ *n.* **1.** the down of the swan used in trimmings etc. **2.** thick cotton cloth with soft nap on one side.

swap /swɒp/ *v.t./i.* (-**pp**-) to exchange or barter. —*n.* **1.** an act of swapping. **2.** a thing suitable for swapping. [orig. = hit (prob. imit.)]

sward /swɔːd/ *n.* an expanse of short grass. [OE, = skin]

swarm[1] /swɔːm/ *n.* **1.** a large number of insects, birds, small animals, or persons moving in a cluster. **2.** a cluster of bees leaving the hive with a queen bee, to form a new home. —*v.i.* **1.** to move in or form a swarm. **2.** (of a place) to be crowded or overrun. [OE]

swarm[2] /swɔːm/ *v.i.* (with *up*) to climb by gripping with the hands or arms and legs. [orig. unkn.]

swarthy /'swɔːðɪ/ *adj.* dark, dark-complexioned. —**swarthily** *adv.*, **swarthiness** *n.* [var. of earlier *swarty* (*swart*, f. OE)]

swashbuckler /'swɒʃbʌklə(r)/ *n.* a person who swaggers aggressively. —**swashbuckling** *adj.* & *n.* [f. *swash* strike noisily + BUCKLER]

swastika /'swɒstɪkə/ *n.* a symbol formed by a cross with equal arms each continued as far again at right angles and all in the same direction, especially as the symbol of the Nazis. [f. Skr. *svastika* (*svasti* well-being f. *sú* good + *asti* being)]

swat /swɒt/ *v.t.* (-**tt**-) to hit hard; to crush (a fly etc.) with a blow. —*n.* an act of swatting. [earlier = sit down, dial. var. of SQUAT]

swatch /swɒtʃ/ *n.* a sample, especially of cloth; a collection of samples. [orig. unkn.]

swath /swɔːθ/ *n.* (*pl.* /swɔːθs, swɔːðz/) a ridge of grass or corn etc. lying after being cut; the space left clear after one passage of a mower etc.; a broad strip. [OE]

swathe[1] /sweɪð/ *v.t.* to wrap in layers of bandage, wrappings, or warm garments etc. [OE]

swathe[2] /sweɪð/ *n.* = SWATH.

swatter /'swɒtə(r)/ *n.* an implement for swatting flies. [f. SWAT]

sway *v.t./i.* **1.** to swing or cause to swing gently; to lean from side to side or to one side. **2.** to influence the opinions, sympathy, or action of. **3.** to waver in one's opinion or attitude. —*n.* **1.** a swaying movement. **2.** influence, power; rule. [cf. LG *swajen* be blown to and fro, Du. *zwaaien* swing, wave]

Swazi /'swɑːzɪ/ *n.* **1.** a member of a people of mixed stock inhabiting Swaziland and parts of eastern Transvaal in the Republic of South Africa. **2.** their language, of the Niger-Congo group, an official language of Swaziland. [f. *Mswati*, name of a former King of the Swazi]

Swaziland /'swɑːzɪlænd/ a small landlocked country of southern Africa, bounded by Transvaal, Natal, and Mozambique; pop. (est. 1981) 572,000; official languages, Swazi and English; capital, Mbabane. The country takes its name from the Swazis who occupied it from the mid-18th c. It was a South African protectorate from 1894 and came under British rule in 1902 after the second Boer War. In 1968 it became a fully independent kingdom within the Commonwealth.

swear /sweə(r)/ *v.t./i.* (*past* **swore**; *p.p.* **sworn**) **1.** to state or promise solemnly or on oath; (*colloq.*) to state emphatically. **2.** to cause to take an oath. **3.** to use profane or obscene language in anger or surprise etc. —**swear by**, to appeal to as a witness in taking an oath; (*colloq.*) to have great confidence in. **swear in**, to induct into an office etc. by administering an oath. **swear off**, (*colloq.*) to promise to abstain from (drink etc.). **swear to**, (*colloq.*) to say that one is certain of. **swear-word** *n.* a profane or obscene word. —**swearer** *n.* [OE]

sweat /swet/ *n.* **1.** moisture exuded through the pores of the skin, especially from heat or nervousness. **2.** a state or period of sweating; (*colloq.*) a state of anxiety. **3.** (*colloq.*) drudgery, an effort, a laborious task or undertaking. **4.** condensed moisture on a surface. —*v.t./i.* (*past* & *p.p.* **sweated**, US **sweat**) **1.** to exude sweat. **2.** to be terrified, suffering, etc. **3.** (of a wall etc.) to exhibit surface moisture. **4.** to emit like sweat. **5.** to make (a horse or athlete etc.) sweat by exercise. **6.** to drudge or toil, to cause to do this. —**sweat-band** *n.* a band of absorbent material inside a hat or round the wrist etc. to soak up sweat. **sweat blood**, to work strenuously; to be extremely anxious. **sweated labour**, labour employed for long hours at low wages. **sweat out**, (*colloq.*) to endure to the end. **sweat-shirt** *n.* a sleeved cotton sweater. **sweat-shop** *n.* a place in which sweated labour is used. —**sweaty** *adj.* [OE]

sweater /'swetə(r)/ *n.* a jumper or pullover. [f. SWEAT]

Swede /swiːd/ *n.* a native of Sweden. [MLG & MDu., prob f. ON]

swede /swiːd/ *n.* a large yellow-fleshed turnip, brought from Sweden to Scotland in the 18th c. [= prec.]

Sweden /'swiːd(ə)n/ a country occupying the eastern part of the Scandinavian peninsula; pop. (1982) 8,327,484; official language, Swedish; capital, Stockholm. Its Germanic and Gothic inhabitants took part in the Viking raids. Originally united in the 12th c., Sweden formed part of the Union of Kalmar with Denmark and Norway from 1397 until its re-emergence as an independent State under Gustavus Vasa in 1523. The following two centuries saw the country's rise and fall as the prominent Baltic power, influence on the European mainland peaking during the reign of Gustavus Adolphus in the early 17th c. and collapsing following the defeat of Charles XII in the Great Northern War at the beginning of the 18th c. Between 1814 and 1905, Sweden was united with Norway. She maintained her neutrality in the two World Wars, while her economy prospered through increasing industrialization, and the political hegemony of the Social Democratic party led to the creation of an extensive system of social security.

Swedenborg /'swi:d(ə)nbɔːg/ Emanuel (1688–1772), Swedish scientist and mystical thinker. Endowed with unusual mental fertility and inventiveness and considerable mathematical ability, he anticipated many subsequent hypotheses and discoveries (nebular theory, magnetic theory, machine-gun, aeroplane), and is also claimed as the founder of crystallography. As time went on he became increasingly concerned to show by scientific means the fundamentally spiritual structure of the universe. In 1743–5 he became conscious of visions both in dreams and while awake, and felt called to make known his doctrines to mankind at large. He spent the rest of his life writing assiduously, with doctrines that were a blend of pantheism and theosophy, and maintaining his scientific interests to the end. Swedenborg himself wished his teaching to be propagated within existing churches but his followers set up an independent body, the New Jerusalem Church. The movement is especially strong in Lancashire.

Swedish /'swi:dɪʃ/ adj. of Sweden or its people or language. —n. the official language of Sweden, spoken by its 8 million inhabitants, by another 300,000 in Finland (where it is one of the two official languages), and by 600,000 in the USA. It belongs to the Scandinavian language group. [f. SWEDE or SWEDEN]

sweep v.t./i. (past & p.p. **swept**) 1. to clear away (dust or litter etc.) with or as with a broom or brush; to clean or clear (a surface or area) thus. 2. to move or remove by pushing; to carry in an impetuous course; to clear forcefully. 3. to go smoothly and swiftly or majestically. 4. to pass or cause to pass quickly over or along; to touch lightly; to affect swiftly. 5. to extend in a continuous line or slope. 6. to make (a bow or curtsy) with a smooth movement. —n. 1. a sweeping movement. 2. a sweeping line or slope. 3. the act of sweeping with a broom etc. 4. a chimney-sweep. 5. a sortie by aircraft. 6. (colloq.) a sweepstake. 7. a long oar. 8. the movement of a beam across the screen of a cathode-ray tube. —**make a clean sweep of,** to abolish or expel completely; to win all the prizes etc. in. **sweep the board,** to win all the money in a gambling-game; to win all the possible prizes etc. **sweep (-second) hand,** an extra hand on a clock or watch, indicating seconds. **swept-wing** adj. (of an aircraft) having the wing placed at an acute angle to the axis. [OE]

sweeper n. 1. one who cleans by sweeping. 2. a device for sweeping a carpet etc. 3. (in football) a defensive player positioned close to the goalkeeper. [f. SWEEP]

sweeping adj. 1. wide in range or effect. 2. taking no account of particular cases or exceptions. —n. (in pl.) dirt etc. collected by sweeping. —**sweepingly** adv. [f. SWEEP]

sweepstake n. a form of gambling on horse-races etc. in which all the competitors' stakes are paid to the winners; a race with betting of this kind; a prize or the prizes won in a sweepstake.

sweet adj. 1. tasting as if containing sugar, not bitter. 2. fragrant. 3. melodious. 4. fresh, (of food) not stale, (of water) not salt. 5. pleasant, gratifying; (colloq.) pretty, charming. —n. 1. a small shaped piece of sweet substance, usually made with sugar or chocolate. 2. a sweet dish forming one course of a meal. 3. (in pl.) delights, gratifications. 4. (esp. as a form of address) darling, sweetheart. —**be sweet on,** (colloq.) to be fond of or in love with. **sweet-and-sour** adj. cooked in a sauce with both sweet and sour ingredients. **sweet-brier** n. a small wild rose (Rosa rubiginosa) with fragrant leaves. **sweet corn,** a sweet-flavoured maize. **sweet pea,** a climbing garden plant (Lathyrus odoratus) with fragrant flowers in many colours. **sweet talk,** (US) flattery. **sweet-talk** v.t. (US) to persuade by flattery. **sweet tooth,** a liking for sweet-tasting things. **sweet-william** n. a garden plant (Dianthus barbatus) with clustered fragrant flowers. —**sweetly** adv., **sweetness** n. [OE]

sweetbread n. the pancreas or thymus gland of an animal, especially as food.

sweeten v.t./i. to make or become sweet or sweeter. [f. SWEET]

sweetener n. 1. (also **sweetening**) a substance used to sweeten food or drink. 2. (colloq.) a bribe. [f. prec.]

sweetheart n. each of a pair of persons who are in love with each other (also as a term of endearment).

sweetie n. (colloq.) 1. a sweet. 2. a sweetheart. [f. SWEET]

sweetmeal adj. (of biscuits) sweetened with wholemeal.

sweetmeat n. a sweet; a small fancy cake.

swell v.t./i. (p.p. **swollen** /'swəʊlən/ or **swelled**) 1. to make or become larger because of pressure from within; to curve or cause to curve outwards. 2. to make or become larger in amount, volume, numbers, or intensity. —n. 1. an act or the state of swelling. 2. a heaving of the sea with waves that do not break. 3. a crescendo; a mechanism in an organ etc. for obtaining a crescendo or diminuendo. 4. (colloq.) a person of distinction or of dashing or fashionable appearance. 5. a protuberant part. —adj. (US colloq.) smart, excellent. —**swelled** or **swollen head,** (colloq.) conceit. [OE]

swelling n. a part raised up from the surrounding surface; an abnormal protuberance. [f. SWELL]

swelter v.i. to be uncomfortably hot. —n. a sweltering condition. [f. OE, = perish]

swept past & p.p. of SWEEP.

swerve v.t./i. to turn or cause to turn aside from a straight course, especially in a sudden movement. —n. a swerving movement or course. [OE, = scour]

Swift, Jonathan (1667–1745), Anglo-Irish poet and satirist, nicknamed 'the Dean'. He was born in Dublin, a cousin of Dryden, and divided his life between London and Ireland. His Journal to Stella (letters to Esther Johnson, 1710–13) give a vivid account of life in London, where he was close to Tory ministers. Swift's relations with Stella have remained obscure; whether he ultimately married her is uncertain. Another woman, Esther Vanhomrigh ('Vanessa'), entered his life in 1708, and their romance is related in the poem Cadenus and Vanessa (1713). While in England he wrote A Tale of a Tub (1697), a satire on 'corruptions in religion and learning'. He also wrote many political pamphlets, and involved himself in Irish affairs. In 1713 he was made Dean of St Patrick's in Dublin, where he wrote his greatest work Gulliver's Travels (1726), a powerful satire on man and human institutions, with a fantastic tale of travels in wonderland which appeals to all ages. Macaulay, Thackeray, and many other writers were alienated by his ferocity and coarseness, but the 20th c. has seen a revival of critical interest stressing his vigour and satirical inventiveness rather than his alleged misanthropy. Nearly all his works were published anonymously and for only one, Gulliver's Travels, did he receive any payment (£200).

swift adj. quick, rapid. —n. a swift-flying bird of the family Apodidae with long wings. —**swiftly** adv., **swiftness** n. [OE]

swig v.t./i. (-gg-) (colloq.) to take a drink or drinks (of). —n. (colloq.) a drink or swallow. [orig. unkn.]

swill v.t./i. 1. to pour water over or through; to wash or rinse. 2. (of water etc.) to pour. 3. to drink greedily. —n. 1. a rinse. 2. a sloppy mixture of waste food fed to pigs. 3. inferior liquor.

swim v.t./i. (-mm-; past **swam**; p.p. **swum**) 1. to propel the body through water by movements of the limbs or fins, tail, etc.; to traverse thus; to cause to swim. 2. to float. 3. to be covered or flooded with a liquid. 4. to seem to be whirling or undulating; to have a dizzy sensation. —n. 1. an act or spell of swimming. 2. a deep pool frequented by fish in a river. 3. the main current of affairs. —**in the swim,** active in or knowing what is going on. **swim-bladder** n. a gas-filled bladder, found in most types of fish, whose size can be adjusted to control buoyancy (ill. FISH). **swimming-bath** or **-pool** n. a pool constructed for swimming. **swim-suit** a bathing-suit. —**swimmer** n. [OE]

swimmingly adv. with easy and unobstructed progress. [f. SWIM]

Swinburne /'swɪnbɜːn/, Algernon Charles (1837–1909), English poet and critic, associated with Rossetti and the Pre-Raphaelite circle. He achieved celebrity with Atalanta in Calydon (1865), a drama in classical Greek form which revealed his great metrical skills. Poems and Ballads (1866) demonstrates his preoccupation with de Sade and masochism, and his outspoken repudiation of Christianity caused the volume to be censured; A Song of Italy (1867) and Songs before Sunrise (1871) expressed his support for Mazzini in the struggle for Italian independence and his hatred of authority. His health was seriously affected by heavy drinking and in 1879 he moved to Putney to be cared for by his friend the critic T. Watts-Dunton. As a critic Swinburne showed perception and originality, contributed to the revival of interest in Elizabethan drama, and influenced modern criticism with his studies of Blake, the Bröntes, and others.

swindle v.t./i. to cheat (a person) in a business transaction; to obtain (money etc.) by fraud. —n. **1.** a piece of swindling. **2.** a fraudulent person or thing. —**swindler** n. [backformation f. *swindler* f. G, = extravagant maker of schemes (*schwindeln* be dizzy)]

swine n. (*pl.* same) **1.** a pig. **2.** (*colloq.*) a disgusting or contemptible person or thing. [OE]

swing v.t./i. (*past & p.p.* **swung**) **1.** to move to and fro while hanging or supported; to cause to do this; (*slang*) to be executed by hanging. **2.** to suspend by its end(s). **3.** to lift with a swinging movement; to move by gripping something and leaping; to walk or run with an easy rhythmical gait. **4.** to turn (a wheel etc.) smoothly; to turn to one side or in a curve. **5.** to change from one opinion or mood etc. to another; to influence (voters or voting etc.) decisively; (*slang*) to deal with, to arrange satisfactorily. **6.** to play (music) with a swing rhythm. **7.** (in *partic.*, *slang*) lively. —n. **1.** a swinging motion or action. **2.** a seat slung by ropes or chains for swinging in; a swing-boat; a spell of swinging in this. **3.** the extent to which a thing swings; the amount by which votes, opinions, points scored, etc., change from one side to another. **4.** a kind of jazz with the time of the melody varied while the accompaniment is in strict time. —**in full swing**, with activity at its greatest. **swing-boat** n. a boat-shaped swing at fairs. **swing bridge**, a bridge that can be swung aside to let ships pass. **swing-door** n. a door able to open in either direction and close itself when released. **swing the lead**, (*slang*) to malinger. **swing-wing** n. an aircraft wing that can move from a right-angled to a rear-slanting position. —**swinger** n. [OE *swingan* to beat]

swingeing /ˈswɪndʒɪŋ/ adj. **1.** (of a blow) forcible. **2.** huge in amount, number, or scope. [f. OE *swengan* shake, shatter]

swinish /ˈswaɪnɪʃ/ adj. bestial; filthy. [f. SWINE]

swipe v.t./i. **1.** (*colloq.*) to hit hard and recklessly. **2.** (*slang*) to steal. —n. (*colloq.*) a reckless hard hit or attempt to hit. [perh. var. of SWEEP]

swirl v.t./i. to move, flow, or carry along with a whirling motion. —n. a swirling motion; a twist, a curl. [orig. Sc., perh. f. LDu.]

swish v.t./i. to strike, move, or cause to move with a hissing sound. —n. a swishing action or sound. —adj. (*colloq.*) smart, fashionable. [imit.]

Swiss adj. of Switzerland or its people. —n. (*pl.* same) a native of Switzerland. —**Swiss guards**, Swiss mercenary troops employed formerly by sovereigns of France etc. and still at the Vatican. **Swiss roll**, a thin flat sponge-cake spread with jam etc. and rolled up. [f. F *Suisse* f. MHG]

switch n. **1.** a device for making and breaking a connection in an electric circuit. **2.** a transfer, a change-over; a deviation. **3.** a flexible shoot cut from a tree; a light tapering rod. **4.** a device at a junction of railway tracks for transferring a train from one track to another. —v.t./i. **1.** to turn (an electrical or other appliance) on or off by means of a switch; to control (an electric current) by means of a switch. **2.** to divert (thoughts or talk etc.) to another subject; to change or exchange (positions, methods, policy, etc.). **3.** to transfer (a train) to another track. **4.** to swing round quickly; to snatch suddenly. **5.** to whip or flick with a switch. [prob. f. LG *swukse* long thin stick)]

switchback n. **1.** a railway used for amusement at fairs etc. in which a train's ascents are effected by the momentum of previous descents. **2.** a road or railway with alternate ascents and descents, or zigzagging on a slope.

switchboard n. a panel with a set of switches for making telephone connections or operating electric circuits.

Swithin /ˈswɪðɪn/, St (d. 862), chaplain to Egbert king of Wessex, and bishop of Winchester from 852. The tradition that any rain on St Swithin's day (15 July) will remain for the next forty days may refer to the heavy rain said to have occurred when his relics were to be transferred to a shrine in the cathedral.

Switzerland /ˈswɪtsələnd/ a small country in central Europe, dominated by the Alps and Jura Mountains; pop. (est. 1982) 6,365,900; official languages, French, German, Italian, and Romansch; capital, Berne. The area (occupied by a Celtic people, the Helvetii) was under Roman rule from the 1st c. BC until the 5th c. AD, and from the 10th c. formed part of the Holy Roman Empire. Switzerland emerged as an independent country in the Middle Ages

when the local cantons joined in league to defeat first their Hapsburg overlords (14th c.) and then their Burgundian neighbours (15th c.). The Swiss Confederation maintained neutrality in international affairs through the 17th and 18th centuries, and after a period of French domination (1798–1815), the Confederation's neutrality was guaranteed by the other European powers. Neutral in both World Wars, Switzerland has emerged as the headquarters of such international organizations as the Red Cross. The population is divided linguistically into French-, German-, and Italian-speaking areas, while the economy is centred on precision engineering, dairy products, and tourism, also benefiting from the country's position as an international financial centre.

swivel /ˈswɪv(ə)l/ n. a coupling between two parts enabling one to revolve without the other. —v.t./i. (**-ll-**) to turn (as) on a swivel. —**swivel chair**, a chair with a seat turning horizontally. [f. OE, = sweep]

swizz n. (*slang*) a swindle, a disappointment. [orig. unkn.]

swizzle n. (*colloq.*) **1.** a compounded intoxicating drink especially of rum or gin and bitters made frothy. **2.** (*slang*) a swizz. —**swizzle-stick** n. a stick used for frothing or flattening drinks. [orig. unkn.]

swollen see SWELL.

swoon v.i. to faint. —n. a faint. [perh. f. OE *geswogen* overcome)]

swoop v.i. to descend with a rushing movement like a bird upon its prey; to make a sudden attack. —n. a swooping or snatching movement or action. [perh. rel. to SWEEP]

swop var. of SWAP.

sword /sɔːd/ n. a weapon with a long blade and a hilt with a hand-guard (see below). —**the sword**, war, military power. **cross swords**, to have a fight or dispute. **put to the sword**, to kill, especially in war. **sword-dance** n. a dance in which the performer brandishes swords or steps about swords laid on the ground. **sword-play** n. fencing, repartee or lively arguing. **sword-stick** n. a hollow walking-stick containing a blade that can be used as a sword. [OE]
The sword evolved in the Bronze Age, when metal-smelting became known, and developed in various forms—as a rapier, for cut-and-thrust, and for slashing; with a straight blade, and with the curved blade which was believed to deal a deeper wound. It became obsolete as an infantry weapon after the development of explosives, but remained in use as a weapon of cavalry units until the early 20th c.

swordfish n. a large sea-fish (*Xiphias gladius*) with the upper jaw prolonged into a sharp sword-like weapon.

swordsman n. (*pl.* **-men**) a person of good or specified skill with a sword. —**swordsmanship** n.

swore past of SWEAR.

sworn p.p. of SWEAR. —adj. bound (as) by an oath.

swot v.t./i. (*slang*) (**-tt-**) to study hard. —n. (*slang*) **1.** a person who swots. **2.** hard study. —**swot up**, to study (a subject) hard or hurriedly. [dial. var of SWEAT]

swum p.p. of SWIM.

swung past & p.p. of SWING.

sybarite /ˈsɪbəraɪt/ n. a person who is extremely fond of comfort and luxury. —**sybaritic** /-ˈrɪtɪk/ adj. [f. *Sybaris*, ancient city in southern Italy, noted for its luxury]

sycamore /ˈsɪkəmɔː(r)/ n. **1.** a large maple (*Acer pseudoplatanus*; ill. TREES). **2.** (*US*) a plane-tree. **3.** the wood of either of these. [var. of *sycomore* kind of fig-tree, f. OF f. L f. Gk]

sycophant /ˈsɪkəfænt/ n. a person who tries to win favour by flattery. —**sycophancy** n., **sycophantic** /-ˈfæntɪk/ adj., **sycophantically** adv. [f. F or L f. Gk, = informer]

Sydenham /ˈsɪd(ə)nəm/, Thomas (c. 1624–89), 'the English Hippocrates', so called for his contemporary reputation as a physician and his scepticism of theoretical medicine. He emphasized the healing power of nature, made a study of epidemics, wrote a treatise on gout (from which he suffered), and explained the nature of chorea (St Vitus's dance).

Sydney /ˈsɪdnɪ/ the capital of New South Wales, the largest city and chief port of Australia; pop. (est. 1983) 3,332,550.

syl- see SYN-.

syllabary /ˈsɪləbərɪ/ n. a list of characters representing syllables and serving the purpose, in some languages or stages of writing, of an alphabet. [as SYLLABLE]

syllabic /sɪˈlæbɪk/ adj. of or in syllables. —**syllabically** adv. [f. F or L f. Gk (as SYLLABLE)]

syllabification /sɪlæbɪfɪˈkeɪʃ(ə)n/ n. a division into or utterance in syllables. [f. L (as foll.)]

syllable /'sɪləb(ə)l/ n. **1.** a unit of pronunciation forming the whole or a part of a word and usually having one vowel-sound often with a consonant or consonants before or after. **2.** a character or characters representing a syllable. **3.** the least amount of speech or writing. —**in words of one syllable**, simply, plainly. [f. AF f. L f. Gk *sullabē* (as SYL-, *lambanō* take)]

syllabub /'sɪləbʌb/ n. a dish of sweetened whipped cream flavoured with wine etc. [orig. unkn.]

syllabus /'sɪləbəs/ n. (pl. **-uses**) a programme or conspectus of a course of study, teaching, etc. [misreading of L *sittybas* f. Gk, = title-slips]

syllepsis /sɪ'lepsɪs/ n. (pl. **-pses** /-iːz/) a figure of speech applying a word to two others in different senses (e.g. *took the oath and his seat*), or to two others of which it grammatically suits one only (e.g. *neither you nor he knows*). [L f. Gk, = taking together (as SYLLABLE)]

syllogism /'sɪlədʒɪz(ə)m/ n. a form of reasoning in which from two given or assumed propositions (the *premisses*) which have a common or middle term a third is deduced (the *conclusion*) from which the middle term is absent, as in 'All As are Bs, all Bs are Cs, therefore all As are Cs,'; 'Some As are Bs, all Bs are not Cs, therefore some As are not Cs'. Aristotle listed the types of syllogism and showed of each whether it was valid. —**syllogistic** /-'dʒɪstɪk/ adj. [f. OF f. L f. Gk f. *sullogizomai* (as SYN-, *logizomai* to reason)]

sylph /sɪlf/ n. **1.** an elemental spirit of the air. **2.** a slender graceful woman or girl. [perh. formed by Paracelsus f. L *sylvestris* of woodland + *nympha* nymph]

sylvan var. of SILVAN.

sym- see SYN-.

symbiosis /sɪmbɪ'əʊsɪs, -baɪ-/ n. (pl. **-oses** /-iːz/) **1.** an association of two different organisms living attached to each other or one within the other, usually to their mutual advantage. **2.** an association of co-operating persons. —**symbiotic** /-'ɒtɪk/ adj. [f. Gk, = living together (as SYM-, *bios* life)]

symbol /'sɪmb(ə)l/ n. **1.** a thing regarded as suggesting something or embodying certain characteristics. **2.** a mark or sign with a special meaning, indicating an idea, object, process, etc. [f. L f. Gk *sumbolon* mark, token (as SYM-, *ballō* throw)]

symbolic /sɪm'bɒlɪk/ adj. (also **symbolical**) of, using, or used as a symbol. [as prec.]

symbolism /'sɪmbəlɪz(ə)m/ n. **1.** use of symbols to represent things; symbols collectively. **2.** a school of painters and of (especially French) poets seeking special symbols to express the essence of things by suggestion (see below). —**symbolist** n. [f. SYMBOL]
In a literary and art historical sense, symbolism is the idealist movement of the 1880s and 1890s in France. Primarily a literary concept, it was launched as an identifiable movement by the radical poet Jean Moréas in 1886. Symbolism was seen as the expression of an idea through form, the word or object represented being no more than a sign to open up the world of the imagination; symbolist poets include Mallarmé, Verlaine, and Rimbaud. In the visual arts, the term is widely applied to both French and non-French painters of the *fin de siècle* who reacted against the prevailing standards of classicism, positivism, and naturalism, preferring to paint enigmatic, mysterious, and dreamlike subjects. Redon, Moreau, Rops, and Ensor are the best known, but the movement was much wider; the critic Aurier in 1891-2 identified Gauguin and the Nabis as symbolist painters. Symbolism was important in the development of later theories of abstraction and surrealism.

symbolize v.t. to be a symbol of; to represent by means of symbols. —**symbolization** /-'zeɪʃ(ə)n/ n. [f. F (as SYMBOL)]

symmetry /'sɪmɪtrɪ/ n. **1.** correct proportion of parts; beauty resulting from this. **2.** a structure that allows an object to be divided into parts of equal shape and size; possession of such a structure; the repetition of exactly similar parts facing each other or a centre. —**symmetric** /-'metrɪk/ adj., **symmetrical** /-'metrɪk(ə)l/ adj., **symmetrically** /-'metrɪkəlɪ/ adv. [f. obs. F or L f. Gk (as SYM-, *metron* measure)]

sympathetic /sɪmpə'θetɪk/ adj. **1.** of, showing, or expressing sympathy; due to sympathy. **2.** likeable. **3.** not antagonistic. —**sympathetic magic**, magic seeking to affect an event etc. by imitating the effect desired. **sympathetic nervous system**, see NERVOUS SYSTEM. **sympathetic string**, (*Mus.*) a string which vibrates with sympathetic

resonance, enriching the tone. —**sympathetically** adv. [f. SYMPATHY]

sympathize /'sɪmpəθaɪz/ v.i. to feel or express sympathy. —**sympathizer** n. [f. F (as foll.)]

sympathy /'sɪmpəθɪ/ n. **1.** sharing or the ability to share another's emotions or sensations. **2.** a feeling of pity or tenderness towards one suffering pain, grief, or trouble. **3.** liking for each other produced in people who have similar opinions or tastes. **4.** (in *sing.* or *pl.*) agreement with another person etc. in an opinion or desire. [f. L f. Gk (as SYM-, *pathos* feeling)]

symphonic /sɪm'fɒnɪk/ adj. of or like a symphony or symphonies.—**symphonic poem,** an orchestral piece usually in one movement and usually descriptive or rhapsodic. —**symphonically** adv. [f. foll.]

symphony /'sɪmfənɪ/ n. **1.** an elaborate composition for a full orchestra, usually with several movements (see below). **2.** (*US*) a symphony orchestra. —**symphony orchestra,** a large orchestra playing symphonies etc. [orig. = harmony of sound, f. OF f. L f. Gk (as SYM-, *phōnē* sound)]
In the 16th c. the term denoted a piece of music for an instrumental ensemble, but since the 18th c. it has been applied to an orchestral work typically in four movements (in the early years, three) in a standard order and each conforming to a certain type. Towards the mid-19th c., after the formidable achievements of Beethoven in the genre, the symphony gave way in popularity to the symphonic poem and concert overture but continued to be an important test of a composer's mastery of form. From the time of Brahms onwards great symphonies have been and are still being written and performed, combining Beethoven's expansion of the terms of reference (adding voices to the orchestra, sharing motives between movements, writing with an extra-musical 'programme' in mind, etc.) with a flexible attitude towards the structure and number of movements.

symposium /sɪm'pəʊzɪəm/ n. (pl. **-ia**) a conference or collection of essays etc. on a particular subject; a philosophical or other friendly discussion. [f. L f. Gk, = drinking-party (as SYM-, *potēs* drinker)]

symptom /'sɪmptəm/ n. a sign of the existence of a condition, especially a perceptible change from what is normal in the body, indicating disease or injury. [f. L f. Gk (*sumpiptō* happen, as SYM-, *piptō* fall)]

symptomatic /sɪmptə'mætɪk/ adj. serving as a symptom. —**symptomatically** adv. [f. prec.]

syn- prefix (**syl-** before l, **sym-** before b, m, p) in senses 'together', 'at the same time', 'alike', etc. [f. Gk (*sun* with)]

synagogue /'sɪnəgɒg/ n. a meeting-place of a Jewish assembly for religious observance and instruction; the assembly itself.—**synagogal** adj., **synagogical** /-'gɒgɪk(ə)l, -'gɒdʒɪk(ə)l/ adj. [f. OF f. L f. Gk, = assembly (as SYN-, *agō* bring)]

sync /sɪŋk/ n. (also **synch**) (*colloq.*) synchronization. —v.t. (*colloq.*) to synchronize. [abbr.]

synchromesh /'sɪŋkrəʊmeʃ/ n. a system of gear-changing, especially in motor vehicles, in which the gear-wheels revolve at the same speed while they are being brought into engagement. —adj. of this system. [abbr. of *synchronized mesh*]

synchronic /sɪŋ'krɒnɪk/ adj. concerned with a subject as it exists at a particular time. —**synchronic linguistics,** = descriptive linguistics. —**synchronically** adv. [as SYN-CHRONOUS]

synchronism /'sɪŋkrənɪz(ə)m/ n. **1.** being or treated as synchronous or synchronic. **2.** synchronizing. [f. Gk (as SYNCHRONOUS)]

synchronize /'sɪŋkrənaɪz/ v.t./i. to make or be synchronous with. —**synchronization** /-'zeɪʃ(ə)n/ n., **synchronizer** n. [f. prec.]

synchronous /'sɪŋkrənəs/ adj. **1.** existing or occurring at the same time. **2.** having the same or a proportional speed and operating simultaneously. [f. L f. Gk (as SYN-, *khronos* time]

synchrotron /'sɪŋkrətrɒn/ n. a cyclotron in which the strength of the magnetic field increases with the energy of the particles, keeping their orbital radius constant. [f. SYNCHRONOUS+ -TRON]

syncline /'sɪŋklaɪn/ n. a land formation in which strata are folded so that they slope up on opposite sides of a trough. —**synclinal** /-'klaɪn(ə)l/ adj. [f. SYN- + Gk *klinō* lean]

syncopate /'sɪŋkəpeɪt/ v.t. **1.** to displace the beats or accents in (music). **2.** to shorten (a word) by dropping an interior letter or letters. —**syncopation** /-'peɪʃ(ə)n/ *n*. [f. L (as foll.)]

syncope /'sɪŋkəpɪ/ *n*. **1.** syncopation. **2.** temporary unconsciousness through a fall in blood-pressure; a faint, fainting. [f. L f. Gk (as SYN-, *koptō* cut off)]

syncretize /'sɪŋkrɪtaɪz/ *v.t./i.* to combine (different beliefs or principles). [f. Gk *sugkrētizō* combine as two parties against a third]

syndic /'sɪndɪk/ *n*. any of various university or government officials. [F f. L f. Gk, = advocate (as SYN-, *dikē* justice)]

syndicalism /'sɪndɪk(ə)lɪz(ə)m/ *n*. a movement among industrial workers (especially in France) aiming at the transfer of the means of production and distribution from their present owners to unions of workers. —**syndicalist** *n*. [f. F (*syndicat* trade union), as prec.]

syndicate /'sɪndɪkət/ *n*. **1.** a combination of persons or commercial firms to promote some common interest. **2.** an association supplying material simultaneously to a number of periodicals. **3.** a committee of syndics. —/-keɪt/ *v.t.* **1.** to form into a syndicate. **2.** to publish (material) through a syndicate. —**syndication** /-'keɪʃ(ə)n/ *n*. [as SYNDIC]

syndrome /'sɪndrəʊm/ *n*. **1.** a set of signs and symptoms that together indicate the presence of a disease or abnormal condition. **2.** a combination of opinions, behaviour, etc., characteristic of a particular condition. [f. Gk (as SYN-, *dram-* run)]

synecdoche /sɪ'nekdəkɪ/ *n*. a figure of speech in which a part is named but the whole is understood, or conversely (e.g. *several new faces in the team* for *new persons*, or *England beat Australia at cricket*). [f. L f. Gk (as SYN-, *ekdekhomai* take up)]

Synge /sɪŋ/, (Edmund) John Millington (1871–1909), Irish dramatist. In Paris he was encouraged by Yeats to observe Irish peasant life in the Aran Islands; this resulted in his description *The Aran Islands* (1907) and his best-known play, *The Playboy of the Western World* (1907), which caused outrage and riots at the Abbey Theatre, Dublin, for its frankness and the implication that Irish peasants would condone a brutal murder, but his skilful fusion of the language of ordinary people with his own dramatic rhetoric has made it a classic. His other plays include *The Tinker's Wedding* (1908) and *Deirdre of the Sorrows* (1910), in which a spare rhythmic prose achieves powerful and resonant effects, but many of his countrymen objected to the ironic wit and realism. Many of the poems in *Poems and Translations* (1909) foreshadow his imminent death from Hodgkin's disease.

synod /'sɪnəd/ *n*. a church council of senior clergy and officials. [f. L f. Gk, = meeting (as SYN-, *hodos* way)]

synonym /'sɪnənɪm/ *n*. a word or phrase that means exactly or nearly the same as another in the same language. [f. L f. Gk (as SYN-, *onoma* name)]

synonymous /sɪ'nɒnɪməs/ *adj*. having the same meaning. [f. prec.]

synopsis /sɪ'nɒpsɪs/ *n*. (*pl*. **synopses** /-iːz/) a summary, a brief general survey. [L f. Gk (as SYN-, *opsis* seeing)]

synoptic /sɪ'nɒptɪk/ *adj*. of or giving a synopsis. —**Synoptic Gospels**, those of Matthew, Mark, and Luke, which have many similarities (whereas that of John differs greatly). —**synoptically** *adv*. [f. Gk (as prec.)]

synovia /saɪ'nəʊvɪə/ *n*. a thick sticky fluid lubricating the body joints etc. —**synovial** *adj*. [formed by Paracelsus, prob. arbitrarily]

syntax /'sɪntæks/ *n*. the arrangement of words and phrases to form sentences; the rules or analysis of this. —**syntactic** /-'tæktɪk/ *adj*., **syntactically** /-'tæktɪkəlɪ/ *adv*. [f. F or L f. Gk, = marshalling (as SYN-, *tassō* arrange)]

synthesis /'sɪnθɪsɪs/ *n*. (*pl*. **syntheses** /-siːz/) **1.** the combination of separate parts or elements into a complex whole. **2.** the artificial production of a substance by a chemical process; the process itself. [L f. Gk (as SYN-, THESIS)]

synthesize /'sɪnθɪsaɪz/ *v.t.* to make by synthesis. [f. prec.]

synthesizer /'sɪnθɪsaɪzə(r)/ *n*. an electronic device for combining sounds so as to reproduce the musical tones of conventional instruments or produce a variety of artificial ones (ill. MUSICAL NOTATION). A musical instrument produces a fundamental pure tone and a series of other pure tones of lesser intensity (the *overtones*, each with its own intensity and frequency; see ill. SOUND) which are characteristic of that instrument and which together give it its timbre.

The synthesizer, by generating a combination of pure tones, can simulate this. Its development as a musical instrument dates from the late 1950s, in the USA. [f. prec.]

synthetic /sɪn'θetɪk/ *adj*. **1.** produced by synthesis; manufactured (opp. produced naturally). **2.** (*colloq*.) affected, insincere. —*n*. a synthetic substance or fabric. —**synthetically** *adv*. [f. F f. Gk (as prec.)]

syphilis /'sɪfɪlɪs/ *n*. a contagious venereal disease. —**syphilitic** /-'lɪtɪk/ *adj*. [f. title of a Latin poem (1530), by a physician of Verona in Italy, about a shepherd *Syphilus*, the supposed first sufferer from the disease]

Syria /'sɪrɪə/ a country in SW Asia with a coastline on the eastern Mediterranean Sea; pop. (est. 1981) 10,400,000; official language, Arabic; capital, Damascus. In ancient times the name was applied to a much wider area, which included also the present countries of Lebanon, Israel, Jordan, and adjacent parts of Iraq and Saudi Arabia. It was the site of various early civilizations, trading with Egypt and Crete; the Phoenicians were settled on the coastal plain. The country was greatly enriched by the transit trade from Babylonia, Arabia, and the Far East. Falling successively within the empires of Persia, Macedon, and Rome it became a centre of Islamic power and civilization from the 7th c. and a province of the Ottoman empire in 1516. After the Turkish defeat in the First World War, Syria was mandated to France and achieved independence with the ejection of Vichy troops by the Allies in 1941. The last three and a half decades of Syrian history have been dominated by continuing antagonism towards Israel, involvement in Middle Eastern wars and in the internal affairs of Lebanon, and domestic political instability. Although largely agricultural, Syria is becoming more industrialized, and has benefited in recent years from increasing oil exports. —**Syrian** *adj*. & *n*.

Syriac /'sɪrɪæk/ *n*. the liturgical language of the Maronite and Syrian Catholic Churches, the Syrian Jacobite Church, and the Nestorian Church. It is descended from the Aramaic spoken near the city of Edessa (now Urfa) in SE Turkey from shortly before the Christian era, and was extensively used in the early Church owing to the active Christian communities in those parts. After Greek it was the most important language in the eastern Roman Empire until the rise of Islam in the 8th c. The Syriac alphabet developed from a late form of Aramaic used at Palmyra in Syria. —*adj*. of this language. [f. L f. Gk (*Suria* Syria)]

syringa /sɪ'rɪŋgə/ *n*. **1.** the mock orange (*Philadelphus coronarius*). **2.** the botanical name for lilac (*Syringa vulgaris*). [as foll., from stems of mock orange being used for pipe-stems]

syringe /'sɪrɪndʒ, -'rɪndʒ/ *n*. a device for drawing in liquid by suction and then ejecting it in a fine stream. —*v.t.* to sluice or spray with a syringe. [f. L *syringa* f. Gk *surigx* pipe]

syrup /'sɪrəp/ *n*. **1.** a thick liquid of water (nearly) saturated with sugar; this flavoured or medicated. **2.** condensed sugar-cane juice, molasses, treacle. **3.** excessive sweetness of manner. —**syrupy** *adj*. [f. OF or L f. Arab. cf. SHERBERT]

system /'sɪstəm/ *n*. **1.** a set of connected things or parts that form a whole or work together; a set of organs in the body with a common function. **2.** an animal body as a whole. **3.** a set of rules, principles, or practices forming a particular philosophy or form of government. **4.** a major group of layers of rock that were deposited during a particular geological period and contain similar fossils. **5.** a method of classification, notation, measurement, etc. **6.** being systematic, orderliness. —**get a thing out of one's system**, to be rid of its effects. **systems analysis**, the analysis of an operation in order to use a computer to improve its efficiency. [f. F or L f. Gk *sustēma* (as SYN-, *histēmi* set up)]

systematic /sɪstə'mætɪk/ *adj*. methodical, according to a system, not casually or at random. —**systematically** *adv*. [as prec.]

systematize /'sɪstəmətaɪz/ *v.t.* to make systematic. —**systematization** /-'zeɪʃ(ə)n/ *n*. [f. prec.]

Système International /sɪstem æteərnæsjɔ̃'nɑːl/ the international system of units): see SI. [F]

systemic /sɪ'stemɪk/ *adj*. **1.** of the bodily system as a whole. **2.** (of an insecticide etc.) entering plant tissues via the roots and shoots. —**systemically** *adv*. [f. SYSTEM]

systole /'sɪstəlɪ/ *n*. the rhythmical contraction of the chambers of the heart, alternating with diastole to form the pulse. —**systolic** /sɪ'stɒlɪk/ *adj*. [L f. Gk (*sustellō* contract)]

T

T, t /tiː/ *n.* (*pl.* **Ts, T's**) **1.** the twentieth letter of the alphabet. **2.** a T-shaped thing. —**cross the t's**, to be minutely accurate. **to a T**, exactly, to a nicety.

T *abbr.* tesla.

T *symbol* tritium.

t. *abbr.* ton(s); tonne(s).

TA *abbr.* Territorial Army.

Ta *symbol* tantalum.

ta /tɑː/ *int.* (*colloq.*) thank you. [infantile form]

TAB *abbr.* typhoid-paratyphoid A and B vaccine.

tab *n.* **1.** a small projecting flap or attached strip, especially one by which a thing can be hung, fastened, or identified. **2.** (*colloq.*) an account, a tally; (*US colloq.*) a bill; a price. —*v.t.* (**-bb-**) to provide with tabs. —**keep a tab** *or* **tabs on**, to keep account of; to have under observation or in check. [prob. f. dial.; cf. TAG]

tabard /ˈtæbəd/ *n.* **1.** a short-sleeved or sleeveless jerkin emblazoned with the arms of the sovereign and forming the official dress of a herald or pursuivant. **2.** (*hist.*) a short surcoat open at the sides and with short sleeves, worn by a knight over armour and emblazoned with armorial bearings. **3.** a woman's or girl's garment of similar shape. [f. OF *tabart*; orig. unkn.]

tabby /ˈtæbɪ/ *n.* **1.** a grey or brownish cat with dark stripes. **2.** a kind of watered silk. [f. F f. Arab., = quarter of Baghdad where tabby silk was produced; connection of sense **1.** uncertain]

tabernacle /ˈtæbənæk(ə)l/ *n.* **1.** (in the Bible) a fixed or movable habitation, usually of light construction; a tent containing the Ark of the Covenant, used as a portable shrine by the Israelites during their wanderings in the wilderness. **2.** a meeting-place for worship used by non-Conformists (e.g. Baptists) or by Mormons; (*hist.*) any of the temporary structures used during the rebuilding of churches after the Fire of London. **3.** a canopied niche or recess in the wall of a church etc.; an ornamental receptacle for the pyx or consecrated elements of the Eucharist. [f. OF or L *tabernaculum* tent dim. of *taberna* hut]

tabla /ˈtæblə, ˈtɑːblə/ *n.* a pair of small Indian drums played with the hands, often to accompany the sitar. [Urdu f. Arab. *tabla* drum]

table /ˈteɪb(ə)l/ *n.* **1.** a piece of furniture with a flat top supported on one or more legs, providing a level surface for putting things on. **2.** the food provided at table. **3.** a set of facts or figures systematically arranged, especially in columns; the matter contained in such a set. **4.** a flat surface for working on or for machinery etc. **5.** a slab of wood or stone etc.; the matter inscribed on it. —*v.t.* **1.** to bring forward for discussion or consideration. **2.** to postpone consideration of (a matter). —**at table**, taking a meal at a table. **on the table**, submitted for discussion or consideration. **table-cloth** *n.* a cloth spread on a table, especially for meals. **table licence**, a licence to serve alcoholic drinks with meals only. **table-linen** *n.* table-cloths, napkins, etc. **Table of the House**, the central table in either of the Houses of Parliament. **table tennis**, an indoor game like lawn tennis, played with small bats and a ball bouncing on a table divided by a net. No precise date of its origin or invention is known; equipment for it is mentioned in a sports goods catalogue of 1884. **turn the tables on**, to reverse one's relations (with), especially to pass from a weaker to a stronger position. **under the table**, drunk. [f. OF f. L *tabula* plank, tablet]

tableau /ˈtæblәʊ/ *n.* (*pl.* **-eaux** /-әʊz/) **1.** a picturesque presentation; a group of silent motionless persons arranged to represent a scene. **2.** a dramatic or effective situation suddenly brought about. [F, dim. of *table* (see prec.)]

table d'hôte /ˌtɑːbl ˈdәʊt/ a meal at a fixed time and price in a hotel etc., with less choice of dishes than à la carte. [F, = host's table]

tableland *n.* a plateau of land.

Table Mountain a flat-topped mountain overlooking Cape Town in South Africa.

tablespoon *n.* a large spoon for serving food; the amount held by this. —**tablespoonful** *n.* (*pl.* **-fuls**)

tablet /ˈtæblɪt/ *n.* **1.** a small measured and compressed amount of a substance, especially of a medicine or drug. **2.** a small flat piece of soap etc. **3.** a small slab or panel, especially for the display of an inscription. [f. OF f. L (as TABLE)]

tabloid /ˈtæblɔɪd/ *n.* a newspaper, usually popular in style, printed on sheets that are half the size of larger newspapers. [orig. name of compressed drug-preparation (as prec.)]

taboo /təˈbuː/ *n.* the system or an act of setting a person or thing apart as sacred or accursed; a prohibition or restriction imposed by social custom. —*adj.* avoided or prohibited, especially by social custom. —*v.t.* to put under a taboo; to exclude or prohibit by authority or social influence. [f. Tongan]

tabor /ˈteɪbә(r)/ *n.* (*hist.*) a small drum, especially used to accompany a pipe. [f. OF, cf. TABLA; Pers. *tabīra* drum]

tabular /ˈtæbjʊlә(r)/ *adj.* of or arranged in tables or lists. [f. L (as TABLE)]

tabulate /ˈtæbjʊleɪt/ *v.t.* to arrange (figures or facts) in tabular form. —**tabulation** /-ˈleɪʃ(ә)n/ *n.* [f. L *tabulare* (*tabula* table)]

tabulator *n.* **1.** a person or thing that tabulates. **2.** a device on a typewriter for advancing to a sequence of set positions in tabular work. [f. prec.]

tachisme /ˈtæʃɪz(ә)m/ *n.* action painting. [F (*tache* stain)]

tacho /ˈtækәʊ/ *n.* (*pl.* **-os**) (*colloq.*) a tachometer. [abbr.]

tachograph /ˈtækәgrɑːf/ *n.* a device in a motor vehicle for recording the speed and travel-time. [f. Gk *takhos* speed + -GRAPH]

tachometer /tæˈkɒmɪtә(r)/ *n.* an instrument for measuring velocity or speed of rotation (especially of a vehicle engine). [as prec. + -METER]

tacit /ˈtæsɪt/ *adj.* understood or implied without being stated. —**tacitly** *adv.* [f. L *tacitus* (*tacēre* be silent)]

taciturn /ˈtæsɪtɜːn/ *adj.* habitually saying very little, uncommunicative. —**taciturnity** /-ˈtɜːnɪtɪ/ *n.* [f. F or L *taciturnus* (as prec.)]

Tacitus /ˈtæsɪtәs/, Cornelius (born *c.*56), Roman senator and historian, whose works are pervaded by a deep pessimism (partly the product of personal experience under Domitian) about the course of Roman history since the end of the Republic. His major works on imperial history, only partially preserved, the *Annals* (covering the period from 14 to 68) and the *Histories* (beginning in 69), are a piercingly ironic but scrupulously accurate record of the period, conveyed in a highly individual style, elevated, rapid, and intense.

tack[1] *n.* **1.** a small sharp broad-headed nail; (*US*) a drawing-pin. **2.** a long stitch used in fastening fabric in position lightly or temporarily. **3.** the direction in which a ship moves as determined by the position of its sails; a temporary change of direction in sailing to take advantage of a side wind etc.; a rope for securing the corner of some sails; the corner to which this is fastened. (See ill. SAILING-SHIPS.) **4.** a course of action or policy. **5.** sticky condition of varnish etc. —*v.t./i.* **1.** to fasten with a tack or tacks. **2.** to stitch with tacks. **3.** to add as an extra thing. **4.** to change a ship's course by turning its head to the wind; to make a series of such tacks. **5.** to change one's conduct or policy etc. [cf. OF *tache* clasp]

tack[2] *n.* riding-harness, saddles etc. [f. TACKLE]

tackle *n.* **1.** the equipment for a task or sport. **2.** a mechanism, especially of ropes, pulley-blocks, hooks, etc., for lifting weights, managing sails, etc.; a windlass with its ropes and hooks. **3.** the act of tackling in football etc. —*v.t.* **1.** to try to deal with (a problem or difficulty); to grapple with or try to overcome (an opponent); to enter into a discussion with (a person, especially about an awkward matter). **2.** (in football etc.) to intercept or stop (a player running with the ball). —**tackler** *n.* [prob. f. MLG (*taken* lay hold of)]

tacky *adj.* (of glue or varnish etc.) in the sticky stage before complete dryness. —**tackiness** *n.* [f. TACK¹]

tact *n.* skill in avoiding giving offence or in winning goodwill by saying or doing the right thing. [F. f. L *tactus* (sense of) touch (*tangere* to touch)]

tactful *adj.* having or showing tact. —**tactfully** *adv.*, **tactfulness** *n.* [f. TACT + -FUL]

tactic /'tæktɪk/ *n.* a piece of tactics. [as TACTICS]

tactical /'tæktɪk(ə)l/ *adj.* **1.** of tactics. **2.** (of bombing) done in immediate support of military or naval operations. **3.** adroitly planning or planned. —**tactical weapons,** see STRATEGIC WEAPONS. —**tactically** *adv.* [as TACTICS]

tactician /tæk'tɪʃ(ə)n/ *n.* an expert in tactics. [f. foll.]

tactics *n.pl.* (also treated as *sing.*) **1.** the art of placing and manœuvring armed forces skilfully in a battle (dist. from *strategy*). **2.** the procedure adopted in carrying out a scheme or achieving some end. [f. Gk *taktika* (*tassō* arrange)]

tactile /'tæktaɪl/ *adj.* of or connected with the sense of touch; perceived by touch. —**tactility** /-'tɪlɪtɪ/ *n.* [f. L *tactilis* (*tangere* touch)]

tactless *adj.* having or showing no tact. —**tactlessly** *adv.*, **tactlessness** *n.* [f. TACT + -LESS]

Tadjikistan /tædʒɪkɪ'stɑːn/ the Tadjik SSR, a constituent republic of the USSR, in central Asia; capital, Dushanbe.

tadpole *n.* the larva of a frog or toad etc. at the stage when it lives in water and has gills and a tail (ill. AMPHIBIANS). [as TOAD + POLL, f. size of head]

taffeta /'tæfɪtə/ *n.* a fine lustrous silk or silklike fabric. [f. OF or L ult. f. Pers., p.p. of *tāftan* twist]

taffrail /'tæfreɪl/ *n.* a rail round a ship's stern (ill. SAILING-SHIPS). [f. Du. *taffereel* panel (as TABLE); assim. to RAIL¹]

Taffy /'tæfɪ/ *n.* (*colloq.*) a nickname for a Welshman. [supposed Welsh pronunc. of *Davy* = *David*]

tag¹ *n.* **1.** a loop, flap, or label for handling, hanging, or marking a thing. **2.** a metal or plastic point of a shoelace etc. used to assist insertion. **3.** a loose or ragged end. **4.** a trite quotation, a stock phrase. —*v.t./i.* (**-gg-**) **1.** to attach a tag to. **2.** to attach, to add as an extra thing. **3.** (*colloq.*) to follow; to trail behind. —**tag along,** (*colloq.*) to go along with another or others. [orig. unkn.]

tag² *n.* a children's game of chasing and touching. —*v.t.* (**-gg-**) to touch in a game of tag. [orig. unkn.]

Tagalog /'tægəlɒg/ *n.* **1.** a member of the principal people of the Philippine Islands. **2.** their language, which belongs to the Malayo-Polynesian language group although its vocabulary has been heavily influenced by Spanish with some adaptions from Chinese and Arabic. [Tagalog (*taga* native, *ilog* river)]

tagliatelle /tɑːljəˈtelɪ/ *n.* a ribbon-shaped form of pasta. [It.]

tagmemics /tægˈmiːmɪks/ *n.* the study and description of language in terms of *tagmemes* (the smallest meaningful units of grammatical form), based on the work of K. L. Pike (1912-), which stresses the functional and structural relations of grammatical units. [f. Gk *tagma* arrangement (after *phoneme*)]

Tagore /təˈgɔː(r)/, Sir Rabindranath (1861–1941), Bengali poet and philosopher, who was awarded the Nobel Prize for literature in 1913 for his *Gitanjali: Song-Offering* (1912), poems modelled on medieval Indian devotional lyrics. He wrote philosophical plays such as *Chitra* (1913), novels (*The Home and the World*, 1919; *Gora*, 1929), and short fiction which often comments powerfully and courageously on Indian national and social concerns. He founded the Santiniketan communal school to encourage links between Eastern and Western educational and philosophical systems.

Tagus /'teɪgəs/ a river of Spain and Portugal, flowing into the Atlantic near Lisbon.

Tahiti /tɑːˈhiːtɪ/ one of the Society Islands in the South Pacific, administered by France; pop. (1971) 79,494; capital, Papeete. The Island is famous as the location of the *Bounty* mutiny in 1789. —**Tahitian** /-ʃ(ə)n/ *adj. & n.*

tail¹ *n.* **1.** the hindmost part of an animal, especially when prolonged beyond the rest of the body. **2.** a thing like a tail in form or position, e.g. the part of a shirt below the waist, the hanging part of the back of a coat, the end of a procession; the part of a dovetail joint that is shaped like a dove's spread tail (ill. CARPENTRY). **3.** the rear part of an aeroplane or rocket. **4.** the luminous train of a comet. **5.** the inferior or weaker part of anything. **6.** (in *pl.*, *colloq.*) a tailcoat; evening dress including this. **7.** (usu. in *pl.*) the reverse of a coin turning up in a toss. **8.** (*slang*) a person

following or shadowing another. —*v.t./i.* **1.** to remove the stalks of (fruit etc.). **2.** (*slang*) to shadow, to follow closely. —**on a person's tail,** closely following him. **tail away** *or* **off,** to become fewer or smaller or slighter; to fall behind or away in a scattered line; to end inconclusively. **tail-back** *n.* a long line of traffic extending back from an obstruction. **tail-board** *n.* a hinged or removable back of a lorry etc. **tail-end** *n.* the hindmost, lowest, or last part. **tail-gate** *n.* a tail-board; a door at the back of a motor vehicle. **tail-light** *or* **-lamp** *n.* a light at the rear of a motor vehicle or bicycle. **tail-spin** *n.* the spin of an aircraft. **tail wind,** a wind blowing in the direction of travel of a vehicle or aircraft etc. **turn tail,** to turn one's back; to run away. **with one's tail between one's legs,** humiliated or dejected by defeat etc. [OE]

tail² *n.* limitation of ownership, especially of an estate limited to a person and his heirs. —*adj.* so limited. —**in tail,** under such limitation. [f. OF *taille* (*taillier* cut f. L *talea* twig)]

tailcoat *n.* a man's coat with a long skirt divided at the back into tails and cut away in front, worn as part of formal dress (ill. DRESS).

tailless *adj.* having no tail. [f. TAIL¹ + -LESS]

tailor /'teɪlə(r)/ *n.* a maker of men's clothes, especially to order. —*v.t.* **1.** to make (clothes) as a tailor; to make in a simple smoothly-fitting shape. **2.** to make or adapt for a special purpose. —**tailor-bird** *n.* a small Asian bird, especially of the genus *Orthotomus*, sewing leaves together to form a nest. **tailor-made** *adj.* made by a tailor; entirely suited to a purpose. [f. AF *taillour* (as TAIL²)]

tailpiece *n.* **1.** the final part of a thing. **2.** a decoration in the blank space at the end of a chapter etc.

tailpipe *n.* the rear section of the exhaust pipe of a motor vehicle.

tailplane *n.* the horizontal aerofoil at the tail of an aircraft (ill. FLIGHT).

tailstock *n.* the adjustable part of a lathe, with a fixed spindle to support one end of the workpiece.

taint *n.* a trace of some bad quality or of decay or infection. —*v.t./i.* to affect or become affected with a taint. [f. OF f. L (*tingere* dye)]

Taipei /taɪˈpeɪ/ the capital of Taiwan; pop. (est. 1981) 2,252,700.

Taiwan /taɪˈwæn/ an island, mountainous and densely forested on its east side, off the SE coast of China; pop. (est. 1982) 18,203,000; official language, Chinese; capital, Taipei. Settled for centuries by the Chinese, the island was discovered by the Portuguese in 1590; they named it Formosa (= beautiful). It was ceded to Japan by China in 1895 but returned to China after the Second World War. General Chiang Kai-shek withdrew there in 1949 with 500,000 troops towards the end of the war with the Communist regime, and it became the headquarters of the Chinese Nationalists. Since the 1950s Taiwan has undergone steady economic growth, particularly in its export-oriented industries. In 1971 it lost its seat in the United Nations to the People's Republic of China, which regards Taiwan as one of its provinces. —**Taiwanese** /-ˈniːz/ *adj. & n.*

Taj Mahal /tɑːʒ məˈhɑːl/ a mausoleum at Agra in northern India, by the river Jumna. Completed *c.*1648, it was built by the Mogul emperor Shah Jahan in memory of his favourite wife who had borne him fourteen children. Set in formal gardens, the domed building in white marble is reflected in a pool flanked by cypresses. [perh. corrupt. of Pers. *Mumtaz Mahal*, title of wife of Shah Jahan, f. *mumtāz* chosen one, *mahal* abode]

take *v.t./i.* (*past* **took** /tʊk/, *p.p.* **taken**) **1.** to get into one's hands; to get possession of, to win. **2.** to obtain after fulfilling the necessary conditions; to obtain the use of by payment; to buy (a specified newspaper etc.) regularly. **3.** to assume possession of; to occupy (a position), especially as one's right; to avail oneself of; to indulge in; to use as a means of transport. **4.** to consume (food or medicine). **5.** to be successful or effective. **6.** to require; to use up. **7.** to cause to come or go with one; to carry; to remove from its place; to dispossess a person of. **8.** to catch or be infected with (fire, fever, etc.); to experience or be affected by; to exert (a feeling or effort). **9.** to find out and note (a name, measurements, temperature, etc.). **10.** to grasp mentally, to understand; to deal with or interpret in a specified way. **11.** to accept, to receive. **12.** to perform; to move round or over; to teach or be taught (a subject); to sit for (an examination). **13.** to make by photography; to photograph. **14.** to use as an instance. **15.** (*Gram.*) to have or require as part of a construction. **16.** to copulate with (a woman). —*n.* **1.** the amount taken or caught. **2.** a scene or sequence of a film photographed at one time without stopping the camera. **take after,** to resemble (a parent etc.). **take against,** to begin to dislike. **take away,** to remove or carry elsewhere; to subtract. **take-away** *adj.* (of food) bought at a restaurant for eating elsewhere; (*n.*) a restaurant selling this. **take back,** to retract (a statement); to carry (a person) in thought to a past time. **take down,** to write down (spoken words); to remove (a structure) by separating it into pieces. **take for,** to regard as being. **take-home pay,** that received by an employee after deduction of tax etc. **take in,** to receive as a lodger etc.; to undertake (work) at home; to include; to visit (a place) en route; to make (a garment etc.) smaller; to understand; to cheat. **take in hand,** to undertake; to start doing or dealing with; to undertake the control or reform of. **take in vain,** to use (a person's name) lightly or profanely. **take it,** to assume; (*colloq.*) to endure punishment etc. bravely. **take it or leave it,** to accept it or not. **take it out of,** to exhaust the strength of; to have revenge on. **take it out on,** to relieve frustration by attacking or treating harshly. **take it on** *or* **upon oneself,** to venture or presume to do a thing. **taken by** *or* **with,** attracted or charmed by. **taken ill,** suddenly affected by illness. **take off,** to remove (clothing) from the body; to deduct; to mimic humorously; to jump from the ground; to become airborne; to have (a day) as a holiday. **take-off** *n.* an act of becoming airborne; an act of mimicking; a place from which one jumps. **take oneself off,** to depart. **take on,** to undertake (work); to engage (an employee); to agree to oppose at a game; to acquire (a new meaning etc.); (*colloq.*) to show strong emotion. **take out,** to remove, to escort on an outing, to get (a licence or summons etc.) issued. **take a person out of himself,** to make him forget his worries etc. **take over,** to succeed to the management or ownership of; to assume control. **take-over** *n.* an assumption of control (especially of a business). **take one's time,** not to hurry. **take to,** to begin or fall into the habit of; to have recourse to; to adapt oneself to; to form a liking for. **take up,** to become interested or engaged in (a pursuit); to adopt as a protégé; to occupy (time or space); to begin (residence etc.); to resume after an interruption; to interrupt or question (a speaker); to accept (an offer etc.); to shorten (a garment). **take a person up on,** to accept (his offer etc.). **take up with,** to begin to associate with. [OE]

taker *n.* one who takes bets or accepts an offer etc. [f. TAKE]

taking *adj.* attractive, captivating. —*n.* (in *pl.*) the amount of money taken in a business. [f. TAKE]

talc *n.* **1.** a translucent mineral often found in thin glasslike plates. **2.** talcum powder. [F or f. L *talcum* f. Arab. f. Pers.]

talcum *n.* talc. —**talcum powder,** powdered talc for toilet use, usually perfumed. [L (as prec.)]

tale *n.* **1.** a narrative or story, especially a fictitious one. **2.** a report of an alleged fact, often malicious or in breach of a confidence. [OE (as TELL)]

talebearer *n.* a person who maliciously gossips or reveals secrets.

talent /ˈtælənt/ *n.* **1.** a special or very great ability; high mental ability. **2.** persons who have this. **3.** an ancient weight and unit of currency, especially among the Greeks. —**talent-scout** *n.* a seeker-out of talent, especially for the entertainment industries. [OE, ult. f. Gk *talanton* balance, weight, sum of money]

talented /ˈtæləntɪd/ *adj.* having great ability. [f. prec.]

talisman /ˈtælɪzmən/ *n.* an object supposed to be endowed with magic powers, especially of averting evil from or bringing good luck to its holder. —**talismanic** /-ˈmænɪk/ *adj.* [F & Sp. f. Gk *telesma* completion, religious rite (*telos* end)]

talk /tɔːk/ *v.t./i.* **1.** to convey or exchange ideas by spoken words. **2.** to have the power of speech. **3.** to express, utter, or discuss in words. **4.** to use (a specified language) in speech. **5.** to affect or influence by talking. **6.** to betray secrets; to gossip. **7.** to have influence. —*n.* **1.** talking, conversation, discussion. **2.** style of speech. **3.** an informal lecture. **4.** rumour, gossip; its theme. **5.** talking or promises etc. without action or results. —**now you're talking,** (*colloq.*) I welcome that offer or suggestion. **talk back,** to reply defiantly. **talk down,** to silence by greater loudness or persistence; to speak patronizingly; to bring (a pilot or aircraft) to a landing by radio instructions from the ground. **talking book,** a recorded reading of a book, especially for the blind. **talk out,** to block the course of (a bill in Parliament) by prolonging the discussion to the time of adjournment. **talk over,** to discuss at length. **talk a person over** *or* **round,** to win him over by talking. **you can** *or* **can't talk,** (*colloq.*) you are just as bad yourself. —**talker** *n.* [f. TALE or TELL]

talkative /ˈtɔːkətɪv/ *adj.* talking very much. [f. TALK]

talkie /ˈtɔːkɪ/ *n.* (*colloq.*) a sound-film. [f. *talking film,* after MOVIE]

talking-to *n.* (*colloq.*) a reproof. [f. TALK]

tall /tɔːl/ *adj.* **1.** of more than average height. **2.** having a specified height. —**talk tall,** to talk extravagantly or boastfully. **tall order,** a difficult task. **tall story,** (*colloq.*) one that is difficult to believe. **walk tall,** to feel justifiable pride. —**tallness** *n.* [f. OE, = swift]

tallboy *n.* a tall chest of drawers.

tallow /ˈtæləʊ/ *n.* the harder kinds of (esp. animal) fat melted down for use in making candles, soap, etc. —**tallowy** *adj.* [f. MLG; orig. unkn.]

tally /ˈtælɪ/ *v.i.* to correspond. —*n.* **1.** the reckoning of a debt or score. **2.** a mark registering a fixed number of objects delivered or received; such a number as a unit. **3.** (*hist.*) a piece of wood scored across with notches for the items of an account. **4.** a ticket or label for identification. **5.** a corresponding thing, a counterpart, a duplicate. [f. AF f. L *talea* twig]

tally-ho /tælɪˈhəʊ/ *int.* a huntsman's cry to the hounds on seeing a fox. —*n.* (*pl.* **tally-hos**) an utterance of this. —*v.t./i.* to utter the cry of 'tally-ho'; to indicate (a fox) or urge (hounds) with this. [cf. F *taïant*]

Talmud /ˈtælmʊd/ *n.* a body of Jewish ceremonial law and legend comprising the Mishnah and the Gemara, dating from the 5th c. BC but including earlier material. —**Talmudic** /-ˈmʊdɪk/ *adj.* [f. Heb., = instruction (*lamad* learn)]

talon /ˈtælən/ *n.* a claw, especially of a bird of prey. [f. OF, = heel, f. L *talus* ankle]

TAM *abbr.* (usu. *attrib.*) television audience measurement, denoting a measure of the number of people watching a particular television programme as estimated by the company Television Audience Measurement Ltd.

tamarind /ˈtæmərɪnd/ *n.* a tropical tree (*Tamarindus indica*) with a fruit whose acid pulp is used for cooling or medicinal drinks; this fruit. [f. L f. Arab., = date of India]

tamarisk /ˈtæmərɪsk/ *n.* an evergreen shrub of the genus *Tamarix* with feathery branches. [f. L *tamarix*]

tambour /ˈtæmbʊə(r)/ *n.* **1.** a drum. **2.** a circular frame for holding a fabric taut while it is being embroidered. **3.** a sloping buttress or projection in a fives-court or real-tennis court etc. [F, f. *tabour* tabor]

tambourine /tæmbəˈriːn/ *n.* a percussion instrument of a hoop with a parchment stretched over one side and jingling discs in slots round the hoop. [f. F *tambourin* (as prec.)]

tame *adj.* **1.** (of an animal) gentle and not afraid of human beings, not wild or fierce. **2.** insipid, not exciting or interesting. **3.** (of a person) docile and available. —*v.t.* to make tame or manageable; to subdue. —**tamely** *adv.*, **tameness** *n.* [f. OE]

tameable *adj.* that may be tamed. [f. TAME]

Tamerlane /ˈtæmələɪn/ (d. 1405) Timur Lenk or Lang (= 'lame Timur'), leader of the Mongols who conquered large parts of Asia in the late 14th and early 15th c., establishing the Mogul dynasty in India.

Tamil /ˈtæmɪl/ *n.* **1.** a member of a Dravidian people inhabiting southern India and Sri Lanka. **2.** their language, of the Dravidian group, one of the major languages of southern India, spoken by about 88 million people together with about another 4 million in Sri Lanka and Malaysia. —*adj.* of the Tamils or their language. [f. native name *Tamil,* rel. to DRAVIDIAN]

Tamil Nadu /ˈtæmɪl næˈduː/ a State in SE India; capital, Madras.

Tammany /ˈtæmənɪ/ a fraternal and benevolent society of New York City, founded in 1789, developed out of one of the earlier patriotic societies; a political organisation of the Democratic Party, identified with this society and notorious in the 19th c. for corruption, maintaining power by the use of bribes etc. It dominated the political life of New York City during the 19th and early 20th c. before being reduced in power by Franklin Roosevelt in 1932. —**Tammany Hall,** any of the successive buildings used as the headquarters of Tammany; the members of Tammany. [f. name of Indian chief (late 17th c.) said to have welcomed William Penn and regarded (*c.*1770–90) as 'patron saint' of Pennsylvania and other northern colonies]

Tammuz /ˈtæmʊz/ a Babylonian or Syrian deity, lover of Astarte, corresponding to the Greek Adonis. He became the personification of the seasonal decay and revival of crops.

tam-o'-shanter /tæməˈʃæntə(r)/ n. a round Scottish cap, usually woollen. [f. hero of Burns's *Tam o' Shanter*]

tamp v.t. to pack or ram down tightly. [perh. f. *tampion* stopper for gun-muzzle (as TAMPON)]

tamper v.i. **tamper with,** to meddle with, to make unauthorized changes in; to exert a secret or corrupt influence upon, to bribe. [var. of TEMPER]

tampon /ˈtæmpən/ n. a plug of cotton-wool etc. used to absorb natural secretions or stop a haemorrhage. —v.t. to plug with a tampon. [F (as TAP¹)]

Tamworth Manifesto /ˈtæmwəθ/ an election speech by Sir Robert Peel in 1834 in his Tamworth constituency, in which he accepted the changes instituted by the Reform Act and expressed his belief in moderate political reform. The manifesto is often held to signal the emergence of the Conservative Party from the old loose grouping of Tory interests.

tan¹ n. **1.** yellowish-brown colour. **2.** the brown colour in skin exposed to sun. **3.** tree-bark used in tanning hides. —adj. yellowish-brown. —v.t./i. (**-nn-**) **1.** to make or become brown by exposure to sun. **2.** to convert (raw hide) into leather by soaking in a liquid containing tannic acid or by the use of mineral salts etc. **3.** (*slang*) to thrash. [OE, perh. f. Celt.]

tan² abbr. tangent.

Tanagra /ˈtænəgrə/ n. a terracotta figurine of a type dating chiefly from the 3rd c. BC, many of which were found at Tanagra in Boeotia, Greece. Carefully modelled and painted, their most usual subject consists of elegantly draped young women.

tandem /ˈtændəm/ n. **1.** a bicycle with seats and pedals for two or more persons one behind another. **2.** a group of two persons or machines etc. with one behind or following the other. **3.** a carriage driven tandem. —adv. with two or more horses harnessed one behind another. —**in tandem,** one behind another. [L, = at length]

tandoor /ˈtænduə(r)/ n. a clay oven. [Hind.]

tandoori /tænˈduərɪ/ n. food cooked over charcoal in a tandoor. [f. prec.]

tang n. **1.** a strong taste, flavour, or smell; a characteristic quality. **2.** a projection on the blade of a tool by which the blade is held firm in the handle. [f. ON *tange* point]

T'ang the name of the dynasty which ruled in China from 618 to c.906, a period noted for territorial conquest and great wealth and regarded as the golden age of Chinese poetry and art.

Tanganyika /tæŋgəˈniːkə/ see TANZANIA. —**Lake Tanganyika,** a large lake in central Africa between Tanzania and Zaïre.

tangent /ˈtændʒ(ə)nt/ n. **1.** a straight line that meets a curve or curved surface at a point, but if extended does not intersect it at that point (ill. SHAPES). **2.** the ratio of the sides opposite and adjacent to the angle in a right-angled triangle. —**at a tangent,** diverging from a previous course of action or thought etc. [f. L *tangere* touch]

tangential /tænˈdʒenʃ(ə)l/ adj. **1.** of or along a tangent. **2.** divergent. **3.** peripheral. —**tangentially** adv. [f. prec.]

tangerine /tændʒəˈriːn/ n. **1.** a kind of small flattened orange from Tangier. **2.** its deep orange-yellow colour. [f. TANGIER]

tangible /ˈtændʒɪb(ə)l/ adj. **1.** perceptible by touch. **2.** definite, clearly intelligible; not elusive or visionary. —**tangibility** /-ˈbɪlɪtɪ/ n., **tangibly** adv. [F or f. L (as TANGENT)]

Tangier /tænˈdʒɪə(r)/ a seaport of Morocco, situated nearly opposite Gibraltar and commanding the western entrance to the Mediterranean. It had its beginning in the Roman port and town of Tingis, but the present walled city was built in the Middle Ages by the Moors. It was taken by the Portuguese towards the end of the 15th c., and given to Britain as part of the dowry of Princess Catherine of Braganza when she married Charles II in 1662. Britain abandoned it twenty-two years later to the sultan of Morocco, who retained control of the port and the surrounding countryside until 1904. From then until 1956 (except for five years in the Second World War, when it was seized by Spain) the zone was under international control. In 1956 it passed to the newly independent monarchy of Morocco.

tangle v.t./i. **1.** to twist or become twisted into a confused mass. **2.** to entangle. **3.** to become involved in conflict. **4.** to complicate. —n. a tangled mass or condition. [orig. unkn.]

tangly adj. tangled. [f. prec.]

tango /ˈtæŋgəʊ/ n. (pl. **-os**) a slow South American ballroom dance; the music for this. —v.i. to dance the tango. [Amer. Sp.]

tangram /ˈtæŋgræm/ n. a Chinese puzzle square cut into seven pieces to be combined into various figures. [orig. unkn.]

tangy /ˈtæŋɪ/ adj. having a strong taste or flavour or smell. [f. TANG]

tank n. **1.** a large receptacle for liquid or gas. **2.** an armoured motor vehicle carrying guns and moving on Caterpillar tracks (see below). —**tank up,** to fill the tank of a vehicle etc.; (*slang*) to drink heavily. [f. Gujarati, perh. f. Skr. *tadaga* pond]
Early designs for a mechanical armoured vehicle include one by Leonardo da Vinci (1484), to be driven by an arrangement of crank handles and geared wheels, and protected by a covering of smooth armour. Later inventors tried to use steam power, but it was not until the invention of the internal-combustion engine and the development of track mechanism that a really successful vehicle was constructed. This tank was a British invention, developed secretly during the First World War with the intention of opening the way to a decisive victory by introducing it suddenly in large numbers. (The name 'tank' for these vehicles was adopted for purposes of secrecy during manufacture.) Many senior army officers, however, were hostile to the new weapon, so that fewer than a dozen tanks effectively took the field in their first battle on the Somme (Sept. 1916), and they were not used in mass until Nov. 1917 when they were immediately successful; their use in battle meant that in the Second World War there was no repetition of the static trench warfare of 1914–18. It was soon apparent that different types of tanks and other armoured vehicles should be designed for different roles in battle. Their importance has increased with the development of tactical nuclear weapons, since they are mobile, have a relatively high weapon-power to manpower, and offer some protection against blast and radioactivity.

tankard /ˈtæŋkəd/ n. a tall mug, especially a silver or pewter mug for beer. [orig. unkn.; cf. MDu. *tanckaert*]

tanker n. a ship, aircraft, or road vehicle for carrying liquids (especially mineral oils) in bulk. [f. TANK]

tanner¹ n. one who tans hides. [f. TAN¹]

tanner² n. (hist.) a sixpence. [orig. unkn.]

tannery /ˈtænərɪ/ n. a place where hides are tanned. [as TANNER¹]

Tannhäuser /ˈtænhɔɪzə(r)/, (c.1200–c.1270), German poet whose work, which reveals humour with irony and an alert sense of parody, marks a historical decline in the minnesinger school. Because of his years in the Near East and the sensuality of his love poetry he became a legendary figure as the knight who visited Venus's grotto, repented, and sought absolution from the pope, and as such he is commemorated in Wagner's opera.

tannic /ˈtænɪk/ adj. of tan. —**tannic acid,** tannin. [f. F (as foll.)]

tannin /ˈtænɪn/ n. any of several astringent substances obtained from oak-galls and various tree-barks, used in preparing leather and in making ink etc. [f. F *tanin* (as TAN¹)]

Tannoy /ˈtænɔɪ/ n. [P] a type of public-address system. [orig. unkn.]

tansy /ˈtænzɪ/ n. an aromatic herb (*Chrysanthemum vulgare*) with yellow flowers. [f. OF f. L f. Gk *athanasia* immortality (*a-* not, *thanatos* death)]

tantalize /ˈtæntəlaɪz/ v.t. to tease or torment by the sight of something that is desired but kept out of reach or withheld. —**tantalization** /-ˈzeɪʃ(ə)n/ n. [as TANTALUS]

tantalum /ˈtæntələm/ n. a rare hard white metallic element, symbol Ta, atomic number 73, first discovered in 1802. It can occur uncombined in nature as well as in a number of ores, where it is usually associated with niobium. The metal, which is very hard and resistant to corrosion, was formerly used for the filaments of electric light bulbs, and it is currently used for manufacturing capacitors, parts of aircraft, and surgical and other equipment. [f. foll., with ref. to its non-absorbent quality]

Tantalus /ˈtæntələs/ (*Gk myth.*) a Lydian king, son of Zeus and father of Pelops. He is represented as being punished eternally (for he was immortal): he is hungry and thirsty, but the water in which he stands recedes when he tries to drink it and the fruit above his head is blown aside from his hand. His crime is variously related: some say that he revealed the secrets of the gods, others than he gave their food to mortals, others that he killed his son Pelops and offered his flesh to the gods. His penalty became almost proverbial to the Greeks for 'tantalizing' in the modern sense.

tantalus /ˈtæntələs/ n. a stand in which decanters of spirits are locked up but visible. [f. prec.]

tantamount /ˈtæntəmaʊnt/ predic. adj. equivalent. [f. It. *tanto montare* to amount to so much]

tantra /ˈtæntrə/ n. each of a class of Hindu, Buddhist, or Jain sacred texts that deal with mystical and magical practices. —**tantric** adj. [Skr., = loom (*tan* stretch, weave)]

tantrum /ˈtæntrəm/ n. an outburst of bad temper or petulance, especially in a child. [orig. unkn.]

Tanzania /tænzəˈniːə/ a country in East Africa with a coastline on the Indian Ocean, consisting of a mainland area (the former republic of Tanganyika) and the island of Zanzibar; pop. (1978) 17,551,925; official languages, Swahili and English; capital, Dodoma. A German colony from the late 19th c., Tanganyika became a British mandate after the First World War and a trust territory, administered by Britain, after the Second, before achieving independence as a member State of the Commonwealth in 1961. It was named Tanzania after its union with Zanzibar in 1964. Like most of its neighbours Tanzania is largely dependent on agriculture, exporting sisal, cloves, cotton, and coffee. —**Tanzanian** adj. & n.

Tao /ˈtaʊ, taʊ/ n. the metaphysical concept central to all systems of Chinese philosophy, the absolute principle underlying the universe, combining within itself the principles of yin and yang. To Confucius, it is the Way of the superior man; to Lao-tzu, it is the Way of nature. The latter interpretation developed into the philosophical religion of Taoism. [Chinese, = road, way]

Taoiseach /ˈtiːʃəx, -k/ n. the prime minister of the Irish Republic. [Ir., = chief, leader]

Taoism /ˈtaːəʊɪz(ə)m, ˈtaʊ-/ n. one of the two major Chinese religious and philosophical systems (the other is Confucianism), traditionally founded by Lao-tzu. The central concept and goal is the Tao, an elusive term denoting here the force inherent in nature and, by extension, the code of behaviour that is in harmony with the natural order. Its most sacred scripture is the Tao-te-Ching (also called Lao-tzu), ascribed to its founder. —**Taoist** n. [f. TAO]

tap¹ n. **1.** a device for drawing liquid from a cask or for allowing liquid or gas to come from a pipe or vessel in a controlled flow. **2.** a device for cutting a screw-thread inside a cavity. **3.** a connection for tapping a telephone. —v.t. (**-pp-**) **1.** to fit a tap into (a cask); to let out (liquid) thus. **2.** to draw sap from (a tree) or fluid from (the body) by incision; to draw (fluid etc.) thus. **3.** to extract or obtain supplies or information from; to establish communication or trade with. **4.** to cut a screw-thread inside (a cavity). **5.** to make a connection in (a circuit etc.) so as to divert electricity or fit a listening-device for overhearing telephone conversations. —**on tap**, ready to be drawn off by tap; (*colloq.*) ready for immediate use. **tap-root** n. a tapering root growing vertically downwards (ill. PLANTS). [OE]

tap² v.t./i. (**-pp-**) **1.** to strike with a quick light but audible blow; to knock gently on (a door etc.). **2.** to strike (a thing) lightly against something. —n. a quick light blow; the sound of this. —**tap-dance** n. a dance with a sharp rhythmical tapping of the feet; (v.i.) to perform this dance. [imit.]

tape n. **1.** a narrow strip of woven cotton etc. used for tying, fastening, or labelling things; such a strip stretched across a race-track at the finishing-line. **2.** a strip of paper or of transparent film etc. coated with adhesive for fastening packages etc. **3.** a magnetic tape; a tape-recording. **4.** a long strip of paper printed or punched to convey messages. **5.** a tape-measure. —v.t. **1.** to tie or fasten with tape. **2.** to record on magnetic tape. **3.** to measure with a tape. —**have a person** *or* **thing taped**, (*slang*) to understand him or it fully. **tape-machine** n. a machine for receiving and recording telegraph messages. **tape-measure** n. a strip of tape or thin flexible metal marked for measuring length. **tape-record** v.t. to record (sounds) on magnetic tape. **tape-recorder** n. an apparatus for recording sounds on magnetic tape and afterwards reproducing them. **tape-recording** n. such a record or reproduction. [OE; orig. unkn.]

taper /ˈteɪpə(r)/ n. a wick coated thinly with wax, burnt to

give a light or to light candles etc. —v.t./i. to make or become gradually narrower. —**taper off**, to make or become gradually less in amount etc.; to cease gradually. [OE f. L *papyrus*, whose pith was used for candle-wicks]

tapestry /ˈtæpɪstrɪ/ n. a thick textile fabric in which coloured weft threads are woven (originally by hand) to form pictures or designs; embroidery imitating this, usually in wools on canvas; a piece of such embroidery. —**tapestried** adj. [f. OF *tapisserie* (*tapissier* to carpet f. *tapis* carpet)]

tapeworm n. a tapelike worm of the genus *Taenia* etc. living as a parasite in the intestines.

tapioca /tæpɪˈəʊkə/ n. a starchy substance in hard white grains obtained from cassava and used for puddings etc. [f. Tupi & Guarani *tipioca* (*tipi* dregs, *og*, *ok* squeeze out)]

tapir /ˈteɪpə(r), -pɪə(r)/ n. a piglike mammal of the genus *Tapirus* of tropical America and Malaya, with a short flexible snout. [f. Tupi]

tappet /ˈtæpɪt/ n. a cam or other projecting part used in machinery to give intermittent motion. [app. f. TAP²]

taproom n. a room in which alcoholic drinks are available on tap.

tar¹ n. a dark thick inflammable liquid distilled from wood, coal, or peat etc. and used as a preservative of wood and iron, an antiseptic, etc.; a similar substance formed in the combustion of tobacco etc. —v.t. (**-rr-**) to cover with tar. —**tar and feather**, to smear with tar and then cover with feathers as a punishment. **tarred with the same brush**, having the same faults. **tar-seal** v.t. (*Austr.*) to surface (a road) with a mixture of tar and broken stone; (n.) a road surfaced thus. [OE]

tar² n. (*colloq.*) a sailor. [abbr. of TARPAULIN]

Tara /ˈtɑːrə/ a hill in County Meath, Ireland, site in early times of the residence of the high kings of Ireland, still marked by ancient earthworks.

taradiddle /ˈtærədɪd(ə)l/ n. (*colloq.*) a petty lie; nonsense. [cf. DIDDLE]

tarantella /tærənˈtelə/ n. a rapid whirling South Italian dance; the music for this. [It. (as foll., because said to cure the dancing mania thought to affect those bitten by tarantulas)]

tarantula /təˈræntjʊlə/ n. **1.** a large black spider of the genus *Lycosa* of southern Europe. **2.** a large hairy tropical spider. [L f. It. (*Taranto* in S. Italy)]

tarboosh /tɑːˈbuːʃ/ n. a cap like a fez, worn alone or as part of a turban. [f. Arab., ult. f. Pers., = head cover]

Tardenoisian /tɑːdəˈnɔɪzɪən/ adj. of a late mesolithic industry of western and central Europe, named after the type-site at Tardenois in NE France. —n. this industry. [f. *Tardenois*]

tardy /ˈtɑːdɪ/ adj. slow to act, move, or happen; delaying or delayed beyond the right or expected time. —**tardily** adv., **tardiness** n. [f. F *tardif* f. L *tardus* slow]

tare¹ n. **1.** a kind of vetch, especially as a cornfield weed (*Vicia hirsuta*) or fodder (*V. sativa*). **2.** (in *pl.*, in the Bible) an injurious cornfield weed, thought to be darnel. [orig. unkn.]

tare² n. an allowance made to the purchaser for the weight of the container in which goods are packed, or for the vehicle transporting them, in instances where the goods are weighed together with their container or vehicle. [f. F, = deficiency, ult. f. Arab., = what is rejected]

target /ˈtɑːgɪt/ n. **1.** an object or mark that a person tries to hit in shooting etc.; a round or rectangular object painted with concentric circles for this purpose, especially in archery. **2.** a person or thing against which criticism or scorn is directed. **3.** an objective, a minimum result aimed at. —v.t. **1.** to aim (a weapon etc.) at a target. **2.** to plan or schedule (a thing) to attain an objective. [dim. of *targe* shield, f. OF]

Targum /ˈtɑːgəm/ n. any of various ancient Aramaic paraphrases or interpretations of the Hebrew scriptures, made from at least the 1st c. AD when Hebrew was ceasing to be a spoken language. [f. Chaldee, = interpretation]

tariff /ˈtærɪf/ n. **1.** a list of fixed charges. **2.** the duty on a particular class of imports or exports; a list of duties or customs to be paid. [f. F ult. f. Arab., = notification]

tarlatan /ˈtɑːlət(ə)n/ n. a thin stiff open kind of muslin. [f. F; prob. of Indian orig.]

Tarmac /ˈtɑːmæk/ n. [P] tarmacadam; a runway etc. made of this. —**tarmac** v.t. (**-ck-**) to surface with tarmacadam. [abbr.]

tarmacadam /tɑːməˈkædəm/ n. road materials of stone or slag bound with tar. [f. TAR¹ + MACADAM]

tarn *n.* a small mountain lake (ill. MOUNTAINS). [f. ON]

tarnish /ˈtɑːnɪʃ/ *v.t./i.* **1.** to lessen or destroy the lustre of (metal etc.). **2.** to stain or blemish (a reputation etc.). **3.** (of metal etc.) to lose its lustre. —*n.* **1.** loss of lustre. **2.** a blemish, a stain. [f. F *ternir* (*terne* dark)]

taro /ˈtɑːrəʊ/ *n.* (*pl.* -os) a tropical plant (*Colocasia esculenta*) of the arum family with a tuberous root used as a food especially in the Pacific islands. [Polynesian]

tarot /ˈtærət/ *n.* **1.** a card (especially one of 22 trumps) in a pack of 78 cards used in a game or for fortune-telling (see below and PLAYING-CARDS). **2.** (also in *pl.*) this game. [f. It & F; orig. unkn.]

Tarot cards are thought to go back to the 12th c. in Europe, though the earliest surviving set is from 1390. Their origin and symbolism is obscure. Part of the tarot pack consisted of 56 cards arranged in 4 suits of 14 each, numbered similarly to a 52-card pack except that a Knight was included among the court cards. The suits were called Cups, Swords, Money, and Batons (Clubs). The rest of the pack was composed of a series of pictures representing various aspects of life and drawn from legend and folklore. The Devil was included, and there were emblematic pictures of Death, the Sun, the Moon, etc. There was also an extra unnumbered card called *Le Fou* (the fool), ancestor of the modern Joker. In the game played the emblem cards always had a special power over the others. In fortune-telling the cards are interpreted according to the meaning assigned to them. Renewed interest in the occult has led to a recent revival in the use of tarots.

tarpaulin /tɑːˈpɔːlɪn/ *n.* a waterproof cloth especially of tarred canvas; a sheet or covering of this. [prob. f. TAR¹ + PALL¹]

Tarpeian rock /tɑːˈpiːən/ a cliff, probably at the SW corner of the Capitoline Hill, over which murderers and traitors were hurled in ancient Rome. [f. *Tarpeia*, legendary daughter of the commander of the citadel, which she betrayed to the Sabines; she is said to be buried at the foot of the hill]

Tarquin /ˈtɑːkwɪn/ the name of two kings of ancient Rome, Tarquinius Priscus and Tarquinius Superbus ('the Proud'; traditionally 534–510 BC). After his expulsion from the city, and the founding of the republic, he engaged in a number of vain attacks on Rome.

tarradiddle var. of TARADIDDLE.

tarragon /ˈtærəgən/ *n.* a plant (*Artemisia dracunculus*) related to wormwood, used to flavour salads and vinegar. [L f. Gk *tarkhōn*, perh. through Arab. f. Gk *drakōn* dragon]

tarry¹ /ˈtɑːrɪ/ *adj.* of or smeared with tar. —**tarriness** *n.* [f. TAR¹]

tarry² /ˈtærɪ/ *v.i.* (*archaic*) to delay in coming or going, to linger. [orig. unkn.]

tarsal /ˈtɑːs(ə)l/ *adj.* of the tarsus. [f. TARSUS]

tarsier /ˈtɑːsɪə(r)/ *n.* a small nocturnal tree-climbing animal of SE Asia, with soft fur and large prominent eyes (especially *Tarsius spectrum*), a primate related to the lemurs. [F (as TARSUS, from the structure of its foot)]

Tarski /ˈtɑːskɪ/, Alfred (1902–), Polish-born mathematician and logician, author of works on a wide variety of topics, especially the concept of truth and the relations between language and the world.

Tarsus /ˈtɑːsəs/ a city in SW Turkey, the home of St Paul.

tarsus /ˈtɑːsəs/ *n.* (*pl.* **tarsi** /-siː/) **1.** the small bones (seven in man) that make up the ankle (ill. BODY1). **2.** the shank of a bird's leg (ill. BIRDS). [f. Gk *tarsos* flat of the foot]

tart¹ *n.* **1.** a small round of pastry with jam etc. on top. **2.** a pie with a fruit or sweet filling. [f. OF *tarte*]

tart² *n.* (*slang*) a prostitute, an immoral woman. —*v.t./i.* (*colloq.*) to dress or decorate gaudily or with cheap finery; to smarten. [prob. abbr. of SWEETHEART]

tart³ *adj.* **1.** sharp-tasting, acid. **2.** sharp in manner, biting. —**tartly** *adv.,* **tartness** *n.* [OE; orig. unkn.]

tartan /ˈtɑːt(ə)n/ *n.* a pattern of coloured stripes crossing at right angles, especially a distinctive pattern worn by Scottish Highlanders to denote their clan; cloth woven in such a pattern. [perh. f. OF *tertaine, tiretaine*]

Tartar /ˈtɑːtə(r)/ *n.* **1.** a member of any of numerous mostly Muslim and Turkic tribes inhabiting various parts of European and Asiatic Russia, especially parts of Siberia, Crimea, N. Caucasus, and districts along the Volga; a member of the mingled host of Central Asian peoples, including Mongols and Turks, who under the leadership of Genghis Khan overran and devastated much of Asia and eastern Europe in the early 13th c., and under Tamerlane

(14th c.) established a large empire in central Europe with its capital at Samarkand. **2.** a descendant of this people. **3.** their Turkic language. **4.** a violent-tempered or intractable person. —*adj.* of the Tartars or their language. [f. OF or L *Tartarus*]

tartar /ˈtɑːtə(r)/ *n.* **1.** a hard chalky deposit that forms on the teeth. **2.** a reddish deposit that forms on the side of a cask in which wine is fermented. [f. L f. Gk *tartaron*]

tartaric /tɑːˈtærɪk/ *adj.* of tartar or tartaric acid. —**tartaric acid,** an organic acid present in many plants, especially unripe grapes. [f. F f. L (as prec.)]

tartar sauce /ˈtɑːtə(r)/ a sauce of mayonnaise containing chopped gherkins etc. [f. TARTAR]

Tartarus /ˈtɑːtərəs/ (*Gk myth.*) the underworld generally, or a part of this.

Tartary /ˈtɑːtərɪ/ the Tartar regions of Asia and eastern Europe, especially the high plateau of Asia and its NW slopes.

tartlet /ˈtɑːtlɪt/ *n.* a small tart. [f. F (as TART¹ + -LET)]

Tarzan /ˈtɑːz(ə)n/ a character in novels by the American author Edgar Rice Burroughs (1875–1950) and subsequent films and television series. He is a white man (Lord Greystoke by birth), orphaned in West Africa in his infancy and reared by apes in the jungle. —*n.* a man of powerful physique and great agility.

task /tɑːsk/ *n.* a piece of work to be done. —*v.t.* to make great demands on (a person's powers etc.). —**take to task,** to rebuke. **task force,** a unit specially organized for a task. [f. OF *tasque* f. L *tasca* (perh. as TAX)]

taskmaster *n.* one who imposes a task or burden.

Tasman /ˈtæzmən/, Abel Janszoon (1603–59), Dutch explorer. Sent from the Dutch East Indies by their Governor, van Diemen, to explore Australian waters (1642–3), Tasman arrived at Tasmania (which he named Van Diemen's Land), New Zealand, and some of the Friendly Islands. On a second voyage in 1644 he also reached the Gulf of Carpentaria on the north coast of Australia.

Tasmania /tæzˈmeɪnjə/ a State of the Commonwealth of Australia consisting of one large and several smaller islands south-east of the continent. Like mainland Australia, Tasmania was inhabited in prehistoric times (see ABORIGINES). The first European explorer to arrive there was Tasman (see prec.), who called the island Van Diemen's Land, a name which it bore until 1855. Settled by a British party from New South Wales in 1803, it became a separate colony in 1825 and was federated with the other States of Australia in 1901; capital, Hobart. —**Tasmanian** *adj. & n.*

Tasman Sea the part of the South Pacific that lies between Australia and New Zealand.

Tass the telegraphic news-agency of the Soviet Union. [f. initials of Russ. title]

tassel /ˈtæs(ə)l/ *n.* **1.** a bunch of threads or cords tied at one end and hanging loosely, attached as an ornament to a cushion, scarf, etc. **2.** a tassel-like catkin or head of certain plants (e.g. maize). [f. OF, = clasp; orig. unkn.]

tasset /ˈtæsɪt/ *n.* (in *pl.*) a series of overlapping plates in armour, hanging from the corslet and protecting the thighs (ill. ARMOUR). [f. OF *tasse* purse, holster; connection of sense not clear]

taste /teɪst/ *n.* **1.** the sensation caused in the tongue by a soluble substance placed on it. **2.** the faculty of perceiving this sensation. **3.** a small portion of food or drink taken as a sample; a slight experience of something. **4.** a liking. **5.** aesthetic discernment in art, literature, or conduct; conformity to its dictates. —*v.t./i.* **1.** to discern or test the flavour of (food etc., or *absol.*) by taking it into the mouth. **2.** to eat or drink a small portion of. **3.** to perceive the flavour of. **4.** to have experience of. **5.** to have a specified flavour. —**taste-bud** *n.* any of the cells on the surface of the tongue by which things are tasted. **to one's taste,** pleasing, suitable. [f. OF *tast* f. *taster* touch, try, perh. f. L *tangere* touch + *gustare* taste]

tasteful *adj.* having or showing good taste. —**tastefully** *adv.,* **tastefulness** *n.* [f. TASTE + -FUL]

tasteless *adj.* **1.** lacking flavour. **2.** having or showing bad taste. —**tastelessly** *adv.,* **tastelessness** *n.* [f. TASTE -LESS]

taster /ˈteɪstə(r)/ *n.* a person employed to judge teas or wines etc. by tasting them. [f. TASTE]

tasty /ˈteɪstɪ/ *adj.* having a strong flavour; appetizing. —**tastily** *adv.,* **tastiness** *n.* [f. TASTE]

tat¹ *n.* tatty things; a tatty person; tattiness. [back-formation f. TATTY]

tat² *v.t./i.* (**-tt-**) to do tatting; to make by tatting. [orig. unkn.]

ta-ta /tæˈtɑ:/ *int.* (*colloq.*) goodbye. [orig. unkn.]

Tatar /ˈtɑ:tə(r)/ var. of TARTAR.

Tate/teɪt/, Nahum (1652–1715), English playwright, whose plays were mainly adaptations from earlier writers. His version of *King Lear* omits the Fool, makes Edgar and Cordelia lovers, and ends happily. He wrote (with Dryden) the second part of *Absalom and Achitophel*, the libretto for Purcell's *Dido and Aeneas*, and in 1696, with Nicholas Brady, published the metrical version of the psalms that bears their names. He was appointed Poet Laureate in 1692.

Tate Gallery a national gallery of British art at Millbank, London, which originated in the dissatisfaction felt at the inadequate representation of English schools in the National Gallery. The Tate Gallery, opened in 1897, was built at the expense of (Sir) Henry Tate (1819–99), sugar manufacturer, to house the collection presented by him (in 1890) and other works accumulated by various bequests (including that of Turner) to the nation. In the 20th c. modern foreign paintings and sculpture (both British and foreign) were added. On foundation the gallery was subordinate to the National Gallery, but it was made fully independent in 1955.

Tati /ˈtɑ:ti/ Jacques (1908–82), real name Tatischeff, French film director and actor. His first full-length film *Jour de Fête* (1947) was followed by *Monsieur Hulot's Holiday* (1951), which saw the creation of a gangling comic hero (played by himself) at odds with modern gadgetry. Financial problems and his passionate perfectionism account for the smallness of his output.

Tatra Mountains /ˈtɑ:trə/ (also **Tatras**) a range of the Carpathians in eastern Czechoslovakia and southern Poland, rising to over 2,460 m (8,000 ft.).

tattered /ˈtætəd/ *adj.* in tatters. [f. foll.]

tatters *n.pl.* rags, irregularly torn pieces of cloth or paper etc. —**in tatters**, (of an argument etc.) ruined, demolished. [f. ON *tötrar* rags]

Tattersalls /ˈtætəsɔ:lz/ an English firm of horse auctioneers founded in 1776 by Richard Tattersall.

tatting /ˈtætɪŋ/ *n.* **1.** a kind of knotted lace made by hand with a small shuttle and used for trimming etc. **2.** the process of making this. [orig. unkn.]

tattle *v.i.* to chatter or gossip idly; to reveal information thus. —*n.* idle chatter or gossip. [f. Flem. *tatelen* (imit.)]

tattoo¹ /təˈtu:/ *n.* **1.** an evening drum or bugle signal recalling soldiers to quarters. **2.** an elaboration of this with music and marching as an entertainment. **3.** a rapping or drumming sound. [f. earlier *tap-too* f. Du., = close the tap (of the cask)]

tattoo² /təˈtu:/ *v.t.* to mark (the skin) with an indelible pattern by puncturing and inserting pigment; to make (a design) thus. —*n.* such a design. —**tattooist** *n.* [f. Polynesian]

tatty /ˈtæti/ *adj.* (*colloq.*) **1.** tattered, shabby and untidy. **2.** tawdry, fussily ornate. —**tattily** *adv.*, **tattiness** *n.* [orig. Sc., = shaggy (app. as TATTER)]

tau /taʊ, tɔ:/ *n.* the nineteenth letter of the Greek alphabet, = t. —**tau cross**, a T-shaped cross (ill. VESTMENTS). [f. Gk]

taught *past* & *p.p.* of TEACH.

taunt *n.* a thing said to anger or wound a person. —*v.t.* to assail with taunts; to reproach (a person with conduct etc.) contemptuously. [f. F *tant pour tant* tit for tat, smart rejoinder]

taupe /təʊp/ *n.* grey with a tinge of another colour, usually brown. [F, = mole (MOLE¹)]

Taurus /ˈtɔ:rəs/ a constellation and the second sign of the zodiac, the Bull, which the sun enters about 21 April. It contains the star Aldebaran, the galactic clusters of the Hyades and Pleiades, and the Crab nebula. —**Taurean** *adj.* & *n.* [L, = bull]

Taurus Mountains /ˈtɔ:rəs/ a range of mountains in SW Turkey, rising to over 3,700 m (12,000 ft.).

taut *adj.* **1.** (of a rope etc.) tight, not slack; (of the nerves) tense. **2.** (of a ship etc.) in good condition. —**tautly** *adv.* [perh. as TOUGH]

tauten /ˈtɔ:t(ə)n/ *v.t./i.* to make or become taut. [f. TAUT]

tautology /tɔ:ˈtɒlədʒɪ/ *n.* the saying of the same thing twice over in different words, especially as a fault of style (e.g. *arrived one after the other in succession*). —**tautological** /tɔ:təˈlɒdʒɪk(ə)l/ *adj.*, **tautologous** /-ləgəs/ *adj.* [f. L f. Gk *tautologia* (*tauto* the same, -LOGY)]

tavern /ˈtæv(ə)n/ *n.* (*literary*) an inn, a public house. [f. OF f. L *taberna* hut, tavern]

tawdry /ˈtɔ:drɪ/ *adj.* showy but worthless, gaudy. —**tawdrily**, *adv.*, **tawdriness** *n.* [short for *tawdry lace* f. *St Audrey's lace* (*Audrey* = Etheldrida, patron saint of Ely, d. 679) from the cheap finery sold at St Audrey's fair]

tawny /ˈtɔ:nɪ/ *adj.* brownish-yellow, brownish-orange. —**tawniness** *n.* [f. AF *tauné* (as TAN)]

tawse /tɔ:z/ *n.* (*Sc.*) a leather strap with a slit end, used for punishing children. [pl. of obs. *taw* leather made without tannin]

tax *n.* **1.** a contribution to State revenue legally levied on persons, property, or business. **2.** a heavy demand made upon a person, resources, etc. —*v.t.* **1.** to impose a tax on; to require to pay tax. **2.** to pay the tax on. **3.** to make heavy demands on. **4.** to accuse in a challenging way. —**tax-deductible** *adj.* (of expenses) that may be paid out of income before the deduction of income tax. **tax-free** *adj.* exempt from taxes. **tax haven,** a place where income tax is low. **tax return,** a declaration of income for taxation purposes. [f. OF f. L *taxare* censure, compute, perh. f. Gk *tassō* fix]

taxable *adj.* that may be taxed. [f. TAX]

taxation /tækˈseɪʃ(ə)n/ *n.* the imposition or payment of tax. [as TAX]

taxi /ˈtæksɪ/ *n.* (in full **taxi-cab**) a motor car plying for hire and usually fitted with a taximeter. —*v.t./i.* (*partic.* **taxiing**) **1.** (of an aircraft or pilot) to go along the ground or surface of the water under the machine's own power before or after flying. **2.** to go or convey in a taxi. [abbr. of *taximeter cab*]

taxidermy /ˈtæksɪdɜ:mɪ/ *n.* the art of preparing, stuffing, and mounting the skins of animals with lifelike effect. —**taxidermist** *n.* [f. Gk *taxis* arrangement + *derma* skin]

taximeter /ˈtæksɪmi:tə(r)/ *n.* an automatic fare-indicator fitted to a taxi. [f. F (as TAX, -METER)]

taxman *n.* (*pl.* **-men**) an inspector or collector of taxes.

taxonomic /tæksəˈnɒmɪk/ *adj.* (also **taxonomical**) of or using taxonomy. —**taxonomically** *adv.* [f. foll.]

taxonomy /tækˈsɒnəmɪ/ *n.* classification, especially in biology; the principles of this. —**taxonomist** *n.* [f. F f. Gk *taxis* arrangement, *-nomia* distribution]

taxpayer *n.* one who pays taxes.

Tay a river of Scotland flowing into the North Sea. The first Tay Bridge, a railway bridge across the Firth of Tay, opened in 1877, was blown down in 1879 while a passenger-train was crossing it.

Tayside a local government region in eastern Scotland.

TB *abbr.* tubercle bacillus; (*colloq.*) tuberculosis.

Tb *symbol* terbium.

T-bone /ˈti:bəʊn/ *n.* a T-shaped bone, especially in a steak from the thin end of the loin.

Tchaikovsky /tʃaɪˈkɒfskɪ/, Pyotr (1840–93), Russian composer, who had embarked on a career as a civil servant before beginning to study music seriously in St Petersburg and then at the Moscow Conservatory. His feeling for Russian nationalism is apparent in such works as his Second ('Little Russian' or 'Ukrainian') Symphony (1872) and the incidental music to *The Snow Maiden* (1873), but an equally important influence, that of classical music and in particular Mozart's, is revealed in the opera *The Queen of Spades* (1890). But before this had come the opera for which he is best known today, *Eugene Onegin* (1879); composition of this work coincided with his marriage to a young admirer, a commitment which was to last no longer than a few days. He is popularly known for the ballets *Swan Lake* (1877), *The Sleeping Beauty* (1890), and *The Nutcracker* (1892), and for the *1812* Overture (1880), but for the darker side of his nature one must look to the six symphonies (1866–93): of the Sixth ('Pathetic') he wrote, 'I have put my whole soul into this work'. It was once thought that Tchaikovsky died from cholera after drinking impure water, but there is now a theory that he took poison because of a potential scandal arising from an alleged homosexual relationship with a member of the royal family.

te /ti:/ *n.* (*Mus.*) the seventh note of the major scale in tonic sol-fa (see entry). [alt. f. *si*, perh. f. *Sancte Iohannes* (see GAMUT)]

tea *n.* **1.** an evergreen shrub or small tree (*Camellia sinensis*) grown in India, China, etc. (see below). **2.** its dried leaves. **3.** a drink made by infusing tea-leaves in boiling water; a similar drink made from the leaves of other plants or from some other substance. **4.** a meal at which tea is a main feature. —**tea-bag** *n.* a small porous bag of tea for infusion.

tea-chest n. a light metal-lined wooden box in which tea is exported. **tea-cloth** n. a cloth for a tea-table. **tea-leaf** n. a leaf of tea especially (in pl.) after infusion or as dregs; (rhyming slang) a thief. **tea-room** or **-shop** n. a place where tea and light refreshments are served to the public. **tea-rose** n. a rose (Rosa odorata) with a scent like tea. **tea-towel** n. a towel for drying washed crockery etc. [orig. tay ult. f. Chin. t'e]

The tea-plant has been cultivated for thousands of years in China. When tea was first introduced into Europe in the 17th c. it was so scarce and costly that tea-caddies were fitted with locks and keys. China continued to be the main tea-producing country until the 19th c., when it was discovered that tea grew also in Assam, a district of NE India. In 1870, when rust destroyed the coffee crop in Sri Lanka, tea was planted there, and later it was introduced into the East Indies, the Transcaucasian region of Russia, and Africa. It grows best in areas of moderate to high rainfall, equable temperatures, and high humidity.

teacake n. a light usually sweet bun eaten at tea, usually served toasted and buttered.

teach v.t./i. (past & p.p. **taught** /tɔːt/) 1. to impart information or skill to (a person) or about (a subject) systematically; to do this as a profession. 2. to put forward as a fact or principle. 3. to induce to adopt a practice etc. by example or experience; (colloq.) to deter by punishment etc. —**teach-in** n. a lecture and discussion, or a series of these, on a subject of public interest. [OE]

teachable adj. 1. apt at learning. 2. (of a subject) that can be taught. [f. TEACH]

teacher n. one who teaches, especially in a school. [f. TEACH]

teaching n. 1. what is taught, a doctrine. 2. the teachers' profession. [f. TEACH]

teacup n. a cup from which tea and other hot drinks are drunk.

teak n. a heavy durable timber; the Asian tree (Tectona grandis) yielding this. [f. Port. f. Malayalam]

teal n. (pl. same) a small freshwater duck of the genus Anas etc. [rel. to MDu. teling; orig. unkn.]

team n. 1. a set of players forming one side in certain games and sports. 2. a set of persons working together. 3. two or more animals harnessed together to draw a vehicle or farm implement. —v.t./i. to combine into a team or set or for a common purpose. —**team-mate** n. a fellow member of a team. **team spirit**, willingness to act for the benefit of one's group rather than oneself. **team-work** n. combined effort, co-operation. [OE, = offspring]

teamster n. 1. a driver of a team of animals. 2. (US) a lorry-driver. [f. TEAM]

teapot n. a pot with a handle, spout, and lid, in which tea is brewed and from which it is poured.

tear[1] /teə(r)/ v.t./i. (past **tore**; p.p. **torn**) 1. to pull forcibly apart, away, or to pieces; to make (a hole or rent) thus. 2. to become torn; to be capable of being torn. 3. to subject to conflicting desires or demands; to disrupt violently. 4. to run, walk, or travel hurriedly or impetuously. —n. a hole or rent caused by tearing. —**tear fault**, a geological fault in which the fracture is approximately vertical and movement is horizontal (ill. GEOLOGY). **tear oneself away**, leave in spite of a strong desire to stay. **tear one's hair**, to pull it in anger or frustration or despair. [OE]

tear[2] /tɪə(r)/ n. a drop of clear salty liquid serving to moisten and wash the eye and falling from it in sorrow or distress etc. —**in tears**, weeping. **tear-drop** n. a single tear. **tear-gas** n. a gas that disables by causing severe irritation to the eyes. **tear-jerker** n. (colloq.) a story etc. calculated to evoke sadness or sympathy. **without tears**, presented so as to be learned or done easily. [OE]

tearaway /ˈteərəweɪ/ n. a reckless hooligan. [f. TEAR[1] + AWAY]

tearful /ˈtɪəfəl/ adj. shedding or ready to shed tears; sad. —**tearfully** adv. [f. TEAR[2] + -FUL]

tearing /ˈteərɪŋ/ adj. extreme, overwhelming. [f. TEAR[1]]

tease /tiːz/ v.t. 1. to try playfully or maliciously to provoke (a person) by jokes, questions, or petty annoyances. 2. to pick (wool etc.) into separate strands. 3. to brush up the nap on (cloth). —n. (colloq.) a person who is fond of teasing others. —**tease out**, to separate by disentangling. [OE]

teasel /ˈtiːz(ə)l/ n. 1. a plant of the genus Dipsacus with prickly flower-heads. 2. such a head dried and used for raising the nap on cloth; a device used thus. [OE, rel. to prec.]

teaser /ˈtiːzə(r)/ n. (colloq.) a hard question or task. [f. TEASE]

teaspoon n. a small spoon for stirring tea; the amount held by this. —**teaspoonful** n. (pl. **-fuls**)

teat n. 1. a mammary nipple, especially of an animal. 2. a device, especially of rubber, for sucking milk from a bottle. [f. OF tete, replacing TIT[3]]

tec n. (slang) a detective. [abbr.]

Tech /tek/ n. (colloq.) a technical college or school. [abbr.]

technetium /tekˈniːʃəm/ n. an artificially produced radioactive metallic element, symbol Tc, atomic number 43. Technetium was the first new element to be created artificially, in 1937. Chemically related to rhenium, it has been used in certain alloys to impart resistance to corrosion. [f. Gk tekhnētos artificial (tekhnē art)]

technical /ˈteknɪk(ə)l/ adj. 1. of or involving the mechanical arts and applied sciences. 2. of or relating to a particular subject or craft etc. or its techniques. 3. (of a book or discourse etc.) using technical language, requiring special knowledge to be understood. 4. such in strict interpretation. —**technically** adv. [f. L f. Gk tekhnikos (tekhnē art)]

technicality /teknɪˈkælɪtɪ/ n. 1. being technical. 2. a technical expression. 3. a technical point or detail. [f. prec.]

technician /tekˈnɪʃ(ə)n/ n. 1. an expert in the techniques of a particular skill or craft. 2. a mechanic; a person employed to look after technical equipment in a laboratory etc. [as TECHNICAL]

Technicolor /ˈteknɪkʌlə(r)/ n. 1. [P] a process of colour cinematography. 2. vivid colour, artificial brilliance. [f. TECHNICAL + COLOUR]

technique /tekˈniːk/ n. the method of doing or performing something, especially in an art or science; skill in this. [F (as TECHNICAL)]

technocracy /tekˈnɒkrəsɪ/ n. government or control of a society or industry by technical experts. [f. Gk tekhnē art + -CRACY]

technocrat /ˈteknəkræt/ n. an exponent or advocate of technocracy. [f. prec.]

technological /teknəˈlɒdʒɪk(ə)l/ adj. of or using technology. —**technologically** adv. [f. foll.]

technology /tekˈnɒlədʒɪ/ n. the study or use of the mechanical arts and applied sciences; these subjects collectively. —**technologist** n. [f. Gk (as TECHNICAL, -LOGY)]

tectonics /tekˈtɒnɪks/ n.pl. (usu. treated as sing.) the study of the earth's structural features as a whole. [f. L f. Gk (tektōn carpenter)]

Ted n. (colloq.) a Teddy boy. [abbr.]

tedder n. a machine for drying hay. [f. ON tethja spread manure]

teddy bear a soft furry toy bear. President Theodore Roosevelt's bear-hunting expeditions occasioned a celebrated comic poem, accompanied by cartoons, in the New York Times of 7 Jan. 1906, concerning the adventures of two bears named 'Teddy B' and 'Teddy G'. These names were transferred to two bears (also known as the 'Roosevelt bears') presented to Bronx Zoo in the same year. Finally, the fame of these bears was turned to advantage by toy dealers, whose toy 'Roosevelt bears', imported from Germany, became an instant fashion in the USA. [f. Teddy pet-name of Theodore Roosevelt (d. 1919)]

Teddy boy /ˈtedɪ/ (colloq.) a youth with a supposedly Edwardian style of dress, especially in the 1950s. [f. Teddy, pet-form of Edward]

Te Deum /tiː ˈdiːəm/ an ancient Latin hymn of praise beginning Te Deum laudamus 'We praise thee, O God', sung at matins, or on special occasions as a thanksgiving; a musical setting of this.

tedious /ˈtiːdɪəs/ adj. tiresomely long, wearisome. —**tediously** adv., **tediousness** n. [f. OF or L (as foll.)]

tedium /ˈtiːdɪəm/ n. tediousness. [f. L taedium (taedēre to weary)]

tee[1] n. the letter T. [phonetic spelling]

tee[2] n. 1. a cleared space from which a golf ball is struck at the beginning of play for each hole. 2. a small support of wood or plastic from which a ball is thus struck. 3. the mark aimed at in bowls, quoits, etc. —v.t. to place (a ball) on a golf tee. —**tee off**, to play a ball from a tee, to start, to begin. [f. earlier teaz (orig. unkn.); in last sense of n. perh. = TEE[1]]

teem[1] v.i. 1. to be abundant. 2. to be full, to swarm (with). [OE (as TEAM)]

teem[2] v.i. (of water etc.) to flow copiously. [f. ON]

-teen suffix forming the numerals 13-19. [OE (as TEN)]

teenage /ˈtiːneɪdʒ/ adj. of or characteristic of teenagers. [f. TEENS + AGE]

teenager /ˈtiːneɪdʒə(r)/ n. a person in his or her teens. [f. prec.]

teens /tiːnz/ n.pl. the years of one's age from 13 to 19. [f. -TEEN]

teeny /ˈtiːnɪ/ adj. (colloq.) tiny. [var. of TINY]

teeny-bopper n. a girl in her teens or younger who is a fan of pop music and follows the latest fashions. [f. TEENS + BOPPER]

teeter v.i. to totter, to move unsteadily. [var. of dial. titter]

teeth pl. of TOOTH.

teethe /tiːð/ v.i. to grow or cut teeth, especially the milk-teeth. —**teething-ring** n. a small ring for an infant to bite on while teething. **teething troubles,** initial troubles in an enterprise etc. [f. prec.]

teetotal /tiːˈtəʊt(ə)l/ adj. abstaining completely from alcoholic drinks. —**teetotalism** n., **teetotaller** n. [redupl. of TOTAL]

Tegucigalpa /teguːsɪˈgælpə/ the capital of Honduras; pop. (est. 1982) 533,600.

Tehran /teəˈrɑːn/ the capital of Iran; pop. 6,200,000.

Teilhard de Chardin /taɪɑːd də ˈʃɑːdæ̃/, Pierre (1881–1955), French Jesuit philosopher and palaeontologist, best known for his evolutionary theory, blending science and theology, that man is evolving mentally and socially towards a perfect spiritual state.

tektite /ˈtektaɪt/ n. a small roundish glassy solid body of unknown origin occurring in various parts of the earth. [f. G f. Gk tēktos molten (tēkō melt)]

telamon /ˈteləmən/ n. (pl. **telamones** /-ˈməʊniːz/) a sculptured male figure used as a pillar to support an entablature. [f. L f. Gk Telamōn, name of a mythical hero]

tele- /telɪ-/ in comb. **1.** far, at a distance. **2.** television. [in first sense f. Gk (tēle far off); in second sense f. TELEVISION]

telecommunication /telɪkəmjuːnɪˈkeɪʃ(ə)n/ n. communication over long distances by cable, telegraph, telephone, or broadcasting; (usu. in pl.) this branch of technology.

telegram /ˈtelɪgræm/ n. a message sent by telegraph and then usually delivered in printed form. [f. TELE- + -GRAM]

telegraph /ˈtelɪgrɑːf/ n. transmitting messages or signals to a distance, especially by making and breaking an electrical connection (see below); an apparatus for this. —v.t./i. to send a message by telegraph (to); to send (a message) thus; to send an instruction to by telegraph. [f. F (as TELE-, -GRAPH)]
Electric telegraphy began just before the middle of the 19th c. The many inventors who helped to devise a working system were spurred on by the demands of the newly built railways for some means of conveying messages between signalmen to ensure the safety of trains. Samuel Morse, inventor of the Morse code, made use of the electromagnet and had made his first working model of a telegraph by 1835. The first practical telegraph in England was set up in 1837, linking Euston railway station in London with Camden station a mile away. A few years later, when the railway telegraph helped to bring about the arrest of a murderer, public interest in the invention was assured, and until c.1880, when telephones became more generally available, the telegraph was the standard means of rapid communication within a district. Telegraph wires and cables may be above or below ground or on the sea bed. Optical fibres and radio waves are also used to carry the signals, and satellites relay them from one part of the globe to another.

telegraphic /telɪˈgræfɪk/ adj. **1.** of telegraphs or telegrams. **2.** worded economically like telegrams. —**telegraphically** adv. [f. prec.]

telegraphist /tɪˈlegrəfɪst/ n. a person skilled or employed in telegraphy. [f. TELEGRAPH]

telegraphy /tɪˈlegrəfɪ/ n. the process of communication by telegraph. [as prec.]

telekinesis /telɪkaɪˈniːsɪs, -kɪ-/ n. movement of or in a body alleged to occur at a distance from, and without material connection with, the motive cause or agent. [f. TELE- + Gk kinēsis motion]

Telemachus /tɪˈleməkəs/ (Gk legend) the son of Ulysses and Penelope.

Telemann /ˈteɪləmæn/, Georg Philipp (1681–1767), German composer and organist. His voluminous output included 600 overtures, 44 Passions, 12 complete services, and 40 operas. In his lifetime his reputation far exceeded that of his contemporary, J. S. Bach.

telemeter /ˈtelɪmiːtə(r)/ n. an apparatus for recording the readings of an instrument and transmitting it by radio. [f. TELE- + -METER]

telemetry /tɪˈlemɪtrɪ/ n. the process of obtaining measurements at a point removed from the place where they are made; transmission of these, usually by radio. [f. TELE- + -METRY]

teleology /telɪˈɒlədʒɪ/ n. the doctrine of final causes, especially as related to the evidence of design or purpose in nature. —**teleological** /-əˈlɒdʒɪk(ə)l/ adj. [f. Gk telos end + -LOGY]

telepath /ˈtelɪpæθ/ n. a person able to communicate by telepathy. [f. foll.]

telepathy /tɪˈlepəθɪ/ n. communication between minds otherwise than by the known senses. —**telepathic** /telɪˈpæθɪk/ adj., **telepathist** n. [f. TELE- + Gk pathos feeling]

telephone /ˈtelɪfəʊn/ n. **1.** an apparatus for transmitting sound (especially speech) to a distance by wire, cord, or radio, usually by converting acoustic vibrations into electrical signals for transmission (see below; ill. SOUND). **2.** the transmitting and receiving instrument used in this. **3.** the system of communication by a network of telephones. —v.t./i. to speak to (a person) by telephone; to send (a message) by telephone; to make a telephone call. —**telephone box, booth,** or **kiosk,** a box-like kiosk containing a telephone for public use. **telephone directory** or **book,** a book listing the names and telephone numbers of people who are connected to a particular telephone system. **telephone number,** a number assigned to a particular telephone and used in making connections to it. —**telephonic** /-ˈfɒnɪk/ adj., **telephonically** /-ˈfɒnɪkəlɪ/ adv. [f. TELE- + Gk phōnē voice]
The 'Electrical Speaking Telephone' was invented by Alexander Graham Bell and patented in the USA in 1875–7. The German experimenter P. Reis had already (in 1861) devised an instrument transmitting sound of constant pitch but did not succeed in reproducing a voice. The three basic essentials of a telephone system are a telephone set to convert sound into electrical signals and back again, a transmission system to carry these signals over a distance, within acceptable limits of distortion and attenuation, and a switching system to connect any two telephone sets. Such connections are now usually made automatically as the caller, by dialling the receiver's number, sends out a series of pulses which actuate the switching system, and are monitored electronically. Methods of transmission of signals are the same as those used for telegraphy (see TELEGRAPH).

telephonist /tɪˈlefənɪst/ n. an operator in a telephone exchange or at a switchboard. [f. prec.]

telephony /tɪˈlefənɪ/ n. the use or system of telephones. [f. TELEPHONE]

telephoto /telɪˈfəʊtəʊ/ adj. telephotographic. [abbr.]

telephotography /telɪfəˈtɒgrəfɪ/ n. the photographing of distant objects with combined lenses giving a large image. —**telephotographic** /-fəʊtəˈgræfɪk/ adj.

teleprinter /ˈtelɪprɪntə(r)/ n. a device for typing and transmitting telegraph messages and for receiving and typing them.

telescope /ˈtelɪskəʊp/ n. **1.** an optical instrument using lenses or mirrors or both to make distant objects appear nearer and larger (see below; ill. LIGHT). **2.** a radio telescope (see separate entry). —v.t./i. **1.** to press or drive (sections of tube, colliding vehicles, etc.) together so that one slides into another like the sections of a telescope; to close or be driven or be capable of closing thus. **2.** to compress so as to occupy less space or time. [f. It. (as TELE-, -SCOPE)]
The optical telescope was probably invented independently many times before Galileo turned it on the heavens in 1609; the claim that it was invented in Holland by Hans Lippershey, a Dutch lens-maker (early 17th c.), is false. Its development not only advanced scientific knowledge but brought consequences for religious and philosophical thought (see COPERNICUS). Subsequent improvements of its design were made by Kepler, Galileo, Huygens, and Newton. Classically made from a collection of lenses mounted in a tube, or with a concave mirror and lens system, modern astronomical telescopes built on similar principles but from different materials are also used to observe radio waves and infrared radiation. Higher energy radiation may also be measured from telescopes carried beyond the atmosphere by artificial satellites. The

largest optical telescope is in Crimea and has a mirror 6 metres in diameter.

telescopic /telɪˈskɒpɪk/ *adj.* **1.** of or made with a telescope. **2.** consisting of sections which telescope. —**telescopic sight**, a telescope used for sighting on a rifle etc. —**telescopically** *adv.* [f. prec.]

teletext /ˈtelɪtekst/ *n.* a news and information service from a computer source transmitted to the television screens of subcribers.

Teletype /ˈtelɪtaɪp/ *n.* [P] a kind of teleprinter.

televise /ˈtelɪvaɪz/ *v.t.* to transmit by television. [back-formation f. foll.]

television /ˈtelɪvɪʒ(ə)n, -ˈvɪʒ(ə)n/ *n.* **1.** a system for reproducing on a screen visual images transmitted (with sound) by radio signals (see below and CATHODE-RAY TUBE). **2.** (in full **television set**) a device for receiving these signals. **3.** television broadcasting generally. —**televisual** /-ˈvɪzjʊəl/ *adj.*

When electric telegraphy came into use in the mid-19th c. inventors began to think of transmitting pictures by electric wire. The broad principle is that of cinematography, reproduction of a series of successive images which the human brain registers as a continuous picture because of the persistence of vision. Variations of light and shade are converted by a television camera into variations of electric current which can then be transmitted by radio or cable and picked up by a receiver to be changed back into variations of light and shade on the screen. For colour television light from the scene is split by the camera into its constituent colours and transmitted from these by the television receiver (see ill. LIGHT). Television was first demonstrated by J. L. Baird in 1926.

telex /ˈteleks/ *n.* a system of telegraphy using teleprinters and the public telecommunication network. A telex service opened in London in 1932. —*v.t.* to send by telex; to communicate with by telex. [f. TELEPRINTER + EXCHANGE]

Telford /ˈtelfəd/, Thomas (1757-1834), called by Southey the 'Colossus of Roads', the greatest road-builder, greatest bridge-builder, and greatest canal-builder, son of a Scottish shepherd. He was responsible for hundreds of miles of new roads in the Scottish Highlands and for the London-Holyhead road, the main route to Ireland, of which the most notable feature is the suspension bridge crossing the Menai Strait, opened in 1826. His canals include the Caledonian Canal across Scotland and the Gotha Canal across Sweden, and he was also responsible for a number of dock and harbour works. It is fitting that such a great civil engineer should have become the first president of the Institution of Civil Engineers, the first such engineering institution.

Tell, William. A legendary hero of the liberation of Switzerland from Austrian oppression, who was required to hit with an arrow an apple placed on the head of his son; this he successfully did. The events are placed in the 14th c. but there is no evidence for a historical person of this name. Similar legends of a marksman shooting at an object placed on the head of a man or child are of widespread occurrence.

tell[1] *v.t./i.* (*past & p.p.* **told** /təʊld/) **1.** to make known, especially in spoken or written words; to utter. **2.** to give information to; to assure; to reveal a secret. **3.** to direct or order. **4.** to decide, to determine; to distinguish. **5.** to produce a noticeable effect. **6.** to count. —**tell off**, (*colloq.*) to reprimand, to scold; to count off or detach for duty. **tell on**, to reveal the activities of (a person) by telling others. **tell tales**, to report a discreditable fact about another. **tell the time**, to read it from the face of a clock or watch. **you're telling me**, (*slang*) I am well aware of what you say. [OE]

tell[2] *n.* an artificial mound in the Middle East etc. formed by accumulated remains of ancient settlements superimposed on earlier ones. [f. Arab., = hillock]

teller *n.* **1.** a person employed to receive and pay out money in a bank etc. **2.** a person appointed to count votes. [f. TELL[1]]

telling *adj.* having a noticeable effect, striking. [f. TELL[1]]

tell-tale *n.* **1.** a person who discloses another's private affairs or misdeeds. **2.** an automatic registering device. **3.** a metal sheet extending across the front wall of a squash court, above which the ball must strike the wall (ill. SPORTS). —*adj.* that reveals or betrays.

tellurium /teˈljʊərɪəm/ *n.* a rare semi-metallic element, symbol Te, atomic number 52, chemically related to sulphur and selenium. First discovered in 1782, tellurium occasionally occurs uncombined in nature but more often in ores with metals. The element has two allotropic forms: a silvery crystalline substance and an amorphous powder. It is used as a catalyst, as a colouring agent, and in some electrical devices and alloys. [f. L *tellus -uris* earth, prob. named in contrast to uranium]

telly /ˈtelɪ/ *n.* (*colloq.*) television; a television set. [abbr.]

Telstar /ˈtelstɑ:(r)/ the first of the active communications satellites (i.e. both receiving and retransmitting signals, not merely reflecting signals from their surface). It was launched by the USA in 1964 and used in the transmission of television broadcasting and telephone communication.

Telugu /ˈteləgu:/ *n.* **1.** a member of a Dravidian people in SE India. **2.** their language, the most widespread of the Dravidian languages in India, spoken by about 45 million people mainly in Andhra Pradesh. [Telugu]

temerity /tɪˈmerɪtɪ/ *n.* audacity, rashness. [f. L *temeritas* (*temere* rashly)]

temp *n.* (*colloq.*) a temporary employee, especially a secretary. [abbr.]

temper *n.* **1.** the state of the mind as regards calmness or anger. **2.** a fit of anger; a tendency to have such fits. **3.** calmness under provocation. **4.** the condition of tempered metal as regards hardness and elasticity. —*v.t.* **1.** to bring (metal or clay) to the proper hardness or consistency. **2.** to moderate or mitigate. [OE f. L *temperare* mingle]

tempera /ˈtempərə/ *n.* a method of painting with powdered colours mixed with egg or size. It was used in Europe from the 12th and early 13th c. until the 15th c., when it began to give way to oil painting. [It., f. L *temperare* mix]

temperament /ˈtemprəmənt/ *n.* **1.** a person's distinct nature and character, especially as determined by physical constitution and permanently affecting his or her behaviour. **2.** (*Mus.*) the adjustment of intervals in the tuning of a piano etc. so as to fit the scale for use in all keys, especially (**equal temperament**) in which the twelve semitones are at equal intervals. [f. L (as TEMPER)]

temperamental /temprəˈment(ə)l/ *adj.* **1.** of the temperament. **2.** liable to erratic or moody behaviour —**temperamentally** *adv.* [f. prec.]

temperance /ˈtempərəns/ *n.* **1.** moderation or self-restraint, especially in eating and drinking. **2.** abstinence or partial abstinence from alcoholic drink. [f. AF f. L (as TEMPER)]

temperate /ˈtempərət/ *adj.* **1.** avoiding excess; moderate. **2.** of mild temperature. —**temperately** *adv.* [f. L (as TEMPER)]

temperature /ˈtemprɪtʃə(r)/ *n.* **1.** the degree or intensity of the heat of a body in relation to others, especially as shown by a thermometer or perceived by touch; (*colloq.*) a body temperature above normal. **2.** a degree of excitement in a discussion etc. [f. L (as TEMPER)]

Tempest /ˈtempɪst/, Dame Marie (1864-1942), English actress, real name Mary Susan Etherington. Though trained as a singer she made her name in comedy, becoming noted for her playing of charming elegant middle-aged women.

tempest /ˈtempɪst/ *n.* a violent storm. [f. OF f. L *tempestas* season, storm (*tempus* time)]

tempestuous /temˈpestjʊəs/ *adj.* stormy, turbulent. [f. L (as prec.)]

Templar /ˈtemplə(r)/ *n.* a member of the Knights Templars (see entry). [f. AF (as TEMPLE[1])]

template /ˈtemplɪt/ *n.* a thin board or metal plate used as a guide in cutting, shaping, or drilling. [orig. *templet*, prob. dim. of *temple* device in loom for keeping cloth stretched, f. OF, orig. same word as TEMPLE[2]]

temple[1] /ˈtemp(ə)l/ *n.* a building devoted to the worship, or treated as a dwelling-place, of a god or gods. —**Inner** and **Middle Temple**, two Inns of Court in London. [OE & f. OF f. L *templum* open or consecrated space]

temple[2] /ˈtemp(ə)l/ *n.* the flat part of either side of the head between the forehead and the ear. [f. OF f. L *tempus*]

tempo *n.* (*pl.* **tempos** or **tempi** /-i:/) **1.** the speed at which music is or should be played, especially as characteristic. **2.** a rate of motion or activity. [It., f. L *tempus* time]

temporal /ˈtempər(ə)l/ *adj.* **1.** of worldly as opposed to spiritual affairs, secular. **2.** of or denoting time. **3.** of the temple(s) of the head (*temporal bone* ill. BODY1). [f. OF or L (as TEMPORARY, TEMPLE[2])]

temporary /ˈtempərərɪ/ *adj.* lasting or meant to last only for a limited time. —*n.* a person employed temporarily. —**temporarily** *adv.*, **temporariness** *n.* [f. L (*tempus* time)]

temporize /ˈtempəraɪz/ *v.i.* to avoid committing oneself,

Temples

A Greek Doric temple

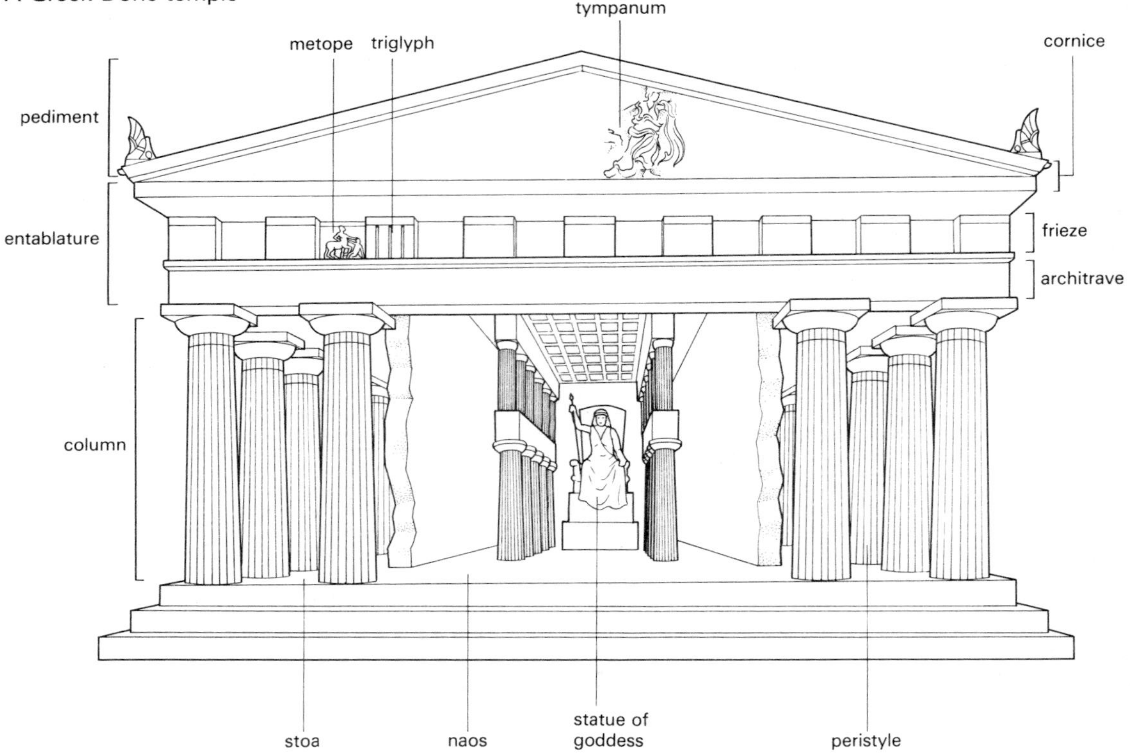

pediment

entablature

column

tympanum

metope   triglyph

cornice

frieze

architrave

stoa

naos

statue of
goddess

peristyle

Orders of architecture: Greek origin

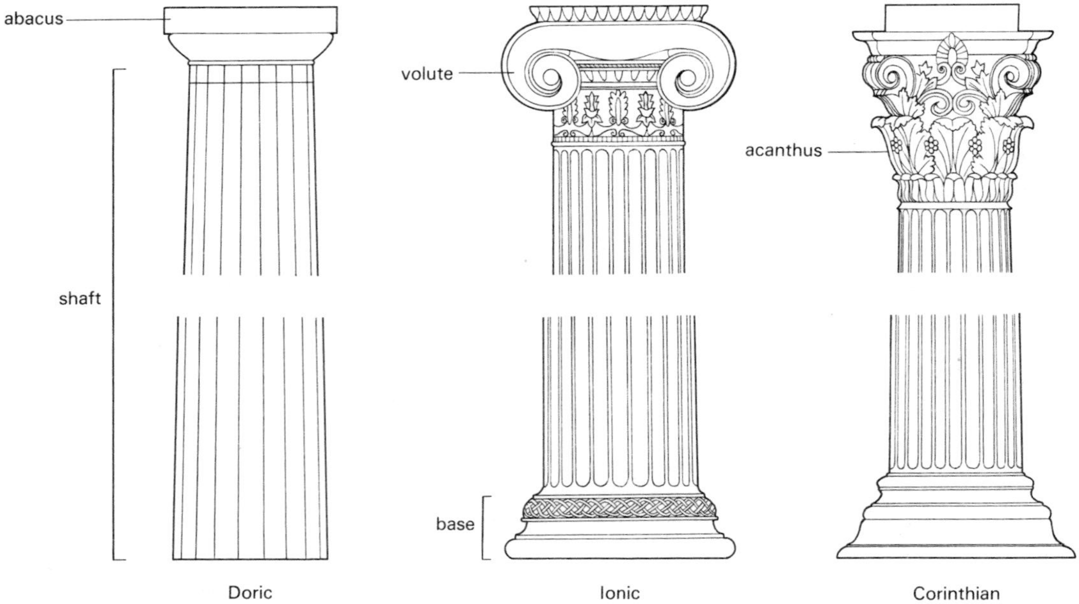

abacus

shaft

volute

acanthus

base

Doric

Ionic

Corinthian

Temples and treasuries at Delphi

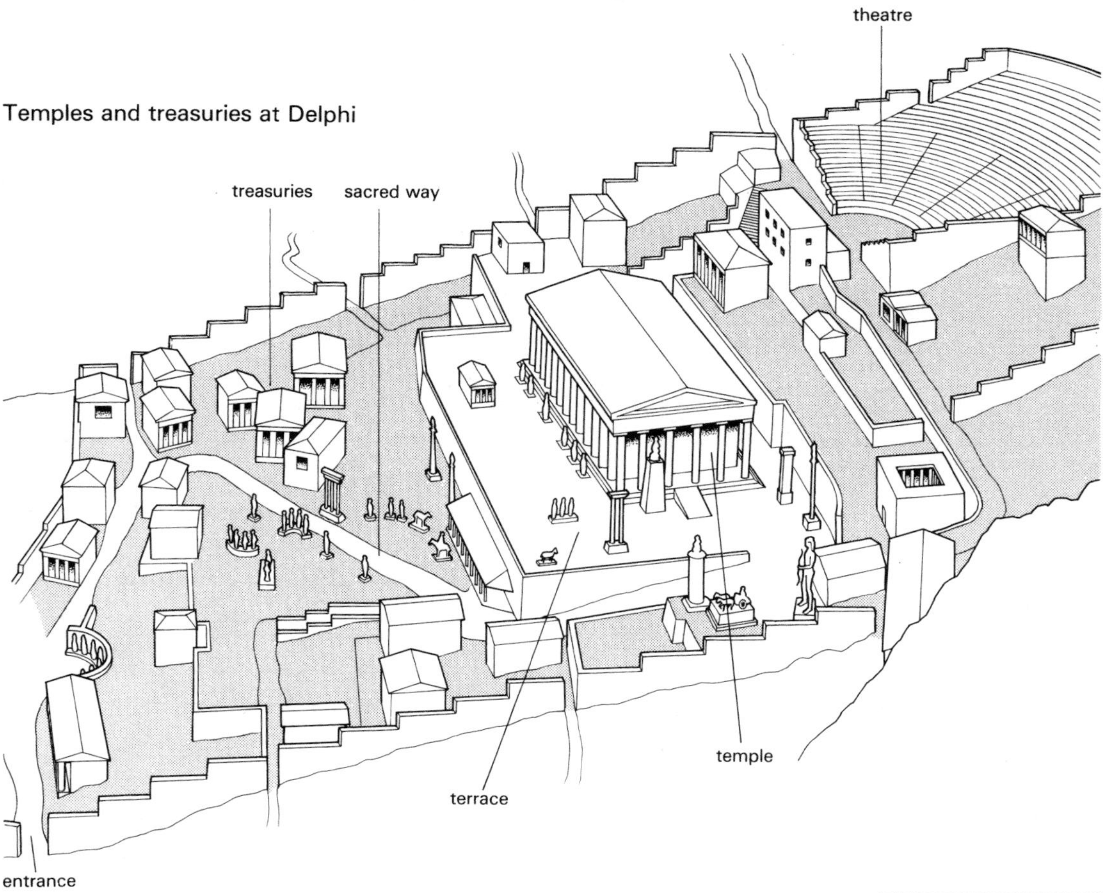

theatre

treasuries   sacred way

temple

terrace

entrance

Orders of architecture: Roman origin

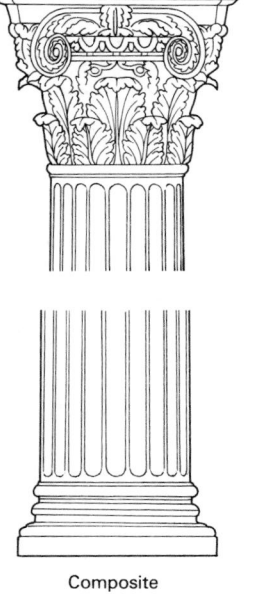

Composite

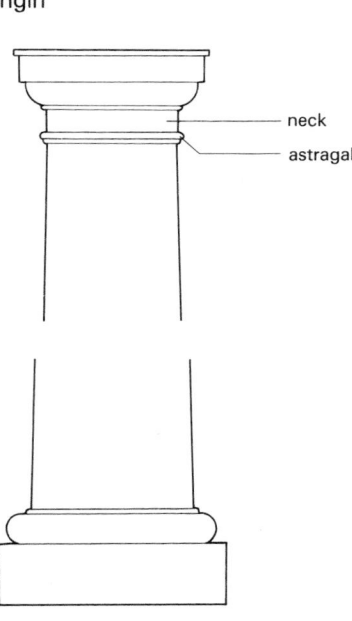

neck

astragal

Tuscan

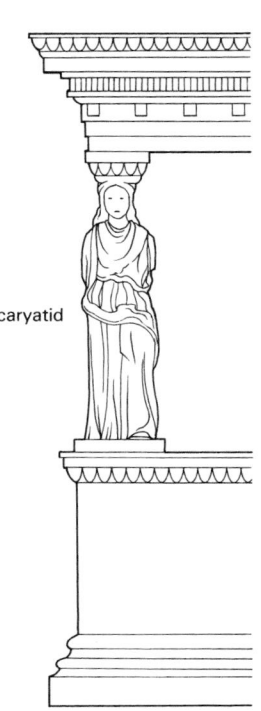

caryatid

to act so as to gain time; to comply temporarily with the requirements of an occasion. —**temporization** /-ˈzeɪʃ(ə)n/ n., **temporizer** n. [f. F f. L (as prec.)]

tempt v.t. **1.** to entice or incite to do a wrong or forbidden thing. **2.** to arouse a desire in, to attract. **3.** to risk provoking (fate or Providence) by deliberate rashness. —**be tempted to,** to be strongly disposed to. —**tempter** n., **temptress** n. fem. [f. OF f. L temptare test]

temptation /tempˈteɪʃ(ə)n/ n. **1.** tempting, being tempted; an incitement, especially to wrongdoing. **2.** an attractive thing or course of action. **3.** (archaic) putting to the test. [as prec.]

tempting adj. attractive, inviting. [f. TEMPT]

ten adj. & n. **1.** one more than nine. **2.** the symbol for this (10, x, X). **3.** a size etc. denoted by ten. [OE]

tenable /ˈtenəb(ə)l/ adj. **1.** that can be maintained against attack or objection. **2.** (of an office etc.) that can be held for a specified period or by a specified class of person. — **tenability** /-ˈbɪlɪtɪ/ n. [F (tenir hold f. L tenēre)]

tenacious /tɪˈneɪʃəs/ adj. **1.** keeping a firm hold (of property, principles, life, etc.). **2.** (of memory) retentive. **3.** holding tightly, not easily separable; tough. —**tenaciously** adv., **tenacity** /tɪˈnæsɪtɪ/ n. [f. L tenax (tenēre hold)]

tenancy n. occupancy as a tenant. [f. foll.]

tenant /ˈtenənt/ n. a person who rents land or property from a landlord; the occupant of a place. —**tenant farmer,** one farming hired land. [f. OF (as TENABLE)]

tenantry n. the tenants of an estate etc. [f. prec.]

tench n. (pl. same) a European freshwater fish (Tinca tinca) of the carp family. [f. OF f. L tinca]

tend[1] v.i. **1.** to be likely to behave in a specified way or to have a specified characteristic or influence. **2.** to take a specified direction (lit. or fig.). [f. OF f. L tendere stretch]

tend[2] v.t. to take care of, to look after. [f. ATTEND]

tendency /ˈtendənsɪ/ n. **1.** the way a person or thing tends to be or behave. **2.** the direction in which something moves or changes, a trend. [f. L (as TEND[1])]

tendentious /tenˈdenʃəs/ adj. (derog., of a speech or piece of writing etc.) designed to advance a cause, not impartial. —**tendentiously** adv., **tendentiousness** n. [as prec.]

tender[1] adj. **1.** easily cut or chewed, not tough. **2.** easily hurt or wounded, susceptible to pain or grief; delicate, fragile, sensitive. **3.** loving, gentle. **4.** requiring tact. **5.** (of age) early, immature. —**tender spot,** a subject on which one is touchy. —**tenderly** adv., **tenderness** n. [f. OF f. L tener]

tender[2] v.t./i. **1.** to make an offer of or present for acceptance. **2.** to send in a tender for the execution of work etc. — n. an offer, especially in writing, to execute work or supply goods at a stated price. —**put out to tender,** to seek offers in respect of (work etc.). [f. OF tendre (as TEND[1])]

tender[3] n. **1.** one who looks after people or things. **2.** a vessel attending a larger one and carrying stores etc. **3.** a truck attached to a steam locomotive and carrying coal etc. [f. TEND[2]]

tenderfoot n. a newcomer who is unused to hardships, an inexperienced person.

tenderize v.t. to make tender; to make (meat) tender by beating etc. —**tenderizer** n. [f. TENDER[1]]

tenderloin n. **1.** the middle part of pork loin. **2.** (US) the undercut of a sirloin.

tendon /ˈtend(ə)n/ n. a band or cord of strong tissue attaching a muscle to a bone etc. (ill. BODY 2). [F or f. L f. Gk tenōn sinew (teinō stretch)]

tendril /ˈtendrɪl/ n. any of the slender leafless shoots by which some climbing plants cling. [prob. f. obs. F tendrillon (tendron young shoot f. L, as TENDER[1])]

tenement /ˈtenɪmənt/ n. **1.** a piece of land held by an owner; (Law) any kind of permanent property held by a tenant. **2.** a flat or room rented as a dwelling-place. **3.** (Sc.) a house divided into and let in tenements. [f. OF f. L (tenēre hold)]

Tenerife /tenəˈriːf/ a volcanic island which is the largest of the Canary Islands, pop. (est., 1978) 664,417; capital, Santa Cruz.

tenet /ˈtenɪt/ n. a doctrine held by a group or person. [L, = he holds (as prec.)]

tenfold /ˈtenfəʊld/ adj. & adv. ten times as much or as many; consisting of ten parts. [f. TEN + -FOLD]

Teniers /ˈtenɪəz/, David (1610–90), Flemish painter known as the Younger in distinction from his father, David the

Elder (1582–1649). A wide-ranging and prolific artist, he worked in Antwerp and Brussels and is best known for his peasant scenes in the style of Brouwer, and scenes of everyday life. In 1651 he was appointed court painter to Archduke Leopold Wilhelm, and was much admired by Philip IV of Spain. The sensitivity and sureness of touch in his paintings was influential until well into the 19th c.

tenner n. (colloq.) a £10 note. [f. TEN]

Tennessee /tenɪˈsiː/ a State in the central south-eastern USA, ceded by Britain to the USA in 1783. It became the 16th State in 1796; capital, Nashville.

Tenniel /ˈtenɪəl/, Sir John (1820–1914), English draughtsman, known chiefly for his work as an illustrator for Lewis Carroll's Alice books. He also worked prolifically for Punch between 1851 and 1901 as a cartoonist.

tennis /ˈtenɪs/ n. **1.** lawn tennis (see LAWN). **2.** (also **real, royal,** or (US) **court tennis**) an indoor game for two or four persons in which a small solid ball is struck with rackets over a net, or rebounds from side walls, in a walled court. A net divides the court into equal but dissimilar halves: the service side, from which service is always delivered, and the hazard side, on which service is received. A similar game was played in monastery cloisters in the 11th c., and early references associate tennis with the clergy. From the Church it spread to the Crown, and became a royal and aristocratic game which spread from France to the rest of Europe. At first it was played with a bare (or gloved) hand, and development to the present sophisticated racket was gradual. Crude wooden boards were followed by the short-handled bat, at first of solid wood, later covered with parchment like a drum. The long-handled racket, strung with sheep's intestines, was not invented until c. 1500. Until c.1700 the stringing was diagonal, and only in 1875 was it strengthened by threading the cross-strings through the main strings, which greatly increased the pace of the game. Its popularity declined partly because of the need for special courts, whose owners found it more profitable to hire them out as theatres: when Molière went on tour in the provinces he acted in tennis courts, and the French theatre still retains the shape of a tennis court. [f. F tenez take, receive, called by server to his opponent]

Tennyson /ˈtenɪs(ə)n/, Alfred, 1st Baron Tennyson (1809–92), English poet, educated by his father, a Lincolnshire rector, and at Cambridge University, where he met A. H. Hallam whose death (1833) he mourned in his greatest work, In Memoriam (1850), which expresses his own anxieties about immortality, change, and evolution. His early volumes of poetry include 'Mariana', 'The Lotos-Eaters', 'The Lady of Shalott', and 'Morte d'Arthur' (1842), the germ of his later Idylls of the King (1859), a series of twelve poems of Arthurian legend. By the middle of the century he was firmly established as the voice of his age, Prince Albert and Queen Victoria being among his admirers, and was made Poet Laureate in 1850. His many later works are the narrative poem Enoch Arden (1864) and several dramas of which Becket (1884) appeared in the year he was made a peer. His reputation in the early 20th c. declined but he is now widely acknowledged for his masterly metrical skill and lyrical genius.

tenon /ˈtenən/ n. a projection shaped to fit into a mortise (ill. CARPENTRY). —**tenon-saw** n. a small saw with a strong brass or steel back, used for fine work (ill. CARPENTRY). [f. F (tenir hold f. L tenēre)]

tenor /ˈtenə(r)/ n. **1.** the highest ordinary adult male singing-voice (see below); a singer with this; a part written for it. **2.** a musical instrument with approximately the range of a tenor voice. **3.** the general routine or course of something. **4.** the general meaning or drift. [f. AF f. L tenor (tenēre hold)]

In music before the 16th c. tenor referred to a voice part (rather than a voice), so called because it formed the basis of a composition, 'holding' a melody (usually pre-existing) against which the other voices were composed. Later, the tenor became the highest male voice using normal voice production, with a range of about two octaves.

tenpin bowling a form of skittles similar to ninepins (see BOWLING).

tense[1] adj. **1.** stretched tightly. **2.** with muscles tight in attentiveness for what may happen; unable to relax, edgy. **3.** causing tenseness. —v.t./i. to make or become tense. —**tensely** adv., **tenseness** n. [f.L tensus (as TEND[1])]

tense[2] n. the form taken by a word to indicate the time (also continuance or completeness) of an action; a set of such forms. In Indo-European languages tense is limited to verbs, but in Japanese, for example, adjectives show tense inflections. [f. OF f. L *tempus* time]

tensile /ˈtensaɪl/ *adj.* **1.** of tension. **2.** capable of being stretched. —**tensile strength,** resistance to breaking under tension. —**tensility** /-ˈsɪlɪtɪ/ *n.* [f. L *tensilis* (as TEND¹)]

tension /ˈtenʃ(ə)n/ *n.* **1.** stretching, being stretched. **2.** tenseness, the condition when feelings are tense. **3.** the effect produced by forces pulling against each other. **4.** electromotive force. **5.** (in knitting) the number of stitches and rows to a unit of measurement. [F or f. L (as TEND¹)]

tent *n.* **1.** a portable shelter or dwelling of canvas or cloth etc. supported by poles and by ropes attached to pegs driven into the ground. **2.** a cover etc. resembling a tent. [as TEND¹]

tentacle /ˈtentək(ə)l/ *n.* **1.** a long slender flexible appendage of an animal, used for feeling or grasping things or for moving. **2.** a thing compared to a tentacle in use. —**tentacled** *adj.* [f. L *tentare* = *temptare* (as TEMPT)]

tentative /ˈtentətɪv/ *adj.* done as a trial, hesitant, not definite. —**tentatively** *adv.* [as prec.]

tenter *n.* a machine for stretching cloth to dry in shape. [f. L *tentorium* (as TEND¹).

tenterhooks *n.pl.* hooks to which cloth is fastened on a tenter. —**on tenterhooks,** in a state of suspense or strain because of uncertainty.

tenth *adj.* next after the ninth. —*n.* each of ten equal parts of a thing. —**tenthly** *adv.* [f. TEN]

tenuous /ˈtenjʊəs/ *adj.* **1.** having little substance or validity, very slight. **2.** very thin in form or consistency. —**tenuity** /-ˈjuːɪtɪ/ *n.*, **tenuously** *adv.*, **tenuousness** *n.* [f. L *tenuis*]

tenure /ˈtenjə(r)/ *n.* the holding of office or of land or other permanent property or of accommodation etc.; the period or condition of this. [f. OF (as TENABLE)]

Tenzing Norgay /ˈtensɪŋ ˈnɔːgeɪ/ (1914–86), Sherpa mountaineer who, with Sir Edmund Hillary, was the first to reach the summit of Mount Everest (1953).

Teotihuacán /teɪəʊtɪwəˈkɑːn/ the largest city of pre-Columban America, about 50 km (33 miles) north-east of Mexico City. Built *c.*300 BC it reached its zenith *c.* AD 300–600, when it was the centre of an influential culture, but by 650 it had declined as a major power and was sacked by the invading Toltec *c.*750. Among its monuments are palatial buildings, plazas, and temples, including the Pyramid of the Sun and of the Moon and the temple of Quetzalcóatl.

tepee /ˈtiːpiː/ *n.* a North American Indian conical tent. [f. Dakota *típí*]

tepid /ˈtepɪd/ *adj.* **1.** slightly warm, lukewarm. **2.** unenthusiastic. —**tepidity** /tɪˈpɪdɪtɪ/ *n.*, **tepidly** *adv.* [f. L *tepidus* (*tepēre* be lukewarm)]

tequila /teˈkiːlə/ *n.* a Mexican liquor made from agave. [f. *Tequila* in Mexico]

tera- /ˈterə-/ *in comb.* one million million. [f. Gk *teras* monster]

terbium /ˈtɜːbɪəm/ *n.* a metallic element of the lanthanide series, symbol Tb, atomic number 65, first discovered in 1843. It has few commercial uses. [as YTTERBIUM]

tercel /ˈtɜːs(ə)l/ *n.* a male hawk. [f. OF, ult. f. L *tertius* third, because believed to come from third egg of clutch]

tercentenary /tɜːsenˈtiːnərɪ/ *n.* a three-hundredth anniversary; a celebration of this. [f. L *ter* thrice + CENTENARY]

terebinth /ˈterɪbɪnθ/ *n.* a South European tree (*Pistacia terebinthus*) yielding turpentine. [f. OF or L f. Gk *terebinthos*]

teredo /teˈriːdəʊ/ *n.* (*pl.* **-os**) a mollusc of the genus *Teredo* that bores into submerged timber. [L f. Gk *terēdōn* (*teirō* rub hard, bore)]

Terence /ˈterəns/ (Publius Terentius Afer, *c.*190–159 BC) Roman comic playwright, originally a slave from North Africa, the author of six comedies based on models from Greek comedy. His plays, all set in Athens, are marked by realism in character and language, consistency of plot, and an urbanity quite different from the extravagance of Plautus. He is an important ancestor of the modern 'comedy of manners'.

Teresa /təˈriːzə/, Mother (1910–), Roman Catholic nun, born in Yugoslavia, founder of an order (Missionaries of Charity) which is noted for its work among the poor and the dying in Calcutta, India, and throughout the world. She was awarded the Nobel Peace Prize in 1979.

Teresa of Ávila /təˈriːzə, ˈævɪlə/, St (1515–82), Spanish Carmelite nun and mystic. Her importance is twofold. As the reformer of the Carmelite Order her work has survived

in the great number of discalced monasteries which venerate her as their foundress; she was a woman of strong character, shrewdness, and great practical ability. As a spiritual writer her influence was epoch-making, giving a description of the entire life of prayer from meditation to the so-called 'mystic marriage' or union with God. Her combination of mystic experience with ceaseless activity as a reformer and organizer make her life the classical instance for those who contend that the highest contemplation is not incompatible with great practical achievements.

Teresa of Lisieux /təˈriːsə, liːzɪˈɜː/, St (1873–97), French Carmelite nun. After her death from tuberculosis her cult grew through the circulation of her autobiography, *L'Histoire d'une âme,* teaching that sanctity can be attained through continual renunciation in small matters, and not only through extreme self-mortification.

tergiversation /tɜːdʒɪvəˈseɪʃ(ə)n/ *n.* a change of party or principles, apostasy; the making of conflicting statements. [f. L (*tergum* the back, *vertere* turn)]

term *n.* **1.** a word used to express a definite concept, especially in a branch of study etc. **2.** (in *pl.*) language used, a mode of expression. **3.** (in *pl.*) a relation between people. **4.** (in *pl.*) conditions offered or accepted; stipulations. **5.** (in *pl.*) the charge or price. **6.** a limited period of some state or activity; a period of action or of contemplated results; a period during which instruction is given in a school or university, or during which a lawcourt holds sessions. **7.** a word or words that may be the subject or predicate of a logical proposition. **8.** (*Math.*) each quantity in a ratio or series; an item of a compound algebraic expression. **9.** (*archaic*) an appointed limit. —*v.t.* to call by a specified term or expression. —**come to terms,** to reach agreement; to reconcile oneself (with a difficulty etc.). **in terms of,** in the language peculiar to; using as a basis of expression or thought. **terms of reference,** the points referred to an individual or body of persons for decision or report; the scope of an inquiry etc.; the definition of this. [f. OF f. L, = TERMINUS]

termagant /ˈtɜːməgənt/ *n.* an overbearing woman, a virago. [f. OF *Tervagan* f. It. *Trivigante* imaginary deity of violent character in morality plays]

terminable /ˈtɜːmɪnəb(ə)l/ *adj.* that may be terminated. [f. TERMINATE]

terminal /ˈtɜːmɪn(ə)l/ *adj.* **1.** of or forming the last part or terminus. **2.** forming or undergoing the last stage of a fatal disease. **3.** of or done etc. each term. —*n.* **1.** a terminating thing, an extremity. **2.** a terminus for trains or long-distance buses; an air terminal (see AIR). **3.** a point of connection for closing an electric circuit. **4.** an apparatus for the transmission of messages to and from a computer or communications system etc. —**terminally** *adv.* [f. L (as TERMINUS)]

terminate /ˈtɜːmɪneɪt/ *v.t./i.* to bring or come to an end. —**terminator** *n.* [f. L *terminare* (as TERMINUS)]

termination /tɜːmɪˈneɪʃ(ə)n/ *n.* an ending; the way something ends; a word's final letter(s). [f. OF or L (as prec.)]

terminology /tɜːmɪˈnɒlədʒɪ/ *n.* **1.** the system of terms used in a particular subject. **2.** the science of the proper use of terms. —**terminological** /-nəˈlɒdʒɪk(ə)l/ *adj.* [f. G (as foll., -LOGY)]

terminus /ˈtɜːmɪnəs/ *n.* (*pl.* **-ni** /-naɪ/) **1.** a station at the end of a railway or bus route. **2.** a point at the end of a pipeline etc. [L, = end, boundary]

termite /ˈtɜːmaɪt/ *n.* a small antlike insect of the order Isoptera, destructive of timber (ill. INSECTS). [f. L *termes, tarmes* (*terere* rub)]

tern *n.* a sea-bird of the genus *Sterna*, like a gull but usually smaller and with a forked tail. [of Scand. orig.]

ternary /ˈtɜːnərɪ/ *adj.* composed of three parts. [f. L *ternarius* (*terni* three each)]

terotechnology /tɪərəʊtekˈnɒlədʒɪ, terəʊ-/ *n.* the branch of technology and engineering concerned with the installation, maintenance, and replacement of industrial plant and equipment and with related subjects and practices. [f. Gk *tērō* watch over, take care of + -LOGY]

Terpsichore /tɜːpˈsɪkərɪ/ (*Gk & Rom. myth.*) the Muse of lyric poetry and dance. [Gk, = delighting in dance]

terrace /ˈterəs/ *n.* **1.** a raised level space, natural or artificial, especially for walking, standing, or cultivation. **2.** a row of houses on a raised level or built in one block of uniform style. **3.** a flight of wide shallow steps as for spectators at a sports ground. [OF f. L *terra* earth]

terraced *adj.* formed into or having a terrace or terraces.

—terraced roof, a flat roof especially of an Eastern house. [f. prec.]

terracotta /terə'kɒtə/ n. **1.** an unglazed usually brownish-red pottery used as an ornamental building-material and in statuary. **2.** a statuette of this. **3.** its colour. [It., = baked earth]

terra firma /terə 'fɜːmə/ dry land, firm ground. [L]

terrain /te'reɪn/ n. a tract of land as regards its natural features. [F f. L *terrenus* (as TERRENE)]

terrapin /'terəpɪn/ n. an edible freshwater tortoise of the family Emydidae of North America. [Algonquian]

terrarium /te'reərɪəm/ n. (pl. **-ums**) **1.** a place for keeping small land animals. **2.** a sealed transparent globe etc. containing growing plants. [f. L *terra* earth, after *aquarium*]

terrazzo /tɪ'rætsəʊ/ n. (pl. **-os**) a flooring-material of stone chips set in concrete and given a smooth surface. [It., = terrace]

terrene /te'riːn/ adj. of the earth, earthly; terrestrial. [f. AF f. L *terrenus* (*terra* earth)]

terrestrial /tə'restrɪəl/ adj. of or on the earth; of or on dry land. [f. L *terrestris* (as prec.)]

terrible /'terɪb(ə)l/ adj. **1.** appalling, distressing; causing or fit to cause terror. **2.** (*colloq.*) extreme, hard to bear. **3.** (*colloq.*) very bad or incompetent. **—terribly** adv. [f. F f. L (*terrere* frighten)]

terrier /'terɪə(r)/ n. a small hardy active dog bred originally for turning out foxes etc. from their earths. [f. OF f. L *terrarius* (as TERRENE)]

terrific /tə'rɪfɪk/ adj. **1.** (*colloq.*) of great size or intensity. **2.** (*colloq.*) excellent. **3.** causing terror. **—terrifically** adv. [f. L (*terrere* frighten, *facere* make)]

terrify /'terɪfaɪ/ v.t. to frighten severely. [as prec.]

terrine /tə'riːn/ n. **1.** a pâté or similar food. **2.** an earthenware vessel holding this. [orig. form of TUREEN]

Territorial /terɪ'tɔːrɪəl/ n. a member of the Territorial Army. **—adj.** of a Territory or Territories. **—Territorial Army,** a trained reserve force organized by localities, for use in an emergency. [= foll.]

territorial /terɪ'tɔːrɪəl/ adj. of a territory or districts. **—territorial waters,** the waters under a State's jurisdiction, especially the part of the sea within a stated distance of the shore. **—territorially** adv. [as foll.]

territory /'terɪtərɪ/ n. **1.** the land under the jurisdiction of a ruler, State, or city etc. **2.** *Territory,* a country or area forming part of the USA, Australia, or Canada, but not ranking as a State or province. **3.** an area for which a person has responsibility or over which a salesman etc. operates. **4.** a sphere of action or thought, a province. **5.** an area claimed or dominated by one person or group and defended against others; an area defended by an animal against others of the same species. [f. L (*terra* land)]

terror /'terə(r)/ n. **1.** extreme fear. **2.** a person or thing causing terror; (*colloq.*) a formidable person, a troublesome person or thing. **—the Terror** *or* **Reign of Terror,** the period of the French Revolution between mid-1793 and July 1794 when the ruling Jacobin faction, dominated by Robespierre, ruthlessly executed opponents and anyone else considered a threat to their regime. It ended with the fall and execution of Robespierre, but in its last six weeks more than 1,300 people were guillotined in Paris alone. **terror-stricken** *or* **-struck** adj. affected with terror. [f. OF f. L *terrēre* frighten]

terrorism n. the practice of using violent and intimidating methods, especially to achieve political ends. **—terrorist** n. [f. F (as prec.)]

terrorize v.t. to fill with terror; to coerce by terrorism. **—terrorization** /-'zeɪʃ(ə)n/ n. [f. TERROR]

Terry /'terɪ/, Dame Ellen Alice (1847–1928), English actress. She was already well known when in 1878 Henry Irving engaged her as his leading lady at the Lyceum, beginning a partnership which was to become one of the outstanding features of the London theatrical scene for the next 25 years. She played many Shakespearian roles, notably Ophelia, Beatrice, Desdemona, Juliet, Viola, Lady Macbeth, and Imogen, and (in 1906) Lady Cicely Waynflete in *Captain Brassbound's Conversion,* a part specially written for her by Shaw. She celebrated her stage jubilee in the same year, but thereafter acted very little.

terry /'terɪ/ n. a pile fabric with the loops uncut, used especially for towels. [orig. unkn.]

terse adj. concise, brief and forcible in style; curt. **—tersely** adv., **terseness** n. [f. L *tersus* (*tergēre* wipe)]

tertiary /'tɜːʃərɪ/ adj. **1.** coming after secondary, of the third order or rank etc. **2.** *Tertiary,* of the first period of the Cainozoic era, so called because it follows the Mesozoic, which was formerly also called *Secondary.* It lasted from about 65 to 2 million years ago, and comprises the Palaeocene, Eocene, Oligocene, Miocene, and Pliocene epochs. World temperatures were generally warm except towards the close of the period, and mammals evolved rapidly, becoming the dominant land vertebrates. **—n. 1.** a bird's flight feather of the third row. **2.** a member of the third order of a monastic body. **3.** *Tertiary,* the Tertiary period. [f. L *tertiarius* (*tertius* third)]

Tertullian /tɜː'tʌlɪən/ (Quintus Septimius Floreas Tertullianus, *c.*160–*c.*240) Latin Church Father from Carthage. Converted to Christianity *c.*195, he was the author of many treaties in which he devoted his gifts of rhetoric and irony to the defence of Christianity and the castigation of pagan idolatry and Gnostic heresy. His enthusiasm for the martyrs, and his puritanism, were intensified when he joined the Montanists.

Terylene /'terɪliːn/ n. [P] a synthetic polyester used as a textile fibre. [f. *terephthalic* acid + ETHYLENE]

tesla /'teslə/ n. the unit of magnetic flux density, = 10,000 gauss. [f. N. *Tesla* Amer. scientist (d. 1943)]

tessellated /'tesəleɪtɪd/ adj. of or resembling a mosaic; having a finely chequered surface. [f. L (*tessella* dim. of TESSERA)]

tessellation /tesə'leɪʃ(ə)n/ n. an arrangement of polygons without gaps or overlapping, especially in a repeating pattern. [f. L *tessellare* (*tessella* dim. of foll.)]

tessera /'tesərə/ n. (pl. **-ae** /-iː/) each of the small cubes or blocks of which a mosaic consists (ill. ARCHAEOLOGY). [L, f Gk *tessares* four]

test[1] n. **1.** a critical examination or trial of a person's or thing's qualities. **2.** the means, standard, or circumstances suitable for or serving such an examination. **3.** a minor examination, especially in a school. **4.** (*colloq.*) a test match. **—v.t. 1.** to subject to a test. **2.** to try severely, to tax. **3.** (*Chem.*) to examine by means of a reagent. **—put to the test,** to cause to undergo a test. **stand the test,** not to fail or incur rejection. **test case,** a case whose decision is taken as settling other cases involving the same question of law. **test match,** a cricket or Rugby match between the teams of certain countries, usually one of a series in a tour. **test paper,** an examination paper used in a test; (*Chem.*) a paper impregnated with a substance changing colour under known conditions. **test pilot,** a pilot who tests the performance of newly designed aircraft. **test-tube** n. a thin glass tube closed at one end used for chemical tests etc. **test-tube baby,** (*colloq.*) a baby developed from an ovum fertilized outside the mother's body. **—tester** n. [f. OF f. L *testu(m)* earthen pot (as foll.)]

test[2] n. the hard continuous shell of some invertebrates. [f. L *testa* tile, shell, etc.; cf. prec.]

testa /'testə/ n. (pl. **testae** /-iː/) a seed-coat. [L (as prec.)]

testaceous /te'steɪʃəs/ adj. having a hard continuous shell. [as prec.]

testacy /'testəsɪ/ n. being testate. [f. TESTATE]

testament /'testəmənt/ n. **1.** (usu. **last will and testament**) a will. **2.** (*colloq.*) a written statement of one's beliefs etc. **3.** a covenant, a dispensation; *Testament,* a portion of the Bible (see OLD, NEW TESTAMENT). [f. L *testamentum* will (as TESTATE); in early Christian Latin rendering Gk *diathēkē* covenant]

testamentary /testə'mentərɪ/ adj. of, by, or in a will. [as prec.]

testate /'testeɪt/ adj. having left a valid will at death. **—n.** a testate person. [f. L (*testari* testify f. *testis* witness)]

testator /te'steɪtə(r)/ n. a person who has made a will, especially one who dies testate. **—testatrix** n.fem. [f. AF f. L (as prec.)]

tester n. a canopy, especially over a four-poster bed. [f. L (*testa* file)]

testicle /'testɪk(ə)l/ n. the male organ that secretes spermatozoa etc., especially one of the pair in the scrotum behind the penis of man and most mammals (ill. BODY 2). [f. L *testiculus* dim. of *testis* witness (or of virility)]

testify /'testɪfaɪ/ v.t./i. to bear witness; to give evidence; to declare; to be evidence of. [f. L (*testis* witness, *facere* make)]

testimonial /testɪ'məʊnɪəl/ n. **1.** a certificate of character, conduct, or qualifications. **2.** a gift presented to a person (esp. in public) as a mark of esteem. [f. OF or L (as foll.)]

testimony /'testɪmənɪ/ n. **1.** a declaration of statement (written or spoken), especially one made under oath. **2.** evidence in support of something. [f. L (*testis* witness)]

testis *n.* (*pl.* **testes**/-i:z/) a testicle. [L, prob. = *testis* witness (cf. TESTICLE)]

testosterone /te'stɒstərəʊn/ *n.* a male sex hormone produced in the testicles and (in very much smaller quantities) in the ovaries and adrenal cortex. [f. prec. + STEROL]

testy *adj.* irascible, short-tempered —**testily** *adv.*, **testiness** *n.* [f. AF *testif* (*teste* head, as TEST²)]

tetanus /'tetənəs/ *n.* a bacterial disease with a continuous painful contraction of some or all voluntary muscles. [L f. Gk *tetanos* (*teinō* stretch)]

tetchy /'tetʃɪ/ *adj.* peevish, irritable, touchy. —**tetchily** *adv.*, **tetchiness** *n.* [prob. f. obs. *tecche*, *tache* blemish, fault, OF]

tête-à-tête /teɪtɑ:'teɪt/ *n.* a private conversation or interview, usually between two persons. —*adv.* & *adj.* together in private. [F, lit. head-to-head]

tether /'teðə(r)/ *n.* a rope or chain by which an animal is tied while grazing. —*v.t.* to tie with a tether. —**at the end of one's tether**, having reached the limit of one's patience or endurance etc. [f. ON]

tetra /tetrə-/ *in comb.* four. [Gk (*tessares* four)]

tetrad /'tetræd/ *n.* a group of four. [f. Gk (as prec.)]

tetragon /'tetrəgən/ *n.* a plane figure with four sides and angles. —**tetragonal** /-'rægən(ə)l/ *adj.* [f. Gk (TETRA-, *-gōnos* -angled)]

tetrahedron /tetrə'hi:drən/ *n.* a four-sided solid, a triangular pyramid (ill. SHAPES). —**tetrahedral** *adj.* [f. Gk (TETRA-, *hedra* base)]

tetralogy /te'trælədʒɪ/ *n.* a group of four related literary or dramatic works. [f. Gk (as TETRA-, -LOGY)]

tetrameter /te'træmɪtə(r)/ *n.* a line of verse of four measures. [f. L Gk (TETRA-, *metron* measure)]

Teuton /'tju:t(ə)n/ *n.* **1.** a member of a Teutonic nation, especially a German. **2.** a member of a north-European tribe mentioned in the 4th c. BC and combining with others to carry out raids on NE and southern France during the Roman period until heavily defeated in 102 BC. [f. L f. Indo-European, = people, country]

Teutonic /tju:'tɒnɪk/ *adj.* **1.** of the Teutons. **2.** of the Germanic peoples or their languages. **3.** German. [as prec.]

Texas /'teksəs/ a State in the southern USA, bordering on the Gulf of Mexico. The area was opened up by Spanish explorers (16th-17th c.) and formed part of Mexico until it became an independent republic in 1836 and the 28th State of the USA in 1845; capital, Austin.

text *n.* **1.** the main body of a book or page etc. as distinct from the notes, illustrations, appendices, etc. **2.** the original words of an author or document, especially as distinct from a paraphrase or commentary. **3.** a passage of Scripture quoted or used as the subject of a sermon etc.; a subject, a theme. **4.** (in *pl.*) books prescribed for study. [f. OF f. L *textus* (*texere* weave)]

textbook *n.* a book of information for use in studying a subject. —*adj.* exemplary, accurate; instructively typical.

textile /'tekstaɪl/ *n.* a woven or machine-knitted fabric. —*adj.* of weaving; woven. [f. L *textilis* (as TEXT)]

textual /'tekstjʊəl/ *adj.* of, in, or concerning a text. —**textually** *adv.* [f. L (as TEXT)]

texture /'tekstʃə(r)/ *n.* the quality of a surface or substance when felt or looked at; the arrangement of threads in a textile fabric. —**textural** *adj.*, **texturally** *adv.* [f. L *textura* (as TEXT)]

textured *adj.* **1.** having a specified texture. **2.** provided with a texture, not smooth or plain. [f. prec.]

Thackeray /'θækəreɪ/, William Makepeace (1811-63), English novelist, no cynic but a satirist, born in Calcutta and educated in England. After leaving Cambridge University (where he made friends with Tennyson and others) without a degree, he entered London literary society as a journalist and illustrator, publishing a variety of works in periodicals. The turning point of his career came with his masterpiece, *Vanity Fair* (1847-8; illustrated by the author), a vivid portrayal of early 19th-c. society, satirizing the pretentions of the upper-middle classes through its central character, the socially ambitious, unscrupulous, low-born Becky Sharp. He consolidated his success with *Pendennis* (1848-50), *The Newcomes* (1853-5), *Henry Esmond* (1852), a virtuoso historical novel set in the 18th c., and its sequel *The Virginians* (1857-9), and *The Rose and the Ring* (1855), one of his Christmas books. In 1860 he became the first editor

of the *Cornhill Magazine* in which appeared many of his later novels.

Thai /taɪ/ *adj.* of Thailand or its people or language. —*n.* **1.** a native or inhabitant of Thailand. **2.** the language of Thailand, a tonal language of the Sino-Tibetan language group, spoken by 35 million people. [Thai, = free]

Thailand /'taɪlænd/ a country in SE Asia on the Gulf of Thailand, with Burma on its western border; pop. (est. 1983) 49,459,000; official language, Thai; capital, Bangkok. The country was known as Siam until 1939, when it changed its name to Thailand (lit. = 'land of the free'). Its early history is uncertain. For centuries Thais had filtered into the area and by the 13th c. had established a number of principalities in what is now Thailand and in adjacent regions. A powerful kingdom emerged in the 14th c. and engaged in a series of wars with its neighbour Burma before increasing exposure to European powers in the 19th c. resulted in the loss of territory in the east to France and in the south to Britain, though Thailand itself succeeded in retaining its independence. Politically unstable for much of the 20th c., Thailand was occupied by the Japanese in the Second World War, and supported the USA in the Vietnam campaign; it has recently had border difficulties with Cambodia (Kampuchea). The country is the world's largest exporter of rice, but mining and industry also play an important role in its economy. —**Thailander** *n.*

thalamus /'θæləməs/ *n.* (*pl.* **-mi** /-maɪ/) the interior region of the brain where the sensory nerves originate (ill. BODY 3). [L f. Gk, = inner room]

Thales /'θeɪli:z/ (early 6th c. BC) Greek philosopher from Miletus in Ionia, universally accounted one of the Seven Sages. Aristotle held him to be the founder of physical science; he is also credited with the founding of geometry. Seeking a primary substance from which all things are derived, he identified this substance as water, and represented the earth as floating on an underlying ocean; his cosmology had Egyptian and Semitic affinities.

Thalia /θə'laɪə/ (*Gk & Rom. myth.*) the Muse of comedy. [Gk, = rich, plentiful]

thalidomide /θə'lɪdəmaɪd/ *n.* a sedative drug found in 1961 to have caused malformation of the limbs of the embryo when taken by the mother early in pregnancy. [f. ph*thal*imidoglutari*mide*]

thallium /'θælɪəm/ *n.* a rare soft white metallic element, symbol Tl, atomic number 81, discovered spectroscopically by Sir William Crookes in 1861. Its compounds were formerly used as insecticides and rat poison and have some use in specialized optical and infra-red equipment. [f. Gk *thallos* green shoot (from the green line in its spectrum)]

Thames /temz/ a river of southern England, flowing eastwards 338 km (210 miles) from the Cotswolds in Gloucestershire through London to the North Sea. A flood barrier across the river to protect London from high tides was completed in 1982.

than /ðən, *emphat.* ðæn/ *conj.* introducing the second element in a comparison (*you are taller than he (is)*; *we like you better than her*), or a statement of difference (*anyone other than me*). [OE, orig. = THEN]

thane *n.* **1.** (in Anglo-Saxon England) one who held land from the king or other superior in return for performing military service. **2.** (in Scotland until the 15th c.) one who held land from a Scottish king and ranked below an earl, a clan-chief. [OE, = servant, soldier]

thank *v.t.* **1.** to express gratitude to. **2.** to hold responsible. —*n.* (in *pl.*) gratitude, an expression of gratitude; (as a formula) thank you. —**thank goodness** *or* **heavens** etc., (*colloq.*) expressions of relief etc. **thank you,** a polite formula acknowledging a gift or service etc. [OE (rel. to THINK)]

thankful *adj.* feeling or expressing gratitude. —**thankfully** *adv.*, **thankfulness** *n.* [f. THANK + -FUL]

thankless *adj.* not likely to win thanks, giving no pleasure or profit. —**thanklessly** *adv.*, **thanklessness** *n.* [f. THANK + -LESS]

thanksgiving *n.* the expression of gratitude, especially to God. —**Thanksgiving (Day),** an annual holiday for giving thanks to God, the fourth Thursday in November in the USA, usually the second Monday in October in Canada. A festival of this kind was first held by Plymouth Colony in 1621 in thankfulness for a successful harvest after a year of hardship. Turkey and pumpkin pie are traditionally eaten.

that /ðət, *emphat.* ðæt/ *pron.* (*pl.* **those** /ðəʊz/) **1.** the person or thing indicated, named, or understood. **2.** the further or less obvious one of two (opp. *this*). **3.** (as *relative pron.*) used instead of *which* or *who* to introduce a defining clause. —*adj.* (*pl.* **those**) designating the person or thing indicated etc. —*adv.* to that degree or extent, so. —*conj.* introducing a dependent clause, especially a statement or hypothesis, purpose, or result. —**all that**, very. **that's that**, that is settled or finished. [OE]

thatch *n.* **1.** roofing of straw, or reeds, or similar material. **2.** (*colloq.*) the hair of the head. —*v.t.* to roof with thatch. —**thatcher** *n.* [OE, = OHG *dach* roof]

Thatcher /ˈθætʃə(r)/, Margaret Hilda (1925–), British stateswoman. She became leader of the Conservative Party in 1975 and the first woman Prime Minister of the UK in 1979.

thaw *v.t./i.* **1.** to pass into a liquid or unfrozen state after being frozen. **2.** to become warm enough to melt ice etc. or to lose numbness. **3.** to become less cool or less formal in manner. **4.** to cause to thaw. —*n.* thawing; warmth of weather that thaws ice etc. [OE]

the /*before a vowel* ðɪ; *before a consonant* ðə; *emphat.* ðiː/ —*adj.* serving to particularize as needing no further identification (*have you seen the newspaper?*), to describe as unique (*the Queen; the Thames*), to assist in defining with an adjective (*Alfred the Great*) or (stressed) distinguish as the best-known (*do you mean the Kipling?*), to indicate a following defining clause or phrase (*the horse you mention*); to confer generic or representative or distributive value on (*diseases of the eye; the stage; 5p in the pound*); or to precede an adjective used *absol.* (*nothing but the best*). —*adv.* (preceding comparatives in expressions of proportional variation) in or by that (or such) degree, on that account (*the more the merrier; am not the more inclined to help him because he is poor*). [OE (as THAT)]

theatre /ˈθɪətə(r)/ *n.* **1.** a building or outdoor area for the performance of plays and similar entertainments (see ill. p. 853 and TEMPLES). **2.** the writing and production of plays. **3.** a room or hall for lectures etc. with seats in tiers. **4.** an operating theatre. —**theatre-in-the-round** *n.* a form of play presentation in which the audience is seated all round the acting area. One of the earliest forms of theatre, it was probably used for open-air performances, street theatres, and such rustic sports as the May Day games and the mummers' play. It was revived in the 20th c.— beginning in the Soviet Union in the 1930s—by those who rebelled against the proscenium arch. **Theatre of the Absurd**, the name given to the works of a group of dramatists, including Beckett, Ionesco, and Pinter, who share the belief that man's life is without meaning or purpose and that human beings cannot communicate. Such dramatists abandoned conventional dramatic form and coherent dialogue, the futility of existence being conveyed by illogical and meaningless speeches and ultimately by complete silence. The first and perhaps most characteristic play in this style was Beckett's *Waiting for Godot* (1952). **theatre weapons**, weapons intermediate between tactical and strategic (see STRATEGIC). [f. OF or L f. Gk *theatron* (*theaomai* behold)]

theatrical /θɪˈætrɪk(ə)l/ *adj.* **1.** of or for the theatre or acting. **2.** (of a person or manner etc.) calculated for effect, showy. —*n.* (in *pl.*) dramatic performances (esp. amateur) or behaviour —**theatricality** /-ˈkælɪtɪ/ *n.*, **theatrically** *adv.* [f. L f. Gk (as prec.)]

Thebes /θiːbz/ **1.** the Greek name for a city of Upper Egypt, about 675 km (420 miles) south of modern Cairo, that was the capital of ancient Egypt under the 18th Dynasty (*c.*1550–1290 BC). Its monuments (on both banks of the Nile) were the richest in the land, with the town and major temples at Luxor and Karnak on the east bank, and the necropolis, with tombs of royalty and nobles, on the west bank. It was already a tourist attraction in the 2nd c. AD. **2.** a city of Greece, about 74 km (46 miles) NW of Athens, leader of the whole of Greece for a short period in the 4th c. BC. —**Theban** *adj. & n.*

thee /ðiː/ *pron.* the objective case of THOU.

theft *n.* stealing; an act or instance of this. [OE (as THIEF)]

their /ðeə(r)/ *poss. adj.* of or belonging to them. [f. ON]

theirs /ðeəz/ *poss. pron.* of or belonging to them; the thing(s) belonging to them. [f. THEIR]

theism /ˈθiːɪz(ə)m/ *n.* belief in the existence of gods or a god, especially a God supernaturally revealed to man (*deism* denies such revelation) and maintaining a personal relation to his creatures. —**theist** *n.*, **theistic** /-ˈɪstɪk/ *adj.* [f. Gk *theos* god]

them /ð(ə)m, *emphat.* ðem/ *pron.* the objective case of THEY; (*colloq.*) they. —*adj.* (*vulgar*) those. [f. ON]

theme /θiːm/ *n.* **1.** the subject or topic of talk, writing, or thought. **2.** (*Mus.*) the leading melody in a composition. **3.** (*US*) a school exercise on a given subject. —**theme song** or **tune**, a recurrent melody in a musical play or film; a signature tune. —**thematic** /θɪˈmætɪk/ *adj.*, **thematically** /θɪˈmætɪkəlɪ/ *adv.* [f. L f. Gk *thema* (*tithēmi* place)]

Themis /ˈθemɪs/ (*Gk myth.*) a goddess originally akin to or even identical with Ge (Earth). Her name probably means 'steadfast'. In Hesiod she is a daughter of Earth and is Zeus's second consort, but, as her name is used also to mean 'firmly established custom or law, justice', she tends to become an abstraction, Justice or Righteousness.

Themistocles /θɪˈmɪstəkliːz/ (*c.*528–462 BC) Athenian democratic statesman who was instrumental in building up the Athenian fleet in the 480s BC, and as a general in 480 BC was responsible for the defeat of the Persian fleet at Salamis. In the following years he lost influence to his conservative opponents, and was ostracized; eventually he fled from Greece to the Persians in Asia Minor, where he died.

themselves /ðəmˈselvz/ *pron.* emphat. & refl. form of THEY and THEM. [f. THEM + pl. of SELF]

then /ðen/ *adv.* **1.** at that time. **2.** next, after that, and also. **3.** in that case, therefore. **4.** used to imply grudging or impatient concession, or to resume a narrative etc. —*adj.* existing at that time. —*n.* that time. —**then and there**, immediately and on the spot. [OE]

thence /ðens/ *adv.* **1.** from that place. **2.** for that reason. [OE]

thenceforth /ðensˈfɔːθ/ *adv.* (also **thenceforward**) from that time on.

theo- *in comb.* God or a god. [Gk (*theos* god)]

theocracy /θɪˈɒkrəsɪ/ *n.* a form of government by God or a god directly or through a priestly order etc. —**theocratic** /θɪəˈkrætɪk/ *adj.*, **theocratically** /θɪəˈkrætɪkəlɪ/ *adv.* [f. Gk (as THEO-, -CRACY)]

Theocritus /θɪˈɒkrɪtəs/ (*c.*300–*c.*260 BC) Hellenistic poet originally from Syracuse, who subsequently wrote in Cos and Alexandria. His poems, known under the title *Idylls*, include hymns, short epic narratives, and dramatic mimes, but he is most famous for the bucolic idylls, hexameter poems in dramatic form presenting the song-contests and love-songs of imaginary shepherds; these poems were immensely influential as the model of Virgil's *Eclogues* and of all subsequent pastoral poetry.

theodolite /θɪˈɒdəlaɪt/ *n.* a surveying-instrument for measuring horizontal and vertical angles, with a rotating telescope. [orig. unkn.]

Theodoric /θɪˈɒdərɪk/ 'the Great' (*c.*454–526), king of the Ostrogoths from 474, who invaded Italy in 488 and completed its conquest in 493, establishing a kingdom with its capital at Ravenna. At its greatest extent his empire included not only the Italian mainland, but Sicily, Dalmatia, and parts of Germany.

Theodosius I /θɪəˈdəʊsɪəs/ 'the Great' (*c.* 346–395), eastern Roman emperor 379–95. War with the Goths was ended by treaty in 382; subsequently he successfully defeated two usurpers, Magnus Maximus and Eugenius, to the western throne, on which he installed his son Honorius. A pious Christian and rigid upholder of Nicene orthodoxy, in 391 he banned all forms of pagan cult, probably under the influence of St Ambrose.

theogony /θɪˈɒgənɪ/ *n.* the genealogy of the gods; an account of this. [f. THEO- + Gk -*gonia* begetting]

theologian /θiːəˈləʊdʒɪən/ *n.* an expert in theology. [as foll.]

theology /θɪˈɒlədʒɪ/ *n.* the study or system of (esp. the Christian) religion. —**theological** /θiːəˈlɒdʒɪk(ə)l/ *adj.*, **theologically** *adv.* [f. OF f. L f. Gk (as THEO-, -LOGY)]

Theophrastus /θɪəˈfræstəs/ (*c.*370–288/5 BC) Greek philosopher and scientist, the pupil and successor of Aristotle, whose method and researches he continued, with a particular emphasis on empirical observation. His few surviving works include treatises on botany and other scientific subjects, and the *Characters*, a collection of sketches of psychological types, which in post-classical times was the most influential of his works.

theorem /ˈθɪərəm/ *n.* **1.** a general proposition not self-evident but demonstrable by argument, especially in mathematics. **2.** a rule in algebra etc., especially one expressed by symbols or formulae. [f. F or L f. Gk (*theōreō* behold)]

Theatre through the Ages

Greek theatre (4th c. BC)

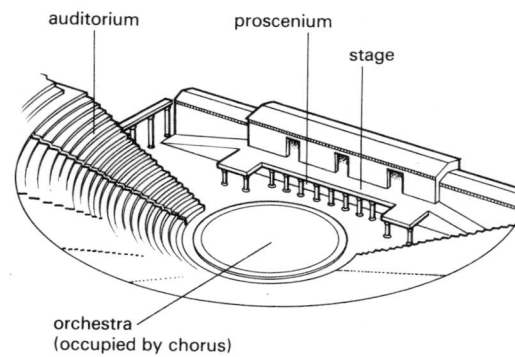

auditorium

proscenium

stage

orchestra
(occupied by chorus)

Roman amphitheatre (1st c. AD)

used for gladiatorial
contests

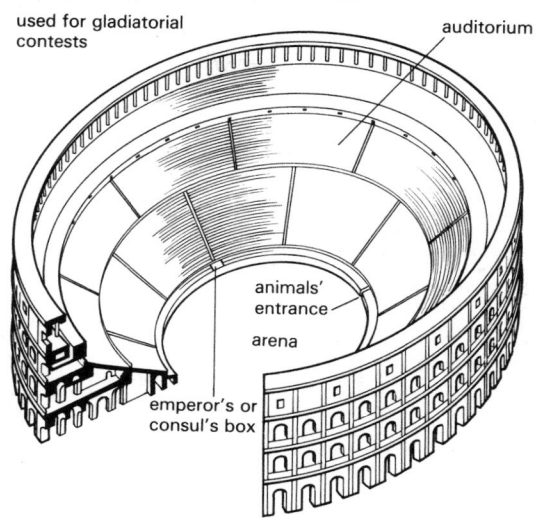

auditorium

animals'
entrance

arena

emperor's or
consul's box

Medieval pageant

mystery play performed on a wagon

Shakespearian theatre

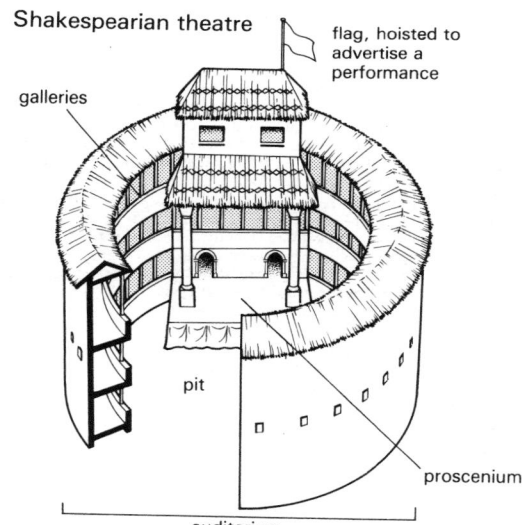

flag, hoisted to
advertise a
performance

galleries

pit

proscenium

auditorium

Traditional European theatre (19th–20th c.)

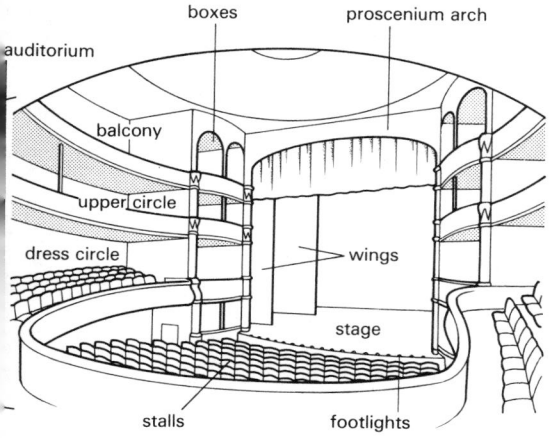

boxes

proscenium arch

auditorium

balcony

upper circle

dress circle

wings

stage

stalls

footlights

Theatre-in-the-round

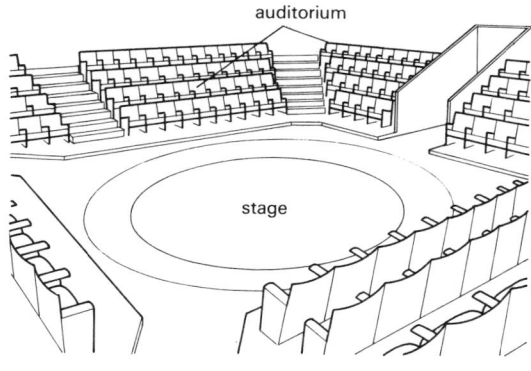

auditorium

stage

theoretical /θɪəˈretɪk(ə)l/ *adj.* **1.** concerned with knowledge but not with its practical application. **2.** based on theory rather than experience. —**theoretically** *adv.* [as THEORY]

theoretician /θɪərɪˈtɪʃ(ə)n/ *n.* a person concerned with the theoretical part of a subject. [as THEORY]

theorist /ˈθɪərɪst/ *n.* a holder or inventor of a theory. [f. THEORY]

theorize /ˈθɪəraɪz/ *v.i.* to evolve or indulge in theories. [f. foll.]

theory /ˈθɪərɪ/ *n.* **1.** a system of ideas formulated (by reasoning from known facts) to explain something. **2.** an opinion, a supposition; ideas or suppositions in general (opp. *practice*). **3.** an exposition of the principles on which a subject is based. [f. L f. Gk (as THEOREM)]

theosophy /θɪˈɒsəfɪ/ *n.* any of various philosophies professing to achieve a knowledge of God by spiritual ecstasy, direct intuition, or special individual relations, especially a modern movement following Hindu and Buddhist teachings and seeking universal brotherhood. It was founded as the Theosophical Society by the Russian adventuress H. P. Blavatsky and Col. H. S. Olcott, teaching the transmigration of souls, the brotherhood of man irrespective of race or creed, and complicated systems of psychology and cosmology, and denying a personal god. —**theosophist** *n.*, **theosophical** /-əˈsɒfɪk(ə)l/ *adj.* [f. L f. Gk, = wise concerning God]

therapeutic /θerəˈpjuːtɪk/ *adj.* of, for, or contributing to the cure of a disease. —**therapeutically** *adv.* [f. F or L f. Gk (*therapeuō* wait on, cure)]

therapeutics *n.pl.* (usu. treated as *sing.*) the branch of medicine concerned with the treatment and remedying of ill health. [f. prec.]

therapy /ˈθerəpɪ/ *n.* **1.** curative medical treatment. **2.** physiotherapy, psychotherapy. —**therapist** *n.* [f. Gk *therapeia* healing]

Theravada /θerəˈvɑːdə/ *n.* the only surviving ancient school of Buddhism (see HINAYANA). It is practised today in Sri Lanka, Burma, Thailand, Cambodia, and Laos. [f. Pali, = doctrine of the elders]

there /ðeə(r)/ *adv.* **1.** in, at, or to that place or position; at that point (in a speech, performance, writing, etc.); in that respect; used for emphasis in calling attention. **2.** used as an introductory word, usually with the verb *to be*, in a sentence where the verb precedes its subject, indicating a fact or the existence of something. —*n.* that place. —*int.* expressing confirmation, satisfaction, reassurance, etc. [OE]

thereabouts /ˈðeərəbaʊts/ *adv.* (also **thereabout**) near that place; near that number, quantity, time, etc.

thereafter /ðeərˈɑːftə(r)/ *adv.* (*formal*) after that.

thereby /ðeəˈbaɪ, ˈðeə-/ *adv.* by that means, as a result of that. —**thereby hangs a tale,** much could be said about that.

therefore /ˈðeəfɔː(r)/ *adv.* for that reason.

therein /ðeərˈɪn/ *adv.* (*formal*) in that place etc.; in that respect.

thereof /ðeərˈɒv/ *adv.* (*formal*) of that or it.

thereto /ðeəˈtuː/ *adv.* (*formal*) to that or it; in addition.

thereupon /ðeərəˈpɒn/ *adv.* in consequence of that; soon or immediately after that.

therm *n.* a unit of heat, in Britain especially the statutory unit of calorific value in a gas-supply (100,000 British thermal units). [f. Gk *thermē* heat]

thermal *adj.* of, for, or producing heat. —*n.* a rising current of heated air, used by gliders to gain height. —**thermal capacity,** the number of heat units needed to raise the temperature of a body by one degree. **thermal unit,** a unit for measuring heat (**British thermal unit,** the amount of heat needed to raise 1lb of water 1°F). —**thermally** *adv.* [F (as prec.)]

thermionic valve /θɜːmɪˈɒnɪk/ a device consisting of a sealed tube containing two or more electrodes, one of which is heated to produce a flow of electrons in one direction. The diode valve (which has two electrodes) functions as a rectifier and was so used by the English scientist, Sir John Ambrose Fleming, in 1904. The triode valve (with two electrodes and a grid) was invented in 1906 by an American engineer Lee de Forest and functioned as an amplifier—a weak signal received in the grid produced a stronger signal in the anode circuit. Before the development of semiconductor devices such as transistors (which have now largely replaced

it) the thermionic tube was used in all electronic equipment such as radio, radar, and computers. [f. THERMO- + ION]

thermo- /θɜːməʊ-/ *in comb.* heat. [Gk (*thermos* hot, *thermē* heat)]

thermocouple /ˈθɜːməʊkʌp(ə)l/ *n.* a device for measuring temperatures by means of the thermoelectric voltage developing between two pieces of wire of different metals joined to each other at each end.

thermodynamics /θɜːməʊdaɪˈnæmɪks/ *n.pl.* (usu. treated as *sing.*) the science of the relations between heat and other forms of energy, and, by extension, of the relationships and interconvertibility of all forms of energy (see below). —**thermodynamic** *adj.*, **thermodynamical** *adj.*, **thermodynamically** *adv.*
Thermodynamics deals with the place of energy in any material system: the forms it takes, its distribution, and the changes liable to take place in the system if the energy distribution is 'unbalanced'. The principles of thermodynamics can therefore be regarded as governing the direction of all physical changes taking place in the universe. Most material systems consist of large numbers of particles (atoms and molecules). Thermodynamics states that, with time, the energy in such a system will inevitably tend to become distributed in the most probable pattern, which consists of all the individual particles of the system engaging in random motion. We perceive such random motion as heat. Other types of change in a system, such as the intermingling of two different types of particles, also lead to greater randomness or disorder. It appears, in fact, that the universe is gradually 'running down' because this randomness or entropy (see ENTROPY) is continually increasing. The historical development of thermodynamics is complicated; it arose from consideration of the efficiency of steam-engines in the early 19th c. (especially by Sadi Carnot), and its main laws were introduced in the 1850s without explicit reference to the random motion of individual particles. The first law states that heat is indeed a form of energy (not a special 'fluid' as had once been thought), and then reaffirms the law of conservation of energy. The second law deals with the tendency of entropy to increase, as described above. Although most, if not all, physical changes are nominally governed by the laws of thermodynamics, many everyday processes of change can be adequately described in terms of ordinary mechanics. Among areas in which the principles and methods of thermodynamics are of great practical importance are the study and design of engines, and the rules governing the direction of chemical and biochemical reactions.

thermoelectric /θɜːməʊɪˈlektrɪk/ *adj.* producing electricity by difference of temperatures.

thermometer /θəˈmɒmɪtə(r)/ *n.* an instrument for measuring temperature by means of a substance whose expansion and contraction under different degrees of heat and cold are capable of accurate measurement (ill. HEAT). The earliest form was an air-thermometer invented and used by Galileo before 1597 for indicating the temperature of the atmosphere; alcohol thermometers were used *c.*1650. The device of a fixed zero (originally the freezing-point) was introduced by Hooke, 1665; the fixing of the zero as an arbitrary point below the freezing-point is attributed to Fahrenheit, who made mercurial thermometers *c.*1720; many other famous figures have contributed to the design of graduated scales. The most familiar type of thermometer consists of a slender hermetically sealed glass tube with a fine bore, having a bulb at the lower end filled with mercury, which rises as a conspicuous column in the tube (which is graduated) on expansion. [f. F (as THERMO-, -METER)]

thermonuclear /θɜːməʊˈnjuːklɪə(r)/ *adj.* relating to nuclear reactions that occur only at very high temperatures; (of a bomb etc.) using such reactions.

thermoplastic /θɜːməʊˈplæstɪk/ *adj.* becoming plastic on heating and hardening on cooling —*n.* a thermoplastic substance.

Thermopylae /θəˈmɒpɪliː/ a pass in Greece, about 200 km (120 miles) NW of Athens, originally narrow but now much widened by the recession of the sea. It was the scene of the heroic defence (480 BC) against the Persian army of Xerxes by 6,000 Greeks including 300 Spartans under their commander Leonidas. The defenders were outflanked then, and by the Gauls in 279 BC, and by Cato in 191 BC.

Thermos /ˈθɜːmɒs/ *n.* [P] a kind of vacuum flask. [f. Gk *thermos* hot]

thermosetting /θɜːməʊˈsetɪŋ/ *adj.* (of plastics) setting permanently when heated.

thermosphere /ˈθɜːməsfɪə(r)/ *n.* the part of the atmosphere between the mesopause and the height at which it ceases to have the properties of a continuous medium, characterized throughout by an increase in temperature with height (ill. WEATHER).

thermostat /ˈθɜːməstæt/ *n.* a device for the automatic regulation of temperature. **—thermostatic** /-ˈstætɪk/ *adj.*, **thermostatically** /-ˈstætɪkəlɪ/ *adv.* [f. THERMO- + Gk *statos* standing]

thesaurus /θɪˈsɔːrəs/ *n.* (*pl.* **-ri** /-raɪ/) a dictionary or encyclopaedia; a list of words or concepts arranged according to sense. [L f. Gk, = treasury]

these *pl.* of THIS.

Theseus /ˈθiːsjəs/ (*Gk legend*) the son of Poseidon (or of Aegeus, king of Athens) and national hero of Athens. He slew the Cretan Minotaur with the help of Ariadne and was successful in numerous other exploits.

thesis /ˈθiːsɪs/ *n.* (*pl.* **theses** /-siːz/) **1.** a proposition to be maintained or proved. **2.** a dissertation, especially by a candidate for a degree. [L f. Gk, = putting (as THEME)]

Thespian /ˈθespɪən/ *adj.* of tragedy or the drama. *—n.* an actor or actress. [f. foll.]

Thespis /ˈθespɪs/ (6th c. BC) Greek dramatic poet, regarded as the father of Greek tragedy.

Thessalonian /θesəˈləʊnɪən/ *adj.* of ancient Thessalonica (modern Salonica), a city in NE Greece. *—n.* a native of ancient Thessalonica. **—(Epistle to the) Thessalonians**, either of two books of the New Testament, the earliest letters of St Paul, written from Corinth to the new Church at Thessalonica.

Thessaly /ˈθesəlɪ/ a district of NE Greece. **—Thessalian** /-ˈseɪlɪən/ *adj. & n.*

theta /ˈθiːtə/ *n.* the eighth letter of the Greek alphabet, = th. [Gk]

Thetis /ˈθetɪs/ (*Gk myth.*) a sea-nymph, mother of Achilles.

thews /θjuːz/ *n.pl.* (*literary*) a person's muscular strength. [OE, = usage, conduct]

they /ðeɪ/ *pron.* (*obj.* THEM; *poss.* THEIR, THEIRS) *pl.* of HE, SHE, IT¹; people in general; those in authority. [f. ON]

thick *adj.* **1.** of great or specified distance in diameter or between opposite surfaces; (of a line etc.) broad, not fine. **2.** arranged closely, crowded together, dense; densely covered or filled; firm in consistency, containing much solid matter; made of thick material; muddy, cloudy, impenetrable by the sight. **3.** (*colloq.*) stupid, dull. **4.** (of the voice) indistinct. **5.** (*colloq.*) intimate, very friendly. *—n.* the thick part of anything. *—adv.* thickly. **—a bit thick**, (*slang*) unreasonable, intolerable. **in the thick of it**, in the busiest part of an activity or fight etc. **thick-headed** *adj.* stupid. **through thick and thin**, under all conditions, in spite of all difficulties. **—thickly** *adv.* [OE]

thicken *v.t./i.* **1.** to make or become thick or thicker. **2.** to become more complicated. **—thickener** *n.* [f. THICK]

thicket /ˈθɪkɪt/ *n.* a tangle of shrubs or trees. [OE (as THICK)]

thickness *n.* **1.** being thick; the extent to which a thing is thick. **2.** a layer of material of known thickness. **3.** the part between opposite surfaces. [f. THICK]

thickset *adj.* **1.** set or growing closely together. **2.** having a stocky or burly body.

thief *n.* (*pl.* **thieves** /θiːvz/) one who steals, esp. stealthily and without violence. [OE]

thieve *v.t./i.* to be a thief; to steal. [OE (as prec.)]

thievery *n.* stealing. [f. THIEF]

thievish *adj.* given to stealing. [f. THIEF]

thigh /θaɪ/ *n.* the part of the leg between the hip and the knee. [OE]

thimble *n.* a metal or plastic cap, usually with a closed end, worn on the end of the finger to protect the finger-tip and push the needle in sewing. [OE (as THUMB)]

thimbleful *n.* (*pl.* **-fuls**) a small quantity, especially of a liquid to drink. [f. prec. + -FUL]

Thimphu /ˈtɪmpuː/ the capital of Bhutan; pop. (approx.) 10,000.

thin *adj.* **1.** having the opposite surfaces close together, of small thickness. **2.** (of a line) narrow, not broad. **3.** made of thin material. **4.** lean, not plump. **5.** not dense or copious; not of thick consistency, (of liquid) flowing easily. **6.** lacking strength or substance or an important ingredient; (of an excuse etc.) feeble, transparent. *—adv.* thinly. *—v.t./i.* to make or become thin or thinner. **—have a thin time**, (*slang*) to have a wretched or uncomfortable time. **thin on**

the ground, few in number, rare. **thin on top**, balding. **thin out**, to make or become fewer or less crowded. **thin-skinned** *adj.* sensitive to reproach or criticism. **—thinly** *adv.*, **thinness** *n.* [OE]

thine /ðaɪn/ *poss. pron.* (*archaic*) of or belonging to thee; the thing(s) belonging to thee. *—poss. adj.* (*archaic*) the form of THY before a vowel. [OE (as THOU)]

thing *n.* **1.** whatever is or may be thought about or perceived. **2.** an inanimate object as distinct from a living creature. **3.** an unspecified object or item. **4.** (expressing pity, contempt, or affection) a creature. **5.** an act, fact, idea, quality, task, etc. **6.** a specimen or type of something. **7.** (*colloq.*) something remarkable. **8.** (in *pl.*) personal belongings, clothing; implement, utensils. **9.** (in *pl.*) affairs in general; circumstances, conditions. **—the thing**, what is conventionally proper or fashionable, what is needed or required, what is most important. **do one's own thing**, (*colloq.*) to pursue one's own interests or inclinations. **have a thing about**, (*colloq.*) to be obsessed or prejudiced about. **make a thing of**, to regard as essential; to cause a fuss about. [OE]

thingummy /ˈθɪŋəmɪ/ *n.* (also **thingumajig** etc.) (*colloq.*) a person or thing whose name one has forgotten or does not know. [f. THING, with meaningless suffix]

think *v.t./i.* (*past & p.p.* **thought** /θɔːt/) **1.** to exercise the mind in an active way, to form connected ideas. **2.** to have as an idea or opinion. **3.** to form as an intention or plan. **4.** to take into consideration. **5.** to call to mind, to remember. *—n.* (*colloq.*) an act of thinking. **—think again**, to revise one's plans or opinions. **think aloud**, to utter one's thoughts as soon as they occur. **think better of**, to change one's mind about (an intention) after reconsideration. **think little** *or* **nothing of**, to consider insignificant. **think much** *or* **well** *or* **highly** etc. **of**, to have a high opinion of. **think out**, to consider carefully; to produce (an idea etc.) by thinking. **think over**, to reflect upon in order to reach a decision. **think through**, to reflect fully upon (a problem etc.). **think twice**, to use careful consideration, to avoid a hasty action etc. **think up**, (*colloq.*) to devise, to produce by thought. [OE]

thinker *n.* one who thinks, especially in a specified way; a person with a skilled or powerful mind. [f. THINK]

thinking *adj.* using thought or rational judgement. *—n.* opinion or judgement. [f. THINK]

think-tank *n.* an organization providing advice and ideas on national and commercial problems; an interdisciplinary group of specialist consultants.

thinner *n.* a volatile liquid used to make paint etc. thinner. [f. THIN]

thiosulphate /θaɪəˈsʌlfeɪt/ *n.* a sulphate in which some oxygen is replaced by sulphur. [f. Gk *theion* sulphur + SULPHATE]

third *adj. & n.* **1.** next after second. **2.** each of three equal parts of a thing. **—third degree**, a long and severe questioning, especially by the police to obtain information or a confession. **third man**, a fielder in cricket near the boundary behind the slips (ill. SPORTS). **third party**, another party besides the two principals; a bystander etc. **third-party** *adj.* (of insurance) covering damage or injury suffered by a person other than the insured. **third person**, a third party; (*Gram.*) see PERSON. **third-rate** *adj.* inferior, very poor. **Third Reich**, see REICH. **Third World**, the under-developed countries of the world; (*orig.*) countries considered as not politically aligned with Communist or Western nations. **—thirdly** *adv.* [OE (as THREE)]

thirst *n.* **1.** the feeling caused by a desire or need to drink. **2.** a strong desire. *—v.i.* to feel a thirst. [OE]

thirsty *adj.* **1.** feeling thirst. **2.** (of a country or season) in need of water, dry. **3.** eager. **4.** (*colloq.*) causing thirst. **—thirstily** *adv.*, **thirstiness** *n.* [OE (as prec.)]

thirteen /θɜːˈtiːn/ *adj. & n.* **1.** one more than twelve; the symbol for this (13, xiii, XIII). **2.** the size etc. denoted by thirteen. **—thirteenth** *adj. & n.* [OE (as THREE, -TEEN)]

thirty /ˈθɜːtɪ/ *adj. & n.* **1.** three times ten; the symbol for this (30, xxx, XXX). **2.** (in *pl.*) the numbers, years, or degrees of temperature from 30 to 39. **—thirtieth** *adj. & n.* [OE (as THREE)]

Thirty-nine Articles the set of doctrinal formulae finally adopted by the Church of England (1571) as a statement of its dogmatic position. Many, perhaps intentionally, allow a wide variety of interpretation. Since 1865 clergy have been asked to give a general assent to them; previously a more particular subscription was demanded.

Thirty Years War a prolonged European war of the

17th c. Beginning as a struggle between the Catholic Holy Roman Emperor and some of his German Protestant States, the war gradually drew in most of the major European military powers and developed into a fight for continental hegemony with France, Sweden, Spain, and the Empire as the major protagonists. The result of three decades of intermittent hostilities was the emergence of Bourbon France as the pre-eminent European power and the devastation of much of Germany, where military activity had remained centred throughout.

this /ðɪs/ *pron.* (*pl.* **these** /ðiːz/) **1.** the person or thing close at hand or indicated or already named or understood. **2.** the nearer or more obvious one of two (opp. *that*). **3.** the present day or time. —*adj.* (*pl.* **these**) designating the person or thing close at hand etc. —*adv.* to this degree or extent. —**this and that,** various things. [OE]

Thisbe /ˈθɪsbɪ/ (*Rom. legend*) lover of Pyramus (see entry).

thistle /ˈθɪs(ə)l/ *n.* **1.** a prickly herbaceous plant of the genus *Carduus*, *Cirsium*, etc., usually with globular heads of purple flowers. **2.** a figure of this as the heraldic emblem of Scotland, and part of the insignia of the distinctively Scottish order of knighthood, the **Order of the Thistle,** instituted in 1687 by James II and revived in 1703 by Queen Anne. [OE]

thistledown *n.* light fluffy stuff containing thistle-seeds and blown about in the wind.

thistly *adj.* overgrown with thistles [f. THISTLE]

thither /ˈðɪðə(r)/ *adv.* (*archaic*) to or towards that place. [OE]

thixotropy /θɪkˈsɒtrəpɪ/ *n.* the property of becoming temporarily liquid when shaken, stirred, etc., and returning to a gel state on standing. —**thixotropic** /-əˈtrɒpɪk/ *adj.* [f. Gk *thixis* touching + *tropē* turning]

thole *n.* (in full **thole-pin**) a pin in the gunwale of a boat as a fulcrum for an oar; each of two such pins forming a rowlock. [OE, = ON *thollr* fir-tree, peg]

Thomas[1] /ˈtɒməs/, Dylan Marlais (1914–53), Welsh-born poet. He moved to London in 1934 and embarked on a career of journalism, broadcasting, and film-making. Thomas's romantic, affirmative, rhetorical style was new and influential and much imitated by his contemporaries. He won recognition with *Deaths and Entrances* (1946), which contains some of his best-known poems, and continued his success with *Collected Poems 1934-1952* (1952), *Portrait of the Artist as a Young Dog* (1955; prose and verse), and *Adventures in the Skin Trade* (1955; stories). Shortly before his death in New York, hastened by wild living and hard drinking, he read his most famous single work, *Under Milk Wood*, a radio drama in which the poetic alliterative prose is interspersed with songs and ballads.

Thomas[2] /ˈtɒməs/, (Philip) Edward (1878–1917), English poet, who produced much biographical and topographical prose before turning to poetry with the encouragement of the American poet Robert Frost. His work combines a loving and accurate observation of the English pastoral scene with colloquial speech-rythms. He was killed at Arras on active service; most of his poems appeared posthumously.

Thomas[3] /ˈtɒməs/, St, an Apostle, who refused to believe that Christ had risen again unless he could see and touch his wounds. Feast day, 21 Dec. —**doubting Thomas,** a sceptic.

Thomas à Kempis /ˈtɒməs ə ˈkempɪs/ (*c*.1380–1471) German ascetical writer. Born Thomas Hemerken at Kempen, near Cologne, he became an Augustinian canon in Holland. He is the probable author of the *Imitation of Christ*, an important manual of spiritual devotion.

Thomas Aquinas see AQUINAS.

Thomism /ˈtəʊmɪz(ə)m/ *n.* the doctrine of Thomas Aquinas or of his followers. —**Thomist** *n.* [f. name *Thomas*]

Thompson /ˈtɒms(ə)n/, Francis (1859–1907), English poet, rescued from destitution by Alice and Wilfred Meynell who secured him literary recognition. His finest work, which conveys intense religious experience in imagery of great power, includes the poems 'The Hound of Heaven' and 'The Kingdom of God'. He published three volumes of verse (1893–7) and much literary criticism in periodicals. Opium addiction together with tuberculosis caused his early death.

Thomson[1] /ˈtɒms(ə)n/, James (1700–48), Scottish poet. He who came to London in 1725, where he met Arbuthnot, Gay, and Pope, found patrons, and through the influence of Lord Lyttelton received a sinecure. *The Seasons* (1726–

30), one of the most popular English poems, both in style and subject inaugurated a new era by its sentiment for nature; the text was adapted for Haydn's oratorio (1801). His other works include his patriotic poem *Liberty* (1735–36), the tragedies *Sophonisba* (1730) and *Tancred and Sigismunda* (1745), the masque *Alfred* (1740), containing 'Rule, Britannia', and *The Castle of Indolence* (1748), which contains a portrait of the poet which mocks his notorious love of idleness.

Thomson[2] /ˈtɒms(ə)n/, Sir Joseph John (1856–1940), English physicist, discoverer of the electron. During his tenure as Cavendish professor of physics at Cambridge from 1884 until 1918 he consolidated the world-wide reputation of the Cavendish Laboratory; seven of his former pupils were to win Nobel Prizes. His own experiments of the bending of cathode rays in magnetic and electric fields began in 1897. He deduced from these deflexions that he was dealing with particles smaller than the atom, which he initially called 'corpuscles' but later 'electrons', adopting the word coined a few years previously by the physicist G. J. Stoney. His model of the atom, incorporating the negatively-charged electron for the first time, was abandoned in favour of Rutherford's more satisfactory model in 1911. Thomson received the 1906 Nobel Prize for physics for his researches into the electrical conductivity of gases and was knighted in 1908. His son Sir George Paget Thomson (1892–1975), also a physicist, shared the 1937 Nobel Prize with Clinton Davisson for his discovery of the effect of electron diffraction.

thong *n.* a narrow strip of hide or leather. [OE]

Thor /θɔː(r)/ (*Scand. myth.*) the god of thunder, the weather, agriculture, and the home. He is represented as armed with a hammer. Thursday is named after him.

thorax /ˈθɔːræks/ *n.* (*pl.* **-races** /-rəsiːz/) the part of the body between the neck or head and the abdomen; the second segment of an insect body (ill. INSECTS). —**thoracic** /-ˈræsɪk/ *adj.* [L f. Gk, orig. = cuirass]

thorium /ˈθɔːrɪəm/ *n.* a radioactive metallic element, symbol Th, atomic number 90, first discovered in 1828. Thorium became economically important after 1885 when its oxide, which can become brightly incandescent, began to be widely used in gas mantles. Thorium's radioactive properties were discovered in 1898. The major isotope found in nature has a very long half-life and is thought, along with uranium and radioactive potassium, to be responsible for most of the heat generated inside the earth. Nowadays thorium has a variety of industrial uses and is of increasing importance as a nuclear fuel. [f. THOR]

thorn *n.* **1.** a stiff sharp-pointed projection on a plant. **2.** a thorn-bearing shrub or tree. —**a thorn in one's flesh** *or* **side,** a constant source of annoyance. [OE]

Thorndike /ˈθɔːndaɪk/, Dame (Agnes) Sybil (1882–1976), English actress, who played a wide range of Shakespearean roles in England and in the USA, and gave one of her finest performances in the title role of the first London production of G. B. Shaw's *St Joan* (1924).

thorny *adj.* **1.** full of thorns. **2.** like a thorn. **3.** (of a subject) hard to handle without offence. —**thornily** *adv.*, **thorniness** *n.* [OE (as THORN)]

thorough /ˈθʌrə/ *adj.* complete and unqualified, not merely superficial; acting or done with great attention to detail; absolute. —**thoroughly** *adv.*, **thoroughness** *n.* [as THROUGH]

thoroughbred *adj.* bred of pure or pedigree stock. —*n.* a thoroughbred animal, especially a horse.

thoroughfare *n.* a road or path open at both ends, especially for traffic.

thoroughgoing *adj.* thorough; extreme.

those *pl.* of THAT.

Thoth /θəʊθ/ (*Egyptian myth.*) a moon-god, the god of wisdom and of scribes and writing, patron of the sciences. He was also regarded as a god of justice, protector of laws. Thoth was closely associated with Ra and was his messenger, which led the Greeks to identify him with Hermes. He is most often represented in human form with the head of an ibis surmounted by the moon's disc and crescent.

thou /ðaʊ/ *pron.* of the second person singular (now replaced by YOU except in some formal, liturgical, and poetic uses). [OE]

though /ðəʊ/ *conj.* despite the fact that; even supposing that; and yet, nevertheless. —*adv.* however, all the same. [f. ON]

thought[1] /θɔːt/ n. **1.** the process, power, or manner of thinking; the faculty of reason. **2.** the way of thinking associated with a particular time or people etc. **3.** sober reflection, consideration. **4.** an idea or chain of reasoning produced by thinking. **5.** an intention. **6.** (usu. in *pl.*) what one is thinking, one's opinion. —**a thought**, somewhat. **in thought**, meditating. **thought-reader** n. a person supposedly able to perceive another's thoughts without their being spoken. [OE (as THINK)]

thought[2] past & p.p. of THINK.

thoughtful adj. **1.** thinking deeply; often absorbed in thought. **2.** (of a book or writer etc.) showing signs of careful thought. **3.** showing thought for the needs of others, considerate. —**thoughtfully** adv., **thoughtfulness** n. [f. THOUGHT[1] + -FUL]

thoughtless adj. careless of consequences or of others' feelings; caused by lack of thought. —**thoughtlessly** adv., **thoughtlessness** n. [f. THOUGHT[1] + -LESS]

thousand /ˈθaʊzənd/ adj. & n. (for plural usage see HUNDRED) **1.** ten hundred; the symbol for this (1,000, m, M) **2.** (in *pl.*) very many. —**thousandth** adj. & n. [OE]

thousandfold adj. & adv. a thousand times as much or as many; consisting of a thousand parts. [f. prec. + -FOLD]

Thrace /θreɪs/ an ancient country lying west of Istanbul and the Black Sea and north of the Aegean, part of modern Turkey, Greece, and Bulgaria, inhabited by a primitive warlike Indo-European people. It became a Roman province in 46. —**Thracian** /ˈθreɪʃ(ə)n/ adj. & n.

thrall /θrɔːl/ n. (*literary*) **1.** a slave (of or to a person or thing). **2.** slavery. —**thraldom** n. [OE f. ON]

thrash v.t./i. **1.** to beat severely with a stick or whip. **2.** to defeat thoroughly in a contest. **3.** to thresh (corn etc.). **4.** to act like a flail, to deliver repeated blows; to move violently. —**thrash out**, to discuss to a conclusion. [OE]

thread /θred/ n. **1.** a thin length of any substance. **2.** a length of spun cotton or wool etc. used in weaving or in sewing or knitting. **3.** anything regarded as threadlike with reference to its continuity or connectedness. **4.** the spiral ridge of a screw. —v.t. **1.** to pass a thread through the eye of (a needle). **2.** to put (beads) on a thread. **3.** to arrange (material in strip form, e.g. film) in the proper position on equipment. **4.** to pick one's way through (a maze, a crowded place, etc.); to make (one's way) thus. —**threader** n. [OE (as THROW)]

threadbare adj. **1.** (of cloth) so worn that the nap is lost and the threads are visible; (of a person) wearing such clothes. **2.** hackneyed.

Threadneedle Street a street in the City of London containing the premises of the Bank of England (the **Old Lady of Threadneedle Street**). [earlier *three-needle*, possibly from a tavern with the arms of the Needlemakers]

threadworm n. a small threadlike worm (*Strongyloides stercoralis*) infesting the intestines.

threat /θret/ n. **1.** a declaration of intention to punish, hurt, or harm a person or thing. **2.** an indication of something undesirable coming. **3.** a person or thing as a likely cause of harm etc. [OE]

threaten /ˈθret(ə)n/ v.t. **1.** to make a threat or threats against. **2.** to be a sign or indication of (something undesirable). **3.** to announce one's intention to do an undesirable or unexpected thing. **4.** to give warning of the infliction of (harm etc.; or *absol.*). [OE (as prec.)]

three adj. & n. **1.** one more than two; the symbol for this (3, iii, III). **2.** the size etc. denoted by three. —**three-cornered** adj. triangular; (of a contest etc.) between three parties each for himself. **three-decker** n. a warship with three gun-decks; a sandwich with three slices of bread; a three-volume novel. **three-dimensional** adj. having or appearing to have length, breadth, and depth. **three-legged race**, a race between pairs with the right leg of one tied to the other's left leg. **three-ply** adj. having three strands or layers; (n.) wool etc. having three strands; plywood having three layers. **three-point turn**, a method of turning a vehicle round in a narrow space by driving forwards, backwards, and forwards. **three-quarter** n. any of the three or four players just behind the half-backs in Rugby football. **three-quarters** n. three parts out of four. **the three Rs**, see R. **three-way** adj. involving three ways or participants. [OE]

threefold adj. & adv. three times as much or as many; consisting of three parts. [f. THREE + -FOLD]

threepence /ˈθrepəns/ n. the sum of three pence.

threepenny /ˈθrepənɪ/ adj. costing or worth three pence. —**threepenny bit**, a former coin worth 3d.

threescore n. (*archaic*) sixty.

threesome /ˈθriːsəm/ n. a group of three persons. [f. THREE + -SOME]

threnody /ˈθrenədɪ/ n. a song of lamentation, especially on a person's death. [f. Gk (*thrēnos* wailing, *ōidē* ode)]

thresh v.t. **1.** to beat out or separate grain from (husks of corn etc.). **2.** to make violent movements. —**threshing-floor** n. a hard level floor for threshing, especially with flails. [var. of THRASH]

threshold /ˈθreʃəʊld/ n. **1.** a strip of wood or stone forming the bottom of a doorway and crossed in entering a house etc. **2.** the point of entry or beginning of something. **3.** the limit below which a stimulus causes no reaction; the magnitude or intensity that must be exceeded for a certain reaction or phenomenon to occur. [OE, rel. to THRASH in sense 'tread']

threw past of THROW.

thrice adv. (*archaic*) **1.** three times, on three occasions. **2.** (esp. in *comb.*) highly. [OE (as THREE)]

thrift n. **1.** economical management of money or resources. **2.** the sea-pink (*Armeria maritima*). [f. ON (as THRIVE)]

thriftless adj. wasteful. [f. prec. + -LESS]

thrifty adj. practising thrift, economical. —**thriftily** adv., **thriftiness** n. [f. THRIFT]

thrill n. a nervous tremor of emotion or sensation; a slight throb or pulsation. —v.t./i. to feel or cause to feel a thrill; to throb or pulsate slightly. [OE, = pierce (rel. to THROUGH)]

thriller n. an exciting or sensational story or play etc., especially one involving crime or espionage. [f. prec.]

thrips n. (*pl.* same) an insect of the order Thysanoptera, many of which injure plants by feeding on their juices (ill. INSECTS). [L f. Gk, = woodworm]

thrive v.i. (*past* **throve** or **thrived**; *p.p.* **thriven** /ˈθrɪv(ə)n/ or **thrived**) **1.** to prosper, to be successful. **2.** to grow or develop well and vigorously. [f. ON]

throat n. **1.** the windpipe, the gullet; the front part of the neck containing this. **2.** a narrow passage entrance or exit. **3.** the forward upper corner of a fore-and-aft sail (ill. SAILING-SHIPS). —**cut one's own throat**, to bring about one's own downfall. **ram** *or* **thrust down a person's throat**, to force (a thing) on his attention. **throat latch** *or* **lash**, the strap of a bridle passing under a horse's throat (ill. HORSE). [OE]

throaty adj. **1.** uttered deep in the throat. **2.** hoarsely resonant. —**throatily** adv., **throatiness** n. [f. prec.]

throb v.i. (**-bb-**) **1.** (of the heart or pulse etc.) to beat with more than usual force or rapidity. **2.** to vibrate or sound with a persistent rhythm; to vibrate with emotion. —n. throbbing. [app. imit.]

throe n. (usu. in *pl.*) a violent pang, especially of childbirth or death. —**in the throes of**, (*colloq.*) struggling with the task of. [alt. f. earlier *throwe*, perh. f. OE *thrēa* calamity]

thrombosis /θrɒmˈbəʊsɪs/ n. (*pl.* **-oses** /-iːz/) a coagulation of blood in a blood-vessel or organ during life. —**thrombotic** /-ˈbɒtɪk/ adj. [f. Gk, = curdling (*thrombos* lump, blood-clot)]

throne n. **1.** a chair of State for a sovereign or bishop etc. **2.** sovereign power. —v.t. to enthrone. [f. OF f. L f. Gk *thronos* high seat]

throng n. a crowded mass of people. —v.t./i. to come, go, or press in a throng; to fill with a throng. [OE]

throstle /ˈθrɒs(ə)l/ n. a song-thrush. [OE (rel. to THRUSH)]

throttle n. **1.** a valve controlling the flow of fuel or steam etc. in an engine; a lever or pedal operating this valve. **2.** the throat, the gullet, the windpipe. —v.t. **1.** to choke, to strangle. **2.** to prevent the utterance etc. of. **3.** to control (an engine or steam etc.) with a throttle. —**throttle back** *or* **down**, to reduce the speed of (an engine or vehicle) by throttling. [perh. f. THROAT]

through /θruː/ prep. **1.** from end to end or side to side of; entering at one side or end and coming out at the other. **2.** between, among. **3.** from beginning to end of. **4.** by reason of; by the agency, means, or fault of. **5.** (*US*) up to and including. —adv. **1.** through a thing; from side to side or end to end; from beginning to end. **2.** so as to be connected by telephone. —adj. going through, especially of travel where the whole journey is made without change of line or vehicle etc. or with one ticket; (of traffic) going through a place to its destination. —**be through**, to have finished; to cease to have dealings; to have no further prospects.

through and through, through again and again; thoroughly, completely. [OE]

throughout /θru:'aʊt/ *prep.* right through, from end to end of. —*adv.* in every part or respect.

throughput *n.* the amount of material put through a process, especially in manufacturing or computing.

throve see THRIVE.

throw /θrəʊ/ *v.t./i.* (*past* **threw** /θru:/; *p.p.* **thrown**) **1.** to propel with some force through the air or in a particular direction. **2.** to force violently into a specified position or state; to compel to be in a specified condition. **3.** to turn or move (a part of the body) quickly or suddenly. **4.** to project or cast (a light, shadow, spell, etc.). **5.** to bring to the ground in wrestling; (of a horse) to unseat (a rider); (*colloq.*) to disconcert. **6.** to put (clothes etc.) on or off carelessly or hastily. **7.** to cause (dice) to fall on a table; to obtain (a specified number) thus. **8.** to cause to pass or extend suddenly. **9.** to move (a switch or lever) so as to operate it. **10.** to shape (round pottery) on a wheel. **11.** to have (a fit or tantrum etc.) **12.** (*slang*) to give (a party). **13.** (*US*) to lose (a contest or race etc.) intentionally. —*n.* **1.** an act of throwing. **2.** the distance a thing is or may be thrown. **3.** being thrown in wrestling. —**throw away,** to part with as useless or unwanted; to fail to make use of (an opportunity etc.). **throw-away** *adj.* meant to be thrown away after use. **throw back,** to revert to ancestral character; (usu. in *pass.*) to compel to rely *on*. **throw-back** *n.* reversion to ancestral character; an instance of this. **throw in,** to interpose (a word or remark); to include with no extra charge; to throw (a football) from the edge of a pitch where it has gone out of play. **throw off,** to discard; to contrive to get rid of or free oneself from; to write or utter easily, as if without effort, or in an offhand way. **throw oneself at,** to seek energetically to win the friendship or love of. **throw oneself into,** to engage vigorously in. **throw oneself on** *or* **upon,** to rely completely on. **throw open,** to cause to be suddenly or widely open; to make accessible. **throw out,** to put out forcibly or suddenly; to throw away; to reject (a proposal etc.); to confuse or distract (a person). **throw over,** to desert, to abandon. **throw together,** to assemble hastily; to bring into casual contact. **throw up,** to abandon; to resign from; to vomit; to erect hastily; to bring to notice. —**thrower** *n.* [OE, = twist]

thrum[1] *v.t./i.* (-mm-) to play (a stringed instrument) monotonously or unskilfully; to drum or tap idly (on). —*n.* such playing; the resulting sound. [imit.]

thrum[2] *n.* an unwoven end of a warp-thread, or the whole of such ends, left when the finished web is cut away; any short loose thread. [OE, = OHG *drum* remnant, end-piece]

thrush[1] *n.* a small bird of the family Turdidae, e.g. the blackbird, nightingale, or especially the song-thrush (*Turdus philomelos*) or missel-thrush. [OE]

thrush[2] *n.* a fungoid infection of the throat (especially in children) or of the vagina. [orig. unkn.]

thrust *v.t./i.* (*past & p.p.* **thrust**) **1.** to push forcibly. **2.** to put forcibly into a specified position or condition; to force the acceptance of. **3.** to make a forward stroke with a sword etc. —*n.* **1.** a thrusting movement or force; the forward force exerted by a propeller or jet etc. (ill. FLIGHT); the stress between parts of an arch etc.; (*Geol.*) a compressive strain in the earth's crust. **2.** a strong attempt to penetrate an enemy's line or territory. **3.** a hostile remark aimed at a person. **4.** the chief theme or gist of remarks etc. —**thruster** *n.* [f. ON]

Thucydides /θju:'sɪdɪdi:z/ (*c.*455–*c.*400 BC) Greek historian from Athens, whose *History* records the events of the Peloponnesian War between Athens and Sparta, in which he himself took part. The work, written to be 'a possession for ever', presents a scientific analysis of the origins and course of the war, based on painstaking inquiry into what actually happened and aided by the application of historical imagination in the reconstruction of political speeches. He does not conceal his admiration for the achievements of Pericles. His idiosyncratic style has a poetic flavour, with an energy and conciseness that matches the power of his thought.

thud *n.* a low dull sound as of a blow on a non-resonant thing. —*v.i.* (-dd-) to make a thud; to fall with a thud. [prob. OE, = thrust]

Thug *n.* a member of an association of professional robbers and murderers in India, who strangled their victims. Their methods were described by travellers from *c.*1665, and their suppression was rigidly prosecuted from 1831. [f. Hindi & Marathi, = swindler]

thug *n.* a vicious or brutal ruffian. —**thuggery** *n.* [f. THUG]

Thule /'θju:lɪ, 'θu:lɪ/ **1.** a name given by the ancient Greek explorer Pytheas (*c.*310 BC) to a country described by him as six days' sail north of Britain, and regarded by the ancients as the northernmost point of the world. It has been variously identified with Iceland, one of the Shetland Islands, and part of Scandinavia. **2.** (usu. *attrib.*) a prehistoric Eskimo culture widely distributed from Alaska to Greenland *c.* AD 500–1400, named after a small Eskimo settlement (now called Dundas) founded in 1910 on the NW coast of Greenland.

thulium /'θju:lɪəm/ *n.* a metallic element of the lanthanide series, symbol Tm, atomic number 69, first discovered in 1879. It has few commercial uses. [f. THULE]

thumb /θʌm/ *n.* **1.** the short thick finger set apart from the other four. **2.** the part of a glove covering the thumb. —*v.t./i.* **1.** to wear or soil (pages etc.) with the thumb. **2.** to turn over pages (as) with the thumb. **3.** to request or get (a lift in a passing vehicle) by indicating the desired direction with the thumb. **4.** to use the thumb (on) in a gesture. —**thumb-index** *n.* a set of lettered grooves cut down the side of a book's leaves to enable the user to open the book directly at a particular section. **thumb-nail sketch,** a brief verbal description. **thumb one's nose,** to cock a snook. **thumbs down,** a gesture of rejection. **thumbs up,** a gesture or exclamation of satisfaction. **under a person's thumb,** completely dominated by him. [OE]

thumbscrew *n.* an instrument of torture for compressing the thumb(s).

thump *v.t./i.* to beat, or strike, or knock heavily, especially with the fist. **2.** to thud. —*n.* a heavy blow; the sound of this. [imit.]

thumping *adj.* (*colloq.*) big. [f. THUMP]

thunder *n.* **1.** a loud noise heard after lightning and due to disturbance of the air by a discharge of electricity. **2.** a resounding loud deep noise. **3.** (in *sing.* or *pl.*) authoritative censure or threats. —*v.t./i.* **1.** to give forth thunder (esp. *it thunders, is thundering*). **2.** to make a noise like thunder; to move with a loud noise. **3.** to utter loudly; to make a forceful verbal attack. —**steal a person's thunder,** to forestall him by using his ideas or words etc. before he can do so himself. [from the remark of John Dennis, English dramatist (*c.*1710), when the stage thunder he had intended for his own play was used for another] **thunder-cloud** *n.* a storm-cloud charged with electricity and producing thunder and lightning. —**thunderer** *n.,* **thundery** *adj.* [OE]

thunderbolt *n.* **1.** a flash of lightning with a crash of thunder. **2.** an imaginary destructive missile thought of as sent to earth with a lighting-flash. **3.** a very startling and formidable event or statement.

thunderclap *n.* **1.** a crash of thunder. **2.** a sudden terrible event or news.

thundering *adj.* (*colloq.*) very big or great. [f. THUNDER]

thunderous *adj.* like thunder; very loud. [as prec.]

thunderstorm *n.* a storm with thunder and lightning and usually heavy rain or hail (ill. WEATHER).

thunderstruck *adj.* amazed.

Thur. *abbr.* Thursday.

Thurber /'θɜ:bə(r)/, James (Grove) (1894–1961), American humourist, writer, and cartoonist. In 1927 began his life-long association with the *New Yorker* in which he published many of his essays, stories, and sketches, including 'The Secret Life of Walter Mitty' (1932). Among his many collections are *Men, Women and Dogs* (1943; drawings) and *The Thurber Carnival* (1945).

thurible /'θjʊərɪb(ə)l/ *n.* a censer (ill. VESTMENTS). [f. OF or L *t(h)uribulum* (*t(h)us* incense)]

Thuringia /θjʊə'rɪndʒɪə/ a region of central Germany, now on the border between East and West Germany.

Thursday /'θɜ:zdeɪ/ *n.* the day of the week following Wednesday. —*adv.* (*colloq.*) on Thursday. [OE, = day of Thor, representing L *Jovis dies* day of Jupiter]

thus /ðʌs/ *adv.* (*formal*) **1.** in this way, like this. **2.** as a result or inference. **3.** to this extent, so. [OE; orig. unkn.]

thwack *v.t.* to hit with a heavy blow. —*n.* a heavy blow. [imit.]

thwart /θwɔ:t/ *v.t.* to frustrate (a person or purpose etc.). —*n.* a rower's seat, placed across the boat. [f. ON = transverse]

thy /ðaɪ/ *poss. adj.* of or belonging to thee; now replaced by YOUR except in some formal, liturgical, and poetic uses. [as THINE]

Thyestes /θaɪˈestiːz/ (*Gk legend*) brother of Atreus (see entry). —**Thyestean** /-ˈestɪən/ *adj.*

thyme /taɪm/ *n.* any of several herbs of the genus *Thymus* with fragrant aromatic leaves. [f. OF f. L f. Gk *thumon* (*thuō* burn sacrifice)]

thymol /ˈθaɪmɒl/ *n.* an antiseptic made from oil of thyme. [f. THYME]

thymus /ˈθaɪməs/ *n.* a lymphoid organ near the base of the neck (in man becoming much smaller at puberty). [f. Gk *thumos*]

thyristor /θaɪˈrɪstə(r)/ *n.* a switch in the form of a semiconductor device in which a small electric current is used to start the flow of a large current. [f. Gk *thura* door + TRANSISTOR]

thyroid /ˈθaɪrɔɪd/ *n.* the thyroid gland. —**thyroid cartilage**, a large cartilage of the larynx, the projection of which in man forms the Adam's apple. **thyroid gland**, a large ductless gland near the larynx secreting a hormone which regulates growth and development; an extract from the thyroid gland of animals used in treating goitre etc. [f. obs. F f. Gk (*thureos* oblong shield)]

thyself *pron.* the emphat. & refl. form of THOU and THEE: now replaced in general use by YOURSELF (cf. at THOU).

Ti *symbol* titanium.

tiara /tɪˈɑːrə/ *n.* **1.** a woman's ornamental crescent-shaped head-dress, worn on ceremonial occasions. **2.** the pope's diadem, pointed at the top and surrounded by three crowns. [L f. Gk; orig. unkn.]

Tiber /ˈtaɪbə(r)/ a river of central Italy, upon which Rome stands, flowing 405 km (252 miles) westwards from the Tuscan Apennines to the sea at Ostia.

Tiberius /taɪˈbɪərɪəs/ (Tiberius Julius Caesar Augustus, 42 BC–AD 37) Roman emperor AD 14–37, the adopted successor of his stepfather Augustus. He pursued a brilliant military career under Augustus, whose policies he faithfully continued when he became emperor. His reign was marked by an increasing number of treason trials. In AD 26 he retired to Capri and never again visited Rome; business with the Senate was conducted by letter. Morose and suspicious, Tiberius was not a popular emperor.

Tibet /tɪˈbet/ a mountainous country on the northern frontier of India, an autonomous region of China since 1965; capital, Lhasa.

Tibetan /tɪˈbet(ə)n/ *adj.* of Tibet or its people or language. —*n.* **1.** a native or inhabitant of Tibet. **2.** the language of Tibet, spoken by 1,250,000 people there, a similar number in neighbouring provinces of China, and a million people in Nepal. It belongs to the Sino-Tibetan language group and is most closely related to Burmese. Its alphabet is based on that of Sanskrit and dates from the 7th c. [f. TIBET]

tibia /ˈtɪbɪə/ *n.* (*pl.* **-ae** /-iː/) the inner and usually larger of the two bones from knee to ankle (ill. BODY 1); the corresponding bone in a bird. —**tibial** *adj.* [L, = shin-bone, flute]

Tibullus /tɪˈbʌləs/, Albius (*c.*50–19 B.C.), Roman poet. His smooth and simply-written verses exalt a nostalgic ideal of peaceful rural life over the harsh realities of war and foreign travel.

tic *n.* a habitual spasmodic contraction of the muscles especially of the face; a kind of neuralgia. [F f. It. *ticchio*]

Tichborne claimant /ˈtɪtʃbɔːn/ Arthur Orton (1834–98), a butcher, who came from Australia to claim the rich Tichborne estate after the heir, eldest son of the 10th baronet, was lost at sea. After a long trial (1871) he lost his claim and was imprisoned for perjury.

tick[1] *n.* **1.** a slight recurring click, especially that of a watch or clock. **2.** (*colloq.*) a moment, an instant. **3.** a small mark set against items in a list etc. in checking. —*v.t./i.* **1.** (of a clock etc.) to make ticks. **2.** to mark (an item) with a tick. —**tick off**, (*slang*) to reprimand. **tick over**, (of an engine or *fig.*) to idle. **tick-tack** *n.* a kind of manual semaphore signalling used by bookmakers on a racecourse. **tick-tock** *n.* the ticking of a large clock etc. *what makes a person tick*, his motivation, what makes him behave as he does. [cf. Du. *tik* touch, tick]

tick[2] *n.* an arachnid of the order Acarina or a similar insect (e.g. *Melophagus*) parasitic on animals. [cf. MDu. or MLG *teke*]

tick[3] *n.* (*colloq.*) credit. [app. abbr. of TICKET in phr. *on the ticket*]

tick[4] *n.* the cover of a mattress or pillow; ticking. [f. MDu. or MLG, ult. f. Gk *thēkē* case]

ticker *n.* (*colloq.*) the heart; a watch; a tape-machine. —**ticker-tape** *n.* (*US*) a paper strip from a tape-machine; this or similar material thrown in long strips from windows to greet a celebrity. [f. TICK[1]]

ticket /ˈtɪkɪt/ *n.* **1.** a written or printed piece of paper or card entitling the holder to enter a place, participate in an event, travel by public transport, etc. **2.** a certificate of discharge from the army or of qualification as a ship's master, pilot, etc. **3.** a label attached to a thing and giving its price etc. **4.** an official notification of a traffic offence etc. **5.** a list of candidates put forward by one group, especially a political party. —*v.t.* to attach a ticket to. —**the ticket**, (*slang*) the correct or desirable thing. [f. obs. F *étiquet* (OF *estiquier* fix, f. MDu.)]

ticking *n.* a stout usually striped linen or cotton material used for covering mattresses etc. [f. TICK[4]]

tickle /ˈtɪk(ə)l/ *v.t./i.* **1.** to apply light touches or stroking to (a person or part of his body) so as to excite the nerves and usually produce laughter and spasmodic movement. **2.** to feel this sensation. **3.** to excite agreeably, to amuse, to divert. —*n.* an act or sensation of tickling. —**tickled pink** or **to death**, (*colloq.*) extremely amused or pleased. [prob. f. *tick* touch lightly (as TICK[1])]

ticklish *adj.* **1.** sensitive to tickling. **2.** (of a matter or person to be dealt with) difficult, requiring careful handling. —**ticklishness** *n.*

tidal /ˈtaɪd(ə)l/ *adj.* of or affected by a tide or tides. —**tidal wave**, an exceptionally large ocean wave (e.g. one caused by an earthquake); a widespread manifestation of feeling etc. —**tidally** *adv.* [f. TIDE]

tidbit *US* var. of TITBIT.

tiddler *n.* (*colloq.*) **1.** a small fish, especially a stickleback or minnow. **2.** an unusually small thing. [perh. rel. to *tiddly* little]

tiddly[1] *adj.* (*colloq.*) very small. [var. of *tiddy* (nursery wd); orig. unkn.]

tiddly[2] *adj.* (*slang*) slightly drunk. [orig. unkn.]

tiddly-winks *n.* a game in which small counters are caused to spring from the table into a cup-shaped or cylindrical receptacle by pressing upon their edges with a larger counter. —**tiddly-wink** *n.* a counter used in this game. [orig. unkn.]

tide *n.* **1.** the regular rise and fall of the sea due to the attraction of the moon and sun; water as moved by this. **2.** a trend of opinion, fortune, or events. **3.** a time or season (*archaic* except in *noontide, Christmastide*, etc.). —*v.i.* to be carried by the tide. —**tide-mark** *n.* the mark made by the tide at high water; (*colloq.*) a line of dirt round a bath showing the level of the water that has been used, or on the body of a person showing the extent of his washing. **tide a person over**, to help him through a temporary need or difficulty. **tide-table** *n.* a list of the times of high tide at a place. **turn the tide**, to reverse the trend of events. [OE, = time]

tideway *n.* the tidal part of a river.

tidings /ˈtaɪdɪŋz/ *n.* (as *sing.* or *pl.*) news. [OE, prob. f. ON, = events]

tidy /ˈtaɪdɪ/ *adj.* **1.** neat and orderly, methodically arranged or inclined. **2.** (*colloq.*) considerable. —*n.* **1.** a receptacle for odds and ends. **2.** a cover for a chair-back etc. —*v.t.* to make tidy. —**tidily** *adv.*, **tidiness** *n.* [orig. = timely, f. TIDE]

tie /taɪ/ *v.t./i.* (*partic.* **tying**) **1.** to attach or fasten with a string or cord etc. **2.** to form (a string, ribbon, shoe-lace, necktie, etc.) into a knot or bow; to form (a knot or bow) thus. **3.** to restrict or limit (a person) in some way. **4.** to make the same score as another competitor. **5.** to bind (rafters etc.) by a cross-piece etc. **6.** (*Mus.*) to unite notes by a tie. —*n.* **1.** a cord or chain etc. used for fastening. **2.** a necktie. **3.** a thing that unites or restricts persons. **4.** equality of score or a draw or dead heat among competitors. **5.** a match between any pair of players or teams. **6.** a rod or beam holding parts of a structure together. **7.** (*Mus.*) a curved line above or below two notes of the same pitch that are to be joined as one. —**tie-beam** *n.* a horizontal beam connecting rafters (ill. BUILDING TECHNIQUES, HOUSES). **tiebreak** *n.* a means of deciding the winner when competitors have tied. **tied cottage**, a dwelling occupied subject to the tenant's working for the owner. **tied house**, a public house bound to supply only a particular brewer's beer. **tie-dyeing** *n.* a method of producing dyed patterns by tying parts of the fabric so that they are protected from the dye. **tie in** or **up**, to agree or be closely associated; to cause to do this.

tie-pin *n.* an ornamental pin holding a tie in place. **tie up,** to bind or fasten with cord etc.; to invest or reserve (capital etc.) so that it is not immediately available for use; to obstruct; (usu. in *pass.*) to occupy (a person) fully. [OE]

Tiepolo /ˈtjeɪpələʊ/, Giovanni Battista or Giambattista (1696-1770), Italian painter and graphic artist, the last of the great Venetian fresco painters. His early work is indebted to Veronese in its sumptuous colour and lavish settings. By the 1740s he had developed an individual style of exotic imagery, translucent colour, and theatrical splendour almost operatic in effect (e.g. the *Antony and Cleopatra* frescoes, Palazzo Labia, Venice, 1746-7). His international fame led to a commission from the Prince-Bishop at Würzburg whose residence he decorated (1751-2) with the greatest fresco cycle of the entire 18th c., a perfect fusion of architecture, painting, and stucco work. In 1762, at the request of Charles III, he moved to Madrid where he spent the rest of his life. His religious paintings for the royal chapel at Aranjuez reveal a more tragic vision and new intensity of feeling. His sons Giandomenico (1727-1804) and Lorenzo (1736-76) worked with him on many commissions, the former working competently in his father's manner as well as producing genre scenes.

tier /tɪə(r)/ *n.* a row, rank, or unit of a structure as one of several placed one above another. **—tiered** *adj.* [f. F *tire* (*tirer* draw, elongate)]

Tierra del Fuego /tɪerə del ˈfweɪɡəʊ/ an archipelago separated from the southern tip of South America by the Strait of Magellan; its main island. It was discovered by Magellan in 1520 and is now divided between Chile and Argentina. [Sp., = land of fire]

tiff *n.* a petty quarrel. [orig. unkn.]

tiffin /ˈtɪfɪn/ *n.* (in India) lunch. [app. f. *tiffing* taking slight drink]

tiger /ˈtaɪɡə(r)/ *n.* **1.** a large Asian animal (*Panthera tigris*) of the cat family, with yellowish and black stripes. **2.** a fierce, energetic, or formidable person. **—tiger-cat** *n.* any moderate-sized feline resembling a tiger, e.g. an ocelot. **tiger-lily** *n.* a tall garden lily (*Lilium tigrinum*) with dark-spotted orange flowers. **tiger-moth** *n.* a moth of the family Arctiidae, especially *Arctia caja*, with richly spotted and streaked wings. [f. OF f. L f. Gk *tigris*]

tight /taɪt/ *adj.* **1.** fixed, fastened, or drawn together firmly and hard to move or undo. **2.** fitting closely, made impermeable to a specified thing. **3.** with things or people arranged closely together. **4.** tense, stretched so as to leave no slack. **5.** (*colloq.*) drunk. **6.** (of money or materials) not easily obtainable. **7.** produced by or requiring great exertion or pressure; (of precautions, a programme, etc.) stringent, demanding; (*colloq.*) presenting difficulties. **8.** (*colloq.*) stingy. **—adv.** tightly. **—tight-fisted** *adj.* stingy. **tight-lipped** *adj.* with the lips compressed to restrain emotion or speech. **—tightly** *adv.*, **tightness** *n.* [prob. f. ON]

tighten *v.t./i.* to make or become tighter. [f. TIGHT]

tightrope *n.* a rope stretched tightly high above the ground, on which acrobats perform.

tights *n.pl.* a thin close-fitting elastic garment covering the legs and the lower part of the body, worn by women in place of stockings; a similar garment worn by a dancer, acrobat, etc. [f. TIGHT]

Tiglath-Pileser /tɪɡlæˈpaɪˈliːzə(r)/ the name of three kings of Assyria.

   Tiglath-Pileser I (reigned *c.*1115-1077 BC), dealt effectively with his enemies, consolidated Assyrian influence, and extended its territory over Armenia, Cappadocia, and modern Lebanon. Best known for his prowess in battle and in hunting, he also built or rebuilt a number of temples, reinforced the city walls of Nineveh, and was a patron of literature, collected in one of the oldest extant libraries.

   Tiglath-Pileser III (reigned 745-727 BC), brought the Assyrian empire to the height of its power, and (under the name Pulu) assumed the position of governor of Babylonia, uniting the two crowns in the person of one ruler bearing different names.

tigress /ˈtaɪɡrɪs/ *n.* a female tiger. [f. TIGER]

Tigris /ˈtaɪɡrɪs/ the more easterly of the two rivers of Mesopotamia, 1850 km (1,150 miles) long, rising in the mountains of eastern Turkey and flowing through Iraq to join the Euphrates, forming the Shatt al-Arab which flows into the Persian Gulf.

tilbury /ˈtɪlbərɪ/ *n.* a light open two-wheeled carriage fashionable in the first half of the 19th c. [f. inventor's name]

tilde /ˈtɪldə/ *n.* the mark (˜) put over a letter, e.g. Spanish *n* when pronounced /nj/ (as in señor). [Sp. f. L (as TITLE)]

tile *n.* **1.** a thin slab of glazed or unglazed baked clay or other material used in series for covering a roof, wall, or floor (ill. BUILDING TECHNIQUES). **2.** a thin flat piece used in a game (especially mah-jong). **—v.t.** to cover with tiles. **— on the tiles,** (*slang*) on a nocturnal spree. [OE f. L *tegula*]

tiling /ˈtaɪlɪŋ/ *n.* **1.** the process of fixing tiles. **2.** an area of tiles. [f. TILE]

till[1] *prep.* & *conj.* until. [f. OE & ON, = to]

till[2] *n.* a drawer for money in a shop or bank etc., especially with a device recording the amount of each purchase. [orig. unkn.]

till[3] *v.t.* to cultivate (land). [OE, = strive for]

tillage *n.* **1.** preparation of land for crop-bearing. **2.** tilled land. [f. TILL[3]]

tiller *n.* a bar by which the rudder is turned (ill. SAILING-SHIPS). [f. AF *telier* weaver's beam]

tilt *v.t./i.* **1.** to move or cause to move into a sloping position. **2.** to run or thrust with a lance in jousting. **—n.** **1.** tilting. **2.** a sloping position. **3.** an attack, especially with argument or satire. **—(at) full tilt,** at full speed; with full force. [perh. f. OE *tealt* unsteady]

timber *n.* **1.** wood prepared for use in building, carpentry, etc. **2.** a piece of wood, a beam, especially as a rib of a vessel. **3.** large standing trees. **4.** (esp. as *int.*) a tree about to fall. **—timber-line** *n.* (on a mountain) the line or level above which no trees grow. [OE, = building]

timbered *adj.* **1.** made wholly or partly of timber. **2.** (of country) wooded. [f. prec.]

timbre /tæbr, ˈtæmbə(r)/ *n.* the distinctive character of a musical sound or a voice apart from its pitch and intensity. [F, ult. f. Gk *tumpanon* drum]

timbrel /ˈtɪmbr(ə)l/ *n.* (*archaic*) a tambourine. [f. OF (as prec.)]

Timbuktu /tɪmbʌkˈtuː/ **1.** a town of Mali in Africa, pop. (est. 1970) 10,000. **2.** (*allusively*) any remote place.

time *n.* **1.** the indefinite continued existence of the universe in the past, present, and future regarded as a whole; the progress of this as affecting persons or things; (also **Father Time**) time personified as an aged man, bald but having a forelock, carrying a scythe and an hourglass. **2.** the portion of time belonging to particular events or circumstances. **3.** a portion of time between two points; the point or period allotted, available, or suitable for something; a prison sentence; an apprenticeship; a period of gestation; the date of childbirth or of death. **4.** a point of time stated in hours and minutes of the day. **5.** any of the standard systems by which time is reckoned. **6.** an occasion or instance; (in *pl.*, expressing multiplication) a specified number of times. **7.** (in *sing.* or *pl.*) the conditions of life or of a period. **8.** measured time spent in work etc. **9.** (*Mus.*) the duration of a note; a style depending on the number and accentuation of beats in the bar; a rate of performance. **—v.t.** **1.** to choose the time or moment for; to arrange the time of. **2.** to measure the time taken by. **—against time,** with the utmost speed so as to finish by a specified time. **at the same time,** in spite of this, however. **at times,** sometimes, intermittently. **behind the times,** old-fashioned. **for the time being,** until some other arrangement is made. **from time to time,** occasionally, at intervals. **half the time,** (*colloq.*) as often as not. **have a time of it,** to undergo trouble or difficulty. **have no time for,** to be unable or unwilling to spend time on; to dislike. **in no time,** very soon or quickly. **in time,** not late, punctual; sooner or later; in accordance with the time of music etc. **keep time,** to move or sing etc. in time. **lose time,** to waste time. **on time,** in accordance with the timetable; punctual, punctually. **pass the time of day,** (*colloq.*) to exchange a greeting or casual remarks. **time after time,** on many occasions; in many instances. **time and (time) again,** on many occasions. **time and a half,** a rate of payment for work at one-and-a-half times the normal rate. **time-and-motion** *adj.* concerned with measuring the efficiency of industrial and other operations. **time bomb,** a bomb designed to explode at a pre-set time. **time-clock** *n.* a clock with a device for recording workers' hours of work. **time exposure,** exposure of a photographic film for longer than an instant. **time-honoured** *adj.* esteemed by tradition or custom. **time-lag** *n.* an interval of time between cause and effect. **time-limit** *n.* a limit of time within which a thing must be done. **time of one's life,** a period of exceptional enjoyment. **time out of mind,** from before anyone can remember. **time-sharing** *n.* the use of a computer by several persons for different operations at one time; the ownership or right to the use of a property for a fixed limited time each year. **time-signal** *n.* an audible indication of the exact time of day. **time signature,** (*Mus.*) see SIGNATURE 3. **time-switch** *n.* a switch acting automatically at a pre-set time. **time was,** there was a time. **time zone,** a range of longitudes where a common standard time is used. [OE]

timekeeper *n.* **1.** one who records the time, especially of workers or in a game. **2.** a watch or clock etc. as regards its accuracy.

timeless *adj.* not affected by the passage of time; not to be thought of as having duration. [f. TIME + -LESS]

timely *adj.* opportune, coming at the right time. —**timeliness** *n.* [f. TIME]

timepiece *n.* a clock or watch.

timer /ˈtaɪmə(r)/ *n.* a person or device that measures the time taken. [f. TIME]

timetable *n.* a list of the times at which events will take place, especially the arrival of buses or trains etc., or the series of lessons in a school etc.

timid /ˈtɪmɪd/ *adj.* easily frightened, not bold; shy. —**timidity** /tɪˈmɪdɪtɪ/ *n.*, **timidly** *adv.* [f. F or L *timidus* (*timēre* fear)]

timing /ˈtaɪmɪŋ/ *n.* the way a thing is timed. [f. TIME]

Timor /ˈtiːmɔː(r)/ an island in the southern Malay Archipelago, divided between Portugal and Indonesia. —**Timor Sea,** the part of the Indian Ocean lying between Timor and NW Australia.

timorous /ˈtɪmərəs/ *adj.* timid; frightened. —**timorously** *adv.*, **timorousness** *n.* [f. AL (as TIMID)]

Timothy /ˈtɪməθɪ/, St (1st c. AD), a convert and colleague of St Paul. —**(Epistle to) Timothy,** either of two Pauline epistles of the New Testament addressed to him.

timpano /ˈtɪmpənəʊ/ *n.* (obs. exc. in *pl.*, **timpani**) a kettle-drum (ill. ORCHESTRA). Its use as an orchestral instrument dates from the 17th c. —**timpanist** *n.* [It., = TYMPANUM]

tin *n.* **1.** a silvery-white malleable metallic element, symbol Sn, atomic number 50 (see below). **2.** a container made of tin or tin plate, or of aluminium, especially one hermetically sealed for preserving food (see CAN²). **3.** tin plate. —*v.t.* (-nn-) **1.** to pack (food) in a tin for preservation. **2.** to cover or coat with tin. —**tin foil,** foil made of tin, aluminium, or tin alloy, and used to wrap food for cooking, keeping fresh, etc. **tin god,** an object of unjustified veneration. **tin-opener** *n.* a tool for opening tins of food. **tin plate,** sheet iron or sheet steel coated with tin. **tin-tack** *n.* a tin-coated iron tack. **tin whistle,** a penny whistle. [OE]
Tin can occur native but is more often found as ores, especially cassiterite. It has two major allotropic forms: white tin, the normal metallic form, and grey tin, a powdery form to which white tin tends to change at low temperatures. The metal takes a high polish and is resistant to corrosion. It is used in a number of important alloys (with lead, copper, or antimony to form solder, white-metal, pewter, bronze, etc.), or for plating iron and steel sheets to form tin plate for containers, kitchen utensils, toys, etc. Its use in making bronze dates from ancient times.

tincture /ˈtɪŋktʃə(r)/ *n.* **1.** a tinge or trace of some element or quality. **2.** a medicinal solution of a drug in alcohol. —*v.t.* to tinge. [as TINGE]

tinder *n.* a dry substance that readily catches fire from a spark. —**tinder-box** *n.* a box containing tinder, flint, and steel, for kindling fires. —**tindery** *adj.* [OE]

tine *n.* each of the points or prongs of a fork, harrow, antler, etc. [OE]

tinge *v.t.* to colour slightly; to give a slight trace of some element or quality to. —*n.* a slight colouring or trace. [f. L *tingere* stain]

tingle *v.i.* to feel a slight pricking, stinging, or throbbing sensation, especially in the ears or hands; to cause this. —*n.* a tingling sensation. [perh. var. of TINKLE]

tinker *n.* **1.** an itinerant mender of kettles and pans etc. **2.** (*Sc.* & *Ir.*) a gypsy. **3.** (*colloq.*) a mischievous person or animal. **4.** a spell of tinkering. —*v.i.* **1.** to work at something casually trying to improve or repair it. **2.** to work as a tinker. [orig. unkn.]

tinkle *n.* **1.** a series of short light ringing sounds. **2.** (*colloq.*) a telephone call. —*v.t./i.* to make or cause to make a tinkle. [f. obs. *tink* to chink (imit.)]

tinny *adj.* **1** of or like tin. **2.** (of a metal object) flimsy, insubstantial. **3.** having a metallic taste or a thin metallic sound. —**tinnily** *adv.*, **tinniness** *n.* [f. TIN]

Tin Pan Alley originally the name given to a district in New York (28th Street, between 5th Avenue and Broadway) where many songwriters, arrangers, and music publishers were based. The district gave its name to the American popular music industry between the late 1880s and the mid-20th c., particularly to such composers as Irving Berlin, Jerome Kern, George Gershwin, Cole Porter, and Richard Rodgers. The term was also applied to Denmark Street in London.

tinpot *adj.* (*colloq.*, *derog.*) cheap, inferior.

tinsel /ˈtɪns(ə)l/ *n.* a glittering metallic substance used in strips or threads to give an inexpensive sparkling effect. —*adj.* superficially showy, gaudy. [prob. f. AF, ult. f. L, = SCINTILLA]

tinsmith *n.* a worker in tin and tin plate.

tint *n.* **1.** a variety of a colour, especially made by adding white. **2.** a slight trace of a different colour. **3.** a faint colour spread over a surface. —*v.t.* to apply a tint to; to colour. —**tinted** *adj.* [f. L *tinctus* (as TINGE)]

Tintagel /tɪnˈtædʒ(ə)l/ a village on the coast of northern Cornwall, with ruins of a castle. It is the traditional birth-place of King Arthur.

tintinnabulation /tɪntɪnæbjʊˈleɪʃ(ə)n/ *n.* a ringing or tinkling of bells. [f. L *tintinnabulum* bell]

Tintoretto /tɪntəˈretəʊ/, Jacopo Robusti (1518-94), Venetian painter, given his nickname because his father was a dyer (*tintore*). Little is known of his early life but he began his artistic career in about 1537 and some sources claim he did work, however briefly, in Titian's studio. He spent nearly all his life in Venice, personally unpopular and considered professionally unscrupulous. Although he received both religious and State commissions, he did not attract aristrocratic patronage as much as he appealed to the monied middle classes. From 1550 the influence of Titian and Veronese can be seen and Tintoretto's works take on a mannerist religious intensity, where the mood dominates. His work can be distinguished by unusual viewpoints, bold colour, lively sometimes rushed brush-work, and the hint of the bizarre, highlighted by bold chiaroscuro effects.

tiny /ˈtaɪnɪ/ *adj.* very small or slight. —**tinily** *adv.*, **tininess** *n.* [orig. unkn.]

tip¹ *n.* **1.** the very end, especially of a small or tapering thing. **2.** a small piece or part attached to an end of a thing. **3.** a leaf-bud of tea. —*v.t.* (-pp-) to provide with a tip. —**on the tip of one's tongue,** just about to be said, or remembered and spoken. **tip of the iceberg,** the small evident part of something much larger. [f. ON (as TOP¹)]

tip² *v.t./i.* (-pp-) **1.** to tilt or topple; to cause to do this. **2.** to overturn, to cause to overbalance; to discharge (the contents of a truck or jug etc.) thus. **3.** to make a small present of money to, especially for service given. **4.** to name as the likely winner of a race or contest etc. **5.** to strike or touch lightly. —*n.* **1.** a small money present, especially for service given. **2.** private or special information (e.g. about a horse-race or stock-market); a small or casual piece of advice. **3.** a slight push or tilt. **4.** a place where material (esp. rubbish) is tipped. **5.** a light stroke. —**tip a person off,** to give him a hint or special information, or a warning. **tip-off** *n.* such information etc. **tip-up** *adj.* able to be tipped, e.g. of a seat in a theatre to allow passage past. **tip a person the wink,** to give him private information. [perh. f. Scand.; partly f. TIP¹]

tippet /ˈtɪpɪt/ *n.* a small cape or collar of fur etc. with the ends hanging down in front. [prob. f. TIP¹]

Tippett /ˈtɪpɪt/, Sir Michael (1905-), English composer. In 1938-39 he composed the *Concerto for Double String Orchestra*, a work which bears many of his stylistic finger-prints—in particular the marked rhythmic drive. He was a conscientious objector in the Second World War, and his concerns with the different strands which make up human nature—light and dark, warm and shrinking, calm and violent—is expressed in much of his music, particularly the oratorio *A Child of our Time* (1939-41) and his four operas (1955-77), as well as in his writings. He has not shunned traditional instrumental forms, and other works include four symphonies (1944-77), four string quartets (1934-79), and three piano sonatas (1936-73).

tipple *v.t./i.* to drink (wine or spirits etc.); to be a habitual drinker. —*n.* (*colloq.*) alcoholic or other drink. —**tippler** *n.* [back-formation f. *tippler*; orig. unkn.]

tipstaff *n.* **1.** a sheriff's officer. **2.** the metal-tipped staff carried by him as a badge of office.

Time

Some early non-mechanical ways of measuring time

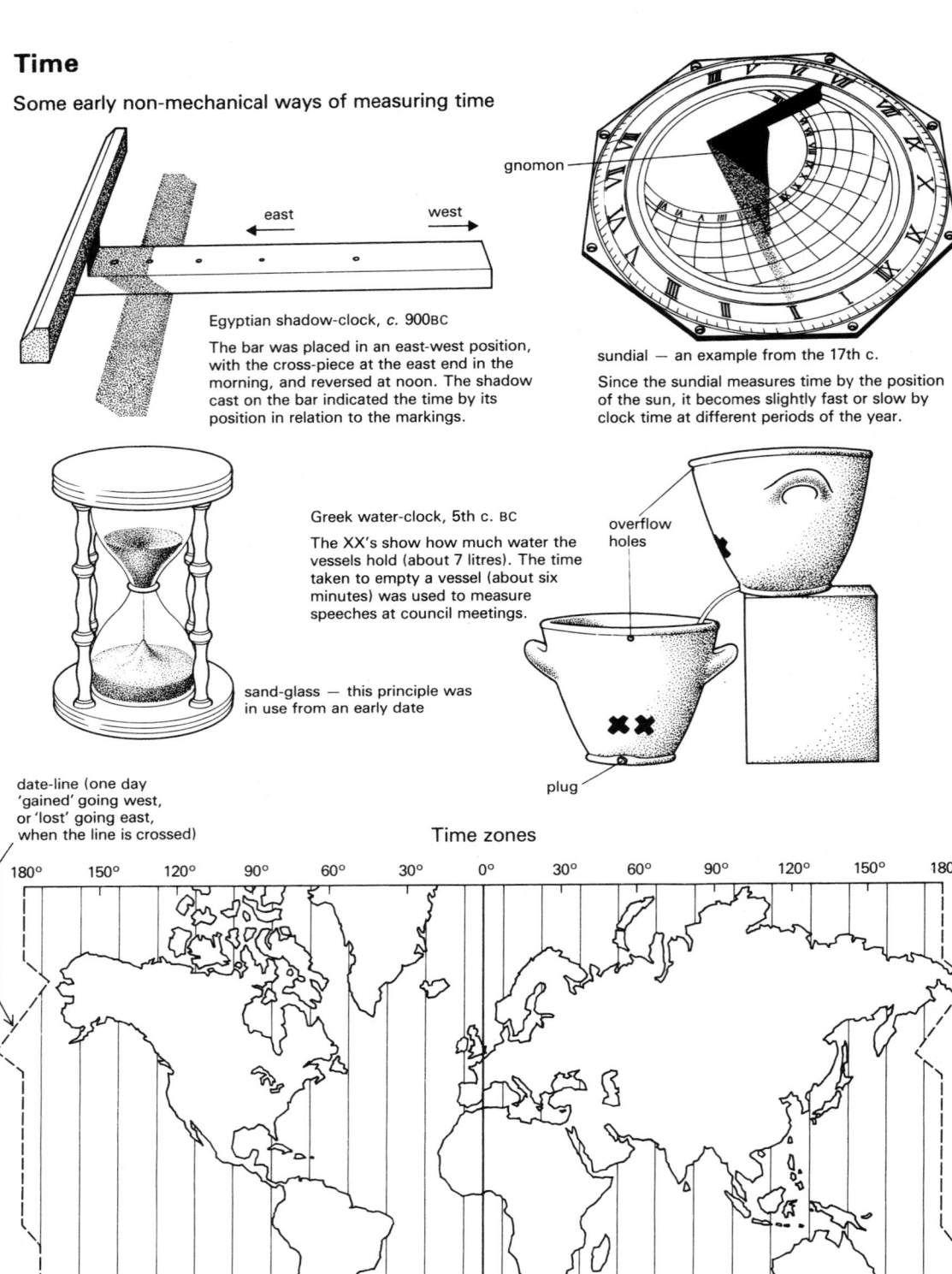

east   west

Egyptian shadow-clock, *c.* 900BC

The bar was placed in an east-west position, with the cross-piece at the east end in the morning, and reversed at noon. The shadow cast on the bar indicated the time by its position in relation to the markings.

gnomon

sundial — an example from the 17th c.

Since the sundial measures time by the position of the sun, it becomes slightly fast or slow by clock time at different periods of the year.

Greek water-clock, 5th c. BC

The XX's show how much water the vessels hold (about 7 litres). The time taken to empty a vessel (about six minutes) was used to measure speeches at council meetings.

overflow holes

sand-glass — this principle was in use from an early date

plug

date-line (one day 'gained' going west, or 'lost' going east, when the line is crossed)

Time zones

| 180° | 150° | 120° | 90° | 60° | 30° | 0° | 30° | 60° | 90° | 120° | 150° | 180° |

−12 −11 −10 −9 −8 −7 −6 −5 −4 −3 −2 −1 GMT +1 +2 +3 +4 +5 +6 +7 +8 +9 +10 +11 +12

0° meridian

hours behind/ahead of GMT

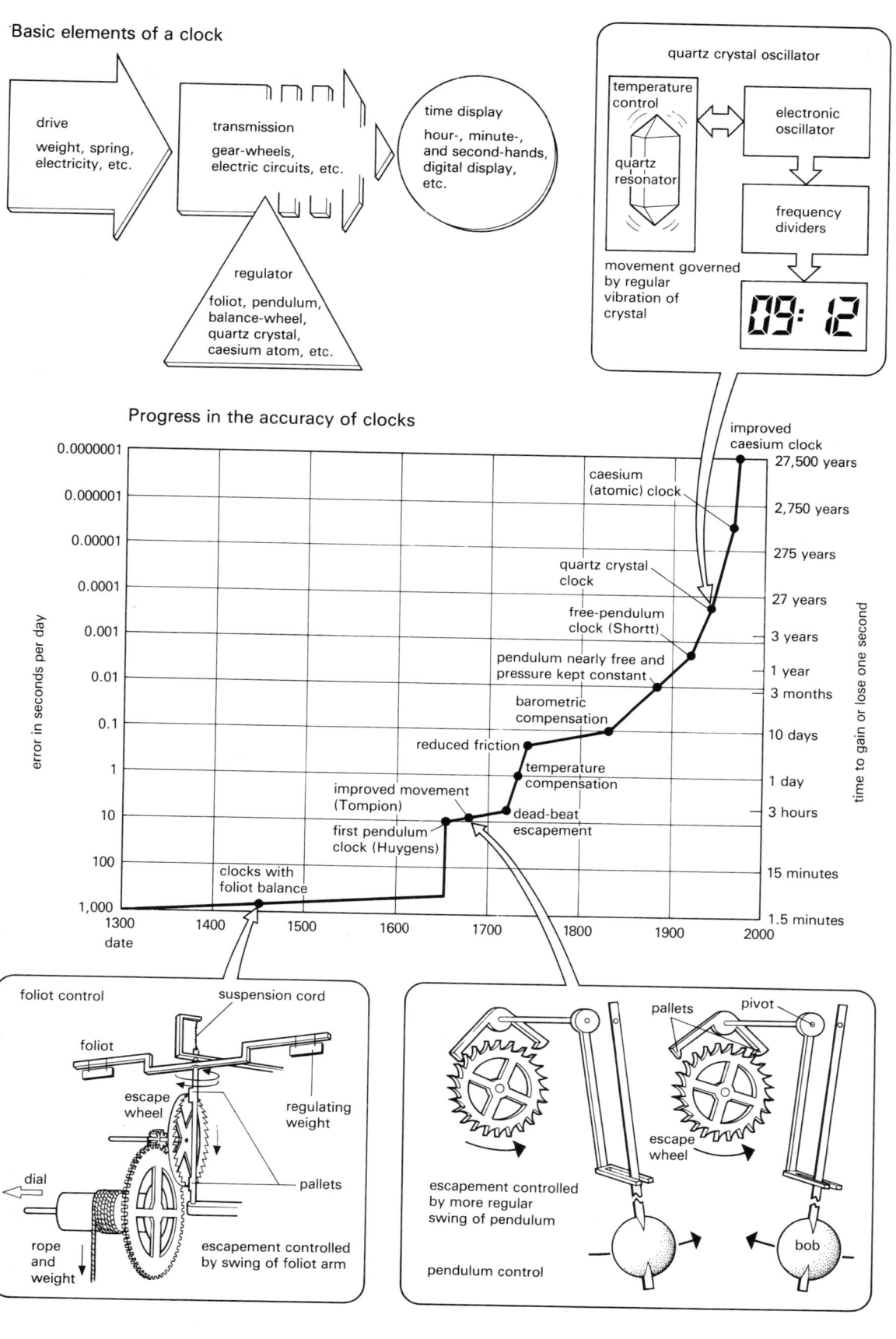

Basic elements of a clock

drive

weight, spring, electricity, etc.

transmission

gear-wheels, electric circuits, etc.

time display

hour-, minute-, and second-hands, digital display, etc.

regulator

foliot, pendulum, balance-wheel, quartz crystal, caesium atom, etc.

quartz crystal oscillator

temperature control

quartz resonator

electronic oscillator

frequency dividers

09:12

movement governed by regular vibration of crystal

Progress in the accuracy of clocks

error in seconds per day

time to gain or lose one second

improved caesium clock — 27,500 years

caesium (atomic) clock — 2,750 years

— 275 years

quartz crystal clock — 27 years

free-pendulum clock (Shortt) — 3 years

pendulum nearly free and pressure kept constant — 1 year

barometric compensation — 3 months

— 10 days

reduced friction

temperature compensation — 1 day

improved movement (Tompion)

dead-beat escapement — 3 hours

first pendulum clock (Huygens)

clocks with foliot balance

— 15 minutes

— 1.5 minutes

date: 1300 1400 1500 1600 1700 1800 1900 2000

foliot control

suspension cord

foliot

escape wheel

regulating weight

dial

pallets

rope and weight

escapement controlled by swing of foliot arm

pallets

pivot

escape wheel

bob

escapement controlled by more regular swing of pendulum

pendulum control

tipster *n.* one who gives tips about horse-races etc. [f. TIP²]
tipsy /ˈtɪpsɪ/ *adj.* slightly intoxicated; caused by or showing slight intoxication. —**tipsy-cake** *n.* a sponge-cake soaked in wine or spirits and served with custard. —**tipsily** *adv.*, **tipsiness** *n.* [prob. f. TIP²]
tiptoe *n.* the tips of the toes. —*v.i.* to walk on tiptoe or very stealthily. —*adv.* on tiptoe, with the heels off the ground.
tiptop /ˈtɪptɒp, -ˈtɒp/ *adj.* (*colloq.*) excellent. —*n.* (*colloq.*) the highest point of excellence. —*adv.* (*colloq.*) excellently.
TIR *abbr.* Transport International Routier. [F, = international road transport]
tirade /taɪˈreɪd, tɪ-/ *n.* a long vehement denunciation or declamation. [F f. It., = volley]
Tiranë /tɪˈrɑːnə/ the capital of Albania; pop. (est. 1978) 198,000.
tire¹ *v.t./i.* to make or become tired. [OE]
tire² *n.* **1.** a band of metal placed round the rim of a wheel to strengthen it. **2.** (*US*) a tyre. [perh. f. ATTIRE]
tired /ˈtaɪəd/ *adj.* **1.** feeling that one would like to sleep or rest. **2.** (of an idea etc.) hackneyed. —**tired of,** having had enough of (a thing or activity) and feeling impatient or bored. [f. TIRE¹]
tireless *adj.* not tiring easily, having inexhaustible energy. —**tirelessly** *adv.* [f. TIRE¹ + -LESS]
Tiresias /taɪˈriːsɪəs/ (*Gk legend*) a blind Theban prophet, so wise that even his ghost had its wits and was not a mere phantom. Legends account variously for his wisdom and blindness.
tiresome *adj.* wearisome, tedious; (*colloq.*) annoying. [f. TIRE¹ + -SOME]
Tir-nan-Og /tɪənæˈnɔʊɡ/ (*Irish myth.*) a land of perpetual youth, the Irish equivalent of Elysium. [f. Ir., = land of the young]
tiro /ˈtaɪərəʊ/ *n.* (*pl.* **tiros**) a beginner, a novice. [L, = recruit]
'tis /tɪz/ (*archaic*) it is.
Tisiphone /tɪˈsɪfənɪ/ (*Gk myth.*) one of the Furies. [Gk, = the avenger of blood]
tissue /ˈtɪʃuː, ˈtɪsjuː/ *n.* **1.** any of the coherent substances of which animal or plant bodies are made. **2.** tissue-paper. **3.** a disposable piece of thin soft absorbent paper for wiping or drying things. **4.** a fine gauzy fabric. **5.** a connected series (of lies etc.). —**tissue-paper** *n.* thin soft unsized paper for wrapping or packing things. [f. OF *tissu* f. L *texere* weave]
tit¹ *n.* any of various small birds (e.g. *blue tit, coal-tit*). [prob. f. Scand.]
tit² *n.* **tit for tat,** blow for blow, retaliation. [= earlier *tip* (TIP²) *for tat*]
tit³ *n.* (*vulgar*) a nipple; (in *pl.*) a woman's breasts. [OE]
Titan /ˈtaɪt(ə)n/ *n.* **1.** (*Gk myth.*) any of the older gods who preceded the Olympians and were the children of Heaven and Earth. They are believed to be pre-Greek gods, but the evidence is slight. **2.** a person of very great strength, intelligence, or importance. [f. L f. Gk]
Titanic /taɪˈtænɪk/ a British passenger liner, the largest ship in the world when she was built, that struck an iceberg in the North Atlantic on her maiden voyage in April 1912 and sank with the loss of 1,490 lives. The disaster led to new regulations requiring ships to carry sufficient lifeboats for all on board, a more southerly liner track across the Atlantic, and an ice patrol which continues to this day.
titanic /taɪˈtænɪk/ *adj.* gigantic, colossal. —**titanically** *adv.* [f. Gk (as TITAN)]
titanium /taɪˈteɪnɪəm, tɪ-/ *n.* a grey metallic element, symbol Ti, atomic number 22, widespread in the earth's crust. It is not found uncombined in nature. First discovered (as the oxide) in 1791, titanium did not become commercially significant until after the Second World War. Since then its lightness, strength, and resistance to corrosion have found use in alloys for parts of aircraft, space vehicles, etc. Of its various compounds, titanium dioxide is noteworthy: it is a very opaque white solid which is widely used in paints and other surface coatings. [f. TITAN, after *uranium*]
titbit *n.* a dainty morsel; a piquant item of news etc. [prob. f. dial. *tid* tender + BIT¹]
titfer *n.* (*slang*) a hat. [abbr. of *tit* (TIT²) *fer* tat, rhyming slang = hat]
tithe /taɪð/ *n.* (*hist.*) a tax of one tenth, especially a tenth part of the annual produce of land or labour formerly levied to support clergy and the Church. —*v.t.* to subject to tithes; to pay tithes. —**tithe barn,** a barn built to hold tithes paid in kind. [OE, = tenth]

Tithonus /tɪˈθəʊnəs/ (*Gk myth.*) a Trojan prince with whom the goddess Aurora fell in love. She asked Zeus to make him immortal but omitted to ask for eternal youth, and he became very old and decrepit although he talked perpetually. Tithonus prayed her to remove him from this world and she changed him into a grasshopper, which chirps ceaselessly.
Titian /ˈtɪʃ(ə)n/ (Tiziano Vecellio, *c.*1488-1576), Italian painter, who dominated Venetian art during its greatest period. Trained in the studio of Giovanni Bellini, he was inspired by Giorgione, after whose early death (1510) it fell to Titian to complete a number of his unfinished paintings. On Bellini's death in 1516 Titian became official painter to the Republic. Among his most famous works are the enigmatic *Sacred and Profane Love* (*c.*1516), the *Assumption* (1516-18), and classical subjects such as *Bacchus and Ariadne* (1518-23). His fame spread throughout Europe; Charles V appointed him court painter and knighted him. Titian painted many noble portraits, conveying the sitters' personalities and not merely recording their features. His last great work was the *Pietà* (1573-6) intended for his own tomb. Titian's influence on later painters has been profound. His greatness as an artist, it appears, was not matched by his character; he was of a mercenary disposition. His name is used to denote the colour of hair which he favoured in his pictures (e.g. *Ariadne, The Magdalene,* and *Flora*), described as 'a bright golden auburn' and more loosely used as a polite or appreciative word for 'red'.
Titicaca /tɪtɪˈkɑːkə/, **Lake** a lake in the Andes, between Peru and Bolivia, at an altitude of 3,809 m (12,497 ft), the highest large lake in the world.
titillate /ˈtɪtɪleɪt/ *v.t.* to excite pleasantly; to tickle. —**titillation** /-ˈleɪʃ(ə)n/ *n.* [f. L *titillare*]
titivate /ˈtɪtɪveɪt/ *v.t.* (*colloq.*) to smarten, to put the finishing touches to. —**titivation** /-ˈveɪʃ(ə)n/ *n.* [earlier *tid-*, perh. f. TIDY after *cultivate*]
title /ˈtaɪt(ə)l/ *n.* **1.** the name of a book, poem, or work of art etc. **2.** the heading of a chapter or legal document etc.; a caption or credit title of a film. **3.** a form of nomenclature indicating a person's status (e.g. *professor, queen*) or used as a form of address or reference (e.g. *Lord, Mr, Your Grace*). **4.** a championship in sport. **5.** the right to the ownership of property with or without possession; the facts constituting this; a just or recognized claim. —**title-deed** *n.* a legal instrument as evidence of a right. **title-page** *n.* a page at the beginning of a book giving the title and particulars of authorship etc. **title-role** *n.* the part in a play etc. that gives it its name (e.g. *Othello*). [f. OF f. L *titulus* placard, title]
titled /ˈtaɪt(ə)ld/ *adj.* having a title of nobility or rank. [f. TITLE]
titmouse *n.* (*pl.* **titmice**) a tit (TIT¹). [f. TIT¹ + obs. *mose* titmouse]
Tito /ˈtiːtəʊ/ (Josip Broz, 1892-1980), Yugoslavian statesman. An NCO in the Austro-Hungarian army, Tito was captured by the Russians in 1915 and after escaping participated in the Russian Revolution and Civil War on the Red side. He returned to Yugoslavia in 1920 and became an active Communist organizer. With the German invasion in 1941 he became a guerrilla leader, gradually establishing his Partisans as the most effective resistance movement, winning Allied support, and emerging as head of the new government at the end of the war. He defied Stalin over policy in the Balkans in 1948 and established Yugoslavia as a non-aligned Communist State, being elected President in 1953 and after successive re-elections being named President for life in 1974.
titrate /taɪˈtreɪt/ *v.t.* to ascertain the amount of a constituent in (a substance) by using a standard reagent. —**titration** /-ˈtreɪʃ(ə)n/ *n.* [f. F *titrer* (*titre* title)]
titter *v.i.* to laugh covertly, to giggle. —*n.* such a laugh. [imit.]
tittle /ˈtɪt(ə)l/ *n.* a small written or printed stroke or dot; a particle, a whit (esp. *not one jot or tittle*). [f. L (as TITLE)]
tittle-tattle *v.i.* to tattle. —*n.* tattle. [redupl. of TATTLE]
tittup /ˈtɪtəp/ *v.i.* to move in a lively or frisky way, to bob up and down. —*n.* such a movement. [perh. imit. of hoof-beats]
titular /ˈtɪtjʊlə(r)/ *adj.* **1.** of or relating to a title. **2.** existing or being such in title only. [f. F (as TITLE)]
Titus¹ /ˈtaɪtəs/ (Titus Flavius Vespasianus, 39-81) Roman emperor 79-81, elder son of Vespasian. In 70 he ended a revolt in Judaea and destroyed Jerusalem. A popular and generous emperor, he completed the Colosseum and pro-

vided relief for the destruction caused by the eruption of Vesuvius in 79.

Titus[2] /ˈtaɪtəs/, St (1st c. AD), a convert and helper of St Paul. —**(Epistle to) Titus,** a Pauline epistle of the New Testament addressed to him.

tizzy /ˈtɪzɪ/ n. (slang) a state of nervous agitation or confusion. [orig. unkn.]

Tl symbol thallium.

Tm symbol thulium.

TNT abbr. trinitrotoluene.

to /tə, before a vowel tʊ, emphat. tuː/ prep. **1.** in the direction of; so as to approach, reach, or be in (a place, position, or state etc.). **2.** as far as, not falling far short of. **3.** as compared with; in respect of. **4.** for (a person or thing) to hold, possess, or be affected etc. by. **5.** (with a verb) introducing an infinitive; expressing purpose, consequence, or cause; used alone when an infinitive is understood (I meant to call but forgot to). —adv. to or in a normal or required position or condition; to a standstill; (of a door) into a nearly closed position. —**to and fro,** backwards and forwards; repeatedly between the same places. [OE]

toad n. **1.** a froglike amphibian of the genus Bufo (ill. AMPHIBIANS). **2.** a repulsive person. —**toad-in-the-hole** n. sausages or other meat baked in batter. [OE]

toadflax n. a plant of the genus Linaria or allied genera with spurred yellow or purple flowers.

toadstool n. a fungus, usually poisonous, with a round top and a slender stalk.

toady n. a sycophant, an obsequious hanger-on. —v.t./i. to behave as a toady (to). [f. toad-eater orig. the attendant of a charlatan, employed to eat or pretend to eat toads (held to be poisonous) to enable his master to exhibit his skill in expelling poison]

toast n. **1.** a toasted slice of bread. **2.** a person or thing in whose honour a company is requested to drink; the call to drink or an instance of drinking in this way. —v.t. **1.** to brown the surface of (bread, a teacake, cheese, etc.) by placing it before a fire or other source of heat. **2.** to warm (one's feet or oneself) thus. **3.** to honour or pledge good wishes by drinking. —**have a person on toast,** (slang) to have him at one's mercy. **toasting-fork** n. a long-handled fork for holding a slice of bread before a fire to toast it.

toast-master n. a person announcing the toasts at a public dinner. **toast-rack** n. a rack for holding slices of toast at table. [f. OF toster f. L torrēre parch]

toaster n. an electrical device for making toast. [f. toast]

tobacco /təˈbækəʊ/ n. (pl. -os) a plant of the genus Nicotiana, native to Central America, with narcotic leaves used for smoking, chewing, or snuff; its leaves, especially as prepared for smoking. Tobacco was introduced into England in the reign of Queen Elizabeth I. Although it can be grown in temperate climates its cultivation as a crop is carried out mainly in tropical and subtropical countries. [f. Sp. tabaco f. Amer. Indian origin]

tobacconist /təˈbækənɪst/ n. a shopkeeper who sells tobacco and cigarettes etc. [f. prec.]

Tobit /ˈtəʊbɪt/ a book of the Apocrypha, a romance of the Jewish captivity telling the story of Tobit, a pious Jew.

toboggan /təˈbɒgən/ n. a long light narrow sledge curved upwards at the front, used for sliding downhill especially over snow or ice. —v.i. to ride on a toboggan. As a winter recreation, tobogganing is recorded in 16th-c. documents. Its development as a racing sport dates from the mid-19th c. [f. Canadian F f. Algonquian]

Toby /ˈtəʊbɪ/ the name of the trained dog introduced (in the first half of the 19th c.) into the Punch and Judy show, which wears a frill round its neck. [familiar form of name Tobias]

toby jug a jug or mug in the form of a stout old man wearing a long full-skirted coat and a three-cornered hat (18th-c. costume). [prob. as prec.]

toccata /təˈkɑːtə/ n. a musical composition for a piano, organ, etc., designed to exhibit a performer's touch and technique. [It., p.p. of toccare touch]

Tocharian /tɒˈkɛərɪən/ n. an extinct Indo-European language of central Asia in the 1st millennium AD. —adj. of this language. [f. F f. L f. Gk Tokharoi Scythian tribe]

tocsin /ˈtɒksɪn/ n. an alarm-signal; a bell used to sound an alarm. [F f. touquesain, toquassen f. Prov. (ult. as touch, sign)]

tod n. (slang) on one's tod, alone, on one's own. [perh. f. on one's Tod Sloan (jockey, d. 1933), rhyming slang]

today /təˈdeɪ/ adv. on this present day; nowadays, in modern times. —n. this present day; modern times. [OE (as to¹, day)]

Todd, Sweeney. A barber who murdered his customers, the central character of a play by George Dibdin Pitt (1799-1855), and of later plays.

toddle v.i. to walk with a young child's short unsteady steps; (colloq., usu. with off) to depart. —n. a toddling walk. [orig. unkn.]

toddler n. a child who has only recently learnt to walk. [f. prec.]

toddy /ˈtɒdɪ/ n. a drink of spirits with hot water and sugar. [f. Hind. (tar palm)]

to-do /təˈduː/ n. a commotion, a fuss. [f. to do as in What's to do?]

toe n. **1.** any of the terminal members (five in man) of the front part of the foot; the corresponding part of an animal or bird. **2.** the part of footwear that covers the toes. **3.** the lower end or tip of an implement etc. —v.t. to touch with the toes. —**on one's toes,** alert, eager. **toe-cap** n. the reinforced toe of a boot or shoe. **toe-hold** n. a slight foothold (lit. & fig.). **toe the line,** to conform (especially under compulsion) to the requirement of one's group or party. [OE]

toff n. (slang) a distinguished or well-dressed person. [perh. f. tuft in archaic sense 'titled undergraduate', who formerly at Oxford and Cambridge Universities wore a gold tassel on the academic cap]

toffee /ˈtɒfɪ/ n. a kind of firm or hard sweet made by boiling sugar, butter, etc.; a small piece of this. —**can't do a thing for toffee,** (slang) is incompetent at it. **toffee-apple** n. a toffee-coated apple on a stick. **toffee-nosed** adj. (slang) snobbish, pretentious. [f. earlier taffy (orig. unkn.)]

tog n. **1.** (usu. in pl., slang) a garment. **2.** a unit expressing the insulating properties of clothes and quilts. —v.t. (-gg-) (with out or up) (slang) to dress. [abbr. of 16th-c. slang togman f. F toge or L toga (see foll.); sense 2 modelled on earlier US term clo (clothes)]

toga /ˈtəʊgə/ n. an ancient Roman citizen's loose flowing outer garment. —**toga'd** adj. [L (rel. to tegere cover)]

together /təˈgeðə(r)/ adv. **1.** in or into company or conjunction; towards each other; so as to unite. **2.** one with another. **3.** simultaneously. **4.** in an unbroken succession. **5.** (colloq.) well organized or controlled. —**together with,** as well as, and also. [OE, (as to¹, gather)]

togetherness n. being together; feeling or belonging together. [f. prec.]

toggle n. a fastening device consisting of a short piece of wood or metal etc. secured by its centre and passed through a loop or hole etc. —**toggle-switch** n. a switch operated by a projecting lever. [orig. unkn.]

Togo /ˈtəʊgəʊ/ a country in West Africa between Ghana and Benin with a short coastline on the Gulf of Guinea; pop. (est. 1979) 2,470,000; official language, French; capital, Lomé. Annexed by Germany in 1884, the district called Togoland was divided between France and Britain after the First World War. The British western section joined Ghana on the latter's independence (1957). The remainder of the area became a United Nations mandate under French administration after the Second World War and achieved independence, as a republic with the name Togo, in 1960. The economy is mainly agricultural but phosphates (of which there are rich deposits) form the principal source of export earnings. —**Togolese** /-ˈliːz/ adj. & n..

toil v.i. to work long or laboriously; to move laboriously. —n. hard or laborious work. —**toiler** n. [f. AF, = dispute, f. L tudiculare stir about (tudicula machine for bruising olives, rel. to tundere beat)]

toilet /ˈtɔɪlɪt/ n. **1.** a lavatory. **2.** the process of washing oneself, dressing, etc. —**toilet-paper** n. paper for cleaning oneself after excreting. **toilet-roll** n. a roll of toilet-paper. **toilet soap,** soap for washing oneself. **toilet-training** n. the training of a young child to use the lavatory. **toilet water,** a scented liquid used in or after cleansing the skin. [f. F toilette (as toils)]

toiletries /ˈtɔɪlɪtrɪz/ n.pl. articles used in making one's toilet. [f. prec.]

toils /tɔɪlz/ n.pl. a snare. [f. OF toile cloth f. L tela web]

toilsome /ˈtɔɪlsəm/ adj. involving toil. [f. toil + -some]

Tokay /ˈtəʊkeɪ/ n. a sweet Hungarian wine; a similar wine from elsewhere. [f. Tokaj in Hungary]

token /ˈtəʊkən/ n. **1.** an indication; a thing serving as a symbol, reminder, keepsake, distinctive mark, or guarantee.

2. a voucher exchangeable for goods. **3.** a thing used to represent something else; a device resembling a coin, bought for use in slot-machines etc. or for making certain payments. —*adj.* serving as a token or pledge but often on a small scale. —**by this** *or* **the same token,** similarly; moreover; in corroboration of what I say. [OE (rel. to TEACH)]

tokenism /'təʊkənɪz(ə)m/ *n.* making only a token effort or granting only minimum concessions, especially to minority or suppressed groups. [f. TOKEN]

Tokyo /'təʊkjəʊ/ the capital of Japan; pop. 11,648,378. The city was formerly called Edo and was the centre of the military government under the shoguns; it was renamed Tokyo in 1868 when it became the imperial capital. [Jap., = eastern capital]

tolbooth /'tɒlbuːθ/ var. of TOLL-BOOTH.

told /təʊld/ *past* & *p.p.* of TELL.

Toledo /tə'leɪdəʊ/ a city of Spain, the Spanish capital 1087-1560, long famous for the manufacture of finely-tempered sword-blades.

tolerable /'tɒlərəb(ə)l/ *adj.* **1.** able to be tolerated, endurable. **2.** fairly good, passable. —**tolerableness** *n.*, **tolerably** *adv.* [f. OF f. L (as TOLERATE)]

tolerance /'tɒlərəns/ *n.* **1.** willingness or ability to tolerate a person or thing. **2.** permissible variation in dimension or weight. [as prec.]

tolerant /'tɒlərənt/ *adj.* having or showing tolerance. —**tolerantly** *adv.* [as prec.]

tolerate /'tɒləreɪt/ *v.t.* **1.** to permit without protest or interference. **2.** to find or treat as endurable. **3.** to be able to take (a medicine) or undergo (a process etc.) without harm. —**toleration** /-'reɪʃ(ə)n/ *n.* [f. L *tolerare*]

Toleration Act an act of 1689 granting freedom of worship to dissenters (excluding Roman Catholics and Unitarians) on certain conditions. Its real purpose was to unite all Protestants under William III against the deposed Roman Catholic James II.

Tolkien /'tɒlkiːn/, John Ronald Reuel (1892-1973), Professor of Anglo-Saxon and later of English Language and Literature at Oxford, born in South Africa, author of *The Hobbit* (1937) and *The Lord of the Rings* (1954-5), two fantasies written for child and adult readers, set in an imaginary Middle Earth peopled by hobbits (shy humanlike creatures of dwarfish stature) and other strange races. The books have attracted a huge following since the mid-1960s.

toll[1] /təʊl/ *n.* **1.** a charge payable for permission to pass a barrier or for the use of a bridge or road etc. **2.** the cost or damage caused by a disaster or incurred in an achievement. —**take its toll,** to be accompanied by loss or injury etc. **toll-booth** *n.* (*archaic*, *Sc.*) a town hall or town gaol. **toll-bridge** *n.* a bridge at which a toll is charged. **toll-gate** *n.* a gate preventing passage until a toll is paid. **toll-house** *n.* (*hist.*) a small house built near a toll-gate for the use of the keeper, usually hexagonal in shape so that the windows commanded a view in all directions. **toll-road** *n.* a road maintained by the tolls collected on it. [OE f. L *toloneum* f. Gk (*telos* tax)]

toll[2] /təʊl/ *v.t./i.* **1.** (of a bell) to sound with a slow uniform succession of strokes. **2.** to ring (a bell or knell) or strike (an hour) or announce or mark (a death etc.) thus. —*n.* the tolling or stroke of a bell. [spec. use of obs. or dial. *toll* pull]

Tollund /'tɒlənd/ a fen in central Jutland, Denmark, where the well-preserved corpse of an Iron Age man (*c.*500 BC-400 AD) was found in a peat bog in 1950. The body was naked save for a leather cap and belt, and round the neck was a plaited leather noose: Tollund Man had met his death by hanging, a victim of murder or ritual slaughter.

Tolpuddle martyrs /'tɒlpʌd(ə)l/ six farm labourers of the village of Tolpuddle, Dorset, who attempted to form a union to obtain an increase in wages and were sentenced in 1834 to seven years' transportation on a charge of administering unlawful oaths. Their harsh sentences caused widespread protests, and two years later they were pardoned and repatriated from Australia.

Tolstoy /'tɒlstɔɪ, -'stɔɪ/, Count Lev Nikolaevich (1828-1910), Russian writer. His first published work, *Childhood* (1852), began the perceptive trilogy of his early years (continued in *Boyhood*, 1854 and *Youth*, 1857). His unromantic view of war, expressed in *Sevastopol Sketches* (1855-6), was inspired by his experiences in the Crimea. The next decade was mainly devoted to the creation of his masterpiece *War and Peace* (1863-9), an epic novel of the Napoleonic

invasion and the lives of three aristocratic families; *Anna Karenina* (1873-7) describes a married woman's passion for a young officer and her tragic fate. His constant concern with moral questions developed into a spiritual crisis which led to radical changes in his life and works, including *The Death of Ivan Ilich* (1886), *The Kreutzer Sonata* (1889), and *Resurrection* (1899). Tolstoy's moral stance regarding non-resistance to evil, renunciation of property, abolition of governments and churches, but a belief in God and man, led to his excommunication from the Russian Orthodox Church (1901) and the banning of many of his works, but brought him a moral authority and influence and his home, Yasnaya Polyana, became a place of pilgrimage.

Toltec /'tɒltek/ *n.* (*pl.* same or **-s**) a member of a Nahuatl-speaking people who dominated central Mexico *c.*900-1200 (see below). —*adj.* of the Toltec. [Sp. f. Nahuatl]
The Toltec were a warrior aristocracy whose period of domination was violent and innovative. They founded or developed cities (their capital was Tula), but were unable to consolidate their hold on the conquered area, which developed into a number of States, mostly independent. In the 12th-13th c. famine and drought (perhaps caused by climatic changes) brought catastrophe, and the disunited area fell to invading barbarian tribes from the north.

tolu /tə'ljuː, 'təʊlju:/ *n.* a fragrant brown balsam from a South American tree (*Myroxylon balsamum*). [f. (Santiago de) *Tolu* in Colombia]

toluene /'tɒljuiːn/ *n.* a colourless aromatic liquid hydrocarbon derivative of benzene, originally obtained from tolu, used in the manufacture of explosives etc. [f. TOLU]

toluol /'tɒljuɒl/ *n.* a commercial grade of toluene. [f. TOLU]

tom *n.* (in full **tom-cat**) a male cat. —**Tom, Dick, and Harry**, (usu. *derog.*) persons taken at random, ordinary people (usu. preceded by *any* or *every*). [abbr. of man's name *Thomas*]

tomahawk /'tɒməhɔːk/ *n.* a North American Indian war-axe. [f. Algonquian (*tämäham* he cuts)]

tomato /tə'mɑːtəʊ/ *n.* (*pl.* **-oes**) the glossy red or yellow fruit of a plant, *Lycopersicon esculentum*, native to tropical America; this plant. Originally called the love-apple because considered to be an aphrodisiac, it arrived in Europe from South America at the end of the 16th c. and became widely cultivated in Italy for use with pasta. In Britain its reputation delayed its acceptability; the Puritans circulated a story that tomatoes were poisonous, and until the 19th c. they were grown as decorative plants, not for eating. [f. F or Sp. & Port. f. Mex. *tomatl*]

tomb /tuːm/ *n.* a grave or other place of burial; a burial-vault; a sepulchral monument. [f. AF, ult. f. Gk *tumbos*]

tombola /tɒm'bəʊlə/ *n.* a kind of lottery with tickets and prizes. [F or f. It. (*tombolare* tumble)]

tomboy *n.* a rough boyish girl.

tombstone *n.* a stone standing or laid over a grave, usually with an epitaph.

tome *n.* a large book or volume. [F f. L f. Gk *tomos*, orig. = section (*temnō* cut)]

tomfool /tɒm'fuːl/ *adj.* extremely foolish. —*n.* a fool.

tomfoolery *n.* foolish behaviour. [f. prec.]

Tommy /'tɒmɪ/ *n.* a British private soldier. [f. *Tommy* (*Thomas*) *Atkins*, name used in specimens of completed official forms]

tommy-gun /'tɒmɪgʌn/ *n.* a sub-machine-gun. [f. co-inventor J. T. *Thompson* (US officer, d. 1940)]

tommy-rot /'tɒmɪrɒt/ *n.* (*slang*) nonsense. [f. *Tommy* (as TOM) + ROT]

tomography /tə'mɒgrəfɪ/ *n.* radiography in which an image of a selected plane in the body or other object is obtained by rotating the detector and the source of radiation in such a way that points outside the plane give a blurred image. The technique, devised in the early 1930s and later sophisticated, is as important in the history of medicine as the discovery of X-rays. —**tomographic** /-'græfɪk/ *adj.* [f. Gk *tomē* cutting + -GRAPHY]

tomorrow /tə'mɒrəʊ/ *adv.* on the day after today; at some future time. —*n.* the day after today; the near future. [f. TO + MORROW]

Tompion /'tɒmpɪən/, Thomas (*c.* 1639-1713), the most famous of the early English clock- and watch-makers, making in 1675 one of the first balance-spring watches invented by Robert Hooke. For the Royal Observatory, Greenwich, he made two large pendulum clocks which needed winding only once a year, and he collaborated with Edward Barlow in patenting the horizontal-wheel cylinder escapement needed to produce flat watches. His achievement in raising the level of the industry was recognized by his burial in Westminister Abbey. Two of his nephews also became famous clockmakers.

Tom Thumb 1. the title of an old nursery tale, of which there are several versions. He was said to be the son of a ploughman in the time of King Arthur, and was as tall as his father's thumb. **2.** a diminutive person. **3.** a dwarf variety of various plants.

tomtit *n.* a tit, especially a blue tit. [f. TOM + TIT¹]

tom-tom /ˈtɒmtɒm/ *n.* a primitive drum beaten with the hands; a tall drum used in jazz bands etc. (ill. MUSICAL NOTATION). [f. Hindi *tamtam* (imit.)]

-tomy /-təmɪ/ *suffix* forming nouns with sense 'cutting', especially in names of surgical operations or incision (*laparotomy*). [f. Gk -*tomia* cutting (*temnō* cut)]

ton /tʌn/ *n.* **1.** a measure of weight, 2,240 lb. (**long ton**) or 2,000 lb. (**short ton**). **2.** a unit of measurement for a ship's tonnage. **3.** (usu. in *pl.*) (*colloq.*) a large number or amount. **4.** (*slang*) a speed of 100 m.p.h. **5.** (*slang*) £100. —**ton-up boys**, motor-cyclists who travel at high speed. **weighs a ton**, is very heavy. [different spelling of TUN]

tonal /ˈtəʊn(ə)l/ *adj.* of or relating to tone or tonality. —**tonal language**, a tone language (see TONE). —**tonally** *adv.* [f. L (as TONE)]

tonality /təˈnælɪtɪ/ *n.* **1.** the relationship between the notes of a musical scale; the observance of a single tonic key as the basis of a composition. **2.** the colour-scheme of a picture. [f. TONAL]

tone *n.* **1.** a musical or vocal sound, especially with reference to its pitch, quality, and strength. **2.** the modulation of the voice to express a particular feeling or mood. **3.** a manner of expression in writing. **4.** (*Mus.*) a musical sound, especially of a definite pitch and character; an interval of a major second, e.g. C-D. **5.** the general effect of colour or of light and shade in a picture; a tint or shade of colour. **6.** the prevailing character of morals and sentiments etc. in a group. **7.** proper firmness of bodily organs and tissues; a state of good or specified health. —*v.t./i.* **1.** to give a desired tone to; to modify the tone of; to attune. **2.** to harmonize in colour. —**tone-deaf** *adj.* unable to perceive differences of musical pitch accurately. **tone down**, to make or become softer in the tone of sound or colour; to make (a statement etc.) less harsh or emphatic. **tone language**, a language which uses variations in pitch to distinguish words which would otherwise sound identical. **tone poem**, an orchestral composition illustrating a poetic idea. **tone up**, to make or become brighter or more vigorous or intense. —**toner** *n.* [f. OF f. L f. Gk, orig. = tension (*teinō* stretch)]

Tonga /ˈtɒŋə/ a country in the South Pacific consisting of over 150 small volcanic and coral islands, SE of Fiji; pop. (est. 1981) 98,000; official languages, Tongan and English; capital, Nukuʻalofa. Discovered by the Dutch in the early 17th c., the islands were visited by Cook who named them the Friendly Islands. The people were converted to Christianity by Methodist missionaries in the early 19th c. and the kingdom became a British protectorate in 1900, gaining independence as a member State of the Commonwealth in 1970. The soil is generally fertile and the main exports are copra and bananas.

Tongan /ˈtɒŋən/ *adj.* of Tonga or its people or language. —*n.* **1.** a native of Tonga. **2.** the Polynesian language spoken in Tonga. [f. TONGA]

tongs /tɒŋz/ *n.pl.* an instrument with two arms joined at one end, used for grasping and holding things. [OE]

tongue /tʌŋ/ *n.* **1.** the fleshy muscular organ in the mouth used in tasting, licking, swallowing, and (in man) speech (ill. BODY 3). **2.** the tongue of an ox etc. as food. **3.** the faculty of or a tendency in speech. **4.** the language of a nation etc. **5.** a thing like a tongue in shape, e.g. a long low promontory, a strip of leather under the laces in a shoe, the clapper of a bell, the pin of a buckle; the projecting strip on a wooden etc. board fitting into the groove of another (ill. CARPENTRY). —**find** (*or* **lose**) **one's tongue**, to be able (or unable) to express oneself after a shock etc. **hold one's tongue**, to remain silent. **tongue-tie** *n.* a speech impediment due to a malformation of the tongue. **tongue-tied** *adj.* too shy or embarrassed to speak; having a tongue-tie. **tongue-twister** *n.* a sequence of words difficult to pronounce quickly and correctly. **with one's tongue in one's cheek**, insincerely or ironically; with sly humour. [OE]

tonguing *n.* (*Mus.*) the use of the tongue to articulate certain notes in playing a wind instrument. [f. prec.]

tonic /ˈtɒnɪk/ *n.* **1.** an invigorating medicine; anything

serving to invigorate. **2.** tonic water. **3.** a keynote in music. —*adj.* **1.** serving as a tonic, invigorating. **2.** of the tonic or keynote in music. —**tonic water**, a carbonated drink flavoured with quinine or another bitter. [f. F f. Gk (as TONE)]

tonic sol-fa /sɒlˈfɑː/ a system of musical notation used especially in teaching the notes in singing. It was developed by Sarah Ann Glover (1785-1867) as *Norwich Sol-fa*, and promulgated by John Curwen (1816-80) in the 1840s. In it the seven notes of the major scale in any key are sung to syllables written *doh, ray, me, fah, soh, lah, te* (modifications of earlier forms; see GAMUT); doh always denotes the tonic or keynote, and the remaining syllables indicate the relation to it of the other notes of the scale. Time-values are shown by vertical lines, colons, etc. *The New Curwen Method*, a revised version aimed at training the ear and leading to reading from standard musical notation, was published in 1980.

tonight /təˈnaɪt/ *adv.* on the present or approaching evening or night. —*n.* the present evening or night, the evening or night of today. [f. TO + NIGHT]

tonnage /ˈtʌnɪdʒ/ *n.* **1.** a ship's internal cubic capacity or freight-carrying capacity. **2.** the charge per ton on cargo or freight. [f. TON]

tonne /tʌn, ˈtʌnɪ/ *n.* a metric ton of 1000 kg. [F (as TON)]

tonsil /ˈtɒns(ə)l/ *n.* either of two small organs, one on each side of the root of the tongue (ill. BODY 3). —**tonsillar** /ˈtɒnsɪlə(r)/ *adj.* [f. F or L *tonsillae*]

tonsillectomy /tɒnsɪˈlektəmɪ/ *n.* surgical removal of the tonsils. [f. prec. + -ECTOMY]

tonsillitis /tɒnsɪˈlaɪtɪs/ *n.* inflammation of the tonsils. [f. TONSIL + -ITIS]

tonsorial /tɒnˈsɔːrɪəl/ *adj.* of a barber or his work. [f. L *tonsor* (*tondēre* shave)]

tonsure /ˈtɒnʃə(r)/ *n.* the rite of shaving the crown of the head (in the RC Church until 1972) or the whole head (in the Orthodox Church), especially of a person entering the priesthood or a monastic order; the part shaved thus. —*v.t.* to give a tonsure to. [f. OF or L (as prec.)]

too *adv.* **1.** to a greater extent than is desirable or permissible. **2.** (*colloq.*) extremely. **3.** in addition, moreover. —**none too**, rather less than. **too much**, intolerable. **too much for**, more than a match for; more than can be endured by. [stressed form of TO]

took *past* of TAKE.

tool *n.* **1.** a thing (usually something held in the hand) for working upon something. **2.** a simple machine, e.g. a lathe. **3.** a thing used in an occupation or pursuit. **4.** a person used as a mere instrument by another. —*v.t./i.* **1.** to dress (stone) with a chisel. **2.** to impress a design on (a leather book-cover etc.). **3.** (*slang*) to drive up or ride in a casual or leisurely manner. —**tool-pusher** *n.* a worker directing drilling on an oil-rig. [OE]

toot *n.* a short sharp sound (as) of a horn or trumpet. —*v.t./i.* to sound (a horn etc.) thus; to give out such a sound. [prob. f. MLG, or imit.]

tooth *n.* (*pl.* **teeth**) **1.** each of the set of hard bony structures in the jaws of most vertebrates, used for biting and chewing things (ill. BODY 1). **2.** a toothlike part or projection, e.g. a cog of a gear-wheel, a point of a saw or comb etc. **3.** sense of taste, an appetite. **4.** (in *pl.*) force or effectiveness. —**armed to the teeth**, completely and elaborately armed or equipped. **fight tooth and nail**, to fight very fiercely. **get one's teeth into**, to devote oneself seriously to. **in the teeth of**, in spite of (opposition or difficulty etc.), in opposition to (instructions etc.); directly against (the wind etc.). **tooth-comb** *n.* a comb with fine close-set teeth (properly a fine-tooth comb; see FINE¹). **tooth-powder** *n.* a powder for cleaning the teeth. [OE]

toothache *n.* pain in a tooth or the teeth.

toothbrush *n.* a brush for cleaning the teeth.

toothless *adj.* having no teeth. [f. TOOTH + -LESS]

toothpaste *n.* paste for cleaning the teeth.

toothpick *n.* a small sharp instrument for removing food etc. lodged between the teeth.

toothsome *adj.* (of food) delicious. [f. TOOTH + -SOME]

toothy *adj.* having large, numerous, or prominent teeth. [f. TOOTH]

tootle *v.i.* **1.** to toot gently or repeatedly. **2.** (*colloq.*) to go in a casual or leisurely way. [f. TOOT]

top¹ *n.* **1.** the highest point or part; **2.** the upper surface; a thing forming the upper part; the cover or cap of a container etc. **3.** the highest rank; the foremost place or position; a person holding such a rank etc. **4.** a garment for the upper part of the body. **5.** (usu. in *pl.*) the leaves etc. of a plant grown chiefly for its root. **6.** the utmost degree or intensity. **7.** top gear. **8.** a platform round the head of the lower mast of a ship. **9.** (*predic.*, in *pl.*) a person or thing of the very best quality. —*adj.* highest in position, degree, or importance. —*v.t.* (**-pp-**) **1.** to furnish with a top or cap. **2.** to be higher than; to be superior to, to surpass. **3.** to be at the top of; to reach the top of (a hill etc.) **4.** to hit (a ball in golf) above its centre. —**at the top,** in the highest rank of a profession etc. **on top,** above, in a superior position. **on top of,** fully in control of; in close proximity to; in addition to. **on top of the world,** exuberant. **over the top,** over the parapet of a trench; into a final or decisive state or a state of excess. **top brass,** (*colloq.*) high-ranking officers. **top dog,** (*colloq.*) the victor, the master. **top drawer,** a high social position or origin. **top-dress** *v.t.* to apply manure or fertilizer on the top of (the earth), not dig it in. **top-flight** *adj.* in the highest rank of achievement. **top gear,** the highest gear. **top hat,** a tall silk hat (ill. DRESS). **top-heavy** *adj.* overweighted at the top and so in danger of falling. **top-hole** *adj.* (*slang*) first-rate. **top-level** *adj.* of or at the highest rank or level. **top-notch** *adj.* (*colloq.*) first-rate. **top off,** to put an end or finishing touch to. **top out,** to put the highest stone on (a building). **top secret,** of the highest secrecy. **top up,** to fill up (a partly empty container); to add extra money or items to. [OE]

top² *n.* a toy, usually conical or pear-shaped, with a sharp point at the bottom on which it rotates when set in motion. [OE]

topaz /ˈtəʊpæz/ *n.* a gem of various colours, especially yellow. [f. OF f. L f. Gk *topazos*]

topcoat *n.* **1.** an overcoat. **2.** an outer coat of paint etc.

tope¹ *n.* a small shark of the genus *Galeorhinus*. [perh. f. Cornish]

tope² *v.i.* (*archaic*) to drink intoxicating liquor to excess, esp. habitually. —**toper** *n.* [perh. f. obs. *top* quaff]

topgallant /tɒpˈgælənt/ *n.* the mast, sail, yard, or rigging immediately above the topmast and topsail (ill. SAILING-SHIPS).

topi /ˈtəʊpɪ/ *n.* (also **topee**) a sun-helmet, especially a sola topi. [f. Hindi]

topiary /ˈtəʊpɪərɪ/ *n.* the art of clipping shrubs etc. into ornamental shapes. —*adj.* of this art. [f. F f. L *topiarius* landscape-gardener ult. f. Gk *topos* place]

topic /ˈtɒpɪk/ *n.* a theme for discussion, a subject of conversation or discourse. [f. L f. Gk (*topos* place, a commonplace)]

topical *adj.* dealing with current topics. —**topicality** /-ˈkælɪtɪ/ *n.*, **topically** *adv.* [f. TOPIC]

topknot *n.* a tuft or crest or bow of ribbon etc. worn or growing on the head.

topless *adj.* without a top; (of a woman's clothing) leaving the breasts bare, (of a woman) so clothed. [f. TOP¹ + -LESS]

topmast *n.* the part of a mast next above the lower mast (ill. SAILING-SHIPS).

topmost *adj.* uppermost, highest. [f. TOP¹ + -MOST]

topography /təˈpɒgrəfɪ/ *n.* the natural and artificial features of a district; the knowledge or description of these. —**topographer** *n.*, **topographical** /tɒpəˈgræfɪk(ə)l/ *adj.* [f. L f. Gk (*topos* place + -GRAPHY)]

topology /təˈpɒlədʒɪ/ *n.* **1.** the study of geometrical properties and spatial relations unaffected by continuous change of shape or size of the figures involved. **2.** the branch of mathematics concerned with the abstract theory of continuity. —**topological** /tɒpəˈlɒdʒɪk(ə)l/ *adj.* [f. G f. Gk *topos* place + -LOGY]

topper *n.* (*colloq.*) a top hat. [f. TOP¹]

topping *n.* decorative cream etc. on top of a cake etc. [f. TOP¹]

topple *v.t./i.* **1.** to fall headlong or as if top-heavy; to cause to do this. **2.** to overthrow, to cause to fall from a position of authority. [f. TOP¹]

topsail /ˈtɒps(ə)l/ *n.* **1.** a square sail next above the lowest (ill. SAILING-SHIPS). **2.** a fore-and-aft sail on a gaff.

topside *n.* **1.** the outer side of a round of beef. **2.** the side of a ship above the water-line.

topsoil *n.* the top layer of soil.

topsy-turvy /tɒpsɪˈtɜːvɪ/ *adv.* & *adj.* **1.** upside-down. **2.** in or into utter confusion..[app. f. TOP¹ + obs. *turve* overturn]

toque /təʊk/ *n.* a woman's close-fitting brimless hat with a high crown. [F; orig. unkn.]

tor *n.* a rocky hill-top. [OE *torr*; cf. Gael. *tòrr* bulging hill]

Torah /ˈtɔːrə/ *n.* the Pentateuch, the Mosaic law; a scroll containing this. [f. Heb., = instruction]

torch *n.* **1.** a small hand-held electric lamp powered by a battery or an electric power cell contained in a case. **2.** a burning piece of resinous wood, or combustible material fixed on a stick and ignited, used as a light for carrying in the hand. —**carry a torch for,** to feel (unreturned) love for. [f. OF f. L *torqua* (*torquēre* twist)]

tore *past* of TEAR¹.

toreador /ˈtɒrɪədɔː(r)/ *n.* a bullfighter, especially on horseback. [Sp. (*toro* bull f. L *taurus*)]

torment /ˈtɔːment/ *n.* severe bodily or mental suffering; a cause of this. —/tɔːˈment/ *v.t.* to subject to torment; to tease or worry excessively. —**tormentor** /-ˈmentə(r)/ *n.* [f. OF f. L *tormentum* (as TORT)]

tormentil /ˈtɔːməntɪl/ *n.* a low-growing herb (*Potentilla erecta*) with yellow flowers. [f. OF f. L]

torn *p.p.* of TEAR¹.

tornado /tɔːˈneɪdəʊ/ *n.* (*pl.* **-oes**) **1.** a violent storm over a small area, especially a rotatory one travelling in a narrow path. **2.** a loud outburst. [app. assim. of Sp. *tronada* thunderstorm]

Toronto /təˈrɒntəʊ/ the capital of Ontario and second largest city in Canada; pop. (1981) 2,998,947.

torpedo /tɔːˈpiːdəʊ/ *n.* (*pl.* **-oes**) a cigar-shaped self-propelled underwater missile fired at a ship from a submarine or surface ship or from an aircraft and exploding on impact (see below). —*v.t.* **1.** to destroy or attack with a torpedo. **2.** to ruin (a policy or institution etc.) suddenly. —**torpedo-boat** *n.* a small fast warship armed with torpedoes. [L, = electric ray (*torpēre* be numb)]

The term was originally applied to a case charged with gunpowder designed to explode under water after a given interval so as to destroy any vessel in its immediate vicinity. This submarine mine was either towed by a ship or moored and allowed to drift. The first self-propelled torpedo was designed in 1866 by Robert Whitehead, a British engineer, and the first successful use of the weapon in war was by the Japanese against the Russians in 1904. Torpedoes can be launched by ships or aircraft but have been used most successfully by submarines, and accounted for heavy shipping losses in the Second World War. Since then developments have included sophisticated acoustic devices that enable the torpedo to home in on its target.

torpid /ˈtɔːpɪd/ *adj.* sluggish, inactive, apathetic; (of a hibernating animal) dormant. —**torpidity** /-ˈpɪdɪtɪ/ *n.*, **torpidly** *adv.* [f. L *torpidus* (as foll.)]

torpor /ˈtɔːpə(r)/ *n.* a torpid condition. [L (*torpēre* be numb)]

torque /tɔːk/ *n.* **1.** a twisting or rotary force especially in a machine. **2.** a necklace or collar usually of twisted metal, worn by the ancient Britons, Gauls, etc. [f. L *torquēre* twist]

Torquemada /tɔːkɪˈmɑːdə/, Tomás de (*c.*1420–98), Spanish cleric, a Dominican monk who became Inquisitor-General of Spain and Grand Inquisitor, and transformed the Inquisition into an instrument of the State. He earned a reputation for ruthlessness and ferocious repression of religious heterodoxy and was the prime mover in the expulsion of the Jews from Spain from 1492 onwards.

torrent /ˈtɒrənt/ *n.* **1.** a rushing stream of water or lava etc. **2.** (usu. in *pl.*) a great downpour of rain. **3.** a violent flow (of abuse, questions, etc.). —**torrential** /təˈrenʃ(ə)l/ *adj.* [F f. It. f. L (as foll.)]

Torricelli /tɒrɪˈtʃelɪ/, Evangelista (1608–47), Italian mathematician and physicist, a disciple of Galileo whom he succeeded as mathematician to the court of Tuscany. A law or theorem that bears his name deals with the velocity of liquids flowing under the force of gravity from orifices. His most important invention was the mercury barometer in 1643, with which he demonstrated that the atmosphere exerts a pressure by showing that it could support a column of mercury in an inverted closed tube, and he was the first person to produce a sustained vacuum.

torrid /ˈtɒrɪd/ *adj.* **1.** (of land etc.) parched by the sun, very hot. **2.** intense, passionate. —**torrid zone,** the tropics. [f. F or L *torridus* (*torrēre* scorch)]

torsion /ˈtɔːʃ(ə)n/ *n.* twisting, especially of one end of a thing while the other is held fixed. —**torsional** *adj.* [f. OF f. L (as TORT)]

torso /ˈtɔːsəʊ/ *n.* (*pl.* **-os**) **1.** the trunk of the human body or of a statue. **2.** a statue lacking the head and limbs. [It., = stalk, stump, f. L *thyrsus*]

tort *n.* a breach of a legal duty, other than under contract, with liability for damages. —**tortious** /'tɔːʃəs/ adj. [f. OF f. L tortum wrong (torquēre twist)]

tortilla /tɔː'tɪlə/ n. a Latin American flat maize cake eaten hot. [Sp. dim. (torta cake f. L)]

tortoise /'tɔːtəs/ n. a slow-moving reptile of the order Chelonia of land or fresh water, with the body encased in a horny shell. [OF f. L tortuca; orig. unkn.]

tortoiseshell /'tɔːtəʃel/ n. **1.** the yellowish-brown mottled and clouded shell of certain turtles. **2.** a cat or butterfly with markings suggesting tortoiseshell. —adj. having such markings.

tortuous /'tɔːtjʊəs/ adj. **1.** full of twists and turns. **2.** devious, not straightforward. —**tortuosity** /-'ɒsɪtɪ/ n., **tortuously** adv. [f. OF f. L (tortus a twist, as TORT)]

torture /'tɔːtʃə(r)/ n. **1.** the infliction of severe bodily pain especially as a punishment or means of coercion; a method of this. **2.** severe physical or mental pain. —v.t. **1.** to subject to torture. **2.** to force out of its natural shape or meaning, to distort. —**torturer** n. [F f. L (as TORT)]

Tory /'tɔːrɪ/ n. **1.** (colloq. or derog.) a member of the Conservative party. **2.** (hist.) a British political party traditionally opposed to the Whigs (see below). **3.** (US derog.) a colonist loyal to the British during the American Revolution. —adj. of Tories or the Tory party. —**Toryism** n. [orig. = Irish outlaw (Ir. tóir pursue). The term was used in the 17th c. of the dispossessed Irish, who became outlaws and subsisted by plundering and killing the English settlers and soldiers. It became used as an abusive nickname (1679-80) for those who opposed the exclusion of James, Duke of York (a Roman Catholic), from the succession to the Crown—reputedly because the Duke was seen to favour Irishmen.]
Historically the Tories were associated with the Church of England and with non-toleration of religious nonconformists and Catholics. They suffered as a result of their links with the Jacobites and were excluded from office in the first half of the 18th c. After 1760 they accepted George III and the established order in Church and State. Their fortunes rose as opponents of the French Revolution, but after the end of the Napoleonic Wars they became increasingly reactionary, a trend which led to their eventual defeat in 1830. In the following decades, particularly under the influence of Peel, the nature of the party changed, and it became known by the name Conservative.

tosh n. (slang) nonsense, rubbish. [orig. unkn.]

toss v.t./i. **1.** to move with an uneven or restless to-and-fro motion. **2.** to throw lightly, carelessly, or easily; to throw back (the head), especially in contempt or impatience. **3.** to send (a coin) spinning in the air to decide a choice etc. by the way it falls; to settle a dispute with (a person) thus. **4.** to coat (food) by gently shaking it in a dressing etc. —n. **1.** a tossing action or movement. **2.** the result obtained by tossing a coin. —**argue the toss**, to dispute a choice already made. **take a toss**, to be thrown by a horse etc. **toss off**, to compose or finish rapidly and effortlessly; to drink (liquor) in one draught. **toss up**, to toss a coin. **toss-up** n. the tossing of a coin; (colloq.) an even chance. [orig. unkn.]

tot¹ n. **1.** a small child. **2.** a dram of liquor. [of dial. orig.]

tot² v.t./i. (-tt-) (usu. with up) to add up; (of items) to mount up. —**totting-up** n. the adding of separate items, especially of convictions towards disqualification from driving. **tot up to**, to amount to. [abbr. of TOTAL or of L totum the whole]

total /'təʊt(ə)l/ adj. **1.** including everything or everyone; comprising the whole. **2.** absolute, unqualified. —n. the total number or quantity. —v.t. (-ll-) to reckon the total of; to amount in number (to). —**total internal reflection**, reflection without refraction, of a light-ray meeting the interface between two media at more than a certain critical angle to the normal. **total war**, war in which all available weapons and resources are employed. [f. OF f. L (totus entire)]

totalitarian /təʊtælɪ'teərɪən/ adj. relating to a form of government permitting no rival loyalties or parties, usually demanding total submission of the individual to the requirement of the State. —**totalitarianism** n. [f. foll.]

totality /təʊ'tælɪtɪ/ n. **1.** the total number or amount. **2.** being total. [f. as TOTAL]

totalizator /'təʊtəlaɪzeɪtə(r)/ n. a device showing the number and amount of the bets staked on a race to enable the total to be divided among those betting on the winner; this betting system. [f. foll.]

totalize v.t. to combine into a total. [f. TOTAL]

totally adv. completely. [f. TOTAL]

tote¹ n. (slang) a totalizator. [abbr.]

tote² v.t. (colloq.) to carry. —**tote bag,** a large bag for parcels etc. [17th-c. US, prob. of dial. orig.]

totem /'təʊtəm/ n. a natural object, especially an animal, adopted as the emblem of a clan or individual, especially among North American Indians; an image of this. —**totem-pole** n. a pole on which totems are carved, painted, or hung. —**totemic** /-'temɪk/ adj. [Algonquian]

totemism /'təʊtəmɪz(ə)m/ n. the stage of cultural development of which totems are characteristic. —**totemistic** /-'mɪstɪk/ adj. [f. TOTEM]

t'other /'tʌðə(r)/ adj. & pron. the other. [f. the tother, for earlier that other 'the other']

totter v.i. **1.** to walk unsteadily or feebly. **2.** to rock or shake as if about to collapse; (of a State or system) to be shaken, to be on the point of collapse. —n. an unsteady or shaky movement or gait. —**tottery** adj. [f. MDu., = swing]

toucan /'tuːkən/ n. a tropical American bird of the family Ramphastidae, with a large bill. [f. Tupi or Guarani]

touch /tʌtʃ/ v.t./i. **1.** to be or come together so that there is no space between; to meet or cause to meet thus. **2.** to put one's hand etc. lightly upon; to press or strike lightly. **3.** to reach as far as; to reach momentarily; to approach in excellence. **4.** (with neg.) to move, harm, affect, or attempt in any degree; to have any dealings with; to eat or drink even a little of. **5.** to arouse sympathy or other emotion in. **6.** to modify; to draw or paint with light strokes. **7.** (slang) to persuade or coax money as a loan or gift. **8.** (in p.p.) slightly crazy. —n. **1.** an act or the fact of touching. **2.** the faculty of perception through the response of the brain to touching things especially with the fingers. **3.** small things done in producing a piece of work. **4.** a small amount, a tinge or trace. **5.** the manner of touching the keys or strings, of an instrument; the response of the keys etc. to this; a distinctive manner of workmanship or procedure. **6.** a relationship of communication or knowledge. **7.** the part of a football field beyond the side limits. **8.** (slang) an act of obtaining money from a person; a person from whom money may be obtained. —**finishing touch(es),** the final details completing and enhancing a piece of work etc. **touch-and-go** adj. uncertain as regards the result, risky. **touch at,** (of a ship) to call at (a port etc.) **touch bottom,** to reach the bottom of the water with the feet; to reach the lowest or worst point. **touch down,** (of an aircraft) to reach the ground in landing. **touch-judge** n. a linesman in Rugby football. **touch-line** n. the side limit of a football field. **touch off,** to explode by touching with a match etc.; to initiate (a process) suddenly. **touch on** or **upon,** to refer to or mention briefly or casually; to verge on. **touch-paper** n. a paper impregnated with nitre to burn slowly and ignite a firework etc. **touch-type** v.t./i. to use a typewriter without looking at the keys. **touch up,** to correct or improve with minor additions. **touch wood,** to put the hand on something wooden in the superstitious belief of averting bad luck (also used as a phrase implying such action). [f. OF tochier (prob. imit.)]

touchdown n. the act of touching down by an aircraft.

touché /'tuːʃeɪ/ int. acknowledging a hit by a fencing-opponent or a justified retort by another in a discussion. [F, = touched (as prec.)]

touching /'tʌtʃɪŋ/ adj. raising sympathy or tender feelings. —prep. concerning. —**touchingly** adv. [f. TOUCH]

touchstone n. **1.** dark schist or jasper for testing alloys by the marks they make on it. **2.** a criterion.

touchwood n. readily inflammable rotten wood or similar substance.

touchy /'tʌtʃɪ/ adj. apt to take offence, over-sensitive. —**touchily** adv., **touchiness** n. [f. TOUCH]

tough /tʌf/ adj. **1.** difficult to break, cut, tear, or chew. **2.** able to endure hardship; not easily hurt, damaged, or injured. **3.** unyielding, stubborn; resolute; (colloq.) acting sternly or viciously. **4.** (colloq., of luck etc.) hard. **5.** (US slang) vicious, rough and violent. **6.** (of clay etc.) stiff, tenacious. —n. a tough person, especially a ruffian. —**toughly** adv., **toughness** n. [OE]

toughen /'tʌf(ə)n/ v.t./i. to make or become tough or tougher. [f. TOUGH]

Toulouse-Lautrec /tuːluːz ləʊ'trek/ Henri de (1864-1901), French painter, draughtsman, and print-maker, the son of Count Alphonse de Toulouse-Lautrec Monfa. His highly original style, often bordering on caricature, adopts the technical apparatus of Post-Impressionism, and his delicate calligraphic line, strongly influenced by Japanese prints, readily reflects the spirit of art nouveau. Lautrec revelled in the Bohemian life, and his depictions of theatre, music-halls, cafés, and brothels sum up the earthier side of the life of Montmartre. Lautrec participated in the 1890s' revival of colour lithography, and his printed works, particularly the large posters, are today regarded as perfect examples of the spirit of the settled and comfortable Parisian life at that time.

toupee /'tu:peɪ/ n. a wig; an artifical patch of hair worn to cover a bald part of the head. [f. *toupet* hair-tuft (as TOP¹)]

tour /tʊə(r)/ n. **1.** a journey through a country, town, or building etc. visiting various places or things of interest or giving performances. **2.** a spell of duty on military or diplomatic service. —v.t./i. to make a tour (of). —**on tour**, touring. [f. OF f. L f. Gk *tornos* lathe (cf. TURN)]

tour de force /tʊə də 'fɔːs/ a great feat of strength or skill. [F]

tourism /'tʊərɪz(ə)m/ n. **1.** visiting places as a tourist. **2.** the business of providing accommodation and services for tourists. [f. TOUR]

tourist /'tʊərɪst/ n. a person who is travelling or visiting a place for recreation. —**tourist class**, a class of passenger accommodation in a ship or aircraft etc. lower than first class. **tourist trap**, a place that exploits tourists. **Tourist Trophy**, motor-cycle races held annually on the Isle of Man from 1907. [f. TOUR]

touristy adj. (derog.) suitable for tourists; frequented by tourists. [f. prec.]

tourmaline /'tʊəməlɪn, -iːn/ n. a mineral with unusual electric properties and used as a gem. [F f. Sinhalese (it was orig. found in Sri Lanka)]

tournament /'tʊənəmənt/ n. **1.** a contest of skill between a number of competitors, involving a series of matches. **2.** a medieval spectacle in which two sides contended with usually blunted weapons. **3.** a modern display of military exercises, contests, etc. [f. OF (as TOURNEY)]

tournedos /'tʊənədəʊ/ n. (pl. same) a small round thick slice of fillet for one person, cooked with a strip of fat round it. [F]

tourney /'tʊənɪ/ n. a tournament. —v.i. to take part in a tournament. [f. OF *tornei*, *torneier* (as TURN)]

tourniquet /'tʊənɪkeɪ/ n. a device or strip of material drawn tightly round a limb to stop the flow of blood through an artery by compression. [F, prob. f. OF *tournicle* coat of mail, infl. by *tourner* turn]

tousle /tauz(ə)l/ v.t. to pull about roughly, to make (the hair or clothes) untidy. [f. dial. *touse*]

tout v.t./i. **1.** to pester possible customers with requests for orders; to solicit the custom of (a person) or for (a thing). **2.** to spy out the movements and condition of racehorses in training. —n. a person who touts; a tipster touting information about racehorses etc. [orig. = look out, = obs. or dial. *toot*]

tow¹ /təʊ/ v.t. to pull along behind, especially with a rope etc. —n. towing, being towed. —**in tow**, being towed; (colloq.) accompanying or under the charge of a person. **on tow**, being towed. **tow-bar** n. the bar by which a caravan is attached to the vehicle towing it. **tow-path** or **towing-path** n. a path beside a river or canal for use when a horse is towing a barge etc. [OE; cf. TUG]

tow² /təʊ/ n. fibres of flax or hemp prepared for spinning. —**tow-headed** adj. having a head of very light-coloured or tousled hair. [f. MLG *touw*]

towards /tə'wɔːdz/ prep. (also **toward**) **1.** in the direction of. **2.** as regards, in relation to. **3.** for the purpose of achieving or promoting; as a contribution to. **4.** near, approaching. [OE, = future (as TO¹, -WARD)]

towel /'taʊəl/ n. an absorbent cloth or paper etc. for drying with after washing. —v.t./i. (-ll-) to wipe or dry with a towel. —**throw in the towel**, to admit defeat. [f. OF *toail(l)e*]

towelling n. material for towels. [f. prec.]

tower n. **1.** a tall usually square or circular structure, either standing alone (e.g. as a fort) or forming part of a castle, church, or other large building; a similar structure housing machinery etc. **2.** a tower block. —v.i. to be of great height; to be taller or more eminent than others. —**the Tower**, the Tower of London (see separate entry). **tower block**, a very tall building containing flats or offices. **tower of strength**, a person who gives strong and reliable support. [OE f. L *turris*]

towering adj. **1.** high, lofty. **2.** (of rage etc.) violent. [f. prec.]

Tower of London a fortress by the Thames just east of the City of London. The oldest part, the White Tower, was begun in 1078. It was later used as a State prison, and is now a repository of ancient armour and weapons and other objects of public interest, including the Crown jewels (which have been kept there since the time of Henry III).

town n. **1.** a collection of dwellings and other buildings, larger than a village, especially one not created a city; its inhabitants. **2.** a town or city as distinct from country. **3.** the central business and shopping area of a neighbourhood. **4.** London. —**go to town**, to act or work with energy and enthusiasm. **on the town**, (colloq.) on a spree in town. **town clerk**, an officer of a town corporation, in charge of records etc. **town crier**, a person making official announcements in public places. **town gas**, manufactured inflammable gas for domestic use. **town hall**, a building for a town's official business, often with a hall that may be used for public events. **town house**, a residence in town as distinct from the country; a terrace house or a house in a compact group in a town. **town planning**, planning for the regulated growth and improvement of towns. [OE *tūn* enclosure]

townee /taʊ'niː/ n. (also **townie** /'taʊnɪ/) (derog.) an inhabitant of a town. [f. TOWN]

townscape n. **1.** a picture of a town. **2.** the visual appearance of a town or towns. [f. TOWN, after *landscape*]

townsfolk n. the inhabitants of a town or towns.

township n. (formerly in the UK) a small town or village that formed part of a large parish. **2.** (US & Canada) an administrative division of a county, or a district six miles square. **3.** (in some other countries) a small town or settlement; (in South Africa) an area set aside for non-White occupation. [f. TOWN + -SHIP]

townsman n. (pl. **-men**) an inhabitant of a town. —**townswoman** n.fem. (pl. **-women**)

townspeople n.pl. the inhabitants of a town.

toxaemia /tɒk'siːmɪə/ n. **1.** blood-poisoning. **2.** the condition of abnormally high blood-pressure in pregnancy. —**toxaemic** adj. [as foll. + Gk *haima* blood]

toxic adj. of, caused by, or acting as a poison. —**toxicity** /tɒk'sɪsɪtɪ/ n. [f. L f. Gk *toxikon pharmakon* poison for arrows (*toxa* arrows)]

toxicology /tɒksɪ'kɒlədʒɪ/ n. the study of poisons. —**toxicological** /-'lɒdʒɪk(ə)l/ adj., **toxicologist** n. [f. TOXIC + -LOGY]

toxin /'tɒksɪn/ n. a poison, especially of animal or vegetable origin; a poison secreted by a micro-organism and causing a particular disease. [f. TOXIC]

toxophilite /tɒk'sɒfɪlaɪt/ n. a student or lover of archery. —adj. of archery. —**toxophily** n. [f. Ascham's *Toxophilus* (1545) f. Gk *toxon* bow + -PHIL]

toy n. **1.** a thing to play with, especially for a child. **2.** a trinket or curiosity; a thing intended for amusement rather than for serious use. —adj. **1.** that is a toy. **2.** (of a dog) of a diminutive breed or variety, kept as a pet. —v.i. (with *with*) to handle or finger idly; to deal with or consider without great seriousness. [orig. unkn.]

Toynbee /'tɔɪnbɪ/, Arnold Joseph (1889-1975), English historian, who held various university posts and became Director of Studies at the Royal Institute of International Affairs (1925-55). His greatest work is his twelve volume *Study of History* (1934-61), in which he surveys the history of 21 civilizations, tracing a pattern of growth, maturity, and decay in them all and concluding that the present Western civilization is in the last of these stages. His suggestion that its fragmentation and waning could be saved by a new universal religion, with one spiritually oriented world society, was not well received.

trace¹ n. **1.** a mark left behind, as the track of an animal, a footprint, or the line made by a moving pen. **2.** a perceptible sign of what has existed or happened. **3.** a very small quantity. —v.t. **1.** to follow or discover by observing marks, tracks, pieces of evidence, etc. **2.** to go along (a path etc.). **3.** to mark out, to sketch the outline of; to form (letters etc.) laboriously. **4.** to copy (a drawing etc.) by marking its lines on a piece of transparent paper placed over it. —**trace element**, a substance occurring or required (especially in soil) only in minute amounts. [f. OF *tracier* f. L *tractus* drawing (see TRACT)]

trace² n. each of the two side-straps, chains, or ropes by which a horse draws a vehicle. —**kick over the traces**, to become insubordinate or reckless. [f. OF *trais*, pl. of TRAIT]

traceable adj. that may be traced. [f. TRACE¹]

tracer /'treɪsə(r)/ n. **1.** a bullet that when ignited by the propellant emits light or a trail of smoke etc. by which its course may be observed, enabling the gunner to correct his aim. **2.** an artificial radioisotope whose course in the human body etc. can be followed by the radiation it produces. [f. TRACE¹]

tracery /ˈtreɪsərɪ/ *n.* stone ornamental open-work especially in the head of a Gothic window; a decorative lacelike pattern suggesting this. [f. TRACE¹]

trachea /trəˈkiːə, ˈtreɪkɪə/ *n.* the windpipe (ill. BODY 3). [f. L f. Gk, = rough artery (*trakhus* rough)]

tracheotomy /treɪkɪˈɒtəmɪ, træk-/ *n.* surgical incision of the trachea. [f. prec. + Gk -*tomia* cutting]

trachoma /trəˈkəʊmə/ *n.* a contagious disease of the eye with inflamed granulation on the inner surface of the eyelids. [f. Gk (*trakhus*) rough)]

tracing /ˈtreɪsɪŋ/ *n.* a traced copy of a map or drawing etc.; the process of making this. —**tracing paper**, transparent paper for making tracings. [f. TRACE¹]

track *n.* **1.** a mark or series of marks left by a person, or animal, or vehicle etc. in passing along. **2.** a path or rough road, especially one established by use. **3.** the course taken. **4.** a course, action, or procedure. **5.** a prepared course for racing etc. **6.** a continuous line of railway. **7.** a continuous band round the wheels of a tank or tractor etc. **8.** a sound-track; a groove on a gramophone record; a particular recorded section of a gramophone record or magnetic tape. —*v.t./i.* **1.** to follow the track or course of; to find or observe by doing this. **2.** (of wheels) to run so that the hinder wheel is exactly in the first wheel's track. **3.** (of a stylus) to follow a groove. **4.** (of a cine-camera) to move along a set path while taking a picture. —**in one's tracks**, (*colloq.*) where one stands, then and there. **keep** (*or* **lose**) **track of,** to follow (or fail to follow) the course or development of. **make tracks,** (*slang*) to go away. **make tracks for,** (*slang*) to go in pursuit of or towards. **off the track,** away from the subject in hand. **track down,** to reach or capture by tracking. **track event,** (in athletics) an event taking place on a track, e.g. running. **track record,** a person's past achievements. **track suit,** a suit worn by athletes etc. while training or before or after competing. [f. OF *trac*, perh. f. L Du. *tre(c)k* draught etc.]

tracker *n.* a person or thing that tracks. —**tracker dog,** a police dog tracing by scent. [f. TRACK]

tracklement /ˈtræk(ə)lmənt/ *n.* an article of food, especially a jelly, for eating with meat. [orig. unkn.]

tract¹ *n.* **1.** a region or area of indefinite (usually large) extent. **2.** a system of connected parts in an animal body, along which something passes. [f. L *tractus* (*trahere* draw, pull)]

tract² *n.* an essay or pamphlet, especially on a religious subject. [app. abbr. of L *tractatus* treatise (as foll.)]

tractable /ˈtræktəb(ə)l/ *adj.* easy to manage or deal with; docile. —**tractability** /-ˈbɪlɪtɪ/ *n.* [f. L (*tractare* handle)]

Tractarian /trækˈteərɪən/ *n.* an adherent or promoter of Tractarianism. —**Tractarianism** *n.* a name for the earlier stages of the Oxford Movement, derived from the *Tracts for the Times*, the series of ninety pamphlets issued under its aegis. [f. TRACT]

traction /ˈtrækʃ(ə)n/ *n.* **1.** pulling or drawing a load along a surface. **2.** a therapeutic sustained pull on a limb etc. —**traction-engine** *n.* a steam or diesel engine for drawing a heavy load on a road or across fields etc. [F or f. L (as TRACT¹)]

tractor /ˈtræktə(r)/ *n.* **1.** a powerful motor vehicle for pulling farm machinery or other heavy equipment. **2.** a traction-engine. [as prec.]

trad *adj.* (*colloq.*) traditional. —*n.* (*colloq.*) traditional jazz. [abbr.]

trade *n.* **1.** the exchange of goods for money or other goods. **2.** business done with a specified class or at a specified time. **3.** business carried on for earnings or profit (especially as distinct from a profession); a skilled handicraft. **4.** the persons engaged in a particular trade. **5.** (usu. in *pl.*) a trade wind. —*v.t./i.* **1.** to engage in trade, to buy and sell. **2.** to exchange (goods) in trade; to have a transaction (*with* a person). —**trade in,** to give (a used article) in part payment for another. **trade-in** *n.* an article given in this way. **trade mark,** a device or word(s) legally registered or established by use to distinguish the goods of a particular manufacturer etc. **trade name,** a name by which a thing is known in the trade, or given by a manufacturer to a proprietary article, or under which a business is carried on. **trade off,** to exchange as a compromise. **trade-off** *n.* a thing given in this way. **trade on** *or* **upon,** to make great use of for one's own advantage. **trade secret,** a technique used in a trade

and giving an advantage because it is not generally known. **trade union, trade wind,** see separate entries. [f. MLG, = track (as TREAD)]

trader /ˈtreɪdə(r)/ *n.* a person or ship engaged in trade. [f. TRADE]

tradescantia /trædɪˈskæntɪə/ *n.* a perennial plant of the genus *Tradescantia* with large blue, white, or pink flowers. [f. J. *Tradescant*, English naturalist (d. 1638)]

tradesman *n.* (*pl.* -**men**) a person engaged in trade, especially a shopkeeper.

Trades Union Congress the official representative body of British trade unions, founded in 1868, which meets annually to discuss matters of common concern. It is made up of delegates of the affiliated unions.

trade union (also **trades union**) an organized association of workers in a trade or group of allied trades or a profession, formed for protection and promotion of their common interests. —**trade-unionism** *n.* this style of association. **trade-unionist** *n.* an advocate of trade-unionism; a member of a trade union.

A product of the Industrial Revolution, the trade unions expanded in size and importance in the 19th c., although often subject, particularly in the earlier years, to repressive legislation (see COMBINATION ACTS), assuming a more aggressive and socialist outlook towards the end of the century and playing a central role in the formation of the Labour Party. The trade-union movement achieved true national power in the early 20th c., with smaller unions tending to amalgamate into organizations with memberships in the hundreds of thousands covering the entire country.

trade wind a constant wind blowing towards the equator from the north-east or south-east. The name had in its origin nothing to do with 'trade' in the commercial sense of 'passage for the purpose of trading', though the importance of those winds to navigation led 18th-c. etymologists (and perhaps even navigators) so to understand the term. It was originally applied to any wind that 'blows trade', i.e. in a constant course or way (a 'track' or 'trodden path'), but as it became gradually known that the only winds of which this is approximately true were the Indian monsoons and the winds now called 'trade winds' on each side of the equator in the Atlantic and Pacific Oceans, the name became restricted to these and eventually to the latter.

trading /ˈtreɪdɪŋ/ *n.* engaging in trade, buying and selling. —**trading estate,** an area designed to be occupied by industrial and commercial firms. **trading stamp,** a stamp given by a tradesman to a customer and exchangeable in quantity for various articles or for cash. [f. TRADE]

tradition /trəˈdɪʃ(ə)n/ *n.* an opinion, belief, or custom handed down from one generation to another, especially orally; this process of handing down; an artistic or literary principle based on usage or experience. [f. OF or L (*tradere* hand on)]

traditional *adj.* of, based on, or obtained by tradition; (of jazz) based on an early style. —**traditionally** *adv.* [f. prec.]

traditionalism *n.* great or excessive respect for tradition. —**traditionalist** *n.* [f. F or prec.]

traduce /trəˈdjuːs/ *v.t.* to misrepresent in an unfavourable way, to slander. —**traducement** *n.* [f. L, = disgrace (as TRANS-, *ducere* lead)]

Trafalgar /trəˈfælgə(r)/ a cape on the south coast of Spain, near which a decisive battle of the Napoleonic Wars was fought on 21 Oct. 1805. The British fleet under Nelson (who was killed in the action) achieved a great victory over the combined fleets of France and Spain which were attempting to clear the way for Napoleon's projected invasion of Britain. Superior British seamanship and gunnery ensured the surrender of more than half the Franco-Spanish fleet after several hours of hard fighting, and after this battle Napoleon was never again able to mount a serious threat to British naval supremacy.

traffic /ˈtræfɪk/ *n.* **1.** vehicles, ships, or aircraft moving along a route. **2.** trade, especially in illicit goods. **3.** the number of persons or amount of goods conveyed. **4.** the use of a service, the amount of this. **5.** dealings between persons etc. —*v.t./i.* (**-ck-**) to trade; to deal in. —**traffic island,** a paved etc. area in a road to direct the traffic and provide a refuge for pedestrians. **traffic-light** *n.* a signal controlling road traffic by coloured lights (see below). **traffic warden,** a person employed to assist the police in controlling the movement and parking of road vehicles. —**trafficker** *n.* [f. F or Sp. f. It.]

A traffic signal, with an official in charge, was tried out in Westminster, London, in 1868; this seems to be the first instance of the use of a mechanical device for street-traffic control. It was a modification of the railway signalling system and consisted of a semaphore arm with red and green gas lamps for night use. The experiment was terminated by the explosion of the lamps. Electric traffic lights were introduced in Cleveland, Ohio, in 1914, and in New York in 1918; c.1925 an attempt was made to co-ordinate the actions of the police in Piccadilly in London by a series of railway colour-light signals. In 1926 a traffic signal was installed at a busy road junction in Wolverhampton, but was not retained in use because there was no legislation to enforce obedience to its indications. Early road signals were manually operated, and were followed by fixed-time signals; modern traffic-actuated systems of control sometimes involve the processing of information by means of a computer.

tragacanth /'trægəkænθ/ n. a white or reddish gum from plants of the genus *Astragalus*, used in pharmacy etc. [f. F f. L f. Gk *tragacantha*, name of shrub (*tragos* goat, *acantha* thorn)]

tragedian /trə'dʒiːdɪən/ n. **1.** a writer of tragedies. **2.** an actor in tragedy. [as TRAGEDY]

tragedienne /trədʒiːdɪ'en/ n. an actress in tragedy. [F (as prec.)]

tragedy /'trædʒɪdɪ/ n. **1.** a serious drama with unhappy events or a sad ending. **2.** the branch of drama consisting of such plays. **3.** a sad event; a serious accident; a calamity. [f. OF f. L f. Gk *tragōidia*, app. = goat-song (*tragos* goat, *ōidē* song). Many theories have been offered to account for the name (e.g. that a goat was given as a prize for a play at the ancient Greek festival of Dionysus, at which tragedies were presented), but some dispute the connection with 'goat'.]

tragic /'trædʒɪk/ adj. **1.** of or in the style of tragedy. **2.** sorrowful. **3.** causing great sadness; calamitous. [f. F f. L f. Gk (*tragos* goat)]

tragical /'trædʒɪk(ə)l/ adj. **1.** sorrowful. **2.** causing great sadness. —**tragically** adv. [as prec.]

tragicomedy /trædʒɪ'kɒmɪdɪ/ n. a drama of mixed tragic and comic events. —**tragicomic** adj., **tragicomically** adv. [f. F or It. f. L (as TRAGIC, COMEDY)]

Traherne, /trə'hɜːn/, Thomas (1637–74), English writer of religious works in prose and verse. *Centuries*, his major achievement, is written in unconventional verse expressing rapturous joy; manuscripts of these and many of his poems were discovered on a London bookstall in 1896–7 and published as *Poetical Works* (1903) and *Centuries of Meditation* (1908). The boundless potential of man's mind and spirit is his recurrent theme, as is the need for man to regain the wonder and simplicity of childhood.

trail v.t./i. **1.** to drag or be dragged along behind, especially on the ground. **2.** to move wearily; to lag or straggle. **3.** to hang or float loosely; (of a plant) to hang or spread downwards. **4.** to be losing in a contest; to be losing to a (specified team etc.). **5.** to diminish, to become fainter. **6.** to follow the trail of, to track. —n. **1.** a mark left where something has passed; a track or scent followed in hunting. **2.** a beaten path, especially through a wild region. **3.** a thing that trails or hangs trailing. **4.** a line of people or things following behind something. —**trailing edge,** the rear edge of a moving body. [f. OF or MLG f. L *tragula* drag-net]

trailer n. **1.** a truck etc. drawn by a vehicle and used to carry a load. **2.** a set of short extracts from a film, shown in advance to advertise it. **3.** a person or thing that trails. **4.** (*US*) a caravan. [f. TRAIL]

train n. **1.** a series of railway carriages or trucks drawn by a locomotive. **2.** a succession or series of persons or things; a set of parts in machinery, actuating one another in a series. **3.** a body of followers, a retinue. **4.** a thing drawn along behind or forming the hinder part, especially the elongated part of a long dress or robe that trails on the ground behind the wearer. **5.** a line of combustible material placed to lead fire to an explosive. —v.t./i. **1.** to bring to a desired standard of performance or behaviour by instruction and practice; to undergo such a process; to teach and accustom (a person or animal) to do something. **2.** to bring or come to physical efficiency by exercise and diet. **3.** to cause (a plant) to grow in the required direction. **4.** to aim (a gun or camera etc.). —**in train,** in preparation; arranged. **train-bearer** n. an attendant holding up the train of a person's robe. **train-spotter** n. a collector of the identification-numbers of railway engines seen. [f. OF ult. f. L *trahere* draw]

trainable adj. that may be trained. [f. TRAIN]

trainee /treɪ'niː/ n. a person being trained, especially for an occupation. [f. TRAIN]

trainer n. **1.** a person who trains horses or athletes etc. **2.** an aircraft or device simulating it to train pilots. **3.** a training shoe. [f. TRAIN]

training n. the process by which one is trained for a sport or contest or for an occupation. —**training shoe,** a soft running-shoe without spikes. [f. TRAIN]

traipse v.i. (*colloq.*) to trudge; to go about on errands etc. [orig. unkn.]

trait /treɪ/ n. a distinguishing feature in a character, appearance, habit, or portrayal. [F, f. L *tractus* (as TRACT¹)]

traitor /'treɪtə(r)/ n. a person who behaves disloyally; one who betrays his country. —**traitorous** adj., **traitress** n.fem. [f. OF f. L *traditor* (as TRADITION)]

Trajan /'treɪdʒ(ə)n/ (Marcus Ulpius Traianus, 53–117) Roman emperor 98–117, born in Spain, the adopted successor of Nerva. He was a popular and respected emperor, efficient in administration and energetic in public works. The Dacian wars of 101–6 ended in the annexation of Dacia as a province (the campaigns are illustrated on Trajan's Column in Rome); his final years were taken up with a war against the Parthians.

trajectory /'trædʒɪktərɪ, trə'dʒek-/ n. the path of a body (e.g. a comet or bullet) moving under given forces. [f. L (*traicere* throw across, TRANS-, *jacere* throw)]

tram n. **1.** (also **tramcar**) a passenger vehicle running on rails laid in a public road (see below). **2.** a four-wheeled truck used in coal-mines. [f. MLG & MDu. *trame* beam] The tram (or tramcar, *US* streetcar) was invented in New York in 1830 by John Stephenson, an Irish coach-builder. Trams were originally horse-drawn (see RAILWAYS), and then steam power was used so that they were either self-propelled or hauled by cables using stationary engines. The great expansion in their use came with electric traction in the 1890s, with current collected either from overhead wires or sometimes from a conductor rail beneath the road surface. The rise of the motor bus and the electric trolleybus with their greater flexibility of the course caused a decline in the use of trams in both Britain and the USA, but some transport planners forecast a return to the tram on grounds of economy and ability to use electric power rather than the oil fuel needed for buses.

tramlines n.pl. **1.** the rails for a tram. **2.** (*colloq.*) the pair of parallel lines at the edge of a tennis or badminton court (ill. SPORTS).

trammel /'træm(ə)l/ n. **1.** a kind of drag-net in which a fine net is hung loosely between vertical walls of coarser net, so that fish passing through carry some of the fine net through the coarser and are trapped in the pocket thus formed. **2.** (usu. in *pl.*) things that hamper one's activities. —v.t. (**-ll-**) to hamper. [f. OF f. L *tramaculum*, perh. as TRI- + *macula* mail]

tramp v.t./i. **1.** to walk with a firm heavy tread; to walk laboriously; to travel on foot across (an area or distance) thus. **2.** to trample. **3.** to live as a tramp. —n. **1.** a person who goes from place to place as a vagrant. **2.** the sound of heavy footsteps. **3.** a long walk. **4.** (*slang*) a dissolute woman. **5.** a freight-vessel, especially a steamer, that does not travel on a regular route. [prob. f. Gmc]

trample v.t./i. to tread repeatedly with heavy or crushing steps; to crush or harm thus. [f. prec.]

trampoline /'træmpəliːn/ n. a stretched canvas sheet connected by springs to a horizontal frame, used for jumping on in acrobatic leaps. Trampolining as a sport was introduced into Britain from the USA, though it was known in Europe as a circus act centuries before the earliest competitions, which were held in the USA in the late 1940s. —v.i. to use a trampoline. [f. It. *trampolino* (*trampoli* stilts)]

tramway n. the rails for a tram.

trance /trɑːns/ n. a sleeplike state without response to stimuli; a hypnotic or cataleptic state; mental abstraction from external things, rapture, ecstasy. [f. OF *transe* (*transir* depart f. L, as TRANSIT)]

tranche /trɑːnʃ/ n. a portion, especially of income or of a block of shares. [F, = slice (as TRENCH)]

tranny /'trænɪ/ n. (*slang*) a transistor radio. [abbr.]

tranquil /'træŋkwɪl/ adj. calm and undisturbed, not agitated. —**tranquillity** /-'kwɪlɪtɪ/ n., **tranquilly** adv. [f. F or L *tranquillus*]

tranquillize /'træŋkwɪlaɪz/ v.t. to make tranquil, to calm, especially by a drug. [f. prec.]

tranquillizer *n.* a drug used to diminish anxiety and induce calmness. [f. prec.]

trans- /trænz-, trɑːnz-/ *prefix* across, through, beyond; to or on the farther side of. [f. L *trans* across]

transact /trænˈzækt, trɑː-/ *v.t.* to perform or carry out (business). —**transactor** *n.* [f. L (as TRANS-, ACT)]

transaction /trænˈzækʃ(ə)n, trɑː-/ *n.* **1.** transacting. **2.** business transacted. **3.** (in *pl.*) the reports of discussions and lectures at the meetings of a learned society. [as prec.]

transalpine /trænzˈælpaɪn, trɑː-/ *adj.* on the north side of the Alps. [f. L (as TRANS-, ALPINE)]

transatlantic /trænsətˈlæntɪk, trɑː-/ *adj.* **1.** crossing the Atlantic. **2.** on or from the other side of the Atlantic; American; (*US*) European.

transceiver /trænˈsiːvə(r), trɑː-/ *n.* a combined radio transmitter and receiver. [f. TRANSMITTER + RECEIVER]

transcend /trænˈsend, trɑː-/ *v.t.* **1.** to go or be beyond the range or grasp of (human experience, belief, description, etc.). **2.** to surpass. [f. OF or L *transcendere* (TRANS-, *scandere* climb)]

transcendent *adj.* **1.** transcending human experience. **2.** of supreme merit or quality, surpassing. **3.** (of God) existing apart from, or not subject to the limitations of, the material universe. —**transcendence** *n.*, **transcendency** *n.*, **transcendently** *adv.* [as prec.]

transcendental /trænsenˈdent(ə)l, trɑː-/ *adj.* **1.** not based on experience, intuitively accepted, innate in the mind. **2.** consisting of, dealing in, or inspired by abstraction, visionary. —**Transcendental Meditation,** a technique of meditation and relaxation based on yoga. **transcendental numbers,** see NUMBER. —**transcendentally** *adv.* [f. L (as prec.)]

transcendentalism *n.* a philosophy or belief taking account of transcendental things. —**transcendentalist** *n.* [f. prec.]

transcontinental /trænzkɒntɪˈnent(ə)l, trɑː-/ *adj.* extending or travelling across a continent.

transcribe /trænˈskraɪb, trɑː-/ *v.t.* **1.** to copy in writing. **2.** to write out (shorthand etc.) in ordinary characters. **3.** (*Mus.*) to adapt (a composition) for a voice or instrument other than that for which it was originally written. —**transcriber** *n.* [f. L *transcribere* (TRANS-, *scribere* write)]

transcript /ˈtrænskrɪpt, ˈtrɑː-/ *n.* a written copy. [f. OF f. L (as prec.)]

transcription /trænˈskrɪpʃ(ə)n, trɑː-/ *n.* **1.** transcribing, the written representation of sounds. **2.** a transcript; something transcribed. [F or f. L (as TRANSCRIBE)]

transducer /trænzˈdjuːsə(r), trɑː-/ *n.* any device which produces an output signal (e.g. a voltage) in response to a different sort of input signal (e.g. pressure). [f. L *transducere* lead across (TRANS-, *ducere* lead)]

transept /ˈtrænsept, ˈtrɑː-/ *n.* the part of a cruciform church at right angles to the nave; either arm of this (ill. CHURCH). [as TRANS- + SEPTUM]

transfer /trænsˈfɜː(r), trɑː-/ *v.t./i.* (**-rr-**) **1.** to convey, move, or hand over from one person, group, or place to another; to make over possession of (property or rights etc.). **2.** to convey (a design etc.) from one surface to another. **3.** to change or be moved to another group or occupation. **4.** to go from one station or route or conveyance to another in order to continue a journey. **5.** to change (a meaning) by extension or metaphor. —/ˈtrænsfɜː(r), ˈtrɑː-/ *n.* **1.** transferring, being transferred. **2.** a document effecting the conveyance of property or a right. **3.** a design or picture that is or can be conveyed from one surface to another. —**transference** /ˈtræ-, ˈtrɑː-/ *n.* [f. F or L *transferre* (TRANS-, *ferre* bear)]

transferable /trænsˈfɜːrəb(ə)l, trɑː-/ *adj.* that may be transferred. [f. prec.]

transfiguration /trænsfɪɡəˈreɪʃ(ə)n, trɑː-/ *n.* **1.** transfiguring, being transfigured. **2. Transfiguration,** that of Christ (Matt. 17: 2), celebrated on 6 Aug. [as foll.]

transfigure /trænsˈfɪɡə(r), trɑː-/ *v.t.* to change the appearance of, especially to something nobler or more beautiful. [f. OF or L (as TRANS-, FIGURE)]

transfinite /trænsˈfaɪnaɪt/ *adj.* beyond or surpassing what is finite; (*Math.*, of a number) exceeding all finite numbers.

transfix /trænsˈfɪks, trɑː-/ *v.t.* **1.** to pierce with or impale on something sharp-pointed. **2.** to make motionless with fear or astonishment etc. [f. L (as TRANS-, FIX)]

transform /trænsˈfɔːm, trɑː-/ *v.t.* **1.** to make a considerable change in the form, appearance, or character of. **2.** to change the voltage of (an electric current). —**transformation**

/-fəˈmeɪʃ(ə)n/ *n.*, **transformational** /-fəˈmeɪʃən(ə)l/ *adj.* [f. OF or L (as TRANS-, FORM)]

transformer *n.* an apparatus for reducing or increasing the voltage of an alternating current. [f. prec.]

transfuse /trænsˈfjuːz, trɑː-/ *v.t.* **1.** to cause (a fluid, colour, influence, etc.) to permeate; to imbue thus. **2.** to inject (blood or other liquid) into a blood-vessel to replace that lost. —**transfusion** /-ˈfjuːʒ(ə)n/ *n.* [f. L *transfundere* (TRANS-, *fundere* pour)]

transgress /trænsˈgres, trɑː-/ *v.t./i.* **1.** to break (a rule or law etc.); to go beyond (a limitation). **2.** to sin. —**transgression** *n.*, **transgressor** *n.* [f. F or L *transgredi* (TRANS-, *gradi* step, go)]

transient /ˈtrænsɪənt, ˈtrɑː-/ *adj.* quickly passing away, fleeting. —**transience** *n.* [f. L *transire* (as TRANSIT)]

transistor /trænˈsɪstə(r), trɑː-/ *n.* **1.** a semiconductor device, usually having three terminals and two junctions, in which the load current can be made to be proportional to a small input current, so that it is functionally equivalent to a valve but is much smaller and more robust, operates at lower voltages, and consumes less power and produces less heat (see below). **2.** (in full **transistor radio**) a portable radio set equipped with transistors. [f. TRANSFER + RESISTOR]
   Transistors were developed at the Bell Telephone Laboratories in the USA in 1947 after an intensive programme of research; the inventors were awarded the Nobel Prize for physics in 1956. They are used to amplify electronic signals, are the active elements of silicon integrated circuits, and have now largely replaced thermionic valves.

transistorize *v.t.* to equip with transistors (rather than valves). [f. prec.]

transit /ˈtrænsɪt, ˈtrɑː-/ *n.* **1.** the process of going, conveying, or being conveyed across, over, or through. **2.** a passage or route. **3.** the apparent passage of a heavenly body across the disc of another or across the meridian of a place. —**transit camp,** a camp for the temporary accommodation of soldiers, refugees, etc. [f. L *transitus* (*transire* go across)]

transition /trænˈsɪʒ(ə)n, trɑː-/ *n.* **1.** the process of changing from one state or subject etc. to another. **2.** a period during which one style of art develops into another, especially of architecture between Norman and Early English. —**transitional** *adj.*, **transitionally** *adv.* [F or f. L (as prec.)]

transitive /ˈtrænsɪtɪv, ˈtrɑː-/ *adj.* (of a verb) taking a direct object expressed or understood. —**transitively** *adv.* [as TRANSIT]

transitory /ˈtrænsɪtərɪ, ˈtrɑː-/ *adj.* existing for a time but not long-lasting, merely temporary. —**transitorily** *adv.*, **transitoriness** *n.* [f. AF f. L (as TRANSIT)]

Transjordan /trænʒˈdɔːd(ə)n/ *n.* the former name of an area of Palestine east of the Jordan, now the major part of the Hashemite Kingdom of Jordan.

translate /trænsˈleɪt, trɑː-/ *v.t.* **1.** to express the sense of (a word or text etc.) in another language, in plainer words, or in another form of representation. **2.** to infer or declare the significance of, to interpret. **3.** to move from one person, place, or condition to another; to remove (a bishop) to another see; to move (a saint's relics etc.) to another place; (in the Bible) to convey to heaven without death. —**translation** *n.*, **translator** *n.* [f. L *translatus* p.p. of *transferre* (see TRANSFER)]

transliterate /trænsˈlɪtəreɪt, trɑː-/ *v.t.* to represent (a letter or word) in the corresponding character(s) of another alphabet or language. —**transliteration** *n.*, **transliterator** *n.* [f. TRANS- + L *littera* letter]

translucent /trænsˈluːsənt, trɑː-/ *adj.* allowing light to pass through, especially without being transparent. —**translucence** *n.*, **translucency** *n.* [f. L *translucēre* (TRANS-, *lucēre* shine)]

transmigrate /trænsmaɪˈgreɪt, trɑː-/ *v.i.* **1.** (of a soul) to pass into a different body. **2.** to migrate. —**transmigration** *n.* [f. L (as TRANS-, MIGRATE)]

transmissible /trænsˈmɪsɪb(ə)l, trɑː-/ *adj.* transmittable. [as TRANSMIT]

transmission /trænsˈmɪʃ(ə)n, trɑː-/ *n.* **1.** transmitting, being transmitted. **2.** a broadcast programme. **3.** the gear transmitting power from the engine to the axle in a motor vehicle. [f. L (as TRANS-, MISSION)]

transmit /trænsˈmɪt, trɑː-/ *v.t.* (**-tt-**) **1.** to send or pass on from one person, place, or thing to another. **2.** to allow to pass through or along, to be a medium for. **3.** to send out (a message, signal, or programme etc.) by telegraph wire or radio waves. [f. L *transmittere* (TRANS-, *mittere* send)]

transmittable /trænsˈmɪtəb(ə)l/ *adj.* that may be transmitted. [f. prec.]

transmitter *n.* **1.** the equipment used to transmit a message, signal, etc. **2.** a person or thing that transmits. [f. TRANSMIT]

transmogrify /trænsˈmɒɡrɪfaɪ, trɑː-/ *v.t.* to transform, especially in a magical or surprising manner. —**transmogrification** /-fɪˈkeɪʃ(ə)n/ *n.* [orig. unkn.]

transmutation /trænsmjuːˈteɪʃ(ə)n, trɑː-/ *n.* transmuting, being transmuted. —**transmutation of metals**, the turning of other metals into gold as the alchemists' aim. [f. OF or L (as foll.)]

transmute /trænsˈmjuːt, trɑː-/ *v.t.* to change the form, nature, or substance of, to convert into a different thing. [f. L *transmutare* (TRANS-, *mutare* change)]

transoceanic /trænsəʊʃɪˈænɪk, trɑː-/ *adj.* **1.** crossing the ocean. **2.** on or from the other side of the ocean.

transom /ˈtrænsəm/ *n.* a cross-beam, especially a horizontal bar of wood or stone above a door or above or in a window (ill. HOUSES); a window above this. [f. OF *traversin* (as TRAVERSE)]

transparency /trænsˈpærənsɪ, trɑː-/ *n.* **1.** being transparent. **2.** a picture (especially a photographic slide) to be viewed by light passing through it. [f. L (as foll.)]

transparent /trænsˈpærənt, trɑː-/ *adj.* **1.** transmitting rays of light without diffusion so that bodies behind can be distinctly seen (cf. *translucent*). **2.** (of a disguise or pretext etc.) easily seen through. **3.** clear and unmistakable; easily understood; free from affectation or disguise. —**transparently** *adv.* [f. OF f. L *transparēre* shine through (TRANS-, *parēre* appear)]

transpire /trænsˈpaɪə(r), trɑː-/ *v.t./i.* **1.** (of a secret or fact etc.) to become known. **2.** (D) to happen. **3.** to emit (vapour or moisture) through leaves or the pores of the skin etc.; to be emitted thus. —**transpiration** /-pɪˈreɪʃ(ə)n/ *n.* [f. F or L *transpirare* (TRANS-, *spirare* breathe)]

transplant /trænsˈplɑːnt, trɑː-/ *v.t.* **1.** to uproot and replant or establish elsewhere (often *fig.*). **2.** to transfer (living tissue or an organ) and implant in another part of the body or in another (human or animal) body. —/ˈtræ-, ˈtrɑː-/ *n.* transplanting of tissue or an organ; a thing transplanted. —**transplantation** /-plɑːnˈteɪʃ(ə)n/ *n.* [f. L *transplantare* (as TRANS-. PLANT)]

transport /trænsˈpɔːt, trɑː-/ *v.t.* **1.** to take (a person or goods etc.) from one place to another. **2.** (*hist.*) to deport (a criminal) to a penal colony. **3.** (esp. in *p.p.*) to affect with strong emotion. —/ˈtræ-, trɑː-/ *n.* **1.** transporting. **2.** means of conveyance; a ship or aircraft employed to carry soldiers, stores, etc. **3.** vehement emotion. —**transport café**, a café catering chiefly for long-distance lorry drivers. —**transportation** /-ˈteɪʃ(ə)n/ *n.* [f. OF or L *transportare* (TRANS-, *portare* carry)]

transportable /trænsˈpɔːtəb(ə)l, trɑː-/ *adj.* that may be transported. [f. prec.]

transporter /trænsˈpɔːtə(r), trɑː-/ *n.* a vehicle used to transport other vehicles, heavy machinery, etc. —**transporter bridge**, a bridge carrying vehicles across water on a suspended platform. [f. TRANSPORT]

transpose /trænsˈpəʊz, trɑː-/ *v.t.* **1.** to cause (two or more things) to change places; to change the position of (a thing) in a series; to change the natural or existing order or position of (a word or words) in a sentence. **2.** to put (music) into a different key. —**transposition** /-pəˈzɪʃ(ə)n/ *n.* [f. OF (as TRANS-, POSE)]

transsexual /trænzˈseksjʊəl, trɑː-/ *adj.* having the physical characteristics of one sex and the psychological characteristics of the other. —*n.* a transsexual person. —**transsexualism** *n.*

trans-ship /trænsˈʃɪp, trɑː-/ *v.t.* (**-pp-**) to transfer from one ship or conveyance to another. —**trans-shipment** *n.*

transubstantiation /trænsəbstænʃɪˈeɪʃ(ə)n/ *n.* the Roman Catholic doctrine that in the Eucharist the whole substance of the bread and wine, after consecration, is converted into the body and blood of Christ, only the 'accidents' (i.e. appearances) of bread and wine remaining. The belief was defined in 1215, and the terminology is based on medieval philosophy with its acceptance of Aristotelian theories on the nature of substance. (See CONSUBSTANTIATION.) [f. L *transubstantiare* (as TRANS-, SUBSTANCE)]

transuranic /trænsjʊˈrænɪk, ˈtrɑː-/ *adj.* (of an element) having a higher atomic number than uranium. There are at least 13 transuranic elements known, all of which are radioactive and were first obtained artificially in nuclear reactors or after nuclear explosions.

Transvaal /trænzˈvɑːl/ a province of the Republic of South Africa, lying north of the Orange Free State and separated from it by the River Vaal; capital, Pretoria. [f. L *trans* across + *Vaal* name of river]

transverse /ˈtrænzvɜːs, ˈtrɑː-, -ˈvɜːs/ *adj.* situated, arranged, or acting in a crosswise direction. —**transversely** *adv.* [f. L (TRANS-, *vertere* turn)]

transvestism /trænzˈvestɪz(ə)m, trɑː-/ *n.* clothing oneself in the garments of the opposite sex as a form of psychological abnormality. [f. TRANS- + L *vestire* clothe]

transvestite /trænzˈvestaɪt, trɑː-/ *n.* a person who indulges in transvestism. [as prec.]

Transylvania /trænsɪlˈveɪnɪə/ a large tableland region in Romania. Its name means 'beyond the forest'. —**Transylvanian** *adj.* & *n.*

trap[1] *n.* **1.** a device, often baited, for catching and holding animals. **2.** a trick betraying a person into speech or an act. **3.** an arrangement to catch an unsuspecting person, e.g. a speeding motorist. **4.** a device for effecting the sudden release e.g. of a greyhound in a race, of a ball to be struck at, of a clay pigeon to be shot at. **5.** a curve in a drainpipe etc. serving when filled with liquid to seal it against the return of a gas. **6.** a two-wheeled carriage. **7.** a trapdoor. **8.** (*slang*) the mouth. —*v.t.* (**-pp-**) **1.** to catch in a trap to stop and retain (as) in a trap. **2.** to furnish (a place) with traps. [OE]

trap[2] *n.* a kind of dark volcanic rock. [f. Sw. *trapp* (*trappa* stair, from its stairlike appearance)]

trapdoor *n.* a door in a floor, ceiling, or roof.

trapeze /trəˈpiːz/ *n.* a crossbar suspended by cords as a swing for acrobatics etc. [f. F f. L (as foll.)]

trapezium /trəˈpiːzɪəm/ *n.* (*pl.* **-ia** or **-iums**) **1.** a quadrilateral with only one pair of sides parallel (ill. SHAPES). **2.** (*US*) a trapezoid. [L f. Gk *trapezion* (*trapeza* table)]

trapezoid /ˈtræpɪzɔɪd/ *n.* **1.** a quadrilateral with no sides parallel (the term *quadrilateral* is preferred). **2.** (*US*) a trapezium. —**trapezoidal** /-ˈzɔɪd(ə)l/ *adj.* [f. Gk (as prec.)]

trapper *n.* a person who traps wild animals, especially for furs. [f. TRAP[1]]

trappings /ˈtræpɪŋz/ *n.pl.* ornamental accessories; the harness of a horse, especially when ornamental. [f. obs. *trap* f. OF *drap* cloth (as DRAPE)]

Trappist /ˈtræpɪst/ *n.* a member of the branch of the Cistercian order founded in 1664 at La Trappe in Normandy, following an austere rule and noted (at least until recently) for abstinence from meat and for practice of perpetual silence. —**Trappistine** /-tɪn/ *n.* a member of an affiliated order of nuns. [f. F f. La *Trappe*]

traps *n.pl.* (*colloq.*) baggage, belongings. [perh. f. TRAPPINGS]

trash *n.* **1.** worthless or waste stuff, rubbish. **2.** a worthless person; worthless people. —**trash-can** *n.* a dustbin. —**trashy** *adj.* [orig. unkn.]

trattoria /trætəˈriːə/ *n.* an Italian eating-house. [It.]

trauma /ˈtrɔːmə/ *n.* (*pl.* **-as**) **1.** an emotional shock producing a lasting effect. **2.** a wound or injury; the condition caused by this. [Gk, = wound]

traumatic /trɔːˈmætɪk/ *adj.* **1.** of or causing trauma. **2.** (*colloq.*) very unpleasant. [f. L f. Gk (as prec.)]

travail /ˈtræveɪl/ *n.* **1.** (*literary*) painful or laborious effort. **2.** (*archaic*) the pains of childbirth. —*v.i.* **1.** (*literary*) to make a painful or laborious effort. **2.** (*archaic*) to suffer the pains of childbirth. [f. OF f. L *trepalium* instrument of torture]

travel /ˈtræv(ə)l/ *v.t./i.* (**-ll-**) **1.** to go from one place or point to another; to make a journey, especially of some length or abroad. **2.** to journey along or through (a country); to cover (a distance) in travelling. **3.** (*colloq.*) to withstand a long journey. **4.** to go from place to place as a salesman. **5.** to move or proceed in a specified manner or at a specified rate. **6.** (*colloq.*) to move quickly. **7.** (of a machine part) to move. —*n.* **1.** travelling, especially in foreign countries. **2.** the range, rate, or mode of movement of a machine part. —**travel agency** (*or* **agent**), an agency (or agent) making arrangements for travellers. **travelling crane**, a crane able to move along an overhead support. [orig. = prec.]

travelled *adj.* experienced in travelling. [f. prec.]

traveller *n.* **1.** a person who travels or is travelling. **2.** a commercial traveller. **3.** a gypsy. —**traveller's cheque**, a cheque for a fixed amount, encashable on a signature usually in many countries. **traveller's joy,** wild clematis (*Clematis vitalba*). **traveller's tale,** an incredible and probably untrue story. [f. TRAVEL]

travelogue /'trævəlɒg/ *n.* a film or illustrated lecture with a narrative of travel. [f. TRAVEL, after *monologue* etc.]

traverse /trə'vɜːs/ *v.t./i.* **1.** to travel or lie across. **2.** to consider or discuss the whole extent of (a subject). **3.** to turn (a large gun) horizontally. —/'trævəs/ *n.* **1.** a sideways movement or course; traversing. **2.** a thing that crosses another. —**traversal** /trə'vɜːs(ə)l/ *n.* [f. OF f. L (as TRANSVERSE)]

travesty /'trævɪstɪ/ *n.* a grotesque misrepresentation or imitation. —*v.t.* to make or be a travesty of. [f. F *travestir* change clothes of, f. It. (as TRANSVESTISM)]

trawl *n.* a large wide-mouthed fishing-net dragged by a boat along the bottom of the sea etc. —*v.t./i.* to catch with a trawl or seine; to catch by trawling. [prob. f. MDu. *tragelen* drag]

trawler *n.* a boat for use with a trawl. [f. TRAWL]

tray *n.* **1.** a flat utensil, usually with a raised edge, on which small articles are placed for display or carrying. **2.** a meal on a tray. **3.** an open receptacle for holding a person's correspondence etc. in an office. **4.** a tray-like (often removable) receptacle forming a compartment in a trunk, cabinet, or other container. [OE]

treacherous /'tretʃərəs/ *adj.* **1.** guilty of or involving treachery. **2.** (of the weather, ice, memory, etc.) not to be relied on, likely to fail or give way. —**treacherously** *adv.*, **treacherousness** *n.* [f. OF (*trechier*, *trichier* deceive, as TRICK)]

treachery /'tretʃərɪ/ *n.* violation of faith or trust, especially by secret desertion of the cause to which one professes allegiance. [as prec.]

treacle /'triːk(ə)l/ *n.* the syrup produced in refining sugar; molasses. —**treacly** *adj.* [orig. = antidote for snake-bite, f. OF f. L *theriaca* f. Gk]

tread /tred/ *v.t./i.* (*past* **trod**; *p.p.* **trodden** or **trod**) **1.** to set one's foot down; to walk or step; (of a foot) to be set down. **2.** to walk on; to press or crush with the feet; to perform (steps etc.) by walking; to make (a path or hole etc.) by treading. **3.** (of a male bird) to copulate with (a hen, or *absol.*). —*n.* **1.** the manner or sound of walking. **2.** the top surface of a step or stair (ill. HOUSES). **3.** the part of a wheel that touches the ground or rails; the part of a rail that the wheels touch; a thick moulded part of a vehicle tyre for gripping the road; a part of the sole of a boot etc. similarly moulded. —**tread the boards,** to be an actor. **tread on air,** to feel elated. **tread on a person's corns** *or* **toes,** to offend his feelings or encroach upon his privileges. **tread water,** to maintain an upright position in water by making treading movements with the feet and hands. [OE]

treadle /'tred(ə)l/ *n.* a lever worked by the foot and imparting motion to a machine. [OE (as prec.)]

treadmill *n.* **1.** a wide mill-wheel turned by people treading on steps fixed along the length of its circumference, formerly worked by prisoners as a punishment. The treadmill, which enforced monotonous and hard work, was first introduced as a prison punishment in 1817. The machines it operated were used for pumping or grinding, or often as mere labour without any other purpose. **2.** tiring monotonous routine work.

treason /'triːz(ə)n/ *n.* violation by a subject of his allegiance to a sovereign or the State; a breach of faith, disloyalty. —**treasonous** *adj.* [f. AF *treisoun* f. L (as TRADITION)]

treasonable *adj.* involving or guilty of treason. —**treasonableness** *n.*, **treasonably** *adv.* [f. prec.]

treasure /'treʒə(r)/ *n.* **1.** precious metals or gems; a hoard of these, accumulated wealth. **2.** a thing valued for its rarity, workmanship, associations, etc. **3.** (*colloq.*) a beloved or highly valued person. —*v.t.* to store as valuable (*lit.*, or *fig.* in the memory); to value highly. —**treasure-hunt** *n.* a search for treasure; a game in which the players seek a hidden object. **treasure trove,** gold or silver coins, plate, or bullion found hidden and of unknown ownership; something very useful or desirable that a person finds. [f. OF f. L *thesaurus* f. Gk]

treasurer *n.* a person in charge of the funds of a society or municipality etc. [f. AF & OF (as prec.)]

treasury *n.* **1.** a place where treasure is kept. **2.** the funds or revenue of a State, or institution, or society. **3. Treasury,** the department managing the public revenue of a country (see below); the offices and officers of this. —**Treasury bench,** the front bench in Parliament occupied by the

Prime Minister, the Chancellor of the Exchequer, etc. **treasury bill,** a bill of exchange issued by a government to raise money for temporary needs. [as TREASURE]

In Britain, the Treasury began to supersede the functions of the Exchequer from the time of Elizabeth I, under Lord Burghley, and in the 18th c. the First Lord gradually assumed the role of Prime Minister. The office of First Lord of the Treasury is now always held by the Prime Minister, but the functions of the office are carried out by the Chancellor of the Exchequer. (See EXCHEQUER.)

treat *v.t./i.* **1.** to act or behave towards (a person or thing) in a specified way. **2.** to deal with or act upon (a person or thing) with a view to obtaining a particular result; to subject to a chemical or other process; to give medical or surgical treatment to. **3.** to present or deal with (a subject). **4.** to provide with food or entertainment at one's own expense. **5.** to negotiate terms. —*n.* **1.** a thing that gives pleasure, especially something unexpected or unusual; an entertainment designed to do this. **2.** the treating of others to something at one's own expense. —**stand treat,** to bear the expense of an entertainment etc. [f. AF *treter* f. L *tractare* handle]

treatise /'triːtɪs, -ɪz/ *n.* a written work dealing formally and systematically with a subject. [as prec.]

treatment *n.* **1.** the process or manner of behaving towards or dealing with a person or thing. **2.** something done to relieve or cure an illness or abnormality etc. [f. TREAT]

treaty /'triːtɪ/ *n.* **1.** a formally concluded and ratified agreement between States. **2.** an agreement between persons, especially for the purchase of property. [f. AF f. L *tractatus* (as TREAT)]

Trebizond /'trebɪzɒnd/ a city and port of Turkey, on the Black Sea, once the capital of an empire (1204-1461) founded by Alexis Comnenus.

treble /'treb(ə)l/ *adj.* **1.** threefold; triple; three times as much or many. **2.** (of the voice) high-pitched; (*Mus.*) soprano (esp. of a boy or boy's voice; or of an instrument). —*n.* **1.** a treble quantity or thing. **2.** a hit at darts on the narrow ring between the two middle circles on the board, scoring treble. **3.** a soprano, especially a boy or boy's voice; a high-pitched voice. —*v.t./i.* to multiply or be multiplied by three. —**trebly** *adv.* [f. OF f. L, = TRIPLE]

Treblinka /tre'blɪŋkə/ a Nazi concentration camp in Poland in the Second World War, where the Jews of the Warsaw ghetto were put to death.

tree *n.* **1.** a perennial plant with a single woody self-supporting stem (*trunk*) usually unbranched for some distance above the ground (see ill. pp. 876-7). **2.** a Christmas tree. **3.** a piece or frame of wood for various purposes. **4.** a family tree. —*v.t.* to force (an animal, or (also *fig.*) a person) to take refuge up a tree. —**grow on trees,** to be plentifully available without effort. **tree-creeper** *n.* a small creeping bird of the family Certhiidae feeding on insects in the tree-bark. **tree-fern** *n.* a large fern with an upright woody stem. **tree-house** *n.* a structure in a tree for children to play in. **tree-ring** *n.* a ring in the cross-section of a tree, from one year's growth. **tree surgeon,** one who specializes in the care of trees. [OE]

trefoil /'trefɔɪl, 'triː-/ *n.* **1.** a kind of plant with leaves of three leaflets (clover, shamrock, etc.). **2.** a three-lobed thing, especially an ornamentation in tracery. [f. AF f. L (TRI-, *folium* leaf)]

trek *v.i.* (-**kk**-) (orig. *S.Afr.*) **1.** to travel arduously. **2.** to migrate or journey with one's belongings in ox-wagons. —*n.* (orig. *S.Afr.*) **1.** such a journey; each stage of it. **2.** an organized migration of a body of persons. [f. S.Afr. Du. *trekken* draw, pull]

trellis /'trelɪs/ *n.* a lattice or grating of light wooden or metal bars used especially as a support for fruit-trees or creepers and often fastened against a wall. [f. OF f. L *trilix* three-ply]

trematode /'tremətəʊd/ *n.* a parasitic flatworm of the class Trematoda. [f. Gk, = perforated (*trēma* hole)]

tremble *v.i.* to shake involuntarily with fear, excitement, weakness, etc.; to be in a state of apprehension; to move in a quivering manner. —*n.* trembling, a quiver. [f. OF f. L *tremulare* (as TREMULOUS)]

trembler *n.* an automatic vibrator for making and breaking an electric circuit. [f. prec.]

trembly *adj.* (*colloq.*) trembling. [f. TREMBLE]

tremendous /trɪ'mendəs/ *adj.* **1.** immense. **2.** (*colloq.*) remarkable, excellent. —**tremendously** *adv.*, **tremendousness** *n.* [f. L, = to be trembled at (as TREMOR)]

Trees

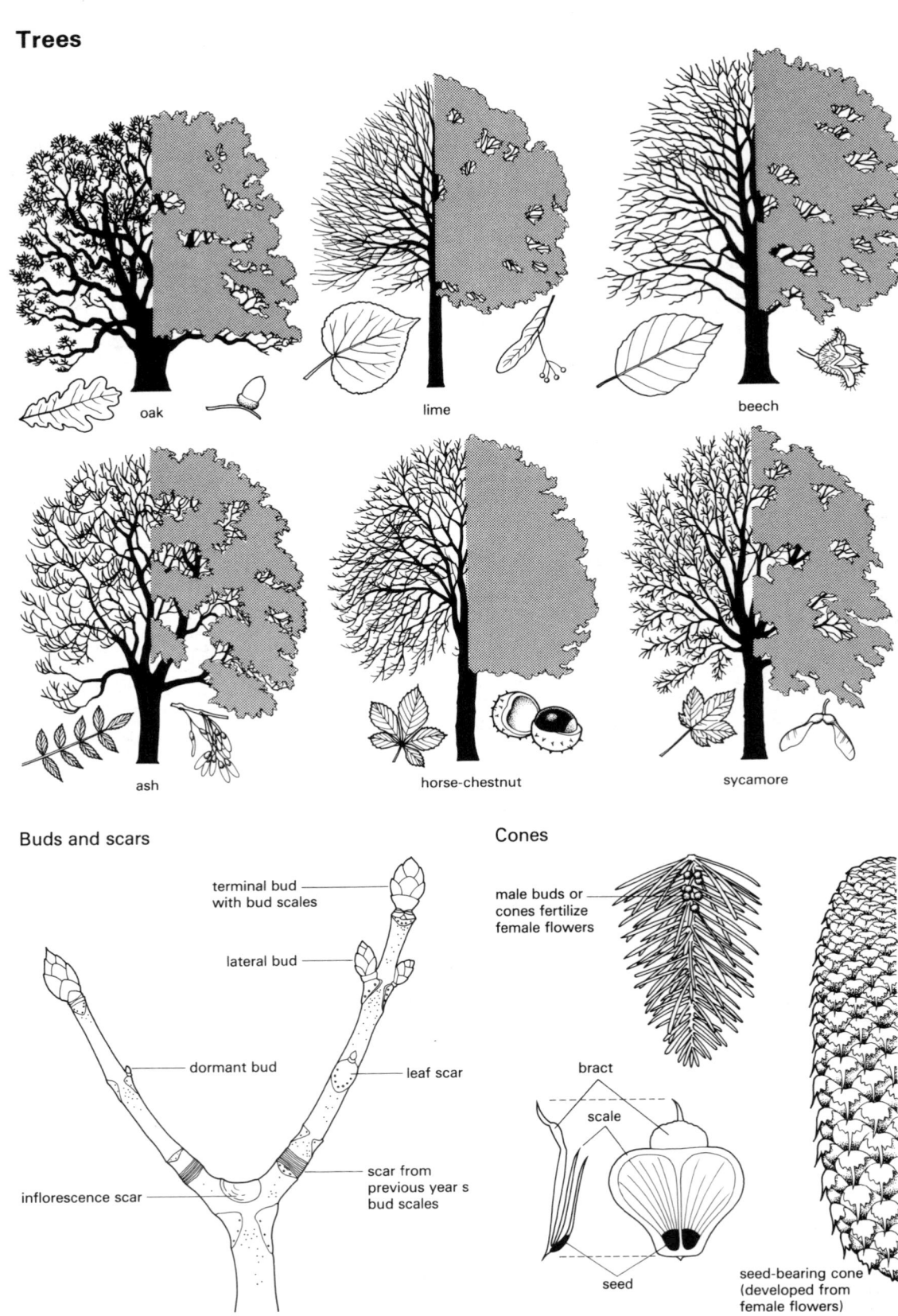

oak

lime

beech

ash

horse-chestnut

sycamore

Buds and scars

terminal bud with bud scales

lateral bud

dormant bud

leaf scar

inflorescence scar

scar from previous year's bud scales

Cones

male buds or cones fertilize female flowers

bract

scale

seed

seed-bearing cone (developed from female flowers)

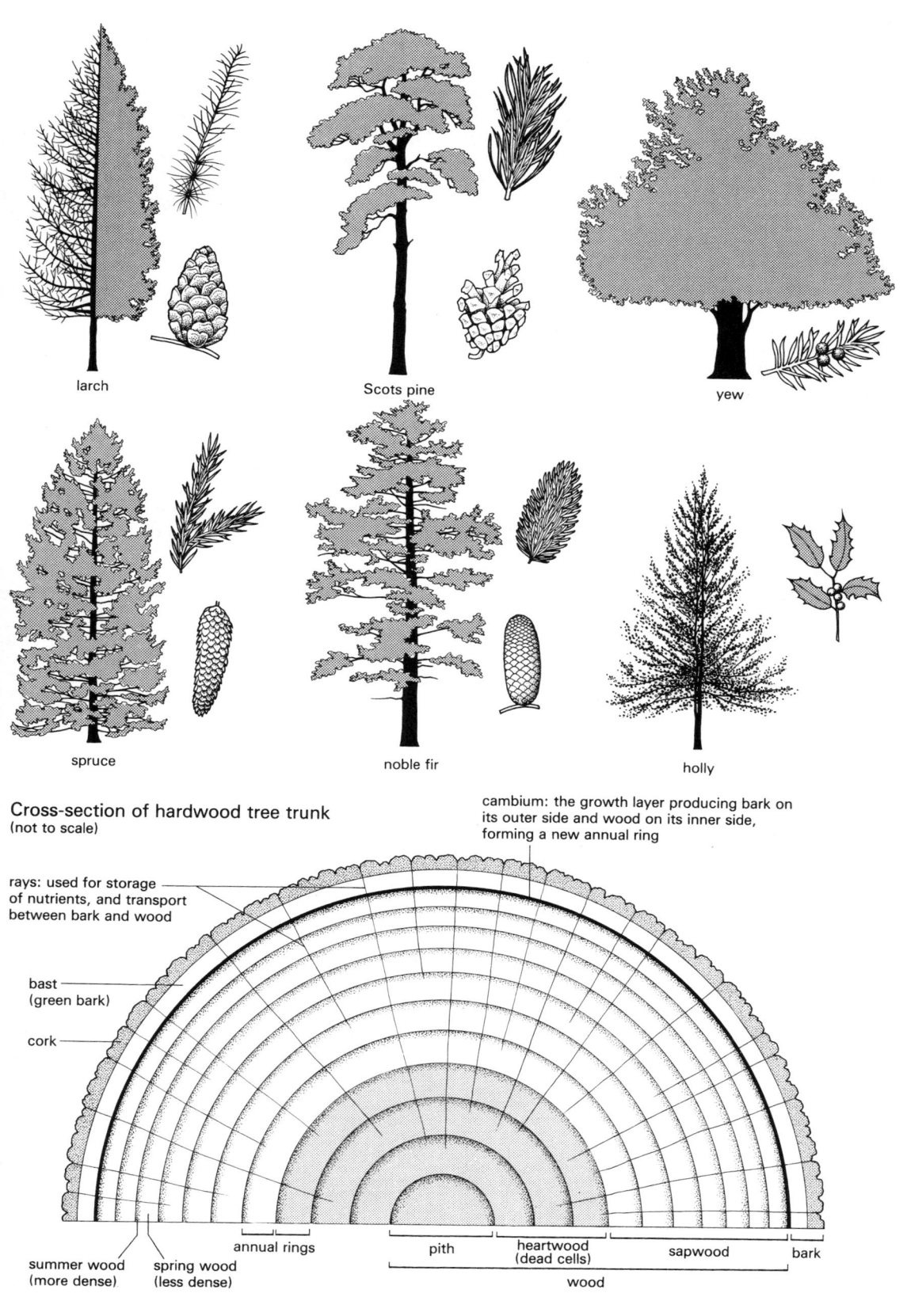

larch

Scots pine

yew

spruce

noble fir

holly

Cross-section of hardwood tree trunk
(not to scale)

cambium: the growth layer producing bark on
its outer side and wood on its inner side,
forming a new annual ring

rays: used for storage
of nutrients, and transport
between bark and wood

bast
(green bark)

cork

summer wood
(more dense)

spring wood
(less dense)

annual rings

pith

heartwood
(dead cells)

sapwood

bark

wood

tremolo /ˈtreməlaʊ/ n. (pl. **-os**) a tremulous effect in playing music or in singing. [It. (as TREMULOUS)]

tremor /ˈtremə(r)/ n. **1.** a slight shaking or trembling movement, a vibration; a slight earthquake. **2.** a thrill of fear or other emotion. [f. OF & L (*tremere* tremble)]

tremulous /ˈtremjʊləs/ adj. **1.** trembling from nervousness or weakness. **2.** easily made to quiver. —**tremulously** adv. [f. L *tremulus* (as TREMOR)]

trench n. a long narrow usually deep ditch, especially one dug by troops to stand in and be sheltered from an enemy's fire. —v.t. to dig a trench or trenches in (the ground); to dig (soil or a garden) thus so as to bring the subsoil to the top. —**trench coat**, a belted coat or raincoat with pockets and flaps like those of a military uniform coat. [f. OF, = cut, f. L (as TRUNCATE)]

trenchant /ˈtrentʃənt/ adj. (of style or language etc.) incisive, strong and effective. —**trenchancy** n., **trenchantly** adv. [as prec.]

trencher n. (hist.) a wooden platter for serving food. [f. AF *trenchour* (as TRENCH)]

trencherman n. (pl. **-men**) a person with regard to the amount he usually eats.

trend n. the general direction that something takes; a continuing tendency.—v.i. to have a specified trend. —**trend-setter** n. a person who leads the way in a fashion etc. [OE, = revolve]

trendy adj. (colloq.) up to date, following the latest trends of fashion. —n. (colloq.) a trendy person. —**trendily** adv., **trendiness** n. [f. TREND]

Trent the anglicized name of Trento, a city of northern Italy, scene of an ecumenical Church council, meeting from time to time between 1545 and 1563, which defined the doctrines of the Church in opposition to those of the Reformation, reformed discipline, and strengthened the authority of the papacy.

trepan /trɪˈpæn/ n. a surgeon's cylindrical saw for removing part of the skull. —v.t. (**-nn-**) to perforate (a skull) with a trepan. [f. L f. Gk *trupanon* auger (*trupē* hole)]

trephine /trɪˈfiːn/ n. an improved form of trepan with a guiding centre-pin. —v.t. to operate on with this. [orig. *trafine*, f. L *tres fines* three ends, app. after TREPAN]

trepidation /trepɪˈdeɪʃ(ə)n/ n. a state of fear and anxiety, nervous agitation. [f. L (*trepidare* be agitated)]

trespass /ˈtrespəs/ v.i. **1.** to enter a person's land or property unlawfully. **2.** to intrude or make use of unreasonably. **3.** (archaic) to sin, to do wrong. —n. **1.** an act of trespassing. **2.** a sin, wrongdoing. —**trespasser** n. [f. OF f. L (as TRANS-, PASS)]

tress n. a lock of human (especially female) hair; (in pl.) a head of such hair. [f. OF, perh. ult. f. Gk *trikha* threefold]

trestle /ˈtres(ə)l/ n. **1.** each of a pair or set of supports on which a board is rested to form a table. **2.** a trestle-work. —**trestle-table** n. a table consisting of a board or boards laid on trestles or other supports. **trestle-work** n. an open braced framework to support a bridge etc. [f. OF ult. f. L *transtrum* cross-beam]

Trevithick /ˈtreviθɪk/, Richard (1771–1833), known as the Cornish Giant, the most notable and original engineer to emerge from the Cornish mining industry, where steam-engines were first widely used. His particular contribution was in the use of high-pressure steam to drive a piston which then could send out exhaust against atmospheric pressure, giving a compact and therefore portable engine; this led to the first railway locomotive in 1804, at a colliery in South Wales. He also applied it to a steam-dredger, a threshing machine, and a cultivator. In 1816 he sailed for Peru to apply steam-power in the silver-mines, but this proved a disastrous enterprise and he returned penniless in 1827. Trevithick was a man of boundless energy, with schemes for refrigeration, tunnelling, wreck salvage, agricultural machinery, land reclamation, and gun-mountings.

trews /truːz/ n.pl. close-fitting usually tartan trousers. [f. Ir. or Gael.; cf. TROUSERS]

TRH abbr. Their Royal Highnesses.

tri- in comb. three, three times. [L & Gk (L *tres* & Gk *treis* three)]

triad /ˈtraɪæd, -əd/ n. **1.** a group of three (especially notes in a chord). **2.** the number three. **3.** a Chinese secret usually criminal organization. —**triadic** /-ˈædɪk/ adj., **triadically** adv. [f. F or L f. Gk (as TRI-)]

trial /ˈtraɪəl/ n. **1.** a judicial examination and determination of issues between parties by a judge with or without a jury.

2. the process of testing qualities or performance by use and experience. **3.** a sports match to test the ability of players who may be selected for an important team. **4.** a test of individual ability on a motor cycle over rough ground or on a road. **5.** a trying thing, experience, or person. —**on trial**, undergoing a trial; to be chosen or retained only if suitable. **trial and error**, the process of trying repeatedly and learning from one's errors until one succeeds. **trial run**, a preliminary testing of a vehicle or vessel etc. [AF (as TRY)]

triangle /ˈtraɪæŋg(ə)l/ n. **1.** a plane figure with three sides and angles (ill. SHAPES). **2.** any three things not in a straight line, with the imaginary lines joining them. **3.** an implement etc. of this shape; a musical instrument of a steel rod bent into a triangle sounded by striking with a small steel rod (ill. ORCHESTRA). **4.** a situation etc. involving three persons. [f. OF or L (as TRI-, ANGLE[1])]

triangular /traɪˈæŋgjʊlə(r)/ adj. **1.** triangle-shaped, three-cornered. **2.** (of a contest or treaty etc.) between three persons or parties. **3.** (of a pyramid) having a three-sided base. [f. L (as prec.)]

triangulate /traɪˈæŋgjʊleɪt/ v.t. to divide (an area) into triangles for surveying purposes (ill. NAVIGATION). —**triangulation** /-ˈleɪʃ(ə)n/ n. [as prec.]

Trianon /ˈtriːənɔ̃/ either of two small palaces in the great park at Versailles. The larger (**Grand Trianon**) was built by Louis XIV in 1687; the smaller (**Petit Trianon**), built by Louis XV 1762–8, belonged first to Madame du Barry and afterwards to Marie Antoinette.

Triassic /traɪˈæsɪk/ adj. of the first period of the Mesozoic era, following the Permian and preceding the Jurassic, lasting from about 248 to 213 million years ago. Dinosaurs became numerous during this period, which also saw the appearance of the first mammals. —n. the Triassic period. [f. L (as TRIAD), f. a threefold subdivision in Germany]

tribe n. **1.** a group of families (especially in a primitive or nomadic culture) living as a community under one or more chiefs and usually claiming descent from a common ancestor; any similar natural or political division; any of the twelve divisions of the people of ancient Israel, each traditionally descended from one of the patriarchs. **2.** (usu. derog.) a set or number of persons, especially of one profession etc. or family. —**tribal** adj., **tribally** adv. [f. OF or L *tribus*]

tribesman n. (pl. **-men**) a member of a tribe or one's own tribe.

tribology /trɪˈbɒlədʒɪ, traɪ-/ n. the study of the friction, wear, lubrication, and design of bearings. [f. Gk *tribos* rubbing + -LOGY]

tribulation /trɪbjʊˈleɪʃ(ə)n/ n. great affliction. [f. OF f. L (*tribulare* oppress f. *tribulum* threshing-sledge)]

tribunal /traɪˈbjuːn(ə)l, trɪ-/ n. **1.** a board appointed to adjudicate in or to investigate some matter. **2.** a seat or bench for a judge or judges. [F or f. L (as foll.)]

tribune[1] /ˈtrɪbjuːn/ n. **1.** a popular leader or demagogue. **2.** (in ancient Rome) an official chosen by the people to protect their liberties; an officer commanding a legion for two-month periods. —**tribunate** n. [f. L *tribunus* (prob. as TRIBE)]

tribune[2] /ˈtrɪbjuːn/ n. **1.** a bishop's throne in a basilica; an apse containing this. **2.** a dais, a rostrum. [F f. It. f. L (as TRIBUNAL)]

Tribune Group a group within the Labour Party consisting of supporters of the extreme left-wing views put forward in the weekly journal *Tribune*.

tributary /ˈtrɪbjʊtərɪ/ n. **1.** a river or stream flowing into a larger river or lake (ill. RIVERS). **2.** a person or State paying or subject to tribute. —adj. **1.** that is a tributary. **2.** contributory. [as foll.]

tribute /ˈtrɪbjuːt/ n. **1.** a thing said, done, or given as a mark of respect or affection etc. **2.** a payment formerly made periodically by one State or ruler to another as a sign of dependence. [f. L *tributum* (*tribuere* assign, orig. divide between tribes)]

trice n. **in a trice**, in an instant. [f. *trice* haul up, f. MDu. & MLG]

triceps /ˈtraɪseps/ n. a muscle (especially in the upper arm) with three points of attachment. [L (TRI-, *caput* head)]

trichinosis /trɪkɪˈnəʊsɪs/ n. a disease caused by hairlike worms in the muscles. [f. *trichina* hairlike worm f. Gk *trikhinos* hairlike]

trichology /trɪˈkɒlədʒɪ/ n. the study of hair.—**trichologist** n. [f. Gk *thrix* hair + -LOGY]

trichromatic /traɪkrə'mætɪk/ *adj.* **1.** three-coloured. **2.** (of vision) having the normal three colour-sensations (red, green, purple). [f. TRI- + CHROMATIC]

trick *n.* **1.** a thing done to fool, outwit, or deceive someone. **2.** an optical or other illusion. **3.** a special technique; the exact or best way to do something. **4.** a feat of skill done for entertainment. **5.** a mischievous, foolish, or discreditable act; a practical joke. **6.** a peculiar or characteristic habit. **7.** the cards played in one round of a card-game; the winning of a round. **8.** (*attrib.*) done to deceive or mystify. —*v.t.* to deceive or persuade by a trick. —**do the trick,** (*colloq.*) to achieve what is required. **how's tricks?** (*slang*) how are things? **trick or treat?** (*US*) a phrase said by children who call at houses at Hallowe'en seeking to be given sweets etc. and threatening to do mischief if these are not provided. **trick out** *or* **up,** to deck, to decorate. [f. OF *trique, triche* (*trichier* deceive; orig. unkn.)]

trickery *n.* deception, the use of tricks. [f. TRICK]

trickle *v.t./i.* **1.** to flow in drops or in a small stream; to cause to do this. **2.** to come or go slowly or gradually. —*n.* a trickling flow. —**trickle charger,** an accumulator-charger that works at a steady slow rate from the mains. [prob. imit.]

trickster *n.* a person who tricks or cheats people. [f. TRICK]

tricksy *adj.* full of tricks, playful. [f. TRICK]

tricky *adj.* **1.** requiring skilful handling. **2.** crafty, deceitful. —**trickily** *adv.*, **trickiness** *n.* [f. TRICK]

tricolour /'trɪkələ(r)/ *n.* a flag of three colours, especially the French national flag of blue, white, and red. [f. F f. L (as TRI-, COLOUR)]

tricorne /'traɪkɔːn/ *adj.* (of a hat) with the brim turned up to give a three-cornered appearance. —*n.* such a hat (ill. DRESS). [f. F or L (TRI-, *cornu* horn)]

tricot /'trɪkəʊ, 'triː-/ *n.* a fine jersey fabric. [F, = knitting]

tricycle /'traɪsɪk(ə)l/ *n.* **1.** a three-wheeled pedal-driven vehicle. **2.** a three-wheeled motor vehicle for a disabled driver. —*v.i.* to ride on a tricycle. —**tricyclist** *n.* [f. TRI- + CYCLE]

trident /'traɪd(ə)nt/ *n.* a three-pronged spear; the three-pronged fish-spear carried by Neptune and by Britannia as a symbol of power over the sea. [f. L (TRI-, *dens* tooth)]

Tridentine /trɪ'dentaɪn/ *adj.* of the Council of Trent (see TRENT), especially as a basis of Roman Catholic orthodoxy. [f. L (*Tridentum* Trento)]

triennial /traɪ'enɪəl/ *adj.* **1.** lasting for three years. **2.** recurring every third year. —**triennially** *adv.* [f. L (TRI-, *annus* year)]

trier /'traɪə(r)/ *n.* **1.** one who perseveres in his attempts. **2.** a tester. [f. TRY]

trifle /'traɪf(ə)l/ *n.* **1.** a thing of only slight value or importance. **2.** a very small amount, especially of money. **3.** a sweet dish made of sponge-cake soaked in wine or jelly with fruit and topped with custard and cream. —*v.i.* to talk or behave frivolously. —**trifle with,** to treat with flippancy or derision; to toy with. —**trifler** *n.* [f. OF *truf(f)le* = *truf(f)e* deceit]

trifling /'traɪf(ə)lɪŋ/ *adj.* trivial. [f. prec.]

trifoliate /traɪ'fəʊlɪət/ *adj.* (of a compound leaf) with three leaflets (ill. PLANTS); (of a plant) having such leaves.

triforium /traɪ'fɔːrɪəm/ *n.* (*pl.* **-ia**) an arcade or gallery above the nave and choir arches (ill. CHURCH). [L; orig. unkn.]

trigeminal /traɪ'dʒemɪn(ə)l/ *adj.* of the fifth and (in man) largest pair of cranial nerves, dividing into three main branches (ophthalmic, maxillary, and mandibular nerves). [f. L, = born as a triplet (TRI-, *geminus* born at same birth)]

trigger *n.* **1.** a movable device for releasing a spring or catch and so setting a mechanism (especially that of a gun) in motion. **2.** an agent that sets off a chain reaction. —*v.t.* (often with *off*) to set (an action or process) in motion; to be the immediate cause of. —**quick on the trigger,** quick to respond. **trigger-happy** *adj.* apt to shoot on slight provocation. [f. Du. *trekker* (as TREK)]

triglyph /'trɪɡlɪf/ *n.* an ornament of a frieze in the Doric order, consisting of a block or tablet with two vertical grooves and a half-groove on each side of these, alternating with metopes (ill. TEMPLES). [f. L f. Gk (TRI-, *gluphe* carving)]

trigonometry /trɪɡə'nɒmɪtrɪ/ *n.* the part of geometry that deals primarily with angles and their functions (e.g. sine, cosine, tangent); (formerly) the study of triangles. —**spherical trigonometry,** the theory of triangles that are formed by segments of great circles on a spherical surface, important in navigation and astronomy. —**trigonometric** /-nə'metrɪk/ *adj.*, **trigonometrical** /-nə'metrɪk(ə)l/ *adj.*, **trigonometrically** /-nə'metrɪkəlɪ/ *adv.* [f. Gk *trigōnon* triangle (TRI-, *-gōnos* cornered) + -METRY]

trike *n.* (*colloq.*) a tricycle. [abbr.]

trilateral /traɪ'lætər(ə)l/ *adj.* **1.** of, on, or having three sides. **2.** affecting or between three parties. [f. L (TRI-, *latus* side)]

trilby /'trɪlbɪ/ *n.* a soft felt hat with a narrow brim and a lengthwise dent in the crown. [f. name of heroine of G. du Maurier's novel *Trilby* (1894), in the stage version of which such a hat was worn]

trilingual /traɪ'lɪŋɡw(ə)l/ *adj.* **1.** speaking or able to speak three languages. **2.** written in three languages. [f. TRI- + L *lingua* tongue]

trill *n.* a quavering or vibratory sound (e.g. a rapid alternation of the main note and the note above in music, a bird's warbling, a pronunciation of *r* with vibration of the tongue). —*v.t./i.* to produce a trill; to warble (a song) or pronounce (*r* etc.) with a trill. [f. It. *trillo, trillare*]

trillion /'trɪljən/ *n.* (for plural usage see HUNDRED) **1.** a million million million. **2.** (*US* and increasingly in British use) a million million. **3.** (in *pl.*) very many. —**trillionth** *adj.* & *n.* [F or f. It. (as TRI-, MILLION)]

trilobite /'traɪləbaɪt/ *n.* a kind of fossil marine arthropod of Palaeozoic times, characterized by a three-lobed body. [f. TRI- + Gk *lobos* lobe]

trilogy /'trɪlədʒɪ/ *n.* a group of three related items, especially literary or operatic works. [f. Gk (as TRI-, -LOGY)]

trim *v.t./i.* (**-mm-**) **1.** to set in good order; to make neat or of the required size and form, especially by cutting away irregular or unwanted parts; (with *off* or *away*) to remove (such parts). **2.** to ornament. **3.** to adjust the balance of (a ship or aircraft) by the arrangement of its cargo etc. **4.** to arrange (sails) to suit the wind. **5.** (*colloq.*) to rebuke sharply; to thrash. **6.** (*colloq.*) to get the better of in a bargain etc. —*n.* **1.** a state of readiness or fitness. **2.** the trimming on a dress or furniture etc.; the colour or type of upholstery and other fittings in a vehicle. **3.** the trimming of hair etc. **4.** the balance or the even horizontal position of a boat or aircraft etc. —*adj.* neat and orderly; having a smooth outline or compact structure. —**trimly** *adv.*, **trimmer** *n.*, **trimness** *n.* [OE, = make firm]

trimaran /'traɪməræn/ *n.* a vessel like a catamaran, with three hulls side by side. [f. TRI- + CATAMARAN]

trimeter /'trɪmɪtə(r)/ *n.* a line of verse of three measures. [f. L f. Gk (as TRI-, METRE)]

trimming *n.* **1.** an ornamentation, a decoration. **2.** (in *pl.*, *colloq.*) the usual accompaniments, especially of the main course of a meal. **3.** (in *pl.*) pieces cut off when something is trimmed. [f. TRIM]

trine *n.* (in astrology) the aspect of two planets one third of the zodiac (= 120°) apart, regarded as having a favourable influence. —*adj.* having this aspect. [f. OF f. L *trinus* threefold (*tres* three)]

Trinidad and Tobago /'trɪnɪdæd, tə'beɪɡəʊ/ a country in the West Indies consisting of the main island of Trinidad, off the NE coast of Venezuela, and the much smaller island of Tobago (further to the north-east); pop. (est. 1980) 1,055,800; official language, English; capital, Port of Spain. Discovered by Columbus in 1498, the islands became British during the Napoleonic Wars and were formally amalgamated as a Crown Colony in 1888. After a short period as a member of the West Indies Federation between 1958 and 1962, Trinidad and Tobago became an independent member State of the Commonwealth in 1962 and finally a republic in 1976. A substantial part of the national income is generated by the export of petroleum products, while the capital Port of Spain is a major seaport. —**Trinidadian** /-'deɪdɪən/ *adj.* & *n.*, **Tobagan** *adj.* & *n.*, **Tobagonian** /-'ɡəʊnɪən/ *adj.* & *n.*

Trinitarian /trɪnɪ'teərɪən/ *n.* a person who believes in the doctrine of the Trinity, as contrasted with a Unitarian. —**Trinitarianism** *n.* [f. TRINITY]

trinitrotoluene /traɪnaɪtrəʊ'tɒljuːiːn/ *n.* (also **trinitrotoluol**) a high explosive. [f. TRI- + NITRO- + TOLUENE]

trinity /'trɪnɪtɪ/ *n.* being three; a group of three. —**the (Holy) Trinity,** the union of three persons (Father, Son, Holy Spirit) in one Godhead; the doctrine of this. **Trinity Sunday,** the Sunday next after Whit Sunday, celebrated in honour of the Holy Trinity. **Trinity term,** the university and law term beginning after Easter. [f. OF f. L (*trinus* threefold)]

Trinity House a corporation founded in 1514, in the reign of Henry VIII, which has official responsibility for the licensing of ships' pilots in the UK and the erection and maintenance of lighthouses, buoys, etc., round the coasts of England and Wales. In Scotland this latter function is discharged by the Commissioners of Northern Lighthouses.

trinket /'trɪŋkɪt/ n. a small fancy article or piece of jewellery. [orig. unkn.]

trio /'triːəʊ/ n. **1.** a musical composition for three performers; these performers. **2.** any group of three. [F & It. f. L *tres* three, after *duo*]

triode /'traɪəʊd/ n. **1.** a thermionic valve having three electrodes. **2.** a semiconductor rectifier having three terminals. [f. TRI- + ELECTRODE]

triolet /'triːəlɪt, 'traɪ-/ n. a poem of eight (usually eight-syllabled) lines, rhyming *abaaabab*, in which the first line recurs as the fourth and seventh and the second as the eighth. [F (as TRIO + -LET)]

trip v.t./i. (**-pp-**) **1.** to walk, run, or dance with quick light steps; (of rhythm) to run lightly. **2.** to stumble, to catch one's foot in something and fall; to cause to do this. **3.** (often with *up*) to make a slip or blunder; to cause to do this; to detect in a blunder. **4.** to take a trip to a place. **5.** (*colloq.*) to have a visionary experience caused by a drug. **6.** to release (a switch or catch) so as to operate a machine etc. —n. **1.** a journey or excursion, especially for pleasure. **2.** a stumble or blunder, tripping or being tripped up. **3.** a nimble step. **4.** (*colloq.*) a visionary experience caused by a drug; a device for tripping a mechanism. —**trip-hammer** n. a large hammer mounted on a pivot and operated by releasing a catch, used in metal forging. **trip-wire** n. a wire stretched close to the ground, operating a trap or alarm etc. when tripped against. [f. OF f. MDu. *trippen* skip, hop]

tripartite /traɪ'pɑːtaɪt/ adj. **1.** consisting of three parts. **2.** shared by or involving three parties. [f. L (TRI-, *partiri* divide)]

tripe n. **1.** the first or second stomach of a ruminant, especially an ox, as food. **2.** (*slang*) nonsense; a worthless thing. [f. OF]

Tripitaka /trɪpɪ'tɑːkə/ n. the sacred canon of Theravada Buddhism, written in the Pali language. [f. Skr., = the three baskets or collections]

triple adj. **1.** threefold, consisting of three parts or involving three parties. **2.** being three times as many or as much. **3.** (of time in music) having three beats in the bar. —n. **1.** a threefold number or amount. **2.** a set of three. —v.t./i. to make or become three times as many or as much. —**triple jump,** an athletic contest comprising a hop, a step, and a jump. **triple point,** the temperature and pressure at which the solid, liquid, and vapour phases of a pure substance can coexist in equilibrium. —**triply** adv. [OF or f. L *triplus* f. Gk]

Triple Alliance an alliance of three States etc.: in 1668, between England, the Netherlands, and Sweden against France; in 1717, between Britain, France, and the Netherlands against Spain; in 1865, between Argentina, Brazil, and Uruguay against Paraguay; in 1882, between Germany, Austria-Hungary, and Italy against France and Russia.

Triple Entente an early 20th-c. alliance between Great Britain, France, and Russia. Originally a series of loose agreements, the Entente began to assume the nature of a more formal alliance as the prospect of war with the Central Powers became more likely. The original Entente Cordiale with France was signed in 1904, the agreement with Russia in 1907.

triplet /'trɪplɪt/ n. **1.** each of three children or animals born at a birth. **2.** a set of three things, especially of notes played in the time of two, or of three lines of verse rhyming together. [f. prec., after *doublet*]

triplex adj. triple, threefold. [L, (TRI-, *plex* f. *plic-* fold)]

triplicate /'trɪplɪkət/ adj. **1.** existing in three examples. **2.** having three corresponding parts. **3.** tripled. —n. each of three things exactly alike. —/-keɪt/ v.t. to make in three copies; to multiply by three. —**triplication** /-ˈkeɪʃ(ə)n/ n. [f. L *triplicare* (as prec.)]

tripod /'traɪpɒd/ n. **1.** a three-legged stand for a camera etc. **2.** a stool, table, or utensil resting on three feet or legs. [f. L f. Gk (TRI-, *pous* foot)]

Tripoli /'trɪpəlɪ/ the capital and chief port of Libya; pop. (est. 1980) 994,000.

tripos /'traɪpɒs/ n. the honours examination for the BA

degree at Cambridge University. [as prec., with ref. to stool on which a BA sat to deliver satirical speech]

tripper n. a person who goes on a pleasure trip or excursion. —**trippery** adj. [f. TRIP]

triptych /'trɪptɪk/ n. a picture or carving on three panels, usually hinged vertically together. [f. TRI- after *diptych*]

Tripura /'trɪpʊrə/ a State in NE India; capital, Agartala.

trireme /'traɪriːm/ n. an ancient warship, perhaps with three men at each oar. [f. F or L (TRI-, *remus* oar)]

trisect /traɪ'sekt/ v.t. to divide into three (usually equal) parts. —**trisection** n. [f. TRI- + L *secare* cut]

Tristram /'trɪstrəm/ (in medieval legend) a knight who was the lover of Iseult (see ISEULT).

trite adj. (of a phrase, opinion, etc.) hackneyed, worn out by constant repetition. [f. L *tritus* (*terere* rub)]

tritium /'trɪtɪəm/ n. a heavy radioactive isotope of hydrogen with a mass about three times that of ordinary hydrogen. [f. Gk *tritos* third]

Triton /'traɪt(ə)n/ (*Gk myth.*) **1.** the son of Poseidon and Amphitrite. **2.** (as n.) a member of a class of minor sea-gods, usually represented as a man with a fish's (sometimes a horse's) tail carrying a trident and shell-trumpet. (See MERMAID.)

triumph /'traɪəmf/ n. **1.** the state of being victorious; a great success or achievement. **2.** a supreme example. **3.** joy at a success, exultation. **4.** the processional entry of a victorious general into ancient Rome. —v.i. **1.** to gain a victory, to be successful; to prevail. **2.** to exult. **3.** (of a Roman general) to ride in a triumph. [f. OF f. L *triump(h)us*, prob. f. Gk *thriambos* hymn to Bacchus]

triumphal /traɪ'ʌmf(ə)l/ adj. of, used in, or celebrating a triumph. [f. OF or L (as prec.)]

triumphant /traɪ'ʌmfənt/ adj. **1.** victorious, successful. **2.** rejoicing at success etc. —**triumphantly** adv. [as prec.]

triumvir /'traɪəmvɪə(r), -'ʌmvɪ(r)/ n. a member of a triumvirate. [L (*tres viri* three men)]

triumvirate /traɪ'ʌmvərət/ n. a board or ruling group of three men, especially in ancient Rome. The term is used specifically of the office to which Antony, Lepidus, and Octavian were appointed in 43 BC (the **Second Triumvirate**) and, improperly, of the unofficial coalition of Julius Caesar, Pompey, and Crassus in 60 BC (the **First Triumvirate**). [f. L (as prec.)]

trivalent /traɪ'veɪlənt/ adj. having a valence of three. [f. TRI- + VALENCE]

trivet /'trɪvɪt/ n. an iron tripod or bracket for a cooking-pot or kettle to stand on. —**as right as a trivet,** (*colloq.*) in a perfectly good state. [app. f. L *tripes* three-footed (TRI-, *pes* foot)]

trivia /'trɪvɪə/ n.pl. trivial things. [as foll.]

trivial /'trɪvɪəl/ adj. of only small value or importance, trifling; (of a person) concerned only with trivial things. —**triviality** /-'ælɪtɪ/ n., **trivially** adv. [f. L, = commonplace (*trivium* place where three roads meet f. TRI-, *via* road)]

Troad /'trəʊæd/ an ancient region of NW Asia Minor of which ancient Troy was the chief city.

trochee /'trəʊkiː/ n. a metrical foot consisting of one long or stressed syllable followed by one short or unstressed syllable. —**trochaic** /trə'keɪɪk/ adj. [f. L f. Gk, = running (*trekhō* run)]

trod, trodden see TREAD.

troglodyte /'trɒglədaɪt/ n. a cave-dweller, especially in prehistoric times. [f. L f. Gk f. name of Ethiopian people, after *troglē* hole]

troika /'trɔɪkə/ n. **1.** a Russian vehicle with a team of three horses abreast; such a team. **2.** a group of three persons especially as an administrative council. [Russ. (*troe* three)]

Troilus /'trɔɪləs/ **1.** (*Gk legend*) the son of Priam and Hecuba, killed by Achilles. **2.** (in medieval legend) the forsaken lover of Cressida.

Trojan /'trəʊdʒ(ə)n/ adj. of Troy or its people. —n. **1.** an inhabitant of Troy. **2.** a person who works, fights, or endures courageously. —**Trojan horse,** the hollow wooden horse used by the Greeks to enter Troy; a person or device insinuated to bring about an enemy's downfall. **Trojan War,** the ten-year siege of Troy by the Greeks in Greek legend (see TROY), which ended with the capture of the city after a band of Greek warriors had entered by a trick, concealed in a hollow wooden horse so large that the city walls had had to be breached for it to be drawn inside. [f. L *Troianus*]

troll[1] /'trəʊl/ n. (*Scand. myth.*) a member of a race of supernatural beings formerly conceived as giants but now (in Denmark and Sweden) as friendly but mischievous dwarfs. [f. ON & Sw. *troll*, Da. *trold*]

troll[2] /trəʊl/ v.t./i. **1.** to sing out in a carefree jovial manner. **2.** to fish by drawing bait along in the water. [orig. = stroll, roll; cf. OF *troller* to quest]

trolley /'trɒlɪ/ n. **1.** a platform on wheels for transporting goods; a small cart or truck. **2.** a small table on wheels or castors for transporting food or small articles. **3.** a trolley-wheel. —**trolley-bus** n. a bus powered by electricity from an overhead wire to which it is linked by a trolley-wheel. **trolley-wheel** n. a wheel attached to a pole etc. for collecting current from an overhead electric wire to drive a vehicle. [dial., perh. f. prec.]

trollop /'trɒləp/ n. a disreputable girl or woman. [perh. rel. to archaic *trull* prostitute]

Trollope /'trɒləp/, Anthony (1815-82), English novelist. His career in the General Post Office began in London in 1834 and took him to Ireland (1841-59) and other parts of the world; in this capacity he introduced the pillar-box for letters. He retired in 1867 and stood unsuccessfully for Parliament as a Liberal candidate in 1868. His literary career became established with his fourth novel *The Warden* (1855), the first of the six 'Barsetshire' novels which included *Barchester Towers* (1857) and ended with *The Last Chronicle of Barset* (1867); they are set in an imaginary English West Country and portray a solid rural society of curates and landed gentry, with characters who reappear in one or more of the series. This technique he developed in his six political 'Palliser' novels; in these, which begin with *Can You Forgive Her?* (1864) and include *The Eustace Diamonds* (1873), he expresses his own political views. Trollope was admired for his treatment of family and professional life, the variety and delicacy of his heroines, and his accurate pictures of social life. His remarkable output included 47 novels, travel books, biographies, and short stories.

trombone /trɒm'bəʊn/ n. a brass wind instrument with a forward-pointing extendable slide, the oldest brass instrument to possess a full chromatic compass (ill. ORCHESTRA). The trombone was introduced towards the mid-15th c., when it was often called 'sackbut', and was a favourite member of both instrumental and sacred and secular vocal music, particularly in Italy. It never really lost its early popularity, and its association with church music developed in 18th-c. Germany and Austria, leading Mozart to bring it in for dramatic and solemn effect in *Don Giovanni* and in the 'Tuba mirum' of his Requiem Mass. [F or f. It. (*tromba* trumpet, as TRUMP[2])]

trompe l'œil /trɔp 'lʌi:/ adj. (of a still-life painting etc.) designed to make a spectator think the objects represented are real. —n. such a painting etc. [F, lit. 'deceives the eye']

-tron suffix forming nouns denoting elementary particles or particle accelerators. [f. ELECTRON]

troop n. **1.** an assemblage of persons or animals, especially when moving. **2.** (in pl.) soldiers, armed forces. **3.** a cavalry unit commanded by a captain. **4.** a unit of artillery. **4.** a unit of three or more Scout patrols. —v.i. to assemble or go as a troop or in great numbers. —**troop the colour**, to show the regimental flag ceremonially along ranks of soldiers. [f. F *troupe* ult. f. L *troppus* flock]

trooper n. **1.** a private soldier in a cavalry or armoured unit. **2.** (Austral. hist. & US) a mounted or motor-borne policeman. **3.** a cavalry horse. **4.** a troop-ship. —**swear like a trooper**, to swear extensively or forcefully. [f. TROOP]

trophy /'trəʊfɪ/ n. **1.** a thing taken in war or hunting etc. as a souvenir of success. **2.** an object awarded as a prize or token of victory. [f. F f. L f. Gk *tropaion* (*tropē* rout f. *trepō* turn)]

tropic /'trɒpɪk/ n. the parallel of latitude 23° 27′ north (**tropic of Cancer**) or south (**tropic of Capricorn**) of the equator; the corresponding circle on the celestial sphere where the sun appears to turn after reaching its greatest declination. —adj. **1.** tropical. **2.** of or showing tropism. —**the tropics**, the region between the tropics of Cancer and Capricorn, with a hot climate. [f. L f. Gk (*tropē* turning)]

tropical /'trɒpɪk(ə)l/ adj. of, peculiar to, or suggestive of the tropics. —**tropically** adv. [as prec.]

tropism /'trəʊpɪz(ə)m/ n. the turning or movement of an organism in response to an eternal stimulus, e.g. that of plant leaves etc. in response to light. [f. Gk *-tropos* turning (*trepō* turn)]

tropopause /'trɒpəpɔ:z/ n. the interface between the troposphere and the stratosphere (ill. WEATHER). [f. foll. + PAUSE]

troposphere /'trɒpəsfɪə(r)/ n. the layer of atmospheric air extending about seven miles upwards from the earth's surface, in which the temperature falls with increasing height (ill. WEATHER). [f. Gk *tropos* turning + SPHERE]

trot v.t./i. (-tt-) **1.** (of a quadruped) to proceed at a steady pace faster than a walk lifting each diagonal pair of legs alternately, often with brief intervals during which the body is unsupported (ill. HORSE). **2.** (of a person) to run at a moderate pace, especially with short strides; (colloq.) to walk, to go. **3.** to cause to trot. **4.** to traverse (a distance) at a trot. —n. the action or exercise of trotting. —**on the trot**, (colloq.) continually busy; in succession. **trot out**, to produce, to bring out for inspection or approval etc. [f. OF f. L *trottare*]

troth /trəʊθ/ n. (archaic) faith, loyalty; truth. —**pledge or plight one's troth**, to pledge one's word, especially in marriage or betrothal. [as TRUTH]

Trotsky /'trɒtskɪ/, Leon, originally Lev Davidovich Bronstein (1879-1940), Russian revolutionary. An early member of the Bolshevik party, Trotsky became Lenin's principal lieutenant in the troubled years following the Russian Revolution, organizing the Red Armies which eventually defeated the opposing Whites in the Russian Civil War. After Lenin's death, he unsuccessfully contested the leadership with Stalin and was eventually banished in 1929. For some years he moved around the world, settling in Mexico in 1937, but was murdered there by a Stalinist assassin three years later.

Trotskyist /'trɒtskɪɪst/ n. a supporter of Leon Trotsky, who believed in the theory of continuing revolution rather than the more pragmatic ideas of State Communism generally accepted in Russia in the post-Revolutionary era. With the defeat and disgrace of their leader in the power struggle following the death of Lenin, the Trotskyists were generally branded by the successful Stalinists as perverters of the Revolution. Trotskyism has generally included a fair mixture of anarchist-syndicalist ideology, but the term has come to be used indiscriminately to describe all forms of radical left-wing Communism. —**Trotskyism** n. [f. prec.]

trotter n. **1.** a horse bred or trained for trotting-races. **2.** (usu. in pl.) an animal's foot as food. [f. TROT]

trotting n. a form of horse-racing (also called *harness-racing*) in which a horse pulls a two-wheeled vehicle (a *sulky*) and its driver. Trotting-races were held in Asia Minor as early as 1350 BC. In the Roman Empire chariot racing became one of the favourite sports, and it is probably from the Romans that trotting took its roots as a world-wide sport. [f. TROT]

troubadour /'tru:bədʊə(r)/ n. a member of a class of lyric poets composing in Provençal during the 12th and early 13th c. (and perhaps earlier), famous for the complexity of their verse forms and for the conception of chivalry and courtly love which prevails in their poems. They flourished in the courts of Spain, Italy, and France and through their influence on the northern French poets and on the German Minnesingers they had a major effect on all the subsequent development of European lyric poetry. As well as love poetry they also composed moralizing, satirical, and political poems (*sirventes*), and military poems. [F f. Prov. *trovador* (*trovar* find, compose)]

trouble /'trʌb(ə)l/ n. **1.** difficulty, inconvenience, distress, vexation, misfortune; a cause of any of these; unpleasant exertion. **2.** faulty functioning of mechanism or of the body or mind. **3.** conflict; (in pl.) public disturbances; **the Troubles**, any of various rebellions, civil wars, and unrest in Ireland, especially in 1919-23 and (in Northern Ireland) from 1968. **4.** unpleasantness involving punishment or rebuke. —v.t./i. **1.** to cause trouble or pain to; to distress. **2.** to be disturbed or worried; to be disturbed to inconvenience or unpleasant exertion. —**ask or look for trouble**, (colloq.) to behave rashly, incautiously, indiscreetly, etc. **in trouble**, involved in a matter likely to bring censure or punishment; (colloq.) pregnant while unmarried. **troublemaker** n. a person who habitually causes trouble. **troubleshooter** n. a person who traces and corrects faults in machinery etc.; a mediator in a dispute. [f. OF, ult. as TURBID]

troublesome adj. causing trouble, annoying. [f. prec. + -SOME]

troublous /'trʌbləs/ adj. (literary) full of troubles, agitated, disturbed. [as TROUBLE]

trough /trɒf/ n. **1.** a long narrow open receptacle for water, animal feed, etc. **2.** a channel or hollow comparable to this. **3.** an elongated region of low barometric pressure. [OE]

trounce /ˈtraʊns/ *v.t.* **1.** to defeat heavily. **2.** to beat, to thrash; to punish severely. [orig. unkn.]

troupe /truːp/ *n.* a company of actors or acrobats etc. [F, = TROOP]

trouper /ˈtruːpə(r)/ *n.* **1.** a member of a theatrical troupe. **2.** a staunch colleague. [f. prec.]

trousers /ˈtraʊzəz/ *n.pl.* a two-legged outer garment reaching from the waist usually to the ankles. —**trouser-suit** *n.* a woman's suit of trousers and jacket. —**trousered** *adj.* [extended form of archaic *trouse*, f. Ir. & Gael. (as TREWS)]

trousseau /ˈtruːsəʊ/ *n.* (*pl.* -**eaus**) a bride's collection of clothes etc. [F, = bundle (as TRUSS)]

trout *n.* (*pl.* usu. same) a small fish of the genus *Salmo* in northern rivers and lakes, valued as food and game; a similar fish of the family Salmonidae (**salmon** or **sea trout**). —**old trout**, (*slang, derog.*) an old woman. [OE]

trove *n.* treasure trove. [f. AF *trové* (*trover* find)]

trow /traʊ, trəʊ/ *v.t.* (*archaic*) to think, to believe. [OE, rel. to TRUCE]

trowel /ˈtraʊ(ə)l/ *n.* **1.** a small tool with a flat blade for spreading mortar or splitting bricks. **2.** a small garden tool with a curved blade for lifting small plants or scooping earth etc. [f. OF f. L *trulla* scoop, dim. of *trua* ladle]

Troy /trɔɪ/ also called Ilium, in Homeric legend the city of King Priam that was besieged for ten years by the Greeks in their endeavour to recover Helen, wife of Menelaus, who had been abducted. It was believed to be a figment of Greek legend until a stronghold called by the Turks Hissarlik was identified as the site of Troy by the German archaeologist H. Schliemann, who in 1870 began excavations of the mound which proved to be composed of 46 strata, dating from the early Bronze Age to the Roman era. The stratum known as Troy VII, believed to be that of the Homeric city, was sacked *c.*1210 BC. Again destroyed *c.*1100 BC, the site was resettled by the Greeks *c.*700 BC and finally abandoned in the Roman period.

troy *n.* (in full **troy weight**) a system of weights used for precious metals and gems, with a pound of 12 ounces or 5760 grains. [prob. f. *Troyes* in France]

truant /ˈtruːənt/ *n.* a child who absents himself from school; a person missing from work etc. —*adj.* (of a person or his conduct etc.) shirking, idle, wandering. —**play truant**, to stay away as a truant. —**truancy** *n.* [f. OF prob. f. Celt. (Welsh *truan*, Gael. *truaghan* wretched)]

truce /truːs/ *n.* a temporary cessation of hostilities; an agreement for this. [orig. pl.; OE, = covenant]

truck[1] *n.* **1.** an open container on wheels for transporting heavy loads; an open railway wagon; a hand-cart. **2.** a lorry. [perh. short for TRUCKLE]

truck[2] *n.* dealings; barter, exchange. —*v.t./i.* (*archaic*) to barter, to exchange. —**Truck Acts,** a series of Acts directed, from 1830 onwards, against the 'truck system', common in the 19th c., whereby workmen received their wages in the form of vouchers for goods redeemable only at a special shop (often run by the employer). The Acts required wages to be paid in cash. [f. F *troquer* f. L *trocare*; orig. unkn.]

truckle *v.i.* to submit obsequiously. —**truckle-bed** *n.* a low bed on wheels so that it may be pushed under another, especially as formerly used by servants etc. [f. AF *trocle* f. L *trochlea* pulley]

truculent /ˈtrʌkjʊlənt/ *adj.* defiant and aggressive. —**truculence** *n.*, **truculency** *n.*, **truculently** *adv.* [f. L *truculentus* (*trux* fierce)]

trudge /trʌdʒ/ *v.t./i.* to walk laboriously; to traverse (a distance) thus. —*n.* a trudging walk. [orig. unkn.]

true /truː/ *adj.* **1.** in accordance with fact. **2.** in accordance with correct principles or an accepted standard; rightly or strictly so called; genuine, not false. **3.** exact, accurate; (of the voice etc.) in good tune. **4.** accurately placed, balanced, or shaped; upright; level. **5.** loyal, faithful. —**come true,** to happen in the way that was prophesied or hoped. **true-blue** *adj.* completely true to one's principles; firmly loyal; (*n.*) such a person. **true north**, north according to the earth's axis, not the magnetic north. —**trueness** *n.* [OE]

truffle *n.* **1.** an edible subterranean fungus of the genus *Tuber*, with a rich flavour. **2.** a round soft sweet made of a chocolate mixture covered with cocoa etc. [prob. f. Du. f. obs. F, perh. f. L *tubera* pl. of TUBER]

trug *n.* a shallow oblong basket usually of wood strips, used by gardeners. [perh. dial. var. of TROUGH]

truism /ˈtruːɪz(ə)m/ *n.* **1.** a statement too obviously true or too hackneyed to be worth making. **2.** a statement that repeats an idea already implied in one of its terms (e.g. *there is no need to be unnecessarily careful*). [f. TRUE]

truly /ˈtruːlɪ/ *adv.* **1.** sincerely, genuinely. **2.** faithfully, loyally. **3.** accurately, truthfully. [OE (as TRUE)]

trump[1] *n.* **1.** a playing-card of a suit temporarily ranking above the others. **2.** an advantage, especially involving surprise. **3.** (*colloq.*) a helpful or excellent person. —*v.t.* to defeat (a card or its player) with a trump. —**trump card,** a card belonging to, or turned up to determine, the trump suit; a valuable resource. **trump up,** to invent (an accusation or excuse etc.) fraudulently. **turn up trumps** (*colloq.*) to turn out better than expected; to be greatly successful or helpful. [corruption of TRIUMPH in same (now obs.) sense]

trump[2] *n.* (*archaic*) a trumpet-blast. —**the last trump,** a trumpet-blast to wake the dead on Judgement Day. [f. OF *trompe* (prob. imit.)]

trumpery /ˈtrʌmpərɪ/ *adj.* showy but worthless. —*n.* worthless finery etc. [f. OF *tromperie* (*tromper* deceive)]

trumpet /ˈtrʌmpɪt/ *n.* **1.** a metal tubular or conical wind instrument with a flared mouth and a bright penetrating tone (see below; ill. ORCHESTRA). **2.** a trumpet-shaped thing. **3.** a sound (as) of a trumpet. —*v.t./i.* **1.** to blow a trumpet. **2.** (of an elephant etc.) to make a loud sound as of a trumpet. **3.** to proclaim (a person's or thing's merit) loudly. —**trumpet-call** *n.* an urgent summons to action. **trumpet-major** *n.* the chief trumpeter of a cavalry regiment. [f. OF *trompette* (as TRUMP[2])]

One of the ancient instruments (two are preserved from the tomb of Tutankhamun), in its early days it produced only 'natural' notes and was particularly associated with fanfares and flourishes, from pageantry to stirring military music. In the 18th c. crooks were added to allow a wider selection of notes, and in the early 19th c. the valved trumpet made possible a far greater and less type-cast contribution to orchestral music.

trumpeter *n.* one who sounds a trumpet, especially a cavalry soldier giving signals. [f. prec.]

truncate /trʌŋˈkeɪt/ *v.t.* to cut the top or end from. —**truncation** /-ˈkeɪʃ(ə)n/ *n.* [f. L *truncare* maim (as TRUNK)]

truncheon /ˈtrʌntʃ(ə)n/ *n.* **1.** a short club carried by a policeman. **2.** a staff or baton as a symbol of authority. [f. OF *tronchon* stump f. L (as TRUNK)]

trundle *v.t./i.* to roll along; to move heavily on a wheel or wheels. [var. of obs. or dial. *trendle* f. OE *trendel* circle (as TREND)]

trunk *n.* **1.** the main stem of a tree as distinct from the branches and roots. **2.** a person's or animal's body apart from the limbs and head. **3.** a large box with a hinged lid, used for transporting or storing clothes etc. **4.** (*US*) the boot of a motor car. **5.** an elephant's elongated prehensile nose. **6.** (in *pl.*) men's close-fitting shorts worn for swimming, boxing, etc. —**trunk-call** *n.* a telephone call on a trunk-line with charges according to distance. **trunk-line** *n.* a main line of a railway, telephone system, etc. **trunk-road** *n.* an important main road. [f. OF *tronc* f. L *truncus*]

trunnion /ˈtrʌnjən/ *n.* **1.** a supporting cylindrical projection on each side of a cannon or mortar. **2.** a hollow gudgeon supporting the cylinder in a steam-engine and giving passage to steam. [f. F *trognon* core, tree-trunk; orig. unkn.]

truss *n.* **1.** a framework of beams or bars supporting a roof or bridge etc. (ill. BRIDGES). **2.** a padded belt or other device worn to support a hernia. **3.** a bundle of hay or straw. **4.** a compact cluster of flowers or fruit. —*v.t.* **1.** to tie or bind securely; to tie (a fowl) compactly for cooking. **2.** to support (a roof or bridge etc.) with a truss or trusses. [f. OF *trusser* v., *trusse* n. (orig. unkn.)]

trust *n.* **1.** firm belief in the reliability, truth, strength, etc., of a person or thing; the state of being relied on. **2.** confident expectation. **3.** a thing or person committed to one's care; the resulting obligation. **4.** (*Law*) trusteeship; a board of trustees; property committed to a trustee or trustees. **5.** an association of several companies for the purpose of united action to reduce or defeat competition. —*v.t./i.* **1.** to have or place trust in; to treat as reliable. **2.** to entrust. **3.** to hope earnestly. —**in trust,** held as a trust (see sense 4). **on trust,** accepted without investigation. **trust to,** to place reliance on. [f. ON (*traustr* strong)]

trustee /trʌsˈtiː/ *n.* **1.** a person or a member of a board given possession of property with a legal obligation to administer it solely for the purposes specified. **2.** a State made responsible for the government of an area. —**trusteeship** *n.* [f. TRUST]

trustful *adj.* full of trust or confidence, not feeling or showing suspicion. —**trustfully** *adv.*, **trustfulness** *n.* [f. TRUST + -FUL]

trusting *adj.* having trust, trustful. [f. TRUST]

trustworthy *adj.* deserving of trust, reliable. —**trustworthiness** *n.*

trusty *adj.* (*archaic*) trustworthy. —*n.* a prisoner who is given special privileges or responsibilities because of continuous good behaviour. —**trustily** *adv.*, **trustiness** *n.* [f. TRUST]

truth /tru:θ/ *n.* (*pl.* /-ðz, -θs/) 1. the quality or state of being true or truthful. 2. what is true. —**in truth,** (*literary*) truly, really. [OE (as TRUE)]

truthful *adj.* 1. habitually telling the truth. 2. (of a story etc.) true. —**truthfully** *adv.*, **truthfulness** *n.* [f. TRUTH + -FUL]

try /traɪ/ *v.t./i.* 1. to make an effort with a view to success; to use effort to achieve or perform. 2. to test (the quality of a thing) by use or experiment; to test the qualities of (a person or thing); to examine the effectiveness or usefulness of for a purpose. 3. to make severe demands on. 4. to investigate and decide (a case or issue) judicially; to subject (a person) to trial. —*n.* 1. an effort to accomplish something. 2. (in Rugby football) a touching-down of the ball by a player behind the goal-line, scoring points and entitling his side to a kick at goal. —**try and,** (*colloq.*) try to. **try for,** to apply or compete for; to seek to reach or attain. **try one's hand,** to see how skilful one is, especially at a first attempt. **try it on,** (*colloq.*) to test another's patience. **try on,** to put on (clothes etc.) to see if they are suitable. **try-on** *n.* (*colloq.*) an act of 'trying it on', an attempt to deceive or outwit. **try out,** to put to the test, to test thoroughly. **try-out** *n.* an experimental test. [orig. = separate, distinguish, f. OF *trier* sift]

trying *adj.* putting a strain on one's temper, patience, or endurance; annoying. [f. TRY]

trypanosome /ˈtrɪpənəsəʊm/ *n.* a flagellate protozoan parasite infesting the blood etc. and causing diseases of a group that includes sleeping sickness. [f. Gk *trupanon* borer, *sōma* body]

tryst /trɪst, traɪst/ *n.* (*archaic*) a time and place for a meeting, especially of lovers. [f. OF *triste* appointed station in hunting]

tsar /zɑ:(r)/ *n.* the title of the former emperor of Russia. It was formally assumed as a title by Ivan the Terrible in 1547; some earlier uses exist. [f. Russ., ult. f. L *Caesar*]

tsetse /ˈtsetsɪ, ˈtetsɪ/ *n.* a fly of the genus *Glossina*, found only in tropical Africa, carrying disease (especially sleeping sickness) to man and animals by biting. [Tswana]

T-shirt /ˈti:ʃɜ:t/ *n.* a short-sleeved shirt for casual wear, having the form of T when spread out.

T-square /ˈti:skweə(r)/ *n.* a T-shaped instrument for drawing or testing right angles.

tsunami /tsʊˈnɑ:mɪ/ *n.* 1. a series of long high sea-waves caused by disturbance of the ocean floor or seismic movement. 2. an exceptionally large tidal wave. [Jap. (*tsu* harbour, *nami* wave)]

Tswana /ˈtswɑ:nə/ *n.* 1. a member of a Negroid people living in Africa between the Orange and Zambezi rivers. 2. their Bantu language (also called *Sechuana*). [native name]

TT *abbr.* 1. Tourist Trophy. 2. tuberculin-tested. 3. teetotal; teetotaller.

Tuareg /ˈtwɑ:reg/ *n.* (*pl.* same or **-s**) 1. a member of a Berber group of nomadic pastoralists of North Africa, the legendary blue-veiled warriors of Timbuktu and the romance of *Beau Geste*. The main concentrations of Tuareg population are now in Algeria, Mali, Niger, and Western Libya, with smaller groups to be found in Nigeria, the Sudan, etc. 2. their Berber dialect, which is the only Berber language to have an indigenous written form (its alphabet is related to ancient Phoenician script). —*adj.* of this people or their language. [native name]

tub *n.* 1. an open flat-bottomed usually round vessel used for washing or for holding liquids or containing soil for plants etc. 2. (*colloq.*) a bath. 3. (*colloq.*) a clumsy slow boat. —*v.t./i.* (**-bb-**) to plant, bath, or wash in a tub. —**tub-thumper** *n.* a ranting preacher or orator. [prob. f. LDu.]

tuba /ˈtju:bə/ *n.* a low-pitched brass wind instrument (ill. ORCHESTRA). [It. f. L, = trumpet]

tubal /ˈtju:b(ə)l/ *adj.* of a tube or tubes, especially the bronchial or Fallopian tubes. [f. TUBE]

tubby *adj.* tub-shaped; (of a person) short and fat. —**tubbiness** *n.* [f. TUB]

tube *n.* 1. a long hollow cylinder; a natural or artificial structure having approximately this shape with open or closed ends and serving for the passage of fluid etc. or as a receptacle. 2. (*colloq.*) the London underground railway. 3. an inner tube. 4. a cathode-ray tube, e.g. in a television set. 5. (*US*) a thermionic valve. —*v.t.* 1. to equip with a tube or tubes. 2. to enclose in a tube. —**the tube,** (*US*) television. [F or f. L *tubus*]

tuber /ˈtju:bə(r)/ *n.* a thick round root (e.g. of a dahlia) or underground stem (e.g. of a potato), frequently bearing buds (ill. PLANTS). [L, = hump, swelling]

tubercle /ˈtju:bək(ə)l/ *n.* a small rounded swelling in a plant or organ of the body, especially as characteristic of tuberculosis in the lungs. —**tubercle bacillus,** the bacillus causing tuberculosis. [f. L *tuberculum*, dim. of prec.]

tubercular /tju:ˈbɜ:kjʊlə(r)/ *adj.* of or affected with tuberculosis. [as prec.]

tuberculin /tju:ˈbɜ:kjʊlɪn/ *n.* a preparation from cultures of the tubercle bacillus used for the treatment and diagnosis of tuberculosis. —**tuberculin-tested** *adj.* (of milk) from cows shown by a tuberculin test to be free of tuberculosis. [as foll.]

tuberculosis /tju:bɜ:kjʊˈləʊsɪs/ *n.* an infectious bacterial wasting disease affecting various parts of the body, in which tubercles appear on body tissue; (in full **pulmonary tuberculosis**) this disease of the lungs. (See below.) [f. TUBERCLE + -OSIS]

The disease occurs throughout the world and has grave social importance because some three million people die from it each year and many more suffer long incapacitating illnesses. It was common in Europe in the 19th c.; Keats developed the illness shortly after nursing his sick brother, and Anne and Emily Brontë and their brother Branwell died of it. Today in the countries that enjoy good living conditions and medical services the situation is very different, but the disease is still widespread in the developing countries. The most common form, formerly popularly known as consumption, affects the lungs, which are invaded by bacteria (tubercle bacilli) first identified by the German bacteriologist Robert Koch in 1882. Tuberculosis was once called the 'white plague' and considered to be incurable, but now treatment, which has been transformed by the use of new drugs and by lung operations, can arrest the disease and restore the patient to normal health. In consequence the death-rate from it has been dramatically reduced. This decline is due also to early diagnosis of the disease by X-rays, to the use of vaccines, and to improved standards of living and hygiene, for tuberculosis flourishes among the overcrowded and underfed. Its control by public health authorities is one of the finest examples of the success of a carefully planned and well-directed campaign against a disease.

Tuberculosis can affect parts of the body other than the lungs, in particular the bones and joints and the central nervous system. There is also a type known as bovine tuberculosis which attacks cattle, and infection can be passed on to human beings by the milk of infected cows. Elimination of tuberculosis from dairy herds, and pasteurization of milk, have greatly reduced such transmission of the disease.

tuberculous /tju:ˈbɜ:kjʊləs/ *adj.* of, having, or caused by tubercles or tuberculosis. [as prec.]

tuberose /ˈtju:bərəʊz/ *n.* a plant (*Polianthes tuberosa*) with fragrant creamy-white flowers. [f. L (as TUBER)]

tuberous *adj.* having tubers; of or like a tuber. [f. F or L (as prec.)]

tubing /ˈtju:bɪŋ/ *n.* a length of tube; a quantity of tubes. [f. TUBE]

tubular /ˈtju:bjʊlə(r)/ *adj.* tube-shaped; having or consisting of tubes; (of furniture etc.) made of tubular pieces. [as foll.]

tubule /ˈtju:bju:l/ *n.* a small tube. [f. L *tubulus* dim. of *tubus* tube]

TUC *abbr.* Trades Union Congress.

tuck *v.t.* 1. to turn (edges or ends) or fold (a part) in, into, or under something so as to be concealed or held in place. 2. to cover snugly and compactly. 3. to put away compactly. 4. to put a tuck or tucks in (a garment etc.). 5. (in *p.p.*, of a dive or somersault etc.) with the knees drawn up to the chest (ill. SPORTS). —*n.* 1. a flattened usually stitched fold in material or a garment etc. to make it smaller or as an ornament. 2. (*slang*) food, especially sweets, cakes, and pastry etc. that children enjoy. —**tuck in,** (*slang*) to eat food heartily. **tuck-in** n. (slang) a large meal. **tuck into,** (slang) to eat (food) heartily. **tuck-shop** n. a shop selling sweets etc. to schoolchildren. [f. MDu. and MLG tucken (rel. to TUG)]

tucker n. **1.** a piece of lace or linen etc. in or on a woman's bodice (hist. exc. in **best bib and tucker,** one's best clothes). **2.** (Austral. colloq.) food. —v.t. (US colloq.) to tire. [f. TUCK]

Tudor /'tju:də(r)/ the name of the English royal house descended from Owen Tudor who married Catherine, widowed queen of Henry V, which ruled England from 1485 (Henry VII) until the death of Elizabeth I (1603). —attrib. or adj. of the architectural style (the latest development of Perpendicular) prevailing in England during the reigns of the Tudors; of or resembling the domestic architecture of this period, with much half-timbering, brickwork frequently in patterns, elaborate chimneys, many gables, rich oriel windows, and much interior panelling and moulded plasterwork. —**Tudor rose,** a conventionalized five-lobed decorative figure of a rose, especially a combination of the red and white roses of York and Lancaster adopted as a badge by Henry VII.

Tue. abbr. Tuesday.

Tuesday /'tju:zdeɪ, -dɪ/ n. the day of the week following Monday. —adv. (colloq.) on Tuesday. [OE, = day of Tiw (Teutonic god of war)]

tufa /'tju:fə/ n. **1.** porous rock formed round springs of mineral water. **2.** tuff. [It. (as foll.)]

tuff n. rock formed from volcanic ashes. [f. F f. It. f. L tofus loose porous stones]

tuffet /'tʌfɪt/ n. a small mound; a tussock. [var. of TUFT]

tuft n. a bunch or collection of threads, grass, feathers, or hair etc. held or growing together at the base. —**tufty** adj. [prob. f. OF tof(f)e]

tufted adj. having or forming a tuft or tufts; (of a bird) with a tuft of feathers on its head; (of a mattress or cushion) with depressions formed by stitching tightly through it at intervals to hold the filling in place. [f. TUFT]

Tu Fu /tu: 'fu:/ (712–70), a major (according to some, the greatest) Chinese poet, noted for his bitter satiric poems attacking social injustice and corruption at court. Intense personal suffering during the turbulent 750s added a note of universal pathos to his verse and inspired some of his finest work.

tug v.t./i. (-gg-) **1.** to pull vigorously or with great effort. **2.** to tow by means of a tugboat. —n. **1.** a vigorous pull (lit. or fig.). **2.** a tugboat. —**tug of love,** (colloq.) a dispute over the custody of a child. **tug of war,** a contest in which two teams hold a rope at opposite ends and pull until one team hauls the other over a central point; a struggle between two persons etc. for power. [rel. to TOW¹]

tugboat n. a small powerful steam-vessel for towing others.

tuition /tju:'ɪʃ(ə)n/ n. teaching instruction, especially as a thing to be paid for. [f. OF f. L (tueri look after)]

tulip /'tju:lɪp/ n. a spring-flowering plant of the genus Tulipa, growing from a bulb, with showy cup-shaped flowers; its flower. —**tulip-tree** n. a tree (Liriodendron tulipifera) with tulip-like flowers. [f. Turk. tul(i)band f. Pers., = TURBAN (from the shape of the flowers)]

Tull /tʌl/, Jethro (1674–1741), the progenitor of the agricultural revolution in England, which preceded the Industrial Revolution, whose major invention in 1701 was the seed-drill for sowing seeds in accurately spaced rows at a controlled rate. This made possible the control of weeds by horse-drawn hoe and so reduced the need for farm labourers, freeing them to work in factories. His methods were adopted abroad also, particularly in France and the USA.

tulle /tju:l/ n. a soft fine silk net for veils and dresses. [f. Tulle in SW France]

tum n. (colloq.) the stomach. [abbr. of TUMMY]

tumble v.t./i. **1.** to fall helplessly or headlong; to cause to do this. **2.** to fall in value or amount. **3.** to roll or toss over and over in a disorderly way. **4.** to move or rush in a hasty careless way. **5.** to throw or push carelessly in a confused mass. **6.** to rumple, to disarrange. **7.** to perform somersaults or other acrobatic feats. **8.** (of a pigeon) to throw itself over backwards in flight. —n. **1.** a tumbling fall. **2.** an untidy state. —**tumble-drier** n. a machine for drying washing in a heated rotating drum. **tumble to,** (colloq.) to realize or grasp the meaning of. [f. MLG tummelen, frequent. of tūmōn]

tumbledown adj. falling or fallen into ruin, dilapidated.

tumbler n. **1.** a drinking-glass with no handle or foot. **2.** an acrobat. **3.** a pivoted piece in a lock that holds the bolt until lifted by a key; any of various kinds of pivoted or swivelling parts in a mechanism. **4.** a pigeon that tumbles in its flight. [f. prec.]

tumbrel /'tʌmbr(ə)l/ n. (also **tumbril**) an open cart in which condemned persons were conveyed to the guillotine during the French Revolution. [f. OF tomberel (tomber fall)]

tumescent /tjʊ'mesənt/ adj. swelling. —**tumescence** n. [f. L tumescere (as TUMOUR)]

tumid /'tju:mɪd/ adj. swollen, inflated; (of style etc.) bombastic. —**tumidity** /-'mɪdɪtɪ/ n. [f. L tumidus (as TUMOUR)]

tummy /'tʌmɪ/ n. (colloq.) the stomach. —**tummy-button** n. (colloq.) the navel. [childish pronunc.]

tumour /'tju:mə(r)/ n. an abnormal mass of new tissue growing on or in the body. —**tumorous** adj. [f. L tumor (tumēre swell)]

tumult /'tju:mʌlt/ n. **1.** an uproar, a public disturbance. **2.** a state of confusion and agitation. [f. OF or L tumultus]

tumultuous /tjʊ'mʌltjʊəs/ adj. making a tumult. —**tumultuously** adv. [as prec.]

tumulus /'tju:mjʊləs/ n. (pl. **-li** /-laɪ/) an ancient burial mound. [L, = mound]

tun n. **1.** a large cask for wine; a brewer's fermenting-vat. **2.** a measure of capacity (usually about 210 gallons). [OE f. L tunna, prob. of Gaulish origin]

tuna /'tju:nə/ n. (pl. same) the tunny; (also **tuna-fish**) the flesh of the tunny as food. [Amer. Sp.]

tundra /'tʌndrə/ n. a vast level treeless Arctic region where the subsoil is frozen. [Lappish]

tune n. **1.** a melody with or without harmony. **2.** the correct pitch or intonation in singing or playing; an adjustment of a musical instrument to obtain this. —v.t. **1.** to put (a musical instrument) in tune. **2.** to adjust (a radio receiver etc.) to a particular wavelength of signals. **3.** to adjust (an engine etc.) to run smoothly and efficiently. **4.** to adjust or adapt (a thing to a purpose etc.). —**call the tune,** to have control of events. **change one's tune,** to change one's style of language or manner, especially from an insolent to a respectful tone. **in** (or **out of**) **tune with,** harmonizing (or clashing) with. **to the tune of,** to the considerable sum or amount of. **tune in,** to set a radio receiver to the right wavelength to receive a certain signal. **tune up,** (of an orchestra) to bring the instruments to the proper or a uniform pitch; to bring to the most efficient condition; to begin to play or sing. **tuning-fork** n. a two-pronged steel fork giving a particular note when struck. [var. of TONE]

tuneful adj. melodious, having a pleasing tune. —**tunefully** adv., **tunefulness** n. [f. TUNE + -FUL]

tuneless adj. not melodious; without a tune. [f. TUNE + -LESS]

tuner /'tju:nə(r)/ n. a person who tunes instruments, especially pianos. [f. TUNE]

tungsten /'tʌŋst(ə)n/ n. a heavy metallic element (also known as wolfram), symbol W, atomic number 74, first isolated in 1783. Tungsten is a strong hard metal with a very high melting-point. It has become of importance in the 20th c. as the chief material from which electric light bulb filaments are made. Tungsten is also used in special steels, and the compound tungsten carbide, which is extremely hard, is used to form the cutting edges of saws, the tips of drill-bits, etc. [Swedish (tung heavy, sten stone)]

Tungus /'tʌŋʌs/ n. **1.** a Mongoloid people of eastern Siberia; a member of this people. **2.** an Altaic language or group of languages, spoken in parts of Siberia, since 1931 set down in an alphabet based on the Russian alphabet. —**Tungusian** /tʌŋ'gju:sɪən/ adj. & n., **Tungusic** /-'gju:sɪk/ adj. & n. [native name]

tunic /'tju:nɪk/ n. **1.** the close-fitting short coat of a police or military uniform. **2.** a loose garment, often sleeveless, reaching to the hips or knees. [f. F or L tunica]

tunicate /'tju:nɪkət/ n. a member of the subphylum Urochorda of marine animals with a hard outer coat. [f. L tunicare clothe with a tunic (as prec.)]

Tunis /'tju:nɪs/ the capital of Tunisia, situated near the Mediterranean coast; pop. (1981) 1,133,000.

Tunisia /tju:'nɪsɪə/ a country in North Africa, on the Mediterranean Sea; pop. (est. 1981) 6,520,000; official language, Arabic; capital, Tunis. Phoenician settlements on the coast developed into the Carthaginian commercial empire which came into conflict with Rome, and after defeat in the Punic Wars became a Roman province. The area was conquered by the Vandals in the 5th c. AD and subsequently by the Arabs (7th c.); in the 16th c. it became part of the Ottoman empire. Under loose Turkish rule, Tunisia became a centre of piratical activity in the 16th–19th c. before its establishment as a French protectorate in 1886. The rise of nationalist activity after the Second World War led to independence and the establishment of a republic in 1956–7. Considerable efforts have been made to improve the economy, which is based almost entirely on agriculture and mining (there are large deposits of phosphates) in the better-watered coastal strip, but economic difficulties have recently led to severe social problems. —**Tunisian** *adj. & n.*

tunnel /ˈtʌn(ə)l/ *n.* an underground passage; a passage dug through a hill or under a road etc., especially for a railway or road; a passage made by a burrowing animal. —*v.t./i.* (**-ll-**) to make a tunnel through (a hill etc.); to make one's way thus. [f. OF *tonel* dim. of *tonne* tun]

tunny /ˈtʌnɪ/ *n.* a large edible sea-fish, especially of the genus *Thunnus*. [f. F *thon* f. L f. Gk *thunnos*]

tup *n.* a male sheep, a ram. —*v.t.* (**-pp-**) (of a ram) to copulate with (a ewe). [orig. unkn.]

Tupi /ˈtuːpɪ/ *n.* **1.** a member of an American Indian people in the Amazon valley. **2.** their language. —*adj.* of this people or their language. [Tupi]

tuppence /ˈtʌpəns/ *n.* = TWOPENCE. [phonetic spelling]

tuppenny /ˈtʌpənɪ/ *adj.* = TWOPENNY. [phonetic spelling]

turban /ˈtɜːbən/ *n.* **1.** a man's head-dress of cotton or silk wound round a cap, worn especially by Muslims and Sikhs. **2.** a woman's head-dress or hat resembling this (ill. DRESS). [ult. f. Turk. f. Pers. (as TULIP)]

turbid /ˈtɜːbɪd/ *adj.* **1.** (of a liquid or colour) muddy, not clear. **2.** (of style etc.) not lucid. —**turbidity** /-ˈbɪdɪtɪ/ *n.*, **turbidly** *adv.* [f. L *turba* crowd, disturbance)]

turbine /ˈtɜːbaɪn/ *n.* a device for producing continuous mechanical power, in which a fluid (water, steam, air, or a gas) is accelerated to a high speed in a channel or nozzle and the resulting jet(s) directed at a rotating wheel with vanes or scoop-shaped buckets round its rim. A force is created on the wheel and hence a torque on its shaft, as in a water-wheel (used to work machinery), and in the 19th c. these were developed (chiefly in France and Germany) to drive machinery in factories. The steam turbine was invented 2,000 years ago by Hero of Alexandria, but the first practical one was devised by Sir Charles Parsons in 1884, and contributions to its development were made by the Swedish engineer de Laval and others. Steam-driven turbines have replaced the steam-engine in electrical power stations. Gas turbines are a form of internal-combustion engine in which air is compressed, heated by means of fuel sprayed into a combustion chamber, then expanded in a turbine to produce enough power both to drive the compressor and to provide a surplus. They are much used for aircraft propulsion, having a high specific power output (i.e. high power for low weight). [F f. L *turbo* spinning-top, whirlwind]

turbo- /ˈtɜːbəʊ/ *in comb.* turbine.

turbofan *n.* a jet engine with additional thrust from cold air drawn in by a fan. [f. TURBO- + FAN]

turbo-jet *n.* a jet engine in which jet gases also operate a turbine-driven compressor for supplying compressed air to the combustion chamber; an aircraft with such an engine. The turbo-jet engine was experimentally devised in the decade before the Second World War by a young RAF officer, Frank Whittle, who at first found it difficult to interest British aircraft engine manufacturers in the design or to secure financial backing for his experiments. German designers, starting slightly later than Whittle, were more fortunate, since the German Air Ministry (unlike the British) appreciated the military potential of the engine, and they were able to develop an engine reliable enough to propel the first turbo-jet aeroplane in 1939. [f. TURBO- + JET¹]

turbo-prop *n.* a jet engine in which a turbine is used as in a turbo-jet and also to drive a propeller; an aircraft with such an engine. [f. TURBO- + PROP²]

turbot /ˈtɜːbət/ *n.* a large European flat-fish (*Scophthalmus maximus*) valued as food. [f. OF]

turbulent /ˈtɜːbjʊlənt/ *adj.* **1.** in a state of commotion or unrest; (of air or water) moving violently and unevenly. **2.** unruly. —**turbulence** *n.*, **turbulently** *adv.* [as TURBID]

Turco- /ˈtɜːkəʊ-/ *in comb.* Turkish. [f. L (as TURK)]

turd *n.* (*vulgar*) a ball or lump of excrement. [OE]

tureen /tjʊəˈriːn/ *n.* a deep covered dish from which soup is served. [f. F *terrine* earthenware dish f. L *terra* earth]

turf *n.* (*pl.* **turfs** or **turves**) **1.** the layer of grass etc. with earth and matted roots as the surface of grassland. **2.** a piece of this cut from the ground. **3.** a slab of peat for fuel. —*v.t.* to plant (ground) with turf. —**the turf,** the racecourse, horse-racing. **turf-accountant** *n.* a bookmaker. **turf out,** (*slang*) to throw out. —**turfy** *adj.* [OE]

Turgenev /tɜːˈɡeɪnjef/, Ivan Sergievich (1818–83), Russian novelist and playwright, who studied at Moscow and St Petersburg Universities and in Berlin (1838–41), then served in the Russian Civil Service which he abandoned for literature in 1845. His first major prose work *A Hunter's Notes* (1847–51) led to a period of confinement at his country estate for its evocative portrayal of Russian serfdom. Partly because of his love for the singer Pauline Garcia Viardot he spent most of his remaining life abroad (mainly in Baden-Baden and Paris) where he met Flaubert and other literary figures, and thus developed a closeness in both sensibility and literary practice to Western Europe. His series of novels in which individual lives are examined to illuminate the social, political, and philosophical issues of the day includes *Rudin* (1856), *On the Eve* (1860), *Fathers and Sons* (1862) in which in Bazarov he created a Nihilist hero, and *Virgin Soil* (1877). His short stories include 'Asya' (1858) and 'First Love' (1860); his greatest play was *A Month in the Country* (1850).

turgescent /tɜːˈdʒesənt/ *adj.* becoming turgid. —**turgescence** *n.* [f. L *turgescere* (as foll.)]

turgid /ˈtɜːdʒɪd/ *adj.* **1.** swollen or distended and not flexible. **2.** (of language or style) pompous, not flowing easily. —**turgidity** /-ˈdʒɪdɪtɪ/ *n.* [f. L *turgidus* (*turgēre* swell)]

Turk *n.* **1.** a native of Turkey. **2.** a member of the Central Asian people from whom the Ottomans derived, speaking Turkic languages. **3.** (esp. **young Turk**) a ferocious, wild, or unmanageable person. —**Turk's head,** a turban-like ornamental knot. [= F *Turc* etc., Pers. & Arab. *Turk*]

Turkey /ˈtɜːkɪ/ a country in SW Asia comprising the whole of the Anatolian peninsula, extending from the Aegean Sea to the western boundaries of the USSR and Iran, and with a small enclave in SE Europe; pop. (1980) 45,217,556; official language, Turkish; capital, Ankara. (See ANATOLIA.) Modern Turkey is descended from the Ottoman empire, established in the late Middle Ages and largely maintained until its collapse at the end of the First World War. The nationalist leader Kemal Ataturk moulded a new westernized State, centred upon Anatolia, from the ruins of the empire, and Turkey successfully avoided involvement in the Second World War. The economy is predominantly agricultural, although the land is generally poor for such purposes, but some industrialization has taken place using its oil and mineral resources. The country suffers from a certain degree of political instability, resulting most recently in the imposition of military rule.

turkey /ˈtɜːkɪ/ *n.* **1.** a large American bird of the genus *Meleagris*, especially *M. gallopavo* which was found domesticated in the Aztec civilization in Mexico when that country was discovered in 1518. It was soon introduced into Europe and thence to Britain, where it ousted peacock and swan as a table food. **2.** its flesh as food. —**talk turkey,** (*US colloq.*) to talk in a frank and businesslike way. **turkey-cock** *n.* a male turkey. [short for *turkey-cock*, orig. applied to the guinea-fowl with which the American turkey was confused) because imported into Europe through Turkey]

Turkey carpet a woollen carpet with a thick pile and a bold design. [f. TURKEY]

Turki /ˈtɜːkɪ/ *adj.* of the Turkic languages or the peoples who speak these. [f. Pers. *Turkī* (as TURK)]

Turkic /ˈtɜːkɪk/ *adj.* of a group of about 20 Altaic languages (including Turkish) and their speakers. —*n.* this group of languages, spoken in Turkey, Iran, and the southern part of the Soviet Union. [f. prec.]

Turkish /ˈtɜːkɪʃ/ *adj.* of Turkey or the Turks or their language. —*n.* the official language of Turkey, spoken by about 40 million people, the most important of the Turkic group. It was originally written in Arabic script but changed over to the Roman alphabet in 1928. —**Turkish bath,** a hot air or steam bath followed by washing, massage, etc.; (in *sing.* or *pl.*) a building for this. **Turkish carpet,** a Turkey carpet. **Turkish coffee,** strong usually sweet black coffee made from very finely ground beans and boiled so that it becomes very thick. **Turkish delight,** a sweet consisting of lumps of flavoured gelatine coated in powdered sugar. **Turkish towel,** a towel made of cotton terry. [f. TURK]

Turkistan /tɜːkɪˈstɑːn/ a region of central Asia east of the Caspian Sea, largely in the USSR.

Turkmenistan /tɜːkmenɪˈstɑːn/ the Turkoman SSR, a constituent republic of the USSR, lying between the Caspian Sea and Afghanistan; capital, Ashkhabad.

Turko- var. of TURCO-.

Turkoman /ˈtɜːkəmən/ n. a member or the language of any of various Turkic tribes. [f. Pers. (as TURK, *mānistan* resemble)]

Turks and Caicos Islands /tɜːks, ˈkeɪkɒs/ a British dependency in the Caribbean, a group of over 30 islands (of which 8 are inhabited) about 80 km (50 miles) SE of the Bahamas.

turmeric /ˈtɜːmərɪk/ n. **1.** an East Indian plant (*Curcuma longa*) of the ginger family. **2.** its aromatic root powdered and used as a flavouring, stimulant, or dye. [perh. f. F *terre mérite*]

turmoil /ˈtɜːmɔɪl/ n. great disturbance or confusion. [orig. unkn.]

turn v.t./i. **1.** to move or cause to move round a point or axis; to perform (a somersault) with a rotary motion. **2.** to change or cause to change in position so that a different side becomes uppermost or faces a certain direction. **3.** to give a new direction to; to take a new direction; to aim or become aimed in a certain way; to seek help, to have recourse. **4.** to move to the other side of, to go round. **5.** to pass (a certain hour or age). **6.** to cause to go, to send or put. **7.** to change or become changed in form, nature, appearance, colour, etc.; to translate. **8.** to make or become sour. **9.** to make or become nauseated. **10.** to shape in a lathe; to give an elegant form to. —n. **1.** turning, being turned; a turning movement. **2.** a change of direction or condition etc.; the point at which this occurs. **3.** an angle; a bend or corner in a road. **4.** character, tendency of mind etc. **5.** an opportunity or obligation etc. that comes successively to each of a number of people or things. **6.** a short performance in an entertainment. **7.** a service of a specified kind; a purpose. **8.** (*colloq.*) an attack of illness; a momentary nervous shock. **9.** (*Mus.*) an ornament consisting of the principal note with those above and below it, in various sequences. **10.** each round in a coil of rope, wire, etc. —**at every turn,** in every place; continually. **by turns,** in rotation of individuals or groups; alternately. **in turn,** in succession. **in one's turn,** when one's turn comes. **out of turn,** before or after one's turn; at an inappropriate moment; presumptuously. **take turns,** to act etc. alternately. **to a turn,** so as to be cooked perfectly. **turn-about** n. turning to face a new direction; an abrupt change of policy etc. **turn against,** to make or become hostile to. **turn and turn about,** alternately. **turn away,** to send away; to reject. **turn-buckle** n. a device for tightly connecting parts of metal rod or wire. **turn down,** to reject; to reduce the volume or strength of (sound or heat etc.) by turning a knob etc.; to fold down. **turn in,** to hand in or return; to register (a score etc.); (*colloq.*) to go to bed; (*colloq.*) to abandon (a plan etc.). **turn in his grave,** (of a dead person) to be disturbed in his eternal rest if he knew of a specified fact which would have shocked or distressed him while he was alive. **turn off,** to stop the flow or operation of by means of a tap or switch etc.; to move (a tap etc.) thus; to enter a side-road; (*colloq.*) to cause to lose interest. **turn on,** to start the flow or operation of by means of a tap or switch etc.; to move (a tap etc.) thus; to be suddenly hostile to; (*colloq.*) to arouse the interest or emotion of, to excite sexually or with drugs etc.; to depend on. **turn out,** to expel; to extinguish (an electric light etc.); to dress or equip; to produce (goods etc.); to empty or clean out (a room etc.); to empty (a pocket); (*colloq.*) to get out of bed; (*colloq.*) to go out of doors; to prove to be the case, to result. **turn-out** n. the number of people at a meeting etc.; a set of clothes or equipment. **turn over,** to reverse the position of; to hand over; to transfer; to consider carefully; to start the running of (an engine etc.); (of an engine) to start running. **turn over a new leaf,** to improve one's conduct. **turn round,** to face in a new direction; to unload and reload (a ship etc.), to process and return (a piece of work etc.). **turn-round** n. the process or time taken in unloading and reloading etc. **turn to,** to set about one's work. **turn up,** to increase the volume or strength of (sound or heat etc.) by turning a knob etc.; to discover or reveal; to be found; to happen or present itself; to fold over or upwards. **turn-up** n. the lower turned-up end of a trouser leg; (*colloq.*) an

unexpected happening. [OE & f. OF f. L *tornare* turn on lathe (*tornus* lathe)]

turncoat n. one who changes his allegiance or principles.

Turner /ˈtɜːnə(r)/, Joseph Mallord William (1775–1851), English landscape painter, eccentric, recognized in his own day as a revolutionary genius. The son of a barber, he trained as a topographical draughtsman, but made his name with paintings of mountain scenery, seascapes, and classical compositions, influenced by Claude Lorraine. His most characteristic work is dominated by the power of light, expressed through the primary colours (especially yellow) and often arranged in a swirling vortex. Throughout his career he made careful studies from nature, but he is also seen as a forerunner of abstract art. In the 1830s and 1840s he adopted watercolour techniques for his 'colour-beginnings' in oil, which he worked up to finished paintings during varnishing days at the Royal Academy. Turner left the entire contents of his studio to the nation: some 300 paintings (now at the Tate Gallery and National Gallery) and 20,000 watercolours and drawings (British Museum).

turner n. a lathe-worker. [f. TURN]

turnery n. **1.** objects made on a lathe. **2.** work with a lathe. [f. TURN]

turning n. **1.** a place where one road meets another, forming a corner. **2.** the use of a lathe. **3.** (in *pl.*) chips or shavings from a lathe. —**turning-circle** n. the smallest circle in which a vehicle can turn. **turning-point** n. the point at which a decisive change occurs. [f. TURN]

turnip /ˈtɜːnɪp/ n. a plant (*Brassica rapa*) with a globular root used as a vegetable and as fodder; its root. —**turnip-tops** n.pl. its leaves used as a vegetable. —**turnipy** adj. [first element of uncertain origin; second element f. dial. *neep* (OE f. L *napus*)]

turnkey n. a gaoler.

turnover n. **1.** turning over. **2.** the amount of money taken in a business; the amount of business done. **3.** a pie or tart made by folding half the pastry over so as to enclose the filling. **4.** the number of persons entering or leaving employment etc.

turnpike /ˈtɜːnpaɪk/ n. **1.** (*hist.*) a toll-gate. **2.** (*hist.* & *US*) a road on which toll is or was collected at gates. In Britain private companies were authorized by separate Acts of Parliament to build and maintain roads between set points and to charge a small toll for usage at turnpike gates at each end of the road. The first Turnpike Act was passed in 1663, but most became law in the 18th c. in response to the increasing need for good roads. The turnpikes fell into decline during the 19th c. through competition from the railways and were progressively abolished between the 1870s and 1890s. The road system remained in a state of neglect until the advent of the motor car in the early 20th c. [orig. = defensive frame of spikes]

turnstile n. an admission-gate with arms revolving on a post.

turntable n. a circular revolving platform or support, e.g. for a gramophone record being played or to turn a locomotive to face in the opposite direction.

turpentine /ˈtɜːpəntaɪn/ n. **1.** a resin obtained from various trees (originally the terebinth). **2.** (in full **oil of turpentine**) a volatile pungent oil distilled from this resin, used in mixing paints and varnishes and in medicine. [f. OF *ter(e)-bentine* f. L (as TEREBINTH)]

Turpin /ˈtɜːpɪn/, Dick (1706–39), English highwayman, hanged at York for horse-stealing in 1739. Turpin was the most famous of the 18th-c. highwaymen, whose exploits, which were in reality criminal and often bloody, were made legendary by the popular literature of the day.

turpitude /ˈtɜːpɪtjuːd/ n. wickedness. [F or f. L (*turpis* shameful)]

turps n. (*colloq.*) oil of turpentine. [abbr.]

turquoise /ˈtɜːkwɔɪz, -kwɑːz/ n. **1.** a precious stone, usually opaque and greenish-blue. **2.** greenish-blue colour. —adj. greenish-blue. [f. OF, = Turkish (stone) (as TURK)]

turret /ˈtʌrɪt/ n. **1.** a small tower, especially as a decorative addition to a building. **2.** a low flat usually revolving armoured tower for a gun and gunners in a ship, aircraft, fort, or tank. **3.** a rotating holder for tools in a lathe etc. —**turreted** adj. [f. OF *to(u)rete* dim. of *to(u)r* tower]

turtle /ˈtɜːt(ə)l/ n. **1.** a marine or (*US*) freshwater reptile of the order Chelonia with flippers and a horny shell. **2.** its flesh used for soup. —**turn turtle,** to capsize. **turtle-neck** n. a high close-fitting neck of a knitted garment. [alt. of OF *tortue* as (TORTOISE)]

turtle-dove *n*. a wild dove of the genus *Streptopelia*, especially *S. turtur*, noted for its soft cooing and its affection for its mate. [f. *turtle* (OE f. L *turtur*) + DOVE]

Tuscan /'tʌskən/ *adj*. **1.** of Tuscany. **2.** (*Archit*.) of a simple unornamented order (ill. TEMPLES). —*n*. an inhabitant or the classical Italian language of Tuscany. [f. L (*Tuscus* Etruscan)]

Tuscany /'tʌskənɪ/ a region of west central Italy; capital, Florence.

tusk *n*. a long pointed tooth, especially one projecting from the mouth as in the elephant, walrus, or boar. [alt. of OE *tux*]

Tussaud /'tu:səʊ/, Marie (*née* Gresholtz, 1760–1850), Swiss founder of 'Madame Tussaud's', a permanent exhibition in London of wax models of eminent or notorious people (originally victims of the French Revolution) from 1802 onwards.

tussle *n*. a struggle, a scuffle. —*v.i.* to engage in a tussle. [orig. Sc. & N.Engl., perh. dim. of *touse* (as TOUSLE)]

tussock /'tʌsək/ *n*. a clump of grass etc. —**tussocky** *adj*. [perh. f. dial. *tusk* tuft]

tut *int*., *n*., & *v.i.* = TUT-TUT. [imit. of click of tongue]

Tutankhamun /tu:tənkɑ:'mu:n/ (1333–1323 BC) an Egyptian pharaoh of the 18th Dynasty, who acceded to the throne while still a boy. He abandoned the worship of the sun-god, instituted by Akhenaten, and reinstated the worship of Amun, with Thebes once again the capital city. Although insignificant in the history of Egypt he has become world-famous because of the variety and richness of the contents of his tomb, discovered by the English archaeologist Howard Carter in 1922, which was found virtually intact, its entrance having remained covered by debris from the building of the tomb of Rameses VI near by.

tutelage /'tju:tɪlɪdʒ/ *n*. **1.** guardianship, being under this. **2.** instruction, tuition. [f. L *tutela* (*tuēri* watch over)]

tutelary /'tju:tɪlərɪ/ *adj*. serving as a guardian, giving protection. [as prec.]

Tuthmosis /tʌθ'məʊsɪs/ the name of three Egyptian pharaohs:

    Tuthmosis III (1479–1425 BC, 18th Dynasty), initially co-ruler with his aunt Hatshepsut. He launched campaigns in Palestine and Syria and in Nubia, and built extensively.

tutor /'tju:tə(r)/ *n*. **1.** a private teacher, especially one in general charge of a person's education. **2.** a university teacher supervising the studies or welfare of assigned undergraduates. **3.** a book of instruction in a subject. —*v.t./i.* **1.** to act as tutor to; to work as a tutor. **2.** to restrain, to discipline. —**tutorship** *n*. [f. AF or L (as TUTELARY)]

tutorial /tju:'tɔ:rɪəl/ *adj*. of or as a tutor. —*n*. a period of individual tuition given by a college tutor. —**tutorially** *adv*. [f. L (as prec.)]

tutti /'tʊti:/ *adv*. (*Mus*.) with all voices or instruments together. —*n*. a passage to be performed this way. [It., pl. of *tutto* all]

tutti-frutti /tʊti'frʊti/ *n*. ice-cream containing or flavoured with mixed fruits. [It., = all fruits]

tut-tut *int*. expressing rebuke, impatience, or contempt. —*n*. such an exclamation. —*v.i.* (**-tt-**) to exclaim thus. [as TUT]

tutu /'tu:tu:/ *n*. a ballet dancer's short skirt made of layers of stiffened frills. [F]

Tuvalu /tu:'vɑ:lu:/ a small country in the SW Pacific, consisting of a group of nine islands, the former Ellice Islands; pop. (1979) 7,349; official languages, English and Tuvaluan; capital, Funafuti. The islands formed part of the British colony of the Gilbert and Ellice Islands until they separated after a referendum (see KIRIBATI) and became independent within the Commonwealth in 1978. —**Tuvaluan** *adj*. & *n*.

tu-whit, tu-whoo /tʊ'wɪt tʊ'wu:/ *n*. the cry of an owl. [imit.]

tuxedo /tʌk'si:dəʊ/ *n*. (*pl*. **-os**) (*US*) a dinner-jacket. [f. *Tuxedo* Park, New York]

TV *abbr*. television.

twaddle /'twɒd(ə)l/ *n*. useless or dull writing or talk. —*v.i.* to indulge in this. [f. earlier *twattle*, alt. of TATTLE]

Twain /tweɪn/, Mark (pseudonym of Samuel Langhorne Clemens, 1835–1910), American writer, brought up in Missouri. After working as a printer's apprentice and a river pilot on the Mississippi (later related in his autobiographical *Life on the Mississippi*, 1883), he established himself as a leading humourist in *The Celebrated Jumping Frog of Calvaleras County, and Other Sketches* (1867), a reputation consolidated by *The Innocents Abroad* (1869). England provided the background for his democratic historical fantasy *The Prince and the Pauper* (1882). His most famous works, both deeply rooted in his own childhood, were *The Adventures of Tom Sawyer* (1876) and its sequel *The Adventures of Huckleberry Finn* (1885), which powerfully evoke Mississippi frontier life, combining picaresque adventure with satire and great technical innovative power.

twain *adj*. & *n*. (*archaic*) two. [OE, masc. nom. & acc. (as TWO)]

twang *n*. the sound made by a plucked string of a musical instrument or by a bowstring; a quality of voice compared to this (esp. *nasal twang*). —*v.t./i.* to emit a twang; to cause to twang. [imit.]

'twas /twɒz, twəz/ (*archaic*) it was. [contr.]

tweak *v.t.* to pinch and twist or jerk. —*n*. such an action. [prob. f. dial. *twick* & TWITCH]

twee *adj*. affectedly dainty or quaint. [childish pronunc. of SWEET]

tweed *n*. a rough-surfaced woollen cloth, frequently of mixed colours; (in *pl*.) a suit of tweed. —**tweedy** *adj*. [orig. misreading of *tweel*, Sc. form of TWILL]

Tweedledum and Tweedledee /twi:d(ə)l'dʌm, -'di:/ two persons or things differing only or chiefly in name (originally applied to the composers Handel and Bononcini in a satire by John Byrom containing the lines 'Strange all this Difference should be Twixt Tweedle-dum and Tweedle-dee!').

'tween *prep*. between. [f. BETWEEN]

tweet *n*. the chirp of a small bird. —*v.i.* to utter a tweet. [imit.]

tweeter *n*. a loudspeaker for accurately reproducing high-frequency signals. [f. TWEET]

tweezers /'twi:zəz/ *n.pl*. a small pair of pincers for taking up small objects, plucking out hairs, etc. [f. obs. *tweezes* pl. of obs. *tweeze* case for small instruments, f. F *étui*]

twelfth *adj*. next after the eleventh. —*n*. each of twelve equal parts of a thing. —**the Twelfth**, 12 August, on which grouse-shooting legally begins. **Twelfth-day** *n*. 6 January, the twelfth day after Christmas, the feast of Epiphany. **Twelfth-night** *n*. the night before this, formerly the last day of Christmas festivities and observed as a time of merrymaking. —**twelfthly** *adv*. [OE (as foll.)]

twelve *adj*. & *n*. **1.** one more than eleven; the symbol for this (12, xii, XII). **2.** a size etc. denoted by twelve. —**the Twelve**, the twelve Apostles. **twelve-note** *adj*. (*Mus*.) using the twelve chromatic notes of the octave arranged in a chosen order without a conventional key. This technique of musical composition was developed by the composer Schoenberg (see entry). **Twelve Tables**, a set of laws drawn up in ancient Rome in 451 and 450 BC, embodying the most important rules of Roman law. **Twelve Tribes**, those of ancient Israel (see TRIBE 1). [OE]

twelvefold *adj*. & *adv*. twelve times as much or as many; consisting of twelve parts. [f. prec. + -FOLD]

twelvemonth *n*. a year.

twenty *adj*. & *n*. **1.** twice ten; the symbol for this (20, xx, XX). **2.** (in *pl*.) the numbers, years, or degrees of temperature from 20 to 29. —**twentieth** *adj*. & *n*. [OE]

'twere /twɜ:(r), twə(r)/ (*archaic*) it were. [contr.]

twerp *n*. (*slang*) a stupid or objectionable person. [orig. unkn.]

Twi /twi:/ *n*. **1.** the chief language spoken in Ghana, consisting of several mutually intelligible dialects. **2.** its speakers.

twice *adv*. **1.** two times, on two occasions. **2.** in double degree or quantity. [OE (as TWO)]

twiddle *v.t.* to twirl or handle aimlessly; to twist quickly to and fro. —*n*. **1.** an act of twiddling. **2.** a twirled mark or sign. —**twiddle one's thumbs**, to make them rotate round each other, especially for want of anything to do. —**twiddler** *n*., **twiddly** *adj*. [app. imit., after *twirl*, *fiddle*]

twig[1] *n*. a small branch or shoot of a tree or shrub. —**twiggy** *adj*. [OE]

twig[2] *v.t.* (**-gg-**) (*colloq*.) to understand, to realize or grasp the meaning or nature (of). [orig. unkn.]

twilight /'twaɪlaɪt/ *n*. **1.** the light from the sky when the sun is below the horizon, especially in the evening; the period of this. **3.** a faint light. **3.** a state of imperfect understanding. **4.** a period of decline or destruction. —**twilight of the gods**, (*Scand. myth*.) the destruction of the gods and of the world in conflict with the powers of evil.

twilight zone, a decrepit urban area; an area between others in position and character. [f. *twi-* (as TWO) + LIGHT[1]]

twilit /'twaɪlɪt/ *adj.* dimly illuminated (as) by twilight. [f. prec.]

twill *n.* a fabric so woven as to have a surface of parallel ridges. —**twilled** *adj.* [f. OE *twili* two-thread]

'twill (*archaic*) it will. [contr.]

twin *n.* **1.** each of a closely related or associated pair, especially of children or animals born at a birth; **the Twins,** the constellation or sign of the zodiac Gemini. **2.** an exact counterpart of a person or thing. —*adj.* forming or being one of such a pair. —*v.t./i.* (**-nn-**) **1.** to join intimately together; to pair (with). **2.** to bear twins. —**twin bed,** each of a pair of single beds. **twin-engined** *adj.* having two engines. **twin set,** a woman's matching cardigan and jumper. **twin towns,** two towns, usually in different countries, establishing special cultural and social links. [OE, = double (as TWO)]

twine *n.* **1.** strong thread or string made of two or more strands twisted together. **2.** a coil, a twist. —*v.t./i.* to twist; to wind or coil. [OE]

twinge /twɪndʒ/ *n.* a slight or brief pang. [f. *twinge* v. = pinch, wring, f. OE]

twinkle *v.i.* **1.** to shine with a light that flickers rapidly; to sparkle. **2.** (of the eyes) to sparkle with amusement. **3.** (of the feet in dancing etc.) to move rapidly. —*n.* a twinkling light, look, or movement. —**in the twinkling of an eye** or **in a twinkling,** in an instant. [OE]

twirl *v.t./i.* to twist lightly or rapidly. —*n.* **1.** a twirling movement. **2.** a twirled mark or sign. —**twirly** *adj.* [prob. alt. (after *whirl*) f. obs. *tirl* trill]

twist *v.t./i.* **1.** to change the form of by rotating one end and not the other or the two ends in opposite ways; to undergo such a change; to make or become spiral; to distort, to warp; to wrench; (with *off*) to break off by twisting. **2.** to wind (strands) about each other; to make (a rope etc.) thus. **3.** to take a curved course; to make one's way in a winding manner. **4.** to distort or misrepresent the meaning of (words). **5.** (*colloq.*) to swindle. —*n.* **1.** twisting; a twisted state. **2.** a thing formed by twisting. **3.** the point at which a thing twists or bends. **4.** a peculiar tendency of mind or character. **5.** (*colloq.*) a swindle. —**round the twist,** (*slang*) crazy. **twist a person's arm,** (*colloq.*) to coerce him. **twist a person round one's little finger,** to persuade or manage him very easily. [rel. to TWIN, TWINE]

twister *n.* (*colloq.*) an untrustworthy person, a swindler. [f. TWIST]

twisty *adj.* full of twists. —**twistily** *adv.*, **twistiness** *n.* [f. TWIST]

twit[1] *n.* (*slang*) a foolish person. [dial., perh. f. foll.]

twit[2] *v.t.* (**-tt-**) to taunt, usually good-humouredly. [OE]

twitch *v.t./i.* **1.** to pull with a light jerk. **2.** to quiver or contract spasmodically. —*n.* **1.** a twitching movement. **2.** (*colloq.*) a state of nervousness. [= LG *twikken*]

twitter *v.t./i.* **1.** to make a series of light chirping or tremulous sounds. **2.** to talk or utter rapidly in an anxious or nervous way. —*n.* **1.** twittering. **2.** (*colloq.*) an excited or nervous state. [imit.]

'twixt *prep.* (*archaic*) betwixt. [abbr.]

two /tuː/ *adj.* & *n.* **1.** one more than one; the symbol for this (2, ii, II). **2.** a size etc. denoted by two. —**in two,** in or into two pieces. **put two and two together,** to make an inference from known facts. **two-dimensional** *adj.* having or appearing to have length and breadth but no depth. **two-edged** *adj.* having two cutting edges. **two-faced** *adj.* insincere. **two-handed** *adj.* used with both hands or by two persons. **two-piece** *n.* a suit of clothes or a woman's bathing-suit comprising two separate parts. **two-ply** *adj.* (of wool etc.) of two strands, layers, or thicknesses. **two-step** *n.* a ballroom dance in march or polka time. **two-stroke** *adj.* (of an internal-combustion engine) having its power cycle completed in one up-and-down movement (i.e. two strokes) of the piston, with the fuel/air mixture entering and exhaust gases leaving the cylinder through inlet and exhaust ports in its walls, opened and closed by movements of the piston, instead of through the more complicated valves used in a four-stroke engine. **two-time** *v.t.* (*slang*) to swindle; to deceive, especially by infidelity. **two-up** *n.* (*Austral.* & *NZ*) a gambling game played by tossing two coins, bets being laid on the showing of two heads or two tails. [OE]

twofold *adj.* & *adv.* **1.** twice as much or as many. **2.** consisting of two parts. [f. TWO + -FOLD]

twopence /'tʌpəns/ *n.* the sum of two pence.

twopenny /'tʌpənɪ/ *adj.* **1.** costing two pence. **2.** cheap, worthless. —**twopenny-halfpenny** *adj.* insignificant, contemptible.

twosome /'tuːsəm/ *n.* two people together, a pair or couple of persons. [f. TWO + -SOME]

'twould /twʊd/ (*archaic*) it would. [contr.]

Tyburn /'taɪbəːn/ a place in London, near the site of Marble Arch, where public hangings were held *c.*1300-1783.

tycoon /taɪˈkuːn/ *n.* a business magnate. [f. Jap., = great prince]

tying *partic.* of TIE.

tyke /taɪk/ *n.* a low or objectionable fellow. [f. ON, = bitch]

Tyler /'taɪlə(r)/, Wat (d. 1381), the leader of the English Peasants' Revolt of 1381, who successfully led the rebels from Kent into London but was killed during a parley with the young king Richard II by the Lord Mayor of London and several other royal supporters.

tympanum /'tɪmpənəm/ *n.* (*pl.* **-a**) **1.** the ear-drum; the middle-ear. **2.** the space enclosed in a pediment or between a lintel and the arch above (ill. TEMPLES). [L, f. Gk *tumpanon* drum]

Tyndale /'tɪnd(ə)l/, William (*c.*1494-1536), English translator of the Bible and a leading figure of the Reformation in England. Faced with ecclesiastical opposition to his project for translating the Bible, Tyndale went abroad, never to return to his own country, and his translation of the New Testament was published in Germany. His vigorous translations from the Greek and Hebrew became widely popular in England and were the basis of both the Authorized and the Revised Version. In 1535 he was arrested on a charge of heresy, and later strangled and burnt at the stake.

Tyne and Wear /taɪn, wɪə(r)/ a metropolitan county of NE England.

Tynwald /'tɪnwɒld/ the legislative assembly of the Isle of Man, which meets annually to proclaim newly enacted laws. It consists of the governor (representing the sovereign) and council acting as the upper house, and the House of Keys (an elective assembly).

type /taɪp/ *n.* **1.** a class of people or things that have characteristics in common, a kind. **2.** a typical example or instance. **3.** (*colloq.*) a person of specified character. **4.** a piece of metal etc. with a raised letter or character on its upper surface for use in printing; a kind or size of such pieces; a set or supply of these. —*v.t./i.* **1.** to write with a typewriter. **2.** to classify according to type. **3.** to be a type or example of. —**type-cast** *v.t.* to cast (an actor) in the kind of part which he has the reputation of playing successfully or which seems to fit his personality. **type site,** an archaeological site where objects regarded as defining the characteristics of an industry etc. are found. [f. F or L f. Gk *tupos* impression (*tuptō* strike)]

typeface *n.* **1.** a set of printing types in one design. **2.** an inked surface of such types.

typescript *n.* a typewritten text or document.

typesetter *n.* **1.** a compositor. **2.** a machine for setting type. —**typesetting** *n.*

typewriter *n.* a machine for producing characters similar to those of print, with keys that are pressed to cause raised metal characters to strike the paper, usually through inked ribbon. As early as 1714 an Englishman, Henry Mill, was granted a patent for a machine to impress or transcribe letters singly, as in writing, but it is not certain whether he ever made one. For a long time inventors concentrated on writing-machines for the use of blind people, but the first practical typewriter was produced in 1873 when the firm of Remington and Sons manufactured that designed by two Americans, Scholes and Gliddon. It had 44 keys, so arranged that the letters which most commonly occur together were placed far apart in order to slow the typist down and prevent the bars which carried the letters from jamming as they struck to and from the roller carrying the paper—an arrangement which has survived in spite of technological advances which make it unnecessary. The history of the typewriter has consisted mainly of a series of improvements upon the original device; the electric typewriter dates from 1935. Typing was considered an acceptable occupation for women at a time when 'working' was thought to be unbecoming but being 'in business' was socially acceptable, and 'lady typewriters' (as they were then called) became a feature of office life.

typewritten *adj.* produced with a typewriter.

typhoid /'taɪfɔɪd/ *adj.* like typhus. —*n.* (also **typhoid fever**) an infectious bacterial fever with eruption of red spots on the chest and abdomen and severe intestinal irritation; a similar disease of animals. Prince Albert died of typhoid fever in 1861, and the disease was formerly a scourge of armies, spread by contaminated water and by infection; in the Boer War more lives were lost by this than by enemy action. A vaccine has been developed which gives temporary immunity. [f. TYPHUS]

typhoon /taɪ'fuːn/ *n.* a violent hurricane in the East Asian seas. [partly f. Chin., = great wind, partly f. Port. f. Arab.]

typhus /'taɪfəs/ *n.* a rickettsial infectious fever with eruption of purple spots, great prostration, and usually delirium. Until 1849 it was confused with typhoid fever, a quite different disease. Formerly known as gaol fever, ship fever, putrid fever, and camp fever, it was always associated with conditions of squalor and overcrowding, spread by lice; prevalent in Europe in the 18th–19th c., it became rare when people became more fastidious. Other forms of the disease are spread by rat fleas, ticks, and mites. A vaccine is now available. [f. Gk *tuphos* smoke, stupor]

typical /'tɪpɪk(ə)l/ *adj.* **1.** having the distinctive qualities of a particular type of person or thing; serving as a representative specimen. **2.** characteristic. —**typically** *adv.* [f. L (as TYPE)]

typify /'tɪpɪfaɪ/ *v.t.* to be a representative specimen of; to represent by a type. —**typification** /-fɪ'keɪʃ(ə)n/ *n.* [f. L *typus* type]

typist /'taɪpɪst/ *n.* a person who types, especially one employed to do so. [f. TYPE]

typography /taɪ'pɒɡrəfɪ/ *n.* **1.** printing as an art. **2.** the style and appearance of printed matter. —**typographical** /-'ɡræfɪk(ə)l/ *adj.*, **typographically** /-'ɡræfɪkəlɪ/ *adv.* [f. F (as TYPE, -GRAPHY)]

Tyr /tɪə(r)/ (*Scand. myth.*) the god of battle.

tyrannical /tɪ'rænɪk(ə)l/ *adj.* given to or characteristic of tyranny. —**tyrannically** *adv.* [f. OF f. L f. Gk (as TYRANT)]

tyrannize /'tɪrənaɪz/ *v.t./i.* to exercise tyranny; to rule as or like a tyrant. [f. F (as TYRANT)]

tyrannosaur /tɪ'rænəsɔː(r)/ *n.* a dinosaur (*Tyrannosaurus rex*) with very short front legs and a large head, that walked on its hind legs, the largest known carnivorous animal. [as TYRANT, after *dinosaur*]

tyrannous /'tɪrənəs/ *adj.* tyrannical. [f. L (as TYRANT)]

tyranny /'tɪrənɪ/ *n.* **1.** the oppressive and arbitrary use of authority. **2.** rule by a tyrant; a period of this; a State thus ruled. [as foll.]

tyrant /'taɪrənt/ *n.* **1.** an oppressive or cruel ruler. **2.** a person exercising power arbitrarily or oppressively. **3.** (*Gk hist.*) an absolute ruler who seized power without legal right. [f. OF f. L f. Gk *turannos*]

Tyre /taɪə(r)/ a city and seaport of the Phoenicians, south of Sidon, now in Lebanon.

tyre /taɪə(r)/ *n.* a rubber covering, usually inflated, placed round a wheel to form a soft contact with a road (see below). [var. of TIRE²]
  Early wheels were of wood, with protection given (when iron-working technology was available) by a strip of iron attached round the felloe. In the mid-19th c. tyres for carriage wheels began to be made of solid rubber, which mitigated the damage to road-surfaces but still gave a hard 'ride'. It was a Belfast veterinary surgeon, John Dunlop (see entry), who in 1888 devised (for use on his son's tricycle) the first practical type of pneumatic tyre, consisting of an air-filled tube inside a canvas cover with rubber treads, and by the early 20th c. such tyres had superseded solid rubber tyres on motor vehicles. Modern tyre design has dispensed with the inner tube.

Tyrian /'tɪrɪən/ *adj.* of ancient Tyre. —*n.* a native of ancient Tyre. —**Tyrian purple**, see PURPLE. [f. L *Tyrius* (*Tyrus* Tyre, f. Semitic, = the rock)]

tyro var. of TIRO.

Tyrol /'tɪr(ə)l, -'rɒl/ an Alpine province of western Austria, the southern part of which was ceded to Italy after the First World War. —**Tyrolean** /-'liːən/ *adj.*, **Tyrolese** /-'liːz/ *adj.* & *n.*

Tyrone /tɪ'rəʊn/ a county of Northern Ireland.

U

U, u /juː/ *n.* (*pl.* **Us, U's**) **1.** the twenty-first letter of the alphabet. **2.** a U-shaped object or curve.

U *symbol* uranium.

U /juː/ *adj.* (*colloq.*) upper-class; supposedly characteristic of the upper class. [abbr.; coined by A. S. C. Ross (1954)]

UAE *abbr.* United Arab Emirates.

ubiquitous /juːˈbɪkwɪtəs/ *adj.* present everywhere or in several places simultaneously; often encountered. —**ubiquity** *n.* [f. L *ubique* everywhere]

U-boat /ˈjuːbəʊt/ *n.* (*hist.*) a German submarine, especially in the First and Second World War. [f. G (*unterseeboot* under-sea boat)]

udder *n.* the baglike milk-secreting organ of the cow, ewe, female goat, etc., with two or more teats. [OE]

UDI *abbr.* Unilateral Declaration of Independence.

Uffizi /uːˈfiːtsɪ/ the chief public art gallery in Florence, illustrating primarily the development of Italian painting from the 13th to the 18th c. The nucleus of the collection derives from the collections of the Medici family, and the Uffizi Palace, in which it is now housed, was built by Vasari in 1560–74.

UFO *abbr.*, **ufo** /ˈjuːfəʊ/ *n.* (*pl.* **-os**) an unidentified flying object. The term is often applied to supposed vehicles ('flying saucers') piloted by beings from outer space, for which no convincing evidence has ever been produced. Most UFO sightings are eventually identified as weather balloons, aircraft, or high-flying birds. A small number are reported in the Press as encounters with intelligent denizens of other worlds, but these are of so sensational a nature as to provoke widespread scepticism about their veracity.

Uganda /juːˈgændə/ a landlocked country in East Africa, a member State of the Commonwealth, of which a large part is covered by lakes, notably Lake Victoria; pop. (est. 1980) 12,600,000; official language, English; capital, Kampala. First explored by Europeans in the mid-19th c., Uganda became a British protectorate in 1894 and achieved full independence in 1962. Since that time the country has been severely troubled by political instability (largely owing to tribal divisions), which continues today, despite the overthrow of the dictator Idi Amin in 1979. Nevertheless, the Ugandan economy is relatively well developed, particularly with regard to the production of agricultural commodities such as tea, coffee, tobacco, and cotton for export. —**Ugandan** *adj.* & *n.*

Ugarit /ˈuːgærɪt/ (modern Ras Shamra) an ancient North Syrian seaport occupied from neolithic times until its destruction by the Sea Peoples in about the 12th c. BC. Ugarit was an important commercial city during the Late Bronze Age, to which period belong a palace, temples, and private residences containing legal, religious, and administrative cuneiform texts in Sumerian, Akkadian, Hurrian, Hittite, and Ugaritic languages. The last of these was written in an early form of the alphabet which is related to Phoenician. —**Ugaritic** /-ˈrɪtɪk/ *adj.* & *n.*

ugh /ʌh, ʊh/ *int.* expressing disgust or horror, or the sound of a cough or grunt. [imit.]

ugli /ˈʌglɪ/ *n.* a mottled green and yellow citrus fruit, a hybrid of the grapefruit and tangerine developed in Jamaica *c.*1930. [f. UGLY]

uglify /ˈʌglɪfaɪ/ *v.t.* to make ugly. [f. UGLY]

ugly /ˈʌglɪ/ *adj.* **1.** unpleasing or repulsive to see or hear. **2.** unpleasant in any way; hostile and threatening; discreditable. —**ugly customer**, an unpleasantly formidable person. **ugly duckling**, a person who at first seems unpromising but later becomes much admired or very able (like the cygnet in the brood of ducks in Hans Andersen's story). —**ugliness** *n.* [f. ON, = to be dreaded]

Ugric /ˈuːgrɪk/ *adj.* of an originally eastern branch of the Finnic peoples, especially the Magyars, or their languages, of which the most important is Hungarian. —*n.* a member of these peoples or their languages. —**Ugrian** *adj.* & *n.* [f. Russ. *Ugri* name of a people dwelling east of the Urals]

UHF *abbr.* ultra-high frequency.

UHT *abbr.* ultra heat treated (of milk, for long keeping).

UK *abbr.* United Kingdom.

ukase /juːˈkeɪz/ *n.* **1.** an arbitrary command. **2.** (*hist.*) an edict of the Russian government. [f. Russ. *ukaz*]

ukiyo-e /uːkiˈjəʊjeɪ/ *n.* a school of Japanese art using subjects from everyday life and simple treatment. [Jap., = genre picture]

Ukraine /juːˈkreɪn/ formerly the name of a district (*the Ukraine*) north of the Black Sea, now the Ukrainian SSR, the third largest constituent republic of the USSR; capital, Kiev. —**Ukrainian** *adj.* & *n.* [f. Russ., = frontier region (*u* at, *krai* edge)]

ukulele /juːkəˈleɪlɪ/ *n.* a small four-stringed (originally Portuguese) guitar. [Hawaiian]

Ulan Bator /ʊˈlɑːn ˈbɑːtɔː(r)/ the capital of Mongolia; pop. (est. 1981) 435,400.

ulcer *n.* **1.** an open sore on the external or internal surface of the body or one of its organs. **2.** a corroding or corrupting influence. —**ulcerous** *adj.* [f. L *ulcus*]

ulcerate /ˈʌlsəreɪt/ *v.t./i.* to form an ulcer (in or on). —**ulceration** /-ˈreɪʃ(ə)n/ *n.* [f. L *ulcerare* (as prec.)]

Ulfilas /ˈʊlfɪlæs/ (311–81), a Christian of Cappadocian origin, who became bishop of the Arian Visigoths in 341. He translated the Bible from the Greek into Gothic, inventing (it is said) an alphabet for the purpose and omitting the Books of Kings as their warlike deeds might have a bad influence upon a nation so fond of war as the Goths. Fragments of this translation survive.

ulna /ˈʌlnə/ *n.* (*pl.* **-ae** /-iː/) the thinner and longer bone in the forearm on the side opposite to the thumb (ill. BODY 1); a corresponding bone in an animal's foreleg or bird's wing. —**ulnar** *adj.* [L, rel. to Gk *ōlenē* and ELL]

Ulpian /ˈʌlpɪən/ (Domitius Ulpianus, d. 223) Roman jurist active under Caracalla. His numerous legal writings, chiefly syntheses of earlier learning, provided one of the chief sources for the *Digest* of Justinian.

Ulster /ˈʌlstə(r)/ a former province of Ireland comprising the present Northern Ireland and the counties of Cavan, Donegal, and Monaghan (which are now in the Republic of Ireland; (*loosely*) Northern Ireland (see entry). —**Ulster Unionist, Ulster Democratic Unionist,** a member of the political parties in Northern Ireland seeking to maintain the union of Northern Ireland with Britain. After the rest of Ireland gained its independence in 1920, Unionist politicians continued to dominate Northern Ireland and still provide much of its representation at Westminster.

ulster *n.* a long loose overcoat of rough cloth, often with a belt, of a kind originally sold in Belfast. [f. prec.]

Ulsterman /ˈʌlstəmən/ *n.* (*pl.* **-men**) a native of Ulster. —**Ulsterwoman** *n. fem.* (*pl.* **-women**)

ult. *abbr.* ultimo.

ulterior /ʌlˈtɪərɪə(r)/ *adj.* (esp. of a motive) beyond what is obvious or admitted. [L, = further (as ULTRA-)]

ultimate /ˈʌltɪmət/ *adj.* **1.** last, final, beyond which no other exists or is possible. **2.** basic, fundamental. —**ultimately** *adv.* [f. L (*ultimus* last)]

ultimatum /ʌltɪˈmeɪtəm/ *n.* (*pl.* **-ums**) a final statement of terms, the rejection of which may lead to war or the end of co-operation etc. [L (as prec.)]

ultimo /ˈʌltɪməʊ/ *adj.* (in commerce) of last month. [L, = in the last (*mense* month)]

ultra- *prefix* **1.** extremely, excessively (*ultra-conservative, ultra-modern*). **2.** beyond. [f. L *ultra* beyond]

ultracentrifuge /ʌltrəˈsentrɪfjuːdʒ/ *n.* a high-speed centrifuge used to determine the size of small particles and large molecules by their rate of sedimentation.

ultra-high /ˈʌltrəhaɪ/ *adj.* (of frequency) between 300 and 3,000 MHz.

ultramarine /ʌltrəməˈriːn/ *n.* a brilliant blue pigment originally obtained from lapis lazuli; the colour of this. —*adj.* of this colour. [f. obs. It. & L, = beyond the sea (because imported)]

ultramicroscope /ʌltrəˈmaɪkrəskəʊp/ *n.* an optical microscope used to detect particles smaller than a wavelength of light by illuminating them at an angle, so that the light scattered by the particles can be observed against a dark background.

ultramicroscopic /ˌʌltrəmaɪkrəˈskɒpɪk/ *adj.* **1.** of such minute size as to be invisible under the ordinary microscope. **2.** of or involving the use of the ultramicroscope.

ultramontane /ˌʌltrəˈmɒnteɪn/ *adj.* **1.** situated south of the Alps. **2.** asserting the absolute authority of the papacy in matters of faith and discipline (cf. GALLICAN). The principle was firmly established by the declaration of papal infallibility (1870). —*n.* one holding such views. —**ultramontanism** *n.* [f. L (*ultra* beyond, *mons* mountain)]

ultrasonic /ˌʌltrəˈsɒnɪk/ *adj.* of or using sound waves with a pitch above the upper limit of human hearing (see below). —**ultrasonics** *n.* the science and application of ultrasonic waves; (as *pl.*) these waves. —**ultrasonically** *adv.*

Methods of producing ultrasonic waves include certain applications of magnetism and application of a rapidly alternating voltage across a piezoelectric crystal. Uses of ultrasonic waves include sonar, detection of faults or cracks in metals, cleaning processes, and destruction of bacteria. Cutting-tools of relatively soft metals can be ultrasonically vibrated to cut shapes or holes in glassy or ceramic materials that cannot be machined by conventional techniques.

ultrasound /ˈʌltrəsaʊnd/ *n.* ultrasonic waves (see SOUND).

ultraviolet /ˌʌltrəˈvaɪələt/ *adj.* (of radiation) just beyond the violet end of the visible spectrum; of or using such radiation.

ululate /ˈjuːljʊleɪt/ *v.i.* to howl, to wail. —**ululation** /-ˈleɪʃ(ə)n/ *n.* [f. L *ululare* (imit.)]

Ulyanov /ʊlˈjɑːnɒf/, Vladimir Ilyich, see LENIN.

Ulysses /ˈjuːlɪsiːz/ the Roman name for Odysseus (see entry).

Umayyad /ʊˈmaɪjæd/ *adj.* of a Muslim dynasty, which included the family of the prophet Muhammad, that ruled Islam from 660 (or 661) to 750 and later ruled Moorish Spain 756-1031. —*n.* a member of this dynasty.

umbel /ˈʌmb(ə)l/ *n.* a flower-cluster in which stalks nearly equal in length spring from a common centre and form a flat or curved surface, as in the carrot (ill. PLANTS). —**umbellate** *adj.* [f. obs. F or L *umbella* sunshade]

umbellifer /ʌmˈbelɪfə(r)/ *n.* a plant of the order Umbelliferae, bearing umbels, to which the carrot, parsnip, celery, etc., belong. —**umbelliferous** /-bəˈlɪfərəs/ *adj.* [as prec. + -*fer* f. L *ferre* bear]

umber *n.* a pigment like ochre but darker and browner; the colour of this. —*adj.* of this colour. [f. F or It., = shadow, or f. L, = of the province Umbria]

umbilical /ʌmˈbɪlɪk(ə)l/ *adj.* of the navel. —**umbilical cord**, the flexible cordlike structure attaching the foetus to the placenta; an essential connecting-line in various technologies. [obs. F, or f. foll.]

umbilicus /ʌmˈbɪlɪkəs/ *n.* the navel; a navel-like formation. [L]

umbra /ˈʌmbrə/ *n.* (*pl.* -**ae** /-iː/ or -**as**) **1.** a region of complete shadow where no light reaches a surface etc. (ill. LIGHT), especially that cast by the moon or the earth in an eclipse. **2.** the dark central part of a sunspot. [L, = shadow]

umbrage /ˈʌmbrɪdʒ/ *n.* a sense of being offended. [f. OF f. L *umbraticus* (as prec.)]

umbrella /ʌmˈbrelə/ *n.* **1.** a light collapsible usually circular canopy of cloth mounted on radial ribs attached to a central stick, used for protection against sunshine or (especially) as a portable protection against rain, or as a symbol of rank and authority in some Oriental and African countries. **2.** any kind of general protecting force or influence; a co-ordinating or unifying agency. [f. It. *ombrella* dim. of *ombra* shade f. L *umbra*]

Umbria /ˈʌmbrɪə/ a district of ancient central Italy; a corresponding region of modern Italy; capital, Perugia. —**Umbrian** *adj. & n.*

umlaut /ˈʊmlaʊt/ *n.* **1.** a vowel-change in related words in Germanic languages, e.g. *man/men* in English, *mann/männer* in German. **2.** the mark like a diaeresis used to mark this in German etc. [G (*um* about, *laut* sound)]

umpire /ˈʌmpaɪə(r)/ *n.* a person appointed to see that the rules of a game or contest are observed and to settle disputes (e.g. in a game of cricket or baseball), or to give a decision on any disputed question. —*v.t./i.* to act as umpire (in). [later form of *noumpere* f. OF *non per* not equal (*non* NON-, *per* PEER[2])]

umpteen /ʌmpˈtiːn, ˈʌm-/ *adj.* (*slang*) many; an indefinite number of. —**umpteenth** *adj.* [joc. formation on -TEEN]

UN *abbr.* United Nations.

'un /ən/ *pron.* (*colloq.*) one (*a good 'un*). [dial. var. of ONE]

un- *prefix* added to (1) adjectives and their derivative nouns and adverbs, in the sense 'not' (*unusable, uneducated, unyielding, unofficial*), or in the sense 'the reverse of' with the implication of praise or blame (*unselfish, unsociable*); (2) verbs, denoting an action contrary to or annulling that of the simple verb (*unlock, untie*); (3) nouns, forming verbs in the senses 'deprive of', 'divest (oneself) of', 'release from' (*unfrock, unleash*), or 'cause to be no longer' (*unman*); (4) nouns, in the senses 'lack of' or 'the reverse of' (*unbelief, unemployment*). [OE]

The number of words that can be formed with this prefix is unlimited and only a selection can be given here.

unable /ʌnˈeɪb(ə)l/ *adj.* not able (to do a specified thing).

unaccompanied /ˌʌnəˈkʌmpənɪd/ *adj.* **1.** not accompanied; alone, without an escort. **2.** without musical accompaniment.

unaccountable /ˌʌnəˈkaʊntəb(ə)l/ *adj.* **1.** that cannot be explained or accounted for. **2.** not accountable for one's actions etc. —**unaccountably** *adv.*

unaccustomed /ˌʌnəˈkʌstəmd/ *adj.* not accustomed; not usual.

unadopted /ˌʌnəˈdɒptɪd/ *adj.* (of a road) not taken over for maintenance by a local authority.

unadulterated /ˌʌnəˈdʌltəreɪtɪd/ *adj.* pure.

unadvised /ˌʌnədˈvaɪzd/ *adj.* **1.** indiscreet, rash. **2.** not advised. —**unadvisedly** /-zɪdlɪ/ *adv.*

unalloyed /ˌʌnəˈlɔɪd/ *adj.* (of pleasure etc.) pure, sheer.

un-American *adj.* **1.** not in accordance with American characteristics. **2.** contrary to the ideals and interests of the USA.

unanimous /juːˈnænɪməs/ *adj.* all agreeing in an opinion or decision; (of an opinion or decision etc.) held or given by all. —**unanimity** /juːnəˈnɪmɪtɪ/ *n.*, **unanimously** *adv.* [f. L (*unus* one, *animus* mind)]

unanswerable /ʌnˈɑːnsərəb(ə)l/ *adj.* that cannot be refuted. —**unanswerably** *adv.*

unarmed /ʌnˈɑːmd/ *adj.* not armed, without weapons.

unashamed /ˌʌnəˈʃeɪmd/ *adj.* feeling no guilt, shameless. —**unashamedly** /-mɪdlɪ/ *adv.*

unasked /ʌnˈɑːskt/ *adj.* not asked (for), not requested or invited.

unassailable /ˌʌnəˈseɪləb(ə)l/ *adj.* that cannot be attacked or questioned. —**unassailably** *adv.*

unassuming /ˌʌnəˈsjuːmɪŋ/ *adj.* not arrogant, unpretentious.

unattached /ˌʌnəˈtætʃt/ *adj.* **1.** not engaged or married. **2.** not belonging to a particular regiment, church, club, college, etc.

unattended /ˌʌnəˈtendɪd/ *adj.* **1.** not attended (*to*). **2.** not accompanied; (of a vehicle) with no person in charge of it.

unavailing /ˌʌnəˈveɪlɪŋ/ *adj.* ineffectual.

unavoidable /ˌʌnəˈvɔɪdəb(ə)l/ *adj.* unable to be avoided. —**unavoidably** *adv.*

unaware /ˌʌnəˈweə(r)/ *adj.* not aware.

unawares /ˌʌnəˈweəz/ *adv.* unexpectedly, without noticing.

unbacked /ʌnˈbækt/ *adj.* **1.** not supported, having no backers (especially in betting). **2.** having no back or no backing.

unbalanced /ʌnˈbælənst/ *adj.* **1.** not balanced. **2.** mentally unsound.

unbar /ʌnˈbɑː(r)/ *v.t.* (-**rr**-) to remove the bar from (a gate etc.); to unlock.

unbearable /ʌnˈbeərəb(ə)l/ *adj.* that cannot be endured. —**unbearably** *adv.*

unbeatable /ʌnˈbiːtəb(ə)l/ *adj.* impossible to defeat or surpass.

unbeaten /ʌnˈbiːt(ə)n/ *adj.* not beaten; (of a record etc.) not surpassed.

unbecoming /ˌʌnbɪˈkʌmɪŋ/ *adj.* **1.** not suitable, not befitting a person's status etc. **2.** not suited to the wearer.

unbeknown /ˌʌnbɪˈnəʊn/ *adj.* (also **unbeknownst**) (*colloq.*) not known. —**unbeknown to**, without the knowledge of. [f. UN- + archaic *beknown* known]

unbelief /ˌʌnbɪˈliːf/ *n.* incredulity, disbelief especially in divine revelation or in a particular religion. —**unbeliever** *n.*

unbelievable /ˌʌnbəˈliːvəb(ə)l/ *adj.* not believable. —**unbelievably** *adv.*

unbeliever /ʌnbɪ'li:və(r)/ *n.* a person who does not believe, especially one not believing in Christianity or Islam.

unbelieving /ʌnbɪ'li:vɪŋ/ *adj.* **1.** atheistic; agnostic. **2.** unduly incredulous.

unbend /ʌn'bend/ *v.t./i.* (*past & p.p.* **unbent**) **1.** to change or become changed from a bent position, to straighten. **2.** to relax (the mind etc.) from strain, exertion, or severity; to become affable. **3.** (*Naut.*) to unfasten (a cable), to untie (a rope).

unbending *adj.* **1.** inflexible; refusing to alter one's demands. **2.** austere; not becoming relaxed or affable.

unbidden /ʌn'bɪd(ə)n/ *adj.* not commanded or invited.

unbind /ʌn'baɪnd/ *v.t.* (*past & p.p.* **unbound**) to release from bonds or from binding; to unfasten, to untie.

unblock /ʌn'blɒk/ *v.t.* to remove an obstruction from.

unblushing /ʌn'blʌʃɪŋ/ *adj.* shameless.

unbolt /ʌn'bəʊlt/ *v.t.* to release (a door etc.) by drawing back the bolt(s).

unborn /ʌn'bɔ:n/ *adj.* not yet born; future.

unbosom /ʌn'bʊz(ə)m/ *v.t.* to disclose (secrets etc.). —**unbosom oneself,** to disclose one's thoughts, feelings, secrets, etc.

unbounded /ʌn'baʊndɪd/ *adj.* infinite.

unbreakable /ʌn'breɪkəb(ə)l/ *adj.* not breakable.

unbridle /ʌn'braɪd(ə)l/ *v.t.* to remove the bridle from (a horse) or (*fig.*) restraint from (the tongue etc.).

unbridled /ʌn'braɪd(ə)ld/ *adj.* (of insolence, the tongue, etc.) unrestrained.

unbroken /ʌn'brəʊkən/ *adj.* **1.** not broken. **2.** not tamed. **3.** not interrupted. **4.** not surpassed.

unbuckle /ʌn'bʌk(ə)l/ *v.t.* to release the buckle(s) of (a strap, shoe, etc.).

unburden /ʌn'bɜ:d(ə)n/ *v.t.* to relieve (oneself or one's conscience etc.) by confession.

unbutton /ʌn'bʌt(ə)n/ *v.t.* to unfasten the buttons of.

uncalled-for /ʌn'kɔ:ldfɔ:(r)/ *adj.* offered or intruded impertinently or unjustifiably.

uncanny /ʌn'kænɪ/ *adj.* **1.** strange and rather frightening. **2.** extraordinary, beyond what is reckoned to be normal. —**uncannily** *adv.*, **uncanniness** *n.*

uncared-for /ʌn'keədfɔ:(r)/ *adj.* neglected.

unceasing /ʌn'si:sɪŋ/ *adj.* not ceasing. —**unceasingly** *adv.*

unceremonious /ʌnserɪ'məʊnɪəs/ *adj.* without proper formality or dignity; abrupt in manner. —**unceremoniously** *adv.*

uncertain /ʌn'sɜ:t(ə)n/ *adj.* **1.** not certainly knowing or known. **2.** not to be depended on. **3.** changeable. —**uncertainly** *adv.*

uncertainty *n.* being uncertain. —**uncertainty principle,** the principle that the momentum and position of a particle cannot both be precisely determined at the same time (see HEISENBERG and QUANTUM); any of various similar restrictions on the accuracy of measurement.

unchain /ʌn'tʃeɪn/ *v.t.* to release from chains.

unchangeable /ʌn'tʃeɪndʒəb(ə)l/ *adj.* that may not be changed.

uncharitable /ʌn'tʃærɪtəb(ə)l/ *adj.* censorious, severe in judgement. —**uncharitably** *adv.*

unchristian /ʌn'krɪstjən/ *adj.* contrary to Christian principles, uncharitable.

uncial /'ʌnsɪəl, 'ʌnʃ(ə)l/ *adj.* of or written in the kind of writing with characters partly resembling modern capitals, found in manuscripts of 4th-8th c. —*n.* an uncial letter or manuscript. [f. L (*uncia* inch)]

uncivil /ʌn'sɪvɪl/ *adj.* ill-mannered, rude. —**uncivilly** *adv.*

unclasp /ʌn'klɑ:sp/ *v.t.* **1.** to loosen the clasp(s) of. **2.** to release the grip of (the hand(s) etc.).

uncle /'ʌŋk(ə)l/ *n.* **1.** a brother or brother-in-law of one's father or mother. **2.** (*colloq.*) an unrelated friend of a parent. **3.** (*slang*) a pawn broker. —**Uncle Sam,** see separate entry. **Uncle Tom,** the name of the hero of Harriet Beecher Stowe's novel *Uncle Tom's Cabin* (1851-2), used allusively for a Black man who is submissively loyal or servile to Whites. [f. AF & OF f. L *avunculus*]

unclean /ʌn'kli:n/ *adj.* **1.** not clean; foul. **2.** ceremonially impure. **3.** unchaste.

Uncle Sam a personification of the government or people of the United States of America. The suggestion that it arose as a facetious interpretation of the letters US is as old as the first recorded instance, and later statements

connecting it with different government officials of the name of Samuel appear to be unfounded.

unclose /ʌn'kləʊz/ *v.t./i.* to open.

unclothe /ʌn'kləʊð/ *v.t.* to remove the clothes from, to uncover.

uncoil /ʌn'kɔɪl/ *v.t./i.* to draw out or become drawn out after having been coiled, to unwind.

uncommon /ʌn'kɒmən/ *adj.* not common, unusual, remarkable.

uncommunicative /ʌnkə'mju:nɪkətɪv/ *adj.* not inclined to give information or an opinion etc., silent.

uncompromising /ʌn'kɒmprəmaɪzɪŋ/ *adj.* refusing to compromise, unyielding, inflexible.

unconcern /ʌnkən'sɜ:n/ *n.* **1.** freedom from anxiety. **2.** indifference, apathy. —**unconcerned** *adj.*, **unconcernedly** /-nɪdlɪ/ *adv.*

unconditional /ʌnkən'dɪʃən(ə)l/ *adj.* not subject to conditions or limitations, absolute. —**unconditionally** *adv.*

unconditioned *adj.* not subject to or determined by conditions. —**unconditioned reflex,** an instinctive response to a stimulus.

unconformity /ʌnkən'fɔ:mɪtɪ/ *n.* an instance of a break in the chronological sequence of layers of rock (ill. GEOLOGY, OIL).

unconscionable /ʌn'kɒnʃənəb(ə)l/ *adj.* **1.** having no conscience, unscrupulous. **2.** contrary to what one's conscience feels is right; unreasonably excessive. —**unconscionably** *adv.* [f. UN- + *conscion* obs. var. of CONSCIENCE]

unconscious /ʌn'kɒnʃəs/ *adj.* **1.** not conscious, not aware. **2.** done or spoken etc. without conscious intention. —*n.* the part of the mind not normally accessible to consciousness. —**unconsciously** *adv.*, **unconsciousness** *n.*

unconstitutional /ʌnkɒnstɪ'tju:ʃən(ə)l/ *adj.* (of measures or acts etc.) not in accordance with a country's constitution. —**unconstitutionally** *adv.*

uncooperative /ʌnkəʊ'ɒpərətɪv/ *adj.* not co-operative.

uncoordinated /ʌnkəʊ'ɔ:dɪneɪtɪd/ *adj.* not co-ordinated.

uncork /ʌn'kɔ:k/ *v.t.* **1.** to draw the cork from (a bottle). **2.** (*colloq.*) to give vent to (feelings).

uncouple /ʌn'kʌp(ə)l/ *v.t.* to release from couples or couplings.

uncouth /ʌn'ku:θ/ *adj.* awkward or clumsy in manner, boorish. [OE, = unknown (UN- + *cūth* p.p. of *cunnan* know, CAN[1])]

uncover /ʌn'kʌvə(r)/ *v.t./i.* **1.** to remove the cover or covering from. **2.** to reveal, to disclose. **3.** to take off one's cap or hat.

uncrowned /ʌn'kraʊnd/ *adj.* not crowned. —**uncrowned king,** a person having the power but not the title of a king.

unction /'ʌŋkʃ(ə)n/ *n.* **1.** anointing for medical purposes or as a religious rite. **2.** a substance used in this. **3.** soothing words, thought, or quality. **4.** pretended earnestness; excessive politeness. [f. L (*unguere* anoint)]

unctuous /'ʌŋktjʊəs/ *adj.* **1.** having an oily manner; smugly earnest or virtuous. **2.** greasy, oily. —**unctuously** *adv.*, **unctuousness** *n.* [as prec.]

uncurl /ʌn'kɜ:l/ *v.t./i.* to straighten out from a curled state or position.

uncut /ʌn'kʌt/ *adj.* not cut; (of a book) with the leaves not cut open or with untrimmed margins; (of a film) not censored; (of a diamond) not shaped; (of a fabric) with the loops of the pile not cut.

undeceive /ʌndɪ'si:v/ *v.t.* to disillusion.

undecided /ʌndɪ'saɪdɪd/ *adj.* **1.** not yet settled or certain. **2.** not yet having made up one's mind, irresolute. —**undecidedly** *adv.*

undemonstrative /ʌndɪ'mɒnstrətɪv/ *adj.* not given to showing strong feelings, reserved.

undeniable /ʌndɪ'naɪəb(ə)l/ *adj.* that cannot be denied or disputed. —**undeniably** *adv.*

under *prep.* **1.** in or to a position lower than; below; within or on the inside of (a surface etc.); at the foot of (a high wall). **2.** less than. **3.** inferior to; of lower rank than. **4.** in the position or act of supporting or sustaining. **5.** governed or commanded by. **6.** on condition of; subject to an obligation imposed by. **7.** in accordance with; as determined by; designated or indicated by. **8.** in the category of. **9.** (of a field etc.) planted with (a crop). **10.** propelled by. **11.** attested by. —*adv.* **1.** in or into a lower position or subordinate condition. **2.** in or into unconsciousness. **3.** below a certain quantity, rank, age, etc. —*adj.* lower, situated underneath. [OE]

under- *prefix* in the senses (1) UNDER; (2) lower, inner; (3) inferior, subordinate; (4) insufficient, insufficiently; incomplete, incompletely. [OE (as prec.)]

underachieve /ˌʌndərəˈtʃiːv/ *v.i.* to do less well than was expected (esp. scholastically). —**underachiever** *n.*

underarm *adj.* & *adv.* **1.** in the armpit. **2.** (in cricket etc.) bowling or bowled etc. with the hand brought forward and upwards and not raised above shoulder level; (in tennis etc.) with the racket moved similarly.

underbelly *n.* the under-surface of an animal etc., especially as vulnerable to attack.

underbid /ˌʌndəˈbɪd/ *v.t.* (**-dd-**; *past & p.p.* **underbid**) **1.** to make a lower bid than. **2.** (in bridge) to bid less on (one's hand, or *absol.*) than its strength warrants. —/ˈʌndəbɪd/ *n.* such a bid.

undercarriage *n.* **1.** an aircraft's landing-wheels etc. and their supports (ill. FLIGHT). **2.** the supporting frame of a vehicle.

undercharge /ˌʌndəˈtʃɑːdʒ/ *v.t.* **1.** to charge too little for (a thing) or to (a person). **2.** to put too little (explosive, electric, etc.) charge into.

underclass *n.* a subordinate social class; the lowest social stratum in a community, consisting of the poor and the unemployed.

undercliff *n.* a terrace or lower cliff formed by a landslip.

underclothes *n.pl.* garments worn under indoor clothing.

underclothing *n.* underclothes collectively.

undercoat *n.* **1.** a layer of paint under a finishing coat; the paint used for this. **2.** (in animals) a coat of hair under another. —*v.t.* to apply an undercoat to.

undercover /ˌʌndəˈkʌvə(r)/ *adj.* **1.** surreptitious. **2.** spying, especially by working among those observed.

undercroft *n.* a crypt. [f. UNDER- + *obs. croft* (f. MDu. f. L, = CRYPT)]

undercurrent *n.* **1.** a current that is below the surface or below another current. **2.** an underlying trend, influence, or feeling, especially one opposite to the one perceived.

undercut /ˌʌndəˈkʌt/ *v.t.* (**-tt-**; *past & p.p.* **undercut**) **1.** to sell or work at a lower price than. **2.** to strike (a ball) to make it rise high. **3.** to cut away a part below. —/ˈʌndəkʌt/ *n.* an under-side of sirloin.

underdeveloped /ˌʌndədɪˈveləpt/ *adj.* not fully developed; (of a film) not developed enough to give a satisfactory image; (of a country) not having reached its potential level in economic development.

underdog *n.* a person etc. losing a fight or in a state of inferiority or subjection.

underdone /ˌʌndəˈdʌn/ *adj.* not thoroughly done; (of meat) not completely cooked throughout.

underemployed /ˌʌndərɪmˈplɔɪd/ *adj.* not fully employed. —**underemployment** *n.*

underestimate /ˌʌndəˈrestɪmeɪt/ *v.t.* to form too low an estimate of. —/-mət/ *n.* an estimate that is too low. —**underestimation** /-ˈmeɪʃ(ə)n/ *n.*

underexpose /ˌʌndərɪkˈspəʊz/ *v.t.* to expose for too short a time. —**underexposure** *n.*

underfed /ˌʌndəˈfed/ *adj.* insufficiently fed.

underfelt *n.* felt for laying under a carpet.

underfloor *adj.* situated beneath the floor.

underfoot /ˌʌndəˈfʊt/ *adv.* under one's feet, on the ground.

undergarment *n.* a piece of underclothing.

undergo /ˌʌndəˈɡəʊ/ *v.t.* (*past* **underwent**; *p.p.* **undergone** /-ˈɡɒn/) to be subjected to, to experience, to endure.

undergraduate /ˌʌndəˈɡrædʊət/ *n.* a member of a university who has not yet taken a first degree.

underground /ˌʌndəˈɡraʊnd/ *adv.* **1.** beneath the surface of the ground. **2.** in secret; into secrecy or hiding. —/ˈʌn-/ *adj.* **1.** situated underground. **2.** secret, hidden; of a secret political organization or one for resisting enemy forces controlling a country. **3.** (of the press, cinema, etc.) involved in producing unconventional or experimental material. —/ˈʌn-/ *n.* **1.** an underground railway. **2.** an underground organization.

undergrowth *n.* a dense growth of shrubs etc., especially under large trees.

underhand *adj.* **1.** acting or done in a sly or secret way. **2.** (in cricket etc.) underarm. —**underhanded** *adj.*

underlay /ˌʌndəˈleɪ/ *v.t.* (*past & p.p.* **underlaid**) to lay a thing under (another) in order to support or raise it.

—/ˈʌn-/ *n.* a layer of material (e.g. felt, rubber) laid under another as a protection or support.

underlie /ˌʌndəˈlaɪ/ *v.t.* (*past* **underlay**; *p.p.* **underlain**; *partic.* **underlying**) **1.** to lie under (a stratum etc.). **2.** to be the basis of (a doctrine or conduct etc.). **3.** to exist beneath the superficial aspect of.

underline /ˌʌndəˈlaɪn/ *v.t.* **1.** to draw a line under (a word etc.). **2.** to emphasize. —/ˈʌndəlaɪn/ *n.* **1.** a line placed under a word. **2.** a caption below an illustration.

underling /ˈʌndəlɪŋ/ *n.* (usu. *derog.*) a subordinate. [f. UNDER- + -LING]

undermanned /ˌʌndəˈmænd/ *adj.* having too few people as crew or staff.

undermentioned /ˌʌndəˈmenʃənd/ *adj.* mentioned at a later place in a book etc.

undermine /ˌʌndəˈmaɪn/ *v.t.* **1.** to make an excavation under; to wear away the base of. **2.** to weaken or wear out (the health etc.) gradually. **3.** to injure (a person etc.) by secret or insidious means.

undermost *adj.* lowest, furthest underneath. —*adv.* in or to the undermost position.

underneath /ˌʌndəˈniːθ/ *prep.* **1.** at or to a lower place than. **2.** on the inside of. —*adv.* **1.** at or to a lower place. **2.** inside. —*n.* a lower surface or part. [OE (as UNDER, BENEATH)]

undernourished /ˌʌndəˈnʌrɪʃt/ *adj.* insufficiently nourished. —**undernourishment** *n.*

underpants *n.pl.* a man's undergarment covering the lower body and part of the legs.

under-part *n.* a lower or subordinate part.

underpass *n.* a road etc. passing under another; a crossing of this kind.

underpay /ˌʌndəˈpeɪ/ *v.t.* (*past & p.p.* **underpaid**) to pay too little to (a person) or for (a thing).

underpin /ˌʌndəˈpɪn/ *v.t.* (**-nn-**) **1.** to support from below with masonry etc. **2.** to strengthen.

underprivileged /ˌʌndəˈprɪvɪlɪdʒd/ *adj.* less privileged than others, not enjoying a normal standard of living or rights in a community.

underproof *adj.* containing less alcohol than proof spirit does.

underrate /ˌʌndəˈreɪt/ *v.t.* to have too low an opinion of.

underscore /ˌʌndəˈskɔː(r)/ *v.t.* to underline. —/ˈʌn-/ *n.* an underline below a word etc.

undersea *adj.* below the sea, below its surface.

underseal *v.t.* to coat the under-part of (a motor vehicle etc.) with a protective sealing layer. —*n.* a substance used for this.

under-secretary *n.* an official who is directly subordinate to one with the title 'secretary', especially a senior civil servant.

undersell /ˌʌndəˈsel/ *v.t.* (*past & p.p.* **undersold**) to sell at a lower price than (another seller).

under-sexed /ˌʌndəˈsekst/ *adj.* having less than the normal degree of sexual desire.

undershirt *n.* an undergarment worn under a shirt, a vest.

undershoot /ˌʌndəˈʃuːt/ *v.t.* (*past & p.p.* **undershot**) (of an aircraft) to land short of (a runway etc.).

undershot *adj.* **1.** (of a water-wheel) turned by water flowing under it. **2.** (of the lower jaw) projecting beyond the upper jaw.

under-side *n.* the side or surface underneath.

undersigned *adj.* whose signature(s) is or are appended.

undersized *adj.* of less than the usual size.

underskirt *n.* a skirt worn under another, a petticoat (ill. DRESS).

underslung *adj.* supported from above.

underspend /ˌʌndəˈspend/ *v.t./i.* (*past & p.p.* **underspent**) to spend less than (a specified amount); to spend too little.

understaffed /ˌʌndəˈstɑːft/ *adj.* having too few staff.

understand /ˌʌndəˈstænd/ *v.t./i.* (*past & p.p.* **understood**) **1.** to perceive the meaning of (words, a language, or a person). **2.** to perceive the significance, explanation, or cause of. **3.** to be sympathetically aware of the character or nature of, to know how to deal with. **4.** to infer, especially from information received; to take as implied or granted; to supply (a word or words) mentally. **5.** to have understanding in general or in particular. [OE (as UNDER-, STAND)]

understandable *adj.* that may be understood. —**understandably** *adv.* [f. prec.]

understanding *n.* **1.** the power of thought, intelligence. **2.** the ability to understand. **3.** an agreement; a thing agreed upon. **4.** harmony in opinion or feeling. **5.** sympathetic awareness or tolerance. —*adj.* having or showing understanding, insight, or good judgement; able to be sympathetic to others' feelings or points of view. [f. UNDERSTAND]

understate /ʌndəˈsteɪt/ *v.t.* to express in greatly or unduly restrained terms, to represent as being less than it really is. —**understatement** *n.*

understeer *v.i.* (of a vehicle) to have a tendency to turn less sharply than was intended. —*n.* this tendency.

understudy *n.* one who studies the role in a play or the duties etc. of another in order to be able to take his or her place at short notice if necessary. —*v.t.* to study (a role etc.) thus; to act as understudy to (a person).

undertake /ʌndəˈteɪk/ *v.t.* (*past* **undertook** /-ˈtʊk/; *p.p.* **undertaken**) **1.** to agree or promise to do something; to make oneself responsible for, to engage in. **2.** to guarantee, to affirm.

undertaker /ˈʌndəteɪkə(r)/ *n.* one who professionally makes arrangements for funerals.

undertaking /ʌndəˈteɪkɪŋ/ *n.* **1.** work etc. undertaken, an enterprise. **2.** a promise or guarantee. **3.** /ˈʌn-/ the management of funerals.

undertone *n.* **1.** a low or subdued tone. **2.** a colour that modifies another. **3.** an underlying quality or implication; an undercurrent of feeling.

undertow *n.* a current below the surface of the sea, moving in a direction opposite to that of the surface current.

undervalue /ʌndəˈvælju:/ *v.t.* to value insufficiently. —**undervaluation** /-ˈeɪʃ(ə)n/ *n.*

undervest *n.* a vest (undergarment).

underwater /ʌndəˈwɔ:tə(r)/ *adj.* situated, used, or done beneath the surface of water. —*adv.* beneath the surface of water.

underwear *n.* underclothes.

underweight /ʌndəˈweɪt/ *adj.* below the normal, required, or suitable weight. —/ˈʌn-/ *n.* insufficient weight.

underwood *n.* undergrowth.

underworld *n.* **1.** (also **Underworld**; in mythology) the abode of the spirits of the dead, under the earth. **2.** the section of society that is habitually engaged in crime.

underwrite *v.t.* (*past* **underwrote**; *p.p.* **underwritten**) **1.** to sign and accept liability under (an insurance policy, especially on shipping etc.); to accept (a liability) thus. **2.** to undertake to finance or support. **3.** to agree to take up, in a new company or new issue (a certain number of shares if not applied for by the public). —**underwriter** *n.*

undeserved /ʌndɪˈzɜ:vd/ *adj.* not deserved (as a reward or punishment). —**undeservedly** /-vɪdlɪ/ *adv.*

undesirable /ʌndɪˈzaɪərəb(ə)l/ *adj.* not desirable, objectionable. —*n.* an undesirable person. —**undesirability** /-ˈbɪlɪtɪ/ *n.*, **undesirably** *adv.*

undetermined /ʌndɪˈtɜ:mɪnd/ *adj.* undecided.

undies /ˈʌndɪz/ *n.pl.* (*colloq.*) women's underclothes. [abbr.]

undignified /ʌnˈdɪgnɪfaɪd/ *adj.* not dignified.

undine /ˈʌndi:n/ *n.* a female water-spirit. [invented by Paracelsus f. L *unda* wave]

undo /ʌnˈdu:/ *v.t.* (*past* **undid**; *p.p.* **undone** /-ˈdʌn/) **1.** to unfasten; to unfasten the garment(s) of. **2.** to annul, to cancel the effect of. **3.** to ruin the prospects, reputation, or morals etc. of. [OE (as UN-, DO¹)]

undoing /ʌnˈdu:ɪŋ/ *n.* **1.** ruin; a cause of this. **2.** a reversal of what has been done. [f. UNDO]

undone /ʌnˈdʌn/ *adj.* **1.** not done. **2.** not fastened. **3.** (*archaic*) brought to ruin. [f. UNDO]

undoubted /ʌnˈdaʊtɪd/ *adj.* not regarded as doubtful, not disputed. —**undoubtedly** *adv.*

undreamed /ʌnˈdri:md/ *adj.* (also **undreamt** /-ˈdremt/) not (even) dreamed; (with *-of*) not imagined, not thought to be possible.

undress /ʌnˈdres/ *v.t./i.* to take off one's clothes; to take off the clothes of (a person). —*n.* ordinary dress or uniform as opposed to full dress or uniform for ceremonial occasions; casual or informal dress. —/ˈʌn-/ *adj.* constituting such dress or uniform.

undue /ʌnˈdju:/ *adj.* excessive, disproportionate. —**unduly** *adv.*

undulate /ˈʌndjʊleɪt/ *v.i.* to have a wavy motion or look. —**undulation** /-ˈleɪʃ(ə)n/ *n.*, **undulatory** *adj.* [f. L (*unda* wave)]

undying /ʌnˈdaɪɪŋ/ *adj.* immortal; everlasting, never-ending.

unearned /ʌnˈɜ:nd/ *adj.* not earned. —**unearned income,** income from interest payments etc. as opposed to salary, wages, or fees.

unearth /ʌnˈɜ:θ/ *v.t.* **1.** to uncover or obtain from the ground or by digging. **2.** to bring to light, to find by searching.

unearthly /ʌnˈɜ:θlɪ/ *adj.* **1.** not earthly. **2.** supernatural, mysterious and frightening. **3.** (*colloq.*) absurdly early or late, inconvenient. —**unearthliness** *n.*

uneasy /ʌnˈi:zɪ/ *adj.* **1.** not comfortable. **2.** not confident, worried. **3.** worrying. —**uneasily** *adv.*, **uneasiness** *n.*

uneatable /ʌnˈi:təb(ə)l/ *adj.* not fit to be eaten, especially because of its condition.

uneconomic /ʌni:kəˈnɒmɪk/ *adj.* not profitable, not likely to be profitable.

uneducated /ʌnˈedjʊkeɪtɪd/ *adj.* not educated, ignorant.

unemployable /ʌnɪmˈplɔɪəb(ə)l/ *adj.* unfitted by character etc. for paid employment.

unemployed /ʌnɪmˈplɔɪd/ *adj.* **1.** temporarily out of work; lacking employment. **2.** not in use. —**unemployment** *n.*

unencumbered /ʌnɪnˈkʌmbəd/ *adj.* (of an estate) having no liabilities on it.

unending /ʌnˈendɪŋ/ *adj.* having or apparently having no end.

unequal /ʌnˈi:kw(ə)l/ *adj.* **1.** not equal. **2.** of varying quality. **3.** not with equal advantage to both sides; not well matched. —**unequally** *adv.*

unequalled *adj.* superior to all others.

unequivocal /ʌnɪˈkwɪvək(ə)l/ *adj.* not ambiguous, clear and unmistakable. —**unequivocally** *adv.*

unerring /ʌnˈɜ:rɪŋ/ *adj.* not erring, not failing or missing the mark. —**unerringly** *adv.*

UNESCO /ju:ˈneskəʊ/ *abbr.* (also **Unesco**) United Nations Educational, Scientific, and Cultural Organization, an agency of the United Nations set up in 1945 to promote the exchange of information, ideas, and culture. Its headquarters are in Paris.

unethical /ʌnˈeθɪk(ə)l/ *adj.* not ethical; unscrupulous in professional conduct. —**unethically** *adv.*

uneven /ʌnˈi:v(ə)n/ *adj.* **1.** not level or smooth. **2.** not uniform or equable, varying. **3.** (of a contest) unequal. —**unevenly** *adv.*, **unevenness** *n.*

unexampled /ʌnɪgˈzɑ:mp(ə)ld/ *adj.* having no precedent or nothing else that can be compared with it.

unexceptionable /ʌnɪkˈsepʃnəb(ə)l/ *adj.* with which no fault can be found. —**unexceptionably** *adv.*

unexceptional /ʌnɪkˈsepʃən(ə)l/ *adj.* not exceptional, quite ordinary. —**unexceptionally** *adv.*

unexpected /ʌnɪkˈspektɪd/ *adj.* not expected. —**unexpectedly** *adv.*

unfailing /ʌnˈfeɪlɪŋ/ *adj.* not failing; not running short; constant; reliable.

unfair /ʌnˈfeə(r)/ *adj.* not impartial; not in accordance with justice. —**unfairly** *adv.*, **unfairness** *n.*

unfaithful /ʌnˈfeɪθful/ *adj.* **1.** not loyal, not keeping one's promise. **2.** adulterous. —**unfaithfully** *adv.*, **unfaithfulness** *n.*

unfamiliar /ʌnfəˈmɪljə(r)/ *adj.* not familiar. —**unfamiliarity** /-lɪˈærɪtɪ/ *n.*

unfasten /ʌnˈfɑ:s(ə)n/ *v.t./i.* to make or become loose; to open the fastening(s) of; to detach.

unfeeling /ʌnˈfi:lɪŋ/ *adj.* **1.** lacking the power of sensation or sensitivity. **2.** unsympathetic, not caring about the feelings of others. —**unfeelingly** *adv.*, **unfeelingness** *n.*

unfetter /ʌnˈfetə(r)/ *v.t.* to release from fetters.

unfit /ʌnˈfɪt/ *adj.* **1.** not fit, unsuitable. **2.** not in perfect health or physical condition. —*v.t.* (**-tt-**) to make unsuitable.

unfix /ʌnˈfɪks/ *v.t.* to release or loosen from a fixed state; to detach.

unflappable /ʌnˈflæpəb(ə)l/ *adj.* (*colloq.*) imperturbable. —**unflappability** /-ˈbɪlɪtɪ/ *n.*

unfledged /ʌnˈfledʒd/ *adj.* **1.** (of a bird) not fledged. **2.** (of a person) inexperienced.

unfold /ʌnˈfəʊld/ *v.t./i.* **1.** to open the fold(s) of; to spread or become spread out. **2.** to reveal (thoughts etc.). **3.** to become visible or known; (of a story etc.) to develop.

unforgettable /ʌnfəˈgetəb(ə)l/ *adj.* that may not be forgotten.

unformed /ʌnˈfɔːmd/ *adj.* not formed; shapeless.

unfortunate /ʌnˈfɔːtjʊnət, -tʃənət/ *adj.* **1.** unlucky; unhappy. **2.** regrettable. —*n.* an unfortunate person. —**unfortunately** *adv.*

unfounded /ʌnˈfaʊndɪd/ *adj.* with no foundation of fact(s).

unfreeze /ʌnˈfriːz/ *v.t./i.* (*past* **unfroze**; *p.p.* **unfrozen**) **1.** to thaw; to cause to thaw. **2.** to make (frozen assets) available again.

unfrock /ʌnˈfrɒk/ *v.t.* to deprive (a clergyman) of ecclesiastical status.

unfurl /ʌnˈfɜːl/ *v.t./i.* to unroll; to spread out.

unfurnished /ʌnˈfɜːnɪʃt/ *adj.* **1.** without furniture. **2.** not supplied *with*.

ungainly /ʌnˈɡeɪnlɪ/ *adj.* awkward-looking, clumsy, ungraceful. —**ungainliness** *n.* [f. UN- + obs. *gain* (OE f. ON *gegn* straight)]

unget-at-able /ʌnɡetˈætəb(ə)l/ *adj.* (*colloq.*) inaccessible.

ungird /ʌnˈɡɜːd/ *v.t.* to release the girdle of.

ungodly /ʌnˈɡɒdlɪ/ *adj.* **1.** not giving reverence to God; not religious; wicked. **2.** (*colloq.*) absurdly early or late, inconvenient. —**ungodliness** *n.*

ungovernable /ʌnˈɡʌvənəb(ə)l/ *adj.* uncontrollable, violent.

ungracious /ʌnˈɡreɪʃəs/ *adj.* not kindly or courteous.

ungrammatical /ʌnɡrəˈmætɪk(ə)l/ *adj.* contrary to the rules of grammar. —**ungrammatically** *adv.*

ungrateful /ʌnˈɡreɪtf(ə)l/ *adj.* feeling no gratitude.

unguarded /ʌnˈɡɑːdɪd/ *adj.* **1.** not guarded. **2.** incautious, thoughtless.

unguent /ˈʌŋɡwənt/ *n.* an ointment; a lubricant. [f. L *unguentum* (*unguere* anoint)]

ungulate /ˈʌŋɡjʊlət/ *adj.* hoofed. —*n.* a hoofed mammal. [f. L (*ungula* hoof)]

unhallowed /ʌnˈhæləʊd/ *adj.* not consecrated; not sacred, wicked.

unhand /ʌnˈhænd/ *v.t.* (*rhetorical*) to take one's hands off (a person), to let go of.

unhappy /ʌnˈhæpɪ/ *adj.* **1.** not happy, sad. **2.** unfortunate. **3.** unsuitable; unsuccessful. —**unhappily** *adv.*, **unhappiness** *n.*

unharness /ʌnˈhɑːnɪs/ *v.t.* to remove the harness from.

unhealthy /ʌnˈhelθɪ/ *adj.* **1.** not having or not showing good health. **2.** unwholesome. **3.** (of a place etc.) harmful to health; unwholesome; (*slang*) dangerous to life. —**unhealthily** *adv.*, **unhealthiness** *n.*

unheard *adj.* not heard. —**unheard-of** *adj.* unprecedented.

unhinge /ʌnˈhɪndʒ/ *v.t.* **1.** to take (a door etc.) off its hinges. **2.** (esp. in *p.p.*) to cause to become mentally unbalanced.

unhitch /ʌnˈhɪtʃ/ *v.t.* to release from a hitched state; to unhook, to unfasten.

unholy /ʌnˈhəʊlɪ/ *adj.* **1.** impious, wicked. **2.** (*colloq.*) very great, outrageous. —**unholiness** *n.*

unhook /ʌnˈhʊk/ *v.t.* **1.** to remove from a hook or hooks. **2.** to unfasten by releasing a hook or hooks.

unhoped-for /ʌnˈhəʊptfɔː(r)/ *adj.* not hoped for, not expected.

unhorse /ʌnˈhɔːs/ *v.t.* to throw or drag (a rider) from a horse.

unhuman /ʌnˈhjuːmən/ *adj.* not human; superhuman; inhuman.

uni- /juːnɪ-/ *in comb.* one, having or consisting of one. [L (*unus* one)]

Uniat /ˈjuːnɪæt/ *adj.* of the Churches in eastern Europe and the Near East that acknowledge the pope's supremacy and are in communion with Rome but retain their respective languages, rites, and canon law in accordance with the terms of their union. —*n.* a member of such a Church. [f. Russ. *uniyat* f. L *unio* union]

unicameral /juːnɪˈkæmər(ə)l/ *adj.* with one legislative chamber. [f. UNI- + L *camera* chamber]

UNICEF /ˈjuːnɪsef/ *abbr.* United Nations (International) Children's (Emergency) Fund, established in 1946 to assist governments to meet the long-term needs of maternal and child welfare.

unicellular /juːnɪˈseljʊlə(r)/ *adj.* (of an organism) consisting of one cell. [f. UNI- + CELLULAR]

unicorn /ˈjuːnɪkɔːn/ *n.* **1.** a mythical animal usually regarded as having the body of a horse with a single straight horn projecting from its forehead, first portrayed on Assyrian

reliefs. Its horn was reputed to have medicinal or magical properties. The unicorn has been identified at various times with the rhinoceros, certain species of antelope, etc. **2.** a heraldic representation of this (ill. HERALDRY), usually with a deer's legs and lion's tail, especially as a supporter of the royal arms of Great Britain or Scotland. [f. OF f. L, transl. Gk *monocerōs* (= single horn)]

unidentified /ʌnaɪˈdentɪfaɪd/ *adj.* not identified.

unification /juːnɪfɪˈkeɪʃ(ə)n/ *n.* unifying, being unified. [f. UNIFY]

uniform /ˈjuːnɪfɔːm/ *adj.* **1.** not changing in form or character, unvarying. **2.** conforming to the same standard or rule. —*n.* distinctive clothing worn by members of the same school or organization. —**uniformly** *adv.* [f. F or L *uniformis* (UNI-, *forma* form)]

uniformed *adj.* wearing a uniform. [f. prec.]

uniformity /juːnɪˈfɔːmɪtɪ/ *n.* being uniform, sameness, consistency. —**Act of Uniformity**, legislation for securing uniformity in public worship and use of a particular Book of Common Prayer. The first such Acts, establishing the foundations of the English Protestant Church, were passed in the reign of Edward VI but repealed under his Catholic successor Mary I; a third was passed in the reign of Elizabeth I, and a final Act in 1662 after the Restoration.

unify /ˈjuːnɪfaɪ/ *v.t.* to form into a single unit, to unite. [f. F or L *unificare* (UNI-, *facere* make)]

unilateral /juːnɪˈlætər(ə)l/ *adj.* done by or affecting only one side or party. —**Unilateral Declaration of Independence**, the declaration of independence from the United Kingdom made by Rhodesia under Ian Smith in 1965. —**unilaterally** *adv.* [f. UNI- + LATERAL]

unimpeachable /ʌnɪmˈpiːtʃəb(ə)l/ *adj.* not open to doubt or question, completely trustworthy. —**unimpeachably** *adv.*

uninformed /ʌnɪnˈfɔːmd/ *adj.* not informed; ignorant.

uninhabitable /ʌnɪnˈhæbɪtəb(ə)l/ *adj.* not suitable for habitation.

uninhibited /ʌnɪnˈhɪbɪtɪd/ *adj.* not inhibited; having no inhibitions.

uninspired /ʌnɪnˈspaɪəd/ *adj.* not inspired; (of a speech or performance etc.) commonplace, not outstanding.

unintelligible /ʌnɪnˈtelɪdʒəb(ə)l/ *adj.* not intelligible, impossible to understand. —**unintelligibly** *adv.*

uninterested /ʌnˈɪntrəstɪd/ *adj.* not interested; showing or feeling no concern.

uninviting /ʌnɪnˈvaɪtɪŋ/ *adj.* unattractive, repellent.

union /ˈjuːnjən, ˈjuːnɪən/ *n.* **1.** uniting, being united. **2.** a whole formed by uniting parts; an association formed by the uniting of people or groups. **3.** a trade union. **4.** a coupling for pipes or rods. **5.** (*Math.*) the set containing every element that is a member of at least one of two or more other sets. —**the Union**, the union of the English and Scottish crowns under James II in 1603 or of their parliaments in 1707, or of Great Britain and Ireland in 1801. **union catalogue**, a catalogue showing the combined holdings of several libraries. **Union Jack** *or* **flag**, see separate entry. **Union Territory**, any of the nine administrative territories within the Republic of India. [f. OF or L *unio* union (*unus* one)]

unionist /ˈjuːnjənɪst/ *n.* **1.** (in specific uses **Unionist**) an advocate of political or organizational union; (*US*) a supporter or advocate of the Federal Union of the United States of America, especially one who during the Civil War (1861-5) was opposed to secession; (in British politics) a member of the political party which advocated or supported maintenance of the parliamentary Union between Great Britain and Ireland. This party was formed in 1886 by the coalition of the Conservatives with those Liberals (Liberal Unionists) who were opposed to Gladstone's policy of home rule for Ireland. While the chief tenet of this party was the maintenance of the Union, its general policy and principles gradually became identified with those of the Conservative Party, and in 1909 the coalition officially adopted the name of 'Conservative and Unionist Party'. **2.** a member of a trade union. —**unionism** *n.* [f. UNION]

unionize /ˈjuːnjənaɪz/ *v.t.* to bring under trade-union organization or rules. —**unionization** /-ˈzeɪʃ(ə)n/ *n.* [f. UNION]

Union Jack (also **Union flag**) the national flag or ensign of the United Kingdom (formerly of Great Britain), formed by combining the crosses of the three patron saints St George, St Andrew, and St Patrick, retaining the blue ground of the banner of St Andrew. This flag was introduced to symbolize the union of the crowns of England and

Scotland (1603) and was formed by surmounting the cross saltire of St Andrew by the cross of St George; the cross saltire of St Patrick was added on the union of the parliaments of Great Britain and Ireland (1801). Originally and properly the term 'Union Jack' denoted a small British Union flag flown as the jack of a ship; in later and more extended use it denoted any size or adaptation of the Union flag (even when not used as a jack).

Union of Soviet Socialist Republics the world's largest country, with 15 constituent republics, occupying the northern half of Asia (part of it lies within the Arctic Circle) and part of eastern Europe; pop. (1984) 273,843,000; official language, Russian; capital, Moscow. (For its history before 1917 see RUSSIA.) The overthrow of the Tsar in the Russian Revolution of 1917 led to the triumph of the Bolsheviks, the withdrawal of Russia from the First World War, and the establishment of a Communist State. Between the wars Russian history was dominated by the attempted economic overhaul of the country, the imposition of Communist systems and values throughout the country, and Soviet involvement in attempted Communist revolutions elsewhere in the world. The German invasion of 1941 led to a long and bloody campaign in western Russia, leaving millions dead and resulting in the Russian conquest of eastern Europe. In the post-war era, the USSR has emerged as one of two antagonistic superpowers, rivalling the USA, in the polarization of the Communist and non-Communist worlds. The Soviet economy is characterized by strong central planning and continued attempts to open up the large Russian hinterlands.

unique /juˈniːk/ *adj.* **1.** being the only one of its kind, having no like or equal or parallel. **2.** (D) unusual. —**uniquely** *adv.* [F f. L *unicus* (*unus* one)]

unisex /ˈjuːnɪseks/ *n.* the tendency of the human sexes to become indistinguishable in dress etc. —*adj.* designed to be suitable for both sexes. [f. UNI- + SEX]

unison /ˈjuːnɪs(ə)n/ *n.* **1.** (*Mus.*) coincidence in pitch of sounds or notes; (esp. **in unison**) combination of voices or instruments at the same pitch or in a different octave. **2.** agreement. [OF or f. L *unisonus* (UNI-, *sonus* sound)]

unit /ˈjuːnɪt/ *n.* **1.** an individual thing, person, or group regarded for purposes of calculation etc. as single and complete or as part of a complex whole. **2.** a quantity chosen as a standard in terms of which other quantities may be expressed, or for which a stated charge is made. **3.** the smallest share in a unit trust. **4.** a part or group with a specified function within a complex machine or organization. **5.** a piece of furniture for fitting with others like it or made of complementary parts. —**unit price**, the price charged for each unit of goods supplied. **unit trust**, an investment company investing contributions from a number of people in varied stocks and paying contributors a dividend (calculated on the average return on the stocks) in proportion to their holdings. [f. L *unus* one, prob. after *digit*]

unitarian /juːnɪˈteərɪən/ *n.* **1.** an advocate of unity or centralization, e.g. in politics. **2. Unitarian**, a person who believes that God is one person not a Trinity; a member of a religious body maintaining this (see below). —**Unitarianism** *n.* [f. L *unitas* unity]
   Unitarians have no formal creed; originally their teaching was based on scriptural authority, but now reason and conscience have become their criteria for belief and practice. A similar doctrine was voiced in the early Church, but modern Unitarianism dates historically from the Reformation era; as an organized community it became established in the 16th–17th c. in Poland, Hungary, and England, emerging as a full denomination in England when T. Lindsey seceded from the Church of England in 1773.

unitary /ˈjuːnɪtərɪ/ *adj.* **1.** of a unit or units. **2.** marked by unity or uniformity. [f. UNIT or UNITY]

unite /juˈnaɪt/ *v.t./i.* **1.** to join together, to make or become one. **2.** to agree, combine, or co-operate. [f. L *unire* (*unus* one)]

United Arab Emirates an independent State formed in 1971 by the union of seven independent sheikhdoms (formerly called the Trucial States and enjoying special treaty relations with Britain) along the south coast of the Persian Gulf westwards from the entrance to the Gulf of Oman. The member States are Abu Dhabi, Ajman, Dubai, Fujairah, Ras al Khaimah (which joined early in 1972), Sharjah, and Umm al Qaiwain; total pop. (est. 1984) approx. 1,300,000.

United Kingdom the kingdom of Great Britain (see

BRITAIN) and, since 1922, Northern Ireland. The term referred to Great Britain and the whole of Ireland from 1801 (when the two countries were united by Act of Parliament) until 1920, when Ireland was partitioned.

United Nations an international organization of countries set up in 1945, in succession to the League of Nations, to promote international peace, security, and co-operation, with its headquarters in New York. Its members, originally the countries that fought against the Axis in the Second World War, now number 157 and include most sovereign States of the world, the chief exceptions being Switzerland and North and South Korea. Administration is by the Secretariat, headed by the Secretary-General. The chief deliberative body is the General Assembly, in which each member State has one vote; recommendations are passed but the UN has no power to impose its will. The Security Council bears the primary responsibility for the maintenance of peace and security; other bodies carry out the functions of the UN with regard to international economic, social, judicial, cultural, educational, health, and other matters.

United Provinces (*hist.*) the seven Dutch provinces of Friesland, Gelderland, Groningen, Holland, Overijssel, Utrecht, and Zeeland which formed a union under the Treaty of Utrecht in 1579 following their successful rebellion against Spanish rule, leading to the formation of the Dutch Republic or the Netherlands.

United Reformed Church the Church formed in 1972 by the union of the greater part of the Congregational Church in England and Wales with the Presbyterian Church in England.

United States of America a country occupying most of the southern half of North America and including also Alaska in the north and Hawaii in the Pacific Ocean, comprising 50 States and the Federal District of Columbia; pop. (1980) 231,106,727; official language, English; capital, Washington DC. The east coast of North America was colonized by the British in the 17th c., while the south was penetrated by the Spanish from Mexico and the centre taken possession of, but barely colonized, by the French. The modern USA grew out of the successful rebellion of the east coast colonies against British rule in 1775–83. The Louisiana territory was purchased from France in 1803 and the south-west was taken from Mexico after the war of 1846–8. The second half of the 19th c. saw the gradual opening up of the western half of the country after the interruption caused by the Civil War between the northern States and those of the south. In the 20th c. the United States has been the world's principal economic power, participating on the Allied side in both World Wars and becoming one of the two antagonistic superpowers, dominating the non-Communist world in the era following the Second World War.

unity /ˈjuːnɪtɪ/ *n.* **1.** the state of being one or a unit. **2.** a thing forming a complex whole. **3.** (*Math.*) the number 'one'. **4.** harmony; agreement in feelings, ideas, or aims etc. [f. OF f. L *unitas* (*unus* one)]

univalent /juːnɪˈveɪlənt/ *adj.* having a chemical valence of one. [f. UNI- + VALENCE]

univalve /ˈjuːnɪvælv/ *adj.* having one valve. —*n.* a univalve mollusc. [f. UNI- + VALVE]

universal /juːnɪˈvɜːs(ə)l/ *adj.* of, for, or done by all; applicable to all cases. —*n.* (*Philos.*) a general notion or idea; a thing that by its nature may be predicated of many. —**universal coupling** *or* **joint**, one that can transmit power by a shaft coupled at any selected angle. **universal time**, that used for astronomical reckoning at all places. —**universality** /-ˈsælɪtɪ/ *n.*, **universally** *adv.* [f. OF or L (as foll.)]

Universal Postal Union a UN inter-governmental agency that regulates international postal affairs, founded in 1875.

universe /ˈjuːnɪvɜːs/ *n.* (also **Universe**) all existing things including the Earth and its creatures and all the heavenly bodies (see below); all mankind. [f. F f. L *universus* combined into one (UNI-, *vertere* turn)]
   Ancient and medieval ideas confined all known things to the surface of Earth, apart from the relatively few heavenly bodies visible to the naked eye, which were supposed to orbit Earth on idealized crystal spheres. This geocentric world-picture was replaced by the system of Copernicus, which placed the sun at the centre of the system of worlds. In turn, the privileged position of the sun was displaced by the realization of Herschel that the Milky Way was a great

host of stars, of which our sun was part. Only in the 20th c. was it conclusively shown that even this system of stars occupied no special position, and that there were millions of other star systems, or galaxies, many bigger than our own. The known Universe is believed to be at least ten thousand million light-years in diameter; its formation and evolution are the province of the science of cosmology (see also HUBBLE'S LAW).

university /juːnɪ'vɜːsɪtɪ/ *n.* an educational institution that provides instruction and facilities for research in many branches of advanced learning, and confers degrees; its members collectively. [f. OF f. L (as prec.)]

unjust /ʌn'dʒʌst/ *adj.* not just, not fair. —**unjustly** *adv.*

unkempt /ʌn'kempt/ *adj.* of untidy or uncared-for appearance. [f. UN- + archaic *kempt* combed]

unkind /ʌn'kaɪnd/ *adj.* not kind; harsh, cruel. —**unkindly** *adv.*, **unkindness** *n.*

unknot /ʌn'nɒt/ *v.t.* (-tt-) to release the knot(s) of, to untie.

unknown /ʌn'nəʊn/ *adj.* not known, unfamiliar; not identified. —*n.* **1.** an unknown thing or person. **2.** an unknown quantity. —**unknown quantity**, a person or thing whose nature or significance etc. cannot be determined. **Unknown Soldier** *or* **Warrior**, an unnamed representative of a country's armed services killed in battle, buried in a tomb serving as a national memorial. In Britain the tomb of the Unknown Warrior (a term which conceals which of the services he belonged to), a representative of those killed in the First World War, is in Westminster Abbey. **unknown to**, without the knowledge of.

unlace /ʌn'leɪs/ *v.t.* to undo the lace(s) of; to unfasten or loosen thus.

unladen /ʌn'leɪd(ə)n/ *adj.* not laden. —**unladen weight**, the weight of a vehicle etc. when not loaded with goods.

unlatch /ʌn'lætʃ/ *v.t.* to release the latch of; to open thus.

unlearn /ʌn'lɜːn/ *v.t.* to discard from one's memory; to rid oneself of (a habit, false information, etc.).

unlearned[1] /ʌn'lɜːnɪd/ *adj.* not well educated.

unlearned[2] /ʌn'lɜːnd/ *adj.* (also **unlearnt**) (of a lesson etc.) not learnt.

unleash /ʌn'liːʃ/ *v.t.* **1.** to release from a leash or restraint. **2.** to set free to engage in pursuit or attack (*lit.* or *fig.*).

unleavened /ʌn'lev(ə)nd/ *adj.* not leavened; made without yeast or other raising agent.

unless /ʌn'les/ *conj.* if not; except when. [f. LESS preceded by *on* or *in*]

unlettered /ʌn'letəd/ *adj.* illiterate.

unlike /ʌn'laɪk/ *adj.* **1.** not like, different from. **2.** uncharacteristic of. —*prep.* differently from. —**unlike signs,** (*Math.*) plus and minus.

unlikely /ʌn'laɪklɪ/ *adj.* **1.** not likely to happen or be true; not to be expected (to do a specified thing). **2.** not likely to be successful.

unlimited /ʌn'lɪmɪtɪd/ *adj.* not limited; very great or numerous.

unlined /ʌn'laɪnd/ *adj.* **1.** not marked with lines. **2.** without a lining.

unlisted /ʌn'lɪstɪd/ *adj.* not in a published list, especially of telephone numbers or Stock Exchange prices.

unload /ʌn'ləʊd/ *v.t.* **1.** to remove the load from (a ship etc., or *absol.*); to remove (the load) from a ship etc. **2.** to remove the charge from (a firearm etc.). **3.** (*colloq.*) to get rid of.

unlock /ʌn'lɒk/ *v.t.* to release the lock of (a door etc.); to release (as if) by unlocking.

unlooked-for /ʌn'lʊktfɔː(r)/ *adj.* unexpected.

unloose /ʌn'luːs/ *v.t.* (also **unloosen**) to loose.

unlucky /ʌn'lʌkɪ/ *adj.* **1.** not lucky; wretched; having or bringing bad luck. **2.** ill-judged. —**unluckily** *adv.*

unmake /ʌn'meɪk/ *v.t.* (*past* & *p.p.* **unmade**) **1.** to destroy, to annul. **2.** (in *p.p.*) not made.

unman /ʌn'mæn/ *v.t.* (-nn-) to weaken the manly qualities (e.g. self-control, courage) of; to cause to weep etc.

unmanageable /ʌn'mænɪdʒəb(ə)l/ *adj.* not (easily) managed or manipulated or controlled. —**unmanageably** *adv.*

unmanned /ʌn'mænd/ *adj.* not manned; operated without a crew.

unmannerly /ʌn'mænəlɪ/ *adj.* without good manners, showing a lack of good manners. —**unmannerliness** *n.*

unmarked /ʌn'mɑːkt/ *adj.* **1.** not marked. **2.** not noticed.

unmarried /ʌn'mærɪd/ *adj.* not married.

unmask /ʌn'mɑːsk/ *v.t./i.* **1.** to remove the mask from; to remove one's mask. **2.** to expose the true character of.

unmeaning /ʌn'miːnɪŋ/ *adj.* without meaning.

unmeant /ʌn'ment/ *adj.* not intended.

unmentionable /ʌn'menʃənəb(ə)l/ *adj.* so bad, embarrassing, or shocking that it cannot (properly) be spoken of.

unmistakable /ʌnmɪ'steɪkəb(ə)l/ *adj.* that cannot be mistaken for another or doubted, clear and obvious. —**unmistakably** *adv.*

unmitigated /ʌn'mɪtɪgeɪtɪd/ *adj.* not modified; absolute.

unmoral /ʌn'mɒr(ə)l/ *adj.* not concerned with morality. —**unmorally** *adv.*

unmoved /ʌn'muːvd/ *adj.* not moved; not changed in one's purpose; not affected by emotion.

unmusical /ʌn'mjuːzɪk(ə)l/ *adj.* **1.** not pleasing to the ear. **2.** unskilled in or indifferent to music. —**unmusically** *adv.*

unmuzzle /ʌn'mʌz(ə)l/ *v.t.* to remove the muzzle from.

unnameable /ʌn'neɪməb(ə)l/ *adj.* too bad etc. to be named.

unnatural /ʌn'nætʃər(ə)l/ *adj.* **1.** not natural, not normal. **2.** lacking natural feelings of affection; extremely cruel, wicked, monstrous. **3.** artificial; affected. —**unnaturally** *adv.*

unnecessary /ʌn'nesəsərɪ/ *adj.* **1.** not necessary. **2.** more than is necessary. —**unnecessarily** *adv.*

unnerve /ʌn'nɜːv/ *v.t.* to cause to lose courage or resolution.

unnumbered /ʌn'nʌmbəd/ *adj.* not marked with a number; not counted; countless.

unobtrusive /ʌnəb'truːsɪv/ *adj.* not making oneself or itself noticed. —**unobtrusively** *adv.*

unoccupied /ʌn'ɒkjʊpaɪd/ *adj.* not occupied.

unoffending /ʌnə'fendɪŋ/ *adj.* harmless, innocent.

unofficial /ʌnə'fɪʃ(ə)l/ *adj.* not officially authorized or confirmed. —**unofficial strike**, a strike not formally approved by the strikers' trade union. —**unofficially** *adv.*

unpack /ʌn'pæk/ *v.t.* to open and remove the contents of (luggage etc., or *absol.*); to take (a thing) out thus.

unpaged /ʌn'peɪdʒd/ *adj.* with the pages not numbered.

unpaid /ʌn'peɪd/ *adj.* **1.** (of a debt) not yet paid. **2.** (of a person) not receiving payment.

unparalleled /ʌn'pærəleld/ *adj.* not yet parallelled or equalled.

unparliamentary /ʌnpɑːlə'mentərɪ/ *adj.* contrary to parliamentary custom. —**unparliamentary language,** oaths, abuse.

unperson /'ʌnpɜːsən/ *n.* one whose name or existence is denied or ignored.

unpick /ʌn'pɪk/ *v.t.* to undo the stitching of.

unpin /ʌn'pɪn/ *v.t.* (-nn-) to unfasten or detach by removing a pin or pins.

unplaced /ʌn'pleɪst/ *adj.* not placed as one of the first three in a race etc.

unplayable /ʌn'pleɪəb(ə)l/ *adj.* (of a ball in games) that cannot be played or returned etc.

unpleasant /ʌn'plezənt/ *adj.* not pleasant. —**unpleasantly** *adv.*, **unpleasantness** *n.*

unplug /ʌn'plʌg/ *v.t.* (-gg-) **1.** to disconnect (an electrical device) by removing its plug from the socket. **2.** to unstop.

unplumbed /ʌn'plʌmd/ *adj.* **1.** not plumbed. **2.** not fully explored or understood.

unpointed /ʌn'pɔɪntɪd/ *adj.* **1.** having no point(s). **2.** not punctuated; (of written Hebrew etc.) having no vowel points marked. **3.** (of masonry) not pointed.

unpolitical /ʌnpə'lɪtɪk(ə)l/ *adj.* not concerned with politics.

unpopular /ʌn'pɒpjʊlə(r)/ *adj.* not popular; disliked by the public or by people in general. —**unpopularity** /-'lærɪtɪ/ *n.*, **unpopularly** *adv.*

unpractical /ʌn'præktɪk(ə)l/ *adj.* not practical; (of a person) without practical skill.

unpractised /ʌn'præktɪst/ *adj.* **1.** not experienced or skilled. **2.** not put into practice.

unprecedented /ʌn'presɪdentɪd/ *adj.* for which there is no precedent; unparalleled; novel.

unpredictable /ʌnprɪ'dɪktəb(ə)l/ *adj.* impossible to predict.

unpremeditated /ʌnprɪ'medɪteɪtɪd/ *adj.* not deliberately planned.

unprepared /ʌnprɪ'peəd/ *adj.* not prepared beforehand, not ready or equipped to do something.

unprepossessing /ʌnpriːpə'zesɪŋ/ *adj.* unattractive, not making a good impression.

unpretending /ʌnprɪˈtendɪŋ/ *adj.* unpretentious.

unpretentious /ʌnprɪˈtenʃəs/ *adj.* not pretentious, not showy or pompous.

unprincipled /ʌnˈprɪnsɪpəld/ *adj.* lacking or not based on good moral principles, unscrupulous.

unprintable /ʌnˈprɪntəb(ə)l/ *adj.* too indecent, libellous, or blasphemous to be printed.

unprofessional /ʌnprəˈfeʃən(ə)l/ *adj.* **1.** contrary to professional etiquette. **2.** not belonging to a profession. —**unprofessionally** *adv.*

unprofitable /ʌnˈprɒfɪtəb(ə)l/ *adj.* **1.** not producing a profit. **2.** serving no useful purpose. —**unprofitably** *adv.*

unprompted /ʌnˈprɒmptɪd/ *adj.* spontaneous.

unputdownable /ʌnpʊtˈdaʊnəb(ə)l/ *adj.* (*colloq.*) (of a book) so engrossing that the reader cannot put it down.

unqualified /ʌnˈkwɒlɪfaɪd/ *adj.* **1.** not competent; not legally or officially qualified. **2.** not restricted or modified, complete.

unquestionable /ʌnˈkwestʃənəb(ə)l/ *adj.* too clear to be questioned or doubted. —**unquestionably** *adv.*

unquestioning /ʌnˈkwestʃənɪŋ/ *adj.* asking no questions; done etc. without asking questions.

unquote /ʌnˈkwəʊt/ *v.imper.* (in dictation etc.) end the quotation, close the quotation-marks.

unravel /ʌnˈræv(ə)l/ *v.t.* (**-ll-**) **1.** to disentangle. **2.** to undo (knitted fabric etc.). **3.** to probe and solve (a mystery etc.). **4.** to become unravelled.

unread /ʌnˈred/ *adj.* **1.** (of a book etc.) not read. **2.** (of a person) not well read.

unreadable /ʌnˈriːdəb(ə)l/ *adj.* not readable; too dull or too difficult to be worth reading.

unready /ʌnˈredɪ/ *adj.* not ready; not prompt in action. —**unreadily** *adv.*, **unreadiness** *n.*

unreal /ʌnˈrɪəl/ *adj.* not real; imaginary, illusory. —**unreality** /-ˈælɪtɪ/ *n.*

unreason /ʌnˈriːz(ə)n/ *n.* lack of reasonable thought or action.

unreasonable /ʌnˈriːz(ə)nəb(ə)l/ *adj.* **1.** not reasonable in attitude etc. **2.** excessive, going beyond the bounds of what is reasonable or just. —**unreasonably** *adv.*

unreel /ʌnˈriːl/ *v.t./i.* to unwind from a reel.

unrelenting /ʌnrɪˈlentɪŋ/ *adj.* **1.** not relenting or yielding; unmerciful. **2.** not abating or relaxing.

unrelieved /ʌnrɪˈliːvd/ *adj.* lacking the relief given by contrast or variation.

unremitting /ʌnrɪˈmɪtɪŋ/ *adj.* incessant, never slackening.

unremunerative /ʌnrɪˈmjuːnərətɪv/ *adj.* not (sufficiently) profitable.

unrepeatable /ʌnrɪˈpiːtəb(ə)l/ *adj.* **1.** that cannot be repeated or done etc. again. **2.** too indecent etc. to be said again.

unrequited /ʌnrɪˈkwaɪtɪd/ *adj.* (of love etc.) not returned or rewarded.

unreserved /ʌnrɪˈzɜːvd/ *adj.* **1.** not reserved. **2.** without reserve or reservation. —**unreservedly** /-vɪdlɪ/ *adv.*

unrest /ʌnˈrest/ *n.* disturbed or agitated condition.

unrighteous /ʌnˈraɪtʃəs/ *adj.* not righteous, wicked.

unrip /ʌnˈrɪp/ *v.t.* (**-pp-**) to open by ripping.

unripe /ʌnˈraɪp/ *adj.* not yet ripe.

unrivalled /ʌnˈraɪvəld/ *adj.* having no equal, peerless.

unroll /ʌnˈrəʊl/ *v.t./i.* to open out from a rolled-up state; to display or be displayed thus.

unruly /ʌnˈruːlɪ/ *adj.* not easily controlled or disciplined, refractory. —**unruliness** *n.* [f. UN- + RULE]

unsaddle /ʌnˈsæd(ə)l/ *v.t.* **1.** to remove the saddle from. **2.** to throw (a rider) from the saddle.

unsaid /ʌnˈsed/ *adj.* not spoken or expressed.

unsaleable /ʌnˈseɪləb(ə)l/ *adj.* not saleable.

unsalted /ʌnˈsɔːltɪd, -ˈsɒltɪd/ *adj.* not seasoned with salt.

unsaturated /ʌnˈsætʃəreɪtɪd/ *adj.* (*Chem.*) able to combine with hydrogen to form a third substance by the joining of molecules.

unsavoury /ʌnˈseɪvərɪ/ *adj.* **1.** disagreeable to taste or smell. **2.** morally unpleasant or disgusting. —**unsavouriness** *n.*

unsay /ʌnˈseɪ/ *v.t.* (*past & p.p.* **unsaid** /ʌnˈsed/) to retract (a statement).

unscathed /ʌnˈskeɪðd/ *adj.* without suffering injury.

unscientific /ʌnsaɪənˈtɪfɪk/ *adj.* not in accordance with scientific principles. —**unscientifically** *adv.*

unscramble /ʌnˈskræmb(ə)l/ *v.t.* to restore from a scrambled state, to make (a scrambled transmission etc.) intelligible.

unscreened /ʌnˈskriːnd/ *adj.* (of coal) not passed through a sieve.

unscrew /ʌnˈskruː/ *v.t.* to unfasten by removing a screw or screws; to loosen (a screw).

unscripted /ʌnˈskrɪptɪd/ *adj.* (of a speech etc.) delivered without a prepared script.

unscrupulous /ʌnˈskruːpjʊləs/ *adj.* having no moral scruples, not prevented from doing wrong by scruples of conscience. —**unscrupulously** *adv.*, **unscrupulousness** *n.*

unseal /ʌnˈsiːl/ *v.t.* to break the seal of, to open (a sealed letter, receptacle, etc.).

unseasonable /ʌnˈsiːz(ə)nəb(ə)l/ *adj.* not seasonable; untimely, inopportune. —**unseasonably** *adv.*

unseat /ʌnˈsiːt/ *v.t.* **1.** to dislodge (a rider) from a seat on horseback or a bicycle etc. **2.** to remove from a parliamentary seat.

unseeded /ʌnˈsiːdɪd/ *adj.* (of a tennis-player etc.) not seeded (see SEED *v.* 5).

unseeing /ʌnˈsiːɪŋ/ *adj.* unobservant; blind.

unseemly /ʌnˈsiːmlɪ/ *adj.* not seemly, improper. —**unseemliness** *n.*

unseen /ʌnˈsiːn/ *adj.* **1.** not seen, invisible. **2.** (of translation) to be done without preparation. —*n.* an unseen translation.

unselfconscious /ʌnselfˈkɒnʃəs/ *adj.* not self-conscious.

unselfish /ʌnˈselfɪʃ/ *adj.* not selfish, considering the interests of others before one's own. —**unselfishly** *adv.*, **unselfishness** *n.*

unsettle /ʌnˈset(ə)l/ *v.t.* to make uneasy, to disturb the settled calm or stability of.

unsex /ʌnˈseks/ *v.t.* to deprive of the qualities of her or his sex.

unshackle /ʌnˈʃæk(ə)l/ *v.t.* to release from shackles; to set free.

unshakeable /ʌnˈʃeɪkəb(ə)l/ *adj.* not shakeable, firm.

unsheathe /ʌnˈʃiːð/ *v.t.* to remove (a knife etc.) from a sheath.

unshockable /ʌnˈʃɒkəb(ə)l/ *adj.* not able to be shocked.

unshrinkable /ʌnˈʃrɪŋkəb(ə)l/ *adj.* (of a fabric etc.) not liable to shrink.

unshrinking /ʌnˈʃrɪŋkɪŋ/ *adj.* unhesitating, fearless.

unsightly /ʌnˈsaɪtlɪ/ *adj.* unpleasant to look at, ugly. —**unsightliness** *n.*

unskilled /ʌnˈskɪld/ *adj.* not having or needing special skill or training.

unsociable /ʌnˈsəʊʃəb(ə)l/ *adj.* not sociable, withdrawing oneself from the company of others. —**unsociably** *adv.*

unsocial /ʌnˈsəʊʃ(ə)l/ *adj.* **1.** not social. **2.** not suitable for or seeking society. **3.** outside the normal working day(s). —**unsocially** *adv.*

unsolicited /ʌnsəˈlɪsɪtɪd/ *adj.* not asked for; given or done voluntarily.

unsophisticated /ʌnsəˈfɪstɪkeɪtɪd/ *adj.* not sophisticated, simple and natural or naïve.

unsound /ʌnˈsaʊnd/ *adj.* not sound or strong; not free from defects or mistakes; ill-founded. —**of unsound mind,** insane.

unsparing /ʌnˈspeərɪŋ/ *adj.* **1.** giving freely and lavishly. **2.** merciless. —**unsparingly** *adv.*

unspeakable /ʌnˈspiːkəb(ə)l/ *adj.* that words cannot express; indescribably bad or good. —**unspeakably** *adv.*

unspecified /ʌnˈspesɪfaɪd/ *adj.* not specified.

unstable /ʌnˈsteɪb(ə)l/ *adj.* **1.** not stable, changeable. **2.** mentally or emotionally unbalanced. —**unstably** *adv.*

unsteady /ʌnˈstedɪ/ *adj.* not steady or firm; changeable, fluctuating; not uniform or regular. —**unsteadily** *adv.*, **unsteadiness** *n.*

unstick /ʌnˈstɪk/ *v.t.* (*past & p.p.* **unstuck**) to separate (a thing stuck to another). —**come unstuck,** (*colloq.*) to fail, to suffer disaster.

unstinted /ʌnˈstɪntɪd/ *adj.* given freely and lavishly.

unstitch /ʌnˈstɪtʃ/ *v.t.* to undo the stitches of.

unstop /ʌnˈstɒp/ *v.t.* (**-pp-**) **1.** to free from an obstruction. **2.** to remove the stopper from.

unstoppable /ʌnˈstɒpəb(ə)l/ *adj.* that cannot be stopped or prevented.

unstressed /ʌnˈstrest/ *adj.* not pronounced with a stress.

unstring /ʌnˈstrɪŋ/ v.t. (past & p.p. **unstrung**) 1. to remove or relax the string(s) of (a bow, harp, etc.). 2. to take (beads etc.) off a string. 3. (esp. in p.p.) to unnerve.

unstructured /ʌnˈstrʌktʃəd/ adj. not structured, informal.

unstudied /ʌnˈstʌdɪd/ adj. natural in manner, not affected.

unsubstantial /ʌnsəbˈstɑːnʃ(ə)l/ adj. 1. not substantial, flimsy. 2. having little or no factual basis.

unsuitable /ʌnˈsuːtəb(ə)l, -sjuːt-/ adj. not suitable. —**unsuitably** adv.

unsuited /ʌnˈsjuːtɪd/ adj. not fit (for a purpose); not adapted (to a specified thing).

unsullied /ʌnˈsʌlɪd/ adj. not sullied, pure.

unsung /ʌnˈsʌŋ/ adj. not celebrated in song.

unsuspecting /ʌnsəˈspektɪŋ/ adj. feeling no suspicion.

unswerving /ʌnˈswɜːvɪŋ/ adj. not turning aside; unchanging.

untangle /ʌnˈtæŋg(ə)l/ v.t. to free from a tangle, to disentangle.

untapped /ʌnˈtæpt/ adj. not (yet) tapped or used.

untaught /ʌnˈtɔːt/ adj. 1. not instructed by teaching. 2. not acquired by teaching.

untenable /ʌnˈtenəb(ə)l/ adj. (of a theory) not tenable, not able to be held, because strong arguments can be produced against it.

untether /ʌnˈteðə(r)/ v.t. to release from a tether.

unthink /ʌnˈθɪŋk/ v.t. (past & p.p. **unthought** /ʌnˈθɔːt/) to retract in thought.

unthinkable /ʌnˈθɪŋkəb(ə)l/ adj. 1. that cannot be imagined or grasped by the mind. 2. (colloq.) highly unlikely or undesirable.

unthinking /ʌnˈθɪŋkɪŋ/ adj. thoughtless; unintentional, inadvertent. —**unthinkingly** adv.

unthread /ʌnˈθred/ v.t. to take the thread out of (a needle).

unthrone /ʌnˈθrəʊn/ v.t. to dethrone.

untidy /ʌnˈtaɪdɪ/ adj. not tidy. —**untidily** adv., **untidiness** n.

untie /ʌnˈtaɪ/ v.t. (partic. **untying**) 1. to undo (a knot etc.); to undo the cords of (a parcel etc.). 2. to liberate from bonds or an attachment.

until /ʌnˈtɪl/ prep. up to (a specified time); as late as; up to the time of. —conj. 1. up to the time when. 2. so long that. [f. ON und as far as + TILL¹]

untimely /ʌnˈtaɪmlɪ/ adj. 1. happening at an unsuitable time. 2. happening too soon or sooner than is normal. —**untimeliness** n.

unto /ˈʌntʊ, ˈʌntə/ prep. (archaic) = TO (in all uses except as a sign of the infinitive). [formed f. UNTIL, with substitution of to for til]

untold /ʌnˈtəʊld/ adj. 1. not told. 2. not counted, too much or too many to be measured or counted.

untouchable /ʌnˈtʌtʃəb(ə)l/ adj. that may not be touched; non-caste. —n. a member of a hereditary Hindu group (non-caste), held to defile members of a caste on contact. Use of the term, and the social restrictions which accompany it, were declared illegal in India in 1949 and in Pakistan in 1953.

untoward /ʌntəˈwɔːd/ adj. inconvenient, awkward, unlucky; perverse, refractory. [f. UN- + toward docile (as TOWARDS)]

untraceable /ʌnˈtreɪsəb(ə)l/ adj. that may not be traced.

untrammelled /ʌnˈtræm(ə)ld/ adj. not trammelled, not hampered.

untravelled /ʌnˈtrævəld/ adj. 1. that has not travelled. 2. that has not been travelled over or through.

untried /ʌnˈtraɪd/ adj. not yet tried or tested; inexperienced.

untroubled /ʌnˈtrʌbəld/ adj. not troubled; calm, tranquil.

untrue /ʌnˈtruː/ adj. 1. not true; contrary to fact. 2. not faithful or loyal. 3. deviating from an accepted standard. —**untruly** adv.

untruth /ʌnˈtruːθ/ n. 1. lack of truth, being untrue. 2. an untrue statement, a lie.

untruthful /ʌnˈtruːθf(ə)l/ adj. not truthful. —**untruthfully** adv.

untuck /ʌnˈtʌk/ v.t. to free (bedclothes etc.) from being tucked in or up.

untwine /ʌnˈtwaɪn/ v.t./i. to untwist, to unwind.

untwist /ʌnˈtwɪst/ v.t./i. to open from a twisted or spiralled state.

unused /ʌnˈjuːzd/ adj. 1. not in use; not yet used. 2. /-ˈjuːst/ not accustomed.

unusual /ʌnˈjuːʒʊəl/ adj. not usual; remarkable. —**unusually** adv.

unutterable /ʌnˈʌtərəb(ə)l/ adj. inexpressible, beyond description. —**unutterably** adv.

unvarnished /ʌnˈvɑːnɪʃt/ adj. 1. not varnished. 2. (of a statement etc.) plain and straightforward.

unveil /ʌnˈveɪl/ v.t./i. 1. to remove the veil from; to remove one's veil. 2. to remove concealing drapery from (a statue etc.) as part of a ceremony when the statue etc. is displayed to the public for the first time. 3. to disclose; to make publicly known.

unversed /ʌnˈvɜːst/ adj. not experienced or not skilled (in a specified thing).

unvoiced /ʌnˈvɔɪst/ adj. 1. not spoken. 2. (of a consonant etc.) not voiced.

unwanted /ʌnˈwɒntɪd/ adj. not wanted.

unwarrantable /ʌnˈwɒrəntəb(ə)l/ adj. unjustifiable. —**unwarrantably** adv.

unwarranted /ʌnˈwɒrəntɪd/ adj. unauthorized; unjustified.

unwary /ʌnˈweərɪ/ adj. 1. not cautious. 2. not aware (of a possible danger etc.). —**unwarily** adv., **unwariness** n.

unwearying /ʌnˈwɪərɪɪŋ/ adj. not tiring; persistent.

unwell /ʌnˈwel/ adj. not in good health; indisposed.

unwholesome /ʌnˈhəʊlsəm/ adj. 1. harmful to or not promoting health or moral well-being. 2. unhealthy-looking. —**unwholesomeness** n.

unwieldy /ʌnˈwiːldɪ/ adj. awkward to move or control because of its size, shape, or weight. —**unwieldily** adv., **unwieldiness** n. [UN- + dial. wieldy active (f. WIELD)]

unwilling /ʌnˈwɪlɪŋ/ adj. not willing; reluctant, hesitating to do something. —**unwillingly** adv.

unwind /ʌnˈwaɪnd/ v.t./i. (past & p.p. **unwound**) 1. to draw out or become drawn out after being wound. 2. (colloq.) to relax.

unwinking /ʌnˈwɪŋkɪŋ/ adj. 1. not winking; gazing or (of a light) shining steadily. 2. watchful. —**unwinkingly** adv.

unwisdom /ʌnˈwɪzdəm/ n. lack of wisdom.

unwise /ʌnˈwaɪz/ adj. not wise, foolish. —**unwisely** adv.

unwished /ʌnˈwɪʃt/ adj. not wished (usu. for).

unwitting /ʌnˈwɪtɪŋ/ adj. 1. unaware of the state of the case. 2. unintentional. —**unwittingly** adv. [OE (as UN-, WIT)]

unwonted /ʌnˈwəʊntɪd/ adj. not customary or usual. —**unwontedly** adv.

unworkable /ʌnˈwɜːkəb(ə)l/ adj. not workable.

unworkmanlike /ʌnˈwɜːkmənlaɪk/ adj. amateurish.

unworldly /ʌnˈwɜːldlɪ/ adj. not worldly; spiritually-minded. —**unworldliness** n.

unworn /ʌnˈwɔːn/ adj. 1. that has not yet been worn. 2. not impaired by wear.

unworthy /ʌnˈwɜːðɪ/ adj. 1. not worthy, lacking worth or excellence. 2. not deserving. 3. unsuitable to the character of a person or thing. —**unworthily** adv., **unworthiness** n.

unwrap /ʌnˈræp/ v.t./i. (-pp-) to open or become opened after being wrapped.

unwritten /ʌnˈrɪt(ə)n/ adj. 1. not written. 2. (of a law etc.) resting on custom or judicial decision, not on statute.

unyielding /ʌnˈjiːldɪŋ/ adj. firm, not yielding to pressure or influence.

unyoke /ʌnˈjəʊk/ v.t./i. 1. to release (as) from a yoke. 2. to cease work.

unzip /ʌnˈzɪp/ v.t./i. (-pp-) to open or become opened by the undoing of a zip-fastener.

up adv. 1. at, in, or towards a higher place, level, value, or condition, or a place etc. regarded as higher; to a larger size; northwards, further north; at or towards a central place or capital city; at or to a university; in a stronger or winning position or condition; (of a jockey) mounted, in the saddle. 2. in or to an erect or vertical position. 3. so as to be inflated. 4. to the place or time in question or where the speaker etc. is. 5. into a condition of activity, progress, efficiency, etc.; out of bed. 6. apart, into pieces; (of a road) with the surface broken or removed during repairs. 7. into a compact or accumulated state; securely. 8. so as to be finished. 9. happening, especially of an unusual or undesirable event etc. —prep. 1. upwards along, through, or into; from the bottom to the top of; along. 2. at or in a higher part of. —adj. 1. directed upwards. 2. (of travel) towards a capital or centre. —v.t./i. (-pp-) (colloq.) 1. to begin abruptly or unexpectedly to say or do something. **2.** to raise, to pick up. **3.** to increase. —*n.* a spell of good fortune. —**all up with,** hopeless for (a person). **on the up-and-up,** (*colloq.*) steadily improving; honest, honestly. **up against,** close to; in or into contact with; (*colloq.*) confronted with (a difficulty etc.). **up and about** *or* **up and doing,** having risen from bed; active. **up-and-coming** *adj.* (*colloq.*, of a person) making good progress and likely to succeed. **up and down,** to and fro (along). **up-and-over** *adj.* (of a door) opened by being raised and pushed back into a horizontal position. **up for,** available for or being considered for (sale, office, etc.). **up in,** (*colloq.*) knowledgeable about. **ups and downs,** rises and falls; alternate good and bad fortune. **up stage,** at or to the back of a theatre stage. **up to,** until; not more than; equal to; incumbent on; capable of; occupied or busy with. **up to date,** see DATE[1]. **up (with),** may (the stated person or thing) prosper. [OE]

up- *prefix* in the senses of UP, added (1) as an adverb to verbs and verbal derivatives, = 'upwards' (*upcurved*, *update*); (2) as a preposition to nouns forming adverbs and adjectives (*up-country*, *uphill*); (3) as an adjective to nouns (*upland*, *up-stroke*). [OE]

Upanishad /ʊˈpænɪʃæd/ *n.* each of a series of esoteric Sanskrit treatises based on the Vedas, dating from 400 BC onwards. Held to teach 'the conclusion of the Veda' (Vedanta), the Upanishads mark the transition from ritual sacrifice to a mystical concern with the nature of reality. Polytheism is superseded by a pantheistic monism derived from the basic concepts of atman and Brahman. [f. Skr., = sitting near, i.e. at the feet of a master]

upas /ˈjuːpəs/ *n.* **1.** (also **upas-tree**) a Javanese tree yielding a poisonous sap. **2.** (in mythology) a Javanese tree thought to be fatal to whatever came near it. **3.** the poisonous sap of the upas and other trees. [Malay *ūpas* poison]

upbeat *n.* an unaccented beat in music, when the conductor's baton moves upwards. —*adj.* (*colloq.*) optimistic, cheerful.

upbraid /ʌpˈbreɪd/ *v.t.* to reproach. [OE (UP-, BRAID in obs. sense 'brandish')]

upbringing *n.* the bringing up (of a child), education and training during childhood.

up-country *adv.* & *adj.* inland.

update /ʌpˈdeɪt/ *v.t.* to bring up to date.

Updike /ˈʌpdaɪk/, John Hoyer (1932–), American novelist and short-story writer. His novels include the trilogy *Rabbit, Run* (1960), *Rabbit Redux* (1971), and *Rabbit is Rich* (1981), a small-town domestic tragedy which traces the career of an ex-basketball-player from his marriage through the social upheavals of the 1960s to the compromise of middle age; *Couples* (1968), a portrait of sexual passion and realignment amongst a group of couples in Massachusetts; and *The Coup* (1979), an exotic first-person narration by the fictitious ex-dictator of an African State. His writing is marked by an ornate highly charged prose.

up-end /ʌpˈend/ *v.t./i.* to set or rise up on end.

upfield *adv.* in or to a position further along the field.

upgrade /ʌpˈgreɪd/ *v.t.* to raise to a higher grade or rank.

upheaval /ʌpˈhiːv(ə)l/ *n.* **1.** a sudden heaving upwards. **2.** a violent change or disruption. [f. foll.]

upheave /ʌpˈhiːv/ *v.t.* to lift forcibly.

uphill /ʌpˈhɪl/ *adv.* up a slope. —/ˈʌphɪl/ *adj.* **1.** sloping upwards; ascending. **2.** arduous.

uphold /ʌpˈhəʊld/ *v.t.* (*past* & *p.p.* **upheld**) **1.** to support, to keep from falling. **2.** to confirm (a decision etc.).

upholster /ʌpˈhəʊlstə(r)/ *v.t.* to provide (a chair etc.) with upholstery. —**upholsterer** *n.* [back-formation f. *upholsterer* f. UPHOLD in obs. sense 'keep in repair']

upholstery *n.* **1.** textile covering, padding, springs, etc., for furniture. **2.** the work of upholstering. [f. prec.]

upkeep *n.* maintenance in good condition; the cost or means of this.

upland /ˈʌplənd/ *n.* (usu. in *pl.*) the higher part of a country. —*adj.* of this part.

uplift /ʌpˈlɪft/ *v.t.* to raise. —/ˈʌp-/ *n.* (*colloq.*) a mentally or morally elevating influence.

upon /əˈpɒn/ *prep.* on (*upon* is sometimes more formal, and is preferred in *once upon a time* and *upon my word*). [f. UP + ON]

upper *adj.* **1.** higher in place or position. **2.** situated on higher ground or to the north. **3.** ranking above others. **4.** (of a geological or archaeological period) later (called 'upper' because its rock formations or remains lie above those of

the period called 'lower'. —*n.* the upper part of a boot or shoe, above the sole. —**on one's uppers,** (*colloq.*) extremely short of money. **upper case,** see CASE[2]. **Upper Chamber,** = Upper House. **upper circle,** that next above the dress circle in a theatre (ill. THEATRE). **upper crust,** (*colloq.*) the aristocracy. **upper-cut** *n.* a hit upwards with the arm bent; (*v.t.*) to hit thus. **the upper hand,** dominance, control. **Upper House,** the higher (sometimes non-elected) body in a legislature, especially the House of Lords. [compar. of UP]

uppermost *adj.* highest in place or rank; predominant. —*adv.* at or to the highest or most prominent position. [f. prec. + -MOST]

uppish *adj.* self-assertive, arrogant. [f. UP]

uppity /ˈʌpɪtɪ/ *adj.* (*colloq.*) uppish. [fancifully f. UP]

upright *adj.* **1.** in a vertical position; having such a posture or attitude. **2.** (of a piano) with the strings mounted vertically. **3.** strictly honest or honourable. —*n.* **1.** a post or rod fixed upright, especially as a support. **2.** an upright piano. —**uprightness** *n.*

uprising *n.* an insurrection.

uproar *n.* an outburst of noise and excitement or anger. [f. Du. (*op* up, *roer* confusion)]

uproarious /ʌpˈrɔːrɪəs/ *adj.* very noisy; provoking loud laughter. —**uproariously** *adv.*

uproot /ʌpˈruːt/ *v.t.* **1.** to pull (a plant) up from the ground together with its roots. **2.** to force to leave a native or accustomed place. **3.** to eradicate.

uprush *n.* an upward rush.

upset /ʌpˈset/ *v.t.* (**-tt-**; *past* & *p.p.* **upset**) **1.** to overturn; to become overturned. **2.** to disturb the feelings, composure, or digestion of. **3.** to disrupt. —/ˈʌpset/ *n.* **1.** upsetting, being upset. **2.** a surprising result in a contest etc.

upshot *n.* an outcome.

upside-down /ʌpsaɪdˈdaʊn/ *adv.* & *adj.* **1.** with the upper part where the lower part should be, inverted. **2.** in or into great disorder. [orig. *up so down*, perh. = 'up as if down']

upsilon /ʌpˈsaɪlən/ *n.* the twentieth letter of the Greek alphabet, = u. [Gk, = slender U (*psilos* slender), to distinguish it from the diphthong *oi* (*n* and *oi* being pronounced alike in late Gk)]

upstage /ʌpˈsteɪdʒ/ *adj.* & *adv.* **1.** nearer the back of a theatre stage. **2.** snobbish, snobbishly. —*v.t.* to move upstage from (an actor) and thus make him face away from the audience; to divert attention from (a person) to oneself.

upstairs /ʌpˈsteəz/ *adv.* up the stairs; to or on an upper floor. —*adj.* situated upstairs. —*n.* an upper floor.

upstanding /ʌpˈstændɪŋ/ *adj.* **1.** standing up. **2.** strong and healthy. **3.** honest.

upstart *n.* a person who has risen suddenly to prominence, especially one who behaves arrogantly. —*adj.* that is an upstart; of upstarts.

upstate *adj.* (*US*) of the part of a State remote from large cities, especially the northern part. —*n.* this part.

upstream *adv.* against the flow of a stream etc. —*adj.* moving upstream.

up-stroke *n.* a stroke made or written upwards.

upsurge *n.* an upward surge.

upswept *adj.* (of the hair) combed to the top of the head.

upswing *n.* an upward movement or trend.

upsy-daisy /ˈʌpsɪdeɪzɪ/ *int.* of encouragement to a child who is rising after a fall or who is being lifted. [orig. *up-a-daisy*, f. UP]

uptake *n.* (*colloq.*) understanding (usu. in **quick** or **slow in the uptake**).

upthrust *n.* an upward thrust; an upward displacement of part of the earth's crust.

uptight /ˈʌptaɪt, ʌpˈtaɪt/ *adj.* **1.** (*colloq.*) nervously tense, annoyed. **2.** (*US colloq.*) rigidly conventional.

uptown *adj.* (*US*) of the residential part of a town or city. —*adv.* (*US*) in or into this part. —*n.* (*US*) this part.

upturn /ˈʌptɜːn/ *n.* **1.** an upward trend, an improvement. **2.** an upheaval. —/ʌpˈtɜːn/ *v.t.* to turn up or upside-down.

upward /ˈʌpwəd/ *adv.* (also **upwards**) towards what is higher, superior, more important, or earlier. —*adj.* moving or extending upwards. [OE (as UP, -WARD)]

upwind *adj.* & *adv.* against the wind; in the direction from which the wind is blowing.

Ur /ɜː(r)/ an ancient Sumerian city in what is now southern Iraq, formerly (until the river changed its course) on the Euphrates, a city of the moon-god Nanna (Sin) and his spouse Ningal. There is no evidence supporting the Biblical statement that it was Abraham's place of origin, and the connection of Ur with the people known as 'Chaldees' (Chaldeans) dates only from *c.*8th c. BC, many centuries later than any plausible date for Abraham as a historical figure. The site was excavated in 1922-34 by Sir Leonard Woolley, who discovered there spectacularly rich royal tombs of *c.*2600-2000 BC. The city was sacked by invaders *c.*2000 BC, and superseded by Babylon.

uraeus /ˈjʊərɪəs/ *n.* a religious symbol of ancient Egypt, shown as a cobra with its neck puffed and ready to strike, representing the royal power and magic and often shown on the brow of the pharaoh. It was also the symbol of various divinities.

Ural-Altaic *adj.* **1.** of the Urals and the Altai mountain ranges. **2.** of a group of languages, thought to be sufficiently close to be considered together, comprising the Uralic and Altaic languages. —*n.* this group of languages.

Uralic /jʊəˈrælɪk/ *adj.* of a family of languages comprising the Finno-Ugric group and Samoyed, spoken over a wide area in Europe, Asia, and the Scandinavian countries. —*n.* this family of languages. [f. foll.]

Ural Mountains /ˈjʊər(ə)l/ (also **Urals**) a mountain range in the USSR. It extends 1,600 km (1,000 miles) south from within the Arctic Circle to Kazakhstan, and forms a natural boundary between Europe and Asia.

Urania /jʊəˈreɪnɪə/ (*Gk & Rom. myth.*) the Muse of astronomy. [Gk, = heavenly]

uranium /jʊəˈreɪnɪəm/ *n.* a heavy grey radioactive metallic element, symbol U, atomic number 92, used as a source of nuclear energy. Not found uncombined in nature, it was discovered in 1789 and first isolated in 1841, but did not become economically important until the 20th c. Becquerel discovered radioactivity in uranium in 1896, and its capacity to undergo fission, first revealed in 1938, pointed the way to its use as a source of energy. The main natural isotope of uranium, uranium 238, is not fissile, however, and the fissile isotope, uranium 235, had to be separated from it by a laborious process before it could be used. The atomic bomb exploded over Hiroshima in 1945 contained uranium 235. This isotope has since been used to produce power in nuclear reactors, as has the more common uranium 238, which can be transmuted into the artificial fissile element plutonium. Uranium compounds have been used as colouring agents for ceramics, glass, etc. —**uranic** /jʊəˈrænɪk/ *adj.* [f. foll. (name of planet); cf. *tellurium*]

Uranus /ˈjʊərənəs, -ˈreɪnəs/ **1.** (*Gk myth.*) a personification of the sky, the most ancient of the Greek gods and first ruler of the universe. In a cosmological myth he was overthrown by his son Cronus. **2.** (*Astron.*) the seventh of the major planets, the first planet to be discovered by the telescope, by Sir William Herschel in 1781. [Gk, = sky]

urban /ˈɜːbən/ *adj.* of, living in, or situated in a town or city. —**urban guerrilla**, a terrorist operating in an urban area. [f. L (*urbs* city)]

urbane /ɜːˈbeɪn/ *adj.* having manners that are courteous and elegant. —**urbanely** *adv.*, **urbanity** /ɜːˈbænɪtɪ/ *n.* [f. F or L, = prec.]

urbanize /ˈɜːbənaɪz/ *v.t.* to render urban; to remove the rural quality of (a district). —**urbanization** /-ˈzeɪʃ(ə)n/ *n.* [f. F (as URBAN)]

urchin /ˈɜːtʃɪn/ *n.* **1.** a mischievous or needy boy. **2.** a sea-urchin. [orig. = hedgehog, f. OF *herichon* f. L (*h*)*ericius*]

Urdu /ˈʊədu:, ˈɜː-/ *n.* an Indic language allied to Hindi, which it resembles in grammar and structure, but with a large admixture of Arabic and Persian words, having been built up from the language of the early Muslim invaders, and usually written in Persian script. It is the language of the Muslim population, spoken as a first language by about 5 million people in Pakistan (where it is an official language), as a second language by another 40 million there, and by about 30 million in India. [f. Hindustani, = (language of the) camp, rel. to HORDE]

urea /ˈjʊərɪə, -ˈrɪə/ *n.* a soluble colourless crystalline compound contained especially in urine. [f. F *urée* f. Gk *ouron* urine]

ureter /jʊəˈriːtə(r)/ *n.* a duct by which urine passes from the kidney to the bladder or cloaca (ill. BODY 2, 3). [f. F f. Gk (*oureō*)]

urethra /jʊəˈriːθrə/ *n.* the duct by which urine passes from the bladder (ill. BODY 2). [L f. Gk (as prec.)]

urge *v.t.* **1.** to drive onward, to encourage to proceed. **2.** to try hard or persistently to persuade. **3.** to recommend strongly with reasoning or entreaty; to mention earnestly as a reason or justification. —*n.* an urging impulse or tendency; a strong desire. [f. L *urgēre*]

urgent *adj.* **1.** requiring immediate action or attention. **2.** importunate. —**urgency** *n.*, **urgently** *adv.* [f. F (as prec.)]

Uriah /jʊəˈraɪə/ an officer in David's army, husband of Bathsheba, whom David caused to be killed in battle (2 Sam. 11).

uric /ˈjʊərɪk/ *adj.* of urine. —**uric acid,** a constituent of urine. [f. F *urique* (as URINE)]

urinal /jʊəˈraɪn(ə)l, ˈjʊərɪn(ə)l/ *n.* a place or receptacle for urination. [as URINE]

urinary /ˈjʊərɪnərɪ/ *adj.* of or relating to urine. [as URINE]

urinate /ˈjʊərɪneɪt/ *v.i.* to discharge urine. —**urination** /-ˈneɪʃ(ə)n/ *n.* [f. L (as foll.)]

urine /ˈjʊərɪn/ *n.* the pale-yellow fluid secreted by the blood from the kidneys and (in man and the higher animals) stored in the bladder and discharged at intervals. [f. OF f. L *urina*]

urn *n.* **1.** a vase with a foot and usually a rounded body, especially for storing the ashes of the dead or as a vessel or measure. **2.** a large vessel with a tap, in which tea or coffee etc. is made or kept hot. [f. L *urna*]

urnfield /ˈɜːnfiːld/ *n.* a necropolis in which cremated remains are placed in pottery vessels (cinerary urns) and buried, especially one belonging to a group of Bronze Age cultures of central Europe and associated with peoples who were later identified as Celts.

urogenital /jʊərəˈdʒenɪt(ə)l/ *adj.* of the urinary and reproductive systems. [as foll. + GENITAL]

urology /jʊəˈrɒlədʒɪ/ *n.* the study of the urinary system. [f Gk *ouron* urine + -LOGY]

Ursa Major /ˈɜːsə ˈmeɪdʒə(r)/ the most familiar of the constellations, variously named the Great Bear, Plough, Big Dipper, or Charles's Wain. According to legend Callisto, daughter of Lycaon, was transformed by Zeus into a bear to escape the wrath of Juno. Her son Arcas, not recognizing her, was about to slay the bear when both were transported into the heavens, Callisto as the Great Bear, Arcas as the Little Bear. [L, = greater (she-)bear]

Ursa Minor /ˈɜːsə ˈmaɪnə(r)/ the constellation of the Little Bear, containing the north celestial pole and Polaris. It is known also as the Little Dipper, and its two bright stars beta and gamma are known as Guardians of the Pole. [L, = lesser (she-)bear]

ursine /ˈɜːsaɪn/ *adj.* of or like a bear. [f. L (*ursus* bear)]

Ursula /ˈɜːsjʊlə/, St, legendary British saint and martyr, said to have been put to death with 11,000 virgins after being captured by Huns near Cologne while on a pilgrimage. The legend developed from the veneration of some nameless virgin martyrs at Cologne, dating from before the 4th-5th c.; in later forms of the story Ursula, whose name now came to be affixed to their leader, was a British princess.

Ursuline /ˈɜːsjʊlaɪn/ *adj.* of an order of nuns founded by St Angela Merici at Brescia in 1537 for nursing the sick and teaching girls. It is the oldest teaching order of women in the Roman Catholic Church. —*n.* a nun of this order. [f. prec.]

Uruguay /ˈjʊərəgwaɪ/ a country in South America lying south of Brazil, with a coastline on the Atlantic Ocean; pop. (est.) 2,886,187; official language, Spanish; capital, Montevideo. Not permanently settled by Europeans until the 17th c., Uruguay became an area of long-standing Spanish-Portuguese rivalry. Liberated in 1825, it remained relatively backward and disunited through the 19th c., but in the 20th c., despite its small size (it is the smallest of the South American republics) it has emerged as one of the most prosperous and literate nations in the continent, boasting an extensive social welfare system and a balanced economy. —**Uruguayan** *adj. & n.*

Uruk /ˈʊrək/ (Biblical *Erech*, modern Arabic *Warka*) a leading city of Sumer and Babylonia, founded in the 5th millennium BC and associated with the legendary hero Gilgamesh and the god Dumuzi.

US *abbr.* United States (of America).

us /əs, *emphat.* ʌs/ *pron.* **1.** the object case of WE. **2.** (*colloq.*) we. **3.** (*colloq.*) me. [OE]

USA *abbr.* United States of America.

usable /ˈjuːzəb(ə)l/ *adj.* that may be used.

usage /ˈjuːsɪdʒ/ *n.* **1.** the manner of using or treating something. **2.** a customary practice, especially in the use of a language. [f. OF (as USE²)]

use[1] /juːz/ *v.t./i.* **1.** to cause to act or serve for a purpose; to bring into service. **2.** to treat in a specified manner; to behave towards. **3.** to exploit selfishly. **4.** (in *past*; often /juːst/) had as one's or its constant or frequent practice or state. —**be used to** /juːst/, to be familiar with by practice or habit. **use up,** to use the whole of; to find a use for (remaining material or time); to exhaust or tire out. [f. OF, ult. f. L *uti* use]

use[2] /juːs/ *n.* **1.** using, being used. **2.** the right or power of using. **3.** ability to be used; the purpose for which a thing can be used. **4.** custom, usage. —**have no use for,** to be unable to find a use for; to dislike; to be contemptuous of. **in use,** being used. **make use of,** to use; to benefit from; to exploit. **out of use,** not being used. [f. OF f. L *usus* (as prec.)]

used /juːzd/ *adj.* second-hand.

useful /ˈjuːsf(ə)l/ *adj.* **1.** able to be used for some practical purpose; producing or able to produce good results. **2.** (*colloq.*) creditable, efficient. —**make oneself useful,** to perform useful services. —**usefully** *adv.*, **usefulness** *n.* [f. USE[2] + -FUL]

useless /ˈjuːslɪs/ *adj.* serving no practical purpose; not able to produce good results. —**uselessly** *adv.*, **uselessness** *n.* [f. USE[2] + -LESS]

user /ˈjuːzə(r)/ *n.* one who uses something. —**user-friendly** *adj.* (in computers) easy to use; designed with the needs of users in mind. [f. USE[1]]

ushabti /ʊˈʃæbtɪ/ *n.* each of a set of wooden, stone, or faience figurines, in the form of mummies, placed in an ancient Egyptian tomb to serve the dead person by taking his place in any work that he might be called upon to do in the after-life. They were often 365 in number, one for each day of the year, with a number of overseers. [f. Egyptian, = answerer]

usher *n.* **1.** a person who shows people to their seats in a hall or theatre etc. **2.** the door-keeper of a lawcourt etc. **3.** an officer walking before a person of rank. —*v.t.* **1.** to escort as an usher. **2.** to announce or show (in or out etc.; *lit.* or *fig.*). [f. AF f. L *ostiarius* (*ostium* door)]

usherette /ʌʃəˈret/ *n.* a female usher, especially in a cinema. [f. prec. + -ETTE]

usquebaugh /ˈʌskɪbɔː/ *n.* whisky. [f. Ir. & Sc. Gael. *uisge beatha* water of life]

USSR *abbr.* Union of Soviet Socialist Republics.

usual /ˈjuːʒʊəl/ *adj.* such as occurs or is done or used etc. in many or most instances. —**as usual,** as commonly occurs. —**usually** *adv.* [f. OF or L (as USE[2])]

usurer /ˈjuːʒərə(r)/ *n.* one who practises usury. [as USURY]

usurious /jʊˈzʊərɪəs/ *adj.* of, involving, or practising usury. [f. USURY]

usurp /jʊˈzɜːp/ *v.t.* to seize or assume (a throne or power etc.) wrongfully or by force. —**usurpation** /juːzəˈpeɪʃ(ə)n/ *n.*, **usurper** *n.* [f. OF f. L *usurpare* seize for use]

usury /ˈjuːʒərɪ/ *n.* the lending of money at interest, especially at an exorbitant or illegal rate; interest at this rate. [f. AF f. L *usura* (as USE[1])]

UT *abbr.* universal time.

Utah /ˈjuːtɑː, *US* -tɔː/ a State in the western USA. The area was ceded to the USA by Mexico in 1848 and was settled by Mormons; statehood was refused until these abandoned their practise of polygamy—a dispute which led to a brief war (1857) of settlers against US troops. Utah became the 45th State of the USA in 1896; capital, Salt Lake City.

Utamaro /uːtəˈmɑːrəʊ/, Kitagawa (1753-1806), Japanese print-maker, one of the greatest masters of ukiyo-e. His books of woodblock prints range from his *Insects* (1788) to his better-known *The Poem of the Pillow* (1788), and *The Twelve Hours of the Green Houses* (1795) with its sensual and elegant depictions of women. His expressive simple design was greatly admired by the modern movement in Europe in the second half of the 19th c.

UTC *abbr.* co-ordinated universal time (see GREENWICH).

utensil /juːˈtens(ə)l/ *n.* an implement or vessel, especially for domestic use. [f. OF f. L, = usable (as USE[1])]

uterine /ˈjuːtəraɪn/ *adj.* of the uterus. [f. L (as foll.)]

uterus /ˈjuːtərəs/ *n.* (*pl.* **-i** /-aɪ/) the womb (ill. BODY 2). [L]

Uther Pendragon /juːθə penˈdrægən/ (in Arthurian legend) king of the Britons and father of Arthur.

utilitarian /juːtɪlɪˈteərɪən/ *adj.* **1.** designed to be useful for a purpose rather than decorative or luxurious; severely practical. **2.** of utilitarianism. —*n.* an adherent of utilitarianism. [f. UTILITY]

utilitarianism /juːtɪlɪˈteərɪənɪz(ə)m/ *n.* the theory, famously advocated by Bentham and J. S. Mill, that the guiding principle of conduct should be to achieve the greatest happiness of the greatest number; the theory that the usefulness (or otherwise) of an action is the criterion of whether it is right (or wrong). [f. prec.]

utility /juːˈtɪlɪtɪ/ *n.* **1.** usefulness, profitableness. **2.** a useful thing; a public service such as the supply of water, gas, or electricity. —*adj.* severely practical and standardized; made or serving for utility. —**utility room,** a room containing large fixed domestic appliances, e.g. a washing-machine. **utility vehicle,** a vehicle serving various functions. [f. OF f. L (*utilis* useful, as USE[1])]

utilize /ˈjuːtɪlaɪz/ *v.t.* to make use of, to turn to account. —**utilization** /-ˈzeɪʃ(ə)n/ *n.* [f. F f. It. (as prec.)]

utmost /ˈʌtməʊst/ *adj.* furthest, extreme, greatest. —*n.* the utmost point or degree etc. —**do one's utmost,** to do all that one can. [OE, = OUTMOST]

Utopia /juːˈtəʊpɪə/ *n.* an imagined perfect place or state of things. —**Utopian** *adj.* [name of imaginary island, governed on a perfect political and social system, in book of that title by Sir Thomas More (1516)]

Utrecht /juːˈtrext/ a city and province of the Netherlands. —**Peace of Utrecht,** a series of treaties (1713) ending the War of the Spanish Succession. By their terms the disputed throne of Spain was given to the French aspirant Philip V, but the union of the French and Spanish thrones was forbidden, while the succession of the House of Hanover to the British throne was secured and the former Spanish territories in Italy were ceded to the Hapsburgs.

utricle /ˈjuːtrɪk(ə)l/ *n.* a cell or small cavity in an animal or plant. [f. F or L *utriculus* dim. of *uter* leather bag)]

Utrillo /uːˈtrɪləʊ, -ˈtriːəʊ/, Maurice (1883-1955), French painter, an alcoholic from an early age, noted for his paintings of Parisian street scenes.

Uttar Pradesh /ʊtə prəˈdeʃ/ a State in Northern India, bordering on Tibet and Nepal; capital, Lucknow.

utter[1] *attrib. adj.* complete, absolute. —**utterly** *adv.* [OE, = OUTER]

utter[2] *v.t./i.* **1.** to make (a sound or words) with the mouth or voice. **2.** to speak. **3.** to put (a forged banknote or coin etc.) into circulation. [f. MDu. *ūteren* make known]

utterance /ˈʌtərəns/ *n.* **1.** uttering. **2.** the power or manner of speaking. **3.** a thing spoken. [f. prec.]

uttermost *adj.* utmost. [f. UTTER[1]]

U-turn /ˈjuːtɜːn/ *n.* **1.** turning a vehicle in a U-shaped course so as to face the opposite direction. **2.** a reversal of policy.

UV *abbr.* ultraviolet.

uvula /ˈjuːvjʊlə/ *n.* (*pl.* **-ae** /-iː/) the fleshy part of the soft palate hanging from the back of the roof of the mouth above the throat. —**uvular** *adj.* [L, dim. of *uva* grape]

uxorious /ʌkˈsɔːrɪəs/ *adj.* greatly or obsessively fond of one's wife. [f. L (*uxor* wife)]

Uzbek /ˈʊzbek, ˈʌ-/ *n.* **1.** a native of Uzbekistan. **2.** the language of Uzbekistan, the most widely spoken non-Slavonic language in the USSR with some 9 million speakers, a Turkic language belonging to the Altaic language group. Originally it was written in the Arabic script but that was replaced by the Roman alphabet in 1927 and the Cyrillic in 1940. [Uzbek]

Uzbekistan /ʊzbekɪˈstɑːn, ʌ-/ the Uzbek SSR, a constituent republic of the USSR, lying south and south-east of the Aral Sea; capital, Tashkent.

V

V, v /viː/ n. (pl. **Vs, V's**) 1. the twenty-second letter of the alphabet. 2. a V-shaped thing. 3. (as a Roman numeral) 5.

V symbol vanadium.

V abbr. volt(s).

v. abbr. 1. verse. 2. versus. 3. very. 4. vide.

vac n. (colloq.) 1. a vacation. 2. a vacuum cleaner. [abbr.]

vacancy /ˈveɪkənsɪ/ n. 1. being vacant, emptiness. 2. an unoccupied position of employment or place of accommodation. [f. foll. or L vacantia]

vacant /ˈveɪkənt/ adj. 1. empty, not filled or occupied. 2. not mentally active, having a blank expression. —**vacant possession,** (of a house etc.) the state of being empty of occupants and available for the purchaser to occupy immediately. —**vacantly** adv. [f. OF or L (as foll.)]

vacate /vəˈkeɪt/ v.t. to cease to occupy (a place or position). [f. L vacare be empty]

vacation /vəˈkeɪʃ(ə)n/ n. 1. any of the intervals between terms in universities and lawcourts. 2. (US) a holiday. 3. vacating. —v.i. (US) to take a holiday. [f. OF or L (as prec.)]

vaccinate /ˈvæksɪneɪt/ v.t. to inoculate with a vaccine. —**vaccination** /-ˈneɪʃ(ə)n/ n., **vaccinator** n. [f. foll.]

vaccine /ˈvæksiːn, -sɪn/ n. a preparation of cowpox virus introduced into the bloodstream to procure immunity against smallpox; any preparation of an organism or substance causing a disease, specially treated or synthesized and injected or administered orally against an infection. [f. L (vacca cow)]

vacillate /ˈvæsɪleɪt/ v.i. to fluctuate in opinion or resolution. —**vacillation** /-ˈleɪʃ(ə)n/ n., **vacillator** n. [f. L vacillare sway]

vacuole /ˈvækjʊəʊl/ n. a tiny cavity in an organ or cell, containing air or fluid etc. [F, dim. of L vacuus empty]

vacuous /ˈvækjʊəs/ adj. 1. expressionless; unintelligent. 2. empty. —**vacuity** /vəˈkjuːɪtɪ/ n., **vacuously** adv., **vacuousness** n. [f. L vacuus empty]

vacuum /ˈvækjʊəm/ n. (pl. **vacua** or **vacuums**) 1. space entirely devoid of matter; a space or vessel from which the air has been completely or partly removed by a pump etc. 2. absence of normal or previous contents. 3. (pl. **-s**) (colloq.) a vacuum cleaner. —v.t./i. (colloq.) to use a vacuum cleaner (on). —**vacuum brake,** a brake in which pressure is produced by exhaustion of air. **vacuum flask,** a vessel with a double wall enclosing a vacuum so that liquid in the inner receptacle retains its temperature (ill. HEAT). The modern flask was invented by Sir James Dewar, Scottish physicist, in the 1890s. **vacuum-packed** adj. sealed after partial removal of the air. **vacuum tube,** a tube with a near-vacuum for the free passage of electric current. [neut. of L vacuus empty]

vacuum cleaner an electric appliance for taking up dust, dirt, etc., by suction. The first vacuum cleaner was invented and named by H. C. Booth (1871–1955), English engineer, in 1901. He founded a company providing a cleaning service using his machines, which were large and cumbersome and required a horse-drawn cart to convey the electric motor which powered them. Smaller domestic models were developed some years later.

vade-mecum /vɑːdɪˈmeɪkəm, veɪdɪˈmiːkəm/ n. a handbook or other small useful work of reference. [F f. L, = go with me]

vagabond /ˈvægəbɒnd/ n. a wanderer, especially an idle or dishonest one. —adj. having no fixed habitation, wandering. [f. OF or L vagabundus (vagari wander)]

vagary /ˈveɪgərɪ/ n. a capricious act, idea, or fluctuation. [f. L vagari wander]

vagina /vəˈdʒaɪnə/ n. (pl. **-ae** /-iː/ or **-as**) the passage leading from the vulva to the womb in a female mammal (ill. BODY 2). —**vaginal** adj. [L, = sheath]

vagrant /ˈveɪgrənt/ n. a person without a settled home or regular work. —adj. wandering, roving. —**vagrancy** n. [f. AF vag(a)raunt (cf. L vagari wander)]

vague /veɪg/ adj. 1. of uncertain or ill-defined meaning or character. 2. (of a person or mind) imprecise, inexact in thought, expression, or understanding —**vaguely** adv., **vagueness** n. [F or f. L vagus wandering]

vain adj. 1. conceited, especially about one's appearance. 2. having no value or significance, unsubstantial. 3. useless, futile, followed by no good result. —**in vain,** without result or success. —**vainly** adv. [f. OF f. L vanus empty]

vainglory /veɪnˈglɔːrɪ/ n. extreme vanity, boastfulness. —**vainglorious** adj. [after OF vaine gloire, L vana gloria]

vair n. 1. (archaic) a squirrel-fur widely used in medieval times for linings and trimmings. 2. (in heraldry) a fur represented by small shield-shaped or bell-shaped figures usually alternately azure and argent (ill. HERALDRY). [f. OF f. L (as VARIOUS)]

Vaisya /ˈvaɪsjə/ n. a member of the third of the four great Hindu castes, the farmer and merchant class. [f. Skr., = peasant, labourer]

valance /ˈvæləns/ n. a short curtain round the frame or canopy of a bedstead or above a window or under a shelf. [perh. f. AF valer descend]

vale n. (archaic exc. in place-names) a valley. [f. OF val f. L vallis]

valediction /vælɪˈdɪkʃ(ə)n/ n. bidding farewell; the words used in this. —**valedictory** adj. [f. L valedicere bid farewell (vale farewell, dicere say; after benediction]

valence /ˈveɪləns/ n. the combining or replacing power of an atom as compared with that of the hydrogen atom. [f. L valentia power]

Valencia /vəˈlensɪə/ 1. a city and port of eastern Spain, capital of the former Moorish kingdom of Valencia; pop. (1981) 744,748. 2. a region of eastern Spain, on the Mediterranean, a Moorish Kingdom 1021–1238.

valency /ˈveɪlənsɪ/ n. the unit of the combining power of an atom; this power. [as VALENCE]

Valentine /ˈvæləntaɪn/, St. The name of an early Italian saint (or possibly two saints), traditionally commemorated on 14 Feb.—a Roman priest martyred c.269, and a bishop of Terni martyred at Rome. St Valentine was regarded as the patron of lovers, a tradition which may be connected with the old belief that birds pair on 14 Feb., or with the pagan fertility festival of Lupercalia (mid-Feb.).

valentine /ˈvæləntaɪn/ n. 1. a card or picture etc. sent (often anonymously) to a person of the opposite sex on St Valentine's day (14 Feb.; see prec. and below). 2. a sweetheart chosen on this day. [f. prec.]

Valentines as we know them first appeared in the 18th c., and were cards with drawings and verses made by the sender. In the 19th c. shop-made valentines appeared and became increasingly elaborate, adorned with lace, real flowers, feathers, and moss. Today the custom offers an opportunity for indulging in gentle or humorous sentimentality and for manufacturers of greetings cards to boost their profits.

Valentino /vælənˈtiːnəʊ/, Rudolph (1895–1926), real name Rodolfo Guglielmi di Valentino, Italian-born American film actor who in his short career held an unrivalled place in the imagination of female audiences. The dismissive description 'Latin lover' fails to convey his audacious yet fundamentally romantic sexuality in The Sheikh (1921) and subsequent films. At his funeral there were scenes of mass hysteria and his death was said to be the cause of several suicides.

valerian /vəˈlɪərɪən/ n. 1. any of various herbaceous plants of the widely-distributed genus Valeriana, many of which have been used medicinally as stimulants or antispasmodics. 2. the dried roots of such a plant used in medicine or scents etc. [f. OF f. L, app. f. Valerianus of Valerius]

valet /ˈvælɪt, -leɪ/ n. a man's personal attendant who takes care of clothes etc. —v.t./i. to act as valet (to). [F, = VARLET]

valetudinarian /vælɪtjuːdɪˈneərɪən/ n. a person who pays excessive attention to preserving his health. —adj. that is a valetudinarian. —**valetudinarianism** n. [f. L (valetudo health)]

Valhalla /vælˈhælə/ n. (Scand. myth.) the hall assigned to heroes who have died in battle, in which they feast with Odin. [f. ON (*valr* the slain, *höll* hall)]

valiant /ˈvæljənt/ *adj.* (of a person or conduct) brave, courageous. —**valiantly** *adv.* [f. AF f. L *valēre* be strong]

valid /ˈvælɪd/ *adj.* **1.** (of a reason, objection, etc.) sound and to the point, logical. **2.** legally acceptable or usable; executed with the proper formalities. —**validity** /vəˈlɪdɪtɪ/ *n.*, **validly** *adv.* [f. F or L *validus* strong]

validate /ˈvælɪdeɪt/ *v.t.* to make valid, to ratify. —**validation** /-ˈdeɪʃ(ə)n/ *n.* [f. L (as prec.)]

valise /vəˈliːz/ *n.* a kitbag; (*US*) a small suitcase. [F f. It. *valigia*; orig. unkn.]

Valkyrie /ˈvælkɪrɪ, -ˈkɪərɪ/ *n.* (*Scand. myth.*) each of Odin's twelve handmaidens hovering over battlefields and carrying slain warriors designated by the gods to Valhalla. [f. ON, = chooser of the slain (*valr* the slain)]

Valletta /vəˈletə/ the capital and port of Malta; pop. (est. 1979) 14,042.

valley /ˈvælɪ/ *n.* **1.** a long low area between hills. **2.** a region drained by a river. **3.** the internal angle formed by intersecting planes of a roof (ill. HOUSES). [f. AF f. L. *vallis* (as VALE)]

Valois[1] /ˈvælwɑː/ a medieval duchy of France; the name of the French royal family from the time of Philip VI (1328) to the death of Henry III (1589), when the throne passed to the Bourbons.

Valois[2] /ˈvælwɑː/, Ninette de (1898–), real name Edris Stannus, British dancer, choreographer, teacher, and ballet director, born in Ireland. In 1931 she opened the official ballet school of the Sadler's Wells Theatre, where her company, the Vic-Wells Ballet, appeared, later becoming the Sadler's Wells Ballet and then the Royal Ballet in 1956. As a choreographer her most successful years were the 1930s, when she created such works as *Job* (1931), *The Rake's Progress* (1935), *The Gods Go a-Begging* (1936), and *Checkmate* (1937).

valour /ˈvælə(r)/ *n.* courage, especially in battle. —**valorous** *adj.* [f. OF f. L *valor* (*valēre* be strong)]

valuable /ˈvæljʊəb(ə)l/ *adj.* of great value, price, or worth. —*n.* (usu. in *pl.*) a valuable thing. —**valuably** *adv.* [f. VALUE]

valuation /væljʊˈeɪʃ(ə)n/ *n.* estimation of a thing's value (especially by a professional valuer) or of a person's merit; the value so estimated. [f. foll.]

value /ˈvæljuː/ *n.* **1.** the amount of money, goods, or services etc. considered to be equivalent to a thing or for which it can be exchanged. **2.** desirability, usefulness, importance. **3.** the ability of a thing to serve a purpose or cause an effect. **4.** (in *pl.*) one's principles or standards; one's judgement of what is valuable or important in life. **5.** the amount or quantity denoted by a figure etc.; the duration of a musical sound indicated by a note; the relative importance of each playing-card, chess piece, etc., in a game; (in painting) the relative lightness and darkness of tones. —*v.t.* **1.** to estimate the value of; to appraise professionally. **2.** to have a high or specified opinion of; to attach importance to. —**value added tax,** a tax on the amount by which the value of an article has been increased at each stage of its production. **value judgement,** a subjective estimate of quality etc. [f. OF, p.p. of *valoir* be worth f. L *valēre* be strong]

valueless *adj.* having no value. [f. VALUE + -LESS]

valuer *n.* one who estimates or assesses values, especially as a professional. [f. VALUE]

valve *n.* **1.** a device for controlling the passage of a fluid through a pipe etc., especially an automatic device allowing movement in one direction only. **2.** a membranous structure in the heart or in a blood-vessel allowing blood to flow in one direction only. **3.** a thermionic valve (see THERMIONIC). **4.** a device to vary the length of tube in a trumpet etc. **5.** each of the two shells of an oyster or mussel etc. [f. L. *valva* leaf of folding-door]

valvular /ˈvælvjʊlə(r)/ *adj.* **1.** of or like a valve. **2.** forming or having a valve or valves. [f. dim. of L *valva* (see prec.)]

vambrace /ˈvæmbreɪs/ *n.* (*hist.*) a piece of defensive armour for the forearm (ill. ARMOUR). [f. AF & OF (*avant* before, *bras* arm)]

vamoose /vəˈmuːs/ *v.i.* (*US slang*) to depart hurriedly. [f. Sp. *vamos* let us go]

vamp[1] *n.* the upper front part of a boot or shoe. —*v.t./i.* **1.** to repair, to furbish. **2.** to make by patching or from odds and ends. **3.** to improvise (a musical accompaniment). [f. OF *avantpié* (*avant* before, *pied* foot)]

vamp[2] *n.* (*colloq.*) a seductive woman who uses her attrac-

tiveness to exploit men; an unscrupulous flirt. —*v.t./i.* (*colloq.*) to exploit or flirt with (a man) unscrupulously; to act as a vamp. [abbr. of foll.]

vampire /ˈvæmpaɪə(r)/ *n.* **1.** a ghost or reanimated corpse supposed to leave a grave at night and suck the blood of living persons (see below). **2.** a person who preys ruthlessly on others. —**vampire bat,** a tropical bat, especially of South America, actually or supposedly biting animals and persons and lapping their blood. [F or G f. Magyar perh. f. Turk. *uber* witch]

The vampire legend is widespread in Europe and Asia but is particularly associated with the folklore of eastern Europe, and its continual popularity in the 20th c. is largely due to the success of Bram Stoker's novel *Dracula* (1897). A number of superstitions have arisen: that vampires cast no shadow, are not reflected in mirrors, attack only at night, and can be warded off by garlic or by a crucifix; that the body of a vampire can be destroyed by being beheaded or burnt, or by a stake being driven through its heart.

van[1] *n.* **1.** a covered vehicle for transporting goods or horses etc. or prisoners. **2.** a railway carriage for luggage or for the use of the guard. [abbr. of CARAVAN]

van[2] *n.* the vanguard; the forefront. [abbr.]

vanadium /vəˈneɪdɪəm/ *n.* a hard grey metallic element, symbol V, atomic number 23, discovered in 1801 and first isolated in 1867. It is not found in the uncombined state in nature. The main use of the metal is in certain steels, where it improves strength and hardness. Its compounds are widely employed as catalysts and in the ceramic and glass industries. [f. ON *vanadis* name of the Scandinavian goddess Freya]

Van Allen belt /væn ˈælən/ (also **Van Allen layer**) each of the two regions of intense radiation partly surrounding the earth at heights of several thousand kilometres. [f. J. A. *Van Allen*, Amer. physicist (1914–)]

Vanbrugh /ˈvænbrə/, Sir John (1664–1726), English architect, one of the chief exponents of the baroque in England. In early life he was a soldier and a playwright, author of two famous comedies *The Relapse* or *Virtue in Danger* and *The Provok'd Wife* (1697), but from 1699 became known chiefly as an architect. His masterpieces, produced in collaboration with Hawksmoor, were Castle Howard in Yorkshire, Blenheim Palace in Oxfordshire, and Seaton Delaval Hall in Northumberland.

Vancouver[1] /vænˈkuːvə(r)/, George (1757–98), English explorer who commanded a naval expedition exploring the coasts of Australia, New Zealand, and Hawaii in 1791-2, and then went on to circumnavigate Vancouver Island and chart the west coast of North America (1792-4).

Vancouver[2] /vænˈkuːvə(r)/ a city and seaport of British Columbia, Canada; pop. (1981) 1,268,183. —**Vancouver Island,** a large island off the Pacific coast of Canada, opposite Vancouver. [f. prec.]

Vandal /ˈvænd(ə)l/ *n.* a member of a Germanic people who overran part of Roman Europe in the 4th-5th c., establishing kingdoms in Gaul and Spain and finally (428-9) migrated to North Africa. They sacked Rome in 455 in a marauding expedition, but were eventually defeated by the Byzantine general Belisarius, after which their North African kingdom fell prey to Muslim invaders. [f. L f. Gmc]

vandal /ˈvænd(ə)l/ *n.* one who wilfully or ignorantly destroys or damages works of art or other property or the beauties of nature. —**vandalism** *n.* [f. prec.]

vandalize /ˈvændəlaɪz/ *v.t.* to destroy or damage (property etc.) as a vandal. [f. prec.]

Van de Graaff generator /væn də ˈɡrɑːf/ a machine for generating electrostatic charge by means of a vertical endless belt which collects charge at its lower end from needle points connected to a voltage source and carries it to similar points at the top connected to the inside of a metal dome, whose potential is thereby increased; a particle accelerator based on this machine. [f. R. J. *Van de Graaff* (d. 1967), US physicist]

Van de Velde see VELDE.

Van Diemen's Land /væn ˈdiːmənz/ the former name of Tasmania (see entry). Its name commemorates Anthony van Diemen (1593-1645), Dutch governor of Java, who sent Tasman on his voyage.

Van Dyck /daɪk/, Sir Anthony (1599-1641), Flemish painter. From 1618-20 he worked in Rubens's workshop, rapidly becoming his most brilliant pupil. In 1621-8 he was in Italy where he studied Titian and the Venetians. The portraits he produced at Genoa marked the onset of his artistic maturity in their acute characterization, superlative brushwork, and shimmering colour. In 1628-32 he worked in Antwerp, at the height of his powers, and was then invited to England by Charles I, who knighted him. His subsequent portraits of the Caroline court determined the course of portraiture in England for over 200 years with their sensitivity and refinement of style, glittering surface, and elegant composition.

Vandyke /væn'daɪk/ *adj.* in the style of dress etc. common in portraits by Van Dyck. —**Vandyke beard,** a neat pointed beard. **Vandyke brown,** deep rich brown. [anglicized f. prec.]

vane *n.* **1.** a weather-vane. **2.** the blade of a screw propeller, sail of a windmill, or similar device acted on or moved by water or wind. **3.** the flat part of a bird's feather formed by barbs (ill. BIRDS). [var. of obs. *fane* f. OE *fana* banner]

Van Eyck /væn 'aɪk/, Jan (1390-1441), Flemish painter. Vasari attributes to him the invention of oil painting, and though it is known that oils were used as a medium in the Middle Ages long before his time there is no doubt that he made an innovative contribution to the technique of their use, bringing greater flexibility, richer and denser colour, and a wider range from light to dark. His most famous works, the Ghent altarpiece and the portrait *Arnolfini and his Wife* (1434), justify his contemporary fame with their superb control of oil paint, clarity of exposition, and representational skill. His brother Hubert (d. 1426) remains a shadowy figure but may have collaborated on the Ghent altarpiece.

Van Gogh /gɒf/, Vincent Willem (1853-90), Dutch Post-Impressionist painter, who lived as art dealer, lay preacher, and tramp before deciding to become an artist in 1881. After a period of study at Antwerp, where his humanitarian ideals were reflected in paintings of peasants such as *The Potato Eaters*, he moved to Paris in 1886, coming under the influence of the impressionists and of Japanese woodcuts. Rejecting the optical realism of the impressionists he began to use colours for their expressive or symbolic values, and abandoned the delicate manner of the pointillists for broad, vigorous, swirling brushstrokes. In 1888 he settled at Arles, where he produced many paintings but suffered poverty, depression, and hallucinations. There he was joined by Gauguin, but they quarrelled, precipitating a crisis in which Van Gogh cut off his own ear; he subsequently spent a year in an asylum near by, where he painted *Starry Night*. His prodigious activity continued—he painted 70 canvases in the last 70 days of his life—but his acute depression culminated in his suicide. His letters to his brother Theo, of which more than 750 are extant, provide abundant information about his aesthetic aims and mental disturbances.

vanguard /'vængɑːd/ *n.* **1.** the foremost part of an army or fleet advancing or ready to do so. **2.** the leaders of a movement, opinion, etc. [f. OF *avan(t)garde (avant* before, *garde* guard)]

vanilla /və'nɪlə/ *n.* **1.** a substance obtained from the vanilla-pod or synthetically and used to flavour ices, chocolate, etc. **2.** a tropical climbing orchid of the genus *Vanilla* with fragrant flowers; the fruit of this. —**vanilla-pod** *n.* this fruit. [f. Sp. *vainilla* pod, dim. of *vaina* sheath, pod, f. L *vagina* sheath]

vanish /'vænɪʃ/ *v.t./i.* **1.** to disappear completely; to cease to exist. **2.** to cause to disappear. —**vanishing-point** *n.* the point at which receding parallel lines viewed in perspective appear to meet; the stage of complete disappearance. [f. OF *evanir* f. L (as EVANESCE)]

vanity /'vænɪtɪ/ *n.* **1.** conceit, especially about one's appearance. **2.** futility, worthlessness; something vain. —**vanity bag** *or* **case,** a bag or case carried by a woman and containing a small mirror, cosmetics, etc. [f. OF f. L *vanitas* (as VAIN)]

vanquish /'væŋkwɪʃ/ *v.t.* (literary) to conquer. [f. OF f. L *vincere*]

vantage /'vɑːntɪdʒ/ *n.* advantage, especially as a score in tennis. —**vantage-point** *n.* a place from which one has a good view of something. [f. AF (as ADVANTAGE)]

Vanuatu /vænwɑː'tuː/ a country consisting of a group of islands in the SW Pacific; pop. (1980) 117,000; official languages, English and French; capital, Vila. Discovered by the Portuguese in the early 17th c., the islands were administered jointly by Britain and France as the condominium of the New Hebrides. They became an independent republic within the Commonwealth in 1980.

vapid /'væpɪd/ *adj.* insipid, uninteresting. —**vapidity** /və'pɪdɪtɪ/ *n.,* **vapidly** *adv.,* **vapidness** *n.* [f. L. *vapidus*]

vaporize /'veɪpəraɪz/ *v.t./i.* to convert or be converted into

vapour. —**vaporization** /-'zeɪʃ(ə)n/ *n.,* **vaporizer** *n.* [f. foll.]

vapour /'veɪpə(r)/ *n.* **1.** moisture or other substance diffused or suspended in air. **2.** the gaseous form of a normally liquid or solid substance. —**vaporous** *adj.,* **vapoury** *adj.* [f. OF or L *vapor* steam]

Varanasi /və'rɑːnəsɪ/ (formerly Benares) a Hindu holy city on the Ganges in the State of Uttar Pradesh, India; pop. (1971) 560,296. Said to contain 1,500 temples and shrines, it is a place of pilgrimage for devout Hindus, who undergo ritual purification in the river.

Varangian /və'rændʒɪən/ *n.* a Norse rover, especially one of those who penetrated into Russia in the 9th-10th c. —*adj.* of the Varangians. [f. L, ult. f. ON, = confederate]

Varèse /'væerez/, Edgard (1883-1965), French-born composer. He emigrated to the USA in 1915, and it is the works composed in his adopted country that are known today, virtually all others being lost. His music employed traditional forces until the 1950s, when he began to experiment with tape-recordings and electronic instruments.

variable /'veərɪəb(ə)l/ *adj.* **1.** varying, changeable. **2.** that may be varied. **3.** (of a mathematical quantity) indeterminate, that may assume different numerical values. —*n.* a variable thing or quantity. —**variable star,** any star whose brightness changes, either irregularly because of unpredictable changes in the physical state of the star, or regularly. Irregular variables include those which undergo a single outburst, such as novae or supernovae. Periodic variables show regular changes in light intensity either because of eclipses by binary companions or because of regular changes within the stellar interior, as in the case of Cepheid variables. The period of variability may range from a few hours to several years. —**variability** /-'bɪlɪtɪ/ *n.,* **variably** *adv.* [f. OF f. L (as VARY)]

variance /'veərɪəns/ *n.* a discrepancy. —**at variance,** disagreeing, conflicting; in a state of discord or enmity. [f. OF f. L (as VARY)]

variant /'veərɪənt/ *adj.* differing in form or details from that named or from a standard; differing thus among themselves. —*n.* a variant form, spelling, type, etc. [as VARY]

variation /veərɪ'eɪʃ(ə)n/ *n.* **1.** varying; the extent to which a thing varies. **2.** a thing that varies from a type. **3.** music produced by repeating a theme in a different (usually more elaborate) form. [as VARY]

varicoloured /'veərɪkʌləd/ *adj.* **1.** variegated in colour. **2.** of various or different colours. [f. L *varius* (as VARIOUS) + COLOURED]

varicose /'værɪkəʊs/ *adj.* (of a vein etc.) permanently and abnormally dilated. —**varicosity** /-'kɒsɪtɪ/ *n.* [f. L (*varix* varicose vein)]

varied /'veərɪd/ *adj.* showing variety. [f. VARY]

variegated /'veərɪgeɪtɪd/ *adj.* marked with irregular patches of different colours. —**variegation** /-'geɪʃ(ə)n/ *n.* [f. L *variegare* (as VARIOUS)]

variety /və'raɪətɪ/ *n.* **1.** absence of uniformity; the quality of not being the same or of not being the same at all times. **2.** a quantity, collection, or range of different things. **3.** a class of things differing from others in the same general group; a specimen or member of such a class; a different form of a thing, quality, etc. **4.** an entertainment consisting of a mixed series of short performances of different kinds (e.g. singing, dancing, comedy acts, acrobatics). [f. F or L (as foll.)]

various /'veərɪəs/ *adj.* **1.** of several kinds, unlike one another. **2.** more than one, several; individual and separate. —**variously** *adv.* [f. L *varius* changing, diverse]

varlet /'vɑːlɪt/ *n.* (archaic) a menial, a rascal. [f. OF, var. of *vaslet* (cf. VALET)]

varna /'vɑːnə/ *n.* any of the four great Hindu castes. In Vedic religion, the first three classes of Aryan society were Brahmin, Kshatriya, and Vaisya. The fourth class, Sudra, was probably recruited later from the indigenous people of India. Each class was considered equally necessary to the social order, the separate functions being complementary. In modern India, varna has largely given way to the more specific requirements of caste and sub-caste. [Skr., = colour, class]

varnish /'vɑːnɪʃ/ *n.* **1.** a resinous solution used to give a hard shiny transparent coating; some other preparation for a similar purpose. **2.** an external appearance or display without underlying reality. —*v.t.* **1.** to apply varnish to. **2.** to gloss over (a fact). [f. OF *vernis* f. L or Gk, prob. f. *Berenice* in Cyrenaica]

Varro /ˈværəʊ/, Marcus Terentius (116–27 BC), Roman scholar and encyclopaedist. Of his voluminous works, which covered almost every branch of ancient knowledge and were a mine of information for later pagan and Christian authors, there survive (apart from fragments) only a work on agriculture and part of a work on the Latin language. He was also the author of literary satires and dialogues.

varsity /ˈvɑːsɪtɪ/ n. **1.** (colloq., esp. with ref. to sports) university. **2.** (US) the team representing a school or college etc. in a sport. [abbr.]

Varuna /ˈvʌrʊnə/ (Hinduism) one of the oldest of the gods in the Rig-Veda. Originally the sovereign lord of the universe and guardian of cosmic law, he is known in later Hinduism as god of the waters.

varve n. a pair of layers of silt deposited in lakes where a glacier melts, one being of fine silt (deposited in winter, when there is little melting) and one of coarser silt (deposited in summer, when the ice melts more freely). [f. Sw. varv layer]

vary /ˈveərɪ/ v.t./i. **1.** to make or become different. **2.** to be different or of different kinds. [f. OF or L variare (as VARIOUS)]

vas /væs/ n. (pl. **vasa** /ˈveɪsə/) a duct, a vessel. —**vas deferens** /ˈdefərenz/ (pl. **vasa deferentia** /defəˈrentɪə/), the spermatic duct of the testicle (ill. BODY 2). [L, = vessel]

Vasari /vəˈsɑːrɪ/, Giorgio (1511–74), Italian painter, architect, and biographer whose pioneering Lives of the Most Excellent Painters, Sculptors and Architects (1550, enlarged 1568) remains influential today and the starting-point for the study of Renaissance art, tracing the rise of Renaissance naturalism and humanism from the experiments of Cimabue and Giotto to the sophisticated styles of the 16th c.; he celebrated the art of Leonardo, Raphael, and particularly Michelangelo, whom he knew and admired, as the pinnacle of achievement. His own considerable achievements as painter and architect have sometimes been overshadowed by his importance as 'the first art historian worthy of the title'. His painting style can be classified as mannerist, and his major works are the vast frescoes, depicting the history of Florence and the Medici, in the Palazzo Vecchio in Florence, and those in the Sala Regia in the Vatican. Vasari was the architect of the Uffizi Palace in Florence and designed the tomb of Michelangelo in Sta Croce.

Vasco da Gama see GAMA.

vascular /ˈvæskjʊlə(r)/ adj. of or containing vessels for conveying blood, sap, etc. [f. L vasculum, dim. of VAS]

vase /vɑːz/ n. an open usually tall vessel of glass, pottery, etc., used for holding cut flowers or as an ornament. [F f. L vas vessel]

vasectomy /vəˈsektəmɪ/ n. surgical removal of a part of each vas deferens, especially to sterilize a patient. [f. VAS + -ECTOMY]

Vaseline /ˈvæsəliːn/ n. [P] a type of petroleum jelly used as an ointment etc. [f. G wasser water + Gk elaion oil]

vaso- /ˈveɪsəʊ/ comb. form vessel, blood-vessel. —**vasomotor** adj. causing constriction or dilatation of blood-vessels. [f. L vas vessel]

vassal /ˈvæs(ə)l/ n. **1.** a humble servant or dependant. **2.** (hist.) a holder of land by feudal tenure. —**vassalage** n. [f. OF f. L vassallus retainer; of Celtic origin]

vast /vɑːst/ adj. immense, very great in area or size. —**vastly** adv., **vastness** n. [f. L vastus]

VAT /vi: eɪ ˈtiː, væt/ abbr. value added tax.

vat n. a tank or other great vessel, especially for holding liquids in the process of brewing, tanning, dyeing, etc. —**vatful** n. [dial. var. of obs. fat, OE fæt]

Vatican /ˈvætɪkən/ the pope's palace and official residence in Rome; papal government. —**Vatican City,** an independent papal State in Rome, the seat of government of the Roman Catholic Church. The former papal States became incorporated into a unified Italy in 1870, and the temporal power of the pope was in suspense until the Lateran Treaty of 1929, signed between Pope Pius XI and Mussolini, which recognized the full and independent sovereignty of the Holy See in the City of the Vatican. It covers an area of 44 hectares (109 acres), and has its own police force, diplomatic service, postal service, coinage, and radio station. **Vatican Council,** the ecumenical council of the Roman Catholic Church held in 1869–70 and proclaiming the infallibility of the pope when speaking ex cathedra; a similar council held 1962–5. [F or f. L Vaticanus name of hill in Rome]

vaudeville /ˈvɔːd(ə)vɪl, ˈvəʊ-/ n. variety entertainment, popular from about 1880 to 1932, by which time films and radio had driven it into decline. [F, orig. of convivial song, esp. any of those composed by O. Basselin, 15th-c. poet born at Vau de Vire in Normandy]

Vaughan /vɔːn/, Henry (1621–95), British poet, born in Wales, who probably studied law and is known to have practised medicine. One of the Metaphysical Poets, his volumes of religious poetry include Silex Scintillans (1650, 1655), in which he acknowledges his debt to George Herbert, and The Mount of Olives, or Solitary Devotions (1652). His poems have a distinctive limpid ethereal quality which has classed him as a mystic.

Vaughan Williams /vɔːn ˈwɪljəmz/, Ralph (1872–1958), English composer. His music is often thought of as quintessentially English, and this is only partly due to the influence of folk music: he had a keen interest in English folk-songs, which he collected and arranged. He composed in almost every genre, from operas and symphonies to choral works for amateurs and for professional choirs, concertos for neglected instruments such as harmonica and tuba, a suite for pipes, etc. The basis of his work is melody; its visionary quality, broad humanity, and appeal at several levels make it a remarkable expression of the national spirit in music, just as the man himself personified all that was best in the English 19th-c. tradition of which he was a scion.

vault¹ /vɔːlt, vɒlt/ n. **1.** an arched roof (ill. CHURCH). **2.** a vault-like covering. **3.** an underground room used as a place of storage. **4.** a burial chamber. —v.t. (esp. in p.p.) to make in the form of a vault; to furnish with a vault or vaults. [f. OF, ult. f. L volvere roll]

vault² /vɔːlt, vɒlt/ v.t./i. to leap (over), especially while resting on the hand(s) or with the help of a pole. —n. a leap performed thus. —**vaulting-horse** n. a padded structure for vaulting over in a gymnasium. [f. OF vo(u)lter leap (as prec.)]

vaulting n. the arched work in a vaulted roof or ceiling. [f. VAULT¹]

vaunt v.t./i. (literary) to boast. —n. (literary) a boast. [f. AF f. L vanitare (vanus vain)]

VC abbr. Victoria Cross.

VD abbr. venereal disease.

VDU abbr. visual display unit.

've v.t./i. (colloq., usu. after pronouns) = HAVE. [abbr.]

veal n. calf's flesh as food. [f. AF f. L vitellus dim. of vitulus calf]

vector /ˈvektə(r)/ n. **1.** a quantity having direction as well as magnitude (e.g. velocity = speed in a given direction). **2.** a carrier of disease or infection. —**vectorial** /-ˈtɔːrɪəl/ adj. [L, = carrier (vehere convey)]

Veda /ˈveɪdə, ˈviː-/ n. (also **Vedas**) the most ancient and sacred literature of the Hindus, believed to have been revealed directly to the early seers. It contains ritual utterances of the early Aryans in India, composed in old Sanskrit and preserved by oral tradition, manuals for the priests of Vedic religion. The term applies first to the Rig-Veda; the 'triple Veda' includes the Sama-Veda and Yajur-Veda; the Atharva-Veda was added later. In its wider sense, the term also includes the Brahmanas and the mystical Aranyakas and Upanishads. [f. Skr., = (sacred) knowledge]

Vedanta /viːˈdɑːntə, vɪˈdæ-/ n. **1.** the Upanishads. **2.** a monistic Hindu philosophy founded on these. —**Vedantic** adj. [f. Skr. veda knowledge, anta end)]

Vedda /ˈvedə/ n. (pl. same) an aboriginal of Sri Lanka. [f. Sinhalese, = hunter]

Vedic /ˈveɪdɪk, ˈviː-/ adj. of the Veda(s). —n. the language of the Vedas, an old form of Sanskrit. —**Vedic religion,** the ancient religion of the Aryan tribes who entered NW India c. 1500 BC; the religious beliefs and practices contained in the Veda. It was a religion of ritual sacrifice to many gods, especially Indra, Varuna, Soma, and Agni; animal, vegetable, and human sacrifice are described. Vedic society is divided into four distinct classes (varna) that are still in evidence in Hinduism today. The increasing complexity of Vedic ritual led to the dominance of the specialist priesthood, the composition of the Brahmanas, and the rigidity of orthodox Brahmanism (c. 900 BC onwards). The transition to classical Hinduism began in about the 5th c. BC.

veer v.i. to change direction or course; (of the wind) to change gradually in a clockwise direction. —n. a change of direction. [f. F virer, perh. ult. f. L gyrare gyrate]

veg /vedʒ/ n. (colloq.) vegetable(s). [abbr.]

Vega /ˈviːgə/ the brightest star in the constellation Lyra, discovered to have a system of tiny particles (gathered round the star) which may eventually coalesce into planets.

[f. Arab., = the falling (vulture), i.e. the constellation Lyra]

Vega Carpio /ˈveɪgə ˈkɑːpɪəʊ/, Lope Felix de (1562-1635), Spanish poet and playwright, who sailed with the Armada in 1588, an experience which inspired one of his less-regarded works, an epic which violently attacked England and Drake. A celebrated wit, idolized by his contemporaries, he was immensely prolific in many genres. He is said to have written 1,500 plays, of which several hundred survive, and is regarded as the founder of Spanish drama.

vegan /ˈviːgən/ n. a strict vegetarian who eats neither meat nor animal products (e.g. eggs). —adj. of vegans or their diet. [f. VEGETARIAN]

vegetable /ˈvedʒɪtəb(ə)l/ n. 1. a plant of which some part is used (raw or cooked) for food, especially as an accompaniment to meat. 2. a person living a dull monotonous life; one who is physically alive but mentally inert owing to injury, illness, or abnormality. —adj. of, from, or relating to plant life. [f. OF or L (as VEGETATE)]

vegetal /ˈvedʒɪt(ə)l/ adj. of plants; of the nature of plants. [as VEGETATE]

vegetarian /vedʒɪˈteərɪən/ n. a person who eats no meat and whose diet includes vegetables, cereals, seeds, fruit, and nuts, with (or in strict observance without) eggs and dairy products. —**vegetarianism** n. [f. VEGETABLE]

vegetate /ˈvedʒɪteɪt/ v.i. 1. to lead a dull existence devoid of intellectual or social acitivity; to live in comfortably uneventful retirement or seclusion. 2. to grow as plants do. [f. L vegetare to animate (vegetus active)]

vegetation /vedʒɪˈteɪʃ(ə)n/ n. plants collectively, plant life. [as prec.]

vegetative /ˈvedʒɪtətɪv/ adj. 1. concerned with growth and development rather than (sexual) reproduction. 2. of vegetation. [f. OF or L (as VEGETATE)]

vehement /ˈviːəmənt/ adj. showing or caused by strong feeling, ardent. —**vehemence** n., **vehemently** adv. [f. F or L vehemens]

vehicle /ˈviːɪk(ə)l/ n. 1. a conveyance for transporting passengers or goods on land or in space. 2. a medium by which thought, feeling, or action is expressed or displayed. 3. a liquid etc. as a medium for suspending pigments, drugs, etc. —**vehicular** /vɪˈhɪkjʊlə(r)/ [f. F or L vehiculum (as VECTOR)]

veil /veɪl/ n. 1. a piece of fine net or other fabric worn as part of a head-dress or to protect or conceal the face. 2. a piece of linen etc. as part of a nun's head-dress. 3. a curtain, especially that separating the sanctuary in the Jewish Temple. 4. a disguise, a pretext. —v.t. 1. to cover (as) with a veil. 2. to conceal partly. —**beyond the veil**, in the unknown state of life after death. **draw a veil over**, to avoid discussing or calling attention to. **take the veil**, to become a nun. [f. AF f. L velum]

vein /veɪn/ n. 1. any of the tubes by which blood is conveyed from all parts of the body to the heart; (pop.) any blood-vessel. 2. a rib of a leaf or insect's wing. 3. a streak or stripe of a different colour in wood, marble, cheese, etc. 4. a fissure in rock filled with ore. 5. a distinctive character or tendency, a mood. —**veined** adj., **veiny** adj. [f. OF f. L vena]

Velázquez /vɪˈlæskwɪz/, Diego Rodríguez de Silva y (1599-1660), Spanish painter. His religious works are naturalistic portraits rather than idealized types, and at the same time he painted a series of everyday subjects from Spanish domestic life and still-lifes before becoming court painter to Philip IV in 1623. There his portraits humanized the stiff and formal Spanish tradition of idealized figures and tended towards naturalness and simplicity, rendering the character of the sitter with startling perception. In Las Meninas (The Maids of Honour, c.1656) the Infanta and her attendants are shown watching a sitting for a portrait of the king and queen, with the royal couple reflected in a mirror in the background, and the painter himself at work; it so impressed Picasso (who saw it at the age of 15) that in 1957 he painted 44 variations upon its theme.

Velcro /ˈvelkrəʊ/ n. [P] a fastener for clothes etc., consisting of two strips of fabric with tiny loops on one and hooks on the other which cling together when pressed one upon the other. [f. F velours croché hooked velvet]

veld /velt/ n. (also **veldt**) open grassland in southern Africa. [Afrik., = FIELD]

Velde /velt/, van de, Dutch family of painters. Willem I (1611-93) executed detailed portraits of ships and was for a time official artist to the Dutch fleet; his sons were Adriaen

(1636-72) and Willem II (1633-1707). Adriaen, the more versatile and gifted of the brothers, painted landscapes, biblical and genre scenes, and portraits, producing hundreds of paintings and also etchings. Willem II was one of Holland's greatest marine painters, known for the sensitive details of weather and light on his paintings of ships at sea. He went to England in 1672 and from 1674 Charles II gave him a retaining fee of £100 yearly, royal patronage enjoyed by his father before him.

veleta /vəˈliːtə/ n. an old-fashioned ballroom dance in triple time. [Sp., = weather-vane (vela cloth, veil)]

Velleius Paterculus /veˈleɪəs pəˈtɜːkjʊləs/ (c.19 BC- after AD 30) Roman historian who in early life served abroad with the future emperor Tiberius. His Roman History in two books, reaching from the early history of Greece and Rome to AD 30, is notable for its rhetorical manner and for its adulation of Tiberius.

vellum /ˈveləm/ n. 1. fine parchment originally from the skin of the calf; a manuscript on this. 2. smooth writing-paper imitating vellum. [f. OF velin (as VEAL)]

velocipede /vɪˈlɒsɪpiːd/ n. (hist.) a light vehicle propelled by the rider, especially an early form of bicycle or tricycle (see BICYCLE). [f. F f. L velox swift + pes foot]

velocity /vɪˈlɒsɪtɪ/ n. speed, especially in a given direction (usually of inanimate things). [f. F or L (velox swift)]

velour /vəˈlʊə(r)/ n. (also **velours**) a plush-like woven fabric or felt. [F, = velvet]

velvet /ˈvelvɪt/ n. 1. a closely woven fabric (originally of silk) with a thick short pile on one side. 2. a furry skin on a growing antler. —adj. of, like, or as soft as velvet. —**on velvet**, in an advantageous or prosperous position. **velvet glove**, outward gentleness cloaking sternness or inflexibility. —**velvety** adj. [f. OF veluotte, ult. f. L villus down]

velveteen /velvɪˈtiːn/ n. cotton velvet. [f. prec.]

Ven. abbr. Venerable (as the title of an archdeacon).

vena cava /viːnə ˈkeɪvə/ each of the (usually two) veins carrying deoxygenated blood into the heart (ill. BODY 3). [L, = hollow vein]

venal /ˈviːn(ə)l/ adj. (of a person) that may be bribed; (of conduct etc.) characteristic of a venal person. —**venality** /viːˈnælɪtɪ/ n., **venally** adv. [f. L venalis (venum thing for sale)]

vend v.t. to offer (small wares) for sale. —**vending-machine** n. a slot-machine for the automatic retail of small articles. [f. F or L vendere sell (as VENAL)]

vendetta /venˈdetə/ n. a blood feud; prolonged bitter hostility. [It. f. L vindicta (as VINDICTIVE)]

vendor n. 1. (esp. Law) one who sells. 2. a vending-machine. [f. AF (as VEND)]

veneer /vɪˈnɪə(r)/ v.t. 1. to cover (wood) with a thin layer of a finer wood. 2. (esp. in p.p.) to disguise (character etc.) superficially. —n. 1. a layer used in veneering. 2. a superficial show of some good quality. [earlier fineer f. G furni(e)ren f. OF (as FURNISH)]

venerable /ˈvenərəb(ə)l/ adj. 1. entitled to veneration on account of character, age, associations, etc. 2. the title of an archdeacon in the Church of England. —**venerability** /-ˈbɪlɪtɪ/ n., **venerably** adv. [f. OF or L (as foll.)]

venerate /ˈvenəreɪt/ v.t. to regard with deep respect; to honour as hallowed or sacred. —**veneration** /-ˈreɪʃ(ə)n/ n., **venerator** n. [f. L venerari adore, revere]

venereal /vɪˈnɪərɪəl/ adj. of sexual desire or intercourse; relating to venereal disease. —**venereal disease**, a disease contracted chiefly by sexual intercourse with a person already infected. —**venereally** adv. [f. L venereus (venus sexual love)]

Venetian /vɪˈniːʃ(ə)n/ adj. of Venice. —n. a native or the dialect of Venice. —**venetian blind**, a window-blind of horizontal slats that can be adjusted to let in or exclude light. [f. OF, assim. to L Venetianus (Venetia Venice)]

Venezuela /veneˈzweɪlə/ a country on the north coast of South America, with a coastline on the Caribbean Sea; pop. (1981) 14,516,735; official language, Spanish; capital, Caracas. Columbus discovered the mouth of the Orinoco River in 1498, and in the following year Vespucci explored the coast. It was the early Italian explorers who gave the country its name (= little Venice), when they saw native Indian houses built on stilts over water and were reminded of the city of Venice. Settled by the Spanish in the 16th c., Venezuela won its independence in 1821 after a ten-year struggle, but did not finally emerge as a separate nation until its secession from the Federation of Grand Colombia in 1830. Its history since then has been characterized by endemic political instability, civil war, and dictatorship, and by the generation of considerable wealth from its well-established oil industry. —**Venezuelan** adj. & n.

vengeance /ˈvendʒəns/ n. revenge for hurt or harm to oneself or to a person etc. whose cause one supports. —**with a vengeance,** to an extreme degree, more than was expected. [f. OF (venger avenge f. L, as VINDICATE)]

vengeful adj. vindictive, seeking vengeance. —**vengefully** adv., **vengefulness** n. [f. obs. venge avenge (as prec.) + -FUL]

venial /ˈviːnɪəl/ adj. (of a sin or fault) pardonable, excusable, not mortal. —**veniality** /viːnɪˈælɪtɪ/ n., **venially** adv. [f. OF f. L (venia forgiveness)]

Venice /ˈvenɪs/ a city of NE Italy, on a lagoon of the Adriatic Sea, built on numerous islands that are separated by canals and linked by bridges; pop. (est. 1981) 362,494. It was a powerful republic in the Middle Ages, and from the 13th to the 16th c. a leading sea-power, controlling trade to the Levant and ruling parts of the eastern Mediterranean. Its commercial importance declined after the Cape route to India was discovered at the end of the 16th c., but it remained an important centre of art and music. After the Napoleonic Wars Venice was placed under Austrian rule; it was incorporated into a unified Italy in 1866.

venison /ˈvenɪsən/ n. deer's flesh as food. [f. OF f. L venatio hunting]

Venn diagram a diagram using overlapping and intersecting circles etc. to show the relationships between mathematical sets. [f. J. Venn, British logician (d. 1923)]

venom /ˈvenəm/ n. **1.** poisonous fluid secreted by certain snakes, scorpions, etc., and injected into a victim by a bite or sting. **2.** virulence of feeling, language, or conduct. [f. OF f. L venenum poison]

venomous /ˈvenəməs/ adj. **1.** secreting venom. **2.** full of venom in feeling etc. —**venomously** adv. [as prec.]

venous /ˈviːnəs/ adj. of, full of, or contained in veins. [f. L venosus (vena vein)]

vent¹ n. **1.** a hole or opening allowing air, gas, or liquid to pass out of or into a confined space. **2.** the anus, especially of a lower animal. **3.** an outlet; free passage or play. —v.t. **1.** to make a vent in. **2.** to give vent or free expression to. —**vent light,** a small window, hinged at the top edge (ill. HOUSES). [f. F f. L ventus wind]

vent² n. a slit in a garment, especially in the lower edge of the back of a coat. [f. OF fente f. L findere cleave]

ventilate /ˈventɪleɪt/ v.t. **1.** to cause air to circulate freely in (a room etc.). **2.** to express (a question, grievance, etc.) publicly for consideration and discussion. —**ventilation** /-ˈleɪʃ(ə)n/ n. [f. L ventilare blow, winnow (ventus wind)]

ventilator n. **1.** an appliance or aperture for ventilating a room etc. **2.** equipment for maintaining breathing artificially. [f. prec.]

ventral /ˈventr(ə)l/ adj. of or on the abdomen. —**ventrally** adv. [f. L venter abdomen]

ventricle /ˈventrɪk(ə)l/ n. a cavity in the body, the hollow part of an organ, especially each of four in the brain or of two in the heart that pump blood into the arteries by contracting (ill. BODY 3). —**ventricular** /-ˈtrɪkjʊlə(r)/ adj. [f. L ventriculus dim. of venter belly]

ventriloquist /venˈtrɪləkwɪst/ n. an entertainer who produces voice-sounds so that they seem to come from a source other than himself. —**ventriloquism** n. [f. L ventriloquus (venter belly, loqui speak)]

ventriloquize /venˈtrɪləkwaɪz/ v.i. to use ventriloquism. [f. prec.]

venture /ˈventʃə(r)/ an undertaking that involves risk; a commercial speculation. —v.t./i. **1.** to dare, not to be afraid; to dare to go, do, or utter. **2.** to expose to risk, to stake. **3.** to take risks. —**at a venture,** at random; without previous consideration. **venture on,** to dare to engage in or make etc. **Venture Scout,** a member of the senior section of the Scout Association. [as ADVENTURE]

venturesome adj. **1.** willing to take risks, daring. **2.** risky. [f. prec. + -SOME]

venturi tube /venˈtjʊərɪ/ a device consisting of a short section of tube which is narrower than the parts at each end, so that gas or liquid under pressure flows through it faster, used to produce an effect of suction or in measuring the rate of flow. [f. G. B. Venturi, Italian physicist (d. 1822)]

venue /ˈvenjuː/ n. **1.** an appointed place of meeting, especially for a sports match. **2.** the county etc. within which a jury must be gathered and a cause tried. [F, = coming (venir come)]

Venus /ˈviːnəs/ **1.** (Rom. myth.) an Italian goddess, not originally Roman. In classical Rome she was identified with Aphrodite, though she seems to have been formerly a spirit of kitchen gardens and their fertility. Famous statues of her include the Venus of Milo (see separate entry). **2.** (Astron.) the second planet of the solar system, almost equal in size to Earth and orbiting 108 million km from the sun, known to the Greeks as 'Hesperus' and 'Phosphorus'—the morning and evening star—in recognition of its appearances in the twilight sky, where it outshines all celestial objects other than the sun and moon. The early telescopic observations of Galileo revealed its phases clearly, demonstrating that it did orbit the sun. Because of the total cloud cover no surface detail can be seen through even the largest telescope. The clouds, rich in sulphuric acid, are supported in a dense atmosphere of carbon dioxide which traps the light and heat of the sun to produce surface temperatures of 460 °C. The topography of the planet is largely flat, but with two raised 'continental' plateaux. The surface has been revealed by space probes to be a rocky plain, sweltering under a dull orange sky.

Venus of Milo /ˈmaɪləʊ, ˈmiː-/ a classical sculpture of Aphrodite dated to c.100 BC. It was discovered on the Greek island of Melos in 1820 and is now in the Louvre, having formed part of the war loot acquired by Napoleon on his campaigns. The most famous antique sculpture, it is essentially an eclectic piece, the head being in 5th-c. style while the spiral movement of the body betrays a Hellenistic concern for dynamic sculptural effect.

veracious /vəˈreɪʃəs/ adj. **1.** truthful. **2.** (of a statement etc.) that is or is meant to be true. —**veraciously** adv., **veracity** /vəˈræsɪtɪ/ n. [f. L verax (verus true)]

veranda /vəˈrændə/ n. a roofed terrace along the side of a house. [f. Hindi f. Port. varanda]

verb n. a word used to indicate an action, state, or occurrence (e.g. bring, become, happen). [f. OF or L verbum, lit. 'word']

verbal adj. **1.** of or in words. **2.** spoken, not written. **3.** of a verb. **4.** (of a translation) literal. —n. (colloq.) a verbal statement, especially one made to the police. —**verbal noun,** a noun (e.g. singing, dancing, or other nouns ending in -ing) derived from a verb and partly sharing its constructions. —**verbally** adv. [f. F or L (as prec.)]

verbalism /ˈvɜːbəlɪz(ə)m/ n. minute attention to words. [f. prec.]

verbalize /ˈvɜːbəlaɪz/ v.t./i. **1.** to express in words. **2.** to be verbose. —**verbalization** /-ˈzeɪʃ(ə)n/ n. [f. VERBAL]

verbatim /vɜːˈbeɪtɪm/ adv. & adj. in exactly the same words, word for word. [f. L (verbum word)]

verbena /vɜːˈbiːnə/ n. a herb or small shrub of the genus Verbena. —**lemon verbena,** a similar plant (Lippia citriodora) with lemon-scented leaves. [L, orig. = sacred bough of olive]

verbiage /ˈvɜːbɪdʒ/ n. an excessive number of words used to express an idea. [F (obs. verbeier chatter f. verbe word, as VERB)]

verbose /vɜːˈbəʊs/ adj. using or expressed in more words than are needed. —**verbosely** adv., **verbosity** /vɜːˈbɒsɪtɪ/ n. [f. L verbosus (verbum word)]

verdant /ˈvɜːd(ə)nt/ adj. (of grass etc.) green, fresh-coloured; (of a field etc.) covered with green grass etc. —**verdancy** n. [perh. f. OF verdoier be green f. L viridis green]

Verdi /ˈveədiː/, Giuseppe (1813–1901), Italian composer. His first major operatic success was Nabucco (Nabucodonosor, 1842); he followed it with a period of sustained activity which he described as his 'years in the galleys', which resulted in a series of operas. The 1850s saw the completion of two further masterpieces, Rigoletto (1851), based on Hugo's Le Roi s'amuse, and La Traviata (1853), a failure on its first production but since then known as one of the most popular of operas. He was involved in the movement for Italian unity, his name being identified with the cause as an acrostic (VIVA VERDI, 'Viva Vittorio Emanuele, Re d'Italia'), and in 1868 accepted a commission to compose an opera in honour of the opening of the Suez Canal: Aida was in the event first performed at La Scala in 1871. Two operas based on Shakespeare followed, Otello (1884–7) and the glorious comedy Falstaff (1889–93), the contradiction to any accusation that Verdi's talents were limited to tragedy and high drama. Indeed, Verdi's strength lies in his strong feeling for characterization as much as in his original and nearly always effective orchestration, and more than in his gift for memorable tunes, so often the butt of unsympathetic criticism. His Requiem Mass (1873–4) is a powerful work which offsets the dramatic force of the Day of Judgement against a moving expression of human faith.

verdict /ˈvɜ:dɪkt/ n. **1.** the decision of a jury on an issue of fact in a civil or criminal cause. **2.** a decision or opinion given after examining, testing, or experiencing something. [f. AF *verdit* (*veir* true f. L *verus*, *dit* = DICTUM)]

verdigris /ˈvɜ:dɪgrɪs, -ri:s/ n. a green deposit on copper or brass. [f. OF, = green of Greece]

Verdon-Roe /ˈvɜ:d(ə)n ˈrəʊ/, Sir Edwin Alliott Verdon (1877–1958), English engineer and aircraft designer. He built the first British seaplane to rise from the water and (in 1912) the first cabin aircraft, and invented anti-dazzle car headlights. With his brother H. V. Roe he founded the Avro Company (1910–28) and built a number of planes of which the Avro 504 was the most successful; in 1928 he formed the Saunders-Roe Company to design and manufacture flying-boats.

verdure /ˈvɜ:djə(r), -djʊə(r)/ n. green vegetation; the greenness of this. —**verdurous** adj. [f. OF (*verd* green f. L *viridis*)]

verge[1] n. **1.** a brink or border (usu. *fig.*). **2.** a grass edging of a road, flower-bed, etc. **3.** (in the mechanism of a clock) the spindle or arbor of the balance in a vertical escapement (ill. TIME). [f. OF f. L *virga* rod]

verge[2] v.i. to incline downwards or in a specified direction. —**verge on**, to border on, to approach closely. [f. L *vergere* incline]

verger n. an official in a church who acts as caretaker and attendant; an officer who bears a staff before a bishop or other dignitary. [as VERGE[1]]

verifiable /ˈverɪfaɪəb(ə)l/ adj. that may be verified. [f. foll.]

verify /ˈverɪfaɪ/ v.t. to establish the truth or correctness of by examination or demonstration; (of an event etc.) to bear out, to fulfil (a prediction or promise). —**verification** /-fɪˈkeɪʃ(ə)n/ n., **verifier** n. [f. OF f. L *verificare* (*verus* true, *facere* make)]

verily /ˈverɪli/ adv. (*archaic*) really, truly. [f. VERY]

verisimilitude /verɪsɪˈmɪlɪtjuːd/ n. the appearance of being true or real. [f. L, = resemblance to the truth (*verus* true, *similis* like)]

veritable /ˈverɪtəb(ə)l/ adj. real, rightly so called. —**veritably** adv. [OF (as foll.)]

verity /ˈverɪti/ n. a true statement; truth. [f. OF f. L *veritas* truth (*verus* true)]

Vermeer /vɜ:ˈmɪə(r)/, Jan (Johannes) (1632–75), Dutch painter whose short life was spent in Delft. Little is known of him other than that he took over the family silk business in 1655 in order to support his ever-growing family of children. It appears that he made no money from his art in his lifetime, and as few as 36 paintings are known to be by his hand. Most of these are simple genre pictures, often with a single figure (his wife as the model) or views of streets and towns; his work is distinguished by its clear design and simple form, and its harmonious balance of predominant yellows, blues, and greys. No other artist has enjoyed so dramatic a change from obscurity to fame. Virtually unknown, until the later 19th c. Vermeer was as neglected after his death as he had apparently been in his lifetime.

vermicelli /vɜ:mɪˈseli, -tʃeli/ n. pasta made in long slender threads. [It., dim. of *verme* f. L *vermis* worm]

vermicide /ˈvɜ:mɪsaɪd/ n. a drug that kills worms. [f. L *vermis* worm + -CIDE]

vermiform /ˈvɜ:mɪfɔ:m/ adj. worm-shaped. —**vermiform appendix**, a small blind tube extending from the caecum in man and some other mammals. [f. L *vermis* worm + FORM]

vermilion /vəˈmɪljən/ n. **1.** cinnabar. **2.** a brilliant red pigment made by grinding this or artificially. **3.** the colour of this. —adj. of this colour. [f. OF *vermeillon* (*vermeil* f. L *vermiculus* dim. of *vermis* worm)]

vermin /ˈvɜ:mɪn/ n. **1.** (usu. treated as *pl.*) common mammals and birds injurious to game, crops, etc., e.g. foxes, mice, owls. **2.** noxious or parasitic worms or insects. **3.** vile persons, those harmful to society. [f. OF, ult. f. L *vermis* worm]

verminous /ˈvɜ:mɪnəs/ adj. of the nature of vermin; infested with vermin. [f. prec. or L *verminosus*]

Vermont /vɜ:ˈmɒnt/ a State in the north-eastern USA bordering on Canada. Explored and settled by the French (17th–18th c.) it became an independent republic in 1777 and the 14th State of the USA in 1791; capital, Montpelier.

vermouth /ˈvɜ:məθ/ n. a wine flavoured with aromatic herbs. [f. F f. G *wermut* wormwood]

vernacular /vəˈnækjʊlə(r)/ n. **1.** the language or dialect of the country. **2.** the language of a particular class or group. **3.** homely speech. —adj. (of a language) of one's native country, not of foreign origin or of learned formation. [f. L *vernaculus* domestic, native (*verna* home-born slave)]

vernal /ˈvɜ:n(ə)l/ adj. of, occurring in, or appropriate to spring. —**vernally** adv. [f. L *vernalis* (*vernus* f. *ver* spring)]

Verne /veən/, Jules (1828–1905), French novelist who achieved great and enduring popularity by the combination of adventure and popular science in his tales, which included *De la terre à la lune* (1865), a story of an earth-to-moon journey, launched by a cannon. His work anticipates the principle adopted by later writers of science fiction: a hypothesis, and an examination of its consequences, made interesting by a story woven around it.

vernicle /ˈvɜ:nɪk(ə)l/ n. a cloth with a representation of Christ's face, especially one miraculously so impressed after its use by St Veronica (see entry). [f. OF f. L *veronica* (used in same sense) f. VERONICA]

vernier /ˈvɜ:nɪə(r)/ n. a small movable graduated scale for obtaining fractional parts of subdivisions on the fixed scale of a barometer etc. [f. P. *Vernier*, French mathematician (d. 1637)]

Veronese /verəˈneɪzi/ (Paolo Caliari, c.1528–88), Italian painter, born at Verona, whose use of cool silvery colours and soft yellows persisted in all his work. By about 1553 he had established himself in Venice and was already popular. Apart from his frescoes, his masterpieces were great feast-scenes of pageantry and splendour (e.g. *The Marriage Feast at Cana*, 1562). With the help of a large workshop, including three of his sons and his brother, his output was enormous. Unfortunately the treatment of religious themes was not always felt to be sufficiently respectful, and in 1573 Veronese was summoned before the Inquisition on a charge of irreverence in his painting of the *Feast in the House of Levi*.

Veronica /vəˈrɒnɪkə/, St, a woman of Jerusalem said to have offered her headcloth to Christ on the way to Calvary, to wipe the blood and sweat from his face. The cloth is said to have retained the image of his features.

veronica /vəˈrɒnɪkə/ n. **1.** a plant of the genus *Veronica*, speedwell. **2.** a vernicle. [L, f. woman's name *Veronica*]

verruca /vəˈru:kə/ n. (*pl.* **-cae** /-si:/ or **-cas**) a wart or similar protuberance. [L]

Versailles /veəˈsaɪ/ a town SW of Paris, noted for its royal palace, of which the central portion was built by Louis XIII and the wings and other edifices by Louis XIV. The grandeur of its design in the French classical style, and the elaborate gardens full of fountains and statuary, embody the whole spirit of the French monarchy and the courtly culture for which it stood. Its active life terminated and its *raison d'être* was gone when in October 1789 the Paris revolutionaries forced Louis XVI to leave for the city. —**Treaty of Versailles**, a treaty which terminated the American War of Independence in 1783; a treaty signed in 1919 which, along with a series of associated agreements, brought a formal end to the First World War, redivided the territory of the defeated Central Powers, and restricted Germany's armed forces. The Treaty in fact represented an unhappy compromise between conciliation and punishment, leaving Germany smarting under what she considered a vindictive settlement while not sufficiently restricting her ability eventually to rearm and seek forcible redress.

versatile /ˈvɜ:sətaɪl/ adj. able to do or to be used for many different things. —**versatility** /-ˈtɪlɪti/ n. [F, or f. L *versare* turn]

verse n. **1.** a metrical form of composition. **2.** a stanza of metrical lines; a metrical line. **3.** each of the short numbered divisions of the Bible. [OE & f. OF f. L *versus* turn of plough, furrow, line of writing (*vertere* turn)]

versed /vɜ:st/ adj. (with *in*) experienced or skilled in, having a knowledge of. [f. F or L *versatus* (*versari* be engaged in)]

versicle /ˈvɜ:sɪk(ə)l/ n. each of the short sentences in a liturgy said or sung by a priest etc. and alternating with the responses. [f. OF or L *versiculus* dim. of *versus* (see VERSE)]

versify /ˈvɜ:sɪfaɪ/ v.t./i. to turn into or express in verse; to compose verses. —**versification** /-fɪˈkeɪʃ(ə)n/ n. [f. OF f. L *versificare* (as VERSE, *facere* make)]

version /ˈvɜ:ʃ(ə)n/ n. **1.** an account of a matter from a particular person's point of view. **2.** a book or work etc. in

Vestments and Church Furniture

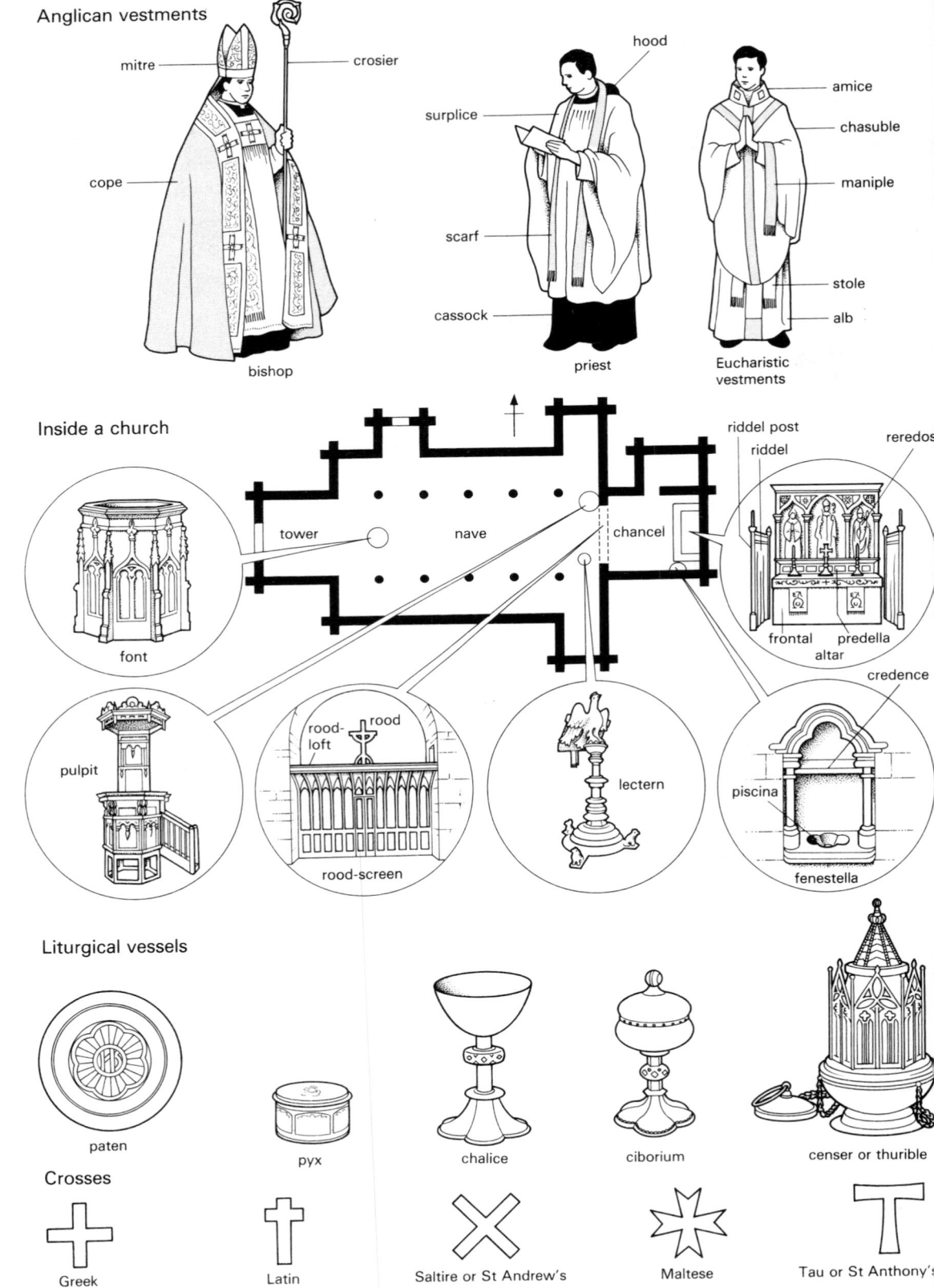

Anglican vestments

mitre — crosier

cope

bishop

hood

surplice

scarf

cassock

priest

amice

chasuble

maniple

stole

alb

Eucharistic
vestments

Inside a church

riddel post
riddel
reredos

tower

nave

chancel

frontal   predella
altar

credence

font

rood-
loft   rood

pulpit

lectern

piscina

rood-screen

fenestella

Liturgical vessels

paten

pyx

chalice

ciborium

censer or thurible

Crosses

Greek

Latin

Saltire or St Andrew's

Maltese

Tau or St Anthony's

a particular edition or translation. **3.** a particular variant. [F or f. L (*vertere* turn)]

verso *n*. (*pl*. **-os**) the left-hand page of an open book, the back of a leaf of a book etc. (cf. RECTO). [f. L *verso* (*folio*) = turned (leaf) (*vertere* turn)]

versus /ˈvɜːsəs/ *prep*. (esp. *Law* and in sport) against. [L, = against]

vert *n*. (in heraldry) green. [f. OF f. L *viridis* green]

vertebra /ˈvɜːtɪbrə/ *n*. (*pl*. **-ae** /-iː/) each segment of the backbone (ill. BODY 1). —**vertebral** *adj*. [L (*vertere* turn)]

vertebrate /ˈvɜːtɪbrət, -reɪt/ *adj*. having a spinal column, and thus belonging to the subphylum Vertebrata of the phylum Chordata, which includes fish, amphibians, reptiles, birds, and mammals. —*n*. a vertebrate animal. [f. L. *vertebratus* jointed (as prec.)]

vertex /ˈvɜːteks/ *n*. (*pl*. **vertices** /-ɪsiːz/ or **vertexes**) **1.** the highest point of a hill or structure; the apex. **2.** each angular point of a triangle, polygon, etc. (ill. SHAPES); the meeting-point of the lines that form an angle. [L, = whirlpool, crown of head]

vertical /ˈvɜːtɪk(ə)l/ *adj*. **1.** at right angles to the plane of the horizon. **2.** in the direction from top to bottom of a picture etc. **3.** of or at the vertex. —*n*. a vertical line or plane. —**vertical take-off,** the take-off of an aircraft directly upwards. —**vertically** *adv*. [F or f. L (as prec.)]

vertiginous /vɜːˈtɪdʒɪnəs/ *adj*. of or causing vertigo. [f. L (as foll.)]

vertigo /ˈvɜːtɪɡəʊ/ *n*. (*pl*. **-os**) dizziness. [L, = whirling (*vertere* turn)]

vervain /ˈvɜːveɪn/ *n*. a herbaceous plant of the genus *Verbena*, especially *V. officinalis* with small blue, white, or purple flowers. [f. OF f. L, = VERBENA]

verve *n*. enthusiasm, vigour, especially in artistic or literary work. [F, orig. = form of expression, f. L *verba* words]

very /ˈverɪ/ *adv*. **1.** in a high degree. **2.** (with superlative adjectives or *own*) in the fullest sense. **3.** exactly. **4.** (*archaic*) genuine, truly so called, —*adj*. **1.** itself or himself etc. and no other; actual, truly such. **2.** extreme, utter. —**not very,** in a low degree; far from being. **very good** *or* **well,** an expression of approval or consent. **very high frequency,** (in radio) 30–300 megahertz. [f. OF *verai* f. L *verus* truth]

Very light /ˈverɪ, ˈvɪərɪ/ a flare projected from a pistol for signalling or temporarily illuminating part of a battlefield etc. [f. E. W. *Very*, Amer. inventor (d. 1910)]

Vesalius /vɪˈseɪlɪəs/, Andreas (1514–64), Flemish anatomist who challenged traditional theories of anatomy which he held to be seriously flawed in being based upon the bodies of apes. This was a guess, but one borne out by later studies. His major work *De humani corporis fabrica* (1543), containing accurate descriptions of human anatomy, owed its great historical impact, however, more to the woodcuts of his dissections (drawn and engraved by someone else) than to Vesalius' text. He became physician to the emperor Charles V but died at the age of 49 as the result of a shipwreck.

vesica /ˈvesɪkə, vɪˈsaɪkə/ *n*. a pointed oval used as an aureole in medieval sculpture and painting. [L, = bladder, blister]

vesicle /ˈvesɪk(ə)l/ *n*. a small bladder, blister, or bubble. [f. F or L *vesicula* dim. of *vesica* bladder]

Vespasian /vesˈpeɪʒ(ə)n/ (Titus Flavius Vespasianus, AD 9–79) the first Flavian Roman emperor 69–79. A distinguished general (he played a leading part in Claudius' invasion of Britain), he was acclaimed emperor by the legions in Egypt during the civil wars that followed the death of Nero, and gained control of Italy after the defeat of Vitellius. He restored financial and military order after the chaos of civil war and was able to restore the Capitol, build his Forum and Temple of Peace, and start work on the Colosseum.

vespers /ˈvespəz/ *n.pl*. the evening service in the Western (Roman Catholic) Church. [f. OF f. L (*vesper* evening, evening star]

Vespucci /veˈspuːtʃɪ/, Amerigo (1451–512), Florentine merchant and explorer. While in the service of the king of Portugal, Vespucci made several voyages to the New World and claimed, on dubious authority, to have been the first to sight the mainland of South America (1497). The name America is said to have been derived from his own first name, but there are other suggestions of its origin.

vessel /ˈves(ə)l/ *n*. **1.** a hollow receptacle, especially for liquid. **2.** a hollow structure designed to travel on water and carry people or goods, a ship or boat. **3.** a tubelike structure holding or conveying blood or sap etc. in the body of an animal or plant. [f. AF f. L *vascellum* dim. of *vas* vessel]

vest¹ *n*. **1.** a knitted or woven undergarment covering the trunk of the body. **2.** (*US* & in commerce) a waistcoat. —**vest-pocket** *adj*. of a very small size, as if suitable for carrying in a waistcoat pocket. [f. F f. It. f. L *vestis* garment]

vest² *v.t./i*. **1.** to confer (on) as a firm or legal right. **2.** (of property or a right etc.; with *in*) to come into the possession of. **3.** (usu. *archaic*) to clothe. —**vested interest** *or* **right,** one securely held by right or by long association. **a vested interest in,** an expectation of benefiting from. [f. OF f. L *vestire* clothe (as prec.)]

Vesta /ˈvestə/ **1.** (*Rom. myth*.) goddess of the hearth and household. Her State worship was not in a temple but in a round building (doubtless an imitation in stone of the ancient round hut), which contained no image but a fire which was kept constantly burning and was tended by the Vestal Virgins. **2.** (*Astron*.) one of the minor planets, with orbit between Mars and Jupiter, discovered in 1807. [L f. Gk *hestia* hearth]

Vestal /ˈvest(ə)l/ *adj*. of the Roman goddess Vesta. —*n*. a Vestal Virgin, a virgin consecrated to Vesta and vowed to chastity. In historical times there were normally six, serving for 30 years. Vestals wore the old sacral dress otherwise reserved for brides. Their duty was to tend the undying fire burning in the shrine of Vesta in the Forum of ancient Rome, and to remain virgin: an unchaste Vestal was punished by being entombed alive. [f. prec.]

vestibule /ˈvestɪbjuːl/ *n*. **1.** an antechamber, entrance hall, or lobby next to the outer door of a building. **2.** (*US*) an enclosed entrance to a railway-carriage. [F, or f. L *vestibulum* entrance-court]

vestige /ˈvestɪdʒ/ *n*. **1.** a trace, a small remaining part of what once existed. **2.** a very small amount. **3.** a part or organ (of a plant or animal) that is now degenerate but was well developed in the ancestors. —**vestigial** /-ˈtɪdʒɪəl/ *adj*. [F, f. L *vestigium* footprint]

vestment /ˈvestmənt/ *n*. **1.** any of the official garments of the clergy, choristers, etc., worn during divine service, especially the chasuble (see ill. p. 910). **2.** a garment, especially an official or State robe. [f. OF f. L *vestimentum* (as VEST²)]

vestry /ˈvestrɪ/ *n*. **1.** a room or building attached to a church, where vestments are kept and where clergy and choir robe themselves. **2.** (*hist*.) a meeting of parishioners, usually in the vestry, for parochial business; the body of parishioners meeting thus. [f. OF f. L *vestiarium* (as VEST¹)]

Vesuvius /vɪˈsuːvɪəs/ an active volcano near Naples in Italy, 1,277 m (4,190 ft.) high. It erupted violently in AD 79, burying the towns of Pompeii and Herculaneum.

vet *n*. (*colloq*.) a veterinary surgeon. —*v.t*. (**-tt-**) **1.** to examine carefully and critically for faults or errors etc. **2.** to examine or treat (an animal). [abbr.]

vetch *n*. a plant of the pea family especially of the genus *Vicia*, largely used for fodder. [f. AF f. L *vicia*]

vetchling *n*. a plant of the genus *Lathyrus*, allied to vetch. [f. VETCH + -LING]

veteran /ˈvetərən/ *n*. **1.** a person with long experience, especially in the armed forces. **2.** (*US*) an ex-serviceman. —**veteran car,** a car made before 1916, especially before 1905. [f. F or L *veteranus* (*vetus* old)]

veterinarian /vetərɪˈneərɪən/ *n*. a veterinary surgeon. [as foll.]

veterinary /ˈvetərɪnərɪ/ *adj*. of or for the diseases of farm and domestic animals or their treatment. —*n*. a veterinary surgeon. —**veterinary surgeon,** one skilled in such treatment. [f. L *veterinarius* (*veterinae* cattle)]

veto /ˈviːtəʊ/ *n*. (*pl*. **-oes**) **1.** the constitutional right to reject a legislative enactment; the right of a permanent member of the UN Security Council to reject a resolution. **2.** such a rejection; an official message conveying this. **3.** a prohibition. —*v.t*. to exercise one's veto against; to forbid authoritatively. [L, = I forbid]

vex *v.t*. **1.** to annoy, to irritate. **2.** (*archaic*) to grieve, to afflict. —**vexed question,** a problem that is much discussed. [f. OF f. L *vexare* shake, disturb]

vexation /vekˈseɪʃ(ə)n/ *n*. **1.** vexing, being vexed; a state of irritation or worry. **2.** an annoying or distressing thing. [f. OF or L (as prec.)]

vexatious /vekˈseɪʃəs/ *adj*. causing vexation, annoying; (*Law*) not having sufficient grounds for action and seeking only to annoy the defendant. —**vexatiously** *adv*., **vexatiousness** *n*. [as prec.]

VHF *abbr.* very high frequency.

via /ˈvaɪə/ *prep.* by way of, through. [L, abl. of *via* way]

viable /ˈvaɪəb(ə)l/ *adj.* capable of living or existing successfully; (of a foetus) sufficiently developed to be able to survive after birth; (of a plan etc.) feasible, especially from an economic standpoint. —**viability** /-ˈbɪlɪtɪ/ *n.*, **viably** *adv.* [F *vie* life f. L *vita*)]

viaduct /ˈvaɪədʌkt/ *n.* a bridgelike structure, especially a series of arches, carrying a railway or road across a valley or dip in the ground. [f. L *via* way, after *aqueduct*]

vial /ˈvaɪəl/ *n.* a small (usually cylindrical glass) vessel especially for holding liquid medicines. [as PHIAL]

viand /ˈvaɪənd/ *n.* (*archaic*, usu. in *pl.*) an article of food. [f. OF f. L *vivenda* (gerundive of *vivere* live)]

viaticum /vaɪˈætɪkəm/ *n.* the Eucharist given to a person dying or in danger of death. [L, = provision for a journey (*via* way)]

vibes /vaɪbz/ *n.pl.* (*colloq.*) **1.** a vibraphone. **2.** mental or emotional vibrations. [abbr.]

vibrant /ˈvaɪbrənt/ *adj.* vibrating, resonant; thrilling with energy or activity. [as VIBRATE]

vibraphone /ˈvaɪbrəfəʊn/ *n.* a percussion instrument of metal bars and tubular resonators surmounted by small circular fans mechanically rotated to give a vibrato effect. [f. VIBRATO + -PHONE]

vibrate /vaɪˈbreɪt/ *v.t./i.* **1.** to move rapidly and continuously to and fro; to move to and fro like a pendulum, to oscillate. **2.** to cause to do this. **3.** to resound; to sound with a rapid slight variation of pitch. [f. L *vibrare* shake]

vibration /vaɪˈbreɪʃ(ə)n/ *n.* **1.** vibrating; a vibrating movement, sensation, or sound. **2.** (in *pl.*) mental stimuli thought to be given out by a person or place; the emotional sensations these produce. [as prec.]

vibrato /vɪˈbrɑːtəʊ/ *n.* (*pl.* **-os**) the slight wavering of pitch used to enrich and intensify the tone of the voice and of many (esp. stringed) instruments. [It. (as VIBRATE)]

vibrator /vaɪˈbreɪtə(r)/ *n.* a thing that vibrates or causes vibration, especially an electric or other instrument used in massage. [f. VIBRATE]

vibratory /ˈvaɪbrətərɪ/ *adj.* causing vibration. [as prec.]

viburnum /vɪˈbɜːnəm/ *n.* a shrub of the genus *Viburnum*, usually with white flowers. [L, = wayfaring-tree]

vicar /ˈvɪkə(r)/ *n.* an incumbent of a Church of England parish where the tithes formerly belonged to a chapter or religious house or to a layman. —**vicar apostolic**, a Roman Catholic missionary or titular bishop. **vicar-general** *n.* an official assisting or representing a bishop, especially in administrative matters. **Vicar of Christ**, the pope. [f. AF f. L *vicarius* substitute]

vicarage /ˈvɪkərɪdʒ/ *n.* the house provided for a vicar. [f. VICAR]

vicarious /vɪˈkeərɪəs/ *adj.* **1.** experienced through sharing imaginatively in the feelings or emotions etc. of another person. **2.** acting or done for another; deputed, delegated. —**vicariously** *adv.*, **vicariousness** *n.* [f. L (as VICAR)]

vice[1] *n.* **1.** evil or grossly immoral conduct, depravity. **2.** an evil habit; a particular form of depravity. **3.** a defect or blemish. —**vice squad**, the police department enforcing the laws against criminal and immoral practices such as prostitution. [f. OF f. L *vitium*]

vice[2] *n.* an instrument with two jaws between which a thing may be gripped so as to leave the hands free to work on it. [orig. = screw, f. OF *vis* f. L *vitis* vine]

vice[3] /ˈvaɪsɪ/ *prep.* in the place of, in succession to. [L, abl. of (*vix*) *vicis* change]

vice- *prefix* forming nouns in the senses 'acting as a substitute or deputy for' (*vice-president*), 'next in rank to' (*vice-admiral*). [f. VICE[3]]

vice-chancellor /vaɪsˈtʃɑːnsələ(r)/ *n.* a deputy chancellor (especially of a university), discharging most of the chancellor's administrative duties.

vicegerent /vaɪsˈdʒerənt/ *adj.* exercising delegated power. —*n.* a vicegerent person, a deputy. [f. L (VICE-, *gerere* carry on)]

Vicente /vɪˈsentɪ/, Gil (c.1465–1536), Portuguese poet and playwright. His plays (some in Portuguese, some in Spanish) include dramas on religious themes and comedies which satirize the nobility and clergy. He has been identified with a goldsmith of the same name, and has sometimes been called the Portuguese Shakespeare.

viceregal /vaɪsˈriːg(ə)l/ *adj.* of a viceroy. —**viceregally** *adv.* [f. REGAL, after VICEROY]

vicereine /ˈvaɪsreɪn/ *n.* a viceroy's wife; a woman viceroy. [F (VICE-, *reine* queen)]

viceroy /ˈvaɪsrɔɪ/ *n.* a ruler on behalf of a sovereign in a colony, province, etc. [F (VICE-, *roy* king)]

viceroyalty /vaɪsˈrɔɪəltɪ/ *n.* the office of viceroy. [f. F (as prec.)]

vice versa /ˈvaɪsɪ ˈvɜːsə/ with the order of the terms changed, the other way round. [L, = the position being reversed]

Vichy /ˈviːʃiː/ a town in central France noted for its mineral waters. It was the headquarters of the French government under Pétain administering Southern France following the Franco-German armistice in 1940.

vicinage /ˈvɪsɪnɪdʒ/ *n.* **1.** the neighbourhood, the surrounding district. **2.** the relation of neighbours. [f. OF f. L *vicinus* neighbour]

vicinity /vɪˈsɪnɪtɪ/ *n.* **1.** the surrounding district. **2.** nearness, closeness. —**in the vicinity (of)**, near. [f. L *vicinitas* (as prec.)]

vicious /ˈvɪʃəs/ *adj.* **1.** acting or done with evil intentions. **2.** brutal, strongly spiteful; bad-tempered; (of animals) savage and dangerous. **3.** violent, severe. **4.** (of language or reasoning) faulty, unsound. —**vicious circle**, a state of affairs in which a cause produces an effect which itself produces or intensifies the original cause. **vicious spiral**, a similar interaction causing a continuous increase or decrease (see SPIRAL 2). —**viciously** *adv.*, **viciousness** *n.* [f. OF f. L *vitiosus* (as VICE[1])]

vicissitude /vɪˈsɪsɪtjuːd/ *n.* a change of circumstances, especially of fortune. [F or f. L *vicissitudo* (*vicissim* by turns)]

Vicksburg /ˈvɪksbɜːg/ a city on the Mississippi, successfully besieged by Federal forces under General Grant in 1863. It was the last Confederate-held outpost on this river and its loss effectively split the secessionist States in half, bringing the end of the American Civil War much nearer.

victim /ˈvɪktɪm/ *n.* **1.** a person who is injured or killed by another or as the result of an event or circumstance. **2.** a prey; a person who suffers because of a trick. **3.** a living creature sacrificed to a deity or in a religious rite. [f. L *victima*]

victimize *v.t.* to single out (a person) for punishment or unfair treatment; to make (a person etc.) a victim. —**victimization** /-ˈzeɪʃ(ə)n/ *n.* [f. prec.]

victor /ˈvɪktə(r)/ *n.* the winner in a battle or contest. [f. AF or L (*vincere* conquer)]

Victor Emmanuel /vɪktər ɪˈmænjʊəl/ the name of three kings of Sardinia, two of whom became kings of Italy:
Victor Emmanuel II (1820–78), first king of a unified Italy (1861–78).
Victor Emmanuel III (1869–1947), king of Italy 1900–46, forced to abdicate after the defeat and death of Mussolini, whose policies he had supported.

Victoria[1] /vɪkˈtɔːrɪə/ (1819–1901), queen of the United Kingdom 1837–1901, the longest reign in British history. Brought up in stifling seclusion, she succeeded to the throne on the death of her uncle, William IV, and at once showed qualities of determination and obstinacy coupled with a pleasure-loving disposition. After her marriage to her cousin Prince Albert in 1840 Victoria became more serious, more conscious of her responsibilities, and more business-like; she took an active interest in the policies of her ministers in both home and foreign affairs, ably advised by the Prince, who persuaded her that the Crown should not be aligned with any political party—a principle that has endured. The idea of duty, rather solemnly performed, came to the forefront of her life; the age of Victorian respectability had begun. She was hostile to Palmerston and never liked or understood Gladstone; Melbourne was her trusted adviser, and Disraeli (who in 1876 gained for her the title of Empress of India) was similarly esteemed. Albert's death in 1861 was a shock from which Victoria never recovered; her ensuing retirement from public life was unpopular, but from Disraeli's time onwards she gradually emerged and the old lady in her widow's weeds became a national figure, grandmother (through her nine children) to half the royal houses of Europe, and her Diamond Jubilee in 1897 was made an occasion for a demonstration of public loyalty and imperial splendour. During Queen Victoria's reign Britain reached the summit of her power and prosperity, and the Crown became the link between parts of an Imperial Commonwealth. Her death was rightly felt to be the end of an era.

Victoria² /vɪkˈtɔːrɪə/ a State of south-east Australia. Originally known as the Port Philip district of New South Wales, it became a separate colony in 1851 and was federated with the other States of Australia in 1901; capital, Melbourne.

Victoria³ /vɪkˈtɔːrɪə/, Tomás Luis de (1548–1611), the leading Spanish composer of his generation. While working in Rome he may have studied with Palestrina, and his music, all of it sacred, resembles that of the Roman composer in its smoothly flowing counterpoint, undisturbed by subjective emotion, although where called for by the text an impassioned depiction of anguish and drama is one of the notable features of his style.

Victoria⁴ /vɪkˈtɔːrɪə/, **Lake** (also **Victoria Nyanza** /nɪˈænzə/) the largest lake in Africa and the chief reservoir of the Nile, discovered by Speke in 1858. Sections of it lie within the boundaries of Uganda, Tanzania, and Kenya.

victoria /vɪkˈtɔːrɪə/ n. **1.** a low light four-wheeled horse-drawn carriage with a seat for two and a raised driver's seat and with a collapsible top. **2.** (in full **victoria plum**) a large red luscious variety of plum. [f. VICTORIA¹]

Victoria and Albert Museum a national museum of fine and applied art in South Kensington, London, created out of the surplus funds of the Great Exhibition of 1851 from which a nucleus of objects was purchased. This 'Museum of Ornamental Art', linked with an art library, was moved to its present site in 1857. In 1899 it was renamed after Queen Victoria and her consort, and the foundation-stone of the present building was laid by her. Its principal collections are of pictures (including the Raphael cartoons belonging to the Crown), textiles, ceramics, and furniture.

Victoria Cross a decoration awarded to members of the Commonwealth armed services for a conspicuous act of bravery, founded by Queen Victoria in 1856 and struck from the metal of guns captured at Sebastopol during the Crimean War. The most prized of all decorations, it consists of a bronze cross, with the royal crown surmounted by a lion in the centre, and with the words 'For Valour' beneath.

Victoria Falls a spectacular waterfall 109 m (355 ft.) high on the River Zambezi at the border of Zimbabwe and Zambia, discovered by David Livingstone in 1855.

Victorian /vɪkˈtɔːrɪən/ adj. belonging to or characteristic of the reign of Queen Victoria. Among the characteristics of the age in allusion to which the term is sometimes used are its improved standards of decency and morality; a self-satisfaction engendered by the great increase of wealth, the prosperity of the nation as a whole, and the immense industrial and scientific development; conscious rectitude and deficient sense of humour; an unquestioning acceptance of authority and orthodoxy. —n. a person of this period. —**Royal Victorian Order,** an order founded by Queen Victoria in 1896 and awarded for personal service to the sovereign. [f. VICTORIA¹]

Victoriana /vɪktɔːrɪˈɑːnə/ n.pl. objects from Victorian times. [as prec.]

victorious /vɪkˈtɔːrɪəs/ adj. having gained the victory. [as VICTORY]

Victory the flagship of Lord Nelson at the battle of Trafalgar, now restored and on display in dry-dock at Portsmouth.

victory /ˈvɪktərɪ/ n. success in a battle, contest, or game etc. achieved by gaining mastery over one's opponent(s) or by achieving the highest score. [f. AF f. L victoria (as VICTOR)]

victual /ˈvɪt(ə)l/ n. (usu. in pl.) food, provisions. —v.t./i. (-ll-) **1.** to supply with victuals. **2.** to obtain stores; to eat victuals. [f. OF vitaille f. L victualia (victus food)]

victualler /ˈvɪtlə(r)/ n. one who furnishes victuals. —**licensed victualler,** an innkeeper licensed to sell alcoholic liquor etc. [as prec.]

vicuña /vɪˈkjuːnə/ n. **1.** a South American mammal (Vicugna vicugna) related to the llama, with fine silky wool. **2.** cloth made from its wool; an imitation of this. [Sp. f. Quechua]

vide /ˈvɪdeɪ, ˈvaɪdɪ/ v.t. (as an instruction in a reference to a passage in a book etc.) see, consult. [L, imper. of vidēre see]

videlicet /vɪˈdeliset/ adv. = VIZ. [L, = it is permitted to see]

video /ˈvɪdɪəʊ/ adj. relating to the recording or broadcasting of photographic images. —n. (pl. -os) **1.** such a recording or broadcasting. **2.** an apparatus for recording or playing videotapes. **3.** a videotape. —**video game,** a game played by electronically manipulating images displayed on a television screen. [L, = I see]

videotape n. a magnetic tape containing or suitable for records of television pictures and sound. —v.t. to make a recording of (broadcast material etc.) with this.

vie /vaɪ/ v.i. (partic. **vying** /ˈvaɪɪŋ/) to carry on a rivalry, to compete. [prob. as ENVY]

Vienna /vɪˈenə/ the capital of Austria, situated on the River Danube; pop. 1,531,346. It was an important military centre (Vindobona) under the Romans, and from 1278 to 1918 the seat of the Hapsburgs. It has long been a centre of the arts and especially music, Mozart and Beethoven being among the great composers associated with it. —**Vienna Circle,** a group of empiricist philosophers, scientists, and mathematicians, active in Vienna from the 1920s to 1938, who were concerned chiefly with methods of verification of statements (see LOGICAL POSITIVISM), the formalization of language, and the unifying of scientific systems. —**Viennese** /vɪəˈniːz/ adj. & n.

Vientiane /vɪentɪˈɑːn/ the capital of Laos; pop. (est. 1978) 90,000.

Vietcong /vjetˈkɒŋ/ n. (pl. same) a member of the Communist guerrilla force(s) active in Vietnam 1954–76. [Vietnamese, lit. = Vietnamese Communist]

Vietminh /vjetˈmɪn/ n. (pl. same) **1.** a nationalist independence movement (1941–50) in French Indo-China; the movement succeeding this. **2.** a member of one of these movements. [f. Vietnamese Viet-Nam Dôc-Lâp Dong-Minh Vietnamese Independence League]

Vietnam /vjetˈnæm/ a country in SE Asia, with its eastern coastline on the South China Sea; pop. (est. 1984) 60,000,000; official language, Vietnamese; capital, Hanoi. Traditionally dominated by China, Vietnam came under increasing French influence in the second half of the 19th c. The country was occupied by the Japanese during the Second World War, and post-war hostilities between the French and the Communist Vietminh ended with French defeat and the partition of Vietnam along the 17th parallel in 1954. A prolonged war between North and South Vietnam, fought largely as a guerrilla campaign in the south, ended with the withdrawal of direct American military assistance to South Vietnam and its conquest by Communist forces in 1976, after which a reunited socialist republic was proclaimed. Since then Vietnam has been involved in border disputes with China and military intervention in Cambodia, while its predominantly agricultural economy, now largely collectivized, has been slowly recovering from wartime destruction and dislocation. [f. Vietnamese Viet tribal name, nam south]

Vietnamese /vjetnəˈmiːz/ adj. of Vietnam or its people or language. —n. (pl. same) **1.** a native or inhabitant of Vietnam. **2.** the language of Vietnam, spoken by about 50 million people. Its origin is uncertain but it may be distantly related to Chinese, from which it derives about half its vocabulary. [f. prec.]

view /vjuː/ n. **1.** what can be seen from a specified point; fine natural scenery. **2.** range of vision. **3.** visual inspection of something. **4.** a mental survey of a subject etc. **5.** a manner of considering a subject; a mental attitude; an opinion. —v.t./i. **1.** to survey with the eyes or mind. **2.** to inspect, to look over (a house etc.) with the idea of buying it. **3.** to watch television. **4.** to regard or consider. —**have in view,** to have as one's object; to bear in mind in forming a judgement etc. **in view of,** having regard to, considering. **on view,** being shown (for observation or inspection). **with a view to,** with the hope or intention of. [f. AF f. L vēoir see f. L vidēre]

viewdata n. a news and information service provided by a computer source to which a television screen is connected by a telephone link.

viewer n. **1.** one who views. **2.** a person watching television. **3.** a device for looking at photographic transparencies etc. [f. VIEW]

viewfinder n. a device on a camera showing the area that will be included in a photograph.

viewpoint n. a point of view, a standpoint.

vigil /ˈvɪdʒɪl/ n. **1.** staying awake during the time usually given to sleep, especially to keep watch or pray. **2.** the eve of a religious festival, especially an eve that is a fast. [f. OF f. L vigilia (vigil wakeful)]

vigilance /ˈvɪdʒɪləns/ n. watchfulness, being on the lookout for possible danger etc. —**vigilance committee,** (US) a self-appointed body for the maintenance of order etc. —**vigilant** adj., **vigilantly** adv. [F or f. L (as prec.)]

vigilante /vɪdʒɪˈlænti/ n. a member of a vigilance committee or similar body. [Sp., = vigilant]

vignette /viːnʲjet/ *n.* **1.** an illustration not in a definite border. **2.** a photograph etc. with the background gradually shaded off. **3.** a short description, a character-sketch. —*v.t.* to shade off in the style of a vignette. [F, dim. of *vigne* vine]

Vigny /ˈviːnjɪ/, Alfred de (1797–1863), French poet, novelist, and dramatist. His ten-year undistinguished career as an army officer ended in 1827. His poems (collected in *Les Destinées*, 1864) reveal his philosophy of stoical resignation to the world, a place of suffering, as the only valid response to the inflexibility of Divine Justice. Other works include his historical novel *Cinq-Mars* (1826) and the play *Chatterton* (1835), his masterpiece.

vigorous /ˈvɪɡərəs/ *adj.* full of vigour. —**vigorously** *adv.*, **vigorousness** *n.* [as foll.]

vigour /ˈvɪɡə(r)/ *n.* **1.** active physical or mental strength, energy; flourishing physical condition. **2.** forcefulness of language or composition etc. [f. OF f. L *vigor* (*vigēre* be lively)]

Viking /ˈvaɪkɪŋ/ *n.* a member of the Scandinavian traders and pirates who ravaged much of northern Europe, and spread eastwards to Russia and Byzantium, between the 8th and 11th centuries. While their early expeditions were generally little more than raids in search of plunder, in later years they tended to end in conquest and colonization. Much of eastern England was occupied by the Vikings and eventually Cnut, king of Denmark, succeeded to the English throne. [f. ON perh. f. OE (*wīc* camp)]

vile *adj.* **1.** extremely disgusting. **2.** despicable on moral grounds. **3.** (*colloq.*) abominably bad. —**vilely** *adv.*, **vileness** *n.* [f. OF f. L *vilis* cheap, base]

vilify /ˈvɪlɪfaɪ/ *v.t.* to defame, to speak evil of. —**vilification** /-fɪˈkeɪʃ(ə)n/ *n.* [f. L *vilificare* (as prec.)]

Villa /ˈviːjə/, Francisco ('Pancho') (1877–1923), Mexican revolutionary. Pancho Villa was one of the strongest revolutionary leaders during the chaotic period of Mexican history at the beginning of the 20th c., playing a prominent role in the Madero revolution of 1910 and the uprising against Carranzo in 1914–15. Driven out of the country, he invaded the USA but was forced back into Mexico by the American army in 1916. He was eventually assassinated.

villa /ˈvɪlə/ *n.* **1.** a detached or semi-detached house in a residential district. **2.** a country residence, especially in Italy or southern France. **3.** a house for holiday-makers at the seaside etc. [It. & L]

village /ˈvɪlɪdʒ/ *n.* a group of houses etc. in a country district, smaller than a town and usually having a church. [f. OF f. L *villa*]

villager /ˈvɪlɪdʒə(r)/ *n.* an inhabitant of a village. [f. prec.]

villain /ˈvɪlən/ *n.* **1.** a person who is guilty of or capable of great wickedness; a wrongdoer, a criminal. **2.** a character in a story or play whose evil actions or motives are important in the plot. **3.** (*colloq.*) a rascal. —**villainy** *n.* [f. OF f. L *villa*; cf. VILLEIN]

villainous /ˈvɪlənəs/ *adj.* **1.** worthy of a villain; wicked. **2.** (*colloq.*) abominably bad. —**villainously** *adv.* [f. prec.]

villein /ˈvɪlɪn/ *n.* (*hist.*) a feudal tenant entirely subject to a lord or attached to a manor. —**villeinage** *n.* [var. of VILLAIN]

vim *n.* (*colloq.*) vigour. [perh. L, accusative of *vis* energy]

vina /ˈviːnə/ *n.* an Indian four-stringed musical instrument with a fretted finger-board and a half-gourd at each end. In its most common (northern Indian) form it comprises a wide bamboo tube about a yard long to which are attached towards each end half-gourds acting as resonators; the strings, of steel and brass, are plucked with wire finger-picks and the sound, while delicate in tone, is characteristically bright, with a slightly 'buzzing' quality. [f. Skr. & Hindi]

vinaigrette /vɪnɪˈɡret/ *n.* **1.** vinaigrette sauce. **2.** a small bottle for smelling-salts. —**vinaigrette sauce,** a salad dressing of oil and vinegar. [F, dim. of *vinaigre* vinegar]

Vincent de Paul /ˈvɪns(ə)nt də ˈpɔːl/, St (*c.*1580–1660), French priest who devoted his life to work among the poor, the sick, and the oppressed, and inspired similar devotion in others. In 1625 he established the Congregation of the Mission (or Lazarists), secular priests living under vows, for missions to rural areas, and in 1633 was co-founder of the Sisters of Charity, the first congregation of 'unenclosed' women devoted entirely to the care of the poor and the sick. He was strongly opposed to Jansenism.

vindicate /ˈvɪndɪkeɪt/ *v.t.* **1.** to clear of blame or suspicion. **2.** to establish the existence, merits, or justice of (one's courage, conduct, assertion, etc.). —**vindication** /-ˈkeɪʃ(ə)n/

n., **vindicator** *n.*, **vindicatory** *adj.* [f. L *vindicare* (*vindex* claimant, avenger)]

vindictive /vɪnˈdɪktɪv/ *adj.* tending to seek revenge. —**vindictively** *adv.*, **vindictiveness** *n.* [f. L *vindicta* vengeance (as prec.)]

vine *n.* **1.** a climbing or trailing plant of the genus *Vitis* (especially *V. vinifera*) with a woody stem, bearing grapes. **2.** a slender stem or climbing stem. [f. OF f. L *vinea* vineyard (*vinum* wine)]

vinegar /ˈvɪnɪɡə(r)/ *n.* **1.** a sour liquid made from wine, cider, etc., by fermentation and used as a condiment or for pickling. **2.** sour behaviour or character. —**Vinegar Bible,** the edition of 1717 with *parable of the vinegar* (for *vineyard*) in the heading above Luke 20. —**vinegary** *adj.* [f. OF *vyn egre* f. *vinum* wine, *acer* sour]

vinery /ˈvaɪnərɪ/ *n.* a greenhouse for grape-vines. [f. VINE]

vineyard /ˈvɪnjɑːd/ *n.* a plantation of grape-vines, especially for wine-making.

vingt-et-un /væ̃teɪˈœ̃/ pontoon (PONTOON[1]). [F, = twenty-one]

Vinland /ˈvɪnlənd/ a region of North America, probably near Cape Cod, discovered and briefly settled in the 11th c. by Norsemen under Leif Ericsson. It was so named from the report that grape-vines were found growing there.

vinous /ˈvaɪnəs/ *adj.* **1.** of, like, or due to wine. **2.** addicted to wine. [f. L *vinosus* (*vinum* wine)]

vintage /ˈvɪntɪdʒ/ *n.* **1.** the gathering of grapes for wine-making; the season of this. **2.** the season's produce of grapes; wine made from this. **3.** wine of high quality (from a single year) kept separate from others. **4.** the year or period when a thing was made or existed; a thing made etc. in a particular year etc. —*adj.* of high quality, especially of a past season. —**vintage car,** a car made between 1917 and 1930. [f. OF f. L *vindemia* (*vinum* wine, *demere* remove)]

vintner /ˈvɪntnə(r)/ *n.* a wine-merchant. [f. AF *vineter* f. L *vinetarius* (*vinetum* vineyard)]

vinyl /ˈvaɪnɪl/ *n.* one of a group of plastics, made by polymerization, especially polyvinyl chloride. [f. L *vinum* wine]

viol /ˈvaɪəl/ *n.* a bowed string instrument of the Renaissance and baroque periods, with six strings and (unlike the instruments of the violin family) gut frets tied round the neck. The music for viol consort from 16th- and 17th-c. England by such composers as William Byrd, Orlando Gibbons, and Henry Purcell represents the heyday of the instrument, but already in other countries the violin was assuming greater popularity, and the viol fell into disuse until its revival in the early 20th c. [f. OF f. Prov., prob. ult. f. L *vitulari* be joyful; cf. FIDDLE]

viola[1] /vɪˈəʊlə/ *n.* **1.** a bowed stringed instrument of the violin family, larger and deeper-pitched than the violin itself, and sometimes known as the 'alto' or 'tenor violin' because of this (ill. ORCHESTRA). **2.** a viol. —**viola da gamba,** a viol held between a seated player's legs, especially corresponding to the modern cello. **viola d'amore** /dæˈmɔːreɪ/, a sweet-toned tenor viol. [It. & Sp., prob. f. Prov. (see prec.)]

viola[2] /ˈvaɪələ/ *n.* any plant of the group including the violet and pansy, especially a cultivated hybrid. [L, = violet]

violable /ˈvaɪələb(ə)l/ *adj.* that may be violated. [f. foll.]

violate /ˈvaɪəleɪt/ *v.t.* **1.** to break or act contrary to (an oath, treaty, conscience, etc.). **2.** to treat (a sacred place) with irreverence or disrespect. **3.** to disturb (a person's privacy etc.). **4.** to rape. —**violation** /-ˈleɪʃ(ə)n/ *n.*, **violator** *n.* [f. L *violare* treat violently]

violence /ˈvaɪələns/ *n.* being violent; violent acts, conduct, or treatment; the unlawful use of force. —**do violence to,** to act contrary to, to be a breach of. [f. OF f. L *violentia* (as foll.)]

violent /ˈvaɪələnt/ *adj.* **1.** involving great force, strength, or intensity. **2.** (of a death) caused by physical force or by poison, not natural. —**violently** *adv.* [f. OF f. L *violentus*]

violet /ˈvaɪələt/ *n.* **1.** a plant of the genus *Viola* with usually purple, blue, or white flowers. **2.** the colour seen at the end of the spectrum opposite red, blue with a slight admixture of red. **3.** a pigment, clothes or material of this colour. —*adj.* of this colour. [f. OF, dim. of *viole* = VIOLA[2]]

violin /vaɪəˈlɪn/ *n.* **1.** a musical instrument of treble pitch with four strings played with a bow (see below; ill. ORCHESTRA). **2.** a player of this. —**violinist** *n.* [f. It. *violino* dim. of VIOLA[1]]
   The violin family comprises the double-bass, cello, viola, and the violin itself. All the instruments are bowed and

have four strings, smooth unfretted necks (unlike the viol), and *f*-shaped sound-holes. The violin is the treble of the family, with a compass of over three-and-a-half octaves and a magnificent range of expression and technique. Many of the instruments of the great Italian makers such as the Amatis (including Andrea, early 16th c.), Antonio Stradivari (d. 1737), and the Guarneri family (including Giuseppe 'del Gesù', d. 1744), are still in use today and are taken as models for new instruments. The violin is perfectly suited to the baroque style of melody and more or less subordinate accompaniment, and soon replaced the viol, first in Italy and then in France and elsewhere. Its solo repertory is immense and it is an indispensable member of the orchestra.

violist¹ /ˈvaɪəlɪst/ *n.* a viol-player. [f. VIOL]

violist² /vɪˈoʊlɪst/ *n.* a viola-player. [f. VIOLA¹]

violoncello /vaɪələnˈtʃeloʊ, viː-ə-/ *n.* (*pl.* -os) a cello. [It., dim. of foll.]

violone /viːəˈloʊni/ *n.* a double-bass viol. [It. (as VIOLA¹)]

VIP *abbr.* very important person.

viper /ˈvaɪpə(r)/ *n.* 1. a small venomous snake of the family Viperidae, especially the common viper or adder, the only poisonous snake in Great Britain. 2. a malignant or treacherous person. [f. F or L *vipera* (*vivus* alive, *parere* bring forth)]

virago /vɪˈrɑːgoʊ/ *n.* (*pl.* -os) a fierce or abusive woman. [L, = female warrior (*vir* man)]

viral /ˈvaɪər(ə)l/ *adj.* of or caused by a virus. [f. VIRUS]

Virchow /ˈvɜːkoʊ/, Rudolf Carl (1821-1902), German physician and pathologist, who laid the basis of cellular pathology. He was a great believer in the use of the microscope and saw the cell as the basis of life, and he stated that diseases were equivalent to particular types of cellular abnormality. In 1858 he published *Die Cellularpathologie* where he set out different types of abnormal cell, thus giving a scientific basis to pathology. Of a liberal if somewhat dogmatic character, Virchow joined in the 1848 uprising in Berlin. His interest in society and politics showed itself in his work on improving the sanitary conditions in Berlin and more generally in his view that social conditions played a crucial role in causing disease. Despite his wish to marry science to medicine, Virchow believed that environmental factors such as poor living conditions could cause disease just as much as specific agents such as germs. As professor of pathological anatomy in Berlin from 1856 Virchow helped to make the city a European centre of medicine.

Virgil /ˈvɜːdʒɪl/ (Publius Vergilius Maro, 70-19 BC) Roman poet. Born near Mantua and educated in Cremona, Milan, and Rome, he studied Epicureanism in Naples. The loss of his paternal estate in the confiscations of 41 BC, following the civil war, is reflected in the imaginary scenes of his first major work, the *Eclogues*, ten pastoral poems in which the traditional themes of Greek bucolic poetry are blended with contemporary political and literary themes. His next work, the *Georgics*, is a didactic poem on farming, which also treats the wider themes of the relationship between man and nature and outlines an ideal of national revival after civil war. His last and most famous work was the *Aeneid*, an epic poem in twelve books (see AENEID). He died at Brindisi while returning from a journey to Greece. His works quickly established themselves as the greatest classics of Latin poetry and exerted an immense influence on later classical and post-classical literature.

virgin /ˈvɜːdʒɪn/ *n.* 1. a person (especially a woman) who has never had sexual intercourse. 2. a picture or statue of the Virgin Mary. 3. **the Virgin,** the constellation or sign of the zodiac Virgo. —*adj.* 1. virginal. 2. spotless, undefiled. 3. untouched, in its original state; not yet used. —**the (Blessed) Virgin (Mary),** the mother of Christ. **Virgin birth,** the doctrine that Christ had no human father but was conceived by the Virgin Mary by the power of the Holy Spirit. **Virgin Queen,** Elizabeth I of England. —**virginity** /vəˈdʒɪnɪtɪ/ *n.* [f. AF & OF f. L *virgo*]

virginal *adj.* that is or befits a virgin. —*n.* (usu. in *pl.*) a legless spinet in a box. [f. OF or L (as prec.)]

Virginia /vəˈdʒɪnjə/ a State on the Atlantic coast of the USA, site of the first permanent English settlement in North America (1607) and named in honour of Elizabeth I, the 'Virgin Queen'. It was one of the original 13 States of the USA; capital, Richmond.

Virginia creeper a North American climbing plant of the genus *Parthenocissus*, cultivated for ornament. [f. prec.]

Virgin Islands a group of Caribbean islands at the eastern extremity of the Greater Antilles, discovered by Columbus

in 1493 and now divided between British and US administration. Those which are a British dependency number about 42 (the largest is Tortola); capital, Road Town. The remainder constitute an overseas territory of the USA; pop. (1980) 95,591; capital, Charlotte Amalie. These were purchased from Denmark in 1917 for strategic reasons. The small population is concentrated on the three major islands of St Thomas, St John, and St Croix. All the islands are increasingly dependent on tourism.

Virgo /ˈvɜːgoʊ/ a constellation and the sixth sign of the zodiac, the Virgin, which the sun enters about 23 Aug., containing the bright star Spica and a rich cluster of galaxies. —**Virgoan** *adj.* & *n.* [OE f. L, = virgin]

virile /ˈvɪraɪl/ *adj.* 1. having masculine vigour or strength. 2. of or having procreative power. 3. of a man as distinct from a woman or child. —**virility** /vɪˈrɪlɪtɪ/ *n.* [f. F or L *virilis* (*vir* man)]

virology /vaɪəˈrɒlədʒɪ/ *n.* the study of viruses. —**virological** /-rəˈlɒdʒɪk(ə)l/ *adj.*, **virologist** *n.* [f. VIRUS + -LOGY]

virtual /ˈvɜːtjʊəl/ *adj.* that is such in effect though not in name or according to strict definition. —**virtually** *adv.* [f. L (as VIRTUE)]

virtue /ˈvɜːtjuː/ *n.* 1. moral excellence, goodness; a particular form of this. 2. chastity, especially in a woman. 3. a good quality, an advantage. —**by** or **in virtue of,** by reason of; because of. [f. OF f. L *virtus* (*vir* man)]

virtuoso /vɜːtjʊˈoʊsoʊ/ *n.* (*pl.* -si /-siː/) a person skilled in the technique of a fine art, especially music. —**virtuosity** /-ˈɒsɪtɪ/ *n.* [It., = skilful, f. L (as foll.)]

virtuous /ˈvɜːtjʊəs/ *adj.* having or showing moral virtue, chaste. —**virtuously** *adv.*, **virtuousness** *n.* [f. OF f. L *virtuosus* (as VIRTUE)]

virulent /ˈvɪrʊlənt/ *adj.* 1. (of poison or disease) extremely strong, violent. 2. strongly and bitterly hostile. —**virulence** *n.*, **virulently** *adv.* [f. L *virulentus* (as foll.)]

virus /ˈvaɪərəs/ *n.* any of a group of minute infective and disease-producing agents consisting essentially of a length of DNA (or RNA) enveloped in a protein coat. Different viruses may infect animals, plants, and bacteria; in man, viruses cause, for example, the common cold, influenza, measles, rabies, and smallpox. Viruses can reproduce only within a host cell, utilizing the cell's own biochemical 'machinery' to assemble replica viruses which are then released into the organism. Outside the cell they are inert and show no metabolism of their own, so that it is arguable whether they are really 'alive' or not. The electron microscope reveals them to be mainly cylindrical or polyhedral in form, but systematic classification is difficult, and their origin (in evolutionary terms) remains obscure. [L, = poison]

visa /ˈviːzə/ *n.* an endorsement on a passport etc. especially as permitting the holder to enter or leave a country. —**visaed** *adj.* [F f. L, p.p. of *vidēre* see]

visage /ˈvɪzɪdʒ/ *n.* (*literary*) a person's face, a countenance. [f. OF f. L *visus* sight]

vis-à-vis /viːzɑːˈviː/ *prep.* 1. in relation to. 2. so as to face, opposite to. —*adv.* facing one another. —*n.* a person or thing facing another. [F, = face to face (as prec.)]

viscera /ˈvɪsərə/ *n.pl.* the internal organs of the body. —**visceral** *adj.* [L, pl. of *viscus*]

viscid /ˈvɪsɪd/ *adj.* (of liquid) thick and gluey. —**viscidity** /-ˈsɪdɪtɪ/ *n.* [f. L *viscidus* (*viscum* birdlime)]

Visconti /vɪsˈkɒntɪ/, Luchino (1906-76), Italian film director, of aristocratic family background and professed Marxist sympathies. He worked for a time with Renoir, absorbing his naturalistic technique, and his first film *Ossessione* (*Obsession*, 1942) was hailed as a masterpiece of realism. Visconti worked also in the theatre, an innovative director of plays and later of operas. His best work in the cinema is characterized by a distinctive visual richness and formality which developed as his theatrical experience tended more towards the grandiose.

viscose /ˈvɪskoʊz/ *n.* cellulose in a highly viscous state (for making into rayon etc.); fabric made from this. [f. L (as VISCOUS)]

viscosity /vɪsˈkɒsɪtɪ/ *n.* the quality or degree of being viscous. [f. OF or L (as VISCOUS)]

viscount /ˈvaɪkaʊnt/ *n.* 1. a British nobleman ranking between earl and baron. 2. the courtesy title of an earl's eldest son. —**viscountcy** *n.* [f. AF f. L (as VICE-, COUNT²)]

viscountess /ˈvaɪkaʊntɪs/ *n.* a viscount's wife or widow; a woman holding the rank of viscount in her own right.

viscous /ˈvɪskəs/ adj. thick and gluey; semifluid; not flowing freely. [f. AF or L viscosus (as VISCID)]

Vishnu /ˈvɪʃnuː/ one of the major gods of modern Hinduism. Originally a minor Vedic god, he became the preserver in the Hindu triad with Siva and Brahma. To his devotees, he is the supreme being from whom the whole universe emanates. His consort is Lakshmi; his mount, the eagle Garuda. According to the avatar doctrine, Vishnu has descended to earth nine times to save the world: as a fish, a tortoise, a boar, half-man half-lion, a dwarf, the legendary Parasurama, Rama (the perfect hero of the Ramayana), the god Krishna, and the historical Buddha. The tenth incarnation, Kalkin, depicted as a man on a white horse carrying a flaming sword, will herald the end of the world. [f. Skr., = pervader (vis pervade)]

visibility /vɪzɪˈbɪlɪtɪ/ n. 1. being visible. 2. the range or possibility of vision as determined by conditions of light and atmosphere. [f. F or L (as foll.)]

visible /ˈvɪzɪb(ə)l/ adj. 1. that can be seen or noticed. 2. (of exports etc.) consisting of actual goods. —**visibly** adv. [f. OF or L visibilis (vidēre see)]

Visigoth /ˈvɪzɪgɒθ/ n. a West Goth, a member of the western branch of the Goths who invaded the Roman Empire between the 3rd and 5th c. and eventually established in Spain a kingdom that was overthrown by the Moors in 711-12. —**Visigothic** adj. [f. L]

vision /ˈvɪʒ(ə)n/ n. 1. the faculty of seeing, sight. 2. a thing seen in the imagination or in a dream etc. 3. imaginative insight into a subject or problem etc.; foresight and wisdom in planning. 4. a person etc. of unusual beauty. 5. what is seen on a television screen. [f. OF f. L (as prec.)]

visionary /ˈvɪʒənərɪ/ adj. 1. given to seeing visions or to indulging in fanciful theories. 2. existing only in vision or in imagination; not practicable. —n. a visionary person. [f. prec.]

visit /ˈvɪzɪt/ v.t./i. 1. to go or come to see (a person or place etc., or absol.) socially or on business etc. 2. to reside temporarily with (a person) or at (a place). 3. to be a visitor. 4. (of a disease or calamity etc.) to come upon, to attack. 5. to inflict punishment for (a sin) upon a person. —n. an act of visiting; temporary residence with a person or at a place. [f. OF or L visitare go to see, frequent. of visare view f. vidēre see]

visitant /ˈvɪzɪt(ə)nt/ n. 1. a visitor, especially a supposedly supernatural one. 2. a migratory bird that is a visitor to an area. [F, or f. L visitare (see prec.)]

visitation /vɪzɪˈteɪʃ(ə)n/ n. 1. an official visit of inspection. 2. trouble or disaster regarded as divine punishment. 3. **the Visitation**, the visit of the Virgin Mary to her kinswoman Elizabeth; the festival on 2 July commemorating this. [as VISIT]

visitor /ˈvɪzɪtə(r)/ n. 1. one who visits a person or place. 2. a migratory bird that lives in an area temporarily or at a certain season. 3. (in a college etc.) an official with the right or duty of occasionally inspecting and reporting. —**visitors' book**, a book in which visitors to a hotel or church etc. record their visit by writing their names and addresses and sometimes remarks. [f. AF & OF (as VISIT)]

visor /ˈvaɪzə(r)/ n. 1. a movable part of a helmet covering the face (ill. ARMOUR). 2. a shield at the top of a vehicle windscreen to protect the eyes from bright sunshine. 3. the projecting front part of a cap. [f. AF viser (as VISAGE)]

vista /ˈvɪstə/ n. 1. a long narrow view as between rows of trees. 2. a mental view of a long succession of events. [It., = view]

Vistula /ˈvɪstjʊlə/ a river of Poland flowing from the Carpathians to the Baltic at Gdansk.

visual /ˈvɪzjʊəl, ˈvɪʒ-/ adj. of or used in seeing; received through sight. —**visual aid**, a film etc. as an aid to learning. **visual display unit**, a device containing a screen, used for output or input in a computer. —**visually** adv. [f. L visualis (visus sight)]

visualize /ˈvɪzjʊəlaɪz, ˈvɪʒ-/ v.t. 1. to form a mental picture of. 2. to make visible to the eye. —**visualization** /-ˈzeɪʃ(ə)n/ n. [f. prec.]

vital /ˈvaɪt(ə)l/ adj. 1. of, concerned with, or essential to organic life. 2. essential to the existence of a thing or to the matter in hand. 3. full of vitality. 4. affecting life; fatal to life or to success etc. —n. (in pl.) the vital organs of the body (e.g. heart, lungs, brain). —**vital statistics**, statistics relating to population figures or births and deaths; (colloq.) the measurements of a person's bust, waist, and hips. [f. OF f. L vitalis (vita life)]

vitalism /ˈvaɪtəlɪz(ə)m/ n. the doctrine that life originates in a vital principle distinct from physical forces. —**vitalist** n., **vitalistic** /-ˈlɪstɪk/ adj. [f. F or prec.]

vitality /vaɪˈtælɪtɪ/ n. liveliness, vigour, persistent energy; the ability to sustain life. [f. L (as VITAL)]

vitalize /ˈvaɪtəlaɪz/ v.t. to endow with life; to infuse with vitality. —**vitalization** /-ˈzeɪʃ(ə)n/ n. [f. VITAL]

vitally /ˈvaɪtəlɪ/ adv. essentially, indispensably. [f. VITAL]

vitamin /ˈvɪtəmɪn, ˈvaɪ-/ n. any of a number of unrelated organic compounds, essential for normal growth and nutrition, which are required in small quantities in the diet because they cannot be synthesized by the body. A lack of any specific vitamin leads to a characteristic deficiency disease. Substances that are vitamins for one animal need not be so for another — vitamin C, for example, is required in the diet of only a few animals other than man. **vitamin A** (retinol) contributes to the pigments of the eye. Deficiency causes night-blindness and other symptoms. It can be obtained from various animal products, especially liver, and from vegetables such as carrots. **vitamin B** is a general term for any of a group of vitamins, formerly thought to be one substance, that are essential for the working of various different enzymes. They are found in a wide variety of animal and plant foods. **vitamin C** (ascorbic acid) serves to aid cells to adhere to one another and to maintain connective tissue. Deficiency results in scurvy. It is found mainly in fresh fruits and vegetables. **vitamin D** (calciferol) is involved in the absorption and deposition in the bone of calcium and phosphorus. It is obtained especially from fish oils and liver, but can be synthesized in the skin in the presence of sunlight. Deficiency results in rickets. **vitamin E** protects some types of molecule in the body from oxidation. It is found in a wide variety of foods. **vitamin K**, also widely distributed in foods, is needed to synthesize a substance essential for blood clotting. [f. G f. L vita life + AMINE, because orig. thought to contain an amino acid]

vitaminize /ˈvɪtəmɪnaɪz, ˈvaɪ-/ v.t. to add vitamins to (food). [f. prec.]

Vitellius /vɪˈtelɪəs/, Aulus (15-69), Roman emperor in 69. Acclaimed emperor by the legions in Germany during the civil wars that followed the death of Nero, he entered Rome after the defeat of Otho but was in turn defeated and killed by the supporters of Vespasian. His gluttony was notorious.

vitiate /ˈvɪʃɪeɪt/ v.t. 1. to impair the quality or efficiency of, to debase. 2. to make invalid or ineffectual. —**vitiation** /-ˈeɪʃ(ə)n/ n. [f. L vitiare (as VICE¹)]

viticulture /ˈvɪtɪkʌltʃə(r), ˈvaɪt-/ n. grape-growing. [f. L vitis vine + CULTURE]

Vitoria /vɪˈtɔːrɪə/ a town in NE Spain where in 1813 the British army under Wellington defeated a French force under Napoleon's brother, Joseph Bonaparte, and thus freed Spain from French domination. The French were forced back over the Pyrenees, leaving the way clear for Wellington's invasion of France early in 1814.

vitreous /ˈvɪtrɪəs/ adj. of or like glass. —**vitreous humour,** see HUMOUR. [f. L vitreus (vitrum glass)]

vitrify /ˈvɪtrɪfaɪ/ v.t./i. to change into glass or a glassy substance, especially by heat. —**vitrifaction** /-ˈfækʃ(ə)n/ n., **vitrification** /-fɪˈkeɪʃ(ə)n/ n. [f. F (as prec.)]

vitriol /ˈvɪtrɪəl/ n. 1. sulphuric acid or a sulphate. 2. caustic or hostile speech or criticism. —**vitriolic** /-ˈɒlɪk/ adj. [f. OF or L vitriolum (as VITREOUS)]

Vitruvius /vɪˈtruːvɪəs/ (Vitruvius Pol(l)io or Mamurra, late 1st c. BC) Roman architect and military engineer, who wrote a comprehensive treatise on architecture, based on Greek sources and on his own experience. He dealt with all aspects of building, including the health aspects of planning, and with acoustics, water supply, sundials, water-clocks, and many other mechanical contrivances as well as the more obvious aspects of architectural design, decoration, and building. His influence was profound, both immediately and in the Renaissance.

vituperate /vɪˈtjuːpəreɪt, vaɪ-/ v.t./i. to revile, to abuse; to use abusive language. —**vituperation** /-ˈreɪʃ(ə)n/ n., **vituperative** /-ətɪv/ adj., **vituperator** n. [f. L vituperare (vitium VICE¹)]

Vitus /ˈvaɪtəs/, St (c.300), a martyr of the persecution in the reign of Diocletian. He was invoked against epilepsy and certain nervous diseases, including 'St Vitus's dance' (= chorea), and against rabies. Feast day, 15 June.

viva /ˈvaɪvə/ n. & v.t. (past & p.p. **vivaed**) (colloq.) = VIVA VOCE. [abbr.]

viva /ˈviːvə/ *int.* long live. —*n.* a cry of this as a salute etc. [It., pres. subj. of *vivere* live]

vivacious /vɪˈveɪʃəs/ *adj.* lively, high-spirited. —**vivaciously** *adv.*, **vivacity** /vɪˈvæsɪtɪ/ *n.* [f. L *vivax* (*vivere* live)]

Vivaldi /vɪˈvældɪ/, Antonio (1678–1741), Italian composer and violinist, known in his lifetime as 'Il prete rosso' (the red priest; he entered the Church in 1703) because of his red hair. Throughout his life he served an orphanage for girls in Venice as violin teacher and composer, but he also travelled a good deal in Italy and abroad where his reputation was higher than at home; he died in Vienna, being buried in a pauper's grave. Bach studied his music and copied and arranged several of the concertos, which number around 500. His feeling for texture and melody is evident not only in his most popular works, *L'Estro armonico* (*Harmonic inspiration*, 1711), a set of concertos for violins, and *The Four Seasons* (1725), but also in the surviving operas and in the solo motets that he wrote for the orphanage. Vivaldi's prolific output has led to his being accused of over-facility and repetitiveness, but the 20th c. has seen his work re-estimated, especially since the revival of interest in authentic methods of performing baroque music.

vivarium /vaɪˈveərɪəm/ *n.* (*pl.* **-ia**) a place artificially prepared for keeping animals in (nearly) their natural state. [L (*vivere* live)]

viva voce /ˌvaɪvə ˈvəʊtʃɪ/ *adj.* oral. —*adv.* orally. —*n.* an oral examination. —**viva-voce** *v.t.* to examine viva voce. [L, = with the living voice]

vivid /ˈvɪvɪd/ *adj.* **1.** (of light or colour) bright and strong, intense. **2.** (of a description etc.) producing strong and clear mental pictures; (of a mental impression) clearly produced; (of the imagination) creating ideas etc. in an active and lively way. —**vividly** *adv.*, **vividness** *n.* [f. L *vividus* (*vivere* live)]

vivify /ˈvɪvɪfaɪ/ *v.t.* to give life to (esp. *fig.*), to enliven, to animate. [f. F f. L *vivificare* (*vivus* alive, *facere* make)]

viviparous /vɪˈvɪpərəs, vaɪ-/ *adj.* bringing forth young that are in a developed state when they leave the mother's body, not hatching by means of an egg (cf. *oviparous*). [f. L (*vivus* alive, *parere* bear)]

vivisect /ˈvɪvɪsekt/ *v.t.* to perform vivisection on. [f. foll.]

vivisection /ˌvɪvɪˈsekʃ(ə)n/ *n.* performance of surgical or other experiments on living animals for scientific research. —**vivisectionist** *n.*, **vivisector** /ˈvɪvɪsektə(r)/ *n.* [f. L *vivus* alive, after *dissection*]

vixen /ˈvɪks(ə)n/ *n.* **1.** a female fox. **2.** a spiteful woman. [f. earlier *fixen*, fem. of FOX]

viz. /vɪz, or by substitution ˈneɪmlɪ/ *adv.* namely, that is to say, in other words. [abbr. of VIDELICET]

vizier /vɪˈzɪə(r), ˈvɪz-/ *n.* an official of high rank in some Muslim countries. [ult. f. Arab. *wazīr* caliph's chief counsellor]

Vladimir /ˈvlædɪmɪə(r)/, St (956–1015), apostle of the Russians and Ruthenians. In 978 he took Kiev from the rule of his elder brother and conquered large areas of White Russia. After marrying a sister of the Greek emperor Basil II he became an ardent promoter of Christianity, which he imposed by force.

V neck a V-shaped neckline on a pullover or other garment.

vocable /ˈvəʊkəb(ə)l/ *n.* a word, especially with reference to its form not its meaning. [F or f. L *vocabulum* (*vocare* call)]

vocabulary /vəˈkæbjʊlərɪ/ *n.* **1.** the words used in a language, book, or branch of science, or by an author. **2.** a list of these arranged alphabetically with definitions or translations. **3.** the range of words known to an individual person. **4.** a set of artistic or stylistic forms or techniques. [f. L *vocabularius* (as prec.)]

vocal /ˈvəʊk(ə)l/ *adj.* **1.** of, for, or uttered by the voice. **2.** expressing one's feelings freely in speech. —*n.* (in *sing.* or *pl.*) the sung part or a sung piece of music. —**vocal cords**, the folds of the lining membrane of the larynx at the opening of the glottis, with edges that vibrate in the air-stream to produce the voice (ill. BODY 2). —**vocally** *adv.* [f. L *vocalis* (as VOICE)]

vocalic /vəˈkælɪk/ *adj.* of or consisting of a vowel or vowels. [f. VOCAL]

vocalist /ˈvəʊkəlɪst/ *n.* a singer. [f. VOCAL]

vocalize /ˈvəʊkəlaɪz/ *v.t.* to form (a sound) or utter (a word) with the voice. —**vocalization** /-ˈzeɪʃ(ə)n/ *n.* [f. VOCAL]

vocation /vəˈkeɪʃ(ə)n/ *n.* **1.** a divine call to or a sense of one's fitness for a certain career or occupation. **2.** a person's trade or profession. —**vocational** *adj.* [f. OF or L (*vocare* call)]

vocative /ˈvɒkətɪv/ *n.* the case of a noun used in addressing or invoking a person or thing. —*adj.* of or in the vocative. [f. OF or L (*vocare* call)]

vociferate /vəˈsɪfəreɪt/ *v.t./i.* to utter noisily; to shout. —**vociferation** /-ˈreɪʃ(ə)n/ *n.*, **vociferator** *n.* [f. L *vociferari* (*vox* voice, *ferre* bear)]

vociferous /vəˈsɪfərəs/ *adj.* making a great outcry; expressing one's views loudly and insistently in speech. —**vociferously** *adv.*, **vociferousness** *n.* [as prec.]

vodka /ˈvɒdkə/ *n.* an alcoholic spirit distilled especially in Russia from rye etc. [Russ., dim. of *voda* water]

vogue /vəʊg/ *n.* prevailing fashion; popular favour or acceptance. —**in vogue**, in fashion; generally current. **vogue-word** *n.* a word currently fashionable. [F f. It. *voga* rowing, fashion]

voice *n.* **1.** sound formed in the larynx and uttered by the mouth, especially human utterance in speaking or singing etc.; ability to produce this. **2.** use of the voice; an utterance in spoken or (*fig.*) written form; an opinion so expressed; the right to express an opinion; the agency by which an opinion is expressed. **3.** (*Gram.*) a set of verbal forms showing whether a verb is active or passive. —*v.t.* **1.** to give utterance to; to express in words. **2.** to utter with vibration of the vocal cords (e.g. *b*, *d*). —**in good voice**, in proper vocal condition for singing or speaking. **voice-over** *n.* narration in a film etc. not accompanied by a picture of the speaker. **with one voice**, unanimously. [f. AF *voiz* f. L *vox*]

voiceless *adj.* **1.** dumb, speechless, mute. **2.** (of a sound) uttered without vibration of the vocal cords (e.g. *f*, *p*). [f. VOICE + -LESS]

void *adj.* **1.** empty, vacant. **2.** (of a contract etc.) invalid, not legally binding. —*n.* empty space, a vacuum. —*v.t.* **1.** to render void. **2.** to excrete. —**void of**, lacking; free from. [f. OF, ult. f. L (as VACATE)]

voile /vɔɪl, vwɑːl/ *n.* a thin semi-transparent dress-material. [F, = veil]

vol. *abbr.* volume.

volatile /ˈvɒlətaɪl/ *adj.* **1.** evaporating rapidly. **2.** changing quickly or easily from one mood or interest to another; transient; lively; apt to break out into violence. —**volatility** /-ˈtɪlɪtɪ/ *n.* [f. OF or L *volatilis* (*volare* fly)]

volatilize /vəˈlætɪlaɪz/ *v.t./i.* to turn into vapour. —**volatilization** /-ˈzeɪʃ(ə)n/ *n.* [f. prec.]

vol-au-vent /ˈvɒlaʊvɑ̃/ *n.* a (usually small) round case of puff pastry filled with a savoury mixture. [F, lit. 'flight in the wind']

volcanic /vɒlˈkænɪk/ *adj.* of, like, or produced by a volcano. —**volcanically** *adv.* [f. F (as foll.)]

volcano /vɒlˈkeɪnəʊ/ *n.* (*pl.* **-oes**) **1.** an opening in the earth's crust through which lava, steam, etc., are or have been expelled; a mountain or hill formed round such an opening. **2.** a state of things likely to cause a violent outburst. [It. f. L *Volcanus* Vulcan]

vole *n.* a small herbivorous rodent of the family Cricetidae. [orig. *vole-mouse*, f. Norw. *voll* field]

Volga /ˈvɒlgə/ the longest river in Europe (3,688 km, 2,292 miles) rising in the north-west of the USSR and flowing to the Caspian Sea. It has been dammed at several points to provide a water supply and hydroelectric power.

volition /vəˈlɪʃ(ə)n/ *n.* the act or faculty of willing. —**volitional** *adj.*, **volitionally** *adv.* [F or f. L (*volo* I wish)]

volley /ˈvɒlɪ/ *n.* **1.** a simultaneous discharge of a number of weapons; the bullets etc. thus discharged. **2.** a noisy emission of questions or curses etc. in quick succession. **3.** return of a ball in tennis, football, etc., before it touches the ground; a full toss. —*v.t.* **1.** to discharge or fly in a volley. **2.** to return (a ball) by a volley. [f. F *volée* f. L *volare* fly]

volley-ball *n.* a game for two teams of 6 persons, volleying a large ball by hand over a net. It was developed in the USA from 1895, when W. G. Morgan, a physical fitness instructor at the YMCA at Holyoke, Massachusetts, formulated the game for middle-aged men who found basketball too vigorous.

volt /vəʊlt/ *n.* a unit of electromotive force, the difference of potential that would carry one ampere of current against one ohm resistance. [f. foll.]

Volta /ˈvɒltə/, Alessandro Giuseppe Antonio Anastasio, Count (1745–1824), Italian physicist, the discoverer of a number of important electrical instruments, including the electrophorus (for generating static electricity), the condensing electroscope, and, most significant of all, the voltaic pile or electrochemical battery, the first device to produce a continuous electric current, which he announced in 1800. The impetus for this invention was Galvani's contention in 1791 that he had discovered a new kind of electricity, 'animal electricity', produced in animal tissue, which Volta ascribed to normal electricity produced by the contact of two dissimilar metals. He was made a Count when he demonstrated his battery to Napoleon in 1801. The volt is named in his honour.

voltage /ˈvəʊltɪdʒ/ n. electromotive force expressed in volts. [f. VOLT]

Voltaire /ˈvɒlteə(r)/ (pseudonym of François-Marie Arouet, 1694–1778) French writer, author of plays, poetry, and histories, not so much a philosopher as a publicizer of the philosophical ideas of others. During a period in the Bastille (as author of a pungent political satire) he completed his tragedy *Oedipe* (1719) and his epic poem *La Henriade* (1723, 1728); both reveal his nascent political revolt. He spent a period in exile in England (1726–9) and was introduced there to the scientific theories of Newton and the empiricist philosophy of Locke. He also became acquainted with the political institutions of England, and extolled them as against the royal autocracy and nobles' privileges of France. Much of the rest of his life was spent outside France, or in a house from which he could make a quick escape across the border. He rejected all claims to revelation and came to be openly and fiercely hostile to Christianity and the Roman Catholic Church. His relentless attacks on the civil and ecclesiastical establishments, with every resource of wit and satire, were the source of both his immense prestige and his persecution.

volte-face /vɒltˈfɑːs/ n. a complete reversal of position in an argument or opinion. [F f. It. *voltafaccia* (*voltare* to turn f. L *volvere* roll)]

voltmeter /ˈvəʊltmiːtə(r)/ n. an instrument measuring electric potential in volts. [f. VOLT + -METER]

voluble /ˈvɒljʊb(ə)l/ adj. with a vehement or incessant flow of words. —**volubility** /-ˈbɪlɪtɪ/ n., **volubly** adv. [F or f. L *volubilis* (*volvere* roll)]

volume /ˈvɒljuːm/ n. 1. a book, especially one of a set. 2. the amount of space (often expressed in cubic units) that a three-dimensional object occupies or contains or that a gas or liquid occupies. 3. the amount of a thing, a quantity. 4. the strength or power of a sound. [f. OF f. L *volumen* (as prec., ancient books being in roll form)]

volumetric /vɒljʊˈmetrɪk/ adj. of measurement by volume. —**volumetrically** adv. [f. prec. + METRIC]

voluminous /vəˈljuːmɪnəs, vɒˈluː-/ adj. 1. having great volume, bulky; of (drapery etc.) loose and ample. 2. (of writings) great in quantity; (of a writer) producing many works, copious. —**voluminously** adv., **voluminousness** n. [f. L (as VOLUME)]

voluntary /ˈvɒləntərɪ/ adj. 1. acting, done, or given etc. of one's own free will, not under compulsion. 2. working or done without payment. 3. (of an institution) maintained by voluntary contributions or voluntary workers; (of a school) originally built by such an institution but maintained by a Local Education Authority. 4. (of a movement, muscle, or limb) controlled by the will. —n. an organ solo played before, during, or after a church service. —**voluntarily** adv., **voluntariness** n. [f. OF or L *voluntarius* (*voluntas* will)]

volunteer /vɒlənˈtɪə(r)/ n. a person who voluntarily undertakes a task or enters military etc. service. —v.t./i. 1. to undertake or offer voluntarily. 2. to be a volunteer. [f. F *volontaire* (as prec.)]

voluptuary /vəˈlʌptjʊərɪ/ n. a person given up to luxury and sensual pleasure. [f. L (as foll.)]

voluptuous /vəˈlʌptjʊəs/ adj. of, tending to, occupied with, or derived from sensuous or sensual pleasure; (of a woman) having a full and attractive figure. —**voluptuously** adv., **voluptuousness** n. [f. OF or L (*voluptas* pleasure)]

volute /vəˈljuːt/ n. a spiral scroll in stonework forming the chief ornament of Ionic capitals and used also in Corinthian and composite capitals (ill. TEMPLES). [F, or f. L *voluta* (*volvere* roll)]

vomit /ˈvɒmɪt/ v.t./i. 1. to eject (matter) from the stomach through the mouth; to be sick. 2. (of a volcano, chimney, etc.) to eject violently, to belch forth. —n. matter vomited from the stomach. [f. OF or L *vomitus*, *vomitare*]

von Neumann see NEUMANN.

voodoo /ˈvuːduː/ n. 1. use of or belief in a form of religious witchcraft practised among Blacks in Haiti and elsewhere in the Caribbean area (see below). 2. a person skilled in this. 3. a voodoo spell. —v.t. to affect by voodoo, to bewitch. —**voodooism** n., **voodooist** n. [f. Dahomey *vodu*]
In voodoo some debased elements of Roman Catholic ritual, dating from the French colonial period before 1804, are blended with African religious and magical elements derived from the former slave population. Trances induced by spirit possession are central to its ritual. Professed belief in a supreme God is combined with service to the *loa*, who are local (or African) gods, deified ancestors, or Catholic saints. The cult is strongly opposed by both the Catholic and the Protestant Church.

voracious /vəˈreɪʃəs/ adj. 1. greedy in eating, ravenous. 2. very eager in some activity. —**voraciously** adv., **voracity** /vəˈræsɪtɪ/ n. [f. L *vorax* (*vorare* devour)]

vortex /ˈvɔːteks/ n. (pl. **vortexes** or **vortices** /-ɪsiːz/) 1. a whirlpool, a whirlwind, a whirling motion or mass. 2. a thing viewed as swallowing those who approach it. —**vortical** /-ɪk(ə)l/ adj., **vortically** /-ɪkəlɪ/ adv. [L *vortex* -*icis* eddy, var. of VERTEX]

vorticism /ˈvɔːtɪsɪz(ə)m/ n. an aggressive literary and artistic movement that flourished from 1912 to 1915. It attacked the sentimentality of 19th-c. art and celebrated violence, energy, and the machine. The vorticists, dominated by Wyndham Lewis, included Ezra Pound (who suggested the idea of a vortex from which ideas were constantly rushing), the sculptor Gaudier-Brzeska, and the painter Edward Wadsworth; they were associated with the philosopher T. E. Hulme, the novelist Ford Madox Ford, and the sculptor Jacob Epstein. In the visual arts their style was expressed in bold abstract compositions and was indebted to cubism and futurism. A vorticist exhibition was held in 1915 at which there was manifested a tendency towards simplification into angular machine-like objects, but owing to wartime conditions the movement did not persist. —**vorticist** n. [as prec.]

Vosges /vəʊʒ/ a mountain system of eastern France.

votary /ˈvəʊtərɪ/ n. a person vowed or devoted to the service of a god, cult, or pursuit. —**votaress** n.fem. [f. L (as foll.)]

vote n. 1. a formal expression of choice of opinion in the election of a candidate, passing of a law, etc., signified by a ballot or show of hands etc. 2. the right to vote, especially in a State election. 3. an opinion expressed by a majority of votes; the collective votes given by or for a particular group. —v.t./i. 1. to give one's vote. 2. to enact or resolve by a majority of votes; to grant (a sum of money etc.) by a vote. 3. (colloq.) to pronounce by general consent; to announce one's proposal (that). —**vote down**, to defeat (a proposal etc.) by votes. **vote in**, to elect by votes. —**voter** n. [f. L *votum* (*vovēre* vow)]

votive /ˈvəʊtɪv/ adj. given or consecrated in fulfilment of a vow. [f. L *votivus* (as VOTE)]

vouch v.i. (with *for*) to guarantee the certainty, accuracy, or reliability of. [f. OF *vo(u)cher* summon, ult. f. L *vocare* call]

voucher n. 1. a document (issued in token of payment made or promised) exchangeable for certain goods or services. 2. a document establishing that money has been paid or goods etc. delivered. [AF or f. prec.]

vouchsafe /vaʊtʃˈseɪf/ v.t. to condescend to grant or do a thing. [f. VOUCH in sense 'warrant' + SAFE]

voussoir /ˈvuːswɑː(r)/ n. each of the wedge-shaped or tapered stones forming an arch (ill. BRIDGES, BUILDING TECHNIQUES). [f. OF, ult. f. L *volvere* roll]

vow n. a solemn promise especially in the form of an oath to a deity or saint. —v.t. 1. to promise solemnly. 2. (archaic) to declare solemnly. [f. AF *vou* f. L (as VOTE)]

vowel /ˈvaʊəl/ n. a speech-sound made with vibration of the vocal cords but without audible friction (cf. CONSONANT); a letter or letters representing this, as *a, e, i, o, u, aw, ah*. [f. OF f. L *vocalis* (*littera*) vocal (letter)]

vox populi /vɒks ˈpɒpjʊliː, -laɪ/ public opinion, the general verdict, popular belief. [L, = the people's voice]

voyage /ˈvɔɪɪdʒ/ n. an expedition to a distance, especially by water or in space. —v.i. to make a voyage. —**voyager** n. [f. AF f. L *viaticum* (*via* road)]

Voyager each of two US space probes launched in 1977 to Jupiter, Saturn, Uranus, and Neptune.

voyeur /vwɑːˈjɜː(r)/ n. one who obtains sexual gratification from looking at others' sexual actions or organs. —**voyeur-ism** *n.* [F (*voir* see)]

vs. *abbr.* versus.

V sign a gesture made with the raised hand with the first and second fingers forming a V, expressing victory or approval, or vulgar derision.

VTO *abbr.* vertical take-off.

VTOL *abbr.* vertical take-off and landing.

Vulcan /ˈvʌlkən/ (*Rom. myth.*) the god of fire (see HEPHAESTUS).

Vulcanist /ˈvʌlkənɪst/ *n.* a holder of the plutonic theory in geology (see PLUTONIST). [f. prec.]

vulcanite /ˈvʌlkənaɪt/ *n.* hard black vulcanized rubber. [as foll.]

vulcanize /ˈvʌlkənaɪz/ *v.t.* to make (rubber etc.) stronger and more elastic by treating with sulphur at a high temperature. —**vulcanization** /-ˈzeɪʃ(ə)n/ *n.* [f. VULCAN]

vulcanology /vʌlkəˈnɒlədʒɪ/ *n.* the study of volcanoes. [as prec. + -LOGY]

vulgar /ˈvʌlgə(r)/ *adj.* **1.** characteristic of the common people; lacking in refinement or good taste, coarse. **2.** commonly used. **3.** (of a fraction) a fraction expressed by a numerator and a denominator, not decimally. **vulgar tongue,** *the* national or vernacular language. —**vulgarity** /-ˈgærɪtɪ/ *n.*, **vulgarly** *adv.* [f. L *vulgaris* (*vulgus* common people)]

vulgarian /vʌlˈgeərɪən/ *n.* a vulgar person, especially a rich one. [f. prec.]

vulgarism *n.* a word or expression in coarse or uneducated use; an instance of coarse or uneducated behaviour. [f. VULGAR]

vulgarize /ˈvʌlgəraɪz/ *v.t.* **1.** to make vulgar. **2.** to spoil by making too common or frequented or too well known. —**vulgarization** /-ˈzeɪʃ(ə)n/ *n.* [as prec.]

Vulgate /ˈvʌlgət/ *n.* the Latin version of the Bible prepared mainly by Jerome in the late 4th c., translated directly from the Hebrew text of the Old Testament. It is used by the Roman Catholic Church in the recension of 1592, the Council of Trent having decreed in 1546 that the Vulgate was to be the sole Latin authority for the Bible. [f. L (*editio*) *vulgata* (*vulgare* make public)]

vulnerable /ˈvʌlnərəb(ə)l/ *adj.* **1.** that may be hurt, wounded, or injured. **2.** unprotected, exposed to danger, attack, or criticism etc. **3.** having won a game towards a rubber at contract bridge and therefore liable to higher penalties. —**vulnerability** /-ˈbɪlɪtɪ/ *n.*, **vulnerably** *adv.* [f. L *vulnerabilis* (*vulnus* wound)]

vulpine /ˈvʌlpaɪn/ *adj.* of or like a fox; crafty, cunning. [f. L *vulpinus* (*vulpes* fox)]

vulture /ˈvʌltʃə(r)/ *n.* **1.** a large bird of prey of the order Raptores, feeding chiefly on carrion and reputed to gather with others in anticipation of a death. **2.** a rapacious person seeking to profit from the misfortunes of others. [f. AF f. L]

vulva /ˈvʌlvə/ *n.* the external parts of the female genitals. [L, = womb]

vv. *abbr.* **1.** verses. **2.** volumes.

vying *partic.* of VIE.

W

W, w /'dʌb(ə)lju:/ *n.* (*pl.* **Ws, W's**) the twenty-third letter of the alphabet.

W *abbr.* **1.** watt(s). **2.** west(ern).

W *symbol* tungsten. [f. *wolframium*, Latinized name]

W. *abbr.* **1.** wicket(s). **2.** wide(s). **3.** with.

WA *abbr.* Western Australia.

wacky *adj.* (*slang*) crazy. —*n.* (*slang*) a crazy person. [orig. dial., = left-handed]

wad /wɒd/ *n.* **1.** a lump or bundle of soft material to keep things apart or in place or to block a hole. **2.** a collection of banknotes or documents placed together. **3.** (*slang*) a bun; a sandwich. —*v.t.* (**-dd-**) to fix or stuff with a wad; to stuff, line, or protect with wadding. [perh. rel. to Du. *watten*, F *ouate* padding]

wadding /'wɒdɪŋ/ *n.* soft fibrous material used for padding, packing, or lining things. [f. WAD]

waddle /'wɒd(ə)l/ *v.i.* to walk with short steps and a swaying motion. —*n.* a waddling walk. [perh. frequent. of WADE]

Wade /weɪd/, George (1673–1748), British field-marshal and road-builder, responsible for the construction of a network of modern roads and bridges in the 1720s and 1730s in the Highlands of Scotland in order to enable the government to control the Jacobite clans, who had hitherto enjoyed a certain freedom from interference owing to the inaccessibility of their homeland.

wade *v.t./i.* **1.** to walk through water or some impeding medium; to cross (a stream) thus. **2.** to progress slowly or with difficulty. —*n.* a spell of wading. —**wade in,** (*colloq.*) to make a vigorous intervention or attack. **wade into,** (*colloq.*) to attack (a person or task) vigorously. **wade through,** to read through (a book etc.) in spite of its difficulty, dullness, or length. **wading-bird** *n.* a long-legged water-bird that wades in shallow water. [OE]

wader *n.* **1.** a wading-bird. **2.** (in *pl.*) high waterproof fishing-boots. [f. WADE]

wadi /'wɒdɪ/ *n.* a rocky watercourse in North Africa and neighbouring countries that is dry except in the rainy season. [f. Arab.]

wafer /'weɪfə(r)/ *n.* **1.** a kind of thin light crisp sweet biscuit. **2.** a thin disc of unleavened bread used in the Eucharist. **3.** a disc of red paper stuck on law papers instead of a seal. —*v.t.* to fasten or seal with a wafer. —**wafer-thin** *adj.* very thin. [f. AF *wafre* f. MLG *wāfel* WAFFLE²]

waffle¹ /'wɒf(ə)l/ *n.* aimless verbose talk or writing. —*v.i.* to indulge in waffle. [orig. dial., f. *waff* yelp (imit.)]

waffle² /'wɒf(ə)l/ *n.* a small crisp batter cake. —**waffle-iron** *n.* a utensil, usually of two hinged shallow metal pans, for baking waffles. [f. Du. *wafel* f. MLG; cf. WAFER]

waft /wɒft/ *v.t.* to convey smoothly (as) through air or along water. —*n.* a wafted odour. [orig. = convoy (ship), f. obs. *wafter* armed convoy-ship f. Du. or LG *wachter* (*wachten* guard)]

wag *v.t./i.* (**-gg-**) to shake or move briskly to and fro. —*n.* **1.** a single wagging movement. **2.** a person who is given to joking or playing practical jokes. —**tongues wag,** there is talk. [f. root of OE *wagian* sway]

wage *n.* (in *sing.* or *pl.*) a regular payment to an employee in return for his work or services. —*v.t.* to carry on (a war etc.). —**wage-earner** *n.* one who works for a wage. **wage freeze,** a ban on wage-increases. [f. AF; cf. GAGE¹, WED]

wager /'weɪdʒə(r)/ *n.* a bet. —*v.t./i.* to bet. [f. AF (as prec.)]

waggish *adj.* playful, facetious. —**waggishly** *adv.*, **waggishness** *n.* [f. WAG]

waggle /'wæg(ə)l/ *v.t./i.* (*colloq.*) to wag. —*n.* (*colloq.*) a waggling movement. —**waggle dance,** a movement performed by honey-bees at their hive or nest, believed to indicate to other bees the site of a source of food (ill. INSECTS). —**waggly** *adj.* [f. WAG]

Wagner /'vɑ:gnə(r)/, Richard (1813–83), German composer and conductor. His life has attracted notoriety—because of his marriage to Liszt's daughter Cosima after an affair which involved deceiving her husband, his association

with the deranged Ludwig II of Bavaria, his anti-Semitism, and the way in which his music and the festival opera-house he built at Bayreuth became a focal point for all that Hitler intended for the new Germany. In *The Flying Dutchman* (1841), inspired by a sea journey to London in which the ship was driven into a Norwegian fjord, *Tannhäuser* (1845), and *Lohengrin* (1848) can be seen the basic concerns of Wagner's approach to opera: myth and legend, often as recounted by early German writers; redemption through love, both Christian and secular; and above all unification of music and drama. The sheer mastery of *The Ring*, the sustaining of such an imposing achievement at a white-heat of inspiration for something like twenty hours of music, is among the most amazing triumphs of the human spirit.

wagon /'wægən/ *n.* (also **waggon**) **1.** a four-wheeled vehicle for heavy loads drawn by horses or oxen. **2.** an open railway truck. **3.** a trolley for carrying food etc. —**hitch one's wagon to a star,** to utilize powers higher than one's own. **on the (water-)wagon,** (*slang*) abstaining from alcohol. [f. Du. *wag(h)en*, rel. to WAIN]

wagoner *n.* (also **waggoner**) the driver of a wagon. [f. prec.]

wagonette /wægə'net/ *n.* (also **waggonette**) a four-wheeled open horse-drawn carriage with facing side-seats. [f. WAGON + -ETTE]

wagtail *n.* a kind of small bird of the genus *Motacilla* with a long tail that is in frequent motion when the bird is standing.

Wahabi /wə'hɑ:bɪ/ *n.* a member of a sect of Muslim puritans, following strictly the original words of the Koran, named after Muhammad ibn Abd al-Wahab (1703–92), a native of Najd in central Arabia. Dissatisfied with the practices of his contemporaries in the capitals of Islamic learning, Abd al-Wahab called for a return to the earliest doctrines and practices of Islam as embodied in the Koran and Sunna, and for the abolition of accretions and corruptions which had pervaded the medieval Muslim community through the activities and preachings of mystical groups (see SUFI) and also through the blind subservience of the ulama—scholars and legislators of the community—to the dictates of earlier scholars. Forming an alliance with Muhammad ibn Saud, prince of a small adjacent kingdom, he showed his awareness of the inseparability of spiritual and temporal in Islam. The two leaders forged a State which came to encompass most of the Arabian peninsula, but their expansion and especially their attacks on sites holy to followers of Islam brought a response in the form of a successful military campaign undertaken by Muhammad Ali, Viceroy of Egypt, acting for the Ottoman government, which was nominal sovereign over the Arabian peninsula. The reconquest of Ottoman territory and dissolution of the Wahabi State was completed in 1919. The term 'Wahabi', however, was appropriated by various movements seeking reform and purification of the faith in the 19th c., and became almost a generic name for such movements.

waif *n.* **1.** a homeless and helpless person, especially an abandoned child. **2.** an ownerless object or animal. —**waifs and strays,** homeless or neglected children; odds and ends. [f. AF, prob. of Scand. orig.]

wail *n.* a long sad inarticulate cry of pain or grief; a sound resembling this. —*v.i.* **1.** to utter a wail; to make such a sound. **2.** to lament or complain persistently. [f. ON (rel. to WOE)]

Wailing Wall a high wall in Jerusalem, known in Jewish tradition as the 'Western Wall'. Originally part of the Temple structure erected by Herod the Great, since the 7th c. it has formed the western wall of the sanctuary enclosing the Dome of the Rock and other buildings, the third most holy place to Muslims after Mecca and Medina. Jews have been accustomed, probably since the Middle Ages, to lament at this wall the destruction of the Temple and the Holy City in AD 70 and to pray for its restoration.

wain *n.* (*archaic*) a wagon. —**the Wain** (also **Charles's Wain**), the constellation Ursa Major. In its name, Charles = Charlemagne; it was originally called the Wain of

Arcturus (a neighbouring star); Arcturus was confused with Arturus, King Arthur, who is associated with Charlemagne in legend. [OE]

wainscot /ˈweɪnskət/ n. the boarding or wooden panelling on the lower part of a room-wall. [f. MLG *wagenschot* (app. as WAGON)]

wainscoting n. wainscot; material for this. [f. prec.]

waist n. **1.** the part of the human body below the ribs and above the hips; the narrowness marking this; its circumference. **2.** a similar narrow part in the middle of a long object (e.g. a violin) or of a wasp etc. **3.** the part of a garment corresponding to the waist. **4.** (*US*) a blouse; a bodice. —**waist-deep** or **-high** adjs. & advs. immersed up to the waist; so high as to reach the waist. [orig. *wast*, perh. f. root of WAX²]

waistband n. a strip of cloth forming the waist of a garment.

waistcoat n. a close-fitting waist-length garment without sleeves or a collar, worn (especially by men) over a shirt and under a jacket (ill. DRESS).

waistline n. the outline or size of the body at the waist.

wait v.t./i. **1.** to defer an action or departure until an expected event occurs; to do this for (a specified time). **2.** to await (an opportunity, one's turn, etc.). **3.** to defer (a meal) until a person's arrival. **4.** to park a vehicle for a short time at the side of the road etc. **5.** to act as a waiter or attendant. —n. **1.** an act or period of waiting. **2.** waiting for an enemy. **3.** (in *pl.*) street singers of Christmas carols. —**lie in wait**, to be hidden and ready. **wait and see**, to await the progress of events. **waiting-game** n. postponing an action for greater effect. **waiting-list** n. a list of applicants etc. for a thing not immediately available. **waiting-room** n. a room where people can wait, e.g. at a railway station or surgery. **wait on** or **upon**, to await the convenience of; to be an attendant or respectful visitor to. **wait up (for)**, not to go to bed (until the arrival or happening of). **you wait!** an expression of threat or warning. [f. OF (rel. to WAKE¹)]

Waitangi /waɪˈtæŋɪ/ a settlement in New Zealand at which in 1840 was negotiated the **Treaty of Waitangi**, forming the basis of British annexation of New Zealand, by which the Maori chiefs of North Island accepted British sovereignty in exchange for protection. Subsequent encroachment on the lands set aside for them led eventually to the Maori Wars of 1860-72 in which Maori independence was finally destroyed. —**Waitangi Day**, 6 Feb., celebrated in New Zealand since 1960 as a public holiday.

waiter n. a man who takes orders and brings food etc. at hotel or restaurant tables. —**waitress** n.fem. [f. WAIT]

waive v.t. to refrain from insisting on or using (a right or claim etc.). [f AF *weyver*, OF *gaiver* allow to become a waif, abandon]

waiver n. the waiving of a legal right; a document recording this. [f. prec.]

wake¹ v.t./i. (*past* woke or waked; *p.p.* waked or woken) **1.** (often with *up*) to cease or cause to cease to sleep; to make or become alert or attentive. **2.** (archaic exc. in **waking**) to be awake. **3.** to disturb with noise. **4.** to evoke (an echo). —n. **1.** (in Ireland) a watch by a corpse before burial; the attendant lamentations and merry-making. **2.** (usu. in *pl.*) an annual holiday in (industrial) northern England. [OE (rel. to WATCH)]

wake² n. **1.** the track left on the water's surface by a moving ship etc. **2.** turbulent air left by a moving aircraft. **in the wake of**, following; as a result of; in imitation of. [prob. f. MLG f. ON, = hole or opening in ice]

wakeful /ˈweɪkfʊl/ adj. **1.** unable to sleep; (of a night etc.) with little sleep. **2.** vigilant. —**wakefully** adv. [f. WAKE¹ + -FUL]

waken /ˈweɪkən/ v.t./i. to wake (*lit.* or *fig.*). [f. ON (as WAKE¹)]

Walachia /wɒˈleɪkjə/ a former principality of SE Europe, united in 1859 with Moldavia to form Romania. —**Walachian** adj. & n.

Waldenses /wɒlˈdensiːz/ n.pl. a Puritanical religious sect founded in southern France *c.*1173 by Peter Waldo (L *Valdus*), a merchant of Lyons, and despite much former persecution by the Roman Catholic Church still surviving, notably in Piedmont.

wale n. **1.** a weal (WEAL¹). **2.** a ridge on corduroy etc. **3.** (*Naut.*) a broad thick timber along a ship's side. [OE, = stripe, ridge]

Wales /weɪlz/ the western part of Great Britain; pop. (1981)

2,791,851; capital Cardiff. The earliest inhabitants appear to have been overrun by Celtic peoples in the Bronze and Iron Age. The Romans fortified the north and south of Wales and established a system of forts and outposts linked by roads that traversed the country. After the Roman withdrawal in the 5th c., the Celtic inhabitants of Wales successfully maintained their independence against the Anglo-Saxons who settled in England, and in the 8th c. Offa king of Mercia built an earthwork (see OFFA'S DYKE) marking the frontier established by his struggles against them. Largely isolated from historical developments in the rest of England until the Middle Ages, Wales was conquered by Edward I in the late 13th c. but continued a sporadic resistance to English rule until finally incorporated into the larger country by Henry VIII in 1536. Despite its absorption into the British State, Wales has retained a distinct cultural identity, but has suffered increasingly in recent years from the stagnation of its coal and steel industries.

walk /wɔːk/ v.t./i. **1.** to move by lifting and setting down each foot in turn so that one foot is always on the ground at any time. **2.** to travel or go on foot; to take exercise thus. **3.** to traverse (a distance) in walking. **4.** to tread the floor or surface of. **5.** to cause to walk with one, to accompany in walking; to ride or lead (a horse) or lead (a dog) at a walking pace. —n. **1.** the act or style of walking; a walking pace. **2.** a journey on foot, especially for pleasure or exercise. **3.** a route or track for walking. —**walk (all) over**, (*colloq.*) to defeat easily; to take advantage of. **walk away from**, to outdistance easily. **walk away** or **off with**, (*colloq.*) to steal; to win easily. **walk into**, (*colloq.*) to encounter through unwariness. **walk of life**, one's occupation. **walk on air**, to feel elated. **walk-on part**, a part involving an appearance on stage but no speaking. **walk out**, to depart suddenly or angrily. **walk-out** n. a sudden angry departure, especially as a protest or strike. **walk out on**, to desert, to leave in the lurch. **walk-over** n. an easy victory. **walk the streets**, to be a prostitute. [OE, = roll, toss]

walkabout n. **1.** an informal stroll among a crowd by a visiting royal person etc. **2.** a period of wandering by an Australian Aboriginal.

walker /ˈwɔːkə(r)/ n. **1.** one who walks. **2.** a framework for a person unable to walk without support. [f. WALK]

Walker Cup /ˈwɔːkə(r)/ a golf tournament played between teams of men amateurs of the USA and Great Britain and Ireland, held every second year in May, alternately in the USA and Great Britain, from 1922; the trophy for this, donated by George H. Walker, a former president of the US Golf Association, who organized the competition.

walkie-talkie /ˈwɔːkɪˈtɔːkɪ/ n. a small portable radio transmitting and receiving set. [f. WALK + TALK]

walking-stick n. a stick held or used as a support when walking. The walking-stick with a pommel held in the hand seems to have been introduced during the 15th c., but it was not until the 17th c. that the cane, or walking-stick, became an essential part of the dress of a fine gentleman. In the early 19th c. such sticks were notably fashionable, having entirely replaced swords which were no longer carried, and remained popular up to the beginning of the First World War, but now the traditional 'stick and gloves' of the man about town have almost completely vanished.

walkway n. a passage for walking along, especially one connecting sections of a building; a wide path in a garden etc.

wall /wɔːl/ n. **1.** a continuous upright structure of stone or brick etc. enclosing, protecting, or separating a building, room, field, or town etc. **2.** a thing like a wall in appearance or effect; the steep side of a mountain; the outermost part of a hollow structure; the outermost layer of an animal or plant organ or cell. —v.t. to surround, enclose, or block with a wall. —**go to the wall**, to suffer defeat, failure, or ruin. **up the wall**, (*colloq.*) crazy, furious. **wall-board** n. board made from wood-pulp etc. and used to cover walls. **wall game**, a ball-game played at Eton beside a wall (see ETON). **walls have ears**, beware of eavesdroppers. **wall-to-wall** adj. covering the whole floor of a room. **with one's back to the wall**, at bay. —**wall-less** adj. [OE]

wallaby /ˈwɒləbɪ/ n. **1.** a kind of small kangaroo. **2.** **Wallabies**, an Australian international Rugby Union team, so called from the animal found extensively in Australia. [f. Aboriginal *wolabā*]

Wallace¹ /ˈwɒlɪs/, Alfred Russel (1823-1913), British naturalist who independently formulated a theory of the origin of species that was identical with that of Charles Darwin, to whom he communicated his conclusions. He travelled extensively in South America and the East Indies, collecting specimens and studying the geographical distribution of animals. In 1858 a summary of the joint views of Wallace and Darwin concerning natural selection was read to the Linnaean Society in London, and credit for the theory has attached somewhat unfairly to Darwin. —**Wallace's line,** a hypothetical line, proposed by Wallace, extending from the Indian Ocean northward between Borneo and the Celebes into the Philippine Sea, dividing the regions where Australasian fauna are found from those of Asian fauna. The former are (in evolutionary terms) more primitive than the latter, and the line indicates the stage at which the continents became separated.

Wallace[2] /ˈwɒlɪs/, (Richard Horatio) Edgar (1875-1932), English novelist, playwright, and journalist. After working as a newspaper correspondent in South Africa he became the first editor of the *Rand Daily Mail* in Johannesburg before returning to England and embarking on the novels that were to make him famous. His *Sanders* stories, set in West Africa, are among the best of his writings, but it is for his thrillers that he is chiefly remembered. In 28 years of authorship more than 170 of his books were published; his style was simple and racy, his plots varied, the speed of his output was a byword, and meanwhile he sometimes had two or three plays running simultaneously in London. Notable among his works are *The Four Just Men* (1905) and its sequels, *The Ringer* (novel 1925; play 1926), *The Crimson Circle* (1922), and *The Mind of Mr. J. G. Reeder* (1925). He died in Hollywood, California, where he had been writing motion picture stories, the first of which, *King Kong*, was produced shortly after his death.

Wallace[3] /ˈwɒlɪs/, Sir William (c.1270-1305), a national hero of Scotland, a leader of Scottish resistance to Edward I. Following his victory over an English army at Stirling in 1297 he briefly became official Guardian of the Realm, but his defeat at Falkirk a year later reduced him to little more than a guerrilla leader. He was eventually captured and executed by the English.

Wallace Collection /ˈwɒlɪs/ a museum in Manchester Square, London, containing a fine representation of French 18th-c. paintings and furniture, English 18th-c. portraits, and medieval armour. The collection was built up by the Seymour-Conway family, Earls and later Marquesses of Hertford, and was given to the nation in 1897.

wallah /ˈwɒlə/ n. (slang) a person employed or concerned in a specific occupation or task. [f. HINDI]

wallet /ˈwɒlɪt/ n. a small flat folding case for holding banknotes or small documents etc. [earlier *walet*; orig. unkn.]

wall-eye /ˈwɔːlaɪ/ n. an eye with the iris whitish or streaked, or with an outward squint. —**wall-eyed** adj. [f. ON; cf. Icel. *vagl* film over eye]

wallflower n. 1. a plant of the genus *Cheiranthus*, especially *C. cheiri*, with fragrant flowers. 2. (colloq.) a woman sitting out dances for lack of partners.

Wallis /ˈwɒlɪs/, Sir Barnes Neville (1887-1979), English inventor who patented over 140 designs. He designed the R100 airship, used geodetic construction on his famous Wellington bomber of the Second World War, invented radio telescopes and range-finders for use over water, worked on guided missiles and swing-wing aircraft, and later designed supersonic aircraft. His bomb designs included the famous bouncing bomb used to destroy the Ruhr dams in Germany in 1943.

Walloon /wɒˈluːn/ n. 1. a member of a people, of Gaulish origin and speaking a French dialect, living in southern Belgium (where they form the chief part of the population) and neighbouring parts of France. 2. their language. —adj. of the Walloons or their language. [f. F f. L (rel. to WELSH)]

wallop /ˈwɒləp/ v.t. (slang) 1. to thrash, to beat. 2. (in partic.) big. —n. (slang) 1. a heavy resounding blow. 2. beer or other drink. [earlier sense 'gallop', 'boil', f. OF *waloper* (as GALLOP)]

wallow /ˈwɒləʊ/ v.i. 1. to roll about in mud, sand, water, etc. 2. to take unrestrained pleasure in a specified thing. —n. 1. the act of wallowing. 2. a place where animals go to wallow. [OE]

wallpaper n. paper for pasting on the interior walls of rooms, often decoratively printed.

Wall Street a street at the south end of Manhattan, New York, where the New York Stock Exchange and other leading American financial institutions are located, whence the allusive use of its name to refer to the American money-market or financial interests. (See STOCK EXCHANGE.)

walnut /ˈwɔːlnʌt/ n. 1. a nut containing an edible kernel with a wrinkled surface. 2. the tree (*Juglans regia*) bearing this; its timber used in making furniture. [OE, = foreign nut]

Walpole[1] /ˈwɔːlpəʊl/, Horace, 4th Earl of Orford (1717-97), English writer and connoisseur, an MP 1741-67. In 1747, supported by various sinecures, he settled in Twickenham at Strawberry Hill which he made into his 'little Gothic castle'. There he collected curios, established his own printing press, and printed Gray's Pindaric Odes and his own *Anecdotes of Painting in England* (1762). His novel *The Castle of Otranto* (1764) set a fashion for 'Gothic' tales of mystery and horror. His literary reputation rests largely on his letters which are remarkable for their charm and wit and for their autobiographical, political, and social interest.

Walpole[2] /ˈwɔːlpəʊl/, Sir Hugh (1884-1941), British novelist, born in New Zealand, educated in England. His short experience as a schoolmaster is reflected in *Mr. Perrin and Mr. Traill* (1911) which set a vogue for novels and plays about schoolmasters. Among his many novels are *The Dark Forest* (1916), based on his war-time service with the Russian Red Cross, and *The Herries Chronicle* (1930-3), a historical sequence set in Cumberland (where he lived from 1924).

Walpole /ˈwɔːlpəʊl/, Sir Robert, 1st Earl of Orford (1676-1745), British statesman. A career Whig politician, whose colourful career included a spell in the Tower of London on a charge of venality in office, Walpole is generally recognized as the first modern British Prime Minister. He held office between 1715-17 and 1721-42, presiding over a period of considerable peace and prosperity, although eventually failing to prevent war with Spain in 1739.

Walpurgis Night /vælˈpʊəgɪs/ the eve of 1 May, on which, according to German legend, a witches' Sabbath took place on the Brocken, a peak of the Harz mountains. It is named after St Walburga, an English nun who in the 8th c. helped to convert the Germans to Christianity; one of her feast days coincided with an ancient pagan feast with rites protecting from witchcraft.

walrus /ˈwɔːlrəs/ n. a large amphibious mammal (*Odobenus rosmarus*) of Arctic seas, with two long tusks (ill. MAMMALS). —**walrus moustache,** a long thick drooping moustache. [prob. f. Du.]

Walton[1] /ˈwɔːltən/, Izaak (1593-1683), English writer, chiefly known for *The Compleat Angler* (1653, largely rewritten in the second edition, 1655), a discourse on fishing which combines practical information with folklore, pastoral interludes of songs and ballads, and glimpses of an idyllic rural life. His biographies of Donne (1640), Wotton (1651), Hooker (1665), and George Herbert (1670) are gentle and admiring in tone.

Walton[2] /ˈwɔːlt(ə)n/, Sir William (1902-83), English composer. He was a chorister and later an undergraduate at Christ Church, Oxford, but left without taking a degree and was unofficially adopted by the Sitwell family. *Façade* (1921-3), his music for a recitation of poems by Edith Sitwell, won him a reputation as a musical wit and iconoclast. There followed the bustling overture *Portsmouth Point* (1925), the deeply serious Viola Concerto (1928-9), then the flamboyantly-scored cantata *Belshazzar's Feast* (1930-1) to words arranged by Osbert Sitwell from the Bible, and the First Symphony (1932-5). Two Coronation Marches (1937 and 1953), skilful scores for the films of three Shakespeare plays, the opera *Troilus and Cressida* (1950-4), and further orchestral, chamber, and choral works have confirmed Walton's importance in the history of 20th-c. English music.

waltz /wɔːls, wɒls/ n. a ballroom dance for couples, with a graceful flowing melody in triple time; the music for this. In its early years in the late 18th c. the waltz was seen as conducive to lasciviousness and immorality because of the physical closeness of the couples. The most famous examples today are those by 19th-c. Viennese composers, particularly Joseph Lanner and Johann Strauss I and II, father and son. —v.t./i. 1. to dance a waltz. 2. to move (a person) in or as in a waltz. 3. to dance round in joy etc.; to move easily or casually. [f. G *walzer* (*walzen* revolve)]

wampum /ˈwɒmpəm/ n. strings of shell-beads formerly used by North American Indians for money or ornament. [f. Algonquin]

wan /wɒn/ *adj.* pallid, especially from illness or exhaustion. —**wanly** *adv.*, **wanness** *n.* [OE, = dark]

wand /wɒnd/ *n.* a slender rod for carrying in the hand, especially one associated with the working of magic; a music conductor's baton; a slender rod or staff carried as a sign of office etc. [f. ON]

wander /ˈwɒndə(r)/ *v.i.* **1.** to go from place to place without a settled route or aim; to go aimlessly *in*, *off*, etc. **2.** to diverge from the right way (*lit.* or *fig.*). **3.** to digress from a subject; to be inattentive or incoherent through illness or weakness. —**wanderer** *n.* [OE (as WEND)]

Wandering Jew 1. a person of medieval legend condemned to wander the earth until the Day of Judgement, as a punishment for having insulted Christ on the way to the Crucifixion. **2.** a climbing plant especially of the genus *Tradescantia*.

wanderlust *n.* an eager desire or fondness for travelling or wandering. [G]

wane *v.i.* **1.** (of the moon) to show a gradually decreasing area of brightness after being full. **2.** to decrease in vigour, strength, or importance. —*n.* **1.** the process of waning. **2.** a defect in a plank etc. when the corners are not square. —**on the wane,** declining. [OE *wanian* lessen]

wangle *v.t.* (*slang*) to obtain or arrange by using trickery, improper influence, or persuasion etc. —*n.* (*slang*) an act of wangling. [19th-c. printers' slang; orig. unkn.]

wank *v.i.* (*vulgar*) to masturbate. —*n.* (*vulgar*) an act of masturbation. —**wanker** *n.* [orig. unkn.]

Wankel /ˈwæŋk(ə)l/, Felix (1902–), German engineer, inventor of a rotary-piston internal-combustion engine which bears his name. Its main advantage over the conventional reciprocating-piston design is its freedom from vibration, which enables it to be used at a higher rotational speed and so to be more compact and lighter for a given capacity, but its many problems include sealing at the tips of the rotor lobes, higher fuel consumption, and increased pollutants in the exhaust.

want /wɒnt/ *v.t./i.* **1.** to desire, to wish for. **2.** to require or need; should, ought. **3.** to lack; to be insufficiently supplied with; to fall short of. **4.** to be without the necessaries of life. —*n.* **1.** a desire for something, a requirement. **2.** lack or need of something, deficiency. **3.** lack of the necessaries of life. —**in want of,** needing. **wanted (by the police),** sought by the police as a suspected criminal. [f. ON (*vanr* lacking), OE *wana* (as WANE)]

wanting *adj.* lacking; deficient; not equal to requirements. [f. WANT]

wanton /ˈwɒnt(ə)n/ *adj.* **1.** licentious, unchaste. **2.** (of cruelty, damage, etc.) purposeless, unprovoked. **3.** capricious, playful; unrestrained, luxuriant. —*n.* a licentious person. —*v.i.* to behave capriciously or playfully. —**wantonly** *adv.*, **wantonness** *n.* [orig. *wantowen* = undisciplined (as UN-, *tēon* team)]

wapentake /ˈwæpənteɪk, ˈwɒp-/ *n.* (*hist.*) a hundred or division of a shire (in areas of England that had a large Danish population). [OE f. ON (*vápn* weapon, *tak* taking); perh. with ref. to voting in assembly by show of weapons]

wapiti /ˈwɒpɪtɪ/ *n.* a North American elk (*Cervus canadensis*) resembling the red deer but larger. [f. Cree, = white deer]

war /wɔː(r)/ *n.* **1.** strife (especially between countries) involving military, naval, or air attacks; the period of this. **2.** open hostility between persons. **3.** strong efforts to combat crime, disease, poverty, etc. —*v.i.* (**-rr-**) (*archaic*) to make war. —**at war,** engaged in a war. **go to war,** to begin hostile operations. **have been in the wars,** (*colloq.*) to show signs of injury. **war-cry** *n.* a phrase or name shouted in battle; the slogan of a political or other party. **war-dance** a dance performed by certain primitive peoples before war or after victory. **war-game** *n.* a game simulating warfare, using models or blocks moved about on a map etc.; a set of military exercises designed to examine or test a military strategy. **war-horse** *n.* a trooper's horse; a veteran soldier. **war-lord** *n.* (in China, esp. in 1916–28) a military commander with a regional power base, acting independently of the central government. **war memorial,** a monument to those killed in a war. **War of American Independence,** see AMERICAN REVOLUTION. **war of nerves,** an attempt to wear down an opponent by gradual destruction of his morale. **war-paint** *n.* paint put on the body (especially by North American Indians) before battle. **war-path** *n.* a march of North American Indians to make war; *on the war-path,* engaged in conflict, taking a hostile attitude. [f. AF, OF *guerre* (cf. OHG *werra* confusion, strife)]

War. *abbr.* Warwickshire.

Warbeck /ˈwɔːbek/, Perkin (1474–99), the second of two pretenders to the English Crown in the reign of Henry VII, both claiming to be Richard Duke of York. Warbeck presented a far more formidable threat to Henry than had Lambert Simnel before him, chiefly because various foreign powers were willing to recognize him for their own diplomatic ends. After a series of abortive plots and uprisings he was finally captured. At first he was treated leniently, but he continued to intrigue in captivity and was executed.

warble /ˈwɔːb(ə)l/ *v.t./i.* to sing, especially with a gentle trilling note as certain birds do. —*n.* a warbling sound. [f. OF *werbler* f. Frankish, = whirl, trill]

warble-fly *n.* a kind of fly whose larvae burrow under the skin of cattle etc. and produce tumours. [orig. unkn.]

warbler *n.* any of several small birds of the family Sylviidae or (*US*) Parulidae (not necessarily one noted for its song). [f. WARBLE]

Ward /wɔːd/, Mrs Humphry (née Mary Augusta Arnold, 1851–1920), English novelist, granddaughter of Thomas Arnold and niece of Matthew Arnold from whom she inherited a sense of high moral purpose. A leading figure in the intellectual life of her day, an active philanthropist and supporter of higher education for women, she wrote several novels dealing with social and religious themes, including *Robert Elsmere* (1888), a vivid evocation, in part, of the varieties of religious faith and doubt which succeeded the ferment of the Oxford Movement.

ward /wɔːd/ *n.* **1.** a separate room or division in a hospital or (*hist.*) workhouse. **2.** an administrative division, especially for elections. **3.** a minor etc. under the care of a guardian or court. **4.** (in *pl.*) the notches and projections in a key and lock designed to prevent opening by a key other than the right one. **5.** (*archaic*) guarding, defending, guardianship; the bailey of a castle (ill. CASTLES). —*v.t.* **1.** (usu. with *off*) to parry (a blow), to avert (a danger etc.). **2.** (*archaic*) to guard, to defend. [OE, = guard]

-ward /-wɔːd/ *suffix* (also **-wards**) added to nouns of place or destination and to adverbs of direction and forming adverbs (usu. in *-wards*) meaning 'towards the place etc.' (*backwards, homewards*), adjectives (usu. in *-ward*) meaning 'turned or tending towards' (*downward, onward*), and less commonly nouns meaning 'the region towards or about' (*look to the eastward*). [OE]

warden /ˈwɔːd(ə)n/ *n.* **1.** the president or governor of an institution (e.g. a hospital or college). **2.** an official with supervisory duties. **3.** a churchwarden. [f. AF & OF, = guardian]

warder /ˈwɔːdə(r)/ *n.* an official in charge of prisoners in a prison. —**wardress** *n.fem.* [f. AF (as GUARD)]

wardrobe /ˈwɔːdrəʊb/ *n.* **1.** a place where clothes are kept, especially a large cupboard usually with pegs or rails etc. from which they hang. **2.** a person's or persons' stock of clothes. —**wardrobe master** *or* **mistress,** one who has charge of an actor's or a company's costumes. [f. OF (as GUARD, ROBE)]

wardroom /ˈwɔːdruːm/ *n.* a room for commissioned officers in a warship.

-wards see -WARD.

wardship *n.* tutelage, a guardian's care. [f. WARD + -SHIP]

ware *n.* **1.** manufactured articles (especially pottery) of the kind specified. **2.** (in *pl.*) what one has for sale. [OE, perh. orig. = 'object of care']

warehouse /ˈweəhaʊs/ *n.* a building in which goods are stored or shown for sale. —/also -haʊz/ *v.t.* to place or keep in warehouses.

warfare *n.* making war, fighting; a particular form of this.

warhead *n.* the explosive head of a missile, torpedo, or similar weapon.

Warhol /ˈwɔːhəʊl/ Andy (1930–), American painter, graphic artist, and film maker whose work played a definitive role in New York pop art of the 1960s. Warhol's background in commercial art and advertising illustration was central to the pop movement's concern with the imagery of the mass media; his famous statement 'I like boring things' was expressed in the standardized, consciously banal, nature of his work. In the early 1960s he achieved notoriety for a series of silk-screen prints and acrylic paintings whose subjects included familiar objects (such as Campbell's soup tins), car accidents, and Marilyn Monroe, treated with industrial precision and complete artistic detachment. These interests were readily extended to film, and Warhol played an important part in the new American underground cinema. His first films were silent and (deliberately) technically unsophisticated, treating repetitive and often voyeuristic themes. Later films such as *Flesh* (1968) and *Trash* (1970) were technically smoother, more conventional in structure, and intended for wide commercial release.

warlike *adj*. **1**. fond of or skilful in war, aggressive. **2**. of or for war.

warlock /ˈwɔːlɒk/ *n*. (*archaic*) a sorcerer. [OE, = traitor]

warm /wɔːm/ *adj*. **1**. moderately hot, not cold or cool. **2**. (of clothes etc.) keeping the body warm; (of exertion) making one warm. **3**. enthusiastic, hearty; (of a reception) vigorous by being either heartily friendly or strongly hostile. **4**. kindly and affectionate. **5**. (of colours) suggesting warmth, especially by containing reddish shades. **6**. (of the scent in hunting) still fairly fresh and strong; (of the seeker in a children's game etc.) close to the object sought or guessed at. —*v.t./i.* to make or become warm or warmer. —*n*. **1**. the act of warming. **2**. warmth of atmosphere. —**keep a position warm**, to occupy it temporarily so that it can be available (for a specified person) at a later date. **warm-blooded** *adj*. having blood that remains warm (36–42 °C) permanently; passionate. **warm-hearted** *adj*. having a kindly and affectionate disposition. **warming-pan** *n*. a covered metal pan with a long handle, formerly filled with live coals and used for warming beds. **warm to**, to become cordial or well-disposed to (a person) or more animated about (a task). **warm up**, to make or become warm; to reach or cause to reach the temperature of efficient working; to prepare for a performance by exercise or practice; to reheat (food). **warm-up** *n*. the process of warming up. —**warmly** *adv*., **warmness** *n*. [OE]

warmonger /ˈwɔːmʌŋgə(r)/ *n*. one who seeks to cause war.

warmth /wɔːmθ/ *n*. warmness, being warm. [f. WARM]

warn /wɔːn/ *v.t.* to inform (a person) about a present or future danger or about something to be reckoned with; to advise about action in such circumstances. —**warn off**, to tell (a person) to keep away (from); to prohibit from taking part in race-meetings (at). [OE]

warning /ˈwɔːnɪŋ/ *n*. what is said or done or occurs to warn a person. [f. WARN]

warp /wɔːp/ *v.t./i.* **1**. to make or become crooked or twisted especially by uneven shrinkage or expansion. **2**. to distort or pervert (a person's judgement or principles); to suffer such distortion. **3**. to haul (a ship) along by means of a rope fixed to an external point; to progress thus. —*n*. **1**. a warped condition. **2**. threads stretched lengthwise in a loom, to be crossed by the weft. **3**. a mental perversion or bias. **4**. a rope used in warping a ship. [OE, = throw]

warrant /ˈwɒrənt/ *n*. **1**. a thing that authorizes an action; a written authorization to receive or supply money, goods, or services, or to carry out an arrest or search. **2**. a certificate of the service rank held by a warrant-officer. —*v.t.* **1**. to serve as a warrant for, to justify. **2**. to guarantee, to answer for the genuineness etc. of. —**I('ll) warrant (you)**, I am certain, I assure you. **warrant-officer** *n*. an officer ranking between commissioned officers and NCOs. [f. OF *warant* f. Frankish (*giweren* be surety for)]

warranty *n*. **1**. authority or justification for doing something. **2**. a seller's undertaking that a thing sold is his and fit for use etc., often accepting responsibility for repairs needed over a specified period. [f. AF *warantie* (as prec.)]

warren /ˈwɒrən/ *n*. **1**. a piece of ground abounding in rabbit burrows. **2**. a densely populated or labyrinthine building or district. [f. AF *warenne*, OF *garenne*, game-park]

warring /ˈwɔːrɪŋ/ *adj*. engaged in a war; rival, antagonistic. [f. WAR]

warrior /ˈwɒrɪə(r)/ *n*. a person who fights in battle; a distinguished or veteran soldier; a member of any of the armed services. [f. OF (*guerreier* make war)]

Warsaw /ˈwɔːsɔː/ the capital of Poland, on the River Vistula; pop. (est. 1980) 1,576,600. The city was systematically razed to the ground by German occupying forces in the Second World War.

Warsaw Pact a treaty of mutual defence and military aid signed at Warsaw on 14 May 1955 by Communist States of Europe, under Russian leadership, in answer to the creation of NATO. The alliance is currently composed of the USSR, East Germany, Poland, Czechoslovakia, Hungary, Bulgaria and Romania. One other original member, Albania, left in 1968, another potential candidate for membership, Yugoslavia, refused to join.

warship *n*. a ship for use in war.

Wars of the Roses a general name (popularized by Sir Walter Scott in the 19th c.) for the civil wars of the dynastic struggle between the followers of the house of York (with the white rose as its emblem) and the house of Lancaster (with the red rose) in 15th-c. England during the reigns of Henry VI, Edward IV, and Richard III. The struggle was ended (except for the rebellion of Lambert Simnel) by the accession in 1485 of the Lancastrian Henry Tudor (Henry VII) who united the two houses by marrying Elizabeth, daughter of Edward IV. (For the reputed adoption of the emblems of the roses see Shakespeare *I Henry VI* II iv. 27ff.)

wart /wɔːt/ *n*. **1**. a small hard roundish growth on the skin, caused by a virus. **2**. a protuberance on the skin of an animal or on the surface of a plant. **3**. (*colloq*.) an objectionable person. —**wart-hog** *n*. an African wild pig of the genus *Phacochoerus*, with warty lumps on the face and large curved tusks. **warts and all**, (*colloq*.) with no attempt to conceal blemishes or inadequacies. —**warty** *adj*. [OE]

wartime *n*. a period when war is being waged.

Warwick /ˈwɒrɪk/, Richard Neville, Earl of (1428–71), English statesman, known as 'the Kingmaker'. During the Wars of the Roses he fought first on the Yorkist side, and was instrumental in placing Edward IV on the throne in 1461, then (having lost influence at court) he changed sides and briefly restored Henry VI in 1470. Warwick was killed in the following year when the Lancastrians were defeated at Barnet.

Warwickshire /ˈwɒrɪkʃɪə(r)/ a midland county of England.

wary /ˈweərɪ/ *adj*. cautious, in the habit of looking out for possible danger or difficulty. —**warily** *adv*., **wariness** *n*. [f. *ware* cognizant (as AWARE)]

was see BE.

wash /wɒʃ/ *v.t./i.* **1**. to cleanse with water or other liquid. **2**. to remove (a stain) by washing; (of a stain) to be removed thus. **3**. to wash oneself; to wash clothes etc. **4**. to be washable; (of reasoning) to be valid. **5**. to moisten; (of a river etc.) to flow past or against. **6**. (of a moving liquid) to carry in a specified direction; to go splashing or flowing. **7**. to sift (ore) by the action of water. **8**. to coat with a wash of paint or wall-colouring etc. —*n*. **1**. washing, being washed; the process of laundering; clothes etc. that are being washed or to be washed or have just been washed. **2**. the motion of disturbed water or air behind a moving ship or aircraft etc. **3**. liquid food or swill for pigs etc. **4**. a thin coating of colour painted over a surface; a cleansing or healing liquid for external use. —**come out in the wash**, (of mistakes etc.) to be eliminated during the process of work etc. **wash-basin** *n*. a basin (usually fixed to a wall) for washing one's hands etc. in. **wash dirty linen in public**, to discuss private quarrels or difficulties publicly. **wash down**, to clean by washing; to accompany or follow (food) with a drink. **washed out**, faded by washing; faded-looking; pallid; enfeebled. **washed up**, (*slang*) defeated, having failed. **wash one's hands (of)**, to renounce responsibility (for). **wash-leather** *n*. chamois or similar leather for washing windows etc.; a piece of this. **wash out**, to clean the inside of by washing; (*colloq*.) to cancel. **wash-out** *n*. a breach in a railway or road caused by a flood; (*slang*) a complete failure. **wash up**, to wash (dishes etc., or *absol*.) after use; (of the sea) to cast up on the shore. [OE]

washable *adj*. that may be washed without being damaged. [f. WASH]

washer /ˈwɒʃə(r)/ *n*. **1**. a flat ring of leather, rubber, or metal etc. to tighten a joint and prevent leakage. **2**. a washing-machine. [f. WASH]

washerwoman *n*. (*pl*. **-women**) a woman whose occupation is washing clothes etc.

washing /ˈwɒʃɪŋ/ *n*. clothes etc. that are being washed or to be washed or have just been washed. —**washing-machine** *n*. a machine for washing clothes. **washing-powder** *n*. a powder of soap or detergent for washing clothes etc. **washing-soda** *n*. sodium carbonate, used (dissolved in water) for washing and cleaning things. **washing-up** *n*. the process of washing dishes etc. after use; the dishes etc. for washing. [f. WASH]

Washington[1] /ˈwɒʃɪŋt(ə)n/ the capital and administrative centre of the USA, coterminous with the District of Columbia, founded in the presidency of George Washington and named after him.

Washington[2] /ˈwɒʃɪŋt(ə)n/ the most northerly of the Pacific States of the USA, occupied jointly by Britain and the USA in the first half of the 19th c. It became the 42nd State of the USA in 1889; capital, Olympia.

Washington[3] /ˈwɒʃɪŋt(ə)n/, George (1732-99), 1st President of the USA 1789-96. A soldier with a distinguished record in the French and Indian War, Washington was chosen as commander of the Continental Army in 1775 and served in that capacity throughout the War of Independence, contributing greatly to the eventual American victory through his military ability and strength of character. After a brief retirement he returned to public life and was unanimously elected first President after the adoption of the Constitution. He served two terms, following a policy of neutrality in international affairs, before declining a third term and retiring once again to private life. Rightly known as the father of his country, Washington probably did more than any other man to secure the independence of the United States.

washy /ˈwɒʃɪ/ adj. **1.** (of liquids) thin, watery. **2.** (of colours) washed-out. **3.** lacking vigour. —**washily** adv., **washiness** n. [f. WASH]

wasn't /ˈwɒz(ə)nt/ (colloq.) was not.

WASP /wɒsp/ abbr. (US, usu. derog.) White Anglo-Saxon Protestant, a member of the American white Protestant middle or upper class descended from early European settlers in North America.

wasp /wɒsp/ n. a stinging insect of the superfamily Vespoidea, especially the common kind (of the genus Vespa) with black and yellow stripes, a slender waist, and buzzing flight. —**wasp-waist** n. a very slender waist. [OE]

waspish /ˈwɒspɪʃ/ adj. snappish, making sharp comments. —**waspishly** adv., **waspishness** n. [f. WASP]

wassail /ˈwɒseɪl/, -s(ə)l/ n. (archaic) merry-making, festive drinking. —v.i. (archaic) to make merry. [f. ON ves heill 'be in good health', form of salutation (cf. HALE[1])]

Wassermann /ˈvɑːsəmɑːn/, August Paul von (1866-1925), German bacteriologist, remembered chiefly for his introduction of a diagnostic test for syphilis owing to his discovery of a distinctive reaction in the blood serum when that disease is present.

wastage /ˈweɪstɪdʒ/ n. **1.** loss by waste; the amount of this. **2.** (in full **natural wastage**) loss of employees through retirement or resignation, not by redundancy. [f. foll.]

waste /weɪst/ v.t./i. **1.** to use to no purpose, for an inadequate result, or extravagantly; to fail to use (an opportunity). **2.** to give (advice etc.) without effect on a person. **3.** to run to waste. **4.** to wear away gradually; to make or become gradually weaker. **5.** to lay waste; to treat as waste. —adj. **1.** superfluous, no longer serving a purpose; not wanted. **2.** (of land) not used, not cultivated or built on. —n. **1.** an act of wasting. **2.** waste material. **3.** a waste region. **4.** diminution by use or wear. **5.** a waste-pipe. —**go** or **run to waste,** to be wasted. **waste paper,** spoiled or valueless paper. **waste-paper basket,** a receptacle for waste paper. **waste-pipe** n. a pipe to carry off waste liquid, especially from washing etc. **waste product,** a useless by-product of an organism or manufacture. [f. OF waster f. L vastare (as VAST)]

wasteful adj. using more than is needed, causing or showing waste. —**wastefully** adv., **wastefulness** n. [f. prec. + -FUL]

wasteland n. an unproductive or useless area of land.

waster n. **1.** a wasteful person. **2.** (slang) a wastrel. [f. WASTE]

wastrel /ˈweɪstr(ə)l/ n. a good-for-nothing person. [f. WASTE]

watch /wɒtʃ/ n. **1.** a small portable device indicating the time, usually worn on the wrist or carried in the pocket (see CLOCK[1]). **2.** the act of watching, especially to see that all is well; constant observation or attention. **3.** (Naut.) a spell of duty (usually four hours) on board ship; the part of a crew taking this. **4.** (hist.) a watchman or watchmen. —v.t./i. **1.** to look at, to keep one's eyes fixed on; to keep under observation. **2.** to be on the alert; to take heed. **3.** to be careful about; to safeguard, to exercise protective care. **4.** to look out for (an opportunity). **5.** (archaic) to remain awake for devotions etc. —**on the watch,** alert for an occurrence. **watch-dog** n. a dog kept to guard property etc.; a person etc. acting as guardian of others' rights etc. **watches of the night,** a time when one lies awake. **watching brief,** the brief of a barrister who follows a case for a client not directly concerned. **watch it,** (colloq.) be careful. **watch-night service,** a religious service on the last day of the year. **watch out,** to be on one's guard. **watch over,** to look after, to protect. **watch-tower** n. a tower from which observation can be kept. —**watcher** n. [OE (as WAKE[1])]

watchful adj. watching or observing closely; on the watch. —**watchfully** adv., **watchfulness** n. [f. prec. + -FUL]

watchmaker n. a person who makes and repairs watches and clocks.

watchman n. (pl. **-men**) a man employed to look after an empty building etc. at night.

watchword n. a phrase summarizing a principle of a party etc.

water /ˈwɔːtə(r)/ n. **1.** a colourless odourless tasteless liquid that is a compound of hydrogen and oxygen, convertible into steam by heat and into ice by cold; liquid consisting chiefly of this (in seas and rivers, rain, tears, sweat, saliva, urine), (usu. in pl.) amniotic fluid, etc.); a body of this as a sea, lake, or river; water as supplied for domestic use; (in pl.) part of a sea or river, the mineral water at a spa etc. **2.** the state of the tide. **3.** a solution of specified substance in water. **4.** the transparency and brilliance of a diamond or other gem. —attrib. **1.** found in or near water. **2.** of, for, or worked by water. **3.** involving, using, or yielding water. —v.t./i. **1.** to give drinking-water to (an animal); to supply (a plant etc.) with water. **2.** to take in a supply of water. **3.** to dilute with water. **4.** to secrete saliva or tears. **5.** (in p.p., of silk etc.) having irregular wavy markings. —**by water,** using a ship etc. for travel or transport. **like water,** lavishly, recklessly. **make one's mouth water,** to cause a flow of saliva; to create an appetite or desire. **make** or **pass water,** to urinate. **mouth-watering** adj. appetizing. **under water,** in or covered by water. **water-bed** n. a mattress of rubber or plastic etc. filled with water. **water-bird** n. a bird that swims on or wades in water. **water-biscuit** n. a thin crisp unsweetened biscuit made from flour and water. **water-buffalo** n. the common domestic Indian buffalo. **water bus,** a boat carrying passengers on a regular route on a lake or river. **water-cannon** n. a device giving a powerful water-jet to disperse a crowd etc. **Water-carrier** n. the constellation and sign of the zodiac Aquarius. **water-clock** n. see separate entry. **water-closet** n. see separate entry. **water-colour** n. a pigment diluted with water and not oil; a picture painted or the art of painting with this. **water-cooled** adj. cooled by the circulation of water. **water down,** to dilute; to make less forceful or horrifying. **water-glass** n. a solution of sodium or potassium silicate, especially for preserving eggs. **water-hammer** n. a knocking noise in a pipe when a tap is turned off. **water-hole** n. a shallow depression in which water collects. **water-ice** n. an edible concoction of frozen flavoured water. **watering-can** n. a portable container with a long tubular spout, holding water for watering plants. **watering-place** n. a pool where animals drink; a spa or seaside resort. **water-jump** n. a place where a horse must jump over water in a steeplechase etc. must jump over water. **water-level** n. the surface of water in a reservoir etc.; the height of this; the water-table; a level using water to determine the horizontal. **water-lily** n. an aquatic plant of the family Nymphaeaceae with floating leaves and flowers. **water-line** n. the line along which the surface of the water touches a ship's side. **water-main** n. a main pipe in a water-supply system. **water-meadow** n. a meadow periodically flooded by a stream. **water-melon** n. a large melon (Citrullus vulgaris) with a smooth green skin, red pulp, and watery juice. **water-mill** n. a mill worked by a water-wheel. **water-pistol** n. a toy pistol shooting a jet of water. **water polo,** a game played by swimmers with a ball like a football. The game originated in Britain as far back as 1870 or earlier, though the early rules were primitive and varied from area to area. It was played at the Olympic Games in 1900. **water-power** n. mechanical force from the weight or motion of water. **water-rat** n. a water-vole. **water-rate** n. a charge for the use of a public water-supply. **water-ski** n. a ski on which a person towed by a motor boat can skim the water-surface. **water-softener** n. an apparatus for softening hard water. **water-table** n. the plane below which the ground is saturated with water. **water-tower** n. a tower with an elevated tank to give pressure for distributing water. **water under the bridge,** the irrevocable past. **water-vole** n. an aquatic rat-like vole (Arvicola amphibius). **water-wheel** n. a wheel driven by water to work machinery, or used to raise water. **water-wings** n.pl. inflated supports worn on the shoulders by a person learning to swim. [OE]

water-clock n. a device for measuring time by the flow of water. In ancient Egypt (c.1400 BC) these consisted of round vessels from which water flowed through a hole in the base, with a time-scale marked on the inside of the vessel; the sloping sides helped to regulate the pressure of the outflow. Similar vessels were used in ancient Greece (see ill. TIME). The Romans had a cylinder into which water dripped, with a float for taking readings against a scale. By the 1st c. BC they had developed one with a shaft, attached to the float, with teeth that engaged a cogwheel to which was fixed a pointer moving over a dial. Similar clocks were used in Europe until the 16th c.

water-closet *n.* a lavatory with a pan that is flushed by water. Some ancient civilizations had elaborate systems of drainage and lavatories which in construction surpass anything of later periods up to the 19th c. The Elizabethan poet Sir John Harington designed the first English water-closet and installed it in his home near Bath; water pumped into a cistern descended through a pipe to flush the pan, the flow being regulated by a hand-operated tap and then released from the pan by means of a valve. Although Queen Elizabeth I is said to have had a model installed at her Richmond Palace, most of Sir John's contemporaries regarded the innovation as a joke and it was never patented. The first patent for a water-closet was taken out in 1755 by Alexander Cumming, a watchmaker, and in 1778 Joseph Bramah patented one with an improved valve. By mid-Victorian times most middle-class homes had indoor water-closets, but as there was no adequate water-supply and sewage system until near the end of the 19th c. these drained into cesspools, which were later connected by pipes to town sewers, and the inadequate water supply was insufficient to keep the complicated workings clean. Improvements on the basic design included ceramic pans to replace the earlier metal ones, an S-bend in the outlet pipe (in which trapped water prevented drain odours from rising), improved flushing systems, and the use of non-corroding plastic to replace metal parts.

watercourse *n.* a brook or stream; the bed of this.

watercress *n.* a cress of the genus *Rorippa* growing in springs etc., with pungent leaves used in salads.

waterfall *n.* a stream falling over a precipice or down a steep height.

waterfowl *n.* (usu. as *pl.*) water birds, especially game-birds that can swim.

waterfront *n.* the part of a town that borders on a river or lake or on the sea.

Watergate /ˈwɔːtəgeɪt/ a building in Washington, DC, housing the offices of the Democratic Party, the scene of a bungled bugging attempt by Republicans during the US election campaign of 1972. The attempted cover-up and subsequent inquiry caused a massive political scandal, gravely weakened the prestige of the government, and finally led to the resignation of President Richard Nixon in August 1974.

waterlogged *adj.* saturated with water; (of a boat etc.) barely able to float from being saturated or filled with water. [f. WATER + LOG¹; connection with *log* obscure]

Waterloo /wɔːtəˈluː/ a village in Belgium, south of Brussels, where on 18 June 1815 Napoleon's army was defeated by the British (under the Duke of Wellington) and Prussians. Attempting to exploit the temporary separation of the British and Prussian armies after the battles of Ligny and Quatre Bras, Napoleon attacked the outnumbered British force. Wellington was able to hold off the French until the arrival of the Prussians on his left flank forced them to retreat. Under the pressure of the Allied pursuit Napoleon's army disintegrated completely, effectively ending his bid to return to power. —**meet one's Waterloo**, to lose a decisive contest.

waterman *n.* (*pl.* **-men**) 1. a boatman plying for hire. 2. an oarsman as regards skill in keeping the boat balanced.

watermark *n.* a manufacturer's design in some kinds of paper, visible when the paper is held against light. —*v.t.* to mark with this.

waterproof *adj.* impervious to water. —*n.* a waterproof coat, cape or covering. —*v.t.* to make waterproof.

watershed *n.* 1. a line of high land where streams on one side flow into one river or sea and streams on the other side flow into another. 2. a turning-point in the course of events.

waterside *n.* the margin of a river, lake, or sea.

waterspout *n.* a funnel-shaped column of water and spray between sea and cloud, formed when a whirlwind draws up a gyrating mass of water.

watertight *adj.* 1. closely fastened or fitted so as to prevent the passage of water. 2. (of an argument etc.) unassailable; (of an agreement) with inescapable provisions.

waterway *n.* a route for travel by water; a navigable channel.

waterworks *n.* 1. an establishment for the management of a water-supply. 2. (*slang*) the shedding of tears. 3. (*slang*) the urinary system.

watery *adj.* 1. of or like water. 2. containing too much water; thin in consistency. 3. full of water or moisture. 4. (of a colour) pale; (of the sun, moon, or sky) looking as if rain will come. —**watery grave**, death by drowning. —**wateriness** *n.* [f. OE]

Watling Street /ˈwɒtlɪŋ/ a Roman road running NW across England from Richborough in Kent through London and St Albans to Wroxeter in Shropshire.

Watson¹ /ˈwɒts(ə)n/, Dr. A doctor who is the companion and assistant of Sherlock Holmes in stories by Sir Arthur Conan Doyle. A stolid upright citizen of sterling qualities, he is a foil to his friend's brilliance, being slightly (but only slightly) more stupid than the average reader.

Watson² /ˈwɒts(ə)n/, James Dewey (1928-), American biologist who together with F. H. C. Crick proposed a model for the structure of the DNA molecule, for which he was awarded a Nobel Prize in 1962.

Watson³ /ˈwɒts(ə)n/, John Broadus (1878-1958), American psychologist and founder of the school of behaviourism. He viewed behaviour as determined by an interplay between genetic endowment and environmental influences, and held that the role of the psychologist was to discern through observation and experimentation just which behaviour was innate and which was acquired. Seeking an objective study of psychology, he set the stage for the empirical study of animal and human behaviour which was to dominate the field of psychology, particularly in the USA, throughout the 20th c.

Watt /wɒt/, James (1736-1819), Scottish engineer, not the inventor but the great improver of the steam-engine. While repairing a Newcomen engine in 1764 he realized that it could be made more efficient by condensing the spent steam in a separate chamber, allowing the cylinder to remain hot. Progress in its development was slow until eventually he found a good business partner in Matthew Boulton, whose hearty enthusiasm balanced Watt's own tendency towards despondency and pessimism, and the improved engines became used for a variety of purposes. Watt continued inventing until the end of his life. He introduced rotatory engines and the centrifugal governor to control them, devised a chemical method of copying documents, and introduced the term 'horsepower' (see entry). The metric unit of power is named in his honour.

watt /wɒt/ *n.* a unit of power, the rate of working of one joule per second, corresponding to an electric circuit where the electromotive force is one volt and the current one ampere. —**watt-hour** *n.* the energy of one watt applied for one hour. [f. WATT]

wattage /ˈwɒtɪdʒ/ *n.* an amount of electrical power expressed in watts. [f. WATT]

Watteau /ˈwɒtəʊ/, Jean Antoine (1684-1721), French painter, of Flemish descent, an initiator of the rococo style in painting, who achieved fame with his new genre of elegant richly-coloured *fêtes galantes* (scenes of gallantry) and pastorals. Watteau deliberately created an imaginary rather theatrical world; his novel imagery, based largely on themes of the game of love and the pursuit of pleasure, was the antithesis of the serious religious and classical subject-matter approved by the French Academy. His finest and most characteristic work is *L'Embarquement pour l'Île de Cythère* (1717).

wattle¹ /ˈwɒt(ə)l/ *n.* 1. an Australian acacia with pliant boughs and golden flowers, used as the national emblem. 2. interlaced rods and twigs for fences etc. —**wattle and daub,** this plastered with mud or clay to make huts etc. [OE; orig. unkn.]

wattle² /ˈwɒt(ə)l/ *n.* a red fleshy fold of skin on the head or throat of certain birds (e.g. the turkey). [orig. unkn.]

Watts¹ /wɒts/, George Frederick (1817-1904), English painter and sculptor, from the 1880s a dominant figure in the Victorian art world, one of the first holders of the Order of Merit (1902). Like many of his contemporaries he saw his art as a vehicle for moral purpose. His allegorical pictures (e.g. *Hope*), once immensely popular, have lasted less well than the great series of portraits of Gladstone, Tennyson, J. S. Mill, etc. His first wife was the actress Ellen Terry, whom he married in 1864.

Watts² /wɒts/, Isaac (1674-1748), English hymn-writer and poet, who published four volumes of verse including *Divine*

Songs for the Use of Children (1715) and is remembered for his well-known hymns such as 'O God, our help in ages past', and his songs for children ('How doth the little busy bee'), some of which foreshadow Blake. He also wrote theological works and Pindaric odes and made daring experiments with metre.

Waugh /wɔː/, Evelyn Arthur St John (1903–66), English novelist. Educated at Oxford, he then worked as a schoolmaster, a background which provided material for his first and immensely successful novel *Decline and Fall* (1928); he became a Roman Catholic in 1930. His novels *Vile Bodies* (1930), *Black Mischief* (1932), *A Handful of Dust* (1934), and *Scoop* (1938) were works of high comedy and social satire which capture the brittle, cynical, determined frivolity of the post-war generation; *Brideshead Revisited* (1945), a complex story of an ancient Roman Catholic family, struck a more serious note. Waugh's career continued to prosper with *The Loved One* (1948) and *The Ordeal of Gilbert Pinfold* (1957), a self-caricature which ends in salvation. His wartime experiences in Crete and Yugoslavia appear in his trilogy *Men at Arms* (1952), *Officers and Gentlemen* (1955), *Unconditional Surrender* (1961). Waugh also wrote travel books, biographies, and an autobiography (1964).

wave *v.t./i.* **1.** to move (the arm, hand, or something held) to and fro as a signal or in greeting; to signal or express thus. **2.** to move loosely to and fro or up and down. **3.** to give a wavy form to; to have such a form. —*n.* **1.** a ridge of water moving along the surface of the sea etc. or curling into an arched form and breaking on the shore (ill. COASTS). **2.** a thing compared to this, e.g. an advancing group of attackers, a temporary increase of an influence or condition; a spell of hot or cold weather. **3.** a wave-like curve or arrangement of curves; waving of the hair. **4.** a gesture of waving. **5.** a rhythmic disturbance of a fluid or solid substance in which successive portions of it undergo alternate displacement and recovery, so that a state of motion travels through it without any continued advance of the substance itself; an analogous variation of an electromagnetic field in the propagation of light or other radiation (see below); a single curve in this plotted graphically against time. —**wave aside,** to dismiss as intrusive or irrelevant. **wave down,** to wave to (a vehicle or driver) as a signal to stop. **wave mechanics,** a particular mathematical formulation of quantum mechanics introduced by E. Schrödinger in which particles such as electrons are regarded as having some of the properties of waves. [OE]
Waves can be longitudinal, transverse, or torsional. In longitudinal waves (e.g. sound waves) the to-and-fro vibration is parallel to the direction of propagation; in transverse waves (e.g. water waves or light waves) the vibration is at right angles to the direction of propagation; in torsional waves a 'twist' is propagated. Waves display their characteristic properties of reflection, refraction, diffraction, and interference, under appropriate conditions. When two waves travelling in opposite directions meet, a 'standing wave' can result, which vibrates up and down but is not propagated. Wave phenomena are of great importance throughout physics. In the 20th c. quantum theory has introduced the seemingly paradoxical idea of 'wave-particle duality', in which photons of light and subatomic particles such as electrons are considered to have a dual nature, sharing characteristics of both waves and particles.

waveband *n.* a range of wavelengths between specified limits.

wavelength *n.* the distance between the crests of successive waves; a corresponding distance between points in a sound wave or electromagnetic wave (ill. SOUND); this as a distinctive feature of waves from a particular transmitter or (*fig.*) of a person's way of thinking.

wavelet *n.* a small wave. [WAVE + -LET]

waver /ˈweɪvə(r)/ *v.i.* **1.** to be or become unsteady, to begin to give way. **2.** to show hesitation or uncertainty. **3.** (of light) to flicker. —**waverer** *n.* [f. ON, = flicker; cf. WAVE]

wavy /ˈweɪvɪ/ *adj.* having waves or alternate contrary curves. —**wavily** *adv.*, **waviness** *n.* [f. WAVE]

wax[1] *n.* **1.** a sticky plastic yellowish substance secreted by bees as the material of honeycomb; this bleached and purified for candles, modelling, etc., or used in polishes. **2.** any similar substance. —*v.t.* to cover or treat with wax. —**be wax in a person's hands,** to be entirely subservient to him. [OE]

wax[2] *v.i.* **1.** (of the moon) to show a gradually increasing area of brightness before becoming full. **2.** to increase in

vigour, strength, or importance. **3.** (*archaic*) to pass into a specified state, to become. —**wax and wane,** to undergo alternate increases and decreases. [OE]

wax[3] *n.* (*slang*) a fit of anger. [orig. unkn.]

waxen *adj.* **1.** like wax, having a smooth pale translucent surface as of wax. **2.** (*archaic*) made of wax. [f. WAX[1]]

waxwing *n.* any of several small birds of the genus *Bombycilla* with red tips like sealing-wax to some wing-feathers.

waxwork *n.* an object modelled in wax; a model of a person with the face etc. made in wax, clothed to look lifelike and to be exhibited; (in *pl.*) an exhibition of such models.

waxy *adj.* **1.** resembling wax in consistency or surface. **2.** (*slang*) angry; easily enraged. —**waxily** *adv.*, **waxiness** *n.* [f. WAX[1,3]]

way *n.* **1.** a line of communication, e.g. a road or track. **2.** a course or route for reaching a place; the best route, the one taken or intended. **3.** a method or plan for attaining an object; a person's desired or chosen course of action. **4.** travelling-distance; the amount of difference between two states or conditions. **5.** an unimpeded opportunity to advance; a space free of obstacles so that people etc. can pass; a region over which advance is proceeding, desired, or natural. **6.** an advance in some direction, impetus, progress. **7.** a specified direction. **8.** a manner; habitual manner; the normal course of action or events; a talent or skill. **9.** a scope or range; a line of occupation or business. **10.** a specified condition or state; a respect. **11.** (in *pl.*) a structure of timber etc. down which a new ship is launched. —*adv.* (*colloq.*) far. —**by the way,** by the roadside during a journey; incidentally, as a more or less irrelevant comment. **by way of,** by means of; as a form of or substitute for; as a method of; passing through. **come one's way,** to become available to one. **go out of one's way,** to make a special effort; to act without compulsion. **in a way,** to a limited extent; in some respects. **in no way,** not at all. **in the way,** forming an obstacle or hindrance. **lead** or **show the way,** to act as guide or leader. **look the other way,** to ignore deliberately. **make one's way,** to go; to prosper. **make way for,** to allow to pass; to be superseded by. **on one's way,** in the process of travelling or approaching. **on the way,** travelling or approaching; having progressed; (of a baby) conceived but not yet born. **on the way out,** (*colloq.*) going down in status or favour; disappearing. **out of the way,** unusual; not obstructing; remote; disposed of. **under way,** in motion or progress. **way back,** (*colloq.*) long ago. **way-bill** *n.* a list of the passengers or parcels conveyed. **way-leave** *n.* a right of way rented to another. **way of life,** the principles or habits governing one's actions. **way-out** *adj.* (*colloq.*) exaggeratedly unusual in style, exotic; progressive. **ways and means,** methods of achieving something; (in Parliament) a means of providing money. [OE; adv. f. AWAY]

wayfarer /ˈweɪfeərə(r)/ *n.* a traveller, especially on foot. —**wayfaring** *n.*

wayfaring-tree *n.* a shrub (*Viburnum lantana*) that grows commonly along roadsides, with white flowers and with berries that turn red and then black.

Wayland the Smith /ˈweɪlənd/ (*Scand. myth.*) a smith with supernatural powers, in English legend supposed to have his forge in a dolmen on the downs in SW Oxfordshire.

waylay /weɪˈleɪ/ *v.t.* (*past* & *p.p.* **waylaid**) to lie in wait for, especially so as to talk to or rob.

-ways *suffix* forming adjectives and adverbs of direction or manner (*sideways*). [f. WAY]

wayside *n.* the side of a road; the land bordering a road.

wayward *adj.* childishly self-willed, capricious. —**waywardness** *n.* [f. obs. *awayward* turned away (AWAY, -WARD)]

Wb *abbr.* weber.

WC *abbr.* **1.** water-closet. **2.** West Central.

we /wiː, wɪ/ *pron.* (obj. US; poss. OUR, OURS). **1.** pl. of I, used by a person referring to himself and another or others, or speaking on behalf of a nation, group, firm, etc. **2.** used instead of 'I' by a royal person in formal proclamations and by the writer of a newspaper editorial etc. [OE]

weak *adj.* **1.** lacking strength, power, or number; easily broken, bent, or defeated. **2.** lacking vigour, not acting strongly. **3.** not convincing or forceful. **4.** (of a solution or drink) dilute, having a large proportion of water or other solvent. —**weaker sex,** women. **weak-kneed** *adj.* lacking determination, giving way easily when intimidated. **weak-minded** *adj.* mentally deficient; lacking determination. **weak verb,** a verb forming inflexions by a suffix, not by vowel-change only. —**weakly** adv. [f. ON veikr = OE wāc pliant, insignificant]

weaken v.t./i. to make or become weaker. [f. WEAK]

weakling n. a feeble person or animal. [f. WEAK + -LING]

weakly adj. sickly, not robust. —**weakliness** n. [f. WEAK]

weakness n. 1. being weak. 2. a weak point, a defect or fault. 3. a self-indulgent liking, inability to resist a particular temptation. [f. WEAK]

weal[1] n. a ridge raised on the flesh by a stroke of a whip etc. —v.t. to mark with a weal. [var. of WALE]

weal[2] n. welfare. [OE (as WELL[1])]

weald /wiːld/ n. the formerly wooded district including parts of Kent, Surrey, and East Sussex. [OE, = wold]

wealth /welθ/ n. 1. riches, possession of these. 2. a great quantity, plenty. [f. prec. or WELL[1], after health]

wealthy /ˈwelθɪ/ adj. having wealth, rich. —**wealthily** adv., **wealthiness** n. [f. prec.]

wean v.t. 1. to accustom (an infant or other young mammal) to take food other than (its mother's) milk. 2. (with of) to cause (a person) to give up a habit or interest etc. gradually. [OE, = accustom]

weapon /ˈwepən/ n. 1. a thing designed, used, or usable as a means of inflicting bodily harm. 2. a means employed for getting the better of someone in a conflict. [OE]

weaponry /ˈwepənrɪ/ n. weapons collectively. [f. prec.]

wear /weə(r)/ v.t./i. (past **wore**; p.p. **worn**) 1. to have on one's body, e.g. as clothing, ornaments, or make-up. 2. to have (a specified look) on one's face. 3. (colloq., usu. with neg.) to accept or tolerate. 4. to injure the surface of or become injured by rubbing, stress, or use; to make (a hole etc.) thus. 5. to exhaust or (with down) overcome by persistence. 6. to endure continued use or life (well or badly etc.). 7. (of time) to pass gradually. 8. (of a ship) to fly (a specified flag). —n. 1. wearing or being worn as clothing etc. 2. (esp. as suffix) clothing, suitable apparel (sportswear). 3. (also **wear and tear**) damage resulting from ordinary use. 4. capacity to endure being worn. —**wear one's heart on one's sleeve**, to show one's affections openly. **wear off**, to lose effectiveness or intensity. **wear out**, to use or to be used until no longer usable; to tire or be tired out. **wear thin**, (of patience etc.) to begin to fail. —**wearer** n. [OE]

wearable /ˈweərəb(ə)l/ adj. that may be worn. [f. WEAR]

wearisome /ˈwɪərɪsəm/ adj. tedious, tiring by monotony or length. [f. foll. + -SOME]

weary /ˈwɪərɪ/ adj. 1. very tired, especially from exertion or endurance. 2. (with of) tired of (a specified thing). 3. tiring, tedious. —v.t./i. to make or become weary. —**wearily** adv., **weariness** n. [OE]

weasel /ˈwiːz(ə)l/ n. a small fierce carnivorous animal (Mustela nivalis) with a slender body and reddish-brown fur, living on small animals, birds' eggs, etc. —**weasel word**, an equivocating or ambiguous word that takes away the force of the expression containing it (said to allude to the weasel's alleged habit of sucking out the contents of an egg and leaving only the shell). [OE]

weather /ˈweðə(r)/ n. 1. the state of the atmosphere at a certain place and time, with reference to heat, cloudiness, dryness, sunshine, wind, rain, etc. (see ill. pp. 930-1). 2. (attrib.) windward. —v.t./i. 1. to expose to or affect by atmospheric changes; to be discoloured or worn thus. 2. to come safely through (a storm, lit. or fig.). 3. to get to windward of (a cape etc.). —**keep a weather eye open**, to be watchful. **make heavy weather of**, to find trying or needlessly difficult. **under the weather**, (colloq.) indisposed. **weather-beaten** adj. affected by exposure to the weather. **weather-board** n. a sloping board at the bottom of a door to keep out rain; (in pl., also **weatherboarding**) a series of boards each overlapping the one below, fixed to the outside walls of light buildings (ill. BUILDING TECHNIQUES). **weather-vane** n. a weathercock. [OE]

weathercock n. 1. a revolving pointer, often in the form of a cockerel, mounted in a high place and turning easily in the wind to show from which direction the wind is blowing. 2. an inconstant person.

weatherly adj. (Naut.) making little leeway, capable of keeping close to the wind. —**weatherliness** n. [f. WEATHER]

weatherman n. (pl. -men) a meteorologist, especially one who broadcasts a weather forecast.

weatherproof adj. resistant to wind and rain.

weave[1] v.t./i. (past **wove**; p.p. **woven**) 1. to make (fabric etc.) by passing crosswise threads or strips under and over

lengthwise ones; to form (thread etc.) into fabric thus. (See LOOM.) 2. to put (facts etc.) together into a story or connected whole; to make (a story etc.) thus. —n. a style or pattern of weaving. [OE]

weave[2] v.i. to move repeatedly from side to side; to take an intricate course to avoid obstructions. —**get weaving**, (slang) to begin an action, to hurry. [prob. f. ON (as WAVE)]

weaver n. 1. one whose occupation is weaving. 2. a tropical bird of the family Ploceidae that builds a nest of elaborately interwoven twigs etc. [f. WEAVE[1]]

web n. 1. the network of fine strands made by a spider etc. 2. a network. 3. woven fabric; an amount woven in one piece. 4. a membrane filling the spaces between the toes of swimming birds (e.g. ducks) and animals (e.g. frogs). 5. a large roll of paper for printing. 6. a thin flat connecting part in machinery. —**web-footed** adj. having the toes connected by a web. —**webbed** adj. [OE (as WEAVE)]

Webb[1], (Gladys) Mary (1881-1927), English novelist. Her tales of rustic life, romantic, passionate, morbid, and frequently naïve, are written in a fervid prose easily ridiculed by Stella Gibbons in Cold Comfort Farm (1932), but retain a certain emotional power. They include Gone to Earth (1917) and Precious Bane (1924). Public praise of the latter by the Prime Minister Stanley Baldwin, after her death, brought her posthumous fame.

Webb[2], Sidney James (1859-1947), English socialist, who with his wife Beatrice (1858-1943), in a life of public service and private happiness, exerted considerable influence on political theory and social reform. They were prominent members of the Fabian Society, and launched the idea which culminated in the founding of the London School of Economics (1895), to which they gave unwearying service. Together they produced several important books on sociopolitical theory and history, most notably The History of Trade Unionism (1894) and Industrial Democracy (1897). Sidney's involvement with the Labour Party led to his decision to stand for Parliament; he became an MP in 1922 and was made a peer (Baron Passfield) in 1929.

webbing n. strong narrow closely-woven fabric used for belts or in upholstery etc. [f. WEB]

Weber[1] /ˈveɪbə(r)/, Carl Maria von (1786-1826), German composer, especially of operas, orchestral works, and piano music. His first major operatic success was Der Freischütz (The Freeshooter, 1817-21). The importance of this work for German opera was considerable: it became immensely popular at a time when Italian opera dominated, and it formed the focal point of Weber's influence on Wagner with its anticipation of Wagner's leitmotiv technique. His subsequent works were less successful as self-contained forms but contain some fine music; they include Euryanthe (1822-3) and Oberon (1825-6), composed for London, where he died of tuberculosis. In 1844 his coffin was shipped back to Germany and buried in Dresden after a funeral oration by Wagner.

Weber[2] /ˈveɪbə(r)/, Max (1864-1920), German economist, successively professor at Berlin, Freiburg, Heidelberg, and Munich, most famous for his work on the relationship between economy and society, which established him as one of the founders of modern sociology. His influential The Protestant Ethic and the Spirit of Capitalism (1904-5) put forward the theory that there was a direct relationship between the Calvinist work ethic and the rise of Western capitalism.

weber /ˈveɪbə(r)/ n. a unit of magnetic flux, causing an electromotive force of one volt in a circuit of one turn when generated or removed in one second. [f. W. E. Weber, German physicist (d. 1891)]

Webern /ˈveɪbən/, Anton (1883-1945), Austrian composer, an important pupil of Schoenberg. His music is marked by its brevity and clarity of expression—from the atonality of his three sets of songs to verses by Stefan George (1907-17) and increasingly concise orchestral works, to the strict serialism of the Symphony (1928), the String Quartet (1937-8), and the Orchestral Variations (1940). Webern survived the Second World War in Vienna, despite having his music proscribed by the Nazis, but was shot, accidentally, by an American soldier during the post-war occupation of Austria.

Webster[1] /ˈwebstə(r)/, John (c.1578-c.1632), English dramatist, son of a London coachmaker. Little is known of his life. He wrote several plays in collaboration with other dramatists but his great reputation rests on his own two major tragedies The White Devil (1609-12) and The Duchess of Malfi (1623), both of which are marked by a rich poetic texture and an intense tragic power. In the 19th c. critics complained about Webster's excessive use of horror, but in recent years there has been a revival of interest in his plays as drama and in Webster as a satirist and moralist.

Webster[2] /ˈwebstə(r)/, Noah (1758-1843), American lexicographer and philologist, remembered for his scholarly *American Dictionary of the English Language* (2 vols., 1828; there were many subsequent revisions) in which he challenged the parochialism of British dictionaries and, with a strong national pride and spirit, recorded Americanisms and American usages.

wed v.t./i. (-dd-; p.p. occas. **wed**) **1.** to marry. **2.** (fig.) to unite; **3.** (in p.p.) of marriage; (with *to*) devoted to and unable to abandon (an occupation or opinion etc.). [OE, = pledge]

Wed. abbr. Wednesday.

wedding n. a marriage ceremony and festivities. —**wedding breakfast,** a meal after the wedding ceremony and before departure for the honeymoon. **wedding-cake** n. a rich iced cake cut and eaten at a wedding. **wedding march,** a march (especially one by Mendelssohn) for a wedding procession. **wedding-ring** n. a ring worn by a married person from the time of the wedding ceremony. [OE (as WED)]

wedge n. **1.** a piece of wood or metal etc. thick at one end and tapered to a thin edge at the other, thrust between things to force them apart or prevent free movement etc. **2.** a wedge-shaped thing. —v.t. **1.** to force apart or fix firmly by using a wedge. **2.** to thrust or pack tightly between other things or people or in a limited space; to be made immovable thus. —**thin end of the wedge,** a change or procedure etc. that appears small or insignificant but will open the way to greater changes etc. [OE]

Wedgwood[1] /ˈwedʒwʊd/, Josiah (1730-95), English potter, whose artistic and entrepreneurial skills helped to establish a Staffordshire factory of international repute. He produced china which could be afforded by all classes, and his productions document the rise of neo-classical taste in England; his designs were often based on antique relief sculptures. The factory is perhaps best known for powder-blue pieces with white embossed cameos or patterns. Among the artists employed to produce designs were George Stubbs and John Flaxman.

Wedgwood[2] /ˈwedʒwʊd/ n. **1.** [P] a kind of fine pottery, especially with a white cameo design. **2.** its characteristic blue colour. [f. prec.]

wedlock /ˈwedlɒk/ n. the married state. —**born in wedlock,** legitimate. **born out of wedlock,** illegitimate. [OE, = marriage vow]

Wednesday /ˈwenzdeɪ, -dɪ/ n. the day of the week following Tuesday. —adv. (colloq.) on Wednesday. [OE, = day of (the god) Odin, transl. of L *Mercurii dies* day of the planet Mercury]

wee adj. **1.** (esp. Sc.) little. **2.** (colloq.) tiny. [orig. Sc., f. obs. *wei* (small) quantity (as WEIGH)]

weed n. **1.** a wild plant growing where it is not wanted. **2.** a thin weak-looking person or horse. **3.** (slang) marijuana. **4.** (archaic) tobacco. —v.t./i. **1.** to remove weeds from; to uproot weeds. **2.** (with *out*) to remove as inferior or undesirable. —**weed-killer** n. a substance used to destroy weeds. [OE; orig. unkn.]

weeds /wiːdz/ n.pl. the deep mourning formerly worn by widows. [OE, = garment]

weedy adj. **1.** full of weeds. **2.** growing freely like a weed. **3.** thin and weak-looking. [f. WEED]

week n. **1.** a period of seven successive days, especially one reckoned from midnight at the end of Saturday. **2.** the six days between successive Sundays; the five days other than Saturday and Sunday. **3.** the period for which one regularly works during a week. —**a week (from) today, Monday,** etc. (or **today, Monday,** etc., **week**), seven days after today, Monday, etc. [OE]

weekday n. a day other than Sunday.

weekend /wiːkˈend, ˈwiː-/ n. Sunday and (part of) Saturday (or a slightly longer period) especially for a holiday or visit.

weekly adj. done, produced, occurring, or payable etc. every week. —adv. every week. —n. a weekly newspaper or periodical. [f. WEEK]

weeny /ˈwiːnɪ/ adj. (colloq.) tiny. [f. WEE, after *tiny*]

weep v.t./i. (past & p.p. **wept**) **1.** to shed tears. **2.** to shed or ooze moisture in drops; to send forth in drops. **3.** (of a tree, usu. in *partic.*) to have drooping branches. —n. a spell of weeping. —**Weeping Cross,** (hist.) a wayside cross for penitents to pray at. [OE]

weepy adj. (colloq.) inclined to weep, tearful. [f. WEEP]

weevil /ˈwiːvɪl/ n. a destructive granary-beetle of the family Curculionidae. [f. MLG *wevel* = OE *wifel* beetle]

wee-wee /ˈwiːwiː/ n. (children's colloq.) urination; urine. —v.i. (children's colloq.) to urinate. [orig. unkn.]

weft n. crosswise threads woven over and under the warp threads to make fabric. [OE (as WEAVE)]

Wegener /ˈveɪɡənə(r)/, Alfred Lothar (1880-1930), German meteorologist and geologist, who from 1910 onwards propounded a detailed theory of continental drift (see CONTINENTAL). The theory was not accepted by most geologists during his lifetime, partly because he could not provide a convincing motive force to account for continental movements, but it is now accepted as correct in principle. As well as his geological studies Wegener wrote a standard textbook of meteorology. He died on the Greenland ice-cap in 1930 during an expedition.

Wei /weɪ/ the name of several dynasties which ruled in China, especially that of 386-535.

weigh /weɪ/ v.t./i. **1.** to measure the weight of, especially by means of scales or a similar instrument. **2.** to have (a specified weight). **3.** to consider carefully the relative importance or value of; to compare (a thing with or against another). **4.** to have importance or influence. **5.** to be burdensome. —**weigh anchor,** see ANCHOR. **weigh down,** to bring or keep down by weight; to depress or make troubled. **weigh in,** to be weighed (of a boxer before a contest, or a jockey after a race). **weigh in with,** (colloq.) to advance (an argument etc.) confidently. **weigh out,** to take a specified weight of; (of a jockey) to be weighed before a race. **weigh up,** (colloq.) to form an estimate of. **weigh one's words,** to choose those which precisely express one's meaning. [OE; rel. to WAIN, WAY]

weighbridge n. a weighing-machine set into a road etc., with a plate on to which vehicles can be driven to be weighed.

weight /weɪt/ n. **1.** the force with which a body tends to a centre of gravitational attraction, especially the tendency of bodies to fall to earth. **2.** relative mass giving such force; (pop.) mass. **3.** a quantitative expression of a body's mass; a scale for expressing weights. **4.** a heavy object, especially one used to bring or keep something down; an object of known weight for use in weighing. **5.** a load to be supported; a burden of responsibility or worry. **6.** influence, importance. **7.** (in athletics) a shot (SHOT[1]). —v.t. **1.** to attach a weight to; to hold down with a weight or weights. **2.** to burden with a load. **3.** to bias or arrange the balance of. —**throw one's weight about,** (colloq.) to use one's influence aggressively. **weight-lifting** n. see separate entry. **weight training,** a system of physical training using weights in the form of barbells or dumb-bells. [OE (as WEIGH)]

weighting /ˈweɪtɪŋ/ n. extra pay given in special cases. [f. prec.]

weightless adj. having no weight, or with no weight relative to the surroundings (e.g. in a spacecraft moving under the action of gravity). —**weightlessness** n. [f. WEIGHT + -LESS]

weight-lifting n. the athletic sport of lifting heavy objects. The ancient Greeks lifted heavy stones as a pastime, and the custom persisted in many parts of Europe through the Middle Ages. Modern weight-lifting with barbells and dumb-bells became popular towards the end of the 19th c. and was fostered by strong-man acts in circuses and music-halls.

weighty /ˈweɪtɪ/ adj. **1.** having great weight, heavy. **2.** burdensome. **3.** showing or deserving earnest thought. **4.** important, influential. —**weightily** adv., **weightiness** n. [f. WEIGHT]

Weill /vaɪl/, Kurt (1900-50), German composer. He studied in Berlin, where he remained until 1933, employing the art of the cabaret in his collaborations with the dramatist Bertolt Brecht to produce satirical works such as *The Rise and Fall of the City of Mahagonny* (1930), *The Threepenny Opera* (1928), and *The Seven Deadly Sins* (1933). He married the Austrian-born singer Lotte Lenya, the supreme exponent of his songs, most memorably 'Pirate Jenny' and 'Surabaya Johnny'. Weill continued to compose after settling in the USA but produced nothing to equal the works of his Berlin years, which brilliantly evoke the harsh decadence of the period leading up to Hitler's rise to power.

Weather

The atmosphere

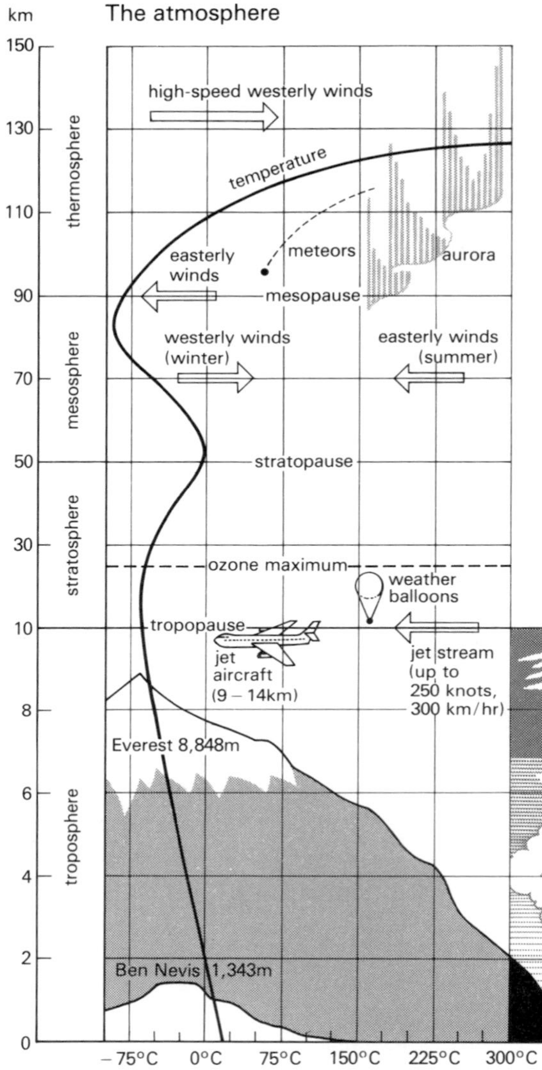

km

150 —

130 —

thermosphere

high-speed westerly winds

temperature

110 —

easterly winds

meteors

aurora

mesopause

90 —

mesosphere

westerly winds (winter)

easterly winds (summer)

70 —

50 —

stratopause

stratosphere

30 —

ozone maximum

weather balloons

10 —

tropopause

jet aircraft (9 – 14km)

jet stream (up to 250 knots, 300 km/hr)

Everest 8,848m

8 —

6 —

troposphere

4 —

2 —

Ben Nevis 1,343m

0 —

−75°C   0°C   75°C   150°C   225°C   300°C

temperature in the atmosphere in a temperate zone, varying with altitude (°C)

Winds and pressure systems

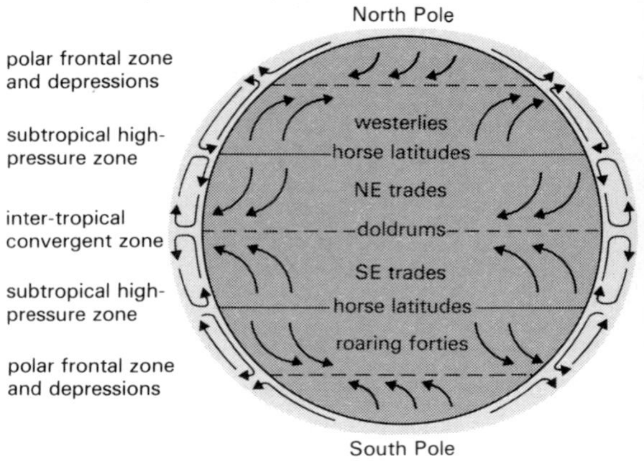

North Pole

polar frontal zone and depressions

subtropical high-pressure zone

westerlies

horse latitudes

NE trades

inter-tropical convergent zone

doldrums

subtropical high-pressure zone

SE trades

horse latitudes

polar frontal zone and depressions

roaring forties

South Pole

Clouds

high level (5 – 13km)
  Cs cirrostratus
  Cc cirrocumulus
  Ci cirrus

middle level (2 – 7km)
  Cb cumulonimbus
  Ac altocumulus
  As altostratus

low level (0 – 3km)
  St stratus
  Ns nimbo-stratus

  Cu cumulus
  Sc stratocumulus

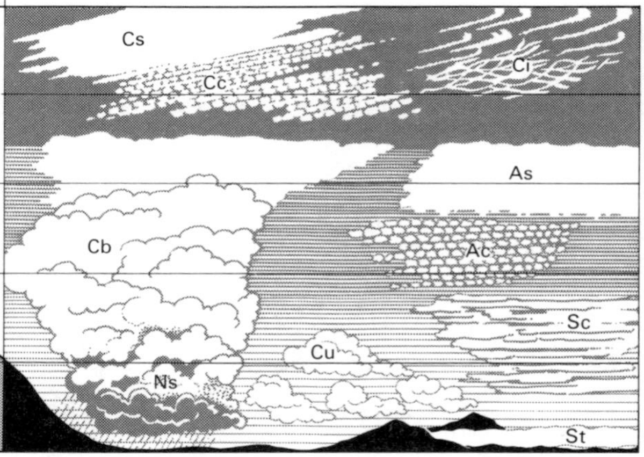

Cs   Ci   Cc   As   Ac   Sc   Cb   Cu   Ns   St

Thunderstorms

When the upper part of the cloud becomes positively charged and the lower part negatively charged to a sufficient extent, a giant spark of lightning occurs and the air expands rapidly, producing a thunderclap. Rain is typically (but not essentially) present.

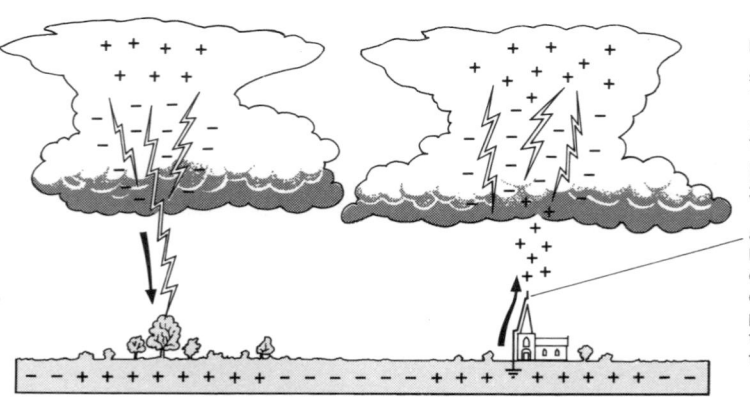

lightning

speed approx. 140,000km/sec

current up to 100,000 amps

heat release up to 30,000°C

a lightning-conductor lowers the charge difference by concentrating a positive 'electric wind' towards the base of the cloud

Precipitation from convective clouds

When warm air is forced upwards it cools and can hold less water-vapour, producing rain, hail, and snow.

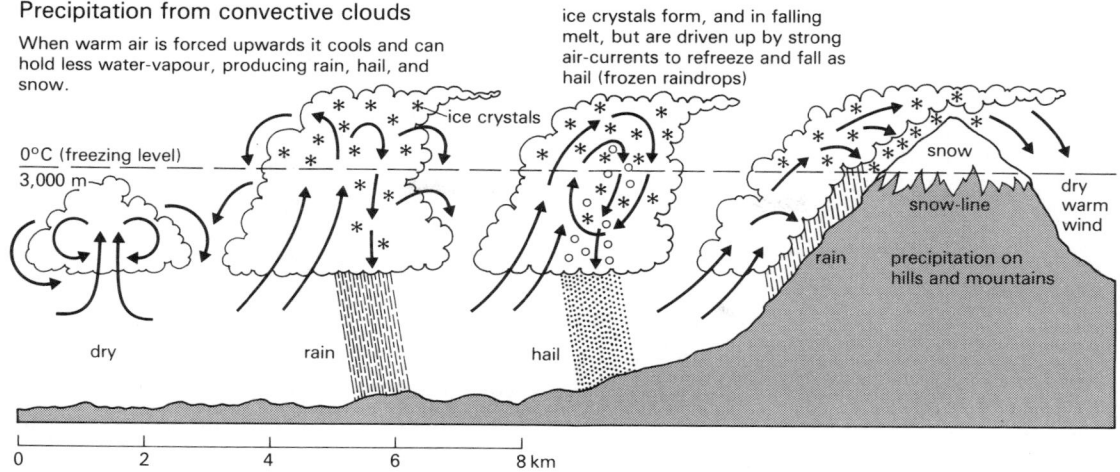

Development of depressions with warm, cold, and occluded fronts

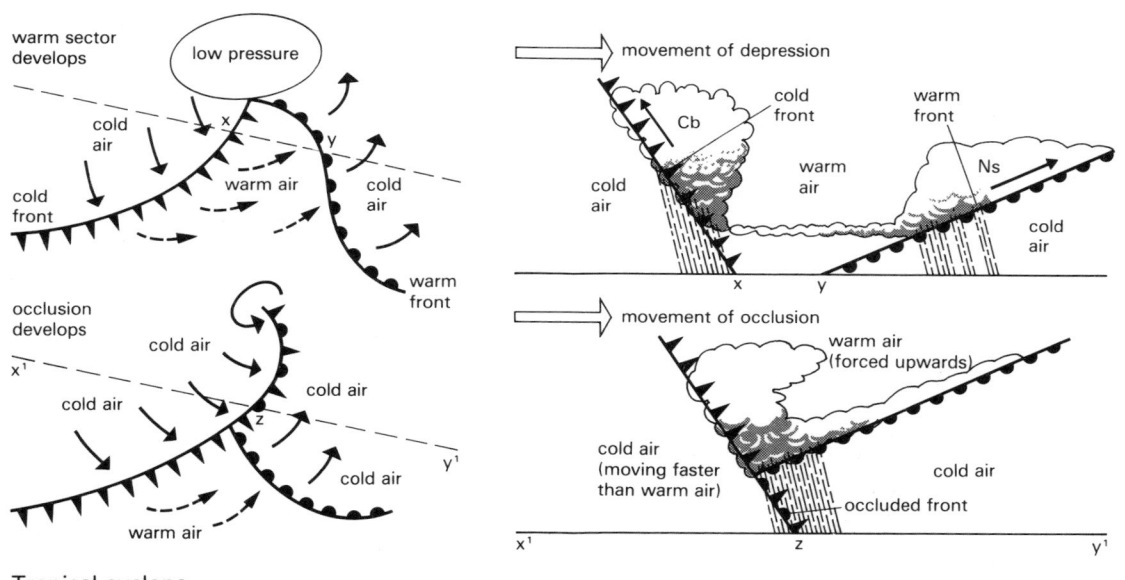

Tropical cyclone

(called hurricane in the Atlantic, typhoon in the Pacific)

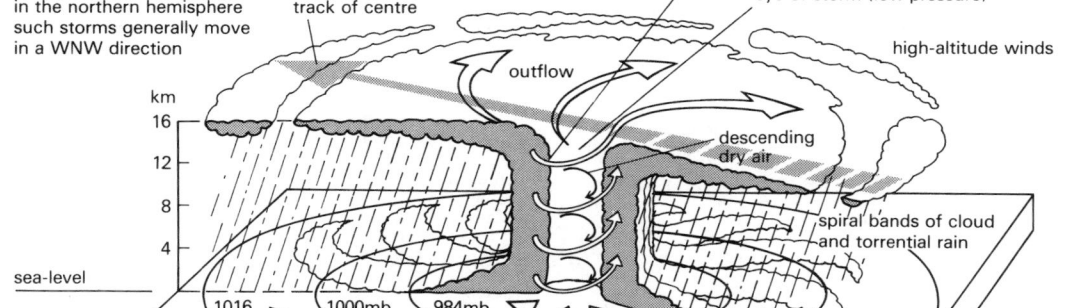

Weimar /'vaɪmɑː(r)/ a town in central Germany, famous as the residence of Goethe and Schiller and as the seat of the National Assembly of Germany 1919-33. —**Weimar Republic,** the German republic of this period, so called because its constitution was drawn up at Weimar.

weir /wɪə(r)/ n. a small dam built across a river or canal to raise the level of water upstream or regulate its flow. [OE wer f. werian dam up]

weird /wɪəd/ adj. **1.** strange and uncanny or bizarre. **2.** connected with fate (obs. exc. in **the weird sisters,** the Fates; witches). —**weirdly** adv., **weirdness** n. [f. OE wyrd destiny]

Weismann /'vaɪsmən/, August Friedrich Leopold (1834-1914), German biologist, one of the founders of modern genetics. He expounded a theory of heredity which assumed the continuity of 'germ-plasm', a substance which he postulated bore the factors that determine the transmission of characters from parent to offspring, carried by the gametes and itself unchanged from generation to generation. The theory rules out transmission of acquired characteristics.

welcome /'welkəm/ int. of greeting expressing pleasure at a person's coming. —n. saying 'welcome'; a kind or glad reception. —v.t. to receive with signs of pleasure. —adj. that one receives with pleasure; (predic.) ungrudgingly permitted or given the right (to a thing). [orig. OE wilcuma one whose coming is a pleasure (as WILL, COME)]

weld v.t. **1.** to unite or fuse (pieces of metal) by hammering or pressure, usually after softening by heat. **2.** to make (an article) thus. **3.** to be able to be welded. **4.** to unite effectively into a whole. —n. a welded joint. —**welder** n. [alt. f. WELL² in obs. sense 'melt']

welfare /'welfeə(r)/ n. **1.** good health, happiness, and prosperity. **2.** the maintenance of persons in such a condition; money given for this purpose. —**Welfare State,** a country ensuring the welfare of its citizens by social services operated by the government. **welfare work,** organized efforts for the welfare of a class or group. [f. WELL¹ + FARE]

welkin n. (poetic) the sky. [OE, = cloud]

well¹ adv. (compar. BETTER; superl. BEST) **1.** in the right or a satisfactory way. **2.** favourably, kindly. **3.** thoroughly, carefully. **4.** to a considerable extent. **5.** with good reason; easily; probably. —adj. **1.** in good health. **2.** (attrib.) in a satisfactory state or position. **3.** (attrib.) advisable. —int. expressing surprise or resignation etc., used especially after a pause in speaking. —**let well alone,** to avoid needless change or disturbance. **well-advised** adj. prudent. **well and truly,** decisively, completely. **well away,** having made considerable progress. **well-being** n. welfare. **well-born** adj. born of good family. **well-bred** adj. having or showing good breeding or manners. **well-connected** adj. related to good families. **well-disposed** adj. having kindly or favourable feelings (towards a person or plan etc.). **well done!** a cry of commendation. **well-groomed** adj. with carefully tended hair, clothes, etc. **well-heeled** adj. (colloq.) wealthy. **well-intentioned** adj. having or showing good intentions. **well-judged** adj. opportunely, skilfully, or discreetly done. **well-known** adj. known to many; known thoroughly. **well-mannered** adj. having good manners. **well-meaning** or **-meant** adj. well-intentioned (but ineffective). **well off,** fortunately situated; fairly rich. **well-oiled** adj. (slang) drunk. **well-preserved** adj. in good condition; (of an old person) showing little sign of age. **well-read** adj. having read much literature. **well-spoken** adj. speaking in a polite and correct way. **well-to-do** adj. fairly rich. **well-tested** adj. often tested with good results. **well-trodden** adj. much frequented. **well-wisher** n. a person who wishes one well. **well-worn** adj. much worn by use; (of a phrase etc.) hackneyed. [OE]

well² n. **1.** a shaft sunk into the ground to obtain water or oil from below the earth's surface. **2.** an enclosed space like a well-shaft, e.g. in the middle of a building for stairs (ill. HOUSES) or a lift, or to admit light and air. **3.** (fig.) a source. **4.** (in pl.) a spa. **5.** an ink-well. **6.** (archaic) a water-spring. —v.i. to spring as from a fountain. [OE]

Welles /welz/, (George) Orson (1915-), American film director and actor, a man of wayward talents whose career was both brilliant and erratic. The classic Citizen Kane (1941) was one of the peaks of his achievement.

wellies /'weliz/ n.pl. (colloq.) wellingtons. [abbr.]

Wellington¹ /'welɪŋt(ə)n/ the capital of New Zealand, situated at the south end of North Island; pop. (1981) 343,982.

Wellington² /'welɪŋt(ə)n/ Arthur Wellesley, 1st Duke of (1769-1852), British soldier and statesman, known as the

'Iron Duke'. The son of an Irish peer, Wellesley first achieved prominence as a result of his victory over the Marathas in India in 1803. As commander of British forces in the Spanish Peninsula (1809-14) he won a series of victories against French forces and finally drove them across the Pyrenees into southern France, then in 1815 he decisively defeated Napoleon at the Battle of Waterloo, bringing the Napoleonic Wars to an end. A convinced conservative, Wellington served in a variety of political posts between 1819 and 1846, including that of Prime Minister (1828-30 and briefly in 1834), often accepting change against his personal inclinations. He served as Commander-in-Chief of the army from 1842 until his death, being widely considered in his later years the senior statesman on the British scene.

wellington /'welɪŋt(ə)n/ n. a boot of rubber or similar waterproof material, usually reaching almost to the knee. [f. prec.]

Wells, Herbert George (1866-1946), English novelist, the son of a tradesman and professional cricketer. He was apprenticed to a draper, and studied science under the influence of T. H. Huxley. In 1903 he joined the Fabian Society but his provocative independence caused a rift with Shaw and the Webbs. His vast and varied literary output included early examples of science fiction, such as The Time Machine (1895), The Invisible Man (1897), and The War of the Worlds (1898), which combine political satire, warnings about the dangers of scientific advancement, and a hope for the future. He also wrote novels evoking, in comic realistic style, the lower-middle-class world of his youth: Kipps (1905) and The History of Mr Polly (1910). Among his other writings are the highly successful Tono-Bungay (1909), which he described as 'a social panorama in the vein of Balzac', and many works of scientific and political speculation (including The Shape of Things to Come, 1933) which confirmed his position as a great popularizer and one of the most influential voices of his age.

Wells, Fargo & Co. US express company founded in 1852 by an American business man, Henry Wells (1805-78), William Fargo (1818-81), and others. It carried mail to and from the newly developed West, originally by sea from New York to San Francisco (travelling overland at the Isthmus of Panama), founded a San Francisco bank, and later ran a stagecoach service (having bought the Pony Express and Southern Overland Mail empire) until the development of a transcontinental railway service. In 1918 it merged with other companies to form the American Railway Express Company.

Welsh adj. of Wales or its people or language. —n. the Celtic language of Wales (see below). —**the Welsh,** the Welsh people. **Welsh rabbit** (or by folk etym. **rarebit**), a dish of melted cheese on toast. [OE, ult. f. L Volcae name of a Celtic people]

Welsh belongs to the Brythonic group of the Celtic languages. It is spoken by about 500,000 people in Wales and has a substantial literature dating from the medieval period. When Wales was united with England in 1536 it seemed likely that Welsh would disappear as a living language, but the publication of a Bible in Welsh in 1588 played an important part in preserving it. Although under great pressure from English, Welsh is widely used and taught in Wales. It is written almost phonetically, each letter (except y) having one standard sound only.

welsh v.i. **1.** (of one who loses a bet, esp. a bookmaker at a racecourse) to decamp without paying out winnings. **2.** (with on) to break an agreement with (a person); to fail to honour (an obligation). —**welsher** n. [orig. unkn.]

Welshman n. (pl. **-men**) one who is Welsh by birth or descent. —**Welshwoman** n.fem. (pl. **-women**).

welt n. **1.** a leather rim sewn to a shoe-upper for the sole to be attached to. **2.** a weal (WEAL¹). **3.** a heavy blow. **4.** a ribbed or reinforced border of a garment. —v.t. **1.** to provide with a welt. **2.** to raise weals on; to thrash. [orig. unkn.]

welter¹ v.i. **1.** (of a ship) to be tossed to and fro on the waves. **2.** to roll or lie prostrate, to be soaked (in blood etc.). —n. a state of turmoil; a disorderly mixture. [f. MDu. or MLG]

welter² n. a heavy rider or boxer. [orig. unkn.]

welterweight n. the boxing-weight between lightweight and middleweight (see BOXING-WEIGHT).

wen n. a benign tumour on the skin, esp. of the scalp. [OE]

Wenceslas¹, **-laus** /'wensɪsləs/, St (907-29), prince of Bohemia and patron saint of Czechoslovakia. He worked for the religious and cultural improvement of his people but was murdered by his brother and became venerated as a martyr. The story told in J. M. Neale's carol 'Good King Wenceslas' appears imaginary. Feast day, 28 Sept.

Wenceslas², **-laus** /ˈwensɪsləs/ (1361–1419), king of Bohemia (as Wenceslaus IV) 1378–1419. He became king of Germany and Holy Roman Emperor at the same time as he succeeded to the throne of Bohemia, but was deposed by the German electors in 1400 and afterwards imprisoned in Vienna. He regained the Bohemian throne in 1404 and held it until his death.

wench *n.* (*archaic*) a girl or young woman. [f. OE *wencel* child]

wend *v.t.* **wend one's way**, to go. [OE, = turn]

Wendy house /ˈwendɪ/ a children's small houselike structure for playing in. [character in J. M. Barrie's *Peter Pan* (1904)]

went *past* of GO¹.

wept *past & p.p.* of WEEP.

were see BE.

weren't /wɜːnt/ (*colloq.*) = were not.

werewolf /ˈwɪəwʊlf/ *n.* (also **werwolf**; *pl.* **-wolves**) a mythical being who at times changes from a person to a wolf. [OE; first element perh. f. *wer* man = L *vir*]

Werner¹ /ˈvɜːnə(r)/, Abraham Gottlob (1749–1817), German geologist, the chief exponent of the Neptunian theory (see NEPTUNIAN) which included the belief that rocks such as granites (now known to be of igneous origin) were formed as precipitates from a primeval ocean. Although this theory was invalid, the controversy that it stimulated prompted a rapid increase in geological research, and Werner's was probably the first attempt to establish a universal stratigraphic sequence.

Werner² /ˈvɜːnə(r)/, Alfred (1866–1919), French-born Swiss chemist, founder of co-ordination chemistry. He demonstrated that stereochemistry was not just the property of carbon compounds, but was general to the whole of organic and inorganic chemistry. In 1893 he announced the theory of 'co-ordinating compounds' which had come to him in a flash of inspiration and in which he proposed two types of valency bonds. This theory, which gave fresh insight into the structure of chemical compounds, is fundamental not only to modern inorganic chemistry but also to the analytical, organic, physical, and biochemical fields, and the related ones of mineralogy and crystallography. In 1913 he became the first Swiss to be awarded the Nobel Prize for chemistry.

Wesker /ˈweskə(r)/, Arnold (1932–), English playwright. His plays are avowedly socialist in outlook; a frequent theme is the working class's need for a cultural identity, as in *Roots* (1959).

Wesley /ˈwezlɪ/, John (1703–91), founder of Methodism. An Anglican priest, he was the leader of an earnest, devout, and scholarly group in Oxford who became known by various names including 'Methodists', and included his brother Charles (1707–88), who later became the composer of many well-known hymns. In 1738 the brothers experienced a spiritual conversion on a visit to the Moravian Church in Saxony, and determined to devote their lives to evangelistic work. Finding the churches closed to him through Anglican opposition, John Wesley began preaching out of doors; his success led him to organize a body of lay pastors to follow up his evangelism, and societies for their many working-class converts. Thenceforward he travelled the British Isles on horseback, averaging 8,000 miles a year; despite some hostility from the clergy he was mostly received with enthusiasm. Wesley himself wished his movement to remain within the Church of England, but an increasingly independent system grew up.

Wesleyan /ˈwezlɪən/ *adj.* (*hist.*) of the Protestant denomination founded by John Wesley. —*n.* a member of this denomination. [f. prec.]

Wessex /ˈwesɪks/ the kingdom of the West Saxons, established in Hampshire in the early 6th c. and gradually extended by conquest to include much of southern England. Under Alfred the Great and his successors it formed the nucleus for the Anglo-Saxon kingdom of England. The name was revived by Thomas Hardy to designate the south-western counties of England (especially Dorset) in which his novels are set, and is used in the titles of certain present-day regional authorities.

West¹, Benjamin (1738–1820), American painter who settled in England in 1763, becoming historical painter to George III and second President of the Royal Academy in 1792. West made his reputation with large historical can-

vases in the neo-classical style. Later paintings, such as *Saul and the Witch of Endor* (1777) and *Death on a Pale Horse* (1802), are early examples of the Romantic taste for melodrama and fantasy.

West², Dame Rebecca (real name Cicily Isabel Fairfield, 1892–1983), English novelist, journalist, and feminist, much influenced by the Pankhursts and the Women's Suffrage Movement. She chose the name 'Rebecca West' (one of Ibsen's heroines) when writing for *The Freewoman*, a fiercely feminist journal. In her younger days she became known for her beauty and for her shrewd, witty, and combative pieces. Her outspoken review of H. G. Wells's novel *Marriage* (1912) led to their secret love affair and the birth of a son. Among her many novels are *The Return of the Soldier* (1918), describing the return home of a shell-shocked soldier, *The Judge* (1922), and *The Birds Fall Down* (1966). Her non-fiction works include *Black Lamb and Grey Falcon* (1941), a two-volume study on Yugoslavia, and *The Meaning of Treason* (1949; updated in 1965 to include more recent spy scandals), and reports of the Nuremberg war-crimes trials after the Second World War. She continued to write with exceptional vigour almost until her death at the age of 90.

west *n.* **1.** the point of the horizon where the sun sets at the equinoxes, opposite east; the compass point corresponding to this; the direction in which this lies. **2.** (usu. **West**) the western part of a country etc.; European civilization; the non-Communist States of Europe and North America. —*adj.* towards, at, or facing the west; (of a wind) blowing from the west. —*adv.* towards, at, or near the west. —**go west**, (*slang*) to be killed or destroyed etc. **West Country**, south-western England. **West End**, the part of London near Piccadilly, containing famous theatres, restaurants, shops, etc. **West Side**, (*US*) the western part of Manhattan. **west-north-west, west-south-west** *adjs. & advs.* midway between west and south-west; (*ns.*) the compass point in this position. [OE]

West Bengal a State in eastern India, formed in 1947 from the Hindu area of former Bengal; capital, Calcutta.

westering *adj.* (of the sun) nearing the west. [f. WEST]

westerly /ˈwestəlɪ/ *adj. & adv.* in a western position or direction (of a wind) blowing from the west (approximately). [as prec.]

western /ˈwestən/ *adj.* of or in the west. —*n.* a film or novel about life in western North America during the wars with the Indians, or involving cowboys etc. (see below). —**Western Church**, the Churches of western Christendom as distinct from the Eastern or Orthodox Church. **Western Empire**, see ROMAN EMPIRE. —**easternmost** *adj.* [OE (as WEST)]

Westerns are the oldest and most enduring genre in cinema, their historical setting being traditionally the 1850s to 1890s. In 1908–14 D. W. Griffith made a number of one-reel westerns, and by the 1920s the western was an internationally accepted convention. In the late 1930s and early 1940s it reached maturity, led by *Stagecoach* (1939) directed by John Ford, the greatest director of the genre, and starring John Wayne, its most popular star. From the early 1950s its accepted modes provided a 20th-c. mythology within which a wide variety of ideas could be developed, and its conventions have influenced action films of other cultures.

Western Australia a State comprising the western part of Australia. It was first settled by the British in 1826 and 1829, and was federated with the other States of Australia in 1901; capital, Perth.

westerner *n.* a native or inhabitant of the west. [f. WESTERN]

Western Isles 1. the Hebrides. **2.** an islands area of Scotland consisting of the Outer Hebrides.

westernize /ˈwestənaɪz/ *v.t.* to make (an Oriental person etc.) more like the West in ideas and institutions etc. —**westernization** /-ˈzeɪʃ(ə)n/ *n.* [f. WESTERN]

Western Samoa /səˈməʊə/ a country consisting of a group of nine islands in the SW Pacific; pop. (1981) 158,130; official languages, Samoan and English; capital, Apia. Discovered by the Dutch in the early 18th c., the islands were administered by Germany from 1900. After the First World War they were mandated to New Zealand, and became an independent republic within the Commonwealth in 1962. Robert Louis Stevenson settled there in 1890 and died at Apia in 1894.

West Glamorgan /gləˈmɔːgən/ a county of South Wales.

West Indies a chain of islands extending from the coast

of Florida in North America to that of Venezuela in South America, enclosing the Caribbean Sea. Discovered by Columbus in 1492 and named in the belief that he had discovered the Asian coast, the islands were opened up by the Spanish in the 16th c. and thereafter were the theatre of rivalry between the European colonial powers. Cultivation of sugar was introduced and the population was transformed by the mass importation of West African slaves to work the agricultural plantations; their descendants form the largest group in the population. —**West Indian** adj. & n.

westing n. (Naut. etc.) **1.** a distance travelled or measured westward. **2.** a westerly direction. [f. WEST]

Westinghouse /ˈwestɪŋhaʊs/, George (1846–1914), American engineer whose achievements covered several different fields: vacuum-operated brakes for railway vehicles which enabled the driver to apply brakes throughout the train and which would act automatically in case of failure in any part of the system; electrically controlled signals for railways; this led him into the generation and transmission of electric power and (through Nikola Tesla) he championed the use of alternating current rather than the direct current used by Thomas Edison. Westinghouse built up a huge enterprise to manufacture his products, both in the USA and abroad. He also pioneered the use of natural gas and pneumatic power (compressed air), and installed water turbines at Niagara Falls; altogether he had over 400 patents to his name.

West Midlands a metropolitan county of central England.

Westminster /ˈwestmɪnstə(r)/ an inner London borough containing the Houses of Parliament (*Palace of Westminster*; see below) and many government offices etc., whence its allusive use to mean British parliamentary life or politics. —**Palace of Westminster,** a palace, supposed to date from Edward the Confessor, on the site now occupied by the Houses of Parliament. It was destroyed by fire in 1512 and ceased to be a royal residence, but a great part of it remained. The Houses of Lords and Commons for a long time sat in its buildings, until these were destroyed by fire in 1834. **Statute of Westminster,** the statute of 1931 recognizing the equality of status of the Dominions as autonomous communities within the British Empire, and giving their legislatures independence from British control.

Westminster Abbey the collegiate church of St Peter in Westminster, London, originally the abbey church of a Benedictine monastery. The present building, begun by Henry III in 1245 and altered and added to by successive rulers, replaced an earlier church built by Edward the Confessor. Nearly all the kings and queens of England have been crowned in Westminster Abbey; it is also the burial-place of many of England's monarchs (up to George II) and of the nation's leading statesmen, poets (in the section called Poets' Corner), and other celebrities, and of the Unknown Warrior.

Westphalia /westˈfeɪlɪə/ a former province of NW Germany which from 1815 formed part of Prussia, now part of the West German Land ('State') of North Rhine-Westphalia; capital, Dusseldorf. —**Peace of Westphalia,** the peace (1648) which ended the Thirty Years War. —**Westphalian** adj. & n.

West Sussex /ˈsʌsɪks/ a county of SE England.

West Virginia /vəˈdʒɪnjə/ a State of the USA, to the west of Virginia. It separated from Virginia during the American Civil War (1861), and became the 35th State of the USA in 1863; capital, Charleston.

westward /ˈwestwəd/ adj. & (also **westwards**) adv. towards the west. —n. a westward direction or region. [f. WEST + -WARD]

West Yorkshire a metropolitan county of northern England.

wet adj. **1.** soaked, covered, or moistened with water or other liquid. **2.** (of weather etc.) rainy. **3.** (of ink or paint etc.) not yet dried. **4.** used with water. **5.** (slang) lacking good sense or mental vitality, feeble, dull. —v.t. (-tt-; past & p.p. **wet** or **wetted**) to make wet. —n. **1.** liquid that wets something. **2.** rainy weather. **3.** (slang) a dull or feeble person. **4.** (slang) a drink. —**wet behind the ears,** immature, inexperienced. **wet blanket,** a person or thing damping or discouraging enthusiasm, cheerfulness, etc. **wet dream,** an erotic dream with involuntary emission of semen. **wet-nurse** n. a woman employed to suckle another's child; (v.t.) to suckle thus; to treat as if helpless. **wet suit,** a rubber garment worn by skin-divers etc. to keep warm.

wet through or **to the skin,** with one's clothes soaked. —**wetly** adv., **wetness** n. [OE, rel. to WATER]

wether /ˈweðə(r)/ n. a castrated ram. [OE]

Weyden /ˈvaɪd(ə)n/, Rogier van der (c.1400–64), the leading Flemish painter of the 15th c. In 1435 he was appointed official painter to the city of Brussels, where he settled. An enigmatic figure, he produced no signed or dated works, but his paintings became widely known in Europe during his lifetime. Major works include the *Deposition*, showing the influence of Jan van Eyck, and the *Entombment*, which may show Italian influences from his visit to Italy in 1450. His influence on other artists was great, and Netherlands portraiture of the 15th c. looked to his lead.

whack v.t. (colloq.) to strike or beat forcefully. —n. **1.** (colloq.) a sharp or resounding blow. **2.** (slang) a share. —**have a whack at,** (slang) to attempt. [imit.]

whacked adj. (colloq.) tired out. [f. prec.]

whacking adj. (slang) very large. —adv. (slang) very (great etc.). [f. WHACK]

whale n. a marine mammal of the order Cetacea, especially a large one hunted for oil, whalebone, etc. —v.i. to hunt whales. —**a whale of a time,** (colloq.) an exceedingly good or fine etc. time. **whale-oil** n. oil from the blubber of whales. [OE]
There are about 83 living species of whales. Unlike seals, whales spend no time on land, and they have a very fishlike appearance with a tapering body, fins, and no trace of hind limbs. There are two main groups: the toothed whales, comprising the majority of species, are carnivorous and include dolphins, porpoises, and the sperm whale; the baleen whales, of which the largest species, the blue whale, is the biggest animal that has ever lived, feed by sieving plankton through fibrous plates in their mouths. Although air-breathing, some whales can dive to great depths and stay under water for an hour or more. They navigate by using a form of sonar, and also communicate by sound, sometimes over very long distances. Most whales are intelligent and sociable creatures. In recent decades whaling has threatened some species with extinction.

whalebone n. an elastic horny substance from the upper jaw of some whales, formerly used as stiffening.

whaler /ˈweɪlə(r)/ n. a person or ship engaged in hunting whales. [f. WHALE]

wham int. expressing forcible impact. [imit.]

whang v.t./i. to strike heavily and loudly. —n. a whanging sound or blow. [imit.]

wharf /wɔːf/ n. (pl. **wharfs**) a platform to which a ship may be moored to load and unload. —v.t. to moor (a ship) at or store (goods) on a wharf. [OE]

wharfage n. accommodation at a wharf; the fee for this. [f. prec.]

wharfinger /ˈwɔːfɪndʒə(r)/ n. the owner or keeper of a wharf. [f. WHARF; cf. messenger]

Wharton /ˈwɔːt(ə)n/, Edith (née Newbold Jones, 1862–1937), American novelist who settled in France in 1907 and devoted considerable energy to a cosmopolitan social life, which included a close friendship with Henry James, and to a literary career. She established her reputation as a leading novelist with *The House of Mirth* (1905) and continued with other novels, short stories, poems, and an autobiography (*A Backward Glance*, 1934). Her chief preoccupation is with the conflict between social and individual fulfilment (which frequently leads to tragedy), and her observant satiric portrayal of social nuance, both in Europe and America, shows a keen interest in the 'tribal behaviour' of various groups.

what interrog. adj. asking for a choice from an indefinite number (what books have you read?) or for a statement of amount, number, or kind (what stores have we got?); (colloq.) which? (what book have you chosen?). —excl. adj. how great or remarkable. —rel. adj. the or any . . . that. —interrog. pron. **1.** what thing(s)? **2.** (a request for a remark to be repeated) what did you say? —excl. pron. what thing(s)!, how much!, etc. —rel. pron. that or those which; the thing(s) or anything that. —adv. to what extent or degree. —int. expressing surprise. —**what about,** what is the news about (a subject); what is your opinion of (an activity, etc.); shall we do or have etc. **what d'you call it** or **what's his (or its) name?** a substitute for a name that one cannot remember. **what for?** for what reason or purpose? (give a person what for, (slang) to punish or scold him or her). **what have you,** anything else similar. **what not,** other similar things. **what's what,** what is useful or important etc. **what with,** because of (various specified causes). [OE]

whatever /wɒtˈevə(r)/ *adj. & pron.* **1.** = WHAT (in relative uses) with emphasis on indefiniteness. **2.** though anything. **3.** (with neg. or interrog.) at all, of any kind.

whatnot *n.* **1.** something trivial or indefinite. **2.** a stand with shelves for small objects.

whatsoever /wɒtsəʊˈevə(r)/ *adj. & pron.* = WHATEVER.

wheat *n.* a cereal of the genus *Triticum* bearing dense four-sided seed-spikes from which much bread is made; its grain. [OE]

wheatear *n.* a small migratory bird of the genus *Oenanthe*, especially a species with a white belly and rump. [app. f. *wheatears* (as WHITE, ARSE)]

wheaten *adj.* made of wheat. [as WHEAT]

wheatmeal *n.* wholemeal flour made from wheat.

Wheatstone /ˈwiːtstəʊn/, Sir Charles (1802–75), English physicist and inventor in acoustics, optics, electricity, and telegraphy, a member of a family of musical instrument-makers and dealers. He invented the kaleidoscope, stereoscope, and the concertina, but is probably best known for his electrical inventions, including an electric clock. In the 1830s he collaborated with Sir William Fothergill Cooke to develop the electric telegraph, and in 1843 he devised the Wheatstone bridge (see foll.; based on an idea of the mathematician Samuel Christie) and the rheostat for measuring electrical resistance.

Wheatstone bridge an apparatus for measuring electrical resistance by equalizing the potential at two points of a circuit. [f. prec.]

wheedle *v.t.* to coax; to persuade or obtain by coaxing. [perh. f. G *wedeln* fawn, cringe (*wedel* tail)]

wheel *n.* **1.** a circular frame or disc arranged to revolve on an axle and used to facilitate the motion of a vehicle or for various mechanical purposes (see below); a wheel-like thing. **2.** a machine etc. of which a wheel is an essential part. **3.** motion like that of a wheel; movement of a line of men that pivots on one end. —*v.t./i.* **1.** to turn or cause to turn like a wheel; to change direction and face another way. **2.** to push or pull (a bicycle or cart etc. with wheels, or its contents) along. **3.** to move in circles or curves. —**at the wheel,** driving a vehicle or directing a ship's course; in control of affairs. **on (oiled) wheels,** smoothly. **wheel and deal,** (*US*) to engage in political or commercial scheming so as to exert influence. **wheel-spin** *n.* rotation of a vehicle's wheels without traction. **wheels within wheels,** secret or indirect motives and influences interacting with one another. [OE]
The wheel is regarded as one of the most important of man's inventions, first recorded in Mesopotamia about 3500 BC, made of solid wood; it was unknown in the pre-Columbian civilizations of Central America other than Mexico. Spoked wheels appeared soon after 2000 BC and were gradually improved and refined; iron tyres were used to protect and strengthen the rim, and the dished wheel of slightly conical form greatly increased strength and stiffness. A wheel using wire spokes in tension only was evolved for the bicycle: by arranging alternate spokes to lead to opposite flanges of the hub and be tangential to the hub in the forward and backward directions the result was a strong lightweight wheel able to transmit a torque from hub to rim. The final evolution of the wheel was in the use of pneumatic tyres, making it easier for vehicles to traverse uneven surfaces.

wheelbarrow *n.* an open container for moving small loads in gardening, building, etc., with a wheel beneath one end and two handles (by which it is pushed) at the other.

wheelbase *n.* the distance between the axles of a vehicle.

wheelchair *n.* a disabled person's chair on wheels.

wheel-house *n.* **1.** a steersman's shelter. **2.** a stone-built circular house with inner partition walls radiating like the spokes of a wheel, found in western and northern Scotland and dating chiefly from *c.*100 BC–*c.*100 AD.

wheelie *n.* the stunt of riding a bicycle or motor cycle for a short distance with the front wheel off the ground.

wheelwright *n.* a maker or repairer of wooden wheels.

wheeze *v.i.* to breathe with an audible hoarse whistling sound. —*n.* **1.** a sound of wheezing. **2.** (*slang*) a clever scheme. —**wheezy** *adj.* [prob. f. ON = hiss]

whelk *n.* a spiral-shelled marine mollusc of the genus *Bucinum* etc., especially one used as food. [OE; orig. unkn.]

whelm *v.t.* (*poetic*) to engulf, to crush with a weight. [cf. OE *hwylfan*]

whelp *n.* **1.** a young dog, a pup. **2.** (*archaic*) a cub. —*v.t./i.* to give birth to (a whelp or whelps). [OE]

when *interrog. adv.* at what time?, on what occasion?, how soon? —*rel. adv.* (with ref. to time) at or on which. —*conj.* **1.** at the or any time that; as soon as. **2.** although; considering that; since. —*pron.* what or which time. —*n.* the time, the occasion (*fix the where and when*). [OE]

whence *interrog. adv.* from what place or source? —*rel. adv., & conj.* (with ref. to place) from which; to the place from which. —*pron.* what place?; which place. —*n.* source. [OE, rel. to prec.]

whenever /wenˈevə(r)/ *conj. & adv.* at whatever time, on whatever occasion; every time that.

whensoever /wensəʊˈevə(r)/ *conj. & adv.* = WHENEVER.

where /weə(r)/ *interrog. adv.* in or to what place or position (*lit. or fig.*)?; in what direction?; in what respect? —*rel. adv., & conj.* (with ref. to place) in or to which; in the direction, part, or respect, in which; and there. —*pron.* what place? —*n.* the place (see WHEN). [OE]

whereabouts /weərəˈbaʊts/ *adv.* approximately where. —/ˈweər-/ *n.* (as *sing.* or *pl.*) a person's or thing's location roughly defined.

whereas /weərˈæz/ *conj.* **1.** in contrast or comparison with the fact that. **2.** (esp. in legal preambles) taking into consideration the fact that.

whereby /weəˈbaɪ/ *conj.* by what or which means.

wherefore *adv.* (*archaic*) for what reason?; for which reason. —*n.* a reason (see WHY).

wherein /weərˈɪn/ *conj.* (*formal*) in what or which place or respect.

whereof /weərˈɒv/ *adv. & conj.* (*formal*) of what or which.

whereupon /weərəˈpɒn/ *conj.* immediately after which.

wherever /weərˈevə(r)/ (also **wheresoever**) *adv.* in or to whatever place. —*conj.* in every place that.

wherewithal /ˈweəwɪðɔːl/ *n.* (*colloq.*) the money or things needed for a purpose.

wherry /ˈwerɪ/ *n.* a light rowing-boat usually for carrying passengers; a light barge. [orig. unkn.]

whet *v.t.* (**-tt-**) **1.** to sharpen by rubbing against a stone etc. **2.** to stimulate (an appetite or interest). [OE]

whether /ˈweðə(r)/ *conj.* introducing the first or both of alternative possibilities. —**whether or no,** whether it is so or not. [OE]

whetstone *n.* a shaped stone for sharpening tools.

whew /hwjuː/ *int.* expressing surprise, consternation, or relief. [imit.]

whey /weɪ/ *n.* the watery liquid left when milk forms curds. [OE]

which *interrog. adj.* asking for a choice from a definite or known number (*which way shall we go?*). —*rel. adj.* (usu. with noun) being the one just referred to, and this or these (*for ten years, during which time he spoke to nobody*). —*interrog. pron.* which person(s) or thing(s)? —*rel. pron.* which thing(s), used (esp. of an incidental description rather than a defining one) of the thing, or animal, or (*archaic*) person referred to (*the house, which is empty, has been damaged*; *Our Father, which art in heaven*), or in place of THAT after *in* or *that*. [OE]

whichever /wɪtʃˈevə(r)/ *adj. & pron.* any which, that or those which.

whiff *n.* **1.** a puff of air, smoke, or odour; a trace of scandal etc. **2.** a small cigar. [imit.]

Whig /wɪg/ *n.* (*hist.*) **1.** a 17th-c. Scottish Presbyterian. **2.** a member of a former British political group (see below). **3.** (*US*) a supporter of the American Revolution. **4.** (*US*) a member of a political party of 1834–56, succeeded by the Republicans. —*adj.* of the Whigs. —**Whiggery** *n.* [prob. abbr. of *whiggamer*, Scottish rebel of 1648 (*whig* drive)].
The British political interest group (not really a party in the modern sense of the word) was composed of a loose alliance of the country aristocracy and various trading interests, functioning largely through patronage. Opponents of Jacobitism and advocates of the supremacy of Parliament and the Hanoverian succession, the Whigs dominated the English political scene in the late 17th and first half of the 18th c. In the early 19th c. they experienced a revival as the advocates of parliamentary reform, passing the Reform Bill of 1832, and in the middle of the century gradually metamorphosed into the modern Liberal party.

while *n.* a space of time, the time spent in some action. —*conj.* **1.** during the time that, for as long as, at the same time as. **2.** in spite of the fact that, at the same time. —*v.t.* (with *away*) to pass (time etc.) in a leisurely or interesting manner. —*adv.* (preceded by *time* etc.) during which. —**between whiles,** in the intervals. **for a while,** for some time. **in a while,** soon. **once in a while,** occasionally. **the while,** during some other action. **worth (one's) while,** worth the time or effort spent. [OE]

whiles /waɪlz/ *conj.* (*archaic*) while. [f. prec.]

whilom /ˈwaɪləm/ *adv.* (*archaic*) formerly. —*adj.* (*archaic*) former. [f. WHILE]

whilst /waɪlst/ *adv.* & *conj.* while. [f. WHILES]

whim *n.* a sudden unreasoning desire or impulse, a caprice. [orig. unkn.]

whimper *v.i.* to make feeble querulous or frightened sounds. —*n.* such a sound. [imit.]

whimsical /ˈwɪmzɪk(ə)l/ *adj.* **1.** impulsive and playful. **2.** fanciful, quaint. —**whimsicality** /-ˈkælɪtɪ/ *n.*, **whimsically** *adv.* [f. foll.]

whimsy /ˈwɪmzɪ/ *n.* a whim. [rel. to *whim-wham* toy; orig. unkn.]

whin *n.* (in *sing.* or *pl.*) furze. [prob. Scand.]

whinchat *n.* a small brownish songbird (*Saxicola rubetra*).

whine *v.t./i.* **1.** to make a long-drawn complaining cry like that of a child or dog. **2.** to make a similar shrill sound. **3.** to complain in a petty or feeble way; to utter thus. —*n.* a whining cry, sound, or complaint. —**whiner** *n.*, **whiny** *adj.* [OE]

whinge /wɪndʒ/ *v.i.* to whine, to grumble persistently. [OE]

whinny /ˈwɪnɪ/ *n.* a gentle or joyful neigh. —*v.i.* to give a whinny. [imit.]

whip *n.* **1.** a cord or strip of leather fastened to a stick that serves as a handle, used for urging animals on or for striking a person or animal in punishment. **2.** an official of a political party in Parliament with authority to maintain discipline among members of his party; his written notice requesting attendance at a division etc. (variously underlined according to the degree of urgency: *three-line whip*); party discipline and instructions. **3.** a food made with whipped cream etc. **4.** a whipper-in. —*v.t./i.* (**-pp-**) **1.** to strike or urge on with a whip. **2.** to beat (cream or eggs etc.) into a froth. **3.** to move suddenly, or unexpectedly, or rapidly. **4.** (*slang*) to excel, to defeat. **5.** to bind with spirally wound twine. **6.** to sew with overcast stitches. —**have the whip hand,** to have the advantage or control. **whip in,** to bring (hounds) together. **whip on,** to urge into action. **whip-round** *n.* (*colloq.*) an appeal for contributions from a group of people. **whip up,** to incite, to stir up. [prob. f. MLG & MDu. *wippen* swing]

whipcord *n.* **1.** cord made of tightly twisted strands. **2.** a kind of twilled fabric with prominent ridges.

whiplash *n.* the lash of a whip. —**whiplash injury,** injury to the neck caused by a jerk of the head in a collision.

whipper-in *n.* a huntsman's assistant who manages hounds.

whipper-snapper /ˈwɪpəsnæpə(r)/ *n.* a small child; an insignificant but presumptuous person.

whippet /ˈwɪpɪt/ *n.* a cross-bred dog of greyhound type used for racing. [perh. f. obs. *whippet* move briskly, f. *whip it*]

whipping-boy *n.* a scapegoat; (*hist.*) a boy educated with a young prince and punished for the prince's faults.

whipping-top *n.* a top kept spinning by blows of a lash.

whippoorwill /ˈwɪpʊəwɪl/ *n.* the American nightjar (*Caprimulgus vociferus*). [imit. of its cry]

whippy *adj.* flexible, springy. —**whippiness** *n.* [f. WHIP]

whipstock *n.* the handle of a whip.

whirl *v.t./i.* **1.** to swing round and round, to revolve rapidly. **2.** to send or travel swiftly in a curved course. **3.** to convey or go rapidly in a vehicle. **4.** (of the brain, senses, etc.) to seem to spin round. —*n.* **1.** a whirling movement. **2.** a state of intense activity or confusion. [f. ON (*hvirfill* circle) or MLG & MDu. *wervel* spindle]

whirligig /ˈwɜːlɪɡɪɡ/ *n.* **1.** a spinning or whirling toy. **2.** a merry-go-round. **3.** a revolving motion. [f. prec. + obs. *gig* whipping-top]

whirlpool *n.* a circular eddy of water, often drawing floating objects towards its centre.

whirlwind *n.* **1.** a whirling mass or column of air. **2.** (*attrib.*) very rapid.

whirlybird /ˈwɜːlɪbɜːd/ *n.* (*slang*) a helicopter.

whirr *n.* a continuous rapid buzzing or softly clicking sound. —*v.i.* to make this sound. [prob. Scand.]

whisk *v.t./i.* **1.** to brush or sweep lightly from a surface. **2.** to move with a quick light sweeping movement; to convey or go rapidly. **3.** to beat (eggs etc.) into a froth. —*n.* **1.** a whisking movement. **2.** a utensil for beating eggs etc. **3.** a bunch of strips of straw etc. tied to a handle, used for flicking flies away. [prob. Scand.]

whisker *n.* **1.** (usu. in *pl.*) the hair growing on a man's face, especially on the cheeks. **2.** bristle(s) on the face of a cat etc. **3.** (*colloq.*) a very small distance. —**whiskery** *adj.* [f. prec.]

whiskey var. of foll. (esp. *US* and of Irish whisky).

whisky *n.* spirit distilled from malted grain, especially barley; a drink of this. [abbr. of obs. *whiskybae*, var. of USQUEBAUGH]

whisper *v.t./i.* **1.** to speak or utter softly, using the breath but not the vocal cords. **2.** to converse confidentially or secretly; to spread (a tale) thus. **3.** (of leaves or fabric etc.) to rustle. —*n.* **1.** a whispering sound or remark; whispering speech. **2.** a rumour. —**whispering gallery,** a gallery or dome in which the slightest sound made at a particular point can be heard at another far off. [OE (imit.)]

whist *n.* a card-game of mingled skill and chance, using a pack of 52 cards, usually played between two pairs of players. It was in vogue in the 18th c.; Swift alluded to it as a favourite pastime for clergymen. —**whist drive,** a progressive whist party, usually with prizes. [f. earlier *whisk,* influenced by the cry of *whist!* for silence in the game]

whistle /ˈwɪs(ə)l/ *n.* **1.** a clear shrill sound made by forcing the breath through a small hole between nearly closed lips; a similar sound made by a bird, wind, missile, or instrument. **2.** an instrument used to produce this sound as a signal etc. —*v.t./i.* to emit a whistle; to summon or signal thus; to produce (a tune) by whistling. —**whistle for,** (*colloq.*) to seek or desire in vain. **whistle-stop** *n.* (*US*) a small unimportant town on a railway; a politician's brief pause for an electioneering speech on a tour. —**whistler** *n.* [OE (imit.)]

Whistler /ˈwɪslə(r)/, James Abbott McNeill (1834–1903), American-born, French-educated, and (mainly) English-domiciled painter and etcher. In Paris he became a devotee of the cult of the Japanese print and of Oriental art and decoration in general, and met Courbet, whose realism inspired much of his early work. Settling in London in 1859 he was immediately successful, specializing in portraits (e.g. *The Artist's Mother,* 1872) and landscapes, often mainly in one or two colours and showing a harmonious relationship between colour and tone. In 1877 Ruskin denounced his *Nocturne in Black and Gold,* accusing him of 'flinging a pot of paint in the public's face', and the costs of the subsequent libel action (which he won) left him bankrupt. After a year devoted mostly to making etchings and pastels in Venice he returned to London. A dandy, a wit, and an inveterate conversationalist, he there conducted a series of campaigns against the public and critics in the form of pamphlets, annotated exhibition catalogues, and letters to newspapers.

Whit *adj.* connected with, belonging to, or following Whit Sunday. —**Whit Sunday,** the seventh Sunday after Easter, commemorating the descent of the Holy Spirit upon the Apostles at Pentecost. [OE, = White (Sunday), prob. f. white robes of newly-baptized; in the Western Church the festival became a date for baptisms]

whit *n.* the least possible amount. [app. alt. f. WIGHT]

Whitby /ˈwɪtbɪ/, **Synod of** a conference held in 664 chiefly to settle the method of calculating the date of Easter. The Northumbrian Christians had followed the Irish custom while those of the South had adopted the Roman system. King Oswy of Northumbria decided in favour of Rome and England effectively severed her connection with the Irish Church.

White, Patrick Victor Martindale (1912–), Australian novelist, born in England. After service in the RAF during the Second World War he returned to Australia, which was the setting of his first published novel *Happy Valley* (1939) and many others. White won an international reputation with two epics, *The Tree of Man* (1955) and *Voss* (1957); the latter, set in the heroic Australian past, relates the doomed attempt of visionary German hero Johann Voss to lead an expedition across the continent. He has also published plays, short stories, and a self-portrait *Flaws in the*

Glass (1981). He was awarded the Nobel Prize for literature in 1973.

white *adj.* **1.** reflecting all light, of the colour of fresh snow or common salt; approaching this colour; pale from illness, fear, or other emotion. **2. White,** of the human group characterized by light-coloured skin; of or reserved for such persons. **3.** (of magic etc.) of a harmless kind. —*n.* **1.** white colour or pigment; white clothes or material. **2.** the white part of something (e.g. of the eyeball round the iris); the translucent or white part round the yolk of an egg. **3.** a white ball or piece in a game; the player using this. **4. White,** a White person. —**white admiral,** see ADMIRAL. **white ant,** a termite. **white Christmas,** one with snow. **white coffee,** coffee with milk or cream. **white-collar worker,** one not engaged in manual labour. **white dwarf,** a star of high density, formed when a low-mass star has exhausted all its central nuclear fuel, losing its outer layers as a planetary nebula. Although as massive as many stars, the radius of a typical white dwarf is no greater than that of Earth, implying densities so great that a matchbox full of white dwarf material must weigh several tons. **white elephant,** a useless possession. [from the story that the kings of Siam were accustomed to present an elephant of a rare white albino kind (venerated in some Asian countries) to courtiers who had rendered themselves obnoxious, in order to ruin the recipient by the cost of its maintenance] **white feather,** a symbol of cowardice. **white flag,** a symbol of surrender. **White Friars,** Carmelites (so called from their white cloaks). **white gold,** a pale alloy of gold with nickel etc. **white-headed boy,** a highly favoured person. **white heat,** the temperature at which metal looks white; a state of intense passion or activity. **white hope,** a person expected to achieve much. **white horses,** white-crested sea-waves. **white-hot** *adj.* at white heat. **white lead,** a mixture of lead carbonate and hydrated lead oxide used as a pigment. **white lie,** a harmless or trivial untruth. **white light,** colourless light, e.g. ordinary daylight. **white noise,** noise containing many frequencies with about equal energies. **white-out** *n.* a dense blizzard, especially in polar regions. **White Paper,** a government report giving information on a subject. **white pepper,** pepper made by grinding the ripe or husked berry. **White Russia(n),** Belorussia(n). **white sale,** a sale of household linen. **white sauce,** a sauce of flour, melted butter, and milk or cream. **white slave,** a woman tricked or forced into prostitution. **white spirit,** light petroleum as a solvent. **white sugar,** purified sugar. **white tie,** a man's white bow-tie worn with full evening dress. **white whale,** a northern whale (*Delphinapterus leucas*), white when adult. —**whitely** *adv.*, **whiteness** *n.*, **whitish** *adj.* [OE]

whitebait *n.* a small silvery-white food-fish, probably the young of herring, sprat, etc.

whiten /ˈwaɪt(ə)n/ *v.t./i.* to make or become white or whiter. [f. WHITE]

Whitehall /ˈwɔɪthɔːl/ a street in Westminster, London, in which many important government offices are located, whence the allusive use of its name to refer to the British government or its offices or policy. The name is taken from the former royal palace of White Hall, originally a residence of Cardinal Wolsey confiscated by Henry VIII.

Whitehead /ˈwaɪthed/, Alfred North (1861-1947), English philosopher and mathematician. He is remembered chiefly for *Principia Mathematica* (1910-13), on which he collaborated with his pupil Bertrand Russell, but he was concerned to explain more generally the connections between mathematics, theoretical science, and ordinary experience. The work on geometry which arose from *Principia* led to an interest in the philosophy of science, and he proposed an alternative to Einstein's theories of relativity. In his later years he developed a general and systematic metaphysical view, which has had little direct influence, in part because of its obscurity.

White House the official residence of the US President in Washington, DC. It was built in 1792-9 of greyish-white limestone from designs of the Irish-born architect James Hoban (1762-1831) on a site chosen by George Washington; President John Adams took up residence there in 1800. The building was restored in 1814 after being burnt by British troops, the smoke-stained walls being painted white. Although known informally as the White House from the early 19th c., it was not formally so designated until the time of Theodore Roosevelt (1902).

whitewash *n.* **1.** a solution of lime or whiting for whitening walls etc. **2.** the concealing of mistakes or faults. —*v.t.* **1.**

to cover with whitewash. **2.** to conceal the mistakes or faults of or in.

whitewood *n.* a light-coloured wood, especially one prepared for staining etc.

whither /ˈwɪðə(r)/ *adv.* (*archaic*) to what place or state?; (preceded by *place* etc.) to which. —*conj.* (*archaic*) to the or any place to which; and thither. [OE]

whiting[1] /ˈwaɪtɪŋ/ *n.* a small white-fleshed food-fish (*Merlangus merlangus*). [f. MDu., app. as WHITE]

whiting[2] *n.* (also **whitening**) ground chalk used in whitewashing, plate-cleaning, etc. [f. WHITE]

whitlow /ˈwɪtləʊ/ *n.* a small abscess under or near a nail. [earlier *whitflaw*, app. = WHITE + FLAW[1] in sense 'crack']

Whitman /ˈwɪtmən/, Walt (1819-92) American poet, with little formal education, who worked as a printer, wandering school-teacher, journalist, and politician. His experience of the frontier resulted in the first edition of *Leaves of Grass* (1855) which aimed at liberating the American mind from the 'anti-democratic authorities of Asiatic and European past'. His prose *Memoranda during the War* (1875) is a moving account of his experience as a hospital visitor during the Civil War, as are the poems collected in *Drum-Taps* (1865). Whitman's free vigorous verse, conveying subjects at once national, mystically sexual, and personal, proved a liberating force to many of his literary successors.

Whitney /ˈwɪtnɪ/, Eli (1765-1825), American inventor. He is chiefly remembered for his mechanical cotton-gin, which was immediately successful but brought him little money because his design was so simple to copy. More important (and more lucrative) was his concept of interchangeable parts. Having obtained a US government contract to supply muskets he manufactured these in standardized parts for reassembly—a pioneer invention, since for the first time worn parts could be replaced by spares and the weapons repaired instead of being wholly replaced.

Whitsun /ˈwɪts(ə)n/ *n.* (also **Whitsuntide**) the weekend or week including Whit Sunday. [f. *Whitsun Day* = Whit Sunday]

Whittington /ˈwɪtɪŋt(ə)n/, Sir Richard (d. 1423), medieval Mayor of London. Whittington was a London mercer who rose to become Lord Mayor of London in 1397-8, 1406-7, and 1419-20, and left substantial sums to the city for the rebuilding of Newgate Prison and the establishment of a city library. His early career later became the subject of a very popular folk tale.

Whittle /ˈwɪt(ə)l/, Sir Frank (1907-   ), English engineer, inventor of the turbo-jet engine.

whittle /ˈwɪt(ə)l/ *v.t./i.* **1.** to pare (wood) with repeated slicings of a knife; to use a knife thus. **2.** reduce by repeated subtractions. [var. of dial. *thwittle*]

Whitworth /ˈwɪtwɜːθ/, Sir Joseph (1803-87), English engineer whose name is chiefly remembered for his introduction in 1841 of standard screw-threads.

whiz *n.* the sound made by a body moving through the air at great speed. —*v.i.* (**-zz-**) to move with or make this sound; to move very quickly. —**whiz-kid** *n.* (*colloq.*) a brilliant or highly successful young person. [imit.]

WHO *abbr.* World Health Organization.

who /huː/ *pron.* (*obj.* **whom,** *colloq.* **who;** *poss.* **whose** /huːz/) **1.** (*interrog.*) what or which person(s)? **2.** (*rel.*) the particular person(s) that; and or but he, they, etc. (*sent it to Jones, who sent it on to Smith*). —**who's who,** who or what each person is; a list with facts about notable persons. [OE]

whoa /wəʊ/ *int.* used to stop a horse etc. [var. of HO]

whodunit /huːˈdʌnɪt/ *n.* (*colloq.*) a detective or mystery story or play etc. [= *who done* (illiterate for *did*) *it?*]

whoever /huːˈevə(r)/ *pron.* (*obj.* **whomever,** (*colloq.*) **whoever;** *poss.* **whosever** /huːz-/ **1.** the or any person(s) who. **2.** though anyone.

whole /həʊl/ *adj.* **1.** with no part removed or left out. **2.** not injured or broken. —*n.* **1.** the full or complete amount, all the parts or members. **2.** a complete system made up of parts. —**on the whole,** taking everything relevant into account; in respect of the whole though some details form exceptions. **whole foods,** foods not processed or refined. **whole-hearted** *adj.* without doubts or reservations; done with all possible effort. **a whole lot,** (*colloq.*) a great amount. **whole number,** a number consisting of one or more units with no fractions. **whole wheat,** wheat not separated into parts by bolting. [OE]

wholemeal *adj.* made from the whole grain of (unbolted) wheat etc.

wholesale *n.* the selling of things in large quantities to be retailed by others. *—adj. & adv.* **1.** by wholesale. **2.** on a large scale. *—v.t.* to sell wholesale. **—wholesaler** *n.* [orig. *by whole sale*]

wholesome /'həʊlsəm/ *adj.* promoting good physical or mental health or moral condition; showing good sense. **—wholesomeness** *n.* [as WHOLE, -SOME]

wholly /'həʊllɪ/ *adv.* entirely, with nothing excepted or removed. [as WHOLE]

whom *pron.* the objective case of WHO.

whoop /huːp/ *n.* **1.** a loud cry (as) of excitement etc. **2.** a long rasping indrawn breath in whooping cough. *—v.i.* to utter a whoop. **—whooping cough,** an infectious bacterial disease, especially of children, with a short violent cough followed by a whoop. **whoop it up,** (*colloq.*) to engage in revelry; (*US*) to make a stir. [imit.]

whoopee /woʊ'piː/ *int.* expressing exuberant joy. **—make whoopee** /'wʊpɪ/, (*colloq.*) to rejoice noisily or hilariously. [f. prec.]

whoops /wʊps/ *int.* on making an obvious mistake or losing balance. [var. of OOPS]

whop *v.t.* (**-pp-**) (*slang*) to thrash, to defeat. [var. of (dial.) *wap*; orig. unkn.]

whopper *n.* (*slang*) a big specimen; a great lie. [f. WHOP]

whopping *adj.* (*slang*) very big. [f. WHOP]

whore /hɔː(r)/ *n.* a prostitute; a sexually immoral woman. **—whore-house** *n.* a brothel. [OE]

whorl /wɜːl/ *n.* **1.** a coiled form; one turn of a spiral. **2.** a ring of leaves or petals round a stem or central point. **3.** a complete circle formed by ridges in a fingerprint. [app. var. of WHIRL]

whortleberry /'wɜːt(ə)lberɪ/ *n.* a bilberry. [dial. form of *hurtleberry*]

whose /huːz/ *interrog. & rel. pron. & adj.* of whom; of which. [OE, genitive case of WHO]

whosoever /huːsəʊ'evə(r)/ *pron.* (*obj.* **whomsoever**; *poss.* **whosesoever** /huːzsəʊ'evə(r)/) = WHOEVER.

why /waɪ/ *interrog. adv.* for what reason or purpose? *—rel. adv.* preceded by *reason* etc.) for which. *—int.* expressing surprised discovery or recognition, impatience, reflection, objection, etc. *—n.* a reason (*the whys and wherefores*). [OE]

Whymper /'wɪmpə(r)/, Edward (1840–1911), English pioneer mountaineer. In 1860 he was commissioned to make drawings of the Alps to illustrate a record of the adventures of members of the Alpine Club, and in the following year returned to climb mountains as well as draw them, making his first reconnaissance of the Matterhorn which was then considered impregnable. After a series of first ascents in the Dauphiné and Mont Blanc regions, he attained his life's ambition by climbing the Matterhorn in 1865, at the age of 25, only to see it turn to tragedy when on the way down four of his fellow climbers hurtled to their death. Whymper never recovered from the experience, which for a time aroused public opposition to mountain-climbing.

WI *abbr.* **1.** West Indies. **2.** Women's Institute.

wick *n.* a strip or thread feeding a flame with fuel. [OE]

wicked /'wɪkɪd/ *adj.* **1.** morally bad, offending against what is right. **2.** (*colloq.*) very bad or formidable, severe. **3.** malicious, mischievous. **—wicked Bible,** the edition of 1631 with *not* omitted in the seventh commandment. **—wickedly** *adv.*, **wickedness** *n.* [f. obs. *wick* in same sense]

wicker *n.* thin canes or osiers woven together as material for making furniture, baskets, etc. [f. Scand.; cf. Sw. *viker* willow rel. to *vika* bend]

wickerwork *n.* wicker; things made of this.

wicket /'wɪkɪt/ *n.* **1.** a small door or gate especially beside or in a larger one or closing the lower part only of a doorway. **2.** (in cricket) the stumps (orig. two, now three) with the bails in position defended by a batsman (ill. SPORTS); the ground between the two wickets; the state of this; a batsman's tenure of the wicket. **—wicket-keeper** *n.* a fieldsman stationed close behind the batsman's wicket (ill. SPORTS). [f. AF *wiket*, OF *guichet*; orig. unkn.]

widdershins var. of WITHERSHINS.

wide *adj.* **1.** having the sides far apart, not narrow. **2.** extending far; having great range. **3.** open to the full extent. **4.** far from the target etc., not within a reasonable distance. **5.** (appended to a measurement) in width; (as *suffix*) extending to the whole of (*worldwide*). *—adv.* widely, to the full extent; far from the target etc. *—n.* a wide ball. **—give a**

wide berth to, see BERTH. **to the wide,** completely. **wide awake,** (*colloq.*) wary, knowing. **wide ball,** (in cricket) one judged by an umpire to be beyond the batsman's reach. **wide-eyed** *adj.* with eyes wide open in amazement or innocent surprise. **wide of the mark,** incorrect; irrelevant. **wide open,** exposed to attack; (of a contest) with no contestant who can be predicted as a certain winner. **the wide world,** the whole world, great as it is. **—widely** *adv.*, **wideness** *n.* [OE]

widen /'waɪd(ə)n/ *v.t./i.* to make or become wider. [f. WIDE]

widespread *adj.* widely distributed.

widgeon /'wɪdʒ(ə)n/ *n.* a kind of wild duck, especially *Anas penelope* or (US) *A. americana.* [perh. f. imit. *wi-*, after *pigeon*]

widow /'wɪdəʊ/ *n.* a woman who has lost her husband by death and not married again. *—v.t.* to make into a widow or widower; (in *p.p.*) bereft by the death of a husband or wife. **—widowhood** *n.* [OE]

widower *n.* a man who has lost his wife by death and not married again. [f. prec.]

width *n.* **1.** distance or measurement from side to side. **2.** a strip of material of full width as woven. **3.** a large extent. **4.** liberality of views etc. **—widthways** *adv.* [f. WIDE]

wield /wiːld/ *v.t.* **1.** to hold and use (a weapon or tool etc.). **2.** to have and use (power). [OE]

Wiener schnitzel /'viːnə 'ʃnɪts(ə)l/ a veal cutlet breaded, fried, and garnished. [G, = Viennese cutlet]

wife *n.* (*pl.* **wives**) **1.** a married woman, especially in relation to her husband. **2.** (*archaic*) a woman. **—wifely** *adv.* [OE]

wig¹ *n.* an artificial head of hair. [abbr. of PERIWIG]

wig² *v.t.* (**-gg-**) (*colloq.*) to rebuke lengthily (esp. in *a wigging*). [app. slang use of prec.]

wiggle *v.t./i.* (*colloq.*) to move or cause to move repeatedly from side to side; to wriggle. *—n.* a wiggling movement. [f. MLG & MDu. *wiggelen*; cf. WAG, WAGGLE]

wight /waɪt/ *n.* (*archaic*) a person. [OE, = thing, creature]

Wightman Cup /'waɪtmən/ an annual lawn tennis contest between women players of the USA and Britain, inaugurated in 1923; the trophy for this, a silver vase donated by the US player Mrs H. H. Wightman.

wigwam /'wɪgwæm/ *n.* a hut or tent made by fastening skins or mats over a framework of poles, as formerly used by American Indians. [Amer. Ind., = their house]

Wilberforce /'wɪlbəfɔːs/, William (1759–1833), English philanthropist. A prominent Evangelical who sought, as an MP, to give practical expression to his Christian beliefs, he is best known for his work for the abolition of the slave trade, achieved in 1807.

wilco /'wɪlkəʊ/ *int.* expressing compliance or agreement. [abbr. of *will comply*]

Wilcox /'wɪlkɒks/, Ella Wheeler (1850–1919), American poet whose many volumes of romantic, sentimental, and mildly erotic verse were enjoyed by a vast readership. She also wrote short stories, novels, and two volumes of autobiography.

wild /waɪld/ *adj.* **1.** living or growing in its original natural state, not domesticated or tame or cultivated. **2.** not civilized, barbarous. **3.** unrestrained, disorderly, uncontrolled. **4.** tempestuous, stormy. **5.** full of strong unrestrained feeling, intensely eager, frantic; (*colloq.*) infuriated. **6.** extremely foolish or unreasonable; random, ill-aimed. *—adv.* in a wild manner. *—n.* a wild tract, a desert. **in the wilds,** (*colloq.*) far from towns etc. **run wild,** to grow or stray unchecked or undisciplined. **sow one's wild oats,** to indulge in youthful follies before maturity. **wild-goose chase,** a foolish or useless search; a hopeless quest. **wild silk,** silk from wild silkworms; an imitation of this. **Wild West,** the western regions of the USA at the time when they were lawless frontier districts. **—wildly** *adv.*, **wildness** *n.* [OE]

wildcat *n.* a hot-tempered or violent person. *—adj.* **1.** reckless, financially unsound. **2.** (of a strike) sudden and unofficial.

Wilde /waɪld/, Oscar Fingal O'Flahertie Wills (1854–1900), British dramatist and poet, born in Dublin. His flamboyant aestheticism attracted attention, much of it hostile; he proclaimed himself a disciple of Pater and the cult of 'Art for Art's sake'. Early publications include the fairy stories *The Happy Prince and other tales* (1888) and his only novel, *The Picture of Dorian Gray* (1890), a Gothic melodrama which aroused scandalized protest. His epigrammatic brilliance and shrewd social observation brought theatrical success with *Lady Windermere's Fan* (1892), *A Woman of No Importance* (1893), *An Ideal Husband* (1895), and his masterpiece *The Importance of Being Earnest* (1895). Lord Alfred Douglas's father, the Marquess of Queensberry, disapproved of his son's friendship with Wilde and publicly insulted the playwright; this started a chain of events which led to Wilde's imprisonment (1895-7) for homosexual offences. In prison he was declared bankrupt, and his letter of bitter reproach to Lord Alfred was published in part as *De Profundis* (1905), providing an apologia for his own conduct; his prison experiences provided material for *The Ballad of Reading Gaol* (1898) written in France after his release.

wildebeest /ˈwɪldəbiːst, v-/ *n.* the gnu. [Afrik. (as WILD, BEAST)]

wilderness /ˈwɪldənɪs/ *n.* **1.** a desert, an uncultivated region. **2.** a confused assemblage. —**voice in the wilderness,** an unheeded advocate of reform (with ref. to Matt. 3: 3 etc.). [f. OE (*wil(d)deor* wild deer)]

wildfire *n.* (*hist.*) a combustible liquid used in war. —**spread like wildfire,** to spread with extraordinary speed.

wildfowl *n.* a game-bird or game-birds (e.g. ducks and geese, quail, pheasants).

wildlife *n.* wild animals collectively.

wile *n.* (usu. in *pl.*) a piece of trickery intended to deceive or attract. —*v.t.* to lure. [perh. f. Scand. (ON *vél* craft)]

wilful /ˈwɪlfʊl/ *adj.* **1.** intentional, deliberate. **2.** self-willed. —**wilfully** *adv.,* **wilfulness** *n.* [f. WILL² + -FUL]

Wilkie /ˈwɪlkɪ/, Sir David (1785-1841), Scottish painter, who attained wide popularity with pictures of village life in a style influenced by 17th-c. Dutch and Flemish genre painters. After travel abroad in 1825-8 his style was revolutionized by Spanish painting, and he began to work on historical subjects on a larger scale and in a broader technique. His success did much to establish the popularity of anecdotal or 'subject' painting, esteemed in an age which looked first to the 'story' of a painting and the moral lesson it contained.

will¹ *v.aux.* (3 *sing. pres.* **will**; 2 *sing.* (*archaic*) **wilt**; *past* WOULD) **1.** (strictly only in 2nd and 3rd persons) expressing a future statement or an order (*they will attack at dawn; you will do as you are told*). **2.** expressing the speaker's intention (*I will support you!*). [OE]

will² *n.* **1.** the mental faculty by which a person decides or conceives himself as deciding upon and initiating his actions. **2.** (also **will-power**) control exercised by one's will. **3.** determination, fixed desire or intention. **4.** (*archaic*) that which is desired or ordained. **5.** a person's disposition in wishing good or bad to others. **6.** written directions made by a person for the disposal of his or her property after his or her death. —*v.t.* **1.** to exercise one's will-power; to influence or compel thus. **2.** to intend unconditionally. **3.** to bequeath by a will. —**at will,** however one pleases. [OE]

William¹ /ˈwɪljəm/ the name of four kings of England:
    William I 'the Conqueror' (*c.*1027-87), reigned 1066-87, the first Norman king of England, illegitimate son of Robert ('the Devil') Duke of Normandy. William claimed the English throne on the death of Edward the Confessor (who had no children), stating that Edward had promised it to him and that Harold Earl of Wessex (Harold II) had agreed to be his 'liege man'. He landed in England and defeated and killed Harold at the battle of Hastings (1066), successfully repressed a series of uprisings in the following years, and imposed his rule on England, introducing Norman institutions and customs (including feudalism and administrative and legal practices); the effect on English culture was considerable.
    William II (*c.*1060-1100), son of William I, reigned 1087-1100, known as Rufus because of his ruddy complexion. The chroniclers have transmitted a hostile picture of an irreligious and homosexual king, but in fact he seemed to have been blunt but shrewd though unpopular for his temper and high-handedness. He was a good soldier, campaigning in the north of England, where he secured the frontier against the Scots along a line from the Solway Firth to the Tweed, and in Normandy, which he finally acquired peacefully by purchase. His death while out hunting may well have been at the hands of an assassin rather than by accident.
    William III (1650-1702), grandson of Charles I, reigned 1689-1702, known as William of Orange. Son of the Prince of Orange and Mary, daughter of Charles I, William was Stadholder (chief magistrate) of the Netherlands from 1672

and married Mary, daughter of the future James II, in 1677. In 1688 he landed in England at the behest of disaffected politicians, deposed James II, and, having accepted the Declaration of Rights, was crowned along with his wife early in the following year. In 1689-90 he successfully defeated James's supporters in Scotland and Ireland, and thereafter devoted most of his energies towards opposing the territorial ambitions of Louis XIV of France.
    William IV (1765-1837), son of George III, reigned 1830-7, known as 'the sailor king'. William IV succeeded his unpopular brother George IV in 1830. In political terms, William IV's reign was significant for his reluctant agreement to create 50 new peers to overcome the House of Lords' opposition to the First Reform Bill, and for his attempt in 1834 to choose a Prime Minister to his own taste (Peel) without regard to the composition of Parliament.

William² /ˈwɪljəm/ (1143-1214), king of Scotland (as William I) 1165-1214, known as 'the Lion', grandson of David I. He attempted to reassert Scottish independence but was captured by Henry II of England and forced to become his 'liege man'.

William³ /ˈwɪljəm/ (Ger. *Wilhelm*) the name of two German emperors and kings of Prussia:
    William I (1797-1888), king of Prussia 1861-88, first German emperor 1871-88.
    William II (1859-1941), 'the Kaiser', emperor of Germany 1888-1918. A weak and unsteady leader, he was unable to exercise a strong or consistent influence over German policies and tended to be dominated by politicians and soldiers. Vilified by Allied propaganda as the plotter of the First World War, William was in reality more the pawn of others and fell increasingly under the dominance of the army as the war progressed. With Germany on the verge of collapse in November 1918, he went into exile in Holland and abdicated his throne, leaving the way clear for the formation of the Weimar Republic.

William of Occam /ˈwɪljəm, ˈɒkəm/ (*c.*1285-1349) English Franciscan friar who spent the first part of his career (until 1324) studying and teaching philosophy in Oxford and the last part (1333-47) in Munich writing anti-papal pamphlets. He is remembered for a maxim which has acquired the name of *Occam's razor*—'it is vain to do with more what can be done with fewer', i.e. the fewest possible assumptions should be made in explaining a thing. Occam distinguished sharply between faith and reason, advocated a radical separation of the Church from the world, denied the pope all temporal authority, and conceded large powers to the laity and its representatives. Occam was the last of the great scholastic philosophers. His ideas influenced Luther, and paved the way for the Reformation.

Williams /ˈwɪljəmz/, Tennessee (real name Thomas Lanier Williams, 1911-83), American dramatist, born in Mississippi, brought up there and in St Louis. He achieved success with the semi-autobiographical *The Glass Menagerie* (1944), a poignant and painful family drama set in St Louis; the young heroine's cherished glass animals stand for the bright vulnerable creatures found in all his plays, subjected to increasingly harsh pressures. His next success was *A Streetcar Named Desire* (1947), a study of sexual frustration, violence, and aberration, set in New Orleans. He continued to write prolifically, largely in a Gothic and macabre vein, with deep insight into human passion and its perversions. Other works include *Cat on a Hot Tin Roof* (1955), *Suddenly Last Summer* (1958), *The Night of the Iguana* (1962), the novella *The Roman Spring of Mrs Stone* (1950), collections of poems, and his *Memoirs* (1975).

willies /ˈwɪlɪz/ *n.pl.* (*slang*) nervous discomfort. [orig. unkn.]

willing *adj.* **1.** ready to consent to or to undertake what is required. **2.** given or done etc. by a willing person. —*n.* a cheerful intention (*to show willing*). —**willingly** *adv.,* **willingness** *n.* [f. WILL²]

will-o'-the-wisp /wɪləðəˈwɪsp/ *n.* **1.** a phosphorescent light seen on marshy ground. **2.** an elusive person. **3.** a delusive hope or plan. [orig. *Will* (William) *with the wisp* (*wisp* = bundle of (lighted) hay)]

willow /ˈwɪləʊ/ *n.* a waterside tree of the genus *Salix* with pliant branches yielding osiers and timber for cricket-bats. —**willow-herb** *n.* a plant of the genus *Epilobium* with leaves like the willow. [OE]

willow-pattern *n.* a conventional 'Chinese' design of blue on white china etc., in which a willow-tree is a prominent feature. Origination of the pattern is attributed to Thomas Turner of Caughley *c.*1780 and also to Thomas Minton.

The pattern was widely copied in the 19th c. As it became standardized *c.*1830 it shows a pagoda, two birds in the sky, a fence in the foreground, a boat, a three-arched bridge across which walk three Chinese figures, and a willow-tree overhanding the bridge.

willowy /ˈwɪləʊɪ/ *adj.* **1.** full of willow trees. **2.** lithe and slender. [f. prec.]

Wills /wɪlz/, William John (1834–61), English explorer of Australia (see BURKE³).

willy-nilly /ˌwɪlɪˈnɪlɪ/ *adv.* whether one likes it or not. [= *will I, nill* (obs. for *will not*) *I*]

Wilson¹ /ˈwɪls(ə)n/, Sir Angus (Frank Johnstone) (1913–), English novelist and short-story writer. Born in Durban, South Africa, and educated in England, he became Deputy Superintendent of the Reading Room of the British Museum. His works include the novels *Hemlock and After* (1952), *Anglo-Saxon Attitudes* (1956), *The Middle Age of Mrs. Eliot* (1958), *No Laughing Matter* (1967), *Setting the World on Fire* (1980), and several volumes of short stories. These display a brilliant satiric wit, acute social observation, and a love of the macabre and the farcical. He has also written on Zola (1950), Dickens (1970), and Kipling (1977).

Wilson² /ˈwɪls(ə)n/, Thomas Woodrow (1856–1924), 28th President of the USA 1913–21. Already possessed of a reputation as the pre-eminent American academic expert on law and political economy, as President he carried out a series of successful administrative and fiscal reforms. He was re-elected in 1916 on a platform of keeping America out of the First World War, but, following the German reintroduction of unrestricted submarine warfare, entered the war on the Allied side in April 1917. Wilson's 14 Points and plan for the formation of the League of Nations were crucial in the international negotiations surrounding the end of the war, but political opposition at home blocked full American participation in the peace settlement and Wilson's health collapsed before he could overcome Senatorial opposition to his policies.

wilt *v.t./i.* **1.** (of plants) to lose freshness and droop. **2.** to cause to do this. **3.** (of persons) to become limp from exhaustion. —*n.* a plant-disease that causes wilting. [orig. dial., perh. f. LDu.]

Wilton /ˈwɪlt(ə)n/ *n.* a kind of carpet with loops cut into thick pile, first made at Wilton in Wiltshire.

Wilts. *abbr.* Wiltshire.

Wiltshire /ˈwɪltʃɪə(r)/ a county of SW England.

wily /ˈwaɪlɪ/ *adj.* full of wiles, crafty, cunning. —**wilily** *adv.*, **wiliness** *n.* [f. WILE]

Wimbledon /ˈwɪmb(ə)ld(ə)n/ a suburb of London, the most famous of all lawn tennis centres, containing the headquarters of the All England Lawn Tennis and Croquet Club, scene of 'The Lawn Tennis Championships on Grass', the oldest tournament of this kind, since 1877.

wimple *n.* a head-dress of linen or silk folded round the head and neck so as to cover all but the front of the face, worn by women in medieval times and retained in the dress of nuns. [OE]

Wimsey /ˈwɪmzɪ/, Lord Peter (Death Bredon), an aristocratic amateur detective in the novels of D. L. Sayers.

win *v.t./i.* (-nn-; *past* & *p.p.* **won** /wʌn/) **1.** to obtain or achieve as the result of a battle, contest, bet, or effort; to be the victor. **2.** to be victorious in (a battle, game, race, etc.). **3.** to make one's way or become (free etc.) by successful effort. —*n.* victory in a game or contest. —**win over**, to gain the favour or support of. **win one's spurs**, (*hist.*) to gain a knighthood; (*fig.*) to prove one's ability, to gain distinction. **win through** *or* **out**, to overcome obstacles. **you can't win**, (*colloq.*) there is no way to succeed. [OE]

wince *n.* a start or involuntary shrinking movement showing pain or distress. —*v.i.* to make such a movement. [cf. OF *guenchir* turn aside]

wincey /ˈwɪnsɪ/ *n.* a lightweight fabric of wool and cotton or linen. [app. f. *woolsey* in LINSEY-WOOLSEY]

winceyette /ˌwɪnsɪˈet/ *n.* a soft napped fabric woven of cotton and wool. [f. prec. + -ETTE]

winch *n.* **1.** the crank of a wheel or axle. **2.** a windlass. —*v.t.* to lift with a winch. [OE]

wind¹ /wɪnd/ *n.* **1.** air in natural motion; a scent carried by this and indicating a presence. **2.** an artificially produced air-current especially for sounding a wind instrument. **3.** the wind instruments in an orchestra etc. **4.** breath as needed in exertion or speech; the power of breathing without difficulty. **5.** a point below the centre of the chest where a blow temporarily paralyses the breathing. **6.** gas

generated in the stomach or bowels. **7.** empty talk. —*v.t.* **1.** to exhaust the wind of by exertion or a blow. **2.** to renew the wind of by a rest. **3.** to make breathe quickly and deeply by exercise. **4.** to detect the presence of by scent. —**get wind of**, to begin to suspect. **get** *or* **have the wind up**, (*slang*) to feel frightened. **in the wind**, about to happen. **like the wind**, swiftly. **put the wind up**, (*slang*) to frighten. **take the wind out of a person's sails**, to frustrate him by anticipating his action or remark. **wind-break** *n.* a row of trees etc. to break the force of the wind. **wind-cheater** *n.* a jacket designed to give protection against the wind. **wind instrument**, a musical instrument sounded by a current of air, especially that produced by the player's breath. **wind-jammer** *n.* a merchant sailing-ship. **wind-sock** *n.* a canvas cylinder or cone on a mast to show the direction of the wind. **wind-swept** *adj.* exposed to high winds. **wind-tunnel** *n.* a tunnel-like device to produce an air-stream past models of aircraft etc. for the study of wind effects. [OE]

wind² /waɪnd/ *v.t./i.* (*past* & *p.p.* **wound**) **1.** to go or cause to go in a curving, twisting, or spiral course; to make (one's way) thus. **2.** to coil; to wrap closely; to provide with a coiled thread etc.; to surround (as) with a coil. **3.** to haul, hoist, or move by turning a handle or windlass etc. **4.** to wind up (a clock etc.). —*n.* **1.** a bend or turn in a course. **2.** a single turn in winding. —**wind down**, to unwind (*lit.* or *fig.*). **winding-sheet** *n.* a sheet in which a corpse is wrapped for burial. **wind off**, to unwind. **wind up**, to set or keep (a clock etc.) going by tightening its spring or adjusting its weights; to bring or come to an end; to settle and finally close the business affairs of (a company); (*colloq.*) to arrive finally. —**winder** *n.* [OE]

windbag *n.* (*colloq.*) a person who talks at length and without value.

windfall *n.* **1.** a fruit blown to the ground by the wind. **2.** a piece of unexpected good fortune, especially a sum of money acquired.

Windhoek /ˈvɪnthuːk/ the capital of Namibia; pop. (1970) 61,260.

windlass /ˈwɪndləs/ *n.* a machine with a horizontal axle for hauling or hoisting things. [f. AF f. ON (*vinda* WIND², *áss* pole)]

windmill *n.* a mill worked by the wind acting on its sails (see below). —**tilt at windmills**, to attack an imaginary enemy (with ref. to Don Quixote, who attacked windmills, thinking they were giants).

The windmill uses the power of the wind to drive a corn mill or for purposes such as pumping water or generating electricity. Originating in Persia in the 7th c., it spread to Europe in the 12th c. and was gradually improved, especially in England during the 18th c. where the millwrights evolved remarkably effective self-acting control mechanisms. The wind-pump was first developed in Holland for drainage purposes, while the deep-well pump for raising water for stock-watering originated in the USA and was further developed in Australia. Most windmills use a rotor with a near-horizontal axis; the sails were originally of canvas, a type still used in Crete. English windmills adopted wooden sails, with pivoted slats for control, while US wind-pumps use a large number of sheet-metal sails; they are controlled by a tail vane which points the rotor into the wind but turns it edge-on to dangerously strong winds. Some windmills have a vertical axis, such as the Savonius rotor, which uses blades of S shape. The Darrieus windmill has flexible blades of aerofoil section which form catenaries; its high rotational speed makes it suitable for electricity generation. Since the energy crisis of the 1970s there has been a revival of interest in the windmill.

window /ˈwɪndəʊ/ *n.* **1.** an opening in a wall etc. usually with glass for the admission of light etc. (ill. HOUSES); the glass itself; the space for display behind the window of a shop. **2.** a window-like opening. **3.** an interval during which the positions of planets etc. allow a specified journey by a spacecraft. —**window-box** *n.* a trough fixed outside a window for cultivating ornamental plants. **window-dressing** *n.* the art of arranging a display in a shop-window etc.; adroit presentation of facts etc. to give a falsely favourable impression. **window-shopping** *n.* looking at the goods displayed in shop-windows without buying anything. [f. ON (as WIND¹, EYE)]

windpipe *n.* the air-passage from the larynx to the bronchial tubes.

windscreen *n.* a screen of glass at the front of a motor vehicle.

Windsor /ˈwɪnzə(r)/ the name assumed by the British royal house in 1917. —**Duke of Windsor,** the title conferred on Edward VIII on his abdication in 1936. **Windsor Castle,** a royal residence in Berkshire, founded by William the Conqueror and extended by his successors, particularly Edward III.

Windsurfer n. [P] a board like a surf-board with a sail. —**windsurfer** n. one engaged in the sport of riding on such a board. —**windsurfing** n.

windward /ˈwɪndwəd/ adj. & adv. in the direction from which the wind is blowing. —n. the windward direction. [f. WIND¹ + -WARD]

Windward Islands a group of islands in the eastern Caribbean Sea which constitute the southern part of the Lesser Antilles. The largest are Dominica, Martinique, St Lucia, and Barbados. Their name refers to the fact that they are nearest to the direction of the prevailing winds, which are easterly.

windy adj. 1. with much wind. 2. exposed to wind. 3. generating or characterized by flatulence. 4. full of useless talk. 5. (slang) nervous, frightened. —**windily** adv., **windiness** n. [f. WIND¹]

wine n. 1. fermented grape-juice as an alcoholic drink; a fermented drink resembling it made from other fruits etc. 2. the dark red colour of red wine. —v.t./i. 1. to drink wine. 2. to entertain to wine. —**wine-bibber** n. a tippler. **wine-cellar** n. a cellar for storing wine; its contents. [OE f. L vinum]

wineglass n. a glass for wine, usually with a stem and foot.

winepress n. a press in which grapes are squeezed in making wine.

wineskin n. the whole skin of a goat etc. sewn up and used to hold wine.

wing n. 1. each of a pair of projecting parts by which a bird (ill. BIRDS), bat, or insect etc. is able to fly; a corresponding part in a non-flying bird or insect. 2. a winglike part of an aircraft, supporting it in flight. 3. a part resembling a wing in appearance or position; a projecting part of a building, battle array, etc.; (in pl.) the sides of a theatre stage out of sight of the audience (ill. THEATRE). 4. (in football etc.) the player at either end of the forward line; the side part of the playing area. 5. a section of a political party or other group, with more extreme views than those of the majority. 6. the mudguard of a motor vehicle, the part of the bodywork immediately above each wheel. 7. an air-force unit of several squadrons or groups. —v.t./i. 1. to fly, to travel by means of wings; to make (its way) thus. 2. to equip with wings; to enable to fly; to send in flight. 3. to wound in the wing or arm. —**on the wing,** flying. **spread one's wings,** to develop one's powers fully. **take under one's wing,** to treat as a protégé. **take wing,** to fly away. **wing-case** n. the horny cover of an insect's wing. **wing-chair** n. one with side pieces at the top of a high back. **wing-collar** n. a high stiff collar with turned-down corners. **wing commander,** an RAF officer next below group captain. **wing-nut** n. a nut with projections for the finger to turn it on a screw. **wing-span** or **-spread** n. the measurement right across the wings. [f. ON]

Winged Victory a winged statue of Nike, the Greek goddess of victory, especially the Nike of Samothrace (c.200 BC) preserved in the Louvre.

winger n. (in football etc.) a wing player.

wink v.t./i. 1. to close and open one eye deliberately, especially as a private signal to someone. 2. (of a light) to twinkle. —n. 1. an act of winking. 2. a short sleep. —**tip a person the wink,** to give him information privately. **wink at,** to pretend not to notice (something that should be stopped or condemned). [OE; cf. WINCE]

winker n. a flashing indicator on a motor vehicle. [f. WINK]

winkle n. a small edible sea snail of the genus Littorina. —v.t. (with out) to extract or eject. —**winkle-picker** n. (slang) a shoe with a long pointed toe. [abbr. of PERIWINKLE]

winner n. 1. one who wins. 2. a successful thing. [f. WIN]

winning adj. 1. having or bringing victory. 2. attractive. —n. (in pl.) money won. —**winning-post** n. a post marking the end of a race. [f. WIN]

Winnipeg /ˈwɪnɪpeg/, **Lake** a large lake in Manitoba, Canada, north of the city of Winnipeg.

winnow /ˈwɪnəʊ/ v.t. 1. to expose (grain) to a current of air by tossing or fanning it so that the loose dry outer part is blown away; to separate (chaff) thus. 2. to sift or separate (evidence etc.) from worthless or inferior elements. [OE (as WIND¹)]

wino /ˈwaɪnəʊ/ n. (pl. -os) (slang) an alcoholic. [f. WINE]

winsome /ˈwɪnsəm/ adj. (of a person, looks, or manner) winning, engaging. [OE (wyn joy)]

winter n. the coldest and last season of the year, from December to February in the northern hemisphere. —adj. characteristic of or fit for winter. —v.i. to spend the winter. —**winter garden,** a garden or conservatory of plants kept flourishing in winter. **winter sports,** sports performed on snow or ice, e.g. skiing. [OE]

wintergreen n. any of various creeping or low shrubby plants with leaves remaining green in winter, especially the North American Gaultheria procumbens with drooping white flowers, edible scarlet berries, and aromatic leaves yielding an oil used in medicine and for flavouring.

Winterhalter /ˈvɪntəhæltə(r)/, Franz Xavier (1806–73), German artist and international court-painter, whose sitters included Napoleon III, the emperor Francis Joseph, and Queen Victoria and her family. His work still has a clear-cut, waxen, decorative charm but is remembered as a reflection of the high society that he portrayed rather than as creative art.

Winter Palace the former Russian imperial residence in Leningrad (St Petersburg), stormed in the Revolution of 1917, later used as a museum and art gallery.

wintry adj. 1. characteristic of winter. 2. (of a smile etc.) lacking warmth or vivacity. —**wintriness** n. [f. WINTER]

winy /ˈwaɪnɪ/ adj. wine-flavoured. [f. WINE]

wipe v.t./i. 1. to clean or dry the surface of by rubbing; to rub (a cloth) over a surface; to put (a liquid etc.) on to a surface by rubbing. 2. to clear or remove by wiping. —n. the act of wiping. —**wipe the floor with,** (slang) to inflict a humiliating defeat on. **wipe off,** to annul (a debt). **wipe out,** to avenge (an insult etc.); to destroy, to annihilate. [OE]

wiper /ˈwaɪpə(r)/ n. a device for keeping a windscreen clear of rain etc. [f. WIPE]

wire n. 1. metal drawn out into a slender flexible rod or thread; a piece of this. 2. a length of wire used for fencing or to carry an electric current etc. 3. (colloq.) a telegram. —v.t./i. 1. to provide, fasten, or strengthen with wire. 2. (colloq.) to telegraph. —**get one's wires crossed,** to become confused and misunderstand. **wire-haired** adj. (esp. of a dog) with stiff or wiry hair. **wire-tapping** n. the tapping of telephone wires. **wire wheel,** a vehicle wheel with wire spokes. **wire wool,** a mass of fine wire for cleaning kitchen utensils etc. **wire-worm** n. the destructive larva of a beetle of the family Elateridae. [OE]

wireless n. radio, a radio receiving set. [f. WIRE + -LESS]

wiring /ˈwaɪrɪŋ/ n. a system of wires providing electrical circuits. [f. WIRE]

wiry /ˈwaɪrɪ/ adj. tough and flexible as wire; (of a person) lean and strong. —**wirily** adv., **wiriness** n. [f. WIRE]

Wisconsin /wɪsˈkɒnsɪn/ a State in the northern USA, bordering on Lakes Superior and Michigan, ceded to Britain by the French in 1763 and acquired by the USA in 1783. It became the 30th State of the USA in 1848; capital, Madison.

wisdom /ˈwɪzdəm/ n. 1. experience and knowledge together with the power of applying them; sagacity, prudence, common sense. 2. wise sayings. —**Wisdom of Solomon,** see SOLOMON. **wisdom tooth,** the third and hindmost molar tooth on each side of the upper and lower jaws, usually cut (if at all) after the age of 20. [OE (as WISE¹)]

wise¹ /waɪz/ adj. 1. having, or showing, or dictated by wisdom; having knowledge; suggestive of wisdom. 2. (US slang) alert, crafty. —**none the wiser,** knowing no more than before. **wise man,** a wizard; each of the Magi. —**wisely** adv. [OE]

wise² /waɪz/ n. (archaic) way, manner, degree. —**in no wise,** not at all. [OE]

-wise /-waɪz/ suffix forming adjectives and adverbs of manner (clockwise, crosswise, lengthwise) or respect (moneywise). [as prec.]

wiseacre /ˈwaɪzeɪkə(r)/ n. one who affects to be wise. [f. MDu., = soothsayer]

wisecrack n. (colloq.) a smart pithy remark. —v.i. (colloq.) to make a wisecrack.

wish n. 1. a desire or ambition. 2. an expression of desire about another person's welfare. —v.t./i. 1. to have or express as a wish; to formulate a wish. **2.** to hope or express hope for (specified fortune) to befall someone; to hope that (a person) will fare (*well* or *ill*). **3.** (*colloq.*) to foist (a specified thing etc. on a person). [OE]

wishbone *n.* **1.** a forked bone between the neck and breast of a bird (pulled in two between two persons, the one who gets the larger part having the supposed right to magic fulfilment of any wish). **2.** a thing shaped like this.

wishful *adj.* desiring. —**wishful thinking,** belief founded on wishes rather than facts. —**wishfully** *adv.* [f. WISH + -FUL]

wishy-washy /ˈwɪʃɪwɒʃɪ/ *adj.* feeble in quality or character. [redupl. of WASHY]

wisp *n.* **1.** a small bundle or twist of straw etc.; a small separate quantity of smoke or hair etc. **2.** a small thin person. —**wispy** *adj.* [orig. unkn.]

wistaria /wɪˈsteərɪə/ *n.* (also **wisteria**) a climbing shrub of the genus *Wistaria* with blue, purple, or white hanging flowers. [f. C. *Wistar* (or *Wister*), Amer. anatomist (d. 1818)]

wistful *adj.* full of sad or vague longing. —**wistfully** *adv.*, **wistfulness** *n.* [app. assim. of obs. *wistly* adv. (= intently) to *wishful*]

wit *n.* **1.** (in *sing.* or *pl.*) intelligence, quick understanding. **2.** the ability to combine words or ideas etc. ingeniously so as to produce a kind of clever humour that appeals to the intellect. **3.** a person with such ability. —*v.t./i.* (*sing. pres.* **wot**; *past & p.p.* **wist**; *partic.* **witting**) (*archaic*) to know. —**at one's wit's** (or **wits'**) **end,** utterly at a loss or in despair. **have** or **keep one's wits about one,** to be alert. **live by one's wits,** to live by ingenious or crafty expedients, without a settled occupation. **out of one's wits,** mad. **to wit,** that is to say, namely. [OE]

witch *n.* **1.** a sorceress, a woman supposed to have dealings with the Devil or evil spirits. **2.** an ugly old woman. **3.** a fascinating woman. —**witch ball,** a coloured glass ball of the kind formerly hung up to keep witches away. **witch-doctor** *n.* a tribal magician of a primitive people. **witches' sabbath,** a supposed midnight orgy of the Devil and witches. **witch-hunt** *n.* a search for and the persecution of supposed witches or persons suspected of unpopular or unorthodox views. [OE]

witch- var. of WYCH-.

witchcraft *n.* the use of magic. Witchcraft, which has a long history around the world, rests on belief in a person's ability to injure others by occult means. Most witch-trials in early modern Europe arose from harm which a villager claimed had been inflicted on him by a neighbour (usually female). What was distinctive in this period was the concern of the Church and intellectuals, both Catholics and Protestants defining the witch as a heretic who obtained her power through a pact with the Devil. The papal bull of 1484 led to fierce persecution for about a century and a half. In England roughly a thousand people were hanged for witchcraft, mostly under Elizabeth and James I; the last execution was in 1685. On the Continent, and in Scotland, the use of torture produced far more victims and bizarre confessions of sabbaths and night-flying. The Church's concern with devil-worship probably grew out of a misinterpretation of late medieval heresies and popular practices and superstitions. Inflation and population increases produced social pressures which encouraged allegations, and in Protestant countries the Church's traditional remedies, such as holy water, were no longer available. Educated opinion came to reject witchcraft in the course of the 17th c., though popular rural belief survived much longer.

witchery *n.* witchcraft, the power exercised by beauty or eloquence or the like. [f. WITCH]

with /wɪð/ *prep.* expressing (1) instrumentality or means, cause, possession, circumstances, manner, material, agreement and disagreement, (2) company and parting of company, (3) antagonism. —**in** (or **out** etc.) **with,** take, send, or put (a person or thing) in (or out etc.). **with it,** (*colloq.*) up to date, conversant with modern ideas etc. [OE]

withal /wɪˈðɔːl/ *adv.* (*archaic*) in addition, moreover. [f. WITH + ALL]

withdraw /wɪðˈdrɔː/ *v.t./i.* (*past* **-drew**; *p.p.* **-drawn**) **1.** to pull or take back or away. **2.** to remove (deposited money) from a bank etc. **3.** to discontinue; to cancel (a promise or statement etc.). **4.** to go away from company or from a place etc. **5.** (in *p.p.*), of a person) unresponsive, unsociable. —**withdrawal** *n.* [f. *with-* away (as WITH) + DRAW]

withe /wɪθ, wɪð, waɪð/ *n.* a tough flexible shoot used for tying a bundle of wood etc. [OE]

wither /ˈwɪðə(r)/ *v.t./i.* **1.** to make or become dry and shrivelled; to lose or cause to lose vigour or freshness. **2.** to blight with scorn etc. [app. var. of WEATHER]

withers /ˈwɪðəz/ *n.pl.* the ridge between a horse's shoulder-blades (ill. HORSE). [app. f. obs. *widersome* (*wider-*, *wither-* against)]

withershins /ˈwɪðəʃɪnz/ *adv.* (esp. *Sc.*) in a direction contrary to the apparent course of the sun (considered unlucky), anticlockwise. [f. MLG f. MHG (*wider* against, *sin* direction)]

withhold /wɪðˈhəʊld/ *v.t.* (*past & p.p.* **-held**) **1.** to hold back, to restrain. **2.** to refuse to give or grant or allow. [f. *with-* away (as WITH) + HOLD]

within /wɪˈðɪn/ *adv.* inside; indoors. —*prep.* **1.** inside, not out of or beyond. **2.** not transgressing or exceeding. **3.** not further off than. —**within one's grasp,** close enough to be grasped or obtained. **within reach** (or **sight**) **of,** near enough to be reached (or seen). [OE (as WITH, IN)]

without /wɪˈðaʊt/ *prep.* **1.** not having, not feeling or showing; with freedom from. **2.** in the absence of. **3.** with neglect or avoidance of. **4.** (*archaic*) outside. —*adv.* (*archaic*) outside. [OE (as WITH, OUT)]

withstand /wɪðˈstænd/ *v.t.* (*past & p.p.* **-stood** /-ˈstʊd/) to endure successfully, to resist. [OE (as WITH, STAND)]

withy /ˈwɪðɪ/ *n.* = WITHE.

witless *adj.* foolish, crazy. —**witlessly** *adv.*, **witlessness** *n.* [f. WIT + -LESS]

witness /ˈwɪtnɪs/ *n.* **1.** a person giving sworn testimony; a person attesting another's signature to a document. **2.** a person present, one who sees or hears what happens. **3.** testimony, evidence, confirmation. **4.** a person or thing whose existence etc. serves as testimony or proof. —*v.t./i.* **1.** to be a witness to the authenticity of (a document or signature). **2.** to be a spectator of. **3.** to serve as evidence or indication of. **4.** to be a witness. —**bear witness to** or **of,** to attest the truth of. **call to witness,** to appeal to for confirmation etc. **witness-box** or (*US*) **-stand** *n.* an enclosure in a lawcourt from which a witness gives evidence. [OE (as WIT)]

Wittenberg /ˈvɪtənbɜːg/ a German university town on the Elbe, famous as the place where Luther taught.

witter *v.i.* (*colloq.*) to speak with annoying lengthiness on trivial matters. [prob. imit.]

Wittgenstein /ˈvɪtgənstaɪn/, Ludwig Josef Johann (1889–1951), Austrian-born philosopher who came to England in 1911, studied at Cambridge under Bertrand Russell in 1912–13, and abandoned philosophy until the late 1920s, returning to Cambridge in 1929. From early training in engineering and a philosophical interest in mathematics he passed to the study of language and its relationship to the things of the world. In his earlier work, the *Tractatus Logico-philosophicus* (1921), he held that language 'pictures' things by established conventions. In his later works the topic is again language, which he now saw as a response to, not merely a reproduction of, what is real; traditional philosophical problems were seen as caused by mistaken analogies and simplistic generalizations, chiefly in attempts to understand the workings of language. The positive view which emerges is that correctness in any use of language is determined solely by the role of that use in human activities and practices. None of the work of this later period was published in his lifetime; the breadth of his influence was largely due to the powerful effect of his personality on friends, pupils, and colleagues at philosophical meetings.

witticism /ˈwɪtɪsɪz(ə)m/ *n.* a witty remark. [coined by Dryden f. WITTY]

wittingly /ˈwɪtɪŋlɪ/ *adv.* with knowledge of what one is doing. [f. WIT]

witty /ˈwɪtɪ/ *adj.* showing verbal wit. —**wittily** *adv.*, **wittiness** *n.* [OE (as WIT)]

wives *pl.* of WIFE.

wizard /ˈwɪzəd/ *n.* **1.** a magician. **2.** a person of extraordinary ability. —**wizardry** *n.* [f. WISE¹]

wizened /ˈwɪzənd/ *adj.* (of a person or face) full of wrinkles. [p.p. of *wizen* shrivel, f. OE]

WNW *abbr.* west-north-west.

woad *n.* a plant (*Isatis tinctoria*) of the mustard family, yielding a blue dye; the dye itself. [OE]

wobble *v.i.* **1.** to rock from side to side; to stand or go unsteadily. **2.** (of the voice) to quiver. —*n.* a wobbling movement; a quiver. —**wobbly** adj. [cf. LG wabbeln, ON vafla waver]

Wodehouse /'wʊdhaʊs/, Sir Pelham Grenville (1881–1975), English humorous writer, an American citizen from 1955. In a writing career that spanned more than 70 years his prolific output included over 120 volumes, and he became Broadway's leading writer of musical comedy lyrics. His best-known characters include Jeeves, Bertie Wooster, and the vague absent-minded Lord Emsworth, owner of the prize sow the Empress of Blandings. Wodehouse's stories, told with exuberant vitality, most of them set in an upper-class world of his own invention, exist in a realm that is as oblivious of the external world as the author was when writing them. They are musical comedies without music, their plots ingenious and finely wrought, their construction faultless, cadence and nuance displaying fineness of ear and taste, the work of a consummate stylist, while the reader is treated to gleanings from a remarkable variety of poets, philosophers, and classical writers. Wodehouse has been the subject of overstated praise, and of stupid attacks during the Second World War when he was unjustly accused of being a traitor and producing propaganda for the Axis powers.

wodge n. (colloq.) a chunk, a lump. [alt. f. WEDGE]

woe n. **1.** sorrow, distress. **2.** (in pl.) trouble causing this, misfortune. [OE]

woebegone /'wəʊbɪgɒn/ adj. dismal-looking. [f. WOE + obs. bego surround (BE-, GO)]

woeful adj. **1.** full of woe, sad. **2.** deplorable. —**woefully** adv. [f. WOE + -FUL]

wok n. a bowl-shaped frying-pan used especially in Chinese cookery. [Chinese]

woke past of WAKE¹.

woken p.p. of WAKE¹.

wold /wəʊld/ n. a high open uncultivated or moorland tract. [OE, = OHG wald forest, ON völlr field]

Wolf /vɒlf/, Hugo (1860–1903), Austrian composer. Although his opera Der Corregidor (1895) is occasionally given, Wolf is known as a lieder composer. In under 20 years he produced some 300 songs, making full use of the resources of chromaticism but maintaining an essentially small scale. In his early songs he took the verse of German writers, especially Goethe, very often setting the same texts as his great predecessor Schubert but bringing to them an entirely different approach, introspective and complex, capable of expressing the celestial eroticism of Gannymede as well as the anguished cry of the mad harpist in the three Harfenspieler. In 1889–96 he turned to translations of Spanish and Italian verse for the three volumes of his Spanish Songbook and the two volumes of his Italian Songbook, but his composing career was cut short by mental illness resulting from a syphilitic infection, and his last years were spent in an asylum.

wolf /wʊlf/ n. (pl. **wolves**) **1.** a carnivorous doglike mammal of the genus Canis (esp. Canis lupus), with coarse tawny-grey fur and erect ears, preying on sheep etc. or combining in packs to hunt larger animals. **2.** (slang) a man who aggressively seeks to attract women for sexual purposes. —v.t. to devour greedily. —**cry wolf**, to raise a false alarm (like the shepherd-boy in the fable, so that eventually a genuine alarm is ignored). **keep the wolf from the door**, to avert starvation. **wolf in sheep's clothing**, a hypocrite. [OE]

wolf-whistle n. a whistle by a man sexually admiring a woman. [OE]

Wolfe /wʊlf/, James (1727–59), British general, captor of Quebec. As one of the leaders of the expedition sent to capture French Canada, he played a vital part in the siege of Louisburg before being charged with the attack on the enemy capital, Quebec City. He was mortally wounded while leading his troops to victory on the Plains of Abraham, the battle which effectively sealed the fate of France's Canadian empire.

wolfhound n. a dog of a kind used (originally) to hunt wolves.

wolfram /'wʊlfrəm/ n. tungsten (ore). [G, perh. f. wolf wolf + rahm cream, or MHG rām dirt, soot]

Wollaston /'wʊləst(ə)n/, William Hyde (1766–1828), English chemist and physicist, pioneer of powder metallurgy, developed when attempting to produce malleable platinum, in the course of which he discovered palladium (1802) and rhodium (1804). The income he derived from his platinum process allowed him to devote himself entirely to scientific research. He demonstrated in 1801 that frictional electricity

(electrostatics) and current electricity were the same, was the first to observe the dark (Fraunhofer) lines in the solar spectrum, and invented a chemical slide-rule and several optical instruments, including the reflecting goniometer (for measuring the angles of crystals), a double-image prism, and an aberration-free lens. He supported Dalton's atomic theory and the wave theory of light. The mineral wollastonite is named after him.

Wolsey /'wʊlzɪ/, Thomas (c.1474–1530), English cardinal, archbishop of York (1514–30), Lord Chancellor (1515–29), a statesman rather than a churchman. Favoured by Henry VIII, he wielded an almost royal power and dominated foreign and domestic policy until he occurred royal displeasure through his failure to secure the papal dispensation necessary for the king's divorce from Catherine of Aragon, which led to his arrest on a charge of treason; he died on his way to trial in London. Wolsey had devoted his life to the aggrandizement of king and country, fostering the development of royal absolutism in politics as well as in ecclesiastical matters. His main interest was in foreign politics, in which he frequently changed sides, skilfully holding the balance of power between the Holy Roman Empire and France in a boldly conceived (but disastrously expensive) attempt to make England the arbiter of Europe, a dream that remained unrealized in his age.

wolverine /'wʊlvəriːn/ n. an animal (Gulo gulo), also known as the glutton, that is the largest of the weasel family, living in the cold pine forests of the northern continents, especially North America. The coarse shiny hairs of its brown fur are remarkable in that they do not collect and hold moisture; for this reason the fur is prized for trimming the openings of Eskimo clothing. [orig. wolvering f. WOLF]

woman /'wʊmən/ n. (pl. **women** /'wɪmɪn/) **1.** an adult human female. **2.** women in general. **3.** feminine emotions. **4.** (attrib.) female. **5.** (colloq.) a charwoman. —**Women's Lib**, a movement urging the liberation of women from domestic duties and subservient status. **women's rights**, the right of women to have a position of legal and social equality with men. [OE (as WIFE, MAN)]

-woman suffix denoting a woman concerned or skilful with (needlewoman) or describable as (Welshwoman).

womanhood n. **1.** female maturity. **2.** womanly instinct. **3.** womankind. [f. WOMAN + -HOOD]

womanish adj. like a woman; (usu. derog.) effeminate, unmanly. [f. WOMAN]

womanize v.i. to philander, to consort illicitly with women. —**womanizer** n. [as prec.]

womankind n. (also **womenkind**) women in general.

womanly adj. having or showing the qualities befitting a woman. —**womanliness** n. [f. WOMAN]

womb /wuːm/ n. the hollow organ (in women and other female animals) in which children or young are conceived and nourished while developing before birth, the uterus. [OE]

wombat /'wɒmbæt/ n. a burrowing herbivorous Australian marsupial, especially of the genus Phascolomis, resembling a small bear. [Aboriginal]

women pl. of WOMAN.

womenfolk n. **1.** women in general. **2.** the women in a family.

Women's Institute an organization of women to enable those in rural areas to meet regularly and engage in crafts, cultural activities, social work, etc. Now world-wide, it was first set up in Ontario, Canada, in 1895, and in Britain in 1915.

won past & p.p. of WIN.

wonder /'wʌndə(r)/ n. **1.** a feeling of surprise mingled with admiration, curiosity, or bewilderment. **2.** something that arouses this, a marvel, a remarkable thing or event. —v.t./i. **1.** to feel wonder or surprise. **2.** to feel curiosity about; to desire to know; to try to form an opinion about. —**for a wonder**, as a welcome exception. **I wonder!** I very much doubt it. **no or small wonder**, it is not surprising. **work or do wonders**, to produce remarkably successful results. [OE]

wonderful /'wʌndəf(ə)l/ adj. remarkable, surprisingly fine or excellent. —**wonderfully** adv. [f. prec. + -FUL]

wonderland n. a land or place full of marvels or wonderful things.

wonderment n. surprise. [f. WONDER]

wondrous /'wʌndrəs/ adj. (poetic) wonderful. —adv. (poetic) wonderfully. —**wondrously** adv. [f. obs. wonders (f. WONDER), after marvellous]

wonky *adj.* (*slang*) unsteady; unreliable. [fanciful formation]

wont /wəʊnt/ *predic. adj.* (*archaic*) accustomed. —*n.* (*archaic*) what is customary, one's habit. [OE]

won't /wəʊnt/ (*colloq.*) = will not.

wonted /ˈwəʊntɪd/ *attrib. adj.* habitual, usual. [f. WONT]

woo *v.t.* **1.** (*archaic*) to court (a woman). **2.** to try to achieve or obtain (fame, fortune, etc.). **3.** to seek the favour of; to try to coax or persuade. [OE]

Wood /wʊd/, Sir Henry (1869–1944), English conductor. He had many posts as a conductor before becoming, in 1894, music adviser to Felix Mottl's Wagner concerts at the new Queen's Hall, the setting a year later for the first of the Promenade Concerts re-established by Robert Newman and with Wood as conductor. He retained the conductorship until the year he died, building the concerts from rudimentary beginnings to form a central feature of English musical life. He was a tireless champion of contemporary music, conducting the first performance of Schoenberg's Five Orchestral Pieces in 1912 and introducing the music of Janáček to England. He made many orchestral transcriptions and arranged the *Fantasia on British Sea Songs* which for many years was performed, with the participation of the audience, on the last night of every Prom season.

wood /wʊd/ *n.* **1.** the hard fibrous substance in the trunks and branches of a tree or shrub; timber or fuel of this. **2.** (in *sing.* or *pl.*) growing trees densely occupying a tract of land. **3.** a wooden cask for wine etc. **4.** a wooden-headed golf-club. **5.** a bowl (BOWL²). —**cannot see the wood for the trees,** cannot get a clear view of the main issue because of over-attention to details. **out of the wood,** out of danger or difficulty. **wood-louse** *n.* a small land crustacean of the genus *Oniscus* etc. with many legs, found in old wood etc. **wood-pigeon** *n.* the ring-dove. **wood-pulp** *n.* wood fibres prepared for paper-making. **wood-shed** *n.* a shed where wood for fuel is stored. **wood sorrel,** a plant of the genus *Oxalis* with trifoliate leaves and white or pink flowers. [OE]

woodbine *n.* honeysuckle.

woodchuck *n.* a reddish-brown and grey North American marmot (*Marmota monax*). [f. Amer. Ind. name]

woodcock *n.* a game-bird (*Scolopax rusticola*) related to the snipe.

woodcut *n.* a relief cut on wood; a print made from this.

wooded *adj.* having woods or many trees. [f. WOOD]

wooden /ˈwʊd(ə)n/ *adj.* **1.** made of wood. **2.** stiff and unnatural in manner, showing no expression or animation. —**wooden horse,** that by use of which Troy was taken. **wooden spoon,** a spoon made of wood, used in cookery or given as a prize to the competitor with the lowest score. —**woodenly** *adv.*, **woodenness** *n.* [f. WOOD]

woodland *n.* wooded country, woods.

woodman *n.* (*pl.* **-men**) a forester.

woodpecker *n.* a bird of the family Picidae that clings to tree-trunks and taps them in search of insects.

woodwind *n.* orchestral wind instruments made (originally) of wood.

woodwork *n.* the making of things in wood; things made of wood.

woodruff *n.* a white-flowered plant (*Galium odoratum*) with fragrant leaves.

woodworm *n.* the larva of a beetle (*Anobium punctatum*) that bores into wooden furniture and fittings.

woody /ˈwʊdɪ/ *adj.* **1.** like wood; consisting of wood. **2.** wooded. —**woodiness** *n.* [f. WOOD]

woof¹ /wʊf/ *n.* the gruff bark of a dog. —*v.i.* to give a woof. [imit.]

woof² /wuːf/ *n.* the weft. [OE as A³, WEB]

woofer /ˈwʊfə(r)/ *n.* a loudspeaker for accurately reproducing low-frequency signals. [f. WOOF¹]

wool /wʊl/ *n.* **1.** the fine soft hair that forms the fleece of sheep and goats etc. **2.** yarn made from this; fabric made from such yarn. **3.** something resembling wool in texture. —**pull the wool over a person's eyes,** to deceive him. **wool-gathering** *n.* being in a dreamy or absent-minded state. [OE]

Woolf /wʊlf/, (Adeline) Virginia (1882–1941), English novelist, whose London house became the centre of the Bloomsbury Group. She began her literary career as a critic for the *Times Literary Supplement* and in 1912 married Leonard Woolf with whom she founded the Hogarth Press

(1917), which published some of her finest works. Her third novel, *Jacob's Room* (1922), was recognized as a new development in the art of fiction and in her succeeding novels she firmly established her stream-of-consciousness technique and poetic impressionism, becoming a principal exponent of modernism; these include *Mrs. Dalloway* (1925), *To the Lighthouse* (1927), *The Waves* (1931), and *The Years* (1937), interspersed with slighter works and her feminist classic *A Room of One's Own* (1929). She had meanwhile suffered recurring attacks of acute mental disturbance and shortly after completing her final and most experimental novel, *Between the Acts* (1941), drowned herself in the River Ouse. She is now acclaimed as one of the great innovative novelists of the 20th c. and many of her techniques have been absorbed into mainstream fiction. Her published letters and diaries are a dazzling evocation of the literary world of her time.

woollen /ˈwʊlən/ *adj.* made wholly or partly of wool. —*n.* a woollen fabric; (in *pl.*) woollen garments. [OE (as WOOL)]

Woolley /ˈwʊlɪ/, Sir Charles Leonard (1880–1960), English archaeologist, noted for his excavations at Ur.

woolly /ˈwʊlɪ/ *adj.* **1.** covered with wool or wool-like hair. **2.** like wool; woollen. **3.** not thinking clearly; not clearly expressed or thought out, vague. —*n.* (*colloq.*) a knitted woollen garment; a jumper or cardigan etc. —**woolly-bear** *n.* a hairy caterpillar, especially of the tiger-moth. —**woolliness** *n.* [f. WOOL]

Woolsack *n.* the usual seat, without back or arms, of the Lord Chancellor in the House of Lords, made of a large square bag of wool and covered with cloth. It is said to have been adopted in Edward III's reign as a reminder to the Lords of the importance to England of the wool trade.

Woolworth /ˈwʊlwəθ/, Frank Winfield (1852–1919), American business man who from 1879 onwards opened a chain of shops, in the USA and other countries, selling low-priced goods.

Worcester /ˈwʊstə(r)/ a city in the county of Hereford and Worcester, on the River Severn, scene of a battle (1651) in which Cromwell defeated a Scottish army under Charles II. —**Worcester china** (also **Royal Worcester**), porcelain made at Worcester in a factory founded in 1751. **Worcester sauce,** a pungent sauce containing soy, vinegar, and condiments, first made at Worcester.

word /wɜːd/ *n.* **1.** any sound or combination of sounds (or its written or printed symbol, usually shown with a space on either side of it but none within it) forming a meaningful element of speech, conveying an idea or alternative ideas, and capable of serving as a member of, the whole of, or a substitute for a sentence; a unit of expression in a computer. **2.** speech, especially as distinct from action. **3.** one's promise or assurance. **4.** (in *sing.* or *pl.*) a thing said, a remark; a conversation. **5.** (in *pl.*) the text of a song or of an actor's part. **6.** (in *pl.*) angry talk. **7.** news; a message. **8.** a command; a password; a motto. —*v.t.* to put into words, to select words to express. —**in a** *or* **one word,** briefly. **in other words,** expressing the same thing differently. **in so many words,** explicitly, bluntly. **take a person's word for it,** to believe his statement without investigation etc. **take a person at his word,** to act on the assumption that he meant exactly what he said. **(upon) my word,** an exclamation of surprise or consternation. **word for word,** in exactly the same or (of a translation) corresponding words. **word-game** *n.* a game involving the making, selection, or guessing etc. of words. **the Word (of God),** the Bible or a part of it; the title of the Second Person of the Trinity, = LOGOS. **word of honour,** an assurance given upon one's honour. **word of mouth,** speech (only). **word-perfect** *adj.* knowing one's part etc. by heart. **word processor,** a device for storing text entered from a keyboard, incorporating corrections, and providing a printout. [OE]

wording /ˈwɜːdɪŋ/ *n.* the form of words used. [f. WORD]

wordless *adj.* without words, not expressed in words. —**wordlessly** *adv.* [f. WORD + -LESS]

Wordsworth /ˈwɜːdzwəθ/, William (1770–1850), English poet, an enthusiastic worshipper of nature and simplicity and, with Coleridge, the creator of the English Romantic movement. He was born in the Lake District and describes the profound effect of his country childhood and sense of the living landscape in his posthumously published poetic autobiography *The Prelude* (1850). He spent some time in France, where he became an enthusiastic republican until disillusioned by the Terror, and had a love affair with Annette Vallon, who bore him a daughter, and then in Somerset, where, with Coleridge, he composed the *Lyrical*

Ballads, 1798, which attacked conventional poetry of the 18th c. Then he settled with his sister Dorothy in Grasmere in 1799; with his wife (Mary Hutchinson, whom he married in 1802) they lived a life of 'plain living and high thinking', and he composed the poems that made him (after initial hostility) revered as the greatest poet of his time. These include his 'Immortality' ode (1807), many fine sonnets, and pastoral poems such as 'Michael' (1800). Radical in his youth, he became conservative with age, and in 1843 was made Poet Laureate.

wordy /'wɜːdɪ/ adj. using many or too many words. —**wordily** adv., **wordiness** n. [f. WORD]

wore past of WEAR.

work /wɜːk/ n. 1. the application of mental or physical effort in order to do or make something, especially as contrasted with play or recreation; use of energy. 2. (in physics) the exertion of force overcoming resistance or producing molecular change. 3. something to be undertaken; the materials for this. 4. a thing done or produced by work; the result of action; a piece of literary or musical composition. 5. doings or experiences of a specified kind. 6. employment or occupation, what a person does to earn a living. 7. things or parts made of specified material or with specified tools; ornamentation of a specified kind. 8. (in pl.) operations in building etc. 9. (in pl.) the operative parts of a clock or machine; (slang) all that is available. 10. (in pl., often treated as sing.) a place where industrial or manufacturing processes are carried out. 11. (usu. in pl. or comb.) a defensive structure (earthwork). —v.t./i. 1. to perform work, to be engaged in bodily or mental activity. 2. to make efforts. 3. to be employed, to have a job. 4. to operate or function; to do this effectively. 5. to carry on, to manage, to control. 6. to put or keep in operation so as to obtain material or benefit etc.; to cause to work or function. 7. to bring about, to accomplish. 8. to shape, knead, or hammer etc. into the desired shape or consistency. 9. to do or make by needlework, fretwork, etc. 10. to make (a way) or cause to pass gradually or by effort; to become (loose etc.) through repeated stress, movement, or pressure. 11. to excite artificially. 12. to solve (a sum) by mathematics. 13. to purchase with one's labour instead of with money. 14. to be in motion or agitated; to ferment; to have an influence. —**at work**, in action; engaged in work. **give a person the works**, to give or tell him everything; to treat him harshly. **have one's work cut out**, to be faced with a hard task. **make short work of**, to accomplish or dispose of quickly. **work-basket** n. a basket containing sewing materials. **work-force** n. the workers engaged or available; the number of these. **work in**, to find a place for in a composition or structure. **work-load** n. the amount of work to be done. **work of art**, a fine picture, poem, building, etc. **work off**, to get rid of by work or activity. **work out**, to solve (a sum) or find (an amount) by calculation; to be calculated; to have a result; to provide for all the details of; to attain with difficulty; to exhaust with work. **work-out** n. a practice or test, especially in boxing. **work over**, to examine thoroughly; (colloq.) to treat with violence. **work-room** n. a room in which work is done. **work-shy** adj. disinclined to work. **work study**, a system of assessing jobs so as to get the best results for employees and employers. **work to rule**, to follow the rules of one's occupation with excessive strictness so as to reduce efficiency, usually as a protest. **work-to-rule** n. this process. **work up**, to bring gradually to an efficient state; to advance gradually (to a climax); to elaborate or excite by degrees; to mingle (ingredients); to learn (a subject) by study. [OE]

workable /'wɜːkəb(ə)l/ adj. that may be worked, used, or acted upon successfully. [f. WORK]

workaday adj. ordinary, everyday, practical.

workaholic /wɜːkə'hɒlɪk/ n. (colloq.) a person who is addicted to working. [f. WORK, after alcoholic]

workday n. a day on which work is regularly done.

worker /'wɜːkə(r)/ n. 1. a person who works; one who works well or in a specified way. 2. a neuter or undeveloped bee or ant etc. that does the work of the hive or colony but cannot reproduce. 3. a member of the working class. [f. WORK]

workhouse n. (hist.) a public institution where people unable to support themselves were housed and (if able-bodied) made to work. Under the new Poor Law of 1834, able-bodied paupers could obtain public relief only by staying at workhouses, where conditions were made as uncomfortable as possible with a view to discouraging idlers; families were split up. Conditions gradually improved in the face of public protest, but workhouses were always dreaded as places of humiliation until their disappearance c.1930.

working /'wɜːkɪŋ/ adj. 1. engaged in work, especially in manual or industrial labour; working-class. 2. functioning, able to function. —n. 1. the activity of work. 2. functioning. 3. a mine or quarry etc.; a part of this in which work is or has been carried on. —**working capital**, capital actually used in a business. **working class**, the class of people who are employed for wages, especially in manual or industrial work. **working day**, a workday; the part of the day devoted to work. **working knowledge**, knowledge adequate to work with. **working order**, the condition in which a machine works satisfactorily. **working party**, a group of people appointed to advise on some question. [f. WORK]

workman n. (pl. **-men**) 1. a man employed to do manual labour. 2. a person in respect of his skill in a job.

workmanlike adj. showing practised skill.

workmanship n. degree of skill in doing a task or of finish in a product made. [f. WORKMAN + -SHIP]

workmate n. one engaged in the same work as another.

workpeople n.pl. people employed in labour for wages.

workpiece n. a thing worked on with a tool or machine.

worksheet n. 1. a paper for recording work done or in progress. 2. a paper listing questions or activities for students etc. to work through.

workshop n. 1. a room or building in which manual work or manufacture is done. 2. a place for concerted activity; such activity.

world /wɜːld/ n. 1. the earth, or a heavenly body like it. 2. the universe, all that exists. 3. the time, state, or scene of human existence. 4. secular interests and affairs. 5. human affairs; the active life. 6. average or respectable people; their customs or opinions. 7. all that concerns or all who belong to a specified class or sphere of activity. 8. a vast amount. 9. (attrib.) affecting many nations; of all nations. —**bring** (or **come**) **into the world**, to give birth to (or be born). **in the world**, of all or at all. **man** or **woman of the world**, a person experienced and practical in human affairs. **out of this world**, (colloq.) extremely good etc. **think the world of**, to have a very high regard for. **world-beater** n. a person or thing surpassing all others. **world-famous** adj. known throughout the world. **world-wide** adj. covering or known in all parts of the world. [OE]

World Bank the popular name of the International Bank for Reconstruction and Development, an agency set up by the United Nations in 1945 to promote the economic development of member nations by facilitating the investment of capital for productive purposes, encouraging private foreign investment, and if necessary lending money from its own funds. Its headquarters are in Washington, DC.

World Cup any of various international sports competitions, or the trophies awarded for these; (in Association football) a competition instituted in 1930 and held every fourth year between teams who are winners from regional competitions.

World Health Organization an agency of the United Nations, established in 1948. Its aim is the attainment by all peoples of the world of the highest possible level of health, and to this end its activities include co-operation with member governments in their efforts to promote health and control communicable diseases, and the advancement of biomedical research through some 500 collaborating research centres throughout the world. Its headquarters are in Geneva.

worldly /'wɜːldlɪ/ adj. 1. of or belonging to life on earth, not spiritual. 2. engrossed in worldly affairs, especially the pursuit of pleasure or material gains. —**worldly-wise** adj. prudent in dealing with worldly affairs. —**worldliness** n. [OE (as prec.)]

World Meteorological Organization an agency of the United Nations, established in 1950. Its aim is to facilitate world-wide co-operation in meteorological observations, research, and services. Its headquarters are in Geneva.

world war a war involving many important nations. The name is commonly given to the wars of 1914–18 and 1939–45, although only the second of these was truly global.

First World War (1914–18), a war between the Central Powers (Germany and Austria-Hungary, joined later by Turkey and Bulgaria) and the Allies (Britain, France, Russia, and minor European nations, joined later by Italy and the USA). Most of the fighting took place in Europe, being characterized by a long and bloody stalemate in the west and the eventual collapse of Russia in the east. The war was ended by a series of armistices in late 1918, the most important being that with Germany on 11 November, and peace terms were finally settled at Versailles in 1919. One of the most important consequences of the war was the collapse of the German, Austro-Hungarian, and Russian empires.

Second World War (1939-45), a war between the Axis Powers (Germany, Italy, and Japan) and the Allies, including the three major powers Britain, Russia, and the USA. It began with the German attack on Poland in September 1939, within a year of which the Germans had overrun most of Europe, including France, the Low Countries, Scandinavia (excluding neutral Sweden and allied Finland), and Poland. Fighting spread to the Mediterranean where Italy had joined Germany and finally to Russia, which Germany attacked in June 1941. The war became worldwide following the Japanese attack on the US naval base at Pearl Harbor in December 1941. From 1942 onwards the Allies gradually began to turn the tide against the Axis, but although Italy surrendered in 1943, Germany did not give up until invaded (surrendering in May 1945) and Japan resisted until the first atomic bombs were dropped on the country in August 1945.

worm /wɜ:m/ n. 1. any of many types of invertebrate slender burrowing or creeping animal; the wormlike larva of an insect, especially one feeding on fruit or wood etc.; (in pl.) internal (intestinal) parasites. 2. an insignificant or contemptible person. 3. the spiral part of a screw. —v.t./i. 1. to move with a twisting movement like a worm; to make (one's way) by wriggling or with slow or patient progress. 2. to obtain (a secret) by crafty persistence. 3. to rid of parasitic worms. 4. (Naut.) to make (a rope etc.) smooth by winding thread between the strands. —**worm-cast** n. a convoluted pile of earth set up by an earthworm on to the surface of the ground. **worm-eaten** adj. full of worm-holes. **worm-hole** n. a hole left in fruit or wood etc. by the passage of a worm. **worm's-eye view**, a view from below or from a humble position. [OE]

wormwood /ˈwɜ:mwʊd/ n. 1. a plant (Artemisia abrotanum) with a bitter aromatic taste. 2. bitter mortification; the source of this. [alt. f. obs. wormod f. OE (ult. orig. unkn.); cf. VERMOUTH]

wormy /ˈwɜ:mɪ/ adj. full of worms; worm-eaten. —**worminess** n. [f. WORM]

worn p.p. of WEAR. —adj. 1. damaged by use or wear. 2. looking tired and exhausted. —**worn-out** adj. [f. WEAR]

worrisome /ˈwʌrɪsəm/ adj. causing worry. [f. foll. + -SOME]

worry /ˈwʌrɪ/ v.t./i. 1. to give way to anxiety. 2. to harass, to importune; to be a trouble or anxiety to. 3. (of a dog etc.) to shake or pull about with the teeth. 4. (in p.p.) feeling or showing worry, uneasy. —n. 1. a state of worrying, mental uneasiness. 2. a thing that causes this. —**worry beads**, a string of beads manipulated by the fingers to occupy or calm oneself. **worry out**, to obtain (a solution to a problem etc.) by persistent effort. —**worrier** n. [OE, = strangle]

worse /wɜ:s/ adj. 1. more bad. 2. (predic.) in or into worse health; in a worse condition. —adv. more badly or ill. —n. a worse thing or things. —**from bad to worse**, into an even worse state. **the worse**, a worse condition. **the worse for wear**, damaged by use; injured or exhausted. **worse luck**, see LUCK. [OE]

worsen /ˈwɜ:s(ə)n/ v.t./i. to make or become worse. [f. prec.]

worship /ˈwɜ:ʃɪp/ n. 1. homage or service paid to a deity. 2. the acts, rites, or ceremonies of this. 3. adoration of or devotion to a person or thing. —v.t./i. (-pp-) 1. to honour as a deity, to pay worship to. 2. to take part in an act of worship. 3. to idolize, to regard with adoration. —**Your** (or **His** etc.) **Worship**, the title of respect used to or of a mayor or certain magistrates. —**worshipper** n. [OE (as WORTH, -SHIP)]

worshipful /ˈwɜ:ʃɪpf(ə)l/ adj. (archaic, esp. in old titles of companies or officers) honourable, distinguished. —**worshipfully** adv. [f. prec. + -FUL]

worst /wɜ:st/ adj. most bad. —adv. most badly. —n. the worst part or possibility. —v.t. to get the better of, to defeat. —**at its** etc. **worst**, in the worst state. **at (the) worst**, in the worst possible case. **do your worst**, an expression of defiance. **get the worst of it**, to be defeated. **if the worst comes to the worst**, if the worst happens. [OE (as WORSE)]

worsted /ˈwʊstɪd/ n. fine smooth yarn spun from long strands of wool which has been combed so that the fibres lie parallel; fabric made from this. [f. Worste(a)d in Norfolk]

wort /wɜ:t/ n. 1. (archaic exc. in names) a plant (liverwort). 2. an infusion of malt before it is fermented into beer. —**St John's wort**, a plant of the genus Hypericum, with yellow flowers. [f. OE, rel. to ROOT]

worth /wɜ:θ/ predic. adj. (governing a noun like a prep.) 1. of a value equivalent to. 2. such as to justify or repay. 3. possessing, having property amounting to. —n. 1. what a person or thing is worth; (high) merit; usefulness. 2. the amount that a specified sum will buy. —**for all one is worth**, (colloq.) making every effort. **for what it is worth**, with no guarantee of its truth or value. **worth one's salt**, having merit. **worth (one's) while**, see WHILE. [OE]

worthless adj. without value or merit. —**worthlessly** adv., **worthlessness** n. [f. prec. + -LESS]

worthwhile /wɜ:θˈwaɪl/ adj. that is worth the time or effort spent.

worthy /ˈwɜ:ðɪ/ adj. 1. having great merit, deserving respect or support. 2. having sufficient worth or merit, deserving (of); adequate or suitable to the dignity etc. (of a specified person or thing). 3. (as suffix forming adjectives) deserving of, suitable for (noteworthy, seaworthy). —n. a worthy person; a person of some distinction in his country, time, etc. —**worthily** adv., **worthiness** n. [f. WORTH]

wot see WIT.

would /wʊd, emphat. wʊd/ v. aux. (3 sing. **would**) past tense of WILL, used especially in reported speech or to express a habitual action or a condition, question, polite request, or probability. —**would-be** adj. desiring or aspiring to be. [as WILL]

wouldn't /ˈwʊd(ə)nt/ (colloq.) = would not.

wound[1] /wu:nd/ n. 1. an injury done to living tissue by a cut or blow etc. 2. an injury to a person's reputation or feelings. —v.t. to inflict a wound on. [OE]

wound[2] past & p.p. of WIND[2].

wove past of WEAVE[1].

woven p.p. of WEAVE[1].

wow[1] int. expressing astonishment or admiration. —n. (slang) a sensational success. [imit.]

wow[2] n. a slow pitch-fluctuation in sound-reproduction, perceptible in long notes. [imit.]

w.p.b. abbr. waste-paper basket.

WPC abbr. woman police constable.

w.p.m. abbr. words per minute.

WRAC abbr. Women's Royal Army Corps.

wrack n. 1. seaweed cast up or growing on the shore, used for manure. 2. destruction. [f. MDu. or MLG; cf. WRECK, RACK[2]]

WRAF abbr. Women's Royal Air Force.

wraith n. a ghost; a spectral appearance of a living person supposed to portend his death. [orig. unkn.]

wrangle n. a noisy angry argument or quarrel. —v.i. to engage in a wrangle. —**wrangler** n. [prob. f. LDu.; cf. LG wrangelen frequent. of wrangen to struggle]

wrap v.t./i. (-pp-) 1. to enclose in soft or flexible material used as a covering. 2. to arrange (such a covering or a garment etc.) round a person or thing. —n. a shawl, coat, or cloak etc. worn for warmth. —**under wraps**, in concealment or secrecy. **wrap over**, (of a garment) to overlap at the edges when worn. **wrapped up in**, with one's attention deeply occupied by; deeply involved in. **wrap up**, to envelop in wrappings; to put on warm clothing; (slang) to finish, to cease talking. [orig. unkn.]

wrapper n. 1. a cover of paper etc. wrapped round something. 2. a loose enveloping robe or gown. [f. WRAP]

wrapping n. (esp. in pl.) wraps, wrappers, enveloping garments. —**wrapping paper** strong or decorative paper for wrapping parcels. [f. WRAP]

wrasse /ræs/ n. a bright-coloured sea-fish of the family Labridae with thick lips and strong teeth. [f. Cornish wrach mutated rel. to Welsh gwrach (lit. 'old woman')]

wrath /rɒθ, rɔ:θ/ n. extreme anger. [OE (as WROTH)]

wrathful adj. extremely angry. —**wrathfully** adv. [f. prec. + -FUL]

wreak v.t. to give play to (vengeance, anger, etc.) upon an enemy etc.; to inflict (damage etc.). [OE, = drive, avenge]

wreath n. (pl. /ri:θs, ri:ðz/) 1. flowers or leaves fastened in a ring especially as an ornament for the head or a building or for laying on a grave etc. as a mark of respect. **2.** a curl or ring of smoke, cloud, or soft fabric. [OE (as WRITHE)]

wreathe /riːð/ v.t./i. **1.** to encircle as, with, or like a wreath. **2.** to wind (one's arms etc.) round a person etc. **3.** (of smoke etc.) to move in wreaths. [partly back-formation f. earlier *wrethen* writhe, partly f. prec.]

wreck n. **1.** destruction or disablement, especially of a ship by storm or accidental damage. **2.** a ship that has suffered wreck. **3.** a greatly damaged or disabled building, thing, or person; a wretched remnant. —v.t./i. **1.** to cause the wreck of (a ship, hopes, etc.). **2.** to suffer wreck; (in p.p.) involved in a wreck. [f. AF *wrec* etc.; cf. WREAK]

wreckage n. wrecked material; the remnants of a wreck. [f. prec.]

wrecker n. **1.** one who wrecks something, one who tries from the shore to bring about a shipwreck in order to plunder or profit by wreckage. **2.** a person employed in demolition work. [f. WRECK]

Wren[1] /ren/ n. a member of the Women's Royal Naval Service. [orig. in pl., f. abbr. WRNS]

Wren[2] /ren/, Sir Christopher (1632–1723), English architect and scientist, founder-member and later President of the Royal Society (1680). His early scientific training may well be responsible for the lucid and elegant architectural style Wren developed with St Paul's Cathedral (1675–1710) and the City churches (1670–86), whose spatial relations were clearly and logically expressed at a time when baroque exuberance tended towards a surcharged emotionalism. His unrealized town-plan for the rebuilding of London after the Great Fire (1666) would have made it one of the great European show-pieces of baroque architecture.

Wren[3] /ren/, Percival Christopher (1885–1941), English novelist, who had a varied and much-travelled life, working at one time as a member of the French Foreign Legion. He achieved popular success with the first of his Foreign Legion novels, *Beau Geste* (1924), a romantic adventure story.

wren n. a small short-winged usually brown songbird of the family Troglodytidae, with a short erect tail. [OE]

wrench n. **1.** a violent twist or oblique pull. **2.** an adjustable tool like a spanner for gripping and turning nuts, bolts, etc. **3.** a painful parting. —v.t. **1.** to twist or pull violently round; to damage or pull (away etc.) thus. **2.** to distort (facts) to suit a theory etc. [f. OE, = twist]

wrest v.t. **1.** to wrench away. **2.** to obtain by effort or with difficulty. **3.** to distort into accordance with one's own views or interests etc. [OE, rel. to WRIST]

wrestle /ˈres(ə)l/ v.t./i. **1.** to fight (especially as a sport) by grappling with a person and trying to throw him to the ground (see below); to fight with (a person) thus. **2.** (with *with*) to struggle to deal with or overcome. —n. **1.** a wrestling-match. **2.** a hard struggle. —**wrestler** n. [OE]. Wrestling is one of the oldest and most basic of all sports. Many of the holds and throws used now in international championship events are the same as those of ancient Egypt, China, and Greece. It was introduced to the Olympic Games in 704 BC.

wretch n. **1.** an unfortunate or pitiable person. **2.** a despicable person; (in playful use) a rascal. [OE, = OHG *reccho* exile, adventurer]

wretched /ˈretʃid/ adj. **1.** unhappy, miserable. **2.** of bad quality or no merit, contemptible. **3.** unsatisfactory, displeasing. —**wretchedly** adv., **wretchedness** n. [f. prec.]

wriggle v.t./i. to move with short twisting movements; to make (one's way) thus. —n. a wriggling movement. —**wriggle out of**, to avoid on some pretext. —**wriggly** adj. [f. MLG]

Wright[1] /rait/, Frank Lloyd (1869–1959), American architect, the leading exponent of 'organic' architecture, advocating a close relationship between building and landscape and the nature of the materials used. His 'prairie' style houses revolutionized American domestic architecture in the first decade of the 20th c. with their long low horizontal lines and visual merging of an unbroken interior with the surrounding landscape. Pupils gathered round him and during his long and prolific career, which extended over a period of 74 years, he influenced whole generations of architects. His lecture *The Art and Craft of the Machine* (1901) carried his belief, that art must dominate the machine in an industrial society, to a wide audience.

Wright[2] /rait/, Orville (1871–1948) and Wilbur (1867–1912), American brothers who were the first to make brief powered sustained and controlled flights in an aeroplane (Kitty Hawk, North Carolina, 17 Dec. 1903). They were also the first to make and fly a fully practical powered aeroplane (1905) and passenger-carrying aeroplane (1908). With the profits from their bicycle-manufacturing business at Dayton, Ohio, they experimented first with gliders, developed their aerofoils in their own wind tunnel, invented wing-warping, and designed and built their own petrol engine for their *Flyer*. Both brothers became skilled pilots and in 1908 demonstrated in France that their aircraft was capable of long flights and manoeuvrability.

wright /rait/ n. (archaic exc. in comb.) a maker or builder (playwright, wheelwright). [OE (as WORK)]

wring v.t. (past & p.p. **wrung**) **1.** to twist and squeeze in order to remove liquid; to remove (liquid) thus. **2.** to squeeze firmly or forcibly; to clasp (one's hands) together emotionally. **3.** to extract or obtain (a promise etc.) with effort or difficulty. —n. a wringing movement; a squeeze or twist. —**wringing wet**, so wet that water can be wrung out. **wring the neck of**, to kill (a chicken etc.) by twisting its head round. [OE, rel. to WRONG]

wringer n. a device with a pair of rollers between which washed clothes etc. are passed so that water is squeezed out. [f. prec.]

wrinkle n. **1.** a small crease; a small furrow or ridge in the skin such as is produced by age. **2.** (colloq.) a useful hint about how to do something. —v.t./i. to make wrinkles in; to form wrinkles. —**wrinkly** adj. [f. OE, = sinuous]

wrist n. **1.** the joint connecting the hand with the arm (ill. BODY 1). **2.** the part of a garment covering this. **3.** (also **wrist-work**) working the hand without moving the arm. —**wrist-watch** n. a small watch worn on a strap etc. round the wrist. [OE, = ON *rist* instep]

wristlet n. a band or bracelet etc. worn round the wrist. [f. prec. + -LET]

writ[1] n. a form of written command to act or not act in some way. [OE (as WRITE)]

writ[2] archaic p.p. of WRITE. —**writ large**, in a magnified or emphasized form. [f. foll.]

write /rait/ v.t./i. (past **wrote**; p.p. **written**) **1.** to mark letters or other symbols or words on a surface, especially with a pen or pencil on paper. **2.** to form (such symbols etc. or a message) thus; to fill or complete (a sheet or cheque etc.) with writing. **3.** to put (data) into a computer store. **4.** to compose for written or printed reproduction or publication; to be engaged in such literary composition. **5.** to write and send a letter; (US or colloq.) to write and send a letter to (a person); to convey (news etc.) by letter. **6.** to state in a book etc. —**write down**, to record in writing; to write as if for inferiors; to disparage in writing; to reduce the nominal value of. **write off**, to write and send a letter; to cancel the record of (a bad debt, sum absorbed by depreciation, etc.); to ignore (a person) as now of no account. **write-off** n. a thing written off; a vehicle too badly damaged to be worth repairing. **write out**, to write in full or in a finished form. **write up**, to write a full account of; to praise in writing. **write-up** n. a written or published account, a review. [OE, = scratch, score, write; orig. of symbols inscribed with sharp tools on stone or wood]

writer n. one who writes or has written something; one who writes books, an author. —**writer's cramp**, a muscular spasm caused by excessive writing. [f. prec.]

writhe /raið/ v.i. **1.** to twist or roll oneself about (as) in acute pain; to suffer. **2.** to suffer because of great shame or embarrassment. [OE]

writing /ˈraitiŋ/ n. **1.** the process of marking letters or other symbols or words on a surface (see below). **2.** written symbols or words; a written document; (in pl.) an author's works; **the Writings**, the Jewish name for the parts of the Old Testament other than the Law and the Prophets. —**in writing**, in written form. **writing on the wall**, an ominous event or sign that something is doomed (with allusion to the Biblical story of the writing that appeared on the wall at Belshazzar's feast (Dan. 5: 5, 25–8), foretelling his doom). **writing-paper** n. paper for writing (especially letters) on. [f. WRITE]
Primitive drawings, as records of ideas, were the forerunners of writing which began in Mesopotamia with pictographic signs and developed into a formalized system of linear and then cuneiform signs representing first words or ideas, then syllables, and finally sounds. The cuneiform system was adopted from the Sumerians by the Akkadians and passed on to Syria, the Elamites, and the Hurrians in the 3rd millennium BC, the Assyrians, Hittites, Canaanites,

and Egyptians in the 2nd millennium BC, and the Achaemenid Persians in the 1st millennium BC when it was gradually superseded by the alphabetic system of writing (see ALPHABET).

written *p.p.* of WRITE.

WRNS *abbr.* Women's Royal Naval Service.

wrong *adj.* **1.** (of conduct etc.) morally bad, contrary to justice, equity, or duty. **2.** incorrect, not true; less or least desirable; (of a side of a fabric) not meant for show or use. **3.** not in a normal condition, not functioning normally. —*adv.* in a wrong manner or direction; with an incorrect result. —*n.* what is morally wrong; a wrong or unjust action or treatment. —*v.t.* **1.** to do wrong to, to treat unjustly. **2.** to attribute bad motives to (a person) mistakenly. —**get (hold of) the wrong end of the stick,** to misunderstand completely. **get a person wrong,** to misunderstand him or her. **go wrong,** to take the wrong path; to stop functioning properly; to cease virtuous behaviour. **in the wrong,** not having justice or truth on one's side. **on the wrong side of,** out of favour with or not liked by (a person); somewhat more than (a stated age). **wrong-foot** *v.t.* to catch (a person) unprepared. **wrong-headed** *adj.* perverse and obstinate. **wrong 'un,** (*colloq.*) a person of bad character. —**wrongly** *adv.*, **wrongness** *n.* [OE]

wrongdoer *n.* a person guilty of a breach of law or morality. —**wrongdoing** *n.*

wrongful *adj.* contrary to what is fair, just, or legal. —**wrongfully** *adv.* [f. WRONG + -FUL]

wrote *past* of WRITE.

wroth /rəʊθ, rɒθ/ *predic. adj.* (*literary*) angry. [OE]

wrought /rɔːt/ *archaic past & p.p.* of WORK. —*adj.* (of metals) beaten out or shaped by hammering. —**wrought iron,** see IRON. [as WORK]

wrung *past & p.p.* of WRING.

WRVS *abbr.* Women's Royal Voluntary Service.

wry /raɪ/ *adj.* (*compar.* **wryer**; *superl.* **wryest**) **1.** distorted, turned to one side. **2.** (of a face, smile, etc.) contorted in disgust, disappointment, or mockery. **3.** (of humour) dry and mocking. —**wryly** *adv.*, **wryness** *n.* [f. *wry* v. f. OE, = tend, incline (later = deviate, contort)]

wryneck *n.* a small bird of the genus *Jynx*, able to turn its head over its shoulder.

WSW *abbr.* west-south-west.

wt. *abbr.* weight.

Wulfila /ˈwʊlfɪlə/ var. of ULFILAS.

Wundt /vʊnt/, Wilhelm (1832-1920), German philosopher, physiologist, and founder of psychology as an independent and scientific discipline in Leipzig, where he established a laboratory devoted to its study. He felt that the major task of the psychologist was to analyse human consciousness, which could be broken down into simpler fundamental units. He required subjects to report their sensory impressions under controlled conditions, and although this method of inquiry (*introspection*) was later rejected by experimental psychologists, Wundt's legacy includes the rigorous methodology upon which he insisted.

wych- *prefix* in names of trees with pliant branches (*wych-alder, -elm*). —**wych-hazel** *n.* an American shrub of the genus *Hamamelis* whose bark yields an astringent lotion; this lotion. [OE, = bending (rel. to WEAK)]

Wyclif /ˈwɪklɪf/, John (c.1330-84), English reformer, a philosopher and theologian. A lecturer at Oxford (1361-82) and prolific writer, he criticized the wealth and power of the visible Church (which he constrasted with the eternal ideal Church), upheld the Bible as the sole guide for doctrine, and questioned the scriptural basis of the papacy. He instituted the first translation into English of the whole Bible, himself translating the Gospels and probably other parts. After his attacks on the doctrine of transubstantiation (1381) and on the Peasants' Revolt, widely but erroneously attributed to his teaching, he was compelled to retire from Oxford. His teaching cut at the roots of medieval theocracy and at current faith and dogma, and he has been called the 'Morning Star of the Reformation'.

Wyoming /waɪˈəʊmɪŋ/ a State in the western central USA, acquired as part of the Louisiana Purchase in 1803. It became the 44th State of the USA in 1890; capital, Cheyenne.

wyvern /ˈwaɪvən/ *n.* (in heraldry) a winged two-legged dragon with a barbed tail (ill. HERALDRY). [f. OF f. L *vipera* viper]

X

X, x /eks/ *n.* (*pl.* **Xs, X's**) **1.** the twenty-fourth letter of the alphabet. **2.** (as a Roman numeral) 10. **3.** (in algebra) **x,** the first unknown quantity. **4.** a cross-shaped symbol, especially used to indicate a position or incorrectness or to symbolize a kiss or vote, or as the signature of a person who cannot write.

Xanthian Marbles /ˈzænθɪən/ sculptures found in 1838 at Xanthus in ancient Lycia, which are now in the British Museum. The figures are Assyrian in character and it is believed they were executed before 500 BC; the subjects include processions, athletic activity, sieges, and tomb scenes.

Xanthippe /zænˈθɪpɪ/ (5th c. BC) wife of the philosopher Socrates. Her bad-tempered behaviour towards her husband has made her proverbial as a shrew.

Xavier /ˈzævɪə(r), ˈzeɪ-/, St Francis (1506–52), Spanish missionary, known as the 'Apostle of the Indies' and 'of Japan'. While studying in Paris he met St Ignatius Loyola and became with him one of the orginal seven Jesuits, pledged to follow Christ and evangelize the heathen. He set out on a remarkable series of missionary journeys: to southern India, Malacca, the Molucca Islands, Sri Lanka and Japan, and is said to have made more than 700,000 converts. He died, worn out from his labours, while on his way to China.

Xe *symbol* xenon.

Xenakis /zeˈnɑːkɪs/, Iannis (1922–), French composer, born in Romania of Greek parents. He moved to Paris in 1947 and established the School of Mathematical and Automated Music there in 1965. He had had an early training as an engineer and architect, and his music employs the mathematical laws of probability, computer-aided calculations, and electronic instruments. In the works which make up *Polytope* he combined electronic sound with laser beams and other visual effects.

xenon /ˈzenɒn/ *n.* a colourless odourless element of the noble gas group, symbol Xe, atomic number 54, discovered in 1898 by Sir William Ramsay and M. W. Travers. It is obtained by the distillation of liquefied air and is used in certain specialized electric lamps. A radioactive isotope produced in nuclear reactors is important in the control of the chain reaction. [Gk, neut. of *xenos* strange]

Xenophanes /zeˈnɒfəniːz/ (*c.*570–490 BC) Greek philosopher and poet, the first writer to consider the impact of natural theology on conduct. In ruthless criticism of Homer and Hesiod he denied that the gods resemble men in conduct, shape, or understanding, and argued that there is a single eternal self-sufficient Consciousness which sways the universe (with which it is identical) through thought.

xenophobia /zenəˈfəʊbɪə/ *n.* strong dislike or distrust of foreigners. —**xenophobic** *adj.* [f. Gk *xenos* foreigner + -PHOBIA]

Xenophon /ˈzenəfən/ (*c.*428/7–*c.*354 BC) Greek writer from Athens who spent many years in the service of Sparta. His writings reflect the viewpoint of a conventional and practical-minded gentleman who supported aristocratic ideals and virtues. His historical works include the *Anabasis*, an eye-witness account of the expedition of the Persian prince Cyrus II against Artaxerxes (401–399 BC) in which he led the Greek mercenaries in their retreat to the Black Sea after they had been left in a dangerous situation between the Tigris and Euphrates; the *Apology, Memorabilia,* and *Symposium* recall the life and teachings of his friend Socrates; the *Cyropaedia* is a historical romance on the education of Cyrus II, seen as the ideal prince. He also wrote treatises on politics, war, hunting, and horsemanship.

xerography /zɪəˈrɒgrəfɪ, zeˈr-/ *n.* a dry copying process in which powder adheres to areas remaining electrically charged after exposure of the surface to light from the image of the document to be copied. [f. Gk *xēros* dry + -GRAPHY]

Xerox /ˈzɪərɒks, ˈzer-/ *n.* [P] a certain process of xerography; a copy made by this. —**xerox** *v.t.* to reproduce by a process of this kind. [f. prec.]

Xerxes I /ˈzɜːˌksiːz/ son of Darius, king of Persia 486–465 BC, who inherited the task of punishing the Greeks for their support of the cities of Ionia that had revolted against Persian rule. After victories in 480 BC by sea at Artemisium and by land at Thermopylae his fleet was defeated at Salamis, and his land forces were defeated at Plataea in the following year.

Xhosa /ˈkəʊsə, ˈkɔː-/ *n.* a member or the language of a Bantu people of Cape Province, South Africa. —*adj.* of this people or their language. [native name]

xi /ksaɪ, gzaɪ, zaɪ/ *n.* the fourteenth letter of the Greek alphabet, = x. [Gk]

Ximenes /hiˈmeɪneɪθ, *pop.* ˈzɪmɪniːz/ = Jiménes de CISNEROS.

Xiphias /ˈzɪfɪæs/ a southern constellation, also called Dorado. [f. Gk *xiphos* sword]

Xmas /ˈkrɪsməs/ *n.* = CHRISTMAS. [abbr., with X for initial chi of Gk *Khristos* Christ]

X-ray /ˈeksreɪ/ *n.* (in *pl.*) **1.** electromagnetic radiation of short wavelength, able to pass through opaque bodies (see below). **2.** a photograph made by X-rays, especially one showing the position of bones etc. by their greater absorption of the rays. —*v.t.* to photograph, examine, or treat with X-rays. [transl. of G *X-strahlen*, so called from their unknown nature]

X-rays were discovered in 1895 by Wilhelm Röntgen, who noticed the fluorescence of certain crystals in the vicinity of an operating cathode-ray tube. He attributed this to a new kind of radiation from the tube which he called X-rays. He discovered that the rays travel in straight lines, that they are not electrical, that they affect photographic plates, and that they have a considerable power of penetrating matter. Röntgen produced the first X-ray photograph or radiograph of the human hand. By 1912 it was recognized that X-rays are electromagnetic radiation of a very high frequency with wavelengths more than a thousand times smaller than those of visible light. The shorter the wavelength of the X-ray, the greater its penetrating power. X-rays are produced when very high velocity electrons are stopped suddenly by a target, as in an X-ray tube; the rapid deceleration of the electrons at the target produces a pulse of X-radiation. X-rays now have a great variety of applications in science, medicine, and industry. The best known of these include radiology, the spectroscopic analysis of the structure of solid crystalline materials, and the study of the structure of organic molecules. High doses of X-radiation can be damaging to living tissue and, in particular, can be used to treat cancerous tissue.

X-ray astronomy the observation of celestial objects with instruments capable of detecting and measuring high-energy electromagnetic radiation. Because the atmosphere absorbs practically all cosmic X-rays, it is necessary to place X-ray telescopes and spectrometers in Earth orbit aboard artificial satellites. Objects known to emit X-rays include the sun, certain cataclysmic variable stars, and clusters of galaxies which have been found to be permeated by a rarefied, but extremely hot, intergalactic gas. Temperatures characteristic of X-ray emitting regions of stars and galaxies are in the millions of degrees. The detection of X-rays from certain close binary stars offers the best hope of detecting black holes.

xylem /ˈzaɪləm/ *n.* woody tissue (opp. PHLOEM) in the stem of a plant, that carries water and dissolved minerals upwards from the ground. [f. Gk *xulon* wood]

xylophone /ˈzaɪləfəʊn/ *n.* a musical instrument of graduated wooden bars with tubular resonators suspended vertically beneath them, struck with small wooden etc. hammers. Its first appearance was in Africa and in Java, where it was known before the 9th c. In central Europe a different type was a popular instrument from the 15th c., known as the straw-fiddle because the bars lay on straw. It was first used in orchestral music by Saint-Saëns in *Danse macabre* (1874), its sound being particularly apt for the representation of rattling skeletons. —**xylophonist** /-ˈlɒfənɪst/ *n.* [f. Gk *xulon* wood + -PHONE]

Y

Y, y /waɪ/ *n.* (*pl.* **Ys, Y's**) **1.** the twenty-fifth letter of the alphabet. **2.** (in algebra) **y**, the second unknown quantity. **3.** a Y-shaped thing.

Y *symbol* yttrium.

yacht /yɒt/ *n.* **1.** a light sailing-vessel kept, and usually specially built and rigged, for racing; a similar vessel for use on sand or ice. **2.** a vessel propelled by sails, steam, electricity, or motive power other than oars, and used for private pleasure excursions, cruising, travel, etc. [f. Du. *jachte* = *jaghtship* fast pirate-ship (*jagen* to hunt)]

yachting /ˈjɒtɪŋ/ *n.* racing or cruising in a yacht. Modern yachting was pioneered in Holland in the 17th c. when travel along the miles of sheltered Dutch waterways was difficult without boats. An early convert to the pastime was Charles II of England, who spent nearly ten years in exile in the Low Countries until the Restoration in 1660. His brother James (later James II) was almost as keen, and Pepys records that the royal brothers delighted in working the ship themselves 'like common seamen'. In the early 18th c. yachting (because of its inevitable discomforts) was regarded as an eccentric occupation, but in 1775 a revival of royal patronage and 'water parties' on the Thames gave rise to the organized yachting of today.

yachtsman *n.* (*pl.* **-men**) a person who goes yachting.

yah *int.* expressing derision or defiance. [imit.]

yahoo /jəˈhuː/ *n.* a bestial person. [name of race of brutes in Swift's *Gulliver's Travels*]

Yahveh /ˈjɑːveɪ/ *n.* (also **Yahweh**) = JEHOVAH.

Yajur-Veda /ˈjʌdʒʊəveɪdə, -viː-/ *n.* one of the four Vedas, a collection of sacrificial formulae in Old Sanskrit, used in the Vedic religion by the priest in charge of sacrificial ritual. [f. Skr., *yajus* ritual worship, *vēda* knowledge]

yak *n.* a long-haired Tibetan ox (*Bos grunniens*), wild or domesticated. [f. Tibetan *gyag*]

Yale *n.* [P] (in full **Yale lock**) a type of lock for doors etc., with a revolving barrel. [f. L. *Yale*, Amer. inventor (d. 1868)]

Yale University an American university, now non-sectarian, originally a 'collegiate school' founded in 1701 at Killingworth and Saybrook, Connecticut, by a group of Congregational ministers. In 1716 it moved to its present site at New Haven and soon afterwards was renamed Yale College after Elihu Yale, a notable benefactor. In 1887 it became Yale University.

Yalta /ˈjɒltə/ a port on the Black Sea in the USSR, site of a conference in February 1945 between the Allied leaders Churchill, Roosevelt, and Stalin, who met to plan the final stages of the Second World War and to agree the subsequent territorial division of Europe. In spite of the friendship displayed at the time the scene was set for East/West polarization; the Iron Curtain and the Cold War were to follow.

yam *n.* **1.** a tropical or subtropical climbing plant of the genus *Dioscorea*; its edible starchy tuber. **2.** the sweet potato. [f. Port. or Sp. *iñame* (orig. unkn.)]

Yama /ˈjæmə/ (in Hindu mythology) the first man to die. He became the guardian, judge, and ruler of the dead, and is represented as carrying a noose and riding a buffalo. [f. Skr. *yama* restraint (*yam* restrain)]

Yamato /jæˈmɑːtəʊ/ *n.* the style or school in Japan which culminated in the 12th and 13th c. and dealt with Japanese subjects in a distinctively Japanese (rather than Chinese) way. [Jap., = Japanese]

yammer *n.* (*colloq.* or *dial.*) a lament, a wail, a grumble; voluble talk. —*v.i.* (*colloq.* or *dial.*) to utter a yammer. [OE (*geōmor* sorrowful)]

yang *n.* (in Chinese philosophy) the active principle of the universe, characterized as heaven, male, light, and penetrating (complemented by YIN). [Chinese]

Yangshao /yæŋˈʃaʊ/ *adj.* of an ancient civilization of northern China during the 3rd millennium BC, characterized by painted pottery with naturalistic designs of fish and human faces, and abstract patterns of triangles, spirals, arcs, and dots.

Yangtze Kiang /jæŋtsɪ ˈkjæŋ/ the principal river of China, which rises in Tibet and flows 6,380 km (3,964 miles) through central China to the East China Sea. [Chinese *kiang* river]

Yank *n.* (*colloq.*) a Yankee. [abbr.]

yank *v.t.* (*colloq.*) to pull with a jerk. —*n.* (*colloq.*) such a pull. [orig. unkn.]

Yankee /ˈjæŋkɪ/ *n.* **1.** (*colloq.*) an American. **2.** (*US*) an inhabitant of New England; an inhabitant of the northern States, a Federal soldier in the Civil War. **3.** a type of bet on four or more horses to win (or be placed) in different races. —**Yankee Doodle**, a burlesque song to a jolly tune, first used by British troops, in the American War of Independence, to deride the American colonial revolutionaries. It was subsequently adopted by the Americans and turned to their own advantage, and is now regarded as a national air. [perh. f. Du. *Janke* dim. of *Jan* John used derisively, or perh. f. *Jengees*, Amer. Ind. pronunc. of *English*]

Yaoundé /jæˈʊndeɪ/ the capital of Cameroon; pop. 337,000.

yap *v.i.* (**-pp-**) **1.** to bark shrilly or fussily. **2.** (*colloq.*) to chatter. —*n.* a sound of yapping. [imit.]

yapp *n.* a bookbinding with a projecting limp leather cover. [name of London bookseller *c.*1860, for whom it was first made]

yarborough /ˈjɑːbərə/ *n.* a whist or bridge hand with no card above a 9. [f. Earl of *Yarborough* (d. 1897), said to have betted against its occurrence]

yard[1] *n.* **1.** a unit of linear measure, = 3 ft. or 36 inches (0.9144 metre); this length of material; a square or cubic yard. The earlier standard was the ell (= 45 inches), and this was succeeded in 1353 by the *verge* of which 'yard' is the English equivalent; the yard was defined as the distance between two marks on a certain metallic bar, kept in the Tower of London, when this is at a temperature of 60 °F. **2.** a spar slung across a mast for a sail to hang from (ill. SAILING-SHIPS). —**yard-arm** *n.* a ship's yard; either end of this. [OE, = OS *gerdia* twig]

yard[2] *n.* **1.** a piece of enclosed ground, especially one attached to a building or used for a particular purpose. **2.** (*US*) the garden of a house. [OE (as GARTH, GARDEN)]

yardage *n.* the number of yards of material etc. [f. YARD[1]]

yardstick *n.* **1.** a rod a yard long, usually divided into inches etc. **2.** a standard of comparison.

yarmulka /ˈjɑːmʌlkə/ *n.* a skull-cap worn by Jewish men. [Yiddish]

yarn *n.* **1.** spun thread, esp. of the kinds prepared for knitting or weaving etc. **2.** (*colloq.*) a tale, esp. one that is exaggerated or invented. —*v.i.* (*colloq.*) to tell yarns. [OE]

yarrow /ˈjærəʊ/ *n.* a perennial herb of the genus *Achillea*, especially milfoil (*A. millefolium*). [OE]

yashmak /ˈjæʃmæk/ *n.* a veil concealing the face except the eyes, worn in public by Muslim women in certain countries. [f. Arab.]

yaw *v.i.* **1.** (of a ship or aircraft etc.) to fail to hold a straight course, to go unsteadily, esp. turning from side to side (ill. FLIGHT). **2.** a yawing course or movement. [orig. unkn.]

yawl *n.* **1.** a two-masted fore-and-aft sailing-boat with the mizen-mast stepped far aft. **2.** a kind of small fishing-boat. [f. MLG or Du. *jol* (orig. unkn.); cf. *jolly-boat*]

yawn *v.i.* **1.** to open the mouth wide and inhale, especially in sleepiness or boredom. **2.** to have a wide opening, to form a chasm. —*n.* the act of yawning. [OE]

yaws /jɔːz/ *n.pl.* (usu. treated as *sing.*) a contagious tropical skin-disease with raspberry-like swellings. [orig. unkn.]

Yayoi /jəˈjɔɪ/ *adj.* of a neolithic industry of Japan, dating from the 3rd c. BC, named after a street in Tokyo where its characteristic chiefly wheel-made pottery was first discovered. It is marked by the introduction of rice cultivation to Japan, and the appearance of large burial mounds has suggested the emergence of an increasingly powerful ruling class. —*n.* this industry. [Jap.]

Yb *symbol* ytterbium.

yd(s) *abbr.* yard(s).

ye[1] /jɪ, jiː/ *pron.* (*archaic*) *pl.* of THOU.

ye[2] /jiː; or as THE/ *adj.* (*pseudo-archaic*) = THE (*ye olde tea-shoppe*). [f. old use of obs. y-shaped letter for *th*]

yea /jeɪ/ *adv.* (*archaic*) yes. —*n.* the word 'yea'. —**yeas and nays,** affirmative and negative votes. [OE]

yeah /jeə/ *adv.* (*colloq.*) yes. [casual pronunc. of YES]

year /jɪə(r), jɜː(r)/ *n.* **1.** the time occupied by the earth in one revolution round the sun, approximately 365¼ days. **2.** the period from 1 Jan. to 31 Dec. inclusive. **3.** a period of the same length as this starting at any point. **4.** (in *pl.*) age, time of life. **5.** (usu. in *pl.*) a very long time. **6.** a group of students entering a college etc. in the same acedamic year. —**year-book** *n.* an annual publication containing current information about a specified subject. [OE]

yearling /ˈyɜːlɪŋ/ *n.* an animal between one and two years old. [f. YEAR]

yearly /ˈyɜːlɪ/ *adj.* **1.** done, produced, or occurring etc. every year. **2.** of, for, or lasting a year. —*adv.* once every year. [OE (as YEAR)]

yearn /jɜːn/ *v.i.* to be filled with great longing. [OE]

yeast *n.* a greyish-yellow fungous substance that causes alcohol and carbon dioxide to be produced when it is developing, used to cause fermentation in making beer and wines and as a raising agent in baking. —**yeast cake,** one in which the raising agent used is yeast. [OE]

yeasty *adj.* frothy like yeast when it is developing. —**yeastiness** *n.* [f. prec.]

Yeats /jeɪts/, William Butler (1865-1939), Irish poet and dramatist, son of J. B. Yeats and brother of Jack Yeats (both celebrated painters). Yeats developed a fascination for mystic religion and the supernatural while studying at the School of Art in Dublin. With Lady Gregory and others he established the Irish National Theatre (later based at the Abbey Theatre) and his play *The Countess Cathleen* (1892) began the Irish revival in the theatre. Irish lore and legend predominate in *The Celtic Twilight* (1893; stories) which became a generic phrase for the Irish literary revival of which Yeats is the acknowledged leader. Irish traditional and national themes and his unrequited love for revolutionary patriot Maude Gonne inspired *The Wanderings of Oisin and other Poems* (1889) and other volumes. In his later works he moved further from his early elaborate Pre-Raphaelite style towards a new spare colloquial lyricism. In 1917 he married Georgie Hyde-Lees, whose power of automatic writing stimulated his occultism; her 'communicators' ultimately provided him with the system of symbolism (described in *A Vision*, 1925) which underlies many of the poems in *The Tower* (1928) and *The Winding Stair* (1929). Yeats served as senator of the Irish Free State (1922-8) and was awarded the Nobel Prize for literature in 1923.

yell *n.* a loud sharp cry of pain, anger, fright, encouragement, delight, etc.; a shout. —*v.t./i.* to make or utter with a yell. [OE]

yellow /ˈjeləʊ/ *adj.* **1.** of the colour of buttercups and ripe lemons, or a colour approaching this. **2.** having a yellow skin or complexion. **3.** (*colloq.*) cowardly. —*n.* **1.** yellow colour or pigment. **2.** yellow clothes or material. —*v.t./i.* to turn yellow. —**yellow card,** such a card shown by the referee at a football match to a player whom he is cautioning. **yellow flag,** that displayed by a ship in quarantine. **yellow pages,** a section of a telephone directory, printed on yellow paper, listing business subscribers according to the goods or services they offer. —**yellowish** *adj.*, **yellowness** *n.* [OE (rel. to GOLD)]

yellow fever a tropical disease with fever and jaundice, the notorious 'yellow jack' of the old sea-stories, carried from infected persons by the bite of a female mosquito of the genus *Aëdes aegyptii*. Primarily a disease of monkeys, it became established in humans many centuries ago and was probably carried from Africa to the West Indies when African slaves were first taken there. Yellow fever is often fatal; its prevention and control (as by inoculation) are all-important.

yellowhammer *n.* a bunting (*Emberiza citrinella*), the male of which has a yellow head, neck, and breast.

Yellowstone /ˈjeləʊstəʊn/ an area of Wyoming and Montana in the USA, reserved as a National Park since 1872. It is famous for its scenery, geysers, and wildlife. The Yellowstone River, which rises in the park, is a tributary of the Missouri.

yelp *n.* a sharp shrill cry or bark. —*v.i.* to utter a yelp. [OE, = boast (imit.)]

Yemen /ˈjemən/ a country in the south and south-west of the Arabian peninsula, now divided into the People's Democratic Republic of Yemen (South Yemen; pop. (est. 1977) 1,800,000; official language, Arabic; capital, Aden) and the Yemen Arab Republic (North Yemen; pop. approx. 8,556,974; official language, Arabic; capital, Sana'a). An Islamic country since the mid-7th c., Yemen was part of the Ottoman empire from the 16th c. In the 19th c. it came under increasing British influence as a result of the strategic importance of Aden at the mouth of the Red Sea. Civil war between royalist and republican forces in the era following the Second World War ended with the British withdrawal and South Yemen's declaration of independence in 1967. Relations between the two countries, with their antagonistic political systems, remain bad. —**Yemenite** /-naɪt/ *adj.* & *n.*

yen[1] *n.* (*pl.* same) the Japanese monetary unit. [Jap. f. Chin. *yuan* round, dollar]

yen[2] *n.* a longing or yearning. —*v.i.* (**-nn-**) to feel a longing. [Chin. dial.]

yeoman /ˈjəʊmən/ *n.* (*pl.* **-men**) **1.** a man holding and cultivating a small landed estate. **2.** a member of a yeomanry force. —**Yeoman of the Guard,** a member of the British sovereign's bodyguard, first established by Henry VII. Their functions are now entirely ceremonial, and along with the warders of the Tower of London (who, like them, wear Tudor dress as uniform) they are commonly known as beefeaters. —**yeoman('s) service,** efficient or useful help in need. —**yeomanly** *adj.* [prob. f. YOUNG + MAN]

yeomanry /ˈjəʊmənrɪ/ *n.* **1.** a body of yeomen. **2.** (*hist.*) a volunteer cavalry force raised from the yeoman class. [f. prec.]

yes *adv.* **1.** serving to indicate that the answer to the question is affirmative, the statement etc. made is correct, the request or command will be complied with, or the person summoned or addressed is present. **2.** (*interrog.*) indeed?; is that so?; what do you want? —*n.* the word or answer 'yes'. —**yes-man** *n.* (*colloq.*) a weakly acquiescent person. [OE, prob. = yea let it be]

yester- *in comb.* (*literary*) of yesterday, that is last past (*yester-eve, yestermorn*). —**yester-year** *n.* last year; the recent past. [OE]

yesterday /ˈjestədeɪ, -dɪ/ *adv.* on the day before today; in the recent past. —*n.* the day before today; the recent past. [OE (as prec. + DAY)]

yet *adv.* **1.** up to this or that time and continuing, still. **2.** (with neg. or interrog.) by this or that time, so far. **3.** besides, in addition. **4.** before the matter is done with, eventually. **5.** (with compar.) even. **6.** nevertheless. —*conj.* nevertheless, but in spite of that. [OE]

yeti /ˈjetɪ/ *n.* the Abominable Snowman (see ABOMINABLE). [Tibetan]

yett *n.* (*Sc.*) a type of gate or portcullis with interlocking bands. [= GATE]

yew *n.* a dark-leaved evergreen coniferous tree (*Taxus baccata*) with needle-like leaves and red berries (ill. TREES); its wood, used formerly as material for bows and still in cabinet-making. [OE]

Yggdrasil /ˈɪgdrəsɪl/ (*Scand. myth.*) the ash-tree whose roots and branches connect heaven, earth, and hell. The Norns sit beneath it. [f. ON (*Yggr* Odin, *drasill* horse)]

Yiddish /ˈjɪdɪʃ/ *n.* a language used by Jews of or from central Europe. Until 1939 it was widely spoken, but since the Second World War the number of speakers has declined in the face of the use of Hebrew as a spoken language. It originated in the 9th c. among Jewish emigrants who settled in cities along the Rhine in Germany and adopted the German dialect of the area. Their German was heavily influenced by Hebrew which remained their literary language. In the 14th c. it was carried eastwards where it was again influenced by the Slavonic languages. From this amalgam arose Yiddish. When it was written down, the Hebrew characters were used with the difference that vowels were written with separate signs. —*adj.* of this language. [f. G *jüdisch* Jewish]

yield *v.t./i.* **1.** to give or return as fruit or as gain or result. **2.** to surrender; to do what is requested or ordered. **3.** to be inferior, to confess inferiority. **4.** (of traffic) to give the right of way to other traffic. **5.** to be able to be forced out of the natural or usual shape, e.g. under pressure. —*n.* the amount yielded or produced. [OE, = pay]

yin *n.* (in Chinese philosophy) the passive principle of the universe, characterized as earth, female, dark, and absorbing (complemented by YANG). [Chinese]

yippee /ˈjɪpɪ/ *int.* expressing delight or excitement. [cf. HIP³]

YMCA *abbr.* Young Men's Christian Association.

Ymir /ˈiːmə(r)/ (*Scand. myth.*) the primeval giant from whose body the gods created the world.

yob *n.* (also **yobbo** /ˈjɒbəʊ/) (*pl.* **-os**) (*slang*) a lout, a hooligan. [back slang for BOY]

yodel /ˈjəʊd(ə)l/ *v.t./i.* (**-ll-**) to sing, or utter a musical call, with the voice alternating continually between falsetto and its normal pitch, in the manner of Swiss and Tyrolean mountain-dwellers. —*n.* a yodelling cry. —**yodeller** *n.* [f. G *jodeln*]

yoga /ˈjəʊgə/ *n.* a Hindu system of philosophic meditation and asceticism designed to effect reunion with the universal spirit; the system of physical exercises and breathing-control used in this. [Hind. f. Skr., = union]

yoghurt /ˈjɒgət/ *n.* a semi-solid sourish food prepared from milk fermented by added bacteria. [f. Turk.]

yogi /ˈjəʊgɪ/ *n.* a devotee of yoga. [Hind. (as YOGA)]

yoicks *int.* used by a fox-hunter to urge on hounds. [orig. unkn.]

yoke *n.* **1.** a wooden cross-piece fastened over the necks of two oxen etc. and attached to a plough or wagon to be drawn. **2.** a pair of oxen etc. **3.** an object like a yoke in form or function; a piece of wood shaped to fit a person's shoulders and to hold a pail or other load slung from each end; the top section of a dress or skirt etc. from which the rest hangs. **4.** oppression, burdensome restraint. **5.** a bond of union, especially of marriage. —*v.t./i.* **1.** to put a yoke upon; to harness by means of a yoke. **2.** to unite, to link. [OE]

yokel /ˈjəʊk(ə)l/ *n.* a rustic, a country bumpkin. [perh. f. dial. *yokel* green woodpecker]

yolk /jəʊk/ *n.* the yellow internal part of an egg. [OE as YELLOW)]

Yom Kippur /jɒm kɪˈpʊə(r)/ the Day of Atonement (see ATONE). [Heb.]

yomp *v.i.* to march with heavy equipment over difficult terrain. [orig. unkn.]

yon *adj. & adv.* (*archaic* or *dial.*) yonder. —*n.* (*archaic* or *dial.*) yonder person or thing. [OE]

yonder *adv.* over there. —*adj.* situated or able to be seen over there. [cf. OS *gendra*]

yore *n.* **of yore**, formerly, in or of old days. [OE]

York **1.** a city in North Yorkshire, seat of the archbishop, Primate of England. **2.** the name of the English royal house descended from Edmund of Langley (1341-1402), 5th son of Edward III and (from 1385) 1st Duke of York, which ruled England from 1461 (Edward IV) until the death of Richard III (1485). It was united with the House of Lancaster when Henry VII married the eldest daughter of Edward IV (1486).

yorker *n.* (in cricket) a ball that pitches immediately under the bat. [prob. as foll., with ref. to practice of Yorkshire cricketers]

Yorkist /ˈjɔːkɪst/ *adj.* of the family descended from the 1st Duke of York (see YORK) or of the White Rose party supporting it in the Wars of the Roses (cf. LANCASTRIAN). —*n.* a member or adherent of the Yorkist family. [f. YORK]

Yorkshire pudding /ˈjɔːkʃə(r)/ baked batter eaten with roast beef. [*Yorkshire*, former county of England]

Yorkshire terrier /ˈjɔːkʃə(r)/ a small shaggy blue and tan toy kind of terrier. [as prec.]

Yoruba /ˈjɒrəbə/ *n.* (*pl.* same or **-s**) **1.** a member of a Black people on the coast of West Africa, especially in Nigeria where they are numerically the largest ethnic group. **2.** their language, which is one of the major languages of Nigeria and is spoken by 10 million people in the south-west of the country. It is a tonal language of the Niger-Congo language group. [native name]

Yosemite /jəʊˈsemɪtɪ/ a National Park in eastern California in the USA, named after the Yosemite River which flows through it.

you /juː, jʊ/ *pron.* of the second person singular and plural (*obj.* **you**; *poss.* YOUR, YOURS) **1.** the person(s) or thing(s) addressed; (as *voc.* with a noun in an exclamatory statement: *you fools!*). **2.** (in general statements) one, a person, anyone, everyone. —**you and yours**, you together with your family, property, etc. [OE, orig. acc. & dat. of YE¹]

Young /jʌŋ/, Brigham (1801-77), Mormon leader (see MORMON).

young /jʌŋ/ *adj.* **1.** having lived or existed for only a short

time, not yet old; (of the night or a year etc.) still near its beginning. **2.** immature; having little experience. **3.** representing young people; characteristic of youth. **4.** distinguishing the son from the father or (in *compar.*) one person from another of the same name. —*n. collect.* offspring, especially of animals before or soon after birth. —**the young**, young people. **Young Pretender**, see PRETENDER. [OE]

youngster *n.* a child, a young person. [f. prec.]

your /jɔː(r), jʊə(r)/ *poss. adj.* of or belonging to you. [OE, orig. gen. of YE¹]

yours /jɔːz, jʊəz/ *poss. pron.* of or belonging to you; the thing or things belonging to you. —**yours ever, faithfully, sincerely, truly**, etc., formulas preceding the signature of a letter. [f. YOUR]

yourself /jɔːˈself, jʊəˈself/ *pron.* (*pl.* **yourselves**) the emphatic and reflexive form of YOU.

youth /juːθ/ *n.* (*pl.* /juːðz/) **1.** being young; the period between childhood and adult age; the vigour, enthusiasm, inexperience, or other characteristic of this period. **2.** a young man. **3.** (as *pl.*) young people collectively. —**youth club**, a place where leisure activities are provided for young people. **youth hostel**, a place where (young) holiday-makers can stay cheaply for the night. **youth hosteller**, a user of a youth hostel. [OE (as YOUNG)]

youthful *adj.* young or (still) having the characteristics of youth. —**youthfully** *adv.*, **youthfulness** *n.* [f. prec. + -FUL]

yowl *n.* a loud wailing cry, a howl. —*v.i.* to utter a yowl. [imit.]

Yo-Yo /ˈjəʊjəʊ/ *n.* (*pl.* **Yo-Yos**) [P] a toy consisting of a pair of discs with a deep groove between them in which a string is attached and wound, and which can be made to fall and rise on the string when this is jerked by a finger. [orig. unkn.]

Ypres /ˈiːprə, *joc.* ˈwaɪpəz/ a town in Belgium, scene of some of the bitterest fighting on the Western Front during the First World War.

yr. *abbr.* **1.** year(s). **2.** younger. **3.** your.

yrs. *abbr.* **1.** years. **2.** yours.

ytterbium /ɪˈtɜːbɪəm/ *n.* a soft metallic element of the lanthanide series, symbol Yb, atomic number 70. It has few commercial uses. [f. *Ytterby* village in Sweden]

yttrium /ˈɪtrɪəm/ *n.* a metallic element, symbol Y, atomic number 39, included among the rare-earth metals. Yttrium compounds have a variety of uses, the most important being to make red phosphors for colour-television tubes. The metal itself is used in certain alloys. [as prec.]

yucca /ˈjʌkə/ *n.* a tall American plant of the genus *Yucca*, with white bell-like flowers and spiky leaves. [Carib]

Yugoslavia /juːgəʊˈslɑːvɪə/ a country in SE Europe with a coastline on the Adriatic Sea and with frontiers that border seven nations; pop. (1981) 22,420,000; no official language since all are constitutionally equal, but Serbo-Croat serves as the lingua franca; capital, Belgrade. The country was formed, as a kingdom, as a result of the peace settlement at the end of the First World War from Serbia, Montenegro, and the former Slavic provinces of the Austro-Hungarian empire. Invaded by the Axis powers during the Second World War, Yugoslavia emerged from a long guerrilla war as a Communist State but refused to accept Soviet domination. Composed of a mixture of racial and religious groups, the country has maintained well-developed links with the west and has benefited from major industrialization and the promotion of tourism. —**Yugoslav** /ˈjuː-/ *adj. & n.*, **Yugoslavian** *adj. & n.* [f. G *Jugoslav* f. Serbian *jug* south + SLAV]

Yukatan /juːkəˈtɑːn/ a peninsula in SE Mexico between the Gulf of Mexico and the Gulf of Honduras.

Yukon /ˈjuːkɒn/ a river of North America 3,020 km (1,870 miles) long, rising in Canada on the border between Yukon Territory and British Columbia and flowing through Alaska into the Bering Sea.

Yukon Territory a territory of NW Canada, where gold was discovered in the Klondike River in 1896. It was constituted a separate political unit in 1898, with its capital at Dawson.

yule *n.* (in full **yule-tide**) (*archaic*) the Christmas festival. —**yule-log** *n.* a large log traditionally burnt on the hearth on Christmas Eve. [OE]

yummy *adj.* (*colloq.*) tasty, delicious. [f. foll.]

yum-yum /jʌmˈjʌm/ *int.* expressing pleasure from eating or the prospect of eating. [natural excl.]

YWCA *abbr.* Young Women's Christian Association.

Z

Z, z /zed/ n. (pl. **Zs, Z's**) **1.** the twenty-sixth letter of the alphabet. **2.** (in algebra) **z**, the third unknown quantity.

zabaglione /zɑ:bɑ:ˈljəʊneɪ/ n. an Italian sweet of whipped and heated egg yolks, sugar, and Marsala or other wine. [It.]

Zaïre¹ /zɑ:ˈɪə(r)/ a major river of central Africa flowing into the Atlantic. It lies largely within the republic of Zaïre and is 4,630 km (2,880 miles) long.

Zaïre² /zɑ:ˈɪə(r)/ a country in central Africa with a short coastline on the Atlantic Ocean; pop. (est. 1981) 28,400,000; official language, French; capital, Kinshasa. Only gradually opened up by European exploration, the area became a Belgian colony known as the Belgian Congo in the late 19th and early 20th c. Independence (as a republic) in 1960 was followed by civil war and UN intervention and an even reasonably stable State was some time in emerging; the name Zaïre was adopted in 1971. The economy is largely based on mineral exports, particularly of copper, of which Zaïre is one of the world's major producers. —**Zaïrean** /-rɪən/ adj. & n.

Zambezi /zæmˈbiːzɪ/ an African river 2,655 km (1,650 miles) long, flowing through Angola, Zambia, and Mozambique to the Indian Ocean. It forms the border between Zambia and Zimbabwe.

Zambia /ˈzæmbɪə/ a landlocked country in central Africa, a member State of the Commonwealth; pop. (est. 1982) 6,050,000; official language, English; capital, Lusaka. Explored by Livingstone in the mid-19th c., the area was administered by the British South Africa Company from 1889 until taken over as a protectorate by the British government in 1924, having been named Northern Rhodesia in 1911. After some disturbances full independence was gained in 1964, as a republic under President Kenneth Kaunda, subsequent economic reconstruction being assisted by Chinese financial aid and the redevelopment of the copper-mining industry. Zambia is the third-largest copper-producing country in the world after the USA and USSR. —**Zambian** adj. & n.

zany /ˈzeɪnɪ/ adj. crazily funny or ridiculous. —n. **1.** a comical or eccentric person. **2.** (hist.) an attendant clown awkwardly mimicking the chief clown in shows. [f. F or It. zan(n)i, Venetian form of Giovanni John]

Zanzibar /ˈzænzɪbɑ:(r)/ an island off the coast of East Africa that was (together with the islands of Pemba and Latham) a sultanate from 1856 and a British protectorate from 1890 until it gained independence as a member State of the Commonwealth in 1963. In the following year the Sultan's government was overthrown and the country became a republic, uniting with Tanganyika (see TANZANIA).

zap v.t. (-pp-) (slang) to hit, to attack, to kill. [imit.]

Zapata /səˈpɑ:tə/, Emiliano (c.1877-1919), Mexican revolutionary. Unlike most of the other Mexican leaders of the period Zapata was not associated with any particular faction, earning his fame as a champion of agrarianism. Like most of his contemporaries, however, he met a violent end, being assassinated in 1919.

Zapotec /ˈzæpətek/ n. (pl. same or **-s**) a member or the language of an Indian people centred at Oaxaca in SW Mexico. [Sp. f. Nahuatl]

Zarathustra /zærəˈθʊstrə, -ˈθu:-/ the Old Iranian name for Zoroaster. —**Zarathustrian** adj. & n.

zeal n. enthusiasm, hearty and persistent effort. [f. L f. Gk zēlos]

zealot /ˈzelət/ n. **1.** a zealous person; an uncompromising or extreme partisan, a fanatic. **2. Zealot**, a member of a Jewish sect aiming at world Jewish theocracy and resisting the Romans until AD 70. —**zealotry** n. [as prec.]

zealous /ˈzeləs/ adj. full of zeal. —**zealously** adv. [f. ZEAL]

zebra /ˈzebrə, ˈziːbrə/ n. **1.** an African quadruped of the genus Equus, related to the ass and the horse, with a body entirely covered by black and white (or dark-brown and cream) stripes. **2.** (attrib.) with alternate dark and pale stripes. —**zebra crossing**, a striped street-crossing where pedestrians have precedence over vehicles. [It. or Port. f. Congolese]

zebu /ˈziːbuː/ n. a humped ox (Bos indicus) of India, East Asia, and Africa. [f. F zébu; orig. unkn.]

Zebulun /ˈzebjuːlən/ **1.** Hebrew patriarch, son of Jacob and Leah (Gen. 30: 20). **2.** the tribe of Israel traditionally descended from him.

Zechariah /zekəˈraɪə/ **1.** a Hebrew minor prophet of the 6th c. BC. **2.** a book of the Old Testament containing his prophecies, urging the restoration of the Temple, and some later material.

zed n. the letter Z. [f. F f. L f. Gk, = ZETA]

Zedekiah /zedɪˈkaɪə/ the last king of Judah, who rebelled against Nebuchadnezzar and was carried off to Babylon into captivity (2 Kings 24-5, 2 Chron. 36).

zee n. (US) the letter Z. [var. of ZED]

Zeeman /ˈziːmən/, Pieter (1865-1943), Dutch physicist, who in 1886 discovered the phenomenon now named after him—the Zeeman effect, the splitting of the spectral lines of a substance by a magnetic field. It has been used to detect and measure the magnetic fields of stars, and in studying atomic particles and nuclei. For this discovery Zeeman shared the 1902 Nobel Prize for physics with Lorentz, his former teacher, who had predicted the existence of such an effect.

Zen n. a sect of Japanese Buddhism that teaches the attainment of enlightenment through meditation and intuition rather than through study of the scriptures. [Jap., = meditation]

zenana /zɪˈnɑ:nə/ n. the part of the house for the seclusion of women of high-caste families in India and Iran. [f. Hind. f. Pers. (zan woman)]

Zend /zend/ n. an interpretation of the Avesta, each Zend being part of the **Zend-Avesta**, Zoroastrian scriptures consisting of Avesta (= text) and Zend (= commentary). [f. Pers. zand interpretation]

zenith /ˈzenɪθ, ˈziː-/ n. **1.** the point of the heavens directly above the observer (ill. NAVIGATION). **2.** the highest point (of power or prosperity etc.). [f. OF or L ult. f. Arab., = path (over the head)]

Zeno /ˈziːnəʊ/ (5th c. BC) Greek philosopher from Elea in southern Italy, pupil of Parmenides whose theories he supported by demonstrating the paradoxical conclusions that follow from the premisses of its opponents—the paradox of Achilles and the tortoise, for example, by which it is shown that once Achilles has given the tortoise a start he can never overtake it, since by the time he arrives where it was it has already moved on.

Zenobia /zeˈnəʊbɪə/ (3rd c.) queen of Palmyra, who succeeded her murdered husband as ruler and then conquered Egypt and much of Asia Minor. When she proclaimed her son emperor, the Roman emperor Aurelian marched against her and eventually defeated and captured her. She was later given a pension and a villa in Italy.

Zephaniah /zefəˈnaɪə/ **1.** a Hebrew minor prophet of the 7th c. BC. **2.** a book of the Old Testament containing his prophecies.

zephyr /ˈzefə(r)/ n. a soft mild gentle wind or breeze. [f. F or L f. Gk zephuros (god of the) west wind]

Zeppelin /ˈzepəlɪn/, Ferdinand Adolf August Heinrich, Count von (1838-1917), German airship pioneer who both designed and built airships as well as forming the world's first commercial passenger service. In the First World War his airships, known as Zeppelins, were used to bomb England. Later designs by the company he formed included the Graf Zeppelin and the Hindenburg (see AIRSHIP), and in the 1920s and 1930s achieved success with transatlantic commercial flights.

zero /ˈzɪərəʊ/ n. (pl. **-os**) **1.** nought; the figure 0. **2.** the point on the graduated scale of a thermometer etc. from which a positive or negative quantity is reckoned. **3.** (in full **zero-hour**) the hour at which a planned military or other operation is timed to begin; the crucial or decisive moment. —**zero in on**, to take aim at; to focus attention on. **zero-rated** *adj.* on which no value added tax is charged. [f. F or It. ult. f. Arab. (as CIPHER)]

zest *n.* **1.** piquancy, stimulating flavour or quality. **2.** keen enjoyment or interest. **3.** the coloured part of orange or lemon peel as flavouring. —**zestful** *adj.*, **zestfully** *adv.* [f. F *zeste* orange or lemon peel; orig. unkn.]

zeta /ˈziːtə/ *n.* the sixth letter of the Greek alphabet, = z. [f. Gk]

zeugma /ˈzjuːgmə/ *n.* a figure of speech using a verb or adjective with two nouns, to one of which it is strictly applicable while the word appropriate to the other is not used (e.g. *with weeping eyes and* [sc. *grieving*] *hearts*); (*loosely*) syllepsis. [L f. Gk (*zeugnumi* to yoke, *zugon* yoke)]

Zeus /zjuːs/ (*Gk myth.*) the supreme god, whose epithet is 'father' and whose name means 'sky'. He was the god of weather and atmospheric phenomena (rain, thunder, etc.), protector and ruler of the family, son of Cronus whom he dethroned after being brought up in Crete (see CRONUS). The Romans identified him with Jupiter. [Gk f. Skr., = sky]

Zeuxis /ˈzjuːksɪs/ (latter 5th c. BC) Greek painter, born at Heraclea in southern Italy. Our only knowledge of his works (none of which survive) comes through the records of ancient writers, who make reference to monochrome techniques and his use of shading to create an illusion of depth. There are many anecdotes about his verisimilitude; his paintings of grapes are said to have deceived the birds.

Zhou Enlai = CHOU EN-LAI.

Ziegfeld /ˈziːgfeld/, Florenz (1867-1932), American theatre manager, creator of a series of revues entitled the *Ziegfeld Follies* which began in 1907 and continued annually until his death, being seen intermittently thereafter until 1957. He based his show on that of the *Folies Bergère*, with the emphasis on scenic splendour, comic sketches, vaudeville specialities, and attractive young women.

ziggurat /ˈzɪgəræt/ *n.* a pyramidal stepped tower in ancient Mesopotamia, built in several stages which diminish in size towards the summit on which there may have been a shrine. Possibly derived from earlier platform temples, the ziggurat is first attested in the late 3rd millennium BC; the one at Babylon may be the 'Tower of Babel' of early Hebrew legend (Gen. 11: 1-9). [f. Assyrian, = pinnacle]

zigzag /ˈzɪgzæg/ *adj.* with abrupt alternate right and left turns. —*n.* a zigzag line; a thing forming this or having sharp turns. —*adv.* with a zigzag course. —*v.i.* (**-gg-**) to move in a zigzag course. [F f. G *zickzack* (symbolic formation)]

zillion /ˈzɪljən/ *n.* (*US*) an indefinite large number. [f. *z* (perh. = unknown quantity) + MILLION]

Zimbabwe /zɪmˈbɑːbwɪ/ a landlocked country in SE Africa, south of the River Zambezi, bordered by Zambia, Botswana, the Transvaal, and Mozambique; pop. (est. 1982) 7,539,000; official language, English; capital Harare. Known as Southern Rhodesia and then as Rhodesia, the country was a self-governing British colony from 1923. The ruling White minority sought independence from Britain when Northern Rhodesia became independent (as Zambia) in 1964, but Britain refused to grant this unless Black majority rule was to be guaranteed within a definite period. Led by its prime minister, Ian Smith, Rhodesia issued a unilateral declaration of independence (UDI) in 1965, which was countered by the imposition of economic sanctions by Britain and the UN. These, and even more the growing activity of nationalist guerrillas, forced Smith eventually to concede the principle of Black majority rule, and after an unsuccessful attempt to introduce this under the moderate Bishop Muzorewa, whose regime failed to come to terms with the guerrilla movement, national elections were held under British supervision in 1980. These resulted in the election of Robert Mugabe as prime minister and were followed by the formal granting of independence to the country as a republic and member State of the Commonwealth, taking its name from Great Zimbabwe. —**Great Zimbabwe,** a complex of imposing stone ruins in a fertile valley *c.*270 km (175 miles) south of Harare, discovered in 1868 and at first optimistically believed to be the city of Ophir, mentioned in the Bible as a place from which Solomon brought gold in great quantity, and of King Solomon's Mines, a belief which led to a great staking of mining claims. The buildings consist of an acropolis, a stone enclosure, and scattered remains between these, covering an area of 24 hectares (60 acres). The city probably grew up as a focus of trade routes, and in the 14th-15th c. was the

centre of a powerful and wealthy empire, where a Black civilization flourished centuries before the arrival of Europeans. What eventually happened to this place and the skills that built it remains unexplained. —**Zimbabwean** *adj.* & *n.* [Bantu, = stone house]

zinc *n.* a white metallic element, symbol Zn, atomic number 30 (see below). —*v.t.* to coat or treat with zinc. [f. G *zink*, orig. unkn.]
   In ancient times the metal was known only in brass, an alloy of copper and zinc. It is now used as a component in a number of alloys, as well as for coating (galvanizing) iron and steel to protect against corrosion; its compounds have numerous industrial uses. Trace amounts of zinc are essential to the human body and to many other living organisms.

zing *n.* (*colloq.*) vigour, energy. —*v.i.* (*colloq.*) to move swiftly or shrilly. [imit.]

Zinjanthropus /zɪnˈdʒænθrəpəs/ *n.* a species of Australopithecus (*A. boisei*). [f. Arab. *Zinj* E. Africa + Gk *anthropos* man]

zinnia /ˈzɪnɪə/ *n.* a garden plant of the genus *Zinnia* with brightly-coloured flowers. [f. J. G. *Zinn*, German botanist (d. 1759)]

Zion /ˈzaɪən/ **1.** one of the two hills and also the citadel of ancient Jerusalem, taken by David from the Jebusites (2 Sam. 5: 6-7). The name came to signify Jerusalem itself (Is. 1: 27) and, allegorically, the heavenly city or kingdom of heaven (Heb. 12: 22). **2.** the Jewish religion. **3.** the Christian Church. **4.** a non-conformist chapel. [OE f. L f. Heb.]

Zionism /ˈzaɪənɪz(ə)m/ *n.* a political movement founded in 1897 under the leadership of Theodore Herzl that sought and has achieved the re-establishment of a Jewish nation in Palestine, reflecting the continuing nationalist attachment of the Jews and their religion to that country. —**Zionist** *n.* [f. ZION]

zip *n.* **1.** a short sharp sound like that of a bullet going through the air. **2.** energy, vigour. **3.** a zip-fastener (see entry). —*v.t./i.* (**-pp-**) **1.** to move with a zip or at high speed. **2.** to fasten with a zip-fastener. [imit.]

Zip code (*US*) a system of postal codes. [f. *z*one *i*mprovement *p*lan]

zip-fastener *n.* a fastening device of two flexible strips with interlocking projections closed or opened by a sliding clip pulled along them. Slide fasteners using hooks and eyes were exhibited at Chicago in 1893; a similar device using spring clips followed in 1912 in the USA and in Europe, and in 1917 the US Navy used such fasteners on windproof flying-suits for its airmen. The zipper (patented under this name) was used in 1923 on boots made of rubber and fabric, and in the late 1920s these fasteners began to appear on other clothing.

zipper *n.* a zip-fastener. [f. ZIP]

zircon /ˈzɜːkən/ *n.* zirconium silicate of which some translucent varieties are used as gems. [f. G *zirkon*]

zirconium /zɜːˈkəʊnɪəm/ *n.* a grey metallic element, symbol Zr, atomic number 40, chemically related to titanium. First discovered (as the oxide) in 1789, zirconium and its compounds now have a variety of industrial uses. The metal's resistance to heat and corrosion and its transparency to neutrons have led to its becoming an important structural material within nuclear reactors. [f. prec.]

zither /ˈzɪðə(r)/ *n.* **1.** a plucked stringed folk instrument of Austria and Bavaria, in its present most common form comprising a shallow wooden sound-box over which are stretched five melody strings and two sets of accompaniment strings tuned to form chords (ill. MUSICAL NOTATION). The zither features in Anton Karas's theme music to the film *The Third Man* (1949). **2.** any of various instruments in which the strings are stretched between the two ends of a flat body, such as a board or a stick. Members of the family include the psaltery, dulcimer, and vina. [G, ult. f. Gk *kithara* kind of harp (cf. GUITAR)]

zloty /ˈzlɒtɪ/ *n.* the monetary unit of Poland. [Polish lit. 'golden']

Zn *symbol* zinc.

zodiac /ˈzəʊdɪæk/ *n.* **1.** a band of the heavens close to the sun's apparent annual path through the celestial sphere, as viewed from Earth, and including about 8° on each side of the ecliptic. This band is divided into twelve equal parts (the **signs of the zodiac**), each named after a prominent constellation situated in it (see ill. ASTRONOMY), through which the sun appears to move at the approximate rate of one per month. **2.** a diagram of these signs. [f. OF f. L f. Gk (*zōidion* animal-figure)]

The zodiac, comprising stars immensely distant, appeared from Earth to be immutable. All the seven moving stars or planets known before modern times—the Sun, Moon, Mercury, Venus, Mars, Jupiter, and Saturn—moved within the zodiacal band, constantly changing their positions in relation to the Earth and each other, and these movements formed the basis of astrological science. Each sign governed a different part of the body, and a planet's influence changed as it moved from one to another. Many physicians thought it vital to choose the appropriate astrological moment in letting blood, giving medicines, or attempting surgery. The constellations are no longer located in the zodiacal signs named after them, a consequence of the fact that the Earth is not a perfect sphere and the polar axis changes slightly each year (see PRECESSION).

zodiacal /zə'daɪək(ə)l/ *adj.* of or in the zodiac. —**zodiacal light,** a diffuse band of light seen in the night sky on either side of the ecliptic and thought to be due to reflection of sunlight from minute particles of ice and dust within the plane of the solar system. It is best observed in the darkness of tropical skies. [F (as prec.)]

Zoffany /'zɒfəni/, Johann (1734/5–1810), German-born painter who had settled in England by 1758. His introduction to Garrick led to his painting scenes from the contemporary theatre (e.g. *The Clandestine Marriage*), which brought him immediate success. Zoffany received several royal commissions, the most important being *The Tribune of the Uffizi* for Queen Charlotte in 1770; in Vienna he painted portraits of the Austrian imperial family. In 1783–9 he made an extended sojourn in India. His paintings are for the most part of indifferent artistic merit.

Zola /'zəʊlə/, Émile (1840–1902), French novelist, the leading figure of the naturalist school of fiction, of which *Thérèse Raquin* (1867) is his earliest example. His principal work *Les Rougon-Macquart* (1871–93), a series of 20 novels, influenced by contemporary theories of heredity and experimental science, presents a panorama of mid-19th c. French life through two branches of his family, focusing on vice, misery, and the powerful claims of human appetites and instincts; the prevailing pessimism is relieved by passages of lyrical beauty. Zola moves to a heightened symbolism in his trilogy *Les trois villes* (1894–8) which is concerned with social and religious problems; his final unfinished work *Les quatre Evangiles* (1899–1903) is inspired by optimistic humanitarian ideals. He intervened vigorously in the Dreyfus case in his letter 'J'accuse', and foiled the sentence of imprisonment for libel by spending 11 months in exile in England (1898–9).

Zöllner /'tsœlnə(r)/, Johann Karl Friedrich (1834–82), German pioneer in astrophysics. He gave up managing the family's cotton-printing factory so that he could devote himself to science. He invented a sophisticated photometer (1860), and a type of spectroscope (1869), both used in early studies in astrophysics. He correctly described how the nuclei of comets gradually vaporize as the sun is approached. Like Crookes, he became increasingly interested in spiritualism. A visual illusion which he discovered is named after him: parallel lines appear not to be so when crossed by short diagonal lines slanting in opposite directions (see ill. SHAPES).

zombie /'zɒmbɪ/ *n.* **1.** (in voodoo) a corpse said to be revived by witchcraft. **2.** (*colloq.*) a dull or apathetic person. [West African]

zone *n.* **1.** an area having particular features, properties, purpose, or use. **2.** any well-defined region of more or less beltlike form. **3.** the area between two concentric circles. **4.** an encircling band of colour etc. **5.** (*archaic*) a girdle or belt. —*v.t.* **1.** to encircle as or with a zone. **2.** to arrange or distribute by zones; to assign to a particular area. —**zonal** *adj.* [F or f. L f. Gk *zōnē* girdle]

zoo *n.* a zoological garden. [abbr.]

zoological /zəʊə'lɒdʒɪk(ə)l, zu:ə-/ *adj.* of zoology. —**zoological garden(s),** a public garden or park with a collec-

tion of animals for exhibition and study. —**zoologically** *adv.* [f. foll.]

zoology /zəʊ'ɒlədʒɪ, zu:-/ *n.* the study of animal structure, physiology, classification, habits, behaviour, and distribution. —**zoologist** *n.* [f. Gk *zōïon* animal + -LOGY]

zoom *v.i.* **1.** to move quickly, especially with a buzzing sound. **2.** to rise quickly or steeply. **3.** (in photography) to alter the size of the image continuously from long shot to close-up. —*n.* an aeroplane's steep climb. —**zoom lens,** a lens allowing a camera to zoom by varying the focus. [imit.]

zoomorphic /zəʊə'mɔːfɪk/ *adj.* **1.** imitating or representing animal forms; having the form of an animal. **2.** attributing the form or nature of an animal to a deity etc. —**zoomorphism** *n.* [f. Gk *zōïon* animal + *morphē* form]

zoophyte /'zəʊəfaɪt/ *n.* a plantlike animal, especially a coral, jellyfish, or sponge. [f. Gk (*zōïon* animal, *phuton* plant)]

Zoroaster /zɒrəʊ'æstə(r)/ (? *c.*628–551 BC, or perhaps considerably earlier) the Greek name for the Persian prophet Zarathustra, founder of Zoroastrianism.

Zoroastrianism /zɒrəʊ'æstrɪənɪz(ə)m/ *n.* a monotheistic religion of ancient Iran founded by Zoroaster (or Zarathustra) in the 6th c. BC. According to Zoroastrian mythology the supreme god, Ahura Mazda, created twin spirits, one of which chose truth and light, the other untruth and darkness. Later formulations pit Ahura Mazda (now called Ormazd) against his own evil twin (Ahriman). Zoroastrianism survives today in isolated areas of Iran and in India, where followers are known as Parsees. —**Zoroastrian** *adj.* & *n.* [f. prec.]

Zr *symbol* zirconium.

zucchini /zu:'ki:nɪ/ *n.* (*pl.* same or **-is**) a courgette. [It., pl. of *zucchino* dim. of *zucca* gourd]

Zuider Zee /zaɪdə 'zi:/ a large shallow inlet of the North Sea in the Netherlands, large parts of which have been reclaimed for agricultural use in a programme started in 1924. [Du., = southern sea]

Zulu /'zu:lu:/ *n.* **1.** a member of a South African Bantu people inhabiting the north-eastern part of Natal. **2.** their language, one of the major Bantu languages of southern Africa, spoken by about 5 million people in the Zulu homeland in Natal. —*adj.* of the Zulus or their language. [native name]

Zululand /'zu:lu:lænd/ the South African homeland of the Zulus, conquered by the British after heavy fighting in the Zulu War of 1879. It was annexed to Natal in 1897.

Zurbarán /θʊərbə'rɑːn/, Francisco (1598–1664), Spanish painter who became official painter to the town of Seville in 1628 and remained there until 1658, when he moved to Madrid. The influence of Caravaggio is evident in his works, which include narrative series of scenes from the lives of the saints, with simple colour and form in a profoundly realistic style. Philip IV employed him in 1634 on a series *The Labours of Hercules* and a historical scene *The Defence of Cadiz*. In Spain Zurbarán was eclipsed during his lifetime by Murillo, but Courbet, Manet, and Picasso are among those who have paid tribute to him.

Zurich /'zjʊərɪk/ the largest city in Switzerland, situated on Lake Zurich; pop. 367,900.

Zwingli /'zvɪŋglɪ/, Ulrich (1484–1531), Swiss Protestant reformer, minister of Zurich from 1518, where he sought to carry through his political and religious ideals and met with strong local support. From 1522 he published articles advocating the liberation of believers from the control of the papacy and bishops, and upholding the Gospel as the sole basis of truth. His attacks on purgatory, invocation of saints, monasticism, and other orthodox doctrines seem to have owed little directly to Luther, of whose influence he always betrayed some jealousy, and he differed irreconcilably from Luther in his doctrine of the Eucharist, upholding a purely symbolic interpretation. The movement spread over Switzerland but met fierce resistance in some parts, and Zwingli was killed in the resulting civil war, when as chaplain of the Zurich forces he carried the banner.

zygote /'zaɪɡəʊt/ *n.* a cell formed by the union of two gametes. [f. Gk *zugōtos* yoked (as ZEUGMA)]

APPENDIX I
COUNTRIES OF THE WORLD

Country	Capital	Area	Currency unit
Afghanistan	Kabul	652,090 sq. km (251,773 sq. miles)	afghani = 100 puls
Albania	Tiranë	28,748 sq. km (11,000 sq. miles)	lek = 100 qindarka
Algeria	Algiers	2,381,741 sq. km (919,595 sq. miles)	dinar = 100 centimes
Andorra	Andorra la Vella	464 sq. km (179 sq. miles)	{ franc = 100 centimes / peseta = 100 céntimos
Angola	Luanda	1,246,700 sq. km (481,353 sq. miles)	kwanza = 100 lweis
Antigua and Barbuda	St John's	442 sq. km (171 sq. miles)	dollar = 100 cents
Argentina	Buenos Aires	2,758,829 sq. km (1,065,189 sq. miles)	austral
Australia	Canberra	7,682,300 sq. km (2,966,200 sq. miles)	dollar = 100 cents
Austria	Vienna	83,853 sq. km (32,376 sq. miles)	schilling = 100 groschen
Bahamas	Nassau	13,864 sq. km (5,353 sq. miles)	dollar = 100 cents
Bahrain	Manama	669 sq. km (258 sq. miles)	dinar = 1,000 fils
Bangladesh	Dhaka	143,998 sq. km (55,598 sq. miles)	taka = 100 poisha
Barbados	Bridgetown	430 sq. km (166 sq. miles)	dollar = 100 cents
Belgium	Brussels	30,521 sq. km (11,784 sq. miles)	franc = 100 centimes
Belize	Belmopan	22,965 sq. km (8,867 sq. miles)	dollar = 100 cents
Benin	Porto Novo	112,600 sq. km (43,475 sq. miles)	franc
Bhutan	Thimphu	46,100 sq. km (17,800 sq. miles)	ngultrum = 100 paisa
Bolivia	La Paz	1,098,581 sq. km (424,165 sq. miles)	peso = 100 centavos
Botswana	Gaborone	581,700 sq. km (224,600 sq. miles)	pula = 100 thebe
Brazil	Brasilia	8,512,000 sq. km (3,286,500 sq. miles)	cruzado = 1,000 cruzeiros
Brunei	Bandar Seri Begawan	5,765 sq. km (2,226 sq. miles)	dollar = 100 sen
Bulgaria	Sofia	110,912 sq. km (42,823 sq. miles)	lev = 100 stotinki
Burkina	Ouagadougou	274,122 sq. km (105,839 sq. miles)	franc
Burma	Rangoon	678,000 sq. km (261,789 sq. miles)	kyat = 100 pyas
Burundi	Bujumbura	27,834 sq. km (10,747 sq. miles)	franc
Cameroon	Yaoundé	475,499 sq. km (183,591 sq. miles)	franc
Canada	Ottawa	9,976,147 sq. km (3,851,809 sq. miles)	dollar = 100 cents
Cape Verde Islands	Praia	4,033 sq. km (1,557 sq. miles)	escudo = 100 centavos
Central African Republic	Bangui	622,996 sq. km (240,540 sq. miles)	franc
Chad	N'Djamena	1,270,994 sq. km (490,733 sq. miles)	franc
Chile	Santiago	756,943 sq. km (292,257 sq. miles)	peso = 100 centavos
China	Peking	9,560,948 sq. km (3,691,500 sq. miles)	yuan = 10 jiao or 100 fen
Colombia	Bogotá	1,138,907 sq. km (439,734 sq. miles)	peso = 100 centavos
Comoros	Moroni	2,274 sq. km (878 sq. miles)	franc
Congo	Brazzaville	348,999 sq. km (134,749 sq. miles)	franc
Costa Rica	San José	50,899 sq. km (19,652 sq. miles)	colón = 100 céntimos
Cuba	Havana	114,524 sq. km (44,218 sq. miles)	peso = 100 centavos
Cyprus	Nicosia	9,251 sq. km (3,572 sq. miles)	pound = 1,000 mils
Czechoslovakia	Prague	127,870 sq. km (49,371 sq. miles)	koruna = 100 haléru
Denmark	Copenhagen	43,030 sq. km (16,614 sq. miles)	krone = 100 öre
Dominica	Roseau	751 sq. km (290 sq. miles)	dollar = 100 cents
Dominican Republic	Santo Domingo	48,441 sq. km (18,703 sq. miles)	peso = 100 centavos
Ecuador	Quito	455,502 sq. km (175,870 sq. miles)	sucre = 100 centavos
Egypt	Cairo	1,000,250 sq. km (386,198 sq. miles)	pound = 100 piastres or 1,000 millièmes
El Salvador	San Salvador	20,865 sq. km (8,056 sq. miles)	colón = 100 centavos
Equatorial Guinea	Malabo	45,392 sq. km (17,526 sq. miles)	franc
Ethiopia	Addis Ababa	1,221,895 sq. km (471,776 sq. miles)	birr = 100 cents
Fiji	Suva	18,272 sq. km (7,055 sq. miles)	dollar = 100 cents
Finland	Helsinki	360,317 sq. km (139,119 sq. miles)	markka = 100 penniä
France	Paris	549,619 sq. km (212,209 sq. miles)	franc = 100 centimes
Gabon	Libreville	265,000 sq. km (102,317 sq. miles)	franc
Gambia	Banjul	10,368 sq. km (4,003 sq. miles)	dalasi = 100 bututs
German Democratic Republic (East Germany)	East Berlin	107,860 sq. km (41,645 sq. miles)	Ostmark = 100 pfennig
Germany, Federal Republic of (West Germany)	Bonn	248,528 sq. km (95,957 sq. miles)	Deutschmark = 100 pfennig
Ghana	Accra	238,538 sq. km (92,100 sq. miles)	cedi = 100 pesewa
Greece	Athens	131,955 sq. km (50,948 sq. miles)	drachma = 100 lepta
Grenada	St George's	345 sq. km (133 sq. miles)	dollar = 100 cents
Guatemala	Guatemala	108,888 sq. km (42,042 sq. miles)	quetzal = 100 centavos
Guinea	Conakry	245,855 sq. km (94,925 sq. miles)	franc
Guinea-Bissau	Bissau	36,125 sq. km (13,948 sq. miles)	peso = 100 centavos
Guyana	Georgetown	214,969 sq. km (83,000 sq. miles)	dollar = 100 cents

Country	Capital	Area	Currency unit
Haiti	Port-au-Prince	27,749 sq. km (10,714 sq. miles)	gourde = 100 centimes
Honduras	Tegucigalpa	112,087 sq. km (43,277 sq. miles)	lempira = 100 centavos
Hungary	Budapest	93,030 sq. km (35,919 sq. miles)	forint = 100 fillér
Iceland	Reykjavík	102,828 sq. km (39,702 sq. miles)	króna = 100 aurer
India	New Delhi	3,166,829 sq. km (1,261,816 sq. miles)	rupee = 100 paise
Indonesia	Jakarta	1,919,263 sq. km (741,031 sq. miles)	rupiah = 100 sen
Iran	Teheran	1,648,184 sq. km (636,367 sq. miles)	rial = 100 dinars
Iraq	Baghdad	433,999 sq. km (167,568 sq. miles)	dinar = 1,000 fils
Ireland, Republic of	Dublin	70,282 sq. km (27,136 sq. miles)	pound (punt) = 100 pence
Israel	Jerusalem	20,770 sq. km (8,017 sq. miles)	new shekel
Italy	Rome	301,190 sq. km (116,290 sq. miles)	lira
Ivory Coast	Abidjan	319,820 sq. km (123,483 sq. miles)	franc
Jamaica	Kingston	11,425 sq. km (4,411 sq. miles)	dollar = 100 cents
Japan	Tokyo	369,698 sq. km (142,741 sq. miles)	yen
Jibuti	Jibuti	21,699 sq. km (8,378 sq. miles)	franc
Jordan	Amman	97,739 sq. km (37,737 sq. miles)	dinar = 1,000 fils
Kampuchea	Phnom Penh	181,035 sq. km (69,898 sq. miles)	riel = 100 sen
Kenya	Nairobi	582,644 sq. km (224,960 sq. miles)	shilling = 100 cents
Kiribati	Bairiki	655 sq. km (253 sq. miles)	dollar = 100 cents
Korea, North	Pyongyang	121,248 sq. km (46,814 sq. miles)	won = 100 chon
Korea, South	Seoul	99,590 sq. km (38,452 sq. miles)	won = 100 jeon
Kuwait	Kuwait	20,150 sq. km (7,780 sq. miles)	dinar = 1,000 fils
Laos	Vientiane	236,798 sq. km (91,428 sq. miles)	kip = 100 ats
Lebanon	Beirut	10,399 sq. km (4,015 sq. miles)	pound = 100 piastres
Lesotho	Maseru	30,344 sq. km (11,716 sq. miles)	maluti
Liberia	Monrovia	111,370 sq. km (43,000 sq. miles)	dollar = 100 cents
Libya	Tripoli	1,759,530 sq. km (679,358 sq. miles)	dinar = 1,000 dirhams
Liechtenstein	Vaduz	161 sq. km (62 sq. miles)	franc = 100 centimes
Luxemburg	Luxemburg	2,587 sq. km (999 sq. miles)	franc = 100 centimes
Madagascar	Antananarivo	587,042 sq. km (226,658 sq. miles)	franc malgache
Malawi	Lilongwe	94,485 sq. km (36,481 sq. miles)	kwacha = 100 tambala
Malaysia	Kuala Lumpur	330,669 sq. km (127,672 sq. miles)	dollar (ringgit) = 100 cents
Maldives, the	Malé	298 sq. km (115 sq. miles)	rufiyaa = 100 laris
Mali	Bamako	1,204,022 sq. km (464,875 sq. miles)	franc
Malta	Valletta	316 sq. km (122 sq. miles)	lira = 100 cents
Mauritania	Nouakchott	1,118,604 sq. km (431,895 sq. miles)	ouguiya = 5 khoums
Mauritius	Port Louis	1,865 sq. km (720 sq. miles)	rupee = 100 cents
Mexico	Mexico City	1,972,355 sq. km (761,530 sq. miles)	peso = 100 centavos
Monaco	Monaco	1.6 sq. km (0.6 sq. mile)	franc = 100 centimes
Mongolia	Ulan Bator	1,565,001 sq. km (604,250 sq. miles)	tugrik = 100 mongo
Morocco	Rabat (summer capital, Tangier)	622,012 sq. km (240,160 sq. miles)	dirham = 100 centimes
Mozambique	Maputo	784,961 sq. km (303,075 sq. miles)	metical = 100 centavos
Namibia	Windhoek	824,293 sq. km (318,261 sq. miles)	rand = 100 cents
Nauru	Yaren	21 sq. km (8 sq. miles)	dollar = 100 cents
Nepal	Kathmandu	141,414 sq. km (54,600 sq. miles)	rupee = 100 paisa
Netherlands	Amsterdam (seat of government, The Hague)	36,174 sq. km (13,967 sq. miles)	guilder = 100 cents
New Zealand	Wellington	268,675 sq. km (103,736 sq. miles)	dollar = 100 cents
Nicaragua	Managua	148,005 sq. km (57,145 sq. miles)	córdoba = 100 centavos
Niger	Niamey	1,188,994 sq. km (459,073 sq. miles)	franc
Nigeria	Lagos	923,769 sq. km (356,669 sq. miles)	naira = 100 kobo
Norway	Oslo	324,218 sq. km (125,181 sq. miles)	krone = 100 öre
Oman	Muscat	212,379 sq. km (82,000 sq. miles)	rial = 1,000 baiza
Pakistan	Islamabad	803,941 sq. km (310,403 sq. miles)	rupee = 100 paisa
Panama	Panama	75,648 sq. km (29,208 sq. miles)	balboa = 100 cents
Papua New Guinea	Port Moresby	461,692 sq. km (178,260 sq. miles)	kina = 100 toea
Paraguay	Asunción	406,750 sq. km (157,047 sq. miles)	guarani = 100 céntimos
Peru	Lima	1,285,215 sq. km (496,224 sq. miles)	inti = 1,000 soles
Philippines	Manila	299,765 sq. km (115,740 sq. miles)	peso = 100 centavos
Poland	Warsaw	311,700 sq. km (120,348 sq. miles)	zloty = 100 groszy
Portugal	Lisbon	91,970 sq. km (35,510 sq. miles)	escudo = 100 centavos
Qatar	Doha	10,360 sq. km (4,000 sq. miles)	riyal = 100 dirhams
Romania	Bucharest	237,500 sq. km (91,699 sq. miles)	leu = 100 bani
Rwanda	Kigali	26,338 sq. km (10,169 sq. miles)	franc
St Kitts and Nevis	Basseterre	311 sq. km (120 sq. miles)	dollar = 100 cents
St Lucia	Castries	616 sq. km (238 sq. miles)	dollar = 100 cents
St Vincent	Kingstown	389 sq. km (150 sq. miles)	dollar = 100 cents
San Marino	San Marino	60 sq. km (23 sq. miles)	lira
São Tomé and Principé	São Tomé	964 sq. km (372 sq. miles)	dobra = 100 centimos
Saudi Arabia	Riyadh	2,263,579 sq. km (873,972 sq. miles)	riyal = 20 qursh or 100 halalas

Country	Capital	Area	Currency unit
Senegal	Dakar	197,160 sq. km (76,124 sq. miles)	franc
Seychelles	Victoria	443 sq. km (171 sq. miles)	rupee = 100 cents
Sierra Leone	Freetown	72,326 sq. km (27,925 sq. miles)	leone = 100 cents
Singapore	Singapore	580 sq. km (224 sq. miles)	dollar = 100 cents
Solomon Islands	Honiara	29,785 sq. km (11,500 sq. miles)	dollar = 100 cents
Somalia	Mogadishu	637,539 sq. km (246,155 sq. miles)	shilling = 100 cents
South Africa	Pretoria (administrative); seat of Legislature, Cape Town	1,221,038 sq. km (471,445 sq. miles)	rand = 100 cents
Spain	Madrid	504,745 sq. km (194,883 sq. miles)	peseta = 100 céntimos
Sri Lanka	Colombo	65,610 sq. km (25,332 sq. miles)	rupee = 100 cents
Sudan	Khartoum	2,505,792 sq. km (967,491 sq. miles)	pound = 100 piastres or 1,000 millièmes
Surinam	Paramaribo	163,820 sq. km (63,251 sq. miles)	guilder = 100 cents
Swaziland	Mbabane	17,366 sq. km (6,705 sq. miles)	lilangeni = 100 cents
Sweden	Stockholm	449,791 sq. km (173,665 sq. miles)	krona = 100 öre
Switzerland	Berne	41,287 sq. km (15,941 sq. miles)	franc = 100 centimes
Syria	Damascus	185,179 sq. km (71,498 sq. miles)	pound = 100 piastres
Tanzania	Dodoma	939,762 sq. km (362,844 sq. miles)	shilling = 100 cents
Thailand	Bangkok	513,517 sq. km (198,270 sq. miles)	baht = 100 stangs
Togo	Lomé	56,591 sq. km (21,850 sq. miles)	franc
Tonga	Nuku'alofa	699 sq. km (270 sq. miles)	pa'anga = 100 seniti
Trinidad and Tobago	Port of Spain	5,128 sq. km (1,980 sq. miles)	dollar = 100 cents
Tunisia	Tunis	164,148 sq. km (63,378 sq. miles)	dinar = 1,000 millimes
Turkey	Ankara	780,576 sq. km (301,382 sq. miles)	lira = 100 kurus
Tuvalu	Funafuti	24.6 sq. km (9.5 sq. miles)	dollar = 100 cents
Uganda	Kampala	236,036 sq. km (91,134 sq. miles)	shilling = 100 cents
Union of Soviet Socialist Republics	Moscow	22,272,000 sq. km (8,599,341 sq. miles)	rouble = 100 copecks
United Arab Emirates	Abu Dhabi	86,449 sq. km (33,378 sq. miles)	dirham = 100 fils
United Kingdom:	London	244,019 sq. km (94,216 sq. miles)	pound = 100 pence
England	London	130,362 sq. km (50,333 sq. miles)	
Northern Ireland	Belfast	14,147 sq. km (5,462 sq. miles)	
Scotland	Edinburgh	78,749 sq. km (30,405 sq. miles)	
Wales	Cardiff	20,761 sq. km (8,016 sq. miles)	
United States of America	Washington	9,363,132 sq. km (3,615,123 sq. miles)	dollar = 100 cents
Uruguay	Montevideo	186,925 sq. km (72,172 sq. miles)	peso = 100 centésimos
Vanuatu	Vila	15,469 sq. km (6,050 sq. miles)	vatu
Vatican City	—	0.44 sq. km (0.17 sq. mile)	lira
Venezuela	Caracas	912,047 sq. km (352,143 sq. miles)	bolivar
Vietnam	Hanoi	334,331 sq. km (129,086 sq. miles)	dong = 10 hào or 100 xu
Western Samoa	Apia	2,841 sq. km (1,097 sq. miles)	tala = 100 sene
Yemen Arab Republic	Sana'a	195,000 sq. km (75,290 sq. miles)	riyal = 100 fils
Yemen, People's Democratic Republic of	Aden	290,273 sq. km (112,075 sq. miles)	dinar = 1,000 fils
Yugoslavia	Belgrade	255,803 sq. km (98,766 sq. miles)	dinar = 100 paras
Zaïre	Kinshasa	2,344,104 sq. km (905,063 sq. miles)	zaire = 100 makuta or 10,000 senghi
Zambia	Lusaka	752,620 sq. km (290,586 sq. miles)	kwacha = 100 ngwee
Zimbabwe	Harare	390,308 sq. km (150,699 sq. miles)	dollar = 100 cents

APPENDIX II

STATES OF THE UNITED STATES OF AMERICA

(with official and postal abbreviations)

State	Capital	Popular name
Alabama (Ala., AL)	Montgomery	Yellowhammer State, Heart of Dixie, Cotton State
Alaska (Alas., AK)	Juneau	Great Land
Arizona (Ariz., AZ)	Phoenix	Grand Canyon State
Arkansas (Ark., AR)	Little Rock	Land of Opportunity
California (Calif., CA)	Sacramento	Golden State
Colorado (Col., CO)	Denver	Centennial State
Connecticut (Conn., CT)	Hartford	Constitution State, Nutmeg State
Delaware (Del., DE)	Dover	First State, Diamond State
Florida (Fla., FL)	Tallahassee	Sunshine State
Georgia (Ga., GA)	Atlanta	Empire State of the South, Peach State
Hawaii (HI)	Honolulu	The Aloha State
Idaho (ID)	Boise	Gem State
Illinois (Ill., IL)	Springfield	The Inland Empire
Indiana (Ind., IN)	Indianapolis	Hoosier State
Iowa (Ia., IA)	Des Moines	Hawkeye State
Kansas (Kan., KS)	Topeka	Sunflower State
Kentucky (Ky., KY)	Frankfort	Bluegrass State
Louisiana (La., LA)	Baton Rouge	Pelican State
Maine (Me., ME)	Augusta	Pine Tree State
Maryland (Md., MD)	Annapolis	Old Line State, Free State
Massachusetts (Mass., MA)	Boston	Bay State, Old Colony
Michigan (Mich., MI)	Lansing	Great Lake State, Wolverine State
Minnesota (Minn., MN)	St Paul	North Star State, Gopher State
Mississippi (Miss., MS)	Jackson	Magnolia State
Missouri (Mo., MO)	Jefferson City	Show Me State
Montana (Mont., MT)	Helena	Treasure State
Nebraska (Nebr., NB)	Lincoln	Cornhusker State
Nevada (Nev., NV)	Carson City	Sagebush State, Battleborn State, Silver State
New Hampshire (NH)	Concord	Granite State
New Jersey (NJ)	Trenton	Garden State
New Mexico (N. Mex., NM)	Santa Fe	Land of Enchantment
New York (NY)	Albany	Empire State
North Carolina (NC)	Raleigh	Tar Heel State, Old North State
North Dakota (N. Dak., ND)	Bismarck	Peace Garden State
Ohio (OH)	Columbus	Buckeye State
Oklahoma (Okla., OK)	Oklahoma City	Sooner State
Oregon (Oreg., OR)	Salem	Beaver State
Pennsylvania (Pa., PA)	Harrisburg	Keystone State
Rhode Island (RI)	Providence	Little Rhody, Ocean State
South Carolina (SC)	Columbia	Palmetto State
South Dakota (S. Dak., SD)	Pierre	Coyote State, Sunshine State
Tennessee (Tenn., TN)	Nashville	Volunteer State
Texas (Tex., TX)	Austin	Lone Star State
Utah (UT)	Salt Lake City	Beehive State
Vermont (Vt., VT)	Montpelier	Green Mountain State
Virginia (Va., VA)	Richmond	Old Dominion
Washington (Wash., WA)	Olympia	Evergreen State
West Virginia (W. Va., WV)	Charleston	Mountain State
Wisconsin (Wis., WI)	Madison	Badger State
Wyoming (Wyo., WY)	Cheyenne	Equality State

APPENDIX III

COUNTIES OF THE UNITED KINGDOM

(with abbreviations in general use)

England

Avon
Bedfordshire (Beds.)
Berkshire (Berks.)
Buckinghamshire (Bucks.)
Cambridgeshire (Cambs.)
Cheshire (Ches.)
Cleveland
Cornwall (Corn.)
Cumbria
Derbyshire (Derby.)
Devon
Dorset
Durham (Dur.)
East Sussex
Essex
Gloucestershire (Glos.)

Greater London
Greater Manchester
Hampshire (Hants)
Hereford & Worcester
Hertfordshire (Herts.)
Humberside
Isle of Wight (IOW)
Kent
Lancashire (Lancs.)
Leicestershire (Leics.)
Lincolnshire (Lincs.)
Merseyside
Norfolk
Northamptonshire (Northants)
Northumberland (Northumb.)

North Yorkshire
Nottinghamshire (Notts.)
Oxfordshire (Oxon.)
Shropshire
Somerset (Som.)
South Yorkshire
Staffordshire (Staffs.)
Suffolk
Surrey
Tyne and Wear
Warwickshire (War.)
West Midlands
West Sussex
West Yorkshire
Wiltshire (Wilts.)

Northern Ireland

Antrim
Armagh

Down
Fermanagh (Ferm.)

Londonderry
Tyrone

(For administrative purposes smaller unit areas are used.)

Scotland

Regions

Borders
Central
Dumfries & Galloway
Fife
Grampian

Highland
Lothian
Strathclyde
Tayside

Islands Areas

Orkney
Shetland
Western Isles

Wales

Clwyd
Dyfed
Gwent

Gwynedd
Mid Glamorgan
Powys

South Glamorgan
West Glamorgan

APPENDIX IV · THE BRITISH CONSTITUTION

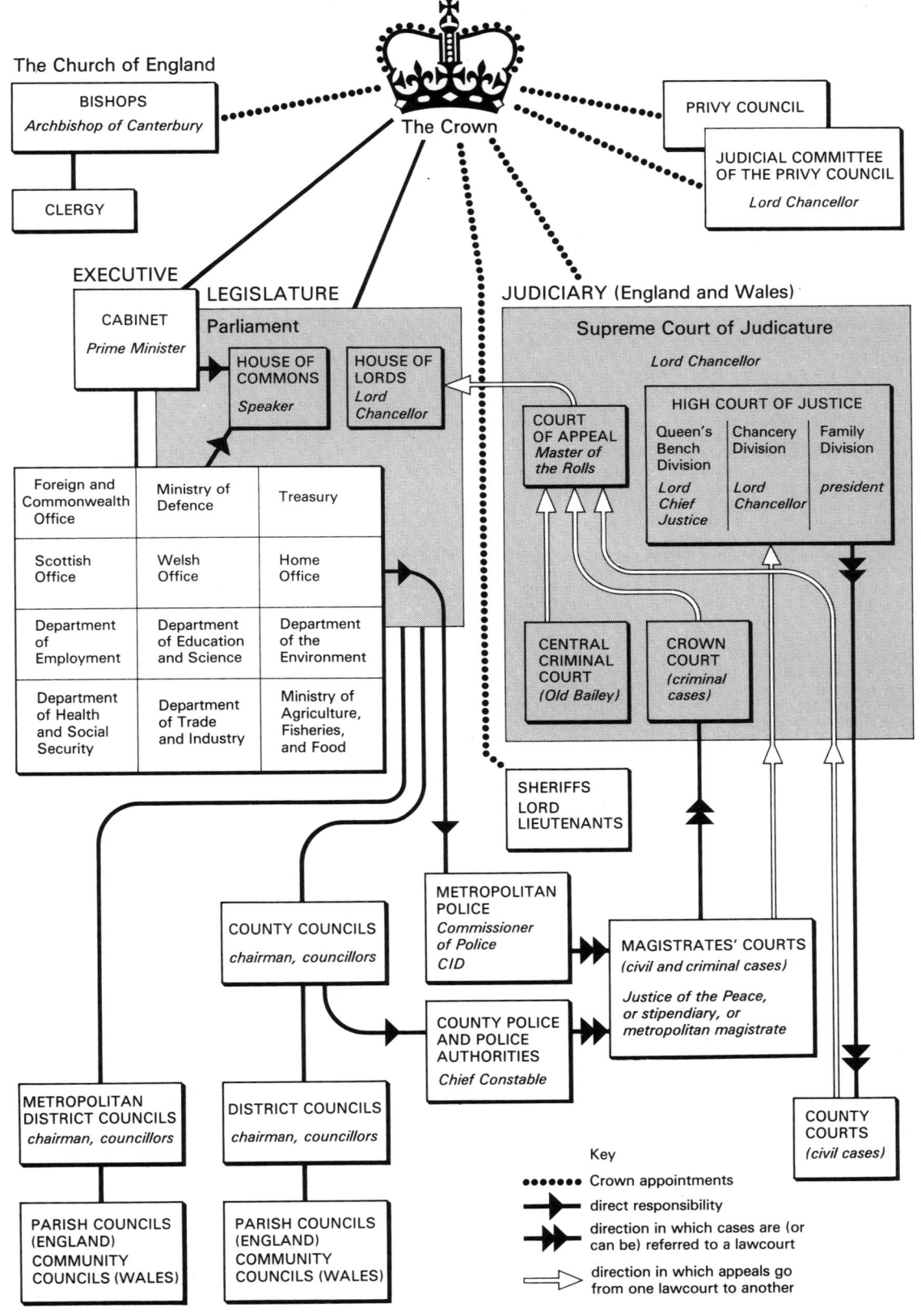

APPENDIX V

RULERS OF ENGLAND AND OF THE UNITED KINGDOM

Saxon Line

Edwy	955–959
Edgar	959–975
Edward the Martyr	975–978
Ethelred the Unready	978–1016
Edmund Ironside	1016

Danish Line

Canute (Cnut)	1017–1035
Harold I	1035–1040
Hardicanute (Harthacnut)	1040–1042

Saxon Line

Edward the Confessor	1042–1066
Harold II (Godwinson)	1066

House of Normandy

William I (the Conqueror)	1066–1087
William II	1087–1100
Henry I	1100–1135
Stephen	1135–1154

House of Plantagenet

Henry II	1154–1189
Richard I	1189–1199
John	1199–1216
Henry III	1216–1272
Edward I	1272–1307
Edward II	1307–1327
Edward III	1327–1377
Richard II	1377–1399

House of Lancaster

Henry IV	1399–1413
Henry V	1413–1422
Henry VI	1422–1461

House of York

Edward IV	1461–1483
Edward V	1483
Richard III	1483–1485

House of Tudor

Henry VII	1485–1509
Henry VIII	1509–1547
Edward VI	1547–1553
Mary I	1553–1558
Elizabeth I	1558–1603

House of Stuart

James I of England and VI of Scotland	1603–1625
Charles I	1625–1649

Commonwealth (declared 1649)

Oliver Cromwell, Lord Protector	1653–1658
Richard Cromwell	1658–1659

House of Stuart

Charles II	1660–1685
James II	1685–1688
William III and Mary II (Mary d. 1694)	1689–1702
Anne	1702–1714

House of Hanover

George I	1714–1727
George II	1727–1760
George III	1760–1820
George IV	1820–1830
William IV	1830–1837
Victoria	1837–1901

House of Saxe-Coburg-Gotha

Edward VII	1901–1910

House of Windsor

George V	1910–1936
Edward VIII	1936
George VI	1936–1952
Elizabeth II	1952–

APPENDIX VI

PRIME MINISTERS OF GREAT BRITAIN AND OF THE UNITED KINGDOM

Sir Robert Walpole	Whig	[1721]–1742	Viscount Palmerston	Liberal	1859–1865
Earl of Wilmington	,,	1742–1743	Earl Russell	,,	1865–1866
Henry Pelham	,,	1743–1754	Earl of Derby	Conservative	1866–1868
Duke of Newcastle	,,	1754–1756	Benjamin Disraeli	,,	1868
Duke of Devonshire	,,	1756–1757	William Ewart Gladstone	Liberal	1868–1874
Duke of Newcastle	,,	1757–1762	Benjamin Disraeli	Conservative	1874–1880
Earl of Bute	Tory	1762–1763	William Ewart Gladstone	Liberal	1880–1885
George Grenville	Whig	1763–1765	Marquis of Salisbury	Conservative	1885–1886
Marquis of Rockingham	,,	1765–1766	William Ewart Gladstone	Liberal	1886
Earl of Chatham	,,	1766–1768	Marquis of Salisbury	Conservative	1886–1892
Duke of Grafton	,,	1768–1770	William Ewart Gladstone	Liberal	1892–1894
Lord North	Tory	1770–1782	Earl of Rosebery	,,	1894–1895
Marquis of Rockingham	Whig	1782	Marquis of Salisbury	Conservative	1895–1902
Earl of Shelburne	,,	1782–1783	Arthur James Balfour	,,	1902–1905
Duke of Portland	coalition	1783	Sir Henry Campbell-Bannerman	Liberal	1905–1908
William Pitt	Tory	1783–1801	Herbert Henry Asquith	,,	1908–1916
Henry Addington	,,	1801–1804	David Lloyd George	coalition	1916–1922
William Pitt	,,	1804–1806	Andrew Bonar Law	Conservative	1922–1923
Lord William Grenville	Whig	1806–1807	Stanley Baldwin	,,	1923–1924
Duke of Portland	Tory	1807–1809	James Ramsay MacDonald	Labour	1924
Spencer Perceval	,,	1809–1812	Stanley Baldwin	Conservative	1924–1929
Earl of Liverpool	,,	1812–1827	James Ramsay MacDonald	coalition	1929–1935
George Canning	,,	1827	Stanley Baldwin	,,	1935–1937
Viscount Goderich	,,	1827–1828	Neville Chamberlain	,,	1937–1940
Duke of Wellington	,,	1828–1830	Winston Spencer Churchill	,,	1940–1945
Earl Grey	Whig	1830–1834	Clement Richard Attlee	Labour	1945–1951
Viscount Melbourne	,,	1834	Sir Winston Spencer Churchill		
Duke of Wellington	Tory	1834		Conservative	1951–1955
Sir Robert Peel	Conservative	1834–1835	Sir Anthony Eden	,,	1955–1957
Viscount Melbourne	Whig	1835–1841	Harold Macmillan	,,	1957–1963
Sir Robert Peel	Conservative	1841–1846	Sir Alexander Douglas-Home	,,	1963–1964
Lord John Russell	Whig	1846–1852	Harold Wilson	Labour	1964–1970
Earl of Derby	Conservative	1852	Edward Heath	Conservative	1970–1974
Earl of Aberdeen	coalition	1852–1855	Harold Wilson	Labour	1974–1976
Viscount Palmerston	Liberal	1855–1858	James Callaghan	,,	1976–1979
Earl of Derby	Conservative	1858–1859	Margaret Thatcher	Conservative	1979–

APPENDIX VII

PRIME MINISTERS OF AUSTRALIA

Edmund Barton	1901–1903	James H. Scullin	1929–1931
Alfred Deakin	1903–1904	Joseph A. Lyons	1932–1939
John C. Watson	1904	Robert Gordon Menzies	1939–1941
George Houstoun Reid	1904–1905	Arthur William Fadden	1941
Alfred Deakin	1905–1908	John Curtin	1941–1945
Andrew Fisher	1908–1909	Joseph Benedict Chifley	1945–1949
Alfred Deakin	1909–1910	Robert Gordon Menzies	1949–1966
Andrew Fisher	1910–1913	Harold Edward Holt	1966–1967
Joseph Cook	1913–1914	John Grey Gorton	1968–1971
Andrew Fisher	1914–1915	Gough Whitlam	1972–1975
William M. Hughes	1915–1923	J. Malcolm Fraser	1975–1983
Stanley M. Bruce	1923–1929	Robert J. L. Hawke	1983–

PRIME MINISTERS OF CANADA

John A. Macdonald	1867–1873	W. L. Mackenzie King	1926–1930
Alexander Mackenzie	1873–1878	Richard B. Bennett	1930–1935
John A. Macdonald	1878–1891	W. L. Mackenzie King	1935–1948
John J. C. Abbott	1891–1892	Louis Stephen St Laurent	1948–1957
John S. D. Thompson	1892–1894	John George Diefenbaker	1957–1963
Mackenzie Bowell	1894–1896	Lester B. Pearson	1963–1968
Charles Tupper	1896	Pierre Elliott Trudeau	1968–1979
Wilfrid Laurier	1896–1911	Joseph Clark	1979–1980
Robert L. Borden	1911–1920	Pierre Elliott Trudeau	1980–1984
Arthur Meighen	1920–1921	John Turner	1984
W. L. Mackenzie King	1921–1926	Brian Mulroney	1984–
Arthur Meighen	1926		

PRIME MINISTERS OF NEW ZEALAND

Henry Sewell	1856	Robert Stout	1884–1887
William Fox	1856	Harry Albert Atkinson	1887–1891
Edward William Stafford	1856–1861	John Ballance	1891–1893
William Fox	1861–1862	Richard John Seddon	1893–1906
Alfred Domett	1862–1863	William Hall-Jones	1906
Frederick Whitaker	1863–1864	Joseph George Ward	1906–1912
Frederick Aloysius Weld	1864–1865	Thomas Mackenzie	1912
Edward William Stafford	1865–1869	William Ferguson Massey	1912–1925
William Fox	1869–1872	Francis Henry Dillon Bell	1925
Edward William Stafford	1872	Joseph Gordon Coates	1925–1928
George Marsden Waterhouse	1872–1873	Joseph George Ward	1928–1930
William Fox	1873	George William Forbes	1930–1935
Julius Vogel	1873–1875	Michael J. Savage	1935–1940
Daniel Pollen	1875–1876	Peter Fraser	1940–1949
Julius Vogel	1876	Sidney G. Holland	1949–1957
Harry Albert Atkinson	1876–1877	Walter Nash	1957–1960
George Grey	1877–1879	Keith J. Holyoake	1960–1972
John Hall	1879–1882	John R. Marshall	1972
Frederick Whitaker	1882–1883	Norman Kirk	1972–1974
Harry Albert Atkinson	1883–1884	Wallace Rowling	1974–1975
Robert Stout	1884	Robert D. Muldoon	1975–1984
Harry Albert Atkinson	1884	Hon. David Lange	1984–

APPENDIX VIII

PRESIDENTS OF THE UNITED STATES OF AMERICA

1. George Washington	Federalist	1789-1797	
2. John Adams	,,	1797-1801	
3. Thomas Jefferson			
	Democratic-Republican	1801-1809	
4. James Madison	,,	1809-1817	
5. James Monroe	,,	1817-1825	
6. John Quincy Adams	Independent	1825-1829	
7. Andrew Jackson	Democrat	1829-1837	
8. Martin Van Buren	,,	1837-1841	
9. William H. Harrison	Whig	1841	
10. John Tyler	Whig, then Democrat	1841-1845	
11. James K. Polk	Democrat	1845-1849	
12. Zachary Taylor	Whig	1849-1850	
13. Millard Fillmore	,,	1850-1853	
14. Franklin Pierce	Democrat	1853-1857	
15. James Buchanan	,,	1857-1861	
16. Abraham Lincoln	Republican	1861-1865	
17. Andrew Johnson	Democrat	1865-1869	
18. Ulysses S. Grant	Republican	1869-1877	
19. Rutherford B. Hayes	,,	1877-1881	
20. James A. Garfield	,,	1881	
21. Chester A. Arthur	Republican	1881-1885	
22. Grover Cleveland	Democrat	1885-1889	
23. Benjamin Harrison	Republican	1889-1893	
24. Grover Cleveland	Democrat	1893-1897	
25. William McKinley	Republican	1897-1901	
26. Theodore Roosevelt	,,	1901-1909	
27. William H. Taft	,,	1909-1913	
28. Woodrow Wilson	Democrat	1913-1921	
29. Warren G. Harding	Republican	1921-1923	
30. Calvin Coolidge	,,	1923-1929	
31. Herbert Hoover	,,	1929-1933	
32. Franklin D. Roosevelt	Democrat	1933-1945	
33. Harry S Truman	,,	1945-1953	
34. Dwight D. Eisenhower	Republican	1953-1961	
35. John F. Kennedy	Democrat	1961-1963	
36. Lyndon B. Johnson	,,	1963-1969	
37. Richard M. Nixon	Republican	1969-1974	
38. Gerald R. Ford	,,	1974-1977	
39. James Earl Carter	Democrat	1977-1981	
40. Ronald W. Reagan	Republican	1981-	

APPENDIX IX
WEIGHTS AND MEASURES

Note. The conversion factors are not exact unless so marked. They are given only to the accuracy likely to be needed in everyday calculations.

1. BRITISH AND AMERICAN, WITH METRIC EQUIVALENTS

Linear Measure

1 inch	= 25.4 millimetres exactly
1 foot = 12 inches	= 0.3048 metre exactly
1 yard = 3 feet	= 0.9144 metre exactly
1 (statute) mile = 1,760 yards	= 1.609 kilometres

Square Measure

1 square inch	= 6.45 sq. centimetres
1 square foot = 144 sq. in.	= 9.29 sq. decimetres
1 square yard = 9 sq. ft.	= 0.836 sq. metre
1 acre = 4,840 sq. yd.	= 0.405 hectare
1 square mile = 640 acres	= 259 hectares

Cubic Measure

1 cubic inch	= 16.4 cu. centimetres
1 cubic foot = 1,728 cu. in.	= 0.0283 cu. metre
1 cubic yard = 27 cu. ft.	= 0.765 cu. metre

Capacity Measure

British

1 pint = 20 fluid oz.	= 0.568 litre
= 34.68 cu. in.	
1 quart = 2 pints	= 1.136 litres
1 gallon = 4 quarts	= 4.546 litres
1 peck = 2 gallons	= 9.092 litres
1 bushel = 4 pecks	= 36.4 litres
1 quarter = 8 bushels	= 2.91 hectolitres

American dry

1 pint = 33.60 cu. in.	= 0.550 litre
1 quart = 2 pints	= 1.101 litres
1 peck = 8 quarts	= 8.81 litres
1 bushel = 4 pecks	= 35.3 litres

American liquid

1 pint = 16 fluid oz.	= 0.473 litre
= 28.88 cu. in.	
1 quart = 2 pints	= 0.946 litre
1 gallon = 4 quarts	= 3.785 litres

Avoirdupois Weight

1 grain	= 0.065 gram
1 dram	= 1.772 grams
1 ounce = 16 drams	= 28.35 grams
1 pound = 16 ounces	= 0.4536 kilogram
= 7,000 grains	(0.45359237 exactly)
1 stone = 14 pounds	= 6.35 kilograms
1 quarter = 2 stones	= 12.70 kilograms
1 hundredweight = 4 quarters	= 50.80 kilograms
1 (long) ton = 20 hundred-weight	= 1.016 tonnes
1 short ton = 2,000 pounds	= 0.907 tonne

2. METRIC, WITH BRITISH EQUIVALENTS

Linear Measure

1 millimetre	= 0.039 inch
1 centimetre = 10 mm	= 0.394 inch
1 decimetre = 10 cm	= 3.94 inches
1 metre = 10 dm	= 1.094 yards
1 decametre = 10 m	= 10.94 yards
1 hectometre = 100 m	= 109.4 yards
1 kilometre = 1,000 m	= 0.6214 mile

Square Measure

1 square centimetre	= 0.155 sq. inch
1 square metre = 10,000 sq. cm	= 1.196 sq. yards
1 are = 100 sq. metres	= 119.6 sq. yards
1 hectare = 100 ares	= 2.471 acres
1 square kilometre = 100 hectares	= 0.386 sq. mile

Cubic Measure

1 cubic centimetre	= 0.061 cu. inch
1 cubic metre = 1,000,000 cu. cm	= 1.308 cu. yards

Capacity Measure

1 millilitre	= 0.002 pint (British)
1 centilitre = 10 ml	= 0.018 pint
1 decilitre = 10 cl	= 0.176 pint
1 litre = 10 dl	= 1.76 pints
1 decalitre = 10 l	= 2.20 gallons
1 hectolitre = 100 l	= 2.75 bushels
1 kilolitre = 1,000 l	= 3.44 quarters

Weight

1 milligram	= 0.015 grain
1 centigram = 10 mg	= 0.154 grain
1 decigram = 10 cg	= 1.543 grain
1 gram = 10 dg	= 15.43 grain
1 decagram = 10 g	= 5.64 drams
1 hectogram = 100 g	= 3.527 ounces
1 kilogram = 1,000 g	= 2.205 pounds
1 tonne (metric ton) = 1,000 kg	= 0.984 (long) ton

3. POWER NOTATION

This expresses concisely any power of ten (any number that is composed of factors 10), and is sometimes used in the dictionary. 10^2 or ten squared $= 10 \times 10 = 100$; 10^3 or ten cubed $= 10 \times 10 \times 10 = 1,000$. Similarly, $10^4 = 10,000$ and $10^{10} = 1$ followed by ten noughts $= 10,000,000,000$. Proceeding in the opposite direction, dividing by ten and subtracting one from the index, we have $10^2 = 100$, $10^1 = 10$, $10^0 = 1$, $10^{-1} = \frac{1}{10}$, $10^{-2} = \frac{1}{100}$, and so on; $10^{-10} = 1/10^{10} = 1/10,000,000,000$.

4. TEMPERATURE

Fahrenheit: Water boils (under standard conditions) at 212° and freezes at 32°.

Celsius or Centigrade: Water boils at 100° and freezes at 0°.

Kelvin: Water boils at 373.15 K and freezes at 273.15 K.

Celsius	Fahrenheit
−17.8°	0°
−10°	14°
0°	32°
10°	50°
20°	68°
30°	86°
40°	104°
50°	122°
60°	140°
70°	158°
80°	176°
90°	194°
100°	212°

To convert Celsius into Fahrenheit: multiply by 9, divide by 5, and add 32.

To convert Fahrenheit into Celsius: subtract 32, multiply by 5, and divide by 9.

5. METRIC PREFIXES

	Abbreviation or Symbol	Factor
deca-	da	10
hecto-	h	10^2
kilo-	k	10^3
mega-	M	10^6
giga-	G	10^9
tera-	T	10^{12}
peta-	P	10^{15}
exa-	E	10^{18}
deci-	d	10^{-1}
centi-	c	10^{-2}
milli-	m	10^{-3}
micro-	μ	10^{-6}
nano-	n	10^{-9}
pico-	p	10^{-12}
femto-	f	10^{-15}
atto-	a	10^{-18}

Pronunciations and derivations of these are given at their alphabetical places in the dictionary. They may be applied to any units of the metric system: hectogram (abbr. hg) = 100 grams; kilowatt (abbr. kW) = 1,000 watts; megahertz (MHz) = 1 million hertz; centimetre (cm) = $\frac{1}{100}$ metre; microvolt (μV) = one millionth of a volt; picofarad (pF) = 10^{-12} farad, and are sometimes applied to other units (megabit, microinch).

6. CHEMICAL NOTATION

The symbol for a molecule (such as H_2O, CH_4, H_2SO_4) shows the symbols for the elements contained in it (C = carbon, H = hydrogen, etc.), followed by a subscript numeral denoting the number of atoms of each element in the molecule where this number is more than one. For example, the water molecule (H_2O) contains two atoms of hydrogen and one of oxygen.

7. SI UNITS

Base Units

Physical quantity	Name	Abbreviation or Symbol
length	metre	m
mass	kilogram	kg
time	second	s
electric current	ampere	A
temperature	kelvin	K
amount of substance	mole	mol
luminous intensity	candela	cd

Supplementary Units

Physical quantity	Name	Abbreviation or Symbol
plane angle	radian	rad
solid angle	steradian	sr

Derived Units with Special Names

Physical quantity	Name	Abbreviation or Symbol
frequency	hertz	Hz
energy	joule	J
force	newton	N
power	watt	W
pressure	pascal	Pa
electric charge	coulomb	C
electromotive force	volt	V
electric resistance	ohm	Ω
electric conductance	siemens	S
electric capacitance	farad	F
magnetic flux	weber	Wb
inductance	henry	H
magnetic flux density	tesla	T
luminous flux	lumen	lm
illumination	lux	lx

8. BINARY SYSTEM

Only two units (0 and 1) are used, and the position of each unit indicates a power of two.

One to ten written in binary form:

	eights (2^3)	fours (2^2)	twos (2^1)	one
1				1
2			1	0
3			1	1
4		1	0	0
5		1	0	1
6		1	1	0
7		1	1	1
8	1	0	0	0
9	1	0	0	1
10	1	0	1	0

i.e. ten is written as 1010 (2^3+0+2^1+0); one hundred is written as 1100100 ($2^6+2^5+0+0+2^2+0+0$)

APPENDIX X · THE BEAUFORT

Equivalent speed at 10 m above ground

Beaufort Number	Knots		Miles per hour		Metres per second		Description of wind
	Mean	Limits	Mean	Limits	Mean	Limits	
0	0	<1	0	<1	0.0	0.0–0.2	Calm
1	2	1–3	2	1–3	0.8	0.3–1.5	Light air
2	5	4–6	5	4–7	2.4	1.6–3.3	Light breeze
3	9	7–10	10	8–12	4.3	3.4–5.4	Gentle breeze
4	13	11–16	15	13–18	6.7	5.5–7.9	Moderate breeze
5	19	17–21	21	19–24	9.3	8.0–10.7	Fresh breeze
6	24	22–27	28	25–31	12.3	10.8–13.8	Strong breeze
7	30	28–33	35	32–38	15.5	13.9–17.1	Near gale
8	37	34–40	42	39–46	18.9	17.2–20.7	Gale
9	44	41–47	50	47–54	22.6	20.8–24.4	Strong gale
10	52	48–55	59	55–63	26.4	24.5–28.4	Storm
11	60	56–63	68	64–72	30.5	28.5–32.6	Violent storm
12	—	≥64	—	≥73	—	≥32.7	Hurricane

SCALE OF WIND FORCE

Specifications for use at sea	*Specifications for use on land*	*Beaufort Number*
Sea like a mirror	Calm: smoke rises vertically	0
Ripples with the appearance of scales are formed but without foam crests	Direction of wind shown by smoke drift but not by wind vanes	1
Small wavelets, still short but more pronounced; crests have a glassy appearance and do not break	Wind felt on face; leaves rustle; ordinary vanes moved by wind	2
Large wavelets; crests begin to break; foam of glassy appearance; perhaps scattered white horses	Leaves and small twigs in constant motion; wind extends light flag	3
Small waves, becoming longer; fairly frequent white horses	Dust and loose paper raised; small branches are moved	4
Moderate waves, taking a more pronounced long form; many white horses are formed; chance of some spray	Small trees in leaf begin to sway; crested wavelets form on inland waters	5
Large waves begin to form; the white foam crests are more extensive everywhere; probably some spray	Large branches in motion; umbrellas used with difficulty	6
Sea heaps up and white foam from breaking waves begins to be blown in streaks along the direction of the wind	Whole trees in motion; inconvenience felt when walking against wind	7
Moderately high waves of greater length; edges of crests begin to break into spindrift; the foam is blown in well-marked streaks along the direction of the wind	Twigs broken off trees; progress generally impeded	8
High waves; dense streaks of foam along the direction of the wind; crests of waves begin to topple, tumble, and roll over; spray may affect visibility	Slight structural damage occurs (chimney-pots and slates removed)	9
Very high waves with long overhanging crests; the resulting foam, in great patches, is blown in dense white streaks along the direction of the wind; on the whole, the surface of the sea takes a white appearance; the tumbling of the sea becomes heavy and shock-like; visibility affected	Seldom experienced inland; trees uprooted; considerable structural damage occurs	10
Exceptionally high waves (small and medium-sized ships might be for a time lost to view behind the waves); the sea is completely covered with long white patches of foam lying along the direction of the wind; everywhere the edges of the wave crests are blown into froth; visibility affected	Very rarely experienced; accompanied by widespread damage	11
The air is filled with foam and spray; sea completely white with driving spray; visibility very seriously affected	——	12

APPENDIX XI
THE CHEMICAL ELEMENTS

Element	Symbol	Atomic number	Element	Symbol	Atomic number	Element	Symbol	Atomic number
actinium	Ac	89	hafnium	Hf	72	praseodymium	Pr	59
aluminium	Al	13	hahnium	Ha	105	promethium	Pm	61
americium	Am	95	helium	He	2	protactinium	Pa	91
antimony	Sb	51	holmium	Ho	67	radium	Ra	88
argon	Ar	18	hydrogen	H	1	radon	Rn	86
arsenic	As	33	indium	In	49	rhenium	Re	75
astatine	At	85	iodine	I	53	rhodium	Rh	45
barium	Ba	56	iridium	Ir	77	rubidium	Rb	37
berkelium	Bk	97	iron	Fe	26	ruthenium	Ru	44
beryllium	Be	4	krypton	Kr	36	rutherfordium	Rf	104
bismuth	Bi	83	lanthanum	La	57	samarium	Sm	62
boron	B	5	lawrencium	Lr	103	scandium	Sc	21
bromine	Br	35	lead	Pb	82	selenium	Se	34
cadmium	Cd	48	lithium	Li	3	silicon	Si	14
caesium	Cs	55	lutetium	Lu	71	silver	Ag	47
calcium	Ca	20	magnesium	Mg	12	sodium	Na	11
californium	Cf	98	manganese	Mn	25	strontium	Sr	38
carbon	C	6	mendelivium	Md	101	sulphur	S	16
cerium	Ce	58	mercury	Hg	80	tantalum	Ta	73
chlorine	Cl	17	molybdenum	Mo	42	technetium	Tc	43
chromium	Cr	24	neodymium	Nd	60	tellurium	Te	52
cobalt	Co	27	neon	Ne	10	terbium	Tb	65
copper	Cu	29	neptunium	Np	93	thallium	Tl	81
curium	Cm	96	nickel	Ni	28	thorium	Th	90
dysprosium	Dy	66	niobium	Nb	41	thulium	Tm	69
einsteinium	Es	99	nitrogen	N	7	tin	Sn	50
erbium	Er	68	nobelium	No	102	titanium	Ti	22
europium	Eu	63	osmium	Os	76	tungsten	W	74
fermium	Fm	100	oxygen	O	8	uranium	U	92
fluorine	F	9	palladium	Pd	46	vanadium	V	23
francium	Fr	87	phosphorus	P	15	xenon	Xe	54
gadolinium	Gd	64	platinum	Pt	78	ytterbium	Yb	70
gallium	Ga	31	plutonium	Pu	94	yttrium	Y	39
germanium	Ge	32	polonium	Po	84	zinc	Zn	30
gold	Au	79	potassium	K	19	zirconium	Zr	40

APPENDIX XII
BOOKS OF THE BIBLE

Old Testament

Genesis (Gen.)
Exodus (Exod.)
Leviticus (Lev.)
Numbers (Num.)
Deuteronomy (Deut.)
Joshua (Josh.)
Judges (Judg.)
Ruth
First Book of Samuel (1 Sam.)
Second Book of Samuel (2 Sam.)
First Book of Kings (1 Kgs.)
Second Book of Kings (2 Kgs.)
First Book of Chronicles (1 Chr.)
Second Book of Chronicles (2 Chr.)

Ezra
Nehemiah (Neh.)
Esther
Job
Psalms (Ps.)
Proverbs (Prov.)
Ecclesiastes (Eccles.)
Song of Songs, Song of Solomon, Canticles (S. of S., Cant.)
Isaiah (Isa.)
Jeremiah (Jer.)
Lamentations (Lam.)
Ezekiel (Ezek.)

Daniel (Dan.)
Hosea (Hos.)
Joel
Amos
Obadiah (Obad.)
Jonah
Micah (Mic.)
Nahum (Nah.)
Habakkuk (Hab.)
Zephaniah (Zeph.)
Haggai (Hag.)
Zechariah (Zech.)
Malachi (Mal.)

Apocrypha

First Book of Esdras (1 Esd.)
Second Book of Esdras (2 Esd.)
Tobit
Judith
Rest of Esther (Rest of Esth.)
Wisdom of Solomon (Wisd.)

Ecclesiasticus, Wisdom of Jesus the Son of Sirach (Ecclus., Sir.)
Baruch
Song of the Three Children (S. of III Ch.)

Susanna (Sus.)
Bel and the Dragon (Bel & Dr.)
Prayer of Manasses (Pr. of Man.)
First Book of Maccabees (1 Macc.)
Second Book of Maccabees (2 Macc.)

New Testament

Gospel according to St Matthew (Matt.)
Gospel according to St Mark (Mark)
Gospel according to St Luke (Luke)
Gospel according to St John (John)
Acts of the Apostles (Acts)
Epistle to the Romans (Rom.)
First Epistle to the Corinthians (1 Cor.)
Second Epistle to the Corinthians (2 Cor.)

Epistle to the Galatians (Gal.)
Epistle to the Ephesians (Eph.)
Epistle to the Philippians (Phil.)
Epistle to the Colossians (Col.)
First Epistle to the Thessalonians (1 Thess.)
Second Epistle to the Thessalonians (2 Thess.)
First Epistle to Timothy (1 Tim.)
Second Epistle to Timothy (2 Tim.)
Epistle to Titus (Tit.)

Epistle to Philemon (Philem.)
Epistle to the Hebrews (Heb.)
Epistle of James (Jas.)
First Epistle of Peter (1 Pet.)
Second Epistle of Peter (2 Pet.)
First Epistle of John (1 John)
Second Epistle of John (2 John)
Third Epistle of John (3 John)
Epistle of Jude (Jude)
Revelation, Apocalypse (Rev., Apoc.)

APPENDIX XIII
SOME TERMS FOR GROUPS OF ANIMALS, BIRDS, ETC.

Terms marked † belong to 15th-c. lists of 'proper terms', notably that in the *Book of St Albans* attributed to Dame Juliana Barnes (1486). Many of these are fanciful or humorous terms which probably never had any real currency, but have been taken up by Joseph Strutt in *Sports and Pastimes of England* (1801) and by other antiquarian writers.

a †shrewdness of apes
a herd or †pace of asses
a †cete of badgers
a †sloth or †sleuth of bears
a hive of bees; a swarm, drift, or bike of bees
a flock, flight, (*dial.*) parcel, pod (= small flock), †fleet, or †dissimulation of (small) birds; a volary of birds in an aviary
a sounder of wild boar
a †blush of boys
a herd or gang of buffalo
a †clowder or †glaring of cats; a †dowt (= ?do-out) or †destruction of wild cats
a herd, drove, (*dial.*) drift, or (*US & Austral.*) mob of cattle
a brood, (*dial.*) cletch or clutch, or †peep of chickens
a †chattering or †clattering of choughs
a †drunkship of cobblers
a †rag or †rake of colts
a †hastiness of cooks
a †covert of coots
a herd of cranes
a litter of cubs
a herd of curlew
a †cowardice of curs
a herd of deer
a pack or kennel of dogs
a trip of dotterel
a flight, †dole, or †piteousness of doves
a raft, bunch, or †paddling of ducks on water; a team of wild ducks in flight
a fling of dunlins
a herd of elephants
a herd or (*US*) gang of elk
a †business of ferrets
a charm or †chirm of finches
a shoal of fish; a run of fish in motion
a cloud of flies
a †stalk of foresters
a †skulk of foxes
a gaggle or (in the air) a skein, team, or wedge of geese
a herd of giraffes
a flock, herd, or (*dial.*) trip of goats
a pack or covey of grouse
a †husk or †down of hares
a cast of hawks let fly
an †observance of hermits
a †siege of herons
a stud or †haras of (breeding) horses; (*dial.*) a team of horses
a kennel, pack, cry, or †mute of hounds
a flight or swarm of insects
a mob or troop of kangaroos
a kindle of kittens
a bevy of ladies
a †desert of lapwing

an †exaltation or bevy of larks
a †leap of leopards
a pride of lions
a †tiding of magpies
a †sord or †sute (= suit) of mallard
a †richesse of martens
a †faith of merchants
a †labour of moles
a troop of monkeys
a †barren of mules
a †watch of nightingales
a †superfluity of nuns
a covey of partridges
a †muster of peacocks
a †malapertness (= impertinence) of pedlars
a rookery of penguins
a head or (*dial.*) nye of pheasants
a kit of pigeons flying together
a herd of pigs
a stand, wing, or †congregation of plovers
a rush or flight of pochards
a herd, pod, or school of porpoises
a †pity of prisoners
a covey of ptarmigan
a litter of pups
a bevy or drift of quail
a string of racehorses
an †unkindness of ravens
a bevy of roes
a parliament or †building of rooks
a hill of ruffs
a herd or rookery of seals; a pod (= small herd) of seals
a flock, herd, (*dial.*) drift or trip, or (*Austral.*) mob of sheep
a †dopping of sheldrake
a wisp or †walk of snipe
a †host of sparrows
a †murmuration of starlings
a flight of swallows
a game or herd of swans; a wedge of swans in the air
a herd of swine; a †sounder of tame swine, a †drift of wild swine
a †glozing (= fawning) of taverners
a †spring of teal
a bunch or knob of waterfowl
a school, herd, or gam of whales; a pod (= small school) of whales; a grind of bottle-nosed whales
a company or trip of widgeon
a bunch, trip, or plump of wildfowl; a knob (less than 30) of wildfowl
a pack or †trout of wolves
a gaggle of women (*derisive*)
a †fall of woodcock
a herd of wrens

1. **British Isles**

1	Belfast
2	Newtownabbey
3	Carrickfergus
4	Castlereagh
5	North Down
6	Ards
7	Down
8	Newry & Mourne
9	Banbridge
10	Lisburn
11	Craigavon
12	Armagh
13	Dungannon
14	Fermanagh
15	Omagh
16	Cookstown
17	Magherafelt
18	Strabane
19	Derry
20	Limavady
21	Coleraine
22	Ballymoney
23	Moyle
24	Ballymena
25	Larne
26	Antrim

Shetland

Orkney

Scotland

Western Isles

Highland

Grampian

Tayside

Fife

Central

Lothian

Strathclyde

Borders

0   50   100   150 km

North Sea

Northern
Ireland

North
Atlantic
Ocean

Donegal

Dumfries and
Galloway

Northumberland

Tyne and Wear

Durham

Cleveland

Cumbria

North Channel

Sligo

Leitrim

Cavan

Monaghan

Louth

Mayo

Roscommon

Longford

West-
meath

Meath

N. Yorks.

Isle of Man

Lancs.

W.Yorks.

Humberside

Galway

Offaly

Dublin

Merseyside

G.
Manch.

S.Yorks.

England

Irish Sea

Clare

Laois

Kildare

Wicklow

Cheshire

Derby

Notts.

Lincolnshire

Gwyn.

Clwyd

Limerick

Tipperary

Kilkenny

Carlow

Wexford

Staffs.

Shropshire

Leics.

Norfolk

Kerry

Cork

Waterford

Wales

Powys

Here. and
Worc.

W. Mid.

War.

Northants.

Cambs.

Suffolk

Irish
Republic

St George's
Channel

Dyfed

Gwent

Glos.

Oxon.

Bucks.

Beds.

Herts.

Essex

North
Atlantic
Ocean

W.
Glam.

Mid
Glam.

S.Glam.

Avon

Wilts.

Berks.

G.
London

Surrey

Kent

Bristol Channel

Somerset

Hants

W. Susx.

E.Susx.

Strait of Dover

Devon

Dorset

Cornwall

Isle of Wight

Isles
of Scilly

English Channel

Iceland
Reykjavík

ARCTIC CIRCLE

Murmansk

Archangel

0 250 500 750 km

Faeroe Islands
(*Denmark*)

Shetland
Islands(*UK*)

Sweden

Finland

N o r w a y

Orkney
Islands (*UK*)

Oslo

Helsinki

Leningrad

Stockholm

*North
Sea*

**Irish
Republic**

Belfast   Edinburgh

Dublin

**United
Kingdom**

Denmark
Copenhagen

Baltic Sea

Moscow

*North
Atlantic
Ocean*

Cardiff

London

Hamburg

Amsterdam

Gdańsk

U n i o n   o f   S o v i e t
S o c i a l i s t   R e p u b l i c s

The
Hague

Netherlands

East Berlin

Warsaw

English Channel

Brussels

Belg.

Bonn

**German
Democratic
Republic**

P o l a n d

Channel Islands (*UK*)

Paris

Lux.

**Federal
Republic
of Germany**

Prague

Czechoslovakia

Vienna

Bay of Biscay

F r a n c e

Berne

Munich

Switz. **Liecht.**

Austria

Budapest

Odessa

Bordeaux

Lyons

*Mont
Blanc*

Milan

Venice

Hungary

R o m a n i a

Bucharest

Constanta

Sevastopol

Turin

Black Sea

Oporto

Portugal

Madrid

Andorra

Marseilles

Monaco

Italy

Belgrade

**San
Marino**

Yugoslavia

Black Sea

Istanbul

Lisbon

S p a i n

Barcelona

*Corsica
(Fr)*

Rome

Bulgaria

Sofia

Ankara

Turkey

Seville

*Balearic
Islands
(Spain)*

*Sardinia
(Italy)*

Naples

Tiranë

Albania

Greece

Gibraltar
(*UK*)

M e d i t e r r a n e a n

Palermo

Mt. Etna

*Sicily
(Italy)*

Athens

Nicosia

Cyprus

S e a

*Crete
(Greece)*

2. Europe

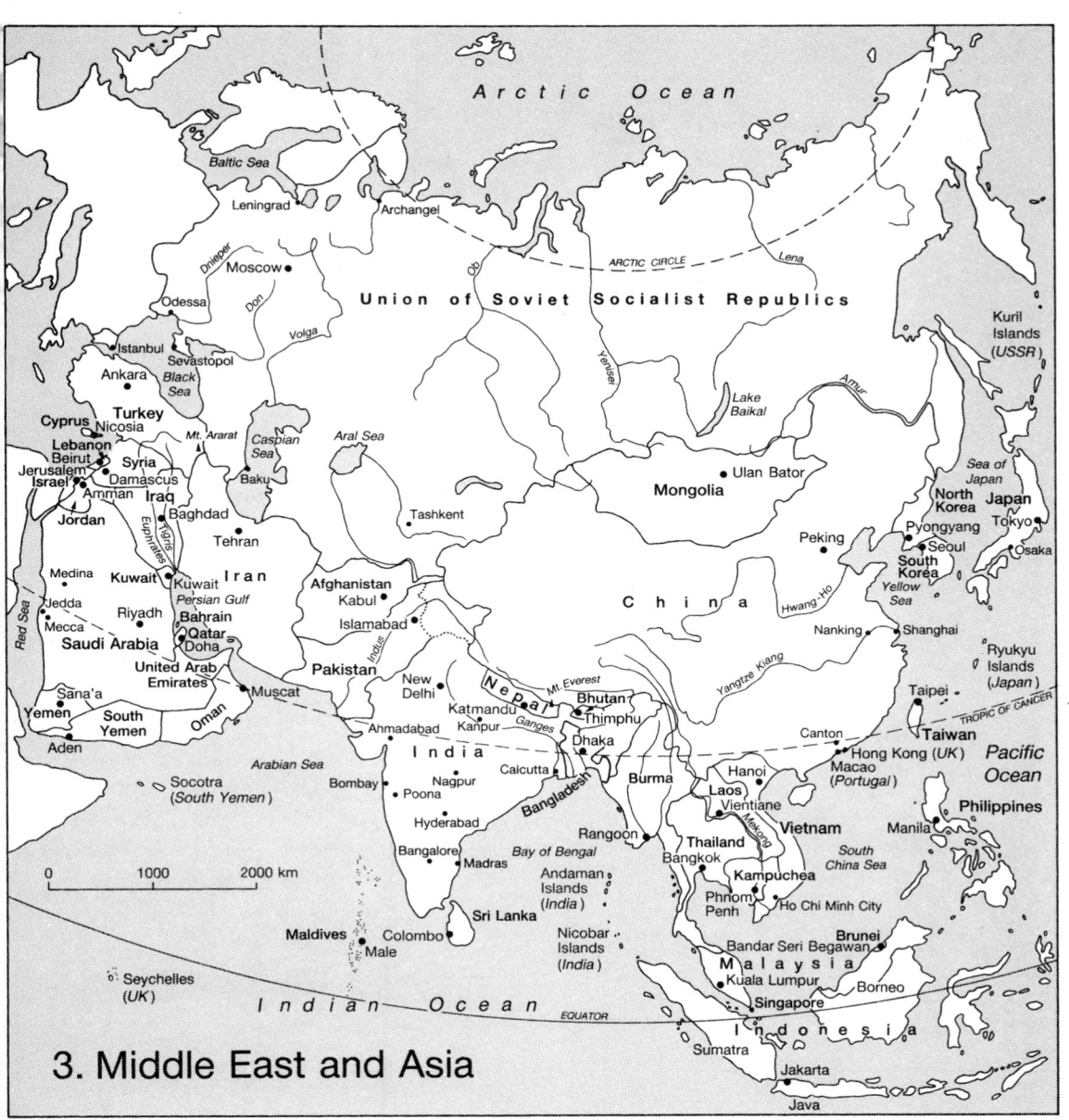

Arctic Ocean

Baltic Sea

Leningrad
Archangel

ARCTIC CIRCLE

Dnieper
Moscow
Odessa
Don
Volga

Union of Soviet Socialist Republics

Ob
Lena
Yenisei

Kuril
Islands
(USSR)

Istanbul
Sevastopol
Black Sea
Ankara

Mt. Ararat
Caspian Sea
Aral Sea

Lake Baikal

Amur

Sea of
Japan

Turkey
Cyprus Nicosia
Lebanon
Beirut
Syria
Jerusalem Damascus
Israel
Amman
Jordan
Baghdad

Baku

Tashkent

Ulan Bator

Mongolia

Peking

North
Korea
Pyongyang
Seoul
South
Korea
Yellow
Sea

Japan
Tokyo
Osaka

Tigris
Euphrates
Tehran

Iraq

Iran

Afghanistan
Kabul

China

Hwang-Ho

Ryukyu
Islands
(Japan)

Medina
Jedda
Mecca
Riyadh

Kuwait
Kuwait
Persian Gulf
Bahrain
Qatar
Doha

Islamabad

Nanking
Shanghai

Saudi Arabia

United Arab
Emirates

Pakistan
New
Delhi

Indus

Nepal
Mt. Everest

Katmandu
Kanpur Ganges
Ahmadabad

Bhutan
Thimphu

Dhaka

Yangtze Kiang

Canton

Taipei
Taiwan

TROPIC OF CANCER

Red Sea
Sana'a
South
Yemen

Muscat
Oman

Hong Kong (UK)
Macao
(Portugal)

Pacific
Ocean

Yemen
Aden

Arabian Sea
Socotra
(South Yemen)
Bombay
Poona

India

Nagpur

Hyderabad

Bangalore
Madras

Calcutta

Bangladesh

Burma

Rangoon

Hanoi
Laos
Vientiane

Mekong

Vietnam

Manila

Philippines

Thailand
Bangkok

South
China Sea

Bay of Bengal

Andaman
Islands
(India)

Kampuchea
Phnom
Penh

Ho Chi Minh City

0   1000   2000 km

Sri Lanka

Nicobar
Islands
(India)

Brunei
Bandar Seri Begawan

Maldives
Male

Colombo

Seychelles
(UK)

Indian   Ocean

EQUATOR

Malaysia
Kuala Lumpur

Borneo

Singapore

Indonesia

Sumatra

Jakarta

Java

3. Middle East and Asia

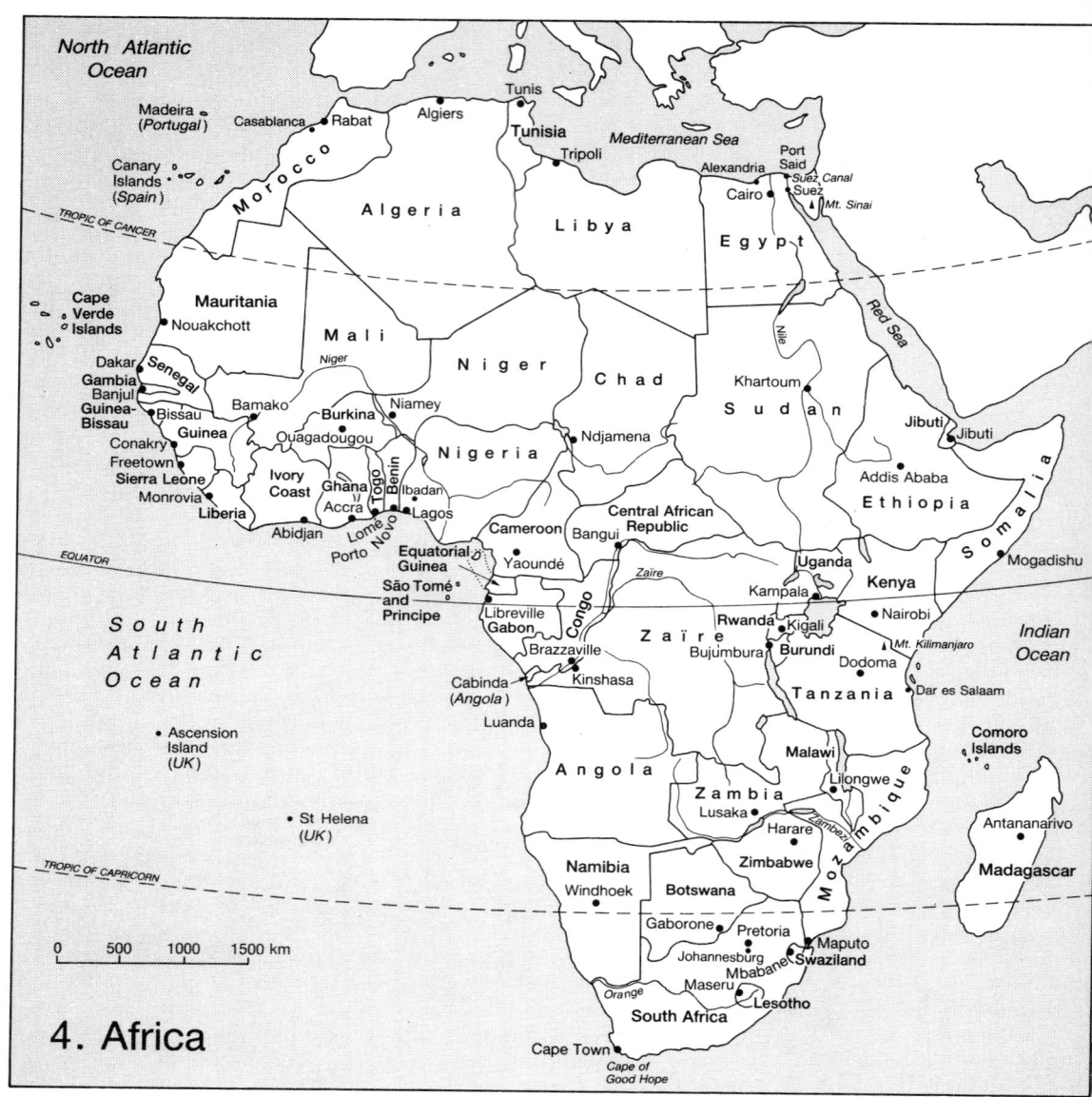

North Atlantic Ocean

Madeira (*Portugal*)
Casablanca • Rabat
Algiers
Tunis
Tunisia
Tripoli
Mediterranean Sea
Alexandria
Port Said
Suez Canal
Suez
Cairo
▲ *Mt. Sinai*

Canary Islands (*Spain*)

TROPIC OF CANCER

Morocco
Algeria
Libya
Egypt

Red Sea

Cape Verde Islands

Mauritania
• Nouakchott
Mali
Niger
Chad
Sudan
Khartoum •
Nile

Dakar •
Senegal
Niger
Niamey
Ouagadougou
Burkina
Bamako •
Gambia
Banjul
Guinea-Bissau
Bissau •
Guinea
Conakry
Freetown
Sierra Leone
Monrovia •
Liberia
Ivory Coast
Ghana
Accra
Togo
Benin
Lomé
Porto Novo
Abidjan •
Nigeria
Ibadan •
Lagos
Ndjamena •
Cameroon
Bangui •
Central African Republic
Addis Ababa •
Ethiopia
Somalia
Jibuti
Jibuti

Yaoundé •
Equatorial Guinea
São Tomé and Principe
Libreville
Gabon
Zaïre
Congo
Brazzaville •
Uganda
Kampala •
Rwanda
Kigali •
Burundi
Bujumbura •
Kenya
Nairobi •
Mogadishu •

EQUATOR

South Atlantic Ocean

Kinshasa •
Zaïre
Cabinda (*Angola*)
Luanda •
Dodoma •
▲ *Mt. Kilimanjaro*
Dar es Salaam •
Tanzania

Indian Ocean

• Ascension Island (*UK*)

Angola

Malawi
Lilongwe •
Comoro Islands

Zambia
Lusaka •
Zambezi
Harare •
Antananarivo •

• St Helena (*UK*)

Namibia
Windhoek •
Botswana
Zimbabwe
Mozambique
Madagascar

TROPIC OF CAPRICORN

Gaborone •
Pretoria •
Johannesburg •
Maputo
Mbabane
Swaziland
Maseru
Lesotho
Orange
South Africa

0 500 1000 1500 km

Cape Town •
Cape of Good Hope

4. Africa

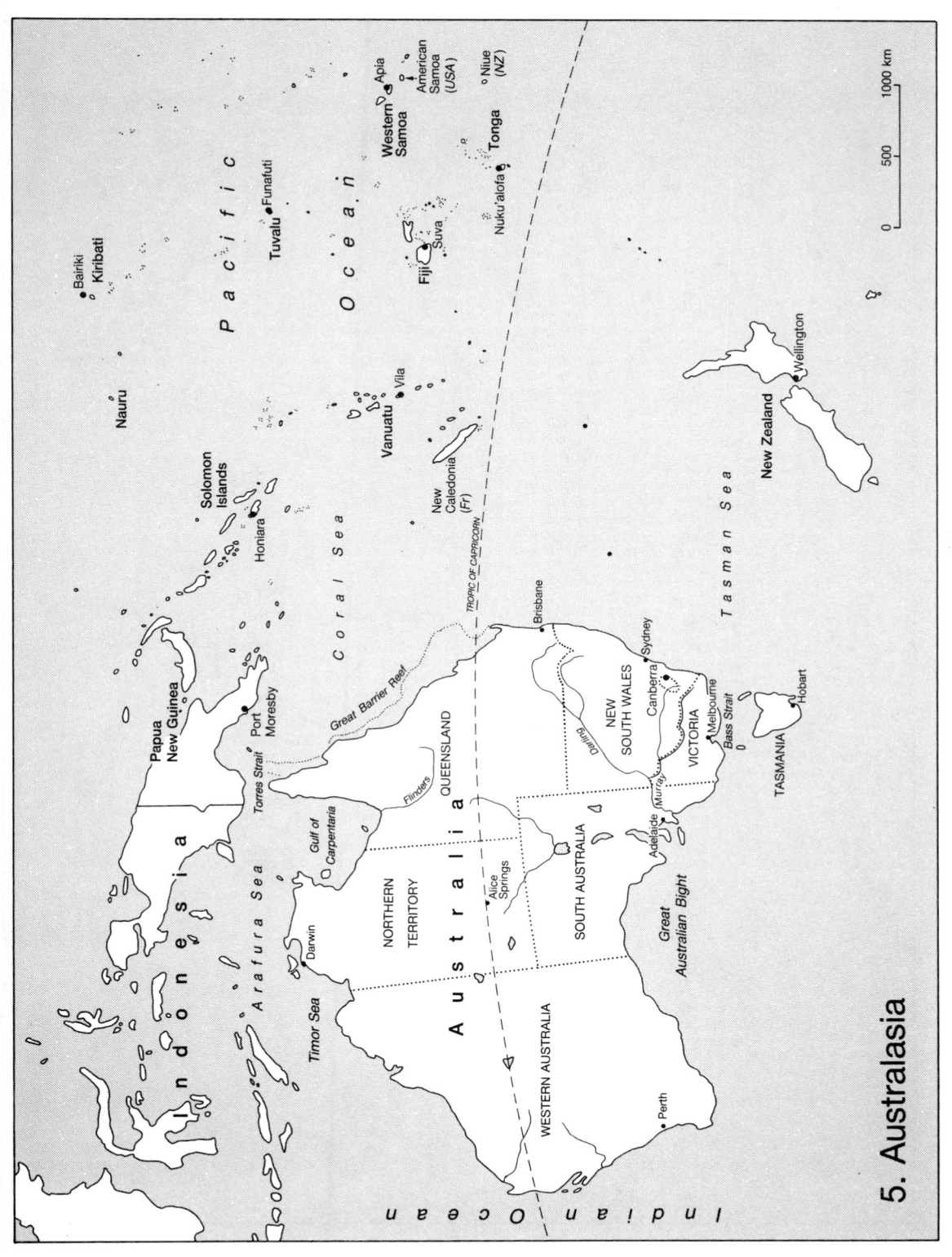

5. Australasia

Indonesia

Timor Sea

Arafura Sea

Darwin

Gulf of
Carpentaria

Torres Strait

Papua
New Guinea

Port
Moresby

Coral Sea

Great Barrier Reef

Flinders

Brisbane

QUEENSLAND

NORTHERN
TERRITORY

Australia

WESTERN AUSTRALIA

Alice
Springs

SOUTH AUSTRALIA

Great
Australian Bight

Perth

Adelaide

Murray

Darling

NEW
SOUTH WALES

Canberra

Sydney

VICTORIA

Melbourne

Bass Strait

TASMANIA

Hobart

Tasman Sea

New Zealand

Wellington

Indian Ocean

TROPIC OF CAPRICORN

Solomon
Islands

Honiara

Nauru

Bairiki
Kiribati

Pacific

Ocean

Tuvalu Funafuti

Western
Samoa

Apia

American
Samoa
(USA)

Niue
(NZ)

Tonga

Nuku'alofa

Fiji Suva

Vanuatu Vila

New
Caledonia
(Fr)

0   500   1000 km

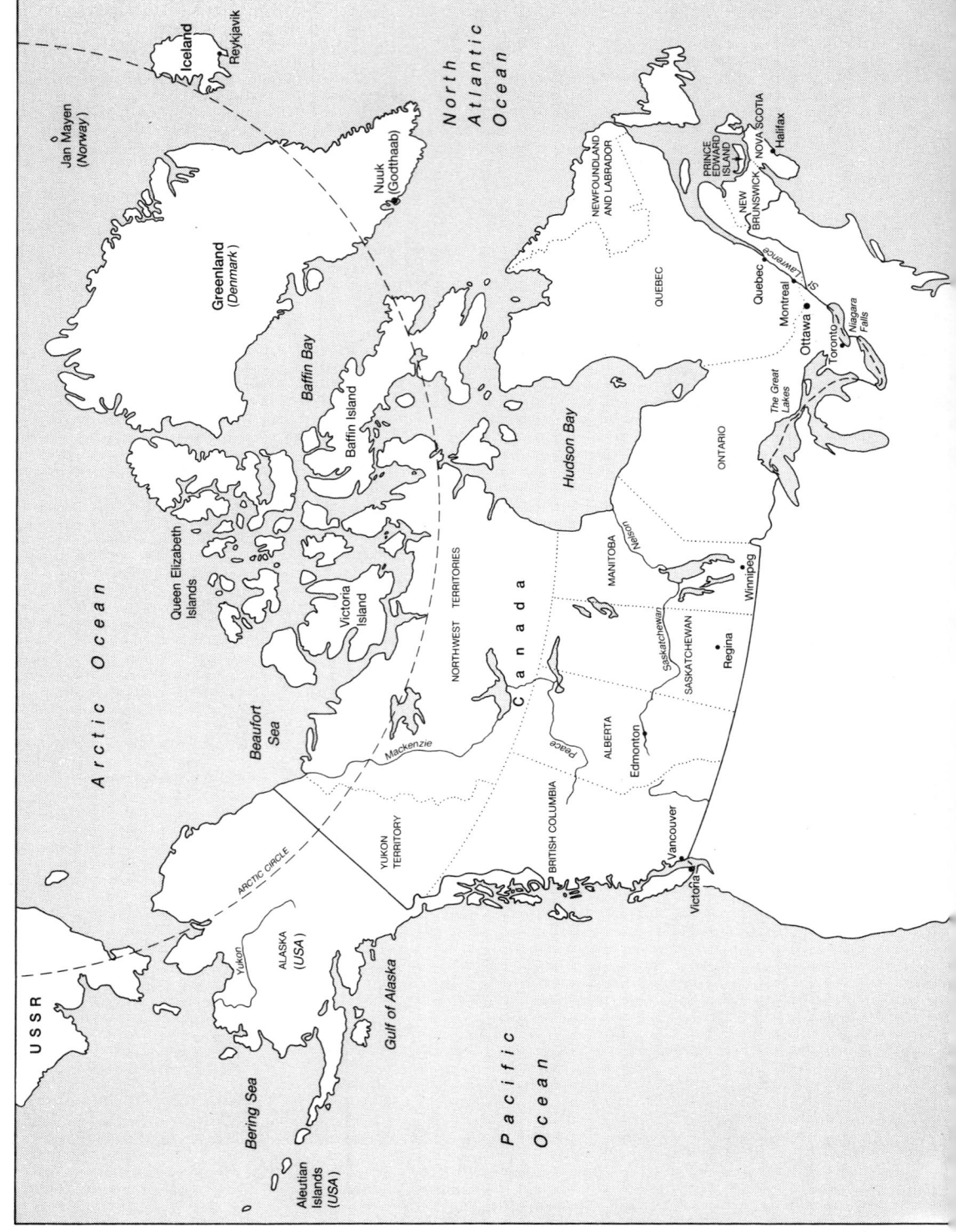

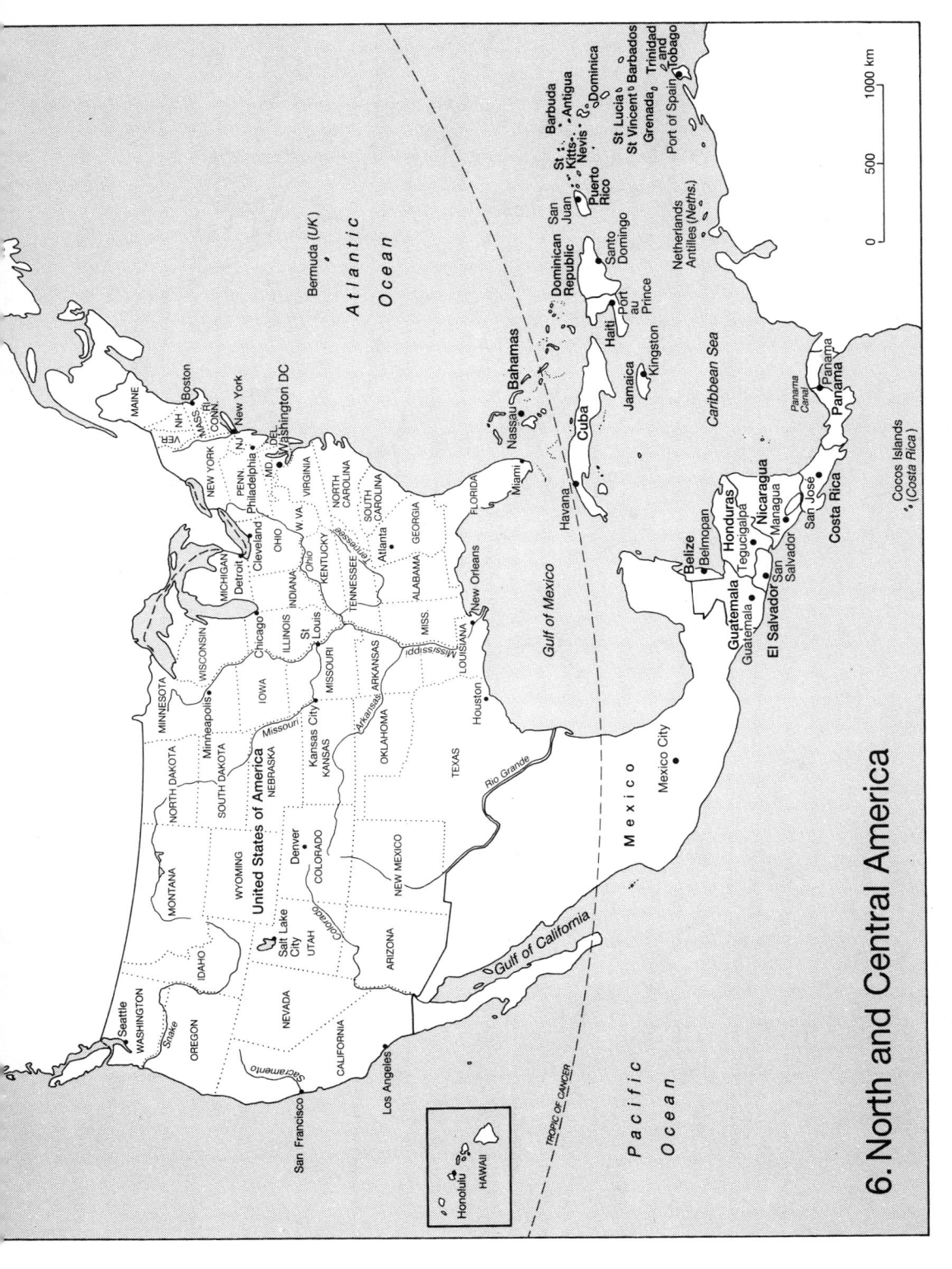

6. North and Central America

United States of America

Seattle · WASHINGTON
OREGON
IDAHO
MONTANA
Sacramento · NEVADA
San Francisco · CALIFORNIA
Los Angeles · WYOMING
Salt Lake City · UTAH
Denver · COLORADO
ARIZONA
NEW MEXICO
NORTH DAKOTA
SOUTH DAKOTA
NEBRASKA
KANSAS
OKLAHOMA
TEXAS
MINNESOTA
Minneapolis
IOWA
Kansas City
MISSOURI
St Louis
ARKANSAS
Chicago
WISCONSIN
MICHIGAN
ILLINOIS
INDIANA
OHIO
KENTUCKY
TENNESSEE
MISS.
ALABAMA
LOUISIANA
New Orleans
Houston
Cleveland
Detroit
Ohio
W. VA.
VIRGINIA
NORTH CAROLINA
SOUTH CAROLINA
GEORGIA
Atlanta
FLORIDA
Miami
MAINE
NH
VER.
MASS.
CONN.
Boston
New York
NEW YORK
PENN.
Philadelphia
NJ
DEL.
MD.
Washington DC
RI

Snake
Colorado
Missouri
Arkansas
Mississippi
Rio Grande
Gulf of California
TROPIC OF CANCER

Honolulu · HAWAII

Pacific Ocean

Atlantic Ocean

Bermuda (UK)

Bahamas
Nassau

Havana
Cuba

Mexico City
Mexico

Gulf of Mexico

Jamaica
Kingston

Haiti
Port au Prince

Dominican Republic
Santo Domingo
San Juan
Puerto Rico

St Kitts · Nevis
Barbuda · Antigua
Dominica
St Lucia
St Vincent · Barbados
Grenada · Trinidad and Tobago
Port of Spain

Netherlands Antilles (Neths.)

Caribbean Sea

Belize
Belmopan
Guatemala
Guatemala
El Salvador
San Salvador
Honduras
Tegucigalpa
Nicaragua
Managua
San José
Costa Rica
Panama Canal
Panama
Panama

Cocos Islands (Costa Rica)

1000 km
500
0

Caribbean Sea

North
Atlantic
Ocean

Caracas

Venezuela
Georgetown
Guyana Paramaribo
Cayenne
Surinam French
Guiana

Bogotá

Colombia

EQUATOR

Quito
Amazon

Ecuador

Galapagos Islands
(*Ecuador*)

B r a z i l

P e r u
Lima
Cuzco

Brasilia

La Paz

B o l i v i a

Pacific Ocean

Paraguay
Paraná
São Paulo
Rio de Janeiro

TROPIC OF CAPRICORN

Asunción

Mt. Aconcagua

Uruguay
Montevideo
Valparaiso
Buenos
Aires
River Plate
Estuary

South
Atlantic
Ocean

Santiago

Juan Fernandez
Islands (*Chile*)

A r g e n t i n a

Stanley
Falkland
Islands (*UK*)

South Georgia (*UK*)

Tierra del Fuego

Cape Horn

South
Shetland
Islands
(*UK*)

South Orkney
Islands
(*UK*)

ANTARCTIC CIRCLE

0   500   1000   1500 km

7. South America

ALI BABA AMPHIBIAN ANAESTHETIC **ANTHROP**
OLOGY **ARMADA** ASTROLOGY ASTRON
BOMB ATOMIC ENERGY AURORA AUTH
OCK BAALBEK **BACTERIUM** BALLOON
OURISM BESSEMER PROCESS BICYCLE
BLACK DEATH BLACK HOLE BLIND MAN
GONE BOOK OF COMMON PRAYER BOTA
MUSEUM **BROCKEN SPECTRE** BRONZ
ING SOCIETY CABINET CALAMITY JANE
RSITY CAMERA CANAL CANCER **CANNIB**
ANDRA **CHESS** CHRISTIANITY CHRISTIAN
STMAS TREE CHURCH OF ENGLAND CINE
T CRICKET CRIMEAN WAR CULTURAL
AGES **DAVY LAMP** DEAD SEA
TIONARY DIVINE RIGHT
ME OF THE ROCK **DOM**
UID DR WATSON DYNA
ECTRICITY ELECTRON
GLISH **EXISTENTIALISM**
COND WORLD WAR FISH
RANKENSTEIN FREEMASO
GENEVA CONVENTIONS G
QUEEN **GOLDEN FLEECE**
GUNPOWDER PLOT GYPSY H
HELICOPTER HITTITES HO
RED YEARS WAR **HY**
VOLUTION
INE IRO
EVES JE
ARTING
D'S MAC
AISE **MARS**
TRIC SYST
MOSQUE
PLAY NAZI
LON OPER
TOMIME
LTDOWN

DEN FLEECE G
PLOT GYPSY H
HITTITES HO
HYDROGEN
REVOLUTION
N ENGINE IRO
ZZ JEEVES JI
BA KARTINC
LLOYD'S M
MARSUPIA
METRIC SYSTEM
MON MOSQUE MOTORC
AZISM **NEANDERTHAL MAN**
NYLON OPERA OXFORD UNIV
ANTOMIME PAPER-MAKING
HY **PILTDOWN MAN** PLANET
EM PREHISTORY PRINTING
LISHING PUNCH AND JUDY
HEORY RADAR **RADIO** RAIL
VAN WINKLE ROBINSON CR
ARY CLUB RUSSIAN SALVA
CHINE **SHERLOCK HOLMES**
SHORTHAND SILHOUETTE
RIENDS SPECTACLES SPIRITUALISM
HANGE **STONEHENGE** SUBMARINE SURGER
REALISM TANK TAROT TEA TELEGRAPHY TEL
NE TELESCOPE TELEVISION TENNIS THERMO
AMICS TIN **TORPEDO** TRAFFIC LIGHTS **TRAN**
PIST TREADMILL TUBERCULOSIS TURBO-JE
BO-PROP UFO UNCLE SAM UNICORN UTILI
ANISM VALENTINE VAMPIRE VANDAL VAT

Tongue action of a toad

Magnetism

Magnets

bar magnet

poles

north south

horseshoe magnet

keeper (prevents loss of magnetism)

Magnetic fields

the earth

magnetic north

geographical north (earth's axis)

magnetic field

The Body: 1.

Skull

Skeleton

Teeth

Spine

Genetics

Genes, chromosomes, and heredity

Fractures

simple fracture

comminuted fracture

impacted fracture